MACQUARIE
COMPACT DICTIONARY

MACQUARIE

MACQUARIE
COMPACT DICTIONARY

Published by Macquarie Dictionary Publishers, an imprint of Pan Macmillan Australia Pty Ltd
1 Market Street, Sydney, New South Wales, Australia 2000

First edition published 2014
Second edition published 2017

© Copyright Macquarie Dictionary Publishers 2017
ISBN: 9781743549520

Cover design: Natalie Bowra
Cover photograph: Colin Leonhardt, Birdseye View Photography
Typeset by Macmillan Publishing Solutions, Bangalore-25
Printed in China

Macquarie Dictionary at

A Cataloguing-in-Publication entry is available from the National Library of Australia
http://catalogue.nla.gov.au

CONTENTS

EXPLANATORY NOTES

Headword

The headword is the item being defined in a particular entry.

Separate entries are made for all words which, although spelt identically, are of quite distinct derivation. In such cases, each headword is followed by a small superscript number, as, for example, in **gum**[1] and **gum**[2].

Entries are arranged in strict alphabetical order. A particular headword can be located by taking each successive letter of the headword in alphabetical order, ignoring hyphens, apostrophes and word spaces. For example, the words **whitebait** and **white-collar** are found between **white** and **white noise**. A special case is the treatment of numbers which form part of a headword, as is the case of **catch 22**. For the purpose of alphabetical ordering the number is regarded as spelt out (as **catch twenty-two**), so that **catch 22** comes between **catchphrase** and **catch-up**.

An exception to the alphabetical ordering of headwords occurs with those beginning with **St**. These are arranged as though the **St** is spelt out as **Saint**. For example, **St Vitus dance** is treated as though it were spelt **Saint Vitus dance**.

Variant spellings

Definitions always appear under the most common spelling of a word. Less common variants cross-refer to the main headword. For example, the word **cipher** has a variant **cypher** which appears as a headword followed by **→ cipher** to show that the entry is at the main spelling **cipher**.

Hyphens are a variable detail in the writing of words, and subject to diversity of opinion. Australian practice is variable and the dictionary reflects this. In the headword list hyphens are shown where they are most necessary to link or separate the elements of a word which would otherwise be difficult to read or ambiguous, as in **re-count** ('to count again', as opposed to **recount**) and **re-entry**, but writers are at liberty to add them as they see fit. Note that hyphens should be added whenever a compound is used in a new grammatical role, as, for example, when **upper class** becomes a compound adjective in **upper-class background**.

For compound headwords in which one word has a spelling variant, this variant form is not given since it is deemed to be adequately covered at the entry for that individual word. For example, **call centre** does not have a variant form **call center** because at **centre** the US variant **center** is given.

Pronunciation

The appropriate pronunciation of a headword is indicated by the sequence of symbols from the International Phonetic Alphabet which appear between slant brackets, usually immediately following the headword. A key to the pronunciation symbols appears on page x.

If the pronunciation of a headword differs according to its part of speech, or a particular sense, the appropriate pronunciation is placed before the relevant definition(s).

Headwords consisting of two or more words are not given pronunciation guides if the pronunciation for each word in the headword can be found elsewhere in the dictionary. A pronunciation guide is given for one of these multi-word headwords if there are variant pronunciations for any of the individual words, and only one applies to that word in the multi-word entry. Hyphenated compounds are treated as multi-word headwords.

Grammar

The grammatical category of the headword is indicated by an italic part-of-speech or word-class label, such as *n.* (noun), *adv.* (adverb), *conj.* (conjunction), etc.

If the headword is used in more than one grammatical form, the part-of-speech label precedes each set of definitions to which it applies.

Inflected forms

If a headword has irregularly inflected forms (any form not made by the simple addition of the suffix to the main entry), the summary of these forms is given immediately after the relevant part of speech. Regularly inflected forms, not generally shown, include:

1. Nouns forming a plural merely by the addition of *-s* or *-es*, such as **dog** (**dogs**) or **class** (**classes**);
2. Verbs forming the past tense by adding *-ed*, such as **halt** (**halted**);
3. Verbs forming the present tense by adding *-s* or *-es*, such as **talk** (**talks**) or **smash** (**smashes**);
4. Verbs forming the present participle by adding *-ing*, such as **walk** (**walking**);
5. Adjectives forming the comparative and superlative by adding *-er* and *-est*, such as **black** (**blacker, blackest**).

Regular forms are given, however, when necessary for clarity or the avoidance of confusion.

The past tense, past participle and present participle are given as the inflected forms of verbs. Where, as commonly happens, the past tense and past participle are the same in form, this form is shown once. For example, the inflected forms indicated for **love** are **loved, loving**, where **loved** is both the past tense and past participle.

Restrictive labels

Entries that are limited to a particular style, region, time or subject, are marked with such labels as *Colloq.* (Colloquial), *Archaic*, *US*, *Agric.* (Agriculture), etc.

If the restrictive label applies to the entire entry, it appears before the definition(s) at the beginning of the entry. If however the restrictive label applies to only one grammatical form, it appears after the part-of-speech label to which it applies and before the definition(s). If the restrictive label applies to only one definition, it appears before that definition, after the definition number.

Some headwords are marked with the restrictive label *taboo*. This indicates that the word itself may give offence essentially because of its taboo nature. This label is also used if there is a particularly crass and offensive meaning given to a usually neutral word. Taboo words are to be differentiated from words which are intended to denigrate another person (labelled *derogatory*), and words which are racist (labelled *racist*). Some words can attract a combination of these restrictive labels.

Definitions

Definitions are individually numbered, with numbers appearing in a single sequence which does not begin afresh with each grammatical form. The central meaning of each part of speech is put first – this is generally the most common meaning.

In some cases in which two definitions are very closely related, usually within the same field of information, they are marked with bold-face letters of the alphabet under the same definition number.

Secondary headwords

Idiomatic phrases, prepositional phrases, etc., are placed at the entry for the key word, and are listed in secondary bold-face type alphabetically at the end of the entry following the label *phr.* (phrase).

Illustrative material

Illustrative phrases, showing how the word is used in context, appear in italics after a colon at the end of a definition.

Cross-referencing

There are several forms of cross-referencing in this dictionary. The arrow → indicates that the headword which precedes it is not defined in this place but that a suitable definition is to be found under the headword which follows the arrow.

The word 'See' directs the reader to information relevant to the current definition but to be found within a different part of the dictionary.

The word 'Compare' is similar in function but limited to those cases where the information is in some way complementary or matching.

Run-on headwords

Words which are derivatives of the headword and which are simple extensions of the meaning are run on after the last definition in the entry. Such headwords appear in bold-face type followed by an indication of their grammatical word class. Occasionally, a pronunciation guide is given if the pronunciation of the derived form is not clear from the pronunciation given for the headword.

STRUCTURE OF ENTRIES

headword — **backblocks** /'bækblɒks/ *pl. n.* **1.** *Aust., NZ.* remote, sparsely inhabited inland country. **2.** *Aust. Colloq.* the outer suburbs of a city. –**backblock**, *adj.* –**backblocker**, *n.* — *labels*

back-burn /'bæk-bɜn/ *Aust., NZ –verb* (**-burnt** or **-burned, -burning**) *–v.t.* **1.** to clear (land, grass or scrub) by burning into or against the wind. *–v.i.* **2.** to control a fire by burning off an area in advance of it, often into or against the wind. *–n.* **3.** the act or process of back-burning. –**back-burning,** *n.* — *run-on headword*

secondary headword — **backburner** /'bækbɜnə/ *n.* **1.** the rear burner of a stove, often used to keep food warm. *–phr.* **2. put on the backburner**, to take no further action on for the time being; postpone.

superscripted headwords — **backtrack¹** /'bæktræk/ *v.i.* **1.** to return over the same course or route. **2.** to withdraw from an undertaking, position, etc.; pursue a reverse policy. –**backtracker**, *n.*

backtrack² /'bæktræk/ *n.* a minor road in worse condition than the main road and passing through less populated areas.

bad cholesterol *n.* low-density lipoprotein (LDL), seen as being undesirable because it has a tendency to clog blood vessels; a high level of this component of cholesterol in the blood is associated with an increased risk of coronary artery disease. Compare **good cholesterol**. — *part of speech* ... *cross-reference*

bails /beilz/ *pl. n. Aust., NZ* **1.** → **bail³** (def. 3). **2. the bails**, the milking shed. — *cross-reference*

ballot /'bælət/ *n.* **1.** a ticket or paper used in voting. **2.** the number of votes placed or recorded: *a large ballot.* **3.** Also, **secret ballot.** secret voting with printed or written ballots or voting machines. **4.** the right to vote: *to give the ballot to 18 year-olds.* **5.** a small ball used in voting or drawing lots. *–v.i.* (**-loted, -loting**) **6.** to vote by ballot. **7.** to draw lots: *to ballot for places.* –**balloter**, *n.* — *variant* ... *illustrative phrase*

inflected forms
pronunciation —

balm /bam/ *n.* **1.** any of various oily, fragrant, resinous substances, often of medicinal value, exuding from certain plants, especially tropical trees of the genus *Commiphora.* See **balsam** (def. 1). **2.** any aromatic or fragrant ointment. **3.** aromatic fragrance; sweet smell. **4.** any of various aromatic plants, especially of the genus *Melissa*, as *M. officinalis*, a lemon-scented perennial herb. **5.** anything which heals, soothes, or mitigates pain. — *cross-reference*

definition —

ABBREVIATIONS

The following is a list of abbreviations used in the dictionary.

abbrev.	abbreviation	**Geog.**	Geography	**Psychol.**	Psychology
ACT	Australian Capital Territory	**Geol.**	Geology	**Qld**	Queensland
		Geom.	Geometry	**S**	South, Southern
adj.	adjective	**Govt**	Government	**SA**	South Australia
adv.	adverb	**Gram.**	Grammar	**Scot.**	Scottish
Agric.	Agriculture	**Hist.**	History	**sing.**	singular
Alg.	Algebra	**Hort.**	Horticulture	**Surg.**	Surgery
Anat.	Anatomy	**interj.**	interjection	**Telecom.**	Telecommunications
Anthrop.	Anthropology	**It.**	Italian		
Archaeol.	Archaeology	**L**	Latin	**ult.**	ultimate, ultimately
Archit.	Architecture	**Ling.**	Linguistics		
Astrol.	Astrology	**lit.**	literally	**uncert.**	uncertain
Astron.	Astronomy	**Lit.**	Literature	**US**	United States of America
Aust.	Australian	**Maths**	Mathematics		
aux.	auxiliary	**Med.**	Medicine	**usu.**	usually
b.	blend; born	**Meteorol.**	Meteorology	**v.**	verb
Bacteriol.	Bacteriology	**Mil.**	Military	**var.**	variant
Biochem.	Biochemistry	**Mineral.**	Mineralogy	**v.i.**	intransitive verb
Biol.	Biology	**Myth.**	Mythology	**v.t.**	transitive verb
Bot.	Botany	**N**	North, Northern	**W**	West, Western
Brit.	British	**n.**	noun	**WA**	Western Australia
c.	circa	**Naut.**	Nautical	**Zool.**	Zoology
cf.	compare	**Navig.**	Navigation		
Chem.	Chemistry	**NSW**	New South Wales		
Colloq.	Colloquial	**NT**	Northern Territory		
conj.	conjunction	**NZ**	New Zealand		
def.	definition	**Obs.**	Obsolete		
derog.	derogatory	**Obsolesc.**	Obsolescent		
E	English; East, Eastern	**oft.**	often		
		orig.	origin, original, originally		
Eccles.	Ecclesiastical				
Ecol.	Ecology	**Ornith.**	Ornithology		
Econ.	Economics	**Pathol.**	Pathology		
Educ.	Education	**Philos.**	Philosophy		
Elect.	Electricity	**phr.**	phrase		
Eng.	Engineering	**Physiol.**	Physiology		
esp.	especially	**pl.**	plural		
F	French	**p.p.**	past participle		
fol.	followed	**prep.**	preposition		
gen.	genitive	**pron.**	pronoun		

PRONUNCIATION GUIDE

Vowels

i	as in 'peat'	/pit/		ʊ	as in 'put'	/pʊt/
ɪ	as in 'pit'	/pɪt/		u	as in 'pool'	/pul/
ɛ	as in 'pet'	/pɛt/		ɜ	as in 'pert'	/pɜt/
æ	as in 'pat'	/pæt/		ə	as in 'apart'	/ə'pat/
a	as in 'part'	/pat/		ɒ̃	as in 'bon voyage'	/bɒ̃ vwa'jaʒ/
ɒ	as in 'pot'	/pɒt/		æ̃	as in French 'vin'	/væ̃/
ʌ	as in 'putt'	/pʌt/		y	as in French 'rue'	/ry/
ɔ	as in 'port'	/pɔt/				

Diphthongs

aɪ	as in 'buy'	/baɪ/		oʊ	as in 'hoe'	/hoʊ/
eɪ	as in 'bay'	/beɪ/		ɪə	as in 'here'	/hɪə/
ɔɪ	as in 'boy'	/bɔɪ/		ɛə	as in 'hair'	/hɛə/
aʊ	as in 'how'	/haʊ/		ʊə	as in 'tour'	/tʊə/

Consonants

Plosives

p	as in 'pet'	/pɛt/
b	as in 'bet'	/bɛt/
t	as in 'tale'	/teɪl/
d	as in 'dale'	/deɪl/
k	as in 'came'	/keɪm/
g	as in 'game'	/geɪm/

Fricatives

f	as in 'fine'	/faɪn/
v	as in 'vine'	/vaɪn/
θ	as in 'thin'	/θɪn/
ð	as in 'then'	/ðɛn/
s	as in 'seal'	/sil/
z	as in 'zeal'	/zil/
ʃ	as in 'show'	/ʃoʊ/
ʒ	as in 'pleasure'	/'plɛʒə/
h	as in 'heal'	/hil/
r	as in 'real'	/ril/

Affricates

tʃ	as in 'choke'	/tʃoʊk/
dʒ	as in 'joke'	/dʒoʊk/

Nasals

m	as in 'mail'	/meɪl/
n	as in 'nail'	/neɪl/
ŋ	as in 'sing'	/sɪŋ/

Semi-vowels

j	as in 'you'	/ju/
w	as in 'woo'	/wu/

Laterals

l	as in 'love'	/lʌv/

Stress

Primary stress: ' as in 'clatter' /'klætə/
Secondary stress: ˌ as in 'encyclopedia' /ɛnˌsaɪklə'pidiə/

A a

A, a /eɪ/ *n.* **1.** the first letter of the English alphabet. **2.** the first in any series. **3.** the highest mark for school, college, or university work; alpha. **4.** *Music* **a.** the sixth degree in the scale of C major, or the first in the relative minor scale (A minor). **b.** a written or printed note representing this tone. **c.** a string, key, or pipe tuned to this note. **d.** (in the fixed system of solmisation) the sixth note of the scale, called *la*. **e.** the note to which concert performers tune their instruments; concert A. –*phr.* **5. from A to Z**, from beginning to end.

a¹ /ə/, *emphatic* /eɪ/ *adj. or indefinite article* used especially before nouns beginning with a consonant sound to mean: **1.** some (indefinite singular referring to one individual of a class): *a child; a house; a star.* **2.** another: *he is a Cicero in eloquence.* **3.** one: *two of a kind; a thousand.* **4.** any (a single): *not a one.* **5.** indefinite plural: *a few; a great many.* Also, (*before a vowel sound*), **an.**

a² /ə/ *adj. or indefinite article* each; every: *three times a day.*

a-¹ a prefix, a reduced form of Old English preposition *on*, meaning 'on', 'in', 'into', 'to', 'towards', preserved before a noun in a prepositional phrase, forming a predicate adjective or an adverbial element, as in *afoot, abed, ashore, apart, aside,* and in archaic and dialectal use before a present participle in *-ing*, as in *to set the bells aringing.*

a-² a prefix, a reduced form of Old English *of*, as in *akin, afresh, anew.*

a-³ a prefix indicating: **1.** up, out, or away, as in *arise, awake.* **2.** intensified action, as in *abide, amaze.*

a-⁴ variant of **ab-** before *m*, *p*, and *v*, as in *amove, aperient, avert.*

a-⁵ variant of **ad-**, used: **1.** before *sc, sp, st*, as in *ascend.* **2.** in words of French derivation (often with the sense of increase, addition), as in *amass.*

a-⁶ variant of **an-¹** before consonants, as in *achromatic.*

aardvark /ˈɑdvak/ *n.* a large, nocturnal, burrowing mammal of Africa, subsisting largely on termites, and having a long, extensile tongue, claws, and conspicuously long ears. There is only one genus, *Orycteropus*, constituting a separate order, Tubulidentata.

ab- a prefix meaning 'off', 'away', 'from', as in *abduct, abjure.*

aback /əˈbæk/ *phr.* **taken aback, 1.** suddenly disconcerted. **2.** (of a ship) caught by the wind so as to press the sails back against the mast. **3.** (of sails) caught by a wind on the forward surface.

abacus /ˈæbəkəs/ *n.* (*pl.* **-ci** /-si/ *or* **-cuses**) a contrivance for calculating, consisting of beads or balls strung on wires or rods set in a frame.

abalone /æbəˈloʊni/ *n.* (*pl.* **-lone** *or* **-lones**) any of the various univalve, marine molluscs of the genus *Haliotis*, having a bowl-like, nacre-lined shell bearing a row of respiratory holes. The flesh is used for food and the shell for mother-of-pearl ornaments.

abandon¹ /əˈbændən/ *v.t.* **1.** to leave completely and finally; forsake utterly; desert: *to abandon one's home.* **2.** to give up (something begun) without finishing: *to abandon a cricket match because of rain.* **3.** to yield (oneself) unrestrainedly: *to abandon oneself to grief.* –**abandoner**, *n.* –**abandonment**, *n.*

abandon² /əˈbændən/ *n.* a giving up to natural impulses; freedom from constraint or conventionality: *to do something with abandon.*

abase /əˈbeɪs/ *v.t.* (*chiefly reflexive*) to reduce or lower, as in rank, office, estimation; humble; degrade. –**abasement**, *n.* –**abaser**, *n.*

abashed /əˈbæʃt/ *adj.* embarrassed; mortified.

abate /əˈbeɪt/ *v.t.* **1.** to reduce in amount, intensity, etc.; lessen; diminish: *to abate a tax; to abate one's enthusiasm.* **2.** *Law* to put an end to or suppress (a nuisance); suspend or extinguish (an action); annul (a writ). –*v.i.* **3.** to decrease or become less in strength or violence: *the storm has abated.* –**abatement**, *n.* –**abater**; *Law*, **abator**, *n.* –**abatable**, *adj.*

abattoir /ˈæbətwa, -tɔ/ *n.* a building or place where animals are slaughtered for food; a slaughterhouse. Also, **abattoirs.**

abbess /ˈæbɛs/ *n.* the female superior of a convent, regularly in the same religious orders in which monks are governed by an abbot.

abbey /ˈæbi/ *n.* (*pl.* **-beys**) **1.** the religious body or establishment under an abbot or abbess; a monastery or convent. **2.** the monastic buildings.

abbot /ˈæbət/ *n.* the male head or superior of a monastery. –**abbotship**, **abbotric**, *n.*

abbreviate /əˈbriviˌeɪt/ *v.t.* to make brief; make shorter by contraction or omission: *to abbreviate 'company' to 'co.'.* –**abbreviation**, *n.* –**abbreviator**, *n.*

abdicate /ˈæbdɪkeɪt/ *v.i.* **1.** to renounce a throne or some claim; relinquish a right, power, or trust. –*v.t.* **2.** to give up or renounce (office, duties, authority, etc.), especially in a public or formal manner. –**abdication**, *n.* –**abdicable**, *adj.* –**abdicative** /əbˈdɪkətɪv/, *adj.* –**abdicator, abdicant**, *n.*

abdomen /ˈæbdəmən, əbˈdoʊmən/ *n.* **1.** the part of the body of a mammal between the thorax and the pelvis; the visceral cavity containing most of the digestive organs; the belly. **2.** *Zool.* the posterior section of the body of an arthropod animal, behind the thorax or the crustacean cephalothorax. –**abdominal** /æbˈdɒmənəl/, *adj.*

abduct /əbˈdʌkt, æb-/ *v.t.* **1.** to carry off surreptitiously or by force, especially to kidnap. **2.** *Physiol.* to draw away from the original position (opposed to *adduct*). –**abductor**, *n.* –**abduction**, *n.*

Aberdeen Angus /æbədin ˈæŋgəs/ *n.* one of a breed of hornless beef cattle with smooth black hair, originally bred in Scotland and now found in Australia, especially in higher rainfall areas.

aberrant /ˈæbərənt, əˈbɛrənt/ *adj.* **1.** straying from the right or usual course. **2.** deviating from the ordinary or normal type. –**aberrance, aberrancy**, *n.*

aberration /æbəˈreɪʃən/ *n.* **1.** a lapse from a sound mental state. **2.** a momentary departure from a usual practice. **3.** deviation from truth or moral rectitude. **4.** *Optics* any disturbance of the rays of a pencil of light such that they can no longer be brought to a sharp focus or form a clear image. –**aberrational**, *adj.*

abet /əˈbɛt/ *v.t.* (**abetted, abetting**) to encourage or allow to happen by aid or approval (used chiefly in a bad sense): *to abet evildoers; to abet a crime or offence.* –**abetment**, *n.* –**abetter**; *Law*, **abettor**, *n.*

abeyance /əˈbeɪəns/ n. 1. temporary inactivity or suspension. –phr. 2. in abeyance, in an inactive or suspended state.

abhor /əbˈhɔ/ v.t. (-horred, -horring) to regard with repugnance; loathe. –abhorrer, n.

abhorrent /əbˈhɒrənt/ adj. exciting horror; detestable. –abhorrence, n. –abhorrently, adv.

abide /əˈbaɪd/ verb (abided or, Archaic, abode /əˈboʊd/, abiding) –v.t. 1. to put up with; tolerate: I can't abide such people. –v.i. 2. Archaic or Poetic to remain; continue; stay: abide with me. –phr. 3. abide by, a. to accept and continue to observe (an undertaking, promise, agreement, rule, law, etc.) b. to await or accept the consequences of: to abide by the decision. –abider, n. –abidance, n. –abiding, adj.

ability /əˈbɪləti/ n. (pl. -ties) 1. power or capacity to do or act in any relation. 2. competence in any occupation or field of action, from the possession of capacity, skill, means, or other qualification. 3. (pl.) talents; mental gifts or endowments.

abiotic /eɪbaɪˈɒtɪk/ adj. of or relating to the non-living components of an ecosystem.

abject /ˈæbdʒɛkt/ adj. 1. utterly hopeless or disheartening: abject poverty. 2. contemptible; despicable: an abject liar. 3. humble; servile: an abject apology. –abjection /æbˈdʒɛkʃən/, n. –abjectly, adv. –abjectness, n.

abjure /əbˈdʒuə/ v.t. 1. to renounce or repudiate; retract, especially with solemnity: to abjure one's errors. 2. to forswear: to abjure allegiance. –abjuratory, adj. –abjurer, n. –abjuration, n.

ablation /əˈbleɪʃən/ n. 1. Med. removal, especially of organs, abnormal growths, or harmful substances from the body by mechanical, physical or chemical means, as surgery or irradiation. 2. Physics erosion of a solid body by a fluid. 3. Geol. the removal of surface structures of the earth by wind or water, especially the wastage or removal of surface snow or ice. 4. Aerospace the melting or wearing away of some expendable part of a space vehicle upon re-entry into the earth's atmosphere.

ablaze /əˈbleɪz/ adj. 1. on fire. 2. gleaming as if on fire: ablaze with light. 3. charged with emotion: ablaze with anger; ablaze with enthusiasm.

able /ˈeɪbəl/ adj. (abler, ablest) 1. having sufficient power, strength, or qualifications; qualified: she is ready, willing and able. 2. exhibiting outstanding abilities: an able minister. 3. showing talent or knowledge: an able speech. –phr. 4. be able to, to have the capability or capacity to: I wasn't able to attend; a device able to bear heavy loads.

-able a suffix used to form adjectives, especially from verbs, to denote ability, liability, tendency, worthiness, or likelihood. Also, -ble, -ible.

able-bodied adj. 1. physically healthy; robust. 2. not having a physical disability.

able-bodied seaman n. an experienced seaman who has passed certain tests in the practice of seamanship.

able seaman n. Navy 1. a sailor in the Royal Australian Navy ranking below leading seaman and above seaman. 2. the rank. Abbrev.: AB

ablution /əˈbluʃən/ n. 1. a cleansing with water or other liquid, as in ceremonial purification. 2. (pl.) the act of washing oneself: do one's ablutions. –ablutionary, adj.

ably /ˈeɪbli/ adv. 1. competently; well. 2. with a will; energetically.

ABN /eɪ bi ˈɛn/ n. → Australian Business Number.

abnegate /ˈæbnəgeɪt/ v.t. to refuse or deny to oneself; reject; renounce. –abnegation /æbnəˈgeɪʃən/, n. –abnegator, n.

abnormal /æbˈnɔməl/ adj. not conforming to rule; deviating from the type or standard. –abnormality, n. –abnormally, adv.

aboard /əˈbɔd/ adv. 1. on board; on or in a ship, train, bus, etc. 2. Naut. alongside. –prep. 3. on board of.

abode /əˈboʊd/ n. 1. a dwelling place; a habitation. 2. continuance in a place; sojourn; stay. –v. 3. a past tense and past participle of abide.

abolish /əˈbɒlɪʃ/ v.t. to do away with; put an end to; annul; destroy: to abolish slavery. –abolishable, adj. –abolisher, n. –abolishment, n.

abolition /æbəˈlɪʃən/ n. annulment; abrogation: the abolition of a capital gains tax; the abolition of slavery. –abolitionary, adj.

A-bomb /ˈeɪ-bɒm/ n. → atomic bomb.

abominable /əˈbɒmənəbəl, əˈbɒmnəbəl/ adj. 1. detestable; loathsome. 2. shocking; unpleasant; bad. –abominableness, n. –abominably, adv.

abominate /əˈbɒmɪneɪt/ v.t. to regard with intense aversion; dislike strongly; abhor.

abomination /əbɒməˈneɪʃən/ n. 1. something greatly disliked or abhorred. 2. a detestable action; shameful vice. 3. intense aversion; detestation: to hold in abomination.

aboriginal /æbəˈrɪdʒənəl/ adj. of or relating to aborigines.

Aboriginal /æbəˈrɪdʒənəl/ adj. 1. of or relating to the Australian Aborigines. –n. 2. an Australian Aborigine.

Aboriginal land rights pl. n. the land rights of Aboriginal people with regard to their traditional land.

aborigine /æbəˈrɪdʒəni/ n. (generally) one of the first inhabitants of a country; one of the people living in a country at the earliest known period.

Aborigine /æbəˈrɪdʒəni/ n. 1. one of a race of tribal peoples, the earliest known inhabitants of Australia. 2. a descendant of this people, sometimes of mixed descent.

abort /əˈbɔt/ v.i. 1. a. (of a pregnancy) to come to an end by the expulsion of the fetus before it is viable. b. (of a fetus) to be born prematurely, before it is viable. c. (of a woman) to have a pregnancy ended by the expulsion of the fetus before it is viable; miscarry; have a miscarriage: this drug has been known to cause women to abort. 2. to develop incompletely; come to nothing; fail. 3. to decide not to complete a mission, test, experiment, etc. –v.t. 4. to cause to abort. 5. to bring (a mission, test, experiment, etc.) to a sudden and premature end. –abortive, adj.

abortion /əˈbɔʃən/ n. 1. a. the removal of a fetus from the mother's womb before it is viable. b. Also, spontaneous abortion. the involuntary expulsion of a fetus before it is viable. 2. Biol. the arrested development of an embryo or an organ at its (more or less) early stage. 3. anything which fails in its progress before it is matured or perfected, as a design or project. 4. a total failure. –abortionist, n.

abound /əˈbaʊnd/ v.i. 1. to be in great plenty; be very prevalent: the discontent which abounds in the world. –phr. 2. abound in, to be rich in: some languages abound in figurative expressions. 3. abound with, to be filled with; teem with: the ship abounds with rats. –abounding, adj.

about /əˈbaʊt/ prep. 1. of; concerning; in regard to: to talk about secrets. 2. connected with: instructions about the work. 3. somewhere near or in: she is about the house. 4. near; close to: about my height. 5. on every side of; around: the railing about the tower. 6. on or near (one's person): they had lost all they had about them. 7. here and there in or on: wander about the place. 8. concerned with; engaged in doing. –adv. 9. near in time, number, degree, etc.; approximately: about a hundred kilometres. 10. nearly; almost: about ready. 11. nearby:

he is somewhere about. **12.** on every side in every direction: *look about.* **13.** half round; in the reverse direction: *to spin about.* **14.** *Naut.* on the opposite tack. **15.** to and fro; here and there: *move furniture about.* **16.** in rotation or succession; alternately: *turn about is fair play.* **17.** at large; around: *there are lots of ailments about.* –*phr.* **18. about to,** on the point of (doing something): *about to leave.* **19. up and about,** astir; active (after sleep or illness).

about face *interj. US* → **about turn.**

about-face *n.* **1.** → **about-turn.** –*v.i.* (**-faced, -facing**) **2.** → **about-turn.**

about turn *interj.* **1.** a military command to turn, face in the opposite direction, usually in a prescribed manner, as *right about turn, left about turn.* –*n.* **2.** this manoeuvre. Also, *US,* **about face.**

about-turn *n.* **1.** *Chiefly Mil.* the performance of an about turn as a manoeuvre. **2.** a complete sudden change in position, principle, attitude, etc.; volte-face. –*v.i.* **3.** *Chiefly Mil.* to perform an about turn. **4.** to turn in the opposite direction. Also, **about-face.**

above /əˈbʌv/ *adv.* **1.** in or to a higher place; overhead: *the blue sky above.* **2.** higher in rank or power: *appeal to the courts above.* **3.** before in order, especially in a book or writing: *from what has been said above.* **4.** in heaven. –*prep.* **5.** in or to a higher place than: *fly above the earth.* **6.** more in quantity or number than: *the weight is above a tonne.* **7.** superior to, in rank or authority. **8.** not capable of (an undesirable thought, action, etc.). **9.** beyond the reach of: *above reproach.* **10.** in preference to: *to favour one child above another.* –*adj.* **11.** said, mentioned, or written above; foregoing: *the above explanation.* –*phr.* **12. above all,** principally; most importantly of all. **13. above and beyond the call of duty,** beyond what a person would normally be expected to do. **14. above suspicion,** of such probity as never to invite suspicion of wrongdoing. **15. get above oneself,** to adopt a superior air; have expectations out of keeping with one's status or position. **16. the above,** that which was said, mentioned, or written previously.

aboveboard /əbʌvˈbɔd/ *adv.* **1.** openly; without tricks, deceit or disguise. –*adj.* **2.** open; frank: *open and aboveboard actions.* Also, (*especially in predicative use*), **above board.**

abrade /əˈbreɪd/ *v.t.* **1.** to scrape off. –*v.i.* **2.** to wear down by friction. –**abradant,** *adj., n.* –**abrader,** *n.*

abrasion /əˈbreɪʒən/ *n.* **1.** the result of rubbing or abrading; an abraded spot or place. **2.** the act or process of abrading.

abrasive /əˈbreɪsɪv, -zɪv/ *n.* **1.** any material or substance used for grinding, polishing, lapping, etc., as emery or sand. –*adj.* **2.** tending to produce abrasion. **3.** (of a personality) irritating; tending to annoy. –**abrasiveness,** *n.*

abreast /əˈbrɛst/ *adv.* **1.** side by side. –*phr.* **2. abreast of** (or **with**), up to date in knowledge of; conversant with: *to keep abreast of discoveries in science.* **3. come abreast of,** to move into position alongside of.

abridge /əˈbrɪdʒ/ *v.t.* (**abridged, abridging**) **1.** to shorten by condensation or omission, or both; rewrite or reconstruct on a smaller scale. **2.** to lessen; diminish. **3.** to deprive; cut off. –**abridgeable, abridgable,** *adj.* –**abridged,** *adj.* –**abridger,** *n.*

abroad /əˈbrɔd/ *adv.* **1.** in or to a foreign country or countries: *to live abroad.* **2.** outdoors: *the owl ventures abroad at night.* **3.** astir; at large; in circulation: *rumours of disaster are abroad.* **4.** broadly; widely.

abrogate /ˈæbrəgeɪt/ *v.t.* to abolish summarily; annul by an authoritative act; repeal: *to abrogate a law.* –**abrogative,** *adj.* –**abrogator,** *n.* –**abrogable** /ˈæbrəgəbəl/, *adj.* –**abrogation** /æbrəˈgeɪʃən/, *n.*

abrupt /əˈbrʌpt/ *adj.* **1.** sudden; without warning: *an abrupt entrance.* **2.** changing from one subject to another suddenly: *an abrupt style of writing.* **3.** brief and impolite in speech or manner; brusque. **4.** steep; precipitous: *an abrupt climb.* –**abruptly,** *adv.* –**abruptness,** *n.*

abs- variant of **ab-** before *c, q, t,* as in *abscond, abstergent.*

ABS /eɪ bi ˈɛs/ *n.* **1.** a type of anti-lock braking system in motor vehicles and aircraft which incorporates electronic means to prevent a wheel from locking and sliding under heavy braking. –*adj.* **2.** of or relating to this system.

abscess /ˈæbsəs, ˈæbsɛs/ *n.* a localised collection of pus in a cavity, caused by disintegration of body tissue, often accompanied by swelling and inflammation and usually caused by bacteria.

abscind /əbˈsɪnd/ *v.t.* to cut off; sever. –**abscission,** *n.*

abscissa /æbˈsɪsə/ *n.* (*pl.* **-cissas** *or* **-cissae** /-ˈsɪsi/) (in plane Cartesian coordinates) the *x*-coordinate of a point, i.e., its horizontal distance from the *y*-axis measured parallel to the *x*-axis.

abscond /æbˈskɒnd, əb-/ *v.i.* to depart in a sudden and secret manner, especially to avoid legal process. –**absconder,** *n.*

abseil /ˈæbseɪl/ *v.i. Mountaineering* to descend a vertical cliff or wall by means of a rope attached to a harness, and a friction device to control downward movement; rappel. –**abseiling,** *n.* –**abseiler,** *n.*

absent *adj.* /ˈæbsənt/ **1.** not in a certain place at a given time; away (opposed to *present*). **2.** lacking: *revenge is absent from his mind.* **3.** absent-minded. –*phr.* /əbˈsɛnt/ **4. absent oneself, a.** to take or keep (oneself) away: *to absent oneself from the party for a short time.* **b.** *Aust. Hist.* (of a convict) to escape from custody, usually for a short period of time. –**absence,** *n.* –**absenter,** *n.* –**absently,** *adv.*

absentee /æbsənˈti/ *n.* **1.** someone who is absent. **2.** someone who habitually lives away from his or her country, place of work, etc.

absenteeism /æbsənˈtiɪzəm/ *n.* **1.** the practice of absenting oneself from duties, studies, employment, etc., often for inadequate reasons. **2.** the practice of living away from one's estates, country, employment, source of income, etc.

absentee vote *n.* a vote lodged by a voter who, on election day, is outside the division in which they are enrolled but still within their state or territory. Also, **absent vote.**

absent-minded /ˈæbsənt-ˈmaɪndəd/ *adj.* forgetful of one's immediate surroundings; preoccupied. –**absent-mindedly,** *adv.* –**absent-mindedness,** *n.*

absinthe /ˈæbsɪnθə/ *n.* a strong, bitter, green-coloured, aromatic liqueur made with wormwood, anise, and other herbs, having a pronounced liquorice flavour. Also, **absinth.**

absolute /ˈæbsəlut/ *adj.* **1.** free from imperfection; complete; perfect: *absolute liberty.* **2.** not mixed; pure. **3.** free from restriction or limitation; unqualified: *absolute command.* **4.** arbitrary or despotic: *an absolute monarchy.* **5.** viewed independently; not comparative or relative: *absolute position.* **6.** *Gram.* **a.** (of a phrase) not explicitly connected with any other element in the sentence, as *It being Monday* in *It being Monday, she had to start work early.* **b.** (of a transitive verb) used with no object expressed, as *to give* in *the collectors for the charity asked him to give.* **c.** (of an adjective) having its noun understood, not expressed, as *poor* in *the poor are always with us.* **d.** (of a possessive pronoun) used independently as a noun phrase, as *mine* in *mine was the objection.* **e.** characterising the phonetic or phonemic form of a word or phrase occurring by itself, not influenced by surrounding forms. Example: *not* in *is not* as opposed to *isn't*, or *will* in *they will* as opposed to *they'll*. **7.** *Physics* **a.** as nearly independent as possible of arbitrary standards or of properties of special substances or systems: *absolute zero of temperature*. **b.** relating to a system of units based on some primary units, especially units of length, mass, and time: *SI units are absolute units*. **c.** relating to a measurement based on an absolute zero or unit: *absolute pressure*. **8.** *Law* (of a court order, decree, etc.) unconditional; having full effect immediately (opposed to *nisi*). *–phr.* **9. the Absolute**, *Metaphysics* (*sometimes lower case*) **a.** that which is free from any restriction, or is unconditioned; the ultimate ground of all things. **b.** that which is independent of some or all relations. **c.** that which is perfect or complete. **–absolutely**, *adv.* **–absoluteness**, *n.*

absolute majority *n.* → **majority** (def. 2).

absolute zero *n.* the unattainable lower limit to temperature, or that temperature at which the particles whose motion constitutes heat would be at rest, being defined as **zero kelvin** (-273.15 degrees Celsius or -459.67 degrees Fahrenheit).

absolution /ˌæbsəˈluʃən/ *n.* **1.** the act of absolving; release from consequences, obligations, or penalties. **2.** the state of being absolved. **3.** *Roman Catholic Theology* a remission of sin or of the punishment due to sin, which the priest, on the ground of authority received from Christ, makes in the sacrament of penance.

absolve /əbˈzɒlv/ *v.t.* **1.** (sometimes fol. by *from*) to free from the consequences or penalties of actions: *to absolve someone from blame*. **2.** (sometimes fol. by *from*) to set free or release, as from some duty, obligation, or responsibility: *absolved from his oath*. **3.** to grant pardon for. **–absolvable**, *adj.* **–absolvent**, *adj.*, *n.* **–absolver**, *n.*

absorb /əbˈsɔb, -ˈzɔb/ *v.t.* **1.** to suck up or drink in (liquids): *this cloth will absorb the milk*. **2.** to take in; assimilate: *the newcomers were quickly absorbed into the group; the student absorbed all the facts*. **3.** to take up or receive in by chemical or molecular action. **4.** to take in without echo or reaction: *to absorb sound*. **–absorbable**, *adj.* **–absorbability** /əbˌsɔbəˈbɪləti, -ˌzɔb-/, *n.*

absorbent /əbˈsɔbənt, -ˈzɔ-/ *adj.* **1.** capable of absorbing; performing the function of absorption. *–n.* **2.** a thing that absorbs. **–absorbency**, *n.*

absorption /əbˈsɔpʃən, -ˈzɔp-/ *n.* **1.** the act or process of absorbing. **2.** the state of being absorbed. **3.** preoccupation. **–absorptive**, *adj.* **–absorptiveness**, *n.*

abstain /əbˈsteɪn/ *v.i.* **1.** to refrain deliberately from casting one's vote. **2. abstain from**, to refrain voluntarily, especially from drinking or enjoying something: *abstain from drinking alcohol*. **–abstainer**, *n.*

abstemious /əbˈstimiəs/ *adj.* **1.** sparing in diet; moderate in the use of food and drink; temperate. **2.** characterised by abstinence: *an abstemious life*. **3.** sparing: *an abstemious diet*. **–abstemiously**, *adv.* **–abstemiousness**, *n.*

abstention /əbˈstɛnʃən/ *n.* **1.** a holding off or refraining; abstinence from action. **2.** a deliberate withholding of one's vote. **–abstentious**, *adj.*

abstinence /ˈæbstənəns/ *n.* **1.** forbearance from any indulgence of appetite, especially from the drinking of alcohol: *total abstinence*. **2.** self-restraint; forbearance. **–abstinent**, *adj.* **–abstinently**, *adv.*

abstract *adj.* /ˈæbstrækt/ **1.** conceived apart from matter and from special cases: *an abstract number*. **2.** theoretical; not applied: *abstract science*. **3.** of or relating to abstract art. *–n.* /ˈæbstrækt/ **4.** a summary of a statement, document, speech, etc. **5.** that which concentrates in itself the essential qualities of anything more

extensive or more general, or of several things; essence. **6.** an idea or term considered apart from some material basis or object. *–v.t.* **7.** /əbˈstrækt/ to draw or take away; remove. **8.** /əbˈstrækt/ to withdraw or divert (the attention). **9.** /əbˈstrækt/ to consider as a general object apart from special circumstances: *to abstract the notions of time, space, or matter*. **10.** /ˈæbstrækt/ to summarise. *–phr.* /ˈæbstrækt/ **11. the abstract**, the ideal. **–abstracter** /əbˈstræktə/, *n.* **–abstractly**, *adv.* **–abstractness**, *n.*

abstracted /əbˈstræktəd/ *adj.* lost in thought; preoccupied. **–abstractedly**, *adv.* **–abstractedness**, *n.*

abstraction /əbˈstrækʃən/ *n.* **1.** an abstract or general idea or expression. **2.** an impractical idea. **3.** an act of abstracting. **4.** a state of being lost in thought; reverie. **5.** *Art* a work of abstract art either without any relation to natural objects (**pure abstraction**) or with representation of them through geometrical or generalised forms (**near abstraction**).

abstract noun *n.* a noun having an abstract meaning, as *honesty*. Compare **concrete noun**.

abstruse /əbˈstrus/ *adj.* difficult to understand; esoteric: *abstruse questions*. **–abstrusely**, *adv.* **–abstruseness**, *n.*

absurd /əbˈsɜd, -ˈzɜd/ *adj.* **1.** contrary to reason or common sense; obviously false or foolish; logically contradictory; ridiculous: *an absurd statement*. **2.** comical; laughable. **–absurdity, absurdness**, *n.* **–absurdly**, *adv.*

abundant /əˈbʌndənt/ *adj.* **1.** present in great quantity; fully sufficient: *an abundant supply*. *–phr.* **2. abundant in**, possessing in great quantity; abounding in: *a river abundant in salmon*. **–abundance**, *n.* **–abundantly**, *adv.*

abuse *v.t.* /əˈbjuz/ **1.** to use wrongly or improperly; misuse: *he abused his position of authority*. **2.** to do wrong to; injure. **3.** to speak insultingly to. **4.** to inflict a sexual act on (a person), especially one whose relationship or proximity makes them vulnerable. *–n.* /əˈbjus/ **5.** wrong or improper use; misuse. **6.** consumption or use of something specified to an excessive degree or in an inappropriate manner: *drug abuse*; *alcohol abuse*. **7.** insulting or violent language. **8.** ill treatment of a person. **9.** sexual violation, as rape or sexual assault, especially of a child. **–abusive**, *adj.* **–abuser**, *n.*

abut /əˈbʌt/ *v.i.* (**abutted, abutting**) (sometimes fol. by *on* or *against*) to be adjacent to: *this piece of land abuts on a street*. **–abuttal**, *n.*

abysmal /əˈbɪzməl/ *adj.* **1.** of or like an abyss. **2.** immeasurable: *abysmal ignorance*. **3.** immeasurably bad: *an abysmal performance*. **–abysmally**, *adv.*

abyss /əˈbɪs/ *n.* **1.** a very deep chasm. **2.** any deep, immeasurable space. **3.** anything profound and unfathomable: *the abyss of time*. **–abyssal**, *adj.*

ac- variant of **ad-** (by assimilation) before *c* and *qu*, as in *accede, acquire*, etc.

-ac an adjective suffix meaning 'relating to', as in *elegiac, cardiac*.

acacia /əˈkeɪʃə, əˈkeɪsiə/ *n.* **1.** any tree or shrub of the mimosaceous genus *Acacia*, native in warm regions; usually known as wattle in Australia. **2.** any of certain related plants. **3.** → **gum arabic**.

academic /ˌækəˈdɛmɪk/ *adj.* **1.** relating to higher education, as at a college, university, or academy. **2.** theoretical or intellectual; not related to practical skills: *an academic subject*; *an academic question*. **3.** having an aptitude for learning or study. *–n.* **4.** a teacher or researcher in a university or college. **–academically**, *adv.*

academy /əˈkædəmi/ *n.* (*pl.* **-mies**) **1.** an association or institution for the promotion of literature, science, or art: *the Academy of Arts and Letters*. **2.** a school for instruction in a particular art or science: *a military academy.*

accede /ək'sid/ *v.i.* (-ceded, -ceding) **1.** to give consent; agree; yield: *to accede to terms.* **2.** to come, as to an office or dignity: *to accede to the throne.* –**accedence**, *n.* –**acceder**, *n.*

accelerate /ək'sɛləreɪt, æk-/ *v.t.* **1.** to cause to move or advance faster: *accelerate growth.* **2.** *Physics* to change the magnitude and/or direction of the velocity of (a body). **3.** *Educ.* to cause (a child) to move through grades of learning faster than is the norm, because of their greater aptitude. –*v.i.* **4.** to become faster; increase in speed. –**acceleration**, *n.* –**accelerative**, *adj.*

accelerator /ək'sɛləreɪtə, æk-/ *n.* **1.** Also, **accelerant**. *Chem.* any substance that increases the speed of a chemical change. **2.** *Motor Vehicles* a device which increases the speed of the machine by opening the throttle, especially one operated by the foot. **3.** *Physics* a device for producing high-energy particles, as a cyclotron.

accent *n.* /'æksənt/ **1.** the degree or pattern of stress or pitch that forms the special character of a vowel or syllable. **2.** *Gram.* a mark showing stress, pitch, or vowel quality, etc. **3.** *Poetry* regularly repeated stress. **4.** a characteristic style of pronunciation: *foreign accent.* **5.** *Music* **a.** (a mark showing) stress or emphasis given to certain notes. **b.** stress or emphasis regularly repeated as part of rhythm. **6.** (*pl.*) words or tones expressing some emotion: *he spoke in the accents of love.* **7.** a special character of something, as taste, style, etc. **8.** particular attention or emphasis: *she puts a lot of accent on studying.* –*v.t.* /æk'sɛnt/ **9.** to pronounce with a particular accent. **10.** to mark (writing, music) with an accent. **11.** to stress; accentuate. –**accentual**, *adj.*

accentuate /ək'sɛntʃueɪt/ *v.t.* **1.** to emphasise. **2.** to mark or pronounce with an accent. –**accentuation** /ək,sɛntʃu-'eɪʃən/, *n.*

accept /ək'sɛpt/ *v.t.* **1.** to take or receive (something offered) usually with approval or agreement: *to accept a gift; accept an invitation.* **2.** to agree to; admit as valid or satisfactory: *to accept an excuse; accept the report of a committee.* **3.** to take responsibility for (duties of office, order for payment, etc.). **4.** to put up with; accommodate oneself to: *I will have to accept the situation.* **5.** to believe: *to accept a fact.* –**acceptance**, *n.*

acceptable /ək'sɛptəbəl/ *adj.* **1.** capable or worthy of being accepted. **2.** pleasing to the receiver; agreeable; welcome. –**acceptability** /əksɛptə'bɪləti/, **acceptableness**, *n.* –**acceptably**, *adv.*

acceptable daily intake *n.* a measure of the amount of a particular substance which can be ingested daily over a long period of time without risk to human health; used of food additives, etc., rather than contaminants. *Abbrev.*: ADI Compare **tolerable daily intake**.

accepted /ək'sɛptəd/ *adj.* customary; established; approved.

access /'æksɛs/ *n.* **1.** (sometimes fol. by *to*) the act or privilege of coming; admittance; approach: *to gain access to a person.* **2.** way, means, or opportunity of approach. **3.** a parent's right to see a child. –*v.t.* **4.** to gain admittance to: *You can access the foyer through this door.* **5.** *Computers* to locate and provide means of getting (information) out of or into a computer storage. –*adj.* **6.** *Radio, TV, etc.* run by special-interest or minority groups who wish to transmit their own programs.

accessible /ək'sɛsəbəl/ *adj.* **1.** easy of access; approachable. **2.** attainable: *accessible evidence.* –*phr.* **3. accessible to**, open to being influenced by: *accessible to bribery.* **4. accessible to** (or **for**), affording easy entry to: *a building accessible to the disabled.* –**accessibility** /əksɛsə'bɪləti/, *n.* –**accessibly**, *adv.*

accession /ək'sɛʃən/ *n.* **1.** the act of coming into the possession of a right, dignity, office, etc.: *accession to the throne.* **2.** an increase by something added: *an accession of territory.* **3.** consent: *accession to a demand.* **4.** *International Law* formal acceptance of a treaty, international convention, or other agreement between states. **5.** the act of coming near; approach. –**accessional**, *adj.*

accessory /ək'sɛsəri/ *n.* (*pl.* -**ries**) **1.** a subordinate part or object; something added or attached for convenience, attractiveness, etc., such as a spotlight, heater, driving mirror, etc., for a vehicle. **2.** (*pl.*) the additional parts of an outfit, as shoes, gloves, hat, handbag, etc. **3.** Also, **accessary**. *Law* the person who is not the chief actor at a felony, nor present at its perpetration, but yet is in some way concerned therein (either before or after the fact committed). –*adj.* **4.** contributing to a general effect; subsidiary: *accessory sounds in music.* –*phr.* *Law* **5. an accessory before the fact**, a person who encourages, counsels or assists a perpetrator before a crime is committed. **6. an accessory after the fact**, a person who assists a perpetrator after a crime is committed. –**accessorial**, *adj.* –**accessorily**, *adv.* –**accessoriness**, *n.*

accident /'æksədənt/ *n.* **1.** an undesirable or unfortunate happening; casualty; mishap. **2.** anything that happens unexpectedly, without design, or by chance. **3.** the operation of chance: *I was there by accident.* **4.** *Philos.* a non-essential circumstance; occasional characteristic. **5.** *Colloq.* a person born from an unplanned pregnancy: *I was definitely an accident.*

accidental /æksə'dɛntl/ *adj.* **1.** happening by chance or accident, or unexpectedly: *an accidental meeting.* **2.** non-essential; incidental; subsidiary: *accidental gains.* **3.** *Music* of or relating to sharps, flats, or naturals not in the key signature. –*n.* **4.** a non-essential or subsidiary circumstance or feature. **5.** *Music* a sign placed in front of a note indicating a sharp, flat, or natural not in the key signature. –**accidentally**, *adv.*

acclaim /ə'kleɪm/ *v.t.* **1.** to salute with words or sounds of joy or approval; applaud. **2.** to announce or proclaim by acclamation. –*n.* **3.** an oral vote, often unanimous, usually taken after the sense of a meeting is clear and unmistakable. –**acclaimer**, *n.*

acclamation /æklə'meɪʃən/ *n.* **1.** a shout or other demonstration of welcome, goodwill, or applause. **2.** the act of acclaiming. **3.** → **acclaim** (def. 3). –**acclamatory** /ə'klæmətri/, *adj.*

acclimatise /ə'klaɪmətaɪz/ *v.t.* **1.** to habituate to a new climate or environment. –*v.i.* **2.** to become habituated to a new climate or environment. Also, **acclimatize**. –**acclimatisable**, *adj.* –**acclimatisation** /əklaɪmətaɪ-'zeɪʃən/, *n.* –**acclimatiser**, *n.*

acclivity /ə'klɪvəti/ *n.* (*pl.* -**ties**) an upward slope, as of ground; an ascent.

accolade /'ækəleɪd/ *n.* **1.** any award, acclamation, or honour. **2.** a ceremony used in conferring knighthood.

accommodate /ə'kɒmədeɪt/ *v.t.* **1.** to do a kindness or a favour to; oblige: *to accommodate a friend.* **2.** to provide with lodging, sometimes including food. **3.** to make suitable or consistent; adapt: *to accommodate oneself to circumstances.* **4.** to bring into harmony; adjust; reconcile: *to accommodate differences.* **5.** to find or provide space for (something). –*v.i.* **6.** to become or be conformable; act conformably; agree. –*phr.* **7. accommodate someone with something**, to supply something suitably to someone. **8. accommodate to**, to adapt to: *his eyes had not accommodated to the glare.* –**accommodator**, *n.*

accommodating /ə'kɒmədeɪtɪŋ/ *adj.* easy to deal with; obliging. –**accommodatingly**, *adv.*

accommodation /əkɒməˈdeɪʃən/ *n.* **1.** the act or process of people or things adapting to a situation or to each other. **2.** a room for a visitor to stay, especially in hotel; lodgings. **3.** a willingness to help others. *–phr.* **4. make accommodation(s) for,** to adjust to suit or to encompass: *to make accommodation for changes of plans.*

accompaniment /əˈkʌmpnimənt/ *n.* **1.** something incidental or added for ornament, symmetry, etc. **2.** *Music* the part of a composition which provides the harmonic and rhythmic backing to a melodic line, especially a song.

accompany /əˈkʌmpəni, əˈkʌmpni/ *v.t.* **(-nied, -nying) 1.** to go in company with; join in action: *to accompany a friend on a walk.* **2.** to be or exist in company with: *thunder accompanies lightning.* **3.** *Music* to play or sing an accompaniment to. *–phr.* **4. accompany with,** to put in company with; associate with: *he accompanies his speech with gestures.* **–accompanist,** *n.*

accomplice /əˈkʌmpləs, -ˈkɒm-/ *n.* an associate in a crime; partner in wrongdoing.

accomplish /əˈkʌmplɪʃ, -ˈkɒm-/ *v.t.* **1.** to bring to pass; carry out; perform; finish: *to accomplish one's mission.* **2.** to complete (a distance or period of time). **3.** to make complete; equip perfectly. **–accomplishable,** *adj.* **–accomplisher,** *n.*

accomplished /əˈkʌmplɪʃt, -ˈkɒm-/ *adj.* **1.** completed; effected: *an accomplished fact.* **2.** perfected in knowledge or training; expert: *an accomplished scholar.* **3.** perfected in the graces and attainments of polite society.

accomplishment /əˈkʌmplɪʃmənt, -ˈkɒm-/ *n.* **1.** the act of carrying into effect; fulfilment: *the accomplishment of our desires.* **2.** anything accomplished; achievement: *the accomplishments of scientists.* **3.** *(oft. pl.)* an acquired art or grace; polite attainment.

accord /əˈkɔd/ *v.t.* **1.** to make to agree or correspond; adapt. **2.** to grant; concede: *to accord due praise. –n.* **3.** just correspondence of things; harmony of relation. **4.** consent or concurrence of opinions or wills; agreement. **5.** an international agreement; settlement of questions outstanding between nations. *–phr.* **6. accord with,** to be in agreement or harmony with; correspond: *this accords with my understanding of the situation.* **7. in accord,** in harmony or agreement. **8. of one accord,** in agreement. **9. of one's own accord,** voluntarily. **10. with one accord,** with spontaneous agreement. **–accordable,** *adj.* **–accorder,** *n.*

accordance /əˈkɔdns/ *n.* **1.** agreement; conformity. *–phr.* **2. in accordance with,** in line with: *in accordance with your wishes.* **–accordant,** *adj.*

according /əˈkɔdɪŋ/ *adj.* **1.** agreeing. *–phr.* **2. according as,** conformably or proportionately as. **3. according to, a.** in accordance with: *according to the instructions.* **b.** proportionately with. **c.** on the authority of; as stated by. **–accordingly,** *adv.*

accordion /əˈkɔdiən/ *n.* **1.** a portable wind instrument with bellows and button-like keys sounded by means of metallic reeds. **2.** a piano accordion. *–adj.* **3.** having folds like the bellows of an accordion: *accordion pleats; accordion door.* **–accordionist,** *n.*

accost /əˈkɒst/ *v.t.* **1.** to approach, especially to ask a question, make a request, or confront with an accusation, etc. **2.** (of a prostitute) to solicit (a client).

accouchement /əˈkuʃmənt, -ˈkuʃ-/ *n.* period of confinement in childbirth; labour.

account /əˈkaʊnt/ *n.* **1.** a verbal or written recital of particular transactions and events; narrative: *an account of everything as it happened.* **2.** an explanatory statement of conduct, as to a superior. **3.** a statement of reasons, causes, etc., explaining some event. **4.** consequence; importance: *things of no account.* **5.** estimation; reckoning: *by his own account.* **6.** profit; advantage: *to turn something to account.* **7.** a statement of pecuniary transactions. **8.** a bill, as for service rendered or goods purchased: *the petrol account; the electricity account.* **9.** *Bookkeeping* **a.** a formal record of the debits and credits relating to the person named (or caption placed) at the head of the ledger account. **b.** a balance of a specified period's receipts and expenditures. **10.** a relationship between a person and a financial institution which implies regularity of trading between the two and the keeping of formal records of this trading by the financial institution: *I have an account with the Commonwealth Bank.* **11.** such a relationship with a department store, garage, etc., which allows the provision of goods and services without immediate cash payment and sometimes with special privileges. **12.** *Computers* an authorisation to access a database, network, website, etc. *–v.i.* **13.** to render an account, especially of money. *–v.t.* **14.** to count; consider as: *I account myself well paid. –phr.* **15. account for, a.** to give an explanation of: *to account for the accident.* **b.** to take responsibility for: *to account for shortages.* **c.** to cause the death, defeat, etc., of: *he accounted for ten of the enemy.* **16. account to,** to assign or impute to. **17. bring** (or **call**) **to account,** to demand explanation or justification of the actions of (someone). **18. by all accounts,** according to all reports. **19. give a good account of oneself,** to acquit oneself well. **20. on account of, a.** because of; by reason of. **b.** for the sake of. **21. on all accounts,** for all reasons or considerations. **22. on** (or **to**) **account,** as an interim payment. **23. on someone's account,** on someone's behalf: *I was acting on your account at the time.* **24. of little account,** of little worth or value. **25. take into account,** to take into consideration; allow for.

accountable /əˈkaʊntəbəl/ *adj.* **1.** liable to be called to account; responsible (*to* a person, *for* an act, etc.): *I am not accountable to any man for my deeds.* **2.** capable of being explained. **–accountability** /əkaʊntəˈbɪləti/, **accountableness,** *n.* **–accountably,** *adv.*

accountant /əˈkaʊntənt/ *n.* a person whose profession is analysing and communicating financial information and maintaining financial records for an organisation. **–accountancy,** *n.* **–accountantship,** *n.*

accounting /əˈkaʊntɪŋ/ *n.* the theory and system of setting up, maintaining, and auditing the books of a firm; the art of analysing the financial position and operating results of a business firm from a study of its sales, purchases, overheads, etc. (distinguished from *bookkeeping* in that a bookkeeper only makes the proper entries in books set up to the accountant's plan).

accoutrement /əˈkutrəmənt/ *n.* **1.** *(pl.)* equipage; trappings. **2.** *(pl.)* the equipment of a soldier except arms and clothing. **3.** a particular item of dress (def. 2) or equipment. Also, *US,* **accouterment.**

accredit /əˈkrɛdət/ *v.t.* **1.** to furnish (an officially recognised agent) with credentials: *to accredit an envoy.* **2.** to certify as meeting official requirements. **3.** to bring into credit; invest with credit or authority. **4.** to believe. *–phr.* **5. accredit to,** to attribute to; consider as belonging to: *a discovery accredited to Edison.* **6. accredit someone with something,** to ascribe or attribute to: *she was accredited with having said it.* **–accreditation** /əkrɛdəˈteɪʃən/, *n.*

accretion /əˈkriʃən/ *n.* **1.** an increase by natural growth or by gradual external addition; growth in size or extent. **2.** the result of this process. **3.** an extraneous addition: *the last part of the legend is a later accretion.* **4.** the growing together of separate parts into a single whole. **–accretive,** *adj.*

accrue /əˈkru/ *verb* **(-crued, -cruing)** *–v.i.* **1.** to accumulate in the course of time. *–v.t.* **2.** to collect over a period of time: *to accrue points.* –**accrual, accrue-ment**, *n.*

acculturation /əkʌltʃə'reɪʃən/ *n.* **1.** the process of borrowing between cultures, marked by the continuous transmission of elements and traits between different peoples and resulting in new and blended patterns. **2.** the modification of one culture through direct and prolonged contact with another, usually more technologically complex, culture (distinguished from *assimilation*). **3.** the process of socialisation. –**acculturative** /ə'kʌltʃərətɪv/, *adj.*

accumulate /ə'kjumjəleɪt/ *v.t.* **1.** to heap up; gather as into a mass; collect. –*v.i.* **2.** to grow into a heap or mass; form an increasing quantity: *public evils accumulate.* –**accumulation**, *n.* –**accumulative**, *adj.*

accumulator /ə'kjumjəleɪtə/ *n. Elect.* a secondary cell, or battery of secondary cells connected in series or parallel, used for storing electrical energy; a storage battery.

accurate /'ækjərət/ *adj.* **1.** exactly conforming to truth, to a standard or rule, or to a model; free from error or defect: *an accurate account of the incident.* **2.** showing precision; meticulous: *an accurate typist.* –**accuracy, accurateness**, *n.* –**accurately**, *adv.*

accursed /ə'kɜsəd, ə'kɜst/ *adj.* **1.** subject to a curse; ruined. **2.** worthy of curses; detestable. Also, **accurst**. –**accursedly** /ə'kɜsədli/, *adv.* –**accursedness** /ə'kɜsədnəs/, *n.*

accusation /ˌækju'zeɪʃən/ *n.* **1.** a charge of wrongdoing; imputation of guilt or blame. **2.** the specific offence charged: *the accusation is murder.* **3.** the act of accusing or charging.

accusatory /ə'kjuzətəri, -tri/ *adj.* containing an accusation; accusing: *he looked at the jury with an accusatory expression.*

accuse /ə'kjuz/ *v.t.* **1.** to bring a charge against; charge with the fault or crime (*of*). **2.** to blame. –**accuser**, *n.* –**accusing**, *adj.* –**accusingly**, *adv.*

accused /ə'kjuzd/ *adj.* **1.** charged with a crime or the like. –*n.* **2.** the defendant or defendants in a criminal law case.

accustom /ə'kʌstəm/ *v.t.* to familiarise by custom or use; habituate: *to accustom oneself to cold weather.*

accustomed /ə'kʌstəmd/ *adj.* **1.** customary; habitual: *in their accustomed manner.* –*phr.* **2. accustomed to, a.** in the habit of: *accustomed to rising early.* **b.** used to or inured to: *accustomed to chronic pain.*

ac-dc /ˌeɪsiˌsiˈdiˌsiˈ/ *adj.* **1.** of or relating to an electric device, as a radio, which can operate from either an alternating current or direct current power source. **2.** *Colloq.* bisexual; attracted to both males and females as sexual partners.

ace /eɪs/ *n.* **1.** a playing card or die marked with a single spot. **2.** *Tennis, etc.* a successful serve which the opponent fails to touch. **3.** a very small amount or degree: *within an ace of winning.* **4.** a highly skilled person; expert: *an ace at dancing.* **5.** a fighter pilot who has shot down five or more enemy aeroplanes. –*adj.* **6.** excellent; agreeable; outstanding.

-aceous a suffix of adjectives used in scientific terminology, indicating: **1.** of or relating to, as in *sebaceous.* **2.** of the nature of, or similar to, as in *cretaceous.* **3.** belonging to a scientific grouping, especially a botanic family, as in *liliaceous.*

acerbity /ə'sɜbəti/ *n.* **1.** sourness, with roughness or astringency of taste. **2.** harshness or severity, as of temper or expression. –**acerbic**, *adj.*

acetate /'æsəteɪt/ *n.* a salt or ester of acetic acid.

acetic /ə'sitɪk, ə'sɛtɪk/ *adj.* of or relating to vinegar or acetic acid.

acetic acid *n.* a colourless liquid, CH_3COOH, the essential constituent of vinegar, used in the manufacture of acetate rayon and the production of numerous esters as solvents and flavouring agents. –**acetous**, *adj.*

acetone /'æsətoʊn/ *n.* a colourless, volatile, flammable liquid, CH_3COCH_3, (a ketone) formed in the distillation of acetates, etc., used as a solvent and in smokeless powders, varnishes, etc.

acetylene /ə'sɛtəlin, -lən/ *n.* a colourless gas, C_2H_2, prepared by the action of water on calcium carbide, used in metal welding and cutting, as an illuminant, and in organic synthesis.

ache /eɪk/ *v.i.* (**ached, aching**) **1.** to suffer pain; have or be in continuous pain: *his whole body ached.* **2.** to be eager; yearn; long. –*n.* **3.** pain of some duration, in opposition to sudden twinges or spasmodic pain. **4.** a longing. –**achingly**, *adv.* –**achage**, *n.* –**achy, achey**, *adj.*

achieve /ə'tʃiv/ *v.t.* **1.** to bring to a successful end; carry through; accomplish. **2.** to bring about, as by effort; gain or obtain: *to achieve victory.* –*v.i.* **3.** to accomplish some enterprise; bring about a result intended. –**achievable**, *adj.* –**achiever**, *n.*

achievement /ə'tʃivmənt/ *n.* **1.** something accomplished, especially by valour, boldness, or superior ability; a great or heroic deed. **2.** the act of achieving; accomplishment: *the achievement of one's object.*

Achilles heel /ə,kɪliz 'hil/ *n.* a single major weakness or point of vulnerability.

Achilles tendon /əkɪliz 'tɛndən/ *n.* the tendon joining the calf muscles to the heel bone.

achkan /'atʃkan/ *n.* a type of long coat reaching to the knees and having buttons down the front, worn by Indian men.

achromatic /eɪkrə'mætɪk/ *adj.* of colour perceived to have no saturation, and therefore no hue, such as neutral greys. –**achromatically**, *adv.*

acid¹ /'æsəd/ *n.* **1.** *Chem.* a compound (usually having a sour taste and capable of neutralising alkalis and reddening blue litmus paper) containing hydrogen which can be replaced by certain metals or an electropositive group to form a salt. Acids are proton donors, and yield hydronium ions in water solution. **2.** a substance with a sour taste. –*adj.* **3.** *Chem.* **a.** belonging or relating to acids or the anhydrides of acids. **b.** having only a part of the hydrogen of an acid replaced by a metal or its equivalent: *an acid phosphate.* **4.** tasting sharp or sour. **5.** sour; sharp; ill-tempered. –*phr.* *Colloq.* **6. come the acid over**, *NZ* to act sharply or viciously towards. **7. put the acid on**, *Aust., NZ* to ask something of (someone) in such a manner that refusal is difficult; pressure (someone). **8. take the acid off**, *Aust., NZ* to cease to pressure (someone). –**acidic** /ə'sɪdɪk/, *adj.* –**acidify**, *v.* –**acidity**, *n.*

acid² /'æsəd/ *n.* **1.** *Colloq.* LSD. –*phr.* **2. drop acid**, to take LSD.

acid house *n.* a blend of rap music and disco with a heavy beat, which incorporates sampled industrial sounds, vocal phrases, laughs and screams, and which is played at dance parties, often as a background to drug taking.

acid rain *n.* highly acidic rain, caused by pollution in the atmosphere.

acid test *n. Colloq.* a critical test; final analysis.

acidulous /ə'sɪdʒələs/ *adj.* slightly acid.

-acious an adjective suffix made by adding **-ous** to nouns ending in **-acity** (the *-ty* being dropped), indicating a tendency towards or abundance of something, as *audacious.*

-acity a suffix of nouns denoting quality or a state of being, and the like.

acknowledge /ək'nɒlɪdʒ/ v.t. (**-edged, -edging**) **1.** to admit to be real or true; recognise the existence of: *to acknowledge the need for help.* **2.** to show recognition of: *she acknowledged him with a wave.* **3.** to recognise the authority or claims of: *to acknowledge his right to vote.* **4.** to indicate thanks for: *I gratefully acknowledge your help.* **5.** to admit the receipt of: *to acknowledge a letter.* –**acknowledgement, acknowledgment,** *n.* –**acknowledgeable, acknowledgable,** *adj.* –**acknowledger,** *n.*

acknowledgement of country *n.* the official recognition of the Indigenous traditional custodians of a locality, given in the preamble to a public event, meeting, etc.

acme /'ækmi/ *n.* the highest point; culmination.

acne /'ækni/ *n.* an inflammatory disease of the sebaceous glands, characterised by an eruption (often pustular) of the skin, especially of the face. –**acned,** *adj.*

acolyte /'ækəlaɪt/ *n.* **1.** an altar attendant of minor rank. **2.** *Roman Catholic Church* one of the two minor orders, the other being that of lector. **3.** an attendant; an assistant.

acorn /'eɪkɔn/ *n.* the fruit of the oak, a nut in a hardened scaly cup.

acoustic /ə'kustɪk/ *adj.* **1.** Also, **acoustical.** of or relating to to the sense or organs of hearing, or with the science of sound. **2.** *Music* of or relating to instruments whose sound is not electronically amplified, as acoustic guitar, acoustic bass, as opposed to electric guitar and electric bass. –**acoustically,** *adv.*

acoustics /ə'kustɪks/ *n.* **1.** *Physics* the science of sound. **2.** (*construed as pl.*) acoustic properties, as of an auditorium. –**acoustician** /æku'stɪʃən/, *n.*

acquaint /ə'kweɪnt/ *v.t.* (sometimes fol. by *with*) to make familiar or conversant; furnish with knowledge; inform: *to acquaint him with our plan; to acquaint a friend with one's efforts.*

acquaintance /ə'kweɪntəns/ *n.* **1.** a person (or persons) known to one, especially a person with whom one is not on terms of great intimacy. **2.** the state of being acquainted; personal knowledge. –**acquaintanceship,** *n.*

acquiesce /ˌækwi'ɛs/ *v.i.* (**-esced, -escing**) to assent tacitly; comply quietly; agree; consent. –**acquiescence,** *n.* –**acquiescent,** *adj.* –**acquiescently,** *adv.*

acquire /ə'kwaɪə/ *v.t.* **1.** to come into possession of; get as one's own: *to acquire property, a title, etc.* **2.** to gain for oneself through one's actions or efforts: *to acquire learning, a reputation, etc.* –**acquirement,** *n.* –**acquirable,** *adj.* –**acquirer,** *n.*

acquired immune deficiency syndrome *n.* → AIDS.

acquisition /ækwə'zɪʃən/ *n.* **1.** the act of acquiring or gaining possession: *the acquisition of property.* **2.** something acquired: *a valued acquisition.* –*v.t.* **3.** to order and acquire (new material, as books for a library). –**acquisitionist,** *n.*

acquisitive /ə'kwɪzətɪv/ *adj.* tending to make acquisitions; fond of acquiring possessions: *an acquisitive society.* –**acquisitively,** *adv.* –**acquisitiveness,** *n.*

acquit /ə'kwɪt/ *v.t.* (**-quitted, -quitting**) **1.** (sometimes fol. by *of*) to relieve from a charge of fault or crime; pronounce not guilty. **2.** to release or discharge (a person) from an obligation. **3.** to settle (a debt, obligation, claim, etc.). –*phr.* **4. acquit oneself, a.** to behave; bear or conduct oneself. **b.** to clear oneself: *she acquitted herself of suspicion.* –**acquittal,** *n.* –**acquitter,** *n.*

acre /'eɪkə/ *n.* **1.** a unit of land measurement in the imperial system, equal to 4840 square yards or 160 perches, and equivalent to 4046.856 422 4 m² (approximately 0.405 hectares). *Symbol:* ac **2.** (*pl.*) fields or land in general. **3.** (*pl. construed as sing.*) *Colloq.* a large amount: *there was acres of food at the picnic.*

acreage /'eɪkərɪdʒ/ *n.* **1.** acres collectively; extent in acres. **2.** *Aust.* a large allotment of land comprising a number of acres, in a rural area: *they've built on acreage.*

acrid /'ækrəd/ *adj.* **1.** sharp or biting to the smell or taste; bitterly pungent; irritating. **2.** irritating to the feelings; sharp: *acrid remarks.* –**acridity** /ə'krɪdəti/, **acridness,** *n.* –**acridly,** *adv.*

acrimony /'ækrəməni/, *Orig. US* /-mooni/ *n.* sharpness or severity of temper; bitterness of expression proceeding from anger or ill nature. –**acrimonious** /ækrə'mooniəs/, *adj.*

acro- a word element meaning 'tip', 'top', 'apex', or 'edge', as in *acrogen.* Also, (*before vowels*), **acr-.**

acrobat /'ækrəbæt/ *n.* **1.** a skilled performer who can walk on a tightrope, perform on a trapeze, or do other similar feats. **2.** someone who makes striking changes of opinion, as in politics, etc. –**acrobatic** /ækrə'bætɪk/, *adj.* –**acrobatically** /ækrə'bætɪkli/, *adv.*

acrobatics /ækrə'bætɪks/ *n.* **1.** (*construed as sing.*) the feats of an acrobat; gymnastics. **2.** (*construed as pl.*) skilled tricks like those of an acrobat.

acronym /'ækrənɪm/ *n.* **1.** a word formed from the initial letters of a sequence of words, as *radar* (from *radio detection and ranging*) or *ANZAC* (from *Australian and New Zealand Army Corps*). **2.** an initialism.

acropolis /ə'krɒpələs/ *n.* the citadel of an ancient Greek city.

across /ə'krɒs/ *prep.* **1.** from side to side of: *a bridge across a river.* **2.** on the other side of: *across the sea.* **3.** unexpectedly into contact with: *we came across our friends.* –*adv.* **4.** from one side to another: *I came across in a boat.* **5.** on the other side: *we'll soon be across.* –*phr.* **6. be across,** to have an understanding of: *to be across the complexities of the design.*

across-the-board *adj.* embracing all categories; general: *an across-the-board increase.*

acrostic /ə'krɒstɪk/ *n.* a series of lines or verses in which the first, last, or other particular letters form a word, phrase, the alphabet, etc.

acrylic /ə'krɪlɪk/ *adj.* **1.** of or relating to fibres formed by the polymerisation of acrylonitrile. **2.** of or relating to fabrics woven from such fibres. **3.** of or relating to items, such as pieces of furniture, kitchen utensils, etc., made from such fibres. –*n.* **4.** an acrylic fabric, such as orlon. **5.** → **acrylic colour.**

acrylic acid *n.* a colourless, corrosive liquid, $CH_2=CH-CO_2H$, used in the manufacture of polymerised fibres and coatings; propenoic acid.

acrylic colour *n.* → acrylic paint. Also, **acrylic color.**

acrylic paint *n.* artist's colour based on acrylic polymer resin and mixed with water or an acrylic medium. Also, **acrylic, acrylic colour, acrylic polymer colour, polymer colour.**

acrylic resin *n.* one of the group of thermoplastic resins formed by polymerising the esters or amides of acrylic acid, used chiefly when transparency is desired. Perspex and plexiglas are in this group.

acrylonitrile /ˌækrɪloʊ'naɪtraɪl/ *n.* a colourless toxic organic chemical, $CH_2.CHCN$, used in the manufacture of acrylic fibres, thermoplastics, synthetic rubber, etc.

act /ækt/ *n.* **1.** anything done or performed; a doing; deed. **2.** the process of doing: *caught in the act.* **3.** (*oft. upper case*) a decree, edict, law, statute, judgement, resolve, or award, especially a decree passed by a legislature: *an act of Parliament.* **4.** a deed of instrument recording a transaction. **5.** one of the main divisions of a play or opera. **6.** an individual performance forming part of a variety show, radio program, etc.: *a juggling act.* **7.** behaviour which is contrived and artificial, somewhat in the manner of a theatrical performance: *he's not really an ocker – it's just an act.* *–v.i.* **8.** to do something; exert energy or force; be employed or operative: *her mind acts quickly.* **9.** to be employed or operate in a particular way; perform specific duties or functions: *to act as chairperson.* **10.** to have effect; perform a function: *the medicine failed to act.* **11.** to perform a specific function: *the stick will act as a lever.* **12.** to behave: *to act well under pressure.* **13.** to pretend. **14.** to perform as an actor: *did she ever act on the stage?* **15.** to be capable of being acted on the stage: *his plays don't act well.* *–v.t.* **16.** to represent (an imaginary or historical character) with one's person: *to act Macbeth.* **17.** to feign; counterfeit: *to act outraged virtue.* **18.** to behave as suitable for: *act your age.* **19.** to behave as: *he acted the fool.* *–phr.* **20.** act for, to serve or substitute for. **21. act of defiance,** a deliberate action calculated to disobey or offend someone who is attempting to establish their authority. **22. act on** (or **upon**), **a.** to act in accordance with; follow: *she acted on my suggestion.* **b.** to affect: *alcohol acts on the brain.* **23. act out, a.** to give expression to (an idea, emotion, etc.), either consciously (as in acting or mime) or unconsciously. **b.** to misbehave as a response to an underlying psychological state. **24. act up,** *Colloq.* **a.** to misbehave. **b.** (of a motor vehicle, machine, etc.) to malfunction. **25. bung** (or **stack**) **on an act, a.** to display bad temper. **b.** to behave in a manner especially put on for the occasion. **26. clean up one's act,** *Colloq.* to improve one's behaviour, practices, etc., to meet an acceptable standard. **27. get one's act together,** to become organised and effective.

acting /ˈæktɪŋ/ *adj.* **1.** serving temporarily; substitute: *acting governor.* **2.** that acts; functioning. **3.** provided with stage directions; designed to be used for performance: *an acting version of a play.* *–n.* **4.** performance as an actor. **5.** the occupation of an actor.

action /ˈækʃən/ *n.* **1.** the process or state of acting or of being active. **2.** something done; an act; deed. **3.** (*pl.*) habitual or usual acts; conduct. **4.** energetic activity. **5.** an exertion of power or force: *the action of wind upon a ship's sails.* **6. the action,** the centre of all the excitement: *close to the action.* **7.** *Physiol.* a change in organs, tissues, or cells leading to performance of a function, as in muscular contraction. **8.** way or manner of moving. **9.** the mechanism by which something is operated, as that of a breech-loading rifle or a piano. **10.** *Physics* **a.** a force exerted by one object on a second object (as opposed to *reaction*, the equal and opposite force exerted by the second object on the first). **b.** the difference between the kinetic and potential energies of a mechanical system integrated over time. **11.** a small battle. **12.** military and naval combat. **13.** the main subject or story, as distinguished from an incidental episode. **14.** *Law* **a.** a proceeding instituted by one party against another. **b.** the right of bringing it. *–v.t.* **15.** to take action concerning: *I will action your request.* **16.** to bring about a desired action in relation to (something). *–interj.* **17.** *Film, TV* a cue to actors or subjects after the camera and sound recorder have begun to roll, signalling them to commence their action. *–phr.* **18. be out of action, a.** to be not functional. **b.** to be unable to participate, especially as a result of injury. **19. take action,** to commence legal proceedings. **–actionless,** *adj.*

actionable /ˈækʃənəbəl/ *adj.* furnishing ground for a law suit. **–actionably,** *adv.*

action verb *n. Gram.* → **dynamic verb**.

activate /ˈæktəveɪt/ *v.t.* **1.** to make active. **2.** *Physics* to render radioactive. **3.** to aerate (sewage) as a purification measure. **–activation** /æktəˈveɪʃən/, *n.*

activated carbon *n.* granulated charcoal heated to 800°–1000°C in a current of steam to remove hydrocarbons; highly absorbent of gases and vapours because of its enormous surface area; used in solvent recovery, deodorisation, and as an antidote to certain poisons. Also, **activated charcoal**.

active /ˈæktɪv/ *adj.* **1.** in a state of action; in actual progress or motion: *active hostilities.* **2.** constantly engaged in action; busy: *an active toddler.* **3.** having the power of quick motion; nimble: *an active animal.* **4.** highly involved in some area, activity, etc.: *active in the community; an active environmentalist.* **5.** causing change; capable of exerting influence: *active treason.* **6.** *Gram.* denoting a voice of verb inflection in which the subject is represented as performing the action expressed by the verb (opposed to *passive*). For example, *he writes the letter* (active); *the letter was written* (passive) **7.** requiring action; practical: *the intellectual and the active mental powers.* **8.** (of a volcano) erupting. **9.** *Electronics* (of an electronic component, or a complete circuit) able to amplify or switch a signal. **10.** capable of acting or reacting, especially in some specific manner: *active carbon.* **11.** (of a communications satellite) able to retransmit signals. *–n.* **12.** *Gram.* the active voice. *–phr.* **13. be active,** to be in such good physical health as to be able to undertake customary pursuits and exercise. **–actively,** *adv.* **–activeness,** *n.*

active euthanasia *n.* → **euthanasia**.

activist /ˈæktəvəst/ *n.* a zealous worker for a cause, especially a political cause. **–activism,** *n.*

activity /ækˈtɪvəti/ *n.* (*pl.* **-ties**) **1.** the state of action; doing. **2.** the quality of acting promptly; energy. **3.** a specific deed or action; sphere of action: *social activities.* **4.** liveliness; agility. *–adj.* **5.** of or relating to educational provision made for children or adults with intellectual disabilities, usually involving methods of learning and teaching associated with practical activities: *an activity class.*

act of God *n.* a direct, sudden, and irresistible action of natural forces, such as could not humanly have been foreseen or prevented, for example, tornado, tidal wave, flood, and earth movements.

actor /ˈæktə/ *n.* **1.** someone who plays the part of a character in a dramatic performance. **2.** someone who acts; doer.

actress /ˈæktrəs/ *n.* a female actor.

actual /ˈæktʃuəl/ *adj.* **1.** existing in act or fact; real. **2.** now existing; present: *the actual position of the moon.* **–actualness,** *n.*

actuality /æktʃuˈæləti/ *n.* (*pl.* **-ties**) **1.** actual existence; reality. **2.** (*pl.*) actual conditions or circumstances; facts: *he had to adjust to the actualities of life.*

actually /ˈæktʃuəli, ˈæktʃəli/ *adv.* **1.** as an actual or existing fact; really. **2.** as a matter of fact; indeed: *to actually enjoy oneself.* **3.** as a matter of interest; moreover: *actually, I'm not feeling well.*

actuary /ˈæktʃuəri/, *Orig. US* /ˈæktʃuɛri/ *n.* (*pl.* **-ries**) a statistician who computes risks, rates, etc., according to probabilities indicated by recorded facts. **–actuarial** /æktʃuˈɛəriəl/, *adj.* **–actuarially** /æktʃuˈɛəriəli/, *adv.*

actuate /ˈæktʃueɪt/ *v.t.* **1.** to incite to action: *actuated by selfish motives.* **2.** to put into action. **–actuation** /æktʃuˈeɪʃən/, *n.* **–actuator,** *n.*

acuity /əˈkjuəti/ *n.* sharpness; acuteness: *acuity of vision.*

acumen /ˈækjəmən/ *n.* quickness of perception; mental acuteness; keen insight. **–acuminous** /əˈkjumənəs/, *adj.*

acupressure /ˈækjəprɛʃə, ˈækə-/ *n.* the massage of muscles and application of pressure to acupuncture points to promote wellbeing or to cure illness; shiatsu.

acupuncture /ˈækjəpʌŋktʃə, ˈækə-/ *n.* a Chinese medical practice to treat disease, establish diagnosis or relieve pain, by puncturing specific areas of skin with long sharp needles. **–acupuncturist,** *n.*

acute /əˈkjut/ *adj.* **1.** ending in a sharp point. **2.** sharp in effect; intense: *acute sorrow.* **3.** severe; crucial: *an* *acute shortage.* **4.** (of disease, etc.) brief and severe (opposed to *chronic*). **5.** keen of mind; perceptive: *an acute observer.* **6.** sensitive and accurate: *acute eyesight.* **7.** *Geom.* (of an angle) less than 90°. **8.** *Gram.* of or having a particular accent (´). –**acutely,** *adv.* –**acuteness,** *n.*

-acy a suffix of nouns of quality, state, office, etc., many of which accompany adjectives in *-cious* or nouns or adjectives in *-ate,* as in *efficacy, fallacy,* etc., *advocacy, primacy,* etc., *accuracy, delicacy,* etc.

acyclic /eɪˈsaɪklɪk, eɪˈsɪklɪk/ *adj.* not occurring in cycles; not periodic.

ad /æd/ *n.* **1.** an advertisement. –*adj.* **2.** of or relating to advertising: *an ad agency; in the ad business.*

ad- a prefix of direction, tendency, and addition, attached chiefly to stems not found as words themselves, as in *advert, advent.*

-ad **1.** a suffix forming nouns denoting a collection of a certain number, as in *triad.* **2.** a suffix found in words and names proper to Greek myth, as in *dryad.*

adage /ˈædɪdʒ/ *n.* a proverb.

adagio /əˈdaʒioʊ, -dʒioʊ/ *adv. Music* in a leisurely manner; slowly.

adamant /ˈædəmənt/ *adj.* firm in purpose or opinion; unyielding. –**adamantly,** *adv.*

Adam's apple /ˈædəmz æpəl/ *n.* a projection of the thyroid cartilage at the front of the (male) throat.

adapt /əˈdæpt/ *v.t.* **1.** to make suitable to requirements; adjust or modify fittingly. –*v.i.* **2.** to adjust oneself: *to adapt to new surroundings.* –**adaptation,** *n.* –**adaptive,** *adj.*

adaptable /əˈdæptəbəl/ *adj.* **1.** capable of being adapted. **2.** able to adapt oneself easily to new conditions. –**adaptability** /ədæptəˈbɪləti/, **adaptableness,** *n.*

adaptor /əˈdæptə/ *n.* **1.** a device for fitting together parts having different sizes or designs. **2.** an accessory to convert a machine, tool, etc., to a new or modified use. Also, **adapter.**

add /æd/ *v.t.* **1.** to unite or join so as to increase the number, quantity, size, or importance: *to add another stone to the pile.* **2.** Also, **add up.** to find the sum of. **3.** to say or write further. –*v.i.* Also, **add up. 4.** to perform the arithmetical operation of addition. –*phr.* **5. add in,** to include. **6. add to,** to be or serve as an addition to: *to add to someone's grief.* **7. add up,** **a.** to make the desired or expected total. **b.** to make sense or be logically consistent: *the facts don't add up.* **8. add up to,** to amount to. –**addable, addible,** *adj.*

ADD /eɪ di ˈdi/ *n.* → **attention deficit disorder.**

added value *n.* something added to a product or process which increases its value.

addendum /əˈdɛndəm/ *n.* (*pl.* **-da** /-də/) **1.** a thing to be added; an addition. **2.** an appendix to a book.

adder /ˈædə/ *n.* **1.** the common European viper, *Vipera berus,* a small venomous snake, widespread in northern Eurasia. **2.** any of various other snakes, venomous or harmless, resembling the viper.

addict /ˈædɪkt/ *n.* someone who is addicted to a practice or habit: *a drug addict.* –**addicted,** *adj.* –**addiction,** *n.* –**addictive,** *adj.*

addition /əˈdɪʃən/ *n.* **1.** the act or process of adding or uniting. **2.** the process of uniting two or more numbers into one sum, denoted by the symbol + . **3.** anything added. –*phr.* **4. in addition,** besides. **5. in addition to,** as well as. –**additional,** *adj.*

additive /ˈædətɪv/ *n.* **1.** a substance added to a product, usually to preserve or improve its quality. **2.** something added. –*adj.* **3.** to be added; of the nature of an addition; characterised by addition: *an additive process.* –**additively,** *adv.*

addle /ˈædl/ *v.t.* **1.** to muddle or confuse. –*v.i.* **2.** to become spoiled or rotten, as eggs. –*adj.* **3.** mentally confused; muddled, as in the combination *addlebrained.*

address *n.* /əˈdrɛs, ˈædrɛs/ **1.** a direction as to name and residence inscribed on a letter, etc. **2.** a place where a person lives or may be reached. **3.** *Computers* a number or symbol which identifies a particular register in the memory of a digital computer. **4.** a formal speech or writing directed to a person or a group of persons: *an address on current problems.* **5.** manner of speaking to persons; personal bearing in conversation. **6.** skilful management; adroitness: *to handle a matter with address.* **7.** (*usu. pl.*) attentions paid by a lover; courtship. –*v.t.* /əˈdrɛs/ **8.** to direct for delivery; put a direction on: *to address a letter.* **9.** to make a formal speech to: *the leader addressed the assembly.* **10.** to direct to the ear or attention: *to address a warning to someone.* **11.** to deal with (a problem, question, etc.): *these are the issues you should address in your essay.* **12.** *Golf* to adjust and apply the club to (the ball) in preparing for a stroke. –*phr.* **13. address oneself to,** **a.** to apply in speech to: *she addressed herself to the president.* **b.** to direct one's attention or energy to: *he addressed himself to the work in hand.* –**addresser, addressor,** *n.* –**addressee,** *n.*

adduce /əˈdjus/ *v.t.* (**-duced, -ducing**) to bring forward in argument; cite as pertinent or conclusive: *to adduce reasons.* –**adducible,** *adj.* –**adducer,** *n.*

adduct /əˈdʌkt/ *v.t. Physiol.* to draw towards the main axis (opposed to *abduct*). –**adductive,** *adj.* –**adductor,** *n.*

-ade¹ **1.** a suffix found in nouns denoting action or process, product or result of action, person or persons acting, often irregularly attached, as in *blockade, escapade, masquerade.* **2.** a noun suffix indicating a drink made of a particular fruit, as in *orangeade.*

-ade² a collective suffix, variant of **-ad** (def. 1), as in *decade.*

adeno- a word element meaning 'gland'. Also, (*before vowels*), **aden-.**

adenoid /ˈædənɔɪd/ *n.* **1.** (*oft. in the pl.*) a mass or nodule of lymphoid tissue in the upper pharynx; enlargement can prevent nasal breathing, especially in young children. –*adj.* Also, **adenoidal** /ædəˈnɔɪdl/ **2.** relating to the lymphatic glands.

adept *adj.* /əˈdɛpt/ **1.** highly skilled; proficient; expert. –*n.* /ˈædɛpt/ **2.** someone who has attained proficiency; someone fully skilled in anything. –**adeptly,** *adv.* –**adeptness,** *n.*

adequate /ˈædəkwət/ *adj.* (sometimes fol. by *to* or *for*) equal to the requirement or occasion; fully sufficient, suitable, or fit. –**adequately,** *adv.* –**adequacy, adequateness,** *n.*

ADHD /eɪ di eɪtʃ ˈdi/ *n.* → **attention deficit hyperactivity disorder.**

adhere /ədˈhɪə/ *v.i.* (**-hered, -hering**) **1.** (sometimes fol. by *to*) to stick fast; cleave; cling. –*phr.* **2. adhere to,** **a.** to be devoted to; be attached to as a follower or upholder: *to adhere to a leader; to adhere to a creed.* **b.** to hold closely or firmly to: *to adhere to a plan.* –**adherence,** *n.* –**adherent,** *n.,* *adj.* –**adherer,** *n.*

adhesion /ədˈhiʒən/ *n.* **1.** the act or state of adhering, or of being united: *the adhesion of parts united by growth.* **2.** *Physics* the molecular force exerted across the surface of contact between unlike liquids and solids which resists their separation. **3.** *Pathol.* the abnormal union of adjacent tissues due to inflammation.

adhesive /ədˈhisɪv, -ˈhizɪv/ *adj.* **1.** clinging; tenacious; sticking fast. –*n.* **2.** a substance for sticking things together. –**adhesively,** *adv.* –**adhesiveness,** *n.*

ad hoc /æd ˈhɒk/ *adj.* **1.** for this (special purpose); an **ad hoc committee** is one set up to deal with one subject only. **2.** impromptu; an **ad hoc decision** is one made with regard to the exigencies of the moment. –*adv.* **3.** with respect to this (subject or thing).

adiabatic /ˌædiəˈbætɪk, ˌeɪdaɪəˈbætɪk/ *adj.* without gain or loss of heat (distinguished from *isothermal*). –**adiabatically,** *adv.*

adieu /əˈdju, əˈdjɜ/ *interj.* **1.** goodbye; farewell. –*n.* (*pl.* **adieus** /əˈdjuz, əˈdjɜz/ or **adieux** /əˈdju, əˈdjɜ/) **2.** the act of taking one's leave; a farewell.

ad infinitum /ˌæd ɪnfəˈnaɪtəm/ to infinity; endlessly; without limit.

adipose /ˈædəpoʊs/ *adj.* fatty; of or relating to fat. –**adiposeness, adiposity** /ædəˈpɒsəti/, *n.*

adjacent /əˈdʒeɪsənt/ *adj.* lying near, close, or contiguous; adjoining; neighbouring: *a field adjacent to the main road.* –**adjacency,** *n.* –**adjacently,** *adv.*

adjacent angle *n.* one of two angles having the same vertex and having a common side between them.

adjective /ˈædʒəktɪv/ *n.* **1.** *Gram.* **a.** one of the major word classes in many languages, comprising words that typically modify a noun. **b.** such a word, as *wise* in *a wise ruler,* or in *she is wise.* –*adj.* **2.** *Gram.* relating to an adjective; functioning as an adjective; adjectival. –*phr.* **3. the great Australian adjective,** (*humorous*) bloody (def. 4). –**adjectival** /ædʒəkˈtaɪvəl/, *adj.* –**adjectivally** /ædʒəkˈtaɪvəli/, *adv.*

adjoin /əˈdʒɔɪn/ *v.t.* **1.** to be in connection or contact with; abut on: *his house adjoins the lake.* –*v.i.* **2.** to lie or be next, or in contact. –**adjoining,** *adj.*

adjourn /əˈdʒɜn/ *v.t.* **1.** to suspend the meeting of (a public or private body) to a future day or to another place: *adjourn the court.* –*v.i.* **2.** to postpone, suspend, or transfer proceedings. –**adjournment,** *n.*

adjudge /əˈdʒʌdʒ/ *v.t.* (**-judged, -judging**) **1.** to pronounce formally; decree: *the will was adjudged void.* **2.** to award judicially; assign: *the prize was adjudged to him.* **3.** to deem: *it was adjudged wise to avoid war.* –**adjudgement,** *n.*

adjudicate /əˈdʒudəkeɪt/ *v.t.* **1.** to pronounce or decree by judicial sentence; settle judicially; pass judgement on; to determine (an issue or dispute) judicially. –*v.i.* **2.** (sometimes fol. by *on* or *upon*) to sit in judgement. **3.** to act as a judge in a competition, especially a debating competition. –**adjudication,** *n.* –**adjudicator,** *n.* –**adjudicative** /əˈdʒudəkətɪv/, *adj.*

adjunct /ˈædʒʌŋkt/ *n.* **1.** something added to another thing but not essentially a part of it. **2.** a person joined to another in some duty or service; an assistant. **3.** *Gram.* a modifying form, word, phrase, etc., depending on some other form, word, phrase, etc. –*adj.* **4.** joined to a thing or person, especially subordinately; associated; auxiliary. –**adjunctive,** *adj.*

adjure /əˈdʒʊə/ *v.t.* **1.** to charge, bind, or command, earnestly and solemnly, often under oath or the threat of a curse. **2.** to entreat or request earnestly. –**adjuration** /ædʒəˈreɪʃən/, *n.* –**adjuratory** /əˈdʒʊərətri/, *adj.* –**adjurer, adjuror,** *n.*

adjust /əˈdʒʌst/ *v.t.* **1.** to fit, as one thing to another, make correspondent or conformable; adapt; accommodate: *to adjust things to a standard.* **2.** to put in working order; regulate; bring to a proper state or position: *to adjust an instrument.* **3.** to settle or bring to a satisfactory state, so that parties are agreed in the result: *to adjust differences.* **4.** *Insurance* to fix (the sum to be paid on a claim); settle (a claim). –*v.i.* **5.** to adapt oneself; become adapted. –**adjuster, adjustor,** *n.* –**adjustment,** *n.* –**adjustable,** *adj.* –**adjustably,** *adv.*

adjutant /ˈædʒətənt/ *n.* **1.** *Mil.* a staff officer who assists the commanding officer. **2.** an assistant. –**adjutancy,** *n.*

ad lib /æd ˈlɪb/ *adv.* **1.** freely; in an impromptu manner. –*adj.* **2.** of or relating to an improvised performance. Also, **ad-lib.**

ad-lib /ædˈlɪb/ *verb* (**-libbed, -libbing**) –*v.t.* **1.** to improvise and deliver extemporaneously. –*v.i.* **2.** to improvise, as notes, words or actions, during rehearsal or performance.

administer /ədˈmɪnəstə, æd-/ *v.t.* **1.** to manage (affairs, a government, etc.); have charge of the execution of: *to administer laws.* **2.** to bring into use or operation; dispense: *to administer justice.* **3.** to make application of; give: *to administer medicine.* **4.** to supervise or impose the taking of (an oath, etc.): *to administer an oath.* –*v.i.* **5.** to perform the duties of an administrator. –*phr.* **6. administer to,** to contribute assistance to; bring aid or supplies to: *to administer to the needs of the poor.* –**administrable** /ədˈmɪnəstrəbəl/, *adj.* –**administrant,** *adj., n.*

administration /ədmɪnəsˈtreɪʃən/ *n.* **1.** the management or direction of any office or employment. **2.** the function of a political state in exercising its governmental duties. **3.** any body of people entrusted with administrative powers. **4.** *Chiefly US* the period of service of a government.

administrative /ədˈmɪnəstrətɪv/ *adj.* of or relating to administration; executive: *administrative ability*; *administrative problems.* –**administratively,** *adv.*

administrator /ədˈmɪnəstreɪtə/ *n.* **1.** someone who directs or manages affairs of any kind. **2.** *Law* someone appointed by a court to take charge of the estate of a person who died without appointing an executor. **3.** (*oft. upper case*) **a.** (in Australia) the person exercising the powers of the governor-general or a state governor when they are temporarily absent or incapacitated. **b.** the chief executive of an Australian dependent territory. **4.** *Internet* a person who manages the technical details of a website, in terms of creating levels of access and the structure of the site.

admirable /ˈædmərəbəl/ *adj.* worthy of admiration, exciting approval, reverence or affection; excellent. –**admirableness,** *n.* –**admirably,** *adv.*

admiral /ˈædmərəl/ *n.* **1.** *Navy* **a.** a commissioned officer of the highest rank in the Royal Australian Navy. **b.** the rank. *Abbrev.*: ADML **2.** a naval officer of high rank. **3.** the ship of an admiral; flagship. **4.** any of various butterflies, as the **Australian admiral,** *Vanessa itea.* –**admiralship,** *n.* –**admiralty,** *n.*

admire /ədˈmaɪə/ *v.t.* **1.** to regard with wonder, pleasure, and approbation. –*v.i.* **2.** to feel or express admiration. –**admiration,** *n.* –**admirer,** *n.* –**admiringly,** *adv.*

admissible /ədˈmɪsəbəl/ *adj.* **1.** that may be allowed or conceded; allowable. **2.** *Law* allowable as evidence. –**admissibility** /ədmɪsəˈbɪləti/, **admissibleness,** *n.* –**admissibly,** *adv.*

admission /ədˈmɪʃən/ *n.* **1.** the act of allowing to enter; entrance afforded by permission, by provision or existence of means, or by the removal of obstacles: *the admission of aliens into a country.* **2.** Also, **admission fee, admission charge.** the price paid for entrance, as to an exhibition, museum, etc. **3.** the act or condition of being received or accepted in a position or office; appointment: *admission to the practice of law.* **4.** confession of a charge, an error, or a crime. **5.** an acknowledgement of the truth of something. **6.** a point or statement admitted; concession. **7.** a person admitted into a hospital. **8.** (*pl.*) the section of an institution, as a hospital, university, etc., where people are received, as for treatment, enrolment in a course, etc.

admit /ədˈmɪt/ *verb* (**-mitted, -mitting**) –*v.t.* **1.** to allow to enter; grant or afford entrance to: *to admit a student to college.* **2.** to permit; allow. **3.** to permit to exercise a certain function or privilege: *to admit a lawyer to the bar.* **4.** to allow as valid: *to admit the force of an argument.* **5.** to have capacity for the admission of at one time: *this passage admits two abreast.* **6.** to acknowledge; confess: *he admitted his guilt. –v.i.* **7.** to give access; grant entrance: *this gate admits to the garden. –phr.* **8. admit of,** to leave room for: *this situation admits of no other solution.* **–admittance,** *n.* **–admitter,** *n.*

admittedly /əd'mɪtədli/ *adv.* by acknowledgement; confessedly: *he was admittedly the one who had lost the documents.*

admonish /əd'mɒnɪʃ/ *v.t.* **1.** to counsel against something; caution or advise. **2.** to notify of or reprove for a fault, especially mildly: *to admonish someone as a brother.* **3.** to recall or incite to duty; remind: *to admonish someone about their obligations.* **–admonisher,** *n.* **–admonishingly,** *adv.* **–admonishment,** admonition, *n.*

ad nauseam /æd 'nɔziəm, æd 'nɔsiəm/ *adv.* to a sickening or disgusting extent.

ado /ə'du/ *n.* **1.** activity; bustle; fuss. *–phr.* **2. much ado about nothing,** a great fuss about very little.

adobe /ə'doʊbi/ *n.* a yellow silt or clay, deposited by rivers, used to make bricks.

adolescence /ædə'lɛsəns/ *n.* **1.** the transition period between puberty and adult stages of development; youth. **2.** the quality or state of being in this period; youthfulness. **–adolescent,** *n., adj.*

adopt /ə'dɒpt/ *v.t.* **1.** to choose for or take to oneself; make one's own by selection or assent: *to adopt a name or idea.* **2.** to take (a child born to someone else) to be legally your own child, specifically by a formal legal act. **3.** to vote to accept: *the House adopted the report.* **–adoptable,** *adj.* **–adopter,** *n.* **–adoption,** *n.*

adoptive /ə'dɒptɪv/ *adj.* **1.** related by adoption: *an adoptive father; an adoptive son.* **2.** tending to adopt. **3.** (of children) for adoption. **–adoptively,** *adv.*

adorable /ə'dɔrəbəl/ *adj.* **1.** worthy of being adored. **2.** arousing strong liking: *her coat was absolutely adorable.* **–adorableness,** adorability /ədɔrə'bɪləti/, *n.* **–adorably,** *adv.*

adore /ə'dɔ/ *v.t.* **1.** to regard with the utmost esteem, love, and respect. **2.** to honour as divine; worship: *to be adored as gods.* **3.** to like greatly: *I adore Mexican food.* **–adoration,** *n.* **–adorer,** *n.* **–adoring,** *adj.* **–adoringly,** *adv.*

adorn /ə'dɔn/ *v.t.* **1.** to make pleasing or more attractive; embellish; add lustre to: *the piety which adorns his character.* **2.** to increase or lend beauty to, as by dress or ornaments; decorate: *garlands of flowers adorning her hair.* **–adornment,** *n.* **–adorner,** *n.* **–adorningly,** *adv.*

adrenal /ə'rinəl/ *adj.* **1.** situated near or on the kidneys. **2.** of or relating to the adrenal glands. *–n.* **3.** one of the adrenal glands.

adrenaline /ə'drɛnələn, -lin/ *n.* **1.** a hormone, epinephrine, $C_9H_{13}NO_3$, produced by the medulla of the adrenal gland. **2.** this substance purified from the suprarenal secretion of animals and used as a drug to speed heart action, contract blood vessels, etc. Also, **adrenalin.**

adrift /ə'drɪft/ *adj.* **1.** not fastened by any kind of moorings; at the mercy of winds and currents. **2.** swayed by any chance impulse. **3.** missing the point; wide of the mark. *–phr.* **4. cut adrift,** to isolate or expel.

adroit /ə'drɔɪt/ *adj.* expert in the use of the hand or mind; ingenious. **–adroitly,** *adv.* **–adroitness,** *n.*

ADSL /ˌeɪ di ɛs 'ɛl/ *n.* Asymmetric Digital Subscriber Line service; a telecommunications system which downloads data at a speed faster than the speed at which it uploads data; a common form of broadband internet access, running via a telephone line as opposed to a coaxial cable.

adsorb /əd'sɔb/ *v.t. Chem.* to gather (a gas, liquid, or dissolved substance) on a surface in a condensed layer, as is the case when charcoal adsorbs gases. **–adsorbent,** *adj., n.* **–adsorption,** *n.* **–adsorptive,** *adj., n.*

adulate /'ædʒəleɪt/ *v.t.* to show pretended or undiscriminating devotion to; flatter servilely. **–adulation** /ædʒə'leɪʃən/, *n.* **–adulator,** *n.* **–adulatory,** *adj.*

adult /ə'dʌlt, 'ædʌlt/ *adj.* **1.** having attained full size and strength; grown up; mature. **2.** of or relating to adults: *adult education.* **3.** having reached the age at which a person is considered legally an adult (def. 4b). *–n.* **4. a.** a person who has attained full physical maturity. **b.** a person who has reached the age, variously defined in different political systems and legal contexts, at which an individual is considered to be fully legally responsible and can assume certain civic duties, such as voting (in Australia, the age of 18). **5.** a full-grown animal or plant. **–adulthood,** *n.* **–adultness,** *n.*

adulterate /ə'dʌltəreɪt/ *v.t.* to debase by adding inferior materials or elements; make impure by admixture; use cheaper, inferior, or less desirable goods in the production or marketing of (any professedly genuine article): *to adulterate food.* **–adulterator, adulterant,** *n.* **–adulteration** /ədʌltə'reɪʃən/, *n.*

adultery /ə'dʌltəri/ *n.* voluntary sexual intercourse between a married person and anyone other than the lawful spouse. **–adulterous,** *adj.* **–adulterer,** *n.* **–adulteress**

adult onset diabetes *n. Med.* type 2 diabetes. See **diabetes** (def. 1).

adumbrate /'ædəmbreɪt/ *v.t.* **1.** to give a faint shadow or resemblance of; outline or shadow forth. **2.** to foreshadow; prefigure. **3.** to darken or conceal partially; overshadow. **–adumbration** /ædəm'breɪʃən/, *n.*

advance /əd'væns, -'vɑns/ *verb* **(-vanced, -vancing)** *–v.t.* **1.** to move or bring forwards in place: *the troops were advanced to the new position.* **2.** to bring to view or notice; propose. **3.** to improve; further: *to advance one's interests.* **4.** to raise in rank; promote. **5.** to raise in rate: *to advance the price.* **6.** to bring forwards in time; accelerate: *to advance growth.* **7.** to supply beforehand; furnish on credit, or before goods are delivered or work is done. **8.** to supply or pay in expectation of reimbursement: *to advance money on loan. –v.i.* **9.** to move or go forwards in place or time; proceed. **10.** to improve or make progress; grow: *to advance in knowledge; to advance in rank.* **11.** to increase in quantity, value, price, etc.: *stocks advanced three points. –n.* **12.** a moving forwards; progress in space: *advance to the sea.* **13.** advancement; promotion: *an advance in rank.* **14.** a step forwards; actual progress in any course of action. **15.** *(usu. pl.)* **a.** an effort to bring about acquaintance, accord, understanding, etc. **b.** an indication of a wish to engage in sexual activity. **16.** addition to price; rise in price: *an advance in cottons.* **17.** *Commerce* **a.** a giving beforehand; a furnishing of something before an equivalent is received. **b.** the money or goods thus provided. **c.** a loan against securities, or in advance of payment due. **18.** *Mil. Obs.* the order or a signal to advance. **19.** *US* the leading body of an army. *–adj.* **20.** made or given in advance: *an advance payment.* **21.** issued in advance: *an advance copy. –phr.* **22. advance against** (or **on**), (of an army) to attack. **23. advance on,** to move towards, especially threateningly. **24. in advance, a.** before; in front. **b.** beforehand; ahead of time: *he insisted on paying his rent in advance.* **–advancement,** *n.* **–advancer,** *n.*

advance directive *n.* an instruction as to the type and level of health care a person wishes to receive in the case of the person being no longer able to indicate his or her wishes, usually applying to the situation of terminal illness or injury and forming part of a living will. Also, **advance care directive, advance medical directive.**

advantage /əd'vɑːntɪdʒ, -'van-/ *n.* **1.** any state, circumstance, opportunity, or means specially favourable to success, interest, or any desired end: *the advantage of a good education.* **2.** benefit; gain; profit: *it is to her advantage.* **3.** (sometimes fol. by *over* or *of*) superiority or ascendancy: *her height gave her an advantage over her opponents*; *you have the advantage of me.* **4.** *Tennis* the first point scored after deuce, or the resulting state of the score. *–v.t.* (**-taged, -taging**) **5.** to be of service to; yield profit or gain to; benefit. *–phr.* **6. take advantage of, a.** to make use of: *to take advantage of an opportunity.* **b.** to impose upon: *to take advantage of someone.* **7. to advantage,** with good effect; advantageously. *–advantageous* /ædvæn'teɪdʒəs/, *adj.*

advent /'ædvɛnt/ *n.* **1.** a coming into place, view, or being; arrival: *the advent of scientific methods of treatment.* **2.** (*upper case*) *Christianity* a season of the liturgical year (including four Sundays) preceding Christmas, commemorative of Christ's coming.

adventitious /ædvɛn'tɪʃəs/ *adj.* **1.** accidentally or casually acquired; added extrinsically; foreign. **2.** *Bot., Zool.* appearing in an abnormal or unusual position or place, as a root. *–adventitiously, adv. –adventitiousness, n.*

adventure /əd'vɛntʃə/ *n.* **1.** an undertaking of uncertain outcome; a hazardous enterprise. **2.** an exciting experience. **3.** participation in exciting undertakings or enterprises: *the spirit of adventure.* **4.** a commercial or financial speculation of any kind; a venture. *–v.t.* **5.** to venture. *–adventurer, n. –adventurous, adj.*

adventure sport *n.* an exhilarating sport, usually for individuals, which involves a degree of danger, as parachuting, white water canoeing, abseiling, etc.

adverb /'ædvɜːb/ *n.* one of the major parts of speech comprising words used to modify or limit a verb, a verbal noun (also, in Latin, English, and some other languages, an adjective or another adverb), or an adverbial phrase or clause. An adverbial element expresses some relation of place, time, manner, attendant circumstance, degree, cause, inference, result, condition, exception, concession, purpose, or means. *–adverbial* /əd'vɜːbiəl/, *adj. –adverbially* /əd'vɜːbiəli/, *adv.*

adversary /'ædvəsri, -səri, əd'vɜːsəri/, *Orig. US* /'ædvəsɛri/ *n.* (*pl.* **-ries**) **1.** an unfriendly opponent. **2.** an opponent in a contest; a contestant. *–adversarial, adj.*

adverse /'ædvɜːs, əd'vɜːs/ *adj.* **1.** antagonistic in purpose or effect: *adverse criticism*; *adverse to slavery.* **2.** opposing one's interests or desire: *adverse fate*; *adverse fortune*; *adverse influences*; *adverse circumstances.* **3.** being or acting in a contrary direction; opposed or opposing: *adverse winds.* **4.** opposite; confronting: *the adverse page.* **5.** *Bot.* turned towards the axis, as a leaf. **6.** *Law* **a.** opposed to the examining party in a law suit: *an adverse witness.* **b. adverse possession,** an occupation or possession of land by someone who has no lawful title to it, which, if unopposed for a certain period, extinguishes the right and title of the true owner. *–adversity, n. –adversely, adv. –adverseness, n.*

advert[1] /əd'vɜːt/ *phr.* **advert to,** to make a remark or refer to: *he adverted briefly to the occurrences of the day.*

advert[2] /'ædvɜːt/ *n. Colloq.* an advertisement.

advertise /'ædvətaɪz/ *v.t.* **1.** to give information to the public concerning; make public announcement of, by publication in periodicals, by printed posters, by broadcasting over the radio, television, etc.: *to advertise a reward.* **2.** to offer (an article) for sale or (a vacancy) to applicants, etc., by placing an advertisement in a newspaper, magazine, etc.: *he advertised the post of private secretary.* **3.** *Obs.* to praise the good qualities of, in order to induce the public to buy or invest in. *–v.i.* **4.** to ask (*for*) by placing an advertisement in a newspaper, magazine, etc.: *to advertise for a house to rent. –advertiser, n. –advertising, n.*

advertisement /əd'vɜːtəsmənt/ *n.* any device or public announcement, as a printed notice in a newspaper, a commercial film on television, a neon sign, etc., designed to attract public attention, bring in custom, etc.

advertorial /ædvə'tɔːriəl/ *n.* a media piece that looks like a news or feature article but which is written and paid for by an advertiser.

advertorialise /ædvə'tɔːriəlaɪz/ *v.i.* to advertise a product or service by means of an advertorial. Also, **advertorialize.**

advice /əd'vaɪs/ *n.* **1.** an opinion recommended, or offered, as worthy to be followed: *I shall act on your advice.* **2.** a communication, especially from a distance, containing information: *advice from abroad.* **3.** a formal or professional opinion given, especially by a barrister. *–phr.* **4. take advice,** to listen to and follow advice.

advisable /əd'vaɪzəbəl/ *adj.* proper to be advised or to be recommended: *it is advisable to go to bed early if you are sick. –advisability* /ədˌvaɪzə'bɪləti/, *advisableness, n.*

advise /əd'vaɪz/ *v.t.* **1.** to give counsel to; offer an opinion to, as worthy or expedient to be followed: *I advise you to be cautious.* **2.** to recommend as wise, prudent, etc.: *he advised secrecy. –v.i.* **3.** to offer counsel; give advice: *I shall act as you advise. –phr.* **4. advise someone of something,** to give someone information or notice about something: *the merchants were advised of the risk. –adviser, advisor, n.*

advisedly /əd'vaɪzədli/ *adv.* after due consideration; deliberately.

advisory /əd'vaɪzəri/ *adj.* **1.** of, or giving, advice; having power to advise: *an advisory council. –n.* (*pl.* **-sories**) **2.** a statement of advice.

advocate *v.t.* /'ædvəkeɪt/ **1.** to plead in favour of; support or urge by argument; recommend publicly: *he advocated isolationism. –n.* /'ædvəkət, -keɪt/ **2.** (sometimes fol. by *of*) someone who defends, vindicates, or espouses a cause by argument; an upholder; a defender: *an advocate of peace. –advocator, n. –advocacy* /'ædvəkəsi/, *n. –advocatory* /əd'vɒkətri/, *adj.*

adze /ædz/ *n.* **1.** a heavy chisel-like steel tool fastened at right angles to a wooden handle, used to dress timber, etc. *–v.t.* **2.** to carve out using an adze. Also, *US,* **adz.**

ae a digraph or ligature appearing in Latin and Latinised Greek words. In English words of Latin or Greek origin, it is now usually reduced to *e*, except generally in proper names (*Caesar*), in words belonging to Roman or Greek antiquities (*aegis*), and in modern words of scientific or technical use (*aecium*).

ae- For words beginning with **ae-**, see also spellings under **e-**.

aegis /'idʒəs/ *n.* protection; sponsorship: *under the imperial aegis.*

-aemia a suffix referring to the state of the blood, as in *toxaemia.* Also, **-emia, -haemia, -hemia.**

aeon /'iən/ *n.* **1.** an indefinitely long period of time; an age. **2.** *Geol.* the largest division of geological time, comprising two or more eras. Also, **eon.**

aerate /'ɛəreɪt/ *v.t.* **1.** to charge or treat with air or a gas, especially with carbon dioxide. **2.** to expose to the free action of the air: *to aerate milk in order to remove unpleasant smells. –aeration* /ɛə'reɪʃən/, *n.*

aerial /'ɛəriəl/ *n.* **1.** that part of a radio or television system which radiates or receives electromagnetic or microwave signals into or from free space and which may consist of a simple wire, a single metal rod, or a complex metal framework; an antenna. *–adj.* **2.** of, in, or produced by the air: *aerial currents.* **3.** living in the air: *aerial creatures.* **4.** reaching high into the air; lofty:

aerial spires. **5.** of the nature of air; airy: *aerial beings.* **6.** unreal; visionary: *aerial fancies.* **7.** *Biol.* growing in the air, as roots of some trees. –**aerially,** *adv.*

aero- a word element indicating: **1.** air; atmosphere. **2.** gas. **3.** aeroplane.

aerobatics /ɛərə'bætɪks/ *pl. n.* stunts carried out by aircraft; aerial acrobatics. –**aerobatic,** *adj.*

aerobic /ɛə'roʊbɪk, ə'roʊbɪk/ *adj.* **1.** (of organisms or tissues) living or active only in the presence of free oxygen. **2.** relating to or caused by the presence of oxygen: *aerobic respiration.* Compare **anaerobic.** **3.** relating to or making use of aerobics: *an aerobic work-out.* –**aerobically,** *adv.*

aerobic exercise *n.* physical exercise during which energy is derived from glucose produced by the reaction of oxygen in the blood with stored glycogen, and which typically involves moderate activity over a relatively long period of time, such as walking, gently paced running, swimming, gymnastic exercises, etc.; benefits are improved blood circulation, and strengthened respiratory and cardiac muscles. See **anaerobic exercise.**

aerobics /ɛə'roʊbɪks, ə'roʊbɪks/ *pl. n.* physical exercises which stimulate the respiratory and circulatory systems to improve and maintain physical fitness.

aerobic threshold *n.* the physiological state of the body induced by a level of physical exercise just short of that required to cross the anaerobic threshold. *Abbrev.:* AeT

aerodrome /'ɛərədroʊm/ *n.* a landing field for aeroplanes, especially private aeroplanes, having permanent buildings, equipment, hangars, etc., but usually smaller than an airport. Also, *US,* **airdrome.**

aerodynamic /ˌɛəroʊdaɪ'næmɪk/ *adj.* **1.** of or relating to aerodynamics. **2.** able to travel through the air; designed for air travel. **3.** of or relating to a shape that reduces drag (def. 12), as of an aeroplane or sports car. –**aerodynamically,** *adv.*

aerodynamics /ˌɛəroʊdaɪ'næmɪks/ *n.* **1.** the study of air in motion and of the forces acting on solids in motion relative to the air through which they move. **2.** the properties of a solid object in relation to these forces acting on it: *the aerodynamics of the new-model car.* –**aerodynamicist,** *n.*

aerofoil /'ɛərəfɔɪl/ *n.* any surface, such as a wing, aileron, or stabiliser, designed to help in lifting or controlling an aircraft or sailing boat by making use of the current of air through which it moves.

aeronautics /ɛərə'nɔtɪks/ *n.* the science or art of flight.

aeroplane /'ɛərəpleɪn/ *n.* an aircraft, heavier than air, kept aloft by the upward thrust exerted by the passing air on its fixed wings, and driven by propellers, jet propulsion, etc. Also, *Chiefly US,* **airplane.**

aerosol /'ɛərəsɒl/ *n.* **1.** *Physics, Chem.* a system consisting of colloidal particles dispersed in a gas; a smoke or fog. **2.** an aerosol container; spray can.

aerosol can *n.* → **spray can.**

aerosol container *n.* a metal container for storing a substance under pressure and subsequently dispensing it as a spray.

aerospace /'ɛəroʊˌspeɪs/ *n.* **1.** the earth's envelope of air and the space beyond it. –*adj.* **2.** of or relating to aeronautics and astronautics considered together.

aesthetic /əs'θɛtɪk, is-/ *adj.* **1.** relating to the sense of the beautiful or the science of aesthetics. **2.** having a sense of the beautiful; characterised by a love of beauty. –*n.* **3.** an artistic expression, viewed as reflective of a personal or cultural ideal of what is aesthetically valid. Also, **esthetic.**

aesthetics /əs'θɛtɪks, is-/ *n. Philos.* the science which deduces from nature and taste the rules and principles of art; the theory of the fine arts; the science of the

beautiful, or the branch of philosophy that deals with its principles or effects; the doctrines of taste. Also, **esthetics.**

aestivate /'ɛstəveɪt/ *v.i. Zool.* to enter into a dormant condition in response to high temperatures and aridity. Also, **estivate.** –**aestivation,** *n.* –**aestivator,** *n.*

aetiology /iti'ɒlədʒi/ *n.* the study of the causes of anything, especially of diseases. Also, **etiology.** –**aetiological,** *adj.* –**aetiologically,** *adv.* –**aetiologist,** *n.*

af- variant of **ad-** (by assimilation) before *f,* as in *affect.*

afar /ə'fɑ/ *adv.* **1.** (usu. preceded by *from*) from a distance: *he came from afar.* **2.** **afar off,** far away; at or to a distance: *he saw the plane afar off.*

affable /'æfəbəl/ *adj.* **1.** easy to talk to or to approach; polite; friendly: *an affable and courteous gentleman.* **2.** expressing affability, mild; benign: *an affable countenance.* –**affability** /æfə'bɪləti/, **affableness,** *n.* –**affably,** *adv.*

affair /ə'fɛə/ *n.* **1.** anything done or to be done: *an affair of great importance; affairs of state.* **2.** (*usu. pl.*) matters of interest or concern: *put your affairs in order.* **3.** an event or particular action, operation, etc. **4.** a love affair. **5.** a social function: *a big affair at the town hall.*

affect[1] *v.t.* /ə'fɛkt/ **1.** to act on; produce an effect or a change in: *cold affects the body.* **2.** (of pain, disease, etc.) to attack or lay hold of. –*n.* /'æfɛkt/ **3.** *Psychol.* observable feeling or emotion, as linked to a thought process or as a response to a stimulus (opposed to *conation*).

affect[2] /ə'fɛkt/ *v.t.* **1.** to make a show of; put on a pretence of; pretend; feign: *to affect ignorance.* **2.** to assume or imitate, especially in a pretentious fashion: *to affect an Oxford accent.* **3.** to use or adopt by preference; choose; prefer: *the peculiar costume which he affected.* **4.** *Obs.* to assume the character or attitude of: *to affect the freethinker.* –*v.i.* **5.** to profess; pretend: *he affected to be wearied.* –**affecter,** *n.*

affectation /ˌæfɛk'teɪʃən/ *n.* **1.** (sometimes fol. by *of*) a striving for the appearance of (a quality not really or fully possessed); pretence of the possession or character; effort for the reputation: *an affectation of wit; affectation of great wealth.* **2.** artificiality of manner or conduct; effort to attract notice by pretence, assumption, or any assumed peculiarity: *his affectations are insufferable.*

affected[1] /ə'fɛktəd/ *adj.* **1.** acted upon; influenced. **2.** influenced injuriously; impaired; attacked, as by climate, disease or pollution, etc. **3.** moved; touched: *she was deeply affected.*

affected[2] /ə'fɛktəd/ *adj.* **1.** assumed artificially: *affected airs; affected diction.* **2.** assuming or pretending to possess characteristics which are not natural: *an affected lady.* **3.** inclined or disposed: *well affected towards a project.* –**affectedly,** *adv.* –**affectedness,** *n.*

affection /ə'fɛkʃən/ *n.* **1.** a settled goodwill, love, or attachment: *the affection of a father for his child.* **2.** the state of having one's feelings affected; emotion or feeling: *over and above our reason and affections.* **3.** *Pathol.* a disease, or the condition of being diseased; a morbid or abnormal state of body or mind: *a gouty affection.* **4.** the act of affecting; act of influencing or acting upon. **5.** the state of being affected.

affectionate /ə'fɛkʃənət/ *adj.* **1.** characterised by or manifesting affection; possessing or indicating love; tender: *an affectionate embrace.* **2.** having great love or affection; warmly attached: *your affectionate brother.* –**affectionately,** *adv.* –**affectionateness,** *n.*

affiance /æfi'ɒns, ə'faɪəns/ *v.t.* (**-anced, -ancing**) to bind by promise of marriage; betroth: *to affiance a daughter.* –**affianced,** *adj.*

affidavit /æfəˈdeɪvət/ *n.* a written statement on oath, sworn to before an authorised official, often used as evidence in court proceedings.

affiliate *v.t.* /əˈfɪlieɪt/ **1.** (sometimes fol. by *with*) to attach as a branch or part; unite; associate: *affiliated with the church.* **2.** to bring into association or close connection: *the two banks were affiliated.* –*v.i.* /əˈfɪlieɪt/ **3.** to associate oneself; be intimately united in action or interest. –*n.* /əˈfɪliət/ **4.** a person or thing that is affiliated; associate or auxiliary. **–affiliation** /əfɪliˈeɪʃən/, *n.*

affinity /əˈfɪnəti/ *n.* **1.** a natural liking for, or attraction to, a person or thing. **2.** inherent likeness or agreement as between things; close resemblance or connection. **3.** relationship by marriage or by ties other than those of blood (distinguished from *consanguinity*). **4.** *Chem.* the force by which the atoms of dissimilar nature unite in certain definite proportions to form a compound. –**affinitive**, *adj.*

affirm /əˈfɜm/ *v.t.* **1.** to state or assert positively; maintain as true: *to affirm one's loyalty to one's country.* **2.** to establish, confirm, or ratify: *the appellate court affirmed the judgement of the lower court.* –*v.i.* **3.** to declare positively; assert solemnly. **4.** *Law* to declare solemnly before a court or magistrate, but without oath (a practice allowed where the affirmant has scruples, usually religious, against taking an oath). **–affirmation** /æfəˈmeɪʃən/, *n.* **–affirmer, affirmant**, *n.* **–affirmable**, *adj.* **–affirming**, *adj.*

affirmative /əˈfɜmətɪv/ *adj.* **1.** giving affirmation or assent; confirmatory; not negative: *an affirmative answer.* **2.** *Logic* denoting a proposition or judgement that asserts a relation between its terms, or asserts that the predicate applies to the subject. –*n.* **3.** that which affirms or asserts; a positive proposition: *two negatives make an affirmative.* **4.** an affirmative word or phrase, as *yes* or *I do.* –*phr.* **5. the affirmative**, the agreeing or concurring side. **–affirmatively**, *adj.*

affirmative action *n.* action designed to provide increased employment opportunities for groups who have previously suffered from discrimination, especially women and minority racial groups.

affix *v.t.* /əˈfɪks/ **1.** (sometimes fol. by *to*) to fix; fasten, join, or attach: *to affix stamps to a letter.* **2.** to impress (a seal or stamp). **3.** to attach (blame, reproach, ridicule, etc.). –*n.* /ˈæfɪks/ **4.** something that is joined or attached. **5.** *Gram.* any meaningful element (prefix, infix, or suffix) added to a stem or base, as *-ed* added to *want* to form *wanted.* **–affixation** /ˌæfɪkˈseɪʃən/, *n.* **–affixer** /əˈfɪksə/, *n.* **–affixture** /əˈfɪkstʃə/, *n.*

afflict /əˈflɪkt/ *v.t.* to distress with mental or bodily pain; trouble greatly or grievously: *to be afflicted with the gout.* **–affliction**, *n.* **–afflicter**, *n.* **–afflictive**, *adj.*

affluent /ˈæfluənt/ *adj.* **1.** having a lot of money or possessions; rich: *an affluent person.* **2.** abounding in anything; abundant. –*n.* **3.** a tributary stream. **–affluence**, *n.* **–affluently**, *adv.*

afford /əˈfɔd/ *v.t.* **1.** (usu. with *can* or *may*) to have enough money (to do something): *we can afford to eat well.* **2.** (usu. with *can* or *may*) to have enough money to pay for; to be able to spare the price of: *he can't afford a car.* **3.** (usu. with *can* or *may*) to be able to give or spare: *I can't afford the loss of a day.* **4.** to give; supply: *it affords me great pleasure.* **–affordable**, *adj.*

affray /əˈfreɪ/ *n.* a public fight; a noisy quarrel; a brawl.

affront /əˈfrʌnt/ *n.* **1.** a personally offensive act or word; an intentional slight; an open manifestation of disrespect; an insult to the face: *an affront to the king; some passages in the work were interpreted as an affront to their religion.* **2.** an offence to one's dignity, self-respect or sensibilities. –*v.t.* **3.** to offend by an open manifestation of disrespect or insolence. **4.** to make ashamed or confused. **–affronter**, *n.* **–affrontingly**, *adv.*

Afghan hound /ˈæfgæn ˈhaʊnd/ *n.* one of a breed of greyhound with a very long silky coat.

aficionado /əfɪʃiəˈnadoʊ/ *n.* (*pl.* **-dos**) **1.** an ardent devotee. **2.** a person who is very knowledgeable about something. Also, **afficionado.**

afield /əˈfild/ *adv.* **1.** abroad; away from home. **2.** off the beaten path; far and wide: *to stray far afield in one's reading.*

afire /əˈfaɪə/ *adj.* **1.** on fire; alight. **2.** involved; enthusiastic.

aflame /əˈfleɪm/ *adj.* **1.** on fire; ablaze: *the house was all aflame.* **2.** inflamed; aroused; glowing: *aflame with curiosity.*

aflatoxin /æfləˈtɒksən/ *n.* a naturally occurring carcinogenic toxin produced by many species of the *Aspergillus* fungus; a contaminant of grains, peanuts, etc., before harvesting or in storage.

afloat /əˈfloʊt/ *adj.* **1.** borne on the water; in a floating condition. **2.** flooded: *the main deck was afloat.* **3.** moving without guide or control: *our affairs are all afloat.* **4.** surviving financially; solvent. –*adv.* **5.** on board ship; at sea. **6.** in a boat on the water. –*phr.* **7. set afloat**, to put (an enterprise, business, etc.) in operation; launch.

afocal /eɪˈfoʊkəl/ *adj.* having no finite focal point, as a telescope.

afoot /əˈfʊt/ *adj.* astir; in progress: *there is mischief afoot.*

aforesaid /əˈfɔsɛd/ *adj.* said or mentioned previously.

afraid /əˈfreɪd/ *adj.* **1.** feeling fear; filled with apprehension: *afraid to go.* **2.** reluctantly or regretfully of the opinion: *I am afraid you will have to wait.*

afresh /əˈfrɛʃ/ *adv.* anew; again: *to start afresh.*

African violet /æfrɪkən ˈvaɪələt/ *n.* a plant, *Saintpaulia ionantha*, with violet, pink, or white flowers, popular in cultivation.

afro /ˈæfroʊ/ *n.* a hairstyle in which the hair, which is frizzy or frizzed, is allowed to grow to considerable length, then cut to form a large rounded shape.

aft /aft/ *adv. Naut.* at, in, or towards the stern.

after /ˈaftə/ *prep.* **1.** behind; following. **2.** in search or pursuit of: *run after him.* **3.** about; concerning: *to inquire after a person.* **4.** later in time than; at the end of. **5.** following and because of: *after what has happened I can never return.* **6.** below in rank or standard; next to. **7.** in the style of: *to make something after a model; after Raphael.* **8.** with the name of: *he was named after his uncle.* **9.** according to: *arranged after the first letter of their names.* –*adv.* **10.** behind; in the rear: *Jill came tumbling after.* **11.** later in time; afterwards: *happy ever after.* –*adj.* **12.** later in time; next; following; subsequent: *in after years.* **13.** *Naut.* rear: *the after deck.* –*conj.* **14.** following the time that: *after the boys left.* –*phr.* **15. day after day, week after week**, etc., an expression where a measure of time is specified twice over to imply the triggering of boredom, weariness, frustration, etc. **16. the after years**, the period after a specified event.

afterbirth /ˈaftəbɜθ/ *n.* the placenta and fetal membranes expelled from the uterus after parturition.

afterlife /ˈaftəlaɪf/ *n.* **1.** life after death. **2.** later life.

aftermath /ˈaftəmæθ, -maθ/ *n.* resultant conditions, especially of a catastrophe: *the aftermath of the storm.*

afternoon /aftəˈnun/ *n.* **1.** the time from noon until evening. **2.** the latter part: *the afternoon of life.* –*adj.* **3.** relating to the latter part of the day.

afternoon tea *n.* **1.** a light, but sometimes quite formal, meal, at which cakes, sandwiches, etc. are served with tea, usually at about three or four o'clock in the afternoon. **2.** any small quantity of food or drink taken after the midafternoon, as by children when returning from school.

aftertaste /ˈaftəteɪst/ *n.* **1.** a taste remaining after the substance causing it is no longer in the mouth. **2.** a slight lingering after-effect, often an unpleasant one.

afterwards /ˈaftəwədz/ *adv.* in later or subsequent time; subsequently. Also, **afterward** /ˈaftəwəd/.

afterword /ˈaftəwɜd/ *n.* a section of text coming after the main body; epilogue.

ag- variant of **ad-** (by assimilation) before *g*, as in *agglutinate*.

again /əˈgɛn, əˈgeɪn/ *adv.* **1.** once more; in addition; another time; anew: *he did it all over again.* **2.** in an additional case or instance; moreover; besides; furthermore. **3.** on the other hand: *it might happen and again it might not.* **4.** in the opposite direction; to the same place or person: *to return again.* *–phr.* **5. again and again**, often; with frequent repetition. **6. as much again**, twice as much.

against /əˈgɛnst, əˈgeɪnst/ *prep.* **1.** in an opposite direction to, so as to meet; towards; upon: *to ride against the wind; the rain beats against the window.* **2.** touching or pressing on: *to lean against a wall.* **3.** in opposition to; hostile to: *twenty votes against ten; against reason.* **4.** in resistance to or defence from: *protection against burglars.* **5.** in preparation for; providing for: *he saved money against losing his job.* **6.** in exchange for; in return for: *to draw out money against a cheque.* **7.** (sometimes preceded by *as*) compared to; as an alternative to; in contrast with: *the advantages of flying against going by train.*

agape¹ /əˈgeɪp/ *adv.* **1.** in an attitude of wonder or eagerness; with the mouth wide open. *–adj.* **2.** wide open.

agape² /ˈægəpeɪ, əˈgapi/ *n.* altruistic love.

agar-agar /eɪgər-ˈeɪgə/ *n.* a gelatine-like product of certain seaweeds, used to solidify culture media and, especially in Asia, for soups, etc. Also, **agar**.

agate /ˈægət/ *n.* a variegated variety of quartz (chalcedony) showing coloured bands or other markings (clouded, moss-like, etc.).

age /eɪdʒ/ *n.* **1.** the length of time during which a being or thing has existed; length of life or existence to the time spoken of or referred to: *his age is 20 years; a tree or building of unknown age.* **2.** a period of human life, usually marked by a certain stage of physical or mental development, especially a degree of development, measured by years from birth, which involves legal responsibility and capacity: *the age of discretion; the age of consent.* **3.** the particular period of life at which one becomes naturally or conventionally qualified or disqualified for anything: *under age for conscription.* **4.** one of the periods or stages of human life: *a person of middle age.* **5.** old age: *his eyes were dim with age.* **6.** a particular period of history, as distinguished from others; a historical epoch: *the age of Pericles; the Stone Age; the Middle Ages.* **7.** the people who live at a particular period. **8.** a generation or a succession of generations: *ages yet unborn.* **9.** *Colloq.* a great length of time: *it's been an age since I saw you; it could be ages before we go back there again.* **10.** *Geol.* a long or short part of the world's history distinguished by special features: *the Ice Age.* **11.** any one of the stages in the history of humankind divided, according to Hesiod, into the golden, silver, bronze, heroic, and iron ages. The happiest and best was the first (or golden) age, and the worst the iron age. *–verb* (**aged**, **ageing** *or* **aging**) *–v.i.* **12.** to grow old; develop the characteristics of old age: *he is ageing rapidly.* *–v.t.* **13.** to make old; cause to grow old or to seem old: *fear aged him overnight.* **14.** to bring to maturity or to a state fit for use: *to age wine.* *–phr.* **15. act** (or **be**) **one's age**, *Colloq.* to behave in a manner in keeping with that expected of someone's age. **16. for an age** or **for ages**, for a long period of time. **17. of age**, *Law* being of an age, usually 21 or 18,

at which certain legal rights, as of voting or marriage, are acquired.

-age a noun suffix, common in words taken from French, as in *baggage, language, savage, voyage*, etc., now a common English formative, forming: **1.** collective nouns from names of things, as in *fruitage, leafage.* **2.** nouns denoting condition, rank, service, fee, etc., from personal terms, as in *bondage, parsonage.* **3.** nouns expressing various relations, from verbs, as in *breakage, cleavage.* **4.** nouns denoting an amount or charge, as in *postage, corkage.*

aged *adj.* **1.** /eɪdʒd, ˈeɪdʒəd/ having lived or existed long: *an aged man; an aged tree.* **2.** /eɪdʒd/ relating to old age: *the aged sector.* **3.** /eɪdʒd/ of the age of: *a man aged 40 years.* **4.** /eɪdʒd/ (of a product, as wine, cheese, etc.) having been subjected to an ageing process; matured.

ageism /ˈeɪdʒɪzəm/ *n.* an attitude which stereotypes a person, especially an elderly person, according to age rather than individual abilities. *–***ageist**, *adj.*, *n.*

agency /ˈeɪdʒənsi/ *n.* (*pl.* **-cies**) **1.** a commercial or other organisation furnishing some form of service for the public: *an advertising agency.* **2.** the place of business of an agent. **3.** the office of agent; the business of an agent entrusted with the concerns of another. **4.** the state of being in action or of exerting power; action; operation: *the agency of Providence.* **5.** a mode of exerting power; a means of producing effects; instrumentality: *by the agency of friends.*

agenda /əˈdʒɛndə/ *n.* **1.** a program or list of things to be done, discussed, etc. **2.** a list of matters to be brought before a committee, council, board, etc., as things to be done. **3.** a set of motivating factors: *a political agenda behind the recent grant to the farmers.*

agender /eɪˈdʒɛndə/ *adj.* identifying as having no gender, whether male, female or non-binary.

agent /ˈeɪdʒənt/ *n.* **1.** a person authorised to act on behalf of another: *my agent has power to sign my name.* **2.** someone or something that acts or has the power to act: *a free agent.* **3.** something with an effect or used for a particular purpose: *a cleansing agent.* **4.** an active cause: *an agent of destruction.* **5.** an official or representative of a business firm, especially a travelling salesperson. **6.** a secret agent; spy. **7.** *Chem.* a substance which causes a reaction. *–***agential** /eɪˈdʒɛnʃəl/, *adj.*

Agent Orange *n.* a 50:50 mixture of n-butyl esters of 2,4-D and 2,4,5-T, used as a defoliant.

agent provocateur /ˌaʒɒ̃ prəvɒkəˈtɜ/ *n.* (*pl.* **agents provocateurs** /ˌaʒɒ̃ prəvɒkəˈtɜz/) a person who tries to incite dissatisfaction or unrest, especially one who incites to an illegal action.

age spot *n.* → **liver spot**.

agflation /ægˈfleɪʃən/ *n.* an increase in the price of food caused by an increase in demand either for human consumption or for use as an alternative source of energy. *–***agflationary**, *adj.*

agglomerate *v.t.* /əˈglɒməreɪt/ **1.** to collect or gather into a mass. *–v.i.* /əˈglɒməreɪt/ **2.** to take the shape of a mass. *–n.* /əˈglɒmərət/ **3.** a mass of things clustered together. **4.** *Geol.* a rock formation composed of large angular volcanic fragments. *–***agglomeration**, *n.* *–***agglomerative**, *adj.*

agglutinate /əˈglutəneɪt/ *v.t.* to unite or cause to adhere. *–***agglutinant**, *adj.* *–***agglutination**, *n.*

aggrandise /əˈgrændaɪz/ *v.t.* **1.** to widen in scope; increase in size or intensity; enlarge; extend. **2.** to make great or greater in power, wealth, rank, or honour. **3.** to make (something) appear greater. Also, **aggrandize**. *–***aggrandisement** /əˈgrændəzmənt/, *n.* *–***aggrandiser**, *n.*

aggravate /ˈægrəveɪt/ *v.t.* **1.** to make worse or more severe; intensify, as anything evil, disorderly, or troublesome: *to aggravate guilt; grief aggravated her* illness. **2.** to provoke; irritate; exasperate: *threats will only aggravate her.* –**aggravated**, *adj.* –**aggravating**, *adj.* –**aggravation**, *n.* –**aggravator**, *n.* –**aggravatingly**, *adv.*

aggregate *adj.* /ˈægrəgət/ **1.** formed by adding together single things into a mass or sum; combined: *the aggregate mark for all six subjects.* –*n.* /ˈægrəgət/ **2.** sum or collection of single things; total: *the aggregate of all past experience.* **3.** *Geol.* mixture of different mineral substances that can be separated mechanically, e.g. granite. **4.** any hard material added to cement to make concrete. –*v.t.* /ˈægrəgeɪt/ **5.** to bring together; collect into one sum, mass, or body. **6.** to amount to a certain number: *the guns captured will aggregate five or six hundred.* –*v.i.* /ˈægrəgeɪt/ **7.** to combine and form a collection or mass. –*phr.* **8. in the aggregate**, considered together; collectively. –**aggregation**, *n.* –**aggregately**, *adv.* –**aggregative**, *adj.*

aggression /əˈgrɛʃən/ *n.* **1.** the practice of making assaults or attacks; offensive action in general. **2.** *Psychol.* the emotional drive to attack; an offensive mental attitude (rather than defensive). **3.** the action of a state in violating by force the rights of another state, particularly its territorial rights. **4.** any offensive action or procedure; an inroad or encroachment: *an aggression upon one's rights.* –**aggressor**, *n.*

aggressive /əˈgrɛsɪv/ *adj.* **1.** tending to aggress; making the first attack. **2.** characterised by or prone to aggression: *an aggressive personality.* **3.** energetic; vigorous. **4.** (of a disease such as cancer) fast-growing and tending to spread quickly to different parts of the body. **5.** (of a medical treatment) vigorous and intensive: *an aggressive course of chemotherapy.* **6.** of or relating to a high-risk investment strategy which has the potential to bring a high profit. –**aggressively**, *adv.* –**aggressiveness**, *n.*

aggro /ˈægroʊ/ *adj. Aust. Colloq.* aggressive; dominating.

aghast /əˈgast/ *adj.* struck with amazement; stupefied with fright or horror: *they stood aghast at this unforeseen disaster.*

agile /ˈædʒaɪl/ *adj.* **1.** quick and light in movement: *a robust and agile frame.* **2.** active; lively: *an agile mind.* –**agility** /əˈdʒɪləti/, *n.* –**agilely**, *adv.*

agist /əˈdʒɪst/ *v.t.* **1.** to take in and feed on pasture (livestock) for payment. **2.** to lay a public burden, as a tax, on (land or its owner). –**agistment**, *n.* –**agistor**, *n.*

agitate /ˈædʒəteɪt/ *v.t.* **1.** to move or force into violent irregular action; shake or move briskly: *the wind agitates the sea.* **2.** to move to and fro; impart regular motion to: *to agitate a fan, etc.* **3.** to disturb, or excite into tumult; perturb: *his mind was agitated by various emotions.* –*v.i.* **4.** to arouse or attempt to arouse public feeling as in some political or social question: *to agitate for the repeal of a tax.* –**agitator**, *n.* –**agitation** /ædʒəˈteɪʃən/, *n.* –**agitatedly**, *adv.*

agnostic /ægˈnɒstɪk/ *n.* **1.** someone who holds that the ultimate cause (God) and the essential nature of things are unknown or unknowable or that human knowledge is limited to experience. –*adj.* **2.** relating to the agnostics or their doctrines. **3.** asserting the relativity and uncertainty of all knowledge. **4.** not committed to any particular point of view, especially any political alignment. –**agnosticism**, *n.* –**agnostically**, *adv.*

ago /əˈgoʊ/ *adv.* in past time; past: *some time ago*; *long ago.*

agog /əˈgɒg/ *adj.* **1.** in a state of wonder and amazement; astonished: *they were agog to learn of her remarkable success.* **2.** in an anticipatory state of interest; eager. **3.** in a state of excited interest. –*phr.* **4. agog with**, in a state of keen interest as a result of: *agog with excitement.* **5. all agog**, in a state of excited interest: *they were all agog to hear the results.*

-agogue a word element meaning 'leading' or 'guiding', found in a few agent nouns (often with pejorative value), as in *demagogue, pedagogue.*

agonise /ˈægənaɪz/ *v.i.* **1.** to suffer anxiety in the process of making a difficult decision or choice. **2.** to make great effort of any kind. **3.** *Obs.* to writhe with extreme pain; suffer violent anguish. –*v.t.* **4.** *Obs.* to distress with extreme pain; torture. –*phr.* **5. agonise over** (or **about**), to worry excessively about. Also, **agonize.** –**agonisingly**, *adv.*

agony /ˈægəni/ *n.* **1.** extreme, and generally prolonged, pain; intense suffering. **2.** intense mental excitement of any kind. **3.** the struggle preceding natural death: *mortal agony.*

agoraphobia /ægərəˈfoʊbiə/ *n.* a morbid fear of being in open or public spaces. –**agoraphobic**, *adj., n.*

agrarian /əˈgrɛəriən/ *adj.* **1.** relating to land, land tenure, or the division of landed property: *agrarian laws.* **2.** relating to the advancement of agricultural groups: *an agrarian experiment.* **3.** rural; agricultural. –**agrarianism**, *n.*

agree /əˈgri/ *verb* (**agreed**, **agreeing**) –*v.i.* **1.** (sometimes fol. by *to*) to yield assent; consent: *do you agree to the conditions?* **2.** (sometimes fol. by *with*) to be of one mind; harmonise in opinion or feeling: *I don't agree with you.* **3.** to live in concord or without contention; harmonise in action. **4.** (sometimes fol. by *upon*) to come to one opinion or mind; come to an arrangement or understanding; arrive at a settlement. **5.** (sometimes fol. by *with*) to be consistent; harmonise: *this story agrees with others.* **6.** (sometimes fol. by *with*) to be applicable or appropriate; resemble; be similar: *the picture does not agree with the original.* **7.** *Gram.* (sometimes fol. by *with*) to correspond in inflectional form, as in number, case, gender, or person. –*v.t.* **8.** to yield assent; consent: *he agreed to accompany the ambassador.* **9.** to concede; grant: *I agree that she is the ablest of us.* **10.** to determine; settle: *to agree a price; to agree that a meeting should be held.* –*phr.* **11. agree to**, to accept: *I agree to your conditions.* **12. agree with**, to be accommodated or adapted to; suit: *the same food does not agree with every person.* –**agreed**, *adj.*

agreeable /əˈgriəbəl/ *adj.* **1.** to one's liking; pleasing: *agreeable manners.* **2.** willing or ready to agree or consent: *are you agreeable?* **3.** (sometimes fol. by *to*) suitable; conformable. –**agreeability** /əgriəˈbɪləti/, **agreeableness**, *n.* –**agreeably**, *adv.*

agreement /əˈgrimənt/ *n.* **1.** the act of coming to a mutual arrangement. **2.** the arrangement itself. **3.** unanimity of opinion; harmony in feeling: *agreement among the members.* **4.** the state of being in accord; concord; harmony; conformity: *agreement between observation and theory.* **5.** *Gram.* correspondence in inflectional form, as in number, case, gender, person.

agribusiness /ˈægribɪznəs/ *n.* the businesses, collectively, which are involved in the production, distribution and sale of agricultural produce. Also, **agribusiness.**

agriculture /ˈægrəkʌltʃə/ *n.* the cultivation of land, including crop-raising, forestry, stock-raising, etc.; farming. –**agricultural** /ægrəˈkʌltʃərəl/, *adj.* –**agriculturalist**, *n.* –**agriculturally** /ægrəˈkʌltʃərəli/, *adv.*

agro- a word element meaning 'soil', 'field', as in *agrology.*

agronomy /əˈgrɒnəmi/ *n.* **1.** the applied aspects of both soil science and the several plant sciences, often limited to applied plant sciences dealing with crops. **2.** → **agriculture.** –**agronomist**, *n.* –**agronomic** /ægrəˈnɒmɪk/, **agronomical** /ægrəˈnɒmɪkəl/, *adj.*

aground /əˈgraʊnd/ *adv.* onto the ground or shore: *the ship ran aground.*

ague /ˈeɪgju/ n. 1. Pathol. a malarial fever characterised by regularly returning paroxysms, marked by successive cold, hot, and sweating fits. 2. a fit of shaking or shivering as if with cold; a chill. –**agued**, adj. –**aguish**, adj. –**aguishly**, adv.

ahead /əˈhɛd/ adv. 1. Also, **on ahead**. in or to the front; in advance; before. 2. forward; onward. –phr. 3. **be ahead**, to be at an advantage; be winning: I was well ahead in the deal. 4. **get ahead**, to progress; prosper; be successful. 5. **get ahead of**, to surpass. 6. **see one's way ahead to**, to plan on.

ahoy /əˈhɔɪ/ interj. a call used in hailing, especially on ships.

aid /eɪd/ v.t. 1. to afford support or relief to; help. 2. to promote the course of accomplishment of; facilitate. 3. to give financial support to: a state-aided school. –v.i. 4. to give help or assistance. –n. 5. help; support; assistance. 6. someone or something that aids or yields assistance; a helper; an auxiliary: a nursing aid; a hearing aid; an aid to understanding. 7. US → **aide-de-camp**. –phr. 8. **in aid of**, directed towards; intended to achieve. –**aider**, n.

aide-de-camp /eɪd-də-ˈkɒ̃/ n. (pl. **aides-de-camp**) a military or naval officer acting as a confidential assistant to a superior, especially a general, governor, etc.

AIDS /eɪdz/ n. a disease caused by a virus (HIV) which destroys the body's white cells, resulting in reduced immunity, and therefore severe infections, tumours, and ultimately death.

aikido /aɪˈkidoʊ, ˈaɪkɪdoʊ/ n. a Japanese martial art in which the attacker's energy or force is deflected and used against them.

ail /eɪl/ v.t. 1. to affect with pain or uneasiness; trouble. –v.i. 2. to feel pain; be ill (usually in a slight degree); be unwell. –**ailing**, adj. –**ailment**, n.

aileron /ˈeɪlərɒn/ n. a hinged, movable flap of an aeroplane wing, usually part of the trailing edge, used primarily to maintain lateral balance.

aim /eɪm/ v.t. 1. to give a certain direction and elevation to (a gun or the like), for the purpose of causing the projectile, when the weapon is discharged, to hit the object. 2. to direct or point (something) at something: the satire was aimed at the Church –v.i. 3. to level a gun; give direction to a blow, missile, etc. 4. to strive; try: we aim to give the best possible service. 5. to intend: she aims to go tomorrow. –n. 6. the act of aiming or directing anything at or towards a particular point or object. 7. the direction in which a missile is pointed; the line of sighting: to take aim. 8. the point intended to be hit; thing or person aimed at. 9. something intended or desired to be attained by one's efforts; purpose. –phr. 10. **aim at** (or **towards**), to direct or point (something) in the direction of: to aim the gun at the target. 11. **aim for**, **a.** to direct or point (something) in the direction of: to aim for the target. **b.** to direct one's action or energies towards: to aim for perfection. –**aimless**, adj. –**aimer**, n.

air /ɛə/ n. 1. a mixture of oxygen, nitrogen and other gases, which surrounds the earth and forms its atmosphere. 2. the body of air immediately surrounding the earth, especially as regarded as the medium for the operation of aircraft or any airborne object or for the functioning of any creature relying on aerial power, as a bird. 3. a movement of the atmosphere; a light breeze. 4. the general character or complexion of anything; appearance. 5. the peculiar look, appearance, and bearing of a person. 6. (pl.) Also, **airs and graces**. an affected manner; manifestation of pride or vanity; assumed haughtiness: to put on airs. 7. Music **a.** a tune; a melody. **b.** the soprano or treble part. **c.** an aria. **d.** an Elizabethan song. 8. Radio the medium through which radio waves are sent. 9. Motor Vehicles air

conditioning. –v.t. 10. to expose to the air; give access to the open air; ventilate. 11. to expose to warm air; to dry with heated air: to air sheets. 12. to expose ostentatiously; bring into public notice; display: to air a pet theory. 13. Communications to broadcast or telecast. –phr. 14. **clear the air**, to eliminate dissension, ambiguity, or tension from a discussion, situation, etc. 15. **give oneself airs**, to behave in a conceited, haughty, or high-handed manner. 16. **in the air**, **a.** without foundation or actuality; visionary or uncertain. **b.** (of a rumour) in circulation. **c.** Also, **up in the air**. undecided or unsettled. 17. **into** (or **in**) **thin air**, completely or entirely out of sight or reach. 18. **off the air**, **a.** Also, **off air**. no longer being broadcast; not on the air. **b.** Colloq. incapacitated as a result of taking drugs or alcohol. **c.** Colloq. in a dreamy or vague state of mind, as if under the influence of drugs or alcohol. 19. **on** (the) **air**, in the act of broadcasting; being broadcast. 20. **take the air**, to go outdoors; walk or ride a little distance. 21. **walk** (or **tread**) **on air**, to feel very happy or elated. –**airing**, n.

airbag /ˈɛəbæg/ n. a safety device in a motor vehicle consisting of a bag which inflates instantly in front of the driver or front-seat passenger on collision.

airborne /ˈɛəbɔn/ adj. borne up, carried, or transported by air.

air brake n. 1. Aeronautics a hinged flap or other extendible device for reducing the speed of an aircraft. 2. a brake or system of brakes operated by compressed air.

airbrush /ˈɛəbrʌʃ/ n. 1. a small pencil-type spray gun used for very fine paint work or stencilling. –v.t. 2. to use an airbrush on (a motor body, sign, etc.): to airbrush the aircraft's tail wing. 3. to use an airbrush to touch up (a photograph).

air chief marshal n. Air Force 1. a commissioned officer of the highest rank in the Royal Australian Air Force. 2. the rank. Abbrev.: ACM

air commodore n. Air Force 1. a commissioned officer in the Royal Australian Air Force ranking below air vice-marshal and above group captain. 2. the rank. Abbrev.: AIRCDRE

air-condition v.t. to furnish with an air-conditioning system. –**air-conditioned**, adj.

air conditioner n. an apparatus for air-conditioning a room, house, car, etc.

air conditioning n. a system of treating air in buildings or vehicles to assure temperature, humidity, dustlessness, and movement at levels most conducive to personal comfort, manufacturing processes, or preservation of items stored, as books, etc. Also, **air-conditioning**.

air corridor n. an air route established by international agreement or government regulation.

aircraft /ˈɛəkrɑft/ n. any machine supported for flight in the air by buoyancy (such as balloons and other lighter-than-air craft) or by dynamic action of air on its surfaces (such as aeroplanes, helicopters, gliders, and other heavier-than-air craft).

aircraft carrier n. a large naval ship, designed to serve as an air base at sea, with a long strip of deck for the taking off and landing of aircraft.

aircraftman /ˈɛəkrɑftmən/ n. (pl. **-men**) Air Force 1. a man of the lowest rank in the Royal Australian Air Force. 2. the rank. Abbrev.: AC

aircraftwoman /ˈɛəkrɑftwʊmən/ n. (pl. **-women**) Air Force 1. a woman of the lowest rank in the Royal Australian Air Force. 2. the rank. Abbrev.: ACW

airfare /ˈɛəfɛə/ n. the price of a flight in a commercial aircraft.

airfield /ˈɛəfild/ n. a level area, usually equipped with hard-surfaced runways, buildings, etc., for the operation and maintenance of aircraft.

air force *n.* the branch of the armed forces of any country concerned with military aircraft.

air guitar *n.* an imaginary guitar which someone pretends to hold and play, usually to rock music.

air gun *n.* a gun operated by compressed air.

air kiss *n. Colloq.* a formalised kiss of greeting or farewell in which one's lips do not make contact with the other person.

airlift /'ɛəlɪft/ *n.* **1.** a system of transporting people, supplies, equipment, etc., by aircraft when surface routes are blocked, as during a military blockade, or at a time of national emergency. **2.** the act or process of transporting such a load. –*v.t.* **3.** to transport by airlift.

airline /'ɛəlaɪn/ *n.* **1.** a system furnishing scheduled air transport between specified points. **2.** the aeroplanes, airports, navigational aids, etc., of such a system. **3.** a company that owns or operates such a system.

airlock /'ɛəlɒk/ *n.* **1.** *Civil Eng., etc.* an airtight transition compartment at the entrance of a pressure chamber, as in a spacecraft or a submerged caisson. **2.** *Eng.* an obstruction to or stoppage of a flow of liquid in a pipe caused by an air bubble. **3.** *Archit.* an area between doors which impedes the flow of air between sections of a building.

airmail /'ɛəmeɪl/ *n.* the system of transmitting mail by aircraft.

airman /'ɛəmən/ *n.* (*pl.* **-men**) an aviator, especially a member of an air force. –**airmanship**, *n.*

air marshal *n.* **1.** an officer in the Royal Australian Air Force ranking below air chief marshal and above air vice-marshal. **2.** the rank. *Abbrev.*: AIRMSHL

air mass *n. Meteorol.* a large body of air, up to thousands of kilometres in extent, of uniform temperature and humidity, and impacting on an adjacent air mass at a well-defined front.

airplay /'ɛəpleɪ/ *n.* the amount of public exposure a recording receives on radio or television.

air pocket *n.* **1.** *Aeronautics* a downward current of air, usually causing a sudden loss of altitude. **2.** any pocket of air, as in a mine, where gas or water is held back by the air pressure in the pocket.

airport /'ɛəpɔt/ *n.* a large airfield usually equipped with a control tower, hangars, and accommodation for the receiving and discharging of passengers and cargo.

airport novel *n.* a style of popular fiction, presented usually as a thick paperback with a colourful cover, designed as light reading for long periods of travel.

air pressure *n.* **1.** the pressure of the atmosphere. **2.** the pressure exerted by the air, as inside a tyre.

air quotes *pl. n.* the representation of quotation marks during speech, made by a movement of the fingers in the air, and used to indicate that an expression is a quotation, is intended ironically, or is one that the speaker would not normally use.

air rage *n.* uncontrolled aggressive behaviour in an aeroplane, resulting from the tensions of air travel.

air raid *n.* a raid by hostile aircraft, especially for dropping bombs or other missiles. –**air-raider**, *n.*

airship /'ɛəʃɪp/ *n.* a self-propelled, lighter-than-air craft with means of controlling the direction of flight, usually classed as rigid, semi-rigid, or nonrigid.

air show *n.* an exhibition of aircraft, often including a display of air formations and stunts. Also, **airshow**.

airspace /'ɛəspeɪs/ *n.* **1.** the part or region of the atmosphere above the territory of a nation or other political division which is considered under its jurisdiction. **2.** the space directly above a building which can be sold for the construction of another building on or over the first. **3.** the space between the cork and the wine in a wine bottle. **4.** any defined space, as in a

room, vehicle, etc., especially when considered in terms of ventilation. **5.** → **airtime** (def. 1).

air strike *n.* an attack by fighters, bombers or attack aircraft on a specific objective. Also, **airstrike**.

airstrip /'ɛəstrɪp/ *n.* a runway, especially a single runway forming a landing ground in a remote place.

air terminal *n.* a place of assembly for air passengers, not necessarily at an airport, with administrative offices, etc.

airtight /'ɛətaɪt/ *adj.* **1.** so tight or close as to be impermeable to air. **2.** having no weak points or openings of which an opponent may take advantage.

airtime /'ɛətaɪm/ *n.* **1.** Also, **airspace**. the amount of television or radio broadcasting time dedicated to a particular subject, person, recording, etc. **2.** the amount of time a mobile phone is able to be used, especially that allocated under a mobile phone service provision contract: *unlimited airtime*. Also, **air time**.

air traffic control *n.* direction of airborne aircraft movement by ground-based personnel via a radiotelephone link or, in emergencies, by light signals.

air vice-marshal *n. Air Force* **1.** a commissioned officer in the Royal Australian Air Force ranking below air marshal and above air commodore. **2.** the rank. *Abbrev.*: AVM

airwaves /'ɛəweɪvz/ *pl. n.* (*in non-technical use*) the medium used for transmission of television, radio and wireless communications signals.

airy /'ɛəri/ *adj.* (**airier**, **airiest**) **1.** open to a free current of air; breezy: *airy rooms*. **2.** light in appearance; thin: *airy lace*. **3.** light in manner or movement; lively; graceful: *an airy walk*. **4.** light as air; insubstantial; imaginary: *airy dreams*. **5.** careless; superficial; flippant: *an airy wave goodbye*. –**airily**, *adv.* –**airiness**, *n.*

aisle /aɪl/ *n.* **1. a.** a passageway between seats in a church, hall, etc. **b.** a passageway between seats in a bus, train, aeroplane, etc. **c.** a passageway between shelves in a supermarket, etc. **2.** *Archit.* **a.** a lateral division of a church or other building separated from the nave by piers or columns. **b.** a similar division at the side of the choir or transept. **c.** any of the lateral divisions of a church or hall, as the nave. –*phr.* **3. lay them in the aisles**, *Colloq.* to impress people favourably. –**aisled** /aɪld/, *adj.*

ajar[1] /ə'dʒa/ *adv.* **1.** neither quite open nor shut; partly opened: *leave the door ajar*. –*adj.* **2.** partly open.

ajar[2] /ə'dʒa/ *adj.* out of harmony; jarring: *ajar with the world*.

aka[1] /'aka/ *n.* any of several species of woody, climbing vines of the genus *Metrosideros* native to New Zealand; rata.

aka[2] /'æka/ *adv.* also known as: *Smith aka Jones*.

akeake /'aki,aki/ *n.* **1.** a large, tropical, hard-wooded shrub, *Dodonaea viscosa*, with young twigs compressed or triangular and viscid. **2.** either of two New Zealand trees, *Olearia avicenniaefolia* and *O. traversii*. Also, **ake**.

AK-47 /eɪ keɪ-fɔti 'sɛvən/ *n.* a type of Kalashnikov automatic rifle.

akimbo /ə'kɪmboʊ/ *adv.* with hands on hips and elbows bent outwards: *to stand with arms akimbo*.

akin /ə'kɪn/ *adj.* **1.** related by blood. **2.** allied by nature; partaking of the same properties.

al- variant of **ad-** before *l*, as in *allure*.

-al[1] an adjective suffix meaning 'relating to', 'connected with', 'being', 'like', 'befitting', etc., occurring in numerous adjectives and in many nouns of adjectival origin, as *annual, choral, equal, regal*.

-al[2] a suffix forming nouns of action from verbs, as in *refusal, denial, recital, trial*.

-al[3] a suffix indicating that a compound includes an aldehyde group, as in *chloral*.

ala /ˈeɪlə/ *n.* (*pl.* **alae** /ˈeɪli/) **1.** a wing. **2.** a winglike part, process, or expansion, as of a bone, a shell, a seed, a stem, etc.

alabaster /ˈæləbæstə, æləˈbæstə, ˈæləbastə/ *n.* **1.** a finely granular variety of gypsum, often white and translucent, used for ornamental objects or work, such as lamp bases, figurines, etc. **2.** a variety of calcite, often with a banded structure, used for similar purposes (**oriental alabaster**). *—adj.* Also, **alabastrine** /ælə'bæstrɒn/ **3.** made of alabaster: *an alabaster column*. **4.** resembling alabaster; smooth and white as alabaster: *her alabaster throat*.

à la carte /a la ˈkat/ *adv.* according to the menu; with a stated price for each dish: *dinner à la carte*.

alacrity /əˈlækrəti/ *n.* **1.** liveliness; briskness; sprightliness. **2.** cheerful readiness or willingness. **–alacritous**, *adj.*

alarm /əˈlam/ *n.* **1.** a sudden fear or painful suspense caused by recognition of danger; apprehension; fright. **2.** any sound or message to warn of approaching danger: *a false alarm; to give the alarm*. **3.** (a sound from) a device of any kind used to call attention, wake from sleep, warn of danger, etc. *–v.t.* **4.** to fill with sudden fear or worry. **5.** to fit (a house, motor vehicle, etc.) with an alarm system. **–alarmed**, *adj.* **–alarmingly**, *adv.*

alarmist /əˈlaməst/ *n.* someone given to raising alarms, especially without sufficient reason, as by exaggerating dangers, prophesying calamities, etc. **–alarmism**, *n.*

alas /əˈlæs, əˈlas/ *interj.* an exclamation expressing sorrow, grief, pity, concern, or apprehension of evil.

alb /ælb/ *n.* a loose-fitting white linen robe with long sleeves, worn by an officiating priest.

albatross /ˈælbətrɒs/ *n.* **1.** any of various large webfooted seabirds related to the petrels, especially of the genera *Diomedea* and *Thalassarche*, of the Pacific and southern waters, noted for their powers of flight. **2.** *Golf* a score of three strokes below the par figure for a hole.

albeit /ɔlˈbiət, æl-/ *conj.* notwithstanding that: *to choose a strategic albeit inglorious retreat*.

albino /ælˈbinoʊ, -ˈbaɪnoʊ/ *n.* (*pl.* **-nos**) **1.** a person with a pale, milky skin, light hair, and pink eyes, resulting from a congenital absence of pigmentation. **2.** an animal or plant with a marked deficiency in pigmentation. *—adj.* **3.** of or relating to albinos or albinism. **–albinism** /ˈælbənɪzəm/, *n.*

album /ˈælbəm/ *n.* **1.** a book consisting of blank leaves for the insertion or preservation of photographs, stamps, autographs, etc. **2.** long-playing recording on which there is a collection of songs or pieces: *an album of Puccini arias*.

albumen /ˈælbjəmən/ *n.* **1.** the white of an egg. **2.** *Bot.* the nutritive matter around the embryo in a seed.

albumin /ˈælbjəmən/ *n.* any of a class of water-soluble proteins occurring in animal and vegetable fluids and tissues.

alchemy /ˈælkəmi/ *n.* **1.** the medieval chemical science which sought in particular to transmute baser metals into gold, and to find a universal solvent and an elixir of life. **2.** any magical power or process of transmuting. **–alchemic** /ælˈkɛmɪk/, **alchemical**, *adj.* **–alchemically**, *adv.*

alcheringa /æltʃəˈrɪŋgə/ *n.* → **Dreaming** (def. 1). Also, **alchera** /ˈæltʃərə/.

alcohol /ˈælkəhɒl/ *n.* **1.** a colourless, flammable liquid (**ethyl alcohol**, C_2H_5OH), the intoxicating principle of fermented liquors, formed from certain sugars (especially glucose) by fermentation, now usually prepared by treating grain with malt and adding yeast. **2.** any intoxicating beverage containing this spirit. **3.** *Chem.* any of a class of chemical compounds derived from the

hydrocarbon by replacement of a hydrogen atom by the hydroxyl radical, OH.

alcoholic /ælkəˈhɒlɪk/ *adj.* **1.** relating to or containing alcohol. **2.** caused by alcohol: *alcoholic poisoning*. **3.** suffering from alcoholism. *–n.* **4.** a person suffering from alcoholism.

alcoholism /ˈælkəhɒlɪzəm/ *n.* **1.** an addiction to alcohol. **2.** a diseased condition due to the excessive consumption of alcoholic beverages.

alcopop /ˈælkoʊpɒp/ *n.* a commercially-sold alcoholic drink based on a soft drink, such as lemonade, etc., to which alcohol has been added.

alcove /ˈælkoʊv/ *n.* **1.** a recess opening out of a room. **2.** a recess in a room for a bed, for books in a library, or for other similar furnishings. **3.** any recessed space, as in a garden.

aldehyde /ˈældəhaɪd/ *n.* one of a group of organic compounds with the general formula R-CHO, which yield acids when oxidised and alcohols when reduced. **–aldehydic** /ældəˈhaɪdɪk/, *adj.*

alderman /ˈɔldəmən/ *n.* (*pl.* **-men**) **1.** (in various countries, as Australia and the US) an elected local government representative having powers varying according to locality; councillor. **2.** (formerly, in Britain) a senior member of a county council or other local government body, elected by other members of the council. **–aldermanity** /ɔldəˈmænəti/, **aldermanship**, *n.* **–aldermanic** /ɔldəˈmænɪk/, *adj.*

ale /eɪl/ *n.* **1.** any of various English types of beer brewed by the top-fermentation method. **2.** any beer.

aleatory /æliˈeɪtəri/ *adj.* dependent on chance.

alert /əˈlɜt/ *adj.* **1.** vigilantly attentive: *an alert mind*. **2.** quick to react. *–n.* **3.** an attitude of vigilance, wariness or caution. **4.** an alarm or warning, especially an air-raid warning. **5.** the period during which such a warning is in effect. *–v.t.* **6.** to prepare (troops, etc.) for action. **7.** to warn of an impending raid or attack. *–phr.* **8. on the alert**, (sometimes fol. by *for*) watchful and attentive; on the lookout: *on the alert for danger*. **–alerted**, *adj.* **–alertly**, *adv.* **–alertness**, *n.*

Alexandrine /ælɪgˈzændrin, -draɪn/ *Prosody* *–n.* **1.** a verse or line of poetry of six iambic feet. *–adj.* **2.** designating such a verse or line.

alfalfa /ælˈfælfə/ *n.* **1.** *Chiefly US* → **lucerne** (def. 1). **2.** → **alfalfa sprouts**.

alfalfa sprouts *pl. n.* the sprouts of alfalfa seeds, used in salads. Also, **alfalfa**.

alfresco /ælˈfrɛskoʊ/ *adv.* **1.** in the open air; out-of-doors: *to dine alfresco*. *–adj.* **2.** open-air: *an alfresco cafe*. Also, **al fresco**.

alga /ˈælgə/ *n.* the singular form of **algae**. **–algal**, *adj.*

algae /ˈældʒi, ˈælgi/ *pl. n.* (*sing.* **alga**) chlorophyll-containing plants belonging to the phylum Thallophyta, comprising the seaweeds and various freshwater forms and varying in form and size, from single microscopic cells, sometimes single and sometimes large and branching, to forms with trunk-like stems many metres in length. They constitute a subphylum, the Algae.

algebra /ˈældʒəbrə/ *n.* **1.** the mathematical art of reasoning about (quantitative) relations by means of a systematised notation including letters and other symbols; the analysis of equations, combinatorial analysis, theory of fractions, etc. **2.** any special system of notation adapted to the study of a special system of relationships: *algebra of classes*. **3.** *Maths* **a.** the study of mathematical systems possessing operations analogous to those of addition and multiplication. **b.** a particular system of the above type: *vector algebra; matrix algebra*. **–algebraic**, *adj.*

-algia a noun suffix meaning 'pain', as in *neuralgia*.

algo- a word element meaning 'pain', as in *algolagnia*.

ALGOL /ˈælɡɒl/ *n.* an internationally accepted language in which computer programs are written, in algebraic notation following the rules of Boolean algebra. Also, **Algol.**

algorithm /ˈælɡərɪðəm/ *n.* an effective procedure for solving a particular mathematical problem in a finite number of steps. –**algorithmic** /ælɡəˈrɪðmɪk/, *adj.*

alias /ˈeɪliəs/ *adv.* **1.** known sometimes as: *Simpson alias Smith.* –*n.* (*pl.* **aliases**) **2.** an assumed name; another name: *living under an alias.*

alibi /ˈæləbaɪ/ *n.* (*pl.* **-bis**) **1.** *Law* a defence by an accused person that he or she was elsewhere at the time the offence with which he or she is charged was committed. **2.** the evidence that proves one was elsewhere. **3.** *Colloq.* an excuse.

alien /ˈeɪliən/ *n.* **1.** someone born in or belonging to another country who has not acquired citizenship by naturalisation and is not entitled to the privileges of a citizen. **2.** someone who has been estranged or excluded; an outsider. **3.** (in science fiction) an extraterrestrial being. **4.** *Biol.* an organism introduced by humans into a region which is outside the range of its natural distribution, as the rabbit or the prickly pear in Australia. –*adj.* **5.** belonging or relating to aliens: *alien property.* **6.** (in science fiction) of or relating to an extraterrestrial being, life-form, etc.: *alien spacecraft.* –*phr.* **7.** alien to, opposed to; incompatible with; repugnant to: *ideas alien to our way of thinking.*

alienate /ˈeɪliəneɪt/ *v.t.* **1.** to make indifferent or averse; estrange. **2.** to turn away: *to alienate the affections.* **3.** to cause to feel hostility or antipathy: *a council decision that alienates the community.* **4.** *Law* to transfer or convey, as title, property, or other right, to another: *to alienate lands.* –**alienator**, *n.* –**alienation** /eɪliənˈeɪʃən/, *n.*

alight[1] /əˈlaɪt/ *v.i.* (**alighted** or **alit** /əˈlɪt/, **alighting**) **1.** to get down from a horse or out of a vehicle; dismount. **2.** to settle or stay after descending: *a bird alights on a tree.* **3.** (of aircraft) to land. –*phr.* **4.** alight on (or upon), to come on accidentally, or without design.

alight[2] /əˈlaɪt/ *adv., adj.* provided with light; lighted up; burning.

align /əˈlaɪn/ *v.t.* **1.** to adjust to a line; lay out or regulate by line; form in line. **2.** to adjust (mechanical items such as car wheels) so that as a group they are in positions favouring optimum performance. –*v.i.* **3.** to fall or come into line; be in line. **4.** to join with others in a cause. –**aligner**, *n.* –**alignment**, *n.*

alike /əˈlaɪk/ *adv.* **1.** in the same manner, form, or degree; in common; equally: *known to treat all customers alike.* –*adj.* **2.** having resemblance or similarity; having or exhibiting no marked or essential difference (used regularly of a plural substantive or idea, and only in the predicate): *he thinks all politicians are alike.*

alimentary /æləˈmɛntri/ *adj.* **1.** concerned with the function of nutrition. **2.** providing sustenance or maintenance.

alimentary canal *n.* the digestive passage in any animal from mouth to anus. Also, **alimentary tract.**

alimony /ˈæləmənɪ/, *Orig. US* /-moʊni/ *n. Chiefly US* → **maintenance** (def. 4).

aliphatic /æləˈfætɪk/ *adj.* relating to or concerned with those organic compounds which are open chains, as the paraffins.

A-list /ˈeɪ-lɪst/ *n. Colloq.* a list, often unwritten, of the most desirable celebrities or other public figures sought for prestigious or spectacular social events, etc. Also, **A list.**

alive /əˈlaɪv/ *adj.* (*rarely used attributively*) **1.** in life or existence; living. **2.** (by way of emphasis) of all living: *the proudest person alive.* **3.** in a state of action; in force or operation; unextinguished: *keep a memory*

alive. 4. full of life; lively: *alive with excitement.* **5.** filled as with living things; swarming; thronged; teeming. –*phr.* **6.** alive and kicking, *Colloq.* in good health and active. **7.** alive to, attentive to; awake or sensitive to. **8.** be alive and well, *Colloq.* an expression confirming someone's continued existence: *she's alive and well and living in Nunawading.* –**aliveness**, *n.*

alkali /ˈælkəlaɪ/ *n.* (*pl.* **-lis** or **-lies**) *Chem.* **1.** any of various bases, the hydroxides of the alkali metals and of ammonium, which neutralise acids to form salts and turn red litmus paper blue. **2.** any of various other more or less active bases, as calcium hydroxide. –**alkaline**, *adj.* –**alkalinity** /ælkəˈlɪnəti/, *n.*

all /ɔl/ *adj.* **1.** the whole of (with reference to quantity, extent, duration, amount, or degree): *all Australia*; *all the year round.* **2.** the whole number of (with reference to individuals or particulars, taken collectively): *all women.* **3.** a large number of; many: *he collects all kinds of things*; *all sorts of people were there.* **4.** any; any whatever: *beyond all doubt.* **5.** the greatest possible: *with all speed.* –*pron.* **6.** the whole quantity or amount: *all of the cake.* **7.** the whole number: *all of us.* **8.** everything: *is that all?* –*n.* **9.** a whole; a totality of things or qualities. **10.** one's whole interest, concern, or property: *to give one's all*; *to lose one's all.* –*adv.* **11.** wholly; entirely; quite: *all alone.* **12.** each; apiece: *the score was all one all.* **13.** by so much; to that extent: *rain made conditions all the worse.* –*phr.* **14.** above all, before everything else. **15.** after all, **a.** after everything has been considered; notwithstanding: *it's not her fault after all.* **b.** in spite of all that was done, said, etc.: *he lost the fight after all.* **16.** all aboard, **a.** an exclamation warning intending passengers, used by transport attendants, conductors, etc. **b.** *NZ* a cry given by shearers when shearing is about to begin. **17.** all in, *Colloq.* exhausted. **18.** all in all, **a.** taking everything together: *all in all, we're better off now.* **b.** someone's sole and exclusive concern in life: *she is his all in all.* **19.** all or nothing, a deep commitment or no involvement at all: *with me it's all or nothing.* **20.** all over, **a.** representatively; typically: *that's him all over.* **b.** completely finished: *the game's all over.* **c.** everywhere: *to look all over for something.* **d.** over the whole extent: *he has spots all over.* **21.** all over the place, in a state of confusion and disorder. **22.** all that, *Colloq.* of exceptional worth. **23.** all up, *Colloq.* with everything included: *the cost is $25 all up.* **24.** and all, as well as everything else; moreover. **25.** and all that, and so on; et cetera. **26.** as all get out, (*placed after an adjective*) *Colloq.* in the extreme: *as angry as all get out.* **27.** at all, **a.** in any degree: *not bad at all.* **b.** for any reason: *I was surprised at his coming at all.* **c.** in any way: *no offence at all.* **28.** for all that, notwithstanding; nevertheless. **29.** for all to see, open to public gaze. **30.** for good and all, forever; finally. **31.** in all, included: *a hundred people in all.*

Allah /ˈælə/ *n. Islam* God; the Supreme Being.

allay /əˈleɪ/ *v.t.* **1.** to put at rest; quiet (tumult, fear, suspicion, etc.); appease (wrath). **2.** to mitigate; relieve or alleviate: *to allay pain.* –**allayer**, *n.*

allege /əˈlɛdʒ/ *v.t.* (**-leged, -leging**) **1.** to assert without proof. **2.** to declare before a court, or elsewhere as if upon oath. **3.** to declare with positiveness; affirm; assert. **4.** to plead in support of; urge as a reason or excuse. –**allegation** /æləˈɡeɪʃən/, *n.* –**allegeable**, *adj.* –**allegedly**, *adv.* –**alleger**, *n.*

allegiance /əˈlidʒəns/ *n.* **1.** the obligation of a subject or citizen to his or her sovereign or government; duty owed to a sovereign or state. **2.** observance of obligation; faithfulness to any person or thing.

allegory /ˈæləɡəri, -gri/ *n.* (*pl.* **-ries**) **1.** figurative treatment of one subject under the guise of another; a presentation of an abstract or spiritual meaning under concrete or material forms. **2.** a symbolic narrative: *the political allegory of Piers Plowman.* –**allegorical** /ælə-ˈgɒrɪkəl/, *adj.* –**allegorist,** *n.*

allegro /əˈlɛgroʊ, əˈleɪgroʊ/ *adv. Music* in rapid tempo.

alleluia /ælɪˈluːjə/ *interj.* **1.** praise to the Lord; hallelujah. –*n.* **2.** a song of praise to God.

allergen /ˈælədʒən/ *n.* any substance which might induce an allergy. –**allergenic** /ælɪˈdʒɛnɪk/, *adj.*

allergy /ˈælədʒi/ *n.* (*pl.* **-gies**) **1.** a state of physical hypersensitivity to certain things, as pollens, food, fruits, etc., which are normally harmless. Hay fever, asthma, and hives are common allergies. **2.** the symptoms produced by reaction to an allergen, as oedema and inflammation. **3.** *Colloq.* a dislike or antipathy: *an allergy to hard work.* –**allergic** /əˈlɜːdʒɪk/, *adj.*

alleviate /əˈliːvieɪt/ *v.t.* to make easier to be endured; lessen; mitigate: *to alleviate sorrow, pain, punishment, etc.* –**alleviation** /əliːviˈeɪʃən/, *n.* –**alleviator,** *n.*

alley /ˈæli/ *n.* (*pl.* **-leys**) **1.** a narrow enclosed lane. **2.** a narrow backstreet. **3.** a long narrow enclosure with a smooth wooden floor for bowling, etc. –*phr.* **4. up someone's alley,** *Colloq.* in the sphere that someone knows or likes best.

alliance /əˈlaɪəns/ *n.* **1.** the state of being allied or connected. **2.** a formal agreement by two or more nations to work together for special purposes. **3.** a joining of efforts or interests by persons, families, states, or organisations: *an alliance between church and state.* **4.** a marriage, or union brought about between families through marriage.

allied /ˈælaɪd/ *adj.* **1.** joined by treaty. **2.** related: *allied species.*

allied angle *n. Maths* one of a pair of angles formed by the intersection of two parallel lines with a transversal, such that both angles lie on the same side of the transversal and are between the parallel lines. Also, **co-interior angle.**

alligator /ˈælɪgeɪtə/ *n.* **1.** any broad-snouted representative of the order Crocodylia found in America. **2.** used erroneously for crocodiles and gavials found in other parts of the world, such as the Australian saltwater crocodile *Crocodylus porosus.*

alligator weed *n.* a weed with broad leaves and white flowers, *Alternanthera philoxeroides,* commonly found in Australian waterways.

alliteration /əlɪtəˈreɪʃən/ *n.* **1.** the commencement of two or more stressed syllables of a word group: **a.** with the same consonant sound or sound group (**consonantal alliteration**), as in *from stem to stern.* **b.** with a vowel sound which may differ from syllable to syllable (**vocalic alliteration**), as in *each to all.* **2.** the commencement of two or more words of a word group with the same letter, as in *apt alliteration's artful aid.* –**alliterative** /əˈlɪtərətɪv/, *adj.*

allo- a word element indicating difference, alternation, or divergence, as in *allonym, allomerism.* Also, **all-.**

allocate /ˈæləkeɪt/ *v.t.* **1.** to set apart for a particular purpose; assign or allot: *to allocate shares.* **2.** to fix the place of; locate. –**allocation** /æləˈkeɪʃən/, *n.*

All Ordinaries Index *n.* (*sometimes lower case*) (on the Australian Stock Exchange) an index which gives a weighted average of the ordinary share prices of a specified large group of companies expressed in relation to a base period. Also, **All Ords.**

allot /əˈlɒt/ *v.t.* (**-lotted, -lotting**) **1.** to divide or distribute as by lot; distribute or parcel out; apportion: *to allot shares.* **2.** to appropriate to a special purpose: *to allot money for a new park.* **3.** to assign as a portion (*to*); set apart; appoint. –**allotter,** *n.*

allotment /əˈlɒtmənt/ *n.* **1.** the act of allotting; distribution; apportionment. **2.** a portion, share, or thing

allotted. **3.** a block of land: *vacant allotment.* **4.** *Brit.* a small plot of land let out by a public authority to an individual for gardening, especially vegetable growing.

allotrope /ˈælətroʊp/ *n.* one of two or more existing forms of a chemical element: *charcoal, graphite, and diamond are allotropes of carbon.*

all-out *adj.* using all one's resources; complete; total: *an all-out effort.*

allow /əˈlaʊ/ *v.t.* **1.** to grant permission to or for; permit: *to allow a student to be absent; no smoking allowed.* **2.** to let have; grant or give as one's share or suited to one's needs; assign as one's right: *to allow someone $100 for expenses; to allow someone so much a year.* **3.** to permit involuntarily, by neglect or oversight: *to allow an error to occur.* **4.** to admit; acknowledge; concede: *to allow a claim.* **5.** to take into account; set apart; abate or deduct: *to allow an hour for changing trains.* **6.** *US* to say or think. –*v.i.* **7.** to permit; make possible: *to spend more than one's salary allows.* –*phr.* **8. allow for,** to make concession, allowance, or provision for: *to allow for breakage.* –**allowable,** *adj.*

allowance /əˈlaʊəns/ *n.* **1.** a definite amount or share given or set apart; ration. **2.** a definite sum of money allotted or granted to meet expenses or requirements. **3.** an addition, as to a wage, etc., on account of some extenuating or qualifying circumstance: *a travel allowance.* **4.** a deduction: *allowance for breakages.* **5.** acceptance; admission: *the allowance of a claim.* **6.** tolerance: *we made allowance for his youth.* **7.** *Mechanics* a prescribed variation in dimensions (size). See **tolerance.** –*phr.* **8. make allowance(s)**, (*sometimes fol. by for*) **a.** to take special circumstances into account in mitigating a judgement: *to make allowances for her broken arm.* **b.** to include relevant factors in reaching a conclusion: *to make allowance for increased humidity.*

alloy *n.* /ˈælɔɪ/ **1.** a substance composed of two or more metals (or, sometimes, a metal and a nonmetal) which have been intimately mixed by fusion, electrolytic deposition, or the like. **2.** a less costly metal mixed with a more valuable one. **3.** *Obs.* standard; quality; fineness. –*v.t.* /əˈlɔɪ, ˈælɔɪ/ **4.** to mix (metals) so as to form an alloy. **5.** to debase, impair, or reduce by admixture.

all right *adj.* **1.** in good condition; not harmed, damaged or sick. **2.** satisfactory but not outstanding: *his work is all right, but not worth a raise.* **3.** acceptable or permissible: *is it all right if I leave early?* –*adv.* **4.** satisfactorily; acceptably; correctly: *he did his job all right.* Also, **alright.**

all-round *adj.* **1.** able to do many things. **2.** having general use; not too specialised. –**all-rounder,** *n.*

allspice /ˈɔːlspaɪs/ *n.* **1.** the berry of a tropical American myrtaceous tree, *Pimenta dioica.* **2.** a mildly sharp and fragrant spice made from it; pimento.

allude /əˈluːd/ *phr.* **allude to, 1.** to make an allusion to, refer casually or indirectly to: *he often alluded to his poverty.* **2.** to contain a casual or indirect reference: *the letter alludes to something now forgotten.*

all-up *adj.* **1.** total, inclusive: *the all-up weight is three tonnes.* **2.** cumulative: *an all-up bet.*

allure /əˈluə, əˈljuə/ *v.t.* **1.** to attract by the offer of some real or apparent good; tempt by something flattering or acceptable. **2.** to fascinate; charm. –*n.* **3.** fascination; charm. –**allurer,** *n.* –**alluring,** *adj.*

allusion /əˈluːʒən/ *n.* a passing or casual reference; an incidental mention of something, either directly or by implication: *a classical allusion.* –**allusive,** *adj.*

alluvial /əˈluːviəl/ *adj.* **1.** of or relating to alluvium. **2.** of or relating to a mine, claim, diggings, etc., on alluvial soil. –*n.* **3.** soil deposited by flowing water. **4. the alluvial,** gold-bearing alluvial ground.

alluvium /əˈluːviəm/ *n.* (*pl.* **-viums** *or* **-via** /-viə/) **1.** a deposit of sand, mud, etc., formed by flowing water.

2. the sedimentary matter deposited thus within recent times, especially in the valleys of large rivers.

all-wheel drive *n.* **1.** a system which gives a constant connection of all four wheels of a motor vehicle to the source of power. **2.** a motor vehicle which has such a system. *Abbrev.*: AWD

ally *verb* /ə'laɪ/ (**-lied, -lying**) *–v.t.* **1.** to bind together; connect by some relation, as by resemblance or friendship; associate. *–v.i.* **2.** to enter into an alliance; join or unite. *–n.* /'ælaɪ/ (*pl.* **-lies**) **3.** one united or associated with another, especially by treaty or league; an allied nation, sovereign, etc. **4.** someone who cooperates with another; supporter; associate. *–phr.* **5. ally to** (or **with**), to unite with by marriage, treaty, league, or confederacy; connect with by formal agreement.

alma mater /ælmə 'meɪtə, ælmɑ 'mɑtə/ *n.* (*sometimes upper case*) one's school, college, or university.

almanac /'ɔlmənæk, 'æl-/ *n.* a calendar of the days of the year, in weeks and months, indicating the time of various events or phenomena during the period, as anniversaries, sunrise and sunset, changes of the moon and tides, etc., or giving other pertinent information. Also, **almanack**.

almighty /ɔl'maɪti/ *adj.* **1.** possessing all power; omnipotent: *God Almighty.* **2.** having great might; overpowering: *the almighty power of the press.* **3.** *Colloq.* great; extreme *–adv.* **4.** an intensifier **–almightily,** *adv.* **–almightiness,** *n.*

almond /'amənd/ *n.* **1.** the stone (nut) or kernel (sweet or bitter) of the fruit of the almond tree, *Prunus dulcis,* which grows in warm temperate regions. **2.** a flavour or flavouring of or like almonds. **3.** a delicate pale tan colour. *–adj.* **4.** of an almond colour. **5.** shaped like an almond: *almond eyes.*

almost /'ɔlmoʊst/ *adv.* very nearly; all but.

alms /amz/ *n.* (*construed as sing. or pl.*) that which is given to the poor or needy; anything given as charity.

aloe /'æloʊ/ *n.* (*pl.* **aloes**) **1.** any plant of the liliaceous genus *Aloe,* chiefly African, various species of which yield a drug (**aloes**) and a fibre. **2.** (*oft. pl. construed as sing.*) a bitter purgative drug, made from the juice of the leaves of several species of *Aloe.* **3.** American aloe; the century plant. **4.** (*pl. construed as sing.*) a fragrant resin of wood from the heart of a tropical Asian tree, the eaglewood.

aloe vera /æloʊ 'vɪərə/ *n.* an aloe plant, *Aloe barbadensis,* having fleshy leaves from which a vulnerary agent is derived which is used in skin lotions, gels, etc.

aloft /ə'lɒft/ *adv., adj.* high up; in or into the air; above the ground.

alone /ə'loʊn/ *adj.* (*used in the predicate or following the noun*) **1.** apart from another or others: *to be alone.* **2.** to the exclusion of all others or all else: *man shall not live by bread alone. –adv.* **3.** solitarily. **4.** only; merely. *–phr.* **5. leave** (or **let**) **alone,** to refrain from bothering or interfering with. **6. let alone,** not to mention: *let alone his other failings.* **7. stand alone,** to be unique by virtue of one's talents, ability, etc. **–aloneness,** *n.*

along /ə'lɒŋ/ *prep.* **1.** implying motion or direction through or by the length of; from one end to the other of: *to walk along a road.* **2.** by the length of; parallel to or in a line with the length of: *a row of poppies along the path.* **3.** in accordance with: *along the lines suggested. –adv.* **4.** in a line, or with a progressive motion; onwards. **5.** by the length; lengthways. **6.** as a companion; with one: *he took his sister along. –phr.* **7. all along, a.** all the time. **b.** throughout; continuously. **c.** from end to end. **d.** at full length. **8. along with,** in addition to. **9. be along,** to come to a place: *he will soon be along.* **10. get along, a.** *Colloq.* to go; depart. **b.** (*sometimes fol. by with*) to be on amicable terms.

c. to manage successfully; cope: *to get along okay.* **11. get along with you,** *Colloq.* an exclamation of dismissal or disbelief. **12. go along with, a.** to agree with. **b.** to go in company with or together with: *I'll go along with you a little way.*

alongside /əlɒŋ'saɪd/ *adv.* **1.** along or by the side; at or to the side of anything: *we brought the boat alongside. –prep.* **2.** beside; by the side of.

aloof /ə'luf/ *adv.* **1.** at a distance, but within view; withdrawn: *to stand aloof. –adj.* **2.** reserved and undemonstrative: *to appear aloof and unfriendly.* **–aloofly,** *adv.* **–aloofness,** *n.*

alopecia /ælə'piʃə/ *n.* loss of hair; baldness.

aloud /ə'laʊd/ *adv.* **1.** with the natural tone of the voice as distinguished from a whisper or silently: *to read aloud.* **2.** with a loud voice; loudly: *to cry aloud.*

alp /ælp/ *n.* **1.** a high mountain. **2.** (*pl.*) a high mountain system, usually covered with snow. **–alpine,** *adj.*

alpaca /æl'pækə/ *n.* **1.** a domesticated South American ruminant, *Lama pacos,* raised for its long, soft, silky hair or wool, thought to be descended from the guanaco. **2.** a fabric made of the hair.

alpha /'ælfə/ *n.* **1.** the first letter in the Greek alphabet (A, α = English A, a), often used to designate the first in a series, especially in scientific classifications as: **a.** (*upper case*) *Astron.* a star, usually the brightest of a constellation: *Alpha Centauri.* **b.** *Chem.* (of a compound) one of the possible positions of substituted atoms or groups. **c.** (in examinations, etc.) the highest mark. **2.** the first; beginning. *–adj.* **3.** *Zool.* holding the dominant position in a group of social animals: *alpha pair; alpha wolf.*

alphabet /'ælfəbɛt/ *n.* **1.** the letters of a language in their customary order. **2.** any system of characters or signs for representing sounds or ideas. **–alphabetical,** *adj.*

alpha male *n.* **1.** *Zool.* the dominant male in a group of social animals. **2.** *Colloq.* an assertive or dominant man.

alphanumeric /ˌælfənju'mɛrɪk/ *adj.* Also, **alphanumerical. 1.** (of a set of characters) conveying information by using both letters and numbers. **2.** (of a character) being either a letter or a number. *–n.* **3.** a character which is either a letter or a number. **–alphanumerically,** *adv.*

already /ɔl'rɛdi/ *adv.* by this (or that) time; previously to or at some specified time.

alright /ɔl'raɪt/ *adj.* **1.** in good condition; not harmed, damaged or sick. **2.** satisfactory but not outstanding: *his work is alright, but not worth a raise.* **3.** acceptable or permissible: *is it alright if I leave early? –adv.* **4.** satisfactorily; acceptably; correctly: *he did his job alright.* Also, **all right.**

Alsatian /æl'seɪʃən/ *n.* → **German shepherd.**

also /'ɔlsoʊ/ *adv.* in addition; too; further.

also-ran *n.* **1.** an unplaced horse in a race. **2.** a nonentity.

alt- variant of **alto-** before vowels.

altar /'ɔltə, 'ɒl-/ *n.* **1.** an elevated place or structure, on which sacrifices are offered or at which religious rites are performed. **2.** (in most Christian churches) the communion table. *–phr.* **3. lead to the altar,** to marry.

alter /'ɔltə, 'ɒl-/ *v.t.* **1.** to make different in some particular; modify. **2.** *Colloq.* to castrate or spay. *–v.i.* **3.** to become different in some respect. *–n.* **4.** → **alter ego** (def. 3). **–alteration** /ɔltə'reɪʃən, ɒl-/, *n.* **–alterability** /ɔltrə'bɪləti, ɒl-/, *n.* **–alterative,** *adj.* **–alterable,** *adj.*

altercation /ɔltə'keɪʃən, ɒl-/ *n.* a heated or angry dispute; a noisy wrangle. **–altercative** /'ɔltəkeɪtɪv, 'ɒl-/, *adj.*

alter ego *n.* **1.** a second self. **2.** an inseparable friend. **3.** Also, **alter.** *Psychiatry* an alternative identity existing for a person who has dissociative identity disorder.

alternate *v.i.* /'ɔltəneɪt, 'ɒl-/ **1.** (usu. fol. by *with*) to follow one another in time or place: *day and night* *alternate with each other.* **2.** to change about by turns between points, states, actions, etc.: *he alternates between hope and despair.* –*v.t.* /ˈɔltəneɪt, ˈɒl-/ **3.** to use or perform by turns, or one after another. –*adj.* /ɔlˈtɜnət, ɒl-/ **4.** arranged or following each after the other, in succession: *alternate winter and summer.* **5.** every other one of a series: *read only alternate lines.* **6.** (*not considered standard by some*) affording a choice between two things, possibilities, etc.; alternative. **7.** *Bot.* (of leaves, etc.) placed singly at different heights on the axis, on each side, in turn or at certain distances from one another. –**alternation** /ɔltəˈneɪʃən, ɒl-/, *n.* –**alternateness** /ɔlˈtɜnətnəs, ɒl-/, *n.* –**alternately**, *adv.*

alternating current *n. Elect.* a current that reverses direction in regular cycles. *Abbrev.*: AC, a.c. Compare **direct current.**

alternative /ɔlˈtɜnətɪv, ɒl-/ *n.* **1.** a possibility of one out of two (or, less strictly, more) things: *the alternative of remaining neutral or attacking.* –*adj.* **2.** affording a choice between two things, or a possibility of one thing out of two. **3.** (of two things) mutually exclusive, so that if one is chosen the other must be rejected: *alternative results of this or that course.* **4.** offering standards and criteria of behaviour of a minority group within and opposed to an established western society: *alternative society; alternative medicine.* **5.** (of any aspect of popular culture) not having a mainstream following. –**alternatively**, *adv.* –**alternativeness**, *n.*

alternative energy *n.* energy which is not derived from fossil fuels, such as wind energy, solar energy, geothermal energy, etc.; usually not including nuclear power.

alternative medicine *n.* the range of practices and treatments, often based on traditional remedies, which fall outside the scope of mainstream medicine.

alternator /ˈɔltəneɪtə, ˈɒl-/ *n. Elect.* a generator of alternating current.

although /ɔlˈðoʊ/ *conj.* even though (practically equivalent to *though*, but often preferred to it in stating fact). Also, *Poetic*, **altho'**.

altimeter /ˈæltəmitə/ *n.* a sensitive aneroid barometer calibrated and graduated to measure altitudes by the decrease of atmospheric pressure with height, used in aircraft for finding distance above sea level, terrain, or some other reference point. –**altimetry** /ælˈtɪmətri/, *n.*

altitude /ˈæltətjud, -tʃud/ *n.* **1.** the height above sea level of any point on the earth's surface or in the atmosphere. **2.** extent or distance upwards. **3.** *Geom.* the perpendicular distance from the base of a figure to its highest point. **4.** a high point or region: *mountain altitudes.* **5.** high or exalted position, rank, etc.

alto /ˈæltoʊ/ *Music* –*n.* (*pl.* **-tos**) **1.** the lowest female voice or voice part; contralto. **2.** the highest male voice or voice part; countertenor. **3.** a singer with an alto voice. **4.** an instrument of a range between soprano and tenor, as alto saxophone. –*adj.* **5.** of the alto; having the compass of the alto.

alto- a word element meaning 'high', as in *altostratus.* Also, **alt-, alti-.**

altogether /ɔltəˈgɛðə/ *adv.* **1.** wholly; entirely; completely; quite: *altogether bad.* **2.** in all: *the debt amounted altogether to twenty dollars.* **3.** on the whole: *altogether, I'm glad it's over.* –*phr.* **4. in the altogether**, *Colloq.* in the nude.

altruism /ˈæltru.ɪzəm/ *n.* the principle or practice of seeking the welfare of others. –**altruistic** /ˌæltruˈɪstɪk/, *adj.* –**altruist** /ˈæltruəst/, *n.* –**altruistically**, *adv.*

alum /ˈæləm/ *n.* an astringent crystalline substance, a double sulphate of aluminium and potassium, $K_2SO_4.Al_2(SO_4)_3.24H_2O$, or $KAl(SO_4)_2.12H_2O$, used in medicine, dyeing, and many technical processes.

alumina /əˈlumənə/ *n. Mineral.* the oxide of aluminium, Al_2O_3, occurring widely in nature as corundum (in the ruby and sapphire, emery, etc.).

aluminium /ˌæljəˈmɪniəm, ˌælju-/ *n.* a silver-white metallic element, light in weight, ductile, malleable, and not readily oxidised or tarnished, occurring combined in nature in igneous rocks, shales, clays, and most soils. It is much used in alloys and for lightweight utensils, castings, aeroplane parts, etc. *Symbol*: Al; *relative atomic mass*: 26.9815; *atomic number*: 13; *density*: 2.70 at 20°C. Also, *US*, **aluminum** /əˈlumənəm/.

always /ˈɔlweɪz, -wəz/ *adv.* **1.** all the time; uninterruptedly. **2.** every time; on every occasion: *he always works on Saturday.* **3.** often, especially with monotonous regularity; repeatedly: *you always say that.*

Alzheimer's disease /ˈæltshaɪməz dəˈziz/ *n.* a progressive, organic brain disease which appears usually in middle age or old age and which results in confusion, memory failure, disorientation, etc.

am /æm/, *weak forms* /əm, m/ *v.* first person singular present indicative of **be.**

amalgam /əˈmælgəm/ *n.* **1.** a mixture or combination. **2.** an alloy of mercury with another metal or metals.

amalgamate /əˈmælgəmeɪt/ *v.t.* **1.** to mix so as to make a combination; blend; unite; combine: *to amalgamate two companies.* **2.** *Metallurgy* to mix or alloy (a metal) with mercury. –*v.i.* **3.** to combine, unite, or coalesce. **4.** to blend with another metal, as mercury. –**amalgamation** /əmælgəˈmeɪʃən/, *n.* –**amalgamable**, *n.* –**amalgamable**, *adj.* –**amalgamative**, *adj.* –**amalgamator**, *n.*

amanuensis /əmænjuˈɛnsəs/ *n.* (*pl.* **-enses** /-ɛnsiz/) someone employed to write or type what another dictates, or to copy what has been written by another.

amass /əˈmæs/ *v.t.* **1.** to gather for oneself; collect as one's own: *to amass a fortune.* **2.** to collect into a mass or pile; bring together. –**amassable**, *adj.* –**amasser**, *n.* –**amassment**, *n.*

amateur /ˈæmətə, ˈæmətʃə/ *n.* **1.** someone who cultivates any study or art or other activity for personal pleasure instead of professionally or for gain. **2.** an athlete who has never competed for money. **3.** a superficial or unskilful worker; dabbler. –*adj.* **4.** of or relating to an amateur or amateurs. –**amateurish**, *adj.* –**amateurism**, *n.* –**amateurship**, *n.*

amatory /ˈæmətri/ *adj.* relating to lovers or lovemaking; expressive of love: *amatory poems; an amatory look.*

amaze /əˈmeɪz/ *v.t.* to overwhelm with surprise; astonish greatly. –**amazedly** /əˈmeɪzədli/, *adv.* –**amazedness**, *n.*

ambassador /æmˈbæsədə/ *n.* **1.** a diplomatic agent of the highest rank who represents his or her country's interests in another country. **2.** an authorised messenger or representative. **3.** a person of some personal distinction as a sportsperson, actor, etc., who wins goodwill for his or her country in another: *she was a real ambassador for Australia in Sweden.* –**ambassadorial** /æmbæsəˈdɔriəl/, *adj.* –**ambassadorship**, *n.*

amber /ˈæmbə/ *n.* **1.** a pale yellow, sometimes reddish or brownish, fossil resin of vegetable origin, translucent, brittle, and capable of gaining a negative electrical charge by friction. **2.** the yellowish brown colour of resin. **3.** an amber light used as a warning in signalling. –*adj.* **4.** made of or resembling amber.

ambergris /ˈæmbəgris, -grɪs/ *n.* an opaque, ash-coloured substance, a morbid secretion of the sperm whale, fragrant when heated, usually found floating on the ocean or cast ashore, used chiefly in perfumery.

ambi- a word element meaning 'both', 'around', 'on both sides', as in *ambidextrous.*

ambidextrous /æmbiˈdɛkstrəs/ *adj.* **1.** able to use both hands equally well. **2.** unusually skilful; facile. –**ambidextrously**, *adv.* –**ambidexterity, ambidextrousness**, *n.*

ambience /'æmbiəns/ n. 1. environment; surrounding atmosphere. 2. the mood, character, quality, atmosphere, etc., as of a place or milieu.

ambient /'æmbiənt/ adj. 1. completely surrounding: *ambient air.* 2. circulating. 3. of or relating to the surrounding air, especially with regard to temperature, pressure, humidity, etc. 4. of or relating to a style of music designed to induce a calm and reflective mood in the listener.

ambiguous /æm'bɪgjuəs/ adj. 1. open to various interpretations; having a double meaning; equivocal: *an ambiguous answer.* 2. of doubtful or uncertain nature; difficult to comprehend, distinguish, or classify: *a rock of ambiguous character.* 3. lacking clearness or definiteness; obscure; indistinct. −**ambiguity**, n. −**ambiguously**, adv.

ambit /'æmbət/ n. 1. scope; extent: *the ambit of the legislation.* 2. *Rare* boundary; limits.

ambit claim n. *Aust.* a claim made by employees to a conciliation and arbitration court which anticipates bargaining and compromise with the employer and is therefore extreme in its demands.

ambition /æm'bɪʃən/ n. 1. an eager desire for distinction, preferment, power, or fame. 2. the object desired or sought after: *the crown was his ambition.* −**ambitious**, adj. −**ambitionless**, adj.

ambivalence /æm'bɪvələns/ n. 1. the coexistence in one person of opposite and conflicting feelings towards someone or something. 2. uncertainty or ambiguity, especially due to inability to make up one's mind. Also, **ambivalency**. −**ambivalent**, adj.

amble /'æmbəl/ v.i. 1. to move with the gait of a horse, when it lifts first the two legs on one side and then the two on the other. 2. to go at an easy pace. −n. 3. an ambling gait. −**ambler**, n. −**ambling**, adj.

ambrosia /æm'brouziə/ n. 1. the food of the gods of classical mythology, imparting immortality. 2. anything imparting the sense of divinity, as poetic inspiration, music, etc. 3. something especially delicious to taste or smell. 4. a mild, originally Swedish, cheese with a tangy flavour and smooth, buttery texture.

ambulance /'æmbjələns/ n. a vehicle specially equipped for carrying sick or wounded persons.

ambulance officer n. a person, often a paramedic, who attends the sick or injured in an ambulance and provides emergency primary care.

ambulant /'æmbjələnt/ adj. 1. moving from place to place; shifting. 2. *Med.* → **ambulatory** (def. 4).

ambulatory /'æmbjələtri/ adj. 1. relating to or capable of walking. 2. adapted for walking, as the limbs of many animals. 3. moving about; not stationary. 4. *Med.* not confined to bed: *ambulatory patient.*

ambush /'æmbʊʃ/ n. 1. the act of lying concealed so as to attack by surprise. 2. the act of attacking unexpectedly from a concealed position. 3. a secret or concealed position from which a surprise attack is made. 4. a person or persons lying in wait. −v.t. 5. to attack from ambush. −**ambusher**, n.

ameliorate /ə'miliəreɪt, ə'miljəreɪt/ v.i. 1. to become better; improve. −v.t. 2. to make better; improve. −**amelioration** /ə,miliə'reɪʃən, -jə'reɪʃən/, n. −**ameliorator**, n. −**ameliorable**, adj. −**ameliorant**, n. −**ameliorative**, adj.

amen /eɪ'mɛn, a-/ interj. 1. it is so; so be it (used after a prayer, creed, or other formal statement). −n. 2. an expression of concurrence or assent.

amenable /ə'mɛnəbəl, ə'min-/ adj. 1. disposed or ready to answer, yield, or submit; submissive; tractable. 2. liable to be called to account; answerable; legally responsible. 3. liable or exposed (to charge, claim, etc.): *amenable to criticism.* −**amenability** /ə,mɛnə'bɪləti/, **amenableness**, n. −**amenably**, adv.

amend /ə'mɛnd/ v.t. 1. to alter (a motion, bill, constitution, etc.) by due formal procedure. 2. to change for the better; improve: *to amend one's ways.* 3. to remove or correct faults in; rectify: *an amended spelling.* −v.i. 4. to grow or become better by reforming oneself. −**amendment**, n. −**amendable**, adj. −**amender**, n.

amends /ə'mɛndz/ phr. **make amends**, to offer reparation or compensation for a loss, damage or injury of any kind; recompense.

amenity /ə'mɛnəti/ n. (pl. **-ties**) 1. the quality of being pleasant or agreeable in situation, prospect, etc.: *the amenity of the climate.* 2. (pl.) the equipment or services of a house, area, etc., including basic utilities such as toilets, showers, etc., or extra facilities such as a swimming pool.

American football /ə,mɛrɪkən 'fʊtbɔl/ n. a game similar to Rugby football, in which two teams of eleven players each try to score touchdowns and field goals.

amethyst /ˈæməθəst/ n. *Mineral.* 1. a crystallised purple or violet quartz used in jewellery. 2. a purplish colour. −**amethystine** /ˌæmə'θɪstɪn, -taɪn/, adj.

amiable /'eɪmiəbəl/ adj. 1. having or showing agreeable personal qualities, as sweetness of temper, kind-heartedness, etc. 2. friendly; kindly: *an amiable mood.* −**amiability** /ˌeɪmiə'bɪləti/, **amiableness**, n. −**amiably**, adv.

amicable /'æmɪkəbəl/ adj. characterised by or exhibiting friendliness; friendly; peaceable: *an amicable settlement.* −**amicability** /æmɪkə'bɪləti/, **amicableness**, n. −**amicably**, adv.

amid /ə'mɪd/ prep. in the midst of or surrounded by; among; amidst.

amidst /ə'mɪdst/ prep. amid.

amine /ə'min, 'æmin/ n. *Chem.* any of a class of compounds prepared from ammonia by replacing one, two, or all hydrogen atoms with organic radicals.

amino- a prefix denoting an amino group.

amino acid /ə,minoʊ 'æsəd, ,æmənoʊ 'æsəd / n. any of a group of organic compounds containing an amino group and a carboxyl group. Up to twenty alpha-amino acids are considered the building blocks from which proteins are formed, while others can be found in some antibiotics.

amiss /ə'mɪs/ adv. 1. out of the proper course or order; in a faulty manner; wrongly. −adj. 2. (*used only predicatively*) (sometimes fol. by *with*) wrong; faulty; out of order; improper. −phr. 3. **come amiss**, to be unwelcome; be received with ingratitude; be inopportune. 4. **take amiss**, to be offended at; resent.

amity /'æməti/ n. friendship; harmony; good understanding, especially between nations.

ammeter /'æmitə/ n. an instrument for measuring the strength of electric currents in amperes.

ammonia /ə'moʊnjə, -iə/ n. 1. a colourless, pungent, suffocating gas, NH_3, a compound of nitrogen and hydrogen, very soluble in water. 2. Also, **ammonia water, aqueous ammonia**. this gas dissolved in water, the common commercial form. −**ammoniacal** /æmə'naɪəkəl/, adj.

ammonium carbonate /ə,moʊniəm 'kɑbəneɪt/ n. an ammonium salt of carbonic acid.

ammunition /,æmjə'nɪʃən/ n. 1. all the material used in discharging all types of firearms or any weapon that throws projectiles; powder, shot, shrapnel, bullets, cartridges, and the means of igniting and exploding them, as primers and fuses. Chemicals, bombs, grenades, mines, pyrotechnics are also ammunition. 2. any material or means used in combat. 3. evidence used to support an argument.

amnesia /æm'niʒə, -ziə/ n. loss of a large block of interrelated memories. −**amnesiac** /æm'niziæk/, adj., n. −**amnesic** /æm'nisɪk, -zɪk/, **amnestic** /æm'nɛstɪk/, adj.

amnesty /ˈæmnəsti/ n. (pl. **-ties**) **1.** a general pardon for offences against a government. **2.** the granting of immunity for past offences against the laws of war. –v.t. (**-tied, -tying**) **3.** to grant amnesty to; pardon.

amniocentesis /ˌæmnioʊsɛnˈtisəs/ n. (pl. **-teses** /-tisiz/) removal of some amniotic fluid, especially to diagnose chromosomal abnormality in a fetus.

amnion /ˈæmniən/ n. (pl. **amnia** /ˈæmniə/) the innermost of the embryonic or fetal membranes of insects, reptiles, birds, and mammals; the sac containing the amniotic fluid and the embryo. –**amniotic** /ˌæmniˈɒtɪk/, **amnionic** /ˌæmniˈɒnɪk/, adj.

amoeba /əˈmibə/ n. (pl. **-bas** or **-bae** /-bi/) **1.** a protozoon of irregular and protean shape, moving and feeding by the use of pseudopodia. **2.** any protozoan of the genus *Amoeba.* Also, **ameba.** –**amoebic**, adj. –**amoeba-like**, adj.

amok /əˈmʌk/ phr. **run amok, 1.** to rush about in a murderous frenzy. **2.** to rush about wildly. Also, **amuck.**

among /əˈmʌŋ/ prep. **1.** surrounded by; in or into the midst of: *you are among friends.* **2.** one of; included in a group of: *that's among the things we must do.* **3.** from; out of (a group): *choose among these; you are only one among many.* **4.** to, by, for or with (more than two people): *divide these among you; let them settle it among themselves.*

amongst /əˈmʌŋst/ prep. among.

amoral /eɪˈmɒrəl, æ-/ adj. without moral quality; neither moral nor immoral. –**amorality** /eɪməˈrælətɪ, æm-/, n. –**amorally**, adv.

amorous /ˈæmərəs/ adj. **1.** inclined or disposed to love: *an amorous disposition.* **2.** in love; enamoured. **3.** showing love: *amorous sighs.* **4.** relating to love: *amorous poetry.* –**amorously**, adv. –**amorousness**, n.

amorphism /əˈmɔfɪzəm/ n. the state or quality of being amorphous.

amorphous /əˈmɔfəs/ adj. **1.** lacking definite form; having no specific shape. **2.** of no particular kind or character; indeterminate; formless; unorganised: *an amorphous style.* **3.** Geol. occurring in a mass, as without stratification or crystalline structure. **4.** Chem. non-crystalline. –**amorphously**, adv. –**amorphousness**, n.

amortise /əˈmɔtaɪz, ˈæmətaɪz/ v.t. to liquidate or extinguish (an indebtedness or charge) usually by periodic payments (or by entries) made to a sinking fund, to a creditor, or to an account. Also, **amortize.** –**amortisable**, adj.

amount /əˈmaʊnt/ n. **1.** quantity or extent: *the amount of resistance.* **2.** the full effect, value, or import. **3.** the sum total of two or more sums or quantities; the aggregate: *the amount of 7 and 9 is 16.* **4.** the sum of the principal and interest of a loan. –phr. **5. amount to,** to reach, extend, or be equal to in number, quantity, effect, etc.

amour /əˈmʊə/ n. a love affair, especially a clandestine one.

amp /æmp/ n. Colloq. **1.** an amplifier. **2.** an ampere.

ampere /ˈæmpɛə/ n. the base SI unit of current, defined as the current which, if maintained in two parallel conductors of infinite length, of negligible cross-section, and separated by one metre in a vacuum, would produce a force of 2×10^{-7} newtons per metre. *Symbol:* A

ampersand /ˈæmpəsænd/ n. the character &, meaning *and.*

amphetamine /æmˈfɛtəmin, -mən/ n. any of a class of drugs which have stimulant and vasoconstrictor activity.

amphi- a word element meaning 'on both sides', 'on all sides', 'around', 'round about', as in *amphicoelous.*

amphibian /æmˈfibiən/ n. **1.** the class of vertebrate animals, as the frog, newt, etc., that live on land but breed in water, the young metamorphosing (changing) into adult form from an early fish-like (tadpole) stage. **2.** an amphibious plant. **3.** an aeroplane that can take off from and land on either land or water. **4.** an amphibious vehicle. –**amphibious**, adj.

amphitheatre /ˈæmfiθɪətə/ n. **1.** a level area of oval or circular shape surrounded by rising ground. **2.** any place for public contests or games; an arena. **3.** a building with tiers of seats around an arena or central area, such as those used in ancient Rome for gladiatorial contests. **4.** a semicircular sloping gallery in a modern theatre. Also, *US,* **amphitheater.**

amphora /ˈæmfərə/ n. (pl. **-rae** /-ri/ or **-ras**) a two-handled, narrow-necked vessel, commonly big-bellied and narrowed at the base, used by the ancient Greeks and Romans for holding wine, oil, etc. –**amphoral**, adj.

ample /ˈæmpəl/ adj. **1.** of great extent, size, or amount; large; spacious. **2.** in full or abundant measure; copious; liberal. **3.** fully sufficient for the purpose or for needs; enough and to spare. **4.** rather bulky or full in form or figure. –**ampleness**, n.

amplifier /ˈæmpləfaɪə/ n. **1.** Elect. a device for increasing the amplitudes of electric waves or impulses by means of the control exercised by the input over the power supplied to the output from a local source of energy. Commonly it is a radio valve or transistor, or a device using them. **2.** such a device used to magnify the sound produced by a radio, record-player, or any of certain musical instruments, such as an electric guitar. **3.** Photography an additional lens for expanding the field of vision.

amplify /ˈæmpləfaɪ/ verb (**-fied, -fying**) –v.t. **1.** to make larger or greater; enlarge; extend. **2.** to expand in stating or describing, as by details, illustration, etc. **3.** Elect. to increase the amplitude of (impulses or waves). **4.** to make louder; magnify (a sound). –v.i. **5.** (sometimes fol. by *on*) to discourse at length; expatiate or dilate. –**amplification**, n.

amplitude /ˈæmpləˌtjud, -tʃud/ n. **1.** extension in space, especially breadth or width; largeness; extent. **2.** large or full measure; abundance; copiousness. **3.** Physics the distance or range from one extremity of an oscillation to the middle point or neutral value. **4.** Elect. the maximum strength of an alternating current during its cycle, as distinguished from the mean or effective strength.

amplitude modulation n. Radio a broadcasting system in which the carrier wave is modulated by changing its amplitude (distinguished from *frequency modulation*). *Abbrev.:* AM

ampoule /ˈæmpul/ n. a sealed glass bulb used to hold hypodermic solutions.

amputate /ˈæmpjəteɪt/ v.t. to cut off (a limb, etc.) by a surgical operation. –**amputation** /æmpjəˈteɪʃən/, n. –**amputator**, n.

amulet /ˈæmjələt/ n. an object superstitiously worn to ward off evil; a protecting charm.

amuse /əˈmjuz/ v.t. **1.** to hold the attention of agreeably; entertain; divert. **2.** to excite mirth in. –phr. **3. amuse oneself,** to while away one's time pleasantly. –**amused**, adj. –**amusement**, n. –**amuser**, n. –**amusing**, adj.

an /æn/, weak form /ən/ adj. or indefinite article the form of **a** before an initial vowel sound. See **a**[1].

an-[1] a prefix meaning 'not', 'without', 'lacking', used before vowels and *h*, as in *anarchy.* Also, **a-**[6].

an-[2] variant of **ad-**, before *n*, as in *announce.*

an-[3] variant of **ana-**, used before vowels, as in *anaptotic.*

-an a suffix meaning: **1.** belonging to', 'pertaining or relating to', 'adhering to', and commonly expressing connection with a place, person, leader, class, order, sect, system, doctrine, or the like, serving to form adjectives, many of which are also used as nouns, as

Australian, Christian, Elizabethan, republican, and hence serving to form other nouns of the same type, as *historian, theologian.* **2.** *Zool.* 'relating to a certain class of organisms', as in *mammalian.*

ana- a prefix meaning 'up', 'throughout', 'again', 'back', occurring originally in words from the Greek, but used also in modern words (English and other) formed on the Greek model, as in *anabatic.*

-ana a noun suffix denoting a collection of material relating to a given subject, as in *Shakespeariana, Australiana.* Also, **-iana.**

anabolic steroid *n.* any of a group of synthetic androgens which accelerate bone and muscle growth.

anabolism /ə'næbəlɪzəm/ *n. Physiol.* constructive metabolism (opposed to *catabolism*). –**anabolic** /ænə-'bɒlɪk/, *adj.*

anabranch /'ænəbræntʃ/ *n. Geog.* a branch of a river which leaves the main stream and enters it again further on.

anachronism /ə'nækrənɪzəm/ *n.* **1.** an error assigning a custom, event, person, or thing to an age other, especially earlier, than the correct one. **2.** something placed or occurring out of its proper time. –**anachronistic** /ənækrə'nɪstɪk/, *adj.*

anaconda /ænə'kɒndə/ *n.* **1.** a large South American snake, *Eunectes murinus,* of the boa family. **2.** any boa constrictor.

anaemia /ə'nimiə/ *n.* **1.** a quantitative deficiency of the haemoglobin, often accompanied by a reduced number of red blood cells, and causing pallor, weakness, and breathlessness. **2.** bloodlessness; paleness. Also, **anemia.** –**anaemic,** *adj.*

anaerobic /ænə'roʊbɪk/ *adj.* **1.** *Biol., Physiol.* (of organisms or tissues) requiring the absence of free oxygen or not destroyed by its absence. **2.** relating to or caused by the absence of oxygen. **3.** affected by or involving the activities of anaerobes. –**anaerobically,** *adv.*

anaerobic exercise *n.* physical exercise of sufficient intensity to trigger anaerobic metabolism; typically involves a short burst of intense muscular activity, as in weightlifting, sprinting, etc. See **aerobic exercise.**

anaerobic threshold *n.* the point at which the body begins to accumulate unmetabolised lactic acid in the bloodstream, in response to the demands of intense physical exercise. *Abbrev.:* AT

anaesthesia /ænəs'θiʒə, -ziə/ *n.* **1.** *Med.* general or local insensibility, as to pain and other sensation, induced by certain drugs. **2.** *Pathol.* general loss of the senses of feeling, such as pain, heat, cold, touch, and other less common varieties of sensation. **3.** the science of anaesthetics. Also, **anesthesia.**

anaesthetic /ænəs'θetɪk/ *n.* **1.** a substance which induces anaesthesia, especially one injected or applied as a preliminary to a medical procedure. See **general anaesthetic, local anaesthetic.** –*adj.* **2.** relating to or causing physical insensibility. Also, **anesthetic.**

anaesthetise /ə'nisθətaɪz/ *v.t.* to make (someone) unable to feel pain, etc., by or as by an anaesthetic. Also, **anaesthetize, anesthetise, anesthetize.** –**anaesthetisation,** *n.* –**anaesthetist,** *n.*

anagram /'ænəgræm/ *n.* **1.** a transposition of the letters of a word or sentence to form a new word or sentence, as *caned* is an anagram of *dance.* –*v.t.* **2.** to transpose into an anagram. –*v.i.* **3.** to make anagrams.

anal /'eɪnəl/ *adj.* **1.** of or relating to the anus. **2.** relating to a stage of psychosexual development during which the child's interest is concentrated on the anal region and excremental function. **3.** *Colloq.* obsessive; finicky; fussy: *don't be so anal.* –**anally,** *adv.*

analgesic /ænəl'dʒizɪk, -sɪk/ *n.* **1.** *Med.* a remedy that relieves or removes pain. –*adj.* **2.** relating to or causing analgesia.

analog /'ænəlɒg/ *adj.* **1.** *Electronics, Broadcasting, etc.* relating to any device or procedure which encodes physical properties such as those of sound, sight, etc., in terms of frequencies and their amplitudes. **2.** of or relating to any device which represents a variable by a continuously moving or varying entity, such as a clock, the hands of which move to represent time, or a VU meter, the needle of which moves to represent varying amplifier output energy. Compare **digital.** Also, **analogue.**

analog broadcasting *n.* broadcasting by the use of an analog system (opposed to *digital broadcasting*).

analog computer *n.* a type of computer in which information is represented by directly measurable, continuously varying quantities (as voltages, resistances, or rotations). Also, **analogue computer.**

analogous /ə'næləgəs, -dʒəs/ *adj.* **1.** having analogy; corresponding in some particular. **2.** *Biol.* corresponding in function, but not evolved from corresponding organs, as the wings of a bee and those of a hummingbird. –**analogously,** *adv.* –**analogousness,** *n.*

analog-to-digital converter *n.* a device which converts an analog signal to a digital equivalent. Also, **analog-digital converter.**

analogue /'ænəlɒg/ *n.* **1.** something having analogy to something else. **2.** *Biol.* an organ or part analogous to another. –*adj.* **3.** → **analog.**

analogy /ə'nælədʒi/ *n.* (*pl.* **-gies**) **1.** an agreement, likeness, or correspondence between the relations of things to one another; a partial similarity in particular circumstances on which a comparison may be based: *the analogy between the heart and a pump.* **2.** agreement; similarity. **3.** *Biol.* an analogous relationship. **4.** (in linguistic change) the tendency of inflections and formations to follow existing models and regular patterns, as when the more common '-s' plural *brothers* replaces the older *brethren.* **5.** *Logic* a form of reasoning in which similarities are inferred from a similarity of two or more things in certain particulars. –*phr.* **6. by analogy,** by a comparison to a similar pattern.

analyse /'ænəlaɪz/ *v.t.* **1.** to resolve into elements or constituent parts; determine the elements or essential features of: *to analyse an argument.* **2.** to examine critically, so as to bring out the essential elements or give the essence of: *to analyse a poem.* **3.** to subject to mathematical, chemical, grammatical, etc., analysis. **4.** → **psychoanalyse.** Also, *US,* **analyze.** –**analysable,** *adj.*

analysis /ə'næləsəs/ *n.* (*pl.* **-lyses** /-ləsiz/) **1.** separation of something into its basic parts in order to discover its nature, meaning, etc.: *the grammatical analysis of a sentence.* **2.** a short statement of results of this; outline or summary, as of a book. **3.** *Chem.* **a.** separation of a substance into its elements to find their kind or quantity. **b.** the finding out of the kind or amount of one or more of the constituents of a substance, whether actually obtained in separate form or not. **4.** → **psychoanalysis.** –**analyst,** *n.*

analytic /ænə'lɪtɪk/ *adj.* **1.** relating to or proceeding by analysis (opposed to *synthetic*). **2.** (of languages) characterised by the use of separate words (free forms) rather than of inflectional adjuncts (bound forms) to show syntactic relationships, as in English or Chinese (opposed to *synthetic*). **3.** → **analytical.** –**analytically,** *adv.*

analytical /ænə'lɪtɪkəl/ *adj.* **1.** proceeding by way of analysis: *an analytical approach.* **2.** inclined towards analysis: *an analytical mind.* **3.** exclusively preoccupied with the search for understanding in terms of elements, relations, structure, etc. Also, **analytic**. **–analytically**, *adv*.

Anangu /ə'naŋgu/ *n.* an Aboriginal person from Central Australia. Compare **Koori** (def. 1), **Murri**, **Nunga**, **Nyungar**, **Yamatji**, **Yolngu**.

anaphylactic shock /ænəfəlæktɪk 'ʃɒk/ *n.* an acute systemic reaction produced by an allergen to which the victim has become sensitised.

anarchy /'ænəki/ *n.* **1.** a state of society without government or law. **2.** political and social disorder due to absence of governmental control. **3.** absence of government or governmental restraint. **4.** a theory which regards the union of order with the absence of all direct or coercive government as the political ideal. **5.** confusion in general; disorder. **–anarchist**, *n.* **–anarchism**, *n.*

anathema /ə'næθəmə/ *n.* (*pl.* **-mas**) **1.** a formal ecclesiastical curse involving excommunication. **2.** any imprecation of divine punishment. **3.** a curse; an execration. **4.** a person or thing accursed or consigned to damnation or destruction. **5.** a person or thing detested or loathed.

anatomy /ə'nætəmi/ *n.* **1.** the structure of an animal or plant, or of any of its parts. **2.** the science of the structure of animals and plants. **3.** the cutting up of animals or plants for study of their structure. **4.** any detailed examination. **5.** *Colloq.* the body; bodily form; figure. **–anatomical** /ænə'tɒmɪkəl/, *adj.*

-ance a suffix of nouns denoting action, state, or quality, or something exemplifying one of these, often corresponding to adjectives in *-ant*, as *brilliance*, *distance*, or formed directly from verbs, as in *assistance*, *defiance*. Compare **-ence**.

ancestor /'ænsestə/ *n.* **1.** someone from whom a person is descended, usually distantly; a forefather; a progenitor. **2.** *Biol.* the actual or hypothetical form or stock of an earlier and presumably lower type, from which any organised being is known or inferred to have developed. **–ancestral**, *adj.* **–ancestress**

ancestry /'ænsəstri, -sɛs-/ *n.* **1.** ancestral descent. **2.** honourable descent. **3.** a series of ancestors.

anchor /'æŋkə/ *n.* **1.** a device for holding boats, vessels, floating bridges, etc., in place. **2.** any similar device for holding fast or checking motion. **3.** a key person; mainstay. **4.** (in a tug-of-war team) the person, usually the one who is most effective because of superior weight, strength or skill, placed at the end of the rope. **5.** the person who is most heavily relied upon in a team, as the last runner in a relay race. **6.** *Radio*, *TV* the host or main presenter of a program. **7.** a means of stability: *hope is his anchor.* **8.** *Mil.* a key defensive position. **9.** (*pl.*) *Colloq.* brakes: *hit the anchors.* **–v.t. 10.** to hold fast by an anchor. **11.** to fix or fasten; affix firmly. **12.** to act as the anchor (def. 6) of (a radio or television broadcast). **–v.i. 13.** to drop anchor. **14.** to lie or ride at anchor. **15.** to keep hold or be firmly fixed. **16.** *Colloq.* to take up residence (in a place); settle. **–phr. 17. at anchor**, held still by an anchor; anchored. **18. cast anchor**, to put down or drop the anchor. **19. drop anchor**, to make a halt to a journey by ship. **20. weigh anchor**, to take up the anchor. **–anchorless**, *adj.* **–anchor-like**, *adj.*

anchorage /'æŋkərɪdʒ/ *n.* **1.** a place for anchoring. **2.** a charge for anchoring. **3.** that to which anything is fastened. **4.** something that can be depended upon.

anchorite /'æŋkəraɪt/ *n.* someone who has retired to a solitary place for a life of religious seclusion; a hermit; a recluse. **–anchoritic** /æŋkə'rɪtɪk/, *adj.*

anchorman /'æŋkəmæn/ *n.* (*pl.* **-men**) a male anchor (defs 3–6).

anchovy /'æntʃəvi, æn'tʃoʊvi/ *n.* (*pl.* **-vies** *or* **-vy**) **1.** a small, herring-like, marine fish, *Engraulis australis*, occurring in bays and estuaries of the Australian coastline south of the Tropic of Capricorn. **2.** any of a number of fishes of the same family (Engraulidae) found elsewhere, especially *Engraulis encrasicholus*, abundant in southern Europe, much used pickled and in the form of a salt paste.

ancient /'eɪnʃənt, 'eɪntʃənt/ *adj.* **1.** of or in time long past, especially before the end of the Western Roman Empire, AD 476: *ancient history.* **2.** very old; of great age: *an ancient monument; an ancient woman.* **3.** *Law* having existed for a particular period of time, often 20 years: *an ancient matter.* **–n. 4.** (*usu. pl.*) a person, especially a classical writer, who lived in ancient times, as an ancient Greek, Roman, Hebrew, etc. **–ancientness**, *n.*

ancillary /æn'sɪləri/ *adj.* **1.** accessory; auxiliary. **–n.** (*pl.* **-aries**) **2.** an accessory, subsidiary or helping thing or person.

-ancy an equivalent of **-ance**, used chiefly in nouns denoting state or quality, as in *buoyancy*.

and /ænd/, *weak forms* /ənd, ən, n/ *conj.* (*connecting words, phrases or clauses*) **1.** with; along with; also: *pens and pencils.* **2.** as a result: *concentrate and your work will improve.* **3.** afterwards: *do the shopping and come straight home.* **4.** as well as: *nice and warm.* **5.** to (used between verbs): *try and do it.*

andante /æn'dænteɪ, -ti/ *adv. Music* moderately slowly and evenly.

andiron /'ændaɪən/ *n.* one of a pair of metallic stands used to support wood in an open fire; a firedog.

andro- a word element meaning 'man', 'male', as contrasted with 'female', as in *androsphinx*. Also, **andr-**.

androgen /'ændrədʒən/ *n.* any steroid which promotes masculine characteristics.

androgynous /æn'drɒdʒənəs/ *adj.* **1.** being both male and female; hermaphroditic. **2.** having both masculine and feminine characteristics. **3.** *Bot.* having staminate and pistillate flowers in the same inflorescence. **4.** not conforming to a male or a female stereotype in appearance or behaviour. **–androgyny**, *n.*

-androus a word element meaning 'male', as in *polyandrous*.

-ane **1.** a noun suffix used in chemical terms, especially names of hydrocarbons of the methane or paraffin series, as *decane*, *pentane*, *propane*. **2.** an adjective suffix used when a similar form (with a different meaning) exists in **-an**, as *human*, *humane*.

anecdote /'ænəkdoʊt/ *n.* a short narrative of a particular incident or occurrence of an interesting nature. **–anecdotal**, **anecdotic** /ænək'dɒtɪk/, *adj.*

anemo- a word element meaning 'wind', as in *anemometer*.

anemometer /ænə'mɒmətə/ *n.* **1.** an instrument for indicating wind velocity; wind gauge. **2.** any instrument for measuring the rate of flow of a fluid. **–anemometric** /ænəmə'mɛtrɪk/, **anemometrical** /ænəmə'mɛtrɪkəl/, *adj.* **–anemometry**, *n.*

anemone /ə'nɛməni/ *n.* **1.** any plant of the genus *Anemone*, especially *A. coronaria*, a native of the Mediterranean area, widely cultivated for its mostly red and blue flowers. **2.** → **sea anemone**.

aneroid /'ænərɔɪd/ *adj.* **1.** using no fluid. **–n. 2.** → **aneroid barometer**.

aneroid barometer *n.* an instrument for measuring atmospheric pressure and, indirectly, altitude, by registering the pressure exerted on the elastic top of a box or chamber exhausted of air.

aneurysm /'ænjərɪzəm/ *n.* a permanent cardiac or arterial dilation usually caused by weakening of the vessel wall by diseases such as syphilis or arteriosclerosis. Also, **aneurism**. **–aneurysmal** /ˌænjə'rɪzməl/, *adj.*

anew /ə'nju/ *adv.* **1.** over again; once more: *to write a story anew.* **2.** in a new form or manner.

angel /ˈeɪndʒəl/ n. **1.** (in Judaism, Christianity and Islam) one of a class of spiritual beings, attendants of God (in medieval Christianity divided, according to their rank, into nine orders, ranging from highest to lowest as follows: seraphim, cherubim, thrones, dominations or dominions, virtues, powers, principalities or princedoms, archangels, angels). **2.** the usual representation of such a being, in human form, with wings. **3.** a person, especially a woman, who is thought to be like an angel in beauty, kindliness, etc. **4.** a protecting or guardian spirit. **5.** *Colloq.* a person who supports a project with money, especially a theatrical play. –**angelic** /ænˈdʒɛlɪk/, **angelical** /ænˈdʒɛlɪkəl/, *adj.* –**angelhood**, *n.*

anger /ˈæŋgə/ n. **1.** a strongly felt displeasure aroused by real or supposed wrongs, often accompanied by an impulse to retaliate; wrath; ire. –*v.t.* **2.** to excite to anger or wrath.

angina /ænˈdʒaɪnə/ n. **1.** → **angina pectoris**. **2.** any inflammatory affection of the throat or fauces, as quinsy, croup, mumps, etc. –**anginal**, *adj.*

angina pectoris /ænˈdʒaɪnə ˈpɛktərəs/ n. a syndrome characterised by paroxysmal, constricting pain below the sternum, most easily precipitated by exertion or excitement and caused by ischaemia of the heart muscle, usually due to a coronary artery disease, such as arteriosclerosis.

angio- a word element meaning 'vessel', or 'container', as in *angiology.*

angioplasty /ˌændʒioʊˈplæsti/ n. *Surg.* the repairing of a blood vessel, as by the insertion of a balloon to unblock it or by the replacement of part of it.

angiosperm /ˈændʒiəˌspɜm/ n. *Bot.* a plant having its seeds enclosed in an ovary (opposed to *gymnosperm*). –**angiospermous** /ˌændʒiəˈspɜməs/, *adj.*

angle¹ /ˈæŋgəl/ n. **1. a.** the space within two lines or three planes diverging from a common point, or within two planes diverging from a common line. **b.** the figure so formed. **c.** the amount of rotation needed to bring one line or plane into coincidence with another. **2.** an angular projection; a projecting corner: *the angles of a building.* **3.** an angular recess; a nook, corner. **4. a.** a point from which an object may be viewed. **b.** a cognitive standpoint. **5.** an aspect, side: *to consider all angles of the question.* **6.** *Colloq.* a devious, artful scheme, method, etc. **7.** *Eng.* → **angle iron**. –*v.t.* **8.** to move, direct, bend or present at an angle or in an angular course. **9.** to put a slant or bias on (a question, statement, etc.). –*v.i.* **10.** to move or bend in angles. –*phr.* **11. at an angle,** (sometimes fol. by *to* or *from*) slanting; not perpendicular.

angle² /ˈæŋgəl/ v. **1.** to fish with hook and line. –*phr.* **2. angle for,** to try to get (something) by scheming, using tricks or artful means: *to angle for a compliment.*

angle iron n. **1.** a bar of iron in the form of an angle. **2.** a rolled iron or steel bar with an L-shaped cross-section, used mainly in iron constructions. Also, **angle, angle section**.

Anglican /ˈæŋglɪkən/ adj. *Eccles.* **1.** of or relating to the Church of England. **2.** of or relating to any church related in origin to, or in communion with the Church of England, as the Anglican Church of Australia. –*n.* **3.** a member of an Anglican church. **4.** (formerly) a High-Churchman or Anglo-Catholic. –**Anglicanism**, *n.*

Anglo /ˈæŋgloʊ/ n. **1.** a person of Anglo-Celtic ancestry. **2.** a person of English ancestry. **3.** a person who is a native speaker of English and who appears to be of Anglo-Celtic ancestry. –*adj.* **4.** of or relating to such a person.

Anglo- a word element meaning 'relating to England or the English', as in *Anglo-American.*

Anglo Celt /æŋgloʊ ˈkɛlt/ n. *Aust.* someone who is of Anglo-Celtic origin. Also, **Anglo-Celt**.

Anglo-Celtic /ˌæŋgloʊ-ˈkɛltɪk/ adj. *Aust.* of or relating to a person whose origin was in the British Isles. Also, **Anglo Celtic**.

Angora /æŋˈgɔrə/ n. (*sometimes lower case*) **1. a.** the hair of the Angora rabbit. **b.** the hair of the Angora goat; mohair. **c.** a yarn or fabric made from such hair. **2.** → **Angora rabbit**. **3.** → **Angora goat**. **4.** → **Angora cat**.

Angora cat n. a long-haired variety of the domestic cat. Also, **Angora**.

Angora goat n. one of a breed of domestic goat principally reared for its long, silky fleece known as mohair. Also, **Angora**.

Angora rabbit n. any of various long-haired breeds of domestic rabbit the hair of which is used to make Angora yarn or fabric. Also, **Angora**.

angry /ˈæŋgri/ adj. (**-grier**, **-griest**) **1.** feeling or showing anger or resentment (*with* or *at* a person, *at* or *about* a thing). **2.** characterised by anger; wrathful: *angry words.* **3.** *Pathol.* inflamed, as a sore; exhibiting inflammation. –**angrily** /ˈæŋgrəli/, *adv.* –**angriness**, *n.*

angst /æŋst/ n. a feeling or outlook of dread, fear, etc.

angstrom /ˈæŋstrəm/ n. a unit of length for measuring very short wavelengths and distances between atoms in molecules, equal to 10^{-10} metres. *Symbol:* Å

anguish /ˈæŋgwɪʃ/ n. **1.** excruciating or agonising pain of either body or mind; acute suffering or distress: *the anguish of grief.* –*v.t.* **2.** to affect with anguish. –*v.i.* **3.** to suffer anguish.

angular /ˈæŋgjələ/ adj. **1.** having angle or angles. **2.** consisting of, found at, or forming an angle. **3.** of, relating to, or measured by an angle. **4.** acting or moving awkwardly. **5.** stiff in manner; unbending. –**angularly**, *adv.* –**angularity** /æŋgʊəˈlærəti/, **angularness**, *n.*

anhydride /ænˈhaɪdraɪd, -drəd/ n. **1.** a compound formed by abstraction of water, an oxide of a nonmetal (**acid anhydride**) or a metal (**basic anhydride**) which forms an acid or a base, respectively, when united with water. **2.** a compound from which water has been abstracted.

anhydrous /ænˈhaɪdrəs/ adj. *Chem.* having lost all water, especially water of crystallisation.

aniline /ˈænəlɪn/ n. **1.** an oily liquid, $C_6H_5NH_2$, obtained first from indigo but now prepared from benzene, and serving as the basis of many brilliant dyes, and in the manufacture of plastics, resins, etc. –*adj.* **2.** relating to or derived from aniline: *aniline colours.*

animadvert /ænəmædˈvɜt/ v.t. **1.** to remark. –*phr.* **2. animadvert on** (or **upon**), to comment critically on. –**animadversion** /ænəmædˈvɜʒən/, *n.*

animal /ˈænəməl/ n. **1.** any living thing that is not a plant, generally capable of voluntary motion, sensation, etc. **2.** any animal other than a human. **3.** an inhuman person; brutish or beastlike person. –*adj.* **4.** of, relating to, or derived from animals: *animal life, animal fats.* **5.** relating to the physical or carnal nature of humans, rather than their spiritual or intellectual nature: *animal needs.*

animal companion n. → **companion animal**.

animal husbandry n. the practice or science of breeding, feeding, and care of animals, especially on a farm.

animate v.t. /ˈænəmeɪt/ **1.** to give life to; make alive. **2.** to make lively; vivacious; vigorous. **3.** to encourage. **4.** to create an animated film of. –*adj.* /ˈænəmət/ **5.** alive; possessing life: *animate creatures.* –**animateness**, *n.* –**animator**, **animater**, *n.* –**animatingly**, *adv.*

animated /ˈænəmeɪtəd/ adj. **1.** full of life, action, or spirit; lively; vigorous: *an animated debate.* **2.** moving or made to move as if alive. **3.** of or relating to a film, or part of a film, which consists of a series of drawings, each slightly different from the ones before and after it, run through a projector. –**animatedly,** adv.

animateur /ænəməˈtɜ/ n. a person who leads a group activity by giving creative input, direction, facilitation and organisation, as in community projects, artistic ventures, etc. –**animateuring,** n.

animation /ænəˈmeɪʃən/ n. 1. the act of creating an animated film. 2. an animated film.

anime /ˈænəmeɪ/ n. 1. → **manga** movie. 2. the genre of Japanese animation.

animism /ˈænəmɪzəm/ n. the belief that all natural objects and the universe itself possess a soul. –**animist,** n., adj. –**animistic** /ænəˈmɪstɪk/, adj.

animosity /ænəˈmɒsəti/ n. (pl. **-ties**) (sometimes fol. by *between* or *towards*) a feeling of ill will or enmity tending to display itself in action.

anion /ˈænaɪən/ n. Chem. a negatively charged ion which is attracted to the anode in electrolysis.

anise /ˈænəs, ˈænɪs, əˈnis/ n. 1. a herbaceous plant, *Pimpinella anisum*, of Mediterranean regions, yielding aniseed. 2. → **aniseed**.

aniseed /ˈænəsid/ n. 1. the aromatic seed of the anise, used in medicine, in cookery, etc. 2. a stout aromatic New Zealand herb, *Gingidia montana*.

aniso- a word element meaning 'unlike' or 'unequal'.

ankle /ˈæŋkəl/ n. 1. the aggregate joint connecting the foot with the leg. 2. the slender part of the leg above the foot.

anklebiter /ˈæŋkəlbaɪtə/ n. Colloq. a child.

annals /ˈænəlz/ pl. n. 1. a history or relation of events recorded year by year. 2. historical records generally. 3. a periodical publication containing formal reports of learned societies, etc.

anneal /əˈnil/ v.t. 1. to heat (glass, earthenware, metals, etc.) to remove or prevent internal stress. 2. to toughen or temper: *to anneal the mind*.

annex v.t. /ˈænɛks, əˈnɛks/ 1. to attach, join, or add, especially to something larger or more important; unite; append; subjoin. 2. to invade and take possession of (a neighbouring country, territory, etc.). 3. to take possession of, take to one's own use permanently. 4. Colloq. to take without permission; appropriate. –n. /ˈænɛks/ 5. something annexed or added, especially a supplement to a document: *an annex to a treaty*. 6. an annexe. –**annexation** /ænɛkˈseɪʃən/, n. –**annexure** /əˈnɛkʃə/, n.

annexe /ˈænɛks/ n. 1. a subsidiary building or an addition to a building. 2. something annexed. Also, **annex**.

annihilate /əˈnaɪəleɪt/ v.t. 1. to reduce to nothing; destroy utterly: *the bombing annihilated the city*. 2. to destroy the form or collective existence of: *to annihilate an army*. 3. to cancel the effect of; annul: *to annihilate a law*. 4. to defeat utterly, as in argument, competition, or the like. –**annihilation** /ənaɪəˈleɪʃən/, n. –**annihilator,** n. –**annihilative** /əˈnaɪəleɪtɪv/, adj. –**annihilable,** adj.

anniversary /ænəˈvɜsəri/ n. (pl. **-ries**) 1. the yearly recurrence of the date of a past event. 2. the celebration of such a date. –adj. 3. returning or recurring each year. 4. relating to an anniversary: *an anniversary gift*.

annotate /ˈænəteɪt/ v.t. 1. to supply with notes; remark upon in notes: *to annotate the works of Bacon*. –v.i. 2. to make annotations or notes. –**annotation** /ænəˈteɪʃən/, n. –**annotator,** n.

announce /əˈnaʊns/ verb (**announced, announcing**) –v.t. 1. to make known publicly; give notice of. 2. to state the approach or presence of: *to announce guests*; *to announce dinner*. 3. to make known to the mind or senses. –v.i. 4. to work as an announcer. –**announcement,** n.

announcer /əˈnaʊnsə/ n. a person who announces, especially one who reads the news, etc., on radio or television.

annoy /əˈnɔɪ/ v.t. 1. to disturb in a way that is displeasing, troubling, or slightly irritating. –v.i. 2. to be disagreeable or troublesome. –**annoyance,** n. –**annoyer,** n. –**annoyed,** adj. –**annoying,** adj.

annual /ˈænjuəl/ adj. 1. of, for, or relating to a year; yearly. 2. taking place or returning once a year: *annual celebration*. 3. Bot. living only one growing season, as beans or wheat. 4. performed during one year: *annual course of the sun*. –n. 5. a plant living only one year or season. 6. a book or magazine published once a year. –**annually,** adv.

annual general meeting n. 1. the obligatory annual meeting of the shareholders and directors of a registered company. 2. an annual meeting of the members of any organisation, as a club, sporting group, school committee, etc. Also, **AGM**.

annuity /əˈnjuəti/ n. (pl. **-ties**) 1. a specified income payable at stated intervals for a fixed or a contingent period, often for the recipient's life, in consideration of a stipulated premium paid either in prior instalment payments or in a single payment. 2. the right to receive such an income, or the duty to make such a payment or payments. –**annuitant,** n.

annul /əˈnʌl/ v.t. (**annulled, annulling**) 1. to make void or null; abolish (used especially of laws or other established rules, usages, and the like): *to annul a marriage*. 2. to reduce to nothing; obliterate. –**annulment,** n. –**annullable,** adj.

annular /ˈænjələ/ adj. 1. having the form of a ring. 2. bearing a ring. –**annularity** /ænjəˈlærəti/, n. –**annularly,** adv.

annunciate /əˈnʌnsieɪt/ v.t. to announce.

Annunciation /ənʌnsiˈeɪʃən/ n. Christianity 1. (*sometimes lower case*) the announcement by the angel Gabriel to the Virgin Mary of the incarnation of Christ. 2. the church festival (25 March) instituted in memory of this.

anode /ˈænoʊd/ n. 1. the electrode which gives off positive ions, or towards which negative ions or electrons move or collect in electrolysis, as a voltaic cell, radio valve, etc. 2. the positive pole of a battery or other source of current (opposed to *cathode*).

anodyne /ˈænədaɪn/ n. 1. a medicine, especially a drug, that relieves or removes pain. 2. anything relieving distress. –adj. 3. relieving pain. 4. soothing to the feelings. 5. insipid; bland: *an anodyne, inane and instantly forgettable song*.

anoint /əˈnɔɪnt/ v.t. 1. to put oil on; apply an unguent or oily liquid to. 2. to consecrate by applying a holy oil. –**anointer,** n. –**anointment,** n.

anomaly /əˈnɒməli/ n. (pl. **-lies**) 1. deviation from the common rule or analogy. 2. something that deviates in this way: *the anomalies of human nature*. –**anomalous,** adj.

anonymous /əˈnɒnəməs/ adj. 1. without any name acknowledged, as that of author, contributor, or the like: *an anonymous pamphlet*. 2. of unknown name; whose name is withheld: *an anonymous author*. 3. lacking individuality; without distinguishing features; without identity. –**anonymity** /ænəˈnɪməti/, **anonymousness,** n. –**anonymously,** adv.

anopheles /əˈnɒfəliz/ n. (pl. **-pheles**) any mosquito of the genus *Anopheles*, which, when infested with the organisms causing malaria, may transmit the disease to human beings.

anorak /ˈænəræk/ n. → **parka**.

anorectic /ænəˈrɛktɪk/ adj. 1. → **anorexic** (def. 1). 2. Also, **anorexic**. Colloq. extremely thin, as if suffering from anorexia nervosa. –n. 3. → **anorexic** (def. 3).

anorexia /ænəˈrɛksiə/ n. lack of appetite. Also, **anorexy**.

anorexia nervosa /ænərɛksiə nɜˈvoʊsə/ n. a mental disorder, most common in adolescent girls, causing an aversion to food, which may lead to serious malnutrition.

anorexic /ænəˈrɛksik/ *adj.* **1.** Also, **anorectic.** suffering from anorexia nervosa. **2.** *Colloq.* → **anorectic** (def. 2). –*n.* Also, **anorectic. 3.** someone suffering from anorexia nervosa.

another /əˈnʌðə/ *adj.* **1.** a second; a further; an additional: *another piece of cake.* **2.** a different; a distinct; of a different kind: *at another time; another man.* –*pron.* **3.** one more; an additional one: *try another.* **4.** a different one; something different: *going from one house to another.* –*phr.* **5. one another,** one the other; each other: *love one another.*

answer /ˈænsə, ˈan-/ *n.* **1.** a spoken or written reply to a question, request, letter, etc. **2.** a reply or response in act: *the answer was a volley of fire.* **3.** a reply to a charge or an accusation. **4.** *Law* a pleading of facts by a defendant in opposition to those stated in the plaintiff's declaration; defence to a divorce petition. **5.** a solution to a doubt or problem, especially in mathematics. **6.** a piece of work (written or otherwise) performed as a demonstration of knowledge or ability in a test or examination. **7.** a re-echoing, imitation, or repetition of sounds. **8.** *Music* the entrance of a fugue subject, usually on the dominant, after its first presentation in the main key. –*v.i.* **9.** to make answer; reply. **10.** to respond by a word or act: *to answer with a nod.* –*v.t.* **11.** to make answer to; to reply or respond to: *to answer a person; to answer a question.* **12.** to give as an answer. **13.** to make a defence against (a charge); meet or refute (an argument). **14.** to act in reply or response to: *to answer the bell; answer a summons.* **15.** to serve or suit: *this will answer the purpose.* **16.** to conform or correspond to; be similar or equivalent to: *to answer a description.* –*phr.* **17. answer back,** to make a rude or impertinent reply. **18. answer for, a.** to be or declare oneself responsible or accountable for: *I will answer for his safety.* **b.** to give assurance of; vouch for: *he answered for the truth of the statement.* **c.** to act or suffer in consequence of: *to answer for one's sins.* **d.** to be satisfactory or serve for: *to answer for a particular purpose.* **19. answer to, a.** to respond to (a stimulus, direction, command, etc.); obey; acknowledge: *to answer to the whip; to answer to one's name.* **b.** to correspond to; conform to: *to answer to a description.* **c.** to be directly inferior to or in a chain of command. –**answerer,** *n.* –**answerless,** *adj.*

answerable /ˈænsərəbəl/ *adj.* **1.** capable of being answered. –*phr.* **2. answerable for,** accountable for, responsible for: *I am answerable for his safety.* **3. answerable to,** liable to be called to account to or asked to defend one's actions to: *she is answerable to her employer.*

ant /ænt/ *n.* **1.** any of certain small hymenopterous insects constituting the family Formicidae, very widely distributed in thousands of species, all of which have some degree of social organisation. –*phr. Colloq.* **2. have ants in one's pants,** to be restless or impatient. **3. the ant's pants,** someone or something considered the ultimate in style, novelty or cleverness. –**antlike,** *adj.*

ant- variant of **anti-,** especially before a vowel or *h,* as in *antacid.*

-ant **1.** adjective suffix, originally participial, as in *ascendant, pleasant.* **2.** noun suffix used in words of participial meaning, denoting agency or instrumentality, as in *servant, irritant.*

antacid /ˈæntˈæsəd/ *adj.* **1.** neutralising acids; counteracting acidity, as of the stomach. –*n.* **2.** an antacid agent or remedy.

antagonise /ænˈtægənaɪz/ *v.t.* to make hostile; make an antagonist of: *his speech antagonised half the voters.* Also, **antagonize.**

antagonism /ænˈtægənɪzəm/ *n.* **1.** the activity or the relation of contending parties or conflicting forces; active opposition. **2.** an opposing force, principle, or tendency.

antagonist /ænˈtægənəst/ *n.* **1.** someone who is opposed to or strives with another in any kind of contest; opponent; adversary. **2.** *Physiol.* a muscle which acts in opposition to another (the *agonist*). –**antagonistic** /ænˌtægəˈnɪstɪk/, *adj.*

antarctic /ænˈtaktɪk/ *adj.* **1.** (*usu. upper case*) of, at, or near the South Pole. **2.** extremely cold.

Antarctic Circle *n.* an imaginary circle around the earth forming the northern boundary of the South Frigid Zone, at latitude 66°32′S.

ante /ˈæntɪ/ *n.* **1.** *Poker* a stake put into the pool by each player after seeing their hand but before drawing new cards, or, sometimes, before seeing their hand. **2.** the amount paid as one's share. **3.** a payment, usually monetary, extracted as part of a bargain. –*v.t.* (**-ted** *or* **-teed, -teing**) **4.** *Poker* to put (one's stake) into the pool. –*phr.* **5. ante up, a.** to pay one's share as contribution. **b.** to put up (the price or amount to be paid or contributed): *he will ante up $1000.* **6. raise** (or **up**) **the ante, a.** to increase suddenly the price to be paid, as for goods or services. **b.** to raise the requirements, as for a job, etc. **c.** to increase what is at stake.

ante- a prefix meaning 'before in space or time'.

anteater /ˈæntitə/ *n.* **1.** any of the echidnas or spiny anteaters of Australia and New Guinea. **2.** → **numbat. 3.** any of various edentates of tropical America, feeding chiefly on termites. **4.** → **aardvark. 5.** any of the pangolins or scaly anteaters of Africa and tropical Asia.

antecedent /æntəˈsidnt/ *adj.* **1.** (sometimes fol. by *to*) going or being before; preceding; prior: *an antecedent event.* –*n.* **2.** (*pl.*) **a.** ancestry. **b.** one's personal history, especially in the early stages of one's life. **3.** a preceding circumstance, event, etc. **4.** *Gram.* the word or phrase, usually a noun or its equivalent, which is replaced by a pronoun or other substitute later (or rarely, earlier) in the sentence or in a subsequent sentence. In *Jack lost a hat and he can't find it, Jack* is the antecedent of *he,* and *hat* is the antecedent of *it.* –**antecedently,** *adv.* –**antecedence,** *n.*

antechinus /æntəˈkaɪnəs/ *n.* (*pl.* **-nuses**) a type of Australian marsupial mouse of the family Dasyuridae, as the widespread **yellow-footed antechinus,** *Antechinus flavipes,* having a grey head, orange-brown rump and feet, and a black tip on the tail.

antedate /ˈæntideɪt, ænti'deɪt/ *v.t.* **1.** to be of older date than; precede in time: *the Peruvian empire antedates that of Mexico.* **2.** to affix a date earlier than the true one to (a document, etc.): *to antedate a cheque.* **3.** to assign to an earlier date: *to antedate a historical event.*

antediluvian /ˌæntidəˈluviən/ *adj.* **1.** belonging to the period before the Flood, that is, the universal deluge recorded in the Bible as having occurred in the days of Noah. **2.** antiquated; primitive: *antediluvian ideas.*

antelope /ˈæntəloup/ *n.* (*pl.* **-lopes** *or, especially collectively,* **-lope**) a slenderly built, hollow-horned ruminant allied to cattle, sheep, and goats, found chiefly in Africa and Asia.

ante meridiem /ˌænti məˈrɪdiəm/ **1.** before noon. **2.** the time between 12 midnight and 12 noon. *Abbrev.:* a.m., am –**antemeridian,** *adj.*

antenatal /ænti'neɪtl/ *adj., n.* → **prenatal.**

antenna /ænˈtɛnə/ *n.* (*pl.* **-tennae** /-'tɛni/ *for def. 1,* **-tennas** *for def. 2*) **1.** *Zool.* one of the jointed appendages occurring in pairs on the heads of insects, crustaceans, etc., often called feelers. **2. a.** an electrical device that receives, and sometimes sends, electromagnetic and microwave signals. **b.** such a device designed to be attached to a vehicle, phone, television, etc., for the reception of information conveyed in this way. –**antennal, antennary,** adj. –**antenniform,** adj.

antepenultimate /ˌæntɪpə'nʌltəmət/ adj. **1.** last but two. –n. **2.** the last but two; the third from the end.

anterior /æn'tɪəriə/ adj. **1.** placed before; situated more to the front (opposed to *posterior*). **2.** going before in time; preceding; earlier: *an anterior age.* –**anteriority** /ˌæntɪ'ɒrəti/, n. –**anteriorly,** adv.

anteroom /'æntirum/ n. **1.** a smaller room through which access is had to a main room. **2.** a waiting room.

anthem /'ænθəm/ n. **1.** a hymn, as of praise, devotion, or patriotism. **2.** a piece of sacred vocal music, usually with words taken from the Scriptures. **3.** a recorded song or piece of music which achieves cult status with its audience: *a disco anthem; a gay anthem.*

anther /'ænθə/ n. Bot. the pollen-bearing part of a stamen.

antho- a word element meaning 'flower', as in *anthocyanin*.

anthology /æn'θɒlədʒi/ n. (pl. **-gies**) a collection of literary pieces, especially poems, of varied authorship. –**anthologist,** n. –**anthological** /ænθə'lɒdʒɪkəl/, adj.

anthracite /'ænθrəsaɪt/ n. a hard, black, lustrous coal containing little of the volatile hydrocarbons and burning almost without flame; hard coal. –**anthracitic** /ænθrə'sɪtɪk/, adj.

anthrax /'ænθræks/ n. a malignant infectious disease of cattle, sheep, and other animals and of humans, caused by *Bacillus anthracis.* –**anthracic** /æn'θræsɪk/, adj.

anthropo- a word element meaning 'person', 'human being', as in *anthropocentric.* Also, **anthrop-.**

anthropogenic /ˌænθrəpə'dʒɛnɪk/ adj. caused by human beings: *anthropogenic stress on coral reefs.*

anthropoid /'ænθrəpɔɪd/ adj. Also, **anthropoidal. 1.** resembling a human. –n. **2.** an anthropoid ape.

anthropology /ænθrə'pɒlədʒi/ n. the systematic study that deals with the origin, development (physical, intellectual, cultural, moral, etc.) and varieties of humanity. –**anthropologist,** n. –**anthropological** /ænθrəpə'lɒdʒɪkəl/, **anthropologic** /ænθrəpə'lɒdʒɪk/, adj. –**anthropologically** /ænθrəpə'lɒdʒɪkli/, adv.

anthropomorphic /ænθrəpə'mɔfɪk/ adj. ascribing human form or attributes to beings or things not human, especially to a deity. –**anthropomorphism,** n.

anti- a prefix meaning 'against', 'opposed to'. Also, **ant-.**

antibiotic /ˌæntibaɪ'ɒtɪk/ n. **1.** a chemical substance produced by microorganisms which, in dilute solutions, may inhibit the growth of and even destroy bacteria and other microorganisms. **2.** such a substance isolated and purified (as penicillin, streptomycin) and used in the treatment of infectious diseases of humans, animals, and plants.

antibody /'æntibɒdi/ n. (pl. **-dies**) any of various proteins which are produced by a vertebrate as a result of the presence of a foreign substance in the body and which act to neutralise or remove that substance.

anticipate /æn'tɪsəpeɪt/ v.t. **1.** to realise beforehand; foretaste or foresee: *to anticipate pleasure.* **2.** to expect: *to anticipate an acquittal.* **3.** to be before (another) in doing something; forestall: *anticipated by his predecessors.* **4.** to consider or mention before the proper time: *to anticipate more difficult questions.* –v.i. **5.** to think, speak, act, etc., in advance or prematurely. –**anticipation** /æntɪsə'peɪʃən/, n. –**anticipative, anticipatory,** adj. –**anticipatively,** adv. –**anticipator,** n.

anticlimax /ænti'klaɪmæks/ n. **1.** Theatre a noticeable or ludicrous descent in discourse from lofty ideas or expressions to what is much less impressive. **2.** an abrupt descent in dignity; an inglorious or disappointing conclusion. –**anticlimactic** /ˌæntiklaɪ'mæktɪk/, adj.

anticlockwise /ænti'klɒkwaɪz/ adv. **1.** in a direction opposite to that of the rotation of the hands of a clock. –adj. **2.** of or relating to movement in this direction.

antics /'æntɪks/ pl. n. odd, amusing or ridiculous behaviour.

anticyclone /ænti'saɪkloʊn/ n. Meteorol. an extensive horizontal movement of the atmosphere spirally around and away from a gradually progressing central region of high barometric pressure, the spiral motion being clockwise in the Northern Hemisphere, anticlockwise in the Southern. –**anticyclonic** /ˌæntisaɪ'klɒnɪk/, adj.

antidepressant /ˌæntidə'prɛsənt/ Med. –n. **1.** any of a class of drugs used in treating depression. –adj. **2.** of or relating to this class of drugs.

antidote /'æntidoʊt/ n. **1.** a medicine or other remedy for counteracting the effects of poison, disease, etc. **2.** whatever prevents or counteracts injurious effects. –**antidotal,** adj.

antigen /'æntidʒən, 'æntə-/ n. any substance which when injected into animal tissues will stimulate the production of antibodies. –**antigenic** /ænti'dʒɛnɪk/, adj.

antihistamine /ænti'hɪstəmɪn, -maɪn/ n. any of certain medicines or drugs which neutralise or inhibit the effect of histamine in the body, used mainly in the treatment of allergic conditions, as hay fever, asthma, etc. –**antihistaminic** /ˌæntihɪstə'mɪnɪk/, adj.

antilogarithm /ænti'lɒgərɪðəm/ n. the number corresponding to a logarithm.

antinomy /æn'tɪnəmi/ n. **1.** opposition between laws and principles; contradiction in law. **2.** Philos. the mutual contradiction of two principles or correctly drawn inferences, each of which is supported by reason. –**antinomian,** n., adj. –**antinomianism,** n.

antioxidant /ænti'ɒksədənt/ n. **1.** any substance inhibiting oxidation. **2.** any substance which inhibits oxidative deterioration in certain materials, including many foods. **3.** such a substance in the body, which neutralises free radicals formed when body cells burn oxygen for energy, keeping the immune system healthy and reducing the risk of cancer and other diseases. Also, **anti-oxidant.**

antipasto /ænti'pæstoʊ/ n. (in Italian cookery) an assortment of meats, cheeses, olives, etc., served as an appetiser: *we ordered antipasto.*

antipathy /æn'tɪpəθi/ n. (pl. **-thies**) **1.** a natural or settled dislike; repugnance; aversion. **2.** an instinctive contrariety or opposition in feeling. **3.** an object of natural aversion or settled dislike. –**antipathetic** /ˌæntipə'θɛtɪk/, adj. –**antipathetically** /æntipə'θɛtɪkəli/, adv.

antiperspirant /ænti'pɜspərənt/ n. any preparation for decreasing or preventing perspiration.

antipodes /æn'tɪpədiz/ pl. n. points diametrically opposite to each other on the earth or any globe. –**antipodean** /æn,tɪpə'diən/, adj., n.

antiquary /'æntəkwəri/ n. (pl. **-ries**) an expert on ancient things; a student or collector of antiquities.

antiquate /'æntəkweɪt/ v.t. **1.** to make old and useless by substituting something newer and better. **2.** to make antique. –**antiquated,** adj. –**antiquation** /æntə'kweɪʃən/, n.

antique /æn'tik/ adj. **1.** belonging to former times, as contrasted with modern. **2.** dating from an early period: *antique furniture.* **3.** Colloq. very old-fashioned. –n. **4.** an object of art or a furniture piece of a former period. –v.t. (**-tiqued, -tiquing**) **5.** to make appear antique. –**antiquely,** adv. –**antiqueness,** n.

antiquity /æn'tɪkwəti/ n. (pl. **-ties**) **1.** the quality of being ancient; great age: *a family of great antiquity.* **2.** ancient times; former ages: *the errors of dark antiquity.* **3.** the time before the Middle Ages. **4.** the ancients collectively; the people of ancient times. **5.** (usu. pl.) something belonging to or remaining from ancient times.

antiseptic /æntəˈsɛptɪk/ *adj.* **1.** relating to or causing antisepsis. –*n.* **2.** an antiseptic agent. –**antiseptically**, *adv.*

anti-siphoning law /ænti-ˈsaɪfənɪŋ lɔ/ *n.* (in telecommunications and broadcasting legislation) a provision ensuring that particular events of cultural significance will be available on free-to-air television for viewing by the general public, the aim being to prevent these events from being siphoned off to pay TV.

antisocial /æntiˈsoʊʃəl/ *adj.* **1.** unwilling or unable to associate normally with one's fellows. **2.** opposed, damaging, or motivated by antagonism to social order, or to the principles on which society is constituted. –**antisocially**, *adv.*

antithesis /ænˈtɪθəsəs/ *n.* (*pl.* **-theses** /-θəsiz/) **1.** opposition; contrast: *the antithesis of theory and fact.* **2.** (sometimes fol. by *of* or *to*) the direct opposite. –**antithetic** /ˌæntəˈθɛtɪk/, *adj.*

antitoxin /æntiˈtɒksən/ *n.* the antibody formed in immunisation with a given toxin, used in treating or immunising against certain infectious diseases. –**antitoxic**, *adj.*

antivenene /ˌæntivəˈnin/ *n.* **1.** an antitoxin produced in the blood by repeated injections of venom, as of snakes. **2.** the antitoxic serum obtained from such blood. Also, **antivenin**, **antivenom**.

antler /ˈæntlə/ *n.* one of the solid deciduous horns, usually branched, of an animal of the deer family.

antonym /ˈæntənɪm/ *n.* a word opposed in meaning to another (opposed to *synonym*): '*good*' *is the antonym of* '*bad*'. –**antonymic**, *adj.*

anus /ˈeɪnəs/ *n. Anat.* the opening at the lower end of the alimentary canal, through which the solid refuse of digestion is excreted.

anvil /ˈænvəl/ *n.* **1.** a heavy iron block with a smooth face, frequently of steel, on which metals, usually red-hot or white-hot, are hammered into desired shapes. **2.** anything on which blows are struck.

anxiety /æŋˈzaɪəti/ *n.* **1.** distress or uneasiness of mind caused by apprehension of danger or misfortune. **2.** solicitous desire; eagerness. **3.** *Psychol.* a state of apprehension and psychic tension found in some forms of mental disorder.

anxious /ˈæŋʃəs, ˈæŋk-/ *adj.* **1.** full of anxiety or solicitude; greatly troubled or solicitous: *to be anxious about someone's safety.* **2.** earnestly desirous: *anxious to please; anxious for your safety.* **3.** attended with or showing solicitude or uneasiness: *anxious forebodings.* **4.** causing anxiety or worry; difficult: *an anxious business, an anxious time.* –**anxiously**, *adv.* –**anxiousness**, *n.*

any /ˈɛni/ *adj.* **1.** one, a, an, or (with plural noun) some, whatever or whichever it may be: *if you have any witnesses, produce them.* **2.** in whatever quantity or number, great or small: *have you any butter?* **3.** every: *any schoolchild would know that.* **4.** (with a negative) none at all. **5.** a great or unlimited (amount): *any number of things.* –*pron.* **6. a.** (*construed as sing.*) any person; anybody: *he does better than any before him* **b.** (*construed as pl.*) any persons: *unknown to any.* **7.** any single one or any one's; any thing or things; any quantity or number: *I haven't any.* –*adv.* **8.** in any degree; to any extent; at all: *do you feel any better?; will this route take any longer?* –*phr.* **9. any one ...,** any single or individual (person or thing): *any one part of the town.* **10. get any,** *Colloq.* to have sexual intercourse: *are you getting any?*

anybody /ˈɛnibɒdi, -bədi/ *pron.* **1.** any person. –*n.* (*pl.* **-bodies**) **2.** a person of little importance.

anyhow /ˈɛnihaʊ/ *adv.* **1.** in any case; at all events. **2.** in a careless manner. **3.** in any way whatever.

anyone /ˈɛniwʌn/ *pron.* any person; anybody.

anything /ˈɛniθɪŋ/ *pron.* **1.** any thing whatever; something, no matter what. –*adv.* **2.** in any degree; to any extent. –*phr.* **3. if anything,** if it is possible to make a judgement at all: *the patient is worse, if anything; if anything she's too lenient.* **4. like anything,** *Colloq.* greatly; with great energy or emotion.

any way *adv.* **1.** in any way or manner. **2.** carelessly; haphazardly; anyhow.

anyway /ˈɛniweɪ/ *adv.* in any case; anyhow.

anywhere /ˈɛniwɛə/ *adv.* in, at, or to any place.

anywise /ˈɛniwaɪz/ *adv.* in any way or respect.

Anzac /ˈænzæk/ *n.* **1.** a member of the Australian and NZ Army Corps during World War I. **2.** a soldier from Australia or NZ. **3.** an Anzac biscuit.

Anzac biscuit *n.* a biscuit made from wheat flour, rolled oats, desiccated coconut, and golden syrup. Also, **anzac biscuit**.

Anzac Day *n.* 25 April, the anniversary of the Anzac landing on Gallipoli in 1915.

A-1 /eɪ-ˈwʌn/ *adj.* **1.** registered as a first-class vessel in a shipping register, as Lloyd's Register. **2.** *Colloq.* first-class; excellent. Also, **A1**, **A-one**.

aorta /eɪˈɔtə/ *n.* (*pl.* **-tas** *or* **-tae** /-ti/) *Anat.* the main trunk of the arterial system, conveying blood from the left ventricle of the heart to all of the body except the lungs. –**aortic**, **aortal**, *adj.*

ap- variant of **apo-**.

apart /əˈpat/ *adv.* **1.** in pieces, or to pieces: *to take a watch apart.* **2.** separately or aside in motion, place, or position. **3.** to or at one side, with respect to purpose or function: *to set something apart.* **4.** separately or individually in consideration. **5.** aside (used with a noun or gerund): *joking apart, what do you think?* –*adj.* **6.** separate; independent: *a class apart.* –*phr.* **7. apart from,** leaving aside: *apart from other considerations.* **8. set apart,** to isolate, often because of superiority: *the ocean views set this restaurant apart.*

apartheid /əˈpataɪd, əˈpateɪt/ *n.* (especially as applied to the former policy in South Africa) racial segregation.

apartment /əˈpatmənt/ *n.* a flat or unit.

apathy /ˈæpəθi/ *n.* **1.** lack of feeling; absence or suppression of passion, emotion, or excitement. **2.** lack of interest in things which others find moving or exciting. –**apathetic** /æpəˈθɛtɪk/, *adj.* –**apathetically**, *adv.*

apatosaurus /əˈpætəsɔrəs/ *n.* a very large, amphibious, herbivorous dinosaur (popularly known as a brontosaurus), having a long neck and tail and a relatively small head, existing in parts of North America in the late Jurassic period.

ape /eɪp/ *n.* **1.** a non-human anthropoid. **2.** an imitator; a mimic. **3.** any monkey. –*v.t.* (**aped, aping**) **4.** to imitate servilely; mimic. –*phr.* **5. go ape,** *Colloq.* (sometimes fol. by *over*) to react with excessive and unrestrained pleasure, excitement, etc. –**apelike**, *adj.*

aperient /əˈpɪəriənt/ *adj.* **1.** purgative; laxative. –*n.* **2.** a medicine or an article of diet that acts as a mild laxative.

aperitif /əˈpɛrətif/ *n.* a small alcoholic drink, such as a cocktail or glass of sherry, often taken as an appetiser. Also, **aperitive** /əˈpɛrətɪv/.

aperture /ˈæpətʃə/ *n.* a hole, slit, crack, gap, or other opening.

apex /ˈeɪpɛks/ *n.* (*pl.* **apexes** *or* **apices** /ˈeɪpəsiz/) **1.** the tip, point, or vertex of anything; the summit. **2.** climax; acme.

aphasia /əˈfeɪʒə, -ziə/ *n.* loss or impairment of the faculty of symbolic formulation to a lesion of the central nervous system resulting in inhibition of speech. –**aphasic**, *adj.*, *n.*

aphid /'eɪfəd/ n. any of the plant-sucking insects of the family Aphididae; greenfly; plant louse. –**aphidian** /ə'fɪdiən/, adj., n.

aphorism /'æfərɪzəm/ n. a terse saying embodying a general truth. –**aphorismic, aphorismatic,** adj.

aphrodisiac /æfrə'dɪziæk/ adj. **1.** arousing sexual desire. –n. **2.** a drug or food that arouses sexual desire.

apiary /'eɪpiəri/ n. (pl. **-ries**) a place in which bees are kept; a stand or shed containing a number of beehives. –**apiarist,** n.

apical /'æpɪkəl, 'eɪ-/ adj. **1.** of, at, or forming the apex. **2.** Phonetics relating to speech sounds formed with the tip of the tongue as articulator, such as [t], [s], [n]. –**apically,** adv.

apices /'eɪpəsiz/ n. a plural of **apex.**

apiculture /'eɪpɪkʌltʃə/ n. the rearing of bees. –**apicultural,** adj. –**apiculturist,** n.

apiece /ə'pis/ adv. for each piece, thing, or person; for each one; each: an orange apiece; costing a dollar apiece.

apivorous /eɪ'pɪvərəs/ adj. feeding on bees, as certain birds.

aplomb /ə'plɒm/ n. imperturbable self-possession, poise, or assurance.

apo- a prefix meaning 'from', 'away', 'off', 'asunder', as in apomorphine, apophyllite. Also, **ap-, aph-.**

apocalypse /ə'pɒkəlɪps/ n. discovery; revelation; disclosure. –**apocalyptic,** adj.

apocryphal /ə'pɒkrəfəl/ adj. **1.** of doubtful authorship or authenticity. **2.** false; spurious. **3.** fabled; fictitious; mythical. –**apocryphally,** adv. –**apocryphalness,** n.

apogee /'æpədʒi/ n. **1.** Astron. the point in the orbit of a heavenly body or artificial satellite most distant from the earth (opposed to perigee). **2.** the highest or most distant point; climax. –**apogeal, apogean,** adj.

apolitical /eɪpə'lɪtɪkəl/ adj. **1.** having no interest in political issues. **2.** not involving obligations to a particular political party: the vote on this issue is apolitical.

apologetic /əpɒlə'dʒɛtɪk/ adj. **1.** making apology or excuse for fault, failure, etc. **2.** defending by speech or writing. Also, **apologetical.** –**apologetically,** adv.

apologia /æpə'loʊdʒiə/ n. a formal defence or justification in speech or writing, as of a cause or doctrine.

apologise /ə'pɒlədʒaɪz/ v.i. **1.** to offer excuses or regrets for some fault, insult, failure, or injury. **2.** to make a formal defence in speech or writing. Also, **apologize.** –**apologiser,** n.

apology /ə'pɒlədʒi/ n. (pl. **-gies**) **1.** an expression of regret offered for some fault, failure, insult, or injury. **2.** an apologia. **3.** a poor specimen or substitute; a makeshift: a sad apology for a hat.

apoplexy /'æpəplɛksi/ n. **1.** marked loss of bodily function due to cerebral haemorrhage. **2.** a fit of rage. –**apoplectic,** adj.

apostasy /ə'pɒstəsi/ n. (pl. **-tasies**) a total desertion of, or departure from, one's religion, principles, party, cause, etc. –**apostate,** n.

apostle /ə'pɒsəl/ n. **1.** one of the twelve disciples sent forth by Christ to preach the gospel. **2.** any important Christian teacher or missionary, especially in the early period of the spread of Christianity. **3.** a pioneer of any great moral reform. **4.** a vigorous and zealous upholder (of a principle, cause, etc.). –**apostleship,** n.

apostrophe[1] /ə'pɒstrəfi/ n. the sign (') used to indicate: **1.** the omission of one or more letters in a word, as in o'er for over, halo'd for haloed. **2.** the possessive case, as in lion's, lions'. **3.** certain plurals, as in several MD's. –**apostrophic** /æpə'strɒfɪk/, adj.

apostrophe[2] /ə'pɒstrəfi/ n. Rhetoric a digression from a discourse, especially in the form of a personal address

to someone not present. –**apostrophic** /æpə'strɒfɪk/, adj.

apothecary /ə'pɒθəkri, -kəri/ n. (pl. **-ries**) Archaic a chemist; a pharmacist.

app /æp/ n. Computers **1.** an application (def. 7). **2.** a digital product which can be downloaded onto a smart phone, tablet, etc.

appal /ə'pɔl/ v.t. (**-palled, -palling**) **1.** to overcome with fear; fill with consternation and horror. **2.** to shock; dismay; displease. Also, **appall.** –**appalling,** adj. –**appallingly,** adv.

apparatus /æpə'ratəs, -'reɪtəs/ n. (pl. **-tus** or **-tuses**) **1.** an assemblage of instruments, machinery, appliances, materials, etc., for a particular use. **2.** an organisation or subdivision of an organisation.

apparel /ə'pærəl/ n. **1.** a person's outer clothing; raiment. –v.t. (**-relled** or, Chiefly US, **-reled, -relling** or, Chiefly US, **-reling**) **2.** Archaic to dress or clothe; adorn; ornament.

apparent /ə'pærənt/ adj. **1.** capable of being clearly perceived or understood; plain or clear. **2.** seeming; ostensible: the apparent motion of the sun. **3.** (of a scientific measurement) not corrected to allow for factors such as the position of observation, which affect the measurement (as opposed to true). **4.** exposed to the sight; open to view. –**apparently,** adv. –**apparentness,** n.

apparition /æpə'rɪʃən/ n. **1.** a ghostly appearance; a spectre or phantom. **2.** anything that appears, especially something remarkable or phenomenal. **3.** the act of appearing. –**apparitional,** adj.

appeal /ə'pil/ n. **1.** a call for help, support, mercy, money, etc.: the prisoners made an appeal for mercy; a Red Cross appeal. **2.** a request to some person or group for support, decision, etc. **3.** Sport a call from a player to the referee or umpire for a decision on a point of play. **4.** Law a formal request for review by a higher court. **5.** the power to attract or to move the feelings; charm: the game has lost its appeal; sex appeal. –v.i. **6.** to make an appeal. –phr. **7. appeal to,** to offer a peculiar attraction, interest, enjoyment, etc., to: this colour appeals to me. –**appealable,** adj. –**appealer,** n. –**appealingly,** adv.

appear /ə'pɪə/ v. (copular) **1.** to have an appearance; seem; look: to appear wise. **2.** to come into sight; become visible: a cloud appeared on the horizon. **3.** to be obvious; be clear or made clear by evidence: it eventually appeared that the man was her uncle. **4.** to come or be placed before the public: his biography appeared last year. **5.** Law to come formally before a tribunal, authority, etc., as defendant, plaintiff, or counsel. –phr. **6. appear in,** (of a theatrical performer) to have a part in (a play, film, etc.).

appearance /ə'pɪərəns/ n. **1.** the act or fact of appearing, as to the eye, the mind, or the public. **2.** Law **a.** the formal coming into court of a party to a suit. **b.** formal notice of intent to defend an action. **3.** outward look or aspect; mien: a woman of noble appearance. **4.** outward show or seeming; semblance: to avoid the appearance of coveting an honour. **5.** (pl.) outward signs; indications; apparent conditions or circumstances: don't judge by appearances. –phr. **6. keep up appearances,** to maintain a socially acceptable outward show (often to conceal shortcomings). **7. to all appearances,** apparently; so far as can be seen.

appease /ə'piz/ v.t. **1.** to bring to a state of peace, quiet, ease, or content: to appease an angry king. **2.** to satisfy: to appease one's hunger. **3.** to accede to the belligerent demands of (a country, government, etc.) by a sacrifice of justice. –**appeasable,** adj. –**appeasement,** n. –**appeaser,** n. –**appeasing,** adj. –**appeasingly,** adv.

appellant /ə'pɛlənt/ n. someone who appeals.

appellate /ə'pɛlət/ adj. Law relating to appeals.

appellation /æpə'leɪʃən/ *n.* 1. a name, title, or designation. 2. the act of naming.

append /ə'pɛnd/ *v.t.* 1. to add, as an accessory; subjoin; annex. 2. to attach as a pendant. **–appendage,** *n.*

appendectomy /ˌæpɛn'dɛktəmi/ *n.* (*pl.* **-mies**) the surgical excision of the vermiform appendix. Also, **appendicectomy** /əpɛndə'sɛktəmi/.

appendicitis /əpɛndə'saɪtəs/ *n.* inflammation of the vermiform appendix.

appendix /ə'pɛndɪks/ *n.* (*pl.* **-dixes** *or* **-dices** /-dəsiz/) 1. matter which supplements the main text of a book, generally explanatory, statistical, or bibliographic material. 2. *Anat.* **a.** a process or projection. **b.** the vermiform appendix.

appertain /æpə'teɪn/ *v.i.* (sometimes fol. by *to*) to belong as a part, member, possession, attribute, etc.; pertain.

appetiser /'æpətaɪzə/ *n.* a food or drink that stimulates the desire for food. Also, **appetizer.**

appetising /'æpətaɪzɪŋ/ *adj.* exciting or appealing to the appetite. Also, **appetizing. –appetisingly,** *adv.*

appetite /'æpətaɪt/ *n.* 1. a desire for food or drink: *to work up an appetite.* 2. a desire to supply any bodily want or craving: *the natural appetites.* 3. an innate or acquired demand or propensity to satisfy a want: *an appetite for reading.* 4. (*oft.* used in the negative) an enthusiasm for a particular course of action: *to have no appetite for budget cuts.*

applaud /ə'plɔd/ *v.i.* 1. to express approval by clapping the hands, shouting, etc. 2. to give praise; express approval. *–v.t.* 3. to praise or show approval of by clapping the hands, shouting, etc.: *to applaud an actor.* 4. to praise in any way; commend; approve: *to applaud one's conduct.* **–applauder,** *n.* **–applause,** *n.*

apple /'æpəl/ *n.* 1. the edible fruit, usually round and with red, yellow or green skin, of the tree *Malus pumila.* 2. Also, **apple tree.** the tree, cultivated in most temperate regions. 3. the fruit of any of certain other species of tree of the same genus. 4. Also, **apple tree.** any of these trees. 5. the forbidden fruit of the tree in the Garden of Eden. *–phr.* 6. **compare apples to oranges,** to try to compare two things which are so essentially different that any comparison is misleading. 7. **she's apples** or **she'll be apples,** *Aust., NZ Colloq.* all is well.

applet /'æplət/ *n.* a small Java computer program which can be transferred over the internet and which runs on the client machine rather than the server.

appliance /ə'plaɪəns/ *n.* 1. an instrument, apparatus, or device, especially one operated by electricity and designed for household use. 2. a vehicle designed primarily for firefighting, as a water tanker, a pumper, a rescue vehicle, etc. 3. the act of applying; application.

applicable /ə'plɪkəbəl, 'æp-/ *adj.* capable of being applied; fit; suitable; relevant. **–applicability** /ə,plɪkə'bɪləti/, **applicableness,** *n.* **–applicably,** *adv.*

applicant /'æplɪkənt/ *n.* someone who applies; a candidate: *an applicant for a position.*

application /æplə'keɪʃən/ *n.* 1. the act of putting to special use: *application of common sense to a problem.* 2. the quality of being usable for a particular purpose; relevance: *this has no application to the case.* 3. the act of applying: *application of paint to a wall.* 4. the thing applied. 5. (the act of making) a written or spoken request. 6. close attention; continuous effort: *application to one's studies.* 7. *Computers* a program which is written specifically to perform a specialised task. **–applicator,** *n.*

application program *n.* → **application** (def. 7).

applied /ə'plaɪd/ *adj.* 1. put to practical use, as a science when its laws are concrete phenomena (distinguished from *abstract, theoretical,* or *pure* science). 2. laid flat against.

appliqué /'æpləkeɪ/ *adj.* 1. formed with ornamentation of one material sewn or otherwise applied to another. *–n.* 2. the ornamentation used to make an appliqué material. 3. work so formed. *–v.t.* (**-quéd, -quéing**) 4. to apply or form as in appliqué work.

apply /ə'plaɪ/ *verb* (**-plied, -plying**) *–v.t.* 1. to lay on; bring into physical closeness: *to apply a match to powder.* 2. to bring to bear; put into practical operation, as a principle, law, rule, etc. 3. to put to use, often with reference to some person or thing: *they know how to apply their labour; to apply the finding to the case.* 4. to give with full attention; set: *I apply my mind to my lessons.* *–v.i.* 5. to have a bearing; be relevant: *the arguments apply to the case.* 6. to make request; ask: *they can apply for a job.* **–applier,** *n.*

appoint /ə'pɔɪnt/ *v.t.* 1. to nominate or assign to a position, or to perform a function; set apart; designate: *to appoint a new secretary.* 2. to constitute, ordain, or fix by decree, order, or decision; decree: *laws appointed by God.* 3. to determine by authority or agreement; fix; settle: *to appoint a time for the meeting.* 4. *Law* to designate (a person) to take the benefit of an estate created by a deed or will. 5. to provide with what is requisite; equip. **–appointee,** *n.* **–appointer,** *n.*

appointment /ə'pɔɪntmənt/ *n.* 1. the act of appointing, designating, or placing in office: *to fill a vacancy by appointment.* 2. an office held by a person appointed. 3. the act of fixing by mutual agreement; engagement: *an appointment to meet at six o'clock.* 4. (*usu. pl.*) equipment, as for a ship, hotel, etc. 5. decree; ordinance.

apportion /ə'pɔʃən/ *v.t.* to divide and assign in just proportion or according to some rule; distribute or allocate proportionally: *to apportion expenses.* **–apportionable,** *adj.* **–apportionment,** *n.*

apposite /'æpəzət/ *adj.* suitable; well-adapted; pertinent: *an apposite answer.* **–appositely,** *adj.* **–appositeness,** *n.*

apposition /æpə'zɪʃən/ *n.* 1. the act of adding to or together; a placing together; juxtaposition. 2. *Gram.* a syntactic relation between expressions, usually consecutive, which have the same function and the same relation to other elements in the sentence, the second expression identifying or supplementing the first. For example: *Adam, the first man,* has *the first man* in apposition to *Adam.* **–appositional, appositive** /ə'pɒzətɪv/, *adj.* **–appositionally,** *adv.*

appraise /ə'preɪz/ *v.t.* 1. to estimate generally, as to quality, size, weight, etc. 2. to value in current money; estimate the value of. **–appraisable,** *adj.* **–appraisal,** *n.* **–appraiser,** *n.* **–appraisingly,** *adv.*

appreciable /ə'priʃəbəl/ *adj.* 1. capable of being perceived or estimated; noticeable. 2. fairly large. **–appreciably,** *adv.*

appreciate /ə'priʃieɪt, ə'prisi-/ *v.t.* 1. to place a sufficiently high estimate on: *her great ability was not appreciated.* 2. to be fully conscious of; be aware of; detect: *to appreciate the dangers of a situation.* 3. to be aware of the good qualities (of a person, thing, or action); be pleased with or grateful for. 4. to raise in value. *–v.i.* 5. to increase in value. **–appreciative, appreciatory,** *adj.* **–appreciation** /əpriʃi'eɪʃən, əprisi-/, *n.* **–appreciator,** *n.*

apprehend /æprə'hɛnd/ *v.t.* 1. to take into custody; arrest by legal warrant or authority. 2. to grasp the meaning of; understand; conceive. 3. to entertain suspicion or fear of; anticipate: *I apprehend no violence.* *–v.i.* 4. to understand. 5. to be apprehensive; fear. **–apprehender,** *n.*

apprehension /æprə'hɛnʃən/ *n.* 1. anticipation of adversity; dread or fear of coming evil. 2. the faculty of apprehending; understanding. 3. a view, opinion, or idea on any subject. 4. the act of arresting; seizure.

–**apprehensive**, *adj.* –**apprehensively**, *adv.* –**apprehensiveness**, *n.*

apprentice /ə'prɛntəs/ *n.* **1.** someone who works for another with obligations to learn a trade. **2.** a learner; a novice. **3.** *Horseracing* a trainee jockey under 21 years of age. –*v.t.* (**-ticed, -ticing**) **4.** to bind to or put under the care of an employer for instruction in a trade. –**apprenticeship**, *n.*

apprise /ə'praɪz/ *v.t.* (sometimes fol. by *of*) to give notice to; inform; advise.

appro /'æproʊ/ *phr.* **on appro**, *Colloq.* on approval; for examination, without obligation to buy.

approach /ə'proʊtʃ/ *v.t.* **1.** to come nearer or near to: *to approach the city; approaching Homer as a poet.* **2.** to make advances or a suggestion to: *to approach the minister with a plan.* –*v.i.* **3.** to come nearer; draw near: *the storm approaches.* –*n.* **4.** the act of drawing or being near: *the approach of a horseman; a fair approach to the truth.* **5.** any means of reaching: *the approach to a city; an approach to a problem.* **6.** (*sing.* or *pl.*) advances made to a person. **7.** (*pl.*) Mil. cover for protecting forces in an advance against a strong position.

approachable /ə'proʊtʃəbəl/ *adj.* **1.** capable of being approached; accessible. **2.** (of a person) easy to approach. –**approachability** /əproʊtʃə'bɪləti/, **approachableness**, *n.*

approbation /æprə'beɪʃən/ *n.* approval; commendation. –**approbatory, approbative**, *adj.*

appropriate *adj.* /ə'proʊpriət/ **1.** suitable or fitting for a particular purpose, person, occasion, etc.: *an appropriate example.* **2.** belonging or peculiar to one: *each played their appropriate part.* –*v.t.* /ə'proʊprieɪt/ **3.** to set apart for some specific purpose or use: *parliament appropriated funds for the university.* **4.** to take to or for oneself; take possession of. **5.** to filch; annex; steal. –**appropriation** /əproʊpri'eɪʃən/, *n.* –**appropriately**, *adv.* –**appropriateness**, *n.* –**appropriative**, *adj.* –**appropriator**, *n.*

approval /ə'pruvəl/ *n.* **1.** the act of approving; approbation. **2.** sanction; official permission. –*phr.* **3. on approval**, for examination, without obligation to buy.

approve /ə'pruv/ *v.t.* **1.** to pronounce or consider good; speak or think favourably of: *to approve the policies of the government.* **2.** to confirm or sanction officially; ratify. –*v.i.* **3.** (sometimes fol. by *of*) to speak or think favourably: *they don't approve of him; we'll leave at once if you approve.* –**approvable**, *adj.* –**approver**, *n.* –**approvingly**, *adv.*

approximate *adj.* /ə'prɒksəmət/ **1.** nearly exact, equal, or perfect: *that is an approximate kilo.* **2.** inaccurate; rough. **3.** near; close together. –*v.t.* /ə'prɒksəmeɪt/ **4.** to come near to; approach closely to. –*v.i.* /ə'prɒksəmeɪt/ **5.** (usu. fol. by *to*) to come near in position, quality, amount, etc.: *his answer approximated to the truth.* –**approximately**, *adv.* –**approximation** /əprɒksə'meɪʃən/, *n.*

appurtenance /ə'pɜtənəns/ *n.* **1.** something accessory to another and more important thing; an adjunct. **2.** *Law* a right, privilege, or improvement belonging to and passing with a principal property.

après-ski /,æpreɪ-'ski/ *adj.* of or relating to a party or social occasion held at the end of a day spent skiing.

apricot /'eɪprɪkɒt, -prə-/ *n.* **1.** the downy yellow fruit, somewhat resembling a small peach, of the tree *Prunus armeniaca.* **2.** the tree. **3.** a pinkish yellow or yellowish pink.

April /'eɪprəl/ *n.* the fourth month of the year, containing 30 days.

a priori /eɪ pri'ɔri, a praɪ'ɔraɪ/ **1.** from cause to effect; from a general law to a particular instance; valid independently of observation. **2.** claiming to report

matters of fact but actually not supported by factual study. –**apriority** /eɪpraɪ'ɒrəti/, *n.* –**aprioristic** /eɪpraɪə-'rɪstɪk/, *adj.* –**aprioristically**, *adv.*

apron /'eɪprən/ *n.* **1.** a piece of clothing made in various ways for covering, and usually also protecting, the front of the person more or less completely. **2.** a flat continuous conveyor belt. **3.** a paved or hard-packed area abutting on airfield buildings and hangars. **4.** the part of the stage in front of the proscenium arch. –*v.t.* **5.** to put an apron on; furnish with an apron. –**apronlike**, *adj.*

apropos /æprə'poʊ/ *adv.* **1.** to the purpose; opportunely. **2.** by the way. –*adj.* **3.** opportune; pertinent: *apropos remarks.* –*phr.* **4. apropos of**, with reference or regard to; in respect of: *apropos of nothing.*

apse /æps/ *n. Archit.* a vaulted semicircular or polygonal recess in a building, especially at the end of the choir of a church. –**apsidal** /'æpsədl/, *adj.*

apt /æpt/ *adj.* **1.** unusually intelligent; quick to learn: *an apt pupil.* **2.** suited to the purpose or occasion; *an apt metaphor.* –*phr.* **3. apt to**, inclined or disposed to: *the baby is apt to cry when we leave the room.* –**aptly**, *adv.* –**aptness**, *n.*

apteryx /'æptərɪks/ *n.* (*pl.* **-teryxes** /-tərɪksəz/) any of several flightless birds of New Zealand, constituting the genus *Apteryx*, allied to the extinct moa; kiwi.

aptitude /'æptətjud, -tʃud/ *n.* **1.** a natural tendency or acquired inclination; both capacity and propensity for a certain course. **2.** readiness in learning; intelligence; talent. **3.** the state or quality of being apt; special fitness.

aquaculture /'ækwəkʌltʃə/ *n.* **1.** cultivation of the food resources of the sea or of inland waters. **2.** the cultivation of fish in tank or pond systems. Also, **aquiculture**. –**aquacultural**, *adj.* –**aquaculturalist, aquaculturist**, *n.*

aqualung /'ækwəlʌŋ/ *n.* (*from trademark*) a cylinder of compressed air, usually strapped on to the back, with a tube leading to a special mouthpiece or watertight mask, which enables a swimmer to move about freely at a considerable depth for an extended length of time.

aquamarine /ækwəmə'rin/ *n.* **1.** a transparent light-blue or greenish blue variety of beryl, used as a gem. **2.** a light blue-green or greenish blue.

aquaplane /'ækwəpleɪn/ *n.* **1.** a single broad water-ski. –*v.i.* **2.** to ride an aquaplane. **3.** Also, **hydroplane**. (of a motor vehicle, etc.) to ride up at high speed on water on the road surface so that the wheels lose contact with the surface.

aquarium /ə'kwɛəriəm/ *n.* (*pl.* **-riums** *or* **-ria** /-riə/) a pond, tank, or establishment in which living aquatic animals or plants are kept, as for exhibition.

Aquarius /ə'kwɛəriəs/ *n.* the eleventh sign of the zodiac, which the sun enters about 20 January; the Waterbearer. –**Aquarian**, *n., adj.*

aquatic /ə'kwɒtɪk/ *adj.* **1.** of or relating to water. **2.** living or growing in water. **3.** practised on or in water: *aquatic sports.*

aqueduct /'ækwədʌkt/ *n.* **1.** *Civil Eng.* **a.** a conduit or artificial channel for conducting water from a distance, the water usually flowing by gravity. **b.** a structure which carries a conduit or canal across a valley or over a river. **2.** *Anat.* a canal or passage through which liquids pass.

aqueous /'ækwiəs, 'eɪkwi-/ *adj.* **1.** of, like, or containing water; watery. **2.** *Geol.* (of rocks) formed of matter deposited in or by water.

aquifer /'ækwəfə/ *n. Geol.* a geological formation which holds water and allows water to percolate through it. Also, **aquafer**.

aquiline /'ækwəlaɪn/ *adj.* **1.** of or like the eagle. **2.** (of the nose) curved like an eagle's beak; hooked.

ar- variant of **ad-** (by assimilation) before *r*, as in *arrear*.

-ar¹ **1.** an adjective suffix meaning 'relating to', 'being', 'like', as in *linear*, *regular*. **2.** a suffix forming adjectives not directly related to nouns, as *similar*, *singular*.

-ar² a noun suffix, as in *vicar*, *scholar*, *collar*.

-ar³ a noun suffix denoting an agent (replacing regular **-er¹**), as in *beggar*, *liar*.

arabesque /ærə'bɛsk/ *n.* **1.** a kind of ornament in which flowers, foliage, fruits, vases, animals, and figures (in strict Muslim use, no animate objects) are represented in a fancifully combined pattern. **2.** a pose in ballet in which one leg is stretched horizontally behind and the body lowered forward from the hips. **3.** *Music* a short composition with florid decoration.

Arabic numerals /ˌærəbɪk 'njumərəlz/ *pl. n.* the characters 0, 1, 2, 3, 4, 5, 6, 7, 8, 9, in general Western use since the 12th century. Also, **Arabic figures.**

arable /'ærəbəl/ *adj.* capable, without much modification, of producing crops by means of tillage. —**arability** /ærə'bɪləti/, *n.*

arachnid /ə'ræknɪd/ *n.* any arthropod of the class Arachnida, which includes the spiders, scorpions, mites, etc. —**arachnidan** /ə'ræknɪdən/, *adj., n.*

arachnophobia /ə'ræknəfoʊbiə/ *n.* fear of spiders. —**arachnophobic,** *adj.*

araucaria /ærə'kɛəriə/ *n.* any tree of the coniferous genus *Araucaria* of the Southern Hemisphere, such as the hoop pine, klinki pine and monkey puzzle.

arbiter /'abətə/ *n.* **1.** someone empowered to decide points at issue. **2.** someone who has the sole or absolute power of judging or determining.

arbitrary /'abətrəri, 'abətri/, *Orig. US* /'abətrɛri/ *adj.* **1.** subject to individual will or judgement; discretionary. **2.** not attributable to any rule or law; accidental. **3.** capricious; uncertain; unreasonable: *an arbitrary interpretation.* **4.** selected at random or by convention: *an arbitrary constant.* —**arbitrarily** /'abətrərəli/, *adv.* —**arbitrariness,** *n.*

arbitrate /'abətreɪt/ *v.t.* **1.** to submit to arbitration; settle by arbitration: *to arbitrate a dispute.* **2.** to decide as arbiter or arbitrator; determine. —**arbitrator,** *n.* —**arbitrative,** *adj.*

arbitration /abə'treɪʃən/ *n.* **1.** *Law* the hearing or determining of a dispute between parties by a person or persons chosen, agreed between them, or appointed by virtue of a statutory obligation. **2.** *Industrial Law* the presentation of legal argument by parties (for whom conciliation has failed), before a government-appointed arbitrator who is empowered to make a binding decision. —**arbitrable** /'abətrəbəl/, **arbitral** /'abətrəl/, **arbitrational,** *adj.*

arboreal /a'bɔriəl/ *adj.* **1.** relating to trees; treelike. **2.** *Zool.* adapted for living and moving about in trees, as the limbs and skeleton of possums, monkeys, and apes.

arbour /'abə/ *n.* a bower formed by trees, shrubs, or vines, often on a trellis. Also, **arbor.**

arc /ak/ *n.* **1.** any part of a circle or other curved line. **2.** *Elect.* the luminous bridge formed by the passage of a current across a gap between two conductors or terminals, due to the incandescence of the conducting vapours. **3.** anything bow-shaped. —*v.i.* (**arced** /akt/, **arcing** /'akɪŋ/) **4.** to form an electric arc. —*phr.* **5. arc up, a.** to increase suddenly in intensity: *the fire arced up.* **b.** *Colloq.* to react angrily.

arcade /a'keɪd/ *n.* **1.** *Archit.* **a.** a series of arches supported on piers or columns. **b.** an arched, roofed-in gallery. **2.** a pedestrian way with shops on one side or both sides.

Arcadian /a'keɪdiən/ *adj.* pastoral; rustic; simple; innocent.

arcane /a'keɪn/ *adj.* mysterious; secret; obscure: *poor writing can make even the most familiar things seem arcane.*

arch¹ /atʃ/ *n.* **1.** a curved structure resting on supports at both ends, used to support weight, or to bridge or roof an open space, etc. **2.** Also, **archway.** such a structure built as an ornamental gateway. **3.** something curved like an arch: *the arch of the foot; the arch of the heavens.* —*v.t.* **4.** to build an arch across (an opening). **5.** to make into the shape of an arch; curve: *a horse arches its neck.*

arch² /atʃ/ *adj.* **1.** chief; most important; principal: *the arch rebel.* **2.** cunning; sly; roguish: *an arch smile.* —**archly,** *adv.* —**archness,** *n.*

arch- a prefix meaning 'first', 'chief', as in *archbishop*, *arch-priest*.

-arch a suffix meaning 'chief', as in *monarch*.

archaeo- a word element meaning 'primeval', 'primitive', 'ancient', as in *archaeology*, *archaeopteryx*. Also, (*especially before a vowel*), **archeo-**, **archae-**, **arche-**.

archaeology /aki'plədʒi/ *n.* the systematic study of any culture, especially a prehistoric one, by excavation and description of its remains. Also, **archeology.** —**archaeological** /akiə'lɒdʒɪkəl/, *adj.* —**archaeologist,** *n.*

Archaeozoic /ˌakiə'zoʊɪk/ *adj., n.* (relating to) the most ancient period of the earth's history (preceding the Proterozoic), during which the earliest forms of life probably appeared.

archaic /a'keɪɪk/ *adj.* **1.** marked by the characteristics of an earlier period; old-fashioned. **2.** no longer used in ordinary speech or writing; borrowed from older usage (distinguished from *obsolete*). —**archaise,** *v.* —**archaiser,** *n.* —**archaically,** *adv.*

archaism /'akeɪˌɪzəm/ *n.* something archaic, as a word or expression. —**archaist,** *n.* —**archaistic** /ˌakeɪ'ɪstɪk/, *adj.*

archangel /'akeɪndʒəl/ *n.* a chief or principal angel; one of a particular order of angels. See **angel** (def. 1). —**archangelic** /ˌakæn'dʒɛlɪk/, *adj.*

archbishop /atʃ'bɪʃəp/ *n.* a bishop of the highest rank.

archenemy /atʃ'ɛnəmi/ *n.* a chief enemy.

archer /'atʃə/ *n.* someone who shoots with a bow and arrow; a bowman. —**archery,** *n.*

archetype /'akətaɪp/ *n.* **1.** a model or first form; the original pattern or model after which a thing is made. **2.** (in Jungian psychology) an inherited mode of perception or response linked to the instincts, which is part of the collective unconscious. **3.** someone or something adhering closely to the model or first form. —**archetypal, archetypical** /akə'tɪpɪkəl/, *adj.*

archipelago /akə'pɛləgoʊ/ *n.* (*pl.* **-gos** *or* **-goes**) **1.** any large body of water with many islands. **2.** the island groups in such a body of water. —**archipelagic** /akəpə-'lædʒɪk/, *adj.*

architect /'akətɛkt/ *n.* **1.** someone whose profession is to design buildings and superintend their construction. **2.** the deviser, maker, or creator of anything.

architecture /'akətɛktʃə/ *n.* **1.** the art or science of building, including plan, design, construction, and decorative treatment. **2.** the style of building. **3.** the action or process of building; construction. **4.** a building or buildings. **5.** the structure or design of something, as a computer, a novel, etc. —**architectural,** *adj.* —**architecturally,** *adv.*

architrave /'akətreɪv/ *n. Archit.* a band of mouldings or other ornamentation around a rectangular door or other opening or a panel.

archive /'akaɪv/ *n.* (*oft. pl.*) **1.** the non-current documents or records relating to the activities, rights, claims, treaties, constitutions, etc., of a family, corporation, community, or nation. **2.** a place where public records or other historical documents are kept. **3.** the agency or organisation responsible for collecting and storing such documents. –**archival**, *adj.* –**archivist** /'akəvəst/, *n.*

arch rival *n.* the chief rival. Also, **archrival**.

archway /'atʃweɪ/ *n.* **1.** an entrance or passage under an arch. **2.** a covering or enclosing arch.

-archy a word element meaning 'rule', 'government', as in *monarchy*.

arc light *n.* **1.** Also, **arc lamp.** a lamp in which the light source of high intensity is an electric arc, usually between carbon rods. **2.** the light produced.

arctic /'aktɪk/ *adj.* **1.** (*oft. upper case*) of, at, or near the North Pole; frigid. **2.** extremely cold.

Arctic Circle *n.* an imaginary circle around the earth forming the southern boundary of the North Frigid Zone, at latitude 66°32′N.

-ard a noun suffix, originally intensive but now often depreciative or without special force as in *coward, drunkard, wizard*. Also, **-art**.

ardent /'adnt/ *adj.* **1.** glowing with feeling, earnestness, or zeal; passionate; fervent: *ardent vows, an ardent patriot.* **2.** glowing; flashing. **3.** burning, fiery, or hot. –**ardency**, *n.* –**ardently**, *adv.*

ardour /'adə/ *n.* **1.** warmth of feeling; fervour; eagerness; zeal. **2.** burning heat. Also, **ardor**.

arduous /'adʒuəs/ *adj.* **1.** requiring great exertion; laborious; strenuous: *an arduous enterprise.* **2.** hard to endure; severe; full of hardships: *an arduous winter.* **3.** hard to climb; steep: *an arduous path.* –**arduously**, *adv.* –**arduousness**, *n.*

are[1] /a/, *weak form* /ə/ *v.* present indicative plural of the verb **be**.

are[2] /ɛə/ *n.* a non-SI metric surface measure equal to 100 square metres; one hundredth of a hectare.

area /'ɛəriə/ *n.* **1.** any particular extent of surface; region; tract: *the settled area.* **2.** a piece of unoccupied ground; an open space. **3.** extent, range or scope: *the whole area of science.* **4.** a field of study, interest, or knowledge: *her area is 19th century Australian history.* **5.** *Maths* amount of surface (plane or curved); two-dimensional extent; the SI unit of area is the square metre (m²). –**areal**, *adj.*

area code *n.* a sequence of numbers preceding a telephone subscriber's number, indicating the area or exchange.

arena /ə'rinə/ *n.* **1.** the oval space in a Roman amphitheatre for combats or other performances. **2.** an enclosure for sports contests, shows, etc. **3.** a field of conflict or endeavour: *the arena of politics.*

areola /ə'rɪələ/ *n.* (*pl.* **-lae** /-li/) **1.** a small ring of colour, as around a pustule or the human nipple. **2.** a small interstice, as between the fibres of connective tissue. –**areolar**, *adj.* –**areolate**, *adj.* –**areolation** /əriə-'leɪʃən/, *n.*

argent /'adʒənt/ *n. Archaic* silver.

Argentine ant /ˌadʒəntin 'ænt/ *n.* a very destructive small brown ant, *Iridomyrmex humilis*, now spread widely throughout the world from its original centre in South America.

argon /'agɒn/ *n.* a colourless, odourless, chemically inactive, gaseous element. *Symbol:* Ar; *relative atomic mass:* 39.948; *atomic number:* 18.

argot /'agoʊ/ *n.* the peculiar language or jargon of any class or group; cant; originally, that of thieves and vagabonds, devised for purposes of disguise and concealment. –**argotic** /a'gɒtɪk/, *adj.*

arguable /'agjuəbəl/ *adj.* **1.** capable of being maintained; plausible. **2.** open to dispute or argument. **3.** capable of being argued. –**arguably**, *adv.*

argue /'agju/ *verb* (**-gued, -guing**) –*v.i.* **1.** to present reasons for or against a thing: *to argue for or against a proposed law.* **2.** to contend in argument; dispute: *to argue with someone about something.* –*v.t.* **3.** to state the reasons for or against: *counsel argued the cause.* **4.** to maintain in reasoning: *to argue that something must be so.* **5.** to argue in favour of; support by argument: *his letter argues restraint.* **6.** to persuade, prove, etc., by reasoning: *to argue someone out of a plan.* **7.** to show; prove or imply: *his clothes argue poverty.* –*phr.* **8. argue the toss, a.** to go on arguing after a dispute has been settled. **b.** to debate or discuss, especially at length. –**arguer**, *n.*

argument /'agjəmənt/ *n.* **1.** a disagreement; quarrel. **2.** a discussion in which reasons for and against something are stated. **3.** a fact or series of reasons, stated in support of something. **4.** a summary of the subject matter of a book, etc.

argumentation /agjəmən'teɪʃən/ *n.* **1.** debate; discussion; reasoning. **2.** the setting forth of reasons together with the conclusion drawn from them; formal or logical reasoning.

argumentative /agjə'mɛntətɪv/ *adj.* **1.** given to argument; disputatious. **2.** controversial. **3.** presenting an argument or point of view: *argumentative writing.* –**argumentatively**, *adv.* –**argumentativeness**, *n.*

aria /'ariə/ *n.* an elaborate melody for a single voice, with accompaniment, in an opera, oratorio, etc., especially one consisting of a principal and a subordinate section, and a repetition of the first with or without alterations.

-arian a compound suffix of adjectives and nouns, often referring to pursuits, doctrines, etc., or to age, as in *antiquarian, humanitarian, octogenarian.*

arid /'ærəd/ *adj.* **1.** dry; without moisture; parched with heat. **2.** uninteresting; dull; unrewarding. **3.** barren; unproductive; lacking spiritual or creative life. –**aridity** /ə'rɪdəti/, **aridness**, *n.* –**aridly**, *adv.*

Aries /'ɛəriz/ *n.* the first sign of the zodiac, which the sun enters about 21 March; the Ram. –**Arian**, *n.*, *adj.*

arise /ə'raɪz/ *v.i.* (**arose, arisen, arising**) **1.** to come into being or action; originate; appear: *new questions arise.* **2.** to move upwards. **3.** to rise; get up from sitting, lying, or kneeling. –*phr.* **4. arise from**, to result or proceed from.

aristo- a word element meaning 'best', 'superior', as in *aristocratic.*

aristocracy /ærə'stɒkrəsi/ *n.* (*pl.* **-cies**) **1.** a government or a state characterised by the rule of a nobility, elite, or privileged upper class. **2.** a body of persons holding exceptional prescriptive rank or privileges; a class of hereditary nobility. **3.** government by the best people in the state.

aristocrat /'ærəstəkræt, ə'rɪstəkræt/ *n.* **1.** someone who has the tastes, manners, etc., of the members of a superior group or class. **2.** (one of) the best of its kind. –**aristocratic** /ærəstə'krætɪk/, *adj.*

arithmetic *n.* /ə'rɪθmətɪk/ **1.** the art or skill of computation with figures (the most elementary branch of mathematics). **2.** Also, **theoretical arithmetic.** the theory of numbers; the study of the divisibility of whole numbers, the remainder after division, etc. **3.** a book on this subject. –*adj.* /ærə'θ'mɛtɪk/ **4.** of or relating to arithmetic. –**arithmetical** /ærəθ'mɛtɪkəl/, *adj.* –**arithmetically**, *adv.*

arithmetical progression *n.* a sequence in which each term is obtained by the addition of a constant number to the preceding term. For example, 1, 4, 7, 10, 13, and 6, 1, -4, -9, -14. Also, **arithmetic series.**

arithmetic unit /ˌærəθmɛtɪk 'junət/ *n.* the section of a computer which does arithmetical processes.

ark /ak/ *n.* **1.** the vessel built by Noah for safety during the Flood. Gen. 6-9. **2.** Also, **ark of the covenant.** a chest or box of great sanctity representing the presence of the Deity, the most sacred object of the tabernacle and of the temple in Jerusalem.

arm[1] /am/ *n.* **1.** the upper limb of the human body from the shoulder to the hand. **2.** this limb, exclusive of the hand. **3.** the forelimb of any four-legged vertebrate. **4.** some part of an organism like or likened to an arm. **5.** any armlike part, as of a lever or of the yard (**yard-arm**) of a ship. **6.** a covering for the arm, as the sleeve of a garment. **7.** a branch or subdivision of an organisation or structure. **8.** a projecting support for the forearm at the side of a chair, sofa, etc. **9.** an area of water that branches off from the main body of water: *an arm of the sea.* –*phr.* **10. arm in arm**, with the arm of one person linked with the arm of another usually as an expression of friendship. **11. at arm's length**, at a distance, yet almost within reach. **12. chance one's arm**, *Colloq.* to take a risk. **13. in arms**, **a.** carried in the arms, as a child. **b.** not yet independent or fully developed. **14. keep someone at arm's length**, (sometimes fol. by *from*) to keep someone at a distance, in terms of emotions, alliances, business dealings, etc. **15. the long arm of the law**, *Colloq.* (*humorous*) the police. **16. with open arms**, cordially. –**armless**, *adj.* –**armlike**, *adj.*

arm[2] /am/ *n.* **1.** (*usu. pl.*) a weapon. **2.** See **arms**. –*v.i.* **3.** to prepare for war by making or supplying arms. –*v.t.* **4.** to supply (a person, military unit, etc.) with arms. **5.** to cover or provide with whatever will add strength, force, or security. **6.** to fit or prepare (a thing) for any specific purpose or effective use: *to arm the cabin doors.*

armada /a'mada/ *n.* **1.** a fleet of warships. **2.** a large number of boats or ships.

armadillo /ama'diloʊ/ *n.* (*pl.* **-los**) any armoured mammal of the family Dasypodidae, from South America and southern North America.

Armageddon /ama'gɛdn/ *n.* **1.** the place where the final cataclysmic battle will be fought between the forces of good and evil, prophesied in the Bible to occur at the end of the world. **2.** any great crucial armed conflict.

armament /'amamant/ *n.* **1.** the weapons with which a military unit, especially a plane, vehicle, or warship, is equipped. **2.** a land, sea, or air force equipped for war. **3.** the process of equipping or arming for war.

armature /'amatʃa/ *n.* **1.** *Biol.* the protective covering of an animal or plant, or any part serving for defence or offence. **2.** *Elect.* **a.** the iron or steel applied across the poles of a permanent magnet to close it, or to the poles of an electromagnet to communicate mechanical force. **b.** the part of an electrical machine which includes the main current-carrying winding (distinguished from the *field*). **c.** a pivoted part of an electrical device as a buzzer or relay, activated by a magnetic field.

armchair /'amtʃɛa/ *n.* **1.** a chair with arms to support the forearms or elbows. –*adj.* **2.** amateur: *an armchair critic.* **3.** seen or enjoyed at home: *the armchair theatre.*

armed services *pl. n.* all of the principal military forces of a country or countries including the army, navy, marines, air force, etc. Also, **armed forces.**

armistice /'amastas/ *n.* a temporary suspension of hostilities by agreement of the parties, as to discuss peace; a truce.

armorial /a'mɔrial/ *adj.* belonging to heraldry or to heraldic bearing.

armour /'ama/ *n.* **1.** defensive equipment; any covering worn as a protection against offensive weapons. **2.** a metallic sheathing or protective covering, especially metal plates used on warships, armoured vehicles, aeroplanes, and fortifications. **3.** something that serves as a protection or safeguard. –*v.t.* **4.** to cover with armour or armour plate. Also, **armor.** –**armoured**, *adj.*

armoury /'amari/ *n.* (*pl.* **-ries**) a storage place for weapons and other war equipment. Also, **armory.**

armpit /'ampɪt/ *n.* the hollow under the arm at the shoulder; the axilla.

arms /amz/ *pl. n.* **1.** → **arm**[2] (def. 1). **2.** *Mil.* small arms. **3.** heraldic bearings. –*phr.* **4. bear arms**, to perform military service. **5. call to arms**, **a.** a summons to battle. **b.** a rallying cry usually seeking support or particular action, as an inflammatory political speech, a policy statement, etc. **6. take arms**, to resort to fighting; fight. **7. under arms**, armed. **8.** (**up**) **in arms**, **a.** armed and prepared to resist. **b.** very angry and indignant.

army /'ami/ *n.* (*pl.* **-mies**) **1.** the military forces of a nation, exclusive of the naval and, in some countries, the air forces. **2.** a large body of troops trained and armed for war. **3.** any body of persons organised for any cause: *an army of temporary workers will be needed for the Census.* **4.** a host; a great multitude: *an army of relatives descended on us at Christmas.*

army reserve *n.* the part of a country's fighting force not in active service, but used as a further means of defence in case of necessity. Also, **reserve.**

aroma /a'roʊma/ *n.* **1.** a smell arising from spices, plants, etc., especially an agreeable smell; fragrance. **2.** (of wines and spirits) the smell or bouquet. **3.** a characteristic, subtle quality. –**aromatic** /æra'mætɪk/, *adj.* –**aromatically** /æra'mætɪkli/, *adv.* –**aromaticity** /æramə'tɪsəti/, *n.*

aromatherapy /aroʊma'θɛrapi/ *n.* a type of therapy using scented oils. –**aromatherapist**, *n.*

arose /a'roʊz/ *v.* past tense of **arise.**

around /a'raʊnd/ *adv.* **1.** in a circle on every side: *a crowd gathered around; The land is mine for 20 km around.* **2.** here and there; about: *to travel around.* **3.** somewhere about or near: *to wait around.* **4.** with a circular movement: *the wheels go around.* **5.** at or to a place understood, as a shop, a friend's house, office, etc.: *I'll be around at three.* **6.** active; in circulation: *that singer has been around for a long time.* –*prep.* **7.** on all sides of; surrounding: *a belt around her waist.* **8.** on the other side of: *the house around the corner.* **9.** here and there, in, or near: *to drive around the country; stay around the house.* **10.** near to in time, amount, etc.; approximately: *around ten o'clock.*

arouse /a'raʊz/ *v.t.* **1.** to excite into action; stir or put in motion; call into being: *aroused to action, arousing suspicion.* **2.** to wake from sleep. **3.** to awaken sexual excitement and readiness in. –*v.i.* **4.** to become aroused. –**arousal**, *n.* –**arouser**, *n.*

arpeggio /a'pɛdʒioʊ/ *n.* (*pl.* **-gios**) the sounding of the notes of a chord separately and in succession instead of simultaneously.

arraign /a'reɪn/ *v.t. Law* to call or bring before a court to answer to a charge or accusation. –**arraignment**, *n.* –**arraigner**, *n.*

arrange /a'reɪndʒ/ *verb* (**-ranged**, **-ranging**) –*v.t.* **1.** to put in order: *to arrange books on a shelf.* **2.** to come to an agreement about; settle: *to arrange a sale.* **3.** to prepare or plan: *to arrange a wedding; to arrange to meet a friend.* **4.** *Music* to change (a composition) to make it suitable for a particular kind of performance, especially for different instruments or voices. –*v.i.* **5.** to make preparations or agreements: *I arranged for her to come early.* –**arrangement**, *n.* –**arranger**, *n.*

arrant /'ærant/ *adj.* downright; thorough: *an arrant fool.* –**arrantly**, *adv.*

arras /'æras/ *n.* **1.** rich tapestry. **2.** a wall hanging.

array /a'reɪ/ *v.t.* **1.** to place in position for battle, as soldiers, etc. **2.** to dress, especially with show; bedeck. –*n.* **3.** the proper or desired order, as of troops drawn up on a parade ground or for battle. **4.** a group of things on show: *the shop had a good array of books.* **5.** clothing. –**arrayal**, *n.*

arrest /əˈrɛst/ *v.t.* **1.** to seize or capture by legal authority: *the police arrested the criminal.* **2.** to catch and fix: *the shouting arrested her attention.* **3.** to stop the movement or growth of (something): *to arrest the current of a river; arrest a disease.* −*n.* **4.** the act of arresting (a person, etc.): *the police have made an arrest.* **5.** the state of being arrested: *the criminal was put under arrest.* **6.** a stopping of movement or growth: *cardiac arrest.* **7.** anything used for stopping the motion of a machine. −**arrester**, *n.*

arresting /əˈrɛstɪŋ/ *adj.* catching the attention; striking: *an arresting painting.*

arrive /əˈraɪv/ *v.i.* **1.** to come to a certain point in the course of travel; reach one's destination. **2.** to come: *the time has arrived.* **3.** to happen; occur. **4.** to attain a position of success in the world. −*phr.* **5. arrive at**, to reach in any course or process; attain: *to arrive at a conclusion.* −**arrival**, *n.*

arrogant /ˈærəgənt/ *adj.* **1.** making unwarrantable claims or pretensions to superior importance or rights; overbearingly assuming; insolently proud. **2.** characterised by or proceeding from arrogance: *arrogant claims.* −**arrogance, arrogancy**, *n.* −**arrogantly**, *adv.*

arrow /ˈærou/ *n.* **1.** a slender, straight, generally pointed, missile weapon made to be shot from a bow. The shaft is nearly always made of light wood, fitted with feathers at the neck end to help guide it. **2.** anything resembling an arrow in form, such as the inflorescence of a sugar cane. **3.** a figure of an arrow used to indicate direction. −**arrowy, arrow-like, arrow-shaped**, *adj.* −**arrowless**, *adj.*

arrowroot /ˈærəruːt/ *n.* **1.** a tropical American plant, *Maranta arundinacea*, or related species, whose rhizomes yield a nutritious starch. **2.** the starch itself. **3.** a similar starch from other plants, used in puddings, biscuits, etc.

arse /as/ *Colloq.* (*taboo*) −*n.* **1.** the rump; bottom; buttocks; posterior. **2.** a despised person. **3.** impudence: *what arse!* −*phr.* (*v.* **arsed, arsing**) **4.** a bit (or piece) of **arse**, a person considered as a sexual object. **5. a boot up the arse**, swift punishment or retribution. **6. arse about**, in reverse or illogical order: *he did the exercise completely arse about.* **7. arse about** (or **around**), to act like a fool; waste time. **8. arse about face**, changed in direction; back to front. **9. arse over tit** (or **apex**), fallen heavily and awkwardly, usually in a forward direction. **10. arse up**, to spoil; cause to fail. **11. cover one's arse**, to protect oneself. **12. down on one's arse**, out of luck; destitute. **13. get one's arse into gear**, to become organised and ready for action. **14. get the arse**, **a.** to be dismissed, especially from employment. **b.** to be rejected or rebuffed. **15. give someone the arse**, **a.** to dismiss someone, especially from employment. **b.** to reject or rebuff someone. **16. kick arse**, **a.** to assert authority by being violent and aggressive towards people. **b.** to defeat opponents soundly. **17. kick someone's arse**, **a.** to beat someone convincingly. **b.** to reprimand someone severely. **18. kiss my arse**, an expression of derision. **19. pain in the arse**, an annoying person, thing, event, etc.: *this computer is a pain in the arse.* **20. up Cook's arse**, *NZ* an expression of disgust.

arsenal /ˈasənəl/ *n.* **1.** a repository or magazine of arms and military stores of all kinds for land or naval service. **2.** a public establishment where military equipment or munitions are manufactured.

arsenic /ˈasənɪk, ˈasnɪk/ *n.* a greyish white element having a metallic lustre, volatilising when heated, and forming poisonous compounds. *Symbol*: As; *relative atomic mass*: 74.9216; *atomic number*: 33.

arson /ˈasən/ *n.* the act of maliciously setting fire to someone else's property, or to one's own property, for illegal purposes. −**arsonist**, *n.*

art /at/ *n.* **1.** the production or expression of what is beautiful (especially visually), appealing, or of more than ordinary significance. **2.** *Journalism* any illustration in a newspaper or magazine. **3.** a department of skilled performance: *industrial art.* **4.** (*pl.*) a branch of learning or university study. **5.** (*pl.*) liberal arts. **6.** skilled workmanship, execution, or agency (often opposed to *nature*). **7.** a skill or knack; a method of doing a thing, especially if it is difficult. **8.** craft; cunning: *glib and oily art.* **9.** studied action; artificiality in behaviour. **10.** (*usu. pl.*) an artifice or artful device: *the arts and wiles of politics.* **11.** learning or science.

-art variant of **-ard**, as in *braggart*.

artefact /ˈatəfækt/ *n.* **1.** any object made by humans with a view to subsequent use. **2.** *Biol.* a substance, structure, or the like, not naturally present in tissue, but formed by reagents, death, etc. Also, **artifact**.

arterial /aˈtɪəriəl/ *adj.* **1.** *Anat.* of or relating to the arteries: *arterial blood.* **2.** having a main channel and many branches: *arterial drainage.* **3.** carrying the main flow of traffic between large towns: *an arterial road.*

arteriosclerosis /aˌtɪəriouskləˈrousəs/ *n.* *Pathol.* an arterial disease occurring especially in the elderly, characterised by inelasticity and thickening of the vessel walls, with lessened blood flow. −**arteriosclerotic** /aˌtɪəriouskləˈrɒtɪk/, *adj.*

artery /ˈatəri/ *n.* (*pl.* **-ries**) **1.** *Anat.* a blood vessel which conveys blood from the heart to any part of the body. **2.** a main channel in any ramifying system of communications or transport, as in drainage or roads.

artesian basin /aˌtiʒən ˈbeɪsən/ *n.* a geological structural feature or combination of such features in which water is confined under pressure.

artesian bore /aˌtiʒən ˈbɔ/ *n.* a bore whose shaft penetrates an aquifer and in which the water level rises above ground by hydrostatic pressure. Also, **artesian well**.

artful /ˈatfəl/ *adj.* **1.** crafty; cunning; tricky: *artful schemes.* **2.** skilful in adapting means to ends; ingenious. −**artfully**, *adv.* −**artfulness**, *n.*

arthritis /aˈθraɪtəs/ *n.* *Pathol.* inflammation of a joint, as in gout or rheumatism. −**arthritic**, *adj.*

arthro- a word element meaning 'joint', as in *arthropod*. Also, **arthr-**.

arthropod /ˈaθrəpɒd/ *n.* any of the Arthropoda, the phylum of segmented invertebrates, having jointed legs, as the insects, arachnids, crustaceans, and myriapods.

arthroscope /ˈaθrəskoup/ *n.* a thin, tubular instrument which is inserted into the cavity between bones to examine a joint and perform surgical procedures.

arthroscopy /aˈθrɒskəpi/ *n.* *Med.* **1.** the examination of a joint using an arthroscope. **2.** Also, **arthroscopic debridement**. the use of this technique to facilitate the removal of damaged tissue or foreign matter in a joint. −**arthroscopic**, *adj.*

artichoke /ˈatətʃouk, ˈatɪtʃouk/ *n.* **1.** a herbaceous, thistlelike plant, *Cynara scolymus*, with an edible flower head; globe artichoke. **2.** the edible portion, used as a table vegetable. **3.** → **Jerusalem artichoke**.

article /ˈatɪkəl/ *n.* **1.** a particular or separate thing: *an article of food; an article of dress.* **2.** a thing in general: *what is that article?* **3.** a piece of writing on a particular subject, complete in itself but forming part of a book, newspaper, magazine, etc. **4.** (in some languages) any word, as the English words *a* or *an* (**indefinite article**) and *the* (**definite article**), which come before nouns to indicate their particularity, etc. **5.** a separate section, clause, item in an agreement, contract, law, etc. −*v.t.* **6.** to bind by contract, etc.: *to article an apprentice; an articled clerk in a lawyer's office.*

articled clerk *n.* a person under articles of agreement to serve a solicitor in return for training.

articulate *v.t.* /aˈtɪkjəleɪt/ **1.** to speak (words, etc.) clearly. **2.** *Phonetics* to make the movements of the speech organs necessary to produce (speech). **3.** to unite with joints. *–v.i.* /aˈtɪkjəleɪt/ **4.** to speak with clearly pronounced syllables or words: *he articulates well.* **5.** to form a joint. *–adj.* /aˈtɪkjələt/ **6.** clear; distinct. **7.** able to express ideas clearly: *she is very articulate on that subject.* **8.** having the power of speech. **9.** Also, **articulated.** having joints or segments. **–articulately,** *adv.* **–articulateness,** *n.* **–articulation,** *n.* **–articulator,** *n.*

articulated /aˈtɪkjəleɪtəd/ *adj.* **1.** connected by a joint or joints. **2.** (of a road vehicle) consisting of sections connected by a flexible joint, as a prime mover and trailer.

artifice /ˈatəfəs/ *n.* **1.** a crafty device or expedient; a clever trick or stratagem. **2.** craft; trickery. **3.** skilful or apt contrivance.

artificial /atəˈfɪʃəl/ *adj.* **1.** made by human skill and labour (opposed to *natural*). **2.** made in imitation of or as a substitute; not genuine. **3.** feigned; fictitious; assumed. **4.** full of affectation; affected. **–artificially,** *adv.* **–artificiality** /ˌatəfɪʃiˈæləti/, **artificialness,** *n.*

artificial insemination *n.* a method of inducing pregnancy by artificial introduction of viable sperm into the canal of the cervix, widely practised on cattle and horses for the purpose of selective breeding.

artificial intelligence *n.* decision-making computers.

artificial language *n.* **1.** a language invented for a particular purpose, for which the rules are explicitly established prior to its use, as Esperanto. **2.** in the area of communication between people and computers, a language conveying instructions to machines for which the rules are explicitly established prior to its use.

artificial respiration *n.* any of various methods for restarting the breathing of a person whose breathing has stopped, as by expired air resuscitation or by the application of rhythmic pressure to the rib cage.

artillery /aˈtɪləri/ *n.* **1.** mounted guns, movable or stationary, light or heavy, as distinguished from small arms. **2.** the troops, or the branch of an army, concerned with the use and service of such guns. **3.** the science that deals with the use of such guns.

artisan /ˈatəzən/ *n.* **1.** someone skilled in an industrial or applied art; a craftsman. *–adj.* **2.** of, relating to, or designating an artisan food: *artisan recipe*; *artisan bread.* **–artisanry,** *n.*

artisanal /aˈtɪzənəl/ *adj.* **1.** produced by human labour rather than machines; handmade. **2.** of or relating to artisan food: *artisanal bread.*

artisan food *n.* food which is made by traditional, often labour-intensive methods and usually in small batches, rather than by large-scale factory processing.

artist /ˈatəst/ *n.* **1.** someone who practises one of the fine arts, especially a painter or sculptor. **2.** someone who practises one of the performing arts, such as an actor or singer. **3.** someone who exhibits art in their work, or makes an art of their employment.

artistic /aˈtɪstɪk/ *adj.* **1.** conformable to the standards of art; aesthetically excellent or admirable. **2.** stormy, emotional, and capricious, as temperament or behaviour popularly ascribed to artists. **3.** naturally gifted to be an artist. **–artistically,** *adv.*

artistry /ˈatəstri/ *n.* **1.** artistic workmanship, effect, or quality. **2.** artistic pursuits.

artless /ˈatləs/ *adj.* **1.** free from deceit, cunning, or craftiness; ingenuous: *an artless mind.* **2.** natural; simple: *artless beauty.* **3.** lacking art, knowledge, or skill. **–artlessly,** *adv.* **–artlessness,** *n.*

art union *n.* *Aust., NZ* a lottery, especially one with goods as prizes.

arty /ˈati/ *adj.* (**-tier, -tiest**) **1.** artistic: *an arty advertisement.* **2.** ostentatious in display of artistic interest.

arvo /ˈavoʊ/ *n.* *Aust., NZ Colloq.* afternoon. Also, **afto.**

-ary¹ 1. an adjective suffix meaning 'pertaining to', attached chiefly to nouns (*honorary*) and to stems appearing in other words (*voluntary*). **2.** a suffix forming nouns from other nouns or adjectives indicating location or repository (*dictionary, granary, apiary*), officers (*functionary, secretary*), or other relations (*adversary*). **3.** a suffix forming collective numeral nouns, especially in time units (*centenary*).

-ary² variant of **-ar¹**, as in *exemplary, military.*

as /æz/, *weak form* /əz/ *adv.* **1.** to such a degree or extent: *as good as gold* [the first *as*]. *–conj.* **2.** the consequent in the correlations *as* (*or so*) ... *as*, *same* ... *as*, etc., denoting degree, extent, manner, etc. (*as good as gold* [the second *as*], *in the same way as before*). **3.** (without antecedent) in the degree, manner, etc., of or that: *quick as thought*; *speak as he does.* **4.** according to what, or the manner in which, or the extent to which: *as I hear*; *we help as we are able.* **5.** though: *bad as it is, it could be worse.* **6.** as if, as though: *she spoke quietly, as to herself*; *the car was sold as new.* **7.** when or while: *I arrived as she was leaving.* **8.** since; because: *I hesitated as she seemed upset.* **9.** in the way that: *I may fail you, as you realise*; *as is well known, he died soon after.* **10.** for instance: *a variety of colours, as red, blue, and green.* *–pron.* (*relative*) **11.** (esp. after *such* and *the same*) that; who; which: *that is the same as I thought.* *–prep.* **12.** in the role, function, status, or manner of: *to appear as Othello*; *serve as a warning.* *–phr.* **13.** as for (or **to**), with regard or respect to. **14.** as if, an exclamation expressing disbelief or disagreement. **15. as if** ..., expressing incredulity about what is stated: *as if anyone would do that!* **16. as if** (or **though**), as it would be if. **17. as is,** *Colloq.* as it is; unaltered: *I sold it as is.* **18. as it were,** in some sort; so to speak. **19. as well, a.** also; too: *beautiful, and good as well.* **b.** better; advisable: *it is as well to avoid trouble.* **20. as well as,** in addition to: *goodness as well as beauty.* **21. as yet, a.** up to now: *the new director has not as yet been appointed.* **b.** for the moment: *as yet he's still a young man.*

as- variant of **ad-** before *s*, as in *assert.*

asbestos /əsˈbɛstəs, æs-, -tɒs/ *n.* **1.** *Mineral.* any of various silicate minerals having a fibrous structure, in particular, the amphibole group and chrysotile; used in fire-retardant devices and clothing and in building materials, but now banned in many countries as known to cause mesothelioma and asbestosis. **2.** a fire-resistant fabric woven from asbestos fibres.

asbestosis /æsbɛsˈtoʊsəs/ *n.* inflammation of the lungs caused by the inhalation of asbestos particles.

ascend /əˈsɛnd/ *v.i.* **1.** to climb or go upwards; mount; rise. **2.** to rise to a higher point or degree; proceed from an inferior to a superior degree or level. **3.** to go towards the source or beginning; go back in time. **4.** *Music* to rise in pitch; pass from any tone to a higher one. *–v.t.* **5.** to go or move upwards upon or along; climb; mount: *to ascend a hill*; *to ascend the staircase.* **–ascendable, ascendible,** *adj.*

ascendancy /əˈsɛndənsi/ *n.* the state of being in the ascendant; governing or controlling influence; domination. Also, **ascendency, ascendance, ascendence.**

ascendant /əˈsɛndənt/ *n.* **1.** a position of dominance or controlling influence; superiority; predominance: *in the ascendant.* **2.** an ancestor (opposed to *descendant*). **3.** *Astrology* **a.** the point of the ecliptic or the sign of the zodiac rising above the horizon at the time of a birth, etc. **b.** the horoscope. *–adj.* **4.** superior; predominant. Also, **ascendent**.

ascension *n.* **1.** the act of ascending; ascent. **2.** (*upper case*) *Christianity* the ascending of Christ into heaven. **3.** (*upper case*) *Islam* the ascending of Mohammed into heaven.

ascent /ə'sɛnt/ *n.* **1.** the act of ascending; upward movement; rise. **2.** a rising from a lower to a higher state, degree, or grade; advancement. **3.** the act of climbing or travelling up. **4.** gradient.

ascertain /æsə'teɪn/ *v.t.* to find out by trial, examination, or experiment, so as to know as certain; determine. **–ascertainable**, *adj.* **–ascertainableness**, *n.* **–ascertainably**, *adv.* **–ascertainment**, *n.*

ascetic /ə'sɛtɪk/ *n.* **1.** someone who lives a life of austerity, especially for religious reasons. **2.** someone who leads an abstemious life. *–adj.* **3.** rigorously abstinent; austere. **–ascetical**, *adj.* **–ascetically**, *adv.* **–asceticism**, *n.*

asco- a word element meaning 'bag'.

ascorbic acid /əskɔbɪk 'æsəd/ *n.* a water-soluble vitamin, vitamin C, which has a major role in the formation of collagen, bones, blood vessels and connective tissues; occurring naturally in citrus fruits, tomatoes, capsicum, and green vegetables, but also produced synthetically.

ascribe /ə'skraɪb/ *v.t.* **1.** to attribute impute, or refer, as to a cause or source; assign: *the alphabet is usually ascribed to the Phoenicians.* **2.** to consider or allege to belong. **–ascribable**, *adj.*

asdic /'æzdɪk/ *n.* a device to determine the presence and location of objects under water by measuring the direction and return time of a sound echo.

-ase a noun suffix used in names of enzymes, as in *lactase, pectase*.

asexual /eɪ'sɛkʃuəl/ *adj.* **1.** not sexual. **2.** having no sex or no sexual organs. **3.** independent of sexual processes. **–asexuality** /ˌeɪsɛkʃu'æləti/, *n.* **–asexually**, *adv.*

ash¹ /æʃ/ *n.* **1.** the powdery residue of matter that remains after burning: *hot ashes, soda ash.* **2.** *Geol.* finely pulverised lava thrown out by a volcano in eruption. *–v.t.* **3.** to cause the ash collected on the tip of (a cigar or cigarette) to fall, usually by giving a light tap: *don't ash your cigarette on the carpet!* See **ashes**.

ash² /æʃ/ *n.* **1.** any tree of the genus *Fraxinus*, family Oleaceae, of the Northern Hemisphere. **2.** any of many Southern Hemisphere trees whose timber or foliage resembles that of the ash, especially species of the genera *Eucalyptus, Flindersia*, and *Elaeocarpus*.

ashamed /ə'ʃeɪmd/ *adj.* **1.** feeling shame; abashed by guilt. **2.** unwilling or restrained through fear of shame: *ashamed to speak. –phr.* **3. ashamed of, a.** feeling guilty about: *ashamed of his action; you should be ashamed of yourself.* **b.** embarrassed about: *ashamed of her husband; a foreign accent is nothing to be ashamed of.* **–ashamedly** /ə'ʃeɪmədli/, *adv.* **–ashamedness**, *n.*

ashen /'æʃən/ *adj.* **1.** ash-coloured; grey. **2.** consisting of ashes.

ashes /'æʃəz/ *pl. n.* **1.** → **ash**¹ (def. 1). **2.** the embers of a camp fire. **3.** ruins, as from destruction by burning: *the ashes of an ancient empire.* **4.** the remains of a corpse after cremation.

ashore /ə'ʃɔ/ *adv.* **1.** to shore; on or to the land. *–adj.* **2.** on land (opposed to *aboard* or *afloat*).

ashram /'æʃræm, 'ʊʃrəm/ *n.* a community of people, together for spiritual development, as through yoga, meditation, etc.

ashtray /'æʃtreɪ/ *n.* a small tray, saucer, or bowl for tobacco ash.

Asian pear /eɪʒən 'pɛə/ *n.* → **nashi pear**.

aside /ə'saɪd/ *adv.* **1.** on or to one side; to or at a short distance; apart; away from some position or direction:

to turn aside. **2.** away from one's thoughts or consideration: *to put one's cares aside. –n.* **3.** words spoken in an undertone, so as not to be heard by some of the people present. **4.** a remark or comment which is incidental to the main subject.

asinine /'æsənaɪn/ *adj.* stupid; obstinate. **–asininely**, *adv.* **–asininity** /æsə'nɪnəti/, *n.*

ask /ask/ *v.t.* **1.** to put a question to: *ask him.* **2.** to seek to be informed about: *to ask the way.* **3.** to seek by words to obtain; request: *to ask advice; to ask a favour.* **4.** (with a personal object, and with or without *for* before the thing desired) to solicit; request of: *I ask you a great favour; you should ask her for advice.* **5.** to demand; expect: *to ask a price for something.* **6.** to invite: *to ask guests. –phr.* **7. a big ask**, *Aust.*, *NZ* an expectation which it would be extremely difficult to meet. **8. ask after** (or **about**), to make inquiry about: *she asked after him; she asked about him.* **9. ask around**, to make general enquiries. **10. ask for**, to request or petition for: *to ask for bread.* **11. ask for it** (or **trouble**), *Colloq.* to behave so as to invite trouble. **12. ask someone out**, to ask someone to accompany one on an outing or to a social engagement, especially with a view to forming a romantic or sexual relationship. **13. I ask you**, an exclamation indicating surprise, disgust, disdain, etc. **14. if you ask me**, a rhetorical phrase meaning 'in my opinion'. **–asker**, *n.*

askance /əs'kæns/ *adv.* **1.** with suspicion, mistrust, or disapproval: *he looked askance at my offer.* **2.** with a side glance; sideways.

askew /əs'kju/ *adv.* **1.** to one side; out of line; obliquely; awry. *–adj.* **2.** oblique.

asleep /ə'slip/ *adv.* **1.** in or into a state of sleep. *–adj.* **2.** sleeping. **3.** dormant; inactive. **4.** (of the foot, hand, leg, etc.) numb.

asp /æsp/ *n.* **1.** any of several poisonous snakes, especially the Egyptian cobra, *Naja naja*, said to have caused Cleopatra's death, and much used by snakecharmers. **2.** the common European viper or adder.

asparagus /ə'spærəgəs/ *n.* **1.** any plant of the genus *Asparagus*, especially *A. officinalis*, cultivated for its edible shoots. **2.** the shoots, used as a table vegetable.

aspect /'æspɛkt/ *n.* **1.** the way a thing appears to the eye or mind; look: *the physical aspect of the country; both aspects of a question.* **2.** the side or surface facing a given direction: *the dorsal aspect of a fish.* **3.** view; direction; exposure: *the house has a southern aspect.* **4.** *Gram.* (in some languages) the part of the sense of a verb's meaning which shows the relation of the action of the verb to the passage of time, as in continuous aspect (e.g. *was eating*), completed aspect (e.g. *had eaten*), etc.

aspen /'æspən/ *n.* **1.** any of various species of poplar, as *Populus tremula* of Europe, and *P. tremuloides* (**quaking aspen**) or *P. alba* (**white aspen**) in America, with leaves that tremble in the slightest breeze. *–adj.* **2.** of or relating to the aspen. **3.** trembling or quivering, like the leaves of the aspen.

Asperger's syndrome /'æspɜgəz sɪndroʊm, 'æspɜdʒɜz, æs'pɜgəz, æs'pɜdʒɜz/ *n.* a form of autism characterised by a tendency to social isolation and eccentric behaviour with some distinctive speech patterns and noticeable clumsiness in gross motor movements. Also, **Asperger syndrome, Asperger's**.

asperity /æs'pɛrəti, əs-/ *n.* **1.** roughness or sharpness of temper; severity; acrimony. **2.** hardship; difficulty; rigour. **3.** roughness of surface; unevenness. **4.** something rough or harsh.

aspersion /ə'spɜʒən, -spɜʃən/ *n.* a damaging imputation; a derogatory criticism: *to cast aspersions on one's character.*

asphalt /'æffelt, 'æsfelt/ *n.* **1.** any of various dark-coloured, solid bituminous substances, composed mostly of mixtures of hydrocarbons, occurring native in various parts of the earth. **2.** a similar artificial substance, the by-product of petroleum-cracking operations. **3.** a mixture of such a substance with crushed rock, etc., used for roads, etc. *–v.t.* **4.** to cover or pave with asphalt. Also, **asphaltum.** –**asphaltic,** *adj.* –**asphalt-like,** *adj.*

asphyxia /əs'fɪksiə/ *n. Pathol.* the extreme condition caused by lack of oxygen and excess of carbon dioxide in the blood, caused by sufficient interference with respiration, as in choking. –**asphyxiate,** *v.* –**asphyxiation,** *n.*

aspic /'æspɪk/ *n.* **1.** a cold dish of meat, fish, etc., served set in a jellied mould. **2.** the jellied garnish, made from fish or meat stock, sometimes with added gelatine.

aspidistra /æspə'dɪstrə/ *n.* a smooth, stemless Asian herb, *Aspidistra elatior*, family Liliaceae, bearing large evergreen leaves often striped with white, once widely grown as a house plant; often seen as a symbol of genteel respectability.

aspirate /'æspəreɪt/ *v.t.* **1.** *Phonetics* **a.** to release (a stop) in such a way that the breath escapes with audible friction, as in *title* where the first *t* is aspirated, the second is not. **b.** to begin (a word or syllable) with an *h* sound, as in *when* (pronounced *hwen*), *howl*, opposed to *wen*, *owl*. **2.** *Med.* to remove (fluids) from body cavities by use of an aspirator. **3.** *Med.* to inhale (foreign matter) into the lungs.

aspiration /æspə'reɪʃən/ *n.* **1.** the act of aspiring; lofty or ambitious desire. **2.** something aspired to; an ambition: *her aspiration is to travel through Africa*. **3.** an act of aspirating; a breath. **4.** *Med.* the act of aspirating (def. 2). –**aspirational,** *adj.*

aspirator /'æspəreɪtə/ *n.* **1.** an apparatus or device using suction. **2.** a jet pump used in laboratories to produce a partial vacuum. **3.** *Med.* an instrument for removing fluids from the body by suction.

aspire /ə'spaɪə/ *phr.* **aspire to,** to aim at (something, usually something great or lofty): *aspiring to greatness.* –**aspirant** /'æspərənt, ə'spaɪrənt/, *n.*, *adj.* –**aspirer,** *n.* –**aspiring,** *adj.*

aspirin /'æspərən/ *n.* (*from trademark*) **1.** acetylsalicylic acid, $C_9H_8O_4$, used to relieve the pain of headache, rheumatism, gout, neuralgia, etc. **2.** a tablet of aspirin.

ass /æs/ *n.* **1.** a long-eared, usually ash-coloured mammal, *Equus asinus*, related to the horse, serving as a slow, patient, sure-footed beast of burden; donkey. **2.** any allied wild species, as the **Mongolian wild ass,** *E. hemionus*. **3.** a fool; a blockhead.

assail /ə'seɪl/ *v.t.* **1.** to set upon with violence; assault. **2.** to set upon vigorously with arguments, entreaties, abuse, etc. **3.** to undertake with the purpose of mastering. –**assailant,** *n.*, *adj.* –**assailable,** *adj.* –**assailer,** *n.* –**assailment,** *n.*

assassin /ə'sæsən/ *n.* someone who undertakes to murder, especially from fanaticism or for a reward.

assassinate /ə'sæsəneɪt/ *v.t.* **1.** to kill by sudden or secret, premeditated assault, especially for political or religious motives. **2.** to blight or destroy treacherously: *to assassinate a person's character.* –**assassination** /əsæsə'neɪʃən/, *n.* –**assassinator,** *n.*

assault /ə'sɒlt, -'sɔlt/ *n.* **1.** the act of assailing; an attack; onslaught. **2.** *Law* an unlawful physical attack upon another; an attempt or offer to do violence to another, with or without a battery, as by holding a stone or club in a threatening manner. *–v.t.* **3.** to make an assault upon; attack; assail. –**assaulter,** *n.*

assay /ə'seɪ/ *v.t.* **1.** to examine by trial; put to test or trial: *to assay one's strength.* **2.** *Metallurgy* to test (ores or minerals) by chemical methods. **3.** to attempt;

endeavour; essay. **4.** to judge the quality of; evaluate. –**assayer,** *n.* –**assayable,** *adj.*

assemblage /ə'sɛmblɪdʒ/ *n.* **1.** a number of persons or things assembled; an assembly. **2.** the act of assembling. **3.** the state of being assembled.

assemble /ə'sɛmbəl/ *v.t.* **1.** to bring together; gather into one place, company, body or whole. **2.** to put or fit (parts) together; put together the parts of (a mechanism, etc.). *–v.i.* **3.** to come together; gather; meet.

assembler /ə'sɛmblə/ *n. Computers* a program which converts symbolic language to machine language on a word-for-word basis.

assembly /ə'sɛmbli/ *n.* (*pl.* **-lies**) **1.** a company of persons gathered together, usually for the same purpose, whether religious, political, educational, or social. **2.** (*upper case*) *Govt* a legislative body, especially a lower house of a legislature. **3.** the putting together of complex machinery, as aeroplanes, from interchangeable parts of standard dimensions.

assembly line *n.* a sequential arrangement of machines, tools, and workers in which each worker performs a special operation on an incomplete unit, which passes down a line of workers until it is finished.

assent /ə'sɛnt/ *v.i.* **1.** (sometimes fol. by *to*) to agree by expressing acquiescence or admitting truth; express agreement or concurrence: *to assent to a statement.* *–n.* **2.** agreement, as to a proposal; acquiescence; concurrence. **3.** → **royal assent.** –**assenter,** *n.*

assert /ə'sɜt/ *v.t.* **1.** to state as true; affirm; declare: *to assert that one is innocent.* **2.** to maintain or defend (claims, rights, etc.). *–phr.* **3. assert oneself,** to put oneself forward boldly and insistently. –**assertable,** *adj.* –**asserter, assertor,** *n.* –**assertive,** *adj.*

assertion /ə'sɜʃən/ *n.* **1.** a positive statement; an unsupported declaration. **2.** the act of asserting.

assess /ə'sɛs/ *v.t.* **1.** to estimate officially the value of (property, income, etc.) as a basis for taxation: *the property was assessed at two million dollars.* **2.** to fix or determine the amount of (damages, a tax, a fine, etc.). **3.** to impose a tax or other charge on. –**assessment,** *n.* –**assessable,** *adj.*

assessor /ə'sɛsə/ *n.* **1.** someone who assesses. **2.** someone who makes assessments of value or cost, as of damage for insurance purposes, or of property, etc., for taxation purposes. **3.** an advisory associate or assistant. –**assessorial** /æsɛ'sɔriəl/, *adj.*

asset /'æsɛt/ *n.* **1.** a useful thing or quality: *neatness is an asset.* **2.** a single item of property.

assets /'æsɛts/ *pl. n.* **1.** *Commerce* resources of a person or business consisting of such items as real property, machinery, inventories, notes, securities, cash, etc. **2.** property or effects (opposed to *liabilities*). **3.** any property available for paying debts, etc.

asseverate /ə'sɛvəreɪt/ *v.t.* to declare earnestly or solemnly; affirm positively. –**asseveration** /əsɛvə'reɪʃən/, *n.*

assiduous /ə'sɪdʒuəs/ *adj.* **1.** constant; unremitting: *assiduous reading.* **2.** constant in application; attentive; devoted. –**assiduously,** *adv.* –**assiduity** /æsə'djuəti/, **assiduousness,** *n.*

assign /ə'saɪn/ *v.t.* **1.** to make over or give, as in distribution; allot: *assign rooms at a hotel.* **2.** to appoint, as to a post or duty: *assign to stand guard.* **3.** *Aust. Hist.* to allocate (a convict) for employment by a private individual, as an officer or settler, generally as a shepherd, domestic servant, labourer, etc. **4.** to designate; specify: *to assign a day.* **5.** to ascribe; attribute; refer: *to assign a reason.* –**assigner;** *Chiefly Law,* **assignor** /æsɪ'nɔ/, *n.* –**assignable,** *adj.*

assignation /æsɪg'neɪʃən/ *n.* **1.** an appointment for a meeting, now especially an illicit love-meeting. **2.** the act of assigning; assignment.

assignee /əsaɪˈniː/ *n.* **1.** *Law* someone to whom some right or interest is transferred, either for his or her own enjoyment or in trust. **2.** *Aust. Hist.* a private individual, as a settler, officer, etc., to whom a convict was assigned.

assignment /əˈsaɪnmənt/ *n.* **1.** something assigned, such as a particular task or duty. **2.** the act of assigning. **3.** a task set for a student to do in private study for a course.

assimilate /əˈsɪməleɪt/ *v.t.* **1.** to take in and incorporate as one's own; absorb: *to assimilate a minority group; to assimilate information.* **2.** *Physiol.* to convert (food, etc.) into a substance suitable for absorption into the system. –*v.i.* **3.** to be or become absorbed. **4.** (usu. fol. by *into* or *with*) to become like; blend into: *to assimilate with the rest of the community.* –**assimilable**, *adj.*

assimilation /əsɪməˈleɪʃən/ *n.* **1.** the act or process of assimilating. **2.** the state or condition of being assimilated. **3.** *Physiol.* the conversion of absorbed food into the substance of the body. **4.** the process whereby individuals or groups of differing ethnic heritage, as migrant groups, or minority groups, acquire the basic attitudes, habits and mode of life of another all-embracing national culture (distinguished from *acculturation*).

assist /əˈsɪst/ *v.t.* **1.** to give support, help, or aid to in some undertaking or effort, or in time of distress. **2.** to be associated with in an assisting capacity. –*v.i.* **3.** to give aid or help. –**assistance**, *n.* –**assistant**, *n.* –**assister**; *Law*, **assistor**, *n.* –**assistive**, *adj.*

associate *v.t.* /əˈsoʊʃieɪt, əˈsoʊsieɪt/ **1.** to connect, as in thought: *I associate camping with discomfort.* **2.** to join as a companion, or partner: *I associated myself with the group.* **3.** to unite; combine: *coal is associated with shale.* –*v.i.* /əˈsoʊʃieɪt, əˈsoʊsieɪt/ **4.** to enter into an association or group; unite. **5.** to keep company: *to associate only with wealthy people.* –*n.* /əˈsoʊʃiət, əˈsoʊsiət/ **6.** a partner in some interest or someone who shares a common purpose. **7.** a companion: *my closest associate.* **8.** anything usually associated with another. **9.** someone with a lower rank of membership in an association. –*adj.* /əˈsoʊʃiət, əˈsoʊsiət/ **10.** associated, especially as a companion or partner: *an associate partner.* **11.** having lower rank of membership. –**associative**, *adj.*

association /əsoʊsiˈeɪʃən/ *n.* **1.** an organisation of people with a common purpose. **2.** the act of associating. **3.** companionship or partnership. **4.** connection or combination. **5.** the connection of ideas in thought. –**associational**, *adj.*

assonance /ˈæsənəns/ *n.* **1.** resemblance of sounds. **2.** a substitute for rhyme, in which the same vowel sounds, though with different consonants, are used in the terminal words of lines, as *penitent* and *reticence*. **3.** partial agreement. –**assonant**, *adj.*, *n.* –**assonantal** /æsəˈnæntl/, *adj.*

assorted /əˈsɔtəd/ *adj.* **1.** consisting of selected kinds; arranged in sorts or varieties. **2.** consisting of various kinds; miscellaneous. **3.** matched; suited.

assortment /əˈsɔtmənt/ *n.* **1.** the act of assorting; distribution; classification. **2.** an assorted collection.

assuage /əˈsweɪdʒ/ *v.t.* (**-suaged, -suaging**) **1.** to make milder or less severe; mitigate; ease: *to assuage grief or wrath.* **2.** to appease; satisfy: *to assuage appetite, thirst, craving, etc.* –**assuagement**, *n.* –**assuager**, *n.*

assume /əˈsjum/ *v.t.* **1.** to take for granted: *can you assume it will work?* **2.** to agree to do; undertake: *to assume office, a responsibility, etc.* **3.** to take on: *to assume new habits of life.* **4.** to pretend to have or be; feign: *to assume a false modesty.* **5.** to take over: *to assume a right to oneself.* –**assumable**, *adj.* –**assumed**, *adj.* –**assumer**, *n.* –**assumption**, *n.*

assurance /əˈʃɔrəns, -ˈʃʊə-/ *n.* **1.** a declaration intended to give confidence or guarantee. **2.** full confidence or trust; certainty. **3.** freedom from fearfulness; self-reliance. **4.** forwardness; impudence. **5.** insurance (now usually only life insurance).

assure /əˈʃɔ/ *v.t.* **1.** to declare earnestly to. **2.** to make sure or certain; convince, as by a promise or declaration. **3.** to make (an event or position) sure: *this assures the success of our work.* **4.** to give confidence to; encourage. **5.** to insure, especially against death. –**assurer**; *Law*, **assuror**, *n.*

astatine /ˈæstətin, -taɪn/ *n.* *Chem.* a rare element of the halogen family. *Symbol:* At; *atomic number:* 85. See **halogen.**

asterisk /ˈæstərɪsk/ *n.* **1.** the figure of a star (*), used in writing and printing as a reference mark or to indicate omission, doubtful matter, etc. **2.** something in the shape of a star or asterisk. –*v.t.* **3.** to identify or mark by means of this sign.

asteroid /ˈæstərɔɪd/ *n.* **1.** *Astron.* one of several hundred small celestial bodies with orbits lying mostly between those of Mars and Jupiter; minor planet. **2.** *Zool.* any of the Asteroidea, a class of echinoderms characterised by a starlike body with radiating arms or rays, as the starfishes.

asthma /ˈæsmə/ *n.* *Pathol.* a paroxysmal disorder of respiration with laboured breathing, a feeling of constriction in the chest, and coughing. –**asthmatic** /æsˈmætɪk/, *adj.*, *n.*

astigmatism /əˈstɪgmətɪzəm/ *n.* a defect of the eye or of a lens whereby rays of light from an external point converge unequally in different meridians, thus causing imperfect vision or images.

astir /əˈstɜ/ *adj.* **1.** in a stir; in motion or activity. **2.** up and about; out of bed.

astonish /əˈstɒnɪʃ/ *v.t.* to strike with sudden and overpowering wonder; surprise greatly; amaze.

astound /əˈstaʊnd/ *v.t.* to overwhelm with amazement; astonish greatly. –**astoundingly**, *adv.*

astral /ˈæstrəl/ *adj.* **1.** of or relating to the stars; stellar. **2.** *Biol.* of, relating to, or resembling an aster; star-shaped. **3.** *Theosophy* of or relating to a substance, beyond the reach of human senses, supposedly pervading all space and form the substance of a second body belonging to each individual. –*n.* **4.** an astral body or spirit.

astray /əˈstreɪ/ *adv.* **1.** out of the right way or away from the right; straying; wandering. –*phr.* **2.** **go astray**, **a.** to slip from morality into immorality. **b.** to become lost or mislaid. **3.** **lead astray**, to cause another to take a wrong path.

astride /əˈstraɪd/ *adv.* **1.** in the posture of striding or straddling. –*prep.* **2.** with a leg on each side of.

astringent /əˈstrɪndʒənt/ *adj.* **1.** (as affecting the skin) refreshing, tightening, drying: *an astringent after-shave lotion.* **2.** severe, sharp, austere: *an astringent style.* **3.** (of tastes) unpleasantly dry, hard (in wines, from the presence of tannin). **4.** *Med.* contracting; constrictive; styptic. –*n.* **5.** an astringent agent (especially cosmetic). –**astringency**, *n.* –**astringently**, *adv.*

astro- a word element meaning 'star', as in *astrology*.

astrology /əsˈtrɒlədʒi/ *n.* **1.** a study which assumes, and professes to interpret, the influence of the heavenly bodies on human affairs. **2.** (formerly) practical astronomy, the earliest form of the science. –**astrologer**, **astrologist**, *n.* –**astrological** /æstrəˈlɒdʒɪkəl/, **astrologic**, *adj.* –**astrologically**, *adv.*

astronaut /ˈæstrənɔt/ *n.* a person trained as a pilot, navigator, etc., to take part in the flight of a spacecraft.

astronautics /æstrəˈnɔtɪks/ *n.* the science and technology of flight outside the atmosphere of the earth.

astronomical /æstrə'nɒmɪkəl/ adj. **1.** of, relating to, or connected with astronomy. **2.** very large, like the numbers used in astronomical calculations. Also, **astronomic.** –**astronomically,** adv.

astronomy /əs'trɒnəmi/ n. the science of the celestial bodies, their motions, positions, distances, magnitudes, etc. –**astronomer,** n.

astute /əs'tjut/ adj. of keen penetration or discernment; sagacious; shrewd; cunning. –**astutely,** adv. –**astuteness,** n.

asunder /ə'sʌndə/ adv. **1.** into separate parts; in or into pieces: to tear asunder. **2.** apart or widely separated: as wide asunder as the poles.

asylum /ə'saɪləm/ n. **1.** an institution for the maintenance and care of the insane, the blind, orphans or the like. **2.** an inviolable refuge, as formerly for criminals and debtors; a sanctuary. **3.** International Law protection, usually right of residence, granted by the government of a country to one or more refugees who have left their own country because of war or because of political or other persecution: political asylum.

asymmetric /eɪsə'metrɪk/ adj. not symmetrical; without symmetry. Also, **asymmetrical.** –**asymmetry** /eɪ'sɪmətri/, n. –**asymmetrically,** adv.

asystole /eɪ'sɪstəli/ n. Med. a state of the heart in which there is an absence of systole, and hence no contraction of the myocardium and no blood flow, leading to death. –**asystolic** /eɪsɪs'tɒlɪk/, adj.

at /æt, weak form /ət/ prep. **1.** a particle specifying a point occupied, attained, sought, or otherwise concerned, as in place, time, order, experience, etc., and hence used in many idiomatic phrases expressing circumstantial or relative position, degree or rate, action, manner: to stand at the door; to aim at a mark; at home; at hand; at noon; at zero; at work; at ease; at length; at a risk; at cost; at one's best. –phr. **2. at it again,** acting in a characteristic manner. **3. at that,** as things stand: let it go at that; she's only an amateur, and an untalented one at that. **4. be at,** Colloq. engaged in, occupied with: what are you at these days? **5. be at someone,** to be critical of someone.

at- variant of **ad-** before t, as in attend.

atavism /'ætəvɪzəm/ n. **1.** Biol. the reappearance in an individual of characteristics of some more or less remote ancestor that have been absent in intervening generations. **2.** reversion to an earlier type. –**atavist,** n. –**atavistic** /ætə'vɪstɪk/, adj.

ataxia /ə'tæksiə/ n. Pathol. loss of coordination of the muscles, especially of the extremities. –**ataxic, atactic,** adj.

ate /eɪt, ɛt/ v. past tense of **eat.**

-ate¹ a suffix forming: **1.** adjectives equivalent to **-ed²** (in participial and other adjectives), as in accumulate, separate. **2.** nouns denoting especially persons charged with some duty or function, or invested with some dignity, right, or special character, as in advocate, candidate, curate, legate, prelate. **3.** nouns denoting some product or result of action, as in mandate (lit., a thing commanded). **4.** verbs, originally taken from Latin past participles but now formed from any Latin or other stem, as in actuate, agitate, calibrate.

-ate² a suffix forming nouns denoting a salt formed by action of an acid on a base, especially where the name of the acid ends in -ic, as in acetate.

-ate³ a suffix forming nouns denoting condition, estate, office, officials, or an official, etc., as in consulate, senate.

atheism /'eɪθi,ɪzəm/ n. **1.** the doctrine that there is no god. **2.** disbelief in the existence of a god (or gods) (opposed to theism).

athlete /'æθlit/ n. **1.** someone trained to exercises of physical agility and strength. **2.** someone trained to track and field events only.

athlete's foot n. tinea of the foot, especially of the skin between the toes.

athletic /æθ'letɪk/ adj. **1.** physically active and strong. **2.** of or relating to an athlete. **3.** of a physical type characterised by long limbs, a large build, and well-developed muscles. **4.** of or relating to athletics. –**athletically,** adv. –**athleticism,** n.

athletics /æθ'letɪks/ n. **1.** (usu. construed as pl.) athletic sports, such as running, rowing, boxing, etc. **2.** (usu. construed as sing.) track and field events only. **3.** (usu. construed as sing.) the practice of athletic exercises; the principles of athletic training.

-athon a suffix indicating an endurance test of a specified kind, as in walkathon, swimathon, often associated with a fundraising campaign. Also, **-thon.**

athwart /ə'θwɔt/ adv. **1.** from side to side (often in an oblique direction); transversely. **2.** perversely; awry; wrongly. –prep. **3.** from side to side of; across. **4.** in opposition to; contrary to.

-ation a suffix forming nouns denoting action or process, state or condition, a product or result, or something producing a result, often accompanying verbs or adjectives of Latin origin ending in -ate, as in agitation, decoration, elation, migration, separation, but also formed in English from any stem, as in botheration, flirtation, starvation. See **-ion, -tion.**

-ative an adjective suffix expressing tendency, disposition, function, bearing, connection, etc., as in affirmative, demonstrative, talkative.

atlas /'ætləs/ n. **1.** a bound collection of maps. **2.** a book of photographs or tables covering any subject.

ATM /eɪ ti 'ɛm/ n. → automatic teller machine.

atmosphere /'ætməsfɪə/ n. **1.** the gaseous fluid surrounding the earth; the air. **2.** this medium at a given place. **3.** Astron. the gaseous envelope surrounding any of the heavenly bodies. **4.** environing or pervading influence: an atmosphere of freedom. **5.** the quality in a work of art which produces a predominant mood or impression. –**atmospheric,** adj.

atmospheric pressure n. the pressure exerted on an object by the atmosphere; at sea level a column of air 1 square metre across weighs 100 kilonewtons.

atoll /'ætɒl/ n. a ringlike coral island enclosing a lagoon.

atom /'ætəm/ n. **1.** Physics, Chem. the smallest unitary constituent of a chemical element, composed of a more or less complex aggregate of protons, neutrons, and electrons, whose number and arrangement determine the element. **2.** (especially formerly) a hypothetical particle of matter so minute as to not allow any division. **3.** anything extremely small; a minute quantity.

atomic /ə'tɒmɪk/ adj. **1.** relating to atoms. **2.** propelled or driven by atomic energy. **3.** using or having developed atomic weapons. **4.** Chem. existing as free uncombined atoms. **5.** extremely minute. –**atomically,** adv.

atomic bomb n. a bomb whose potency is derived from nuclear fission of atoms of fissionable material, with consequent conversion of part of their mass into energy; its explosion is extremely violent and attended by great heat, brilliant light and strong gamma-ray radiation. Compare **hydrogen bomb.** Also, **atom bomb, A-bomb.**

atomic clock n. a highly accurate clock in which an electric oscillator, such as a crystal, is regulated by the vibration of an atomic system.

atomic energy n. **1.** the energy obtained from changes within the atomic nucleus, chiefly from nuclear fission, or fusion. **2.** this energy regarded as a source of power, as for industrial usage.

atomic mass *n.* the mass of an isotope of an element measured in atomic mass units.

atomic number *n.* the number of protons in the nucleus of an atom of a given element. *Abbrev.*: at. no.

atomic power *n.* **1.** energy released in nuclear reactions. **2.** a world power having developed its own atomic weapons. Also, **nuclear power**.

atomic theory *n. Physics* **1.** *Chem.* the modern theory of the atom having a complex internal structure and electrical properties. **2.** the mathematical and geometrical description of the motions of the electrons in the atom around the nucleus. Also, **atomic hypothesis**.

atomic weight *n.* → **relative atomic mass**.

atomise /ˈætəmaɪz/ *v.t.* **1.** to reduce to atoms. **2.** to reduce to fine particles or spray. Also, **atomize**. –**atomisation** /ˌætəmaɪˈzeɪʃən/, *n.*

atomiser /ˈætəmaɪzə/ *n.* an apparatus for reducing liquids to a fine spray, as for medicinal application. Also, **atomizer**.

atonal /eɪˈtoʊnəl/ *adj. Music* having no key or tonal centre. –**atonalism**, *n.* –**atonalistic** /ˌeɪtoʊnəˈlɪstɪk/, *adj.* –**atonally**, *adv.*

atone /əˈtoʊn/ *v.i.* (sometimes fol. by *for*) to make amends or reparation. –**atonement**, *n.*

atrium /ˈætriəm, ˈeɪ-/ *n.* (pl. **-tria** /-triə/) **1.** *Archit.* **a.** the central main room of an ancient Roman private house. **b.** an open area which is central to the design of a building, especially one designed for public use. **2.** *Zool.* an internal cavity or space; applied variously to different cavities in different organisms. **3.** *Anat.* one of the two chambers of the heart through which blood from the veins passes into the ventricles. –**atrial** /ˈeɪtriəl/, *adj.*

atrocious /əˈtroʊʃəs/ *adj.* **1.** extremely or shockingly wicked or cruel; heinous. **2.** shockingly bad or lacking in taste; execrable. –**atrociously**, *adv.* –**atrociousness**, *n.*

atrocity /əˈtrɒsəti/ *n.* (pl. **-ties**) **1.** the quality of being atrocious. **2.** an atrocious deed or thing.

atrophy /ˈætrəfi/ *n.* **1.** *Pathol.* wasting away of the body or of an organ or part, as from defective nutrition or other cause. **2.** degeneration; reduction in size and functional power through lack of use. –*verb* (**-phied**, **-phying**) –*v.t.* **3.** to affect with atrophy. –*v.i.* **4.** to undergo atrophy. –**atrophied**, *adj.* –**atrophic** /əˈtroʊfɪk/, *adj.*

atropine /ˈætrəpən, -in/ *n.* a poisonous crystalline alkaloid, $C_{17}H_{23}NO_3$, obtained from belladonna (deadly nightshade) and related plants, which prevents the response of various body structures to certain types of nerve stimulation; it is used medicinally to prevent spasm, to dilate the pupil of the eye, or as premedication, before an anaesthetic.

attach /əˈtætʃ/ *v.t.* **1.** to fasten; affix; join; connect: *to attach a cable.* **2.** to join in action or function. **3.** to connect as an adjunct; associate: *a curse is attached to this treasure.* **4.** to assign or attribute: *to attach significance to a gesture.* **5.** to bind by ties of affection or regard. **6.** *Law* to arrest (a person) or distrain (property) in payment of a debt by legal authority. –*phr.* **7. attach to**, to adhere or pertain to: *no blame attaches to him.* –**attachable**, *adj.* –**attachment**, *n.*

attaché /əˈtæʃeɪ/ *n.* a person attached to an official staff, especially that of an embassy or legation.

attaché case *n.* a small rectangular briefcase with a hinged lid, for documents, etc.

attack /əˈtæk/ *v.t.* **1.** to set upon with force or weapons; begin war against: *attack the enemy.* **2.** to direct unfavourable argument, etc., against; blame violently. **3.** to set about (a task) or go to work on (a thing) forcefully. **4.** (of disease, destructive agencies, etc.) to begin to affect. –*v.i.* **5.** to make an attack; begin war. –*n.* **6.** a military operation with the aim of overcoming an

enemy and destroying its forces and will to resist. **7.** the initial (offensive) movement in a contest; onset. **8.** the act or manner of presenting a musical work; vigour; precision; flair. –**attacker**, *n.*

attain /əˈteɪn/ *v.t.* **1.** to reach, achieve, or accomplish by continued effort: *to attain one's ends.* **2.** to come to or arrive at in due course: *to attain the opposite shore.* –*phr.* **3. attain to**, to arrive at; succeed in reaching or obtaining. –**attainment**, *n.* –**attainable**, *adj.*

attempt /əˈtempt, əˈtemt/ *v.t.* **1.** to make an effort at; try; undertake; seek: *to attempt a conversation, to attempt to study.* –*n.* **2.** effort put forth to accomplish something; a trial or essay. –*phr.* **3. attempt on someone's life**, a murderous attack. **4. attempt someone's life**, to attack someone with the intent of murdering them. **5. make an attempt**, to try to do something. –**attemptability** /əˌtemptəˈbɪləti, -temt-/, *n.* –**attemptable**, *adj.* –**attempter**, *n.*

attend /əˈtend/ *v.t.* **1.** to be present at: *to attend school; to attend a meeting.* **2.** to accompany as a result: *a cold attended with fever.* **3.** to look after; serve. –*v.i.* **4.** to apply oneself: *to attend to our work.* **5.** to take care of or charge of: *to attend to a task.* **6.** to wait (*on*) with service. –**attendee**, *n.*

attendance /əˈtendəns/ *n.* **1.** the act of attending. **2.** the number of persons present. **3.** the number of times (out of a maximum) that a person is present.

attendant /əˈtendənt/ *n.* **1.** someone who attends another, as for service or company. **2.** someone employed to take care or charge of someone or something, especially when this involves directing or assisting the public: *a cloakroom attendant.* –*adj.* **3.** concomitant; consequent: *attendant evils.*

attention /əˈtenʃən/ *n.* **1.** the act or faculty of attending. **2.** observant care; consideration; notice: *your letter will receive early attention.* **3.** civility or courtesy: *attention to a stranger.* **4.** (*pl.*) acts of courtesy indicating regard, as in courtship. **5.** *Mil.* **a.** a position held by soldiers in a formal drill of motionless attentiveness with the body held erect, the eyes to the front, the arms stiffly by the sides, and the heels together with toes turned outwards at an angle of 45 degrees. **b.** /əˈtenʃən, əˌtenˈʃʌn/ a command given in formal drill to take the position of attention. –*phr.* **6. call attention to**, to bring to the notice of other people; emphasise; highlight. **7. centre** (or **focus**) **of attention**, someone or something upon which everyone's gaze or concentration is fixed. **8. draw attention to**, to cause others to take notice of. **9. draw attention to oneself**, to behave in a way that causes others to notice, usually with disapproval. **10. pay attention** (**to**), **a.** to concentrate. **b.** to focus particularly on: *to pay attention to every detail.* **c.** to make one's attraction to another known; court. **11. pay no attention** (**to**), **a.** to withhold one's interest or gaze. **b.** to fail to be offended by.

attention deficit disorder *n. Obs.* → **attention deficit hyperactivity disorder**. Also, **ADD**.

attention deficit hyperactivity disorder *n.* a genetic disorder resulting in biochemical imbalances in the brain which cause symptoms which may include inattentiveness, hyperactivity, and impulsivity. Also, **ADHD**, **attention-deficit/hyperactivity disorder**; *Obs.*, **attention deficit disorder**.

attentive /əˈtentɪv/ *adj.* **1.** characterised by or giving attention; observant. **2.** assiduous in service or courtesy; polite; courteous. –**attentively**, *adv.* –**attentiveness**, *n.*

attenuate /əˈtenjueɪt/ *v.t.* **1.** to make thin; make slender or fine; rarefy. –*v.i.* **2.** to become thin or fine. –**attenuation** /əˌtenjuˈeɪʃən/, *n.*

attest /əˈtest/ *v.t.* **1.** to bear witness to; certify; declare to be correct, true, or genuine; declare the truth of, in words or writing; especially, affirm in an official capacity: *to attest the truth of a statement.* **2.** to give proof or evidence of; manifest: *his works attest his industry.* –*v.i.* **3.** to certify to the genuineness of a document by signing as witness. –**attester, attestor,** *n.*

attic /'ætɪk/ *n.* **1.** the part of a building, especially a house, directly under a roof; a garret. **2.** a room or rooms in that part, frequently used for storage.

attire /ə'taɪə/ *v.t.* **1.** to dress, array, or adorn, especially for special occasions, ceremonials, etc. –*n.* **2.** clothes or apparel, especially rich or splendid garments.

attitude /'ætɪtjud, -tʃud/ *n.* **1.** position, disposition, or manner with regard to a person or thing: *a menacing attitude.* **2.** position of the body appropriate to an action, emotion, etc. **3.** *Aeronautics* the inclination of the three principal axes of an aircraft relative to the wind, to the ground, etc. –**attitudinal** /ætə'tjudənəl/, *adj.*

attorney /ə'tɜni/ *n.* (*pl.* **-neys**) **1.** a person duly appointed or empowered by another to transact any business for him or her (**attorney in fact**). **2.** *Now Chiefly US* → **lawyer.**

attorney-general *n.* (*pl.* **attorneys-general** *or* **attorney-generals**) the chief law officer of a government and the minister responsible for the administration of justice.

attract /ə'trækt/ *v.t.* **1.** to act upon by a physical force causing or tending to cause approach or union (opposed to *repel*). **2.** to draw by other than physical influence; invite or allure; win: *to attract attention; to attract admirers.* –*v.i.* **3.** to possess or exert the power to attract someone or something. –**attractable,** *adj.* –**attracter, attractor,** *n.* –**attraction,** *n.*

attractive /ə'træktɪv/ *adj.* **1.** appealing to one's liking or admiration; engaging; alluring; pleasing. **2.** having the quality of attracting. –**attractively,** *adv.* –**attractiveness,** *n.*

attribute *v.t.* /ə'trɪbjut/ **1.** (sometimes fol. by *to*) to consider as belonging; regard as owing, as an effect to a cause. –*n.* /'ætrəbjut/ **2.** something attributed as belonging; a quality, character, characteristic, or property: *wisdom is one of his attributes.* **3.** *Gram.* a word or phrase grammatically subordinate to another, serving to limit (identify, particularise, describe, or supplement) the meaning of the form to which it is attached. For example: in *the red house*, *red* limits the meaning of *house*; it is an attribute of *house.* –**attribution** /ætrə'bjuʃən/, *n.* –**attributable,** *adj.* –**attributer, attributor,** *n.*

attrition /ə'trɪʃən/ *n.* **1.** a rubbing against; friction. **2.** a wearing down or away by friction; abrasion. **3.** a natural, gradual reduction in membership or personnel, as by retirement, resignation or death.

attune /ə'tjun, -tʃun/ *v.t.* **1.** to adjust to tune or harmony; bring into accord. **2.** (*usu. in the passive*) to adjust (a person) to accept their surroundings, situation, environment, etc.: *he has become attuned to the office politics.*

atypical /eɪ'tɪpɪkəl/ *adj.* not typical; not conforming to the type; irregular; abnormal. –**atypically,** *adv.*

aubergine /'oʊbəʒin, -dʒin/ *n.* **1.** → **eggplant.** –*adj.* **2.** of the colour of the dark-fruited eggplant, ranging from reddish-purple to bluish-purple.

auburn /'ɔbən/ *n.* **1.** a reddish-brown or golden-brown colour. –*adj.* **2.** having auburn colour: *auburn hair.*

auction /'ɒkʃən/ *n.* **1.** a public sale at which property or goods are sold to the highest bidder. –*v.t.* Also, **auction off.** **2.** to sell by auction: *they auctioned off their furniture.* –**auctioneer,** *n.*

audacious /ɔ'deɪʃəs/ *adj.* **1.** bold or daring; spirited; adventurous: *audacious warrior.* **2.** reckless or bold in wrongdoing; impudent and presumptuous. –**audaciously,** *adv.* –**audaciousness, audacity,** *n.*

audiation /ɔdi'eɪʃən/ *n.* the process by which one imagines or recalls music, playing it over in one's mind.

audible /'ɔdəbəl/ *adj.* capable of being heard; actually heard; loud enough to be heard. –**audibility** /ɔdə'bɪləti/, **audibleness,** *n.* –**audibly,** *adv.*

audience /'ɔdiəns/ *n.* **1.** an assembly of hearers or spectators: *the audience applauded warmly.* **2.** the persons reached by a book, radio or television broadcast, website, etc.; public: *you need to know your target audience.* **3.** liberty or opportunity of being heard or of speaking with or before a person or group: *we must give audience to both sides; an audience with the Pope.* **4.** *Govt* admission of a diplomatic representative to a sovereign or high officer of government; formal interview.

audio /'ɔdioʊ/ *adj.* **1.** of or relating to sound or hearing: *an audio frequency.* **2.** designating an electronic apparatus using audio frequencies in the transmission, reception or reproduction of sound: *audio amplifier.* **3.** operating at audio frequencies. –*n.* **4.** such apparatus.

audio- a word element meaning 'hear', 'of or for hearing', as in *audiometer.*

audiology /ɔdi'ɒlədʒi/ *n.* the science of the hearing mechanism, especially the measurement, diagnosis, and management of impaired function. –**audiological** /ɔdiə'lɒdʒɪkəl/, *adj.* –**audiologist,** *n.*

audiovisual /ɔdioʊ'vɪʒuəl/ *adj.* involving or directed simultaneously at the faculties of seeing and hearing: *an audiovisual aid to teaching.*

audit /'ɔdət/ *n.* **1.** an official examination and verification of accounts and records, especially of financial accounts. **2.** a thorough examination or inspection, particularly in relation to an approved standard measure. –*v.t.* **3.** to make audit of; examine (accounts, etc.) officially. **4.** to attend (lectures, classes, etc.) with official approval, but not for credit and without obligation to do the work of the course.

audition /ɔ'dɪʃən/ *n.* **1.** the act, sense, or power of hearing. **2.** a hearing given to a musician, speaker, etc., to test voice qualities, performance, etc. –*v.t.* **3.** to give (someone) an audition. –*v.i.* **4.** to be tested or to perform in an audition.

auditor /'ɔdətə/ *n.* **1.** a hearer; listener. **2.** someone appointed and authorised to examine accounts and accounting records, compare the charges with the vouchers, verify balance sheet and income items, and state the result.

auditorium /ɔdə'tɔriəm/ *n.* (*pl.* **-toriums** *or* **-toria** /-'tɔriə/) **1.** the space for the audience in a concert hall, theatre, school, or other building. **2.** a large building or room for meetings, assemblies, theatrical performances, etc.

auditory /'ɔdətri, -təri/ *adj.* relating to hearing, to the sense of hearing, or to the organs of hearing: *the auditory nerve.* –**auditorily,** *adv.*

auger /'ɔgə/ *n.* **1.** a carpenter's tool larger than a gimlet, with a spiral groove for boring holes in wood. **2.** a large tool for boring holes deep in the ground. **3.** a tool, often simply the thread of a drill bit, used for extracting small sample of a mineral deposit from a depth without actual excavation.

aught /ɔt/ *n.* anything whatever; any part: *for aught I know.*

augment /ɔg'mɛnt/ *v.t.* **1.** to make larger; enlarge in size or extent; increase. –*v.i.* **2.** to become larger. –**augmentable,** *adj.* –**augmenter,** *n.*

augur /'ɔgə/ *n.* **1.** a soothsayer; prophet. –*v.t.* **2.** to divine or predict, as from omens; prognosticate. –*v.i.* **3.** to be a sign; bode (*well* or *ill*). –**augural** /'ɔgjərəl/, *adj.* –**augury,** *n.*

august /ɔ'gʌst/ *adj.* **1.** inspiring reverence or admiration; of supreme dignity or grandeur; majestic: *an august spectacle.* **2.** venerable: *your august father.* –**augustly,** *adv.* –**augustness,** *n.*

August /ˈɔɡəst/ n. the eighth month of the year, containing 31 days.

au lait /oʊ ˈleɪ/ adj. prepared or served with milk.

au naturel /oʊ nætʃəˈrɛl/ adj. 1. in the natural state; naked. 2. cooked plainly. 3. uncooked.

aunt /ant/ n. 1. the sister of one's father or mother. 2. the wife of one's uncle. 3. a term of address used by children to a female friend of the family.

aunty /ˈanti/ n. (pl. **aunties**) 1. a familiar or diminutive form of **aunt**. 2. Aboriginal English **a.** a female relative of an older generation. **b.** a closely connected non-Aboriginal woman. 3. (upper case) a title of respect for a female elder of an Aboriginal community. Also, **auntie**.

aura /ˈɔrə/ n. (pl. **auras** or **aurae** /ˈɔri/) 1. a distinctive air, atmosphere, character, etc.: an aura of culture. 2. a subtle emanation proceeding from a body and surrounding it as an atmosphere. 3. Pathol. a sensation, as of a current of cold air, or other sensory experience, preceding an attack of epilepsy, hysteria, etc.

aural /ˈɔrəl/ adj. of or relating to an aura.

aureole /ˈɔrioʊl, ˈɔ-/ n. 1. a radiance surrounding the head or the whole figure in the representation of a sacred personage. 2. any encircling ring of light or colour; a halo.

auric /ˈɔrɪk/ adj. of or containing gold, especially in the trivalent state.

auricle /ˈɔrɪkəl, ˈɒr-/ n. 1. Anat. **a.** the projecting outer portion of the ear; the pinna. **b.** an ear-shaped sac forming part of an atrium of the heart. **c.** (esp. in nontechnical use) an atrium of the heart. 2. Bot., Zool. a part like or likened to an ear. –**auricled, auriculate** /ɔˈrɪkjələt, -leɪt/, adj.

auriferous /ɔˈrɪfərəs/ adj. yielding or containing gold.

aurora /əˈrɔrə/ n. an atmospheric display in skies of moving streamers or bands of light, usually green, red or yellow, probably caused by streams of charged particles from the sun passing into the Earth's magnetic field.

Auskick /ˈɒzkɪk/ n. a form of Australian Rules modified for children, with a reduced playing area and playing time, and modified equipment.

auspices /ˈɔspəsəz/ n. (sometimes sing.) favouring influence; patronage: under the auspices of the Australian Red Cross Society.

auspicious /ɔˈspɪʃəs, ə-/ adj. 1. of good omen; betokening success; favourable: an auspicious moment. 2. favoured by fortune; prosperous; fortunate. –**auspiciously**, adv. –**auspiciousness**, n.

Aussie /ˈɒzi/ Colloq. –adj. 1. Australian. –n. 2. an Australian. Also, **Ozzie**.

austere /ɒsˈtɪə, ɔs-/ adj. 1. harsh in manner; stern in appearance; forbidding. 2. severe in disciplining or restraining oneself; morally strict. 3. grave; sober; serious. 4. severely simple; without ornament: austere writing. –**austerely**, adv. –**austerity** /ɒsˈtɛrəti/, **austereness**, n.

Australasian bittern /ɒstrəˌleɪʒən ˈbɪtən/ n. the bittern, Botaurus poiciloptilus, with a camouflaging brown plumage, of southern Australia, New Caledonia and New Zealand.

Australian /əsˈtreɪljən, ɒs-/ adj. 1. of or relating to Australia. –n. 2. a person native to or resident in Australia. 3. the English language as spoken in Australia. See **Australian English**. –phr. 4. **the great Australian adjective**, (humorous) bloody (def. 4).

Australiana /əstreɪliˈanə, ɒs-/ n. items, especially of historical interest, originating in or relating to Australia, as early books, furniture, paintings, etc.

Australian Business Number n. an 11-digit number allocated by the government to a business, which must be displayed on invoices, receipts, letterhead, etc. Also, **ABN**.

Australian cattle dog n. a purebred dog with black or red face and ears and dark blue body speckled with lighter blues, developed in Australia for work with cattle; blue heeler.

Australian crawl n. → **freestyle** (def. 1).

Australian English n. 1. the English language as used in Australia, including all varieties whether regional or social. 2. the national dialect of the English language used in Australia, characterised by the pronunciation, lexis, and idiom typical of those born and educated in Australia. Abbrev.: AE

Australian fur seal n. an Antarctic and southern Australian eared seal, Arctocephalus doriferus.

Australian Rules pl. n. (construed as sing.) a code of football requiring two teams of 18 players, which originated in Australia in 1859; influenced by the various forms of football played at the time, as association football, Gaelic football, Rugby football, etc., and also possibly by marngrook. Also, **Australian National Football, Australian Football, Aussie Rules**.

Australian terrier n. a small, sturdy, low-set and rather elongated dog with erect ears and a short, coarse coat, usually grey-blue with rich tan markings on face and legs.

Australoid /ˈɒstrəlɔɪd/ Ethnology –adj. 1. (in a system devised in the 19th century) of or relating to an ethnic classification of humankind which includes the Australian Aboriginal people and certain peoples of Asia and the Pacific islands. –n. 2. a person having the physical characteristics of this group. Compare **Caucasian, Mongoloid, Negroid**.

australopithecine /ˌɒstrəloʊˈpɪθəsin/ n. a primate of the extinct genus Australopithecus, of the Pliocene epoch, found first in southern Africa, having jaws resembling those of humans and a skull resembling that of the apes.

aut- variant of **auto-**¹ before most vowels, as in autacoid.

autarchy /ˈɔtaki/ n. (pl. **-chies**) 1. absolute sovereignty. 2. self-government. –**autarchic** /ɔˈtakɪk/, adj.

autarky /ˈɔtaki/ n. (pl. **-kies**) 1. the condition of self-sufficiency, especially economic, as applied to a state. 2. a national policy of economic independence. –**autarkical** /ɔˈtakɪkəl/, adj. –**autarkist**, n., adj.

authentic /ɔˈθɛntɪk/ adj. 1. entitled to acceptance or belief; reliable; trustworthy: an authentic story. 2. of the authorship or origin reputed; of genuine origin: authentic documents. 3. Law executed with all due formalities: an authentic deed. –**authenticity** /ˌɔθɛnˈtɪsəti/, n. –**authentically**, adv.

authenticate /ɔˈθɛntəkeɪt/ v.t. 1. to make authoritative or valid. 2. to establish as genuine. –**authenticable** /ɔˈθɛntɪkəbəl/, adj. –**authentication** /ɔˌθɛntəˈkeɪʃən/, n. –**authenticator**, n.

author /ˈɔθə/ n. 1. someone who writes a novel, poem, essay, etc.; the composer of a literary work, as distinguished from a compiler, translator, editor, or copyist. 2. the originator, beginner, or creator of anything. –**authoress** /ˈɔθərəs/, fem. n. –**authorial** /ɔˈθɔriəl/, adj. –**authorless**, adj.

authorise /ˈɔθəraɪz/ v.t. 1. to give authority or legal power to; empower (to do something). 2. to give authority for; formally sanction (an act or proceeding). 3. to establish by authority or usage: authorised by custom. Also, **authorize**. –**authorisation** /ˌɔθəraɪˈzeɪʃən/, n. –**authoriser**, n.

authoritarian /ɔˌθɒrəˈtɛəriən, ə-/ adj. 1. favouring the principle of subjection to authority as opposed to that of individual freedom. 2. assuming the commanding style of one in a position of authority; dictatorial. –n. 3. someone who favours authoritarian principles. –**authoritarianism**, n.

authority /ɔ'θɒrəti, ə-/ n. (pl. **-ties**) **1.** (of a person) the right to determine, judge or settle; right to control, command; warrant. **2.** an accepted source of information, advice, etc.; testimony; witness. **3.** (the writings of) an expert on a subject. **4.** a statute, court rule, or legal decision which establishes a rule or principle of law; ruling. –**authoritative**, adj.

autism /'ɔtɪzəm/ n. **1.** Psychiatry a neurodevelopmental syndrome of unknown aetiology, chiefly characterised by some degree of inability to comprehend or communicate, failure to relate emotionally, and inappropriate or obsessive behaviour. **2.** Psychol. fantasy; introverted thought; daydreaming; marked subjectivity of interpretation. –**autistic** /ɔ'tɪstɪk/, adj.

autism spectrum disorder n. a disorder encompassing a wide range of symptoms including those identified as autism, Asperger's syndrome and atypical autism. Abbrev.: ASD

auto-¹ a word element meaning 'self', 'same', as in autograph. Also, **aut-**.

auto-² a combining form of **automobile**.

autobiography /,ɔtəbaɪ'ɒɡrəfi/ n. (pl. **-phies**) an account of a person's life written by himself or herself. –**autobiographical** /,ɔtəbaɪə'ɡræfəl/, adj. –**autobiographer**, n.

autochthon /ɔ'tɒkθən/ n. (pl. **-thons** or **-thones** /-θəniz/) **1.** an aboriginal inhabitant. **2.** Ecol. one of the indigenous animals or plants of a region. –**autochthonous**, adj.

autocracy /ɔ'tɒkrəsi/ n. (pl. **-cies**) **1.** uncontrolled or unlimited authority over others, invested in a single person; the government or power of an absolute monarch. **2.** a country governed by a person with such authority. –**autocratic** /ɔtə'krætɪk/, adj. –**autocrat** /'ɔtəkræt/, n.

auto-electrician /,ɔtoʊ-ɛlɛk'trɪʃən/ n. someone who specialises in the repair and servicing of the electrical circuits of motor cars.

autograph /'ɔtəgræf, -graf/ n. **1.** a person's own signature. **2.** a person's own handwriting. –v.t. **3.** to write one's name on or in: to autograph a book. **4.** to write with one's own hand. –**autographic** /,ɔtə'græfɪk/, **autographical** /,ɔtə'græfəkəl/, adj. –**autographically** /,ɔtə'græfɪkli/, adv.

autoimmune system /ɔtoʊɪm'jun sɪstəm/ n. Med. the system within the body which produces antibodies.

autoinjector /ɔtoʊɪn'dʒɛktə/ n. a hypodermic syringe preloaded with a single dose of a medication for use in emergency situations, such as the provision of instant treatment for anaphylactic shock. Also, **auto-injector**.

automate /'ɔtəmeɪt/ v.t. **1.** to apply the principles of automation to (a mechanical process). **2.** to operate or control by automation.

automatic /ɔtə'mætɪk/ adj. **1.** having the power of self-motion; self-moving or self-acting; mechanical. **2.** Physiol. occurring independently of volition, as certain muscular actions. **3.** (of a firearm, pistol, etc.) utilising the recoil, or part of the force of the explosive, to eject the spent cartridge shell, introduce a new cartridge, cock the arm, and fire it repeatedly. **4.** done unconsciously or from force of habit; mechanical (opposed to voluntary). –n. **5.** a machine which operates automatically, as a motor vehicle with automatic gear shift. –**automatically**, adv.

automatic teller machine n. computerised equipment located outside banks and building societies, in shopping areas, etc., offering basic banking facilities and operated by inserting a plastic card with a magnetised strip and keying in a personal identification number. Also, **ATM**, **automated teller machine**.

automatic transmission n. a transmission system on a motor vehicle in which gear-changing is operated automatically in accordance with car engine speed rather than manually by the driver.

automation /ɔtə'meɪʃən/ n. **1.** the science of applying automatic control to industrial processes; the replacement of manpower by sophisticated machinery. **2.** the process or act of automating a mechanical process. **3.** the degree to which a mechanical process is automatically controlled.

automaton /ɔ'tɒmətən/ n. (pl. **-tons** or **-ta** /-tə/) **1.** a mechanical figure or contrivance constructed to act as if spontaneously through concealed motive power. **2.** someone who acts in a monotonous routine manner, without active intelligence. **3.** something capable of acting spontaneously or without external impulse.

automobile /'ɔtəməbil/ n. Chiefly US a car (or other self-propelled road transport vehicle). –**automobilist** /ɔtə'moʊbələst, ɔtəmə'biləst/, n.

automotive /ɔtə'moʊtɪv/ adj. **1.** propelled by a self-contained power plant. **2.** of or relating to motor vehicles.

autonomic /ɔtə'nɒmɪk/ adj. **1.** autonomous. **2.** of or relating to the autonomic nervous system. –**autonomically**, adv.

autonomic nervous system n. Physiol., Anat. the part of the peripheral nervous system which controls the involuntary functions of the glands, blood vessels, the viscera, and the heart and smooth muscles. Compare **somatic nervous system**.

autonomous /ɔ'tɒnəməs/ adj. self-governing; independent; subject to its own laws only. –**autonomously**, adv.

autonomy /ɔ'tɒnəmi/ n. **1.** Govt the condition of being autonomous; self-government, or the right of self-government. **2.** independence; self-sufficiency; self-regulation. –**autonomist**, n.

autopilot /'ɔtoʊ,paɪlət/ n. **1.** a device in an aircraft's control system that can be engaged to keep an aircraft flying on a pre-set course. –phr. **2. on autopilot, a.** (of an aircraft) flying under the control of the autopilot. **b.** (of a person) acting in a reasonably competent way but without giving full attention, as a result of shock, fatigue, absent-mindedness, etc. Also, **automatic pilot**, **automatic control**.

autopsy /'ɔtɒpsi/ n. (pl. **-sies**) inspection and dissection of a body after death, as for determination of the cause of death; a post-mortem examination.

autumn /'ɔtəm/ n. **1.** the season of the year between summer and winter; in the Southern Hemisphere, March, April, and May. **2.** a period of maturity passing into decline. –**autumnal** /ɔ'tʌmnəl/, adj.

auxiliary /ɒɡ'zɪljəri, ɔɡ-/ adj. **1.** giving support; helping; aiding; assisting. **2.** additional; subsidiary: auxiliary soldiers. **3.** used as a reserve: auxiliary engine. –n. (pl. **-ries**) **4.** someone or something that gives aid of any kind; helper. **5.** → **auxiliary verb**.

auxiliary verb n. a verb customarily preceding certain forms of other verbs, used to express distinctions of time, aspect, mood, etc., as do, am, etc., in I do think; I am going; we have spoken; may we go?; can they see?; we shall walk.

avail /ə'veɪl/ v.i. **1.** to have force or efficacy; be of use; serve. **2.** to be of value or profit. –v.t. **3.** to be of use or value to; profit; advantage. –n. **4.** efficacy for a purpose; advantage to an object or end: of little or no avail. –phr. **5. avail oneself of**, to give oneself the advantage of; make use of. **6. to no avail**, with no good result; to no purpose. –**availingly**, adv.

available /ə'veɪləbəl/ adj. suitable or ready for use; at hand; of use or service: available resources. –**availability** /əveɪlə'bɪləti/, **availableness**, n. –**availably**, adv.

avalanche /'ævəlænʃ, -lanʃ, -læntʃ, -lantʃ/ n. **1.** a large mass of snow, ice, etc., detached from a mountain slope and sliding or falling suddenly downwards. **2.** anything like an avalanche in suddenness and destructiveness: *an avalanche of misfortunes.* –*v.i.* (**-lanched, -lanching**) **3.** to come down in, or like, an avalanche.

avant-garde /ˌævɒnt-ˈgad/ *n.* **1.** the vanguard; the leaders in progress in any field, especially the arts; the new ideas or thinkers. –*adj.* **2.** modern; experimental; (affectedly) ultra-modern.

avarice /ˈævərəs/ *n.* insatiable greed for riches; inordinate, miserly desire to gain and hoard wealth. –**avaricious** /ævəˈnʃəs/, *adj.*

avatar /ˈævəta/ *n.* **1.** *Hindu Myth.* the descent of a deity to the earth in an incarnate form or some manifest shape; the incarnation of a god. **2.** *Internet* the representation of a person in virtual reality.

avenge /əˈvɛndʒ/ *v.t.* (**avenged, avenging**) to take vengeance or exact satisfaction for: *to avenge a death.* –**avenger,** *n.* –**avengement,** *n.*

avenue /ˈævənju/ *n.* **1.** a street or road, especially one which is wide and lined with a double row of trees. **2.** any street so called. **3.** a way or opening for entrance into a place: *the avenue to India.* **4.** means of access or attainment: *avenue of escape, avenues of success.*

aver /əˈvɜ/ *v.t.* (**averred, averring**) to affirm with confidence; declare in a positive or peremptory manner. –**averment,** *n.*

average /ˈævərɪdʒ, -vrɪdʒ/ *n.* **1.** an arithmetical mean. **2.** a quantity intermediate to a set of quantities. **3.** the ordinary, normal, or typical amount, rate, quality, kind, etc.; the common run. **4.** *Commerce* **a.** a small charge paid by the master on account of the ship and cargo, such as pilotage, towage, etc. **b.** an expense, partial loss, or damage to ship or cargo. **c.** the incidence of such an expense or loss on the owners or their insurers. **d.** an equitable apportionment among all the interested parties of such an expense or loss. **5.** the number of sheep a shearer expects to shear in a typical day. –*adj.* **6.** of or relating to an average; estimated by average; forming an average. **7.** intermediate, medial, or typical in amount, rate, quality, etc. **8.** mediocre in quality or performance. –*verb* (**-raged, -raging**) –*v.t.* **9.** to find an average value for; reduce to a mean. **10.** to result in, as an arithmetical mean; amount to, as a mean quantity: *the profit averages $50 a week.* –*v.i.* **11.** to have or show an average: *in general, the weekly profits have averaged as expected.* –*phr.* **12. average out,** *Colloq.* to divide or sort out, more or less evenly. –**averagely,** *adv.*

averse /əˈvɜs/ *adj.* having strong feelings of antipathy or repugnance; opposed: *averse to flattery.* –**aversely,** *adv.* –**averseness,** *n.*

aversion /əˈvɜʒən, -ˈvɜʃən/ *n.* **1.** (sometimes fol. by *to*) an averted state of the mind or feelings; repugnance, antipathy, or rooted dislike **2.** a cause of dislike; an object of repugnance.

avert /əˈvɜt/ *v.t.* **1.** to turn away or aside: *to avert one's eyes.* **2.** to ward off; prevent: *to avert evil.*

avi- a word element meaning 'bird'.

avian /ˈeɪviən/ *adj.* of or relating to birds.

avian flu *n.* → **avian influenza.**

avian influenza *n.* any of a wide range of influenza viruses affecting birds, some strains of which, such as the H5N1 virus, are transmittable from birds to humans, this being recognised for the first time in Hong Kong in 1997. Also, **avian flu, bird flu.**

aviary /ˈeɪvjəri, ˈeɪviəri/ *n.* (*pl.* **-ries**) a large cage or enclosure in which birds are kept.

aviation /ˌeɪviˈeɪʃən/ *n.* **1.** the act, art, or science of flying by mechanical means, especially with heavier-than-air craft. **2.** the aircraft (with equipment) of an air force. –**aviational,** *adj.*

aviator /ˈeɪvieɪtə/ *n.* a pilot of an aeroplane or other heavier-than-air craft. –**aviatrix** /ˈeɪviˌeɪtrɪks/, **aviatress** /ˈeɪviˌeɪtrəs/, *fem. n.*

avid /ˈævəd/ *adj.* **1.** keenly desirous; eager; greedy: *an avid reader.* **2.** keen; sharp: *avid hunger.* –**avidly,** *adv.* –**avidity** /əˈvɪdəti/, *n.*

avocado /ævəˈkadoʊ/ *n.* (*pl.* **-dos**) **1.** a tropical American fruit, green to black in colour and commonly pearshaped, borne by the tree *Persea americana*, eaten raw, especially as a salad fruit. **2.** the tree. Also, **avocado pear.**

avocation /ævəˈkeɪʃən/ *n.* **1.** a minor or occasional occupation; hobby. **2.** (*also pl.*) one's regular occupation, calling, or vocation. **3.** diversion or distraction.

avoid /əˈvɔɪd/ *v.t.* to keep away from; keep clear of; shun; evade: *to avoid a person; to avoid danger.* –**avoidance,** *n.* –**avoidable,** *adj.* –**avoidably,** *adv.* –**avoider,** *n.*

avoirdupois weight /ˌævwadjuˈpwa weɪt/ *n.* a system of weights formerly used in most English-speaking countries for goods other than gems, precious metals and drugs.

avow /əˈvaʊ/ *v.t.* **1.** to admit or acknowledge frankly or openly; own; confess. **2.** to state; assert; affirm; declare. –**avowal,** *n.* –**avowed,** *adj.* –**avower,** *n.*

avuncular /əˈvʌŋkjələ/ *adj.* like or characteristic of an uncle: *avuncular affection.*

await /əˈweɪt/ *v.t.* **1.** to wait for; look for or expect. **2.** to be in store for; be ready for. –*v.i.* **3.** to wait, as in expectation.

awake /əˈweɪk/ *verb* (**awoke, awoken, awaking**) –*v.t.* **1.** to rouse (someone) from sleep; wake up. **2.** to stir the interest of; excite: *to awake them to the realities of life.* **3.** to stir, disturb (the memories, fears, etc.). –*v.i.* **4.** to wake up; come out of sleep. –*adj.* **5.** waking, not sleeping. **6.** watchful; alert: *awake to a danger.*

awakening /əˈweɪkənɪŋ/ *adj.* **1.** rousing; reanimating; alarming. –*n.* **2.** the act of awaking from sleep. **3.** an arousal or revival of interest or attention; a waking up, as from indifference, ignorance, etc. –**awaken,** *v.*

award /əˈwɔd/ *v.t.* **1.** to adjudge to be due or merited; assign or bestow: *to award prizes.* **2.** to bestow by judicial decree; assign or appoint by deliberate judgement, as in arbitration. –*n.* **3.** something awarded, as a medal, rate of pay, particular working conditions, etc. –**awardable,** *adj.* –**awarder,** *n.*

award wage *n.* (in Australia and NZ) a wage arrived at by mutual consent or arbitration and fixed by an industrial court, payable by law to all employees in a particular occupation.

aware /əˈwɛə/ *adj.* **1.** cognisant or conscious: *aware of the danger.* **2.** informed or up-to-date. –**awareness,** *n.*

awash /əˈwɒʃ/ *adj.* **1.** covered with water. **2.** washing about; tossed about by the waves.

away /əˈweɪ/ *adv.* **1.** from this or that place; off: *to go away.* **2.** apart; at a distance: *to stand away from the wall.* **3.** aside: *turn your eyes away.* **4.** out of possession, notice, use, or existence: *to give money away.* **5.** continuously; on: *to blaze away.* **6.** without hesitation: *fire away.* **7.** immediately; forthwith: *right away.* –*adj.* **8.** absent: *away from home.* **9.** distant: *six kilometres away.* **10.** on the move; having started; in full flight. **11.** *Colloq.* in a state of uncontrollable excitement, hilarity, etc.: *the guests were well away.* **12.** *Sport* **a.** of or relating to a game not played on one's home ground: *an away match.* **b.** of or relating to a team, player, etc., participating in a game not played on their home ground: *the away team.* –*interj.* **13.** go away! depart! –*phr.* **14. away with ...,** a command to remove someone or something: *away with this man!* **15. away with the fairies,** *Aust., NZ Colloq.* no longer in tune with reality. **16. do** (or **make**) **away with,** to put out of existence; get rid of; kill. **17. make away with,** to run off with; steal.

awe /ɔ/ *n.* **1.** respectful or reverential fear, inspired by what is grand or sublime: *to regard the works of nature with awe.* −*v.t.* (**awed, awing**) **2.** to inspire with awe. **3.** to influence or restrain by awe.

awesome /'ɔsəm/ *adj.* **1.** inspiring awe. **2.** characterised by awe. **3.** *Colloq.* extremely impressive; of high quality. −**awesomely,** *adv.* −**awesomeness,** *n.*

awful /'ɔfəl/ *adj.* **1.** extremely bad; unpleasant; ugly. **2.** *Colloq.* very great: *an awful lot.* **3.** inspiring fear; dreadful; terrible. **4.** full of awe; reverential. **5.** inspiring reverential awe; solemnly impressive. −**awfulness,** *n.*

awfully /'ɔfəli/ *adv.* **1.** very badly: *he treats his dogs awfully.* **2.** used as an intensifier: *awfully good*; *an awfully long way.*

awhile /ə'waɪl/ *adv.* for a short time or period.

awkward /'ɔkwəd/ *adj.* **1.** lacking skill; clumsy. **2.** ungraceful; ungainly; uncouth: *awkward gestures.* **3.** difficult to handle; dangerous: *an awkward customer.* **4.** embarrassing or trying: *an awkward moment.* **5.** deliberately difficult; perverse; obstructive. −**awkwardly,** *adv.* −**awkwardness,** *n.*

awl /ɔl/ *n.* a pointed instrument for piercing small holes in leather, wood, etc.

awn /ɔn/ *n.* a bristle-like appendage of a plant, especially on the glumes of grasses. −**awned,** *adj.* −**awnless,** *adj.*

awning /'ɔnɪŋ/ *n.* **1.** a roof-like shelter of canvas, etc., in front of a window or door, over a deck, etc., as for protection from the sun. **2.** a shelter.

awoke /ə'woʊk/ *v.* past tense of **awake.**

AWOL /eɪ ˌdʌbəlju oʊ 'ɛl, 'eɪwɒl/ −*adj.* **1.** absent without leave. −*phr.* **2. go AWOL,** *Colloq.* to leave without permission or notice.

awry /ə'raɪ/ *adv.* **1.** with a turn or twist to one side; askew: *to glance or look awry.* **2.** away from reason or the truth. **3.** amiss; wrong: *our plans went awry.*

axe /æks/ *n.* (*pl.* **axes**) **1.** an instrument with a bladed head on a handle or helve, used for hewing, cleaving, chopping, etc. **2.** *Colloq.* a guitar, usually electric. −*v.t.* (**axed, axing**) **3.** to shape or trim with an axe. **4.** *Colloq.* to cut down; reduce (expenditure, prices, etc.) sharply. **5.** *Colloq.* to dismiss from a position. **6.** *Colloq.* to bring (a project, etc.) to an end; discontinue. −*phr.* **7. have an axe to grind,** to have a private purpose or selfish end to attain. **8. the axe,** *Colloq.* **a.** a drastic cutting down (of expenses). **b.** dismissal from a job, position, or the like; the sack. Also, *Chiefly US,* **ax.** −**axelike,** *adj.*

axes¹ /'æksiz/ *n.* plural of **axis.**

axes² /'æksəz/ *n.* plural of **axe.**

axial /'æksiəl/ *adj.* **1.** of, relating to, or forming an axis. **2.** situated in an axis or on the axis.

axilla /æk'sɪlə/ *n.* (*pl.* **axillae** /æk'sɪli/) *Anat.* the armpit. −**axillary,** *adj.*

axiom /'æksiəm/ *n.* **1.** a recognised truth. **2.** an established and universally accepted principle or rule. **3.** *Logic, Maths, etc.* a proposition which is assumed without proof for the sake of studying the consequences that follow from it. −**axiomatic** /æksiə'mætɪk/, *adj.*

axis /'æksəs/ *n.* (*pl.* **axes** /'æksiz/) **1.** the line about which a rotating body, such as the earth, turns. **2.** the central line of any symmetrical, or nearly symmetrical, body: *the axis of a cylinder, of the building, etc.* **3.** a fixed line adopted for reference, as in plotting a curve on a graph, in crystallography, etc. **4.** an alliance of two or more nations to coordinate their foreign and military policies, and to draw in with them a group of dependent or supporting powers.

axle /'æksəl/ *n.* *Machinery* the pin, bar, shaft, or the like, on which or with which a wheel or pair of wheels rotate.

axolotl /æksə'lɒtl, 'æksəlɒtl/ *n.* any of several Mexican salamanders that breed in the larval stage, in Mexico prized as food.

axon /'æksɒn/ *n.* *Physiol.* the appendage of a neuron which transmits impulses from the neuron to other cells. Also, **axone** /'æksoʊn/.

ayatollah /aɪə'tɒlə/ *n.* **1.** a high-ranking religious leader in the Shiite division of Islam, the official religion of Iran. **2.** *Colloq.* (*derog.*) an autocratic leader.

azalea /ə'zeɪljə, -liə/ *n.* any plant of a particular group (Azalea) of the genus *Rhododendron,* family Ericaceae, comprising species with handsome, variously coloured flowers, some of which are familiar in cultivation. *Azalea was once considered a botanical genus but is now a nursery or horticultural classification.*

azimuth /'æzəməθ/ *n.* **1.** *Astron., Navig.* the arc of the horizon from the celestial meridian to the foot of the great circle passing through the zenith, the nadir, and the point of the celestial sphere in question (in astronomy commonly reckoned from the south point of the horizon towards the west point; in navigation reckoned from the north point of the horizon towards the east point). **2.** *Surveying, Gunnery, etc.* an angle measured clockwise from the south or north. −**azimuthal** /æzə-'mjuθəl/, *adj.* −**azimuthally** /æzə'mjuθəli/, *adv.*

azo- a prefix indicating the presence of a divalent nitrogen group.

azure /'eɪʒə, æ'zjʊə/ *adj.* of a sky blue colour. −**azury,** *adj.*

B b

B, b /biː/ *n.* **1.** the second letter of the English alphabet. **2.** the second in any series: *schedule B.* **3.** the second highest mark for school, college, or university work; beta. **4.** *Music* the seventh degree in the scale of C major or the second degree in the relative minor scale (A minor).

babaco /bəˈbakoʊ/ *n.* the seedless, five-sided fruit of the hybrid *Carica pentagonia,* similar to the pawpaw and originally from Ecuador.

baba ganoush /babə ɡəˈnʊʃ/ *n.* a paste of cooked eggplant seasoned with herbs and garlic. Also, **baba ghanoush, babaganoush, baba ghannouj.**

babble /ˈbæbəl/ *v.i.* **1.** to speak words quickly and unclearly. **2.** to talk foolishly or without purpose; chatter. **3.** to make a continuous soft sound; murmur: *the stream babbled along.* –*v.t.* **4.** to speak (words) quickly and unclearly. **5.** to tell thoughtlessly: *he babbled the whole secret.* –*n.* **6.** unclear speaking, as when many are talking at once. **7.** foolish talk; chatter. **8.** a soft, gentle sound.

babbler /ˈbæblə/ *n.* **1.** someone or something that babbles. **2.** any of several noisy, gregarious, insectivorous birds of the family Pomatostomidae, common in scrub and open forest of Australia, as the **grey-crowned babbler,** *Pomatostomus temporalis.* **3.** any of numerous other tropical and subtropical birds of the family Timaliidae, many of which have noisy, babbling calls.

babe /beɪb/ *n.* **1.** a baby. **2.** *Colloq.* a familiar term of address, especially to a woman. **3.** *Colloq.* a sexually attractive person. –*phr.* **4. a babe in arms,** a young baby. **5. a babe in the woods,** an innocent or inexperienced person.

babel /ˈbeɪbəl/ *n.* **1.** a confused mixture of sounds. **2.** a scene of noise and confusion.

baboon /bæˈbun, bə-/ *n.* any of various large, terrestrial monkeys, of the genera *Papio* and *Theropitheeus,* of Africa and Arabia, with a doglike muzzle, large cheek pouches, and a short tail. –**baboonish,** *adj.*

baby /ˈbeɪbi/ *n.* (*pl.* -**bies**) **1.** an infant; young child. **2.** a young animal. **3.** the youngest member of a family, group, etc. **4.** a childish person. **5.** *Colloq.* an invention, creation, or project of which one is particularly proud or for which one has a special responsibility. **6.** *Colloq.* (often used as a form of address) a lover or spouse. –*adj.* **7.** of, like, or suitable for a baby: *baby clothes.* **8.** infantile; babyish: *a baby face.* **9.** comparatively small: *baby carrots; a baby grand.* –*v.t.* (-**bied, -bying**) **10.** to treat like a young child; pamper. –*phr.* **11. leave someone holding the baby,** *Colloq.* to abandon someone with a problem or responsibility not rightly theirs. **12. make babies,** *Colloq.* (*humorous*) to have sexual intercourse. **13. throw the baby out with the bathwater,** to toss out what is valued along with what is considered to be rubbish. –**babyhood,** *n.* –**babyish,** *adj.* –**babyishly,** *adv.* –**babyishness,** *n.*

baby boom *n.* a sudden and marked increase in the number of babies born in a specified community.

baby boomer *n.* a person born in the baby boom following World War II.

baby capsule *n.* a plastic container for carrying a baby, which slots into a base, the whole structure being anchored into a motor vehicle and incorporating various safety design features.

babysit /ˈbeɪbɪsɪt/ *verb* (-**sat, -sitting**) –*v.i.* **1.** to take charge of a child while the parents are temporarily absent. –*v.t.* **2.** to mind (a child). **3.** to look after (something) while the owners are away: *we babysat the house while they were overseas.* –**babysitter,** *n.* –**babysitting,** *n.*

baccarat /ˈbækərə, bækəˈra/ *n.* a gambling card game played by a banker and two or more punters. Also, **baccara.**

bach /bætʃ/ *v.i. Aust., NZ Colloq.* to keep house alone or with a companion when neither is accustomed to housekeeping: *she was baching with a friend at North Sydney.* Also, **batch.** –**bacher,** *n.* –**baching,** *n.*

bachelor /ˈbætʃələ/ *n.* **1.** an unmarried man of any age. **2.** a person who has taken the first degree at a university: *Bachelor of Arts.* **3.** an unmated mature male animal, especially a young male fur seal kept from the breeding grounds by the older males. –**bachelordom** /ˈbætʃələdəm/, *n.* –**bachelorhood,** *n.*

bacillus /bəˈsɪləs/ *n.* (*pl.* -**cilli** /-ˈsɪli/) any of the group of rod-shaped bacteria which produce spores in the presence of free oxygen.

back[1] /bæk/ *n.* **1.** the hinder part of the human body, extending from the neck to the end of the spine. **2.** the part of the body of animals corresponding to the human back. **3.** the rear portion of any part or organ of the body: *the back of the head.* **4.** the whole body, with reference to clothing: *the clothes on his back.* **5.** the part opposite to or farthest from the face or front; the hinder side; the rear part: *the back of a hall.* **6.** the part covering the back, as of clothing. **7.** the spine: *to break one's back.* **8.** any rear part of an object serving to support, protect, etc.: *the back of a book.* **9.** *Naut.* the keel and keelson of a vessel. **10.** the strength to carry a burden or responsibility. **11.** *Football, etc.* one of the defending players behind the forwards. –*v.t.* **12.** to support, as with authority, influence, or money. **13.** to cause to move backwards; reverse the action of: *to back a car.* **14.** to bet in favour of: *to back a horse in the race.* **15.** to furnish with a back. **16.** to lie at the back of; form a back or background for: *sandhills back the beach.* –*v.i.* **17.** to go backwards. **18.** *Naut.* (of wind) to change direction anticlockwise. –*adj.* **19.** lying or being behind: *a back door.* **20.** relating to the back, especially the spine: *back pain.* **21.** away from the front position or rank: *the back seats of the theatre.* **22.** remote: *back country.* **23.** relating to the past: *back issues; back pay.* **24.** coming or going back; backward: *back current.* **25.** *Phonetics* pronounced with the tongue drawn back in the mouth as the vowel /ɔ/ in *bought* /bɒt/ or the consonant /k/ in *cup* /kʌp/. –*phr.* **26. at the back of, a.** in the part furthest from the front of: *at the back of the room; at the back of my mind.* **b.** behind: *the shed at the back of the house.* **c.** beyond: *at the back of Boree.* **d.** responsible for: *at the back of this confusion.* **27. back and fill, a.** *Naut.* to manoeuvre a sailing vessel to and fro in a channel by trimming the sails to be alternately full and then slack. **b.** *Colloq.* to drive a motor vehicle backwards and forwards, usually while parking. **c.** *Colloq.* to vacillate. **28. back away,** (sometimes fol. by *from*) to draw back, especially in alarm. **29. back away from,** to go back on; renege on: *to back away from one's promise.* **30. back down, a.** to retreat from or abandon an argument, opinion, claim, etc. **b.** *Rowing* to row a boat backwards. **31. back off,** (sometimes fol. by *from*) to retreat or withdraw. **32. back out, a.** to go or cause to move out backwards. **b.** (sometimes fol. by *of*) to withdraw; retreat: *to back out of a deal.* **c.** *Surfing* to slide off a wave by manoeuvring so that the front of the surfboard lifts out of the water. **33. back to back, a.** with the back of one (person or thing) opposed to the back of another (person or thing). **b.** consecutively: *the team won three matches back to back.* **34. back up, a.** to go backwards: *when he saw the snake, he started to back up.* **b.** to cause to move backwards: *she backed the car up.* **c.** to encourage; support: *please back me up at the meeting.* **d.** to give corroboration or credence to: *the evidence backs up her statement.* **e.** (of water) to cease to flow freely. **f.** *Computers* to copy (data) on to a tape, disk, etc., as a safety measure: *back up all the day's work.* **g.** *Computers* to back up data: *have you backed up yet?* **h.** *Mountaineering* to climb a chimney or cleft by pressing the feet on one side and the back on the other. **i.** *Cricket* (of the person batting who is not playing the ball) to advance down the wicket in readiness to run as the ball is bowled. **j.** *Cricket* (of a fielder) to cover a player receiving a return of the ball to prevent an overthrow. **35. back up for,** to seek a second share of (a commodity being distributed). **36. back water,** *Naut.* to reverse the forward thrust of a vessel. **37. behind someone's back,** in secret; deceitfully; in someone's absence. **38. be on someone's back,** *Colloq.* to urge someone constantly to further action: *she's always on my back to get a job.* **39. break the back of, a.** to deal with or accomplish the most difficult or arduous part of (a task, etc.). **b.** to overburden or overwhelm. **40. get off someone's back,** *Colloq.* to cease to annoy or harass someone. **41. get one's back up,** *Colloq.* to become annoyed. **42. get on someone's back,** *Colloq.* to begin to nag someone: *my parents got on my back when I failed the exam.* **43. on the back foot,** at a disadvantage. **44. on the back of,** close behind; immediately following in space or time. **45. out the back,** *Colloq.* in the rear part of a building or property, such as in the backyard. **46. put one's back into,** to perform with all one's energy and strength. **47. put someone's back up,** *Colloq.* to arouse someone's resentment. **48. see the back of, a.** to be rid of (a person). **b.** to be finished with (a situation, task, etc.). **49. turn one's back on,** to disregard, neglect, or ignore. **50. with one's back to the wall,** in a very difficult predicament. **–backer,** *n.*

back² /bæk/ *adv.* **1.** at, to, or towards the rear; backwards: *to step back.* **2.** towards the past: *to look back on one's youth.* **3.** ago: *a long while back.* **4. a.** later in time: *to move the launch back from June to August.* **b.** earlier in time: *to move the launch back from June to May.* **5.** towards the original starting point, place, or condition: *to go back to the old home.* **6.** returned home; in the original starting point, place, or condition again: *back where she started from*; *back in style*; *back in the saddle.* **7.** in reply; in return: *to pay back a loan.* **8.** in reversal of the usual course: *to take back a gift.* **9.** at an original starting point or place: *meanwhile, back in Australia.* *–phr.* **10. back and forth,** from side to side, to and fro. **11. back to ... week (day,** etc.**),** a time when former inhabitants of a town, students of a college, etc., return and join with present inhabitants, etc., in celebration of former and present times: *back to Mudgee week.* **12. go back,** to return. **13. make back,** to go in a direction to the rear of one's present position: *you make back to the house.*

backbench /'bækbɛntʃ/ *n.* Also, **back bench**. **1.** the non-office-holding parliamentary members of a political party who by tradition occupy the seats at the back of the legislature, behind the front benches where the ministers and members of the shadow cabinet sit: *the Labor backbench gave him hearty applause.* *–adj.* **2.** of or relating to the backbench. **–backbencher,** *n.*

backbite /'bækbaɪt/ *verb* (**-bit, -bitten** *or*, *Colloq.*, **-bit, -biting**) *–v.t.* **1.** to attack the character or reputation of secretly. *–v.i.* **2.** to speak evil of the absent; gossip. **–backbiter,** *n.* **–backbiting,** *n.*

backblocks /'bækblɒks/ *pl. n.* **1.** *Aust.*, *NZ* remote, sparsely inhabited inland country. **2.** *Aust. Colloq.* the outer suburbs of a city. **–backblock,** *adj.* **–backblocker,** *n.*

backbone /'bækboʊn/ *n.* **1.** the spinal or vertebral column; the spine. **2.** strength of character; resolution. *–phr.* **3. to the backbone,** in all respects: *loyal to the backbone.*

backbreaking /'bækbreɪkɪŋ/ *adj.* extremely arduous; physically exhausting.

back-burn *Aust.*, *NZ –verb* (**-burnt** *or* **-burned, -burning**) *–v.t.* **1.** to clear (land, grass or scrub) by burning into or against the wind. *–v.i.* **2.** to control a fire by burning off an area in advance of it, often into or against the wind. *–n.* **3.** the act or process of back-burning. **–back-burning,** *n.*

backburner /'bækbɜnə/ *n.* **1.** the rear burner of a stove, often used to keep food warm. *–phr.* **2. put on the backburner,** to take no further action on for the time being; postpone.

backchat /'bæktʃæt/ *n.* *Colloq.* impertinent talk; answering back.

back country *n. Aust.*, *NZ* **1.** sparsely populated rural regions. **2.** the remoter and less developed parts of a large rural property.

backdate /'bækdeɪt/ *v.t.* to date (something) earlier; apply retrospectively: *we shall backdate the pay rise.*

backdrop /'bækdrɒp/ *n.* the painted curtain or hanging at the back of a theatrical set.

backfire /bæk'faɪə/ *v.i.* **1.** (of an internal-combustion engine) to have a premature explosion in the cylinder or in the admission or exhaust passages. **2.** to bring results opposite to those planned: *the plot backfired.* *–n.* **3.** (in an internal-combustion engine) premature ignition of fuel, resulting in loss of power and loud explosive sound in the manifold. **4.** an explosion coming out of the breech of a firearm.

backgammon /'bækgæmən, bæk'gæmən/ *n.* a game played by two persons at a board with pieces or men moved in accordance with throws of dice.

background /'bækgraʊnd/ *n.* **1.** the ground or parts situated in the rear. **2. a.** the surface or ground against which the parts of a picture are relieved. **b.** the portions of a picture represented as in the distance. **3.** the social, historical and other antecedents which explain an event or condition: *the background of the war.* **4.** a person's origin and education, in relation to present character, status, etc. **5.** *Physics* the counting rate of a Geiger counter or other counter tube due to radioactive sources other than the one being measured. *–adj.* **6.** of or relating to the background; in the background. **7.** *Computers* of or relating to background processing. *–v.t.* **8.** to provide background information for. *–phr.* **9. in the background,** out of sight or notice; in obscurity.

background processing *n.* *Computers* the processing of a task at the same time as another task is being performed, as printing one document while another is being edited.

backhand /'bækhænd/ *n.* **1.** the hand turned backwards in making a stroke, as in tennis. **2. a.** a stroke, as in tennis, by a right-handed player from the left of the body (or the reverse for a left-handed player). **b.** *Bowls* a delivery of a bowl by a right-handed player in a left-hand direction with the bias inwards (or the reverse for a left-handed player). **3.** writing which slopes backwards or to the left. **-backhanded,** *adj.*

backhander /'bækhændə/ *n.* **1.** a backhanded blow or stroke. **2.** *Colloq.* an indirectly insulting remark. **3.** *Colloq.* a bribe: *he slipped the witness a backhander.*

backing /'bækɪŋ/ *n.* **1.** aid or support of any kind. **2.** something that forms the back or is placed at or attached to the back of anything to support or strengthen it. **3.** musical background for a singer. *-adj.* **4.** providing a backing. **5.** of, relating to, or designating an instrumentalist or singer who provides an accompaniment to a lead instrumentalist or singer.

backlash /'bæklæʃ/ *n.* **1.** any sudden, violent, or unexpected reaction. **2.** an antagonistic political or social reaction, sometimes sudden and violent, to a previous action construed as a threat.

backlight /'bæklaɪt/ *n.* **1.** light that illuminates the subject of a photograph, film, etc., from behind. *-v.t.* **(-lit, -lighting)** **2.** to illuminate in such a way.

backload /'bækloʊd/ *v.t.* **1.** to transport (cargo, passengers, etc.) on a return trip from a major destination: *to backload cargo from America into Australian ports.* *-adj.* **2.** of or relating to such cargo, passengers, etc. **-backloading,** *n.*

backlog /'bæklɒg/ *n.* **1.** an accumulation of business resources, stock, etc., acting as a reserve. **2.** an accumulation of work, correspondence, etc., awaiting attention. **3.** a log at the back of a fire.

back number *n.* **1.** an out-of-date issue of a serial publication. **2.** anything out of date.

back of beyond *Aust., NZ Colloq.* *-n.* **1.** a remote, inaccessible place. **2.** the far outback. *-adv.* **3.** in the outback. **4.** to the outback. Also, **back o' beyond.**

backpack /'bækpæk/ *n.* **1.** a light, strong bag designed to be carried on the back. **2.** portable equipment carried on the back, as television or film cameras, or firefighting, hiking, camping equipment, etc. *-v.i.* **3.** to travel from place to place, carrying one's possessions in a backpack.

backpacker /'bækpækə/ *n.* a traveller who carries their personal belongings in a backpack, and usually stays in lower priced accommodation.

back-pedal *v.i.* **1.** to press the pedals of a bicycle backwards, as in slowing down. **2.** to make an effort to slow down, or reverse one's course, as to avoid danger. **3.** to retreat in argument by moderating one's view or tone.

backroom /'bækrum/ *adj.* **1.** doing or relating to important work behind the scenes. *-phr.* **2. backroom boys,** *Colloq.* people operating behind the scenes, usually in enterprises which they do not wish to make public.

back-seat driver *n.* **1.** a passenger in a car who offers unsolicited advice to the driver. **2.** someone who gives advice or orders in matters which are not their responsibility.

backside /bæk'saɪd/ *n.* **1.** the back part. **2.** *Colloq.* the buttocks.

backslash /'bækslæʃ/ *n.* a short diagonal line (\), either printed or on a computer screen.

backslide /'bækslaɪd, bæk'slaɪd/ *v.i.* **(-slid, -slidden** *or* **-slid, -sliding)** to relapse into error or sin. **-backslider,** *n.*

backstab /'bækstæb/ *v.t.* **(-stabbed, -stabbing)** to do harm to (someone), especially someone defenceless or unsuspecting, as by making a treacherous attack upon their reputation. **-backstabber,** *n.*

backstage /bæk'steɪdʒ/ *adv.* **1.** out of the view of the audience in a theatre; in the wings or dressing rooms, or behind the backdrop or back flats. **2.** towards the rear of the stage; upstage. **3.** behind the scenes; in private.

backstop /'bækstɒp/ *n.* **1.** *Sport* a person, screen, or fence placed to prevent a ball going too far. **2.** a person or thing relied on for assistance when all else fails: *I have $500 as a backstop.*

backstreet /'bækstrit/ *n.* **1.** a small, unimportant street. *-adj.* **2.** illegal, illicit or improper.

backstroke /'bækstroʊk/ *n.* **1.** a backhanded stroke. **2.** a blow or stroke in return; recoil. **3.** a swimming stroke in which the swimmer is on his or her back performing a flutter-kick and rotating the arms alternately backwards.

back-to-back *adj.* **1.** consecutive: *she had four back-to-back wins.* *-adv.* **2.** consecutively: *they played two games back-to-back.*

back-to-front *adj.* reversed; disordered.

backtrack¹ /'bæktræk/ *v.i.* **1.** to return over the same course or route. **2.** to withdraw from an undertaking, position, etc.; pursue a reverse policy. **-backtracker,** *n.*

backtrack² /'bæktræk/ *n.* a minor road in worse condition than the main road and passing through less populated areas.

backup /'bækʌp/ *n.* **1.** support given subsequently; corroboration: *backup to the doctors' warnings.* **2.** a pent-up accumulation, especially of a liquid: *the backup of flood water.* **3.** a reserve supply or resource; a second means of support. **4.** *Computers* **a.** the process of copying data to a tape, CD-ROM, etc., so that a version is available if the original data is lost, corrupted, etc.: *to do the daily backup.* **b.** the data so copied: *to retrieve files from the backup.* *-adj.* **5.** of or relating to support given subsequently: *a backup campaign.* **6.** *Computers* of or relating to the process of backing up: *a backup tape.* Also, **back-up.**

backward /'bækwəd/ *adj.* **1.** Also, **backwards.** directed towards the back or past: *a backward glance.* **2.** Also, **backwards.** reversed; returning: *a backward movement.* **3.** behind others in growth, progress, or ability to learn: *a backward child.* **4.** reluctant; hesitating; bashful. *-adv.* **5.** → **backwards.** **-backwardly,** *adv.* **-backwardness,** *n.*

backwards /'bækwədz/ *adv.* **1.** towards the back or rear. **2.** with the back foremost. **3.** in reverse of the usual or right way: *to spell backwards.* **4.** towards the past. **5.** towards a worse or less advanced condition; retrogressively. *-phr.* **6. backwards and forwards,** to and fro. **7. bend** (or **lean**) (or **fall**) **over backwards,** *Colloq.* to go to a great deal of trouble. Also, **backward.**

backwash /'bækwɒʃ/ *n.* **1.** *Naut.* the water thrown back by a motor, oars or paddlewheels. **2.** *Aeronautics* the air which flows back from the propellers of an aircraft. **3.** a condition lasting after the event which caused it. **4.** the water which is backwashed from a swimming pool. *-v.t.* **5.** to send the water of (a swimming pool) through its filtering system in a reverse direction, so as to clean the filters.

backwater /'bækwɒtə/ *n.* **1.** *Naut.* water held or forced back, as by a dam, flood, tide, or current. **2.** a body of stagnant water connected to a river. **3.** a place or state considered to be stagnant or backward. **4.** a quiet, peaceful place. *-v.i.* **5.** to move a boat backwards by paddling with the oars.

backwoods /'bækwʊdz/ *pl. n.* **1.** sparsely populated rural regions. **2.** any unfamiliar or unfrequented area: *the backwoods of English literature.* *-adj.* Also, **backwood.** **3.** of or relating to the backwoods. **4.** rustically unsophisticated and uncouth.

backyard /bæk'jad/ *n.* **1.** an area, often of some size with gardens and lawn, at the back of a building, usually a house. **2.** *Colloq.* one's own neighbourhood, community, or society. *-adj.* **3.** of or relating to a small or part-time business conducted from a place of residence: *a backyard motor mechanic.* **4.** illegal, illicit, improper or unqualified: *backyard abortionist.*

bacon /'beɪkən/ n. 1. meat from the back and sides of the pig, salted and dried or smoked. –phr. 2. **bring home the bacon**, a. to support a family; provide for material needs. b. to succeed in a specific task. 3. **save someone's bacon**, to save someone from a dangerous or awkward situation.

bacteria /bæk'tɪərɪə/ pl. n. (sing. **bacterium**) a group of prokaryotes which are the simplest living organisms, exhibiting a wide range of genetic and metabolic variation and occurring in a wide range of habitats, various species of which are concerned in fermentation and putrefaction, the production of disease, and the fixing of atmospheric nitrogen. –**bacterial**, adj. –**bacterially**, adv.

bacteriology /bæk‚tɪəri'ɒlədʒi/ n. the branch of microbiology that deals with the identification of bacteria. –**bacteriological**, adj. –**bacteriologically**, adv. –**bacteriologist**, n.

bacterium /bæk'tɪəriəm/ n. the singular of **bacteria**.

bad /bæd/ adj. (**worse, worst**) 1. not good: bad conduct, a bad life. 2. defective; worthless: a bad coin. 3. unsatisfactory; poor; below standard; inadequate: bad heating; a bad businessman. 4. incorrect; faulty: a bad shot. 5. not valid; not sound: a bad claim. 6. having an injurious or unfavourable tendency or effect: bad air; bad for you. 7. in ill health; sick: to feel bad. 8. regretful; contrite; sorry; upset: to feel bad about an error. 9. unfavourable; unfortunate: bad news. 10. offensive; disagreeable; painful: a bad temper. 11. severe: a bad sprain. 12. rotten; decayed. 13. (**badder, baddest**) Colloq. wonderful; excellent; good. –n. 14. that which is bad. –adv. 15. badly. –phr. 16. **bad at**, unskilful or incompetent at (a specified activity): bad at tennis. 17. **go bad**, to decay; rot. 18. **go to the bad**, to become morally ruined or corrupt. 19. **in bad with**, Colloq. out of favour with. 20. **not bad**, Colloq. a. fair; mediocre. b. (rhetorical understatement) excellent. 21. **too bad**, Colloq. a. an expression used to indicate lack of sympathy or unwillingness to compromise. b. an expression used to indicate sympathy at some misfortune. 22. **to the bad**, in deficit; out of pocket: two hundred dollars to the bad. –**badness**, n.

bad blood n. hate; long-standing enmity; dislike.

bad cholesterol n. low-density lipoprotein (LDL), seen as being undesirable because it has a tendency to clog blood vessels; a high level of this component of cholesterol in the blood is associated with an increased risk of coronary artery disease. Compare **good cholesterol**.

bade /bæd/ v. past tense of **bid**.

badge /bædʒ/ n. 1. a mark, token or device worn as a sign of allegiance, membership, authority, achievement. 2. any emblem, token, or distinctive mark. –v.t. (**badged, badging**) 3. to mark with an insignia or brand: to badge a website. –phr. 4. **badge of honour**, evidence of an action for which one has earned respect, and of which one is consequently proud: he regarded his arrest at the demonstration as a badge of honour.

badger /'bædʒə/ n. 1. any of the various burrowing carnivorous mammals of the Mustelidae, as Meles meles, a European species, and Taxidea taxus, a similar American species. –v.t. 2. to harass; torment.

badinage /'bædənaʒ, -adʒ/ n. light, playful banter or raillery.

badly /'bædli/ adv. 1. in a bad manner; ill. 2. very much: to need badly; to want badly. –phr. 3. **badly off**, poor; impoverished: the Smiths are very badly off. 4. **badly off for**, badly supplied with: the school is badly off for money.

badminton /'bædmɪntən/ n. a game, similar to lawn tennis, but played with a high net and shuttlecock.

baffle /'bæfəl/ v.t. 1. to thwart or frustrate disconcertingly; baulk; confuse. 2. to puzzle or mystify. –n. 3. an artificial obstruction for checking or deflecting a flow, as of gases (as in a boiler), sounds (as in a radio), air as in a paraglider, etc. –**bafflement**, n. –**baffler**, n. –**baffling**, adj. –**bafflingly**, adv.

bag /bæg/ n. 1. a receptacle of leather, cloth, plastic, paper, etc. 2. a suitcase or other portable receptacle for carrying articles. 3. a handbag. 4. the contents of a bag. 5. a baggy part. 6. tally; score: a bag of five goals. 7. a. Hunting a hunter's take of game, etc. b. Angling a fisherman's take of fish. 8. Colloq. an unattractive woman. 9. Colloq. a chosen occupation, hobby, pursuit, etc.: golfing is his bag. –verb (**bagged, bagging**) –v.i. 10. to swell or bulge. 11. to hang loosely like an empty bag. –v.t. 12. to put into a bag. 13. to cause to swell or bulge; distend. 14. to kill or catch, as in hunting. 15. to grab; seize; steal. 16. Colloq. to arrest and jail. 17. Aust. Colloq. to criticise sarcastically. –phr. 18. **bag and baggage**, Colloq. with all one's possessions; completely. 19. **bag of bones**, Colloq. an animal or person emaciated through want. 20. **bag of tricks**, Colloq. a. a miscellaneous collection of items. b. a person never at a loss. 21. **bag of wind**, Colloq. a loquacious person. b. a football. 22. **bags of**, Colloq. a lot of: bags of money. 23. **carry the bag**, Colloq. to bear the responsibility; take the blame. 24. **in the bag**, Colloq. a. secured; certain to be accomplished: the contract is in the bag. b. Horseracing (of a horse, jockey, etc.) running to lose. 25. **rough as bags**, Aust., NZ Colloq. (of a person) extremely rough in either manners or looks. 26. **the bag**, Colloq. the breathalyser.

baggage /'bægɪdʒ/ n. 1. luggage, especially as for transportation in bulk. 2. Colloq. a pert or impudent young woman. 3. emotions, beliefs, etc., retained from previous experience, especially as influencing one's behaviour.

baggy /'bægi/ adj. (**-gier, -giest**) bag-like; hanging loosely. –**baggily**, adv. –**bagginess**, n.

bag lady n. a homeless, often elderly, woman, typically one who carries all her belongings in a shopping bag.

bagpipes /'bægpaɪps/ pl. n. a reed instrument consisting of a melody pipe and one or more accompanying drone pipes protruding from a windbag into which the air is blown by the mouth or a bellows. –**bagpipe**, adj. –**bagpiper**, n.

bags /bægz/ v.t. (**bagsed, bagsing**) Colloq. (usually in children's speech) to make a claim for: I bags sitting on the outside.

baht /bat/ n. the principal monetary unit of Thailand.

bail[1] /beɪl/ n. 1. (in criminal proceedings) the release of a prisoner from legal custody into the custody of persons acting as sureties, undertaking to produce the prisoner to the court at a later date or forfeit the security deposited as a condition of the release. 2. property given as security that a person released on bail will appear in court at the appointed time. 3. the person acting as surety or providing security for a person released on bail. 4. the position or privilege of being bailed. –v.t. Also, **bail out**. 5. a. to grant or to obtain the liberty of (a person under arrest) on security given for his or her appearance when required, as in court for trial. b. Colloq. to save (someone) who is under threat. –phr. 6. **jump bail**, to forfeit one's bail by absconding or failing to appear in court at the appointed time. 7. **stand** (or **go**) **bail for**, to supply bail for (someone).

bail[2] /beɪl/ verb (**bailed, bailing**) –v.t. 1. to remove (water) especially from a boat, as with a bucket or a can. –v.i. 2. to bail water in this manner. 3. Colloq. a. to depart; leave: come on, let's bail. b. to withdraw from or fail to honour a commitment, agreement, social engagement, etc.; renege: we had plans for tonight, but she bailed; don't bail on me this time. –n. 4. a bucket or other vessel for bailing. –phr. 5. **bail out**, a. to empty (a boat) of water by dipping: *to bail out a boat*. **b.** to make a parachute jump from a plane. **c.** *Colloq.* to abandon a dangerous position or course. Also, **bale**. –**bailer**, *n.*

bail³ /beɪl/ *n.* **1.** *Cricket* either of the two small bars or sticks laid across the tops of the stumps which form the wicket. **2.** a bar for separating horses in a stable. **3.** Also, **bails**. a framework for securing a cow's head during milking. **4.** Also, **bail rod**, **paper bail**. (in a typewriter) the rod which holds paper in place. –*phr.* **5. bail up**, **a.** to bring (a wild pig, etc.) to bay with dogs. **b.** to secure the head of (a cow) in a bail. **c.** to hold up and rob. **d.** to delay (someone) unnecessarily, as in conversation.

bailiff /ˈbeɪləf/ *n.* **1.** an officer employed by a sheriff to serve writs and summonses, execute processes, make arrests, fulfil court orders, collect payments of judgement debts, etc. **2.** an overseer of a landed estate.

bails /beɪlz/ *pl. n. Aust., NZ* **1.** → **bail³** (def. 3). **2. the bails**, the milking shed.

bain-marie /bæn-məˈriː/ *n.* a cooking vessel containing hot water into which another vessel is placed to heat its contents gently.

bait /beɪt/ *n.* **1.** food, etc., used on a hook or trap to catch fish or animals. **2.** food containing poison, etc., used to kill or drug animals. **3.** anything that is used to attract or tempt. –*v.t.* **4.** to put bait on (a hook or trap). **5.** to add harmful substances to (food) to kill or drug animals. **6.** to set dogs upon (an animal) for sport. **7.** to make (someone) angry for amusement by making rude remarks, etc. –**baiter**, *n.*

baize /beɪz/ *n.* a soft, usually green, woollen fabric resembling felt, used chiefly for the tops of billiard and card tables.

bake /beɪk/ *v.t.* **1.** to cook by dry heat in an oven, under coals, or on heated metals or stones. **2.** to harden by heat. –*v.i.* **3.** to bake bread, etc. **4.** to become baked. **5.** to become very hot, especially by sunbathing. –**baker**, *n.* –**bakery**, *n.*

baker's dozen *n.* thirteen, reckoned as a dozen.

baking powder *n.* any of various powders used as a leavening agent in baking, composed of sodium bicarbonate and an acid substance (such as cream of tartar) which together react with moisture to release carbon dioxide.

baking soda *n.* → **sodium bicarbonate**.

baklava /ˈbæklavə, ˈbaː-/ *n.* a Middle Eastern dessert made from filo pastry layered with chopped walnuts, and soaked in a honey and sugar syrup.

balalaika /bæləˈlaɪkə/ *n.* a Russian musical instrument with a triangular body and guitar-like neck, and usually three strings.

balance /ˈbæləns/ *n.* **1.** an instrument for weighing, usually a swaying bar with scales (pans) hanging at the ends. **2.** a condition in which all parts are equal in weight, amount, etc.; equilibrium. **3.** the habit of calm behaviour, judgement, etc. **4.** a pleasing arrangement of elements in a work of art. **5.** something used to produce balance. **6.** what remains or is left over. **7.** *Accounting* **a.** equality between totals of two sides of an account. **b.** the difference between the totals of money received and paid out in an account. –*verb* (**-anced, -ancing**) –*v.t.* **8.** to weigh in a balance. **9.** to compare the weight or importance of: *let's balance these arguments*. **10.** to serve as equal weight or force to; counterbalance: *your calmness balances my temper*. **11.** to put or hold in a state of balance: *balance a book on your head; balance the shapes in a design*. **12.** *Accounting* to find or equalise the difference between the two sides of an account. –*v.i.* **13.** to be equal in weight, parts, etc.; be in equilibrium: *the account doesn't balance; do these scales balance?* **14.** *Accounting* to arrange accounts in

order to make the totals of both sides equal. –*phr.* **15. balance the books**, *Accounting* to achieve a situation where the debit total of an account equals the credit total. **16. lose one's balance**, to fall over as a result of failing to maintain the equilibrium of one's body.

balanced /ˈbælənst/ *adj.* **1.** having a balance; having weight evenly distributed or being in good proportion. **2.** (of a discussion, opinion, etc.) taking everything into account in a fair, well-judged way; not biased. **3.** (of a diet) having different kinds of food in the correct proportion to maintain health.

balance of payments *n.* an account of a nation's total payments to foreign countries (debits) and its total receipts from foreign sources (credits).

balance of trade *n.* the difference between the value of the exports and imports of a country, said to be favourable or unfavourable as exports are greater or less than imports.

balance sheet *n.* *Accounting* the analysis at a given date of an enterprise's financial position, in accordance with which the total equities listed on one side are balanced by the assets listed on the other.

balcony /ˈbælkəni/ *n.* (*pl.* **-nies**) **1.** a balustraded or raised and railed platform projecting from the wall of a building. **2.** (in some cinemas and theatres) the highest gallery. –**balconied**, *adj.*

bald /bɔld/ *adj.* **1.** lacking hair (on the head): *bald head; bald person*. **2.** lacking some natural growth or covering: *bald mountain*. **3.** (of tyres) having the outer rubber worn off. **4.** bare; plain; unadorned: *bald style of writing*. **5.** open; undisguised: *bald lie*. **6.** *Zool.* having white on the head: *bald eagle*. –**balding**, *adj.* –**baldish**, *adj.* –**baldly**, *adv.* –**baldness**, *n.*

bale¹ /beɪl/ *n.* **1.** a large bundle or package prepared for storage or transportation, especially one closely compressed and secured by cords, wires, hoops or the like, sometimes with a wrapping: *a bale of wool*. –*v.t.* **2.** to make into bales. –**baler**, *n.*

bale² /beɪl/ *v.t.*, *v.i.*, *n.* → **bail²**. –**baler**, *n.*

baleful /ˈbeɪlfəl/ *adj.* full of menacing or malign influences; pernicious. –**balefully**, *adv.* –**balefulness**, *n.*

ball¹ /bɔl/ *n.* **1.** a spherical or approximately spherical body; a sphere. **2.** a round or roundish body, of different materials and sizes, hollow or solid, for use in various games, as cricket, football, tennis, or golf. **3.** any game played with a ball, especially an informal or unstructured ball game as played by children. **4.** a throw, play, action, movement, etc., of a ball: *a low ball; a flighted ball*. **5.** *Baseball, Softball* a pitch by the pitcher that passes above the batter's shoulder, below the knee or outside his or her reach, four of which entitle the batter to walk (def. 5). **6.** any part of a thing that is rounded or protuberant: *the ball of the thumb*. **7.** *Colloq.* a testicle. –*v.t.* **8.** to make into a ball or balls. **9.** *Colloq.* (*taboo*) to have sexual intercourse with. –*v.i.* **10.** to form or gather into a ball. –*phr.* **11. a ball of muscle** (or **strength**) (or **style**), *Colloq.* a person who is very healthy (very strong) (very stylish). **12. do one's balls on**, *Colloq.* (of a man) to become infatuated with. **13. grab someone by the balls**, *Colloq.* to impress someone favourably. **14. have someone by the balls**, *Colloq.* to have someone in one's power. **15. have the ball at one's feet**, to be in a position of immediate opportunity or obligation to act. **16. have the ball in one's court**, to have the opportunity or obligation to act. **17. keep the ball rolling**, to keep something going; keep up the rate of progress or activity. **18. on the ball**, in touch with a situation, reality, etc.; alert; sharp. **19. play ball**, *Colloq.* (sometimes fol. by *with*) to work together; cooperate. **20. play hard ball**, *Orig. US Colloq.* to behave aggressively and with ruthless determination. **21. start** (or **set**) **the ball rolling**, to start an operation; set an activity in motion. **22. that's the way the ball bounces,** *Chiefly US Colloq.* that's how things are.

ball[2] /bɔl/ *n.* **1.** a social gathering (usually formal) at which people dance. *–phr.* **2. have (oneself) a ball,** *Colloq.* to have an extremely pleasurable experience.

ballad /'bæləd/ *n.* **1.** a simple narrative poem, often of popular origin, composed in short stanzas, especially one of romantic character and adapted for singing. **2.** any light, simple song, especially one of sentimental or romantic character, having two or more stanzas, all sung to the same melody. **3.** the musical setting for a ballad. **4.** a style of pop song with a romantic or sentimental theme, often narrative in form and usually sung at a relatively slow tempo. *–***balladist,** *n.*

ballast /'bæləst/ *n.* **1.** heavy material carried by a ship to keep it steady, or by a balloon to control height. **2.** anything that gives mental, moral, or political steadiness. **3.** broken stone, etc., placed under railway sleepers for support and drainage. *–v.t.* **4.** to supply with ballast: *to ballast a ship.* **5.** to give steadiness to.

ball bearing *n.* **1.** a bearing in which the shaft or journal of a machine turns upon a number of steel balls running in an annular track. **2.** (*in non-technical use*) any of the steel balls so used.

ballerina /bælə'rinə/ *n.* (*pl.* **-nas**) **1.** the principal female dancer in a ballet company. **2.** any female ballet-dancer.

ballet /'bæleɪ/ *n.* **1.** a style of European formal dancing, often designed to tell a story, using graceful, precise movement. **2.** a performance in this style of dancing. **3.** a company of dancers.

ballistic /bə'lɪstɪk/ *adj.* **1.** of or relating to ballistics. **2.** of or relating to projectiles. **3.** of or relating to the motion of projectiles proceeding under no power and acted on only by gravitational force, etc. *–phr.* **4. go ballistic,** *Colloq.* to become extremely angry. *–***ballistics,** *n.*

balloon /bə'lun/ *n.* **1.** a bag, usually round or roundish, filled with a lighter-than-air gas, designed to rise and float in the atmosphere. It may have a basket for passengers, etc. **2.** a blow-up rubber bag, usually brightly coloured, used for decoration and as a children's toy. **3.** something shaped like a balloon. **4.** a balloon shape containing words said by speaker shown in a comic strip picture. *–v.i.* **5.** to go up or ride in a balloon. **6.** to swell like a balloon. *–v.t.* **7.** to inflate with air. *–phr.* **8. burst someone's balloon,** *Colloq.* to destroy someone's daydream or fantasy. *–***balloonist,** *n.*

ballot /'bælət/ *n.* **1.** a ticket or paper used in voting. **2.** the number of votes placed or recorded: *a large ballot.* **3.** Also, **secret ballot.** secret voting with printed or written ballots or voting machines. **4.** the right to vote: *to give the ballot to 18 year-olds.* **5.** a small ball used in voting or drawing lots. *–v.i.* (**-loted, -loting**) **6.** to vote by ballot. **7.** to draw lots: *to ballot for places.* *–***balloter,** *n.*

ballpark /'bɔlpak/ *–n.* **1.** *US* a park in which games, especially baseball, are played. *–adj.* **2.** *Colloq.* broadly estimated: *a ballpark figure.* *–phr.* **3. in the ballpark,** *Colloq.* within acceptable limits; relatively close to a desired target.

ballpoint pen /,bɔlpɔɪnt 'pɛn/ *n.* a pen in which the point is a fine ball bearing, depositing an extremely thin film of ink, which is stored in a cartridge. Also, **ballpoint.**

balls /bɔlz/ *Colloq.* *–n.* **1.** boldness; forcefulness: *you have to have balls to win through.* *–interj.* **2.** an exclamation of repudiation, ridicule, etc. *–phr.* **3. balls something up,** to bring something to a state of hopeless confusion or difficulty: *you've really ballsed the whole thing up now.* **4. balls up,** to make an error.

ball-up *n.* *Aust. Rules* the bouncing of the ball by the field umpire to restart play after the ball has been smothered in a pack.

ballyhoo /bæli'hu/ *n.* (*pl.* **-hoos**) **1.** a clamorous attempt to win customers or advance any cause; blatant advertising or publicity. **2.** clamour or outcry. *–v.t.* (**-hooed, -hooing**) **3.** to advertise by sensational methods.

balm /bam/ *n.* **1.** any of various oily, fragrant, resinous substances, often of medicinal value, exuding from certain plants, especially tropical trees of the genus *Commiphora*. See **balsam** (def. 1). **2.** any aromatic or fragrant ointment. **3.** aromatic fragrance; sweet smell. **4.** any of various aromatic plants, especially of the genus *Melissa*, as *M. officinalis*, a lemon-scented perennial herb. **5.** anything which heals, soothes, or mitigates pain.

Balmain bug /,bælmeɪn 'bʌg/ *n.* an edible, curiously flattened, marine crustacean, *Ibacus incisus*, first discovered in Sydney Harbour; closely related to the shovel-nosed lobster.

balmy /'bami/ *adj.* (**-mier, -miest**) **1.** mild and refreshing; soft; soothing: *balmy weather.* **2.** having the qualities of balm; aromatic; fragrant: *balmy leaves.* **3.** *US →* **barmy.** *–***balmily,** *adv.* *–***balminess,** *n.*

baloney /bə'louni/ *n.* *Colloq.* nonsense; insincere or idle talk; eyewash; waffle. Also, **boloney.**

balsa /'bɔlsə/ *n.* **1.** a tree, *Ochroma lagopus*, of the family Bombacaceae, of tropical America. **2.** the extremely light wood of this tree, formerly used in life-preservers, rafts, etc., now much used in crafts.

balsam /'bɔlsəm, 'bɒl-/ *n.* **1.** any of various fragrant exudations from certain trees, especially of the genus *Commiphora*, as the balm of Gilead (**balsam of Mecca**). See **balm** (def. 1). **2.** a similar product (**balsam of Peru** and **balsam of Tolu**) yielded by the trees, *Myroxylon pereirae* and *M. balsamum* of Central and South America. **3.** a plant or tree yielding a balsam. **4.** any of various plants of the genus *Impatiens*, as *I. balsamina*, a common garden annual and *I. sultanii*, a common garden perennial with red, pink or white flowers. **5.** any aromatic ointment, whether for ceremonial or medicinal use. **6.** any healing or soothing agent or agency. *–***balsamaceous** /bɔlsə'meɪʃəs, bɒl-/, *adj.*

balustrade /bælə'streɪd/ *n.* a railing or coping with the row of balusters supporting it. *–***balustraded,** *adj.*

bamboo /bæm'bu/ *n.* (*pl.* **-boos**) **1.** any of the woody or treelike tropical and subtropical grasses of the genus *Bambusa* and allied genera. **2.** the hollow woody stem of such a plant, used for building purposes and for making furniture, poles, etc. *–adj.* **3.** made with bamboo: *bamboo ladder.*

bamboozle /bæm'buzəl/ *v.t.* **1.** to deceive by trickery; impose upon. **2.** to perplex; mystify. *–***bamboozlement,** *n.* *–***bamboozler,** *n.*

ban[1] /bæn/ *v.t.* (**banned, banning**) **1.** to prohibit; interdict: *to ban a meeting*; *to ban a book.* *–n.* **2.** a prohibition by law or decree.

ban[2] /bæn/ *n.* a public proclamation or edict.

banal /'beɪnəl, bə'nal/ *adj.* hackneyed; trite. *–***banality** /bə'næləti/, *n.* *–***banally,** *adv.*

banana /bə'nanə/ *n.* **1.** a plant of the tropical genus *Musa*, of which various species are cultivated for their nutritious fruit. **2.** the pulpy fruit, especially that of *M. × paradisiaca*, with yellow skin when ripe, growing in clusters. *–phr. Colloq.* **3. cool bananas,** an exclamation of understanding and agreement. **4. go bananas,** to become uncontrollably angry. **5. top bananas,** an exclamation indicating approval, admiration, etc.

banana bender *n.* *Colloq.* a Queenslander. Also, **banana-bender, bananabender.**

banana republic *n.* **1.** any small tropical country, especially of South or Central America, considered as backward, politically unstable, etc., and dependent on the trade of rich foreign nations. **2.** any country or state considered as backward.

band[1] /bænd/ *n.* **1. a.** a company of persons associated or acting together; company, party or troop. **b.** a group of animals. **2.** a company of musicians constituted according to the kind of music played, usually playing for performance or as an accompaniment to dancing. –*v.t.* **3.** to unite in a group, troop, company or confederacy. –*phr.* **4. band together**, to unite; form a group; confederate.

band[2] /bænd/ *n.* **1.** any strip that contrasts with its surroundings in colour, texture, or material. **2.** a thin, flat strip of some material for binding, confining, reinforcing, trimming, or some other purpose. **3.** *Radio* a range of frequencies lying between any two well-defined limits. **4.** a ring, especially one which is wide and flat: *a plain wedding band.* –*v.t.* **5.** to mark or fasten with a band or bands.

bandage /'bændɪdʒ/ *n.* **1.** a strip of cloth or other material used to bind up a wound, hold a dressing in place, etc. **2.** anything used as a band or ligature. –*v.t.* (**-daged**, **-daging**) **3.** to bind or cover with a bandage. –**bandager**, *n.*

bandaid /'bændeɪd/ (*from trademark*) –*n.* **1.** a light adhesive dressing for covering superficial wounds. –*adj.* **2.** palliative; superficially helpful and short-term.

bandana /bæn'dænə/ *n.* a large coloured handkerchief or scarf with spots or figures, usually white on a red or blue background. Also, **bandanna**.

B & B *n.* → **bed and breakfast**. Also, **b & b**.

bandeau /bæn'doʊ/ *n.* (*pl.* **-deaux** /-doʊz/) **1.** a band worn around the head. **2.** a strapless top, usually made of elastic material.

bandicoot /'bændɪkut/ *n.* **1.** any of various small, omnivorous, somewhat rat-like Australian and New Guinean marsupials of the families Paramelidae and Peroryctidea. **2.** any of the very large rats of the genus *Bandicota*, of India and Sri Lanka, as *B. bandicota*; Malabar rat. –*v.t.* **3.** *Colloq.* to dig up (root vegetables, potatoes, etc.) with the fingers, leaving the top of the plant undisturbed. –*phr.* **4. bald as a bandicoot**, *Aust. Colloq.* remarkably bald. **5. bandy as a bandicoot**, *Aust. Colloq.* remarkably bandy-legged. **6. barmy as a bandicoot**, *Aust.*, *NZ Colloq.* remarkably irrational or eccentric. **7. like a bandicoot on a burnt ridge**, *Aust. Colloq.* lonely and forlorn. **8. lousy as a bandicoot**, *Aust. Colloq.* miserly. **9. miserable as a bandicoot**, *Aust.*, *NZ Colloq.* extremely miserable.

bandit /'bændət/ *n.* **1.** a robber, especially one who robs by violence. **2.** an outlaw.

bandstand /'bændstænd/ *n.* a platform, for band performances, often roofed when outdoors.

bandwagon /'bændwægən/ *n.* **1.** *US* a wagon often elaborately decorated, used to transport musicians, as at the head of a procession or parade. –*phr.* **2. climb** (or **jump**) **on the bandwagon**, to join the winning side; take advantage of a popular movement or fashion; follow the crowd.

bandy[1] /'bændi/ *v.t.* (**-died**, **-dying**) **1.** to pass from one to another, or back and forth; give and take: *to bandy blows.* **2.** to throw or strike to and fro, or from side to side, as a ball in tennis. –*phr.* **3. bandy about**, to talk about in a non-specific way, often without a full grasp of the facts: *bandying about figures in the millions.* **4. bandy words**, to engage in an argument, with each person countering the position held by the other.

bandy[2] /'bændi/ *adj.* (**-dier**, **-diest**) (of legs) having a bend or crook outward.

bandy-legged /'bændi-lɛgəd, -lɛgd/ *adj.* having crooked legs; bow-legged.

bane /beɪn/ *n.* **1.** something that causes death or destroys life. **2.** a deadly poison. **3.** a person or thing that ruins or destroys: *he was the bane of her life.* **4.** ruin; destruction; death.

bang[1] /bæŋ/ *n.* **1.** a loud, sudden explosive noise, as the discharge of a gun. **2.** a resounding stroke or blow. **3.** *Colloq.* (*taboo*) an instance of sexual intercourse. **4.** *US Colloq.* energy; spirit. **5.** *Colloq.* a thrill; excitement. –*v.t.* **6.** to strike or beat resoundingly: *she banged the desk with her fist.* **7.** to slam: *he always bangs the door.* **8.** to knock or bump: *he banged his head.* **9.** to place or move with a bang: *to bang a plate down.* **10.** *Colloq.* (*taboo*) to have sexual intercourse with. –*v.i.* **11.** to strike violently or noisily: *to bang on the door.* **12.** to make a loud noise, as of violent blows: *the guns banged away.* **13.** to slam; to slam repeatedly: *the door banged.* **14.** *Colloq.* (*taboo*) to have sexual intercourse. –*adv.* **15.** *Colloq.* exactly; precisely; just: *bang in the middle.* –*phr.* **16. bang on, a.** dead-centre. **b.** perfectly correct. **c.** to dwell on a topic persistently or tediously. **17. bang one's head against a brick wall**, to make repeated attempts to do something without ever achieving success. **18. bang the drum, a.** to promote a cause, etc., with fervour. **b.** to present one's case in an unwarrantedly emphatic and longwinded fashion. **19. bang up**, to make pregnant. **20. go off with a bang**, to be a considerable success: *the party went off with a bang.* **21. the whole bang lot** (or **circus**), everything. **22. with a (big) bang**, in a highly visible and noticeable manner.

bang[2] /bæŋ/ *n.* **1.** (*oft. pl.*) a fringe of banged hair. –*v.t.* **2.** to cut (the hair) so as to form a fringe over the forehead. **3.** to cut the hair of the tail of (a horse, etc.) straight across, just below the dock.

bangalay /bæŋ'æli/ *n.* a tree, *Eucalyptus botryoides*, family Myrtaceae, of New South Wales and eastern Victoria, growing near the coast, and yielding durable red timber.

banger /'bæŋə/ *Colloq.* –*n.* **1.** a sausage. –*phr.* **2. three bangers short of a barbie**, dimwitted.

bangle /'bæŋgəl/ *n.* a bracelet in the form of a ring, without a clasp.

bangtail muster /'bæŋteɪl mʌstə/ *n.* **1.** a round-up of animals for counting, during which the tails of the animals are docked as they are counted so that none is counted more than once. **2.** a carnival or sports day in an Australian country town.

banish /'bænɪʃ/ *v.t.* **1.** to condemn to exile; expel from or relegate to a country or place by authoritative decree. **2.** to compel to depart; send, drive, or put away: *to banish sorrow.* –**banisher**, *n.* –**banishment**, *n.*

banister /'bænəstə/ *n.* **1.** one of the supports of a stair rail, either plain or resembling a pillar. **2.** (*oft. pl.*) a stair rail and its supports. Also, **bannister**.

banjo /'bændʒoʊ/ *n.* (*pl.* **-jos**) **1.** a musical instrument of the guitar family, having a circular body covered in front with tightly stretched parchment, and played with the fingers or a plectrum. **2.** *Colloq.* a shovel or spade. **3.** *Colloq.* a frying pan. –**banjoist**, *n.*

bank[1] /bæŋk/ *n.* **1.** a long pile or mass: *bank of earth*; *bank of snow*; *bank of clouds.* **2.** a slope or acclivity. **3.** *Physical Geog.* the slope immediately bordering the course of a river along which the water normally runs. **4.** the lateral inclination of an aeroplane, especially during a curve. **5.** the lateral inclination of a road at curves. –*v.t.* **6.** to border with or like a bank; embank. **7.** to tip or incline (an aeroplane) laterally. **8.** to cover up (a fire) with ashes or fuel and close the dampers, to make it burn long and slowly. –*v.i.* **9.** to tip or incline laterally, as an aircraft, road, cycle racing track, etc. –*phr.* **10. bank and dank**, *NZ* (of a river) in flood. **11. bank up, a.** to rise in or form banks, as clouds or snow: *the snow is banking up.* **b.** to accumulate: *the line of cars banked up.* **c.** to form into a bank or mass: *to bank up the snow.*

bank² /bæŋk/ *n.* **1.** an institution for receiving and lending money (in some cases, issuing notes or holding current accounts that serve as money) and transacting other financial business. **2.** the office or quarters of such an institution. **3.** (in games) **a.** the stock or fund of pieces from which the players draw. **b.** the fund of the manager or the dealer. **5.** any store place. **5.** any store or reserve: *a blood bank*. *–v.i.* **6.** to exercise the functions of a bank or banker. **7.** to keep money in, or have an account with, a bank. **8.** (in games) to hold the bank. *–v.t.* **9.** to deposit in a bank. *–phr.* **10. bank on**, to rely or count on.

bank³ /bæŋk/ *n.* **1.** an arrangement of objects in line. **2.** *Music* a row of keys in an organ. **3.** a row or tier of oars.

bank bill *n.* a commercial bill which has been accepted or endorsed by a trading bank.

banker /'bæŋkə/ *n.* **1.** someone who manages a bank or is in the banking business. **2.** someone who holds or supplies money for another. **3.** (in games) the keeper or holder of the bank.

banknote /'bæŋknoʊt/ *n.* a promissory note, payable on demand, issued by a central bank and intended to circulate as money.

bankroll /'bæŋkroʊl/ *n.* **1.** a roll of money notes. *–v.t.* **2.** to provide funds for; act as backer for.

bankrupt /'bæŋkrʌpt/ *n.* **1.** *Law* a person judged insolvent by a court, whose property is therefore to be managed by a trustee for the benefit of the creditors, under bankruptcy law. **2.** any person unable to pay money owed to others. **3.** a person completely lacking some human quality: *a moral bankrupt*. *–adj.* **4.** *Law* subject to having (one's) property managed by a trustee for the benefit of the creditors, under bankruptcy law. **5.** completely lacking some human quality: *hack politicians bankrupt of ideas and imagination*. *–v.t.* **6.** to make bankrupt. *–phr.* **7. go bankrupt**, **a.** to submit oneself to being declared officially bankrupt. **b.** to become insolvent and unable to pay one's debts.

banksia /'bæŋksiə/ *n.* **1.** any plant of the Australian genus *Banksia* comprising shrubs and trees with leathery leaves and dense cylindrical heads of flowers, sometimes called a bottlebrush. **2.** Also, **Banksia rose**, **Banksian rose**. a Chinese species of climbing rose, *Rosa banksiae*, having yellow or white flowers.

banner /'bænə/ *n.* **1.** the flag of a country, army, troop, etc. **2.** an ensign or the like bearing some device or motto, as one borne in processions. **3.** anything displayed as a profession of principles: *the banner of freedom*. **4.** *Journalism* a headline which extends across the width of the newspaper, usually at the top of the first page. **5.** Also, **web banner**. *Internet* a large rectangular section on a web page, often for branding or advertising purposes. *–bannered, adj.*

banns /bænz/ *pl. n. Eccles.* notice of an intended marriage, formerly required by English law to be given three times in the parish church of each of the betrothed. Also, **bans**.

banquet /'bæŋkwət/ *n.* **1.** a formal and ceremonious meal, often one given to celebrate an event or to honour a person. **2.** (in a restaurant) a meal consisting of a fixed number of set dishes eaten communally. *–banqueter, n.*

bantam /'bæntəm/ *n.* **1.** (*oft. upper case*) a domestic fowl of any of certain varieties or breeds characterised by very small size. **2.** a small person, especially a quarrelsome one.

bantamweight /'bæntəmweɪt/ *n.* **1.** a light weight division in boxing. **2.** a boxer of this weight class.

banter /'bæntə/ *n.* **1.** playfully teasing language; good-humoured raillery. *–v.t.* **2.** to address with banter; chaff. *–v.i.* **3.** to use banter. *–banterer, n. –bantering, adj. –banteringly, adv.*

banyan /'bænjæn/ *n.* any of various figs of India or Indonesia, especially *Ficus benghalensis*, whose branches send out adventitious roots to the ground, sometimes causing the tree to spread over a wide area. Also, **banian**.

baobab /'beɪoʊbæb/ *n.* → **boab**.

baptise /bæp'taɪz/ *v.t.* **1.** to immerse in water, or sprinkle or pour water on, in the Christian rite of baptism. **2.** to cleanse spiritually; initiate or dedicate by purifying. **3.** to christen. Also, **baptize**. *–baptiser, n.*

baptism /'bæptɪzəm/ *n.* **1.** a ceremonial immersion in water, or application of water, as an initiatory rite or sacrament of the Christian church. **2.** any similar ceremony or action of initiation, dedication, etc. *–baptismal /bæp'tɪzməl/, adj. –baptismally, adv.*

bar¹ /ba/ *n.* **1.** a relatively long and evenly shaped piece of some solid substance, especially one of wood or metal used as a guard or obstruction, or for some mechanical purpose: *the bars of a fence*. **2.** *Athletics* the cross-piece of wood, metal, or plastic which jumpers must clear in the high jump or the pole vault. **3.** an oblong piece of any solid material: *a bar of soap*; *a bar of toffee*. **4.** the amount of material in a bar. **5.** an ingot, lump, or wedge of gold or silver. **6.** *Mining* a band of rock or gravel which traps gold in a stream. **7.** a ridge of sand or gravel, usually just below the surface of the water, formed by currents such as those in a river or at the mouth of a harbour or just offshore in the ocean. **8.** anything which obstructs, hinders, or impedes; an obstacle; a barrier: *a bar to vice*. **9.** *Music* **a.** Also, **bar line**. the vertical line drawn across the stave to mark the metrical accent. **b.** that which is included between two bars. **10.** a counter or a room where alcoholic drinks, etc., are served to customers. **11.** any counter or place specialising in the sale of one particular commodity: *wine bar*. **12.** *Heraldry* a wide horizontal band crossing the field. **13.** a strip of silver or some other metal added to a medal below the clasp as a further distinction. *–v.t.* (**barred**, **barring**) **14.** to provide or fasten with a bar or bars: *to bar the door*. **15.** to shut in or out by or as by bars. **16.** to block (a way, etc.) as with a barrier; prevent or hinder, as access. **17.** to exclude; except. **18.** to forbid; preclude: *no holds barred*. **19.** to mark with bars, stripes, or bands. *–prep.* **20.** except; omitting; but: *bar none*. *–phr.* **21. all over bar the shouting**, settled or concluded except for some minor details. **22. lower the bar**, to lower the level of performance required. **23. not to be able to have** (or **stand**) **a bar of**, *Aust.*, *NZ* to dislike strongly; detest. **24. not to have a bar of**, *Aust.*, *NZ* not to tolerate: *I won't have a bar of it*. **25. raise the bar**, to raise the level of performance required. **26. the bar**, practising barristers collectively.

bar² /ba/ *n.* a unit of pressure equal to 100 000 pascals.

barb /bab/ *n.* **1.** a point or pointed part projecting backwards from a main point, as of a fishhook, an arrowhead, or a fence wire. **2.** a sharp or unkind implication in a remark; cutting comment. **3.** any of a large number of small, cyprinoid fishes of the genera *Barbus* or *Puntius*, widely cultivated for home aquariums. *–v.t.* **4.** to furnish with a barb or barbs. *–barbed, adj.*

barbarian /ba'bɛəriən/ *n.* **1.** a person belonging to a non-literate culture regarded as uncivilised, especially any of the ancient European peoples other than the Greeks and Romans. **2.** an ignorant and uncouth person. *–adj.* **3.** belonging to a culture regarded as uncivilised. **4.** ignorant and uncouth. *–barbaric, adj. –barbarism, barbarity, n. –barbarous, adj. –barbarously, adv.*

barbecue /'babəkju/ *n.* **1.** a fireplace or metal frame for cooking meat, etc., over open fire. **2.** meat cooked in this way. **3.** a rack or spit on which animals, as pig or lamb, are roasted. **4.** a social occasion, usually outdoors, where barbecued food is served *–v.t.* (**-cued**,

-cuing) 5. to cook on barbecue. Also, **barbeque, bar-b-q.**

barbecue stopper *n.* a topic of conversation or issue for discussion which is of general concern, especially one of political significance.

barbed wire /babd ˈwaɪə, bab ˈwaɪə/ *n.* steel wire on which barbs are located at short intervals, used largely for fencing in livestock, protecting a defensive military position, etc. Also, **barbwire.**

barbell /ˈbabɛl/ *n.* an apparatus used in weightlifting, consisting of a steel bar, about 2 metres long, to the ends of which disc-shaped weights are attached.

barber /ˈbabə/ *n.* **1.** someone whose occupation it is to cut and dress the hair of customers, especially men, and to shave or trim the beard. **2.** *NZ* a cold, keen, cutting wind. *–v.t.* **3.** to trim or dress the beard and hair of.

barbie /ˈbabi/ *n. Aust., NZ Colloq.* a barbecue.

barbiturate /baˈbɪtʃərət, -eɪt/ *n.* a derivative of barbituric acid, especially a sedative drug.

barcode /ˈbakoʊd/ *n.* **1.** a product code containing information about prices, destinations, etc., which is in the form of a series of bars of varying thickness, designed to be read by an optical scanner. *–v.t.* **2.** to identify by means of a bar code. Also, **bar code.** **–barcoding,** *n.*

barcode reader *n.* a device which optically scans a barcode and interprets the information in the code. Also, **barcode scanner.**

bard /bad/ *n.* **1.** a member of the order of poets in the ancient and medieval Celtic societies. **2.** *Archaic* any poet. **–bardic,** *adj.*

bare /bɛə/ *adj.* (**barer, barest**) **1.** uncovered; naked: *bare knees; bare walls.* **2.** unornamented; plain: *the bare facts.* **3.** worn smooth; threadbare. **4.** only just enough. *–v.t.* (**bared, baring**) **5.** to make bare. *–phr.* **6. the bare necessities,** provisions or facilities that are scarcely or just sufficient. **–bareness,** *n.*

bareback /ˈbɛəbæk/ *adv.* without a saddle: *we rode bareback.*

barebelly /ˈbɛəbɛli/ *n.* (*pl.* **-bellies**) *Aust., NZ* a sheep with bare belly and legs, as a result of defective wool growth. **–barebellied,** *adj.*

barefaced /ˈbɛəfeɪst/ *adj.* **1.** with the face uncovered. **2.** undisguised; boldly open. **3.** shameless; impudent; audacious: *a barefaced lie.* **–barefacedly** /ˈbɛəˌfeɪsədli, -ˌfeɪstli/, *adv.* **–barefacedness,** *n.*

barely /ˈbɛəli/ *adv.* **1.** only; just; no more than: *she is barely sixteen.* **2.** without disguise or concealment; openly: *a question barely put.*

bargain /ˈbagən/ *n.* **1.** an agreement between parties settling what each shall give and take, or perform and receive, in a transaction. **2.** such an agreement as affecting one of the parties: *a losing bargain.* **3.** *Stock Exchange* an agreement to sell or to purchase; a sale or purchase. **4.** that which is acquired by bargaining. **5.** an advantageous purchase. *–v.i.* **6.** to discuss the terms of a bargain; haggle over terms. **7.** to come to an agreement; make a bargain. *–v.t.* **8.** to arrange by bargain; stipulate. *–phr.* **9. bargain for,** to be prepared for; expect: *he got more than he bargained for.* **10. bargain on,** to count on; expect: *I hadn't bargained on thirty people for dinner.* **11. into the bargain,** over and above what is stipulated; moreover; besides. **12. strike a bargain,** to make a bargain; come to terms. **–bargainer,** *n.*

barge /badʒ/ *n.* **1.** a large flat-bottomed vessel, usually moved by towing, used for transporting freight. **2.** a ceremonial vessel of state. **3.** a naval boat reserved for a flag officer. *–verb* (**barged, barging**) *–v.t.* **4.** to transport by barge. *–v.i.* **5.** to move aggressively or with undue energy (*through, past, etc.*) often knocking others out of the way: *to barge through a crowd.* *–phr.* **6. barge in,** to intrude clumsily, as unexpectedly into a

room or a social situation: *the door opened and George barged in.* **7. barge into,** to bump or collide with.

barge pole *n.* **1.** a pole used to propel a barge. *–phr.* **2. not touch with a (ten foot or forty foot) barge pole,** to have nothing to do with; not to go near.

bariatrics /bæriˈætrɪks/ *n.* the branch of medical science concerned with the causes and treatment of obesity. **–bariatric,** *adj.* **–bariatrician** /bæriəˈtrɪʃən/, *n.*

barista /bəˈrɪstə/ *n.* (*pl.* **baristas** *or* **baristi**) a person skilled in making espresso coffee in a cafe or restaurant.

baritone /ˈbærətoʊn/ *n.* **1.** a male voice or voice part intermediate between tenor and bass. **2.** a singer with such a voice. **3.** a large, valved brass instrument, slightly smaller in bore than a euphonium, used chiefly in military bands. *–adj.* **4.** of or relating to the baritone; having the compass of a baritone. Also, **barytone.**

barium /ˈbɛəriəm/ *n.* a whitish, malleable, active, divalent, metallic element occurring in combination chiefly as barytes or as witherite. *Symbol*: Ba; *relative atomic mass*: 137.34; *atomic number*: 56; *density*: 3.5 at 20°C.

barium enema *n.* a preparation of barium sulphate ingested before a radiological examination to show up any abnormality in the colon or rectum.

barium meal *n.* a preparation of barium sulphate ingested before a radiological examination to show up any abnormality of the stomach or duodenum.

bark[1] /bak/ *n.* **1.** the abrupt, explosive cry of a dog. **2.** a similar sound made by another animal or by a person. *–v.i.* **3.** to utter an abrupt, explosive cry or a series of such cries, as a dog. **4.** to speak or cry out sharply or gruffly. *–v.t.* **5.** to utter or give forth with a bark: *he barked an order. –phr.* **6. bark up the wrong tree,** to mistake one's object; assail or pursue the wrong person or purpose.

bark[2] /bak/ *n.* **1.** the external covering of the woody stems, branches, and roots of plants, as distinct and separable from the wood itself. *–v.t.* **2.** to strip off the bark of; peel. **3.** to remove a circle of bark from; ringbark. **4.** to treat with a bark infusion; tan. **5.** to rub off the skin of: *to bark one's shins.* **–barker,** *n.*

barley /ˈbali/ *n.* **1.** a widely distributed cereal plant of the genus *Hordeum*, whose awned flowers grow in tightly bunched spikes, with three small additional spikes at each node. **2.** the grain of this plant, used as food, and in the making of beer and whisky.

bar mitzvah /ba ˈmɪtsvə/ *n.* (in Judaism) **1.** a boy at the age of thirteen, when he acquires religious obligations. **2.** the ceremony and feast marking this. Also, **bar mitzvah.**

barmy /ˈbami/ *adj.* (**-mier, -miest**) *Colloq.* lacking reason; irrational.

barn /ban/ *n.* **1.** a building for storing hay, grain, etc., and often for stabling livestock. **2.** a large shop or supermarket which keeps prices down by providing minimum service to the customers.

barnacle /ˈbanəkəl/ *n.* **1.** any of certain crustaceans of the group Cirripedia, as the **goose barnacles,** stalked species which cling to ship bottoms and floating timber, and the **rock barnacles,** species which attach themselves to marine rocks. **2.** a thing or person that clings tenaciously. **–barnacled,** *adj.*

barney /ˈbani/ *Colloq.* *–n.* **1.** an argument; fight. **2.** humbug; cheating. *–v.i.* **3.** to argue or fight.

barn owl *n.* a predatory, nocturnal bird, *Tyto alba*, having light brown and white plumage, and commonly frequenting barns, where it destroys mice; one of the most widespread birds in the world, found in Europe, Africa, the Americas, Australia and much of Asia; introduced into New Zealand and some Pacific islands.

barnstorm /ˈbanstɔm/ *v.i.* **1.** to conduct a vigorous political campaign in rural regions, making many stops and frequent speeches: *both candidates went barnstorming for the farm vote.* **2.** (of an aviator in the early years of aviation) to fly from one country show or fair to the next, making a living by taking passengers for short joy flights. –*v.t.* **3.** to canvass (a region or group) by such a campaign: *the candidate barnstormed New South Wales.* –**barnstormer,** *n.* –**barnstorming,** *adj.*

baro- a word element meaning 'weight', 'pressure', as in *barogram.*

barometer /bəˈrɒmətə/ *n.* **1.** an instrument for measuring atmospheric pressure, thus determining height, weather changes, etc. **2.** anything that indicates changes: *the barometer of public opinion.* –**barometric** /bærəˈmɛtrɪk/, *adj.*

baron /ˈbærən/ *n.* **1.** a man holding a peerage of the lowest titular rank. **2.** a feudal tenant-in-chief holding lands directly from a king. **3.** a rich and powerful man; magnate: *a squatter baron.*

baronet /ˈbærənət, -nɛt/ *n.* a member of a British hereditary order of commoners, ranking below the barons and made up of commoners, designated by *Sir* before the name, and *Baronet,* usually abbreviated to *Bart.,* after: *Sir Thomas Mitchell, Bart.*

baroque /bəˈrɒk, bəˈrouk/ *adj.* **1.** *Art* of or relating to a style developed in Italy in the 16th century, characterised by the use of asymmetry, florid illusionism, direct imagery and lavish ornamentation. **2.** *Music* of or relating to the ornate style of composition of the 17th and early 18th centuries. **3.** extravagantly ornamented. **4.** (of a pearl) irregularly shaped. –*n.* **5.** the baroque style or period.

barque /bak/ *n.* **1.** *Naut.* a sailing vessel having three or more masts, square-rigged on all but the aftermost mast, which is fore-and-aft rigged. **2.** *Poetic* any boat or sailing vessel. Also, **bark.**

barrack[1] /ˈbærak/ *n.* (*usu. pl.*) **1.** a building or range of buildings for lodging soldiers, especially in garrison. **2.** any large, plain building in which many people are lodged.

barrack[2] /ˈbærak/ *v.t.* **1.** *Obs.* to jeer, shout derisively at (a player, team, etc.). –*phr.* **2. barrack for,** to support; shout encouragement and approval for: *to barrack for the local team.* –**barracker,** *n.*

barracouta /bærəˈkutə/ *n.* (*pl.* **-couta** *or* **-coutas**) **1.** Also, **couta.** an elongated, cold water, sport and food fish, *Thyrsites atun,* widespread in southern seas. **2.** *NZ Colloq.* a long, raised bread loaf.

barracuda /bærəˈkudə/ *n.* (*pl.* **-cuda** *or* **-cudas**) any of various species of elongated, predacious, tropical and subtropical marine fishes of the family Sphyraenidae, some of which are used extensively for food; sea pike.

barrage /ˈbæraʒ, -adʒ/ *n.* **1.** *Mil.* a barrier of artillery fire used to prevent the enemy from advancing, to enable troops behind it to operate with a minimum of casualties, or to cut off the enemy's retreat in one or more directions. **2.** a sustained attack: *a barrage of questions.* –*v.t.* (**-raged, -raging**) **3.** to cut off by or subject to a barrage.

barramundi /bærəˈmʌndi/ *n.* (*pl.* **-mundi** *or* **-mundis**) **1.** a large, silvery-grey food fish of excellent quality, *Lates calcarifer,* found in coastal rivers and estuaries of tropical northern Australia and the Indo-Pacific; giant perch. **2.** a primitive freshwater fish of the genus *Scleropages* of northern Australia.

barrel /ˈbærəl/ *n.* **1.** a wooden cylindrical vessel made of staves hooped together, and having slightly bulging sides and flat parallel ends. **2.** a unit of quantity in the imperial system, equal to $159.11315 \times 10^{-3} \text{m}^3$, and in the US, to $158.9873 \times 10^{-3} \text{m}^3$. **3.** the tube of a gun. –*v.t.* (**-relled** *or, Chiefly US,* **-reled, -relling** *or, Chiefly US,* **-reling**) **4.** to put or pack in a barrel or barrels. **5.** *Colloq.* to knock over or run into (as in football): *I'll barrel*

the bloke. –*phr.* **6. barrel along,** *Colloq.* to move along swiftly and confidently. **7. over a barrel,** at a disadvantage; in difficulty.

barren /ˈbærən/ *adj.* **1.** incapable of producing, or not producing, offspring; sterile: *a barren woman.* **2.** unproductive; unfruitful: *barren land.* **3.** destitute of interest or attraction. **4.** mentally unproductive; dull; stupid. **5.** not producing results; fruitless: *barren years.* –*phr.* **6. barren of,** lacking in: *barren of feeling.* –**barrenly,** *adv.* –**barrenness,** *n.*

barrette /bəˈrɛt/ *n.* a metal or plastic clasp for fastening hair in position, usually comprising two parts joined with a hinge.

barricade /ˈbærəkeɪd, bærəˈkeɪd/ *n.* **1.** a defensive barrier hastily constructed, as in a street, to stop an enemy. **2.** any barrier or obstruction to passage: *a barricade of rubbish.* –*v.t.* **3.** to obstruct or block with a barricade. **4.** to shut in and defend with or as with a barricade.

barrier /ˈbæriə/ *n.* **1.** anything built or serving to bar passage, as a stockade or fortress, or a railing. **2.** any natural bar or obstacle: *a mountain barrier.* **3.** anything that restrains or obstructs progress, access, etc.: *a trade barrier.* **4.** a limit or boundary of any kind: *the barriers of caste.* **5.** *Horseracing* a gate which keeps horses in line before the start of a race.

barrier reef *n.* a long narrow ridge of coral close to or above the surface of the sea off the coast of a continent or island.

barring /ˈbarɪŋ/ *prep.* excepting; except for: *barring accidents, I'll be there.*

barringtonia /bærɪŋˈtouniə, -jə/ *n.* a tree, *Barringtonia asiatica,* of tropical sea beaches in Asia, tropical Australia, and the western Pacific.

barrister /ˈbærəstə/ *n.* a legal practitioner whose main function is to act as an advocate in court.

barrow[1] /ˈbærou/ *n.* **1.** a pushcart or horse-drawn cart used by street vendors, especially those selling fruit and vegetables. **2.** → **wheelbarrow** (defs 1 and 2). –*phr. Aust.* **3. push one's barrow,** to campaign vigorously in one's own interest. **4. push someone's barrow,** to take up someone's cause.

barrow[2] /ˈbærou/ *n.* an ancient or prehistoric burial mound.

barrow[3] /ˈbærou/ *v.i. Aust., NZ* (of a shedhand who is learning to become a shearer) to finish shearing a sheep left partly shorn by a shearer at the end of a shearing run. –**barrower,** *n.* –**barrowing,** *n.* –**barrowman,** *n.*

barter /ˈbatə/ *v.i.* **1.** to trade by exchange of commodities rather than by the use of money. –*v.t.* **2.** to exchange in trade as one commodity for another; trade. –*n.* **3.** the act of bartering. **4.** the thing bartered. –*phr.* **5. barter away,** to bargain away unwisely or dishonourably. –**barterer,** *n.*

barytes /bəˈraitiz/ *n.* a common mineral, barium sulphate, $BaSO_4$, the principal ore of barium, occurring in tabular crystals.

BAS /bæz, bæs/ *n.* → **business activity statement.**

basal cell carcinoma *n.* a cancer of the deep layers of the skin, caused by prolonged exposure to sunlight, and occurring as a shiny, rounded lump that may change in size and colour. Compare **squamous cell carcinoma.** Also, **BCC.**

basalt /ˈbæsɔlt, ˈbæsɒlt/ *n.* the dark, dense igneous rock of a lava flow or minor intrusion, composed essentially of plagioclase and pyroxene, and often displaying a columnar structure. –**basaltic** /bəˈsɔltɪk/, *adj.*

base[1] /beɪs/ *n.* **1.** the bottom of anything, considered as its support; that on which a thing stands or rests. **2.** a fundamental principle or groundwork; foundation; basis. **3.** *Archit.* **a.** the part of a column on which the shaft immediately rests. **b.** the lower elements of a complete structure. **4.** the principal element or ingredient of anything, considered as its fundamental part. **5.** *Baseball* one of the four fixed stations to which players run. **6.** *Mil.* a fortified or protected area or place used by any of the armed services. **7.** *Maths* **a.** the number which serves as a starting point for a logarithmic or other numerical system. **b.** the side or face of a geometric figure to which an altitude is thought to be drawn. **8.** a primary place of residence, employment, etc.: *his base is Hong Kong but he travels widely.* **9.** → **baseline. 10.** *Chem.* any of numerous compounds which react with an acid to form a salt, as metallic oxides and hydroxides, amines, alkaloids and ammonia. –*adj.* **11.** serving as a base. –*v.t.* **12.** to make or form a base or foundation for. **13.** to place or establish on a base or basis; ground; found; establish. **14.** to locate the main part of (a business, enterprise, etc.): *to base the operations in Albury.* **15.** to locate (a person) somewhere as their primary place of residence or employment: *to base the CEO in Hong Kong.* –*phr.* **16. base on** (or **upon**), **a.** to arrive at as a result of: *I based my conclusion on the facts available.* **b.** to create after the pattern of: *the character of Viola is based on his mother.* **17. base over apex**, *Colloq.* fallen heavily and awkwardly, usually in a forward direction. **18. touch base with**, to make contact with.

base² /beɪs/ *adj.* **1.** morally low; mean; selfish; cowardly. **2.** of little value: *base metals.* **3.** debased or counterfeit: *base coin.* **4.** *Archaic* low, short or poor. –**basely**, *adv.* –**baseness**, *n.*

baseball /ˈbeɪsbɔl/ *n.* **1.** a game played with a wooden bat and a hard ball, by two opposing teams of nine players, each team batting and fielding alternately, and each batter having to run a course of four bases laid out in a diamond pattern in order to score. **2.** the ball used in playing this game. –**baseballer**, *n.*

BASE-jump /ˈbeɪs-dʒʌmp/ *n.* a parachute jump from a structure such as a tall building, bridge, etc., as opposed to a jump from an aeroplane. –**BASE-jumper**, *n.* –**BASE-jumping**, *n.*

baseline /ˈbeɪslaɪn/ *n.* **1.** a line at the base of anything. **2.** a basic standard or level, usually regarded as a reference point for comparison: *baseline data.* **3.** *Surveying* an accurately measured line forming one side of a triangle or system of triangles from which all other sides are computed. **4.** *International Law* the line from which the breadth of a coastal state's territorial sea is measured (normally, the low-water line). **5.** *Tennis* a line at the end of the court. **6.** *Baseball* a line joining bases.

baseline-and-credit *adj.* of or relating to an emissions trading scheme in which polluters earn credits for emissions below agreed baselines, such credits being available to be sold to other polluters. See **cap-and-trade.**

base load *n.* the power in an electricity grid available to meet minimum expected requirements at a given time. Also, **baseload.**

basement /ˈbeɪsmənt/ *n.* **1.** a storey of a building partly or wholly underground. **2.** the portion of a structure which supports those portions which come above it.

bases¹ /ˈbeɪsɪz/ *n.* plural of **basis.**

bases² /ˈbeɪsəz/ *n.* plural of **base¹.**

bash /bæʃ/ *v.t.* **1.** to strike with a crushing or smashing blow. **2.** Also, **bash up.** *Colloq.* to assault: *he was bashed outside the pub.* **3.** *Colloq.* to criticise severely. **4.** *Colloq.* to use greatly or excessively: *bash the bottle.* –*n.* **5.** a crushing blow. **6.** *Colloq.* a party, especially a large one. **b.** a drinking spree. –*phr.* **7. give it a bash**, **a.** to make an attempt. **b.** to go on a drinking spree. **8. have a bash**, (sometimes fol. by *at*) to make an attempt: *I'll have a bash at fixing the car.*

bashful /ˈbæʃfəl/ *adj.* **1.** uncomfortably diffident or shy; timid and easily embarrassed. **2.** indicative of, accompanied with, or proceeding from bashfulness. –**bashfully**, *adv.* –**bashfulness**, *n.*

bashing /ˈbæʃɪŋ/ *n. Colloq.* **1.** excessive attention, exposure or use: *that song's had a bashing on air lately.* **2.** activity evincing hostility towards a group thought to be behaving in an undesirable way: *union bashing.*

basic /ˈbeɪsɪk/ *adj.* **1.** of, relating to, or forming a base; fundamental: *a basic principle; a basic ingredient.* –*n.* **2.** something that is basic or essential. –*phr.* **3. back to basics**, back to first principles; back to the origins. –**basically**, *adv.*

basic wage *n.* (in Australia and NZ) the minimum wage payable to an adult employee under an award or agreement.

basil /ˈbæzəl/ *n.* any of various herbs of the genus *Ocimum*, family Labiatae, of tropical and subtropical regions, having aromatic leaves used in cookery, as **sweet basil**, *O. basilicum*, of tropical Asia.

basilica /bəˈsɪlɪkə, -ˈzɪl-/ *n.* **1.** an oblong building, especially a church with a nave higher than its aisles. **2.** one of the seven main churches of Rome or another Roman Catholic church accorded certain religious privileges.

basilisk /ˈbæsəlɪsk, ˈbæz-/ *n.* **1.** a tropical American lizard of the genus *Basiliscus*, of the family Iguanidae, with a crest on the back of the head and along the back and tail. **2.** a legendary reptile, the glance and breath of which could kill.

basin /ˈbeɪsən/ *n.* **1.** a circular container of greater width than depth, contracting towards the bottom, used chiefly to hold water or other liquid, especially for washing. **2.** a sink; washbasin. **3.** a small circular container of approximately equal width and depth, used chiefly for mixing, cooking, etc. **4.** a natural or artificial hollow place containing water, especially one in which ships are docked. **5.** *Physical Geog.* a hollow or depression in the earth's surface, wholly or partly surrounded by higher land: *ocean basin, lake basin, river basin.* –**basined**, *adj.* –**basin-like**, *adj.*

basis /ˈbeɪsəs/ *n.* (*pl.* **bases** /ˈbeɪsiz/) **1.** the bottom or base of anything, or that on which it stands or rests. **2.** a groundwork or fundamental principle. **3.** the principal constituent; a fundamental ingredient.

basis point *n. Commerce* a measure used in financial markets, equal to one hundredth of one percentage point (0.01%).

bask /bask/ *v.i.* **1.** to lie in or be exposed to a pleasant warmth: *to bask in the sunshine.* **2.** to enjoy a pleasant situation: *he basked in royal favour.*

basket /ˈbaskət/ *n.* **1.** a receptacle of twigs, rushes, thin strips of wood, or other flexible material, woven together. **2.** a container made of pieces of thin veneer, used for packing berries, vegetables, etc.; punnet. **3.** the contents of a basket. **4.** *Basketball* **a.** a short open net, suspended before the backboard, through which the ball must pass to score points. **b.** a score, counting one point on a free throw and two or three for a field goal. **5.** *Econ.* a list of retail goods from which the consumer price index is calculated. **6.** *Finance* a group of currencies or investments: *a basket of five leading currencies.* –**basketful**, *n.* –**basketlike**, *adj.*

basketball /ˈbaskətbɔl/ *n.* **1.** a game played by two teams of five players each, in which points are scored by throwing the ball through the elevated baskets at the opponents' end of a rectangular court. **2.** the large round inflated ball used in this game. –**basketballer**, *n.*

basket case *n.* **1.** a person in an advanced state of nervous tension or mental instability. **2.** something which has been dealt a crippling blow: *the economy is a basket case after the last budget.*

basmati rice /bæz'mati rais, bas'mati rais/ n. an Indian long-grain rice variety which, when cooked, produces light dry grains which separate easily.

basque /bask/ n. 1. (upper case) one of a people of unknown origin inhabiting the western Pyrenees region of Spain and France. 2. (upper case) their language, historically connected only with Iberian. 3. a woman's close-fitting top, sometimes with a part reaching over the hips. 4. this part or skirt hanging from the waist of a garment. 5. a tightly knitted band on the lower edge and cuffs of a jumper, etc.

bas-relief /ba-rə'lif/ n. sculpture in low relief, in which the figures project only slightly from the background.

bass[1] /beis/ adj. 1. low in pitch; of the lowest pitch or range: a bass voice; a bass singer; a bass instrument; a bass part. –n. 2. a bass voice, singer, or instrument

bass[2] /bæs/ n. (pl. **bass** or **basses**) 1. an Australian freshwater fish of genus Percalates. 2. elsewhere, any of the spiny-finned sea fish of the family Serranidae, or similar fish of other families.

basset /'bæsət/ n. a long-bodied, short-legged dog resembling a dachshund but larger and heavier. Also, **basset hound**.

bassinet /bæsə'nɛt/ n. a basket in which a baby sleeps. Also, **bassinette**.

bassoon /bə'sun/ n. a double-reed woodwind instrument, the bass of the oboe class, having a wooden tubular body doubled back on itself and a curved metallic crook and mouthpiece.

bastard /'bastəd/ n. 1. a person whose parents were not married; an illegitimate child. 2. Colloq. (offensive) an unpleasant or hateful person. 3. Aust., NZ Colloq. any person (without offensive meaning). 4. Colloq. something which causes difficulty or annoyance. –**bastardy**, n.

bastardise /'bastədaiz/ v.t. 1. to debase; adulterate. 2. Aust. to seek to humiliate, as part of initiation into a regiment, college, etc. Also, **bastardize**. –**bastardisation**, n.

baste[1] /beist/ v.t. to sew with temporary stitches, as a garment in the first stages of making; tack.

baste[2] /beist/ v.t. to moisten (meat, etc.) while cooking, with dripping, butter, etc.

bastion /'bæstiən/ n. 1. a fortified place. 2. any person or object which affords support or defence. –**bastioned**, adj.

bat[1] /bæt/ n. 1. Sport a. the club used in certain games, as cricket and baseball, to strike the ball. b. a racquet, especially one used in table tennis. 2. Cricket a player who bats: he is a good bat. 3. a heavy stick, club, or cudgel. 4. → kip[2]. 5. Colloq. rate of motion: to go at a fair bat. 6. Colloq. a spree; binge: to go on a bat. 7. → batt. –verb (**batted**, **batting**) –v.t. 8. to strike or hit with or as with a bat or club. –v.i. 9. Colloq. to rush (away, around, etc.). 10. Cricket, etc. a. to strike at the ball with the bat. b. to take one's turn at batting. –phr. 11. **bat along**, to travel at speed. 12. **bat for the other side** (or **team**), Colloq. a. to switch sides in a debate or argument. b. (from a heterosexual perspective) to be homosexual. c. (from a homosexual perspective) to be heterosexual. 13. **bat on**, to continue; persevere. 14. **carry one's bat**, a. Cricket to continue batting undismissed to the end of an innings. b. Colloq. to accomplish any difficult, lengthy, or dangerous task. 15. (**go in to**) **bat for**, to take action in support of: I'm glad you're going in to bat for me. 16. **off one's own bat**, independently; without prompting or assistance.

bat[2] /bæt/ n. 1. any of the nocturnal or crepuscular flying mammals constituting the order Chiroptera, characterised by modified forelimbs which serve as wings and are covered with a membranous skin extending to the hind limbs. –phr. Colloq. 2. **blind as a bat**, very blind.

3. **have bats in the belfry**, to have mad notions; be crazy or peculiar. 4. **like a bat out of hell**, at speed; quickly. 5. **old bat**, an unpleasant or eccentric woman, usually old. –**batlike**, adj.

bat[3] /bæt/ v.t. (**batted**, **batting**) 1. to wink or flutter (one's eyelids). –phr. 2. **not bat an eye** (or **eyelid**), to show no emotion or surprise.

batch /bætʃ/ n. 1. a quantity or a number taken together; a group: a batch of prisoners. 2. the quantity of material prepared or required for one operation or that quantity produced by one operation. 3. the quantity of bread made at one baking. –v.t. 4. to put into batches. 5. Computers to process (data or programs) by batch processing.

bate /beit/ v.t. to moderate or restrain (the breath): to wait with bated breath.

bath /baθ/ n. 1. the washing, especially of a body, in water, other liquid, steam, etc. 2. the water or other liquid used for a bath. 3. a container for this liquid, etc., especially a large metal or plastic one for bathing a body. –v.t. 4. to put or wash in a bath. –phr. 5. **take a bath**, Colloq. to suffer a defeat or misfortune, especially a financial loss. –**bathless**, adj.

bathe /beið/ verb (**bathed**, **bathing**) –v.t. 1. to dip or soak in water or other liquid to clean, etc. 2. to wash. 3. to moisten or wet with any liquid. –v.i. 4. to have a bath. 5. to swim for pleasure. –n. 6. Chiefly Brit. the act of bathing, as in the sea. –**bather**, n.

bathers /'beiðəz/ pl. n. Aust. Colloq. → **swimming costume**.

batho- a word element meaning 'deep', as in batholith. Also, **bathy-**.

bathos /'beiθɒs/ n. 1. a ludicrous descent from the elevated to the commonplace; anticlimax. 2. triteness or triviality in style. 3. insincere pathos; sentimentality. –**bathetic** /bə'θɛtik/, adj.

bathroom /'baθrum/ n. 1. a room fitted with a bath or a shower (or both), and sometimes with a toilet and washbasin. 2. a. a room fitted with a toilet. b. (euphemistic) a toilet.

baths /baðz/ pl. n. 1. Obsolesc. a public swimming pool. 2. a building containing apartments for washing or bathing, or fitted up for bathing.

bathy- → **batho-**.

bathyscaphe /'bæθəskeif/ n. a small submarine for deep-sea exploration and research, having a spherical cabin on its underside. Also, **bathyscaph**.

bathysphere /'bæθəsfiə/ n. a spherical diving apparatus from which to study deep-sea life. Also, **bathyscape** /'bæθəskeip/, **bathyscope** /'bæθəskoup/.

batik /'batik, 'bætik/ n. 1. a method of printing cloth by applying wax to the fabric in a desired pattern, thus sealing it off from the dye. 2. the fabric so decorated. Also, **battik**.

batman /'bætmən/ n. (pl. -**men**) a soldier assigned to an army officer as a servant.

bat mitzvah /bat 'mitsvə/ n. (in Judaism) 1. a girl at the age of twelve, when she acquires religious obligations. 2. the ceremony and feast marking this. Also, **bas mitzvah**.

baton /'bætn/ n. 1. a staff, club, or truncheon, especially as a mark of office or authority. 2. Music the wand used by a conductor. 3. Athletics (in relay racing) a metal or wooden tube, handed on by one relay runner to the next.

bat-pad n. Cricket → **short leg**.

batt /bæt/ n. a rectangular sheet of matted fibreglass, cottonwool, etc., used for insulating houses, filling quilts, etc. Also, **bat**.

battalion /bə'tæljən/ n. 1. Mil. a ground-force unit composed of three or more companies or similar units. 2. an army in battle array. 3. (oft. pl.) a large number; force.

batten[1] /ˈbætn/ v.i. **1.** to become fat. –phr. **2. batten on,** to live in luxury or prosper at the expense of (others).

batten[2] /ˈbætn/ n. **1.** a light strip of wood usually having an oblong cross-section and used to fasten main members of a structure together. **2.** Naut. **a.** a thin strip of wood inserted in a sail to keep it flat. **b.** a strip of wood, as one used to secure the edges of a tarpaulin over a hatchway. –v.t. **3.** to furnish with battens. **4.** Also, **batten down.** Naut. to fasten (as hatches) with battens and tarpaulins. –phr. **5. batten down (the hatches),** to prepare for imminent difficulty.

batter[1] /ˈbætə/ v.t. **1.** to beat persistently or hard; pound. **2.** to damage by beating or hard usage. –v.i. **3.** to deal heavy, repeated blows; pound.

batter[2] /ˈbætə/ n. a mixture of flour, milk or water, eggs, etc., beaten together for use in cookery.

batter[3] /ˈbætə/ n. **1.** someone or something that bats. **2.** Cricket, Baseball, etc. a player whose role is to strike the ball with the bat or whose turn it is to do this.

battery /ˈbætəri/ n. (pl. **-ries**) **1.** Elect. a series of cells for producing or storing electricity. **2.** a set of guns, machines, instruments, or other things to be used together. **3.** a large number of cages in which chickens, etc., are reared. **4.** the act of beating or battering.

battle /ˈbætl/ n. **1.** a hostile encounter or engagement between opposing forces. **2.** any extended or intense fight, struggle, or contest: the battle between sand-miners and conservationists. –v.i. **3.** to engage in battle. **4.** to struggle; strive: to battle for freedom. **5.** Aust. to live the life of a battler. –v.t. **6.** to fight. –phr. **7. battle on, a.** to continue to struggle for existence. **b.** to maintain one's efforts to do or achieve something despite setbacks. **8. battle one's way through,** to force a path through: I battled my way through the surf. **9. battle through,** to struggle on despite hardship.

battleaxe /ˈbætəlæks/ n. **1.** an axe for use as a weapon of war. **2.** Colloq. a domineering woman. Also, US, **battleax.**

battleaxe block n. a block or section of land, behind those with street frontages and accessible through a drive or lane. Also, **battleaxe section.**

battlefield /ˈbætlfild/ n. **1.** the field or ground on which a battle is fought. **2.** any sphere in which conflict occurs. Also, **battleground.**

battlement /ˈbætlmənt/ n. an indented parapet, having a series of openings, originally for shooting through; a crenellated upper wall.

battler /ˈbætlə/ n. Aust. **1.** NZ someone who struggles continually and persistently against heavy odds. **2.** a conscientious worker, especially one living at subsistence level. **3.** (formerly) an itinerant worker reduced to living as a swagman.

bauble /ˈbɔbl/ n. a cheap but showy ornament; trinket.

baud /bɔd/ n. a unit for measuring the speed with which electronic data is transmitted, especially in computers.

baud rate n. the rate measured in bauds at which electronic data is transmitted, as for a modem.

bauhinia /bouˈhɪniə/ n. any shrub or tree of the genus Bauhinia, family Caesalpiniaceae, of tropical regions, widely cultivated for their variously coloured flowers.

baulk /bɔk/ v.i. **1.** to stop or pull up as if barred or blocked: he baulked at making the speech. –v.t. **2.** to block; thwart. **3.** to miss; let slip; fail to use: to baulk a catch. –n. **4.** a stop or disappointment. **5.** a block; a hindrance. **6.** a cross-beam in the roof of a house which unites and supports the rafters. –**baulker,** n.

bauxite /ˈbɔksaɪt/ n. a rock, the principal ore of aluminium, consisting chiefly of aluminium oxide or hydroxide with various impurities.

bawdy /ˈbɔdi/ adj. (**-dier, -diest**) **1.** rollickingly vulgar; lewd. –n. **2.** promiscuous sexual behaviour. **3.** indecent or lewd talk. –**bawdily,** adv. –**bawdiness,** n.

bawl /bɔl/ v.i. **1.** to cry loudly and vigorously. **2.** to cry out loudly. –v.t. **3.** to utter or proclaim by outcry. –n. **4.** a loud shout; a wail; an outcry. –phr. **5. bawl out, a.** to yell out loudly. **b.** to scold. –**bawler,** n.

bay[1] /beɪ/ n. a recess or inlet in the shore of a sea or lake between two capes or headlands, not as large as a gulf but larger than a cove.

bay[2] /beɪ/ n. **1. a.** a recessed space projecting outwards from the line of a wall, as to contain a window. **b.** a space or division of a wall, building, etc., between two vertical architectural features or members. **2.** the aisle between parallel shelving as in a library. **3.** a compartment in an aircraft: a bomb bay; an engine bay. **4.** a recess or marked-out area set back from the general flow of traffic beside a road or in a car park.

bay[3] /beɪ/ n. **1.** a deep, prolonged bark, as of a hound or hounds in hunting. **2.** a stand made by a hunted animal to face or repel pursuers, or of a person forced to face a foe or difficulty: to stand at bay, be brought to bay. **3.** the position of the pursuers or foe thus kept off. –v.i. **4.** to bark, especially with a deep prolonged sound, as a hound in hunting. –v.t. **5.** to bring to or hold at bay.

bay[4] /beɪ/ n. **1.** the European laurel, Laurus nobilis, the leaves of which are used in cooking. **2.** a West Indian tree, Pimenta racemosa, whose leaves are used in making bay rum. **3.** any of various laurel-like trees.

bay[5] /beɪ/ n. **1.** a reddish-brown colour. –adj. **2.** (of horses, etc.) of the colour bay.

bayonet /ˈbeɪnət, ˈbeɪənət/ n. **1.** a stabbing or slashing instrument of steel, made to be attached to or at the muzzle of a rifle. –v.t. (**-neted, -neting**) **2.** to kill or wound with a bayonet.

bazaar /bəˈzɑ/ n. **1.** a marketplace or quarter containing shops, especially in the Middle East. **2.** a sale of miscellaneous articles, as for some charitable purpose.

bazooka /bəˈzukə/ n. a cylindrical rocket-launcher, an individual infantry weapon that fires a rocket capable of penetrating several centimetres of armour-plate, used to destroy tanks and other armoured military vehicles.

BBQ barbecue.

be /bi/ verb (copular) **1.** a link connecting a subject with predicate or qualifying words in declarative interrogative, and imperative sentences, or serving to form infinitive and participial phrases: you are late; he is much to blame; is he here?; try to be just; the art of being agreeable. **2.** to be suitable for or characteristic of: that dress is really you; insulting the mayor was Dick all over. –v. (aux.) **3.** used with the present participle of a principal verb to form the progressive: I am waiting, or with a past participle in passive forms of transitive verbs: the date was fixed; it must be done. –v. (substantive) **4.** to be found or located: where are the children? **5.** (used in the perfect and pluperfect) to pay a visit; go: I have been to Spain; have you been to the shops today? **6.** (used in the perfect and pluperfect) Colloq. (with children) to defecate or urinate: have you been yet? –v.i. **7.** to exist; have reality; live; take place; occur; remain as before: he is no more; it was not to be; think what might have been.

Usage: The different forms of the verb **be** are:

Present tense: I am, you are, he/she/it is, we are, they are

Past tense: I was, you were, he/she/it was, we were, they were

Past participle: been

Present participle: being

Some archaic forms are also retained:

Present tense: thou art

Past tense: thou wast, thou wert

The subjunctive form were, as in If I were to go, I would be happy, is rarely used now.

be- a prefix of western Germanic origin, meaning 'about', 'around', 'all over', and hence having an intensive and often disparaging force, much used as an English formative of verbs (and their derivatives), as in *besiege*, *becloud*, *bedaub*, *beplaster*, *bepraise*, and often serving to form transitive verbs from intransitives or from nouns or adjectives, as in *begrudge*, *belabour*, *befriend*, *belittle*.

beach /biːtʃ/ *n.* **1.** the sand or loose water-worn pebbles of the seashore. **2.** the part of the shore of the sea, or of a large river or lake, washed by the tide or waves. **3.** the seaside as a place of recreation. –*v.t.* **4.** *Naut.* to run or haul up (a ship or boat) on the beach.

beach buggy *n.* a light vehicle with wide tyres for travelling over sand.

beach bum *n. Colloq.* someone who spends most of their time lazing on a beach.

beachcomber /ˈbiːtʃkoʊmə/ *n.* **1.** someone who lives by gathering articles along the beaches, as from wreckage. **2.** a vagrant of the beach or coast, especially a European in South Pacific regions. **3.** a long wave rolling in from the ocean.

beachhead /ˈbiːtʃhɛd/ *n.* the area of lodgement which is the first objective of a military force landing on an enemy shore.

beacon /ˈbiːkən/ *n.* **1.** a guiding or warning signal, such as a fire, especially one on a pole, tower, hill, etc. **2.** a tower or hill used for such purposes. **3.** a lighthouse, signal buoy, etc., on a coast or over dangerous spots at sea to warn and guide vessels. **4.** a radio beacon. **5.** any person, thing, or act that warns or guides.

bead /biːd/ *n.* **1.** a small ball of glass, pearl, wood, etc., with a hole through it, strung with others like it, and used as an ornament or in a rosary. **2.** (*pl.*) a necklace. **3.** (*pl.*) a rosary. **4.** any small globular or cylindrical body. **5.** a bubble rising through effervescent liquid. **6.** a drop of liquid: *beads of sweat*. **7.** the front sight of a gun. **8.** *US* aim: *to take a bead on a target*. **9.** Also, **beading.** *Archit., etc.* **a.** a narrow convex moulding, usually more or less semicircular in section. **b.** any of various pieces similar in some sections to this type of moulding. –*v.t.* **10.** to ornament with beads. –*v.i.* **11.** to form beads; form in beads or drops. –*phr.* **12. say** (or **tell**) (or **count**) **one's beads**, to say prayers and count them off by means of the beads on the rosary. –**beaded**, *adj.* –**beadlike**, *adj.* –**beady**, *adj.*

beading /ˈbiːdɪŋ/ *n.* **1.** material composed of or adorned with beads. **2.** narrow lacelike trimming. **3.** narrow openwork trimming through which ribbon may be run. **4.** a narrow ornamental strip of wood used on walls, furniture, etc.

beagle /ˈbiːgəl/ *n.* one of a breed of small hounds with short legs and drooping ears, used especially in hunting.

beak[1] /biːk/ *n.* **1.** the horny bill of a bird. **2.** the membranous mouthparts of the platypus and protruding jaws of certain whales and dolphins. **3.** *Colloq.* a person's nose. **4.** anything beaklike or ending in a point, as the lip of a pitcher or a beaker. –**beaked**, *adj.* –**beakless**, *adj.* –**beaklike**, *adj.* –**beaky**, *adj.*

beak[2] /biːk/ *n. Colloq.* a magistrate; judge.

beaker /ˈbiːkə/ *n.* **1.** a large drinking vessel with a wide mouth. **2.** a flat-bottomed cylindrical vessel usually having a pouring lip, used in laboratories.

beam /biːm/ *n.* **1.** a thick, long piece of timber, shaped for structural use. **2.** a similar piece of metal, stone, etc. **3.** *Building Trades* one of the main horizontal supporting members in a building or the like, as for supporting a roof or floor. **4.** *Shipbuilding* one of the strong transverse pieces of timber or metal stretching across a ship to support the deck, hold the sides in place, etc. **5.** *Naut.* **a.** the side of a vessel, or the direction at right angles to the keel, with reference to the wind, sea, etc. **b.** the greatest breadth of a ship. **6.** *Machinery* **a.** an oscillating lever of a steam engine, transferring the motion from piston rod to crankshaft. **b.** a roller or cylinder in a loom, on which the warp is wound before weaving. **c.** a similar cylinder on which cloth is wound as it is woven. **7.** the transverse bar of a balance from the ends of which the scales or pans are suspended. **8.** a ray, or bundle of parallel rays, of light or other radiation. **9.** *Radio, Aeronautics* a signal transmitted along a narrow course, used to guide pilots through darkness, bad weather, etc. –*v.t.* **10.** to emit in or as in beams or rays. **11.** *Radio* to transmit (a signal) on a narrow beam. –*v.i.* **12.** to emit beams, as of light. **13.** to look or smile radiantly. –*phr.* **14. broad in the beam**, (of a person) very wide across the buttocks. **15. off (the) beam**, **a.** not on the course indicated by a radio beam. **b.** wrong; incorrect; out of touch with the situation. **c.** *Colloq.* crazy. **16. on the beam**, **a.** *Naut.* at right angles with the keel. **b.** on the course indicated by a radio beam. **c.** *Colloq.* just right; exact; correct; in touch with the situation. –**beamed**, *adj.* –**beamless**, *adj.* –**beamlike**, *adj.*

bean /biːn/ *n.* **1.** the edible fruit or seed of various species of the family Fabaceae especially of the genus *Phaseolus* used either fresh or dried. **2.** a plant producing such seeds. **3.** any of various other beanlike seeds or plants, as the coffee bean. **4.** *Colloq.* a coin; anything of the least value: *I haven't a bean*. **5.** *Colloq.* the human head. –*v.t.* **6.** *Colloq.* to hit on the head. –*phr.* **7. count beans**, *Colloq.* to practise as an accountant. **8. full of beans**, *Colloq.* energetic; vivacious. **9. give someone beans**, *Aust., NZ Colloq.* to berate or attack someone. **10. know how many beans make five**, *Colloq.* to be aware; be well informed. **11. not add up** (or **amount**) **to a row of beans**, *Colloq.* not to amount to anything significant. **12. spill the beans**, *Colloq.* to divulge information, often unintentionally. –**beanlike**, *adj.*

beanbag /ˈbiːnbæg/ *n.* **1.** a small cloth bag filled with beans, used as a toy. **2.** a large triangular cushion used as a chair, filled with pellets of synthetic material, as expanded polystyrene, which yields to accommodate the shape of the body.

bean curd *n.* → tofu. Also, **beancurd**.

beanie /ˈbiːni/ *n.* a small close-fitting knitted cap, often having a pompom or other decoration on top.

bean sprout *n.* the very young shoot of any of certain beans, especially the mung bean or the soybean, used in Chinese and some other Asian cookery and as a salad vegetable. Also, **beansprout, bean shoot**.

bean tree *n.* any of several trees bearing pods resembling those of a bean, as the catalpa and the carob tree.

bear[1] /bɛə/ *verb* (**bore** /bɔː/ or, *Archaic,* **bare**, **borne** or **born**, **bearing**) –*v.t.* **1.** to hold up; support: *to bear the weight of the roof*. **2.** to carry: *to bear gifts*. **3.** to conduct; guide; take: *they bore him to his quarters*. **4.** to render; afford; give: *to bear witness*. **5.** to transmit or spread (gossip, tales, etc.). **6.** to undergo; suffer: *to bear pain*. **7.** to sustain without yielding or suffering injury (usually negative unless qualified): *I can't bear your scolding*. **8.** to accept or have as an obligation: *to bear responsibility; to bear the cost; to bear the blame*. **9.** to hold up under; sustain: *his claim doesn't bear close examination*. **10.** to be fit for or worthy of: *the story doesn't bear repeating*. **11.** to have and be entitled to: *to bear title*. **12.** to possess as a quality, characteristic, etc.; have in or on: *to bear traces; to bear an inscription*. **13.** to stand in (a relation or ratio): *the relation that price bears to profit*. **14.** to carry in the mind: *to bear love; to bear a grudge*. **15.** to exhibit; show. **16.** to manage (oneself, one's body, head, etc.): *to bear oneself erectly*. **17.** to give birth to: *to bear quintuplets*. **18.** to produce by natural growth: *plants bear leaves*. –*v.i.* **19.** to tend in course or direction; move; go: *the* *ship bears due west.* **20.** to be located or situated: *the headland bears due west from us. –phr.* **21. bear away,** *Naut.* to alter course away from the wind. **22. bear down, a.** (of a woman in labour) to make a voluntary muscular expulsive effort. **b.** (sometimes fol. by *on*) to press down heavily. **c.** (sometimes fol. by *on*) (of a ship, car, etc.) to approach, usually at speed. **23. bear on, a.** to continue without pause or interruption. **b.** to have an effect, reference, or bearing on: *time bears heavily on him.* **24. bear out,** to confirm; prove right: *the facts bear me out.* **25. bear up, a.** to hold, or remain firm, as under pressure: *will the wall bear up under the weight of the roof?* **b.** to remain strong in a time of difficulty: *how are you bearing up after your accident?* **26. bear with,** to be patient with. **27. bring to bear,** to bring into effective operation. **–bearable,** *adj.* **–bearableness,** *n.* **–bearably,** *adv.* **–bearer,** *n.*

bear² /bɛə/ *n.* **1.** any of the carnivorous or omnivorous mammals of the family Ursidae, having massive bodies, coarse, heavy fur, relatively short limbs, and almost rudimentary tails. **2.** any of various animals resembling the bear, as the ant bear. **3.** a gruff, clumsy, or rude person. **4.** *Stock Exchange* someone who sells (often what they do not possess) with the expectation of buying in at a lower price and making a profit of the difference (opposed to a *bull*). **5.** someone who believes that conditions are or will be unfavourable. *–adj.* **6.** *Stock Exchange* of, relating to, or caused by declining prices in stocks, etc.: *a bear market. –v.t.* **7.** *Stock Exchange* to attempt to lower the price of (stocks). *–phr.* **8. like a bear with a sore head,** *Colloq.* intensely irritable; grumpy. **–bearish,** *adj.*

beard /bɪəd/ *n.* **1.** the growth of hair on the face of an adult male, sometimes exclusive of the moustache. **2.** *Bot.* a tuft or growth of awns or the like, as in wheat, barley, etc. **3.** a barb or catch on an arrow, fishhook, knitting needle, crochet hook, etc. *–v.t.* **4.** to oppose boldly; defy. **–bearded,** *adj.* **–beardless,** *adj.* **–beardlessness,** *n.*

beardy /ˈbɪədi/ *n.* (*pl.* **-dies**) any plant of the terrestrial orchid genus *Calochilus* of Australia, New Zealand, and New Caledonia, with a labellum covered with long, dense, bright red hairs. Also, **beard orchid.**

bearing /ˈbɛərɪŋ/ *n.* **1.** the manner in which one bears or carries oneself, including posture, gestures, etc.: *a person of dignified bearing.* **2.** *Archit.* **a.** a supporting part, as in a structure. **b.** the contact area between a load-carrying member and its support. **3.** *Machinery* a part in which a journal, pivot, or the like, turns or moves. **4.** *Geog.* a horizontal angle measured from 0° to 90° fixing the direction of a line with respect to either the north or south direction. **True bearings** are referred to the true north direction, **magnetic bearings** to magnetic north (or south). **5.** (*oft. pl.*) direction or relative position, determined by reference to known points: *the pilot took his bearings.* **6.** *Heraldry* any single device on a coat of arms; a charge. *–phr.* **7. have a bearing on,** to have an effect on or relevance to. **8. get one's bearings,** to establish one's position in or as in relation to one's environment, circumstances, etc. **9. lose one's bearings,** to become lost, especially by losing one's sense of relative position in or as in a particular environment, set of circumstances, etc.

bear market *n. Stock Exchange* a period of depressed trading during and after a fall in share prices, when traders consider there is little chance of quick recovery.

beast /bist/ *n.* **1.** any animal except a human, but especially a large four-footed one. **2.** a steer, bullock, cow or heifer raised for meat production. **3.** the animal nature common to humans and non-humans. **4.** a coarse, filthy, or otherwise beastlike person. **–beastlike,** *adj.*

beastly /ˈbistli/ *adj.* (**-lier, -liest**) **1.** *Obs.* of or like a beast; bestial. **2.** *Chiefly Brit. Colloq.* nasty; disagreeable. **–beastliness,** *n.*

beat /bit/ *verb* (**beat, beaten** *or* **beat, beating**) *–v.t.* **1.** to strike repeatedly and usually violently. **2.** to thrash, cane, or flog, as a punishment. **3.** to whisk; stir, as in order to thicken or aerate: *to beat cream; beat egg white.* **4.** to dash against: *rain beating the trees.* **5.** to flutter or flap: *a bird beating its wings.* **6.** to sound as on a drum. **7.** to make (a path) by repeated treading. **8.** *Music* to mark (time) by strokes, as with the hand or a metronome. **9.** *Hunting* to scour (forest, grass, bush, etc.) in order to rouse game. **10.** to overcome in a contest; defeat. **11.** to break or destroy (a habit or the like). **12.** to be superior to. **13.** *Colloq.* to frustrate or baffle; be too difficult for. **14.** to take measures to counteract or offset: *leaving early to beat the rush hour.* **15.** to anticipate (someone) in reaching or achieving a goal: *she beat him to the corner.* **16.** *US* to swindle or cheat: *to beat someone out of five hundred dollars. –v.i.* **17.** to strike repeated blows; pound. **18.** to throb or pulsate. **19.** to radiate intense light or heat; glare: *the sun beat down on his head.* **20.** to fall violently: *the rain beat down on the roof.* **21.** to dash (*against*, etc.). **22.** *Physics* to make a beat or beats. **23.** *Naut.* to make progress to windward by sailing full and by, first on one tack and then on the other. *–n.* **24.** a stroke or blow. **25.** the sound made by it. **26.** a throb or pulsation. **27.** a beaten path or habitual round, as of a police officer. **28.** *Colloq.* a similar habitual round or path followed by a prostitute looking for clients, or people looking for a sexual partner. **29.** *Colloq.* a place, as a club, men's toilet, etc., used for anonymous male homosexual intercourse. **30.** the area of land a musterer must clear of sheep or cattle. **31.** *Music* **a.** the audible, visual, or mental marking of the metrical divisions of music. **b.** a stroke of the hand, baton, etc., marking time division or accent for music during performance. **32.** *Prosody* the accent, stress, or ictus, in a foot or rhythmical unit of poetry. **33.** *Physics* a periodic fluctuation caused by simultaneous occurrence of two waves, currents, or sounds of slightly different frequency. *–adj.* **34.** *Colloq.* exhausted; worn out: *I'm beat after working all day.* **35.** *Colloq.* defeated. **36.** of or relating to the beat generation or their culture. *–phr.* **37. beat about the bush,** to approach a matter in a roundabout way; avoid coming to the point. **38. beat a retreat,** to withdraw hurriedly, as from an unpleasant situation. **39. beat down, a.** to subdue; subject; overcome. **b.** to suppress or override (opposition, etc.) **c.** to secure a lower price from by haggling. **40. beat it,** *Colloq.* to go away; depart. **41. beat off, a.** to repulse; thrust aside. **b.** *Colloq.* (*taboo*) to masturbate. **42. beat out, a.** to hammer (metal) thin; flatten. **b.** to forge or make by repeated blows. **c.** to put out (a fire) by beating it: *to beat out the flame.* **d.** to mark out (a rhythm) with the hand. **43. beat the count,** *Boxing* to rise from the floor of the ring before the referee has counted ten. **44. beat the drum, a.** to promote a cause, etc., with fervour. **b.** to present one's case in an unwarrantedly emphatic and longwinded fashion. **45. beat the gun, a.** (of a competitor in a race) to begin before the starting gun has fired. **b.** *Colloq.* to begin prematurely; be overeager. **46. beat up, a.** to assault (someone). **b.** to damage (something). **c.** *Journalism* to exaggerate (a story). **–beatable,** *adj.*

beatific /biəˈtɪfɪk/ *adj.* **1.** bestowing blessedness or beatitude: *a beatific gesture.* **2.** blissful: *a beatific vision; a beatific smile.* **–beatifically,** *adv.*

beatify /biˈætəfaɪ/ *v.t.* (**-fied, -fying**) *Roman Catholic Church* to declare (a deceased person) to be among the blessed, and thus entitled to specific religious honour. **–beatification,** *n.*

beatitude /biˈætəˌtjud, -tʃud/ *n.* **1.** supreme blessedness; exalted happiness. **2.** (*oft. upper case*) *Christianity* any one of the declarations of blessedness pronounced by Christ in the Sermon on the Mount, such as 'Blessed are the poor'.

beatnik /ˈbitnɪk/ *n. Colloq.* someone who avoids traditional conventions of behaviour, dress, etc.

beau /boʊ/ *n.* (*pl.* **beaus** /boʊz/ *or* **beaux** /boʊ, boʊz/) **1.** a boyfriend or lover of a girl or woman. **2.** an escort of a girl or woman. **3.** *Chiefly Brit.* a dandy; fop.

Beaufort scale /ˈboʊfət skeɪl/ *n.* a numerical scale for indicating the force or velocity of the wind, ranging from 0 for calm to 12 for hurricane, or velocities above 120 km/h.

beaujolais /boʊʒəˈleɪ/ *n.* (*sometimes upper case*) **1.** a light red or white wine from the Beaujolais region in south-eastern France. **2.** (in unofficial use) a similar light red wine.

beaut /bjut/ *Aust., NZ Colloq.* –*adj.* **1.** fine; good: *a beaut car.* –*interj.* Also, **you beaut!**. **2.** an exclamation of approval, delight, enthusiasm, etc. –*n.* Also, **beauty**. **3. a.** something successful or highly valued. **b.** a pleasant, agreeable, trustworthy person.

beauteous /ˈbjutiəs/ *adj.* beautiful. –**beauteously,** *adv.* –**beauteousness,** *n.*

beautician /bjuˈtɪʃən/ *n.* a person skilled in cosmetic treatment and beauty aids.

beautiful /ˈbjutəfʊl/ *adj.* **1.** having or exhibiting beauty. **2.** very pleasant: *a beautiful meal.* **3.** perfect: *a beautiful example.* –*phr.* **4. the beautiful,** an aesthetic or philosophical concept of beauty. **5. the beautiful people, a.** a fashionable social set of wealthy, well-groomed, usually young people. **b.** hippies. –**beautifully,** *adv.*

beautify /ˈbjutəfaɪ/ *v.t.* (**-fied, -fying**) to decorate, adorn or make more beautiful: *a plan to beautify the city.* –**beautification** /bjutəfəˈkeɪʃən/, *n.* –**beautifier,** *n.*

beauty /ˈbjuti/ *n.* (*pl.* **-ties**) **1.** that quality which causes pleasure or admiration or delights the aesthetic sense. **2.** something or someone beautiful. **3.** a particular advantage: *the beauty of this job is the long holidays.* –*phr.* **4. (you) (little) beauty,** *Aust., NZ* an exclamation of approval, delight, etc.

beauty spot *n.* **1.** a patch worn on the face or elsewhere to set off the fairness of the skin. **2.** a mole or other small mark on the skin. **3.** a place of scenic beauty.

beaver /ˈbivə/ *n.* **1.** an amphibious rodent of the genus *Castor*, of Europe, Asia and North America, valued for its fur and formerly for castor, and noted for its ingenuity in damming streams with trees, branches, stones, mud, etc. **2.** a flat, round hat made of beaver fur or a similar fabric. –*phr.* **3. beaver away,** (sometimes fol. by *at*) to work hard, like a beaver. –**beaver-like,** *adj.*

bebop /ˈbibɒp/ *n.* a style of jazz composition and performance characterised by dissonant harmony, complex rhythmic devices, and experimental, often bizarre, instrumental effects. Also, **bop, rebop.** –**bebopper,** *n.*

became /bəˈkeɪm/ *v.* past tense of **become**.

because /biˈkɒz, -ˈkɒz, bə-/ *conj.* **1.** for the reason that; due to the fact that: *the game was abandoned because it rained.* –*phr.* **2. because of,** by reason of; on account of: *the game was abandoned because of rain.*

beck /bɛk/ *phr.* **at someone's beck and call,** ready to obey someone immediately; subject to someone's slightest wish.

beckon /ˈbekən/ *v.t.* **1.** to signal, summon, or direct by a gesture of the hand. **2.** to lure; entice. –*v.i.* **3.** to make a summoning gesture. –**beckoner,** *n.*

become /bəˈkʌm, bi-/ *verb* (**became, become, becoming**) –*v. (copular)* **1.** to come or grow to be: *he became tired.* **2.** to develop into: *he became a director.* –*v.t.* **3.** to befit; suit: *that dress becomes you.* –*phr.* **4. become of,** to be the fate of: *what will become of him?*

becoming /bəˈkʌmɪŋ, bi-/ *adj.* **1.** attractive: *a becoming dress.* **2.** suitable; proper: *a becoming sentiment.* –**becomingly,** *adv.* –**becomingness,** *n.*

bed /bɛd/ *n.* **1.** a piece of furniture upon which or within which a person sleeps. **2.** the use of a bed for the night; lodging. **3.** a place for sexual relations: *she took him to her bed.* **4.** a piece of ground (in a garden) in which plants are grown. **5.** the ground under a body of water: *the bed of a lake.* **6.** a piece or part forming a foundation or base. **7.** *Geol.* a sedimentary rock unit with essentially uniform composition, marked by a more or less well-defined divisional plane from its neighbours above and below. –*v.t.* (**bedded, bedding**) **8.** *Hort.* to plant in or as in a bed. **9.** to lay flat, or in a bed or layer. **10.** to embed, as in a substance. **11.** to go to bed with (someone) for sexual intercourse. –*phr.* **12. a bed of roses,** an extremely pleasant situation. **13. bed down, a.** to provide (someone) with a bed. **b.** to put (someone) to bed. **c.** to make a bed for (a horse, cattle, domestic animal, etc.). **d.** to go to bed. **14. put to bed, a.** to ensure (someone) goes to bed. **b.** *Printing* to lock up (a publication) in formes in a press before printing. **c.** to consign (a publication) to the printing process. –**beddable,** *adj.*

bed and breakfast *n.* **1.** (in a motel or the like) the provision of sleeping accommodation and breakfast. **2.** an establishment providing sleeping accommodation and breakfast to paying guests. *Abbrev.:* B & B

bed bug *n.* a small flat, wingless, hemipterous, blood-sucking insect, *Cimex lectularius*, that infests houses and especially beds.

bedding /ˈbedɪŋ/ *n.* **1.** blankets, sheets, for a bed; bedclothes. **2.** litter; straw, etc., as a bed for animals.

bedeck /bəˈdɛk, bi-/ *v.t.* to deck out; showily adorn.

bedevil /bəˈdɛvəl, bi-/ *v.t.* (**-illed** *or, Chiefly US,* **-iled, -illing** *or, Chiefly US,* **-iling**) **1.** to treat diabolically; torment maliciously. **2.** to possess as with a devil; bewitch. **3.** to confound; muddle; spoil. –**bedevilment,** *n.*

bedlam /ˈbedləm/ *n.* **1.** a scene of wild uproar and confusion. **2.** *Archaic* any lunatic asylum; a madhouse.

bedpan /ˈbedpæn/ *n.* **1.** a shallow toilet pan for use by persons confined to bed. **2.** a warming pan.

bedraggled /bəˈdrægəld, bi-/ *adj.* wet and dishevelled.

bedridden /ˈbedrɪdn/ *adj.* confined to bed.

bedrock /ˈbedrɒk/ *n.* **1.** *Geol.* unbroken solid rock, overlaid in most places by soil or rock fragments. **2.** any firm foundation. –*phr.* **3. get down to bedrock,** to come to the essentials.

bedroom /ˈbedrum/ *n.* **1.** a room set aside to sleep in. –*adj.* **2.** of or relating to sexually explicit scenes in a film, play, etc., usually taking place in a bedroom.

bedspread /ˈbedsprɛd/ *n.* an outer covering, usually decorative, for a bed.

bedstead /ˈbedstɛd/ *n.* the framework of a bed supporting the springs and a mattress.

bedwetting /ˈbedwetɪŋ/ *n.* → **enuresis.** –**bedwetter,** *n.*

bee[1] /bi/ *n.* **1.** any of various hymenopterous insects of the superfamily Apoidea, which includes many social and solitary bees of several families, as the bumblebees, honey bees, etc. **2.** the common honey bee, *Apis mellifera.* –*phr.* **3. a bee in one's bonnet,** an obsession. **b.** a slightly crazy idea, attitude, fad, etc. **4. the bee's knees,** *Colloq.* someone or something arousing great admiration. –**beelike,** *adj.*

bee[2] /bi/ *n.* a local gathering for work, entertainment, contests, etc.: *sewing bee; spelling bee.*

beech /bitʃ/ *n.* **1.** any tree of the genus *Fagus*, of temperate regions, having a smooth grey bark, and bearing small edible triangular nuts. **2.** the wood of such a tree. **3.** any species of the genus *Nothofagus* of southern temperate regions. **4.** any of certain unrelated species thought to be similar in appearance or timber, as the **white beech.** **–beechen,** *adj.*

beef /biːf/ *n.* **1.** the flesh of an animal of the genus *Bos*, used for food. **2.** (*pl.* **beeves** /biːvz/) a bull, cow, or steer, especially if intended for meat. **3.** *Colloq.* brawn; muscular strength. **4.** *Colloq.* weight, as of human flesh. **5.** (*pl.* **beefs**) *Chiefly US Colloq.* a complaint. *–v.i.* **6.** *Chiefly US Colloq.* to complain; grumble. *–phr.* **7. beef up,** *Colloq.* to strengthen; make more worthy of attention or interest as by increasing the volume, length, dramatic interest. **–beefy,** *adj.*

beefcake /ˈbiːfkeɪk/ *n. Colloq.* **1.** photographs of attractive men, posed so as to display their bodies and emphasise their sex appeal, as in magazines, newspapers, etc. **2.** men's bodies viewed as sex objects suitable for such photographs. Compare **cheesecake** (def. 2).

beef tea *n.* a beverage made by boiling chopped, lean beef in water and straining it; often given to invalids.

beehive /ˈbiːhaɪv/ *n.* **1.** a hive or receptacle, traditionally dome-shaped but now generally box-like, in which bees live. **2.** a crowded, busy place. **3.** a hat, house, or other object shaped like a traditional beehive.

beeline /ˈbiːlaɪn/ *n.* a direct line, like the course of bees returning to a hive: *the hungry children made a beeline for the food.*

been /biːn/, *weak form* /bən/ *v.* past participle of **be.**

beep /biːp/ *n.* **1.** the sound made by a horn on a car or other vehicle. **2.** a short, high-pitched sound often electronically produced.

beer /bɪə/ *n.* **1.** an alcoholic beverage made by brewing and fermentation from cereals, usually malted barley and flavoured with hops, etc., to give a bitter taste. **2.** any of various beverages, whether alcoholic or not, made from roots, molasses, or sugar, yeast, etc.: *root beer, ginger beer.* **3.** a glass, can, etc., of beer: *let's have a beer.* **–beery,** *adj.*

beet /biːt/ *n.* any of various biennial plants of the genus *Beta*, whose varieties include the red beet, which has a fleshy edible root, and the sugar beet, which yields sugar. **–beetlike,** *adj.*

beetle /ˈbiːtl/ *n.* **1.** any insect of the order Coleoptera, characterised by having forewings modified as hard, horny structures (elytra), not vibrated in flight. **2.** any of various insects resembling beetles, as the common cockroach. **3.** (*also upper case*) *Colloq.* a dice game in which the aim is to assemble or draw a beetle-shaped figure. *–phr.* **4. beetle along,** to move rapidly along, especially in a motor vehicle.

beetroot /ˈbiːtruːt/ *n.* the edible root of the red beet.

befall /bəˈfɔːl/ *verb* (**-fell, -fallen, -falling**) *–v.i.* **1.** to happen or occur. *–v.t.* **2.** to happen to.

befit /bəˈfɪt/ *v.t.* to be fitting or appropriate for; be suited to: *his clothes befit the occasion.*

before /bəˈfɔː/ *adv.* **1.** in front; in advance; ahead. **2.** in time preceding; previously. **3.** earlier or sooner: *begin at noon, not before.* *–prep.* **4.** in front of; ahead of; in advance of: *before the house.* **5.** previously to; earlier than: *before the war.* **6.** ahead of; in the future of; awaiting: *the golden age is before us.* **7.** in preference to; rather than: *they would die before yielding.* **8.** in precedence of, as in order or rank: *we put freedom before fame.* **9.** in the presence or sight of: *before an audience.* **10.** under the jurisdiction or consideration of: *before a magistrate.* *–conj.* **11.** previously to the time when: *before we go.* **12.** sooner than; rather than: *I will die before I submit.* **13.** as a condition under which: *students must achieve an exam result of at least 80 per cent before they will be considered for entry into the program.* *–phr.* **14. before the wind,** *Naut.* blown along by the wind.

beforehand /bəˈfɔːhænd/ *adv.* in anticipation; in advance; ahead of time.

befriend /bəˈfrɛnd, biː-/ *v.t.* to act as a friend to; aid.

befuddle /bəˈfʌdl, biː-/ *v.t.* **1.** to make stupidly drunk. **2.** to confuse, as with glib argument.

beg /bɛg/ *verb* (**begged, begging**) *–v.t.* **1.** to ask for in charity; ask as alms. **2.** to ask for, or of, with humility or earnestness, or as a favour: *to beg forgiveness; to beg him to forgive me.* **3.** to assume or demand permission (to say or do something): *to beg to differ; to beg to point out an error.* *–v.i.* **4.** to ask alms or charity; live by asking alms. **5.** (sometimes fol. by *for*) to ask humbly or earnestly: *to beg for help.* *–phr.* **6. beg off,** to excuse oneself from: *to beg off going to the pictures.* **7. beg the question, a.** to assume something which supports a point of view, even though this assumption may not be proven: *Saying that criminal parents produce criminal children begs the question of the influence of heredity on the development of a child.* **b.** to prompt or raise the question: *saying that women should be paid to stay at home begs the question of who is to fund it.* **c.** to evade the point at issue. **8. beg your pardon, a.** an exclamation of polite apology. **b.** a request for the repetition of something not clearly heard. **9. go begging,** to be unwanted; be unclaimed.

began /bəˈgæn, biː-/ *v.* past tense of **begin.**

beget /bəˈgɛt, biː-/ *v.t.* (**begot, begotten** *or* **begot, begetting**) **1.** to procreate or generate (used chiefly of the male parent). **2.** to cause; produce as an effect. **–begetter,** *n.*

beggar /ˈbɛgə/ *n.* **1.** someone who begs alms, or lives by begging. **2.** a penniless person. **3.** *Chiefly Brit. Colloq.* a person: *a lucky beggar.* *–v.t.* **4.** to reduce to beggary; impoverish. **5.** to exhaust the resources of: *to beggar description.* *–phr.* **6. a beggar for punishment,** someone who consistently exerts himself or herself. **7. beggar belief,** to cause astonishment to the point of disbelief. **–beggarly,** *adv.* **–beggary,** *n.* **–beggardom** /ˈbɛgədəm/, **beggarhood,** *n.* **–beggarman,** *n.*

begin /bəˈgɪn/ *verb* (**began, begun, beginning**) *–v.i.* **1.** to enter upon an action; take the first step; commence; start. **2.** to come into existence; arise; originate. *–v.t.* **3.** to take the first step in; set about; start; commence. **4.** to originate; be the originator of. *–phr.* **5. to begin with, a.** in the first place; firstly. **b.** as a start. **–beginner,** *n.*

beginning /bəˈgɪnɪŋ/ *n.* **1.** the act or fact of entering upon an action or state. **2.** the point of time or space at which anything begins: *the beginning of the Christian era.* **3.** the first part or initial stage of anything: *the beginnings of science.* **4.** origin; source; first cause: *humility is the beginning of wisdom.*

begone /bəˈgɒn, biː-/ *v.i.* (*usu. imperative*) to go away, depart.

begonia /bəˈgoʊniə, -jə/ *n.* any plant of the tropical genus *Begonia*, including species much cultivated for their handsome, succulent, often varicoloured leaves and waxy flowers.

begrudge /bəˈgrʌdʒ, biː-/ *v.t.* **1.** to be discontented at seeing (a person) have (something): *to begrudge someone their good fortune.* **2.** to be reluctant to give, grant, or allow: *to begrudge him the money he earned.*

beguile /bəˈgaɪl, biː-/ *v.t.* (**-guiled, -guiling**) **1.** to influence by guile; mislead; delude. **2.** to charm or divert. **–beguilement,** *n.* **–beguiler,** *n.* **–beguilingly,** *adv.*

begun /bəˈgʌn, biː-/ *v.* past participle of **begin.**

behalf /bəˈhaf, biː-/ *n.* (preceded by *on*) side, interest, or aid: *on behalf of his country.*

behave /bəˈheɪv, biː-/ *v.i.* **1.** to conduct oneself or itself; act: *the ship behaves well.* **2.** to act in a socially acceptable manner: *did the child behave?* *–phr.* **3. behave oneself, a.** to conduct oneself in a specified way. **b.** to conduct oneself properly.

behaviour /bəˈheɪvjə, biː-/ *n.* **1.** manner of behaving or acting. **2.** *Psychol.* the actions or activities of the individual as matters of psychological study. Also, **behavior.** –**behavioural,** *adj.* –**behaviourally,** *adv.*

behaviourism /bə'heɪvjəˌrɪzəm, bi-/ *n.* the study, in humans and animals, of externally observable behavioural responses as functions or environmental stimuli; mental states are either ignored or redefined in stimulus/response terms. Also, **behaviorism.** –**behaviourist,** *n., adj.*

behead /bə'hɛd, bi-/ *v.t.* to cut off the head of; kill or execute by decapitation.

beheld /bə'hɛld, bi-/ *v.* past tense and past participle of **behold.**

behest /bə'hɛst, bi-/ *n.* bidding or injunction; mandate or command.

behind /bə'haɪnd, bi-/ *prep.* **1.** at the back of: *behind the house.* **2.** after; later than: *behind schedule.* **3.** less advanced than: *behind his class in science.* **4.** on the far side of; beyond: *behind the mountain.* **5.** supporting; promoting: *the council is behind the idea.* **6.** hidden by: *bitterness lay behind her smile.* –*adv.* **7.** at or towards the back: *she pushed him behind.* **8.** in a place, state or stage already passed: *he left his wallet behind.* **9.** late: *behind with the rent.* **10.** slow, as a watch or clock. –*n.* **11.** the buttocks. **12.** *Aust. Rules* a score of one point, achieved by putting the ball between a goal post and an outer post.

behindhand /bə'haɪndhænd, bi-/ *adj.* **1.** late. **2.** behind in progress; backward. **3.** in arrears: *behindhand with payments.*

behold /bə'hoʊld, bi-/ *v.t.* (**-held, -holding**) **1.** to observe; look at; see. –*interj.* **2.** look! see! –**beholder,** *n.*

beholden /bə'hoʊldn, bi-/ *adj.* under an obligation; indebted.

behove /bə'hoʊv, bi-/ *v.t.* (**-hoved, -hoving**) to be needful or proper for or incumbent on (now only in impersonal use): *it behoves me to see him.* Also, *Chiefly US,* **behoove** /bə'huːv/.

beige /beɪʒ/ *n.* a very light brown, as of undyed wool; light grey with brownish tinge.

being /'biːɪŋ/ *n.* **1.** existence; life: *what is the purpose of our being?* **2.** nature; self: *she threw her whole being into the task.* **3.** something that lives or exists: *beings on a strange planet; a human being.* **4.** *Philos.* **a.** that which has reality either materially or in idea. **b.** absolute existence in a complete or perfect state, lacking no necessary characteristic; essence.

belabour /bə'leɪbə, bi-/ *v.t.* **1.** to beat vigorously; ply with heavy blows. **2.** to assail persistently, as with ridicule. Also, **belabor.**

belated /bə'leɪtəd, bi-/ *adj.* coming or being late or too late. –**belatedly,** *adv.* –**belatedness,** *n.*

belay /bə'leɪ, bi-/ *verb* (**-layed, -laying**) –*v.t.* **1.** *Naut.* to fasten (a rope) by winding around a pin or short rod inserted in a holder so that both ends of the rod are clear. **2.** *Mountaineering* to secure (a rope or person) by a turn of rope round a rock or piton. –*v.i.* **3.** (*used chiefly in the imperative*) to stop. **4.** to make a rope fast.

belch /bɛltʃ/ *v.i.* **1.** to eject wind spasmodically and noisily from the stomach through the mouth; eructate; burp. **2.** to emit contents violently, as a gun, geyser, or volcano. –*v.t.* **3.** to eject spasmodically or violently; give forth. –*n.* **4.** a belching; eructation. –**belcher,** *n.*

beleaguer /bə'liːgə, bi-/ *v.t.* **1.** to surround with an army. **2.** to surround: *to beleaguer the city.* **3.** to beset with troubles and annoyances. –**beleaguerer,** *n.*

beleaguered /bə'liːgəd, bi-/ *v.* **1.** past tense and past participle of **beleaguer.** –*adj.* **2.** surrounded by hostile forces: *the beleaguered city.* **3.** oppressed by problems that threaten one's position, role, status, prospects, etc.: *the beleaguered minister.*

belfry /'bɛlfri/ *n.* (*pl.* **-ries**) **1.** a belltower, either attached to a church or other building or standing apart. **2.** the

part of a steeple or other structure in which a bell is hung. **3.** a frame of timberwork which may sustain a bell. –*phr.* **4. have bats in the belfry,** *Colloq.* to have mad notions; be crazy or peculiar.

belie /bə'laɪ, bi-/ *v.t.* (**-lied, -lying**) **1.** to misrepresent: *his face belied his thoughts.* **2.** to show to be false: *his trembling belied his calm words.* –**belier,** *n.*

belief /bə'liːf, bi-/ *n.* **1.** something that is believed; an accepted opinion. **2.** conviction of the truth or reality of a thing, based upon grounds insufficient to afford positive knowledge: *statements unworthy of belief.* **3.** confidence; faith; trust: *a child's belief in his or her parents.*

believe /bə'liːv, bi-/ *v.t.* **1.** to have belief in: *to believe a person.* **2.** to think: *I believe he has left the city.* **3.** to credit; accept as true: *to believe a story.* –*phr.* **4. believe in, a.** to have confidence in; trust; rely through faith on: *I believe in you implicitly.* **b.** to be persuaded of the truth or existence of: *he still believes in Santa Claus.* **c.** to accept (a doctrine, principle, system, etc.): *I don't believe in private education.* –**believable,** *adj.* –**believer,** *n.* –**believingly,** *adv.* –**believably,** *adv.*

belittle /bə'lɪtl, bi-/ *v.t.* to make little or less important; depreciate; disparage.

bell /bɛl/ *n.* **1.** a sounding instrument, usually of metal, cup-shaped with a flaring mouth, rung by the strokes of a clapper, tongue, or hammer suspended within it. **2.** any instrument emitting a ringing signal, especially an electrical device in which an electromagnet causes a hammer to strike repeatedly a hollow metal hemisphere, producing a continuous ringing sound, as a doorbell. **3.** the stroke, sound, or signal emitted by such an instrument. **4.** *Colloq.* a telephone call: *to give someone a bell.* **5.** *Naut.* the half-hourly subdivisions of a watch of four hours, each being marked by single or double strokes of a bell. **6.** any object in the shape of a traditional bell (def. 1). **7.** the end of a musical wind instrument, or any tube when its edge has been turned out and enlarged. **8.** *Zool.* → **umbrella** (def. 2). –*v.t.* **9.** to put a bell on (grazing cattle, etc.), so as to know where they are: *the horses had been hobbled and belled for the night.* **10.** *Colloq.* to make a telephone call to. –*phr.* **11. bells and whistles,** additional features, especially those which are of a frivolous and a superficially attractive nature. **12. bell the cat,** to undertake a dangerous enterprise for the common good. **13. ring a bell,** to jog the memory. **14. with bells on,** *Colloq.* **a.** in all one's finery. **b.** ready and eager. –**bell-like,** *adj.*

belladonna /bɛlə'dɒnə/ *n.* **1.** a poisonous plant, *Atropa belladonna,* of the family Solanaceae; deadly nightshade. **2.** either of two drugs, atropine and hyoscyamine, obtained from this plant, and used as a cardiac or respiratory stimulant, or an antispasmodic.

bellbird /'bɛlbɜːd/ *n.* **1.** Also, **bell miner.** a yellowish-green honeyeater, *Manorina melanophrys,* with a distinctive, tinkling, bell-like call, found especially near water in wooded coastal and mountain areas from southern Qld to Victoria. **2.** a New Zealand honeyeater, *Anthornis melanura.*

bellboy /'bɛlbɔɪ/ *n.* a young employee in a hotel who carries luggage, runs errands, etc.

belle /bɛl/ *n.* a woman or girl admired for her beauty; a reigning beauty.

bellicose /'bɛləkoʊs/ *adj.* inclined to war; warlike; pugnacious. –**bellicosely,** *adv.* –**bellicosity** /bɛlə-'kɒsəti/, *n.*

belligerent /bə'lɪdʒərənt/ *adj.* **1.** warlike; given to waging war. **2.** of warlike character: *a belligerent tone.* **3.** relating to war, or to those engaged in war: *belligerent rights.* **4.** aggressive; argumentative. –*n.* **5.** a state or nation at war, or a member of the military forces of such a state. —**belligerence**, **belligerency**, *n.* —**belligerently**, *adv.*

bell jar *n.* a bell-shaped glass vessel or cover, as for protecting delicate instruments, bric-a-brac, etc., or for holding gases in chemical operations. Also, **bell glass**.

bell miner *n.* → **bellbird** (def. 1).

bellow /'bɛloʊ/ *v.i.* **1.** to make a hollow, loud, animal cry, as a bull or cow. **2.** to roar; bawl: *bellowing with rage.* —*v.t.* **3.** to utter in a loud deep voice: *to bellow forth an answer.* —*n.* **4.** the act or sound of bellowing. —**bellower**, *n.*

bellows /'bɛloʊz/ *n. (construed as sing. or pl.)* **1.** an instrument or machine for producing a strong current of air, as for a draught for a fire or sounding an organ or other musical instrument, consisting essentially of an air-chamber which can be expanded to draw in air through a valve and contracted to expel the air through a tube or tubes. **2.** anything resembling or suggesting a bellows, as the collapsible part of a camera or enlarger.

bellwether /'bɛlwɛðə/ *n.* **1.** a wether or other male sheep which leads the flock, on which a bell is hung to facilitate tracking. **2.** a person whom others follow blindly. **3.** a social group which is the leader in a particular trend, thus indicating directions for the future for the mass of people.

belly /'bɛli/ *n. (pl.* **bellies)** **1.** the front or underneath part of a vertebrate animal from the chest to the thighs, containing the stomach, bowel, etc.; the abdomen. **2.** the stomach. **3.** appetite for food; gluttony. **4.** the inside of anything: *the belly of a ship.* **5.** a raised section of anything, as of a bottle, etc. **6.** the front, inner, or underneath part (opposed to *back*). —*verb* (**bellied**, **bellying**) —*v.i.* **7.** to become swollen: *the sails bellied in the wind.* —*v.t.* **8.** to make swollen: *the wind bellied the sails.* —*phr.* **9. go belly up**, *Colloq.* to fail: *the business went belly up after devaluation.*

bellyache /'bɛli-eɪk/ *Colloq.* —*n.* **1.** a pain in the stomach, especially colic. **2.** a complaint. —*v.t.* (**-ached**, **-aching**) **3.** to complain or grumble. —**bellyacher**, *n.*

belong /bə'lɒŋ, bi-/ *v.i.* **1.** to be usually or rightly placed: *the knives belong in the drawer.* **2.** to have the proper social qualifications: *he doesn't belong.* **3.** to be proper or due. —*phr.* **4. belong to, a.** to bear a relation to as a member, adherent, inhabitant, etc.: *to belong to the soccer club.* **b.** to be the property of: *the book belongs to him.* **c.** to be an appurtenance, adjunct, or part of: *that lid belongs to this jar.* **d.** to be a property, function, or concern of: *attributes which belong to nature.*

beloved /bə'lʌvəd, -'lʌvd, bi-/ *adj.* **1.** greatly loved; dear to the heart. —*n.* **2.** someone who is greatly loved.

below /bə'loʊ, bi-/ *adv.* **1.** in or to a lower place; beneath. **2.** on or to a lower floor; downstairs. **3.** at a later point on a page or in writing: *see below for further notes.* **4.** in a lower rank or grade: *the class below.* —*prep.* **5.** lower than: *below the knee; below the usual cost.* **6.** unworthy of.

belt /bɛlt/ *n.* **1.** a band of flexible material, as leather, worn around the waist to support clothing, for decoration, etc. **2.** *Sport* such a band as a token of honour or achievement. **3.** *Surf Lifesaving* a wide canvas belt which is worn by the member of the surf lifesaving team who swims out to effect a rescue, and which is attached to the surf-line. **4.** any encircling or transverse band, strip, or strips: *a belt of storms moving along the coast.* **5.** a strip of a city comprising a suburb or number of suburbs in which a specified group of people tend to predominate: *the stockbroker belt.* **6.** a large strip of land having distinctive properties or characteristics: *the wheat belt.* **7.** *Machinery* a flexible band or cord connecting and pulling about each of two or more wheels, pulleys or the like, to transmit or change the direction of motion. **b.** conveyor belt. **8.** *Mil.* **a.** a cloth

strip with loops, or a series of metal links with grips, for holding cartridges which are fed into an automatic gun. **b.** a band of leather or webbing, worn around the waist and used as a support for weapons, ammunition, etc. **9.** *Boxing* an imaginary line round the body at the level of the navel below which the boxer must not strike. —*v.t.* **10.** to gird or furnish with a belt. **11.** to surround or mark as if with a belt. **12.** to fasten on (a sword, etc.) by means of a belt. **13.** to beat with a belt, strap, etc. —*phr.* **14. below the belt**, against the rules; unfairly. **15. belt along**, *Colloq.* to move quickly or expeditiously. **16. belt into, a.** to begin with speed and vigour. **b.** *Colloq.* to eat or drink quickly: *belt that food into you.* **17. belt out**, to sing very loudly and often raucously. **18. belt up**, *Colloq.* **a.** to be quiet; shut up. **b.** to fasten a safety belt. **c.** to beat; strike.

bemoan /bə'moʊn, bi-/ *v.t.* **1.** to moan over; bewail; lament. **2.** to express pity for.

bemused /bə'mjuzd, bi-/ *adj.* **1.** confused; muddled; stupefied. **2.** lost in thought; preoccupied.

bench /bɛntʃ/ *n.* **1.** a long seat with or without a back to accommodate several people. **2.** a seat on which members sit in a house of parliament. **3.** a seat occupied by a person in his or her official capacity. **4.** the strong work-table of a carpenter or other mechanic. **5.** → **kitchen bench**. **6.** *Mining* a step or working elevation in a mine. **7. the bench**, **a.** the position or office of a judge: *appointed to the bench.* **b.** the body of persons sitting as judges. **c.** *Sport* the reserve players present at a game. —*v.t.* **8.** to place in exhibition: *to bench a dog.* **9.** *Sport* to relegate to the bench. —**benchless**, *adj.*

benchmark /'bɛntʃmak/ *n.* **1.** a point of reference from which quality or excellence is measured. —*adj.* **2.** of or relating to a benchmark. —*v.t.* **3.** to set a benchmark for: *this case will benchmark all future judgements in the wages area.*

bend /bɛnd/ *verb* (**bent**, **bending**) —*v.t.* **1.** to force into a different or particular, especially curved, shape, as by pressure. **2.** to cause to submit: *to bend someone to one's will.* **3.** to turn in a particular direction. —*v.i.* **4.** to become curved, crooked, or bent. **5.** to assume a bent posture; stoop. **6.** to bow in submission or reverence; yield; submit. —*n.* **7.** the act of bending. **8.** a bent thing or part; curve; crook. **9.** *Naut.* a knot by which a rope is fastened to another rope or to something else. —*phr.* **10. bend over backwards**, to exert oneself to the utmost; make a strenuous effort. **11. bend the elbow**, *Colloq.* to drink alcoholic liquor, usually to excess. **12. bend towards**, to incline mentally: *to bend towards an innovative approach.* **13. round the bend**, *Colloq.* mad. —**bendable**, *adj.*

bender /'bɛndə/ *n.* **1.** *Colloq.* a heavy bout of alcoholic consumption to the point of intoxication, usually lasting several days and involving loss of control. **2.** an imaginary character who has supernatural powers to summon an element such as fire or water to their defence.

bends /bɛndz/ *pl. n.* **the**, a dangerous disorder where nitrogen bubbles form in the blood because of a too rapid decrease in surrounding pressure, found especially in divers who have surfaced too quickly.

bene- a word element meaning 'well', as in *benediction.*

beneath /bə'niθ, bi-/ *adv.* **1.** below; in a lower place, position, state, etc. **2.** underneath: *the heaven above and the earth beneath.* —*prep.* **3.** below; under: *beneath the same roof.* **4.** further down than; underneath. **5.** lower in position, power, etc., to: *a captain is beneath a general.* **6.** unworthy of; below the level of: *beneath your notice.*

benediction /bɛnə'dɪkʃən/ *n.* **1.** the act of uttering a blessing. **2.** the form of blessing pronounced by an officiating minister, as at the close of Christian worship. **3.** the advantage conferred by blessing; a mercy or benefit. –**benedictional**, *adj.* –**benedictory** /bɛnə-'dɪktəri/, *adj.*

benefactor /'bɛnəfæktə, bɛnə'fæktə/ *n.* **1.** someone who confers a benefit; kindly helper. **2.** someone who makes a bequest or endowment. –**benefactress** /'bɛnəfæktrəs, bɛnə'fæktrəs/, *fem. n.*

beneficent /bə'nɛfəsənt/ *adj.* doing good or causing good to be done; conferring benefits; kindly in action or purpose. –**beneficence**, *n.* –**beneficently**, *adv.*

beneficial /bɛnə'fɪʃəl/ *adj.* **1.** conferring benefit; advantageous; helpful. **2.** *Law* helpful in the meeting of needs: *a beneficial association.* –**beneficially**, *adv.* –**beneficialness**, **beneficiality**, *n.*

beneficiary /bɛnə'fɪʃəri/ *n.* (*pl.* -**ries**) someone who receives benefits, profits, or advantages.

benefit /'bɛnəfət/ *n.* **1.** an act of kindness. **2.** anything that is for the good of a person or thing. **3.** any public performance to raise money for a worthy purpose. **4.** payment or other assistance given by an insurance company, public agency, etc. –*verb* (-**fited**, -**fiting**) –*v.t.* **5.** to do good to: *the holiday will benefit her.* –*v.i.* **6.** to gain advantage: *he will benefit from the will.*

benevolent /bə'nɛvələnt/ *adj.* **1.** desiring to do good for others. **2.** intended for benefits rather than profit: *a benevolent institution.* –**benevolence**, *n.* –**benevolently**, *adv.*

benighted /bə'naɪtəd/ *adj.* **1.** intellectually or morally ignorant; unenlightened. **2.** overtaken by darkness or night.

benign /bə'naɪn/ *adj.* **1.** of a kind disposition; kind. **2.** showing or caused by gentleness or kindness: *a benign smile.* **3.** favourable; propitious: *benign planets.* **4.** *Pathol.* not malignant: *a benign tumour.* –**benignity** /bə'nɪgnəti/, *n.* –**benignly**, *adv.*

benign neglect *n.* neglect which has beneficial results, possibly better results than if there had been active involvement or concern: *a foreign policy of benign neglect.*

bent /bɛnt/ *adj.* **1.** curved; crooked: *a bent stick, bow, etc.* **2.** *Colloq.* dishonest; corrupt: *a bent cop.* **3.** *Colloq.* diverging from what is considered to be normal or conservative behaviour. **4.** *Colloq.* stolen: *to sell bent goods.* **5.** *Music* of a tone, slightly altered from the pitch of the diatonic scale, as a bent note. –*n.* **6.** bent state or form. **7.** direction taken; inclination; leaning; bias: *a bent for painting.* **8.** capacity of endurance. **9.** *Civil Eng.* a transverse frame of a bridge or a building, designed to support either vertical or horizontal loads. –*phr.* **10. bent on** (or **upon**), set on: *bent on having fun; bent upon escape.*

bento box /'bɛntoʊ bɒks/ *n.* a selection of Japanese foods served in a compartmentalised container, traditionally an elaborately decorated lacquered box.

benumb /bə'nʌm, bi-/ *v.t.* **1.** to make numb; deprive of sensation: *benumbed by cold.* **2.** to render inactive; stupefy.

benzene /'bɛnzin, bɛn'zin/ *n.* a colourless, volatile, flammable, liquid, aromatic hydrocarbon, C_6H_6, obtained chiefly from coal tar, and used as a solvent for resins, fats, etc., and in the manufacture of dyes, etc.

benzine /'bɛnzin, bɛn'zin/ *n.* a colourless, volatile, flammable liquid, a mixture of various hydrocarbons, obtained in the distillation of petroleum, and used in cleaning, dyeing, etc.

bequeath /bə'kwið, -'kwiθ/ *v.t.* **1.** *Law* to dispose by last will of (personal property, especially money). **2.** to hand down; pass on. –**bequeathal** /bə'kwiðəl/, *n.*

bequest /bə'kwɛst, bi-/ *n.* **1.** *Law* a disposition in a will concerning personal property, especially money. **2.** a legacy.

berate /bə'reɪt/ *v.t.* to scold.

bereave /bə'riv, bi-/ *v.t.* (-**reaved** *or* -**reft**, -**reaving**) **1.** (*usu. in the passive*) to deprive ruthlessly, especially of hope, joy, etc.: *bereft of all their lands.* **2.** (*usu. in the passive*) to make desolate through loss, especially by death: *bereaved of their mother.* –**bereavement**, *n.*

bereft /bə'rɛft/ *v.* **1.** past participle of **bereave**. –*adj.* **2.** suffering loss; deprived of possession: *bereft of his family.* **3.** lacking: *bereft of meaning.*

beret /'bɛreɪ, bə'reɪ/ *n.* a soft, round, peakless cap that fits closely.

beri-beri /'bɛri-bɛri/ *n.* a disease of the peripheral nerves caused by deficiency in vitamin B_1 and marked by pain in and paralysis of the extremities, and severe emaciation or swelling of the body.

berley /'bɜli/ *n. Aust., NZ* any bait, as chopped fish or broken bread or chopped green weed mixed with sand, spread on the water by fishermen to attract fish.

Bermuda jacket /bəmjudə 'dʒækət/ *n.* → **reefer jacket**.

berry /'bɛri/ *n.* (*pl.* -**ries**) **1.** any small, (usually) stoneless and juicy fruit, irrespective of botanical structure, as the gooseberry, strawberry, holly berry, rosehip, etc. **2.** a dry seed or kernel, as of wheat. **3.** *Bot.* a simple fruit having a pulpy pericarp in which the seeds are embedded, as the grape, gooseberry, currant, tomato, etc. –**berryless**, *adj.* –**berrylike**, *adj.*

berserk /bə'zɜk/ *adj.* **1.** violently and destructively frenzied. –*phr.* **2. go berserk**, to behave in an emotional and extravagant fashion, as from anger or grief.

berth /bɜθ/ *n.* **1.** a shelf-like space, bunk, or whole room allotted to a traveller on a vessel or a train as a sleeping space. **2.** *Naut.* **a.** room for a vessel to moor at a dock or ride at anchor. **b.** a space allowed for safety or convenience between a vessel and other vessels, rocks, etc. **3.** any place allotted to a person. **4.** *Colloq.* a job; position. –*v.t.* **5.** *Naut.* to assign or allot anchoring ground to; give space to lie in, as a ship in a dock. –*v.i.* **6.** *Naut.* to come to a dock, anchorage, or mooring. –*phr.* **7. give a wide berth to**, to avoid; keep away from.

beryl /'bɛrəl/ *n.* **1.** a mineral, beryllium aluminium silicate, $Be_3Al_2Si_6O_{18}$, usually green (but also blue, rose, white, and golden) and either opaque or transparent, the latter variety including the gems emerald and aquamarine; the principal ore of beryllium. **2.** pale bluish green; sea green. –**beryline** /'bɛrəlin, -laɪn/, *adj.*

beseech /bə'sitʃ, bi-/ *v.t.* (-**sought** *or* -**seeched**, -**seeching**) **1.** to implore urgently. **2.** to beg eagerly for; solicit. –**beseecher**, *n.* –**beseechingness**, *n.* –**beseeching**, *adj.* –**beseechingly**, *adv.*

beset /bə'sɛt, bi-/ *v.t.* (-**set**, -**setting**) to attack on all sides; assail; harass: *beset by enemies; beset by difficulties.* –**besetment**, *n.*

beside /bə'saɪd, bi-/ *prep.* **1.** by or at the side of; near: *sit down beside me.* **2.** compared with. **3.** apart from; not connected with: *beside the point; beside the question.* –*adv.* **4.** in addition; besides. –*phr.* **5. beside oneself**, out of one's senses through strong emotion.

besides /bə'saɪdz, bi-/ *adv.* **1.** moreover. **2.** in addition. **3.** otherwise; else. –*prep.* **4.** over and above; in addition to. **5.** other than; except.

besiege /bə'sidʒ, bi-/ *v.t.* (-**sieged**, -**sieging**) **1.** to lay siege to. **2.** to crowd round. **3.** to assail or ply, as with requests, etc. –**besiegement**, *n.* –**besieger**, *n.*

besotted /bə'sɒtəd, bi-/ *adj.* **1.** filled with foolish love: *he was besotted with her.* **2.** stupid or drunk.

besought /bə'sɔt, bi-/ *v.* past tense and past participle of **beseech**.

bespoke /bə'spoʊk, bi-/ *adj.* made to order: *bespoke goods.*

best /bɛst/ *adj.* (*superlative of* **good**) **1.** of the highest quality, excellence, or standing: *the best judgement.* **2.** most advantageous, suitable, or desirable: *the best way.* **3.** largest; most: *I haven't seen her for the best* part of an hour. **4.** favourite: *best friend.* *–adv.* (*superlative of* **well**) **5.** most excellently or suitably; with most advantage or success. **6.** in or to the highest degree; most fully. *–n.* **7.** the best thing, state, or part. **8.** one's finest clothing. **9.** utmost or best quality. *–v.t.* **10.** to defeat; beat. **11.** to outdo; surpass. *–phr.* **12. all the best,** an expression of good will, used as a farewell or a toast. **13. at best, a.** in the best circumstances. **b.** in the most favourable view. **14. at one's best,** appearing or performing as well as possible. **15. for the best, a.** having an unexpectedly good result: *it all turned out for the best.* **b.** with good intentions or motives: *I'm sure she meant it for the best.* **16. get** (or **have**) **the best of,** to defeat. **17. get the best out of,** to so manage or operate as to coax the best performance from: *to get the best out of a car; to get the best out of a player.* **18. give someone** (or **something**) **best,** to admit defeat to someone or something. **19. had best,** would be wiser, safer, etc., to. **20. have the best of both worlds,** to combine or enjoy the benefits of two different situations. **21. make the best of,** to manage as well as one can with (unfavourable or adverse circumstances). **22. the best thing since sliced bread,** *Colloq.* something worthy of great admiration.

bestial /ˈbɛstiəl/ *adj.* **1.** of or belonging to a beast. **2.** brutal; inhuman; irrational. **3.** depravedly sensual; carnal. *–bestially, adv.*

bestiality /bɛstiˈæləti/ *n.* **1.** bestial character or conduct; beastliness. **2.** excessive appetites or indulgence. **3.** sexual relations of a human with an animal.

bestie /ˈbɛsti/ *Colloq.* *–n.* **1.** a best friend. *–phr.* **2. become besties with,** to form a close friendship with.

best man *n.* the man who acts as the chief attendant of the bridegroom at a wedding.

bestow /bəˈstoʊ, bi-/ *v.t.* **1.** to present as a gift; give; confer. **2.** to dispose of; apply to some use. **3.** to put; stow; deposit; store. *–bestowal, bestowment, n.* *–bestower, n.*

bet /bɛt/ *verb* (**bet** or **betted, betting**) *–v.t.* **1.** to pledge as a forfeit to another who makes a similar pledge in return, in support of an opinion; stake; wager. *–v.i.* **2.** to lay a wager. **3.** to make a practice of betting. **4.** to predict a certain outcome: *I bet it rains on the weekend.* *–n.* **5.** a pledge of something to be forfeited, in case one is wrong, to another who has the opposite opinion. **6.** that which is pledged. **7.** a thing, person, or course of action on which to gamble or stake one's hopes: *he's a bad bet.* *–phr.* **8. bet London to a brick** (**on**), *Colloq.* an expression used to emphasise the fact that you are firmly convinced about something. **9. one's best bet,** the best option for a person to choose: *catching the bus is your best bet.* **10. the best bet,** the best option: *living on campus is the best bet for students.* **11. you bet,** *Colloq.* an exclamation of agreement, confirmation, etc.

beta /ˈbitə/ *n.* the second letter of the Greek alphabet (B, β = English B, b), often used to designate the second in a series, especially in scientific classification, as: **1.** (*upper case*) *Astron.* the second brightest star of a constellation: *Rigel is β (or Beta) Orionis.* **2.** *Chem.* (of a compound) one of the possible positions of substituted atoms or groups. **3.** (in examinations, etc.) the second highest mark or grade.

beta- *Chem.* a combining form designating one of two or more possible allotropes, as in *beta-endorphin.*

beta test *n.* a final test of a newly developed product prior to its official release. *–beta testing, n.*

beta version *n.* the version of a product used in a beta test.

betel nut /ˈbitl nʌt/ *n.* the fruit of the betel palm, chewed in New Guinea and many parts of tropical Asia with lime derived from burnt coral or shells, and with any of various hot substances.

bête noire /bɛt ˈnwa/ *n.* something that one especially dislikes or dreads, such as a person, task, or object; bugbear.

betide /bəˈtaɪd, bi-/ *v.t.* **1.** *Archaic* to happen to; befall; come to: *woe betide the villain!* *–v.i.* **2.** to come to pass.

betoken /bəˈtoʊkən, bi-/ *v.t.* **1.** to give evidence of; indicate. **2.** to be or give a token of; portend.

betray /bəˈtreɪ, bi-/ *v.t.* **1.** to deliver or expose to an enemy by treachery or disloyalty. **2.** to be disloyal to; disappoint the hopes or expectations of. **3.** to be unfaithful in keeping or upholding: *to betray a trust.* **4.** to reveal or disclose in violation of confidence: *to betray a secret.* **5.** to reveal unconsciously (something one would preferably conceal). **6.** to show; exhibit. *–phr.* **7. betray oneself,** to reveal one's real character, plans, etc. *–betrayal, n.* *–betrayer, n.*

betroth /bəˈtroʊð, -ˈtroʊθ, bi-/ *v.t.* *Archaic* **1.** (of a man) to promise to marry (a woman). **2.** to arrange for the marriage of; affiance. *–betrothal, n.*

better /ˈbɛtə/ *adj.* (*comparative of* **good**) **1.** of superior quality or excellence: *a better position.* **2.** of superior value, use, fitness, desirability, acceptableness, etc.: *a better time for action.* **3.** larger; greater: *the better part of a lifetime.* **4.** improved in health; healthier. **5.** completely recovered in health; well. *–adv.* (*comparative of* **well**) **6.** in a more excellent way or manner: *to behave better.* **7.** to a superior degree: *nature does it better.* **8.** more: *better than a kilometre to town.* *–v.t.* **9.** to make better; improve; increase the good qualities of. *–n.* **10.** that which has superior excellence, etc.: *the better of two choices.* **11.** (*usu. pl.*) one's superior in wisdom, wealth, etc. *–phr.* **12. better off,** in better circumstances. **13. get the better of, a.** to prove superior to. **b.** to overcome: *to allow one's imagination to get the better of one's judgement.* **14. had better,** would be wiser, safer, etc., to. **15. one's better half,** *Colloq.* one's spouse. **16. think better of, a.** to reconsider and decide more wisely. **b.** to think more favourably of. *–betterment, n.*

bettong /ˈbɛtɒŋ/ *n.* any of various small nocturnal marsupials of the genus *Bettongia,* and related genera, which resemble a small wallaby with brown-grey fur above and white below, as the woylie or eastern bettong.

between /bəˈtwin, bi-/ *prep.* **1.** in the space separating (two or more points, objects, etc.). **2.** intermediate in time, quantity, or degree: *between 12 and 1 o'clock; between pink and red.* **3.** connecting: *a link between parts.* **4.** involving; concerning: *war between nations; a choice between parts.* **5.** by joint action or possession of: *own land between them.* **6.** distinguishing one thing from another: *he can't tell the difference between butter and margarine.* *–adv.* **7.** in the intervening space or time; in an intermediate position or relation: *visits far between.* *–phr.* **8. between you and me** or **between ourselves,** in confidence. **9. come between,** to act as a barrier or obstruction to affection, ambition, etc., between (people): *don't let your aunt come between us.* **10. in between,** after one item, event, etc., and before another.

bevel /ˈbɛvəl/ *n.* **1.** the inclination that one line or surface makes with another when not at right angles. **2.** an adjustable instrument used by woodworkers for laying out angles or adjusting the surface of work to a particular inclination. *–verb* (**-elled** or, *Chiefly US,* **-eled, -elling** or, *Chiefly US,* **-eling**) *–v.t.* **3.** to cut at a bevel. *–v.i.* **4.** to slant at a bevel. *–beveller, n.*

beverage /ˈbɛvrɪdʒ, ˈbɛvərɪdʒ/ *n.* any kind of drink, other than water: *intoxicating beverages.*

bevy /ˈbɛvi/ *n.* (*pl.* **-vies**) **1.** a flock of birds, especially larks or quails. **2.** a group, especially of girls or women. **3.** a large number: *a bevy of new companies.*

bewail /bə'weɪl, bi-/ v.t. **1.** to express deep sorrow for; lament. –v.i. **2.** to express grief.

beware /bə'wɛə, bi-/ v.i. **1.** to be wary, cautious, or careful: *let the buyer beware!*; *beware of the dog.* –v.t. **2.** be wary of: *beware the dangers of isolation.*

bewilder /bə'wɪldə, bi-/ v.t. **1.** to confuse or puzzle completely; perplex. –**bewilderment**, n. –**bewildered**, adj. –**bewildering**, adj. –**bewilderingly**, adv. –**bewilderedly**, adv.

bewitch /bə'wɪtʃ, bi-/ v.t. **1.** to affect by witchcraft or magic; throw a spell over. **2.** to enchant. –**bewitcher**, n. –**bewitchment**, n. –**bewitching**, adj. –**bewitchingly**, adv.

beyond /bə'jɒnd, bi-/ prep. **1.** on or to the farther side of: *beyond the house.* **2.** farther on than; more distant than: *beyond the horizon.* **3.** later than: *they stayed beyond the time limit.* **4.** outside the understanding, limits, or reach of; past: *beyond human comprehension.* **5.** superior to; surpassing; above: *wise beyond all others.* **6.** more than; in excess of; over and above. –adv. **7.** farther on or away: *as far as the house and beyond.* –phr. **8. the beyond**, the life after the present one.

bezel /'bɛzəl/ n. **1.** a sloping face or edge of a chisel or other cutting tool. **2.** the upper oblique faces of a brilliant-cut gem.

bi- a prefix meaning 'twice, doubly, two', as in *bilateral*, *binocular*, *biweekly*. Also, **bin-**.

biannual /baɪ'ænjuəl/ adj. occurring twice a year. –**biannually**, adv.

bias /'baɪəs/ n. **1.** an oblique or diagonal line of direction, especially across a woven fabric: *to cut cloth on the bias.* **2.** a particular tendency or inclination, especially one which prevents unprejudiced consideration of a question. **3.** *Bowls* bulge or a greater weight on one side of the bowl, causing it to swerve. –adj. **4.** cut, set, folded, etc., diagonally. –v.t. (**biased**, **biasing**) **5.** to influence, usually unfairly; prejudice; warp.

bias binding n. a binding for cloth, cut on the bias, used especially in hems.

biased /'baɪəst/ adj. having or showing an opinion based on personal prejudice.

bib /bɪb/ n. **1.** an article of clothing worn under the chin by a child, especially while eating, to protect the clothes. **2.** the part of an apron, overalls, etc., above the waist. –phr. *Colloq.* **3. keep one's bib out**, to refrain from interfering with or inquiring into the affairs of another. **4. put** (or **stick**) **one's bib in**, to interfere in the affairs of another. –**bibless**, adj.

Bible /'baɪbəl/ n. **1. the Bible**, **a.** the collection of sacred writings of the Christian religion, comprising the Old Testament and the New Testament. **b.** the Old Testament only. **2.** a copy of the text of these writings: *an old, worn Bible.* **3.** (*oft. lower case*) the sacred writings of any religion. **4.** (*lower case*) any book accepted as authoritative –**biblical** /'bɪblɪkəl/, adj.

biblio- a word element meaning: **1.** book, as in *bibliophile.* **2.** Bible, as in *bibliolatry.*

bibliography /bɪbli'ɒɡrəfi/ n. (pl. **-phies**) **1.** a complete or selective list of literature on a particular subject. **2.** a list of works by a given author. **3.** a list of source materials used or consulted in the preparation of a work. **4.** the systematic description, history, classification, etc., of books and other written or printed works. –**bibliographer**, **bibliograph** /'bɪbliəɡræf/, n. –**bibliographic** /ˌbɪbliə'ɡræfɪk/, **bibliographical**, adj.

bicameral /baɪ'kæmərəl/ adj. having two branches, chambers, or houses, as a legislative body. Compare **unicameral**.

bicarbonate /baɪ'kabənət, -neɪt/ n. a salt of carbonic acid, containing the HCO_3^- ion; an acid carbonate, as *sodium bicarbonate*, $NaHCO_3$.

bicentenary /baɪsən'tinəri, -'tɛnəri/ adj. **1.** of or relating to a 200th anniversary. –n. (pl. **-naries**) **2.** a 200th anniversary. **3.** its celebration.

bicentennial /baɪsən'tɛniəl/ adj. **1.** consisting of or lasting 200 years: *a bicentennial period.* **2.** recurring every 200 years. –n. **3.** *US* a bicentenary.

biceps /'baɪsəps, -sɛps/ n. a muscle having two heads or origins, especially **biceps brachii**, the muscle on the front of the upper arm, which bends the forearm, and **biceps femoris**, the hamstring muscle on the back of the thigh.

bicker /'bɪkə/ v.i. **1.** to engage in petulant argument; wrangle. –n. **2.** an angry dispute; squabble. –**bickerer**, n.

bicuspid /baɪ'kʌspəd/ adj. Also, **bicuspidate** /baɪ'kʌspədeɪt/ **1.** having two cusps or points, as certain teeth. –n. **2.** *Anat.* one of eight such teeth in humans, four on each jaw between the cuspid and the first molar teeth.

bicycle /'baɪsɪkəl/ n. **1.** a vehicle with two wheels, one in front of the other, and having a saddle-like seat for the rider. It is steered by handlebars and driven by pedals. –v.i. **2.** to ride a bicycle. –**bicyclist**, n.

bid /bɪd/ verb (**bade** /bæd/ or **bad** /bæd/ or **bid**, **bidden** or **bid**, **bidding**) –v.t. **1.** to command; order; direct: *bid them depart.* **2.** to say as a greeting or benediction: *to bid farewell.* **3.** to invite. **4.** *Commerce* to offer, as a price at an auction or as terms in a competition to secure a contract. **5.** *Cards* to enter a bid of a given quantity or suit; call: *to bid two no-trumps.* –v.i. **6.** to make an offer to purchase at a price. **7.** *Cards* to make a bid: *your turn to bid.* –n. **8.** an offer, as at an auction. **9.** the price or terms offered. **10.** *Cards* **a.** the number of points or tricks a player undertakes to make. **b.** the turn of a person to bid. **11.** an attempt to attain some goal or purpose: *a bid for power.* –phr. **12. bid fair to**, to seem likely to. –**bidder**, n.

biddable /'bɪdəbəl/ adj. willing to do what is asked; obedient; docile.

bidding /'bɪdɪŋ/ n. **1.** invitation; command; order. **2.** bids collectively.

biddy-biddy /'bɪdi-bɪdi/ n. *NZ* any low-growing herb of the genus *Acaena*, family Rosaceae, bearing a clinging burr. Also, **bidi-bidi**, **biddy-bid**, **bid-a-bid**, **biddy**, **biddy bush**, **piripiri**.

bide /baɪd/ v.t. **1.** *Archaic* to endure; bear. –v.i. **2.** *Archaic* to dwell; abide; wait; remain; continue. –phr. **3. bide one's time**, to wait for a favourable opportunity.

bidet /'bideɪ/ n. a small low bath, straddled by the user, for washing the external genitals, anus, and surrounding area.

biennial /baɪ'ɛniəl/ adj. **1.** happening every two years: *the biennial Adelaide festival.* **2.** *Bot.* (especially in cool temperate regions) completing the normal term of life in two years, flowering and fruiting in the second year, as parsnip. –n. **3.** a biennial plant. –**biennially**, adv.

bier /bɪə/ n. a frame or stand on which a corpse, or the coffin containing it, is laid before burial.

bifid /'baɪfəd/ adj. cleft into two parts or lobes.

bifocal /baɪ'foʊkəl/ adj. *Optics* **1.** having two foci. **2.** (of spectacle lenses) having two portions, one for near and the other for far vision.

bifocals /baɪ'foʊkəlz/ pl. n. spectacles with bifocal lenses.

bi-fold /'baɪ-foʊld/ adj. of or relating to usually narrow doors which are hinged together and open by folding sideways. Also, **bifold**.

bifurcate /'baɪfəkeɪt/ v.t. **1.** to divide or fork into two branches. –v.i. **2.** to separate into two parts. –**bifurcation**, n.

big /bɪg/ adj. (**bigger**, **biggest**) **1.** large in size or amount: *a big house*; *a big payment.* **2.** intense: *a big noise*; *a big storm.* **3.** important; operating on a large scale: *big business*; *a big financier.* **4.** magnanimous; generous;

liberal: *a big heart*; *a big gesture*; *it was big of him to agree*. **5.** pompous; boastful: *big words*; *a big talker*. *–adv. Colloq.* **6.** boastfully: *to talk big*. **7.** on a grand scale; liberally: *to think big*. *–phr.* **8. big on**, knowledgeable and enthusiastic about: *she's big on wine*. **9. big with child**, pregnant. **10. in a big way**, with obvious enthusiasm: *to go in for hats in a big way*. **11. in big with**, highly favoured by (a person): *he got in big with the boss*. **12. the big one**, **a.** *Colloq.* the ultimate test or obstacle: *this exam is the big one*. **b.** the most important item in a set or list: *I have many vices but smoking is the big one*. *–biggish, adj. –bigness, n.*

bigamy /ˈbɪɡəmi/ *n.* the offence of purporting to marry while already legally married to another. *–bigamous, adj.*

big bang *n.* **the**, (*also upper case*) the initial explosion of matter postulated as the beginning of the universe.

Big Brother *n.* a dictator, especially one who tries to control people's private lives and thoughts.

big bucks *pl. n. Colloq.* a large amount of money.

big game *n.* **1.** large animals, especially when hunted for sport. **2.** an important prize or objective.

bight /baɪt/ *n.* **1.** the loop or bent part of a rope, as distinguished from the ends. **2.** an inward bend or curve in the shore of a sea or a river.

big mouth *n. Colloq.* a garrulous or conceited person.

big-note *v.t. Colloq.* to boast of or promote (oneself): *he big-notes himself at every committee meeting*. *–big-noter, n. –big-noting, n.*

bigot /ˈbɪɡət/ *n.* someone who is intolerantly convinced of the rightness of a particular creed, opinion, practice, etc. *–bigoted, adj. –bigotry, n.*

big-time *Colloq. –adj.* **1.** at the top level in any business or pursuit: *big-time boys*. *–adv.* **2.** an intensifier used after the verb: *she loves you big-time*.

big top *n.* **1.** the main tent in a circus. **2.** the circus.

bigwig /ˈbɪɡwɪɡ/ *n. Colloq.* a very important person.

bike /baɪk/ *n.* **1.** a bicycle, tricycle, or motorcycle. **2.** *Colloq.* (*derog.*) a promiscuous woman: *the town bike*. *–v.i.* **3.** to ride a bike, as a means of transport or as a sporting activity. *–phr. Colloq.* **4. get off one's bike**, to become angry; lose control of oneself. **5. on your bike**, an exclamation of dismissal.

biker /ˈbaɪkə/ *n.* someone who rides a motorbike but who is not a member of a motorbike gang. Compare **bikie**.

bikie /ˈbaɪki/ *n. Colloq.* a member of a gang of motorcycle riders. Compare **biker**.

bikini /bəˈkini/ *n.* **1.** a two-piece swimming costume for women, especially a very brief one. *–adj.* **2.** (of underpants) very brief.

bilateral /baɪˈlætrəl/ *adj.* relating to, involving, or affecting two sides or parties. *–bilateralism, bilateralness, n. –bilaterally, adv.*

bilby /ˈbɪlbi/ *n.* (*pl.* **-bies**) either of the rabbit-eared bandicoots of genus *Macrotis* of the regions west of the Australian Great Dividing Range.

bile /baɪl/ *n.* **1.** *Physiol.* a bitter yellow or greenish liquid secreted by the liver and aiding in digestion, principally by emulsifying fats. **2.** ill nature; peevishness.

bilge /bɪldʒ/ *n.* **1.** *Naut.* **a.** either of the rounded underportions at either side of a ship's hull. **b.** the lowest portion of a ship's interior. **c.** Also, **bilge water**. foul water that collects in a ship's bilge. **2.** *Colloq.* nonsense; rubbish.

bilingual /baɪˈlɪŋɡwəl/ *adj.* **1.** able to speak two languages with approximately equal facility. **2.** expressed or contained in two different languages. *–bilingualism, n. –bilingually, adv.*

bilious /ˈbɪliəs/ *adj.* **1.** *Physiol., Pathol.* relating to bile or to an excess secretion of bile. **2.** peevish; testy; cross.

3. sick; nauseated. **4.** sickly; nauseating: *a bilious colour*. *–biliously, adv. –biliousness, n.*

-bility a suffix forming nouns from adjectives ending in *-ble*, as in *nobility*.

bilk /bɪlk/ *v.t.* **1.** to evade payment of (a debt). **2.** to defraud; cheat. **3.** to frustrate. **4.** to escape from; elude. *–bilker, n.*

bill¹ /bɪl/ *n.* **1.** an account of money owed for goods or services supplied: *bill of charges*. **2.** a slip or ticket showing the amount owed for goods consumed or purchased, especially in a restaurant. **3.** *Govt* a form or draft of a proposed Act of Parliament. **4.** a written or printed public notice or advertisement. **5. →** **bill of exchange**. **6.** a printed theatre program or similar. *–v.t.* **7.** to announce by bill or public notice: *a new actor was billed for this week*. **8.** to include as part of a program. **9.** to send (someone) a bill (def. 1).

bill² /bɪl/ *n.* **1.** that part of the jaws of a bird covered with a horny sheath; a beak. **2.** *Geog.* a beaklike promontory or headland. *–v.i.* **3.** to join bills or beaks, as doves. *–phr.* **4. bill and coo**, **a.** (of doves, etc.) to join beaks and make soft murmuring sounds. **b.** *Colloq.* to kiss and talk fondly.

billabong /ˈbɪləbɒŋ/ *n. Aust.* a waterhole in an anabranch, replenished only in flood time.

billboard /ˈbɪlbɔd/ *n.* **→** **hoarding** (def. 2).

billet¹ /ˈbɪlət/ *n.* **1.** **a.** a lodging for a soldier, especially in a private house. **b.** private, usually unpaid, short-term lodgings for members of a group or team. **2.** *Mil.* an official order (to a householder) to provide such lodging. **3.** a job; appointment; position. *–v.t.* (**-eted**, **-eting**) **4.** *Mil.* to direct (a soldier) by note, or spoken order, where to lodge. **5.** to provide lodging for; quarter.

billet² /ˈbɪlət/ *n.* **1.** a small thick stick of wood, especially one cut for fuel. **2.** *Metallurgy* a bar or slab of iron or steel, especially when obtained from an ingot by forging, etc.

billiards /ˈbɪljədz/ *n.* a game played by two or more persons on a rectangular table enclosed by an elastic ledger or cushion, with balls (**billiard balls**) of ivory or other hard material, driven by means of cues. *–billiardist, n.*

billing /ˈbɪlɪŋ/ *n.* **1.** the relative position in which a performer or act is listed on handbills, posters, etc. **2.** publicity or advertising, especially for consumer goods. **3.** the total business of an advertising agency during a given period.

billion /ˈbɪljən/ *n.* (*pl.* **-lions**, *as after a numeral*, **-lion**) **1.** a thousand times a million, or 10^9. **2.** *Obsolesc.* a million times a million, or 10^{12}. **3.** *Colloq.* a large amount. *–adj.* **4.** amounting to a billion in number. *–billionth, adj., n.*

billionaire /bɪljəˈnɛə/ *n.* the owner of a billion dollars, pounds, euros, etc.

bill of exchange *n.* a written authorisation or order to pay a specified sum of money to a specified person.

bill of fare *n.* a list of foods that are served; menu.

bill of lading *n.* a document recording particulars of a contract for the carriage of goods by sea, serving also as a document of title to the goods.

bill of rights *n.* a formal statement of the fundamental rights of the people of a nation.

bill of sale *n.* a document transferring title in personal property from one person to another, either temporarily as security against a loan or debt (**conditional bill of sale**), or permanently (**absolute bill of sale**).

billow /ˈbɪloʊ/ *n.* **1.** a great wave or surge of the sea. **2.** any surging mass: *billows of smoke*. *–v.i.* **3.** to rise or roll in or like billows; surge. *–billowy, adj.*

billposter /ˈbɪlpoʊstə/ *n.* someone who pastes up bills and advertisements. Also, **billsticker** /ˈbɪlstɪkə/.

billy[1] /'bɪli/ *Aust., NZ –n.* (*pl.* **-lies**) **1.** a cylindrical container for liquids, sometimes enamelled, usually having a close-fitting lid. **2.** any container, often makeshift, for boiling water, making tea, etc. *–adj.* **3.** made in a billy: *billy tea, billy bread. –phr.* **4. boil the billy,** *Aust., NZ* **a.** *Colloq.* to prepare billy tea. **b.** (*humorous*) to make tea; take a break.

billy[2] /'bɪli/ *n.* (*pl.* **-lies**) → **billy goat.**

billycart /'bɪlikat/ *n. Aust., NZ* A small four-wheeled cart, usually homemade, consisting essentially of a box on a board and steered by ropes attached to its movable front axle. Also, *Esp. WA and SA,* **soapbox.**

billy goat *n.* **1.** a male goat. **2.** *Colloq.* a man or boy who is incompetent. Also, **billygoat.**

billyo /'bɪlioʊ/ *phr. Colloq.* **1. go to billyo,** an exclamation of dismissal. **2. like billyo,** **a.** with gusto. **b.** with great speed: *she rode like billyo.* **3. off to billyo, a.** off course; astray; in error. **b.** a long way away. Also, **billy-o.**

bimbo /'bɪmboʊ/ *n. Colloq.* **1.** an attractive but unintelligent young woman. **2.** *Obs.* a male homosexual.

bimonthly /baɪ'mʌnθli/ *adj., adv.* **1.** every two months. **2.** twice a month; semi-monthly.

bin /bɪn/ *n.* **1.** a box or enclosed space used for storing grain, wool as it is shorn, coal, refuse, etc. **2.** a container for rubbish or waste material. **3.** a partitioned stand used by a winemaker for storing wine in bottles. **4.** (of wine) a particular bottling, usually of above average quality. **5.** *Colloq.* a jail. *–v.t.* (**binned, binning**) **6.** to throw into a rubbish bin: *you should bin stale food.* **7.** to discard as worthless: *to bin the campaign strategy.*

binary /'baɪnəri/ *adj.* **1.** of or relating to the number two. **2.** of or relating to the binary number system. **3.** *Maths* having two variables. *–n.* (*pl.* **-ries**) **4.** a whole composed of two.

binary code *n.* any means of representing information by a sequence of the digits 1 and 0.

binary digit *n.* a single digit in a binary number.

binary number system *n.* a number system which uses only the digits 1 and 0, based on the rules $1 + 0 = 1$, $1 + 1 = 10$. Also, **binary system.**

bind /baɪnd/ *verb* (**bound, binding**) *–v.t.* **1.** to make fast with a band or bond. **2.** to encircle with a band or ligature: *bind up one's hair.* **3.** to swathe or bandage. **4.** to cause to cohere or harden. **5.** to unite by any legal or moral tie: *bound by debt; bound by duty.* **6.** to hold to a particular state, place, employment, etc. **7.** (*usu. passive*) to place under obligation or compulsion: *all are bound to obey the laws.* **8.** to make compulsory or obligatory: *to bind an order with a deposit.* **9.** Also, **bind out.** to indenture as an apprentice. **10.** *Pathol.* to hinder or restrain (the bowels) from their natural operations; constipate. **11.** to fasten or secure within a cover, as a book. **12.** to cover the edge of, as for protection or ornament. *–v.i.* **13.** to become compact or solid; cohere. **14.** to have power to oblige: *an obligation that binds.* **15.** to tie up anything, especially sheaves of grain. *–n.* **16.** something that binds. **17.** an irritating circumstance; nuisance. **18.** *Music* a tie. *–phr.* **19. bind over,** *Law* to put under legal obligation: *to bind someone over to keep the peace.* **20. bind up, a.** to encircle with a band or ligature: *bind up your hair.* **b.** to bandage. **21. in a bind,** awkwardly placed; in a dilemma.

binder /'baɪndə/ *n.* **1.** a detachable cover for loose papers. **2.** a machine that both cuts and binds grain. **3.** *Metallurgy* a substance used to hold crushed ore dust together before and during sintering or refining. **4.** *Building Trades* a material, as cement, used to join masonry.

bindi-eye /'bɪndi-aɪ/ *n.* any of a number of plants of the genus *Calotis* which have small burrs with fine barbed awns. Also, **bindi, bindy.**

binding /'baɪndɪŋ/ *n.* **1.** anything that binds, as the covering around pages of a book, the band along edge of cloth, etc. *–adj.* **2.** having the power to bind (someone to do something): *a binding agreement.* **–bindingly,** *adv.* **–bindingness,** *n.*

binge /bɪndʒ/ *Colloq. –n.* **1.** a spree; a period of excessive indulgence, as in eating or drinking. *–v.i.* (**binged, binging**) **2.** to engage in such a binge.

binge drinking *n.* **1.** a pattern of alcohol consumption in which a person punctuates periods of total abstinence with sessions in which alcohol is consumed to the point of intoxication. **2.** a similar pattern in which the drinking lasts for some days. See **bender. –binge drinker,** *n.*

binocular /bə'nɒkjələ/ *adj.* **1.** involving (the use of) two eyes: *binocular vision. –n.* **2.** (*pl.*) a double telescope used by both eyes at once; field-glasses. **–binocularity** /bənɒkjə'lærəti/, *n.* **–binocularly,** *adv.*

binomial /baɪ'noʊmiəl/ *Maths –n.* **1.** an expression which is a sum or difference of two terms, as $3x + 2y$ and $x^2 - 4x$. *–adj.* **2.** of or relating to two terms or a binomial.

bio- a word element meaning 'life', 'living things', as in *biology.*

bioaccumulate /baɪoʊə'kjumjəleɪt/ *v.i.* (of a substance, especially a toxin) to remain within an organism, increasing in concentration with repeated doses, as mercury, PCBs, some pesticides, etc. **–bioaccumulation,** *n.*

biochar /'baɪoʊtʃa/ *n.* charcoal produced from the imperfect burning of biomass; able to store carbon dioxide and fertilise the soil.

biochemistry /baɪoʊ'kemɪstri/ *n.* the chemistry of living matter. *Abbrev.:* biochem. **–biochemical** /baɪoʊ-'kɛmɪkəl/, *adj.* **–biochemically,** *adv.* **–biochemist,** *n.*

biocontrol /ˌbaɪoʊkən'troʊl/ *n.* → **biological control.**

biodegradable /ˌbaɪoʊdə'greɪdəbəl/ *adj.* capable of being decomposed by the action of living organisms, especially of bacteria: *a biodegradable detergent.* **–biodegradability,** *n.* **–biodegradation,** *n.*

biodiesel /'baɪoʊdizəl/ *n.* a biodegradable fuel, being a methyl ester produced from field crop oils, especially from recycled cooking oil. Compare **petrodiesel.**

biodiverse /ˌbaɪoʊdaɪ'vɜs, ˌbaɪoʊdə'vɜs/ *adj.* exhibiting biodiversity: *a biodiverse region.*

biodiversity /baɪoʊdə'vɜsəti/ *n.* the variety of species of plants, animals and microorganisms, their genes, and the ecosystems they comprise, often considered in relation to a particular area: *threats to coastal biodiversity.*

biodynamic /baɪoʊdaɪ'næmɪk/ *adj.* of or relating to agricultural or horticultural techniques and management which aim to improve the soil and vegetation without chemical fertilisers and in a way that is environmentally sound and sustainable.

bioethanol /baɪoʊ'ɛθənɒl/ *n.* ethanol produced from the starch or sugar in various crops, such as corn, for use as a biofuel.

biofuel /'baɪoʊfjuəl/ *n.* a fuel, such as biogas, methane, biodiesel, ethanol, etc., derived from renewable sources such as biological matter.

biogenesis /ˌbaɪoʊ'dʒɛnəsəs/ *n.* **1.** Also, **biogeny** /baɪ-'ɒdʒəni/ the doctrine that living organisms come from other living organisms only. **2.** the development of living organisms from prior living organisms. **–biogenetic** /ˌbaɪoʊdʒə'nɛtɪk/, *adj.* **–biogenetically,** *adv.*

biography /baɪ'ɒɡrəfi/ *n.* (*pl.* **-phies**) **1.** a written account of a person's life. **2.** such writings collectively. **3.** the study of the lives of individuals. **4.** the art of writing a biography. **–biographer,** *n.* **–biographical,** *adj.*

biohazard /ˈbaɪoʊhæzəd/ *n.* any biological material likely to cause human or animal disease or environmental contamination. Also, **bio-hazard.** **–biohazardous,** *adj.*

bioinformatics /ˌbaɪoʊɪnfəˈmætɪks/ *n.* a scientific discipline which applies computer science to the analysing of biological data.

biolistics /baɪoʊˈlɪstɪks/ *n.* a genetic engineering technique whereby genetic material is impelled directly into a living cell.

biological clock *n.* a hypothetical mechanism controlling the timing of the development of an organism through the various stages of its life span.

biological control *n.* a method of controlling pests by introducing one of their natural enemies.

biological family *n.* a family which is linked by having the same biological parents for all the children.

biological parent *n.* a person whose parenthood is based on actual conception rather than performance of the role and whose genes have therefore been handed down to the child.

biological warfare *n.* warfare which makes use of biologically produced poisons that affect humans, domestic animals, or food crops, especially bacteria or viruses.

biology /baɪˈɒlədʒi/ *n.* **1.** the science of life or living matter in all its forms and phenomena, especially with reference to origin, growth, reproduction, structure, etc. **2.** the living organisms of a particular region: *the biology of the wetlands.* **–biological,** *adj.* **–biologist,** *n.*

biomass /ˈbaɪoʊmæs/ *n.* **1.** the quantity of living matter contributed to a given habitat by one or several kinds of organism, and usually expressed as weight for unit area or volume. **2.** organic matter used as a source of energy, as the residue from farming activity, landfill, compressed household waste, etc.

biome /ˈbaɪoʊm/ *n.* a major regional ecological community of plants and animals adapted to a particular climate or environment and extending over a large geographical area, as coral reef, tropical rainforest, etc.

biometric /baɪəˈmɛtrɪk/ *adj.* of or relating to biometric data: *biometric authorisation; biometric technology.* Also, **biometrical.** **–biometrically,** *adv.*

biometric data *n.* biological data, especially that identifying aspects of the face which cannot be altered and which can be scanned and matched to a passport.

biomimetics /baɪoʊmɪˈmɛtɪks/ *n.* a systematic approach to problem-solving in design engineering, etc., that looks to living creatures to provide a model.

biomimicry /baɪoʊˈmɪməkri/ *n.* the use of a naturally occurring model as the basis for the design of a manufactured product.

bionic /baɪˈɒnɪk/ *adj.* **1.** of or relating to bionics. **2.** of or relating to body parts or functions replaced or improved by electronic equipment: *a bionic hand.*

bionic ear *n.* → **cochlear implant.**

bionic eye *n. Med.* an implanted device which restores basic vision in patients with some degenerative eye diseases by transmitting images from a small camera fitted to a pair of glasses to a silicon chip implanted into the eye and acting as an artificial retina.

bionics /baɪˈɒnɪks/ *n.* the study of biological systems as an aid to the development of such electronic or mechanical equipment as artificial limbs.

biophysical /baɪoʊˈfɪzɪkəl/ *adj.* of or relating to the physical environment which includes the living organisms which inhabit it.

biopiracy /baɪoʊˈpaɪrəsi/ *n.* the patenting of genetic materials from plants and other biological resources that have long been identified with, developed and used

by, the people to whom these resources are indigenous. **–biopirate,** *n.*

bioplastic /baɪoʊˈplæstɪk/ *n.* **1.** a plastic in the manufacture of which renewable sources such as vegetable oils and corn starch are used, resulting in less involvement of fossil fuels. **–adj. 2.** of, relating to, or made from such a plastic.

biopsy /ˈbaɪɒpsi/ *n.* (*pl.* **-sies**) *Med.* the excision and diagnostic study of a piece of tissue from a living body.

bioretention /baɪoʊrəˈtɛnʃən/ *n.* the removal of pollutants from stormwater by means of vegetation, from large trees to surface plants, that slow and filter the run-off, absorbing the pollutants.

biorhythm /ˈbaɪoʊrɪðəm/ *n.* **1.** a theory that our well-being is affected by three internal cycles, the physiological, emotional, and intellectual. **2.** (*pl.*) the rhythms themselves. **3.** (*pl.*) the cycle of biological processes, as eating, sleeping, etc., that occur in a living organism at specific intervals of time; circadian rhythms.

biosecurity /baɪoʊsəˈkjʊrəti/ *n.* **1.** security measures against the transmission of disease to the plants or animals of a particular region. **2.** security measures taken against bioterrorism.

-biosis a word element meaning 'way of life', as in *symbiosis.*

biosolid /baɪoʊˈsɒlɪd/ *n.* a solid end product of the wastewater treatment process, used as a fertiliser in agriculture and forestry.

biosphere /ˈbaɪəsfɪə/ *n.* the part of the earth where living organisms are to be found.

biosurgery /baɪoʊˈsɜdʒəri/ *n.* the branch of medicine which treats infected or necrotic wounds, especially those infected with antibiotic-resistant strains of bacteria, by the use of living creatures, such as larvae, to clean the wound and help new tissue to grow. **–biosurgical,** *adj.*

biosystem /ˈbaɪoʊsɪstəm/ *n.* **1.** an interactive group of living things forming an interdependent community. **2.** a lifelike system that includes at least some living elements as the main entities within the system, or that imitates a living system, as in robotics.

biota /baɪˈoʊtə/ *n. Biol.* the total animal and plant life of a habitat or region, or sometimes an epoch, viewed collectively.

biotech /ˈbaɪoʊtɛk/ *n.* **1.** biotechnology. **–adj. 2.** of or relating to biotechnology.

biotechnology /baɪoʊtɛkˈnɒlədʒi/ *n.* **1.** *US* → **ergonomics. 2.** any technology which introduces organisms or parts of organisms into industrial processes, agriculture or pharmacology, or into services such as waste recycling. **–biotechnological** /ˌbaɪoʊtɛknəˈlɒdʒɪkəl/, *adj.* **–biotechnologically** /ˌbaɪoʊtɛknəˈlɒdʒɪkli/, *adv.* **–biotechnologist,** *n.*

bioterrorism /baɪoʊˈtɛrərɪzəm/ *n.* terrorism involving the use of biological agents such as bacteria, viruses, etc., that affect humans, domestic animals or food crops. **–bioterrorist,** *n.*

biotite /ˈbaɪətaɪt/ *n.* a very common mineral of the mica group, occurring in dark brown or green or black sheets and scales, an important constituent of igneous rocks. **–biotitic** /baɪəˈtɪtɪk/, *adj.*

bioweapon /ˈbaɪoʊwɛpən/ *n.* a weapon which uses a living organism to cause the death of humans or the destruction of crops.

bipartisan /baɪˈpatəzən, -zæn/ *adj.* representing, supported, or characterised by two parties, especially political parties. **–bipartisanship,** *n.*

bipartite /baɪˈpataɪt/ *adj.* **1.** *Law* being in two corresponding parts: *a bipartite contract.* **2.** *Bot.* divided into two parts nearly to the base, as a leaf. **–bipartitely,** *adv.* **–bipartition** /ˌbaɪpaˈtɪʃən/, *n.*

biped /ˈbaɪpɛd/ n. **1.** a two-footed animal. –adj. **2.** having two feet.

biplane /ˈbaɪpleɪn/ n. an aeroplane or glider with two pairs of wings, one above and usually slightly forward of the other.

bipolar /baɪˈpoʊlə/ adj. **1.** having two poles. **2.** relating to or found at both poles. **3.** of or relating to bipolar disorder. **4.** suffering bipolar disorder: a bipolar child; bipolar patients. –**bipolarity** /baɪpəˈlærəti/, n.

bipolar disorder n. a mental disorder marked by alternating periods of excitation and depression; manic depression. Also, **bipolar affective disorder**, **bipolar mood disorder**.

birch /bɜtʃ/ n. **1.** any tree or shrub of the genus Betula, comprising species with a smooth, laminated outer bark and close-grained wood. **2.** the wood itself. **3.** any of various unrelated trees with similar timbers. **4.** NZ any species of Nothofagus, beech. **5.** a birch rod, or a bundle of birch twigs, used as a whip.

Bircher muesli /bɜtʃə ˈmjuzli/ n. a style of muesli in which rolled oats and fruit are soaked overnight in milk and yoghurt.

bird /bɜd/ n. **1.** any of the Aves, a class of warm-blooded vertebrates having a body more or less completely covered with feathers, and the forelimbs so modified as to form wings by means of which most species fly. **2.** Colloq. **a.** a young woman. **b.** a girlfriend. –phr. **3. bird in the hand**, that which is sure, although perhaps not entirely satisfactory. **4. birds of a feather**, people of similar character or like tastes. **5. for the birds**, trivial, worthless. **6. the birds and the bees**, (euphemistic) human sexual relations. –**birdless**, adj. –**birdlike**, adj.

birdcage /ˈbɜdkeɪdʒ/ n. a wicker or wire cage for tame birds.

bird flu n. → avian influenza.

birdie /ˈbɜdi/ n. **1.** Colloq. a bird; small bird. **2.** Golf a score of one stroke under par on a hole.

bird of paradise n. **1.** any bird of the family Paradiseidae of Australia and New Guinea, noted for magnificent plumage. **2.** a perennial tropical plant, Strelitzia reginae, with purple and orange flowers.

bird of passage n. **1.** a bird that migrates seasonally. **2.** a restless person; someone who does not stay in one place for long.

bird of prey n. any of numerous predatory, flesh-eating birds such as the eagles, hawks, kites, vultures, owls, etc., most of which have strong beaks and claws for catching, killing and tearing to pieces the animals on which they feed.

bird's-eye view n. **1.** a view from above, as of terrain, landscape, etc: a bird's-eye view of a city. **2.** an overview which is broad in scope but lacks detail: a bird's-eye view of history.

biretta /bəˈrɛtə/ n. a stiff, square cap with three (or four) upright projecting pieces extending from the centre of the top to the edge; worn by Roman Catholic ecclesiastics.

biro /ˈbaɪroʊ/ n. (from trademark) a ballpoint pen.

birth /bɜθ/ n. **1.** the fact of being born: the day of his birth. **2.** the act of bearing or bringing forth; parturition. **3.** lineage; extraction; descent: of Grecian birth. **4.** supposedly natural heritage: a musician by birth. **5.** any coming into existence; origin: the birth of Protestantism. –phr. **6. give birth**, to bring forth young. **7. give birth to**, to produce (an offspring).

birth certificate n. a certificate issued by a registrar upon the birth of each person, recording sex, parentage, date and place of birth.

birth control n. the regulation of birth through the deliberate control or prevention of conception.

birthday /ˈbɜθdeɪ/ n. **1.** (of persons) the day of one's birth. **2.** (of things) origin or beginning. **3.** the anniversary of one's birth or the origin of something.

birthmark /ˈbɜθmak/ n. a congenital mark on the body.

birthrate /ˈbɜθreɪt/ n. the proportion of the number of births in a place in a given time to the total population.

birthright /ˈbɜθraɪt/ n. any right or privilege to which a person is entitled by birth.

birthstone /ˈbɜθstoʊn/ n. a precious stone associated with a person's month of birth and worn as a lucky charm.

bis /bɪs/ adv. twice: used in music to mean that a part is to be repeated.

biscuit /ˈbɪskət/ n. **1. a.** a stiff, sweet mixture of flour, liquid, shortening and other ingredients, shaped into small pieces before baking or sliced after baking. **b.** a savoury, unleavened similar mixture, rolled, sliced and baked crisp. **2.** a pale brown colour. **3.** pottery after the first baking and before glazing. –**biscuity**, adj.

bisect /baɪˈsɛkt/ v.t. to cut or divide into two parts. –**bisection**, n. –**bisectional**, adj. –**bisectionally**, adv.

bisexual /baɪˈsɛkʃuəl/ adj. **1.** of both sexes. **2.** combining male and female organs in one individual; hermaphroditic. **3.** attracted to both sexes as sexual partners. –n. **4.** Biol. an organism with the reproductive organs of both sexes. **5.** a person sexually attracted to both sexes. –**bisexualism**, n. –**bisexuality** /ˌbaɪsɛkʃuˈæləti/, n. –**bisexually**, adv.

bishop /ˈbɪʃəp/ n. **1.** a member of the clergy consecrated for the spiritual direction of a diocese, being in the Greek, Anglican, and certain other churches a member of the highest order in the ministry. **2.** a spiritual overseer in the early Christian church, either of a local church or of a number of churches. **3.** Chess a piece which moves obliquely on squares of the same colour.

bishopric /ˈbɪʃəprɪk/ n. the see, diocese, or office of a bishop.

bismuth /ˈbɪzməθ/ n. a brittle, metallic element, having compounds used in medicine. Symbol: Bi; atomic number: 83; relative atomic mass: 208.98; density: 9.8 at 20°C. –**bismuthal**, adj.

bison /ˈbaɪsən/ n. (pl. **bison**) a large North American bovine ruminant, Bison bison, with high, well-haired shoulders; also popularly but erroneously known as the buffalo. Also, **American bison**.

bisque¹ /bɪsk/ n. **1.** any smooth, creamy soup. **2.** a thick soup made of shellfish or game stewed long and slowly. Also, **bisk**.

bisque² /bɪsk/ n. a point, extra turn, or the like, allowed to a player as odds in tennis and other games.

bisque³ /bɪsk/ n. **1.** pottery which has been baked but not glazed; biscuit. **2.** a variety of white unglazed porcelain.

bistro /ˈbɪstroʊ/ n. (pl. **-tros**) **1.** a wine bar. **2.** a small casual restaurant.

bit¹ /bɪt/ n. **1.** the metal mouthpiece of a bridle, with the adjacent parts to which the reins are fastened. **2.** Machinery the cutting or penetrating part of various tools. **3.** the part of a key which enters the lock and acts on the bolt and tumblers. –phr. **4. take the bit between one's teeth**, **a.** to tackle a task, problem, etc., in a determined and energetic fashion. **b.** to throw off control; rush headlong. –**bitless**, adj.

bit² /bɪt/ n. **1.** a small piece or quantity of anything. **2.** a short time: wait a bit. **3.** the smallest amount; jot; whit. **4.** one's share or part of a duty, task, etc. **5.** Colloq. (taboo) a woman, considered as a sex object. **6.** US Colloq. twelve and a half cents. –phr. **7. a bit**, to a small extent, degree, time, etc.: a bit funny. **8. a bit of**, **a.** rather; to a small degree: a bit of a shock; a bit of a nuisance. **b.** someone who is representative of a specified style or class of people: a bit of rough; a bit of *skirt*. **9. a bit of all right**, something or someone exciting admiration, especially a sexually attractive person. **10. a bit on the side**, *Colloq*. **a.** something beyond the usual arrangement. **b.** an extra-marital affair. **11. bit by bit**, slowly; gradually; in stages. **12. get a bit**, *Colloq*. (*taboo*) to have sexual intercourse. **13. have a bit both ways**, *Colloq*. to attempt to cover oneself against any eventuality. **14. not a bit of it**, not at all; by no means.

bit³ /bɪt/ *n*. a single, basic unit of information stored by a computer, being the smallest possible unit, and having one of only two possible values, 0 or 1; more complex information is represented by combinations of consecutive bits.

bit⁴ /bɪt/ *v*. past tense of **bite**.

bitch /bɪtʃ/ *n*. **1.** a female dog, fox, wolf, etc. **2.** *Colloq*. (*offensive*) a woman, especially an unpleasant or bad-tempered one. –*v.i.* **3.** *Colloq*. to complain. –**bitchiness**, **bitchery**, *n*. –**bitchily**, *adv*.

bitcoin /ˈbɪtkɔɪn/ *n*. a unit of digital currency in the Bitcoin online payment system, introduced in 2009.

bite /baɪt/ *verb* (**bit**, **bitten** *or*, *Archaic*, **bit**, **biting**) –*v.t.* **1.** to cut into or wound, with the teeth: *the dog bit me*. **2.** to grip with the teeth. **3.** to sting, as an insect. **4.** to cause to smart or sting. **5.** to eat into or corrode, as an acid does. **6.** to make a great impression on: *bitten by the love of music*. **7.** to take firm hold or act effectively on. **8.** to cheat; deceive. **9.** *Colloq*. to trouble; worry; disturb: *what's biting him?* –*v.i.* **10.** to cut into something with the teeth; snap. **11.** to act effectively; grip; hold. **12.** *Angling* (of fish) to bite on the bait. **13.** *Colloq*. to accept a deceptive offer or suggestion. **14.** *Colloq*. to react angrily: *don't tease her, she bites*. –*n*. **15.** the act of biting. **16.** a wound made by biting. **17.** *Dentistry* the angle at which the upper and lower teeth meet. **18.** a cutting, stinging, or nipping effect. **19.** pungency; sharpness. **20.** a small piece bitten off. **21. a.** *Angling* the pull on a fishing line which indicates that a fish is attempting to take the bait. **b.** *Colloq*. an expression of interest in a proposal. **22.** *Machinery* **a.** the catch or hold that one object or one part of a mechanical apparatus has on another. **b.** a surface brought into contact to obtain a hold or grip, as in a lathe, chuck, or similar device. **23.** *NZ Colloq*. a nagging person. **24.** a brazen attempt to borrow: *go the bite*. **25.** *Colloq*. a person from whom one anticipates borrowing money: *he'd be a good bite*. **26.** a reaction: *did you get a bite from Robin?* –*phr*. **27. a bite (to eat)**, *Colloq*. a small meal or snack. **28. bite back**, **a.** to restrain: *she bit back her angry reply*. **b.** *Colloq*. to reply sharply. **c.** to retaliate. **29. bite into**, to make an initial incision into with the teeth. **30. bite off** (or **out**), to remove with the teeth. **31. bite off more than one can chew**, to attempt something that is beyond one's abilities. **32. bite on**, to grip with the teeth. **33. bite someone for**, to cadge off someone: *I'll bite you for five bucks*. **34. bite someone's head off**, *Colloq*. to respond angrily to someone. **35. bite something off**, to beg or borrow something from. **36. bite the dust**, *Colloq*. **a.** to fall dead, especially in combat. **b.** to lose a contest or competition: *Essendon bit the dust in the grand final*. **c.** (of a plan, enterprise, etc.) to fail. **37. bite the hand that feeds one**, to attack or in some way turn on someone to whom one owes a debt of gratitude. **38. bite through**, to cut or pierce with or as with the teeth. **39. on the bite**, (of fish) taking the bait. **40. put the bite on**, *Aust*., *NZ Colloq*. to attempt to cadge from. –**biter**, *n*.

biting /ˈbaɪtɪŋ/ *adj*. **1.** nipping; keen: *biting cold*. **2.** cutting; sarcastic: *a biting remark*. –**bitingly**, *adv*.

bitmap /ˈbɪtmæp/ *n*. a computer graphics image consisting of rows and columns of dots stored as bits. –**bitmapped**, *adj*. –**bitmapping**, *n*.

bitter /ˈbɪtə/ *adj*. **1.** having a sharp, disagreeable taste. **2.** hard to accept or bear: *a bitter lesson*; *bitter sorrow*. **3.** bitingly cold: *a bitter wind*. **4.** filled with sour feeling; resentful: *he is bitter towards his family*; *bitter words*. **5.** sharp; harsh: *bitter cold*; *a bitter landscape*. –*n*. **6.** something bitter; bitter things in general. **7.** *Chiefly Brit*. a bitter type of beer. –**bitterish**, *adj*. –**bitterly**, *adv*. –**bitterness**, *n*.

bitterbark /ˈbɪtəbak/ *n*. a tree of inland Australia, *Alstonia constricta*, with bark which may be used in a tonic preparation.

bittern /ˈbɪtən/ *n*. any of several small or medium-sized birds of the tribe Botaurini, family Ardeidae, closely related to herons and egrets.

bitters /ˈbɪtəz/ *pl. n*. a spirituous or other drink in which bitter herbs or roots are steeped.

bittersweet /ˈbɪtəˈswit/ *adj*. **1.** both bitter and sweet to the taste. **2.** both pleasant and painful.

bitumen /ˈbɪtʃəmən/ *n*. **1.** any of various natural substances, as asphalt, maltha, etc., consisting mainly of hydrocarbons, and used in surfacing roads, roofing, etc. **2. the bitumen**, a. a tarred or sealed road. **b.** any bituminised area. **3.** a brown tar or asphalt-like substance used in painting. –**bituminous** /bəˈtʃumənəs/, **bituminoid** /bəˈtʃumənɔɪd/, *adj*.

bitzer /ˈbɪtsə/ *n*. *Aust*., *NZ Colloq*. **1.** a mongrel. **2.** any contrivance the parts of which come from miscellaneous sources, as a billycart. Also, **bitser**.

bivalent /baɪˈveɪlənt/ *adj*. *Chem*. **1.** having a valency of 2. **2.** having two valencies, as mercury, with valencies 1 and 2. –**bivalence**, **bivalency**, *n*.

bivalve /ˈbaɪvælv/ –*n*. **1.** *Zool*. a mollusc having two shells hinged together, as the oyster, clam, mussel; a lamellibranch. –*adj*. **2.** *Bot*. having two valves, as a seed case. –**bivalvular** /baɪˈvælvjulə/, *adj*.

bivouac /ˈbɪvəwæk/ *n*. **1.** a temporary camp, especially a military one, made out in the open with little or no equipment. –*v.i.* (**-acked**, **-acking**) **2.** to sleep out; make a bivouac.

biweekly /baɪˈwikli/ *adj*., *adv*. **1.** every two weeks. **2.** twice a week.

bizarre /bəˈza/ *adj*. singular in appearance, style, or general character; whimsically strange; odd. –**bizarrely**, *adv*. –**bizarreness**, *n*.

blab /blæb/ *verb* (**blabbed**, **blabbing**) –*v.t.* **1.** to reveal indiscreetly and thoughtlessly. –*v.i.* **2.** to talk or chatter indiscreetly and thoughtlessly.

black /blæk/ *adj*. **1.** without brightness or colour; absorbing all or nearly all the rays emitted by a light source. **2.** wearing black or dark clothing, armour, etc.: *the black prince*. **3.** relating or belonging to an ethnic group characterised by dark skin pigmentation. **4.** soiled or stained with dirt. **5.** characterised by absence of light; involved or enveloped in darkness: *a black night*. **6.** gloomy; dismal: *a black outlook*. **7.** boding ill; sudden; forbidding: *black words*; *black looks*. **8.** without any moral light or goodness; evil; wicked. **9.** caused or marked by ruin or desolation. **10.** indicating censure, disgrace, or liability to punishment: *a black mark on one's record*. **11.** illicit: *black market*. **12.** prohibited or banned by a trade union. **13.** (of coffee or tea) without milk or cream. **14.** superficially humorous but pursuing an underlying theme related to the darker side of life. –*n*. **15.** a colour without hue at one extreme end of the scale of greys, opposite to white. A black surface absorbs light of all hues equally. **16.** (*sometimes upper case*) a member of an ethnic group characterised by dark skin pigmentation. **17.** a black speck, flake, or spot, as of soot. **18.** black clothing, especially as a sign of mourning: *to be in black*. **19.** *Chess*, *Draughts* the dark-coloured pieces. **20.** black pigment. –*v.t.* **21.** to make black; put black on. **22.** (of a trade union) to ban or prevent normal industrial working in (a factory, industry, or the like). *–phr.* **23. black out, a.** to obscure by concealing all light in defence against air raids. **b.** to jam (a radio). **c.** to suppress (news). **d.** to impose a blackout on (a particular area). **e.** to lose consciousness. **24. in the black, a.** financially solvent. **b.** (of betting odds) any bet above or including even money. **25. on one's blacks,** on an unrestricted driver's licence. –**blackish,** *adj.* –**blackness,** *n.* –**black,** *v.*

black-and-blue *adj.* discoloured, as by bruising. Also, (*especially in predicative use*), **black and blue.**

black armband *n.* **1.** a band of black material worn around one's left arm as a sign of mourning. *–adj.* Also, **black-armband. 2.** (*derog.*) of or relating to an interpretation of Australian history which foregrounds past injustices and wrongs, especially those committed against Indigenous Australians: *a black armband view of history.* Compare **white blindfold.**

blackball /'blækbɔl/ *v.t.* **1.** to ostracise. **2.** to vote against. **3.** to reject (a candidate) by placing a black ball in the ballot box. *–n.* **4.** *NZ* a hard, round, black sweet. –**blackballer,** *n.*

black ban *n. Aust.* a refusal by a group, as of producers, trade unions, consumers, etc., to supply or purchase goods or services, in an attempt to force a particular change or action.

black beat *n.* rhythmic drive which is derived from black African music.

black belt *n. Judo* a belt worn by an experienced contestant ranking up to tenth Dan.

blackberry /'blækbəri, -bri/ *n.* (*pl.* -**ries**) **1.** the fruit, black or very dark purple when ripe, of *Rubus fruticosus* and other species of the genus *Rubus.* **2.** the plant bearing this fruit; the bramble. –**blackberry-like,** *adj.*

blackbird /'blækbɜd/ *n.* **1.** a Eurasian songbird of the thrush family, *Turdus merula,* introduced into southeastern Australia and New Zealand, the male of which is all black with a yellow beak and eye-ring. **2.** any of various unrelated birds having black plumage in the male. **3.** (formerly) a Pacific islander kidnapped and transported as a slave labourer. *–v.t.* **4.** (formerly) to kidnap (a Pacific islander) to be transported and used as a slave labourer.

blackboard /'blækbɔd/ *n.* a smooth dark board, used in schools, etc., for writing or drawing on with chalk.

black box *n.* **1.** → **flight recorder. 2.** any device, invention, etc., the workings of which are mysterious or kept secret.

black boy *n.* → **grass tree** (def. 1). Also, **blackboy.**

black coal *n.* ordinary coal containing more than 80 per cent of carbon; includes bituminous coal and anthracite; formed from peat or brown coal by increased temperature and pressure.

black cockatoo *n.* any of various large, primarily black-plumed cockatoos endemic to Australia, such as the **red-tailed black cockatoo,** *Calyptorhynchus banksii.*

black comedy *n.* a comedy expressing an underlying pessimism or bitterness, or one dealing with a tragic or gruesome subject.

blackcurrant /blæk'kʌrənt/ *n.* **1.** the small, black edible fruit of the shrub *Ribes nigrum.* **2.** the shrub itself.

black duck *n.* → **Pacific black duck.**

black economy *n.* the part of a country's economy in which payment for goods and services is made in cash without receipts, usually as a means of tax evasion. Also, **cash economy.**

black eye *n.* bruising round the eye, resulting from a blow, etc.

black-eyed Susan /ˌblæk-aɪd 'suzən/ *n.* any of many unrelated flowers with dark centres, as species of

Tetratheca, Australian plants with nodding pink flowers with dark stamens, and *Thunbergia alata,* a twining plant whose orange flowers have a dark throat.

blackfella /'blækfɛlə/ *Chiefly Aboriginal English –n.* **1.** an Indigenous Australian. *–adj.* **2.** of or relating to or characteristic of an Indigenous Australian: *blackfella business; blackfella talk.* Also, **blackfeller, blackfellow.**

blackfellow /'blækfɛloʊ/ *n., adj.* → **blackfella.** Also, **blackfeller.**

blackguard /'blægad/ *n.* **1.** a coarse, despicable person; a scoundrel. *–v.t.* **2.** to revile in scurrilous language. *–v.i.* **3.** to behave like a blackguard. –**blackguardism,** *n.*

blackhead /'blækhɛd/ *n.* a small, black-tipped, fatty mass in a follicle, especially of the face.

black hole¹ *n. Colloq.* any small, overcrowded room.

black hole² *n.* **1.** a region postulated as arising from the collapse of a star under its own gravitational forces and from which no radiation or matter can escape. **2.** anything into which things seem to disappear, usually without making any impression or leaving any trace.

black ice *n.* a thin, barely visible coating of newly formed ice, as on a road, etc.

blackjack /'blækdʒæk/ *n.* **1.** the black flag of a pirate. **2.** a short club, usually leather covered, consisting of a heavy head and a flexible shaft or strap. **3.** *Cards* → **pontoon².**

black knight *n.* a company, or group of companies, which targets another company for an unwelcome takeover bid. Compare **white knight** (def. 2).

blackleg /'blæklɛg/ *n.* **1.** → **scab** (def. 3). **2.** a swindler especially in racing or gambling.

black light *n.* ultraviolet light.

blacklist /'blæklɪst/ *n.* **1.** a list of persons under suspicion, disfavour, censure, etc., or a list of fraudulent or unreliable customers or firms. *–v.t.* **2.** to put on a blacklist. –**blacklisted,** *adj.*

black magic *n.* magic used for evil purposes.

blackmail /'blækmeɪl/ *n.* **1.** *Law* **a.** any payment extorted by intimidation, as by threats of injurious revelations or accusations. **b.** the extortion of such payment. *–v.t.* **2.** to extort blackmail from. –**blackmailer,** *n.*

black maria /blæk mə'raɪə/ *n. Colloq.* → **paddy wagon.** Also, **Black Maria.**

black market *n.* an illegal market violating price controls, rationing, etc.

black mass *n.* a travesty of the mass, as performed by devil-worshippers.

blackout /'blækaʊt/ *n.* **1.** the extinguishing of all visible lights in a city, etc., as a wartime protection. **2.** the extinguishing or failure of light as in a power failure. **3.** temporary loss of consciousness or vision, especially in aviation due to high acceleration. **4.** loss of memory. *–adj.* **5.** of or relating to a blackout.

black power *n.* a movement originating in the US advocating the advancement of blacks (in Australia especially of the Aboriginal population) through violence or political means.

black pudding *n.* a dark sausage made from pig's blood, finely minced pork fat, herbs and other ingredients of which oatmeal may be one. Also, **blood pudding, blood sausage.**

black sheep *n.* a person regarded as a disappointment or failure in comparison to the other members of his family or group.

blacksmith /'blæksmɪθ/ *n.* someone who shapes or processes iron or, in the modern era, steel, using a forge, anvil, hammer, etc.; traditionally someone who made horseshoes, hoops for casks, coach wheels, etc.

black spot *n.* any of various fungal infections causing black spots on plant foliage.

blackspot /'blækspɒt/ *n.* any dangerous or difficult place where accidents frequently occur, especially on a road.

black stump *n.* **1.** *Aust. Colloq.* a point at which known territory or established settlement ends. *–phr.* **2. beyond** (or **back of**) **the black stump**, in the far outback; in outback or wilderness areas beyond the reach of civilisation. **3. this side of the black stump,** anywhere in the community: *the best barber this side of the black stump.*

black swan *n.* a large, stately swimming bird, *Cygnus atratus,* with black plumage and a red bill, found throughout Australia and introduced in NZ.

black tie *n.* **1.** a black bow tie for men, worn with a formal style of evening dress. **2.** a formal style of evening dress for men, of which the characteristic garments are a black bow tie and a dinner jacket (distinguished from *white tie*).

blacktracker /'blæktrækə/ *n.* an Aboriginal tracker used by police to track down missing or wanted persons. Also, **black tracker.**

bladder /'blædə/ *n.* **1.** *Zool., Anat.* **a.** a distensible pelvic sac with membranous and muscular walls, for storage and expulsion of urine excreted by the kidneys. **b.** any similar sac or receptacle. **2.** *Bot.* a sac or the like containing air, as in certain seaweeds. **3.** any inflatable or distensible bag, as the inner bag of a football, or the bellows of bagpipes. *–phr.* **4. have a weak bladder,** to suffer from the need to urinate frequently. **–bladderless,** *adj.* **–bladdery,** *adj.*

blade /bleɪd/ *n.* **1.** the flat cutting part of a sword, knife, etc. **2.** (*pl.*) a hand-held tool like scissors for shearing sheep. **3.** a leaf of a plant, especially of grass. **4.** *Bot.* the broad part of a leaf, not including the stem, etc. **5.** a cut of beef from the shoulder. **6.** a thin, flat part of something, as of a bone, oar, etc. **7.** a blade-shaped prosthetic leg, adapted for running. **–bladed,** *adj.* **–bladeless,** *adj.* **–bladelike,** *adj.*

blame /bleɪm/ *v.t.* **1.** to lay the responsibility of (a fault, error, etc.) on a person: *I blame the accident on him.* **2.** to find fault with; censure: *I blame you for that.* **3.** (*as a humorous imperative or optative*) *US Colloq.* to blast: *blame my hide if I go. –n.* **4.** imputation of fault; censure. **5.** responsibility for a fault, error, etc. *–phr.* **6. to blame,** responsible for a fault or error; blamable; culpable. **–blamable, blameable,** *adj.* **–blameless,** *adj.* **–blameworthy,** *adj.*

blanch /blæntʃ, blantʃ/ *v.t.* **1.** to whiten by removing colour. **2.** to remove the skin from (nuts, fruits, etc.) by immersion in boiling water, then in cold. *–v.i.* **3.** to become white; turn pale. **–blancher,** *n.*

blancmange /blə'mɒnʒ, -'mɒndʒ/ *n.* a jelly-like preparation of milk thickened with cornflour, gelatine, or the like, and flavoured.

bland /blænd/ *adj.* **1.** (of a person's manner) suave; deliberately agreeable or pleasant but often without real feeling. **2.** soothing or balmy, as air. **3.** mild, as food or medicines: *a bland diet.* **–blandly,** *adv.* **–blandness,** *n.*

blandish /'blændɪʃ/ *v.t.* to treat flatteringly; coax; cajole. **–blandisher,** *n.* **–blandishment,** *n.*

blank /blæŋk/ *adj.* **1.** (of paper, etc.) free from marks; not written or printed on. **2.** not filled in: *a blank cheque.* **3.** unrelieved or unbroken by ornament or opening: *a blank wall.* **4.** lacking some usual or completing feature; empty. **5.** void of interest, results, etc. **6.** showing no attention, interest, or emotion: *a blank face.* **7.** disconcerted; nonplussed: *a blank look.* **8.** complete, utter, or unmitigated: *blank stupidity.* **9.** Also, **blanky, blankety.** *Colloq.* euphemistic for any vulgar or taboo epithet. *–n.* **10.** a place where something is lacking: *a blank in one's memory.* **11.** a void; emptiness. **12.** a space left (to be filled in) in written or printed matter. **13.** a printed form containing such spaces. **14.** a dash put in place of an omitted letter or word, especially to disguise a profanity or obscenity: *instead of her age, she wrote blanks.* **15.** *Machinery* a piece of metal prepared to be stamped or cut into a finished object, such as a coin or key. **16.** *Archery* the white mark in the centre of a butt or target at which an arrow is aimed. **17.** a blank cartridge. **18.** a domino unmarked on one or both of its halves. **19.** a lottery ticket which does not win. *–v.t.* **20.** *Machinery* to stamp or punch out of flat stock as with a die. *–phr.* **21. blank out, a.** to make blank or void: *to blank out an entry.* **b.** to lose attention, consciousness, memory, etc., momentarily: *to blank out for a minute.* **22. draw a blank, a.** to draw from a lottery an unmarked counter, one not associated with any prize. **b.** to be unsuccessful, especially when looking for someone or something, or trying to find out about something. **23. go blank, a.** (of a screen) to become clear of any image. **b.** (of the mind) to lose conscious thought. **24. fire** (or **shoot**) **blanks,** *Colloq.* (of a man) to be sterile. **–blankness,** *n.* **–blankly,** *adv.*

blank cartridge *n.* a cartridge containing powder only, without a bullet.

blank cheque *n.* **1.** a cheque bearing a signature but no stated amount, allowing the payee to write in the amount. **2.** a free hand; carte blanche.

blanket /'blæŋkət/ *n.* **1.** a large rectangular piece of soft fabric, usually wool, used especially as a bed covering. **2.** any layer or covering that hides something: *a blanket of clouds. –v.t.* **3.** to cover with or as if with a blanket. *–adj.* **4.** covering or intended to cover a group or class of things, conditions, etc.: *blanket approval.*

blank verse *n.* **1.** unrhymed verse. **2.** the unrhymed iambic pentameter verse most frequently used in English dramatic, epic, and reflective poems.

blare /blɛə/ *verb* (**blared, blaring**) *–v.i.* **1.** to emit a loud raucous sound. *–v.t.* **2.** to sound loudly; proclaim noisily. *–n.* **3.** a loud raucous noise.

blarney /'blani/ *n.* flattering or wheedling talk; cajolery.

blasé /bla'zeɪ, 'blazeɪ/ *adj.* **1.** indifferent to and bored by pleasures of life. **2.** (sometimes fol. by *about*) unmoved or unperturbed; indifferent: *to be blasé about the amount of work to be done.*

blaspheme /blæs'fim/ *v.t.* **1.** to speak impiously or irreverently of (God or sacred things). *–v.i.* **2.** to utter impious words. **–blasphemy,** *n.* **–blasphemous,** *adj.* **–blasphemer,** *n.*

blast /blast/ *n.* **1.** a sudden blowing or gust of wind. **2.** the blowing of a trumpet, whistle, etc. **3.** the sound produced by this. **4.** a forcible stream of air from the mouth, from bellows, or the like. **5.** *Mining, Civil Eng., etc.* the charge of dynamite or other explosive used at one firing in blasting operations. **6.** the act of exploding; explosion. **7.** the forcible movement of air, or the shock wave, caused by an explosion. **8.** any pernicious or destructive influence, especially on animals or plants; blight. **9.** *Colloq.* **a.** something that is very funny; hoot; laugh: *what a blast!* **b.** an extremely exciting or exhilarating experience. **10.** *Colloq.* severe criticism, especially noisy or choleric. *–v.t.* **11.** to cause to shrivel or wither; blight. **12.** to affect with any pernicious influence; ruin; destroy: *to blast someone's hopes.* **13.** to tear (rock, etc.) to pieces with an explosive. **14.** to criticise abusively. *–interj.* **15.** an exclamation of anger or irritation. *–phr.* **16. blast from the past,** *Colloq.* someone or something, such as a song, fashion, etc., which is from the past or reminiscent of the past. **17. blast off, a.** to fire the rockets of a rocket ship, spacecraft, etc., in order to leave a planet's surface. **b.** *Colloq.* to depart rapidly or immediately. **18. full blast, a.** to or at the loudest volume: *she turned the radio up full blast.* **b.** with the utmost energy and vigour. **–blaster,** *n.*

blast furnace *n.* a vertical, steel cylindrical furnace using a forced blast to produce molten iron which may be converted into steel or formed into pig iron.

blastoma /blæs'toʊmə/ *n.* a cancer of primitive or pre-cursor cells, usually found in children.

blatant /'bleɪtnt/ *adj.* **1.** (of actions, etc.) flagrantly obvious or undisguised: *a blatant error, a blatant lie.* **2.** (of persons) offensively conspicuous in or un-concerned by (bad) behaviour; brazen; barefaced. –**blatancy**, *n.* –**blatantly**, *adv.*

blather /'blæðə/ *n.* **1.** foolish talk. –*v.i.* **2.** to talk fool-ishly. –*v.t.* **3.** to utter foolishly. Also, **blether**.

blaze¹ /bleɪz/ *n.* **1.** a bright flame or fire. **2.** a bright, hot gleam or glow: *a blaze of sunshine.* **3.** a sparkling brightness: *a blaze of jewels.* **4.** a sudden passion or fury. –*v.i.* **5.** to burn brightly. **6.** to shine like flame. **7.** (of guns) to fire continuously.

blaze² /bleɪz/ *n.* **1.** a spot or mark made on a tree, as by removing a piece of the bark, to indicate a boundary or a path in a forest. **2.** a white mark on the face of a horse, cow, etc. –*v.t.* **3.** to mark with blazes. –*phr.* **4. blaze a trail, a.** to mark out a trail with blazes. **b.** to break new ground; pioneer.

blazer /'bleɪzə/ *n.* **1.** a lightweight jacket, often brightly coloured, as worn by sportsmen. **2.** a jacket, usually bearing some badge or crest, as worn by schoolchil-dren.

blazes /'bleɪzəz/ *Colloq.* –*pl. n.* **1.** hell. –*phr.* **2. go to blazes**, an exclamation of dismissal, contempt, anger, etc. **3.** (**in**) **the** (**blue**) **blazes**, an intensifier. **4. like blazes**, with great energy or at great speed.

blazon /'bleɪzən/ *v.t.* **1.** to set forth conspicuously or publicly; display; proclaim. –*n.* **2.** a heraldic shield; armorial bearings.

-ble variant of **-able**, as in *noble*; occurring first in words of Latin origin which came into English through French, later in words taken directly from Latin. Also, (*after consonant stems*), **-ible**.

bleach /blitʃ/ *v.t.* **1.** to make white, pale, or colourless. –*v.i.* **2.** to become white, pale or colourless. –*n.* **3.** a bleaching agent.

bleak /blik/ *adj.* **1.** bare, desolate, and windswept: *a bleak plain.* **2.** cold and piercing: *a bleak wind.* **3.** dreary: *a bleak prospect.* –**bleakly**, *adv.* –**bleakness**, *n.*

bleary /'bliəri/ *adj.* (**-rier, -riest**) **1.** (of the eyes) dim from a watery discharge, or from tiredness. **2.** dull of perception. **3.** misty; dim; indistinct. –**blearily**, *adv.* –**bleariness**, *n.*

bleat /blit/ *v.i.* **1.** to cry as a sheep, goat, or calf. **2.** to complain; moan. –*n.* **3.** the cry of a sheep, goat, or calf. **4.** any similar sound. –**bleater**, *n.* –**bleatingly**, *adv.*

bleed /blid/ *verb* (**bled** /blɛd/, **bleeding**) –*v.i.* **1.** to lose blood, from the body or internally from the vascular system. **2.** to die, as in battle: *he bled for the cause.* **3.** (of blood, etc.) to flow out. **4.** (of colour) to run. **5.** to give out sap, juice, etc. **6.** to feel pity, sorrow: *the na-tion bleeds for its dead soldiers.* –*v.t.* **7.** to cause to lose blood, especially from surgery. **8.** to drain, draw sap, liquid, air, etc., from: *to bleed the brakes of a car.* **9.** to extort money from: *they bled him white.* –*n.* **10.** a bleeding from part of the body.

bleep /blip/ *v.i.* to emit a high-pitched broken sound, or a radio signal.

blemish /'blɛmɪʃ/ *v.t.* **1.** to destroy the perfection of. –*n.* **2.** a defect; a disfigurement; stain. –**blemisher**, *n.*

blench /blɛntʃ/ *v.i.* to shrink; flinch; quail. –**blencher**, *n.*

blend /blɛnd/ *verb* (**blended, blending**) –*v.t.* **1.** to mix smoothly and inseparably together. **2.** to mix (various sorts or grades) in order to obtain a particular kind or quality. –*v.i.* **3.** to mix or intermingle smoothly and inseparably. –*n.* **4.** a mixture or kind produced by blending. **5.** *Ling.* a word made by putting together parts of other words, as *motel*, from *motor* and *hotel*.

blended family *n.* a family formed from the members of separate families, usually as a result of the parents' remarriage.

blender /'blɛndə/ *n.* an electric device, usually with very rapidly rotating sharp blades in the base of a cylindrical container, used for chopping or pulverising dry ingre-dients, and for combining and mixing dry and liquid food ingredients.

bless /blɛs/ *v.t.* **1.** to consecrate by a religious rite; make or pronounce holy. **2.** to request of God the bestowal of divine favour on. **3.** to bestow good of any kind upon: *a nation blessed with peace.* **4.** *Eccles.* to make the sign of the cross over.

blessed /'blɛsəd, blɛst/ *adj.* **1.** consecrated; sacred; holy. **2.** divinely or supremely favoured; fortunate; happy. **3.** (*euphemistic*) damned: *blessed if I know*; *it's a blessed nuisance.* –**blessedly**, *adv.* –**blessedness**, *n.*

blessing /'blɛsɪŋ/ *n.* **1.** the act or words of someone who blesses. **2.** a special favour, mercy, or benefit. **3.** a fa-vour or gift bestowed by God, thereby bringing hap-piness. **4.** the invoking of God's favour upon a person. –*phr.* **5. blessing in disguise**, a misfortune which subsequently turns out to have unexpected advantages.

blew /blu/ *v.* past tense of **blow²**.

blight /blaɪt/ *n.* **1.** any cause of destruction, ruin, or frustration. **2.** → **sandy blight**. –*v.t.* **3.** to destroy; ruin; frustrate.

blimp /blɪmp/ *n.* **1.** a small, nonrigid airship, used for military surveillance, scientific applications, the display of advertising and the filming of sporting events. **2.** *Colloq.* any dirigible.

blind /blaɪnd/ *adj.* **1.** lacking the sense of sight. **2.** un-willing or unable to try to understand: *blind to all arguments.* **3.** not controlled by reason: *blind tenacity.* **4.** not possessing or proceeding from intelligence. **5.** lacking all awareness: *a blind stupor.* **6.** drunk. **7.** hard to see or understand: *blind reasoning.* **8.** that cannot be seen round; obstructing vision: *a blind cor-ner.* **9.** having no outlets. **10.** closed at one end: *a blind street.* **11.** done without seeing: *blind flying.* **12.** made without knowledge in advance: *a blind date.* **13.** relat-ing to sightless people. –*v.t.* **14.** to make blind, as by injuring, dazzling, or bandaging the eyes. **15.** to deprive of discernment or judgement. –*n.* **16.** a shade for a window, as a strip of cloth on a roller, or a venetian blind. **17.** a lightly built structure of brush or other growths, especially one in which hunters conceal themselves; a hide. **18.** a cover for masking action or purpose; decoy. **19.** *Colloq.* a bout of excessive drink-ing; drinking spree. –*adv.* **20.** without being able to see one's way: *to fly blind.* **21.** without assessment or prior consideration: *to enter into a deal blind.* –*phr.* **22. on the blind**, in a situation where not all the conditions can be known: *small-time opal seekers sink shafts on the blind.* **23. the blind**, sightless people. **24. the blind side**, the side of a vehicle, location, etc., which is obscured from view: *the blind side of the car.* –**blinding**, *adj.* –**blindingly**, *adv.* –**blindly**, *adv.* –**blindness**, *n.*

blind-bake *v.t.* to bake (a pastry case) before it is filled.

blindfold /'blaɪndfoʊld/ *v.t.* **1.** to prevent sight by cov-ering (the eyes); cover the eyes of. **2.** to impair the clear thinking of. –*n.* **3.** a bandage over the eyes.

blindside /'blaɪndsaɪd/ *v.t.* **1.** *Football* to manoeuvre (a player) into a position where an approaching opponent is not visible. **2.** to surprise with an unforeseen deci-sion, strategy, etc.

blindsided /'blaɪndsaɪdəd/ *adj.* caught off guard: *the government was blindsided by the revelations.*

blindsight /'blaɪndsaɪt/ *n.* the visual awareness which a visually-impaired person has, created by a response to stimuli that falls short of actual sight but which allows the person to sense aspects of visual stimuli such as movement, location, etc. **–blindsighted**, *adj.* **–blindsightedly**, *adv.*

blind snake *n.* a small, subterranean, non-venomous snake of the family Typhlopidae; worm snake.

blind spot *n.* **1.** *Anat.* a small area on the retina, insensitive to light, at which the optic nerve leaves the eye. **2.** a matter about which one is ignorant, unintelligent, or prejudiced, despite knowledge of related things. **3.** *Radio, TV, etc.* an area in which signals are weak and their reception poor. **4.** (in a car) a line of sight obscured by a window column or other obstruction.

bling /blɪŋ/ *n.* showy jewellery, especially when worn in large quantity. Also, **bling-bling**.

blink /blɪŋk/ *v.i.* **1.** to wink, especially rapidly and repeatedly. **2.** to look with winking or half-shut eyes. **3.** to shine unsteadily or dimly; twinkle. *–n.* **4.** a blinking. **5.** a gleam; glimmer. *–phr.* **6. don't blink or you'll miss it,** *Colloq.* a phrase indicating that something will last for a very short time. **7. in the blink of an eye,** *Colloq.* very quickly. **8. not blink (an eye) at,** to show no surprise or concern about. **9. on the blink,** *Colloq.* not working properly.

blinker /'blɪŋkə/ *n.* **1.** an indicator (def. 1) on a motor vehicle. **2.** either of two flaps on a bridle, to prevent a horse from seeing sideways or backwards.

blintz /blɪnts/ *n.* a pancake with either a sweet or a savoury filling, and fried or baked.

bliss /blɪs/ *n.* **1.** lightness of heart; blitheness; gladness. **2.** supreme happiness or delight. **–blissful**, *adj.*

blister /'blɪstə/ *n.* **1.** a bubble-like swelling under the skin, containing watery matter especially from a burn or other injury. **2.** any similar swelling. *–v.t.* **3.** to raise blisters on. *–v.i.* **4.** to form blisters; become blistered. **–blistery**, *adj.*

blithe /blaɪð/ *adj.* joyous or merry in disposition; glad; cheerful. **–blithely**, *adv.*

blithering /'blɪðərɪŋ/ *adj.* **1.** nonsensical; jabbering. **2.** *Colloq.* blinking.

blitz /blɪts/ *n.* **1.** Also, **blitzkrieg** /'blɪtskriɡ/ *Mil.* war waged by surprise, swiftly and violently, as by the use of aircraft. **2.** *Colloq.* any swift, vigorous attack: *a blitz on litterbugs. –v.t.* **3.** to attack with a blitz. **4.** *Colloq.* to deal with vigorously: *to blitz the housework.* **5.** *Colloq.* to defeat decisively.

blizzard /'blɪzəd/ *n.* **1.** a violent windstorm with dry, driving snow and intense cold. **2.** a widespread and heavy snowstorm.

bloat /bloʊt/ *v.t.* **1.** to make distended, as with air, water, etc.; cause to swell. **2.** to puff up; make vain or conceited. *–v.i.* **3.** to become swollen; be puffed out or dilated. *–n.* Also, **bloating. 4.** *Vet. Science* (in cattle and other livestock) a distension of the stomach by gases of fermentation, caused by ravenous eating of green forage, especially legumes.

bloated /'bloʊtəd/ *adj.* **1.** swollen: *bloated features.* **2.** suffering from flatulence. **3.** suffering from excessive size: *a bloated bureaucracy.*

blob /blɒb/ *n.* a small lump, drop, splotch, or daub.

bloc /blɒk/ *n.* **1.** a group of states or territories united by some common factor. **2.** *Politics* a coalition of factions or parties for a particular measure or purpose.

block /blɒk/ *n.* **1.** a solid mass of wood, stone, etc., usually with one or more plane or approximately plane faces. **2.** a child's building brick. **3.** a mould or piece on which something is shaped or kept in shape, as a hat block. **4.** a piece of wood prepared for cutting, or as cut, for wood engraving. **5.** a (wooden) bench or board for chipping or cutting on. **6.** the support on which a person about to be beheaded lays his or her head. **7.** a platform from which an auctioneer sells. **8.** *Mechanics* **a.** a

device consisting of one or more grooved pulleys mounted in a casing or shell, to which a hook or the like is attached, used for transmitting power, changing direction of motion, etc. **b.** the casing or shell holding the pulley. **9.** an obstacle or hindrance. **10.** a blocking or obstructing, or blocked or obstructed state or condition. **11.** *Pathol.* an obstruction, as of a nerve. **12.** *Sport* a hindering of an opponent's actions. **13.** *Cricket* a mark made on the crease by the person batting when taking guard. **14.** a quantity, portion, or section taken as a unit or dealt with at one time: *block of tickets.* **15.** *Computers* a set of data or instructions. **16.** *Aust., NZ* a fairly large area of land, especially for settlement, mining, farming, etc. **17.** *Aust.* a section of land, frequently suburban, as for building a house, etc.: *a block of land; a building block.* **18.** *NZ* the area of land, especially Crown or State forest, over which a trapper or hunter is licensed to operate. **19. a.** one large building, divided into offices, apartments, etc.: *an office block; a block of flats.* **b.** a building containing a number of units of a particular type: *a toilet block; a shower block; a cell block.* **20. a.** a portion of a city, town, etc., enclosed by (usually four) neighbouring and intersecting streets. **b.** the length of one side of this; distance between one intersection and the next. **21.** a stage direction added to a script. **22.** a writing or sketching pad. **23.** *Athletics* a starting block. *–adj.* **24.** organised as a block (def. 14): *block teaching for two weeks. –v.t.* **25.** to fit with blocks; mount on a block. **26.** to shape or prepare on or with a block. **27.** to cut into blocks. **28.** to write in stage directions on (a script). **29.** to obstruct (a space, progress, etc.); check or hinder (a person, etc.) by placing obstacles in the way. **30.** to restrict the use of (a currency, etc.) **31.** *Pathol., Physiol.* to stop the passage of impulses in (a nerve, etc.). *–v.i.* **32.** to act so as to obstruct an opponent (as in football, boxing, etc.). **33.** *Cricket* to stop the ball with the bat; to bat defensively. *–phr.* **34. block in, a.** to draw or paint roughly without detail or elaboration. **b.** to outline or explain in a general way. **35. block out, a.** to obscure from view: *the smoke blocked out the sun.* **b.** to conceal by screening in some way: *to block out the silence with noise; to block out the image with a red spot.* **c.** to prevent penetration by: *this cream blocks out radiation.* **36. do the block,** *Colloq.* to promenade the fashionable area of town. **37. knock someone's block off,** *Colloq.* to punch someone in the head. **38. lose (or do) one's block,** *Colloq.* to become very angry. **39. new kid (or boy) (or girl) on the block,** a newcomer arriving into an established group, as a particular field, organisation, etc., especially one who attracts attention as a force in the group. **40. off one's block,** *Colloq.* insane.

blockade /blɒ'keɪd/ *n.* **1.** *Navy, Mil.* the shutting up of a place, especially a port, harbour, or part of a coast by hostile ships or troops to prevent entrance or exit. **2.** a similar barricading of a place carried out by any group, usually as a form of protest. **3.** any obstruction of passage or progress. *–v.t.* **4.** to subject to a blockade. **–blockader**, *n.*

blockage /'blɒkɪdʒ/ *n.* an obstruction.

block and tackle *n.* the block (def. 8) and associated ropes used for hoisting.

blockbuster /'blɒkbʌstə/ *n.* anything large and spectacular, as a lavish theatrical production, impressive political campaign, etc. **–blockbusting**, *adj.*

blocked shoe *n.* a dance shoe with a stiffened toe, worn by a ballet dancer to enable dancing on the tip of the toes.

blockhead /'blɒkhɛd/ *n.* a stupid person; a dolt.

blockhouse /'blɒkhaʊs/ *n. Mil.* a fortified structure with ports or loopholes for gunfire, used against bombs, artillery, and small-arms fire.

block letter *n.* a plain capital letter. Also, **block capital**.

blockout /'blɒkaʊt/ *n.* (*from trademark*) → **sunscreen** (def. 2).

blog /blɒg/ *n.* **1.** a record of items of interest found on the internet, edited and published as a website with comments and links. **2.** a personal diary published on the internet. **3.** an online forum. *–verb* (**blogged, blogging**) *–v.i.* **4.** to post entries on a blog: *to blog all day.* *–v.t.* **5.** to communicate by means of a blog: *to blog a film review.* **–blogger,** *n.*

bloke /bloʊk/ *n. Colloq.* a man; fellow; guy. **–blokeish, blokish,** *adj.*

blokey /'bloʊki/ *adj. Colloq.* illustrative of essential masculinity, especially as defined in a crude and stereotypical way: *blokey behaviour is to drink beer and watch the footy.* **–blokeyness,** *n.*

blond /blɒnd/ *adj.* **1.** (of a person or a people) having light-coloured hair and skin. **2.** (of hair) of a light yellow or golden colour. **3.** (of furniture, wood, etc.) light-coloured. *–n.* **4.** a blond person, especially a male. **–blondness,** *n.*

blonde /blɒnd/ *n.* **1.** a female with light-coloured hair. *–adj.* **2.** (of a female) having light-coloured hair and skin. **3.** (of a female's hair) light; fair. **4.** (of a beer) clear rather than cloudy, with a light gold colour; sometimes with the addition of citrus flavours. **–blondeness,** *n.*

blood /blʌd/ *n.* **1.** the fluid that circulates in the arteries and veins or principal vascular system of animals, in humans being of a red colour and consisting of a pale yellow plasma containing semisolid corpuscles. **2.** bloodshed; slaughter; murder. **3.** temper or state of mind: *a person of hot blood.* **4.** descent from a common ancestor: *related by blood.* **5.** people of a kind specified: *young blood; to introduce new blood.* *–v.t.* **6.** to cause to bleed. **7.** *Hunting* **a.** to give (hounds, etc.) a first taste or sight of blood. **b.** to smear with blood, as after a hunt. **8.** to initiate in the ways of a group, organisation, etc., by real experience. *–phr.* **9. get blood from a stone,** to extract value from a source previously considered incapable of such. **10. in cold blood,** calmly, coolly, and deliberately. **11. one's blood is up,** one's anger or belligerence is aroused. **12. one's blood is worth bottling,** *Aust., NZ Colloq.* one is exceptionally meritorious or praiseworthy.

blood bank *n.* a place where blood is stored for later use.

bloodbath /'blʌdbɑθ/ *n.* a massacre.

bloodborne /'blʌdbɔn/ *adj.* **1.** (of a pathogen) transported in the blood. **2.** (of a disease) transmitted from one person to another by contact with the blood of the person who already has the disease. Also, **blood-borne.**

blood count *n.* the count of the number of red or white blood cells in a specific volume of blood.

bloodcurdling /'blʌd,kɜdlɪŋ/ *adj.* frightening; terrifyingly horrible.

blood diamond *n.* a rough diamond that is sourced by unscrupulous or illicit means in an area where there is military conflict, the sale of which is then used to perpetuate the conflict. Also, **conflict diamond.**

blood doping *n.* the practice of increasing the number of red blood cells in the body to improve sporting performance, either by transfusion of stored blood or by hormone treatment which causes the body to increase its own production of red blood cells; banned by sports associations internationally. **–blood doper,** *n.*

blood group *n.* one of several classifications into which the blood may be grouped according to its clotting reactions, the commonest being A (A antigens in the blood), B (B antigens in the blood), AB (both A and B antigens in the blood) and O (neither A nor B antigens in the blood). Also, **blood type.**

bloodhound /'blʌdhaʊnd/ *n.* **1.** one of a breed of large, powerful dogs with a very acute sense of smell, used for tracking game, human fugitives, etc. **2.** *Colloq.* a detective; sleuth. Also, **sleuthhound.**

bloodless /'blʌdləs/ *adj.* **1.** without blood; pale. **2.** free from bloodshed: *a bloodless victory.* **3.** spiritless; without energy. **–bloodlessly,** *adv.* **–bloodlessness,** *n.*

bloodletting /'blʌdlɛtɪŋ/ *n.* **1.** the act of letting blood by opening a vein or artery; formerly regarded as a remedy for many illnesses. **2.** → **bloodshed.**

blood money *n.* **1.** a fee paid to a hired murderer. **2.** compensation paid to the survivors of a murder victim. **3.** small remuneration earned by unreasonably great effort. **4.** riches acquired through dishonourable or distasteful means.

blood-poisoning *n.* a morbid condition of the blood due to the presence of toxic matter or microorganisms; toxaemia; septicaemia.

blood pressure *n.* the pressure of the blood against the inner walls of the blood vessels, varying in different parts of the body, during different phases of contraction of the heart, and under different conditions of health, exertion, etc.

blood relation *n.* someone related to another by birth. Also, **blood relative.**

bloodshed /'blʌdʃɛd/ *n.* destruction of life; slaughter.

bloodshot /'blʌdʃɒt/ *adj.* (of the eyes) red from dilated blood vessels.

blood sport *n.* a sport involving bloodshed, as hunting. Also, **bloodsport.**

bloodstock /'blʌdstɒk/ *n.* thoroughbred stock, especially stud horses.

bloodstream /'blʌdstrim/ *n.* the blood flowing through a circulatory system.

bloodsucker /'blʌdsʌkə/ *n.* **1.** any animal that sucks blood, especially a leech. **2.** *Colloq.* an extortionist. **–bloodsucking,** *adj.*

blood sugar *n.* glucose in the blood, which, after overnight fasting, is normally between 70 and 100 mg/dL.

bloodthirsty /'blʌdθɜsti/ *adj.* eager to shed blood; murderous. **–bloodthirstily,** *adv.* **–bloodthirstiness,** *n.*

blood type *n.* → **blood group.**

blood vessel *n.* any of the vessels (arteries, veins, capillaries) through which the blood circulates.

bloody /'blʌdi/ *adj.* (**-dier, -diest**) **1.** stained with blood: *bloody handkerchief.* **2.** causing bloodshed: *bloody battle.* **3.** of the nature of, or relating to blood. **4.** *Colloq.* a word indicating approval or disapproval: *bloody miracle; bloody idiot.* *–v.t.* (**-died, -dying**) **5.** to stain with blood. *–adv.* **6.** *Colloq.* very; extremely: *bloody awful.* **–bloodily,** *adv.* **–bloodiness,** *n.*

bloody-minded *adj. Colloq.* **1.** obstructive; unhelpful; difficult. **2.** deliberately cruel or unpleasant. **–bloody-mindedness,** *n.*

bloom /blum/ *n.* **1.** the flower of a plant. **2.** the state of having the buds opened. **3.** a glowing, healthy condition: *bloom of youth.* **4.** a state of full development; prime; perfection. **5.** *Bot.* a whitish powdery coating on the surface of certain fruits and leaves. **6.** any similar surface coating or appearance. *–v.i.* **7.** to produce or yield flowers. **8.** to be in a state of healthy beauty and vigour; flourish. **9.** to reach the stage of full development. **–bloomless,** *adj.*

bloomers /'bluməz/ *pl. n.* **1.** loose trousers gathered at the knee, formerly worn by women for gymnastics, riding, or other active exercise. **2.** a woman's undergarment so designed.

blossom /'blɒsəm/ *n.* **1.** the flower of a plant, especially of one producing an edible fruit. **2.** the state of flowering: *the apple tree is in blossom.* *–v.i.* **3.** *Bot.* to produce or yield blossoms. **4.** to reach the stage of full development. **5.** Also, **blossom out.** to flourish; develop. –**blossomless**, *adj.* –**blossomy**, *adj.*

blot /blɒt/ *n.* **1.** a spot or stain, especially of ink on paper. **2.** a blemish or reproach on character or reputation. –*verb* (**blotted, blotting**) –*v.t.* **3.** to spot, stain, or bespatter. **4.** to dry with absorbent paper or the like. –*v.i.* **5.** (of ink, etc.) to spread in a stain. **6.** to become blotted or stained: *this paper blots easily.* –*phr.* **7. blot out, a.** to make indistinguishable: *cloud blotted out the mountains.* **b.** to destroy; wipe out completely: *to blot out a memory* –**blotless**, *adj.*

blotch /blɒtʃ/ *n.* a large irregular spot or blot. –**blotchy**, *adj.*

blotting paper *n.* **1.** a soft, absorbent, unsized paper, used especially for drying ink on paper. **2.** *Colloq.* food taken while drinking alcoholic beverages, to mitigate the effects of the alcohol.

blotto /ˈblɒtəʊ/ *adj. Colloq.* under the influence of alcoholic drink.

blouse /blaʊz/ *n.* **1.** a light, loosely fitting bodice or shirt, especially one that is gathered or held in at the waist. –*v.i.* **2.** to hang loose and full. –*v.t.* **3.** to drape loosely.

blow[1] /bloʊ/ *n.* **1.** a sudden stroke with hand, fist, or weapon. **2.** a sudden shock, or a calamity or reverse. **3.** a sudden attack or drastic action. **4.** a stroke of the shears made in shearing a sheep. **5.** an outcrop of discoloured quartz-rich rock, sometimes thought to indicate mineral deposits below. –*phr.* **6. at one blow,** with a single act. **7. come to blows,** to start to fight. **8. strike a blow,** to begin or resume work.

blow[2] /bloʊ/ *verb* (**blew** /blu/, **blown, blowing**) –*v.i.* **1.** (of the wind or air) to be in motion. **2.** to move along, carried by or as by the wind: *the dust was blowing.* **3.** to produce or emit a current of air, as with the mouth, a bellows, etc.: *blow on your hands.* **4.** *Colloq.* to boast; brag. **5.** *Colloq.* to depart. **6.** *Zool.* (of a whale) to spout. **7.** (of a fuse, gasket, light bulb, radio valve, etc.) to burn out or perish; become unusable. **8.** *Colloq.* (taboo) (usually of a man) to experience orgasm. **9.** Also, **blow out.** *Horseracing Colloq.* (of odds on a horse offered by bookmakers) to lengthen. –*v.t.* **10.** to drive by means of a current of air. **11.** to divulge (a secret). **12.** to shape (glass, etc.) with a current of air. **13.** to cause to sound, especially by a current of air. **14.** to destroy by explosion: *to blow the bridge.* **15.** to put (a horse) out of breath by fatigue. **16.** to register (a level of blood alcohol concentration) by breathing into a breathalyser or the like: *she blew .25.* **17.** *Colloq.* to waste; squander: *to blow one's money.* **18.** *Colloq.* to exceed the spending limits of (a budget). **19.** *Colloq.* to fail in: *to blow an exam.* **20.** *Colloq.* (taboo) to perform fellatio on. –*n.* **21. a.** a storm with a high wind. **b.** a high wind. **22.** *Colloq.* a boasting or bragging. **23.** *Colloq.* a rest: *we'll have a blow now.* –*interj.* **24.** *Colloq.* an expression of frustration: *Blow! I've missed the train.* –*phr.* **25. blow away,** *Colloq.* **a.** to kill by shooting. **b.** to amaze, usually with delight: *that concert really blew me away.* **26. hot and cold,** to change attitudes frequently; vacillate. **27. blow in,** *Colloq.* to make an unexpected visit; drop in; call. **28. blow it,** *Colloq.* an exclamation of frustration, dissatisfaction, etc. **29. blow me (down),** *Colloq.* an exclamation indicating astonishment, wonder, etc. **30. blow off, a.** to remove, carried by or as by a current of air: *the steam blew the lid off.* **b.** to allow (a gas under pressure) to escape. **c.** to allow gas under pressure to escape. **d.** *Colloq.* to fart noisily. **31. blow one's mind,** *Colloq.* to achieve a state of euphoria, especially with drugs: *I blew my mind on LSD.* **32. blow one's stack** (or **top**), *Colloq.* to lose one's temper. **33. blow out, a.** to be extinguished, as by the wind: *the candle blew out.* **b.** (of a tyre) to burst, especially as a result of the high speed of the vehicle.

c. (of an oil or gas well) to lose oil or gas suddenly in a way that is not controlled. **d.** (of a budget) to exceed the spending limits set: *the budget has blown out by a million dollars.* **e.** Also, **blow.** *Horseracing Colloq.* (of odds on a horse offered by bookmakers) to lengthen. **f.** to extinguish (a flame, etc.) with a puff of air. **34. blow over, a.** (of a storm, etc.) to cease; subside. **b.** to be forgotten **35. blow someone's head off,** *Colloq.* **a.** to shoot someone through the head. **b.** to speak very angrily to someone. **36. blow someone's mind,** *Colloq.* to amaze or delight someone: *this film will blow your mind.* **37. blow the whistle on,** *Colloq.* to inform upon; report to authority. **38. blow through,** *Colloq.* to depart, especially to evade a responsibility. **39. blow to bits** (or **smithereens**), *Colloq.* to cause to explode into small fragments. **40. blow up, a.** to come into being: *a storm blew up.* **b.** to explode: *the ship blew up.* **c.** to cause to explode. **d.** to cause to inflate: *to blow up balloons.* **e.** *Colloq.* to scold or abuse (someone). **f.** *Photography* to reproduce by enlargement. **41. blow wide open,** to make a matter for general discussion, public scrutiny, etc., as via media reporting. **42. blow you** (or **him, her,** etc.), *Colloq.* **a.** an expression of dissatisfaction with someone. **b.** an expression indicating an intention to disregard someone.

blow-dry *v.t.* (**-dried, -drying**) **1.** to style hair by brushing it into shape while drying it with a blow dryer. –*n.* (*pl.* **-dries**) **2.** an instance of blow-drying: *a wash and blow-dry.* Also, **blowdry.**

blow dryer *n.* a handheld machine which blows out warm air and is used to dry the hair. Also, **blow drier.**

blowfly /ˈbloʊflaɪ/ *n.* (*pl.* **-flies**) **1.** any of various true flies, of the order Diptera, family Calliphoridae, which deposit their eggs or larvae on carcasses or meat, or in sores, wounds, etc., especially the **green blowfly**, *Lucilia cuprina.* **2.** *Colloq.* an officious person, especially one in authority, as a police officer.

blowfly strike *n.* → **flystrike.**

blowhole /ˈbloʊhoʊl/ *n.* **1.** an air or gas vent. **2.** a hole in a coastal rock formation through which compressed air and sea water are forced violently up by tide or wave.

blown /bloʊn/ *adj.* **1.** inflated; distended. **2.** out of breath; fatigued; exhausted. **3.** flyblown. **4.** formed by blowing: *blown glass.*

blowout /ˈbloʊaʊt/ *n.* **1.** a rupture of a motor vehicle tyre. **2.** the blowing of a fuse. **3.** a sudden or violent escape of air, steam, crude oil, or gas from a well, or the like. **4.** *Econ.* an excess on the limits of a budget, usually as a result of inflation. **5.** *Colloq.* a big meal or lavish entertainment; spree. Also, **blow-out.**

blowpipe /ˈbloʊpaɪp/ *n.* a pipe or tube through which missiles are blown by the breath.

blowtorch /ˈbloʊtɔtʃ/ *n.* a portable apparatus which gives an extremely hot flame by forcing oxyacetylene under pressure through a small nozzle and burning it in air; used in welding, etc.

blow-up *n.* **1.** an explosion or other drastic trouble. **2.** a violent outburst of temper or scolding. **3.** *Photography* an enlargement. –*adj.* **4.** inflatable: *a blow-up mattress.*

blowzy /ˈblaʊzi/ *adj.* (**-zier, -ziest**) dishevelled; unkempt: *blowzy hair.*

blubber /ˈblʌbə/ *n.* **1.** *Zool.* the fat found between the skin and muscle of whales and other cetaceans, from which oil is made. –*v.i.* **2.** to weep, usually noisily and with contorted face. –**blubberer**, *n.* –**blubberingly**, *adv.*

bludge /blʌdʒ/ *Aust., NZ Colloq.* –*verb* (**bludged, bludging**) –*v.i.* **1.** to evade responsibilities. **2.** to be idle; do nothing: *we spent Saturday just bludging around the house.* –*v.t.* **3.** to cadge. –*n.* **4.** a job which entails next to no work. **5.** a period of not working or not working conscientiously. –*phr.* **6. bludge on,** to impose on (someone). **7. on the bludge**, imposing on others. **–bludger**, *n*.

bludgeon /ˈblʌdʒən/ *n.* **1.** a short, heavy club with one end loaded, or thicker and heavier than the other. *–v.t.* **2.** to strike or fell with a bludgeon. **3.** to force (someone) into something; bully. **–bludgeoner**, *n.*

blue /bluː/ *n.* **1.** the pure hue of clear sky; deep azure (between green and violet in the spectrum). **2.** Also, **washing blue**. a substance, as indigo, used to whiten clothes in laundering them. **3.** a blue thing. **4.** a person who wears blue, or is a member of a group characterised by a blue symbol. **5. a.** a sportsperson who represents another. **b.** the honour awarded for this. **c.** the colours awarded for this. **6.** *Aust., NZ Colloq.* a fight; dispute. **7.** *Aust., NZ Colloq.* a mistake. **8.** *Aust., NZ Colloq.* a summons in law. *–adj.* **(bluer, bluest) 9.** of the colour blue. **10.** tinged with blue. **11.** (of the skin) discoloured by cold, contusion, fear, rage, or vascular collapse. **12.** (of a steak) quickly seared on the outside and rare inside. **13.** *Colloq.* depressed in spirits: *to feel blue.* **14.** *Colloq.* out of tune: *a blue note.* **15.** *Colloq.* obscene, or relating to obscenity. *–verb* **(blued, blueing or bluing)** *–v.t.* **16.** *Colloq.* to spend wastefully; squander. *–v.i.* **17.** *Aust., NZ Colloq.* to fight. *–phr.* **18. cop the blue**, *Aust., NZ Colloq.* to take the blame. **19. once in a blue moon**, rarely and exceptionally. **20. out of the blue (yonder)**, unexpectedly. **21. scream blue murder**, **a.** (of a child) to scream loudly. **b.** to protest vociferously. **22. stack on a blue**, *Colloq.* to instigate a fight or a brawl. **23. the blue**, **a.** the sky. **b.** the sea. **c.** the unknown; the dim distance; nowhere: *out of the blue.* **–bluely**, *adv.* **–blueness**, *n.* **–bluish, blueish**, *adj.*

bluebell /ˈbluːbel/ *n.* **1.** any Australian or New Zealand herb of the genus *Wahlenbergia*, family Campanulaceae, chiefly of southern temperate regions, having blue bell-shaped flowers, as the Australian bluebell, *W. trichogyna*, of temperate mainland Australia. **2.** any herb of the genus *Campanula*, family Campanulaceae, of northern temperate regions and tropical mountains, having similar flowers.

blueberry /ˈbluːbəri/ *n.* (*pl.* **-ries**) the edible berry, usually bluish-black, of any of various shrubs of the genus *Vaccinium*.

blue blood *n.* aristocratic descent. **–blue-blooded**, *adj.*

blue bonnet *n.* **1.** an endemic Australian parrot, *Northiella haematogaster*, predominantly brown, with a blue face and yellow and red underparts, found in semi-arid woodlands of south-eastern Australia and the Nullarbor Plain. **2.** → **red-collared lorikeet**.

bluebottle /ˈbluːbɒtl/ *n.* **1.** a hydrozoan of genus *Physalia* found in warm seas and having an elongated, deep blue, gas-filled bladder typically up to 13 centimetres long, from which trail numerous tentacles, extending many metres in length and capable of inflicting a painful sting. **2.** any of several large, metallic blue and green flies of the dipterous family Calliphoridae; the larvae of some are parasites of domestic animals.

blue chip *n.* **1.** *Stock Exchange* a stock in which investment is secure, though less secure than in gilt-edged. **2.** a valuable asset. **–blue-chip**, *adj.*

blue-collar *adj.* belonging or relating to workers involved in some sort of manual labour, as distinct from clerical or professional workers (who are sometimes referred to as *white-collar*).

blue duck *n.* **1.** a New Zealand native mountain duck, *Hymenolaimus malacorhynchus*; whio. **2.** *Chiefly NZ Mil.* **a.** a baseless rumour. **b.** a failure.

bluefish /ˈbluːfɪʃ/ *n.* **1.** an Australian and New Zealand marine fish, *Girella cyanea*, of violet-blue colouring. **2.** a predacious marine food fish, *Pomatomus saltatrix*,

bluish or greenish in colour, of the Atlantic coast of the Americas.

bluegrass /ˈbluːgrɑːs/ *n.* **1.** any of various grasses of the genus *Poa*, as the Kentucky bluegrass, *P. pratensis*, etc. **2.** music of the south-eastern US characterised by instruments such as steel-string acoustic guitar, bottle-neck guitar, and fiddle, with emphasis on the solo banjo. Also, **blue grass**.

blue-green algae *pl. n.* a poisonous blue-green growth resembling algae occurring in stagnant fresh water in hot weather. See **cyanobacteria**.

blue gum *n.* any of several species of *Eucalyptus* with smooth and often bluish-coloured bark or leaves.

blue heeler *n.* → **Australian cattle dog**.

blue metal *n.* *Aust.* crushed dark igneous rock used in construction work.

blue peter *n.* a blue flag with a white square in the centre, symbol of the letter P in the International Code of Signals, hoisted by a ship as a signal that it is ready to leave port.

blueprint /ˈbluːprɪnt/ *n.* **1.** a process of photographic printing, based on ferric salts, in which the prints are white on a blue ground; used chiefly in making copies of technical drawings, plans, etc. **2.** a detailed outline or plan.

blue ribbon *n.* a high distinction, especially a prize in an exhibition or show: *her cake won a blue ribbon.* **–blue-ribbon**, *adj.*

blue-ringed octopus *n.* a small octopus, *Octopus maculosus*, of eastern Australia, with a highly venomous bite and distinctive blue to purple banding on the tentacles appearing when the octopus is disturbed.

blue-rinse *adj.* (*derog.*) of or relating to well-off, middle-aged women of conservative and trivial outlook: *the blue-rinse set.*

blues /bluːz/ *pl. n.* **1.** *Colloq.* despondency; melancholy. **2.** a style of folk music, of African American origin, predominantly melancholy in character and usually performed in slow tempo.

blue screen *n.* a large blue background for a film or video shot which is then filled in with an image of the desired background.

blue shift *n.* *Astron.* a shift of spectral lines toward the blue end of the visible spectrum of the light emitted by an approaching celestial body; thought to be a consequence of the Doppler effect of red shift.

bluestocking /ˈbluːstɒkɪŋ/ *n.* **1.** a woman who devotes herself to intellectual pursuits to the exclusion of other interests such as fashion, social life, etc. **2.** a member of the London literary circle of the mid-18th century.

blue swimmer *n.* an edible Australian crab, *Portunus pelagicus*, of blue-green colour and capable of powerful sustained swimming.

blue-tongue *n.* **1.** Also, **blue-tongue lizard**. any of several large, stout-bodied Australian skinks of the genus *Tiliqua*, as the common *T. scincoides*, which are harmless but display their broad blue tongues in a threatening manner when disturbed. **2.** *Aust.* → **rouseabout**.

bluetooth wireless technology *n.* (*from trademark*) a short-range radio technology that provides connectivity between mobile phones, mobile computers, portable handheld devices and the internet. Also, **bluetooth**.

blue vein *n.* a type of semi-soft ripened cheese with blue-green veins of *Penicillium* mould culture throughout the ripened curd.

blue water *n.* water drawn from ground or surface supplies. Compare **green water**.

bluewater /ˈbluːwɔːtə/ *adj.* of or relating to the open sea, as opposed to enclosed or sheltered waters: *bluewater sailing; bluewater craft; bluewater charts.*

blue whale *n.* a whale, *Balaenoptera musculus*, of northern and southern oceans, bluish-grey with yellowish underparts, the largest mammal that has ever lived.

blue wren *n.* any of various fairy-wrens in which the males acquire blue adult or breeding plumage.

bluey /ˈbluːi/ *adj.* **1.** somewhat blue; bluish. –*n.* **2.** *Aust., NZ* → **swag** (def. 1). **3.** *Aust., NZ Colloq.* a summons in law. **4.** *Aust. Colloq.* → **blue swimmer**.

bluff¹ /blʌf/ *adj.* **1.** somewhat abrupt and unconventional in manner; hearty; frank. –*n.* **2.** a cliff, headland, or hill with a broad, steep face. –**bluffly**, *adv.* –**bluffness**, *n.*

bluff² /blʌf/ *v.t.* **1.** to mislead by presenting a bold front. **2.** to gain by bluffing: *he bluffed his way*. **3.** *Poker* to deceive by a show of confidence in the strength of one's cards. –*v.i.* **4.** to present a bold front in order to mislead someone. –*n.* **5.** an act of bluffing. –*phr.* **6. call someone's bluff**, to challenge or expose someone's deception. –**bluffer**, *n.*

blunder /ˈblʌndə/ *n.* **1.** a gross or stupid mistake. –*v.i.* **2.** to move or act blindly, stupidly, or without direction or steady guidance. –**blunderer**, *n.* –**blunderingly**, *adv.*

blunt /blʌnt/ *adj.* **1.** having an obtuse, thick, or dull edge or tip; rounded; not sharp. **2.** abrupt in address or manner; forthright; plain-spoken. –*v.t.* **3.** to weaken or impair the force, keenness, or susceptibility of. –**bluntly**, *adv.* –**bluntness**, *n.*

blur /blɜ/ *verb* (**blurred, blurring**) –*v.t.* **1.** to obscure or sully as by smearing with ink, etc. **2.** to obscure by making confused in form or outline; make indistinct. –*v.i.* **3.** to become indistinct: *the vision blurred.* –*n.* **4.** a blurred condition; indistinctness. –**blurry**, *adj.*

blurb /blɜb/ *n.* an announcement or advertisement, usually an effusively laudatory one, especially on the jacket flap of a book or the cover of a CD, record, etc.

blurt /blɜt/ *v.t.* **1.** to say suddenly or inadvertently. **2.** Also, **blurt out**. to divulge unadvisedly.

blush /blʌʃ/ *v.i.* **1.** to redden as from embarrassment, shame, or modesty. **2.** (of the sky, flowers, etc.) to become rosy. –*n.* **3.** a rosy or pinkish tinge. –*adj.* **4.** pale pink. –**blushful**, *adj.* –**blushless**, *adj.* –**blushingly**, *adv.*

bluster /ˈblʌstə/ *v.i.* **1.** to roar and be tumultuous, as wind. **2.** to be loud, noisy, or swaggering; utter loud, empty menaces or protests. –*n.* **3.** noisy, empty menaces or protests; inflated talk. –**blusterer**, *n.* –**blusteringly**, *adv.* –**blustery, blusterous**, *adj.*

BMX /bi ɛm ˈɛks/ *adj.* **1.** of or relating to the racing of small sturdily-built bicycles on circuits presenting a variety of surfaces and terrain. –*n.* **2.** a bicycle designed for such a use.

BO /bi ˈoʊ/ *n. Colloq.* body odour, especially due to excessive perspiration.

boa /ˈboʊə/ *n.* (*pl.* **boas**) **1.** any of various non-venomous snakes of the family Boidae, notable for their vestiges of hind limbs, as the boa constrictor of the American tropics. **2.** a long, snake-shaped wrap of silk, feathers, or other material, worn around the neck by women.

boab /ˈboʊæb/ *n.* a large tree with a very thick trunk, native to northern Australia and tropical Africa; bottle tree. Also, **baobab**.

boa constrictor *n.* **1.** a boa, *Constrictor constrictor*, of Central and South America, noted for its size and crushing power. **2.** any large python or other snake of the boa family.

boar /bɔ/ *n.* **1.** an uncastrated male pig. **2.** a wild male pig.

board /bɔd/ *n.* **1.** a piece of timber sawn thin, and of considerable length and breadth compared with the thickness. **2.** (*pl.*) *Theatre* the stage. **3. a.** Also, **shearing board**. in a shearing shed, the clear part of the floor on which the sheep are shorn. **b.** the complement of shearers employed in a woolshed: *they had a full board.* **4.** a flat slab of wood for some specific purpose: *ironing-board*; *jigger board.* **5.** a blackboard. **6.** daily meals, especially as provided for pay, often as part of accommodation. **7.** an official body of people who direct or supervise some activity: *a board of directors*; *board of trade.* –*v.t.* **8.** to cover or close with boards. **9.** to go aboard or enter (a ship, train, etc.). –*v.i.* **10.** to occupy a room in a dwelling, often with meals provided, in return for payment. –*phr.* **11. across the board**, in a comprehensive fashion. **12. board out**, to place out for meals and lodgings. **13. go by the board**, to be discarded, neglected, or destroyed. **14. on board**, on or in a ship, aeroplane, or vehicle. **15. take on board**, **a.** to grasp the significance of. **b.** to accept and use, as an idea, etc. –**boarder**, *n.*

boarding house *n.* a place, usually a home, at which board and lodging are provided.

boarding school *n.* a school at which board and lodging are furnished for the pupils.

boardroom /ˈbɔdrum/ *n.* a room in which a board (def. 7) meets to carry out business.

board shorts *pl. n.* shorts with an extended leg, often made of quick-drying fabric, originally designed to protect surfers against waxed surfboards.

boast /boʊst/ *v.i.* **1.** to speak exaggeratedly and objectionably, especially about oneself. –*v.t.* **2.** to speak of with pride, vanity, or exultation. **3.** to be proud in the possession of: *the town boasts a new school.* –*n.* **4.** a thing boasted of. –*phr.* **5. boast of**, to lay claim to; claim credit for: *he boasted of his success.* –**boaster**, *n.* –**boastingly**, *adv.* –**boastful**, *adj.*

boat /boʊt/ *n.* **1.** a vessel for transport by water, constructed to provide buoyancy by excluding water and shaped to give stability and permit propulsion. **2.** a small ship, generally for specialised use. **3.** a small vessel carried for use by a large one. **4.** a ship. **5.** an open dish resembling a boat: *a gravy boat.* –*v.i.* **6.** to go in a boat. –*phr.* **7. burn one's boats**, to commit oneself; make an irrevocable decision. **8. in the same boat**, faced with the same circumstances, especially unfortunate ones.

boater /ˈboʊtə/ *n.* a straw hat with a flat crown and a flat hard brim.

boat people *pl. n.* people who leave their own country and travel in small boats to seek refuge in another country.

boatswain /ˈboʊsən/ *n.* a warrant officer on a warship, or a petty officer on a merchant vessel, in charge of rigging, anchors, cables, etc. Also, **bo's'n, bosun**.

bob¹ /bɒb/ *n.* **1.** a short jerky motion: *a bob of the head.* **2.** a quick curtsy. –*verb* (**bobbed, bobbing**) –*v.t.* **3.** to move quickly down and up: *to bob the head.* –*v.i.* **4.** to curtsy. **5.** to move up and down with a bouncing motion, as a boat. –*phr.* **6. bob up**, to rise to the surface or into view suddenly or jerkily: *a face bobbed up in front of him.*

bob² /bɒb/ *n.* **1.** a style of short haircut for women and children. **2.** a horse's tail cut short. **3.** a small dangling or terminal object, as the weight on a pendulum or a plumbline.

bobbin /ˈbɒbɪn/ *n.* a reel, cylinder, or spool upon which yarn or thread is wound, as used in spinning, machine sewing, etc.

bobby pin /ˈbɒbi pɪn/ *n.* a metal hairpin with two slender prongs which clamp together in order to hold the hair; hairgrip.

bobcat /ˈbɒbkæt/ *n.* **1.** a medium-sized American wild cat, *Felis rufus*, with a spotted grey, brown or red coat, ranging from southern Canada through western USA to Mexico. **2.** (*from trademark*) *Aust., NZ* a small, rubber-tyred, four-wheeled loader used in underground and trench work.

bobsleigh /'bɒbsleɪ/ *n.* a racing sledge carrying two or more people, having two sets of runners, one at the back and one at the front.

bocconcini /bɒkən'tʃini/ *n.* a small fresh cheese of the stretched curd variety, usually packed in its own whey.

bod /bɒd/ *n. Colloq.* **1.** a person: *an odd bod.* **2.** a body: *he's got a cute bod!*

bode /boʊd/ *verb* (**boded**, **boding**) –*v.t.* **1.** to be an omen of; portend. –*v.i.* **2.** to portend: *to bode well.* –**bodement**, *n.*

bodgie /'bɒdʒi/ *Colloq.* –*adj.* **1.** *Colloq.*, *Aust.*, *NZ* inferior; worthless. –*n.* **2.** *Aust.* a worthless person. **3.** an alias. –*v.t.* (**bodgied**, **bodgying**) Also, **bodgie up.** **4.** *Aust.* to repair superficially.

bodice /'bɒdəs/ *n.* the fitted upper part of or body of a woman's dress.

bodily /'bɒdəli/ *adj.* **1.** of or relating to the body. **2.** corporeal or material, in contrast with spiritual or mental. –*adv.* **3.** as a whole; without taking apart.

bodkin /'bɒdkən/ *n.* a blunt needle-like instrument for drawing tape, cord, etc., through a loop, hem, or the like.

body /'bɒdi/ *n.* (*pl.* **-dies**) **1.** the physical structure of an animal (and sometimes, of a plant) living or dead. **2.** a corpse; carcass. **3.** the trunk or main mass of a thing. **4.** *Zool.* the physical structure of an animal minus limbs and head. **5.** *Archit.* the central structure of a building, especially the nave of a church; the major mass of a building. **6.** a vehicle minus wheels and other appendages. **7.** *Naut.* the hull of a ship. **8.** *Aeronautics* the fuselage of an aeroplane. **9.** *Printing* the shank of a type, supporting the face. **10.** *Geom.* a figure having the dimensions, length, breadth, and thickness; a solid. **11.** *Physics* anything having inertia; a mass. **12.** any of the larger visible spherical objects in space, as a sun, moon, or planet: *heavenly bodies.* **13.** the major portion of an army, population, etc. **14.** the central part of a speech or document, minus introduction, conclusion, indexes, etc. **15.** *Colloq.* a person. **16.** a number of things or people taken together: *the student body.* **17.** a separate or distinct mass, as of water: *a large body of water swept down in the flood.* **18.** consistency or density; substance; strength as opposed to thinness: *wine of a good body.* **19.** (of hair) springiness; resilience. **20.** matter or physical substance (as opposed to *spirit* or *soul*). **21.** that part of a dress which covers the trunk, or the trunk above the waist. **22.** *Agric.* the quality possessed by wool when the staple appears full and bulky. –*phr.* **23. body and soul**, completely: *she owned him body and soul.* **24. keep body and soul together**, to remain alive. –**bodied**, *adj.*

body art *n.* the decorative modification of the body by piercing, tattooing, scarring, painting, etc.

body bag *n.* a large bag or sack with features such as waterproofing and zippers, designed to facilitate the transportation of a corpse.

body building *n.* the performance of regular exercises designed to increase the power and size of the body's muscles. –**body builder**, *n.*

body corporate *n.* (*pl.* **bodies corporate** *or* **body corporates**) (in Australia) the governing body of a block of units (def. 4) consisting of the unit owners or their representatives.

bodyguard /'bɒdigad/ *n.* **1.** a personal or private guard, as for a high official. **2.** a retinue; escort.

body image *n.* the perception that a person has of their own body, particularly in relation to whether they see themselves as fat or thin, good-looking or not.

body jewellery *n.* any of various rings, bars, and other adornments used in body piercing.

body language *n.* the non-linguistic communication of attitudes or feelings by movements or postures of the body, usually unintentional.

body mass index *n.* a measure of body mass that is calculated as weight divided by height squared; used to define nutritional status in relation to health risk. *Abbrev.*: BMI

body politic *n.* a people as forming a political body under an organised government.

body sculpting *n.* the shaping of the body by loss of fat and toning of muscles to an ideal form. –**body sculptor**, *n.*

bodysurfing /'bɒdi,sɜfɪŋ/ *n.* the sport of swimming in the surf, and especially of riding waves, by holding the body stiff, usually with the arms outstretched, and allowing oneself to be carried along by the force of the water. Also, **surfing**.

body temperature *n.* → **temperature** (def. 2a).

body wave *n.* a type of soft perm with very little wave, designed to give more fullness to the hair.

bodywork /'bɒdiwɜk/ *n.* the outer shell of the body of a vehicle, or its construction.

boffin /'bɒfən/ *n. Colloq.* someone who is enthusiastic for and knowledgeable in any pursuit, activity, study, etc., especially a research scientist.

bog /bɒg/ *n.* **1.** wet, spongy ground, with soil composed mainly of decayed vegetable matter. **2.** an area or stretch of such ground. **3.** *Colloq.* a type of putty used to fill dents in the bodywork of vehicles. –*verb* (**bogged**, **bogging**) –*v.t.* **4.** to cause (a vehicle) to run into mud, sand, etc., stopping its progress. –*v.i.* **5.** (of a vehicle) to run into mud, sand, etc., thereby having its progress halted. –*phr.* **6. bog down, a.** to falter or lose momentum, especially as the result of a series of delays. **b.** to impede the progress of (someone), especially by creating innumerable small difficulties and restraints. **c.** to be prevented from progressing, as from or as if from sinking in mud. **7. bog in**, *Colloq.* **a.** to eat voraciously. **b.** to attack a task vigorously: *if we all bog in, it will be done quickly.* –**boggish**, *adj.* –**boggy**, *adj.*

bogan /'boʊgən/ *n. Colloq.* (*mildly derog.*) a person, generally from an outer suburb of a city or town and from a lower socio-economic background, viewed as uncultured.

bogey[1] /'boʊgi/ *Golf* –*n.* (*pl.* **-geys**) **1.** a score of one over par. –*v.t.* (**-geyed**, **-geying**) **2.** to score a bogey on (a certain hole).

bogey[2] /'boʊgi/ *n.* (*pl.* **-geys**) *Aust.* **1.** a swim or bath. **2.** a swimming hole. Also, **bogie**.

bogeyman /'boʊgimæn, 'bugimæn, 'bugimæn/ *n.* (*pl.* **-men**) **1.** an evil spirit in the guise of a man. **2.** anything that is persistently frightening. Also, **bogyman**, **boogieman**.

boggle /'bɒgəl/ *v.i.* **1.** to take alarm; start with fright. **2.** to hesitate, as if afraid to proceed; waver; shrink: *the mind boggles.* –**boggler**, *n.*

bogie[1] /'boʊgi/ *n.* **1.** a low truck or trolley. **2.** one of a pair of pivoted trucks supporting a railway locomotive, carriage, tram, etc.

bogie[2] /'boʊgi/ *n.* → **bogey[2]**.

bog-standard *adj.* ordinary or basic; run-of-the-mill.

bogus /'boʊgəs/ *adj.* counterfeit; spurious; sham.

bogy /'boʊgi/ *n.* (*pl.* **-gies**) **1.** a hobgoblin; evil spirit. **2.** anything that haunts, frightens or annoys one.

bogyman /'boʊgimæn, 'bugimæn, 'bugimæn/ *n.* (*pl.* **-men**) → **bogeyman**.

bohemian /boʊ'himiən/ *n.* **1.** a person with artistic or intellectual tendencies or pretensions who lives and acts without regard for conventional rules of behaviour. **2.** a Gypsy. –*adj.* **3.** relating to or characteristic of bohemians. –**bohemianism**, *n.*

boil[1] /bɔɪl/ v.i. **1.** to change from liquid to gaseous state, producing bubbles of gas that rise to the surface of the liquid, agitating it as they rise. **2.** to be in a similarly agitated state: *the sea was boiling.* **3.** to be agitated by angry feeling. **4.** to contain, or be contained in, a liquid that boils: *the pot is boiling*; *the meat is boiling.* **5.** *Colloq.* to feel very hot. –*v.t.* **6.** to cause to boil. **7.** to cook by boiling. **8.** to separate (sugar, salt, etc.) from something containing it by heat. –*n.* **9.** the act of boiling. **10.** the state or condition of boiling. –*phr.* **11. boil down, a.** to reduce by boiling. **b.** to boil (the carcasses of animals) so as to extract the fat. **c.** to shorten; abridge. **12. boil down to,** to be in essence: *it all boils down to this.* **13. boil over, a.** to overflow while boiling. **b.** to be unable to suppress excitement, anger, etc. **14. boil up,** to make tea. **15. off the boil, a.** (of a liquid) cooled so as not to boil. **b.** no longer ready to engage effectively or enthusiastically in an activity or undertaking. **c.** ceasing to command attention, interest, or enthusiasm. **16. on the boil, a.** (of a liquid) in a simmering state leading up to boiling. **b.** about to happen; imminent.

boil[2] /bɔɪl/ n. a painful, suppurating, inflammatory sore forming a central core, caused by microbic infection, *Staphylococcus aureus.*

boiler /ˈbɔɪlə/ n. **1.** a closed vessel together with its furnace, in which steam or other vapour is generated for heating or for driving engines. **2.** a vessel for boiling or heating, especially a copper one. **3.** a fowl which is or appears to be fit to be eaten only when boiled. **4.** *Colloq.* an old woman.

boilermaker /ˈbɔɪləmeɪkə/ n. a tradesman who marks out, develops and fabricates boilers or metal cylinders.

boilersuit /ˈbɔɪləsut/ n. a one-piece garment of some cheap tough material for rough work.

boiling point n. **1.** the equilibrium temperature of the liquid and vapour phases of the substance, usually at a pressure of 101 325 pascals. **2.** the peak of excitement or emotion.

boisterous /ˈbɔɪstrəs/ adj. **1.** rough and noisy; clamorous; unrestrained. **2.** (of waves, weather, wind, etc.) rough and stormy. –**boisterously,** adv. –**boisterousness,** n.

bok choy /bɒk ˈtʃɔɪ/ n. a vegetable, *Brassica rapa* subsp. *chinensis,* with white stalks and dark green leaves; celery cabbage. Also, **buk choy.**

bold /boʊld/ adj. **1.** not hesitating in the face of actual or possible danger or rebuff. **2.** not hesitating to breach the rules of propriety; forward. **3.** overstepping usual bounds or conventions. **4.** conspicuous to the eye: *bold handwriting.* **5.** *Printing* (of type, etc.) with heavy lines. –**boldly,** adv. –**boldness,** n.

bole /boʊl/ n. the stem or trunk of a tree up to the first branch.

bolero /bəˈlɛəroʊ, bəˈlɪəroʊ/ n. (pl. **-ros**) **1.** a lively Spanish dance in three-four time. **2.** the music for it. **3.** a short jacket ending above or at the waistline.

boll /boʊl/ n. a rounded seed vessel or pod of a plant, as of flax or cotton.

bollard /ˈbɒlad/ n. *Naut.* a vertical post on which hawsers are made fast.

bollocky /ˈbɒləki/ adj. **1.** *Colloq.* naked: *stark bollocky.* –*phr.* **2. in the bollocky,** naked. Also, **bollicky.**

bolognaise /bɒləˈneɪz/ adj. of or relating to a sauce for pasta, made with minced meat, onions, garlic, tomato paste and seasonings. Also, **bolognese.**

Bolshevik /ˈbɒlʃəvɪk/ n. (pl. **-viks** or **-viki**) **1.** (*also lower case*) a member of a communist party. **2.** (*derog.*) (*usu. lower case*) any person with radical socialist ideas. –**bolshevism,** n.

bolster /ˈboʊlstə/ n. **1.** a long ornamental pillow for a bed, sofa, etc. **2.** a support, as one for a bridge truss.

–*v.t.* **3.** to support with or as with a pillow. **4.** Also, **bolster up.** to prop, support, or uphold (something weak, unworthy, etc.). –**bolsterer,** n.

bolt /boʊlt/ n. **1.** a movable bar which when slid into a socket fastens a door, gate, etc. **2.** the part of a lock which is protruded from and drawn back into the case, as by the action of the key. **3.** a strong metal pin, often with a head at one end and with a screw thread at the other to receive a nut. **4. a.** a woven length of cloth. **b.** a roll of wallpaper. **5.** the uncut edge of a sheet folded to make a book. **6.** a sudden swift motion or escape. **7.** any sudden dash, run, flight, etc. **8.** a jet of any liquid, especially molten glass. **9.** an arrow, especially one for a crossbow. **10.** a rod or bar which closes the breech of a rifle. **11.** a shaft of lightning; a thunderbolt. –*v.t.* **12.** to fasten with or as with bolts. **13.** to shoot; discharge (a missile). **14.** to blurt; utter hastily. **15.** to swallow (one's food) hurriedly or without chewing. **16.** to make (cloth, wallpaper, etc.) into bolts. –*v.i.* **17.** to run away in alarm and uncontrollably, especially of horses and rabbits. **18.** to abscond in order to evade one's debt or to escape with illegal gains. –*adv.* **19.** suddenly; with sudden meeting or collision. –*phr.* **20. bolt from** (or **out of**) **the blue,** a sudden and entirely unexpected occurrence. **21. bolt upright,** stiffly upright. **22. do the bolt,** *Colloq.* to run away, especially when caught committing a misdemeanour. **23. have shot one's bolt,** *Colloq.* to have reached the limit of one's endurance or effort. **24. shoot one's bolt,** *Colloq.* **a.** to do one's utmost. **b.** (*taboo*) to ejaculate prematurely. –**bolter,** n. –**boltless,** adj.

bomb /bɒm/ n. **1.** a hollow projectile filled with an explosive charge. **2.** any similar missile or explosive device. **3.** *Aust., NZ Colloq.* an old car. **4.** *Colloq.* a failure, as in an examination. **5.** *Colloq.* a jump into water, made in a crouched position. **6.** *Rugby League* an up-and-under directed near or over the opponents' goal line. –*v.t.* **7.** to hurl bombs at; drop bombs upon, as from an aeroplane; bombard. **8.** *Colloq.* to jump onto (someone) in water. **9.** *Colloq.* to fail; perform badly at: *she bombed the exam.* –*v.i.* **10.** to explode a bomb or bombs. **11.** to hurl or drop bombs. **12.** *Colloq.* to jump into a pool, waterhole, etc., in a tucked up position so as to create a large splash. **13.** *Colloq.* to perform badly; fail. –*phr.* **14. bomb out, a.** to err; to fail. **b.** to be heavily under the influence of drugs. **15. go like a bomb, a.** to turn out successfully. **b.** (of a motor vehicle, etc.) to go rapidly.

bombard /bɒmˈbad/ v.t. **1.** to attack or batter with artillery. **2.** to attack with bombs. **3.** to assail vigorously: *bombard someone with questions.* –**bombardment,** n.

bombardier /bɒmbəˈdɪə/ n. **1.** *Mil.* the lowest rank of NCO in an artillery regiment. **2.** *Mil.* the member of a bomber crew who operates the bomb release mechanism. **3.** *Hist.* an artilleryman.

bombast /ˈbɒmbæst/ n. high-sounding and often insincere words; verbiage. –**bombastic,** adj.

bomber /ˈbɒmə/ n. **1.** someone who throws or places bombs. **2.** a plane used to carry and drop bombs.

bomber jacket n. a waist-length jacket, sometimes made out of leather, with a fitted waistband and usually a zipper down the front.

bombie /ˈbɒmi/ n. *Colloq.* → **bommie.**

bombora /bɒmˈbɔrə/ n. *Aust.* **1.** a submerged reef of rocks. **2.** a dangerous current over a reef.

bombshell /ˈbɒmʃel/ n. **1.** a bomb. **2.** a sudden or devastating action or effect: *his resignation was a bombshell.* **3.** *Colloq.* a very attractive woman. –*phr.* **4. drop a bombshell,** to make a startling or unexpected announcement.

bommie /ˈbɒmi/ n. *Colloq.* a bombora. Also, **bombie, bommy.**

bona fide /ˌboʊnə ˈfaɪdi/ *adj.* **1.** genuine; real: *a bona fide doctor.* **2.** undertaken or carried out in good faith: *a bona fide agreement.* Also, **bona-fide.**

bonanza /bəˈnænzə/ *n.* **1.** a mine of wealth; good luck. **2.** any fortunate and profitable occasion.

bonbon /ˈbɒnbɒn/ *n.* **1.** a piece of confectionery. **2.** a small firework made from a paper roll twisted at each end and containing a gift, joke, motto, etc., which makes a loud report when pulled sharply at both ends. Also, **bon bon, bon-bon.**

bond /bɒnd/ *n.* **1.** something that binds, fastens, or holds together: *a bond of feeling; the bonds of a prisoner.* **2.** any binding written agreement, such as a promise to work for a certain time made when accepting a scholarship. **3.** *Law* **a.** a contract under seal to pay a debt, or to pay a sum of money in default of fulfilling some condition. **b.** an undertaking by an offender to be of good behaviour for a certain period. **4.** the state of taxable goods kept in storage until tax is paid: *goods in bond.* **5.** a certificate of government debt to an individual, usually at a fixed rate of interest. **6.** → **bond money.** **7.** a substance that causes particles to stick; binder. **8.** *Chem.* any connection between atoms in any molecule, or between atoms and molecules in any substance. **9.** → **bond paper.** **10.** *Building Trades* an arrangement of stones or bricks in a wall, etc., made in an overlapping pattern in order to bind them strongly. −*v.t.* **11.** to hold or join with a bond. **12.** to put (goods, a person) in or under bond. **13.** *Finance* to place a bonded debt on; mortgage. **14.** *Building Trades* to cause (bricks, etc.) to hold together firmly by overlapping them. **15.** to unite (members of a group, etc.). −*v.i.* **16.** to hold together by being bonded, as bricks in wall. **17.** to establish a close interpersonal relationship with another or others. −**bonder,** *n.*

bondage /ˈbɒndɪdʒ/ *n.* **1.** slavery or involuntary servitude; serfdom. **2.** the state of being bound by or subjected to external control. **3.** a form of sexual play in which a person submits to being bound.

Bondaian /bɒnˈdaɪən/ *n.* a cultural period of Aboriginal development recognised in eastern Australia and reaching a climax about 1600 years ago (it follows the Capertian but overlaps to some extent).

bond money *n.* money additional to any rent which a new tenant pays as surety against damages to the premises rented.

bond paper *n.* a superior variety of white paper.

bond store *n.* a warehouse licensed for the storage of goods on which duty has not yet been paid.

bone /boʊn/ *n.* **1.** *Zool., Anat.* **a.** any of the separate pieces of which the skeleton of a vertebrate is composed. **b.** the hard tissue which composes the skeleton. **2.** a bone or piece of a bone with the meat adhering to it, as an article of food. **3.** any of various similar substances, such as ivory, whalebone, etc. **4.** a strip of whalebone used to stiffen corsets, etc. **5.** a white colour with a touch of yellowish beige; the colour of dry bones. **6.** Also, **boner.** *Colloq. (taboo)* an erect penis. **7.** (*pl.*) the skeleton. **8.** (*pl.*) a body. −*v.t.* **9.** to take out the bones of: *to bone a fish.* **10.** to put whalebone into (clothing). **11.** *Aboriginal English* (in tribal culture) to intend the death of (someone) by pointing a bone at them: *he died ten days after being boned.* −*phr.* **12. bare bones,** the essentials without any trimming. **13. bone of contention,** a matter which causes disagreement. **14. bone up,** *Colloq.* (sometimes fol. by *on*) to study hard; acquire information. **15. close to** (or **near**) **the bone,** indecent; risqué. **16. feel in one's bones,** to understand intuitively. **17. have a bone to pick with,** to have a point of dispute or a matter for complaint with. **18. jump** (**on**) **someone's bones,** *Colloq.* to have sexual intercourse with someone.

19. make no bones about, to be absolutely frank about. **20. make old bones,** (*usu. in the negative*) *Colloq.* to live to an old age. **21. point the bone at, a.** (in tribal Aboriginal culture) to intend the death of (someone) by pointing a bone at them. **b.** *Aust. Colloq.* to bring or wish bad luck upon. **c.** *Aust. Colloq.* to indicate as guilty. **22. to the bone,** through and through; thoroughly: *chilled to the bone; bad to the bone.* −**boned,** *adj.* −**boneless,** *adj.* −**bonelike,** *adj.*

bone china *n.* a kind of china in which bone ash is used.

bonfire /ˈbɒnfaɪə/ *n.* a large fire in an open place, for entertainment, celebration, or as a signal.

bong[1] /bɒŋ/ *Colloq.* −*v.t.* **1.** to hit, especially on the head. −*n.* **2.** a blow.

bong[2] /bɒŋ/ *n. Colloq.* a hookah.

bongo /ˈbɒŋgoʊ/ *n.* (*pl.* **-gos**) one of a pair of small drums, played by beating with the fingers.

bonhomie /bɒnˈɒmi/ *n.* frank and simple good-heartedness; a good-natured manner. Also, **bonhommie.**

bonito /bəˈnitoʊ/ *n.* (*pl.* **-tos**) any of several fishes belonging to the tuna family, *Sarda chiliensis australis* found along the eastern Australian coast.

bonk /bɒŋk/ *Colloq.* −*v.t.* **1.** to administer a blow to (someone); hit: *she bonked her little brother on the head.* **2.** (*taboo*) to have sexual intercourse with (someone). −*v.i.* **3.** to collide with a thud. **4.** (*taboo*) to have sexual intercourse. −*n.* **5.** a sharp blow. **6.** (*taboo*) an act of sexual intercourse.

bonkers /ˈbɒŋkəz/ *adj. Colloq.* crazy.

bonnet /ˈbɒnət/ *n.* **1.** a woman's or child's outdoor head covering, commonly fitting down over the hair, and often tied under the chin. **2.** any of various hoods, covers, or protective devices. **3.** a hinged cover over the engine (in some makes over the luggage section) at the front of a motor vehicle.

bonny /ˈbɒni/ *adj.* (**-nier, -niest**) radiant with health; handsome; pretty. Also, **bonnie.** −**bonnily,** *adv.* −**bonniness,** *n.*

bonobo /ˈbɒnəboʊ, bəˈnoʊboʊ/ *n.* a chimpanzee, *Pan paniscus,* found in humid forests of the Congo region, and forming communities which are female-centred and typified by the frequency of sexual encounters engaged in freely between all adults; pygmy chimpanzee.

bonsai /ˈbɒnsaɪ/ *n.* **1.** the practice, originally Chinese and later Japanese, of growing very small examples of trees and shrubs in ornamental pots, by skilful pruning of roots and branches. **2.** a tree or shrub so grown.

bonus /ˈboʊnəs/ *n.* **1.** something given or paid over and above what is due. **2.** *Insurance* **a.** dividend. **b.** free additions to the sum assured. **3.** any unsolicited or unexpected gift. −*adj.* **4.** of or relating to something given as a bonus.

bonus issue *n.* a free issue of shares to shareholders of a company. Also, **bonus.**

bon voyage /bɒ̃ vwaˈjaʒ, bɒ̃ vɔɪˈjaʒ/ *interj.* pleasant trip.

bony /ˈboʊni/ *adj.* (**-nier, -niest**) **1.** of or like bone. **2.** full of bones. **3.** having prominent bones; big-boned. **4.** emaciated; skeletal: *bony limbs.* −**boniness,** *n.*

bonzer /ˈbɒnzə/ *Aust., NZ Colloq.* (*dated*) −*adj.* **1.** excellent; attractive; pleasing. −*adv.* **2.** excellently; pleasingly: *the beer went down bonzer.* −*interj.* **3.** an exclamation indicating pleasure, agreement, etc. Also, **bonz, bonze, bonza, boshter, bosker.**

boo /bu/ *interj.* **1.** an exclamation used to express contempt, disapproval, etc., or to frighten. −*n.* (*pl.* **boos**) **2.** this exclamation. −*verb* (**booed, booing**) −*v.i.* **3.** to cry 'boo'. −*v.t.* **4.** to cry 'boo' at; show disapproval of by booing. −**booer,** *n.*

boob[1] /bub/ *n. Colloq.* **1.** a fool; a dunce. **2.** a foolish mistake.

boob² /bub/ *n. Colloq.* a woman's breast.

boo-boo /'bu-bu/ *n.* **1.** *Colloq.* an error, usually of judgement: *he made a classic boo-boo. –v.i.* **2.** to make an error.

boobook /'bubʊk/ *n.* a small owl, *Ninox novaeseelandiae*, brownish, with white-spotted back and wings and large dark patches behind the eyes; widely distributed in Australia, New Guinea, New Zealand, and adjacent islands.

booby /'bubi/ *n. (pl.* **-bies) 1.** a stupid or awkward person. **2.** the worst student, player, etc., of a group. **3.** a large, robust, seabird with long wings and a wedge-shaped tail, and which plunges into the sea to catch prey, as the **brown booby,** *Sula leucogaster,* of tropical seas and northerly parts of the Australian coastline. **–boobyish,** *adj.*

booby prize *n.* a prize given in consolation or good-natured ridicule to the worst player in a game or contest.

booby trap *n.* **1.** an object so placed as to fall on or trip up an unsuspecting person. *–v.t.* **2.** to set with a booby trap. Also, **booby-trap.**

boogie /'bʊgi, 'bugi/ *v.i.* **(-gied, -gieing)** to dance to rock music.

boogie board /'bugi bɔd, 'bʊgi bɔd/ *n. (from trademark)* a small flexible lightweight surfboard, usually ridden lying down.

boogie-woogie /ˌbʊgi-'wʊgi, ˌbugi-'wugi/ *n.* a form of instrumental blues using melodic variations over a constantly repeated bass figure. Also, **boogie.**

book /bʊk/ *n.* **1.** a text of some length, comprising a whole work as a treatise or other literary composition. **2.** such a text in printed form on consecutive sheets fastened or bound together. **3.** such a text in digital form; ebook. **4.** a number of sheets of writing paper bound together and used for making entries, as of commercial transactions. **5.** a division of a literary work, especially one of the larger divisions. **6.** *Music* the text of an opera, operetta, etc. **7.** a record of bets, as on a horserace. **8.** a set of tickets, cheques, stamps, etc., bound together like a book. **9.** *Colloq.* someone's intentions, plans, or arrangements: *it doesn't suit my book.* **10.** *Horseracing Colloq.* a bookmaker. *–v.t.* **11.** to enter in a book or list; record; register. **12.** to engage (a place, passage, etc.) beforehand. **13.** to put (somebody, something) down for a place, passage, etc. **14.** to engage (a person or company) for a performance or performances. **15.** to record the name of, with a view to possible prosecution for a minor offence: *the police booked him for speeding. –v.i.* **16.** to engage a place, services, etc. *–phr.* **17. a closed book, a.** something which is incomprehensible: *maths is a closed book to me.* **b.** a matter which is to be discussed no further. **18. an open book, a.** someone whose feelings, motives, etc., can be clearly interpreted. **b.** something which can be clearly understood or interpreted. **19. book in, a.** to register one's name for service, accommodation, etc. **b.** to register (someone) for service, accommodation, etc.: *to book the children in.* **20. bring to book,** to bring to account. **21. by the book, a.** formally. **b.** authoritatively; correctly. **22. in someone's bad books,** out of favour with someone. **23. in someone's good books,** in favour with someone. **24. make a book,** *Horseracing* to lay and receive bets in the expectation that the odds are such that whichever horse wins, a profit is made. **25. on the books,** entered on the list of members. **26. take a leaf out of someone's book,** to emulate someone. **27. the Book,** the Bible. **28. the books,** a record of commercial transactions. **29. throw the book at,** *Colloq.* **a.** to bring all possible charges against (an offender). **b.** to sentence (an offender) to the

maximum penalties. **c.** to punish (someone) severely. **–bookless,** *adj.* **–bookable,** *adj.*

bookcase /'bʊkkeɪs/ *n.* a set of shelves for books.

bookend /'bʊkɛnd/ *n.* **1.** a support placed at the end of a row of books to hold them upright. *–v.t.* **2.** to act as a marker at the beginning and end of (a process, activity, etc.): *a concert bookended by Beethoven sonatas.*

booking /'bʊkɪŋ/ *n.* **1.** advance engagement of a place or passage. **2.** an engagement to perform.

bookish /'bʊkɪʃ/ *adj.* **1.** given to reading or study. **2.** stilted; pedantic. **–bookishly,** *adv.* **–bookishness,** *n.*

bookkeeping /'bʊkkipɪŋ/ *n.* the work or skill of keeping account books or systematic records of money transactions. **–bookkeeper,** *n.*

booklet /'bʊklət/ *n.* a little book, especially one with paper covers; pamphlet.

bookmaker /'bʊkmeɪkə/ *n.* a professional betting person, who accepts the bets of others, as on horses in racing. **–bookmaking,** *n.*

bookmark /'bʊkmak/ *n.* **1.** a strip of cardboard, ribbon, or the like placed between the pages of a book to mark a place. **2.** *Internet* a URL reference stored in a file by a browser for future reference. *–v.t.* **3.** *Internet* to store (a URL) in a file for future reference by a browser.

book value *n. Econ.* the amount which a trader shows in his or her accounts as the value of an item. Also, **book figure.**

bookworm /'bʊkwɜm/ *n.* **1.** any of various insects that feed on books. **2.** a person fond of reading or study.

Boolean /'buliən/ *adj.* **1.** of or relating to Boolean algebra: *Boolean logic.* **2.** expressed or executed by means of Boolean algebra: *a Boolean equation.*

Boolean algebra *n.* a mathematical system of representing statements in logic using operators such as 'and', 'or' and 'not', in which each element or variable has one of only two possible values, as 'true' or 'false'; used extensively in computer science for programming and information retrieval.

Boolean operator *n.* an operator (def. 4), as 'and', 'or', or 'not', used in computer programming and to phrase queries in database searches.

Boolean search *n.* a search of a computer database in which Boolean operators may be used.

boom¹ /bum/ *v.i.* **1.** to make a deep, resounding noise. **2.** to develop, progress or flourish, as a business, city, etc. *–v.t.* **3.** (usu. fol. by *out*) to give forth with booming sound: *the clock boomed out 12. –n.* **4.** a loud, deep sound as of waves or distant guns. **5.** a period of high economic growth and general prosperity. **–booming,** *adj.*

boom² /bum/ *n.* **1.** *Naut.* a long pole or spar used to extend the foot of certain sails. **2.** a chain or cable or a series of connected floating timbers, etc., serving to obstruct navigation, to confine floating timber, etc. **3.** the area thus shut off. **4.** *Machinery* a spar or beam projecting from the mast of a derrick, supporting or guiding the weights to be lifted. **5.** (in a television or film studio) a movable arm supporting a microphone or floodlight above the actors, or an aerial camera. *–phr.* **6. lower the boom on,** to prohibit; refuse: *he lowered the boom on further discussion.*

boomer /'bumə/ *n. Aust.* **1.** *NZ Colloq.* something large, as a surfing wave. **2.** *NZ Colloq.* something successful or popular, as a party or song. **3.** a large male kangaroo.

boomerang /'buməræŋ, 'buməræŋ/ *n.* **1.** a bent or curved piece of hard wood traditionally used by Aboriginal people as a missile in hunting and fighting or as a clap stick; one form can be thrown so as to return to the thrower. **2.** *Colloq.* something that is expected to be returned by a borrower. *–v.i.* **3.** to return to, or recoil upon, the originator: *the argument boomeranged; the cheque boomeranged.*

boom gate *n.* a barrier to traffic, usually consisting of a long beam pivoted at one end and raised or lowered as required.

boon /buːn/ *n.* **1.** a benefit enjoyed; a thing to be thankful for; a blessing. **2.** *Archaic* a favour sought.

boong /bʊŋ/ *n. Colloq. (derog.) (racist)* **1.** *Aust.* an Aborigine. **2.** *NZ* a Maori or Pacific Islander. **3.** *Aust., NZ* any black person.

boor /bɔ, bʊə/ *n.* **1.** a rude or unmannerly person. **2.** a peasant; a rustic. **–boorish,** *adj.*

boost /buːst/ *v.t.* **1.** to lift or raise by pushing from behind or below. **2.** to increase; push up: *to boost prices.* **3.** *Aeronautics, Motor Vehicles* to supercharge. **–n. 4.** an upward shove or push. **5.** an aid that helps one to rise in the world.

booster /ˈbuːstə/ *n.* **1.** *Elect.* a device connected in series with a current for increasing or decreasing the nominal circuit voltage. **2.** *Aeronautics, Motor Vehicles* a supercharger in an internal-combustion engine. **3.** *Astronautics* **a.** a rocket engine used as the main supply of thrust in a missile flight. **b.** the stage of a missile containing this engine, usually detached when its fuel has been consumed. **4.** *Pharmacology* a substance, usually injected, for prolonging a person's immunity to a specific infection.

boot[1] /buːt/ *n.* **1.** a heavy shoe, especially one reaching above the ankle. **2.** a covering, usually of leather, rubber or a similar synthetic material, for the foot and leg, reaching up to and sometimes beyond the knee. **3.** a place for baggage, usually at the rear of a vehicle. **4.** *Colloq.* a kick. **–v.t. 5.** to put boots on. **6.** *Colloq.* to kick; drive by kicking. **7.** *Colloq.* to dismiss; discharge. **–phr. 8. be too big for one's boots,** to hold too high an opinion of oneself; be conceited. **9. bet one's boots,** to be certain. **10. boot home,** *Colloq.* **a.** *Horseracing* to ride (a horse) to win, kicking it to greater speed. **b.** to push (something) into position forcibly. **c.** to emphasise strongly. **11. boots and all,** completely; with all one's strength or resources. **12. get the boot,** *Colloq.* to be discharged. **13. give someone (or something) the boot,** *Colloq.* to reject or dismiss someone or something. **14. have one's heart in one's boots,** to be extremely despondent. **15. put in the boot,** *Colloq.* **a.** to make an assault by kicking as in a street brawl. **b.** to make a malicious verbal attack. **16. put the boot into someone,** *Colloq.* **a.** to assault someone by kicking as in a street brawl. **b.** to make a malicious verbal attack on someone. **17. the boot's on the other foot,** the situation has been reversed, as when a person who was at an advantage is now at a disadvantage.

boot[2] /buːt/ *phr.* **to boot,** into the bargain; in addition.

boot[3] /buːt/ *v.t.* Also, **boot up. 1.** to start (a computer), as by activating the operating system. **–phr. 2. boot up,** (of a computer) to become operational.

boot camp *n.* **1.** *US Mil.* a training camp for recruits. **2.** a prison camp for young offenders which places emphasis on military-style discipline. **3.** *Sport* a training camp of high physical intensity, involving strenuous outdoor activities.

bootee /ˈbuːti/ *n.* a baby's knitted shoe. Also, **bootie.**

booth /buːð, buːθ/ *n.* **1.** a stall or light structure for the sale of goods or for display purposes, as at a market or fair. **2.** a small compartment for a telephone, film projector, etc. **3. → polling booth. 4.** an alcove or small compartment in a restaurant, milk bar, etc., with seating arranged on either side of a long table or around three sides.

bootleg /ˈbuːtlɛg/ *Chiefly US* **–n. 1.** something secretly and unlawfully made, sold, or transported, especially alcohol. **2.** the part of a boot which covers the leg. **–v.t. (-legged, -legging) 3.** to deal in (spirits or other goods)

illicitly. **–adj. 4.** made, sold, or transported unlawfully. **–bootlegger,** *n.*

bootless /ˈbuːtləs/ *adj.* without advantage; unavailing; useless. **–bootlessly,** *adv.* **–bootlessness,** *n.*

bootstrap /ˈbuːtstræp/ *n.* **1.** a loop sewn on the side of a boot to assist in pulling it on. **2.** *Computers* a program or procedure by which a computer can be made to translate progressively more complex programs. **–phr. 3. pull oneself up by the bootstraps,** to advance to success solely by one's own efforts.

booty /ˈbuːti/ *n.* **1.** spoil taken from an enemy in war; plunder; pillage. **2.** a prize or gain, without reference to use of force.

booze /buːz/ *Colloq.* **–n. 1.** alcoholic drink. **2.** a drinking bout; spree. **–v.i. 3.** to drink alcohol, especially immoderately: *they were boozing all night.* **–phr. 4. hit the booze,** to drink alcoholic liquor with the intention of getting drunk. **5. on the booze,** drinking immoderately. **–boozer,** *n.*

booze bus *n. Colloq.* **1.** *Aust.* a bus used by a mobile police unit engaged in breath analysis. **2.** a vehicle with a sober driver, organised to take drinkers home from a hotel or a party. **3.** a courtesy bus which conveys the clientele of a hotel, club, etc., to their homes because they may be over the alcohol limit for driving.

borage /ˈbɒrɪdʒ, ˈbɔ-/ *n.* **1.** a plant, *Borago officinalis,* native to southern Europe, with hairy leaves and stems, used in salads and medicinally. **2.** any of various allied or similar plants.

borax /ˈbɔːræks/ *n.* a white, crystalline compound of sodium, $Na_2B_4O_7.10H_2O$, occurring naturally or prepared artificially and used as a flux, cleansing agent, in the manufacture of glass, etc.

bordello /bɔːˈdɛloʊ/ *n.* a brothel.

border /ˈbɔːdə/ *n.* **1.** a side, edge, or margin. **2. a.** the line that separates one country, state, or province from another; frontier line. **b.** *Aust. Hist.* the margin of land surveyed and ready for tenure. **3. a.** the district or region that lies along the boundary line of a country. **b.** *Aust. Hist.* the land lying along the boundary of land surveyed and ready for tenure. **4.** brink; verge. **5.** an ornamental strip or design around the edge of a printed page, a drawing, etc. **6.** a piece of ornamental trimming around the edge of a garment, cap, etc. **7.** *Hort.* a narrow strip of ground in a garden, enclosing a portion of it. **–v.t. 8.** to make a border about; adorn with a border. **9.** to form a border or boundary to. **10.** to lie on the border of; adjoin. **–phr. 11. border on (or upon), a.** to touch or abut at the border. **b.** to approach closely in character; verge on. **–bordered,** *adj.* **–borderless,** *adj.*

border collie *n.* a medium-sized dog, originating in the English-Scottish borderlands, with white markings on the chest, feet and tail, recognised as a breed in Australia.

borderline /ˈbɔːdəlaɪn/ *adj.* **1.** on or near a border or boundary. **2.** uncertain; indeterminate. **3.** (in examinations, etc.) qualifying or failing to qualify by a narrow margin. **4.** verging on indecent or obscene. **–n. 5.** a line that determines or marks a border.

bore[1] /bɔ/ *v.t.* **1.** to pierce (a solid substance) or make (a round hole, etc.) with an auger, drill, or other rotated instrument. **2.** to force by persistent forward thrusting. **–v.i. 3.** to make a hole, as with an auger or drill. **–n. 4.** a hole made by boring, or as if by boring. **5.** a deep hole of small diameter bored to the aquifer of an artesian basin, through which water rises under hydrostatic pressure. **6.** the inside diameter of a hollow cylindrical object or device, such as a bush or bearing, or the barrel of a gun. **–phr. 7. bore into, a.** to pierce as by drilling. **b.** to attack violently. **c.** to put great effort into. **8. bore it up someone,** *Aust. Colloq.* to upbraid or rebuke someone vehemently. **9. bore it up (you)**, *Aust. Colloq.* an offensive retort expressing contempt, dismissal, etc.

bore² /bɔ/ *v.t.* **1.** to weary by tedious repetition, dullness, unwelcome attentions, etc. –*n.* **2.** a dull, tiresome, or uncongenial person. **3.** a cause of ennui or annoyance. –**bored**, *adj.* –**boring**, *adj.* –**boredom**, *n.*

bore³ /bɔ/ *v.* past tense of **bear¹**.

borer /ˈbɔrə/ *n.* **1.** *Machinery* a tool used for boring; an auger. **2.** *Entomology* any insect that burrows in trees, fruits, etc., especially any beetle of certain groups. **3.** *Zool.* any of various molluscs, etc., that bore into wood, etc. **4.** *Zool.* a cyclostome, as a hagfish, that bores into moribund fish to feed on their flesh.

born /bɔn/ *v.* **1.** a past participle of **bear¹**, now normally replaced in all senses by **borne**. –*adj.* **2.** brought forth into independent being or life, from or as from the womb. **3.** possessing from birth the quality or character stated: *a born fool.* –*phr.* **4. be born with a silver spoon in one's mouth**, to inherit social or financial advantages and privileges. **5. not born yesterday**, not easily deceived.

borne /bɔn/ *v.* a past participle of **bear¹**.

boron /ˈbɔrɒn/ *n.* a nonmetallic element present in borax, etc. *Symbol*: B; *relative atomic mass*: 10.811; *atomic number*: 5.

boronia /bəˈrouniə, -jə/ *n.* any of a number of Australian shrubs of the genus *Boronia*, as *B. megastigma*, with brown flowers and a strong perfume, and *B. heterophylla*, with rose-pink flowers.

borough /ˈbʌrə/ *n.* **1.** (in Victoria) an area of land corresponding to a municipality in the other states of Australia. **2.** *Brit.* **a.** an urban community incorporated by royal charter. **b.** an urban electoral constituency, usually subdivided. **3.** *Brit.* (formerly) a fortified town, or a town possessing municipal organisation. **4.** *US* **a.** one of the five administrative divisions of New York City. **b.** (in certain states) a municipality smaller than a city.

borrow /ˈbɒrou/ *v.t.* **1.** to take or obtain (a thing) on the promise to return it or its equivalent; obtain the temporary use of. **2.** to get from another or from a foreign source; appropriate or adopt: *borrowed words.* **3.** *Arithmetic* (in subtraction) to take from one denomination to add to the next lower. –**borrower**, *n.*

borsch /bɔʃ/ *n.* a Russian stock soup containing beetroot, served hot or chilled. Also, **borscht**, **bortsch**.

bosom /ˈbuzəm/ *n.* **1.** the chest or breast of a human being. **2. a.** a woman's breasts; bust. **b.** a woman's breast. **3.** the breast, conceived as the seat of thought or emotion. **4.** something likened to the human bosom as a source or place of comfort or security: *the bosom of the earth.* –*adj.* **5.** intimate or confidential: *a bosom friend.*

boss¹ /bɒs/ *Colloq.* –*n.* **1.** someone who employs or superintends workers. **2.** anyone who asserts command over others. –*v.t.* **3.** Also, **boss about**, **boss around**. **3.** to order around. –*v.i.* **4.** to be domineering. –*adj.* **5.** chief; master: *boss cook.* –*phr.* **6. boss it over**, to be master of or over; manage; direct; control. –**bossy**, *adj.*

boss² /bɒs/ *n.* **1.** *Bot., Zool.* a protuberance or roundish excrescence on the body or on some organ of an animal or plant. **2.** an ornamental protuberance of metal, ivory, etc.

bosun /ˈbousən/ *n.* → **boatswain**.

bot¹ /bɒt/ *n. Colloq.* bottom; the buttocks.

bot² /bɒt/ *n.* **1.** an insect larva infecting the skin, sinuses, nose, eye, stomach, or other parts of animals or humans. **2.** *Aust., NZ Colloq.* a person who cadges persistently. –*v.t.*, *v.i.* (**botted**, **botting**) **3.** *Aust., NZ Colloq.* → **cadge**. –*phr. Aust., NZ Colloq.* **4. on the bot**, cadging: *on the bot for a cigarette.* **5. the bot**, a minor ailment, as a bad cold.

botanical garden *n.* (*oft. pl.*) a large garden usually open to the public where trees, shrubs and plants, typically from many lands, are grown and studied. Also, **botanic garden**.

botany /ˈbɒtəni/ *n.* (*pl.* **-nies**) **1.** the science of plants; the branch of biology that deals with plant life. **2.** the plant life of an area: *the botany of the Simpson Desert.* **3.** the biology of a plant or plant group: *the botany of deciduous trees.* –**botanical** /bəˈtænɪkəl/, *adj.*

botch /bɒtʃ/ *v.t.* Also, **botch up. 1.** to spoil by poor work; bungle. **2.** to do or say in a bungling manner. **3.** to mend or patch in a clumsy manner. –*n.* Also, **botch-up. 4.** a clumsy or poor piece of work; a bungle: *his carpentry was a complete botch.* –**botched**, *adj.* –**botcher**, *n.* –**botchery**, *n.*

both /bouθ/ *adj.* **1.** the one and the other: *give both dates.* –*pron.* **2.** the two together: *both had been there.* –*adv.* **3.** alike; equally: *she is both ready and willing; both men and women.* –*phr.* **4. have it both ways**, to attempt to maintain both of two mutually exclusive possibilities.

bother /ˈbɒðə/ *v.t.* **1.** to give trouble to; annoy; pester; worry. **2.** to confuse; bewilder. –*v.i.* **3.** to bother oneself. **4.** to cause annoyance or trouble. –*n.* **5.** a worried or perplexed state. –*interj.* **6.** a mild exclamation. –**bothersome**, *adj.*

botox /ˈboutɒks/ *(from trademark)* –*n.* **1.** a preparation of botulinum toxin which causes muscle relaxation and paralysis, used for medical and cosmetic purposes, in the latter case to treat wrinkles. –*v.t.* **2.** to apply botox to (a part of the face or body).

bottle /ˈbɒtl/ *n.* **1.** a portable vessel with a neck or mouth, now commonly made of glass, used for holding liquids. **2.** the contents of a bottle; as much as a bottle contains: *a bottle of wine.* **3.** a bottle with a rubber nipple from which a baby sucks milk, etc. **4.** (in hospitals, etc.) a portable container with a wide tilted neck into which bed-ridden males urinate. **5.** a compressed air cylinder. –*v.t.* **6.** to put into or seal in a bottle; to preserve (fruit or vegetables) in bottles. **7.** *Colloq.* to knock over (someone) as though they were a bottle: *bottle 'im!* –*phr.* **8. bottle up**, to shut in or restrain closely: *to bottle up one's feelings.* **9. hit the bottle**, *Colloq.* **a.** to drink heavily; become an alcoholic. **b.** to be on a drinking spree: *they really hit the bottle the night before the wedding.* **10. on the bottle**, **a.** *Colloq.* drinking alcohol heavily and habitually. **b.** *Colloq.* on a drinking spree; intoxicated. **c.** (of babies) feeding on bottled milk (opposed to *on the breast*): *raised on the bottle.* **11. the bottle**, intoxicating drink. **12. the full bottle**, *Aust. Colloq.* an expert. –**bottlelike**, *adj.*

bottlebrush /ˈbɒtlbrʌʃ/ *n.* **1.** a brush for cleaning bottles. **2.** any species of the Australian genus *Callistemon* whose flower spikes resemble a cylindrical brush. **3.** a member of other related, and occasionally unrelated, species with similar flowers.

bottleneck /ˈbɒtlnɛk/ *n.* **1.** a narrow entrance or passage way. **2.** a place, or stage in a process, where progress is retarded. **3. a.** a narrow part of a road between two wide stretches. **b.** a congested junction, road, town, etc., fed by several roads, where traffic is likely to be held up. **4.** a slide made from the neck of a bottle and used for stopping the strings of a steel guitar.

bottler /ˈbɒtlə/ *n. Aust., NZ Colloq.* something or someone exciting admiration or approval: *you little bottler.*

bottle tree *n.* **1.** any of various tree species with bottle-shaped trunks, especially some Australian species of *Brachychiton*, but also *Adansonia gregorii* of Australia and *Cavanillesia arborea* of Brazil. **2.** → **boab**.

bottom /ˈbɒtəm/ *n.* **1.** the lowest or deepest part of anything, as distinguished from the top: *the bottom of a hill, of a page, etc.* **2.** the place of least honour, dignity, or achievement: *the bottom of the class*; *the bottom of the table*. **3.** the underside: *the price was marked on the bottom of the plate*. **4.** the buttocks. **5.** the lowest gear of a motor; first gear. **6.** the ground under any body of water: *the bottom of the sea*. **7.** the fundamental part; basic aspect: *from the bottom of my heart*. **8.** *Mining* a stratum carrying a sought-after mineral: *the hole reached three bottoms*. **9.** the inmost part or inner end of a recess, bay, lane, etc. **10.** (*sometimes pl.*) the part of a two-piece garment designed to be worn on the lower half of the body: *pyjama bottom*; *bikini bottom*. *–v.t.* **11.** to get to the bottom of; fathom. **12.** to dig (a mine) to sufficient depth to reach paydirt. *–adj.* **13.** lowest; undermost. **14.** fundamental: *the bottom cause*. *–phr.* **15. at bottom**, in reality; fundamentally. **16. bottom on, a.** to reach (gold, etc.) at depth. **b.** Also, **bottom upon**. to base or found on (an idea, belief, etc.). **17. bottom out**, to reach the lowest level thought likely: *the recession in the economy has bottomed out*. **18. bottoms up**, an exclamation used as an encouragement to finish a drink. **19. get to the bottom of**, to understand fully. *–bottomless, adj. –bottommost, adj.*

bottom-dweller /'bɒtəm-dwelə/ *n.* **1.** a creature that lives on the bottom of an ocean, lake, pond, etc. **2.** *Colloq.* a person who is at the bottom of civilised society.

bottom feeder *n.* **1.** a freshwater or saltwater animal, especially a fish, which feeds on plants and animals living on the bottom of a river, lake, bay, etc. **2.** a person who takes advantage of what others provide while making no contribution themselves.

bottom fermentation *n.* a brewing method using a strain of yeast that sinks to the bottom of the vessel at the completion of fermentation, producing new beer or lager.

bottom line *n.* **1.** the last line of a financial statement where overall cost, profit, loss, etc., is likely to be found. *–phr.* **2. the bottom line, a.** financial considerations. **b.** the basic requirement or precondition: *the bottom line is talent*.

botulinum /bɒtʃə'laɪnəm/ *n.* the toxin derived from the *Clostridia* genus of anaerobic bacteria, causing botulism. Also, **botulin** /'bɒtʃələn/.

botulism /'bɒtʃəlɪzəm/ *n.* a disease of the nervous system caused by a toxin developed in spoiled sausage, preserved and other foods eaten by animals and humans, often fatal.

boudoir /'budwa/ *n.* a woman's bedroom or private room.

bouffant /'bufɒ/ *adj.* puffed out; full, as sleeves, hairstyle, or draperies.

bougainvillea /bougən'vɪliə, -vɪljə/ *n.* any shrub or spiny climber of the tropical American genus *Bougainvillea* with brightly coloured bracts, widely cultivated in tropical and subtropical Australia.

bough /baʊ/ *n.* a branch of a tree, especially one of the larger of the main branches. *–boughless, adj.*

bought /bɔt/ *v.* past tense and past participle of **buy**.

bouillon /'bujɒn/ *n.* a plain unclarified stock or broth made by boiling beef, veal or chicken in water, with herbs.

boulder /'boʊldə/ *n.* a detached and rounded or worn rock, especially a large one.

boulevard /'buləvad/ *n.* **1.** a broad avenue of a city, often having trees and used as a promenade. **2.** a street. Also, **boulevarde**.

bounce /baʊns/ *verb* (**bounced**, **bouncing**) *–v.i.* **1.** to move with a bound, and rebound, as a ball: *a ball bounces back from the wall*. **2.** to burst ebulliently (*into* or *out of*): *to bounce into a room*. **3.** *Colloq.* (of cheques) to be dishonoured; to be returned unpaid. **4.** (of electronic mail) to return to the sender when not received at the intended address. *–v.t.* **5.** to cause to

bound or rebound: *to bounce a ball*; *to bounce a child on one's knee*. **6.** *Aust. Rules* to bounce (the ball) high, as at the beginning of the game and to restart it in a ball-up. **7.** *Colloq.* to eject or discharge summarily. **8.** *Colloq.* to persuade (someone) by bluff: *they bounced him into signing*. **9.** *Colloq.* to arrest. *–n.* **10.** a rebound or bound: *catch the ball on the first bounce*. **11.** a sudden spring or leap. **12.** impudence; bluster; swagger. **13.** ability to bounce; resilience. **14.** *Aust. Rules* → **ball-up**. *–phr.* **15. bounce back**, to recover health, prosperity, form, etc., after a temporary setback. **16. bounce off, a.** to rebound away from. **b.** to outline (an idea, proposal, etc.) to, in order to get a reaction.

bouncer /'baʊnsə/ *n.* **1.** Also, **baby bouncer**. a spring seat or harness in which a baby may bounce up and down. **2.** *Colloq.* someone employed in a place of public resort to eject disorderly persons. **3.** *Cricket* a bumper.

bouncing /'baʊnsɪŋ/ *adj.* **1.** stout, strong, or vigorous: *a bouncing baby*. **2.** exaggerated; big; hearty; noisy: *a bouncing lie*.

bound¹ /baʊnd/ *adj.* **1.** tied; in bonds: *a bound prisoner*. **2.** made fast as by a band or bond: *bound by one's word*. **3.** secured within a cover, as a book. **4.** constipated; costive. *–phr.* **5. bound to, a.** under obligation to, legally or morally: *in duty bound to help*. **b.** destined or sure to: *it is bound to happen*. **c.** determined or resolved to: *he is bound to go*. **6. bound up in** (or **with**), **a.** inseparably connected with. **b.** having the affections centred in: *his life is bound up in his children*.

bound² /baʊnd/ *v.i.* **1.** to move by leaps; leap; jump; spring. **2.** to rebound, as a ball. *–v.t.* **3.** to cause to bound. *–n.* **4.** a leap onwards or upwards; a jump. **5.** a rebound.

bound³ /baʊnd/ *n.* **1.** (*usu. pl.*) **a.** a limiting line, or boundary: *the bounds of space and time*. **b.** that which limits, confines, or restrains: *within the bounds of reason*. **2.** (*pl.*) territory on or near a boundary: *the outer bounds*. *–v.t.* **3.** to limit as by bounds. **4.** to form the boundary or limit of. *–v.i.* **5. bound on**, to have boundaries on; abut. **6. out of bounds, a.** forbidden to certain persons or to the general public to access. **b.** *Sport* outside the playing area. **c.** *Colloq.* not to be discussed or mentioned: *that subject is strictly out of bounds*. *–boundless, adj. –boundlessly, adv. –boundlessness, n.*

bound⁴ /baʊnd/ *adj.* going or intending to go; on the way (*to*); destined (*for*): *the train is bound for Bathurst*.

-bound¹ a suffix used to mean constrained, kept in, as in *housebound, culturebound*.

-bound² a suffix used to mean headed in the direction of, as in *westbound*.

boundary /'baʊndri/ *n.* (*pl.* **-ries**) **1.** something that indicates bounds or limits; a limiting or bounding line. **2.** *Agric.* a fence which serves to indicate the limits of a property. **3.** *Cricket* **a.** the marked limits of the field within which the game is played. **b.** a stroke which drives the ball up to or beyond those limits. *–adj.* **4.** of or relating to a boundary.

bounder /'baʊndə/ *n. Brit. Colloq.* an obtrusive, ill-bred person; a vulgar upstart.

bounteous /'baʊntiəs/ *adj.* **1.** giving or disposed to give freely; generously liberal. **2.** freely bestowed; plentiful; abundant. *–bounteously, adv. –bounteousness, n.*

bountiful /'baʊntəfəl/ *adj.* **1.** liberal in bestowing gifts, favours, or bounties; munificent; generous. **2.** abundant; ample: *a bountiful supply*. *–bountifully, adv. –bountifulness, n.*

bounty /'baʊnti/ *n.* (*pl.* **-ties**) **1.** generosity in giving. **2.** whatever is given bounteously; a benevolent, generous gift. **3.** a premium or reward, especially one offered by a government.

bouquet /buˈkeɪ, booˈkeɪ/ *n.* **1.** a bunch of flowers; a nosegay. **2.** the characteristic aroma of wine, liqueurs, etc.; nose. **3.** approval, applause: *to get no bouquets.* *–phr.* **4. bouquets and brickbats,** compliments and insults. **5. throw** (or **toss**) **a bouquet** (or **bouquets**) **at,** to compliment; flatter.

bouquet garni /bukeɪ gaˈni/ *n.* a bunch of herbs, usually including a bay-leaf, thyme and parsley, and used to give flavour to sauces, stews, etc., tied together so that it can be removed later.

bourbon /ˈbɜbən/ *n.* a kind of whisky distilled from a mash containing 51 per cent or more maize. Also, **bourbon whisky.**

bourgeois /ˈbʊəʒwa, ˈbu-/ *n.* (*pl.* **-geois**) **1.** a member of the middle class. **2.** a shopkeeper or other trader. **3.** someone whose outlook is said to be determined by a concern for property values; a capitalist, as opposed to a member of the wage-earning class. *–adj.* **4.** of or relating to the middle class. **5.** lacking in refinement or elegance; conventional.

bourgeoisie /bʊəʒwaˈzi/ *n.* **1.** the bourgeois class. **2.** (in Marxist ideology) the class opposed to the proletariat or wage-earning class.

bout /baʊt/ *n.* **1.** a contest, especially a boxing or wrestling match; a trial of strength. **2.** a turn at work or any action. **3.** period; spell: *a bout of illness.*

boutique /buˈtik/ *n.* **1.** a small shop selling fashionable or luxury articles. *–adj.* **2.** designed for or directed to a small, specialised, fashionable market: *boutique beers.*

bouzouki /bəˈzuki/ *n.* a stringed instrument from Greece, related to a mandolin, played by plucking.

bovine /ˈboʊvaɪn/ *adj.* **1.** of the ox family (Bovidae), as the cow, buffalo, etc. **2.** resembling such an animal. **3.** stolid; dull.

bow¹ /baʊ/ *v.i.* **1.** to bend or curve downwards; stoop: *the pines bowed low.* **2.** to yield; submit: *to bow to the inevitable.* **3.** to bend or incline the body or head in worship, reverence, respect, or submission. *–v.t.* **4.** to bend or incline in worship, reverence, respect, or submission: *to bow one's head.* **5.** to cause to stoop: *age had bowed his head.* **6.** to cause to bend; make curved or crooked. *–n.* **7.** an inclination of the body or head in reverence, respect, or submission. *–phr.* **8. bow and scrape,** to be servile. **9. bow out,** to retire; leave the scene. **10. take a bow,** to acknowledge compliments, admiration, applause, etc. **–bowed** /baʊd/, *adj.*

bow² /boʊ/ *n.* **1.** a piece of wood or other material easily bent by a string stretched between its ends, used for shooting arrows. **2.** a bend or curve: *a bow in the road.* **3.** a knot, as of ribbon, consisting of one or two loops and two ends. **4.** *Music* a device, originally curved, but now almost always straight, with horse hairs stretched upon it, designed for playing any stringed instrument. *–adj.* **5.** curved; bent like a bow: *bow legs.* *–v.t.* **6.** *Music* to perform by means of a bow upon a stringed instrument. *–v.i.* **7.** *Music* to play with a bow. **–bowless,** *adj.* **–bowlike,** *adj.* **–bower,** *n.*

bow³ /baʊ/ *n.* **1.** (*sometimes pl.*) the front or forward part or end of a ship, boat, airship, etc. **2.** the foremost oar used in rowing a boat.

bowdlerise /ˈbaʊdləraɪz/ *v.t.* to expurgate prudishly. Also, **bowdlerize.** **–bowdlerism,** *n.* **–bowdlerisation** /ˌbaʊdləraɪˈzeɪʃən/, *n.* **–bowdleriser,** *n.*

bowel /ˈbaʊəl/ *n.* **1.** *Anat.* **a.** an intestine. **b.** (*usu. pl.*) the parts of the alimentary canal below the stomach; the intestines or entrails. **2.** the inward or interior parts: *the bowels of the ship.*

bower¹ /ˈbaʊə/ *n.* **1.** a leafy shelter or recess; an arbour. **2.** *Archaic* a chamber; a boudoir. **–bowerlike,** *adj.*

bower² /ˈbaʊə/ *n.* an anchor carried at a ship's bow. Also, **bower anchor.**

bower³ /ˈbaʊə/ *n.* (in euchre and other card games) the knave of trumps (**right bower**) or the other knave of the same colour (**left bower**); the highest cards in the game, unless the joker (often called the **best bower**) is used.

bowerbird /ˈbaʊəbɜd/ *n.* **1.** any of various birds of the family Ptilonorhynchidae, of Australia and New Guinea, the males of which build bowerlike structures and decorate them with bright objects to attract females for mating. **2.** *Aust. Colloq.* someone who collects useless objects.

bowl¹ /boʊl/ *n.* **1.** a rather deep, round dish or basin, used mainly for holding liquids, food, etc. **2.** the contents of a bowl. **3.** anything shaped like a bowl: *the bowl of a pipe.* **–bowl-like,** *adj.*

bowl² /boʊl/ *n.* **1.** one of the biased or weighted balls used in the game of bowls; wood. **2.** one of the balls, having little or no bias, used in playing ninepins or tenpin bowling. **3.** *Machinery* a rotating cylindrical part in a machine, as one to reduce friction. *–v.i.* **4.** to play with bowls, or at bowling. **5.** to roll a bowl, as in the game of bowls. **6.** *Cricket* to deliver the ball with a straight arm, usually with the intention that it should bounce once before reaching the person batting. *–v.t.* **7.** to roll or trundle, as a hoop, etc. **8.** *Cricket* to dismiss (the person batting) by delivering a ball which breaks their wicket. *–phr.* **9. bowl along,** to move along smoothly and rapidly. **10. bowl down,** to knock down, as by a ball in bowling: *he bowled down everyone in his path.* **11. bowl over,** to knock over, as by the ball in bowling. **12. bowl someone over,** **a.** to disconcert; upset. **b.** to impress greatly.

bowleg /ˈboʊlɛg/ *n.* outward curvature of the legs causing a separation of the knees when the ankles are close or in contact. **–bow-legged** /boʊˈlɛgəd, ˈboʊ-lɛgd/, *adj.*

bowler¹ /ˈboʊlə/ *n.* a hard felt hat with a rounded crown and narrow brim.

bowler² /ˈboʊlə/ *n.* *Cricket* a member of a team who specialises in bowling.

bowline /ˈboʊlaɪn, ˈboʊlən/ *n.* a knot which forms a non-slipping loop. Also, **bowline knot.**

bowls /boʊlz/ *n.* **1.** → **lawn bowls.** **2.** → **carpet bowls.** **3.** skittles, ninepins, or tenpin bowling.

bowser /ˈbaʊzə/ *n.* *Aust., NZ* (*from trademark*) a pump at a service station for putting fuel into motor vehicles.

bowyang /ˈboʊjæŋ/ *n.* *Aust., NZ* a string or strap round the trouser leg to prevent the turn-up from dragging and to allow freedom of movement when crouching or bending.

box¹ /bɒks/ *n.* **1.** a case or receptacle, usually rectangular, of wood, metal, cardboard, etc., with a lid or removable cover. **2.** the quantity contained in a box. **3.** a present or gift, especially as given at Christmas to people who provide services such as milk delivery, garbage collection, etc.; Christmas box. **4.** a compartment or place shut or railed off for the accommodation of a small number of people in a public place, especially in theatres, opera houses, sporting venues, etc. **5.** (in a court of law) a stand or pew reserved for witnesses, the accused, or the jury. **6.** a small shelter: *a watchman's box.* **7.** *Aust. Hist.* **a.** a portable, sometimes wheeled, box-like structure in which numbers of convicts working outdoors were confined for the night. **b.** a similar accommodation used by shepherds allowing them to remain close to their flocks. **8.** the driver's seat on a horse-drawn carriage. **9.** a loosebox. **10.** part of a page of a periodical set off by lines, border, or white space. **11.** *Machinery* an enclosing, protecting, or hollow part. **12.** *Cricket, etc.* → **protector** (def. 4). **13.** Also, **boxing, box-up.** a mixing up of separate flocks of sheep. **14.** *Colloq.* (*taboo*) the vagina and external female genitalia. *–v.t.* **15.** to put into a box. **16.** to enclose or confine as in a box. **17.** to furnish with

box 95 **bracket**

a box. **18.** to form into a box or the shape of a box. **19.** *Horseracing, etc.* to modify (a bet on two or more competitors) so that any combination of these competitors in the first placings of the race wins. **20.** Also, **box up.** to allow (separate mobs of sheep) to become indiscriminately mixed. –*phr.* **21. be a box of birds,** *NZ* to be happy and in good health. **22. box in, a.** to build a box around. **b.** to surround; hem in: *to be boxed in by traffic.* **c.** *Athletics, Horseracing, etc.* to join with other competitors in preventing (a rival) from forging ahead by hemming them in. **23. box of tricks,** *Colloq.* **a.** a person who is lively, inventive, and unpredictable. **b.** a container holding equipment or tools: *what have you got in your box of tricks?* **24. box up, a.** Also, **box.** to mix indiscriminately (as separate mobs of sheep). **b.** to confine; hem in. **25. make a box of,** *Aust.* to muddle. **26. nothing out of the box,** *Aust., NZ Colloq.* not remarkable; mediocre. **27. one out of the box,** *Aust. Colloq.* an outstanding person or thing. **28. the box,** *Colloq.* a television set. **29. the whole box and dice,** *Aust., NZ Colloq.* the whole; the lot. –**boxful,** *n.* –**boxlike,** *adj.*

box² /bɒks/ *n.* **1.** a blow as with the hand or fist. –*v.t.* **2.** to strike with the hand or fist, especially on the ear. **3.** to fight in a boxing match. –*v.i.* **4.** to fight with the fists; spar.

box³ /bɒks/ *n.* **1.** an evergreen shrub or small tree of the genus *Buxus*, especially *B. sempervirens*, used for ornamental borders, hedges, etc., and yielding a hard, durable wood. **2.** the wood itself. See **boxwood**. **3.** any tree of a group of species in the genus *Eucalyptus* with a characteristic close, short-fibred bark.

boxer /'bɒksə/ *n.* **1.** someone who boxes; a pugilist. **2.** a smooth-coated, brown dog of medium size, related to the bulldog and terrier.

boxers /'bɒksəz/ *pl. n.* → **boxer shorts.**

boxer shorts *pl. n.* loose-fitting men's underpants with an elasticised waist, resembling shorts.

box girder *n.* a hollow girder which is square or rectangular in cross-section.

boxing /'bɒksɪŋ/ *n.* the act or art of fighting with the fists, with or without boxing gloves.

Boxing Day *n.* the day after Christmas Day, observed as a holiday.

boxing glove *n.* a padded mitten worn in boxing.

box jellyfish *n.* a type of jellyfish found in tropical seas, which instead of the more usual umbrella shape is a cuboidal mass with tentacles hanging from each of the lower corners. The common Australian species *Chironex fleckeri* (the sea wasp or stinger) is highly venomous.

box office *n.* **1.** the office in which tickets are sold at a theatre or other place of public entertainment. –*adj.* **2.** relating to the size of the audience: *a box office success.*

box seat *n.* **1.** a seat in a theatre box, etc. **2.** the driving seat of a horse-drawn coach **3.** *Horseracing* (in trotting races) a position just behind the leader. **4.** any position of advantage. –*phr.* **5. be in the box seat,** to have reached a peak of success; be in the most favourable position.

boxwood /'bɒkswʊd/ *n.* **1.** the hard, fine-grained, compact wood of species of *Buxus*, especially *B. sempervirens*, used for wood engravers' blocks, musical and mathematical instruments, etc. **2.** the tree or shrub itself. **3.** any of several trees of the families Celastraceae, Pittosporaceae and others with timber similar to that of box (**box³**), *Buxus sempervirens*.

boy /bɔɪ/ *n.* **1.** a male child or young person. **2.** an immature young man. **3.** a young male servant. –*interj.* Also, **oh boy, boy oh boy. 4. a.** an exclamation indicating surprise, delight, etc. **b.** an exclamation indicating dismay, trepidation, etc. –**boyish,** *adj.* –**boyishly,** *adv.* –**boyishness,** *n.* –**boyhood,** *n.*

boy band *n.* an all-male pop music group comprising young members and usually appealing to a young audience.

boycott /'bɔɪkɒt/ *v.t.* **1.** to combine in abstaining from, or preventing dealings with, as a means of intimidation or coercion: *to boycott official functions*; *to boycott non-complying companies.* **2.** to abstain from buying or using: *to boycott a commercial product.* –*n.* **3.** the practice or an instance of boycotting.

boyfriend /'bɔɪfrɛnd/ *n.* **1.** a man with whom one has a steady romantic relationship. **2.** any young male friend.

Boy Scout *n.* (*sometimes lower case*) (becoming obsolete except in the US) → **Scout.**

boysenberry /'bɔɪzənbɛri, -bri/ *n.* (*pl.* **-ries**) a red blackberry-like fruit with a flavour similar to that of raspberries, developed by crossing various species of *Rubus*.

boysie /'bɔɪzi/ *adj. Colloq.* excessively masculine in behaviour, dress, speech, etc., in a way that reflects a male stereotype. Compare **girlie** (def. 4).

BPA *n.* bisphenol-A; a synthetic oestrogen, used in the production of hard, transparent plastic, which can mimic the body's hormones and act as an endocrine disrupter; thought to leach into foods stored in tins with a plastic lining; possibly causing conditions ranging from obesity to infertility.

bra /brɑ/ *n.* a woman's undergarment which supports the breasts.

brace /breɪs/ *n.* **1.** something that holds parts together or in place, as a clasp or clamp. **2.** anything that imparts rigidity or steadiness. **3.** *Machinery* a device for holding and turning tools for boring or drilling. **4.** *Building Trades* a piece of timber, metal, etc., used to support or position another piece or portion of a framework. **5.** (*oft. pl.*) *Dentistry* **a.** a round or flat metal wire placed against surfaces of the teeth, and used to straighten irregularly arranged teeth. **b.** an orthodontic appliance of an arch wire attached to brackets bonded to teeth, which can be tightened to correct bad alignment of the teeth. **6.** *Med.* an appliance for supporting a weak joint or joints. **7.** (*pl.*) straps or bands worn over the shoulders for holding up the trousers. **8.** a pair; a couple. **9.** See **bracket** (def. 3). **10.** (*pl.*) *Maths* → **bracket** (def. 4). **11.** *Music* connected staves. –*v.t.* **12.** to furnish, fasten, or strengthen with or as with a brace. **13.** to fix firmly; make steady. **14.** to make tight; increase the tension of. **15.** to act as a stimulant to. –*phr.* **16. brace up,** to rouse one's strength or vigour. **17. in a brace of shakes,** *Colloq.* immediately.

brace and bit *n.* a boring tool consisting of a bit and a handle for rotating it.

bracelet /'breɪslət/ *n.* **1.** an ornamental band or circlet for the wrist or arm. **2.** *Colloq.* a handcuff.

brachial /'breɪkiəl, 'bræk-/ *adj.* **1.** belonging to the arm, foreleg, wing, pectoral fin, or other forelimb of a vertebrate. **2.** belonging to the upper part of such member, from the shoulder to the elbow. **3.** armlike, as an appendage.

brachio- a word element meaning 'arm', as in *brachiopod.* Also, (*before a vowel*), **brachi-.**

brachy- a word element meaning 'short', as in *brachycephalic.*

bracing /'breɪsɪŋ/ *adj.* **1.** strengthening; invigorating. –*n.* **2.** a brace. **3.** braces collectively. –**bracingly,** *adv.*

bracken /'brækən/ *n.* **1.** a large, coarse fern, especially *Pteridium esculentum*, a perennial native which is widespread throughout the higher rainfall areas of Australia. **2.** a clump of ferns.

bracket /'brækət/ *n.* **1.** a support of wood, metal, etc., often in the shape of a right angle, placed under a shelf or the like. **2.** *Archit.* an ornamental support for a statue, etc. **3.** one of a pair of marks used in writing or printing to enclose parenthetical matter, interpolations, etc., as a **square bracket**, [or], or a **curly bracket**, { or } (also called a **brace**), or a **round bracket**, (or) (also called a **parenthesis**), or an **angle bracket**, < or >. **4.** (*pl.*) *Maths* parentheses of various forms indicating that the enclosed quantity is to be treated as a unit. **5.** a grouping of persons, musical items, etc.: *low income bracket*; *a bracket of songs.* –*v.t.* **6.** to furnish with or support by a bracket or brackets. **7.** to place within brackets; enclose. **8.** to group together; classify.

bracket creep *n.* the gradual shift as a result of inflation of an income subject to a progressive income tax from one tax bracket to another where more tax is paid despite the real level of the income (its purchasing power) remaining unchanged.

brackish /'brækɪʃ/ *adj.* **1.** slightly salt; having a salty or briny flavour. **2.** distasteful. –**brackishness**, *n.*

bract /brækt/ *n.* a specialised leaf or leaf-like part, usually situated at the base of a flower or inflorescence. –**bracteal** /'bræktɪəl/, *adj.*

brag /bræg/ *v.i.* (**bragged**, **bragging**) to use boastful language; boast. –**braggart**, **bragger**, *n.*

Brahma /'brɑːmə/ *n.* (in later Hinduism) the personal Creator, one of a trinity together with Vishnu the Preserver and Shiva the Destroyer, usually represented holding a goblet, a bow, a sceptre, and the Vedas; seldom worshipped today.

Brahman /'brɑːmən/ *n.* (*pl.* -mans) **1.** a member of the highest, or priestly, Hindu caste. **2.** (*oft. lower case*) a person of great culture and intellect. **3.** (*oft. lower case*) a snobbish or aloof intellectual. **4.** one of a breed of cattle originating in India, derived from the Zebu, and used widely in Australia for crossbreeding. Also, **Brahmin.** –**Brahmanic** /brɑːˈmænɪk/, **Brahmanical** /brɑːˈmænɪkəl/, *adj.*

braid /breɪd/ *v.t.* **1.** to weave together strips or strands of; plait. –*n.* **2.** a braided length of hair; plait. **3.** a narrow band or tape, formed by weaving together silk, cotton, wool, or other material, used as a trimming for garments, etc. –**braider**, *n.*

braided stream *n.* a stream, usually shallow, with a water flow insufficient to carry along all the silt, etc., in it, resulting in interconnecting channels and intervening shingle bars as this load is precipitated.

braille /breɪl/ *n.* a system of writing or printing for the blind, in which combinations of tangible points are used to represent letters, etc.

brain /breɪn/ *n.* **1.** (*sometimes pl.*) the soft convoluted mass of greyish and whitish nerve tissue which fills the cranium of humans and other vertebrates; centre of sensation, body coordination, thought, emotion, etc. **2.** *Zool.* (in many invertebrates) a part of the nervous system more or less corresponding to the brain of vertebrates. **3.** (*usu. pl.*) understanding; intellectual power; intelligence. **4.** *Colloq.* a highly intelligent or well-informed person. **5.** *Colloq.* a diminished mental capacity, attributed to a specified cause: *chemo brain*; *baby brain.* –*v.t.* **6.** to dash out the brains of. **7.** *Colloq.* to hit (someone) hard, especially about the head; cuff. –*phr.* **8. go off one's brain**, *Colloq.* to become frenzied (with worry, anger, etc.). **9. have something on the brain**, to have an obsession about or be preoccupied with something. **10. pick someone's brains**, to get the benefit of another person's work or ideas.

brain attack *n.* → **stroke**[1] (def. 4).

brain bank *n.* a collection of human brain tissue and related samples, acquired by donation, for the conduct of research into neurological and psychiatric conditions.

brainchild /'breɪntʃaɪld/ *n.* a product of one's creative work or thought.

brain dead *adj.* **1.** having no further electrical activity in the brain as evidenced by an electroencephalograph, even though other organs such as the heart or lungs may still be functioning. **2.** *Colloq.* (*derog.*) very stupid. Also, **brain-dead.**

brain explosion *n.* *Colloq.* a moment of foolishness or wrongheadedness.

brain-fever bird *n.* **1.** → **pallid cuckoo. 2.** an Indian cuckoo, *Cuculus varius*, having a loud repetitive cry.

brainiac /'breɪniæk/ *n.* *Colloq.* a very intelligent person.

brainpower /'breɪnpaʊə/ *n.* capacity to think; intelligence.

brain scan *n.* an examination of the brain by means of a CAT scan to detect abnormalities.

brain scanner *n.* a CAT scanner used to diagnose abnormalities in the brain.

brainstorm /'breɪnstɔːm/ *n.* **1.** a sudden inspiration, idea, etc. **2.** a sudden, violent attack of mental disturbance. –*v.i.* **3.** to take part in a session of brainstorming. –*v.t.* **4.** to use brainstorming as a means to address or solve (a problem, etc.).

brainteaser /'breɪntiːzə/ *n.* *Colloq.* a mental puzzle.

brainwashing /'breɪnwɒʃɪŋ/ *n.* systematic indoctrination that changes or undermines one's convictions, especially political. –**brainwash**, *v.*

brainwave /'breɪnweɪv/ *n.* a sudden idea or inspiration.

brainy /'breɪni/ *adj.* (**-nier, -niest**) having brains; intelligent; clever. –**braininess**, *n.*

braise /breɪz/ *v.t.* (**braised**, **braising**) to cook (meat or vegetables) by sautéing in fat and then cooking slowly in very little moisture.

brake[1] /breɪk/ *n.* **1.** (*sometimes pl.*) any mechanical device for stopping the motion of a wheel, motor, or vehicle, mainly by means of friction or pressure. **2.** a tool or machine for breaking up flax or hemp, to separate the fibre. –*v.t.* **3.** to slow or stop the motion of (a wheel, motor vehicle, etc.) as by a brake. **4.** to process (flax or hemp) by crushing it in a brake. –*v.i.* **5.** to use or apply a brake. **6.** to slow down. –**brakeless**, *adj.*

brake[2] /breɪk/ *n.* a place overgrown with bushes, shrubs, brambles, or cane; a thicket.

brake drum *n.* the steel or cast-iron drum attached to the wheel hub or propeller shaft of a motor vehicle, etc., against which the brake lining is forcefully applied to arrest its turning when the brake is operated.

bramble /'bræmbəl/ *n.* any rough prickly shrub. –**brambly**, *adj.*

bran /bræn/ *n.* **1.** the ground husk of wheat or other grain, separated from flour or meal by bolting. **2.** by-products of grain processing used as feed.

branch /brɑːntʃ, bræntʃ/ *n.* **1.** *Bot.* a division or subdivision of the stem or axis of a tree, shrub, or other plant. **2.** a limb, offshoot, or ramification: *the branches of a deer's horns.* **3.** any member or part of a body or system; a section or subdivision: *the various branches of learning.* **4.** a local operating division of a company, chain store, library, or the like. **5.** a line of family descent, in distinction from some other line or lines from the same stock. **6.** (in the classification of languages) a subdivision of a family; a group. –*v.i.* **7.** to put forth branches; spread in branches. **8.** to divide into separate parts or subdivisions; diverge. –*phr.* **9. branch out**, to expand in a new direction. –**branchless**, *adj.* –**branchlike**, *adj.* –**branchy**, *adj.*

branch stacking *n.* *Politics* the arranging for a large number of one's supporters to join a branch of a political party, in order to achieve a desired preselection or policy decision. –**branch stacker**, *n.*

brand /brænd/ *n.* **1.** a trademark or trade name to identify a product. **2.** the company identified by such a brand: *to battle the big brands.* **3.** such an image or name or slogan used to identify a place or event or organisation, especially in a marketing context: *to develop Sydney's brand as a leading global city.* **4.** a kind, grade, or make, as shown by a brand, stamp, etc. **5.** a mark made by burning, etc., to indicate the ownership of cattle. **6.** any mark of disgrace; stigma. **7.** an iron for branding. **8.** *Archaic or Poetic* a sword. *–v.t.* **9.** to mark with a brand. **10.** to name as being disgraceful; stigmatise. **–brander,** *n.*

brandish /'brændɪʃ/ *v.t.* **1.** to shake or wave, as a weapon; flourish. *–n.* **2.** a wave or flourish, as of a weapon. **–brandisher,** *n.*

brand name *n.* → **trade name** (def. 3).

brand-new *adj.* completely new.

brandy /'brændi/ *n.* (*pl.* **-dies**) **1.** the spirit distilled from the fermented juice of grapes or, sometimes, of apples, peaches, plums, etc. *–v.t.* (**-died, -dying**) **2.** to mix, flavour, or preserve with brandy.

brash /bræʃ/ *adj.* **1.** impertinent; impudent; forward. **2.** headlong; hasty; rash. *–n.* **3.** loose fragments of rock. **–brashly,** *adv.* **–brashness,** *n.*

brass /bras/ *n.* **1.** an alloy of copper and zinc which is long-lasting and easily worked. **2.** an article made of brass. **3.** a collective term for musical instruments of the trumpet and horn families, blown through a funnel or cup mouthpiece, and not having a reed. **4.** a memorial plaque. **5.** a metallic yellow colour. **6.** Also, **top brass.** *Colloq.* high-ranking people in an organisation, especially in the army. **7.** *Colloq.* too much confidence; effrontery. **8.** *Colloq.* money. *–adj.* **9.** of brass or brass instruments. **–brasslike,** *adj.* **–brassy,** *adj.*

brassiere /'bræziə, -siə/ *n.* a woman's undergarment which supports the breasts.

brat /bræt/ *n.* **1.** (*derog.*) a child. **2.** a badly behaved child. **–brattish,** *adj.*

bravado /brə'vadou/ *n.* boasting; swaggering pretence.

brave /breɪv/ *adj.* **1.** possessing or exhibiting courage or courageous endurance. **2.** making a fine appearance. *–n.* **3.** a Native American warrior from one of the peoples of North America. *–v.t.* **4.** to meet or face courageously: *to brave misfortunes.* *–phr.* **5. brave it out,** to ignore or defy suspicion, blame, or impudent gossip. **6. the brave,** brave people collectively. **–bravely,** *adv.* **–braveness,** *n.*

bravo /bra'vou/ *interj.* **1.** well done! good! *–n.* (*pl.* **-vos**) **2.** a shout of 'bravo!'

bravura /brə'vurə, -'vju-/ *n.* **1.** *Music* a florid passage or piece, requiring great skill and spirit in the performer. **2.** a display of daring; brilliant performance. *–adj.* **3.** *Music* spirited; florid; brilliant.

brawl /brɔl/ *n.* **1.** a noisy quarrel; a squabble. **2.** a rough, noisy fight, often involving more than two people: *a drunken brawl outside the pub.* **3.** a bubbling or roaring noise; a clamour. **–brawler,** *n.*

brawn /brɔn/ *n.* **1.** well-developed muscles. **2.** muscular strength. **3.** meat, especially pork, boiled, pickled, and pressed into a mould. **–brawny,** *adj.*

bray /breɪ/ *n.* **1.** a harsh, breathy cry, as of the donkey. **2.** any similar loud, harsh sound. *–v.i.* **3.** to utter a harsh, noisy sound, as a protest or laugh. **–brayer,** *n.*

braze /breɪz/ *v.t.* to unite (pieces of brass, steel, aluminium, etc.) by heating the parts to be joined and fusing them together with a layer of an alloy with a lower melting point than the parts to be joined.

brazen /'breɪzən/ *adj.* **1.** made of brass. **2.** like brass, as in sound, colour, strength, etc. **3.** shameless or impudent: *brazen effrontery.* *–v.t.* **4.** to make brazen or bold. **–brazenly,** *adv.* **–brazenness,** *n.*

brazier¹ /'breɪziə/ *n.* someone who works in brass.

brazier² /'breɪziə/ *n.* a metal receptacle for holding burning charcoal or other fuel.

brazil nut /brə'zɪl nʌt/ *n.* the triangular edible seed (nut) of the tree *Bertholletia excelsa* and related species, of Brazil and elsewhere.

breach /britʃ/ *n.* **1.** the act or result of breaking; a break or rupture. **2.** a gap made in a wall, dyke, fortification, etc.; rift; fissure. **3.** an infraction or violation, as of law, trust, faith, promise, etc. **4.** a severance of friendly relations. *–v.t.* **5.** to make a breach or opening in. **6.** to violate (trust, a law, etc.): *to breach someone's trust; to breach the rules.* *–v.i.* **7.** (of a whale) to thrust itself above the water. **–breaching,** *n.*

breach of contract *n.* the breaking, by action or omission, of an obligation imposed by a contract.

breach of privilege *n.* an abuse of any of the privileges accorded to members of parliament.

bread /brɛd/ *n.* **1.** a food made of flour or meal, milk or water, etc., made into a dough or batter, with or without yeast or the like, and baked. **2.** food or sustenance; livelihood: *to earn one's bread.* **3.** *Eccles.* the wafer or bread used in the Eucharist. **4.** *Colloq.* money; earnings. *–v.t.* **5.** *Cookery* to cover or dress with breadcrumbs or meal. *–phr.* **6. bread and water,** subsistence rations, especially as a punishment. **7. break bread, a.** to partake of or share food. **b.** *Eccles.* to administer or join in Communion. **–breadless,** *adj.*

bread-and-butter *adj.* **1.** of or relating to the means of living; mercenary: *bread-and-butter issues.* **2.** practical; matter-of-fact; basic: *a bread-and-butter approach to life.* **3.** expressing thanks for hospitality, as a letter.

breadcrumb trail *n.* the information which visitors to a website leave about who they are and their patterns of behaviour, in particular their buying patterns.

breadfruit /'brɛdfrut/ *n.* a large, round, starchy fruit yielded by the tree *Artocarpus altilis,* of the Pacific islands, etc., much used, baked or roasted, for food.

breadline /'brɛdlaɪn/ *n.* **1.** *US Obs.* a line of needy persons assembled to receive food given as charity. *–phr.* **2. on the breadline, a.** living at subsistence level **b.** sustained by public assistance or charity.

breadth /brɛdθ/ *n.* **1.** *Maths* the measure of the second principal dimension of a surface or solid, the first being length, and the third (in the case of a solid) thickness; width. **2.** an extent or piece of something as measured by its width, or of definite or full width: *a breadth of cloth.* **3.** freedom from narrowness or restraint; liberality: *breadth of understanding.* **4.** size in general; extent. **5.** *Art* broad or general effect due to subordination of details or non-essentials.

breadthways /'brɛdθweɪz/ *adv.* in the direction of the breadth. Also, *esp. US,* **breadthwise** /'brɛdθwaɪz/.

breadwinner /'brɛdwɪnə/ *n.* someone who earns a livelihood for a family or household.

break /breɪk/ *verb* (**broke, broken, breaking**) *–v.t.* **1.** to divide into parts violently; reduce to pieces or fragments. **2.** to fracture a bone of: *to break your arm.* **3.** to lacerate; wound: *to break the skin.* **4.** to cause to stop functioning properly: *I've broken the camera.* **5.** to fail to observe; violate: *to break a law or promise.* **6.** to dissolve or annul: *to break an engagement.* **7.** to discontinue abruptly; interrupt; suspend: *to break the silence.* **8.** to destroy the regularity of: *to break a rhythm.* **9.** to put an end to; overcome. **10.** to interrupt the uniformity or sameness of: *to break the monotony.* **11.** to destroy the unity, continuity, or arrangement of. **12.** to exchange for a smaller amount or smaller units. **13.** to make one's way through; penetrate. **14.** to make one's way out of: *to break jail.* **15.** to surpass; outdo: *to break a record.* **16.** to disclose or divulge, with caution or delicacy. **17.** to disable or destroy by or as by shattering or crushing. **18.** to open the breech of (a gun) either for safety or for unloading. **19.** to ruin financially, or make bankrupt. **20.** to reduce in rank. **21.** to impair or weaken in strength, spirit, force, or effect. **22.** to be the first to publish (a news item). **23.** to defeat the purpose of (a strike) as by hiring non-union labour. **24.** to train to obedience; tame. **25.** *Cricket* to strike (a wicket) so as to dislodge the bails. **26.** *Elect.* to render (a circuit) incomplete; stop the flow of (a current). –*v.i.* **27.** to become broken or separated into parts or fragments, especially suddenly and violently. **28.** to stop functioning properly: *the camera broke.* **29.** to happen: *it broke just the way I wanted*; *things broke very nicely for him.* **30.** to free oneself or escape suddenly (*away, from,* etc.) as from restraint: *he broke and ran.* **31.** to stop work, etc., especially temporarily: *we'll break for lunch at 1.00 p.m.* **32.** (of a ball) to change direction on bouncing. **33.** (of a sea swell) to develop into white crested waves, the water of which, unlike the water which carries an unbroken swell, moves forcibly forward; usually caused by the water becoming shallower, as over a reef, near the shore, etc. **34.** (of a wave) to topple forward after developing a crest through the opposing pull of an undertow in shallow water. **35.** (of a news item) to appear for the first time in a newspaper, on television, etc. **36.** (of stock) to stampede: *the cattle broke at night.* **37.** to force a way (*in, through, out,* etc.) **38.** to burst (*in, forth, from,* etc.): *a cry broke from her lips.* **39.** to come suddenly, as into notice. **40.** to dawn, as the day. **41.** to give way or fail as under strain. **42.** (of the heart) to be crushed or overwhelmed, especially by grief. **43.** (of the voice) to vary between two registers, especially in emotion or during adolescence. **44.** *Billiards* to make a break (def. 67a). **45.** *Boxing* to discontinue a clinch. **46.** *Rugby Football* to disband, as a scrum or maul. **47.** *Cycling* to suddenly outdistance the rest of the field. **48.** (in a race) to start before the signal to do so has been given. –*n.* **49.** a forcible disruption or separation of parts; a breaking; a fracture, rupture, or shattering. **50.** an opening made by breaking; a gap. **51.** an opportunity; chance. **52.** a rush away from a place; an attempt to escape: *a break for freedom.* **53.** an interruption of continuity; suspension, stoppage. **54.** an abrupt or marked change, as in sound or direction. **55.** a brief rest, as from work, especially a midmorning pause, usually of fifteen minutes, between school classes. **56.** a short holiday: *a three-day break.* **57.** a stampede of stock. **58.** *Surfing* a section of water as over a reef, near the shore, etc., where the sea swell breaks: *the beach break was about a metre high.* **59.** *Wool* a distinct weakness in one part of the wool staple caused by a temporary interference with the growth of the staple. **60.** *Prosody* a pause or caesura. **61.** *Music* **a.** *Jazz* a solo passage, usually marked by improvisation. **b.** *Pop Music* an instrumental passage in a song. **62.** *Music* the point in the scale where the quality of voice of one register changes to that of another, as from chest to head. **63.** *Elect.* an opening or discontinuity in a circuit. **64.** *Printing* a wordbreak. **65. a.** a series of successful shots, strokes, or the like, in a game. **b.** *Billiards* the score made in such a series. **66.** any continuous run, especially of good fortune. **67.** *Billiards* **a.** the shot that breaks or scatters the balls at the beginning of the game. **b.** the right to the first shot. **68.** a premature start in racing. **69.** *Cricket, etc.* a change in the direction of a ball when it bounces, usually caused by a spinning motion imparted by the bowler. **70.** *CB Radio* access to a radio channel. –*phr.* **71. break and enter,** *Law* to open or force one's way into (a dwelling, store, etc.). **72. break away, a.** to free oneself or escape suddenly, as from restraint. **b.** (in racing) to start prematurely. **c.** *Football* to elude defending players and run towards the opposing goal. **d.** to move away from a crowd. **e.** (of a sheep or cow)

to run away from the flock or herd. **f.** (of a cyclist) to leave the rest of a group behind. **g.** to secede. **h.** (sometimes fol. by *from*) to remove oneself with effort from undesirable contact or influence. **73. break bulk, a.** to open a ship's hatch and discharge the first sling of cargo. **b.** to open a fully enclosed container and unload the first part of the load. **74. break camp,** to pack up tents and equipment and resume a march. **75. break down, a.** to take down or destroy by breaking. **b.** to overcome. **c.** to be overcome by emotion. **d.** to analyse. **e.** *Timber Industry* to cut (logs) into flitches; make the first cuts in (heavy logs). **f.** to add water to (spirits, etc.), to reduce the alcoholic strength. **g.** (of a person) to collapse physically or mentally. **h.** to cease to function: *the car broke down.* **i.** to be in a vehicle that ceases to function: *I broke down on the way to work.* **76. break even** (or **square**), to neither win nor lose on a transaction. **77. break in, a.** to enter a house or the like forcibly, as an intruder. **b.** to adapt to one's convenience by use: *to break in a new pair of shoes.* **c.** to accustom (a horse) to harness and use. **d.** to cultivate (virgin land): *to break in a new paddock.* **e.** (sometimes fol. by *on* or *upon*) to interrupt. **78. break into, a.** to interrupt. **b.** to enter (a house or the like) forcibly. **c.** to suddenly begin (an activity): *she broke into laughter.* **d.** to open for consumption and use: *to break into a packet of biscuits.* **79. break it down,** an exclamation which is an appeal to someone to desist from behaviour which is annoying, embarrassing, upsetting, etc. **80. break new ground,** to venture into a new area of activity. **81. break of,** to train (a person, animal, etc.) away from (a habit or practice). **82. break off, a.** to put a sudden stop to; discontinue: *to break off smoking.* **b.** to cease suddenly: *the music broke off.* **c.** to leave off abruptly. **d.** to become detached. **e.** to dissolve or annul. **83. break one's duck,** *Cricket* (of the person batting) to score one's first run in an innings. **84. break out, a.** *Pathol.* (of certain diseases) to appear in eruptions. **b.** to produce for use or enjoyment, as for a special occasion: *to break out the champagne.* **c.** (sometimes fol. by *of*) to force one's way out; escape: *to break out of prison.* **d.** *Goldmining* (of a particular field) to become the site of a gold rush: *next the Palmerston broke out.* **85. break out in,** (of a person) to have a sudden appearance of (various eruptions on the skin): *to break out in pimples.* **86. break service** (or **serve**), *Tennis* to win a game when receiving the service. **87. break someone's way,** to come about to someone's advantage: *the market finally broke her way.* **88. break step,** *Mil.* to cease marching in step. **89. break up, a.** to separate; disband (especially of a school at end of term). **b.** to dissolve and separate. **c.** *Colloq.* to collapse with laughter. **d.** *Colloq.* to cause to laugh uncontrollably; amuse greatly. **e.** (of a personal relationship) to end: *many marriages break up in the first year.* **f.** (sometimes fol. by *with*) to discontinue a relationship: *to break up with one's partner.* **g.** to put an end to; discontinue. **h.** to cut up (fowl, etc.). **90. break wind,** to expel flatulence. **91. give someone a break,** *Colloq.* to give someone a fair chance. **92. them's the breaks,** *Colloq.* that is how life is. –**breakable,** *adj.*

breakage /ˈbreɪkɪdʒ/ *n.* **1.** an act of breaking; a break. **2.** the amount or quantity of things broken. **3.** an allowance or compensation for loss or damage of articles broken in transit or in use.

breakaway /ˈbreɪkəweɪ/ *n.* **1.** the act of breaking away, becoming separate. **2.** the formation of a splinter group in a political party, or similar group: *there was a breakaway in the Victorian Labor party.* **3.** *Rugby Union* either of two players who pack down on either side of the back row in a scrum. **4.** a panic rush of or among a mob of cattle, horses, etc. –*adj.* **5.** being or relating to a person or thing that has broken away or seeks to break away.

breakdance /ˈbreɪkdæns/ n. **1.** a style of acrobatic dancing originally performed by black male street gangs in the US in the 1970s, performed usually on the streets to rap music, and involving spectacular movements such as spinning the body on the ground or floor. –v.i. (**-danced, -dancing**) **2.** to dance in this style.

breakdancer /ˈbreɪkdænsə/ n. someone who is skilled in breakdancing.

breakdown /ˈbreɪkdaʊn/ n. **1.** a ceasing to function, as of a motor vehicle, machine, etc. **2.** a collapse of physical or mental health.

breaker /ˈbreɪkə/ n. **1.** a person or thing that breaks something. **2.** a wave that breaks or dashes into foam. **3.** a person who breaks in horses: *brumby breaker; Breaker Morant.*

breakfast /ˈbrɛkfəst/ n. **1.** the first meal of the day; a morning meal. **2.** the food eaten at the first meal. –**breakfaster,** n.

breakneck /ˈbreɪknɛk/ adj. dangerous; hazardous.

breakpoint /ˈbreɪkpɔɪnt/ n. **1.** an instruction inserted by a debug program. **2.** the point in a program at which such an instruction operates.

breakthrough /ˈbreɪkθru/ n. any development, as in science, technology, or diplomacy, which removes a barrier to progress.

breakwater /ˈbreɪkwɔtə/ n. a barrier, either artificial, as a wall, or natural, as an island, which breaks the force of waves, as in front of a harbour.

bream /brɪm/ n. (pl. **bream** or **breams**) **1.** in Australia, any of various marine sparid fishes of the genera *Mylio* and *Acanthopagrus,* highly prized as food and for sport, as the **black bream,** *A. australis* of eastern Australian waters. **2.** elsewhere, **a.** any of various freshwater cyprinoid fishes of the genus *Abramis,* as *A. brama* of Europe, with a compressed, deep body. **b.** any of various related and similar species, as the **white bream,** *Blicca bjoerkna.*

breast /brɛst/ n. **1.** Anat., Zool. the outer front part of the thorax, or the front part of the body from neck to belly; the chest. **2.** Zool. the corresponding part in lower animals. **3.** a standard cut of meat from this area. **4.** Anat., Zool. a mammary or milk gland, especially of a woman, or of female animals whose milk glands are similarly formed. **5.** that part of a garment which covers the chest. **6.** the bosom regarded as the seat of thoughts and feelings. –v.t. **7.** to meet or oppose with the breast, as in racing: *to breast the finishing tape.* **8.** to walk through, submerged up to the chest (a body of water, river, etc.). **9.** to lean on (a bar, counter, etc.): *six men were breasting the bar.* **10.** to face; meet boldly or advance against: *the ship breasted the waves.* **11.** to reach the top when travelling over (a hill, rise, etc.). –phr. **12. at** (or **on**) **the breast,** (of a baby) being fed human breast milk (opposed to *on the bottle*). **13. make a clean breast of,** to make a full confession of. **14. the breast,** a woman's breast considered as a source of milk.

breastbone /ˈbrɛstboʊn/ n. → **sternum.**

breastfeed /ˈbrɛstfid/ v.t. (**-fed, -feeding**) to feed (a baby) with the breast. –**breastfeeding,** adj., n.

breastplate /ˈbrɛstpleɪt/ n. armour for the front of the torso.

breaststroke /ˈbrɛststroʊk/ n. Swimming a stroke made in the prone position in which both hands move simultaneously forwards, outwards and rearwards from in front of the chest, and the legs move in a frog-like manner. –**breast-stroke,** v.

breath /brɛθ/ n. **1.** Physiol. the air inhaled and exhaled in respiration. **2.** respiration, especially as necessary to life. **3.** ability to breathe, especially freely: *out of breath.* **4.** a single respiration. **5.** the brief time required for it; an instant. **6.** an utterance; whisper. **7.** a light current of air. **8.** Phonetics voiceless expiration of air, used in the production of many speech sounds, such as *p* or *f.* **9.** moisture emitted in respiration, especially when condensed and visible. –phr. **10. a breath of fresh air,** an original or innovative influence, person, etc. **11. below** (or **under**) **one's breath,** in a low voice or whisper. **12. don't hold your breath,** Colloq. a phrase indicating that an expected event will not happen soon. **13. draw breath, a.** to breathe; to be alive. **b.** to take a deep breath as after strenuous exercise, a long speech, etc. **14. hold one's breath,** to deliberately refrain from exhaling. **15. out of breath,** gasping for breath as the result of some exertion; breathless. **16. take someone's breath away,** to astonish someone. **17. waste one's breath,** to speak to no effect.

breathalyse /ˈbrɛθəlaɪz/ v.t. to administer a breath test to (someone).

breathalyser /ˈbrɛθəlaɪzə/ n. a breath-analysing device which contains chemicals in ampoules which react with alcohol and which change colour in proportion to the amount of alcohol in the breath.

breathe /brið/ verb (**breathed** /briðd/, **breathing**) –v.i. **1.** to inhale and exhale air; respire. **2.** (in speech) to control the outgoing breath in producing voice and speech sounds. **3.** (only in infinitive) to pause, as for breath; take rest: *give me a chance to breathe.* **4.** to live; exist. –v.t. **5.** to inhale and exhale in respiration. **6.** to give utterance to; whisper. **7.** to express; manifest. **8.** to exhale: *dragons breathing fire.* **9.** to inject by breathing; infuse. –phr. **10. breathe hard,** to inhale and exhale deeply, especially after strenuous exertion. **11. breathe heavily,** to inhale and exhale deeply, as with sickness, pain, emotion. **12. breathe in,** to inhale. **13. breathe more freely,** to be freed from anxiety or fear; relax. **14. breathe out,** to exhale. –**breathable,** adj.

breather /ˈbriðə/ n. **1.** a pause for rest. **2.** someone who breathes.

breathless /ˈbrɛθləs/ adj. **1.** out of breath: *the blow left him breathless.* **2.** with the breath held, as in suspense: *breathless listeners.* **3.** that takes away the breath: *a breathless ride.* **4.** motionless, as the air. –**breathlessly,** adv. –**breathlessness,** n.

breathtaking /ˈbrɛθteɪkɪŋ/ adj. causing amazement: *a breathtaking performance.* –**breathtakingly,** adv.

breath test n. any test of the breath from which an estimate of the amount of alcohol in the bloodstream can be made.

breath-test v.t. → **breathalyse.**

breathy /ˈbrɛθi/ adj. (**-thier, -thiest**) (of the voice) characterised by excessive emission of breath. –**breathily,** adv. –**breathiness,** n.

bred /brɛd/ v. past tense and past participle of **breed.**

breech /britʃ/ n. **1.** the lower part of the trunk of the body behind; the posterior or buttocks. **2.** the hinder or lower part of anything.

breech birth n. a birth in which the baby's posterior, not its head, is first presented.

breeches /ˈbrɪtʃəz/ pl. n. **1.** a garment worn by men (and by women for riding, etc.), covering the hips and thighs. **2.** trousers.

breed /brid/ verb (**bred,** **breeding**) –v.t. **1.** to produce (offspring). **2.** to obtain (offspring) by the mating of parents. **3.** to raise (livestock, etc.). **4.** to bring about; produce: *dirt breeds disease.* –v.i. **5.** to produce offspring. **6.** to be produced; grow; develop: *they will breed under perfect conditions.* –n. **7.** a relatively similar group within a species, developed by man. **8.** lineage; strain. **9.** sort; kind. –**breeder,** n.

breeding /'briːdɪŋ/ n. 1. the rearing of livestock to improve their quality or merit. 2. the results of training as shown in behaviour and manners; good manners.

breeze /briːz/ n. 1. a wind or current of air, especially a light or moderate one. 2. *Meteorol.* any wind of Beaufort scale numbers 2 to 6 inclusive, comprising velocities from 4 to 27 knots, i.e. 6 to 49 km/h. 3. *Colloq.* an easy task: *it's a breeze.* –v.i. 4. *Colloq.* (sometimes fol. by *along, in, through,* etc.) to move or proceed in a casual, quick, carefree manner: *to breeze in after dinner.* –phr. *Colloq.* 5. **bat the breeze,** to engage in idle conversation. 6. **breeze through,** to perform without effort. 7. **have the breeze up,** to be afraid. 8. **put the breeze up,** to make afraid.

breezy /'briːzi/ adj. (**-zier, -ziest**) 1. abounding in breezes; windy. 2. fresh; sprightly; cheerful. –**breezily,** adv. –**breeziness,** n.

brekkie /'brɛki/ n. *Colloq.* breakfast. Also, **brekky.**

brethren /'brɛðrən/ n. 1. *Archaic* plural of **brother.** 2. fellow members of a particular group, community, etc., especially of a Christian religious denomination.

breve /briːv/ n. 1. a mark (˘) placed over a vowel to show that it is pronounced short, as in ŭ. 2. a writ, as one issued by a court of law.

brevi- a word element meaning 'short', as in *brevirostrate.*

breviary /'brɛvjəri, 'bri-, -vəri/ n. (*pl.* **-ries**) *Roman Catholic Church* a book of daily prayers and readings to be read by those in major orders.

brevity /'brɛvəti/ n. 1. shortness of time or duration; briefness: *the brevity of human life.* 2. condensation in speech; conciseness.

brew /bruː/ v.t. 1. to make (beer, ale, etc.) from malt, etc., by steeping, boiling, and fermentation. 2. Also, **brew up.** to make (a hot beverage). 3. to concoct or contrive; bring about: *to brew mischief.* –v.i. Also, **brew up.** 4. to be in preparation; be forming or gathering: *trouble was brewing.* –n. 5. a quantity brewed in a single process. –**brewer,** n.

brewery /'bruːəri/ n. (*pl.* **-ries**) an establishment for brewing beer, ale, etc.

briar /'braɪə/ n. 1. the white heath, *Erica arborea,* of France and Corsica, whose woody root is used for making tobacco pipes. 2. a prickly shrub or plant, especially the sweetbriar, *Rosa rubiginosa.* –**briary,** adj.

bribe /braɪb/ n. 1. anything of value, as money or preferential treatment, privilege, etc., given or promised for corrupt behaviour in the performance of official or public duty. 2. anything given or serving to persuade or induce. –v.t. 3. to influence or corrupt by a bribe. –**bribable,** adj. –**bribability** /ˌbraɪbə'bɪləti/, n. –**bribery,** n. –**briber,** n.

bric-a-brac /'brɪk-ə-bræk/ n. miscellaneous ornamental articles of antiquarian, decorative, or other interest. Also, **bric-à-brac.**

brick /brɪk/ n. 1. a block of clay, usually rectangular, hardened by drying in the sun or burning in a kiln, and used for building, paving, etc. 2. such blocks collectively. 3. the material. 4. any similar block, especially a small one of painted wood, used as a child's toy. –v.t. 5. *Colloq.* to falsify evidence against (someone) to substantiate a criminal charge. –adj. 6. constructed of brick: *a brick barbecue.* –phr. 7. **a brick** (or **a few bricks**) **short** (**of a load**), *Colloq.* simple-minded. 8. **be a brick,** *Colloq.* to be a person deserving of special thanks or approbation. 9. **brick up,** to lay, line, wall, build, or shut up with brick. 10. **built like a brick,** *Colloq.* (of a person) well-built; stocky. 11. **drop a brick,** *Colloq.* to make a social blunder or solecism. 12. **like a ton of bricks,** *Colloq.* heavily. –**bricklike,** adj.

brickie /'brɪki/ n. *Colloq.* a bricklayer.

bricklayer /'brɪkleɪə/ n. someone who is employed to do bricklaying or who is skilled in bricklaying.

bricklaying /'brɪkleɪɪŋ/ n. the art or occupation of laying bricks in construction.

brick veneer n. a building whose external walls each consist of a timber framework faced with a single skin of bricks, the brickwork being non-structural. –**brick-veneer,** adj.

bridal registry n. (*pl.* **-stries**) a list of suggested gifts compiled by a couple before their wedding, and held by a retailer as a guide for wedding guests. Also, **bridal register.**

bridal shower n. a party for a bride-to-be to which the guests, usually other women, bring a present for her future home; shower tea; kitchen tea.

bride /braɪd/ n. a woman newly married, or about to be married. –**bridal,** adj.

bridegroom /'braɪdɡruːm/ n. a man newly married, or about to be married.

bridesmaid /'braɪdzmeɪd/ n. a woman who attends the bride at a wedding.

bridge[1] /brɪdʒ/ n. 1. a structure standing over a river, road, etc., providing a way of passage for cars, etc. 2. *Naut.* a raised platform on a ship for the officer in charge. 3. *Anat.* the upper line of the nose. 4. *Dentistry* a replacement for a missing tooth or teeth, which may be fixed or removable. 5. *Music* a thin support across which the strings of a stringed instrument are stretched. 6. *Elect.* an instrument for measuring electrical resistance. 7. *Billiards* a notched piece of wood with a long handle, used to support a cue when the distance is otherwise too great to reach; rest. –v.t. (**bridged, bridging**) 8. to make a bridge over; span. –**bridgeable,** adj. –**bridgeless,** adj.

bridge[2] /brɪdʒ/ n. *Cards* a game for four players, derived from whist, in which the trump suit is decided by bidding amongst players and in which one partnership plays to fulfil a certain declaration against the other partnership which tries to prevent this.

bridle /'braɪdl/ n. 1. the part of the harness of a horse, etc., around the head, consisting usually of head strap, bit, and reins, and used to restrain and guide the animal. 2. anything that restrains or curbs. –v.i. 3. (sometimes fol. by *at*) to draw up the head and draw in the chin, as in disdain or resentment. 4. (sometimes fol. by *at*) to react with anger or resentment. –**bridler,** n.

brie /briː/ n. a kind of salted, white, soft cheese, ripened through bacterial action, waxy to semiliquid, as made in Brie, a district in northern France.

brief /briːf/ adj. 1. of little duration. 2. using few words; concise; succinct. 3. abrupt or curt. 4. close-fitting and short in length or extent: *brief underpants.* –n. 5. an outline, the form of which is determined by set rules, of all the possible arguments and information on one side of a controversy: *a debater's brief.* 6. *Law* a summary prepared by a solicitor for a barrister, containing all the information and documents relevant to the presentation of a case in court. 7. *Colloq.* a barrister. 8. a briefing. –v.t. 9. to instruct by a brief or briefing. 10. *Law* to retain as advocate in a suit. –phr. 11. **hold a brief for,** to espouse. 12. **in brief,** in few words; in short. –**briefly,** adv. –**briefness,** n.

briefcase /'briːfkeɪs/ n. a flat, rectangular case of leather or other material used for carrying documents, books, manuscripts, etc. Also, **dispatch case.**

briefing /'briːfɪŋ/ n. a short, accurate summary of the details of a plan or operation, as one given to a military unit, crew of an aeroplane, etc., before it undertakes the operation.

briefs /briːfs/ n. close-fitting, legless underpants.

brig /brɪg/ n. Naut. **1.** a two-masted vessel square-rigged on both masts. **2.** the compartment of a ship where prisoners are confined.

brigade /brə'geɪd/ n. **1.** a unit consisting of several regiments, squadrons, groups, or battalions. **2.** a large body of troops. **3.** a body of individuals organised for a special purpose: *a fire brigade*; *a brigade of chefs*.

brigadier /brɪgə'dɪə/ n. Army **1.** a commissioned officer in the Australian Army ranking below major general and above colonel. **2.** the rank. Abbrev.: BRIG

brigalow /'brɪgəloʊ/ n. a species of Acacia, A. harpophylla, extending over large areas of northern NSW and Qld.

brigand /'brɪgənd/ n. a bandit; one of a gang of robbers in mountain or forest regions. –**brigandish**, adj. –**brigandage**, n.

brigantine /'brɪgəntin/ n. a two-masted vessel in which the foremast is square-rigged and the mainmast bears a fore-and-aft mainsail and square topsails.

bright /braɪt/ adj. **1.** radiating or reflecting light; luminous; shining. **2.** filled with lights. **3.** (of a colour) strong, clear and vivid. **4.** glorious or splendid. **5.** clever or witty. **6.** lively; cheerful, as a person. **7.** favourable or hopeful: *bright prospects*. –**brighten**, v. –**brightly**, adv. –**brightness**, n.

brilliant /'brɪljənt/ adj. **1.** shining brightly; sparkling; glittering; lustrous. **2.** distinguished; illustrious: *a brilliant achievement*. **3.** having or showing great intelligence or mental ability. –n. **4.** a diamond (or other gem) of a particular cut, typically round in outline and shaped like two pyramids united at their bases, the top one cut off near the base and the bottom one close to the apex, with many facets on the slopes. –**brilliance**, n. –**brilliantly**, adv. –**brilliantness**, n.

brim /brɪm/ n. **1.** the upper edge of anything hollow; rim: *the brim of a cup*. **2.** a projecting edge: *the brim of a hat*. –v.i. (**brimmed, brimming**) **3.** to be full to the brim; to be full to overflowing: *a brimming glass*.

brindled /'brɪndld/ adj. grey or tawny with darker streaks or spots. Also, **brinded** /'brɪndəd/.

brine /braɪn/ n. water saturated or strongly impregnated with salt. –**brinish**, adj.

bring /brɪŋ/ v.t. (**brought, bringing**) **1.** to cause to come with oneself; take along to the place or person sought; conduct or convey. **2.** to cause to come, as to a recipient or possessor, to the mind or knowledge, into a particular position or state, to a particular opinion or decision, or into existence, view, action, or effect. **3.** to lead or induce: *he couldn't bring himself to do it*. **4.** to yield as proceeds; sell for: *the car brought $2000*. –phr. **5. bring about, a.** to cause; accomplish. **b.** Naut. to turn (a ship) on to the opposite tack. **6. bring back, a.** to restore: *to bring back corporal punishment*. **b.** to recall to the mind; remind one of. **7. bring down, a.** to shoot down or cause to fall (a plane, animal, footballer, etc.). **b.** to reduce (a price); lower in price. **c.** to humble, subdue, or cause to fail: *to bring down a government*. **d.** to introduce (proposed legislation): *to bring down a bill*. **8. bring forth, a.** to produce. **b.** to give rise to; cause. **9. bring forward, a.** to produce to view. **b.** to adduce. **c.** Accounting to transfer (a figure) to the top of the next column. **d.** to move or transfer (a meeting, appointment, etc.) to an earlier time or date. **10. bring in, a.** to introduce. **b.** to produce (a verdict). **c.** to produce; yield (an income, cash, etc.). **d.** NZ to bring (land) into cultivation. **11. bring into effect,** to cause to operate or function: *the government will bring into effect new road safety regulations*. **12. bring into the world,** to cause to come into being; give birth to. **13. bring off, a.** to bring to a successful conclusion; achieve. **b.** to bring away from a ship, etc. **c.** to induce an orgasm in. **14. bring on, a.** to induce; cause. **b.** to

cause to advance in growth, development, etc. **c.** to excite sexually, so as to induce orgasm. **15. bring out, a.** to expose; show; reveal. **b.** to encourage (a timid or diffident person). **c.** to publish. **d.** to formally introduce (a young woman) into society. **e.** to instruct (workers, etc.) to leave work and go on strike. **16. bring over,** to convince; convert. **17. bring round, a.** to convince of an opinion. **b.** to restore to consciousness, as after a faint. **18. bring to, a.** to bring (someone) back to consciousness. **b.** Naut. to head (a ship) close to or into the wind and kill its headway by manipulating helm and sails. **19. bring to light,** to reveal or expose, as secret corrupt activities or practices. **20. bring under,** to subdue. **21. bring up, a.** to care for during childhood; rear. **b.** to introduce to notice or consideration. **c.** to cause to advance, as troops. **d.** to vomit. **e.** Naut. to stop (a ship); make fast to a buoy or quay, etc. **22. bring up with a jolt,** to cause to stop suddenly, especially for reappraisal.

brink /brɪŋk/ n. **1.** the edge or margin of a steep place or of land bordering water. **2.** any extreme edge; verge.

brinkmanship /'brɪŋkmənʃɪp/ n. the practice of courting disaster, especially nuclear war, to gain one's ends.

briny /'braɪni/ adj. (**-nier, -niest**) **1.** of or like brine; salty. –phr. **2. the briny,** Colloq. the sea. –**brininess**, n.

briquette /brɪ'kɛt/ n. a moulded block of compacted coal dust for fuel. Also, **briquet**.

brisk /brɪsk/ adj. **1.** quick and active; lively: *a brisk breeze, a brisk walk*. **2.** sharp and stimulating: *brisk weather*. **3.** (of alcoholic drinks) effervescing vigorously: *brisk cider*. –**briskish**, adj. –**briskly**, adv. –**briskness**, n.

brisket /'brɪskət/ n. **1.** the breast of an animal, or the part of the breast lying next to the ribs. **2.** this portion used as meat.

bristle /'brɪsəl/ n. **1.** one of the short, stiff, coarse hairs of certain animals, especially swine, used in making brushes, etc. –v.i. (**-tled, -tling**) **2.** to stand or rise stiffly, like bristles. **3.** to erect the bristles, as an irritated animal: *the dog bristled*. **4.** to be thickly set with something suggestive of bristles: *the plain bristled with bayonets; the enterprise bristled with difficulties*. **5.** to be visibly roused to anger, hostility, or resistance. –**bristly**, adj.

brittle /'brɪtl/ adj. **1.** breaking readily with a comparatively smooth fracture, as glass. **2.** tense; irritable. **3.** strained; insincere. –n. **4.** a sweet made with treacle and nuts: *peanut brittle*. –**brittleness**, n.

broach /broʊtʃ/ n. **1.** Mechanics a long, tapering tool with a notched edge which enlarges a hole as the tool is pulled through. **2.** a spit for roasting meat. **3.** a boring tool for tapping wine containers. –v.t. **4.** to enlarge and finish with a broach. **5.** to tap or pierce. **6.** to mention for the first time: *to broach a subject*. –**broacher**, n.

broad /brɔd/ adj. **1.** wide; of great extent from one side to the other: *a broad street; a broad stripe*. **2.** of great extent in all directions: *a broad plain*. **3.** of extensive range or scope: *broad interests; broad experience*. **4.** main or general: *the broad outlines of a subject*. **5.** plain or clear; not subtle: *a broad hint*. **6.** coarse; indelicate: *a broad joke*. **7.** (of pronunciation) strongly dialectal: *broad Scots*. –adv. **8.** fully: *broad awake*. –n. **9.** the broad part of anything. **10.** Colloq. (taboo) a woman. –phr. **11. broad daylight,** the full light of day. –**broaden**, v. –**broadish**, adj. –**broadly**, adv.

broadband /'brɔdbænd/ n. **1.** high-speed internet access having a bandwidth sufficient to carry multiple voice, video, and data channels simultaneously. –adj. **2.** (of an electronic device or circuit) capable of functioning over a wide range of frequencies. **3.** of or relating to internet broadband access.

broad-based /ˈbrɔd-beɪsd/ *adj.* taking into account a wide range of factors: *a broad-based approach.* Also, **broadbased**.

broad bean *n.* an erect annual herb, *Vicia faba*, of the family Fabaceae, often cultivated for its large edible seeds; faba bean.

broadbill /ˈbrɔdbɪl/ *n.* **1.** any of various birds with a broad bill, as the shoveler and spoonbill. **2.** → **swordfish**.

broadbrush /ˈbrɔdbrʌʃ/ *adj.* wide-ranging and general in treatment: *a broadbrush policy outline.*

broadcast /ˈbrɔdkast/ *verb* (**-cast** *or* **-casted**, **-casting**) –*v.t.* **1.** to send (sound and images) by radio or television. **2.** to sow (seed) by scattering. **3.** to spread (information, gossip, etc.). –*v.i.* **4.** to broadcast radio or television signals. –*n.* **5.** *TV, Radio* **a.** the sending out of sound and images. **b.** a radio or television program. –**broadcaster**, *n.*

broad jump *n.* → **long jump**.

broadleaf /ˈbrɔdlif/ *n.* **1.** any of various trees or shrubs having broad leaves. –*adj.* **2.** having broad leaves.

broad-minded *adj.* free from prejudice or bigotry; liberal; tolerant. –**broad-mindedly**, *adv.* –**broad-mindedness**, *n.*

broadsheet /ˈbrɔdʃit/ *n.* **1.** a sheet of paper, especially of large size, printed on one side only, as for distribution or posting. **2.** a ballad, song, tract, etc., printed or originally printed on a broadsheet. **3.** a newspaper printed on the standard sheet size of paper, usually giving greater depth of reporting than a tabloid. –*adj.* **4.** (of a ballad) printed or originally printed on a broadsheet. **5.** relating to or as in a broadsheet.

broadside /ˈbrɔdsaɪd/ *n.* **1.** *Naut.* the whole side of a ship above the waterline, from the bow to the quarter. **2.** *Navy* all the guns that can be fired to one side of a ship. **3.** any comprehensive attack, as of criticism. **4.** any broad surface or side, as of a house. –*adv.* **5.** broadways.

broadwalk /ˈbrɔdwɔk/ *n.* a wide promenade.

broadways /ˈbrɔdweɪz/ *adv.* (sometimes fol. by *on*) breadthways; along or across the breadth; laterally. Also, *esp. US,* **broadwise** /ˈbrɔdwaɪz/.

brocade /brəˈkeɪd/ *n.* **1.** fabric woven with an elaborate design from any yarn. The right side has a raised effect. –*v.t.* **2.** to weave with a design or figure. –**brocaded**, *adj.*

broccoli /ˈbrɒkəli, -lə/ *n.* **1.** a plant, *Brassica oleracea* var. *italica*, of the mustard family, resembling the cauliflower. **2.** the green head of this plant used as a vegetable. Also, **broccoli sprouts**.

brochure /ˈbroʊʃə, brəˈʃʊə/ *n.* a booklet, or piece of folded paper, containing printed advertising or information.

brogue[1] /broʊg/ *n.* a broad accent, especially Irish, in the pronunciation of English.

brogue[2] /broʊg/ *n.* a strongly made, comfortable type of ordinary shoe, often with decorative perforations on the vamp and upper.

broil /brɔɪl/ *v.t.* **1.** to cook by direct radiant heat, as on a gridiron or griller, or under an electric coil, gas grill or the like; grill. –*v.i.* **2.** to be subjected to great heat. –**broiling**, *n.* –**broiled**, *adj.*

broke /broʊk/ *v.* **1.** past tense of **break**. **2.** *Archaic or Colloq.* past participle of **break**. –*adj.* **3.** *Colloq.* out of money; bankrupt. –*phr. Colloq.* **4. broke to the wide**, completely out of money. **5. flat** (or **stony**) **broke**, completely out of money. **6. go for broke**, **a.** (in gambling, investment, etc.) to risk all one's capital in the hope of very large gain. **b.** to take a major risk in pursuing an activity, objective, etc., to its extreme.

broken /ˈbroʊkən/ *v.* **1.** past participle of **break**. –*adj.* **2.** torn; ruptured; fractured. **3.** not complete;

fragmentary: *a broken set.* **4.** (of a machine, etc.) not working properly. **5.** disregarded or disobeyed; infringed; violated: *a broken law.* **6.** interrupted or discontinuous: *broken sleep.* **7.** (of ground) rough or uneven. **8.** (of water) with a disturbed surface as choppy water, surf, etc. **9.** (of weather) patchy; unsettled. **10.** weakened in strength, spirit, etc. **11.** tamed: *the horse was not yet broken to the saddle.* **12.** imperfectly spoken, as language: *he spoke broken English.* **13.** ruined; bankrupt. –**brokenly**, *adv.* –**brokenness**, *n.*

broken-down *adj.* **1.** shattered or collapsed. **2.** having given way to despair. **3.** unserviceable (of machinery, electronic equipment, etc.).

broker /ˈbroʊkə/ *n.* **1.** an agent who buys or sells for a principal on a commission basis without having title to the property. **2.** a middleman or agent. –*v.t.* **3.** to negotiate (a deal, etc.).

brolga /ˈbrɒlgə/ *n.* a large, silvery-grey crane, *Grus rubicunda*, of northern and eastern Australia which performs an elaborate dance, perhaps as part of a courtship display.

brolly /ˈbrɒli/ *n.* (*pl.* **-lies**) *Colloq.* an umbrella.

bromance /ˈbroʊmæns/ *n. Colloq.* a non-sexual but intense friendship between two males.

bromide /ˈbroʊmaɪd/ *n. Chem.* a compound usually containing two elements only, one of which is bromine.

bromine /ˈbroʊmin, -aɪn/ *n. Chem.* an element, a dark-reddish fuming liquid, resembling chlorine and iodine in chemical properties. *Symbol*: Br; *atomic number*: 35; *relative atomic mass*: 79.909. See **halogen**.

bronchi /ˈbrɒŋki/ *n.* plural of **bronchus**.

bronchial /ˈbrɒŋkiəl/ *adj.* relating to the bronchia or bronchi.

bronchitis /brɒŋˈkaɪtəs/ *n.* a inflammation of the membrane lining of the bronchial tubes. –**bronchitic** /brɒŋˈkɪtɪk/, *adj.*

broncho- a word element meaning 'bronchial'. Also, **bronch-**.

bronchus /ˈbrɒŋkəs/ *n.* (*pl.* **-chi** /-kaɪ/) either of the two air passages connecting the trachea and the lungs.

bronco /ˈbrɒŋkoʊ/ *n.* (*pl.* **-cos**) **1.** *Chiefly US* a pony or mustang, especially one that is not broken, or is only imperfectly broken in. **2.** *Aust.* a strong horse used in cattle branding. Also, **broncho**, **bronc**, **bronk**.

brontosaurus /brɒntəˈsɔrəs/ *n.* a large amphibious herbivorous dinosaur of the American Jurassic, properly called apatosaurus.

bronze /brɒnz/ *n.* **1.** *Metallurgy* **a.** a durable brown alloy, consisting essentially of copper and tin. **b.** any of various other copper base alloys, such as aluminium bronze, manganese bronze, silicon bronze, etc. The term implies a product superior in some way to brass. **2.** a metallic brownish colour. **3.** a work of art, as a statue, statuette, bust, or medal, composed of bronze, whether cast or wrought. –*v.t.* **4.** to give the appearance or colour of bronze to. **5.** to make brown, as by exposure to the sun. –**bronzy**, *adj.* –**bronzed**, *adj.*

Bronze Age *n.* the age in human history (between the Stone and Iron Ages) marked by the use of bronze implements.

brooch /broʊtʃ/ *n.* a clasp or ornament for the dress, having a pin at the back for passing through the clothing and a catch for securing the pin.

brood /brud/ *n.* **1.** a number of young creatures produced or hatched at one time; a family of offspring or young. **2.** breed or kind. –*v.t.* **3.** to sit as a bird over (eggs or young); incubate. **4.** to dwell persistently or moodily in thought on; ponder. –*v.i.* **5.** to meditate with morbid persistence. –**broody**, *adj.*

brook[1] /brʊk/ *n.* a small, natural stream of fresh water; creek.

brook[2] /brʊk/ *v.t.* (*usu. in a negative sentence*) to bear; suffer; tolerate.

broom /brum/ *n.* **1.** a sweeping implement consisting of a flat brush of bristles, nylon, etc., on a long handle. **2.** a sweeping implement consisting of a bunch of twigs or plant stems on a handle; besom. **3.** any of certain plants of the family Fabaceae, especially species with leafless stems and yellow flowers. –**broomy**, *adj.*

broth /brɒθ/ *n.* **1.** thin soup of concentrated meat or fish stock. **2.** a decoction of water in which meat or fish has been boiled, with vegetables or barley added.

brothel /ˈbrɒθəl/ *n.* **1.** a house of prostitution. **2.** *Aust. Colloq.* any room in a disorderly state.

brother /ˈbrʌðə/ *n.* (*pl.* **brothers** *or*, *Archaic*, **brethren**) **1.** a male child of the same parents as another (**full brother** or **brother-german**). **2.** a male child of only one of one's parents (**half-brother**). **3.** a male member of the same kinship group, nationality, profession, etc.; an associate; a fellow countryman, fellow man, etc. **4.** (*pl.*) all members of a particular race, or of the human race in general. **5. a.** a male lay member of a religious organisation which has a priesthood. **b.** a man who devotes himself to the duties of a religious order without taking holy orders, or while preparing for holy orders. **6.** Also, **brudda.** *Aboriginal English* a term used to express solidarity with a man in what is not an actual kin relationship. **7.** a form of address, especially between African American men. **8.** a form of address or a title, especially in politically left-wing organisations. –**brotherhood**, *n.* –**brotherly**, *adj.*

brother-in-law *n.* (*pl.* **brothers-in-law**) **1.** one's husband's or wife's brother. **2.** one's sister's husband. **3.** the husband of one's wife's or husband's sister.

brought /brɔt/ *v.* past tense and past participle of **bring**.

brouhaha /ˈbruhaha/ *n.* **1.** an uproar; turmoil. **2.** a scuffle; disturbance.

brow /braʊ/ *n.* **1.** the ridge over the eye. **2.** the hair growing on that ridge; eyebrow. **3.** (*sing. or pl.*) the forehead: *to knit one's brows.* **4.** the countenance. **5.** the edge of a steep place.

browbeat /ˈbraʊbit/ *v.t.* to intimidate by overbearing looks or words; bully.

brown /braʊn/ *n.* **1.** the colour of earth, a mixture of red, yellow and black. –*adj.* **2.** of the colour brown: *a brown horse.* **3.** having skin of that colour: *the Polynesians are a brown people.* **4.** sunburned or tanned. –*v.t.* **5.** to make brown. –*v.i.* **6.** to become brown. –**brownish**, *adj.* –**brownness**, *n.*

brown coal *n.* → **lignite.**

brown dwarf *n.* an astronomical body which is not of sufficient mass and temperature to produce hydrogen fusion and become a star.

brownfield /ˈbraʊnfild/ *adj.* of or relating to an urban site which has been previously developed or used: *a brownfield redevelopment.* Compare **greenfield.**

brown goods *pl. n.* electronic goods such as televisions, sound systems, videos, etc. Also, **browngoods.**

brown goshawk *n.* a hawk, *Accipiter fasciatus*, common throughout Australia, Indonesia, New Guinea and nearby islands; chickenhawk.

brownie /ˈbraʊni/ *n.* **1.** (in folklore) a little brown elf or sprite, especially one who helps secretly in household work. **2.** a loaf baked in a camp oven from a flour, fat, sugar, and water dough with currants and raisins added to it. **3.** a cake-like biscuit made of flour, butter, eggs, cocoa, and walnuts.

Brownie /ˈbraʊni/ *n.* (*also lower case*) a member of the junior division (ages 8–11) of the Guides; in Australia age divisions of the Guides phased out from 1996.

brownout /ˈbraʊnaʊt/ *n.* a partial blackout, resulting in a dimming of lights, sometimes imposed deliberately to conserve electricity or, as in World War II, to reduce the glare in the sky of big industrial cities.

brown pine *n.* a coniferous tree, *Podocarpus elatus*, of eastern Australia, the seeds of which are borne on a large blue-black fleshy receptacle.

brown rice *n.* rice from which the bran layers and germs have not been removed by polishing.

brown snake *n.* any of certain venomous Australian snakes of the genus *Pseudonaja*, brownish or olive in colour.

brown sugar *n.* unrefined or partially refined sugar.

browse /braʊz/ *v.i.* **1.** (of cattle, deer, etc.) to pasture; graze. **2.** to glance though merchandise in a shop. **3.** to glance at random through a book or books. **4.** *Computers* to search for information on the internet using a browser. –*v.t.* **5.** *Computers* to search for information on (the internet) using a browser.

browser /ˈbraʊzə/ *n.* software designed to facilitate searches on the World Wide Web and access to the contents of web pages. Also, **web browser.**

brucellosis /brusəˈloʊsəs/ *n.* infection with bacteria of the *Brucella* group, frequently causing abortions in animals and undulant fever in humans.

brudda /ˈbrʌdə/ *n.* *Aboriginal English* → **brother** (def. 6).

bruise /bruz/ *verb* (**bruised**, **bruising**) –*v.t.* **1.** to cause a discolouration by striking or pressing, without breaking the skin or drawing blood. **2.** to damage (fruit, etc.) by applying pressure, without breaking the skin. **3.** to hurt on the surface: *to bruise feelings; to bruise fruit.* **4.** to crush (drugs or food) by beating or pounding. –*v.i.* **5.** to develop a discoloured spot on the skin as the result of a blow, fall, etc. **6.** to be hurt: *his feelings bruise easily.* –*n.* **7.** an injury due to bruising; contusion. **8.** a damaged area on a piece of fruit, etc., due to bruising.

bruiser /ˈbruzə/ *n.* **1.** a boxer. **2.** *Colloq.* a rough or violent person, especially a young man; bully.

brumby /ˈbrʌmbi/ *n.* (*pl.* **-bies**) *Aust.*, *NZ* **1.** a wild horse, especially one descended from runaway stock. **2.** *Colloq.* the one thing in a group that is faulty or otherwise no good.

brummy /ˈbrʌmi/ *adj. Colloq.* shoddy; cheap.

brunch /brʌntʃ/ *n.* a midmorning meal that serves as both breakfast and lunch.

brunette /bruˈnet/ *adj.* **1.** (of hair) dark; brown. **2.** (of a person) having dark or brown hair, often with brown eyes and olive skin. –*n.* **3.** a woman or girl with dark hair.

brunt /brʌnt/ *n.* the shock or force of an attack, etc.; the main stress, force, or violence: *to bear the brunt of their criticism.*

bruschetta /brʊsˈketə, broˈʃetə/ *n.* grilled slices of bread brushed with olive oil and fresh garlic, often served with various toppings.

brush[1] /brʌʃ/ *n.* **1.** an instrument consisting of bristles, hair, or the like, set in or attached to a handle, used for painting, cleaning, polishing, rubbing, etc. **2.** an act of brushing; an application of a brush. **3.** the bushy tail of an animal, especially of a fox. **4.** *Colloq.* (*taboo*) **a.** the female pubic area. **b.** a woman, considered a sex object. **5.** the art or skill of a painter of pictures. **6.** a painter. **7.** a slight skimming touch or contact. **8.** a brief hostile encounter; argument; skirmish. **9.** *Elect.* **a.** a conductor serving to maintain electric contact between stationary and moving parts of a machine or other apparatus. **b.** → **brush discharge.** –*v.t.* **10.** to sweep, rub, clean, polish, etc., with or as with a brush. **11.** to touch lightly in passing; pass lightly over. **12.** to dress (the hair) using a brush. –*v.i.* **13.** to move or skim with a slight contact. –*phr.* **14. brush aside, a.** to remove by brushing or by lightly passing over. **b.** to ignore. **15. brush off,** to ignore or shun. **16. brush up, a.** to polish up; smarten. **b.** (sometimes fol. by *on*) to revise and renew or improve one's skill. **17. with a broad brush**, employing a wide-ranging and general approach, so as to cover the most significant features without focusing on detail: *to outline the issue with a broad brush.* –**brushy**, *adj.*

brush² /brʌʃ/ *n.* **1.** a dense growth of low-growing bushes, shrubs, bracken, etc.; scrub; a thicket. **2.** such vegetation cut and used as a building material: *a shed made of brush.* –*adj.* **3.** made of brush (def. 2). –**brushy**, *adj.*

brush discharge *n. Elect.* → **corona discharge**. Also, **brush**.

brush fence *n.* a fence made from brush, wired together in sections.

brush-tailed bettong *n.* → **woylie**.

brush turkey *n.* a large mound-building bird, *Alectura lathami*, of the wooded regions of eastern Australia. Also, **scrub turkey**.

brushwood /'brʌʃwʊd/ *n.* **1.** branches of trees cut or broken off. **2.** densely growing small trees and shrubs. **3.** the branches of various shrubs, especially of *Melaleuca uncinata*, family Myrtaceae, of drier parts of southern Australia, bound with wire and used to make fences.

brusque /brʌsk, brʊsk/ *adj.* abrupt in manner; blunt; rough: *a brusque welcome.* –**brusquely**, *adv.* –**brusqueness**, *n.*

brussels sprout /brʌsəlz 'spraʊt/ *n.* **1.** a plant, *Brassica oleracea* var. *gemmifera*, having small edible heads or sprouts along the stalk, which resemble miniature cabbage heads. **2.** one of the heads or sprouts themselves. Also, **brussel sprout**, **sprout**.

brutal /'brutl/ *adj.* **1.** savage; cruel; inhuman. **2.** crude; coarse; harsh. –**brutalise**, **brutalize**, *v.* –**brutality** /bru-'tælətɪ/, *n.* –**brutish**, *adj.* –**brutally**, *adv.*

brute /brut/ *n.* **1.** a non-human animal; beast. **2.** a brutal person. **3.** *Colloq.* a selfish or unsympathetic person. **4.** the animal qualities, desires, etc., of man: *the brute in him came out.* –*adj.* **5.** lacking reason, consciousness or intelligence; inhuman; irrational: *brute strength*; *the brute mind.*

BSB number /bi ɛs 'bi nʌmbə/ *n.* (in financial transactions) a number which indicates the bank, state and branch of an account.

BSE /bi ɛs 'i/ *n.* → **mad cow disease**.

bubble /'bʌbəl/ *n.* **1. a.** a small ball of gas in or rising through a liquid. **b.** a small ball of gas in a thin liquid envelope. **2.** a cavity filled with air or gas, in amber, glass, etc. **3.** something that is not real or firm, or does not last; a delusion. –*v.i.* **4.** to send up bubbles; effervesce. **5.** (oft. fol. by *over*) to be full of good humour or high spirits: *she bubbled over with enthusiasm.* **6.** to flow or run with a gurgling noise; gurgle: *a bubbling pot.*

bubble-and-squeak *n.* **1.** any mix of left-over vegetables, especially potato and cabbage, fried together. **2.** *Brit.* a dish of beef and cabbage fried together.

bubblegum /'bʌbəlgʌm/ *n.* a type of chewing gum which can be blown into bubbles.

bubbler /'bʌblə/ *n. Aust.* a drinking fountain.

bubble wrap *n.* a plastic wrapping material consisting of innumerable small, sealed air pockets, used for protecting delicate items during transport or storage.

bubble writing *n.* a lettering style in which the characters are given a two-dimensional outline in a fluid rounded shape.

bubbly /'bʌblɪ/ *adj.* (**-lier, -liest**) **1.** containing bubbles; bubbling. **2.** sparkling and effervescent: *a bubbly personality.* –*n.* **3.** *Colloq.* champagne.

bubonic plague /bjuˌbɒnɪk 'pleɪg/ *n.* → **plague** (def. 2).

buccaneer /bʌkə'nɪə/ *n.* a pirate. –**buccaneering**, *n., adj.*

buck¹ /bʌk/ *n.* **1.** the male of certain animals, as the deer, antelope, rabbit, or hare. **2.** a young man viewed as a sexual animal; a fop; dandy. –*adj.* **3.** *Obs.* relating to an all-male performance or attendance: *a buck spree.*

buck² /bʌk/ *v.i.* **1.** (of a saddle or pack animal) to leap with arched back and come down with head low and foregs stiff, in order to dislodge rider or pack. –*v.t.* **2.** to throw or attempt to throw (a rider) by bucking. **3.** *Colloq.* to resist obstinately; object strongly to: *to buck the system.* –*n.* **4.** an act of bucking. –*phr.* **5. buck at**, to resist obstinately; object strongly to. **6. buck up**, *Colloq.* **a.** to become more cheerful, vigorous, etc. **b.** to make (someone) more cheerful, vigorous, etc. **c.** *Chiefly Brit.* to make an effort. **d.** an exclamation urging someone to hurry. **7. give it a buck**, *Aust., NZ Colloq.* to make an attempt; chance it. **8. have a buck at**, *Aust., NZ Colloq.* to try; make an attempt at. –**bucker**, *n.*

buck³ /bʌk/ *phr.* **pass the buck**, *Colloq.* to shift the responsibility or blame to another person.

buck⁴ /bʌk/ *n.* **1.** *Colloq.* a dollar. –*phr.* **2. a fast** (or **quick**) **buck**, money earned with little effort, often by dishonest means.

bucket /'bʌkət/ *n.* **1.** a vessel, usually round with flat bottom and a semicircular handle, for carrying water, sand, etc. **2.** one of the scoops attached to or forming the endless chain in certain types of conveyers or elevators. **3.** a cupped vane of a water wheel, turbine, etc. **4.** a bucketful. **5.** (*pl.*) *Colloq.* a large quantity: *buckets of fun*; *buckets of money.* –*v.t.* (**bucketed, bucketing**) **6.** *Colloq.* to criticise strongly. –*phr.* **7. bucket about**, to shake or toss jerkily. **8. bucket down**, (of rain) to pour down heavily. **9. empty** (or **tip**) **the bucket on**, *Colloq.* to make damaging accusations or derogatory statements about. **10. kick the bucket**, *Colloq.* to die. –**bucketful** /'bʌkətfʊl/, *n.*

bucket list *n. Colloq.* a list of activities or experiences which a person feels they must undertake before they die.

bucket seat *n.* (in a car, etc.) a seat with a rounded or moulded back, to hold one person. Also, **bucket**.

bucket shop *n.* **1.** a firm of share or commodity brokers whose business is speculative and conducted along questionable lines. **2.** a business which offers services at a discount such as a travel agent which sells cheap airline tickets.

buckjump /'bʌkdʒʌmp/ *v.i.* (of a horse) to buck.

buckle /'bʌkəl/ *n.* **1.** a clasp consisting of a rectangular or curved rim with one or more movable tongues, used for fastening together two loose ends, as of a belt or strap. **2.** any similar contrivance used for such a purpose. **3.** a bend, bulge, or kink, as in a saw blade. –*v.t.* **4.** to fasten with a buckle or buckles. **5.** to bend and shrivel, by applying heat or pressure; warp; curl. –*v.i.* **6.** to bend, warp, or give way suddenly, as with heat or pressure. –*phr.* **7. buckle** (**down**) **to**, to set to work at with vigour: *they buckled down to the job.* **8. buckle to**, to resume efforts in the face of difficulty. **9. buckle under**, **a.** to yield; give way. **b.** to give in; despair: *he buckled under to the pressure.* **10. buckle up**, to fix one's seatbelt in position.

Buckley's /'bʌkliz/ *Aust., NZ Colloq.* –*n.* Also, **Buckley's chance**, **Buckley's hope**. **1.** a very slim chance; forlorn hope. –*phr.* **2. Buckley's and none**, (*humorous*) two chances amounting to next to no chance.

buckminsterfullerene /ˌbʌkmɪnstəˌfʊlə'rin/ *n.* a molecule of spheroidal structure consisting of 60 carbon atoms arranged as 12 pentagonal and hexagonal interlocking faces. Also, **buckyball**.

buckram /'bʌkrəm/ *n.* stiff cotton fabric for interlining, binding books, etc.

bucks party *n. Aust.* a party in which only the bridegroom and his male associates participate, held as part of the preliminaries to a wedding. Also, **bucks' party**, **bucks' night**.

bucktooth /bʌk'tuθ/ *n.* (*pl.* **buckteeth** /-'tiθ/) a projecting tooth.

buckyball /'bʌkibɔl/ *n.* → **buckminsterfullerene**.

bucolic /bju'kɒlɪk/ *adj.* **1.** of or relating to shepherds; pastoral. **2.** rustic; rural; agricultural: *bucolic isolation.* Also, **bucolical.** –**bucolically**, *adv.*

bud[1] /bʌd/ *n. Bot.* **a.** a small axillary or terminal protuberance on a plant, containing rudimentary foliage (**leaf bud**), the rudimentary inflorescence (**flower bud**), or both (**mixed bud**). **b.** an undeveloped or rudimentary stem or branch of a plant. **c.** a vegetative outgrowth of yeasts and some bacteria. **2.** *Zool.* (in certain animals of low organisation) a prominence which develops into a new individual, sometimes permanently attached to the parent and sometimes becoming detached; gemma. **3.** *Anat.* any small rounded part, as a tactile bud or a gustatory bud. –*verb* (**budded, budding**) –*v.i.* **4.** to put forth or produce buds, as a plant. **5.** to begin to grow and develop. **6.** to be in an early stage of development. –*v.t.* **7.** to cause to bud. **8.** *Hort.* to graft by inserting a single bud into the stock. –*phr.* **9. nip in the bud**, to stop (something) before it gets under way.

bud[2] /bʌd/ *n. Colloq.* **1.** a friend; mate. **2.** *US Colloq.* an informal term of address.

Buddha Day /'budə deɪ/ *n.* → **Vesak**.

Buddhism /'budɪzəm/ *n.* the religion founded by Gautama Buddha which teaches that life is intrinsically full of suffering and that the supreme felicity (Nirvana) is achieved by destroying greed, hatred, and delusion. –**Buddhist**, *n.*, *adj.* –**Buddhistic** /bu'dɪstɪk/, *adj.*

buddy /'bʌdi/ *n.* (*pl.* **-dies**) **1.** *Colloq.* comrade; mate. **2.** someone who acts as either a mentor or a partner to another, as to provide emotional, physical or practical support with a particular task or undertaking.

buddy tape *v.t.* (**buddy taped, buddy taping**) **1.** to tape (a sprained or broken finger or toe) to the adjacent finger or toe to prevent movement and promote healing. –*n.* **2.** such a splinting of a finger or toe. –**buddy taping**, *n.*

budge /bʌdʒ/ *verb* (**budged, budging**) (*usu. with negative*) –*v.i.* **1.** to move slightly; give way. –*v.t.* **2.** to cause to budge.

budgerigar /'bʌdʒəri,ɡa/ *n.* a small nomadic endemic Australian parrot, *Melopsittacus undulatus*, of arid and semi-arid grasslands and woodlands; green and yellow with a blue tail in the wild, it has been widely domesticated and bred in many coloured varieties.

budget /'bʌdʒət/ *n.* **1.** an estimate, often itemised, of expected income and expenditure, or operating results, for a given period in the future. **2.** (*sometimes upper case*) estimates of government income and expenditure. **3.** a stock; a collection. –*v.t.* (**-eted, -eting**) **4.** to plan allotment of (funds, time, etc.). –*phr.* **5. budget for**, to allocate money, time, resources, etc., towards (something). –**budgetary** /'bʌdʒətri/, *adj.*

budgie /'bʌdʒi/ *n. Colloq.* a budgerigar.

buff[1] /bʌf/ *n.* **1.** a kind of thick leather, originally and properly made of buffalo skin but later also of other skins, light yellow with napped surface, used for making belts, pouches, etc. **2.** yellowish brown; medium or light tan. **3.** an enthusiast; an expert (sometimes self-proclaimed): *a wine buff.* **4.** *Colloq.* the bare skin. –*adj.* **5.** *Colloq.* physically toned; muscular: *buff bodies.* –*v.t.* **6.** to polish (metal) or to give a grainless finish of high lustre to (plated surfaces).

buff[2] /bʌf/ *v.t.* **1.** to reduce or deaden the force of, as a buffer. –*n.* **2.** a blow; a slap; a buffet.

buffalo /'bʌfəloʊ/ *n.* (*pl.* **-loes** *or* **-los** *or, especially collectively,* **-lo**) **1.** any of several species of bovine mammals native to parts of Asia and Africa, especially those valued as draught animals. **2.** (popularly) a bison.

buffalo grass *n.* **1.** a lawn grass, *Stenotaphrum secundatum*, coarse and springy with a dense growth of runners, grown in warm districts. **2.** any of many species of short grasses.

buffer[1] /'bʌfə/ *n.* **1.** anything serving to neutralise the shock of opposing forces. **2.** *Electronics* a circuit which links two electronic systems which cannot be joined directly together. **3.** *Computers* an area of temporary storage where data is held during computer operations. –*v.t.* **4.** *Chem.* to oppose a change of composition, especially of acidity or alkalinity.

buffer[2] /'bʌfə/ *n.* a device for polishing.

buffet[1] /'bʌfət/ *n.* **1.** a blow, as with the hand or fist. –*verb* (**-feted, -feting**) –*v.t.* **2.** to strike, as with the hand or fist. –*v.i.* **3.** to force one's way with a fight, struggle, etc. –**buffeter**, *n.*

buffet[2] /'bʌfeɪ, 'bʊfeɪ/ *n.* **1.** a counter, bar, or the like, for lunch or refreshments. **2.** a restaurant containing such a counter or bar. **3.** a meal so served. **4.** a sideboard or cabinet for holding china, plate, etc. –*adj.* **5.** (of a meal) spread on tables or buffets from which the guests serve themselves.

buffoon /bə'fun/ *n.* someone who amuses others by tricks, odd gestures and postures, jokes, etc. –**buffoonery** /bə'funəri/, *n.* –**buffoonish**, *adj.*

bufo /'bufoʊ/ *n.* **1.** (in Australia) the introduced toad *Bufo marinus*, now widespread and abundant in north-eastern Australia; cane toad. **2.** any toad of the genus *Bufo*.

bug /bʌɡ/ *n.* **1.** loosely, any insect, especially one with the forewings thickened at the base. Sucking mouth parts allow them to suck plant juices or to feed on animals, including humans. **2.** *Aust.* a Moreton Bay bug or Balmain bug. **3.** *Colloq.* an illness due to an infection. **4.** (*oft. pl.*) *Colloq.* a defect or difficulty: *to iron out the bugs.* **5.** *Computers* an error in a program or the machine itself, often undetected by the most stringent tests. **6.** a microphone hidden to record conversation. **7.** *Colloq.* an idea or subject with which one is obsessed: *He has a bug about the unions.* **8.** *Colloq.* an enthusiast; a person obsessed with an idea. –*v.t.* (**bugged, bugging**) **9.** to install a bug (def. 6) in (a room, etc.). **10.** *Colloq.* to annoy (someone).

bugbear /'bʌɡbɛə/ *n.* any source, real or imaginary, of needless fright or fear.

bugger /'bʌɡə/ *n.* **1.** (*taboo*) someone who practises bestiality or sodomy. **2.** *Colloq.* (*humorous*) a person: *come on, you old bugger.* **3.** *Colloq.* a contemptible person. **4.** *Colloq.* a nuisance, a difficulty; something unpleasant or nasty: *that recipe is a real bugger; it's a bugger of a day.* –*v.t.* **5.** (*taboo*) to practise bestiality or sodomy on. **6.** *Colloq.* to render incapable: *exercise buggers me for anything else.* **7.** *Colloq.* to render useless; ruin: *to have buggered the camera.* **8.** *Colloq.* to damn or curse, as an indication of contempt or dismissal: *bugger him, I'm going home; bugger it.* **9.** *Colloq.* to cause inconvenience to someone; delay. –*interj.* **10.** *Colloq.* a strong exclamation of annoyance, disgust, etc.: *oh, bugger!* –*phr. Colloq.* **11. bugger about** (or **around**), to mess about; fiddle around. **12. bugger all**, nothing, or next to nothing. **13. bugger off**, to remove oneself. **14. bugger up**, **a.** to cause damage to: *you've really buggered up the fridge.* **b.** to cause frustration or inconvenience to. **15. play silly** (or **funny**) **buggers**, to engage in time-wasting activities and frivolous behaviour.

buggery /'bʌɡəri/ *n.* **1.** anal intercourse with a human or with an animal; the practice of sodomy or bestiality. –*phr. Colloq.* **2. as** (**all**) **buggery**, an intensifier: *hot as* *buggery.* **3. go to buggery, a.** an exclamation of dismissal, contempt, etc. **b.** to deteriorate: *the school has gone to buggery since the principal left.* **4. like buggery**, an intensifier with adverbial force: *we ran like buggery; my arm hurts like buggery.* **5. off to buggery, a.** greatly off course; in error; astray. **b.** a long way away.

buggy /ˈbʌgi/ *n.* (*pl.* **-gies**) a two-wheeled horse-drawn carriage with or without a hood.

bugle /ˈbjugəl/ *n.* **1.** a cornet-like military wind instrument, usually metal, used for sounding signals and sometimes fitted with keys or valves. **2.** *Colloq.* nose. *–v.i.* **3.** to sound a bugle. **4.** to make a noise similar to the sound produced by a bugle. *–phr.* **5. on the bugle**, *Colloq.* **a.** smelly. **b.** of questionable quality or character; suspect; dubious. **–bugler**, *n.*

build /bɪld/ *verb* (**built** *or*, *Archaic*, **builded**, **building**) *–v.t. –v.i.* **1.** to construct (something relatively complex) by assembling and combining parts: *build a house; build an empire.* **2.** to establish, increase, and strengthen: *to build a business.* **3.** to base; form; construct: *to build one's hopes on promises.* **4.** to increase in number: *a crowd building in the foyer.* **5.** to increase in intensity: *the pressure is building.* **6.** to engage in the art or business of building. *–n.* **7.** manner or style of construction or formation: *a yacht with a sleek build; a person with a heavy build. –phr.* **8. build on, a.** Also, **build upon**. to use as a basis, in forming or constructing a plan, system of thought, etc.: *to build on the ideas of others.* **b.** to add a room or rooms to a house. **9. build out**, to obstruct the view from (a building) by erecting another building close to it. **10. build up, a.** to increase or strengthen: *to build up a business.* **b.** to claim public attention for (a person or product) by means of an advertising campaign. **c.** to fill in with houses: *to build up a new estate.* **11. build up to, a.** to prepare for. **b.** to increase gradually to. **–builder**, *n.*

building /ˈbɪldɪŋ/ *n.* **1.** a substantial structure with a roof and walls, as a shed, house, department store, etc. **2.** the act, business, or art of constructing houses, etc.

building society *n.* an organisation which uses money subscribed by its members as a fund for lending money to members, as for the purchase of homes.

build-up *n.* **1.** a gradual increase. **2.** (in northern Australia) the period just before the wet season when there is a gradual increase in heat and humidity.

built /bɪlt/ *v.* **1.** past tense and past participle of **build**. *–adj.* **2.** *Colloq.* (of a woman) big-breasted.

built-up area *n.* an area with a high density of buildings and habitation, usually one within which speed limits apply to traffic.

buk choy /bʌk ˈtʃɔɪ/ *n.* → **bok choy**.

bulb /bʌlb/ *n.* **1.** *Bot.* **a.** a storage organ, usually subterranean, having fleshy leaves and a stem reduced to a flat disc which roots from the underside, as in the onion, lily, etc. **b.** a plant growing from a bulb. **2.** any round, enlarged part, especially one at the end of a long, slender body: *the bulb of a thermometer.* **3.** *Elect.* the glass housing which contains the filament of an incandescent electric light globe. **–bulbous**, *adj.* **–bulbar** /ˈbʌlbə/, *adj.* **–bulblike**, *adj.*

bulbul /ˈbʊlbʊl/ *n.* any bird of the tropical Asian family Pycnonotidae, noted as songsters.

bulge /bʌldʒ/ *n.* **1.** a rounded part that swells out; protuberance; hump. *–verb* (**bulged**, **bulging**) *–v.i.* **2.** to form a bulge; be protuberant. *–v.t.* **3.** to swell (something) out. **–bulgy**, *adj.*

bulimia /bəˈlimiə/ *n.* **1.** a compulsive eating disorder marked by bouts of overeating followed by induced vomiting. **2.** morbidly voracious appetite. **–bulimic**, *adj., n.*

bulk /bʌlk/ *n.* **1.** magnitude in three dimensions: *a ship of great bulk.* **2.** the greater part; the main mass or body: *the bulk of a debt.* **3.** goods or cargo not in packages, boxes, bags, etc. **4.** the thickness of a printed work or paper relative to its weight. *–v.i.* **5.** to be of bulk, size, weight, or importance. *–adj.* **6.** packaged to be bought in large quantities at wholesale prices. *–phr.* **7. bulk up**, (of an athlete, etc.) to increase one's muscle mass, usually intentionally, as by performing body-building exercises and adjusting one's diet: *a protein powder that helps weightlifters bulk up.* **8. in bulk, a.** unpackaged. **b.** in large quantities. **–bulky**, *adj.*

bulkhead /ˈbʌlkhɛd/ *n.* **1.** *Naut.* one of the upright partitions dividing a ship into compartments. **2.** a similar partition in an aircraft, vehicle, etc.

bull[1] /bʊl/ *n.* **1.** an adult male of the domestic cow, with sexual organs intact and capable of reproduction. **2.** an adult male of any bovine animal, especially of the genus *Bos.* **3.** the male of various other large animals, as the elephant, whale, etc., the female of which is the cow. **4.** a violent or powerful, bull-like person. **5.** *Stock Exchange* someone who buys in the hope of selling later at a profit due to a rise in prices (opposed to *bear*). **6.** (in general business) someone who believes that conditions are or will be favourable. **7.** *Mil. Colloq.* polishing and cleaning of equipment. *–adj.* **8.** male: *a bull elephant.* **9.** bull-like; large. **10.** *Stock Exchange* relating to the bulls; marked by a rise in price: *a bull market.* *–v.t.* **11.** *Colloq.* (*taboo*) to have intercourse with (a woman). **12.** *Stock Exchange* **a.** to endeavour to raise the price of (stocks, etc.). **b.** to operate in, for a rise in price: *to bull the market. –phr.* **13. bull at a gate**, an impatient and headstrong person. **14. bull in a china shop**, an inept or clumsy person in a situation requiring care or tact. **15. not within a bull's roar**, *Aust., NZ* (sometimes fol. by *of*) nowhere near: *not within a bull's roar of Bourke.* **–bullish**, *adj.*

bull[2] /bʊl/ *n.* → **bullseye** (defs 1 and 2).

bull[3] /bʊl/ *Colloq. –n.* **1.** nonsense. *–v.t.* **2.** to lie to; dupe. *–v.i.* **3.** to boast; exaggerate. *–interj.* Also, **bulls**. **4.** an exclamation implying that what has been said is nonsensical or wrong.

bulla /ˈbʊlə, ˈbʌlə/ *n.* (*pl.* **bullae** /ˈbʊli, ˈbʌli/) **1.** a seal attached to an official document. **2.** *Pathol.* **a.** a large vesicle. **b.** a blister-like or bubble-like part of a bone.

Bullamakanka /bʊləməˈkæŋkə/ *n.* an imaginary remote town.

bull ant *n.* any of the large, aggressive, primitive ants of the genus *Myrmecia* having powerful jaws and a painful sting. Also, **bulldog ant**.

bull bar *n.* a metal grid placed in front of a motor vehicle to prevent damage to the vehicle in case of collision, especially with kangaroos, stray cattle, etc., on outback roads. Also, **bullbar**.

bulldog /ˈbʊldɒg/ *n.* a large-headed, short-haired, heavily built variety of dog, of comparatively small size but very muscular and vigorous.

bulldozer /ˈbʊldoʊzə/ *n.* **1.** a large tractor moving on tracks (def. 8) or wheels, having a vertical blade at the front end for moving earth, tree stumps, rocks, etc. **2.** *Colloq.* someone who intimidates. **–bulldoze**, *v.*

bulldust /ˈbʊldʌst/ *n. Colloq.* **1.** *Aust.* fine dust on outback roads. **2.** *Aust., NZ* → **bullshit**.

bullet /ˈbʊlət/ *n.* **1.** a small metal projectile, part of a cartridge, for firing from small arms. **2.** a small ball. **3.** a recording which is moving rapidly up the popularity chart. **4.** a heavy dot used in a document to make a particular passage of text more prominent. **5.** *Colloq.* dismissal from employment: *to get the bullet.*

bulletin /ˈbʊlətən/ *n.* **1.** a short account or statement, as of news or events. **2.** a regular publication, as of a society.

bulletin board *n.* **1.** *US* → **noticeboard**. **2.** an electronic message directory accessible on a computer. **3.** a computer file accessed by users on networked terminals or other computers for posting or reading messages.

bullfight /ˈbʊlfaɪt/ *n.* a combat between men and a bull or bulls in an enclosed arena. **–bullfighter**, *n.* **–bullfighting**, *n.*

bull-headed /bʊl-ˈhɛdəd/ *adj.* **1.** obstinate; blunderingly stubborn; stupid. **–adv. 2.** obstinately. **–phr. 3. go bull-headed at**, to undertake aggressively or blunderingly.

bullion /ˈbʊljən/ *n.* **1.** gold or silver in the mass. **2.** gold or silver in the form of bars or ingots.

bull market *n. Stock Exchange* a period of busy trading during and after a rise in share prices when traders consider that further price rises are likely.

bullock /ˈbʊlək/ *n.* **1.** a castrated male of a bovine animal, not having been used for reproduction; ox; steer. **–v.t. 2.** to force: *to bullock one's way through.*

bullocky /ˈbʊləki/ *n.* (*pl.* **-kies**) *Aust., NZ* the driver of a bullock team.

bullroarer /ˈbʊlrɔrə/ *n.* a long, thin, narrow piece of wood attached to a string, by which it is whirled in the air, making a roaring sound, used for religious rites by some societies, as Australian Aborigines, Native Americans, etc., and as a children's toy.

bullseye /ˈbʊlzaɪ/ *n.* **1.** the central spot, usually black, of a target. **2.** a shot that strikes the bullseye. **3.** a small circular opening or window. **4.** a big, round, hard sweet, often of peppermint. **5.** a reddish-pink, large-eyed, marine fish of the family Priacanthidae common along the eastern coast of Australia.

bull shark *n.* a large and aggressive shark, *Carcharhinus leucas*, with a short blunt snout and triangular serrated teeth; found in tropical and subtropical coastal waters.

bullshit /ˈbʊlʃɪt/ *Colloq.* (*taboo*) **–n. 1.** an account, explanation, creative fantasy, etc., which is fabricated or contrived either to delude oneself or to deceive. **2.** nonsense. **–verb** (**-shitted**, **-shitting**) **–v.t. 3.** to deceive; outwit. **–v.i. 4.** to be untruthful, especially by boastful exaggeration: *to bullshit about sporting achievements.* **–interj. 5.** an expression of contemptuous disbelief. Also, **bulldust**. **–bullshitter**, *n.*

bull-terrier *n.* one of a breed of dogs produced by crossing the bulldog and the terrier.

bully /ˈbʊli/ *n.* (*pl.* **-lies**) **1.** a blustering, quarrelsome, overbearing person who browbeats smaller or weaker people. **2.** someone who intimidates or demeans another, especially as by repeated threats to their person, career, or social standing, or by harassment in person, on social networks, etc. **–verb** (**-lied**, **-lying**) **–v.t. 3.** to act the bully towards. **–v.i. 4.** to be loudly arrogant and overbearing. **phr. 5. bully for ...**, (*now usually ironic*) an exclamation indicating support and praise for a person or persons specified.

bullycide /ˈbʊlisaɪd/ *n. Orig. US* suicide which is a reaction to being bullied.

bulrush /ˈbʊlrʌʃ/ *n.* **1.** (in biblical use) the papyrus, *Cyperus papyrus*. **2.** any of various large rushes or rush-like plants of the genus *Scirpus*, as *S. lacustris*, a tall perennial from which mats, bottoms of chairs, etc., are made. Also, **bull-rush**.

bulwark /ˈbʊlwək/ *n.* **1.** *Fortifications* a defensive mound of earth or other material situated round a place; a rampart. **2.** any protection against annoyance or injury from outside.

bum[1] /bʌm/ *Colloq.* **–n. 1.** the rump; buttocks. **–phr. 2. bums on seats**, the number of people attracted to attend an entertainment or event, watch a television show, etc., or buy seats in a train, aeroplane, etc.

bum[2] /bʌm/ *Colloq.* **–n. 1.** a shiftless or dissolute person. **2.** a habitual loafer or tramp. **–verb** (**bummed**,

bumming) **–v.t. 3.** to get for nothing; borrow without expectation of returning: *to bum a cigarette.* **–v.i. 4.** to live at the expense of others; lead an idle or dissolute life. **–adj. 5.** of poor, wretched, or miserable quality; bad. **6.** (of a musical note) out of tune; badly executed. **–phr. 7. bum a ride** (or **a lift**), to appeal successfully for a free ride in a car, etc.

bumble /ˈbʌmbəl/ *v.i.* **1.** to proceed clumsily or inefficiently: *to bumble along.* **–v.t. 2.** to mismanage: *the government bumbled its way through crisis after crisis.*

bumblebee /ˈbʌmbəlbi/ *n.* **1.** Also, **humblebee**. any of various large, hairy social bees of the family Bombidae. **2.** an Australian gobiid fish, *Lindemanella iota*.

bumfluff /ˈbʌmflʌf/ *n. Colloq.* light hair growing on the face of an adolescent male.

bummer /ˈbʌmə/ *n. Colloq.* something which causes disappointment: *losing my wallet was a real bummer.*

bump /bʌmp/ *v.t.* **1.** to come more or less heavily in contact with; strike; collide with. **2.** to cause to strike or collide: *to bump one's head against the wall.* **–v.i. 3.** (sometimes fol. by *against*) to come in contact; collide. **–n. 4.** the act of bumping; a blow. **5.** a dull thud; the noise of collision. **6.** the shock of a blow or collision. **7.** a swelling or contusion from a blow. **8.** a small area raised above the level of the surrounding surface, as on the skull or on a road. **–phr. 9. bump about**, to jolt in the course of movement. **10. bump and grind**, *Colloq.* a sexually aggressive dance movement, usually performed by female dancers, in which the pelvis is both thrust forwards and backwards and rotated. **11. bump into, a.** to collide with. **b.** to meet by chance. **12. bump off**, *Colloq.* to kill. **13. bump up**, *Colloq.* to increase (in extent, etc.). **–bumpy**, *adj.*

bumper /ˈbʌmpə/ *n.* **1.** → **bumper bar**. **2.** a cup or glass filled to the brim, especially when drunk as a toast. **3.** something unusually large or full. **4.** *Aust., NZ Colloq.* a cigarette end; a discarded cigarette, partly smoked. **5.** *Cricket* a ball which is so bowled that it bounces high when it pitches; bouncer. **–adj. 6.** unusually abundant: *bumper crops.* **7.** large: *a bumper packet of cornflakes.* **–phr. 8. bumper to bumper**, (of traffic) congested and moving very slowly.

bumper bar *n.* a horizontal bar affixed to the front or rear of a vehicle to give some protection in collisions.

bumpkin /ˈbʌmpkən/ *n.* an awkward, clumsy yokel.

bumptious /ˈbʌmpʃəs/ *adj.* offensively self-assertive: *he's a bumptious young upstart.* **–bumptiously**, *adv.* **–bumptiousness**, *n.*

bun /bʌn/ *n.* **1.** a kind of bread roll, usually slightly sweetened and round-shaped, and sometimes containing spice, dried currants, etc. **2.** hair arranged on the head in a bun shape. **3.** (*pl.*) *Colloq.* the buttocks. **–phr. 4. do one's bun**, *NZ Colloq.* to lose one's temper. **5. have a bun in the oven**, *Colloq.* to be pregnant.

bunch /bʌntʃ/ *n.* **1.** a connected group; cluster: *a bunch of bananas.* **2.** a group of things; lot: *a bunch of papers.* **3.** *Colloq.* a group of human beings: *a fine bunch of boys.* **4.** a knob; lump; protuberance. **–v.t. 5.** to group together; make a bunch of. **–bunchy**, *adj.*

bundle /ˈbʌndl/ *n.* **1.** a group loosely held together: *a bundle of hay.* **2.** something wrapped for carrying; package. **3.** a number of things considered together. **–v.t. 4.** to tie or wrap in a bundle. **5. a.** *Computers* to include (software) with computer hardware at the same price. **b.** to include (one or more extra items) with an item at the same price: *to bundle the CD with the book.* **–v.i. 6.** to sleep or lie in the same bed without undressing, especially of lovers. **–phr. 7. bundle off** (or **out**), **a.** to send hurriedly or unceremoniously. **b.** to go hurriedly or unceremoniously. **8. bundle up, a.** to dress (someone) snugly. **b.** to collect in a bundle or bundles: *let's bundle up the newspapers for recycling.* **c.** to dress

warmly: *they bundled up before going out into the cold.*
9. drop one's bundle, *Aust., NZ Colloq.* to give up, especially out of a sense of despair or inadequacy. –**bundler,** *n.* –**bundling,** *n.*

bundy¹ /ˈbʌndi/ (*from trademark*) –*n.* (*pl.* **-dies**) **1.** a clock which marks the time on a card inserted in it, used to record arrival and departure times of employees; time clock. –*phr.* (*v.* **-died, -dying**) **2. bundy off,** to finish work by putting one's card into a bundy. **3. bundy on,** to start work by putting one's card into the bundy. **4. punch the bundy,** *Colloq.* to begin work.

bundy² /ˈbʌndi/ *n.* (*pl.* **-dies**) any of several species of *Eucalyptus,* especially *E. goniocalyx,* a rough-barked tree of south-eastern Australia.

bung¹ /bʌŋ/ *n.* **1.** a stopper, as for the hole of a cask. –*v.t.* **2.** Also, **bung up.** to close up with or as with a bung. **3.** *Colloq.* to put, especially hurriedly or carelessly: *bung it in the cupboard.* **4.** *Colloq.* to toss to another person; throw. –*phr.* **5. bung it on, a.** to behave temperamentally. **b.** to act in a pretentious or ostentatious manner. **6. bung on, a.** to stage; put on. **b.** to prepare or arrange, especially at short notice: *let's bung on a party.*

bung² /bʌŋ/ *adj. NZ Colloq., Aust.* **1.** not in good working order; impaired; injured. **2.** (of an eye) infected, especially when the lids are swollen shut or stuck shut with mucus, as with sandy blight or bung-eye. –*phr.* **3. go bung, a.** to break down; cease to function. **b.** to fail in business; become bankrupt.

bungalow /ˈbʌŋgəloʊ/ *n.* a house or cottage of one storey.

bungee¹ /ˈbʌndʒi/ *n.* **1.** any of various springs or other devices involving elastic tension, as those which facilitate the movement of controls in an aircraft, or the strong rubber rings used by skiers as a kind of shock absorber. –*v.t.* **2.** to launch (a glider) by catapult from the top of a hill. –*v.i.* **3.** → **bungee-jump.** Also, **bungy.**

bungee² /ˈbʌndʒi/ *n.* → **bunji.** Also, **bunge** /bʌndʒ/.

bungee-jump *v.i.* to perform a bungee jump. Also, **bungee.**

bungee jumping *n.* a sport in which one throws oneself from a high place such as a bridge to which one is attached by an elasticised cord (**bungee**). Also, **bungy jumping.** –**bungee jumper,** *n.* –**bungee jump,** *n.*

bunger /ˈbʌŋə/ *n. Aust.* a firework which produces a loud bang.

bungle /ˈbʌŋgəl/ *v.i.* **1.** to do something awkwardly and clumsily. –*v.t.* **2.** to do clumsily and awkwardly; botch. –*n.* **3.** a bungling performance. **4.** a bungled job. –**bungler,** *n.* –**bunglingly,** *adv.*

bunion /ˈbʌnjən/ *n.* a swelling on the foot caused by the inflammation of a synovial bursa, especially of the great toe.

bunji /ˈbʌndʒi/ *n. Chiefly Qld and NT Aboriginal English* a friend; mate: *how're you going, bunji?* Also, **bunjie, bungee, bunge.**

bunk¹ /bʌŋk/ *n.* **1.** a built-in platform bed, as on a ship. **2.** one of a pair of beds built one above the other. **3.** *Colloq.* any bed. –*v.i.* **4.** *Colloq.* to occupy a bunk; sleep, especially in rough quarters. –*phr.* **5. bunk down,** to go to bed, often in a makeshift bed. **6. bunk in,** to share sleeping quarters.

bunker /ˈbʌŋkə/ *n.* **1.** a chest or box; a large bin or receptacle: *a coal bunker.* **2.** a fortified shelter, often underground. **3.** *Golf* a shallow excavation, usually at the side of a green, which has been nearly filled with sand and which serves as a hazard.

bunkum /ˈbʌŋkəm/ *n.* insincere talk; claptrap; humbug. Also, *US,* **buncombe.**

bunny /ˈbʌni/ *n.* (*pl.* **-nies**) *Colloq.* **1.** Also, **bunny rabbit.** a rabbit. **2.** a fool. **3.** someone who bears the blame, usually unwillingly, in a situation in which others were also at fault. **4.** an attractive young woman who is more

interested in parading her good looks than taking part in a particular pursuit, activity, sport, etc.: *a ski bunny; beach bunny.*

Bunsen burner /ˈbʌnsən ˈbɜːnə/ *n.* a type of gas burner with which a very hot, practically non-luminous flame is obtained by allowing air to enter at the base and mix with the gas.

bunting¹ /ˈbʌntɪŋ/ *n.* **1.** a coarse open fabric of worsted or cotton used for flags, signals. **2.** flags, especially a vessel's flags, collectively. **3.** festive decorations made from bunting, paper, etc., usually in the form of draperies, wide streamers, etc.

bunya /ˈbʌnjə/ *n.* a tall, dome-shaped coniferous tree of Australia, *Araucaria bidwillii,* bearing edible seeds. Also, **bunya-bunya, bunya-bunya pine.**

bunyip /ˈbʌnjəp/ *n.* an imaginary creature of Aboriginal legend, said to haunt rushy swamps and billabongs.

buoy /bɔɪ/ *n.* **1.** *Naut.* a distinctively marked and shaped anchored float, sometimes carrying a light, whistle, or bell, marking a channel or obstruction. **2.** → **lifebuoy.** –*v.t.* **3.** to support by or as by a buoy; keep afloat in a fluid. **4.** to bear up or sustain, as hope or courage does.

buoyant /ˈbɔɪənt/ *adj.* **1.** tending to float or rise in a fluid. **2.** capable of keeping a body afloat, as a liquid. **3.** not easily depressed; cheerful. **4.** cheering or invigorating. **5.** (of production levels, prices, etc.) having the capacity of recovering from a reverse. –**buoyancy,** *n.* –**buoyantly,** *adv.*

burble /ˈbɜːbəl/ *v.i.* **1.** to make a bubbling sound; bubble. **2.** to speak quickly and unclearly. **3.** to speak incoherently or inconsequentially. –*n.* **4.** a bubbling sound. **5.** a flow of excited, unclear speech.

burden /ˈbɜːdn/ *n.* **1.** something that is carried; a load. **2.** something that is borne with difficulty: *burden of responsibilities.* **3.** *Commerce* the duty to discharge an obligation or responsibility: *the burden of a contract.* –*v.t.* **4.** to load heavily. –**burdensome,** *adj.*

bureau /ˈbjʊroʊ, bjuˈroʊ/ *n.* (*pl.* **-reaus** *or* **-reaux** /-roʊz/) **1.** a desk or writing table with drawers for papers. **2.** a division of a government department or independent administrative unit. **3.** an office for giving out information, etc.: *travel bureau.* **4.** a chest of drawers.

bureaucracy /bjuˈrɒkrəsi/ *n.* (*pl.* **-cies**) **1.** government by administrative officials organised into departments, bureaus, etc. **2.** the body of such officials. **3.** excessive red tape and unnecessary official procedures in any system of government or administration.

bureaucrat /ˈbjʊrəkræt/ *n.* **1.** an official of a bureaucracy. **2.** an official who works by fixed routine without exercising intelligent judgement. –**bureaucratic** /bjʊrə-ˈkrætɪk/, *adj.* –**bureaucratically,** *adv.*

burgeon /ˈbɜːdʒən/ *v.i.* to begin to grow, as a bud; to put forth buds, shoots, as a plant. Also, **burgeon out, burgeon forth.**

burglary /ˈbɜːgləri/ *n.* (*pl.* **-ries**) the offence of breaking into and entering a house or other premises with intent to commit a felony therein. –**burglar,** *n.* –**burgle,** *v.*

burgundy /ˈbɜːgəndi/ *n.* (*pl.* **-dies**) **1.** wine of many varieties, red and white, mostly still, full, and dry, produced in Burgundy, a region in south-eastern France. **2.** (in unofficial use) a similar wine produced elsewhere. **3.** a dull bluish red (colour).

Burgundy /ˈbɜːgəndi/ *n.* (*pl.* **-dies**) (*sometimes lower case*) **1.** wine of many varieties, red and white, mostly still, full, and dry, produced in Burgundy, a region in south-eastern France. **2.** (in unofficial use) a similar wine produced elsewhere.

burial /ˈberiəl/ *n.* the act of burying.

burka /ˈbɜːkə/ *n.* → **burqa.**

burkini /bɜːˈkini/ *n.* (*from trademark*) a swimsuit designed for Muslim women, comprising leggings and a tunic top with a hood. Also, **burqini.**

burl[1] /bɜl/ *n.* a small knot or lump in wool, thread, or cloth. –**burled**, *adj.*

burl[2] /bɜl/ *Colloq.* –*v.i.* **1.** *Colloq., Aust.* to move quickly: *to burl along.* –*v.t.* **2.** *Aust.* to taunt and jeer at: *to burl the science master.* –*n.* **3. give it a burl**, *Aust., NZ* to make an attempt. Also, **birl**.

burlap /'bɜlæp/ *n.* hessian; gunny.

burlesque /bɜ'lɛsk/ *n.* **1.** an artistic composition, especially literary or dramatic, which, for the sake of laughter, vulgarises lofty material or treats ordinary material with mock dignity. **2.** any ludicrous take-off or debasing caricature. **3.** a theatrical or cabaret entertainment featuring coarse, crude, often vulgar comedy and dancing. –**burlesquer**, *n.*

burly /'bɜli/ *adj.* (**-lier, -liest**) **1.** great in bodily size; stout; sturdy. **2.** bluff; brusque. –**burlily**, *adv.* –**burliness**, *n.*

burn /bɜn/ *verb* (**burnt** *or* **burned**, **burning**) –*v.i.* **1.** to be on fire: *the fuel burns.* **2.** (of a furnace, etc.) to contain fire. **3.** to feel heat or a physiologically identical sensation: *his face was burning in the wind.* **4.** to glow like fire. **5.** (in games) to be extremely close to finding a concealed object or guessing an answer. **6.** to feel strong passion: *he was burning with anger.* **7.** *Chem.* to undergo combustion; oxidise. **8.** to become discoloured, tanned, or charred through heat. –*v.t.* **9.** to consume, partly or wholly, with fire. **10.** to cause to feel the sensation of heat. **11.** to injure, discolour, char, or treat with heat. **12.** *Chem.* to cause to undergo combustion; oxidise. **13. a.** to copy (data) onto a CD, DVD, or optical disc: *to burn files for archiving.* **b.** to copy data onto (a CD, DVD, or optical disc): *to burn a disc of your family photos.* **14.** to betray, cheat or dupe: *I'm wary of buying second-hand cars – I've been burnt before.* –*n.* **15.** *Pathol.* an injury produced by heat or by abnormal cold, chemicals, poison gas, electricity, or lightning. A **first-degree burn** is characterised by reddening; a **second-degree burn** by blistering; a **third-degree burn** by charring. **16.** the operation of burning or baking, as in brick-making. **17.** Also, **burn-off. a.** the action or result of clearing land by fire. **b.** the area of land so burnt. –*phr.* **18. burn ahead**, (of bush fires) to intensify and travel in a manner difficult or impossible to control: *the fire's burning ahead on a wide front.* **19. burn off**, **a.** to clear or improve (land) by burning the cover. **b.** *Colloq.* to race on a motorcycle or in a car. **20. burn one's fingers**, to suffer through rash interference or imprudence. **21. burn out**, **a.** (of a fire or flame) to die out for want of fuel. **b.** to lose one's capacity or motivation for effective action, usually through prolonged occupational stress. **22. burn up**, *Colloq.* to pass through or over quickly and easily: *to burn up the kilometres in a car.* **23. to burn**, *Colloq.* in abundance: *money to burn.* –**burning**, *adj.* –**burningly**, *adv.*

burner /'bɜnə/ *n.* **1.** an incinerator. **2.** that part of a gas stove, lamp, etc., from which flame issues or in which it is produced. –*phr.* **3. put on the back burner**, to defer action on.

burnish /'bɜnɪʃ/ *v.t.* **1.** to polish (a surface) by friction. **2.** to make smooth and bright.

burnt /bɜnt/ *v.* **1.** a past tense and past participle of **burn**. –*phr.* **2. burnt out**, **a.** (of a building, etc.) gutted. **b.** (of countryside, bush, etc.) blackened or destroyed by fire, especially bushfire. **c.** (of a person) lacking energy or drive, especially as a result of overwork.

burp /bɜp/ *n.* **1.** → **belch** (def. 4). –*v.i.* **2.** → **belch** (def. 1). –*v.t.* **3.** cause (a baby) to belch, especially to relieve air trapped in the stomach after feeding.

burqa /'bɜkə/ *n.* a traditional Muslim garment for women worn over the usual daily clothing, comprising the jilbab, hijab, and niqab to give full body covering; chador. Also, **burka**.

burqini /bɜ'kini/ *n.* → **burkini**.

burr[1] /bɜ/ *n.* **1.** *Bot.* the rough, prickly case around the seeds of certain plants, as of the chestnut and burdock. **2.** something or someone that adheres like a burr. **3.** any of various knots, knobs, lumps, or excrescences. Also, **bur**.

burr[2] /bɜ/ *n.* **1.** any of various tools and appliances for cutting or drilling. –*v.t.* **2.** to form a rough point or edge on. Also, **bur**.

burr[3] /bɜ/ *n.* **1.** a retracted pronunciation of the letter 'r' (as in certain Northern English dialects). **2.** a whirring noise or sound. –*v.i.* **3.** to speak roughly, indistinctly, or inarticulately. **4.** to make a whirring noise or sound. –*v.t.* **5.** to pronounce with a burr. Also, **bur**.

burrito /bə'ritoʊ/ *n.* (in Mexican cookery) a tortilla folded over a filling of meat, cheese or beans.

burro /'bʌroʊ, 'bʊroʊ/ *n.* (*pl.* **-ros**) a donkey.

burrow /'bʌroʊ/ *n.* **1.** a hole in the ground made by a rabbit, fox, or similar small animal, for refuge and habitation. –*v.i.* **2.** to make a hole or passage (*in*, *into*, or *under* something). –**burrower**, *n.*

bursar /'bɜsə/ *n.* **1.** a treasurer or business officer, especially of a college or university. **2.** a student holding a bursary. –**bursarship**, *n.*

bursary /'bɜsəri/ *n.* (*pl.* **-ries**) a scholarship.

burst /bɜst/ *verb* (**burst**, **bursting**) –*v.i.* **1.** to break open with sudden violence; explode. **2.** to come or go suddenly and forcibly: *he burst out of the room; the idea burst into my mind.* **3.** to give way to an expression of violent emotion: *to burst into speech; to burst into tears.* **4.** to be very full, as if ready to break open: *the bag was bursting with shopping; I am bursting with anger.* –*v.t.* **5.** to cause (something) to burst. –*n.* **6.** an act or result of bursting. **7.** a sudden action or effort: *a burst of clapping; a burst of speed.* **8.** a sudden expression of emotion, etc. –**burster**, *n.*

bury /'beri/ *v.t.* (**buried**, **burying**) **1.** to put in the ground and cover with earth. **2.** to put (a corpse) in the ground or a vault, or into the sea, often with ceremony. **3.** to cause to sink in: *to bury a dagger in someone's heart.* **4.** to cover in order to conceal from sight. –*phr.* **5. bury oneself in**, to occupy oneself completely in: *he buried himself in his work.* **6. bury the hatchet**, to be reconciled after hostilities. –**burier**, *n.*

bus /bʌs/ *n.* (*pl.* **buses** *or* **busses**) **1.** a vehicle with a long body equipped with seats for passengers, usually operating within a scheduled service. **2.** *Colloq.* (*humorous*) a motor car or aeroplane: *the old bus is playing up.* **3.** → **busbar** (def. 2). –*verb* (**bussed** *or* **bused**, **bussing** *or* **busing**) –*v.i.* **4.** to travel by bus. –*v.t.* **5.** to transport (people) by bus. **6.** *Chiefly US* to transport (children) by bus to a more remote school in order to create racially integrated classes. –*phr.* **7. miss the bus**, to miss an opportunity; be too late. **8. throw someone under the** (or **a**) **bus**, *Colloq.* to sacrifice a friend or ally to save one's own interests.

busbar /'bʌsbɑ/ *n.* **1.** an electrical conductor having low resistance connecting several like points in an electrical system, frequently used to supply power to various points. **2.** *Computers* a group of such electrical conductors providing a communication path within a computer or between two or more computerised devices.

busby /'bʌzbi/ *n.* (*pl.* **-bies**) a tall fur hat with a bag hanging from the top over the right side, worn by hussars, etc., in the British Army.

bush /bʊʃ/ *n.* **1.** a woody plant, especially a low one, with many branches which usually arise from or near the ground. **2.** *Bot.* a small cluster of shrubs appearing as a single plant. **3.** something resembling or suggesting this, such as a thick, shaggy head of hair. **4.** terrain covered with bushy vegetation or trees, especially when uncultivated or in its natural state. **5.** a fox's tail. *–adj.* **6.** found in or typical of the bush: *a bush nurse*; *a bush pub*; *bush hospitality*. **7.** *Colloq.* uncivilised; rough; makeshift: *a bush bed*; *bush carpentry*. *–phr.* **8. beat about the bush,** to fail to come to the point; prevaricate. **9. bush it,** to live or camp in the bush: *we were lost and had to bush it for the night.* **10. go bush, a.** (of animals) to stray and live in the bush. **b.** (of people) to reject civilisation and live an isolated life in the bush. **c.** to adopt a way of life which is without the comforts and attractions of the big city, especially one which is close to nature. **11. out bush,** in or to a remote bush region: *I have been out bush for many years.* **12. take to the bush, a.** to go to live in the bush, especially to turn one's back on civilisation and adopt a way of life close to nature. **b.** *Aust. Hist.* to escape custody or leave settlement and become a bushranger. **13. the bush,** *Aust., NZ* **a.** the broad area of bush terrain, especially when contrasted with areas of settlement. **b.** people living in rural areas, considered collectively: *the bush is up in arms about the closure of bank branches.*

bush band *n.* a band which performs Australian folk music, usually with such instruments as the accordion, tea-chest bass, guitar, etc.

bush-burn *n.* NZ **1.** the clearing of bush by fire. **2.** the area of land so cleared.

bush canary *n.* **1.** → **white-throated gerygone.** **2.** a small olive brown and bright yellow bird, *Mohoua ochrocephala*, of the New Zealand rainforest; mohua.

bushcraft /ˈbʊʃkraft/ *n. Aust., NZ* the ability to live in and travel through the bush with a minimum of equipment and assistance.

bushed /bʊʃt/ *adj. Colloq.* **1.** lost. **2.** exhausted. **3.** confused.

bushel /ˈbʊʃəl/ *n.* **1.** a unit of dry measure in the imperial system equal to $36.368\,72 \times 10^{-3}\,\text{m}^3$ (8 gal). **2.** Also, **Winchester bushel.** *US* a unit of dry measure equal to $35.239\,070 \times 10^{-3}\,\text{m}^3$. *–phr.* **3. hide one's light under a bushel,** to conceal one's abilities or good qualities.

bush-faller /ˈbʊʃ-fɔlə/ *n.* NZ someone who fells trees for a living. Also, **bush-feller. –bush-falling,** *n.*

bushfire /ˈbʊʃfaɪə/ *n. Aust., NZ* an unplanned fire in forest, scrub or grassland, often caused by lightning strike.

bushie /ˈbʊʃi/ *n. Colloq.* **1.** *Aust., NZ* (*sometimes derog.*) someone who lives in the country and is familiar with country ways. Compare **townie.** **2.** *Aust.* a person who is experienced in living in the bush. Also, **bushy.**

bush jacket *n.* **1.** Also, **safari jacket.** a belted cotton jacket with buttoned pockets, often khaki in colour. **2.** any protective jacket designed to be worn in the bush.

bush lawyer *n.* **1.** any of several Australian and New Zealand prickly trailing plants, of the genus *Rubus*. **2.** *Colloq.* a person who pretends to a knowledge of the law, especially one who attempts complicated and often specious arguments to prove a point.

bushman /ˈbʊʃmən/ *n.* (*pl.* **-men**) NZ **1.** *Aust.* a man skilled in bushcraft. **2.** → **bush-faller. –bushmanship,** *n.*

bushmeat /ˈbʊʃmit/ *n.* especially in Africa, meat obtained for commercial distribution from wild animals, as apes, monkeys, etc.

bushranger /ˈbʊʃreɪndʒə/ *n. NZ Hist.* **1.** *Aust.* a bandit or criminal who hid in the bush and stole from settlers and travellers at gunpoint. **2.** a European volunteer for bush-warfare against the Maori in the 19th century. **–bushranging,** *n.*

bush rat *n.* any of a number of species of indigenous rodents of genus *Rattus* in Australia, especially *R. fuscipes.*

bush reckoning *n. Colloq.* imprecisely estimated distance or time, usually underestimated or unrealistic: *it takes five days to get there, two days by bush reckoning.*

bush robin *n.* a robin-like forest bird of New Zealand, *Miro australis.*

bush telegraph *n.* **1.** a system of communication over wide distances among tribal peoples, by drumbeats or other means. **2.** *Colloq.* an unofficial chain of communication by which information is conveyed and rumour spread, as by word of mouth. Also, **bush wireless.**

bush turkey *n.* → **brush turkey.**

bushwalk /ˈbʊʃwɔk/ *v.i.* **1.** to hike through the bush for pleasure. *–n.* **2.** such an excursion. **3.** an established route for a bushwalk. **–bushwalker,** *n.* **–bushwalking,** *n.*

bush week *n. Aust. Colloq.* a time when many rural people are in the city (used ironically in phrases such as **what do you think this is – bush week?,** to indicate that one thinks one is being imposed upon, tricked, or taken for a fool). Also, **bushweek.**

bushwhack /ˈbʊʃwæk/ *v.i. Colloq.* **1.** *Aust.* to live as a bushwhacker. **2.** *NZ* to clear land of timber. Also, **bushwack. –bushwhacking,** *n.* **–bushwhacked,** *adj.*

bushwhacker /ˈbʊʃwækə/ *n. Colloq.* **1.** *Aust., NZ* an unsophisticated person who lives in the bush. **2.** *NZ* someone who clears the land of bush, especially an axeman engaged in cutting timber. **3.** *US* someone who lives in a remote wooded area. Also, **bushwacker.**

bush wren *n.* a wren-like forest bird of New Zealand, *Xenicus longipes*; matuhitui.

bushy¹ /ˈbʊʃi/ *adj.* (**bushier, bushiest**) **1.** resembling a bush. **2.** full of or overgrown with bushes.

bushy² /ˈbʊʃi/ *n.* → **bushie.**

business /ˈbɪznəs/ *n.* **1.** one's occupation, profession, or trade. **2.** *Econ.* the purchase and sale of goods and services for the purpose of making a profit. **3.** *Commerce* a person, partnership, or corporation engaged in business; an established or going enterprise or concern: *a clothing business.* **4.** volume of trade; patronage. **5.** one's place of work. **6.** that with which one is principally and seriously concerned. **7.** that with which one is rightfully concerned. **8.** affair; matter. **9.** Also, **stage business.** *Theatre* any deliberate gesture or movement made on stage by an actor which in comedy may be for its own humorous effect, but which more usually advances the dramatic situation. **10.** defecation. **11.** *Colloq.* prostitution. *–phr.* **12. be in business, a.** to earn a living from a commercial activity. **b.** *Colloq.* to be carrying out an activity, enterprise, etc., successfully. **13. business as usual,** the normal state of affairs. **14. mean business,** to be in earnest. **15. the business end, a.** the operational end of a machine, tool, etc. **b.** the final stages of a competition, especially in sport.

business activity statement *n.* a statement which a business is required to submit to the government agency on a regular basis, containing an account of transactions and allowing the calculation of tax, especially GST, payable. Also, **BAS.**

business college *n.* a private institution where subjects of use commercially, as shorthand, typing, bookkeeping, etc., are taught.

businesslike /ˈbɪznəslaɪk/ *adj.* conforming to the methods of business or trade; methodical; systematic.

business model *n.* an outline of the structure and operations of a business, formulating the means by which it aims to generate revenue.

businessperson /ˈbɪznəspɜsən/ *n.* (*pl.* **-people**) a person engaged in business or commerce. **–businessman,** *n.* **–businesswoman,** *n.*

business plan *n.* a plan set out for a commercial organisation which details its projected financial development over a number of years.

busker /ˈbʌskə/ n. an entertainer who gives performances in streets, parks, markets, etc., usually collecting donations from the impromptu audience.

bust¹ /bʌst/ n. 1. the head and shoulders of a person done in sculpture, either in the round or in relief. 2. the chest or breast; the bosom.

bust² /bʌst/ Colloq. –v.i. 1. to burst. 2. to go bankrupt. –v.t. 3. to burst (in, out, through, etc.) 4. to squander: to bust one's pay packet. 5. to bankrupt; ruin. 6. to reduce in rank or grade; demote. 7. US to subdue; break the spirits of (a horse, etc.). 8. to apprehend for an illegal activity, especially for possession of drugs or stolen goods. 9. (of the police) to carry out a raid on (a place): they busted the club last night. –n.10. a complete failure; bankruptcy. 11. a drunken party or spree; brawl. 12. the act of breaking and entering. 13. a police raid, often in search of a specified illegal substance: a drug bust. –adj. 14. Also, **busted**. broken; ruined. 15. bankrupt. –phr. 16. **be busting, a.** to urgently need to urinate or defecate. **b.** to be extremely eager: busting to have a go. 17. **bust a gut**, to overexert oneself: don't bust a gut over that job. 18. **bust one's boiler**, to overexert oneself: don't bust your boiler on the exercise bike. 19. **bust up, a.** to part finally; quarrel and part. **b.** to smash. **c.** to interrupt violently (a political meeting or other gathering). 20. **go bust**, to become bankrupt. 21. **on the bust**, on a drunken spree.

bustard /ˈbʌstəd/ n. a large, heavy bird of the family Otididae, Eupodotis australis, inhabiting grassy plains and open scrub country of Australia and New Guinea; plain turkey.

bustle¹ /ˈbʌsəl/ verb (-tled, -tling) –v.i. 1. to move (in, about, around, etc.) with a great show of energy. –v.t. 2. to cause to bustle. –n. 3. activity with great show of energy; stir, commotion. –**bustlingly**, adv.

bustle² /ˈbʌsəl/ n. (formerly) a pad, cushion, or wire framework worn by women on the back part of the body below the waist, to expand and support the skirt.

busy /ˈbɪzi/ adj. (**busier, busiest**) 1. actively occupied: he is busy with his work; she is too busy to come. 2. full of or marked by activity: a busy time of the day. 3. → **engaged** (def. 4). –v.t. (**busied, busying**) 4. to make or keep busy: I am going to busy myself writing letters. –**busily**, adv. –**busyness**, n.

busybody /ˈbɪzibɒdi/ n. (pl. **-dies**) someone who pries into and meddles in the affairs of others.

busywork /ˈbɪziwɜk/ n. work which causes an employee to appear to be working hard although it is unproductive.

but /bʌt/, weak form /bət/ conj. 1. on the contrary; yet: they all went, but I didn't. 2. except, rather than, or save: anywhere but here. 3. without the circumstance that, or that not: it never rains but it pours. 4. otherwise than: I can do nothing but go. 5. that (especially after doubt, deny, etc., with a negative): I don't doubt but he will do it. 6. Also, **but that**. that not (after a negative or question): the children never played but that a quarrel followed. 7. who or which not: no leader worthy of the name ever existed but was an optimist. –prep. 8. with the exception of; except; save: no one replied but me. –adv. 9. only; just: there is but one God. 10. a mildly adversative addition with the force of 'however' or 'though', used in standard speech at the beginning of a sentence, and in non-standard speech also often at the end of a sentence. –n. 11. a restriction or objection: no buts about it. –phr. 12. **all but**, almost: all but dead. 13. **but for**, except for; had it not been for; were it not for.

butane /ˈbjutein, bjuˈtein/ n. a saturated aliphatic hydrocarbon, C_4H_{10}, existing in two isomeric forms and used as a fuel and a chemical intermediate.

butch /bʊtʃ/ n. Colloq. 1. a homosexual man or woman exhibiting extravagantly masculine characteristics. 2. a

man, especially one of notable physical strength. –adj. 3. exhibiting aggressively masculine characteristics.

butcher /ˈbʊtʃə/ n. 1. a retail dealer in meat. 2. someone who slaughters certain domesticated animals, or dresses their flesh, for food or for market. 3. someone guilty of cruel or indiscriminate slaughter. –v.t. 4. to kill or slaughter for food or for market. 5. to murder indiscriminately or brutally. –**butchery**, n.

butcherbird /ˈbʊtʃəbɜd/ n. 1. any of several birds of the genus Cracticus, of Australia and New Guinea, as the **grey butcherbird**, Cracticus torquatus, so called because they impale their prey of small birds, etc., on spikes or thorns or wedge it in the forks of trees. 2. any of various shrikes of the genus Lanius, as the common European species L. excubitor.

butler /ˈbʌtlə/ n. 1. traditionally, the head male servant of a household. 2. a person performing a similar organisational role in a hotel, large house, etc. –**butlership**, n.

butt¹ /bʌt/ n. 1. the end or extremity of anything, especially the thicker, larger, or blunt end, as of a rifle, fishing rod, whip handle, arrow, log, etc. 2. an end which is not used up: a cigarette butt. 3. Colloq. the buttocks; bottom: shift your butt. –phr. Colloq. 4. **kick butt**, to behave in an aggressive manner to ensure that one's demands are met. 5. **kick someone's butt, a.** to beat someone convincingly **b.** to reprimand someone severely 6. **sit on one's butt**, to be idle. 7. **work one's butt off**, to work very hard or diligently

butt² /bʌt/ n. 1. a person or thing that is an object of wit, ridicule, sarcasm, etc., or contempt. 2. (in rifle or archery practice) a wall of earth behind the targets of a target range, which prevents bullets or arrows from scattering over a wide area. 3. the target for archery practice. 4. a hinge for a door or the like, secured to the butting surfaces or ends instead of the adjacent sides. –v.i. 5. to have an end or projection (on); be adjacent (to).

butt³ /bʌt/ v.t. 1. to strike with the head or horns. –v.i. 2. to strike something or at something with the head or horns. 3. to project. –n. 4. a push with head or horns. –phr. Colloq. 5. **butt in**, to interrupt; interfere; intrude. 6. **butt out**, to mind one's own business and not interfere in something which is not one's proper concern.

butt⁴ /bʌt/ n. a large cask for wine, beer, or ale.

butter /ˈbʌtə/ n. 1. the fatty portion of milk, separating as a soft whitish or yellowish solid when milk or cream is agitated or churned. 2. this substance, processed for cooking and table use. 3. any of various other spreads of similar consistency: butter icing, peanut butter. –v.t. 4. to put butter on or in. –phr. 5. **butter up**, to flatter grossly. 6. **butter wouldn't melt in someone's mouth**, an expression indicating that someone is feigning innocence. –**butter-like**, adj.

buttercup /ˈbʌtəkʌp/ n. any plant of the genus Ranunculus, with yellow or white, usually cup-shaped flowers.

butter-fingers n. Colloq. someone who fails to catch or drops things easily.

butterfish /ˈbʌtəfɪʃ/ n. 1. any of various Australian fishes of genera Selenotoca and Scatophagus, often silvery or butter-coloured and variously banded or spotted and having strong, often venomous dorsal spines. 2. a New Zealand reef fish, Coridodax pullus, often found browsing on kelp; greenbone.

butterfly /ˈbʌtəflaɪ/ n. (pl. **-flies**) 1. any of a group of lepidopterous insects characterised by clubbed antennae, large, broad wings, often conspicuously coloured and marked, and diurnal habits. 2. Also, **social butterfly**. someone who flits gaily but aimlessly from one diversion to another. 3. (pl.) nervousness: butterflies in the stomach. 4. Also, **butterfly stroke**. a swimming stroke made in the prone position in which both arms are lifted simultaneously out of the water and flung forward, usually done in combination with the dolphin kick. –*v.t.* (**-flied**, **-flying**) **5.** to slice (a boneless and usually trimmed and flattened piece of meat, etc.) lengthways about two-thirds of the way through and then open it out flat so as to form a shape resembling that of a butterfly: *ask your butcher to bone and butterfly the leg of lamb.*

butterfly cod *n.* → **red firefish.**

butterfly stroke *n.* → **butterfly** (def. 4).

butter lettuce *n.* a type of lettuce with soft loosely-packed leaves and a mild buttery flavour.

buttermilk /'bʌtəmɪlk/ *n.* the more or less acidulous liquid remaining after the butter has been separated from milk or cream.

butterscotch /'bʌtəskɒtʃ/ *n.* **1.** a kind of toffee made with butter. **2.** a flavour produced in puddings, icing, ice-cream, etc., by a combination of brown sugar, vanilla extract, and butter, with other ingredients.

butthead /'bʌthɛd/ *n. Colloq.* a stupid person.

buttock /'bʌtək/ *n. Anat.* either of the two protuberances which form the rump.

button /'bʌtn/ *n.* **1.** a small solid object, usually round, used as a fastening or ornament on clothing. **2.** anything like a button in shape and size, as a young mushroom or a small knob pressed to ring bell, etc. **3.** *Computers* a small outlined area on a screen which, when selected, performs some function. **4.** *Bot.* a bud or other outgrowth of a plant. –*v.t.* **5.** to fasten with a button or buttons. **6.** *Colloq.* (fol. by *up*) to complete (business, etc.) successfully. **–buttoner**, *n.* **–button-like**, *adj.*

buttonhole /'bʌtnhoʊl/ *n.* **1.** the hole, slit, or loop through which a button is passed. **2.** a small flower or nosegay worn in the buttonhole in the lapel of a jacket. –*v.t.* **3.** to sew with buttonhole stitch. **4.** to seize by or as by the buttonhole in the lapel of the jacket and detain in conversation. **–buttonholer**, *n.*

button quail *n.* any of various birds of the family Turnicidae resembling quails but distinguished by the absence of the hind toe, as the **little button quail,** *Turnix velox,* found throughout continental Australia except in northern and eastern coastal areas.

buttons /'bʌtnz/ *pl. n.* any of a number of plant species, especially of the family Compositae, with button-like flower heads as, **billy buttons** of the genus *Craspedia,* and **water buttons,** *Cotula coronopifolia.*

buttress /'bʌtrəs/ *n.* **1.** *Archit.* a structure built against a wall or building for the purpose of giving it stability. **2.** any prop or support. –*v.t.* **3.** to prop up; support.

buxom /'bʌksəm/ *adj.* **1.** (of a woman) having large breasts. **2.** (usually of a woman) attractively plump and radiantly healthy, with a cheerful, lively disposition. **–buxomly**, *adj., adv.* **–buxomness**, *n.*

buy /baɪ/ *verb* (**bought** /bɔt/, **buying**) –*v.t.* **1.** to acquire the possession of, or the right to, by paying an equivalent, especially in money. **2.** to acquire by giving any kind of recompense: *to buy favour with flattery.* **3.** to hire; bribe. **4.** *Colloq.* to accept: *do you think he'll buy the idea?* –*v.i.* **5.** to be or become a purchaser. –*n.* **6.** *Colloq.* a purchase, especially a good purchase. –*phr.* **7. buy in, a.** *Stock Exchange* (of a broker) to obtain a share scrip from another broker to cover his or her position after a third broker fails to deliver shares. **b.** to join in; become involved. **8. buy into, a.** to acquire shares in (a company): *to buy into BHP.* **b.** to choose to become involved in: *to buy into an argument.* **9. buy into trouble,** *Colloq.* to undertake a course of action against the better judgement of oneself or others. **10. buy it,** *Colloq.* to be killed: *he bought it at Bathurst.* **11. buy off,** to get rid of (a claim, opposition, etc.) by payment; purchase the nonintervention of; bribe. **12. buy out,** to secure all of the share or interest in an

enterprise held by (an owner or partner). **13. buy up,** to buy as much as one can of. **–buyable**, *adj.*

buyback /'baɪbæk/ *n.* **1.** an act or instance of buying back something previously sold. **2.** an agreement between two participants, especially in the money or stock market, whereby the first party sells securities to the second party and at the same time undertakes to buy them back at a specified price at some agreed time in the future.

buyer /'baɪə/ *n.* **1.** someone who buys; a purchaser. **2.** a purchasing agent, as for a chain store.

buyers' market *n.* a situation where, at current prices, supply exceeds demand so that buyers tend to determine price as well as the terms and conditions by which sales are effected.

buzz /bʌz/ *n.* **1.** a low, vibrating, humming sound, as of bees. **2.** *Colloq.* a telephone call. **3.** *Colloq.* **a.** a feeling of exhilaration or pleasure, especially as induced by drugs. **b.** a similar experience of pleasure, delight, etc.: *I get a real buzz out of going sailing.* –*v.i.* **4.** to make a low, vibrating, humming sound. **5.** to move (*around, along,* etc.), especially with energy. –*v.t.* **6.** to make a buzzing sound with: *he buzzed the doorbell.* **7.** *Aeronautics* **a.** to fly an aeroplane very low over: *to buzz a field.* **b.** to signal or greet (someone) by flying an aeroplane low and slowing the motor spasmodically. –*phr. Colloq.* **8. buzz about,** to move busily from place to place. **9. buzz off,** to go away; depart: *I told her to buzz off; buzz off!* **10. the buzz,** rumour; report.

buzzard /'bʌzəd/ *n.* any of various birds of prey related to but smaller than eagles.

buzzword /'bʌzwɜd/ *n. Colloq.* a fashionable jargon word used for its emotive value or its ability to impress the listener. Also, **buzz word.**

by /baɪ/ *prep.* **1.** near to: *a house by the river.* **2.** using as a route: *he came by the main road.* **3.** through or on as a means of conveyance: *she journeyed by water.* **4.** to and past a point near: *he went by the church.* **5.** within the compass or period of: *by day; by night.* **6.** not later than: *by two o'clock.* **7.** to the extent of: *longer by a metre.* **8.** through evidence or authority of: *by his own account.* **9.** with the participation of: *regretted by all.* **10.** in conformity with: *by any standards this is a good book.* **11.** before; in the name of: *by God; by all that's sacred; by crikey.* **12.** through the agency or efficacy of: *founded by Napoleon; done by force.* **13.** after; in serial order: *piece by piece.* **14.** combined with in multiplication or relative dimension: *five metres by six metres.* **15.** involving as unit of measure: *beef by the kilogram.* –*adv.* **16.** near to something: *it's close by.* **17.** to and past a point near something: *the car drove by.* **18.** aside: *put it by for the moment.* **19.** over; past: *in times gone by.* –*n.* **20.** → **bye**[1]. –*phr.* **21. by and by,** at some time in the future; before long; presently. **22. by and large,** in general; on the whole.

by- a prefix meaning: **1.** secondary; incidental, as in *by-product.* **2.** out of the way; removed, as in *byway.* **3.** near, as in *bystander.* Also, **bye-.**

bycatch /'baɪkætʃ/ *n.* the unwanted fish, sea creatures, etc., caught in nets along with the targeted fish.

bye[1] /baɪ/ *n.* **1.** *Sport* the state of having no competitor in a contest where several competitors are engaged in pairs, conferring the right to compete in the next round in an eliminatory competition. **2.** *Golf* the holes of a stipulated course still unplayed after the match is decided. **3.** *Cricket* a run made on a ball not struck by the person batting. **4.** something subsidiary, secondary, or out of the way. –*phr.* **5. by the bye,** incidentally; by the way. Also, **by.**

bye[2] /baɪ/ *interj.* goodbye.

bye-bye *Colloq.* –*interj.* **1.** goodbye. –*n.* (*pl.* **bye-byes**) **2.** (*with children*) (*pl.*) sleep: *go to bye-byes.*

by-election *n.* a parliamentary election held between general elections, to fill a vacancy caused by the death or resignation of a member of parliament. Also, **bye-election**.

bygone /'baɪgɒn/ *adj.* **1.** past; gone by; out of date: *bygone days.* –*n.* **2.** something that is past. –*phr.* **3. let bygones be bygones**, to ignore the past, especially past disagreements or occasions of sadness.

by-law *n.* **1.** an ordinance of an authority having legal effect only within the boundaries of that authority's jurisdiction. **2.** subordinate legislation, generally at the level of local government. **3.** a standing rule, as of a company or society, not in its constitution. Also, **bye-law**.

by-line *n. Journalism* a line under the heading of a newspaper or magazine article giving the writer's name.

byname /'baɪneɪm/ *n.* **1.** a secondary name; cognomen; surname. **2.** a nickname.

BYO /bi waɪ 'oʊ/Also, **BYOG. 1.** an abbreviation used on invitations, indicating that guests should bring their own supply of liquor. –*adj.* Also, **BYOG. 2.** of a party, dinner, etc. to which one brings one's own supply of liquor. –*n.* **3.** *Aust., NZ* a restaurant which allows clients to bring liquor in. –*v.t.* **4.** to bring one's own: *you'll have to BYO sleeping bag.*

bypass /'baɪpas/ *n.* **1.** a road enabling motorists to avoid towns and other heavy traffic points on the main road. **2.** a secondary pipe or other channel connected with the main passage for carrying liquid or gas around a fixed object. –*v.t.* **3.** to avoid (something) by using a bypass. **4.** to go ahead without asking or informing (someone in charge, etc.)

bypass operation *n. Med.* an operation in which a diseased or obstructed segment of the circulatory or digestive systems of the body is circumvented; particularly used to circumvent diseased blood vessels in the heart.

bypass surgery *n.* surgery relating to a bypass operation, especially to circumvent diseased blood vessels in the heart.

by-product *n.* a secondary or incidental product, as in a process of manufacture.

byre /'baɪə/ *n.* a cowhouse or shed; cattle pen.

bystander /'baɪstændə/ *n.* a person present but not involved; a chance looker-on.

byte /baɪt/ *n.* a unit of measurement of computer memory equal to eight bits. Compare **bit³**.

byway /'baɪweɪ/ *n.* **1.** a secluded, or obscure road. **2.** a subsidiary or obscure field of research, endeavour, etc.

byword /'baɪwɜd/ *n.* **1.** the name of a quality or concept which characterises some person or group; the epitome (of): *his name is a byword for courage.* **2.** a word or phrase used proverbially; a common saying; a proverb. **3.** an object of general reproach, derision, scorn, etc. **4.** an epithet, often of scorn.

C c

C, c /siː/ *n.* **1.** the third letter of the English alphabet. **2.** the Roman numeral for 100. **3.** *Music* **a.** the first, or keynote, of the C major scale. **b.** middle C.

C++ /siː plʌs ˈplʌs/ *n.* a computer language based on C, with features enabling object-oriented software development.

cab /kæb/ *n.* **1.** → taxi. **2.** (formerly) any of various one-horse vehicles for public hire, such as the hansom or the brougham. **3.** the covered part of a locomotive or truck where the driver sits.

cabal /kəˈbal, kəˈbæl/ *n.* **1.** the secret schemes of a small group of plotters; an intrigue. **2.** a small group of secret plotters.

cabana /kəˈbanə/ *n.* **1.** a small hut or cabin beside a swimming pool. **2.** a cabin or self-contained unit which is part of a hotel complex.

cabaret /ˈkæbəreɪ/ *n.* a form of musical, variety, or other entertainment at a restaurant, nightclub, etc., often late into the night; a floor show.

cabbage /ˈkæbɪdʒ/ *n.* any of various cultivated varieties of *Brassica oleracea*, var. *capitata*, with short stem and leaves formed into a compact, edible head.

cabbage butterfly *n.* a large European white butterfly, *Pieris rapae*, introduced into Australia, the larvae of which feed on cabbage and related plants. Also, **cabbage white butterfly.**

cabbage gum *n.* a smooth-barked tree, *Eucalyptus amplifolia*, common on swampy ground in coastal NSW.

cabbage tree *n.* **1.** a tall palm with large leaves, *Livistona australis*, of the coastal areas of eastern Australia. **2.** the small tufted tree *Cordyline australis* of New Zealand, frequently cultivated as an ornamental; ti.

caber /ˈkeɪbə/ *n.* a pole or beam, especially one thrown as a trial of strength in the Scottish Highland game of **tossing the caber.**

cabernet sauvignon /ˌkæbəneɪ ˈsoʊvɪnjɒn/ *n.* (*sometimes upper case*) **1.** a highly regarded grape variety widely used in the making of claret-style wines. **2.** a dry red wine made from this variety. Also, *Colloq.,* **cab sav.**

cabin /ˈkæbən/ *n.* **1.** a small house; hut. **2.** such a building for accommodation, as for tourists in a caravan park. **3.** an apartment or room in a ship, as for passengers. **4.** *Aeronautics* the enclosed place in an aircraft for the pilot, passengers, or cargo.

cabinet /ˈkæbənət, ˈkæbnət/ *n.* **1.** a piece of furniture with shelves, drawers, etc., for holding or displaying valuable objects, dishes, etc. **2.** a piece of furniture holding a record-player, radio, television, or the like. **3.** (*also upper case*) **a.** (in Australia, New Zealand, and some other countries with similar parliamentary systems) the main executive organ of government, consisting of the leading parliamentary members of the governing party or coalition. See **shadow cabinet. b.** a council advising a sovereign or chief executive. **4.** a standard size for a sheet of paper or for a photographic print. **5.** *Obs.* a private room.

cable /ˈkeɪbəl/ *n.* **1.** a thick, strong rope, often one of several wires twisted together. **2.** *Elect.* a stranded conductor typically of copper wire or optical fibre, or a combination of such conductors insulated from one another and used for the transmission of electricity or for telecommunication. **3.** (formerly) a message sent by electric signals, especially along submarine cable. –*v.t.* **4.** to send (a message) by submarine cable.

cable television *n.* a system of broadcasting television programs by sending them directly from the distribution centre to the receiving set by means of a linking coaxial cable.

caboodle /kəˈbudl/ *phr.* **the whole (kit and) caboodle,** *Colloq.* the whole lot, pack, or crowd.

cabotage /ˈkæbətaʒ/ *n.* **1.** trade or navigation in coastal waters. **2.** the legal arrangement by which the right to engage in air transportation within a country's borders is restricted to domestic carriers.

cabriolet /ˈkæbriəleɪ/ *n.* **1.** a type of car resembling a coupé, with a folding top; a convertible coupé. **2.** a light, hooded one-horse carriage with two seats.

cacao /kəˈkeɪoʊ, -ˈkaoʊ/ *n.* (*pl.* **-caos**) **1.** a small evergreen tree, *Theobroma cacao*, of the family Sterculiaceae, native to tropical America, cultivated for its seeds, the source of cocoa, chocolate, etc. **2.** the fruit and seeds of this tree.

cache *n.* **1.** /kæʃ/ a store of provisions, treasure, etc., especially one hidden in the ground. **2.** /kæʃ/ a store of food collected by some animals for the winter. **3.** /kæʃ/ a hiding place, especially one in the ground, for provisions, treasure, etc. **4.** /kæʃ/ → cache memory. –*v.t.* (**cached, caching**) **5.** /kæʃ/ to put in a cache; conceal; hide. **6.** /keɪʃ/ *Computers* to put into cache memory: *this information is cached to increase speed.*

cache memory *n. Computers* a section of computer memory which can be accessed at high speed and in which information is stored for fast retrieval.

cackle /ˈkækəl/ *v.i.* **1.** to utter a shrill, broken sound or cry, as a hen after laying an egg. **2.** to laugh brokenly. **3.** to chatter noisily. –**cackler,** *n.*

cacophony /kəˈkɒfəni/ *n.* (*pl.* **-nies**) a harsh sound; dissonance.

cactoblastis /kæktəˈblæstəs/ *n.* a small moth, *Cactoblastis cactorum*, the larvae of which feed on the prickly pear.

cactus /ˈkæktəs/ *n.* (*pl.* **-tuses** *or* **-ti** /-taɪ, -tiː/) any of various fleshy-stemmed plants of the family Cactaceae, usually leafless and spiny, often producing showy flowers, chiefly native to the hot, dry regions of America.

cad /kæd/ *n.* a contemptible, ill-bred person; someone who does not behave like a gentleman.

cadagi /kəˈdadʒi/ *n.* a tropical and subtropical tree, *Corymbia torelliana*, with large roundish leaves and a smooth green trunk. Also, **cadaga** /kəˈdagə/, **cadaghi.**

cadastre /kəˈdæstə/ *n.* an official register of property, with details of boundaries, ownership, etc.

cadaver /kəˈdævə, -ˈdavə/ *n.* a dead body, especially of a human being; a corpse. –**cadaverous, cadaveric,** *adj.*

caddie /ˈkædi/ *n.* **1.** *Golf* an attendant hired to carry the player's clubs, find the ball, etc. **2.** someone who runs errands, does odd jobs, etc. Also, **caddy.**

caddy /ˈkædi/ *n.* (*pl.* **-dies**) **1.** a small box, tin, or chest, especially one for holding tea. **2.** a container or rack for conveniently holding items which are required for a particular purpose: *sewing caddy.* **3.** *Computers* a case which holds a CD-ROM, designed to be inserted into a computer drive so that the CD does not have to be handled.

cadence /'keɪdns/ *n.* **1.** rhythmic flow, as of verses; rhythm. **2.** the beat of any rhythmical movement. **3.** a fall in pitch of the voice, as in speaking. **4.** the general modulation of the voice. **5.** *Music* a sequence of notes or chords which indicates the momentary or complete end of a composition, section, phrase, etc. **–cadenced,** *adj.*

cadenza /kə'dɛnzə/ *n.* an elaborate showy passage, frequently unaccompanied, for a singer usually near the end of an aria or for an instrumentalist usually near the end of a movement of a concerto.

cadet /kə'dɛt/ *n.* **1.** a person undergoing training in the armed services, public service, at sea, etc. **2.** a member of a military training unit in a secondary school. **3.** *NZ* a young person in apprenticeship to farming. **–cadetship,** *n.* **–cadetting,** *n.*

cadge /kædʒ/ *v.t.* **(cadged, cadging) 1.** to obtain by imposing on another's generosity or friendship. **2.** to borrow without intent to repay. **–cadger,** *n.*

cadmium /'kædmiəm/ *n.* a white, ductile, divalent metallic element like tin in appearance, used in plating and in making certain alloys. As it is a good absorber of neutrons it is also used in the control rods of nuclear reactors. *Symbol:* Cd; *relative atomic mass:* 112.410; *atomic number:* 48; *density:* 8.6 at 20°C. **–cadmic,** *adj.*

cadre /'kadə, 'keɪdə/ *n.* **1.** a unit within an organisational framework, especially personnel. **2.** (in communist countries) a group of low-ranking personnel committed to promoting the policies and interests of the party in a particular area. **3.** a member of such a group, especially one with political responsibilities.

caeno- variant of **caino-**.

caesar /'sizə/ *n. Colloq.* → **caesarean section**.

Caesar /'sizə/ *n.* any emperor or dictator.

caesarean /sə'zɛəriən/ *n.* **1.** a caesarean section operation. **–adj. 2.** relating to or involving a caesarean section operation: *a caesarean birth.* Also, **caesarian, cesarean, cesarian.**

caesarean section *n.* the operation by which a fetus is taken from the womb by cutting through the walls of the abdomen and womb. Also, **caesarian section, cesarean section, cesarian section;** *Colloq.,* **caesar;** *US,* **C-section.**

caesar salad *n.* a salad containing lettuce, bread croutons, parmesan cheese and sometimes anchovies, seasoned and dressed with egg, oil and vinegar.

caesura /sə'ʒurə/ *n.* **(pl. -ras** *or* **-rae** /-ri/**) 1.** *English Prosody* a break, especially a sense pause, usually near the middle of a verse, and marked in scansion by a double vertical line, as in *know then thyself* ‖ *presume not God to scan.* **2.** *Greek and Latin Prosody* a division made by the ending of a word within a foot (or sometimes at the end of a foot), especially in certain recognised places near the middle of a verse. Also, **cesura.**

cafe /'kæfeɪ/ *n.* **1.** a room or building where coffee and light refreshments are served. **2.** a restaurant, usually low-priced. Also, **café.**

cafe latte *n.* an Italian style of coffee, typically made by pouring espresso coffee into a large glass of hot milk. Also, **caffe latte, latte.**

cafeteria /kæfə'tɪəriə/ *n.* an inexpensive restaurant or snack-bar, usually self-service.

caffeinated /'kæfəneɪtəd/ *adj.* **1.** containing introduced caffeine, as a beverage. **2.** *Colloq.* in a state of heightened stimulation as a result of consuming caffeine, as in coffee, cola, etc.

caffeine /'kæfin/ *n.* a bitter crystalline alkaloid, $C_8H_{10}N_4O_2.H_2O$, obtained from coffee, tea, etc., used in medicine as a stimulant, diuretic, etc.

caffe latte /kæfeɪ 'lateɪ/ *n.* → **cafe latte**.

caftan /'kæftæn/ *n.* **1.** a long garment having long sleeves and tied at the waist by a girdle, worn under a coat in the Near East. **2.** a loose garment, either short or floor length, with long, bell-shaped sleeves, in imitation of this garment. Also, **kaftan.** **–caftaned,** *adj.*

cage /keɪdʒ/ *n.* **1.** a box-shaped receptacle or enclosure for confining birds or other animals, made with openwork of wires, bars, etc. **2.** anything that confines or imprisons; prison. **3.** the enclosed platform of a lift, especially one in a mine. **4.** any skeleton framework. *–v.t.* **(caged, caging) 5.** to put or confine in or as in a cage.

cagey /'keɪdʒi/ *adj.* **(cagier, cagiest)** *Colloq.* cautious; secretive. Also, **cagy.** **–cagily,** *adv.* **–caginess,** *n.*

caiman /'keɪmən/ *n.* **(pl. caimans)** any of several tropical American crocodilians of the genus *Caiman* and related genera resembling and related to the alligators, but having overlapping abdominal plates. Also, **cayman.**

caino- a word element meaning 'new', 'recent', as in *Cainozoic.* Also, **ceno-, caeno-.**

cairn /kɛən/ *n.* a heap of stones set up as a landmark, monument, tombstone, etc. **–cairned,** *adj.*

caisson /'keɪsən/ *n.* **1.** a structure in which people can work on river beds, etc., consisting essentially of an airtight box or chamber with an open bottom, the water being kept out by the high air pressure maintained within. **2.** a boat-like structure used as a gate for a dock or the like. **3.** a wooden chest containing bombs or explosives, used as a mine; an ammunition chest.

cajole /kə'dʒoʊl/ *v.t.* to persuade by flattery or promises; wheedle; coax. **–cajolery, cajolement,** *n.* **–cajoler,** *n.*

cajuput /'kædʒəpʌt/ *n.* **1.** a small tree, *Melaleuca cajuputi,* found from south-eastern Asia to northern Australia. **2.** a green oil having a distinctive smell, distilled from the leaves of this tree, used medicinally.

cake /keɪk/ *n.* **1.** a sweet baked food in loaf or layer form, made with or without shortening, usually with flour, sugar, eggs, flavouring, and a liquid. **2.** a shaped or compressed mass: *a cake of soap, ice, etc. –v.t.* **3.** to form into a cake or compact mass. *–v.i.* **4.** to become formed into a cake or compact mass: *mud caked on his shoes. –phr.* **5. cakes and ale,** the good things and pleasures of life. **6. have one's cake and eat it,** to have the advantages, and be free of the disadvantages, of a situation. **7. piece of cake,** *Colloq.* something easily accomplished or obtained. **8. piece of the cake,** *Colloq.* a share of the profits, benefits, etc. **9. take the cake,** *Colloq.* **a.** to win the prize. **b.** to surpass all others; excel. **10. the cake,** the total possible material gain: *don't settle for part of the cake.*

calabash /'kæləbæʃ/ *n.* **1.** any of various gourds, especially the fruit of the bottle gourd, *Lagenaria siceraria.* **2.** the dried hollow shell of the calabash used as a vessel or otherwise.

caladenia /kælə'diniə, -jə/ *n.* any of the numerous species of the orchid genus *Caladenia* widespread in temperate Australia.

calamari /kælə'mari/ *n.* squid used as food.

calamata olive /kælə,matə 'ɒləv/ *n.* → **kalamata olive**.

calamine /'kæləmaɪn/ *n.* a liquid soothing to the skin, prepared from zinc oxide with ½ per cent ferric oxide. Also, **calamine lotion.**

calamity /kə'læməti/ *n.* **(pl. -ties) 1.** grievous affliction; adversity; misery. **2.** a great misfortune; a disaster. **–calamitous,** *adj.*

calcareous /kæl'kɛəriəs/ *adj.* of or relating to calcium carbonate; chalky: *calcareous earth.*

calcify /'kælsəfaɪ/ *v.i. Physiol.* to become calcareous or bony; harden by the deposit of calcium salts. **–calcification,** *n.*

calcite /'kælsaɪt/ *n.* one of the commonest minerals, calcium carbonate, $CaCO_3$, occurring in a great variety of crystalline forms; calcspar. Limestone, marble, and chalk consist largely of calcite, and seashells are largely composed of it.

calcium /'kælsiəm/ *n.* a silver-white divalent metal, occurring combined in limestone, chalk, gypsum, etc. *Symbol*: Ca; *relative atomic mass*: 40.08; *atomic number*: 20; *density*: 1.55 at 20°C.

calcium carbonate *n.* a crystalline compound, $CaCO_3$, occurring in nature as calcite, etc.

calculate /'kælkjəleɪt/ *v.t.* **1.** to ascertain by mathematical methods; compute: *we must calculate how much we've spent this month.* **2.** to estimate the possibility of failure before undertaking (a course of action): *to calculate a risk.* –*phr.* **3. calculate on** (or **upon**), to count or rely on. –**calculation** /kælkjə'leɪʃən/, *n.* –**calculable**, *adj.* –**calculative** /'kælkjəlætɪv/, *adj.*

calculated /'kælkjəleɪtəd/ *v.* **1.** past participle of **calculate**. –*adj.* **2.** deliberate or cold-blooded: *a calculated program of extermination.* –**calculatedly**, *adv.*

calculating /'kælkjəleɪtɪŋ/ *adj.* **1.** that performs calculations: *a calculating machine.* **2.** shrewd; cautious. **3.** selfishly scheming.

calculator /'kælkjəleɪtə/ *n.* a machine that performs mathematical operations mechanically, electro-mechanically or electronically.

calculus /'kælkjələs/ *n.* (*pl.* **-luses** *for def. 1*, **-li** /-laɪ/ *for def. 2*) **1. a.** a method of calculation, especially a highly systematic method of treating problems by a special system of algebraic notation. **b.** *Maths* the differential and integral calculus. **2.** *Pathol.* a stone or concretion found in the gall bladder, kidneys, or other parts of the body.

calendar /'kæləndə/ *n.* **1.** any of various systems of reckoning time, especially with reference to the beginning, length, and divisions of the year: *the Gregorian calendar.* **2.** a tabular arrangement of the days of each month and week in a year. **3.** a list, index, or register, especially one arranged chronologically, as a list of the cases to be tried in a court. –**calendric**, *adj.* –**calendrical**, *adj.* –**calendaric**, *adj.*

calf[1] /kaf/ *n.* (*pl.* **calves**) **1.** the young of the cow or of other bovine mammals (in cattle usually under one year of age). **2.** the young of certain other animals, as the elephant, seal, and whale. **3.** calfskin leather. **4.** a mass of ice detached from a glacier, iceberg, or floe. –*phr.* **5. kill the fatted calf**, to prepare an elaborate welcome. **6. worship the golden calf**, to be concerned solely with material wealth and possessions. –**calf-like**, *adj.*

calf[2] /kaf/ *n.* (*pl.* **calves**) the fleshy part of the back of the human leg below the knee.

calibrate /'kæləbreɪt/ *v.t.* **1.** to measure the calibre (def. 1) of. **2.** to check the accuracy or graduation of (any instrument, machine, or gun). –**calibration** /kælə'breɪʃən/, *n.* –**calibrator**, *n.*

calibre /'kæləbə/ *n.* **1.** the diameter of something of circular section, such as a bullet, or especially that of the inside of a tube, such as the bore of a gun. **2.** *Horology* the arrangement of the components of a watch or clock. **3.** degree of capacity or ability; personal character. **4.** degree of merit, or importance; quality. Also, *US,* **caliber.**

calico /'kælɪkoʊ/ *n.* (*pl.* **-coes** *or* **-cos**) **1.** (originally) a type of cotton cloth exported from India. **2.** a white cotton cloth. **3.** *US* a printed cotton cloth, superior to percale. –*adj.* **4.** made of calico. **5.** *Chiefly US* resembling printed calico; spotted; piebald.

caliper /'kæləpə/ *n.* **1.** (*usu. pl.*) a tool in its simplest form having two legs and resembling a draughtsman's compass, used for obtaining inside and outside measurements, especially across curved surfaces. **2.** *Med.* an appliance used on limbs to provide external support or correct deformities. Also, **calliper.**

caliph /'keɪləf/ *n.* the head of a Muslim state. Also, **calif, kaliph, khalif, khalifa.**

call /kɔl/ *v.t.* **1.** to cry out in a loud voice. **2.** (of a bird or other animal) to utter (its characteristic cry). **3.** to announce; proclaim: *to call a halt.* **4.** to attract the attention of by loudly uttering something. **5.** to command or request to come; summon: *the boy was called by his mother; to call a cab; to call a witness.* **6.** to telephone: *to call a friend.* **7.** to give a name to; name: *his parents named him James but the boys call him Jim.* **8.** to designate as something specified: *he called me a liar.* **9.** *Cards* to bid. **10. a.** to nominate (heads or tails) to win the toss of a coin. **b.** to nominate (one of two possible choices, as rough or smooth) using objects other than coins to determine an outcome in a selection process. **11.** to describe (a race, sporting event, etc.) on radio or television, or over the broadcasting system at the venue. –*v.i.* **12.** to speak loudly, as to attract attention; shout; cry: *to call for help.* **13.** (of a bird or animal) to utter its characteristic cry. **14.** to make a short visit; stop at a place on some errand or business: *he called at the shop to pick up the groceries.* **15.** to initiate a telephone communication. **16.** to announce the result of a contest, etc.: *the election was too close to call.* –*n.* **17.** a cry or shout. **18.** the cry of a bird or other animal. **19.** a summons or signal sounded by a bugle, bell, etc. **20.** a short visit: *to make a call on someone.* **21.** a telephone conversation. **22.** a summons; invitation; bidding. **23.** a sense of divine appointment to a vocation or service. **24.** a need or occasion. **25.** the verbal description of a race or other sporting event by a commentator on radio or television, or over the broadcasting system at the venue. **26.** → **call option.** **27.** *Cards* a bid. **28.** (in random selection processes such as tossing a coin) the chance to nominate the winning option: *it's your call.* **29.** a demand for payment of an obligation, especially where payment is at the option of the creditor. **30.** *Stock Exchange* the option of claiming stock at or before a given date. **31.** a decision to say or do something or act in a certain way: *he swore at the footballers drinking at the bar – a dodgy call in anyone's books.* –*adj.* **32.** *Commerce* repayable on demand: *call money; a call loan.* –*phr.* **33. call after**, to hail; recall. **34. call back**, **a.** to recall; summon or bring back. **b.** to telephone a further time or in reply. **35. call down**, **a.** to invoke from above; cause to descend. **b.** to reprimand; scold. **36. call for**, **a.** to go and get. **b.** to require; demand; need. **c.** to advocate: *the minister called for tougher penalties.* **37. call forth**, to bring or summon into action. **38. call in**, **a.** to collect: *to call in debts.* **b.** to withdraw from circulation: *to call in gold; to call in notes.* **c.** to invite; summon to or as to one's assistance. **39. call in** (or **into**) **question**, to throw doubt upon. **40. call into being**, to create. **41. call into play**, to activate. **42. call it a day**, to bring an activity to a close whether temporarily or permanently. **43. call off**, **a.** to order to cease a pursuit: *to call off the dogs.* **b.** to cancel or postpone: *to call off the party.* **c.** to terminate an activity: *to call off the game.* **44. call of nature**, (*euphemistic*) the desire or need to urinate or defecate. **45. call of the wild**, the desire to return to a freer natural habitat or lifestyle: *the caged leopard felt the call of the wild.* **46. call on**, **a.** to appeal to. **b.** to make a short visit to: *to call on friends.* **47. call out**, **a.** to utter in a loud voice. **b.** to summon into service: *to call out the militia.* **48. call someone's attention to**, to bring to someone's notice: *he called the police officer's attention to the disturbance.* **49. call up**, **a.** to bring into action, discussion, etc. **b.** to require payment of. **c.** to ask for payment of (all or part of the unpaid part of a company's share capital). **d.** to summon for military service, jury duty, shiftwork, etc. **e.** to recollect: *to call up my sorrows afresh.* **f.** to telephone. **50. good call**, an exclamation expressing approval for what is considered to be a good decision, analysis, etc. **51. on call**, **a.** Also,

at call. *Commerce* payable or subject to return without advance notice. **b.** (of doctors, etc.) available for duty at short notice. **52. the call, a.** permission from the chair to speak at a meeting: *the minister was given the call.* **b.** *Two-up* the right to call, that is, to nominate either heads or tails to win the toss. –**callable,** *adj.*

call account *n.* a type of deposit account with a financial institution from which the depositor can withdraw all moneys previously deposited at any given time.

call centre *n.* a location at which operators make phone calls for client organisations, as for marketing, information services, etc.

call centre operator *n.* an employee at a call centre who makes or takes phone calls as required.

caller ID *n. Telecommunications* a facility on a telephonic device which displays details of an incoming call, such as the caller's name and telephone number.

callgirl /ˈkɔlgɜl/ *n.* a female prostitute, especially one who makes herself available for appointments by telephone.

calli- a word element meaning 'beauty'.

calligraphy /kəˈlɪgrəfi/ *n.* **1.** the art of beautiful handwriting. **2.** handwriting; penmanship. –**calligrapher, calligraphist,** *n.* –**calligraphic** /kæləˈgræfɪk/, *adj.*

calling /ˈkɔlɪŋ/ *n.* **1.** a vocation, profession, or trade. **2.** a summons. **3.** an invitation.

calliper /ˈkæləpə/ *n.* → **caliper.**

callisthenics /kæləsˈθɛnɪks/ *n.* **1.** (*construed as pl.*) light gymnastic exercises designed to develop grace as well as organic vigour and health. **2.** a team sport incorporating elements of physical culture, marching, simplified ballet, gymnastic exercises, folk dance and modern dance. Also, **calisthenics.** –**callisthenic,** *adj.*

call option *n. Commerce, Stock Exchange* the right to buy a specified commodity, parcel of shares, foreign exchange, etc., at a set price on or before a specified date. Compare **put option.**

callous /ˈkæləs/ *adj.* **1.** hardened. **2.** hardened in mind, feelings, etc. **3.** having a callus; hardened, as parts of the skin exposed to friction. –**callously,** *adv.* –**callousness,** *n.*

callow /ˈkæloʊ/ *adj.* immature or inexperienced: *a callow youth.* –**callowness,** *n.*

callus /ˈkæləs/ *n.* (*pl.* **-luses**) **1.** *Pathol., Physiol.* a hardened or thickened part of the skin; a callosity. **2.** *Bot.* the tissue which forms over the wounds of plants, protecting the inner tissues and causing healing.

calm /kɑm/ *adj.* **1.** without rough motion; still: *a calm sea.* **2.** not windy; of Beaufort scale force nil. **3.** free from excitement or passion; tranquil: *a calm face*; *a calm voice*; *a calm manner.* –*v.t.* **4.** to make calm: *to calm fears*; *to calm an excited dog.* –**calmly,** *adv.* –**calmness,** *n.*

calorie /ˈkæləri, ˈkeɪləri/ *n.* **1.** a non-SI unit used to express the heat output of an organism or the energy value of a food. The recommended SI unit is the kilojoule; 1 calorie is equivalent to 4.1868 kJ. –*phr.* **2. count calories,** to be watchful of the amount of food consumed in order to control one's weight.

caltrop /ˈkæltrəp/ *n.* **1.** any of various plants having spiny heads or fruit, especially of the genera *Tribulus* and *Kallstroemia.* **2.** *Mil.* **a.** (formerly) an iron ball with four projecting spikes so disposed that when the ball is on the ground one of them always points upwards, used to obstruct the passage of cavalry, etc. **b.** a similar device used to puncture the tyres of motor vehicles. Also, **caltrap.**

calumny /ˈkæləmni/ *n.* (*pl.* **-nies**) **1.** a false and malicious statement designed to injure someone's reputation. **2.** slander. –**calumniate** /kəˈlʌmnieɪt/, *v.* –**calumniation** /kəˌlʌmniˈeɪʃən/, *n.* –**calumnious** /kəˈlʌmniəs/, *adj.*

calve /kɑv/ *v.i.* **1.** to give birth to a calf. **2.** (of a glacier, iceberg, etc.) to give off a detached piece.

calves[1] /kɑvz/ *n.* plural of **calf**[1].

calves[2] /kɑvz/ *n.* plural of **calf**[2].

calypso /kəˈlɪpsoʊ/ *n.* (*pl.* **-sos**) a song, based on a musical pattern of West Indian origin, with topical, usually improvised lyrics.

calyx /ˈkeɪlɪks, ˈkæl-/ *n.* (*pl.* **calyces** /ˈkæləsiz, ˈkeɪ-/ *or* **calyxes**) *Bot.* the outermost group of floral parts, usually green; the sepals.

cam /kæm/ *n.* a device for converting regular rotary or straight-line motion into irregular rotary or reciprocating motion, etc., commonly consisting of an oval- or heart-shaped, or other specially shaped flat piece, an eccentric wheel or the like, fastened on and revolving with a shaft, and engaging with another mechanism.

camaraderie /kæməˈrɑdəri/ *n.* comradeship; close friendship.

camber /ˈkæmbə/ *v.t.* **1.** to arch slightly; bend or curve upwards in the middle. –*v.i.* **2.** to cause to arch slightly. –*n.* **3.** a slight arching or convexity above, as of a ship's deck or a road surface.

cambist /ˈkæmbəst/ *n.* a dealer in the foreign exchange market.

camboy /ˈkæmbɔɪ/ *n.* a boy or young man who sets up a webcam site from which he can be viewed by others as an individual living his private life.

came /keɪm/ *v.* past tense of **come.**

camel /ˈkæməl/ *n.* **1.** either of two large ruminant quadrupeds of the genus *Camelus,* native to southern Eurasia, used as beasts of burden, and for meat, milk, hides, and wool: **a.** the **Arabian camel,** with one hump, *C. dromedarius,* now entirely domesticated except for wild populations in Australia which were introduced in the 19th century; used in Arabia for racing; dromedary. **b.** the **Bactrian camel,** with two humps, *C. bactrianus,* domesticated except for a wild population in the Gobi desert. **2.** a brown colour somewhat lighter than fawn. –**camelish, camel-like,** *adj.*

camellia /kəˈmiljə/ *n.* any of eighty or so species of the genus *Camellia,* belonging to the tea family Theaceae, shrubs or trees, native to Asia, with glossy evergreen leaves and white, pink, red, or variegated waxy roselike flowers; familiar in cultivation.

camembert /ˈkæməmbɛə/ *n.* a rich, cream-coloured variety of soft, ripened cheese, usually made in small, flat, round loaves, covered with a thin greyish-white rind.

cameo /ˈkæmioʊ/ *n.* (*pl.* **cameos**) **1.** an engraving in relief upon a gem, stone, etc., with differently coloured layers of the stone often utilised to produce a background of one hue and a design of another. **2.** a short piece of ornate, highly polished writing. **3.** a short performance or appearance in a play or film by a celebrity. –*adj.* **4.** of or relating to a cameo (def. 3): *a cameo appearance.* –*v.i.* (**cameoed, cameoing**) **5.** to make a cameo appearance in a play, film or television show.

camera[1] /ˈkæmrə, ˈkæmərə/ *n.* (*pl.* **-eras**) **1.** a photographic apparatus in which a sensitive plate or film is exposed, the image being formed by means of a lens. **2.** (in a television transmitting apparatus) the device in which the picture to be televised is formed before it is changed into electrical signals.

camera[2] /ˈkæmrə, ˈkæmərə/ *n.* (*pl.* **-erae** /-əri/) **1.** a judge's private room. –*phr.* **2. in camera,** *Law* in the privacy of a judge's chambers, with the public excluded. **b.** in private; in secret: *the meeting was held in camera.*

camgirl /ˈkæmgɜl/ *n.* a girl or young woman who sets up a webcam site from which she can be viewed by others as an individual living her private life.

camisole /ˈkæməsoʊl/ *n.* **1.** a woman's simple top with narrow shoulder straps, now usually worn as an undergarment. **2.** an ornamental bodice, worn under a thin outer bodice.

camomile /ˈkæməmaɪl/ *n.* → **chamomile.**

camouflage /'kæməflaʒ, -flɑdʒ/ *n.* **1.** the means by which any object or creature renders itself indistinguishable from its background, as by assuming the colour, shape, or texture of objects in that background. **2.** disguise; deception; false pretence. *–v.t.* (**-flaged, -flaging**) **3.** to disguise, hide, or deceive by means of camouflage: *camouflaged ships.*

camp[1] /kæmp/ *n.* **1.** a group of tents, caravans, or other temporary shelters in one place. **2.** the persons sojourning in such shelters. **3.** the place where the shelters are situated; a camping ground. **4.** *Aust., NZ* a place where people travelling in the bush stop for the night, usually establishing basic shelter and cooking facilities. **5.** *Aust., NZ* an overnight resting place for livestock. **6.** a site where soldiers are housed, in structures originally intended to be temporary. **7.** army life. **8.** a group of people favouring the same ideals, doctrines, etc.: *the socialist camp. –v.i.* **9.** to establish or pitch a camp. **10.** *Aust., NZ* (of livestock) to assemble or rest at a favoured place. **11.** *Colloq.* to sleep: *you take that bed, I'll camp here. –v.t.* **12.** to put or station (troops, etc.) in a camp shelter. *–phr.* **13. camp out,** to perform or imbue in a tent or similar shelter. **14. make camp,** to establish a camp. **15. strike camp,** to disassemble and remove the tents, equipment, etc., of a camp. **–camping,** *n., adj.* **–camper,** *n.*

camp[2] /kæmp/ *adj.* **1.** exaggeratedly theatrical and flashy in style. **2.** (of a male) homosexual. **3.** (of a male) effeminate; given to acting and speaking with exaggerated mannerisms. *–n.* **4.** an exaggerated effeminate style, often self-parodying or vulgar. **5.** a male homosexual. *–v.i.* **6.** to act in a camp manner. *–phr.* **7. camp as a row of (pink) tents,** *Colloq.* (of a male) ostentatiously homosexual. **8. camp it up,** **a.** to make an ostentatious or affected display. **b.** (of a male) to flaunt one's homosexuality. **9. camp up,** to perform or imbue (something) with a camp quality: *he camped up his performance of Othello.* **10. high camp,** behaviour or performance heavily marked with camp features.

campaign /kæm'peɪn/ *n.* **1.** the military operations of an army in the field during one season or enterprise. **2.** any course of aggressive activities for some special purpose: *a sales campaign.* **3.** the activities of political candidates and organisations aimed at gaining support for themselves or their policies at an election or in a referendum, etc. **–campaigner,** *n.*

camper /'kæmpə/ *n.* **1.** someone who makes camp. **2.** → **campervan.** *–phr.* **3. not a happy camper,** *Colloq.* a person who is displeased for some reason: *he was not a happy camper after losing his wallet.*

campervan /'kæmpəvæn/ *n.* **1.** a motor van in which people may live, usually temporarily, furnished with beds, stove, sink, etc. *–v.i.* (**-vanned, -vanning**) **2.** to live, as for a holiday, in a campervan. **–campervanner,** *n.* **–campervanning,** *n.*

camphor /'kæmfə/ *n.* **1.** a whitish, translucent, crystalline, pleasant-smelling compound, $C_{10}H_{16}O$, obtained chiefly from the camphor laurel and used in medicine, the manufacture of celluloid, etc. **2.** any of various similar substances, used for household use as an insect deterrent. **–camphoric** /kæm'fɒrɪk/, *adj.*

campus /'kæmpəs/ *n.* **1.** the grounds of a university or other institute of higher education. **2.** the grounds of an institution such as a hospital or museum.

can[1] /kæn/, *weak form* /kən/ *or, if followed by k or g,* /kəŋ/ *v. (modal)* (*present sing.* 1 **can,** 2 **can** *or, Archaic,* **canst,** 3 **can; could**) **1.** to know how to: *he can speak Chinese.* **2.** to be able to; have the strength, means, authority to: *I can't reach the top shelf; can you help me?* **3.** to have permission to: *you can go now; can I speak to you a moment?* **4.** used with verbs of perception, etc.: *I can hear music.* **5.** referring to a possible event or situation: *the desk can go here and the lamp*

can go there; we can have another meeting next week; you can go by bus or by train; you can't get blood from a stone. **6.** to happen or be true on certain occasions or in certain instances: *it can get lonely in the evenings; excessive thirst can be a symptom of diabetes.* **7.** used in requests: *can you help me with this?* **8.** used in emphatic commands: *you can mind your own business!; he can get lost! –phr. Colloq.* **9. can do,** an exclamation indicating that a request can be satisfactorily met. **10. no can do,** an exclamation indicating that a request cannot be satisfactorily met.

can[2] /kæn/ *n.* **1.** a container, sometimes sealed, usually for a liquid and made of aluminium or sheet iron coated with tin or other metal. **2.** a tin (def. 4). **3.** the contents of a can. **4.** a drinking vessel. **5.** a rubbish bin (def. 1). **6.** (*pl.*) *Colloq.* a set of earphones. **7.** *US Colloq.* a toilet. **8.** *US Colloq.* the buttocks. *–v.t.* (**canned, canning**) **9. a.** to put in a container, usually sealed for preservation. **b.** to withhold or put aside (a report, film, etc.). **10.** *Colloq.* to dismiss; fire. **11.** *Colloq.* to criticise harshly: *to can a performance –phr.* **12. can it,** *Colloq.* to be or become silent. **13. can of worms,** *Colloq.* a situation, problem, etc., bristling with difficulties. **14. carry the can,** *Colloq.* to take the blame. **15. in the can, a.** (of a film) ready for distribution; filmed, developed, and edited. **b.** completed; made final. **16. kick the … can,** to stir up a predictable reaction of fear and resentment in the community against a particular group ideology, usually to discredit a political opponent: *to kick the communist can.* **17. the can,** *Colloq.* **a.** jail. **b.** the blame for something: *to take the can.* **c.** dismissal. **–canning,** *n.*

canal /kə'næl/ *n.* **1.** an artificial waterway for navigation, drainage, irrigation, etc. **2.** a long, narrow arm of the sea penetrating far inland. **3.** a tubular passage or cavity for food, air, etc., especially in an animal or plant; a duct.

canapé /'kænəpeɪ/ *n.* a thin piece of bread, toast, etc., spread or topped with cheese, caviar, anchovies, or other appetising foods.

canary /kə'nɛəri/ *n.* (*pl.* **-ries**) **1.** Also, **canary bird.** a well-known cage bird, *Serinus canarius,* native to the Canary Islands, and originally of a brownish or greenish colour, but through modification in the domesticated state now usually a bright, clear yellow; noted for its beautiful song. **2.** Also, **canary yellow.** a bright, clear yellow colour.

canasta /kə'næstə/ *n.* a card game of the rummy family in which the main object is to meld sets of seven or more cards.

cancel /'kænsəl/ *verb* (**-celled** *or, Chiefly US,* **-celed, -celling** *or, Chiefly US,* **-celing**) *–v.t.* **1.** to decide not to proceed with (a previously arranged appointment, meeting, event, etc.). **2.** to cross out (writing, etc.) by drawing a line through. **3.** to make (something) no longer legal or effective. **4.** to mark or make a hole in (a postage stamp, bus ticket, etc.) so it cannot be used again. **5.** Also, **cancel out.** to counterbalance; compensate for. **6.** to call off (something arranged): *to cancel a picnic.* **7.** *Maths* to cross out (a factor common to both terms of a fraction, equal terms on opposite sides of an equation, etc.). *–v.i.* **8.** to decide not to proceed with a previously arranged appointment, meeting, event, etc.: *to cancel at the last minute.* **–cancellation** /kænsə'leɪʃən/, *n.* **–canceller,** *n.*

cancer /'kænsə/ *n.* **1.** *Med.* an abnormal and uncontrolled proliferation of cells in some part of the body, tending to prevent normal functioning of surrounding organs and often spreading by means of the circulatory or lymphatic system to other parts of the body. **2.** a disease, often fatal, caused by the presence of such a growth. **3.** any evil condition or thing that spreads destructively. **–cancerous,** *adj.*

Cancer /ˈkænsə/ *n.* **1.** the fourth sign of the zodiac, which the sun enters about 21 June; the Crab. **2. Tropic of,** a parallel of latitude on the terrestrial globe about 23½° north of the equator, being the northern boundary of the Torrid Zone. –**Cancerian,** *n.*, *adj.*

candela /kænˈdiːlə, -ˈdeɪlə/ *n.* the SI base unit of luminous intensity; the luminous intensity in the perpendicular direction of a surface of 1/600 000 of one square metre of a black body radiator at the temperature of solidification of platinum under a pressure of 101 325 pascals. *Symbol:* cd

candelabrum /kændəˈlabrəm/ *n.* (*pl.* **-bra** /-brə/) an ornamental branched candlestick.

candid /ˈkændəd/ *adj.* **1.** frank; outspoken; open and sincere: *a candid account.* **2.** honest; impartial: *a candid mind.* **3.** (of a photograph) unposed or informal. –**candidly,** *adv.* –**candidness,** *n.*

candidate /ˈkændədət, -deɪt/ *n.* **1.** someone who seeks an office, an honour, etc. **2.** someone who is selected by others as a contestant for an office, etc. **3.** someone who seeks an academic qualification or the like, usually by examination. **4.** a suitable subject: *that idea is a candidate for the wastepaper basket.* –**candidacy** /ˈkændədəsi/, **candidature** /ˈkændədətʃə/, **candidateship,** *n.*

candied /ˈkændid/ *adj.* **1.** impregnated or encrusted with or as with sugar. **2.** crystallised, as sugar, honey, etc. **3.** honeyed or sweet; flattering.

candle /ˈkændl/ *n.* **1.** a long, usually slender, piece of tallow, wax, etc., with an embedded wick, burnt to give light. –*v.i.* **2.** to examine (especially eggs for freshness) by holding between the eye and a light. –*phr.* **3. burn the candle at both ends,** to lead a too strenuous existence; attempt to do too much, as by making an excessive demand on one's available energy, rising early and retiring late, etc. **4. not hold a candle to,** to be unable to compete with, or stand comparison to. **5. not worth the candle,** not worth the effort or expense.

candour /ˈkændə/ *n.* **1.** frankness, as of speech; sincerity; honesty. **2.** freedom from bias; fairness; impartiality. Also, **candor.**

candy /ˈkændi/ *n.* (*pl.* **-dies**) **1.** a sweet made of sugar crystallised by boiling. –*v.t.* (**-died, -dying**) **2.** to cook in heavy syrup until transparent, as fruit, fruit peel, or ginger. **3.** to reduce (sugar, etc.) to a crystalline form, usually by boiling down. **4.** to make sweet, palatable, or agreeable.

cane /keɪn/ *n.* **1.** a long, thin, jointed, woody stem of certain plants, such as bamboo. **2.** a stick used for punishing school children. **3.** a walking stick. **4.** rattan used in weaving chairs, etc. –*v.t.* **5.** to beat with a cane. **6.** to make or fit with cane: *to cane chairs.* **7.** *Colloq.* to defeat soundly in a competition. –**caner,** *n.*

cane toad *n.* a large toad, *Bufo marinus,* native to South America and introduced into north-eastern Australia in an unsuccessful attempt to control sugarcane insect pests; now itself a pest; bufo.

canine /ˈkeɪnaɪn/ *adj.* **1.** of or like a dog; relating to or characteristic of dogs. –*n.* **2.** *Anat.* one of the four pointed teeth, especially prominent in dogs, situated one on each side of each jaw, next to the incisors. **3.** any animal of the dog family, the Canidae, including the wolves, jackals, hyenas, coyotes, and foxes.

canine distemper *n.* a highly contagious disease of carnivores caused by a paramyxovirus.

canister /ˈkænəstə/ *n.* a small box, usually of metal, for holding tea, coffee, etc.

canker /ˈkæŋkə/ *n.* **1.** *Med.*, *Vet. Science* an ulcerous sore or disease. **2.** *Bot.* a stem disease. **3.** anything that rots, infects, or destroys. –*v.t.* **4.** to infect; corrupt. –*v.i.* **5.** to become cankered.

cannabin /ˈkænəbən/ *n.* a poisonous resin extracted from Indian hemp.

cannabis /ˈkænəbəs/ *n.* marijuana; the dried pistillate parts of Indian hemp.

cannellini bean /kænəlini ˈbin/ *n.* the white haricot bean, commonly used in Italian cuisine in soups and salads. Also, **cannellini.**

cannelloni /kænəˈləʊni/ *pl. n.* tubular or rolled pieces of pasta usually filled with a mixture of meat or cheese and served with a tomato or cream sauce.

cannery /ˈkænəri/ *n.* (*pl.* **-ries**) a place where meat, fish, fruit, etc., are canned.

cannibal /ˈkænəbəl/ *n.* **1.** a human being who eats human flesh. **2.** any animal that eats its own kind. –**cannibalism,** *n.* –**cannibalistic** /kænəbəˈlɪstɪk/, *adj.*

cannibal star *n.* *Astron.* a small dense star which, because of the attraction it exerts on a larger, less dense mass, is able to draw matter on the periphery of a larger star to itself.

cannon /ˈkænən/ *n.* (*pl.* **-nons** *or, especially collectively,* **-non**) **1.** a large ancient gun for firing heavy projectiles, mounted on a carriage. **2.** a powerful automatic gun for firing explosive shells. **3.** *Machinery* a hollow cylinder fitted over a shaft and capable of revolving independently. **4.** Also, **cannon bit, canon bit.** the part of a bit that is in the horse's mouth. **5.** *Billiards* a shot in which the ball struck with the cue is made to hit two balls in succession. **6.** any strike and rebound, as a ball striking a wall and glancing off. –*phr.* **7. cannon into,** to come into collision with; crash into.

cannot /ˈkænɒt, kæˈnɒt/ *v.* a form of **can not.**

cannula /ˈkænjələ/ *n.* a metal tube for insertion into the body, used to keep a passage open, to draw off fluid, or to introduce medication.

canny /ˈkæni/ *adj.* (**-nier, -niest**) **1.** careful; cautious; wary. **2.** knowing; sagacious; shrewd; astute. –**canniness,** *n.* –**cannily,** *adv.*

canoe /kəˈnu/ *n.* **1.** any light and narrow boat that is propelled by one or more paddles in place of oars. –*v.i.* (**canoed, canoeing**) **2.** to paddle a canoe. **3.** to go in a canoe. –*phr.* **4. paddle one's own canoe,** to be independent; manage on one's own. –**canoeing,** *n.* –**canoeist,** *n.*

canola /kəˈnəʊlə/ *n.* a variety of rapeseed from which is produced an oil extract for human consumption and a meal for livestock feed.

canon¹ *n.* **1.** the law or body of laws of a church. **2.** any rule, law, principle, or standard. **3.** an officially accepted set of holy books. **4.** the books of the Bible recognised by the Christian church as genuine and inspired. **5.** any officially recognised set of representative writings: *the canon of English literature.* **6.** a list of works of a writer generally accepted as genuine. **7.** *Roman Catholic Church* a list of recognised saints. **8.** *Music* a piece in which the same tune is played or sung by two or more parts overlapping each other.

canon² /ˈkænən/ *n.* one of a body of dignitaries or prebendaries attached to a cathedral or a collegiate church; a member of the chapter of a cathedral or a collegiate church. –**canonry,** *n.*

canonise /ˈkænənaɪz/ *v.t.* **1.** *Eccles.* to place in the canon of saints. **2.** to glorify. Also, **canonize.** –**canonisation** /kænənaɪˈzeɪʃən/, *n.*

canopy /ˈkænəpi/ *n.* (*pl.* **-pies**) **1.** a covering suspended or supported over a throne, bed, etc., or held over a person, sacred object, etc. **2.** an overhanging protection or shelter. **3.** the sky. **4.** the fabric body of a parachute.

cant¹ /kænt/ *n.* **1.** insincere statements, especially conventional pretence of enthusiasm for high ideals; insincere expressions of goodness or piety. **2. a.** a secret language or jargon formerly spoken by the criminal class in England in order to deceive, consisting chiefly of invented words of unknown origin. **b.** underworld slang; argot. **3.** the words, phrases, etc., peculiar to a particular class, party, profession, etc.

cant² /kænt/ *n.* **1.** a slope; slant. **2.** a sudden movement that tilts or overturns something. *–v.t.* **3.** to put in an oblique position; tilt; turn. *–v.i.* **4.** to take or have an inclined position; tilt; turn.

can't /kænt/ *v.* contraction of **cannot**.

cantaloupe /ˈkæntəloup, ˈkæntəlup/ *n.* **1.** the edible fruit of the melon *Cucumis melo* var. *cantalupensis*, having a hard, usually ribbed and netted rind, and orange-coloured flesh; rockmelon. **2.** any of several similar melons. Also, *Rare*, **cantaloup**.

cantankerous /kænˈtæŋkərəs/ *adj.* ill-natured; quarrelsome; perverse or contrary, as in disposition: *a cantankerous old maid.* **–cantankerously**, *adv.* **–cantankerousness**, *n.*

cantata /kænˈtatə/ *n.* a vocal and instrumental composition, either sacred or secular, and resembling a short oratorio, such as a lyric drama set to music but not to be acted.

canteen /kænˈtin/ *n.* **1.** a restaurant or cafeteria attached to a factory, office, etc. **2.** a similar food outlet in a school, sportsground, etc., usually staffed by volunteer parents; tuckshop; kiosk. **3.** a temporary food supply set up during an emergency. **4.** a box containing a set of cutlery. **5.** a small container used by soldiers and others for carrying water or other liquids.

canter /ˈkæntə/ *n.* **1.** an easy gait of a horse (or other quadruped) in which in the course of each stride three feet are off the ground at once; between a trot and a gallop in speed. *–v.i.* **2.** to go or ride at a canter.

canticle /ˈkæntɪkəl/ *n.* one of the non-metrical hymns or chants, chiefly from the Bible, used in church services.

cantilever /ˈkæntɪlivə/ *n.* **1.** *Machinery* a free part of any horizontal member projecting beyond a support. **2.** *Civil Eng.* either of two bracket-like arms projecting towards each other from opposite banks or piers, serving to form the span of a bridge (**cantilever bridge**) when united.

canto /ˈkæntou/ *n.* (*pl.* **-tos**) **1.** one of the main or larger divisions of a long poem, as in Dante's *Inferno.* **2.** *Music* a song or melody.

canton /ˈkæntən, kænˈtɒn/ *n.* **1.** a small territorial district, especially one of the states of the Swiss confederation. **2.** a division, part, or portion of anything. **–cantonal** /ˈkæntənəl/, *adj.*

cantor /ˈkæntə/ *n.* an officer whose duty is to lead the singing in a cathedral or in a collegiate or parish church; a precentor.

canvas /ˈkænvəs/ *n.* **1.** a closely woven, heavy cloth of cotton or other fibres, used for tents, sails, etc. **2.** a piece of canvas on which an oil painting is done. **3.** tent(s): *campers living under canvas.* **4.** sails collectively: *a ship under full canvas.* **5.** a fabric, usually stiff, of coarse loose weave, used as a base for embroidery, etc.

canvass /ˈkænvəs/ *v.t.* **1.** to solicit votes, subscriptions, opinions, orders, etc., from (a district, group of people, etc.). **2.** to engage in a political campaign. **3.** to examine carefully; investigate by inquiry: *to canvass the new measure.* **4.** to discuss; debate: *to canvass an idea.* **–canvasser**, *n.*

canyon /ˈkænjən/ *n.* a deep valley with steep sides, often with a stream flowing through it.

canyoning /ˈkænjənɪŋ/ *n.* the sport of following a river down a canyon, usually involving whitewater rafting, rock climbing, abseiling, etc. **–canyoner**, *n.*

cap /kæp/ *n.* **1.** a covering for the head, especially one fitting closely and made of softer material than a hat, and having little or no brim, but often having a peak. **2.** the flat, peaked headdress worn by soldiers and others. **3.** a special headdress denoting rank,

occupation, etc.: *a cardinal's cap*; *a nurse's cap.* **4. a.** a headdress denoting that the wearer has been selected for a special team, as one representing his or her country, in certain sports, as cricket. **b.** membership of such a team. **5.** a close-fitting waterproof headdress worn when swimming, etc. **6.** the detachable protective top of a fountain pen, jar, etc. **7.** *Dentistry* → **crown** (def. 12b). **8.** the top or upper surface, as of a wave, etc. **9.** *Bot.* the pileus of a mushroom. **10.** a noisemaking device for toy pistols and starter's guns, made of a small quantity of explosive wrapped in paper or other thin material. **11.** → **diaphragm** (def. 4). **12.** an upper limit on a price, salary, etc. *–v.t.* (**capped**, **capping**) **13.** to provide or cover with or as with a cap. **14.** to seal off (a gas or oil well). **15.** *Dentistry* → **crown** (def. 16). **16.** to select as a member of a representative team in football, cricket, etc. **17.** *NZ* to confer a degree on. **18.** to complete. **19.** (sometimes fol. by *with*) to surpass; follow up, especially with something as good or better, as a story, sporting achievement, etc. *–phr.* **21. cap and gown**, academic dress. **22. cap in hand**, humbly, submissively; as a suppliant. **23. cap off**, to conclude satisfactorily. **24. if the cap fits, wear it**, if the judgement applies, accept it. **25. set one's cap at**, to try to capture the admiration and attention of; try to secure as a lover.

capable /ˈkeɪpəbəl/ *adj.* **1.** having much intelligence or ability; competent; efficient; able: *a capable instructor.* *–phr.* **2. capable of, a.** having the ability, strength, etc., to; qualified or fitted for. **b.** susceptible to; open to the influence or effect of. **c.** predisposed to; inclined to. **–capability**, *n.* **–capably**, *adv.*

capacious /kəˈpeɪʃəs/ *adj.* capable of holding much. **–capaciously**, *adv.* **–capaciousness**, *n.*

capacitance /kəˈpæsətəns/ *n. Elect.* **1.** the property of a system which enables it to store electrical charge. **2.** the extent of this, usually measured in farads; electrical capacity.

capacitor /kəˈpæsətə/ *n. Elect.* a device for accumulating and holding an electric charge, consisting of two conducting surfaces separated by an insulator or dielectric; a condenser.

capacity /kəˈpæsəti/ *n.* (*pl.* **-ties**) **1.** the ability to contain, absorb, or hold. **2.** volume; content. **3.** mental ability: *a scholar of great capacity.* **4.** (fol. by *of, for,* or infinitive) power, ability, or possibility of doing something: *capacity for self-protection; capacity to act quickly.* **5.** position; function: *in the capacity of a legal adviser.* **6.** maximum output: *factory working at capacity.* **7.** the most that a container, theatre, room, etc., can hold: *the hall was filled to capacity.* **8.** the most that a factory, mine, etc., can produce.

cap-and-trade *adj.* of or relating to an emissions trading scheme in which a cap is set for allowable emissions in a particular area, and individual emitters are given their allocation of emission permits which they can use or sell provided the overall cap is not breached. See **baseline-and-credit**.

cape¹ /keɪp/ *n.* a sleeveless garment fastened round the neck and falling loosely over the shoulders, worn separately or attached to a coat, etc.

cape² /keɪp/ *n.* a piece of land jutting into the sea or some other body of water.

Cape Barren goose *n.* a large goose, *Cereopsis novaehollandiae*, endemic to southern Australia, greyish in colour with pink legs and a black bill; breeds on off-shore islands.

caper¹ /ˈkeɪpə/ *v.i.* **1.** to leap or skip about in a sprightly manner; prance. *–n.* **2.** a prank; capricious action; harebrained escapade. **–caperer**, *n.*

caper² /ˈkeɪpə/ *n.* **1.** a shrub, *Capparis spinosa*, of Mediterranean regions. **2.** its flower bud, which is pickled and used for garnish or seasoning.

caper berry *n.* Also, **scrub caper berry, brush caper berry**. a small tree, *Capparis arborea*, found in dry rainforest from the Hunter Valley in NSW to Cape York in Qld. **2.** the fruit of this tree, globose and green when ripe, with a creamy edible pulp packed with hard seeds. **3.** → **caperberry**.

caperberry /ˈkeɪpəbɛri/ *n.* (*pl.* **-berries**) the semi-mature fruit of the Mediterranean caper shrub (**caper²**), often pickled for use in cooking or for eating as a relish. Also, **caper berry**.

caper bush *n.* any of various bushes belonging to the *Capparis* genus of the Caper family, that grow in the northern parts of inland NSW and in Qld.

capillary /kəˈpɪləri/ *n.* (*pl.* **-laries**) **1.** *Anat.* one of the minute blood vessels between the terminations of the arteries and the beginnings of the veins. *–adj.* **2.** of or relating to a tube of fine bore. **3.** *Physics* of or relating to the property of surface tension. **4.** *Bot.* resembling hair in the manner of growth or in shape. **5.** *Anat.* of or relating to a capillary or capillaries. *–***capillarity**, *n.*

capillary action *n.* the elevation or depression of liquids in fine tubes, etc., due to the relative strengths of the intermolecular forces within the liquid, as by surface tension, and the attraction between the molecules of the liquid and the tube; it accounts for the seeping up of water through the interstices of rock, the rising of sap in trees, the soaking up of water in paper towel, etc.

capital¹ /ˈkæpətl/ *n.* **1.** a city or town which is the official seat of government in a country, state, etc. **2.** a capital (upper case) letter. **3.** the wealth, in money or property, owned by an individual, firm, etc. **4.** any form of wealth used to produce more wealth. **5.** the ownership interest in a business. **6.** any source of profit, advantage, power, etc.: *he tried to make capital out of a chance situation.* **7.** (*oft. upper case*) capitalists as a group or class. *–adj.* **8.** relating to capital: *capital stock.* **9.** highly important. **10.** chief, especially as being the seat of government. **11.** excellent or first-rate. **12.** (of letters) of the large size used at the beginning of a sentence or as the first letter of a proper name(as opposed to *lower-case*). **13.** involving the loss of life, usually as punishment: *a capital offence.*

capital² /ˈkæpətl/ *n. Archit.* the head, or uppermost part, of a column, pillar, etc.

capital expenditure *n.* an addition to the value of a fixed asset, as by the purchase of a new building.

capital gain *n.* a gain, not of the nature of income, but made on the disposal of an asset, such as bonds, real property, etc.

capital-intensive *adj.* of or relating to an industry which, while requiring relatively little labour, requires a high capital investment in plant, etc. (opposed to *labour-intensive*).

capitalise /ˈkæpətəlaɪz/ *v.t.* **1.** to write or print in capital letters, or with an initial capital. **2.** to authorise a certain amount of stocks and bonds in the corporate charter: *to capitalise a company.* **3.** to convert (floating debt) into stock or shares. **4.** *Accounting* to set up (expenditures) as business assets in the books of account instead of treating as expense. **5.** to supply with capital. **6.** to estimate the value of (a stock or an enterprise). *–phr.* **7. capitalise on,** to take advantage of; turn to one's advantage: *capitalise on one's opportunities.* Also, **capitalize**. *–***capitalisation** /kæpətəlaɪˈzeɪʃən/, *n.*

capitalism /ˈkæpətəlɪzəm/ *n.* **1.** a system under which the means of production, distribution, and exchange are in large measure privately owned and directed. **2.** Also, **monopoly capitalism**. (especially in Marxist theory) an economic model representing the Western economic systems as one in which money and power are progressively concentrated in the hands of a few. **3.** a system favouring such concentration of wealth.

capitalist /ˈkæpətəlɪst/ *n.* **1.** someone who has capital, especially extensive capital, used in business enterprises. *–adj.* **2.** of or relating to capital or capitalists; founded on or believing in capitalism. *–***capitalistic** /kæpətəˈlɪstɪk/, *adj.* *–***capitalistically** /kæpətəˈlɪstɪkli/, *adv.*

capital levy *n.* a tax based on total assets.

capital stock *n.* **1.** the total shares issued by a company. **2.** the book value of all the shares of a company, including unissued shares and those not completely paid in.

capital sum *n.* the sum stated to be payable on the happening of some event against which insurance has been effected.

capital surplus *n.* the surplus of a business, exclusive of its earned surplus.

capitation /kæpəˈteɪʃən/ *n.* **1.** a numbering or assessing based on a count of each head or individual person. **2.** a fee or payment of a uniform amount for each person.

capitulate /kəˈpɪtʃəleɪt/ *v.i.* to surrender unconditionally or on stipulated terms. *–***capitulation**, *n.*

cappuccino /kæpəˈtʃinoʊ/ *n.* a coffee drink in which espresso coffee is topped with hot milk which has been frothed up by passing steam through it.

caprice /kəˈpris/ *n.* a sudden change of mind without apparent or adequate motive; whim. *–***capricious** /kəˈprɪʃəs/, *adj.*

Capricorn *n.* **1.** Also, **Capricornus**. the tenth sign of the zodiac, which the sun enters about 22 December; the Goat. **2.** Also, **Capricornian**. a person born under the sign of Capricorn and (according to tradition) exhibiting the typical Capricornian personality traits in some degree. **3. Tropic of,** a parallel of latitude on the terrestrial globe about 23½° south of the equator, being the southern boundary of the Torrid Zone. *–***Capricornian**, *n.*, *adj.*

capri pants /kəˈpri pænts/ *pl. n.* close-fitting calf-length pants for women, originally fashionable in Italy in the 1950s.

capsicum /ˈkæpsəkəm, ˈkæpsɪkəm/ *n.* **1.** any plant of the genus *Capsicum*, as *C. frutescens*, the common pepper of the garden, in many varieties, with mild to hot, pungent seeds enclosed in a podded or bell-shaped pericarp which also ranges from mild to extremely hot. **2. a.** the fruit of any of these plants, used as a vegetable. **b.** a preparation of this fruit, used as a condiment.

capsicum spray *n.* an aerosol spray of oleoresin derived from capsicum, which irritates the skin and eyes; used to disable an attacker. Also, **OC spray, pepper spray**.

capsize /kæpˈsaɪz/ *v.i.* **1.** to overturn: *the boat capsized.* *–v.t.* **2.** to upset: *they capsized the boat.*

capslock key /ˈkæpslɒk ki/ *n. Computers* a toggle key on a keyboard which when depressed determines that letters appear in upper case.

capstan /ˈkæpstən/ *n.* a device resembling a windlass but with a vertical axis, commonly turned by a bar or lever, and winding a cable, for raising weights (as an anchor) or drawing things closer (as a ship to its jetty).

capsule /ˈkæpsjul, ˈkæpful, -fəl/ *n.* **1.** a small case, envelope, or covering. **2.** a gelatinous case enclosing a dose of medicine; the dose itself. **3.** the compartment of a spacecraft containing the crew or instruments. **4.** the part of a spacecraft or aircraft which is detachable. **5.** anything short or condensed, as a story or news item. *–***capsular**, *adj.*

captain /ˈkæptən, ˈkæptn/ *n.* **1.** a person who is in authority over others; leader. **2.** *Army* **a.** a commissioned officer in the Australian Army, ranking below major and above lieutenant. **b.** the rank. *Abbrev.:* CAPT **3.** the commander or master of a merchant ship or other vessel. **4.** *Navy* **a.** a commissioned officer in the Royal

Australian Navy ranking below commodore and above commander, usually in command of a warship. **b.** the rank. *Abbrev.*: CAPT –*v.t.* **5.** to lead or command as a captain. –**captaincy**, *n.* –**captainship**, *n.*

Captain Cooker /'kæptən ˌkʊkə/ *n. NZ* a wild pig.

captain's call *n.* **1.** *Cricket* a decision made by the captain without consultation with other members of the team. **2.** a decision made by a political or business leader without consultation with colleagues.

captcha /'kæptʃə/ *n. Computers (from trademark)* a test that enables the identification of a human response, as opposed to a computer-generated response, by setting a task, such as reading distorted letters, that only a human being can successfully complete.

caption /'kæpʃən/ *n.* **1.** a heading or title, as of a chapter, article, or page. **2.** *Printing* a legend for a picture or illustration. **3.** *Film* the title of a scene, the text of a speech, etc., shown on the screen.

captious /'kæpʃəs/ *adj.* **1.** apt to make much of trivial faults or defects; fault-finding; difficult to please. **2.** proceeding from a fault-finding or cavilling disposition: *captious remarks.* **3.** apt or designed to ensnare or perplex, especially in argument: *captious questions.* –**captiously**, *adv.* –**captiousness**, *n.*

captivate /'kæptəveɪt/ *v.t.* to enthral by beauty or excellence; enchant; charm. –**captivation** /kæptə'veɪʃən/, *n.* –**captivator**, *n.*

captive /'kæptɪv/ *n.* **1.** a prisoner. –*adj.* **2.** made or held prisoner. **3.** enslaved by love, etc.; captivated. –**captivity** /kæp'tɪvəti/, *n.*

captive conservation *n.* a conservation program which relies on breeding animals in captivity.

captor /'kæptə/ *n.* someone who captures.

capture /'kæptʃə/ *v.t.* **1.** to take by force or stratagem; take prisoner; seize: *the chief was captured.* **2.** *Computers* to transfer (information) to computer-readable form. –*n.* **3.** the act of taking by force or stratagem. **4.** the thing or person captured. **5.** inclusion as data, especially data entered into a computer for analysis. –**capturer**, *n.*

car /ka/ *n.* **1.** a vehicle, especially one for passengers, carrying its own power-generating and propelling mechanism, usually an internal-combustion engine, for travel on ordinary roads. **2.** a railway carriage or wagon. **3.** the part of a balloon, lift, etc., in which the passengers, etc., are carried. –*adj.* **4.** of or relating to a motor car: *a car door.*

carabiner /kærə'binə/ *n.* (in mountaineering) a spring-loaded metal clip designed for joining ropes together. Also, **karabiner**.

carafe /kə'raf, -'ræf, 'kæræf/ *n.* **1.** a glass bottle for water, wine, etc. **2.** the contents of such a bottle.

carambola /kærəm'boʊlə/ *n.* the edible fruit of the carambola tree, *Averrhoa carambola*, native to south-eastern Asia, which is yellow-brown in colour with a deeply ridged skin; star fruit.

caramel /'kærəməl/ *n.* **1.** burnt sugar, used for colouring and flavouring food, etc. **2.** a kind of sweet, commonly in small blocks, made from heated sugar, butter, and milk or cream. **3.** any of various sauces and flavourings made in a similar way. **4.** the light brown colour of caramel.

carapace /'kærəpeɪs/ *n.* a shield, test, or shell covering some or all of the dorsal part of an animal.

carat /'kærət/ *n.* Also, **metric carat**. a unit of weight in gemstones, 0.2×10^{-3} kg. *Symbol*: CM **2.** a twenty-fourth part (used in expressing the fineness of gold, pure gold being 24 carats fine).

caravan /'kærəvæn/ *n.* **1.** a vehicle in which people may live, whether temporarily or permanently, usually having two wheels and designed to be drawn by a car. **2.** such a vehicle having four cartwheels and

horse-drawn, traditionally inhabited by Romani people, circus folk, etc. **3.** a group of merchants or others travelling together, as for safety, especially over deserts, etc., in Asia or Africa.

caraway /'kærəweɪ/ *n.* **1.** an umbelliferous condimental herb, *Carum carvi*, bearing aromatic seedlike fruit (**caraway seeds**) used in cookery and medicine. **2.** the fruit or seeds.

carbine /'kabaɪn, 'kabən/ *n.* **1.** (formerly) a short rifle for cavalry use. **2.** a light semi-automatic or fully automatic rifle of a carbine type, as an armalite, useful in circumstances that restrict movement or in difficult terrain.

carbo- a word element meaning 'carbon', as in *carborundum*. Also, **carb-**.

carbohydrate /kabo'haɪdreɪt, kaboʊ'haɪdreɪt/ *n.* any of a class of organic compounds having the general formula $C_x(H_2O)_y$, including cellulose, starch, glycogen, and sugars such as glucose. Cellulose is the main structural material in plants, and the sugars, etc. are the main food and energy source for animals.

carbohydrate loading *n.* a strategy, employed especially by those involved in sports requiring long-term endurance, such as long-distance running and cycling, which involves increasing one's intake of carbohydrate in the days before the endurance exercise in order to maximise the storage of glycogen in the muscles.

carbon /'kabən/ *n.* **1.** *Chem.* a widely distributed element which forms organic compounds in combination with hydrogen, oxygen, etc., and which occurs in a pure state as charcoal. *Symbol*: C; *relative atomic mass*: 12.011; *atomic number*: 6; *density*: (of diamond) 3.51 at 20°C; (of graphite) 2.26 at 20°C. **2.** any of a number of carbon-based compounds found as gases, as carbon dioxide, methane, etc., which are causes of the greenhouse effect, as in *carbon sequestration*, *carbon recovery*. **3.** a sheet of carbon paper. **4.** a carbon copy. –**carbonaceous** /kabə'neɪʃəs/, *adj.*

carbonara /kabə'narə/ *adj.* of or relating to a pasta sauce made from fried bacon or ham with heated egg and cream.

carbonate *n.* /'kabəneɪt, -nət/ **1.** *Chem.* a salt of carbonic acid, as *calcium carbonate*, $CaCO_3$. –*v.t.* /'kabəneɪt/ **2.** to charge or impregnate with carbon dioxide. –**carbonation** /kabə'neɪʃən/, *n.* –**carbonated**, *adj.*

carbon cap *n.* an upper limit, set by a government or international body, of permissible production of carbon dioxide and other greenhouse gases as part of a strategy to limit global production and reduce the risk of climate change.

carbon capture *n.* the process of removing carbon dioxide from a point where it is normally released in large quantities, as from a power plant, so that it can then be prevented from entering the atmosphere. See **carbon sequestration**.

carbon capture and storage *n.* carbon capture, followed by its containment in a holding medium or geological formation so as to prevent its release into the atmosphere. *Abbrev.*: CCS

carbon credit *n.* a credit earned within the carbon tax system for decreasing carbon dioxide in the atmosphere, as by planting forests, etc.

carbon dating *n.* → **radiocarbon dating**.

carbon dioxide /kabən daɪ'ɒksaɪd/ *n.* a colourless, odourless, incombustible gas, CO_2, used extensively in industry as dry ice, and in fizzy drinks, fire-extinguishers, etc. It is present in the atmosphere and is formed during respiration.

carbon dioxide equivalent *n.* a measure of how much global warming a greenhouse gas may give rise to, made by determining the amount of CO_2 required to achieve the equivalent radiative forcing, and using this CO_2 quantity as a reference point. *Abbrev.:* CDE

carbon emission *n.* an amount of carbon dioxide released into the atmosphere by coal-fired power generators, transport, forest burning, slash-and-burn agriculture, etc.

carbon footprint *n.* the carbon dioxide emissions for which an individual or organisation can be held responsible, as by their travel, fuel consumption, diet, energy requirements, etc.

carbon gas *n.* carbon dioxide, the principal greenhouse gas.

carbon monoxide /kabən mə'nɒksaɪd/ *n.* a colourless, odourless, poisonous gas, CO, burning with a pale blue flame, formed when carbon burns with an insufficient supply of air.

carbon-neutral *adj.* having achieved carbon neutrality.

carbon neutrality *n.* a state in which an organisation or country balances its carbon emissions against its carbon reductions to achieve zero net emissions of carbon dioxide.

carbon paper *n.* 1. paper faced with a preparation of carbon or other material, used between two sheets of plain paper in order to reproduce upon the lower sheet that which is written or typed on the upper. 2. a paper for making photographs by the carbon process.

carbon price *n.* a price on carbon as a fuel which takes into account the damage that it does to the environment, as through an emissions trading scheme, a carbon tax, or regulations.

carbon sequestration *n.* the process by which carbon dioxide is removed from the atmosphere, either naturally by plants in their growth, or artificially by various means whereby it is prevented from returning to the atmosphere by the creation of products containing it which have long-term use, as timber from forests, or by storing it in sealed reservoirs, as by injecting it into underground geological formations.

carbon sink *n.* a natural or human-made reservoir able to store carbon for a long period of time, thus reducing the level of greenhouse gases.

carbon tax *n.* a tax on the consumption of fossil fuels, designed to recoup the costs of managing and repairing the environmental damage caused by such fuels.

carbon tetrachloride /ˌkabən tɛtrə'klɔraɪd/ *n.* a non-flammable, colourless liquid, CCl_4, used in medicine, and as a fire-extinguisher, cleaning fluid, solvent, etc.

carbon trading *n.* trading in carbon credits on a carbon market.

carborundum /kabə'rʌndəm/ *n.* (*from trademark*) 1. *Chem.* silicon carbide, SiC, an important abrasive produced in the electric furnace. 2. a block of this or a similar material for sharpening knives, etc.

carb soda *n.* *Colloq.* sodium bicarbonate.

carbuncle /'kabʌŋkəl/ *n.* 1. a painful circumscribed inflammation of the subcutaneous tissue, resulting in suppuration and sloughing, and having a tendency to spread (somewhat like a boil, but more serious in its effects). 2. a garnet cut in a convex rounded form without facets. 3. deep red. –**carbuncled**, *adj.* –**carbuncular** /ka'bʌŋkjələ/, *adj.*

carburettor /'kabjərɛtə, kabjə'rɛtə/ *n.* a device in an internal-combustion engine for mixing a volatile fuel with the correct proportion of air in order to form an explosive gas. Also, *Rare*, **carburetter**; *US*, **carburetor**.

carcase /'kakəs/ *n.* the body of an animal slaughtered for meat, after removal of the offal, etc. Also, **carcass**.

carcass /'kakəs/ *n.* 1. the dead body of an animal or (now only in contempt) of a human being. 2. (*humorous*) a living body. 3. anything from which life and power are gone. 4. → **carcase**.

carcinogen /ka'sɪnədʒən/ *n.* any substance which tends to produce a cancer in a body. –**carcinogenic** /kasənə-'dʒɛnɪk/, *adj.*

carcinoma /kasə'noʊmə/ *n.* (*pl.* **-mas** *or* **-mata** /-mətə/) a malignant and invasive epithelial tumour that spreads by metastasis and often recurs after excision; a cancer. See **basal cell carcinoma**, **squamous cell carcinoma**.

card¹ /kad/ *n.* 1. a piece of stiff paper or thin pasteboard, usually rectangular, for various uses: *a business card.* 2. → **postcard**. 3. a piece of cardboard with more or less elaborate ornamentation, bearing a complimentary greeting: *a Christmas card.* 4. one of a set of small pieces of cardboard with spots or figures, used in playing various games, in prognostication, etc. 5. (*pl.*) a game or games played with such a set. 6. a resource, plan, idea, approach to a problem or proposition, etc.: *that's his best card.* 7. a program of events, as at horseraces. 8. *Computers* a circuit board: *a sound card.* 9. *Colloq.* a likeable, amusing, or facetious person. –*v.t.* 10. to ask (someone) for proof of age, as at a club, bar, etc. –*phr.* 11. **have a card up one's sleeve**, to have a secret plan, resource, etc., that can be used to advantage at a later time. 12. **keep** (or **hold**) (or **play with**) **one's cards close to one's chest**, to be secretive about one's moves. 13. **on the cards**, likely to happen. 14. **put** (or **lay**) **one's cards on the table**, to speak plainly or candidly; disclose all information in one's possession.

card² /kad/ *n.* a toothed implement or wire brush used in disentangling and combing out fibres of wool, flax, etc., preparatory to spinning. –**carder**, *n.*

cardamom /'kadəməm/ *n.* the aromatic seed capsule of various plants of the genera *Amomum* and *Elettaria*, native to tropical Asia, used as a spice or condiment and in medicine.

cardboard /'kadbɔd/ *n.* 1. thin, stiff pasteboard. –*adj.* 2. made of cardboard. 3. resembling cardboard in appearance, texture, etc. 4. existing or performing a function in appearance only; insubstantial: *a cardboard prime minister, a cardboard empire.*

card-carrying *adj.* possessing full membership, as of a trade union or political party.

cardi- variant of **cardio-** before vowels, as in *cardialgia.*

cardiac /'kadiæk/ *adj.* 1. relating to the heart. 2. relating to the oesophageal portion of the stomach.

cardigan /'kadigən/ *n.* a knitted jacket made from wool, synthetics, etc.

cardinal /'kadənəl/ *adj.* 1. of prime importance; chief; principal; fundamental: *of cardinal significance.* 2. deep rich red. –*n.* 3. one of the members of the Sacred College of the Roman Catholic Church, ranking next to the pope. –**cardinally**, *adv.* –**cardinalship**, *n.*

cardinal number *n.* *Maths* a number such as *one, two, three,* etc., which indicates how many things are in a given set, and not the order in which those things occur (the latter is indicated by the ordinal numbers, *first, second, third,* etc.).

cardinal point *n.* one of the four chief directions of the compass; the north, south, east, and west points.

cardio- a word element meaning 'heart'. Also, **cardi-**.

cardiogram /'kadiəgræm/ *n.* *Med.* 1. → **electrocardiogram**. 2. any of various other records of the activity of the heart, as an echocardiogram.

cardiograph /'kadiəgræf, -graf/ *n.* *Med.* 1. → **electrocardiograph**. 2. any of various other devices for recording the activity of the heart, as an echocardiograph. –**cardiographic** /kadiə'græfik/, *adj.* –**cardiography** /kadi'ɒgrəfi/, *n.*

cardiology /kadi'ɒlədʒi/ *n.* the branch of medical science that deals with the heart and its functions. –**cardiologist**, *n.*

cardioplegia /ˌkadioʊˈplidʒiə, -ˈplidʒə/ n. the process of stopping the heartbeat for a short period of time during cardiac surgery.

cardiopulmonary resuscitation /ˌkadioʊˌpʌlmənri rəsʌsəˈteɪʃən/ n. → **CPR**.

cardiovascular /ˌkadioʊˈvæskjələ/ adj. relating to the heart and blood vessels.

card reader n. Computers a device which reads data on a card by sensing or analysing the information coded on it and converting it into electronic messages.

care /kɛə/ n. **1.** worry; anxiety; concern: care had aged him. **2.** a cause of worry, anxiety, distress, etc.: to be free from care. **3.** serious attention; solicitude; heed; caution: devote great care to work. **4.** protection; charge: under the care of a doctor. **5.** an object of concern or attention. –v.i. (**cared, caring**) **6.** to be troubled; to be affected emotionally. **7.** to be concerned or solicitous; have thought or regard. **8.** to be inclined: I don't care to do it today. –phr. **9. care for, a.** (esp. with a negative) to have a liking or taste for: I don't care for cabbage. **b.** to have a fondness or affection for: he cares greatly for her. **c.** to look after; make provision for: the welfare state must care for the needy. **10. care of**, at the address of. Symbol: c/–, C/– Abbrev.: c/o **11. not care less**, to not care at all: I couldn't have cared less when he decided to leave. **12. take care to**, to be sure to: take care to lock the door.

careen /kəˈrin/ v.t. **1.** to cause (a ship) to heel over or lie wholly or partly on its side, as for repairing or the like. –v.i. **2.** to lean, sway, or tip to one side, as a ship. **3.** to careen a ship. **4.** (of a vehicle, aeroplane, etc.) to move rapidly in an uncontrolled way, especially swaying from side to side. –**careenage**, n. –**careener**, n.

career /kəˈrɪə/ n. **1.** general course of action or progress of a person through life, as in some profession, in some moral or intellectual action, etc. **2.** an occupation, profession, etc., followed as one's lifework: a career in law. –v.i. **3.** to run or move rapidly along. –adj. **4.** designating a person in a profession who regards their role as a career (def. 2): a career politician.

carefree /ˈkɛəfri/ adj. without anxiety or worry.

careful /ˈkɛəfəl/ adj. **1.** cautious in one's actions. **2.** taking pains in one's work; exact; thorough. **3.** (of things) done or performed with accuracy or caution. **4.** solicitously mindful. **5.** mean; parsimonious. –**carefully**, adv. –**carefulness**, n.

caregiver /ˈkɛəgɪvə/ n. the person, such as a parent, childcare worker, nurse, etc., who has the responsibility in a paid or unpaid capacity of caring for a dependant.

careless /ˈkɛələs/ adj. **1.** not paying enough attention to what one does. **2.** not exact or thorough: careless work. **3.** done or said heedlessly or negligently; unconsidered: a careless remark. **4.** not caring or troubling; having no care or concern; unconcerned: careless of what people thought; careless about his health. –**carelessly**, adv. –**carelessness**, n.

carer /ˈkɛərə/ n. someone who, in a voluntary or professional capacity, has the care of someone else, as a patient, child, etc.

caress /kəˈrɛs/ n. **1.** an act or gesture expressing affection, as an embrace, pat, kiss, etc. –v.t. **2.** to touch or pat gently to show affection. –**caresser**, n. –**caressingly**, adv.

caret /ˈkærət/ n. **1.** a mark (^) made in written or printed matter to show the place where something is to be inserted. **2.** Computers the symbol ^. **3.** Computers this symbol used to signify the Control key. **4.** Computers → **cursor** (def. 1).

caretaker /ˈkɛəteɪkə/ n. **1.** someone who takes care of a thing or place, especially one whose job is to maintain and protect a building or group of buildings. –adj.

2. holding office temporarily until a new appointment, election, etc., can be made, as an administration.

careworker /ˈkɛəwɜkə/ n. someone employed as a caregiver, such as a nurse, social worker, childcare worker, etc.

cargo /ˈkagoʊ/ n. (pl. **-goes**) **1.** the goods carried on a ship, aircraft, truck, etc. **2.** any load.

cargo pants pl. n. trousers or shorts with pockets sewn onto the outside of the legs, usually at mid-thigh level.

caribou /ˈkærɪbu/ n. (pl. **-bou** or **-bous**) any of several North American subspecies of reindeer, especially those living wild as opposed to domesticated.

caricature /ˈkærəkətʃʊə/ n. a picture, description, etc., ludicrously exaggerating the peculiarities or defects of persons or things. –**caricaturist**, n.

caries /ˈkɛəriz/ n. decay, as of bone or teeth, or of plant tissue.

carillon /kəˈrɪljən/ n. **1.** a set of stationary bells hung in a tower and sounded by manual or pedal action, or by machinery. **2.** a melody played on such bells. **3.** an organ stop which imitates the peal of bells. **4.** a set of horizontal metal plates, struck by hammers, used in the modern orchestra.

carjack /ˈkadʒæk/ v.t. to steal (a car) by forcing the driver to vacate it, or by forcing the driver to drive to a chosen destination. Also, **car-jack**. –**carjacker**, n. –**carjacking**, n.

cark /kak/ Aust., NZ Colloq. –v.i. **1.** to collapse; die. –phr. **2. cark it, a.** to collapse; die. **b.** (of a machine) to fail; break down.

car kit n. a hands-free mobile phone system installed in a vehicle.

carmine /ˈkamaɪn/ n. **1.** a crimson or purplish red colour. **2.** a crimson pigment obtained from cochineal.

carnage /ˈkanɪdʒ/ n. the slaughter of a great number, as in battle; butchery; massacre.

carnal /ˈkanəl/ adj. **1.** not spiritual; merely human; temporal; worldly. **2.** relating to the flesh or the body, its passions and appetites; sensual. **3.** sexual. –**carnality** /kaˈnæləti/, n. –**carnally**, adv.

carnal knowledge n. **1.** sexual intercourse, especially with someone under the age of consent. **2.** Law the penetration, however slight, of the female organ by the male organ.

carnation /kaˈneɪʃən/ n. **1.** any of numerous cultivated varieties of clove pink, Dianthus caryophyllus, with fragrant flowers of various colours. **2.** pink; light red.

carnival /ˈkanəvəl/ n. **1.** revelry and merrymaking, usually riotous and noisy, and accompanied by processions, etc. **2.** a festive procession. **3.** a fair or amusement show, especially one erected temporarily for a period of organised merrymaking. **4.** a series of sporting events as a racing carnival, a surfing carnival, etc.

carnivore /ˈkanəvɔ/ n. **1.** Zool. one of the Carnivora, the order of mammals, chiefly flesh-eating, that includes the cats, dogs, bears, seals, etc. **2.** Bot. a flesh-eating plant.

carnivorous /kaˈnɪvərəs/ adj. flesh-eating. –**carnivorously**, adv. –**carnivorousness**, n.

carob /ˈkærəb/ n. the fruit of a tree, Ceratonia siliqua, of the Mediterranean regions, being a long, dry pod containing hard seeds in a sweet pulp, used as animal fodder, and in cookery as a substitute for chocolate.

carol /ˈkærəl/ n. **1.** a song, especially of joy. **2.** a Christmas song or hymn. –v.i. (**-rolled** or, Chiefly US, **-roled**, **-rolling** or, Chiefly US, **-roling**) **3.** to sing, especially in a lively, joyous manner; warble. –**caroller**, n. –**carolling**, n.

carotid /kəˈrɒtəd/ n. Anat. either of the two great arteries, one on each side of the neck, which carry blood to the head. –**carotidal**, adj.

carouse /kə'raʊz/ *n.* **1.** a noisy or drunken feast; jovial revelry. –*v.i.* **2.** to engage in a carouse; drink deeply. –**carousal,** *n.*

carousel *n.* **1.** Also, **carrousel.** → **merry-go-round** (def. 1). **2.** Also, **carrousel.** a tournament in which horseback riders execute various movements in formation. **3.** Also, **carrousel.** a revolving device by which luggage is returned to travellers after a journey by plane, ship, bus, etc. **4.** Also, **carrousel.** a circular magazine for holding photographic slides. **5.** → **turntable** (def. 2).

carp[1] /kap/ *v.i.* to find fault; cavil; complain unreasonably: *to carp at minor errors.* –**carper,** *n.* –**carping,** *n.*, *adj.* –**carpingly,** *adv.*

carp[2] /kap/ *n.* **1.** a large, coarse freshwater food fish, *Cyprinus carpio* (family Cyprinidæ), commonly bred in ponds and widespread in Australia. **2.** any of various other fishes of the same family.

-carp a word element forming a noun termination meaning 'fruit', used in botanical terms, as *endocarp.*

carpenter /'kapəntə/ *n.* someone whose job is to erect and fix the wooden parts, etc., in the building of houses and other structures. –**carpentry,** *n.*

carpet /'kapət/ *n.* **1.** a heavy fabric, for covering floors. **2.** a covering of such a fabric. **3.** any covering like a carpet: *they walked on the grassy carpet.* –*v.t.* **4.** to cover or furnish with, or as with, a carpet. **5.** to reprimand. –*phr.* **6. on the carpet,** *Colloq.* before an authority for a reprimand.

carpetbagger /'kapətbægə/ *n.* someone who takes up residence in a place and exploits the local people.

carpet bowls *n.* a game similar to lawn bowls but played indoors.

carpet snake *n.* a large, non-venomous Australian python, *Morelia spilotes variegata,* with a particoloured pattern on its skin, often used in silos and barns to control rodent pests.

car phone *n.* a telephone installed in a motor vehicle.

-carpic a word element related to **-carp,** as in *endocarpic.*

carpo- a word element meaning 'fruit' as in *carpology.*

car pool *n.* Also, **carpool. 1.** an arrangement whereby a group of people travel together in one car on a regular basis, taking turns to drive their own car. –*v.i.* **2.** → **carpool.**

carpool /'kapul/ *v.i.* to take part in a car pool: *the parents decided to carpool to reduce traffic around the school.* Also, **car pool.** –**carpooling,** *n.*

carport /'kapɔt/ *n.* a roofed wall-less shed often projecting from the side of a building, used as a shelter for a motor vehicle.

-carpous a combining form related to **-carp,** as in *apocarpous.*

carpus /'kapəs/ *n.* (*pl.* **-pi** /-pi/) the wrist, or the group of bones comprising it. –**carpal,** *adj.*

car rally *n.* → **rally**[1] (def. 10).

carrel /kə'rel, 'kærəl/ *n.* (in a library) a small area or cubicle used by students and others for individual study; a stall.

carriage /'kærɪdʒ/ *n.* **1.** a wheeled vehicle, usually horse-drawn, for carrying people, especially one made for comfort and style. **2.** a passenger-carrying unit on trains. **3.** a wheeled support, for moving something heavy, as a cannon. **4.** a part, as of a machine, designed for carrying something. **5.** a manner of carrying the head and body; bearing: *the carriage of a soldier.* **6.** the act of carrying; conveyance: *the expenses of carriage.* **7.** the cost of carrying.

carriage return *n.* **1.** (on a typewriter) a key or lever which causes the next character typed to be positioned at the left margin and down a line. **2.** (on a computer) a key or character which performs a similar function, as a return key or enter key. **3.** the procedure of activating a carriage return.

carrier /'kæriə/ *n.* **1.** a person, company, etc., that undertakes to convey goods or persons. **2.** a small platform on a bicycle used for carrying luggage. **3.** *Med.* an individual harbouring specific organisms, who, though often immune to the agent harboured, may transmit the disease to others. **4.** an organisation provides telecommunication services.

carrier pigeon *n.* **1.** a pigeon trained to fly home from great distances and thus transport written messages; a homing pigeon. **2.** one of a breed of domestic pigeons characterised by a huge wattle at the base of the beak.

carrion /'kæriən/ *n.* **1.** dead and putrefying flesh. **2.** rottenness; anything vile.

carrot /'kærət/ *n.* **1.** a plant of the umbelliferous genus *Daucus,* especially *D. carota,* in its wild form a widespread, familiar weed, and in cultivation valued for its reddish edible root. **2.** the root of this plant. **3.** an incentive: *to dangle a carrot.*

carry /'kæri/ *verb* (**-ried, -rying**) –*v.t.* **1.** to convey from one place to another in a vehicle, ship, pocket, hand, etc. **2.** to transmit or transfer in any manner; take or bring: *the wind carries sounds; she carries her audience with her.* **3.** to bear the weight, burden, etc., of; sustain. **4.** to take a (leading or guiding part) in acting or singing; bear or sustain (a part or melody). **5.** to hold (the body, head, etc.) in a certain manner. **6.** to behave or comport (oneself). **7.** to take, especially by force; capture; win. **8.** to secure the election of (a candidate) or the adoption of (a motion or bill). **9.** to print or publish in a newspaper or magazine. **10.** to extend or continue in a given direction or to a certain point: *to carry the war into enemy territory.* **11.** to lead or impel; conduct. **12.** to have as an attribute, property, consequence, etc.: *his opinion carries great weight.* **13.** to support or give validity to (a related claim, etc.): *one decision carries another.* **14.** *Maths* to transfer (a number) from one column to the next, as from units to tens, tens to hundreds, etc. **15.** *Commerce* **a.** to keep on hand or in stock. **b.** to keep on one's account books, etc. **16.** to bear, as a crop. **17.** to be pregnant with: *she is carrying her third child.* **18.** to support (livestock): *our grain supply will carry the cattle through the winter.* –*v.i.* **19.** to act as a bearer or conductor. **20.** to have or exert propelling force: *the rifle carries a long way.* **21.** to be transmitted, propelled, or sustained: *my voice carries farther than his.* –*n.* (*pl.* **-ries**) **22.** range, as of a gun. **23.** *Golf* the distance traversed by a ball before it alights. –*phr.* **24. carry away, a.** to cause (someone) to lose control or ordinary restraint: *his passion carried him away.* **b.** to cause (someone) to be engrossed so as to lose some awareness of where they are: *she was carried away by the ballet.* **c.** to remove by force: *the nest was carried away by the storm.* **d.** *Naut.* (of a mast, sail, etc.) to break or tear away from its fastenings. **25. carry forward, a.** to make progress with. **b.** *Bookkeeping* to transfer (an amount, etc.) to the next column, page, etc. **26. carry off, a.** to win (the prize, honour, etc.). **b.** to manage or handle (a difficult situation, etc.): *he carried it off well.* **c.** to cause the death of. **27. carry on, a.** to manage; conduct. **b.** to continue; keep up without stopping. **c.** to behave in an excited or foolish manner. **d.** to exhibit signs of being in a temper. **e.** (sometimes fol. by *with*) to dally amorously; flirt. **28. carry out,** to accomplish or complete (a plan, scheme, etc.): *we carried out the details of her plan.* **29. carry over, a.** to postpone; hold off until later. **b.** *Stock Exchange* to defer completion of (a contract) so that it falls under a different account. **c.** (of vegetables, etc., not sold in a day's trading) to remain for later sale. **30. carry the day,** to succeed; triumph. **31. carry the drinks,** *Cricket Colloq.* to act as twelfth man. **32. carry the fight,** *Boxing* to attack persistently. **33. carry through, a.** to accomplish; complete. **b.** to support or help (in a difficult situation, etc.).

cart /kɑt/ *n.* **1.** a heavy horse-drawn vehicle, usually with solid tyres and made chiefly of wood, without springs, formerly used for carrying heavy goods. **2.** (formerly) a light horse-drawn vehicle especially one used, and sometimes specifically designed, for home delivery of domestic supplies: *a bread cart; a milk cart.* **3.** any small vehicle moved by hand. –*v.t.* **4.** to convey in a cart. **5.** to convey, especially something awkward or cumbersome which is transported with difficulty. –*phr.* **6. put the cart before the horse, a.** to reverse the natural order. **b.** to confuse cause and effect.

carte blanche /kɑt ˈblɒntʃ, kɑt ˈblɒ̃ʃ/ *n. (pl.* **cartes blanches** /kɑts ˈblɒntʃ, kɑts ˈblɒ̃ʃ/) **1.** a signed paper left blank for the person to whom it is given to fill in his or her own conditions. **2.** unconditional authority; full power.

cartel /kɑˈtɛl/ *n.* a collusive syndicate, combine, or trust, generally formed to regulate prices and output in some field of business.

cartilage /ˈkɑtəlɪdʒ, ˈkɑtlɪdʒ/ *n. Zool., Anat.* a firm, elastic, flexible substance of a translucent whitish or yellowish colour, consisting of a connective tissue. –**cartilaginous** /kɑtəˈlædʒənəs/, *adj.*

cartography /kɑˈtɒgrəfi/ *n.* the production of maps, including construction of projections, design, compilation, drafting, and reproduction. –**cartographer,** *n.* –**cartographic** /kɑtəˈgræfɪk/, **cartographical** /kɑtəˈgræfɪkəl/, *adj.* –**cartographically** /kɑtəˈgræfɪkli/, *adv.*

carton /ˈkɑtən/ *n.* a cardboard box, especially one in which food such as eggs, milk, etc., is packaged and sold.

cartoon /kɑˈtun/ *n.* **1.** a sketch or drawing as in a newspaper or periodical, symbolising or caricaturing some subject or current interest, in an exaggerated way. **2.** *Art* a drawing, of the same size as a proposed decoration or pattern in fresco, mosaic, tapestry, etc., for which it serves as a model to be transferred or copied. **3.** a comic strip. **4.** an animated film, often of short duration and with humorous subject matter. –*v.t.* **5.** to represent by a cartoon. –**cartoonist,** *n.* –**cartooning,** *n.*

cartridge /ˈkɑtrɪdʒ/ *n.* **1.** Also, **cartridge case.** a cylindrical case of pasteboard, metal, or the like, for holding a complete charge of powder, and often also the bullet or the shot, for a rifle, machine gun, or other small arm. **2.** the case, charge, and bullet or shot; a round. **3.** a case containing any explosive charge, as for blasting. **4.** anything resembling a cartridge, as the disposable container of ink for some types of fountain pen. **5.** the disposable container for ink in a photocopier, printer, etc. **6. a.** (in a tape recorder) a plastic container enclosing recording tape usually in the form of an endless loop. **b.** a device of similar principle, or more loosely of the cassette principle, with wider tape, as for a video recorder.

carve /kɑv/ *v.t.* **1.** to fashion by cutting: *to carve a block of stone into a statue.* **2.** to produce by cutting: *to carve a design in wood.* **3.** to cut into slices or pieces, as meat. –*phr.* **4. carve out,** to make or establish for oneself by one's own efforts. **5. carve up,** *Colloq.* **a.** to slash (a person) with a knife or razor. **b.** to make a verbal attack on. **c.** to operate on: *the doctors carved me up in hospital.* **d.** to defeat (a person or team) soundly: *the Eagles really carved us up last week.* **e.** to distribute (profits, a legacy, illegal gain, an estate, etc.). **f.** to subdivide (land). **g.** to subject to major earthworks: *the bulldozers carved up the hills.* –**carver,** *n.*

carving /ˈkɑvɪŋ/ *n.* **1.** the act of fashioning or producing by cutting. **2.** carved work; a carved design.

cascade /kæsˈkeɪd/ *n.* **1.** a waterfall over steep rocks, or a series of small waterfalls. **2.** an arrangement of lace, etc., in folds falling one over another in a zigzag fashion. **3.** a type of firework resembling a waterfall in effect. **4.** *Elect.* an arrangement of component devices, each of which feeds into the next in succession. –*v.i.* **5.** to fall in or like a cascade.

case[1] /keɪs/ *n.* **1.** an instance of the occurrence, existence, etc., of something. **2.** the actual state of things. **3.** a question or problem of moral conduct: *a case of conscience.* **4.** situation; condition; plight. **5.** a state of things involving a question for discussion or decision. **6.** a statement of facts, reasons, etc. **7.** an instance of disease, etc., requiring medical or surgical treatment or attention. **8.** a medical or surgical patient. **9.** a person, family, or other social unit receiving any kind of professional social assistance. **10.** *Law* **a.** a proceeding, civil or criminal, in a court of law. **b.** the set of submissions made in support of a party to a proceeding. **11.** *Gram.* **a.** a category in the inflection of nouns, pronouns, and (in languages other than English) adjectives, indicating their syntactic roles within the phrase or clause. **b.** an abstract category expressing any of the underlying syntactic relations which nouns, pronouns, and adjectives contract with each other in a particular phrase or clause. **12.** *Colloq.* a peculiar or unusual person: *he's a case.* –*phr.* **13. in any case,** under any circumstances; anyhow. **14. in case of,** in the event of. **15. (just) in case, a.** if; if it should happen that: *doctors on stand-by just in case there is an emergency.* **b.** as a precaution: *I'll take an umbrella, just in case.*

case[2] /keɪs/ *n.* **1.** a thing for containing or enclosing something; a receptacle. **2.** a sheath or outer covering: *a knife case.* **3.** a box with its contents. –*v.t.* **4.** to put or enclose in a case; cover with a case. **5.** *Colloq.* to examine or survey (a house, bank, etc.) in planning a crime.

casein /ˈkeɪsiən, -sin/ *n.* the major group of proteins in milk, which can be precipitated by rennet, to be used as the basis of cheese, and also in the manufacture of certain plastics.

case law *n.* law established by judicial decisions in particular cases, instead of by legislation.

casement /ˈkeɪsmənt/ *n.* **1.** a window sash opening on hinges which are generally attached to the upright side of its frame. **2.** a casing or covering. –**casemented,** *adj.*

cash /kæʃ/ *n.* **1.** money, especially money on hand, as opposed to a money equivalent (as a cheque). **2.** money paid at the time of making a purchase, or sometimes an equivalent (as a cheque), as opposed to credit. –*v.t.* **3.** to give or obtain cash for (a cheque, etc.). –*phr.* **4. cash in,** to obtain cash for: *to cash in an insurance policy.* **5. cash in on, a.** to gain a return from. **b.** to turn to one's advantage. **6. cash in one's chips, a.** (in poker, etc.) to hand in one's counters, etc., and get cash for them. **b.** *Colloq.* to die. **7. cash up,** (of shopkeepers, etc.) to add up the takings.

cash account *n. Bookkeeping* a record kept of cash transactions.

cash crop *n.* a crop grown for its commercial value rather than for the use of the grower, especially one which offers a quick return of money.

cash economy *n.* → **black economy.**

cashew /ˈkæʃu/ *n.* **1.** a tree, *Anacardium occidentale,* native to tropical America, whose bark yields a medicinal gum. **2.** its fruit, a small, edible, kidney-shaped nut (**cashew nut**).

cash flow *n.* the amount of cash generated by a company in a given period. It equals the net profit after tax, less dividends paid out, plus depreciation in that period.

cashier /kæˈʃɪə/ *n.* a person who has charge of cash or money, especially one who superintends monetary transactions.

cash management trust *n.* a trust that pools the relatively small investments of individuals and invests the funds it receives in short-dated securities, such as treasury notes and bank bills, which have traditionally required large minimum investments. *Abbrev.*: CMT

cashmere /ˈkæʃmɪə/ *n.* the fine downy wool at the roots of the hair of Kashmir goats of India.

cash register *n.* a till with a mechanism for indicating amounts of sales, etc.

casimiroa /kæsəməˈrouə/ *n.* → white sapote.

casing /ˈkeɪsɪŋ/ *n.* **1.** a case or covering. **2.** material for a case or covering. **3.** the framework around a door, window, or staircase, etc. **4.** any frame or framework.

casino /kəˈsinou/ *n.* (*pl.* -nos) a building or large room used for gambling games.

cask /kɑsk/ *n.* **1.** a barrel-like container, usually wooden, and of varying size, for holding liquids, etc., often one larger and stronger than an ordinary barrel. **2.** a light-weight container, usually cardboard with a plastic lining and small tap, used for holding and serving wine for domestic use.

casket /ˈkɑskət/ *n.* **1.** a small chest or box, as for jewels. **2.** a coffin.

cassava /kəˈsavə/ *n.* **1.** any of several tropical plants of the genus *Manihot* of the family Euphorbiaceae, such as *M. esculenta* (**bitter cassava**) and *M. dulcis* (**sweet cassava**), cultivated for their tuberous roots, which yield important food products. **2.** a nutritious starch from the roots, the source of tapioca. Also, **manioc**.

casserole /ˈkæsəroul/ *n.* **1.** a baking dish of glass, pottery, etc., usually with a cover. **2.** any food, usually a mixture, baked in such a dish.

cassette /kəˈsɛt, kæˈsɛt/ *n.* **1. a.** Also, **audiocassette**. (in a tape recorder) a plastic container enclosing both a recording tape and two hubs about which it winds. **b.** a device of similar principle with wider tape, as in a video recorder. **2.** a tape recorder designed to use such a device.

cassia /ˈkæsiə/ *n.* **1.** a variety of cinnamon (**cassia bark**) from the tree *Cinnamomum cassia*, of southern China. **2.** the tree itself. **3.** any of the herbs, shrubs, and trees constituting the genus *Cassia*, as *C. fistula*, an ornamental tropical tree with clusters of bright yellow flowers, and long pods (**cassia pods**) whose pulp (**cassia pulp**) is a mild laxative, and *C. acutifolia* and *C. angustifolia*, which yield senna.

cassock /ˈkæsək/ *n.* a long, close-fitting garment worn by ecclesiastics and others engaged in church functions.

cassowary /ˈkæsəwəri, ˈkæsəweri/ *n.* (*pl.* -ries) any of several large, three-toed, flightless birds constituting the genus *Casuarius*, of Australia, New Guinea and nearby islands, superficially resembling the ostrich but smaller.

cast /kɑst/ *verb* (**cast**, **casting**) –*v.t.* **1.** to throw; fling; hurl (*away, off, out*, etc.) **2.** to throw off or away. **3.** to direct (the eye, a glance, etc.) **4.** to cause (light, etc.) to fall upon something or in a certain direction. **5.** to throw out (a fishing line, anchor, etc.). **6.** to throw down; throw (an animal) on its back or side. **7.** to part with; lose. **8.** to shed or drop (hair, fruit, etc.), especially prematurely. **9.** to bring forth (young), especially abortively. **10.** to throw forth, as from within; emit or eject; vomit. **11.** to throw up (earth, etc.), as with a shovel. **12.** to put or place, especially hastily or forcibly. **13.** to deposit (a vote, etc.) **14.** *Theatre* **a.** to allot parts of (a play) to actors. **b.** to select (actors) for a play. **15.** *Metallurgy* to form (molten metal, etc.) into a particular shape by pouring into a mould; to produce (an object or article) by such a process. **16.** to compute or calculate; add, as a column of figures. **17.** to compute or calculate astrologically, as a horoscope; forecast. **18.** to ponder or consider; contrive, devise, or plan. **19.** to turn or twist; warp. **20.** *Naut.* to let go or let (*loose, off*, etc.) as a vessel from a mooring. –*v.i.* **21.** to warp, as timber. **22.** of a sheepdog, to make a wide sweep to get around sheep without disturbing them. –*n.* **23.** the act of casting or throwing. **24.** the distance to which a thing may be cast or thrown. **25.** *Games* **a.** a throw of dice. **b.** the number rolled. **26.** *Angling* **a.** the act of throwing the line or net on the water. **b.** a line so thrown. **c.** the leader, with flies attached. **27.** the sweep a sheepdog makes when rounding up sheep, the first stage of a sheepdog trial. **28.** the form in which something is made or written; arrangement. **29.** *Theatre* the actors to whom the parts in a play are assigned. **30.** *Metallurgy* **a.** the act of casting or founding. **b.** the quantity of metal cast at one time. **31.** something shaped in a mould while in a fluid or plastic state; a casting. **32.** any impression or mould made from an object. **33.** *Med.* a rigid surgical dressing usually made of plaster-of-Paris bandage. **34.** a reproduction or copy, as a plaster model, made in a mould. **35.** outward form; appearance. **36.** sort; kind; style. **37.** tendency; inclination. **38.** a permanent twist or turn, especially a squint: *to have a cast in one's eye.* **39.** a warp. **40.** a slight tinge of some colour; hue; shade. **41.** a dash or trace; a small amount. **42.** *Zool.* one of the wormlike coils of sand passed by the lugworm or other worms. **43.** *Ornith.* a mass of feathers, furs, bones, or other indigestible matters ejected from the stomach by a hawk or other birds. –*adj.* **44.** discarded; lost: *the cast shoe of a horse.* **45.** (of a sheep) fallen, and unable to rise. **46.** moulded; having a certain shape. **47.** *Theatre* (of a production) having all actors selected. **48.** *NZ Colloq.* drunk. –*phr.* **49.** cast about, **a.** to search this way and that, as for the scent in hunting: *to cast about to find the way.* **b.** (sometimes fol. by *for*) to make a mental effort, as in search for an excuse. **c.** (sometimes fol. by *for*) to scheme. **50.** cast away, **a.** to reject. **b.** to shipwreck. **51.** cast back, **a.** to refer to something past. **b.** to show resemblance to a remote ancestor. **52.** cast down, **a.** to depress; discourage. **53.** cast for age, (of sheep, etc.) culled from the flock or herd because of poor condition due to age. **54.** cast off, **a.** to let (a vessel) loose from a mooring. **b.** to discard or reject. **c.** to let go. **d.** *Printing* to estimate the amount of space necessary for a piece of copy when printed. **e.** *Knitting* to make the final row of stitches. **55.** cast on, *Knitting* to make the initial row of stitches. **56.** cast out, **a.** to throw or set aside; discard or reject; dismiss or disband. **b.** to throw out a fishing line or the like. –**caster**, *n.* –**casting**, *n.*

castanet /kæstəˈnɛt/ *n.* one of a pair of shells of ivory or hard wood held in the palm of the hand and struck together as an accompaniment to music and dancing.

castaway /ˈkɑstəweɪ/ *n.* **1.** a shipwrecked person, especially one who has escaped the wreck and become stranded in a remote, lonely place, as an island. **2.** an outcast. –*adj.* **3.** cast adrift.

caste /kɑst/ *n.* **1.** *Sociology* an endogamous and hereditary social group limited to persons in a given occupation or trade, having mores distinguishing it from other such groups. **2.** one of the divisions or social classes into which the Hindus are separated and by which privileges or disabilities are inherited. **3.** any rigid system of social distinctions.

caster sugar /ˈkɑstə ʃʊgə/ *n.* finely ground white sugar. Also, **castor sugar**.

castigate /ˈkæstəgeɪt/ *v.t.* to punish in order to correct; criticise severely. –**castigation** /kæstəˈgeɪʃən/, *n.* –**castigator**, *n.*

casting vote *n.* the deciding vote of the presiding officer when votes are equally divided.

cast iron *n.* an alloy of iron, carbon, and other elements, cast as a soft and strong, or as a hard and brittle iron, depending on the mixture and methods of moulding.

cast-iron *adj.* **1.** made of cast iron. **2.** strong; hardy. **3.** inflexible; rigid; unyielding. **4.** incontrovertible: *a cast-iron alibi.*

castle /'kasəl, 'kæsəl/ *n.* **1.** a fortified residence, as of a prince or noble in feudal times. **2.** a strongly fortified, permanently garrisoned stronghold. **3.** a large and stately residence, especially one which imitates the forms of a medieval castle. **4.** *Chess* the rook. *–v.i.* (**-tled, -tling**) **5.** *Chess* to move the king sideways two squares and bring the castle to the first square the king passed over. **–castled**, *adj.*

castor[1] /'kastə/ *n.* a brownish unctuous substance with a strong, penetrating smell, secreted by certain glands in the groin of the beaver, used in medicine and perfumery. Also, **castoreum** /kas'tɔriəm/.

castor[2] /'kastə/ *n.* **1.** a small wheel on a swivel, set under a piece of furniture, etc., to facilitate moving it. **2.** a bottle or cruet with a perforated top, for holding sugar or a condiment. **3.** the forward and downward inclination of the kingpin as a means of stabilising the front wheels of a car. Also, **caster**.

castor oil *n.* an oil obtained from the seeds of the castor-oil plant, used as a cathartic, lubricant, etc.

castor-oil plant *n.* a tall plant, *Ricinus communis*, native to India but widely naturalised, yielding castor seeds.

castor sugar *n.* → **caster sugar**.

castrate /'kæstreɪt, 'kas-/ *v.t.* **1.** to deprive of the testicles; emasculate. **2.** to deprive of the ovaries. **3.** to mutilate (a book, etc.) by removing parts; expurgate. **4.** (of a woman) to deprive (a man) of his vigour and self-esteem. **–castration** /kæs'treɪʃən, kas-/, *n.*

casual /'kæʒuəl/ *adj.* **1.** happening by chance: *a casual meeting.* **2.** offhand; without any definite thought: *a casual remark, etc.* **3.** careless; unconcerned: *a casual attitude.* **4.** informal: *casual clothes.* **5.** employed only irregularly: *a casual worker.* *–n.* **6.** a worker employed only irregularly. **7.** (*pl.*) comfortable, informal clothes, shoes, etc. **–casually**, *adv.* **–casualness**, *n.*

casual racism *n.* racism which is ostensibly unintended by the speaker because it takes the form of humorous stereotyping, or common assumptions and misconceptions with regard to other people and other cultures, which is nonetheless hurtful to the people who see themselves typified in this way in the jokes or observations. **–casual racist**, *n.*

casual sexism *n.* sexism which is ostensibly unintended by the speaker because it takes the form of humorous stereotyping, or common assumptions and misconceptions with regard to a particular sex, which is nonetheless hurtful to members of that sex who see themselves typified in this way in the jokes or observations.

casualty /'kæʒjuəlti/ *n.* (*pl.* **-ties**) **1.** *Mil.* **a.** a soldier who is missing in action, or who has been killed, wounded, or captured as a result of enemy action. **b.** (*pl.*) loss in numerical strength through any cause, such as death, wounds, sickness, capture, or desertion. **2.** someone who is injured or killed in an accident. **3.** an unfortunate accident, especially one involving bodily injury or death; a mishap. **4.** Also, **casualty ward**. the section of a hospital to which accident or emergency cases are taken.

casuarina /kæʒjə'rinə/ *n.* any member of the genus *Casuarina*, a group of trees and shrubs with few species outside Australia, characterised by jointed stems with leaves reduced to whorls of teeth at the joints; she-oak; native oak.

casuist /'kæʒjuəst/ *n.* someone who studies and resolves cases of conscience or conduct. **–casuistic** /kæʒju'ɪstɪk/, **casuistical** /kæʒju'ɪstɪkəl/, *adj.* **–casuistry**, *n.* **–casuistically**, *adv.*

cat[1] /kæt/ *n.* **1.** a domesticated carnivore, *Felis sylvestris catus* (formerly *Felis catus*), thought to be descended from the African wildcat, *Felis sylvestris lybica*, and now widely distributed in a number of breeds; feral populations exist throughout all habitats in Australia. **2.** any carnivore of the family Felidae, as the lion, tiger, leopard, jaguar, lynx, bobcat, puma, cheetah, wildcat, ocelot, etc. **3.** *Colloq.* a spiteful and gossipy woman. *–phr.* **4. have too much of what the cat licks itself with**, *Colloq.* to be very talkative. **5. kick the cat**, *Colloq.* to give way to suppressed feelings of frustration by venting one's irritation on someone. **6. let the cat out of the bag**, to disclose information, usually unintentionally. **7. look like something the cat dragged in**, *Colloq.* to be very unkempt or badly dressed. **8. no room to swing a cat**, *Colloq.* an expression indicating a confined, cramped, or cluttered place. **9. put** (or **set**) **the cat among the pigeons**, to cause a disturbance; introduce a disrupting factor. **10. rain cats and dogs**, to rain heavily. **11. see which way the cat jumps**, to await the outcome of events (before committing oneself to a decision). **12. the cat's pyjamas** (or **whiskers**), *Colloq.* someone or something arousing great admiration. **–catlike**, *adj.*

cat[2] /kæt/ *n.* a catamaran.

cat[3] /kæt/ *n.* a person, especially a young jazz musician or devotee of jazz.

cata- a prefix meaning 'down', 'against', 'back', occurring originally in words from the Greek, but used also in modern words (English and other) formed after the Greek type, as in *catabolism*, *catalogue*, *catalysis*, *catastrophe*. Also, (*in scientific use*), **kata-**; (*before a vowel*), **cat-**; (*before an aspirate*), **cath-**.

catabolism /kə'tæbəlɪzəm/ *n.* *Biol.*, *Physiol.* a breaking down process; destructive metabolism (opposed to *anabolism*). Also, **katabolism**. **–catabolic** /kætə'bɒlɪk/, *adj.* **–catabolically** /kætə'bɒlɪkli/, *adv.*

cataclysm /'kætəklɪzəm/ *n.* any violent upheaval, especially one of a social or political nature. **–cataclysmic** /kætə'klɪzmɪk/, *adj.*

catacomb /'kætəkoʊm, -kum/ *n.* **1.** (*usu. pl.*) an underground cemetery, especially one consisting of tunnels and rooms with recesses dug out for coffins and tombs. **2.** any series of underground tunnels and caves.

catafalque /'kætəfælk/ *n.* a raised structure on which the body of a deceased personage lies or is carried in state.

catalepsy /'kætələpsi/ *n.* *Psychol.*, *Pathol.* a morbid bodily condition marked by suspension of sensation, muscular rigidity, fixity of posture, and often by loss of contact with environment. **–cataleptic** /kætə'lɛptɪk/, *adj.*, *n.*

catalogue /'kætəlɒg/ *n.* **1.** a list, usually in alphabetical order, with brief notes on the names, articles, etc., listed. **2.** a record of the books and other resources of a library or a collection, indicated on cards, or, occasionally, in book form. *–v.t.* (**-logued, -loguing**) **3.** to make a catalogue of; enter in a catalogue. **4.** to describe the bibliographical and technical features of (a publication and the subject matter it treats). Also, *US*, **catalog**. **–cataloguer**, **cataloguist**, *n.*

catalyst /'kætələst/ *n.* **1.** *Chem.* a substance that causes catalysis. **2.** the manipulating agent of any event, unaffected by the completion of the action or by its consequences.

catamaran /'kætəməræn/ *n.* **1.** *Naut.* **a.** a float or raft, usually of several logs or pieces of wood lashed together. **b.** any craft with twin parallel hulls. **2.** *NZ* a kauri-timber sledge, resembling a catamaran craft, used in the bush. Also, **cat**.

catapult /'kætəpʌlt/ *n.* **1.** an ancient military engine for hurling darts, stones, etc. **2.** a Y-shaped stick with an elastic strip between the prongs for propelling stones, etc. **3.** a device for launching an aeroplane from the deck of a ship, especially a ship not equipped with a flight deck. –*v.t.* **4.** to hurl as from a catapult. –*v.i.* **5.** to move rapidly into the highest position or status: *she catapulted to fame.*

cataract /ˈkætərækt/ *n.* **1.** a descent of water over a steep surface; a waterfall, especially one of considerable size. **2.** any furious rush or downpour of water; deluge. **3.** *Pathol.* an abnormality of the eye, characterised by opacity of the lens.

catarrh /kəˈtɑ/ *n. Pathol.* inflammation of a mucous membrane, especially of the respiratory tract, accompanied by excessive secretions. –**catarrhal**, *adj.*

catastrophe /kəˈtæstrəfi/ *n.* **1.** a sudden and widespread disaster. **2.** a final event or conclusion, usually an unfortunate one; a disastrous end. **3.** (in a drama) the point at which the circumstances overcome the central motive, introducing the close or conclusion; the denouement. **4.** a sudden violent disturbance, especially of the earth's surface; a cataclysm. –**catastrophic** /kætəˈstrɒfik/, *adj.* –**catastrophically** /kætəˈstrɒfikli/, *adv.*

catatonia /kætəˈtouniə/ *n. Psychol.* abnormal behaviour showing unusual limitations of movement and speech, as well as resistance to suggestions from others. –**catatonic** /kætəˈtɒnik/, *adj.*

catcall /ˈkætkɔl/ *n.* a cry like that of a cat, or an instrument for producing a similar sound, used to express disapproval, at a theatre, meeting, etc.

catch /kætʃ/ *verb* (**caught**, **catching**) –*v.t.* **1.** to capture, especially after pursuit; take captive. **2.** to ensnare, entrap, or deceive. **3. a.** to be in time to reach (a train, boat, etc.): *I barely caught the 5.03.* **b.** to board; travel on: *I caught a cab to Bondi.* **4.** to come upon suddenly; surprise or detect, as in some action: *I caught him doing it.* **5.** to strike; hit: *the blow caught him on the head.* **6.** to intercept and seize (a ball, etc.). **7.** *Surfing* to join (a wave) at such a time and in such a manner that it carries the surfer with it towards the beach. **8.** *Cricket* to dismiss (the person batting) by intercepting and holding the ball after it has been struck by the bat and before it touches the ground. **9.** to check (one's breath, etc.). **10.** to get, receive, incur, or contract: *to catch a cold; I caught the spirit of the occasion.* **11.** to lay hold of; grasp, seize, or snatch; grip or entangle: *a nail caught his sleeve.* **12.** to allow to be caught; be entangled with: *to catch one's finger in a door; to catch one's coat on a nail.* **13.** to fasten with or as with a catch. **14.** to get by attraction or impression: *to catch the eye; to catch someone's attention.* **15.** to hear or see (a radio or television program): *did you catch that program on the Great Barrier Reef?* **16.** to captivate; charm. **17.** to understand by the senses or intellect: *to catch a speaker's word.* –*v.i.* **18.** to become fastened or entangled: *the kite caught in the trees.* **19.** to take hold: *the door lock catches.* **20.** to become lit, take fire, ignite: *the wood caught instantly.* –*n.* **21.** the act of catching. **22.** anything that catches, especially a device for checking motion. **23.** that which is caught, as a quantity of fish. **24.** anything worth getting. **25.** *Colloq.* a catch of either sex regarded as a desirable matrimonial prospect. **26.** *Music* a round, especially one in which the words are so arranged as to produce ludicrous effects. **27.** *Cricket* **a.** the catching and holding of the ball after it has been struck and before it touches the ground. **b.** the wicket so gained. **28.** *Rowing* the beginning of a stroke. **29.** *Colloq.* a difficulty, usually unseen: *what's the catch?* –*phr.* **30. catch at**, **a.** to grasp or snatch. **b.** to be glad to get: *he caught at the chance.* **31. catch it**, *Colloq.* to get a scolding or a beating. **32. catch on**, **a.** to become popular. **b.** *Colloq.* to grasp mentally; understand. **33. catch out**, **a.** to trap (somebody), as into revealing a secret or displaying ignorance. **b.** to surprise. **34. catch up**, **a.** to seize quickly: *he caught up the child in his arms.* **b.** to

embroil or entangle: *they were caught up in the crowd.* **c.** to follow and reach, become level with; overtake: *he caught her up by running.* **d.** (sometimes fol. by *to* or *with*) to reach or become level with others: *I'm so far behind I'll never catch up; he caught up to the field at the bend; she has caught up with the rest of the class by hard work.* **e.** (sometimes fol. by *with* or *on*) to make up a deficiency in: *since my holiday I've been trying to catch up; I must catch up with my sewing; she caught up on her sleep.* **35. catch you later**, *Colloq.* an expression of farewell. –**catcher**, *n.*

catchcry /ˈkætʃkraɪ/ *n.* (*pl.* **-cries**) an ear-catching expression or group of words, voicing a popular sentiment.

catching /ˈkætʃɪŋ/ *adj.* **1.** infectious. **2.** attractive; fascinating; captivating; alluring.

catchment area /ˈkætʃmənt ˌɛəriə/ *n.* **1.** Also, **catchment basin**. *Geog.* a drainage area, especially of a reservoir or river. **2.** *Sociology* the area from which persons may come to a central institution, such as a school or hospital.

catchphrase /ˈkætʃfreɪz/ *n.* **1.** a phrase caught up and repeated because it is fashionable. **2.** a slogan. Also, **catch phrase.**

catch 22 /ˌkætʃ twɛnti-ˈtu/ *n.* **1.** a rule or condition which prevents the completion of a sequence of operations and which may establish a futile self-perpetuating cycle. –*adj.* **2.** of or relating to something that involves such a rule or condition: *a catch 22 situation.* Also, **catch-22.**

catch-up *adj.* of or relating to a price rise, award increase, etc., which is an attempt to compensate for related increases elsewhere in the economy.

catch-up TV *n.* a facility offered by a television station by which programs that have been telecast are made available for viewing online.

catchy /ˈkætʃi/ *adj.* (**-chier**, **-chiest**) **1.** pleasing and easily remembered: *a catchy tune.* **2.** tricky; deceptive: *a catchy question.* **3.** occurring in snatches; fitful: *a catchy wind.*

catechise /ˈkætəkaɪz/ *v.t.* **1.** to instruct orally by means of questions and answers, especially in Christian doctrine. **2.** to question with reference to belief. **3.** to question closely or excessively. Also, **catechize**. –**catechisation** /kætəkaɪˈzeɪʃən/, *n.* –**catechiser**, *n.*

catechism /ˈkætəkɪzəm/ *n.* **1.** an elementary book containing a summary of the principles of the Christian religion, especially as maintained by a particular church, in the form of questions and answers. **2.** a series of formal questions designed to bring out a person's views. –**catechismal**, *adj.*

categorical /kætəˈgɒrɪkəl/ *adj.* not involving a condition, qualification, etc.; explicit; direct: *a categorical answer.* –**categorically**, *adv.* –**categoricalness**, *n.*

category /ˈkætəgəri, -təgri/, *Orig. US* /-gɔri/ *n.* (*pl.* **-ries**) **1.** a classificatory division in any field of knowledge, as a phylum or any of its subdivisions in biology. **2.** any general or comprehensive division; a class. –**categorise**, **categorize**, *v.* –**categorisation**, *n.*

cater /ˈkeɪtə/ *v.i.* **1.** to provide food and service, means of amusement, or the like at functions. –*phr.* **2. cater for**, **a.** to provide food and service at (a function): *to cater for a wedding.* **b.** to provide what is necessary for: *to cater for the expanding population in the area.* **3. cater to**, to go out of one's way to placate or provide for; accommodate: *to cater to the master's taste.* –**caterer**, *n.* –**cateress**, *fem. n.*

caterpillar[1] /ˈkætəpɪlə/ *n.* the wormlike larva of a butterfly or a moth.

caterpillar[2] /ˈkætəpɪlə/ *n.* (*from trademark*) **1.** a tractor having the driving wheels moving inside endless tracks on either side, thus being capable of hauling heavy loads over rough or soft ground. **2.** any device, as a tank or steam shovel, moving on endless tracks. Also, **caterpillar tractor.**

caterwaul /ˈkætəwɔːl/ *v.i.* **1.** to cry as cats on heat. **2.** to utter a similar sound; howl or screech. **3.** to quarrel like cats. –*n.* Also, **caterwauling. 4.** the cry of a cat on heat. **5.** any similar sound.

cat fever *n.* → **feline infectious enteritis.**

catgut /ˈkætɡʌt/ *n.* the intestines of sheep or other animals, dried and twisted, used in surgery as ligatures, as strings for musical instruments, etc.

cath- variant of **cata-** before an aspirate, as in *cathode.*

catharsis /kəˈθɑːsəs/ *n.* **1.** *Aesthetics* the effect of art in purifying the emotions (applied by Aristotle to the relief or purgation of the emotions of the audience or performers effected through pity and terror by tragedy and certain kinds of music). **2.** *Psychol.* an affective discharge with symptomatic relief but not necessarily a cure of the underlying pathology. **3.** *Med.* purgation. –**cathartic** /kəˈθɑːtɪk/, *adj.*

cathedral /kəˈθiːdrəl/ *n.* **1.** the principal church of a diocese, containing the bishop's throne. –*adj.* **2.** relating to or emanating from a chair of office or authority.

catheter /ˈkæθətə/ *n. Med.* a flexible or rigid hollow tube used to drain fluids from body cavities or to distend body passages, especially one for passing into the bladder through the urethra to draw off urine.

cathode /ˈkæθoʊd/ *n.* **1.** the electrode which emits electrons or gives off negative ions and towards which positive ions move or collect in electrolysis, a radio valve, semiconductor diode, etc. **2.** the negative pole of a battery or other source of current (opposed to *anode*). –**cathodic** /kəˈθɒdɪk/, *adj.*

cathode ray *n.* a stream of electrons generated at the cathode during an electric discharge in an evacuated tube.

cathode-ray oscilloscope /ˌkæθoʊd-ˌreɪ əˈsɪləskoʊp/ *n. Physics* an instrument which displays the shape of a voltage or current wave on a cathode-ray tube. *Abbrev.*: CRO Also, **cathode-ray oscillograph.**

cathode-ray tube *n. Electronics* a vacuum tube in which is generated a focused beam of electrons which can be deflected by electric and/or magnetic fields. The terminus of the beam is visible as a spot or line of luminescence caused by its impinging on a sensitised screen at one end of the tube. Cathode-ray tubes are used to study the shapes of electric waves, to reproduce pictures in television receivers, as an indicator in radar sets, etc.

catholic /ˈkæθlɪk, -əlɪk/ *adj.* **1.** relating to the whole Christian body or Church. **2.** universal in extent; involving all; of interest to all. **3.** having sympathies with all; broad-minded; liberal: *to be catholic in one's tastes*; *to be catholic in one's interests.* –**catholically** /kəˈθɒlɪkli/, *adv.*

Catholic /ˈkæθlɪk, -əlɪk/ *adj.* **1.** *Theology* **a.** claiming to possess exclusively the characteristics of the one, only, true, and universal Church, i.e., unity, visibility, indefectibility, apostolic succession, universality, and sanctity (used in this sense, with these qualifications, only by the Church of Rome, as applicable only to itself and its adherents, and to their faith and organisation; often qualified, especially by those not acknowledging these claims, by prefixing the word *Roman*). **b.** (especially among Anglicans) denoting or relating to the conception of the Church as the body representing the ancient undivided Christian witness, comprising all the orthodox churches which have kept the apostolic succession of bishops, and including the Anglican Church, the Roman Catholic Church, the Eastern Orthodox Church, Church of Sweden, the Old Catholic Church (in the Netherlands and elsewhere), etc.

2. relating to the Western Church. –*n.* **3.** a member of a Catholic Church, especially of the Church of Rome. –**Catholicism** /kəˈθɒləsɪzm/, *n.*

Catholic Church *n.* **1.** the universal Christian church; the entire body of Christians, especially up to the point of separation of the Eastern and Western Churches. **2.** Also, **Roman Catholic Church, Church of Rome.** a Christian church maintaining apostolic succession, with a hierarchy of priests and bishops, the pope as head, and administrative headquarters in the Vatican.

cation /ˈkætaɪən/ *n. Chem.* a positively charged ion which is attracted to the cathode in electrolysis. Also, **kation.**

catnap /ˈkætnæp/ *n.* a short, light nap or doze.

cat-o'-nine-tails /ˌkæt-ə-ˈnam-ˌteɪlz/ *n.* (*pl.* **cat-o'-nine-tails**) (formerly) a whip, usually having nine knotted lines or cords fastened to a handle, used to flog offenders.

CAT scanner /ˈkæt skænə/ *n.* a machine which produces a series of X-rays by the process of computerised axial tomography with the resultant image in the axial plane.

cat's paw *n.* **1.** someone used by another to serve their purpose; a tool. **2.** *Naut.* a light breeze which ruffles the surface of the water over a comparatively small area. Also, **catspaw.**

cattle /ˈkætl/ *n.* **1.** ruminants of the bovine kind, of any age, breed, or sex. **2.** human beings considered contemptuously or in a mass.

cattle bush *n.* any of various Australian trees or shrubs on which cattle may feed in drought periods.

cattle egret *n.* a common, widespread, small egret, *Bubulcus coromandus*, all white but having rusty plumage in the breeding season; found in pastures, often among stock, in Southern and Eastern Asia to the Indian subcontinent, Australia and New Zealand.

cattle grid *n.* a pit covered by a grid set in a roadway, designed to prevent the passage of animals, at the same time allowing the passage of wheeled traffic. Also, **cattle pit, cattle ramp;** *NZ,* **cattle stop.**

cattle stop *n. NZ* → **cattle grid.**

catty /ˈkæti/ *adj.* (**-tier, -tiest**) **1.** cat-like. **2.** quietly or slyly malicious; spiteful: *a catty gossip.* –**cattily,** *adv.* –**cattiness,** *n.*

catwalk /ˈkætwɔk/ *n.* **1.** any narrow walking space, as on a bridge, above the stage of a theatre, or in an aircraft. **2.** a long narrow platform on which fashion models parade clothes.

Caucasian /kɔˈkeɪʒən/ *adj.* **1.** *Ethnology* (in a system devised in the 19th century) relating to the so-called 'white race', including the peoples of Europe, southwestern Asia, and northern Africa. **2.** relating to a person of white-skinned or European appearance. –*n.* **3.** *Ethnology* a member of the Caucasian race. **4.** a person of white-skinned or European appearance. Compare **Australoid, Mongoloid, Negroid.** Also, **Caucasoid.**

caucus /ˈkɔkəs/ *n.* **1.** the parliamentary members of a political party or faction of a political party. **2.** a private meeting of the parliamentary members of a political party or faction to discuss policy or tactics.

caudal /ˈkɔdl/ *adj. Zool.* **1.** of, at, or near the tail. **2.** tail-like: *caudal appendages.* –**caudally,** *adv.*

caudate /ˈkɔdeɪt/ *adj. Zool.* having a tail or tail-like appendage. Also, **caudated.**

caught /kɔt/ *v.* past tense and past participle of **catch.**

caul /kɔl/ *n.* a part of the amnion sometimes covering the head of a child at birth, superstitiously supposed to bring good luck and to be an infallible preservative against drowning.

cauldron /ˈkɔldrən/ *n.* a large kettle or boiler, usually spherical, with a lid and handle. Also, **caldron.**

cauliflower /ˈkɒliflaʊə/ *n.* **1.** a cultivated plant, *Brassica oleracea* var. *botrytis*, whose inflorescence forms a compact, fleshy head. **2.** the head of this plant, used as a vegetable.

caulk /kɔk/ *v.t.* **1.** to fill or close (a seam, joint, etc.), as in a boat. **2.** to make (a vessel) watertight by filling the seams between its planks with oakum or other materials driven snug. **3.** to drive the edges of (plating) together to prevent leakage. **4.** to fill or close seams or crevices of (a tank, window, etc.) in order to make watertight, airtight, etc. Also, **calk**.

causal /ˈkɔzəl/ *adj.* of, constituting, or implying a cause. –**causally**, *adv.*

causality /kɔˈzæləti/ *n.* (*pl.* **-ties**) **1.** the relation of cause and effect. **2.** causal quality or agency.

causation /kɔˈzeɪʃən/ *n.* **1.** the action of causing or producing. **2.** the relation of cause to effect. **3.** anything that produces an effect; a cause. –**causative**, *adj.*

cause /kɔz/ *n.* **1.** something that produces an effect; the thing, person, etc., from which something results. **2.** the ground of any action or result; reason; motive. **3.** any subject of discussion or debate. **4.** the side of a question which a person or party supports; the aim, purpose, etc., of a group. –*v.t.* **5.** to be the cause of; bring about. –**causable**, *adj.* –**causeless**, *adj.* –**causer**, *n.*

cause célèbre /kɔz səˈlɛbrə/ *n.* **1.** an issue arousing public debate and partisanship. **2.** *Colloq.* a cause espoused.

causeway /ˈkɔzweɪ/ *n.* a raised road or path, as across low or wet ground.

caustic /ˈkɒstɪk, ˈkɔstɪk/ *adj.* **1.** capable of burning, corroding, or destroying living tissue: *caustic soda.* **2.** severely critical or sarcastic: *a caustic remark.* –*n.* **3.** a caustic substance: *lunar caustic.* –**caustically**, *adv.* –**causticity** /kɒsˈtɪsəti/, *n.*

caustic soda *n.* sodium hydroxide, NaOH, used in metallurgy and photography.

cauterise /ˈkɔtəraɪz/ *v.t.* to burn with a hot iron, or with fire or a caustic, especially for curative purposes; treat with a cautery. Also, **cauterize**. –**cauterisation** /ˌkɔtəraɪˈzeɪʃən/, *n.*

caution /ˈkɔʃən/ *n.* **1.** care in regard to danger or evil; prudence; wariness: *go forward with caution.* **2.** a warning (especially in law) to a person, that their words or actions may be used against them. **3.** *Colloq.* someone or something unusual, odd, amazing, etc. –*v.t.* **4.** to give a warning to; suggest or urge to take heed. **5.** *Law* to warn (someone) that their words may be used against them. –**cautionary**, *adj.*

cautious /ˈkɔʃəs/ *adj.* having or showing caution or prudence to avoid danger or evil; very careful. –**cautiously**, *adv.* –**cautiousness**, *n.*

cavalcade /ˈkævəlkeɪd, kævəlˈkeɪd/ *n.* **1.** a procession of persons on horseback or in horse-drawn carriages. **2.** any procession.

cavalier /kævəˈlɪə/ *n.* **1.** (formerly) a horseman, especially a mounted soldier; knight. **2.** (especially formerly) a courtly gentleman; gallant. –*adj.* **3.** haughty, disdainful, or supercilious. **4.** offhand towards matters of some importance; casual.

cavalry /ˈkævəlri/ *n.* (*pl.* **-ries**) *Mil.* a unit, or units collectively, of an army, which in the past were mounted on horseback, and are now equipped with armoured vehicles in either an armoured or a reconnaissance role. –**cavalryman** /ˈkævəlrimən/, *n.*

cave /keɪv/ *n.* **1.** a hollow in the earth, especially one opening more or less horizontally into a hill, mountain, etc. –*v.t.* **2.** to hollow out. –*v.i.* **3.** to engage in speleology, especially as a sport. –*phr.* **4. cave in, a.** to cause to fall or collapse. **b.** to fall or sink. **c.** to give in, yield, or submit: *he had caved in to the power of the press.* –**caver**, *n.*

caveat /ˈkeɪviət/ *n.* **1.** *Law* a legal notice to a court or public officer to suspend a certain proceeding until the notifier is given a hearing: *a caveat filed against the probate of a will.* **2.** any warning or caution.

caveat emptor /keɪviat ˈɛmptɔ/ let the buyer beware (since he or she buys without recourse).

cave-in *n.* **1.** a collapse, as of a mine, etc. **2.** a sudden yielding, especially after demonstrated resistance.

cavern /ˈkævən/ *n.* a cave, especially a large cave. –**cavernous**, *adj.*

caviar /ˈkævia, kæviˈa/ *n.* **1.** the salted roe of sturgeon or other large fish, considered a great delicacy. –*phr.* **2. caviar to the general**, something beyond appeal to the popular taste. Also, *Rare*, **caviare**.

cavil /ˈkævəl/ *v.i.* (**-illed** *or*, *Chiefly US*, **-iled**, **-illing** *or*, *Chiefly US*, **-iling**) **1.** to raise irritating and trivial objections; find fault unnecessarily. –*n.* **2.** a trivial and annoying objection. **3.** the raising of such objections. –**caviller**; *Chiefly US*, **caviler**, *n.*

cavity /ˈkævəti/ *n.* (*pl.* **-ties**) **1.** any hollow place; a hollow: *a cavity in the earth.* **2.** *Anat.* a hollow space within the body, an organ, a bone, etc. **3.** *Dentistry* the loss of tooth structure, most commonly produced by caries; a cavity may be artificially made to support dental restorations.

cavort /kəˈvɔt/ *v.i. Colloq.* to prance or caper about.

cay /keɪ, ki/ *n.* a small island; key.

cayenne /keɪˈɛn/ *n.* a hot, biting condiment composed of the ground pods and seeds of any of several varieties of *Capsicum*; red pepper. Also, **cayenne pepper**.

cayman /ˈkeɪmən/ *n.* (*pl.* **caymans**) → **caiman**.

CBD /si bi ˈdi/ *n.* that area of a city in which the major business offices are located. Also, **central business district**.

CB radio /si bi ˈreɪdioʊ/ *n.* citizen band radio. Also, **CB**.

CCD /si si ˈdi/ *n. Photography* (in digital cameras) charged coupled device; a light-sensitive chip that converts the light entering through the aperture into electronic signals that can be digitally processed.

CCTV /si si ti ˈvi/ *n.* → **closed-circuit television**.

CCV number *n.* credit card verification number; the three-digit number printed on the back of a credit card to provide added protection against fraud.

CD /si ˈdi/ *n.* **1.** a disc, usually 12 cm in diameter, on which digitally-encoded information is stored, and which can then be read by a laser beam and transmitted to a playback system, computer or television set. –*adj.* **2.** of or relating to a CD. Also, **compact disc**.

CD burner *n.* a device which copies digitally encoded text, audio or visual data onto a CD.

CD-ROM *n.* a laser disc designed for storing digitised text and graphics, a large amount of which can be stored on one disc and displayed on a visual display unit.

cease /sis/ *v.i.* **1.** to stop (moving, speaking, etc.): *he ceased crying.* **2.** to come to an end: *the noise ceased.* –*v.t.* **3.** to put a stop or end to; discontinue: *to cease work.* –**ceaseless**, *adj.*

ceasefire /sisˈfaɪə/ *n.* a cessation of active hostilities; truce.

cedar /ˈsidə/ *n.* **1.** any of the coniferous trees constituting the genus *Cedrus*, native to the Mediterranean region and the Himalayas, as *C. libani* (**cedar of Lebanon**), a stately tree native to Lebanon, Turkey, etc. **2.** any of various other coniferous trees as *Libocedrus decurrens*, the **incense cedar** of the south-western US. **3.** → **red cedar** (def. 1). **4.** any of various other non-coniferous trees, as the New Zealand tree *Dysoxylum spectabile*. **5.** any of various junipers, as *Juniperus virginiana* (**red cedar**), an American tree with a fragrant reddish wood used for making lead pencils, etc. **6.** the wood of any of these trees.

cede /sid/ *v.t.* to yield or formally resign and surrender to another; make over, as by treaty: *to cede territory.*

cedilla /sə'dɪlə/ n. a mark placed under c before a, o, or u, as in façade, to show that it has the sound of s.

ceiling /'siːlɪŋ/ n. **1.** the overhead interior lining of a room; the surface of a room opposite the floor. **2.** top limit: a ceiling on charges. –adj. **3.** at a maximum level: ceiling price.

-cele[1] a word element meaning 'tumour', as in varicocele.

-cele[2] variant of -coele.

celebrant /'sɛləbrənt/ n. **1. a.** the priest who officiates at the performance of a religious rite. **b.** a secular official who conducts civil marriages, funerals, naming ceremonies, etc. **2.** a participant in any celebration. –celebrancy, n.

celebrate /'sɛləbreɪt/ v.t. **1.** to observe (a day or an event) with ceremonies or festivities. **2.** to praise publicly; honour. **3.** to perform with special rites and ceremonies; solemnise: to celebrate mass. –v.i. **4.** to engage in a festive activity; have a party. –celebration /sɛlə'breɪʃən/, n. –celebrator, n. –celebratory, adj.

celebrated /'sɛləbreɪtəd/ adj. famous; renowned; well-known.

celebrity /sə'lɛbrəti/ n. (pl. -ties) **1.** a famous or well-known person. **2.** fame; renown.

celerity /sə'lɛrəti/ n. swiftness; speed.

celery /'sɛləri/ n. a plant, Apium graveolens, of the parsley family, whose leafstalks are used raw for salad, and cooked as a vegetable.

celestial /sə'lɛstiəl/ adj. **1.** relating to the spiritual or invisible heaven; heavenly; divine: celestial bliss. **2.** relating to the sky or visible heaven. –n. **3.** an inhabitant of heaven. –celestially, adv.

celibacy /'sɛləbəsi/ n. **1.** the unmarried state. **2.** (of priests, etc.) abstention by vow from marriage. **3.** abstention from sexual intercourse; chastity. –celibate, n., adj.

cell /sɛl/ n. **1.** a small room in a convent, prison, etc., typically designed to accommodate one person in a solitary existence. **2.** any small compartment, bounded area, receptacle, case, etc. **3.** a small group acting as a unit within a larger organisation. **4.** Biol. **a.** a plant or animal structure, usually microscopic, containing nuclear and cytoplasmic material, enclosed by a semipermeable membrane (animal) or cell wall (plant); the structural unit of plant and animal life. **b.** a minute cavity or interstice, as in animal or plant tissue. **5.** Elect. a device which generates electricity and which forms the whole, or a part of, a voltaic battery, consisting in one of its simplest forms of two plates, each of a different metal, placed in a jar containing a dilute acid or other electrolyte (**voltaic cell**). **6.** Physical Chem. a device for producing electrolysis, consisting essentially of the electrolyte, its container, and the electrodes (**electrolytic cell**). **7.** the area covered by a radio transmitter for cellular telephones. –cellular, adj.

cellar /'sɛlə/ n. **1.** an underground room or store; basement. **2.** a supply or stock of wines.

cello /'tʃɛloʊ/ n. (pl. -los or -li) a four-stringed instrument of the violin family, with a pitch between that of the viola and the double bass, which is rested vertically on the floor between the player's knees. Also, 'cello, violoncello. –cellist, n.

cellophane /'sɛləfeɪn/ n. (from trademark) a transparent, paper-like product of viscose, impervious to moisture, germs, etc., used to wrap sweets, tobacco, etc.

cell phone n. → cellular telephone. Also, cell.

cellular telephone n. a type of telephone, usually portable for use in a car, which sends or receives signals controlled by a low-powered radio transmitter, each transmitter covering a specific area (**cell**) but linked to other such transmitters via a computer network so that the service is available over a large area overall. Also, cellular phone, cell phone.

cellulite /'sɛljəlaɪt/ n. deposits of fat and fibrous tissue, resulting in a dimply appearance of the overlying skin.

celluloid /'sɛljəlɔɪd/ (from trademark) –n. **1.** Chem. a plastic consisting essentially of a solid solution of soluble guncotton (cellulose nitrate) and camphor, usually highly flammable, used for toys, toilet articles, photographic film and as a substitute for amber ivory, vulcanite, etc. **2.** films; the cinema. –adj. **3.** made of celluloid. **4.** of or relating to films; appearing in a film: the celluloid hero of my dreams. **5.** unreal; synthetic.

cellulose /'sɛljəloʊs/ n. Chem. an inert substance, a carbohydrate, the chief constituent of the cell walls of plants, and forming an essential part of wood, cotton, hemp, paper, etc.

Celsius /'sɛlsiəs/ adj. **1.** of or relating to a scale of temperature on which the temperature in degrees Celsius (°C) is numerically equal to the temperature in kelvins (K) reduced by 273.15. On this scale the triple point of water is 0.01°C and the boiling point of water under a pressure of 101.325 kPa is approximately 100°C. The degree Celsius is the unit of temperature equal to the kelvin. –n. **2.** the Celsius scale. Symbol: C

cement /sə'mɛnt/ n. **1.** any of various substances which are soft when first prepared but later become hard or stone-like, used for joining stones, making floors, etc. **2.** a material of this kind (the ordinary variety, often called **Portland cement**) commonly made by burning a mixture of clay and limestone, used for making concrete for foundations or the like, covering floors, etc. **3.** (in non-technical use) → concrete (def. 4). **4.** anything that binds or unites. **5.** Dentistry an adhesive plastic substance used to fill teeth or to pack fillings or inlays into teeth. –v.t. **6.** to unite by, or as by, cement. **7.** to coat or cover with cement. –v.i. **8.** to become cemented; join together or unite; cohere. –cementer, n.

cemetery /'sɛmətri/, Orig. US /'sɛmətɛri/ n. (pl. -ries) a burial ground, especially one not attached to a church; graveyard.

-cene a word element meaning 'recent', 'new', as in Pleistocene.

ceno-[1] variant of **caino-**.

ceno-[2] variant of **coeno-**. Also, (before vowels), **cen-**.

cenotaph /'sɛnətaf/ n. **1.** a sepulchral monument in memory of a deceased person whose body is elsewhere. **2.** a municipal, civic, or national memorial to those killed in war. –cenotaphic, adj.

censer /'sɛnsə/ n. a container in which incense is burnt.

censor /'sɛnsə/ n. **1.** an official who examines books, plays, news reports, films, radio programs, etc., for the purpose of suppressing parts deemed objectionable on moral, political, military, or other grounds. **2.** any person who supervises the manners or morality of others. **3.** an adverse critic; someone who finds fault. –v.t. **4.** to examine and act upon as a censor does. –censorial /sɛn'sɔriəl/, adj. –censorship, n.

censorious /sɛn'sɔriəs/ adj. severely critical; fault-finding; carping. –censoriously, adv. –censoriousness, n.

censure /'sɛnʃə/ n. **1.** an expression of disapproval; adverse or hostile criticism; blaming. –v.t. **2.** to criticise adversely; disapprove; find fault with; condemn. –v.i. **3.** to give censure, adverse criticism, or blame. –censurer, n.

census /'sɛnsəs/ n. an official enumeration of inhabitants, with details as to age, sex, occupation, etc. –censual, adj.

cent /sɛnt/ n. **1.** a unit of currency equal to one hundredth part of a dollar or other unit of decimal currency. **2.** (formerly, in Australia) a coin of the value of a cent. **3.** the hundredth part of various other monetary units.

cent- → centi-.

centaur /ˈsɛntɔ/ *n.* (in Greek legend) one of a race of monsters having the head, trunk, and arms of a man, and the body and legs of a horse.

centenary /sɛnˈtinəri, -ˈtɛn-/ *adj.* **1.** of or relating to a 100th anniversary. *–n.* (*pl.* **-ries**) **2.** a 100th anniversary. **3.** its celebration. **4.** a period of 100 years; a century.

centennial /sɛnˈtɛniəl/ *adj.* **1.** consisting of, or marking the completion of, 100 years. **2.** lasting 100 years. **3.** recurring every 100 years. **4.** 100 years old. *–n.* **5.** *US, NZ* → **centenary**. –**centennially**, *adv.*

centi- a prefix denoting 10^{-2} of a given unit, as in *centigram. Symbol:* c Also, (*before vowels*), **cent-**.

Centigrade /ˈsɛntəɡreɪd/ *n.* **1.** (*lower case*) a non-SI unit of plane angle, equal to one hundredth of a grade (def. 4) or 10^{-4} of a right angle. *–adj.* **2.** *Obs.* Celsius.

centigram /ˈsɛntəɡræm/ *n.* a unit of mass equal to 0.01 gram. *Symbol:* cg

centimetre /ˈsɛntəmitə/ *n.* a unit of length equal to 0.01 metre. *Symbol:* cm Also, *US*, **centimeter**.

centipede /ˈsɛntəpid/ *n.* any member of the class Chilopoda, active, predacious, and mostly nocturnal arthropods having an elongated flattened body of numerous segments each with a single pair of legs, the first pair of which is modified into poison fangs. Few are dangerous to humans.

centr- variant of **centro-** before vowels.

central /ˈsɛntrəl/ *adj.* **1.** of or forming the centre. **2.** in, at, or near the centre. **3.** principal; chief; dominant: *the central idea, the central character in a novel.* –**centrally**, *adv.* –**centrality** /sɛnˈtræləti/, *n.*

central business district *n.* → **CBD**.

centralise /ˈsɛntrəlaɪz/ *v.t.* **1.** to draw to or towards a centre. **2.** to bring under one control, especially in government. *–v.i.* **3.** to come together at a centre. Also, **centralize**. –**centraliser**, *n.* –**centralisation** /ˌsɛntrəlaɪˈzeɪʃən/, *n.* –**centralism**, *n.*

central nervous system *n. Physiol., Anat.* the brain and spinal cord considered together. Compare **peripheral nervous system**.

central processing unit *n. Computers* the arithmetical and logical computing part of a computer considered separately from input/output devices. Also, **central processor unit**.

centre /ˈsɛntə/ *n.* **1.** *Geom.* the middle point, as the point within a circle or sphere equidistant from all points of the circumference or surface, or the point within a regular polygon equidistant from the vertices. **2.** a point, pivot, axis, etc., round which anything rotates or revolves. **3.** a building or building complex which houses a number of related specified services: *a shopping centre; a sports centre; a medical centre.* **4.** a person, thing, group, etc., occupying the middle position, especially troops. **5.** (*usu. upper case*) (in continental Europe) **a.** that part of a legislative assembly which sits in the centre of the chamber, a position customarily assigned to representatives holding views intermediate between those of the conservatives or right and the progressives or left. **b.** a party holding such views. **6.** *Basketball, etc.* **a.** the position of the player in the centre of the court, where the centre jump takes place at the beginning of play. **b.** the player who holds this position. **7.** *Rugby Football* → **centre three-quarter**. **8.** *Aust. Rules* **a.** the centre of the playing area, especially the centre circle. **b.** → **centreman** (def. 1). **9.** *Two-up* **a.** the central part of the ring where the spinner stands and bets with the spinner are taken. **b.** Also, **centreman**. the person who holds all bets made by the spinner. **10.** *Physiol.* a cluster of nerve cells governing a specific organic process: *the vasomotor centre.* **11.** *Machinery* **a.** a pointed rod mounted in the headstock spindle or tailstock of a lathe. A tailstock centre is a **dead centre** if non-rotating, a **live centre** if

free to rotate with the work. **b.** one of two similar points on some other machine, as a planing machine, enabling an object to be turned on its axis. **c.** a tapered indentation in a piece to be turned on a lathe into which the centre is fitted. *–verb* (**-tred, -tring**) *–v.t.* **12.** to place in or on a centre. **13.** to adjust, shape, or modify (an object, part, etc.) so that its axis or the like is in a central or normal position. *–v.i.* **14.** to be at or come to a centre. *–phr.* **15. centre (a)round**, to be concerned principally with. **16. centre on**, to focus on. Also, *US*, **center**.

centreboard /ˈsɛntəbɔd/ *n.* a movable fin keel in a boat, especially a sailing dinghy, that can be drawn up in shallow water. Also, **centreplate**.

centrefold /ˈsɛntəfoʊld/ *n.* the folded pages in the centre of a magazine, designed to be lifted out and unfolded, so as to display a large photograph sometimes of a nude male or female, a pop group, etc.

centreman /ˈsɛntəmæn/ *n.* (*pl.* **-men**) **1.** *Aust. Rules* the player occupying the centre of the playing area. **2.** → **centre** (def. 9b).

centre of gravity *n. Physics* the point of a body (or system of bodies) from which it could be suspended or on which it could be supported and be in equilibrium in any position in a uniform gravitational field.

centrepiece /ˈsɛntəpis/ *n.* **1.** an ornamental object used in a central position, especially on the centre of a dining table. **2.** the most important or conspicuous item in an exhibition, or in a collection.

centre three-quarter *n. Rugby Football* one of two middle players in the three-quarter line. Also, **centre**.

centri- variant of **centro-**, as in *centrifugal*.

centrifugal /sɛnˈtrɪfjəɡəl, sɛntrəˈfjuɡəl/ *adj.* **1.** moving or directed outwards from the centre. **2.** relating to or operated by centrifugal force: *a centrifugal pump.* –**centrifugally**, *adv.*

centrifugal force *n. Physics* an effect of inertia, in that the natural tendency of a moving object is to travel in a straight line, which is mistakenly perceived to be a force pulling the object outwards. Compare **centripetal force**. Also, **centrifugal action**.

centripetal /sɛnˈtrɪpətl/ *adj.* **1.** proceeding or directed towards the centre. **2.** operating by centripetal force. –**centripetally**, *adv.*

centripetal force *n. Physics* a force, directed towards the centre of a circle or curve, which causes a body to move in a circular or curved path. Also, **centripetal action**.

centro- a word element meaning 'centre'. Also, **centr-**, **centri-**.

centuple /ˈsɛntʃəpəl/ *adj.* **1.** a hundred times as great; hundredfold. *–v.t.* (**-pled, -pling**) **2.** to increase a hundred times.

centurion /sɛnˈtjuriən/ *n.* (in the Roman army) the commander of a century (def. 4).

century /ˈsɛntʃəri/ *n.* (*pl.* **-ries**) **1.** a period of one hundred years. **2.** one of the successive periods of 100 years reckoned forwards or backwards from a recognised chronological epoch, especially from the assumed date of the birth of Jesus. **3.** any group or collection of 100, such as 100 runs in cricket. **4.** (in the Roman army) a company, consisting of approximately one hundred men.

cephalic /səˈfælɪk/ *adj.* of or relating to the head.

-cephalic a word element meaning 'head', as in *brachycephalic* (related to **cephalo-**).

cephalo- a word element denoting the 'head', as in *cephalopod*. Also, **cephal-**.

cephalopod /ˈsɛfələpɒd/ *n.* a member of the class Cephalopoda, the most highly organised class of molluscs, including the cuttlefish, squid, octopus, etc., the members of which have tentacles attached to the head. –**cephalopodan** /sɛfəˈlɒpədən/, *adj., n.*

-cephalous a word element related to **cephalo-**.

-ceptor a word element meaning 'taker', 'receiver', as in *preceptor*.

cer- variant of **cero-**, used before vowels, as in *ceraceous*.

ceramic /sə'ræmɪk/ *adj.* **1.** relating to products made from clay and similar materials, such as pottery, brick, etc., or to their manufacture: *ceramic art.* –*n.* **2.** such a product.

ceramics /sə'ræmɪks/ *n.* **1.** (*construed as sing.*) the art and technology of making clay products and similar ware. **2.** such a product. –**ceramist** /sə'ræməst/, **ceramicist**, *n.*

cerato- a word element meaning **1.** *Zool.* horn, horny, or horn-like. **2.** *Anat.* the cornea. Also, (*before a vowel*), **cerat-**.

cereal /'sɪəriəl/ *n.* **1.** any gramineous plant yielding an edible farinaceous grain, such as wheat, rye, oats, rice, maize, etc. **2.** the grain itself. **3.** some edible preparation of it, especially a breakfast food made from some grain. –*adj.* **4.** of or relating to grain or the plants producing it.

cerebellum /sɛrə'bɛləm/ *n.* (*pl.* **-bella** /-'bɛlə/) *Anat.* a large expansion of the hindbrain, concerned with the coordination of voluntary movements, posture, and equilibration. In humans it lies at the back of and below the cerebrum and consists of two lateral lobes and a central lobe. –**cerebellar**, *adj.*

cerebral /'sɛrəbrəl, sə'ribrəl/ *adj.* **1.** of or relating to the cerebrum or the brain. **2.** requiring thought; intellectual. **3.** requiring much thought: *these puzzles are too cerebral for this time of night.* –**cerebrally**, *adv.*

cerebral palsy *n. Pathol.* a form of paralysis caused by injury to the brain, most marked in certain motor areas. It is characterised by involuntary motions and difficulty in control of the voluntary muscles.

cerebrospinal /ˌsɛrəbrouˈspaɪnəl/ *adj.* **1.** relating to or affecting both the brain and the spinal cord. **2.** relating to the central nervous system (distinguished from *autonomic*).

cerebrovascular /ˌsɛrəbrouˈvæskjələ/ *adj.* of or relating to blood vessels and the supply of blood to the brain.

cerebrum /'sɛrəbrəm/ *n.* (*pl.* **-bra** /-brə/) *Anat.* the anterior and upper part of the brain, consisting of two hemispheres, partially separated by a deep fissure but connected by a broad band of fibres, and concerned with voluntary and conscious processes.

ceremonial /sɛrə'mouniəl/ *adj.* **1.** relating to, used for, marked by, or of the nature of ceremonies or ceremony; ritual; formal. –*n.* **2.** a system of ceremonies, rites, or formalities prescribed for or observed on any particular occasion; a rite or ceremony. –**ceremonialism**, *n.* –**ceremonialist**, *n.* –**ceremonially**, *adv.*

ceremony /'sɛrəməni/, *Orig. US* /-mouni/ *n.* (*pl.* **-nies**) **1.** the formalities observed on some solemn or important public or state occasion. **2.** a formal religious or sacred observance; a solemn rite. **3.** any formal act or observance, especially a meaningless one. **4.** formal observances or gestures collectively; ceremonial observances. **5.** strict adherence to conventional forms; formality: *to leave a room without ceremony.* –*phr.* **6. stand on ceremony**, to be excessively formal or polite. –**ceremonious** /sɛrə'mounios/, *adj.*

cerise /sə'ris, -riz/ *adj., n.* mauve-tinged cherry red.

cero- a word element meaning 'wax', as in *cerotype*. Also, **cer-**.

cert /sɜt/ *n. Colloq.* a certainty. Also, **dead cert**.

certain /'sɜtn/ *adj.* **1.** (sometimes fol. by *of*) having no doubt; confident or assured: *I am certain of being able to finish it by tomorrow.* **2.** sure; inevitable; bound to come. **3.** established as true or sure; unquestionable; indisputable. **4.** fixed; agreed upon: *on a certain day.* **5.** definite or particular, but not named or specified.

6. able to be depended on; trustworthy; unfailing; reliable: *their allegiance is certain.* **7.** some though not much: *a certain reluctance.* –*phr.* **8. for certain**, without any doubt; surely. –**certainty**, *n.*

certainly /'sɜtnli/ *adv.* **1.** with certainty; without doubt; assuredly. –*interj.* **2.** yes! of course!

certificate *n.* /sə'tɪfəkət/ **1.** a writing on paper certifying to the truth of something or to status, qualifications, privileges, etc. **2.** a document issued to a person passing a particular examination. **3.** *Law* a statement, written and signed, which is by law made evidence of the truth of the facts stated, for all or for certain purposes. –*v.t.* /sə'tɪfəkeɪt/ **4.** to attest by a certificate. –**certification** /sɜtəfə'keɪʃən/, *n.*

certify /'sɜtəfaɪ/ *v.t.* (**-fied, -fying**) **1.** to guarantee as certain; give reliable information of. **2.** to testify to or vouch for in writing. **3.** to declare insane. –**certifier**, *n.* –**certifiable**, *adj.*

certitude /'sɜtətjud, -tʃud/ *n.* sense of absolute conviction; certainty.

cervic- a combining form of **cervical**. Also, **cervico-**.

cervical /'sɜvɪkəl, sə'vaɪkəl/ *adj.* **1.** of or relating to the neck. **2.** of or relating to the cervix of the uterus.

cervico- variant of **cervic-** used before consonants.

cervix /'sɜvɪks/ *n.* (*pl.* **cervixes** *or* **cervices** /sə'vaɪsiz/) *Anat.* **1.** the neck. **2.** the neck of the uterus, which dilates just before parturition.

cesarean /sə'zɛəriən/ *n., adj.* → **caesarean**. Also, **cesarian**.

cessation /sɛ'seɪʃən/ *n.* a ceasing; discontinuance; pause: *a cessation of hostilities.*

cession /'sɛʃən/ *n.* **1.** the act of ceding, as by treaty. **2.** the voluntary surrender by a debtor of his or her effects to his or her creditors.

cesspit /'sɛspɪt/ *n.* a pit containing a cesspool.

cesspool /'sɛspul/ *n.* **1.** a cistern, well, or pit for retaining the sediment of a drain, or for receiving waste from a sewerage system, etc. **2.** any filthy receptacle or place: *a cesspool of iniquity.*

cet- a word element meaning 'whale'.

cetacean /sə'teɪʃən/ *adj.* **1.** belonging to the Cetacea, an order of aquatic, chiefly marine, mammals, including the whales, dolphins, porpoises, etc. –*n.* **2.** a cetacean mammal. –**cetaceous**, *adj.*

cevapcici /tʃɛvəp'tʃɪtʃi/ *n.* a spicy, skinless sausage made from beef, pork and lamb, seasoned with black pepper and spices.

cevapi /tʃə'vapi/ *n.* → **cevapcici**.

C generation *n.* → **generation C**.

chablis /'ʃæbli, 'ʃabli/ *n.* (*sometimes upper case*) **1.** a very dry white table wine from the Burgundy wine region in France. **2.** (in unofficial use) a similar wine made elsewhere.

chador /'tʃadə/ *n.* → **burqa**.

chafe /tʃeɪf/ *v.t.* **1.** to warm by rubbing: *they chafed his cold feet.* **2.** to wear down or make sore by rubbing: *this saddle chafes my horse.* **3.** to annoy; irritate: *her words chafed him.* –*v.i.* **4.** to become worn or sore by rubbing: *this kind of leather chafes easily.* **5.** to be annoyed or irritated: *he chafed at her words.* **6.** to become impatient; fret: *she chafed at the delay.* –*n.* **7.** a sore caused by rubbing.

chaff[1] /tʃaf/ *n.* **1.** the husks of grains and grasses separated from the seed. **2.** straw cut small for fodder. –**chafflike**, *adj.* –**chaffy**, *adj.*

chaff[2] /tʃaf/ *v.t.* **1.** to ridicule or tease good-naturedly. –*v.i.* **2.** to engage in good-natured teasing; banter. –*n.* **3.** good-natured ridicule or teasing; raillery. –**chaffer**, *n.*

chagrin /'ʃægrən, ʃə'grɪn/ *n.* **1.** a feeling of vexation and disappointment or humiliation. –*v.t.* **2.** to vex by disappointment or humiliation.

chai /tʃaɪ/ n. a sweet milky tea flavoured with spices such as cardamom, cinnamon, cloves, vanilla, etc.

chain /tʃeɪn/ n. **1.** a connected series of metal or other links for connecting, drawing, confining, restraining, etc., or for ornament. **2.** something that binds or restrains. **3.** (*pl.*) bonds or fetters. **4.** (*pl.*) bondage. **5.** a series of things connected or following in succession: *the river was just a chain of ponds.* **6.** a range of mountains. **7.** a number of similar establishments, as banks, theatres, hotels, etc., under one ownership and management. **8.** (*pl.*) → **snow chains**. **9.** *Chem.* a linkage of atoms of the same element, as carbon to carbon. **10.** *Surveying* (formerly) **a.** a measuring instrument consisting of 100 wire rods or links, each 7.92 inches long (**surveyor's chain** or **Gunter's chain**), or one foot long (**engineer's chain**). **b.** the length of a surveyor's chain (66 feet or 20.1168 metres) or engineer's chain (100 feet or 30.48 metres), a unit of measurement in the imperial system. **11. a.** the overhead moving chain in a meatworks, on which carcases are passed to various specialist hands for dressing and processing. **b.** the specialist hands who work on such a chain, regarded as a group or gang. –*v.t.* **12.** to fasten or secure with a chain. **13.** to fetter; confine: *chained to his desk.* –*phr.* **14. drag the chain**, *Aust. Colloq.* to shirk or fall behind in one's share of work or responsibility. **15. on the chain**, *Aust. Hist.* serving one's sentence as part of a chain gang. –**chainless**, *adj.*

chain gang n. a group of convicts chained together, usually while at work.

chain reaction n. **1.** *Physics* a nuclear reaction which produces enough neutrons to sustain itself. **2.** *Chem.* a reaction which results in a product necessary for the continuance of the reaction. **3.** a series of reactions provoked by one event, each reaction causing the next: *a pay increase for rail workers would provoke a chain reaction of wage claims.*

chain-smoke *v.i.* **1.** to smoke continually, as by lighting one cigarette from the preceding one. –*v.t.* **2.** to smoke (cigarettes) in this manner. –**chain-smoker**, *n.*

chain store n. one of a group of retail stores under the same ownership and management and stocked from a common supply point or points.

chair /tʃeə/ n. **1.** a seat with a back and legs or other support, often with arms, usually for one person. **2.** a seat of office or authority. **3.** the position of a judge, chairperson, presiding officer, etc. **4.** the person occupying a seat of office, especially the chairperson of a meeting. **5.** a professorship. –*v.t.* **6.** to conduct as chairperson; preside over. **7.** to place in a chair and carry aloft, especially in triumph. –*phr.* **8. be in the chair**, **a.** to preside at a meeting. **b.** *Colloq.* be the person in a group of drinkers whose turn it is to buy drinks. **9. take the chair**, to assume the position of chair (def. 4) of a meeting; begin or open a meeting.

chairlift /ˈtʃeəlɪft/ n. a series of chairs suspended from an endless cable driven by a motor, for conveying people up or down mountains.

chairman /ˈtʃeəmən/ n. (*pl.* **-men**) **1.** → **chairperson**. **2.** a male chairperson. –**chairmanship**, *n.*

chairperson /ˈtʃeəpɜsən/ n. the presiding officer of a meeting, committee, board, etc.

chakra /ˈtʃʌkrə/ n. (in yoga) one of the six (or seven) major centres of spiritual power in the body for which there are specific physical and mental exercises designed to balance the flow of energy in the body, cultivate the ability to make use of these energies, and enhance wellbeing.

chalcedony /kæl'sɛdəni/ n. a microcrystalline translucent variety of quartz, often milky or greyish. –**chalcedonic** /kælsə'dɒnɪk/, *adj.*

chalet /ˈʃæleɪ/ n. **1.** a kind of cottage, low and with wide eaves, common in alpine regions. **2.** *Aust.*

(in Tasmania) a self-contained flat detached from a house. **3.** Also, **ski chalet**. a ski lodge.

chalice /ˈtʃæləs/ n. **1.** *Eccles.* a cup for the wine of the Eucharist or mass. **2.** *Poetic* a drinking cup. –**chaliced** /ˈtʃæləst/, *adj.*

chalk /tʃɔk/ n. **1.** *Geol.* a soft, white, pure limestone consisting of calcareous fossilised skeletal fragments of microscopic algae. **2.** a prepared piece of chalk or chalklike substance, especially calcium sulphate, for marking. **3.** a mark made with chalk. –*v.t.* **4.** to mark or write with chalk. **5.** to rub over or whiten with chalk. **6.** to treat or mix with chalk. –*phr.* **7. by a long chalk** or **by long chalks**, by far; by a considerable extent or degree. **8. chalk out**, *Brit.* to outline (a plan, etc.). **9. chalk up**, to score: *they chalked up 360 runs in the first innings.* **10. chalk up to**, **a.** to ascribe to, regard as the cause of: *I chalked my failure up to nervousness.* **b.** to regard as having contributed towards the accumulation of: *chalk it up to experience.* **11. like chalk and cheese**, complete opposites. –**chalklike**, **chalky**, *adj.* –**chalkiness**, *n.*

chalkie /ˈtʃɔki/ n. *Colloq.* a schoolteacher. Also, **chalky**.

challenge /ˈtʃæləndʒ/ n. **1.** a call to take part in a test of skill, strength, etc. **2.** a call to fight, as to a duel, etc. **3.** something that makes demands upon one's skills, etc.: *this job is a challenge.* **4. a.** a calling into question (as of rights to join in, be present at, etc.). **b.** *Mil.* a demand by a guard for someone to show who they are. **c.** *Law* a formal objection to a juror or to an entire jury. –*v.t.* (**-lenged**, **-lenging**) **5.** to invite (someone) to compete in a test of skill, strength, etc. **6.** to make demands upon: *this job will challenge your abilities.* **7.** *Mil.* to stop (someone) and demand identification or a password. **8.** *Law* to make formal objection to (a juror or jury). –**challenging**, *adj.* –**challengeable**, *adj.*

chalwar /ˈʃalˈwa/ n. → **salwar**.

chamber /ˈtʃeɪmbə/ n. **1.** (formerly) a private room, especially a bedroom. **2.** (the meeting hall of) a law-making body: *they are meeting in the chamber; the upper chamber is discussing their request.* **3.** (*pl.*) a place where a judge hears matters not requiring action in court. **4.** (*pl.*) the rooms of barristers and others. **5.** a closed-in space; cavity: *a chamber of the heart.* **6.** that part of the barrel of a gun which receives the charge. –**chambered**, *adj.*

chamberlain /ˈtʃeɪmbələn/ n. an official charged with the management of a sovereign's or noble's living quarters.

chamber magistrate n. (in Australia) a qualified solicitor employed in a Court of Petty Sessions, who gives free legal advice.

chambermaid /ˈtʃeɪmbəmeɪd/ n. a female servant who takes care of bedrooms.

chamber music n. music suited for performance in a room or a small concert hall, especially for two or more (but usually less than ten) solo instruments.

chamber of commerce n. an association, primarily of business people, to protect and promote the business activities of a city, etc.

chamber-pot n. a portable vessel used chiefly in bedrooms as a toilet.

chameleon /kə'miliən, ʃə-/ n. **1.** any of a group of lizards, Chamaeleontidae, especially of the genus *Chamaeleon*, found mainly in Africa and Madagascar, characterised by the greatly developed power of changing the colour of the skin, very slow locomotion, and a projectile tongue. **2.** an inconstant person. –**chameleonic** /kəmili'ɒnɪk, ʃə-/, *adj.* –**chameleon-like**, *adj.*

chamfer /ˈtʃæmfə/ n. an oblique surface cut on the edge or corner of a solid, usually a board, made by removing the arris and usually sloping at 45°.

chamois n. (*pl.* **chamois** /ˈʃæmwa/ *for def. 1*, /ˈʃæmiz/ *for defs 2 and 3*) **1.** /ˈʃæmwa/ either of two agile goat-like antelopes **a.** the **alpine chamois**, *Rupicapra rupicapra*, of high mountains of Europe and southwestern Asia. **b.** the **Pyrenean chamois**, *R. pyrenaica*, of the Pyrenees, and the Apennines of central Italy. **2.** /ˈʃæmi/ Also, **shammy**. a soft, pliable leather made from various skins dressed with oil (especially fish oil), originally prepared from the skin of the chamois. **3.** /ˈʃæmi/ Also, **shammy**. **a.** a piece of chamois used for drying glass, motor vehicle paintwork, etc., after washing. **b.** an absorbent cloth made of synthetic material, similarly used.

chamomile /ˈkæməmaɪl/ *n.* **1.** any plant of the genus *Anthemis*, a herb with strongly scented foliage and flowers which are used medicinally. **2.** any of various allied plants, especially of the genus *Matricaria*. Also, **camomile**.

champ¹ /tʃæmp/ *v.t.* **1.** to bite upon, especially impatiently: *horses champing the bit*. **2.** to crush with the teeth and chew vigorously or noisily; munch. –*v.i.* **3.** to make vigorous chewing or biting movements with the jaws and teeth. –*phr.* **4. champ at the bit**, to be keen to see action.

champ² /tʃæmp/ *n. Colloq.* a champion.

champagne /ʃæmˈpeɪn/ *n.* **1.** a sparkling white wine produced in the wine region of Champagne, France. **2.** (in unofficial use) a similar wine produced elsewhere. **3.** the non-sparkling (still) dry white table wine produced in the region of Champagne. **4.** a very pale yellow or cream colour. –*adj.* **5.** having the colour of champagne.

champagne melon *n.* a variety of melon originating in Asia, which is small and round with dark green stripes and a sweet yellow flesh with a slight fizzy taste.

champignon /ˈʃæmpɪnjɒ̃/ *n.* a mushroom (defs 2 and 3), picked for market when very small, that is, before the gills are showing.

champion /ˈtʃæmpiən/ *n.* **1.** someone who holds first place in any sport, etc., having defeated all opponents. **2.** anything that takes first place in competition. **3.** someone who fights for or defends any person or cause: *a champion of the oppressed.* –*v.t.* **4.** to act as champion of; defend; support. –*adj.* **5.** *Colloq.* first-rate. –**championship**, *n.*

chance /tʃæns, tʃɑns/ *n.* **1.** the absence of any known reason why an event should turn out one way rather than another, spoken of as if it were a real agency: *chance governs all.* **2.** fortune; fate; luck. **3.** a possibility or probability of anything happening: *the chances are two to one against us.* **4.** an opportunity: *now is your chance.* **5.** a risk or hazard: *take a chance.* –*verb* (**chanced**, **chancing**) –*v.i.* **6.** to happen or occur by chance. –*v.t.* **7.** *Colloq.* to take the chances or risks of; risk. –*adj.* **8.** due to chance: *a chance occurrence.* –*phr.* **9. by chance**, accidentally. **10. chance it**, to take a risk. **11. chance on** (or **upon**), to come upon by chance. **12. chance one's arm**, to make an attempt, often in spite of a strong possibility of failure. **13. half a chance**, any opportunity at all. **14. the main chance**, **a.** the opportunity to further one's own interests: *he had a constant eye to the main chance.* **b.** the most likely prospect for success. –**chanceful**, *adj.* –**chanceless**, *adj.*

chancel /ˈtʃænsəl, ˈtʃɑnsəl/ *n.* the space around the altar of a church, usually enclosed, for the clergy, choir, etc.

chancellor /ˈtʃænsələ, ˈtʃɑnsələ/ *n.* **1.** the title of various important judges and other high officials. **2.** the chief minister of state in any of various European countries, such as Germany. **3.** the titular, honorary head of a university. –**chancellorship**, *n.*

chancre /ˈʃæŋkə/ *n. Pathol.* the initial lesion of syphilis, commonly a more or less distinct ulcer or sore with a hard base. –**chancrous**, *adj.*

chancy /ˈtʃænsi, ˈtʃɑnsi/ *adj.* (**-cier**, **-ciest**) *Colloq.* uncertain; risky. Also, **chancey**. –**chanciness**, *n.*

chandelier /ʃændəˈlɪə/ *n.* a branched support for a number of lights, especially one suspended from a ceiling.

chandler /ˈtʃændlə, ˈtʃɑndlə/ *n.* **1.** a dealer or trader: *a ship's chandler.* **2.** someone who makes or sells candles.

change /tʃeɪndʒ/ *verb* (**changed**, **changing**) –*v.t.* **1.** (sometimes fol. by *into*) to make different; alter in condition, appearance, etc.; turn: *to change one's habits.* **2.** to substitute another or others for; exchange for something else: *to change one's job.* **3.** to give or get smaller money in exchange for: *to change a twenty-dollar note.* **4.** to give or get different currency in exchange for: *to change dollars into euros.* **5.** to give and take reciprocally; exchange: *to change places with someone.* **6.** to remove and replace the coverings of: *to change a baby.* **7.** to select a higher or lower (gear of a motor vehicle). –*v.i.* **8.** to become different; alter: *to change to a new person; to change into a magician.* **9.** to make a change or an exchange. **10.** to change trains or other conveyances. **11.** to change one's clothes. –*n.* **12.** variation; alteration; modification; deviation; transformation. **13.** the substitution of one thing for another. **14.** (of weather) an alteration usually towards lower temperatures, rain, etc.: *take a jumper in case there's a change.* **15.** variety or novelty. **16.** the passing from one place, state, form, or phase to another: *change of the moon.* **17.** the supplanting of one thing by another. **18.** that which is or may be substituted for another. **19.** a fresh set of clothing. **20.** useful information. **21.** a balance of money that is returned when the sum tendered is larger than the sum due. **22.** coins of low denomination. **23.** (*usu. pl.*) any of the various sequences in which a peal of bells may be rung. **24.** *Music* a harmonic progression. –*phr.* **25. change down**, to select a lower gear while driving a motor vehicle. **26. change front**, *Mil.* to shift a military force in another direction. **27. change hands**, to pass from one possessor to another. **28. change one's mind**, to alter one's intentions or opinion. **29. change one's tune**, to change one's mind; reverse previously held views, attitudes, etc. **30. change up**, to select a higher gear. **31. ring the changes**, to vary the manner of performing an action, especially one that is often repeated; execute a number of manoeuvres or variations. –**changeable**, *adj.*

changeling /ˈtʃeɪndʒlɪŋ/ *n.* a child supposedly substituted secretly for another, especially by fairies; an elfchild.

change of life *n.* → menopause.

channel /ˈtʃænəl/ *n.* **1.** the bed and banks of a river, stream, creek or gully. **2.** the deeper part of a river, ocean passage, etc. **3.** a wide strait, as between a continent and an island. **4.** a sea passage which ships can use to travel between two larger bodies of water such as the English Channel. **5.** a means of approach. **6.** a course into which something may be directed: *he will put his energy into better channels when he is older.* **7.** a way through which anything passes: *channels of communication.* **8.** a means of communication: *through official channels.* **9.** a frequency band for one-way communication, its width depending on the type of transmission (as telephone, radio, television, etc.). **10.** a television station. **11.** a tube for passing through liquids or fluids. **12.** a groove. –*v.t.* (**-nelled** *or, Chiefly US*, **-neled**, **-nelling** *or, Chiefly US*, **-neling**) **13.** to make pass through a channel. **14.** to direct towards some course: *to channel interests.* **15.** to form a channel in; groove.

channelling /ˈtʃænəlɪŋ/ *n.* the supposed process of conveying information or energy of a supernatural origin.

chant /tʃænt, tʃɑnt/ *n.* **1.** a song; singing. **2.** a short, simple melody, specifically one characterised by single notes to which an indefinite number of syllables are intoned, used in singing the psalms, canticles, etc., in the church service. **3.** a monotonous intonation of the voice in speaking. *–v.t.* **4.** to sing to a chant, or in the manner of a chant, especially in the church service.

chaord /ˈkeɪɔd/ *n.* a system in which chaos and order coexist, there being sufficient order to give stability but also sufficient creativity and unpredictability to prevent stagnation. **–chaordic,** *adj.*

chaos /ˈkeɪɒs/ *n.* utter confusion or disorder, wholly without organisation or order. **–chaotic** /keɪˈɒtɪk/, *adj.* **–chaotically** /keɪˈɒtɪkli/, *adv.*

chap¹ /tʃæp/ *verb* (**chapped, chapping**) *–v.t.* **1.** to cause to open in small slits or cracks. **2.** (of cold or exposure) to crack, roughen, and redden (the skin). *–v.i.* **3.** to become chapped. *–n.* **4.** a fissure or crack, especially in the skin.

chap² /tʃæp/ *n. Colloq.* a man.

chapatti /ˈtʃʌpəti, tʃəˈpati/ *n.* a flat Indian unleavened bread made from wholemeal flour and cooked on a griddle. Also, **chapati.**

chapel /ˈtʃæpəl/ *n.* **1.** a separately dedicated part of a church, or a small independent churchlike edifice, devoted to special services. **2.** a room or building for worship in a college or school, royal court, etc. **3.** the body of members of a trade union in a printing or publishing house.

chaperone /ˈʃæpəroʊn/ *n.* **1.** an adult who accompanies one or more children or young people on a public outing, as to ensure their safety, to ensure that they behave appropriately, etc. **2.** an older person, usually a married woman, who, for propriety, attends a young unmarried woman in public or accompanies a party of young unmarried men and women. *–v.t.* **3.** to attend ·or accompany as chaperone. Also, **chaperon. –chaperonage** /ˈʃæpəˈroʊnɪdʒ/, *n.*

chaplain /ˈtʃæplən/ *n.* an ecclesiastic attached to the chapel of a royal court, or, formerly, a noble family, or to a college, school, etc., or to a military unit. **–chaplaincy, chaplainry, chaplainship,** *n.*

chaplet /ˈtʃæplət/ *n.* **1.** a wreath or garland for the head. **2.** a string of beads. **–chapleted,** *adj.*

chapter /ˈtʃæptə/ *n.* **1.** a main division, usually numbered, of a book, treatise, or the like. **2.** a branch, usually localised, of a society or fraternity. **3.** *Eccles.* **a.** an assembly of the monks in a monastery, or of those in a province, or of the entire order. **b.** a general assembly of the canons of a church. **c.** a meeting of the elected representatives of the provinces or houses of a religious community. **d.** the body of such canons or representatives collectively. *–phr.* **4. chapter and verse, a.** an exact reference. **b.** precise details. **5. chapter of accidents,** a series of closely following misfortunes.

char¹ /tʃɑ/ *v.t.* (**charred, charring**) **1.** to burn or reduce to charcoal. **2.** to burn slightly; scorch. **–charry,** *adj.*

char² /tʃɑ/ *n. Brit. Colloq.* → **charwoman.**

char³ /tʃɑ/ *n. Colloq.* tea.

character /ˈkærəktə/ *n.* **1.** the aggregate of qualities that distinguishes one person or thing from others. **2.** moral constitution, as of a person or people. **3.** good moral constitution or status. **4.** reputation. **5.** good repute. **6.** status or capacity. **7.** a person: *a strange character.* **8.** an odd or interesting person. **9.** a person represented in a drama, story, etc. **10.** *Theatre* a part or role. **11.** a significant visual mark or symbol. **12.** a symbol as used in a writing system, as a letter of the alphabet, or a written sign representing a syllable or word. **13.** *Computers* a group of bits representing such a symbol or a numeral. *–v.t.* **14.** to portray; describe. *–phr.* **15. in character,** consistent with what is known of previous character, behaviour, etc. **16. out of character,** inconsistent with what is known of previous character, behaviour, etc. **–characterless,** *adj.*

characterise /ˈkærəktəraɪz/ *v.t.* **1.** to mark or distinguish as a characteristic; be a characteristic of. **2.** to describe the characteristic or peculiar quality of. Also, **characterize. –characteriser,** *n.* **–characterisation,** *n.*

characteristic /ˌkærəktəˈrɪstɪk/ *adj.* **1.** relating to, constituting, or indicating the character or peculiar quality; typical; distinctive. *–n.* **2.** a distinguishing feature or quality. **–characteristically,** *adv.*

charade /ʃəˈrɑd/ *n.* **1.** a game in which a player or players act out in pantomime a word or phrase which the others try to guess. **2.** a ridiculous or pointless act or series of acts.

charcoal /ˈtʃɑkoʊl/ *n.* **1.** the carbonaceous material obtained by the imperfect combustion of wood or other organic substances. **2.** a drawing pencil of charcoal. **3.** a drawing made with charcoal. *–v.t.* **4.** to blacken, write or draw with charcoal.

chardonnay *n.* /ˈʃadəneɪ/ (*sometimes upper case*) **1.** a dry white table wine. *–adj.* **2.** (*derog.*) of, relating to, or designating the comfortably well-off members of society who expound fashionable middle-class ideas and politics: *the chardonnay set.*

chardonnay socialist *n.* (*derog.*) a person with a comfortable upper middle-class income who espouses left-wing views that have no real impact on their own life.

charge /tʃɑdʒ/ *verb* (**charged, charging**) *–v.t.* **1.** to put a load or burden on or in. **2.** to fill or furnish (something) with the appropriate quantity of what it is designed to receive. **3.** to supply a quantity of electricity to (a battery) usually sufficient to make it fully operational again. **4.** to fill (air, water, etc.) with other matter in a state of diffusion or solution. **5.** to load (a weapon) prior to firing: *they waited with muskets charged.* **6.** to fill (a glass, etc.) with drink, especially in preparation for a toast: *please charge your glasses.* **7.** to load or burden (the mind, heart, etc.). **8.** to lay a command or injunction upon. **9.** to instruct authoritatively, as a judge does a jury. **10.** (sometimes fol. by *with*) to find fault in: *charge him with carelessness.* **11.** (sometimes fol. by *with*) to lay blame upon; blame: *to charge someone with negligence.* **12.** to hold liable for payment; enter a debit against. **13.** to list or record as a debt or obligation; enter as a debit. **14.** to postpone payment on (a service or purchase) by having it recorded on one's charge account. **15.** to impose or ask as a price. **16. a.** to attack by rushing violently against. **b.** *Aust. Rules* to so rush against (an opposing player) illegally. *–v.i.* **17.** to make an onset; rush, as to an attack. *–n.* **18.** a load or burden. **19.** the quantity of anything which an apparatus is fitted to hold, or holds, at one time. **20.** a quantity of explosive to be set off at one time. **21.** a duty or responsibility laid upon or entrusted to one. **22.** care, custody, or superintendence: *to have charge of a thing.* **23.** anything or anybody committed to one's care or management. **24.** *Eccles.* a parish or congregation committed to the spiritual care of a minister or priest. **25.** a command or injunction; exhortation. **26.** *Law* an address by a judge to a jury at the close of a trial, instructing them as to the legal points, the weight of evidence, etc., affecting their verdict in the case. **27.** an accusation or imputation of guilt: *he was arrested on a charge of murder.* **28.** expense or cost: *improvements made at a tenant's own charge.* **29.** a sum or price charged: *a charge of $2 for admission.* **30.** a pecuniary burden, encumbrance, tax, or lien; cost; expense; liability to pay. **31.** an entry in an account of something due. **32. a.** an impetuous onset or attack, as of soldiers. **b.** *Aust. Rules* an illegal violent pushing of an opposing player. **33.** a signal by bugle, drum, etc., for a military charge. **34.** *Elect.* an electric charge. **35.** *Physics, Electronics* the quantity of electricity stored in a capacitor or electrical storage battery. **36.** *Heraldry* → **bearing**

(def. 6). **37.** *Colloq.* a thrill; a kick. *–phr.* **38. charge like a wounded bull,** *Colloq.* to fix prices that are excessive. **39. charge up, a.** to recharge (a battery). **b.** to postpone payment on (a service or purchase) by having it recorded on one's charge account. **40. give in charge,** to deliver to the police. **41. in charge,** in command; having supervisory powers. **42. in charge of, a.** having the care or supervision of: *in charge of the class.* **b.** *US* under the care or supervision of: *in charge of the teacher.* **43. in the charge of,** in the care of; under the supervision of. **44. lay** (or **press**) **charges,** *Law* to pursue a conviction in a court of law. **45. take charge,** to put oneself in control of people or events.

charge account *n.* a credit arrangement with a department store, service station, etc., whereby the purchase of goods is charged to the customer's account.

chargé d'affaires /ˌʃaʒeɪ dəˈfɛə/ *n.* (*pl.* **chargés d'affaires**) **1.** (in full: **chargé d'affaires ad interim**) an official placed in charge of diplomatic business during the temporary absence of the ambassador or minister. **2.** an envoy to a state to which a diplomat of higher grade is not sent. Also, **chargé.**

charger[1] /ˈtʃadʒə/ *n.* **1.** a horse intended or suitable to be ridden in battle. **2.** *Elect.* an apparatus which charges storage batteries.

charger[2] /ˈtʃadʒə/ *n.* **1.** a platter. **2.** a large, shallow dish for liquids.

chargrill /ˈtʃagrɪl/ *v.t.* to grill (food) over charcoal. **–chargrilled,** *adj.*

chariot /ˈtʃæriət/ *n.* **1.** a two-wheeled vehicle used by the ancients in war, racing, processions, etc. **2.** any more or less stately carriage.

charisma /kəˈrɪzmə/ *n.* (*pl.* **-mata** /-mətə/) **1.** the special personal qualities that give an individual influence or authority over large numbers of people. **2.** an ability to influence or impress people, especially when visible in politicians or public figures; personality. **–charismatic,** *adj.*

charitable /ˈtʃærətəbəl/ *adj.* **1.** generous in gifts to relieve the needs of others. **2.** kindly or lenient in judging others. **3.** relating to or concerned with charity: *a charitable institution.* **–charitableness,** *n.* **–charitably,** *adv.*

charity /ˈtʃærəti/ *n.* (*pl.* **-ties**) **1.** almsgiving; the private or public relief of unfortunate or needy persons; benevolence. **2.** a charitable fund, foundation, or institution. **3.** benevolent feeling, especially towards those in need. *–adj.* **4.** of or relating to organisations, fundraising activities, etc., of a charitable nature.

charlatan /ˈʃalətən/ *n.* someone who pretends to more knowledge or skill than he or she possesses; a quack. **–charlatanic** /ˌʃaləˈtænɪk/, *adj.*

charleston /ˈtʃalstən/ *n.* a kind of foxtrot, of African American origin, popular in the 1920s.

charlotte /ˈʃalət/ *n.* a hot pudding with a framework of thinly sliced and buttered bread filled with apples or other fruit.

charm /tʃam/ *n.* **1.** a power to please and attract; fascination. **2.** some quality or feature exerting a fascinating influence: *feminine charms.* **3.** a trinket to be worn on a chain, bracelet, etc. **4.** something worn for its supposed magical effect; an amulet. **5.** a verse or formula credited with magical power. *–v.t.* **6.** to attract powerfully by beauty, etc.; please greatly. **7.** to act upon with or as with a charm; enchant. **8.** to calm, soothe, etc. *–phr.* **9. like a charm,** successfully; perfectly. **–charmer,** *n.* **–charming,** *adj.*

charnel-house /ˈtʃanəl-haʊs/ *n.* a house or place in which the bodies or bones of the dead are deposited.

chart /tʃat/ *n.* **1.** a sheet giving information, often in table or graph form. **2.** a map, especially one showing sea and waterways. **3.** an outline map showing special information: *a weather chart.* **4.** (*usu. pl.*) a list of the

best-selling popular recordings for a particular period. *–v.t.* **5.** to make a chart of. **6.** to plan a course of action. **–chartless,** *adj.*

charter /ˈtʃatə/ *n.* **1.** a written instrument or contract, especially relating to land transfers. **2.** a treaty between countries. **3.** a formal agreement, as between an organisation and its clients. **4. a.** a written undertaking, given by a ruler or law-making body, giving certain rights, etc. **b.** a written grant by a governing power creating a university, company, etc. *–v.t.* **5.** to establish by charter. **6.** to hire or make available for hire. *–adj.* **7.** founded or protected by a charter. **8.** hired for a particular purpose or journey: *a charter plane.*

chartered accountant *n.* an accountant who is a full member of one of the institutes of accountants granted a royal charter which have branches in Australia.

charter member *n.* one of the original members.

chartreuse /ʃaˈtrɜz, -ˈtruz, -ˈtrus/ *n.* **1.** one of two aromatic liqueurs made by the Carthusian monks, at Grenoble, France, and (1901–46) in Tarragona, Spain. **2.** a clear, light green with a yellowish tinge. *–adj.* **3.** of the colour chartreuse.

charwoman /ˈtʃawʊmən/ *n.* (*pl.* **-women**) *Brit.* a woman hired to do odd jobs of household work, or to do such work by the hour or day.

chary /ˈtʃɛəri/ *adj.* (**charier, chariest**) **1.** careful; wary. **2.** shy. *–phr.* **3. chary of,** sparing of: *chary of his praise.* **–charily,** *adv.* **–chariness,** *n.*

chase[1] /tʃeɪs/ *v.t.* **1.** to pursue in order to seize, overtake, etc. **2.** (in sport) to attempt to equal or better (an opponent's score): *the Australians were chasing the Poms' first innings score of 401.* **3.** to pursue with intent to capture or kill, as game; hunt. **4.** to drive by pursuing. *–v.i.* **5.** *Colloq.* to run or hasten. *–n.* **6.** the act of chasing; pursuit. **7.** the occupation or sport of hunting. *–phr.* **8. chase after,** to follow in pursuit: *to chase after someone.* **9. chase away,** to chase (someone) so as to cause them to run away. **10. chase off,** to chase (someone) so as to cause them to leave a position or location. **11. chase up, a.** to stimulate to action: *I'll have to chase her up on that.* **b.** to locate or find: *I'll chase up some help.*

chase[2] /tʃeɪs/ *n.* Also, **chasing. 1.** a groove, furrow, or trench; a lengthened hollow. *–v.t.* **2.** to groove or indent, so as to make into a screw.

chaser /ˈtʃeɪsə/ *n.* **1.** someone who chases or pursues. **2.** a drink of water, beer, or other mild beverage taken after a drink of spirits.

chasm /ˈkæzəm/ *n.* **1.** a yawning fissure or deep cleft in the earth's surface; a gorge. **2.** a wide difference of feeling, interest, etc., between persons, groups, nations. **–chasmal** /ˈkæzməl/, *adj.*

chassis /ˈʃæzi/ *n.* (*pl.* **chassis** /ˈʃæziz/) **1.** the frame, wheels, and machinery of a motor vehicle, on which the body is supported. **2.** *Ordnance* the frame or rails on which a gun carriage moves backwards and forwards.

chaste /tʃeɪst/ *adj.* **1.** not having had sexual intercourse; virgin, especially when considered as being virtuous. **2.** free from obscenity; decent. **3.** pure in style; subdued; simple. **–chastity** /ˈtʃæstəti/, **chasteness,** *n.* **–chastely,** *adv.*

chasten /ˈtʃeɪsən/ *v.t.* **1.** to inflict suffering upon for purposes of moral improvement; chastise. **2.** to restrain; subdue. **–chastener,** *n.*

chastise /tʃæsˈtaɪz/ *v.t.* **1.** to punish, especially physically. **2.** to scold or rebuke. **–chastisement** /ˈtʃæstəzmənt, -ˈtaɪzmənt/, *n.* **–chastiser,** *n.*

chat[1] /tʃæt/ *v.i.* (**chatted, chatting**) **1.** to converse in a familiar or informal manner. **2.** *Internet* to take part in real-time communication using internet relay chat. *–n.* **3.** informal conversation. **4.** *Internet* a session of real-time communication using internet relay chat. *–phr.*

5. chat up, *Colloq.* to talk persuasively or to flirt with: *to chat up a woman.*

chat[2] /tʃæt/ *n.* **1.** (in Australia) any of several small, ground-feeding, endemic birds of the genus *Epthianura*, family Meliphagidae, having brush-tipped tongues and walking rather than hopping; Australian chat. **2.** (elsewhere) any of several birds of the subfamily Turdinae, especially of the genus *Saxicola*, known for their harsh chattering cries.

chat room *n. Internet* a virtual venue on the internet for conversation, discussion, etc., using internet relay chat. Also, **chatroom.**

chattels /ˈtʃætlz/ *pl. n. n.* **1.** movable articles of property. **2.** (*sing.*) a slave.

chatter /ˈtʃætə/ *v.i.* **1.** to utter a succession of quick, inarticulate, speech-like sounds: *a chattering monkey.* **2.** to talk rapidly and to little purpose; jabber. **3.** to make a rapid clicking noise by striking together, as the teeth from cold. –*n.* **4.** idle or foolish talk. **5.** the act or sound of chattering.

chatterbox /ˈtʃætəbɒks/ *n.* a very talkative person.

chatterer /ˈtʃætərə/ *n.* **1.** someone who chatters. **2.** any of several noisy, gregarious babblers of the genus *Pomatostomus*, as the **grey-crowned babbler,** *P. temporalis,* which frequent scrub and open forest in various parts of Australia.

chatty /ˈtʃæti/ *adj.* (**-tier, -tiest**) given to or full of chat or familiar talk; conversational: *a chatty letter; a chatty person.* –**chattily,** *adv.* –**chattiness,** *n.*

chauffeur /ˈʃoufə, ʃouˈfɜ/ *n.* **1.** someone employed as a driver for a private car. –*v.t.* **2.** to act as chauffeur to.

chauvinism /ˈʃouvənɪzəm/ *n.* narrow-minded belief in the superiority of one's own gender, group, ideology, etc. –**chauvinist,** *n.,* *adj.* –**chauvinistic** /ʃouvəˈnɪstɪk/, *adj.* –**chauvinistically** /ʃouvəˈnɪstɪkli/, *adv.*

cheap /tʃip/ *adj.* **1.** of a relatively low price; at a bargain. **2.** costing little labour or trouble. **3.** charging low prices: *a very cheap shop.* **4.** of poor quality: *that material is cheap and nasty.* **5.** obtainable at a low rate of interest. **6.** of decreased value or purchasing power, as currency depreciated due to inflation. **7.** of little account; of small value. **8.** base; mean. **9.** *Colloq.* miserly; stingy; mean. **10.** *Colloq.* (of a woman) unrefined or promiscuous. –*adv.* **11.** at a low price; at small cost. –*phr.* **12.** (**as**) **cheap as chips,** *Aust. Colloq.* extremely cheap. **13.** (**as**) **cheap as dirt,** *Colloq.* extremely cheap. **14. cheap drunk,** *Colloq.* someone who becomes intoxicated after taking only a little alcoholic liquor. **15. on the cheap,** *Colloq.* at a low price. –**cheaply,** *adv.* –**cheapness,** *n.*

cheapen /ˈtʃipən/ *v.t.* **1.** to make cheap or cheaper. **2.** to belittle; bring into contempt. –**cheapener,** *n.*

cheat /tʃit/ *n.* **1.** a fraud; swindle; deception. **2.** someone who cheats or defrauds. **3.** *Computer Games* a tip on how to progress in a computer game. –*v.t.* **4.** to defraud; swindle. –**cheatable,** *adj.* –**cheater,** *n.* –**cheatingly,** *adv.* –**cheating,** *n.*

check /tʃɛk/ *v.t.* **1.** to stop or arrest the motion of suddenly or forcibly. **2.** to restrain; hold in restraint or control. **3.** to investigate or verify as to correctness. **4.** Also, **check off.** *US* to tick. **5.** Also, **check in.** to leave in temporary custody: *check your coat and hat.* **6.** to accept for temporary custody: *small parcels checked here.* **7.** *US* to send (luggage, etc.) through to a final destination, but allowing the accompanying passenger to break the journey: *we checked two trunks through to New York.* **8.** *US* to accept for conveyance, and to convey to a final destination: *check this trunk to New York.* **9.** *Chess* to place (an opponent's king) under direct attack. **10.** *Colloq.* to take a look at: *check the nose on that guy!* –*v.i.* **11.** to prove to be right; to correspond accurately: *the reprint checks with the*

original item for item. –*n.* **12.** a person or thing that checks or restrains. **13.** a sudden arrest or stoppage; repulse; rebuff. **14.** control with a view to ascertaining performance or preventing error. **15.** a controlled and carefully observed operation or test procedure to determine actual and potential performance. **16.** a means or standard to prevent error, fraud, etc. **17.** a pattern formed of squares, as on a draughtboard. **18.** a fabric having a check pattern. **19.** *Chess* the exposure of the king to direct attack. **20.** *US* a counter used in card games; the chip in poker. **21.** *US* → **tick**[1] (def. 3). **22.** *US* → **cheque. 23.** *US* a bill, especially for a meal in a restaurant. **24.** *US* → **ticket** (def. 1). –*adj.* **25.** serving to check, control, verify, etc. **26.** ornamented with a checked pattern; chequered. –*interj.* **27.** *Chess* an optional call to inform one's opponent that their king is exposed to direct attack. –*phr.* **28. check in,** to register one's arrival, as at a hotel, work, etc. **29. check out, a.** to ascertain the truth or correctness of: *to check out the arrangements.* **b.** *Colloq.* to inspect and evaluate: *we're going to check out the talent at the party.* **c.** to complete the procedures for leaving a hotel, motel, etc., by paying the bill, returning the room key, etc. **d.** *Colloq.* to depart. **30. check up,** to make an inquiry or investigation for verification, etc. **31. check you later,** *Colloq.* a phrase of farewell. **32. in check, a.** under restraint. **b.** *Chess* (of a player) having a king which is exposed to direct attack, or (of the king) being exposed to direct attack. –**checkable,** *adj.* –**checker,** *n.*

checkmate /ˈtʃɛkmeɪt/ *n.* **1.** *Chess* the act of putting the opponent's king into an inextricable check, thus bringing the game to a close. **2.** defeat; overthrow.

check-out *n.* **1.** the cash desk in a supermarket. **2.** the act of registering one's departure, as at work, at a hotel, etc. –*adj.* **3.** of or relating to the people, equipment or procedure operating at a check-out. Also, **checkout.**

checkpoint /ˈtʃɛkpɔɪnt/ *n.* a place where traffic is halted for inspection.

check-up *n.* **1.** an examination or close scrutiny for purposes of verification as to accuracy, comparison, etc. **2.** a comprehensive physical examination. **3.** an overhaul.

cheddar /ˈtʃɛdə/ *n.* **1.** a smooth white or yellow cheese, with a firm texture, sometimes cracked, the flavour of which depends on the age of the cheese. –*phr.* **2. hard** (or **stiff**) (or **tough**) **cheddar,** *Colloq.* an exclamation indicating a lack of sympathy for another's misfortune.

cheek /tʃik/ *n.* **1.** either side of the face below eye level. **2.** the side wall of the mouth between the upper and lower jaws. **3.** a buttock. **4.** one side of the head of a hammer. **5.** *Machinery* either of the sides of a pulley or block. **6.** *Colloq.* impudence or effrontery. –*v.t.* **7.** *Colloq.* to address saucily; to be impudent. –*phr.* **8. cheek by jowl,** close together; adjacent; in close intimacy. **9. turn the other cheek,** to accept provocation without taking any retaliatory action. **10. with one's tongue in one's cheek,** mockingly; insincerely.

cheeky /ˈtʃiki/ *adj.* (**-kier, -kiest**) **1.** impudent: *a cheeky little boy* **2.** pushing boundaries; irreverent: *a cheeky advertising campaign.* –**cheekily,** *adv.* –**cheekiness,** *n.*

cheep /tʃip/ *v.i.* to chirp; peep.

cheer /tʃɪə/ *n.* **1.** a shout of encouragement, approval, congratulation, etc. **2.** that which gives joy or gladness; encouragement; comfort. **3.** *Obs.* gladness, gaiety, or animation: *an atmosphere of cheer.* –*v.t.* **4.** to salute with shouts of approval, congratulation, etc. **5.** to inspire with cheer; gladden. –*v.i.* **6.** to utter cheers of approval, etc. –*phr.* **7. cheer on,** to encourage or incite. **8. cheer up, a.** to cause to feel cheerful. **b.** to become cheerful. **9. in good cheer,** in good spirits; cheerful. **10. three cheers,** (sometimes fol. by *for*) an encouragement to give three shouts of hurray as a token of approval for someone or something. –**cheerful, cheery,**

adj. **–cheerless,** *adj.* **–cheerfully, cheerily,** *adv.* **–cheerer,** *n.* **–cheeringly,** *adv.*

cheerio /tʃɪəri'ou/ *interj. Colloq.* goodbye.

cheers /tʃɪəz/ *interj. Colloq.* **1.** to your health! **2.** thank you. **3.** goodbye.

cheese /tʃiz/ *n.* **1.** the curd of milk separated from the whey and prepared in any of various ways as a food. **2.** a cake or definite mass of this substance. **3.** a conserve of fruit of the consistency of cream cheese. *–phr. Colloq.* **4. cheese off,** to irritate; annoy: *that really cheeses me off!* **5. hard** (or **stiff**) (or **tough**) **cheese,** an exclamation indicating a lack of sympathy for another's misfortune. **–cheesy,** *adj.* **–cheesiness,** *n.*

cheesecake /'tʃizkeɪk/ *n.* **1.** a kind of cake or open pie filled with a rich, sweet mixture containing a soft cheese, such as cream cheese, and other flavourings. **2.** *Colloq.* **a.** photographs of attractive women in newspapers, magazines, etc., posed to display their bodies, and emphasising their sex appeal. **b.** the women who pose for such photographs. **c.** the titillating display of female bodies. Compare **beefcake.**

cheesecloth /'tʃizklɒθ/ *n.* a coarse cotton fabric of open texture, originally used in cheese-making, now also for clothing, etc.

cheeseparing /'tʃizpɛərɪŋ/ *adj.* **1.** meanly economical; parsimonious. *–n.* **2.** niggardly economy.

cheetah /'tʃitə/ *n.* a slim, long-limbed, long-tailed wild cat, *Acinonyx jubatus,* of south-western Asia and Africa, having a pale yellow coat covered with small black spots, and with heavy black lines (tear lines) from the inner eyes to the outer corners of the mouth; formerly also in India; reputed to be the fastest four-legged animal. Also, **chetah.**

chef /ʃɛf/ *n.* a cook, especially a head cook.

cheiro- variant of **chiro-.**

cheli- a word element meaning 'claws', as in *cheliferous.*

chem- a word element representing **chemical** used before vowels. Also, (*especially before a consonant*), **chemo-.**

chemical /'kɛmɪkəl/ *n.* **1.** a substance produced by or used in a chemical process. *–adj.* **2.** of or concerned with the science or the operations or processes of chemistry. **–chemically,** *adv.*

chemical peel *n.* a beauty treatment in which a weak acid solution is applied to the skin, the idea being that the superficial layer will peel away, taking with it unwanted blemishes.

chemical warfare *n.* warfare with asphyxiating, poisonous, or corrosive gases, oil flames, etc.

chemise /ʃə'miz/ *n.* **1.** a woman's loose-fitting shirt-like undergarment. **2.** (in women's fashions) a dress, suit, etc., designed to fit loosely at the waist and more tightly at the hips.

chemist /'kɛmɪst/ *n.* **1.** someone who studies or is professionally qualified in the science of chemistry. **2.** a retailer of medicinal drugs and toilet preparations.

chemistry /'kɛmɪstri/ *n.* (*pl.* **-ries**) **1.** the science concerned with the composition of substances, the various elementary forms of matter, and the interactions between them. **2.** chemical properties, reactions, etc.: *the chemistry of carbon.*

chemo /'kimoʊ/ *n. Colloq.* chemotherapy.

chemo- variant of **chem-** used especially before a consonant.

chemosynthesis /kɛmoʊ'sɪnθəsəs/ *n. Bot.* production by plants of nutritive substances from carbon dioxide and water with energy derived from other chemical reactions. **–chemosynthetic** /kɛmoʊsɪn'θɛtɪk/, *adj.* **–chemosynthetically** /kɛmoʊsɪn'θɛtɪkli/, *adv.*

chemotherapy /kimoʊ'θɛrəpi/ *n. Med.* treatment of disease by means of chemicals which have a specific toxic effect upon the disease-producing microorganisms. **–chemotherapist,** *n.*

chenille /ʃə'nil/ *n.* a fabric with a pile created by the use of chenille yarns.

chenille yarn *n.* a yarn with a pile protruding all around at right angles; originally from China.

cheque /tʃɛk/ *n.* **1.** *Banking* a written order, usually on a standard printed form directing a bank to pay a specified sum of money to, or to the order of, some particular person or the bearer, either *crossed* (payable only through a bank account) or *uncrossed* (payable on demand). **2.** wages, pay. Also, *US,* **check. –chequing,** *adj.*

cheque account *n.* a bank account from which money may be withdrawn by cheque at any time by the customer.

chequer /'tʃɛkə/ *n.* **1.** a pattern of squares. **2.** a marble or similar token used in Chinese chequers. *–v.t.* **3.** to diversify in colour; variegate. **4.** to diversify in character; subject to alterations. Also, *US,* **checker.**

cherish /'tʃɛrɪʃ/ *v.t.* **1.** to hold or treat as dear. **2.** to care for tenderly; nurture. **3.** to cling fondly to (ideas, etc.): *cherishing no resentment.* **–cherisher,** *n.* **–cherishment,** *n.* **–cherishingly,** *adv.*

cheroot /ʃə'rut/ *n.* a cigar having open, unpointed ends.

cherry /'tʃɛri/ *n.* (*pl.* **-ries**) **1.** the fruit of any of various trees of the genus *Prunus,* consisting of a pulpy, globular drupe enclosing a one-seeded smooth stone. **2.** the tree itself. **3.** its wood. **4.** a bright red. **5.** *Colloq.* **a.** the hymen as a symbol of virginity. **b.** virginity. **c.** a virgin. *–phr.* **6. two bites of** (or **at**) **the cherry,** *Colloq.* two attempts.

cherub /'tʃɛrəb/ *n.* (*pl.* **cherubim** /'tʃɛrəbɪm, 'kɛ-/ *for defs 1 and 2,* **cherubs** *for defs 3 and 4*) **1.** *Bible* a kind of celestial being. **2.** *Theology* a member of the second order of angels, distinguished by knowledge, often represented as a beautiful winged child or as a winged head of a child. See **angel** (def. 1). **3.** a beautiful or innocent person, especially a child. **4.** a person with a chubby, innocent face. **–cherubic** /tʃə'rubɪk/, *adj.* **–cherubically,** *adv.*

chess /tʃɛs/ *n.* a game played by two persons, each with sixteen pieces, on a chequered board.

chess boxing *n.* a sport which alternates a round of boxing with a round of chess. Also, **chessboxing.** **–chess boxer,** *n.*

chessman /'tʃɛsmæn, -mən/ *n.* (*pl.* **-men** /-mɛn, -mən/) one of the pieces used in the game of chess.

chest /tʃɛst/ *n.* **1.** the trunk of the body from the neck to the belly; the thorax. **2.** a box, usually a large, strong one, for the safekeeping of valuables. **3.** the place where the funds of a public institution, etc., are kept. **4.** a box in which certain goods, as tea, are packed for transit. **5.** the quantity contained in such a box. *–phr.* **6. get something off one's chest,** to bring a pressing worry into the open.

chest cold *n.* a form of the common cold that mainly involves inflammation or infection of the respiratory tract. Compare **head cold.**

chestnut /'tʃɛsnʌt/ *n.* **1.** (the edible nut of) a tree of the beech family. **2.** any of various fruits or trees like the chestnut, especially the **horse chestnut. 3.** a reddish brown colour. **4.** a horse of this colour. **5.** *Colloq.* an old or stale joke, anecdote, etc. *–adj.* **6.** reddish brown.

chevapchichi /tʃɛvəp'tʃɪtʃi/ *n.* → **cevapcici.**

chevapi /tʃə'vapi/ *n.* → **cevapcici.**

chevre /'ʃɛavrə/ *n.* cheese made from goat's milk. Also, **chèvre.**

chevron /'ʃɛvrən/ *n.* a badge consisting of stripes meeting at an angle, worn on the sleeve (by non-commissioned officers, police officers, etc.) as an indication of rank, of service, etc.

chew /tʃu/ *v.t.* **1.** to crush or grind with the teeth; masticate. **2.** to damage or destroy by or as if by chewing. –*v.i.* **3.** to perform the act of crushing or grinding with the teeth. –*n.* **4.** the act of chewing. **5.** that which is chewed; a portion, as of tobacco, for chewing. **6.** *NZ* (*with children*) a sweet; lolly. –*phr.* **7. chew out**, *Colloq.* to scold or castigate (someone). **8. chew over**, to meditate on; consider deliberately. **9. chew someone's ear**, *Colloq.* to talk to someone insistently and at length. **10. chew the buns off someone**, *Colloq.* to berate or abuse someone. **11. chew the fat**, *Colloq.* to gossip. **12. chew the rag**, *Colloq.* **a.** to gossip. **b.** to argue or grumble. **c.** to brood or grieve. **13. chew up**, to damage or destroy by or as if by chewing: *this machine has chewed up the carpet*. –**chewer**, *n.*

chewing gum *n.* a preparation for chewing, usually made of sweetened and flavoured gum.

chewy /'tʃui/ *adj.* (**-wier, -wiest**) requiring chewing; tough: *this steak is too chewy*.

chez /ʃeɪ/ *prep.* at the home of.

chi /kaɪ/ *n.* the twenty-second letter (X, χ, = English Ch, ch) of the Greek alphabet.

chia /'tʃiə/ *n.* a plant of the mint family with seeds high in antioxidants and dietary fibre.

chic /ʃik/ *adj.* **1.** cleverly attractive in style; stylish. –*n.* **2.** cleverly attractive style, especially in dress.

chicanery /ʃə'keɪnəri/ *n.* (*pl.* **-ries**) **1.** legal trickery, quibbling, or sophistry. **2.** a quibble or subterfuge.

chick /tʃik/ *n.* **1.** a young chicken or other bird. **2.** *Colloq.* a young woman. **3.** *Obs.* a child.

chicken /'tʃikən/ *n.* **1.** a common domesticated gallinaceous bird, *Gallus gallus domesticus*, of the family Phasianidae, having a prominent comb and wattles and farmed for its eggs, flesh and feathers or kept for cockfighting; bred into numerous breeds and varieties. **2.** the young of the domestic fowl; chick. **3.** a slaughtered and dressed chicken, either raw or cooked. **4.** the flesh of this bird used as food. **5.** *Colloq.* a coward. **6.** *Colloq.* a young person, especially a young girl. –*adj.* **7.** *Colloq.* cowardly. –*phr.* **8.** (*all*) **one's chickens come home to roost**, the consequences of an action are visited on its perpetrator. **9. chicken out**, *Colloq.* to withdraw because of cowardice, tiredness, etc. **10. count one's chickens before they are hatched**, to act on an expectation which has not yet been fulfilled. **11. play chicken**, *Colloq.* **a.** to perform a dangerous dare. **b.** to stand in the path of an approaching vehicle daring the driver to run one down. **c.** (of the drivers of two vehicles) to proceed along a collision course, as a test of courage.

chickenhawk /'tʃikənhɔk/ *n.* **1.** → **brown goshawk**. **2.** any of various hawks regarded as a threat to poultry.

chickenpox /'tʃikənpɔks/ *n. Pathol.* a mild, contagious eruptive disease, commonly of children, caused by a virus; varicella.

chick flick *n. Colloq.* a film thought to appeal more to female than to male viewers, especially a romance.

chick lit *n. Colloq.* a genre of popular fiction appealing typically to young women, often set in a stylish urban business environment and usually featuring romance.

chickpea /'tʃikpi/ *n.* a leguminous plant, *Cicer arietinum*, bearing edible pea-like seeds, much used for food in southern Europe, Asia, and Africa.

chickweed /'tʃikwid/ *n.* any of various herbs of the genus *Stellaria*, especially *S. media*.

chicory /'tʃikəri/ *n.* (*pl.* **-ries**) a perennial herb, *Cichorium intybus*, with blue flowers, native to Europe and western Asia; the blanched shoots are used in salads, and, in the southern US, the roasted, powdered roots added to coffee.

chide /tʃaɪd/ *verb* (**chided** *or* **chid, chided** *or* **chid** *or* **chidden, chiding**) –*v.i.* **1.** to scold; find fault. –*v.t.* **2.** to drive, impel, etc., by chiding. **3.** to express disapproval of. –**chider**, *n.* –**chidingly**, *adv.*

chief /tʃif/ *n.* **1.** the head or leader of a body of people; the person highest in authority. **2.** the head or ruler of a clan or tribe. **3.** *Colloq.* boss. –*adj.* **4.** highest in rank or authority. **5.** most important: *its chief merit; the chief difficulty*. **6.** standing at the head. –*phr. Colloq.* **7. chief cook and bottle-washer**, a person who, as well as being responsible for some enterprise, also does much of the work, especially manual work. **8. too many chiefs and not enough Indians**, a phrase expressing the opinion that there are too many people organising and not enough people doing the real work. –**chiefly**, *adv.*

chief justice *n.* the senior justice of any court, who presides over that court.

chief petty officer *n. Navy* **1.** a non-commissioned officer in the Royal Australian Navy ranking below warrant officer and above petty officer. **2.** the rank. *Abbrev.*: CPO

chieftain /'tʃiftən/ *n.* **1.** the chief of a clan or a tribe. **2.** a leader of a group, band, etc. –**chieftaincy, chieftainship**, *n.*

chiffon /ʃə'fɒn, 'ʃifɒn/ *n.* **1.** sheer fabric of silk, nylon, or rayon in plain weave. **2.** any bit of decorative finery, as of ribbon or lace. –*adj.* **3.** (of food) having a light, fluffy consistency.

chiffonier /ʃifə'nɪə/ *n.* **1.** an elegant waist-high cupboard with a sideboard top and usually a decorated board rising above it at the back. **2.** a high chest of drawers. **3.** a low cupboard with shelves for books. Also, *Rare*, **chiffonnier**.

chignon /'ʃinjɒn/ *n.* a large rolled arrangement of the hair, worn at the back of the head by women.

Chihuahua /tʃə'waʊwə, tʃə'wawə/ *n.* (*also lower case*) a dog belonging to one of the smallest breeds, originating in Mexico.

chil- variant of **chilo-**, used before vowels.

chilblain /'tʃilbleɪn/ *n. Pathol.* (*usu. pl.*) an inflammation on the hands and feet caused by exposure to cold and moisture. –**chilblained**, *adj.*

child /tʃaɪld/ *n.* (*pl.* **children**) **1.** a baby or infant. **2.** a boy or girl. **3.** a son or daughter. **4.** *Law* a young person within a certain age determined by statute. In Australia, for some purposes in law a young person less than 17 years is a child; for others, under 18 or 21 years. **5.** a childish person. **6.** any person or thing regarded as the product or result of particular agencies, influences, etc.: *Satan's followers are the children of darkness*. **7.** (in computer programming) an object (def. 10) contained within another object (the parent) and retaining all the attributes and functions assigned to the parent. See **parent** (def. 7). –**childhood**, *n.* –**childless**, *adj.* –**childlessness**, *n.*

childbirth /'tʃaɪldbɜθ/ *n.* the act of giving birth to a child; parturition.

child care *n.* professional superintendence of children.

childcare centre *n.* a place where children, especially young children, may be minded while their parents work or are otherwise occupied.

childcare worker *n.* a person who is professionally employed in child care.

childish /'tʃaɪldɪʃ/ *adj.* **1.** of, like, or befitting a child. **2.** puerile; weak; silly. –**childishly**, *adv.* –**childishness**, *n.*

childproof /'tʃaɪldpruf/ *adj.* **1.** of or relating to a device designed to be beyond the ability of a child to manipulate or access, thus protecting the child from danger. **2.** of or relating to a device designed so that a child cannot damage it by clumsy handling.

children /'tʃildrən/ *n.* plural of **child**.

child restraint *n.* any of various devices, as a seatbelt, baby capsule, etc., which may be fitted to a motor vehicle to secure a child against injury in the event of collision or sudden braking.

chill /tʃɪl/ *n.* **1.** coldness, especially a moderate but penetrating coldness. **2.** a sensation of cold, usually with shivering. **3.** a cold stage, as a first symptom of illness. **4.** a depressing influence or sensation. **5.** a coldness of manner, lack of friendliness. *–adj.* **6.** cold; tending to cause shivering. **7.** shivering with cold. **8.** depressing or discouraging. **9.** not warm or hearty: *a chill reception.* *–v.i.* **10.** to become cold. **11.** to be seized with a chill. **12.** *Metallurgy* to become hard, especially on the surface, by sudden cooling, as a metal mould. **13.** Also, **chill out.** *Colloq.* to let go of emotional tension and stressful engagement; relax. *–v.t.* **14.** to affect with cold; make chilly. **15.** to make cool, but not freeze: *to chill wines.* **16.** to harden by sudden cooling. **17.** to depress; discourage: *to chill his hopes.* **–chiller,** *n.* **–chillness,** *n.* **–chillingly,** *adv.* **–chilled,** *adj.* **–chilly,** *adj.*

chillax /tʃɪlˈæks/ *v.i. Colloq.* to spend time in complete relaxation.

chilli /ˈtʃɪli/ *n.* (*pl.* **-lies**) **1.** the pungent fruit of some species of capsicum, usually small and hot to the taste. **2.** a capsicum bearing such a fruit, sometimes grown as an ornamental plant. Also, **chile, chili, chilli pepper.**

chilo- a word element meaning 'lip', 'labial'. Also, **chil-.**

chime /tʃaɪm/ *n.* **1.** a device for striking a bell or bells so as to produce a musical sound: *a door chime; the chimes of Big Ben.* **2.** a set of vertical metal tubes struck with a hammer, as used in the modern orchestra. **3.** harmonious sound in general; music; melody. **4.** harmonious relation; accord. *–v.i.* **5.** to sound harmoniously or in chimes, as a set of bells. **6.** to produce a musical sound by striking a bell, etc.; ring chimes. **7.** to harmonise; agree. *–v.t.* **8.** to give forth (music, etc.), as a bell or bells. **9.** to strike (a bell, etc.), so as to produce musical sound. **10.** to indicate by chiming: *the clock chimed three o'clock.* *–phr.* **11. chime in, a.** to break suddenly into a conversation, especially to express agreement. **b.** to join in harmoniously (in music).

chimera /kɪˈmɪərə, kə-/ *n.* (*pl.* **-ras**) **1.** (*oft. upper case*) a mythological fire-breathing monster, commonly represented with a lion's head, a goat's body, and a serpent's tail. **2.** a grotesque monster, as in decorative art. **3.** a horrible or unreal creature of the imagination; a vain or idle fancy. Also, **chimaera.**

chimney /ˈtʃɪmni/ *n.* (*pl.* **-neys**) **1.** a structure, usually vertical, containing a passage or flue through which the smoke, gases, etc., of a fire or furnace escape. **2.** that part of such a structure which rises above a roof. **3.** a glass tube, around the flame of a lamp. **4.** *Mountaineering* a narrow opening in a rock face. **–chimneyless,** *adj.*

chimneysweep /ˈtʃɪmniswip/ *n.* someone whose business is to clean out chimneys. Also, **chimneysweeper.**

chimpanzee /tʃɪmpænˈzi/ *n.* an anthropoid ape, *Pan troglodytes,* of equatorial Africa, smaller, with larger ears, and more arboreal than the gorilla.

chin /tʃɪn/ *n.* **1.** the lower extremity of the face, below the mouth. **2.** the point of the lower jaw. *–phr.* **3. keep one's chin up,** to remain cheerful, especially under stress. **4. take it on the chin,** to take suffering or punishment stalwartly.

china /ˈtʃaɪnə/ *n.* **1.** porcelain (orig. from China) used for making dishes, etc. **2.** plates, cups, etc., collectively: *bring out the best china.* *–adj.* **3.** made of china.

chinchilla /tʃɪnˈtʃɪlə/ *n.* **1.** a small South American rodent of the genus *Chinchilla,* whose valuable skin is dressed as a fur. **2.** the fur itself. **3.** a thick, napped, woollen fabric for coats, especially children's coats. **4.** one of a variety of any of certain animals, such as a cat or rabbit, with long, soft, grey fur.

Chinese broccoli *n.* → **gai lan.**

Chinese cabbage *n.* a vegetable, *Brassica rapa,* which is cabbage-shaped but with crinkly leaves that are a lighter green than ordinary cabbage.

Chinese gooseberry *n.* → **kiwifruit.**

Chinese New Year *n.* a festival lasting two weeks, beginning with the new moon of the first day of the new year in the Chinese calendar (in January or February); parade and celebrations on the final day, the Festival of the Lanterns. Also, (*as the festival occurs at the beginning of spring in China*), **Spring Festival, Lunar New Year.**

Chinese opera *n.* opera as it has developed in the Chinese musical and theatrical tradition, featuring a falsetto singing style, elaborate costumes, masks, and headdresses, and energetic swordplay and acrobatics.

Chinese parsley *n.* → **coriander** (def. 3).

Chinese Wall *n.* a barrier of convention within a financial institution, business organisation, etc., which separates those people who are involved in trading on the stock exchange from those who are involved in corporate finance, so that there can be no question of insider trading.

chink[1] /tʃɪŋk/ *n.* **1.** a crack, cleft, or fissure. **2.** a narrow opening.

chink[2] /tʃɪŋk/ *v.i.* **1.** to make a short, sharp, ringing sound, as of coins or glasses striking together. *–v.t.* **2.** to cause (something) to make this sound. *–n.* **3.** a chinking sound.

chintz /tʃɪnts/ *n.* (*pl.* **-zes**) a printed cotton fabric, glazed or unglazed, used especially for draperies. **–chintzy,** *adj.*

chip /tʃɪp/ *n.* **1.** a small piece, as of wood, separated by chopping, cutting, or breaking. **2.** a very thin slice or piece of food, etc.: *chocolate chips.* **3. a.** a deep-fried finger of potato. **b.** a thin slice of potato, fried and salted, usually eaten cold; crisp. **4.** a mark made by chipping. **5.** *Games* a counter or disc used to represent money in certain gambling games. **6.** *Electronics* a minute square of semiconductor material, processed in various ways to have certain electrical characteristics; especially such a square before being made into an integrated circuit. **7.** a small cut or uncut piece of diamond or crystal. **8.** wood, straw, etc., in thin strips for weaving into hats, baskets, etc. **9.** *Golf* → **chip shot. 10.** *Colloq.* a reprimand. **11.** (*pl.*) *Colloq.* money. *–verb* (**chipped, chipping**) *–v.t.* **12.** to hew or cut with an axe, chisel, etc. **13.** *Agric.* to use a hoe or similar implement to clear weed growth without disturbing the soil surface. **14.** to reduce trees, logs, etc., to small pieces for wood pulp. **15.** to taunt, chaff, poke fun at; to reprimand. **16.** to kick or hit (a ball) so as to loft it a short distance. *–v.i.* **17.** to break off in small pieces; to become chipped. **18.** *Golf* to make a chip shot. *–phr.* **19. cash in one's chips,** to die. **20. chip in, a.** *Colloq.* to contribute money, help, etc. **b.** *Colloq.* to interrupt; enter uninvited into a debate or argument being conducted by others. **c.** *Agric.* to turn seed in (with a harrow, etc.). **d.** *Games* to bet by means of chips, as in poker. **21. chip off the old block,** a person inheriting marked family characteristics. **22. chip on the shoulder,** a long-standing resentment; grievance. **23. have had one's chips,** to have lost one's opportunity. **24. the chips are down,** the moment of decision has been reached.

chipboard /ˈtʃɪpbɔd/ *n.* **1.** a resin-bonded artificial wood made from wood chips, sawdust, etc., used in sheets for light structural work. **2.** a board, usually made of wastepaper, used in box-making, etc. Also, **particle board.**

chip heater *n.* a water heater fuelled by wood chips.

chipmunk /ˈtʃɪpmʌŋk/ *n.* any of various small striped terrestrial squirrels of the North American genus

Tamias, and the Asian and American genus *Eutamias*, especially *T. striatus* of eastern North America.

chip shot *n.* **1.** *Golf* a short shot using a wrist motion, made in approaching the green. **2.** *Tennis* → **chop stroke.**

chiro- a word element meaning 'hand', as in *chiropractic.*

chiropody /kə'rɒpədi, ʃə'rɒpədi/ *n.* the diagnosing and treatment of foot disorders. **–chiropodist,** *n.*

chiropractic /kaɪrə'præktɪk/ *n.* **1.** a therapeutic system based upon the premise that disease is caused by interference with nerve function, the method being to restore normal condition by adjusting the segments of the spinal column. **2.** a chiropractor.

chiropractor /'kaɪrəpræktə/ *n.* someone who practises chiropractic.

chirp /tʃɜp/ *v.i.* **1.** to make a short, sharp sound, as small birds and certain insects. **2.** to make any similar sound. *–v.t.* **3.** to sound or utter in a chirping manner. *–n.* **4.** a chirping sound. **–chirper,** *n.*

chirpy /'tʃɜpi/ *adj.* **(-pier, -piest)** cheerful; lively. **–chirpily,** *adv.*

chirrup /'tʃɪrəp/ *v.i.* **(-ruped, -ruping) 1.** to chirp. **2.** to make a chirping sound, as to a pet bird or a horse. *–n.* **3.** the act or sound of chirruping. **–chirruper,** *n.*

chisel /'tʃɪzəl/ *n.* **1.** a tool, as of steel, with a cutting edge at the extremity, usually transverse to the axis, for cutting or shaping wood, stone, etc. *–verb* **(-elled** *or, Chiefly US,* **-eled, -elling** *or, Chiefly US,* **-eling)** *–v.t.* **2.** to cut, shape, etc., with a chisel. **3.** *Colloq.* to cheat; swindle. *–v.i.* **4.** to work with a chisel. **5.** *Colloq.* to use trickery; cheat. **–chiseller;** *Chiefly US,* **chiseler,** *n.*

chit¹ /tʃɪt/ *n.* **1.** a slip or voucher entitling the bearer to goods or services as food, lodgings, transport, etc. **2.** a note; a short memorandum. Also, **chitty.**

chit² /tʃɪt/ *n.* a young child, especially a cheeky or impudent one.

chivalry /'ʃɪvəlri/ *n.* **1.** good manners and considerate behaviour towards others, especially of men towards women. **2.** the ideal qualifications of a knight, such as courtesy, generosity, valour, dexterity in arms, etc. **3.** the rules and customs of medieval knighthood. **4.** gallant warriors or gentlemen. **–chivalrous,** *adj.* **–chivalrously,** *adv.*

chives /tʃaɪvz/ *pl. n.* a small bulbous plant, *Allium schoenoprasum*, related to the leek and onion, with long, slender leaves which are used as a seasoning in cookery.

chlamydia /klə'mɪdiə/ *n. Pathol.* a sexually-transmitted disease caused by the microorganism *Chlamydia trachomatis*, which is responsible for infections of the eye and the urogenital system, which may cause urethritis in men, and cervical infection, pelvic inflammatory disease and infertility in women.

chlor-¹ a word element meaning 'green', as in *chlorine.* Also, **chloro-.**

chlor-² a combining form denoting 'chlorine', as in *chloral.* Also, **chloro-.**

chloride /'klɔraɪd/ *n.* **1.** a compound usually of two elements only, one of which is chlorine. **2.** a salt of hydrochloric acid.

chlorinate /'klɔrəneɪt, 'klɔ-/ *v.t.* **1.** *Chem.* to combine or treat with chlorine. **2.** to disinfect (water) by means of chlorine. **–chlorination** /klɔrə'neɪʃən, klɔ-/, *n.* **–chlorinator,** *n.*

chlorine /'klɔrin/ *n.* a greenish yellow gaseous element (occurring combined in common salt, etc.), incombustible, and highly irritating to the organs of respiration. It is used as a powerful bleaching agent and in various industrial processes. *Symbol:* Cl; *relative atomic mass:* 35.453; *atomic number:* 17. See **halogen.**

chloro-¹ variant of **chlor-¹**, used before consonants, as in *chlorophyll.*

chloro-² variant of **chlor-²**, used before consonants, as in *chloroform.*

chlorofluorocarbon /ˌklɔrou̩fluərou'kabən/ *n.* any of several volatile compounds of carbon, fluorine, chlorine, and sometimes hydrogen, the use of which as refrigerants and aerosol propellants is being gradually phased out because of the damage they cause to the ozone layer. Also, **CFC.**

chloroform /'klɔrəfɔm/ *n.* **1.** a colourless volatile liquid, $CHCl_3$, used as an anaesthetic and solvent. *–v.t.* **2.** to administer chloroform to. **3.** to put chloroform on (a cloth, etc.).

chlorophyll /'klɔrəfɪl/ *n.* the green colouring substance of leaves and plants, having various forms, **chlorophyll a, b, c, d** and **e**, distinguished by minor differences in chemical structure. It traps energy from sunlight which is necessary for the production of carbohydrates by photosynthesis in plants and is used as a dye for cosmetics and oils.

chock /tʃɒk/ *n.* **1.** a block or wedge of wood, etc., for filling in a space, especially for preventing movement, as of a wheel or a cask. **2.** *Naut.* a shaped standard on which a boat, barrel, or other object rests. *–v.t.* **3.** to furnish with or secure by a chock or chocks. *–adv.* **4.** as close or tight as possible; quite: *chock against the edge.*

chocolate /'tʃɒklət, 'tʃɒkələt/ *n.* **1.** a preparation of the seeds of cacao, roasted, husked, and ground (without removing any of the fat), often sweetened and flavoured, as with vanilla. **2.** a beverage or confection made from this. **3.** dark brown. *–adj.* **4.** made, flavoured or covered with chocolate. **5.** having the colour of chocolate. **–chocolatey, chocolaty,** *adj.*

choice /tʃɔɪs/ *n.* **1.** the act of choosing; selection. **2.** power of choosing; option. **3.** the person or thing chosen: *this book is my choice.* **4.** an abundance and variety from which to choose: *a wide choice of candidates.* **5.** an alternative. *–adj.* **(choicer, choicest) 6.** worthy of being chosen; excellent; superior. **7.** carefully selected: *delivered in choice words.* *–phr.* **8. choice language,** colourfully vulgar language. **–choicely,** *adv.* **–choiceness,** *n.*

choir /'kwaɪə/ *n.* **1.** a company of singers, especially an organised group employed in church service. **2.** any company or band, or a division of one: *a woodwind choir.* **3.** *Archit.* (in cathedrals, etc.) the area between the nave and the main altar.

choke /tʃouk/ *v.t.* **1.** to stop the breath of, by squeezing or blocking the windpipe; strangle; stifle; suffocate. **2.** to stop the breath or speech, etc., by or as by strangling or stifling. **3.** to stop the growth or action of: *to choke off discussion.* **4.** to stop by filling; obstruct; clog; congest. **5.** to fill to the top. **6.** (in internal-combustion engines) to enrich the fuel mixture by decreasing the air to the carburettor to help in starting a motor, etc. *–v.i.* **7.** to suffer strangling or suffocation. **8.** to be blocked or clogged. **9.** to be temporarily overcome with emotion. *–n.* **10.** the act or sound of choking. **11.** (in internal-combustion engines) the device by which the air supply to a carburettor is decreased or stopped. **12.** *Machinery* any device which, by blocking a passage, controls the flow of air, etc. *–phr.* **13. choke down,** to swallow with difficulty. **–choking,** *adj.* **–chokingly,** *adv.*

choker /'tʃoukə/ *n.* **1.** a necklace worn tightly round the neck. **2.** *Colloq.* a cravat or high collar.

choko /'tʃoukou/ *n.* (*pl.* **-kos**) a perennial vine, *Sechium edule*, bearing pear-shaped green fruit used as a vegetable. Also, **chayote.**

chol- a word element meaning 'gall' or 'bile'. Also, **chole-, cholo-.**

choler /'kɒlə/ *n.* irascibility; anger; wrath; irritability. –**choleric**, *adj.*

cholera /'kɒlərə/ *n.* **1.** *Pathol.* an acute, infectious disease, due to a specific microorganism, endemic in India and China, and epidemic generally, marked by profuse diarrhoea, vomiting, cramp, etc., and often fatal. **2.** *Vet. Science* any disease characterised by violent diarrhoea. –**choleraic** /kɒlə'reɪk/, *adj.*

cholesterol /kə'lɛstərɒl/ *n.* a sterol, $C_{27}H_{45}OH$, widely distributed in higher organisms, found in bile and gallstones, and in the blood and brain, the yolk of eggs, etc. Also, **cholesterin**, /kɒ'lɛstərən/.

choli /'tʃoʊli/ *n.* a short top, cut to just above the waist, with short sleeves.

cholo- variant of **chol-** before consonants.

chook /tʃʊk/ *Aust., NZ Colloq.* –*n.* **1.** Also, **chookie**, **chooky**. a domestic chicken. **2.** chicken meat. **3.** an older woman: *silly old chook.* –*phr.* **4. like a chook with its head cut off**, in a foolish and erratic manner.

choose /tʃuz/ *verb* (**chose**, **chosen**, **choosing**) –*v.t.* **1.** to select from a number, or in preference to another or other things or persons. **2.** to prefer and decide (to do something): *she chose to stand for election.* **3.** to want; desire. –*v.i.* **4.** to make a choice. –*phr.* **5. cannot choose but**, cannot do otherwise than: *he cannot choose but hear.* –**chooser**, *n.*

choosy /'tʃuzi/ *adj.* (**-sier**, **-siest**) *Colloq.* hard to please, particular, fastidious, especially in making a choice: *choosy about food.* Also, **choosey**.

chop¹ /tʃɒp/ *verb* (**chopped**, **chopping**) –*v.t.* **1.** to cut with a quick, heavy blow or series of blows, using an axe, etc. **2.** to make by so cutting. **3.** to cut in pieces. **4.** *Tennis, Cricket, etc.* to hit (a ball) with a chop stroke. **5.** *Colloq.* to dismiss; give the sack to; fire. –*v.i.* **6.** to make a quick heavy stroke or a series of strokes, as with an axe. –*n.* **7.** the act of chopping. **8.** a cutting blow. **9.** a short, downward cutting blow. **10.** → **chop stroke**. **11.** a slice of lamb, veal, pork, mutton, etc., with the bone still attached. –*phr.* **12. chop in, a.** to move suddenly into the way; intervene. **b.** to interrupt. **13. chop off, a.** to cut off: *to chop off a dead branch.* **b.** to cut short: *to chop off negotiations.* **c.** to remove from: *to chop a second off his time.* **14. chop out**, *Colloq.* **a.** to remove suddenly; omit: *to chop out a whole section.* **b.** to cease to do: *to chop out smoking.* **15. in for one's chop**, eager to claim a portion or share. **16. the chop**, *Colloq.* **a.** a deathblow. **b.** the sack; dismissal.

chop² /tʃɒp/ *v.i.* (**chopped**, **chopping**) **1.** to turn, shift, or change suddenly, as the wind. –*phr.* **2. chop and change**, to be unreasonably variable; to make frequent changes to arrangements. **3. chop logic**, to reason or dispute argumentatively; argue.

chop³ /tʃɒp/ *n.* **1.** (in Asia) **a.** a personal seal or stamp, used to authorise transactions, verify documents, etc. **b.** a design, corresponding to a brand or trademark, stamped on goods to indicate their special identity. –*v.t.* (**chopped**, **chopping**) **2.** to mark with a seal, stamp, or design. –*phr.* **3. not much chop**, *Colloq.* no good.

chopper /'tʃɒpə/ *n.* **1.** a short axe with a large blade used for cutting up meat, etc.; a butcher's cleaver. **2.** (*pl.*) *Colloq.* teeth. **3.** *Colloq.* a helicopter. **4.** *Colloq.* a modified motorcycle with the front wheel moved forward and high handlebars. –*v.t.* **5.** to fly (someone) in a helicopter: *the injured man was choppered to hospital.* –*v.i.* **6.** to fly by helicopter: *to chopper over the scene.* –*phr.* **7. chopper in**, *Colloq.* **a.** to arrive by helicopter: *the prime minister choppered in for the summit.* **b.** to bring by helicopter: *the accident victims were choppered in to the hospital.*

choppy /'tʃɒpi/ *adj.* (**-pier**, **-piest**) **1.** (of the sea, etc.) forming short, irregular, broken waves. **2.** (of the wind) shifting or changing suddenly or irregularly; variable.

chopstick /'tʃɒpstɪk/ *n.* one of a pair of thin sticks, as of wood, ivory, or plastic, to raise food to the mouth; the traditional eating utensil of China, Japan, etc.

chop stroke *n. Cricket, Tennis, etc.* a downward stroke made with the racquet or bat at an angle.

chop suey /tʃɒp 'sui/ *n.* a dish consisting of small pieces of meat or chicken cooked with bean sprouts or other vegetables, served in Chinese restaurants in Western countries.

choral /'kɔrəl, 'kɔrəl/ *adj.* sung by or adapted for a chorus or a choir. –**chorally**, *adv.*

chorale /kɒ'ral/ *n.* a simple hymn-like tune in slow tempo usually sung by choir and congregation together.

chord¹ /kɔd/ *n.* **1.** a string of a musical instrument. **2.** a feeling or emotion: *to strike a chord.* **3.** *Geom.* the part of a straight line between two of its intersections with a curve. –**chordal**, **chorded**, *adj.*

chord² /kɔd/ *n. Music* a combination of three or more tones, mostly in harmonic relation, sounded either simultaneously or in quick succession.

chore /tʃɔ/ *n.* **1.** a small or odd job; a piece of minor domestic work. **2.** (*pl.*) routine work around a house or farm. **3.** a hard or unpleasant task.

chorea /kɔ'riə/ *n.* a neurological disorder characterised by brief, involuntary, jerky movements. See **Huntington's disease**.

choreography /kɒri'ɒgrəfi/ *n.* **1.** the art of composing ballets, etc., and arranging separate dances. **2.** the art of representing the various movements in dancing by a system of notation. Also, **choregraphy** /kə'rɛgrəfi/. –**choreograph** /'kɒriəgræf, -graf/, *v.* –**choreographer**, *n.* –**choreographic** /kɒriə'græfik/, *adj.*

chorister /'kɒrəstə/ *n.* a singer in a choir.

chortle /'tʃɔtl/ *v.i.* to chuckle with glee. –**chortler**, *n.*

chorus /'kɔrəs/ *n.* (*pl.* **-ruses**) **1. a.** a group of persons singing in concert. **b.** a part of a song in which others join the principal singer or singers. **c.** any recurring refrain. **2.** simultaneous utterance in singing, speaking, etc. **3.** (in musical shows) **a.** the company of dancers and singers. **b.** a company of singers, dancers, or narrators supplementing the performance of the main actors. –*v.i.* (**-rused**, **-rusing**) **4.** to sing or speak in chorus. –**choric**, *adj.*

chose /tʃoʊz/ *v.* past tense of **choose**.

chosen /'tʃoʊzən/ *v.* **1.** past participle of **choose**. –*adj.* **2.** selected from a number; preferred. **3.** → **elect**.

chough /tʃʌf/ *n.* **1.** any of various glossy black corvine birds of the genus *Pyrrhocorax*, of Eurasia and north-western Africa. **2. white-winged chough**, a sooty black bird with white wing patches, *Corcorax melanorhamphos*, endemic to eastern Australia.

chow¹ /tʃaʊ/ *n.* one of a Chinese breed of dogs of medium size, with a thick, even coat of brown or black hair and a black tongue. Also, **chow-chow**.

chow² /tʃaʊ/ *n. Colloq.* food: *let's go to the fish and chip shop for some chow.*

chowder /'tʃaʊdə/ *n.* a kind of soup or stew made of clams, fish, or vegetables, with potatoes, onions, other ingredients and seasoning.

chow mein /tʃaʊ 'mɪn/ *n.* a dish of noodles mixed with shredded vegetables such as carrots, cabbage, mushrooms, etc., and with small quantities of meat and/or poultry.

christen /'krɪsən/ *v.t.* **1.** to receive into the Christian church by baptism; baptise. **2.** to give a name to at baptism. **3.** to name and dedicate; give a name to; name. **4.** *Colloq.* to make use of for the first time.

Christendom /'krɪsəndəm/ *n.* the Christian world.

Christian /'krɪstʃən/ *adj.* **1.** relating to or derived from Jesus Christ, born c.4 BC, crucified c.AD 29, or his teachings. **2.** believing in or belonging to the religion of Jesus Christ. **3.** exhibiting a spirit proper to a follower of Jesus Christ; Christlike. **4.** *Colloq.* decent or respectable. *–n.* **5.** someone who believes in the sanctity of Jesus Christ; an adherent of Christianity. **6.** someone who exemplifies in his or her life the teachings of Christ. **7.** *Colloq.* a decent or presentable person.

Christianity /krɪstiˈænəti/ *n.* Christian beliefs or practices; Christian quality or character.

Christian name *n.* the name given one at baptism or at birth, as distinguished from the family name; given name; forename; first name.

Christmas /ˈkrɪsməs/ *n.* **1.** the annual festival of the Christian church commemorating the birth of Jesus, celebrated on 25 December. **2.** 25 December (**Christmas Day**), now generally observed as an occasion for gifts, greetings, etc. **3.** the season when this occurs. *–adj.* **4.** given on, held on, or connected with Christmas. *–phr. Colloq.* **5.** **have all one's Christmases come at once**, to have extreme good fortune. **6.** **think one is Christmas**, to be pleased with oneself; be elated.

Christmas bush *n.* any of various Australian shrubs or small trees flowering at Christmas and used for decoration, especially *Ceratopetalum gummiferum* of NSW with red fruiting calyces and *Prostanthera lasianthos* of Victoria with white, somewhat bell-shaped flowers.

Christmas in July *n.* in Australia, a celebration with Christmas-like festivities held in July or any of the winter months of the year, reflecting the traditional European season for Christmas; Yulefest.

Christmas tree *n.* **1.** a tree, or part of a tree, especially of a conifer, hung with decorations at Christmas. **2.** an artificial tree made for this purpose. **3.** *NZ* → **pohutukawa**.

-chroic an adjectival word element indicating colour (of skin, plants, etc.). Also, **-chrous**.

chrom-[1] **1.** a combining form referring to colour, as in *chromatic, chromatin*. **2.** a combining form in chemistry used to distinguish a coloured compound from its colourless form. Also, **chromo-**.

chrom-[2] a word element referring to chromium, as in *chromic, bichromate*. Also, **chromo-**.

chromatic /krəˈmætɪk/ *adj.* **1.** relating to colour or colours. **2.** *Music* involving a modification of the diatonic scale by the use of accidentals. **–chromatically**, *adv.*

chromatin /ˈkroʊmətɪn/ *n.* the portion of the animal or plant cell nucleus which readily takes on stains.

chromato- **1.** a word element referring to colour. **2.** a word element meaning 'chromatin'.

chromatography /kroʊməˈtɒgrəfi/ *n. Chem.* the separation of mixtures into their constituents by preferential absorption by a solid such as a column of silica (**column chromatography**), or a thin film of silica (**thin layer chromatography**). **–chromatographic** /ˌkroʊmətəˈgræfɪk/, *adj.*

chrome /kroʊm/ *n.* chromium, especially as a source of various pigments, such as chrome yellow and chrome green.

-chrome a word element meaning 'colour', as in *polychrome*.

chromium /ˈkroʊmiəm/ *n.* a lustrous, hard, brittle metallic element occurring in compounds which are used for making pigments in photography, to harden gelatine, as a mordant, etc.; also used in corrosion-resisting chromium plating. *Symbol*: Cr, *relative atomic mass*: 51.996; *atomic number*: 24; *density*: 7.1.

chromo-[1] variant of **chrom-**[1], used before consonants, as in *chromogen*.

chromo-[2] variant of **chrom-**[2], used before consonants.

chromosome /ˈkroʊməsoʊm, -zoʊm/ *n. Genetics* any of several threadlike, rodlike, or beadlike bodies which contain the chromatin during the meiotic and the

mitotic processes. **–chromosomal** /kroʊməˈsoʊməl, -ˈzoʊməl/, *adj.*

chron- a word element meaning 'time', as in *chronaxie*. Also, **chrono-**.

chronic /ˈkrɒnɪk/ *adj.* **1.** inveterate; constant: *a chronic smoker*. **2.** continuing a long time: *chronic civil war*. **3.** (of disease) long continued (opposed to *acute*). **–chronically**, *adv.*

chronic fatigue syndrome *n. Pathol.* a severe, systemic illness acquired after an apparently mild viral infection, and characterised chiefly by incapacitating fatigue but also by neurological, immunological and endocrinological dysfunction; post-viral syndrome; ME. *Abbrev.*: CFS

chronicle /ˈkrɒnɪkəl/ *n.* **1.** a record or account of events in the order of time; a history. *–v.t.* (**-cled, -cling**) **2.** to record in or as in a chronicle. **–chronicler**, *n.*

chrono- variant of **chron-**, used before consonants, as in *chronogram*.

chronograph /ˈkrɒnəgræf, -ɡrɑf/ *n.* a clock-driven instrument for recording the exact instant of occurrences, or for measuring small intervals of time. **–chronographic** /krɒnəˈgræfɪk/, *adj.*

chronological /krɒnəˈlɒdʒɪkəl/ *adj.* arranged in the order of time: *chronological tables.* **–chronologically**, *adv.*

chronology /krəˈnɒlədʒi/ *n.* **1.** the sequential order in which events occur or have occurred. **2.** a statement or proposition of such an order. **3.** the systematic study of the arrangement of time in periods in order to determine the dates and historical order of past events. **4.** a reference work organised according to the dates of events.

chronometer /krəˈnɒmətə/ *n.* a timepiece with some special mechanism for ensuring accuracy, for use in determining longitude at sea or for any purpose where very exact measurement of time is required. **–chronometric** /krɒnəˈmɛtrɪk/, **chronometrical** /krɒnəˈmɛtrɪkəl/, *adj.* **–chronometrically** /krɒnəˈmɛtrɪkli/, *adv.*

chronoscope /ˈkrɒnəskoʊp/ *n.* an instrument for measuring accurately very small intervals of time, as in determining the velocity of projectiles.

-chroous → **-chroic**.

chrysalis /ˈkrɪsələs/ *n.* (*pl.* **chrysalises** *or* **chrysalids** /krəˈsælədɪz/) the hard-shelled pupa of a moth or butterfly.

chrysanthemum /krəˈsænθəməm, krəˈzænθ-/ *n.* **1.** any of the perennial plants constituting the genus *Chrysanthemum*, such as *C. leucanthemum*, the oxeye daisy. **2.** any of many cultivated varieties of *C. morifolium*, native to China, and of other species of *Chrysanthemum*, notable for the diversity of colour and size of their autumnal flowers.

chrysoprase /ˈkrɪsəpreɪz/ *n.* a nickel-stained, apple-green chalcedony, much used in jewellery.

chubby /ˈtʃʌbi/ *adj.* (**-bier, -biest**) round and plump: *a chubby face; chubby cheeks.*

chuck[1] /tʃʌk/ *v.t.* **1.** to pat or tap lightly, as under the chin. **2.** to throw with a quick motion, usually a short distance. **3.** *Colloq.* to compel to go, especially forcibly: *they chucked him out of the nightclub.* **4.** *Colloq.* to resign from. **5.** *Colloq.* to vomit. **6.** *Aust. Colloq.* to do; perform: *to chuck a U-ey.* *–v.i. Colloq.* **7.** to vomit. **8.** *Cricket* → **throw** (def. 24). *–n.* **9.** a light pat or tap, as under the chin. **10.** a toss; a short throw. *–phr.* **11.** **chuck in**, *Colloq.* to contribute: *I'll chuck in ten dollars.* **12.** **chuck it (in)**, *Colloq.* to abandon an occupation, job, activity, etc., especially suddenly. **13.** **chuck off**, *Aust., NZ Colloq.* (sometimes fol. by *at*) to speak sarcastically or critically: *to chuck off at the teacher.* **14.** **chuck one's hand in**, *Colloq.* to give up; refuse to go on. **15.** **chuck one's weight about**, *Colloq.*

to be overbearing; interfere forcefully and unwelcomely. **16. chuck up,** *Colloq.* to vomit. **17. the chuck,** *Colloq.* dismissal.

chuck² /tʃʌk/ *n.* **1.** Also, **chuck steak.** the cut of beef between the neck and the shoulderblade. **2.** a block or log used as a chock. **3.** a mechanical device for holding tools in a drill, etc., or work in a machine: *lathe chuck.*

chuckle /ˈtʃʌkəl/ *v.i.* **1.** to laugh in a soft, amused manner, usually with satisfaction. **2.** to laugh to oneself. –*n.* **3.** a soft, amused laugh, usually with satisfaction. –**chuckler,** *n.*

chucky chucky /ˈtʃʌki tʃʌki/ *n.* the edible but bitter fruit of the snowberry.

chuffed /tʃʌft/ *adj. Colloq.* pleased; delighted.

chug /tʃʌg/ *n.* **1.** a short, dull explosive sound: *the steady chug of an engine.* –*v.i.* (**chugged, chugging**) **2.** to move while making this sound: *the train chugged along.*

chug-a-lug /ˈtʃʌg-ə-ˈlʌg/ *v.i. Colloq.* to down a drink quickly without pause.

chukka /ˈtʃʌkə/ *n.* (in polo) one of the periods of play. Also, **chukker.**

chum¹ /tʃʌm/ *n.* **1.** an intimate friend or companion: *boyhood chums.* **2.** a companion; someone who has shared the same experience. –*phr.* **3. chum up,** (sometimes fol. by *with*) to become friendly. **4. chum up to,** to behave obsequiously towards. –**chummy,** *adj.* –**chummily,** *adv.*

chum² /tʃʌm/ *n.* refuse from fish, especially that remaining after expressing oil.

chump /tʃʌmp/ *n.* **1.** the thick blunt end of anything. **2.** *Meat Industry* a section of lamb, hogget, or mutton, between the leg and the loin, each chump containing approximately four chops.

chunder /ˈtʃʌndə/ *v.i. Aust., NZ Colloq.* to vomit. –**chundering,** *n.* –**chunderer,** *n.*

chunk /tʃʌŋk/ *n.* a thick mass or lump of anything: *a chunk of bread.* –**chunky,** *adj.*

church /tʃɜtʃ/ *n.* **1.** a building for public Christian worship. **2.** the public worship of God in a church: *he goes to church twice on Sundays.* **3.** (*oft. upper case*) the whole body of Christian believers: *the church is united in prayer.* **4.** (*oft. upper case*) any division of this body adhering to the same particular beliefs and acknowledging the same religious authority; a Christian denomination: *the Uniting Church.* **5.** (*sometimes upper case*) the ecclesiastical organisation or power as distinguished from the state. **6.** the clerical profession: *the third son went into the church.*

Church of England *n.* the established Church in England, Catholic in faith and order but incorporating Protestant features, and having the monarch as head.

churidar /ˈtʃʊrɪdɑ/ *n.* tight-fitting long pants with folds at the bottom of the legs, worn by Indian women with a long shirt or kurta, and by Indian men with a long coat or achkan.

churl /tʃɜl/ *n.* **1.** a peasant; a rustic. **2.** a rude, boorish, or surly person. –**churlish,** *adj.*

churn /tʃɜn/ *n.* **1.** a vessel or machine in which cream or milk is agitated to make butter. **2.** a large metal container for milk. –*v.t.* **3.** to stir or agitate in order to make into butter: *to churn cream.* **4.** to shake or agitate with violence or continued motion. –**churner,** *n.*

chute /ʃut/ *n.* **1.** a channel, trough, tube, shaft, etc., for conveying water, grain, coal, etc., to a lower level; a shoot. **2.** a waterfall; a steep descent, as in a river; a rapid. **3.** an inclined board, with sides, down which a swimmer may slide into the water. **4.** a parachute. **5.** *Agric.* a narrow passage through which animals are moved for branding, drenching, or loading, often having a very steep incline. Also, **shoot, shute.**

chutney /ˈtʃʌtni/ *n.* a relish of Indian origin which consists of fruit or vegetable cooked with sugar, spices, and vinegar or lime juice. Also, **chutnee.**

cicada /səˈkadə, səˈkeɪdə/ *n.* (*pl.* **-das** *or* **-dae** /-di/) any insect of the family Cicadidae, which comprises large homopterous insects noted for the shrill sound produced by the male by means of vibrating membranes or drums on the underside of the abdomen.

cicatrice /ˈsɪkətrəs/ *n.* (*pl.* **cicatrices** /sɪkəˈtraɪsiz/ *or* **cicatrixes**) **1.** the new tissue which forms over a wound or the like, and later contracts into a scar. **2.** *Bot.* the scar left by a fallen leaf, seed, etc. Also, **cicatrix** /ˈsɪkətrɪks/. –**cicatricial** /sɪkəˈtrɪʃəl/, *adj.* –**cicatricose** /ˈsɪkətrəkous/, *adj.*

-cidal adjective form of **-cide.**

-cide a word element meaning 'killer' or 'act of killing'.

cider /ˈsaɪdə/ *n.* the expressed juice of apples (or formerly of some other fruit), used for drinking, either before fermentation (**sweet cider**) or after fermentation (**rough cider**), or for making applejack, vinegar, etc.

cigar /səˈgɑ/ *n.* a small, shaped roll of tobacco leaves prepared for smoking.

cigarette /sɪgəˈrɛt/ *n.* a roll of finely cut tobacco for smoking, usually enclosed in thin paper.

cilia /ˈsɪliə/ *pl. n.* **1.** the eyelashes. **2.** *Zool.* minute hairlike processes of cells which by their movement produce locomotion of the cell or a current that passes over the surface of the cell. **3.** *Bot.* minute hairlike processes embedded in the surface of some cells, usually numerous and arranged in rows.

cinch /sɪntʃ/ *n.* **1.** a strong girth for a saddle or pack. **2.** *Colloq.* something certain or easy. –*v.t.* **3.** to gird with a cinch; gird or bind firmly. –**cinchy,** *adj.*

cincture /ˈsɪŋktʃə/ *n.* **1.** a belt or girdle. **2.** something surrounding or encompassing like a girdle; a surrounding border.

cinder /ˈsɪndə/ *n.* **1.** a burnt-out or partially burnt piece of coal, wood, etc. **2.** (*pl.*) any residue of combustion; ashes. **3.** (*pl.*) *Geol.* coarse scoriae thrown out of volcanoes. –*v.t.* **4.** to reduce to cinders: *cindering flame.* –**cindery,** *adj.*

cinderella /sɪndəˈrɛlə/ *n.* a neglected, ignored, or despised person.

cine- a word element meaning 'motion', used of films, etc., as in *cinecamera.*

cinecamera /ˈsɪnikæmrə/ *n.* a camera used for taking moving films.

cinema /ˈsɪnəmə/ *n.* **1.** a theatre where films are shown; picture theatre. **2.** a showing of a film (def. 4b): *let's go to the cinema tonight.* **3.** films in general: *the history of Australian cinema.* **4.** the art of making films: *this director is one of the icons of cinema.*

cinematic /sɪnəˈmætɪk/ *adj.* **1.** of or relating to the cinema. **2.** suited to a film treatment or presentation: *the cinematic quality of the landscape.* –**cinematically,** *adv.*

cinematography /sɪnəməˈtogrəfi/ *n.* the art or practice of film photography. –**cinematographer,** *n.* –**cinematographic** /sɪnəmætəˈgræfɪk/, *adj.*

cineraria /sɪnəˈrɛəriə/ *n.* any of various horticultural varieties of the plant *Senecio cruentus*, native to the Canary Islands, with heart-shaped leaves and clusters of flowers with white, blue, purple, red, or variegated rays.

cinnamon /ˈsɪnəmən/ *n.* **1.** the aromatic inner bark of any of several trees of the genus *Cinnamomum* of Asia, especially **Ceylon cinnamon,** *C. verum*, much used as a spice, and **Saigon cinnamon,** *C. loureiri*, used in medicine as a cordial and carminative. **2.** yellowish or reddish brown.

-cion a suffix having the same function as **-tion**, as in *suspicion.*

cipher /ˈsaɪfə/ *n.* **1.** the arithmetical symbol (0) meaning nought, or no quantity or magnitude. **2.** any of the Arabic numbers 1 to 9. **3.** a person or thing of no value or importance. **4. a.** a secret (method of) writing; code: *the enemy's cipher was broken by our experts.* **b.** the key to this. **5.** combination initials in a design; monogram. *–v.i.* **6.** to use figures or numerals arithmetically. *–v.t.* **7.** to calculate numerically; figure. **8.** to write in, or as in, code or cipher. Also, **cypher.**

circa /ˈsɜːkə/ /ˈsɜːsə/ *prep.* about (used especially in approximate dates). *Abbrev.:* c., c, ca

circadian /sɜːˈkeɪdɪən/ *adj.* of or relating to physiological activity which occurs approximately every 24 hours.

circadian rhythm *n.* the roughly 24-hour cycle in which physiological processes occur, some being affected by external factors such as sunlight and temperature.

circle /ˈsɜːkəl/ *n.* **1.** a (flat round area enclosed by) a curved line which is everywhere equally distant from a fixed point within it, called the centre. **2.** anything with the shape of a circle: *a circle of trees; dark circles under the eyes from lack of sleep*; *a circle of gold sat on the king's head.* **3.** the upper section of seats in a theatre: *the dress circle.* **4.** the area within which something acts, has influence, etc.: *she is well-known in political circles.* **5.** a series ending where it began, and forever repeated: *this kind of thinking is just a vicious circle.* **6.** a complete series forming a connected whole; cycle: *the circle of the seasons.* **7.** a number of people bound by a common tie; coterie: *John's little circle has such interesting people in it.* **8.** *Law* the group of people involved in circle sentencing. **9.** *Geog.* a parallel of latitude: *the Antarctic circle.* *–v.t.* **10.** → **encircle**. **11.** to move in a circle or circuit around: *he circled the house cautiously.* *–v.i.* **12.** to move in a circle. *–phr.* **13. come full circle,** to come back to one's starting point. **–circler,** *n.*

circle sentencing *n.* a form of court process for some types of crimes in which the case is heard by a circle comprising Aboriginal elders, a police prosecutor and a defence solicitor, with the offender and the victim contributing to a presentation of the facts and an evaluation of the appropriate sentence.

circlet /ˈsɜːklət/ *n.* **1.** a small circle. **2.** a ring. **3.** a ring-shaped ornament, especially for the head.

circuit /ˈsɜːkət/ *n.* **1.** the act of going or moving round: *the circuit of the enemy's position was nearly complete.* **2.** any circular or roundabout journey; a round: *the tour made a circuit of the city.* **3.** a circular racing track. **4.** a journey from place to place, made at regular periods, to perform certain duties, etc.: *the district judge's circuit.* **5.** way followed, places visited, or area covered by such a journey: *the travelling theatre has a new circuit this year.* **6.** a street which is circular or roughly so (usually as street name). **7.** a number of races in a season or series. **8.** a number of venues or events at which an entertainer, etc., performs in turn: *the RSL circuit; the talk show circuit.* **9.** a course regularly travelled: *the airline now flies the Perth-Singapore-London circuit twice weekly.* **10.** *Elect.* the complete path of an electric current. *–v.t.* **11.** to go or move round; make the circuit of: *to circuit the city.* **–circuitry,** *n.*

circuit-breaker *n.* **1.** *Elect.* a device for interrupting an electric circuit between separable contacts under normal or abnormal conditions. **2.** an event, activity, etc., which acts as a distraction from previous preoccupations and tensions.

circuitous /sɜːˈkjuːətəs/ *adj.* roundabout; not direct: *they took a circuitous route to the house.* **–circuitously,** *adv.* **–circuitousness,** *n.*

circular /ˈsɜːkjələ/ *adj.* **1.** of or relating to a circle. **2.** having the form of a circle; round. **3.** circuitous; roundabout; indirect. **4.** (of a letter, etc.) addressed to a number of persons or intended for general circulation.

–n. **5.** a letter, notice, advertisement, or statement for circulation among the general public. **–circularity** /sɜːkjəˈlærəti/, *n.* **–circularly,** *adv.*

circulate /ˈsɜːkjəleɪt/ *v.i.* **1.** to move in a circle or circuit; move or pass through a circuit back to the starting point, as the blood in the body. **2.** to move among the guests at a social function. **–circulative,** *adj.* **–circulator,** *n.* **–circulatory** /sɜːkjəˈleɪtəri/, *adj.*

circulation /sɜːkjəˈleɪʃən/ *n.* **1.** the act of circulating or moving in a circle or circuit. **2.** *Physiol.* the recurrent movement of the blood through the various vessels of the body. **3.** any similar circuit or passage, as of the sap in plants. **4.** the transmission or passage of anything from place to place, person to person, etc. **5.** the distribution of copies of a publication among readers. **6.** the number of copies of each issue of a newspaper, magazine, etc., distributed. **7.** coin, notes, bills, etc., in use as currency; currency. *–phr.* **8. in circulation,** **a.** (especially of a currency or a publication) available or in general use. **b.** *Colloq.* (of a person) socially active. **9. out of circulation,** **a.** (especially of a currency or a publication) not available or not in general use. **b.** *Colloq.* (of a person) socially inactive.

circum- a prefix referring to movement round or about something, or motion on all sides, as in *circumvent, circumnavigate, circumference.*

circumcise /ˈsɜːkəmsaɪz/ *v.t.* to remove the foreskin of (males), sometimes as a religious rite. **–circumciser,** *n.* **–circumcision,** *n.*

circumference /səˈkʌmfərəns/ *n.* the outer boundary, especially of a circular area. **–circumferential** /səkʌmfəˈrɛnʃəl/, *adj.*

circumflex /ˈsɜːkəmflɛks/ *n.* a mark (^) used over a vowel in certain languages or in phonetic keys to indicate quality of pronunciation. **–circumflexion** /sɜːkəmˈflɛkʃən/, *n.*

circumlocution /sɜːkəmləˈkjuːʃən/ *n.* a roundabout way of speaking; the use of too many words. **–circumlocutory** /sɜːkəmˈlɒkjətəri, -tri/, *adj.*

circumnavigate /sɜːkəmˈnævəgeɪt/ *v.t.* to sail round; make the circuit of by navigation: *he circumnavigated the world.* **–circumnavigation** /ˌsɜːkəmnævəˈgeɪʃən/, *n.* **–circumnavigator,** *n.*

circumscribe /ˈsɜːkəmskraɪb, sɜːkəmˈskraɪb/ *v.t.* **1.** to draw a line round; encircle; surround. **2.** to enclose within bounds; limit or confine, especially narrowly. **–circumscriber,** *n.*

circumspect /ˈsɜːkəmspɛkt/ *adj.* watchful; cautious; prudent: *circumspect in behaviour.* **–circumspectly,** *adv.* **–circumspectness,** *n.*

circumstance /ˈsɜːkəmstæns, -stəns/ *n.* **1.** a condition, with respect to time, place, manner, agent, etc., which accompanies, determines, or modifies a fact or event. **2.** (*usu. pl.*) the existing condition or state of affairs surrounding and affecting an agent: *forced by circumstances to do a thing.* **3.** (*pl.*) the condition or state of a person with respect to material welfare: *a family in reduced circumstances.* **4.** an incident or occurrence: *his arrival was a fortunate circumstance.* **5.** ceremonious accompaniment or display: *pomp and circumstance.* *–v.t.* (**-stanced, -stancing**) **6.** to place in particular circumstances or relations. *–phr.* **7. in** (or **under**) **no circumstances,** never; regardless of events. **8. in** (or **under**) **the circumstances,** because of the conditions; such being the case. **–circumstanced,** *adj.* **–circumstantial,** *adj.*

circumstantiate /sɜːkəmˈstænʃieɪt/ *v.t.* **1.** to set forth or support with circumstances or particulars. **2.** to describe fully or minutely. **–circumstantiation** /ˌsɜːkəmstænʃiˈeɪʃən/, *n.*

circumvent /sɜːkəmˈvɛnt, ˈsɜːkəmvɛnt/ *v.t.* **1.** to get around or avoid: *to circumvent a problem.* **2.** to surround or encompass as by stratagem; entrap. **3.** to gain advantage over by artfulness or deception; outwit; overreach. –**circumventer, circumventor,** *n.* –**circumvention,** *n.* –**circumventive,** *adj.*

circus /ˈsɜːkəs/ *n.* **1.** a travelling company of performers, animals, etc. **2.** the performance itself. **3.** (in ancient Rome) an open enclosure, surrounded by tiers of seats, for chariot races, public games, etc. **4.** *Chiefly Brit.* a place, originally circular, with several streets leading from it: *Piccadilly Circus.* **5.** noisy and rough behaviour or activity; uproar: *last Saturday's match was just a circus.*

cirrhosis /sɪˈrəʊsəs, sə-/ *n. Pathol.* a disease of the liver characterised by increase of connective tissue and alteration in gross and microscopic make-up. –**cirrhotic** /sɪˈrɒtɪk/, *adj.*

cirro- a combining form of **cirrus** as in *cirrocumulus.*

cirrus /ˈsɪrəs/ *n.* (*pl.* **cirri** /ˈsɪriː/) **1.** *Bot.* a tendril. **2.** *Zool.* a filament or slender appendage serving as a barbel, tentacle, foot, arm, etc. **3.** *Meteorol.* a variety of cloud having a thin, fleecy or filamentous appearance, normally occurring at great altitudes and consisting of minute ice crystals.

cisgender /ˈsɪsdʒɛndə/ *adj.* **1.** of or relating to, or designating a person whose gender identity matches their physical sex, that is, women with female bodies and men with male bodies, this being regarded as normal. –*n.* **2.** such a person. –**cisgendered,** *adj.* –**cisgenderism,** *n.*

cistern /ˈsɪstən/ *n.* a reservoir, tank, or vessel for holding water or other liquid.

citadel /ˈsɪtədɛl/ *n.* **1.** a fortress in or near a city, intended to keep the inhabitants in subjection, or, in a siege, to form a final point of defence. **2.** any strongly fortified place; a stronghold.

cite /saɪt/ *v.t.* **1.** to quote (a passage, book, etc.), especially as an authority. **2.** to mention in support, proof, or confirmation; refer to as an example. **3.** to summon officially or authoritatively to appear in court. –**citeable, citable,** *adj.* –**citation,** *n.*

citified /ˈsɪtɪfaɪd/ *adj.* having city habits, fashions, etc.

citizen /ˈsɪtəzən/ *n.* **1.** a member, native or naturalised, of a state or nation (as distinguished from *alien*). **2.** someone owing allegiance to a government and entitled to its protection. **3.** an inhabitant of a city or town, especially one entitled to its privileges or franchises. **4.** a civilian, as distinguished from a soldier, police officer, etc. –**citizenship,** *n.*

citizen band radio *n.* point-to-point broadcasting on an assigned frequency band, with transmitters and receivers appropriate to individual use, as by truck drivers, etc.

citric acid /sɪtrɪk ˈæsəd/ *n.* an organic acid containing three carboxyl groups, $C_6H_8O_7$, occurring in small amounts in almost all living cells as a component of the citric acid cycle, and in greater amounts in many fruits, especially in limes and lemons.

citron /ˈsɪtrən/ *n.* **1.** a pale yellow fruit resembling the lemon but larger and with thicker rind, borne by a small tree or large bush, *Citrus medica,* allied to the lemon and lime. –*adj.* **2.** pale yellow: *a citron dress.*

citrus /ˈsɪtrəs/ *n.* any tree or shrub of the genus *Citrus,* which includes the citron, lemon, lime, orange, grapefruit, etc.

city /ˈsɪti/ *n.* (*pl.* **-ties**) **1.** a large or important town; a town so nominated. **2.** the central business area of a city. **3.** the inhabitants of a city collectively.

city council *n.* the local administrative body which serves a capital city or large country town. Compare **municipal council, shire council.**

civet /ˈsɪvət/ *n.* **1.** a yellowish, unctuous substance with a strong musk-like smell, obtained from a pouch in the

genital region of civets and used in perfumery. **2.** Also, **civet cat.** any of the catlike, carnivorous mammals of southern Asia and Africa (family Viverridae) having glands in the genital region that secrete civet.

civic /ˈsɪvɪk/ *adj.* **1.** of or relating to a city; municipal: *civic problems.* **2.** of or relating to citizenship; civil: *civic duties.* **3.** of or relating to citizens: *civic pride.*

civil /ˈsɪvəl/ *adj.* **1.** of or consisting of citizens: *civil life; civil society.* **2.** of or relating to the state or state authorities, as opposed to religious or other authorities: *civil affairs.* **3.** of citizens in their ordinary capacity, or the ordinary life and affairs of citizens (distinguished from *military, ecclesiastical, etc.*): *civil aviation.* **4.** of the citizen as an individual: *civil liberty.* **5.** civilised or polite; courteous. –**civilly,** *adv.*

civil celebrant *n.* a secular official who conducts civil marriages, funerals, naming ceremonies, etc.

civil defence *n.* the emergency measures to be taken by an organised body of civilian volunteers for the protection of life and property in the case of a natural disaster or an attack or invasion by an enemy.

civil disobedience *n.* a refusal, usually on political grounds, to obey laws, pay taxes, etc.

civil engineer *n.* an engineer specialising in the design, construction, and maintenance of public works, such as roads, bridges, dams, canals, aqueducts, harbours, large buildings, etc.

civilian /səˈvɪljən/ *n.* **1.** someone engaged in civil pursuits, distinguished from a soldier, etc. –*adj.* **2.** relating to non-military life and activities.

civilisation /sɪvəlaɪˈzeɪʃən/ *n.* **1.** an advanced state of human society, in which a high level of art, science, religion, and government has been reached. **2.** the people or nations that have reached such a state. **3.** the type of culture, society, etc., of a specific group: *Greek civilisation.* **4.** the act or process of civilising. Also, **civilization.**

civilise /ˈsɪvəlaɪz/ *v.t.* to make civil; elevate in social and individual life; enlighten; refine. Also, **civilize.** –**civilisable,** *adj.* –**civiliser,** *n.*

civilised /ˈsɪvəlaɪzd/ *adj.* **1.** having an advanced culture, society, etc. **2.** polite; well-bred; refined. Also, **civilized.**

civility /səˈvɪləti/ *n.* (*pl.* **-ties**) **1.** courtesy; politeness. **2.** a polite attention or expression. **3.** (*usu. pl.*) polite conversation.

civil law *n.* **1.** the laws of a state or nation regulating ordinary private matters (distinguished from criminal, military, or political matters). **2.** the law of a state (distinguished from other kinds of law, as *international law*).

civil liberty *n.* complete liberty of opinion, etc., restrained only as much as is necessary for the public good.

civil marriage *n.* a marriage performed by a government official rather than a minister of religion.

civil rights *pl. n.* the personal rights of the individual in society.

civil war *n.* a war between parties, regions, etc., within their own country.

civvies /ˈsɪviz/ *pl. n. Colloq.* civilian clothes, as opposed to military dress.

clack /klæk/ *v.i.* **1.** to make a quick, sharp sound, or a succession of such sounds, as by striking or cracking. **2.** to talk rapidly and continuously, or with sharpness and abruptness; chatter. **3.** to cluck or cackle. –**clacker,** *n.*

clad /klæd/ *v.* a past tense and past participle of **clothe.**

cladding /ˈklædɪŋ/ *n.* a covering of any kind, especially one attached to a building structure, or the like.

clade /kleɪd/ *n. Biol.* a group of organisms which are considered to have evolved from a common ancestor.

clado- a word element meaning 'sprout', 'branch'. Also, (*before vowels*), **clad-**.

cladogram /'klædəgræm/ *n.* a taxonomic diagram of inferred relationships within a clade.

claim /kleɪm/ *v.t.* **1.** to demand by or as a right. **2.** to declare as fact. **3.** to need or require: *her plight claims our attention.* –*n.* **4.** a demand for something as due. **5.** an assertion of something as fact. **6.** a right to something. **7.** something claimed, as a piece of land for mining purposes, or a payment in accordance with an insurance policy, etc. –**claimable**, *adj.* –**claimer**, *n.*

claimant /'kleɪmənt/ *n.* someone who makes a claim.

clairvoyant /kleə'vɔɪənt/ *adj.* **1.** having the power of seeing objects or actions beyond the natural range of the senses. –*n.* **2.** a clairvoyant person. –**clairvoyance**, *n.*

clam /klæm/ *n.* **1.** any of various bivalve molluscs, such as the giant clams of the family Tridacnidae of tropical waters, or certain smaller edible species, such as the quahog. **2.** *Colloq.* a secretive or silent person. –*phr.* *Colloq.* **3.** clam up, to refuse to talk further. **4.** clam up on, to refuse to talk to (someone).

clamber /'klæmbə/ *v.i.* to climb, using both feet and hands; climb with effort or difficulty. –**clamberer**, *n.*

clammy /'klæmi/ *adj.* (**-mier, -miest**) covered with a cold, sticky moisture; cold and damp. –**clamminess**, *n.*

clamorous reed-warbler *n.* a warbler of the family Acrocephalidae, *Acrocephalus stentoreus*, inhabiting freshwater reedy areas throughout Australasia, Africa and Asia, and noted for its loud and varied song.

clamour /'klæmə/ *n.* **1.** a loud outcry. **2.** a vehement expression of desire or dissatisfaction. **3.** popular outcry. **4.** any loud and continued noise. –*v.i.* **5.** to make a clamour; raise an outcry. Also, **clamor**. –**clamorous**, *adj.* –**clamorously**, *adv.* –**clamourer**, *n.*

clamp /klæmp/ *n.* **1.** a device, usually of some rigid material, for strengthening or supporting objects or fastening them together. **2.** an appliance with opposite sides or parts that may be screwed or otherwise brought together to hold or compress something. –*v.t.* **3.** to fasten with or fix in a clamp. **4.** to press firmly. –*phr.* **5.** clamp down, to become more strict. **6.** put a clamp on, *Colloq.* to put a stop to.

clan /klæn/ *n.* **1.** a group of people tracing their descent from a common ancestor, as among Australian Aboriginal people or Scottish people. **2.** *Colloq.* a group of people sharing some interest or activity.

clandestine /klæn'dɛstən, klæn'dɛstaɪn, 'klændəstaɪn/ *adj.* secret; private; concealed (generally implying craft or deception): *a clandestine marriage.* –**clandestinely**, *adv.* –**clandestineness**, *n.*

clang /klæŋ/ *v.i.* **1.** to give out a loud, resonant sound, as metal when struck; ring loudly or harshly. **2.** to emit a harsh cry, as geese. –*n.* **3.** a clanging sound.

clanger /'klæŋə/ *n. Colloq.* a glaring error or mistake, such as an embarrassing remark: *to drop a clanger.*

clangour /'klæŋə, 'klæŋgə/ *n.* a loud, resonant sound, as of pieces of metal struck together or of a trumpet; a clang. Also, **clangor**. –**clangorous**, *adj.* –**clangorously**, *adv.*

clank /klæŋk/ *n.* **1.** a sharp, hard, metallic sound: *the clank of chains.* –*v.i.* **2.** to move with such sounds.

clannish /'klænɪʃ/ *adj.* **1.** of, relating to, or characteristic of a clan. **2.** disposed to adhere closely, as the members of a clan. –**clannishly**, *adv.* –**clannishness**, *n.*

clap¹ /klæp/ *verb* (**clapped, clapping**) –*v.t.* **1.** to strike with a quick, smart blow, producing an abrupt, sharp sound; slap; pat. **2.** to strike together resoundingly, as the hands to express applause. **3.** to applaud in this manner. **4.** to flap (the wings). **5.** to put, place, apply, etc., promptly and effectively. –*v.i.* **6.** to make an abrupt, sharp sound, as of bodies in collision. **7.** to move or strike with such a sound. **8.** to clap the hands, as in applause. –*n.* **9.** a resounding blow; slap. **10.** a loud and

abrupt or explosive noise, as of thunder. **11.** an applauding; applause. –*phr.* **12.** clap eyes on, to catch sight of. **13.** clap on, to increase: *to clap on speed.* **14.** clap out, *Colloq.* to break down; cease to function: *the car clapped out on the way home.*

clap² /klæp/ *n. Colloq.* (usu. preceded by *the*) gonorrhoea, or any other venereal disease.

clapper /'klæpə/ *n.* **1.** someone or something that claps. **2.** the tongue of a bell. **3.** a percussion instrument in which two flexible pieces of wood are attached to a handle and shaken so that they impact to make a clapping sound. –*phr.* **4.** go like the clappers, *Colloq.* to move very rapidly.

claret /'klærət/ *n.* **1.** the red (originally the light red or yellowish) table wine of Bordeaux, France. **2.** (in unofficial use) a similar wine made elsewhere. **3.** Also, **claret red.** a deep purplish red.

clarify /'klærəfaɪ/ *verb* (**-fied, -fying**) –*v.t.* **1.** to make clear, pure, or intelligible. **2.** to make clear by removal of sediment, often over low heat: *to clarify butter.* –*v.i.* **3.** to become clear, pure, or intelligible. **4.** to become clear by having sediment removed. –**clarification** /klærəfə'keɪʃən/, *n.* –**clarifier**, *n.*

clarinet /klærə'nɛt/ *n.* a wind instrument in the form of a cylindrical tube with a single reed attached to its mouthpiece. –**clarinettist**, *n.*

clarion /'klæriən/ *adj.* **1.** clear and shrill. **2.** inspiring; rousing.

clarity /'klærəti/ *n.* clearness: *clarity of thinking.*

clash /klæʃ/ *v.i.* **1.** to make a loud, harsh noise. **2.** to collide, especially noisily. **3.** to disagree; conflict. **4.** to coincide unfortunately (especially of events). –*n.* **5.** a loud, harsh noise. **6.** conflict; opposition, especially of views or interests.

clasp /klæsp, klasp/ *n.* **1.** a device, usually of metal, for fastening things or parts together; any fastening or connection; anything that clasps. **2.** a grasp; an embrace. –*v.t.* **3.** to take hold of with an enfolding grasp: *they clasped hands.*

class /klas/ *n.* **1.** a number of people, things, etc., regarded as forming one group through possession of similar qualities; kind; sort. **2.** any division of people or things according to rank or grade. **3. a.** a group of pupils taught together. **b.** the period or year during which they are taught. **4.** → **year** (def. 11). **5.** a section of society sharing essential economic, political or cultural characteristics, and having the same social position: *middle class.* **6.** a social rank, especially high rank. **7.** high quality in style, dress or manner. **8.** (in travel) a grade or standard in ships, planes, etc.: *business class.* **9.** *Zool., Bot.* a major subdivision of a phylum, usually consisting of many different orders, as gastropods, mammals, angiosperms. –*v.t.* **10.** to put into a class; rate. –*adj.* **11.** relating to class: *class warfare.* **12.** *Colloq.* stylish: *a class act.* –**classable**, *adj.* –**classer**, *n.* –**classless**, *adj.*

class action *n. Law* a legal proceeding brought on by a group of people all with the same grievance or claim.

classic /'klæsɪk/ *adj.* **1.** of first or highest class or rank. **2.** serving as a standard, model, or guide: *a classic example.* **3.** of ancient Greek and Roman times, especially relating to literature and art; classical. **4.** relating to an established set of artistic or scientific standards and methods. –*n.* **5.** a work of literature, music or art which is regarded as having an enduring quality or significance. **6. a.** any one of a body of texts in ancient Greek or Latin, traditionally considered as a model for literary works. **b.** the classics, the literature of ancient Greece and Rome; the Greek and Latin languages. **7.** someone or something regarded as the best of their kind. **8.** *Colloq.* (*ironic*) one of a kind; something or someone excellent. –**classical**, *adj.*

classicism /ˈklæsəsɪzəm/ *n.* **1.** the principles of classical literature or art, or adherence to them. **2.** the classical style in literature or art, characterised especially by attention to form with the general effect of regularity, simplicity, balance, proportion, and controlled emotion. Also, **classicalism** /ˈklæsɪkəˌlɪzəm/. **–classicist,** *n.*

classified /ˈklæsəfaɪd/ *adj.* **1.** arranged or distributed in classes; placed according to class. **2.** (of military and other government information) placed in categories in relation to security risk. **3.** (of roads) having a classification number and receiving government financial assistance. *–n.* **4.** → **classified ad.**

classified ad *n. Colloq.* a newspaper advertisement, usually single-column, placed in an appropriately headed set, as for job vacancies, objects for sale, etc.

classify /ˈklæsəfaɪ/ *v.t.* (**-fied, -fying**) **1.** to arrange or distribute in classes; place according to class. **2.** to mark or otherwise declare (a document, paper, etc.) of value to an enemy, and limit and safeguard its handling and use. **–classifiable,** *adj.* **–classification,** *n.* **–classifier,** *n.*

classroom /ˈklɑsrum/ *n.* a room in a school, etc., in which classes meet.

classy /ˈklɑsi/ *adj.* (**-sier, -siest**) *Colloq.* of high class, rank, or grade; stylish; fine.

clastic /ˈklæstɪk/ *adj.* **1.** *Biol.* breaking up into fragments or separate portions; dividing into parts; causing or undergoing disruption or dissolution: *clastic action, the clastic pole of an ovum.* **2.** of or relating to an anatomical model made up of detachable pieces. **3.** of or relating to rock or rocks composed of fragments of older rocks; fragmental.

clatter /ˈklætə/ *v.i.* **1.** to make a rattling sound, as of hard bodies striking rapidly together. **2.** to move rapidly with such a sound. **3.** to talk fast and noisily; chatter. *–n.* **4.** a clattering noise; disturbance.

clause /klɔz/ *n.* **1.** *Gram.* a group of words containing a subject and a predicate, forming part of a compound or complex sentence, or coextensive with a simple sentence. **2.** part of a written composition containing complete sense in itself, as a sentence or paragraph (in modern use commonly limited to such parts of legal documents, as of statutes, contracts, wills, etc.). **–clausal,** *adj.*

claustrophobia /klɒstrəˈfoʊbiə, klɔs-/ *n. Psychol.* a morbid dread of confined places. **–claustrophobic,** *adj.*

claves /kleɪvz, ˈklaveɪz/ *pl. n. Music* a musical instrument consisting of two resonant wooden sticks which are struck together; clapping sticks.

clavichord /ˈklævəkɔd/ *n. Music* an ancient keyboard instrument, in which the strings were softly struck with metal blades vertically projecting from the rear ends of the keys.

clavicle /ˈklævɪkəl/ *n. Anat.* **1.** a bone of the pectoral arch. **2.** (in humans) either of two slender bones each articulating with the sternum and a scapula and forming the anterior part of a shoulder; the collarbone. **–clavicular** /kləˈvɪkjələ/, *adj.*

claw /klɔ/ *n.* **1.** a sharp, usually curved, nail on foot of animal. **2.** a foot with such nails. **3.** anything that looks like a claw. **4.** the pincers of some shellfish and insects. *–v.t.* **5.** to tear, scratch, seize, pull, etc., with or as with claws. *–v.i.* **6.** (fol. by *at*) to tear or scratch.

claw hammer *n.* a hammer having a head with one end curved and cleft for drawing out nails.

clay /kleɪ/ *n.* **1.** a natural earthy material of many varieties which is plastic when wet, consisting essentially of hydrated silicates of aluminium, and used for making bricks, pottery, etc. **2.** earth; mud. **–clayey** /ˈkleɪi/, *adj.* **–clayish,** *adj.*

clay court *n. Tennis* a court with a surface prepared from a red or green clay, designed to produce a slower

ball speed and a shallow bounce. Compare **composition court, grass court, hardcourt.**

claymation /kleɪˈmeɪʃən/ *n.* (*from trademark*) an animation technique using clay figures as the basis for the film rather than drawn figures.

claypan /ˈkleɪpæn/ *n.* a depression in the ground of hardened impervious clay which intermittently retains water; caused by deflation of the topsoil to expose the impermeable subsoil.

Clayton's /ˈkleɪtɒnz/ *adj. Aust., NZ Colloq.* (*from trademark*) serving as a substitute; imitation. Also, **Claytons.**

-cle variant of **-cule.**

clean /klin/ *adj.* **1.** free from dirt or filth; unsoiled; unstained. **2.** free from foreign or extraneous matter: *the wool was sold at $4.27 a kilogram clean.* **3.** free from defect or blemish. **4.** (of stock and grazing land) free of disease, animal pests, etc. **5.** free from addiction to drugs. **6.** free of radioactivity. **7.** not polluting the environment. **8.** free from any form of defilement; morally pure; innocent; upright; honourable. **9.** uncorrupted: *a clean cop.* **10.** free from dirty habits, as an animal. **11.** neatly or evenly made or proportioned; shapely; trim. **12.** even; with a smooth edge or surface. **13.** free from awkwardness; not bungling; dexterous; adroit: *a clean leap.* **14.** complete; perfect: *a clean sweep.* **15.** *Weightlifting* (of a lift) without touching the barbell against the body. **16.** *Colloq.* carrying no weapons, stolen goods, drugs, etc. Compare **dirty** (def. 5). *–adv.* **17.** in a clean manner; cleanly. **18.** wholly; completely; quite. *–v.t.* **19.** to make clean. *–v.i.* **20.** to perform or to undergo a process of cleaning. *–phr.* **21. clean as a whistle,** *Colloq.* extremely clean. **22. clean bowled,** *Cricket* bowled by a ball which breaks the wicket without touching the person batting or the bat. **23. clean out, a.** to rid of dirt, etc. **b.** to use up; exhaust. **c.** to drive out by force. **d.** to empty or rid (a place) of contents, etc. **e.** *Colloq.* to take all money from, especially illegally. **24. clean up, a.** to rid of dirt, etc.: *to clean up the kitchen.* **b.** to get rid of dirt, etc. **c.** to finish up; reach the end of. **d.** *Colloq.* to make (money, or the like) as profit, gain, etc. **e.** *Colloq.* to make money or the like, as profit or gain: *to clean up at the races.* **f.** *Sport, etc.* to defeat soundly: *Carlton cleaned up Richmond last Saturday.* **g.** *Sport* to win decisively: *Australia cleaned up at the SCG.* **25. clean up one's act,** *Colloq.* to improve one's behaviour, practices, etc., to meet an acceptable standard. **26. come clean,** *Colloq.* to make a full confession. **–cleanly,** *adv.* **–cleanable,** *adj.* **–cleanness,** *n.*

clean coal *n.* coal which has been processed to make it environmentally less damaging.

clean-cut *adj.* **1.** distinctly outlined. **2.** definite. **3.** neatly dressed, wholesome: *a clean-cut gentleman.*

cleaner /ˈklinə/ *n.* **1.** a person who cleans, especially for a living. **2.** an apparatus or preparation for cleaning. **3.** (*pl.*) → **drycleaners.** *–phr.* **4. take someone to the cleaners,** to strip someone of all assets, money, etc., usually in gambling.

clean fuel *n.* a fuel which produces minimal greenhouse gas emissions.

cleanliness /ˈklɛnlinəs/ *n.* the condition or quality of being clean or cleanly; freedom from dirt or filth or anything that contaminates: *high standards of cleanliness.*

cleanse /klɛnz/ *v.t.* (**cleansed, cleansing**) **1.** to make clean. **2.** to remove by, or as by, cleaning: *his leprosy was cleansed.* **–cleanser,** *n.*

cleanskin /ˈklinskɪn/ *n.* **1.** an unbranded animal. **2.** someone who is free from blame, or has no record of police conviction. **3.** a bottle of wine labelled as a generic wine type from a particular region but with no brand name.

clear /klɪə/ *adj.* **1.** free from darkness, obscurity, or cloudiness; light. **2.** bright; shining. **3.** transparent; pellucid: *good, clear wine.* **4.** of a pure, even colour: *a clear complexion.* **5.** distinctly perceptible to the eye, ear, or mind; easily seen, heard or understood. **6.** distinct; evident; plain. **7.** free from confusion, uncertainty, or doubt. **8.** perceiving or discerning distinctly: *a clear thinker.* **9.** convinced; certain. **10.** free from guilt or blame; innocent. **11.** serene; calm; untroubled. **12.** free from obstructions; open: *a clear space.* **13.** (sometimes fol. by *of*) unentangled or disengaged; free. **14.** not in code; in plain language. **15.** having no parts that protrude, are rough, etc. **16.** freed or emptied of contents, cargo, etc. **17.** without limitation or qualification: *a clear victory.* **18.** without obligation or liability; free from debt. **19.** without deduction or diminution: *a clear $100.* **20.** (of vowel sounds) light; resembling a front vowel in quality. –*adv.* **21.** in a clear manner; clearly; distinctly; entirely. –*v.t.* **22.** to make clear; free from darkness, cloudiness, muddiness, indistinctness, confusion, uncertainty, obstruction, contents, entanglement, obligation, liability, etc. **23.** to free from imputation, especially of guilt; prove or declare to be innocent. **24.** to pass or get over without entanglement or collision. **25.** to pay (a debt) in full. **26.** to pass (cheques, etc.) through a clearing house. **27.** to free (a person, etc.) from debt. **28.** to gain as clear profit: *to clear $1000 in a transaction.* **29.** to free (a ship, cargo, etc.) from legal detention at a port by satisfying the customs and other required conditions. **30.** *Football, etc.* to get (the ball) away from the area of one's own goal. **31.** to approve or authorise, or to obtain approval or authorisation for, a thing or person. **32.** to remove objects from: *to clear the table.* **33.** to remove trees, undergrowth, etc., from (an area of land). **34.** to sell off, as in a clearance sale. –*v.i.* **35.** to become clear. –*n.* **36.** plain language; not code: *the orders were radioed in clear.* **37.** (*pl.*) *NZ* barren peat-land. –*phr.* **38. clear as mud,** *Colloq.* not clear; confused. **39. clear off, a.** to remove objects from so as to leave (a table, etc.) clear. **b.** (*oft. used imperatively*) *Colloq.* to leave; go away. **40. clear out, a.** to empty or remove, in order to make clear. **b.** *Colloq.* to leave; go away. **41. clear the air, a.** to relieve tension. **b.** to remove misunderstanding. **42. clear up, a.** to make clear. **b.** to solve; explain. **c.** to put things in order; tidy up. **d.** (of weather) to become brighter, lighter, etc. **43. clear with,** to obtain approval for (something) from (someone): *to clear the deal with the boss.* **44. in the clear,** free from the imputation of blame, censure, or the like. –**clearly,** *adv.* –**clearable,** *adj.* –**clearer,** *n.* –**clearage,** *n.*

clear air turbulence *n. Aviation* sudden atmospheric turbulence occurring under cloudless conditions, causing aircraft to be buffeted.

clearance /'klɪərəns/ *n.* **1.** the act of clearing. **2.** a clear space; a clearing. **3.** an intervening space, as between machine parts for free play. **4.** distance or extent of an object to be passed over or under. **5.** official approval; permission to go ahead with a proposal.

clear-cut *adj.* having clearly defined outlines; distinctly defined.

clearing /'klɪərɪŋ/ *n.* a tract of cleared land, as in a forest.

clearing house *n.* **1.** a place or institution where mutual claims and accounts are settled, as between banks. **2.** a central office for receiving and distributing information.

clearway /'klɪəweɪ/ *n.* a stretch of road, especially in a built-up area, on which, between stated times, motorists may stop only in emergencies.

cleat /klit/ *n.* **1.** a small wedge-shaped block, such as one fastened to a spar or the like as a support, etc. **2.** a piece of wood or iron fastened across anything for support, security, etc. **3.** *Mining* a vertical plane of breakage in coal. The planes of easier breakage are **face cleats,**

lesser planes at right angles are **butt cleats. 4. a. a** projecting piece of iron fastened under a shoe to increase grip or to preserve the sole. **b.** → **sprig** (def. 5).

cleavage /'klivɪdʒ/ *n.* **1.** the act of cleaving. **2.** the state of being cleft or split; division. **3.** the cleft between a woman's breasts.

cleave[1] /kliv/ *v.i.* (**cleaved** *or, Archaic,* **clave, cleaved, cleaving**) **1.** (sometimes fol. by *to*) to stick or adhere; cling or hold fast. **2.** (sometimes fol. by *to*) to be attached or faithful.

cleave[2] /kliv/ *verb* (**cleft** *or* **cleaved** *or* **clove, cleft** *or* **cleaved** *or* **cloven, cleaving**) –*v.t.* **1.** to part by, or as by, a cutting blow, especially along the grain or any other natural line of division. **2.** to split; rend apart; rive. **3.** to penetrate or pass through (air, water, etc.). **4.** to make by or as by cutting: *to cleave a path through the wilderness.* **5.** to separate or sever by, or as by, splitting. –*v.i.* **6.** to part or split, especially along a natural line of division. –*phr.* **7. cleave through,** to penetrate or pass through.

cleaver /'klivə/ *n.* a heavy knife or long-bladed hatchet used by butchers for cutting up carcasses.

clef /klɛf/ *n.* a symbol in music notation placed upon a stave to indicate the name and pitch of the notes corresponding to its lines and spaces. The **G clef** (or **treble clef**) indicates that the second line of the stave corresponds to the G next above middle C. The **F clef** (or **bass clef**) indicates that the fourth line of the stave corresponds to the F next below middle C. The **C clef** (or **alto clef**) indicates middle C on the third line of the stave.

cleft[1] /klɛft/ *n.* **1.** a space or opening made by cleavage; a split. **2.** a division formed by cleaving.

cleft[2] /klɛft/ *v.* **1.** a past tense and past participle of **cleave**[2]. –*adj.* **2.** cloven; split; divided.

cleft palate *n.* a congenital defect of the palate in which a longitudinal fissure exists in the roof of the mouth.

clematis /klə'meɪtəs, 'klɛmətəs/ *n.* any of the flowering vines or erect shrubs constituting the genus *Clematis*, such as *C. glycinoides*, traveller's joy of eastern Australia, and *C. vitalba*, the traveller's joy of Europe and western Asia.

clement /'klɛmənt/ *adj.* **1.** mild or merciful in disposition; lenient; compassionate. **2.** (of the weather, etc.) mild or pleasant. –**clemency,** *n.* –**clemently,** *adv.*

clench /klɛntʃ/ *v.t.* **1.** to close (the hands, teeth, etc.) tightly. **2.** to grasp firmly; grip. **3.** to settle decisively; clinch.

clergy /'klɜdʒi/ *n.* (*pl.* **-gies**) the body of ministers ordained for religious duties, especially in the Christian church.

clergyman /'klɜdʒimən/ *n.* (*pl.* **-men**) a male member of the clergy, especially a Christian minister or priest. –**clergywoman,** *n.*

cleric /'klɛrɪk/ *n.* someone whose office is to perform religious rites; a member of a priesthood.

clerical /'klɛrɪkəl/ *adj.* **1.** relating to a clerk or to clerks: *a clerical error.* **2.** of, relating to, or characteristic of the clergy. **3.** upholding the power or influence of the clergy in politics. –**clerically,** *adv.*

clerical collar *n.* a stiff, narrow, white collar, fastened at the back of the neck, worn by certain members of the clergy.

clerk /klak/, *Chiefly US* /klɜk/ *n.* **1.** someone employed in an office, shop, etc., to keep records or accounts, attend to correspondence, etc. **2.** someone who keeps the records and performs the routine business of a court, legislature, board, etc. **3.** the administrative officer, and chief executive of a town or borough council. **4.** *Obs.* a scholar. –**clerkly,** *adj.* –**clerkship,** *n.*

clerk of works *n.* the representative of the owner of the building during day to day supervision of construction works.

clever /ˈklɛvə/ *adj.* **1.** bright mentally; having quick intelligence; able. **2.** dexterous or nimble with the hands or body. **3.** showing adroitness or ingenuity: *a clever remark, a clever device.* **4.** *Aboriginal English* holding knowledge of medicinal plants and traditional healing practices. –**cleverish**, *adj.* –**cleverly**, *adv.* –**cleverness**, *n.*

clever dick *n. Colloq.* a conceited, smug person, who displays prowess at the expense of others.

clianthus /kliˈænθəs/ *n.* any plant of the small genus *Clianthus*, family Fabaceae, especially *C. puniceus*, of New Zealand, and Sturt's desert pea, *C. formosus*, of inland Australia.

cliché /ˈkliʃeɪ/ *n.* (*pl.* **-chés** /-ʃeɪz/) a trite, stereotyped expression, idea, practice, etc., such as *trials and tribulations.*

click /klɪk/ *n.* **1.** a slight, sharp sound: *the click of a door latch.* **2.** *Computers* a single activation of a digital device to open a link. –*v.i.* **3.** to make a click or series of clicks. **4.** *Colloq.* to fall into place or be understood: *his story suddenly clicked.* **5.** *Colloq.* to understand: *I finally clicked and realised that he was lying.* **6.** *Computers* to operate the mouse button: *you have to click firmly.* –*v.t.* **7.** *Computers* to open (a link) by a single activation of a digital device: *click one of the following boxes to select payment method.*

click-and-mortar *adj.* of or relating to a company which has operations both online and offline, as by having both a commercial website and a physical store.

clickbait /ˈklɪkbeɪt/ *n.* an attention-grabbing link on a website which turns out to be of spurious value or interest.

client /ˈklaɪənt/ *n.* **1.** someone who applies to a solicitor for advice or commits his or her cause or legal interests to a solicitor's management. **2.** someone who employs or seeks advice from a professional adviser. **3.** a customer. **4.** someone under the patronage of another; a dependant. **5.** a recipient of a social welfare payment. **6.** a computer which accesses the resources of another computer via a network. –**cliental** /klaɪˈɛntl/, *adj.*

clientele /klaɪənˈtɛl, kliən-/ *n.* **1.** the customers, clients, etc. (of a solicitor, business person, etc.) as a whole. **2.** dependants or followers. Also, **clientage** /ˈklaɪəntɪdʒ/.

cliff /klɪf/ *n.* the high, steep face of a rocky mass; precipice.

cliffhanger /ˈklɪfhæŋə/ *n.* **1.** a play, novel, serial, etc., characterised by suspense. **2.** a contest, election, etc., so closely matched that the outcome is uncertain until the end. –**cliff-hanging**, *adj.*

climacteric /klaɪˈmæktərɪk, klaɪməkˈtɛrɪk/ *adj.* **1.** relating to a critical period; crucial. –*n.* **2.** *Physiol.* a period of decrease of reproductive activity in men and women, culminating, in women, in the menopause.

climactic /klaɪˈmæktɪk/ *adj.* relating to or forming a climax: *climactic arrangement.*

climate /ˈklaɪmət/ *n.* **1.** the composite or generalisation of weather conditions of a region, such as temperature, pressure, humidity, precipitation, sunshine, cloudiness, and winds, throughout the year, averaged over a series of years. **2.** an area of a particular kind of climate. **3.** the general attitude and prevailing opinions of a group of people. –**climatic**, *adj.* –**climatically**, *adv.* –**climatology**, *n.* –**climatologist**, *n.*

climate change *n.* a significant change in the usual climatic conditions persisting for an extended period, especially one thought to be caused by global warming.

climate porn *n.* predictions, thought to be exaggeratedly alarmist, about the progress of global warming and its effects on the world.

climate refugee *n.* someone who flees for refuge, especially to a foreign country, due to catastrophic climate change in their own country.

climate wars *pl. n.* international conflict caused by the effects of climate change, such as reduced resources, population shifts, failing economies, etc., theorised as likely to occur in the future if measures are not taken to control global warming.

climax /ˈklaɪmæks/ *n.* **1.** the highest point of anything; the culmination. **2.** the point in the drama in which it is clear that the central motive will or will not be successful. **3.** an orgasm. –*v.i.* **4.** to reach the climax.

climb /klaɪm/ *v.i.* **1.** to mount or ascend, especially by using both hands and feet. **2.** to rise slowly by, or as by, continued effort. **3.** to move or progress in a specified direction, especially with some effort, or by using both hands and feet; clamber: *to climb through a window.* **4.** to slope upward. **5.** to ascend by twining or by means of tendrils, adhesive tissues, etc., as a plant. **6.** to rise, or attempt to rise, in social position. –*v.t.* **7.** to ascend, go up, or get to the top of, especially by the use of hands and feet. –*n.* **8.** a climbing; an ascent by climbing. **9.** a place to be climbed. –*phr.* **10. climb down**, **a.** to descend, especially by using both hands and feet. **b.** to withdraw from an untenable position; retract an indefensible argument. –**climbable**, *adj.*

clinch /klɪntʃ/ *v.t.* **1.** to secure (a driven nail, etc.) by beating down the point. **2.** to fasten (work) together thus. **3.** to settle (a matter) decisively. –*n.* **4.** *Boxing, etc.* the act or an instance of one or both contestants holding the other in such a way as to hinder the other's punches. **5.** *Colloq.* an embrace or passionate kiss.

cling /klɪŋ/ *v.i.* (**clung**, **clinging**) **1.** to adhere closely; stick. **2.** to hold fast, as by grasping or embracing; cleave. **3.** to be or remain close. **4.** to remain attached (to an idea, hope, memory, etc.). –**clinger**, *n.* –**clingingly**, *adv.*

cling wrap *n.* thin, clear plastic wrapping, usually for packaging food. Also, **cling film**.

clinic /ˈklɪnɪk/ *n.* **1.** any medical centre devoted to a particular type of treatment or health care, as child health care, vaccinations, prenatal care, etc. **2.** one of a number of out-patient sections of a hospital for the specialised treatment of particular conditions and diseases. **3.** a hospital for private patients. **4.** a class of medical students which takes place in a hospital ward, where practical instruction in examining and treating patients is given. **5.** an organised session of instruction in a particular activity or subject: *a maths clinic; a basketball clinic.*

clinical /ˈklɪnɪkəl/ *adj.* **1.** relating to a clinic, sick room or hospital. **2.** concerned with the observation and personal treatment of disease in a patient. **3.** scientific; detached, unemotional: *he has a clinical attitude to death.* –**clinically**, *adv.*

clink[1] /klɪŋk/ *v.i.* **1.** to make a light, sharp, ringing sound. **2.** to rhyme or jingle. **3.** to move with a clinking sound.

clink[2] /klɪŋk/ *n. Colloq.* a prison; jail.

clinker[1] /ˈklɪŋkə/ *n.* **a.** a hard brick, used for paving, etc. **b.** an overburnt face brick. **2.** a partially vitrified mass of brick.

clinker[2] /ˈklɪŋkə/ *adj.* made of pieces, such as boards or plates of metal, which overlap one another. Also, **clinker-built** /ˈklɪŋkə-bɪlt/.

clip[1] /klɪp/ *verb* (**clipped**, **clipping**) –*v.t.* **1.** to cut, or cut off or out, as with shears; trim by cutting. **2.** to cut or trim the hair or fleece of; shear. **3.** to punch a hole in (a ticket). **4.** to pronounce (words) in a brisk and precise manner. **5.** *Colloq.* to hit with a sharp, glancing blow: *the punch clipped his shoulder.* **6.** *Colloq.* to cheat. –*v.i.* **7.** to clip or cut something; make the motion of clipping something. –*n.* **8.** the act of clipping. **9.** → **wool clip**.

10. an extract from a film. **11.** → **video clip. 12.** *Colloq.* rate; pace: *at a rapid clip.*

clip² /klɪp/ *n.* **1.** a device for gripping and holding tightly; a metal clasp, especially one for papers, letters, etc. **2.** a holder for ammunition ready for insertion into the magazine of certain weapons. *–v.t.* (**clipped**, **clipping**) **3.** to grip tightly; hold together by pressure.

clip art *n. Computers* a collection of graphical images designed to be copied and inserted into other applications.

clipjoint /ˈklɪpdʒɔɪnt/ *n. Colloq.* a nightclub or restaurant, etc., where prices are exorbitant and customers are swindled.

clipper /ˈklɪpə/ *n.* **1.** (*oft. pl.*) a cutting tool, especially shears. **2.** (*oft. pl.*) a tool with rotating or reciprocating knives for cutting hair. **3.** something that moves swiftly, as a horse. **4.** a sailing vessel built and rigged for speed.

clipping /ˈklɪpɪŋ/ *n.* **1.** a piece clipped off or out. **2.** → **cutting** (def. 3). **3.** (*pl.*) grass from a mown lawn. *–adj.* **4.** that clips. **5.** *Colloq.* swift: *a clipping pace.*

clique /klik, klɪk/ *n.* **1.** a small set or coterie, especially one that is snobbishly exclusive. *–v.i.* (**cliqued**, **cliqu-ing**) **2.** *Colloq.* to form, or associate in, a clique. **–cliquey, cliquish,** *adj.*

clitoris /ˈklɪtərəs, ˈklaɪ-/ *n.* the erectile organ of the vulva.

cloak /kloʊk/ *n.* **1.** a loose outer garment. **2.** something that covers or conceals; disguise; pretext. *–v.t.* **3.** to cover with, or as with a cloak. **4.** to hide; conceal. **5.** to place in a cloakroom: *to cloak your bags.*

cloak-and-dagger *adj.* melodramatic; concerned with espionage, intrigue, etc.

cloakroom /ˈkloʊkrum/ *n.* **1.** a room where overcoats and other personal belongings may be left temporarily, as at a theatre, hotel, etc. **2.** a toilet.

clobber¹ /ˈklɒbə/ *v.t. Colloq.* to batter severely; maul.

clobber² /ˈklɒbə/ *n. Colloq.* clothes or gear, especially special clothing such as a uniform.

clock¹ /klɒk/ *n.* **1.** an instrument for measuring and indicating time, having either pointers on a numbered dial or a digital display to show the hour, etc. **2.** *Colloq.* a piece of measuring equipment having a dial, as an odometer, taxi-meter, etc. **3.** the dial itself. **4.** *Electronics* a circuit producing regular pulses which control the operations of a system. *–v.t.* **5.** to time, test, or ascertain by the clock, especially in races by athletes, horses, cars, etc. **6.** (on pinball machines, computer games, etc.) to make (the digital read-out of the scoreboard) return to the initial position of zeros in a single game of continuous play. *–phr.* **7. against the clock, a.** in haste, as to meet a deadline. **b.** (in a competitive sport) in an attempt to beat a record time rather than another contestant. **8. around the clock,** continuously; 24 hours a day. **9. clock off** (or **out**), to register the time of departure at a place of work. **10. clock on** (or **in**), to register the time of arrival at a place of work.

clock² /klɒk/ *Colloq.* *–n.* **1.** a punch. *–v.t.* **2.** to hit; strike.

clockwise /ˈklɒkwaɪz/ *adv.* **1.** in the direction of rotation of the hands of a clock. *–adj.* **2.** of, relating to, or indicating movement in this direction.

clockwork /ˈklɒkwɜːk/ *n.* **1.** the mechanism of a clock. **2.** any mechanism similar to that of a clock. *–phr.* **3. like clockwork,** with perfect regularity or precision.

clod /klɒd/ *n.* **1.** a lump or mass, especially of earth or clay. **2.** earth; soil. **3.** anything earthy or base, such as the body in comparison with the soul: *this corporeal clod.* **4.** a stupid person; blockhead; dolt. **–cloddish,** *adj.* **–cloddy,** *adj.* **–cloddishness,** *n.*

clodhopper /ˈklɒdhɒpə/ *n.* **1.** a clumsy boor; rustic; bumpkin. **2.** (*pl.*) strong, heavy shoes.

clog /klɒg/ *v.t.* (**clogged**, **clogging**) **1.** to encumber; hamper; hinder. **2.** to hinder or obstruct, especially by sticky matter; choke up. *–n.* **3.** anything that impedes motion or action; an encumbrance; a hindrance. **4.** a heavy block, as of wood, fastened to a person or animal to impede movement. **5.** a kind of shoe with a thick sole usually of wood. **–cloggy,** *adj.*

cloister /ˈklɔɪstə/ *n.* **1.** a covered walk, especially one adjoining a building, such as a church, commonly running round an open court (garth) and opening on to it with an open arcade or colonnade. **2.** a place of religious seclusion; a monastery or nunnery; a convent. **3.** any quiet, secluded place. *–v.t.* **4.** to confine in a cloister or convent. **–cloistral, cloister-like,** *adj.*

clone /kloʊn/ *v.t.* **1.** to bring about the asexual reproduction of (an individual), as by implanting the nucleus of a body cell from a donor individual into an egg cell from which the nucleus has been removed, and allowing the egg cell to develop, the resulting individual being identical with the donor, but having no cells in common with the female providing or harbouring the egg cell. *–n.* **2.** an asexually produced descendant. **3.** *Hort.* a group of plants originating as parts of the same individual, from buds or cuttings. **4.** a product, especially a computer, which replicates in design or function an existing model produced by another manufacturer: *an IBM clone.* **5.** a person whose appearance and behaviour is clearly modelled on another specified person: *a Michael Jackson clone.*

clop /klɒp/ *n.* the sound made by a horse's hoofs.

close *v.t.* /kloʊz/ **1.** to stop or obstruct (a gap, entrance, aperture, etc.). **2.** to stop or obstruct the entrances, apertures, or gaps in. **3.** to shut in or surround on all sides; enclose; cover in. **4.** to refuse access to or passage across: *lifesavers closed the beach because of heavy seas.* **5.** to bring together the parts of; join; unite: *to close the ranks of troops.* **6.** to bring to an end; to shut down, either temporarily or permanently: *to close a debate; to close a shop.* **7.** to bring (a sale) to a successful completion. *–v.i.* /kloʊz/ **8.** to become closed; shut. **9.** to come together; unite. **10.** to come close. **11.** to come to an end; terminate. **12.** *Stock Exchange* to have a certain value at the end of a trading period: *gold closed at $280 an ounce. –adj.* /kloʊs/ **13.** shut; shut tight; not open. **14.** shut in; enclosed. **15.** completely enclosing. **16.** without opening; with all openings covered or closed. **17.** confined; narrow: *close quarters.* **18.** lacking fresh or freely circulating air: *a close room.* **19.** heavy; oppressive: *a spell of close weather.* **20.** narrowly confined, as a prisoner. **21.** practising secrecy; secretive; reticent. **22.** parsimonious; stingy. **23.** scarce, as money. **24.** having the parts near together: *a close texture.* **25.** compact; condensed. **26.** near, or near together, in space, time, or relation: *in close contact.* **27.** *Ball Games* characterised by short passes and cautious tactics: *they played a close game.* **28.** intimate; confidential: *close friendship.* **29.** based upon a strong uniting feeling of love, honour, etc.: *a close union of nations.* **30.** fitting tightly, as a cap. **31.** (of a haircut, shave, etc.) having the hair cut very near to the roots: *a crew cut is a close haircut.* **32.** not deviating from the subject under consideration: *close attention; keep a close eye on.* **33.** strict; searching; minute: *close investigation.* **34.** not deviating from a model or original: *a close translation.* **35.** nearly even or equal: *a close contest.* **36.** strictly logical: *close reasoning.* **37.** *Phonetics* pronounced with a relatively small opening of the tongue, as *beet* and *boot* which have the closest English vowels. *–adv.* /kloʊs/ **38.** in a close manner; closely. **39.** near: *he lived close to the shops.* **40.** near the base, as in haircutting, shaving, etc.: *the barber shaved his beard close. –n.* **41.** /kloʊz/ the act of closing. **42.** /kloʊz/ the end or conclusion. **43.** /kloʊz/ *Music* → **cadence** (def. 5). **44.** /kloʊz/ a junction; union. **45.** /kloʊs/ an enclosed place; an enclosure; any piece of land held as private property. **46.** /kloʊs/ an enclosure about or beside a building, cathedral, etc. **47.** /kloʊs/ a narrow entry or alley, or a courtyard to which it leads; cul-de-sac. *–phr.* **48. close at hand,** within reach; nearby. **49. close at** (or **on**) **someone's heels,** following someone closely; just behind someone. **50. close down, a.** to cease operation. **b.** to cause to cease operation. **51. close in,** to surround and approach a place gradually, as in making a capture. **52. close on** (or **upon**), to agree on. **53. close out, a.** to nullify one's position in the futures market either by selling (from a bought position) or by buying (from a sold position). **b.** *Surfing* (of a wave) to break simultaneously along the entire face, offering no surface on which a surfer might manoeuvre. **c.** *Sport* to bring (a match) effectively to a close by making it impossible for an opponent to better one's score. **54. close up,** *Printing* to remove or reduce spacing between (set type). **55. close with, a.** to grapple with; engage in close encounter with. **b.** to come to terms with. **c.** *Naut.* to come close to. **56. keep a close eye on,** to maintain a careful scrutiny of. **–closely** /'kloʊsli/, *adv.* **–closeness** /'kloʊsnəs/, *n.* **–closer** /'kloʊzə/, *n.*

close call *n. Colloq.* a narrow escape.

closed /kloʊzd/ *adj.* restricted or exclusive in any of various ways.

closed-circuit television *n.* a television system in which cameras and receivers are linked by wire, used to watch what is happening in another part of a building for security, monitoring production operations, etc. Also, **CCTV.**

closed shop *n.* **1.** a workshop, factory, or the like, in which all employees must belong to a particular trade union. *–adj.* **2.** inflexible: *closed shop mentality.*

close quarters *pl. n.* **1.** a small, cramped place or position. **2.** direct and close contact in a fight.

closet /'klɒzət/ *n.* **1.** a small room, enclosed recess, or cabinet for clothing, food, utensils, etc. **2.** a water closet; toilet. *–adj.* **3.** secret: *a closet smoker; a closet romantic.* *–phr.* **4. come out of the closet,** to make public something about oneself which one has previously concealed, in particular to make one's homosexuality publicly known.

close-up /'kloʊs-ʌp/ *n.* **1.** a picture taken at close range or with a long focal length lens, on a relatively large scale. **2.** an intimate view or presentation of anything.

closure /'kloʊʒə/ *n.* **1.** the act of closing or shutting. **2.** the state of being closed. **3.** a bringing to an end; conclusion. **4.** a sense of completion or finality experienced upon the resolution of a conflict, acceptance of a loss, etc. **5.** a metal or plastic cap for a bottle. **6.** *Psychol.* the tendency to see a complete figure even though a part or parts are missing, the gaps being filled from the viewer's past experience of what is depicted.

clot /klɒt/ *n.* **1.** a mass or lump. **2.** a semisolid mass, as of coagulated blood. **3.** *Colloq.* a stupid person.

cloth /klɒθ/ *n.* (*pl.* **cloths** /klɒθs/) **1.** a fabric formed by weaving, felting, etc., from wool, hair, silk, flax, cotton, or other fibre, used for garments, upholstery, and many other purposes. **2.** a piece of such a fabric for a particular purpose: *a tray cloth.* **3.** in theatre, a painted fabric used as a curtain or as scenery. **4.** a particular profession, especially that of a clergyman.

clothe /kloʊð/ *v.t.* **1.** to dress; attire. **2.** to provide with clothing. **3.** to cover with, or as with, clothing. **4.** to endow; invest (as with meaning). **5.** to conceal.

clothes /kloʊðz/ *pl. n.* **1.** garments for the body; articles of dress; wearing apparel. **2.** bedclothes.

clothes hoist *n.* a device consisting of a square, rotating frame, which may be raised or lowered, supporting wires on which clothes may be hung to dry.

clothes horse *n.* **1.** a frame on which to hang clothes, etc., especially for drying. **2.** *Colloq.* someone who pays particular attention to dress and who wears clothes well, especially a model or mannequin.

clothes line *n.* **1.** a rope or wire on which clothes, etc., may be hung to dry. **2.** a device, such as a clothes hoist, on which to hang clothes to dry.

clothing /'kloʊðɪŋ/ *n.* **1.** garments collectively; clothes; raiment; apparel. **2.** a covering.

cloud /klaʊd/ *n.* **1.** a visible collection of particles of water or ice suspended in the air, usually at an elevation above the earth's surface. **2.** any similar mass, especially of smoke or dust. **3.** a dim or obscure area in something otherwise clear or transparent. **4.** *Obs.* a patch or spot, differing in colour from the surrounding surface. **5.** anything that obscures, darkens, or causes gloom, trouble, suspicion, disgrace, etc. **6.** a great number of insects, birds, etc., flying together: *a cloud of locusts.* **7.** a multitude; a crowd. *–adj.* **8.** of, relating to, or employing cloud computing: *cloud storage; cloud templates.* *–v.t.* **9.** to overspread or cover with, or as with, a cloud or clouds. **10.** to overshadow; obscure; darken. **11.** to make gloomy. **12.** to place under suspicion, disgrace, etc. **13.** to variegate with patches of another colour. *–v.i.* **14.** to grow cloudy; become clouded. *–phr.* **15. cloud over,** to become cloudy and dull. **16. have one's head in the clouds,** to be divorced from reality; be in a dreamlike state. **17. in the clouds, a.** imaginary; unreal. **b.** impractical. **18. on cloud nine,** in a state of bliss. **19. the cloud,** *Computers* the software resources and other services, particularly storage, made available through the internet or other network. See **cloud computing. 20. under a cloud, a.** under suspicion. **b.** in doubt: *the club's future is under a cloud because funds are short.* **–cloudless,** *adj.* **–cloudy,** *adj.*

cloudburst /'klaʊdbɜst/ *n.* a sudden and very heavy rainfall.

cloud computing *n.* the provision of computer applications over the internet as a service to users of a particular site.

clout /klaʊt/ *Colloq.* *–n.* **1.** a blow, especially with the hand; a cuff. **2.** effectiveness; force: *the committee has no political clout.* *–v.t.* **3.** to strike, especially with the hand; cuff. **4.** Also, **clout on.** *Aust.* to cheat by evading payment, especially of a gambling debt; to welsh.

clove[1] /kloʊv/ *n.* the dried flower bud of a tropical tree, *Syzygium aromaticum,* used whole or ground as a spice.

clove[2] /kloʊv/ *n.* one of the small bulbs formed in the axils of the scales of a mother bulb, as in garlic.

clove[3] /kloʊv/ *v.* past tense of **cleave**[2].

cloven /'kloʊvən/ *v.* **1.** past participle of **cleave**[2]. *–adj.* **2.** cleft; split; divided: *cloven feet; cloven hoofs.*

clover /'kloʊvə/ *n.* **1.** any of various herbs of the genus *Trifolium,* with trifoliolate leaves and dense flower heads, many species of which, such as *T. pratense* (the common **red clover**), are cultivated as forage plants or as a pasture improvement plant, such as **subterranean clover.** *–phr.* **2. in clover,** in comfort or luxury.

clown /klaʊn/ *n.* **1.** a jester or buffoon in a circus, pantomime, etc. **2.** *Colloq.* a fool; an idiot. **3.** a peasant; a rustic. **4.** a coarse, ill-bred person; a boor. *–v.i.* **5.** to act like a clown. **–clownish,** *adj.* **–clownishly,** *adv.* **–clownishness, clownery,** *n.*

cloy /klɔɪ/ *v.t.* to weary by an excess of food, sweetness, pleasure, etc.; surfeit; satiate. **–cloyingly,** *adv.* **–cloyingness,** *n.*

club /klʌb/ *n.* **1.** a heavy stick, usually thicker at one end than at the other, suitable for a weapon; a cudgel. **2.** a stick or bat used to drive a ball, etc., in various games. **3.** a stick with a crooked head used in golf, etc. **4.** a group of persons organised for a social, literary, sporting, political, or other purpose, regulated by rules agreed by its members. **5.** the building or rooms owned by or associated with such a group, sometimes lavishly decorated and furnished, and offering dining, gambling, theatrical, and other facilities to members. **6.** *Insurance* a friendly society. **7.** a black trifoliate figure on a playing card. *–verb* (**clubbed, clubbing**) *–v.t.* **8.** to beat with, or as with, a club. **9.** to unite; combine; join together. **10.** to defray by proportional shares: *to club the expense.* **11.** to invert (a rifle, etc.) so as to use as a club. *–v.i.* **12.** to combine or join together as for a common purpose. **13.** to gather into a mass. *–phr.* **14. club in, a.** to contribute as one's share of a general expense. **b.** to contribute to a common fund. **15. club together,** to combine one's resources, especially financial: *to club together to hire a boat.* **16. join the club,** *Colloq.* an acknowledgement that a person shares an experience or state with others.

club foot *n.* a deformed or distorted foot. **–clubfooted,** *adj.*

cluck /klʌk/ *v.i.* **1.** to utter the cry of a hen brooding or calling her chicks. **2.** to make a similar sound. *–n.* **3.** any clucking sound.

clucky /ˈklʌki/ *adj. Aust., NZ* **1.** (of a hen) broody. **2.** *Colloq.* feeling disposed to have children. **3.** *Colloq.* fussy and over-protective of children.

clue /klu/ *n.* **1.** anything that serves to guide or direct in the solution of a problem, mystery, etc. *–phr.* **2. clue someone up,** to give someone the facts. **3. not have a clue, a.** to be completely ignorant or without ideas on a subject. **b.** to be completely out of touch with what is happening.

cluey /ˈklui/ *adj. Colloq.* **1.** well-informed. **2.** showing good sense and keen awareness.

clump /klʌmp/ *n.* **1.** a cluster, especially of trees, or other plants. **2.** a lump or mass. **3.** a clumping tread, sound, etc. *–v.i.* **4.** to walk heavily and clumsily. **–clumpy, clumpish,** *adj.*

clumsy /ˈklʌmzi/ *adj.* (**-sier, -siest**) **1.** awkward in movement or action; without skill or grace: *a clumsy workman.* **2.** awkwardly done or made; unwieldy; ill-contrived: *a clumsy apology.* **–clumsily,** *adv.* **–clumsiness,** *n.*

clung /klʌŋ/ *v.* past tense and past participle of **cling.**

cluster /ˈklʌstə/ *n.* **1.** a number of things of the same kind, growing or held together; a bunch: *a cluster of grapes.* **2.** a group of things or persons near together: *a cluster of bombs.* *–v.i.* **3.** to form a cluster or clusters. **–clustery,** *adj.*

cluster headache *n.* a type of severe, recurrent, vascular headache, typically experienced as intense pain behind one eye or temple, and accompanied by the localised release of histamine, leading to runny nose and eyes and flushed skin.

clutch[1] /klʌtʃ/ *v.t.* **1.** to seize with, or as with, the hands or claws; grasp. **2.** to grip or hold tightly or firmly. *–v.i.* **3.** (fol. by *at*) to try to seize. *–n.* **4.** (*usu. pl.*) power or control; mastery: *in the clutches of the enemy.* **5.** the act of clutching; a snatch; a grasp. **6.** a tight hold; grip. **7.** (of a motor) a device which engages and disengages the engine from transmission, or the pedal which operates this device. **8.** → **clutch bag.**

clutch[2] /klʌtʃ/ *n.* **1.** a hatch of eggs; the number of eggs produced or incubated at one time. **2.** a brood of chickens. **3.** a group; a bunch.

clutch bag *n.* a woman's handbag with no handles.

clutter /ˈklʌtə/ *v.t.* **1.** to heap, litter, or strew in a disorderly manner. *–v.i.* **2.** to run in disorder; move with bustle and confusion. **3.** to make a clatter. *–n.* **4.** a disorderly heap or assemblage; litter.

co- **1.** a prefix signifying association and accompanying action, occurring mainly before vowels and *h* and *gn*, as in *coadjutor, cohabit, cognate.* **2.** a prefix signifying partnership, joint responsibility or ownership, as in *co-producer, co-writer.*

coach /kəʊtʃ/ *n.* **1.** a large, enclosed, four-wheeled carriage, used especially on state occasions. **2.** a stagecoach. **3.** a bus, especially a single-decker, used for long journeys or for sightseeing. **4.** a railway carriage. **5.** a person who trains athletes for games, contests, etc. **6.** a private tutor, especially one who prepares a student for an examination. *–v.t.* **7.** to give instruction or advice to in the capacity of a coach.

coachman /ˈkəʊtʃmən/ *n.* (*pl.* **-men**) someone employed to drive a coach or carriage.

coagulate /kəʊˈægjəleɪt/ *v.i.* **1.** to change from a fluid into a thickened mass; curdle; congeal. *–v.t.* **2.** to change (a fluid) into a thickened mass; curdle; congeal. **–coagulant,** *n.* **–coagulation** /kəʊˌægjəˈleɪʃən/, *n.* **–coagulative** /kəʊˈægjələtɪv/, *adj.* **–coagulator,** *n.*

coal /kəʊl/ *n.* **1.** a black or brown carbon-based sedimentary rock formed by the accumulation and decomposition of plant material and used as a fuel; main types are **hard coal** (anthracite), **soft coal** (bituminous coal), **brown coal** (lignite). *–phr.* **2. add coals to the fire,** to make a bad situation, dissension, etc., worse. **3. coals of fire, a.** good actions or the like in return for bad, giving rise to feelings of remorse. **b.** reproaches. **4. coals to Newcastle,** anything supplied unnecessarily. **5. haul over the coals,** to scold; reprimand.

coalesce /kəʊəˈlɛs/ *v.i.* (**-lesced, -lescing**) **1.** to grow together or into one body. **2.** to unite so as to form one mass, community, etc. **–coalescence,** *n.* **–coalescent,** *adj.*

coalface /ˈkəʊlfeɪs/ *n.* **1.** the part of the coal seam from which coal is cut. **2.** the place where ideas and theories have to be put into practice. *–phr.* **3. at the coalface,** at the place where the real work is done, as opposed to the administration, theorising, etc.

coalition /kəʊəˈlɪʃən/ *n.* **1.** a combination or alliance, especially, a temporary union between persons, political parties, states, etc. **2.** union into one body or mass; fusion. *–adj.* **3.** of, relating to, or deriving from such a union. **–coalitionist,** *n.*

coal seam gas *n.* gas, mostly methane, coming from fractures and cleats in coal seams and released when pressure on the coal seam is reduced, usually by the removal of water; mined as a source of energy. *Abbrev.*: CSG

coal washing *n.* a process in which coal is washed to remove pyritic sulphur, reducing sulphur dioxide pollution as the coal is burnt.

coarse /kɔs/ *adj.* **1.** of inferior or faulty quality; not pure or choice; common; base. **2.** composed of relatively large parts or particles: *coarse sand.* **3.** lacking in fineness or delicacy of texture, structure, etc. **4.** lacking delicacy of feeling, manner, etc.; not refined: *coarse manners.* **5.** rude or offensive: *coarse language.* **–coarsely,** *adv.* **–coarseness,** *n.*

coast /kəʊst/ *n.* **1.** the land next to the sea; the seashore. **2.** the region adjoining it. **3.** *US* **a.** the slope down which a sled travels. **b.** a slide or ride down a hill, etc. *–v.i.* **4.** to proceed or sail along, or sail from port to port of, a coast. **5.** to slide on a sledge down a snowy or icy hillside or incline. **6.** to travel on a downward slope, as on a bicycle, without using pedals, or in a motor vehicle with the engine switched off. **7.** to move along after effort has ceased; keep going on acquired momentum. **8.** to drift along without aim or effort: *the child is coasting at school.* *–phr.* **9. coast along,** to act or perform with minimal effort. **10. the coast is clear,** the danger has gone. **–coastal,** *adj.*

coaster /ˈkəʊstə/ *n.* **1.** a ship which trades from port to port along a coast. **2.** a small dish or mat placed under glasses, etc., to protect the table from moisture or heat.

coastguard /'koʊstgad/ *n.* a coastal police force responsible for preventing smuggling, watching for ships in distress or danger, etc.

coat /koʊt/ *n.* **1.** an outer garment with sleeves; an overcoat, dress coat, etc. **2.** a natural integument or covering, as the hair, fur, or wool of an animal, the bark of a tree, or the skin of a fruit. **3.** anything that covers or conceals: *a coat of paint.* –*v.t.* **4.** to cover with a layer or coating; cover as a layer or coating does. –**coatless**, *adj.*

coathanger /'koʊthæŋə/ *n.* a curved piece of wood, plastic, etc., with a hook attached, on which clothes are hung.

coat of arms *n.* **1.** a surcoat or tabard embroidered with heraldic devices, worn by medieval knights over their armour. **2.** the heraldic bearings of a person, corporation, city, etc.; hatchment; escutcheon.

coax /koʊks/ *v.t.* **1.** to influence by gentle persuasion, flattery, etc. **2.** to get or win by coaxing. –*v.i.* **3.** to use gentle persuasion, etc. –**coaxer**, *n.* –**coaxingly**, *adv.*

coaxial /koʊ'æksiəl/ *adj.* having a common axis or coincident axes.

cob /kɒb/ *n.* **1.** a corncob. **2.** a male swan. **3.** a short-legged, thickset horse. **4.** a small lump of coal, ore, etc. **5.** a roundish mass, lump, or heap.

cobalt /'koʊbɔlt, -bɒlt/ *n.* **1.** *Chem.* a silver-white metallic element with a faint pinkish tinge, occurring in compounds the silicates of which afford important blue colouring substances for ceramics. It is also used in alloys, particularly in cobalt steel. *Symbol*: Co; *relative atomic mass*: 58.9332; *atomic number*: 27; *density*: 8.9 at 20°C. **2.** a blue pigment containing cobalt. **3.** the isotope, cobalt 60; used in the treatment of cancer.

cobber /'kɒbə/ *n. Aust., NZ Colloq.* a mate; friend.

cobbler[1] /'kɒblə/ *n.* **1.** someone who mends shoes. **2.** a clumsy worker. **3.** an iced drink made of wine, fruit, sugar, etc. **4.** a fruit pie with a biscuit dough topping, usually made in a deep dish.

cobbler[2] /'kɒblə/ *n.* a wrinkled sheep that is difficult to shear, often shorn last in the day; snob. Also, **sandy cobbler**.

cobblestone /'kɒbəlstoʊn/ *n.* a rounded brick used in paving.

cobra /'kɒbrə, 'koʊbrə/ *n.* any snake of the genus *Naja*, exceedingly venomous and characterised by the ability to expand the skin of its neck so that it assumes a hood-like form.

cobweb /'kɒbwɛb/ *n.* **1.** a web or net spun by a spider to catch its prey. **2.** anything fine-spun, flimsy, or unsubstantial. **3.** anything obscure or confused: *the cobwebs of early medieval scholarship.* –**cobwebbed**, *adj.* –**cobwebby**, *adj.*

cocaine /koʊ'keɪn/ *n.* a bitter crystalline alkaloid, $C_{17}H_{21}NO_4$, obtained from coca leaves, though now replaced by synthetic derivatives, and formerly used in medicine as a local anaesthetic; also used illicitly as a central nervous system stimulant.

coccyx /'kɒksɪks, 'kɒksɪks/ *n.* (*pl.* **coccyges** /kɒk'saɪdʒiz/) *Anat.* **1.** a small triangular bone forming the lower extremity of the spinal column in humans, consisting of four ankylosed rudimentary vertebrae. **2.** a corresponding part in certain other animals. –**coccygeal** /kɒksə'dʒiəl, kɒk'sɪdʒiəl/, *adj.*

cochineal /kɒtʃə'nil, 'kɒtʃənil/ *n.* **1.** a red dye prepared from the dried bodies of the females of a scale insect, *Dactylopius coccus*, which lives on cacti of Mexico and other warm regions of Central America. **2.** the insect itself. **3.** the crimson colour of this dye.

cochlea /'kɒkliə/ *n.* (*pl.* **-leae** /-lii/ *or* **-leas**) *Anat.* a division, spiral in form, of the internal ear, in humans and most other mammals. –**cochlear**, *adj.*

cochlear implant *n.* an artificial hearing device which produces hearing sounds by stimulating inner-ear nerves by means of a pad of electrodes implanted into the cochlea which process sounds received from an external speech processor, and which is designed to restore some hearing ability to those with severe damage to the inner-ear nerves; bionic ear.

cock[1] /kɒk/ *n.* **1.** a male chicken. **2.** the male of any bird, especially of the gallinaceous kind. **3.** a device for permitting or arresting the flow of a liquid or gas from a receptacle or through a pipe; a tap or stop valve. **4.** (in a firearm) **a.** that part of the lock which by its fall or action causes the discharge; the hammer. **b.** the position into which the cock or hammer is brought by being drawn partly or completely back, preparatory to firing. **5.** *Colloq.* (*taboo*) the penis. –*v.t.* **6.** to pull back and set the cock or hammer of (a firearm) preparatory to firing. –*phr.* **7. cock and bull**, *Colloq.* nonsense; an incredible story. **8. cock of the walk**, a struttingly domineering person, as the leader of a gang.

cock[2] /kɒk/ *v.t.* **1.** to set or turn up or to one side, often in an assertive, jaunty, or significant manner. –*n.* **2.** the act of turning the head, a hat, etc., up or to one side in a jaunty or significant way. **3.** the position of anything thus placed. **4.** the angle to the wrist at which something is held: *the cock of the racquet.* –*phr.* **5. cock a snook** (or **snoot**), *Colloq.* to put a thumb to the nose, in a contemptuous gesture. **6. cock up**, to make a mess of; ruin: *you really cocked that up.*

cockade /kɒ'keɪd/ *n.* a knot of ribbon, rosette, etc., worn on the hat as a badge or a part of a uniform. –**cockaded**, *adj.*

cockamamie /kɒkə'meɪmi/ *adj. Colloq.* crazy; ridiculous; muddled.

cockatiel /kɒkə'tiəl/ *n.* a small, crested, long-tailed, Australian cockatoo, *Nymphicus hollandicus*, common in inland areas of the mainland.

cockatoo /kɒkə'tu/ *n.* **1.** any of various large gregarious parrots of the family Cacatuidae, of Australia, New Guinea and eastern Indonesia, having powerful hooked bills, erectile crests, and loud screeching calls; many species are commonly kept caged as pets and can be taught to talk. **2.** *Aust., NZ* a farmer, especially one who farms in a small way. **3.** *Aust. Colloq.* someone who keeps watch during a two-up game, or other illegal activity.

cockatoo apple *n.* a small tree, *Planchonia careya*, common in northern Australia, with bark used as a fish poison. Also, **cocky apple**.

cockerel /'kɒkərəl, 'kɒkrəl/ *n.* a young domestic cock.

cocker spaniel /kɒkə 'spænjəl/ *n.* one of a breed of small spaniels trained for use in hunting or kept as pets.

cockeyed /'kɒkaɪd/ *adj.* **1.** having a squinting eye; cross-eyed. **2.** *Colloq.* twisted or slanted to one side. **3.** *Colloq.* foolish; absurd.

cockfight /'kɒkfaɪt/ *n.* **1.** a fight between gamecocks, often with metal spurs attached to their legs, on the outcome of which spectators place bets. **2.** a game, often in water, in which contestants on piggyback try to unseat one another by grappling, etc. –**cockfighting**, *n.*

cockle /'kɒkəl/ *n.* **1.** any of the bivalve molluscs with somewhat heart-shaped, radially ribbed valves which constitute the genus *Cardium*, especially *C. edule*, the common edible species of Europe. **2.** any of the similar bivalve molluscs which constitute the Australian genus *Andara*. **3.** any of various allied or similar molluscs. **4.** a wrinkle; pucker. **5.** a small shallow or light boat. –*v.i.* **6.** to contract into wrinkles; pucker. –*v.t.* **7.** to cause to wrinkle or pucker: *a book cockled by water.* –*phr.* **8. cockles of the heart**, the depths of one's emotions or feelings.

cockney /'kɒkni/ n. 1. (oft. upper case) a native of London, especially the East End (often with reference to someone who has marked peculiarities of pronunciation and dialect). 2. this pronunciation or dialect. –**cockneyish**, adj.

cockpit /'kɒkpɪt/ n. 1. (in some aeroplanes) an enclosed space containing seats for the pilot and copilot. 2. the driver's seat in a racing car. 3. a recess aft, in the deck of a yacht or other boat, which provides a small amount of deck space at a lower level. 4. a pit or enclosed space for cockfights. 5. a place where a contest is fought, or which has been the scene of many contests or battles: Belgium, the cockpit of Europe.

cockroach /'kɒkroʊtʃ/ n. any of various insects of the order Blattodea, usually nocturnal, and having a flattened body, especially the dark brown or black **oriental cockroach**, Blatta orientalis, a common household pest.

cockscomb /'kɒkskoʊm/ n. 1. the comb or caruncle of a cock. 2. (formerly) the cap of a professional fool, resembling a cock's comb.

cocksure /'kɒkʃə/ adj. 1. perfectly certain; completely confident in one's own mind. 2. too certain; overconfident. –**cocksureness**, n.

cocktail /'kɒkteɪl/ n. 1. any of various short mixed drinks, consisting typically of gin, whisky, or brandy, mixed with vermouth, fruit juices, etc. often shaken, usually chilled and frequently sweetened, often served as an aperitif. 2. any mix of ingredients, especially one considered potent or dangerous: a cocktail of drugs; a dangerous cocktail of enthusiasm and ignorance. 3. a small piece of chicken, fish, etc., served as a savoury.

cocky¹ /'kɒki/ adj. (-kier, -kiest) Colloq. arrogantly smart; pertly self-assertive; conceited: a cocky fellow; a cocky air; a cocky answer. –**cockily**, adv. –**cockiness**, n.

cocky² /'kɒki/ n. (pl. cockies) Aust. Colloq. 1. a cockatoo, or other parrot. 2. NZ a farmer, especially one who farms in a small way. Also, **cockie**.

cocoa /'koʊkoʊ/ n. 1. the roasted, husked, and ground seeds of the cacao, Theobroma cacao, from which much of the fat has been removed. 2. a beverage made from cocoa powder. 3. brown; reddish brown.

coconut /'koʊkənʌt/ n. 1. the seed of the coconut palm, large, hard-shelled, lined with a white edible meat, and containing a milky liquid. 2. the edible white flesh of this seed, which may be eaten fresh or dried and used in cookery.

cocoon /kə'kun/ n. 1. the silky envelope spun by the larvae of many insects, such as silkworms, serving as a covering while they are in the chrysalis or pupal state. –v.t. 2. to enclose within a protective covering. 3. to put (a person) in an environment safe from bad news, violence, etc.

cod /kɒd/ n. 1. any of a number of largely unrelated fishes both freshwater and marine, such as the **Murray cod**, Maccullochella peeli, **butterfly cod**, Pterois volitans, **black rock cod**, Epinephelus damelii, etc., belonging to several different families and widely distributed in Australian waters. 2. any of a number of marine species of southern Australia belonging or related to the European cod family Gadidae, especially the **rock cod** and the ling. 3. one of the most important North Atlantic food fishes, Gadus callarias or G. morhua. 4. US any of several other gadoid fishes, such as the **Pacific cod**, Gadus macrocephalus.

coda /'koʊdə/ n. Music a more or less independent passage, at the end of a musical composition, introduced to bring it to a satisfactory close.

coddle /'kɒdl/ v.t. 1. to cook (eggs, fruit, etc.) slowly in water just below boiling point. 2. to treat tenderly; nurse or tend indulgently; pamper.

code /koʊd/ n. 1. any ordered collection of existing laws of a country, or of those relating to a particular subject: civil code of France. 2. any system or collection of rules and regulations: code of honour. 3. a system of symbols into which messages can be translated, for communication by telegraph, etc., or for secrecy: morse code; secret code. 4. a symbol (made up of signs, numbers, letters, sounds, etc.) in such a system. 5. a system of symbols for giving information or instructions to an electronic computer. –v.t. 6. to arrange in code; enter in code. 7. to translate into code.

codeine /'koʊdin/ n. a white, crystalline, slightly bitter alkaloid, $C_{18}H_{21}NO_3H_2O$, obtained from opium, used in medicine as an analgesic, sedative, and hypnotic.

co-dependent /koʊ-də'pɛndənt/ adj. 1. reliant on another to the extent that independent action is no longer possible. –n. 2. such a person. Also, **codependent**. –**co-dependency**, n.

coder /'koʊdə/ n. 1. someone who translates a text into a coded form. 2. Computers a device or application which converts data into a coded form. 3. Computers a person who writes code for a computer; programmer.

codeshare /'koʊdʃeə/ v.i. 1. (of an airline) to take part in codesharing. –adj. 2. of or relating to codesharing.

codesharing /'koʊdʃeərɪŋ/ n. a commercial agreement between two or more airlines that allows one airline to carry the passengers of the other on a particular route.

codger /'kɒdʒə/ n. Colloq. a man, especially elderly: a lovable old codger.

codicil /'kɒdəsɪl/ n. 1. a supplement to a will, containing an addition, explanation, modification, etc., of something in the will. 2. some similar supplement. –**codicillary** /kɒdə'sɪləri/, adj.

codify /'koʊdəfaɪ, 'kɒdə-/ v.t. (-fied, -fying) 1. to reduce (laws, etc.) to a code. 2. to digest; arrange in a systematic collection. –**codification** /koʊdəfə'keɪʃən, kɒdə-/, n. –**codifier**, n.

cod-liver oil /ˌkɒd-lɪvər 'ɔɪl/ n. a fixed oil, extracted from the liver of the common cod (def. 3) or of allied species, extensively used in medicine as a source of vitamins A and D.

co-education /ˌkoʊɛdʒə'keɪʃən/ n. joint education, especially of both sexes in the same institution and classes. Also, **coeducation**. –**co-educational**, **coeducational**, adj.

coefficient /koʊə'fɪʃənt/ n. 1. something that acts together with another thing to produce a result. 2. Maths a number or quantity placed (generally) before and multiplying another quantity: 3 is the coefficient of x in 3x. 3. Physics a quantity, constant for a given substance, body, or process under certain specified conditions, that serves as a measure of one of its properties: coefficient of friction.

-coele a word element referring to some small cavity of the body, as in neurocele, cystocele, etc. Also, **-cele**, **-coel**.

coelenterate /sə'lɛntəreɪt, -tərət/ n. 1. a member of the Coelenterata, a phylum of invertebrate animals that includes the hydras, jellyfishes, sea anemones, corals, etc., and is characterised by a single internal cavity serving for digestion, excretion, and other functions. –adj. 2. belonging to the Coelenterata.

coeliac /'siliæk/ adj. 1. of or relating to the cavity of the abdomen. 2. of or relating to coeliac disease. –n. 3. a person suffering from coeliac disease. Also, **celiac**.

coeliac disease /'siliæk dəziz/ n. a congenital disorder characterised by diarrhoea due to intolerance of the bowels to gluten. Also, **celiac disease**.

coemption /koʊ'ɛmpʃən, -'ɛmfən/ n. the buying up of the whole of a particular commodity, especially in order to acquire a monopoly.

coeno- a word element meaning 'common'. Also, **ceno-**; (*before vowels*) **coen-**.

coerce /koʊ'ɜs/ *v.t.* (**-erced, -ercing**) **1.** to restrain or constrain by force, law, or authority; force or compel, as to do something. **2.** to compel by forcible action: *coerce obedience.* **–coercion,** *n.* **–coercer,** *n.* **–coercive,** *adj.* **–coercible,** *adj.*

coeval /koʊ'ivəl/ *adj.* **1.** of the same age, date, or duration; equally old. **2.** contemporary; coincident. Also, **coaeval.** **–coevally,** *adv.*

coexist /koʊəg'zɪst/ *v.i.* to exist together or at the same time. **–coexistence,** *n.* **–coexistent,** *adj.*

coffee /'kɒfi/ *n.* **1.** a beverage, consisting of a decoction or infusion of the roasted and ground or crushed seeds (**coffee beans**) of the two-seeded fruit (**coffee berry**) of *Coffea arabica* and other species of *Coffea*, trees and shrubs of tropical regions. **2.** roasted coffee beans or a preparation of them made by grinding or crushing, used for making this beverage. **3.** the berry or seed of such plants. **4.** the tree or shrub itself. **5.** light brown.

coffee plunger *n.* a jug in which coffee can be brewed and the grounds pushed down to the base by means of a plunger.

coffer /'kɒfə/ *n.* **1.** a box or chest, especially one for valuables. **2.** (*pl.*) a treasury; funds. **3.** any of various boxlike enclosures. **4.** an ornamental sunken panel in a ceiling or soffit. *–v.t.* **5.** to deposit or lay up in or as in a coffer or chest.

coffin /'kɒfən/ *n.* the box or case in which a corpse is placed for burial.

cog /kɒg/ *n.* **1.** a tooth or projection (usually one of a series) on a wheel, etc., for transmitting motion to, or receiving motion from, a corresponding tooth or part with which it engages. **2.** a person of little importance, in a large organisation. **3.** *Carpentry* a rectangular piece of wood let into notches in two adjacent timbers to prevent sliding.

cogent /'koʊdʒənt/ *adj.* compelling assent or belief; convincing; forcible: *a cogent reason.* **–cogently,** *adv.*

cogitate /'kɒdʒəteɪt/ *v.i.* to think hard; ponder; meditate. **–cogitator,** *n.*

cognac /'kɒnjæk/ *n.* **1.** (*oft. upper case*) the brandy distilled in and shipped from the legally delimited area surrounding the town of Cognac, France. **2.** any brandy, especially one made in France.

cognate /'kɒgneɪt/ *adj.* **1.** related by birth; of the same parentage, descent, etc. **2.** related in origin: *cognate languages; cognate words.* **3.** allied in nature or quality.

cognisance /'kɒgnəzəns, 'kɒnə-/ *n.* **1.** knowledge; notice; perception: *to have cognisance of a fact; to take cognisance of a remark.* **2.** the right of taking judicial notice, as possessed by a court. Also, **cognizance.** **–cognisant,** *adj.*

cognition /kɒg'nɪʃən/ *n.* **1.** the act or process of knowing; perception. **2.** the product of such a process; thing thus known, perceived, etc. **–cognitive** /'kɒgnətɪv/, *adj.*

cognitive behaviour therapy *n.* a therapy for a range of behavioural, emotional and psychiatric problems which trains individuals to identify unhelpful thoughts or behaviours and to learn healthier thought patterns and behaviours to replace them; used to treat phobias, obsessive compulsive disorder, panic attacks and various other disorders. *Abbrev.*: CBT

cognomen /kɒg'noʊmən/ *n.* (*pl.* **-nomens** or **-nomina** /-'nɒmənə, -'noʊmənə/) **1.** a surname. **2.** any name, especially a nickname. **–cognominal** /kɒg'nɒmənəl, -'noʊmə-/, *adj.*

cogwheel /'kɒgwil/ *n.* a wheel with cogs, for transmitting or receiving motion.

cohabit /koʊ'hæbət/ *v.i.* **1.** to live together in a sexual relationship. **2.** (of things) to exist together. **–cohabitant, cohabiter,** *n.* **–cohabitation** /ˌkoʊhæbə'teɪʃən/, *n.*

cohabitation agreement *n.* an agreement between two people living or intending to live together in relation to property, specifying what each partner brings to the relationship and how it is to be divided if they should separate.

cohere /koʊ'hɪə/ *v.i.* (**-hered, -hering**) **1.** to stick together; be united; hold fast, as parts of the same mass. **2.** to agree; be congruous. **–coherence, coherency,** *n.*

coherent /koʊ'hɪərənt/ *adj.* **1.** cohering; sticking together. **2.** having a natural or due agreement of parts; connected. **3.** consistent; logical. **4.** *Physics* (of electromagnetic radiation, especially light) having its waves in phase. **–coherently,** *adv.*

cohesion /koʊ'hiʒən/ *n.* **1.** the act or state of cohering, uniting, or sticking together. **2.** *Physics* the state or process by which the particles of a body or substance are bound together, especially the attraction between the molecules of a liquid. **–cohesive,** *adj.*

cohort /'koʊhɔt/ *n.* **1.** any group or company. **2.** a crony; ally; supporter: *the union leader and his cohorts.* **3.** a group of people at the same level, as in education, skill development, etc.

coiffure /kwʌ'fjʊə/ *n.* a style of arranging or combing of hair.

coil /kɔɪl/ *v.t.* **1.** to wind into loops one above another; twist or wind spirally: *to coil a rope.* *–n.* **2.** a connected series of spirals or loops into which a rope or the like is wound. **3.** a single such loop. **4.** an arrangement of pipes, coiled or in a series, as in a radiator. **5.** *Elect.* a conductor, such as a copper wire, wound up in a spiral or other form.

coin /kɔɪn/ *n.* **1.** a piece of metal stamped and issued by the authority of the government for use as money. **2.** such pieces collectively. *–v.t.* **3.** to make (money) by stamping metal. **4.** to convert (metal) into money. **5.** *Colloq.* to make or gain (money) rapidly. **6.** to make; invent; fabricate: *to coin words.* *–v.i.* **7.** to counterfeit money, etc. *–phr.* **8. coin a phrase,** (*humorous*) to use an acknowledged cliché. **9. coin it,** *Colloq.* to make a lot of money. **10. pay someone in their own coin,** to treat someone as they have treated others. **11. the other side of the coin,** the other side of the argument; the opposing point of view. **–coinable,** *adj.* **–coinage,** *n.* **–coiner,** *n.*

coincide /koʊən'saɪd/ *v.i.* **1.** to occupy the same place in space, the same point or period in time, or the same relative position. **2.** to correspond exactly (in nature, character, etc.). **3.** to agree or concur (in opinion, etc.).

coincidence /koʊ'ɪnsədəns/ *n.* **1.** the condition or fact of coinciding. **2.** a striking occurrence of two or more events at one time apparently by mere chance. **3.** exact agreement in nature, character, etc. **–coincidental** /koʊˌɪnsə'dɛntl/, *adj.* **–coincidentally** /koʊˌɪnsə'dɛntəli/, *adv.*

co-interior angle /koʊ-ɪnˌtɪəriər 'æŋgəl/ *n.* *Maths* → **allied angle.**

coir /'kɔɪə/ *n.* **1.** the prepared fibre of the husk of the coconut fruit, used in making rope, matting, etc. *–adj.* **2.** made from coir.

coitus /'koʊətəs, 'kɔɪtəs/ *n.* sexual intercourse. Also, **coition** /koʊ'ɪʃən/. **–coital** /'koʊətl, 'kɔɪtl/, *adj.*

coke¹ /koʊk/ *n.* the solid product resulting from the distillation of coal in an oven or closed chamber, or by imperfect combustion, used as a fuel, in metallurgy, etc. It contains about 80 per cent carbon.

coke² /koʊk/ *n.* *Colloq.* cocaine.

col /kɒl/ *n.* **1.** *Physical Geog.* a saddle or pass between two higher-standing parts of a mountain range or ridge. **2.** *Meteorol.* the region of relatively low pressure between two anticyclones.

col-¹ variant of **com-**, by assimilation before *l*, as in *collateral.*

col-² variant of **colo-** before vowels, as in *colectomy*.

cola /ˈkoʊlə/ *n.* **1.** the cola nut. **2.** an extract prepared from it. **3.** a carbonated soft drink containing such an extract. **4.** the tree producing it. Also, **kola**.

colander /ˈkʌləndə, ˈkɒl-/ *n.* a strainer for draining off liquids, especially in cookery. Also, **cullender**.

cold /koʊld/ *adj.* **1.** having a relatively low temperature; having little or no warmth: *a cold day.* **2.** having a temperature lower than the normal temperature of the body: *cold hands.* **3.** producing or feeling, especially in a high degree, a lack of warmth: *I am cold.* **4.** dead. **5.** *Colloq.* unconscious because of a severe blow, shock, etc. **6.** deficient in passion, emotion, enthusiasm, ardour, etc.: *cold reason.* **7.** not affectionate, cordial, or friendly; unresponsive: *a cold reply.* **8.** lacking sensual desire; frigid. **9.** failing to excite feeling or interest. **10.** imperturbable. **11.** depressing; dispiriting: *cold misgivings.* **12.** having become faint or weak: *a cold scent.* **13.** distant from the object of search. **14.** unprepared: *he started cold in the race.* **15.** (of colours) blue in effect, or inclined towards blue in tone: *a picture cold in tone.* **16.** slow to absorb heat, as a soil containing a large amount of clay and hence retentive of moisture. –*n.* **17.** the relative absence of heat. **18.** the sensation produced by loss of heat from the body, as by contact with anything having a lower temperature than that of the body. **19.** Also, **the common cold.** an indisposition caused by a virus, characterised by catarrh, hoarseness, coughing, etc. –*phr.* **20. catch** (or **take**) **cold**, to suffer from a cold (def. 19). **21. cold comfort**, almost no consolation; negligible comfort. **22. cold feet**, loss of courage or confidence for carrying out some undertaking. **23. cold sweat**, perspiration and coldness caused by fear, nervousness, etc. **24. in cold blood**, calmly; coolly and deliberately. **25. in the cold**, neglected; ignored. **26. leave someone cold**, to fail to affect someone, as with enthusiasm, sympathy, etc.: *her ravings left him cold.* **27. the cold**, cold weather. **28. throw cold water on**, **a.** to dampen the enthusiasm of (a person); discourage. **b.** to dampen enthusiasm for (a plan, etc.). –**coldish**, *adj.* –**coldly**, *adv.* –**coldness**, *n.*

cold-blooded /ˈkoʊld-blʌdəd/ *adj.* **1.** without feeling; unsympathetic; cruel: *a cold-blooded murder.* **2.** *Zool.* of or relating to animals, such as fishes and reptiles, whose body temperature approximates to that of the surrounding medium. –**cold-bloodedly**, *adv.* –**cold-bloodedness**, *n.*

cold-call *v.t.* to attempt to sell a product or service by making an unsolicited call to (a prospective customer), usually by telephone. –**cold-calling**, *n.*

cold case *n.* a criminal investigation which has proved impossible to bring to a conclusion, usually for lack of evidence.

cold cream *n.* an emollient of oily heavy consistency, used to soothe and cleanse the skin, especially of the face and neck.

cold front *n.* *Meteorol.* the contact surface between two air masses where the cooler mass is advancing against and under the warmer mass.

cold-pressed /ˈkoʊld-prɛst/ *adj.* of or relating to an unrefined, high-grade oil produced from the first pressing of fruit, seeds, etc., such as olives, almonds, canola, etc., which are heated to produce the next output.

cold-shoulder *v.t.* to ignore; show indifference to.

cold sore *n.* *Pathol.* a vesicular eruption on the face often accompanying a cold or a febrile condition; herpes simplex.

cold storage *n.* **1.** the storage of food, furs, etc., in an artificially cooled place. **2.** abeyance; indefinite postponement.

cold turkey *Colloq.* –*n.* **1.** the sudden and complete withdrawal of narcotics as a treatment of drug addiction. –*adv.* **2.** without the aid of other drugs. **3.** without warning, rehearsal, preliminaries, or cushioning of any kind.

cold war *n.* intense economic and political rivalry just short of military conflict.

coleslaw /ˈkoʊlslɔ/ *n.* a dressed salad of finely sliced white cabbage. Also, **slaw**.

coleus /ˈkoʊliəs/ *n.* any plant of the genus *Coleus*, of tropical Asia and Africa, species of which are cultivated for their showy, coloured foliage.

colic /ˈkɒlɪk/ *n.* **1.** *Pathol.* paroxysmal pain in the abdomen or bowels. –*adj.* **2.** relating to or affecting the colon or the bowels. –**colicky** /ˈkɒlɪki/, *adj.*

coliform /ˈkɒləfɔm/ *n.* **1.** one of a group of rod-shaped bacteria of the intestine, such as *E. coli*, whose presence in water, for instance, is an indication of faecal contamination. –*adj.* **2.** of or relating to such bacteria.

-coline → **-colous**.

colitis /kɒˈlaɪtəs, kə-/ *n.* *Pathol.* inflammation of the mucous membrane of the colon.

collaborate /kəˈlæbəreɪt/ *v.i.* **1.** to work, one with another; cooperate, as in literary work. **2.** to cooperate treacherously: *collaborating with the Nazis.* –**collaboration** /kəlæbəˈreɪʃən/, *n.* –**collaborator**, **collaborationist** /kəlæbəˈreɪʃənəst/, *n.* –**collaborative**, *adj.* –**collaboratively**, *adv.*

collaborative economy *n.* → **sharing economy**.

collaborative law *n.* the practice of law based on a cooperative rather than an adversarial process, by which the disputing parties are helped by legal professionals to reach agreement without going to court; often used in divorce cases.

collage /kəˈlaʒ, kɒˈlaʒ, ˈkɒlaʒ/ *n.* a pictorial composition made from any or a combination of various materials, such as newspaper, cloth, etc., affixed in juxtaposition to a surface, and often combined with colour and lines from the artist's own hand.

collagen /ˈkɒlədʒən/ *n.* the protein contained in connective tissue and bones which yields gelatine on boiling.

collapsar /kəˈlæpsa/ *n.* a star which exhausts its fuel and then collapses, creating a black hole.

collapse /kəˈlæps/ *v.i.* (**-lapsed**, **-lapsing**) **1.** to fall or cave in; crumble suddenly: *the roof collapsed.* **2.** to break down; come to nothing; fail: *the project collapsed.* **3. a.** to sink into extreme weakness. **b.** (of lungs) to come into an airless state. –*n.* **4.** a sudden, complete failure; a breakdown.

collapsible /kəˈlæpsəbəl/ *adj.* **1.** designed to fold into a more compact or manageable size, as a pram, bicycle, etc. **2.** designed to collapse or give way under pressure or in an emergency, as a steering column in a motor vehicle. Also, **collapsable**. –**collapsibility** /kəlæpsəˈbɪləti/, *n.*

collar /ˈkɒlə/ *n.* **1.** something worn or placed round the neck, especially part of a garment such as a shirt, coat, etc. **2.** a leather or metal band put round an animal's neck to hold or identify it. **3.** the part of a harness round a horse's neck. **4.** *Machinery* an enlargement around a rod or shaft, serving usually as a holding or bearing piece. –*v.t.* **5.** to put a collar on. **6.** to seize by the collar or neck. **7.** *Colloq.* to seize, take or gain control of. **8.** to gain a monopoly over: *to collar the market in wool.* –**collarless**, *adj.*

collarbone /ˈkɒləboʊn/ *n.* → **clavicle**.

collate /kəˈleɪt, kɒ-/ *v.t.* **1.** to compare (texts, statements, etc.) in order to note points of agreement or disagreement. **2.** to put together (a document) by sorting its pages into the correct order. –**collator**, *n.*

collateral /kəˈlætərəl/ adj. **1.** positioned at the side. **2.** running side by side; parallel. **3.** accompanying or supporting the main thing; secondary: collateral security. **4.** descended from the same ancestor, but through a different line; not directly related. −n. **5.** property, etc., pledged as additional security for the payment of a loan. −**collaterally**, adv.

collateral damage n. unintended destruction or injury, especially unintended civilian casualties in a military operation.

collation /kəˈleɪʃən/ n. **1.** the act of collating. **2.** a description of the technical features of a book (volumes, size, pages, illustrations, etc.). **3.** a light meal.

colleague /ˈkɒlig/ n. an associate in office, professional work, etc. −**colleagueship**, n.

collect[1] /kəˈlɛkt/ v.t. **1.** to gather together; assemble: please collect all the books in the room. **2.** to gather and keep examples of (something): he collects stamps as a hobby. **3.** to gather (money) for rent, debts, winnings, gifts, etc. **4.** to regain control of (oneself, one's thoughts, etc.). **5.** to call for and take away: I'll collect it tomorrow. **6.** Colloq. to run into or hit, especially in a car, etc. −v.i. **7.** to gather together; assemble: a crowd collected to watch the fire. **8.** to build up in amount; accumulate: rainwater is collecting in the drainpipe. −**collection**, n.

collect[2] /ˈkɒlɛkt/ n. a brief written prayer to be used in Christian worship, usually preceding the lesson or epistle in the Communion service.

collectable /kəˈlɛktəbəl/ n. **1.** an object of great antiquarian value, such as a rare coin, often collected as an investment. **2.** an object of no intrinsic value, such as a matchbox or beer can, collected as a hobby or as a memento. −adj. **3.** of or relating to such an object. **4.** suitable for acquisition as a collectable. Also, **collectible**.

collective /kəˈlɛktɪv/ adj. **1.** forming a collection or aggregate; aggregate; combined. **2.** relating to a group of individuals taken together. −n. **3.** a collective body; aggregate. **4.** a communal enterprise or system, working towards the common good, as opposed to one admitting competition between individuals. −**collectively**, adv.

collective bargaining n. a non-institutionalised system of negotiation between employers and employees on matters such as pay and working conditions.

collective noun n. a noun that under the singular form expresses a grouping of individual objects or persons, such as herd, jury, and clergy. The singular verb is used when the noun is thought of as naming a single unit, acting as one, as family in his family is descended from Edward III. The plural verb is used when the noun is thought of as composed of individuals who retain their separateness, as my family are all at home.

collectivism /kəˈlɛktəvɪzəm/ n. the socialist principle of control by the people collectively, or the state, of all means of production or economic activities. −**collectivist**, n., adj. −**collectivistic** /kəlɛktəˈvɪstɪk/, adj.

collector /kəˈlɛktə/ n. **1.** someone employed to collect debts, tickets, taxes, etc. **2.** someone who collects books, paintings, stamps, etc., as a hobby.

college /ˈkɒlɪdʒ/ n. **1.** an educational institution, attended usually after high school, which gives certificates, diplomas and degrees in technical, professional and academic areas. **2.** an institution set up by members of a profession, as the Royal Australian College of Surgeons. **3.** a residence within a university, often established for students by churches. **4.** any of certain large private schools. **5.** an organised association of people having certain powers and duties: an electoral college.

collegial /kəˈlɪdʒiəl, kəˈlɪdʒəl/ adj. **1.** belonging or relating to a college. **2.** involving shared responsibility, as among a group of people working together.

collide /kəˈlaɪd/ v.i. **1.** to come together with force; come into violent contact; crash: the two cars collided. **2.** to clash; conflict.

collider /kəˈlaɪdə/ n. **1.** someone who or something which collides. **2.** Physics an accelerator (def. 3) in which the particles are made to collide.

collie /ˈkɒli/ n. a dog of any of certain intelligent varieties much used for tending sheep, especially one of Scottish breed, usually with a heavy coat of long hair and a bushy tail.

collier /ˈkɒliə/ n. **1.** a ship for carrying coal. **2.** a sailor in such a ship. **3.** a coalminer.

colliery /ˈkɒljəri/ n. (pl. -ries) a coalmine, including all buildings and equipment.

collision /kəˈlɪʒən/ n. **1.** the act of colliding; a coming violently into contact; crash. **2.** a clash; conflict.

collocate /ˈkɒləkeɪt/(-cated, -cating) **1.** to set or place together. −n. **2.** → **collocation** (def. 3c).

collocation /kɒləˈkeɪʃən/ n. **1.** the act of collocating. **2.** the state or manner of being collocated. **3.** Ling. **a.** the recurrent juxtaposition of certain words, as in broad daylight. **b.** the habitual co-occurrence of certain words, as for example hospital and nurse. **c.** Also, **collocate**. a word so regularly juxtaposed or co-occurring. −**collocational**, adj.

colloid /ˈkɒlɔɪd/ n. **1.** Chem. a substance present in solution in the colloidal state. See **colloidal state**. **2.** Pathol. a homogeneous gelatinous substance occurring in some diseased states. −**colloidal**, adj.

colloidal state n. Chem. a system of particles in a dispersion medium in which the particle diameters are between 10^{-7}m and 10^{-9}m, i.e. between a true molecular solution and a coarse suspension.

colloquial /kəˈloʊkwiəl/ adj. **1.** appropriate to or characteristic of conversational speech or writing in which the speaker or writer is under no particular constraint to choose standard, formal, conservative, deferential, polite, or grammatically unchallengeable words, but feels free to choose words as appropriate from the informal, slang, vulgar, or taboo elements of the lexicon. **2.** conversational. −**colloquialism**, n. −**colloquially**, adv. −**colloquialness**, **colloquiality**, n.

colloquium /kəˈloʊkwiəm/ n. (pl. -quia or -quiums) an informal conference or group discussion.

colloquy /ˈkɒləkwi/ n. (pl. -quies) **1.** a speaking together; a conversation. **2.** a literary composition in dialogue form. −**colloquist**, n.

collude /kəˈlud/ v.i. **1.** to act together through a secret understanding. **2.** to conspire in a fraud.

collusion /kəˈluʒən/ n. agreement or cooperation, usually secret, for the purpose of fraud, deception, or the gaining of an advantage at the expense of others.

colo- a combining form of **colon**[2] as in colostomy.

cologne /kəˈloʊn/ n. a perfumed toilet water; eau de Cologne.

colon[1] /ˈkoʊlən/ n. a point of punctuation (:) marking off a main portion of a sentence (intermediate in force between the semicolon and the period).

colon[2] /ˈkoʊlən/ n. (pl. -lons or -la /-lə/) Anat. the portion of the large intestine which extends from the caecum to the rectum.

colonel /ˈkɜnəl/ n. Army **1.** a commissioned officer in the Australian Army ranking below brigadier and above lieutenant colonel. **2.** the rank. Abbrev.: COL. −**colonelcy**, **colonelship**, n.

colonial /kəˈloʊniəl/ adj. **1.** of or relating to a colony or colonies. **2.** of or relating to a colonist: paternalism is something demanded by the colonial outlook. **3.** Ecol.

forming a colony. **–colonialism,** *n.* **–colonialist,** *adj.*, *n.* **–colonially,** *adv.*

colonise /'kɒlənaɪz/ *v.t.* to plant or establish a colony in; form into a colony; settle: *England colonised Australia.* Also, **colonize.** **–colonisation,** *n.* **–coloniser,** *n.*

colonnade /'kɒləneɪd, kɒlə'neɪd/ *n.* **1.** a series of columns set at regular intervals, and usually supporting an entablature, a roof, or a series of arches. **2.** a long row of trees. **–colonnaded,** *adj.*

colony /'kɒləni/ *n.* (*pl.* **-nies**) **1.** a group of people who leave their native country to form a settlement in a new land ruled by, or connected with, the parent state. **2.** the area thus settled. **3.** any of several settlements in Australia before the achievement of responsible government. **4.** a group of people from a particular foreign country or with a common occupation living in a city or country, especially close together. **5.** a group of bacteria growing together as descendants of a single cell. **6.** *Ecol.* group of animals or plants of the same kind, existing close together. **–colonist,** *n.*

colophon /'kɒləfɒn, -fən/ *n.* **1.** an inscription at the close of a book, used especially in the 15th and 16th centuries, giving the title, author, and other publication facts. **2.** a publisher's distinctive emblem.

color /'kʌlə/ *n.*, *v.t.*, *v.i.* → **colour.** **–colored,** *adj.* **–colorer,** *n.* **–colorful,** *adj.* **–colorist,** *n.* **–colorless,** *adj.*

coloratura /kɒlərə'tjʊrə/ *n.* *Music* runs, trills, and other florid decorations in vocal music. Also, **colorature** /'kɒlərətʃʊə/.

colossal /kə'lɒsəl/ *adj.* **1.** gigantic; huge; vast. **2.** great in amount, extent, degree, or importance: *a colossal waste of time.* **–colossally,** *adv.*

colossus /kə'lɒsəs/ *n.* (*pl.* **-lossi** /-'lɒsaɪ/ *or* **-lossuses**) **1.** a huge statue. **2.** a thing or person of great size or importance.

colostomy /kə'lɒstəmi/ *n.* (*pl.* **-tomies**) the surgical formation of an artificial anus from an opening in the colon fixed onto the abdominal wall.

colour /'kʌlə/ *n.* **1.** the evaluation by the visual sense of that quality of light (reflected or transmitted by a substance) which is basically determined by its spectral composition; that quality of a visual sensation distinct from form. **2.** complexion. **3.** a ruddy complexion. **4.** skin pigmentation as an indication of ethnicity or race. **5.** a blush. **6.** vivid or distinctive quality, as of literary work. **7.** details in description, customs, speech, habits, etc., of a place or period, included for the sake of realism: *a novel about the Rum Rebellion with much local colour.* **8.** something that is used for colouring; pigment; paint; dye. **9.** the general effect of all the hues entering into the composition of a picture. **10.** in printing, the amount and quality of ink used. **11.** (*pl.*) any distinctive colour, symbol, badge, etc., of identification: *the colours of a school*; *the colours of a jockey.* **12.** (*pl.*) an award made to outstanding members of a school team: *cricket colours.* **13.** (*pl.*) a flag, ensign, etc., as of a military body or ship. **14.** outward appearance or aspect; guise or show. **15.** a pretext. **16.** kind; sort; variety; general character. **17.** timbre of sound. **18.** an apparent or prima-facie right or ground (especially in legal sense): *to hold possession under colour of title.* **19. a.** a trace or particle of valuable mineral, especially gold, as shown by washing auriferous gravel, etc. **b.** (*oft. pl.*) traces or particles of opal in the potch. **20.** heraldic tincture. **–v.t. 21.** to give or apply colour to; tinge; paint; dye. **22.** to cause to appear different from the reality. **23.** to give a special character or distinguishing quality to: *an account coloured by personal feelings.* **–v.i. 24.** to take on or change colour. **25.** to flush; blush. **–phr. 26. change colour,** (of a person) to turn pale or red. **27. colour in,** to colour (an outline drawing) with paint, crayon, etc. **28. give** (or **lend**) **colour to,** to make probable or realistic. **29. join**

the colours, to enlist in the army. **30. lose colour,** to turn pale. **31. nail one's colours to the mast,** to commit oneself to a party, action, etc. **32. off colour,** not well; indisposed. **33. person** (**man,** **woman,** **etc.**) **of colour,** *Chiefly US* a person (man, woman, etc.,) who is not white (def. 5), especially an African American. **34. show one's true colours,** to reveal one's true nature, opinions, etc. **35. with flying colours,** with dash and brilliance. Also, **color.** **–colourer,** *n.*

colour blindness *n.* defective colour perception, independent of the capacity for distinguishing light and shade, and form. Also, **color blindness.** **–colourblind,** *adj.*

coloured /'kʌləd/ *adj.* **1.** having colour. **2.** (*likely to give offence*) wholly or partly of non-white descent, as a person native to Africa, India, the Pacific islands, etc. **3.** specious; deceptive: *a coloured statement.* **4.** influenced or biased. **–n. 5.** (*likely to give offence*) a person wholly or partly of non-white descent. **6.** Also, **Cape Coloured.** (in the Western Cape province of South Africa) a person of mixed descent who speaks either English or Afrikaans. Also, **colored.**

colourfast /'kʌləfɑst/ *adj.* **1.** (of fabric dyes) lasting. **2.** (of materials) able to be washed without the colours running or fading. Also, **colorfast.** **–colourfastness,** *n.*

colourful /'kʌləfəl/ *adj.* **1.** characterised by bright colour or by many different colours. **2.** richly picturesque: *a colourful historical period.* **3.** (*euphemistic*) known for activities which are unconventional and possibly illegal. **4.** (*euphemistic*) characterised by taboo words: *colourful language.* Also, **colorful.** **–colourfully,** *adv.*

colouring /'kʌlərɪŋ/ *n.* **1.** the act or method of applying colour. **2.** appearance as to colour. **3.** specious appearance; show. **4.** a substance used to colour something. Also, **coloring.**

-colous a word element indicating habitat.

colt /koʊlt/ *n.* **1.** a male horse not past its fourth birthday. **2.** a young or inexperienced man. **–coltish,** *adj.* **–coltishly,** *adv.* **–coltishness,** *n.*

column /'kɒləm/ *n.* **1.** *Archit.* an upright, usually cylindrical, structure of greater length than thickness, usually used as a support; pillar. **2.** any column-like object, mass, or formation: *a column of smoke*; *a column of troops.* **3.** *Geol.* a sequence of rock units deposited through various periods of geological time. **4.** *Geol.* a cylindrical formation made by the union of a stalactite and stalagmite. **5.** one of two or more rows of printed matter going down a page. **6.** a vertical row of numbers. **7.** a regular article in a newspaper, etc., usually signed, and often dealing with a particular subject: *a political column.* **–columnar** /kə'lʌmnə/, *adj.* **–columniation,** *n.* **–columned** /'kɒləmd/, *adj.*

columnist /'kɒləmnəst, 'kɒləməst/ *n.* the editor, writer, or organiser of a special column in a newspaper.

com- a prefix meaning 'with', 'jointly', 'in combination' and (with intensive force) 'completely', occurring in this form before *p* and *b*, as in *compare*, and (by assimilation) before *m*, as in *commingle*. Compare **co-** (def. 1). Also, **con-, col-, cor-.**

coma¹ /'koʊmə/ *n.* (*pl.* **comas**) a state of prolonged unconsciousness, due to disease, injury, poison, etc.

coma² /'koʊmə/ *n.* (*pl.* **comae** /'koʊmi/) **1.** *Astron.* the nebulous envelope round the nucleus of a comet. **2.** *Optics* the aberration of optical systems by which rays of an oblique pencil cannot be brought to a sharp focus. **3.** *Bot.* a tuft of silky hairs at the end of a seed. **4.** the leafy branches forming the head of a tree.

comatose /'koʊmətoʊs/ *adj.* **1.** affected with coma; unconscious. **2.** *Colloq.* **a.** extremely lethargic. **b.** affected by alcohol, drugs, etc. **–comatosely,** *adv.*

comb /koʊm/ *n.* **1.** a piece of plastic, metal, etc., with teeth for arranging or cleaning hair, or for holding it in place. **2.** a card for dressing wool, etc. **3.** a fleshy comb-shaped growth on the head of a domestic fowl. **4.** → **honeycomb.** –*v.t.* **5.** to tidy or arrange (the hair, etc.) with a comb. **6.** (oft. fol. by *out*) to remove or separate as with a comb. **7.** to search thoroughly: *she combed the desk for the missing letter.* –*v.i.* **8.** (of a wave) to roll over or break.

combat *verb* (**-bated, -bating**) –*v.t.* /ˈkɒmbæt, kəmˈbæt/ **1.** to fight or contend against; oppose vigorously. –*v.i.* /ˈkɒmbæt, kəmˈbæt/ **2.** (sometimes fol. by *with* or *against*) to fight; battle; contend. –*n.* /ˈkɒmbæt/ **3.** a fight between two people, armies, etc. –**combatable** /kəmˈbætəbəl/, *adj.* –**combater**, *n.* –**combative**, *adj.*

combatant /kəmˈbætənt, ˈkɒmbətənt/ *n.* **1.** a person or group that fights. –*adj.* **2.** combating; fighting. **3.** disposed to combat.

combination /kɒmbəˈneɪʃən/ *n.* **1.** the act of combining. **2.** the state of being combined. **3.** a number of things combined. **4.** something formed by combining. **5.** the set or series of numbers or letters used in setting the mechanism of a certain type of lock (**combination lock**) used on safes, etc. **6.** *Maths* a selection of a specified number of different objects from a given larger number of different objects. –**combinational**, *adj.*

combine *v.t.* /kəmˈbaɪn/ **1.** to bring or join into a close union or whole; unite; associate; coalesce. –*v.i.* /kəmˈbaɪn/ **2.** to enter into chemical union. –*n.* /ˈkɒmbaɪn/ **3.** a combination. **4.** a combination of persons or groups for the furtherance of their political, commercial, or other interests. **5.** → **combine harvester.** –**combinable**, *adj.* –**combiner**, *n.*

combine harvester *n.* a machine that simultaneously combines the operations of reaping, threshing, and winnowing grain crops.

comb-over *n.* a hairstyle favoured by balding men in which the hair is parted low on the side and combed over to cover the top of the head. Also, **comb-across.**

combustible /kəmˈbʌstəbəl/ *adj.* **1.** capable of catching fire and burning; flammable. **2.** easily excited. –**combustibility** /kəmbʌstəˈbɪləti/, **combustibleness**, *n.*

combustion /kəmˈbʌstʃən/ *n.* the act or process of burning. –**combustive**, *adj.*

come /kʌm/ *verb* (**came, come, coming**) –*v.i.* **1.** to move towards the speaker or towards a particular place; approach. **2.** to arrive by movement or in course of progress; approach or arrive in time, succession, etc. (sometimes in subjunctive use preceding its subject): *when Christmas comes*; *come Christmas.* **3.** to move into view; appear: *the light comes and goes.* **4.** to extend; reach: *the shorts will come to your knees.* **5.** to take place; occur; happen. **6.** to occur at a certain point, position, etc. **7.** to be available, produced, offered, etc.: *toothpaste comes in a tube.* **8.** to occur to the mind. **9.** to befall a person. **10.** to issue; emanate; be derived. **11.** to arrive or appear as a result: *this comes of carelessness.* **12.** to enter or be brought into a specified state or condition: *to come into use.* **13.** to enter into being or existence; be born. **14.** *Colloq.* to have an orgasm. –*v.* (*copular*) **15.** to become: *to come untied.* **16.** to turn out to be: *his dream came true.* –*v.t.* *Colloq.* **17.** to produce; cause: *don't come that rubbish.* **18.** to play the part of. –*interj.* **19. a.** used to call attention, express remonstrance, etc.: *come, that will do.* **b.** often repeated in order to comfort, calm, etc.: *come, come, what's all the fuss.* –*n.* Also, **cum. 20.** semen. –*phr.* **21. as ... they come,** as (good, bad, typical, etc.) as can be found: *this computer is as fast as they come.* **22. come about, a.** to arrive in due course; come to pass. **b.** to tack (in a boat). **23. come across, a.** to meet with, especially by chance. **b.** to communicate successfully; be understood. **c.** *Colloq.* to pay or give. **d.** *Colloq.* to agree to have sexual intercourse. **24. come again, a.** to return. **b.** *Colloq.* a request that the speaker repeat what he or she has just said. **25. come along,** to make haste; hurry. **26. come and ...,** a phrase creating an imperative: *come and see what I have done.* **27. come around, a.** to relent. **b.** to recover consciousness; revive. **c.** to change direction, point of view, etc. **28. come at, a.** to reach. **b.** to rush at; attack. **c.** *Colloq.* to agree to do: *he won't come at that.* **29. come back, a.** to return, especially in memory. **b.** to return to a former position or state. **c.** to retort. **d.** to be reincarnated: *to come back as a dog.* **30. come back at,** to retaliate against. **31. come by, a.** to obtain; acquire. **b.** to stop for a brief visit. **32. come clean,** *Colloq.* to confess: *after years of lying they have finally come clean.* **33. come down, a.** to lose wealth, rank, etc. **b.** to be handed down by tradition or inheritance. **c.** to travel, especially from a town. **d.** to cease to be under the effects of a drug. **e.** *Brit.* to leave a university. **34. come down (heavily) on,** to punish severely. **35. come down off,** to cease to feel the heightened effects of (a drug, an exhilarating experience, etc.). **36. come down with,** to become afflicted with, especially with a disease. **37. come forward,** to offer one's services, etc.; volunteer. **38. come from, a.** to derive or be obtained from. **b.** to live in, or to have been born or brought up in: *I come from Perth.* **39. come from behind,** to improve (in sport, business, etc.) so as to overtake rivals. **40. come good,** *Colloq.* to improve after an unpromising beginning. **41. come in, a.** to enter. **b.** to arrive. **c.** to become useful, fashionable, etc. **d.** to finish in a race or competition. **e.** (of odds on a horse, dog, etc.) to become lower. **42. come in handy,** *Colloq.* to be useful. **43. come in spinner,** *Colloq.* in two-up, a call to the spinner to toss the coins. **44. come into, a.** to get. **b.** to inherit. **45. come of age, a.** to reach the age of legal responsibility. **b.** to become mature: *the nation has come of age.* **46. come off, a.** to happen; occur. **b.** to be completed; result: *how did the game come off?* **c.** to reach the end; acquit oneself: *to come off with honours.* **d.** to become detached or unfastened. **47. come off it,** *Colloq.* a request that someone be reasonable: *Come off it, mate!* **48. come on, a.** to meet unexpectedly. **b.** to make progress; develop. **c.** to appear onstage. **d.** to begin; start. **e.** to hurry. **f.** to germinate; grow, as grain. **49. come on (a bit) strong,** to express oneself rather too forcefully. **50. come on to,** *Colloq.* to make sexual advances to. **51. come out, a.** to appear; be published. **b.** to be revealed; show itself. **c.** to make a debut in society, on the stage, etc. **d.** to emerge; reach the end. **e.** (of a photograph) to be developed successfully. **f.** to declare one's homosexuality. **g.** to turn out (as specified): *the clothes came out clean.* **52. come out of the woodwork,** to appear as from nowhere. **53. come out with, a.** to tell; say. **b.** to bring out; publish. **c.** to blurt out. **54. come over,** to happen to; affect: *what's come over him?* **55. come round, a.** to relent. **b.** to recover consciousness; revive. **c.** to change direction, point of view, etc. **56. come the ... on,** to attempt a specified deception: *don't come the martyr on me.* **57. come the raw prawn,** *Colloq.* (sometimes fol. by *with*) to try to put over a deception. **58. come through, a.** to succeed; reach an end. **b.** to do as expected or hoped. **c.** to pass through. **59. come to, a.** to recover consciousness. **b.** to amount to; equal. **c.** to take the way off a vessel, as by bringing its head into the wind, anchoring, etc. **60. come to light,** to be found after a lapse of time. **61. come to pass,** to occur. **62. come undone** (or **unstuck**) (or **unglued**), *Colloq.* (of a plan or a person) to be shown to be a failure. **63. come up, a.** to arise; present itself. **b.** to be presented for discussion or consideration. **c.** to arrive; travel, especially to a town. **d.** to finish up (as specified), especially after cleaning or polishing: *the table came up shiny.* **e.** *Brit.* to come into residence at a school or university. **64. come up against,** to meet, as a difficulty or opposition. **65. come**

up to, **a.** to equal. **b.** to approach; near. **66. come up trumps,** to be successful; perform well. **67. come up with, a.** to produce; supply. **b.** to present; propose. **c.** to come level with (another person, vehicle, boat, etc.). **68. come upon,** to meet unexpectedly. **69. how come,** a question asking how a situation described has arisen: *how come you're not going?*

comeback /'kʌmbæk/ *n.* **1.** a return to a former position, prosperity, etc., as after a period of retirement. **2.** *Colloq.* a retort; repartee. **3.** *Colloq.* an opportunity for redress.

comedian /kə'midiən/ *n.* **1.** an actor in comedy. **2.** a writer of comedy. **3.** a very amusing person.

comedown /'kʌmdaʊn/ *n.* **1.** an unexpected or humiliating descent from dignity, importance, or prosperity. **2.** a let-down; disappointment. **3.** a flash flooding of a dry creek.

comedy /'kɒmədi/ *n.* (*pl.* **-dies**) **1.** a play, film, etc., of light and humorous character, typically with a happy or cheerful ending; a drama in which the central motive of the play triumphs over circumstances and is therefore successful. **2.** that branch of the drama which concerns itself with this form of composition. **3.** the comic element of drama, of literature generally, or of life. **4.** any literary composition dealing with a theme suitable for comedy, or employing the methods of comedy. **5.** any comic or humorous incident or series of incidents. *–phr.* **6. comedy of errors,** a series of mistakes, with a comic effect.

comely /'kʌmli/ *adj.* (**-lier, -liest**) pleasing in appearance; fair. **–comeliness,** *n.*

come-on *n.* *Colloq.* **1.** a behaviour which indicates a desire to engage in sexual activity with someone: *she was insulted by his blatant come-on.* **2.** inducement; lure.

comestible /kə'mɛstəbəl/ *n.* something edible; an article of food.

comet /'kɒmət/ *n.* *Astron.* a celestial body moving around the sun in an elongated orbit, usually consisting of a central mass (the *nucleus*) surrounded by a misty envelope (the *coma*) which extends into a stream (the *tail*) in the direction away from the sun. **–cometary** /'kɒmətəri/, *adj.* **–cometic** /kɒ'mɛtɪk/, *adj.*

comeuppance /kʌm'ʌpəns/ *n.* *Colloq.* a well-deserved punishment or retribution; one's just deserts.

comfort /'kʌmfət/ *v.t.* **1.** to soothe when in grief; console; cheer. *–n.* **2.** relief in affliction; consolation; solace. **3.** the feeling of relief or consolation. **4.** a person or thing that affords consolation. **5.** a state of ease, with freedom from pain and anxiety, and satisfaction of bodily wants. **–comfortingly,** *adv.* **–comfortless,** *adj.* **–comfortlessly,** *adv.* **–comfortlessness,** *n.*

comfortable /'kʌmftəbəl, 'kʌmfətəbəl/ *adj.* **1.** producing or attended with comfort or ease of mind or body. **2.** being in a state of comfort or ease; easy and undisturbed. **3.** having adequate income or wealth. **4.** easily achieved, as a victory. **–comfortableness,** *n.* **–comfortably,** *adv.*

comfort zone *n.* a set of conditions within which someone feels comfortable in their ability to handle a situation, giving them a sense of being in control.

comic /'kɒmɪk/ *adj.* **1.** of or relating to comedy, as distinguished from tragedy. **2.** provoking laughter; humorous; funny; laughable. *–n.* **3.** a comic actor. **4.** a magazine containing one or more stories in comic strip form.

comical /'kɒmɪkəl/ *adj.* provoking laughter, or amusing; funny. **–comicality** /kɒmə'kæləti/, **comicalness,** *n.* **–comically,** *adv.*

comics /'kɒmɪks/ *pl. n.* comic strips, especially as a genre.

comic strip *n.* a series of cartoon drawings, in colour or black and white, relating a comic incident, an adventure story, etc.

comma /'kɒmə/ *n.* a mark of punctuation (,) used to indicate the smallest interruptions in continuity of thought or grammatical construction.

command /kə'mænd, -'mand/ *v.t.* **1.** to order, direct or demand, usually with the right to be obeyed: *she commanded him to go home; he commanded silence.* **2.** to have charge of or control over. **3.** to overlook: *a hill commanding the sea.* **4.** to deserve and get: *his position commands respect.* *–v.i.* **5.** to give orders or be in charge. *–n.* **6.** the act of commanding or ordering. **7.** an order; direction. **8.** *Mil.* **a.** an order given by an officer to a person of lower military rank. **b.** a body of soldiers, etc., or area, station, etc., under a commander. **9.** power to command or control; mastery. **–commanding,** *adj.* **–commandingly,** *adv.*

commandant /'kɒməndænt, -dant/ *n.* the commanding officer of a place, group, etc.; a commander.

commandeer /kɒmən'dɪə/ *v.t.* **1.** to order or force into active military service. **2.** to seize (private property) for military or other public use. **3.** to seize arbitrarily.

commander /kə'mændə, -'mand-/ *n.* **1.** someone who exercises authority; a leader; a chief officer. **2.** the chief commissioned officer (irrespective of rank) of a military unit. **3.** *Navy* **a.** a commissioned officer of the Royal Australian Navy ranking below captain and above lieutenant commander. **b.** the rank. *Abbrev.*: CMDR **4.** a rank in certain modern orders of knighthood. **–commandership,** *n.*

command line *n.* a line of keyed-in instructions to a computer, activated by pressing the carriage return.

commandment /kə'mændmənt, kə'mand-/ *n.* **1.** a command or edict. **2.** any one of the precepts (the **Ten Commandments**) recorded in the Old Testament as being spoken by God to Israel or delivered to Moses on Mount Sinai.

commando /kə'mændoʊ, -'man-/ *n.* (*pl.* **-dos** *or* **-does**) **1.** a member of a small specially trained fighting force used for making quick, destructive raids against enemy-held areas. **2.** a member of such a force. *–phr.* **3. go commando,** *Colloq.* to not wear underpants under one's outer clothing.

commemorate /kə'mɛməreɪt/ *v.t.* **1.** to serve as a memento of. **2.** to honour the memory of by some solemnity or celebration. **–commemoration** /kəmɛmə-'reɪʃən/, *n.* **–commemorative,** *adj.* **–commemorator,** *n.*

commence /kə'mɛns/ *verb* (**-menced, -mencing**) *–v.t.* **1.** to begin; start. *–v.i.* **2.** to have a beginning; come into being. **–commencement,** *n.* **–commencer,** *n.*

commend /kə'mɛnd/ *v.t.* **1.** to present or mention as worthy of confidence, notice, kindness, etc.; recommend. **2.** to entrust; give in charge; deliver with confidence: *into Thy hands I commend my spirit.* **–commendable,** *adj.* **–commendableness,** *n.* **–commendably,** *adv.* **–commendation,** *n.*

commensurate /kə'mɛnʃərət/ *adj.* **1.** having the same measure; of equal extent or duration. **2.** proportionate. **–commensurately,** *adv.* **–commensuration** /kəmɛnʃə-'reɪʃən/, *n.*

comment /'kɒmɛnt/ *n.* **1.** a note in explanation, expansion, or criticism of a passage in a writing, book, etc.; an annotation. **2.** a remark, observation, or criticism. *–v.i.* **3.** to make spoken or written remarks. **–commenter,** *n.*

commentary /'kɒməntəri, -tri/ *n.* (*pl.* **-ries**) **1.** a series of comments or annotations. **2.** an explanatory essay or treatise: *a commentary on the Bible* **3.** anything serving to illustrate a point; comment. **4.** a description of a public event, as a state occasion, sporting match, etc., broadcast or televised as it happens. **5.** a description accompanying a documentary film. **–commentarial** /kɒmən'teəriəl/, *adj.*

commentate /'kɒmənteɪt/ *v.i.* to act as a commentator.

commentator /'kɒmənteɪtə/ *n.* a writer or broadcaster who makes critical or explanatory remarks about news events, or describes sporting events etc.: *sports commentator.*

commerce /'kɒmɜːs/ *n.* **1.** interchange of goods or commodities, especially on a large scale between different countries (**foreign commerce**) or between different parts of the same country (**domestic commerce** or **internal commerce**); trade; business. **2.** social relations.

commercial /kə'mɜːʃəl/ *adj.* **1.** of or relating to commerce. **2.** likely to be sold in great numbers: *is the invention commercial?* **3.** setting profits or immediate gains above artistic considerations. **4.** not completely or chemically pure: *commercial soda.* **5.** *Radio, TV* dependent on the income from advertising. *–n.* **6.** *Radio, TV* an advertisement. **–commerciality** /kəmɜːʃi'æləti/, *n.* **–commercially**, *adv.*

commercial artist *n.* an artist who makes a living from creating artwork for commercial use, as for advertising, publishing, etc.

commercial bill *n. Finance* a security acknowledging a debt, signed by both the borrower (the drawer) and the lender (the acceptor) and stating the date on which repayment is due.

commercial-in-confidence *adj.* (of a business relationship, enterprise, etc.) based on the premise that commercial transactions undertaken are required to be regarded as being in confidence.

commercialise /kə'mɜːʃəlaɪz/ *v.t.* to make commercial in character, methods, or spirit; make a matter of profit. Also, **commercialize**. **–commercialisation** /kəmɜːʃəlaɪ'zeɪʃən/, *n.*

commercialism /kə'mɜːʃəlɪzəm/ *n.* **1.** the principles, methods, and practices of commerce. **2.** commercial spirit. **3.** a commercial custom or expression. **4.** (*often derog.*) preoccupation with profits or immediate gains. **–commercialist**, *n.* **–commercialistic** /kəmɜːʃə'lɪstɪk/, *adj.*

commercial law *n.* the principles and rules drawn chiefly from custom, determining the rights and obligations of commercial transactions.

commercial traveller *n.* a travelling agent, especially for a wholesale business house, who solicits orders for goods.

commiserate /kə'mɪzəreɪt/ *v.i.* **1.** (sometimes fol. by *with*) to sympathise. *–v.t.* **2.** to feel or express sorrow or sympathy for; pity. **–commiseration** /kəmɪzə'reɪʃən/, *n.* **–commiserative** /kə'mɪzərətɪv/, *adj.* **–commiseratively**, *adv.*

commissar /'kɒmɪsɑː/ *n.* (formerly) the head of a government department (commissariat) in any republic of the Soviet Union.

commissariat /kɒmə'seəriət, -iæt/ *n.* **1.** the department of an army charged with supplying provisions, etc. **2.** the organised method or manner by which food, equipment, transport, etc., is delivered to the armies. **3.** (formerly) any of the governmental divisions of the Soviet Union.

commissary /'kɒməsəri/ *n.* (*pl.* **-ries**) *Mil.* an officer of the commissariat. **–commissarial** /kɒmə'seəriəl/, *adj.*

commission /kə'mɪʃən/ *n.* **1.** the act of committing or giving in charge. **2.** an authoritative order, charge, or direction. **3.** authority granted for a particular action or function. **4.** a document or warrant granting authority to act in a given capacity or conferring a particular rank. **5.** a body of persons authoritatively charged with particular functions. **6.** the condition of being placed under special authoritative charge. **7.** the condition of anything in active service or use: *to be in commission; to be out of commission.* **8.** a task or matter committed

to one's charge. **9.** authority to act as agent for another or others in commercial transactions. **10.** the committing or perpetrating of a crime, error, etc. **11.** something that is committed. **12.** a sum or percentage allowed to an agent, salesperson, etc., for services. **13.** the amount or percentage charged for exchanging money, collecting a bill, or the like. **14.** the position or rank of an officer in the army or navy: *to hold a commission; to resign a commission. –v.t.* **15.** to give a commission to. **16.** to authorise; send on a mission. **17.** to put (a ship, etc.) in commission. **18.** to give a commission or order for. *–phr.* **19. put in** (or **into**) **commission**, *Navy* to transfer (a ship) to active service.

commissionaire /kəmɪʃə'neə/ *n.* a uniformed messenger or doorkeeper at a hotel, office, theatre, etc.

commissioner /kə'mɪʃənə/ *n.* **1.** someone commissioned to act officially; a member of a commission. **2.** a government official in charge of a department. **–commissionership**, *n.*

commit /kə'mɪt/ *verb* (**-mitted, -mitting**) *–v.t.* **1.** to give in trust or charge; entrust; consign. **2.** to commit for preservation: *to commit to writing; to commit to memory.* **3.** to hand over custody of to an institution, as a jail, etc. **4.** (of a magistrate) to send (an accused) to trial by jury: *to commit for trial.* **5.** to hand over for treatment, removal, etc.: *to commit papers to the flames.* **6.** to do; perform; perpetrate: *to commit murder; to commit an error.* **7.** to bind as by promise; pledge. *–v.i.* **8.** to enter into a long-term relationship with a sexual partner. **–commitment**, *n.* **–committable**, *adj.* **–committal**, *n.*

committed /kə'mɪtəd/ *v.* **1.** past tense and past participle of **commit**. *–adj.* **2.** devoted; wholeheartedly engaged: *a committed member of Amnesty International.* **3.** prepared to enter into a long-term relationship with a sexual partner. **4.** characterised by commitment: *a committed relationship. –phr.* **5. committed to, a.** obligated to: *committed to finishing the project.* **b.** strongly supportive of: *deeply committed to a cause.*

committee /kə'mɪti/ *n.* a person or a group of persons elected or appointed from a larger body to investigate, report, or act in special cases.

commode /kə'moʊd/ *n.* **1.** a piece of furniture containing drawers or shelves. **2.** a stand or cupboard containing a chamber-pot or washbasin.

commodious /kə'moʊdiəs/ *adj.* **1.** convenient and roomy; spacious: *a commodious harbour.* **2.** convenient or satisfactory for the purpose. **–commodiously**, *adv.* **–commodiousness**, *n.*

commodities market *n.* a market in which commodities are bought and sold, either immediately (the **spot market**) or more commonly for delivery at a future date (the **futures market**).

commodity /kə'mɒdəti/ *n.* (*pl.* **-ties**) an article of trade or commerce.

commodore /'kɒmədɔː/ *n.* **1.** *Navy* **a.** a commissioned officer in the Royal Australian Navy ranking below rear admiral and above captain. **b.** the rank. *Abbrev.*: CDRE **2.** the senior captain of a line of merchant vessels. **3.** the president or head of a yacht club or boat club. **4.** the ship of a commodore.

common /'kɒmən/ *adj.* **1.** belonging equally to, or shared alike by, two or more or all in question: *common property.* **2.** joint; united: *to make common cause against the enemy.* **3.** relating or belonging to the whole community; public: *common council.* **4.** generally or publicly known; notorious: *a common thief.* **5.** widespread; general; ordinary: *common knowledge.* **6.** of frequent occurrence; familiar; usual: *a common event; common salt.* **7.** hackneyed; trite. **8.** of mediocre or inferior quality; mean; low. **9.** coarse; vulgar: *his language is so common.* **10.** ordinary; having no rank, etc.: *a common soldier; the common people.* **11.** *Gram.* **a.** (in English grammar) denoting the gender of a noun or pronoun which can be used of both male and female referents, such as *student*, *artist*. **b.** denoting the case of English nouns and some pronouns which keep the same form of the word for both subject and object roles. **12.** *Prosody* (of a syllable) either long or short. *–n.* Also, **town common**. **13.** (*also pl.*) **a.** an unenclosed tract of land available for public pasture. **b.** an area of public land used by the community for recreation. **c.** (in Australia) a tract of land comprising a number of individual landholdings, managed and worked collectively by the group of landholders. *–phr.* **14. in common**, in joint possession, use, etc.; jointly. **–commonly**, *adv.* **–commonness**, *n.*

common denominator *n.* **1.** *Maths* an integer, usually the least, divisible by all the denominators of a set of fractions. **2.** an interest, belief, etc., shared by a group of people.

commoner /ˈkɒmənə/ *n.* one of the common people; a member of the commonalty.

common fraction *n.* *Maths* a fraction having the numerator above and the denominator below a horizontal or diagonal line (as opposed to a *decimal fraction*).

common gateway interface *n.* *Computers* a standard piece of communications software linking a web server to a program on a host machine. *Abbrev.*: CGI

common law *n.* **1.** the system of law originating in England, as distinguished from the civil or Roman law and the canon or ecclesiastical law. **2.** the unwritten law, especially of England, based on custom or court decision, as distinguished from statute law. **3.** the law administered through the system of writs, as distinguished from equity, etc.

common-law *adj.* **1.** based on or relating to the common law. **2. a.** relating to a marriage that is deemed in law to exist because the partners have cohabited for a certain period of time, though not having taken part in a formal marriage. **b.** relating to one of the partners in such a marriage: *a common-law wife*.

common market *n.* a group of countries which agree to trade with one another without tariffs, and to impose common tariffs on countries outside the group.

common noun *n.* *Gram.* (in English and some other languages) a noun that can be preceded by an article or other limiting modifier, in meaning applicable to any one or all the members of a class, such as *man*, *men*, *city*, *cities*, in contrast to *Shakespeare*, *Hobart*. Compare **proper noun**.

commonplace /ˈkɒmənpleɪs/ *adj.* **1.** ordinary; uninteresting; without individuality: *a commonplace person*. *–n.* **2.** a well-known, customary, or obvious remark; a trite or uninteresting saying. **–commonplaceness**, *n.*

common room *n.* (in schools, universities, etc.) a sitting room for the use of the teaching staff, or, in some cases, of the students.

commons /ˈkɒmənz/ *pl. n.* **1.** the common people as distinguished from their rulers or a ruling class; the commonalty. **2.** (*upper case*) the elective house of the parliament of Britain, Canada, and some of the other Commonwealth countries. **3. a.** → **common** (def. 13). **b.** *Internet* a website where material is freely available: *information commons*; *software commons*.

common sense *n.* sound, practical perception or understanding. Also, **commonsense**. **–commonsensical**, *adj.*

commonsense /kɒmənˈsɛns/ *adj.* (of an approach, solution, etc.) showing evidence of common sense. Also, **common-sense**.

common share *n.* → **ordinary share**. Also, *US*, **common stock**.

commonweal /ˈkɒmənwil/ *n.* the common welfare; the public good.

commonwealth /ˈkɒmənwɛlθ/ *n.* **1.** the whole body of people of a nation or state; the body politic. **2.** a federation of states and territories with powers and responsibilities divided between a central government and a number of smaller governments, each controlling certain responsibilities in a defined area. **3.** any body of persons united by some common interest.

commotion /kəˈmoʊʃən/ *n.* **1.** violent or tumultuous motion; agitation. **2.** political or social disturbance; sedition; insurrection.

communal /ˈkɒmjunəl, ˈkɒmjənəl/ *adj.* **1.** relating to a commune or a community. **2.** of or belonging to the people of a community: *communal land*. **–communalism**, *n.* **–communality** /kɒmjuˈnælɪti/, *n.* **–communally** /kəˈmjunəli, ˈkɒmjənəli/, *adv.*

commune[1] *v.i.* /kəˈmjun/ **1.** to converse; talk together; interchange thoughts or feelings. *–n.* /ˈkɒmjun/ **2.** interchange of ideas or sentiments; friendly conversation.

commune[2] /ˈkɒmjun/ *n.* **1.** the smallest administrative division in France, Italy, Switzerland, etc., governed by a mayor assisted by a municipal council. **2.** any community organised for the protection and promotion of local interests, and subordinate to the state. **3.** any community of like-minded people choosing to live independently of the state, often cherishing ideals differing from those held in the society: *hippy commune*.

communicate /kəˈmjunəkeɪt/ *v.t.* **1.** to give to another as a partaker; impart; transmit. **2.** to impart knowledge of; make known. **3.** (in writing, painting, etc.) to convey (one's feelings, thoughts, etc.) successfully to others. *–v.i.* **4.** to have interchange of thoughts. **5.** to have or form a connecting passage. **–communicator**, *n.* **–communicable**, *adj.*

communication /kəmjunəˈkeɪʃən/ *n.* **1.** the act or fact of communicating; transmission. **2.** the passing on or sharing of thoughts, opinions, or information. **3.** something which is communicated. **4.** an official paper or message containing views, information, etc. **5.** the passage or a means of passage between places. **6.** the science or process of sending information, especially by electronic or mechanical means. **7.** (*pl.*) the means of passing on information by telephone, radio, television, etc.

communicative /kəˈmjunəkətɪv/ *adj.* **1.** inclined to communicate or impart. **2.** talkative; not reserved. **3.** of or relating to communication. **–communicatively**, *adv.* **–communicativeness**, *n.*

communion /kəˈmjunjən/ *n.* **1.** the act of sharing, or holding in common; participation. **2.** the state of things so held. **3.** interchange of thoughts or interests; communication; intimate talk. **4.** *Eccles.* **a.** a body of persons having one common religious faith; a religious denomination. **b.** (*sometimes upper case*) the celebration of the Lord's Supper; the reception of the Eucharist.

communiqué /kəˈmjunəkeɪ/ *n.* an official bulletin or communication as of war news, events at a conference, etc., usually to the press or public.

communism /ˈkɒmjənɪzəm/ *n.* **1.** a theory or system of social organisation based on the holding of all property in common, actual ownership being ascribed to the community as a whole or to the state. **2.** a system of social organisation in which all economic activity is conducted by a totalitarian state dominated by a single and self-perpetuating political party. **–communist**, *n.*, *adj.* **–communistic** /kɒmjəˈnɪstɪk/, *adj.*

community /kəˈmjunəti/ *n.* (*pl.* **-ties**) **1.** all the people of a specific locality or country: *the new transport service is for the benefit of the whole community*. **2.** a particular locality, considered together with its inhabitants: *a small rural community*. **3.** a group of people within a society with a shared ethnic or cultural background, especially within a larger society: *the Aboriginal* *community*; *Sydney's Chinese community.* **4.** a group of people with a shared profession, etc.: *the scientific community.* **5.** a group of people living together and practising common ownership. **6.** a group of organisms, both plant and animal, living together in an ecologically related fashion in a definite region. **7.** joint possession, enjoyment, liability, etc.: *community of property.* **8.** similar character; agreement; identity: *community of interests.* –*adj.* **9.** (of a radio or television station) owned and operated by the community which uses it. –*phr.* **10. the community,** the public.

community bank *n.* (*from trademark*) a bank which is owned and managed locally and which serves the needs of the local community.

community correction order *n.* an order issued by a judge and encompassing a range of provisions such as home detention, drug treatment, community service, etc., carried out by the person sentenced who is released into the community rather than sent to jail.

community house *n.* → **group house.**

community medicine *n.* that branch of medicine that deals with the identification and solution of health problems which particular communities experience.

community policing *n.* a policing policy involving cooperation between police and a broad range of community organisations and representatives in forming arrangements for community safety.

community service order *n.* a court order which requires a person found guilty of a minor offence to perform some community service, often in lieu of going to jail.

commutation /kɒmjuˈteɪʃən/ *n.* **1.** the act of substituting one thing for another; substitution; exchange. **2.** the substitution of one kind of payment for another. **3.** the changing of a penalty, etc., for another less severe. **4.** *Elect.* **a.** the act of reversing the direction of the current. **b.** the act of converting an alternating current into a direct current.

commute /kəˈmjuːt/ *v.t.* **1.** to exchange (a thing, especially a payment) for another or something else. **2.** to change (a punishment, etc.) for one less severe: *the death sentence was commuted to life imprisonment.* –*v.i.* **3.** to travel some distance regularly between home and work, as from an outer suburb to the city. –*n.* **4.** a trip undertaken as a commuter: *a long commute to work.* –**commutable,** *adj.* –**commuter,** *n.*

comorbid /koʊˈmɔːbəd/ *adj. Med.* (of a medical condition) occurring with another medical condition: *comorbid alcoholism and psychiatric disorder.* –**comorbidity,** *n.*

compact¹ *adj.* /kɒmˈpækt, ˈkɒmpækt/ **1.** joined or packed together; closely and firmly united; dense; solid. **2.** arranged within a relatively small space. **3.** expressed concisely; pithy; terse; not diffuse. –*v.t.* /kɒmˈpækt/ **4.** to join or pack closely together; consolidate; condense. –*n.* /ˈkɒmpækt/ **5.** a small case containing a mirror, face powder, a puff, and (sometimes) rouge. –**compactness,** *n.*

compact² /ˈkɒmpækt/ *n.* an agreement between parties; a covenant; a contract.

compact disc *n.* → **CD.** Also, *Chiefly US,* **compact disk.**

compact fluorescent light bulb *n.* a small fluorescent light with its tube shaped in various compact ways, so as to fit into most standard light fittings; using less energy and having a longer life than a traditional light bulb. *Abbrev.:* CFL

companion /kəmˈpænjən/ *n.* **1.** someone who associates with another. **2.** a person, usually a woman, employed to be with or help another. **3.** someone or something that matches or goes with another. **4.** an information booklet: *the Golfer's Companion.* **5.** a member of the

lowest rank in an order of knighthood. –**companionship,** *n.* –**companionless,** *adj.*

companionable /kəmˈpænjənəbəl/ *adj.* fitted to be a companion; sociable. –**companionableness,** *n.* –**companionably,** *adv.*

companion animal *n.* a domestic animal, as a cat, dog, etc., kept primarily for companionship. Also, **animal companion.**

companionway /kəmˈpænjənˌweɪ/ *n. Naut.* **1.** the space or shaft occupied by the steps leading down from the deck to a cabin. **2.** the steps themselves.

company /ˈkʌmpəni/ *n.* (*pl.* **-nies**) **1.** a number of individuals assembled or associated together; a group of people. **2.** an assemblage of persons for social purposes. **3.** companionship; fellowship; association. **4.** a guest or guests. **5.** society collectively. **6.** an association, such as a corporation, formed by a group of people with a common purpose, such as the acquisition of profit by means of commercial enterprise: *a publishing company.* **7.** the member or members of a firm not specifically named in the firm's title: *John Jones and Company.* **8.** a number of persons associated for the purpose of presenting theatrical productions, etc. **9.** *Mil.* **a.** a subdivision of a regiment or battalion. **b.** any relatively small group of soldiers. **10.** *Naut.* a ship's crew, including the officers. –*phr.* **11. bear** (or **keep**) **someone company,** to associate or go with someone. **12. part company, a.** to cease association or friendship. **b.** to leave or separate from each other.

company tax *n.* a tax imposed on the profits of limited companies, intended to separate the taxation of companies from that of individuals.

company title *n. Law* (in Australia) a form of interest in property, particularly multi-storey buildings, where the whole of the building is owned by a company, shares in which are held by tenants.

comparable /ˈkɒmprəbəl, -pərəbəl/, *Orig. US* /kəmˈpærəbəl/ *adj.* **1.** capable of being compared. **2.** worthy of comparison. –**comparability** /kɒmprəˈbɪləti/, **comparableness,** *n.* –**comparably,** *adv.*

comparative /kəmˈpærətɪv/ *adj.* **1.** of or relating to comparison. **2.** proceeding by or founded on comparison: *comparative anatomy.* **3.** estimated by comparison; not positive or absolute; relative. **4.** *Gram.* denoting the intermediate degree of the comparison of adjectives and adverbs. –*n.* **5.** *Gram.* **a.** the comparative degree. **b.** a form in it, such as English *lower* in contrast to *low* and *lowest*, *more gracious* in contrast to *gracious* and *most gracious*. –**comparatively,** *adv.*

compare /kəmˈpɛə/ *verb* (**-pared, -paring**) –*v.t.* **1.** to represent as similar or analogous; liken (*to*). **2.** to note the similarities and differences of: *to compare apples with pears.* **3.** to bring together for the purpose of noting points of likeness and difference: *to compare two pieces of cloth.* **4.** *Gram.* to form or display the degrees of comparison of (an adjective or adverb). –*v.i.* **5.** to bear comparison; be held equal. –*n.* **6.** comparison: *joy beyond compare.* –*phr.* **7. compare notes,** to exchange views, ideas, impressions, etc. –**comparer,** *n.*

comparison /kəmˈpærəsən/ *n.* **1.** the act of comparing. **2.** the state of being compared. **3.** a likening; an illustration by similitude; a comparative estimate or statement. **4.** *Gram.* the function of an adverb or adjective used to indicate degrees of superiority or inferiority in quality, quantity, or intensity.

compartment /kəmˈpɑːtmənt/ *n.* **1.** a part or space marked or partitioned off. **2.** a separate room, section, etc.: *the compartment of a railway carriage*; *a watertight compartment in a ship.* –*v.t.* **3.** to divide into compartments. –**compartmental,** *adj.* –**compartmentalise, compartmentalize,** *v.*

compass /ˈkʌmpəs/ *n.* **1.** an instrument for determining directions, the chief part of which is a freely moving magnetised needle pointing to magnetic north and south. **2.** a line enclosing any area; measurement round. **3.** the space within limits; area; extent; range; scope. **4.** the total range of notes of a voice or musical instrument. **5.** (*usu. pl.*) an instrument for drawing circles, measuring distances, etc., consisting of two legs hinged together at one end. *–v.t.* **6.** to go or move round: *the sun compassed the earth.* **7.** to extend around. **8.** to understand. **–compassable**, *adj.*

compassion /kəmˈpæʃən/ *n.* a feeling of sorrow or pity for the sufferings or misfortunes of another; sympathy. **–compassionate**, *adj.* **–compassionately**, *adv.*

compatible /kəmˈpætəbəl/ *adj.* **1.** capable of existing together in harmony. **2.** capable of orderly, efficient integration with other elements in a system. **3.** (of a drug) capable of tolerating another drug without undesirable chemical reaction or effect. **4.** (of a computer peripheral) able to work in conjunction with another specified device. **–compatibility** /kəmpætəˈbɪləti/, **compatibleness**, *n.* **–compatibly**, *adv.*

-compatible a combining element meaning 'able to work in conjunction with another specified computer device', as in *IBM-compatible.*

compatriot /kəmˈpeɪtriət, -ˈpæt-/ *n.* **1.** a fellow countryman or fellow countrywoman. *–adj.* **2.** of the same country. **–compatriotism**, *n.*

compel /kəmˈpɛl/ *v.t.* (**-pelled**, **-pelling**) **1.** to force or drive, especially to a course of action. **2.** to secure or bring about by force. **–compellable**, *adj.* **–compeller**, *n.*

compelling /kəmˈpɛlɪŋ/ *adj.* **1.** (of a person, writer, actor, book, etc.) demanding attention or interest. **2.** convincing: *a compelling argument.* **–compellingly**, *adv.*

compendium /kəmˈpɛndiəm/ *n.* (*pl.* **-diums** *or* **-dia** /-diə/) **1.** a comprehensive summary of a subject; a concise treatise; an epitome. **2.** a boxed packet of stationery for letter writing.

compensate /ˈkɒmpənseɪt/ *v.t.* **1.** to counterbalance; offset; make up for. **2.** to make up for something to (a person); recompense. **3.** *Mechanics* to counterbalance (a force or the like); adjust or construct so as to offset or counterbalance variations or produce equilibrium. *–v.i.* **4.** to provide or be an equivalent. **5.** (sometimes fol. by *for*) make up; make amends. **–compensatory**, **compensative**, *adj.* **–compensator**, *n.*

compensation /kɒmpənˈseɪʃən/ *n.* **1.** the act of compensating. **2.** something given or received as an equivalent for services, debt, loss, suffering, etc.; indemnity. **3.** *Psychol.* behaviour which compensates for some personal trait, such as a weakness or inferiority. **–compensational**, *adj.*

compere /ˈkɒmpeə/ *n.* **1.** someone who introduces and links the acts in an entertainment. *–verb* (**-pered**, **-pering**) *–v.t.* **2.** to act as a compere in (a show, etc.). *–v.i.* **3.** to introduce and link together the acts of an entertainment.

compete /kəmˈpit/ *v.i.* to contend with another for a prize, etc.; engage in a contest; vie: *to compete in a race; to compete in business.*

competent /ˈkɒmpətənt/ *adj.* **1.** properly qualified; capable. **2.** fitting, suitable, or sufficient for the purpose; adequate. **3.** *Law* (of a witness, a party to a contract, etc.) having legal capacity or qualification. **–competence**, *n.* **–competently**, *adv.*

competition /kɒmpəˈtɪʃən/ *n.* **1.** the act of competing; rivalry. **2.** a contest for some prize or advantage. **3.** the rivalry between two or more business enterprises to secure the patronage of prospective buyers. **4.** a competitor or competitors.

competitive /kəmˈpɛtɪtɪv/ *adj.* of, relating to, involving, or decided by competition: *competitive examination.* **–competitively**, *adv.* **–competitiveness**, *n.*

competitor /kəmˈpɛtətə/ *n.* someone who competes; a rival.

compile /kəmˈpaɪl/ *v.t.* **1.** to put together (literary materials) in one book or work. **2.** to make (a book, etc.) of materials from various sources. **3.** *Computers* to create (a set of computer instructions) from a high-level language, using a compiler. **–compilation** /kɒmpəˈleɪʃən/, *n.*

compiler /kəmˈpaɪlə/ *n.* *Computers* a computer program which translates programming languages into the basic commands which activate the computer.

complacent /kəmˈpleɪsənt/ *adj.* pleased, especially with oneself or one's own merits, advantages, etc.; self-satisfied. **–complacency**, *n.* **–complacently**, *adv.*

complain /kəmˈpleɪn/ *v.i.* **1.** to express grief, pain, uneasiness, censure, resentment, or dissatisfaction; find fault. **2.** to tell of one's pains, ailments, etc. **3.** to state a grievance; make a formal accusation. **–complainer**, *n.* **–complainingly**, *adv.*

complainant /kəmˈpleɪnənt/ *n.* someone who makes a complaint, as in a legal action.

complaint /kəmˈpleɪnt/ *n.* **1.** an expression of grief, regret, pain, censure, resentment, or discontent; lament; fault-finding. **2.** a cause of grief, discontent, lamentation, etc. **3.** a cause of bodily pain or ailment; a malady.

complaisant /kəmˈpleɪsənt, -zənt/ *adj.* disposed to please; obliging; agreeable; gracious; compliant. **–complaisantly**, *adv.*

complement *n.* /ˈkɒmpləmənt/ **1.** something which completes or makes perfect. **2.** the quantity or amount that completes anything. **3.** either of two parts or things needed to make the other whole. **4.** the full quantity or amount. **5.** the full number of officers and crew required to operate a ship. **6.** *Gram.* the words used to complete a grammatical structure, especially in the predicate, as an object (*woman* in *He saw the woman*), predicate adjective (*tall* in *The tree is tall*), or predicate noun (*John* in *His name is John*). **7.** *Geom.* the angle needed to bring a given angle to a right angle. **8.** *Maths* all members of any set, class or space of elements, that are not in a given subset. *–v.t.* /ˈkɒmpləˌmɛnt/ **9.** to complete; form a complement to. **–complementary**, *adj.*

complementary medicine *n.* the range of treatments and procedures of an alternative nature which are considered, on scientific evidence, to assist mainstream medical treatments and procedures.

complete /kəmˈplit/ *adj.* **1.** having all its parts or elements; whole; entire; full. **2.** finished; ended; concluded. **3.** perfect in kind or quality; consummate. **4.** total; absolute: *I've been a complete fool.* *–v.t.* **5.** to make complete; make whole or entire. **6.** to make perfect. **7.** to bring to an end; finish; fulfil. **–completion** /kəmˈpliʃən/, *n.* **–completely**, *adv.* **–completeness**, *n.* **–completer**, *n.* **–completive**, *adj.*

complex /ˈkɒmplɛks/ *adj.* **1.** composed of interconnected parts; compound; composite. **2.** complicated; intricate. *–n.* **3.** a complex whole or system; a complicated assembly of particulars: *a complex of ideas.* **4.** the buildings and ancillary equipment required for a specified purpose: *shopping complex; launch complex.* **5.** *Psychol.* a group of related ideas, feelings, memories, and impulses which operate together and may be repressed or inhibited together. **6.** (in popular use) a fixed idea; an obsessing notion. **–complexly**, *adv.* **–complexity**, **complexness**, *n.*

complex carbohydrate *n.* any polysaccharide present in grains, vegetables, fruits, legumes and dairy products, broken down by the body into simple sugars and used as a source of energy. Compare **simple carbohydrate**.

complexion /kəmˈplɛkʃən/ *n.* **1.** the natural colour and appearance of the skin, especially of the face. **2.** appearance; aspect; character. **–complexional**, *adj.*

compliance /kəmˈplaɪəns/ *n.* **1.** the act of complying; an acquiescing or yielding. **2.** base subservience. *–phr.* **3. in compliance with,** in keeping or accordance with. *–***compliant,** *adj.* *–***compliantly,** *adv.*

complicate /ˈkɒmpləkeɪt/ *v.t.* to make complex, intricate, or involved.

complicated /ˈkɒmpləkeɪtəd/ *adj.* **1.** composed of interconnected parts; not simple; complex. **2.** consisting of many parts not easily separable; difficult to analyse, understand, explain, etc. *–***complicatedly,** *adv.* *–***complicatedness,** *n.*

complication /kɒmpləˈkeɪʃən/ *n.* **1.** the act of complicating. **2.** a complicated or involved state or condition. **3.** a complex combination of elements or things. **4.** a complicating element. **5.** *Pathol.* a concurrent disease or a fortuitous condition which aggravates the original disease.

complicit /kəmˈplɪsət/ *adj.* involved with a degree of guilt: *a company complicit in safety abuses.*

complicitous /kəmˈplɪsətəs/ *adj.* having complicity: *complicitous governments.*

complicity /kəmˈplɪsəti/ *n.* (*pl.* **-ties**) the state of being an accomplice; partnership in wrongdoing.

compliment *n.* /ˈkɒmpləmənt/ **1.** an expression of praise, commendation, or admiration: *he paid you a great compliment.* **2.** a formal act or expression of civility, respect, or regard: *the compliments of the season.* *–v.t.* /ˈkɒmpləˌment/ **3.** to pay a compliment to: *to compliment the chef on the meal.*

complimentary /kɒmpləˈmentri/ *adj.* **1.** of the nature of, conveying, or addressing a compliment. **2.** politely flattering. **3.** free: *a complimentary ticket.* *–***complimentarily,** *adv.*

comply /kəmˈplaɪ/ *v.i.* (**-plied, -plying**) **1.** to do as required or requested. *–phr.* **2. comply with,** to act in accordance with (wishes, commands, requirements, conditions, etc.).

compo /ˈkɒmpoʊ/ *Aust., NZ Colloq.* *–n.* **1.** compensation for injury at or in connection with a person's work; workers compensation. *–phr.* **2. on compo,** in receipt of such payment.

component /kəmˈpoʊnənt/ *adj.* **1.** composing; constituent. *–n.* **2.** a constituent part. **3.** *Electronics* one of the devices which may be used to make up an electronic circuit, as a resistor, capacitor, inductor, semiconductor device or vacuum tube, etc.

comport /kəmˈpɔt/ *v.t.* **1.** to bear or conduct (oneself); behave. *–phr.* **2. comport with,** to agree or accord with; suit.

comportment /kəmˈpɔtmənt/ *n.* bearing; demeanour; behaviour.

compose /kəmˈpoʊz/ *v.t.* **1.** to make by uniting parts or elements of. **2.** to be the parts or elements of. **3.** to make up; constitute. **4.** to put in proper form or order. **5.** to arrange the parts or elements of (a picture, etc.). **6.** to create (a literary or musical production). **7.** to arrange or settle, as a quarrel, etc. **8.** to bring (the body or mind) to a condition of calmness, etc.; calm; quiet. **9.** *Printing* to set (type). *–v.i.* **10.** to create, especially musical works.

composed /kəmˈpoʊzd/ *adj.* calm; tranquil; serene. *–***composedly** /kəmˈpoʊzədli/, *adv.* *–***composedness,** *n.*

composer /kəmˈpoʊzə/ *n.* **1.** a writer of music. **2.** an author.

composite /ˈkɒmpəzət/ *adj.* **1.** made up of various parts or elements; compound. *–n.* **2.** something composite; a compound. *–***compositely,** *adv.* *–***compositeness,** *n.*

composite rating *n.* a property rating system based on both unimproved capital value and the commercial value.

composition /kɒmpəˈzɪʃən/ *n.* **1.** the act of combining parts to form a whole, as in the composition of works of music and literature. **2.** the resulting state or product, as

musical works, etc. **3.** make-up; constitution. **4.** a compound substance. **5.** a short essay written as a school exercise. **6.** *Printing* the setting up of type for printing.

composition court *n.* *Tennis* a type of clay court in which crushed material, such as rock, is mixed in with the clay, designed to produce a fast ball speed but a normal bounce. Compare **clay court, grass court, hardcourt.**

compositor /kəmˈpɒzətə/ *n.* *Printing* someone whose job is to assemble the type for a printed page.

compos mentis /kɒmpəs ˈmentəs/ *adj.* sane.

compost /ˈkɒmpɒst/ *n.* **1.** a mixture of various kinds of organic matter, as dung, dead leaves, etc., undergoing decay, used for fertilising land. *–v.t.* **2.** to fertilise with compost. **3.** to change (vegetable matter) to compost. *–***composting,** *n.*

composure /kəmˈpoʊʒə/ *n.* serene state of mind; calmness; tranquillity.

compote /ˈkɒmpɒt/ *n.* a preparation or dish of fruit stewed in a syrup.

compound¹ *adj.* /ˈkɒmpaʊnd/ **1.** made of two or more parts or elements, or involving two or more actions, etc.; composite. **2.** *Gram.* (of a word) consisting of two or more parts which are also words, e.g. *housetop, blackberry, well-heeled, stir-crazy,* historically also *cupboard, breakfast.* *–n.* /ˈkɒmpaʊnd/ **3.** something formed by combining parts, elements, etc. **4.** *Chem.* a substance made up of two or more elements, joined chemically in a fixed proportion, whose properties, when so joined, are different from those of the original elements. **5.** *Gram.* a compound word. *–v.t.* /kəmˈpaʊnd/ **6.** to put together into a whole; combine. **7.** to settle by agreement, especially for a reduced amount, as a debt. **8.** *Law* to agree, for a fee or benefit, not to punish a wrongdoer for: *to compound a crime*; *compound a felony.* **9.** to increase or make worse: *the rain compounded their problems.* *–v.i.* /kəmˈpaʊnd/ **10.** to make a bargain; compromise. **11.** to settle a debt, etc., by agreement. *–***compoundable,** *adj.* *–***compounder,** *n.*

compound² /ˈkɒmpaʊnd/ *n.* **1.** (formerly in India, China, and elsewhere) an enclosure containing a residence or other establishment of Europeans. **2.** (formerly in South Africa and elsewhere) an enclosure for housing indigenous and other non-European labourers during the term of their employment. **3.** (in Asia) an enclosed area containing several buildings or houses with some empty space. **4.** an enclosure in which prisoners of war are held. **5.** an enclosure in which animals are held.

compound fracture *n.* a break in a bone such that the fracture line communicates with an open wound.

compound interest *n.* interest paid, not only on the principal, but on the interest after it has periodically come due and, remaining unpaid, been added to the principal.

comprehend /kɒmprəˈhend/ *v.t.* **1.** to understand the meaning or nature of; conceive; know. **2.** to take in or embrace; include; comprise. *–***comprehensible,** *adj.* *–***comprehendible,** *adj.* *–***comprehendingly,** *adv.*

comprehension /kɒmprəˈhenʃən/ *n.* **1.** the act or fact of comprehending. **2.** inclusion; comprehensiveness; perception or understanding. **3.** capacity of the mind to understand; power to grasp ideas, ability to know. **4.** (in schools) a formal exercise in reading and understanding, usually tested with a series of short questions.

comprehensive /kɒmprəˈhensɪv/ *adj.* inclusive; comprehending much; of large scope. *–***comprehensively,** *adv.* *–***comprehensiveness,** *n.*

comprehensive car insurance *n.* insurance on a car for accidental damage, theft and fire, with limited liability cover for damage the vehicle may cause to someone else's vehicle or property.

comprehensive insurance *n.* a form of insurance covering a wide range of instances in which the insured asset or property may be lost or damaged.

compress *v.t.* /kəmˈprɛs/ **1.** to press together; force into less space. **2.** *Computers* to encode (data) into a form that uses less storage. *–n.* /ˈkɒmprɛs/ **3.** *Med.* a soft pad of lint, linen, or the like, held in place by a bandage, used as a means of pressure or to supply moisture, cold, heat, or medication. **4.** an apparatus or establishment for compressing cotton bales, etc. **–compressible**, *adj.* **–compressibility** /kəmprɛsəˈbɪləti/, *n.* **–compressor**, *n.*

compression /kəmˈprɛʃən/ *n.* **1.** the act of compressing. **2.** a compressed state. **3.** (in some internal-combustion engines) the reduction in volume and increase of pressure of the air or combustible mixture in the cylinder prior to ignition, produced by the motion of the piston towards the cylinder head after intake. **4.** *Computers* the process of compressing data. *–adj.* **5.** designed to compress, especially to compress part of the body as a preventive measure against deep vein thrombosis: *compression bandage*; *compression stockings*.

comprise /kəmˈpraɪz/ *v.t.* **1.** to comprehend; include; contain: *an analysis comprising all the data to hand.* **2.** to consist of; be composed of: *a house comprising seven rooms.* **3.** (*not considered standard by some*) to combine to make up: *ten short stories that comprise a book.* **–comprisable**, *adj.* **–comprisal**, *n.*

compromise /ˈkɒmprəmaɪz/ *n.* **1.** the settlement of differences by a giving way on both sides; arbitration. **2.** anything resulting from a compromise. **3.** something intermediate between two different things. *–v.t.* **4.** to settle by a compromise. **5.** to lay open to danger, dishonour, suspicion, scandal, etc.: *to cheat would compromise your standing in the class.* *–v.i.* **6.** to make a compromise. **–compromiser**, *n.* **–compromisingly**, *adv.*

compulsion /kəmˈpʌlʃən/ *n.* **1.** the act of compelling; constraint; coercion. **2.** the state of being compelled. **3.** *Psychol.* **a.** a strong irrational impulse to carry out a given act. **b.** the act.

compulsive /kəmˈpʌlsɪv/ *adj.* **1.** → **compulsory**. **2.** *Chiefly Psychol.* relating to compulsion. **3.** addicted. **4.** compelling one to continue, especially of pleasurable and repetitive activities: *these chips are compulsive*. **–compulsively**, *adv.*

compulsory /kəmˈpʌlsəri/ *adj.* **1.** using compulsion; compelling; constraining: *compulsory measures*. **2.** compelled; forced; obligatory. **–compulsorily**, *adv.* **–compulsoriness**, *n.*

compulsory conference *n.* (in Australia) a meeting to which parties to an industrial dispute and, on occasion, other interested parties, are summoned by an industrial tribunal.

compulsory unionism *n.* the requirement that people become and remain financial members of the union covering their calling as a precondition of employment.

compunction /kəmˈpʌŋkʃən, -ˈpʌnʃən/ *n.* uneasiness of conscience or feelings; regret for wrongdoing or giving pain to another; contrition; remorse.

compute /kəmˈpjut/ *v.t.* **1.** to determine by calculation; reckon; calculate: *to compute the distance of the moon from the earth.* *–v.i.* **2.** to reckon; calculate. **3.** (*usu. in the negative*) *Colloq.* to make sense; seem likely or reasonable. **–computability** /kəmpjutəˈbɪləti/, *n.* **–computation**, *n.* **–computational**, *adj.*

computer /kəmˈpjutə/ *n.* an apparatus for performing mathematical computations electronically according to a series of stored instructions called a program. See **analog computer, digital computer.**

computer-aided design *n.* the use of computers in design allowing the designer greater flexibility in formulating projects on screen. Also, **CAD.**

computer-aided engineering *n.* engineering which uses computers to assist especially in the collection and analysis of data but also in the production of graphics as in computer-aided design. Also, **CAE.**

computer-aided manufacturing *n.* the use of computers in the manufacturing process for networking machines and computerised devices such as robots. Also, **CAM.**

computer crime *n.* crime, usually fraud, involving illegal access to a computer system for personal gain, as in transferring funds or gaining unauthorised access to data or making alterations to data in order to benefit.

computerese /kəmpjutəˈriz/ *n.* the jargon used in relation to computers.

computer geek *n. Colloq.* → **geek²** (def. 2).

computerise /kəmˈpjutəraɪz/ *v.t.* **1.** to process or store (data) in a computer. **2.** to furnish or provide with a computer system. Also, **computerize.** **–computerisation** /kəmˌpjutəraɪˈzeɪʃən/, *n.*

computer language *n.* any artificial language coded in text or graphics that can be interpreted by a machine, particularly a computer. Also, **programming language.**

computer piracy *n.* the production of a computer software package for sale, usually at a cheaper price, which is a direct copy of an existing package developed and marketed by a software company, such a practice usually being in total contravention of copyright laws. **–computer pirate**, *n.*

computer program *n.* → **program** (def. 6).

computer programming *n.* the process of writing, testing, debugging, and maintaining the source code of computer programs to achieve a specified outcome using a computer. **–computer programmer**, *n.*

computer terminal *n.* an input or output device connected to a computer but at a distance from it.

computer virus *n.* → **virus** (def. 3).

computing /kəmˈpjutɪŋ/ *n.* **1.** the science or study of the principles and uses of computers. **2.** the field of computer technology: *to have a job in computing.* *–adj.* **3.** relating to computers: *computing skills.*

comrade /ˈkɒmreɪd, ˈkɒmrəd/ *n.* **1.** an associate in occupation or friendship; a close companion; a fellow; a mate. **2.** a fellow member of a political party (especially a communist party); fraternal group, etc. **–comradeship**, *n.* **–comradely**, *adv.*

con¹ /kɒn/ *adv.* **1.** against a proposition, opinion, etc. (opposed to *pro*). *–n.* **2.** the argument, arguer, or voter against a proposition (opposed to *pro*).

con² /kɒn/ *v.t.* to learn; study; commit to memory; peruse or examine carefully. Also, **con up.**

con³ /kɒn/ *v.t. Naut.* to direct the steering of (a ship). Also, **conn.**

con⁴ /kɒn/ *adj.* **1.** of, relating to, or employing a confidence trick: *con game*; *con email.* *–n.* **2.** a confidence trick; swindle. *–v.t.* (**conned, conning**) **3.** to swindle; defraud. **4.** to deceive with intent to gain some advantage.

con⁵ /kɒn/ *n. Colloq.* a convict.

con- variant of **com-**, before consonants except *b, h, l, p, r, w,* as in *convene, condone,* and, by assimilation, before *n,* as in *connection.* Compare **co-** (def. 1).

concatenate /kɒnˈkætəneɪt/ *v.t.* **1.** to link together; unite in a series or chain. *–v.i.* **2.** to join together in a series or chain.

concave /ˈkɒnkeɪv/ *adj.* **1.** curved like the interior of a circle or hollow sphere; hollow and curved, especially of optical lenses and mirrors. *–n.* **2.** a concave surface, part, line, etc. **–concavely**, *adv.* **–concavity** /kɒnˈkævəti/, **concaveness**, *n.*

conceal /kənˈsiːl/ v.t. **1.** to hide; withdraw or remove from observation; cover or keep from sight. **2.** to forbear to disclose or divulge. –**concealable**, adj. –**concealer**, n.

concede /kənˈsiːd/ verb (**-ceded, -ceding**) –v.t. **1.** to admit as true, just, or proper; admit. **2.** to grant as a right or privilege; yield. –v.i. **3.** to make concession; yield; admit. –**concededly**, adv. –**conceder**, n.

conceit /kənˈsiːt/ n. **1.** an exaggerated estimate of one's own ability, importance, wit, etc. **2.** something that is conceived in the mind; a thought; an idea. **3.** a fanciful thought, idea, or expression, especially of a strained or far-fetched nature. –**conceited**, adj.

conceivable /kənˈsiːvəbəl/ adj. capable of being conceived; imaginable. –**conceivability** /kənsiːvəˈbɪləti/, **conceivableness**, n. –**conceivably**, adv.

conceive /kənˈsiːv/ verb (**-ceived, -ceiving**) –v.t. **1.** to form (a notion, opinion, purpose, etc.). **2.** to form a notion or idea of; imagine. **3.** to apprehend in the mind; understand. **4.** to hold as an opinion; think; believe. **5.** to experience or entertain (a feeling). **6.** to express, as in words. **7.** to become pregnant with. –v.i. **8.** to become pregnant. –phr. **9. conceive of**, to form an idea of; think of. –**conceiver**, n.

concentrate /ˈkɒnsəntreɪt/ v.t. **1.** to bring to bear on one point; direct towards one object; focus: *she concentrated the light on his face.* **2.** to make stronger or purer by removing or reducing what is foreign. **3.** Chem. to increase the strength of a solution, as by evaporation. –v.i. **4.** to bear on a centre. **5.** to become stronger or purer. **6.** to direct one's thoughts or actions towards one subject. –n. **7.** a concentrated form of something. –**concentration**, n. –**concentrative** /ˈkɒnsənˌtreɪtɪv/, adj. –**concentrator**, n.

concentrated /ˈkɒnsəntreɪtəd/ adj. **1.** applied with great energy and intensity; focused: *concentrated attention.* **2.** reduced to the essential ingredient, as by removing water: *concentrated juice.* **3.** clustered densely together: *concentrated population.*

concentration camp n. a guarded enclosure for the detention or imprisonment of political prisoners, racial minority groups, refugees, etc., especially any of the camps established by the Nazis before and during World War II for the confinement, persecution, and mass execution of prisoners.

concentric /kənˈsɛntrɪk/ adj. having a common centre, as circles or spheres. –**concentrically**, adv. –**concentricity** /kɒnsənˈtrɪsəti/, n.

concept /ˈkɒnsɛpt/ n. **1.** a thought, idea, or notion, often one deriving from a generalising mental operation. **2.** a theoretical construct: *the concept of the solar system.* **3.** an idea that includes all that is associated with a word or other symbol. **4.** an idea for something new, as a procedure: *a new concept in roof maintenance.* –**conceptual** /kənˈsɛptʃuəl/, adj.

conception /kənˈsɛpʃən/ n. **1.** the act of conceiving. **2.** the state of being conceived. **3.** the beginning of pregnancy; fertilisation. **4.** a beginning. **5.** an idea; concept. –**conceptional**, adj. –**conceptive**, adj.

concern /kənˈsɜːn/ v.t. **1.** to relate to; be connected with; be of interest or importance to; affect: *the problem concerns us all.* **2.** (*used in the passive*) to disquiet or trouble: *to be concerned about a person's health.* –n. **3.** something that relates or pertains to one; business; affair. **4.** a matter that engages one's attention, interest, or care, or that affects one's welfare or happiness: *it's no concern of mine.* **5.** solicitude or anxiety. **6.** important relation or bearing. **7.** a commercial or manufacturing firm or establishment. **8.** Colloq. any material object or contrivance: *fed up with the whole concern.* –phr. **9. concern oneself**, (sometimes fol. by *with* or *in*) to interest, engage, or involve oneself: *to concern oneself with a matter*; *to concern oneself in a plot.*

concerned /kənˈsɜːnd/ adj. **1.** interested. **2.** involved. **3.** troubled or anxious: *a concerned look.*

concert n. **1.** /ˈkɒnsət/ **a.** a public performance, usually by two or more musicians. **b.** a solo recital. **c.** a series of individual items not necessarily all musical, as in a school concert. **2.** /ˈkɒnsɜːt, ˈkɒnsət/ agreement of two or more in a design or plan; combined action; accord or harmony. –v.t. /kənˈsɜːt/ **3.** to contrive or arrange by agreement. **4.** to plan; devise. –v.i. /kənˈsɜːt/ **5.** to plan or act together. –phr. **6. in concert, a.** in a coordinated or organised way; together. **b.** (of musicians) performing live.

concerted /kənˈsɜːtəd/ adj. contrived or arranged by agreement; prearranged; planned or devised: *concerted action.* –**concertedly**, adv.

concertina /kɒnsəˈtiːnə/ n. **1.** a small accordion, usually hexagonal in cross-section. –v.i. (**-naed, -naing**) **2.** to fold up or collapse like a concertina.

concertmaster /ˈkɒnsətmɑːstə/ n. the first violinist of an orchestra, who acts as assistant to the conductor; leader.

concerto /kənˈtʃɛətoʊ, kənˈtʃɜːtoʊ/ n. (pl. **-tos** or **-ti** /-tiː/) Music a composition for one or more principal instruments, with orchestral accompaniment, now usually in symphonic form.

concession /kənˈsɛʃən/ n. **1.** the act of conceding or yielding, as a right or privilege, or as a point or fact in an argument. **2.** the thing or point yielded. **3.** something conceded by a government or a controlling authority, as a grant of land, a privilege, or a franchise. **4.** an outlet, especially a food outlet, at a sporting or entertainment venue, etc.: *the concessions inside the swimming centre.* **5.** a discount on a ticket, entrance fee, etc., given to people qualifying by virtue of their status as students, pensioners, etc.

conch /kɒntʃ, kɒŋk/ n. (pl. **conches** /ˈkɒntʃəz/ or **conchs** /kɒŋks/) **1.** the spiral shell of a gastropod, often used as a trumpet. **2.** any of several marine gastropods, especially *Strombus gigas.*

conchie /ˈkɒntʃi/ Colloq. –n. **1.** a conscientious objector. **2.** someone who is overconscientious. –adj. **3.** overconscientious. Also, **conchy, conshie, conchy, conch.**

concierge /kɒnsiˈɛəʒ, -ˈɜːʒ/ n. a hotel employee whose job is to assist guests with their travel arrangements, theatre and restaurant reservations, etc.

conciliate /kənˈsɪliˌeɪt/ v.t. **1.** to overcome the distrust or hostility of, by soothing or pacifying means; placate; win over. **2.** to win or gain (regard or favour). **3.** to render compatible; reconcile. –**conciliatory, conciliative**, adj. –**conciliator**, n.

conciliation /kənsɪliˈeɪʃən/ n. **1.** the act of conciliating. **2.** a procedure for the resolution of a dispute. **3.** a system of resolving industrial disputes between employees and employers by official talks in the presence of a government-appointed third party. See **arbitration** (def. 2).

concise /kənˈsaɪs/ adj. expressing much in few words; brief and comprehensive; succinct; terse: *a concise account.* –**concisely**, adv. –**conciseness**, n.

conclave /ˈkɒnkleɪv, ˈkɒŋ-/ n. **1.** any private meeting. **2.** the body of cardinals of the Roman Catholic Church; the Sacred College.

conclude /kənˈkluːd, kəŋ-/ v.t. **1.** to bring to an end; finish; terminate: *to conclude a speech.* **2.** to bring to a decision; settle or arrange finally: *to conclude a treaty.* **3.** to decide by reasoning; deduce; infer. –v.i. **4.** to come to an end; finish. **5.** to arrive at an opinion or judgement; come to a decision; decide. –**concluder**, n.

conclusion /kənˈkluːʒən, kəŋ-/ n. **1.** the end or close; the final part. **2.** the last main division of a discourse, containing a summing up of the points. **3.** a result, issue, or outcome: *a foregone conclusion.* **4.** final settlement or arrangement. **5.** final decision. **6.** a deduction or inference. *–phr.* **7. in conclusion,** finally. **8. leap (or jump) to conclusions,** to reach a conclusion hastily, before one has all the facts. **9. try conclusions with,** to engage (a person) in a contest or struggle for victory or mastery.

conclusive /kən'klusɪv, kəŋ-/ *adj.* serving to settle or decide a question; decisive; convincing: *conclusive evidence.* **–conclusively,** *adv.* **–conclusiveness,** *n.*

concoct /kən'kɒkt, kəŋ-/ *v.t.* **1.** to make by combining ingredients, as in cookery: *to concoct a soup*; *to concoct a dinner.* **2.** to prepare; make up; contrive: *to concoct a story.* **–concoction** /kən'kɒkʃən, kəŋ-/, *n.* **–concocter, concoctor,** *n.* **–concoctive,** *adj.*

concomitant /kən'kɒmətənt, kəŋ-/ *adj.* **1.** accompanying; concurrent; attending. *–n.* **2.** a concomitant quality, circumstance, person, or thing. **–concomitance, concomitancy,** *n.* **–concomitantly,** *adv.*

concord /'kɒnkɔd, 'kɒŋ-/ *n.* **1.** agreement between persons; concurrence in opinions, sentiments, etc.; unanimity; accord. **2.** peace. **3.** a compact or treaty. **4.** agreement between things; mutual fitness; harmony.

concordance /kən'kɔdns, kəŋ-/ *n.* **1.** the state of being concordant; agreement; harmony. **2.** an alphabetical index of the principal words of a book, as of the Bible, with a reference to the passage in which each occurs and usually some part of the context. **–concordant,** *adj.*

concourse /'kɒnkɔs, 'kɒŋ-/ *n.* **1.** a flocking together of people; a throng so drawn together; an assembly. **2.** an open space or main hall in a public building, especially a railway station. **3.** grounds for racing, athletic sports, etc. **4.** a running or coming together; confluence. **5.** a building in which airline passengers assemble, often designed with bays and projections so that aeroplanes may be docked adjacent to it.

concrete /'kɒnkrit, 'kɒŋ-/ *adj.* **1.** existing as an actual thing or instance; real. **2.** concerned with realities or actual examples rather than abstractions; particular (as opposed to general): *a concrete idea.* **3.** made of concrete (def. 4): *a concrete pavement.* *–n.* **4.** a material used in building, etc., made by mixing cement, sand, and small broken stones, etc., with water, and allowing the mixture to harden. See **cement.** *–v.t.* **5.** to treat or lay with concrete. **6.** to form into a mass by coalescence of particles; render solid. *–v.i.* **7.** to coalesce into a mass; become solid; harden. **8.** to use or apply concrete. **–concretely,** *adv.* **–concreteness,** *n.* **–concretive,** *adj.* **–concretively,** *adv.* **–concreter,** *n.*

concrete fatigue *n.* the cumulative damage suffered by concrete which is subjected to repeated exposure to water which leaches through it, resulting in the gradual destruction and loosening of the concrete structure, and finally a fracture.

concrete noun *n.* a noun applied to an actual substance or thing, as *dog, star, land.* Compare **abstract noun.**

concretion /kən'kriʃən, kəŋ-/ *n.* **1.** the act or process of concreting. **2.** a solid mass formed by or as by coalescence or cohesion. **3.** a hard solid mass of foreign material in a cavity in the body or within an organism. **4.** the act of becoming solid or calcified. **5.** an adhesion of two parts.

concubine /'kɒŋkjubaɪn/ *n.* **1.** (among polygamous peoples) a secondary wife. **2.** a woman who cohabits with a man without being married to him. **–concubinage** /kɒn'kjubənɪdʒ, kəŋ-/, *n.*

concur /kən'kɜ, kəŋ-/ *v.i.* **1.** to accord in opinion; agree. **2.** to cooperate; combine; be associated. **3.** to coincide.

concurrent /kən'kʌrənt, kəŋ-/ *adj.* **1.** occurring or existing together or side by side. **2.** acting together; cooperating. **3.** in agreement; accordant. **4.** *Geom.* passing through the same points: *four concurrent lines.* **–concurrently,** *adv.* **–concurrence,** *n.*

concussion /kən'kʌʃən, kəŋ-/ *n.* **1.** the act of shaking or shocking, as by a blow. **2.** shock occasioned by a blow or collision. **3.** *Pathol.* jarring of the brain, spinal cord, etc., from a blow, fall, etc. **–concuss,** *v.* **–concussive,** *adj.*

condemn /kən'dɛm/ *v.t.* **1.** to express strong disapproval of; censure. **2.** to judge (a person) to be guilty; sentence to punishment. **3.** to judge (something) to be unfit for use or service: *the old ship was condemned.* **4.** to force into a certain state or action: *the injury condemned him to a life of inactivity.* **–condemnable,** *adj.* **–condemnation,** *n.* **–condemner,** *n.* **–condemningly,** *adv.*

condense /kən'dɛns/ *verb* **(-densed, -densing)** *–v.t.* **1.** to make more dense or compact; reduce the volume or compass of. **2.** to reduce to another and denser form, as a gas or vapour to a liquid or solid state. **3.** to compress into fewer words; abridge. **4.** *Optics* to concentrate (light); focus (a ray) on to a smaller space. *–v.i.* **5.** to become liquid or solid, as a gas or vapour. **–condensation,** *n.*

condescend /kɒndə'sɛnd/ *v.i.* **1.** to stoop or deign (to do something). **2.** to behave as if one is conscious of descending from a superior position, rank, or dignity. **–condescending,** *adj.* **–condescendingly,** *adv.* **–condescension** /kɒndə'sɛnʃən/, **condescendence,** *n.*

condiment /'kɒndəmənt/ *n.* something used to give a special or additional flavour to food, such as a sauce or seasoning. **–condimental** /kɒndə'mɛntl/, *adj.*

condition /kən'dɪʃən/ *n.* **1.** particular mode of being of a person or thing; situation with respect to circumstances; existing state or case. **2.** state of health. **3.** fit or requisite state. **4.** *Agric.* **a.** the degree of fatness of a beast or carcase. **b.** the amount of yolk (def. 4) and other impurities present in raw wool. **c.** the amount of moisture present in scoured wool expressed as a percentage of clean dry weight. **5.** social position. **6.** a restricting, limiting, or modifying circumstance. **7.** a circumstance indispensable to some result; a prerequisite; that on which something else is contingent. **8.** something demanded as an essential part of an agreement. *–v.t.* **9.** to put in fit or proper state. **10.** to form or be a condition of; determine, limit, or restrict as a condition. **11.** to subject to something as a condition; make conditional (*on* or *upon*). **12.** to subject to particular conditions or circumstances. **13.** to make it a condition; stipulate. **14.** *Psychol.* to cause a conditioned response in. **15.** to use conditioner on: *to condition one's hair.* *–v.i.* **16.** to make conditions. *–phr.* **17. on condition that,** if; provided that. **–conditioner,** *n.*

conditional /kən'dɪʃənəl/ *adj.* **1.** imposing, containing, or depending on a condition or conditions; not absolute; made or granted on certain terms: *a conditional agreement*; *a conditional jail sentence.* **2.** *Gram.* (of a sentence, clause, or mood) involving or expressing a condition. For example: *If the suit is expensive* (conditional clause), *don't buy it.* *–n.* **3.** *Computers* an instruction which is acted upon only when a certain condition pertains; an example of a conditional is *transfer control to X if A equals zero.* **–conditionality** /kəndɪʃən'æləti/, *n.* **–conditionally,** *adv.*

conditional clause *n. Gram.* a clause which expresses the condition which must be met for the action of the main verb to take place, as in *If you visit, we will meet.* Also, **if-clause.**

conditioned response *n. Psychol.* an acquired response elicited by a stimulus, object, or situation (conditioned stimulus) other than that to which it is the natural or normal response (unconditioned stimulus). Also, **conditioned reflex.**

condole /kən'doʊl/ *v.i.* (sometimes fol. by *with*) to express sympathy with one in affliction; grieve. **–condolence,** *n.* **–condolatory,** *adj.* **–condoler,** *n.* **–condolingly,** *adv.*

condom /ˈkɒndɒm/ *n.* a sheath, usually made of thin rubber, worn over the penis during intercourse to prevent conception or the spreading of infection.

condominium /kɒndəˈmɪniəm/ *n.* **1.** joint or concurrent dominion. **2.** *International Law* joint sovereignty over a territory by several foreign states. **3.** Also, *Colloq.*, **condo.** *Chiefly US* **a.** a block of high-rise apartments or units. **b.** an apartment or unit in such a block.

condone /kənˈdoʊn/ *v.t.* **1.** to pardon or overlook (an offence). **2.** to atone for; make up for. –**condoner**, *n.*

condor /ˈkɒndə/ *n.* a large vulture of the Americas, as the **Andean condor**, *Vultur gryphus*, or the **California condor**, *Gymnogyps californianus*.

conduce /kənˈdjuːs/ *phr.* **conduce to**, to lead or contribute to (a result). –**conducive**, *adj.*

conduct *n.* /ˈkɒndʌkt/ **1.** personal behaviour; way of acting: *good conduct*. **2.** direction or management; execution: *the conduct of a business.* –*v.t.* /kənˈdʌkt/ **3.** to behave (oneself). **4.** to carry on; manage; direct: *to conduct a campaign.* **5.** to direct as leader: *to conduct an orchestra.* **6.** to lead or guide; escort. **7.** to serve as a channel or medium for (heat, electricity, sound, etc.). –*v.i.* /kənˈdʌkt/ **8.** to lead. **9.** to act as a conductor.

conductance /kənˈdʌktəns/ *n.* *Physics* the conducting power of a conductor; the derived SI unit of conductance is the siemens.

conduction /kənˈdʌkʃən/ *n.* **1.** a conducting, as of water through a pipe. **2.** *Physics* **a.** a conducting, as of heat, electricity, or sound through a medium. **b.** → **conductivity**. **3.** *Physiol.* the carrying of an impulse up a nerve or other tissue.

conductivity /ˌkɒndʌkˈtɪvəti/ *n.* (*pl.* **-ties**) *Physics* the property or power of conducting heat, electricity, or sound.

conductor /kənˈdʌktə/ *n.* **1.** someone who conducts; a leader, guide, director, or manager. **2.** the person on a public transport vehicle, who collects fares, issues tickets, etc. **3.** the director of an orchestra or chorus, who communicates to the performers by motions of a baton, etc., his or her interpretation of the music. **4.** *Physics* a substance, body, or device that readily conducts heat, electricity, sound, etc. –**conductorship**, *n.* –**conductress**, *fem. n.*

conduit /ˈkɒndʒuət, ˈkɒndjuət, ˈkɒndɪt/ *n.* **1.** a pipe, tube, or the like, for conveying water or other fluid. **2.** some similar natural passage. **3.** *Elect.* a pipe that encases electrical wires or cables to protect them from damage.

cone /koʊn/ *n.* **1.** *Geom.* a solid with a round base, the sides of which meet at the top in a point. **2.** any object shaped like this: *an ice-cream cone.* **3.** *Bot.* the cone-like fruit of the pine, fir, etc., consisting of partly separated seed-bearing scales overlapping each other. **4.** *Zool.* a light-sensitive nerve-cell present in the retina of the eye. –**conic** /ˈkɒnɪk/, **conical** /ˈkɒnɪkəl/, *adj.*

confabulate /kənˈfæbjuleɪt/ *v.i.* to talk together; converse. –**confabulation** /kənfæbjuˈleɪʃən/, *n.*

confection /kənˈfɛkʃən/ *n.* **1.** a sweet or bonbon. **2.** the process of compounding, preparing, or making. **3.** a sweet preparation (liquid or dry) of fruit or the like, as a preserve or sweetmeat. –**confectioner**, *n.*

confectionery /kənˈfɛkʃənri/ *n.* (*pl.* **-ries**) **1.** confections or sweets collectively. **2.** the work or business of a confectioner.

confederacy /kənˈfɛdərəsi, -ˈfɛdrəsi/ *n.* (*pl.* **-cies**) **1.** an alliance of persons, parties, or states for some common purpose. **2.** a group of persons, parties, etc., united by such an alliance. **3.** a combination for unlawful purposes; a conspiracy.

confederate /kənˈfɛdərət/ *for defs 1 and 2*, /kənˈfɛdəreɪt/ *for defs 3 and 4* –*adj.* **1.** united in a league or alliance, or a conspiracy. –*n.* **2.** an accomplice. –*v.t.* **3.** to form into a confederacy. –*v.i.* **4.** to unite in a league

or alliance, or a conspiracy. –**confederation** /kənfɛdəˈreɪʃən/, *n.*

confer /kənˈfɜ/ *verb* (**-ferred**, **-ferring**) –*v.t.* **1.** (sometimes fol. by *on* or *upon*) to bestow as a gift, favour, honour, etc. –*v.i.* **2.** consult together; compare opinions; carry on a discussion or deliberation. –**conferment**, **conferral**, *n.* –**conferrable**, *adj.* –**conferrer**, *n.*

conference /ˈkɒnfərəns/ *n.* **1.** a meeting for consultation or discussion. **2.** the act of conferring or consulting together; consultation, especially on an important or serious matter. **3.** *Eccles.* **a.** an official assembly of clergy, or of clergy and laymen, customary in many Christian denominations. **b.** a group of churches the representatives of which regularly meet in such an assembly. **4.** a cartel of shipping interests. **5.** an act of conferring; a bestowal. –**conferential** /kɒnfəˈrɛnʃəl/, *adj.*

confess /kənˈfɛs/ *v.t.* **1.** to acknowledge or avow: *to confess a secret; to confess a fault; to confess a crime.* **2.** to own or admit; admit the truth or validity of: *I must confess that I haven't read it.* **3.** to acknowledge one's belief in; declare adherence to. **4.** to declare (one's sins) or declare the sins of (oneself), especially to a priest, for the obtaining of absolution. **5.** (of a priest) to hear the confession of. –*phr.* **6. confess to**, to make confession of; own to. –**confessedly**, *adv.* –**confession**, *n.*

confessional /kənˈfɛʃənəl/ *adj.* **1.** of, or of the nature of, confession. –*n.* **2.** the place set apart for the hearing of confessions by a priest.

confessor /kənˈfɛsə/ *n.* a priest authorised to hear confessions.

confetti /kənˈfɛti/ *pl. n.* small bits of coloured paper, thrown at carnivals, weddings, etc.

confidant /kɒnfəˈdænt, ˈkɒnfədənt/ *n.* someone to whom secrets are confided or with whom intimate problems are discussed. –**confidante**, *fem. n.*

confide /kənˈfaɪd/ *v.i.* **1.** to show trust *in* by imparting secrets. **2.** to have full trust: *confiding in that parting promise.* –*v.t.* **3.** to tell in assurance of secrecy. **4.** to entrust; commit to the charge, knowledge, or good faith of another. –**confider**, *n.*

confidence /ˈkɒnfədəns/ *n.* **1.** full trust; belief in the trustworthiness or reliability of a person or thing. **2.** self-reliance, assurance, or boldness. **3.** certitude or assured expectation. **4.** a confidential communication; a secret. –*phr.* **5. in confidence**, as a secret or private matter, not to be divulged to others: *I told him in confidence.* **6. vote of confidence**, **a.** a vote which determines the right of a government or minister to continue in office. **b.** any general expression of support.

confidence trick *n.* a swindle in which the victim's confidence is gained in order to induce them to part with money or property. Also, *US*, **confidence game**. –**confidence trickster**, *n.*

confident /ˈkɒnfədənt/ *adj.* **1.** having strong belief or full assurance; sure: *confident of victory.* **2.** sure of oneself; bold: *a confident bearing.* –**confidently**, *adv.*

confidential /kɒnfəˈdɛnʃəl/ *adj.* **1.** spoken or written in confidence; secret: *a confidential document.* **2.** betokening confidence or intimacy; imparting private matters: *a confidential tone.* **3.** enjoying another's confidence; entrusted with secrets or private affairs: *a confidential secretary.* –**confidentiality** /ˌkɒnfədɛnʃiˈæləti/, **confidentialness**, *n.* –**confidentially**, *adv.*

configuration /kənfɪgəˈreɪʃən, -fɪgju-/ *n.* **1.** the relative disposition of the parts or elements of a thing. **2.** external form, as resulting from this; conformation. **3.** *Computers* a configured system. –**configurational**, **configurative** /kənˈfɪgərətɪv/, *adj.*

confine *v.t.* /kənˈfaɪn/ **1.** to enclose within bounds; limit or restrict. **2.** to shut or keep in; imprison. –*n.* /ˈkɒnfaɪn/ **3.** (*usu. pl.*) a boundary or bound; a border or frontier.

–phr. **4. be confined,** (of a woman) to be kept indoors or in bed for the period immediately before childbirth. **–confinement,** *n.* **–confiner,** *n.*

confirm /kənˈfɜm/ *v.t.* **1.** to make certain or sure; corroborate; verify: *this confirms my suspicions.* **2.** to make certain or definite, often by some legal act; ratify: *to confirm an agreement.* **3.** to make firm or more firm; add strength to: *the news confirmed my ideas.* **4.** *Eccles.* to administer the religious ceremony that admits a person as a full member of a church. **–confirmatory** /kɒnfəˈmeɪtəri, kənˈfɜmətri/, *adj.* **–confirmable,** *adj.* **–confirmation,** *n.*

confiscate /ˈkɒnfəskeɪt/ *v.t.* **1.** to seize as forfeited to the public treasury; appropriate, by way of penalty, to public use. **2.** to seize as if by authority; appropriate summarily. **–confiscation** /kɒnfəsˈkeɪʃən/, *n.* **–confiscatory,** *adj.* **–confiscator,** *n.*

conflagration /kɒnfləˈɡreɪʃən/ *n.* a large and destructive fire.

conflict *v.i.* /kənˈflɪkt/ **1.** to come into collision; clash, or be in opposition or at variance; disagree. **2.** to contend; do battle. *–n.* /ˈkɒnflɪkt/ **3.** a battle or struggle, especially a prolonged struggle; strife. **4.** controversy; a quarrel: *conflicts between church and state.* **5.** discord of action, feeling, or effect; antagonism, as of interests or principles: *a conflict of ideas.* **–confliction,** *n.* **–conflictive,** *adj.* **–conflicting,** *adj.*

conflict diamond *n.* → **blood diamond.**

conflicted /kənˈflɪktəd/ *v.* **1.** past tense and past participle of **conflict.** *–adj.* **2.** placed in a situation which causes a conflict of interest. **3.** experiencing mental conflict; torn: *conflicted over an issue.*

confluent /ˈkɒnfluənt/ *adj.* flowing or running together; blending into one. **–confluence,** *n.*

conform /kənˈfɔm/ *v.i.* **1.** (sometimes fol. by *to*) to act in accord or harmony; comply. **2.** to become similar in form or character. *–v.t.* **3.** to make similar in form or character. **4.** to bring into correspondence or harmony. **–conformist,** **conformer,** *n.* **–conformity,** *n.* **–conformism,** *n.*

conformation /kɒnfəˈmeɪʃən/ *n.* **1.** the manner of formation; structure; form. **2.** symmetrical disposition or arrangement of parts. **3.** the act of conforming; adaptation; adjustment.

confound /kənˈfaʊnd/ *v.t.* **1.** to mix so that the elements cannot be separated. **2.** to treat or regard mistakenly as the same; confuse. **3.** to surprise or perplex. **4.** to damn: *confound it!* **–confounder,** *n.*

confounded /kənˈfaʊndəd/ *adj.* **1.** discomfited; astonished. **2.** *Colloq.* damned: *a confounded lie.* **–confoundedly,** *adv.*

confrère /ˈkɒnfreə/ *n.* a fellow member of a profession, association, etc.; a colleague.

confront /kənˈfrʌnt/ *v.t.* **1.** to stand or come in front of; stand or meet facing; stand in the way of. **2.** to face in hostility or defiance; oppose. **3.** to set face to face. **4.** to bring together for examination or comparison. **–confrontation** /ˌkɒnfrənˈteɪʃən/, **confrontment,** *n.* **–confronter,** *n.* **–confrontational,** *adj.* **–confrontationalist,** *adj.*

Confucian /kənˈfjuʃən/ *adj.* **1.** of or relating to Confucius, 551–479 BC, Chinese philosopher and teacher of principles of conduct. **2.** of or relating to Confucianism. *–n.* **3.** an adherent of Confucianism.

Confucianism /kənˈfjuʃənɪzəm/ *n.* a system of ethics based on the teachings Confucius, 551–479 BC, Chinese philosopher and teacher of principles of conduct.

confuse /kənˈfjuz/ *v.t.* **1.** to combine without order or clearness; jumble; render indistinct. **2.** to throw into disorder. **3.** to fail to distinguish between; associate by mistake; confound: *to confuse dates.* **4.** to perplex or bewilder. **5.** to disconcert or abash. **–confused,** *adj.*

–confusedly /kənˈfjuzədli/, *adv.* **–confusedness,** *n.* **–confusingly,** *adv.* **–confusion,** *n.*

confute /kənˈfjut/ *v.t.* **1.** to prove to be false or defective; disprove: *to confute an argument.* **2.** to prove to be wrong; convict of error by argument or proof: *to confute one's opponent.* **3.** to confound or bring to naught. **–confutation** /kɒnfjuˈteɪʃən/, *n.* **–confuter,** *n.* **–confutative,** *adj.*

conga /ˈkɒŋɡə/ *n.* **1.** a Latin-American dance consisting of three steps forwards followed by a kick and usually performed by a group following a leader in a single column, each dancer clasping the waist of the person in front. **2.** a large cylindrical drum of African American origin.

congeal /kənˈdʒil/ *v.i.* **1.** to change from a fluid or soft to a solid or rigid state, as by freezing or cooling. **2.** to stiffen or coagulate, as blood. **–congealable,** *adj.* **–congealer,** *n.* **–congealment,** *n.*

congenial /kənˈdʒiniəl/ *adj.* **1.** suited or adapted in spirit, feeling, temper, etc.: *congenial companions.* **2.** agreeable or pleasing; agreeing or suited in nature or character: *a congenial task.* **–congeniality** /kəndʒiniˈæləti/, *n.* **–congenially,** *adv.*

congenital /kənˈdʒɛnətl/ *adj.* existing at or from one's birth: *a congenital defect.* **–congenitally,** *adv.*

congest /kənˈdʒɛst/ *v.t.* **1.** to fill to excess; overcrowd. **2. a.** *Pathol.* to cause an unnatural accumulation of blood in the vessels of (an organ or part). **b.** (*oft. in passive*) to fill (the chest, nose, etc.) with mucus: *my chest is congested.* **–congestible,** *adj.* **–congestive,** *adj.* **–congestion,** *n.*

conglomerate *n.* /kənˈɡlɒmərət, kəŋ-/ **1.** anything composed of heterogeneous materials or elements. **2.** *Geol.* a rock consisting of rounded and waterworn pebbles, etc., embedded in a finer cementing material; consolidated gravel. **3.** a company which controls or undertakes a widely diversified range of activities. *–adj.* /kənˈɡlɒmərət, kəŋ-/ **4.** gathered into a rounded mass; consisting of parts so gathered; clustered. *–v.i.* /kənˈɡlɒməreɪt, kəŋ-/ **5.** to collect or cluster together. **–conglomeration** /kənɡlɒməˈreɪʃən, kəŋ-/, *n.* **–conglomeratic** /kənɡlɒməˈrætɪk, kəŋ-/, **conglomeritic** /-ˈrɪtɪk/, *adj.*

congratulate /kənˈɡrætʃəleɪt, kəŋ-/ *v.t.* **1.** to express sympathetic joy to (a person), as on a happy occasion; compliment with expressions of sympathetic pleasure; felicitate. **2.** to acknowledge the achievement or success of: *to congratulate the winning team.* **3.** to consider (oneself) happy or fortunate. **–congratulatory,** *adj.* **–congratulation,** *n.*

congregate /ˈkɒŋɡrəɡeɪt/ *v.i.* **1.** to come together; assemble, especially in large numbers. *–v.t.* **2.** to bring together in a crowd, body or mass; assemble; collect. **–congregative,** *adj.* **–congregativeness,** *n.* **–congregator,** *n.*

congregation /kɒŋɡrəˈɡeɪʃən/ *n.* **1.** the act of congregating. **2.** a congregated body; an assemblage. **3.** an assembly of persons met for common religious worship.

congregational /kɒŋɡrəˈɡeɪʃənəl/ *adj.* **1.** of or relating to a congregation: *congregational singing.* **2.** (*upper case*) of or relating to a form of church government in which each congregation or local church acts as an independent, self-governing body, while maintaining fellowship with other like congregations.

congress /ˈkɒŋɡrɛs/ *n.* **1.** a formal meeting or assembly of representatives, as envoys of independent states, for the discussion, arrangements, or promotion of some matter of common interest. **2.** the act of coming together; an encounter. **–congressional** /kənˈɡrɛʃənəl/, *adj.*

congruent /ˈkɒŋɡruənt/ *adj.* **1.** agreeing; corresponding; congruous. **2.** *Geom.* coinciding exactly when superposed, as of triangles. **3.** *Maths* of or relating to two or more integers which have the same remainder when divided by a given integer called the modulus: *5 and 12 are congruent to the modulus 7.* –**congruence**, **congruency**, *n.*

congruous /ˈkɒŋgruəs/ *adj.* **1.** (sometimes fol. by *with* or *to*) agreeing or harmonious in character; accordant; consonant; consistent. **2.** exhibiting harmony of parts. **3.** appropriate or fitting. –**congruity** /kənˈgruəti, kəŋ-/, **congruousness**, *n.* –**congruously**, *adv.*

conifer /ˈkɒnəfə, ˈkoʊ-/ *n.* any of the (mostly evergreen) trees and shrubs producing naked seeds, usually on cones, such as pine, spruce, and fir, constituting the gymnospermous order or group Coniferales or Coniferae. –**coniferous** /kəˈnɪfərəs/, *adj.*

conjecture /kənˈdʒɛktʃə/ *n.* **1.** the formation or expression of an opinion without sufficient evidence for proof. **2.** an opinion so formed or expressed. –*v.t.* **3.** to conclude or suppose from grounds or evidence insufficient to ensure reliability. –**conjectural**, *adj.* –**conjecturable**, *adj.* –**conjecturably**, *adv.* –**conjecturer**, *n.*

conjoined twins /kəndʒɔind ˈtwɪnz/ *pl. n.* any twins who are born joined together in any manner. Also, **Siamese twins**.

conjugal /ˈkɒndʒəgəl, -dʒu-/ *adj.* concerning husband and wife; marital. –**conjugality** /kɒndʒəˈgæləti, -dʒu-/, *n.* –**conjugally**, *adv.*

conjugate *v.t.* /ˈkɒndʒəgeɪt/ **1.** *Gram.* **a.** to inflect (a verb). **b.** to recite or display all, or some subset of, the inflected forms of (a verb), in a fixed order: *conjugate the present tense verb 'be' as I am, you are, he is, we are, you are, they are.* –*v.i.* /ˈkɒndʒəgeɪt/ **2.** *Biol.* to unite temporarily. –*adj.* /ˈkɒndʒəgət, -geɪt/ **3.** joined together, especially in a pair or pairs; coupled. **4.** (of words) having a common derivation. **5.** *Maths* (of two points, lines, etc.) so related as to be interchangeable in the enunciation of certain properties. –**conjugation**, *n.* –**conjugative**, *adj.*

conjunction /kənˈdʒʌŋkʃən/ *n.* **1.** the act of conjoining; combination. **2.** the state of being conjoined; union; association. **3.** a combination of events or circumstances. **4.** *Gram.* **a.** (in some languages) one of the major form classes, or 'parts of speech', comprising words used to link together words, phrases, clauses, or sentences. **b.** such a word, as English *and* or *but*. **c.** any form of similar function or meaning. **5.** *Astron.* **a.** the meeting of heavenly bodies in the same longitude or right ascension. **b.** the situation of two or more heavenly bodies when their longitudes are the same. –**conjunctive**, *adj.* –**conjunctional**, *adj.* –**conjunctionally**, *adv.*

conjunctiva /ˌkɒndʒʌŋkˈtaɪvə/ *n.* (*pl.* **-tivas** *or* **-tivae** /-taɪvi/) *Anat.* the mucous membrane which lines the inner surface of the eyelids and is reflected over the forepart of the sclera and the cornea. –**conjunctival**, *adj.*

conjunctivitis /kəndʒʌŋktəˈvaɪtəs/ *n. Pathol.* inflammation of the conjunctiva.

conjure /ˈkʌndʒə, ˈkɒndʒə/ *for defs 1–3, 6–8, 9 and 10*, /kənˈdʒʊə/ *for defs 4 and 5* –*v.t.* **1.** to call upon or command (a devil or spirit) by invocation or spell. **2.** to affect or influence by, or as by, invocation or spell. **3.** to effect, produce, bring, etc., by, or as by, magic. **4.** to appeal to solemnly or earnestly. **5.** to charge solemnly. –*v.i.* **6.** to call upon or command a devil or spirit by invocation or spell. **7.** to practise magic. **8.** to practise legerdemain. –*phr.* **9. conjure up**, **a.** to call, raise up, or bring into existence by magic. **b.** to bring to mind or recall. **10. to conjure with**, likely to be influential if quoted; effective: *a name to conjure with.* –**conjurer**, **conjuror**, *n.*

conk /kɒŋk/ *Colloq.* –*n.* **1.** a nose. **2.** a blow; a violent stroke. –*v.t.* **3.** to hit or strike, especially on the head. –*phr.* **4. conk out**, **a.** (of an engine) to break down. **b.** to faint; collapse. **c.** to die.

connect /kəˈnɛkt/ *v.t.* **1.** to bind or fasten together; join or unite; link. **2.** to think of as related: *the pleasures connected with music.* –*v.i.* **3.** to become connected; join or unite. **4.** *Baseball, Tennis, etc. Colloq.* to hit the ball. –**connectedly**, *adv.* –**connecter**, **connector**, *n.*

connection /kəˈnɛkʃən/ *n.* **1.** the act of joining. **2.** the state of being joined. **3.** anything that joins; a connecting part: *telephone connection.* **4.** an association; relationship. **5.** a meeting of one means of transport with another, as a bus system with a railway. **6.** (*usu. pl.*) influential friends, relatives, etc. **7.** (*pl.*) *Horseracing, etc.* the owners of a horse or dog, or the people close to it such as the trainer, jockey, etc. Also, **connexion**. –**connectional**, *adj.*

connective /kəˈnɛktɪv/ *adj.* serving or tending to connect. –**connectively**, *adv.* –**connectivity** /ˌkɒnɛkˈtɪvəti/, *n.*

conning tower *n.* the superstructure on a submarine which acts as observation tower and main entrance to the interior.

connive /kəˈnaɪv/ *v.i.* **1.** (sometimes fol. by *with*) to co-operate secretly. –*phr.* **2. connive at**, to avoid noticing (that which one should oppose or condemn but secretly approves); give aid to (wrongdoing, etc.), by forbearing to act or speak; be secretly accessory to: *conniving at their escape.* –**conniver**, *n.* –**connivance**, *n.*

connoisseur /kɒnəˈsɜ/ *n.* someone competent to pass critical judgements in an art, especially one of the fine arts, or in matters of taste.

connote /kəˈnoʊt/ *v.t.* **1.** to denote secondarily; signify in addition to the primary meaning; imply. **2.** to involve as a condition or accompaniment. –**connotation**, *n.*

connubial /kəˈnjubiəl/ *adj.* of marriage or wedlock; matrimonial; conjugal. –**connubiality** /kənjubiˈæləti/, *n.* –**connubially**, *adv.*

conquer /ˈkɒŋkə/ *v.t.* **1.** to acquire by force of arms; win in war: *to conquer territories.* **2.** to overcome by force; subdue: *to conquer an enemy.* **3.** to gain or obtain by effort. **4.** to gain the victory over; surmount. –*v.i.* **5.** to make conquests; gain the victory. –**conquerable**, *adj.* –**conqueror**, *n.*

conquest /ˈkɒnkwɛst, ˈkɒŋ-/ *n.* **1.** the act of conquering. **2.** captivation, as of favour or affections. **3.** the condition of being conquered; vanquishment. **4.** territory acquired by conquering. **5.** a person whose favour or affections have been captivated.

consanguineous /kɒnsæŋˈgwɪniəs/ *adj.* related by birth; akin. Also, **consanguine** /kɒnˈsæŋgwən/. –**consanguinity**, *n.* –**consanguineously**, *adv.*

conscience /ˈkɒnʃəns/ *n.* **1.** the internal recognition of right and wrong as regards one's actions and motives; the faculty which decides upon the moral quality of one's actions and motives, enjoining one to conformity with the moral law. **2.** conscientiousness. –*phr.* **3. in conscience**, **a.** in reason and fairness; in truth. **b.** most certainly; assuredly. –**conscienceless**, *adj.*

conscience clause *n.* a clause or article in an act or law or the like, which relieves persons whose conscientious or religious scruples forbid their compliance with it.

conscientious /kɒnʃiˈɛnʃəs/ *adj.* controlled by or done according to conscience; scrupulous: *a conscientious judge, conscientious conduct.* –**conscientiously**, *adv.* –**conscientiousness**, *n.*

conscientious objector *n.* someone who on the grounds of deeply held beliefs refuses to meet a political or communal obligation, such as military service, compulsory voting, the attendance of children at school, etc. –**conscientious objection**, *n.*

conscionable /ˈkɒnʃənəbəl/ *adj.* conformable to conscience; just. –**conscionably**, *adv.*

conscious /ˈkɒnʃəs/ *adj.* **1.** aware of one's own existence, sensations, reasonings, etc.; provided with consciousness. **2.** inwardly aware or awake to something: *conscious of one's own faults*; *conscious of one's feelings.* **3.** intentional: *a conscious liar.* **4.** aware of oneself; self-conscious. **5.** deliberate or intentional. –**consciously**, *adv.*

consciousness /ˈkɒnʃəsnəs/ *n.* **1.** the state of being conscious. **2.** inward sensibility of something; knowledge of one's own existence, sensations, cognitions, etc. **3.** the thoughts and feelings, collectively, of an individual, or of an aggregate of people: *the moral consciousness of a nation.* **4.** activity of mental faculties: *to regain consciousness after fainting.* –*phr.* **5. raise one's consciousness**, to raise the level of one's understanding and sensitivity to cultural and social issues.

conscript *n.* /ˈkɒnskrɪpt/ **1.** a recruit obtained by conscription. –*v.t.* /kənˈskrɪpt/ **2.** to enrol compulsorily for service in the armed forces.

conscription /kənˈskrɪpʃən/ *n.* compulsory enrolment in the armed forces.

consecrate /ˈkɒnsəkreɪt/ *v.t.* **1.** to make or declare sacred; set apart or dedicate to the service of a deity. **2.** to ordain (bishops, etc.). **3.** to devote or dedicate to some purpose: *a life consecrated to science.* **4.** to make an object of veneration: *a custom consecrated by time.* –**consecrator**, *n.* –**consecration**, *n.*

consecutive /kənˈsekjətɪv/ *adj.* **1.** following one another in uninterrupted succession; uninterrupted in course or succession; successive. **2.** marked by logical sequence. **3.** *Law* (of a sentence) commencing on the expiry of a previous sentence. **4.** *Gram.* expressing consequence or result: *a consecutive clause.* **5.** *Maths* (of numbers) following in order without interruption, as 12, 13, 14, 15. –**consecutively**, *adv.* –**consecutiveness**, *n.*

consensus /kənˈsensəs/ *n.* **1.** general agreement or concord. **2.** majority of opinion.

consent /kənˈsent/ *v.i.* **1.** (sometimes fol. by *to*) to give assent; agree; comply or yield: *to consent to the request*; *to consent to do this.* –*n.* **2.** assent; acquiescence; permission; compliance. **3.** agreement in sentiment, opinion, a course of action, etc.: *by common consent.* –*phr.* **4. age of consent**, the age at which consent to certain acts, especially sexual intercourse and marriage, is valid in law. –**consenter**, *n.* –**consenting**, *adj.* –**consentingly**, *adv.*

consent agreement *n.* → **consent award.**

consent award *n.* (in Australia) an award made by an industrial tribunal where the parties have already reached agreement on the terms of a settlement but want it to have the force of an arbitrated award and hence submit it to a tribunal for ratification.

consequence /ˈkɒnsəkwəns/ *n.* **1.** the act or fact of following as an effect or result upon something antecedent. **2.** that which so follows; an effect or result. **3.** the conclusion of an argument or inference. **4.** importance or significance: *a matter of no consequence.* **5.** importance in rank or position; distinction. –*phr.* **6. in consequence**, as a result.

consequent /ˈkɒnsəkwənt/ *adj.* **1.** following as an effect or result; resulting. **2.** logically consistent. –*n.* **3.** anything that follows upon something else, with or without implication of causal relation.

consequential /kɒnsəˈkwenʃəl/ *adj.* **1.** of the nature of a consequence; following as an effect or result, or as a logical conclusion or inference; consequent; resultant. **2.** self-important; pompous. **3.** logically consistent.

4. of consequence or importance. –**consequentiality** /ˌkɒnsəkwenʃiˈæləti/, **consequentialness**, *n.* –**consequentially**, *adv.*

conservation /kɒnsəˈveɪʃən/ *n.* **1.** the preservation of areas which are significant, culturally or scientifically, in their natural state. **2.** the management of the natural environment to ensure that it is not destroyed in the process of development. **3.** the preservation or conserving of natural resources, as water, coal, etc. –**conservationist**, *n.* –**conservational**, *adj.*

conservation farming *n.* a system of farming that adopts methods compatible with land and water conservation, thus achieving more sustainable long-term productivity.

conservative /kənˈsɜvətɪv/ *adj.* **1.** disposed to preserve existing conditions, institutions, etc. **2.** cautious or moderate: *a conservative estimate.* **3.** traditional in style or manner. **4.** of or relating to political conservatism. **5.** having the power or tendency to conserve; preservative. –*n.* **6.** a person of conservative principles. **7.** a supporter or member of a conservative political party, group, or movement. –**conservatism**, *n.* –**conservatively**, *adv.* –**conservativeness**, *n.*

conservatorium /kɒnsəvəˈtɔriəm/ *n.* a place for instruction in music and theatrical arts; a school of music. Also, **conservatoire.**

conservatory /kənˈsɜvətri/, *Orig. US* /kənˈsɜvətɔri/ *n.* (*pl.* **-ries**) a glass-covered house or room into which plants in bloom are brought from the greenhouse.

conserve *v.t.* /kənˈsɜv/ **1.** to keep in a safe or sound state; preserve from loss, decay, waste, or injury; keep unimpaired. –*n.* /ˈkɒnsɜv, kənˈsɜv/ **2.** (*oft. pl.*) a preserve of whole fruit, boiled with sugar and sometimes pectin, especially one in which the fruit retains its shape in whole or in part. Compare **jam²** (def. 1). –**conserver**, *n.*

consider /kənˈsɪdə/ *v.t.* **1.** to think about; meditate; reflect. **2.** to regard as or think to be: *I consider the test to be reasonable.* **3.** to think; suppose. **4.** to make allowance for. **5.** to pay attention to; regard: *he always considers others.* **6.** to think about (a position, purchase, etc.): *to consider buying.* –*v.i.* **7.** to think deliberately or carefully; reflect.

considerable /kənˈsɪdrəbəl/ *adj.* **1.** important; of distinction. **2.** (of an amount, extent, etc.); fairly large or great. –**considerably**, *adv.*

considerate /kənˈsɪdərət/ *adj.* showing consideration or regard for another's circumstances, feelings, etc. –**considerately**, *adv.* –**considerateness**, *n.*

consideration /kənsɪdəˈreɪʃən/ *n.* **1.** the act of considering; meditation or deliberation. **2.** regard or account; something taken, or to be taken, into account. **3.** a thought or reflection. **4.** a recompense for service rendered, etc.; a compensation. **5.** thoughtful or sympathetic regard or respect; thoughtfulness for others. **6.** importance or consequence. **7.** estimation; esteem. –*phr.* **8. in consideration of, a.** in view of. **b.** in return for. **9. take into consideration**, to consider; take into account. **10. under consideration**, being considered.

consign /kənˈsaɪn/ *v.t.* **1.** (sometimes fol. by *to*) to hand over or deliver formally; commit. **2.** (sometimes fol. by *to*) to transfer to another's custody or charge; entrust. **3.** (sometimes fol. by *to*) to set apart, as to a purpose or use; assign. **4.** to transmit, as by public carrier, especially for sale or custody. –**consignable**, *adj.* –**consignation** /kɒnsəˈneɪʃən/, *n.* –**consignor**, *n.* –**consignee**, *n.*

consignment /kənˈsaɪnmənt/ *n.* **1.** the act of consigning. **2.** that which is consigned. **3.** property sent to an agent for sale, storage, or shipment. –*phr.* **4. on consignment**, (of goods) sent to an agent for sale, title being held by the consignor until they are sold.

consist /kən'sɪst/ *v.i.* **1.** to be compatible or consistent; accord. –*phr.* **2. consist in**, to be included or contained in: *happiness consists in doing one's duty.* **3. consist of**, to be made up or composed of.

consistency /kən'sɪstənsi/ *n.* (*pl.* **-cies**) **1.** agreement, harmony, or compatibility; agreement among themselves of the parts of a complex thing. **2.** material coherence with retention of form; solidity or firmness. **3.** degree of density or viscosity: *the consistency of cream.* **4.** constant adherence to the same principles, course, etc. Also, **consistence.** –**consistent**, *adj.*

console¹ /kən'soʊl/ *v.t.* to alleviate the grief or sorrow of; comfort; solace; cheer. –**consolable**, *adj.* –**consoler**, *n.* –**consolingly**, *adv.*

console² /'kɒnsoʊl/ *n.* **1.** a desk-like structure containing the keyboards, pedals, etc., of an organ, from which the organ is played. **2.** a desk on which are mounted the controls of an electrical or electronic system. **3.** a cabinet for television, radio, etc., designed to stand on the floor. **4.** *Computers* a computer operator's control panel or terminal.

consolidate /kən'sɒlədeɪt/ *v.t.* **1.** to make solid or firm; solidify; strengthen: *to consolidate gains.* **2.** to bring together compactly in one mass or connected whole; unite; combine: *to consolidate two companies.* –**consolidator**, *n.* –**consolidation**, *n.*

consommé /'kɒnsɒmeɪ, kən'sɒmeɪ/ *n.* a clear soup made from a concentrated clarified meat or vegetable stock. Also, **consomme.**

consonance /'kɒnsənəns/ *n.* **1.** accord or agreement. **2.** correspondence of sounds; harmony of sounds (opposed to dissonance). Also, **consonancy.**

consonant /'kɒnsənənt/ *n.* **1.** a sound made with more or less obstruction of the breath stream in its passage outwards, as the *l, s,* and *t* of *list.* **2.** a letter which usually represents a consonant sound. –*adj.* **3.** (sometimes fol. by *to* or *with*) in agreement; agreeable or accordant; consistent. **4.** corresponding in sound, as words. **5.** harmonious, as sounds. –**consonantly**, *adv.*

consort *n.* /'kɒnsɔt/ **1.** a husband or wife; a spouse, especially of a reigning monarch. **2.** one vessel or ship accompanying another. **3.** a group of instruments or voices in harmony. –*v.i.* /kən'sɔt/ **4.** to associate; keep company.

consortium /kən'sɔtiəm, -fiəm/ *n.* (*pl.* **-tiums** *or* **-tia** /-tiə, -fə/) **1.** a combination of financial institutions, capitalists, etc., for carrying into effect some financial operation requiring large resources of capital. **2.** an association or union.

conspicuous /kən'spɪkjuəs/ *adj.* **1.** easy to be seen. **2.** readily attracting the attention. –**conspicuously**, *adv.* –**conspicuousness**, *n.*

conspiracy /kən'spɪrəsi/ *n.* (*pl.* **-cies**) **1.** the act of conspiring. **2.** a combination of persons for an evil or unlawful purpose; a plot.

conspiracy theory *n.* (*pejorative*) any theory which proposes that some damaging event or situation which lacks an obvious explanation has been brought about by the unseen and evil machinations of government or covert organisations. –**conspiracy theorist**, *n.*

conspirator /kən'spɪrətə/ *n.* someone who is part of a conspiracy: *the conspirators were caught before they could carry out their plan.* –**conspiratorial**, *adj.* –**conspiratorially**, *adv.*

conspire /kən'spaɪə/ *v.i.* **1.** to agree together, especially secretly, to do something reprehensible or illegal; combine for an evil or unlawful purpose. **2.** to act in combination; contribute jointly to a result. –*v.t.* **3.** to plot (something evil or unlawful). –**conspirer**, *n.* –**conspiringly**, *adv.*

constable /'kʌnstəbəl, 'kɒn-/ *n.* **1.** a police officer ranking below sergeant; the lowest in rank in a police force. **2.** the rank. **3.** an officer of high rank in medieval monarchies, usually the commander of all armed forces, particularly in the absence of the ruler. **4.** the keeper or governor of a royal fortress or castle. –**constableship**, *n.*

constabulary /kən'stæbjələri/, *Orig. US* /kən'stæbjəlɛri/ *n.* the police force of a district or locality.

constant /'kɒnstənt/ *adj.* **1.** uniform; invariable; always present. **2.** continuing without interruption. **3.** continual; persistent. **4.** faithful; steadfast. –*n.* **5.** something constant, invariable, or unchanging. **6.** *Maths, Physics* a numerical quantity expressing a relation or value that remains unchanged under certain conditions. –**constancy**, *n.* –**constantly**, *adv.*

constellation /kɒnstə'leɪʃən/ *n.* **1.** *Astron.* any of various groups of stars to which definite names have been given, as the Southern Cross. **2.** *Astrology* the grouping or relative position of the stars as supposed to influence events, especially at a person's birth. **3.** any brilliant assemblage.

consternation /kɒnstə'neɪʃən/ *n.* amazement and dread tending to confound the faculties.

constipation /kɒnstə'peɪʃən/ *n.* *Pathol.* a condition of the bowels marked by defective or difficult evacuation.

constituency /kən'stɪtfuənsi/ *n.* (*pl.* **-cies**) *Brit.* **1.** → **electorate. 2.** any body of supporters; a clientele.

constituent /kən'stɪtfuənt/ *adj.* **1.** serving to make up a thing; component; elementary: *constituent parts.* **2.** having power to frame or alter a political constitution or fundamental law (as distinguished from lawmaking power): *a constituent assembly.* –*n.* **3.** a constituent element, material, etc.; a component. **4.** a voter, or (loosely) a resident, in a district represented by an elected official.

constitute /'kɒnstətjut/ *v.t.* **1.** (of elements, etc.) to compose; form. **2.** to appoint to an office or function; make or create. **3.** to give legal form to (an assembly, court, etc.). –**constitutor, constituter**, *n.*

constitution /kɒnstə'tjuʃən/ *n.* **1.** the way in which anything is made: *the physical constitution of the sun.* **2.** the physical character of the body as to strength, health, etc.: *a strong constitution.* **3.** the act or state of constituting; establishment. **4.** a system of fundamental laws and principles of a government, state or society: *the Australian constitution.* –**constitutional**, *adj.* –**constitutionalist**, *n.*

constitutional monarchy *n.* a form of monarchy in which the power of the sovereign is limited by a constitution, whether written (as in Australia) or unwritten (as in Britain). Also, **limited monarchy.**

constrain /kən'streɪn/ *v.t.* **1.** to force, compel, or oblige; bring about by compulsion: *to constrain obedience.* **2.** to confine forcibly, as by bonds. **3.** to repress or restrain. –**constrainable**, *adj.* –**constrainer**, *n.*

constraint /kən'streɪnt/ *n.* **1.** confinement or restriction. **2.** repression of natural feelings and impulses. **3.** a forced or unnatural manner; embarrassment. **4.** something that constrains.

constrict /kən'strɪkt/ *v.t.* **1.** to draw together; compress; cause to contract or shrink. **2.** to restrict, or inhibit. –**constriction**, *n.* –**constrictive**, *adj.*

construct *v.t.* /kən'strʌkt/ *v.t.* **1.** to form by putting together parts; build; frame; devise. **2.** *Geom., etc.* to draw, as a figure, so as to fulfil given conditions. –*n.* /'kɒnstrʌkt/ **3.** a complex image or idea resulting from a synthesis by the mind. –**constructor, constructer**, *n.*

construction /kən'strʌkʃən/ *n.* **1.** the act or art of constructing. **2.** the way in which a thing is constructed; structure: *objects of similar construction.* **3.** something that is constructed; a structure. **4.** *Gram.* a word or phrase consisting of two or more forms arranged in a particular way. **5.** explanation or interpretation, as of a law or a text, or of conduct or the like. **–constructional**, *adj.*

constructive /kən'strʌktɪv/ *adj.* **1.** positive; practical; helpful: *a constructive suggestion.* **2.** of, relating to, or of the nature of construction; structural. **–constructively**, *adv.* **–constructiveness**, *n.*

construe /kən'stru/ *v.t.* (**-strued, -struing**) **1.** to show the meaning or intention of; explain; interpret; put a particular interpretation on. **2.** to deduce by construction or interpretation; infer. **3.** to translate, especially literally. **–construable**, *adj.* **–construability**, *n.* **–construer**, *n.*

consubstantial /kɒnsəb'stænʃəl/ *adj.* of one and the same substance, essence, or nature. **–consubstantiality** /ˌkɒnsəbstænʃi'ælɪti/, *n.* **–consubstantially**, *adv.*

consul /'kɒnsəl/ *n.* an agent appointed by an independent state to reside in a foreign state and discharge certain administrative duties. **–consular** /'kɒnsjələ/, *adj.* **–consulship**, *n.*

consulate /'kɒnsjələt/ *n.* **1.** the premises officially occupied by a consul. **2.** consulship.

consult *v.t.* /kən'sʌlt/ **1.** to seek counsel from; ask advice of. **2.** to refer to for information. **3.** to have regard for (a person's interest, convenience, etc.) in making plans. *–v.i.* /kən'sʌlt/ **4.** (sometimes fol. by *with*) to consider or deliberate; take counsel; confer. *–n.* /'kɒnsʌlt/ **5.** a consultation, especially one with a medical practitioner. **–consultative**, *adj.* **–consultable**, *adj.* **–consulter**, *n.*

consultant /kən'sʌltənt/ *n.* **1.** someone who consults. **2.** someone who gives professional or expert advice. **3.** *Med.* a medical or surgical specialist to which patients are referred by another medical practitioner, especially a general practitioner.

consultation /ˌkɒnsəl'teɪʃən/ *n.* **1.** the act of consulting; conference. **2.** a meeting for deliberation. **3.** an application for advice to someone engaged in a profession, especially to a medical practitioner, etc.

consumable /kən'sjuməbəl/ *adj.* **1.** able to be consumed. **2.** (of an item of equipment or supply) normally consumed in use: *consumable fuel*; *consumable paper products.* *–n.* **3.** a consumable product or supply. **–consumability** /kənsjumə'bɪlɪti/, *n.*

consume /kən'sjum/ *v.t.* **1.** to destroy or expend by use; use up. **2.** to eat or drink up; devour. **3.** to destroy, as by decaying or burning. **4.** to spend (money, time, etc.) wastefully.

consumer /kən'sjumə/ *n.* someone who uses a commodity or service.

consumer goods *pl. n.* goods ready for consumption in satisfaction of human wants, such as clothing, food, etc., and which are not utilised in any further production.

consumerism /kən'sjumərɪzəm/ *n.* **1.** a movement which aims at educating consumers to an awareness of their rights and at protecting their interests, as from illegal or dishonest trading practices such as false advertising, misleading packaging, etc. **2.** a theory that the economy of a Western capitalist society requires an ever increasing consumption of goods. **–consumerist**, *adj., n.*

consumer price index *n.* (*also upper case*) an index which provides a measure of the change in the average cost of a standard basket of retail goods by relating the cost in the current period to that of a base period; used as a measure of inflation.

consummate *v.t.* /'kɒnsəmeɪt, 'kɒnsjumeɪt/ **1.** to bring to completion or perfection. **2.** to fulfil (a marriage) through sexual intercourse. *–adj.* /'kɒnsjumət, 'kɒnsəmət/ **3.** complete or perfect; supremely qualified; of the highest quality. **–consummation** /kɒnsə'meɪʃən/, *n.* **–consummately**, *adv.* **–consummative**, *adj.* **–consummator**, *n.*

consumption /kən'sʌmpʃən/ *n.* **1.** the act of consuming; destruction or decay. **2.** destruction by use. **3.** the amount consumed. **4.** *Econ.* the using up of goods and services having an exchangeable value. **5.** *Pathol.* a wasting disease, especially tuberculosis of the lungs.

contact *n.* /'kɒntækt/ **1.** the state or fact of touching; a touching or meeting of bodies. **2.** immediate proximity or association. **3.** *Elect.* the moving part of a switch or relay which completes and breaks the circuit. **4.** *Maths* a meeting of two curves or surfaces so that they have a common tangent at the point where they meet. **5.** a person through whom contact is established, often a business acquaintance. **6.** *Med.* **a.** someone who has lately been exposed to an infected person. **b.** inflammation of the skin due to contact with an irritating agent. **7.** *Hist.* the point at which two different peoples are brought into contact with each other, as by colonisation. *–v.t.* /'kɒntækt, kən'tækt/ **8.** to put or bring into contact. **9.** to initiate communication with (a person). *–v.i.* /'kɒntækt, kən'tækt/ **10.** to enter into or be in contact. *–phr.* **11. make contact,** (sometimes fol. by *with*) to initiate communication. **–contactable**, *adj.* **–contactability**, *n.* **–contactee**, *n.*

contact lens *n.* a small lens, usually of plastic, which covers the eye and is held in place by eye fluid, used to aid defective vision inconspicuously.

contact sport *n.* a sport, such as Rugby football, in which bodies regularly come into contact, creating the possibility of injury.

contagious /kən'teɪdʒəs/ *adj.* **1.** communicable to other individuals by physical contact, as a disease. **2.** carrying or spreading a disease. **3.** tending to spread from one to another: *panic is contagious.* **–contagiously**, *adv.* **–contagiousness**, *n.*

contain /kən'teɪn/ *v.t.* **1.** to have within itself; hold within fixed limits. **2.** to be capable of holding; have capacity for. **3.** to have as contents or constituent parts; comprise; include. **4.** to keep within proper bounds; restrain: *to contain oneself*; *to contain one's feelings.* **5.** (of an enemy force, hostile power, disease, etc.) to keep in check, confine within certain limits. **–containable**, *adj.*

container /kən'teɪnə/ *n.* **1.** anything that contains or can contain, as a carton, box, crate, tin, etc. **2.** a box-shaped unit for carrying goods; its standardised size facilitates easy transference from one form of transport to another.

contaminant /kən'tæmənənt/ *n.* **1.** something which contaminates. *–adj.* **2.** serving to contaminate: *contaminant chemicals.*

contaminate /kən'tæməneɪt/ *v.t.* **1.** to render impure by contact or mixture. **2.** to render harmful or unusable by adding radioactive material to. **3.** *Ecol.* to degrade (an environment) by introducing substances or organisms which are toxic to people, animals or plants. **–contamination** /kəntæmə'neɪʃən/, *n.* **–contaminative**, *adj.* **–contaminator**, *n.*

contango /kən'tæŋgoʊ/ *n. Finance* the position in a futures market where the more distantly traded contracts are selling at a premium over the nearer dated contracts.

contemplate /'kɒntəmpleɪt/ *v.t.* **1.** to look at or view with continued attention; observe thoughtfully. **2.** to consider attentively; reflect upon. **3.** to have as a purpose; intend. **4.** to have in view as a future event. *–v.i.* **5.** to think studiously; meditate; consider deliberately. *–phr.* **6. contemplate one's navel,** to indulge in introspection; daydream. **–contemplator**, *n.* **–contemplation**, *n.*

contemplative /'kɒntəmˌpleɪtɪv, kən'templətɪv/ *adj.* **1.** given to or characterised by contemplation. *–n.* **2.** a person devoted to religious contemplation. **–contemplatively**, *adv.* **–contemplativeness**, *n.*

contemporaneous /kəntempə'reɪniəs/ *adj.* contemporary. **–contemporaneously**, *adv.* **–contemporaneousness**, contemporaneity /kənˌtempərə'niəti, -'neɪɪti/, *n.*

contemporary /kən'tɛmpəri, -pri/, *Orig. US* /kən-'tɛmpərɛri/ *adj.* **1.** belonging to or existing at the same time. **2.** in the most modern style; up-to-date. –*n.* (*pl.* **-aries**) **3.** someone belonging to the same time or period as another or others. **4.** a person of the same age as another.

contempt /kən'tɛmpt/ *n.* **1.** the feeling with which one regards anything considered mean, vile, or worthless. **2.** the state of being despised; dishonour; disgrace. **3.** *Law* **a.** disobedience to, or open disrespect of, the rules or orders of a court or legislature, or conduct likely to prejudice the fair trial of a litigant or an accused person. **b.** an act showing this disrespect.

contemptible /kən'tɛmptəbəl/ *adj.* deserving of or held in contempt; despicable. –**contemptibility, contemptibleness,** *n.* –**contemptibly,** *adv.*

contemptuous /kən'tɛmptʃuəs/ *adj.* manifesting or expressing contempt or disdain; scornful. –**contemptuously,** *adv.* –**contemptuousness,** *n.*

contend /kən'tɛnd/ *v.i.* **1.** to struggle in opposition. **2.** to strive in rivalry; compete; vie. **3.** to strive in debate; dispute earnestly. –*v.t.* **4.** to assert or maintain earnestly. –**contender,** *n.*

content[1] /'kɒntɛnt/ *n.* **1.** the amount contained; capacity; volume. **2.** (*usu. pl.*) (a list of) chapters or chief topics of a book or document. **3.** (*usu. pl.*) that which is contained: *he poured the contents of the bottle on the floor.* **4.** the information which is in a communication, as opposed to the format, design, etc.: *the content of a web page.*

content[2] /kən'tɛnt/ *adj.* **1.** having the desires limited to what one has; satisfied. **2.** easy in mind. **3.** willing or resigned; assenting. –**contentment,** *n.*

contented /kən'tɛntəd/ *adj.* satisfied, as with what one has or with something mentioned; content. –**contentedly,** *adv.* –**contentedness,** *n.*

contention /kən'tɛnʃən/ *n.* **1.** a struggling together in opposition; strife. **2.** a striving in rivalry; competition; a contest. **3.** strife in debate; a dispute; a controversy. **4.** a point contended for or affirmed in controversy. –*phr.* **5. in contention, a.** under dispute; at issue: *his talent is not in contention.* **b.** (of a player, team, etc.) playing well enough to be considered a possible winner. –**contentious,** *adj.*

conterminous /kɒn'tɜmənəs/ *adj.* **1.** having a common boundary; bordering; contiguous. **2.** meeting at their ends. **3.** having the same boundaries or limits; coextensive. Also, **conterminal.** –**conterminously,** *adv.*

contest *n.* /'kɒntɛst/ **1.** a struggle for victory; fight, competition or argument. –*v.t.* /kən'tɛst/ **2.** to struggle or fight for. **3.** to argue against; dispute. –*v.i.* /kən'tɛst/ **4.** to dispute; contend; compete. –**contestable,** *adj.* –**contester,** *n.*

contestant /kən'tɛstənt/ *n.* someone who takes part in a contest or competition.

context /'kɒntɛkst/ *n.* **1.** the parts of a discourse or writing which precede or follow, and are directly connected with, a given passage or word. **2.** the circumstances or facts that surround a particular situation, event, etc. –**contextual,** *adj.*

contiguous /kən'tɪgjuəs/ *adj.* **1.** touching; in contact. **2.** in close proximity without actually touching; near. –**contiguity** /kɒntə'gjuəti/, **contiguousness,** *n.* –**contiguously,** *adv.*

continence /'kɒntənəns/ *n.* **1.** self-restraint, especially in regard to sexual activity; moderation; chastity. **2.** ability to exercise voluntary control over natural functions, especially urinating and defecating. Also, **continency.**

continent /'kɒntənənt/ *n.* **1.** one of the main landmasses of the globe, usually reckoned as seven in number (Europe, Asia, Africa, North America, South America, Australia and Antarctica). **2.** the mainland (as distinguished from islands or peninsulas). **3.** a continuous tract or extent, as of land. –*adj.* **4.** *Pathol.* able to control urination and defecation. **5.** exercising restraint in relation to the desires or passions; temperate. **6.** characterised by the ability to exercise control over natural impulses or functions; chaste. –**continental,** *adj.*

continental climate *n.* a type of climate associated with continental interiors and characterised by extremely hot, sunny summers, bitterly cold winters, and little rainfall occurring mainly in early summer.

continental crust *n. Geol.* that portion of the lithosphere which comprises the earth's continents and the shallow seabeds surrounding the continents. Compare **oceanic crust.**

continental plate *n. Geol.* that part of a tectonic plate which lies underneath a continent; thicker and less dense than an oceanic plate.

continental quilt *n.* → **doona.**

continental shelf *n.* that portion of a continent submerged under relatively shallow sea, in contrast with the deep ocean basins from which it is separated by the relatively steep **continental slope.**

contingency /kən'tɪndʒənsi/ *n.* (*pl.* **-cies**) **1.** a contingent event; a chance, accident, or possibility, conditional on something uncertain. **2.** fortuitousness; uncertainty; dependence on chance or on the fulfilment of a condition. **3.** something incidental to a thing.

contingent /kən'tɪndʒənt/ *adj.* **1.** (oft. fol. by *on* or *upon*) dependent for existence, occurrence, character, etc., on something not yet certain; conditional. **2.** happening by chance or without known cause; fortuitous; accidental. –*n.* **3.** a group of people with a single purpose, as troops sent on a particular mission. –**contingently,** *adv.*

contingent liability *n.* an obligation, associated with a past transaction, which will occur in the future only if some particular event occurs.

continual /kən'tɪnjuəl/ *adj.* **1.** proceeding without interruption or cessation; continuous in time. **2.** of regular or frequent recurrence; often repeated; very frequent. –**continually,** *adv.*

continuation /kəntɪnju'eɪʃən/ *n.* **1.** extension or carrying on to a further point: *the continuation of a road.* **2.** that by which anything is continued; a sequel, as to a story.

continue /kən'tɪnju/ *verb* (**-ued, -uing**) –*v.i.* **1.** to go forwards; keep on. **2.** to go on after an interruption. **3.** to last; endure. **4.** to remain in a place or condition; abide; stay: *he'll continue in his ignorance.* –*v.t.* **5.** to go on with: *to continue action.* **6.** to extend from one point to another; prolong. **7.** to carry on; keep going: *to continue a narrative.* –**continuable,** *adj.* –**continuer,** *n.* –**continuity,** *n.* –**continuous,** *adj.*

continuum /kən'tɪnjuəm/ *n.* (*pl.* **-tinuums** *or* **-tinua** /-'tɪnjuə/) a continuous extent, series, or whole.

contort /kən'tɔt/ *v.t.* to twist; bend or draw out of shape; distort. –**contortion,** *n.*

contortionist /kən'tɔʃənəst/ *n.* **1.** someone who performs gymnastic feats involving contorted postures. **2.** someone who practises contortion: *a verbal contortionist.*

contour /'kɒntuə, -tɔ/ *n.* **1.** the outline of a figure or body; the line that defines or bounds anything. **2.** → **contour line.** –*v.t.* **3.** to mark with contour lines. **4.** to make or form the contour or outline of. **5.** to build (a road, etc.) in conformity to a contour line.

contour line *n.* **1.** a line joining points of equal elevation on a surface. **2.** the representation of such a line on a map.

contra /'kɒntrə/ *n.* goods which are exchanged as part of a contra deal.

contra- a prefix meaning 'against', 'opposite', or 'opposing'.

contraband /'kɒntrəbænd/ *n.* **1.** anything prohibited by law from being imported or exported. **2.** goods imported or exported illegally. **3.** illegal or prohibited traffic; smuggling. –*adj.* **4.** prohibited from export or import. –**contrabandist**, *n.*

contrabass /ˈkɒntrəˌbeɪs/ *n.* (in any family of musical instruments) the member below the bass. –**contrabassist** /-ˈbæsəst/, *n.*

contraception /ˌkɒntrəˈsɛpʃən/ *n.* the prevention of conception by deliberate measures; birth control.

contraceptive /ˌkɒntrəˈsɛptɪv/ *adj.* **1.** tending or serving to prevent conception or impregnation. **2.** relating to contraception. –*n.* **3.** a contraceptive agent or device.

contract *n.* /ˈkɒntrækt/ **1.** (a document containing) an agreement, especially one enforceable by law. –*v.t.* /kənˈtrækt, ˈkɒntrækt/ **2.** to draw together or make smaller: *to contract a muscle.* **3.** to shorten (a word, etc.) by combining or omitting some of its parts. **4.** to acquire: *to contract a disease.* **5.** to incur: *to contract debts.* **6.** to settle or establish by agreement: *to contract a marriage.* –*v.i.* /kənˈtrækt, ˈkɒntrækt/ **7.** to become smaller; shrink. **8.** to enter into an agreement. –**contraction**, *n.* –**contractive**, *adj.* –**contractible**, *adj.* –**contractibility, contractibleness**, *n.* –**contractual**, *adj.*

contractor /ˈkɒntræktə, kənˈtræktə/ *n.* someone who contracts to furnish supplies or perform work at a certain price or rate.

contra deal *n.* an agreement involving an exchange of goods or services, rather than money.

contradict /ˌkɒntrəˈdɪkt/ *v.t.* **1.** to assert the contrary or opposite of; deny directly and categorically. **2.** to deny the words or assertion of (a person). **3.** (of a statement, action, etc.) to be directly contrary to. –*v.i.* **4.** to utter a contrary statement. –**contradiction**, *n.* –**contradictable**, *adj.* –**contradictor**, *n.*

contradictory /ˌkɒntrəˈdɪktəri/ *adj.* **1.** of the nature of a contradiction; asserting the contrary or opposite; contradicting each other; inconsistent. **2.** given to contradiction. –**contradictorily**, *adv.* –**contradictoriness**, *n.*

contralto /kənˈtræltoʊ, -ˈtrɑl-/ *Music* –*n.* (*pl.* **-tos** *or* **-ti**) **1.** the lowest female voice or voice part, intermediate between soprano and tenor. –*adj.* **2.** of or relating to the contralto; having the compass of a contralto.

contraption /kənˈtræpʃən/ *n.* a contrivance; a device.

contrary /ˈkɒntrəri/, /kənˈtrɛəri/ *for def. 5* –*adj.* **1.** opposite in nature or character; diametrically opposed; mutually opposed: *contrary to fact; contrary propositions.* **2.** opposite in direction or position. **3.** being the opposite one of two. **4.** untoward or unfavourable: *contrary winds.* **5.** perverse; self-willed. –*n.* (*pl.* **-ries**) **6.** that which is contrary or opposite: *to prove the contrary of a statement.* **7.** either of two contrary things. **8.** *Logic* a proposition so related to a second that it is impossible for both to be true, though both may be false. For example, *all judges are male* is the contrary of *no judges are male.* –*adv.* **9.** in the opposite way. –*phr.* **10. by contraries, a.** by way of opposition. **b.** contrary to expectation. **11. on the contrary,** in opposition to what has been stated. **12. to the contrary,** to the opposite or a different effect. –**contrarily**, *adv.* –**contrariness**, *n.*

contrast *v.t.* /kənˈtrɑst/ **1.** to set in opposition in order to show unlikeness; compare by observing differences: *contrast these two paintings.* –*v.i.* /kənˈtrɑst/ **2.** to supply or form a contrast; set off: *this shirt contrasts well with your skirt.* **3.** to show unlikeness when compared; form a contrast: *he contrasts with his brother.* –*n.* /ˈkɒntrɑst/ **4.** the act of contrasting. **5.** the condition of being contrasted. **6.** something strikingly unlike: *she's quite a contrast to her brother.* –**contrastive**, *adj.* –**contrastable**, *adj.* –**contrasting**, *adj.* –**contrastingly**, *adv.*

contravene /ˌkɒntrəˈvin/ *v.t.* **1.** to come or be in conflict with; go or act counter to; oppose. **2.** to violate,

infringe, or transgress: *to contravene the law.* –**contravention**, *n.* –**contravener**, *n.*

contribute /kənˈtrɪbjut, ˈkɒntrəbjut/ *v.t.* **1.** to give in common with others; give to a common stock or for a common purpose: *to contribute money, time, help.* **2.** to furnish to a magazine or journal. –*v.i.* **3.** to make contribution; furnish a contribution. –**contributor**, *n.* –**contributable**, *adj.* –**contribution**, *n.* –**contributive**, *adj.* –**contributively**, *adv.* –**contributiveness**, *n.* –**contributory**, *adj.*

contributing share *n. Stock Exchange* an ordinary share which has some part of its capital unpaid.

contrite /kənˈtraɪt, ˈkɒntraɪt/ *adj.* **1.** broken in spirit by a sense of guilt; penitent: *a contrite sinner.* **2.** proceeding from contrition: *contrite tears.* –**contritely**, *adv.* –**contriteness, contrition**, *n.*

contrivance /kənˈtraɪvəns/ *n.* **1.** something contrived; a device, especially a mechanical one. **2.** the act or manner of contriving; the faculty or power of contriving. **3.** a plan or scheme; an expedient.

contrive /kənˈtraɪv/ *v.t.* **1.** to plan with ingenuity; devise; invent. **2.** to plot (evil, etc.). **3.** to bring about or effect by a device, stratagem, plan, or scheme; manage (to do something). –*v.i.* **4.** to form schemes or designs; plan. **5.** to plot. –**contrivable**, *adj.* –**contriver**, *n.*

control /kənˈtroʊl/ *v.t.* (**-trolled, -trolling**) **1.** to exercise restraint or direction over; dominate; command: *control your dog; to control your feelings.* **2.** to direct the working of (a machine, vehicle, etc.). **3.** to hold in check; curb: *to control population growth.* **4.** to test or verify (a scientific experiment) by a parallel experiment or other standard of comparison. –*n.* **5.** the act or power of controlling; domination; command: *keep your dog under control.* **6.** a check or restraint: *the control of population growth.* **7.** a standard of comparison in a scientific experiment. **8.** (*pl.*) a system of knobs, levers, etc., for controlling a machine, etc. **9.** a place at or from which officials control or regulate an event or system: *send a message to control.* –**controllable**, *adj.* –**controllability** /kənˌtroʊləˈbɪləti/, *n.* –**controller**, *n.* –**controlment**, *n.*

controlled burning *n.* the controlled application of fire under specified environmental conditions to a predetermined area and at a planned time, intensity and rate of spread, the object being to reduce the danger of bushfire. Also, **control burning, prescribed burning.**

controlled substance *n.* a chemical substance, such as a drug, the availability or use of which is controlled by law.

control order *n.* an order issued by a court which restricts a person's movements and associations, and may also require home detention, the wearing of a tracking device, reporting to police stations at specified times, etc.

control panel *n.* **1.** a panel in which the controls of a device, vehicle, etc., are fitted. **2.** *Computers* an interface (def. 3) for setting system parameters on a computer, made to resemble a control panel (def. 1) on the screen.

controversy /ˈkɒntrəvɜsi, kənˈtrɒvəsi, ˈkɒntrəvəsi/ *n.* (*pl.* **-sies**) **1.** dispute, debate, or contention; disputation concerning a matter of opinion. **2.** a dispute or contention. –**controversial** /ˌkɒntrəˈvɜʃəl/, *adj.*

contumely /ˈkɒntʃuməli, kənˈtjuməli/ *n.* (*pl.* **-lies**) insulting manifestation of contempt in words or actions; contemptuous or humiliating treatment. –**contumelious** /ˌkɒntʃuˈmiliəs/, *adj.* –**contumeliously** /ˌkɒntʃuˈmiliəsli/, *adv.* –**contumeliousness** /ˌkɒntʃuˈmiliəsnəs/, *n.*

contuse /kənˈtjuz/ *v.t. Pathol.* to injure as by a blow with a blunt instrument, without breaking the skin; bruise. –**contusion**, *n.* –**contusive** /kənˈtjusɪv/, *adj.*

conundrum /kə'nʌndrəm/ n. 1. a riddle the answer to which involves a pun or play on words. 2. anything that puzzles.

conurbation /ˌkɒnɜ'beɪʃən/ n. a large urban agglomeration formed by the growth and gradual merging of formerly separate towns.

convalesce /kɒnvə'les/ v.i. to grow stronger after illness; make progress towards recovery of health.

convalescence /kɒnvə'lesəns/ n. 1. the gradual recovery of health and strength after illness. 2. the period during which one is convalescing. –**convalescent**, adj.

convection /kən'vekʃən/ n. 1. Physics the transference of heat by the circulation or movement of the heated parts of a liquid or gas. 2. Meteorol. a mechanical process thermally produced involving the upward or downward transfer of a limited portion of the atmosphere. Convection is essential to the formation of many types of clouds. –**convectional**, adj. –**convective**, adj. –**convectively**, adv.

convection column n. a column of hot gases rising above a bushfire, acting as a chimney and drawing air into the fire.

convene /kən'vin/ v.i. 1. to come together; assemble, usually for some public purpose. –v.t. 2. to cause to assemble; convoke. 3. to summon to appear, as before a judicial officer. –**convener**, **convenor**, n.

convenience /kən'viniəns/ n. 1. the quality of being convenient; suitability. 2. a situation of affairs or a time convenient for someone: to await one's convenience. 3. advantage, as from something convenient: a shelter for the convenience of travellers. 4. anything convenient; an accommodation; an advantage: a convenient appliance, utensil, or the like. 5. a toilet or urinal, especially in a public building; lavatory.

convenient /kən'viniənt/ adj. 1. agreeable to the needs or purpose; well-suited with respect to facility or ease in use; favourable, easy, or comfortable for use. 2. at hand; easily accessible. –**conveniently**, adv.

convent /'kɒnvənt/ n. 1. a community of persons, especially nuns, devoted to religious life under a superior. 2. the building or buildings occupied by such a community. 3. a nunnery. 4. Also, **convent school**. a Roman Catholic school where children are taught by women religious.

convention /kən'venʃən/ n. 1. a formal meeting or assembly, for discussion and action on particular matters. 2. an agreement or contract. 3. an international agreement, especially one dealing with a specific matter, as postal service, copyright, arbitration, etc. 4. general agreement or consent; accepted usage, especially as a standard of operation.

conventional /kən'venʃənəl/ adj. 1. conforming or adhering to accepted standards, as of conduct or taste. 2. relating to convention or general agreement; established by general consent or accepted usage; arbitrarily determined: conventional symbols. 3. formal, rather than spontaneous or original: conventional phraseology. 4. Law resting on consent, express or implied. 5. (of weapons, warfare, etc.) not chemical, biological, or nuclear. –**conventionalist**, n. –**conventionally**, adv.

converge /kən'vɜdʒ/ verb (-verged, -verging) –v.i. 1. to tend to meet in a point or line; incline towards each other, as lines which are not parallel. 2. to tend to a common result, conclusion, etc. –v.t. 3. to cause to converge. –**convergence**, n.

conversant /kən'vɜsənt, 'kɒnvəsənt/ adj. familiar by use or study: conversant with a subject. –**conversance**, **conversancy**, n. –**conversantly**, adv.

conversation /kɒnvə'seɪʃən/ n. informal interchange of thoughts by spoken words; a talk or colloquy. –**conversational**, adj. –**conversationalist**, n.

converse¹ /kən'vɜs/ v.i. (sometimes fol. by with) to talk informally with another; interchange thought by speech. –**converser**, n.

converse² /'kɒnvɜs/ adj. 1. turned about; opposite or contrary in direction or action. –n. 2. a thing which is the opposite or contrary of another. –**conversely** /kɒn'vɜsli, 'kɒn-/, adv.

conversion /kən'vɜʒən, -vɜʃən/ n. 1. the act or result of being converted. 2. a change in character, form, or purpose. 3. a change from one religion, political belief, etc., to another. 4. Maths a change in the form or units of expression. 5. Rugby a. the act of converting a try. b. the try so converted. 6. Physics the process of changing fertile material into fissile material in a nuclear reactor. –**conversional**, **conversionary**, adj.

convert v.t. /kən'vɜt/ 1. to change into something of different form or properties; transmute; transform. 2. Chem. to cause (a substance) to undergo chemical change: to convert sugar into alcohol. 3. to cause to adopt a different religion, political belief, purpose, etc. 4. Rugby to add a goal to (a try) by kicking the ball over the crossbar of the goalposts. 5. to exchange for an equivalent: to convert banknotes into gold. –n. /'kɒnvɜt/ 6. a person who has been converted, as to religion or opinion.

convertible /kən'vɜtəbəl/ adj. 1. capable of being converted. 2. (of a car) having a removable top. 3. (of currency) capable of being exchanged at a fixed price. 4. (of paper currency) capable of being exchanged for gold on demand to its full value at the issuing bank. –n. 5. a convertible car. –**convertibility** /kənvɜtə'bɪləti/, **convertibleness**, n. –**convertibly**, adv.

convex /'kɒnveks/ adj. (especially of optical lenses and mirrors) curved like a circle or sphere when viewed from without; bulging and curved. –**convexity** /kən'veksəti/, n. –**convexly**, adv.

convey /kən'veɪ/ v.t. 1. to carry or transport from one place to another. 2. to lead or conduct as a channel or medium; transmit. 3. to communicate; impart; make known. 4. Law to transfer; pass the title to. –**conveyable**, adj. –**conveyor**, **conveyer**, n.

conveyance /kən'veɪəns/ n. 1. the act of conveying; transmission; communication. 2. a means of conveyance, especially a vehicle; a carriage, car, etc. 3. Law a. the transfer of property from one person to another. b. the instrument or document by which this is effected.

conveyancing /kən'veɪənsɪŋ/ n. the branch of legal practice that consists of examining titles, giving opinions as to their validity, and preparing deeds, etc., for the conveyance of property from one person to another.

conveyor belt n. a flexible band passing around two or more wheels, etc., used to transport objects from one place to another, especially in a factory. Also, **conveyer belt**.

convict v.t. /kən'vɪkt/ 1. to prove or declare guilty of an offence, especially after a legal trial: to convict the prisoner of a felony. 2. to impress with the sense of guilt. –n. /'kɒnvɪkt/ 3. a person proved or declared guilty of an offence. 4. a person serving a prison sentence. 5. (formerly) a person transported to the British colonies to serve out a prison sentence. –**convictive**, adj.

conviction /kən'vɪkʃən/ n. 1. the act of convicting. 2. the fact or state of being convicted. 3. the act of convincing. 4. the state of being convinced. 5. a fixed or firm belief. –**convictional**, adj.

convince /kən'vɪns/ v.t. (-vinced, -vincing) (sometimes fol. by of) to persuade by argument or proof; cause to believe in the truth of what is alleged: to convince someone of their error. –**convincement**, n. –**convincer**, n. –**convincible**, adj. –**convincingly**, adv. –**convincingness**, n.

convivial /kən'vɪvɪəl/ *adj.* **1.** fond of feasting, drinking, and merry company; jovial. **2.** of or befitting a feast; festive. **3.** agreeable; sociable; merry. –**convivialist**, *n.* –**conviviality** /kənvɪvɪ'æləti/, *n.* –**convivially**, *adv.*

convocation /kɒnvə'keɪʃən/ *n.* **1.** the act of convoking. **2.** the fact or state of being convoked. **3.** a group of persons met in answer to a summons; an assembly. **4.** (*sometimes upper case*) an assembly of the members of a professional college or other institution. –**convocational**, *adj.*

convoke /kən'voʊk/ *v.t.* to call together; summon to meet; assemble by summons. –**convoker**, *n.*

convolution /kɒnvə'luʃən/ *n.* **1.** a rolled up or coiled condition. **2.** a rolling or coiling together. **3.** a turn of anything coiled; whorl; sinuosity. –**convolute**, *v.*

convolvulus /kən'vɒlvjələs/ *n.* (*pl.* -**luses** *or* -**li** /-li/) any plant of the genus *Convolvulus*, mostly of temperate regions, comprising erect, twining, or prostrate herbs with trumpet-shaped flowers; bindweed; morning glory.

convoy /'kɒnvɔɪ/ *v.t.* **1.** to accompany or escort, usually for protection: *The merchant ship was convoyed by a destroyer. –n.* **2.** the act of convoying. **3.** a protecting escort, as for ships or troops. **4.** a train of ships, vehicles, etc., travelling under escort.

convulse /kən'vʌls/ *v.i.* **1.** to shake violently; agitate. **2.** to cause to laugh violently. **3.** to cause to suffer violent muscular spasms; distort (the features) as by strong emotion. –**convulsive**, *adj.*

convulsion /kən'vʌlʃən/ *n.* **1.** *Pathol.* contortion of the body caused by violent muscular contractions of the extremities, trunk, and head. **2.** violent agitation or disturbance; commotion. **3.** a violent fit of laughter. –**convulsionary**, *adj.*

coo /ku/ *verb* (**cooed, cooing**) *–v.i.* **1.** to utter the soft, murmuring sound characteristic of pigeons or doves, or a similar sound. **2.** to murmur or talk fondly or amorously. *–v.t.* **3.** to utter by cooing. *–n.* **4.** a cooing sound. –**cooer**, *n.* –**cooingly**, *adv.*

cooba /'kubə/ *n.* any of several species of the genus *Acacia*, native to Australia, especially *A. salicina*, a pendulous and mainly riparian species. Also, **coobah**, **couba**.

cooee /'kui, ku'i/ *Aust., NZ –n.* **1.** a prolonged clear call, the second syllable of which rises rapidly in pitch, used most frequently in the bush as a signal to attract attention. *–v.i.* (**cooeed, cooeeing**) **2.** to utter such a call. *–phr.* **3. within cooee**, within calling distance. **4. not within cooee**, far from achieving a given goal. Also, **coo-ee, cooey**.

cook /kʊk/ *v.t.* **1.** to prepare (food) by the action of heat, as by boiling, baking, roasting, etc. **2.** to subject (anything) to the action of heat. **3.** *Colloq.* to ruin; spoil. *–v.i.* **4.** to prepare food by the action of heat. **5.** (of food) to undergo cooking. *–n.* **6.** someone who cooks. **7.** someone whose occupation is the preparation of food for the table. *–phr.* **8. cook someone's goose**, to frustrate or spoil someone's plans. **9. cook the books, a.** to falsify accounts. **b.** to falsify a result. **10. cook up**, *Colloq.* to concoct; invent falsely: *to cook up an excuse.* –**cookery**, *n.*

cookie /'kʊki/ *n.* (*pl.* -**kies**) **1.** *Chiefly US* a biscuit. **2.** *Colloq.* a person: *a smart cookie.* **3.** *Internet* a small data file containing details of a user's identification, sent by a web server to a browser for use by the web server when being accessed by that user in the future. Also, **cooky**.

cooktop /'kʊktɒp/ *n.* an assemblage of electric hotplates or gas burners for cooking, designed to be fitted into a benchtop.

Cooktown orchid /,kʊktaʊn 'ɔkəd/ *n.* an attractive, purple orchid, *Dendrobium bigibbum*, found on rocks and trees in far northern Qld; the floral emblem of Qld.

cool /kul/ *adj.* **1.** moderately cold; neither warm nor very cold. **2.** imparting or permitting a sensation of moderate coldness: *a cool dress.* **3.** not excited; calm; unmoved; not hasty; deliberate; aloof. **4.** deficient in ardour or enthusiasm. **5.** lacking in cordiality: *a cool reception.* **6.** calmly audacious or impudent. **7.** (of colours) with green, blue, or violet predominating. **8.** *Colloq.* (of a number or sum) without exaggeration or qualification: *a cool thousand.* **9.** *Jazz* restrained and relaxed (opposed to *hot*). **10.** *Colloq.* smart; up-to-date; fashionable. **11.** *Colloq.* attractive; excellent. **12.** *Colloq.* all right; okay: *don't worry, it's cool. –n.* **13. the cool**, that which is cool; the cool part, place, time, etc. **14.** *Colloq.* composure. **15.** *Colloq.* detachment; rejection of involvement. **16.** *Colloq.* sophistication and stylishness: *the very essence of cool. –v.i.* **17.** to become cool. **18.** to become less ardent, cordial, etc.; become more moderate. *–v.t.* **19.** to make cool; impart a sensation of coolness to. **20.** to lessen the ardour or intensity of; allay; calm; moderate. *–interj. Colloq.* **21.** an expression of understanding and agreement. **22.** an expression of admiration, pleasure, etc. *–phr.* **23. be cool with**, *Colloq.* to be happy to accommodate or go along with (a request, suggestion, etc.). **24. cool it**, *Colloq.* to control one's temper; calm down. **25. cool off** (or **down**), *Colloq.* to become calmer; become more reasonable. **26. cool one's heels**, to be kept waiting. **27. keep** (or **stay**) **cool**, *Colloq.* to refrain from losing one's temper or from panicking. **28. lose** (or **blow**) **one's cool**, *Colloq.* to become angry. **29. play it cool**, *Colloq.* to be cautious and shrewd; keep composure under difficult circumstances. –**coolly**, *adv.* –**coolness**, *n.*

coolabah /'kuləbə/ *n.* → **coolibah**.

coolamon /'kuləmɒn/ *n.* a basin-shaped wooden dish traditionally made and used by some Aboriginal peoples.

coolant /'kulənt/ *n.* **1.** a substance, usually a liquid or gas, used to reduce the temperature of a system below a specified value by conducting away the heat evolved in the operation of the system, as the liquid in a car cooling system. The coolant may be used to transfer heat to a power generator, as in a nuclear reactor. **2.** a lubricant which serves to dissipate the heat caused by friction.

cool burn *n.* a bushfire mitigation procedure in which small fires are lit in circumstances which do not allow them to develop the kind of intense heat which is destructive to vegetation and wildlife, but which reduce the threat of uncontrolled bushfire. –**cool burning**, *n.*

cooler /'kulə/ *n.* **1.** a container or apparatus for cooling or keeping cool: *a water-cooler.* **2.** anything that cools or makes cool; refrigerant. **3.** *Colloq.* prison.

coolibah /'kuləbə/ *n.* a species of eucalypt, *Eucalyptus microtheca*, common in the Australian inland and usually associated with areas subject to occasional inundation. Also, **coolabah**.

coolie /'kuli/ *n.* formerly **1.** (in India, China, etc.) an unskilled indigenous labourer. **2.** (elsewhere) such a labourer employed for cheap service.

cooling-off period *n.* **1.** a period during which opponents or contestants stand back from their conflict in the hope of calming their emotions. **2.** a period in which a person may legally back out of a financial agreement.

cool safe *n. Aust., NZ* a cabinet, for the storage of perishable foodstuffs, which allows a breeze to blow through wet fabric, such as hessian, thus reducing the temperature inside.

cool temperate rainforest *n.* a mainly broad-leaved forest which exists under a mean annual biotemperature of about 12°C; carrying such species as Antarctic beech *Nothofagus spp.*, southern sassafras *Atherosperma moschatum*, and leatherwood *Eucryphia lucida* (in Tasmania). Compare **warm temperate rainforest**. Also, **cool temperate forest**.

co-op /ˈkoʊ-ɒp/ *n.* a cooperative shop, store, or society.

coop /kup/ *n.* **1.** an enclosure, cage, or pen, usually with bars or wires on one side or more, in which fowls, etc., are confined for fattening, transportation, etc. –*v.t.* **2.** to place in, or as in, a coop; confine narrowly. –*phr.* **3. coop up**, to confine in narrow quarters, as in a coop. **4. fly the coop**, to escape from a prison, etc.

cooper /ˈkupə/ *n.* someone who makes or repairs vessels formed of staves and hoops, such as casks, barrels, tubs, etc.

cooperate /koʊˈɒpəreɪt/ *v.i.* **1.** to work or act together or jointly; unite in producing an effect. **2.** to practise cooperation. Also, **co-operate**. –**cooperation**, *n.* –**cooperator**, *n.*

cooperative /koʊˈɒpərətɪv, -ˈɒprətɪv/ *adj.* **1.** cooperating. **2.** showing a willingness to cooperate; helpful. **3.** relating to economic cooperation: *a cooperative farm.* –*n.* **4.** a cooperative society or shop. **5.** a cooperative farm. Also, **co-operative**. –**cooperatively**, *adv.* –**cooperativeness**, *n.*

cooperative society *n.* a business undertaking owned and controlled by its members, and formed to provide them with work or with goods at advantageous prices. Also, **co-operative society**.

coopt /koʊˈɒpt/ *v.t.* to elect into a body by the votes of the existing members. Also, **co-opt**. –**cooption** /koʊˈɒpʃən/, **cooptation**, *n.* –**cooptative**, *adj.*

coordinate *v.t.* /koʊˈɔdəneɪt/ **1.** to place or arrange in due order or proper relative position; combine harmoniously: *to coordinate the work of different people.* –*v.i.* /koʊˈɔdəneɪt/ **2.** to go together with; match. **3.** to act or work together with; cooperate. –*adj.* /koʊˈɔdənət, -neɪt/ **4.** equal in rank or importance; matching. **5.** *Maths* using or relating to systems of coordinates. –*n.* /koʊˈɔdənət, -neɪt/ **6.** an equal. **7.** (*oft. pl.*) clothes that match or go together. **8.** *Maths* any of the magnitudes which define the position of a point, line, etc., by reference to a fixed figure, system of lines, etc. Also, **co-ordinate**. –**coordinately**, *adv.* –**coordinateness**, *n.* –**coordination**, *n.* –**coordinative**, *adj.* –**coordinator**, *n.*

coot /kut/ *n.* **1.** any of the aquatic birds of the genus *Fulica* characterised by lobate toes and short wings and tail, as the **Eurasian coot**, *Fulica atra*, a black bird with a white frontal shield and bill. **2.** Also, **bald coot**. → **swamphen**. **3.** any of various other swimming and diving birds, such as the scoter. **4.** *Colloq.* a fool; simpleton. **5.** *Colloq.* a man.

cop /kɒp/ *Colloq.* –*n.* **1.** a police officer. **2.** an arrest; a state of being caught. –*v.t.* (**copped**, **copping**) **3.** to steal. **4.** to receive in payment. **5.** to accept resignedly; put up with: *would you cop a deal like that?* **6.** to be allotted; receive: *she copped more than her fair share.* **7.** to see; look at: *cop that poster over there.* –*phr.* **8. a sure cop**, something certain. **9. a sweet cop**, an easy job. **10. cop a load**, to contract venereal disease. **11. cop it**, to be punished. **12. cop it sweet**, *Aust.* **a.** to accept something unpleasant, as a punishment, an unfair ruling, etc., without complaint. **b.** to be fortunate; enjoy easy living. **13. cop out**, **a.** to fail to do something which one had a responsibility to do; evade responsibility. **b.** to fail completely. **14. cop the lot**, to bear the brunt of some misfortune. **15. cop this**, a verbal accompaniment of an act of aggression: *cop this, you bastard!* **16. not much cop**, not worthwhile.

cope[1] /koʊp/ *v.i.* (sometimes fol. by *with*) to be able to deal effectively with a situation, especially one that presents difficulties: *he's not coping well on his own with the children.*

cope[2] /koʊp/ *n.* **1.** a long mantle of silk or other material worn by ecclesiastics over the alb or surplice in processions and on other occasions. **2.** any cloak-like or canopy-like covering.

copha /ˈkoʊfə/ *n. Aust.* (*from trademark*) a white waxy solid derived from coconut flesh, a form of purified coconut oil, used as a shortening agent; coconut butter. Also, **copha butter**.

coping /ˈkoʊpɪŋ/ *n.* the uppermost course of a wall or the like, usually made sloping so as to carry off water.

copious /ˈkoʊpiəs/ *adj.* **1.** large in quantity or number; abundant. **2.** having or yielding an abundant supply. **3.** exhibiting abundance or fullness, as of thoughts or words. –**copiously**, *adv.* –**copiousness**, *n.*

cop-out *n. Colloq.* an easy way out of a situation of embarrassment or responsibility.

copper[1] /ˈkɒpə/ *n.* **1.** *Chem.* a reddish-brown malleable, ductile metallic element. *Symbol*: Cu; *atomic number*: 29; *relative atomic mass*: 63.54. **2.** a copper coin, as the English penny or the US cent. **3.** a container made of copper. **4.** a large vessel (formerly of copper) for boiling clothes. **5.** a metallic reddish-brown colour. –*v.t.* **6.** to cover or coat with copper. –*adj.* **7.** made of copper. **8.** copper-coloured. **9.** relating to copper: *copper smelting.*

copper[2] /ˈkɒpə/ *n. Colloq.* a police officer.

copperhead /ˈkɒpəhɛd/ *n.* **1.** a bulky, marsh-dwelling venomous Australian snake, *Austrelaps superbus*, brown to black above with a coppery red band behind the head, and reaching about two metres in length. **2.** a venomous snake, *Ancistrodon contortrix*, of the US, having a copper-coloured head and reaching a length of about one metre.

copperplate /ˈkɒpəpleɪt/ *n.* **1.** a plate of polished copper on which writing, a picture, or a design is made by engraving or etching. **2.** a print or impression from such a plate. **3.** an engraving or printing of this kind. **4.** a formal, rounded, heavily sloping style of handwriting, formerly much used in engravings. –*adj.* **5.** (of handwriting) sloping, rounded and formal; in the style of copperplate.

coppice /ˈkɒpəs/ *n.* Also, **copse**. **1.** a wood, thicket, or plantation of small trees or bushes. –*v.t.* **2.** to cut down (a tree) near the base so as to encourage numerous slender trunks to regenerate from the root-stock; done traditionally to provide a source of wood, but now also to create a desired shape or to increase biomass.

copra /ˈkɒprə/ *n.* the dried kernel or meat of the coconut, from which coconut oil is pressed.

copro- a prefix meaning 'dung' or 'excrement', as in *coprophobia*.

coprosma /kəˈprɒzmə/ *n.* any member of the very large genus *Coprosma* of South-East Asia and the Pacific, especially *C. lucida*, native to New Zealand, often grown as a hedge plant for its glossy leaves.

copse /kɒps/ *n.* → **coppice** (def. 1).

cop shop *n. Colloq.* a police station.

copula /ˈkɒpjələ/ *n.* (*pl.* **-lae** /-li/ *or* **-las**) **1.** something that connects or links together. **2.** *Gram.* a verb that does little more than connect the subject with the predicative complement, including *be* as well as others such as *seem* and *become*, which make the complement a current or resulting attribute, and cannot be used intransitively with the same meaning. **3.** *Logic* a word or words used to connect the subject with the predicate of a proposition. –**copular**, *adj.*

copulate /ˈkɒpjuleɪt/ *v.i.* to unite in sexual intercourse. –**copulation**, *n.* –**copulative**, *adj.*

copy /ˈkɒpi/ *n.* (*pl.* **copies**) **1.** something made to be exactly like another: *we need four copies of the letter.* **2.** one of the various examples of the same book, magazine, etc. **3.** written, typed, or printed matter, or artwork, intended to be printed. *–verb* (**copied**, **copying**) *–v.t.* **4.** to make a thing exactly like another; transcribe; reproduce: *to copy a set of figures.* **5.** to follow as a pattern or model; imitate: *she copied her sister in everything.* **6.** to add (a secondary recipient) to an email address list. *–v.i.* **7.** to make a copy or copies. **8.** to use unfairly another person's written work: *James is always copying from me in history class.*

copybook /'kɒpibʊk/ *n.* **1.** a book in which copies are written or printed for learners to imitate. **2.** *US* a book for or containing copies, as of documents. *–adj.* **3.** according to the rules; excellent; conforming to established principles. *–phr.* **4. blot one's copybook,** to spoil, damage, or destroy one's reputation or record.

copyedit /'kɒpiˌɛdət/ *v.t.* to correct, style, and mark up copy (def. 3) to make it ready for printing. *–***copyeditor,** *n. –***copyediting,** *n.*

copyright /'kɒpiraɪt/ *n.* the exclusive right, granted by law for a certain term of years, to make and dispose of copies of, and otherwise to control, a literary, musical, dramatic, or artistic work. *Symbol:* © *–***copyrightable,** *adj. –***copyrighter,** *n.*

copywriter /'kɒpiraɪtə/ *n.* a writer of copy for advertisements or publicity releases. *–***copywriting,** *n.*

coquette /kouˈkɛt, kɒˈkɛt/ *n.* a woman who tries to gain the admiration and affections of men for mere self-gratification; a flirt. *–***coquettish,** *adj. –***coquettishly,** *adv. –***coquettishness,** *n.*

cor- variant of **com-** before *r*, as in *corrupt*.

coral /'kɒrəl/ *n.* **1.** the hard, limy exoskeletons of small marine animals, the individual polyps of which come forth by budding. **2.** such exoskeletons collectively, forming reefs, islands, etc. **3.** an individual coral animal. **4.** a pinkish or reddish-orange colour. *–adj.* **5.** made of coral: *a coral reef; a coral necklace.* **6.** like coral, especially in colour: *a coral dress.*

coral bleaching *n.* the whitening of coral brought about when the coral host expels its zooxanthellae, the algae which give the coral much of its colour and most of its food, such expulsion most commonly occurring because of an increase in ocean temperature under which conditions the zooxanthellae become toxic; bleaching is reversible if the stress-inducing circumstances do not persist and the zooxanthellae grow again, otherwise the starved coral eventually dies.

coral reef *n.* a reef or bank formed by the growth and deposit of coral polyps.

coral snake *n.* a small, venomous but unaggressive snake, *Brachyurophis australis*, of eastern Australia, red with distinctive black and yellow banding.

coral tree *n.* any of several species of *Erythrina*, tropical trees of the family Fabaceae, cultivated for their showy red or orange flowers.

cor anglais /kɔr ˈɒŋgleɪ/ *n.* the alto of the oboe family, richer in tone and a fifth lower than the oboe; English horn.

cord /kɔd/ *n.* **1.** a string or small rope made of several strands twisted or woven together. **2.** → **flex**[1]. **3.** *Anat.* a cord-like structure: *the spinal cord.* **4. a.** a cord-like rib on the surface of cloth. **b.** a ribbed fabric, especially corduroy. **5.** any influence acting as a tie or bond on someone: *tied by a cord of family love.* *–v.t.* **6.** to bind or fasten with cords. *–***corded,** *adj.*

cordate /'kɔdeɪt/ *adj.* heart-shaped, as a shell. *–***cordately,** *adv.*

cord blood *n.* blood which contains many different types of cells, including stem cells, taken from the umbilical cord.

cordial /'kɔdiəl/ *adj.* **1.** hearty; warmly friendly. **2.** invigorating the heart; stimulating. **3. a.** a sweetened, coloured and flavoured liquid concentrate added to water to make a drink. **b.** a glass of this drink. *–***cordially,** *adv. –***cordialness, cordiality** /kɔdiˈæləti/, *n.*

cordillera /kɔdɪlˈjeərə/ *n.* a series of more or less parallel ranges of mountains together with the intervening plateaux and basins. *–***cordilleran** /kɔdiˈleərən/, *n.*

cordon /'kɔdn/ *n.* **1.** a cord or braid worn for ornament or as a fastening. **2.** a ribbon worn, usually diagonally across the breast, as a badge of a knightly or honorary order. **3.** a line of sentinels, military posts, or the like, enclosing or guarding a particular area. *–phr.* **4. cordon off,** to enclose or cut off with or as with a cordon.

corduroy /'kɔdərɔɪ, 'kɔdʒərɔɪ/ *n.* **1.** a cotton pile fabric with lengthwise cords or ridges. **2.** (*pl.*) trousers made of this. *–adj.* **3.** of or like corduroy.

core /kɔ/ *n.* **1.** the central part of a fleshy fruit. **2.** the central, innermost, or most important part of anything: *the core of a curriculum.* **3.** a cylinder of rock, soil, etc., cut out by boring. **4.** the section of the body from the hips to the shoulders, especially the muscles that run the entire length of the torso, and the muscles of the stomach and mid and lower back. **5.** *Computers* the primary memory of a computer. **6.** *Elect.* a piece of iron, bunch of iron wires, etc., forming the central or inner part of an electromagnet, induction coil, etc. **7.** *Physics* the inner part of a nuclear reactor consisting of the fuel and the moderator. **8.** *Geol.* the central mass of the earth, inside the mantle. *–adj.* **9.** fundamental; central: *core promise; core business.* *–v.t.* **10.** to remove the core of (fruit). **11.** to cut from the central part. *–***coreless,** *adj.*

core dump *n. Computers* **1.** a file containing the contents of memory, usually written when a process is aborted, and used for diagnostic purposes. **2.** the writing of such a file. Also, **memory dump.**

corella /kəˈrɛlə/ *n.* any of three Australian cockatoos having predominantly white plumage tinged with pink or red, the endemic **long-billed corella**, *Cacatua tenuirostris*, of parts of Victoria, SA and Tasmania, the **little corella**, *C. sanguinea*, found also in southern New Guinea, and the **western corella**, *C. pastinator*, endemic to south-western WA.

co-respondent /kou-rəˈspɒndənt/ *n.* the person alleged to have committed adultery with the respondent in a suit for divorce (no longer legally relevant in many jurisdictions).

core time *n.* the part of the working day during which one must be at one's place of work. See **flexitime.**

corgi /'kɔgi/ *n.* a dog of either of two ancient Welsh breeds, having short legs, squat body, and erect ears, the **Cardigan** variety having a long tail and the **Pembroke** a short tail. Also, **Welsh corgi.**

coriander /kɒriˈændə/ *n.* **1.** a herbaceous plant, *Coriandrum sativum*, related to the parsley family, with aromatic seedlike fruit and leaves, used in cookery and medicine. **2.** the fruit or seeds. **3.** the leaves; Chinese parsley.

cork /kɔk/ *n.* **1.** the outer bark of the cork oak, used for making stoppers of bottles, floats, etc. **2.** something made of cork. **3.** a piece of cork, or other material (as rubber), used as a stopper for a bottle, etc. **4.** a small float to buoy up a fishing line or to indicate when a fish bites. *–v.t.* **5.** to provide or fit with cork or a cork. **6.** Also, **cork up.** to stop with, or as with, a cork. *–phr.* **7. put a cork in it,** *Colloq.* to be quiet; cease to talk. *–***corklike,** *adj. –***corky,** *adj.*

corkage /'kɔkɪdʒ/ *n.* a charge made by a restaurant, etc., for serving liquor not supplied by the house, but brought in by the customers.

corker /'kɔkə/ *n. Colloq.* **1.** something striking or astonishing. **2.** something very good of its kind.

corkscrew /'kɔkskru/ *n.* **1.** an instrument consisting of a metal spiral with a sharp point and a transverse handle, used to draw corks from bottles. *–adj.* **2.** resembling a corkscrew; helical; spiral. *–v.t.* **3.** to cause to move in a spiral or zigzag course. *–v.i.* **4.** to move in such a course.

corkscrew grass *n.* any of the many species of *Stipa*, found in Australian grasslands, bearing long, spirally twisted awns; spear grass.

corkwood /'kɔkwʊd/ *n.* any of various trees with light and porous wood or corky bark, especially *Erythrina vespertilio* and species of the genus *Duboisia*.

cormorant /'kɔmərənt/ *n.* any bird of the family Phalacrocoracidae, comprising large, web-footed waterbirds with a long neck and a pouch under the beak in which fish are held; often seen standing in sunlight with outstretched wings to dry out after fishing, as the **little pied cormorant**, *P. melanoleucas*, of Australia, New Guinea and Asia.

corn[1] /kɔn/ *n.* **1.** the seed of various grain plants, especially wheat in England, oats in Scotland and Ireland, and maize in North America and Australia. **2.** a grain plant. **3.** a single seed of the grain plants. **4.** *Colloq.* a trite or sentimental writing or style. *–v.t.* **5.** to preserve with salt or pickle in brine: *corned beef.* **–corned**, *adj.*

corn[2] /kɔn/ *n.* **1.** a horny induration or callosity of the epidermis, usually with a central core, caused by undue pressure or friction, especially on the toes or feet. *–phr.* **2. tread on someone's corns**, to hurt someone's feelings.

corn beef *n.* → **corned beef**.

corn chip *n.* a chip (def. 3b) made from processed corn.

corncob /'kɔnkɒb/ *n.* the elongated woody core in which the grains of an ear of maize are embedded.

cornea /'kɔniə/ *n.* (*pl.* **-neas** /-niəz/ *or* **-neae** /-nii/) *Anat.* the transparent anterior part of the external coat of the eye, covering the iris and the pupil, and continuous with the sclera. **–corneal**, *adj.*

corned beef *n.* a cut of beef that is cured in brine. Also, **corn beef**.

corner /'kɔnə/ *n.* **1.** the meeting place of two or three converging lines or surfaces. **2.** the space between two or three converging lines or surfaces near their intersection; angle. **3.** a projecting angle of a solid object: *I bumped my head on the corner of the cupboard.* **4.** the place where two streets meet. **5.** an end; margin; edge. **6.** an awkward or embarrassing position, especially one from which escape is impossible. **7.** *Finance* a monopolising or a monopoly of the available supply of a stock or commodity, to a point permitting control of price. **8.** a region or quarter, especially if considered remote: *all the corners of the earth.* **9.** a piece to protect the corner of anything. **10.** *Soccer, Hockey, etc.* a free kick or hit from the corner of the field taken by the attacking side when the ball has crossed the goal line after last being touched by a member of the defending side. **11.** *Boxing* the space between the junction of two of the ropes, where the contestants rest between rounds. *–v.t.* **12.** to furnish with corners. **13.** to place in or drive into a corner. **14.** to force into an awkward or difficult position, or one from which escape is impossible. **15.** to gain a monopoly in (a market, supply, stock, etc.). **16.** *Surfing* to stay on the shoulder of (a wave). *–v.i.* **17.** to form a corner in a stock or commodity. **18.** to turn a corner in a motor vehicle, especially at speed. *–adj.* **19.** situated at a junction of two roads. **20.** made to be fitted or used in a corner. *–phr.* **21. cut corners**, **a.** to take short cuts. **b.** to bypass an official procedure, or the like. **22. cut off a corner**, to take a short cut. **23. get one's corner**, *Colloq.* to obtain one's share. **24. round the corner**, very close; within walking distance. **25. turn a corner**, to enter into a state of easy progress after a series of difficulties or obstacles. **26. turn the corner**, to begin to get well; improve.

cornerstone /'kɔnəstoʊn/ *n.* **1.** a stone which lies at the corner of two walls, and serves to unite them. **2.** a stone built into a corner of the foundation of an important edifice as the actual or nominal starting point in building, usually laid with formal ceremonies, and often hollowed out and made the repository of documents, etc. **3.** something or someone of prime or fundamental importance.

corner store *n.* a small local shop selling a range of goods for domestic consumption. Also, **corner shop**; *Chiefly WA and SA*, **deli**; *Chiefly Victoria*, **milk bar**.

cornet /'kɔnət/ *n.* **1.** a wind instrument of the trumpet class, with valves or pistons. **2.** a player of a cornet in an orchestra. **3.** an organ stop. **4.** a cone, as for ice-cream.

cornflour /'kɔnflaʊə/ *n.* a starch, or a starchy flour made from maize, rice, or other grain, used as a thickening agent in cookery.

cornice /'kɔnəs/ *n.* **1.** *Archit.* **a.** a horizontal moulded projection which crowns or finishes a wall, building, etc. **b.** the uppermost division of an entablature, resting on the frieze. **2.** an overhanging crest of snow. **3.** the moulding or mouldings between the walls and ceiling of a room. **4.** any of the various other ornamental horizontal mouldings or bands, as for concealing hooks or rods from which curtains are hung or for supporting picture hooks. *–v.t.* (**-niced**, **-nicing**) **5.** to furnish or finish with, or as with, a cornice.

cornucopia /ˌkɔnjə'koupiə/ *n.* **1.** the mythical horn of the goat Amalthaea, which suckled Zeus, represented as overflowing with flowers, fruit, etc., and symbolising plenty. **2.** an overflowing supply. **3.** a horn-shaped or conical receptacle or ornament. **–cornucopian**, *adj.*

corny /'kɔni/ *adj.* (**-nier**, **-niest**) *Colloq.* **1.** lacking subtlety: *a corny joke.* **2.** sentimental; mawkish and of poor quality.

corolla /kə'rɒlə/ *n. Bot.* the internal envelope or floral leaves of a flower, usually of delicate texture and of some colour other than green; the petals considered collectively.

corollary /kə'rɒləri/ *n.* (*pl.* **-ries**) **1.** *Maths, Logic* a proposition which is an extrapolation from a proposition already proved. **2.** an immediate or easily drawn consequence. **3.** a natural consequence or result.

corona /kə'roʊnə/ *n.* (*pl.* **-nas** *or* **-nae** /-ni/) **1.** a white or coloured circle of light seen round a luminous body, especially the sun or moon (in meteorology, restricted to those circles due to the diffraction produced by thin clouds or mist). **2.** a type of circular chandelier, suspended from the roof of a church. **3.** *Anat.* the upper portion or crown of a part, as of the head. **4.** *Bot.* a crown-like appendage, especially one on the inner side of a corolla, as in the narcissus. **5.** *Elect.* → **corona discharge**.

corona discharge *n. Elect.* a discharge, frequently luminous, at the surface of a conductor, or between two conductors of the same transmission line, accompanied by ionisation of the surrounding atmosphere and power loss; brush discharge. Also, **corona**.

coronary /'kɒrənri/ *adj.* **1.** of or like a crown. **2.** *Anat.* **a.** encircling like a crown, as certain blood vessels. **b.** relating to the arteries which supply the heart tissues and which originate in the root of the aorta. *–n.* (*pl.* **-ries**) **3.** a heart attack.

coronary heart disease *n. Pathol.* a heart condition caused by atherosclerosis of the coronary arteries which can result in a heart attack.

coronary thrombosis *n. Pathol.* the occlusion of a coronary arterial branch by a blood clot within the vessel, usually at a site narrowed by arteriosclerosis.

coronation /kɒrə'neɪʃən/ *n.* the act or ceremony of investing a monarch, etc., with a crown.

coronavirus /kəˈrounəvairəs/ *n.* a virus affecting mammals, the cause in humans of the common cold, but, in other animals, of respiratory and intestinal disorders which can be fatal.

coroner /ˈkɒrənə/ *n.* an officer, as of a county or municipality, whose chief function is to investigate by inquest (often before a **coroner's jury**) any death not clearly due to natural causes. **–coronership**, *n.* **–coronial** /kəˈrouniəl/, *adj.*

coronet /ˈkɒrənət, kɒrəˈnɛt/ *n.* **1.** a small or inferior crown. **2.** an insignia for the head, worn by peers or members of nobility. **3.** a crown-like ornament for the head, as of gold or jewels. **4.** the lowest part of the pastern of a horse, just above the hoof.

coronial inquiry /kərouniəl ɪnˈkwairi/ *n.* a formal inquiry held by a coroner in cases where a death may have occurred from other than natural causes, to determine the cause of death and whether, as a consequence, further proceedings should be instituted.

corpora /ˈkɔpərə/ *n.* a plural of **corpus**.

corporal[1] /ˈkɔpərəl/ *adj.* **1.** of the human body; bodily; physical: *corporal punishment.* **2.** personal: *corporal possession.* **3.** *Zool.* of the body proper (as distinguished from the head and limbs). **–corporality**, *n.* **–corporally**, *adv.*

corporal[2] /ˈkɔpərəl, -prəl/ *n. Army, Air Force* a noncommissioned officer in the Australian Army or Royal Australian Air Force ranking below sergeant.

corporate /ˈkɔpərət, -prət/ *adj.* **1.** forming a corporation. **2.** of a corporation. **3.** united in one body. **4.** relating to a united body, as of persons. **5.** relating to a business organisation: *corporate image.* **–corporately**, *adv.*

corporate citizen *n.* a business viewed as a member of a community with obligations beyond its commercial aspirations.

corporate governance *n.* the system by which a business institution is controlled and directed, especially with regard to regulation of decision-making procedures.

corporate raider *n.* someone who purchases large blocks of a company's shares, thus appearing to threaten a takeover, but in reality hoping to profit by the shares' increase in value when the company or its associates react by attempting to secure control.

corporation /kɔpəˈreɪʃən/ *n.* **1.** a type of organisation, created by law or under authority of law, having a continuous existence irrespective of that of its members, and powers and liabilities distinct from those of its members. **2.** any group of persons united, or regarded as united, in one body.

corporeal /kɔˈpɔriəl/ *adj.* **1.** of the nature of the physical body; bodily. **2.** of the nature of matter; material; tangible: *corporeal property.* **–corporeality, corporealness**, *n.* **–corporeally**, *adv.*

corps /kɔ/ *n.* (*pl.* **corps** /kɔz/) **1.** a military unit of ground combat forces consisting of two or more divisions and other troops. **2.** a group of persons associated or acting together.

corpse /kɔps/ *n.* a dead body, usually of a human being.

corpulent /ˈkɔpjələnt/ *adj.* large or bulky of body; portly; stout; fat. **–corpulence**, *n.* **–corpulently**, *adv.*

corpus /ˈkɔpəs/ *n.* (*pl.* **-puses** *or* **-pora** /-pərə/) **1.** the body of a human or animal. **2.** *Anat.* any of various bodies, masses, or parts of special character or function. **3.** a large or complete collection of writings, laws, etc. **4.** the main part; the bulk.

corpuscle /ˈkɔpʌsəl, ˈkɔpəsəl/ *n. Physiol.* one of the minute bodies which form a constituent of the blood (**blood corpuscles**, both red and white), the lymph (**lymph corpuscles**, white only), etc. **2.** a minute body forming a more or less distinct part of an organism. **3.** a minute particle. **–corpuscular** /kɔˈpʌskjələ/, *adj.*

corpus delicti /ˌkɒpəs dəˈlɪktai/ *n.* the body of essential facts constituting a criminal offence.

corral /kɒˈral/ *n.* **1.** a pen or enclosure for horses, cattle, etc. **–v.t.** (**-ralled, -ralling**) **2.** to confine in, or as in, a corral.

correa /ˈkɒriə/ *n.* any shrub of the genus *Correa*, with large, showy, green-to-white flowers.

correct /kəˈrɛkt/ *v.t.* **1.** to set right; remove the mistakes or faults of: *Susan corrected her sums in class*; *to correct the wheel alignment.* **2.** to point out the errors in: *to correct someone's manners*; *to correct someone's pronunciation.* **3.** to scold (a child, etc.) in order to improve behaviour. **4.** to counteract the working or effect of (something hurtful). **5.** *Physics* to change or adjust so as to make conform with a standard or some desired condition: *to correct a reading to allow for zero error, atmospheric pressure, etc.* **–adj.** **6.** agreeing in fact or truth; free from error, accurate: *a correct statement.* **7.** agreeing with an accepted standard; proper: *correct behaviour.* **–correctly**, *adv.* **–correctness**, *n.* **–corrective**, *adj.* **–corrector**, *n.*

correction /kəˈrɛkʃən/ *n.* **1.** the act of correcting. **2.** something that is substituted or proposed for what is wrong; an emendation. **3.** punishment; chastisement; discipline; reproof. **–correctional**, *adj.*

correctional centre *n.* a prison, usually classified as minimum, medium or maximum security.

correlate /ˈkɒrəleɪt/ *v.t.* **1.** to place in or bring into mutual or reciprocal relation; establish in orderly connection. **–v.i.** **2.** to have a mutual or reciprocal relation; stand in correlation. **–n.** **3.** either of two related things, especially when one implies the other.

correlation /kɒrəˈleɪʃən/ *n.* **1.** mutual relation of two or more things, parts, etc. **2.** *Statistics* the degree of relationship of two attributes or measurements on the same group of elements.

correspond /kɒrəˈspɒnd/ *v.i.* **1.** (sometimes fol. by *with*) to be in agreement or conformity: *his words and actions do not correspond.* **2.** (sometimes fol. by *to*) to be similar or analogous; be equivalent in function, position, amount, etc. **3.** to communicate by exchange of letters. **–correspondingly**, *adv.*

correspondence /kɒrəˈspɒndəns/ *n.* **1.** the act or fact of corresponding. **2.** relation or similarity or analogy. **3.** agreement; conformity. **4.** communication by exchange of letters. **5.** letters that pass between correspondents.

correspondent /kɒrəˈspɒndənt/ *n.* **1.** someone who communicates by letters. **2.** a person employed to contribute news, etc., regularly from a distant place. **3.** someone who has regular business relations with another, especially at a distance. **4.** a thing that corresponds to something else. **–adj.** **5.** matching. **–correspondently**, *adv.*

corridor /ˈkɒrədɔ/ *n.* **1.** a gallery or passage connecting parts of a building. **2.** a passage into which several rooms or apartments open. **3.** a passageway on one side of a railway carriage into which the compartments open. **4.** a narrow tract of land forming a passageway, such as one belonging to an inland country and affording an outlet to the sea: *the Polish Corridor.* **5.** → **migration corridor.** **–adj.** **6.** (of a building) designed with a series of rooms opening off a central passage way, as a corridor school.

corrigendum /kɒrəˈdʒɛndəm/ *n.* (*pl.* **-genda** /-dʒɛndə/) **1.** an error to be corrected, especially an error in print. **2.** (*pl.*) a list of corrections of errors in a book, etc.

corroborate /kəˈrɒbəreɪt/ *v.t.* to make more certain; confirm. **–corroboration**, *n.* **–corroborative** /kəˈrɒbərətɪv/, **corroboratory** /kəˈrɒbərətri/, *adj.* **–corroboratively**, *adv.* **–corroborator**, *n.*

corroboree /kəˈrɒbəri/ n. an Aboriginal assembly of sacred, festive, or warlike character.

corrode /kəˈroʊd/ v.t. **1.** to eat away gradually as if by gnawing. **2.** Chem. to eat away the surface of a solid, especially of metals, by chemical action. **3.** to impair; deteriorate: jealousy corroded his whole being. –v.i. **4.** to become corroded, as by oxidisation. –**corrosion**, n. –**corrosive**, adj. –**corrodible**, adj.

corrugate /ˈkɒrəgeɪt/ v.t. **1.** to draw or bend into folds or alternate furrows and ridges. –v.i. **2.** to wrinkle, as the skin, etc.

corrupt /kəˈrʌpt/ adj. **1.** dishonest; guilty of dishonesty, especially involving bribery: a corrupt judge. **2.** of low character; wicked; evil. **3.** infected or rotting. **4.** inaccurate; containing mistakes or changes: a corrupt text of Shakespeare. **5.** Computers (of data or programs) damaged by errors or electrical interference. –v.t. **6.** to make dishonest, disloyal, or unfair, especially by bribery. **7.** to lower the morals of. **8.** to infect, spoil or rot. **9.** to change (a language, text, etc.) for the worse; debase. **10.** Computers to cause the unintentional alteration or mutilation of (data or programs) in processing, storing or transmission. –**corruptible**, adj. –**corrupter**, n. –**corruptness**, n. –**corruptive**, adj. –**corruptly**, adv.

corruption /kəˈrʌpʃən/ n. **1.** the act or result of corrupting. **2.** the condition of being corrupt; depravity. **3.** bribery. **4.** decay.

corsage /kɔːˈsɑːʒ/ n. **1.** the body or waist of a dress; bodice. **2.** a small bouquet worn by a woman at the waist, on the shoulder, etc.

corset /ˈkɔːsət/ n. (oft. pl.) a shaped, close-fitting inner garment stiffened with whalebone or the like and capable of being tightened by lacing, enclosing the trunk and extending for a distance above and below the waistline, worn (chiefly by women) to give shape and support to the body; stays.

cortege /kɔːˈteɪʒ, -ˈteɪʒ/ n. **1.** a train of attendants; retinue. **2.** a procession. Also, **cortège**.

cortex /ˈkɔːteks/ n. (pl. **-tices** /-təsiːz/) **1.** Bot. the portion of the stem between the epidermis and the vascular tissue; bark. **2.** Zool., Anat. **a.** the rind of an organ, such as the outer wall of the kidney. **b.** the layer of grey matter which covers the surface of the cerebral hemispheres and the cerebellum.

corticoid /ˈkɔːtəkɔɪd/ n. a steroid hormone produced naturally by the adrenal cortex or artificially by synthesising it; with many medical uses, such as reducing swelling and reducing immune-system responses.

cortisol /ˈkɔːtəzɒl/ n. a hormone produced by the adrenal glands; involved in the body's response to stress.

cortisone /ˈkɔːtəzoʊn/ n. a hormone from the adrenal cortex originally obtained by extraction from animal glands, now prepared synthetically from Strophanthus or other plants; used in the treatment of arthritic ailments and many other diseases.

corundum /kəˈrʌndəm/ n. a common mineral, aluminium oxide, Al_2O_3, notable for its hardness. Transparent varieties, including the ruby and sapphire, are prized gems; translucent varieties are used as abrasives.

coruscate /ˈkɒrəskeɪt/ v.i. to emit vivid flashes of light; sparkle; gleam.

corvette /kɔːˈvɛt/ n. a small, lightly armed, fast vessel, used for convoy escort, ranging between a destroyer and a gunboat in size.

cos¹ /kɒz, kɒs/ n. a kind of lettuce, with erect oblong heads and generally crisp leaves. Also, **cos lettuce**.

cos² /kɒz, kɒs/ Maths cosine.

cosech /ˈkoʊsɛʃ/ n. Maths hyperbolic cosecant. See **hyperbolic function**.

cosh /kɒʃ, kɒzˈeɪtʃ/ n. Maths hyperbolic cosine. See **hyperbolic function**.

cosine /ˈkoʊsaɪn/ n. Maths the sine of the complement of a given angle. Abbrev.: cos

cosmeceutical /kɒzməˈsjuːtɪkəl/ n. a pharmaceutical product which has cosmetic benefits.

cosmetic /kɒzˈmɛtɪk/ n. **1.** a preparation for beautifying the complexion, skin, etc. –adj. **2.** serving to beautify; imparting or improving beauty, especially of the complexion. **3.** designed to effect a superficial alteration while keeping the basis unchanged. –**cosmetician**, n. –**cosmetically**, adv.

cosmetic tourism n. travel undertaken for the purpose of undergoing cosmetic surgery, usually at a cheaper price than in the home country and in a pleasant location away from the gaze of family, friends, colleagues, etc.

cosmic /ˈkɒzmɪk/ adj. **1.** of or relating to the cosmos: cosmic philosophy. **2.** characteristic of the cosmos or its phenomena; immeasurably extended in time and space; vast. **3.** forming a part of the material universe, especially outside of the earth. –**cosmically**, adv.

cosmo- a word element representing **cosmos**.

cosmonaut /ˈkɒzmənɔːt/ n. an astronaut, especially one from Russia.

cosmopolitan /kɒzməˈpɒlətn/ adj. **1.** belonging to all parts of the world; not limited to one part of the social, political, commercial, or intellectual world. **2.** Bot., Zool. widely distributed over the globe. **3.** free from local, provincial, or national ideas, prejudices, or attachments; at home all over the world. –n. **4.** someone who is free from provincial or national prejudices. –**cosmopolitanism**, n.

cosmos /ˈkɒzmɒs/ n. **1.** the physical universe. **2.** the world or universe as an embodiment of order and harmony (as distinguished from chaos). **3.** a complete and harmonious system.

cosset /ˈkɒsət/ v.t. to treat as a pet; pamper; coddle.

cossie /ˈkɒzi/ n. Colloq. → swimming costume. Also, **cozzie**.

cost /kɒst/ n. **1.** the price paid to acquire, produce, accomplish, or maintain anything: the cost of a new car is very high. **2.** a sacrifice, loss, or penalty. **3.** (pl.) Law the sums which the successful party is usually entitled to recover for reimbursement of particular expenses incurred in the litigation. **4.** (pl.) Law the charges which a solicitor is entitled to make and recover from the client as remuneration for professional services. –verb (**cost** or, for defs 7 and 8, **costed**, **costing**) –v.t. **5.** to require the expenditure of (money, time, labour, etc.) in exchange, purchase, or payment; be of the price of; be acquired in return for: it cost 50 cents. **6.** to result in a particular sacrifice, loss, or penalty: it may cost him his life. **7.** to estimate or determine the cost of. –v.i. **8.** to estimate or determine costs. –phr. **9.** at all costs or at any cost, regardless of the cost. **10.** at the cost of, incurring the loss of. **11.** cost a bomb, Colloq. to be extremely expensive. **12.** cost an arm and a leg, Colloq. to cost a lot of money. –**costless**, adj.

costal /ˈkɒstl/ adj. of or relating to the ribs or side of the body: costal nerves.

cost-effective adj. offering profits deemed to be satisfactory in view of the costs involved. –**cost-effectively**, adv. –**cost-effectiveness**, n.

costly /ˈkɒstli/ adj. (**-lier**, **-liest**) costing much; of great price or value. –**costliness**, n.

costo- a word element meaning 'rib', as in costoscapular.

cost of living n. the average retail prices of food, clothing, and other necessities paid by a person, family, etc., in order to live at their usual standard.

cost-plus n. the cost of production plus an agreed rate of profit (often used as a basis of payment in government contracts).

cost price *n.* **1.** the price at which a merchant buys goods for resale. **2.** the cost of production.

cost-push inflation *n.* See **inflation** (def. 2c). Compare **demand-pull inflation.**

costume /ˈkɒstʃum/ *n.* **1.** a style of clothing, etc., especially of a particular nation, group of people, period of history, etc.: *Greek national costume.* **2.** clothing or an outfit representing an animal, character, theme, etc.: *a gorilla costume; a clown's costume.* **3.** clothes for a particular time or activity: *a riding costume.* **4.** → **swimming costume.** –*v.t.* **5.** to dress; provide costumes for: *to costume a play.*

costume jewellery *n.* decorative jewellery, often made from cheap materials such as beads, shells, etc., and set with imitation or semiprecious stones, and thus of little monetary value.

cosy /ˈkoʊzi/ *adj.* (**-sier, -siest**) **1.** snug; comfortable. –*n.* (*pl.* **-sies**) **2.** a padded covering for a teapot, boiled egg, etc., to retain the heat. –*phr.* **3. cosy up,** to snuggle together; cuddle. **4. cosy up to,** to ingratiate oneself with. Also, *US,* **cozy.** –**cosily,** *adv.* –**cosiness,** *n.*

cot[1] /kɒt/ *n.* **1.** a child's bed with enclosed sides. **2.** a light, usually portable, bed, especially one of canvas stretched on a frame. –*phr.* **3. hit the cot,** *Colloq.* to go to bed.

cot[2] /kɒt/ *n.* **1.** a small house; cottage; hut. **2.** a small place of shelter or protection.

cotangent /koʊˈtændʒənt/ *n. Maths* the tangent of the complement, and hence the reciprocal of the tangent, of a given angle. *Abbrev.:* cot or cotan –**cotangential** /ˌkoʊtænˈdʒɛnʃəl/, *adj.*

cotanh /ˈkoʊθæn, ˈkoʊtænʃ/ *n. Maths* hyperbolic cotangent. See **hyperbolic function.**

cot case *n. Colloq.* (*humorous*) someone who is exhausted, drunk, or in some way incapacitated, and fit only for bed.

cot death *n.* the sudden and apparently inexplicable death of a child while sleeping. See **sudden infant death syndrome.**

cote /koʊt/ *n.* a shelter for doves, pigeons, sheep, etc.

coterie /ˈkoʊtəri/ *n.* **1.** a group of persons who associate closely, especially for social purposes. **2.** a clique.

cotoneaster /kəˌtoʊniˈæstə/ *n.* any plant of the genus *Cotoneaster,* many of which are cultivated for their usually red berries.

cottage /ˈkɒtɪdʒ/ *n.* a small bungalow.

cottage cheese *n.* a kind of soft unripened white cheese made of skim milk curds without rennet.

cottage industry *n.* an industry, such as knitting, pottery, or weaving, carried out in the home of the worker.

cotter /ˈkɒtə/ *n.* a pin, wedge, key, or the like, fitted or driven into an opening in order to secure something or hold parts together. **2.** → **cotter pin.**

cotter pin *n.* a cotter having a split end which is spread after being pushed through a hole, to prevent the cotter from working loose.

cotton /ˈkɒtn/ *n.* **1.** a soft, white, downy substance, consisting of the hairs of fibres attached to the seeds of plants of the genus *Gossypium,* used in making fabrics, thread, wadding, guncotton, etc. **2.** a plant yielding cotton, as *G. hirsutum* (**upland cotton**) or *G. peruvianum* (**sea-island cotton**). **3.** such plants collectively, as a cultivated crop. **4.** cloth, thread, etc., made of cotton. **5.** any soft, downy substance resembling cotton but growing on some other plant. –*phr. Colloq.* **6. cotton on (to),** to understand; perceive the meaning or purpose (of). **7. cotton to,** to take a liking to.

cotton bud *n.* (*from trademark*) a small thin stick, the ends of which are wound with cottonwool, suitable for cleansing or applying lotions to the nostril, ear, etc.

cotton plant *n.* a sub-alpine New Zealand daisy, *Celmisia spectabilis,* with a soft felted tomentum.

cottontree /ˈkɒtnˌtri/ *n.* a yellow flowered tree of tropical coasts, *Hibiscus tiliaceus,* with bark fibre useful for cordage.

cottonwood /ˈkɒtnwʊd/ *n.* **1.** a medium evergreen tree, *Hibiscus tiliaceus,* with heart-shaped leaves which are downy on the underside, and yellow flowers with a crimson throat; found in coastal areas of northern NSW, Qld and islands of the Pacific. **2.** a shrub of eastern Australia, *Bedfordia salicina,* with downy leaves. **3.** Also, **tauhinu, tawine.** the New Zealand heath-like shrub, *Cassinia leptophylla,* which has a white tomentum on the under surface of leaves and branches. **4.** any of several American species of poplar, such as *Populus deltoides,* with cotton-like tufts on the seeds.

cottonwool /kɒtnˈwʊl/ *n.* **1.** raw cotton for surgical dressings and toilet purposes which has had its natural wax chemically removed. **2.** cotton in its raw state, as on the boll or gathered for use. **3.** *Colloq.* a protected and comfortable state or existence. Also, **cotton wool.**

cotyledon /kɒtəˈlidn/ *n.* **1.** *Bot.* the primary or rudimentary leaf of the embryo of seed plants. **2.** *Zool.* a tuft or patch of villi on the placenta of most ruminants. –**cotyledonal,** *adj.* –**cotyledonary,** *adj.*

couch[1] /kaʊtʃ/ *n.* **1.** an upholstered seat for two or more people, usually with a back and armrests; lounge. **2.** a backless piece of furniture, used especially by doctors for patients. **3.** a bed or other place for resting. –*v.t.* **4.** to put into words; express: *couched in official terms.* **5.** to lay or put down. –*v.i.* **6.** to lie at rest. **7.** to lie in hiding; lurk.

couch[2] /kutʃ/ *n.* **1.** any of various grasses of the genus *Cynodon,* especially *C. dactylon,* characterised by creeping rootstocks, by means of which it multiplies rapidly; popular as lawn grass. **2.** → **twitch**[2]. Also, **couch grass.**

cougar /ˈkuɡə/ *n.* → **puma.**

cough /kɒf/ *v.i.* **1.** to expel the air from the lungs suddenly and with a characteristic noise. **2.** *Colloq.* to confess. –*v.t.* **3.** to expel by coughing: *to cough blood.* –*n.* **4.** the act or sound of coughing. **5.** an illness characterised by frequent coughing. –*phr.* **6. cough one's lungs out,** to suffer a prolonged and violent fit of coughing. **7. cough up, a.** to expel by coughing: *to cough up blood.* **b.** *Colloq.* to give up; hand over: *to cough up five dollars.* **c.** *Colloq.* to divulge: *to cough up information.* **d.** *Colloq.* to make a financial contribution: *to be asked to cough up for a good cause.* –**cougher,** *n.*

could /kʊd/, *weak form* /kəd/ *v.* (*modal*) **1.** past tense of **can**[1]: *he could speak Chinese; I couldn't help overhearing; they said we could go.* **2.** referring to a potential event or situation: *you could do it if you tried; her health could be better; they could take a day's leave.* **3.** indicating inclination: *sometimes I could throttle her.* **4.** expressing uncertainty: *this could indicate instability of mind; they could still be alive.* **5.** used in polite requests: *could you open the door, please?*

coulomb /ˈkulɒm/ *n. Physics* the derived SI unit of electric charge, defined as the quantity of electricity transferred by 1 ampere in 1 second. *Symbol:* C

coulomb force *n.* the force between two electrically charged bodies. If the charges are of the same polarity, either positive or negative, the force is repulsive (**coulomb repulsion**); if they are of opposite polarity the force is attractive (**coulomb attraction**).

council /ˈkaʊnsəl/ *n.* **1.** an assembly of persons convened or appointed for consultation, deliberation, or advice. **2.** the local administrative body of a city, municipality, or shire.

councillor /ˈkaʊnsələ/ *n.* a member of a council, especially a local administrative council. Also, *Chiefly US*, **councilor.** –**councillorship,** *n.*

counsel /ˈkaʊnsəl/ *n.* **1.** advice; opinion or instruction given in directing the judgement or conduct of another. **2.** interchange of opinions as to future procedure; consultation; deliberation: *to take counsel with one's partners.* **3.** deliberate purpose; plan; design. **4.** the barrister or barristers engaged in the direction of a cause in court; a legal adviser. –*verb* (**-selled** *or*, *Chiefly US*, **-seled, -selling** *or*, *Chiefly US*, **-seling**) –*v.t.* **5.** to give counsel to; advise. **6.** to urge the doing or adoption of; recommend (a plan, etc.). **7.** to give official notice to (an employee) of shortcomings in the performance of their duties. –*v.i.* **8.** to give counsel or advice. –*phr.* **9. counsel of perfection,** excellent but impractical advice. **10. keep one's own counsel,** to keep secret one's opinion or plans.

counsellor /ˈkaʊnsələ/ *n.* **1.** someone who counsels; an adviser. **2.** a high-ranking officer in a diplomatic mission. **3.** a professional psychologist employed in a school to advise students on both personal and educational problems; guidance officer. **4.** a person trained to give help and advice, especially to someone experiencing difficulty of some kind: *bereavement counsellor; trauma counsellor.* Also, *US*, **counselor.** –**counsellorship,** *n.*

count¹ /kaʊnt/ *v.t.* **1.** to check over one by one (the individuals of a collection) in order to ascertain their total number; enumerate. **2.** to reckon up; calculate; compute. **3.** to list or name the numerals up to. **4.** to include in a reckoning; take into account. **5.** to reckon to the credit of another; ascribe; impute. **6.** to esteem; consider. –*v.i.* **7.** to count the items of a collection one by one in order to know the total. **8.** to list or name the numerals in order. **9.** to reckon numerically. **10.** to have a numerical value (as specified). **11.** to be accounted or worth: *a book which counts as a masterpiece.* **12.** to enter into consideration: *every effort counts.* –*n.* **13.** the act of counting; enumeration; reckoning; calculation. **14.** the number representing the result of a process of counting, such as the number of sheep shorn by an individual shearer, or the number of cattle in a muster, etc. **15.** an accounting. **16.** *Law* a distinct charge or cause of action in a declaration or indictment. **17.** *Boxing* the calling aloud by the referee of ten seconds, after which, if a boxer is unable to stand up, a loss by knockout is declared. –*phr.* **18. count for,** to be worth; amount to. **19. count in,** to include in a projected enterprise. **20. count off,** to divide into groups by calling off numbers in order. **21. count on** (or **upon**), **a.** to depend or rely on. **b.** to allow for as a possibility: *they didn't count on the visitors coming early.* **22. count out,** **a.** to count (something, especially money), handling each unit individually: *to count out the change.* **b.** to count (sheep or cattle) as they leave the pen or paddock, as after shearing, branding, etc. **c.** to exclude: *count me out.* **d.** *Boxing* to proclaim (someone) the loser because of their inability to stand up before the referee has counted ten seconds. **23. on all counts,** in every respect. **24. out for the count,** *Colloq.* **a.** *Boxing* still knocked out after the referee's count of ten. **b.** completely exhausted. **c.** unable to continue an activity. –**countable,** *adj.*

count² /kaʊnt/ *n.* (in some European countries) a nobleman corresponding in rank to the English earl.

countdown /ˈkaʊntdaʊn/ *n.* **1.** the final check prior to the firing of a missile, detonation of an explosive, etc. With the precise moment of firing or detonation designated as zero, the days, hours, minutes, and seconds are counted backwards from the initiation of a project. **2.** the period of time preceding such an event or the procedure carried out in that time. **3.** the final check or period of time preceding any large-scale project.

countenance /ˈkaʊntənəns/ *n.* **1.** aspect; appearance, especially the look or expression of the face. **2.** the face; visage. **3.** composed expression of face. **4.** appearance of favour; encouragement; moral support. –*v.t.* (**-anced, -ancing**) **5.** to give countenance or show favour to; encourage; support. **6.** to tolerate; permit. –*phr.* **7.** in **countenance,** unabashed. **8. out of countenance,** visibly disconcerted, or abashed. –**countenancer,** *n.*

counter¹ /ˈkaʊntə/ *n.* **1.** a table or board on which money is counted, business is transacted, or goods are laid for examination. **2.** (in a cafe, restaurant or hotel) a long, narrow table, shelf, bar, etc., at which customers eat. **3.** anything used in keeping account, as in games, especially a round or otherwise shaped piece of metal, ivory, wood, or other material. **4.** an imitation coin or token. –*phr.* **5. over the counter,** (of medicines) without a prescription: *you can buy these tablets over the counter.* **6. under the counter,** **a.** clandestine or reserved for favoured customers. **b.** in a manner other than that of an open and honest business transaction; clandestinely and often illegally.

counter² /ˈkaʊntə/ *n.* **1.** someone who counts. **2.** an apparatus for counting. **3. a.** *Electronics* a circuit for counting electrical impulses. **b.** Also, **counter tube.** *Physics* a device for counting ionising events, such as a Geiger counter.

counter³ /ˈkaʊntə/ *adv.* **1.** in the wrong way; in the opposite direction. **2.** in opposition: *to run counter to the rules.* –*adj.* **3.** opposite; opposed. –*n.* **4.** something opposite to, against or in response to something else. –*v.t.* **5.** to go against; oppose. **6.** to meet or answer (a move, blow, etc.) by another in return. –*v.i.* **7.** to make an answering or opposing move.

counter- a prefixal use of **counter³**, as in *counteract.*

counteract /kaʊntərˈækt/ *v.t.* to act in opposition to; frustrate by contrary action. –**counteraction,** *n.* –**counteractive,** *adj.* –**counteractively,** *adv.*

counterattack /ˈkaʊntərətæk/ *n.* an attack made in response or opposition to another attack.

counterfeit /ˈkaʊntəfət, -fit/ *adj.* **1.** made to imitate something else, so as to deceive; not genuine: *counterfeit coins.* **2.** pretended: *counterfeit grief.* –*n.* **3.** an imitation; forgery. –*v.t.* **4.** to look like or imitate. –*v.i.* **5.** to pretend. –**counterfeiter,** *n.*

counterintuitive /kaʊntərɪnˈtjuətɪv/ *adj.* contrary to what one would normally think or expect. Also, **counter-intuitive.** –**counterintuitively,** *adv.* –**counterintuitiveness,** *n.*

countermand /ˌkaʊntəˈmænd, -ˈmɑːnd/ *v.t.* **1.** to revoke (a command, order, etc.). **2.** to recall or stop by a contrary order. –*n.* **3.** a command, order, etc., revoking a previous one.

counterpane /ˈkaʊntəpeɪn/ *n.* a quilt or coverlet for a bed; a bedspread.

counterpart /ˈkaʊntəpat/ *n.* **1.** a copy; duplicate. **2.** a part that answers to another, as each part of a document executed in duplicate. **3.** one of two parts which fit each other; a thing that complements something else. **4.** a person or thing closely resembling another.

counterpoint /ˈkaʊntəpɔɪnt/ *n.* *Music* the art of combining melodies.

countersign *n.* /ˈkaʊntəsaɪn/ **1.** a password given by authorised persons in passing through a guard. **2.** a sign used in reply to another sign. –*v.t.* /ˈkaʊntəsaɪn, kaʊntəˈsaɪn/ **3.** to sign (a document) in addition to another signature, especially in confirmation or authentication.

countertenor /ˈkaʊntətɛnə/ *n.* *Music* **1.** an adult male voice or voice part higher than the tenor. **2.** a singer with such a voice; a high tenor.

counterterrorism /kaʊntə'tɛrərɪzəm/ *n.* **1.** measures taken by a government, etc., involving such activities as intelligence gathering, police operations, maintenance of security provisions, etc., to prevent or control terrorism. **2.** an act of reprisal by a government, etc., against terrorism. –**counterterrorist**, *adj.*, *n.*

countess /'kaʊntɛs/ *n.* **1.** the wife or widow of a count in the nobility of continental Europe, or of an earl in the British peerage. **2.** a woman having the rank of a count or earl in her own right.

countless /'kaʊntləs/ *adj.* incapable of being counted; innumerable: *the countless stars of the unbounded heavens.*

country /'kʌntri/ *n.* (*pl.* **-tries**) **1. a.** a relatively large area of land occupied by a group of people organised under a single, usually independent, government; nation; state; land: *the countries of Asia; to visit a foreign country.* **b.** the people forming such a group: *the whole country rebelled.* **2.** any considerable territory demarcated by geographical conditions or by a distinctive population. **3.** the land of one's birth or citizenship. **4.** *Aboriginal English* traditional land with its embedded cultural values relating to the Dreamtime. **5. a.** land, especially with reference to its character, quality, or use: *sandstone country; farming country.* **b.** land, especially with reference to its association with a person or people: *Lawson country.* –*adj.* **6.** of the country; rural. **7.** rude; unpolished: *country manners.* –*phr.* **8. go to the country**, to call an election. **9. the country, a.** the rural districts (as opposed to towns or cities): *to have a holiday in the country.* **b.** people living in rural areas, considered collectively: *the country votes differently to the city.*

country and western *n.* a type of music originating in the southern and western United States of America, consisting mainly of rural songs accompanied by a stringed instrument such as the guitar or fiddle. Also, **country music.**

county /'kaʊnti/ *n.* (*pl.* **-ties**) **1.** (in NSW) an area of land delineated for administrative convenience or some specific purpose such as development planning or the supply of electricity. **2.** a larger division, as for purposes of local administration, in New Zealand, Canada, etc.

coup /ku/ *n.* (*pl.* **coups** /kuz/) **1.** an unexpected and successfully executed stratagem; masterstroke. **2.** → **coup d'état.**

coup de grâce /ku də 'gras/ *n.* (*pl.* **coups de grâce** /ku də 'gras/) **1.** a deathblow, such as a bullet in the head, to make sure the person being executed is dead. **2.** a finishing stroke.

coup d'état /ku deɪ'ta/ *n.* (*pl.* **coups d'état** /ku deɪ'ta/) a sudden and decisive measure in politics, especially one effecting a change of government illegally or by force.

coupe[1] /kup, 'kupeɪ/ *n.* **1.** a chilled dessert consisting of fruit and ice-cream. **2.** a stemmed glass in which such a dessert may be served. **3.** a shallow, bowl-shaped dish.

coupe[2] /kup/ *n.* a single defined area of forest, usually less than 50 hectares, from which trees are, or will be, harvested for sawlogs or woodchips.

coupe[3] /kup/ *n. Chiefly US* → **coupé.**

coupé /'kupeɪ/ *n.* an enclosed two-door car with only one seat or set of seats. Also, *Chiefly US,* **coupe.**

couple /'kʌpəl/ *n.* **1.** a combination of two; a pair. **2.** two people who live together: *a married couple.* **3.** a small number; a few: *in a couple of minutes; a couple of things to do.* **4.** *Mechanics* a pair of equal, parallel forces acting in opposite directions and tending to produce a circular movement. –*v.t.* **5.** to link together (in a pair). –*v.i.* **6.** to join in a pair; unite. –**coupler**, *n.*

couplet /'kʌplət/ *n.* **1.** a pair of successive lines of verse, especially such as rhyme together and are of the same length. **2.** a pair; couple.

coupling /'kʌplɪŋ/ *n.* **1.** any mechanical device for uniting or connecting parts or things. **2.** a device used in joining railway carriages, etc. **3.** *Elect.* the association of two circuits or systems in such a way that power may be transferred from one to the other.

coupon /'kupɒn/ *n.* **1.** a separable part of a certificate, ticket, advertisement, etc., entitling the holder to something. **2.** one of a number of such parts calling for periodical payments on a bond. **3.** a separate ticket or the like, for a similar purpose. **4.** a printed entry form for football pools, newspaper competitions, etc. **5.** a detachable printed certificate, issued as a means of rationing commodities and goods to ensure fair distribution of short supplies.

courage /'kʌrɪdʒ/ *n.* the quality of mind that enables one to encounter difficulties and danger with firmness or without fear; bravery. –**courageous** /kə'reɪdʒəs/, *adj.*

courgette /kɔ'ʒɛt/ *n.* → **zucchini.**

courier /'kʊriə/ *n.* **1.** a messenger sent in haste. **2.** someone employed to take charge of the arrangements of a journey. **3.** someone who works for a courier service. –*v.t.* **4.** to deliver (a letter, parcel, etc.) as a courier does.

course /kɔs/ *n.* **1.** advance in a particular direction; onward movement. **2.** the path, route or channel along which anything moves: *the course of a stream; the course of a ship.* **3.** the ground, water, etc., on which a race is run, sailed, etc. **4.** the continuous passage or progress through time or a succession of stages: *in the course of a year; the course of a battle.* **5.** customary manner of procedure; regular or natural order of events: *the course of a disease; the course of an argument; a matter of course.* **6.** a mode of conduct; behaviour. **7.** a particular manner of proceeding: *try another course with him.* **8.** a systematised or prescribed series: *a course of studies, lectures, medical treatments, etc.* **9.** any one of the studies in such a series: *the first course in algebra.* **10.** a part of a meal served at one time: *the main course was steak.* **11.** a continuous horizontal (or inclined) range of stones, bricks, or the like, in a wall, the face of a building, etc. –*v.t.* **12.** to run through or over. –*v.i.* **13.** to run; move swiftly; race. –*phr.* **14. in due course**, in the proper or natural order; at the right time. **15. of course, a.** certainly; obviously. **b.** *Obs.* naturally; as to be expected: *a ruling to be applied of course.*

court /kɔt/ *n.* **1.** an open space wholly or partly enclosed by a wall, buildings, etc. **2.** a large building within such a space. **3.** a stately dwelling; manor house. **4.** a short street. **5.** a smooth, level area on which to play tennis, netball, etc. **6.** one of the divisions of such an area. **7.** the residence of a sovereign or other high dignitary; palace. **8.** the collective body of persons forming a sovereign's retinue. **9.** a sovereign and his or her councillors as the political rulers of a state. **10.** a formal assembly held by a sovereign. **11.** homage paid, as to a sovereign. **12.** *Law* **a.** a place where justice is administered. **b.** a judicial tribunal duly constituted for the hearing and determination of cases. **c.** the judge or judges who sit in a court. –*v.t.* **13.** to endeavour to win the favour of. **14.** to seek the affections of; woo. **15.** to attempt to gain (applause, favour, a decision, etc.). **16.** to hold out inducements to; invite. **17.** to provoke or risk provoking as a consequence of one's actions: *to court disaster.* –*v.i.* **18.** to seek another's love; woo. –*phr.* **19. hold court, a.** (of a sovereign) to have a formal assembly. **b.** to preside in regal fashion over a group of followers and admirers. **20. out of court, a.** *Law* without a hearing; privately. **b.** *Colloq.* out of the question; not to be considered. **21. pay court,**

(sometimes fol. by *to*) to give assiduous attention in order to gain favour or affection: *pay court to the new president.*

court card *n.* a king, queen, or knave in a pack of playing cards.

courteous /ˈkɜtiəs/ *adj.* having or showing good manners; polite. **–courteously,** *adv.* **–courteousness,** *n.*

courtesan /ˈkɔtəzæn/ *n.* **1.** a court mistress. **2.** any female prostitute.

courtesy /ˈkɜtəsi/ *n.* **1.** excellence of manners or behaviour; politeness. **2.** a courteous act or expression. **3.** acquiescence; indulgence; consent: *a title by courtesy rather than by right.*

courthouse /ˈkɔthaʊs/ *n.* a building in which courts of law are held.

courtier /ˈkɔtiə/ *n.* **1.** someone in attendance at the court of a sovereign. **2.** someone who seeks favour by obsequiousness.

courtly /ˈkɔtli/ *adj.* (**-lier, -liest**) **1.** polite; elegant; refined. **2.** flattering; obsequious. **–courtliness,** *n.*

court martial *n.* (*pl.* **courts martial** *or* **court martials**) a court consisting of naval, army, or air force officers appointed by a commander to try charges of offence against martial law.

court order *n.* → **order** (def. 2).

court reporter *n.* **1.** Also, **court recorder.** a person whose job is to record the proceedings of a court or court-related hearing, using handwritten shorthand, a stenotype machine or sound equipment. **2.** a news reporter responsible for reporting on court proceedings.

courtship /ˈkɔtʃɪp/ *n.* **1.** the seeking of a person's affections, especially with a view to marriage. **2.** the period during which one seeks another person's affections. **3.** distinctive animal behaviour seen before and during mating.

courtyard /ˈkɔtjad/ *n.* a space enclosed by walls, next to or within a castle, large house, etc.

couscous /ˈkuskʊs/ *n.* small grains comprising largely semolina but with some flour and salt added.

cousin /ˈkʌzən/ *n.* **1.** the son or daughter of an uncle or aunt. **2.** a person related by descent in a diverging line from a known common ancestor. The children of brothers and sisters are to each other **cousins, cousins-german, first cousins,** or **full cousins.** The children of first cousins are **second cousins** to each other. Often, however, the term **second cousin** is used loosely to refer to the son or daughter of one's first cousin, properly a **first cousin once removed. 3.** a kinsman or kinswoman. **4.** a person or thing related to another by similar natures, languages, etc.: *our Canadian cousins.* **5.** a term of address from one sovereign to another or to a great noble. **–cousinhood, cousinship,** *n.* **–cousinly,** *adj., adv.*

couturier /kuˈturiə/ *n.* someone who designs, makes, and sells fashionable clothes for women. **–couturière** /kuˌturiˈɛə/, *fem. n.*

cove¹ /koʊv/ *n.* **1.** a small indentation or recess in the shoreline of a sea, lake, or river. **2.** a sheltered nook. **3.** a hollow or recess in a mountain; cave; cavern. **4.** a recess with precipitous sides in the steep flank of a mountain.

cove² /koʊv/ *n.* **1.** *Colloq.* a man: *a rum sort of cove.* **2.** *Aust., NZ Obs.* a boss (**boss¹** def. 1), especially the manager of a sheep station.

coven /ˈkʌvən/ *n.* **1.** a gathering of witches. **2.** a company of thirteen witches.

covenant /ˈkʌvənənt/ *n.* **1.** an agreement between people; contract. **2.** *Theology* an agreement made by God with humanity, as recorded in the Bible. **3.** *Law* a formal sealed contract. **–v.i. 4.** to enter into a covenant. **–v.t. 5.** to promise by covenant.

cover /ˈkʌvə/ *v.t.* **1.** to put something over or upon as for protection or concealment. **2.** to be or serve as a covering for; extend over; occupy the surface of. **3.** to put a cover or covering on; clothe. **4.** to put one's hat on (one's head). **5.** to invest (oneself): *she covered herself with glory.* **6.** to shelter; protect; serve as a defence to. **7.** *Mil.* **a.** to be in line with by occupying a position directly before or behind. **b.** to protect (a soldier, force, or military position) during an expected period of combat by taking a position from which any hostile troops can be fired upon who might shoot at the soldier, force, or position. **8.** to take charge or responsibility for: *an assistant covered his post while he was ill.* **9.** *Theatre* to understudy: *is anyone covering Lady Macbeth?* **10.** to hide from view; screen. **11.** to spread thickly the surface of. **12.** to aim directly at, as with a pistol. **13.** to have within range, as a fortress does certain territory. **14.** to include; comprise; provide for; take in: *this book covers all common English words.* **15.** to suffice to defray or meet (a charge, expense, etc.); offset (an outlay, loss, liability, etc.). **16.** to deposit the equivalent of (money deposited), as in wagering; accept the conditions of (a bet, etc.). **17.** to insure against risk: *covered by a comprehensive policy.* **18.** to act as reporter of (occurrences, performances, etc.), as for a newspaper, etc. **19.** to pass or travel over. **20.** (of a male animal) to copulate with. **21. a.** to play a card on top of (a card previously played). **b.** to play a higher card than (the cards previously played). **–n. 22.** that which covers, as the lid of a vessel, the binding of a book, etc. **23.** protection; shelter; concealment. **24.** adequate insurance against risk as loss, damage, etc. **25.** woods, underbrush, etc., serving to shelter and conceal wild animals or game; a covert. **26.** vegetation which serves to protect or conceal animals, such as birds, from excessive sunlight or drying, or from predators. **27.** one of a number of plastic sheets brought out in the event of rain falling before or during a game to protect the playing surface. **28.** something which veils, screens, or shuts from sight. **29.** an assumed occupation, identity, or activity adopted to conceal the true one: *her job as an embassy cook was only a cover.* **30.** a set of articles (plate, knife, fork, etc.) laid at table for one person. **31.** *Finance* funds to cover liability or secure against risk of loss. **32.** *Philately* an envelope or outer wrapping for mail, complete with stamp and post mark. **33.** *Cricket* **a.** a fielding position at cover point or extra cover. **b.** the fielder in this position. **34.** → **cover version.** **–phr. 35. break cover,** to emerge, especially suddenly, from a place of concealment. **36. cover for, a.** to conceal the evidence of wrongdoing for (someone), as by providing an alibi. **b.** to serve as a substitute for (someone who is absent): *she covered for the telephonist during lunch hour.* **c.** to provide protection for, as in military operations, team sports, business, etc. **37. cover up, a.** to cover completely; enfold. **b.** to attempt to conceal. **38. take cover,** to seek shelter or safety. **39. under cover, a.** secret. **b.** secretly. **c.** in an envelope. **40. under the covers, a.** in bed: *to get under the covers with a good book.* **b.** *Computers* in the code that produces the visible output. **–coverer,** *n.* **–coverless,** *adj.*

cover charge *n.* a fixed amount paid at a restaurant, nightclub, etc., for service or entertainment, to which other charges are added.

covering /ˈkʌvərɪŋ/ *n.* something laid over or wrapped around a thing, especially for concealment, protection, or warmth.

coverlet /ˈkʌvələt/ *n.* the outer covering of a bed; a bedspread.

cover note *n.* a document given by an insurance company or agent to the insured to provide temporary coverage until a policy is issued.

cover point *n. Cricket* **1.** a fielding position between point and mid-off. **2.** the fielder in this position.

covert /ˈkʌvət, ˈkoʊvɜːt/ *adj.* **1.** covered; sheltered. **2.** concealed; secret; disguised. –*n.* **3.** (*pl.*) *Ornith.* the smaller feathers that cover the bases of the large feathers of the wing and tail. **4.** shelter; concealment; disguise; a hiding place. **5.** *Hunting* a thicket giving shelter to wild animals or game. –**covertly,** *adv.* –**covertness,** *n.*

cover-up *n.* **1.** an attempt at concealment. **2.** a fabrication; an excuse. **3.** a garment designed to go over the top of a swimsuit, usually made of the same material.

cover version *n.* an additional recording of a song, etc., which has already been released by another performer.

covet /ˈkʌvət/ *v.t.* **1.** to desire inordinately, or without due regard to the rights of others; desire wrongfully. **2.** to wish for, especially eagerly. –**covetable,** *adj.* –**coveter,** *n.* –**covetous,** *adj.*

covey /ˈkʌvi/ *n.* a brood or small flock of partridges or similar birds.

cow¹ /kaʊ/ *n.* **1. a.** a large bovine, *Bos taurus*, the **domestic cow**, owing ancestry to both the European aurochs, *B. primigenius* and the Asian zebu, *B. indicus*, domesticated since prehistoric times and bred into many breeds, as the Jersey, Hereford, Friesian, etc., especially for dairy and beef farming. **b.** a mature female domestic cow. **2.** a mature female of any bovine animal, especially of the genus *Bos*. **3.** the female of various other large animals, as the elephant, whale, etc. **4.** *Colloq.* an ugly or bad-tempered woman. **5.** *Colloq.* (*derog.*) any person or thing. **6.** *Colloq.* a person specified as objectionable (*rotten cow*), wretched (*poor cow*), or foolish (*silly cow*), etc. –*phr. Colloq.* **7. a cow of a ...,** an extremely difficult, unpleasant, disagreeable ...: *a cow of a job.* **8. till the cows come home,** for a long time; forever.

cow² /kaʊ/ *v.t.* to frighten with threats, etc.; intimidate.

coward /ˈkaʊəd/ *n.* **1.** someone who lacks courage to meet danger or difficulty; someone who is basely timid. –*adj.* **2.** lacking courage; timid. –**cowardice,** *n.* –**cowardly,** *adj., adv.*

cowboy /ˈkaʊbɔɪ/ *n.* **1.** *Chiefly US* someone employed in the care of cattle; a stockman. **2.** someone who does not feel constrained by the rules that most people conform to and who is in consequence regarded as reckless and dangerous; maverick.

cower /ˈkaʊə/ *v.i.* **1.** to crouch in fear or shame. **2.** to bend with the knees and back; stand or squat in a bent position.

cowl /kaʊl/ *n.* **1.** a hooded garment worn by monks. **2.** a hood-shaped covering for a chimney or ventilating shaft, to increase the draught. **3.** the forward part of the car body supporting the rear of the bonnet and the windscreen, and housing the pedals and dashboard. **4.** a cowling. –**cowled,** *adj.*

cowlick /ˈkaʊlɪk/ *n.* a tuft of hair turned up, usually over the forehead.

cowling /ˈkaʊlɪŋ/ *n.* a streamlined housing for an aircraft engine, usually forming a continuous line with the fuselage or wing.

cow pat *n.* a mass of cow dung, congealed in a more or less circular shape where it has fallen in a paddock, etc. Also, **cowpat, cow cake**.

cowpox /ˈkaʊpɒks/ *n. Vet. Science* an eruptive disease appearing on the teats and udders of cows in which small pustules form which contain a virus used in the vaccination of humans against smallpox.

cowry /ˈkaʊri/ *n.* **1.** the shell of any of the marine gastropods constituting the genus *Cypraea*, such as that of *C. moneta*, a small shell with a fine gloss, formerly used as money in certain parts of Asia, Africa, and the

Pacific Islands, or that of *C. tigris*, a large, handsome shell. **2.** the animal itself. Also, **cowrie**.

cox /kɒks/ *n.* the person who steers a boat and directs the rowers; a coxswain. –**coxless,** *adj.*

coxcomb /ˈkɒkskoʊm/ *n.* a conceited dandy.

coxsackie virus /kɒkˈsæki vaɪrəs, kukˈsaki/ *n.* any of various viruses closely related to the virus of poliomyelitis, causing diseases in humans including meningitis.

coxswain /ˈkɒksən, -sweɪn/ *n.* the person at the helm who steers a lifeboat, racing shell, surfboat, etc. Also, **cockswain**.

coy /kɔɪ/ *adj.* **1.** shy; modest. **2.** affectedly shy or reserved. –**coyly,** *adv.* –**coyness,** *n.*

coyote /kɔɪˈoʊti, kaɪˈoʊti/ *n.* a wild dog, *Canis latrans*, of North and Central America, noted for loud and prolonged howling at night.

cozen /ˈkʌzən/ *v.t.* to cheat; deceive; beguile. –**cozenage,** *n.* –**cozener,** *n.*

CPR /si pi ˈa/ *n.* cardiopulmonary resuscitation; an emergency life-support procedure using a combination of mouth-to-mouth resuscitation and external cardiac massage.

crab¹ /kræb/ *n.* **1.** any of the stalk-eyed decapod crustaceans constituting the suborder Brachyura (**true crabs**) having a short, broad, more or less flattened body, the abdomen or so-called tail being small and folded under the thorax. **2.** any of various other crustaceans (as the **hermit crab**), or other animals (as the **horseshoe crab**), resembling the true crabs. **3.** any of various mechanical contrivances for hoisting or pulling. **4.** → **crablouse.** –*v.i.* (**crabbed, crabbing**) **5.** to move sideways. **6.** to fish for crabs. –*phr.* **7. catch a crab,** *Rowing* to make a faulty stroke, as one in which the blade either enters the water at the wrong angle and sinks too deep, or is held at the wrong angle and fails to enter the water at all. –**crablike,** *adj.*

crab² /kræb/ *n.* **1.** a crabapple. **2.** an ill-tempered or grouchy person. –**crabby,** *adj.*

crabapple /ˈkræbæpəl/ *n.* **1.** a small, sour wild apple. **2.** any of various cultivated species and varieties of apple, small, sour, and astringent or slightly tart, used for making jelly and preserves.

crablouse /ˈkræblaʊs/ *n.* a body louse, *Phthirius pubis*, that generally infests the pubic region and causes severe itching. Also, **crab**.

crabwise /ˈkræbwaɪz/ *adv.* in the manner of a crab; (referring especially to motion) sideways or diagonally. Also, **crabways** /ˈkræbweɪz/.

crack /kræk/ *v.i.* **1.** to make a sudden, sharp sound in, or as in, breaking; snap, as a whip. **2.** to break with a sudden, sharp sound. **3.** to break without complete separation of parts; become fissured. **4.** (of the voice) to break abruptly and discordantly, especially into an upper register. **5.** to fail; give way. **6.** to break with grief. **7.** to become unsound mentally. –*v.t.* **8.** to cause to make a sudden sharp sound; make a snapping sound with (a whip, etc.); strike with a sharp noise. **9.** to break without complete separation of parts; break into fissures. **10.** to break with a sudden sharp sound. **11.** to break (wheat) into coarse particles. **12.** to subject to the process of cracking in the distillation of petroleum, etc. **13.** to damage; impair. **14.** to make (the voice) harsh or unmanageable. **15.** to utter or tell, as a joke. **16.** *Colloq.* to break into (a safe, vault, etc.). **17.** *Colloq.* to open and drink (a bottle of wine, etc.). **18.** *Colloq.* to solve (a mystery, etc.). **19.** *Surfing* to catch and ride (a wave). **20.** *Colloq.* to deal with successfully: *it was a tough assignment but we cracked it.* –*n.* **21.** a sudden, sharp noise, as of something breaking. **22.** the snap of a whip, etc. **23.** a shot, as with a rifle. **24.** a resounding blow. **25.** a break without complete separation of parts; a fissure; a flaw. **26.** a slight opening, as one between door and doorpost. **27.** → **crack cocaine. 28.** *Colloq.* a try; an opportunity or chance. **29.** *Colloq.* a joke; gibe. **30.** *Colloq.* a moment; instant: *he was on his feet again in a crack.* **31.** *Colloq.* the cleft between the buttocks. **32.** *Colloq.* (*taboo*) the vagina and external female genitalia. *–adj.* **33.** *Colloq.* of superior excellence; first-rate. *–phr.* **34. at first crack,** at dawn. **35. crack a smile,** *Colloq.* to smile, though disinclined. **36. crack down,** *Colloq.* (sometimes fol. by *on*) to take severe measures, especially in enforcing discipline. **37. crack hardy** (or **hearty**), *Aust., NZ Colloq.* to endure with patience; put on a brave front. **38. crack it,** *Colloq.* **a.** to be successful in an enterprise, a project, etc. **b.** to have or offer sexual intercourse. **c.** to work as a prostitute. **39. crack of dawn,** the first light of the day. **40. crack of doom,** the end of the world; doomsday. **41. crack on to,** *Colloq.* to strike up a conversation with (someone) with the ultimate purpose of engaging in sexual activity. **42. crack up, a.** to break into pieces. **b.** *Colloq.* to suffer a physical or mental breakdown. **c.** *Colloq.* to laugh uncontrollably. **d.** *Colloq.* to cause to laugh uncontrollably; amuse greatly. **43. get cracking,** *Colloq.* to start an activity, especially energetically. **44. have a crack at,** *Colloq.* to attempt; try.

crack cocaine *n.* a very pure form of cocaine sold in pellet-sized crystalline pieces and prepared with other ingredients for smoking. Also, **crack.**

cracked /krækt/ *adj.* **1.** broken. **2.** broken without separation of parts; fissured. **3.** damaged. **4.** *Colloq.* mentally unsound. **5.** broken in tone, as the voice. *–phr.* **6. be cracked up to be,** *Colloq.* to be reported to be: *not the great actor he's cracked up to be.*

cracker /ˈkrækə/ *n.* **1.** a thin, crisp biscuit. **2.** a kind of firework which explodes with a loud report; firecracker. **3.** → **bonbon** (def. 2). **4.** something which has a particular quality in a high degree: *this pace is a cracker*; *this model is a cracker. –phr. Colloq.* **5. not to have a cracker,** to have no money. **6. not worth a cracker,** of little worth.

cracking /ˈkrækɪŋ/ *n.* **1.** (in the distillation of petroleum or the like) the process of breaking down certain hydrocarbons into simpler ones of lower boiling points, by means of excess heat, distillation under pressure, addition of a catalyst, etc., in order to give a greater yield of low-boiling products than could be obtained by simple distillation. *–adj.* **2.** fast; vigorous: *a cracking pace.* **3.** done with precision: *a cracking salute.* **4.** *Colloq.* first-rate; fine; excellent. *–phr.* **5. get cracking,** *Colloq.* to start an activity, especially energetically.

crackle /ˈkrækəl/ *v.i.* **1.** to make slight, sudden, sharp noises, rapidly repeated. *–v.t.* **2.** to cause to crackle. *–n.* **3.** a crackling noise. **4.** a network of fine cracks, as in the glaze of some kinds of porcelain.

crackling /ˈkræklɪŋ/ *n.* **1.** the making of slight cracking sounds rapidly repeated. **2.** the crisp browned skin or rind of roast pork. **3.** (*usu. pl.*) the crisp residue left when fat, especially that of pigs, is rendered.

crackpot /ˈkrækpɒt/ *Colloq. –n.* **1.** an eccentric or insane person. *–adj.* **2.** eccentric; insane; impractical.

-cracy a word element forming a noun termination meaning 'rule', 'government', 'governing body', as in *autocracy, bureaucracy.*

cradle /ˈkreɪdl/ *n.* **1.** a little bed or cot for a baby, usually on rockers. **2.** the place of early growth of something: *Greece was the cradle of democracy.* **3.** a framework for support or protection. **4.** a kind of box on rockers used to wash gold-bearing gravel or sand to separate the gold. *–v.t.* **5.** to place, hold, or rock (something) as if in a cradle: *cradled in her arms. –cradler, n.*

cradle cap *n.* a manifestation of seborrhoea in infancy, characterised by adherent yellowish plaques on the scalp.

cradle-snatcher *n. Colloq.* someone who shows romantic or sexual interest in a much younger person.

craft /krɑft/ *n.* **1.** skill; ingenuity; dexterity. **2.** skill or art applied to bad purposes; cunning; deceit; guile. **3.** an art, trade, or occupation requiring special skill, especially manual skill; a handicraft. **4.** the members of a trade or profession collectively; a guild. **5.** (*construed as pl.*) boats, ships, and vessels collectively.

craftsman /ˈkrɑftsmən/ *n.* (*pl.* **-men**) **1.** a man who practises a craft; an artisan. **2.** a person skilled in the fine arts, especially one displaying great technical competence. **–craftsmanship,** *n.* **–craftswoman,** *n.*

crafty /ˈkrɑfti/ *adj.* (**-tier, -tiest**) skilful in underhand or evil schemes; cunning, deceitful; sly. **–craftily,** *adv.* **–craftiness,** *n.*

crag /kræg/ *n.* a steep, rugged rock; a rough, broken, projecting part of a rock. **–cragged** /ˈkrægəd/, *adj.*

craggy /ˈkrægi/ *adj.* (**-gier, -giest**) **1.** full of crags or broken rocks. **2.** rugged; rough. **–craggily,** *adv.* **–cragginess,** *n.*

crake /kreɪk/ *n.* any of various small, widely distributed birds of the family Rallidae, frequenting swamps and reedy margins of lakes, as the **spotless crake,** *Porzana tabuensis*, of Australasia, New Zealand and Pacific islands.

cram /kræm/ *verb* (**crammed, cramming**) *–v.t.* **1.** to fill (something) by force with more than it can conveniently hold. **2.** to fill with or as with excess of food. **3.** *Colloq.* to prepare (a person), as for an examination, by assisting them to memorise information quickly. **4.** *Colloq.* to get a knowledge of (a subject) by so preparing oneself. *–v.i.* **5.** to eat greedily or to excess.

cramp¹ /kræmp/ *n.* **1.** a sudden involuntary, persistent contraction of a muscle or a group of muscles, especially of the extremities, sometimes associated with severe pain, as writer's cramp. **2.** (*oft. pl.*) piercing pains in the abdomen. *–v.t.* **3.** to affect with, or as with, a cramp.

cramp² /kræmp/ *n.* **1.** a small metal bar with bent ends, for holding together planks, masonry, etc.; a cramp iron. **2.** a portable frame or tool with a movable part which can be screwed up to hold things together; clamp. **3.** anything that confines or restrains. *–v.t.* **4.** to fasten or hold with a cramp. **5.** to confine narrowly; restrict; restrain; hamper. *–phr.* **6. cramp someone's style,** to hinder someone from displaying their best abilities, or their preferred self-image.

cranberry /ˈkrænbɛri, -bri/ *n.* (*pl.* **-ries**) the red, acid fruit or berry of any plant of the genus *Vaccinium*, such as *V. oxycoccus*, used in making sauce, jelly, etc.

crane /kreɪn/ *n.* **1.** any of a group of large wading birds (family Gruidae) with very long legs, bill, and neck, and elevated hind toe. **2.** (popularly) any of various superficially similar birds of other families, especially any of various tall herons. **3.** a device for moving heavy weights, having two motions, one a direct lift and the other a horizontal movement, and consisting in one of its simplest forms of an upright post turning on its vertical axis and bearing a projecting arm on which the hoisting tackle is fitted. *–v.t.* **4.** to hoist, lower, or move by or as by a crane. **5.** to stretch (the neck) as a crane does.

cranio- a combining form of **cranium.** Also, **crani-.**

cranium /ˈkreɪniəm/ *n.* (*pl.* **-nia** /-niə/ *or* **-niums**) **1.** *Anat.* the skull of a vertebrate. **2.** the part of the skull which encloses the brain. **–cranial,** *adj.*

crank¹ /kræŋk/ *n.* **1.** *Machinery* a device for communicating motion, or for changing rotary motion into reciprocating motion, or vice versa, consisting in its simplest form of an arm projecting from, or secured at right angles at the end of, the axis or shaft which receives or imparts the motion. *–v.t.* **2.** to cause (a shaft) to revolve by applying force to a crank; turn a crank-shaft in (an internal-combustion engine) to start the engine. –*v.i.* **3.** to turn a crank, as in starting a car engine. **4.** to bend. –*phr.* **5. crank up**, to get (something) started or operating smoothly.

crank² /kræŋk/ *Colloq.* –*n.* **1.** an eccentric person, or someone who holds stubbornly to eccentric views. –*adj.* **2.** odd, as typical of a crank: *a crank idea.* **3.** false; phoney: *crank calls*; *a crank letter.*

crankshaft /'kræŋkʃaft/ *n.* a shaft driving or driven by a crank, especially the main shaft of an engine which carries the cranks to which the connecting rods are attached.

cranky /'kræŋki/ *adj.* (**-kier, -kiest**) ill-tempered; cross. –**crankily**, *adv.* –**crankiness**, *n.*

cranny /'kræni/ *n.* (*pl.* **-nies**) a small, narrow opening (in a wall, rock, etc.); a chink; crevice; fissure. –**crannied**, *adj.*

crap /kræp/ *Colloq.* –*n.* **1.** excrement. **2.** nonsense; rubbish. **3.** junk; odds and ends. –*v.i.* (**crapped, crapping**) **4.** to defecate. **5.** Also, **crap on**. to talk nonsense. –*adj.* **6.** of poor quality: *That was a crap movie.* **7.** unpleasant: *I've had a crap day.* –**crappy**, *adj.*

craps /kræps/ *n.* a gambling game played with two dice.

crash /kræʃ/ *v.t.* **1.** to force or impel with violence and noise. **2.** to damage (a car, aircraft, etc.) in a collision. **3.** to fall, hit something or break in pieces noisily. **4.** *Colloq.* to come uninvited or without permission to: *to crash a party.* –*v.i.* **5.** to break or fall to pieces noisily. **6.** to make the noise of something breaking or falling. **7.** to fail suddenly: *the company crashed.* **8.** to move, go or hit with a crash. **9.** (of an aircraft) to fail in flight, hitting the ground with a sudden impact. **10.** (of computers) to shut down because of a fault. **11.** *Colloq.* **a.** to fall asleep when tired out. **b.** to find a place to sleep: *to crash at a friend's house.* –*n.* **12.** a breaking or falling to pieces with a loud noise. **13.** the shock of hitting something and breaking. **14.** a sudden and violent falling to ruin. **15.** the shutting down of a computer system because of a fault. **16.** the sudden failure of a company, etc. **17.** a sudden loud crashing noise. –*adj.* **18.** characterised by all-out, intensive effort, especially to meet an emergency: *a crash course.* –**crasher**, *n.*

crash diet *n.* an extreme dieting regime designed to lose weight very quickly.

crash-hot *adj. Aust. Colloq.* excellent. Also, (*in predicative use*), **crash hot**.

crashing /'kræʃɪŋ/ *adj. Colloq.* complete and utter: *a crashing bore.*

crash tackle *n.* **1.** *Rugby Football* a tactic in which the player with the ball runs directly at the opposition line, attempting to draw the tackle from the opposing players before off-loading the ball to a teammate who can run through the gaps created in the line. **2.** any forceful direct tackle which fells the person tackled.

crash-tackle *v.t.* to bring (someone) down by tackling them forcefully.

crass /kræs/ *adj.* **1.** gross; stupid: *crass ignorance.* **2.** thick; coarse. –**crassly**, *adv.* –**crassness**, *n.*

-crat a word element forming a noun termination meaning 'ruler', 'member of a ruling body', 'advocate of a particular form of rule', as in *aristocrat, autocrat, democrat, plutocrat.* Compare **-cracy**.

crate /kreɪt/ *n.* **1.** a box or framework, usually of wooden slats, for packing and transporting fruit, furniture, etc. **2.** a basket of wickerwork, for the transportation of crockery, etc. **3.** the amount contained by or contents of a crate. **4.** *Colloq.* a motor vehicle, plane, or the like, especially a dilapidated one. –*v.t.* **5.** to put in a crate.

crater /'kreɪtə/ *n.* **1.** the cup-shaped depression or cavity marking the orifice of a volcano. **2.** (in the surface of the earth, moon, etc.) a rounded hollow formed by the

impact of a meteorite. **3.** the hole or pit in the ground where a military mine, bomb, or shell has exploded. –*v.i.* **4.** to form a crater or craters. –*v.t.* **5.** to make a crater or craters in. –**craterlike**, *adj.* –**craterous**, *adj.* –**cratering**, *n.*

cravat /krə'væt/ *n.* a scarf worn by men round the neck as a tie.

crave /kreɪv/ *v.t.* **1.** to long for or desire eagerly. **2.** to need greatly; require. **3.** to ask earnestly for (something); beg for. –**craver**, *n.* –**cravingly**, *adv.*

craven /'kreɪvən/ *adj.* **1.** cowardly; pusillanimous; mean-spirited. –*n.* **2.** a coward. –**cravenly**, *adv.* –**cravenness**, *n.*

craw /krɔ/ *n.* **1.** the crop of a bird or insect. **2.** the stomach of an animal. –*phr.* **3. stick in someone's craw**, to irritate or annoy someone.

crawl /krɔl/ *v.i.* **1.** to move by dragging the body along the ground, as a worm, or on the hands and knees, as a young child. **2.** to progress slowly, laboriously, or timorously: *the work crawled.* **3.** to go stealthily or abjectly. **4.** to behave abjectly and obsequiously. **5.** to be, or feel as if, overrun with crawling things. –*n.* **6.** the act of crawling; a slow, crawling motion. **7.** → **freestyle** (def. 1). –*phr.* **8. crawl with**, to be overrun with: *the city was crawling with tourists.* –**crawler**, *n.* –**crawlingly**, *adv.*

crayfish /'kreɪfɪʃ/ *n.* (*pl.* **-fishes** *or, especially collectively,* **-fish**) **1.** → **lobster** (def. 2). **2.** → **rock lobster**. **3.** → **yabby** (def. 1).

crayon /'kreɪɒn/ *n.* **1.** a pointed stick or pencil of coloured wax, chalk, etc., used for drawing. **2.** a drawing in crayons. –**crayoner, crayonist**, *n.*

craze /kreɪz/ *v.t.* **1.** to impair in intellect; make insane. **2.** to make small cracks on the surface of (pottery, etc.); to crackle. –*v.i.* **3.** to become insane. **4.** to break; shatter. –*n.* **5.** a short-lived fashion, or sudden keenness; fad. **6.** a tiny crack in the glaze of pottery, etc.

crazy /'kreɪzi/ *adj.* (**-zier, -ziest**) **1.** demented; mad. **2.** eccentric; bizarre; unusual. **3.** unrealistic; impractical: *a crazy scheme.* –*phr.* **4. crazy about** (or **for**), intensely enthusiastic or excited about. –**crazily**, *adv.* –**craziness**, *n.*

creak /krik/ *v.i.* **1.** to make a sharp, harsh, grating, or squeaking sound. **2.** to move with creaking. –*v.t.* **3.** to cause to creak. –*n.* **4.** a creaking sound.

cream /krim/ *n.* **1.** the fatty part of milk, which rises to the surface. **2.** any food made with cream or like cream. **3.** any creamlike substance: *face cream.* **4.** the best part. **5.** a yellowish white colour. –*v.i.* **6.** to form cream. **7.** to foam. –*v.t.* **8.** to beat until creamy: *to cream butter and sugar.* **9.** to put cream in or on. –**creamy**, *adj.*

cream cheese *n.* a soft, white, smooth-textured, unripened cheese made of milk and sometimes cream.

crease /kris/ *n.* **1.** a line or mark produced in anything by folding; a fold; a ridge; a furrow. **2.** the sharp vertical ridge in the front and at the back of each leg of a pair of trousers, produced by pressing. **3.** *Cricket* one of three lines near the wicket marking the limits of movement of the bowler or the person batting. –*v.t.* **4.** to make a crease or creases in or on; wrinkle. –**creaser**, *n.* –**creasy**, *adj.*

create /kri'eɪt/ *v.t.* **1.** to make; cause to exist; produce. **2.** to design or invent. **3.** to make into; appoint: *to create someone a peer.* –*v.i.* **4.** *Colloq.* to make a fuss or an uproar. –**creator**, *n.*

creation /kri'eɪʃən/ *n.* **1.** the act or result of creating. **2.** the world; universe. **3.** an original design or invention. –*phr.* **4. the Creation**, the bringing into being of the universe by God. –**creational**, *adj.*

creative /kri'eɪtɪv/ *adj.* **1.** having the quality or power of creating. **2.** resulting from originality of thought or expression. *–phr.* **3. creative of,** productive of. **–creatively,** *adv.* **–creativeness,** *n.*

creature /ˈkritʃə/ *n.* **1.** anything created, animate or inanimate. **2.** an animate being. **3.** an animal, as distinguished from a human. **4.** a human being (often used in contempt, commiseration, or endearment). **5.** a person owing his or her rise and fortune to another, or subject to the will or influence of another.

creche /kreɪʃ, krɛʃ/ *n.* **1.** a nursery where children are cared for while their parents work. **2.** a home for foundlings. **3.** a tableau of Mary, Joseph, and others round the crib of Jesus in the stable at Bethlehem, often built for display at Christmas. Also, **crèche.**

cred /krɛd/ *n. Colloq.* credibility; worthiness of acceptance or respect within a particular group: *street cred.*

credence /ˈkridns/ *n.* **1.** belief: *to give credence to a statement.* **2.** something giving a claim to belief or confidence: *letter of credence.* **3.** Also, **credence table.** a small side table, shelf, or niche for holding articles used in the Eucharist service.

credential /krəˈdɛnʃəl/ *n.* **1.** anything which is the basis for the belief or trust of others in a person's abilities, authority, etc. **2.** (*usu. pl.*) a letter or other testimonial attesting the bearer's right to confidence or authority. *–adj.* **3.** providing the basis for belief or confidence. **–credentialed, credentialled,** *adj.*

credenza /krəˈdɛnzə/ *n.* **1.** a sideboard or small buffet, especially one without legs. **2.** a small side desk attached at right angles to a main desk to facilitate use.

credible /ˈkrɛdəbəl/ *adj.* **1.** capable of being believed; believable. **2.** worthy of belief or confidence; trustworthy. **–credibility, credibleness,** *n.* **–credibly,** *adv.*

credit /ˈkrɛdət/ *n.* **1.** commendation or honour given for some action, quality, etc. **2.** a person or thing being acknowledged as a source of commendation or honour: *a credit to the team.* **3.** influence or authority resulting from the confidence of others or from one's reputation. **4.** repute; reputation. **5.** trustworthiness; credibility: *a story that has credit.* **6.** (*pl.*) a list, appearing at the beginning or end of a film or television program, which shows the names of those who have been associated with its production. **7. a.** official acceptance and recording of the work of a student in a particular course of study. **b.** a unit of a curriculum (short for **credit hour**): *she took the course for four credits.* **8.** Also, **pass with credit.** (in some educational institutions) a result in an examination which indicates performance higher than necessary to pass. **9.** the practice of allowing time for payment for goods, etc., obtained on trust. **10.** reputation of solvency and probity, entitling a person to be trusted in buying or borrowing. **11.** power to buy or borrow on trust. **12.** a sum of money due to a person; anything valuable standing on the credit side of an account. **13.** the balance in one's favour in an account. **14.** *Bookkeeping* **a.** the acknowledgement of payment or value received, in an account by an entry on the right-hand side. **b.** the side (right-hand) of an account on which such entries are made (opposed to *debit*). **c.** any entry, or the total shown, on the credit side. **15.** any deposit or sum against which one may draw. *–v.t.* **16.** to believe; put confidence in; trust; have faith in. **17.** to reflect credit upon; do credit to; give reputation or honour to. **18.** (sometimes fol. by *with*) to accredit: *to credit the child with doing his homework.* **19. a.** *Bookkeeping* to enter upon the credit side of an account; give credit for or to. **b.** to give the benefit of such an entry to (a person, etc.) **20.** to award educational credits to: *credited with three points in history.* *–phr.* **21. be a credit to,** to behave in a way that brings honour to (someone considered a guardian or mentor). **22. do someone credit** or **do credit to someone,** to be a source of honour or distinction to someone. **23. give credit to,** to believe: *to give credit to the theory of*

global warming. **24. give (full) credit to,** to acknowledge the worth of (someone) in achieving something. **25. in good credit with, a.** in a solid financial position in relation to: *in good credit with the bank.* **b.** *Obs.* enjoying the esteem of: *in good credit with the king.* **26. on credit,** by deferred payment. **27. to one's credit,** in acknowledgement of one's good intentions or behaviour.

creditable /ˈkrɛdətəbəl/ *adj.* bringing credit, honour, reputation, or esteem. **–creditableness,** *n.* **–creditably,** *adv.*

credit agency *n.* an organisation that investigates on behalf of a client the creditworthiness of the client's prospective customers.

credit card *n.* a card which identifies the holder as entitled to obtain goods, food, services, etc., without payment of cash, the charges for which are presented in the form of a periodical statement, usually monthly. Compare **debit card.**

creditor /ˈkrɛdətə/ *n.* **1.** someone who gives credit in business transactions. **2.** someone to whom money is due (opposed to *debtor*).

credit rating *n.* an estimation of the extent to which a customer can be granted credit, usually determined by a credit agency.

credit squeeze *n.* **1.** restriction by a government of the amount of credit available to borrowers. **2.** the period during which the restrictions are in operation.

credit union *n.* a financial organisation for receiving and lending money, usually formed by workers in some industry or at some place of employment.

credo /ˈkreɪdoʊ, ˈkridoʊ/ *n.* **1.** any creed or formula of belief. **2.** (*pl.* **credos**)(*also upper case*) the Apostles' or the Nicene Creed.

credulous /ˈkrɛdʒələs/ *adj.* **1.** ready or disposed to believe, especially on weak or insufficient evidence. **2.** marked by or arising from credulity. **–credulity,** *n.* **–credulously,** *adv.* **–credulousness,** *n.*

creed /krid/ *n.* **1.** any system of belief or of opinion. **2.** any formula of religious belief, as of a denomination. **3.** an authoritative formulated statement of the chief articles of Christian belief, such as the Apostles', the Nicene, or the Athanasian Creed. **–creedal, credal,** *adj.* **–creedless,** *adj.*

creek /krik/ *n.* **1.** a small stream, as a branch of a river. **2.** a narrow recess in the shore of the sea; a small inlet or bay. *–phr.* **3. up the creek (without a paddle)** or **up shit creek (without a paddle),** *Colloq.* in a predicament; in trouble.

creep /krip/ *v.i.* (**crept, creeping**) **1.** to move with the body close to the ground, as a reptile or an insect. **2.** to move slowly, imperceptibly, or stealthily. **3.** to enter undetected; to sneak up behind. **4.** to move or behave timidly or servilely. **5.** to move along very slowly, as a motor car in heavy traffic. **6.** (of flesh) to experience a sensation as of something creeping over the skin, especially as a result of feelings of revulsion or horror. *–n.* **7.** the act of creeping. **8.** the slow movement of concrete due to chemical change in concrete over time. **9.** *Eng.* the deformation of metal caused by heat or stress. **10.** *Geol.* the slow and imperceptible down-slope movement of earth or rock. **11.** *Colloq.* an unpleasant, obnoxious, or insignificant person. *–phr.* **12. make someone's flesh creep,** to frighten or repel someone. **13. the creeps,** *Colloq.* a sensation as of something creeping over the skin, usually as a result of feelings of fear or horror.

creeper /ˈkripə/ *n.* **1.** *Bot.* a plant which grows upon or just beneath the surface of the ground, or upon any other surface, sending out rootlets from the stem, such as ivy and couch. **2.** a grappling device for dragging a river, etc.

creepy /ˈkripi/ *adj.* (**-pier**, **-piest**) **1.** that creeps, as an insect. **2.** having or causing a creeping sensation of the skin, as from horror: *a creepy silence.* **3.** *Colloq.* (of a person) unpleasant, obnoxious, or insignificant. –**creepily**, *adv.* –**creepiness**, *n.*

cremains /krəˈmeɪnz/ *pl. n.* the remains of a cremated body; ashes.

cremate /krəˈmeɪt/ *v.t.* **1.** to reduce (a corpse) to ashes by fire. **2.** to consume by fire; burn. –**cremation**, *n.*

crematorium /krɛməˈtɔriəm/ *n.* an establishment for cremating dead bodies.

creole /ˈkrioʊl/ *n.* a language which has developed from a pidgin to become the primary language of a community. Compare **pidgin**.

creosote /ˈkriəsoʊt/ *n.* an oily liquid with a burning taste and a penetrating smell, obtained by the distillation of wood tar, and used as a preservative and antiseptic. –**creosotic** /kriəˈsɒtɪk/, *adj.*

crepe /kreɪp/ *n.* **1.** a thin, light fabric of silk, cotton, or other fibre, with a finely crinkled or ridged surface. **2.** Also, **crepe paper**. thin paper wrinkled to resemble crepe. **3.** a thin pancake. **4.** a black (or white) silk fabric, used for mourning veils, trimmings, etc. –*v.t.* **5.** to cover, clothe, or drape with crepe. Also, **crêpe, crape.**

crept /krɛpt/ *v.* past tense and past participle of **creep**.

crepuscular /krəˈpʌskjələ/ *adj.* relating to or resembling twilight; dim; indistinct.

crescendo /krəˈʃɛndoʊ/ *n.* (*pl.* **-dos**) **1.** a gradual increase in force or loudness. **2.** *Music* a gradual but steady increase in force or loudness.

crescent /ˈkrɛsənt, ˈkrɛzənt/ *n.* **1.** the biconvex figure of the moon in its first quarter, or the similar figure of the moon in its last quarter, resembling a bow terminating in points. **2.** a representation of this shape used as the symbol of Islam. **3.** any crescent-shaped object, as a roll of bread. **4.** a curved street. –*adj.* **5.** increasing; growing.

cress /krɛs/ *n.* **1.** any of various plants of the mustard family with pungent-tasting leaves, often used for salad and as a garnish, especially the **garden cress**, *Lepidium sativum.* **2.** any of various similar plants.

crest /krɛst/ *n.* **1.** a tuft or other natural growth on top of the head of a bird or other animal. **2.** anything like such a tuft. **3.** a (feather) ornament on a helmet. **4.** (the top of) a helmet. **5.** part of a coat of arms, used for badges, etc.: *a school crest.* **6.** the head or top of anything. –*v.t.* **7.** to provide with a crest. **8.** to reach the crest of. –*v.i.* **9.** to form or reach a crest. –**crested**, *adj.* –**crestless**, *adj.*

crested tern *n.* a tern, *Sterna bergii*, with white underparts, grey back wings and tail, and erectile black crown and nape, found around the coast of Australia, and throughout the Indian and Pacific Oceans and south-east Asia.

crestfallen /ˈkrɛstfɔlən/ *adj.* **1.** dejected; dispirited; depressed. **2.** with drooping crest. –**crestfallenly**, *adv.* –**crestfallenness**, *n.*

cretaceous /krəˈteɪʃəs/ *adj.* of the nature of, resembling, or containing chalk.

Cretaceous /krəˈteɪʃəs/ *Geol.* –*adj.* **1.** of or relating to the third and latest of the periods included in the Mesozoic era. –*n.* **2.** Also, **Cretaceous era**. the Cretaceous period. **3.** the system of strata deposited during the Cretaceous period.

cretin /ˈkrɛtn/ *n.* **1.** a fool; a stupid person. **2.** *Pathol. Obsolesc.* a person afflicted with cretinism. –**cretinous**, *adj.*

cretinism /ˈkrɛtənɪzəm/ *n. Pathol. Obsolesc.* a chronic disease, due to absence or deficiency of the normal thyroid secretion, characterised by physical deformity (often with goitre), dwarfism, and idiocy.

crevasse /krəˈvæs/ *n.* a fissure or deep cleft in the ice of a glacier.

crevice /ˈkrɛvəs/ *n.* a crack forming an opening; a cleft; a rift; a fissure. –**creviced**, *adj.*

crew[1] /kru/ *n.* **1.** a group of people working at something together; gang. **2.** a group of people operating a ship, boat, or aircraft. –*v.i.* **3.** to act as (a member of) a crew. –*v.t.* **4.** to provide with a crew. –**crewed**, *adj.*

crew[2] /kru/ *v.* a past tense of **crow**[2] (def. 1).

crew cut *n.* a very closely cropped haircut.

crewel /ˈkruəl/ *n.* a fine worsted yarn used for embroidery, etc. –**crewelwork**, *n.*

crew-neck *adj.* (of garments) having a plain ribbed neckband fitting closely around the neck.

crib /krɪb/ *n.* **1.** a child's cot. **2.** a cattle stall or pen. **3.** a rack or box for food for cattle, horses, etc. **4.** *NZ* (*South Island*) a holiday shack. **5.** *Aust., NZ* (especially among miners, steelworkers, construction workers, etc.) **a.** Also, **crib box**. a bag, metal box, or other container used to carry one's lunch to work. **b.** a packed lunch brought to work. **c.** Also, **crib break**. the lunch break at work. **6.** a framework used in construction. **7.** *Colloq.* an instance of plagiarism. **8. a.** a book which gives a summary of information, sometimes used as a study aid: *she bought a crib on* Jane Eyre *the day before the literature exam.* **b.** a translation or other illicit aid used by students. –*verb* (**cribbed, cribbing**) –*v.t.* **9.** *Colloq.* to copy (another's work); plagiarise. –*v.i.* **10.** *Colloq.* to use a crib.

cribbage /ˈkrɪbɪdʒ/ *n.* a card game basically for two, but also played by three, or four players, a characteristic feature of which is the crib.

crib box *n.* → **crib** (def. 5a).

crib break *n.* → **crib** (def. 5c).

crick /krɪk/ *n.* **1.** a sharp, painful spasm of the muscles, as of the neck or back, making it difficult to move the part. –*v.t.* **2.** to give a crick or wrench to (the neck, etc.).

cricket[1] /ˈkrɪkət/ *n.* any of the orthopterous insects comprising the family Gryllidae, characterised by their long antennae, ability to leap, and the ability of the males to produce shrill sounds by friction of their leathery forewings.

cricket[2] /ˈkrɪkət/ *n.* **1.** an outdoor game played with ball, bats, and wickets, by two sides of eleven players each. –*phr.* **2. not cricket**, *Colloq.* not in accordance with an accepted standard; not fair. –**cricketer**, *n.*

crier /ˈkraɪə/ *n.* **1.** a court or town official who makes public announcements. **2.** someone who cries goods for sale in the streets; a hawker.

crime /kraɪm/ *n.* **1.** an act committed or an omission of duty, injurious to the public welfare, for which punishment is prescribed by law, imposed in a judicial proceeding usually brought in the name of the state. **2.** serious violation of human law: *steeped in crime.* **3.** any offence, especially one of grave character. **4.** serious wrongdoing; sin. **5.** *Colloq.* a foolish or senseless act: *it's a crime to have to work so hard.*

crime ring *n.* an association of criminals or criminal organisations.

crime scene *n.* a place where a crime has been committed, usually cordoned off to protect possible physical evidence.

crime wave *n.* a marked increase in criminal activity in a particular period or place.

criminal /ˈkrɪmənəl/ *adj.* **1.** of or relating to crime or its punishment: *criminal law.* **2.** of the nature of or involving crime. **3.** guilty of crime. –*n.* **4.** a person guilty or convicted of a crime. –**criminally**, *adv.* –**criminality** /krɪməˈnælɪti/, *n.*

criminalise /ˈkrɪmənəlaɪz/ *v.t.* to make into a criminal offence: *to criminalise racism.* Also, **criminalize.** –**criminalisation**, *n.*

criminal law *n.* a body of law dealing with the constituents of criminal behaviour in general, the definition of particular crimes and defences along with the penalties to be applied, and the specific rules relating to criminal legal proceedings. Compare **civil law**.

criminology /ˌkrɪmə'nɒlədʒi/ *n.* the systematic study dealing with the causes of crimes and treatment of criminals. **–criminological** /ˌkrɪmənə'lɒdʒɪkəl/, *adj.* **–criminologist**, *n.*

crimp /krɪmp/ *v.t.* **1.** to press into small regular folds; corrugate; make wavy. **2.** to curl (hair), especially with a hot iron. **–n. 3.** a crimped condition or form. **4.** something crimped. **–crimper**, *n.*

crimson /'krɪmzən/ *adj.* **1.** deep purplish red. **2.** sanguinary. **–n. 3.** a crimson colour, pigment, or dye. **–v.i. 4.** to become crimson; to blush.

cringe /krɪndʒ/ *v.i.* (**cringed, cringing**) **1.** to shrink, bend, or crouch, especially from fear or servility; cower. **2.** to feel embarrassment or discomfort, as when confronted by inappropriate or distasteful social behaviour. **3.** to fawn. **–cringer**, *n.* **–cringingly**, *adv.*

crinkle /'krɪŋkəl/ *v.i.* **1.** to wind or turn in and out. **2.** to wrinkle; crimple; ripple. **3.** to make slight, sharp sounds; rustle. **–crinkly**, *adj.*

crinoline /'krɪnələn/ *n.* **1.** a petticoat of horsehair and flax or other stiff material, formerly worn by women under a full dress skirt. **2.** a hoop skirt.

cripple /'krɪpəl/ *n.* **1.** someone who is partially or wholly deprived of the use of one or more of their limbs; a lame person. **2.** an animal which is disabled by disease, old age, etc., especially one that cannot keep up with the herd. **–v.t. 3.** to disable; impair. **–crippler**, *n.* **–crippled**, *adj.* **–crippling**, *adj.* **–cripplingly**, *adv.*

crisis /'kraɪsəs/ *n.* (*pl.* **crises** /'kraɪsiz/) **1.** a decisive or vitally important stage in the course of anything; a turning point; a critical time or occasion: *a political crisis, a business crisis.* **2.** the point in a play or story at which hostile elements are most tensely opposed to each other. **3.** the point in the course of a disease at which a decisive change occurs, leading either to recovery or to death.

crisp /krɪsp/ *adj.* **1.** hard but dry and easily breakable; brittle: *crisp toast.* **2.** firm and fresh: *crisp lettuce.* **3.** sharp; brisk; decided: *a crisp manner; a crisp reply.* **4.** lively. **5.** cool, dry and refreshing: *crisp air.* **6.** clean and neat: *a crisp uniform.* **7.** wrinkled or curly: *crisp hair.* **–v.t. 8.** to make crisp. **9.** to curl. **–v.i. 10.** to become crisp. **–n. 11.** → **chip** (def. 3b). **12.** something crisp: *burnt to a crisp.* **–crisply**, *adv.* **–crispness**, *n.*

crisscross /'krɪskrɒs/ *adj.* **1.** in crossing lines; crossed; crossing; marked by crossings. **–n. 2.** a crisscross mark, pattern, etc. **–v.i. 3.** to form crossing lines.

criteria /kraɪ'tɪəriə/ *pl. n.* plural of **criterion**.

criterion /kraɪ'tɪəriən/ *n.* (*pl.* **-teria** /-'tɪəriə/) a standard of judgement or criticism; an established rule or principle for testing anything.

critic /'krɪtɪk/ *n.* **1.** someone skilled in judging the qualities or merits of some class of things, especially of literary or artistic work. **2.** someone who judges captiously or with severity; someone who censures or finds fault.

critical /'krɪtɪkəl/ *adj.* **1.** tending to find fault or judge severely. **2.** of, involving, or related to criticism: *a critical article; critical analysis.* **3.** relating to or with the quality of a crisis or turning point: *the critical moment.* **4.** dangerous: *a critical shortage of water.* **5.** serious; severe: *in a critical condition.* **–critically**, *adv.* **–criticalness**, *n.*

critically endangered species *n.* a threatened species that is facing an extremely high risk of extinction in the wild in the immediate future. Compare **endangered species, vulnerable species**.

criticise /'krɪtəsaɪz/ *v.i.* **1.** to make judgements as to merits and faults. **2.** to find fault. **–v.t. 3.** to judge or discuss the merits and faults of. **4.** to find fault with. Also, **criticize**. **–criticisable**, *adj.* **–criticiser**, *n.*

criticism /'krɪtəsɪzəm/ *n.* **1.** an analysis and judging of the quality of something: *literary criticism.* **2.** disapproval; fault-finding. **3.** a critical remark, article, or essay.

critique /krə'tik, krɪ-/ *n.* **1.** an article or essay criticising a literary or other work; a review. **–v.t.** (**-tiqued, -tiquing**) **2.** to review critically; evaluate.

croak /krook/ *v.i.* **1.** to utter a low, hoarse, dismal cry, as a frog or a raven. **2.** to speak with a low, hollow voice. **3.** to talk despondently; forebode evil; grumble. **4.** *Colloq.* to die. **–n. 5.** the act or sound of croaking. **–croaky**, *adj.* **–croaker**, *n.*

crochet /'krooʃə, 'krooʃeɪ/ *n.* **1.** a kind of needlework done with a needle having at one end a small hook for drawing the thread or yarn into intertwined loops. **–verb** (**-cheted** /-ʃəd, -ʃeɪd/, **-cheting** /-ʃəɪŋ, -ʃeɪŋ/) **–v.t. 2.** to form by crochet. **–v.i. 3.** to do crochet.

crock¹ /krɒk/ *n.* an earthen pot, jar, or other vessel.

crock² /krɒk/ *n.* **1.** an old ewe. **2.** an old worn-out horse. **3.** *Colloq.* a worn-out, decrepit old person.

crockery /'krɒkəri/ *n.* **1.** crocks or earthen vessels collectively; earthenware. **2.** china in general, especially as for domestic use.

crocodile /'krɒkədaɪl/ *n.* **1.** a large, lizard-like reptile living in the waters of tropical Africa, Asia, Australia, and America. **2.** crocodile skin, used for shoes, handbags, etc.

crocodile tears *pl. n.* **1.** false or insincere tears, as the tears said to be shed by crocodiles over those they devour. **2.** a hypocritical show of sorrow.

crocus /'krookəs/ *n.* (*pl.* **-cuses**) **1.** any of the small plants constituting the genus *Crocus*, much cultivated for their showy, solitary flowers. **2.** the flower or bulb of the crocus. **3.** a deep yellow; orangey yellow; saffron.

Crohn's disease /'kroonz dəziz/ *n.* a chronic inflammatory disease of the intestine, of unknown cause.

croissant /krwʌ'sɒ̃/ *n.* a roll of leavened dough or puff pastry, shaped into a crescent and baked.

cromlech /'krɒmlɛk/ *n.* **1.** a circle of upright stones or monoliths. **2.** → **dolmen**.

crone /kroon/ *n.* an old woman, especially one who is withered in appearance and disagreeable in manner.

cronut /'kroonʌt/ *n.* (*from trademark*) a pastry which is made from layered dough, formed with a filling into a doughnut shape, then fried, glazed and rolled in cinnamon sugar.

crony /'krooni/ *n.* (*pl.* **-nies**) an intimate friend or companion.

crony capitalism *n.* (*derog.*) a business practice in which contracts and appointments are awarded to friends and family rather than by tender or merit.

cronyism /'kroonizəm/ *n.* unfair partiality shown, especially in political appointments, for one's friends.

crook /krʊk/ *n.* **1.** a bent or curved piece, appendage, etc.; a hook; the hooked part of anything. **2.** an instrument or implement having a bent or curved part, as a shepherd's staff hooked at one end or as the crozier of a bishop or abbot. **3.** any bend, turn, or curve. **4.** *Colloq.* a dishonest person, especially a swindler, or thief. **–adj.** *Aust., NZ Colloq.* **5.** sick; disabled. **6.** bad; inferior. **7.** unpleasant; difficult. **8.** broken; damaged. **–phr.** *Aust., NZ Colloq.* **9. be crook on**, to be annoyed with. **10. go crook, a.** to lose one's temper. **b.** to cease to function properly: *the fridge has gone crook.* **11. go crook at** (or **on**), to upbraid noisily. **12. put someone crook**, to give wrong or bad advice to someone.

crooked /ˈkrʊkəd/ *adj.* **1.** bent; not straight; curved. **2.** deformed. **3.** dishonest: *a crooked deal.* **–crookedly**, *adv.* **–crookedness**, *n.*

croon /krun/ *v.i.* **1.** to sing softly, especially with exaggerated feeling. **2.** to utter a low murmuring sound. *–v.t.* **3.** to sing softly, especially with exaggerated feeling. **–crooner**, *n.*

crop /krɒp/ *n.* **1.** the cultivated produce of the ground, such as grain or fruit, while growing or when gathered. **2.** the yield of such produce for a particular season. **3.** the yield of some other product in a season: *the lamb crop.* **4.** a supply produced. **5.** a collection or group of persons or things occurring together: *a crop of lies.* **6.** the stock or handle of a whip. **7.** a short riding whip with a loop instead of a lash. **8.** an entire tanned hide of an animal. **9.** the act of cropping. **10.** a mark produced by clipping the ears, as of an animal. **11.** a style of wearing the hair cut short. **12.** a head of hair so cut. **13.** an outcrop of a vein or seam. **14.** a special pouch-like enlargement of the gullet of many birds, in which food is held, and may undergo partial preparation for digestion. **15.** a digestive organ in other animals; the craw. *–verb* (**cropped**, **cropping**) *–v.t.* **16.** to cut off or remove the head or top of (a plant, etc.). **17.** to cut off the ends or a part of. **18.** to cut short. **19.** to clip the ears, hair, etc., of. **20.** *Photography* to cut off or mask the unwanted parts of (a print or negative). **21.** to cause to bear a crop or crops. **22.** *Textiles* to cut or shear the nap of (a fabric) so as to give a smooth face or a level nap. *–v.i.* **23.** to bear or yield a crop or crops. *–phr.* **24. crop up**, to appear unintentionally or unexpectedly: *a new problem has cropped up.*

cropper[1] /ˈkrɒpə/ *n.* **1.** someone who raises a crop. **2.** someone who cultivates land for its owner in return for part of the crop. **3.** a plant which furnishes a crop. **4.** a machine that shears the nap of cloth.

cropper[2] /ˈkrɒpə/ *phr.* **come a cropper**, *Colloq.* **1.** to fall heavily, especially from a horse. **2.** to fail; collapse, or be struck by misfortune.

croquembouche /ˈkrɒkəmbuʃ, ˈkrɒkəmbuʃ/ *n.* an elaborate pastry in which small puff balls, usually with a vanilla cream filling, are arranged in a pyramid shape, and then covered with a thin crisp toffee crust topped with threads of spun sugar.

croquet /ˈkroʊkeɪ/ *n.* an outdoor game played by knocking wooden balls through a series of iron arches by means of mallets.

croquette /kroʊˈkɛt/ *n.* a small mass of minced meat or fish, or of rice, potato, or other material, often coated with beaten egg and breadcrumbs and fried in deep fat.

crosier /ˈkroʊziə/ *n.* → **crozier**.

cross /krɒs/ *n.* **1.** a structure consisting essentially of an upright and a transverse piece, upon which persons were formerly put to death. **2.** a figure of the cross as a Christian emblem, badge, etc. **3.** the cross as the symbol of Christianity. **4.** a small cross with a human figure attached to it, as a representation of Jesus crucified; crucifix. **5.** the sign of the cross made with the right hand as an act of devotion. **6.** a structure or monument sometimes in the form of a cross, set up for prayer, as a memorial or a place where proclamations are read. **7.** the place in a town or village where such a monument stands or stood. **8.** any of various conventional representations or modifications of the Christian emblem as used symbolically or for ornament, as in heraldry, art, etc.: *a Latin cross*; *Greek cross*; *St George's cross*; *Maltese cross.* **9.** any burden, affliction, responsibility, etc., that one has to bear. **10.** any object, figure, or mark resembling a cross, as two intersecting lines. **11.** such a mark made instead of a signature by a person unable to write. **12.** a four-way joint or connection used in pipe-fitting, the connections being at right angles. **13.** a crossing. **14.** a place of crossing. **15.** *Boxing* a

blow delivered to the head through an opponent's guard, or over the opponent's arm. **16.** *Soccer* a pass (def. 50) from a wing position towards the centre. **17.** an opposing; thwarting. **18.** a crossing of animals or plants; a mixing of breeds. **19.** an animal, plant, breed, etc., produced by crossing; a crossbreed. **20.** something intermediate in character between two things. *–v.t.* **21.** to move, pass, or extend from one side to the other side of (a street, river, etc.). **22.** to lie or pass across; intersect. **23.** to transport across something. **24.** to meet and pass. **25.** to oppose openly; thwart. **26.** to cause (members of different genera, species, breeds, varieties, or the like) to produce offspring; cross-fertilise. **27.** to mark with a cross. **28.** to place in the form of a cross or crosswise. **29.** to put or draw (a line, etc.) across. **30.** to mark (the face of a cheque) with two vertical parallel lines with or without the words *not negotiable* written between them. **31.** to make the sign of the cross upon or over, as in devotion. *–v.i.* **32.** to lie or be athwart; intersect. **33.** to move, pass, extend from one side or place to another. **34.** to meet and pass. **35.** to interbreed. *–adj.* **36.** lying or passing crosswise or across each other; athwart; transverse: *cross axes.* **37.** involving interchange; reciprocal. **38.** contrary; opposite. **39.** adverse; unfavourable. **40.** ill-humoured; snappish: *a cross word.* **41.** crossbred; hybrid. *–phr.* **42. cross as two sticks**, extremely bad-tempered. **43. cross one's heart**, to pledge; promise; swear. **44. cross out**, **a.** to cancel by marking with a cross or with a line or lines. **b.** to indicate (something) as being incorrect with such a mark. **45. cross someone's mind**, to occur to someone; come to someone as an idea. **46. cross someone's palm with silver**, to give money to someone to tell one's fortune. **47. cross the floor**, (in parliament) to vote with an opposing party. **48. on the cross**, dishonestly. **–crossly**, *adv.* **–crossness**, *n.*

cross- a first element of compounds, modifying the second part, meaning: **1.** going across: *crossroad.* **2.** counter: *cross-examination.* **3.** marked with a cross. **4.** cruciform: *crossbones, etc.* **5.** changing from one state or type to another, as in *crossdress.*

crossbar /ˈkrɒsba/ *n.* **1.** a transverse bar, line, or stripe. **2.** a transverse bar between goalposts, as in soccer, rugby football, etc. **3.** a horizontal bar used in gymnastics. **4.** (in athletics) the transverse bar that a high-jumper, pole-vaulter, etc., must clear.

crossbench /ˈkrɒsbɛntʃ/ *n.* **1.** one of a set of seats, as at the houses of parliament, for those who belong neither to the government nor to opposition parties. *–adj.* **2.** independent. **–crossbencher**, *n.*

crossbones /ˈkrɒsboʊnz/ *pl. n.* two bones placed crosswise, usually below a skull, symbolising death.

crossbow /ˈkrɒsboʊ/ *n.* an old weapon for shooting missiles, consisting of a bow fixed transversely on a stock having a groove or barrel to direct the missile. **–crossbowman** /ˈkrɒsboʊmən/, *n.*

cross-country *adj.* **1.** directed across open or forested country; not following roads. *–n.* **2.** a running race which is routed across open or forested country, often on difficult terrain, as opposed to one held on a prepared track. *–adv.* **3.** across open country.

cross-dresser /ˈkrɒs-drɛsə/ *n.* a transvestite. **–cross-dressing**, *n., adj.*

cross-examine *v.t.* **1.** to examine by questions intended to check a previous examination; examine closely or minutely. **2.** *Law* to examine (a witness called by the opposing side), as for the purpose of disproving his or her testimony. **–cross-examination**, *n.* **–cross-examiner**, *n.*

cross-eye *n.* strabismus, especially the form in which both eyes turn towards the nose. **–cross-eyed**, *adj.*

crossfire /ˈkrɒsfaɪə/ n. 1. Mil. lines of fire from two or more positions, crossing one another, or a single one of such lines. 2. a brisk exchange of words or opinions.

crossholding /ˈkrɒshoʊldɪŋ/ n. among a group of allied commercial companies, the holding of shares in companies within the group, as a mutually protective device.

crossing /ˈkrɒsɪŋ/ n. 1. a place where lines, tracks, etc., cross each other. 2. a place at which a road, river, etc., may be crossed. 3. a railway crossing. 4. the act of opposing or thwarting; contradiction. 5. crossbreeding.

crossover /ˈkrɒsoʊvə/ n. 1. the act of crossing over. 2. Biol. a genotype resulting from crossing over.

cross-purpose n. 1. an opposing or contrary purpose. –phr. 2. be at cross-purposes, (sometimes fol. by with) to be involved in a misunderstanding, such that each person makes a wrong interpretation of the other's interests or intentions.

cross-reference n. 1. a reference from one part of a book, etc., to a word, item, etc., in another part. –verb (-renced, -rencing) –v.t. 2. to relate (an item, passage in a book, etc.) to another by means of a cross-reference. –v.i. 3. to make a cross-reference.

crossroad /ˈkrɒsroʊd/ n. 1. a road that crosses another road, or one that runs transversely to a main road. 2. a minor road, turning off a main road. 3. a. (oft. pl., construed as sing.) the place where roads intersect. b. (usu. pl., construed as sing.) a stage at which a vital decision must be made.

cross-section n. 1. a section made by a plane cutting anything transversely, especially at right angles to the longest axis. 2. a piece so cut off. 3. the act of cutting anything across. 4. a typical selection; a sample showing all characteristic parts, etc.: a cross-section of Australian opinion. 5. Geol. a profile showing an interpretation of a vertical section of the earth explored by geological and by geophysical methods. –cross-sectional, adj.

cross trainer n. 1. a sports shoe which is designed to be suitable for use in a number of different sports. 2. Also, elliptical cross trainer. a stationary exercise machine which stimulates a walking or running motion with little pressure on the user's joints.

crossword /ˈkrɒsw3d/ n. a puzzle in which words corresponding to given meanings are to be supplied and fitted into a particular figure divided into spaces, the letters of the words being arranged across the figure, or vertically, or sometimes otherwise. Also, **crossword puzzle**.

crotalaria /kroʊtəˈlɛəriə/ n. any herb or shrub of the large genus Crotalaria, widely distributed in tropical areas and occasionally the cause of stock-poisoning, the flowers of which are pea-shaped and usually yellow and the pods hard and inflated when dry.

crotch /krɒtʃ/ n. 1. a forked piece, part, support, etc. 2. a forking or place of forking, as of the human body between the legs. 3. the part of a pair of trousers, pants, etc., formed by the joining of the two legs. 4. a piece of material, so used in the join. –**crotched** /krɒtʃt/, adj.

crotchet /ˈkrɒtʃət/ n. 1. a hooklike device or part. 2. a curved surgical instrument with a sharp hook. 3. an odd fancy or whimsical notion. 4. Music a note having one quarter of the time value of a semibreve or half the value of a minim.

crotchety /ˈkrɒtʃəti/ adj. 1. given to crotchets or odd fancies; full of crotchets. 2. Colloq. irritable, difficult, or cross. –**crotchetiness**, n.

crouch /kraʊtʃ/ v.i. 1. (of people) to lower the body with one or both knees bent, in any position which inclines the trunk forward. 2. (of animals) to lie close to or on the ground with legs bent as in the position taken when about to spring. 3. to stoop or bend low. 4. to bend servilely; cringe. –n. Also, **crouch start**. 5. Athletics a method of starting sprint races in which the runner crouches down on all fours.

croup /krup/ n. Pathol. inflammation of the larynx, especially in children leading to laryngeal spasm, characterised by a hoarse cough and difficulty in breathing.

croupier /ˈkrupiə/ n. 1. an attendant who collects and pays the money at a gaming table. 2. someone who at a public dinner sits at the lower end of the table as assistant chairman.

crouton /ˈkrutɒn/ n. a small piece of bread, often cube shaped, crisply fried or toasted, for use in soups, salads, etc.

crow¹ /kroʊ/ n. 1. either of two large, lustrous black, Australian birds of the genus Corvus, having a characteristic harsh call: the **Torresian crow**, C. orru, found in Indonesia, New Guinea, northern Australia and parts of the inland, and the **little crow**, C. bennetti, of arid and semi-arid regions. 2. certain other birds of the genus Corvus as the **carrion crow**, C. corone of Eurasia, and the **American crow**, C. brachyrhynchos. 3. Colloq. an unattractive woman. –phr. 4. **as the crow flies**, in a straight line. 5. **draw the crow**, Colloq. to end up with the least attractive task, option, etc. 6. **eat crow**, Colloq. to be forced to do or say something very unpleasant or humiliating. 7. **stone the crows**, Also, NZ, **stiffen the crows**; Aust., **starve the crows**. Colloq. an exclamation of astonishment, exasperation, or disgust.

crow² /kroʊ/ v.i. (**crowed** or **crew, crowed, crowing**) 1. to utter the characteristic cry of a cock. 2. to utter an inarticulate cry of pleasure, as an infant does. 3. to exult loudly; boast.

crowbar /ˈkroʊbɑ/ n. a bar of iron, often with a wedge-shaped end, for use as a lever, etc.

crowd /kraʊd/ n. 1. a large number of people or things gathered closely together. 2. people in general. 3. a group or set of people; clique: I can't get on with your crowd. –v.i. 4. to gather in large numbers. 5. to press forward; push. –v.t. 6. to press closely together; force into a confined space. 7. to overfill.

crowdfunding /ˈkraʊdfʌndɪŋ/ n. the obtaining of small donations from individuals contacted through social networks, as to fund a project, support a cause, etc. Also, **crowd source funding**. –**crowdfunded**, adj.

crowdsourcing /ˈkraʊdsɔsɪŋ/ n. Internet 1. the issuing of a task to a number of individuals who are otherwise unrelated, either online or offline, as a means of solving a problem, collecting data, providing up-to-date information, etc. 2. the use of individuals who are engaged in an online activity to provide data that is needed, usually without their knowledge and as a by-product of their primary activity. –**crowdsourced**, adj. –**crowdsourcer**, n.

crowd-surf v.i. to engage in crowd-surfing.

crowd-surfing n. an activity at a rock concert or party in which someone is held up by the main group and moved about over their heads. –**crowd-surfer**, n.

crowfoot /ˈkroʊfʊt/ n. (pl. **-foots**) any plant of the genus Ranunculus, especially one with divided leaves suggestive of a crow's foot; buttercup.

crown /kraʊn/ n. 1. an ornamental headdress worn by a king, queen, etc., as a symbol of position, usually made of gold and precious stones, etc. 2. (usu. upper case) a. the power or position of a king, queen, etc. b. the governing power of a state under a monarchical government. 3. a crown-like symbol or design, used in crests, as a badge of rank, etc. 4. a wreath worn on the head as a mark of victory or honour. 5. an honour or reward. 6. a coin of several countries, usually with a crown or crowned head on it; in UK and Australia formerly a five shilling piece. 7. a pre-metric paper size,

15×20 inches. **8.** something crown-shaped, e.g. the corona of a flower. **9.** the top or highest part of anything, as of a head, hat, or mountain. **10.** the top of a bird's head. **11.** the highest or best part or quality: *the crown of his achievements.* **a.** an artificial replacement for this. −*v.t.* **13.** to place a crown or wreath on the head of. **14.** to install a king, queen, etc., in office by crowning. **15.** to honour; reward. **16.** *Dentistry* to place an artificial crown on (a tooth). **17.** to top, or be the top part of: *snow crowned the mountain.* **18.** *Colloq.* to hit on the head. **19.** to complete well or successfully. −**crowner**, *n.*

Crown land *n.* (*sometimes lower case*) land belonging to the government.

crown-of-thorns starfish *n.* a starfish, *Acanthaster planci*, having sharp, stinging spines on the top surface of the body and arms; widely distributed in tropical waters and particularly abundant on the Great Barrier Reef where it is very destructive of certain corals.

crown seal *n.* a metal cap, usually lined with cork or plastic, for stopping bottles of beer, soft drink, etc., and which is fastened to a rim at the mouth of the bottle by crimping its edge over the rim. Also, **crown cap**, **crown cork.**

Crown witness *n.* (*sometimes lower case*) a witness for the Crown in a criminal prosecution.

crow's-foot *n.* (*pl.* **-feet**) (*usu. pl.*) a wrinkle at the outer corner of the eye.

crow's nest *n. Naut.* **1.** a box or shelter for the lookout, secured near the top of a mast. **2.** a similar lookout station ashore.

crozier /'krouziə/ *n.* the pastoral staff of a bishop or an abbot, hooked at one end like a shepherd's crook. Also, **crosier.**

crucial /'kruʃəl/ *adj.* **1.** involving a final and supreme decision; decisive; critical: *a crucial experiment.* **2.** severe; trying. **3.** of the form of a cross; cross-shaped. −**crucially**, *adv.*

cruciate ligament /'kruʃiət ligəmənt/ *n.* one of two major ligaments of the knee which connect the femur to the tibia and give stability to the knee, as either the **anterior cruciate ligament**, lying towards the front of knee joint, or the **posterior cruciate ligament**, lying towards the back of the knee joint.

crucible /'krusəbəl/ *n.* **1.** a vessel of metal or refractory material used for heating substances to high temperatures. **2.** a severe, searching test.

crucifix /'krusəfiks/ *n.* **1.** a cross with the figure of Jesus crucified upon it. **2.** any cross.

crucify /'krusəfaɪ/ *v.t.* (**-fied, -fying**) **1.** to put to death by nailing or binding the body to a cross. **2.** to treat severely, as by ridicule, industrial action, or other means. **3.** to subdue (passion, sin, etc.). −**crucifier**, *n.* −**crucifixion**, *n.*

crude /krud/ *adj.* **1.** in a raw or unprepared state; unrefined: *crude oil; crude sugar.* **2.** unripe; not mature. **3.** lacking finish, polish, proper arrangement, or completeness: *a crude summary.* **4.** lacking culture, refinement, tact, etc.: *crude people; crude behaviour; crude speech.* −*n.* **5.** crude oil. −**crudely**, *adv.* −**crudity**, **crudeness**, *n.*

crude oil *n.* oil as it is found in nature, usually brown or black, and often in association with natural gas which forms a cap above it and saline water which collects underneath it. Also, **crude.**

cruel /'kruəl/ *adj.* **1.** disposed to inflict suffering; indifferent to, or taking pleasure in, the pain or distress of another; hard-hearted; pitiless. **2.** causing, or marked by, great pain or distress: *a cruel remark.* −*v.t.* (**cruelled, cruelling**) **3.** *Colloq.* to impair, spoil: *to cruel someone's chances.* −*phr.* **4. cruel someone's pitch,**

Colloq. to spoil completely someone's opportunity or plan. −**cruelly**, *adv.* −**cruelness**, *n.* −**cruelty**, *n.*

cruet /'kruət/ *n.* **1.** a set, on a stand, of containers for salt, pepper, and mustard or for vinegar and oil. **2.** an individual container.

cruise /kruz/ *verb* (**cruised, cruising**) −*v.i.* **1.** to sail to and fro, or from place to place, as in search of hostile ships, or for pleasure. **2.** (of a car, aeroplane, etc.) to move along easily at a moderate speed. **3.** *Colloq.* to move around an urban area, in search of excitement, casual sex, drugs, etc. **4.** *Colloq.* to continue without great commitment or purpose, as in a job, between relationships, etc. −*v.t.* **5.** to cruise over. −*n.* **6.** a voyage made by cruising.

cruiser /'kruzə/ *n.* **1.** one of a class of warships of medium tonnage, designed for high speed and long cruising radius. **2.** a boat, usually power-driven and with sleeping accommodation, adapted for pleasure trips. **3.** *Colloq.* a very large beer glass.

cruiserweight /'kruzəweɪt/ *n.* **1.** a heavy weight division in boxing. **2.** a boxer of this weight class.

cruising /'kruzɪŋ/ *n.* the frequenting of bars and parties in search of excitement, casual sex, drugs, etc.

cruisy /'kruzi/ *adj.* (**-sier, -siest**) *Colloq.* **1.** easy; not taxing: *a cruisy job.* **2.** (of a person) relaxed and easygoing; laid-back. Also, **cruisey.**

crumb /krʌm/ *n.* **1.** a small particle of bread, cake, etc., such as breaks or falls off. **2.** a small particle or portion of anything. **3.** the soft inner portion of bread (distinguished from *crust*). −*v.t.* **4.** to dress or prepare with breadcrumbs; to bread. **5.** to break into crumbs or small fragments.

crumble /'krʌmbəl/ *v.t.* **1.** to break into small fragments or crumbs. −*v.i.* **2.** to fall into small pieces; break or part into small fragments. **3.** to decay; disappear piecemeal. −*n.* **4.** a sweet dish containing stewed fruit topped by a crumbly pastry of brown sugar, flour, and butter.

crummy /'krʌmi/ *adj.* (**-mier, -miest**) *Colloq.* very inferior, mean, or shabby.

crumpet /'krʌmpət/ *n.* **1.** a kind of soft, moist, flat yeast cake, with a smooth brown base and many small holes on the upper surface, usually served toasted and buttered. **2.** *Colloq.* women regarded as sex objects. **3.** *Colloq.* the head: *soft in the crumpet.* −*phr.* **4. not worth a crumpet,** *Aust. Colloq.* worthless; of little or no value.

crumple /'krʌmpəl/ *v.t.* **1.** to draw or press into irregular folds; rumple; wrinkle. −*v.i.* **2.** to collapse; give way.

crunch /krʌntʃ/ *v.t.* **1.** to crush with the teeth; chew with a crushing noise. **2.** to crush or grind noisily. −*phr.* **3. the crunch,** a moment of crisis, or one requiring decisive action.

crusade /kru'seɪd/ *n.* **1.** a strong group movement to defend or advance some idea or cause. −*v.i.* **2.** to go on, run, or join in a crusade. −**crusader**, *n.*

crush /krʌʃ/ *v.t.* **1.** to press between hard surfaces so as to break or compress. **2.** to break into small pieces: *to crush stone.* **3.** to press (fruit, etc.) in order to force out juice, etc. **4.** to put down or overpower: *to crush a rebellion.* −*v.i.* **5.** to become crushed. **6.** to press or crowd. −*n.* **7.** the act of crushing. **8.** the state of being crushed. **9.** a device for crushing bulk fruit, as grapes, oranges, etc., to extract the juice. **10.** a beverage made by expressing the juice from fruit, as from oranges. **11.** a narrow, funnel-shaped, fenced passage along which stock are driven for handling; race. **12.** a crowd. **13.** a drink made by crushing fruit: *orange crush.* **14.** *Colloq.* a great fondness, often short-lived. −**crusher**, *n.*

crust /krʌst/ *n.* **1.** the hard outer portion of a loaf of bread (distinguished from *crumb*). **2.** a piece of this. **3.** the outside covering of a pie. **4.** any more or less hard external covering or coating. **5.** the hard outer shell or covering of an animal or plant. **6.** the exterior portion of the earth, accessible to examination. **7.** *Colloq.* a livelihood: *what do you do for a crust? –v.t.* **8.** to cover with or as with a crust; encrust. *–v.i.* **9.** to form or contract a crust. **10.** to form into a crust. *–phr.* **11. down to the last crust,** destitute. **12. earn a crust,** to make a living.

crustacean /krʌsˈteɪʃən/ *adj.* **1.** belonging to the Crustacea, a phylum of (chiefly aquatic) arthropod animals, including the lobsters, prawns, crabs, barnacles, slaters, etc., commonly having the body covered with a hard exoskeleton or carapace. *–n.* **2.** a crustacean animal.

crustal plate *n.* → **tectonic plate.**

crusty /ˈkrʌsti/ *adj.* (**-tier, -tiest**) **1.** being or resembling a crust; having a crust. **2.** harsh; surly: *crusty person*; *crusty manner; crusty remark.* **–crustily,** *adv.* **–crustiness,** *n.*

crutch /krʌtʃ/ *n.* **1.** a stick or support to help an injured or old person walk, usually with a piece at the top to fit under the armpit. **2.** a forked support or part. **3.** the part where the legs meet in the body or trousers. **4.** anything leaned or relied on. *–v.t.* **5.** to shear (wool) from a sheep's hindquarters. **6.** to support on a crutch.

crux /krʌks/ *n.* (*pl.* **cruxes** *or* **cruces** /ˈkrusiz/) a vital, basic, or decisive point.

cry /kraɪ/ *verb* (**cried, crying**) *–v.i.* **1.** to utter inarticulate sounds, especially of lamentation, grief, or suffering, usually with tears. **2.** to weep; shed tears, with or without sound. **3.** to call loudly; shout. **4.** to give forth vocal sounds or characteristic calls, as animals; yelp; bark. *–v.t.* **5.** to utter or pronounce loudly; call out. **6.** to beg or implore in a loud voice. *–n.* (*pl.* **cries**) **7.** the act or sound of crying; any loud utterance or exclamation; a shout, scream, or wail. **8.** clamour; outcry. **9.** an entreaty; appeal. **10.** an opinion generally expressed. **11.** a political or party slogan. **12.** a fit of weeping. **13.** the utterance or call of an animal. *–phr.* **14. a far cry, a.** quite some distance; a long way. **b.** only remotely related; very different. **15. cry down,** to disparage; belittle. **16. cry off,** to break (a promise, agreement, etc.). **17. cry up,** to praise; extol. **18. cry wolf,** to give a false alarm, often on a number of occasions as a way of getting attention.

cryo- a word element meaning 'icy cold', 'frost', 'low temperature'.

cryogenics /kraɪəˈdʒɛnɪks/ *n.* the branch of physics that deals with the properties of materials at very low temperatures. **–cryogenic,** *adj.*

cryonics /kraɪˈɒnɪks/ *n.* the practice of storing a dead body at a very low temperature in the hope that some future technology may be able to bring it back to life. **–cryonic,** *adj.*

crypt /krɪpt/ *n.* **1.** a subterranean chamber or vault, especially one beneath the main floor of a church, used as a burial place, etc. **2.** *Anat.* a slender pit or recess; a small glandular cavity. **–cryptal,** *adj.*

cryptic /ˈkrɪptɪk/ *adj.* **1.** hidden; secret; occult. **2.** mysterious; enigmatic. **–cryptically,** *adv.*

crypto- a word element meaning 'hidden', as in *cryptoclastic.* Also, (*before vowels*), **crypt-.**

cryptocurrency /ˈkrɪptoʊkʌrənsi/ *n.* a system of digital currency using data encryption.

crystal /ˈkrɪstl/ *n.* **1.** a clear mineral or glass which looks like ice. **2.** clear crystallised quartz. **3.** *Chem., Mineral.* a substance with a particular geometric form due to the regular arrangement of atoms, ions, or molecules in it. **4.** a single grain or piece of crystalline substance. **5.** clear, brilliant glass. **6.** cut glass. **7.** → **quartz crystal. 8.** Also, **crystal meth.** *Colloq.* a powdered narcotic, especially methamphetamine. *–adj.* **9.** of or like crystal. **–crystal-like,** *adj.* **–crystalline,** *adj.*

crystal ball *n.* a ball into which a fortune-teller looks, supposedly in order to see distant or future events.

crystallise /ˈkrɪstəlaɪz/ *v.t.* **1.** to form into crystals; cause to assume crystalline form. **2.** to give definite or concrete form to. **3.** *Cookery* to coat (fruit or flower petals) with sugar to give an attractive, edible finish. *–v.i.* **4.** to form crystals; become crystalline in form. **5.** to assume definite or concrete form. Also, **crystallize. –crystallisable,** *adj.*

crystallo- a word element meaning 'crystal', as in *crystallographic.* Also, (*before vowels*), **crystall-.**

crystallography /krɪstəˈlɒgrəfi/ *n.* the science dealing with crystallisation and the forms and structure of crystals. **–crystallographer,** *n.*

C-section /ˈsi-sɛkʃən/ *n. US* → **caesarean section.**

cub /kʌb/ *n.* **1.** the young of certain animals, such as the fox, bear, etc. **2.** (*humorous*) an awkward or uncouth youth. **3.** a novice or apprentice, especially a cub reporter. **4.** (*upper case*) → **Cub Scout. –cubbish,** *adj.* **–cubbishness,** *n.*

cubby /ˈkʌbi/ *n.* (*pl.* **-bies**) a snug, confined place; a cubbyhouse.

cubbyhouse /ˈkʌbihaʊs/ *n. Aust.* a children's playhouse.

cube /kjub/ *n.* **1.** a solid bounded by six equal squares, the angle between any two adjacent faces being a right angle. **2.** the third power of a quantity: *the cube of 4 is $4 \times 4 \times 4$, or 64.* **3.** a small block of sugar, concentrated meat, or vegetable extract: *sugar cube; beef cube. –v.t.* **4.** to make into a cube or cubes. **5.** to raise to the third power; find the cube of.

cube root *n.* the quantity of which a given quantity is the cube: *4 is the cube root of 64.*

cubic /ˈkjubɪk/ *adj.* **1.** of three dimensions; solid, or relating to solid content: *a cubic metre* (the volume of a cube whose edges are each a metre long). **2.** having the form of a cube. **3.** *Arithmetic, Algebra, etc.* being of the third power or degree. Also, **cubical. –cubically,** *adv.* **–cubicalness,** *n.*

cubicle /ˈkjubɪkəl/ *n.* **1.** a bedroom, especially one of a number of small ones in a divided dormitory. **2.** any small space or compartment partitioned off.

cubism /ˈkjubɪzəm/ *n.* an art movement, initiated in France in 1907, which was concerned with the analysis of forms and their interrelation and whose proponents made surface arrangements of planes, lines, and shapes, often overlapping and interlocking, in an attempt to represent solidity and extent on a two-dimensional plane. **–cubist,** *n.*, *adj.* **–cubistic** /kjuˈbɪstɪk/, *adj.* **–cubistically,** *adv.*

Cub Scout *n.* (*sometimes lower case*) a member of a junior division (ages 8–10) of the Scout Association.

cuckold /ˈkʌkəld/ *n.* the husband of an unfaithful wife.

cuckoo /ˈkʊku/ *n.* **1.** any of various birds of the widespread family Cuculidae, noted for their habit of laying eggs in the nests of other birds. **2.** any of various other members of the same family especially *Cuculus canorus*, of Africa, Europe and Asia, noted for its characteristic two-note call. **3.** the call of the cuckoo (def. 2), or an imitation of it. **4.** a fool; simpleton. *–adj.* **5.** *Colloq.* crazy; silly; foolish.

cucumber /ˈkjukʌmbə/ *n.* a creeping plant, *Cucumis sativus*, occurring in many cultivated forms, yielding a long fleshy fruit which is commonly eaten green as a salad and used for pickling.

cucurbit /kjuˈkɜbət/ *n.* **1.** a gourd. **2.** any cucurbitaceous plant including pumpkins and melons.

cud /kʌd/ *n.* **1.** the portion of food which a ruminating animal returns from the first stomach to the mouth to chew a second time. *–phr.* **2. chew the cud,** to reflect; meditate.

cuddle /ˈkʌdl/ *v.t.* **1.** to draw or hold close in an affectionate manner; hug tenderly; fondle. *–v.i.* **2.** to lie close and snug; nestle; curl up in going to sleep. –n. **3.** the act of cuddling; a hug; an embrace. –**cuddlesome**, **cuddly**, adj.

cudgel /ˈkʌdʒəl/ n. **1.** a short, thick stick used as a weapon; a club. –v.t. (**-elled** or, Chiefly US, **-eled**, **-elling** or, Chiefly US, **-eling**) **2.** to strike with a cudgel; beat. –phr. **3. cudgel one's brains**, to think hard. **4. take up the cudgels**, to engage in a contest. –**cudgeller**; Chiefly US, **cudgeler**, n.

cue[1] /kjuː/ n. **1.** anything said or done on or behind the stage that is followed by a specific line or action: each line of dialogue is a cue to the succeeding line; an offstage door slam was his cue to enter. **2.** a hint; an intimation; a guiding suggestion. **3.** the part one is to play; a prescribed or necessary course of action. **4.** the one element in a complex event which is crucial to the perception of the whole.

cue[2] /kjuː/ n. a long tapering rod, tipped with a soft leather pad, used to strike the ball in billiards, etc.

cuff[1] /kʌf/ n. **1.** a fold, band, or variously shaped piece serving as a trimming or finish for the bottom of a sleeve or trouser leg. **2.** the part of a gauntlet or long glove that extends over the wrist. –phr. **3. off the cuff**, impromptu; extemporaneously; on the spur of the moment: to speak off the cuff. **4. on the cuff**, Colloq. **a.** on credit. **b.** NZ exclusive; unfair.

cuff[2] /kʌf/ v.t. **1.** to strike with the open hand; beat; buffet. –n. **2.** a blow with the fist or the open hand; a buffet. **3.** a handcuff.

cufflink /ˈkʌflɪŋk/ n. a link which fastens a shirt cuff.

cuisine /kwəˈziːn/ n. style of cooking; cookery.

cul-de-sac /ˈkʌl-də-sæk/ n. a street, lane, etc., closed at one end; blind alley.

-cule a diminutive suffix of nouns, as in animalcule, molecule. Also, **-cle**.

culinary /ˈkʌlənri, -ənəri/, Orig. US /ˈkʌləneri/ adj. relating to the kitchen or to cookery; used in cooking.

cull /kʌl/ v.t. **1.** to choose; select; pick; gather the choice things or parts from. **2.** to collect; gather; pluck. **3.** to remove animals of inferior quality from (a herd or flock). **4.** to kill (animals, as deer, kangaroos, etc.), with a view to controlling numbers.

culminate /ˈkʌlməneɪt/ v.i. (sometimes fol. by in) to reach the highest point, the summit, or highest development. –**culmination**, n.

culottes /kəˈlɒts/ pl. n. a skirt-like garment, separated and sewn like trousers.

culpable /ˈkʌlpəbəl/ adj. deserving blame or censure; blameworthy. –**culpability** /kʌlpəˈbɪləti/, **culpableness**, n. –**culpably**, adv.

culpable driving n. Law a statutory offence, varying from one jurisdiction to another, but generally involving the driving of a motor vehicle in a dangerous manner, or under the influence of drugs or alcohol, resulting in the death or serious injury of another person.

culprit /ˈkʌlprət/ n. **1.** someone arraigned for an offence. **2.** someone guilty of or responsible for a specified offence or fault.

cult /kʌlt/ n. **1.** a particular system of religious worship, especially with reference to its rites and ceremonies. **2.** (derog.) a religious or pseudo-religious movement, characterised by the extreme devotion of its members, who usually form a relatively small, tightly controlled group under an authoritarian and charismatic leader. **3.** an instance of an almost religious veneration for a person or thing, especially as manifested by a body of admirers: a cult of Napoleon. **4.** the object of such devotion. **5.** a popular fashion; fad. –adj. **6.** taken up by a small but enthusiastic group: a cult figure; a cult film. **7.** made up of a small but enthusiastic group: a cult following. –**cultism**, n. –**cultist**, n. –**cultic**, adj.

cultivar /ˈkʌltəvɑː/ n. Bot. a variety of plant that has been produced only under cultivation.

cultivate /ˈkʌltəveɪt/ v.t. **1.** to work (land) in raising crops. **2.** to dig; turn over (earth). **3.** to encourage the growth or development of. **4.** to grow. **5.** to develop or improve by education; train; refine: to cultivate the mind. **6.** to work at or encourage: to cultivate a friendship. **7.** to try to make friends with (someone). –**cultivation**, n. –**cultivator**, n.

cultural /ˈkʌltʃərəl/ adj. of or relating to culture or cultivation. –**culturally**, adv.

cultural cringe n. a feeling that one's country's culture is inferior to that of other countries.

culture /ˈkʌltʃə/ n. **1.** the state or stage of civilisation of a particular people at a certain time: Greek culture. **2.** the skills, arts, beliefs, and customs of a group of people, passed on from one generation to another. **3.** development or improvement by education or training. **4.** the cultivation of soil. **5.** the raising of plants or animals, especially to improve or develop them. **6.** Biol. the growing of cells, e.g. bacteria or human tissue, for scientific studies, medicinal use, etc. –v.t. **7.** to cultivate. –**cultureless**, adj.

cultured /ˈkʌltʃəd/ adj. **1.** cultivated; artificially nurtured or grown. **2.** enlightened; refined.

culvert /ˈkʌlvət/ n. a drain or channel crossing under a road, etc.; a sewer; a conduit.

cum /kʌm, kʊm/ prep. **1.** with; together with; including (used sometimes in financial phrases as cum dividend, cum rights, etc., which are often abbreviated simply cum). **2.** (in combination) serving a dual function as; the functions being indicated by the preceding and following elements: the dwelling-cum-workshop was nearby.

cumbersome /ˈkʌmbəsəm/ adj. **1.** burdensome; troublesome. **2.** unwieldy; clumsy. –**cumbersomely**, adv. –**cumbersomeness**, n.

cumin /ˈkʌmən/ n. **1.** a small plant, Cuminum cyminum, bearing aromatic seedlike fruit used in cookery and medicine. **2.** the fruit or seeds.

cummerbund /ˈkʌməbʌnd/ n. **1.** (in India and elsewhere) a shawl or sash worn as a belt. **2.** (in Western dress) a broad sash worn about the waist, especially as part of male formal dress.

cumquat /ˈkʌmkwɒt/ n. **1.** a small round or oblong citrus fruit with a sweet rind and acid pulp, used chiefly for preserves. It is the fruit of Fortunella japonica and related species, shrubs native to China and cultivated in many other countries. **2.** the plant itself. Also, **kumquat**.

cumulative /ˈkjumjələtɪv/ adj. **1.** increasing or growing by accumulation or successive additions. **2.** formed by or resulting from accumulation or the addition of successive parts or elements. **3.** of or relating to experimental error which increases in magnitude with each successive step. –**cumulatively**, adv. –**cumulativeness**, n.

cumulus /ˈkjumjələs/ n. (pl. **-li** /-li/) **1.** a heap; pile. **2.** Meteorol. a cloud with summit domelike or made up of rounded heaps, and with flat base, seen in fair weather and usually a brilliant white with a smooth, well-outlined structure. –**cumuliform**, adj. –**cumulous**, adj.

cuneiform /ˈkjunəfɔm/ adj. wedge-shaped, as the characters used in writing in ancient Persia, Assyria, etc.

cunjevoi[1] /ˈkʌndʒəvɔɪ/ n. a common Australian littoral tunicate, Pyura stolonifera, popular as a fish bait; sea squirt. Also, **cunje**.

cunjevoi[2] /ˈkʌndʒəvɔɪ/ n. a hastate-leaved perennial herb of the Arum family, Alocasia brisbanensis, native to Asia and the Pacific Islands as well as Australia where it is common in rainforest and along coastal river banks; its poisonous rhizomes were rendered harmless by cooking and eaten by Aboriginal people.

cunnilingus /ˌkʌnəˈlɪŋgəs/ *n.* oral stimulation of the female genitals. Also, **cunnilinctus** /ˌkʌnəˈlɪŋktəs/.

cunning /ˈkʌnɪŋ/ *n.* **1.** ability; skill; expertness. **2.** skill used in a crafty manner; skilfulness in deceiving; craftiness; guile. –*adj.* **3.** exhibiting or wrought with ingenuity. **4.** artfully subtle or shrewd; crafty; sly. –**cunningly,** *adv.* –**cunningness,** *n.*

cunt /kʌnt/ *n. Colloq. (taboo)* **1.** the vagina and external female genitalia. **2.** a contemptible person. **3.** something which causes difficulty or aggravation.

cup /kʌp/ *n.* **1.** a small, open container, especially of porcelain or metal, used mainly to drink from. **2.** *(oft. upper case)* an ornamental cup or other article, especially of precious metal, offered as a prize for a contest: *Melbourne Cup, Davis Cup.* **3.** *(upper case)* the contest in which such a cup is the prize: *he entered in the Cup.* **4.** the containing part of a goblet or the like. **5.** the quantity contained in a cup. **6.** a unit of capacity formerly equal to 8 fluid ounces, now 250 millilitres. **7.** any of various beverages, as a mixture of wine and various ingredients: *claret cup.* **8.** the chalice used in the Eucharist. **9.** the wine of the Eucharist. **10.** something to be partaken of or endured, as suffering. **11.** any cuplike utensil, organ, part, cavity, etc. **12.** that part of a bra which is shaped to hold the breast. **13.** *Golf* **a.** the metal receptacle within the hole. **b.** the hole itself. –*v.t.* (**cupped, cupping**) **14.** to take or place in or as in a cup: *he cupped his ear with the palm of his hand to hear better.* **15.** to form into the shape of a cup. **16.** to use a cupping glass on. –*phr.* **17. in one's cups,** intoxicated; tipsy. –**cuplike,** *adj.*

cupboard /ˈkʌbəd/ *n.* **1.** an enclosed recess of a room for storing foodstuffs, clothing, etc., usually having shelves, hooks or the like. **2.** a free-standing article of furniture for any of these or similar purposes.

cupidity /kjuˈpɪdəti/ *n.* eager or inordinate desire, especially to possess something.

cupola /ˈkjupələ/ *n. Archit.* a rounded vault or dome constituting, or built upon, a roof; a small domelike or tower-like structure on a roof.

cupping /ˈkʌpɪŋ/ *n.* the process of drawing blood from the body by scarification and the application of a cupping glass, or by the application of a cupping glass without scarification, as for relieving internal congestion.

cupping glass *n.* a glass vessel in which a partial vacuum is created, as by heat, used in cupping.

cupr- a word element referring to copper. Also, *(before consonants,)* **cupri-, cupro-.**

cupronickel /ˈkjuproʊˈnɪkəl/ *n.* **1.** an alloy of copper containing nickel. –*adj.* **2.** containing copper and nickel.

cur /kɜ/ *n.* **1.** a snarling, worthless, or outcast dog. **2.** a low, despicable person.

curare /kjuˈrari/ *n.* a blackish resin-like substance from *Strychnos toxifera* and other tropical plants of the genus *Strychnos,* and from *Chondrodendron tomentosum,* used by the indigenous people of South America to add poison to arrow heads, and employed in physiological experiments, etc., for arresting the action of the motor nerves. Also, **curari.**

curate[1] /ˈkjurət/ *n.* a member of the clergy employed as assistant or deputy of a rector or vicar.

curate[2] /kjuˈreɪt/ *v.i.* **1.** to act as a curator. –*v.t.* **2.** to supervise and maintain (an art collection, museum, etc.). **3.** to collect and prepare (paintings, etc.) for exhibition. –**curation,** *n.*

curative /ˈkjurətɪv/ *adj.* **1.** serving to cure or heal; relating to curing or remedial treatment; remedial. –*n.* **2.** a curative agent; a remedy. –**curatively,** *adv.* –**curativeness,** *n.*

curator /kjuˈreɪtə/ *n.* **1.** someone in charge of a museum, art collection, etc.; a custodian. **2.** a manager; overseer; superintendent. **3.** *Chiefly Scottish* a guardian, as of a minor, mentally ill person, etc. –**curatorial** /kjurəˈtɔriəl/, *adj.* –**curatorship,** *n.* –**curatrix** /ˈkjurətrɪks/, *fem. n.*

curb /kɜb/ *n.* **1.** anything that restrains or controls; a restraint; a check. **2.** an enclosing framework or border. **3.** *Chiefly US* → **kerb.** –*v.t.* **4.** to control as with a curb; restrain; check. **5.** *Chiefly US* → **kerb.**

curd /kɜd/ *n.* **1.** *(oft. pl.)* a substance consisting of casein, etc., obtained from milk by coagulation, and used for making into cheese or eaten as food. **2.** any substance resembling this. –*v.t.* **3.** to turn into curd. –*v.i.* **4.** to coagulate; congeal.

curdle /ˈkɜdl/ *v.t.* **1.** to change into curd. –*v.i.* **2.** to coagulate; congeal. –*phr.* **3. curdle the blood,** to terrify with horror or fear.

cure /ˈkjuə, ˈkjʊə/ *n.* **1.** a medicine or treatment to heal or remove disease. **2.** successful treatment; healing. **3.** *Eccles.* responsibility for the spiritual welfare of people in a certain area. –*v.t.* **4.** to restore (someone) to health. **5.** to get rid of (illness, a bad habit, etc.) **6.** to preserve (meat, fish, etc.) by salting, drying, etc. **7.** to prepare, preserve, or finish (a substance) by a chemical or physical process. –**curable,** *adj.* –**curer,** *n.*

curette /kjuˈrɛt/ *n.* **1.** a scoop-shaped surgical instrument used for removing diseased tissue from body cavities such as the uterus, etc. **2.** *Med.* **a.** the scraping of a cavity, especially the uterus, with a curette. **b.** such a procedure for the purpose of an abortion.

curfew /ˈkɜfju/ *n.* a regulation, as enforced during civil disturbances, which establishes strict controls on movement after nightfall.

curio /ˈkjuriou/ *n.* (*pl.* **-rios**) any article, object of art, etc., valued as a curiosity.

curiosity /kjuriˈɒsəti/ *n.* (*pl.* **-ties**) **1.** the desire to learn or know about anything; inquisitiveness. **2.** curious or interesting quality, as from strangeness. **3.** a curious, rare, or novel thing.

curious /ˈkjuriəs/ *adj.* **1.** wanting to learn or know; inquiring. **2.** taking interest in others' affairs; prying. **3.** interesting because strange or new. –**curiously,** *adv.* –**curiousness,** *n.*

curl /kɜl/ *v.t.* **1.** to form into ringlets, as the hair. **2.** to form into a spiral or curved shape; coil. –*v.i.* **3.** to form curls or ringlets, as the hair. **4.** to coil. **5.** to become curved or undulated. –*n.* **6.** a ringlet of hair. **7.** anything of a spiral or curved shape. **8.** a coil. **9.** the act of curling. **10.** the state of being curled. **11.** any of various diseases of plants with which the leaves are distorted, fluted, or puffed because of unequal growth. –*phr.* **12. curl one's lip,** to express disdain. **13. curl up,** *Colloq.* to settle down comfortably: *to curl up with a good book.* **14. make someone's hair curl,** *Colloq.* to cause someone to be frightened or horrified. –**curly,** *adj.*

curlew /ˈkɜlju/ *n.* any of a number of wideranging, largely migratory shorebirds of the genus *Numenius,* family Scolopacidae, having long legs and a long, slender, down-curved bill.

curlicue /ˈkɜlɪkju/ *n.* a fantastic curl or twist. Also, **curlycue.**

curly bracket *n.* See **bracket** (def. 3).

curly endive *n.* a form of endive with narrow leaves, used in salads.

curly-leaf parsley *n.* a variety of parsley which has crinkled leaves. Compare **flat-leaf parsley.** Also, **curly parsley, English parsley.**

currajong /ˈkʌrədʒɒŋ/ *n.* → **kurrajong.**

currant /ˈkʌrənt/ *n.* **1.** a small seedless raisin, produced chiefly in California and in the eastern Mediterranean, used in cookery, etc. **2.** the small, edible, acid, round fruit or berry of certain wild or cultivated shrubs of the genus *Ribes*, as *R. sativum* (**redcurrant** and **white currant**) and *R. nigrum* (**blackcurrant**).

currawang /ˈkʌrəwæŋ/ *n.* **1.** a small tree, *Acacia doratoxylon*, found on dry ridges in inland eastern Australia; lancewood; spearwood. **2.** any of certain similar species of the genus *Acacia*. Also, **currawong**.

currawong[1] /ˈkʌrəwɒŋ/ *n.* any of several large black and white or greyish birds of the genus *Strepera*, with solid bodies, large pointed bills, yellow eyes, and loud, ringing calls, found in many parts of Australia.

currawong[2] /ˈkʌrəwɒŋ/ *n.* → **currawang**.

currency /ˈkʌrənsi/ *n.* (*pl.* **-cies**) **1.** the money in current use in a country. **2.** the fact or quality of being used, passed on, or generally accepted. –*adj.* **3.** *Aust. Hist.* born in Australia; not an immigrant: *a currency lad*; *a currency lass.*

current /ˈkʌrənt/ *adj.* **1.** belonging to the present time; in progress: *the current month.* **2.** generally used or accepted. –*n.* **3.** the flow, as of a river. **4.** part of a large body of water or air moving in one direction. **5.** *Physics* **a.** the flow of an electric charge. **b.** a measure of the rate of flow. The SI unit of current is the ampere. **6.** a general course or tendency. –**currently,** *adv.*

curriculum /kəˈrɪkjələm/ *n.* (*pl.* **-lums** *or* **-la** /-lə/) **1.** the aggregate of courses of study given in a school, college, university, etc. **2.** the regular or a particular course of study in a school, college, etc. –**curricular,** *adj.*

curriculum vitae /kəˌrɪkjələm ˈvitaɪ, kəˌrɪkjələm ˈvitei/ *n.* (*pl.* **curricula vitae** *or* **curriculum vitae**) a brief account of one's career to date; résumé. Also, **CV.**

curry[1] /ˈkʌri/ *n.* (*pl.* **-ries**) **1.** an Indian sauce or relish in many varieties, containing a mixture of spices, seeds, vegetables, fruits, etc., eaten with rice or combined with meat, fish or other food. **2.** a dish prepared with a curry sauce or with curry powder. –*v.t.* (**-ried, -rying**) **3.** to prepare (food) with a curry sauce or with curry powder. –*phr.* **4. give curry,** *Aust., NZ, Colloq.* to abuse angrily.

curry[2] /ˈkʌri/ *v.t.* (**-ried, -rying**) **1.** to rub and clean (a horse, etc.) with a comb; currycomb. **2.** to dress (tanned hides) by soaking, scraping, beating, colouring, etc. **3.** to beat; thrash. –*phr.* **4. curry favour,** to seek favour by a show of kindness, courtesy, flattery, etc.

curry plant *n.* a herb of southern Europe, *Helichrysum angustifolium*, the essential oil of which is used as a condiment.

curse /kɜs/ *n.* **1.** the expression of a wish that evil things will happen to someone. **2.** swearing; a blasphemous or obscene oath. **3.** an evil that has been called upon someone. –*v.t.* **4.** to wish or call evil, accident, or injury upon. **5.** to swear at. **6.** to cause to suffer from. –*v.i.* **7.** to swear; utter curses. –*phr.* **8. the curse,** *Colloq.* menstruation. –**curser,** *n.*

cursive /ˈkɜsɪv/ *adj.* (of writing or printing type) in flowing strokes, with the letters joined together. –**cursively,** *adv.*

cursor /ˈkɜsə/ *n.* **1.** an indicator on a video display unit screen, usually a small rectangle of light, which shows where the next character will form and which can be moved across the screen to the place required by operating the cursor keys or the mouse; caret. **2.** a slider, such as the transparent slider forming part of a slide rule on which are marked one or more reference lines.

cursory /ˈkɜsəri/ *adj.* going rapidly over something, without noticing details; hasty; superficial. –**cursorily,** *adv.* –**cursoriness,** *n.*

curt /kɜt/ *adj.* **1.** short; shortened. **2.** brief in speech, etc. **3.** rudely brief in speech, manner, etc. –**curtly,** *adv.* –**curtness,** *n.*

curtail /kɜˈteɪl/ *v.t.* to cut short; cut off a part of; abridge; reduce; diminish. –**curtailer,** *n.* –**curtailment,** *n.*

curtain /ˈkɜtn/ *n.* **1.** a hanging piece of fabric used to shut out the light from a window, adorn a room, etc.

2. *Theatre* **a.** a set of hanging drapery, etc., for concealing all or part of the set from the view of the audience. **b.** the act or time of raising or opening a curtain at the start of a performance. **c.** the fall of a curtain at the end of a scene or act. **3.** anything that shuts off, covers, or conceals: *a curtain of artillery fire.* **4.** (*pl.*) *Colloq.* the end, especially of a life. –*v.t.* **5.** to provide, shut off, conceal, or adorn with, or as with, a curtain.

curtain call *n.* the appearance of performers at the conclusion of a performance in response to the applause of the audience.

curtsey /ˈkɜtsi/ *n.* (*pl.* **-seys**) **1.** a bow by women in recognition or respect, consisting of bending the knees and lowering the body. –*v.i.* (**-seyed, -seying**) **2.** to make a curtsey. Also, **curtsy.**

curvaceous /kɜˈveɪʃəs/ *adj. Colloq.* (of a woman) having a full and shapely figure.

curvature /ˈkɜvətʃə/ *n.* **1.** the act of curving. **2.** curved condition, often abnormal. **3.** the degree of curving.

curvature of the spine *n.* See **scoliosis.**

curve /kɜv/ *n.* **1.** a continuously bending line, usually without angles. **2.** any curved outline, form, thing, or part. **3.** a line on a graph, diagram, etc., representing a continuous variation in force, quantity, etc. –*v.i.* **4.** to bend in a curve. –**curvedly** /ˈkɜvədli/, *adv.* –**curvedness,** *n.*

curvilinear /kɜvəˈlɪniə/ *adj.* **1.** consisting of or bounded by curved lines: *a curvilinear figure.* **2.** forming or moving in a curved line. **3.** formed or characterised by curved lines. Also, **curvilineal.**

cuscus /ˈkʌskʌs/ *n.* any of various nocturnal, arboreal marsupials of the genus *Phalanger* or related genera of New Guinea and adjacent islands and rainforest areas of northern Qld, having a round head, small ears, thick, woolly fur, and a long, partially scaled, prehensile tail.

cushion /ˈkʊʃən/ *n.* **1.** a soft bag or pad used to sit, kneel, or lie on. **2.** anything similar in appearance or use. **3.** something used to absorb or protect from shock or pressure. –*v.t.* **4.** to place on or support with a cushion. **5.** to provide with a cushion or cushions. **6.** to lessen or soften the force or effect of.

cushy /ˈkʊʃi/ *adj.* (**-shier, -shiest**) *Colloq.* easy; pleasant.

cusp /kʌsp/ *n.* **1.** a point; pointed end. **2.** *Anat., Zool., Bot.* a point, projection or elevation, as on the crown of a tooth. **3.** *Maths* a point at which the direction of a curve is abruptly reversed. **4.** *Archit., etc.* a point or figure formed by the intersection of two small arcs or curved members, such as one of the pointed projections sometimes decorating the internal curve of an arch or a traceried window. **5.** *Astrology* the transitional first or last part of a sign or house when the new sign is gaining ascendancy, but the influence of the old one persists: *to be born on the cusp.*

cuspid /ˈkʌspəd/ *n.* a tooth with a single projection point or elevation; a canine tooth (*cuspid* is preferred for a human canine tooth).

custard /ˈkʌstəd/ *n.* a sauce for sweet puddings, fruit, etc., made from milk, eggs, and sugar, heated and often thickened with cornflour.

custard apple *n.* the fruit of any of a group of shrubs and trees, native to tropical America, and possessing soft edible pulp; often confined to the single species *Annona reticulata.*

custody /ˈkʌstədi/ *n.* (*pl.* **-dies**) **1.** keeping; guardianship; care: *in the custody of her father.* **2.** *Law* legal guardianship of a child: *the mother was given custody.* **3.** imprisonment: *he was taken into custody.* –**custodian** /kʌsˈtoʊdiən/, *n.* –**custodial** /kʌsˈtoʊdiəl/, *adj.*

custom /ˈkʌstəm/ *n.* **1.** habitual practice; the usual way of acting. **2.** usual actions in general; convention. **3.** a long-continued habit so well-established that it has the force of law. **4.** *Sociology* a pattern of habitual activity usually passed on from one generation to another; tradition. **5.** a habit of doing business or shopping at a particular place: *the shopkeeper valued their custom.* **6.** (*pl.*) customs duties. **7.** (*usu. upper case*) (*pl.*) the government department that collects these duties. –**customary**, *adj.*

custom-built *adj.* made to individual order: *a custom-built limousine.*

customer /ˈkʌstəmə/ *n.* **1.** someone who purchases goods from another; a buyer; a patron. **2.** *Colloq.* a person one has to deal with: *a tricky customer.*

customise /ˈkʌstəmaɪz/ *v.t.* to adapt to suit the needs of a particular customer. Also, **customize**. –**customisation**, *n.*

custom-made *adj.* made to individual order: *custom-made shoes.*

customs duty *n.* a duty imposed by law on imported or, less commonly, exported goods.

cut /kʌt/ *verb* (**cut, cutting**) –*v.t.* **1.** to penetrate, with or as with a sharp-edged instrument: *he cut his finger.* **2.** to strike sharply, as with a whip. **3.** to wound severely the feelings of. **4.** to divide, with or as with a sharp-edged instrument; sever; carve: *to cut a rope; to cut bread into slices.* **5.** to hew or saw down; fell: *to cut timber.* **6.** to detach, with or as with a sharp-edged instrument; separate from the main body; lop off. **7.** to reap; mow; harvest: *to cut grain; to cut hay.* **8.** to trim by clipping, shearing, paring, or pruning: *to cut the hair; to cut the nails.* **9.** to intersect; cross: *one line cuts another at right angles.* **10.** to stop; halt the running of, as an engine, a liquid, etc. **11.** to abridge or shorten by omitting a part: *to cut a speech.* **12.** to lower; reduce; diminish; bring down: *to cut rates.* **13.** *Radio, TV* to stop recording or transmitting (a scene, broadcast, etc.). **14.** *Film, TV, etc.* to edit (filmed material) by cutting and rearranging pieces of film. **15. a.** to record (a song, piece of music, etc.): *the group cut three songs last night.* **b.** to produce (a CD, record, etc.) by recording: *they cut two CDs last year.* **16.** to make or fashion by cutting, as a statue, jewel, garment, etc. **17.** to hollow out; excavate; dig: *to cut a trench.* **18.** to perform or execute: *to cut a caper.* **19.** *Colloq.* to renounce; give up. **20.** to refuse to recognise socially. **21.** *Colloq.* to absent oneself from: *to cut school.* **22.** *Cards* **a.** to divide (a pack of cards) at random into two or more parts, by removing cards from the top. **b.** to take (a card) from a pack. **23.** (of sheep) to yield (wool) on being shorn: *the sheep cut a heavy fleece.* **24.** to dilute or adulterate (a drug, as heroin, etc.) with other substances, as talcum powder. –*v.i.* **25.** to penetrate or divide something as with a sharp-edged instrument; make an incision: *this knife won't cut.* **26.** to allow incision or severing: *butter cuts easily.* **27.** to pass, go, or come, especially in the most direct way (*across, through, in*, etc.): *to cut across a field.* **28.** (of the teeth) to grow through the gums. **29.** *Cards* to cut the cards. **30.** *Radio, TV* to stop filming or recording. **31.** *Colloq.* to run away; make off. –*adj.* **32.** that has been subjected to cutting; divided into pieces by cutting; detached by cutting: *cut flowers.* **33.** fashioned by cutting; having the surface shaped or ornamented by grinding and polishing: *cut glass.* **34.** reduced by, or as by, cutting: *cut rates.* **35.** diluted; adulterated; impure: *cut heroin.* **36.** *Colloq.* drunk. **37.** *Colloq.* circumcised. –*n.* **38.** the act of cutting; a stroke or a blow, as with a knife, whip, etc. **39.** a piece cut off, especially of meat. **40.** *Colloq.* share: *his cut was 20 per cent.* **41.** the quantity cut, as wool or timber. **42.** the result of cutting, as an incision, wound, etc. **43.** a passage, channel, etc., made by cutting or digging. **44.** a harvest, especially of sugar cane. **45.** a job as a shearer: *to arrange a cut for the coming season.* **46.** manner or fashion in which anything is cut.

47. manner or style; kind. **48.** a passage or course straight across: *a short cut.* **49.** an excision or omission of a part. **50.** a part excised or omitted. **51.** part of a mob of livestock separated from a main mob: *a cut of 300 steers was taken.* **52.** a reduction in price, salary, staffing, etc. **53.** an engraved block or plate used for printing, or an impression from it. **54.** *Cards* a cutting of the cards. **55.** *TV, Film, etc.* **a.** a quick transition from one shot to another. **b.** an edited version of recorded material: *first cut; director's cut.* **56.** the quantity of wool shorn: *my cut was thirty bales.* –*phr.* **57. a cut above**, *Colloq.* somewhat superior to in some respect: *a student who is a cut above the rest of the class.* **58. cut across**, **a.** to take a short cut. **b.** to interrupt. **59. cut a dash**, *Colloq.* to make an impression by one's ostentatious or flamboyant behaviour or dress. **60. cut and dried**, **a.** fixed or settled in advance. **b.** lacking freshness or spontaneity. **61. cut and paste**, **a.** to edit (a document), originally by cutting it up and pasting it together in a different order. **b.** *Computers* to move (data) from one application or document to another, or from one location in a document to another. **62. cut and run**, *Colloq.* to leave unceremoniously and in great haste. **63. cut and thrust**, **a.** swordplay with the edge as well as the point of the sword. **b.** lively exchange of opinions or arguments: *the cut and thrust of politics.* **64. cut back**, **a.** to shorten or reduce. **b.** (in a novel, film, etc.) to return suddenly to earlier events. **c.** *Football* to reverse direction suddenly by moving in the diagonally opposite course. **d.** *Surfing* to change the direction of one's board by going out of a wave and coming back into it. **65. cut both ways**, **a.** (of an argument, proposal, etc.) to support and oppose the same contention. **b.** to be beneficial in some respects and disadvantageous in others. **66. cut down**, **a.** to bring down by cutting. **b.** to reduce, especially expenses, costs, etc. **67. cut down to size**, to reduce to the proper status or level, or to the frame of mind in keeping with a person's position. **68. cut in**, **a.** to interrupt. **b.** (in traffic) to pull in dangerously soon after overtaking. **c.** to allow (oneself or someone else) a share: *he cut his brother in on the deal.* **d.** to move in between a dancing couple in order to dance with one of them. **e.** *Elect.* to switch on. **f.** to begin to shear sheep. **g.** to join a card game by taking the place of someone who is leaving. **69. cut it**, **a.** *Colloq.* to make the grade; be competent: *she couldn't cut it in her new job.* **b.** to go; leave: *let's cut it.* **70. cut it fine**, to leave only a narrow margin of error. **71. cut it out**, *Colloq.* an interjection telling someone to stop doing something, such as quarrelling. **72. cut no ice**, (sometimes fol. by *with*) to make no impression. **73. cut off**, **a.** to separate from the main body or part. **b.** to intercept. **c.** to interrupt. **d.** to bring to a sudden end. **e.** to shut out. **f.** to disinherit. **g.** (in a telephone conversation) to disconnect. **h.** to go off in another direction. **74. cut one's coat according to one's cloth**, to live within the limits of one's resources or opportunities. **75. cut one's losses**, to abandon a project in which one has already invested some part of one's capital, either material or emotional, for no return, so as not to incur more losses. **76. cut one's teeth on**, *Colloq.* to gain experience on. **77. cut out**, **a.** to omit; delete; excise. **b.** to spend all the money represented by (a cheque). **c.** to oust and replace; supplant (especially a rival). **d.** to move suddenly out of the lane or path in which one has been driving. **e.** *Printing* to remove the background from (an illustration) so that the outline of the subject appears on an unprinted background. **f.** (of an electrical device) to switch off, as when overloaded. **g.** to remove (individual livestock) from a herd or flock. **h.** to clear (a timbered area) completely. **i.** to leave (someone) out of a card game. **j.** (of a shearer) to come to the end of a contract. **k.** to cause (a shearing shed) to cease operation: *several sheds were cut out.* **l.** to stop; cease; come to an end: *the shearing cut out; the electricity cut out.* **m.** to plan or arrange; prepare. **n.** to fashion or shape by cutting. **78. cut out for** (or **to be**), well fitted for (an occupation, role, etc.). **79. cut someone dead,** to ignore someone. **80. cut someone short,** to interrupt someone. **81. cut teeth,** to have the teeth grow through the gums. **82. cut to the chase,** to address the most important issue immediately, without preliminary small talk; get to the point. **83. cut up, a.** to cut into pieces. **b.** *Colloq.* to criticise severely. **c.** *Colloq.* to upset or cause distress to. **d.** *Horseracing:* to adopt cutthroat tactics. **84. cut up rough** (or **nasty**), *Colloq.* to behave badly; become unpleasant. **85. go like a cut cat,** *Colloq.* to go very fast. **86. in for one's cut,** *Colloq.* participating in the expectation of a share in the spoils or profit. **87. make the cut,** (in sports where players or competitors are selected from a large field during preliminary trials) to qualify for the actual game or competition. **88. the cuts,** *Colloq.* a caning.

cutaneous /kju'teɪniəs/ *adj.* of, relating to, or affecting the skin. −**cutaneously,** *adv.*

cutback /'kʌtbæk/ *n.* reduction to an earlier rate, as in production.

cute /kjut/ *adj.* **1.** appealing in manner or appearance, especially of someone or something which is small or which is pretty in a childlike way. **2.** sexually pleasing or attractive. −*phr.* **3. cute as a button,** *Colloq.* extremely cute. −**cutely,** *adv.* −**cuteness,** *n.* −**cutesy,** *adj.*

cut glass *n.* glass ornamented or shaped by cutting or grinding with abrasive wheels. −**cutglass,** *adj.*

cuticle /'kjutɪkəl/ *n.* **1.** the epidermis. **2.** a superficial integument, membrane, or the like. **3.** the non-living epidermis which surrounds the edges of the fingernail or toenail. −**cuticular** /kju'tɪkjələ/, *adj.*

cutlass /'kʌtləs/ *n.* a short, heavy, slightly curved sword, formerly used especially at sea.

cutlery /'kʌtləri/ *n.* **1.** knives, forks, and spoons collectively, as used for eating. **2.** the art or business of a cutler. **3.** cutting instruments collectively.

cutlet /'kʌtlət/ *n.* **1.** a cut of meat, usually lamb or veal, for grilling, frying or roasting, containing a rib, and cut from the neck of the carcase; a rib chop. **2.** a fish steak.

cut-off *n.* **1.** a cutting off, or something that cuts off; a shorter passage or way. **2.** a specified point of termination; limit.

cut-price *adj.* **1.** (of goods) for sale at a price lower than the suggested retail price. **2.** (of a shop, etc.) dealing in such goods.

cutter /'kʌtə/ *n.* **1.** someone or something that cuts. **2.** a hairdresser who specialises in cutting hair. **3.** a single-masted sailing vessel carrying fore-and-aft sails consisting of a mainsail and two or more headsails. **4.** a medium-sized boat for rowing or sailing, or a launch, belonging to a warship. **5.** *Cricket* a ball which strikes the ground on its seam, and suddenly changes direction.

cutthroat /'kʌtθroʊt/ *n.* Also, **cut-throat. 1.** someone who cuts throats; a murderer. −*adj.* **2.** Also, **cut-throat.** (of a razor) having an open blade. **3.** relentless: *cutthroat competition.* **4.** Also, **cut-throat.** relating to a game participated in as by three or more persons, each acting and scoring as an individual.

cutting /'kʌtɪŋ/ *n.* **1.** something cut off. **2.** *Hort.* a piece cut from a plant, usually a root, shoot, or leaf, in order to reproduce a new plant. **3.** a piece cut out of a newspaper; clipping. **4.** something produced by cutting, as a passage cut through high ground. **5.** (*pl.*) *Geol.* small pieces of rock broken or torn off during drilling. −*adj.* **6.** that cuts. **7.** sharply cold, as a wind. **8.** hurting the feelings severely; sarcastic: *a cutting remark.*

cutting edge *n.* the forefront of innovation: *her work was at the cutting edge of research.*

cutting grass *n.* any of various grasses or sedges with leaves sufficiently hard and rough to inflict cuts, especially *Gahnia* species.

cuttlefish /'kʌtlfɪʃ/ *n.* any of various decapod, two-gilled cephalopods, especially of the genus *Sepia*, having sucker-bearing arms and the power of ejecting a black, inklike fluid when pursued. Also, **cuttle.**

cutty-grass /'kʌti-gras/ *n.* *NZ* → **cutting grass.**

CV /si 'vi/ *n.* → **curriculum vitae.** Also, **cv.**

-cy **1.** a suffix of abstract nouns, usually paired with adjectives ending in *-t*, *-te*, *-tic*, especially *-nt*, as *accuracy, expediency,* also paired with other adjectives, as *fallacy* (*fallacious*), or with a noun, as *lunacy,* sometimes forming (in extended suffixes) action nouns, as *vacancy* (*vacate*), *occupancy* (*occupy*). **2.** a suffix of nouns denoting a rank or dignity, sometimes attached to the stem of a word rather than the word itself, as *captaincy, colonelcy, magistracy.*

cyanide /'saɪənaɪd/ *n.* **1.** a highly poisonous salt of hydrocyanic acid, as potassium cyanide, KCN. −*v.t.* **2.** *NZ* to poison (possums) with cyanides.

cyano-¹ a word element indicating dark blue colouring. Also, **cyan-¹.**

cyano-² a combining form of **cyanide** as in cyanogen. Also, **cyan-².**

cyano-³ a word element referring to the cyanide group, CN. Also, **cyan-³.**

cyanobacteria /ˌsaɪənoʊbæk'tɪəriə/ *pl. n.* (*sing.* **cyanobacterium**) unicellular or filamentous photosynthetic organisms classified within the kingdom Monera, containing chlorophyll and accessory pigments; they thrive in marine or fresh water and contribute to bluish-green scum in late summer; no longer considered true algae. −**cyanobacterial,** *adj.*

cyber /'saɪbə/ *adj.* **1.** of, relating to, or typified by an internet culture: *the cyber age.* **2.** in the style associated with the visuals of computer games: *a cyber goth.*

cyber- a prefix popularly used to indicate a connection with computers, in particular with the internet and virtual reality: *cybertech.*

cyber attack *n.* an infiltration of the internet communications system of a country, organisation, etc., with the intent to damage or disrupt the system. Also, **cyberattack.**

cyberbully /'saɪbəbʊli/ *n.* (*pl.* **-bullies**) **1.** a person who bullies another using email, social network sites, online forums, etc. −*v.t.* (**-bullied, -bullying**) **2.** to bully (another) in this way. Also, **cyber bully, cyber-bully.** −**cyberbullying,** *n.*

cyberchondriac /saɪbə'kɒndriæk/ *n.* *Colloq.* a hypochondriac who habitually uses internet medical sites for self-diagnosis.

cyber hacking *n.* the gaining of unauthorised access to a computer network. −**cyber hacker,** *n.*

cybernetics /saɪbə'nɛtɪks/ *n.* the scientific study of those methods of control and communication which are common to living organisms and machines, especially as applied to the analysis of the operations of machines such as computers. −**cybernetic,** *adj.* −**cybernation,** *n.*

cyberpunk /'saɪbəpʌŋk/ *n.* **1.** a genre of science fiction in which the stories are set in a highly-technological, dystopian society of the near future. **2.** a person who is computer-literate and views current society as heading towards such a future. **3.** a genre of punk-style music utilising electronic instrumentation.

cyber safety *n.* safety in an online environment achieved by taking precautions in one's dealings online, as by not providing banking details, personal information, etc., and by making correct responses to inappropriate content, bullying, harassment, etc.

cybersecurity /ˌsaɪbəsəˈkjurəti/ *n.* protection provided for an information system, such as computer and telecommunications networks, against cyberthreats.

cyberspace /ˈsaɪbəspeɪs/ *n.* **1.** a communication network, conceived of as a separate world, access to which is gained through the use of computers. **2.** a world created in virtual reality. **3.** the internet.

cyberstalking /ˈsaɪbəstɔːkɪŋ/ *n.* sustained harassment or threatening behaviour directed at someone through the use of the internet, email, chat rooms, or other digital communications devices. Also, **internet stalking**.

cyberterrorism /saɪbəˈtɛrərɪzm/ *n.* a type of terrorism in which computer networks, data, etc., are damaged or altered to harm a targeted group or country. –**cyberterrorist**, *n.*

cyberthreat /ˈsaɪbəθrɛt/ *n.* an attack on a computer network, as a worm (def. 10), a virus (def. 3), hacker intrusion, etc.

cycad /ˈsaɪkæd/ *n.* any of the Cycadales, an order of gymnospermous plants intermediate in appearance between ferns and the palms, many species having a thick unbranched columnar trunk bearing a crown of large feathery pinnate leaves.

cycl- a word element meaning 'cycle', used especially in the chemical terminology of cyclic compounds, also in referring to wheel turns. Also, **cyclo-**.

cyclamate /ˈsaɪkləmeɪt, -mət/ *n.* any of a group of artificial sweeteners, sometimes used as food additives.

cyclamen /ˈsaɪkləmən, ˈsɪk-/ *n.* any plant of the genus *Cyclamen* which has tuberous rootstocks and nodding white, purple, pink, or crimson flowers with reflexed petals.

cycle /ˈsaɪkəl/ *n.* **1.** a period of time in which certain events repeat themselves in the same order and at the same time apart. **2.** any complete series of operations or events. **3.** any long period of years; an age. **4.** any group of poems or songs about a central event, figure, etc. Compare **sequence** (def. 3). **5.** a bicycle, tricycle, etc. **6.** *Physics* any series of changes in or operations performed by a system which brings it back to its original state, as in alternating electric current. –*v.i.* **7.** to ride a bicycle, etc. **8.** to move or happen in cycles. –**cyclic**, *adj.*

cycle pants *pl. n.* tight-fitting shorts for, or as if for, cycling.

cyclist /ˈsaɪkləst/ *n.* someone who rides or travels by a bicycle, tricycle, etc. Also, *US*, **cycler**.

cyclone /ˈsaɪkloʊn/ *n. Meteorol.* **1.** an atmospheric pressure system characterised by relatively low pressure at its centre, and by clockwise wind motion in the Southern Hemisphere, anticlockwise in the Northern. **2.** a tropical hurricane, especially in the Indian Ocean. –**cyclonic** /saɪˈklɒnɪk/, **cyclonical**, *adj.* –**cyclonal**, *adj.* –**cyclonically**, *adv.*

cyclopedia /saɪkləˈpidiə/ *n.* an encyclopedia. Also, **cyclopaedia**. –**cyclopedic**, *adj.* –**cyclopedist**, *n.*

cyclotron /ˈsaɪklətrɒn/ *n.* a device for imparting very high speed to electrified particles by successive electric impulses at high frequency, space requirements and applied voltage being kept relatively low by causing the particles to move in spiral paths in a strong magnetic field.

cygnet /ˈsɪgnət/ *n.* a young swan.

cylinder /ˈsɪləndə/ *n.* **1.** *Geom.* **a.** a solid bounded by two parallel planes and the surface generated by a straight line moving parallel to a given straight line, and intersecting a given curve lying in one of the planes. When the given curve is a circle, the solid is called a **right circular cylinder** if the given line is perpendicular to the planes, and an **oblique circular cylinder** otherwise. **2.** any cylinder-like object or part, whether solid or hollow. **3.** the rotating part of a revolver, which contains the chambers for the cartridges. **4.** the body of a pump. **5.** the chamber in an engine in which the working medium acts upon the piston. –**cylindrical** /səˈlɪndrɪkəl/, *adj.*

cymbal /ˈsɪmbəl/ *n.* a brass or bronze concave plate giving a metallic sound when struck. –**cymbalist**, *n.*

cymbidium /sɪmˈbɪdiəm/ *n.* any species of the widespread orchid genus *Cymbidium* found in Africa, Asia, and Australia.

cymo- a word element meaning 'wave'.

cynic /ˈsɪnɪk/ *n.* someone who doubts or denies the goodness of human motives, and who often displays this attitude by sneers, sarcasm, etc. –**cynicism**, *n.* –**cynical**, *adj.* –**cynically**, *adv.*

cynosure /ˈsaɪnəʃʊə/ *n.* **1.** something that strongly attracts attention by its brilliance, etc.: *the cynosure of all eyes.* **2.** something serving for guidance or direction.

cypher /ˈsaɪfə/ *n., v.i., v.t.* → **cipher**.

cypress /ˈsaɪprəs/ *n.* **1.** any of the evergreen trees constituting the coniferous genus *Cupressus*, distinguished by dark green scale-like, overlapping leaves, often a very slender tree with a durable wood. **2.** any of various other allied coniferous trees as of the genera *Chamaecyparis*, *Taxodium* (**bald cypress**), etc.

cypress pine *n.* any tree of the mostly Australian genus *Callitris* including several species producing valuable softwood timber.

cyprinoid /ˈsɪprənɔɪd, səˈpraɪnɔɪd/ *adj.* of or relating to or resembling a carp or related fish.

cyrto- a word element meaning 'curved.'

cyst /sɪst/ *n. Pathol.* a closed bladder-like sac formed in animal tissues, containing fluid or semifluid morbid matter. –**cystic**, *adj.*

cyst- a prefixal use of **cyst**. Also, **cysti-**, **cysto-**.

cystitis /sɪsˈtaɪtəs/ *n. Pathol.* inflammation of the urinary bladder.

cyte /saɪt/ *n.* a cell, especially a maturing germ cell. –**cytic**, *adj.*

-cyte a word element referring to cells or corpuscles, as in *leukocyte*.

cyto- a word element referring to cells, as in *cytogenesis*. Also, (*before vowels*), **cyt-**.

cytology /saɪˈtɒlədʒi/ *n.* the scientific study of cells, especially their formation, structure, and functions. –**cytologist**, *n.* –**cytological** /saɪtəˈlɒdʒɪkəl/, *adj.*

czar /zɑ/ *n.* → **tsar**. –**czardom**, *n.*

D d

D, d /di/ *n.* **1.** the fourth letter of the English alphabet. **2.** the Roman numeral for 500. **3.** *Music* the second note of the scale of C major.

'd *v.* (*in representations of speech*) **1.** did: *where'd you go?* **2.** had: *she'd already left.* **3.** would: *I'd never have guessed.*

dab /dæb/ *v.t.* (**dabbed, dabbing**) **1.** to tap lightly, as with the hand: *she dabbed the surface tentatively.* **2.** to apply (a substance) by light strokes: *I dabbed antiseptic on the wound.* –*n.* **3.** a small quantity: *serve the vegetables with a dab of butter.* –*phr.* **4. dab at,** to touch (something) lightly: *he dabbed at the spill with a cloth.*

dabble /'dæbəl/ *v.i.* **1.** to play in water, with or as with the hands: *to dabble in the clear water of the fountain.* –*phr.* **2. dabble in,** to concern oneself with in a slight or superficial manner: *to dabble in literature.* –**dabbler,** *n.*

dabchick /'dæbtʃɪk/ *n.* any of several small grebes.

dachshund /'dæksənd, 'dæʃənd/ *n.* one of a German breed of small dogs with a long body and very short legs.

dack /dæk/ *v.t.* → **dak.**

dacks /dæks/ *pl. n.* → **daks.**

dactyl /'dæktɪl, -tl/ *n.* *Prosody* a foot of three syllables, one long followed by two short, or in modern verse, one accented followed by two unaccented (ˉ ˘ ˘), as in 'Gēntlў ănd hūmănlў'. –**dactylic,** *adj.*

dad /dæd/ *n.* *Colloq.* **1.** father: *my dad's a plumber.* **2.** a term of address to an older man.

daddy /'dædi/ *n.* (*pl.* **-dies**) *Colloq.* **1.** (*with children*) dad; father. **2.** a familiar form of address for a father. –*phr.* **3. the daddy of them all,** the biggest, most powerful, most impressive, etc.

daddy-long-legs /ˌdædi-'lɒŋ-lɛgz/ *n.* (*pl.* **daddy-long-legs**) *Aust., NZ* a small web-spinning spider of the family Pholcidae, with long thin legs, frequently found indoors.

dado /'deɪdoʊ/ *n.* (*pl.* **dados** *or* **dadoes**) **1.** the part of a pedestal between the base and the cornice or cap. **2.** the lower broad part of an interior wall finished in wallpaper, paint, or the like. **3.** a strip of patterned wallpaper just below the picture rail; frieze.

daffodil /'dæfədɪl/ *n.* a plant, *Narcissus pseudo-narcissus,* with single or double yellow nodding flowers, blooming in the spring.

daft /dɑft/ *adj.* **1.** *Colloq.* lacking in common sense; idiotic: *not as daft as I look!* **2.** *Colloq.* stupid; foolish: *a daft idea.* **3.** *Chiefly Brit.* lacking mental acuity; mentally deficient. –**daftly,** *adv.* –**daftness,** *n.*

dag¹ /dæg/ *n. Aust., NZ Colloq.* **1.** someone who dresses or behaves in an unfashionable or unstylish manner. **2.** an odd, eccentric or amusing person. –**daggish,** *adj.*

dag² /dæg/ *n. Aust., NZ* wool on a sheep's rear quarters, which is dirty with mud and excreta.

dag³ /dæg/ *n. Aust., NZ Colloq.* an untidy, slovenly person.

dagger /'dægə/ *n.* **1.** a short, sharp-edged and pointed weapon, like a small sword, used for thrusting and stabbing. **2.** *Printing* a mark (†) used for references, etc.; the obelisk. –*phr.* **3. look daggers at,** to cast angry, threatening, or vengeful glances.

daggy¹ /'dægi/ *adj.* (**-gier, -giest**) *Aust., NZ Colloq.* **1.** conservative and lacking in style, especially in appearance. **2.** stupid; idiotic; eccentric. –**daggily,** *adv.* –**dagginess,** *n.*

daggy² /'dægi/ *adj.* (**-gier, -giest**) *Aust., NZ* **1.** (of sheep or wool) fouled with dags. **2.** *Colloq.* **a.** dirty. **b.** slovenly; unkempt: *a daggy tracksuit.* –**daggily,** *adv.* –**dagginess,** *n.*

dago /'deɪgoʊ/ *n.* (*pl.* **dagos** *or* **dagoes**) *Colloq.* (*derog.*) (*racist*) a person of Mediterranean extraction, especially an Italian. Also, **Dago.**

dahlia /'deɪljə/ *n.* any plant of the genus *Dahlia,* native to Mexico and Central America, widely cultivated for its showy, variously coloured flowers.

daikon /'daɪkɒn/ *n.* a Japanese variety of radish with white flesh and a mild flavour, growing up to 50 cm in length.

daily /'deɪli/ *adj.* **1.** done, occurring, or issued each day or each weekday. –*n.* (*pl.* **-lies**) **2.** a newspaper appearing each day or each weekday. –*adv.* **3.** every day; day by day: *she phoned the hospital daily; the news grows daily more alarming.*

dainty /'deɪnti/ *adj.* (**-tier, -tiest**) **1.** of delicate beauty or charm; exquisite. **2.** pleasing to the palate; toothsome; delicious: *dainty food.* **3.** particular in discrimination or taste; fastidious. –*n.* (*pl.* **-ties**) **4.** something delicious to the taste; a delicacy. –**daintily,** *adv.* –**daintiness,** *n.*

dairy /'dɛəri/ *n.* (*pl.* **dairies**) **1.** a place, such as a room or building, where milk and cream are kept and made into butter and cheese. **2.** a shed equipped with milking machinery where cows, goats, etc., are milked; bails; milking shed. **3.** the business of producing milk, butter, and cheese. –*adj.* **4.** of or relating to a dairy: *the dairy churn.* **5.** (of an animal) kept for milking: *dairy cow; dairy goat.* **6.** of or relating to milk or butter production: *dairy products; dairy industry.*

dais /'deɪəs/ *n.* a raised platform, as at the end of a room, for a throne, seats of honour, a lecturer's desk, etc.

daisy /'deɪzi/ *n.* (*pl.* **-sies**) **1.** any plant of the family Compositae whose flower heads have a yellow disc and white rays. –*phr.* **2. push up daisies,** *Colloq.* to be dead and buried.

dak /dæk/ *v.t.* (**dakked, dakking**) *Colloq.* to forcibly pull down the trousers, and sometimes the underpants, of: *he dakked me in front of everyone.* Also, **dack.**

daks /dæks/ *pl. n.* *Aust. Colloq.* (*from trademark*) trousers. Also, **dacks.**

dale /deɪl/ *n. Chiefly Brit.* a small, open river valley partly enclosed by low hills.

dalliance /'dæliəns/ *n.* amorous toying; flirtation.

dally /'dæli/ *v.i.* (**-lied, -lying**) to waste time; loiter; delay.

Dalmatian /dæl'meɪʃən/ *n.* one of a breed of dogs resembling the pointer, of a white colour profusely marked with black or liver-coloured spots.

dam¹ /dæm/ *n.* **1.** a barrier to obstruct the flow of water, especially one of earth, masonry, etc., built across a river in order to create a reservoir for use as a water supply or in the generation of electricity. **2.** a body of water confined by such a barrier. **3.** *Aust., NZ* an artificial water storage for farm use, constructed by creating a barrier, either a wall or earthworks, to contain run-off from a slope; tank. –*v.t.* (**dammed, damming**) **4.** to stop up; block up.

dam² /dæm/ *n.* a female parent (used especially of horses and other animals).

damage /ˈdæmɪdʒ/ *n.* **1.** injury or harm that impairs value or usefulness. **2.** (*pl.*) *Law* the estimated money equivalent for detriment or injury sustained. **3.** *Colloq.* cost; expense: *what's the damage?* –*v.t.* (**-aged, -aging**) **4.** to cause damage to.

damage control *n.* **1.** measures to limit damage, as during or after a disaster **2.** attempts to mitigate the unpleasant consequence of an event, action, etc. Also, **damage limitation**.

damask /ˈdæməsk/ *n.* **1.** a reversible fabric of linen, silk, cotton, or wool, woven with patterns. **2.** table linen of this material. **3.** the pink colour of the damask rose.

dame /deɪm/ *n.* **1.** (*upper case*) the distinctive title used before the name of a woman who holds one of a number of honours, such as a Dame of the Order of Australia. **2.** the legal title of the wife of a knight or baronet. **3.** *Chiefly US Colloq.* a woman.

damn /dæm/ *v.t.* **1.** to declare (something) to be bad, unfit, invalid, or illegal: *critics damned the play.* **2.** to bring condemnation upon; ruin: *this action damned him in her eyes.* **3.** to doom to eternal punishment, or condemn to hell. –*n.* **4.** a negligible amount: *not worth a damn.* –*interj.* **5.** an expression of anger or annoyance. –*adv.* **6.** extremely. –*adj.* **7.** an intensifier expressing dislike, annoyance, etc.: *a damn fool; a damn nuisance.* –*phr.* **8. not to give** (or **care**) **a damn**, not to care; be unconcerned. –**damnation**, *n.*

damned /dæmd/ *adj.* **1.** condemned, especially to eternal punishment. **2.** *Colloq.* detestable: *the damned car wouldn't start.* **3.** *Colloq.* an intensifier: *he's a damned fool.* –*adv.* **4.** *Colloq.* an intensifier: *a damned fine cup of coffee; a damned silly idea.*

damp /dæmp/ *adj.* **1.** moderately wet; moist. –*n.* **2.** moisture; humidity; moist air: *the damp had warped the timber.* –*v.t.* **3.** to make damp; moisten. **4.** to check or retard the energy, action, etc., of. –**dampen**, *v.* –**dampish**, *adj.* –**damply**, *adv.* –**dampness**, *n.*

dampcourse /ˈdæmpkɔs/ *n.* a horizontal layer of impervious material laid in a wall to stop moisture rising. Also, **damp-proof course**.

damper¹ /ˈdæmpə/ *n.* **1.** a movable plate for regulating the draught in a stove, furnace, ducting system, etc. –*phr.* **2. put a damper on**, *Colloq.* to discourage (a person) or diminish the enjoyment associated with (an occasion).

damper² /ˈdæmpə/ *n.* bread made from a simple flour and water dough with or without a raising agent, traditionally cooked in the coals or in a camp oven.

damsel /ˈdæmzəl/ *n. Archaic* a young woman; girl; maiden, originally one of gentle or noble birth.

dance /dæns, dɑns/ *verb* (**danced, dancing**) –*v.i.* **1.** to move with the feet or body rhythmically, especially to music. **2.** to leap, skip, etc., as from excitement or emotion; move nimbly or quickly: *she was dancing with joy; he danced into the room.* **3.** to bob up and down: *the boat danced on the waves.* –*v.t.* **4.** to perform or take part in (a dance). **5.** to cause to dance: *he danced her round the room.* –*n.* **6.** a successive group of rhythmical steps, generally executed to music. **7.** an act or round of dancing. **8.** a social gathering for dancing; ball. **9.** a piece of music suited in rhythm to a particular form of dancing. **10.** a series of rhythmic movements as performed by some insects or birds, etc. **11.** dancing as an art or profession. –*adj.* **12.** of or relating to dancing: *a dance teacher.* **13.** of or relating to dance music: *dance tracks.* –*phr.* **14. dance attendance on**, to attend (someone) constantly or solicitously. **15. lead someone a merry dance**, *Colloq.* to frustrate someone, as by constantly changing one's moods, intentions, attitudes, etc. –**dancer**, *n.* –**dancingly**, *adv.*

dance music *n.* any of various genres of pop music with a strong beat, designed for dancing at nightclubs, dance parties, etc.

dance party *n.* **1.** an entertainment involving a large space for dancing, dance music, and usually a lightshow, and at which amphetamines are often taken. **2.** a disco (def. 2).

dandelion /ˈdændəlaɪən, -di-/ *n.* **1.** a common plant, *Taraxacum officinale*, abundant as a weed, characterised by deeply toothed or notched leaves and golden yellow flowers. **2.** any other plant of the genus *Taraxacum.*

dandruff /ˈdændrəf, -rʌf/ *n.* a scurf which forms on the scalp and comes off in small scales.

dandy /ˈdændi/ *n.* (*pl.* **-dies**) **1.** a man who is excessively concerned about clothes and appearance; fop. –*adj.* (**-dier, -diest**) **2.** *Colloq.* fine; first-rate. –**dandyish**, *adj.* –**dandyism**, *n.*

danger /ˈdeɪndʒə/ *n.* **1.** liability or exposure to harm or injury; risk; peril. **2.** an instance or cause of peril. **3.** the position (of a signal, etc.) indicating danger: *although the signal was at danger, the train did not stop.* –**dangerous**, *adj.*

dangerous driving *n. Law* the statutory offence of driving on a road or road-related area at a speed that is furious, negligent or reckless and in a manner that is dangerous to the public.

dangle /ˈdæŋgəl/ *v.i.* **1.** to hang loosely with a swaying motion. –*v.t.* **2.** to cause to dangle; hold or carry swaying loosely. –**dangler**, *n.*

dank /dæŋk/ *adj.* unpleasantly moist or humid; damp. –**dankly**, *adv.* –**dankness**, *n.*

daphne /ˈdæfni/ *n.* **1.** any plant of the genus *Daphne*, family Thymeleaceae, of Europe and Asia, comprising small shrubs of which some species, such as *D. mezereum*, are cultivated for their fragrant flowers. **2.** → spurge laurel.

dapper /ˈdæpə/ *adj.* **1.** neat; trim; smart. **2.** small and active. –**dapperly**, *adv.* –**dapperness**, *n.*

dapple /ˈdæpəl/ *n.* **1.** mottled marking, as of an animal's skin or coat. –*adj.* **2.** dappled; spotted: *a dapple grey.* –**dappled**, *adj.*

dare /dɛə/ *verb* (**dared** or, *Archaic*, **durst, dared, daring**) –*v.i.* **1.** to have the necessary courage or boldness for something; be bold enough: *to dare to win; I didn't dare ask him.* –*v.t.* **2.** to challenge or provoke (someone) to action especially by doubting their courage; defy: *go on, I dare you.* –*n.* **3.** *Colloq.* a challenge, as to some dangerous act. –*phr.* **4. dare say**, to assume as probable; no doubt: *I dare say he'll be tired.* –**darer**, *n.*

daredevil /ˈdɛədɛvəl/ *n.* **1.** a recklessly daring person. –*adj.* **2.** recklessly daring.

daring /ˈdɛərɪŋ/ *n.* **1.** adventurous courage; boldness. –*adj.* **2.** bold; intrepid; adventurous. –**daringly**, *adv.* –**daringness**, *n.*

dark /dɑk/ *adj.* **1.** without light; with very little light: *a dark room; what time does it get dark?* **2.** radiating or reflecting little light: *a dark colour; the dark side of the moon.* **3.** approaching black in hue: *dark green; dark eyes.* **4.** not pale or fair: *a dark complexion; dark circles under the eyes.* **5.** (*euphemistic*) black, as an Aboriginal, African, etc.: *the dark people.* **6.** gloomy; cheerless; dismal: *a dark mood; let's not look on the dark side.* **7.** evil; wicked: *dark intentions; the dark side of human nature.* **8.** hidden; obscure: *he kept his win a dark secret.* **9.** destitute of knowledge or culture; unenlightened. **10.** *Phonetics* (of *l* sounds) resembling a back vowel in quality: *English l is darker than French l.* –*n.* **11.** absence of light; darkness: *dark lay all around us.* **12.** night; nightfall: *the possums come out after dark; we should get there before dark.* **13.** a dark colour: *the silver shows up well against the patch of* *dark.* *–phr.* **14. go dark**, to suffer a diminishing or extinguishing of light: *the room went dark.* **15. in the dark**, in obscurity, secrecy, or ignorance: *kept in the dark.* **16. the dark**, **a.** darkness: *scared of the dark.* **b.** a dark place. **–darken**, *v.* **–darkish**, *adj.* **–darkness**, *n.*

Dark Ages *pl. n.* **1.** the time in history from about AD 476 to about AD 1000. **2.** the whole of the Middle Ages, the period preceding the Renaissance. **3.** a state of backwardness or unenlightenment: *you're really living in the Dark Ages, aren't you?*

dark energy *n.* the energy released by dark matter.

dark horse *n.* **1.** a racehorse, competitor, etc., about whom little is known or who unexpectedly wins. **2.** a person whose capabilities may be greater than they are known to be.

dark matter *n.* theoretically postulated matter of unknown nature that comprises 90% or more of the mass of the universe.

darkroom /'dakrum/ *n.* a room from which the chemically active rays of light have been excluded, used in making, handling, and developing photographic film, etc.

darling /'dalɪŋ/ *n.* **1.** a person very dear to another; someone dearly loved. **2.** a person or thing in great favour: *she is the latest media darling.* **3.** a term of endearment. *–adj.* **4.** very dear; dearly loved.

darn¹ /dan/ *v.t.* **1.** to mend (clothes, etc., or a tear or hole) with rows of stitches, sometimes with crossing and interwoven rows to fill up a gap. *–n.* **2.** a darned place in a garment, etc. **–darner**, *n.*

darn² /dan/ *Colloq. –adj., adv.* **1.** → **darned**. *–v.t.* **2.** to confound; curse: *darn him; darn it. –interj.* **3.** a mild expletive.

darned /dand/ *Colloq. –adj.* **1.** detestable; extreme: *it's a darned nuisance. –adv.* **2.** an intensifier: *it's darned inconvenient.*

dart /dat/ *n.* **1.** a long, slender, pointed missile propelled by the hand or otherwise. **2.** something resembling such an object, such as the sting of an insect. **3.** an act of darting; a sudden, swift movement. **4.** (*pl. construed as sing.*) a game in which pointed missiles are thrown at a dartboard. **5.** a stitched tapering fold used to adjust the fit of a garment. **6.** any of several tropical and semitropical marine fishes as the Australian *Trachinotus botla* and the **snub-nosed dart**, *T. blochii. –v.i.* **7.** to move swiftly; spring or start suddenly and run swiftly. **–dartingly**, *adv.*

darter /'data/ *n.* any of various fish-eating birds of the genus *Anhinga*, having small heads, long slender necks, and long pointed bills, such as *A. melanogaster*, widely distributed in Australia and elsewhere.

Darwinism /'dawənɪzəm/ *n.* the body of biological doctrine maintained by Charles Darwin, respecting the origin of species as derived by descent, with variation, from parent forms, through the natural selection of those best adapted to survive in the struggle for existence. **–Darwinian**, **Darwinist**, *n., adj.*

dash /dæʃ/ *v.t.* **1.** to strike violently, especially so as to break to pieces: *she dashed the glass against the wall.* **2.** to throw or thrust violently or suddenly: *he dashed his hand through the ice.* **3.** to ruin or frustrate (hopes, plans, etc.). **4.** to depress or dispirit. *–v.i.* **5.** to strike with violence: *the ship dashed against the rocks.* **6.** to move with violence; rush: *he dashed into the room. –n.* **7.** a small quantity of anything thrown into or mixed with something else: *a dash of salt; a dash of pink.* **8.** a horizontal line of varying length (– or —) used in writing and printing as a mark of punctuation to indicate an abrupt break or pause in a sentence, to begin and end a parenthetic clause, as an indication of omission of letters, words, etc., as a dividing line between distinct portions of matter, and for other

purposes. **9.** *Music* the sign placed above or below a note to indicate that it is to be played staccato. **10.** *Maths* an acute accent, used in algebra and in lettering diagrams as a discrimination mark; prime. **11.** an impetuous movement; a rush; a sudden onset. **12.** *Athletics* a short race or sprint decided in one attempt, not in heats: *a hundred-metre dash.* **13.** spirited action; vigour in action or style. **14.** *Telegraphy* a signal of longer duration than a dot, used in groups of dots and dashes to represent letters, as in morse code. *–interj.* **15.** a mild expletive. *–phr.* **16. cut a dash**, to create a brilliant impression. **17. dash down**, to write or draw hastily: *to dash down a quick sketch.* **18. dash off**, **a.** to hurry away. **b.** to perform hastily, as by writing, drawing, or creating in any way: *to dash off a letter; to dash off a quick omelette.* **19. do one's dash**, *Aust.* to exhaust one's energies or opportunities.

dashboard /'dæʃbɔd/ *n.* the instrument board of a motor vehicle, aeroplane or boat.

dash cam /'dæʃ kæm/ *n.* a camera installed on the dashboard of a motor vehicle, designed to video the road ahead, in particular to provide evidence in the event of an accident.

dashing /'dæʃɪŋ/ *adj.* **1.** impetuous; spirited; lively. **2.** brilliant; showy; stylish. **–dashingly**, *adv.*

dastardly /'dæstədli/ *adj.* cowardly; meanly base; sneaking. **–dastardliness**, *n.*

dasyurid /dæsi'jurəd, dæzi-/ *n.* **1.** a member of the marsupial family Dasyuridae, which includes quolls, dunnarts, planigales, etc. *–adj.* **2.** of or relating to a dasyurid.

data /'deɪtə, 'datə/ *pl. n.* **1.** plural of **datum**. **2.** (*construed as sing. or pl.*) figures, statistics, etc., known or available; information collected for analysis or reference. **3.** (*construed as sing. or pl.*) *Computers* digital information.

database /'deɪtəbeɪs, 'datə-/ *n.* a large volume of information stored in a computer and organised in categories to facilitate retrieval.

datacast /'deɪtəkast/ *v.i.* (**-cast** *or* **-casted**, **-casting**) to broadcast digital information. **–datacaster**, *n.* **–datacasting**, *n.*

data conversion *n.* *Computers* the conversion of data from one format to another, as from SGML to HTML.

data dictionary *n.* *Computers* a dictionary in which metadata is recorded against each attribute of a database.

data encryption /deɪtə ən'krɪpʃən/ *n.* the encoding of data so that it cannot be decoded without appropriate software or hardware, so as to prevent unauthorised access or use.

data entry *n.* the keying of data into a computer.

data haven *n.* *Computers* a digital data storage device, offering complete privacy, especially from government regulation, by means of data encryption and location in a state which does not have laws allowing legal access.

data mining *n.* *Computers* the process of analysing data for known and unknown data patterns.

data processing *n.* the use of computers to store, organise, and perform calculations on large quantities of data with the minimum of human intervention.

data retrieval *n.* the finding of required information from all the data stored in a database.

dataset /'deɪtəset/ *n.* *Computers* assembled data organised and structured for a particular purpose.

date¹ /deɪt/ *n.* **1.** a particular day, as denoted by some system for marking the passage of time: *today's date is 12 May.* **2.** a particular time when something happens or happened: *what was the date of Federation?; there's more to history than memorising dates.* **3.** an inscription on a writing, coin, etc., that shows the day or year of writing, manufacture, etc. **4.** the time or period to which anything belongs: *events of recent date.* **5.** *Colloq.* an appointment made for a particular time. **6.** *Colloq.* a social engagement with someone in whom one has a romantic interest. **7.** *Colloq.* any social engagement. **8.** *Colloq.* a person with whom one has a social engagement, especially someone in whom one has a romantic interest. *–v.i.* **9.** to have its origin at a particular time or period: *the letter dates from 1873; the practice dates back to the Middle Ages.* **10.** *Colloq.* to go out on dates (def. 6) on a regular basis: *how long have you two been dating? –v.t.* **11.** to mark or furnish with a date: *you must date and initial each entry; the painting is dated on the back.* **12.** to assign a probable time of origin to: *Prof. Myer dates the document a decade later.* **13.** to indicate the probable time of origin of: *the dye used dates the fabric to no earlier than the 1870s.* **14.** to show to be of a certain age, old-fashioned, or out of date: *remembering the Beatles really dates you.* **15.** *Colloq.* to go out with on social engagements (a person in whom one has a romantic interest). *–phr.* **16. to date**, up to the present time.

date² /deɪt/ *n.* the oblong, fleshy fruit of the date palm, a staple food in northern Africa, Arabia, etc., and an important export.

dated /ˈdeɪtəd/ *adj.* no longer fashionable; out-of-date.

date line *n.* **1.** a line in a letter, newspaper article, or the like, giving the date (and often the place) of origin. **2.** Also, **International Date Line.** a line, theoretically coinciding with the meridian of 180° from Greenwich, England, the regions on either side of which are counted as differing by one day in their calendar dates.

date rape *n.* rape by someone with whom one has gone on a date.

dative /ˈdeɪtɪv/ *adj. Gram.* of or relating to a case, in some inflected languages, which has as one function indication of the indirect object of a verb. **–datival** /dəˈtaɪvəl/, *adj.* **–datively**, *adv.*

datum /ˈdeɪtəm, ˈdɑtəm/ *n.* (*pl.* **-ta** /-tə/) **1.** any proposition assumed or given, from which conclusions may be drawn. **2.** (*oft. pl.*) any fact assumed to be a matter of direct observation.

daub /dɔb/ *v.t.* **1.** to cover or coat with soft, adhesive matter, such as plaster, mud, etc. **2.** to spread (plaster, mud, etc.) on or over something. **3.** to paint unskilfully. *–n.* **4.** material, especially of an inferior kind, for daubing walls, etc. **5.** a crude, inartistic painting. **–dauber**, *n.*

daughter /ˈdɔtə/ *n.* **1.** a female child or person in relation to her parents. **2.** any female descendant. **3.** a woman considered as a product of a particular place or environment, or having a relationship with a place or situation like that of a daughter to a parent: *daughter of the church.* **–daughterly**, *adj.*

daughter board *n.* See **motherboard**.

daughter-in-law *n.* (*pl.* **daughters-in-law**) the wife of one's son.

daunt /dɔnt/ *v.t.* **1.** to overcome with fear; intimidate. **2.** to lessen the courage of; dishearten: *I was daunted by the scale of the task.* **–daunting**, *adj.* **–dauntingly**, *adv.*

dauntless /ˈdɔntləs/ *adj.* not to be daunted; fearless; intrepid; bold. **–dauntlessly**, *adv.* **–dauntlessness**, *n.*

dawdle /ˈdɔdəl/ *v.i.* **1.** to waste time; idle; trifle. **2.** to walk slowly or lag behind others. **–dawdler**, *n.*

dawn /dɔn/ *n.* **1.** the first appearance of daylight in the morning: *we set off before dawn; from dawn to dusk.* **2.** the beginning or rise of anything; advent. *–v.i.* **3.** to begin to grow light in the morning: *at last the great day dawned.* **4.** to begin to develop: *a new awareness is dawning. –phr.* **5. dawn on**, to begin to be perceived by: *eventually it dawned on me that she was joking.* **–dawning**, *n.*

day /deɪ/ *n.* **1.** the interval of light between two successive nights; the time between sunrise and sunset. **2.** the light of day; daylight. **3.** *Astron.* the period during which the earth (or a heavenly body) makes one revolution on its axis. **4.** the portion of a day allotted to working: *an eight-hour day.* **5.** a day as a point or unit of time, or on which something occurs. **6.** a day assigned to a particular purpose or observance: *New Year's Day.* **7.** a day of contest, or the contest itself: *to win the day.* **8.** (*oft. pl.*) a particular time or period: *the present day, in days of old.* **9.** (*oft. pl.*) period of life or activity. **10.** period of power or influence: *every dog has his day. –phr.* **11. day after day**, for an indefinite but seemingly very long time. **12. day by day**, daily. **13. day in, day out**, for an undetermined succession of days. **14. day one**, the first day of a new undertaking, organisation, system, etc. **15. in this day and age**, at the present time; nowadays. **16. not be someone's day**, *Colloq.* to be a day when nothing goes right for someone: *Jane had the feeling it just wasn't her day.* **17. one of those days**, *Colloq.* a day when nothing goes right. **18. that'll be the day**, *Colloq.* an expression indicating disbelief, cynicism, etc. **19. these days**, nowadays.

daybreak /ˈdeɪbreɪk/ *n.* the first appearance of light in the morning; dawn: *we left shortly before daybreak.*

daydream /ˈdeɪdrim/ *n.* **1.** a visionary fancy indulged in while awake; reverie. **2.** an unrealistic ambition. *–v.i.* (**-dreamed** *or* **-dreamt, -dreaming**) **3.** to indulge in daydreams. **–daydreamer**, *n.*

daylight robbery *n.* a shameless attempt to rob, overcharge, or cheat someone.

daylight saving *n.* **1.** a system of reckoning time one or more hours later than the standard time for a country or community, usually used during summer months to give more hours of daylight to the working day. *–adj.* **2.** of or relating to such a system.

Daylight Saving Time *n.* the time of day established by instituting daylight saving, often set an hour before standard local time. *Abbrev.*: DST

day surgery *n.* **1.** a surgical facility at a hospital or in a doctor's rooms for procedures which do not involve overnight hospitalisation of the patients. **2.** a procedure undergone at such a facility.

day trading *n.* the buying and subsequent selling of stocks or shares on the same day or during the same trading session. Also, **daytrading.** **–day trader**, *n.*

daze /deɪz/ *v.t.* **1.** to stun or stupefy with a blow, a shock, etc. **2.** to confuse; bewilder; dazzle. *–n.* **3.** a dazed condition. **–dazedly** /ˈdeɪzədli/, *adv.*

dazzle /ˈdæzəl/ *v.t.* **1.** to overpower or dim the vision of by intense light: *the headlamps dazzled me.* **2.** to impress or bewilder by brilliance or display of any kind: *we were dazzled by his qualifications. –v.i.* **3.** to excite admiration by brilliance: *a dazzling performance. –n.* **4.** bewildering brightness: *caught in the dazzle of the headlights.* **5.** impressive brilliance: *seduced by the dazzle of Hollywood.* **–dazzler**, *n.* **–dazzlingly**, *adv.*

D-day /ˈdi-deɪ/ *n.* the day, usually unspecified, set for the beginning of a previously planned attack, especially the day (6 June 1944) of the Allied invasion of Normandy.

DDT /di di ˈti/ *n.* a very powerful insecticide, dichlorodiphenyltrichloroethane.

de- a prefix meaning: **1.** privation and separation, as in *dehorn, dethrone.* **2.** negation, as in *demerit, derange.* **3.** descent, as in *degrade, deduce.* **4.** reversal, as in *deactivate.* **5.** intensity, as in *decompound.* **6.** to make an exit from a means of transport, as in *decoach, deplane.*

deacon /ˈdikən/ *n.* **1.** (in the early Christian church) an officer appointed to care for the poor. **2.** (in the Roman Catholic and Anglican churches) a member of the clerical order next below that of a priest. See **order**

(def. 16). **3.** (in the Uniting Church) a person with ministerial office but with duties oriented to social justice and to those who are not members of the church. **4.** (in some other churches) an appointed or elected officer with administrative or supervisory duties. –**deaconship**, *n.*

dead /dɛd/ *adj.* **1.** no longer living; deprived of life. **2.** not endowed with life; inanimate: *dead matter.* **3.** resembling death: *a dead sleep.* **4.** bereft of sensation; insensible; numb: *my foot is dead; dead to all sense of shame.* **5.** no longer in existence or use: *dead languages.* **6.** lacking in vigour, force, motion, etc., or especially in sport, lacking in or deprived of some other characteristic and desirable quality: *dead market; dead track; dead pitch.* **7. a.** without resonance: *a dead room; a dead sound.* **b.** without resilience or bounce: *a dead ball.* **8.** unproductive: *dead capital.* **9.** extinguished: *a dead fire.* **10.** tasteless or flat, as alcoholic drink. **11.** not glossy, bright, or brilliant. **12.** complete; absolute: *dead loss; dead silence.* **13.** sure; unerring: *a dead shot.* **14.** direct, straight: *a dead line.* **15.** *Sport* out of play: *a dead ball.* **16.** *Colloq.* very tired; exhausted. **17.** *Colloq.* empty: *a dead bottle.* **18.** *Colloq.* (of an appliance, device, battery, etc.) no longer operative. –*adv.* **19.** absolutely; completely: *dead right; dead broke; dead beat; dead set.* **20.** with abrupt and complete stoppage of motion, etc.: *he stopped dead.* **21.** directly; exactly: *the wind was dead ahead.* –*phr.* **22. dead as a dodo**, *Colloq.* **a.** completely lifeless. **b.** completely inactive. **23. dead from the neck up**, *Colloq.* lacking intelligence; stupid. **24. dead to rights**, *Colloq.* with the evidence of one's guilt clear; redhanded. **25. dead to the world**, *Colloq.* **a.** unaware of one's surroundings; sleeping heavily. **b.** totally drunk. **c.** utterly tired; exhausted. **26. drop dead**, **a.** to die suddenly. **b.** in the imperative, used to insult the person addressed. **27. over my dead body**, *Colloq.* absolutely against my will. **28. the dead**, dead persons collectively. **29. the dead of night**, the period of greatest darkness at night. **30. the dead of winter**, the period of greatest coldness in winter. **31. wouldn't be seen dead with** (or **in**) (or **at**, etc.), *Colloq.* (someone) refuses to accompany, wear, visit, etc..

deadbeat /'dɛdbit/ *Colloq.* –*n.* **1.** someone down on their luck; vagrant. –*adj.* **2.** of or relating to the life of a vagrant.

deadbolt /'dɛdboʊlt/ *n.* **1.** a locking mechanism which, once locked, will require a key from either the outside or the inside of the building to release it. –*v.t.* **2.** to lock using a deadbolt.

dead centre *n.* **1.** *Machinery* a stationary centre which holds the work to be turned. **2.** → **dead heart**.

dead-centre *adj.* **1.** completely on target. –*adv.* **2.** right in the middle; accurately.

dead cert *n.* → **cert**.

deaden /'dɛdən/ *v.t.* **1.** to make less sensitive, active, energetic, or forcible; dull; weaken: *to deaden sound, the force of a ball, the senses.* **2.** to lessen the velocity of; retard. **3.** to make impervious to sound, as a floor. –**deadener**, *n.*

dead end *n.* **1.** a road which is closed at one end; a no-through road; cul-de-sac. **2.** a point beyond which no progress is made: *my enquiries have come to a dead end.*

dead-end *adj.* **1.** leading nowhere. **2.** offering no future: *a dead-end job.* **3.** having no apparent hopes or future, as a juvenile delinquent: *a dead-end kid.*

dead heart *n.* the arid central regions of Australia; dead centre.

dead heat *n.* a heat or race in which two or more competitors finish together.

dead letter *n.* **1.** a law, ordinance, etc., which has lost its force, though not formally repealed or abolished. **2.** a letter which lies unclaimed for a certain time at a post office, or which, because of faulty address, etc., cannot be delivered. –**dead-letter**, *adj.*

deadline /'dɛdlaɪn/ *n.* **1.** a line or limit that must not be passed. **2.** the latest time for finishing something.

deadlock¹ /'dɛdlɒk/ *n.* **1.** a state of affairs in which progress is impossible; complete standstill. **2.** *Parliamentary Procedure* **a.** a situation in which the two houses of parliament are in disagreement. **b.** a tied vote on a motion with no chance or opportunity for a change in the allocation of votes that would break the tie.

deadlock² /'dɛdlɒk/ *n.* a type of lock which needs a key to open it from both the inside and outside. Also, **dead latch**.

deadly /'dɛdli/ *adj.* (**-lier, -liest**) **1.** causing or tending to cause death; fatal: *a deadly poison.* **2.** aiming to kill or destroy; implacable: *a deadly enemy.* **3.** involving spiritual death: *a deadly sin.* **4.** like death: *a deadly pallor.* **5.** excessive: *deadly haste.* **6.** *Colloq.* wonderful; excellent. –**deadliness**, *n.*

deadly nightshade *n.* → **belladonna**.

deadpan /'dɛdpæn/ *adj.* **1.** (of a person or face) completely lacking expression or reaction. **2.** said without any indication in the speaker's manner or expression that he or she is aware of the force or implication of what is said: *deadpan humour.* –*adv.* **3.** in a deadpan manner.

deadweight tonnage /'dɛdweɪt tʌnɪdʒ/ *n.* the mass of the cargo, fuel, potable water, boiler feed water, ballast, stores, crew, gear, etc., on a ship.

deaf /dɛf/ *adj.* **1.** lacking or deprived of the sense of hearing, wholly or partially; unable to hear. **2.** refusing to listen; heedless; inattentive: *deaf to advice; turn a deaf ear to a plea.* –*phr.* **3. the deaf**, people unable to hear. –**deafen**, *v.* –**deafly**, *adv.* –**deafness**, *n.*

deaf-mute *n. Rare* (*now likely to give offence*) someone who is deaf and dumb, especially one in whom inability to speak is due to congenital or early deafness.

deal¹ /dil/ *verb* (**dealt, dealing**) –*v.i.* **1.** to conduct oneself towards persons: *deal fairly.* **2.** to distribute, especially the cards required in a game. –*v.t.* **3.** to distribute among a number of recipients. **4.** *Cards* **a.** to distribute (the cards) among the players. **b.** to give a player (a specific card) in dealing. **5.** to deliver (blows, etc.). –*n.* **6.** a business transaction. **7.** a bargain or arrangement for mutual advantage, as in commerce or politics, often a secret or underhand one. **8.** treatment; arrangement: *a raw deal; a fair deal.* **9.** a quantity, amount, extent, or degree. **10.** an indefinite but large amount or extent: *a deal of money.* **11.** a unit quantity of marijuana. **12.** act of dealing or distributing. **13.** *Cards* **a.** the distribution to the players of the cards in a game. **b.** the set of cards in one's hand. **c.** the turn of a player to deal. **d.** the period of time during which a deal is played. **14.** any undertaking, organisation, etc.; affair. –*phr.* **15. a big deal**, *Colloq.* an important event; a serious matter. **16. big deal**, *Colloq.* an ironic exclamation indicating contempt or indifference. **17. deal in**, **a.** to trade or do business in **b.** to have as its subject: *this poem deals in ideas of immortality.* **18. deal it out**, *Colloq.* to deliver a sustained verbal attack on someone: *he can really deal it out when he's in a bad mood.* **19. deal out**, to give to someone as their share; apportion. **20. deal with**, **a.** to do business with. **b.** to occupy oneself or itself with: *deal with the first question; botany deals with the study of plants.* **c.** to take action with respect to: *law courts must deal with law-breakers.*

deal² /dil/ *n.* **1.** a board or plank, especially of fir or pine. **2.** such boards collectively. **3.** fir or pine wood.

dealer /ˈdilə/ n. **1.** someone who buys and sells articles without altering their condition; trader or merchant. **2.** someone who buys and sells drugs, as marijuana, heroin, etc., in large quantities. **3.** *Cards* the player distributing the cards.

dealt /dɛlt/ v. past tense and past participle of **deal**¹.

dean /din/ n. **1.** the head of a medical school, university faculty, or the like. **2.** any of various ecclesiastical dignitaries, such as the head of a division of a diocese. **3.** the senior member, in length of service, of any body. –**deanship**, n. –**deanery**, n.

dear /dɪə/ adj. **1.** beloved or loved: *a dear friend of mine.* **2.** (in a letter) highly respected: *Dear Sirs.* **3.** precious: *dear to his heart.* **4.** high-priced; expensive. **5.** charging high prices. –n. **6.** someone who is loved or precious: *my dear.* –adv. **7.** fondly: *I loved her dear.* **8.** at a high price. –*interj.* **9.** said in various exclamatory or emphatic expressions.

dearth /dɜθ/ n. scarcity or scanty supply; lack.

death /dɛθ/ n. **1.** the act of dying; the end of life; the total and permanent cessation of the vital functions of an animal or plant. **2.** (*oft. upper case*) the agent of death personified, sometimes represented as a skeleton. **3.** the state of being dead: *to lie still in death.* **4.** extinction; destruction: *it will mean the death of our hopes.* **5.** the time at which a person dies: *the letters may be published after my death.* **6.** manner of dying: *a hero's death.* **7.** bloodshed or murder. **8.** a cause or occasion of death: *you'll be the death of me.* **9.** a pestilence: *the black death.* –*phr.* **10. at death's door**, in danger of death; gravely ill. **11. do to death**, a. to kill. b. to repeat until hackneyed. **12. fate worse than death**, *Colloq.* (*usually humorous*) a circumstance regarded as particularly horrible. **13. in at the death**, a. *Hunting* present when the hunted animal is caught and killed. b. present at the climax or conclusion of a series of events or a situation. **14. like death (warmed up)**, *Colloq.* appearing, or feeling, extremely ill or exhausted. **15. like grim death**, tenaciously, firmly: *he hung on like grim death.* **16. put to death**, to kill; execute. **17. sick to death**, *Colloq.* irritated or annoyed to an extreme degree –**deathly**, adj.

death adder n. **1.** Also, **deaf adder**. a venomous viperlike snake, *Acanthophis antarcticus*, of Australia and the island of New Guinea, having a stout body and broad head; an elapid rather than a true adder. **2.** a mean, avaricious person.

death duty n. (*usu. pl.*) a tax paid upon the inheritance of property.

debacle /deɪˈbakəl, də-/ n. a general break-up or rout; sudden overthrow or collapse; overwhelming disaster.

debar /diˈba, də-/ v.t. (**-barred**, **-barring**) **1.** to bar out or exclude from a place or condition. **2.** to prevent or prohibit (an action, etc.). –**debarment**, n.

debase /dəˈbeɪs/ v.t. **1.** to reduce in quality or value; adulterate. **2.** to lower in rank or dignity. –**debasement**, n. –**debaser**, n. –**debasingly**, adv.

debate /dəˈbeɪt/ n. **1.** a discussion, especially of a public question in an assembly. **2.** deliberation; consideration. **3.** a systematic contest of speakers in which two opposing points of view of a proposition are advanced. –v.i. **4.** to engage in discussion, especially in a legislative or public assembly. –v.t. **5.** to dispute about. –**debater**, n. –**debatable**, adj.

debauch /dəˈbɔtʃ/ v.t. **1.** to corrupt by sensuality, intemperance, etc.; seduce. **2.** to corrupt or pervert; deprave. –**debauched**, adj. –**debauchee**, **debaucher**, n. –**debauchery**, **debauchment**, n.

debenture /dəˈbɛntʃə/ n. **1.** a note or certificate acknowledging a debt, as given by an incorporated company or other private organisation; the corporate equivalent of a government bond (def. 5). **2.** a deed containing a charge or mortgage on a company's assets; a mortgage debenture. **3.** a certificate of drawback issued at a customs house.

debilitate /dəˈbɪləteɪt/ v.t. to make weak or feeble; weaken; enfeeble. –**debilitation** /dəbɪləˈteɪʃən/, n. –**debilitative** /dəˈbɪlətətɪv/, adj. –**debility**, n.

debit /ˈdɛbət/ n. **1.** the recording of an entry of debt in an account. **2.** the side (left side) of an account on which such entries are made (opposed to *credit*). –v.t. **3.** to charge with a debt. **4.** to charge as a debt. **5.** to enter upon the debit side of an account.

debit card n. a plastic card, issued by a bank or other financial institution, which allows the holder to obtain cash and purchase goods and services, the cost of which is then withdrawn directly from the holder's bank account. Compare **credit card**.

debonair /dɛbəˈnɛə/ adj. **1.** suave; stylish. **2.** of pleasant manners; courteous. **3.** carefree; cheerful. Also, **debonaire**. –**debonairly**, adv. –**debonairness**, n.

debouch /dəˈbuʃ, dəˈbaʊtʃ/ v.i. to issue or emerge from a narrow opening. –**debouchment**, n.

debrief /diˈbrif/ v.t. to interrogate (a soldier, astronaut, diplomat, etc.) on return from a mission in order to assess the conduct and results of the mission. –**debriefing**, n.

debris /ˈdɛbri, ˈdeɪbri, dəˈbri/ n. **1.** the remains of anything broken down or destroyed; ruins; fragments; rubbish. **2.** *Geol.* an accumulation of loose fragments of rock, etc. Also, **débris**.

debt /dɛt/ n. **1.** that which is owed; that which one person is bound to pay to or perform for another. **2.** a liability or obligation to pay or render something. **3.** the condition of being under such an obligation. –*phr.* **4. bad debt**, a debt of which there is no prospect of payment.

debtor /ˈdɛtə/ n. someone who is in debt or under obligations to another (opposed to *creditor*).

debug /diˈbʌg/ v.t. (**-bugged**, **-bugging**) **1.** to detect and remove faults in (an electronic system). **2.** *Computers* to remove errors or incompatible logical conditions from (a program). **3.** to detect and remove electronic listening devices from (a room, etc.). –**debugger**, n.

debunk /diˈbʌŋk/ v.t. *Colloq.* to strip of false sentiment, etc.; to make fun of. –**debunker**, n. –**debunking**, n.

debut /ˈdeɪbju, -bu, dəˈbu/ n. **1.** a first public appearance on a stage, on television, etc. **2.** a formal introduction and entrance into society. **3.** the beginning of a professional career, etc. –v.i. (**debuted** /ˈdeɪbjud/, **debuting** /ˈdeɪbjuɪŋ/) **4. a.** (of an actor) to make a first appearance in a film, television show, etc. **b.** (of a television show, etc.) to be shown for the first time. **5.** to make a first appearance in some official capacity. **6.** to come into existence; begin operations.

debutant /ˈdɛbjətɒnt, -tɒnt/ n. *Sport* a young player making their first appearance at a particular level.

debutante /ˈdɛbjətɒnt/ n. **1.** a young woman making a debut, especially into society. **2.** *Sport* a young player making her first appearance at a particular level. –**debutant**, *masc. n.*

dec- → **deca-**.

deca- **1.** a word element meaning 'ten'. **2.** (in the metric system) → **deka-**. Also, **dec-**.

decade /ˈdɛkeɪd, dəˈkeɪd/ n. **1.** a period of ten years. **2.** a group, set, or series of ten. –**decadal**, adj.

decadence /ˈdɛkədəns/ n. **1.** the act or process of falling into an inferior condition or state, especially moral; decay; deterioration. **2.** luxurious self-indulgence: *the decadence of a weekend on the yacht.* –**decadent**, adj.

decaffeinated /diˈkæfəneɪtəd/ adj. having had the caffeine removed: *decaffeinated coffee.*

decagon /ˈdɛkəgɒn/ n. a polygon having ten angles and ten sides. –**decagonal** /dəˈkægənəl/, adj.

decahedron /dɛkəˈhidrən/ n. (pl. **-drons** or **-dra** /-drə/) a solid figure having ten faces. –**decahedral**, adj.

decamp /diˈkæmp/ v.i. **1.** to depart from a camp; break camp. **2.** to depart quickly, secretly, or unceremoniously. –**decampment**, n.

decant /dəˈkænt/ v.t. **1.** to pour off gently, as liquor, without disturbing the sediment. **2.** to pour from one container into another. –**decantation** /dikænˈteɪʃən/, n.

decanter /dəˈkæntə/ n. **1.** a bottle used for decanting. **2.** a vessel, usually an ornamental bottle, from which wine, water, etc., is served at table.

decapitate /dəˈkæpəteɪt, di-/ v.t. to cut off the head of; behead; kill by beheading. –**decapitation** /dəkæpəˈteɪʃən/, n. –**decapitator**, n.

decapod /ˈdɛkəpɒd/ n. **1.** any crustacean of the order Decapoda, including crabs, lobsters, crayfish, prawns, shrimps, etc., characterised by their five pairs of walking legs. **2.** any ten-armed two-gilled cephalopod, such as the cuttlefish, squid, etc. –**decapodous** /dəˈkæpədəs/, adj.

decathlon /dəˈkæθlɒn, -lən/ n. an athletic contest comprising ten different events, and won by the contestant having the highest total score. –**decathlete**, n.

decay /dəˈkeɪ/ v.i. **1.** to fall away from a state of excellence, prosperity, health, etc.; deteriorate; decline. **2.** to become decomposed; rot. –n. **3.** a gradual falling into an inferior condition; progressive decline. **4.** decomposition; rotting.

decease /dəˈsis/ n. **1.** departure from life; death. –v.i. **2.** to depart from life; die.

deceased /dəˈsist/ adj. **1.** dead. –phr. **2. the deceased**, the dead person or persons

deceit /dəˈsit/ n. **1.** the act or practice of deceiving; concealment or perversion of the truth for the purpose of misleading; fraud; cheating. **2.** an act or device intended to deceive; a trick; stratagem. **3.** deceiving quality; falseness. –**deceitful**, adj.

deceive /dəˈsiv/ verb (**-ceived, -ceiving**) –v.t. **1.** to mislead by a false appearance or statement; delude. **2.** to be unfaithful to; commit adultery against. –v.i. **3.** to practise deceit; act deceitfully. –**deceivable**, adj. –**deceivableness, deceivability** /dəsivəˈbɪləti/, n. –**deceiver**, n. –**deceivably**, adv. –**deceivingly**, adv.

decelerate /diˈsɛləreɪt/ v.i. **1.** to decrease in velocity. –v.t. **2.** to decrease the velocity of. –**deceleration** /di,sɛləˈreɪʃən/, n. –**decelerator**, n.

December /dəˈsɛmbə/ n. the twelfth month of the year, containing 31 days.

decent /ˈdisənt/ adj. **1.** fitting; appropriate. **2.** keeping to recognised standards of behaviour, good taste, modesty, etc. **3.** respectable; worthy: a decent family. **4.** fair; tolerable; passable: a decent wage. **5.** Colloq. kind; obliging: thanks, that's decent of you. –**decency**, n. –**decently**, adv. –**decentness**, n.

decentralise /diˈsɛntrəlaɪz/ v.t. **1.** to disperse (industry, population, etc.) from an area of concentration or density, especially from large cities to relatively undeveloped rural areas. **2.** to undo the centralisation of administrative powers (of an organisation, government, etc.). Also, **decentralize**. –**decentralisation** /di,sɛntrəlaɪˈzeɪʃən/, n.

deception /dəˈsɛpʃən/ n. **1.** the act of deceiving. **2.** the state of being deceived. **3.** something that deceives or is intended to deceive; an artifice; a sham; a cheat. –**deceptive**, adj.

deci- a prefix denoting 10^{-1} of a given unit, as in decigram. Symbol: d

decibel /ˈdɛsəbɛl/ n. a unit expressing difference in power, usually between electric or acoustic signals, or between some particular signal and a reference level understood; equal to one tenth of a bel. Symbol: dB

decide /dəˈsaɪd/ v.t. **1.** to determine or settle (a question, controversy, struggle, etc.) by giving victory to one side. **2.** to adjust or settle (anything in dispute or doubt). **3.** to bring (a person) to a decision. –v.i. **4.** to settle something in dispute or doubt. **5.** to pronounce a judgement; come to a conclusion. –phr. **6. decide on** (or **upon**), to come to a definite conclusion about. –**decidable**, adj.

decided /dəˈsaɪdəd/ adj. **1.** free from ambiguity; unquestionable; unmistakable. **2.** free from hesitation or wavering; resolute; determined. –**decidedly**, adv. –**decidedness**, n.

deciduous /dəˈsɪdʒuəs/ adj. **1.** shedding the leaves annually, as trees, shrubs, etc. **2.** falling off or shed at a particular season, stage of growth, etc., as leaves, horns, teeth, etc. **3.** not permanent; transitory. –**deciduously**, adv. –**deciduousness**, n.

decile /ˈdɛsaɪl/ n. Statistics one of the values of a variable which divides its distribution into ten groups having equal frequencies.

decimal /ˈdɛsəməl/ adj. **1.** relating to tenths, or to the number ten. **2.** proceeding by tens: a decimal system. –n. **3.** a decimal fraction. **4.** a decimal number. –**decimalise, decimalize**, v. –**decimally**, adv.

decimal currency n. **1.** the monetary system introduced into Australia in 1966, consisting of 100 cents to the dollar, replacing pounds, shillings and pence as the units of currency. **2.** any similar monetary system.

decimal fraction n. a fraction whose denominator is some power of ten, usually indicated by a dot (the **decimal point**) written before the numerator, as $0.4 = {}^4/_{10}; 0.126 = {}^{126}/_{1000}$.

decimal number n. Maths any finite or infinite string of digits containing a decimal point: 1.0, 5.23, 3.14159 ... are decimal numbers.

decimal place n. **1.** the position of a digit to the right of a decimal point: in 9.623, 3 is in the third decimal place. **2.** the number of digits to the right of a decimal point: 9.623 is a number in three decimal places.

decimal point n. (in the decimal system) a dot preceding the fractional part of a number.

decimate /ˈdɛsəmeɪt/ v.t. **1.** to destroy a great number or proportion of. **2.** to select by lot and kill every tenth man of. –**decimation** /dɛsəˈmeɪʃən/, n. –**decimator**, n.

decipher /dəˈsaɪfə/ v.t. **1.** to make out the meaning of. **2.** to interpret by the use of a key, as something written in cipher. –**decipherable**, adj. –**decipherer**, n. –**decipherment**, n.

decision /dəˈsɪʒən/ n. **1.** the act of deciding; determination (of a question or doubt). **2.** a judgement, as one formally pronounced by a court. **3.** a making up of one's mind. **4.** something that is decided; a resolution. **5.** the quality of being decided; firmness, as of character.

decisive /dəˈsaɪsɪv/ adj. **1.** having the power or quality of determining; putting an end to controversy: a decisive fact; a decisive battle. **2.** characterised by or displaying decision; resolute; determined. –**decisively**, adv. –**decisiveness**, n.

deck /dɛk/ n. **1.** a horizontal platform extending from side to side of a ship or part of a ship, forming a covering for the space below and itself serving as a floor. **2.** a floor, platform or tier, as in a bus or bridge. **3.** an unenclosed, elevated platform or verandah, usually of wood. **4.** the top surface of a surfboard or skateboard. **5.** the horizontal platform on or in a tape recorder, record player, or the like, above which the turntable or spools revolve, and which often incorporates some of the controls. **6.** a pack of playing cards. –v.t. **7.** Naut. to furnish with or as with a deck, as a vessel. **8.** Colloq. to knock (someone) to the ground. –phr. **9. between decks**, on a deck or decks below the main deck.

10. clear the decks, a. *Naut.* to prepare for combat, as by removing from the deck all unnecessary gear. **b.** *Colloq.* to prepare for action of any kind. **11. deck out,** to decorate or dress up. **12. hit the deck,** *Colloq.* **a.** to fall to the ground or floor. **b.** to rise from bed. **13. not playing with a full deck,** *Colloq.* insane. **14. on deck,** *Colloq.* **a.** on duty; on hand; present at the time. **b.** alive: *is he still on deck?*

deckchair /ˈdɛktʃɛə/ *n.* a portable folding chair with back and seat of canvas or similar material, often in one piece.

-decker a word element meaning 'level': *a double-decker bus.*

declaim /dəˈkleɪm/ *v.i.* **1.** to speak aloud rhetorically; make a formal speech. **2.** to speak or write for oratorical effect, without sincerity or sound argument. –*v.t.* **3.** to utter aloud in a rhetorical manner. –*phr.* **4. declaim against,** to forcefully attack in words. –**declamatory,** *adj.* –**declaimer,** *n.*

declare /dəˈklɛə/ *v.t.* (**-clared, -claring**) **1.** to make known, especially in explicit or formal terms. **2.** to state emphatically; affirm. **3.** to manifest; reveal. **4.** to make due statement of (dutiable goods, etc.). **5.** to make (a dividend) payable. –**declaration,** *n.* –**declarer,** *n.* –**declarable,** *adj.* –**declarative,** *adj.*

declension /dəˈklɛnʃən/ *n.* **1.** *Gram.* **a.** the inflection of nouns, and of words similarly inflected, for categories such as case and number. For example (Latin): *puella, puellam, puellae, puellae, etc.* **b.** a class of such words having similar sets of inflected forms, as the Latin *second declension.* **2.** an act or instance of declining. **3.** a bending, sloping, or moving downward. –**declensional,** *adj.*

decline *v.t.* /dəˈklaɪn/ **1.** to withhold consent to do, enter upon, or accept; refuse: *he declined to say more about it, he declined the offer with thanks.* **2.** to cause to slope or incline downward. **3.** *Gram.* **a.** to inflect (a noun, pronoun, or adjective). In Latin, *puella* is declined *puella, puellam, puellae, puellae, puellā* in the five cases of the singular. **b.** to recite or display all, or some subset, of the inflected forms of a noun, pronoun, or adjective in a fixed order. –*v.i.* /dəˈklaɪn/ **4.** to express courteous refusal; refuse. **5.** to bend or slant down; slope or trend downward; descend. **6.** to draw towards the close, as the day. **7.** to fail in strength, vigour, character, value, etc.; deteriorate. –*n.* /dəˈklaɪn, ˈdiklaɪn/ **8.** a downward incline or slope. **9.** a failing or gradual loss, as in strength, character, value, etc.; deterioration; diminution. **10.** progress downwards or towards a close, as of the sun or the day. **11.** the last part or phase. –*phr.* **12. in decline,** gradually losing power or effectiveness; degenerating. –**declinable,** *adj.* –**decliner,** *n.*

declivity /dəˈklɪvəti/ *n.* (*pl.* **-ties**) a downward slope, as of ground (opposed to *acclivity*).

declutter /diˈklʌtə/ *v.t.* **1.** to remove gradually accumulated but unnecessary books, clothes, appliances, decorative items, etc., from a (house, room, office, etc.). –*v.i.* **2.** to undertake the process of removing these unnecessary items.

decoction /dəˈkɒkʃən/ *n.* **1.** the act of boiling in water, in order to extract the peculiar properties or virtues. **2.** an extract obtained by decocting. **3.** water in which a substance, usually animal or vegetable, has been boiled, and which thus contains the constituents or principles of the substance soluble in boiling water.

decode /diˈkoʊd, dəˈkoʊd/ *v.t.* to translate from code into the original language or form.

décolleté /deɪˈkɒləteɪ/ *adj.* **1.** (of a garment) low-necked. **2.** wearing a low-necked garment. –**décolletage,** *n.*

decommission /dikəˈmɪʃən/ *v.t.* **1.** to remove from service, as a naval vessel, army officer, etc. **2.** to close down (a facility, as a power station, sewerage plant, etc.).

decompose /dikəmˈpoʊz/ *v.t.* **1.** to separate or resolve into constituent parts or elements; disintegrate. –*v.i.* **2.** to rot; putrefy. –**decomposition** /dikɒmpəˈzɪʃən/, *n.* –**decomposable,** *adj.* –**decomposer,** *n.*

decompress /dikəmˈprɛs/ *v.t.* **1.** to cause to undergo decompression. **2.** *Computers* to decode (data) from a compressed storage format into its original format; unzip. –*v.i.* **3.** to undergo decompression.

decompression /dikəmˈprɛʃən/ *n.* **1.** the act or process of relieving pressure. **2.** the gradual return of persons, such as divers or construction workers, to normal atmospheric pressure after working in deep water or in air under compression.

deconflict /dikənˈflɪkt/ *v.t.* *Mil.* **1.** to avoid the co-occurrence and possible conflict of (flights, convoys, etc.) **2.** to ensure the lack of such co-occurrence within (an area): *to deconflict airspace.*

decongestant /dikənˈdʒɛstənt/ *n.* a substance used to relieve congestion especially in the upper respiratory tract. –*adj.* **2.** relieving congestion.

deconstructionism /dikənˈstrʌkʃənɪzm/ *n.* a philosophical and critical theory developed in the 1960s, which denies that there is any ultimate or secure meaning in a text, and asserts that it is necessary to remove preconceptions arising from a cultural or ethnocentric point of view to arrive at possible meanings of a text. Also, **deconstructionist theory.** –**deconstructionist,** *adj.,* *n.*

deconstructionist theory *n.* → **deconstructionism.**

decontaminate /dikənˈtæməneɪt/ *v.t.* to make (any object or area) safe for unprotected personnel by absorbing, making harmless, or destroying chemicals with which they have been in contact. –**decontamination** /ˌdikəntæməˈneɪʃən/, *n.*

decor /ˈdeɪkɔ, ˈdekɔ/ *n.* **1.** decoration in general. **2.** a style of decoration.

decorate /ˈdɛkəreɪt/ *v.t.* **1.** to furnish or deck with something becoming or ornamental; embellish. **2.** to plan and execute the design, wallpaper, etc., and sometimes the furnishings of (a house, room, or the like). **3.** to confer distinction upon by a badge, a medal of honour, etc. –*v.i.* **4.** to be engaged in executing the decoration of a house, room, etc. –**decoration,** *n.* –**decorative,** *adj.* –**decorator,** *n.*

decorum /dəˈkɔrəm/ *n.* **1.** propriety of behaviour, speech, dress, etc. **2.** that which is proper or seemly; fitness; congruity; propriety. **3.** an observance or requirement of polite society. –**decorous,** *adj.*

decoy *n.* /ˈdikɔɪ/ **1.** someone who entices or allures, as into a trap, danger, etc. **2.** something used as a lure. –*v.t.* /ˈdikɔɪ, dəˈkɔɪ/ **3.** to lure by or as by a decoy. –**decoyer,** *n.*

decrease *v.i.* /dəˈkris/ **1.** to diminish gradually in extent, quantity, strength, power, etc. –*v.t.* /dəˈkris/ **2.** to make less; cause to diminish. –*n.* /ˈdikris, dəˈkris/ **3.** a process of growing less, or the resulting condition; gradual diminution. **4.** the amount by which a thing is lessened. –**decreasingly,** *adv.*

decree /dəˈkri/ *n.* **1.** an ordinance or edict promulgated by civil or other authority. **2.** *Law* a judicial decision or order. –*v.t.* (**-creed, -creeing**) **3.** to ordain or decide by decree.

decree nisi /dəkri ˈnaɪsaɪ/ *n.* *Law* See **nisi.**

decrement /ˈdɛkrəmənt/ *n.* **1.** the process or fact of decreasing; gradual diminution. **2.** the amount lost by diminution. –*v.t.* **3.** *Computers* to reduce the numerical contents of (a counter).

decrepit /dəˈkrɛpət/ *adj.* broken down or weakened by old age; feeble; infirm. –**decrepitude,** *n.* –**decrepitly,** *adv.*

decriminalise /diːˈkrɪmənəlaɪz/ v.t. to remove legal restrictions against (an activity, such as smoking marijuana), and thus eliminate the legal penalties previously associated with it. Also, **decriminalize**. –**decriminalisation**, n.

decry /dəˈkraɪ/ v.t. (-**cried, -crying**) to speak disparagingly of; censure as faulty or worthless. –**decrier**, n. –**decrial**, n.

dedicate /ˈdɛdəkeɪt/ v.t. 1. to set apart and consecrate to a deity or to a sacred purpose. 2. to give up wholly or earnestly, as to some person or end; set apart or appropriate. 3. to inscribe or address (a book, piece of music, etc.) to a patron, friend, etc., as in testimony of respect or affection. –**dedicated**, adj. –**dedication**, n. –**dedicator**, n.

deduce /dəˈdjuːs/ v.t. (-**duced, -ducing**) 1. to derive as a conclusion from something known or assumed; infer. 2. to trace the derivation of; trace the course of. –**deducible**, adj.

deduct /dəˈdʌkt/ v.t. to take away, as from a sum or amount. –**deductible, deductable**, adj.

deduction[1] /dəˈdʌkʃən/ n. 1. the act of deducting; subtraction; abatement. 2. something that is deducted.

deduction[2] /dəˈdʌkʃən/ n. 1. the process of drawing a conclusion from something known or assumed. 2. such an inference in which, granted the truth of the premises, the conclusion must be true. –**deductive**, adj.

deed /diːd/ n. 1. something that is done, performed, or accomplished; an act. 2. an exploit or achievement. 3. action or performance, often as contrasted with words. 4. Law a writing or document signed, sealed, and delivered to effect a conveyance, especially of real property. –**deedless**, adj.

deed poll n. a deed in the form of a declaration to all the world of the grantor's act and intention, as, for example, to change one's name.

deem /diːm/ v.i. to form or have an opinion; judge; think.

deep /diːp/ adj. 1. extending far downwards, inwards, or backwards. 2. having a specified dimension downwards, inwards, or backwards: a tank two metres deep. 3. situated far or a certain distance down, in, or back. 4. extending far in width; broad: a deep border. 5. outside the solar system: deep space. 6. extending or advancing far down: a deep dive. 7. coming from far down: a deep breath. 8. lying below a surface. 9. difficult to penetrate or understand; abstruse. 10. not superficial; profound. 11. grave or serious. 12. heartfelt: deep sorrow; deep hostility. 13. absorbing: deep study. 14. great in measure; intense: deep sleep. 15. (of colours) intense; dark and vivid: a deep red. 16. low in pitch, as sound. 17. having penetrating intellectual powers. 18. profoundly cunning or artful. 19. much involved: deep in debt. 20. absorbed: deep in thought. 21. Cricket relatively far from the wicket: the deep field. 22. Tennis (of a shot) landing near the baseline. –n. 23. the deep part of the sea, a river, etc. 24. any deep space or place. 25. the part of greatest intensity, as of winter. –adv. 26. to or at a considerable or specified depth. 27. far on (in time). 28. profoundly; intensely. –phr. 29. **in deep water**, Colloq. in trouble or difficulties. 30. **the deep**, Poetic the sea or ocean. –**deepen**, v. –**deeply**, adv. –**deepness**, n.

Deepavali /diːpəˈvɑːli/ n. an annual four-day Hindu festival, held between October and November, celebrated with feasting and the lighting of lamps to mark the victory of good over evil; Festival of Lights. Also, **Divali, Diwali**.

deep ecology n. a branch of ecosophy that considers humankind as an integral part of the environment, leading to a system of ethical behaviour in relation to the environment.

deep freeze n. (from trademark) a locker or compartment in a refrigerator where food can be quickly frozen and stored at a very low temperature; freezer.

deep-freeze v.t. (-**froze, -frozen, -freezing**) to store or freeze in a deep freeze.

deep vein thrombosis n. Med. a thrombosis occurring in a non-superficial vein, usually in the thigh or calf, which can dislodge from the vein wall and travel to the lungs, causing a life-threatening pulmonary embolism. Also, **deep venous thrombosis, DVT**.

deep well injection n. a method of disposing of liquid pollutants by injecting them into geological formations deep in the earth which are sealed by impermeable strata, the insertion point being plugged by concrete.

deer /dɪə/ n. 1. any animal of the family Cervidae, comprising ruminants most of which have solid deciduous horns or antlers (usually the male only), such as Cervus elaphus of Europe. 2. any of the smaller species of this family, as distinguished from the elk, etc.

deface /dəˈfeɪs/ v.t. (-**faced, -facing**) 1. to mar the face or appearance of; disfigure. 2. to blot out; obliterate; efface. –**defaceable**, adj. –**defacement**, n. –**defacer**, n.

de facto /di ˈfæktoʊ, də ˈfæktoʊ, deɪ ˈfæktoʊ/ adj. 1. in fact; in reality. 2. actually existing, whether with or without right. 3. of or relating to a situation in which two people live together in the relation of husband and wife, although not legally married: a de facto relationship. –n. Aust., NZ 4. Also, **de facto wife**. a woman who lives with a man as his wife, but is not married to him. 5. Also, **de facto husband**. a man who lives with a woman as her husband, but is not married to her.

defame /diˈfeɪm, də-/ v.t. to attack the good name or reputation of, as by uttering or publishing maliciously anything injurious; slander; libel; calumniate. –**defamation**, n. –**defamatory** /dəˈfæmətri, -ətəri/, adj. –**defamer**, n.

default /dəˈfɒlt/ n. 1. failure to act; neglect. 2. failure to pay debts. 3. Law failure to perform an act legally required, especially failure to appear in a law court when required, or failure to pay a debt. 4. failure to take part in or finish something, as a competition. 5. want; lack; absence: owing to default of water. 6. a procedure which has pre-set parameters which operate unless changed by the user. –v.i. 7. to fail in fulfilling or satisfying an engagement, claim, or obligation. 8. to fail to pay debts, or to account properly for money, etc., in one's care. 9. Law to fail to appear in court. 10. **a.** to fail to take part in or finish anything, as a match. **b.** to lose a match by default. –v.t. 11. to fail to do or pay. 12. Law to lose by failure to appear in court. 13. **a.** to fail to take part in (a game, race, etc.). **b.** to lose (a game, etc.) by default. –**defaulter**, n.

defeasance /dəˈfiːzəns/ n. Law a rendering null and void.

defeat /dəˈfiːt/ v.t. 1. to overcome in a contest, battle, etc.; vanquish; win or achieve victory over. 2. to frustrate; thwart. 3. Law to annul. –**defeater**, n.

defeatism /dəˈfiːtɪzəm/ n. the attitude, policy, or conduct of those who admit or expect defeat, usually resulting from a premature decision that further struggle or effort is futile. –**defeatist**, n., adj.

defecate /ˈdɛfəkeɪt/ v.i. 1. to void excrement. 2. to become clear of dregs, impurities, etc. –**defecation** /dɛfəˈkeɪʃən/, n. –**defecator**, n.

defect n. /ˈdifɛkt, dəˈfɛkt/ 1. a falling short; a fault or imperfection. 2. want or lack, especially of something essential to perfection or completeness; deficiency. –v.i. /dəˈfɛkt/ 3. to desert a country, cause, etc. –v.t. /dəˈfɛkt/ 4. to serve a defect notice on: my car was defected. –**defector**, n. –**defection** /dəˈfɛkʃən/, n.

defective /dəˈfɛktɪv/ adj. having a defect; faulty; imperfect. –**defectively**, adv. –**defectiveness**, n.

defect notice *n.* an official notice to a driver that his or her vehicle is defective, indicating the time by which repairs should be made.

defence /dəˈfɛns/ *n.* **1.** resistance against attack; protection. **2.** the defending of a cause or the like by speech, argument, etc. **3.** *Law* the denial or pleading of the defendant in answer to the claim or charge against him or her. **4.** /dəˈfɛns/, *Orig. US* /ˈdifɛns/ **a.** the practice or art of defending oneself or one's goal against attack, as in fencing, boxing, soccer, etc. **b.** the players in a team collectively whose primary function is to defend the goal, etc. Also, *Chiefly US*, **defense.** –**defenceless**, *adj.* –**defencelessly**, *adv.* –**defencelessness**, *n.*

defence mechanism *n.* **1.** *Physiol.* organic activity, such as the formation of an antitoxin, as a defensive measure. **2.** *Psychoanalysis* a group of unconscious processes which oppose the entrance into consciousness or the acting out of unacceptable or painful ideas and impulses.

defend /dəˈfɛnd/ *v.t.* **1.** (sometimes fol. by *from* or *against*) to ward off attack from; guard against assault or injury. **2.** to prepare (a building) against natural disaster, as a bushfire. **3.** to maintain by argument, evidence, etc.; uphold. **4.** to contest (a legal charge, claim, etc.). **5.** to act as counsel for (an accused person). –*v.i.* **6.** *Law* to enter or make a defence. –**defendable**, *adj.* –**defender**, *n.*

defendant /dəˈfɛndənt/ *n. Law* the party against whom a claim or charge is brought in a proceeding.

defensible /dəˈfɛnsəbəl/ *adj.* **1.** capable of being defended against assault or injury. **2.** capable of being defended in argument; justifiable. –**defensibility** /dəfɛnsəˈbɪləti/, **defensibleness**, *n.* –**defensibly**, *adv.*

defensive /dəˈfɛnsɪv/ *adj.* **1.** serving to defend; protective: *defensive armour.* **2.** made or carried on for the purpose of resisting attack. **3.** of or relating to defence: *a defensive attitude.* –*n.* **4.** defensive position or attitude. –*phr.* **5. on the defensive**, in a defensive position or attitude, especially when it is not called for. –**defensively**, *adv.* –**defensiveness**, *n.*

defer¹ /dəˈfɜ/ *verb* (**-ferred**, **-ferring**) –*v.t.* **1.** to put off (action, etc.) to a future time. –*v.i.* **2.** to put off action; delay. –**deferment**, **deferral**, *n.* –**deferrer**, *n.*

defer² /dəˈfɜ/ *v.i.* (sometimes fol. by *to*) to yield in judgement or opinion.

deference /ˈdɛfərəns/ *n.* **1.** submission or yielding to the judgement, opinion, will, etc., of another. **2.** respectful or courteous regard: *in deference to his wishes.* –**deferential** /dɛfəˈrɛnʃəl/, *adj.*

defiance /dəˈfaɪəns/ *n.* **1.** a daring or bold resistance to authority or to any opposing force. **2.** open disregard: *in defiance of criticism.* **3.** a challenge to meet in combat or contest. –**defiant**, *adj.*

deficient /dəˈfɪʃənt/ *adj.* **1.** lacking some element or characteristic; defective. **2.** insufficient; inadequate. –**deficiency**, *n.* –**deficiently**, *adv.*

deficit /ˈdɛfəsət/ *n.* the amount by which a sum of money falls short of the required amount.

defile¹ /dəˈfaɪl/ *v.t.* **1.** to make foul, dirty, or unclean; pollute; taint. **2.** to violate the chastity of. –**defilement**, *n.* –**defiler**, *n.*

defile² /dəˈfaɪl, ˈdifaɪl/ *n.* **1.** any narrow passage, especially between mountains. –*v.i.* **2.** to march in a line, or by files; file off.

define /dəˈfaɪn/ *v.t.* **1.** to state or set forth the meaning of (a word, phrase, etc.). **2.** to explain the nature or essential qualities of; describe. **3.** to determine or fix the boundaries or extent of. **4.** to make clear the outline or form of. **5.** to fix or lay down definitely; specify distinctly. –**definability** /dəfaɪnəˈbɪləti/, *n.* –**definable**, *adj.* –**definably**, *adv.* –**definer**, *n.* –**definition**, *n.*

definite /ˈdɛfənət/ *adj.* **1.** clearly defined or determined; not vague or general; fixed; precise; exact. **2.** having fixed limits; bounded with precision. **3.** defining; limiting. **4.** certain; sure: *he was quite definite about his intentions.* –**definitely**, *adv.* –**definiteness**, *n.*

definitive /dəˈfɪnətɪv/ *adj.* **1.** having the function of deciding or settling; determining; conclusive; final. **2.** serving to fix or specify definitely. **3.** having its fixed and final form. –*n.* **4.** a defining or limiting word, such as an article, a demonstrative, or the like. –**definitively**, *adv.* –**definitiveness**, *n.*

deflate /dəˈfleɪt/ *v.t.* **1.** to release the air or gas from (something inflated, as a tyre). **2.** to reduce (currency, prices, etc.) from an inflated condition. **3.** to reduce in esteem, especially self-esteem (a person or a person's ego).

deflation /dəˈfleɪʃən/ *n.* **1.** the act of deflating. **2.** an abnormal decline in the level of commodity prices, especially one not accompanied by an equal reduction in the costs of production. –**deflationary**, *adj.*

deflect /dəˈflɛkt/ *v.i.* **1.** to bend or turn aside; swerve. –*v.t.* **2.** to cause to turn from a true course or right line. –**deflection**, **deflexion**, *n.* –**deflector**, *n.*

defoliant /dəˈfoʊliənt/ *n.* a chemical preparation used to cause defoliation.

defoliate /dəˈfoʊlieɪt/ *v.t.* **1.** to strip or deprive (a tree, etc.) of leaves. –*v.i.* **2.** to lose leaves. –**defoliation** /dəfoʊliˈeɪʃən/, *n.*

deforestation /diˌfɒrəstˈeɪʃən/ *n.* the permanent removal of forests or trees from a large area, usually for commercial purposes.

deform /dəˈfɔm/ *v.t.* **1.** to mar the natural form or shape of; put out of shape; disfigure. **2.** to make ugly, ungraceful, or displeasing; mar the beauty of; spoil. –**deformation** /difɔˈmeɪʃən/, *n.* –**deformer**, *n.*

deformity /dəˈfɔməti/ *n.* (*pl.* **-ties**) **1.** the quality or state of being deformed, disfigured, or misshapen. **2.** an abnormally formed part of the body, etc.

defrag *Computers Colloq.* –*v.t.* /diˈfræg/ **1.** → **defragment**. –*n.* /ˈdifræg/ **2.** the process of defragmenting a disk.

defragment /difrægˈmɛnt/ *v.t. Computers* to reorganise the data stored on (a disk) so that whole files are stored in the same place, in order to eliminate fragmentation (def. 3). Also, *Colloq.*, **defrag.** –**defragmentation**, *n.*

defraud /dəˈfrɔd/ *v.t.* to deprive of a right or property by fraud; cheat. –**defrauder**, *n.*

defray /dəˈfreɪ/ *v.t.* to bear or pay (the costs, expenses, etc.). –**defrayable**, *adj.* –**defrayer**, *n.*

defriend /diˈfrɛnd/ *v.t.* → **unfriend**. –**defriended**, *adj.* –**defriending**, *n.*

defrost /diˈfrɒst, dəˈ/ *v.t.* **1.** to remove the frost or ice from. **2.** to cause (food, etc.) to thaw, as by removing from a freezer. –**defroster**, *n.*

deft /dɛft/ *adj.* dexterous; nimble; skilful; clever. –**deftly**, *adv.* –**deftness**, *n.*

defunct /dəˈfʌŋkt/ *adj.* **1.** deceased; dead; extinct. **2.** no longer operative; not in use. **3.** no longer existing: *a defunct company.* –**defunctness**, *n.*

defund /diˈfʌnd/ *v.t. Politics* to stop the flow of government funds to (an organisation, enterprise, program, etc.).

defuse /diˈfjuz/ *v.t.* **1.** to remove the fuse from (a bomb). **2.** to calm (a situation or action).

defy /dəˈfaɪ/ *v.t.* (**-fied**, **-fying**) **1.** to challenge the power of; resist boldly or openly. **2.** to challenge (someone) to do something deemed impossible.

degenerate *v.i.* /dəˈdʒɛnəreɪt/ **1.** to decline in physical, mental, or moral qualities; deteriorate. **2.** *Biol.* to revert to a less highly organised or simpler type. –*adj.* /dəˈdʒɛnərət/ **3.** having declined in physical or moral qualities; deteriorated; degraded: *a degenerate king.* –*n.*

/dəˈdʒɛnərət/ **4.** someone who has retrogressed from a normal type or standard, as in morals or character. —**degenerately**, *adv.* —**degenerateness**, *n.* —**degeneration**, *n.* —**degenerative**, *adj.*

degrade /dəˈgreɪd/ *v.t.* **1.** to reduce from a higher to a lower rank, degree, etc.; deprive of office, rank, degree, or title as a punishment. **2.** to lower in character or quality; debase; deprave. **3.** to lower in dignity or estimation; bring into contempt. **4.** to reduce in strength, intensity, etc. —**degrading**, *adj.* —**degradable**, *adj.* —**degradation** /dɛɡrəˈdeɪʃən/, *n.*

degree /dəˈgri/ *n.* **1.** a step or stage in an ascending or descending scale, or in a course or process. **2.** *Genetics, Law, etc.* a certain distance or remove in the line of descent or consanguinity. **3.** a stage in a scale of rank or dignity; relative rank, station, etc.: *a man of high degree.* **4.** a stage in a scale of intensity or amount: *to the last degree.* **5.** the angle between two radii of a circle which cut off on the circumference an arc equal to $\frac{1}{360}$ of that circumference (often indicated by the sign °, as 45°); $17.453\,293 \times 10^{-3}$ radians. **6.** a unit in the measurement of temperature. **7. a.** *Geog.* the unit of measurement of latitude or longitude, usually employed to indicate position on the earth's surface, the position of a line or point being fixed by its angular distance measured in degrees from the equator or a given meridian. **b.** *Astron.* the position of a line or point in the celestial sphere fixed by its angular distance measured from the equator (equinoctial) or a given meridian. **8.** a qualification conferred by a university for successful work, as judged by examination, or as an honorary recognition of achievement. **9.** *Gram.* one of the three parallel formations (positive, comparative, and superlative) of adjectives and adverbs, showing differences in quality, quantity, or intensity in the attribute referred to, as English *low, lower, lowest.* **10.** *Music* **a.** the interval from one note to another on a stave. **b.** one of the eight progressive intervals from the tonic in an octave. **11.** *US* a classification of certain crimes according to their seriousness: *first degree murder.* —*phr.* **12. by degrees**, gradually. **13. to a degree**, to an undefined but not great extent.

degustation /deɪɡʊsˈteɪʃən/ *n.* **1.** a sampling of a variety of different wines. **2.** a sampling of a variety of different food dishes, as in a restaurant, etc.

dehiring /diˈhaɪərɪŋ/ *n.* dismissal from employment for reasons relating to corporate rationalisations, mergers, liquidations, etc., rather than to the performance of the individual concerned.

dehumanise /diˈhjumənaɪz/ *v.t.* to deprive of human character. Also, **dehumanize**. —**dehumanisation**, *n.*

dehydrate /ˈdihaɪdreɪt/ *v.t.* **1.** to deprive of water. **2.** to free (vegetables, etc.) of moisture, for preservation. —*v.i.* **3.** to lose water or moisture. —**dehydration** /dihaɪˈdreɪʃən/, *n.*

deify /ˈdiəfaɪ, ˈdeɪə-/ *v.t.* (**-fied, -fying**) **1.** to make a god of; exalt to the rank of a deity. **2.** to adore or regard as a deity: *to deify prudence.* —**deification** /ˌdiɪfəˈkeɪʃən, ˌdeɪɪ-/, *n.* —**deifier**, *n.*

deign /deɪn/ *v.i.* to think fit or in accordance with one's dignity; condescend.

deism /ˈdiɪzəm, ˈdeɪ-/ *n.* **1.** belief in the existence of a god on the evidence of reason and nature only, with rejection of supernatural revelation (distinguished from *theism*). **2.** belief in a god who created the world but has since remained indifferent to his creation (distinguished from *atheism, pantheism,* and *theism*). —**deist**, *n.*

deity /ˈdeɪəti, ˈdi-/ *n.* (*pl.* **-ties**) **1.** a god or goddess. **2.** divine character or nature. **3.** the estate or rank of a god. **4.** the character or nature of the Supreme Being.

deja vu /deɪʒa ˈvu/ *n.* the sense or illusion of having previously experienced something actually being encountered for the first time. Also, **déjà vu**.

dejected /dəˈdʒɛktəd/ *adj.* depressed in spirits; disheartened; low-spirited. —**dejectedly**, *adv.* —**dejection, dejectedness**, *n.*

deka- (in the metric system) a prefix denoting 10 times a given unit, as in *dekametre. Symbol:* da Also, **deca-**; (*before vowels*), **dec-, dek-**.

dekko /ˈdɛkoʊ/ *n.* (*pl.* **-kos**) *Colloq.* look or view. Also, **dek**.

delay /dəˈleɪ, di-/ *v.t.* **1.** to put off to a later period; defer; postpone. **2.** to impede the progress of; retard; hinder. —*v.i.* **3.** to put off action; linger; loiter: *don't delay!* —*n.* **4.** the act of delaying; procrastination; loitering. **5.** an instance of being delayed. —**delayer**, *n.*

delectable /dəˈlɛktəbəl/ *adj.* delightful; highly pleasing; enjoyable. —**delectableness, delectability** /dəlɛktəˈbɪləti/, *n.* —**delectably**, *adv.*

delectation /ˌdilɛkˈteɪʃən/ *n.* → **delight**.

delegate *n.* /ˈdɛləgət, -geɪt/ **1.** someone delegated to act for or represent another or others; a deputy; a representative, as at a conference, or the like. —*v.t.* /ˈdɛləgeɪt/ **2.** to send or appoint (a person) as deputy or representative. **3.** to commit (powers, functions, etc.) to another as agent or deputy.

delegation /dɛləˈgeɪʃən/ *n.* **1.** the act of delegating. **2.** the fact of being delegated. **3.** a group of persons officially elected or appointed to represent another, or others: *the delegation from Townsville voted with the opposition.*

delete /dəˈlit/ *v.t.* to strike out or take out (anything written or printed); cancel; erase; expunge. —**deletion**, *n.*

deleterious /dɛləˈtɪəriəs/ *adj.* **1.** injurious to health. **2.** hurtful; harmful; injurious. —**deleteriously**, *adv.* —**deleteriousness**, *n.*

deli /ˈdɛli/ *n. Colloq.* **1.** a delicatessen. **2.** *Chiefly WA and SA* → **corner store**.

deliberate *adj.* /dəˈlɪbərət/ **1.** carefully considered; purposeful; intentional. —*v.t.* /dəˈlɪbəreɪt/ **2.** to consider carefully: *to deliberate a question.* —*v.i.* /dəˈlɪbəreɪt/ **3.** to think carefully; reflect. **4.** to meet for formal discussion. —**deliberately**, *adv.* —**deliberateness**, *n.* —**deliberation**, *n.* —**deliberator**, *n.*

deliberative /dəˈlɪbərətɪv, -lɪbrə-/ *adj.* **1.** having the function of deliberating, as a legislative assembly. **2.** of or relating to policy; dealing with the wisdom and expediency of a proposal: *a deliberative speech.* —**deliberatively**, *adv.* —**deliberativeness**, *n.*

delicacy /ˈdɛləkəsi/ *n.* (*pl.* **-cies**) **1.** fineness of texture, quality, etc.; softness: *the delicacy of lace.* **2.** fineness of perception or feeling; sensitiveness. **3.** the quality of requiring or involving great care or tact: *negotiations of great delicacy.* **4.** nicety of action or operation; minute accuracy: *a surgeon's delicacy of touch.*

delicate /ˈdɛləkət/ *adj.* **1.** finely-made: *delicate lace.* **2.** soft or faint, as colour: *a delicate shade of pink.* **3.** so fine or slight that it can hardly be seen; subtle: *a delicate distinction.* **4.** easily damaged; fragile. **5.** needing great care, caution, or tact: *a delicate situation.* **6.** sensitive; fine: *a delicate instrument.* **7.** very sensitive in perception or feeling; fastidious. —**delicately**, *adv.* —**delicateness**, *n.*

delicatessen /dɛləkəˈtɛsən/ *n.* a shop selling cooked or prepared goods ready for serving, usually having a noticeable proportion of specialist items.

delicious /dəˈlɪʃəs/ *adj.* **1.** highly pleasing to the senses, especially to taste or smell. **2.** pleasing in the highest degree; delightful. —*n.* **3.** (*upper case*) any of certain varieties of eating apple. See **Red Delicious, Golden Delicious**. —**deliciously**, *adv.* —**deliciousness**, *n.*

delight /dəˈlaɪt/ *n.* **1.** a high degree of pleasure or enjoyment; joy; rapture. **2.** something that gives great pleasure. –**delighted**, *adj.* –**delighter**, *n.*

delightful /dəˈlaɪtfəl/ *adj.* affording delight; highly pleasing. –**delightfully**, *adv.* –**delightfulness**, *n.*

delimit /diˈlɪmət/ *v.t.* to fix or mark the limits of; demarcate. –**delimiter**, *n.* –**delimitation** /diˌlɪməˈteɪʃən/, *n.* –**delimitative** /diˌlɪməˈteɪtɪv/, *adj.*

delineate /dəˈlɪnieɪt/ *v.t.* **1.** to trace the outline of; sketch or trace in outline; represent pictorially. **2.** to portray in words; describe.

delinquent /dəˈlɪŋkwənt/ *adj.* **1.** failing in or neglectful of a duty or obligation; guilty of a misdeed or offence. **2.** of or relating to delinquents: *delinquent taxes.* –*n.* **3.** someone who is delinquent in fulfilling an obligation, especially by committing an offence against the law: *juvenile delinquent.* –**delinquency**, *n.* –**delinquently**, *adv.*

delirious /dəˈlɪəriəs/ *adj.* **1.** affected with delirium. **2.** characteristic of delirium. **3.** wild with excitement, enthusiasm, etc. –**deliriously**, *adv.* –**deliriousness**, *n.*

delirium /dəˈlɪəriəm/ *n.* (*pl.* -**riums** *or* -**ria** /-riə/) **1.** *Pathol.* a more or less temporary disorder of the mental faculties, as in fevers, disturbances of consciousness, or intoxication, characterised by restlessness, excitement, delusions, hallucinations, etc. **2.** a state of violent excitement or emotion.

delirium tremens /dəˌlɪəriəm ˈtrɛmənz/ *n. Pathol.* a violent restlessness due to excessive indulgence in alcohol, characterised by trembling, terrifying visual hallucinations, etc.

deliver /dəˈlɪvə/ *v.t.* **1.** to give up or surrender; give into another's possession or keeping. **2.** to carry and pass over (letters, goods, etc.) to the intended recipient or recipients. **3.** to direct; cast; cause to move in a certain direction: *the bowler delivers the ball to the batsman.* **4.** to strike: *to deliver a blow.* **5.** to give forth or produce: *our mines are still delivering millions of tonnes of coal each year.* **6.** to give forth in words; utter or pronounce: *to deliver a verdict.* **7.** to bring forth (young); give birth to. **8.** to assist (a female) in giving birth. **9.** to assist at the birth of. **10.** to set free; liberate. **11.** to release or save: *deliver us from evil.* –*v.i.* **12.** to make a delivery or deliveries. **13.** to give birth. **14.** to provide a delivery service. **15.** to perform a task competently and professionally; come up to expectations: *he seems to have the qualifications, but can he deliver?* –*phr.* **16. deliver the goods**, *Colloq.* to bring good results; provide a good outcome. –**deliverable**, *adj.* –**deliverance**, *n.* –**deliverer**, *n.*

delivery /dəˈlɪvəri/ *n.* (*pl.* -**ries**) **1.** the delivering of letters, goods, etc. **2.** a giving up or handing over; surrender. **3.** a manner of speaking: *he has a clear delivery.* **4.** an act or manner of delivering, as of a ball by the bowler in cricket. **5.** the act of being set free. **6.** the act of giving birth to a child; parturition. **7.** something delivered. –*adj.* **8.** of or relating to someone or something that makes deliveries: *delivery truck.*

dell /dɛl/ *n. Poetic* a small valley; a vale, especially a wooded one.

delta /ˈdɛltə/ *n.* **1.** the fourth letter (Δ, δ, = English *D*, *d*) of the Greek alphabet. **2.** anything triangular, like the Greek capital Δ. **3.** a nearly flat plain of alluvial deposit between diverging branches of the mouth of a river, often, though not necessarily, triangular, the Nile delta being the archetypal shape. **4.** the branching and sometimes maze-like network of waterways cutting through such a plain: *to sail across the delta.* –**deltaic** /dɛlˈteɪk/, *adj.*

delude /dəˈlud, -ˈljud/ *v.t.* to mislead the mind or judgement of; deceive. –**deluder**, *n.*

deluge /ˈdɛljudʒ/ *n.* **1.** a great overflowing of water; inundation; flood; downpour. **2.** anything that overwhelms like a flood. –*v.t.* (-**uged**, -**uging**) **3.** to flood; inundate.

delusion /dəˈluʒən, -ˈljuʒən/ *n.* **1.** the act of deluding. **2.** the fact of being deluded. **3.** a false belief or opinion. **4.** *Psychiatry* a false belief which cannot be modified by reasoning or by demonstration of facts. Compare **illusion** (def. 4), **hallucination**. –**delusional**, *adj.*

deluxe /dəˈlʌks/ *adj.* of special elegance, sumptuousness, or fineness. Also, **de luxe**.

delve /dɛlv/ *v.i.* **1.** to carry on intensive or thorough research for information, etc. **2.** to dip; slope suddenly.

demagogue /ˈdɛməgɒg/ *n.* **1.** a leader who uses the passions or prejudices of the populace for his or her own interests; an unprincipled popular orator or agitator. **2.** (historically) a leader of the people. Also, *Chiefly US*, **demagog**.

demand /dəˈmænd, -ˈmand/ *v.t.* **1.** to ask for with authority; claim as a right: *to demand something of a person*; *to demand something from a person.* **2.** to ask for peremptorily or urgently. **3.** to call for or require as just, proper, or necessary: *a task which demands patience.* –*v.i.* **4.** to make a demand; inquire or ask. –*n.* **5.** the act of demanding. **6.** that which is demanded. **7.** an urgent or pressing requirement: *demands upon one's time.* **8.** the state of being in request for purchase or use: *an article in great demand.* **9.** *Econ.* **a.** the desire to purchase and possess, coupled with the power of purchasing. **b.** the quantity of any goods which buyers will take at a particular price. See **supply**[1] (def. 10). –*phr.* **10. on demand**, **a.** subject to payment upon presentation and demand. **b.** as required. –**demandable**, *adj.* –**demander**, *n.*

demand-pull inflation *n. Econ.* See **inflation** (def. 2b). Compare **cost-push inflation**.

demarcation /dimaˈkeɪʃən/ *n.* **1.** the marking off of the boundaries of something. **2.** a division between things, especially the division between types of work carried out by members of different trade unions. Also, **demarkation**. –**demarcate**, *v.*

demean[1] /dəˈmin/ *v.t.* to lower in dignity or standing; debase.

demean[2] /dəˈmin/ *v.t.* to conduct or behave (oneself) in a specified manner.

demeanour /dəˈminə/ *n.* conduct; behaviour; bearing. Also, **demeanor**.

demented /dəˈmɛntəd/ *adj.* out of one's mind; crazed; insane; affected with dementia. –**dementedly**, *adv.* –**dementedness**, *n.*

dementia /dəˈmɛnʃə, -ʃiə/ *n.* a state of mental disorder characterised by impairment or loss of the mental powers; commonly an end result of several mental or other diseases.

demerit /diˈmɛrət/ *n.* **1.** censurable or punishable quality; fault. **2.** a mark against a person for misconduct or deficiency.

demesne /dəˈmeɪn/ *n.* **1.** possession (of land) as one's own. **2.** an estate possessed, or in the actual possession or use of the owner. **3.** a district; region.

demi- a prefix meaning: **1.** half, as in *demilune.* **2.** inferior, as in *demigod.*

demilitarise /diˈmɪlətəraɪz/ *v.t.* **1.** to deprive of military character; free from militarism. **2.** to place under civil instead of military control. **3.** to prevent by treaty or force (an independent state) from arming itself, or maintaining its arms. Also, **demilitarize**. –**demilitarisation** /diˌmɪlətəraɪˈzeɪʃən/, *n.*

demise /dəˈmaɪz/ *n.* **1.** death or decease. –*v.t.* **2.** *Law* to transfer (an estate, etc.) for a limited time; lease. **3.** *Govt* to transfer (sovereignty), as by the death or abdication of the sovereign. –**demisable**, *adj.*

demister /diˈmɪstə/ n. a device for directing air, usually heated, onto the windscreen or other windows of a vehicle to clear them of mist or frost.

demo /ˈdɛmoʊ/ Colloq. –n. **1.** a demonstration. **2.** a demonstration tape, CD or record produced by a performer or band, as an example of their work. **3.** one of a line of products used to demonstrate the qualities of the line. –adj. **4.** produced or used for the purpose of demonstration: a demo tape; a demo model. –v.t. **5.** to demonstrate (a car, etc.).

demo- a word element meaning 'people', 'population', 'common people'.

demobilise /diˈmoʊbəlaɪz/ v.t. **1.** to disband (an army, etc.). –v.i. **2.** (of an army or its members) to disband. Also, **demobilize**. –**demobilisation** /diˌmoʊbəlaɪˈzeɪʃən/, n.

democracy /dəˈmɒkrəsi/ n. (pl. **-cies**) **1.** government by the people, or by their elected representatives. **2.** a state having such a government. **3.** the principle that all people should have equal political rights. –**democratic**, adj.

democrat /ˈdɛməkræt/ n. **1.** an advocate of democracy. **2.** someone who maintains the political or social equality of all people.

demography /dəˈmɒɡrəfi/ n. **1.** the science of vital and social statistics, as of the births, deaths, diseases, marriages, etc., of populations. **2.** the range of different groups existing in a particular populace, as distinguished by factors such as age, ethnicity, social background, etc.: the demography of the outer suburbs. –**demographer**, **demographist**, n. –**demographic** /dɛməˈɡræfɪk/, adj.

demolish /dəˈmɒlɪʃ/ v.t. **1.** to throw or pull down (a building, etc.); reduce to ruins. **2.** to put an end to; destroy; ruin utterly. –**demolisher**, n. –**demolishment**, **demolition** /dɛməˈlɪʃən/, n.

demon /ˈdimən/ n. **1.** an evil spirit; a devil. **2.** an evil passion. **3.** a person of great energy, enthusiasm for a cause, etc. –**demonic** /dəˈmɒnɪk/, **demoniac** /dəˈmoʊniæk/, adj.

demonstrable /dəˈmɒnstrəbəl, ˈdɛmən-/ adj. capable of being demonstrated. –**demonstrability** /dɒmənstrəˈbɪləti/, **demonstrableness**, n. –**demonstrably**, adv.

demonstrate /ˈdɛmənstreɪt/ v.t. **1.** to make evident by arguments or reasoning; prove. **2.** to describe and explain with the help of specimens or by experiment. **3.** to manifest or exhibit. –v.i. **4.** to make, give, or take part in, a demonstration.

demonstration /dɛmənˈstreɪʃən/ n. **1.** the act of demonstrating. **2.** a proof, description or explanation. **3.** the act of showing and explaining a product, in order to advertise it. **4.** a public show of opinion, as a march or mass meeting. –**demonstrational**, adj. –**demonstrationist**, n.

demonstrative /dəˈmɒnstrətɪv/ adj. **1.** characterised by or given to open exhibition or expression of the feelings, etc. **2.** serving to demonstrate; explanatory or illustrative. **3.** serving to prove the truth of anything; indubitably conclusive. **4.** Gram. indicating or specifying the thing referred to. –n. **5.** Gram. a demonstrative word, as this or there. –**demonstratively**, adv. –**demonstrativeness**, n.

demonstrator /ˈdɛmənstreɪtə/ n. **1.** someone who takes part in a public demonstration. **2.** someone who explains or teaches by practical demonstrations. **3.** someone who shows the use and application of a product, etc., to prospective customers. **4.** a new car which has been used only for demonstration.

demoralise /diˈmɒrəlaɪz/ v.t. **1.** to corrupt or undermine the morals of. **2.** to deprive (a person, a body of soldiers, etc.) of spirit, courage, discipline, etc. **3.** to reduce to a state of weakness or disorder. Also,

demoralize. –**demoralisation** /diˌmɒrəlaɪˈzeɪʃən/, n. –**demoraliser**, n.

demote /dəˈmoʊt, di-/ v.t. to reduce to a lower grade or class (opposed to promote). –**demotion**, n.

demotic /dəˈmɒtɪk/ adj. **1.** of or relating to the common people; popular. **2.** of or relating to the ancient Egyptian handwriting of ordinary life, a simplified form of the hieratic characters. **3.** of or relating to the Modern Greek vernacular.

demountable /dəˈmaʊntəbəl/ adj. **1.** able to be dismantled. –n. **2.** a building which can be dismantled and removed from one site and reassembled at another.

demur /dəˈmɜ/ v.i. (**-murred**, **-murring**) **1.** to make objection; take exception; object. **2.** Law to interpose a demurrer. –n. **3.** an objection raised. –**demurral**, n.

demure /dəˈmjʊə, -ˈmjʊə/ adj. **1.** affectedly or unnaturally modest, decorous, or prim. **2.** sober; serious; sedate; decorous. –**demurely**, adv. –**demureness**, n.

demurrage /dəˈmʌrɪdʒ/ n. Commerce the detention of a vessel, as in loading or unloading, beyond the time agreed upon.

demutualise /diˈmjutʃuəlaɪz/ v.i. (of an organisation) to cease to be a mutual society owned by its members and become a public company owned by its shareholders. Also, **demutualize**. –**demutualisation**, n.

den /dɛn/ n. **1.** a secluded place, such as a cave, serving as the habitation of a wild beast. **2.** a cave as a place of shelter, concealment, etc. **3.** a squalid or vile abode or place: dens of misery. **4.** a place devoted to an illicit activity: a gambling den. **5.** a cosy or secluded room for personal use.

denature /diˈneɪtʃə/ v.t. **1.** to deprive (something) of its peculiar nature. **2.** to render (alcohol, etc.) unfit for drinking or eating by adding a poisonous substance without altering the usefulness for other purposes. **3.** Biochem. to treat (a protein, etc.) by chemical or physical means, such as adding acid or heating, so as to cause loss of solubility, biological activity, etc. –**denaturant**, n. –**denaturation** /dineɪtʃəˈreɪʃən/, n.

dendro- a word element meaning 'tree', as in dendrology.

dendrobium /dɛnˈdroʊbiəm/ n. any species of the very large orchid genus Dendrobium, widely distributed in Asia and Australia, such as D. bigibbum, Cooktown orchid, and D. speciosum, rock lily.

dendroclimatology /ˌdɛndroʊklaɪməˈtɒlədʒi/ n. the science of determining climates in previous periods of history by examining tree rings as indicators of good or bad conditions.

dendrology /dɛnˈdrɒlədʒi/ n. the part of botany that deals with trees and shrubs. –**dendrological** /dɛndrəˈlɒdʒɪkəl/, **dendrologous** /dɛnˈdrɒləgəs/, adj. –**dendrologist** /dɛnˈdrɒlədʒəst/, n.

-dendron a word element meaning 'tree', as in rhododendron.

denial /dəˈnaɪəl/ n. **1.** an act of denying. –phr. **2. in denial**, closing one's mind to an unpleasant fact or experience. –**denier**, n.

denigrate /ˈdɛnəgreɪt/ v.t. **1.** to sully; defame. **2.** to blacken. –**denigration** /dɛnəˈgreɪʃən/, n. –**denigrator**, n.

denim /ˈdɛnəm/ n. **1.** a heavy twilled cotton material for overalls, trousers, etc. **2.** a similar fabric of a finer quality used to cover cushions, etc. **3.** (pl.) Colloq. denim trousers or overalls.

denizen /ˈdɛnəzən/ n. **1.** an inhabitant; resident. **2.** an alien admitted to residence and to certain rights of citizenship in a country. **3.** anything adapted to a new place, condition, etc., such as a naturalised foreign word, or an animal or plant not indigenous to a place but successfully naturalised.

denomination /dənɒməˈneɪʃən/ n. **1.** a name or designation, especially one for a class of things. **2.** a class or kind of persons or things distinguished by a specific name. **3.** a religious group, especially an established church. **4.** the act of denominating. **5.** one of the grades or degrees in a series of designations of quantity, value, measure, weight, etc.: *money of small denominations.* –**denominational**, *adj.*

denominator /dəˈnɒməneɪtə/ *n. Maths* the term of a fraction (usually under the line) which shows the number of equal parts into which the unit is divided. Compare **numerator**.

denotation /dinouˈteɪʃən/ *n.* **1.** the meaning of a term when it identifies something by naming it (distinguished from *connotation*). **2.** the act or fact of denoting; indication. **3.** something that denotes; a mark; symbol. –**denotative**, *adj.*

denote /dəˈnout/ *v.t.* **1.** to be a mark or sign of; indicate: *a quick pulse often denotes fever.* **2.** to be a name or designation for. **3.** to represent by a symbol; stand as a symbol for. –**denotable**, *adj.*

denouement /deɪˈnumɒ̃, dəˈnumɒ̃/ *n.* **1.** the final disentangling of the intricacies of a plot, as of a drama or novel. **2.** outcome; solution.

denounce /dəˈnaʊns/ *v.t.* (**denounced, denouncing**) **1.** to condemn openly; assail with censure. **2.** to make formal accusation against; inform against. –**denouncement**, *n.* –**denouncer**, *n.*

dense /dɛns/ *adj.* **1.** having the component parts closely compacted together; compact: *a dense forest, dense population.* **2.** thickheaded; obtuse; stupid. **3.** intense: *dense ignorance.* **4.** *Photography* (of a developed negative) relatively opaque; transmitting little light. –**densely**, *adv.* –**denseness**, *n.*

density /ˈdɛnsəti/ *n.* (*pl.* **-ties**) **1.** the state or quality of being dense; compactness; closely set or crowded condition. **2.** stupidity. **3.** *Physics* the mass per unit of volume. **4.** *Photography* the opacity of any medium, especially of a photographic plate or negative.

dent /dɛnt/ *n.* **1.** a hollow or depression in a surface, as from a blow; ding. –*v.t.* **2.** to make a dent in or on; indent.

dental /ˈdɛntl/ *adj.* **1.** of or relating to the teeth. **2.** of or relating to dentistry.

dental floss *n.* soft, waxed thread used for cleaning between the teeth. Also, **floss**.

denti- a word element meaning 'tooth', as in *dentiform*. Also, (*before vowels*), **dent-**.

dentist /ˈdɛntəst/ *n.* someone whose profession is dentistry.

dentistry /ˈdɛntəstri/ *n.* the science or art dealing with the prevention and treatment of oral disease, including such operations as the filling and crowning of teeth, the construction of dentures, etc.

dentition /dɛnˈtɪʃən/ *n.* **1.** the growing of teeth; teething. **2.** the kind, number, and arrangement of the teeth of an animal, including humans.

denture /ˈdɛntʃə/ *n.* an artificial restoration of teeth.

denude /dəˈnjud/ *v.t.* to make naked or bare; strip.

denunciation /dənʌnsiˈeɪʃən/ *n.* **1.** a denouncing as evil; open and vehement condemnation. **2.** notice of the termination of an international agreement or part thereof. **3.** announcement of impending evil; threat; warning.

deny /dəˈnaɪ/ *v.t.* (**-nied, -nying**) **1.** to assert the negative of; declare not to be true **2.** to refuse to believe (a doctrine, etc.); reject as false or erroneous. **3.** to refuse to grant (a claim, request, etc.) **4.** to refuse to recognise or acknowledge; disown; disavow; repudiate. –*phr.* **5. deny oneself**, to exercise self-denial. –**deniable**, *adj.*

deodorant /diˈoudərənt/ *n.* **1.** an agent for destroying odours. **2.** a substance, often combined with an antiperspirant, for inhibiting or masking perspiration or

other bodily odours. –*adj.* **3.** capable of destroying odours.

deodorise /diˈoudəraɪz/ *v.t.* to deprive of odour, especially of the fetid smell arising from impurities. Also, **deodorize**. –**deodorisation** /diˌoudəraɪˈzeɪʃən/, *n.* –**deodoriser**, *n.*

deoxyribonucleic acid /diˌɒksiˌraɪbounjuˌkliɪk ˈæsəd, diˌɒksiˌraɪbounjuˌklɛɪk ˈæsəd/ *n.* → **DNA**.

depart /dəˈpat/ *v.i.* **1.** to go away, as from a place; take one's leave. **2.** to pass away, as from life or existence. –*phr.* **3. depart from**, to turn aside or away from; diverge from; deviate from. –**departure**, *n.*

department /dəˈpatmənt/ *n.* **1.** a division or separate part of a complex whole or organised system, especially in government or business. **2.** a section of a school, college, or university dealing with a particular field of knowledge: *department of English.* **3.** a section of a retail store selling a particular kind of goods. **4.** an aspect of a person: *a bit light on in the brains department.* –**departmental** /ˌdipatˈmɛntl/, *adj.* –**departmentally** /ˌdipatˈmɛntli/, *adv.*

department store *n.* a large retail shop selling a variety of goods in different departments.

depend /dəˈpɛnd/ *v.i.* **1.** to rely; trust: *you may depend on the accuracy of the report.* **2.** to be conditional or contingent: *we might go, but it depends.* –*phr.* **3. depend on** (or **upon**), **a.** to rely on: *to depend on someone for support.* **b.** to be contingent on: *it depends on what happens today.* –**dependable**, *adj.*

dependant /dəˈpɛndənt/ *n.* **1.** someone who depends on or looks to another for support, favour, etc. **2.** someone to whom one contributes all or a major amount of necessary financial support. **3.** a retainer; servant.

dependency /dəˈpɛndənsi/ *n.* (*pl.* **-cies**) **1.** the state of being dependent; dependence. **2.** something dependent or subordinate; an appurtenance. **3.** a subject territory which is not an integral part of the ruling country.

dependent /dəˈpɛndənt/ *adj.* **1.** depending on something else for help, support, etc. **2.** conditioned (by); contingent (on): *whether we play is dependent on the weather.* **3.** subject; subordinate. **4.** *Maths* (of a quantity or variable) depending upon another for value. –**dependence**, *n.*

depersonalise /diˈpɜsənəlaɪz/ *v.t.* to make impersonal. Also, **depersonalize**. –**depersonalisation** /diˌpɜsənəlaɪˈzeɪʃən/, *n.*

depict /dəˈpɪkt/ *v.t.* **1.** to represent by or as by painting; portray; delineate. **2.** to represent in words; describe. –**depicter**, *n.* –**depiction**, *n.* –**depictive**, *adj.*

depilatory /dəˈpɪlətri/ *adj.* **1.** capable of removing hair. –*n.* (*pl.* **-ries**) **2.** a depilatory agent.

deplete /dəˈplit/ *v.t.* to deprive of that which fills; decrease the fullness of; reduce the stock or amount of. –**depletion**, *n.* –**depletive**, **depletory** /dəˈplitəri/, *adj.*

deplorable /dəˈplɔrəbəl/ *adj.* **1.** causing or being a subject for grief or regret; sad; lamentable. **2.** causing or being a subject for censure or reproach; bad; wretched. –**deplorableness**, **deplorability** /dəplɔrəˈbɪləti/, *n.* –**deplorably**, *adv.*

deplore /dəˈplɔ/ *v.t.* to feel or express deep grief for in regard to; regret deeply. –**deplorer**, *n.* –**deploringly**, *adv.*

deploy /dəˈplɔɪ/ *v.t.* **1.** to spread out (troops or military units) and form an extended front. **2.** to make careful utilisation of (mineral resources). –**deployment**, *n.* –**deployable**, *adj.*

deport /dəˈpɔt/ *v.t.* **1.** to transport forcibly, as to a penal colony or a place of exile. **2.** to expel (an undesirable alien) from a country; banish. –*phr.* **3. deport oneself**, to bear, conduct, or behave oneself in a particular manner. –**deportation**, *n.* –**deportee**, *n.*

deportment /dəˈpɔtmənt/ n. 1. manner of bearing; carriage. 2. demeanour; conduct; behaviour.

depose /dəˈpouz/ v.t. 1. to remove from office or position, especially high office. 2. to declare or testify, especially under oath, usually in writing. –v.i. 3. to bear witness; give sworn testimony, especially in writing. –**deposable**, adj. –**deposer**, n.

deposit /dəˈpɒzət/ v.t. 1. to put or lay down; place; put. 2. to place for safekeeping or in trust: *she deposited her money in a bank.* –n. 3. a coating of metal deposited by electric current. 4. something entrusted to another for safekeeping. 5. money placed in a financial institution. 6. anything given as security or in part payment. –**depositor**, n.

deposition /dɛpəˈzɪʃən, dipə-/ n. 1. removal from an office or position. 2. **a.** the act of depositing. **b.** that which is deposited. 3. *Law* **a.** the giving of testimony under oath. **b.** the testimony so given.

depository /dəˈpɒzətri, -ətəri/ n. (pl. -**ries**) 1. a place where anything is deposited or stored for safekeeping; a storehouse. 2. a trustee.

depot /ˈdɛpou/ n. 1. a depository; storehouse. 2. a place where buses, trams, trucks, etc., are kept when they are not in service.

depraved /dəˈpreivd/ adj. corrupt or perverted, especially morally; wicked. –**deprave**, v. –**depravity**, n.

deprecate /ˈdɛprəkeit/ v.t. to express earnest disapproval of; urge reasons against; protest against (a scheme, purpose, etc.). –**deprecatingly**, adv. –**deprecation** /dɛprəˈkeiʃən/, n. –**deprecator**, n. –**deprecatory**, adj.

depreciate /dəˈpriʃieit, dəˈprisieit/ v.t. 1. to reduce the purchasing value of (money). 2. to lessen the value of. 3. to represent as of little value or merit; belittle. –v.i. 4. to decline in value. –**depreciatingly**, adv. –**depreciator**, n.

depreciation /dəpriʃiˈeiʃən, -prisi-/ n. 1. a decrease in value due to wear and tear, decay, decline in price, etc. 2. the notional amount of money involved in such a decrease, viewed as a cost. 3. a decrease in the purchasing or exchange value of money. 4. a lowering in estimation; disparagement.

depredate /ˈdɛprədeit/ v.t. 1. to prey upon; plunder; lay waste. –v.i. 2. to prey; make depredations. –**depredation** /dɛprəˈdeiʃən/, n. –**depredator**, n. –**depredatory** /dɛprəˈdeitəri, dəˈprɛdətəri, -tri/, adj.

depress /dəˈprɛs/ v.t. 1. to lower in spirits; deject; dispirit. 2. to lower in force, vigour, etc.; weaken; make dull. 3. to lower in amount or value. 4. to put into a lower position: *to depress the muzzle of a gun.* 5. to press down. –**depressed**, adj. –**depressive**, adj. –**depressible**, adj. –**depressingly**, adv.

depressant /dəˈprɛsənt/ adj. 1. having the quality of depressing or lowering the vital activities; sedative. –n. 2. a sedative.

depression /dəˈprɛʃən/ n. 1. an act of depressing. 2. the state of being depressed. 3. a sunken place; a hollow. 4. *Psychol.* a state of despondency marked by feelings of inadequacy, reduced activity, sadness, etc. 5. a time of reduced economic activity and high unemployment. 6. *Weather* an area of low air pressure. –**depressive**, adj.

deprive /dəˈpraiv/ v.t. 1. to divest of something possessed or enjoyed; dispossess; strip; bereave. 2. to keep (a person, etc.) from possessing or enjoying something withheld. 3. to remove (an ecclesiastic) from a benefice; to remove from office. –**deprivable**, adj. –**deprival** /dəˈpraivəl/, n. –**deprivation**, n. –**depriver**, n.

deprived /dəˈpraivd/ adj. (especially of children) without certain benefits of money or social class; lacking educational opportunities, parental affection, etc.

depth /dɛpθ/ n. 1. measure or distance downwards, inwards, or backwards. 2. deepness, as of water, suited to

or safe for a person or thing. 3. abstruseness, as of a subject. 4. gravity; seriousness. 5. emotional profundity: *depth of woe.* 6. (pl.) a low intellectual or moral condition. 7. intensity, as of silence, colour, etc. 8. lowness of pitch. 9. extent of intellectual penetration, sagacity, or profundity. 10. (usu. pl.) a deep part or place, as of the sea. 11. an unfathomable space, or abyss. 12. the remotest or extreme part, as of space. 13. a deep or underlying region, as of feeling. 14. the part of greatest intensity, as of night or winter. 15. (in team sports) a high level of skill based on the inclusion of a good number of relatively skilled players rather than just one or two outstanding players. –*phr.* 16. **beyond** (or **out of**) **one's depth**, **a.** in water too deep for one to touch the bottom. **b.** involved in matters beyond one's capacity or understanding. 17. **in depth**, intensively; thoroughly: *he studied the subject in depth.*

deputation /dɛpjuˈteiʃən/ n. 1. appointment to represent or act for another or others. 2. the person or (usually) body of persons so appointed or authorised.

deputise /ˈdɛpjətaiz/ v.t. 1. to appoint as a deputy. –v.i. 2. to act as a deputy. Also, **deputize**.

deputy /ˈdɛpjəti/ n. (pl. -**ties**) 1. a person appointed or authorised to act for another or others. 2. a person appointed or elected as assistant to a public official such as an alderman or (US) a sheriff, serving as successor in the event of a vacancy. 3. a person representing a constituency in any of certain legislative bodies, such as the French Chamber of Deputies. –adj. 4. acting as deputy for another. –**deputyship**, n.

der /dɜ/ interj. Colloq. an exclamation of feigned and exaggerated stupidity used to mock someone who has said something considered so obvious that to say it demonstrates stupidity.

derail /diˈreil/ v.t. 1. to cause (a train, etc.) to run off the rails. –v.i. 2. (of a train, etc.) to run off the rails of a track. –**derailment**, n.

derange /dəˈreindʒ/ v.t. (deranged, deranging) 1. to unsettle the reason of; make insane. 2. to disturb the condition, action, or functions of. 3. Obs. to throw into disorder; make a mess of. –**derangement**, n.

derby /ˈdabi, ˈdɜbi/ n. (pl. -**bies**) an important race, especially of horses.

deregulate /diˈrɛgjəleit/ v.t. to remove the inhibiting restraints of government regulation from (a commercial enterprise). –**deregulation**, n.

derelict /ˈdɛrəlikt/ adj. 1. left or abandoned, as by the owner or guardian (said especially of a ship abandoned at sea). 2. neglected; dilapidated. 3. guilty of lack of care for one's obligations; remiss: *derelict in one's duty.* –n. 4. a ship abandoned at sea. 5. a person forsaken or abandoned, especially by society.

dereliction /dɛrəˈlikʃən/ n. 1. culpable neglect, as of duty; delinquency; fault. 2. the act of abandoning. 3. the state of being abandoned. 4. Law a leaving dry of land by recession of the waterline.

deride /dəˈraid/ v.t. to laugh at in contempt; scoff or jeer at; mock. –**derider**, n. –**derision**, n. –**derisive**, adj. –**derisory**, adj.

derivation /dɛrəˈveiʃən/ n. 1. the act of deriving. 2. the state of being derived. 3. origination or origin. 4. something that is derived; derivative. 5. the history of a word from its earliest known form. –**derivational**, adj.

derivative /dəˈrivətiv/ adj. 1. coming from something else; derived. 2. not original or first; secondary. –n. 3. something derived. 4. Chem. a substance or compound obtained from, or structurally related to, another compound. 5. Maths the instantaneous rate of change of a function in relation to a variable. –**derivatively**, adv.

derive /dəˈraiv/ v.t. 1. (sometimes fol. by *from*) to receive or obtain from a source or origin. 2. to trace, as from a source or origin. 3. to obtain by reasoning; deduce.

4. *Chem.* to produce (a compound) from another by chemical substitution, etc. *–v.i.* **5.** to come from a source; originate. *–derivable, adj. –deriver, n.*

-derm a word element meaning 'skin', as in *endoderm*.

dermabrasion /dɜmə'breɪʒən/ *n.* a procedure in cosmetic surgery in which a wire brush or a diamond wheel with rough edges is used to remove the upper layers of skin, allowing new smoother skin to replace damaged areas. *–dermabrasive, adj.*

dermatitis /dɜmə'taɪtəs/ *n. Pathol.* inflammation of the skin.

dermato- a word element meaning 'skin', as in *dermatology*. Also, **derm-, dermat-, dermo-**.

dermatology /dɜmə'tɒlədʒi/ *n.* the science of the skin and its diseases. *–dermatological* /dɜmətə'lɒdʒɪkəl/, *adj. –dermatologist, n.*

dero /'dɛroʊ/ *n. Colloq.* a vagrant, especially one with a weird or sinister appearance. Also, **derro**.

derogatory /də'rɒɡətri, -ətəri/ *adj.* tending to derogate or detract, as from authority or estimation; disparaging; depreciatory. *–derogatorily, adv. –derogatoriness, n.*

derrick /'dɛrɪk/ *n.* any of various devices for lifting and moving heavy weights.

derro /'dɛroʊ/ *n.* → **dero.**

dervish /'dɜvɪʃ/ *n.* a member of any of various Muslim ascetic orders, some of which carry on ecstatic observances, such as violent dancing and pirouetting (**dancing dervish, spinning dervish**, or **whirling dervish**) or vociferous chanting or shouting (**howling dervish**).

desalinate /di'sæləneɪt/ *v.t.* to subject (sea water) to a process of desalination. Also, **desalinise**.

desalination /ˌdisælə'neɪʃən/ *n.* the process of removing the dissolved salts from sea water so that it becomes suitable for drinking water or for agricultural irrigation. Also, **desalinisation**.

descant *n.* /'dɛskænt/ **1.** *Music* **a.** a melody or counterpoint accompanying a simple musical theme and usually written above it. **b.** (in part music) the soprano. **c.** a song or melody. **2.** a commentary on a subject. *–adj.* /'dɛskænt/ **3.** *Music* of or relating to the highest-pitched member of an instrumental family, as the descant recorder. *–v.i.* /dɛs'kænt, dəs-/ **4.** *Music* to sing. **5.** to comment or discourse about a subject. *–descanter, n.*

descend /də'sɛnd/ *v.i.* **1.** to move or pass from a higher to a lower place; go or come down; fall; sink. **2.** to pass from higher to lower in any scale. **3.** to go from generals to particulars. **4.** to slope or tend downward. **5.** to come down by transmission, as from ancestors. **6.** to be derived by birth or extraction. *–v.t.* **7.** to move or lead downwards upon or along; go down. *–phr.* **8. descend on** (or **upon**), **a.** to come down on or pounce on, especially in a hostile fashion. **b.** to visit unexpectedly in a manner that is unwelcome. *–descendent, adj.*

descendant /də'sɛndənt/ *n.* someone descended from an ancestor; an offspring, near or remote.

descent /də'sɛnt/ *n.* **1.** the act or fact of descending. **2.** a downward inclination or slope. **3.** a passage or stairway leading down. **4.** derivation from an ancestor; extraction; lineage. **5.** any passing from higher to lower in degree or state.

describe /də'skraɪb/ *v.t.* **1.** to set forth in written or spoken words; give an account of: *to describe a scene; to describe a person.* **2.** *Geom.* to draw or trace, as an arc. *–describable, adj. –describer, n.*

description /də'skrɪpʃən/ *n.* **1.** representation by written or spoken words; a statement that describes. **2.** sort; kind; variety: *persons of that description.*

descriptive /də'skrɪptɪv/ *adj.* **1.** having the quality of describing; characterised by description. **2.** *Ling.* seeking to describe language as it is rather than prescribe what it should be. *–descriptively, adv. –descriptiveness, n.*

desecrate /'dɛsəkreɪt/ *v.t.* to divest of sacred or hallowed character or office; divert from a sacred to a profane purpose; treat with sacrilege; profane. *–desecrater, desecrator, n. –desecration* /dɛsə'kreɪʃən/, *n.*

deselect /disə'lɛkt/ *v.t. Computers* to cancel the selection of (an item, a set of items, highlighted text, etc.) by clicking the mouse outside or inside (depending on the program operating) the target to have its selection cancelled.

desert[1] /'dɛzət/ *n.* **1.** an area so deficient in moisture as to support only a sparse, widely spaced vegetation, or none at all. **2.** any area in which few forms of life can exist because of lack of water, permanent frost, or absence of soil. **3.** any place lacking in something. *–adj.* **4.** of, relating to, or like a desert. **5.** desolate; barren. **6.** uninhabited: *a desert island.*

desert[2] /də'zɜt/ *v.t.* **1.** to leave (a person, place, etc.) without intending to return; to abandon or forsake: *he deserted his wife.* **2.** (of a soldier or sailor) to leave or run away from (the service, duty, etc.) with the intention of never returning. **3.** to fail (one): *all hope deserted him.* *–v.i.* **4.** (especially of a soldier or sailor) to forsake one's duty, etc. *–deserter, n. –desertion, n.*

desert[3] /də'zɜt/ *n.* **1.** that which is deserved; a due reward or punishment. **2.** worthiness of reward or punishment; merit or demerit. **3.** the fact of deserving well; merit; a virtue. *–phr.* **4. just deserts,** a misfortune or punishment viewed as being richly deserved.

deserve /də'zɜv/ *v.t.* **1.** to merit (reward, punishment, esteem, etc.) in return for actions, qualities, etc. *–v.i.* **2.** to be worthy of recompense. *–deserver, n.*

desex /di'sɛks/ *v.t.* to spay or castrate (an animal).

desiccate /'dɛsəkeɪt/ *v.t.* **1.** to dry thoroughly; dry up. **2.** to preserve by depriving of moisture, as foods. *–desiccation* /dɛsə'keɪʃən/, *n. –desiccative* /'dɛsəkətɪv, də'sɪkətɪv/, *adj.*

desiccated /'dɛsəkeɪtəd/ *adj.* **1.** dehydrated or powdered: *desiccated coconut; desiccated milk.* **2.** completely dried out.

design /də'zaɪn/ *v.t.* **1.** to prepare the preliminary sketch or the plans for (a work to be executed). **2.** to plan or fashion artistically or skilfully. **3.** to intend for a definite purpose. **4.** to form or conceive in the mind; contrive; plan. *–v.i.* **5.** to make drawings, preliminary sketches, or plans. **6.** to plan and fashion a work of art, etc. *–n.* **7.** an outline, sketch, or plan, as of a work of art, an edifice, or a machine to be executed or constructed. **8.** the combination of details or features of a picture, building, etc.; the pattern or device of artistic work. **9.** the art of designing: *a school of design.* **10.** a plan; a project; a scheme. **11.** a hostile plan; crafty scheme. **12.** the end in view; intention; purpose. **13.** (*usu. pl.*) evil or selfish intention. *–phr.* **14. by design,** deliberately.

designate *v.t.* /'dɛzɪgneɪt/ **1.** to mark or point out; indicate; show; specify. **2.** to name; entitle; style. **3.** to nominate or select for a duty, office, purpose, etc.; appoint; assign. *–adj.* /'dɛzɪgnət, -neɪt/ **4.** appointed to an office but not yet in possession of it; designated, as *the ambassador designate.* *–designation* /dɛzɪg'neɪʃən/, *n. –designator, n. –designative, adj.*

designated driver *n.* a member of a group of people attending a social event at which alcohol will be drunk, who agrees not to drink alcohol and to be responsible for driving the other members home safely.

designer /də'zaɪnə/ *n.* **1.** someone who devises or executes designs, as for works of art, decorative patterns, dresses, machines, etc. **2.** a schemer or intriguer. *–adj.* **3.** relating to colours, materials, etc., favoured by well-known designers: *a kitchen featuring designer colours.* **4.** (especially of clothes, fabrics, etc.) carrying the label or identification of a particular designer, even though mass-produced: *designer jeans.* **5.** created in a fashionable style: *designer drugs; designer pop.*

designer drug *n.* a synthetically-produced drug, the chemical structure of which differs in minor detail from an illegal drug (especially cocaine or heroin) which it is intended to imitate so as to produce a specific effect on the central nervous system, the new substance being not specifically proscribed by law.

designer gene *n.* a gene created or modified by genetic engineering.

designer steroid *n.* a steroid designed to evade testing for illicit drugs.

designer stubble *n.* stubble on a man's face, kept very short in a fashionable style.

desirable /də'zaɪrəbəl/ *adj.* **1.** worthy to be desired; pleasing, excellent, or fine. **2.** arousing desire: *a desirable woman.* **3.** advisable: *a desirable course of action.* –*n.* **4.** something that is desirable. –**desirability** /dəzaɪrə'bɪləti/, **desirableness**, *n.* –**desirably**, *adv.*

desire /də'zaɪə/ *v.t.* **1.** to wish or long for; crave; want. **2.** to express a wish for, implying a request: *the king desires your presence.* –*n.* **3.** a strong need; craving. **4.** a request. **5.** something desired. **6.** sexual appetite; lust. –**desirer**, *n.*

desirous /də'zaɪrəs/ *phr.* **desirous of**, having or experiencing a wish or hope for: *both leaders are desirous of peace.*

desist /də'zɪst, də'sɪst/ *v.i.* to cease, as from some action or proceeding; stop. –**desistance, desistence**, *n.*

desk /dɛsk/ *n.* **1.** a table specially adapted for convenience in writing or reading, sometimes made with a sloping top, and generally fitted with drawers and compartments. **2.** a section of a complex organisation, such as a government department or newspaper, with responsibilities for a particular area of activities: *the China desk at Foreign Affairs.* **3.** the section of a hotel, office, building, etc., where clients and visitors may be received and assisted; the reception desk.

de-skilling /di-'skɪlɪŋ/ *n.* the process whereby an individual is left without appropriate skills and therefore made unemployable because of changes in work practices, such as the introduction of new technology. Also, **deskilling.** –**de-skilled**, *adj.*

desktop /'dɛsktɒp/ *n.* **1.** *Computers* a graphical interface with the operating system represented as a work space similar to that of a desktop, with windows, icons, folders, toolbars, etc. **2.** a desktop computer. –*adj.* **3.** (of a computer, office equipment, etc.) small enough in design to be used at a desk.

desktop publishing *n.* the production of printed material by means of a computer system comprising a personal computer, software, and a laser printer, all of which can be contained within an office. –**desktop publisher**, *n.*

desolate *adj.* /'dɛsələt, 'dɛz-/ **1.** barren or laid waste; devastated. **2.** deserted; lonely. **3.** hopeless; helpless. **4.** very sad; dreary; dismal. –*v.t.* /'dɛsəleɪt, 'dɛz-/ **5.** to lay waste; devastate. **6.** to make unhappy or disconsolate. **7.** to forsake or abandon. –**desolater, desolator**, *n.* –**desolately**, *adv.* –**desolateness**, *n.*

despair /də'spɛə/ *n.* **1.** loss of hope; hopelessness. **2.** something that causes hopelessness; something of which there is no hope.

despatch /dəs'pætʃ/ *v.t., v.i., n.* → dispatch. –**despatcher**, *n.*

desperado /dɛspə'radoʊ/ *n.* (*pl.* **-does** *or* **-dos**) a desperate or reckless criminal; one ready for any desperate deed.

desperate /'dɛsprət, -pərət/ *adj.* **1.** reckless from despair; ready to run any risk: *a desperate villain.* **2.** leaving little or no hope; very serious or dangerous; extremely bad: *a desperate illness.* **3.** having no hope: *a desperate*

situation. **4.** undertaken as a last resort: *a desperate remedy.* –*phr.* **5. desperate for**, *Colloq.* having a great need or desire for. –**desperation** /dɛspə'reɪʃən/, **desperateness**, *n.* –**desperately**, *adv.*

despicable /də'spɪkəbəl/ *adj.* that is to be despised; contemptible. –**despicability** /dəspɪkə'bɪləti/, **despicableness**, *n.* –**despicably**, *adv.*

despise /də'spaɪz/ *v.t.* to look down upon, as in contempt; scorn; disdain. –**despiser**, *n.*

despite /də'spaɪt/ *prep.* **1.** in spite of; notwithstanding. –*n.* **2.** contemptuous treatment; insult. –*phr.* **3. in despite of**, in contempt or defiance of; in spite of; notwithstanding.

despoil /də'spɔɪl/ *v.t.* to strip of possessions; rob; plunder; pillage. –**despoiler**, *n.* –**despoilment**, *n.*

despondent /də'spɒndənt/ *adj.* desponding; depressed or dejected. –**despondency**, *n.* –**despondently**, *adv.*

despot /'dɛspɒt/ *n.* **1.** an absolute ruler; autocrat. **2.** a tyrant or oppressor. –*phr.* **3. benevolent despot**, a ruler who has the interests of his or her subjects at heart; an enlightened ruler. –**despotic** /dəs'pɒtɪk/, *adj.*

des res /dɛz 'rɛz/ *n. Orig. Brit. Colloq.* a desirable residence.

dessert /də'zɜt/ *n.* the final course of a meal including sweet pies, puddings, etc.

dessertspoon /də'zɜtspun/ *n.* a spoon, intermediate in size between a tablespoon and a teaspoon, used for eating dessert.

destabilise /di'steɪbəlaɪz/ *v.t.* **1.** to make unstable. **2.** *Politics* to deliberately create uncertainty about: *to destabilise the leadership.* Also, **destabilize.** –**destabilising**, *adj.* –**destabilisation**, *n.*

destigmatise /di'stɪgmətaɪz/ *v.t.* to remove the stigma from: *to destigmatise poverty.* Also, **destigmatize.** –**destigmatisation** /di,stɪgmətaɪ'zeɪʃən/, *n.*

destination /dɛstə'neɪʃən/ *n.* **1.** the predetermined end of a journey or voyage. **2.** the purpose for which anything is destined; ultimate end or design. –*adj.* Also, **destinational.** **3.** advertised as a reason to travel to a particular place: *destination shopping; a destination restaurant.*

destine /'dɛstən/ *v.t.* **1.** to set apart for a particular use, purpose, etc.; design; intend. **2.** to appoint or ordain beforehand, as by divine decree; foreordain; predetermine.

destined /'dɛstənd/ *adj.* **1.** bound for a certain destination. **2.** designed; intended. **3.** predetermined.

destiny /'dɛstəni/ *n.* (*pl.* **-nies**) **1.** that which is to happen to a particular person or thing; one's lot or fortune. **2.** the predetermined course of events. **3.** the power or agency which determines the course of events. **4.** (*upper case*) this power personified or represented as a goddess.

destitute /'dɛstətjut/ *adj.* **1.** bereft of means or resources; lacking the means of subsistence. –*phr.* **2. destitute of**, deprived or devoid of: *destitute of hope.* –**destitution** /dɛstə'tjuʃən/, **destituteness**, *n.*

destroy /də'strɔɪ/ *v.t.* **1.** to reduce to pieces or to a useless form; ruin; spoil; demolish. **2.** to put an end to; extinguish. **3.** to kill; slay. **4.** to render ineffective; nullify; invalidate. **5.** to cause the ruination of (someone): *to hate someone enough to destroy them.* –**destroyable**, *adj.*

destroyer /də'strɔɪə/ *n.* a small, fast warship, originally designed to destroy torpedo boats.

destruction /də'strʌkʃən/ *n.* **1.** the act of destroying. **2.** the fact or condition of being destroyed; demolition; annihilation. **3.** a cause or means of destroying. –**destructive**, *adj.*

desultory /'dɛsəltri, -təri, 'dɛz-/ *adj.* **1.** veering about from one thing to another; lacking purpose, method, or enthusiasm: *desultory reading or conversation.*

2. random: *a desultory thought.* –**desultorily,** *adv.* –**desultoriness,** *n.*

detach /dəˈtætʃ/ *v.t.* **1.** to unfasten and separate; disengage; disunite. **2.** to send away (a regiment, ship, etc.) on a special mission: *men were detached to defend the pass.* –**detachability** /dətætʃəˈbɪləti/, *n.* –**detachable,** *adj.* –**detacher,** *n.* –**detachment,** *n.*

detached /dəˈtætʃt/ *adj.* **1.** standing apart; separate; unattached (usually applied to houses): *he lives in a detached house.* **2.** not interested; unconcerned; aloof. **3.** objective; unbiased.

detached retina *n.* a condition in which the retina comes away from the back of the eye, potentially resulting in blindness. Also, **retinal detachment.**

detail /ˈditeɪl/ *n.* **1.** an individual or minute part; an item or particular. **2.** particulars collectively; minutiae. **3.** a dealing with or treating part by part or item by item. **4.** fine, intricate decoration. **5.** a detail drawing. **6.** any small section of a larger structure considered as a unit. **7.** a reproduction of a part or section of something, especially a work of art, often enlarged. **8.** *Mil.* **a.** a detailing or telling off, as of a small force or an officer, for a special service. **b.** the party or person so selected. **c.** a particular assignment of duty. –*v.t.* **9.** to relate or report in particulars; tell fully and distinctly. **10.** *Mil.* to order or appoint for some particular duty, as a patrol, a guard, etc. **11.** to decorate with fine, intricate designs. **12.** to improve the appearance of (a motor vehicle, aeroplane, etc.) before sale by finishing and decorating it, inside and out. –*phr.* **13. in detail,** circumstantially; item by item.

detain /dəˈteɪn/ *v.t.* **1.** to keep from proceeding; keep waiting; delay. **2.** to keep under restraint or in custody. **3.** to keep back or withhold, as from a person. –**detainee,** *n.* –**detainment,** *n.*

detect /dəˈtɛkt/ *v.t.* **1.** to discover or notice a fact, a process, or an action: *to detect someone in a dishonest act.* **2.** to find out the action or character of: *to detect a hypocrite.* –**detectable, detectible,** *adj.* –**detector,** *n.*

detection dog *n.* → **sniffer dog.**

detective /dəˈtɛktɪv/ *n.* **1.** a member of the police force or a private investigator whose job is to obtain information and evidence, as of offences against the law, and to discover the author of a crime. –*adj.* **2.** relating to detection or detectives: *a detective story.* **3.** serving to detect; detecting.

détente /deɪˈtɒnt/ *n.* a relaxing, as of international tension.

detention /dəˈtɛnʃən/ *n.* **1.** the act of detaining. **2.** the state of being detained. **3.** a keeping in custody; confinement. **4.** a keeping in (of a pupil) after school hours, during lunch break, etc., as a form of punishment. **5.** the withholding of what belongs to or is claimed by another.

deter /dəˈtɜ/ *v.t.* (**-terred, -terring**) to discourage or restrain (someone) from acting or proceeding, through fear, doubt, etc. –**determent,** *n.*

detergent /dəˈtɜdʒənt/ *adj.* **1.** cleansing; purging. –*n.* **2.** any cleaning agent, including soap.

deteriorate /dəˈtɪəriəreɪt/ *v.t.* **1.** to make worse; make lower in character or quality. –*v.i.* **2.** to become worse. –**deterioration** /dətɪəriəˈreɪʃən/, *n.* –**deteriorative,** *adj.*

determinate /dəˈtɜmɪnət/ *adj.* **1.** having defined limits; definite. **2.** settled; positive. **3.** determined upon; conclusive; final. **4.** determined; resolute. –**determinately,** *adv.* –**determinateness,** *n.*

determination /dətɜməˈneɪʃən/ *n.* **1.** the act of deciding; fixing or settling of purpose. **2.** a decision made, especially after consideration. **3.** a result brought about; solution. **4.** an official settlement of a problem, quarrel, etc. **5.** the quality of being determined or resolute; firmness of purpose: *she showed great determination.*

6. *Biol.* the fixing of the nature of structured differences in a group of cells before actual, visible differentiation.

determine /dəˈtɜmən/ *v.t.* (**-mined, -mining**) **1.** to settle or decide (an argument, question, etc.) by an official decision. **2.** to reach a decision as after reasoning, examining, etc. **3.** *Geom.* to fix the position of. **4.** to fix or decide causally; condition: *demand determines supply.* –**determinable,** *adj.*

determined /dəˈtɜmənd/ *adj.* **1.** resolute; unflinching; firm. **2.** decided; settled; resolved. –**determinedly,** *adv.* –**determinedness,** *n.*

determiner /dəˈtɜmənə/ *n.* **1.** someone or something that determines. **2.** *Gram.* a word such as an article, a demonstrative or number, which precedes nouns and any modifiers attached to them, and limits their scope. Examples in English include *the* as in *the role, this* as in *this red book,* and *seven* as in *seven dwarfs.*

deterrent /dəˈtɛrənt, -ˈtɜr-/ *adj.* **1.** deterring; restraining. –*n.* **2.** something that deters or is expected to deter. –**deterrence,** *n.*

detest /dəˈtɛst/ *v.t.* to feel abhorrence of; hate; dislike intensely. –**detester,** *n.*

detonate /ˈdɛtəneɪt/ *v.t.* **1.** to cause to explode. –*v.i.* **2.** to explode, especially with great noise, suddenness, or violence.

detonator /ˈdɛtəneɪtə/ *n.* **1.** a device, such as a percussion cap or an explosive, used to make another substance explode. **2.** something that explodes.

detour /ˈdituə, -tuə, -tɔ/ *n.* **1.** a roundabout or circuitous way or course, especially one used temporarily instead of the main route. –*v.i.* **2.** to make a detour; go by way of a detour. –*v.t.* **3.** to cause to make a detour; send by way of a detour.

detox /ˈditɒks/ *n.* **1.** the process of detoxification. –*v.t.* **2.** to assist (a person) to go through the process of detoxification. –*v.i.* **3.** to go through the process of detoxification.

detox centre *n.* a medical centre designed to assist patients in the process of detoxification.

detoxification /ˌditɒksəfəˈkeɪʃən/ *n.* the process of withdrawing from physical or psychological dependency on a substance of abuse, such as drugs, alcohol, etc.

detract /dəˈtrækt/ *v.t.* **1.** to take away (a part): *to detract one's share.* **2.** to draw away or divert: *to detract one's attention.* –*phr.* **3. detract from,** to take away some part from, as from quality, value, or reputation: *the ugly view detracts from the value of the house.* –**detractingly,** *adv.* –**detractor,** *n.*

detriment /ˈdɛtrəmənt/ *n.* **1.** loss, damage, or injury. **2.** a cause of loss or damage.

detritus /dəˈtraɪtəs/ *n.* **1.** particles of rock or other material worn or broken away from a mass, as by the action of water or glacial ice. **2.** any disintegrated material; debris.

detrivore /ˈdɛtrəvɔ/ *n.* an organism which feeds on sizeable dead or decaying organic matter, as beetles, worms, crabs, etc. –**detrivorous** /dəˈtrɪvərəs/, *adj.*

deuce /djus/ *n.* **1.** a card, or the side of a die, having two pips. **2.** *Tennis, etc.* a juncture in a game at which the scores are level and either player (or pair) must gain a lead of two points in order to win the game.

deutschmark /ˈdɔɪtʃmak/ *n.* (formerly, until the introduction of the euro in 2002) the principal monetary unit of Germany; previously (1948–90), the principal monetary unit of West Germany. *Abbrev.*: DM Also, **deutschemark.**

devalue /diˈvælju/ *verb* (**-valued, -valuing**) –*v.t.* **1.** to lower the legal value of (a currency); devaluate. **2.** to diminish the worth or value of: *his advice was devalued by recent developments.* –*v.i.* **3.** (of a currency) to decrease in legal value. –**devaluation,** *n.*

devastate /'dɛvəsteɪt/ v.t. to lay waste; ravage; render desolate.

develop /də'vɛləp/ v.t. **1.** to bring to a more advanced or effective state. **2.** to cause to grow or become larger. **3.** to enlarge upon the detail of: *develop one's ideas.* **4.** to bring into being or activity; generate; evolve. **5.** to build on (land). **6.** *Biol.* to cause to go through the process of natural evolution. **7.** *Photography* to treat (a photographic plate, etc.) with chemical agents so as to bring out the picture. –v.i. **8.** to grow into a more mature or advanced state; advance; expand. **9.** to come gradually into existence or operation; be evolved. **10.** *Biol.* to undergo differences in ontogeny or progress in phylogeny. –**developer**, n. –**developable**, adj.

developed /də'vɛləpt/ adj. **1.** having undergone development. **2.** (of a country or economy) industrialised.

developing /də'vɛləpɪŋ/ adj. **1.** undergoing development. **2.** Also, **underdeveloped**. (of a country or economy) in the early stages of becoming industrialised.

deviant /'diviənt/ adj. **1.** deviating from an accepted norm, especially in sexual behaviour. –n. **2.** a person or thing that is deviant. –**deviance, deviancy**, n.

deviate /'diviɛɪt/ v.i. **1.** to turn aside (from a way or course). **2.** to depart or swerve, as from a procedure, course of action, or acceptable standard. **3.** to digress, as from a line of thought or reasoning. –v.t. **4.** to cause to swerve; turn aside. –**deviator**, n.

deviation /divi'eɪʃən/ n. **1.** the act of deviating; divergence. **2.** departure from an accepted standard. **3.** *Statistics* the difference between one of a set of values and the mean of the set. **4.** *Navig.* the error of a ship's magnetic compass due to local magnetism; the angle between the compass meridian and the magnetic meridian. **5.** a road or rail detour.

device /də'vaɪs/ n. **1.** an invention or contraption. **2.** a crafty scheme; trick. **3.** a design or emblem on a coat of arms. **4.** a motto. –phr. **5. leave to one's own devices**, to allow (someone) to act without interference.

device driver n. Computers a program that enables the operating system of a computer to recognise peripheral devices, such as modems, printers, mouses, etc. Also, **driver**.

devil /'dɛvəl/ n. **1.** (in Jewish, Christian and Islamic theologies) **a.** (*sometimes upper case*) the supreme spirit of evil; Satan. **b.** a subordinate evil spirit at enmity with God, and having power to afflict humankind both with bodily disease and with spiritual corruption. **2.** (in many religions) an evil spirit; demon. **3.** a depiction of the devil as a man with a tail, cloven hoofs, and horns. **4.** an atrociously wicked, cruel, or ill-tempered person. **5.** a person of great cleverness, energy, or recklessness. **6.** Colloq. a person, usually one in unfortunate circumstances. **7.** Colloq. fighting spirit. **8.** a machine designed to do destructive work, especially with spikes or sharp teeth, as a machine for tearing rags, etc. **9.** any of various portable furnaces or braziers. –verb (**-illed** or, Chiefly US, **-iled, -illing** or, Chiefly US, **-iling**) –v.t. **10.** Colloq. to harass, torment or pester. **11.** Cookery to prepare (food) with the addition of hot spices. **12.** to tear (rags, cloth, etc.) with a devil (def. 8). –v.i. **13.** to do work, especially hackwork, for a lawyer or writer; perform arduous or unpaid work or without recognition of one's services. –phr. **14. between the devil and the deep blue sea**, faced with two equally distasteful alternatives. **15. give the devil his due**, to do justice to or give deserved credit to an unpleasant or disliked person. **16. go to the devil, a.** to fail completely; be ruined. **b.** to become depraved. **c.** an exclamation expressing annoyance, disgust, impatience, etc. **17. let the devil take the hindmost**, to leave the least fortunate to suffer unpleasant consequences; abandon or leave others to their fate. **18. play the (very) devil with**, to ruin; do great

harm to. **19. raise the devil, a.** to cause a lot of commotion or trouble. **b.** to complain or protest vociferously. **20. speak** (or **talk**) **of the devil**, here comes the person who has been the subject of conversation. **21. the devil**, an emphatic exclamation or mild oath used to express disgust, anger, astonishment, negation, etc. **22. the devil is in the detail**, an expression indicating that a superficially simple task or attractive offer presents obstacles on closer examination. **23. the devil of a ...**, Colloq. an intensifier: *the devil of a hard time.* **24. the devil to pay**, serious trouble to be faced.

devious /'diviəs/ adj. **1.** departing from the direct or accepted way; circuitous; roundabout. **2.** not straightforward; tricky; deceptive; deceitful. –**deviously**, adv. –**deviousness**, n.

devise /də'vaɪz/ v.t. **1.** to order or arrange the plan of; think out; plan; contrive; invent. **2.** Law to assign or transmit (property, especially real property) by will. –v.i. **3.** to form a plan; contrive. –**deviser**, n. –**devisable**, adj.

devoid /də'vɔɪd/ phr. **devoid of**, not possessing, free from: *devoid of hair; devoid of emotion.*

devolve /də'vɒlv/ v.t. **1.** to transfer or delegate (a duty, responsibility, etc.) to or upon another; pass on. **2.** Law to pass by inheritance or legal succession. –v.i. **3.** to fall as a duty or responsibility on a person. **4.** to be transferred or passed on from one to another. –**devolution**, n. –**devolvement**, n.

devon /'dɛvən/ n. Aust. a large, mild-flavoured, precooked sausage, usually sliced thinly and eaten cold; fritz; luncheon sausage; polony; Strasburg.

devote /də'voʊt/ v.t. **1.** to appropriate to a particular pursuit, occupation, purpose, cause, person, etc.: *to devote evenings to reading.* **2.** to appropriate by or as by a vow; consecrate: *to devote my life to good works.*

devoted /də'voʊtəd/ adj. **1.** zealous or ardent in attachment: *a devoted friend.* **2.** dedicated; consecrated. –**devotedly**, adv. –**devotedness**, n.

devotee /dɛvə'ti, dɛvoʊ'ti/ n. **1.** someone ardently devoted to anything; an enthusiast. **2.** someone zealously or fanatically devoted to religion.

devotion /də'voʊʃən/ n. **1.** dedication; consecration. **2.** earnest attachment to a cause, person, etc. **3.** (oft. pl.) Eccles. religious observance or worship; a form of prayer or worship for special use.

devour /də'vaʊə/ v.t. **1.** to swallow or eat up voraciously or ravenously. **2.** to consume destructively, recklessly, or wantonly. **3.** to swallow up or engulf. **4.** to take in greedily with the senses or intellect. **5.** to absorb or engross wholly: *devoured by fears.* –**devourer**, n. –**devouringly**, adv.

devout /də'vaʊt/ adj. **1.** devoted to divine worship or service; pious; religious. **2.** expressing devotion or piety: *devout prayer.* **3.** earnest or sincere; heartfelt. –**devoutly**, adv. –**devoutness**, n.

dew /dju/ n. **1.** moisture condensed from the atmosphere, especially at night, and deposited in the form of small drops upon any cool surface. **2.** something likened to dew, as serving to refresh or as suggestive of morning. **3.** moisture in small drops on a surface, as tears, perspiration, etc. –v.t. **4.** to wet with or as with dew. –**dewless**, adj.

dexterity /dɛks'tɛrəti/ n. adroitness or skill in using the hands or mind. –**dexterous**, adj.

dextrin /'dɛkstrən/ n. a soluble gummy substance formed from starch by the action of heat, acids, or enzymes. Also, **dextrine**.

dextro- a word element meaning: **1.** right. **2.** Chem. denoting a substance that rotates the plane of planepolarised light to the right. Symbol: **+** Also, **dextr-**.

dextrose /'dɛkstroʊz, -oʊs/ n. See **glucose** (def. 1).

dhow /daʊ/ n. an Arab sailing vessel.

di-[1] a prefix of Greek origin, meaning 'twice', 'doubly', 'two', freely used (like *bi-*) as an English formative, as in *dicotyledon*, *dipolar*, and in many chemical terms, as *diatomic*, *disulphide*. Compare **mono-**. Also, **dis-**.

di-[2] variant of **dis-**[1], before *b, d, l, m, n, r, s*, and *v*, and sometimes *g* and *j*, as in *divide*.

di-[3] variant of **dia-**, before vowels, as in *dioptase*, *diorama*.

dia- a prefix meaning: **1.** passing through, as in *diathermy*. **2.** thoroughly; completely, as in *diagnosis*. **3.** going apart, as in *dialysis*. **4.** opposed in moment (def. 5), as in *diamagnetism*. Also, **di-**.

diabatic /daɪəˈbætɪk/ *adj.* involving a process in which heat leaves or enters a system, as in condensation, evaporation, solar radiation, etc.: *a diabatic thermodynamic process*. Compare **adiabatic**.

diabesity /daɪəˈbiːsəti/ *n.* obesity accompanied by diabetes.

diabetes /daɪəˈbiːtɪz/ *n.* **1.** Also, **diabetes mellitus**. a disease in which the production of insulin in the pancreas is impaired (**type 1 diabetes**), or the body's ability to use the insulin produced is impaired (**type 2 diabetes**); sugar diabetes. **2.** Also, **diabetes insipidus**. a disorder of the pituitary gland causing excessive thirst and the production of a large volume of dilute urine; water diabetes.

diabetes insipidus /daɪəbiːtɪz ɪnˈsɪpədəs/ *n.* → **diabetes** (def. 2).

diabetes mellitus /daɪəbiːtɪz məˈlaɪtəs/ *n.* → **diabetes** (def. 1).

diabetic /daɪəˈbɛtɪk/ *adj.* **1.** of or relating to diabetes. **2.** having diabetes. *–n.* **3.** a person who has diabetes.

diabolical /daɪəˈbɒlɪkəl/ *adj.* **1.** having the qualities of a devil; fiendish; outrageously wicked: *a diabolical plot*. **2.** relating to or actuated by the devil or a devil. **3.** *Colloq.* difficult; unpleasant; very bad. Also, **diabolic**. **–diabolically**, *adv.* **–diabolicalness**, *n.*

diacritic /daɪəˈkrɪtɪk/ *n.* a mark added to a letter or character to distinguish it from a similar one. **–diacritical**, *adj.*

diadem /ˈdaɪədɛm/ *n.* **1.** a crown. **2.** a cloth headband, sometimes adorned with jewels, formerly worn by kings in some countries. **3.** royal dignity or authority.

diagnose /ˈdaɪəgnoʊz/ *v.t.* **1.** to identify by diagnosis (a case, disease, etc.). *–v.i.* **2.** to make a diagnosis.

diagnosis /daɪəgˈnoʊsəs/ *n.* (*pl.* **-noses** /-ˈnoʊsiz/) **1.** *Med.* **a.** the process of determining, by examination of the patient, the nature and identity of a diseased condition. **b.** the decision reached from such an examination. **2.** *Biol.* scientific determination; a description which classifies precisely. **3.** any analysis of events, character, etc.

diagnostic /daɪəgˈnɒstɪk/ *adj.* **1.** relating to a diagnosis. *–n.* **2.** a tool or technique used in the process of reaching a diagnosis. **–diagnostician** /ˌdaɪəgnɒsˈtɪʃən/, **diagnostics** , *n.* **–diagnostically**, *adv.*

diagnostic imaging *n.* the preparation of images of internal organs or parts of the body as by X-ray or CAT scan to assist in the diagnosis of a disease or condition.

diagonal /daɪˈægənəl/ *adj.* **1.** *Maths* connecting, as a straight line, two non-adjacent angles or vertices of a quadrilateral, polygon, or polyhedron. **2.** having an oblique direction. *–n.* **3.** a diagonal line or plane. **–diagonally**, *adv.*

diagram /ˈdaɪəgræm/ *n.* **1.** a figure, or set of lines, marks, etc., to accompany a geometrical demonstration, give the outlines or general features of an object, show the course or results of a process, etc. **2.** a drawing or plan that outlines and explains the parts, operation, etc., of something. **3.** a chart, plan, or scheme. *–v.t.* (**-grammed** *or*, *Chiefly US*, **-gramed**, **-gramming** *or*, *Chiefly US*, **-graming**) **4.** to represent by a diagram; make a diagram of.

dial /ˈdaɪəl/ *n.* **1.** a face of a clock, watch, gauge, etc. **2.** a rotating knob or disc used for tuning a radio, making telephone connections, etc. **3.** *Colloq.* the human face. *–v.t.* (**dialled** *or*, *Chiefly US*, **dialed**, **dialling** *or*, *Chiefly US*, **dialing**) **4.** to measure, select, show or tune in by means of a dial. **5.** to call (a number or person) on a telephone.

dialect /ˈdaɪəlɛkt/ *n.* *Ling.* one of the forms of a given language which differ from one another in details of sound system, lexis, grammar, etc., each of which is usually to be found in a particular region or social class, but the speakers of which are typically mutually intelligible: *Australian English is a regional dialect of English*. **–dialectal** /daɪəˈlɛktl/, *adj.* **–dialectology** /daɪəlɛkˈtɒlədʒi/, *n.*

dialectic /daɪəˈlɛktɪk/ *adj.* **1.** of, or relating to, logical argument or discussion. *–n.* **2.** the examination of ideas by or as if by a debate between the opposing points of view. **3.** any formal system of reasoning or thought.

dialogue /ˈdaɪəlɒg/ *n.* **1.** a conversation between two or more people, especially characters in a novel, play, etc. **2.** an exchange of ideas or opinions on a particular issue. **3.** (especially in diplomacy) a discussion between parties, countries, etc., usually with the aim of agreement: *we need dialogue with China*. **–dialoguer**, *n.*

dialogue partner *n.* a country with which an association of countries engages in consultative discussion on topics of shared interest, even though the country is not a full member of the association.

dial-up *adj.* **1.** able to be accessed by telephone: *a dial-up health service*. **2.** *Computers* able to be accessed via a modem. Also, **dialup**.

dialysis /daɪˈæləsəs/ *n.* (*pl.* **-alyses** /-ˈæləsiz/) **1.** *Chem.* the separation of smaller molecules from larger ones, or of crystalloids from colloids in a solution by selective diffusion through a semipermeable membrane. **2.** (in cases of defective kidney function) the removal of waste products from the blood by causing them to diffuse through a semipermeable membrane; haemodialysis.

diamanté /daɪəˈmɒnti, diə-/ *n.* **1.** a fabric made to sparkle by covering with glittering particles. **2.** such a glittering particle. *–adj.* **3.** (of a fabric) sparkling.

diameter /daɪˈæmətə/ *n.* **1.** *Geom.* **a.** a straight line passing through the centre of a circle or sphere and terminated at each end by the circumference or surface. **b.** a straight line passing from side to side of any figure or body, through its centre. **2.** the length of such a line; thickness.

diametric /daɪəˈmɛtrɪk/ *adj.* **1.** relating to a diameter; along a diameter. **2.** (of opposites) direct; complete; absolute. Also, **diametrical**. **–diametrically**, *adv.*

diamond /ˈdaɪəmənd, ˈdaɪmənd/ *n.* **1.** an extremely hard, and nearly pure form of carbon, used in industry, or as a precious stone. **2.** a tool with an uncut diamond, used for cutting glass. **3.** (a playing card showing) a red rhombus-shaped figure. **4.** a baseball field. *–adj.* **5.** indicating the 75th, or sometimes the 60th, event of a series, as a wedding anniversary: *diamond wedding*.

diamond python *n.* a large Australian python, *Morelia spilotes*, greenish-black in colour with yellow diamond spots on the sides. Also, **diamond snake**.

diaper /ˈdaɪəpə, ˈdaɪpə/ *n.* **1.** *US* a baby's nappy. **2.** a linen or cotton fabric with a woven pattern of small constantly repeated figures, such as diamonds.

diaphanous /daɪˈæfənəs/ *adj.* transparent; translucent. **–diaphanously**, *adv.* **–diaphanousness**, **diaphaneity** /daɪəfəˈniəti/, *n.*

diaphragm /ˈdaɪəfræm/ *n.* **1.** *Anat.* **a.** a muscular, membranous, or ligamentous wall separating two cavities or limiting a cavity. **b.** the partition separating the thoracic cavity from the abdominal cavity in mammals.

2. *Physical Chem., etc.* a semipermeable membrane or the like. **3.** a vibrating membrane or disc, as in a telephone or microphone. **4.** a contraceptive membrane worn in the vagina covering the cervix.

diarrhoea /daɪə'rɪə/ *n.* an intestinal disorder characterised by morbid frequency and fluidity of faecal evacuations. Also, **diarrhea.** –**diarrhoeal, diarrhoeic,** *adj.*

diary /'daɪəri/ *n.* (*pl.* **-ries**) **1.** a daily record, especially of the writer's own experiences or observations. **2.** a book for keeping such a record, or for noting appointments and engagements. –**diarist,** *n.*

diastole /daɪ'æstəli/ *n. Physiol.* the normal rhythmical relaxation and dilatation of the heart, especially that of the ventricles. Compare **systole.** –**diastolic** /daɪə'stɒlɪk/, *adj.*

diatonic /daɪə'tɒnɪk/ *adj. Music* involving only the tones, intervals, or harmonies of a major or minor scale without chromatic alteration. –**diatonically,** *adv.*

diatribe /'daɪətraɪb/ *n.* a bitter and violent denunciation, attack, or criticism.

dibbler /'dɪblə/ *n.* an implement for making holes in the ground for planting seeds, bulbs, etc. Also, **dibber.**

dibs /dɪbz/ *pl. n. Colloq.* **1.** → **marble** (def. 8). **2.** a stake in a game. **3.** funds or money: *in the dibs.* **4.** winnings. –*phr.* **5. dibs in,** taking part; included, especially in a game. **6. play for dibs,** to play with the object of keeping what has been won.

dice /daɪs/ *pl. n.* (*sing.* **die**) **1.** small cubes of plastic, ivory, bone, or wood, marked on each side with a different number of spots (1 to 6), usually used in pairs in games of chance or in gambling. **2.** (*construed as sing.*) a single small cube of such a kind. **3.** any of various games, especially gambling games, played by shaking the dice (in the cupped hand or in a receptacle) and throwing them on to a flat surface. **4.** any small cubes. –*verb* (**diced, dicing**) –*v.t.* **5.** to cut into small cubes. –*v.i.* **6.** to play at dice. –*phr. Colloq.* **7. dice with death,** to act dangerously or take a risk. **8. no dice,** of no use; unsuccessful; out of luck. –**dicer,** *n.*

dicey /'daɪsi/ *adj. Colloq.* unpredictable and thus potentially dangerous; risky; tricky.

dicho- a word element meaning 'in two parts', 'in pairs', as in *dichotomy.*

dichotomy /daɪ'kɒtəmi/ *n.* (*pl.* **-mies**) division into two parts or into twos; subdivision into halves or pairs. –**dichotomous, dichotomic** /ˌdaɪkoʊ'tɒmɪk/, *adj.* –**dichotomously,** *adv.*

dick¹ /dɪk/ *Colloq.* –*n.* **1.** the penis. **2.** a foolish or objectionable person. **3.** nothing: *it means dick.* –*phr.* **4. have had the dick,** to be broken or ruined.

dick² /dɪk/ *n.* a detective.

dickhead /'dɪkhɛd/ *n. Colloq.* **1.** a fool; idiot: *country people are scornful of Sydney dickheads.* **2.** a person who behaves in an objectionable manner.

dicky¹ /'dɪki/ *n.* (*pl.* **-kies**) **1.** a detachable shirt front, or blouse front. **2.** Also, **dicky-seat.** a small additional seat at the outside or back of a vehicle; rumble seat. Also, **dickey, dickie.**

dicky² /'dɪki/ *adj. Colloq.* **1.** unsteady, shaky; in bad health; in poor condition: *a dicky knee.* **2.** difficult; untenable: *a dicky position.*

dictaphone /'dɪktəfoʊn/ *n.* (*from trademark*) an instrument that records and reproduces dictation (def. 2).

dictate *v.t.* /dɪk'teɪt/ **1.** to say or read aloud (something) to be taken down in writing or recorded mechanically. **2.** to prescribe positively; command with authority. **3.** to influence or control (a decision, action, etc.). –*n.* /'dɪkteɪt/ **4.** a commandment, rule or guiding principle: *the dictates of conscience; the dictates of fashion.*

dictation /dɪk'teɪʃən/ *n.* **1.** the act of dictating for reproduction in writing, etc. **2.** words dictated, or taken down as dictated.

dictator /dɪk'teɪtə, 'dɪkteɪtə/ *n.* **1.** someone exercising absolute power, especially one who assumes absolute control in a government without hereditary right or the free consent of the people. **2.** someone who authoritatively prescribes conduct, usage, etc.; a domineering or overbearing person. –**dictatorial** /dɪktə'tɔriəl/, *adj.* –**dictatorship,** *n.* –**dictatress** /dɪk'teɪtrəs/, **dictatrix** /'dɪktətrɪks/, *fem. n.*

diction /'dɪkʃən/ *n.* **1.** style of speaking or writing as dependent upon choice of words: *good diction; a Latin diction.* **2.** the degree of distinctness with which speech sounds are uttered; enunciation.

dictionary /'dɪkʃənri, 'dɪkʃənəri/, *Orig. US* /'dɪkʃənɛri/ *n.* (*pl.* **-ries**) **1.** a reference work containing a selection of the words of a language, usually arranged alphabetically, with explanations of their meanings, pronunciations, etymologies, and other information concerning them, expressed either in the same or in another language. **2.** a reference work giving information on particular subjects or a particular class of words, names or facts, usually under alphabetically arranged headings: *a biographical dictionary.* **3.** *Computers* a wordlist used in a spellchecker.

dictum /'dɪktəm/ *n.* (*pl.* **-tums** *or* **-ta** /-tə/) **1.** an authoritative pronouncement; judicial assertion. **2.** a saying; maxim.

did /dɪd/ *v.* past tense of **do.**

didactic /daɪ'dæktɪk, də-/ *adj.* **1.** intended for instruction; instructive: *didactic poetry.* **2.** inclined to teach or lecture others too much: *a didactic old lady.* –**didactically,** *adv.* –**didacticism,** *n.*

diddle /'dɪdl/ *v.t. Colloq.* to cheat; swindle; victimise. –**diddler,** *n.*

didgeridoo /ˌdɪdʒəri'du/ *n.* → **didjeridu.**

didjeridu /ˌdɪdʒəri'du/ *n.* an Aboriginal wind instrument consisting of a long wooden pipe about five centimetres in diameter on which complex rhythmic patterns are played more or less on one note. Also, **didgeridoo.**

didn't /'dɪdnt, 'dɪdn/ *v.* contraction of *did not.*

die¹ /daɪ/ *v.i.* (**died, dying**) **1.** to cease to live; undergo the complete and permanent cessation of all vital functions. **2.** (of something inanimate) to cease to exist: *the secret died with him.* **3.** to lose force, strength, or active qualities: *traditions die slowly.* **4.** to cease to function; stop: *the engine died.* **5.** to pass gradually: *the echoes slowly died.* **6.** *Colloq.* (of an actor, comedian, etc.) to gradually lose the approval or attention of an audience: *to die on stage.* –*phr.* **7. be dying for,** *Colloq.* to desire or want keenly or greatly: *I'm dying for a drink.* **8. be dying to,** *Colloq.* to desire or want keenly to: *I'm dying to see Venice.* **9. die away, a.** to pass gradually away; subside. **b.** (of a sound) to become weaker or fainter and then cease: *the music gradually died away.* **10. die back,** (of a plant, etc.) to wither from the top downwards to the stem or root. **11. die down, a.** to become calm or quiet; subside. **b.** (of a plant, etc.) to die above the ground, leaving only the root. **12. die hard, a.** to die only after a bitter struggle. **b.** (of a belief, theory, etc.) to persist despite all efforts at suppression. **13. die off,** to die one after another until the number is greatly reduced. **14. die on someone, a.** to die, in circumstances where the death leaves a possibly unexpected responsibility or obligation to someone. **b.** to cease to function for someone: *the engine died on me.* **c.** to fall asleep while in the company of someone. **15. die out, a.** to pass gradually away; fade gradually. **b.** to become extinct; disappear, etc.: *they sell ice-creams to die for.* **16. to die for,** *Colloq.* extremely wonderful, desirable, etc.: *they sell ice-creams to die for.*

die² /daɪ/ *n.* (*pl.* **dies** *for defs 1 and 2,* **dice** *for def. 3*) **1. a.** any of various devices for cutting or forming material in a press or a stamping or forging machine. **b.** a hollow device of steel, often composed of several pieces, to be fitted into a stock, for cutting the threads of bolts, etc. **c.** one of the separate pieces of such a device. **d.** a steel block or plate with small conical holes through which wire, plastic rods, etc., are drawn. **2.** an engraved stamp for impressing a design, etc., upon some softer material, as in coining money. **3.** singular of **dice**. *–phr.* **4. straight as a die**, uncompromisingly honest. **5. the die is cast**, the decision has been irrevocably made.

dieback /ˈdaɪbæk/ *n.* a condition of plants observed to start at the outer leaf tips causing gradual yellowing, loss of leaves and progressive lifelessness; may be caused by a variety of agents including salinity, drought, insect damage or plant pathogens such as the fungus *Phytophthora cinnamomi*.

diehard /ˈdaɪhad/ *n.* **1.** someone who resists vigorously to the last, especially a bigoted conservative. *–adj.* **2.** resisting vigorously to the last.

dieresis /daɪˈɛrəsəs/ *n.* (*pl.* **-reses** /-rəsiz/) **1.** the separation of two adjacent vowels. **2.** a sign (¨) placed over the second of two adjacent vowels to indicate separate pronunciation, as in *Alcinoüs*. **3.** *Prosody* the division made in a line of verse by coincidence of the end of a foot and the end of a word. Also, **diaeresis**.

diesel /ˈdizəl/ *n.* **1.** → **diesel oil**. **2.** → **diesel engine**. **3.** a locomotive, truck, ship, motor vehicle or the like driven by a diesel engine.

diesel engine *n.* an ignition-compression type of internal-combustion engine in which fuel oil is sprayed into the cylinder after the air in it has been compressed to about 550°C, thus causing the ignition of the oil, at substantially constant pressure. Also, **diesel**, **diesel motor**.

diesel oil *n.* the oil which remains after petrol and kerosene have been distilled from crude petroleum; used as a fuel for diesel engines and for carburetting water gas; distillate. Also, **diesel**, **dieseline**, **gas oil**.

diet[1] /ˈdaɪət/ *n.* **1.** food considered in terms of its qualities, composition, and its effects on health: *milk is a wholesome article of diet.* **2.** a particular selection of food, especially as prescribed to improve the physical condition, regulate weight, or cure a disease. **3.** the usual or regular food or foods a person eats most frequently. **4.** anything that is habitually provided. *–v.i.* (**-eted, -eting**) **5.** to select or limit the food one eats to improve one's physical condition or lose weight. *–phr.* **6. be on a diet**, to be following a prescribed diet, especially so as to lose weight. *–***dieter**, *n.* *–***dietary**, *adj.*

diet[2] /ˈdaɪət/ *n.* (*sometimes upper case*) the legislative body of certain countries, as Japan.

dietitian /daɪəˈtɪʃən/ *n.* someone versed in the regulation of diet, or in the planning or supervision of meals. Also, **dietician**.

differ /ˈdɪfə/ *v.i.* **1.** (sometimes fol. by *from* or *between*) to be unlike, dissimilar, or distinct in nature or qualities. **2.** (sometimes fol. by *with* or *from*) to disagree in opinion, belief, etc.; be at variance.

difference /ˈdɪfrəns/ *n.* **1.** the state or relation of being different; dissimilarity. **2.** an instance or point of unlikeness or dissimilarity. **3.** a significant change in or effect upon a situation. **4.** a distinguishing characteristic; distinctive quality or feature. **5.** the degree in which one person or thing differs from another. **6.** a disagreement in opinion; dispute; quarrel. **7.** *Maths* the amount by which one quantity is greater or less than another. **8.** *Logic* a differentia. *–phr.* **9. split the difference**, **a.** to compromise. **b.** to divide the remainder equally.

different /ˈdɪfrənt/ *adj.* **1.** differing in character; having unlike qualities; dissimilar. **2.** not identical; separate or distinct. **3.** various; several. **4.** unusual; not ordinary; striking. *–***differently**, *adv.*

differential /dɪfəˈrɛnʃəl/ *adj.* **1.** of or relating to difference or diversity. **2.** constituting a difference; distinguishing; distinctive: *a differential feature.* **3.** exhibiting or depending upon a difference or distinction. *–n.* **4.** *Machinery* an epicyclic train of gears designed to permit two or more shafts to revolve at different speeds when driven by a third shaft; especially a set of gears in a car which permit the driving wheels to revolve at different speeds when the car is turning. *–***differentially**, *adv.*

differentiate /dɪfəˈrɛnʃieɪt/ *v.t.* **1.** to mark off by differences: *his colouring differentiates him from his brother.* **2.** to see the difference in or between; discriminate: *I can differentiate him from his brother.* **3.** *Maths* to obtain the derivative of. *–v.i.* **4.** to change in character. **5.** to make a distinction; discriminate: *I can differentiate between the two.* **6.** *Biol.* (of cells or tissues) to develop from generalised to specialised kinds. *–***differentiation** /dɪfərɛnʃiˈeɪʃən/, *n.* *–***differentiator**, *n.*

difficult /ˈdɪfəkəlt/ *adj.* **1.** hard to do, perform, or accomplish; not easy; requiring much effort: *a difficult task.* **2.** hard to understand or solve: *a difficult problem.* **3.** hard to deal with or get on with. **4.** hard to please or induce. **5.** disadvantageous; hampering; involving hardships. *–***difficultly**, *adv.*

difficulty /ˈdɪfəkəlti/ *n.* (*pl.* **-ties**) **1.** the fact or condition of being difficult. **2.** (*oft. pl.*) an embarrassing situation, especially of financial affairs. **3.** (a cause of) trouble. **4.** unwillingness; reluctance. **5.** something which is hard to do, understand, etc.: *English is my difficulty.*

diffident /ˈdɪfədənt/ *adj.* lacking confidence in one's own ability, worth, or fitness; timid; shy. *–***diffidence**, *n.* *–***diffidently**, *adv.*

diffract /dəˈfrækt/ *v.t.* to break up or bend by diffraction.

diffraction /dəˈfrækʃən/ *n.* **1.** a modification that light or other radiation undergoes when it passes by the edge of an opaque body, or is sent through small apertures, resulting in the formation of a series of light and dark bands, prismatic colours, or spectra. This effect is an interference phenomenon due to the wave nature of radiation. **2.** the analogous modification produced upon soundwaves when passing by the edge of a building or other large body.

diffuse *v.t.* /dəˈfjuz/ **1.** to pour out or spread (something). *–v.i.* /dəˈfjuz/ **2.** to spread. **3.** *Physics* to mix, move, or spread by diffusion. *–adj.* /dəˈfjus/ **4.** widely spread or scattered. **5.** marked by unnecessary length in speech or writing; wordy. *–***diffusely** /dəˈfjusli/, *adv.* *–***diffuseness**, *n.* *–***diffuser**, **diffusor**, *n.*

diffusion /dəˈfjuʒən/ *n.* **1.** the act of diffusing. **2.** the state of being diffused. **3.** diffuseness or prolixity of speech or writing. **4.** *Physics* the gradual permeation of any region by a fluid, owing to the thermal agitation of its particles or molecules. **5.** *Anthrop.*, *Sociology* the transmission of elements from one culture to another.

dig[1] /dɪg/ *verb* (**dug**, **digging**) *–v.i.* **1.** to break up, turn over, or remove earth, etc., as with a spade; make an excavation. **2.** to make one's way by, or as by, digging. *–v.t.* **3.** to penetrate and loosen (the ground) with a spade, etc. **4.** to make (a hole, tunnel, etc.) by removing material. *–n.* **5.** a thrust; poke. **6.** a cutting, sarcastic remark. **7.** an archaeological site undergoing excavation. **8.** *Cricket* an innings. *–phr.* **9. dig in, a.** to dig trenches, as in order to defend a position in battle. **b.** to maintain one's position or opinion firmly. **c.** *Colloq.* to apply oneself vigorously. **d.** *Colloq.* to begin to eat heartily. **10. dig into, a.** to thrust, plunge, or force into: *he dug his heel into the ground.* **b.** *Colloq.* to apply oneself vigorously to (work, eating, etc.). **11. dig up, a.** to break up and turn over with a spade: *to dig up the* *soil.* **b.** Also, **dig out**. to obtain and remove by digging. **c.** to find or discover by effort or search.

dig[2] /dɪg/ *v.t. Colloq.* **1.** to like, understand or appreciate. **2.** to take notice of; pay attention to.

digest *v.t.* /dəˈdʒɛst, daɪ-/ **1.** to prepare (food) in the stomach and intestines for use by the body. **2.** to take in mentally; think over: *to digest information.* **3.** to shorten considerably; summarise. *–v.i.* /dəˈdʒɛst, daɪ-/ **4.** to digest food. **5.** to be digested as food. *–n.* /ˈdaɪdʒɛst/ **6.** a collection of written matter, often summarised, as a group of laws. **–digestedly**, *adv.* **–digestedness**, *n.* **–digestible** /dəˈdʒɛstəbəl/, *adj.* **–digestive**, *adj.*

digestion /dəˈdʒɛstʃən, daɪ-/ *n. Physiol.* the process by which food is digested.

digger /ˈdɪgə/ *n.* **1.** a tool, part of a machine, etc., for digging. **2.** a miner, especially a gold miner. **3.** *Colloq.* an Australian or New Zealand soldier, especially one who served in World War I. **4.** *Aust., NZ Colloq.* (a term of address among men) cobber; mate. **5.** *NZ Prison Colloq.* a punishment cell.

diggings /ˈdɪgɪŋz/ *pl. n.* **1.** a place where digging is carried on. **2.** a mining operation or locality. **3.** that which is dug out. **4.** *Colloq.* living quarters; lodgings.

digiscope camera *n.* a digital camera fitted to a spotting scope.

digit /ˈdɪdʒət/ *n.* **1.** a finger or toe. **2.** any of the Arabic figures 0, 1…9.

digital /ˈdɪdʒətəl/ *adj.* **1.** of or relating to a digit or finger. **2.** of or relating to digits or numerals. **3.** *Electronics* of or relating to information represented by patterns made up from qualities existing in two states only, on and off, as pulses (opposed to *analog*): *digital signals.* **4.** of or relating to a device which represents a variable as a series of digits, as a digital watch which shows passing time by a series of changing numbers, or a digital tuner which similarly shows the frequencies to which it is being tuned. Compare **analog. 5.** involving or relating to the use of computer technology: *a digital device.* **–digitally**, *adv.*

digital audio *n.* a system of recording and reproduction of sound which is based on digital encoding.

digital broadcasting *n.* broadcasting by the use of digitally compressed signals which are decoded by a specifically designed receiver (opposed to *analog broadcasting*).

digital camera *n.* a camera which stores pictures as digital files.

digital computer *n.* a type of computer in which data is entered as discrete units of information, usually as numbers, characters, etc., represented by on-off states of voltages. Compare **analog computer**.

digital display *n.* a display in which information is represented in digital rather than analog form; readout.

digital fingerprint *n.* **1.** a digitised image of a fingerprint. **2.** the particular digital information that constitutes a web browser identification, as information about cookies, plug-ins, etc., which can be traced to the user. **–digital fingerprinting**, *n.*

digital immigrant *n.* a person who has acquired the skills to deal with digital technology in their adult life. Compare **digital native**.

digitalis /dɪdʒəˈtaləs/ *n.* **1.** any plant of the genus *Digitalis*, especially the common foxglove, *D. purpurea.* **2.** the dried leaves of the common foxglove, used in medicine, especially as a heart stimulant.

digital native *n.* a person who grows up using digital media and communications systems, and thus has complete familiarity with them. Compare **digital immigrant**.

digital recording *n.* **1.** a recording method in which the sound (the audio wave form) is sampled at regular

frequent intervals, usually between 40 000 and 50 000 times per second, and each sample is assigned a numerical value, usually expressed in binary notation. **2.** a recording produced by the process of digital recording.

digital signature *n.* a unique code, in the form of a series of characters, used to verify the identity of the creator or sender of an electronic document, and to ensure that the document has not been altered before reaching the receiver. Also, **e-signature**.

digital-to-analog converter *n.* an electronic device for converting digital signals to analog signals. **–digital-to-analog conversion**, *n.*

digital TV *n.* the technology of sending and receiving television images and sound as digitally-encoded signals. See **HDTV**, **SDTV**. Also, **digital television**, **DTV**.

digital watermark *n.* a copyright notice or other verification which is embedded in digital audio, video or images, which may or may not be visible or audible.

dignified /ˈdɪgnəfaɪd/ *adj.* marked by dignity of aspect or manner; noble; stately: *dignified conduct.* **–dignifiedly**, *adv.*

dignify /ˈdɪgnəfaɪ/ *v.t.* (**-fied**, **-fying**) **1.** to confer honour or dignity upon; honour; ennoble. **2.** to give high-sounding title or name to; confer unmerited distinction upon.

dignitary /ˈdɪgnətri, -nətəri/ *n.* (*pl.* **-ries**) someone who holds a high rank or office, especially in a government or religious organisation.

dignity /ˈdɪgnəti/ *n.* (*pl.* **-ties**) **1.** nobleness of manner or style; stateliness. **2.** nobleness of mind; worthiness. **3.** high rank or title. **4.** degree of excellence or rank. **5.** sense of self-importance or self-respect.

digraph /ˈdaɪgræf, -graf/ *n.* a pair of letters representing a single speech sound, as *ea* in *meat*, or *th* in *path*.

digress /daɪˈgrɛs/ *v.i.* to deviate or wander away from the main purpose in speaking or writing, or from the principal line of argument, study, etc. **–digresser**, *n.*

dike[1] /daɪk/ *n.*, *v.t.* → **dyke**[1].

dike[2] /daɪk/ *n.* → **dyke**[2].

dilapidated /dəˈlæpədeɪtəd/ *adj.* reduced to, or fallen into, ruin or decay.

dilate /daɪˈleɪt, də-/ *v.t.* **1.** to make wider or larger; cause to expand. *–v.i.* **2.** to spread out; expand. *–phr.* **3. dilate on** (or **upon**), to speak about at length; expatiate on. **–dilatability** /daɪˌleɪtəˈbɪləti, də-/, *n.* **–dilatable**, *adj.* **–dilation**, *n.* **–dilator**, *n.*

dilatory /ˈdɪlətri, -təri/ *adj.* **1.** inclined to delay or procrastinate; slow; tardy; not prompt. **2.** intended to bring about delay, gain time, or defer decision: *a dilatory strategy.* **–dilatorily**, *adv.* **–dilatoriness**, *n.*

dilemma /dəˈlɛmə, daɪ-/ *n.* **1.** a situation requiring a choice between equally undesirable alternatives; an embarrassing or perplexing situation. *–phr.* **2. on the horns of a dilemma**, in a difficult situation in which the way forward is not clear. **–dilemmatic** /dɪləˈmætɪk/, *adj.*

dilettante /dɪləˈtɒnt, -ˈtænt, ˈdɪlətɒnt, -tænt, dɪləˈtænteɪ/ *n.* (*pl.* **-tantes** or **-tanti** /-tanti/) **1.** someone who pursues an art or science desultorily or merely for amusement; a dabbler. **2.** a lover of an art or science, especially of a fine art. *–adj.* **3.** of or relating to dilettantes. **–dilettantish**, *adj.*

diligent /ˈdɪlədʒənt/ *adj.* **1.** constant and persistent in an effort to accomplish something. **2.** pursued with persevering attention; painstaking. **–diligently**, *adv.* **–diligence**, *n.*

dill[1] /dɪl/ *n.* a herb of the parsley family, *Anethum graveolens*, with aromatic seeds and finely divided leaves used as a flavouring in cooking.

dill[2] /dɪl/ *n. Colloq.* a fool; an incompetent. Also, **dillpot**.

dillybag /ˈdɪlibæg/ *n.* **1.** *Aust.* any small bag for carrying food or personal belongings. **2.** a bag made of twisted grass or fibre, traditionally used by some Aboriginal peoples. Also, **dilly**.

dillydally /ˈdɪlidæli/ *v.i.* (**-dallied**, **-dallying**) to waste time, especially by indecision; trifle; loiter.

dilute /daɪˈlut, -ˈljut/ *v.t.* **1.** to make thinner or weaker by the addition of water, etc. –*adj.* **2.** reduced in strength, as a chemical with water added; weak: *a dilute solution.* –**diluter**, *n.* –**dilution**, *n.*

dim /dɪm/ *adj.* (**dimmer**, **dimmest**) **1.** not bright; lacking in light: *a dim room.* **2.** not clearly seen or heard; indistinct: *a dim object.* **3.** not clear to the mind; vague: *a dim idea.* **4.** not brilliant; dull: *a dim colour.* **5.** not seeing clearly: *eyes dim with tears.* **6.** disapproving: *to take a dim view of something.* **7.** *Colloq.* (of a person), lacking in understanding; stupid. –*verb* (**dimmed**, **dimming**) –*v.t.* **8.** to make dim. –*v.i.* **9.** to become dim. –**dimly**, *adv.* –**dimmer**, *n.* –**dimness**, *n.*

dime /daɪm/ *n.* **1.** a silver coin of the US, of the value of 10 cents or $^1/_{10}$ dollar. –*phr.* **2. a dime a dozen**, *Colloq.* extremely plentiful and therefore casually cheap.

dimension /dəˈmɛnʃən, daɪ-/ *n.* **1.** magnitude measured in a particular direction, or along a diameter or principal axis. **2.** (*usu. pl.*) measure; extent; size; magnitude; scope; importance. **3.** an aspect; appearance: *the conference took on a more interesting dimension.* –**dimensional**, *adj.* –**dimensionality**, *n.* –**dimensionless**, *adj.* –**dimensionally**, *adv.*

diminish /dəˈmɪnɪʃ/ *v.t.* **1.** to make, or cause to seem, smaller; lessen; reduce. **2.** *Music* to make smaller by a semitone than the corresponding perfect or minor interval. **3.** to detract from; disparage. –*v.i.* **4.** to lessen; decrease. –**diminishable**, *adj.* –**diminishingly**, *adv.*

diminishing returns *pl. n. Econ.* the fact, often stated as a law or principle, that as any factor in production (such as labour, capital, etc.) is increased, the output per unit factor will eventually decrease.

diminuendo /dəˌmɪnjuˈɛndoʊ/ *n.* (*pl.* **-dos** /-doʊz/) *Music* a gradual reduction of force or loudness.

diminutive /dəˈmɪnjətɪv/ *adj.* **1.** small; little; tiny: *a diminutive house.* **2.** *Gram.* relating to or productive of a form denoting smallness, familiarity, affection, or triviality, as the suffix *-let*, in *droplet* from *drop.* –*n.* **3.** *Gram.* a diminutive element or formation. –**diminutively**, *adv.* –**diminutiveness**, *n.*

dimple /ˈdɪmpəl/ *n.* **1.** a small natural hollow, permanent or transient, in some soft part of the human body, especially one produced in the cheek in smiling. **2.** any slight depression like this. –*v.t.* **3.** to mark with, or as with, dimples; produce dimples in. –*v.i.* **4.** to become dimpled. **5.** to cause dimples to form by smiling. –**dimply**, *adj.*

dim sim /dɪm ˈsɪm/ *n.* a dish of Chinese origin, made of seasoned meat wrapped in thin dough and steamed or fried. Compare **dim sum**.

dim sum /dɪm ˈsʊm, dɪm ˈsʌm/ *n.* **1.** (in Chinese cookery) individual servings of food, as offered during yum cha. See **yum cha**. **2.** → **dim sim**.

dimwit /ˈdɪmwɪt/ *n. Colloq.* a stupid or slow-thinking person. –**dimwitted**, *adj.*

din /dɪn/ *n.* **1.** a loud, confused noise; a continued loud or tumultuous sound; noisy clamour. –*verb* (**dinned**, **dinning**) –*v.t.* **2.** to assail with din. **3.** to sound or utter with clamour or persistent repetition. –*v.i.* **4.** to make a din.

dinar /ˈdinɑ/ *n.* the principal monetary unit of various Arab countries, including Iraq, Jordan, Bahrain, and Kuwait, also of Serbia, and formerly of other republics of Yugoslavia, its value varying greatly from country to country.

dine /daɪn/ *verb* (**dined**, **dining**) –*v.i.* **1.** to eat the principal meal of the day; have dinner. **2.** to take any meal. –*v.t.* **3.** to entertain at dinner. –*phr.* **4. dine at the Y**, *Colloq.* (*taboo*) to engage in cunnilingus. **5. dine out**, to

eat dinner away from home. **6. dine out on**, **a.** to be invited to places where one might not otherwise have gone on the strength of (a particular ability, qualification, etc.). **b.** to entertain with (a particular joke, anecdote, etc.) at a dinner or other social occasion.

ding /dɪŋ/ *v.i.* **1.** to strike or beat. **2.** to sound, as a bell; ring, especially repeatedly. –*v.t.* **3.** to cause to ring, as by striking. **4.** *Aust., NZ Colloq.* to smash; damage. –*n.* **5.** a blow or stroke. **6.** the sound of bell, etc. **7.** → **dent** (def. 1). **8.** Also, **dink**. *Aust., NZ Colloq.* a damaged section on a motor vehicle, bike, surfboard, etc. **9.** Also, **dink**. *Aust., NZ Colloq.* a minor accident with a car, bike, surfboard, etc.

dingbat /ˈdɪŋbæt/ *n.* **1.** *Colloq.* an eccentric or peculiar person. **2.** *Printing* any ornamental typographical symbol used for decoration, text division, etc. –*phr.* **3. the dingbats**, *Colloq.* **a.** delirium tremens. **b.** a fit of madness or rage. –**dingbats**, *adj.*

dinghy /ˈdɪŋi, ˈdɪŋɪ/ *n.* (*pl.* **-ghies**) **1.** a small rowing or sailing boat or ship's tender. **2.** an inflatable rubber boat carried by aircraft, for use in emergencies. Also, **dingy**.

dingo /ˈdɪŋɡoʊ/ *n.* (*pl.* **-goes** *or* **-gos**) **1.** a wild dog, *Canis familiaris*, usually tawny-yellow in colour, with erect ears, a bushy tail and distinctive gait, and with a call resembling a howl or yelp rather than a bark, found throughout mainland Australia, New Guinea and South-East Asia; brought to Australia about 4000 years ago probably by Indonesian seafarers; pure populations endangered by hybridisation with feral domestic dog; native dog. **2.** *Aust.* **a.** a contemptible person; coward. **b.** someone who shirks responsibility or evades difficult situations. –*v.i.* **3.** *Aust.* to act in a cowardly manner. –*v.t.* **4.** *Aust.* **a.** to shirk, evade, or avoid. **b.** to spoil or ruin. –*phr.* **5. dingo on someone**, *Aust.* to betray someone.

dingy /ˈdɪndʒi/ *adj.* (**-gier**, **-giest**) **1.** of a dark, dull, or dirty colour or aspect; lacking brightness or freshness. **2.** shabby; disreputable. –**dingily**, *adv.* –**dinginess**, *n.*

dink[1] /dɪŋk/ *Aust. Colloq.* –*n.* **1.** → **double** (def. 18). –*v.t.* **2.** → **double** (def. 25).

dink[2] /dɪŋk/ *n.* → **ding** (defs 8 and 9).

dinkum /ˈdɪŋkəm/ *Aust., NZ Colloq.* –*adj.* **1.** Also, **dinky-di**. true; honest; genuine: *dinkum Aussie.* **2.** seriously interested in a proposed deal, scheme, etc. –*adv.* **3.** true. See **fair dinkum**. –*interj.* Also, **fair dinkum**, **straight dinkum**. **4.** an assertion of truth or genuineness: *dinkum, that's what happened.*

dinky /ˈdɪŋki/ *Colloq.* –*adj.* (**-kier**, **-kiest**) **1.** of small size. **2.** neat; dainty; smart. –*n.* (*pl.* **-kies**) **3.** *Aust.* a small tricycle. **4.** → **dinghy**.

dinky-di /ˈdɪŋki-daɪ/ *adj. Aust., NZ Colloq.* → **dinkum**.

dinner /ˈdɪnə/ *n.* **1.** the evening meal. **2.** (especially formerly) the midday meal; lunch. **3.** a formal meal in honour of some person or occasion. –*phr.* **4. done like a dinner**, *Aust. Colloq.* completely defeated or outwitted. –**dinnerless**, *adj.*

dinner jacket *n.* a jacket worn by men on formal or semi-formal occasions, differing from tails (def. 14a) in not having the tapering skirts at the back.

dinner suit *n.* a man's suit for formal evening wear, usually black and often worn with a bow tie.

dinosaur /ˈdaɪnəsɔ/ *n.* **1.** any member of extinct groups of Mesozoic reptiles, mostly of gigantic size, known in modern classifications as the Saurischia and the Ornithischia. **2.** something completely outdated.

dint /dɪnt/ *n.* **1.** a dent. –*v.t.* **2.** to make a dint or dints in. **3.** to impress or drive in with force. –*phr.* **4. by dint of**, by means of: *by dint of argument.*

diocese /ˈdaɪəsəs/ *n.* (*pl.* **dioceses** /ˈdaɪəsiz/) the district, with its population, falling under the pastoral care of a bishop.

diode /ˈdaɪoʊd/ *n.* a valve or solid-state device that allows electric current to flow in only one direction through it.

diorama /daɪəˈrɑmə/ *n.* **1.** a miniature scene reproduced in three dimensions with the aid of lights, colours, etc. **2.** a spectacular picture, partly translucent, for exhibition through an aperture, made more realistic by various illuminating devices. **3.** a building where such scenes or pictures are exhibited. –**dioramic** /daɪəˈræmɪk/, *adj.*

dioxin /daɪˈɒksən/ *n.* any of a group of chemical compounds present as contaminants in certain herbicides, especially the highly toxic 2,3,7,8-tetrachlorodibenzoparadioxin (TCDD) present in 2,4,5-T.

dip /dɪp/ *verb* (**dipped, dipping**) –*v.t.* **1.** to plunge temporarily into a liquid, as to wet or to take up some of the liquid. **2.** to lower and raise: *to dip a flag in salutation.* **3.** to immerse (a sheep, etc.) in a solution to destroy germs, parasites, or the like. **4.** to direct (motor-car headlights) downwards, as to avoid dazzling oncoming drivers. –*v.i.* **5.** to plunge into water or other liquid and emerge quickly. **6.** to sink or drop down, as if plunging into water. **7.** to incline or slope downwards. **8.** to engage slightly in a subject. **9.** to read here and there in a book. –*n.* **10.** the act of dipping; a plunge into water, etc. **11.** a liquid into which something is dipped. **12.** → **sheep dip**. **13.** a lowering momentarily; a sinking down. **14.** a soft savoury mixture into which biscuits, potato crisps, or the like, are dipped before being eaten, usually served with cocktails. **15.** downward extension, inclination, or slope. **16.** the amount of such extension. **17.** a hollow or depression in the land. **18.** *Geol., Mining* the downward inclination of a stratum, vein, fault, joint, or other planar surface referred to a horizontal plane. **19.** *Surveying* the angular amount by which the horizon lies below the level of the eye. **20.** the angle which a freely poised magnetic needle makes with the plane of the horizon; inclination. **21.** a short downward plunge of an aeroplane or the like. **22.** *Colloq.* a short swim. **23.** *Prison Colloq.* a pickpocket. –*phr.* **24. dip into one's pocket**, to spend money. **25. dip one's lid**, *Aust.* **a.** to lift one's hat as a mark of respect. **b.** (sometimes fol. by *to*) to offer special respect, honour, or congratulations (often in the non-standard form): *I dips me lid to you.* **26. dip out**, *NZ Colloq., Aust.* **a.** (sometimes fol. by *on*) to remain uninvolved. **b.** to miss out. **c.** to fail: *he dipped out in his exams.*

diphtheria /dɪfˈθɪəriə/ *n. Pathol.* a febrile infectious disease caused by a specific bacillus and characterised by the formation of a false membrane in the air passages, especially the throat.

diphthong /ˈdɪfθɒŋ/ *n.* **1.** *Phonetics* a speech sound consisting of a glide from the articulatory position of one vowel towards that of another, and having only one syllabic peak, as /eɪ/ in *vein*. **2.** a digraph as *ea* in *each*. **3.** a ligature representing a vowel. –**diphthongal** /ˈdɪfθɒŋəl, -θɒŋɡəl/, *adj.*

diploid /ˈdɪplɔɪd/ *adj.* **1.** double. **2.** *Biol.* having two similar complements of chromosomes.

diploma /dəˈploʊmə/ *n.* (*pl.* **-mas**) a document as one stating a candidate's success in an examination or some other qualification, etc., usually of a lower standard or more specialised character than a degree.

diplomacy /dəˈploʊməsi/ *n.* **1.** the conduct by government officials of negotiations and other relations between states. **2.** the science of conducting such negotiations. **3.** skill in managing any negotiations; artful management. –**diplomat**, *n.* –**diplomatic**, *adj.*

diplomatic corps *n.* the entire body of diplomats accredited to a particular nation, usually residing in the capital city of that country. Also, **diplomatic body.**

diplomatic immunity *n.* the immunity from local jurisdiction, taxation, etc., which is the privilege of official representatives of a foreign state.

dipper /ˈdɪpə/ *n.* a container with a handle, used for taking up liquids. –**dipperful** /ˈdɪpəfʊl/, *n.*

dire /ˈdaɪə/ *adj.* **1.** causing or attended with great fear or suffering; dreadful; awful: *a dire calamity.* –*phr.* **2. in dire straits**, in extreme difficulty; in danger.

direct /dəˈrɛkt, daɪ-/ *v.t.* **1.** to guide; conduct; manage. **2.** to give instructions to: *I directed him to do it.* **3.** to command; order: *I directed that he do it.* **4.** to tell or show (a person) the way to a place, etc. **5.** to organise and control the production of (a play or film). **6.** to point or aim towards a place or object. **7.** to address (words, a letter, etc.) to a person. –*v.i.* **8.** to act as a guide or director. **9.** to give commands or orders. –*adj.* **10.** going in a straight line or by the shortest course; straight: *a direct route.* **11.** in an unbroken line of descent; lineal. **12.** without anything or anyone in between; immediate. **13.** going straight to the point; straightforward: *a direct insult.* **14.** (of opposites, contrasts, etc.) complete; exact. **15.** *Gram.* (of a quotation or speech) consisting exactly of the words originally used. **16.** *Elect.* of or relating to direct current. –*adv.* **17.** in a direct manner. –*phr.* **18. sell direct**, (of a company) to sell directly to the customer, bypassing retailers. –**directness**, *n.*

direct action *n.* any method of directly pitting the strength of organised workers or any other large group against employers or government, as by strikes, picketing, sabotage, working strictly to rule, civil disobedience, etc. –**direct-actionist**, *n.*

direct current *n. Elect.* a relatively steady current in one direction in a circuit; a continuous stream of electrons through a conductor. *Abbrev.*: DC, d.c. Compare **alternating current.**

direction /dəˈrɛkʃən, daɪ-/ *n.* **1.** the act of directing, pointing, aiming, etc. **2.** the line along which anything lies, faces, moves, etc., towards a certain point or area. **3.** the point or area itself. **4.** a line of action, tendency, etc. **5.** guidance; instruction; management. **6.** (*oft. pl.*) instructions. **7.** an order; command. **8.** a name and address on a letter, etc. **9.** the decisions of the director in a stage or film production. –**directional**, *adj.*

directive /dəˈrɛktɪv, daɪ-/ *adj.* **1.** serving to direct; directing. –*n.* **2.** an authoritative instruction or direction.

directly /dəˈrɛktli, daɪ-/ *adv.* **1.** in a direct line, way, or manner; straight. **2.** without delay; immediately. **3.** presently. **4.** absolutely; exactly; precisely. **5.** as soon as: *directly he arrived, he mentioned the subject.*

direct mail *n.* the system of marketing goods and services by mailing material direct to potential customers, as by using sales letters, postcards, leaflets, brochures, booklets, catalogues or journals. –**direct mailer**, *n.*

direct mailing *n.* the process of using direct mail. Also, **direct marketing.**

direct marketing *n.* a marketing technique in which the producer bypasses retailers and sells directly to the customer by such means as door-to-door selling, home parties, etc. Also, **direct selling.** –**direct marketer**, *n.*

director /dəˈrɛktə, daɪ-/ *n.* **1.** *Commerce* one of a body of persons chosen to control or govern the affairs of a company or corporation. **2.** the manager of the interpretative aspects of a stage or film production who supervises such elements as the acting, photography, etc. –**directorship**, *n.*

directorate /dəˈrɛktərət, -trət, daɪ-/ *n.* **1.** the office of a director. **2.** a body of directors.

directory /dəˈrɛktəri, -tri/ *n.* (*pl.* **-ries**) **1.** a book or the like containing an alphabetical list of the names and addresses of people in a city, district, building, etc., or of a particular class of persons, etc. **2.** a book containing an alphabetical list of telephone subscribers and their numbers. **3.** any book or list which serves to direct the reader. **4.** Also, (*in some operating systems*), **folder**. *Computers* a defined area on a computer disk used to store files. *–adj.* **5.** serving to direct; directing.

direct selling *n.* → **direct marketing**.

direct taxation *n.* the levying of a compulsory monetary contribution such as income tax, demanded by a government for its support and levied directly on the persons who will bear the burden of it (opposed to *indirect taxation*). Also, **direct tax**.

dirge /dɜdʒ/ *n.* a funeral song or tune, or one expressing mourning.

dirigible /ˈdɪrədʒəbəl, dəˈrɪdʒəbəl/ *n.* **1.** an early airship. *–adj.* **2.** capable of being controlled, directed, or steered.

dirt /dɜt/ *n.* **1.** earth or soil, especially when loose. **2.** any foul or filthy substance, as excrement, mud, etc. **3.** something vile, mean, or worthless. **4.** moral filth; vileness. **5.** abusive or scurrilous language. **6.** unsavoury or malicious gossip. *–adj.* **7. dirt cheap**, *Colloq.* extremely inexpensive. **8.** made of dirt: *a dirt floor*. *–phr.* **9. eat dirt**, to accept insult without complaint.

dirt bike *n.* a motorbike designed for cross-country conditions, built with a high engine and exhaust system, often of especially light construction. Also, **dirtbike**, **trail bike**.

dirty /ˈdɜti/ *adj.* (**-tier**, **-tiest**) **1.** soiled with dirt; foul; unclean. **2.** imparting dirt; soiling. **3.** vile; mean. **4.** morally unclean; indecent. **5.** in possession of illegal drugs, stolen goods, etc. Compare **clean** (def. 16). **6.** *Sport* characterised by roughness, unfairness, and frequent fouls: *a dirty game*. **7.** (of devices capable of producing nuclear reactions) having the quality of generating unwanted radioactive by-products: *a dirty bomb*. **8.** stormy; squally, as the weather: *it looks dirty to windward*. **9.** *Aust. Colloq.* angry. *–verb* (**-tied**, **-tying**) *–v.t.* **10.** to make dirty. *–v.i.* **11.** to become dirty. *–adv.* **12.** *Colloq.* an intensifier: *a dirty big truck*. *–phr.* **13. be dirty on**, *Aust. Colloq.* to be angry with. **14. do the dirty on**, *Colloq.* to behave unfairly or wrongly towards. *–dirtily*, *adv.* *–dirtiness*, *n.*

dirty word *n.* **1.** a vulgar word. **2.** something one doesn't mention because it is as objectionable as if it were a vulgar word: *work is a dirty word around here*.

dis-¹ a prefix of Latin origin meaning 'apart', 'asunder', 'away', or having a privative, negative, or reversing force (see **de-** and **un-²**), used freely, especially with these latter significations, as an English formative, as in *disability*, *disaffirm*, *disbar*, *disbelief*, *discontent*, *disentangle*, *dishearten*, *disinfect*, *dislike*, *disown*, *disrelish*. Also, **di-**.

dis-² variant of **di-¹**, as in *dissyllable*.

disability /dɪsəˈbɪləti/ *n.* (*pl.* **-ties**) **1.** lack of competent power, strength, or physical or mental ability; incapacity. **2.** a condition which restricts a person's mental or sensory processes, or their mobility.

disable /dɪsˈeɪbəl/ *v.t.* **1.** to make unable; weaken or destroy the capability of; cripple; incapacitate. **2.** to make legally incapable; disqualify. **3.** to make inoperative: *they soon disabled the alarm*. *–disablement*, *n.*

disabled /dɪsˈeɪbəld/ *adj.* incapacitated in some way, especially by permanent injury or disease.

disabuse /dɪsəˈbjuz/ *v.t.* to free from deception or error; set right.

disadvantage /dɪsədˈvæntɪdʒ/ *n.* **1.** absence or deprivation of advantage; any unfavourable circumstance or condition. **2.** injury to interest, reputation, credit, profit, etc.; loss. *–v.t.* (**-taged**, **-taging**) **3.** to subject to disadvantage. *–disadvantageous* /dɪsædvænˈteɪdʒəs/, *adj.*

disadvantaged /dɪsədˈvæntɪdʒd/ *v.* **1.** past tense and past participle of **disadvantage**. *–adj.* **2.** low in socioeconomic rank or background: *a disadvantaged suburb*. **3.** deprived of financial security, educational background, opportunity, etc., as a result of discrimination.

disaffect /dɪsəˈfɛkt/ *v.t.* to alienate the affection of; make ill-affected, discontented, or disloyal.

disagree /dɪsəˈgri/ *v.i.* (**-greed**, **-greeing**) **1.** (sometimes fol. by *with*) to fail to agree; differ: *the conclusions disagree with the facts*. **2.** to differ in opinion; dissent. **3.** to quarrel. *–phr.* **4. disagree with**, **a.** to hold an opinion contrary to (someone). **b.** to have a bad effect on: *food that disagrees with you*. *–disagreement*, *n.*

disagreeable /dɪsəˈgriəbəl/ *adj.* **1.** contrary to one's taste or liking; unpleasant; offensive; repugnant. **2.** unpleasant in manner or nature; unamiable. *–disagreeableness*, *n.* *–disagreeably*, *adv.*

disallow /dɪsəˈlaʊ/ *v.t.* **1.** to refuse to allow. **2.** to refuse to admit the truth or validity of. *–disallowable*, *adj.* *–disallowance*, *n.*

disappear /dɪsəˈpɪə/ *v.i.* **1.** to cease to appear or be seen; vanish from sight. **2.** to cease to exist or be known; pass away; end gradually. **3.** (of a person) to go missing, especially as a consequence of abduction or arrest for political reasons, followed by secret imprisonment or murder. *–v.t.* **4.** to abduct, and usually subsequently murder or imprison (a political opponent, dissident, etc.), without making their fate known. *–phr.* **5. do a disappearing act**, (*humorous*) to go away rapidly; depart. *–disappearance*, *n.*

disappoint /dɪsəˈpɔɪnt/ *v.t.* **1.** to fail to fulfil the expectations or wishes of (a person): *his conduct disappointed us*. **2.** to defeat the fulfilment of (hopes, plans, etc.); thwart; frustrate. *–disappointer*, *n.* *–disappointingly*, *adv.*

disappointment /dɪsəˈpɔɪntmənt/ *n.* **1.** the act or fact of disappointing: *he has lost hope because of frequent disappointments*. **2.** state or feeling of being disappointed: *great was his disappointment*. **3.** something that disappoints: *the play was a disappointment*.

disapprobation /dɪsæprəˈbeɪʃən/ *n.* disapproval; censure. *–disapprobative* /dɪsəˈprəʊbətɪv/, *adj.* *–disapprobatory* /dɪsəˈprəʊbətri, -təri/, *adj.*

disapprove /dɪsəˈpruv/ *v.i.* **1.** to be full of censure. *–v.t.* **2.** to withhold approval from; decline to sanction: *the court disapproved the verdict*. **3.** *Obs.* to think wrong or reprehensible; censure or condemn in opinion. *–phr.* **4. disapprove of**, to have an unfavourable opinion of. *–disapproval*, *n.* *–disapprover*, *n.* *–disapprovingly*, *adv.*

disarm /dɪsˈam/ *v.t.* **1.** to deprive of weapons. **2.** to deprive of means of attack or defence. **3.** to divest of hostility, suspicion, etc.; make friendly. **4.** to take out of a state of readiness for any specific purpose or effective use: *to disarm the cabin doors*. **5.** (in an aircraft) to release the locking mechanism on (a cabin door). *–v.i.* **6.** (of a country) to reduce or limit the size, equipment, armament, etc., of the army, navy, or air forces. *–disarmer*, *n.*

disarmament /dɪsˈaməmənt/ *n.* **1.** the act of disarming. **2.** the state of being disarmed, as in fencing. **3.** the reduction or limitation of the size, equipment, armament, etc., of an army, navy, or air forces.

disarray /dɪsəˈreɪ/ *v.t.* **1.** to put out of array or order; throw into disorder. *–n.* **2.** disorder; confusion. **3.** disorder of apparel; disorderly dress.

disassociate /dɪsəˈsoʊʃieɪt, -sieɪt/ *v.t.* → **dissociate**. *–disassociation* /dɪsəsoʊʃiˈeɪʃən, -soʊsi-/, *n.* *–disassociative*, *adj.*

disaster /dəˈzastə/ *n.* **1.** any unfortunate event, especially a sudden or great misfortune. **2.** a total failure, as of a person, machine, event, plan, etc. –**disastrous** /dəˈzastrəs/, *adj.*

disavow /disəˈvaʊ/ *v.t.* to disclaim knowledge of, connection with, or responsibility for; disown; repudiate. –**disavower**, *n.*

disband /disˈbænd/ *v.t.* **1.** to break up or disorganise (a band or company); dissolve (a military force) by dismissing from service. –*v.i.* **2.** to break up, as a band or company. –**disbandment**, *n.*

disbar /disˈba/ *v.t.* (**-barred, -barring**) to expel from the legal profession or from the bar. –**disbarment**, *n.*

disbelief /disbəˈlif/ *n.* refusal or inability to believe.

disbelieve /disbəˈliv/ *v.t.* **1.** to reject as false: *I disbelieve your statement.* –*phr.* **2. disbelieve in**, to have no faith in: *I disbelieve in ready-made solutions.* –**disbelieving**, *adj.* –**disbelievingly**, *adv.* –**disbeliever**, *n.*

disbenefit /disˈbɛnəfət/ *n.* **1.** a disadvantage. –*v.t.* (**-fited** *or* **-fitted, -fiting** *or* **-fitting**) **2.** to disadvantage: *to disbenefit the older community.*

disburse /disˈbɜs/ *v.t.* to pay out (money); expend. –**disbursable**, *adj.* –**disburser**, *n.*

disc /disk/ *n.* **1.** any thin, flat, circular plate or object. **2.** a round, flat area. **3.** the apparently flat surface of the sun, etc. **4.** *Computers* → **disk**. **5.** a gramophone record. **6.** *Zool., Anat.* **a. interarticular disc,** a plate of cartilage interposed between the articulating ends of bones. **b. intervertebral disc,** the plate of fibrocartilage interposed between the bodies of adjacent vertebrae. Also, *Chiefly US,* **disk**. –**discal**, *adj.* –**disclike**, *adj.*

discard *v.t.* /disˈkad/ **1.** to cast aside; reject; dismiss, especially from use. **2.** *Cards* **a.** to throw out (a card or cards) from one's hand. **b.** to play (a card, not a trump, of a different suit from that of the card led). –*n.* /ˈdiskad/ **3.** a person or thing that is cast out or rejected. **4.** *Cards* the card or cards discarded. –**discarder**, *n.*

discern /dəˈsɜn/ *v.t.* **1.** to perceive by the sight or some other sense or by the intellect; see, recognise, or apprehend clearly. **2.** to distinguish mentally; recognise as distinct or different; discriminate: *he discerns good and bad, good from bad.* –*v.i.* **3.** to distinguish or discriminate. –**discerner**, *n.* –**discernible**, *adj.*

discerning /dəˈsɜnɪŋ/ *adj.* showing discernment; discriminating. –**discerningly**, *adv.*

discernment /dəˈsɜnmənt/ *n.* **1.** faculty of discerning; discrimination; acuteness of judgement. **2.** the act of discerning.

discharge *verb* (**-charged, -charging**) –*v.t.* /disˈtʃadʒ/ **1.** to unload (a ship, etc.). **2.** to fire; shoot: *to discharge a gun.* **3.** to give out; emit: *the pipe discharged water.* **4.** to fulfil or perform (a duty, responsibility, etc.). **5.** to dismiss from office, employment, service, etc. **6.** (fol. by *from*) to send away or allow to go. **7.** to pay (a debt). **8.** *Law* **a.** to terminate (an obligation): *to discharge a debt by payment.* **b.** to release (someone) from an obligation. **9.** *Elect.* to rid (something) of a charge of electricity: *a short circuit may discharge a battery.* –*v.i.* /disˈtʃadʒ/ **10.** to get rid of a charge or load. **11.** to give out liquid, etc.: *the wound was discharging.* **12.** to go off; explode: *the gun discharged.* **13.** *Elect.* to lose, or give up, a charge of electricity. –*n.* /ˈdistʃadʒ/ **14.** the act of discharging a ship, load, etc. **15.** the act of firing a weapon. **16.** a sending or coming out, as of water from a pipe; emission. **17.** something discharged. **18.** *Law* **a.** the freeing of someone held by police or in prison. **b.** the termination of an obligation. **19.** the payment of a debt. **20.** dismissal from office, employment, service, etc. **21.** a certificate of release, as from service, responsibility, etc. **22.** *Elect.* **a.** the withdrawing or transferring of an electric charge. **b.** the equalisation of potential difference between two terminals, etc. –**dischargeable**, *adj.* –**discharger**, *n.*

disciple /dəˈsaɪpəl/ *n.* **1.** *Bible* one of the twelve personal followers of Jesus Christ. **2.** any follower of Christ. **3.** an adherent of the doctrines of another; a follower. –**discipleship**, *n.*

disciplinarian /disəpləˈnɛəriən/ *n.* **1.** someone who enforces or advocates discipline. –*adj.* **2.** disciplinary.

discipline /ˈdisəplən/ *n.* **1.** training designed to teach proper conduct or behaviour in accordance with rules. **2.** punishment given to correct and train. **3.** the training effect of experience, trouble, etc.: *the army will be good discipline for them.* **4.** a state of order kept by training and control: *to keep good discipline in an army.* **5.** a set or system of rules. **6.** a branch of learning: *the discipline of mathematics.* –*v.t.* (**-plined, -plining**) **7.** to bring to a state of order and obedience by training and control. **8.** to punish; correct; chastise: *I shall have to discipline him severely.* –**disciplinary**, *adj.* –**discipliner**, *n.*

disc jockey *n.* → **DJ** (def. 1).

disclaim /disˈkleim/ *v.t.* **1.** to repudiate or deny interest in or connection with; disavow; disown: *disclaiming all participation.* –*v.i.* **2.** *Law* to renounce or repudiate a legal claim or right.

disclaimer /disˈkleimə/ *n.* **1.** the act of disclaiming; the renouncing, repudiating, or denying of a claim; disavowal. **2.** *Law* a clause added to legal documents, etc., limiting the application of previous clauses.

disclose /disˈkloʊz/ *v.t.* **1.** to cause to appear; allow to be seen; make known; reveal: *to disclose a plot.* **2.** to uncover; lay open to view. –**discloser**, *n.* –**disclosure**, *n.*

disco /ˈdiskoʊ/ *n.* (*pl.* **-cos**) **1.** a place of public entertainment or a club in which patrons may dance, especially to recorded music. **2.** an entertainment event at which patrons may dance to recorded music: *there's a disco at the school hall on Friday night.* –*adj.* **3.** of or relating to music in the style of that used in discos, characterised by a strong dance beat.

discolour /disˈkʌlə/ *v.t.* **1.** to change the colour of; spoil the colour of; stain. –*v.i.* **2.** to change colour; become faded or stained. Also, **discolor**. –**discolouration** /diskʌləˈreɪʃən/, *n.*

discomfit /disˈkʌmfət/ *v.t.* **1.** to defeat utterly; rout. **2.** to frustrate the plans of; thwart; foil. **3.** to throw into perplexity and dejection; disconcert.

discomfiture /disˈkʌmfətʃə/ *n.* **1.** frustration of hopes or plans. **2.** disconcertion; confusion.

discomfort /disˈkʌmfət/ *n.* **1.** absence of comfort or pleasure; uneasiness; disturbance of peace; pain. **2.** anything that disturbs the comfort. –*v.t.* **3.** to disturb the comfort or happiness of; make uncomfortable or uneasy.

discompose /diskəmˈpoʊz/ *v.t.* **1.** to bring into disorder; disarrange; unsettle. **2.** to disturb the composure of; agitate; perturb. –**discomposedly**, *adv.* –**discomposingly**, *adv.*

disconcert /diskənˈsɜt/ *v.t.* **1.** to disturb the self-possession of; confuse; perturb; ruffle. **2.** to throw into disorder or confusion; disarrange. –**disconcertingly**, *adv.* –**disconcertion, disconcertment**, *n.*

disconnect /diskəˈnɛkt/ *v.t.* to sever or interrupt the connection of or between; detach. –**disconnection**, *n.*

disconnected /diskəˈnɛktəd/ *adj.* **1.** not connected; disjointed; broken. **2.** incoherent. –**disconnectedness**, *n.*

disconsolate /disˈkɒnsələt/ *adj.* **1.** without consolation or solace; unhappy; inconsolable. **2.** characterised by or causing discomfort; cheerless; gloomy. –**disconsolately**, *adv.* –**disconsolation** /disˌkɒnsəˈleɪʃən/, **disconsolateness**, *n.*

discontent /diskənˈtɛnt/ *n.* Also, **discontentment**. **1.** lack of content; dissatisfaction. –*v.t.* **2.** to deprive of content; dissatisfy; displease.

discontinue /dɪskən'tɪnjuː/ *verb* (**-tinued**, **-tinuing**) *–v.t.* **1.** to cause to cease; put an end to. **2.** to cease to take, use, etc.: *to discontinue a newspaper. –v.i.* **3.** to come to an end or stop; cease; desist. **–discontinuation** /dɪskəntɪnjuː'eɪʃən/, *n.* **–discontinuer**, *n.* **–discontinuous**, *adj.*

discord /'dɪskɔd/ *n.* **1.** lack of concord or harmony between persons or things; disagreement of relations. **2.** difference of opinions. **3.** strife; dispute; war. **4.** *Music* an inharmonious combination of musical notes sounded together. **5.** any confused or harsh noise; dissonance. **–discordant**, *adj.*

discotheque /'dɪskətɛk/ *n.* → **disco**.

discount /'dɪskaʊnt/ *for defs 1 and 2, 6–11;* /dɪs'kaʊnt/ *for defs 3–5 –v.t.* **1.** to deduct an amount from the purchase price of (an item): *they are discounting refrigerators this week.* **2.** to purchase or sell (a bill or note) before maturity at a reduction based on the interest for the time it still has to run. **3.** to leave out of account; disregard. **4.** to make a deduction from; allow for exaggeration in (a statement, etc.). **5.** to take (an event, etc.) into account in advance, especially with loss of value, effectiveness, etc. *–v.i.* **6.** to advance money after deduction of interest. *–n.* **7.** the act of discounting. **8.** amount deducted for prompt payment or other special reason. **9.** any deduction from the nominal value. *–adj.* **10.** having, showing or offering a discount or discounts: *discount store; discount price. –phr.* **11. at a discount, a.** *Commerce* below par. **b.** in low esteem or regard. **c.** not in demand. **–discountable**, *adj.* **–discounter**, *n.*

discourage /dɪs'kʌrɪdʒ/ *v.t.* (**-raged**, **-raging**) **1.** to deprive of courage; dishearten; dispirit. **2.** to obstruct by opposition or difficulty; hinder: *low prices discourage industry.* **3.** to express disapproval of: *to discourage the expression of enthusiasm. –phr.* **4. discourage from**, to dissuade from: *cold weather discourages some people from going out.* **–discourager**, *n.* **–discouragingly**, *adv.*

discourse *n.* /'dɪskɔs, dɪs'kɔs/ **1.** communication of thought by words; talk; conversation. **2.** a formal discussion of a subject in speech or writing, such as a dissertation, treatise, sermon, etc. *–v.i.* /dɪs'kɔs/ **3.** to communicate thoughts orally; talk; converse. **4.** to treat of a subject formally in speech or writing. **–discourser**, *n.*

discourteous /dɪs'kɜtiəs/ *adj.* lacking courtesy; impolite; uncivil; rude. **–discourteously**, *adv.* **–discourteousness**, *n.*

discover /dəs'kʌvə/ *v.t.* to get knowledge of, learn of, or find out; gain sight or knowledge of (something previously unseen or unknown). **–discoverer**, *n.* **–discovery**, *n.*

discredit /dɪs'krɛdət/ *v.t.* **1.** to injure the credit or reputation of. **2.** to show to be undeserving of credit or belief; destroy confidence in: *the report is discredited. –n.* **3.** loss or lack of belief, of confidence; disbelief; distrust. **4.** loss or lack of repute or esteem; disrepute. **5.** something that damages a good reputation. **–discreditable**, *adj.*

discreet /dəs'krit, dɪs'-/ *adj.* **1.** wise or judicious in avoiding mistakes or faults; prudent; circumspect; cautious; not rash. **2.** not given to careless talk; restrained. **3.** not flamboyant; unobtrusive. **–discreetly**, *adv.* **–discreetness**, *n.*

discrepancy /dɪs'krɛpənsi/ *n.* (*pl.* **-cies**) **1.** the state or quality of being discrepant; difference; inconsistency. **2.** an instance of difference or inconsistency.

discrete /dəs'krit, dɪs-/ *adj.* **1.** detached from others; separate; distinct. **2.** consisting of or characterised by distinct or individual parts; discontinuous. **–discretely**, *adv.* **–discreteness**, *n.*

discretion /dɪs'krɛʃən/ *n.* **1.** power or right of deciding, or of acting according to one's own judgement; freedom of judgement or choice. **2.** the quality of being discreet; discernment of what is judicious or expedient, especially with reference to one's own actions or speech; prudence. *–phr.* **3. at one's discretion**, as one wishes or decides.

discriminate /dəs'krɪməneɪt/ *v.i.* **1.** to make a distinction, as in favour of or against a person or thing: *to discriminate against a minority.* **2.** to note or observe a difference; distinguish accurately: *to discriminate between things.* **3.** *Electronics* to extract a desired frequency from unwanted frequency components in a radio signal. *–v.t.* **4.** to make or constitute a distinction in or between; differentiate: *to discriminate one thing from another.* **–discriminately**, *adv.* **–discrimination**, *n.* **–discriminator**, *n.* **–discriminatory**, *adj.*

discursive /dɪs'kɜsɪv/ *adj.* **1.** passing freely from one subject to another; wideranging; digressive. **2.** proceeding by reasoning or argument; not intuitive. **–discursively**, *adv.* **–discursiveness**, *n.* **–discursion**, *n.*

discus /'dɪskəs/ *n.* (*pl.* **discuses** *or* **disci** /'dɪskaɪ/) a disc, usually made of wood rimmed with metal, thrown by athletes.

discuss /dəs'kʌs/ *v.t.* to examine by argument; sift the considerations for and against; debate; talk over. **–discusser**, *n.* **–discussible**, **discussable**, *adj.*

discussion /dəs'kʌʃən/ *n.* **1.** the act of discussing; critical examination by argument; debate. **2.** a written or spoken text type or form which offers a balanced presentation of different points of view on an issue.

disdain /dɪs'deɪn/ *v.t.* **1.** to look upon or treat with contempt; despise; scorn. **2.** to think unworthy of notice, performance, etc.; consider beneath oneself. *–n.* **3.** a feeling of contempt for anything regarded as unworthy; haughty contempt; scorn. **–disdainful**, *adj.*

disease /də'ziz/ *for defs 1–3, 5;* /dɪs'iz/ *for def. 4 –n.* **1.** a morbid condition of the body, or of some organ or part; illness; sickness; ailment. **2.** a similar disorder in plants. **3.** any deranged or depraved condition, as of the mind, affairs, etc. **4.** uneasiness; anxiety. *–v.t.* **5.** to affect with disease; make ill.

diseconomy /dɪsə'kɒnəmi/ *n.* **1.** the lack of economy; a faulty economy. *–phr.* **2. diseconomy of scale**, a situation where a manufacturer finds that any increase in capital outlay in plant and machinery results in higher costs per unit of production.

disembark /dɪsəm'bak/ *v.t.* **1.** to put on shore from a ship; land. *–v.i.* **2.** to go on shore; land. **–disembarkation** /dɪs,ɛmba'keɪʃən/, *n.*

disembowel /dɪsəm'baʊəl/ *v.t.* (**-elled** *or, Chiefly US*, **-eled**, **-elling** *or, Chiefly US*, **-eling**) to remove the bowels or entrails from; eviscerate. **–disembowelment**, *n.*

disempower /dɪsəm'paʊə/ *v.t.* to take power or authority away from. **–disempowered**, *adj.* **–disempowerment**, *n.*

disenchant /dɪsən'tʃænt/ *v.t.* to disillusion; make discontented. **–disenchanter**, *n.* **–disenchantment**, *n.*

disenchanted /dɪsən'tʃæntəd/ *adj.* (sometimes fol. by *with*) disappointed

disendorse /dɪsən'dɔs/ *v.t.* to withdraw approval or support from. **–disendorsed**, *adj.* **–disendorsement**, *n.*

disenfranchise /dɪsən'fræntʃaɪz/ *v.t.* **1.** to deprive (persons) of rights of citizenship, as of the right to vote. **2.** to deprive of a franchise, privilege, or right. Also, **disfranchise**. **–disenfranchisement** /dɪsən-'fræntʃɒzmənt, ,dɪsənfræn'tʃaɪzmənt/, *n.*

disengage /dɪsən'geɪdʒ/ *verb* (**-engaged**, **-engaging**) *–v.t.* **1.** to release from attachment or connection; loosen; unfasten. **2.** to free from engagement, pledge, obligation, etc. **3.** to break off action with (an enemy). *–v.i.* **4.** to become disengaged; free oneself.

disentangle /dɪsən'tæŋgəl/ *v.t.* **1.** to free from entanglement; untangle; extricate. *–v.i.* **2.** to become free from entanglement. **–disentanglement,** *n.*

disfavour /dɪs'feɪvə/ *n.* **1.** unfavourable regard; displeasure; disesteem: *the minister incurred the king's disfavour.* **2.** lack of favour; state of being regarded unfavourably: *in disfavour at court.* **3.** an act of disregard, dislike, or unkindness: *to dispense disfavours.* *–v.t.* **4.** to regard or treat with disfavour. Also, **disfavor.**

disfigure /dɪs'fɪgə/ *v.t.* **1.** to mar the figure, appearance, or beauty of; deform; deface. **2.** to mar the effect or excellence of. **–disfigurer,** *n.* **–disfigured,** *adj.*

disfranchise /dɪs'fræntʃaɪz/ *v.t.* → **disenfranchise. –disfranchisement** /dɪs'fræntʃəzmənt, ˌdɪsfræn'tʃaɪzmənt/, *n.*

disgorge /dɪs'gɔdʒ/ *verb* **(-gorged, -gorging)** *–v.t.* **1.** to eject or throw out from or as from the gorge or throat; to vomit; discharge. **2.** to give up unwillingly. *–v.i.* **3.** to disgorge something. **–disgorgement,** *n.* **–disgorger,** *n.*

disgrace /dəs'greɪs/ *n.* **1.** the state of being in dishonour; ignominy; shame. **2.** a cause of shame or reproach. **3.** the state of being out of favour; exclusion from favour, confidence, or trust. *–v.t.* **(-graced, -gracing) 4.** to bring or reflect shame or reproach upon. **5.** to dismiss with discredit; put out of grace or favour; treat with disfavour. **–disgracer,** *n.* **–disgraceful,** *adj.*

disgruntled /dɪs'grʌntld/ *adj.* mildly upset; discontented.

disguise /dəs'gaɪz/ *v.t.* **(-guised, -guising) 1.** to change the appearance of, so as to hide identity. **2.** to conceal or cover up the real state or character of: *she may disguise her intentions.* *–n.* **3.** a covering, condition, manner, etc., that serves for concealment of character or quality. **4.** the make-up, mask or costume of an entertainer. **5.** the act of disguising. **6.** the state of being disguised. **–disguisable,** *adj.* **–disguisedly,** *adv.* **–disguiser,** *n.*

disgust /dəs'gʌst/ *v.t.* **1.** to cause nausea or loathing in. **2.** to offend the good taste, moral sense, etc., of; cause aversion or impatient dissatisfaction in. *–n.* **3.** strong distaste; nausea; loathing. **4.** repugnance caused by something offensive; strong aversion; impatient dissatisfaction. **–disgustedly,** *adv.*

dish /dɪʃ/ *n.* **1.** an open, more or less shallow container of pottery, glass, metal, wood, etc., used for various purposes, especially for holding or serving food. **2.** that which is served or contained in a dish. **3.** a particular article or preparation of food. **4.** as much as a dish will hold. **5.** anything like a dish in form or use, as a goldminer's vessel for washing alluvial gold, a concave antenna for satellite television reception, the larger receptors of radio telescopes, etc. **6.** concave state, or the degree of concavity, as of a wheel. **7.** *Colloq.* an attractive woman or man. *–v.t.* **8.** to fashion like a dish; make concave. **9.** *Goldmining* to swirl (dirt and water) in a pan seeking to separate out the gold: *they dished the stuff all morning.* **10.** *Colloq.* to defeat; frustrate; cheat. *–phr.* **11. dish out,** to distribute; share out. **12. dish up, a.** to put into or serve in a dish, as food: *to dish up dinner.* **b.** to present hastily or carelessly.

disharmony /dɪs'haməni/ *n. (pl.* **-nies)** discord; lack of harmony between persons or things.

dishearten /dɪs'hatn/ *v.t.* to depress the spirits of; discourage. **–dishearteningly,** *adv.* **–disheartenment,** *n.*

dishevelled /dɪ'ʃɛvəld/ *adj.* **1.** hanging loosely or in disorder; unkempt: *dishevelled hair.* **2.** untidy; disarranged: *dishevelled appearance.* Also, *Chiefly US,* **disheveled.**

dishonest /dɪs'ɒnəst/ *adj.* **1.** not honest; disposed to lie, cheat, or steal: *a dishonest person.* **2.** proceeding from or exhibiting lack of honesty; fraudulent. **–dishonestly,** *adv.* **–dishonesty,** *n.*

dishonour /dɪs'ɒnə/ *n.* **1.** lack of honour or respect: *his actions show dishonour to his country.* **2.** shame; ignominy; disgrace: *his actions brought dishonour on his country.* *–v.t.* **3.** to bring shame on; disgrace: *his actions dishonour his country.* **4.** to fail or refuse to honour (a cheque, etc.) by payment. Also, **dishonor.**

disillusion /dɪsə'luʒən/ *v.t.* **1.** to free from illusion; disenchant. *–n.* **2.** a freeing or a being freed from illusion; disenchantment. **–disillusionment,** *n.* **–disillusive** /dɪsə'lusɪv/, *adj.*

disincline /ˌdɪsɪn'klaɪn/ *v.t.* **1.** to make averse. *–v.i.* **2.** to be averse or indisposed. **–disinclination,** *n.*

disinfect /ˌdɪsɪn'fɛkt/ *v.t.* to cleanse (rooms, clothing, etc.) from infection; destroy disease germs in. **–disinfector,** *n.*

disinfectant /dɪsən'fɛktənt/ *n.* **1.** any chemical agent that destroys bacteria. *–adj.* **2.** disinfecting.

disinflation /ˌdɪsɪn'fleɪʃən/ *n.* a reduction of prices, generally with attendant increase in the purchasing power of money.

disinformation /dɪsɪnfə'meɪʃən/ *n.* misleading information supplied intentionally, as in counterespionage.

disinherit /ˌdɪsɪn'hɛrət/ *v.t.* **1.** to exclude from inheritance (an heir or a next of kin). **2.** to deprive of the right to inherit. **–disinheritance,** *n.*

disinhibit /dɪsɪn'hɪbət/ *v.t.* (of an outside stimulus, such as alcohol, a drug, etc.) to remove inhibitions from for a temporary period. **–disinhibition,** *n.* **–disinhibited,** *adj.*

disintegrate /dɪs'ɪntəgreɪt/ *v.t.* **1.** to reduce to particles, fragments, or parts; break up or destroy the cohesion of: *rocks are disintegrated by frost and rain.* *–v.i.* **2.** to separate into its component parts; break up. **3.** (of a person) to lose one's judgement, memory, mental grasp, etc., as through senility. **–disintegrable** /dɪs-'ɪntəgrəbəl/, *adj.* **–disintegration** /dɪsˌɪntə'greɪʃən/, *n.* **–disintegrator,** *n.*

disinterest /dɪs'ɪntərəst, -trəst/ *n.* **1.** absence of personal involvement or bias. *–v.t.* **2.** to divest of interest or concern.

disinterested /dɪs'ɪntrəstəd/ *adj.* **1.** unbiased by personal involvement or advantage; not influenced by selfish motives. **2.** (*not considered standard*) uninterested. **–disinterestedly,** *adv.* **–disinterestedness,** *n.*

disjoint /dɪs'dʒɔɪnt/ *v.t.* **1.** to separate or disconnect the joints or joinings of. **2.** to put out of order; derange. *–v.i.* **3.** to come apart. **4.** to be dislocated; to put out of joint. *–adj.* **5.** *Maths* (of two sets) having no elements in common.

disjointed /dɪs'dʒɔɪntəd/ *adj.* **1.** disconnected; incoherent: *a disjointed discourse.* **2.** having the joints or connections separated: *a disjointed fowl.* **–disjointedly,** *adv.* **–disjointedness,** *n.*

disk /dɪsk/ *n.* a storage unit for computers consisting of a rapidly spinning magnetic disc on which information is recorded by magnetising the surface. Also, **disc.**

dislike /dɪs'laɪk/ *v.t.* **1.** not to like; regard with displeasure or aversion: *I dislike him; I dislike having to work.* *–n.* **2.** the feeling of disliking; distaste: *I have taken a strong dislike to him.* **–dislikeable,** *adj.*

dislocate /'dɪsləkeɪt/ *v.t.* **1.** to put out of place; displace; put out of proper relative position. **2.** to put out of joint or out of position, as a limb or an organ. **–dislocation,** *n.*

dislodge /dɪs'lɒdʒ/ *v.t.* **(-lodged, -lodging)** to remove or drive from a place of rest or lodgement; drive from a position occupied. **–dislodgement,** *n.*

disloyal /dɪs'lɔɪəl/ *adj.* not loyal; false to one's obligations or allegiance; faithless; treacherous. **–disloyalty,** *n.* **–disloyally,** *adv.*

dismal /ˈdɪzməl/ *adj.* **1.** causing gloom or dejection; gloomy; dreary; cheerless; melancholy. **2.** terrible; dreadful. –**dismally**, *adv.* –**dismalness**, *n.*

dismantle /dɪsˈmæntl/ *v.t.* **1.** to deprive or strip of apparatus, furniture, equipment, defences, etc.: *to dismantle a ship or a fortress.* **2.** to pull down; take apart; take to pieces. –**dismantlement**, *n.*

dismay /dɪsˈmeɪ/ *v.t.* **1.** to break down the courage of utterly, as by sudden danger or trouble; dishearten utterly; daunt. **2.** to cause to feel strong displeasure or disappointment. –*n.* **3.** sudden or complete loss of courage; utter disheartenment.

dismember /dɪsˈmɛmbə/ *v.t.* **1.** to deprive of members or limbs; divide limb from limb. **2.** to separate into parts; divide and distribute the parts of (a kingdom, etc.). –**dismemberer**, *n.* –**dismemberment**, *n.*

dismiss /dɪsˈmɪs/ *v.t.* **1.** to direct or allow to leave. **2.** to remove, as from office or service. **3.** *Cricket* to cause (the person or team batting) to be out. **4.** to discard or reject. **5.** to lay aside, especially to put aside from consideration. **6.** *Law* to put out of court, as a complaint or appeal. –**dismissal**, *n.* –**dismissive**, *adj.*

dismount /dɪsˈmaʊnt/ *v.i.* **1.** to get off or alight from a horse, bicycle, etc. –*v.t.* **2.** to bring or throw down, as from a horse; unhorse. **3.** to remove (a thing) from its mounting, support, setting, etc. **4.** to take (a piece of mechanism) to pieces. –**dismountable**, *adj.*

disobedient /dɪsəˈbidiənt/ *adj.* neglecting or refusing to obey; refractory. –**disobedience**, *n.* –**disobediently**, *adv.*

disobey /dɪsəˈbeɪ/ *v.t.* **1.** to neglect or refuse to obey (an order, person, etc.). –*v.i.* **2.** to be disobedient. –**disobeyer**, *n.*

disorder /dɪsˈɔdə/ *n.* **1.** a lack of order or regular arrangement; confusion. **2.** something which is different from usual, especially in physical or mental health. **3.** a public disturbance. –*v.t.* **4.** to destroy the order of. **5.** to upset the physical or mental health of. –**disorderly**, *adj.*

disorganise /dɪsˈɔgənaɪz/ *v.t.* to destroy the organisation, systematic arrangement, or orderly connection of; throw into confusion or disorder. Also, **disorganize.**

disorganised /dɪsˈɔgənaɪzd/ *v.* **1.** past tense and past participle of **disorganise**. –*adj.* **2.** prone to disorder: *a disorganised person.* Also, **disorganized.**

disorientate /dɪsˈɔriənteɪt/ *v.t.* **1.** to confuse as to direction. **2.** to perplex; to confuse. Also, **disorient.** –**disorientation** /dɪsˌɔriənˈteɪʃən/, *n.*

disown /dɪsˈoʊn/ *v.t.* to refuse to acknowledge as belonging or relating to oneself; deny the ownership of or responsibility for; repudiate; renounce. –**disowner**, *n.* –**disownment**, *n.*

disparage /dəsˈpærɪdʒ, dɪs-/ *v.t.* (**-raged, -raging**) **1.** to bring reproach or discredit upon; lower the estimation of. **2.** to speak of or treat slightingly; depreciate; belittle. –**disparager**, *n.* –**disparagingly**, *adv.*

disparate /ˈdɪspərət/ *adj.* distinct in kind; essentially different; dissimilar; unlike; having no common genus. –**disparately**, *adv.* –**disparity**, **disparateness**, *n.*

dispassionate /dɪsˈpæʃənət/ *adj.* free from or unaffected by passion; devoid of personal feeling or bias; impartial; calm: *a dispassionate critic.* –**dispassionately**, *adv.* –**dispassionateness**, *n.*

dispatch /dəsˈpætʃ/ *v.t.* **1.** to send off; put under way: *I will dispatch a letter immediately.* **2.** to put to death; kill. **3.** to carry through (business, etc.) speedily; settle quickly. –*n.* **4.** the sending off of a messenger, letter, etc. **5.** a putting to death; killing. **6.** efficient performance or speed: *proceed with all possible dispatch.* **7.** a state or military communication sent by special messenger. **8.** a news account sent by a reporter to a newspaper. –*phr.* **9. mentioned in dispatches,** named

in military reports for special bravery. Also, **despatch.** –**dispatcher**, *n.*

dispel /dɪsˈpɛl/ *v.t.* (**-pelled, -pelling**) to drive off in various directions; scatter; disperse; dissipate: *to dispel vapours, fear, etc.* –**dispeller**, *n.*

dispensable /dɪsˈpɛnsəbəl/ *adj.* able or liable to be dispensed with or done without; unimportant. –**dispensability** /dɪspɛnsəˈbɪləti/, *n.*

dispensary /dɪsˈpɛnsəri, -sri/ *n.* (*pl.* **-ries**) a place where something is dispensed, especially medicines.

dispensation /ˌdɪspɛnˈseɪʃən/ *n.* **1.** the act of dispensing; distribution; administration; management. **2.** something that is distributed or given out. **3.** a certain order, system, or arrangement. **4.** a dispensing with, doing away with, or doing without something. **5.** *Roman Catholic Church* the relaxation of a law by a competent superior in a specific case directly affecting physical matters. –**dispensational**, *adj.*

dispense /dɪsˈpɛns/ *v.t.* **1.** to deal out; distribute: *to dispense justice; to dispense wisdom.* **2.** to administer (laws, etc.). **3.** *Pharmaceutical* to put up and distribute (medicine), especially on prescription. –*phr.* **4. dispense with, a.** to do without; forgo. **b.** to do away with (a need, etc.). **c.** to grant exemption from (a law, promise, etc.): *not even the prime minister can dispense with the common law.*

disperse /dəsˈpɜs/ *v.t.* **1.** to scatter abroad; send or drive off in various directions. **2.** to spread; diffuse: *the wise disperse knowledge.* **3.** to dispel; cause to vanish: *the fog is dispersed.* –*v.i.* **4.** to separate and move apart in different directions without order or regularity; become scattered: *the company dispersed at 10 o'clock.* **5.** to be dispelled; be scattered out of sight; vanish. –**dispersal**, **dispersion**, *n.* –**disperser**, *n.* –**dispersedly**, *adv.* –**dispersive**, *adj.*

dispirit /dɪsˈpɪrət/ *v.t.* to deprive of spirit; depress the spirits of; discourage; dishearten. –**dispirited**, *adj.* –**dispiriting**, *adj.* –**dispiritedly**, *adv.* –**dispiritingly**, *adv.* –**dispiritedness**, *n.*

displace /dɪsˈpleɪs/ *v.t.* (**-placed, -placing**) **1.** to put out of the usual or proper place: *to displace a bone.* **2.** to take the place of; replace. **3.** to remove from a position, office, etc.

displaced person *n.* a civilian who is involuntarily outside the national boundaries of his or her country.

displacement /dɪsˈpleɪsmənt/ *n.* **1.** the act of displacing. **2.** the state of being displaced. **3.** *Psychoanalysis* the transfer of an emotion from the object about which it was originally experienced to another object; transference.

display /dəˈspleɪ/ *v.t.* **1.** to show; exhibit: *the ship will display a flag; his face displayed fear.* –*n.* **2.** the act of displaying; exhibition; show: *a display of goods; a display of skill.* **3.** an ostentatious display: *a display of wealth.* **4.** behaviour used by birds in communication, often before mating. –**displayer**, *n.*

displease /dɪsˈpliz/ *v.t.* **1.** to cause dissatisfaction to; offend; annoy. –*v.i.* **2.** to be unpleasant; cause displeasure. –**displeasingly**, *adv.* –**displeasure**, *n.*

disposable income *n.* the part of a person's income which remains after the deduction of income tax, etc.

disposable nappy *n.* a commercially-made nappy in which a soft absorbent lining is attached to a fitted plastic covering, the nappy being thrown away after use.

disposal /dəsˈpoʊzəl/ *n.* **1.** the act of disposing, or of disposing of, something; arrangement. **2.** power or right to dispose of a thing; control: *left to his disposal.*

dispose /dəsˈpoʊz/ *v.t.* **1.** to put in a particular or the proper order or arrangement; adjust by arranging the parts. **2.** to put in a particular or suitable place. **3.** to give a tendency or inclination to; incline: *to dispose* *someone to listen.* –*phr.* **4. dispose of, a.** to deal with definitely: *to dispose of the matter.* **b.** to get rid of; dump: *to dispose of a corpse.* **c.** *Sport* to eliminate as a competitor. **d.** to make over or part with (property), as by gift or sale. –**disposable**, *adj.* –**disposer**, *n.*

disposition /dɪspəˈzɪʃən/ *n.* **1.** mental or moral constitution; turn of mind. **2.** mental inclination; willingness. **3.** physical inclination or tendency. **4.** *Obs.* power to dispose of a thing; control. –**dispositional**, *adj.*

dispossess /dɪspəˈzɛs/ *v.t.* **1.** to put (a person) out of possession, especially of real property; oust. –**dispossession**, *n.* –**dispossessor**, *n.* –**dispossessory** /dɪspəˈzɛsəri/, *adj.*

disproportionate /dɪsprəˈpɔʃənət/ *adj.* not proportionate; out of proportion, as in size, number, etc. Also, **disproportional.** –**disproportion**, *n.* –**disproportionately**, *adv.* –**disproportionateness**, *n.*

disprove /dɪsˈpruv/ *v.t.* (-**proved**, -**proving**) to prove (an assertion, claim, etc.) to be false or wrong; refute; invalidate. –**disprovable**, *adj.*

dispute /dəsˈpjut/ *v.i.* **1.** to engage in argument or discussion. **2.** to argue vehemently; wrangle or quarrel. –*v.t.* **3.** to argue or debate about; discuss. **4.** to quarrel or fight about; contest. –*n.* **5.** argumentation; verbal contention; a debate or controversy; a quarrel. –**disputable**, *adj.* –**disputer**, *n.*

disqualify /dɪsˈkwɒləfaɪ/ *v.t.* (-**fied**, -**fying**) **1.** to deprive of qualification or fitness; render unfit; incapacitate. **2.** to deprive of legal or other rights or privileges; pronounce unqualified. **3.** *Sport* to deprive of the right to engage or compete in a match because the rules have been broken. –**disqualification**, *n.*

disquiet /dɪsˈkwaɪət/ *v.t.* **1.** to deprive of quiet, rest, or peace; disturb; make uneasy. –*n.* **2.** lack of quiet; disturbance; unrest; uneasiness. –**disquietly**, *adv.*

disregard /dɪsrəˈgad/ *v.t.* **1.** to pay no attention to; leave out of consideration. **2.** to treat without due regard, respect, or attentiveness. –*n.* **3.** lack of regard or attention; neglect. **4.** lack of due or respectful regard. –**disregardful**, *adj.* –**disregarder**, *n.*

disrepair /dɪsrəˈpɛə/ *n.* the state of being out of repair; impaired condition.

disreputable /dɪsˈrɛpjətəbəl/ *adj.* **1.** not reputable; having a bad reputation. **2.** discreditable; dishonourable. –**disreputability** /dɪsˌrɛpjətəˈbɪləti/, **disreputableness**, *n.* –**disreputably**, *adv.*

disrepute /dɪsrəˈpjut/ *n.* (usu. preceded by *in*, *into*) ill repute; discredit: *this would bring the administration of justice into disrepute.*

disrespect /dɪsrəˈspɛkt/ *n.* lack of respect; disesteem; rudeness.

disrobe /dɪsˈroʊb/ *v.i.* **1.** to undress. –*v.t.* **2.** to undress (someone). –**disrobement**, *n.* –**disrober**, *n.*

disrupt /dɪsˈrʌpt/ *v.t.* **1.** to interrupt the continuity of: *the TV transmission was disrupted.* **2.** to cause disorder in: *to disrupt a meeting.* –**disruption**, *n.* –**disruptive**, *adj.* –**disrupter, disruptor**, *n.*

dissatisfy /dɪsˈsætəsfaɪ/ *v.t.* (-**fied**, -**fying**) to make ill-satisfied, ill-pleased, or discontented. –**dissatisfaction**, *n.*

dissect /daɪˈsɛkt, də-/ *v.t.* **1.** to cut apart (an animal body, plant, etc.) to examine the structure, relation of parts, or the like. **2.** to examine minutely part by part; analyse. –**dissectible**, *adj.* –**dissector**, *n.*

dissemble /dəˈsɛmbəl/ *v.t.* **1.** to give a false semblance to; conceal the real nature of. **2.** to put on the appearance of; feign. –*v.i.* **3.** to conceal one's motives, etc., under some pretence; speak or act hypocritically. –**dissembler**, *n.* –**dissemblingly**, *adv.*

disseminate /dəˈsɛməneɪt/ *v.t.* to scatter, as seed in sowing; spread abroad; diffuse; promulgate. –**dissemination**

/dəsɛməˈneɪʃən/, *n.* –**disseminative**, *adj.* –**disseminator**, *n.*

dissension /dəˈsɛnʃən/ *n.* **1.** violent disagreement; discord; a contention or quarrel. **2.** difference in sentiment or opinion; disagreement.

dissent /dəˈsɛnt/ *v.i.* **1.** (sometimes fol. by *from*) to differ in sentiment or opinion; disagree; withhold assent. –*n.* **2.** difference in sentiment or opinion. –**dissenter**, *n.* –**dissenting**, *adj.* –**dissentingly**, *adv.*

dissertation /dɪsəˈteɪʃən/ *n.* **1.** a written essay, treatise, or thesis. **2.** a formal discourse. –**dissertational**, *adj.*

disservice /dɪsˈsɜvəs/ *n.* harm; injury; an ill turn. –**disserviceable**, *adj.*

dissident /ˈdɪsədənt/ *adj.* **1.** differing; disagreeing; dissenting. –*n.* **2.** someone who differs; a dissenter, especially against a particular political system.

dissimilar /dɪˈsɪmələ/ *adj.* not similar; unlike; different. –**dissimilarly**, *adv.*

dissimulate /dəˈsɪmjəleɪt/ *v.t.* **1.** to disguise or conceal under a false semblance; dissemble. –*v.i.* **2.** to use dissimulation; dissemble. –**dissimulative** /dəˈsɪmjələtɪv/, *adj.* –**dissimulator**, *n.*

dissipate /ˈdɪsəpeɪt/ *v.t.* **1.** to scatter in various directions; disperse; dispel; disintegrate. **2.** to scatter wastefully or extravagantly; squander. –*v.i.* **3.** to become scattered or dispersed; be dispelled; disintegrate. **4.** to indulge in extravagant, intemperate, or dissolute pleasure; practise dissipation. –**dissipater**, *n.* –**dissipation**, *n.* –**dissipative**, *adj.*

dissociate /dɪˈsoʊʃieɪt, -ˈsoʊsieɪt/ *v.t.* **1.** to sever the association of; disunite; separate. –*v.i.* **2.** to withdraw from association. Also, **disassociate.** –**dissociation**, *n.*

dissociative /dɪˈsoʊʃətɪv, -ˈsoʊsiətɪv/ *adj.* **1.** of or relating to dissociation. **2.** suffering from a dissociative disorder. Also, **disassociative.**

dissociative identity disorder *n.* a rare psychotic disorder in which the patient develops several distinct, independent personalities which emerge at different times; multiple personality disorder. *Abbrev.:* DID Also, **dissociative disorder.**

dissolute /ˈdɪsəlut/ *adj.* indifferent to moral restraints; given over to dissipation; licentious. –**dissolutely**, *adv.* –**dissoluteness**, *n.*

dissolution /dɪsəˈluʃən/ *n.* **1.** the act of resolving into parts or elements. **2.** the undoing or breaking up of a tie, bond, union, etc. **3.** *Govt* an order issued by the head of the state terminating a parliament and necessitating a new election. **4.** death or decease. **5.** a bringing or coming to an end; destruction. –**dissolutive** /ˈdɪsəlutɪv/, *adj.*

dissolve /dəˈzɒlv/ *v.t.* **1.** to make a solution of in a solvent: *to dissolve sugar in water.* **2.** to undo (a tie or bond); break up (a connection, union, assembly, etc.). **3.** *Govt* to order the termination of a parliament, usually at a regular interval, or in the event of the government being defeated. **4.** to bring to an end; destroy; dispel. –*v.i.* **5.** to become dissolved, as in a solvent: *sugar dissolves in water.* **6.** to break up; disperse. **7.** to disappear gradually: *the figure dissolved into the mist.* –**dissolvability** /dəzɒlvəˈbɪləti/, **dissolvableness**, *n.* –**dissolvable**, *adj.* –**dissolver**, *n.*

dissonance /ˈdɪsənəns/ *n.* **1.** an inharmonious or harsh sound; discord. **2.** disagreement or incongruity. Also, **dissonancy.** –**dissonant**, *adj.*

dissuade /dɪˈsweɪd/ *v.t.* (sometimes fol. by *from*) to deter by advice or persuasion; persuade not to do something: *dissuade him from leaving home.* –**dissuader**, *n.* –**dissuasion**, *n.* –**dissuasive**, *adj.*

distance /ˈdɪstns, ˈdɪstəns/ *n.* **1.** the amount of space between things or points: *the distance between Sydney and Perth*; *we travelled a great distance.* **2.** the condition or fact of being distant; remoteness: *the distance of*

Sydney from Perth makes communication difficult.
3. any kind of gap or space: *the distance between ideas and action*; *the business has covered a lot of distance in a year.* **4.** the far part of a landscape, etc.: *the distance was covered in haze.* –*v.t.* **5.** to leave far behind, as in a race. **6.** to make distant, especially in feelings: *she distanced herself from them.* –*phr.* **7. go the distance,** to complete something. **8. keep one's distance,** to be reserved or aloof.

distant /'dɪstənt/ *adj.* **1.** far off or apart in space or time; remote: *a distant town.* **2.** separate or apart in space: *a place a kilometre distant.* **3.** far apart in any way: *a distant relative.* **4.** not friendly; reserved; aloof. **5.** to a distance: *a distant journey.* –**distantly,** *adv.*

distaste /dɪs'teɪst/ *n.* dislike; disinclination. –**distasteful,** *adj.*

distemper¹ /dɪs'tɛmpə/ *n.* **1.** *Vet. Science* a disease of animals, sometimes causing death. See **canine distemper, feline infectious enteritis, strangle** (def. 5). **2.** deranged condition of mind or body; a disorder or disease. **3.** ill humour; discontent.

distemper² /dɪs'tɛmpə/ *n.* a water paint used for the decoration of interior walls and ceilings, especially one in which the binding medium consists essentially of glue, casein, or a similar sizing material.

distend /dəs'tɛnd/ *v.i.* **1.** to become stretched, or bloated; to swell, as something hollow or elastic. –*v.t.* **2.** to stretch apart or asunder. **3.** to exaggerate, or magnify the importance of. –**distensible,** *adj.*

distil /dəs'tɪl/ *verb* (**-tilled, -tilling**) –*v.t.* **1.** to purify and concentrate (a liquid) by heating it to vapour, and then changing it back to liquid by condensation. **2.** to extract by distillation. **3.** to separate (*off* or *out*) by distillation: *to distil salt out of water.* **4.** to let fall or give forth in or as if in drops: *to distil wisdom.* –*v.i.* **5.** to undergo distillation. **6.** to fall in drops; trickle; exude. Also, *Chiefly US,* **distill.** –**distillable,** *adj.*

distillate /'dɪstələt, -leɪt/ *n.* **1.** the product obtained from the condensation of vapours in distillation. **2.** → **diesel oil.**

distillation /dɪstə'leɪʃən/ *n.* **1.** the volatilisation or evaporation and subsequent condensation of a liquid, as when water is boiled in a retort and the steam is condensed in a cool receiver. **2.** the purification or concentration of a substance; the obtaining of the essence or volatile properties contained in it, or the separation of one substance from another, by such a process. **3.** a product of distilling; a distillate. –**distillatory** /dəs-'tɪlətəri, -tri/, *adj.*

distillery /dəs'tɪləri/ *n.* (*pl.* **-ries**) a place or establishment where distilling, especially the distilling of alcoholic spirits, is carried on.

distinct /dəs'tɪŋkt/ *adj.* **1.** (sometimes fol. by *from*) distinguished as not being the same; not identical; separate. **2.** different in nature or qualities; dissimilar. **3.** clear to the senses or intellect; plain; definite; unmistakable. **4.** distinguishing clearly, as the vision. **5.** more than usually notable; pronounced; effective: *her book is a distinct enrichment of our literature.* –**distinctly,** *adj.* –**distinctness,** *n.*

distinction /dəs'tɪŋkʃən/ *n.* **1.** a marking of something as different: *the distinction between the two sets of marks is plain.* **2.** the recognising or noting of differences; discrimination: *the distinction made between black and white peoples has had some sad results.* **3.** difference: *the distinction between psychology and psychiatry is not always fully understood.* **4.** a distinguishing characteristic: *he has the distinction of being the only one who always comes late.* **5.** a mark of special favour: *she was given the distinction of appearing on the platform with the leaders.* **6.** marked superiority; note; eminence: *a writer of distinction.* **7.** (in certain

examinations) **a.** a high-level grade or mark, in some systems the highest awarded. **b. high distinction,** an award above distinction.

distinctive /dəs'tɪŋktɪv/ *adj.* distinguishing; serving to distinguish; characteristic. –**distinctively,** *adv.* –**distinctiveness,** *n.*

distinguish /dəs'tɪŋgwɪʃ/ *v.t.* **1.** (sometimes fol. by *from*) to mark off as different. **2.** to recognise as distinct or different; discriminate. **3.** to perceive clearly by sight or other sense; discern; recognise. **4.** to serve to separate as different; be a distinctive characteristic of; characterise. **5.** to make prominent, conspicuous, or eminent: *to distinguish oneself in battle.* **6.** to divide into classes; classify. –*v.i.* **7.** to recognise or note differences; discriminate. –*phr.* **8. distinguish between,** to indicate or show a difference between. –**distinguishable,** *adj.* –**distinguishableness,** *n.* –**distinguishably,** *adv.* –**distinguisher,** *n.* –**distinguishingly,** *adv.*

distinguished /dəs'tɪŋgwɪʃt/ *adj.* **1.** conspicuous; marked. **2.** noted; eminent; famous. **3.** having an air of distinction.

distort /dəs'tɔt/ *v.t.* **1.** to twist awry or out of shape; make crooked or deformed. **2.** to pervert; misrepresent. –**distortion, distortedness,** *n.* –**distorted,** *adj.* –**distorter,** *n.*

distract /dəs'trækt/ *v.t.* **1.** to draw away or divert, as the mind or attention. **2.** to divide (the mind, attention, etc.) between objects. **3.** to entertain; amuse; divert. **4.** to disturb or trouble greatly in mind. **5.** to rend by dissension or strife. –**distracted,** *adj.* –**distractedly,** *adv.* –**distracter,** *n.* –**distracting,** *adj.* –**distractingly,** *adv.* –**distraction,** *n.*

distraught /dəs'trɔt/ *adj.* **1.** distracted; bewildered; deeply agitated. **2.** crazed. –**distraughtly,** *adv.*

distress /dəs'trɛs/ *n.* **1.** great pain, anxiety, or sorrow; acute suffering; affliction; trouble. **2.** acute poverty. **3.** physical exhaustion. –**distressful, distressing,** *adj.* –**distressingly,** *adv.*

distribute /dəs'trɪbjut, 'dɪstrəbjut/ *v.t.* **1.** to divide and bestow in shares; deal out; allot. **2.** to disperse through a space or over an area; spread; scatter. **3.** to divide into parts of distinct character. –**distributable,** *adj.*

distributed database *n. Computers* a database, the various sections of which are located in more than one computer.

distribution /dɪstrə'bjuʃən/ *n.* **1.** the act of distributing: *the distribution of presents made everyone happy.* **2.** the state or manner of being distributed: *an unfair distribution of wealth*; *the distribution of coniferous forests.* **3.** arrangement; classification: *distribution into types.* **4.** anything distributed: *a distribution to the poor.* **5.** the process by which goods reach consumers; process of selling a product: *some quality is lost in distribution.* **6.** *Econ.* **a.** the division of the total income of any society among its members, or among the factors of production. **b.** the system of dispersing goods throughout a community. –**distributional,** *adj.*

distributor /dəs'trɪbjətə/ *n.* **1.** a person or thing that distributes something. **2.** *Commerce* a person or firm engaged in the general distribution or marketing of some article or class of goods. **3.** *Machinery* a device in a multicylinder engine which distributes the igniting voltage to the sparking plugs in a definite sequence. **4.** *Aust.* a major arterial road, usually a freeway, designed to take traffic quickly from the centre of the city towards the outer suburbs. Also, **distributer.**

district /'dɪstrɪkt/ *n.* **1.** a region or locality. **2.** an area of land delineated for some administrative or other purpose.

distrust /dɪs'trʌst/ *v.t.* **1.** to feel distrust of; regard with doubt or suspicion. –*n.* **2.** lack of trust; doubt; suspicion. –**distrustful,** *adj.* –**distruster,** *n.*

disturb /dəˈstɜb/ v.t. **1.** to interrupt the quiet, rest, or peace of. **2.** to interfere with; interrupt; hinder. **3.** to throw into commotion or disorder; agitate; disorder; disarrange; unsettle. **4.** to perplex; trouble. –**disturber,** n. –**disturbing,** adj. –**disturbingly,** adv.

disturbance /dəˈstɜbəns/ n. **1.** the act of disturbing. **2.** the state of being disturbed. **3.** an instance of this; commotion. **4.** an outbreak of disorder; a breach of public peace.

disuse n. /dɪsˈjus/ **1.** discontinuance of use or practice. –v.t. /dɪsˈjuz/ (**-used, -using**) **2.** to cease to use.

ditch /dɪtʃ/ n. **1.** a long, narrow hollow made in the earth by digging, as one for draining or irrigating land; trench. **2.** any open passage or trench, as a natural channel or waterway. –v.t. Colloq. **3.** to get rid of; get away from. **4.** to crash-land (an aeroplane), especially in the sea.

dither /ˈdɪðə/ n. **1.** a trembling; vibration. **2.** a state of trembling excitement or vacillation. –v.i. **3.** to be vacillating; uncertain. **4.** to tremble with excitement or fear. –**dithering, dithery,** adj.

ditto /ˈdɪtoʊ/ n. (pl. **-tos**) **1.** the aforesaid; the same (used in accounts, lists, etc., to avoid repetition). Symbol: " Abbrev.: do. **2.** the same thing repeated. –adv. **3.** as already stated; likewise. –v.t. (**-toed, -toing**) **4.** to duplicate; copy.

ditty /ˈdɪti/ n. (pl. **-ties**) **1.** a poem intended to be sung. **2.** a short, simple song.

ditzy /ˈdɪtsi/ adj. (**-zier, -ziest**) Colloq. flighty; empty-headed; scatterbrained. Also, **ditsy.**

diuretic /ˌdaɪjuˈrɛtɪk/ adj. **1.** increasing the volume of the urine, as a medicinal substance. –n. **2.** a diuretic medicine or agent.

diurnal /daɪˈɜnəl/ adj. **1.** occurring each day; daily. **2.** of or relating to the daytime. **3.** active by day, as certain birds and insects. –**diurnally,** adv.

diva /ˈdivə/ n. (pl. **divas** or **dive** /ˈdivi/) **1.** a distinguished female singer. **2.** → **prima donna.**

Divali /diˈvali/ n. → **Deepavali.** Also, **Diwali.**

divan /dəˈvæn/ n. **1.** a low bed with no headboard or tailboard. **2.** a sofa or couch, especially one that can be converted into a bed for occasional use. **3.** (formerly) a council of state in Turkey and other Middle Eastern countries.

dive /daɪv/ v.i. (**dived** or, Chiefly US, **dove, dived,** diving) **1.** to plunge, especially head first, into water, etc. **2.** to go below the surface of the water, as a submarine, scuba diver, etc. **3.** (of an aeroplane) to descend steeply. **4.** to dart; go out of sight: the thief dived behind the cupboard. **5.** to decline rapidly: sales dived in October. –n. **6.** the act of diving. **7.** an instance of diving: he scored highly for that dive. **8.** a session of diving, for work or sport: we have a dive arranged for tomorrow morning. **9.** a sharp drop or fall: profits took a dive this week. **10.** Colloq. a disreputable place, as for drinking, gambling, etc. –phr. **11. dive into, a.** to penetrate suddenly into anything, as with the hand: to dive into one's pockets. **b.** to enter deeply into a subject, business, etc.: to dive into politics. **12. take a dive,** Soccer, Rugby Football, Aust. Rules to fall deliberately to the ground, pretending to be fouled by an opponent.

diver /ˈdaɪvə/ n. **1.** a person or thing that dives. **2.** someone who makes a business of diving, as for pearl oysters, to examine sunken vessels, etc. **3.** any of various birds which habitually dive, as loons, grebes, etc.

diverge /daɪˈvɜdʒ/ v.i. **1.** to move or lie in different directions from a common point; branch off. **2.** to differ in opinion or character; deviate. **3.** to digress, from a plan, discussion, etc. –**divergent,** adj. –**divergence,** n.

diverse /daɪˈvɜs, ˈdaɪvɜs, dəˈvɜs/ adj. **1.** of a different kind, form, character, etc.; unlike. **2.** of various kinds or forms; multiform. –**diversely,** adv. –**diverseness,** n.

diversify /daɪˈvɜsəfaɪ, də-/ verb (**-fied, -fying**) –v.t. **1.** to make diverse, as in form or character; give variety or diversity to; variegate. **2.** to vary (investments); invest in different types of (securities). –v.i. **3.** to extend one's activities, especially in business, over more than one field. –**diversified,** adj. –**diversification,** n. –**diversifiable,** adj.

diversion /dəˈvɜʒən, daɪ-/ n. **1.** the act of diverting or turning aside, as from a course. **2.** a compulsory detour on a road or motorway, to avoid an obstacle, bottleneck, etc. **3.** distraction from business, care, etc.; recreation; entertainment; amusement; a pastime. **4.** Mil. a feint intended to draw off attention from the point of main attack. –**diversionary, diversional,** adj.

diversity /dəˈvɜsəti, daɪ-/ n. (pl. **-ties**) **1.** the state or fact of being diverse; difference; unlikeness. **2.** variety; multiformity. **3.** a point of difference.

divert /dəˈvɜt, daɪ-/ v.t. **1.** to turn aside from a path or course; deflect. **2.** to set (traffic) on a detour. **3.** to draw off to a different object, purpose, etc. **4.** to distract from serious occupation; entertain or amuse. –**diverter,** n. –**divertible,** adj.

diverticulum /daɪvəˈtɪkjələm/ n. (pl. **-la** /-lə/) Anat. a blind tubular sac or process, branching off from a canal or cavity, as the intestine. –**diverticular,** adj.

divest /daɪˈvɛst/ v.t. **1.** to strip of clothing, etc.; disrobe. **2.** to strip or deprive of anything; dispossess.

divide /dəˈvaɪd/ v.t. **1.** to separate into parts; split up: a river divides the city; all that backbiting has divided the staff. **2.** to separate or part from each other or from something else; sunder; cut off. **3.** to deal in parts; share; apportion: to divide a cake; divide an estate; to divide time between work and play. **4.** to separate in opinion or feeling; cause to disagree: the tax issue divided Parliament. **5.** to classify: zoologists divide animals into families. **6.** Maths to separate into equal parts by the process of division: to divide 16 by 4. **7.** Parliamentary Procedure to separate (a legislature, etc.) into two groups to find out the vote on a question. –v.i. **8.** to become divided or separated: to divide into four parts; the staff divided over the issue. **9.** to branch; diverge; fork: the road divides three kilometres out of town. **10.** Maths to do division. **11.** Parliamentary Procedure to vote by separating into two groups. –n. **12.** Geog. a watershed: the Great Divide.

dividend /ˈdɪvədɛnd/ n. **1.** Maths a number to be divided by another number (the divisor). **2.** Finance **a.** a pro rata share in an amount to be distributed, as of a company's profits to shareholders. **b.** interest payable on public funds. **3.** a payment to creditors and shareholders in a liquidated company. **4.** a share of anything divided. **5.** the totalisator payout on a racing bet. **6.** Colloq. a good result or advantage: the way I'm doing it is paying dividends.

dividend imputation n. a taxation system designed to avoid a double taxation on company profits both at the corporate and at the individual level, by allowing the individual to claim the tax on dividends already paid by the company; franking.

divider /dəˈvaɪdə/ n. **1.** a person or thing that divides something. **2.** (pl.) a pair of compasses as used for dividing lines, measuring, etc.

divine /dəˈvaɪn/ adj. **1.** of or relating to God or a god. **2.** addressed or belonging to God; religious; sacred: divine service. **3.** coming from God: the divine right of kings. **4.** supremely good, great, etc.: a person of divine beauty. **5.** Colloq. excellent: what a divine dress! –v.t. **6.** to discover (water, metal, etc.) by a divining rod. **7.** to discover or tell (something unknown or the future), as by supernatural means; prophesy. **8.** to guess or make out (something) by conjecture: *to divine someone's intentions.* *–v.i.* **9.** to use or practise divination; prophesy. **10.** to have perception by intuition or insight; conjecture. **–divination**, *n.* **–divinely**, *adv.* **–divineness**, *n.*

diving bell *n.* a hollow vessel filled with air under pressure, in which persons may work under water.

diving petrel *n.* any of various short-winged, black and white, pelagic birds of the genus *Pelecanoides*, family Procellariidae, especially the **common diving petrel**, *P. urinatrix*, a small, short-tailed bird, with brown eyes, black beak and cobalt blue legs, common in southeastern Australian seas.

divining rod *n.* a rod used in divining, especially a forked stick, commonly of hazel, said to tremble or move when held over a spot where water, metal, etc., is underground.

divinity /dəˈvɪnəti/ *n.* (*pl.* **-ties**) **1.** the quality of being divine; divine nature. **2.** a divine being; a god. **3.** the science of divine things; theology. **4.** godlike character; supreme excellence.

divisible /dəˈvɪzəbəl/ *adj.* capable of being divided. **–divisibility, divisibleness**, *n.* **–divisibly**, *adv.*

division /dəˈvɪʒən/ *n.* **1.** the act of dividing or the state of being divided; partition: *the division of a country after war.* **2.** a distribution; a sharing-out: *a just division of wealth.* **3.** *Maths* the opposite process to multiplication; the finding of a quantity (the quotient) which, when multiplied by a given quantity (the divisor), gives another given quantity (the dividend). *Symbol:* ÷ **4.** something that divides; a dividing line or mark: *the division between NSW and Qld.* **5.** a section, grouping or category: *all the players under 15 will be in A division.* **6.** a separation by difference of opinion or feeling; disagreement; dissension: *the divisions in our society are alarming.* **7.** *Govt* the separation of the members of a legislature, etc., into two groups, in taking a vote. **8.** a semi-independent administrative unit in industry or government. **9.** a major military unit, larger than a regiment or brigade and smaller than a corps, usually commanded by a major general. **–divisional, divisionary**, *adj.* **–divisionally**, *adv.*

division of powers *n.* *Govt* the formal division of legislative powers between the national and state or regional governments in a federal political system.

divisive /dəˈvaɪsɪv, -ˈvɪzɪv/ *adj.* **1.** forming or expressing division or distribution. **2.** creating division or discord. **–divisively**, *adv.* **–divisiveness**, *n.*

divisor /dəˈvaɪzə/ *n.* *Maths* **1.** a number by which another number (the dividend) is divided. **2.** a number contained in another given number a certain number of times, without a remainder.

divorce /dəˈvɔs/ *n.* **1.** the dissolution of the marriage contract. **2.** any formal separation of man and wife according to established custom. **3.** a complete separation of any kind. *–v.t.* (**-vorced, -vorcing**) **4.** to separate; cut off. **–divorceable**, *adj.* **–divorcer**, *n.*

divorcee /dəvɔˈsi/ *n.* a divorced person.

divot /ˈdɪvət/ *n.* *Golf, Cricket, etc.* a piece of turf cut out with a club or bat making a stroke.

divulge /dəˈvʌldʒ, daɪ-/ *v.t.* (**-vulged, -vulging**) to disclose or reveal (something private, secret, or previously unknown). **–divulger**, *n.* **–divulgence**, *n.*

divvy /ˈdɪvi/ *Colloq.* *–n.* (*pl.* **-vies**) **1.** a dividend. **2.** (*pl.*) rewards; profits; gains. *–v.t.* (**-vied, -vying**) **3.** (sometimes fol. by *with*) to share. *–phr.* **4. divvy up**, **a.** to divide (something) into shares. **b.** to hand over portions as shares: *we'll divvy up tomorrow.*

dizzy /ˈdɪzi/ *adj.* (**-zier, -ziest**) **1.** having an unpleasant feeling of spinning around, with a tendency to fall; giddy; vertiginous. **2.** bewildered; confused. **3.** causing a giddy feeling: *a dizzy height.* **4.** *Colloq.* foolish or stupid. *–v.t.* (**-zied, -zying**) **5.** to make dizzy. **–dizzily**, *adv.* **–dizziness**, *n.*

DJ /ˈdi dʒeɪ, di ˈdʒeɪ/ *n.* Also, **disc jockey**. **1.** someone who plays and announces recorded music, as on a radio program, at a disco, nightclub, party, etc. *–v.i.* (**DJ'd, DJ'ing**) **2.** to perform as a DJ. **3.** to create an improvised piece of music using a recorded piece as a base, mixing it with effects created on vinyl records on turntables. *–adj.* **4.** of or relating to such improvised performances: *DJ mixer; DJ music.* Also, **deejay**.

DNA /di ɛn ˈeɪ/ *n.* deoxyribonucleic acid; one of a class of large molecules which are found in the nuclei of cells and in viruses and which are responsible for the transference of genetic characteristics, usually consisting of two interwoven helical chains of polynucleotides.

DNA analysis *n.* the analysis of DNA especially for identification purposes, as in identifying a corpse. See **genetic fingerprinting**. Also, **DNA testing**.

do /du/ *v.t.* **1.** to perform (acts, duty, penance, a part, etc.). **2.** to accomplish; finish. **3.** to put forth; exert: *do your best.* **4.** to be the cause of (good, harm, credit, etc.); bring about; effect. **5.** to render (homage, justice, etc.). **6.** to deal with as the case may require: *to do meat; do the dishes.* **7.** to solve or find the answer to: *to do a maths problem.* **8.** to cover; traverse: *we did thirty kilometres today.* **9.** to travel at (a specified speed): *the car was doing 50 km/h.* **10.** to serve (a period of time in a prison). **11.** to make; create; form: *she will do your portrait.* **12.** to study: *he is doing German.* **13.** to visit as a tourist or sightseer: *they did Spain last year.* **14.** to spay or castrate (an animal). **15.** *Colloq.* to provide; prepare: *this pub does lunches.* **16.** *Colloq.* to attend, especially with someone else as a social event: *we'll meet after work and do a show.* **17.** *Colloq.* to serve; suffice for: *this will do us for the present.* **18.** *Colloq.* to cheat or swindle. **19.** *Colloq.* to treat violently; beat up: *I'll do you.* **20.** *Colloq.* to arrest; to charge with a specified offence: *to do someone for murder.* **21.** *Aust., NZ Colloq.* to use up; expend: *he did his money at the races.* *–v.i.* **22.** to act, especially effectively; be in action. **23.** to behave or proceed (wisely, etc.). **24.** to get along or fare (well or ill); manage (with; without, etc.). **25.** to be as to health: *how are you doing?* **26.** to serve or be satisfactory, as for the purpose; suffice; be enough: *will this do?* *–v.* (*aux.*) **27.** used in interrogative, negative, and inverted constructions, in imperatives with *you* or *thou* expressed, and occasionally as a metric expedient in verse: *do you think so? I don't agree.* **28.** used to lend emphasis to a principal verb: *do come!* **29.** used to avoid repetition of a full verb or verb expression: *I think as you do; did you see him? I did.* *–n.* **30.** *Colloq.* a swindle. **31.** *Colloq.* a festivity or treat: *we're having a big do next week.* **32.** *NZ* a success: *make a do of something.* *–phr.* **33. can** (or **could**) **do with**, to require or be likely to benefit from: *I could do with more sleep.* **34. can** (or **could**) **do without**, to be better off without: *I could do without your sarcasm.* **35. do a ...**, *Colloq.* to imitate or act in the manner of (someone): *he did a Whitlam.* **36. do away with**, **a.** to put an end to; abolish. **b.** to kill. **37. do by**, to deal; treat: *she did well by her employees.* **38. do for**, *Colloq.* **a.** to accomplish the defeat, ruin, death, etc., of. **b.** to cook and keep house for. **39. do in**, *Colloq.* **a.** to kill; murder. **b.** to exhaust; tire out. **c.** to ruin. **40. do lunch**, *Colloq.* to have lunch with someone, especially as a social or business occasion: *to do lunch with a client.* **41. do one's block** (or **nana**), *Colloq.* to lose one's temper. **42. do one's dough**, **a.** to lose money on a bad buy or bet. **b.** to throw away a last chance. **43. do one's thing**, *Colloq.* to act according to one's own self-image. **44. do or die**, a situation in which one must venture all in the knowledge that the outcome will be either victory or complete failure. **45. do out of,** *Colloq.* to deprive, cheat, or swindle of. **46. do over, a.** to redecorate; renovate: *to do a room over.* **b.** to assault. **47. dos and don'ts,** *Colloq.* rules and regulations. **48. do someone proud,** *Colloq.* to treat someone lavishly. **49. do time,** to serve a term in prison. **50. do up, a.** to wrap and tie up. **b.** to fasten. **c.** to renovate. **51. do without, a.** to dispense with; give up: *I will do without sweets for Lent.* **b.** to manage without; cope without: *we can do without butter since we have margarine.* **52. have to do with,** to be connected with: *smoking has a lot to do with cancer.* **53. make do,** to get along with the resources available. –**doable,** *adj.*

Usage: The different forms of the verb **do** are:
Present tense: I **do,** you **do,** he/she/it **does,** we **do,** they **do**
Past tense: I **did,** you **did,** he/she/it **did,** we **did,** they **did**
Past participle: **done**
Present participle: **doing**
Some archaic forms are also retained:
Present tense: thou **doest** or **dost,** he/she/it **doeth** or **doth**
Past tense: thou **didst**

dob /dɒb/ *Colloq.* –*verb* (**dobbed, dobbing**) –*v.t.* **1.** *Aust., NZ* to betray (someone), as by reporting for a misdemeanour. **2.** *Football* to kick, usually accurately, especially in shooting for goal: *he's dobbed another goal.* –*v.i.* **3.** to report another's misdemeanour. –*phr.* **4. dob in, a.** to report (someone) for a misdemeanour. **b.** to nominate (someone absent) for an unpleasant task. **c.** to contribute money to a common fund: *we'll all dob in and buy him a present.* **d.** to contribute: *to dob in a fiver.* **5. dob on,** to inform against; betray. –**dobber,** *n.*

Doberman pinscher /ˈdoʊbəmən ˈpɪntʃə/ *n.* one of a breed of large smooth-coated terriers, usually black-and-tan or brown, with long forelegs, and wide hindquarters. Also, **Doberman.**

docile /ˈdoʊsaɪl/ *adj.* **1.** readily trained or taught; teachable. **2.** easily managed or handled; tractable. –**docilely,** *adv.* –**docility** /doʊˈsɪləti/, *n.*

dock¹ /dɒk/ *n.* **1.** a wharf. **2.** the space or waterway between two piers or wharves, as for receiving a ship while in port. **3.** such a waterway, enclosed or open, together with the surrounding piers, wharves, etc. **4.** → **dry dock. 5.** a semi-enclosed structure which a plane, truck, etc., can enter for the purpose of loading, repair, maintenance, etc. –*v.t.* **6.** to bring into a dock; lay up in a dock. **7.** to put into a dry dock for repairs, cleaning, or painting. **8.** *Aerospace* to close and lock (one spacecraft) into another while in orbit. –*v.i.* **9.** to come or go into a dock or dry dock. **10.** *Aerospace* to close and lock two spacecraft together in orbit.

dock² /dɒk/ *n.* **1.** the solid or fleshy part of an animal's tail, as distinguished from the hair. **2.** the part of a tail left after cutting or clipping. –*v.t.* **3.** to cut off the end of (a tail, etc.). **4.** to deduct a part from (wages, etc.).

dock³ /dɒk/ *n.* an enclosed place in a courtroom where the accused is placed during trial.

dock⁴ /dɒk/ *n.* **1.** any of various plants of the genus *Rumex,* as *R. crispus* (**curled dock**) and *R. obtusifolius* (**broad-leaved dock**), mostly troublesome weeds with long taproots. **2.** any of various other plants, mostly coarse weeds.

docket /ˈdɒkət/ *n.* **1.** an official memorandum or entry of proceedings in a legal cause, or a register of such entries. **2.** a warrant certifying payment of customs duty. **3.** a receipt: *can I have a docket please?*

dockyard /ˈdɒkjad/ *n.* a naval establishment containing docks, shops, warehouses, etc., where ships are built, fitted out, and repaired.

doctor /ˈdɒktə/ *n.* **1.** a person licensed to practise medicine, or some branch of medicine; a physician or medical practitioner other than a surgeon. **2.** a person who has received a doctorate. **3.** (*upper case*) a conventional title of respect for such a person. **4.** *Aust.* any of various fresh sea breezes that arise in the afternoon or evening during summer, as the Esperance doctor, Fremantle doctor. –*v.t. Colloq.* **5.** to tamper with; falsify; adulterate. **6.** to castrate or spay. –*v.i.* **7.** to practise medicine. –*phr.* **8. go for the doctor, a.** to bet all one's money on a race. **b.** to make an all-out effort that consumes all one's resources or lacks all restraint. **9. just what the doctor ordered,** *Colloq.* something agreeable; the perfect solution. –**doctoral,** *adj.*

doctorate /ˈdɒktərət/ *n.* the highest academic degree awarded in any branch of knowledge.

doctrinaire /dɒktrəˈnɛə/ *n.* **1.** someone who tries to apply some doctrine or theory without a sufficient regard to practical considerations; an impractical theorist. –*adj.* **2.** dogmatic. **3.** theoretical and unpractical. **4.** of a doctrinaire. –**doctrinarism,** *n.* –**doctrinarian,** *n.*

doctrine /ˈdɒktrən/ *n.* **1.** a particular moral or religious principle taught or advocated. **2.** teachings collectively. **3.** a body or system of teachings relating to a particular subject. –**doctrinism,** *n.*

document *n.* /ˈdɒkjəmənt/ **1.** a written or printed paper furnishing information or evidence; a legal or official paper. **2.** *Computers* a file produced by an application, especially a text-based file produced by word-processing software. –*v.t.* /ˈdɒkjuˌmɛnt/ **3.** to furnish with documents, evidence, or the like. **4.** to support with documentary evidence. **5.** to record, give an account of: *an attempt to document the period.* –**documentation,** *n.*

documentary /dɒkjuˈmɛntəri, -tri/ *adj.* Also, **documental** /dɒkjuˈmɛntl/ **1.** relating to, consisting of, or derived from documents. –*n.* (*pl.* **-ries**) **2.** a factual presentation of a real event, person's life, etc., in a television or radio program, film, etc.

dodder /ˈdɒdə/ *v.i.* to shake; tremble; totter. –**doddery,** *adj.*

doddle /ˈdɒdl/ *n. Colloq.* something which can be accomplished with little effort; walkover: *this course is a real doddle.*

dodeca- a word element meaning 'twelve'. Also, (*before vowels*), **dodec-.**

dodge /dɒdʒ/ *verb* (**dodged, dodging**) –*v.i.* **1.** to move aside or change position suddenly, as to avoid a blow or to get behind something. **2.** to use evasive methods; prevaricate. –*v.t.* **3.** to elude by a sudden shift of position or by strategy. –*n.* **4.** an act of dodging.

dodgy /ˈdɒdʒi/ *adj.* (**dodgier, dodgiest**) **1.** artful. **2.** *Colloq.* tricky; awkward; unreliable.

dodo /ˈdoʊdoʊ/ *n.* (*pl.* **-does** or **-dos**) **1.** a large, ground-dwelling bird, *Raphus cucullatus,* of the extinct family Raphidae, formerly inhabiting the island of Mauritius. **2.** *Colloq.* a silly or slow-witted person. –*phr.* **3. dead as a dodo,** *Colloq.* **a.** completely lifeless. **b.** completely inactive.

doe /doʊ/ *n.* **1.** the female of the deer and antelope. **2.** the female of certain other animals, such as the kangaroo, goat, and rabbit.

does /dʌz/, *weak form* /dəz/ *v.* **1.** 3rd person singular present indicative of **do.** –*phr.* **2. that does it,** an exclamation indicating exasperation, defeat, etc.

doesn't /ˈdʌzənt/ *v.* contraction of *does not.*

doff /dɒf/ *v.t.* **1.** to put or take off, as dress. **2.** to remove (the hat) in salutation. –**doffer,** *n.*

dog /dɒg/ *n.* **1.** a domesticated carnivore, *Canis familiaris,* descended from the grey wolf; bred in a great many varieties and commonly kept as a pet. **2.** any animal belonging to the same family, Canidae, including the wolves, jackals, foxes, etc. **3.** the male of such an animal (opposed to *bitch*). **4.** *Colloq.* a despicable man. **5.** *Colloq.* an unattractive woman or man. **6.** *Colloq.* something which is disappointing or unsuccessful: *he's produced some good films as well as a few dogs.* **7.** any of various mechanical devices, as for gripping or holding something. **8.** an andiron. **9.** (*pl.*) *Colloq.* feet. *–v.t.* (**dogged, dogging**) **10.** to follow or track constantly like a dog; hound; worry; plague: *he was dogged by misfortune.* *–phr.* **11. a dog tied up,** *Colloq.* an outstanding account. **12. gay dog,** *Colloq.* a rakish, possibly dissolute man. **13. go to the dogs,** *Colloq.* to go to ruin. **14. lame dog,** an unfortunate person; a helpless person. **15. lead a dog's life,** to have a harassed existence; to be continuously unhappy. **16. let sleeping dogs lie,** to refrain from action which might alter the existing situation. **17. put on (the) dog,** to behave pretentiously; put on airs. **18. the dogs,** *Colloq.* greyhound racing.

dogbox /'dɒgbɒks/ *n. Colloq.* **1.** a compartment in a passenger train or tram to which there is no access by corridor from other compartments within the carriage. **2.** cramped quarters; a very small room or building.

dog-collar *n.* **1.** a collar to identify or control a dog. **2.** *Colloq.* → **clerical collar. 3.** *Colloq.* → **choker** (def. 1).

doge /doʊg, doʊʒ/ *n. Internet* a language style which uses a grammatical structure in which a modifier is linked to another word, commonly a noun or a verb, in a way that does not follow the rules of standard grammar, as in *much eat, so respect, such delicious.*

dog-ear *n.* the corner of a page in a book folded over like a dog's ear, as by careless use or to mark a place. *–***dog-eared,** *adj.*

dogfight /'dɒgfaɪt/ *n.* **1.** a fierce fight between two dogs. **2.** a violent engagement of fighter planes at close quarters. **3.** any rough-and-tumble physical battle.

dogged /'dɒgəd/ *adj.* having the pertinacity of a dog; obstinate. *–***doggedly,** *adv. –***doggedness,** *n.*

doggerel /'dɒgərəl/ *adj.* **1.** (of verse) comic or burlesque, and usually loose or irregular in measure. *–n.* **2.** doggerel verse.

doggo /'dɒgoʊ/ *adv.* **1.** *Colloq.* out of sight. *–phr.* **2. lie doggo,** to hide; remain in concealment.

dogleg /'dɒglɛg/ *n.* **1.** an angle in a road, track, etc., resembling that of a dog's hind leg. *–adj.* Also, **dog-legged. 2.** having such a bend.

dogma /'dɒgmə/ *n.* (*pl.* **-mas** *or* **-mata** /-mətə/) **1.** a system of principles or tenets, as of a church. **2.** a tenet or doctrine authoritatively laid down, as by a church. **3.** prescribed doctrine. **4.** a settled opinion; a belief; a principle. *–***dogmatism,** *n. –***dogmatist,** *n.*

dogmatic /dɒg'mætɪk/ *adj.* **1.** of or relating to a dogma or dogmas; doctrinal. **2.** asserting opinions in an authoritative, positive, or arrogant manner; positive; opinionated. Also, **dogmatical.** *–***dogmatically,** *adv.*

dog paddle *n.* **1.** a simple, very slow swimming stroke, in which the arms and legs are flicked below water. *–v.i.* **2.** to perform this swimming stroke. Also, **dogpaddle.**

dog whistling *n.* **1.** the summoning of a dog using a dog whistle. **2.** *Politics* the making of a public statement designed to appeal to a particular group of voters while drawing no response from the rest of the electorate.

doily /'dɔɪli/ *n.* (*pl.* **-lies**) a small ornamental mat, as of embroidery or lace, paper or plastic, often placed under cakes, sandwiches, etc., on a plate. Also, **doiley.**

dojo /'doʊdʒoʊ/ *n.* a room or hall in which judo, karate, and other martial arts are practised.

Dolby system /'dɒlbi sɪstəm/ *n.* (*from trademark*) either of two systems, Dolby A and Dolby B, by means of which noise is reduced in recording and playback of

magnetic tapes; Dolby A treats all sections of the sound spectrum while Dolby B treats only the high frequency end of the spectrum.

doldrums /'dɒldrəmz/ *pl. n.* **the, 1. a.** the region of relatively calm winds near the equator. **b.** the calms or weather variations characteristic of those parts. **2. a.** a period of dullness, gloominess, etc. **b.** a period of stagnation or inactivity.

dole /doʊl/ *n.* **1.** a portion of money, food, etc., given, especially in charity or for maintenance. **2.** a dealing out or distributing, especially in charity. **3.** a payment by a government to an unemployed person. *–v.t.* **4.** to distribute in charity. *–phr.* **5. dole out,** to give out sparingly or in small quantities. **6. go** (or **be**) **on the dole,** to receive the dole (def. 3).

dole bludger *n. Aust., NZ Colloq.* (*derog.*) **1.** someone who is unemployed and lives on social security benefits without making proper attempts to find employment. **2.** any person on social security benefits.

doleful /'doʊlfəl/ *adj.* full of grief; sorrowful; gloomy. *–***dolefully,** *adv. –***dolefulness,** *n.*

doll /dɒl/ *n.* **1.** a toy puppet representing a child or other human being; a child's toy baby. **2.** a pretty but expressionless or unintelligent woman. **3.** *Colloq.* an attractive woman, especially one who is young. *–phr.* Also, **dolly up. 4. doll up,** *Colloq.* **a.** to dress (someone or oneself) in a smart or ostentatiously stylish fashion: *all dolled up in satin.* **b.** to dress (oneself) up rather too smartly or too much. *–***dollish,** *adj. –***dollishly,** *adv. –***dollishness,** *n.*

dollar /'dɒlə/ *n.* **1.** the principal monetary unit of Australia, divided into 100 cents. *Symbol*: $ *Abbrev.*: AUD **2.** the principal monetary unit of various other countries, as in the US, Canada, Hong Kong, Singapore, Brunei, some countries of the West Indies, etc. *–phr.* **3. big dollars,** *Colloq.* a large amount of money. **4. one's bottom dollar,** the last of one's money: *down to his bottom dollar.* **5. top dollar,** a very high price: *to be prepared to pay top dollar.*

dollarbird /'dɒləbɜd/ *n.* a red-billed, insectivorous bird, *Eurystomus orientalis,* family Coraciidae, found in India, South-East Asia and New Guinea; one subspecies, *E. o. pacificus,* is a summer breeding migrant to northern and eastern Australia. Also, **dollar bird.**

dollop /'dɒləp/ *n. Colloq.* a lump; a mass.

dolly /'dɒli/ *n.* (*pl.* **-lies**) **1.** (*with children*) a doll. **2. a.** a low truck with small wheels for moving loads too heavy to be carried by hand. **b.** *Film, TV* a small, mobile platform for carrying cameras, directors, etc., and often running on tracks. **3.** Also, **dolly bird.** *Colloq.* a woman, especially a young, attractive one, who is not particularly intelligent. *–phr.* **4. up to dolly's wax,** *Aust., NZ Colloq.* up to the neck (where a doll's wax head began), in the sense of full of food.

dolmades /dɒl'madiz/ *pl. n.* (*sing.* **dolma**) blanched vine leaves with a savoury filling such as minced lamb, rice and seasonings. Also, **dolmas.**

dolmen /'dɒlmən/ *n.* an ancient structure, usually regarded as a tomb, consisting of two or more large upright stones set with a space between and capped by a horizontal stone. Compare **cromlech.**

dolomite /'dɒləmaɪt/ *n.* **1.** a very common mineral, calcium magnesium carbonate, $CaMg(CO_3)_2$, occurring in crystals and in masses (called **dolomite marble** when coarse-grained). **2.** a rock consisting essentially or largely of this mineral. *–***dolomitic** /dɒlə'mɪtɪk/, *adj.*

dolorous /'dɒlərəs/ *adj.* expressing pain or sorrow. *–***dolorously,** *adv. –***dolorousness,** *n.*

dolour /'dɒlə, 'doʊlə/ *n.* sorrow or grief. Also, **dolor.**

dolphin /'dɒlfən/ *n.* **1.** any of various cetaceans of the family Delphinidae, some of which are commonly called porpoises, especially *Delphinus delphis,* which has a long, sharp nose and abounds in the Mediterranean and the temperate Atlantic. **2.** either of two fishes of tropical and temperate seas *Coryphaena hippurus* and *C. equisetis*, noted for their rapid colour changes when dying.

dolt /doʊlt/ *n.* a dull, stupid person; a blockhead. –**doltish**, *adj.* –**doltishly**, *adv.* –**doltishness**, *n.*

-dom a noun suffix meaning: **1.** domain, as in *kingdom*. **2.** collection of persons, as in *officialdom*. **3.** rank or station, as in *earldom*. **4.** general condition, as in *freedom*.

domain /dəˈmeɪn/ *n.* **1.** *Law* ownership and control over the use of land. **2.** a field of activity, knowledge, etc.: *the domain of commerce; the domain of science.* **3.** a region with specific characteristics, types of growth, animal life, etc. **4.** *Physics* a small region of ferromagnetic substance in which the atoms or molecules have a common direction of magnetic effect. **5.** *Maths* (of a function) the set of values of the independent variables for which the function is defined.

domain name *n. Internet* the name of a server connected to the internet comprising the name of the host, followed by the domain, such as commercial, academic, news, etc., followed by the country of origin with the exception of the USA.

Domain Name System *n.* a system for naming internet-connected devices or services which adopts a hierarchy of discrete types of information to provide a unique location. *Abbrev.*: DNS

dome /doʊm/ *n.* **1.** *Archit.* a large, hemispherical, approximately hemispherical, or spheroidal vault, its form produced by rotating an arch on its radius or vertical radius. **2.** anything shaped like a dome. **3.** *Colloq.* a person's head. –*v.i.* **4.** to rise or swell as a dome. –**domelike**, *adj.*

domestic /dəˈmɛstɪk/ *adj.* **1.** of or relating to the home, the household, or family. **2.** enjoying home life or matters. **3.** living with humans; tame: *domestic animals.* **4.** belonging, existing, or produced within a country; not foreign. –*n.* **5.** a hired household servant. **6.** *Colloq.* an argument with one's spouse or another member of the household. –**domestically**, *adv.*

domesticate /dəˈmɛstəkeɪt/ *v.t.* **1.** to convert to domestic uses; tame. **2.** to attach to home life or affairs. **3.** to cause to be or feel at home; naturalise. –**domestication** /dəmɛstəˈkeɪʃən/, *n.* –**domesticator**, *n.*

domesticated /dəˈmɛstəkeɪtəd/ *adj.* **1.** (of a species or an individual animal) tamed and adapted for use in agriculture, or as a companion animal, etc. **2.** (of a person) adept at household tasks as cooking, cleaning, etc.

domesticity /ˌdɒmɛsˈtɪsəti/ *n.* the state of being domesticated; domestic or home life.

domestic violence *n. Law* violence committed or threatened by one member of a household against the person or property of another, as co-tenants or people in shared housing. Compare **family violence**.

domicile /ˈdɒməsaɪl/ *n.* **1.** a place of residence; an abode; a house or home. **2.** *Law* a permanent legal residence. –*v.i.* **3.** (sometimes fol. by *at, in,* etc.) to have one's domicile; dwell.

dominant /ˈdɒmənənt/ *adj.* **1.** ruling; governing; controlling; most influential. **2.** occupying a commanding position: *the dominant points of the globe.* **3.** main; major; chief: *steel production is the dominant industry in our town.* –*n.* **4.** *Genetics* a hereditary character resulting from a gene with a greater biochemical activity than another, termed the recessive. The dominant masks the recessive. –**dominantly**, *adv.* –**dominance**, *n.*

dominate /ˈdɒməneɪt/ *v.t.* **1.** to rule over; govern; control. **2.** to tower above; overshadow. –*v.i.* **3.** to rule; exercise control; predominate. **4.** to occupy a commanding position. –**dominator**, *n.* –**dominative**, *adj.*

domination /dɒməˈneɪʃən/ *n.* **1.** the act of dominating. **2.** rule or sway, often arbitrary. **3.** Also, **dominion**. *Theology* a member of the fourth order of angels. See **angel** (def. 1).

domineer /dɒməˈnɪə/ *v.i.* **1.** to govern arbitrarily; tyrannise. **2.** to command haughtily; behave arrogantly. **3.** to tower (over or above). –*v.t.* **4.** to rule or command (someone) arrogantly or arbitrarily. –**domineering**, *adj.*

dominion /dəˈmɪnjən/ *n.* **1.** the power or right of governing and controlling; sovereign authority. **2.** rule or sway; control or influence. **3.** a territory, usually of considerable size, in which a single rulership holds sway. **4.** lands or domains subject to sovereignty or control. **5.** a territory constituting a self-governing commonwealth and being one of a number of such territories united in a community of nations, or empire (formerly applied to self-governing divisions of the British Empire, as Australia, Canada, New Zealand, etc.). **6.** *Theology* → **domination** (def. 3).

domino /ˈdɒmənoʊ/ *n.* (*pl.* **-noes**) **1.** (*pl. construed as sing.*) any of various games played with flat, oblong pieces of ivory, bone, or wood, the face of which is divided into two parts, each left blank or marked with pips, usually from one to six. **2.** one of these pieces.

domino theory *n.* a theory that a particular political development or event in one country will lead to its repetition in others, as a Communist takeover of one South-East Asian country leading to a similar takeover of neighbouring countries.

don¹ /dɒn/ *n.* **1.** (*upper case*) a Spanish or Italian title prefixed to the given name of a man of a high rank. **2.** a Spanish lord or gentleman. **3.** a person of great importance. **4.** (in British universities) a head, fellow, or tutor of a college. **5.** the leader of a Mafia family.

don² /dɒn/ *v.t.* to put on (clothing, etc.).

donate /doʊˈneɪt, ˈdoʊneɪt/ *v.t.* (**-nated, -nating**) **1.** to present as a gift; make a gift or donation of, as to a fund or cause. **2.** to provide, as a donor (def. 2) (an organ, sperm, etc.) to another person. –**donator**, *n.* –**donation**, *n.*

done /dʌn/ *v.* **1.** past participle of **do**. –*adj.* **2.** executed; completed; finished; settled. **3.** cooked. **4.** worn out; used up. **5.** in conformity with fashion and good taste. –*interj.* **6.** an exclamation signifying that something has been agreed upon, settled, etc. –*phr.* **7. done and dusted**, completed in every last detail. **8. done for**, *Colloq.* **a.** dead. **b.** close to death. **c.** utterly exhausted. **d.** deprived of one's means of livelihood, etc.; ruined. **9. done in**, *Colloq.* very tired; exhausted. **10. done out of**, *Colloq.* cheated of. **11. done to death**, *Colloq.* hackneyed; trite. **12. done up**, *Colloq.* **a.** dressed in a way that is too formal or showy for the occasion or in contrast with one's usual more casual style. **b.** finished; ruined. **13. get done**, *Colloq.* to be beaten, as in a contest or fight: *the Tigers got done last Saturday.* **14. have** (or **be**) **done with**, to finish relations or connections with. **15. not done**, generally frowned upon; not acceptable.

doner kebab /ˈdoʊnə kəˌbæb, ˈdɒnə kəˌbæb/ *n.* a dish consisting of slices of lamb cut from a vertical spit, and served with onion, tomato, etc., rolled in flat bread. Also, **kebab**.

donga /ˈdɒŋə, ˈdɒŋgə/ *Aust.* –*n.* **1.** a shallow gully or dried-out watercourse. **2.** a makeshift shelter. **3.** a portable prefabricated structure used as a temporary office on a building site, sleeping quarters at a mine, etc. –*phr.* **4. the donga**, *Chiefly SA Colloq.* the bush; the outback.

dongle /ˈdɒŋgəl/ *n. Computers* a hardware device which, when plugged into a computer, can provide software copying protection, as well as wireless connectivity, such as to audio and video sources, printers, mobile phones, GPS devices, etc.

donkey /'dɒŋki/ *n.* (*pl.* **-keys**) **1.** a domesticated ass, *Equus asinus*, used as a beast of burden. **2.** a stupid, silly or obstinate person. *–adj.* **3.** *Machinery* auxiliary: *donkey pump.* *–phr.* **4. donkey's years** (or **ages**), a long time.

donkey vote *n.* (in a compulsory preferential system of voting) a vote in which the voter's apparent order of preference among the candidates listed on the ballot paper corresponds with the order in which the names appear in the list, so that he or she probably is not expressing any preference at all.

donnybrook /'dɒnibrʊk/ *n.* a fight or argument; a brawl. Also, **donneybrook**.

donor /'doʊnə/ *n.* **1.** someone who gives or donates something. **2.** *Med.* **a.** a person or animal furnishing blood for transfusion. **b.** a person from whose body an organ, bone marrow, body part, etc., is transplanted to a recipient. **c.** a person or animal furnishing sperm, ova or an embryo as part of assisted reproduction. **3.** *Law* someone who gives property by gift, legacy, or devise, or who confers a power of appointment. *–adj.* **4.** *Med.* of or relating to the blood, organ, sperm, etc., furnished by a donor (def. 2).

don't /doʊnt/ *v.* contraction of *do not.*

doodle /'dudl/ *v.t.* **1.** to draw (a design, figure, etc.) while preoccupied. *–v.i.* **2.** to scribble idly. *–n.* **3.** a scribbled design, figure, etc., drawn idly.

doom /dum/ *n.* **1.** a terrible fate. **2.** ruin; death. **3.** a judgement or sentence, especially an unfavourable one. *–v.t.* **4.** to destine, especially to a terrible fate. **5.** to pronounce judgement against; condemn.

doona /'dunə/ *n. Aust.* (*from trademark*) a quilted bedspread, filled with down, or synthetic padding, and often used instead of top sheets and blankets; continental quilt; duvet.

door /dɔ/ *n.* **1.** a movable barrier of wood or other material, commonly turning on hinges or sliding in a groove, for closing and opening a passage or opening into a building, room, cupboard, etc. **2.** a doorway. **3.** the building, etc., to which a door belongs: *two doors down the street.* **4.** any means of approach or access, or of exit. *–v.t.* **5.** to open the door of a vehicle in the path of (an oncoming bicyclist). *–phr.* **6. lay something at someone's door**, to attribute something to someone; impute blame for something to someone. **7. next door to, a.** in the next house to. **b.** very near; bordering upon. **8. out of doors**, in the open air; outside a building. **9. show someone the door**, to dismiss someone from the house; turn someone out. **10. the door**, the takings from a show's ticket sales at the door.

doover /'duvə/ *n. Aust. Colloq.* (often used humorously in place of the usual or precise name) any object. Also, **doovah, doofer**.

dopamine /'doʊpəmin/ *n.* a hormone-like substance, $C_8H_{11}NO_2$, with many functions relating to behaviour, cognition, motor activity, motivation and reward, and as a neurotransmitter to the brain; an imbalance in dopamine activity can cause central nervous system disorders such as Parkinson's disease and schizophrenia.

dope /doʊp/ *Colloq.* *–n.* **1.** any drug, especially marijuana. **2.** a stupid person. *–v.t.* **3.** (oft. fol. by *up*) to affect with dope or drugs: *They doped the horses before the race.* *–v.i.* **4.** to take performance-enhancing drugs. *–phr.* **5. the dope**, information or report. *–***doper**, *n.*

Doppler effect /'dɒplər əfɛkt/ *n.* the apparent change in frequency and wavelength of a train of sound or light waves if the distance between the source and the receiver is changing.

dork /dɔk/ *n. Colloq.* a fool, especially someone who is physically or socially clumsy or inept.

dormant /'dɔmənt/ *adj.* **1.** lying asleep or as if asleep; inactive as in sleep; torpid. **2.** in a state of rest or inactivity; quiescent; inoperative; in abeyance.

dormer /'dɔmə/ *n.* Also, **dormer window**. a vertical window in a projection built out from a sloping roof. **2.** the whole projecting structure.

dormitory /'dɔmətri/ *n.* (*pl.* **-ries**) **1.** a room for sleeping, usually large and containing many beds, sometimes in cubicles, for the inmates of a school or other institution. **2.** Also, **dormitory suburb**. a suburb in which a high proportion of the inhabitants are commuters.

dormouse /'dɔmaʊs/ *n.* (*pl.* **dormice** /'dɔmaɪs/) any of the small, furry-tailed rodents of Europe, Asia, and Africa which constitute the family Gliridae, resembling small squirrels in appearance and habits.

Dorothy Dixer /ˌdɒrəθi 'dɪksə/ *n. Colloq.* a question asked in parliament specifically to allow a propagandist reply by a minister.

dorsal /'dɔsəl/ *adj.* **1.** *Zool.* of or relating to the back, as of an organ or part: *dorsal nerves.* **2.** *Bot.* of or relating to the surface away from the axis, as of a leaf; abaxial. *–***dorsally**, *adv.*

dorsi- a combining form of **dorsal**, as in *dorsiferous.* Also, **dorso-**.

dory[1] /'dɔri/ *n.* (*pl.* **-ries**) a small boat with a flat bottom and flaring sides.

dory[2] /'dɔri/ *n.* (*pl.* **dory** or **dories**) **1.** Also, **John Dory**. one of several species of flattened, deep-bodied, spinyrayed, marine food fish, especially *Zeus australis*. **2.** any of several similar species of the family Zeidae found in Australian waters. **3.** any of various species found in European waters, especially *Zeus faber*, the European **John Dory**.

dosage /'doʊsɪdʒ/ *n.* **1.** the administration of medicine in doses. **2.** the amount of a medicine to be given.

dose /doʊs/ *n.* **1.** a quantity of medicine prescribed to be taken at one time. **2.** a definite quantity of anything analogous to medicine, especially of something nauseous or disagreeable.

dose equivalent *n.* a measure of radiation dose, excluding radiation from normal sources; less fundamental than absorbed dose but more significant in terms of physiological effects; used in measuring radiation in radiotherapy. *Symbol:* H_T

doss /dɒs/ *Colloq.* *–n.* **1.** a place to sleep, especially in a cheap lodging house. *–v.i.* Also, **doss down**. **2.** to make a temporary sleeping place for oneself. *–***dosshouse**, *n.*

dossier /'dɒsiə, -ieɪ/ *n.* a bundle of documents on the same subject, especially information about a particular person.

dot /dɒt/ *n.* **1.** a minute or small spot on a surface; a speck. **2.** a small, roundish mark made with or as with a pen. **3.** *Music* **a.** a point placed after a note or rest, to indicate that the duration of the note or rest is to be increased one half. A double dot further increases the duration by one half the value of the single dot. **b.** a point placed under or over a note to indicate that it is to be played staccato, i.e., shortened. **4.** *Telegraphy* a signal of shorter duration than a dash, used in groups of dots, dashes, and spaces, to represent letters in Morse or a similar code. **5. a.** a full stop. **b.** the mark made above a lower-case letter 'i'. **c.** a decimal point. **d.** the keyboard symbol (.), especially as used in domain names. *–v.t.* (**dotted, dotting**) **6.** to mark with or as with a dot or dots. **7.** to stud or diversify, as dots do. *–phr.* **8. dot and carry one, a.** to walk with a limp. **b.** (in simple mathematics) to set down the unit and carry over the tens to the next column. **9. dot one's i's and cross one's t's**, to pay particular attention to detail. **10. on the dot**, punctual; exactly on time. **11. the year dot**, a point in time far in the past (the notional start of time). *–***dotter**, *n.*

dotage /ˈdoʊtɪdʒ/ *n.* **1.** feebleness of mind, especially resulting from old age; senility. **2.** excessive fondness; foolish affection.

dot art *n.* a style of Aboriginal art in which ochre or other pigment is applied as a series of dots to build up a composite picture.

dotcom /ˈdɒtˈkɒm/ *n.* **1.** a company trading over the internet. **2.** a company involved in the information technology industry. *–adj.* **3.** of or relating to a dotcom. **4.** (of a company) trading over the internet. Also, **dot com**, **dot.com**, **dot.com**.

dote /doʊt/ *v.i.* **1.** to be weak-minded, especially from old age. *–phr.* **2. dote on** (or **upon**), to bestow excessive love or fondness on. **–doter**, *n.*

dot-matrix printer *n.* a printer which composes each character out of a series of dots produced by a stylus which moves across the paper.

dot painting *n.* **1.** → **dot art**. **2.** a picture in the style of dot art. **–dot painter**, *n.*

dotty /ˈdɒti/ *adj.* (**-tier, -tiest**) **1.** *Colloq.* crazy; eccentric. **2.** marked with dots; placed like dots.

double /ˈdʌbəl/ *adj.* **1.** twice as great, heavy, strong, etc.: *double pay.* **2.** twofold in form, size, amount, extent, etc.; of extra size or weight: *a double blanket.* **3.** composed of two like parts or members; paired: *a double cherry.* **4.** *Bot.* (of flowers) having the number of petals greatly increased. **5.** (of musical instruments) producing a tone an octave lower than the notes indicate. **6.** twofold in character, meaning, or conduct; ambiguous: *a double interpretation.* **7.** deceitful; hypocritical; insincere. **8.** folded over once; folded in two; doubled. **9.** duple, as time or rhythm. *–pron.* **10.** a twofold size or amount; twice as much. *–n.* **11.** a duplicate; a counterpart. **12.** a sudden backward turn or bend. **13.** *Film, etc.* a substitute actor who takes another's place, as in difficult or dangerous scenes. **14.** *Theatre* an actor with two parts in one play. **15.** *Tennis* two successive faults in serving. **16.** (in darts) **a.** a narrow space between two parallel circles on the outer edge of a dartboard. **b.** a throw which places a dart there. **17.** (in Australia) a form of multiple betting on two horseraces **18.** Also, **dub**. *Aust., NZ* a ride obtained from being doubled (def. 25); dink. *–v.t.* **19.** to make double or twice as great: *to double a sum*; *to double a size.* **20.** *Film, etc.* to act as a double or substitute for (another actor). **21.** to be or have twice as much as. **22.** (sometimes fol. by *over, up, back,* etc.) to bend or fold with one part upon another. **23.** to clench (the fist). **24.** to sail or go round: *to double Cape Horn.* **25.** Also, **dub**. *Aust., NZ* to convey as a second person on a horse, bicycle, or motorcycle; dink. *–v.i.* **26.** to become double. **27.** (sometimes fol. by *up*) to double a stake in gambling or the like. **28.** (sometimes fol. by *up*) to bend or fold. **29.** *Mil.* to march at the double-time pace. **30. a.** *Theatre* to play two stage roles in a small company. **b.** *Music* to play two instruments in a band. *–adv.* **31.** twofold; doubly. *–phr.* **32. at** (or **on**) **the double, a.** *Colloq.* fast; quickly; at a run. **b.** in double time, as in marching troops. **33. double back,** to turn back on a course. **34. double or quits,** *Colloq.* **a.** a bet in which a debt is doubled if the debtor loses, or discharged if the debtor wins. **b.** any of various gambling games based on this principle. **35. double up,** to share quarters, etc. **36. live** (or **lead**) **a double life,** to conduct one's life in an apparently blameless fashion while secretly involved in a dishonourable, immoral, or socially disapproved activity. **–doubleness**, *n.* **–doubler**, *n.* **–doubly**, *adv.*

double agent *n.* a secret agent working simultaneously for two opposed countries, companies, etc., usually without either knowing of the agent's association with the other.

double bass *n.* **1.** Also, **string bass**. the largest instrument of the violin family, having four strings and played resting vertically on the floor. **2.** → **contrabass**.

double-breasted /ˈdʌbəl-brɛstəd/ *adj.* (of a garment) overlapping sufficiently to form two thicknesses of considerable width on the breast. See **single-breasted**.

double chin *n.* a fold of fat beneath the chin.

doublecross /dʌbəlˈkrɒs/ *v.t. Colloq.* to prove treacherous to; betray. **–double-crosser**, *n.*

double dip *v.i.* **1.** to draw income from two sources, sometimes illegally, in Australia especially to receive two types of retirement benefit from public funds as by receiving tax concessions on superannuation savings and then disposing of the superannuation proceeds in such as way as to be eligible for a whole or part age pension. **2.** to use the same implement or food item with which one has already taken and eaten food from a dish for general consumption to dip into the food again. Also, **double-dip**. **–double dipping**, *n.* **–double dipper**, *n.*

double dissolution *n. Govt* (in Australia) the simultaneous dissolving by the governor or governor-general of both houses of parliament prior to the calling of a general election, used as a means of resolving the situation where the upper house consistently opposes the intentions of the lower house.

double-dutch /dʌbəl-ˈdʌtʃ/ *n. Colloq.* nonsense; gibberish; incomprehensible speech.

double-jointed /dʌbəl-ˈdʒɔɪntəd/ *adj.* having unusually flexible joints which enable the appendages and spine to curve in extraordinary ways.

double negative *n. Gram.* a combination of two negative elements in a construction.

double standard *n.* **1.** a code of sexual morality more lenient towards men than towards women. **2.** any rule, judgement, principle, etc., which permits greater freedom to one person or group than to another.

doublet /ˈdʌblət/ *n.* **1.** a close-fitting outer body garment, with or without sleeves, formerly worn by men. **2.** a pair of like things; a couple. **3.** one of a pair of like things; a duplicate. **4.** *Jewellery* a counterfeit gem made by the welding of two pieces of a different nature, as a thin bar of opal with a potch or plastic backing.

double take *n.* a second look, either literal or figurative, given to a person, event, etc., whose significance is suddenly understood.

double-take *v.i.* to be surprised into reconsidering one's judgement.

doubletalk /ˈdʌbəltɔk/ *n. Colloq.* **1.** speech using nonsense syllables together with words in a rapid patter. **2.** evasive or ambiguous language.

double time *n.* **1.** double wages paid to persons who remain at work on certain occasions, such as public holidays, etc. **2.** *US Army* the fastest rate of marching troops, a slow jog in which 180 paces are taken in a minute. *–phr.* **3. in double time,** with speed; quickly.

doubt /daʊt/ *v.t.* **1.** to be uncertain in opinion about; hold questionable; hesitate to believe. **2.** to distrust. *–v.i.* **3.** to feel uncertainty as to something; be undecided in opinion or belief. *–n.* **4.** undecidedness of opinion or belief; a feeling of uncertainty. **5.** distrust; suspicion. **6.** a state of affairs such as to occasion uncertainty. *–phr.* **7. beyond a shadow of doubt,** for certain; definitely. **8. in doubt,** in uncertainty; in suspense. **9. without doubt,** without question; certainly. **–doubtable**, *adj.* **–doubter**, *n.* **–doubtingly**, *adv.*

doubtful /ˈdaʊtfəl/ *adj.* **1.** admitting of or causing doubt; uncertain; ambiguous. **2.** of uncertain issue. **3.** of questionable character. **4.** undecided in opinion or belief; hesitating. **–doubtfully**, *adv.* **–doubtfulness**, *n.*

doubtless /'dautləs/ adv. **1.** without doubt; unquestionably. **2.** probably or presumably. –**doubtlessly,** adv. –**doubtlessness,** n.

douche /duʃ/ n. a jet or current of water applied to a body part, organ, or cavity for medicinal, hygienic, or contraceptive purposes.

dough /dou/ n. **1.** flour or meal combined with water, milk, etc., in a mass for baking into bread, cake, etc. **2.** any soft, pasty mass. **3.** Colloq. money. –phr. **4. do one's dough,** Colloq. to lose one's money, especially in some speculation or gamble.

doughnut /'dounʌt/ n. a small, usually ring-shaped cake of dough, deep-fried in fat and often coated in sugar and cinnamon. Also, **donut.**

dour /'dauə, duə/ adj. hard; severe; stern. –**dourly,** adv. –**dourness,** n.

douse /daus/ v.t. **1.** to plunge into water or the like; drench: to douse someone with water. **2.** Colloq. to put out or extinguish (a light). Also, **dowse.** –**douser,** n.

dove¹ /dʌv/ n. **1.** any of various birds of the pigeon family Columbidae, generally those that are smaller than pigeons, as the **peaceful dove,** Geopelia placida, of Australia and New Guinea. **2.** an innocent, gentle, or tender person. **3.** a politician or political adviser who favours conciliatory policies as a solution to armed conflict. Compare **hawk¹** (def. 3).

dove² /douv/ v. Chiefly US past tense of **dive.**

dovecote /'dʌvkɒt/ n. a structure, usually at a height above the ground, for domestic pigeons, containing recesses for nesting and holes for the birds to enter and leave. Also, **dovecot.**

dovetail /'dʌvteɪl/ n. **1.** Carpentry a joint or fastening formed by one or more tenons and mortices spread in the shape of a dove's tail. –v.t. **2.** to join together compactly or harmoniously.

dowager /'dauədʒə/ n. **1.** a woman who holds some title or property from her deceased husband, especially the widow of a king, duke, or the like; often added to her title to distinguish her from the wife of the present king, duke, or the like. **2.** Colloq. a dignified elderly woman.

dowdy /'daudi/ adj. (**-dier, -diest**) **1.** ill-dressed; not trim, smart, or stylish. –n. (pl. **-dies**) **2.** an ill-dressed woman. –**dowdily,** adv. –**dowdiness,** n. –**dowdyish,** adj.

dowel /'dauəl/ Carpentry –n. **1.** Also, **dowel pin.** a pin, usually round, fitting into corresponding holes in two adjacent pieces to prevent slipping or to align the two pieces. **2.** Also, **dowelling.** long, thin, round strips of wood suitable for making such pins, or for hanging posters, etc. –v.t. (**-elled** or, Chiefly US, **-eled, -elling** or, Chiefly US, **-eling**) **3.** to reinforce with dowels; furnish with dowels.

down¹ /daun/ adv. **1.** from higher to lower; in descending direction or order; into or in a lower position or condition. **2.** on or to the ground. **3.** to a point of submission, inactivity, etc. **4.** to or in a position spoken of as lower, as the south, the country, a business district, etc. **5.** in or into a city, having come from a country area: he was relieved the wool had gone down. **6.** to or at a low point, degree, rate, pitch, volume, etc. **7.** from an earlier to a later time. **8.** from a greater to a lesser bulk, degree of consistency, strength, etc.: to boil down syrup. **9.** in due position or state: to settle down to work. **10.** on paper or in a book: to write something down. **11.** in cash; at once: to pay $40 down. **12.** Boxing touching the ring floor with some part of the body other than the feet. –prep. **13.** to, towards, or at a lower place or on or in: down the stairs. **14.** to, towards, near, or at a lower station, condition, or rank in. **15. a.** away from the source, origin, etc., of: down the river. **b.** down at: I've a cottage down the coast. **16.** in the same course or direction as: to sail down the wind. –adj.

17. downwards; going or directed downwards. **18.** travelling away from a terminus: a down train. **19.** fallen or prostrate. **20.** not in activity: the wind is down. **21.** (of a computer or a computerised system) not operational, usually because of a malfunction. **22.** being a portion of the full price of an article bought on an instalment plan or mortgage, etc., that is paid at the time of purchase. **23.** losing or having lost money at gambling: he was $10 down after a day at the races. **24.** losing or behind an opponent by a specified number of points, holes, etc. **25.** Colloq. depressed; unhappy. **26.** Colloq. in prison: he is down for a few months. –n. **27.** a downward movement; a descent. **28.** a reverse: the ups and downs of fortune. –v.t. **29.** to put or throw down; subdue. **30.** to drink or eat at speed: to down a schooner of beer. –v.i. **31.** to go down; fall. –interj. **32.** a command, especially to a dog, to cease jumping, etc.: down Rover! **33.** a command to take cover, or duck. –phr. **34. down and out,** without friends, money, or prospects. **35. down at heel,** poor; shabby; seedy. **36. down at** (or **in**), at or in any place considered lower, as in altitude, or in the area more southerly located: down in the big smoke. **37. down below,** Colloq. concerning one's genitalia: I've got problems down below. **38. down in the mouth,** discouraged; depressed. **39. down on,** over-severe towards; unnecessarily ready to detect faults in and punish harshly. **40. down on one's luck,** suffering a period of poverty, destitution, etc. **41. down south, a.** in the south. **b.** Colloq. (of money) not spent, but in the bank: put it all down south. **42. down to, a.** to any place considered lower, as in altitude, or being more southerly in geographical location. **b.** attributable to: success down to hard work. **43. down tools,** (of workers) to cease to work, as in starting a strike. **44. down with ...,** an exclamation indicating total resistance, as to a person in power, a law or regulation, a practice, etc.: down with taxes; down with the king! **45. go down,** Colloq. (taboo) (sometimes fol. by on) to perform oral sex. **46. have a down on,** Colloq. to bear a grudge against; be hostile towards. **47. send down,** Brit. **a.** to expel from university. **b.** Colloq. to send to prison: he was sent down for three years.

down² /daun/ n. **1.** the first feathering of young birds. **2.** a soft hairy growth, as the hair on the human face when first beginning to appear.

down³ /daun/ n. (usu. pl.) open, rolling, upland country with fairly smooth slopes usually covered with grass.

down-and-out n. Colloq. a person, usually of disreputable appearance, without friends, money, or prospects.

down beat n. **1.** a downward movement of the conductor's baton indicating the first beat of the bar in a piece of music. **2.** the first beat of a bar.

down-beat adj. **1.** pessimistic; gloomy. **2.** relaxed and understated.

downcast /'daunkast/ adj. **1.** directed downwards, as the eyes. **2.** dejected in spirit; depressed.

downer /'daunə/ n. Colloq. **1.** a depressant or tranquilliser. **2.** a depressing experience.

downfall /'daunfɔl/ n. **1.** descent to a lower position or standing; overthrow; ruin. **2.** a cause of this. **3.** a fall, as of rain or snow. –**downfallen,** adj.

downgrade v.t. /daun'greɪd/ **1.** to assign (a person, job or the like) to a lower status, usually with a smaller salary. **2.** to reduce the security classification of (a classified document, article, etc.). **3.** to denigrate or belittle: politicians are constantly downgraded by the public. –n. /'daungreɪd/ **4.** a downward slope. –adj. /'daungreɪd/ **5.** downhill. –phr. /'daungreɪd/ **6. on the downgrade,** heading for poverty, ruin, etc.

downhill *adv.* /daʊnˈhɪl/ **1.** down the slope of a hill; downwards into a deteriorating or declining position, condition, etc. –*adj.* /ˈdaʊnhɪl/ **2.** going or tending downwards on or as on a hill. –*n.* /ˈdaʊnhɪl/ **3.** *Skiing* a high-speed race downhill in which skiers compete in turn, the winner being the competitor who completes the course in the fastest time.

download *v.t.* /daʊnˈloʊd/ **1.** *Computers* to transfer or copy (data) from one computer to another, or from a computer to a peripheral device. **2.** (of carriers) to transfer (goods) to a second truck before delivering them. –*n.* /ˈdaʊnloʊd/ **3.** the act or process of downloading data. **4.** the data downloaded in such an operation. –**downloadable**, *adj.*

down-market *adj.* **1.** of or relating to commercial services and goods of inferior status, quality, and price. **2.** inferior in style or production. See **up-market**.

down payment *n.* the initial deposit on a purchase made on an instalment plan or mortgage.

downpour /ˈdaʊnpɔ/ *n.* a heavy, continuous fall of water, rain, etc.

downright /ˈdaʊnraɪt/ *adj.* **1.** thorough; absolute; out-and-out. **2.** direct; straightforward. –*adv.* **3.** completely or thoroughly: *he is downright angry.* –**downrightly**, *adv.* –**downrightness**, *n.*

downshift /ˈdaʊnʃɪft/ *v.i.* to take an employment position at a lower salary level than one has already reached, usually in order to have more time for other pursuits and to suffer less stress. –**downshifter**, *n.* –**downshifting**, *n.*

downsize /ˈdaʊnsaɪz/ *v.t.* **1.** to scale down in size, as a work force, space requirements, financial commitment, etc. –*v.i.* **2.** to engage in such scaling down or reduction.

downstairs /daʊnˈstɛəz/ *adv.* **1.** down the stairs. **2.** to or on a lower floor.

downstream *adv.* /daʊnˈstrim/ **1.** with or in the direction of the current of a stream. –*adj.* /ˈdaʊnstrim/ **2.** farther down a stream.

Down syndrome *n.* a genetic condition resulting from a third chromosome on the 21st chromosomal pairing, characterised by varying degrees of intellectual and physical impairment. Also, **Down's syndrome**.

downtime /ˈdaʊntaɪm/ *n.* **1.** time during which a machine is not operational. **2.** time in which a factory, workplace, etc., is not operating because of machine failure or regulated maintenance. **3.** the nonproductive period in a cyclical industry such as sugar growing. **4.** a period of relaxation. Also, **down time**.

down-to-earth *adj.* sensible; without pretensions; realistic.

downtown /daʊnˈtaʊn/ *adv.* to or in the business section of a city.

downtrend /ˈdaʊntrɛnd/ *n.* a downward trend: *a downtrend in interest rates.*

downtrodden /ˈdaʊntrɒdn/ *adj.* trodden down; trampled upon; tyrannised over. Also, **downtrod**.

downturn /ˈdaʊntɜn/ *n.* a decline, deterioration: *a downturn in prosperity.*

Down Under *n. Colloq.* (*also lower case*) Australia or New Zealand (viewed from or as from the Northern Hemisphere).

downward /ˈdaʊnwəd/ *adj.* **1.** moving or tending to a lower place or condition. **2.** descending or deriving from a head, source, or beginning. –*adv.* **3.** downwards. –**downwardly**, *adv.* –**downwardness**, *n.*

downwards /ˈdaʊnwədz/ *adv.* **1.** from a higher to a lower place or condition. **2.** down from a head, source, or beginning. **3.** from more ancient times to the present day. Also, **downward**.

downwind /daʊnˈwɪnd/ *adv.* **1.** in the direction of the wind; with the wind. **2.** towards the leeward side.

dowry /ˈdaʊəri, ˈdaʊri/ *n.* (*pl.* **-ries**) **1.** the money, goods, or estate which a woman brings to her husband at marriage. **2.** any gift or reward given to or for a bride by a man in consideration for the marriage.

dowse /daʊs/ *v.t.* → **douse**. –**dowser**, *n.*

dox /dɒks/ *n.* **1.** an internet-enabled attack on a person's privacy in which their personal details and sometimes those of their family and friends are released online, viewers being invited to use them in whatever way they wish. –*v.t.* (**doxxed** *or* **doxed**, **doxxing** *or* **doxing**) **2.** to publish the private details of (someone) online. –**doxxing**, **doxing**, *n.*

doyen /ˈdɔɪən/ *n.* the senior member of a body, class, profession, etc. –**doyenne**, *fem. n.*

doze /doʊz/ *v.i.* **1.** to sleep lightly or fitfully. **2.** to be dull or half asleep. –*n.* **3.** a light or fitful sleep. –*phr.* **4. doze away**, to pass or spend (time) in drowsiness. **5. doze off**, to fall into a light sleep unintentionally. –**dozer**, *n.*

dozen /ˈdʌzən/ *n.* (*pl.* **-zen** *or* **-zens**) **1.** a group of twelve units or things: *cheaper by the dozen.* –*adj.* **2.** amounting to a dozen in number: *a dozen eggs.*

DP /di ˈpi/ *n.* (*pl.* **DPs** *or* **DP's**) a displaced person.

drab /dræb/ *adj.* (**drabber, drabbest**) **1.** having a dull grey colour. **2.** dull; cheerless. –**drably**, *adv.* –**drabness**, *n.*

drachma /ˈdrækmə/ *n.* (*pl.* **-mas** *or* **-mae** /-mi/) (formerly, until the introduction of the euro in 2002) the principal monetary unit of modern Greece, equal to 100 lepta.

draconian /drəˈkoʊniən/ *adj.* harsh; rigorous; severe. –**draconically**, *adv.*

draft /draft/ *n.* **1.** Also, **draught**. a preliminary plan, sketch, or design. **2.** Also, **draught**. a rough form of any writing, intended to be revised or copied. **3.** → **conscription**. **4.** a written order for the payment of money; bill of exchange. **5.** an animal or animals chosen and separated from the herd or flock. **6.** *Chiefly US* → **draught**. –*v.t.* **7.** Also, **draught**. to draw the outlines or plan of; sketch. **8.** Also, **draught**. to write as a draft. **9.** to conscript. **10.** to separate animals from the herd or flock for a particular purpose, such as branding. –**drafter**, *n.* –**drafting**, *n.*

draftsman /ˈdraftsmən/ *n.* (*pl.* **-men**) **1.** someone who draws up documents. **2.** someone who draws sketches, plans, or designs. **3.** someone employed in making mechanical drawings, as of machines, structures, etc. Also, **draughtsman**.

drag /dræg/ *verb* (**dragged, dragging**) –*v.t.* **1.** to draw with force, effort, or difficulty; pull heavily or slowly along; haul; trail. **2.** to search with a drag, grapnel, or the like. **3.** *Computers* to move (text, a file, etc.) across a computer screen by selecting with the mouse and moving the cursor to another part of the screen. –*v.i.* **4.** to be drawn or hauled along. **5.** to trail on the ground. **6.** to move heavily or with effort. **7.** to proceed or pass with tedious slowness. –*n.* **8.** something used by or for dragging as a dragnet or a dredge. **9.** anything that retards progress. **10.** act of dragging. **11.** slow, laborious movement or procedure; retardation. **12.** the force due to the relative airflow exerted on an aeroplane or other body tending to reduce its forward motion. **13.** *Angling* **a.** a brake on a fishing reel. **b.** the sideways pull on a fishing line as caused by a cross-current. **14.** *Colloq.* somebody or something that is extremely boring. **15.** *Colloq.* a puff or a pull on a cigarette. **16.** *Colloq.* the clothes typically worn by one sex, when worn by the other; transvestite costume. **17.** *Colloq.* → **drag race**. **18.** *Colloq.* a road or street: *the main drag.* –*phr.* **19. drag in**, **a.** to haul in. **b.** to introduce, as an irrelevant matter. **20. drag on**, to pass tediously: *the days dragged on.* **21. drag one's feet**, to hang back deliberately. **22. drag out**, **a.** to haul out. **b.** to protract: *to drag* *out the proceedings.* **23. have a drag with,** *US Colloq.* to have influence with.

dragnet /'drægnet/ *n.* **1.** a net to be drawn along the bottom of a river, pond, etc., or along the ground, to catch something. **2.** anything that serves to catch or drag in, as a police system.

dragon /'drægən/ *n.* **1.** a mythical monster variously represented, generally in the European tradition as a huge winged reptile with crested head and terrible claws, and often spouting fire, but in the Eastern tradition as powerful but beneficent. **2.** a fierce, violent person. **3. a.** a severely watchful woman. **b.** a formidable woman. **4.** → **komodo dragon. 5.** any of various lizards of the family Agamidae, such as the frill-necked lizard, *Chlamydosaurus kingi* of northern Australia, or the bearded dragon, *Amphibolorus barbatus.* –**dragoness,** *fem. n.* –**dragonish,** *adj.*

dragonfly /'drægənflaɪ/ *n.* (*pl.* **-flies**) any of the larger, harmless insects of the order Odonata, which feed on mosquitoes and other insects, and whose immature forms are aquatic.

dragoon /drə'gun/ *n.* **1.** a cavalryman of certain regiments. –*v.t.* **2.** to force by rigorous and oppressive measures; coerce.

drag queen *n.* a male transvestite whose clothing and behaviour are excessively flamboyant.

drag race *n.* a race between cars starting from a standstill, the winner being the car that can accelerate fastest. Also, **drag.** –**drag racer,** *n.*

drain /dreɪn/ *v.t.* **1.** to draw off gradually, as a liquid; remove by degrees, as by filtration. **2.** to draw off or take away completely. **3.** to withdraw liquid gradually from; make empty or dry by drawing off liquid. **4.** to deprive of possessions, resources, etc., by gradual withdrawal; exhaust. –*v.i.* **5.** to flow off gradually. **6.** to become empty or dry by the gradual flowing off of moisture. –*n.* **7.** that by which anything is drained, as a pipe or conduit. **8.** *Electronics* one of the three electrodes of a field effect transistor. **9.** *Surg.* a material or appliance for maintaining the opening of a wound to permit free exit of fluid contents. **10.** gradual or continuous outflow, withdrawal, or expenditure. **11.** the cause of a continual outflow, withdrawal, or expenditure. **12.** act of draining. **13.** *Colloq.* a small drink. –*phr. Colloq.* **14. drain the dragon,** to urinate. **15. go down the drain, a.** to be wasted. **b.** to become worthless. **16. laugh like a drain,** to laugh loudly. –**drainable,** *adj.* –**drainer,** *n.*

drainage /'dreɪnɪdʒ/ *n.* **1.** the act or process of draining. **2.** a system of drains, artificial or natural. **3.** something that is drained off. **4.** *Med.* the draining of body fluids (bile, urine, etc.) or of pus and other morbid products from a wound.

drake /dreɪk/ *n.* the male of any bird of the duck kind.

dram /dræm/ *n.* **1.** a unit of measurement in the imperial system, equal to $\frac{1}{16}$ ounce avoirdupois weight (27.34 grains) or approximately 1.772×10^{-3} kg. **2.** a small quantity of anything.

DRAM /'di ræm/ *n. Computers* dynamic random access memory; a type of memory in which the information gradually decays, the cells needing to be topped up at frequent intervals. Also, **Dram.**

drama /'dramə/ *n.* **1.** a composition in prose or verse presenting in dialogue or pantomime a story involving conflict or contrast of character, especially one intended to be acted on the stage; a play. **2.** *TV* a program, either a one-off or part of a series, which is of a similar nature: *hospital drama; police drama.* **3.** the branch of literature having such compositions as its subject; dramatic art or representation. **4.** the art which deals with plays from their writing to their final production. **5.** any series of events having dramatic interest or results.

dramatic /drə'mætɪk/ *adj.* **1.** of or relating to drama. **2.** using the form or manner of drama. **3.** characteristic of or appropriate to drama; involving conflict or contrast. **4.** showy; ostentatious: *a dramatic display of indignation.* **5.** sudden and marked: *a dramatic rise in unemployment.* –**dramatically,** *adv.*

dramatise /'dræmətaɪz/ *v.t.* **1.** to put into dramatic form. **2.** to express or represent dramatically: *he dramatises his woes.* Also, **dramatize.** –**dramatiser,** *n.*

dramatist /'dræmətəst/ *n.* a writer of dramas or dramatic poetry; a playwright.

drank /dræŋk/ *v.* past tense of **drink.**

drape /dreɪp/ *v.t.* **1.** to cover or hang with cloth or some fabric, especially in graceful folds; adorn with drapery. **2.** to adjust (hangings, clothing, etc.) in graceful folds. **3.** to position in a casual manner: *he draped his legs over the arms of the chair.* –*n.* **4.** (*pl.*) curtains.

draper /'dreɪpə/ *n.* a dealer in textiles and cloth goods, etc.

drapery /'dreɪpəri/ *n.* (*pl.* **-ries**) **1.** cloths or textile fabrics collectively. **2.** the business of a draper. **3.** coverings, hangings, clothing, etc., of some fabric, especially as arranged in loose, graceful folds.

drastic /'dræstɪk/ *adj.* severe or forceful; extreme. –**drastically,** *adv.*

draught /draft/ *n.* **1.** a current of air, especially in a room, chimney, stove, or any enclosed space. **2.** a device for regulating the flow of air in a stove, fireplace, etc. **3.** an act of drawing or pulling, or that which is drawn; a pull; haul. **4.** an animal, or team of animals used to pull a load. **5.** the drawing of a liquid from its receptacle, as of ale from a cask. **6.** → **draught beer. 7.** drinking, or a drink. **8.** an amount drunk as a continuous act. **9.** a dose of medicine. **10.** a catch or take of fish. **11. a.** the action of displacing water with a vessel. **b.** the depth of water a vessel needs to float it. **12.** (*pl. construed as sing.*) a game played by two people each with twelve pieces on a chequered board. Also, **draughtsman.** one of the pieces in this game. **14.** → **draft** (defs 1 and 2). –*adj.* **15.** being on draught; drawn as required: *draught ale.* **16.** used or suited for drawing loads. –*v.t.* **17.** → **draft** (defs 7 and 8). –*phr.* **18. feel the draught,** *Colloq.* to be harmed by conditions becoming unfavourable to one's affairs. Also, *Chiefly US,* **draft.**

draught beer *n.* beer drawn from a cask or keg.

draught horse *n.* a strong heavily built horse, 15 hands or over in height, used for pulling heavy loads. Also, **draughthorse.**

draughts /drafts/ *pl. n.* (*construed as sing.*) a game played by two people each with twelve pieces on a chequered board; chequers.

draughtsman /'draftsmən/ *n.* (*pl.* **-men**) **1.** → **draftsman. 2.** one of the pieces used in draughts, usually a small coloured disc. –**draughtsmanship,** *n.*

draughty /'drafti/ *adj.* (**-tier, -tiest**) characterised by or causing draughts of air. –**draughtiness,** *n.*

draw /drɔ/ *verb* (**drew** /dru/, **drawn, drawing**) –*v.t.* **1.** (sometimes fol. by *along, away, in, out, off,* etc.) to cause to come as by a pulling force; pull; drag; lead. **2.** to bring or take out, as from a receptacle or source: *to draw water; to draw blood; to draw tears; to draw teeth.* **3.** to bring towards oneself or itself, as by inherent force or influence; attract: *draw a crowd; draw flak.* **4.** to pick or choose at random. **5. a.** to be dealt or take (a card) from the pack. **b.** *Bridge* to remove (trumps, or outstanding cards of a given suit) from an opponent's hand. **6.** to sketch in lines or words; delineate; depict: *to draw a picture.* **7.** to mark out; trace. **8.** to frame or formulate, as a distinction. **9.** to take in, as by sucking or inhaling. **10.** to get; derive; deduce: *to draw a conclusion.* **11.** to disembowel (a fowl, etc.). **12.** to pull out to full or greater length; stretch; make by attenuating, as wire. **13.** *Med.* to digest and cause to discharge: *to draw an abscess by a poultice.* **14.** to write or sign (an order, draft, or bill of exchange). **15.** *Naut.* (of a boat) to displace (a certain depth of water). **16.** *Sport* to leave (a contest) undecided. **17.** *Sport* to be placed in (a certain position) for the start of a race: *to draw a good position.* **18.** *Archery* to pull back the bowstring and arrow of (a bow) preparatory to shooting the arrow. –*v.i.* **19.** to exert a pulling, moving, or attracting force: *a sail draws by being filled with wind and properly trimmed.* **20.** to be drawn; move (*on, off, out,* etc.) as under a pulling force: *the day draws near.* **21.** (sometimes fol. by *on*) to take out a sword, pistol, etc., for action: *to draw on an opponent.* **22.** to use or practise the art of tracing figures; practise drawing. **23.** to produce or have a draught of air, etc., as in a pipe or flue. **24.** *Games* to leave a contest undecided. **25.** (of tea) to infuse. –*n.* **26.** the act of drawing. **27.** something that draws or attracts. **28.** that which is drawn, as a lot. **29.** *Sport* a drawn or undecided contest. **30.** the drawing of a gun out of its holster: *Cowboy Dan was quick on the draw.* –*phr.* **31. draw a bath,** *Chiefly Brit.* to fill a bathtub with water in preparation for a bath. **32. draw a bead on,** to take aim at. **33. draw a blank, a.** to draw from a lottery an unmarked counter, one not associated with any prize. **b.** to be unsuccessful, especially when looking for someone or something, or trying to find out about something. **34. draw down,** *Banking* to transfer (funds) from one account to another. **35. draw near,** to approach gradually. **36. draw on, a.** to approach; to near. **b.** to pull on (a garment). **c.** to call on or make a demand on: *to draw on supplies.* **d.** to make a levy or call on (for money, supplies, etc.). **37. draw out, a.** to extract. **b.** to lengthen or prolong. **c.** to encourage or persuade (somebody) to talk. **38. draw stumps,** *Cricket* to pull up the stumps as a sign that the day's play has ended. **39. draw the line,** *Colloq.* **a.** to fix a limit. **b.** to refuse. **40. draw the teeth of,** *Colloq.* to render harmless. **41. draw up, a.** to bring to a halt. **b.** to come to a halt **c.** to prepare or set out (a document, plan, etc.). **d.** to arrange, especially in military formation.

drawback /'drɔbæk/ *n.* **1.** a hindrance or disadvantage. **2.** *Commerce* an amount paid back from a charge made. **3.** *Govt* refund of excise or import duty, as when imported goods are re-exported. See **rebate**[1]. **4.** the full inhalation of tobacco smoke into the lungs.

drawbridge /'drɔbrɪdʒ/ *n.* a bridge of which the whole or a part may be drawn up or aside to prevent access or to leave a passage open for boats, etc.

drawcard /'drɔkad/ *n.* a person, act, entertainment, occasion, etc., that can be relied upon to produce a large attendance; crowd puller.

drawee /drɔ'i/ *n.* someone on whom an order, draft, or bill of exchange is drawn.

drawer /drɔ/ *for defs 1 and 2,* /'drɔə/ *for defs 3 and 4 n.* **1.** a sliding compartment, as in a piece of furniture, that may be drawn out in order to get access to it. **2.** (*pl.*) a garment for the lower part of the body, with a separate portion for each leg; underpants. **3.** a person or thing that draws something. **4.** *Finance* someone who draws an order, draft, or bill of exchange.

drawing /'drɔɪŋ, 'drɔrɪŋ/ *n.* **1.** the act of a person or thing that draws. **2.** representation by lines; delineation of form without reference to colour. **3.** a sketch, plan, or design, especially one made with pen, pencil, or crayon. **4.** the art of making these.

drawing board *n.* **1.** a rectangular board to which paper can be affixed for drawing on. –*phr.* **2. back to the drawing board,** back to the basic essentials; back to the planning stage. **3. on the drawing board,** in preparation.

drawing-pin /'drɔɪŋ-pɪn/ *n.* a short broad-headed tack designed to be pushed in by the thumb; thumbtack.

drawing room *n.* a room for the reception and entertainment of visitors; a living room.

drawl /drɔl/ *v.i.* **1.** to speak with slow, lingering utterance. –*v.t.* **2.** to say or utter with slow, lingering utterance. –*n.* **3.** the act or utterance of someone who drawls. –**drawler,** *n.* –**drawlingly,** *adv.* –**drawly,** *adj.*

drawn /drɔn/ *v.* **1.** past participle of **draw**. –*adj.* **2.** tired; haggard; tense.

dray /dreɪ/ *n.* **1.** a low, strong cart without fixed sides, for carrying heavy loads. **2.** a sledge. –*v.t.* **3.** to convey on a dray.

dread /drɛd/ *v.t.* **1.** to fear greatly; be in shrinking apprehension or expectation of: *to dread death.* –*n.* **2.** terror or apprehension as to something future; great fear. **3.** deep awe or reverence. –*adj.* **4.** greatly feared; frightful; terrible.

dreadful /'drɛdfəl/ *adj.* **1.** extremely bad or unpleasant. **2.** causing great dread, fear, or terror; terrible: *a dreadful storm.* **3.** venerable; awe-inspiring. –**dreadfully,** *adv.* –**dreadfulness,** *n.*

dreadlock /'drɛdlɒk/ *n.* **1.** a single matted lock of hair in the Rastafarian style. **2.** (*pl.*) Also, **dreads.** a hairstyle in which the hair is worn in long, rope-like locks, as that of Rastafarian men. –*v.t.* **3.** to form (hair) into dreadlocks. –**dreadlocked,** *adj.*

dream /drim/ *n.* **1.** a succession of images or ideas present in the mind during sleep. **2.** the sleeping state in which this occurs. **3.** an object seen in a dream. **4.** an involuntary vision occurring to one awake: *a waking dream.* **5.** a vision voluntarily indulged in while awake; daydream; reverie. **6.** a wild or vain fancy. **7.** something or somebody of an unreal beauty or charm. **8.** a hope that gives one inspiration; an aim. –*adj.* **9.** ideal: *my dream home.* –*verb* (**dreamed** *or* **dreamt** /drɛmt/, **dreaming**) –*v.i.* **10.** to have a dream or dreams. **11.** to indulge in daydreams or reveries. –*v.t.* **12.** to see or imagine in sleep or in a vision. **13.** to imagine as if in a dream; fancy; suppose. –*phr.* **14. dream away,** to pass or spend (time, etc.) in dreaming. **15. dream of,** to think or conceive of (something) in a very remote way: *to dream of having a holiday.* **16. dream on,** *Colloq.* an exclamation indicating that someone is being unrealistic. **17. dream up,** *Colloq.* to form or plan in the imagination; invent. **18. in your dreams,** *Colloq.* an exclamation indicating that the person addressed is indulging in wishful thinking or unrealistic fantasy. –**dreamer,** *n.* –**dreamful,** *adj.* –**dreamless,** *adj.* –**dreamlike,** *adj.*

Dreaming /'drimɪŋ/ *n.* (*also lower case*) **1. the,** Also, **the Dreamtime.** (in Aboriginal mythology) the time in which the earth received its present form and in which the patterns and cycles of life and nature were initiated; alcheringa. **2.** a division of an Aboriginal people, based on allegiance to a totemic ancestor.

Dreamtime /'drimtaɪm/ *n.* **the** → **Dreaming** (def. 1).

dreamy /'drimi/ *adj.* (**-mier, -miest**) **1.** full of dreams; characterised by or causing dreams. **2.** of the nature of or characteristic of dreams; visionary. **3.** vague; dim. **4.** soothing; quiet; gentle. **5.** *Colloq.* marvellous; extremely pleasing. –**dreamily,** *adv.* –**dreaminess,** *n.*

dreary /'drɪəri/ *adj.* (**-rier, -riest**) **1.** causing sadness or gloom. **2.** dull. –**drearily,** *adv.* –**dreariness,** *n.*

dredge[1] /drɛdʒ/ *n.* **1.** a dragnet or other contrivance for gathering material or objects from the bed of a river, etc. **2.** any of various powerful machines for dredging up or removing earth, etc., as from the bottom of a river, by means of a scoop, a series of buckets, a suction pipe, or the like. –*verb* (**dredged, dredging**) –*v.t.* **3.** to clear out with a dredge; remove sand, silt, mud, etc., from the bottom of. **4.** to take, catch, or gather with a dredge; obtain or remove by a dredge. *–v.i.* **5.** to use a dredge. *–phr.* **6. dredge up**, to find, usually with some difficulty: *to dredge up an argument.*

dredge[2] /drɛdʒ/ *v.t.* (in cookery) to sprinkle or coat with some powdered substance, especially flour.

dreg /drɛg/ *n.* a small remnant or quantity. **–dreggy,** *adj.*

dregs /drɛgz/ *pl. n.* **1.** sediment of wine or other drink; lees; grounds. **2.** any waste or worthless residue. *–phr.* **3. the dregs (of society),** a person or a class of people considered to be low or despicable, especially irretrievably immoral.

drench /drɛntʃ/ *v.t.* **1.** to wet thoroughly; steep; soak: *the rain drenched my clothes.* **2.** *Vet. Science* to give a dose of medicine to (an animal), by mouth into the stomach: *to drench a horse.* *–n.* **3.** something that drenches: *a drench of rain.* **4.** a dose of medicine for an animal. **–drencher,** *n.*

dress /drɛs/ *n.* **1.** a one-piece outer garment worn by women and girls, comprising a skirt and bodice, with or without sleeves. **2.** clothing; apparel; garb. **3.** fine clothes; formal costume: *full dress.* *–adj.* **4.** of or for a dress or dresses: *dress fabric.* **5.** of or for a formal occasion: *a dress suit; a dress uniform.* *–v.t.* **6.** to equip with clothing, ornaments, etc.; deck; attire. **7.** to put formal or evening clothes on. **8.** to arrange a display in; ornament or adorn: *to dress a shop window.* **9.** to prepare (fowl, game, skins, fabrics, timber, stone, ore, etc.) by special processes. **10.** to comb out and do up (hair). **11.** to cultivate (land, etc.). **12.** to treat (wounds or sores). **13.** to make straight; bring (troops) into line: *to dress ranks.* *–v.i.* **14.** to clothe or attire oneself. **15.** to clothe oneself in formal or evening clothes. **16.** to come into line, as troops. *–phr.* **17. dress down,** *Colloq.* **a.** to scold severely; upbraid and rebuke. **b.** to dress more casually than might be expected for a particular occasion. **18. dressed to kill,** *Colloq.* so well dressed as to make an extremely favourable impression. **19. dress on the left,** (of males) to have the genitals positioned at the inside top of the left trouser leg. **20. dress on the right,** (of males) to have the genitals positioned at the inside top of the right trouser leg. **21. dress ship,** *Naut.* to decorate a ship by hoisting lines of flags running the full length of the ship. **22. dress up, a.** to put on best clothes. **b.** to put on fancy dress, costume, or guise.

dressage /ˈdrɛsaʒ/ *n.* the art of training of a horse in obedience, deportment, and responses.

dress circle *n.* a circular or curving division of seats in a theatre, cinema, etc., usually the first gallery above the floor.

dresser[1] /ˈdrɛsə/ *n.* **1.** someone employed to help to dress actors, etc., at a theatre. **2.** any of several tools or devices used in dressing materials, as a hammer used to dress lead. **3.** an assistant to a surgeon. **4.** a window-dresser.

dresser[2] /ˈdrɛsə/ *n.* a kitchen sideboard with a set of shelves and drawers for dishes and cooking utensils.

dressing /ˈdrɛsɪŋ/ *n.* **1.** that with which something is dressed. **2.** a sauce for food: *salad dressing.* **3.** stuffing for a fowl. **4.** an application for a wound. **5.** manure, compost, or other fertilisers for land.

dressing-gown *n.* a loose gown or robe generally worn over night attire.

dressing table *n.* **1.** a piece of bedroom furniture, consisting of a table or stand, usually with drawers and a mirror. **2.** a small desk-like table, with drawers beneath often screened by curtains.

dressy /ˈdrɛsi/ *adj.* **(-sier, -siest) 1.** smart; stylish. **2.** suitable for formal occasions. **3.** excessively elaborate. **–dressily,** *adv.* **–dressiness,** *n.*

drew /druː/ *v.* past tense of **draw.**

dribble /ˈdrɪbəl/ *v.i.* **1.** to fall or flow in drops or small quantities; trickle. **2.** to let saliva flow from the mouth;

drivel; slaver. **3.** (in certain sports) to move a ball along by a series of rapid kicks, bounces, or pushes. *–v.t.* **4.** to let fall in drops. **5.** *Sport* to move (the ball) along by a quick succession of kicks, bounces, pushes, or hits. *–n.* **6.** a small trickling stream. **7.** a small quantity of anything. **–dribbler,** *n.* **–dribbly,** *adj.*

dried /draɪd/ *v.* past tense and past participle of **dry.**

drier /ˈdraɪə/ *adj.* Also, **dryer. 1.** comparative of **dry.** *–n.* **2.** → **dryer.**

driest /ˈdraɪəst/ *adj.* superlative of **dry.**

drift /drɪft/ *n.* **1.** a driving movement or force; impetus. **2.** *Aeronautics* the deviation of an aircraft, ship, etc., from a set course, due to currents. **3.** a tendency or trend: *the drift to the cities; the drift of public opinion towards improved conservation.* **4.** the course of anything; tenor; general meaning: *the drift of an argument.* **5.** a heap of any matter driven together: *a drift of sand.* **6.** a tapering steel rod used to bring two holes into alignment for riveting or bolting. *–v.i.* **7.** to be carried along by currents of water or air, or by the force of circumstances. **8.** to wander aimlessly. **9.** to collect into heaps: *the sand drifts into ridges.* *–v.t.* **10.** to carry along: *the current drifted the boat out to sea.*

driftwood /ˈdrɪftwʊd/ *n.* wood floating on, or cast ashore by, the water.

drill[1] /drɪl/ *n.* **1.** a tool or machine for boring cylindrical holes. **2.** *Mil.* training in formal marching or other precise military or naval movements. **3.** any strict, methodical training or exercise: *fire drill.* **4.** *Colloq.* the correct procedure; routine: *they showed the new worker the drill.* *–v.t.* **5.** to pierce or bore (a hole). **6.** *Mil.* to train (soldiers) in formation marching, etc. **7.** train (someone) in new work or procedure. *–v.i.* **8.** to pierce or bore with a drill. **9.** to go through an exercise in military or other training. *–phr.* **10. drill down, a.** *Internet* to progress into the layers of information in a website through a series of clicked links. **b.** to make a deep analysis of a text, set of data, etc. **–drillable,** *adj.* **–driller,** *n.*

drill[2] /drɪl/ *n.* **1.** a small furrow made in the soil in which to sow seeds. **2.** a row of seeds or plants thus sown. *–v.t.* **3.** to plant (ground) in drills. **–driller,** *n.*

drill[3] /drɪl/ *n.* strong twilled cotton.

drily /ˈdraɪli/ *adv.* → **dryly.**

drink /drɪŋk/ *verb* (**drank** *or, formerly,* **drunk, drunk** *or, sometimes,* **drank,** *formerly or as predicative adjective,* **drunken, drinking**) *–v.i.* **1.** to swallow water or other liquid; imbibe. **2.** to imbibe alcoholic beverages, especially habitually or to excess; tipple. *–v.t.* **3.** to swallow (a liquid). **4.** to take in (a liquid) in any manner; absorb. **5.** to take in through the senses, especially with eagerness and pleasure. **6.** to swallow the contents of (a cup, etc.). **7.** to drink in honour of or with good wishes for: *to drink one's health.* *–n.* **8.** any liquid which is swallowed to quench thirst, for nourishment, etc.; a beverage. **9. a.** alcoholic liquor. **b.** a measure of this. **10.** excessive indulgence in alcoholic liquor. **11.** a draught of liquid; a potion. **12.** *(pl.)* a small informal party: *do come over for drinks.* *–phr.* **13. drink to,** to salute in drinking; drink in honour of. **14. drink with the flies,** *Colloq.* to drink (def. 2) alone. **15. the drink,** *Colloq.* the sea or a large lake. **–drinker,** *n.* **–drinking,** *n.*

drink-driving *n.* the driving of a motor vehicle while under the influence of alcohol. **–drink-driver,** *n.*

drinking fountain *n.* a small fountain which ejects a jet of water from the drinker's mouth.

drip /drɪp/ *verb* (**dripped, dripping**) *–v.i.* **1.** to let fall drops; shed drops: *a tap drips if the washer is worn out.* **2.** to fall in drops, as a liquid: *water drips from a tap.* *–v.t.* **3.** to let fall in drops: *the tap drips water.* *–n.* **4.** the act or sound of dripping. **5.** *Med.* a continuous slow infusion of liquid into a blood vessel of a patient. **6.** *Colloq.* a dull or boring person. **–drippy,** *adj.*

dripping /'drɪpɪŋ/ *n.* **1.** the act of anything that drips. **2.** fat exuded from meat in cooking and used as shortening, for making gravy, or for basting. *–phr.* **3. dripping wet,** very wet.

drive /draɪv/ *verb* (**drove, driven, driving**) *–v.t.* **1.** to send along, away, off, in, out, back, etc., by compulsion; force along. **2.** to overwork; overtask. **3.** to cause and guide the movement of (an animal, vehicle, etc.). **4.** to convey in a vehicle. **5. a.** to keep (machinery) going. **b.** to keep (an enterprise, activity, etc.) going: *climate change is driving growth in demand for renewable energy.* **6.** to impel; urge; compel: *to drive someone to do something.* **7.** to carry (business, a bargain, etc.) vigorously through. **8.** *Mining, etc.* to excavate horizontally (or nearly so). **9.** *Tennis, Cricket, Golf, Bowls, etc.* to hit or throw (the ball) very swiftly. **10.** *Hunting* to chase (game). *–v.i.* **11.** to go along before an impelling force; be impelled: *the ship drove before the wind.* **12.** to rush or dash violently. **13.** to act as driver. **14.** to go or travel in a driven vehicle: *to drive away, back, in, out, from, to, etc.* *–n.* **15.** the act of driving. **16.** an impelling along, as of game, cattle, or floating logs, in a particular direction. **17.** the animals, logs, etc., thus driven. **18.** (in tree felling) a line of trees on a hillside partly cut so as to fall when the uppermost tree is felled. **19.** *Psychol.* a source of motivation: *the sex drive.* **20.** *Sport* a propelling or forceful action, especially a powerful battery stroke in cricket, tennis, etc., or a forcible delivery in bowls. **21.** a vigorous onset or onward course. **22.** a strong military offensive. **23.** a united effort to accomplish some purpose, especially to raise money for a government loan or for some charity. **24.** vigorous pressure or effort, as in business. **25.** energy and initiative. **26.** a trip, usually short, in a motor vehicle, often undertaken as an excursion or outing. **27.** a road for driving, especially a private access road to a private house. **28.** *Mining* a horizontal tunnel or shaft. **29.** *Machinery* a driving mechanism, as of a motor vehicle: *gear drive, chain drive.* **30.** *Motor Vehicles* point or points of power application to the roadway: *front drive; rear drive; four-wheel drive.* **31.** *Computers* a controlling mechanism for moving magnetic tapes, floppy disks, etc., thus enabling data to be accessed. *–adj.* **32.** relating to a part of a machine used in its propulsion. *–phr.* **33. drive a coach-and-four through,** to go through easily, without opposition or hindrance: *you could drive a coach-and-four through that argument.* **34. drive at,** to make an effort to reach for; aim at: *the idea he was driving at; what is he driving at?* **35. drive away,** to repel. **36. drive back,** to repel (an attack). **37. drive off,** to chase away from a secured location. **38. drive someone up the wall,** *Colloq.* to exasperate someone.

drive-in *n.* **1.** a cinema so designed that patrons drive in to a large area in front of an outdoor screen and view the film while seated in their cars. *–adj.* **2.** (of any shop, food outlet, etc.) catering for customers in cars.

drivel /'drɪvəl/ *v.i.* (**-elled** *or, Chiefly US,* **-eled, -elling** *or, Chiefly US,* **-eling**) **1.** to let saliva flow from the mouth or mucus from the nose; slaver. **2.** to talk childishly or idiotically. *–n.* **3.** idiotic, or silly talk; twaddle. **–driveller,** *n.*

driven /'drɪvən/ *v.* **1.** past participle of **drive.** *–adj.* **2.** pursuing a goal with relentless determination.

driver /'draɪvə/ *n.* **1.** someone who drives an animal or animals, a vehicle, etc.; coachman, drover, chauffeur, etc. **2.** a golf club with a long shaft, used for making long shots, as from the tee. **3.** *Computers* → **device driver. –driverless,** *adj.*

driveway /'draɪvweɪ/ *n.* **1.** a passage along which vehicles may be driven, especially outside a private house. **2.** the area in the front of a service station adjacent to the fuel pumps.

driving /'draɪvɪŋ/ *adj.* **1.** (of a person) energetic or active. **2.** violent; having tremendous force. **3.** relaying or transmitting power. **4.** rhythmic; urgent; in a fast tempo.

drizzle /'drɪzəl/ *v.i.* **1.** to rain gently and steadily in fine drops; sprinkle. *–v.t.* **2.** *Cookery* to pour (viscous liquid) in a thin stream: *to drizzle the oil over the salad.* *–n.* **3.** a very light rain. **4.** *Cookery* a small amount of viscous liquid poured over something: *a drizzle of oil.* **–drizzly,** *adj.*

droll /droʊl/ *adj.* amusingly odd; comical; waggish. **–drollery, drollness,** *n.* **–drolly,** *adv.*

-drome 1. a word element meaning 'running', 'course', 'racecourse', as in *hippodrome.* **2.** a word element referring to a large structure or area for a specific use, as in *aerodrome, cosmodrome.*

dromedary /'drɒmədəri, -dri/ *n.* (*pl.* **-ries**) See **camel** (def. 1a).

drone¹ /droʊn/ *n.* **1.** the male of the honey bee and other bees, stingless and making no honey. **2.** someone who lives on the labour of others; an idler; a sluggard. **3. a.** an unmanned aerial vehicle, used for military purposes in situations when manned flight is considered too risky or difficult. **b.** a remotely controlled aerial device used for various purposes: *surf drone; ag drone; film drone.* **–dronish,** *adj.*

drone² /droʊn/ *v.i.* **1.** to make a dull, continued, monotonous sound; hum; buzz. **2.** to speak in a monotonous tone. *–n.* **3.** *Music* **a.** a continuous low tone produced by the bass pipes or bass strings of musical instruments. **b.** the pipes (especially of the bagpipe) or strings producing this tone. **–droningly,** *adv.*

drongo¹ /'drɒŋgoʊ/ *n.* (*pl.* **-gos**) any of various insectivorous birds of the family Dicruridae, of Africa, Asia, and Australia, usually black in colour, with long forked tails.

drongo² /'drɒŋgoʊ/ *n.* (*pl.* **-gos**) *Aust., NZ Colloq.* a slow-witted or stupid person.

drool /drul/ *n.* **1.** saliva flowing from the mouth or mucus from the nose. *–v.i.* **2.** to produce drool. *–phr.* **3. drool over,** *Colloq.* to show excessive pleasure at (something or the prospect of something).

droop /drup/ *v.i.* **1.** to sink, bend, or hang down, as from weakness or exhaustion. **2.** to fall into a state of physical weakness; flag; fail. **3.** to lose spirit or courage. **–droopingly,** *adv.* **–droopy,** *adj.*

drop /drɒp/ *n.* **1.** a small quantity of liquid which falls or is produced in a more or less spherical mass; a liquid globule. **2.** the quantity of liquid contained in such a mass. **3. a.** a very small quantity of liquid. **b.** a small drink, usually alcoholic. **4.** a minute quantity of anything. **5.** (*usu. pl.*) liquid medicine given in drops. **6.** a lozenge (confection). **7.** a pendant. **8.** act of dropping; fall; descent. **9.** the distance or depth to which anything drops or falls. **10.** a steep slope. **11.** a fall in degree, amount, value, etc.: *a drop in price.* **12.** *Cricket* a falling wicket: *first drop; second drop.* **13.** that which drops or is used for dropping. **14.** a drop curtain. **15.** a trapdoor. **16. a.** a stick of parachutists. **b.** a descent by parachute. **17. a.** the total yield of lambs from a flock of sheep. **b.** the lambing season. *–verb* (**dropped, dropping**) *–v.i.* **18.** to fall in globules or small portions, as water or other liquid: *rain drops from the clouds.* **19.** to fall vertically like a drop; have an abrupt descent. **20.** to sink to the ground as if inanimate. **21.** to fall wounded, dead, etc. **22.** to come to an end; cease; lapse: *there the matter dropped.* **23.** to withdraw; disappear: *to drop out of sight.* **24.** to squat or crouch, as a dog at the sight of game. **25.** to fall lower in condition, degree, etc.;

sink: *the prices dropped sharply.* **26.** to pass without effort into some specified condition: *to drop asleep*; *drop into the habit of doing it.* **27.** to move down gently, as with the tide or a light wind. **28.** to fall or move (*back, behind*, etc.). **29.** (of an unborn child) to change position in the womb so that the head becomes engaged before labour. **30.** (of animals) to give birth, especially of sheep and cattle. –*v.t.* **31.** to let fall in drops or small portions: *drop a tear.* **32.** to let fall; allow to sink to a lower position; lower: *to drop anchor.* **33.** to give birth to (young). **34.** to bring to the ground by a blow or shot. **35.** *Colloq.* to fell (a tree, etc.). **36.** to lengthen by lowering: *to drop a hem.* **37.** to lower (the voice) in pitch or loudness. **38.** to utter or express casually or incidentally, as a hint. **39.** to send or post (a note, etc.): *drop me a line.* **40.** to omit (a letter or syllable) in pronunciation or writing: *he dropped his h's.* **41.** to cease to keep up or have to do with: *I dropped the subject.* **42.** to cease to employ; to dismiss. **43.** *Rugby Football, etc.* to score (a goal) by a drop kick. **44.** *Colloq.* to stop, cease: *drop it!* **45.** *Colloq.* to take (drugs) in tablet or capsule form. **46.** *Cricket* to spill (a caught ball). –*phr.* **47. drop by** (or **across**), to visit briefly. **48. drop in**, (sometimes fol. by *on*) to come casually or unexpectedly into a place; to visit informally: *he drops in on us occasionally.* **49. drop off**, **a.** to decrease; decline: *sales have dropped off.* **b.** to fall asleep. **c.** to set down, as from a ship, motor vehicle, etc. **50. drop out**, **a.** to leave a particular community out of disenchantment with their aims or beliefs. **b.** (of a telecommunication line) to become disconnected. **c.** (of a mobile phone) to lose its connection. **d.** (of a computer) to lose its access to the internet. **51. get** (or **have**) **the drop on**, *US Colloq.* **a.** to pull and aim a gun, etc., before (an antagonist) can. **b.** to get or have at a disadvantage. **52. till one drops**, *Colloq.* until one is exhausted: *shop till you drop.* –**droppable**, *adj.*

drop-dead *adv.* **1.** *Colloq.* an intensifier: *drop-dead gorgeous.* –*adj.* **2.** extremely attractive: *a drop-dead hunk.*

drop-down menu *n.* → **pull-down menu**.

drop kick *n.* **1.** *Football* a kick which connects with the ball just as it rises from the ground after being dropped by the kicker. **2.** Also, **dropkick**. *Aust. Colloq.* an obnoxious person.

dropout /'drɒpaʊt/ *n.* **1.** someone who decides to opt out of conventional society, a given social group, or an educational institution: *student dropouts became more numerous in the sixties.* **2.** *Rugby Football* a drop made from a defending player's quarter line or goal line after the ball has crossed the try line or has been touched down. Also, **drop-out**.

dropper /'drɒpə/ *n.* a glass tube with an elastic cap at one end and a small orifice at the other, for drawing in a liquid and expelling it in drops.

dropsy /'drɒpsi/ *n. Pathol.* an excessive accumulation of serous fluid in a serous cavity or in the subcutaneous cellular tissue. –**dropsical**, *adj.* –**dropsied**, *adj.*

drop zone *n.* the place where skydivers, parachutists, etc., are intended to land. Also, **dropzone**.

dross /drɒs/ *n.* **1.** *Metallurgy* a waste product taken off molten metal during smelting, essentially metallic in character. **2.** waste matter; refuse. –**drossy**, *adj.* –**drossiness**, *n.*

drought /draʊt/ *n.* **1.** dry weather; lack of rain in a region, especially such as would affect the growth of crops or deplete reserves of water for industrial or domestic use. **2.** scarcity. –*phr.* **3. break the drought**, **a.** to end a drought. **b.** to bring to an end a period in which a particular commodity has been in short supply.

droughtproof /'draʊtpruːf/ *v.t.* **1.** to ensure a supply of drinking water for: *to droughtproof the city.* –*adj.*

2. designed so as to be unaffected by drought: *a droughtproof garden.* –**droughtproofing**, *n.*

drove¹ /droʊv/ *v.* past tense of **drive**.

drove² /droʊv/ *n.* **1.** a number of oxen, sheep, or swine driven in a group. **2.** (*usu. pl.*) a large crowd of human beings, especially in motion. –*v.t.* (**droved, droving**) **3.** to herd (cattle or sheep), over long distances, to market or to better pasture, etc. –**droving**, *n.*

drover /'droʊvə/ *n.* someone who drives cattle, sheep, etc., to market, usually over long distances.

drown /draʊn/ *v.i.* **1.** to be suffocated by being under water or other liquid for too long. –*v.t.* **2.** to suffocate (a person, etc.) by holding under water or other liquid. **3.** to destroy; get rid of: *to drown your sorrows.* **4.** to flood. **5.** (fol. by *out*) to overpower (sound) by a louder sound.

drowse /draʊz/ *v.i.* **1.** to be sleepy; be half asleep. **2.** to be dull or sluggish.

drowsy /'draʊzi/ *adj.* (**-sier, -siest**) **1.** inclined to sleep; half asleep. **2.** dull; sluggish. –**drowsily**, *adv.* –**drowsiness**, *n.*

drubbing /'drʌbɪŋ/ *n.* **1.** a beating. **2.** a decisive defeat.

drudge /drʌdʒ/ *n.* **1.** someone who labours at servile or uninteresting tasks; a hard toiler. –*v.i.* (**drudged, drudging**) **2.** to perform servile, distasteful, or hard work. –**drudger**, *n.* –**drudgingly**, *adv.*

drudgery /'drʌdʒəri/ *n.* (*pl.* **-ries**) tedious, hard, or uninteresting work.

drug /drʌg/ *n.* **1.** a chemical substance given with the intention of preventing or curing disease or otherwise enhancing the physical or mental welfare of humans or animals. **2.** a chemical substance taken for non-medical reasons to bring about a change in behaviour, mood or perception, as a narcotic, hallucinogen, etc. –*v.t.* (**drugged, drugging**) **3.** to stupefy or poison with a drug.

drug cheat *n.* a person who takes banned substances to improve their sporting performance.

drug mule *n.* → **mule¹** (def. 6).

druid /'druːɪd/ *n.* **1.** (*sometimes upper case*) one of an order of priests among the ancient Celts of Gaul, Britain, and Ireland. **2.** a member of one of several modern movements to revive druidism, which meet seasonally in special costume to conduct their ceremonies. –**druidic, druidical**, *adj.* –**druidism**, *n.*

drum /drʌm/ *n.* **1.** a musical instrument consisting of a hollow body, often covered at one or both ends with a tightly stretched membrane, or head, which is struck with the hand, a stick, or a pair of sticks. **2.** any hollow tree or similar device used in this way. **3.** the sound produced by either of these. **4.** any noise suggestive of it. **5.** someone who plays the drum. **6.** a natural organ by which an animal produces a loud or bass sound. **7.** *Computers* (formerly) a magnetically coated cylinder revolving at high speed, used for data storage. **8.** a cylindrical part of a machine. **9.** a cylindrical box or receptacle. –*verb* (**drummed, drumming**) –*v.i.* **10.** to beat or play a drum. **11.** to beat on anything rhythmically. **12.** to make a sound like that of a drum; resound. –*v.t.* **13.** to beat rhythmically; perform (a tune) by drumming. **14.** to call or summon by, or as by, beating a drum. **15.** to drive or force by persistent repetition: *to drum an idea into someone.* –*phr.* **16. drum out**, to expel or dismiss in disgrace to the beat of a drum. **17. drum up**, **a.** to solicit or obtain (trade, customers, etc.). **b.** *Colloq.* to give advice or information to: *I drummed him up on the deal.* **18. the drum**, *Aust., NZ Colloq.* information or advice usually confidential or profitable: *to give someone the drum.* –**drummer**, *n.*

drum line *n.* a shark trap comprising a floating drum with a line to anchor it to the seabed and another line and baited hook to catch a shark; often located near popular swimming spots to reduce the number of sharks in the vicinity.

drumstick /ˈdrʌmstɪk/ *n.* **1.** a stick for beating a drum. **2.** the lower part of the leg of a cooked chicken, duck, turkey, etc.

drunk /drʌŋk/ *v.* **1.** past participle of **drink.** *–adj.* **2.** (*usu. used predicatively*) intoxicated with alcoholic drink. *–n.* **3.** *Colloq.* a drunken person. *–phr.* **4. drunk with,** intoxicated with, or as with: *drunk with joy; drunk with success.* **–drunkard** /ˈdrʌŋkəd/, *n.*

drunken /ˈdrʌŋkən/ *adj.* **1.** intoxicated; drunk. **2.** relating to, proceeding from, or marked by intoxication: *a drunken quarrel.*

drupe /drup/ *n.* a fruit, such as the peach, cherry, plum, etc., consisting of an outer skin (epicarp), a (generally) pulpy and succulent layer (mesocarp), and a hard and woody inner shell or stone (endocarp) which encloses usually a single seed. **–drupaceous**, *adj.*

dry /draɪ/ *adj.* (**drier, driest**) **1.** free from moisture; not moist; not wet. **2.** having little or no rain: *a dry climate; a dry season.* **3.** characterised by absence, deficiency, or failure of natural or ordinary moisture. **4.** not under, in, or on water: *dry land.* **5.** not yielding water or other liquid: *a dry well.* **6.** not yielding milk: *a dry cow.* **7.** free from tears: *dry eyes.* **8.** wiped or drained away; evaporated: *a dry river.* **9.** desiring drink; thirsty. **10.** causing thirst: *dry work.* **11.** without butter or the like: *dry toast.* **12.** (of a biscuit) not sweet. **13.** plain; bald; unadorned: *dry facts.* **14.** dull; uninteresting: *a dry subject.* **15.** humorous or sarcastic in an unemotional or impersonal way: *dry humour.* **16.** indifferent; cold; unemotional: *a dry answer.* **17.** (of wine and cider) not sweet. **18.** of or relating to non-liquid substances or commodities: *dry measure.* **19.** characterised by a prohibition of the consumption or sale of alcohol: *a dry ship; a dry community.* **20.** (of a sheep) not rearing a lamb. **21.** (of a cough) not accompanied by the bringing up of mucus, phlegm, etc. *–verb* (**dried, drying**) *–v.t.* **22.** to make dry; to free from moisture: *dry your eyes.* *–v.i.* **23.** to become dry; lose moisture. *–n.* (*pl.* **dries**) **24.** a dry state, condition, or place. **25.** someone within a political party, etc., who maintains a hard, uncompromising fiscal policy, as a monetarist (opposed to *wet*). **26.** *US Colloq.* a prohibitionist. *–phr.* **27. declare dry,** to declare sheep to be sufficiently unaffected by rain to enable shearing to continue. **28. dry out, a.** (of wet things, especially clothes) to dry of their own accord. **b.** to subject (an alcoholic or drug addict) to a systematic process of detoxification. **c.** (of alcoholics and drug addicts) to rid the body of the drug of dependence. **d.** (of drought) to cause (land) to become quite dry: *the plain was dried out.* **e.** (of drought) to afflict (people in rural and outback areas) so severely that they must leave their land. **29. dry up, a.** to become completely dry. **b.** to become intellectually barren. **c.** *Colloq.* to stop talking. **30. the dry,** (*sometimes upper case*) the rainless season in central and northern Australia and in the tropics generally; in Australia usually from May to November (with transition in April). **–dryness**, *n.*

dry-clean *v.t.* to clean (garments, etc.) with benzine, chemical solvents, etc., rather than water. **–drycleaner**, *n.*

drycleaners /draɪˈklinəz/ *n.* a business where clothes, etc., are dry-cleaned. Also, **cleaners.**

dry dock *n.* **1.** a basin-like structure from which the water can be removed after the entrance of a ship, used when making repairs on a ship's bottom, etc. **2.** a floating structure which may be partially submerged to permit a vessel to enter, and then raised to lift the vessel out of the water for repairs, etc.

dryer /ˈdraɪə/ *n.* **1.** a substance added to paints, varnishes, etc., to make them dry quickly. **2.** a mechanical contrivance for removing moisture. *–adj.* **3.** → **drier.**

dry ice *n.* solid carbon dioxide, having a temperature of minus 78°C at atmospheric pressure.

dryland /ˈdraɪlænd/ *adj.* **1.** of or relating to land which is often dry, especially land having sandy soil. *–n.* Also, **drylands. 2.** such a tract of land.

dryland farming *n.* a method of cultivation of land which receives little rainfall, as by careful selection of crops and the leaving of stubble on the ground to provide nutrients and preserve water.

dryly /ˈdraɪli/ *adv.* in a dry or sarcastic manner: *she smiled dryly at the inept remark.* Also, **drily.**

dry measure *n.* the system of units of capacity formerly used in Britain, Australia, and the US for measuring dry commodities, such as grain, fruit, etc.

dry needling *n.* a treatment for muscle pain which involves the insertion of an acupuncture or hypodermic needle into a trigger point with the aim of releasing the tension in the muscle.

dry run *n.* a test exercise or rehearsal.

dry season *n.* the period of an annual cycle in the tropics when there is little rainfall and the days are hot and sunny, usually as a result of the change in the prevailing winds. Compare **wet season.**

DTs /di ˈtiz/ *n.* → **delirium tremens.** Also, **DT.**

dual /ˈdjuəl/ *adj.* **1.** of or relating to the number two. **2.** composed or consisting of two parts; twofold; double: *dual ownership, dual controls on a plane.* **–dually**, *adv.*

dual citizenship *n.* the holding of concurrent citizenship of two nations, either original or acquired. Also, **dual nationality.**

dual occupancy *n.* the erection on a single block of land of two separate dwellings, each with unit title.

duathlon /djuˈæθlɒn/ *n.* an athletic contest comprising two events, cycling and running.

dub¹ /dʌb/ *v.t.* **1.** to strike lightly with a sword in the ceremony of conferring knighthood; make, or designate as, a knight: *the king dubbed him knight.* **2.** to invest with any dignity or title; style; name; call: *he dubbed me charlatan.* **3.** to strike, cut, rub, etc., in order to make smooth, or of an equal surface: *to dub leather, timber.* **4.** to dress (a fly) for fishing.

dub² /dʌb/ *v.t.* **1.** to change the soundtrack of (a film or videotape), as in substituting a dialogue in another language. **2.** to add new sounds on to (an existing recording). **3.** to transfer (recorded sound) on to a new record or tape; rerecord.

dubious /ˈdjubiəs/ *adj.* **1.** doubtful; marked by or occasioning doubt: *a dubious question.* **2.** wavering or hesitating in opinion; inclined to doubt. **–dubiously**, *adv.* **–dubiousness**, *n.*

duchess /ˈdʌtʃɛs, ˈdʌtʃəs/ *n.* **1.** the wife or widow of a duke. **2.** a woman who holds in her own right the sovereignty or titles of a duchy. **3.** *Colloq.* a woman of showy demeanour or appearance. *–v.t.* **4.** *Colloq.* to lavish entertainment on someone in order to gain favour, or to distract their attention from the reality of the situation.

duchy /ˈdʌtʃi/ *n.* (*pl.* **-chies**) the territory ruled by a duke or duchess.

duck¹ /dʌk/ *n.* **1.** any of numerous wild or domesticated aquatic birds of the family Anatidae, especially of the genus *Anas* and allied genera, characterised by a broad, flat bill, short legs, webbed feet, and a squat body with compact, waterproof feathers. **2.** the female of this bird, as distinguished from the male (or *drake*). **3.** the flesh of a duck, eaten as food.

duck² /dʌk/ *v.i.* **1.** to plunge the whole body or the head momentarily under water. **2.** to stoop suddenly; bob.

3. to avoid a blow, unpleasant task, etc. –*phr.* **4. duck out**, to absent oneself for a short time: *to duck out to the shops for a few minutes.* **5. duck out on**, to desert (someone). **–ducker**, *n.*

duck³ /dʌk/ *n.* a military vehicle for amphibious use.

duck⁴ /dʌk/ *Cricket –n.* **1.** a batsman's score of nought. –*phr.* **2. golden duck**, a duck scored by being out on the first ball of an innings. Also, **duck's egg**.

duckbill /'dʌkbɪl/ *n.* → **platypus**. Also, **duck-billed platypus**.

duckling /'dʌklɪŋ/ *n.* a young duck.

duckweed /'dʌkwid/ *n.* **1.** any member of the family Lemnaceae, especially of the genus *Lemna*, comprising small aquatic plants which float free on still water. **2.** a native weed, *Hydrocotyle tripartita*, with small leaves and creeping stems, especially troublesome on lawns; waterweed.

Duckworth-Lewis system /dʌkwɜθ-luəs 'sɪstəm/ *n.* *Cricket* a mathematical system used to determine the winning score in a rain-interrupted one-day match, calculated on the number of overs remaining and the number of wickets that have fallen when rain interruptions occur.

duco /'djukoʊ/ *n.* *Aust.* (*from trademark*) a type of paint, especially as applied to the body work of a motor vehicle.

duct /dʌkt/ *n.* **1.** any tube, canal, or conduit by which fluid or other substances are conducted or conveyed. –*v.t.* **2.** to convey by means of a duct or ducts.

ductile /'dʌktaɪl/ *adj.* **1.** capable of being drawn out into wire or threads, as gold. **2.** capable of being hammered out thin, as certain metals. **3.** able to stand deformation under a load without fracture. **4.** capable of being moulded or shaped; plastic. **5.** susceptible; compliant; tractable. **–ductility** /dʌk'tɪləti/, *n.*

dud /dʌd/ *Colloq. –n.* **1.** any thing or person that proves a failure. –*adj.* **2.** useless; defective.

dude /djud, dud/ *n.* *Colloq.* **1.** a man or boy. **2.** a person who is fashionable and up-to-date. **3.** a person who is well regarded as being exceptional in some way. **4.** a familiar form of address. **5.** *Chiefly US* a person who is stylishly dressed in a somewhat ostentatious way. **6.** *Chiefly US* a city slicker.

dudgeon /'dʌdʒən/ *n.* a feeling of offence or resentment; anger: *we left in high dudgeon.*

duds /dʌdz/ *pl. n.* *Colloq.* **1.** *Aust.* trousers. **2.** clothes, especially old or ragged clothes. **3.** belongings in general.

due /dju/ *adj.* **1.** immediately payable. **2.** owing, irrespective of whether the time of payment has arrived. **3.** rightful; proper; fitting: *due care; in due time.* **4.** adequate; sufficient: *a due margin for delay.* **5.** under engagement as to time; expected to be ready, be present, or arrive. –*n.* **6.** that which is due or owed. **7.** (*usu. pl.*) a payment due, as a charge, a fee, a membership subscription, etc. –*adv.* **8.** directly or straight: *he sailed due east.* –*phr.* **9. due to**, owing to. **10. give someone their due**, to ascribe proper credit to someone. **11. one's due**, what one has earned or merited.

due diligence *n.* the process of acquiring objective and reliable information on a person or a company as required, especially before a commercial acquisition.

duel /'djuəl/ *n.* **1.** a prearranged combat between two persons, fought with deadly weapons according to an accepted code of procedure, especially to settle a private quarrel. **2.** any contest between two persons or parties. –*v.i.* (**-elled** *or, Chiefly US*, **-eled**, **-elling** *or, Chiefly US*, **-eling**) **3.** to fight in a duel. **–dueller, duellist**, *n.*

duet /dju'et/ *n.* a musical composition for two voices or performers. **–duettist**, *n.*

duff¹ /dʌf/ –*n.* **1.** *Brit.* a flour pudding boiled, or sometimes steamed, in a bag. –*v.t.* **2.** *Colloq.* to make

pregnant. –*phr.* **3. up the duff**, *Colloq.* **a.** pregnant. **b.** ruined; broken.

duff² /dʌf/ *v.t.* to steal (cattle, sheep, etc.), usually altering brands in the process.

duffer¹ /'dʌfə/ *n.* someone who steals cattle, sheep, etc., especially by altering the brand.

duffer² /'dʌfə/ *n.* **1.** (*humorous*) a foolish person: *you're a silly duffer!* **2.** a plodding, stupid, or incompetent person.

dug¹ /dʌg/ *v.* past tense and past participle of **dig**¹.

dug² /dʌg/ *v.* past tense and past participle of **dig**².

dug³ /dʌg/ *n.* the breast, udder, or nipple of a female.

dugite /'djugaɪt/ *n.* a medium-sized, venomous snake, *Pseudonaja affinis*, of central and western areas of Australia, related to the common brown snake.

dugong /'djugɒŋ/ *n.* an aquatic herbivorous mammal, *Dugong dugon*, of the order Sirenia, found in tropical coastal areas of the Indian Ocean, having forelimbs adapted as flippers, no hind limbs, and a horizontal lobed tail; sea cow.

dugout /'dʌgaʊt/ *n.* **1.** a rough shelter or dwelling formed by an excavation in the ground or in the face of a bank. **2.** *Mining* an abandoned opal working which has been turned into living quarters. **3.** Also, **dugout canoe**. a boat made by hollowing out a log.

duke¹ /djuk/ *n.* **1.** a sovereign prince, the ruler of a small state called a duchy. **2.** (in Britain) a nobleman of the highest rank after that of a prince and ranking next above marquess. **3.** a nobleman of corresponding rank in certain other countries.

duke² /djuk/ *n.* *Colloq.* a fist. Also, **dook**.

dukkah /'dukə/ *n.* an Egyptian spice blend made from selected toasted nuts and seeds, usually with hazelnuts or chickpeas as a base. Also, **dukka**.

dulcet /'dʌlsət/ *adj.* agreeable to the feelings, the eye, or, especially, the ear; pleasing; soothing; melodious.

dulcimer /'dʌlsəmə/ *n.* **1.** a trapezoidal zither with metal strings struck by light hammers. **2.** *US* a modern folk instrument related to the guitar and plucked with the fingers.

dull /dʌl/ *adj.* **1.** slow of understanding; stupid. **2.** lacking sharpness in the senses or feelings; unfeeling. **3.** not sharply felt: *a dull pain.* **4.** low in spirits; listless. **5.** boring, uninteresting: *a dull talk.* **6.** not sharp; blunt: *a dull knife.* **7.** not bright, or clear; dim: *a dull day; a dull sound.* –*v.t.* **8.** to make dull. –*v.i.* **9.** to become dull. **–dullish**, *adj.* **–dullness**, *n.* **–dully**, *adv.*

duly /'djuli/ *adv.* **1.** in a due manner; properly; fitly. **2.** in due season; punctually. **3.** adequately.

dumb /dʌm/ *adj.* **1.** (*likely to give offence*) without the power of speech. **2.** silent. **3.** *Colloq.* stupid; dull-witted. **4.** *Colloq.* unpleasing; disagreeable: *homework is so dumb.* –*phr.* **5. dumb down**, *Colloq.* **a.** to put (information) in simpler terms, as for a less informed audience: *to dumb down a lecture.* **b.** to cause to become less informed or less intelligent: *calculators have been blamed for dumbing down maths students.* **–dumbly**, *adv.* **–dumbness**, *n.*

dumbbell /'dʌmbel/ *n.* a gymnasium hand apparatus made of wood or metal, consisting of two balls joined by a bar-like handle, used as weights, usually in pairs.

dumbfound /'dʌmfaʊnd/ *v.t.* to strike dumb with amazement. Also, **dumfound**. **–dumbfounder**, *n.*

dumbstruck /'dʌmstrʌk/ *adj.* shocked into speechlessness.

dummy /'dʌmi/ *n.* (*pl.* **-mies**) **1.** an imitation or copy of something, as for display, to indicate appearance, exhibit clothing, etc. **2.** *Colloq.* a stupid person; dolt. **3.** someone who has nothing to say or who takes no active part in affairs. **4.** *Aust., NZ Hist.* (especially in buying land) someone ostensibly acting on their own behalf while actually acting as an agent for others. **5.** a rubber teat given to a baby to suck. **6.** *Printing* sheets folded and made up to show the size, shape, form, sequence, and general style of a contemplated piece of printing. **7.** Also, **dummy pass.** *Football* a feigned or pretended pass intended to deceive an opponent. **8.** *NZ Prison Colloq.* a punishment cell; digger. *–adj.* **9.** acting for others while ostensibly acting for oneself, especially in buying land. **10.** counterfeit; sham; imitation. **11.** (of ammunition) not equipped with a destructive missile, and used chiefly in military training. *–phr.* **12. sell someone the dummy,** *Football* to deceive one's opponent into thinking that one is about to make a pass. **13. spit the dummy,** *Aust. Colloq.* **a.** to give up or opt out of a contest or the like before there is a reasonable cause to do so. **b.** to throw a tantrum.

dump /dʌmp/ *v.t.* **1.** to throw down in a mass; fling down or drop heavily. **2.** to empty out, as from a cart by tilting. **3.** to get rid of; hand over to somebody else. **4.** *Computers* to print out, with minimal editing, the content of computer memory, usually for diagnostic purposes in debugging. **5.** *Commerce* **a.** to put (goods) on the market in large quantities and at a low price, especially to a large or favoured buyer. **b.** to market (goods) thus in a foreign country, as at a price below that charged in the home country. **6.** *Football* to tackle heavily. **7.** (of a wave) to hurl (a body-surfer) onto the churned-up sand at the bottom of the wave. *–v.i.* **8.** to fall or drop down suddenly. **9.** to unload. **10.** to offer for sale at a low price, especially to offer low prices to favoured buyers. *–n.* **11.** anything as rubbish dumped or thrown down. **12.** Also, **rubbish dump.** → tip² (def. 9). **13.** *Mil.* a collection of ammunition, stores, etc., deposited at some point, as near a battle front, to be distributed for use. **14.** the act of dumping. **15.** *Mining* mullock and dirt heaped around mine shafts. **16.** *Colloq.* a place, house, or town that is poorly kept up, and generally of wretched appearance. *–phr. Colloq.* **17. dump on,** to criticise or rebuke. **18. sell the dump,** (sometimes fol. by *from*) **a.** *Football* to pass the ball to avoid being tackled. **b.** to pass on something worthless, or the object of some dispute to avoid trouble.

dumper /'dʌmpə/ *n.* **1.** a person or thing that dumps something. **2.** *Surfing* a wave which, in shallow water, instead of breaking evenly from the top, crashes violently down, throwing surfers to the bottom.

dumpling /'dʌmplɪŋ/ *n.* **1.** a rounded mass of steamed dough (often served with stewed meat, etc.). **2.** a kind of pudding consisting of a wrapping of dough enclosing an apple or other fruit, and boiled or baked.

dumps /dʌmps/ *pl. n.* **1.** *Colloq.* a dull, gloomy state of mind. *–phr.* **2. down in the dumps,** in a dull or depressed state of mind.

dumpy /'dʌmpi/ *adj.* **(-pier, -piest)** short and stout; squat: *a dumpy woman.* **–dumpily,** *adv.* **–dumpiness,** *n.*

dun¹ /dʌn/ *v.t.* **(dunned, dunning)** to make repeated and insistent demands upon, especially for the payment of a debt.

dun² /dʌn/ *adj.* **1.** dull or greyish brown. **2.** dark; gloomy.

dunce /dʌns/ *n.* a dull-witted or stupid person; a dolt.

dune /djun/ *n.* a sand hill or sand ridge formed by the wind, usually in desert regions or near lakes and oceans.

dung /dʌŋ/ *n.* manure; excrement, especially of animals. **–dungy,** *adj.*

dungeon /'dʌndʒən/ *n.* any dark, small prison or cell, especially underground.

dunk /dʌŋk/ *v.t.* **1.** to immerse in water. **2.** to dip (biscuits, etc.) into coffee, milk, etc. **3.** *Basketball* to push (the ball) down through the basket, by jumping so high and so close to the ring that the hand can reach above the ring to achieve this. **–dunker,** *n.*

dunnart /'dʌnat/ *n.* any of the narrow-footed carnivorous dasyurids of genus *Sminthopsis*, being a small nocturnal marsupial resembling a mouse and feeding on small insects, ground-dwelling invertebrates and even small lizards.

dunny /'dʌni/ *n.* (*pl.* **-nies**) *Aust., NZ* **1.** an outside toilet, found in unsewered areas, usually at some distance from the house it serves and consisting of a small shed furnished with a lavatory seat placed over a sanitary can. **2.** *Colloq.* a toilet.

duo /'djuou/ *n.* (*pl.* **duos** or **dui** /'djui/) **1.** *Music* a duet. **2.** a pair of singers, entertainers, etc.

duo- a word element meaning 'two', as in *duologue*.

duodenum /djuə'dinəm/ *n. Anat.* the first portion of the small intestine, from the stomach to the jejunum.

dupe /djup/ *n.* **1.** someone who is imposed upon or deceived; a gull. *–v.t.* **2.** to make a dupe of; deceive; delude; trick. **–dupable,** *adj.* **–dupability** /djupə'bɪləti/, *n.* **–duper,** *n.*

duple /'djupəl/ *adj.* double; twofold.

duplex /'djupleks/ *adj.* **1.** twofold; double. *–n.* **2.** *US, Aust.* a building consisting of two separate dwellings, arranged either on each storey of a two-storey building, or as a pair of semidetached cottages.

duplicate *adj.* /'djupləkət/ **1.** exactly like or corresponding to something else. **2.** double; consisting of or existing in two corresponding parts. *–n.* /'djupləkət/ **3.** a copy exactly like an original. **4.** anything corresponding in all respects to something else. *–v.t.* /'djupləkeɪt/ **5.** to make an exact copy of; repeat. **6.** to double; make twofold. *–phr.* **7. in duplicate,** in two copies, exactly alike. **–duplicative** /'djupləkətɪv/, *adj.* **–duplicator,** *n.*

duplicity /dju'plɪsəti/ *n.* deceitfulness in speech or conduct; speaking or acting in two different ways concerning the same matter with intent to deceive; double-dealing. **–duplicitous,** *adj.*

durable /'djurəbəl/ *adj.* **1.** having the quality of lasting or enduring; not easily worn out, decayed, etc. **n. 2.** (*pl.*) goods which are durable. **–durability** /djurə'bɪləti/, **durableness,** *n.* **–durably,** *adv.*

duration /dju'reɪʃən/ *n.* **1.** continuance in time. **2.** the length of time anything continues. *–phr.* **3. for the duration,** for a long time; for as long as something takes. **–durative,** *adj.*

duress /dju'rɛs/ *n.* **1.** constraint; compulsion. **2.** forcible restraint of liberty; imprisonment. **3.** *Law* such constraint or coercion as will render void a contract or other legal act entered or performed under its influence.

during /'djurɪŋ/ *prep.* **1.** throughout the continuance of. **2.** in the course of.

dusk /dʌsk/ *n.* **1.** partial darkness; a state between light and darkness; twilight; shade; gloom. **2.** the darker stage of twilight. **–duskish,** *adj.*

dusky /'dʌski/ *adj.* **(-kier, -kiest)** **1.** somewhat dark; dark-coloured. **2.** deficient in light; dim. **–duskily,** *adv.* **–duskiness,** *n.*

dusky moorhen *n.* a rail, *Gallinula tenebrosa*, brownish black with white patches on the tail coverts and a red frontal shield, found mainly in swamps and parklands of eastern Australia.

dust /dʌst/ *n.* **1.** earth or other matter in fine, dry particles. **2.** any finely powdered substance, as sawdust. **3.** a cloud of finely powdered earth or other matter in the air. **4.** that to which anything, as the human body, is reduced by disintegration or decay. **5.** the mortal human body. *–v.t.* **6.** (sometimes fol. by *off*) to free from dust; wipe the dust from: *to dust the table.* **7.** to sprinkle (with dust or powder): *to dust plants with powder.* **8.** to strew or sprinkle as dust: *dust powder over plants.* **9.** to soil with dust; make dusty. *–v.i.* **10.** to wipe dust from furniture, a room, etc. **11.** to become dusty. *–phr.* **12. bite the dust,** *Colloq.* **a.** to fall dead, especially in combat. **b.** to lose a contest or competition: *Essendon bit the dust in the grand final.* **c.** (of a plan, enterprise, etc.) to fail. **13. dust off**, to take from storage and make ready for use again; begin to use or practise again. **14. let the dust settle**, let the disturbance die down. **15. lick the dust**, *Colloq.* **a.** to be killed or wounded. **b.** to grovel; humble oneself abjectly. **16. raise** (or **kick up**) **the dust**, *Colloq.* to make a fuss; cause a disturbance. **17. throw dust in someone's eyes**, to mislead someone. **–dustless**, *adj.* **–dusty**, *adj.*

duster /'dʌstə/ *n.* **1.** a cloth, brush, etc., for removing dust. **2.** a felt pad mounted on a wooden block, used in schools for cleaning the blackboard. **3.** an apparatus for sprinkling dust or powder on something.

dust jacket *n.* a jacket (def. 2) for a book. Also, **dust cover**.

dust-up *n.* *Colloq.* a commotion; fight; scuffle.

Dutch courage /dʌtʃ 'kʌrɪdʒ/ *n.* courage inspired by alcoholic drink.

Dutch oven *n.* **1.** a large, heavy pot with a close-fitting lid used for slow cooking. **2.** a metal utensil, open in front, for roasting before an open fire. **3.** a brick oven in which the walls are preheated for cooking.

Dutch treat *n.* a meal or entertainment in which each person pays for himself or herself. Also, **Dutch shout**.

Dutch uncle *n.* someone who offers concerned or disinterested advice at length.

dutiful /'djutəfəl/ *adj.* **1.** performing the duties required of one; obedient: *a dutiful child.* **2.** required by duty; proceeding from or expressive of a sense of duty: *dutiful attention.* **–dutifully**, *adv.* **–dutifulness**, *n.*

duty /'djuti/ *n.* (*pl.* **-ties**) **1.** that which one is bound to do by moral or legal obligation. **2.** the binding or obligatory force of that which is morally right; moral obligation. **3.** action required by one's position or occupation; office; function: *the duties of a soldier; the duties of a clergyman.* **4.** a specific or *ad valorem* levy imposed by law on the import, export, sale, or manufacture of goods, the transference of property, the legal recognition of deeds and documents, etc. **5.** *Agric.* the amount of water necessary to provide for the crop in a given area. *–phr.* **6. do duty for**, to be a substitute for; serve the same function as. **7. off duty**, not at work. **8. on duty**, at work. **–dutiable**, *adj.*

duty of care *n.* *Law* a legal obligation to avoid causing harm to another person by the exercise of reasonable care to avoid foreseeable injury to that person.

duvet /'duveɪ/ *n.* *Brit.*, *NZ* → **doona**.

dux /dʌks/ *n.* *Aust.*, *NZ* the top pupil academically in some division of a school.

DVD /di vi 'di/ *n.* **1.** a high-capacity optical disc, usually 12 cm in diameter, used to store, in digital form, audio, video or text data, especially films, television shows, etc. **2.** the technology related to this storage. *–adj.* **3.** relating to or utilising this technology: *a DVD player; a DVD film.*

DVR /di vi 'a/ *n.* digital video recorder; an electronic device which records video in a digital format, allowing capture and playback to and from a disk.

dwarf /dwɔf/ *n.* (*pl.* **dwarfs** or **dwarves** /dwɔvz/) **1.** any person, animal or plant much below the ordinary height or size. *–adj.* **2.** of unusually small height or size; diminutive. *–v.t.* **3.** to cause to seem small: *the tower dwarfed the surrounding buildings.* **4.** to prevent the proper growth or development of.

dwell /dwɛl/ *v.i.* (**dwelt** or **dwelled**, **dwelling**) **1.** to abide as a permanent resident. **2.** to continue for a time. *–phr.* **3. dwell on** (or **upon**), to linger over in thought, speech, or writing; to emphasise: *to dwell upon a subject; to dwell on a point in argument.* **–dweller**, *n.*

dwelling /'dwɛlɪŋ/ *n.* **1.** a place of residence or abode; a house. **2.** continued or habitual residence.

dwindle /'dwɪndl/ *v.i.* **1.** to become smaller and smaller; shrink; waste away: *his vast fortune has dwindled away.* **2.** to fall away, as in quality; degenerate.

dye /daɪ/ *n.* **1.** a colouring material or matter. **2.** a liquid containing colouring matter for imparting a particular hue to cloth, etc. **3.** colour or hue, especially as produced by dyeing. *–verb* (**dyed**, **dyeing**) *–v.t.* **4.** to colour or stain; treat with a dye; colour (cloth, etc.) by soaking in a liquid containing colouring matter: *to dye cloth red.* *–v.i.* **5.** to impart colour, as a dye. **6.** to become coloured when treated with a dye: *this cloth dyes easily.* *–phr.* **7. of the deepest** (or **blackest**) **dye**, of the worst kind. **–dyer**, *n.*

dying /'daɪɪŋ/ *adj.* **1.** ceasing to live; approaching death: *a dying man.* **2.** relating to or associated with death: *a dying hour.* **3.** given, uttered, or manifested just before death: *dying words.* **4.** drawing to a close: *the dying year.* *–n.* **5.** death. *–phr.* *Colloq.* **6. be dying for**, to desire or want keenly or greatly: *I'm dying for a drink.* **7. be dying to**, to desire or want keenly or greatly: *I'm dying to see Venice.*

dyke¹ /daɪk/ *n.* **1.** an embankment for restraining the waters of the sea or a river. **2.** a ditch. **3.** a ridge or bank of earth as thrown up in excavating. **4.** a causeway. **5.** an obstacle; barrier. **6.** *Geol.* a tabular body of igneous rock which cuts across the structure of adjacent rocks or cuts massive rocks; formed by intrusion of magma. **7.** *Aust.*, *NZ Colloq.* a toilet. *–v.t.* **8.** to drain with a dyke. **9.** to enclose, restrain, or protect by a dyke: *to dyke a tract of land.* Also, **dike**.

dyke² /daɪk/ *n.* *Colloq.* a lesbian. Also, **dike**.

dyna- a word element referring to power, as in *dynameter.* Also, **dynam-**.

dynamic /daɪ'næmɪk/ *adj.* **1.** of or relating to force not in equilibrium (opposed to *static*) or to force in any state. **2.** of or relating to dynamics. **3.** characterised by energy or effective action; active; forceful. *–n.* **4.** a particular state of social or personal interaction: *the interesting dynamic between actor and audience.* **–dynamically**, *adv.*

dynamic random access memory *n.* → **DRAM**.

dynamics /daɪ'næmɪks/ *n.* **1.** *Physics* the branch of mechanics that deals with those forces which cause or affect the motion of bodies. **2.** the science or principles of forces acting in any field. **3.** (*construed as pl.*) the forces, physical or moral, at work in any field. **4.** *Music* variations in the volume of sound.

dynamic verb *n.* *Gram.* a verb which indicates an action or process, as *The child jumps*, or *The light fades.* Compare **stative verb**. Also, **action verb**.

dynamism /'daɪnəmɪzəm/ *n.* the force or active principle on which a thing, person, or movement operates.

dynamite /'daɪnəmaɪt/ *n.* **1.** a high explosive consisting of nitroglycerine mixed with some absorbent substance such as kieselguhr. **2.** *Colloq.* anything or anyone potentially dangerous and liable to cause trouble. **3.** *Colloq.* anything or anyone exceptional. *–v.t.* **4.** to blow up, shatter, or destroy with dynamite. **–dynamitic** /daɪnə'mɪtɪk/, *adj.*

dynamo /'daɪnəmoʊ/ *n.* (*pl.* **-mos**) **1.** any rotating machine in which mechanical energy is converted into electrical energy, especially a direct current generator. **2.** *Colloq.* a forceful, energetic person.

dynasty /'dɪnəsti/, *Chiefly US* /'daɪnəsti/ *n.* (*pl.* **-ties**) **1.** a sequence of rulers from the same family or stock. **2.** the rule of such a sequence. **3.** a sequence of important powerful or wealthy people from the one family. **–dynastic** /də'næstɪk, daɪ-/, **dynastical** /də'næstɪkəl, daɪ-/, *adj.* **–dynastically** /də'næstɪkli, daɪ-/, *adv.*

dyne /daɪn/ n. the unit of force in the centimetre-gram-second system, equal to 10×10^{-6} newtons. *Symbol*: dyn

dys- a prefix, especially medical, indicating difficulty, poor condition, as in *dysphoria*.

dysentery /ˈdɪsəntri/ n. *Pathol.* an infectious disease marked by inflammation and ulceration of the lower part of the bowels, with diarrhoea that becomes mucous and haemorrhagic. –**dysenteric** /dɪsənˈtɛrɪk/, *adj.*

dysfunctional /dɪsˈfʌŋkʃənəl/ *adj.* **1.** not functioning properly or normally: *a dysfunctional engine.* **2.** not functioning in a way that conforms behaviourally, socially, etc., to accepted norms: *a dysfunctional family; a dysfunctional relationship.*

dyslexia /dɪsˈlɛksiə/ n. *Psychol.* impairment in reading ability, often associated with other disorders especially in writing and coordination.

dysmenorrhoea /dɪsˌmɛnəˈriə/ n. *Pathol.* painful menstruation. Also, **dysmenorrhea**.

dysmorphia /dɪsˈmɔfiə/ n. a deformity or abnormality in the shape or size of a part of the body. –**dysmorphic**, *adj.*

dyspepsia /dɪsˈpɛpsiə/ n. *Pathol.* unsettled or impaired digestion; indigestion.

dyspeptic /dɪsˈpɛptɪk/ *adj.* **1.** of or relating to dyspepsia. **2.** morbidly gloomy or pessimistic. –n. **3.** someone subject to or suffering from dyspepsia. –**dyspeptically**, *adv.*

dysphoria /dɪsˈfɔriə/ n. a state of dissatisfaction, anxiety, restlessness, or fidgeting. –**dysphoric**, *adj.*

dysthymia /dɪsˈθaɪmiə, dɪsˈθɪmiə/ n. *Psychol.* a mild form of depression characterised by a chronic inability to get pleasure out of life, usually accompanied by irregularities in the patterns of eating and sleeping, chronic tiredness, and low self-esteem. Also, **dysthymic disorder**. –**dysthymic**, *adj., n.*

dystopia /dɪsˈtoʊpiə/ n. an imaginary world in which everything is as bad as it can possibly be (opposed to *utopia*).

E e

E, e /i/ *n.* **1.** the fifth letter of the English alphabet. **2.** *Music* the third note in the scale of C major.

e-¹ variant of **ex-¹**, used in words of Latin origin before consonants except *c*, *f*, *p*, *q*, *s*, and *t*, as in *emit*.

e-² **1.** a prefix used to indicate that the specified activity is carried out or operates over the internet, or is associated with it in some way: *email*; *e-banking*; *ecommerce*; *e-activism*. **2.** a prefix which indicates that something operates electronically: *e-tag*; *e-ticket*.

each /itʃ/ *adj.* **1.** every, or two or more considered individually or one by one: *each stone in the building.* –*pron.* **2.** each one: *they went his way.* –*adv.* **3.** apiece: *they cost a dollar each.* –*phr.* **4. bet each way, a.** to place an each-way bet. **b.** to be undecided or neutral.

each other *n.* each the other (used to describe a reciprocal relation or action between two or more people, objects, etc.): *they hit each other.*

each-way bet *n.* a bet in which a racehorse, etc., is staked to win the place dividend for a place (def. 27b), or both the win and place dividends for a win.

eager /ˈigə/ *adj.* **1.** keen or ardent in desire or feeling; impatiently longing: *I am eager for or about it*; *eager to do it.* **2.** characterised by great earnestness. –**eagerly,** *adv.* –**eagerness,** *n.*

eagle /ˈigəl/ *n.* **1.** any of certain large, diurnal birds of prey of the family Accipitridae, as the wedge-tailed eagle, noted for their size, strength, powerful flight and keenness of vision. **2.** *Golf* a score two below par on any but par-three holes.

eaglehawk /ˈigəlhɔk/ *n.* **1.** → **wedge-tailed eagle.** –*v.i.* **2.** to pluck wool from a dead sheep.

eaglet /ˈiglət/ *n.* a young eagle.

ear¹ /ɪə/ *n.* **1.** the organ of hearing, in humans and other mammals usually consisting of three parts (**external ear, middle ear,** and **inner ear**). **2.** the external part alone. **3.** the sense of hearing. **4.** keen perception of the differences of sound, especially sensitiveness to the quality and correctness of musical sounds: *an ear for music.* **5.** attention; heed, especially favourable attention: *gain a person's ear.* –*phr.* **6. be all ears,** to listen attentively. **7. bend someone's ear,** *Colloq.* to harangue someone. **8. by ear,** without dependence upon or reference to written music. **9. fall on deaf ears,** to pass unheeded. **10. go in one ear and out the other,** to be heard but ignored; make no impression. **11. have an ear to the ground,** to be well informed about gossip or trends. **12. out on one's (pink) ear,** *Colloq.* dismissed summarily. **13. set by the ears,** to cause to disagree or quarrel. **14. turn a deaf ear,** to refuse to help or consider helping. **15. up to one's ears,** deeply involved; extremely busy. **16. wet behind the ears,** naive; immature or inexperienced. –**earless,** *adj.* –**earlike,** *adj.*

ear² /ɪə/ *n.* the part of a cereal plant, such as wheat or barley, which contains the flowers and hence the fruit, grains, or kernels.

earbash /ˈɪəbæʃ/ *Colloq.* –*v.t.* **1.** to harangue (someone). –*v.i.* **2.** to talk insistently and for a long time. –**earbasher,** *n.* –**earbashing,** *n.*

earbud /ˈɪəbʌd/ *n.* a small earphone designed to sit in the ear canal.

eardrum /ˈɪədrʌm/ *n.* the tympanic membrane.

ear gauging /ˈɪə geɪdʒɪŋ/ *n.* an ear piercing procedure that involves the stretching of the pierced hole with a series of objects, each one larger than the previous one.

earl /ɜl/ *n.* a British nobleman ranked immediately below a marquess and immediately above a viscount, the title now being unconnected with territorial jurisdiction. –**earldom,** *n.*

earlobe /ˈɪəloʊb/ *n.* the soft pendulous lower part of the external ear.

early /ˈɜli/ *adv.* (**-lier, -liest**) **1.** in or during the first part of some division of time, or of some course or series: *early in the year.* **2.** before the usual or appointed time; in good time: *come early.* **3.** far back in time. –*adj.* (**-lier, -liest**) **4.** occurring in the first part of some division of time, or of some course or series: *an early hour.* **5.** occurring before the usual or appointed time: *an early dinner.* **6. a.** belonging to a period far back in time or to the first part of such a period: *the early Norman castles.* **b.** belonging to the period when white settlements were first made in Australia, or in a section of it: *the early days*; *early explorers.* **7.** occurring soon: *an early reply.* –*phr.* **8. early days,** too soon to form an opinion or see an outcome: *it's early days yet.* **9. early on (in the piece),** after very little time has elapsed; before the main part of a project, game, etc., has been completed. –**earliness,** *n.*

early Nancy /ɜli ˈnænsi/ *n.* a wildflower of the lily family, *Anguillaria dioica*, found throughout Australia, the white flower of which has a purple band around the base of each segment, together forming a purple ring.

earmark /ˈɪəmak/ *n.* **1.** a mark of identification made on the ear of an animal. **2.** any identifying or distinguishing mark or characteristic. –*v.t.* **3.** to set aside for a specific purpose or use: *to earmark goods for export.*

earn /ɜn/ *v.t.* (**earned** *or* **earnt, earning**) **1.** to gain by labour or service: *to earn a good salary.* **2.** to merit, as for service; deserve: *to receive more than one has earned.* **3.** to get as one's desert or due: *to earn a reputation for honesty.* **4.** to gain as due return or profit: *defence bonds earn interest.* –*phr.* **5. earn a living,** to receive an income from employment, sufficient to be able to support oneself. –**earner,** *n.*

earnest /ˈɜnəst/ *adj.* **1.** serious in intention, purpose, or effort; sincerely zealous: *an earnest worker.* **2.** showing depth and sincerity of feeling: *earnest words.* –**earnestly,** *adv.* –**earnestness,** *n.*

earphone /ˈɪəfoʊn/ *n.* a small device for converting electric signals into soundwaves, so designed that it is meant to fit into the ear or to be held close to it.

earring /ˈɪərɪŋ/ *n.* a ring or other ornament worn in or on the lobe of the ear.

earshot /ˈɪəʃɒt/ *n.* reach or range of hearing: *within earshot*; *out of earshot.*

earth /ɜθ/ *n.* **1.** (*oft. upper case*) the planet which we inhabit, the third in order from the sun. Its period of revolution is one year, and its mean distance from the sun 149 597 870 km. Its diameter is 12 756 km. It has one satellite, the moon. **2.** the inhabitants of this planet: *the whole earth rejoiced.* **3.** this planet as the habitation of humans, often in contrast to heaven and hell. **4.** the surface of this planet. **5.** the solid matter of this planet: the dry land; the ground. **6.** the softer part of the land, as distinguished from rock; soil. **7.** the hole of a burrowing animal. **8.** any hole in the ground where a fox seeks shelter when being chased. **9.** *Elect.* **a.** a conducting connection between an electric circuit or equipment and the ground or some similar large conducting body. **b.** the terminal to which the earthing connection is attached. *–v.t.* **10.** *Elect.* to establish an earth for (a device, circuit, etc.); join (a conductor) to earth. *–phr.* **11. come down** (or **back**) **to earth,** to return to practical or realistic attitudes. **12. down to earth,** practical; plain; blunt. **13. on earth,** used as an intensifier: *what on earth are you doing?* **14. run to earth,** **a.** to pursue (an animal) to its burrow or hole. **b.** to hunt down; track down. **15. the earth,** everything; a great deal: *cost the earth*; *want the earth.*

earthen /'ɜθən/ *adj.* **1.** composed of earth. **2.** made of baked clay.

earthenware /'ɜθənwɛə/ *n.* **1.** earthen pottery; vessels, etc., of baked or hardened clay. **2.** the material of such vessels (usually the coarse, opaque varieties, the finer, translucent kinds being called *porcelain*). *–adj.* **3.** made of such material. **4.** of or relating to vessels made of such material.

earthly /'ɜθli/ *adj.* **1.** of or relating to the earth, especially as opposed to heaven; worldly. **2.** possible or conceivable: *no earthly use.* *–phr.* **3. an earthly (chance),** (*used with a negative*) any chance whatsoever: *he stood no earthly chance of winning.* **4. not have an earthly,** **a.** to have no idea. **b.** to have no chance. **–earthliness,** *n.*

earthquake /'ɜθkweɪk/ *n.* tremors or earth movements in the earth's crust when fracturing rocks send out a series of three distinct sets of shock waves (earthquake waves).

earthworm /'ɜθwɜm/ *n.* **1.** any of numerous annelid worms that burrow in soil and feed on soil and decaying organic matter. **2.** a mean or grovelling person.

earthy /'ɜθi/ *adj.* (**-thier, -thiest**) **1.** of the nature of or consisting of earth or soil. **2.** (of the flavour of a wine) suggestive of the soil in which the grapes were grown. **3.** coarse or unrefined. **4.** direct; robust; unaffected.

ease /iz/ *n.* **1.** freedom from labour, pain, or physical annoyance of any kind; tranquil rest; comfort: *to take one's ease.* **2.** freedom from concern, anxiety, or solicitude; a quiet state of mind: *be at ease.* **3.** freedom from difficulty or great labour; facility: *it can be done with ease.* **4.** freedom from stiffness, constraint, or formality; unaffectedness: *ease of manner*; *at ease with others.* *–v.t.* **5.** to give rest or relief to; make comfortable. **6.** to free from anxiety or care: *to ease one's mind.* **7.** to mitigate, lighten, or lessen: *to ease the pain.* **8.** to release from pressure, tension, or the like. **9.** (in sewing, etc.) to join (two pieces of material whose edges are of unequal length) in such a way that the extra fullness of the larger section is distributed evenly along the join. **10.** to render less difficult; facilitate. **11.** to move slowly and with great care. **12.** *Finance* to free from the pressure created by financial stringency: *to ease monetary policy.* *–v.i.* **13.** to become less painful or burdensome, etc. **14.** *Gambling* (of betting odds) to lengthen. *–phr.* **15. at ease, a.** comfortable and relaxed. **b.** *Mil.* a position of rest in which soldiers may relax, but may not leave their place or talk. **16. ease along,** to move with great care. **17. ease in,** to insert slowly and with care. **18. ease into,** to commence gradually. **19. ease off** (or **up**), to reduce severity, pressure, tension, etc. **20. put at ease,** to make feel relaxed and free from nervousness or tension. **–easeful,** *adj.* **–easer,** *n.*

easel /'izəl/ *n.* a frame in the form of a tripod, for supporting an artist's canvas, a blackboard, or the like.

easement /'izmənt/ *n.* **1.** an easing; relief. **2.** something that gives ease; a convenience. **3.** *Law* a right held by one person to make use of the land of another.

east /ist/ *n.* **1.** a cardinal point of the compass (90 degrees to the right of north), corresponding to the point where the sun is seen to rise. **2.** the direction in which this point lies. *–adj.* **3.** lying towards or situated in the east: *the east side.* **4.** directed or proceeding towards the east: *the east route.* **5.** coming from the east: *an east wind.* **6.** (*also upper case*) designating the eastern part of a region, nation, etc. **7.** *Eccles.* towards the altar as situated with respect to the nave. *–adv.* **8.** towards or in the east: *he went east.* **9.** from the east. *–phr.* **10. the east,** (*also upper case*) a quarter or territory situated in an eastern direction.

Easter /'istə/ *n.* **1.** an annual Christian festival in commemoration of the resurrection of Jesus Christ, observed on the first Sunday after the full moon that occurs on or next after 21 March (the vernal equinox) or, by some Orthodox or Eastern Rite churches, on dates calculated from the Julian calender, usually occurring after the Western festival but sometimes on the same dates. **2.** Also, **Easter Day, Easter Sunday.** the day on which this festival is celebrated. **3.** the period from Good Friday to the following Monday (Easter Monday).

easterly /'istəli/ *adj.* **1.** moving, directed, or situated towards the east: *an easterly course.* **2.** coming from the east: *an easterly wind.* *–adv.* **3.** towards the east. **4.** from the east. *–n.* (*pl.* **-lies**) **5.** a wind from the east.

eastern /'istən/ *adj.* **1.** lying towards or situated in the east: *the eastern seaboard.* **2.** directed or proceeding towards the east: *an eastern route.* **3.** coming from the east: *an eastern wind.* **4.** (*usu. upper case*) of or relating to the East. **–easterner,** *n.*

easy /'izi/ *adj.* (**-sier, -siest**) **1.** not difficult; requiring no great labour or effort: *easy to read*; *an easy victory.* **2.** free from pain, discomfort, worry, or care: *he has an easy conscience now*; *easy in one's mind.* **3.** conducive to ease or comfort: *an easy stance.* **4.** fond of or given to ease; easygoing. **5.** not harsh or strict; lenient: *an easy master.* **6.** not burdensome or oppressive: *easy terms.* **7.** not difficult to influence; compliant. **8.** *Colloq.* (usually of a woman) sexually promiscuous. **9.** *Colloq.* having no firm preferences in a particular matter: *I'm easy.* **10.** free from formality, constraint, or embarrassment: *easy style*; *easy manners.* **11.** not tight; fitting loosely: *an easy fit.* **12.** not forced or hurried; moderate: *an easy pace.* *–adv.* **13.** *Colloq.* in a less tense manner; comfortably: *take it easy.* *–phr.* **14. easy meat,** *Colloq.* someone who is expected to put up no opposition or resistance. **15. easy on the eyes,** *Colloq.* attractive; good-looking. **16. easy pickings,** profits or advantages which are readily obtainable. **17. easy (up)!, a.** an admonishment, calling for calm and restraint from an over-excited or angry person. **b.** a soothing call to a nervous animal in an attempt to calm its fears. **18. go easy on,** *Colloq.* **a.** to be lenient with. **b.** to use sparingly: *go easy on the honey.* **19. go easy with,** *Colloq.* to handle carefully: *go easy with that valuable jar.* **20. take it easy,** *Colloq.* to proceed at a comfortable pace.

easygoing /'izigoʊɪŋ/ *adj.* **1.** taking matters in an easy way; comfortably unconcerned. **2.** going easily, as a horse.

easy street *Colloq.* *–n.* **1.** a comfortable life surrounded by material possessions: *back to easy street.* *–phr.* **2. on easy street,** in a comfortable financial position.

eat /it/ *verb* (**ate** /eɪt, ɛt/, **eaten** /'itn/, **eating**) *–v.t.* **1.** to take into the mouth and swallow for nourishment; especially to masticate and swallow, as solid food. **2.** to consume by or as by devouring. **3.** to ravage or devastate. **4.** to wear or waste away; corrode. **5.** to make (a hole, passage, etc.) as by gnawing or corrosion. **6.** *Colloq.* to cause to worry; trouble: *what's eating* *you?* **7.** *Colloq.* *(taboo)* to perform fellatio or cunnilingus on. *–v.i.* **8.** to consume food; take a meal. **9.** to make a way as by gnawing or corrosion. *–n.* **10.** *Colloq.* *(pl.)* food. *–phr.* **11.** **eat fit to bust**, *Colloq.* to eat with good appetite. **12.** **eat into**, to remove gradually; erode. **13.** **eat it up, a.** to consume food. **b.** to process or work through rapidly. **14.** **eat one's heart out**, to pine or fret, especially with envy. **15.** **eat one's words**, to take back what one has said. **16.** **eat out**, to dine away from one's home at a restaurant, club, hotel, etc. **17.** **eat out of someone's hand**, to be uncritically compliant and trusting of another, often in a servile or sycophantic manner. **–eater**, *n.*

eating disorder *n.* a pattern of eating which involves compulsive over-eating or abstinence to such an extent that it affects one's physical and mental health.

eaves /ivz/ *pl. n.* the overhanging lower edge of a roof.

eavesdrop /'ivzdrɒp/ *v.i.* (**-dropped, -dropping**) to listen clandestinely. **–eavesdropper**, *n.*

ebb /ɛb/ *n.* **1.** the reflux or falling of the tide (opposed to *flood* and *flow*). **2.** a flowing backwards or away; decline or decay. *–v.i.* **3.** to flow back or away, as the water of a tide (opposed to *flow*). **4.** to decline or decay; waste or fade away: *his life is ebbing. –phr.* **5.** **at a low ebb**, in weak spirits; depressed.

Ebola /ə'boʊlə/ *n.* a virus causing high fever and internal haemorrhaging, often fatal. Also, **Ebola virus.**

ebony /'ɛbəni/ *n.* (*pl.* **-nies**) a hard, heavy, durable wood, most highly prized when black, from various tropical trees usually of the genus *Diospyros*, such as *D. ebenum* of southern India and Sri Lanka, used for cabinetwork, etc., and *Maba humilis* of Qld used for musical instruments.

ebook /'ibʊk/ *n.* a book in an electronic format designed to be read in an ereader. Compare **p-book.** Also, **e-book.**

ebook reader *n.* → **ereader.**

ebullient /ə'bʊljənt, ə'bʌl-, ə'bjul-/ *adj.* **1.** seething or overflowing with fervour, enthusiasm, excitement, etc. **2.** boiling; bubbling like a boiling liquid. **–ebulliently**, *adv.* **–ebullience, ebulliency,** *n.*

ec- variant of **ex-³**, before consonants, as in *eccentric.*

e-card *n.* a greeting card created using digital media instead of paper and sent via email.

eccentric /ək'sɛntrɪk/ *adj.* **1.** deviating from the recognised or usual character, practice, etc.; irregular; peculiar; odd; strange: *eccentric conduct, an eccentric person.* **2.** not having the same centre, as two circles or spheres of which one is within the other or which intersect; not concentric. **3.** not situated in the centre, as an axis. *–n.* **4.** an unusual, peculiar, or odd person or thing. **–eccentricity** /ɛksən'trɪsəti/, *n.* **–eccentrically,** *adv.*

ecclesiastic /əklizi'æstɪk/ *n.* **1.** a member of the clergy, especially of the Christian clergy, or a person in orders. *–adj.* **2.** ecclesiastical.

ecclesiastical /əklizi'æstɪkəl/ *adj.* of or relating to a religious organisation, especially the Christian church or the clergy; clerical; not secular; not lay: *ecclesiastical discipline*; *ecclesiastical affairs*; *ecclesiastical courts.* **–ecclesiastically,** *adv.*

echelon /'ɛʃəlɒn/ *n.* **1.** a level of command: *in the higher echelons.* **2.** any steplike formation, especially of people in movement.

echidna /ə'kɪdnə/ *n.* (*pl.* **-nas** *or* **-nae** /-ni/) any of the spine-covered insectivorous egg-laying monotreme mammals with claws and a slender snout, occurring in two genera, the **long-beaked echidna**, *Zaglossus*, of New Guinea, and the smaller **straight-beaked echidna**, *Tachyglossus*, of mainland Australia, Tasmania, and southern New Guinea; spiny anteater.

echinacea /ɛkə'neɪʃə/ *n.* a North American plant of the genus *Echinacea* (family Asteraceae), extracts of which are used in herbal medicine as a cold remedy, antibiotic, and immune system stimulant.

echo /'ɛkoʊ/ *n.* (*pl.* **echoes**) **1.** a repetition of sound, produced by soundwaves bouncing back from a surface. **2.** a sound heard again near its source, after reflection. **3.** any repetition or close imitation, as of ideas or opinions of another. **4.** *Electronics* the reflection of a radio wave such as is used in sonar, radar or the like. *–verb* (**echoed, echoing**) *–v.i.* **5.** to resound with an echo. **6.** to be repeated by or as if by an echo: *her words echoed in my mind for years.* *–v.t.* **7.** to repeat by or as by an echo: *the hall will echo even faint sounds*; *his followers merely echoed his ideas.* **8.** to repeat the words, etc., of (a person, etc.): *the children echo the teacher.*

echocardiogram /ɛkoʊ'kadiəgræm/ *n. Med.* an ultrasound image of the heart.

echocardiograph /ɛkoʊ'kadiəgræf, -graf/ *n. Med.* an ultrasound device for the examination of the heart. **–echocardiographic** /ɛkoʊˌkadiə'græfɪk/, *adj.* **–echocardiography** /ɛkoʊˌkadi'ɒgrəfi/, *n.*

e-cigarette *n.* an electronic inhaler that has a heating element which vaporises a liquid solution with a particular flavour; designed to look like a cigarette and to be used in the same way but to avoid the harmful effects of smoking tobacco.

eclair /eɪ'klɛə, ə-/ *n.* a light, finger-shaped cake made of pastry, filled with cream or custard, and coated with (usually chocolate) icing. Also, **éclair.**

eclectic /ɛ'klɛktɪk, ə-/ *adj.* **1.** selecting; choosing from various sources. **2.** made up of what is selected from diverse sources. **–eclectically,** *adv.* **–eclecticism,** *n.*

eclipse /ə'klɪps, i-/ *n.* **1.** *Astron.* **a.** the obscuration of the light of a satellite by the intervention of its primary planet between it and the sun, as in a **lunar eclipse** when the moon is partially or wholly within the earth's shadow. **b.** the interception of the light of the sun by the intervention of the moon between it and the observer, as in a **solar eclipse. c.** (in an eclipsing binary system) the partial or complete interception of the light of one component by the other. **2.** any obscuration of light. **3.** any obscuration or overshadowing; loss of brilliance or splendour. *–v.t.* (**eclipsed, eclipsing**) **4.** to cause to suffer eclipse: *the moon eclipses the sun.* **5.** to cast a shadow upon; obscure; darken. **6.** to make dim by comparison; surpass: *to eclipse one's rival.* **–eclipser,** *n.*

ecliptic /ə'klɪptɪk, i-/ *n.* **1.** the great circle formed by the intersection of the plane of the earth's orbit with the celestial sphere; the apparent annual path of the sun in the heavens. **2.** an analogous great circle on a terrestrial globe. *–adj.* Also, **ecliptical. 3.** relating to an eclipse. **4.** relating to the ecliptic. **–ecliptically,** *adv.*

eco /'ikoʊ/ *adj.* of, relating to, or employing environmentally friendly practices, materials, technology, etc.: *eco baby products*; *eco shoes.*

eco- **1.** a prefix denoting 'ecology' or 'ecological', as in *ecosphere.* **2.** protective of or beneficial to the environment: *eco-agriculture.*

ecoactivism /ikoʊ'æktəvɪzəm/ *n.* activism directed towards environmental issues. **–ecoactivist,** *n.*

ecocentrism /ikoʊ'sɛntrɪzəm/ *n.* a philosophy based on the idea that the ecosphere (def. 1) is more central to life than any particular organism, and that human activity, whether it is community or individual activity, must base its morality on this recognition. **–ecocentric,** *adj.* **–ecocentrist,** *n.*

ecofascism /ikoʊ'fæʃɪzəm/ *n.* **1.** *(derog.)* a term for environmentalism used by those who are deeply opposed to it and who see its advocates as being extreme and dictatorial. **2.** a world view that mixes radical environmental concerns with racism and nationalism. **–ecofascist,** *n., adj.*

eco house /ˈikoʊ haʊs/ *n.* a house designed to be environmentally friendly, as by being efficient in the use of energy and minimising any damaging impact on natural surroundings.

ecolabel /ˈikoʊleɪbəl/ *n.* a label for goods or services which gives standardised information with regard to claims for environmental friendliness, thus assisting consumers to make choices based on environmental considerations.

E. coli /ˌi ˈkoʊlaɪ/ *n.* a common rod-shaped bacillus, *Escherichia coli,* normally found in the intestinal tract, which may cause a clinical infection if present in other parts of the body, such as the bladder; also used as an indicator of faecal pollution of water.

ecological footprint *n.* a measure of the demands put on the environment by humans, as in growing food, providing fuel, etc., taking into account the emissions produced in the production of food and in goods and services, as well as those produced in fuel consumption and household requirements such as heating, cooling, etc. Also, **footprint.**

ecological sustainability *n.* the capacity for development that can be sustained into the future without destroying the environment in the process.

ecology /əˈkɒlədʒi/ *n.* **1.** the branch of biology that deals with the relations between organisms and their environment; bionomics. **2.** Also, **human ecology, social ecology.** the branch of sociology that deals with the location of people and of institutions in their natural environment, and their resulting interdependence. **–ecological** /ikəˈlɒdʒɪkəl/, **ecologic** /ikəˈlɒdʒɪk/, *adj.* **–ecologically** /ikəˈlɒdʒɪkli/, *adv.* **–ecologist,** *n.*

ecommerce /ˈiˈkɒmɜs/ *n.* commerce transacted via the internet. Also, **ebusiness.**

econocrat /əˈkɒnəkræt/ *n.* a bureaucrat working in the field of economics, particularly one providing the government with economic data.

economic /ɛkəˈnɒmɪk, ikə-/ *adj.* **1.** of or relating to the production, distribution, and use of income and wealth. **2.** of or relating to the science of economics. **3.** of or relating to an economy, or system of organisation or operation, especially of the process of production. **4.** of or relating to the means of living; utilitarian: *economic entomology; economic botany.*

economical /ɛkəˈnɒmɪkəl, ikə-/ *adj.* **1.** avoiding waste or extravagance; thrifty. **2.** economic. **–economically,** *adv.*

economic rationalism *n.* a theory of economics which opposes government intervention and which maintains that the economy of a country works better when it responds to marketplace forces in such matters as utilisation of resources and industrial relations. **–economic rationalist,** *n.*

economics /ɛkəˈnɒmɪks, ikə-/ *n.* **1.** the science that deals with the production, distribution, and consumption of goods and services, or the material welfare of human beings; political economy. **2.** *(construed as pl.)* economically significant aspects. **–economist,** *n.*

economise /əˈkɒnəmaɪz/ *v.t.* **1.** to manage economically; use sparingly or frugally. *–v.i.* **2.** to practise economy; avoid waste or extravagance. Also, **economize.** **–economisation** /əˌkɒnəmaɪˈzeɪʃən/, *n.* **–economiser,** *n.*

economy /əˈkɒnəmi/ *n.* *(pl.* **-mies)** **1.** the careful management of money, materials, etc. **2.** an act or means of careful saving; a saving. **3.** *Econ.* the interrelationship between the factors of production (land, labour and capital, and possibly also management or enterprise) and the means of production, distribution, and exchange. **4.** the management of the resources of a country, etc., with a view to productiveness and the avoidance of waste: *national economy.* **5.** the efficient and sparing use of something: *economy of effort.* *–adj.* **6.** at the cheaper end of a range of prices: *economy brands; economy fare.* *–adv.* **7.** cheaply; at a cheaper fare: *I'm travelling economy.*

economy class *n.* **1.** a type of lower-priced accommodation, as in a hotel. **2.** the cheapest class of seating on an aircraft, etc., offering less space and often fewer services than business or first class. *–adj.* **3.** of or relating to such accommodation or travel.

economy class syndrome *n. Colloq.* deep vein thrombosis resulting from immobility during a long flight in an aeroplane.

ecosophy /ˈikoʊˌsɒfi/ *n.* a branch of philosophy that deals with humankind in relation to the environment, in particular, with the respect owed to other living beings. Also, **ecophilosophy.** **–ecosophical** /ikəˈsɒfɪkəl/, *adj.*

ecosphere /ˈikoʊsfɪə/ *n.* **1.** the global ecosystem of a planet. **2.** the part of the atmosphere of a planet or other heavenly body which can sustain life.

ecosystem /ˈikoʊsɪstəm/ *n.* a community of organisms interacting with one another and with the environment in which they live, as in a pond, a forest, etc.

ecotax /ˈikoʊtæks/ *n.* a tax levied against companies, organisations, or individuals who cause pollution, with the aim of encouraging the adoption of environmentally cleaner practices; green tax.

ecotourism /ikoʊˈtʊərɪzəm/ *n.* **1.** tourism so arranged that it involves no degradation of the environment. **2.** tourism which takes in places of great ecological interest, such as unusual ecosystems, the habitats of rare species, etc.

ecowarrior /ˈikoʊwɒriə/ *n.* an environmental activist, especially one who takes public action for a cause.

e-crime *n.* a type of computer-related crime, especially crime which involves the use of the internet.

ecstasy /ˈɛkstəsi/ *n.* *(pl.* **-sies)** **1.** overpowering emotion or exaltation; a sudden access of intense feeling. **2.** rapturous delight. **3.** Also, **MDMA.** a synthetic drug, 3,4 methylenedioxymethamphetamine, used illicitly as a stimulant, especially at dance parties. **–ecstatic** /ɛkˈstætɪk/, *adj.*

ecto- a prefix (chiefly in biological words) meaning 'outside', 'outer', 'external', 'lying upon' (opposed to *endo-, ento-*), as in *ectoderm.*

-ectomy a combining form attached to the name of a part of the body and producing a word meaning the operation for the excision of that part, as in *appendectomy, mastectomy.*

ecumenical /ɛkjəˈmɛnɪkəl, ik-/ *adj.* **1.** general; universal. **2.** relating to the whole Christian church. Also, **ecumenic, oecumenical.** **–ecumenicalism,** *n.* **–ecumenically,** *adv.*

eczema /ˈɛksəmə, ˈɛksmə/ *n. Pathol.* an inflammatory disease of the skin attended with itching and the exudation of serous matter. **–eczematous** /ɛkˈsɛmətəs/, *adj.*

-ed¹ a suffix forming the past tense, as in *he crossed the river.*

-ed² a suffix forming: **1.** the past participle, as in *he had crossed the river.* **2.** participial adjectives indicating a condition or quality resulting from the action of the verb, as *inflated balloons.*

-ed³ a suffix serving to form adjectives from nouns, as *bearded, moneyed, tender-hearted.*

edam /ˈidæm, ˈɛdəm/ *n.* a hard, round, yellow cheese, sometimes spiced, with a red wax rind.

eddy /ˈɛdi/ *n.* *(pl.* **eddies)** **1.** a current at variance with the main current in a stream of liquid or gas, especially one having a rotary or whirling motion. **2.** any similar current, as of air, dust, fog, etc.

edge /ɛdʒ/ *n.* **1.** the border or part adjacent to a line of division; a brim or margin: *the horizon's edge.* **2.** a brink or verge: *the edge of a precipice.* **3.** one of the narrow surfaces of a thin, flat object: *a book with gilt edges.* **4.** the line in which two surfaces of a solid object meet: *the edge of a box.* **5.** the thin, sharp side of the blade of a cutting instrument or weapon. **6.** the sharpness proper to a blade. **7.** sharpness or keenness of language, argument, appetite, desire, etc. **8.** *Skiing* a steel edge fitted to skis to make control easier on ice or hard snow. **9.** *Cricket* a stroke off the edge of the bat, usually unintentional; a snick. –*verb* (**edged, edging**) –*v.t.* **10.** to put an edge on; sharpen. **11.** to machine to a straight line or a desired curve. **12.** to provide with an edge or border; border. **13.** to move edgeways; move or force gradually: *to edge one's way through a crowd; to edge a rival off the track.* **14.** *Skiing* to force the edges of (the skis) into the slope to prevent side slipping. **15.** *Cricket* to play (the ball) from the edge of the bat, usually unintentionally; snick. –*v.i.* **16.** to move (*along, down, up,* etc.) edgeways; advance gradually. –*phr.* **17. edge out,** to force (an opponent) out of a race, competition, etc. **18. have the edge,** *Colloq.* (sometimes fol. by *on* or *over*) to have the advantage. **19. on edge, a.** acutely uncomfortable or sensitive **b.** eager or impatient. **20. over the edge,** into a state of imbalance or disorder, especially nervous disorder. –**edged,** *adj.* –**edgeless,** *adj.* –**edger,** *n.*

edgeways /ˈɛdʒweɪz/ *adv.* **1.** with the edge forwards; in the direction of the edge. **2.** with a sideways movement. –*phr.* **3. get a word in edgeways,** to succeed in making oneself heard in conversation. Also, **edgewise.**

edgy /ˈɛdʒi/ *adj.* (**edgier, edgiest**) **1.** sharp-edged; sharply defined, as outlines. **2.** on edge; irritable. **3.** *Colloq.* at the forefront or cutting edge: *edgy fashion designers.* –**edginess,** *n.*

edible /ˈɛdəbəl/ *adj.* **1.** fit to be eaten as food; eatable; esculent. –*n.* **2.** (*usu. pl.*) anything edible; an eatable. –**edibility** /ɛdəˈbɪləti/, **edibleness,** *n.*

edict /ˈidɪkt/ *n.* **1.** a decree issued by a sovereign or other authority. **2.** any authoritative proclamation or command. –**edictal** /iˈdɪktəl/, *adj.* –**edictally** /iˈdɪktəli/, *adv.*

edifice /ˈɛdəfəs/ *n.* a building, especially one of large size or imposing appearance: *a spacious edifice of brick.* –**edificial** /ɛdəˈfɪfəl/, *adj.*

edify /ˈɛdəfaɪ/ *v.t.* (**-fied, -fying**) to build up or increase the faith, morality, etc., of; instruct or benefit, especially morally. –**edifier,** *n.* –**edification** /ɛdəfəˈkeɪʃən/, *n.* –**edifyingly,** *adv.*

edit /ˈɛdət/ *v.t.* **1.** to supervise or direct the preparation of (a newspaper, magazine, etc.); act as editor of; direct the policies of. **2.** to collect, prepare, and arrange (materials) for publication. **3.** to revise and correct. **4.** to make (a cinema or television film, sound recording, or any part of a film or recording) from rushes, by cutting and arranging them, synchronising soundtrack, etc. –**editor,** *n.*

edition /əˈdɪʃən/ *n.* **1.** one of a number of printings of the same book, newspaper, etc., issued at different times, and differing from another by alterations, additions, etc. (as distinguished from *impression*). **2.** the format in which a literary work is published: *a one-volume edition of Shakespeare.* **3.** the whole number of impressions or copies of a book, newspaper, etc., printed from one set of type at one time. **4.** any version of anything, especially one resembling an earlier version.

editorial /ɛdəˈtɔriəl/ *n.* **1.** an article, in a newspaper or the like, presenting the opinion or comment of an editor or a leader-writer in the name of the publication; a leader. –*adj.* **2.** of or relating to an editor. **3.** written by an editor. –**editorially,** *adv.*

educate /ˈɛdʒəkeɪt/ *v.t.* **1.** to develop the faculties and powers of by teaching, instruction, or schooling; qualify by instruction or training for a particular calling, practice, etc.; train: *to educate someone for something*

or to do something. **2.** to provide education for; send to school. **3.** to develop or train (the ear, taste, etc.): *to educate one's palate.* –**educated,** *adj.* –**educative,** *adj.* –**educable,** *adj.* –**educability,** *n.*

education /ɛdʒəˈkeɪʃən/ *n.* **1.** the act or process of educating; the imparting or acquisition of knowledge, skill, etc.; systematic instruction or training. **2.** the result produced by instruction, training, or study. **3.** the science or art of teaching; pedagogics. –**educational,** *adj.*

educology /ɛdʒəˈkɒlədʒi/ *n.* the study of methods of teaching based on the observation of teaching practices and the application of that theory in order to enhance teaching skills. –**educologist,** *n.*

-ee a suffix of nouns denoting someone who is the object of some action, or undergoes or receives something (often as opposed to the person acting), as in *assignee, donee, employee.*

eel /il/ *n.* **1.** any of various elongate, snake-like, freshwater or marine fishes of the order Apodes, such as *Anguilla reinhardtii* of eastern Australian rivers or *A. anguilla* of Europe. **2.** any of several similar but unrelated fishes, such as the lamprey.

EEPROM /ˈiprɒm/ *n.* electrically erasable programmable read-only memory; a computer memory chip the contents of which can be erased electronically and reprogrammed for other purposes. Compare **EPROM.**

-eer a suffix of nouns denoting someone who is concerned with, or employed in connection with, or busies himself or herself with something, as in *auctioneer, engineer, profiteer.* Also, **-ier.**

eerie /ˈɪəri/ *adj.* (**eerier, eeriest**) inspiring fear; weird, strange, or uncanny. –**eerily,** *adv.* –**eeriness,** *n.*

ef- variant of **ex-¹** (by assimilation) before *f*, as in *efferent.*

efface /əˈfeɪs/ *v.t.* (**effaced, effacing**) **1.** to wipe out; destroy; do away with: *to efface a memory.* **2.** to rub out, erase, or obliterate (outlines, traces, inscriptions, etc.). **3.** to make inconspicuous or not noticeable: *to efface oneself.* –**effaceable,** *adj.* –**effacement,** *n.*

effect /əˈfɛkt, i-/ *n.* **1.** that which is produced by some agency or cause; a result; a consequence: *the effect of heat.* **2.** power to produce results; efficacy; force; validity; weight: *of no effect.* **3.** the state of being operative; operation or execution; accomplishment or fulfilment: *to bring a plan into effect.* **4.** a mental impression produced, as by a painting, speech, etc. **5.** the result intended; purport or intent; tenor or significance: *he wrote to that effect.* **6.** (of stage properties) a sight, sound or, occasionally, smell simulated by artificial means to give a particular impression in a theatre. **7.** a scientific phenomenon: *the Doppler effect.* **8.** (*pl.*) goods; movables; personal property. –*v.t.* **9.** to produce as an effect; bring about; accomplish; make happen. **10.** to produce or make. –*phr.* **11. be in effect,** be in operation, as a law. **12. come into effect,** become operative, as a law. **13. for effect,** for the sake of a desired impression; with histrionic intent. **14. in effect,** in fact or reality, although perhaps not formally acknowledged as such: *he is in effect the leader.* **15. take effect,** to begin to operate, as a drug, etc. –**effecter,** *n.* –**effectible,** *adj.*

effective /əˈfɛktɪv, i-/ *adj.* **1.** serving to effect the purpose; producing the intended or expected result: *effective measures, effective steps towards peace.* **2.** actually in effect: *the law becomes effective at midnight.* **3.** producing a striking impression; striking: *an effective picture.* –*n.* **4.** a soldier or sailor fit for duty or active service. **5.** the effective total of a military force. –**effectively,** *adv.* –**effectiveness,** *n.*

effectual /əˈfɛktʃuəl, i-/ *adj.* **1.** producing, or capable of producing, an intended effect; adequate. **2.** valid or binding, as an agreement or document. —**effectuality** /əfɛktʃuˈælətɪ, i-/, **effectualness**, n. —**effectually**, adv.

effeminate /əˈfɛmənət, i-/ adj. **1.** (of a man) soft or delicate to an unmanly degree in traits, tastes, habits, etc.; womanish. **2.** characterised by unmanly softness, delicacy, self-indulgence, etc.: an effeminate life. —n. **3.** a male homosexual. —**effeminately**, adv. —**effeminacy**, **effeminateness**, n.

effervesce /ɛfəˈvɛs/ v.i. (**-vesced, -vescing**) **1.** to give off bubbles of gas, as fermenting liquors; bubble and hiss. **2.** to issue forth in bubbles. **3.** to exhibit fervour, excitement, liveliness, etc. —**effervescent**, adj. —**effervescence, effervescency**, n.

effete /əˈfit/ adj. **1.** weak and ineffectual as a result of over-refinement: an effete intellectual. **2.** that has lost its vigour or energy; exhausted; worn out. **3.** (of animals and plants) unable to produce. —**effetely**, adv. —**effeteness**, n.

efficacy /ˈɛfəkəsɪ/ n. (pl. **-cies**) capacity for serving to produce effects; effectiveness. —**efficacious** /ɛfəˈkeɪʃəs/, adj.

efficient /əˈfɪʃənt, i-/ adj. **1.** effective in the use of energy or resources. **2.** adequate in operation or performance; having and using the requisite knowledge, skill, and industry; competent; capable. **3.** producing an effect, as a cause; causative. —**efficiency**, n. —**efficiently**, adv.

effigy /ˈɛfədʒɪ/ n. (pl. **-gies**) **1.** a representation or image, especially sculptured, as on a monument or coin. **2.** a doll or crude representation of a person, especially one made as an expression of hatred, or to be used in witchcraft.

effloresce /ɛfləˈrɛs/ v.i. (**-resced, -rescing**) **1.** to burst into bloom; blossom. **2.** (of a crystal) to change on the surface to a powder, upon exposure to air, as a result of loss of some water of crystallisation. **3.** (of a rock or mineral) to become encrusted with fine-grain crystals as a result of evaporation or chemical change. —**efflorescent**, adj. —**efflorescence**, n.

effluent /ˈɛfluənt/ adj. **1.** flowing out. —n. **2.** something that flows out, as liquid waste from industry, sewage works, etc. **3.** a stream flowing out of another stream, lake, etc.

effort /ˈɛfət/ n. **1.** exertion of power, physical or mental: an effort to reform. **2.** an attempt. —**effortless**, adj. —**effortful**, adj.

effrontery /əˈfrʌntərɪ/ n. shameless or impudent boldness; barefaced audacity.

effusion /əˈfjuʒən, i-/ n. **1.** the act of effusing or pouring forth. **2.** something that is effused. **3.** unrestrained expression of feelings, etc.: poetic effusions.

effusive /əˈfjusɪv, -zɪv, i-/ adj. unduly demonstrative; without reserve: effusive emotion, an effusive person. —**effusively**, adv. —**effusiveness**, n.

EFTPOS /ˈɛftpɒs/ n. Also, **EFTPOS system**. **1.** a system of electronic funds transfer from a customer's account to a merchant's account, operated by the customer by means of a coded plastic card inserted into a special-purpose terminal and a PIN by which the transaction is authorised. —adj. **2.** of or relating to an EFTPOS system.

egalitarian /əgæləˈtɛərɪən, i-/ adj. **1.** asserting the equality of all people. —n. **2.** someone who asserts the equality of all people. —**egalitarianism**, n.

egg[1] /ɛg/ n. **1.** the roundish reproductive body produced by the female of animals, consisting of the female reproductive cell and its envelopes. The envelopes may be albumen jelly, membranes, egg case, or shell, according to species. **2.** the body of this sort produced by birds, especially the domestic hen. **3.** the contents of an egg, especially that of a domestic hen, used for food. **4.** Also, **egg cell**. the ovum or female reproductive cell. —v.t. **5.** to prepare (food) by dipping in beaten egg.

—phr. **6. bad egg**, a person of reprehensible character. **7. have egg on one's face**, Colloq. to be exposed in an embarrassing situation. **8. in the egg**, in the planning stages. **9. put all one's eggs in one basket**, to devote all one's resources to or risk all one's possessions, etc., on a single undertaking.

egg[2] /ɛg/ phr. **egg on**, to incite or urge; encourage.

eggflip /ˈɛgflɪp/ n. a milk drink containing whipped raw egg, sugar, and sometimes flavouring.

eggplant /ˈɛgplænt/ n. **1.** a plant, Solanum melongena, probably originally of Central Asia, cultivated for its edible, more or less egg-shaped fruit, dark purple (or sometimes white or yellow) in colour; aubergine. **2.** the fruit, used as a table vegetable; aubergine.

eggshell /ˈɛgʃɛl/ n. **1.** the shell of a bird's egg. **2.** a pale yellow colour. —phr. **3. tread on eggshells**, to be very cautious in anticipation of a distressing or disastrous social situation.

ego /ˈigoʊ/ n. (pl. **egos**) **1.** the 'I' or self of any person; a person as thinking, feeling, and willing, and distinguishing itself from the selves of others and from objects of its thought. **2.** Colloq. conceit; egotism.

egocentric /ˈigoʊsɛntrɪk, ˈɛgoʊ-/ adj. **1.** Philos. having or regarding self as the centre of all things, especially as applied to the known world. **2.** self-centred. —n. **3.** an egocentric person. —**egocentricity** /ˌigoʊsɛnˈtrɪsəti, ˌɛgoʊ-/, n.

egotism /ˈigətɪzəm, ˈɛgə-/ n. **1.** the habit of talking too much about oneself; self-conceit; boastfulness. **2.** selfishness. —**egotist**, n. —**egotistical, egotistic**, adj. —**egotistically**, adv.

ego trip n. Colloq. behaviour intended to attract attention and admiration, for the sake of boosting one's own ego.

egregious /əˈgridʒəs/ adj. remarkably or extraordinarily bad; flagrant: an egregious lie, an egregious fool. —**egregiously**, adv. —**egregiousness**, n.

egress /ˈigrɛs/ n. **1.** the act of going or passing out, especially from an enclosed place. **2.** a means or place of going out; an exit. **3.** the right of going out. —**egression** /iˈgrɛʃən/, n.

egret /ˈigrət/ n. any of various birds of the genera Egretta, Ardea and Bubulcus, family Ardeidae, occurring throughout the world near rivers, lakes, or dams and bearing long plumes in the breeding season. See cattle egret, great egret.

eider /ˈaɪdə/ n. any of several large sea ducks of the genus Somateria and allied genera of the Northern Hemisphere, generally black and white, and yielding eiderdown. Also, **eider duck**.

eiderdown /ˈaɪdədaʊn/ n. **1.** down or soft feathers from the breast of the eider duck. **2.** a heavy quilt, properly one filled with eiderdown.

Eid-ul-Adha /id-ʊl-ˈadə/ n. an Islamic festival commemorating the obedience of Abraham in being willing to sacrifice his son; falls on varying dates from November to March and lasts several days, marking the end of the hajj (pilgrimage) season. Also, **Id-ul-Adha**.

Eid-ul-Fitr /id-ʊl-ˈfitrə/ n. an Islamic festival marking the end of Ramadan. Also, **Eid, Id-ul-Fitr, Id**.

eight /eɪt/ n. **1.** a cardinal number, seven plus one (7 + 1). **2.** the symbol for this number, e.g. 8 or VIII. **3.** a set of eight people or things especially a rowing crew. —adj. **4.** amounting to eight: eight apples. —pron. **5.** eight people or things: eight came to the party. —**eighth**, adj.

eighteen /eɪˈtin/ n. **1.** a cardinal number, ten plus eight. **2.** a symbol for this number, as 18 or XVIII. **3.** a team in Australian Rules football: the Carlton eighteen. —adj. **4.** amounting to eighteen in number. —pron. **5.** eighteen people or things. —**eighteenth**, adj.

eighty /ˈeɪtɪ/ n. (pl. **eighties**) **1.** a cardinal number, ten times eight. **2.** a symbol for this number, as 80 or

LXXX or XXC. **3.** (*pl.*) the numbers from 80 to 89 of a series, especially with reference to the years of a person's age, or the years of a century. –*adj.* **4.** amounting to eighty in number. –*pron.* **5.** eighty people or things. –**eightieth**, *adj.*, *n.*

eisteddfod /əˈstɛdfəd/ *n.* (*pl.* **-fods** or **-fodau** /-fədaɪ/) any competitive music festival.

either /ˈaɪðə, ˈiðə/ *adj.* **1.** one or the other of two: *you may sit at either end of the table.* **2.** each of the two; the one and the other: *there are trees on either side of the river.* –*pron.* **3.** one or the other; not both: *take either; either is correct.* –*conj.* **4.** used to indicate one of two coordinate alternatives: *either come or write.* –*adv.* **5.** used after negative sentences coordinated by *and*, *or*, *nor*, or after a negative subordinate clause: *she is not fond of parties and I am not either*; *I am going and nobody can prevent it either*; *if you do not come, he will not come either.*

ejaculate /əˈdʒækjəleɪt, i-/ *v.i.* **1.** to discharge seminal fluid. –*v.t.* **2.** to eject suddenly and swiftly; discharge. **3.** to utter suddenly and briefly; exclaim. –**ejaculation** /ədʒkjəˈleɪʃən, i-/, *n.* –**ejaculator**, *n.* –**ejaculatory**, *adj.*

eject /əˈdʒɛkt, i-/ *v.t.* **1.** to drive or force out; expel, as from a place or position. **2.** to evict, as from property. –*v.i.* **3.** to eject oneself in an emergency from the cockpit of an aircraft, etc., by means of a mechanical device. –**ejective**, *adj.* –**ejection**, **ejectment**, *n.* –**ejector**, *n.*

eke /ik/ *phr.* **eke out**, **1.** to supply what is lacking to; supplement. **2.** to contrive to make (a living) or support (existence) by various makeshifts: *a poor family eking out a miserable existence on a run-down farm.*

elaborate *adj.* /əˈlæbərət/ **1.** worked out with great care and nicety of detail; executed with great minuteness: *elaborate preparations*; *an elaborate scheme.* –*v.t.* /əˈlæbəreɪt, i-/ **2.** to work out carefully or minutely; work up to perfection. **3.** to produce or develop by labour. –*v.i.* /əˈlæbəreɪt, i-/ **4.** to become elaborate. –*phr.* **5. elaborate on**, to add details to; give fuller treatment of. –**elaboration** /əlæbəˈreɪʃən, i-/, *n.* –**elaborately**, *adv.* –**elaborateness**, *n.* –**elaborator**, *n.* –**elaborative**, *adj.*

elan /eɪˈlæn, -ˈlɒ̃/ *n.* dash; impetuous ardour. Also, **élan**.

eland /ˈilənd/ *n.* (*pl.* **elands** or, especially collectively, **eland**) either of two large, heavily built African antelopes, the **common eland**, *Taurotragus oryx*, and the **giant eland**, *T. derbianus*, having spirally twisted horns in both sexes.

elapse /əˈlæps, i-/ *v.i.* (**elapsed**, **elapsing**) **1.** (of time) to slip by or pass away. –*n.* **2.** the passing (of time); lapse.

elastic /əˈlæstɪk, i-/ *adj.* **1.** (of solids) having the property of recovering shape after being pushed, pulled, etc. **2.** (of gases) expanding spontaneously. **3.** flexible, yielding, or adaptable. **4.** (of a person) readily recovering from depression or tiredness. –*n.* **5.** a band or fabric made elastic with strips or threads of rubber. –**elastically**, *adv.* –**elasticity** /əlæsˈtɪsəti, i-/, *n.*

elastomer /əˈlæstəmə, i-/ *n.* an elastic, rubber-like substance occurring naturally (natural rubber) or produced synthetically (butyl rubber, neoprene, etc.). –**elastomeric** /əlæstəˈmɛrɪk, i-/, *adj.*

elate /əˈleɪt, i-/ *v.t.* to put in high spirits; make proud. –**elated**, *adj.* –**elation**, *n.*

elbow /ˈɛlboʊ/ *n.* **1.** the bend or joint of the arm between upper arm and forearm. **2.** something bent like the elbow, as a sharp turn in a road or river, or a piece of pipe bent at an angle. –*v.t.* **3.** to push with or as with the elbow; jostle. **4.** to make (one's way) by so pushing. –*v.i.* **5.** to push; jostle. –*phr.* **6. at one's elbow**, near at hand. **7. bend** (or **raise**) **one's elbow**, to drink (especially to consume beer). **8. out at elbows** or **out at the elbow**, ragged or impoverished. **9. up to the elbows**, very busy; wholly engaged or engrossed.

elbow grease *n.* vigorous, continuous exertion; hard physical labour.

elbow room *n.* sufficient room or scope.

elder[1] /ˈɛldə/ *adj.* **1.** older. **2.** higher in rank; senior. –*n.* **3.** a person older than oneself: *you should be polite to your elders.* **4. a.** a senior person of status in an Aboriginal community, especially one who holds knowledge of traditional language and culture: *my nana's an elder.* **b.** an older and more powerful person in a tribe or social group. **5.** → **presbyter** (defs 1 and 3). –**eldership**, *n.*

elder[2] /ˈɛldə/ *n.* **1.** any plant of the genus *Sambucus* of the Northern Hemisphere, comprising shrubs or trees with clusters of small, usually white, flowers and black to red fruit. **2.** any of various unrelated species, such as **ground elder**, *Aegopodium podagraria*, and **box elder**, *Acer negundo*.

elderly /ˈɛldəli/ *adj.* **1.** quite old; in one's old age. **2.** of or relating to persons in later life. –*phr.* **3. the elderly**, elderly people. –**elderliness**, *n.*

eldest /ˈɛldəst/ *adj.* oldest; now surviving only in the *eldest brother*, *sister*, and *eldest hand.*

elect /əˈlɛkt, i-/ *v.t.* **1.** to select by vote, as for an office. **2.** to determine in favour of (a course of action, etc.). **3.** to pick out or choose. –*adj.* **4.** (*after the noun*) selected for an office, but not yet inducted: *the president elect.* –*n.* **5.** a person or the persons chosen or worthy to be chosen. –*phr.* **6. the elect**, those chosen by God, especially for eternal life.

election /əˈlɛkʃən, i-/ *n.* **1.** the selection of a person or persons for office by vote. **2.** a public vote upon a proposition submitted. **3.** the act of electing.

electioneer /əlɛkʃəˈnɪə, i-/ *v.i.* **1.** to work for the success of a candidate, party, etc., in an election. –*n.* **2.** a person who engages in this activity. –**electioneering**, *adj.*, *n.*

elective /əˈlɛktɪv, i-/ *adj.* **1.** appointed by election. **2.** filled by an election: *elective position.* **3.** having the power to choose. **4.** not required; optional: *an elective subject*; *an elective course.* –*n.* **5.** an optional course of study. –**electively**, *adv.* –**electiveness**, **electivity** /ilɛkˈtɪvəti/, *n.*

elector /əˈlɛktə, i-/ *n.* someone who elects or may elect, especially someone qualified to vote in the election of a government. –**electorship**, *n.*

electoral /əˈlɛktərəl, -trəl, i-/ *adj.* **1.** relating to electors or election. **2.** consisting of electors.

electorate /əˈlɛktərət, -trət, i-/ *n.* **1.** a body of constituents; the body of voters, or, loosely, of residents, in a district represented by an elected member of the legislature. **2.** the district itself. **3.** the body of persons entitled to vote in an electorate.

electr- variant of **electro-**, before vowels, as in *electrode*.

Electra complex /əˈlɛktrə ˌkɒmplɛks/ *n.* (in psychoanalysis) the unresolved desire of a daughter for sexual gratification from her father.

electric /əˈlɛktrɪk/ *adj.* **1.** of or relating to electricity: *an electric current*; *an electric shock.* **2.** producing, transmitting, or operated by electric currents: *an electric bell.* **3.** electrifying; thrilling; exciting; stirring. **4.** of or relating to musical instruments which are amplified by means of a built-in electronic device attached directly to some sounding section of the instrument, as electric guitar, electric bass, etc. –*n.* **5.** (*pl.*) an electrical system, as in a motor vehicle. –**electrical**, *adj.*

electrician /əlɛkˈtrɪʃən, ɛlɛk-, ilɛk-/ *n.* someone who installs, operates, maintains, or repairs electrical devices.

electricity /əlɛkˈtrɪsəti, ɛlɛk-, ilɛk-/ *n.* **1.** *Physics* an agency producing various physical phenomena, such as attraction and repulsion, luminous and heating effects, shock to the body, chemical decomposition, etc., which were originally thought to be caused by a kind of fluid, but are now regarded as being due to the presence and movements of electrons, protons, and other electrically charged particles. **2.** the science dealing with this agency. **3.** electric current.

electrify /ə'lɛktrəfaɪ, i-/ *v.t.* (**-fied, -fying**) **1.** to charge with or subject to electricity; to apply electricity to. **2.** to equip for the use of electric power, as a railway. **3.** to startle greatly; excite or thrill: *to electrify an audience.* **–electrifiable,** *adj.* **–electrification** /əlɛktrəfə-'keɪʃən/, *n.* **–electrifier,** *n.*

electro- a word element meaning 'relating to or caused by electricity', as in *electromagnet, electrotype, electrochemistry, electrolysis, electrocute.* Also, **electr-**.

electrocardiogram /ə,lɛktroʊ'kadiəgræm, i-/ *n. Med.* the graphic record produced by an electrocardiograph. *Abbrev.*: ECG Also, **cardiogram**.

electrocardiograph /ə,lɛktroʊ'kadiəgræf, -graf, i-/ *n. Med.* a device which detects and records the minute differences in electric potential caused by heart action and occurring between different parts of the body; used in the diagnosis of heart disease. *Abbrev.*: ECG Also, **cardiograph**. **–electrocardiographic** /ə,lɛktroʊ,kadiə-'græfɪk, i-/, *adj.* **–electrocardiography** /ə,lɛktroʊ,kadi-'ɒgrəfi/, *n.*

electrocute /ə'lɛktrəkjut, i-/ *v.t.* **1.** to kill by electricity. **2.** to execute (a criminal) by electricity. **–electrocution** /əlɛktrə'kjuʃən/, *n.*

electrode /ə'lɛktroʊd, i-/ *n.* a conductor of electricity belonging to the class of metallic conductors, but not necessarily a metal, through which a current enters or leaves an electrolytic cell, arc generator, radio valve, gaseous discharge tube, or any conductor of the non-metallic class.

electroencephalogram /ə,lɛktroʊɛn'sɛfələgræm, i-/ *n.* the graphic record produced by an electroencephalograph. *Abbrev.*: EEG

electroencephalograph /ə,lɛktroʊɛn'sɛfələgræf, -graf, i-/ *n.* a device which detects and records the electrical activity of the brain. *Abbrev.*: EEG **–electroencephalographic** /ə,lɛktroʊɛn,sɛfələ'græfɪk, i-/, *adj.* **–electroencephalographically** /ə,lɛktroʊɛn,sɛfələ'græfɪkli, i-/, *adv.* **–electroencephalography** /ə,lɛktroʊɛn,sɛfə-'lɒgrəfi, i-/, *n.*

electrolysis /əlɛk'trɒləsəs, ilɛk-, ɛlək-/ *n.* **1.** the decomposition of a chemical compound in solution or as a pure liquid by an electric current. **2.** *Surg.* the destruction of tumours, hair roots, etc., by an electric current. **–electrolytic** /əlɛktrə'lɪtɪk, i-/, *adj.*

electrolyte /ə'lɛktrəlaɪt, i-/ *n.* **1.** an electricity conducting medium in which the flow of current is accompanied by the movement of matter. **2.** *Chem.* any substance which dissociates into ions when dissolved in a suitable medium or when melted, thus forming a conductor of electricity. **3.** such a substance present in the blood and vital to body functions. **–electrolytic** /əlɛktrə'lɪtɪk, i-/, *adj.*

electromagnetism /ə,lɛktroʊ'mægnə,tɪzəm, i-/ *n.* **1.** the phenomena collectively resting upon the relations between electric currents and magnetism. **2.** the science that deals with these relations. **–electromagnetic,** *adj.*

electromotive force /æ,ɛkrə,moʊtɪv 'fɔs/ *n.* a measure of the intensity of a source of electrical energy which produces an electric current in a circuit. The SI unit is the volt. *Abbrev.*: EMF

electron /ə'lɛktrɒn, i-/ *n. Physics* an elementary particle which is a constituent of all atoms, with a minute mass of 9.1083×10^{-28} grams. It has a negative electric charge of approximately 1.6×10^{-19} coulombs. The positively charged electron is called a *positron*.

electronegative /ə,lɛktroʊ'nɛgətɪv, i-/ *adj.* **1.** having a negative charge. **2.** having an affinity for electrons, thus forming anions.

electronic /ɛlək'trɒnɪk, ələk'trɒnɪk, i-/ *adj.* **1.** of or relating to electrons. **2.** of or relating to electronics or any devices or systems based on electronics. **–electronically,** *adv.*

electronica /ɛlək'trɒnɪkə, ələk'trɒnɪkə, i-/ *n.* the broad array of music created electronically.

electronic banking *n.* banking transactions conducted by means of electronic systems or networks, as by EFTPOS.

electronic funds transfer *n.* a computerised banking system for the transfer of funds from one account to another. *Abbrev.*: EFT

electronic game *n.* any of various small, handheld, usually battery-operated devices for playing computerised games, having a screen for the display of graphics and a small range of control buttons.

electronic mail *n.* → **email** (def. 1).

electronic money *n.* a means for making payments without cash, such as a smart card carrying electronically stored credit or a system for debiting an account via a mobile phone. Also, **e-money**.

electronics /əlɛk'trɒnɪks, i-, ɛlək-/ *n.* the investigation and application of phenomena involving the movement of electrons in valves and semiconductors.

electronic signature *n.* → **digital signature**.

electronic whiteboard *n.* a whiteboard that has digital capability and can be connected to the internet, a printer, etc.

electron microscope *n.* a microscope of extremely high power which uses beams of electrons focused by electron lenses instead of rays of light, the magnified image being formed on a fluorescent screen or recorded on a photographic plate. Its magnification and resolving power is substantially greater than that of any optical microscope.

electroplate /ə'lɛktrəpleɪt, i-/ *v.t.* **1.** to plate or coat with a metal by electrolysis. **–n. 2.** electroplated articles or ware. **–electroplater,** *n.* **–electroplating,** *n.*

electro-pop /ə'lɛktroʊ-pɒp/ *n.* a style of pop music originating in Britain and Europe in which the number of musicians is reduced to a minimum in favour of computer-driven synthesised backing tracks.

electropositive /ə,lɛktroʊ'pɒzətɪv, i-/ *adj.* **1.** having a positive charge. **2.** tending to give up electrons, thus forming cations.

elegant /'ɛləgənt, 'ɛlɪ-/ *adj.* **1.** tastefully fine or luxurious in dress, manners, etc.: *elegant furnishings.* **2.** gracefully refined, as in tastes, habits, literary style, etc. **3.** nice, choice, or pleasingly superior in quality or kind, as a contrivance, preparation, or process. **4.** *Colloq.* excellent; fine; superior. **–elegance,** *n.* **–elegantly,** *adv.*

elegy /'ɛlədʒi/ *n.* (*pl.* **-gies**) a mournful, melancholy, or plaintive poem, especially a funeral song or a lament for the dead.

element /'ɛləmənt/ *n.* **1.** a thing or quality that is part of a whole. **2.** *Chem.* one of a class of substances each consisting totally of atoms of the same atomic number. **3.** one of the simple substances, usually earth, water, air, and fire, once thought to make up all matter. **4.** the natural or ideal surroundings of any person or thing: *He's in his element.* **5.** (*pl.*) atmospheric forces; weather: *protected from the elements.* **6.** (*pl.*) the basic principles of an art, science, etc.: *the elements of grammar.* **7.** *Elect.* **a.** a resistance wire, etc., making up the heating unit of an electric heater, cooker, etc. **b.** one of the electrodes of a cell or radio valve. **8.** *Maths* **a.** a member of a set. **b.** part of a geometric figure.

elemental /ɛlə'mɛntl/ *adj.* **1.** simple or basic, unable to be further divided. **2.** of or like forces of nature; basic or powerful. **3.** relating to the four elements (def. 3). **4.** relating to chemical elements. **–elementally,** *adv.*

elementary /ˌɛləˈmɛntri, -təri/ *adj.* **1.** of or relating to elements, rudiments, or first principles: *elementary education*; *an elementary grammar.* **2.** being an ultimate constituent; simple or uncompounded. **3.** of or relating to the four elements or to the great forces of nature; elemental. **–elementarily,** *adv.* **–elementariness,** *n.*

elementary particle *n.* any of a class of entities which are thought to be the indivisible units of which all matter is composed.

elephant /ˈɛləfənt/ *n.* **1.** either of two very large, herbivorous mammals of the family Elephantidae, the *Loxodonta africana* of Africa (**African elephant**) and the somewhat smaller *Elephas maximus* of India and neighbouring regions (**Indian elephant**), having thick, almost hairless skin, a long, prehensile trunk, upper incisors prolonged into long curved tusks and, in the African species, large, flapping ears. **2.** an animal of the order Proboscidea, such as a mammoth. *–phr.* **3. the elephant in the room**, the topic that everyone knows about but no-one wants to discuss openly. **–elephantine, elephantoid,** *adj.*

elevate /ˈɛləveɪt/ *v.t.* **1.** to move or raise to a higher place or position; lift up. **2.** to raise to a higher state or station; exalt. **3.** to raise the spirits of; put in high spirits. **–elevated,** *adj.*

elevation /ɛləˈveɪʃən/ *n.* **1.** height above sea or ground level. **2.** a high or raised place. **3.** grandeur or dignity; nobleness. **4.** the act of lifting. **5.** the state of being raised. **6.** *Archit.* **a.** a scale drawing of an object or structure, especially the face of a building, showing it without perspective, every point being drawn as if looked at horizontally. **b.** the front, side, or back of a building. **7.** *Surveying* the angle between the line from an observer to an object above the observer and a horizontal line.

elevator /ˈɛləveɪtə/ *n.* **1.** a mechanical device for raising articles. **2.** → **lift** (def. 12). **3.** a building for storing grain, the grain being handled by means of mechanical lifting and conveying devices. **4.** a hinged horizontal device on a aeroplane, etc., used to control the longitudinal inclination, generally placed at the tail end of the fuselage. **5.** *Anat.* a muscle for raising part of the body.

eleven /əˈlɛvən/ *n.* **1.** a cardinal number, ten plus one (10 + 1). **2.** the symbol for this number, e.g. 11 or XI. **3.** a set of eleven people or things. **4.** a team of eleven players, as in soccer, cricket, hockey, etc. *–adj.* **5.** amounting to eleven: *eleven apples. –pron.* **6.** eleven people or things: *eleven came to the party.* **–eleventh,** *adj., n.*

eleventh hour *n.* the last possible moment for doing something. **–eleventh-hour,** *adj.*

elf /ɛlf/ *n.* (*pl.* **elves** /ɛlvz/) **1.** one of a class of imaginary beings, especially from mountainous regions, with magical powers, given to capricious interference in human affairs, and usually imagined to be a diminutive being in human form; a sprite; a fairy. **2.** a dwarf or a small child. **3.** a small, mischievous person. **–elfin, elfish, elvish, elflike,** *adj.*

elicit /əˈlɪsət/ *v.t.* to draw or bring out or forth; educe; evoke: *to elicit the truth.* **–elicitation** /əlɪsəˈteɪʃən/, *n.* **–elicitor,** *n.*

elide /əˈlaɪd/ *v.t.* to omit (a vowel, consonant, or syllable) in pronunciation.

eligible /ˈɛlədʒəbəl/ *adj.* **1.** fit or proper to be chosen; worthy of choice; desirable. **2.** legally qualified to be elected or appointed to office. **3.** (of a single person) the desirable object of matrimonial designs: *an eligible bachelor.* **–eligibly,** *adv.* **–eligibility** /ɛlədʒəˈbɪləti/, *n.*

eligible termination payment *n. Aust.* a lump-sum payment made by an employer to an employee on termination of employment. Also, **ETP.**

eliminate /əˈlɪməneɪt, i-/ *v.t.* **1.** to get rid of; expel; remove: *to eliminate errors.* **2.** to omit as irrelevant or unimportant; ignore. **3.** *Physiol.* to void or expel (waste matter) from an organism. **4.** *Maths* to remove (a quantity) from an equation by elimination. **5.** *Colloq.* to murder. **–eliminability** /əlɪmənəˈbɪləti/, *n.* **–eliminable,** *adj.* **–elimination,** *n.* **–eliminative,** *adj.* **–eliminator,** *n.* **–eliminatory,** *adj.*

elision /əˈlɪʒən, i-/ *n.* the omission of a vowel, consonant, or syllable in writing or pronunciation.

elite /əˈlit, eɪ-, i-/ *n.* **1.** the choice or best part, as of a body or class of persons. **2.** (*construed as pl.*) persons of the highest class. **3.** the most privileged or socially advantaged groups in a society, organisation, etc. **4. the elite, a.** the most privileged or advantaged groups in a society, organisation, etc. **b.** the people constituting the group regarded as the most superior. *–adj.* **5.** of or relating to or belonging to an elite: *elite schools.*

elitism /əˈlitɪzəm, eɪ-, i-/ *n.* **1.** practice of or belief in rule by an elite. **2.** consciousness of or pride in belonging to a select or favoured group. **3.** snobbery; anti-democratic sentiment. **–elitist,** *n., adj.*

elixir /əˈlɪksə, ɛ-, i-/ *n.* **1.** an alchemic preparation formerly believed to be capable of transmuting base metals into gold, or of prolonging life (**elixir vitae** or **elixir of life**). **2.** a sovereign remedy; panacea; cureall. **3.** the quintessence or absolute embodiment of anything.

elk /ɛlk/ *n.* (*pl.* **elks** *or, especially collectively,* **elk**) the largest existing deer, *Alces alces*, having a large head with broad, overhanging muzzle, and large palmate antlers in the male, found in moist wooded areas across the Northern Hemisphere. Compare **moose.**

ellipse /əˈlɪps, i-/ *n. Geom.* a plane curve such that the sums of the distances of each point in its periphery from two fixed points, the foci, are equal. It is a conic section formed by the intersection of a right circular cone by a plane which cuts obliquely the axis and the opposite sides of the cone. **–elliptical,** *adj.*

ellipsis /əˈlɪpsɪs, i-/ *n.* (*pl.* **-lipses** /-ˈlɪpsiz/) **1.** *Gram.* the omission from a sentence of a word or words which would complete or clarify the construction. **2.** *Printing* a mark or marks, such as —, or ..., or ***, to indicate an omission or suppression of letters or words.

elm /ɛlm/ *n.* **1.** any tree, mostly deciduous, of the genus *Ulmus*, family Ulmaceae, of northern temperate regions and mountains of tropical Asia, such as the English elm, *U. procera*, a large tree probably once endemic in England, now widely cultivated for shade and ornament, and Chinese elm, *U. parvifolia*, of China, Japan, Korea, and Taiwan. **2.** the wood of any such tree.

elocution /ɛləˈkjuʃən/ *n.* **1.** manner of speaking or reading in public. **2.** the study and practice of spoken delivery, including the management of voice and gesture. **–elocutionary** /ɛləˈkjuʃənri, -ʃənəri/, *adj.* **–elocutionist,** *n.*

elongate /ˈilɒŋgeɪt/ *v.t.* **1.** to draw out to greater length; lengthen; extend. *–v.i.* **2.** to increase in length. **–elongation,** *n.*

elope /əˈloʊp, i-/ *v.i.* to run away with a lover, usually in order to marry without parental consent. **–elopement,** *n.* **–eloper,** *n.*

eloquent /ˈɛləkwənt/ *adj.* **1.** having or exercising the power of fluent, forcible, and appropriate speech: *an eloquent orator.* **2.** characterised by forcible and appropriate expression: *an eloquent speech.* **3.** movingly expressive: *eloquent looks.* **–eloquently,** *adv.* **–eloquence,** *n.*

Eloueran /ɛˈlaʊərən/ *n.* a cultural period of Aboriginal development recognised in eastern Australia, which follows the Bondaian period and extends to the present.

else /ɛls/ *adv.* **1.** (following an indefinite or interrogative pronoun as an appositive). **a.** other than the person or the thing mentioned instead: *somebody else*; *who else?* **b.** in addition: *what else shall I do? who else is going?* **2.** following an indefinite or interrogative pronoun and forming with it an indefinite or compound pronoun with inflection at the end: *somebody else's child*; *nobody else's business*; *who else's child could it be?* **3.** otherwise: *run, or else you will be late.*

elsewhere /ˈɛlswɛə, ɛlsˈwɛə/ *adv.* somewhere else; in or to some other place.

elucidate /əˈluːsədeɪt, i-/ *v.t.* to make lucid or clear; throw light upon; explain. –**elucidation** /əluːsəˈdeɪʃən, i-/, *n.*

elude /əˈluːd, i-/ *v.t.* **1.** to avoid or escape by dexterity or artifice: *to elude pursuit.* **2.** to slip away from; evade: *to elude vigilance.* **3.** to escape the mind of; baffle. –**eluder**, *n.* –**elusion**, *n.* –**elusive, elusory,** *adj.*

elves /ɛlvz/ *n.* plural of **elf**.

em /ɛm/ *n.* (*pl.* **ems**) **1.** the letter M, m. **2.** *Printing* the square of the body size of any type (originally the portion of a line occupied by the letter M). **3.** *Printing* the unit of measurement of the printing on a page equal to 12 points; pica.

em-¹ variant of **en-¹**, before *b*, *p*, and sometimes *m*, as in *embalm*. Compare **im-¹**.

em-² variant of **en-²**, before *b*, *m*, *p*, *ph*, as in *embolism*, *emphasis*.

emaciate /əˈmeɪsieɪt, i-/ *v.t.* to make lean by a gradual wasting away of flesh. –**emaciation**, *n.*

email /ˈiːmeɪl/ *n.* Also, **electronic mail**. the sending of messages over a computer network, especially the internet: *most businesses use email these days.* **2.** messages sent this way: *you've got email.* **3.** such a message: *an email from my mother.* –*v.t.* **4.** to send (a message) by email: *I'll email the information this afternoon.* **5.** to send such messages to (someone): *he emailed me about the party.* –*v.i.* **6.** to communicate by sending emails: *to prefer to email rather than telephone.* –*adj.* **7.** of or relating to email. Also, **e-mail**. –**emailing**, *n.*

email harvester *n.* a program which collects email addresses as for marketing purposes.

emanate /ˈɛməneɪt/ *v.i.* to flow out, issue, or proceed as from a source or origin; come forth; originate. –**emanation** /ɛməˈneɪʃən/, *n.*

emancipate /əˈmænsəpeɪt, i-/ *v.t.* **1.** to free from restraint of any kind, especially the inhibitions of tradition. **2.** *Aust. Hist.* to free (a convict who has received a conditional or absolute pardon as a reward for good conduct). **3.** to free (a slave). –**emancipation**, *n.* –**emancipative,** *adj.* –**emancipator,** *n.*

emancipist /əˈmænsəpəst, i-/ *n.* **1.** an emancipationist. **2.** *Aust. Hist.* a freed convict, as one whose sentence had expired or who had received a conditional or absolute pardon from a colonial governor in Australia as a reward for good conduct. –*adj.* **3.** *Aust. Hist.* of or relating to such a freed convict.

emasculate /əˈmæskjəleɪt, i-/ *v.t.* **1.** to castrate. **2.** to deprive of strength or vigour; weaken; render effeminate. –**emasculation** /əmæskjəˈleɪʃən, i-/, *n.* –**emasculator,** *n.*

embalm /ɛmˈbam/ *v.t.* **1.** to treat (a corpse) with balsams, spices, etc., or (now usually) with drugs or chemicals, in order to preserve from decay. **2.** to preserve from oblivion; keep in memory. –**embalmer**, *n.* –**embalmment,** *n.*

embankment /ɛmˈbæŋkmənt, ə-/ *n.* **1.** a bank, mound, dyke, or the like, raised to hold back water, carry a road, etc. **2.** the act of embanking.

embargo /ɛmˈbagoʊ/ *n.* (*pl.* **-goes**) **1.** an order of a government prohibiting the movement of merchant vessels from or into its ports. **2.** any legal restriction imposed upon commerce, as when a government suspends trade with another country or suspends trade in a particular commodity: *an embargo on uranium shipments.* **3.** a prohibition on the publishing of news about a particular matter, often until after a specified date. **4.** a restraint or hindrance; a prohibition. –*v.t.* (**-goed, -going**) **5.** to impose an embargo on.

embark /ɛmˈbak/ *v.i.* **1.** to board a ship, as for a voyage. **2.** to engage in an enterprise, business, etc. –*v.t.* **3.** to put or receive on board a ship. **4. a.** to involve (a person) in an enterprise. **b.** to venture or invest (money, etc.) in an enterprise. –**embarkation, embarcation** /ɛmbaˈkeɪʃən/, *n.*

embarrass /ɛmˈbærəs/ *v.t.* **1.** to disconcert; abash; make uncomfortable, self-conscious, etc.; confuse. **2.** to beset with financial difficulties; burden with debt. –*v.i.* **3.** to become disconcerted, abashed. –**embarrassing,** *adj.* –**embarrassingly,** *adv.* –**embarrassment,** *n.*

embassy /ˈɛmbəsi/ *n.* (*pl.* **-sies**) **1.** a body of persons entrusted with a mission to a sovereign or government; an ambassador and his or her staff. **2.** the official headquarters of an ambassador. **3.** the function or office of an ambassador.

embattled /ɛmˈbætld/ *adj.* **1.** involved in a battle or argument. **2.** beleaguered; under attack.

embed /ɛmˈbɛd/ *v.t.* (**-bedded, -bedding**) **1.** to fix firmly in a surrounding mass. **2.** to lay in or as in a bed. **3.** *Journalism* to attach (a war correspondent) to a military unit, with the advantage of protection and access but with the risk of compromised objectivity. Also, **imbed**. –**embedding, embedment,** *n.*

embedded water *n.* → **virtual water**.

embellish /ɛmˈbɛlɪʃ/ *v.t.* **1.** to beautify by or as by ornamentation; ornament; adorn. **2.** to enhance (a statement or narrative) with fictitious additions; embroider. –**embellisher**, *n.* –**embellishment,** *n.*

ember /ˈɛmbə/ *n.* **1.** a small live coal, brand of wood, etc., as in a dying fire. **2.** (*pl.*) the smouldering remains of a fire.

embezzle /ɛmˈbɛzəl/ *v.t.* to appropriate fraudulently to one's own use, as money or property entrusted to one's possession. –**embezzlement**, *n.* –**embezzler,** *n.*

embitter /ɛmˈbɪtə/ *v.t.* to make bitter or more bitter. –**embitterer**, *n.* –**embitterment**, *n.* –**embittered,** *adj.*

emblazon /ɛmˈbleɪzən/ *v.t.* **1.** to portray or inscribe on or as on a heraldic shield; to embellish or decorate. **2.** to proclaim; celebrate or extol. –**emblazoner**, *n.* –**emblazonment**, *n.* –**emblazonry**, *n.* –**emblazoned,** *adj.*

emblem /ˈɛmbləm/ *n.* **1.** an object, or a representation of it, symbolising a quality, state, class of persons, etc.; a symbol. **2.** an allegorical drawing or picture, often with explanatory writing. –**emblematic** /ɛmbləˈmætɪk/, **emblematical** /ɛmbləˈmætɪkəl/, *adj.* –**emblematically** /ɛmbləˈmætɪkli/, *adv.*

embody /ɛmˈbɒdi/ *v.t.* (**-bodied, -bodying**) **1.** to invest with a body, as a spirit; incarnate; make corporeal. **2.** to give a concrete form to; express or exemplify (ideas, etc.) in concrete form. **3.** to collect into or include in a body; organise; incorporate. **4.** to embrace or comprise. –**embodiment**, *n.*

embolism /ˈɛmbəlɪzəm/ *n.* *Pathol.* the occlusion of a blood vessel by an embolus. –**embolismic,** *adj.*

embolus /ˈɛmbələs/ *n.* (*pl.* **-li** /-laɪ/) undissolved material carried by the blood current and impacted in some part of the vascular system, as thrombi or fragments of thrombi, tissue fragments, clumps of bacteria, protozoan parasites, fat globules, gas bubbles.

emboss /ɛmˈbɒs/ *v.t.* **1.** to raise or represent (surface designs) in relief. **2.** to cause to bulge out; make protuberant; make umbonate. **3.** to raise a design on (a fabric) by pressing. **4.** to cover or ornament with bosses or studs. **—embosser**, *n.* **—embossment**, *n.* **—embossed**, *adj.*

embrace /ɛmˈbreɪs/ *verb* (**-braced, -bracing**) *—v.t.* **1.** to take or hold in the arms; hug. **2.** to take or receive (an idea, etc.) gladly or eagerly. **3.** to make use of (an opportunity, etc.). **4.** to encircle; surround; enclose. **5.** to include. *—v.i.* **6.** to join in an embrace. *—n.* **7.** the act of embracing; a hug. **—embraceable**, *adj.* **—embracement**, *n.* **—embracer**, *n.* **—embracive**, *adj.*

embroider /ɛmˈbrɔɪdə/ *v.t.* **1.** to decorate with ornamental needlework. **2.** to adorn or embellish rhetorically, especially with fictitious additions. **—embroiderer**, *n.* **—embroidery**, *n.* **—embroidered**, *adj.*

embroil /ɛmˈbrɔɪl, əm-/ *v.t.* **1.** to bring into a state of discord; involve in contention or strife. **2.** to throw into confusion; complicate. **—embroiler**, *n.* **—embroilment**, *n.*

embryo /ˈɛmbrioʊ/ *n.* (*pl.* **-bryos**) **1.** an organism in the earlier stages of its development, as before emergence from the egg or before metamorphosis. **2.** (among mammals and other viviparous animals) a young animal during its earlier stages within the mother's body (including, in humans, the developmental stages up to the end of the seventh week). **3.** the rudimentary plant usually contained in the seed. **4.** the beginning or rudimentary stage of anything.

embryonic /ɛmbriˈɒnɪk/ *adj.* **1.** relating to or in the state of an embryo. **2.** rudimentary; undeveloped. Also, **embryonal** /ˈɛmbriənəl/. **—embryonically**, *adv.*

embryo transfer *n.* a procedure whereby a developing embryo is transplanted, usually into the uterus of a female parent. Also, **embryo transplant**.

emend /əˈmɛnd, i-/ *v.t.* **1.** to free from faults or errors; correct. **2.** to amend (a text) by removing errors. **—emendable**, *adj.* **—emendation** /imənˈdeɪʃən/, *n.* **—emendatory**, *adj.*

emerald /ˈɛmrəld, ˈɛmərəld/ *n.* **1.** a rare green variety of beryl, highly valued as a gem. **2.** clear bright green. *—adj.* **3.** having a clear, bright green colour.

emerge /əˈmɜːdʒ, i-/ *v.i.* **1.** to rise or come forth from or as from water or other liquid. **2.** to come forth into view or notice, as from concealment or obscurity. **3.** to come up or arise, as a question or difficulty.

emergency /əˈmɜːdʒənsi, i-/ *n.* (*pl.* **-cies**) an unforeseen occurrence; a sudden and urgent occasion for action.

emergent /əˈmɜːdʒənt, i-/ *adj.* **1.** (of a nation) recently independent or newly formed as a political entity, and generally in an early stage of economic development. **2.** emerging. **—emergence**, *n.* **—emergently**, *adv.*

emeritus /əˈmɛrətəs, i-/ *adj.* retired or honourably discharged from active duty because of age, infirmity, or long service, but retained on the rolls: *a professor emeritus.*

emery /ˈɛməri/ *n.* a granular mineral substance consisting typically of corundum mixed with an iron oxide, used powdered, crushed, or consolidated for grinding and polishing.

emetic /əˈmɛtɪk/ *adj.* **1.** inducing vomiting, as a medicinal substance. *—n.* **2.** an emetic medicine or agent.

-emia variant of **-aemia**, as in *hyperemia.*

emigrate /ˈɛməɡreɪt/ *v.i.* to leave one country or region to settle in another; migrate. **—emigrant**, *n.* **—emigration** /ɛməˈɡreɪʃən/, *n.*

eminent /ˈɛmənənt/ *adj.* **1.** high in station, rank, or repute; distinguished. **2.** conspicuous, signal, or noteworthy: *eminent services, eminent fairness.* **—eminence**, *n.* **—eminently**, *adv.*

emir /ɛˈmɪə, ˈɛmɪə/ *n.* **1.** a Muslim or Arabian chieftain or prince. **2.** a title of honour of the descendants of Mohammed. **3.** a former title of certain Turkish officials. Also, **emeer.** **—emirate** /ˈɛməreɪt/, *n.*

emissary /ˈɛməsəri, -əsri/, *Orig. US* /ˈɛməsɛri/ *n.* (*pl.* **-ries**) an agent sent on a mission.

emission /əˈmɪʃən, i-/ *n.* **1.** the act of emitting. **2.** something that is emitted; a discharge; an emanation. **3.** such a discharge, especially of pollutants such as greenhouse gases, into the environment.

emission control *n.* the control of polluting gases released into the atmosphere by motor vehicles, incinerators, factories, etc.

emission credit *n.* a credit purchased within an emissions trading scheme, as from a scheme achieving a reduction in carbon dioxide in the atmosphere, to offset the carbon emission of the buyer.

emission factor *n.* the average emission rate of a given pollutant from a given source relative to the intensity of a specific activity, as, for example, carbon dioxide from carbon fuel with complete oxidisation.

emission permit *n.* a permit to release a certain quota of emissions of a pollutant such as carbon dioxide into the atmosphere, usually for a period of time to allow for a transition into a technology which does not produce such emissions.

emission rate *n.* the rate at which a pollutant is emitted, being the product of the measured pollutant concentration and the measured effluent flow, the volumes in each case being measured under the same conditions of temperature and pressure which vary from country to country.

emissions market *n.* a market in which emission permits are bought and sold.

emissions trading *n.* trading in emission permits under a system by which countries or organisations not using their quotas are able to sell their excess permits to others exceeding their quota. See **carbon cap**.

emission tax *n.* a tax set for every unit of pollution produced.

emit /əˈmɪt, i-/ *v.t.* (**emitted, emitting**) **1.** to send forth; give out or forth (liquid, light, heat, sound, etc.); discharge. **2.** to issue, as an order or a decree. **3.** to issue formally for circulation. **4.** to utter, as opinions. **—emitter**, *n.*

emo /ˈiːmoʊ/ *adj.* **1.** of or relating to a music style derived from hardcore punk but with lyrics expressing personal emotional experiences. **2.** of or relating to a style of dress associated with fans of emo music, reminiscent of goth. *—n.* **3.** emo music. **4.** a fan of emo music. **5.** *Colloq.* a person who is overly pessimistic and emotional.

emoji /əˈmoʊdʒi/ *n.* a stylised set of symbols, originally devised in Japan for use in electronic messages.

emollient /əˈmɒliənt, -ˈmoʊ-/ *adj.* having the power of softening or relaxing living tissues, as a medicinal substance; soothing, especially to the skin.

emolument /əˈmɒljəmənt/ *n.* profit arising from office or employment; compensation for services; salary or fees.

e-money *n.* → **electronic money.**

emoticon /əˈmoʊtəkɒn/ *n.* *Computers* an image, created with keyboard characters, used in texts to indicate an emotion, such as :-) to denote happiness and :-(to denote unhappiness.

emotion /əˈmoʊʃən, i-/ *n.* **1.** an affective state of consciousness in which joy, sorrow, fear, hate, or the like, is experienced (distinguished from cognitive and volitional states of consciousness). **2.** any of the feelings of joy, sorrow, fear, hate, love, etc. **3.** a state of agitation of the feelings actuated by experiencing fear, joy, etc. **—emotionless**, *adj.*

emotional /əˈmoʊʃənəl, i-/ *adj.* **1.** relating to emotion or the emotions. **2.** subject to or easily affected by emotion. **3.** appealing to the emotions. **4.** effected or determined by emotion rather than reason: *an emotional* *decision.* **5.** overwrought; displaying undue emotion. —**emotionally,** *adv.* —**emotionality,** *n.*

emotive /ə'moʊtɪv, i-/ *adj.* **1.** characterised by or relating to emotion. **2.** exciting emotion. —**emotively,** *adv.* —**emotiveness, emotivity** /ˌiːmoʊ'tɪvəti/, *n.*

empanel /ɛm'pænəl/ *v.t.* (**-elled** *or, Chiefly US,* **-eled, -elling** *or, Chiefly US,* **-eling**) to enter on a panel or list for jury duty. Also, **impanel.** —**empanelment,** *n.*

empathy /'ɛmpəθi/ *n.* mental entering into the feeling or spirit of a person or thing; appreciative perception or understanding. —**empathetic, empathic** /ɛm'pæθɪk/, *adj.* —**empathically** /ɛm'pæθɪkli/, *adv.* —**empathise, empathize,** *v.*

emperor /'ɛmpərə/ *n.* **1.** the sovereign or supreme ruler of an empire. **2.** a title of dignity given to certain kings not rulers of empires. **3.** any of various Australian fishes of the family Lethrinidae, resembling bream, but having pointed heads and scaleless cheeks. —**emperorship,** *n.*

emphasis /'ɛmfəsəs/ *n.* (*pl.* **-phases** /-fəsiz/) **1.** stress laid upon, or importance or significance attached to anything. **2.** anything upon which great stress is laid. **3.** intensity or force of expression, action, etc. **4.** prominence, as of outline.

emphasise /'ɛmfəsaɪz/ *v.t.* to give emphasis; lay stress upon; stress. Also, **emphasize.**

emphatic /ɛm'fætɪk/ *adj.* **1.** uttered, or to be uttered, with emphasis; strongly expressive. **2.** using emphasis in speech or action. **3.** forcibly significant; strongly marked; striking. —**emphatically,** *adv.*

emphysema /ɛmfə'simə/ *n. Pathol.* abnormal distension of an organ or a part of the body with air or other gas, especially pulmonary emphysema which causes severe restriction of respiratory function. —**emphysematous** /ɛmfə'sɛmətəs, -'simə-/, *adj.*

empire /'ɛmpaɪə/ *n.* **1.** an aggregate of nations or peoples ruled over by an emperor or other powerful sovereign or government; usually a territory of greater extent than a kingdom ruled by a single sovereign: *the Roman empire.* **2.** a government under an emperor: *the first French empire.* **3.** supreme power in governing; imperial power; sovereignty. **4.** supreme control; absolute sway. **5.** a large and powerful enterprise or group of enterprises controlled by a single person or group of people.

empirical /ɛm'pɪrɪkəl/ *adj.* **1.** derived from or guided by experience or experiment. **2.** depending upon experience or observation alone, without using science or theory, especially in medicine. —**empirically,** *adv.*

empiricism /ɛm'pɪrəsɪzəm/ *n.* **1.** empirical method or practice. **2.** *Philos.* the doctrine that all knowledge is derived from experience. **3.** undue reliance upon experience; quackery. —**empiricist,** *n., adj.*

employ /ɛm'plɔɪ/ *v.t.* **1.** to use the services of (a person); have or keep in one's service; keep busy or at work: *this factory employs thousands of workers.* **2.** to make use of (an instrument, means, etc.); use; apply. **3.** to occupy or devote (time, energies, etc.): *I employ my spare time in reading.* —*n.* **4.** employment; service: *to be in someone's employ.* —**employable,** *adj.* —**employment,** *n.*

employee /ɛm'plɔɪi, ɛmplɔɪˈi/ *n.* a person working for another person or a business firm for pay.

employee contribution *n.* an after-tax payment made from one's salary into a regulated superannuation fund. Compare **salary sacrifice.**

employer /ɛm'plɔɪə/ *n.* someone who employs people, especially for wages.

emporium /ɛm'pɔriəm/ *n.* (*pl.* **-poriums** *or* **-poria** /-'pɔriə/) a large store selling a great variety of articles.

empower /ɛm'paʊə/ *v.t.* **1.** to give power or authority to; authorise: *I empowered him to make the deal for me.* **2.** to enable or permit. **3.** to cause (a person or group of

people) to feel confident and in control of their own life: *to empower women.* —**empowerment,** *n.*

empress /'ɛmprəs/ *n.* **1.** a woman ruler of an empire. **2.** the consort of an emperor. **3.** a woman with power to influence or command.

empty /'ɛmpti, 'ɛmti/ *adj.* (**-tier, -tiest**) **1.** containing nothing; void of the usual or appropriate contents: *an empty bottle.* **2.** vacant; unoccupied: *an empty house.* **3.** without burden or load: *an empty wagon.* **4.** without force, effect, or significance: *empty compliments; empty pleasures.* **5.** unsatisfactory; meaningless: *empty promises; empty threat.* **6.** without knowledge or sense; frivolous; foolish. **7.** *Colloq.* hungry. **8.** *Colloq.* drained of emotion; spent. —*verb* (**-tied, -tying**) —*v.t.* **9.** to make empty; deprive of contents; discharge the contents of: *to empty a bucket.* **10.** to discharge (contents): *empty the water out of a bucket.* —*v.i.* **11.** to become empty: *the room emptied rapidly after the lecture.* **12.** to discharge contents, as a river: *the river empties into the sea.* —*n.* (*pl.* **-ties**) **13.** *Colloq.* something empty, as a bottle, can, or the like. —*phr.* **14. empty of,** destitute of (some quality or qualities); devoid of: *a life empty of happiness.* —**emptily,** *adv.* —**emptiness,** *n.*

emu /'imju/ *n.* (*pl.* **emu** or **emus**) a large, flightless, three-toed Australian bird, *Dromaius novaehollandiae,* of the family Casuariidae, closely related to the cassowary, having dark brown shaggy plumage and exposed blue skin on the neck and head.

emu bush *n.* any of a number of shrubs of the endemic Australian genus *Eremophila,* family Myoporaceae, having fruits which are eaten by emus.

emulate /'ɛmjulelt, -jə-/ *v.t.* **1.** to try to equal or excel; imitate with effort to equal or surpass. **2.** to rival with some degree of success. **3.** (of a computer) to imitate (a particular computer system) by means of a software system that allows it to run the same programs as the system imitated. —**emulation** /ɛmju'leɪʃən, -jə-/, *n.* —**emulative** /'ɛmjəlatɪv/, *adj.* —**emulator,** *n.*

emulsify /ə'mʌlsəfaɪ/ *v.t.* (**-fied, -fying**) to make into an emulsion. —**emulsification** /əmʌlsəfə'keɪʃən/, *n.* —**emulsifier,** *n.*

emulsion /ə'mʌlʃən/ *n.* **1.** a liquid preparation of the colour and consistency of milk. **2.** *Chem.* any colloidal suspension of a liquid in another liquid. —**emulsive,** *adj.*

en /ɛn/ *n.* (*pl.* **ens**) **1.** the letter N, n. **2.** *Printing* half of the width of an em.

en-¹ a prefix meaning primarily 'in', 'into', first occurring in words from French, but now used freely as an English formative: **1.** with the old concrete force of putting the object into or on something or of bringing the object into the specified condition, often serving to form transitive verbs from nouns or adjectives, as in *enable, enact, endear, engulf, enshrine, enslave.* **2.** prefixed to verbs, to make them transitive, or, if already transitive, to give them the transitive sign, as in *enkindle, entwine, engild, engird, engrave, enshield.* Compare **in-²,** **im-¹.** Also, **em-.**

en-² a prefix representing Greek en-, corresponding to **en-¹** and occurring chiefly in combinations already formed in Greek, as *energy, enthusiasm.* Also, **em-.**

-en¹ a suffix, forming transitive and intransitive verbs from adjectives, as in *fasten, harden, sweeten,* or from nouns, as in *heighten, lengthen, strengthen.*

-en² a suffix of adjectives indicating material, appearance, as in *ashen, golden, oaken.*

-en³ a suffix used to mark the past participle in many strong and some weak verbs, as in *taken, proven.*

-en⁴ a suffix forming the plural of some nouns, as in *brethren, children, oxen.*

-en⁵ a diminutive suffix, as in *maiden, kitten,* etc.

enable /ɛn'eɪbəl, ən-/ *v.t.* **1.** to make able; give power, means, or ability to; make competent; authorise: *this* *will enable him to do it.* **2.** to make possible or easy. **3.** to assist, actively or passively, (an addicted person) in the pursuit of their addiction. –**enabler**, *n.*

enabling /ɛnˈeɪblɪŋ, ən-/ *adj.* (of an act, statute, or bill) making it possible for a person or a company to do something that would otherwise be illegal.

enact /ɛnˈækt, ən-/ *v.t.* **1.** to make into an act or statute. **2.** to ordain; decree. **3.** to represent on or as on the stage; act the part of: *to enact Hamlet.* –**enactor**, *n.* –**enactment**, *n.*

enamel /əˈnæməl/ *n.* **1.** a glassy substance, usually opaque, applied by fusion to a surface of metal, pottery, etc., as an ornament or for protection. **2.** any of various enamel-like varnishes, paints, etc. **3.** *Anat., Zool.* the hard, glossy, outer structure of the crowns of teeth. –*v.t.* (**-elled** *or, Chiefly US,* **-eled, -elling** *or, Chiefly US,* **-eling**) **4.** to inlay, cover, or ornament with enamel. –**enameller**, *n.* –**enamellist**, *n.* –**enamelwork**, *n.* –**enamelled**, *adj.*

enamoured /ɛnˈæməd, ən-/ *adj.* (sometimes fol. by *of*) inflamed with love; charmed; captivated: *to be enamoured of a lady.* Also, **enamored**.

encapsulate /ɛnˈkæpsjəleɪt, ən-, -ʃə-/ *v.t.* **1.** to enclose in or as in a capsule. **2.** to put in shortened form; condense; abridge. –**encapsulation** /ɛnˌkæpsjəˈleɪʃən, -ʃə-/, *n.*

encase /ɛnˈkeɪs, ən-/ *v.t.* (**-cased, -casing**) to enclose in or as in a case. Also, **incase**. –**encasement**, *n.*

-ence a noun suffix equivalent to **-ance**, and corresponding to **-ent** in adjectives, as in *abstinence, consistence, dependence, difference.*

encephalitis /ɛnsɛfəˈlaɪtəs, ɛnkɛf-, ən-/ *n. Pathol.* inflammation of the substance of the brain. –**encephalitic** /ɛnsɛfəˈlɪtɪk, ɛnkɛf-, ən-/, *adj.*

encephalo- a word element meaning 'brain', as in *encephalomyelitis.* Also, **encephal-**.

encephalogram /ɛnˈsɛfələgræm, ɛnkɛf-/ *n.* an X-ray photograph of the brain.

enchant /ɛnˈtʃænt, ən-, -ˈtʃɑnt/ *v.t.* **1.** to subject to magical influence; cast a spell over; bewitch. **2.** to impart a magic quality or effect to. **3.** to delight in a high degree; charm. –**enchanting**, *adj.* –**enchantment**, *n.*

enchilada /ɛntʃəˈladə/ *n.* **1.** a Mexican dish of a rolled tortilla filled with meat and seasonings, usually including chilli. –*phr.* **2. the whole enchilada**, *Colloq.* the entirety of something possessed or achieved, especially something impressive: *the house has a pool, tennis court, billiard room – the whole enchilada.*

encircle /ɛnˈsɜkəl, ən-/ *v.t.* **1.** to form a circle around; surround; encompass. **2.** to make a circling movement around; make the circuit of. –**encirclement**, *n.*

enclave /ˈɛnkleɪv, ˈɒnkleɪv/ *n.* a country, or, especially, an outlying portion of a country, entirely or mostly surrounded by the territory of another country.

enclose /ɛnˈkloʊz, ən-/ *v.t.* **1.** to shut in; close in on all sides. **2.** to surround as with a fence or wall: *to enclose land.* **3.** to insert in the same envelope, etc., with the main letter, etc.: *he enclosed a cheque.* **4.** to contain (the thing transmitted): *her letter enclosed a cheque.*

enclosure /ɛnˈkloʊʒə, ən-/ *n.* **1.** the act or result of enclosing: *the horses were in a large enclosure.* **2.** (formerly) the practice of taking common land by setting up a fence around it. **3.** that which is enclosed, e.g. paper, money, etc., sent in a letter.

encode /ɛnˈkoʊd/ *v.t.* to put into coded form, as a message, computer program, etc.

encompass /ɛnˈkʌmpəs, ən-/ *v.t.* **1.** to form a circle around; encircle; surround. **2.** to enclose; contain. –**encompassment**, *n.*

encore /ˈɒnkɔ, ˈɒŋkɔ/ *interj.* **1.** again; once more (used by an audience in calling for a repetition of a song, etc., or for an additional number or piece). –*n.* **2.** a demand, as

by applause, for a repetition of a song, etc., or for an additional number or piece. **3.** something that is performed in response to such a demand.

encounter /ɛnˈkaʊntə, ən-/ *v.t.* **1.** to come upon; meet with, especially unexpectedly. **2.** to meet with or contend against (difficulties, opposition, etc.). **3.** to meet (a person, military force, etc.) in conflict. –*n.* **4.** a meeting with a person or thing, especially casually or unexpectedly. **5.** a meeting in conflict or opposition; a battle; a combat.

encourage /ɛnˈkʌrɪdʒ, ən-/ *v.t.* (**-raged, -raging**) **1.** to inspire with courage, spirit, or confidence. **2.** to stimulate by assistance, approval, etc. –**encourager**, *n.* –**encouragingly**, *adv.* –**encouragement**, *n.*

encroach /ɛnˈkroʊtʃ, ən-/ *v.i.* **1.** to advance beyond proper limits; make gradual inroads. **2.** to trespass upon the property or rights of another, especially stealthily or by gradual advances. –**encroacher**, *n.* –**encroachingly**, *adv.* –**encroachment**, *n.*

encrust /ɛnˈkrʌst, ən-/ *v.t.* **1.** to cover or line with a crust or hard coating. **2.** to form into a crust. **3.** to deposit as a crust. –*v.i.* **4.** to form a crust.

encumber /ɛnˈkʌmbə, ən-/ *v.t.* **1.** to impede or hamper; retard; embarrass. **2.** to block up or fill with what is obstructive or superfluous. **3.** to burden with obligations, debt, etc. **4.** to burden or impede with or as with parcels, etc. Also, **incumber**. –**encumbrance**, *n.*

encyclopedia /ɛnˌsaɪkləˈpidiə, ən-/ *n.* **1.** a work treating separately various topics from all branches of knowledge, usually in alphabetical arrangement. **2.** a work treating exhaustively one art or science especially in articles arranged alphabetically; a cyclopedia. Also, **encyclopaedia**.

end /ɛnd/ *n.* **1.** an extremity of anything that is longer than it is broad: *the end of a street; the end of a rope.* **2.** an extreme or farthermost part of anything extended in space. **3.** anything that bounds an object at one of its extremities; a limit. **4.** a place or section adjacent to an extremity or limit: *at the far end of the room.* **5.** the act of coming to an end; termination. **6.** the concluding part. **7.** a purpose or aim: *to gain one's end.* **8.** the object for which a thing exists: *the happiness of the people is the end of government.* **9.** issue or result. **10.** termination of existence; death. **11.** a cause of death, destruction, or ruin. **12.** a remnant or fragment: *odds and ends.* **13.** a part or share of something: *her end of the work.* **14.** a district or locality, especially part of a town: *the West End.* **15.** *Bowls* a part of the game during which the players all deliver their bowls to one end of the green; at the completion of one end the direction of play may reverse. –*v.t.* **16.** to bring to an end or natural conclusion. **17.** to put an end to by force. **18.** to form the end of. –*v.i.* **19.** to come to an end; terminate; cease: *he ended by settling down.* **20.** to issue or result: *extravagance ends in want.* –*phr.* **21. at the end of one's string** (or **rope**) (or **tether**), *Colloq.* completely emotionally exhausted. **22. at the pointy** (or **sharp**) **end**, at the point in a situation of conflict or competition where the important action takes place, hence where the greatest risk exists: *at the pointy end of the race; at the sharp end of negotiations.* **23. end on**, with the end facing, or next to the observer. **24. end to end**, (of two objects) having the ends adjacent. **25. end up**, *Colloq.* to reach a final condition, circumstance, goal: *you'll end up in prison.* **26. get one's end in**, *Colloq.* (taboo) (of a male) to have sexual intercourse. **27. go off the deep end**, *Colloq.* to become violently agitated; lose control of one's emotions. **28. in the end**, as an outcome; at last; finally. **29. keep one's end up**, *Colloq.* to see that one's contribution to a joint undertaking is adequately performed. **30. make** (**both**) **ends meet**, to keep expenditure within one's means. **31. no**

end, *Colloq.* an intensifier: *no end of trouble.* **32. on end**, **a.** upright. **b.** continuously. **c.** into an opposite procedure or tack: *to turn the game on end.* **33. the (living) end**, **a.** the worst thing possible. **b.** a person who is incompetent or insufferable in every way. **34. to the ends of the earth**, a long way away. –**ender**, *n.* –**endless**, *adj.*

endanger /ɛnˈdeɪndʒə, ən-/ *v.t.* to expose to danger; imperil. –**endangerment**, *n.*

endangered species *n.* a threatened species that is facing a very high risk of extinction in the wild in the near future. Compare **critically endangered species**, **vulnerable species**.

endear /ɛnˈdɪə, ən-/ *v.t.* to make dear, esteemed, or beloved: *he endeared himself to his mother.* –**endearingly**, *adv.*

endearment /ɛnˈdɪəmənt, ən-/ *n.* **1.** the act of endearing. **2.** the state of being endeared. **3.** an action or utterance manifesting affection; a caress or an affectionate term.

endeavour /ɛnˈdɛvə, ən-/ *v.i.* **1.** to exert oneself to do or effect something; make an effort; strive. –*v.t.* **2.** to attempt; try: *he endeavours to keep things nice about his place.* –*n.* **3.** a strenuous effort; an attempt. Also, **endeavor**. –**endeavourer**, *n.*

endemic /ɛnˈdɛmɪk/ *adj.* Also, **endemical**. **1.** peculiar to a particular people or locality, as a disease. –*n.* **2.** an endemic disease or plant. –**endemically**, *adv.* –**endemism** /ˈɛndəmɪzəm/, **endemicity** /ɛndəˈmɪsəti/, *n.*

endive /ˈɛndaɪv/ *n.* a herb, *Cichorium endivia*, probably of Indian origin, now widely cultivated for its finely divided curled leaves used in salads and as a cooked vegetable.

endo- a word element meaning 'internal', as in *endocarp*. Also, **end-**.

endocrine /ˈɛndəkrən, -krɪn, -kraɪn/ *adj.* of or relating to the endocrine glands or their secretions: *endocrine function.* –**endocrinal** /ɛndəˈkraɪnəl/, **endocrinic** /ɛndəˈkrɪnɪk/, **endocrinous** /ɛnˈdɒkrənəs/, *adj.*

endocrine gland *n. Physiol.* any of various glands or organs (as the thyroid gland, suprarenal bodies, pituitary body, etc.) which produce certain important internal secretions (products released directly into the blood or lymph) acting upon particular organs, and which, through improper functioning, may cause grave disorders or death; ductless gland.

endorse /ɛnˈdɔs, ən-/ *v.t.* (**-dorsed, -dorsing**) **1.** to add a modifying statement to (a document, licence, etc.). **2.** to sign one's name to (a commercial document, cheque, etc.) as to transfer money, acknowledge receipt, etc. **3.** to give support to; approve: *I don't endorse that sort of behaviour.* **4.** (of a branch of a political party) to select (someone) as a candidate for election: *Labor has endorsed him as its candidate.* **5.** (of a celebrity) to express publicly a positive opinion of (a product, cause, etc.), often for a fee. Also, **indorse**. –**endorsable**, *adj.* –**endorsement**, *n.* –**endorser**, *n.*

endoscope /ˈɛndəskoʊp/ *n.* a slender tubular medical instrument used to examine the interior of a body cavity or hollow organ. –**endoscopic** /ɛndəˈskɒpɪk/, *adj.*

endoscopy /ɛnˈdɒskəpi/ *n.* (*pl.* **-pies**) a medical examination by means of an endoscope. –**endoscopist**, *n.*

endoskeleton /ˌɛndoʊˈskɛlətn/ *n.* the internal skeleton or framework of the body of an animal (opposed to *exoskeleton*). –**endoskeletal**, *adj.*

endow /ɛnˈdaʊ, ən-/ *v.t.* **1.** to provide with a permanent fund or source of income: *to endow a college.* **2.** to furnish as with some gift, faculty, or quality; equip: *Nature has endowed him with great ability.* –**endowment**, *n.* –**endower**, *n.*

end product *n.* final or resulting product.

endue /ɛnˈdju, ən-/ *Rare* –*v.t.* (**-dued, -duing**) **1.** to put on; assume. –*phr.* **2. endue with**, to invest or endow with (some gift, quality, or faculty): *endued with life.* Also, **indue**.

endurance /ɛnˈdjurəns, ən-/ *n.* **1.** the fact or power of enduring or bearing anything. **2.** lasting quality; duration. **3.** something endured, as a hardship. **4.** *Aeronautics* the time an aircraft can continue flying under given conditions without refuelling. –*adj.* **5.** of or relating to something requiring stamina: *an endurance event.*

endure /ɛnˈdjuə/ *v.t.* **1.** to hold out against; sustain without impairment or yielding; undergo. **2.** to bear without resistance or with patience; tolerate: *I cannot endure to listen to that any longer.* –*v.i.* **3.** to continue to exist; last. **4.** to support adverse force or influence of any kind; suffer without yielding; suffer patiently. **5.** to retain a certain stature; maintain recognition of merit. –**endurable**, *adj.* –**enduring**, *adj.*

-ene 1. a noun suffix used in chemistry, in names of hydrocarbons, as *anthracene, benzene, naphthalene*, specifically those of the ethylene series, as *butylene*. **2.** a generalised suffix used in trademarks for substances, often implying synthetic manufacture.

enema /ˈɛnəmə/ *n.* (*pl.* **enemas** or **enemata** /əˈnɛmətə, i-/) *Med.* a fluid injected into the rectum, as to evacuate the bowels.

enemy /ˈɛnəmi/ *n.* (*pl.* **-mies**) **1.** someone who hates another, or has harmful designs against them; adversary; opponent. **2.** an armed foe; opposing military force. **3.** a hostile nation, state, or its people. **4.** something harmful. –*adj.* **5.** belonging to a hostile power or to its people: *enemy property.*

energetic /ɛnəˈdʒɛtɪk/ *adj.* **1.** possessing or exhibiting energy; forcible; vigorous. **2.** powerful in action or effect; effective. –**energetically**, *adv.*

energy /ˈɛnədʒi/ *n.* (*pl.* **-gies**) **1.** capacity or habit of vigorous activity. **2.** the actual exertion of power; operation; activity. **3.** power as exerted. **4.** ability to produce action or effect. **5.** vigour or forcefulness of expression.

energy efficiency rating *n.* an energy labelling approved by a regulatory authority and required for devices such as washing machines, dryers, refrigerators, dishwashers, etc., which indicates the performance level of the device with respect to energy efficiency. *Abbrev.*: EER

energy efficiency ratio *n.* the ratio of the cooling capacity of an air-conditioning system (measured in Btus per hour) to the power input (measured in watts) at a given set of rating conditions, expressed as Btu/h per watt. *Abbrev.*: EER

energy labelling *n.* the system of labelling an appliance, such as a refrigerator, freezer or room air conditioner, to indicate how much electricity it would use annually in kilowatt hours, when tested to an Australian Standard.

energy recovery *n.* the efficient use of materials which are the incidental by-product of a process, as the heat energy produced in the air vented by an air conditioner, or the methane produced in wastewater treatment.

enervate /ˈɛnəveɪt/ *v.t.* to deprive of force, or strength; destroy the vigour of; weaken. –**enervation** /ɛnəˈveɪʃən/, *n.*

enfold /ɛnˈfoʊld, ən-/ *v.t.* **1.** to wrap up; envelop: *enfolded in a magic mantle.* **2.** to clasp; embrace. **3.** to surround with or as with folds. **4.** to form into a fold or folds: *a cambium layer deeply enfolded where it extends downwards.* Also, **infold**. –**enfolder**, *n.* –**enfoldment**, *n.*

enforce /ɛnˈfɔs, ən-/ *v.t.* (**-forced, -forcing**) **1.** to put or keep in force; compel obedience to: *to enforce laws*; *to enforce rules.* **2.** to obtain (payment, obedience, etc.) by force or compulsion. **3.** to impose (a course of action) upon a person. **4.** to support (a demand, etc.) by force. **5.** to impress or urge (an argument, etc.) forcibly; lay stress upon. –**enforceable**, *adj.* –**enforcer**, *n.* –**enforcement**, *n.*

enfranchise /ɛnˈfræntʃaɪz, ən-/ *v.t.* (**-chised, -chising**) **1.** to grant a franchise to; admit to citizenship, especially to the right of voting. **2.** *Law* to invest with the right of being represented in Parliament. **3.** to set free; liberate, as from slavery. –**enfranchisement** /ənˈfræntʃəzmənt/, *n.* –**enfranchiser**, *n.*

engage /ɛnˈɡeɪdʒ, ən-/ *verb* (**engaged, engaging**) –*v.t.* **1.** to obtain the attention or efforts of (a person, etc.): *he engaged her in conversation.* **2.** to obtain for aid, employment, use, etc.; hire: *to engage a workman; to engage a room.* **3.** to attract and hold fast: *to engage the attention; to engage someone's interest.* **4.** to bind as by a promise, contract, oath, etc.: *he engaged to do it in writing.* **5.** (*usu. in passive*) to promise in marriage; betroth. **6.** to bring (troops) into conflict; enter into battle with: *our army engaged the enemy.* **7.** *Mechanics* to cause to become interlocked: *to engage first gear.* –*v.i.* **8.** to occupy oneself; become involved: *to engage in business; to engage in a strategy.* **9.** to pledge one's word; assume an obligation. **10.** to enter into battle. **11.** *Mechanics* to interlock. –**engager**, *n.*

engaged /ɛnˈɡeɪdʒd, ən-/ *adj.* **1.** busy or occupied; involved. **2.** under agreement to marry. **3.** *Mechanics* **a.** interlocked. **b.** (of toothed wheels) in gear with each other. **4.** (of a telephone line) inaccessible because already in use.

engagement /ɛnˈɡeɪdʒmənt, ən-/ *n.* **1.** the act of engaging. **2.** the state of being engaged. **3.** an appointment or arrangement, often of a business nature.

engaging /ɛnˈɡeɪdʒɪŋ, ən-/ *adj.* winning; attractive; pleasing. –**engagingly**, *adv.* –**engagingness**, *n.*

engender /ɛnˈdʒɛndə, ən-/ *v.t.* **1.** to produce, cause, or give rise to: *hatred engenders violence.* **2.** to beget; procreate. –**engenderer**, *n.* –**engenderment**, *n.*

engine /ˈɛndʒən/ *n.* **1.** any mechanism or machine designed to convert energy into mechanical work: *a steam engine; an internal-combustion engine.* **2.** a railway locomotive. **3.** any mechanical contrivance. **4.** a machine or instrument used in warfare, as a battering ram, catapult, piece of artillery, etc. **5.** a driving force.

engineer /ɛndʒəˈnɪə/ *n.* **1.** a person professionally qualified in the design, construction, and use of engines or machines, or in any of the various branches of engineering: *a mechanical engineer; an electrical engineer.* **2.** a skilful manager. –*v.t.* **3.** to plan, construct, or manage as an engineer. **4.** to arrange, manage or carry through by skilful, clever means.

engineering /ɛndʒəˈnɪərɪŋ/ *n.* **1.** the art or science of making practical application of the knowledge of pure sciences such as physics, chemistry, biology, etc. **2.** the action, work, or profession of an engineer. **3.** skilful or artful contrivance; manoeuvring.

English /ˈɪŋɡlɪʃ, ˈɪŋlɪʃ/ *adj.* **1.** of, relating to, or characteristic of England or its inhabitants, institutions, etc. **2.** belonging or relating to, or spoken or written in, the English language. –*n.* **3.** the people of England collectively, especially as distinguished from the Scots, Welsh, and Irish. **4.** the Germanic language of the British Isles, historically termed Old English or Anglo-Saxon (to 1150), Middle English (to 1450) and Modern English. **5.** (*pl.* **Englishes**) a dialect or national variety of English, being one of many such varieties used throughout the world, often specified as in *Australian English, American English, British English.* **6.** straightforward and simple language. –*phr.* **7. the Queen's** (or **King's**) **English**, English which is regarded as being educated or correct in pronunciation or usage.

English muffin *n.* a thick, flat yeast cake, made from a soft, risen dough, baked without browning, served cut open and usually toasted, with butter, etc.

English parsley *n.* → **curly-leaf parsley**.

English spinach *n.* → **spinach** (def. 1).

engrain /ɛnˈɡreɪn/ *v.t., adj.* → **ingrain** (defs 1 and 2).

engrave /ɛnˈɡreɪv, ən-/ *v.t.* **1.** to incise (letters, designs, etc.) on a hard surface, as of metal, stone, or the end-grain of wood. **2.** to print from such a surface. **3.** to mark or ornament with incised letters, designs, etc. **4.** to impress deeply; infix. –**engraver**, *n.*

engraving /ɛnˈɡreɪvɪŋ, ən-/ *n.* **1.** the art of forming designs by cutting, corrosion by acids, a photographic process, etc., on the surface of metal plates or of blocks of wood, etc., for the purpose of taking off impressions or prints of the design so formed. **2.** the design engraved. **3.** an engraved plate or block. **4.** an impression or print from this.

engross /ɛnˈɡroʊs, ən-/ *v.t.* **1.** to occupy wholly, as the mind or attention; absorb. **2.** to write or copy in a fair, large hand or in a formal manner, as a public document or record. –**engrosser**, *n.* –**engrossment**, *n.*

engulf /ɛnˈɡʌlf, ən-/ *v.t.* **1.** to swallow up in a gulf (def. 2). **2.** to immerse. **3.** to overwhelm. Also, **ingulf**. –**engulfment**, *n.*

enhance /ɛnˈhæns, -ˈhans, ən-/ *v.t.* (**-hanced, -hancing**) **1.** to raise to a higher degree; intensify; magnify. **2.** to raise the value or price of. –**enhancement**, *n.* –**enhancer**, *n.* –**enhancive**, *adj.*

enhanced greenhouse effect *n.* → **greenhouse effect** (def. 2b).

enigma /əˈnɪɡmə/ *n.* **1.** somebody or something puzzling or inexplicable. **2.** a saying, question, picture, etc., containing a hidden meaning; a riddle. –**enigmatic** /ɛnɪɡˈmætɪk/, **enigmatical** /ɛnɪɡˈmætɪkəl/, *adj.*

enjoin /ɛnˈdʒɔɪn, ən-/ *v.t.* to order or direct (a person, etc.) to do something; prescribe (a course of action, etc.) with authority or emphasis. –**enjoiner**, *n.* –**enjoinment**, *n.*

enjoy /ɛnˈdʒɔɪ, ən-/ *v.t.* **1.** to experience with joy; take pleasure in. **2.** to have and use with satisfaction; have the benefit of. **3.** to find or experience pleasure for (oneself). **4.** to undergo (an improvement). –*v.i.* **5.** to have a good time: *let's forget our troubles and enjoy.* –**enjoyable**, *adj.* –**enjoyment**, *n.*

enlarge /ɛnˈlɑdʒ, ən-/ *verb* (**-larged, -larging**) –*v.t.* **1.** to make larger; increase in extent, bulk, or quantity; add to. **2.** to increase the capacity or scope of; expand. **3.** *Photography* to make (a print) larger than the negative, by projection printing. –*v.i.* **4.** to speak or write at large; expatiate: *to enlarge upon a point.* –**enlargeable**, *adj.* –**enlargement**, *n.* –**enlarger**, *n.*

enlighten /ɛnˈlaɪtn, ən-/ *v.t.* to give intellectual or spiritual light to; instruct; impart knowledge to. –**enlightener**, *n.* –**enlighteningly**, *adv.* –**enlightenment**, *n.*

enlist /ɛnˈlɪst, ən-/ *v.i.* **1.** to engage for military or naval service by enrolling after mutual agreement. **2.** to enter into some cause, enterprise, etc. –**enlister**, *n.* –**enlistment**, *n.*

enliven /ɛnˈlaɪvən, ən-/ *v.t.* **1.** to make vigorous or active; invigorate. **2.** to make sprightly or cheerful; brighten. –**enlivener**, *n.* –**enlivenment**, *n.*

en masse /ɒn ˈmæs/ *adv.* in a mass or body; all together.

enmity /ˈɛnməti/ *n.* (*pl.* **-ties**) a feeling or condition of hostility; hatred; ill will; animosity; antagonism.

enneagon /ˈɛniəɡən/ *n.* a polygon having nine angles and nine sides; nonagon.

ennui /ɒnˈwi/ *n.* a feeling of weariness and discontent resulting from satiety or lack of interest; boredom.

enormity /əˈnɔməti, i-/ *n.* (*pl.* **-ties**) **1.** outrageous or heinous character; atrociousness: *the enormity of his offences.* **2.** something outrageous or heinous, as an offence. **3.** (*not considered standard by some*) enormousness; hugeness of size, scope, extent, etc.

enormous /ə'nɔːməs, i-/ *adj.* **1.** greatly exceeding the common size, extent, etc.; huge; immense. **2.** outrageous or atrocious: *enormous wickedness.* **—enormously,** *adv.* **—enormousness,** *n.*

enough /ə'nʌf, i-/ *adj.* **1.** adequate for the want or need; sufficient for the purpose or to satisfy desire: *enough food for everyone.* *–pron.* **2.** an adequate quantity or number; a sufficiency: *I've had enough of it.* *–adv.* **3.** in a quantity or degree that answers a purpose or satisfies a need or desire; sufficiently: *you're not pressing hard enough.* **4.** fully or quite: *ready enough.* **5.** tolerably or passably: *he sings well enough.* *–interj.* **6.** an exclamation indicating frustration, anger, extreme irritation, etc. *–phr.* **7. be man enough,** (of a man) to be suitably courageous or honourable: *he was man enough to own up.* **8. enough and to spare,** a comfortable sufficiency. **9. enough's enough** or **that's enough,** an expression indicating that one's limit of toleration has been reached. **10. enough to sink a ship,** *Colloq.* a great deal.

enquire /ɪn'kwaɪə, ən-, ɛn-/ *v.i.*, *v.t.* → **inquire.** **—enquirer,** *n.*

enquiry /ɪn'kwaɪri, ən-, ɛn-/ *n.* (*pl.* **-ries**) → **inquiry.**

enrage /ɛn'reɪdʒ, ən-/ *v.t.* to put into a rage; infuriate.

enrapture /ɛn'ræptʃə, ən-/ *v.t.* to move to rapture; delight beyond measure. **—enrapt,** *adj.*

enrich /ɛn'rɪtʃ, ən-/ *v.t.* **1.** to supply with abundance of anything desirable: *to enrich the mind with knowledge.* **2.** to make finer in quality as by supplying desirable elements or ingredients: *to enrich bread; to enrich soil.* **3.** to enhance; make finer in flavour, colour, or significance. **4.** *Physics* to increase the abundance of a particular isotope in a mixture of isotopes, especially of a fissile isotope in a nuclear fuel, as enriching uranium with the isotope U-235. **—enrichment,** *n.*

enrol /ɛn'roʊl, ən-/ *verb* **(-rolled, -rolling)** *–v.t.* **1.** to write (a name) or insert the name of (a person) in a roll or register; place upon a list. **2.** to place (a person) on a list or register as a preliminary to their joining an organisation **3.** *Educ.* to place on the register of an educational institution, or of a course offered by an educational institution. **4.** *Computers* to place on a list of authorised users of software. **5.** to put in a record, as of a court; record. *–v.i.* **6.** to enrol oneself. Also, *Chiefly US,* **enroll. —enroller,** *n.* **—enrolment,** *n.*

enrolled nurse *n.* a nurse with a non-degree qualification, as from a nursing college, TAFE college, etc. *Abbrev.:* EN Compare **registered nurse.**

en route /ɒn 'ruːt/ *adv.* on the way.

ensconce /ɛn'skɒns, ən-/ *v.t.* **1.** to cover or shelter; hide securely. **2.** to settle securely or snugly: *ensconced in an armchair.*

ensemble /ɒn'sɒmbəl/ *n.* **1.** all the parts of a thing taken together, so that each part is considered only in relation to the whole. **2.** the entire costume of an individual, especially when all the parts are in harmony. **3.** the general effect, as of a work of art. **4.** the united performance of the full number of singers, musicians, etc. **5.** a group of supporting singers, actors, dancers, etc., in a theatrical production.

enshrine /ɛn'ʃraɪn, ən-/ *v.t.* **1.** to enclose in or as in a shrine. **2.** to cherish as sacred. Also, **inshrine. —enshrinement,** *n.*

ensign /'ɛnsən, 'ɛnsaɪn/ *n.* **1.** a flag or banner, as of a nation. **2.** a badge of office or authority. **3.** any sign, token, or emblem. **4.** a standard-bearer. **5.** (formerly) the lowest commissioned rank in the British infantry. **—ensignship, ensigncy,** *n.*

enslave /ɛn'sleɪv, ən-/ *v.t.* to make a slave of; reduce to slavery. **—enslavement,** *n.* **—enslaver,** *n.*

ensnare /ɛn'snɛə, ən-/ *v.t.* **(-snared, -snaring)** to capture in, or involve as in a, snare. **—ensnarement,** *n.* **—ensnarer,** *n.*

ensue /ɛn'sjuː, ən-/ *v.i.* **1.** to follow in order; come afterwards, especially in immediate succession. **2.** to follow as a consequence; result.

en suite /ɒn 'swiːt/ *adj.* in succession; in a series or set.

ensure /ɛn'ʃɔː, ən-/ *v.t.* **1.** to secure, or bring surely, as to a person: *this letter will ensure you a hearing.* **2.** to make sure or certain to come, occur, etc.: *measures to ensure the success of an undertaking.*

-ent a suffix equivalent to **-ant,** in adjectives and nouns, as in *ardent, dependent, different, expedient.*

entail /ɛn'teɪl, ən-/ *v.t.* **1.** to bring on or involve by necessity or consequences: *a loss entailing no regret.* **2.** to impose as a burden. **3.** *Law* to limit the inheritance of (a landed estate) to a specified line of heirs, so that it cannot be bequeathed, alienated, or devised. **4.** to cause (anything) to descend to a fixed series of possessors. *–n.* **5.** *Law* the rule of descent settled for an estate. **—entailer,** *n.* **—entailment,** *n.*

entangle /ɛn'tæŋgəl, ən-/ *v.t.* **1.** (*usu. used in the passive*) to make tangled; complicate. **2.** to involve in anything like a tangle; ensnare; enmesh. **3.** to involve in difficulties; embarrass; perplex. **—entangler,** *n.* **—entanglement,** *n.*

entente /ɒn'tɒnt/ *n.* **1.** understanding. **2.** the parties to an understanding.

enter /'ɛntə/ *v.i.* **1.** to come or go in. **2.** to make an entrance, as on the stage. **3.** to be admitted. *–v.t.* **4.** to come or go into. **5.** to penetrate or pierce: *the bullet entered the flesh.* **6.** to put in or insert: *to enter a wedge.* **7.** to become a member of, or join. **8.** to cause to be admitted, as into a school, competition, etc. **9.** to make a beginning of or in, or begin upon; engage or become involved in. **10.** to make a record of; record or register. **11.** to type (data, text, etc.) into a computer file. **12.** *Law* **a.** to place in regular form before a court, as a writ. **b.** to occupy or to take possession of (lands); make an entrance, entry, ingress in, under claim of a right to possession. **13.** to register formally; submit; put forward: *to enter an objection.* *–phr.* **14. enter into, a.** to take an interest or part in; engage in. **b.** to take up the consideration of (a subject); investigate. **c.** to sympathise with (a person's feelings, etc.). **d.** to assume the obligation of. **e.** to become a party to. **f.** to make a beginning in. **g.** to form a constituent part or ingredient of: *lead enters into the composition of pewter.* **h.** to penetrate; plunge deeply into. **i.** to go into (a specific state): *to enter into a state of hypnosis.* **15. enter on** (or **upon**), to make a beginning in. **—enterable,** *adj.* **—enterer,** *n.*

enteritis /ɛntə'raɪtəs/ *n.* *Pathol.* inflammation of the intestines.

enter key *n.* → **return key.**

entero- a word element meaning 'intestine'.

enterprise /'ɛntəpraɪz/ *n.* **1.** a project undertaken or to be undertaken, especially one that is of some importance or that requires boldness or energy. **2.** engagement in such projects. **3.** boldness or readiness in undertaking, adventurous spirit, or energy. **4.** a company organised for commercial purposes.

enterprise agreement *n.* (in Australia) an agreement between the employees and employers of an enterprise regarding pay and working conditions, which results from enterprise bargaining.

enterprise bargaining *n.* (in Australia) bargaining on wages and conditions conducted between the employer and employees of an enterprise.

enterprise information portal *n.* → **information portal.**

enterprising /ˈɛntəpraɪzɪŋ/ adj. ready to undertake projects of importance or difficulty, or untried schemes; energetic and daring in carrying out any undertaking. –**enterprisingly**, adv.

entertain /ɛntəˈteɪn/ v.t. **1.** to hold the attention of agreeably; divert; amuse. **2.** to receive as a guest. **3.** to have in the mind; consider: he entertained ideas of growing rich. –v.i. **4.** to entertain guests. –**entertaining**, adj. –**entertainment**, n.

entertainer /ɛntəˈteɪnə/ n. **1.** someone who entertains. **2.** a singer, reciter, or the like, who gives, or takes part in, public entertainments.

enthral /ɛnˈθrɔl, ən-/ v.t. (**-thralled, -thralling**) **1.** to captivate; charm. **2.** to put or hold in servitude; subjugate. Also, Chiefly US, **enthrall**. –**enthraller**, n. –**enthralment**, n. –**enthralled**, adj.

enthrone /ɛnˈθroʊn, ən-/ v.t. **1.** to place on or as on a throne. **2.** to invest with sovereign or episcopal authority. **3.** to exalt. –**enthronement**, n.

enthuse /ɛnˈθuz, -ˈθjuz, ən-/ verb (**-thused, -thusing**) –v.i. **1.** to become enthusiastic; show enthusiasm. –v.t. **2.** to move to enthusiasm.

enthusiasm /ɛnˈθuziæzəm, -ˈθjuz-, ən-/ n. **1.** absorbing or controlling possession of the mind by any interest or pursuit; lively interest. **2.** extravagant religious emotion. –**enthusiast**, n. –**enthusiastic**, adj.

entice /ɛnˈtaɪs, ən-/ v.t. (**-ticed, -ticing**) to draw on by exciting hope or desire; inveigle. –**enticer**, n. –**enticement**, n. –**enticingly**, adv.

entire /ɛnˈtaɪə, ən-/ adj. **1.** having all the parts or elements; whole; complete. **2.** not broken, mutilated, or decayed; intact. **3.** unimpaired or undiminished. **4.** being wholly of one piece; undivided; continuous. **5.** full or thorough: entire freedom of choice. –**entirely**, adv. –**entireness**, **entirety**, n.

entitle /ɛnˈtaɪtl, ən-/ v.t. **1.** to give (a person or thing) a title, right, or claim to something; furnish with grounds for laying claim. **2.** to call by a particular title or name; name. **3.** to designate (a person) by an honorary title.

entity /ˈɛntəti/ n. (pl. **-ties**) **1.** something that has a real existence; a thing, especially when considered as independent of other things. **2.** being or existence. **3.** essential nature. **4.** an independent organisation or person, especially when regarded as having legal responsibilities.

ento- variant of **endo-**.

entomology /ɛntəˈmɒlədʒi/ n. the branch of zoology that deals with insects. –**entomological** /ɛntəməˈlɒdʒɪkəl/, **entomologic** /ɛntəməˈlɒdʒɪk/, adj. –**entomologically** /ɛntəməˈlɒdʒɪkli/, adv. –**entomologist**, n.

entourage /ˈɒnturadʒ, -raʒ/ n. **1.** attendants, as of a person of rank. **2.** any group of people accompanying or assisting someone.

entrails /ˈɛntreɪlz/ pl. n. the internal parts of the trunk of an animal body.

entrance[1] /ˈɛntrəns/ n. **1.** the act of entering, as into a place or upon new duties. **2.** a point or place of entering; an opening or passage for entering. **3.** power or liberty of entering; admission.

entrance[2] /ɛnˈtræns, -ˈtrans, ən-/ v.t. (**-tranced, -trancing**) **1.** to fill with delight or wonder; enrapture. **2.** to put into a trance. –**entrancement**, n. –**entrancingly**, adv.

entrant /ˈɛntrənt/ n. **1.** someone who enters. **2.** a new member, as of an association, a university, etc. **3.** a competitor in a contest.

entreat /ɛnˈtrit, ən-/ v.t. **1.** to make supplication to (a person); beseech; implore: to entreat a person for something. **2.** to ask earnestly for (something). –v.i. **3.** to make an earnest request or petition. Also, **intreat**. –**entreatingly**, adv. –**entreaty**, n.

entree /ˈɒntreɪ/ n. **1.** a dish served at dinner before the main course. **2.** US the main course of a dinner. **3.** the right or privilege of entering. Also, **entrée**.

entrench /ɛnˈtrɛntʃ, ən-/ v.t. **1.** to dig trenches for defensive purposes around (oneself, a military position, etc.). **2.** to place in a position of strength; establish firmly: the soldiers entrenched themselves behind a thick concrete wall. **3.** to establish so strongly or securely as to make any change very difficult: the clauses concerning human rights are entrenched in the new constitution. –v.i. **4.** to dig in. –phr. **5.** **entrench on** (or **upon**), **a.** to encroach on; trespass on; infringe on: to entrench on the domain or rights of another. **b.** to verge on: proceedings entrenching on impiety. Also, **intrench**. –**entrencher**, n.

entrepreneur /ɒntrəprəˈnɜ/ n. **1.** (originally in theatrical use) someone who organises and manages any enterprise, especially one involving considerable risk. **2.** Commerce an employer of productive labour; a contractor. –**entrepreneurial**, adj. –**entrepreneurialism**, n. –**entrepreneurship**, n.

entropy /ˈɛntrəpi/ n. a measure of the unavailable energy in a thermodynamic system; it may also be regarded as a measure of the state of disorder of a system. A change of entropy in a reversible process is the ratio of heat absorbed to the absolute temperature.

entrust /ɛnˈtrʌst, ən-/ v.t. **1.** to invest with a trust or responsibility; charge with a specified office or duty involving trust. **2.** to commit (something) in trust (to); confide, as for care, use, or performance: to entrust a secret, money, powers, or work to another. **3.** to commit as if with trust or confidence: to entrust one's life to a frayed rope. Also, **intrust**. –**entrustment**, n.

entry /ˈɛntri/ n. (pl. **-ries**) **1.** the act of entering; entrance. **2.** a way or place of entering. **3.** permission or right to enter; access. **4.** the act of recording something in a book, list, etc. **5.** the statement, name, etc., so recorded. **6.** someone entered in competition. **7.** Music a point in a musical performance where a member of an orchestra or choir or a soloist begins to play or sing after being silent for some time.

entwine /ɛnˈtwaɪn, ən-/ v.t., v.i. to twine with, about, around, or together. Also, **intwine**. –**entwinement**, n.

E number n. one of a set of numbers used as a code to identify food additives.

enumerate /əˈnjuməreɪt, i-/ v.t. **1.** to mention separately as if in counting; name one by one; specify as in a list. **2.** to ascertain the number of; count. –**enumerator**, n. –**enumeration** /ənjuməˈreɪʃən, i-/, n.

enunciate /əˈnʌnsieɪt, i-/ v.t. **1.** to utter or pronounce (words, etc.), especially in a particular manner: he enunciates his words distinctly. **2.** to state precisely and, usually, formally, as a theory, policy, etc. **3.** to announce or proclaim. –v.i. **4.** to pronounce words, especially in an articulate or a particular manner. –**enunciable**, adj. –**enunciability** /ənʌnsiəˈbɪləti, i-/, n. –**enunciatively**, adv. –**enunciator**, n. –**enunciation** /ənʌnsiˈeɪʃən, i-/, n.

enuresis /ɛnjuˈrisəs/ n. Pathol. incontinence or involuntary discharge of urine; bedwetting. –**enuretic** /ɛnjuˈrɛtɪk/, adj.

envelop v.t. /ɛnˈvɛləp, ən-/ **1.** to wrap up in or as in a covering. **2.** to serve as a wrapping or covering for. **3.** to surround entirely. **4.** to obscure or conceal: mountains enveloped in mist. –n. /ˈɛnvəloʊp, ˈɒn-/ **5.** → **envelope**. –**enveloper** /ɛnˈvɛləpə, ən-/, n. –**envelopment**, n.

envelope /ˈɛnvəloʊp, ˈɒn-/ n. **1.** a cover for a letter or the like, usually so made that it can be sealed or fastened. **2.** something that envelops; a wrapper, integument, or surrounding cover. –phr. **3.** **push the envelope**, Colloq. **a.** Aeronautics to operate an aircraft close to its set limits. **b.** to extend one's capabilities, ideas, etc.

enviable /ˈɛnviəbəl/ adj. that is to be envied; worthy to be envied; highly desirable. –**enviableness**, n. –**enviably**, adv.

envious /ˈɛnviəs/ adj. full of, feeling, or expressing envy: *envious of a person's success, an envious attack.* –**enviously**, adv. –**enviousness**, n.

environment /ɛnˈvaɪrənmənt, ən-/ n. **1.** the aggregate of surrounding things, conditions, or influences. **2.** the particular influences on personal development as work conditions, home situation, etc.: *a child in a good environment will do better at school.* **3.** the biological conditions in which an organism lives, especially a balanced system. **4.** the totality of the surrounding conditions, physical and social, of a particular area. **5.** a situation involving a specified factor or factors: *the work environment.* **6.** an art form which is designed to be viewed and touched while the spectator moves around, over, under and through it. –*phr.* **7. the environment**, the broad natural surrounding conditions, such as the bush, the rivers, the air, the sea, in which human beings live: *the burning of fossil fuels harms the environment.* –**environmental**, adj. –**environmentally**, adv.

environmental audit n. a process which identifies for a business or organisation areas of inefficiency and excessive waste in their processes, such as paper usage, energy consumption, etc., thus reducing damage to the environment as well as providing a financial benefit.

environmental equity n. the principle that there should not be gross disparities between groups in a population with regard to exposure to environmental hazards which result from industrial, municipal, commercial, or other human activities.

environmental impact study n. (in Australia) a study undertaken in order to assess the effect on a specified environment of the introduction of any new factor which may upset the ecological balance.

environmental indicator n. a variable factor in the environment, which, when measured over time, can be used to indicate the state of a related aspect of the environment; for example, a dwindling frog population may indicate a problem in a particular ecosystem.

environmentalism /ɛnˌvaɪrənˈmɛntəlɪzəm/ n. the advocacy of the protection and conservation of the natural environment. –**environmentalist**, n.

environmental science n. the study of the environment with regard to its physical aspects, its ecology, and the social issues involved in managing and utilising it.

environment effects statement n. (in Australia) a statement of all matters that significantly affect a specified environment to determine whether to proceed with an environmental impact statement.

environs /ɛnˈvaɪrənz, ən-/ pl. n. immediate neighbourhood; surrounding parts or districts, as of a city; outskirts; suburbs.

envisage /ɛnˈvɪzədʒ, -zɪdʒ, ən-/ v.t. (-aged, -aging) **1.** to contemplate; visualise. **2.** to expect. –**envisagement**, n.

envoy /ˈɛnvɔɪ/ n. **1.** a diplomatic agent of the second rank, next in dignity after an ambassador, commonly called minister (title in full: **envoy extraordinary and minister plenipotentiary**). **2.** a diplomatic agent. **3.** any accredited messenger or representative.

envy /ˈɛnvi/ n. (pl. **-vies**) **1.** a feeling of discontent or mortification, usually with ill will, at seeing another's superiority, advantages, or success. **2.** desire for some advantage possessed by another. **3.** an object of envious feeling. –v.t. (**-vied, -vying**) **4.** to regard with envy; be envious of. –**envier**, n. –**envyingly**, adv.

enzyme /ˈɛnzaɪm/ n. any protein capable of catalysing a chemical reaction necessary to the cell. –**enzymic** /ɛnˈzaɪmɪk/, **enzymatic** /ˌɛnzaɪˈmætɪk/, adj.

eo- a word element meaning 'early', 'primeval', as in *Eocene.*

eon /ˈiɒn/ n. → **aeon**.

-eous variant of **-ous**, occurring in adjectives taken from Latin or derived from Latin nouns.

Eozoic /iouˈzouɪk, iə-/ n. the earliest span of geological time preceding the Archaeozoic and Proterozoic.

epaulet /ˈɛpəlɛt, -lɒt/ n. an ornamental shoulder piece worn on uniforms, chiefly by military and naval officers. Also, **epaulette**.

ephemeral /əˈfɛmərəl, i-/ adj. **1.** lasting only a day or a very short time; short-lived; transitory. –n. **2.** an ephemeral entity, as certain insects. –**ephemerally**, adv.

epi- a prefix meaning 'on', 'to', 'against', 'above', 'near', 'after', 'in addition to', sometimes used as an English formative, chiefly in scientific words, as *epiblast, epicalyx, epizoon.* Also, **ep-**, **eph-**.

epic /ˈɛpɪk/ adj. **1.** of or relating to poetry dealing with a series of heroic achievements or events, in a long narrative in elevated style: *Homer's 'Iliad' is an epic poem.* –n. **2.** an epic poem. **3.** a novel or film resembling an epic, especially one dealing with the adventures and achievements of a single individual. –phr. **4. epic fail**, Colloq. an instance of something that someone has done that has gone badly wrong. –**epically**, adv. –**epic-like**, adj.

epicene /ˈɛpisin, ˈɛpə-/ adj. belonging to, or partaking of the characteristics of, both sexes.

epicentre /ˈɛpisɛntə/ n. a point from which earthquake waves seem to go out, directly above the true centre of disturbance. Also, **epicentrum**; US, **epicenter**. –**epicentral** /ɛpiˈsɛntrəl/, adj.

epicure /ˈɛpəkjuə, ˈɛpi-, -kjuə/ n. **1.** someone who cultivates a refined taste, as in food, drink, art, music, etc. **2.** someone given up to sensuous enjoyment; a glutton or sybarite. –**epicurean**, adj., n.

epidemic /ɛpəˈdɛmɪk/ adj. Also, **epidemical**. **1.** affecting at the same time a large number of people in a locality, and spreading from person to person, as a disease not permanently prevalent there. –n. **2.** a temporary prevalence of a disease. –**epidemical**, adj. –**epidemically**, adv. –**epidemicity** /ɛpədəˈmɪsəti/, n.

epidermis /ɛpiˈdɜməs, ɛpə-, ˈɛpidɜməs/ n. Anat. the outer, non-vascular, non-sensitive layer of the skin, covering the true skin or corium (dermis). –**epidermal, epidermic**, adj.

epidural /ɛpiˈdjurəl/ adj. **1.** Anat. situated on or over the dura. –n. **2.** → **epidural anaesthetic**.

epidural anaesthetic n. **1.** an agent injected into the epidural space of the spinal cord to produce regional anaesthesia, especially in childbirth. **2.** the procedure for doing this. Also, **epidural anesthetic**.

epiglottis /ɛpiˈglɒtəs, ˈɛpiglɒtəs/ n. Anat. a thin, valve-like cartilaginous structure that covers the glottis during swallowing, preventing the entrance of food and drink into the larynx. –**epiglottal, epiglottic**, adj.

epigram /ˈɛpigræm, ˈɛpə-/ n. **1.** any witty, ingenious, or pointed saying tersely expressed. **2.** epigrammatic expression. **3.** a short poem dealing concisely with a single subject, usually ending with a witty or ingenious turn of thought, and often satirical.

epigraph /ˈɛpigraf, -graf, ˈɛpə-/ n. **1.** an inscription, especially on a building, statue, or the like. **2.** an apposite quotation at the beginning of a book, chapter, etc. –**epigraphic** /ɛpiˈgræfik, ɛpə-/, adj. –**epigraphy** /ɛˈpɪgrəfi, ə-/, n. –**epigraphist** /ɛˈpɪgrəfəst, ə-/, n.

epilepsy /ˈɛpəlɛpsi/ n. Pathol. a nervous disease usually characterised by convulsions and almost always by loss of consciousness. –**epileptic** /ɛpəˈlɛptɪk/, adj.

epilogue /ˈɛpilɒg, ˈɛpə-/ n. **1.** a speech, usually in verse, by one of the actors after the conclusion of a play. **2.** the person or persons speaking this. **3.** a concluding part added to a literary work. **4.** the final program, especially one with a religious content, of a day's broadcasting on radio or television. –**epilogist** /ɛˈpɪlədʒəst, ə-/, n.

epinephrine autoinjector /ɛpəˌnɛfrən ɔtoʊɪnˈdʒɛktə/ n. *Med.* a device used to administer a regulated dose of epinephrine (adrenaline) to a person suffering from anaphylactic shock.

epiphany /əˈpɪfəni/ n. (*pl.* **-nies**) **1.** an appearance, revelation, or manifestation of a divine being. **2.** a revelation of the basic nature of something; a perception of some essential truth.

epiphyte /ˈɛpɪfaɪt, ˈɛpə-/ n. *Bot.* a plant which grows upon another but does not get food, water, or minerals from it. –**epiphytic** /ɛpiˈfɪtɪk, ɛpə-/, **epiphytical** /ɛpiˈfɪtɪkəl, ɛpə-/, adj. –**epiphytically** /ɛpiˈfɪtɪkli, ɛpə-/, adv.

episcopal /əˈpɪskəpəl/ adj. **1.** of or relating to a bishop. **2.** *Chiefly US* of or relating to the Anglican Church, or a branch of it.

episode /ˈɛpəsoʊd/ n. **1.** an incident in the course of a series of events, in a person's life or experience, etc. **2.** an incidental narrative or digression in the course of a story, poem, or other writing. **3.** any of a number of loosely connected but generally related scenes or stories comprising a literary work. **4.** (in radio, television, etc.) any of the separate programs constituting a serial. –**episodic** /ɛpəˈsɒdɪk/, **episodical** /ɛpəˈsɒdɪkəl/, adj. –**episodically** /ɛpəˈsɒdɪkli/, adv.

epistemology /əpɪstəˈmɒlədʒi/ n. the branch of philosophy that deals with the origin, nature, methods, and limits of human knowledge. –**epistemological** /əpɪstəməˈlɒdʒɪkəl/, adj. –**epistemologically** /əpɪstəməˈlɒdʒɪkli/, adv. –**epistemologist**, n.

epistle /əˈpɪsəl/ n. **1.** a written communication; a letter, especially one of formal or didactic character. **2.** (*usu. upper case*) one of the apostolic letters found in the New Testament.

epitaph /ˈɛpɪtaf, ˈɛpə-/ n. **1.** a commemorative inscription on a tomb or mortuary monument. **2.** any brief writing resembling such an inscription. –**epitaphic** /ɛpiˈtæfɪk/, adj. –**epitaphist**, n.

epithet /ˈɛpəθɛt, ˈɛpi-, -θət/ n. **1.** an adjective or other term applied to a person or thing to express an attribute, as in Alexander *the Great.* **2.** a word or phrase expressing abuse or contempt: *she hurled choice epithets at his departing figure.* –**epithetic** /ɛpəˈθɛtɪk, ɛpi-/, **epithetical** /ɛpəˈθɛtɪkəl/, adj.

epitome /əˈpɪtəmi/ n. **1.** a summary or condensed account, especially of a literary work; an abstract. **2.** a condensed representation or typical characteristic of something: *the epitome of all mankind.* –**epitomise**, **epitomize**, v.

epoch /ˈipɒk, ˈɛpɒk/ n. **1.** a particular period of time as marked by distinctive character, events, etc. **2.** the beginning of any distinctive period in the history of anything. **3.** a point of time distinguished by a particular event, or state of affairs. **4.** *Geol.* the main division of a geological period, representing the time required for making a geological series. **5.** *Astron.* **a.** an arbitrarily fixed instant of time or date (usually the beginning of a century or half-century) used as a reference in giving the elements of a planetary orbit or the like. **b.** the mean longitude of a planet as seen from the sun at such an instant or date. –**epochal** /ˈɛpəkəl/, adj.

eponym /ˈɛpənɪm/ n. **1.** a name, especially a place name, which is taken, or is supposed to be taken, from a person, real or mythical. **2.** the person, real or mythical, from which a name is taken. –**eponymous** /əˈpɒnəməs/, adj. –**eponymic** /ɛpəˈnɪmɪk/, adj. –**eponymy** /əˈpɒnəmi/, n.

epoxy /ɪˈpɒksi, ə-/ adj. **1.** *Chem.* containing an oxygen atom that bridges two connected atoms, as in *epoxy*

ethene. –n. (*pl.* **epoxies**) Also, **epoxy resin**, **epoxide resin.** **2.** any of a class of substances derived by polymerisation from certain viscous liquid or brittle solid compounds, used chiefly in adhesives, coatings, electrical insulation, solder mix, in the casting of tools and dies, and in experimental sculpture.

EPROM /ˈiprɒm/ n. erasable programmable read-only memory; a computer memory chip whose contents can be erased using a process involving ultraviolet light, and reprogrammed for other purposes. Compare **EEPROM**.

Epsom salts /ɛpsəm ˈsɒlts/ pl. n. hydrated magnesium sulphate, formerly used as a cathartic, etc.

Epstein-Barr virus /ˌɛpstaɪn-ˈba vaɪrəs/ n. a virus that causes glandular fever, characterised by sudden fevers and a benign swelling of the lymph nodes.

equable /ˈɛkwəbəl/ adj. **1.** free from variations; uniform, as motion or temperature. **2.** uniform in operation or effect, as laws. **3.** tranquil, even, or not easily disturbed, as the mind. –**equability** /ɛkwəˈbɪləti/, **equableness**, n. –**equably**, adv.

equal /ˈikwəl/ adj. **1.** (sometimes fol. by *to* or *with*) as great as another: *the velocity of sound is not equal to that of light.* **2.** like or alike in quantity, degree, value, etc.; of the same rank, ability, merit, etc. **3.** evenly proportioned or balanced: *an equal mixture, an equal contest.* **4.** uniform in operation or effect: *equal laws.* **5.** level, as a plain. –n. **6.** a person or thing that is equal to another. –v.t. (**equalled** *or*, *US*, **equaled**, **equalling** *or*, *US*, **equaling**) **7.** to be or become equal to; match. **8.** to make or do something equal to. **9.** to recompense fully: *he will equal your losses.* –phr. **10. equal to, a.** adequate or sufficient in quantity or degree for: *the supply is equal to the demand.* **b.** having adequate powers, ability, or means for: *he was not equal to the task.* –**equality**, n. –**equally**, adv. –**equalise**, **equalize**, v.

equanimity /ɛkwəˈnɪməti, ikwə-/ n. evenness of mind or temper; calmness; composure.

equate /iˈkweɪt, ə-/ v.t. **1.** to state the equality of or between; put in the form of an equation. **2.** to reduce to an average; make such correction or allowance in as will reduce to a common standard of comparison. **3.** to regard, treat, or represent as equivalent.

equation /iˈkweɪʒən, ə-, -ʃən/ n. **1.** the act of making equal; equalisation. **2.** equally balanced state; equilibrium. **3.** *Maths* an expression of, or a proposition asserting, the equality of two quantities, using the sign = between them. –**equational**, adj.

equator /əˈkweɪtə, i-/ n. **1.** the great circle of a sphere or any heavenly body which has its plane perpendicular to the axis joining the poles of that sphere or body, and lies equidistant between them. **2.** the great circle of the earth, equidistant from the North and South Poles. **3.** a circle separating a surface into two congruent parts. –**equatorial** /ɛkwəˈtɔriəl/, adj.

equatorial climate n. a type of climate characterised by consistently high temperatures and rainfall throughout the year; roughly between latitudes 5°N and 5°S.

equerry /ˈɛkwəri/ n. (*pl.* **-ries**) **1.** (formerly) an officer of a royal or similar household, charged with the care of the horses. **2.** an officer who attends on the British sovereign or on a representative of the sovereign, such as an Australian state governor.

equestrian /əˈkwɛstriən, i-/ adj. **1.** of or relating to horseriding or riders. **2.** mounted on horseback. **3.** representing a person on horseback: *an equestrian statue.* –n. **4.** a rider or performer on horseback. –**equestrianism**, n. –**equestrienne**, *fem.* n.

equi- a word element meaning 'equal', as in *equidistant*, *equivalent.*

equidistant /ikwiˈdɪstənt, ikwə-, ɛ-/ adj. equally distant. –**equidistantly**, adv. –**equidistance**, n.

equilateral /ˌikwəˈlætərəl/ *adj.* **1.** having all the sides equal. *–n.* **2.** a figure having all its sides equal. **3.** a side equivalent, or equal to others. **–equilaterally,** *adv.*

equilibrium /ˌikwəˈlibriəm, ɛ-/ *n.* (*pl.* **-riums** *or* **-ria**) **1.** a state of rest due to the action of forces that counteract each other. **2.** equal balance between any powers, influences, etc.; equality of effect. **3.** mental or emotional balance.

equine /ˈɛkwaɪn, ˈi-/ *adj.* **1.** of, relating to, or belonging to the family *Equidae*, which comprises horses, zebras and asses. *–n.* **2.** a horse. **–equinity** /ɛˈkwɪnəti/, *n.*

equine growth hormone *n.* **1.** a growth hormone produced in the pituitary gland of horses. **2.** a synthetic form of this hormone used as a veterinary medicine for ageing horses and used illegally by humans as a performance-enhancing drug in sport. *Abbrev.*: eGH

equine influenza *n.* a viral respiratory disease which causes flu-like symptoms in horses; horse flu. *Abbrev.*: EI

equinox /ˈikwənɒks, ˈɛ-/ *n. Astron.* **1.** the time when the sun crosses the plane of the earth's equator, making night and day all over the earth of equal length, occurring about 21 March and 22 September. **2.** either of the equinoctial points.

equip /əˈkwɪp, i-/ *v.t.* (**equipped, equipping**) **1.** to furnish or provide with whatever is needed for services or for any undertaking; to fit out, as a ship, office, kitchen, etc. **2.** to dress out; array. **–equipper,** *n.*

equipment /əˈkwɪpmənt, i-/ *n.* **1.** anything used in or provided for equipping. **2.** the act of equipping. **3.** the state of being equipped. **4.** knowledge and skill necessary for a task, etc.: *he lacks equipment for the law.* **5.** a collection of necessary implements (such as tools).

equitable /ˈɛkwətəbəl/ *adj.* characterised by equity or fairness; just and right; fair; reasonable. **–equitableness,** *n.* **–equitably,** *adv.*

equity /ˈɛkwəti/ *n.* (*pl.* **-ties**) **1.** the quality of being fair; fairness; impartiality. **2.** anything which is fair and just. **3.** *Law* **a.** a body of law (orig. English), serving to correct and make up for the limitations and inflexibility of common law. **b.** an equitable right or claim. **4.** (*pl.*) a company's ordinary shares not bearing fixed interest. **5.** (*upper case*) the actors' trade union.

equivalent /əˈkwɪvələnt, i-/ *adj.* **1.** equal in value, measure, force, effect, significance, etc. **2.** corresponding in position, function, etc. *–n.* **3.** something that is equivalent. **–equivalently,** *adv.* **–equivalence** /əˈkwɪvələns, i-/, *n.*

equivocal /əˈkwɪvəkəl, i-/ *adj.* **1.** of uncertain significance; not determined: *an equivocal attitude.* **2.** of doubtful nature or character; questionable; dubious; suspicious. **3.** having different meanings equally possible, as a word or phrase; susceptible to double interpretation; ambiguous. **–equivocally,** *adv.* **–equivocalness,** *n.*

equivocate /əˈkwɪvəkeɪt, i-/ *v.i.* to use equivocal or ambiguous expressions, especially in order to mislead; prevaricate. **–equivocatingly,** *adv.* **–equivocator,** *n.* **–equivocatory,** *adj.*

-er¹ a suffix: **1.** forming nouns designating persons from the object of their occupation or labour, as in *hatter*, *tiler*, or from their place of origin or abode, as in *Icelander*, *villager*, or designating either persons or things from some special characteristic or circumstances, as in *two-seater*, *three-master*, *fiver*. **2.** serving as the regular English formative of agent nouns, as in *bearer*, *creeper*, *employer*, *harvester*, *teacher*, *theoriser*.

-er² a suffix of nouns denoting persons or things concerned or connected with something, as in *butler*, *grocer*, *officer*, *garner*.

-er³ a suffix forming the comparative degree of adjectives and adverbs, as in *harder*, *smaller*, *faster*.

-er⁴ a termination of certain nouns denoting action or process, as in *dinner*, *rejoinder*, *remainder*, *trover*.

era /ˈɪərə/ *n.* **1.** a period of time marked by a particular character, events, etc.: *an era of progress.* **2.** the period of time to which anything belongs. **3.** a period where years are counted from a given date: *the Christian era.* **4.** a date or event forming the beginning of any distinctive period. **5.** a major division of geological time: *the Palaeozoic era.*

eradicate /əˈrædəkeɪt, i-/ *v.t.* **1.** to remove or destroy utterly; extirpate. **2.** to pull up by the roots. **–eradication** /əˌrædəˈkeɪʃən, i-/, *n.* **–eradicator,** *n.* **–eradicable,** *adj.*

erase /əˈreɪz, i-/ *v.t.* (**erased, erasing**) **1.** to rub or scrape out, as letters or characters written, engraved, etc.; efface. **2.** to obliterate (material recorded on an electromagnetic tape) by demagnetising it. **3.** to destroy (digital data) as by overwriting it with new data. **–erasable,** *adj.* **–erasion,** *n.*

eraser /əˈreɪzə, i-/ *n.* an instrument, such as a piece of rubber or cloth, for erasing marks made with pen, pencil, chalk, etc.

ereader /ˈiridə/ *n.* a handheld electronic device for reading publications in electronic form. Also, **e-reader, ebook reader.**

erect /əˈrɛkt, i-/ *adj.* **1.** upright in position or posture: *an erect stance.* **2.** raised or directed upwards: *a dog with ears erect.* **3.** *Bot.* upright throughout; not spreading, etc.: *an erect stem; an erect leaf; an erect ovule. –adv.* **4.** in an erect position: *to stand erect. –v.t.* **5.** to build or set up; construct; raise: *to erect a house; to erect social barriers.* **6.** to raise and set in an upright position: *to erect a telegraph pole.* **7.** to set up or establish, as an institution; found. **–erectable,** *adj.* **–erecter,** *n.* **–erectness,** *n.* **–erectly,** *adv.*

erection /əˈrɛkʃən, i-/ *n.* **1.** the act of erecting. **2.** the state of being erected. **3.** something erected, as a building or other structure. **4.** *Physiol.* **a.** a distended and rigid state of an organ or part containing erectile tissue. **b.** an erect penis.

erg¹ /ɜg/ *n.* a unit of work or energy in the centimetre-gram-second system, equal to 0.1×10^{-6} joules. *Symbol*: erg

erg² /ɜg/ *n.* any vast area covered deeply with sand in the form of shifting dunes, as parts of the Sahara Desert.

ergo /ˈɜgoʊ/ *adv.* therefore; consequently.

ergonomics /ɜgəˈnɒmɪks, ɜgoʊ-/ *n.* the study of engineering aspects of the relationship between human workers and their working environment. **–ergonomist,** *n.*

ermine /ˈɜmən/ *n.* (*pl.* **-mines** *or, especially collectively,* **-mine**) **1.** the white colour phase of *Mustela erminea*, a small carnivore of the weasel family found in Europe, Asia and North America; the brown colour phase is called the stoat. Compare **stoat. 2.** the lustrous white winter fur of the ermine, having a black tail tip.

-ern an adjectival suffix occurring in *northern*, etc.

erode /əˈroʊd, i-/ *v.t.* **1.** to eat out or away; destroy by slow consumption. **2.** to form (a channel, etc.) by eating or wearing away (used especially in geology, to denote the action of all the forces of nature that wear away the earth's surface). **–erodent,** *adj.*

erogenous /əˈrɒdʒənəs, ɛ-, i-/ *adj.* arousing or tending to arouse sexual desire. Also, **erogenic** /ɛrəˈdʒɛnɪk/. **–erogeneity** /ˌɛrədʒəˈniəti/, *n.*

erosion /əˈroʊʒən, i-/ *n.* **1.** the act of eroding. **2.** the state of being eroded. **3.** *Geol.* the process by which the surface of the earth is worn away by the action of water, glaciers, winds, waves, etc.

erotic /əˈrɒtɪk, ɛ-, i-/ *adj.* **1.** of or relating to sexual love; amatory. **2.** arousing or satisfying sexual desire.

3. subject to or marked by strong sexual desires. —**erotically**, *adv.*

err /ɜ/ *v.i.* **1.** to go astray in thought or belief; be mistaken; be incorrect. **2.** to go astray morally; sin. **3.** to deviate from the true course, aim, or purpose.

errand /ˈɛrənd/ *n.* **1.** a trip to convey a message or execute a commission; a short journey for a specific purpose: *he was sent on an errand.* **2.** a specific business entrusted to a messenger; a commission. **3.** the purpose of any trip or journey: *his errand was to secure the release of the captives.*

errant /ˈɛrənt/ *adj.* **1.** journeying or travelling, as a medieval knight in quest of adventure; roving adventurously. **2.** deviating from the regular or proper course; erring. **3.** moving in an aimless or quickly changing manner. —**errantly**, *adv.*

erratic /əˈrætɪk, i-/ *adj.* **1.** deviating from the proper or usual course in conduct or opinion; eccentric. **2.** having no certain course; wandering; not fixed: *erratic winds.* **3.** *Geol.* (of boulders, etc.) transported from the original site to an unusual location, as by glacial action. —**erratically**, *adv.*

erratum /əˈrɑtəm, ɛ-/ *n.* (*pl.* **-ta** /-tə/) an error in writing or printing.

erroneous /əˈrouniəs/ *adj.* containing error; mistaken; incorrect. —**erroneously**, *adv.* —**erroneousness**, *n.*

error /ˈɛrə/ *n.* **1.** deviation from accuracy or correctness; a mistake, as in action, speech, etc. **2.** belief in something untrue; the holding of mistaken opinions. **3.** the condition of believing what is not true: *in error about the date.* **4.** a moral offence; wrongdoing. —**errorless**, *adj.*

ersatz /ˈɜsæts, ˈɜsats/ *adj.* serving as a substitute: *an ersatz meat dish made of eggplant and oatmeal.*

erstwhile /ˈɜstwaɪl/ *adj.* former: *erstwhile enemies.*

erudite /ˈɛrədaɪt/ *adj.* characterised by erudition; learned or scholarly: *an erudite professor; an erudite commentary.* —**eruditely**, *adv.* —**eruditeness**, *n.*

erudition /ɛrəˈdɪʃən/ *n.* acquired knowledge, especially in literature, languages, history, etc.; learning; scholarship.

erupt /əˈrʌpt, i-/ *v.i.* **1.** to burst forth, as volcanic matter. **2.** (of a volcano, geyser, etc.) to eject matter. **3.** (of teeth) to break through surrounding hard and soft tissues and become visible in the mouth. **4.** to break out suddenly or violently, as if from restraint. **5.** to break out with or as with a skin rash. —**eruption**, *n.* —**eruptible**, *adj.* —**eruptive**, *adj.*

-ery **1.** an adoption of a French word ending in *-erie*, as in *bravery, nunnery, cutlery.* **2.** a suffix of nouns denoting **a.** a place of employment, as in *bakery, brewery, fishery.* **b.** a class of goods, as in *confectionery, pottery.* **c.** things collectively, as in *machinery, crockery, scenery.* **d.** a state or condition, as in *slavery, foolery, witchery.* **e.** a place where certain animals are kept, as in *piggery, rookery.* **f.** (*humorous*) a place where an article or service may be obtained, as in *eatery, fish and chippery.*

erythro- a word element meaning 'red', as in *erythrocyte.* Also, **erythr-**.

erythrocyte /əˈrɪθrəsaɪt/ /əˈrɪθrou-/ *n.* one of the red corpuscles of the blood; red blood cell.

-es a variant of **-s**¹ and **-s**² after *s, z, ch, sh,* and in those nouns ending in *-f* which take *-v-* in the plural. Compare **-ies**.

escalate /ˈɛskəleɪt/ *v.t.* **1.** to enlarge; intensify, especially a war. —*v.i.* **2.** to grow in size or intensity; develop or increase by stages: *food prices are escalating.* —**escalation** /ɛskəˈleɪʃən/, *n.*

escalator /ˈɛskəleɪtə/ *n.* (*from trademark*) a continuously moving staircase for carrying passengers up or down.

escapade /ˈɛskəpeɪd, ɛskəˈpeɪd/ *n.* **1.** a reckless proceeding; a wild prank. **2.** an escape from confinement or restraint.

escape /əsˈkeɪp/ *v.i.* **1.** to get away from or avoid capture, restraint, danger, evil, etc.: *to escape from prison; they escaped with their lives.* **2.** (of fluid, etc.) to leak or flow out from a container. **3.** *Bot.* (of an introduced plant) to grow wild. —*v.t.* **4.** to succeed in getting free from or avoiding (prison, capture, danger, evil, etc.): *to escape the police; to escape death.* **5.** to not be noticed or remembered by (a person): *his name escapes me.* **6.** to slip from (someone) by accident: *a sigh escaped her.* —*n.* **7.** the act of escaping. **8.** a means of escaping: *a fire escape.* **9.** avoidance of reality. **10.** leakage, especially of water, gas, etc. **11.** *Computers* a key, combination of keys, or a sequence of keys, used to interrupt a command, exit a program, or change levels within a program. —**escapable**, *adj.* —**escapeless**, *adj.*

escapee /ɛskəˈpi/ *n.* someone who has escaped, as from internment, imprisonment, etc. Also, **escaper**.

escapism /əsˈkeɪpɪzəm/ *n.* the avoidance of reality by absorption of the mind in entertainment, or in an imaginative situation, activity, etc. —**escapist**, *adj., n.*

escarpment /əsˈkɑpmənt/ *n.* **1.** a long, cliff-like ridge of rock, or the like, commonly formed by faulting or fracturing of the earth's crust. **2.** ground cut into an escarp around a fortification or defensive position.

-esce a suffix of verbs meaning to begin to be or do something, become, grow, or be somewhat (as indicated by the rest of the word), as in *convalesce, deliquesce.*

-escence a suffix of nouns denoting action or process, change, state, or condition, etc., and corresponding to verbs ending in *-esce* or adjectives ending in *-escent*, as in *convalescence, deliquescence, luminescence, recrudescence.*

-escent a suffix of adjectives meaning beginning to be or do something, becoming or being somewhat (as indicated), as in *convalescent, deliquescent, recrudescent*, often associated with verbs ending in *-esce* or nouns ending in *-escence.*

Escher figure /ˈɛʃə figə/ *n.* a graphic design which alters spatial reality by introducing multiple planes, in a symmetrical pattern, thus producing unusual optical effects.

eschew /əˈʃu/ /ɛˈʃu/ /əsˈtʃu/ /ɛs-/ *v.t.* to abstain from; shun; avoid: *to eschew evil.* —**eschewal**, *n.* —**eschewer**, *n.*

escort *n.* /ˈɛskɔt/ **1.** a body of persons, or a single person, ship or ships, etc., accompanying another or others for protection, guidance, or courtesy. **2.** an armed guard. **3.** protection, safeguard, or guidance on a journey. **4.** a person accompanying another to a dance, party, etc.; partner. —*v.t.* /əsˈkɔt, ɛs-/ **5.** to attend or accompany as an escort.

escutcheon /əsˈkʌtʃən/ *n.* **1.** the shield or shield-shaped surface, on which armorial bearings are depicted. —*phr.* **2. a blot on someone's escutcheon**, a stain on someone's honour or reputation. —**escutcheoned**, *adj.*

-ese a noun and adjective suffix indicating **1.** locality, nationality, language, etc., as in *Japanese, Vietnamese.* **2.** a particular jargon, as in *computerese, journalese, bureaucratese.*

e-signature *n.* → **digital signature**.

esky /ˈɛski/ *n.* (*pl.* **-kies**) *Aust.* (*from trademark*) a portable icebox. Also, **Esky**.

esoteric /ɛsəˈtɛrɪk, isə-/ *adj.* **1.** understood by or meant for a select few; profound; recondite. **2.** belonging to the select few. **3.** private; secret; confidential. **4.** (of philosophical doctrine, etc.) intended to be communicated only to the initiated. —**esoterically**, *adv.* —**esotericism, esotery** /ˈɛsətəri/, *n.*

ESP /i ɛs 'pi/ *n.* extrasensory perception; perception or communication outside of normal sensory activity, as in telepathy and clairvoyance.

espalier /əsˈpælja, əsˈpæliei/ *n.* **1.** a trellis or framework on which fruit trees, vines, or shrubs are trained to grow flat. **2.** a plant trained on such a trellis or framework, or on a fence or wall. –*v.t.* **3.** to train on an espalier. **4.** to furnish with an espalier.

especial /əsˈpɛʃəl/ *adj.* **1.** special; exceptional; outstanding: *of no especial importance, an especial friend.* **2.** of a particular kind, or peculiar to a particular one: *your especial case.*

especially /əsˈpɛʃəli/ *adv.* **1.** particularly; unusually: *be especially watchful.* **2.** principally: *crops diminished due to the drought, especially in Queensland.*

Esperanto /ɛspəˈræntoʊ/ *n.* a constructed language invented in 1887 by LL Zamenhof and intended for international use. It is based on the commonest words in the most important European languages.

espionage /ˈɛspiənaʒ, -nadʒ/ *n.* **1.** the practice of spying on others. **2.** the systematic use of spies by a government to discover the military and political secrets of other nations.

esplanade /ˈɛsplənad, -neɪd/ *n.* any open level space serving for public walks or drives, especially one by a body of water, as a river, lake or ocean.

espouse /əsˈpaʊz, ɛs-/ *v.t.* (**-poused, -pousing**) **1.** to make one's own, adopt, or embrace, as a cause. **2.** to take in marriage; marry. –**espousal,** *n.* –**espouser,** *n.*

espresso /ɛsˈprɛsoʊ/ *n.* coffee made by forcing steam under pressure or boiling water through ground coffee beans. Also, **expresso.**

espy /əsˈpaɪ, ɛs-/ *v.t.* (**-pied, -pying**) to see at a distance; catch sight of; detect. –**espier,** *n.*

-esque an adjective suffix indicating style, manner, or distinctive character, as in *arabesque, picturesque, statuesque.*

-ess a suffix forming distinctively feminine nouns, such as *countess, hostess, lioness.*

essay *n.* **1.** /ˈɛseɪ/ a short literary composition on a particular subject. **2.** /ˈɛseɪ, ɛˈseɪ/ an effort to perform or accomplish something; an attempt. **3.** /ˈɛseɪ, ɛˈseɪ/ a tentative effort. –*v.t.* /ɛˈseɪ/ **4.** to try; attempt. **5.** to put to the test; make trial of. –**essayer,** *n.* –**essayistic,** *adj.*

essence /ˈɛsəns/ *n.* **1.** intrinsic nature; important elements or features of a thing. **2.** a substance obtained from a plant, drug, or the like, by distillation or other process, and containing its characteristic properties in concentrated form. **3.** an alcoholic solution of an essential oil. **4.** a perfume. **5.** something that is, especially a spiritual or immaterial entity. –*phr.* **6. of the essence,** necessary for what needs to be done.

essential /əˈsɛnʃəl/ *adj.* **1.** absolutely necessary; indispensable: *discipline is essential in an army.* **2.** constituting or relating to the essence of a thing. **3.** being the essence of a plant, etc. **4.** being such by its very nature, or in the highest sense: *essential happiness; essential poetry.* –*n.* **5.** an indispensable element; a chief point: *concentrate on essentials rather than details.* –**essentially,** *adv.* –**essentialness,** *n.* –**essentiality,** *n.*

essentialise /əˈsɛnʃəlaɪz/ *v.t.* (**-lised, -lising**) to reduce to the essential features or qualities, especially when this results in a simplistic or stereotyped view: *to essentialise an ethnic identity.* Also, **essentialize.** –**essentialisation,** *n.*

-est a suffix forming the superlative degree of adjectives and adverbs, as in *warmest, fastest, soonest.*

establish /əsˈtæblɪʃ/ *v.t.* **1.** to set up on a firm or permanent basis; institute; found: *to establish a business; to establish a university.* **2.** to settle or install (someone) in a position, business, etc. **3.** to settle (oneself) as if permanently. **4.** to cause to be accepted: *to establish a*

custom; to establish a precedent. **5.** to show (a fact, claim, etc.) to be valid; prove. **6.** to appoint or ordain (a law, etc.). **7.** to bring about: *to establish peace.* **8.** to make (a church) a state institution. –**establisher,** *n.* –**established,** *adj.*

establishment /əsˈtæblɪʃmənt, ɛs-/ *n.* **1.** the act of establishing. **2.** something established, especially an organisation or institution. **3.** office or home and everything connected with it (as furniture, grounds, employees, etc.). –*phr.* **4. the Establishment,** those people collectively, whose opinions are said to have influence in society and government.

estate /əˈsteɪt, ɛs-/ *n.* **1.** a piece of landed property, especially one of large extent: *to have an estate in the country.* **2.** *Law* **a.** an interest in land, traditionally classified either as freehold or of fixable duration, as by lease. **b.** property viewed as an aggregate, as in *partnership estate, trust estate, estate of a deceased person.* **3.** a housing development. **4.** an industrial development area; a trading estate. **5.** period or condition of life: *to attain to man's estate.* **6.** a political or social group or class, as in France, the clergy, nobles, and commons, or in England, the lords spiritual, lords temporal, and commons (the three **estates of the realm**). **7.** condition or circumstances with reference to worldly prosperity, estimation, etc.; social status or rank. **8.** high rank or dignity. –*adj.* **9.** denoting the wine from one particular estate or vineyard.

estate agent *n.* → **real estate agent.**

esteem /əsˈtim/ *v.t.* **1.** to regard as valuable; regard highly or favourably: *I esteem him highly.* **2.** to consider as of a certain value; regard: *I esteem it worthless.* **3.** to set a value on; value: *to esteem lightly.* –*n.* **4.** favourable opinion or judgement; respect or regard: *to hold a person or thing in high esteem.*

ester /ˈɛstə/ *n. Chem.* a compound formed by the reaction between an acid and an alcohol with the elimination of a molecule of water.

estimable /ˈɛstəməbəl/ *adj.* **1.** worthy of esteem; deserving respect. **2.** capable of being estimated. –**estimableness,** *n.* –**estimably,** *adv.*

estimate *v.t.* /ˈɛstəmeɪt/ **1.** to approximately calculate (the value, size, weight, etc.). **2.** to form an opinion of; judge. –*n.* /ˈɛstəmət/ **3.** an approximate calculation of the value, amount, possible cost, etc., of something. **4.** a judgement or opinion. –**estimation,** *n.* –**estimative,** *adj.* –**estimator,** *n.*

estrange /əˈstreɪndʒ/ *v.t.* (**estranged, estranging**) **1.** to turn away in feeling or affection; alienate the affections of. **2.** to remove to or keep (usu. oneself) at a distance. –**estrangement,** *n.*

estuary /ˈɛstʃʊri, ˈɛstʃuəri/, *Orig. US* /ˈɛstʃuɛri/ *n.* (*pl.* **-ries**) **1.** the part of the mouth or lower course of a river in which its current meets the sea's tides, and is subject to their effects. **2.** an arm or inlet of the sea. –**estuarial** /ɛstʃuˈɛəriəl/, **estuarine,** *adj.*

-et a noun suffix having properly a diminutive force (now lost in many words), as in *islet, bullet, facet, midget, owlet, plummet.*

e-tag *n.* **1.** an electronic device attached to a vehicle which transmits information to an electronic reader, causing a toll to be debited from the customer's account. **2.** an external electronic tag used for the identification of animals, as dogs or livestock. Also, **etag, electronic tag.**

e-tailer /ˈi-teɪlə/ *n.* a retailer conducting business over the internet. –**e-tailing,** *n.*

et cetera /ət ˈsɛtrə, ɛt, -ərə/ and others; and so on. *Abbrev.:* etc.

etch /ɛtʃ/ *v.t.* **1.** to engrave (metals, etc.) with an acid or the like, especially to form a design in furrows which when charged with ink will give an impression on paper. **2.** to portray or outline clearly (a character, features, etc.). **3.** to fix (in the memory); to root firmly (in the mind). **4.** to cut, as a geographical feature, by erosion, etc. –*v.i.* **5.** to practise the art of etching. –**etcher,** *n.*

etching /ˈɛtʃɪŋ/ *n.* **1.** a process of making designs or pictures on a metal plate, glass, etc., by the corrosion of an acid. **2.** an impression, as on paper, taken from an etched plate. **3.** the design produced. **4.** the plate on which such a design is etched.

E10 /ˈi ˈtɛn/ *n.* a fuel consisting of ethanol and unleaded petrol, being 10 per cent ethanol and 90 per cent petrol; petranol.

eternal /əˈtɜnəl, i-/ *adj.* **1.** lasting throughout eternity; without beginning or end: *eternal life.* **2.** perpetual; ceaseless **3.** enduring; immutable: *eternal principles.* **4.** *Metaphysics* existing outside of all relations of time; not subject to change. –*n.* **5.** that which is eternal. –**eternally,** *adv.* –**eternalness,** *n.*

eternity /əˈtɜnəti, i-/ *n.* (*pl.* **-ties**) **1.** infinite time; duration without beginning or end. **2.** eternal existence, especially as contrasted with mortal life. **3.** an endless or seemingly endless period of time.

e-text *n.* an electronic text. Also, **etext**.

-eth[1] an ending of the third person singular present indicative of verbs, now occurring only in archaic forms or used in solemn or poetic language, as in *doeth* or *doth, hath, hopeth, sitteth.*

-eth[2] the form of *-th,* the ordinal suffix, after a vowel, as in *twentieth, thirtieth,* etc. See **-th**[2].

ethanol /ˈɛθənɒl, ˈiθ-/ *n.* an alcohol produced from crops and used as a biofuel.

ether /ˈiθə/ *n.* **1.** *Chem.* **a.** a highly volatile and flammable colourless liquid, diethyl ether, $(C_2H_5)_2O$, obtained by the action of sulphuric acid on alcohol, and used as a solvent and anaesthetic; sulphuric ether. **b.** one of a class of organic compounds in which any two organic groups are attached directly to oxygen, having the general formula R_2O, as ethyl ether $(C_2H_5)_2O$. **2.** Also, **aether.** the upper regions of space; the clear sky; the heavens. **3.** Also, **aether.** the medium supposed by the ancients to fill the upper regions. **4.** Also, **aether.** an all-pervading medium postulated for the transmission of light, heat, etc., by the older elastic solid theory. **5.** (*usu. pl.*) certain undefined properties of wine which result in fine flavour and bouquet. –**etheric** /ˈiˈθɛrɪk/, *adj.*

ethereal /əˈθɪəriəl, i-/ *adj.* **1.** light, airy, or tenuous. **2.** extremely delicate or refined: *ethereal beauty.* **3.** heavenly or celestial. **4.** of the ether or upper regions of space. **5.** *Chem.* of or relating to ethyl ether. –**ethereality** /əθiəriˈæləti, i-/, **etherealness,** *n.* –**ethereally,** *adv.*

ethernet /ˈiθənɛt/ *n.* (*from trademark*) a protocol for a local area network covering both software and hardware, which standardises the size of the coaxial cable, the speed of information flow within the system, the type of information to be transmitted through the system, and the number of devices attached to the network. Also, **Ethernet**.

ethical /ˈɛθɪkəl/ *adj.* **1.** relating to or dealing with morals or the principles of morality; relating to right and wrong in conduct. **2.** in accordance with the rules or standards for right conduct or practice, especially the standards of a profession: *it is not considered ethical for doctors to advertise.* –**ethically,** *adv.* –**ethicalness,** *n.*

ethics /ˈɛθɪks/ *pl. n.* **1.** a system of moral principles, by which human actions and proposals may be judged good or bad, or right or wrong. **2.** the rules of conduct recognised in respect of a particular class of human actions: *medical ethics.* **3.** moral principles, as of an individual.

ethnic /ˈɛθnɪk/ *adj.* **1.** relating to a human population or particular group and their history, customs, language, etc. **2.** of or relating to members of the Australian community who are migrants or children of migrants and whose first language is not English. **3.** coming from a particular culture: *ethnic music.* –*n.* **4.** *Colloq.* (*derog.*) (*racist*) a member of an ethnic group whose first language is not English. –**ethnically,** *adv.* –**ethnicity** /ɛθˈnɪsəti/, *n.*

ethnic cleansing *n.* the forcible removal of all ethnic groups in an ethnically mixed population that are not of a particular origin.

ethno- a word element meaning 'race', 'nation', as in *ethnology.*

ethnocentrism /ɛθnoʊˈsɛntrɪzəm/ *n.* the belief in the inherent superiority of one's own group and culture. Also, **ethnicism.** –**ethnocentric,** *adj.* –**ethnocentricity,** *n.*

ethnography /ɛθˈnɒɡrəfi/ *n.* **1.** the scientific description and classification of the various human descriptive and racial groups. **2.** ethnology, especially as descriptive. –**ethnographer,** *n.* –**ethnographic** /ɛθnəˈɡræfɪk/, **ethnographical** /ɛθnəˈɡræfɪkəl/, *adj.* –**ethnographically** /ɛθnəˈɡræfɪkli/, *adv.*

ethnology /ɛθˈnɒlədʒi/ *n.* the systematic study dealing with the distinctive subdivisions of humankind, their origin, relations, speech, institutions, etc. –**ethnological** /ɛθnəˈlɒdʒɪkəl/, **ethnologic** /ɛθnəˈlɒdʒɪk/, *adj.* –**ethnologically** /ɛθnəˈlɒdʒɪkli/, *adv.* –**ethnologist,** *n.*

ethos /ˈiθɒs/ *n.* **1.** character or disposition. **2.** *Sociology* the fundamental spiritual characteristics of a culture.

ethyl alcohol /ɛθəl ˈælkəhɒl/ *n.* See **alcohol**.

etiquette /ˈɛtɪkət/ *n.* **1.** conventional requirements as to social behaviour; proprieties of conduct as established in any class or community or for any occasion. **2.** a prescribed or accepted code of usage in matters of ceremony, as at a court or in official or other formal observances. **3.** conventional and accepted standards and practices in certain professions, as medicine.

-ette a noun suffix, the feminine form of *-et,* occurring especially: **1.** with the original diminutive force, as in *cigarette.* **2.** in trademarks of imitations or substitutes, as in *leatherette.* **3.** as a distinctively feminine ending, as in *coquette, brunette,* etc.

etymology /ɛtəˈmɒlədʒi/ *n.* (*pl.* **-gies**) **1.** the study of historical linguistic change, especially as applied to individual words. **2.** the derivation of a word. –**etymological** /ɛtəməˈlɒdʒɪkəl/, **etymologic** /ɛtəməˈlɒdʒɪk/, *adj.* –**etymologically** /ɛtəməˈlɒdʒɪkli/, *adv.* –**etymologist,** *n.*

eucalypt /ˈjukəlɪpt/ *n.* any tree of the genus *Eucalyptus.*

eucalyptus /jukəˈlɪptəs/ *n.* (*pl.* **-tuses** *or* **-ti** /taɪ/ *or* **-tus**) **1.** any member of the myrtaceous genus *Eucalyptus,* including many tall trees, native to the Australian region and cultivated elsewhere, many yielding valuable timber and some an oil, used in medicine as a germicide and expectorant. –*adj.* **2.** of or relating to a preparation, confection, etc., containing eucalyptus oil.

Eucharist /ˈjukərəst/ *n.* **1.** the sacrament of the Lord's Supper; the communion; the sacrifice of the mass. **2.** the consecrated elements of the Lord's Supper, especially the bread. –**Eucharistic** /jukəˈrɪstɪk/, **Eucharistical** /jukəˈrɪstɪkəl/, *adj.* –**Eucharistically** /jukəˈrɪstɪkli/, *adv.*

euchre /ˈjukə/ –*n.* **1.** *Cards* a game played usually by two, three, or four persons, with the 32 (or 28 or 24) highest cards in the pack. –*v.t.* (**-chred, -chring**) **2.** *Colloq.* to outwit; get the better of, as by scheming.

Euclidean distance /juˌklɪdiən ˈdɪstəns/ *n.* distance as measured in Euclidean space, that is, as one would with a tape measure or ruler.

Euclidean geometry *n.* a system of plane (two-dimensional) and solid (three-dimensional) geometry developed by Greek geometrician Euclid, fl. c. 300 BC, in which all theorems are developed logically from a finite number of axioms.

Euclidean space *n.* space that is described within the rules of Euclidean geometry.

eugenic /juˈdʒɪnɪk, -ˈdʒɛn-/ *adj.* **1.** of or bringing about improvement in the type of offspring produced. **2.** having good inherited characteristics. Also, **eugenical**. **–eugenically**, *adv.*

eukaryote /juˈkærioʊt/ *n.* a microscopic organism, the smallest living thing, which, unlike bacteria, has DNA in its clearly-defined nucleus, and which contains complex organelles which also contain DNA and replicate independently, being the descendants of symbiotic bacteria living within the host. Compare **prokaryote**. Also, **eucaryote**.

eulogy /ˈjulədʒi/ *n.* (*pl.* **-gies**) **1.** a speech or writing in praise of a person or thing, especially an oration in honour of a deceased person. **2.** high praise or commendation.

eunuch /ˈjunək/ *n.* a castrated man, especially (formerly) one employed as a harem attendant, servant or political advisor by the Ottoman sultans or in certain other Asian courts.

euphemism /ˈjufəmɪzəm/ *n.* **1.** the substitution of a mild, indirect, or vague expression for a harsh or blunt one. **2.** the expression so substituted: *'to pass away' is a euphemism for 'to die'.* **–euphemist**, *n.* **–euphemistic** /jufəˈmɪstɪk/, **euphemistical** /jufəˈmɪstɪkəl/, *adj.* **–euphemistically** /jufəˈmɪstɪkli/, *adv.*

euphonium /juˈfoʊniəm/ *n.* a tenor tuba mainly used in brass bands.

euphony /ˈjufəni/ *n.* **1.** agreeableness of sound; pleasing effect to the ear, especially of speech sounds as uttered or as combined in utterance. **2.** *Phonetics* a tendency to change speech sounds for ease and economy of utterance, a former explanation of phonetic change.

euphoria /juˈfɔriə/ *n.* a feeling or state of wellbeing, especially one of unnatural elation. **–euphoric** /juˈfɒrɪk/, *adj.* **–euphorically** /juˈfɒrɪkli/, *adv.*

eureka /juˈrikə/ *interj.* an exclamation of triumph at a discovery or supposed discovery.

Eureka flag *n.* a flag bearing a white cross, with a star at the end of each arm, on a blue field; first raised at the Eureka Stockade in 1854 and more recently associated with the move to make Australia a republic.

eurhythmics /juˈrɪðmɪks/ *n.* the art of interpreting in bodily movements the rhythm of musical compositions, with the aim of developing the sense of rhythm and symmetry; invented by Emile Jaques-Dalcroze. Also, **eurythmics**.

euro[1] /ˈjuroʊ/ *n.* (*pl.* **euros**) → **wallaroo** (def. 2).

euro[2] /ˈjuroʊ/ *n.* (*pl.* **euros** *or* **euro**) the principal monetary unit of the European Union, divided into 100 cents; created in 1999 and introduced as legal tender in most of the member nations in 2002. *Symbol:* €

eurodollar /ˈjuroʊdɒlə/ *n.* a US dollar as part of funds held outside the United States of America.

European wasp /jurəpiən ˈwɒsp/ *n.* a wasp, *Vespula germanica*, which is a native of Europe, North Africa, and parts of western Asia, but which is now also established in the US, Australia, and New Zealand.

eury- a word element meaning 'broad', as in *eurypterid*.

Eustachian tube /juˈsteɪʃən tjub/ *n. Anat.* a canal extending from the middle ear to the pharynx; auditory canal.

eustasy /ˈjustəsi/ *n.* a worldwide change in sea level due to an increase or decrease in the volume of water in the seas, as caused by the melting of ice sheets. **–eustatic** /juˈstætɪk/, *adj.*

euthanase /ˈjuθəneɪz/ *v.t.* (**-nased**, **-nasing**) to subject to euthanasia. Also, **euthanise**.

euthanasia /juθəˈneɪʒə/ *n.* the deliberate bringing about of the death of a person suffering from an incurable disease or condition, as by administering a lethal drug or by withdrawing existing life-supporting treatments. See **passive euthanasia**, **voluntary euthanasia**. Also, **active euthanasia**.

evacuate /əˈvækjueɪt/ *v.t.* **1.** to leave empty; vacate. **2.** to move (persons or things) from a threatened place, disaster area, etc., to a place of greater safety. **3.** *Physiol.* to discharge or eject as through the excretory passages, especially from the bowels. **4.** *Physical Chem.* to pump out, creating a vacuum; exhaust: *the apparatus was evacuated before being filled with oxygen.* *–v.i.* **5.** to leave a town because of air-raid threats, etc.: *they evacuated when the air raids began.* **–evacuation**, *n.* **–evacuator**, *n.*

evacuee /əvækjuˈi/ *n.* someone who is withdrawn or removed from a place of danger.

evade /əˈveɪd, i-/ *v.t.* **1.** to get round or escape from by trickery or cleverness: *to evade the law; to evade pursuit.* **2.** to avoid doing: *to evade a duty; to evade an obligation.* **3.** to keep from answering directly: *to evade a question.* **–evadable**, **evadible**, *adj.* **–evader**, *n.* **–evadingly**, *adv.*

evaluate /əˈvæljueɪt, i-/ *v.t.* to ascertain the value or amount of; appraise carefully. **–evaluation** /əvæljuˈeɪʃən, i-/, *n.* **–evaluative**, *adj.*

evangelical /ivænˈdʒɛlɪkəl/ *adj.* **1.** relating to the gospel and its teachings. **2.** relating to Christians who emphasise the teachings and authority of the Bible, especially in its literal reading and often in contrast to the authority of the church or of the intellect. **3.** relating to Christian movements since the 18th century which stress the importance of personal experience of guilt for sin and the need to be reconciled to God through Christ's atonement. **–evangelicalism**, *n.* **–evangelically**, *adv.*

evangelist /əˈvændʒələst, i-/ *n.* **1.** a preacher of the Christian gospel. **2.** (*upper case*) any of the writers (Matthew, Mark, Luke, and John) of the four Gospels. **3.** one of a class of teachers in the early Christian church, next in rank after apostles and prophets. **4.** someone who speaks enthusiastically about a specified product, brand, etc., and wins over others to its use: *an Apple evangelist.* **–evangelistic**, *adj.* **–evangelism**, *n.*

evaporate /əˈvæpəreɪt, i-/ *v.i.* **1.** to turn to vapour; pass off in vapour. **2.** to give off moisture. **3.** to disappear; vanish; fade: *as soon as his situation became clear to him, his hopes quickly evaporated.* *–v.t.* **4.** to convert into a gaseous state or vapour; drive off or extract in the form of vapour. **–evaporation**, *n.* **–evaporator**, *n.*

evasion /əˈveɪʒən, i-/ *n.* **1.** the act of escaping something by trickery or cleverness: *evasion of one's duty; evasion of responsibilities.* **2.** the avoiding of an argument, accusation, question, or the like, as by a subterfuge. **3.** a means of evading; a subterfuge; an excuse or trick to avoid or get round something. **4.** tax evasion. **–evasive**, *adj.*

eve /iv/ *n.* **1.** the evening, or often the day, before a Christian church festival, and hence before any date or event. **2.** the period just preceding any event, etc.: *the eve of a revolution.*

even[1] /ˈivən/ *adj.* **1.** level; flat; without irregularities; smooth: *an even surface; even country.* **2.** on the same level; in the same plane or line; parallel: *even with the ground.* **3.** free from variations or fluctuations; regular: *even motion.* **4.** uniform in action, character, or quality: *an even colour; to hold an even course.* **5.** equal in measure or quantity: *even quantities of two substances.* **6.** same: *letters of even date.* **7.** divisible by 2, thus, 2, 4, 6, 8, 10, and 12 are *even* numbers (opposed to *odd*, as 1, 3, etc.). **8.** denoted by such a number: *the even pages of a book*. **9.** exactly expressible in integers, or in tens, hundreds, etc., without fractional parts: *an even kilometre*; *an even hundred*. **10.** exactly balanced on each side; equally divided. **11.** leaving no balance of debt on either side, as accounts; square, as one person with another. **12.** calm; placid; not easily excited or angered: *an even temper*. **13.** equitable, impartial, or fair: *an even bargain*; *an even chance*. –*adv.* **14.** evenly. **15.** still; yet (used to emphasise a comparative): *even more suitable*. **16.** used to suggest that something mentioned as a possibility constitutes an extreme case, or one that might not be expected: *the slightest noise, even, disturbs him*; *even if he goes, he may not take part*. **17.** just: *even now*. **18.** *Archaic* fully or quite: *even to death*. **19.** indeed (used as an intensifier for stressing identity or truth of something): *he is willing, even eager, to do it*. –*v.t.* **20.** to make even; level; smooth. **21.** to place in an even state as to claim or obligation; balance: *to even, or even up, accounts*. –*phr.* **22. break even**, to have one's credits or profits equal one's debits or losses. **23. even out** (or **off**), **a.** to make even. **b.** to become even. **24. get even**, to get one's revenge; square accounts. –**evener**, *n.* –**evenness**, *n.* –**evenly**, *adv.*

evening /ˈivnɪŋ/ *n.* **1.** the later part of the day and the early part of the night. **2.** any ending or weakening period: *the evening of life*. **3.** *Qld* (especially in rural areas) the period of the day after midday. –*adj.* **4.** relating to evening.

event /əˈvɛnt, i-/ *n.* **1.** anything that happens or is regarded as happening; an occurrence, especially one of some importance. **2.** the fact of happening: *to wait for the event of a disaster*. **3.** a specified meteorological occurrence of some significance: *a rain event*; *a wind event*. **4.** *Philos.* something which occurs in a certain place during a particular interval of time. **5.** *Sport* each of the items in a program of one sport or a number of sports. –*v.i.* **6.** *Horseriding* to participate in eventing. –*phr.* **7. after the event**, after the outcome of a situation: *to give advice after the event*. **8. at all events** or **in any event**, whatever happens; in any case. **9. in the event of**, in the circumstances of: *in the event of her death*. –**eventless**, *adj.*

eventful /əˈvɛntfəl, i-/ *adj.* **1.** full of events or incidents, especially of a striking character: *an eventful period*. **2.** having important issues or results; momentous. –**eventfully**, *adv.* –**eventfulness**, *n.*

eventing /əˈvɛntɪŋ/ *n.* an equestrian competition in which riders and horses compete in dressage, cross-country and showjumping. –**eventer**, *n.*

eventual /əˈvɛntʃuəl, -tʃəl/ *adj.* **1.** relating to the event or issue; consequent; ultimate. **2.** depending upon uncertain events; contingent.

eventuality /əvɛntʃuˈæləti/ *n.* (*pl.* **-ties**) **1.** a contingent event; a possible occurrence or circumstance. **2.** the state or fact of being eventual; contingent character.

eventually /əˈvɛntʃuəli, -tʃəli/ *adv.* finally; ultimately.

eventuate /əˈvɛntʃueɪt/ *v.i.* **1.** to have issue; result. **2.** to come about. –**eventuation** /əvɛntʃuˈeɪʃən/, *n.*

ever /ˈɛvə/ *adv.* **1.** at all times: *he is ever ready to excuse himself*. **2.** continuously: *ever since then*. **3.** at any time: *did you ever see anything like it?* **4.** (with emphatic force, in various idiomatic constructions and phrases) in any possible case; by any chance; at all: *how ever did you manage to do it?* –*phr.* **5. do I ever!**, *Colloq.* an exclamation used to express a positive answer to a question. **6. ever and again** or **ever and anon**, every now and then, continually. **7. ever so**, **a.** to whatever extent or degree: *be she ever so bold*. **b.** *Colloq.* an intensifier: *he's ever so handsome*.

evergreen /ˈɛvəgrin/ *adj.* **1.** (of trees, shrubs, etc.) having living leaves throughout the entire year, the leaves of the past season not being shed until after the new foliage has been completely formed. **2.** (of leaves) belonging to such a plant. **3. a.** retaining youthful characteristics in maturity: *an evergreen tennis player*. **b.** retaining popularity from an earlier period: *an evergreen play*. –*n.* **4.** an evergreen plant. –*v.t.* **5.** *Chiefly US* to retain the patent rights on (a medicinal drug) beyond their normal term by registering new patents with slight alterations such as different colours, preparations, etc.

everlasting /ˈɛvəlastɪŋ/ *adj.* **1.** always; forever: *everlasting God*. **2.** lasting or continuing for a long time. **3.** constantly happening; incessant: *I seem to have everlasting worries*. –*n.* Also, **everlasting flower**. **4.** any of various plants or flowers which keep their shape, colour, etc., when dried. –*phr.* **5. the everlasting**, eternal duration; eternity. –**everlastingly**, *adv.* –**everlastingness**, *n.*

evermore /ɛvəˈmɔ/ *adv.* (oft. preceded by *for*) from now on for always; forever; eternally.

every /ˈɛvri/ *adj.* **1.** each (referring one by one to all the members of an aggregate): *we go there every day, be sure to remember every word he says*. **2.** all possible; the greatest possible degree of: *every prospect of success*. –*phr.* **3. every bit**, *Colloq.* in every respect; in all points: *every bit as good*. **4. every man and his dog**, a lot of people; the general public. **5. every now and then** or **every now and again** or **every once in a while**, occasionally; from time to time. **6. every other**, every second; every alternate. **7. every which way**, in all directions: *the wind seems to be blowing every which way*.

everybody /ˈɛvribɒdi/ *pron.* **1.** every person. –*phr.* **2. everybody who is anybody**, *Colloq.* everyone important.

everyday /ˈɛvrideɪ/ *adj.* **1.** happening every day; daily: *an everyday occurrence*. **2.** of or for ordinary days, as contrasted with Sundays or special occasions: *everyday clothes*. **3.** such as is met with every day; ordinary; commonplace: *an everyday scene*.

everyone /ˈɛvriwʌn/ *pron.* every person; everybody.

everything /ˈɛvriθɪŋ/ *pron.* **1.** every thing or particular of an aggregate or total; all. **2.** something extremely important: *this news means everything to us*. –*phr.* **3. have everything going for one**, to have every possible advantage. **4. into everything**, involved in a wide number of activities.

everywhere /ˈɛvriwɛə/ *adv.* in every place or part; in all places.

evict /əˈvɪkt, i-/ *v.t.* **1.** to expel (a person, especially a tenant) from land, a building, etc., by legal process. **2.** to recover (property, etc.) by virtue of superior legal title. –**eviction**, *n.* –**evictor**, *n.*

evidence /ˈɛvədəns/ *n.* **1.** ground for belief; that which tends to prove or disprove something; proof. **2.** something that makes evident; an indication or sign. **3.** *Law* the data, in the form of testimony of witnesses, or of documents or other objects (such as a photograph, a revolver, etc.) identified by witnesses, offered to the court or jury in proof of the facts at issue. –*v.t.* (**-denced, -dencing**) **4.** to make evident or clear; show clearly; manifest. **5.** to support by evidence. –*phr.* **6. in evidence**, in a situation to be readily seen; plainly visible; conspicuous. **7. turn queen's** (or **king's**) (or **state's**) **evidence**, *Law* (of an accomplice in a crime) to become a witness for the prosecution against the others involved. –**evidential, evidentiary**, *adj.*

evident /ˈɛvədənt/ *adj.* plain or clear to the sight or understanding: *an evident mistake*.

evidently /ˈɛvədəntli/ *adv.* obviously; apparently.

evil /ˈiːvəl/ *adj.* **1.** violating or inconsistent with the moral law; wicked: *evil deeds, an evil life.* **2.** harmful; injurious: *evil laws.* **3.** characterised or accompanied by misfortune or suffering; unfortunate; disastrous: *to be fallen on evil days.* **4.** due to (actual or imputed) bad character or conduct: *an evil reputation.* **5.** characterised by anger, irascibility, etc. —*n.* **6.** that which is evil; evil quality, intention, or conduct: *to choose the lesser of two evils.* **7.** (*sometimes upper case*) the force which governs and brings about wickedness and sin. **8.** that part of someone or something that is wicked. **9.** harm; mischief; misfortune: *to wish one evil.* **10.** anything causing injury or harm. —**evilly**, *adv.* —**evilness**, *n.*

evince /əˈvɪns, i-/ *v.t.* (**evinced, evincing**) **1.** to show clearly; make evident or manifest; prove. **2.** to reveal the possession of (a quality, trait, etc.). —**evincible**, *adj.*

eviscerate /əˈvɪsəreɪt, i-/ *v.t.* to deprive of vital or essential parts. —**evisceration** /əvɪsəˈreɪʃən, i-/, *n.*

evocative /əˈvɒkətɪv/ *adj.* tending to evoke. —**evocatively**, *adv.*

evoke /əˈvoʊk, i-/ *v.t.* **1.** to call up, or produce (memories, feelings, etc.): *to evoke a memory, a smile, etc.* **2.** to provoke, or elicit. **3.** to call up; cause to appear; summon: *to evoke a spirit from the dead.*

evolution /ɛvəˈluːʃən, ivə-/ *n.* **1.** any process of formation or growth; development: *the evolution of drama; the evolution of the aeroplane.* **2.** *Biol.* the continuous genetic adaptation of organisms or species to the environment by the integrating agencies of selection, hybridisation, inbreeding, and mutation. **3.** something evolved; a product. **4.** a motion incomplete in itself, but combining with coordinated motions to produce a single action, as in a machine. **5.** an evolving or giving off of gas, heat, etc. —**evolutionary**, *adj.* —**evolutionist**, *n.*

evolve /əˈvɒlv, i-/ *v.t.* **1.** to develop gradually: *to evolve a scheme; to evolve a plan; to evolve a theory.* **2.** *Biol.* to develop, as by a process of differentiation, to a more highly organised condition. **3.** to give off or emit, as smells, vapours, etc. —*v.i.* **4.** to come forth gradually into being; develop; undergo evolution. —**evolvable**, *adj.* —**evolvement**, *n.* —**evolver**, *n.*

e-waste *n.* computers and other such electronic devices as computers, television sets, DVD and video players, mobile phones, cameras, game consoles, microwaves, power tools, etc., dumped as garbage.

ewe /juː/ *n.* a female sheep.

ewer /ˈjuːə/ *n.* **1.** a pitcher with a wide spout, especially one to hold water for ablutions. **2.** a decorative vessel having a spout and handle, especially a tall, slender vessel with a base.

ex[1] /ɛks/–*prep.* **1.** *Finance* without, not including, or without the right to have: *ex dividend, ex interest, ex rights.* **2.** *Commerce* out of; free out of: *ex warehouse, ex ship,* etc. (free of charges until the time of removal out of the warehouse, ship, etc.). —*n. Colloq.* **3.** one's former husband or wife. **4.** one's former boyfriend or girlfriend.

ex[2] /ɛks/ *n.* the letter X, x.

ex-[1] a prefix meaning 'out of', 'from', and hence 'utterly', 'thoroughly', and sometimes serving to impart a privative or negative force or to indicate a former title, status, etc.; freely used as an English formative, as in *expatriate, exterritorial,* and especially in such combinations as *ex-president* (former president), *ex-member, ex-wife;* occurring before vowels and *c, p, q, s, t.* See **e-**[1], **ef-, ec-**.

ex-[2] variant of **exo-**.

ex-[3] a prefix identical in meaning with **ex-**[1], occurring before vowels in words of Greek origin, as in *exarch, exegesis.* Also, **ec-**.

exacerbate /əɡˈzæsəbeɪt/ *v.t.* to increase the bitterness or violence of (disease, ill feeling, etc.); aggravate. **2.** to embitter the feelings of (a person); irritate; exasperate.

exact /əɡˈzækt, ɛɡ-/ *adj.* **1.** strictly correct or accurate: *an exact likeness.* **2.** completely right; precise: *the exact date.* **3.** (of laws, discipline, etc.) strict: *he expects exact manners.* —*v.t.* **4.** to call for or demand, sometimes by force: *to exact obedience; to exact money.* —**exactable**, *adj.* —**exacter, exactor**, *n.* —**exactness**, *n.*

exacting /əɡˈzæktɪŋ, ɛɡ-/ *adj.* **1.** severe or rigid in demands or requirements, as a person. **2.** requiring close application, as a task. **3.** given to or characterised by exaction; extortionate. —**exactingly**, *adv.* —**exactingness**, *n.*

exactitude /əɡˈzæktɪtjuːd, -tʃuːd, ɛɡ-/ *n.* the quality of being exact; exactness; preciseness; accuracy.

exactly /əɡˈzæktli, ɛɡ-/ *adv.* **1.** in an exact manner; precisely, according to rule, measure, fact, etc., accurately. **2.** just: *she does exactly as she likes.* —*interj.* **3.** quite so; that's right.

exaggerate /əɡˈzædʒəreɪt, ɛɡ-/ *v.t.* **1.** to magnify beyond the limits of truth; overstate; represent disproportionately: *to exaggerate one's importance; to exaggerate the difficulties of a situation; to exaggerate the size of one's house.* **2.** to increase or enlarge abnormally. —*v.i.* **3.** to use exaggeration, as in speech or writing: *she's always exaggerating.* —**exaggeration**, *n.* —**exaggerative**, *adj.* —**exaggeratingly**, *adv.* —**exaggerator**, *n.*

exalt /əɡˈzɔlt, ɛɡ-/ *v.t.* **1.** to elevate in rank, honour, power, character, quality, etc.: *exalted to the position of president.* **2.** to praise; extol: *to exalt someone to the skies.* **3.** to stimulate, as the imagination. **4.** to intensify, as a colour. —**exaltation**, *n.* —**exalter**, *n.*

exalted /əɡˈzɔltəd, ɛɡ-/ *adj.* **1.** elevated, as in rank or character; of high station: *an exalted personage.* **2.** noble or elevated; lofty: *an exalted style.* **3.** rapturously excited. —**exaltedly**, *adv.* —**exaltedness**, *n.*

exam /əɡˈzæm, ɛɡ-/ *n.* an examination (defs 2 and 3).

examination /əɡzæməˈneɪʃən, ɛɡ-/ *n.* **1.** the act of examining; inspection; inquiry; investigation. **2.** the act or process of testing students, etc., as by questions. **3.** the test itself; list of questions asked. **4.** the statements, etc., made by one examined. **5.** *Law* formal questioning. —**examinational**, *adj.*

examine /əɡˈzæmən, ɛɡ-/ *v.t.* **1.** to inspect or scrutinise carefully; inquire into or investigate. **2.** to test the knowledge, reactions, or qualifications of (a pupil, candidate, etc.), as by questions or assigned tasks. **3.** to subject to legal inquisition; put to question in regard to conduct or to knowledge of facts; interrogate: *to examine a witness or a suspect.* —**examinable**, *adj.* —**examiner**, *n.*

example /əɡˈzæmpəl, -ˈzampəl, ɛɡ-/ *n.* **1.** one of several things, or a part of something, taken to show the character of the whole. **2.** something to be followed; a pattern or model: *to set a good example.* **3.** a model used to show one of a type; specimen. **4.** something used to explain a rule or method, as a mathematical problem to be solved. **5.** a case, especially of punishment, used as a warning.

exasperate /əɡˈzæspəreɪt, ɛɡ-/ *v.t.* to irritate to a high degree; annoy extremely; infuriate. —**exasperation**, *n.* —**exasperatedly**, *adv.* —**exasperatingly**, *adv.* —**exasperator**, *n.*

excavate /ˈɛkskəveɪt/ *v.t.* **1.** to make hollow by removing the inner part; make a hole or cavity in; form into a hollow, as by digging. **2.** to make (a hole, tunnel, etc.) by removing material. **3.** to expose or lay bare by digging; unearth: *to excavate an ancient city.* —**excavation**, *n.* —**excavator**, *n.*

exceed /əkˈsiːd, ɛk-/ *v.t.* **1.** to go beyond the bounds or limits of: *to exceed one's powers.* **2.** to go beyond in

quantity, degree, rate, etc.: *to exceed the speed limit.*
3. to surpass; be superior to; excel. *–v.i.* **4.** to be greater,
as in quantity or degree. **5.** to surpass others, excel,
or be superior. **–exceeder**, *n.* **–exceedence, exceed-
ance**, *n.*

excel /əkˈsɛl, ɛkˈ/ *verb* (**-celled, -celling**) *–v.t.* **1.** to surpass; be superior to; outdo. *–v.i.* **2.** to surpass others or
be superior in some respect.

excellence /ˈɛksələns/ *n.* **1.** the fact or state of excelling;
superiority; eminence. **2.** an excellent quality or feature.
3. (*usu. upper case*) → **excellency** (def. 1).

excellency /ˈɛksələnsi/ *n.* (*pl.* **-cies**) **1.** (*usu. upper case*)
a title of honour given to certain high officials, as
governors and ambassadors. **2.** (*usu. upper case*) a
person so entitled. **3.** excellence.

excellent /ˈɛksələnt/ *adj.* possessing excellence or
superior merit; remarkably good. **–excellently**, *adv.*

except¹ /əkˈsɛpt, ɛkˈ/ *prep.* **1.** with the exclusion of;
excluding; save; but: *they were all there except me.*
–conj. **2.** Also, **except that.** with the exception that:
parallel cases except A is younger than B. **3.** otherwise
than; but: *well fortified except here.*

except² /əkˈsɛpt, ɛkˈ/ *v.t.* **1.** to exclude; leave out: *present
company excepted.* *–v.i.* **2.** to object: *to except against a
statement, a witness, etc.*

exception /əkˈsɛpʃən, ɛkˈ/ *n.* **1.** the act of excepting.
2. the fact of being excepted. **3.** something excepted; an
instance or case not conforming to the general rule.
4. an adverse criticism, especially on a particular point;
opposition of opinion; objection; demurral: *a statement
liable to exception.* *–phr.* **5. exception that proves the
rule,** an apparent exception which can in fact be
accommodated within a rule. **6. take exception,** to take
offence. **7. take exception to,** to make objection to;
demur with respect to.

exceptional /əkˈsɛpʃənəl, ɛkˈ/ *adj.* **1.** forming an
exception or unusual instance; unusual; extraordinary.
2. extraordinarily good, as of a performance or product.
3. extraordinarily skilled, talented, or clever. **–exceptionally**, *adv.* **–exceptionalness**, *n.*

excerpt *n.* /ˈɛksɜpt/ **1.** a passage taken out of a book
or the like; an extract. *–v.t.* /ɛkˈsɜpt/ **2.** to take out
(a passage) from a book or the like; extract. **–excerp-
tion**, *n.*

excess *n.* /əkˈsɛs, ˈɛkˈ/ **1.** the fact of exceeding (going
beyond) something else in amount or degree. **2.** the
amount or degree by which one thing exceeds another.
3. an extreme amount or degree: *to have an excess of
energy; he drank to excess.* **4.** a going beyond ordinary
or proper limits, especially in eating and drinking. *–adj.*
/ˈɛksɛs/ **5.** more than is necessary, or usual; extra:
excess baggage. **–excessive**, *adj.*

exchange /əksˈtʃeɪndʒ, ɛkˈ/ *verb* (**-changed, -changing**)
–v.t. **1.** give up (something) in return for something
else, usually of equal value, quantity, etc.: *to exchange
dollars for pounds.* **2.** to replace by another or something else: *to exchange a faulty tool.* **3.** (of two or more
people) to each give and receive; interchange: *to exchange blows; to exchange gifts.* *–v.i.* **4.** to make an
exchange: *we'll exchange with you.* **5.** to pass or be
taken as an equivalent. *–n.* **6.** the act or process of exchanging: *an exchange of gifts.* **7.** something given or
received in exchange for something else: *the car was a
fair exchange.* **8.** a central office or station where incoming calls, letters, etc., are sorted, and redirected: *a
telephone exchange.* **9.** a method or system by which
debits and credits in different places are settled without
the actual sending of money, by means of documents
representing money values. **10.** the equal interchange of
equivalent sums of money, as in the currencies of two
countries. **11.** *Econ.* the varying rate or sum, in one
country's money, given for a fixed sum in another; rate

of exchange. **–exchangeable**, *adj.* **–exchangeability**, *n.*
–exchanger, *n.*

exchange rate *n.* in international money markets,
the rate at which one currency can be exchanged for
another.

exchequer /əksˈtʃɛkə, ɛksˈ/ *n.* **1.** a treasury, as of a state
or nation. **2.** *Colloq.* funds; finances.

excise¹ *n.* /ˈɛksaɪz, ˈɛksaɪs/ **1.** an inland tax or duty on
certain commodities, such as spirits, tobacco, etc.,
levied on their manufacture, sale, or consumption
within the country. **2.** a tax levied for a licence to carry
on certain types of employment, pursue certain sports,
etc. **3.** *Brit.* that branch of government which collects
excise duties. *–v.t.* /ɛkˈsaɪz/ (**-cised, -cising**) **4.** to impose an excise on. **–excisable**, *adj.*

excise² /ɛkˈsaɪz/ *v.t.* (**-cised, -cising**) **1.** to expunge, as a
passage or sentence. **2.** to cut out or off, as a tumour.
–excision /ɛkˈsɪʒən/, *n.* **–excisable**, *adj.*

excite /əkˈsaɪt, ɛkˈ/ *v.t.* **1.** to arouse or stir up the feelings
of: *Christmas excites children.* **2.** to cause; awaken: *to
excite interest; to excite curiosity.* **3.** to stir to action; stir
up: *to excite a dog.* **4.** *Physiol.* to stimulate: *to excite a
nerve.* **–excitable**, *adj.* **–exciting**, *adj.* **–excited**, *adj.*
–excitement, *n.*

exclaim /əksˈkleɪm, ɛksˈ/ *v.i.* **1.** to cry out or speak suddenly and vehemently, as in surprise, strong emotion,
protest, etc. *–v.t.* **2.** to cry out; say loudly or vehemently. **–exclaimer**, *n.*

exclamation /ɛkskləˈmeɪʃən/ *n.* **1.** the act of exclaiming.
2. an outcry in response to feelings of protest, disgust,
indignation, joy, or surprise. **3.** an interjection.

exclamation mark *n.* **1.** a punctuation mark (!) used
after an exclamation. **2.** *Brit.* a road sign bearing a
symbol resembling this mark, placed to give advance
warning of some hazard. Also, **exclamation point.**

exclosure /ɛksˈkloʊʒə/ *n.* an area fenced to prevent
animals getting into it, as to prevent feral animals from
attacking farm animals, or domestic animals from
stripping vegetation.

exclude /əksˈklud, ɛksˈ/ *v.t.* **1.** to shut or keep out; prevent the entrance of. **2.** to shut out from consideration,
privilege, etc. **3.** to expel and keep out; thrust out; eject.
–excluder, *n.* **–exclusion**, *n.*

exclusive /əksˈklusɪv, ɛksˈ/ *adj.* **1.** not including or admitting of something else; incompatible: *the idea of
masculine is exclusive of the idea of feminine.* **2.** excluding from consideration or account, as from 100 to
121 exclusive (excluding 100 and 121, but including
from 101 to 120). **3.** limited to a given object or objects:
he pays exclusive attention to business. **4.** shutting out
all others from a part or share: *exclusive interview.*
5. single or sole: *a horse was his exclusive means of
transport.* **6.** (of a club, group, etc.) having limited
membership; elitist. **7.** fashionable: *an exclusive club.*
8. *Colloq.* (of a couple) committed to going out with
each other to the exclusion of all others. **–exclusively**,
adv. **–exclusiveness**, *n.* **–exclusivity**, *n.*

excommunicate /ɛkskəˈmjunəkeɪt/ *v.t.* to cut off from
communion or membership, especially from the
sacraments and fellowship of the church by ecclesiastical sentence. **–excommunicable**, *adj.* **–excommunication**, *n.* **–excommunicator**, *n.*

excrement /ˈɛkskrəmənt/ *n.* waste matter discharged
from the body, especially the faeces. **–excrementitious**,
adj. **–excremental** /ɛkskrəˈmɛntl/, *adj.* **–excrementally**
/ɛkskrəˈmɛntli/, *adv.*

excrescence /ɛksˈkrɛsəns/ *n.* **1.** abnormal growth or
increase. **2.** an abnormal outgrowth, usually harmless,
on an animal or vegetable body. **3.** a normal outgrowth
such as hair. **4.** any disfiguring addition.

excreta /əksˈkritə, ɛksˈ/ *pl. n.* excreted matter, as sweat,
urine, etc. **–excretal**, *adj.*

excrete /əks'krit, ɛks-/ *v.t.* to separate and eliminate from an organic body; separate and expel from the blood or tissues, as waste or harmful matters. –**excretive**, **excretory**, *adj.*

exculpate /'ɛkskʌlpeɪt, ɛks'kʌlpeɪt/ *v.t.* to clear from a charge of guilt or fault; free from blame; vindicate. –**exculpatory**, *adj.* –**exculpable** /əks'kʌlpəbəl, ɛk-/, *adj.* –**exculpation** /ɛkskʌl'peɪʃən/, *n.*

excursion /ək'skɜʃən, ɛk-, -ʒən/ *n.* **1.** a short journey or trip to some point for a special purpose: *a pleasure excursion, a scientific excursion.* **2.** a trip in a coach, train, etc., at a reduced rate: *weekend excursions to mountain resorts.* **3.** the persons who make such a journey. **4.** deviation or digression. –**excursionist**, *n.*

excuse *v.t.* /ək'skjuz, ɛk-/ (**-cused, -cusing**) **1.** to pardon or forgive; overlook (a fault, etc.): *we'll excuse your behaviour.* **2.** to try to remove the blame of; apologise for. **3.** to serve as a reason for (a fault, etc.); justify: *his youth does not excuse his behaviour.* **4. a.** to free from duty, punishment, etc.: *he excused her from the washing up.* **b.** to allow to leave: *she excused him from the room.* –*n.* /ək'skjus/ **5.** something which is offered as, or serves as, a reason for being excused. **6.** the act of excusing. **7.** a pretended reason; pretext. **8.** a bad example of a particular thing: *she was wearing a poor excuse for a hat.* –**excusable**, *adj.* –**excusableness**, *n.* –**excusably**, *adv.* –**excusal**, *n.* –**excuseless**, *adj.* –**excuser**, *n.* –**excusive**, *adj.*

execrable /'ɛksəkrəbəl/ *adj.* **1.** deserving to be execrated; detestable; abominable. **2.** very bad: *an execrable pun.* –**execrably**, *adv.*

execrate /'ɛksəkreɪt/ *v.t.* **1.** to detest utterly; abhor; abominate. **2.** to curse; imprecate evil upon. –**execration**, *n.*

executable /ɛksə'kjutəbəl/ *adj.* **1.** that can be executed or carried out. **2.** *Computers* of or relating to a version of an application that can be directly read by a computer: *executable code.* –*n.* **3.** *Computers* (*pl.*) the executable version of a program.

executable code *n. Computers* a machine language which can be interpreted and acted upon by a specific piece of hardware. Compare **machine language**, **source code**.

executable file *n. Computers* a version of an application (def. 7) that can be directly read by the computer.

execute /'ɛksəkjut/ *v.t.* **1.** to carry out; accomplish: *to execute a plan*; *to execute an order.* **2.** to perform or do: *to execute a manoeuvre*; *to execute a gymnastic feat.* **3.** to inflict capital punishment on; put to death according to law. **4.** to produce in accordance with a plan or design: *to execute a statue*; *to execute a still life.* –**executer**, *n.* –**execution**, *n.*

executive /əg'zɛkjətɪv, ɛg-/ *adj.* **1.** suited for execution or carrying into effect; of the kind requisite for practical performance or direction: *executive ability.* **2.** charged with or relating to execution of laws, or administration of affairs. **3.** designed for or used by executives: *an executive aircraft.* –*n.* **4.** a person or body having administrative authority as in a company. **5.** *Govt* the body of people, members of the governing party or parties, drawn from both houses of parliament, who devise policy and control the appropriate government departments and instrumentalities, and who are responsible to parliament for such administration. Compare **legislature**, **judiciary**. –**executively**, *adv.*

executor /əg'zɛkjətə, ɛg-/ *n.* **1.** someone who executes, or carries out, performs, fulfils, etc. **2.** *Law* a person named by a testator in his or her will to carry out its provisions. –**executrix**, *fem. n.* –**executorial** /əgzɛkjə-'tɔriəl, ɛg-/, *adj.* –**executorship**, *n.*

exe file /'ɛksi faɪl/ *n. Computers Colloq.* an executable file.

exegesis /ɛksə'dʒisəs/ *n.* (*pl.* **-geses** /-'dʒisiz/) critical explanation or interpretation, especially of Scripture. –**exegete**, *n.* –**exegetic, exegetical**, *adj.*

exemplary /əg'zɛmpləri, ɛg-/ *adj.* **1.** worthy of imitation; commendable: *exemplary conduct.* **2.** such as may serve as a warning: *an exemplary penalty.* **3.** serving as a model or pattern. **4.** serving as an illustration or specimen; illustrative; typical. **5.** of, relating to, or consisting of exempla. –**exemplarily**, *adv.* –**exemplariness**, *n.*

exemplify /əg'zɛmpləfaɪ, ɛg-/ *v.t.* (**-fied, -fying**) **1.** to show or illustrate by example. **2.** to furnish, or serve as, an example of. –**exemplification**, *n.* –**exemplifier**, *n.*

exempt /əg'zɛmpt, ɛg-/ *v.t.* **1.** to free from an obligation or liability to which others are subject; release: *to exempt someone from military service*; *to exempt a student from an examination.* –*adj.* **2.** released from, or not subject to, an obligation, liability, etc.: *exempt from taxes.* –*n.* **3.** someone who is exempt from, or not subject to, an obligation, duty, etc. –**exemption**, *n.* –**exemptible**, *adj.*

exequies /'ɛksəkwiz/ *pl. n.* (*sing.* **-quy** /-kwi/) funeral rites or ceremonies. –**exequial**, *adj.*

exercise /'ɛksəsaɪz/ *n.* **1.** bodily or mental activity, especially for training or improvement. **2.** something done or performed as practice or training in a particular skill: *French grammar exercises*; *piano exercises.* **3.** a putting into use or operation: *the exercise of care*; *the exercise of willpower.* **4.** a literary, musical or artistic work done for practice or to show a particular technical point. –*verb* (**-cised, -cising**) –*v.t.* **5.** to put through exercises, or forms of practice in order to train, develop, etc.: *to exercise soldiers*; *to exercise a horse*; *to exercise the voice.* **6.** to put into action, practice, or use: *to exercise care*; *to exercise patience*; *to exercise judgement.* **7.** to have as an effect: *to exercise influence on someone.* **8.** to worry; make uneasy: *his poor health exercised his mind.* –*v.i.* **9.** to do exercises; take bodily exercise. –**exercisable**, *adj.* –**exerciser**, *n.*

exert /əg'zɜt, ɛg-/ *v.t.* **1.** to put forth, as power; exercise, as ability or influence; put into vigorous action. –*phr.* **2. exert oneself**, to put forth one's powers; use one's efforts; strive. –**exertive**, *adj.*

exertion /əg'zɜʃən, ɛg-/ *n.* **1.** vigorous action or effort. **2.** an effort. **3.** exercise, as of power or faculties. **4.** an instance of this.

exeunt /'ɛksiʊnt/ a stage direction indicating that the actors named go out or off stage.

exfoliate /ɛks'fouliert/ *v.t.* **1.** to throw off in scales. **2.** to remove dirt, dead skin, etc., from the surface of (human skin). –**exfoliation**, *n.* –**exfoliative**, *adj.*

ex gratia /ɛks 'ɡraʃə, ɛks 'ɡreɪʃə/ *adj.* (of something granted) as a favour and not because of a legal obligation.

exhale /ɛks'heɪl/ *v.i.* to emit breath or vapour. –**exhalation**, *n.*

exhaust /əg'zɔst, ɛg-/ *v.t.* **1.** to wear out, or tire greatly (a person): *I have exhausted myself working.* **2.** to empty by drawing out the contents; drain off completely. **3.** to make a vacuum in. **4.** to use up completely: *I have exhausted my patience.* **5.** to treat or study thoroughly (a subject, etc.). –*n.* **6.** *Machinery* **a.** the escape of gases from the cylinder of an engine after ignition and expansion. **b.** the steam or gases given off. **c.** the parts of an engine through which the exhaust is ejected. –**exhauster**, *n.* –**exhaustible**, *adj.* –**exhaustibility** /əg,zɔstə'bɪləti, ɛg-/, *n.* –**exhaustion**, *n.*

exhaustive /əg'zɔstɪv, ɛg-/ *adj.* **1.** exhausting a subject, topic, etc.; comprehensive; thorough. **2.** tending to exhaust or drain, as of resources or strength. –**exhaustively**, *adv.* –**exhaustiveness**, *n.*

exhibit 286 **expatriate**

exhibit /əgˈzɪbət, ɛg-/ v.t. **1.** to offer or expose to view; present for inspection. **2.** to manifest or display: *to exhibit anger.* **3.** to place on show: *to exhibit paintings.* **4.** *Law* to submit (a document, etc.) in evidence in a court of law. –n. **5.** something that is exhibited. –**exhibitor, exhibiter,** n. –**exhibitory,** adj.

exhibition /ɛksəˈbɪʃən/ n. **1.** an exhibiting, showing, or presenting to view. **2.** a public display of feats of skill, athletic prowess, etc., as a boxing bout in which no decision is reached. **3.** a public show or display. –phr. **4. make an exhibition of oneself,** to behave foolishly or so as to excite ridicule.

exhibitionism /ɛksəˈbɪʃənɪzəm/ n. a tendency to display one's abilities or to behave in such a way as to attract attention. –**exhibitionist,** n.

exhilarate /əgˈzɪləreɪt, ɛg-/ v.t. **1.** to make cheerful or merry. **2.** to enliven; stimulate; invigorate. –**exhilaration,** n. –**exhilarating,** adj. –**exhilarant,** n. –**exhilaratingly,** adv.

exhort /əgˈzɔt, ɛg-/ v.t. **1.** to urge, advise, or caution earnestly; admonish urgently. –v.i. **2.** to make exhortation; give admonition. –**exhortation,** n.

exhume /ɛksˈhjum/ v.t. to dig (something buried, especially a corpse) out of the earth; disinter. –**exhumation** /ɛkshjuˈmeɪʃən/, n. –**exhumer,** n.

exigent /ˈɛksədʒənt/ adj. **1.** requiring immediate action or aid; urgent; pressing. **2.** requiring a great deal, or more than is reasonable. –**exigency, exigence,** n. –**exigently,** adv.

exiguous /əgˈzɪgjuəs, ɛg-/ adj. scanty; small; slender. –**exiguity** /ɛksəˈgjuəti/, **exiguousness,** n. –**exiguously,** adv.

exile /ˈɛgzaɪl, ˈɛksaɪl/ n. **1.** prolonged separation from one's country or home, as by stress of circumstances. **2.** someone separated from his or her country or home. **3.** expulsion from one's native land by authoritative decree. **4.** the fact or state of such expulsion. –v.t. **5.** to separate from country, home, etc.

exist /əgˈzɪst, ɛg-, ɪg-/ v.i. **1.** to have actual being; be. **2.** to have life or animation; live.

existence /əgˈzɪstəns, ɛg-, ɪg-/ n. **1.** the state or fact of existing; being. **2.** continuance in being or life; life: *a struggle for existence.* **3.** mode of existing. **4.** all that exists. **5.** something that exists, an entity, or a being. –**existent,** adj., n.

existentialism /ɛgzɪsˈtɛnʃəlɪzəm/ n. any of a group of doctrines, some theistic, some atheistic, which stress the importance of existence, as such, and of the freedom and responsibility of the finite human individual. –**existential,** adj. –**existentialist,** adj., n.

exit /ˈɛgzət, ˈɛksət/ n. **1.** a way or passage out. **2.** a going out or away; departure: *to make an exit.* **3.** the departure of a player from the stage as part of the action of a play. –verb (**exited, exiting**) –v.i. **4.** to depart; go away. **5.** a stage direction meaning that the actor named goes out or off stage. –v.t. **6.** to depart from: *she exited the stage to great applause.* **7.** *Computers* to get out of (a particular operating system, file, drive, etc.).

exit counselling n. **1.** counselling provided to someone leaving an institution, a course of counselling, a rehabilitation program, etc., with the aim of helping them adjust to the next phase of their life or to the next phase of the program, etc. **2.** counselling provided to someone leaving a situation in which they are perceived to have been indoctrinated, such as a religious cult, with the aim of persuading them that the indoctrinated beliefs are erroneous. –**exit counsellor,** n.

exit poll n. a poll taken of people as they are leaving a polling booth after voting in an election.

exit strategy n. a plan for the termination of a project, especially in a military or business context, which

meets the objective of maintaining political or financial security.

exo- a prefix meaning 'external'. Also, **ex-²**.

exocrine /ˈɛksoʊkraɪn, -rɪn/ adj. **1.** (of a gland, organ, etc.) having external secretion. **2.** relating to the secretion of such a gland.

exodus /ˈɛksədəs/ n. a going out; departure or emigration, usually of a large number of people.

exonerate /əgˈzɒnəreɪt, ɛg-/ v.t. **1.** to clear, as of a charge; free from blame; exculpate. **2.** to relieve, as from an obligation, duty, or task. –**exoneration** /əgzɒnəˈreɪʃən, ɛg-/, n.

exorbitant /əgˈzɔbətənt, ɛg-/ adj. exceeding the bounds of custom, propriety, or reason, especially in amount or extent: *to charge an exorbitant price for something.* –**exorbitance,** n. –**exorbitantly,** adv.

exorcise /ˈɛksɔsaɪz/ v.t. (**-cised, -cising**) **1.** to seek to expel (an evil spirit) by adjuration or religious or solemn ceremonies. **2.** to deliver (a person, place, etc.) from evil spirits or malignant influences. Also, **exorcize.** –**exorcism,** n. –**exorcist,** n.

exoskeleton /ˌɛksoʊˈskɛlətn/ n. an external protective covering or integument, especially when hard, as the shell of crustaceans, the scales and plates of fishes, etc. (opposed to *endoskeleton*). –**exoskeletal,** adj.

exosphere /ˈɛksoʊsfɪə/ n. the outermost region of the atmosphere where collisions between molecular particles are so rare that only the force of gravity will return escaping molecules to the upper atmosphere, extending from an altitude of 500 to 750 km above the earth.

exoteric /ɛksoʊˈtɛrɪk/ adj. **1.** suitable for or communicated to the general public. **2.** not belonging or relating to the inner or select circle, as of disciples. **3.** popular; simple; commonplace. **4.** of or relating to the outside; exterior; external. –**exoterically,** adv. –**exotericism,** n.

exotic /əgˈzɒtɪk, ɛg-/ adj. **1.** of foreign origin or character; not native; introduced from abroad, but not fully naturalised or acclimatised. **2.** *Bot., Zool.* of, relating to, or designating a species which is not native to an area. **3.** strikingly unusual or colourful in appearance or effect; strange; exciting. –**exotically,** adv.

expand /əkˈspænd, ɛk-/ v.t. **1.** to increase in extent, size, volume, scope, etc.: *heat expands metal.* **2.** to spread or stretch out; unfold: *a bird expands its wings.* **3.** to express in fuller form or greater detail; develop: *to expand a short story into a novel.* –v.i. **4.** to increase or grow in extent, bulk, scope, etc.: *most metals expand with heat, the mind expands with experience.* **5.** to spread out; unfold; develop: *the buds had not yet expanded.* –**expandable,** adj. –**expanded,** adj. –**expander,** n. –**expansion,** n.

expanse /əkˈspæns, ɛk-/ n. **1.** something that is spread out, especially over a large area. **2.** an uninterrupted space or area; a wide extent of anything: *an expanse of water; an expanse of sky.* **3.** expansion; extension.

expansive /əkˈspænsɪv, ɛk-/ adj. **1.** tending to expand or capable of expanding. **2.** causing expansion. **3.** having a wide range or extent; comprehensive; extensive. **4.** (of a person's manner or speech) effusive; unrestrained; free; open. –**expansively,** adv. –**expansiveness,** n.

expatiate /əksˈpeɪʃieɪt, ɛk-/ v.i. **1.** to enlarge in discourse or writing; be copious in description or discussion: *to expatiate upon a theme.* **2.** to move or wander about intellectually, imaginatively, etc., without restraint. –**expatiation** /əkspeɪʃiˈeɪʃən, ɛk-/, n. –**expatiator,** n.

expatriate v.t. /ɛksˈpætrieɪt/ **1.** to banish (a person) from his or her native country. **2.** to withdraw (oneself) from residence in and/or allegiance to one's native country. –adj. /ɛksˈpætriət, -rieɪt/ **3.** expatriated; exiled. –n. /ɛksˈpætriət, -rieɪt/ **4.** an expatriated person. –**expatriation** /ɛksˌpætriˈeɪʃən/, n.

expect /əkˈspɛkt, ɛk-/ *v.t.* **1.** to look forward to; regard as likely to happen; anticipate the occurrence or the coming of: *I expect to do it*; *I expect him to come*; *I expect that he will come.* **2.** to look for with reason or justification: *we cannot expect obedience*; *I expect you to do that.* *–v.i.* **3.** to suppose or surmise. *–phr.* **4. be expecting,** *Colloq.* to be pregnant. *–***expected,** *adj.*

expectant /əkˈspɛktənt, ɛk-/ *adj.* **1.** having expectations; expecting. **2.** expecting the birth of a child: *an expectant mother.* **3.** characterised by expectations. **4.** expected or anticipated; prospective. *–n.* **5.** someone who expects or waits in expectation. *–***expectancy,** *n.* *–***expectantly,** *adv.*

expectation /ˌɛkspɛkˈteɪʃən/ *n.* **1.** the act of expecting. **2.** the state of expecting: *he waits in expectation.* **3.** the state of being expected. **4.** something expected; a thing looked forward to. **5.** (*oft. pl.*) a prospect of future good, success, or profit: *to have great expectations.*

expectorate /əkˈspɛktəreɪt, ɛk-/ *v.t.* **1.** to eject or expel (phlegm, etc.) from the throat or lungs by coughing or hawking and spitting; spit. *–v.i.* **2.** to spit. *–***expectorant,** *n.* *–***expectoration,** *n.* *–***expectorator,** *n.*

expedient /əkˈspidiənt, ɛk-/ *adj.* **1.** tending to promote some proposed or desired object; fit or suitable for the purpose; proper in the circumstances: *it is expedient that you go.* **2.** conducive to advantage or interest, as opposed to right. **3.** acting in accordance with expediency. *–n.* **4.** a means to an end. **5.** a means devised or used in an exigency; a resource; a shift: *to resort to expedients to achieve one's purpose.* *–***expediency,** *n.* *–***expediently,** *adv.*

expedite /ˈɛkspədaɪt/ *v.t.* **1.** to speed up the progress of; hasten: *to expedite matters.* **2.** to accomplish promptly, as a piece of business; dispatch. **3.** to issue officially, as a document. *–***expediter,** *n.*

expedition /ɛkspəˈdɪʃən/ *n.* **1.** an excursion, journey, or voyage made for some specific purpose, as of war or exploration. **2.** the body of persons or ships, etc., engaged in it. **3.** promptness or speed in accomplishing something. *–***expeditionary,** *adj.*

expeditious /ɛkspəˈdɪʃəs/ *adj.* quick; characterised by promptness and efficiency. *–***expeditiously,** *adv.* *–***expeditiousness,** *n.*

expel /əkˈspɛl, ɛk-/ *v.t.* (**-pelled, -pelling**) **1.** to drive or force out or away; discharge or eject: *to expel air from the lungs*; *to expel an invader from a country.* **2.** to cut off from membership or relations: *to expel a pupil from a school.* *–***expellant,** *adj.*, *n.* *–***expellable,** *adj.*

expend /əkˈspɛnd, ɛk-/ *v.t.* **1.** to use up: *to expend all one's energy*; *to expend time unnecessarily*; *to expend care on something.* **2.** to pay out; disburse; spend. *–***expender,** *n.*

expendable /əkˈspɛndəbəl, ɛk-/ *adj.* **1.** capable of being expended. **2.** (of an item of equipment or supply) normally consumed in use. **3.** (of troops, equipment, etc.) capable of being sacrificed to achieve an objective.

expenditure /əkˈspɛndətʃə, ɛk-/ *n.* **1.** the act of expending; disbursement; consumption. **2.** something that is expended; expense.

expense /əkˈspɛns, ɛk-/ *n.* **1.** cost or charge. **2.** a cause or occasion of spending: *owning a car is a great expense.* **3.** the act of expending; expenditure. **4.** (preceded by *at*) loss or injury due to any detracting cause: *quantity at the expense of quality.* **5.** (*pl.*) *Commerce* **a.** charges incurred in the execution of an undertaking or commission. **b.** money paid as reimbursement for such charges: *to receive a salary and expenses.* *–v.t.* (**-pensed, -pensing**) **6.** to claim reimbursement for, as part of one's expenses.

expense account *n.* a record of expenditure incurred by an employee in the course of business to be refunded by the employer or claimed against tax.

expensive /əkˈspɛnsɪv, ɛk-/ *adj.* entailing great expense; costly. *–***expensively,** *adv.* *–***expensiveness,** *n.*

experience /əkˈspɪəriəns, ɛk-/ *n.* **1.** a particular instance of personally encountering or undergoing something: *a strange experience.* **2.** the process or fact of personally observing, encountering, or undergoing something: *business experience.* **3.** the observing, encountering, or undergoing of things generally as they occur in the course of time: *to learn from experience, the range of human experience.* **4.** knowledge or practical wisdom gained from what one has observed, encountered, or undergone: *men of experience.* *–v.t.* (**-enced, -encing**) **5.** to have experience of; meet with; undergo; feel. *–***experienced,** *adj.* *–***experiential,** *adj.*

experiment *n.* /əkˈspɛrəmənt, ɛk-/ **1.** a test or trial; a tentative procedure; an act or operation for the purpose of discovering something unknown or testing a principle, supposition, etc.: *a chemical experiment.* **2.** the conducting of such operations; experimentation: *a product that is the result of long experiment.* *–v.i.* /əkˈspɛrəmɛnt, ɛk-/ **3.** to try or test in order to find something out: *to experiment with drugs in order to find a cure for a certain disease.* *–***experimental,** *adj.* *–***experimentation,** *n.* *–***experimenter,** *n.*

expert /ˈɛkspɜt/ *n.* **1.** someone who has special skill or knowledge in some particular field; a specialist; authority: *a language expert*; *an expert on mining.* **2.** *Shearing* the person who sharpens the shearers' cutters. *–adj.* **3.** relating to, coming from, or characteristic of an expert: *expert work, expert advice.* *–***expertly,** *adv.* *–***expertness,** *n.* *–***experting,** *n.*

expertise /ɛkspɜˈtiz/ *n.* expert skill or knowledge; expertness.

expert system *n.* a computing system which is provided with a certain amount of basic information and a general set of rules instructing it how to reason and draw conclusions, which allows it to mimic the thought processes of a human expert in a specialised field, such as diagnostic medicine, in order to reach a conclusion. *–***expert-system,** *adj.*

expiate /ˈɛkspieɪt/ *v.t.* to atone for; make amends or reparation for. *–***expiable,** *adj.* *–***expiatory,** *adj.* *–***expiation,** *n.* *–***expiator,** *n.*

expire /əkˈspaɪə, ɛk-/ *v.i.* **1.** to come to an end; terminate. **2.** to emit the last breath; die. **3.** (of food products) to be beyond the use-by date: *this milk has expired.* *–***expiration,** *n.* *–***expiratory,** *adj.* *–***expirer,** *n.* *–***expiry,** *n.*

expiry date *n.* **1.** the date by which the manufacturer of a product, such as a medication, recommends that it should be used, usually stamped onto the packaging. **2.** the date on which an authorisation, as one on a swipe card, credit card, etc., expires.

explain /əkˈspleɪn, ɛk-/ *v.t.* **1.** to make plain or clear; render intelligible: *to explain an obscure point.* **2.** to make known in detail: *to explain how to do something, to explain a process.* **3.** to assign a meaning to; interpret. *–***explanatory,** *adj.* *–***explainable,** *adj.* *–***explainer,** *n.*

explanation /ɛkspləˈneɪʃən/ *n.* **1.** the act or process of explaining. **2.** something that explains; a statement made to clarify something and make it understandable; an exposition. **3.** a meaning or interpretation: *to find an explanation of a mystery.* **4.** a mutual declaration of the meaning of words spoken, actions, motives, etc., with a view to adjusting a misunderstanding or reconciling differences. **5.** a written or spoken text type or form which describes how something operates or why something happens.

expletive /əkˈsplitɪv, ɛk-/ *adj.* Also, **expletory. 1.** added merely to fill out a sentence or line, give emphasis, etc. *–n.* **2.** an expletive syllable, word, or phrase. **3.** an interjectory word or expression, frequently profane; an exclamatory oath. —**expletively**, *adv.*

explicable /əks'plıkəbəl, ɛk-/ *adj.* capable of being explained.

explicate /'ɛkspləkeıt/ *v.t.* **1.** to develop (a principle, etc.). **2.** to make plain or clear; explain; interpret.

explicit /ək'splısət, ɛk-/ *adj.* **1.** leaving nothing merely implied; clearly expressed; unequivocal: *an explicit statement; explicit instructions.* **2.** clearly developed or formulated: *explicit knowledge or belief.* **3.** definite and unreserved in expression; outspoken: *he was quite explicit on that point.* —**explicitly**, *adv.* —**explicitness**, *n.*

explode /ək'sploʊd, ɛk-/ *v.i.* **1.** to expand with force and noise because of rapid chemical change or decomposition, as gunpowder, nitroglycerine, etc. **2.** to burst, fly into pieces, or break up violently with a loud report, as a boiler from excessive pressure of steam. **3.** to burst forth violently, especially with noise, laughter, violent speech, etc. –*v.t.* **4.** to cause to be rejected; destroy the reputation of; discredit or disprove: *to explode a theory.* —**exploder**, *n.*

exploit[1] /'ɛksploıt/ *n.* a striking or notable deed; a feat; a spirited or heroic act.

exploit[2] /ək'sploıt, ɛk-/ *v.t.* **1.** to turn to practical account; utilise for profit, especially natural resources. **2.** to use selfishly for one's own ends. —**exploitation**, *n.* —**exploiter**, *n.* —**exploitable**, *adj.* —**exploitative**, *adj.*

explore /ək'splɔ, ɛk-/ *v.t.* **1.** to traverse or range over (a region, etc.) for the purpose of discovery. **2.** to look into closely; scrutinise; examine. **3.** *Surg.* to investigate, especially mechanically, as with a probe. –*v.i.* **4.** to engage in exploration. –*phr.* **5.** **explore every avenue**, to try every means. —**exploration**, *n.* —**exploratory**, *adj.* —**explorer**, *n.*

explosion /ək'sploʊʒən, ɛk-/ *n.* **1.** the act of exploding; a violent expansion or bursting with noise, as of gunpowder or a boiler. **2.** the noise itself. **3.** a violent outburst of laughter, anger, etc. **4.** any sudden, rapid, or large increase: *the population explosion.*

explosive /ək'sploʊzıv, ɛk-, -sıv/ *adj.* **1.** tending or serving to explode: *an explosive substance.* **2.** of or relating to an explosion. **3.** liable to flare up suddenly. –*n.* **4.** an explosive agent or substance, as dynamite. —**explosively**, *adv.* —**explosiveness**, *n.*

expo /'ɛkspoʊ/ *n.* a large exhibition of technology, arts and crafts, industrial products, etc., often accompanied by shows, dances, festivals, displays, etc.

exponent /ək'spoʊnənt, ɛk-/ *n.* **1.** a person or thing that expounds, explains, or interprets. **2.** a person or thing that stands as a representative, type, or symbol of something: *the exponent of democratic principles.* **3.** *Maths* a symbol placed above and at the right of another symbol (the base), to denote to what power the latter is to be raised, as in x^3. —**exponential**, *adj.*

export *v.t.* /ək'spɔt, ɛk-, 'ɛkspɔt/ **1.** to send (commodities) to other countries or places for sale, exchange, etc. **2.** *Computers* to copy (data) from one processing system to another in a different format. –*n.* /'ɛkspɔt/ **3.** the act of exporting; exportation. **4.** an article exported. –*adj.* /'ɛkspɔt/ **5. a.** of or relating to the export of goods: *export income.* **b.** of or relating to products good enough in quality to be exported and better than those kept for home consumption: *export beef.* —**exportable**, *adj.* —**exporter**, *n.*

expose /ək'spoʊz, ɛk-/ *v.t.* (**-posed, -posing**) **1.** to lay open to danger, attack, harm, etc.: *to expose soldiers to gunfire, to expose one's character to attack.* **2.** to lay open to something specified: *to expose oneself to misunderstanding.* **3.** to uncover or bare to the air, cold, etc.: *to expose one's head to the rain.* **4.** to present to view; exhibit; display: *the beggar who exposes his sores.* **5.** to make known, disclose, or reveal (intentions,

secrets, etc.) **6.** to reveal or unmask (crime, fraud, an impostor, etc.). **7.** to hold up to public reprehension or ridicule. **8.** to leave in an unsheltered or open place, as (in some societies) an unwanted child to die. **9.** *Photography* to subject (a plate, film or paper) to the action of light or other actinic rays. –*phr.* **10. expose oneself**, to exhibit one's external sexual organs in public.

exposé /ɛkspoʊ'zeı/ *n.* **1.** a formal explanation or exposition. **2.** an exposure, as of something discreditable.

exposition /ɛkspə'zıʃən/ *n.* **1.** an exhibition or show, as of the products of art and manufacture. **2.** an act of expounding, setting forth, or explaining. **3.** a written or spoken text type or form which represents a detailed statement or explanation; an explanatory treatise. **4.** the act of presenting to view; display. —**expository**, *adj.*

expostulate /ək'spɒstʃuleıt, ɛk-/ *v.i.* to reason earnestly with a person against something they intend to do or have done; remonstrate (*on*, or *upon*): *to expostulate with him on the impropriety.* —**expostulation**, *n.*

exposure /ək'spoʊʒə, ɛk-/ *n.* **1.** the act of exposing. **2.** disclosure, as of something private or secret. **3.** revealing or unmasking, as of crime, fraud, an impostor, etc. **4.** presentation to view, especially in an open or public manner. **5.** a laying open or subjecting to the action or influence of something: *exposure to the weather; exposure to danger; exposure to ridicule.* **6.** *Photography* **a.** the act of presenting a sensitive material as film, plate, or paper, to the action of light or other actinic rays. **b.** the duration of this exposure. **7.** contact with a hazardous substance. **8.** situation with regard to sunlight or wind; aspect: *a southern exposure.* **9.** *Finance* the amount that one may lose if an investment fails.

expound /ək'spaʊnd, ɛk-/ *v.t.* **1.** to set forth or state in detail: *to expound theories; to expound principles.* **2.** to explain; interpret. —**expounder**, *n.*

express /ək'sprɛs, ɛk-/ *v.t.* **1.** to put (thought) into words: *to express an idea clearly.* **2.** to show or make known; reveal: *her actions expressed her feelings; he expressed his ideas in his painting.* **3.** to set forth the thoughts, feelings, etc., of (oneself): *he expresses himself in his work; she finds it hard to express herself in English.* **4.** to represent: *the colour in this painting expresses sadness.* **5.** to press out: *to express the juice of a fruit.* –*adj.* **6.** clearly stated; definite; explicit. **7.** special; particular; definite: *an express purpose.* **8.** exactly formed or represented: *an express image.* **9.** sent by express (def. 15): *an express letter.* **10.** specially direct or fast: *an express train.* –*adv.* **11.** by express; unusually fast. **12.** specially; for a particular purpose. –*n.* **13.** an express train, bus, etc. **14.** a messenger or message specially sent. **15.** a system or method for sending parcels, money, etc., quickly: *to send a parcel by express.* —**expresser**, *n.* —**expressible**, *adj.*

expression /ək'sprɛʃən, ɛk-/ *n.* **1.** the act of setting forth in words: *the expression of opinions; the expression of facts.* **2.** a particular word, phrase, or form of words: *a polite expression.* **3.** the manner or form in which a thing is expressed in words. **4.** the showing of feeling, character, etc., on the face, in the voice, in a work of art, etc.: *her loneliness found expression in her writing; she reads with a lot of expression.* **5.** a look or tone of voice that expresses feeling, etc.: *a sad expression.* **6.** the quality or power of expressing feeling, etc.: *a face that lacks expression.* **7.** the act of representing by symbols, etc. **8.** *Maths* a combination of numbers or symbols with no equals sign, which represents a number or mathematical entity. **9.** the act of pressing out. —**expressionless**, *adj.*

expressionism /ək'sprɛʃənızəm, ɛk-/ *n.* a theory of art especially that originating in Europe about the time of World War I, which emphasises free expression of the artist's emotional reactions rather than the representation of the natural appearance of objects. —**expressionist**, *n.*, *adj.* —**expressionistic** /əksprɛʃəˈnɪstɪk, ɛk-/, *adj.*

expressive /əkˈsprɛsɪv, ɛk-/ *adj.* **1.** serving to express; indicative of power to express: *a look expressive of gratitude.* **2.** full of expression, as the face or voice. **3.** of, relating to, or concerned with expression. —**expressively**, *adv.* —**expressiveness**, *n.* —**expressivity** /ɛksprɛsˈɪvəti/, *n.*

expressway /əkˈsprɛsweɪ, ɛk-/ *n.* → **freeway**.

expropriate /ɛksˈprouprieɪt/ *v.t.* **1.** to take, especially for public use by the right of eminent domain, thus divesting the title of the private owner. **2.** to dispossess (a person) of ownership. —**expropriation** /ɛksproupriˈeɪʃən/, *n.* —**expropriator**, *n.*

expulsion /əkˈspʌlʃən, ɛk-/ *n.* **1.** the act of driving out or expelling. **2.** the state of being expelled. —**expulsive**, *adj.*

expunge /əkˈspʌndʒ, ɛk-/ *v.t.* (**-punged**, **-punging**) **1.** to strike or blot out; erase; obliterate. **2.** to efface; wipe out or destroy. —**expunction**, *n.* —**expunger**, *n.*

expurgate /ˈɛkspɜɡeɪt, -pəgeɪt/ *v.t.* **1.** to amend by removing offensive or objectionable matter: *to expurgate a book.* **2.** to purge or cleanse. —**expurgatory**, *adj.* —**expurgation** /ɛkspɜˈɡeɪʃən, -pəˈɡeɪʃən/, *n.*

exquisite /əkˈskwɪzət, ɛk-, ˈɛkskwəzət/ *adj.* **1.** of peculiar beauty or charm, or rare and appealing excellence, as a face, a flower, colouring, music, poetry, etc. **2.** extraordinarily fine, admirable, or consummate. **3.** intense, acute, or keen, as pleasure, pain, etc. **4.** keenly or delicately sensitive or responsive: *an exquisite ear for music.* **5.** of peculiar refinement or elegance, as taste, manners, etc., or persons. —**exquisitely**, *adv.* —**exquisiteness**, *n.*

extant /ɛkˈstænt, ˈɛkstənt/ *adj.* in existence; still existing; not destroyed or lost.

extempore /əkˈstɛmpəri, ɛk-/ *adv.* **1.** on the spur of the moment; without premeditation or preparation; offhand. **2.** without notes: *to speak extempore.* **3.** (of musical performance) by improvisation. —*adj.* **4.** extemporaneous; impromptu. —**extemporaneous**, *adj.* —**extemporaneously**, *adv.*

extend /əkˈstɛnd, ɛk-/ *v.t.* **1.** to stretch; draw out to the full length. **2.** to cause to reach or stretch: *he extended his soldiers along the front line.* **3.** to stretch forth or hold out: *she extended her hand.* **4.** to lengthen; prolong: *they extended the time of play.* **5.** to spread out in area, scope, etc.; expand: *they extended their operations interstate.* **6.** to offer; grant; give: *she extended me an invitation.* —*v.i.* **7.** to be or become extended. **8.** to reach or stretch: *this road extends for miles.* **9.** to increase in length, area, scope, etc. —**extended**, *adj.* —**extendible, extendable**, *adj.*

extended family *n.* a family group or unit comprising not only parents and children but also immediate relatives, and sometimes people not related to the group; responsibility for all the children is shared by all the older members of the group. See **nuclear family**.

extensile /ɛkˈstɛnsaɪl/ *adj. Chiefly Zool., Anat.* capable of being extended; adapted for stretching out; extensible; protrusible.

extension /əkˈstɛnʃən, ɛk-/ *n.* **1.** an extending or being extended. **2.** something extended; an extended object, time or space: *an extension to a house; an extension of time.* **3.** range of extending; extent. **4.** an extra telephone connected to the same line as a main telephone. **5.** *Commerce* a written agreement by someone who is owed a debt to give extra time to the person who owes it. **6.** *Anat.* the act of straightening a limb, or its resulting position. **7.** *Philos.* the class of things to which a term applies; denotation: *the extension of the term 'man' includes individuals as 'Socrates', 'Plato',*

'Aristotle', etc. —*adj.* **8.** of or relating to a course, service, etc., which is outside the normal work of an organisation: *the Department of Agriculture offers an extension service to farmers.* —**extensional**, *adj.* —**extensionally**, *adv.*

extension cord *n.* an electrical cord which can be connected to the cord attached to an appliance, device, etc., to extend its reach.

extensive /əkˈstɛnsɪv, ɛk-/ *adj.* **1.** of great extent; wide; broad; covering a great area; large in amount: *an extensive forest, an extensive influence.* **2.** far-reaching; comprehensive; thorough; lengthy; detailed: *extensive knowledge; extensive inquiries.* **3.** of or having extension. **4.** relating to a system of agriculture involving the use or cultivation of large areas of land (as where land is cheap) with a minimum of labour and expense (opposed to *intensive*). —**extensively**, *adv.* —**extensiveness**, *n.*

extensor /əkˈstɛnsə, ɛk-, -sɔ/ *n. Anat.* a muscle which serves to extend or straighten a part of the body (opposed to *flexor*).

extent /əkˈstɛnt, ɛk-/ *n.* **1.** the space or degree to which a thing extends; length, area, or volume: *the extent of a line, to the full extent of his power.* **2.** something extended; an extended space; a particular length, area, or volume; something having extension.

extenuate /əkˈstɛnjueɪt, ɛk-/ *v.t.* **1.** to represent (a fault, offence, etc.) as less serious: *to extenuate a crime.* **2.** to serve to make (fault, offence, etc.) seem less serious: *extenuating circumstances.* —**extenuation**, *n.*

exterior /əkˈstɪəriə, ɛk-/ *adj.* **1.** outer; being on the outer side: *the exterior side; the exterior surface; exterior decorations.* **2.** situated or being outside; relating to or connected with what is outside: *the exterior possessions of a country.* **3.** *Geom.* (of an angle) outer, as an angle formed outside two parallel lines when cut by a third line. —*n.* **4.** the outer surface or part; the outside; outward form or appearance. **5.** *Film, TV* a sequence shot outdoors. —**exteriority** /əkstɪəriˈɒrəti, ɛk-/, *n.* —**exteriorly**, *adv.*

exterior angle *n. Geom.* an outer angle, as an angle formed outside two parallel lines when cut by a third line.

exterminate /əkˈstɜməneɪt, ɛk-/ *v.t.* to get rid of by destroying; destroy totally; extirpate. —**extermination** /əkstɜməˈneɪʃən, ɛk-/, *n.* —**exterminator**, *n.*

external /əkˈstɜnəl, ɛk-/ *adj.* **1.** of or relating to the outside or outer part; outer. **2.** (of a cream, etc.) to be applied to the outside of a body. **3.** acting or coming from without. **4.** relating to outward appearance or show: *external acts of worship.* **5.** relating to what is outside or foreign: *external commerce.* **6.** *Educ.* studying or studied outside a university, etc.: *an external degree.* —*n.* **7.** (*pl.*) things that are external and not absolutely necessary: *the externals of religion.* —**externality**, *n.* —**externally**, *adv.*

external course *n.* a course provided for external students.

external student *n.* a student who undertakes courses offered by an educational institution, although not physically in attendance at the institution.

extinct /əksˈtɪŋkt, ɛk-/ *adj.* **1.** (of a species) without a living representative. **2.** (of a volcano) no longer active, with no possibility of further eruption. **3.** (of an organisation, etc.) no longer working. **4.** having come to an end. —**extinction**, *n.*

extinguish /əkˈstɪŋɡwɪʃ, ɛk-/ *v.t.* **1.** to put out (a fire, light, etc.); put out the flame of (something burning or alight). **2.** to put an end to or bring to an end; wipe out of existence: *to extinguish a hope; to extinguish a life.* **3.** to obscure or eclipse, as by superior brilliance.

—**extinguisher**, *n.* —**extinguishable**, *adj.* —**extinguishment**, *n.*

extirpate /ˈɛkstɜpeɪt, -stə-/ *v.t.* **1.** to remove utterly; destroy totally; exterminate; do away with. **2.** to pull up by the roots; root up. —**extirpation** /ɛkstɜˈpeɪʃən, -stə-/, *n.* —**extirpative**, *adj.* —**extirpator**, *n.*

extol /əkˈstoʊl, ɛk-/ *v.t.* (**-tolled**, **-tolling**) to praise highly; laud; eulogise. Also, **extoll**. —**extoller**, *n.* —**extolment**, *n.*

extort /əkˈstɔt, ɛk-/ *v.t.* **1.** to wrest or wring (something) from a person by violence, intimidation, or abuse of authority; obtain (money, information, etc.) by force, torture, threat, or the like. **2.** to take illegally under cover of office. —**extorter**, *n.* —**extortive**, *adj.*

extortion /əkˈstɔʃən, ɛk-/ *n.* **1.** the act of extorting. **2.** *Law* the crime of obtaining money or other things of value under abuse of one's office or authority, when none is due or not so much is due, or before it is due. **3.** oppressive or illegal exaction, as of excessive price or interest. **4.** anything extorted. —**extortionate**, *adj.* —**extortionary**, *adj.* —**extortioner**, *n.*

extra /ˈɛkstrə/ *adj.* **1.** beyond or more than what is usual, expected, or necessary; additional: *an extra edition of a newspaper*; *an extra lecture.* **2.** better than usual: *extra fineness.* —*n.* **3.** something extra or additional. **4.** an additional expense. **5.** an edition of a newspaper other than the regular edition or editions. **6.** *Film* a person hired by the day to play a small part. **7.** (*usu. pl.*) *Cricket* a score or run not made from the bat, as a bye or a wide; a sundry. —*adv.* **8.** in excess of the usual or specified amount: *an extra high price.* **9.** beyond the ordinary degree; unusually; uncommonly: *done extra well.*

extra cover *n. Cricket* **1.** the position of a fielder between mid-off and cover point. **2.** a fielder occupying this position. Also, **extra cover point**.

extract *v.t.* /əkˈstrækt, ɛk-/ **1.** to draw forth or get out by force or effort: *The dentist must extract the tooth.* **2.** to draw out (a doctrine, principle, etc.). **3.** to obtain (pleasure, comfort, etc.) from a person, event, etc. **4.** to copy out (passages, etc.), as from a book, etc. **5.** to take by force (information, money, etc.). **6.** to separate or obtain (a juice, ingredient, etc.) from a mixture by pressure, distillation, etc. **7.** *Metallurgy* to separate (a metal) from an ore by any process. —*n.* /ˈɛkstrækt/ **8.** something extracted, as the substance from a drug, plant, etc. **9.** a passage taken from a book, etc. —**extractive**, *adj.* —**extractor**, *n.* —**extractable**, **extractible**, *adj.*

extraction /əkˈstrækʃən, ɛk-/ *n.* **1.** the act of extracting. **2.** the state or fact of being extracted. **3.** descent or lineage. **4.** something extracted; an extract.

extracurricular /ɛkstrəkəˈrɪkjələ/ *adj.* outside the regular curriculum.

extradition /ɛkstrəˈdɪʃən/ *n.* the surrender of a prisoner by one state or authority to another. —**extradite**, *v.*

extramarital /ɛkstrəˈmærətl/ *adj.* of or relating to sexual relations with someone other than one's spouse.

extraneous /əkˈstreɪniəs, ɛk-/ *adj.* introduced or coming from without; not belonging or proper to a thing; external; foreign; not essential. —**extraneously**, *adv.* —**extraneousness**, *n.*

extraordinaire /ɛkstrɔdəˈnɛə/ *adj.* (follows noun) **1.** (of a professional) unusually excellent or skilful: *a tenor extraordinaire.* **2.** extraordinary.

extraordinary /əkˈstrɔdənri, ɛk-/, *Orig. US* /-dənɛri/, *also for def. 4* /ɛkstrəˈɔdənri/, *Orig. US* /-dənɛri/ —*adj.* **1.** beyond what is ordinary; out of the regular or established order: *extraordinary power or expenses.* **2.** exceptional in character, amount, extent, degree, etc.; unusual; remarkable: *extraordinary weather*; *extraordinary weight*; *extraordinary speed*; *an extraordinary*

person; *an extraordinary book.* **3.** (*usu. follows noun*) (of officials, etc.) outside of, additional to, or ranking below an ordinary one: *a professor extraordinary.* **4.** (of a meeting) in addition to the usual scheduled meetings, usually to discuss an urgent item of business that has arisen: *an extraordinary general meeting.* —**extraordinarily**, *adv.* —**extraordinariness**, *n.*

extraordinary rendition *n.* the transfer of a prisoner to a country where there is less legal restraint on torture than in the country in which they were previously held, in order to extract information from them. Also, **rendition**.

extrapolate /ɛkˈstræpəleɪt/ *v.t.* to infer (what is not known) from that which is known; conjecture. —**extrapolation** /ɛkstræpəˈleɪʃən/, *n.*

extrasensory /ɛkstrəˈsɛnsəri/ *adj.* outside the normal sense perception.

extrasensory perception *n.* → ESP.

extraterrestrial /ɛkstrətəˈrɛstriəl/ *adj.* outside or originating outside the earth.

extravagant /əkˈstrævəgənt, ɛk-/ *adj.* **1.** going beyond prudence or necessity in expenditure; wasteful: *an extravagant person.* **2.** excessively high; exorbitant: *extravagant expenses*; *extravagant prices.* **3.** exceeding the bounds of reason, as actions, demands, opinions, passions, etc. **4.** exceedingly elaborate; flamboyant: *an extravagant dress.* —**extravagantly**, *adv.* —**extravagance**, *n.*

extravaganza /əkstrævəˈgænzə, ɛk-/ *n.* **1.** a musical or dramatic composition, as comic opera or musical comedy, marked by wildness and irregularity in form and feeling and elaborateness in staging and costume. **2.** extravagant behaviour or speech.

extra-virgin *adj.* of or relating to an oil, such as olive oil, peanut oil, etc., extracted by cold pressing rather than by chemical treatment, and therefore of the highest quality.

extreme /əkˈstrim, ɛk-/ *adj.* **1.** of a character or kind most removed from the ordinary or average: *an extreme case*; *extreme measures.* **2.** very great in degree: *extreme joy.* **3.** outermost: *at the extreme edge of the forest.* **4.** farthest, or very far in any direction. **5.** going to the utmost lengths: *extreme fashions*; *extreme politics.* —*n.* **6.** the highest degree, or a very high degree: *showy in the extreme*; *to an extreme.* **7.** one of two things as different from each other as possible: *the extremes of joy and grief.* **8.** the farthest length, beyond the ordinary or average: *extreme in dress.* —**extremely**, *adv.* —**extremeness**, *n.*

extreme sport *n.* a sport, such as bungee jumping, canyoning, etc., in which a person contends with the forces of nature, and in so doing incurs a high degree of physical risk.

extremism /əkˈstrimɪzəm, ɛk-/ *n.* a tendency or disposition to go to extremes, especially in political matters. —**extremist**, *n.*

extremity /əkˈstrɛməti, ɛk-/ *n.* (*pl.* **-ties**) **1.** the extreme or terminal point, limit, or part of something. **2.** a limb of the body. **3.** the end part of a limb, as a hand or foot. **4.** (*oft. pl.*) a condition, or circumstances, of extreme need, distress, etc. **5.** the utmost or any extreme degree: *the extremity of joy.*

extricate /ˈɛkstrəkeɪt/ *v.t.* **1.** to disentangle; disengage; free: *to extricate one from a dangerous or embarrassing situation.* **2.** to liberate (gas, etc.) from combination, as in a chemical process. —**extricable** /ɛksˈtrɪkəbəl/, *adj.* —**extrication** /ɛkstrəˈkeɪʃən/, *n.*

extrinsic /ɛksˈtrɪnzɪk/ *adj.* **1.** extraneous; not inherent; unessential. **2.** being outside a thing; outward or external; operating or coming from without. —**extrinsically**, *adv.*

extrovert /ˈɛkstrəvɜt/ *n.* **1.** *Psychol.* someone characterised by extroversion; someone concerned chiefly with what is external or objective. Compare **introvert** (def. 1). *–adj.* **2.** marked by extroversion. *–v.t.* **3.** to direct (the mind, etc.) outwards, or to things outside the self. **–extroversion,** *n.* **–extroverted,** *adj.*

extrude /ɛkˈstrud/ *v.t.* **1.** to thrust out; force or press out; expel. **2.** (in moulding or making metals, plastics, etc.) to form into a desired cross-sectional shape by ejecting through a shaped opening: *to extrude tubing. –v.i.* **3.** to protrude. **–extruder,** *n.* **–extrusion,** *n.*

exuberant /əɡˈzjubərənt, ɛɡ-/ *adj.* **1.** lavish; effusive: *an exuberant welcome.* **2.** full of vigour and high spirits: *the soldiers were exuberant after their victory.* **3.** profuse in growth or production; luxuriant; superabundant: *exuberant vegetation.* **–exuberance,** *n.* **–exuberantly,** *adv.*

exude /əɡˈzjud, ɛɡ-/ *v.i.* **1.** to come out gradually in drops like sweat through pores or small openings; ooze out. *–v.t.* **2.** to send out like sweat; emit through pores or small openings. **–exudation,** *n.* **–exudative,** *adj.*

exult /əɡˈzʌlt, ɛɡ-/ *v.i.* (sometimes fol. by *in, at, over*) to show or feel a lively or triumphant joy; rejoice exceedingly; be highly elated; be jubilant: *he exulted to find that he had won.* **–exultant,** *adj.* **–exultation,** *n.* **–exultingly,** *adv.*

exy /ˈɛksi/ *adj. Colloq.* expensive. Also, **exie, exxy, exxie.**

-ey¹ variant of **-y**¹, used especially after *y,* as in *clayey.*

-ey² variant of **-y**², used especially after *y.*

eye /aɪ/ *n.* (*pl.* **eyes**) **1.** the organ of sight or vision. **2.** this organ with respect to the colour of the iris: *blue eyes.* **3.** the region surrounding the eye: *a black eye.* **4.** sight; vision. **5.** power of seeing; appreciative or discriminating visual perception: *an eye for colour; an eye for detail.* **6.** (*oft. pl.*) look, glance, or gaze: *to cast one's eye on a thing.* **7.** (*oft. pl.*) attentive look, close observation, or watch: *to be all eyes.* **8.** regard, respect, view, aim, or intention: *to have an eye to one's own advantage; with an eye to winning favour.* **9.** (*oft. pl.*) manner or way of looking at a thing, estimation, or opinion: *in the eyes of the law.* **10.** something resembling or suggesting the eye in appearance, shape, etc., as the bud of a tuber, the central spot of a target, the lens of a camera, one of the round spots on the tail feathers of a peacock, the hole of a needle, a hole pierced in a thing for the insertion of some object, a metal or other ring as for a rope to pass through, or the loop into which a hook is inserted (forming together with the hook a **hook and eye**). **11.** *Meteorol.* the central region of low pressure in a tropical hurricane, where calm conditions prevail, often with clear skies. **12.** the central, best portion of a steak, usually round and discernible from the surrounding more fatty section. *–v.t.* (**eyed, eyeing** *or* **eying**) **13.** to fix the eyes upon; view. **14.** to observe or watch narrowly. *–phr.* **15. all my eye,** *Colloq.* nonsense. **16. an eye for an eye,** repayment in kind, as revenge for an injustice. **17. before** (or **under**) **someone's very eyes,** in someone's presence. **18. catch someone's eye,** to attract someone's attention. **19. cry one's eyes out,** to weep copiously. **20. easy on the eye,** *Colloq.* attractive to look at. **21. get one's eye in, a.** (in cricket and other ball games) to be able, through practice, to follow the movement of the ball. **b.** *Colloq.* to adapt oneself to a situation; become accustomed. **22. give someone the glad eye,** *Colloq.* to look amorously at someone. **23. have an eye for,** to be discerning about; be a good judge of. **24. have eyes only for, a.** to look at nothing

else but. **b.** to desire nothing else but. **25. have one's eye on, a.** to watch over carefully, especially for misdemeanour. **b.** to watch with interest in order to take; covet. **c.** to set one's sights on: *to have one's eye on the state archery team.* **26. in the public eye,** often seen in public; well known. **27. keep an eye on,** to watch attentively; mind. **28. keep an eye out for,** to be watchful, or on the lookout for. **29. keep one's eye on the ball,** *Colloq.* **a.** (in cricket, golf, and other ball games) to watch the ball right up to the moment when one strikes it, catches it, etc. **b.** to pay attention to the matter in hand. **30. keep one's eyes open** (or **skinned**) (or **peeled**), to be especially watchful. **31. lay** (or **clap**) (or **set**) **eyes on,** to catch sight of; see. **32. make eyes at,** to gaze flirtatiously at. **33. make someone open their eyes,** to astonish someone; cause someone to stare in surprise. **34. open the eyes of,** to make (someone) aware of the truth of something or of something previously unknown; to enlighten. **35. pick the eyes out of,** to select the best parts, pieces, etc., of (a collection). **36. run one's eye over,** to glance at briefly. **37. see eye to eye,** to have the same opinion; agree. **38. see with half an eye,** to see easily; realise immediately. **39. shut** (or **close**) **one's eyes to,** to refuse to see; disregard. **40. sight for sore eyes,** a welcome sight; an agreeable surprise. **41. the eye of the storm,** the centre of a cyclonic storm where there is no wind or cloud. **42. turn a blind eye on** (or **to**), to pretend not to see; ignore. **43. up to the eyes in,** very busy with; deeply involved in. **44. with one's eyes open,** fully aware of potential risks. **–eyeless,** *adj.*

eyeball /ˈaɪbɔl/ *n.* **1.** the ball or globe of the eye. *–v.t.* **2.** *Colloq.* to look at, especially to observe closely.

eyebrow /ˈaɪbraʊ/ *n.* **1.** the arch or ridge forming the upper part of the orbit of the eye. **2.** the fringe of hair growing upon it.

eye candy *n. Colloq.* any person or thing that is visually appealing but not of intrinsic value.

eyelash /ˈaɪlæʃ/ *n.* one of the short, thick, curved hairs growing as a fringe on the edge of an eyelid.

eyelet /ˈaɪlət/ *n.* **1.** a small, typically round hole, as in cloth or leather, for passing a lace or cord through. **2.** a metal ring for lining a small hole.

eyelid /ˈaɪlɪd/ *n.* the movable lid of skin which serves to cover and uncover the eyeball.

eyeliner /ˈaɪlaɪnə/ *n.* a cosmetic material, usually black or brown, applied to the edges of the eyelids.

eyesight /ˈaɪsaɪt/ *n.* **1.** the power or faculty of seeing. **2.** the action or fact of seeing. **3.** the range of the eye.

eyesore /ˈaɪsɔ/ *n.* something unpleasant to look at: *the broken window was an eyesore to the neighbours.*

eyetooth /ˈaɪtuθ/ *n.* (*pl.* **eyeteeth** /-tiθ/) **1.** a canine tooth, especially of the upper jaw (so named from its position under the eye). *–phr.* **2. cut one's eyeteeth,** to become old and experienced enough to understand things. **3.** (**would**) **give one's eyeteeth for,** *Colloq.* to desire greatly.

eyewitness /ˈaɪwɪtnəs/ *n.* **1.** someone who actually beholds some act or occurrence, and hence can give testimony concerning it. *–adj.* **2.** given by an eyewitness.

eyrie /ˈɪəri, ˈɛəri/ *n.* **1.** the nest of a bird of prey, as an eagle or a hawk. **2.** a lofty nest of any large bird. **3.** an elevated habitation or situation. Also, **aerie, aery, eyry.**

ezine /ˈiˈzin/ *n.* a magazine published on the internet. Also, **e-zine.**

F f

F, f /ɛf/ *n.* **1.** the sixth letter of the English alphabet. **2.** the sixth in order or in a series. **3.** *Music* the fourth degree in the scale of C major or the sixth in the relative scale of A minor.

faba bean /ˈfɑbə bin/ *n.* → **broad bean**.

fable /ˈfeɪbəl/ *n.* **1.** a short tale to teach a moral, often with animals or inanimate objects as characters: *the fable of the tortoise and the hare.* **2.** a story not founded on fact. **3.** an untruth; a falsehood. –**fabler,** *n.*

fabric /ˈfæbrɪk/ *n.* **1.** a cloth made by weaving, knitting, or felting fibres: *woollen fabrics.* **2.** framework; structure: *fabric of society.*

fabricate /ˈfæbrəkeɪt/ *v.t.* **1.** to make by art and labour; construct. **2.** to make by assembling standard parts or sections. **3.** to devise or invent (a legend, lie, etc.). **4.** to fake; forge (a document). –**fabrication** /fæbrəˈkeɪʃən/, *n.* –**fabricator,** *n.*

fabulous /ˈfæbjuləs/ *adj.* **1.** almost unbelievable: *a fabulous price.* **2.** *Colloq.* wonderful; exceptionally pleasing. **3.** told about in fables; legendary; not true or real: *the fabulous exploits of Hercules.* –**fabulously,** *adv.* –**fabulousness,** *n.*

facade /fəˈsad, fæ-/ *n.* **1.** *Archit.* a face or front, or the principal face, of a building. **2.** an appearance, especially a misleading one: *behind his facade of benevolence he hides a cruel nature.* Also, **façade.**

face /feɪs/ *n.* **1.** the front part of the head, from the forehead to the chin inclusive. **2.** a person, especially with regard to familiarity or some other quality: *it's time for some fresh faces on council.* **3.** a look or expression on the face: *sad face.* **4.** an expression, indicating ridicule, disgust, etc.: *to make faces.* **5.** *Colloq.* boldness; impudence: *to have the face to ask.* **6.** outward appearance: *old problems with new faces.* **7.** outward show; pretence: *to put a good face on the matter.* **8.** a well-known person, especially one on whom a publicity drive, campaign, etc., depends; identity. **9.** an aspect of a hill, mountain, etc.: *the sheep were on the southern face.* **10.** the surface: *face of the earth.* **11.** the side or part of a side upon which the use of a thing depends: *the face of a cloth; the face of a document; the face of a playing card; the face of a watch.* **12.** the most important side; the front: *the face of a building; the face of an arch.* **13.** the acting, striking, or working surface of an implement, tool, bat, club, etc. **14.** *Geom.* any one of the bounding surfaces of a solid figure: *a cube has six faces.* **15.** *Mining* the front or end of a drift or excavation, where the material is being or was last mined; workface. **16.** *Printing* **a.** the working surface of a type, plate, etc. **b.** the style or appearance of type; typeface: *broad face; narrow face.* –*verb* (**faced, facing**) –*v.t.* **17.** to look towards: *to face the light.* **18.** to have the front towards or in the direction of: *the apartment faces the park.* **19.** to meet face to face; confront: *faced with a problem.* **20.** to see a matter through despite embarrassment: *to face a thing out.* **21.** to oppose confidently or defiantly: *to face fearful odds.* **22.** to cover or partly cover with a different material in front: *a brick house faced with wood.* **23.** to cover some part of (a garment) with another material. –*v.i.* **24.** (sometimes fol. by *to, towards,* or *on*) to be turned or positioned: *the houses face to the south; the house faces on the square.* **25.** to turn in a specified direction: *to face right.* –*phr.*

26. come face to face with, to be confronted with: *to come face to face with death.* **27. face down,** *Colloq.* to overcome (opponents) by confidently and persistently maintaining that one is right: *the prime minister faced down a rowdy opposition.* **28. face it out,** *Colloq.* to ignore or defy blame, hostility, etc. **29. face off,** (of two people) to confront each other. **30. face someone out,** to stand up to someone: *to face out a bully* **31. face to face,** opposite: *the buildings are face to face.* **32. face up to,** to meet courageously; acknowledge; deal with. **33. in one's face,** *Colloq.* demanding attention: *I can't concentrate because she's always in my face.* **34. in the face of, a.** notwithstanding: *in the face of many obstacles.* **b.** when confronted with: *to keep up prices in the face of a falling market.* **35. look someone in the face,** *Colloq.* to meet someone without fear or embarrassment. **36. lose face,** to suffer embarrassment and loss of prestige. **37. off one's face,** *Colloq.* **a.** mad; insane. **b.** incapacitated as a result of taking drugs, alcohol, etc. **38. on the face of it,** to all appearances; seemingly. **39. put on one's face,** *Colloq.* to put on make-up. **40. save face,** to avoid potential embarrassment or loss of prestige. **41. set one's face against,** to oppose implacably. **42. show one's face,** to make an appearance; be seen. **43. to someone's face,** in the presence of someone. –**faceable,** *adj.*

face lift *n.* **1.** a session or course of plastic surgery on the face for the elimination of wrinkles, etc. **2.** any improvement in appearance: *to give an ancient building a face lift.* Also, **facelift.** –**facelifting,** *n., adj.*

face mask *n.* Also, **facial mask.** a cosmetic preparation left on the face for a number of minutes to tone and clean the skin. **2.** → **mask** (def. 5).

face peel *n.* a chemical peel of the face. See **chemical peel.**

facer /ˈfeɪsə/ *n.* **1.** a person or thing that faces, especially a cutter for smoothing a surface. See **face** (def. 22). **2.** *Colloq.* a sudden and severe check; a disconcerting difficulty, problem, etc. **3.** *Colloq.* a blow in the face.

facet /ˈfæsət/ *n.* **1.** one of the small plane polished surfaces of a cut gem. **2.** aspect; phase: *a facet of the mind.*

facetious /fəˈsiʃəs/ *adj.* **1.** intended to be amusing: *his facetious remarks are often merely offensive.* **2.** trying to be amusing: *a facetious person.* –**facetiously,** *adv.* –**facetiousness,** *n.*

face value *n.* **1.** the value stated on the face of a financial instrument or document. **2.** the value shown on a ticket, price tag, etc. –*phr.* **3. at face value,** taken at the apparent value or significance: *to accept a promise at face value; at face value it seemed a good idea.*

face washer *n.* a small piece of towelling or similar material used for washing the face or body. Also, **flannel, washer.**

facial /ˈfeɪʃəl/ *adj.* **1.** of or relating to the face. –*n.* **2.** a massage or treatment for the face. –**facially,** *adv.*

facial mask *n.* → **face mask** (def. 1).

-facient a suffix forming adjectives meaning 'that makes or causes (something)' and nouns meaning 'one that makes or causes (something)', as in *absorbefacient,* noun and adjective.

facile /ˈfæsaɪl/ *adj.* **1.** moving, acting, working, proceeding, etc., with ease: *a facile hand; a facile tongue; a facile pen.* **2.** easily done, performed, used, etc.: *a facile* *victory*; *a facile method*. **3.** easy or unconstrained, as manners or persons; affable, agreeable, or complaisant; easily influenced. **4.** glib: *a facile expression*. —**facilely**, *adv*. —**facileness**, *n*.

facilitate /fəˈsɪləteɪt/ *v.t.* to make easier or less difficult; help forward (an action, a process, etc.). —**facilitation** /fəsɪləˈteɪʃən/, *n*.

facility /fəˈsɪləti/ *n.* (*pl.* -**ties**) **1.** something that makes possible the easier performance of any action; advantage: *they will provide every facility for the undertaking*. **2.** freedom from difficulty; ease: *facility of understanding*. **3.** readiness because of skill or practice; dexterity: *he has a facility with tools*; *to have a facility with words*. **4.** (in electronic devices) a specific capability or function. **5.** (*pl.*) Also, **toilet facilities**. bathroom and toilet. **6.** a building or buildings designed for a particular purpose, as for the holding of sporting events.

facing /ˈfeɪsɪŋ/ *n.* **1.** a covering in front, for ornament, protection, etc., as an outer layer of different stone forming the face of a wall. **2.** material applied on the edge of a garment for ornament or protection. **3.** *NZ* an open hillside; face.

facsimile /fækˈsɪməli/ *n.* **1.** an exact copy. **2. a.** (formerly) a method of transmitting pictures by radio telegraph. **b.** → **fax**.

fact /fækt/ *n.* **1.** what has really happened or is the case; truth; reality: *in fact rather than theory*; *the fact of the matter is*. **2.** something known to have happened; a truth known by actual experience or observation: *scientists working with facts*. **3.** something said to be true or supposed to have happened: *the facts are as follows*. **4.** *Law* **a.** an actual or alleged physical or mental event or existence, as distinguished from a legal effect or consequence. Thus, whether certain words were spoken is *a question of fact*; whether, if spoken, they constituted a binding promise, is usually *a question of law*. **b.** a wrongful deed (now only in certain legal phrases): *before the fact*; *after the fact*. —*phr.* **5. in fact**, really; indeed. —**factual**, *adj*.

factbox /ˈfæktbɒks/ *n.* an insert on a printed page, computer screen, etc., which contains detail relevant to an item mentioned in the main text.

fact check *n.* a verification of the accuracy of information, as in a publication, document, etc. —**fact checker**, *n.* —**fact-check**, *v*.

faction /ˈfækʃən/ *n.* **1.** a smaller group of people within a larger group, often one using unscrupulous methods to accomplish selfish purposes. **2.** party strife or intrigue: *faction has no regard for national interests*. —**factionary**, **factionist**, *n*.

factious /ˈfækʃəs/ *adj.* **1.** acting only in the interests of a group or faction: *factious opposition*. **2.** caused by factional spirit or strife: *factious quarrels*. —**factiously**, *adv*. —**factiousness**, *n*.

factitious /fækˈtɪʃəs/ *adj.* **1.** artificial; not spontaneous or natural: *a factitious value, factitious enthusiasm*. **2.** made; manufactured. —**factitiously**, *adv*. —**factitiousness**, *n*.

factor /ˈfæktə/ *n.* **1.** one of the elements that contribute to bringing about any given result. **2.** *Maths* one of two or more numbers, algebraic expressions, or the like, which when multiplied together produce a given product; a divisor: *6 and 3 are factors of 18*. **3.** someone who acts, or transacts business, for another. **4.** an agent entrusted with possession of goods for sale. —**factorship**, *n*.

factorial /fækˈtɔriəl/ *Maths* —*n.* **1.** the product of an integer multiplied by all the lower integers: *the factorial of 4 (written 4!) is $4 \times 3 \times 2 \times 1 = 24$*. —*adj.* **2.** of or relating to factors or factorials.

factory /ˈfæktri, -təri/ *n.* (*pl.* -**ries**) **1.** a building or group of buildings, usually with equipment, where things are made. —*phr.* **2. the factory floor**, **a.** the part of a factory in which the manufacturing processes are carried out: *the noise of the factory floor*. **b.** an industrial workplace or the people who work there, when viewed as separate from management, administration, promotions, etc.: *productivity can only be improved by incentives offered to the factory floor*.

factotum /fækˈtoutəm/ *n.* someone employed to do all kinds of work for another.

faculty /ˈfækəlti/ *n.* (*pl.* -**ties**) **1.** an ability, natural or acquired, for a particular kind of action. **2.** one of the powers of the mind, as memory, reason, speech, etc.: *the mental faculties, be in full possession of all one's faculties*. **3.** an inherent capability of the body: *the faculties of sight and hearing*. **4.** *Educ.* **a.** one of the branches of learning, as arts, law, or medicine, in a university. **b.** the teaching body, sometimes with the students, in any of these branches. **5.** the members of a learned profession, especially the medical profession.

fad /fæd/ *n.* a temporary, usually irrational pursuit, by numbers of people, of some action that excites attention and has prestige.

fade /feɪd/ *v.i.* **1.** to lose freshness, vigour, strength, or health: *the flower faded*. **2.** to lose brightness or vividness, as light or colour. —*v.t.* **3.** to cause to fade: *sunshine faded the tapestry*. —*phr.* **4. fade away**, to disappear or die gradually: *her smile faded*. **5. fade in** (or **up**), *TV*, *Radio*, *Film* to cause (sound or vision) to increase gradually. **6. fade out**, **a.** *TV*, *Radio*, *Film* to cause (sound or vision) to decrease gradually. **b.** to ease oneself out of a difficult situation. —**fader**, *n*.

faeces /ˈfiːsiz/ *pl. n.* waste matter discharged from the intestines; excrement. Also, **feces**. —**faecal** /ˈfiːkəl, ˈfiːsəl/, *adj*.

fag¹ /fæg/ *v.i.* (**fagged**, **fagging**) **1.** *Colloq.* to work till wearied; work hard: *to fag away at French*. —*n.* **2.** *Brit.* a younger boy at a public school required to perform certain services for an older pupil. —*phr.* **3. fag out**, to tire by labour; exhaust: *we were fagged out*.

fag² /fæg/ *n. Colloq.* (*derog.*) a male homosexual.

fag³ /fæg/ *n. Colloq.* a cigarette.

faggot /ˈfægət/ *n.* **1.** a bundle of sticks, twigs, or small branches, etc. bound together, used for fuel, etc. **2.** a bundle of pieces of iron or steel to be welded. **3.** *Colloq.* (*derog.*) a male homosexual. Also, *US*, **fagot**.

Fahrenheit /ˈfærənhaɪt/ *adj.* **1.** of or relating to a scale of temperature in which the melting point of ice is 32 degrees above zero (32°F) and the boiling point of water is 212 degrees above zero (212°F). The relation of the degree Fahrenheit to the degree Celsius (°C) is expressed by the formula $°F = \frac{9}{5} \times °C + 32$. —*n.* **2.** the Fahrenheit scale.

fail /feɪl/ *v.i.* **1.** to come short or be wanting in action, detail, or result; disappoint or prove lacking in what is attempted, expected, desired, or approved. **2.** to be or become deficient or lacking; fall short; be insufficient or absent: *our supplies failed*. **3.** to fall off; dwindle; pass or die away. **4.** to lose strength or vigour; become weaker. **5.** to become unable to meet one's engagements, especially one's debts or business obligations; become insolvent or bankrupt. —*v.t.* **6.** to neglect to perform or observe: *he failed to come*. **7.** to prove of no use or help to, as some expected or usual resource: *his friends failed him; words failed her*. **8.** to take (an examination, etc.) without passing. **9.** to declare (a person) unsuccessful in a test, course of study, etc. **10.** to declare (a vehicle, train, etc.) unroadworthy. —*n.* **11.** an examination score which is classified as a failure. **12.** *Colloq.* an instance of failing: *a memory fail*. —*phr.* **13. without fail**, for certain; with certainty. —**failed**, *adj*.

failing /ˈfeɪlɪŋ/ *n.* **1.** a defect; shortcoming; weakness. —*adj.* **2.** becoming weaker or poorer: *failing eyesight*.

–prep. **3.** in the absence or default of: *failing payment, we shall sue.* *–***failingly,** *adv.*

fail-safe *adj.* ensuring safety in the event of failure or accident: *a fail-safe system.*

failure /ˈfeɪljə/ *n.* **1.** an act of failing; lack of success: *his effort ended in failure.* **2.** non-performance of something due or required: *a failure to do as promised.* **3.** a running short; insufficiency: *failure of crops; failure of supplies.* **4.** loss of strength, etc.: *the failure of health.* **5.** inability to meet financial commitments. **6.** someone or something that proves unsuccessful.

faint /feɪnt/ *adj.* **1.** lacking brightness, clearness, loudness, strength, etc.: *a faint light; a faint sound; a faint similarity.* **2.** half-hearted: *faint resistance; faint praise.* **3.** feeling weak, dizzy, or exhausted: *faint with hunger.* *–v.i.* **4.** to lose consciousness for a short time; swoon. *–n.* **5.** short loss of consciousness; a swoon. *–***fainter,** *n.* *–***faintish,** *adj.* *–***faintly,** *adv.* *–***faintness,** *n.*

fair[1] /feə/ *adj.* **1.** free from bias, dishonesty, or injustice: *a fair decision; a fair judge.* **2.** that is legitimately sought, pursued, done, given, etc.; proper under the rules: *a fair game; a fair stroke; a fair fight.* **3.** moderately good, large, or satisfactory; not undesirable, but not excellent: *a fair income; a fair education; a fair reputation.* **4.** marked by favouring conditions; likely; promising: *in a fair way to succeed.* **5.** *Meteorol.* **a.** (of the sky) bright; sunny; cloudless to half-cloudy. **b.** (of the weather) fine; with no aspect of rain, snow, or hail; not stormy. **6.** free from blemish, imperfection, or anything that impairs the appearance, quality, or character: *a fair copy.* **7.** clear; easy to read: *fair handwriting.* **8.** of a light hue; not dark: *fair skin.* **9.** beautiful; pleasing in appearance; attractive. **10.** seemingly good or sincere but not so: *fair promises.* **11.** courteous; civil: *fair words.* *–adv.* **12.** in a fair manner: *he doesn't play fair.* **13.** straight; directly, as in aiming or hitting. **14.** *Colloq.* completely: *I was fair flabbergasted; it fair took my breath away.* *–phr.* **15. a fair cop,** *Colloq.* the discovery of a wrongdoer in the act or with guilt apparent. **16. a fair treat,** *Colloq.* excellently; splendidly. **17. fair and square,** *Colloq.* **a.** honest; just; straightforward: *a fair and square deal.* **b.** directly; accurately: *I hit him fair and square on the chin.* **c.** honestly; justly; straightforwardly: *to be beaten fair and square.* **18. fair call,** *Colloq.* an expression acknowledging the reasonableness of an attitude stated by another. **19. fair crack of the whip,** *Aust. Colloq.* an appeal for fairness or reason. **20. fair enough,** *Colloq.* an expression of agreement. **21. fair's fair,** an exclamation offered as a plea for fair play. **22. fair suck (of the sauce bottle),** *Aust. Colloq.* an appeal for fairness or reason. **23. fair to middling,** *Colloq.* reasonably good; so-so. **24. in a fair way to,** likely to; on the way to: *you're in a fair way to becoming an alcoholic, the amount you drink.* *–***fairness,** *n.*

fair[2] /feə/ *n.* **1.** a collection of amusements, such as merry-go-rounds, dodgems, etc., often travelling from place to place. **2.** a periodic gathering of buyers and sellers, as of livestock, books, antiques, etc., in an appointed place. **3.** an exhibition, especially an international one, for the display of national industrial and other achievements: *International Trade Fair.*

fair dinkum *Aust., NZ Colloq. –adj.* **1.** true; genuine: *the fair dinkum article.* **2.** in earnest: *to be fair dinkum about an issue.* **3.** typically Australian: *fair dinkum blokes and sheilas.* *–adv.* **4.** well and truly: *to be fair dinkum drunk.* **5.** truly: *I'll go. Fair dinkum I will.* *–interj.* Also, **fair dink. 6.** an assertion of truth or genuineness: *it's true, mate, fair dinkum.* *–phr.* **7. be fair dinkum,** (sometimes fol. by *about*) to be in earnest.

fair enough *Colloq. –adj.* **1.** acceptable; passable. **2.** justified; reasonable. *–interj.* **3.** a statement of acquiescence, or agreement.

fair game *n.* a legitimate, suitable, or likely subject of attack.

fair go *Aust., NZ Colloq. –n.* **1.** a fair or reasonable course of action: *do you think that's a fair go?* **2.** a chance to get on with something without interference or distraction: *the chairperson pleaded for silence and a fair go for the speaker.* *–interj.* **3.** an appeal for fairness or reason: *fair go, mate!*

fairly /ˈfeəli/ *adv.* **1.** in a fair manner; justly; impartially. **2.** moderately; tolerably: *fairly good.* **3.** actually; completely: *the wheels fairly spun.* **4.** properly; legitimately.

fairway /ˈfeəweɪ/ *n.* **1.** an unobstructed passage or way. **2.** *Golf* the part of the links between tees and putting greens where the grass is kept short.

fairy /ˈfeəri/ *n.* (*pl.* **-ries**) **1.** one of a class of supernatural beings, generally conceived of as of diminutive human form, having magical powers capriciously exercised for good or evil in human affairs. **2.** such beings collectively. **3.** *Colloq.* (*derog.*) a homosexual male *–adj.* **4.** of or relating to fairies. **5.** of the nature of a fairy; fairy-like. *–phr. Colloq.* **6. away** (or **off**) **with the fairies,** no longer in tune with reality. **7. shoot a fairy,** to fart.

fairy penguin *n.* a small penguin, *Eudyptula minor,* steely blue on top and white underneath, with silver-grey eyes and a black bill, found in the southern coastal regions of Australia and in New Zealand. Also, **little penguin.**

fairytale /ˈfeəriteɪl/ *n.* **1.** a traditional story, usually involving magical happenings, as told to children. **2.** a statement or account of something imaginary or incredible. **3.** a lie; fabrication. *–adj.* **4.** relating to or likely to occur in a fairytale; unreal.

fairy-wren *n.* any of various Australian wrens of the genus *Malurus,* found throughout Australia, New Guinea and adjacent islands.

faith /feɪθ/ *n.* **1.** confidence or trust in someone or something. **2.** belief which is not based on proof. **3.** belief in the teachings of religion. **4.** a system of religious belief: *Christian faith; Jewish faith.* **5.** a duty or obligation of loyalty (to a person, promise, engagement, etc.): *to keep or break faith with; to act in good faith; act in bad faith.* *–***faithless,** *adj.*

faithful /ˈfeɪθfəl/ *adj.* **1.** strict or thorough in the performance of duty. **2.** true to one's word, promises, vows, etc. **3.** full of or showing loyalty or fidelity. **4.** able to be relied upon, trusted, or believed. **5.** adhering or true to fact or an original: *a faithful account; a faithful copy.* *–phr.* **6. the faithful, a.** the believing members of the Christian church or of some branch of it. **b.** the adherents of the Muslim faith. **c.** the body of loyal members of any party or group. *–***faithfully,** *adv.* *–***faithfulness,** *n.*

fake /feɪk/ *v.t.* **1.** to prepare or make (something) deceptive, or fraudulent: *to fake money.* **2.** to pretend; simulate: *to fake illness.* *–n.* **3.** someone who fakes: *you can tell he's a fake.* **4.** something faked or not genuine: *that diamond's a fake.* *–adj.* **5.** artificial: *a fake tan.* *–phr.* **6. fake it,** *Colloq.* to simulate a reaction, mood, etc.

fakir /ˈfeɪkɪə/ *n.* a Muslim or Hindu religious ascetic or mendicant monk. Also, **fakeer.**

falcon /ˈfælkən, ˈfɔlkən/ *n.* **1.** any of various diurnal birds of prey of the family Falconidae, especially the genus *Falco,* having long, pointed wings and a notched bill, and taking its quarry as it moves. **2.** any of various hawks used in falconry, and trained to hunt other birds and game (properly, the female only, the male being known as a tercel).

fall /fɔl/ *verb* (**fell, fallen, falling**) *–v.i.* **1.** to descend from a higher to a lower place or position through loss or lack of support; drop. **2.** to come down suddenly from a standing or erect position: *to fall on one's knees.* **3.** to become less or lower: *the temperature fell ten degrees.* **4.** to hang down; extend downwards: *her hair falls to her waist.* **5.** to be cast down, as the eyes. **6.** to succumb to temptation. **7.** to lose high position, dignity, character, etc. **8.** to succumb to attack: *the city fell to the enemy.* **9.** to be overthrown, as a government. **10.** to drop down wounded or dead; be slain: *to fall in battle.* **11.** to come as if by dropping, as stillness, night, etc. **12.** to come by lot or chance: *their choice fell upon him.* **13.** to come by chance into a particular position: *to fall among thieves.* **14.** to come to pass; occur; happen: *Christmas falls on a Monday this year.* **15.** to have proper place: *the accent falls on the first syllable.* **16.** come by right: *the inheritance fell to the only surviving relative.* **17.** (of speech, etc.) to issue or proceed: *the words that fall from his lips.* **18.** to lose animation, as the face. **19.** to slope, as land. **20.** to be directed, as light, sight, etc., on something. **21.** to come down in fragments, as a building. *–v. (copular)* **22.** to pass into some condition or relation: *to fall asleep; to fall in love; to fall into ruin.* **23.** to become: *to fall sick; to fall pregnant; to fall vacant; to fall due.* *–v.t. Aust., NZ* to fell (trees, etc.) *–n.* **25.** the act of falling, or dropping from a higher to a lower place or position; descent, as of rain, snow, etc. **26.** the quantity that descends. **27.** a becoming less; a lowering; a sinking to a lower level. **28.** the distance through which anything falls. **29.** (*usu. pl.*) a cataract or waterfall. **30.** downward slope or declivity. **31.** a falling from an erect position, as to the ground: *to have a bad fall.* **32.** a hanging down. **33.** a succumbing to temptation; lapse into sin. **34.** surrender or capture, as of a city. **35.** proper place: *the fall of an accent on a syllable.* **36.** *Wrestling* **a.** the fact or a method of being thrown on one's back by an opponent and held down with both shoulders on the canvas for a specific period of time, usually a count of three; a pinfall. **b.** a bout, or one of the best of three victories which go to make up a bout: *to try a fall.* **37.** *Chiefly US* autumn. **38.** a stand of trees suitable for felling. *–phr.* **39. fall about,** *Colloq.* to laugh immoderately. **40. fall apart,** (of an organisation, business, scheme, etc.) to cease to operate or function effectively, resulting in failure. **41. fall away, a.** to withdraw support or allegiance. **b.** to decline; decay; perish. **c.** to lose flesh; become lean. **d.** *Naut.* to deviate from the course to which the head of the ship is directed. **42. fall back,** to recede; give way; retreat. **43. fall back on, a.** *Mil.* to retreat to. **b.** to have recourse to. **44. fall behind,** to slacken in pace or progress; lag: *to fall behind in work; to fall behind in payments.* **45. fall down,** to fail: *to fall down on the job.* **46. fall flat,** to fail to have a desired effect: *his jokes fell flat.* **47. fall for, a.** to be deceived by. **b.** to fall in love with. **48. fall in, a.** to sink inwards; fall to pieces inwardly. **b.** to take one's proper place in line, as a soldier. **c.** to agree. **d.** to make a mistake, especially when tricked into doing so. **49. fall into,** to be naturally divisible into: *the nut falls into halves.* **50. fall into place,** to eventuate in a satisfactory way. **51. fall in with, a.** to meet and become acquainted with. **b.** to agree to. **52. fall off, a.** to drop off. **b.** to separate or withdraw. **c.** to become estranged; withdraw from allegiance. **d.** to decline in vigour, interest, etc. **e.** to decrease in number, amount, intensity, etc.; diminish. **53. fall off the back of a truck,** *Colloq.* to be obtained by questionable or illegal means. **54. fall on hard times,** to experience difficulties in one's life, especially of a financial nature. **55. fall on (or upon), a.** to assault; attack. **b.** to light upon; chance upon. **56. fall on one's feet,** to emerge from a difficult or adverse situation without serious harm. **57. fall on one's sword, a.** to commit suicide by falling on one's sword, thought to be a traditional Roman way. **b.** to step down from office or

from a position of power for honourable motives. **58. fall out, a.** to drop out of one's place in line, as a soldier. **b.** to disagree; quarrel. **c.** to occur; happen; turn out. **59. fall out of the air,** (of an aircraft) to have a complete loss of power resulting in a crash landing. **60. fall over oneself, a.** to become confused in attempting to take some action. **b.** to be very enthusiastic: *people were falling over themselves to sign up.* **61. fall short, a.** to fail to reach a particular amount, degree, standard, etc. **b.** to prove insufficient; give out. **62. fall through,** to come to naught; fail; miscarry. **63. fall to, a.** to apply oneself to; begin: *to fall to work; to fall to argument; to fall to blows, etc.* **b.** to begin to eat. **64. fall under,** to be classed as; be included in. **65. the fall,** (*sometimes upper case*) *Theology* **a.** the transgression of Adam and Eve from which ensued the lapse of humankind into a state of natural or innate sinfulness: *the fall of humankind.* **b.** this lapsed state of humanity.

fallacy /ˈfæləsi/ *n.* (*pl.* **-cies**) **1.** a deceptive, misleading, or false notion, belief, etc.: *a popular fallacy.* **2.** a misleading or unsound argument. **3.** deceptive, misleading, or false nature. **4.** *Logic* any of various types of erroneous reasoning that render arguments logically unsound. *–***fallacious,** *adj.*

fallible /ˈfæləbəl/ *adj.* **1.** liable to be deceived or mistaken; liable to err. **2.** liable to be erroneous or false. *–***fallibility** /fælə'bɪləti/, **fallibleness,** *n.* *–***fallibly,** *adv.*

fallopian tube /fə'loʊpiən tjub/ *n. Anat.* one of the uterine tubes, a pair of slender oviducts leading from the ovaries to the uterus, for transport and fertilisation of ova. Also, **Fallopian tube.**

fallout /ˈfɔlaʊt/ *n.* **1.** the descent of airborne particles of dust, soot, or more particularly, of radioactive materials resulting from a nuclear explosion. **2.** the indirect effects of a decision, event, etc.

fallow /ˈfæloʊ/ *adj.* ploughed and left unseeded for a season or more; uncultivated. *–***fallowness,** *n.* *–***fallowing,** *n.*

false /fɔls, fɒls/ *adj.* (**falser, falsest**) **1.** not true or correct; erroneous: *a false statement; a false accusation.* **2.** uttering or declaring what is untrue: *false prophets; a false witness.* **3.** deceitful; treacherous; faithless: *a false friend.* **4.** deceptive; used to deceive or mislead: *false weights; to give a false impression.* **5.** not genuine: *a false signature; false diamonds; false teeth.* **6.** *Biol.* improperly so called, as from deceptive resemblance to something that properly bears the name: *the false acacia.* **7.** inaccurate in pitch, as a musical note. *–phr.* **8. play someone false,** to behave disloyally towards someone. *–***falsely,** *adv.* *–***falseness,** *n.* *–***falsity,** *n.*

falsehood /ˈfɔlshʊd/ *n.* **1.** lack of conformity to truth or fact. **2.** something false; an untrue idea, belief, etc.

false memory *n.* a memory believed to be of a real event but shown to be without foundation and prompted by suggestion from an individual or from the community culture.

false pretences *pl. n.* the use of false representations, forged documents, or similar illegal devices to obtain money or property.

falsetto /fɔl'sɛtoʊ/ *n.* (*pl.* **-tos**) **1.** an unnaturally or artificially high-pitched voice or register, especially in a man. **2.** someone who sings with such a voice.

falsify /ˈfɔlsəfaɪ/ *v.t.* (**-fied, -fying**) **1.** to make false or incorrect, especially so as to deceive. **2.** to alter fraudulently. **3.** to represent falsely; misrepresent. **4.** to show or prove to be false; disprove. *–***falsifiable,** *adj.* *–***falsification** /fɔlsəfə'keɪʃən/, *n.* *–***falsifier,** *n.*

falter /ˈfɔltə/ *v.i.* **1.** to hesitate or waver in action, purpose, etc.; give way. **2.** to speak hesitatingly or brokenly. **3.** to become unsteady in movement, as a person, an animal, or the legs, steps, etc.: *with faltering steps.* *–***falteringly,** *adv.*

fame /feɪm/ *n.* **1.** widespread reputation, especially of a favourable character: *literary fame.* **2.** reputation; common estimation; opinion generally held. **–fameless,** *adj.*

familiar /fəˈmɪljə/ *adj.* **1.** well-known: *a familiar sight.* **2.** well-acquainted: *to be familiar with a subject.* **3.** easy; informal: *to write in familiar style.* **4.** close; intimate: *a familiar friend; to be on familiar terms.* **5.** unduly intimate; taking liberties; presuming. *–n.* **6.** a close friend. **–familiarise, familiarize,** *v.* **–familiarly,** *adv.* **–familiarity,** *n.*

family /ˈfæmli, ˈfæməli/ *n.* (*pl.* **-lies) 1.** parents and their children, whether dwelling together or not. **2.** one's children collectively. **3.** any group of persons closely related by blood, as parents, children, uncles, aunts, and cousins. **4.** all those persons descended from a common progenitor. **5.** descent, especially good or noble descent: *young men of family.* **6.** a group of persons who form a household and who regard themselves as having familial ties. **7.** *US* an independent unit of the Mafia. **8.** *Biol.* the usual major subdivision of an order or suborder, commonly comprising several genera, as Equidae (horses), Formicidae (ants), Orchidaceae (orchids). Names of animal families end in *-idae*, of plant families in *-aceae*. **9.** any group of related things. **10.** (in the classification of languages) a number of languages all of which are more closely related to each other than any of them are to any language outside the group, usually a major grouping admitting of subdivisions: *English is of the Indo-European family.* *–adj.* **11.** of, relating to, or used by a family: *the family car; a family pack.* **12.** (of a film, television program, etc.) of a type suitable in subject matter and treatment for all members of the family to see. *–phr.* **13. in the family way,** *Colloq.* pregnant. **–familial,** *adj.*

family law *n.* the body of law relating to the rights of parents and their children, especially at the time of the break-up of the family unit.

family planning *n.* the regulation of the number of children born into a family by the use of various methods of birth control.

family tree *n.* a genealogical chart showing the ancestry, descent, and relationship of the members of a family, as of people, animals, languages, etc.

family violence *n. Law* violence committed or threatened by one member of a family against the person or property of another member of the family. Compare **domestic violence.**

famine /ˈfæmən/ *n.* **1.** extreme and general scarcity of food. **2.** any extreme and general scarcity.

famished /ˈfæmɪʃt/ *adj.* very hungry.

famous /ˈfeɪməs/ *adj.* celebrated in fame or public report; renowned; well known: *a famous victory.* **–famously,** *adv.* **–famousness,** *n.*

fan¹ /fæn/ *n.* **1.** any device for causing a current of air by the movement of a broad surface or a number of such surfaces. **2.** such an object made of feathers, leaves, paper, cloth, etc., designed to be handheld. **3.** anything resembling such an implement, as the tail of a bird. **4.** any of various devices consisting essentially of a series of radiating vanes or blades attached to and revolving with a central hub-like portion, and used to produce a current of air. **5.** a series of revolving blades supplying air for winnowing or cleaning grain. **6.** *Geol.* a fan-shaped shingle, deposit, etc. *–v.t.* (**fanned, fanning) 7.** to move or agitate (the air) with, or as with, a fan. **8.** to cause air to blow upon, as from a fan; cool or refresh with, or as with, a fan. **9.** to stir to activity with, or as with, a fan: *to fan a flame; to fan emotions.* **10.** (of a breeze, etc.) to blow upon, as if driven by a fan. **11.** to spread out like a fan. **12.** *Agric.* to winnow, especially by an artificial current of air. *–phr.* **13. fan out, a.** to

spread out like a fan: *the peacock's tail fans out.* **b.** (of people, especially soldiers) to spread out in pursuance of a plan, especially one which involves covering a wide terrain. **14. fan the flames, a.** to fan a fire so as to make it burn brighter. **b.** to exacerbate hostility between people. **–fanlike,** *adj.* **–fanner,** *n.*

fan² /fæn/ *n.* an enthusiastic devotee or follower: *a football fan; a film fan.* **–fandom,** *n.*

fanatic /fəˈnætɪk/ *n.* **1.** a person who is extremely enthusiastic about or devoted to an activity, practice, etc.: *a skiing fanatic; a health fanatic.* **2.** a person with an extreme and unreasoning enthusiasm or zeal, especially in religious matters. *–adj.* **3.** fanatical. **–fanatical,** *adj.*

fanbelt /ˈfænbɛlt/ *n.* the belt which drives the cooling fan of a motor, especially a car motor.

fanciful /ˈfænsəfəl/ *adj.* **1.** exhibiting fancy; quaint or odd in appearance: *a fanciful design.* **2.** suggested by fancy; imaginary; unreal. **3.** led by fancy rather than by reason and experience; whimsical: *a fanciful mind.* **–fancifully,** *adv.* **–fancifulness,** *n.*

fancy /ˈfænsi/ *n.* (*pl.* **-cies) 1.** imagination, especially as exercised in a capricious or desultory manner. **2.** a mental image or conception. **3.** an idea or opinion with little foundation; a hallucination. **4.** a caprice; whim; vagary. **5.** capricious preference; inclination; a liking: *to take a fancy to something.* *–adj.* (**-cier, -ciest) 6.** adapted to please the taste or fancy; of delicate or refined quality: *fancy goods; fancy fruits.* **7.** ornamental. **8.** depending on fancy or caprice; whimsical; irregular. **9.** bred to develop points of beauty or excellence, as an animal. *–v.t.* (**-cied, -cying) 10.** to form a conception of; picture to oneself: *fancy living with him all your life!* **11.** to believe without being sure or certain. **12.** to have a desire or appetite for: *I fancy a cold beer just now.* **13.** to be sexually attracted to: *I think she fancies you, mate!* **14.** to place one's hopes or expectations on: *I fancy her for our next MP.* *–interj.* **15.** an expression of mild surprise. *–phr.* **16. fancy oneself,** *Colloq.* to hold an excessively good opinion of one's own merits.

fancy dress *n.* **1.** dress chosen in accordance with the wearer's fancy, for wear at a ball or the like, as that characteristic of a particular period or place, class of persons, or historical or fictitious character. **2.** any bizarre or unusual costume.

fanfare /ˈfænfeə/ *n.* **1.** a flourish or short air played on trumpets or the like. **2.** an ostentatious flourish or parade.

fanfic /ˈfænfɪk/ *n. Colloq.* fiction written by fans of a popular television show or other work, involving characters and settings from that work, and often published on the internet or in a fan magazine. Also, **fan fiction.**

fang¹ /fæŋ/ *n.* **1.** one of the long, sharp, hollow or grooved teeth of a snake, by which venom is injected. **2.** a canine tooth. **3.** the root of a tooth. **4.** a pointed tapering part of a thing. **5.** *Colloq.* a tooth. **–fanged,** *adj.* **–fangless,** *adj.*

fang² /fæŋ/ *Colloq.* *–v.t.* **1.** to drive (a motor vehicle) at high speed. *–v.i.* **2.** to move (*along, down,* etc.) in a motor vehicle at high speed.

fanlight /ˈfænlaɪt/ *n.* a fan-shaped or other window above a door or other opening.

fanny /ˈfæni/ *n.* (*pl.* **-nies)** *Colloq.* **1.** the vagina and external female genitalia. **2.** *Chiefly US* the buttocks.

fantail /ˈfænteɪl/ *n.* **1.** a tail, end, or part shaped like a fan. **2.** one of a fancy breed of domestic pigeons with a fan-shaped tail. **3.** any of various small insectivorous Asian and Australasian birds of the genus *Rhipidura,* family Dicruridae, having fanlike tails, as the **grey fantail,** *R. fuliginosa,* and the willie wagtail. **4.** one of an artificially bred variety of goldfish with double anal and caudal fins.

fantasise /ˈfæntəsaɪz/ *v.i.* to indulge in an extended and elaborate daydream. Also, **fantasize.** –**fantasiser,** *n.*

fantastic /fænˈtæstɪk/ *adj.* **1.** peculiar or strange in character, design, movement, etc.: *fantastic ornaments.* **2.** fanciful or unexpected, as persons or their ideas, actions, etc. **3.** imaginary; groundless; not real: *fantastic fears.* **4.** very fanciful; irrational: *fantastic reasons.* **5.** *Colloq.* large, great: *a fantastic sum of money.* **6.** *Colloq.* very good; fine; wonderful. Also (for defs 1–4), **fantastical.** –**fantastically,** *adv.* –**fantasticalness, fantasticality** /fænˌtæstəˈkæləti/, *n.*

fantasy /ˈfæntəsi, -zi/ *n.* (*pl.* **-sies**) **1.** imagination, especially when unrestrained. **2.** the forming of grotesque mental images. **3.** a hallucination. **4.** an imagined event that one hopes will happen in reality. **5.** an ingenious or odd thought, design, or invention. **6.** a genre of literature, film, computer games, etc., featuring magic and the supernatural, often set in an imaginary world and involving heroic quests and battles. **7.** *Colloq.* → **GHB.** –*adj.* **8.** ideal: *a fantasy holiday.*

fantasy fiction *n.* a fiction genre based on fantasy worlds. See **fantasy** (def. 6).

FAQ /ɛf eɪ ˈkju, fæk/ *n.* **1.** frequently asked question. **2.** an electronic file of frequently asked questions and the corresponding answers on a given topic.

far /fɑ/ *adv.* (**further** *or* **farther, furthest** *or* **farthest**) **1.** at or to a great distance; a long way off; to a remote point: *far ahead.* **2.** to or at a remote time, etc.: *to see far into the future.* **3.** to a great degree; very much: *far better; far worse; far different.* **4.** at or to a definite distance, point of progress, or degree: *we've come this far – why turn back?* –*adj.* (**further** *or* **farther, furthest** *or* **farthest**) **5.** at a great distance; remote in place: *the far scrub.* **6.** extending to a great distance. **7.** more distant of the two: *the far side.* **8.** remote in time, degree, scope, purpose, etc. **9.** greatly different or apart. –*phr.* **10. as far as**, to the distance, extent, or degree that. **11. by far**, very much. **12. far and away**, very much. **13. far and near**, over great distances. **14. far and wide**, over great distances. **15. far be it from me**, I do not wish or dare. **16. far gone, a.** in an advanced or extreme state. **b.** *Colloq.* extremely mad. **c.** *Colloq.* extremely drunk. **d.** *Colloq.* almost exhausted. **e.** *Colloq.* dying. **17. far out**, *Colloq.* an exclamation indicating astonishment, admiration, etc. **18. few and far between**, rare; infrequent. **19. go far**, **a.** to be successful; do much. **b.** to tend greatly. **20. how far**, to what distance, extent, or degree. **21. in so far**, to such an extent. **22. so far, a.** up to now. **b.** up to a certain point, extent, etc. **23. so far so good**, no trouble yet. **24. the far north**, (*also upper case*) **a.** the remote northern regions of Australia. **b.** *NZ* the northern part of the north Auckland region in New Zealand. **25. the far south**, (*also upper case*) *NZ* the southern part of the South Island in New Zealand, or the offshore islands near it. **26. the far west**, (*also upper case*) *Qld, NSW* the remote western regions of Queensland and New South Wales. –**farness,** *n.*

farad /ˈfærəd/ *n. Elect.* the derived SI unit of the electric capacitance that exists between two conductors when the transfer of an electric charge of one coulomb from one to the other changes the potential difference between them by one volt. *Symbol:* F

faraway /ˈfɑrəweɪ/ *adj.* **1.** distant; remote. **2.** abstracted or dreamy, as a look.

farce /fɑs/ *n.* **1.** a light, humorous play in which the plot depends upon situation rather than character. **2.** the branch of drama that is concerned with this form of composition. **3.** foolish show; mockery; a ridiculous sham. –**farcical,** *adj.*

fare /fɛə/ *n.* **1.** the price of passage in a vehicle. **2.** the person or persons who pay to be conveyed in a vehicle. **3.** food. –*v.i.* (**fared, faring**) **4.** to experience good or bad fortune, treatment, etc.; get on: *he fared well.* **5.** (*used impersonally*) to go; turn out; happen: *it fared ill with him.* –**farer,** *n.*

farewell /fɛəˈwɛl/ *interj.* **1.** goodbye; adieu; may you fare well. –*n.* **2.** good wishes at parting. **3.** leave-taking; departure: *a fond farewell.* –*adj.* **4.** parting; valedictory: *a farewell sermon*; *a farewell performance.* –*v.t.* **5.** to say goodbye to.

far-fetched /ˈfa-fetʃt/ *adj.* remotely connected; forced; strained: *a far-fetched example.*

farinaceous /færəˈneɪʃəs/ *adj.* consisting or made of flour or meal, as food.

farm /fɑm/ *n.* **1.** a tract of land devoted to agriculture. **2.** a farmhouse. **3.** a tract of land or water devoted to some other industry, especially the raising of livestock, fish, etc.: *a chicken farm; an oyster farm.* –*v.t.* **4.** to cultivate (land). **5.** to raise (livestock, fish, etc.) on a farm (def. 3). –*v.i.* **6.** to cultivate the soil; operate a farm. –*phr.* **7. buy back the farm**, to reverse a trend towards excessive foreign ownership of companies, by means of legislation or other government control. **8. farm out**, to distribute (responsibilities, duties, etc.): *he farmed out the difficult questions to the supervisor.* **9. sell off the farm**, to sell to foreign interests the capital assets of a country. –**farmable,** *adj.*

farmer /ˈfɑmə/ *n.* someone who farms; someone who cultivates land or operates a farm.

farmstay /ˈfɑmsteɪ/ *n.* a holiday spent on a farm, learning about life on the farm and taking part in farm activities. Also, **farm stay.**

farrier /ˈfæriə/ *n.* **1.** a blacksmith who shoes horses. **2.** a veterinary surgeon for horses. –**farriery,** *n.*

farrow /ˈfærəʊ/ *n.* **1.** a litter of pigs. –*v.t.* **2.** (of swine) to bring forth (young). –*v.i.* **3.** to produce a litter of pigs.

far-sighted /ˈfa-saɪtəd/ *adj.* **1.** seeing to a great distance. **2.** seeing objects at a distance more clearly than those near at hand; long-sighted; hypermetropic. **3.** foreseeing future results wisely: *a far-sighted statesman.* –**farsightedly,** *adv.* –**far-sightedness,** *n.*

fart /fɑt/ *Colloq.* –*n.* **1.** an emission of intestinal gas from the anus, especially an audible one. **2.** a foolish or ineffectual person: *an old fart.* –*v.i.* **3.** to emit intestinal gas from the anus. –*phr.* **4. fart around** (*or* **about**), to behave stupidly or waste time.

farther /ˈfaðə/ (*comparative of* **far**) –*adv.* **1.** at or to a greater distance, degree, point. **2.** additionally; further. –*adj.* **3.** more distant or remote. **4.** additional; further.

farthest /ˈfaðəst/ (*superlative of* **far**) –*adj.* **1.** most distant or remote. **2.** longest. –*adv.* **3.** to or at the greatest distance.

farthing /ˈfaðɪŋ/ *n.* **1.** a former British coin of bronze, worth one quarter of a penny. **2.** something of very small value.

fascia *n.* (*pl.* **fascias** *or* **fasciae**) **1.** /ˈfeɪʃə, ˈfeɪʃiə/ a band or fillet. **2.** /ˈfeɪʃə, ˈfeɪʃiə/ *Archit.* a long, flat member or band. **3.** /ˈfæʃiə/ *Anat., Zool.* a band or sheath of connective tissue surrounding, supporting, or binding together internal organs or parts of the body. **4.** /ˈfeɪʃə, ˈfeɪʃiə/ the plastic covering for the face of a mobile phone, often coloured, decorated or branded. Also, **facia.**

fascia board *n.* a long flat board covering the ends of rafters. Also, **facia board.**

fascinate /ˈfæsəneɪt/ *v.t.* **1.** to attract and hold irresistibly by delightful qualities. **2.** to deprive of the power of resistance or movement, as through terror. –*v.i.* **3.** to hold the attention. –**fascination** /fæsəˈneɪʃən/, *n.* –**fascinating,** *adj.*

fascism /ˈfæʃɪzəm, ˈfæsɪzəm/ *n.* **1.** (*oft. upper case*) a theory of social organisation based on the idea that those most suited to hold power should do so. **2.** (*oft. upper case*) a pattern of social organisation embracing this theory which usually exalts a people or nation, has centralised autocratic government under a dictator and forcibly suppresses all opposition; adopted between the World Wars by several European countries, such as Italy, Germany, etc. **3.** (*derog.*) any extreme right-wing ideology, sometimes involving racism. –**fascist**, *n.*, *adj.*

fashion /ˈfæʃən/ *n.* **1.** a prevailing custom or style of dress, etiquette, procedure, etc.: *the latest fashion in hats.* **2.** conventional usage in dress, manners, etc., especially of polite society, or conformity to it: *dictates of fashion; out of fashion.* **3.** manner; way; mode: *in a warlike fashion.* **4.** the make or form of anything. **5.** a kind; sort. –*v.t.* **6.** to give a particular shape or form to; make. **7.** to accommodate; adapt. –*adj.* **8.** relating to or displaying new fashions in clothes, etc. –*phr.* **9.** after (or in) a fashion, in some manner or other, but not particularly well.

fashionable /ˈfæʃənəbəl, ˈfæʃnəbəl/ *adj.* **1.** observant of or conforming to the fashion. **2.** of, characteristic of, or patronised by the world of fashion. –**fashionableness**, **fashionability**, *n.* –**fashionably**, *adv.*

fashion victim *n.* a person who slavishly follows current fashions even though the styles do not suit them personally or are worn without flair or true fashion sense.

fast[1] /fast/ *adj.* **1.** moving or able to move quickly; quick; swift; rapid: *a fast horse.* **2.** done in comparatively little time: *a fast race; fast work.* **3.** indicating a time in advance of the correct time, as a clock. **4.** extremely energetic and active, especially in pursuing pleasure immoderately or without restraint, as a person. **5.** characterised by such energy or pursuit of pleasure, as a mode of life. **6.** firmly fixed in place; not easily moved; securely attached: *to make fast.* **7.** that cannot escape or be extricated. **8.** firmly tied, as a knot. **9.** closed and made secure, as a door. **10.** such as to hold securely: *to lay fast hold on a thing.* **11.** firm in adherence: *fast friends.* **12.** permanent; lasting: *a fast colour.* **13.** deep or sound, as sleep. **14.** *Photography* permitting very short exposure, as by having a wide shutter opening or high film sensitivity: *a fast lens; a fast film.* **15.** (of the surface of a cricket pitch, racecourse, etc.) hard and dry, and therefore conducive to fast movement. –*adv.* **16.** tightly: *to hold fast.* **17.** soundly: *fast asleep.* **18.** quickly, swiftly, or rapidly. **19.** in quick succession. **20.** in an energetic or dissipated way. –*phr.* **21.** play fast and loose, (oft. fol. by *with*) to behave in a way in which obligations are acknowledged at one moment and denied or ignored in the next. **22.** pull a fast one, *Colloq.* to act unfairly or deceitfully.

fast[2] /fast/ *v.i.* **1.** to abstain from all food. **2.** to eat only sparingly or of certain kinds of food, especially as a religious observance. –*n.* **3.** a fasting; an abstinence from food, or a limiting of one's food, especially when voluntary and as a religious observance. –**faster**, *n.*

-fast an adjective suffix meaning 'lasting', 'not fading', as in *colourfast.*

fasten /ˈfasən/ *v.t.* **1.** to make fast; fix firmly or securely in place or position; attach securely to something else. **2.** to make secure, as an article of dress with buttons, clasps, etc., or a door with a lock, bolt, etc. **3.** to attach by any connecting agency: *to fasten a nickname or a crime upon one.* **4.** to direct (the eyes, thoughts, etc.) intently. –*phr.* **5.** fasten in, to enclose securely, as a person or an animal. **6.** fasten on, to take firm hold of; seize. –**fastener**, *n.*

fast forward *n.* **1.** the mode on a video or audio tape recorder which runs the tape forward quickly, or, on a

DVD player, advances quickly through the DVD. **2.** a state in which things move at a rapid pace. –*adv.* **3.** in this mode or state.

fast-forward /fast-ˈfɔwəd/ *adj.* **1.** of or relating to fast forward. –*v.t.* **2.** to run (a videotape or audio tape or DVD, or a specific section thereof) at fast forward. –*v.i.* **3.** to advance at fast forward through a videotape or audio tape or DVD. **4.** to move rapidly forward in the imagination to a future time.

Fast4 /fast'fɔ/ *n.* a format for a tennis competition in which matches are played to the best of three sets, each set comprising four games, with a tie breaker to be played at three sets all, and other rules adjusted to ensure swift progress through the game.

fastidious /fæsˈtɪdiəs/ *adj.* **1.** hard to please; excessively critical: *a fastidious taste.* **2.** anxious to achieve the best result; particular: *fastidious attention to detail.* –**fastidiously**, *adv.* –**fastidiousness**, *n.*

fast lane *n.* **1.** the right-hand lane on a highway, often used for overtaking. –*phr.* **2.** life in the fast lane, an urban lifestyle characterised by activity and pace.

fast-track *v.t.* **1.** to move (people, oneself, etc.) into or through a system with unusual speed. **2.** to bring (something) about with unusual speed: *the government fast-tracked the construction of the bridge.* –*v.i.* **3.** to move at unusual speed towards a goal. –*adj.* **4.** relying on or relating to a fast track.

fat /fæt/ *adj.* (**fatter, fattest**) **1.** having much flesh other than muscle; fleshy; corpulent; obese. **2.** having much edible flesh; well-fattened: *to kill a fat lamb.* **3.** consisting of, resembling, or containing fat. **4.** fertile, as land. **5.** profitable, as an office: *a fat job in government.* **6.** yielding excess: *a fat profit.* **7.** thick; broad; extended. **8.** plentiful. **9.** plentifully supplied. –*n.* **10.** any of several white or yellowish substances, greasy to the touch, forming the chief part of the adipose tissue of animals and also found in plants. **11.** animal or human tissue containing much of this substance, lying under the skin and having the function of storing energy and maintaining body warmth. **12.** the richest or best part of anything. **13.** especially profitable or advantageous work. **14.** (*pl.*) livestock fattened for sale. **15.** *Colloq.* (*taboo*) an erection. **16.** *Colloq.* overtime. –*phr.* **17. a fat chance**, *Colloq.* little or no chance. **18. a fat lot of ...**, *Colloq.* little or no ... **19. crack a fat**, *Colloq.* (*taboo*) to get an erection. **20. it isn't over till the fat lady sings**, *Colloq.* the outcome is unknown until the very end. **21. live on one's fat**, to consume reserves; live on one's capital. **22. the fat is in the fire**, an irrevocable step has been taken, resulting in dire consequences. **23. the fat of the land**, the trappings of luxury, especially rich food and drink. –**fatly**, *adv.* –**fatness**, *n.* –**fatten**, *v.* –**fatty**, *adj.*

fatal /ˈfeɪtl/ *adj.* **1.** causing death: *a fatal accident.* **2.** causing destruction or ruin: *an action that is fatal to the success of a project.* **3.** decisively important; fateful: *the fatal day finally arrived.* **4.** proceeding from or decreed by fate; inevitable. –**fatally**, *adv.* –**fatalness**, *n.*

fatalism /ˈfeɪtəlɪzəm/ *n.* **1.** the doctrine that all events are subject to fate or inevitable predetermination. **2.** the acceptance of all things and events as inevitable; submission to fate. –**fatalist**, *n.* –**fatalistic** /feɪtəˈlɪstɪk/, *adj.* –**fatalistically** /feɪtəˈlɪstɪkli/, *adv.*

fatality /fəˈtæləti, feɪ-/ *n.* (*pl.* -**ties**) **1.** a disaster resulting in death; a calamity or misfortune. **2.** someone who is killed in an accident or disaster.

fate /feɪt/ *n.* **1.** fortune; lot; destiny. **2.** a divine decree or a fixed sentence by which the order of things is prescribed. **3.** something that is inevitably predetermined. **4.** a prophetic declaration of what must be. –*v.t.* **5.** (*now only in the passive*) to predetermine as by the decree of fate; destine.

fateful /'feɪtfəl/ adj. **1.** involving momentous consequences; decisively important. **2.** fatal, deadly, or disastrous. **3.** controlled by irresistible destiny. **4.** prophetic; ominous. –**fatefully**, adv. –**fatefulness**, n.

father /'faðə/ n. **1.** a male parent. **2.** any male ancestor, especially the founder of a people, family, or line. **3.** a father-in-law, stepfather, or adoptive father. **4.** someone who exercises paternal care over another; a fatherly protector or provider: *a father to the poor.* **5.** one of the leading men of a city, etc. **6. a.** (*oft. upper case*) a title of reverence, as for Church dignitaries, officers of monasteries, monks, confessors, and priests. **b.** a person bearing this title. –v.t. **7.** to be the father of; procreate or generate; give origin or rise to (a child). **8.** to originate; be the author of. –phr. **9. how's your father**, *Chiefly Brit. Colloq.* sexual play; hanky-panky **10. the father of a ...**, *Colloq.* the biggest; a very big: *the father of a hiding.* –**fatherhood**, n. –**fatherly**, adj.

father-in-law n. (pl. **fathers-in-law**) the father of one's husband or wife.

fathom /'fæðəm/ n. (pl. **fathoms** or, *especially collectively*, **fathom**) **1.** a unit of depth in the imperial system equal to 6 ft or 1.8288 m, used in nautical measurements. *Symbol*: fm –v.t. **2.** to reach in depth by measurement in fathoms; sound; try the depth of; penetrate to or find the bottom or extent of. **3.** to measure the depth of by sounding. **4.** to penetrate to the bottom of; understand thoroughly. –**fathomable**, adj. –**fathomless**, adj. –**fathomer**, n.

fatigue /fə'tig/ n. **1.** (a cause of) weariness from bodily or mental exertion. **2.** *Physiol.* a temporary lessening of the proper functioning of organs, tissues, cells, etc., after too much use. **3.** (*usu. with a modifier*) a reduced capacity to respond in an appropriate way to a specified need, duty, etc., due to prolonged and repeated exposure to the same situation or emotion, or to messages of exhortation on the issue, etc.: *compassion fatigue*; *safe-sex fatigue.* **4.** *Mechanics* the weakening of material subjected to stress. **5.** Also, **fatigue duty.** *Mil.* labour of a generally non-military kind such as cleaning or cooking. –verb (**-tigued, -tiguing**) –v.t. **6.** to weary with bodily or mental effort; drain. –v.i. **7.** to grow weary as a result of exertion; tire. –**fatigued**, adj. –**fatigueless**, adj.

fatuous /'fætʃuəs/ adj. **1.** foolish, especially in an unconscious, complacent manner; silly. **2.** unreal; illusory. –**fatuously**, adv. –**fatuousness**, n.

fatwa /'fætwa/ n. a religious decree issued by a Muslim scholar qualified to issued such decrees. Also, **fatwah.**

faucet /'fɔsət/ n. *Chiefly US* any device for controlling the flow of liquid from a pipe or the like by opening or closing an orifice; a tap; a cock.

fault /fɔlt, fɒlt/ n. **1.** a defect or imperfection; a flaw; a failing. **2.** an error or mistake. **3.** a misdeed or transgression. **4.** delinquency; culpability; cause for blame. **5.** *Geol., Mining* a break in the continuity of a body of rock or of a vein, with dislocation along the plane of fracture. **6.** *Tennis, etc.* **a.** a failure to serve the ball legitimately within the prescribed limits. **b.** a ball which when served does not land in the proper section of the opponent's court. **7.** *Showjumping* a scoring unit used in recording improper execution of jumps by contestants. **8.** *Sport* an infringement of the rules which results in a warning or a penalty. –v.i. **9.** *Geol.* to undergo a fault or faults. **10.** to commit a fault. –v.t. **11.** *Geol.* to cause a fault in. **12.** to find fault with, blame, or censure. –phr. **13. at fault, a.** open to censure; blamable. **b.** puzzled; astray. **c.** (of hounds) unable to pick up a lost scent. **14. find fault**, (sometimes fol. by *with*) find something wrong; complain. **15. in fault**, open to censure; blamable. **16. to a fault**, excessively. –**faulty**, adj. –**faultless**, adj.

fault line n. **1.** *Geol.* the line along which the movement in an earthquake is liable to occur. **2.** *Sociology* a difference which may become socially divisive, such as class, gender, race, etc. Also, **faultline.**

faun /fɔn/ n. (in Roman mythology) one of a class of rural deities represented as men with the ears, horns, and tail, and later also the hind legs, of a goat.

fauna /'fɔnə/ n. (pl. **-nas** or **-nae**) **1.** the animals of a given region or period, taken collectively (as distinguished from the plants or *flora*). **2.** a treatise on the animals of a given region or period. –**faunal**, adj.

faux fur /foʊ 'fɜ/ n. **1.** imitation fur: *the resurgence of the popularity of leather and faux fur.* **2.** a garment, especially a coat, made of faux fur: *resplendent in a full-length faux fur.*

faux pas /foʊ pa/ n. (pl. **faux pas** /foʊ paz, 'foʊ pa/) a false step; a slip in manners; a breach of etiquette.

favour /'feɪvə/ n. **1.** a kind act; something done or granted out of goodwill, rather than from justice or for remuneration: *ask a favour.* **2.** kindness; kind approval. **3.** a state of being approved, or held in regard: *in favour, out of favour.* **4.** excessive kindness; unfair partiality: *show undue favour to someone.* **5.** a gift bestowed as a token of goodwill, kind regard, love, etc. **6.** (pl.) consent to sexual intimacy. –v.t. **7.** to regard with favour. **8.** to have a preference for; treat with partiality. **9.** to be favourable to; facilitate. **10.** to deal with gently: *favour a lame leg.* **11.** to aid or support. –phr. **12. in favour of, a.** in support of; on the side of. **b.** to the advantage of. **c.** (of a cheque, etc.) payable to. Also, **favor. –favourer**, n. –**favouringly**, adv. –**favourless**, adj.

favourable /'feɪvərəbəl, -vrəbəl/ adj. **1.** affording aid, advantage, or convenience: *a favourable position.* **2.** manifesting favour; inclined to aid or approve. **3.** (of an answer) granting what is desired. **4.** promising well: *the signs are favourable.* Also, **favorable.** –**favourableness**, n. –**favourably**, adv.

favourite /'feɪvərət, -vrət/ n. **1.** a person or thing regarded with special favour or preference. **2.** *Sport* a competitor considered likely to win. **3.** *Racing* the horse, dog, etc., which is most heavily backed. **4.** a person treated with special (especially undue) favour, as by a ruler. –adj. **5.** regarded with particular favour or preference: *a favourite child.* Also, **favorite.**

favouritism /'feɪvərətɪzəm, -vrə-/ n. **1.** the favouring of one person or group over others having equal claims. **2.** the state of being a favourite. **3.** the state of being the favourite in a race, competition, etc.: *suffering from favouritism, the horse ran at low odds.* Also, **favoritism.**

fawn¹ /fɔn/ n. **1.** a young deer. **2.** a buck or doe of the first year. **3.** a light yellowish colour. –v.i. **4.** (of deer) to bring forth young.

fawn² /fɔn/ v.i. **1.** to seek notice or favour by servile demeanour. **2.** to show fondness by crouching, wagging the tail, licking the hand, etc. (said especially of dogs). –**fawner**, n. –**fawningly**, adv.

fax /fæks/ n. Also, **facsimile. 1.** a method of transmitting documents or pictures along a telephone line. **2.** a document so transmitted. **3.** a machine which transmits and receives graphic data along a telephone line. –v.t. **4.** to send (a document, picture, etc.) by fax. –v.i. **5.** to send a fax.

faze /feɪz/ v.t. *Colloq.* to disturb; discomfit; daunt.

fear /fɪə/ n. **1.** a painful feeling of impending danger, evil, trouble, etc.; the feeling or condition of being afraid. **2.** a specific instance of such a feeling. **3.** anxiety; solicitude. **4.** reverential awe, especially towards God. **5.** a cause for fear. –v.t. **6.** to regard with fear; be afraid of. **7.** to have reverential awe of. –v.i. **8.** to have fear; be afraid. –phr. **9. fear for**, to be fearful or anxious concerning: *they feared for their lives; I fear for his health.*

10. for fear of, in order to avoid or prevent. **11. no fear**, *Colloq.* certainly not. **–fearer**, *n.* **–fearless**, *adj.*

fearful /'fɪəfəl/ *adj.* **1.** causing, or apt to cause, fear. **2.** feeling fear, dread, or solicitude: *I am fearful of him doing it.* **3.** full of awe or reverence. **4.** showing or caused by fear. **5.** *Colloq.* extremely bad, large, etc. **–fearfully**, *adv.* **–fearfulness**, *n.*

fearsome /'fɪəsəm/ *adj.* **1.** causing fear. **2.** afraid; timid. **–fearsomely**, *adv.* **–fearsomeness**, *n.*

feasible /'fizəbəl/ *adj.* **1.** capable of being done, effected, or accomplished: *a feasible plan.* **2.** likely; probable: *a feasible theory, a feasible excuse.* **–feasibility** /fizə-'bɪləti/, **feasibleness**, *n.* **–feasibly**, *adv.*

feast /fist/ *n.* **1.** a periodical celebration or festival having special religious or other significance. **2.** a rich and elaborate meal or entertainment especially one for many or important guests; banquet. **3.** an abundant quantity of anything eaten or giving pleasure: *a feast of oysters; a feast of music.* **4.** something highly agreeable: *a feast for the eyes.* *–v.i.* **5.** to have or eat a feast (def. 2); eat sumptuously: *to feast for a week.* **6.** to look with delight at something pleasing: *to feast on someone's beauty.* *–v.t.* **7.** to provide or entertain with a feast. **8.** to delight; gratify. **–feaster**, *n.* **–feasting**, *n.*

feat /fit/ *n.* **1.** a noteworthy or extraordinary act or achievement, usually displaying boldness, skill, etc. **2.** an action; deed.

feather /'fɛðə/ *n.* **1.** one of the epidermal appendages which together constitute the plumage of birds, being typically made up of a hard, tubelike portion (the quill) attached to the body of the bird, which passes into a thinner, stemlike distal portion (the rachis) bearing a series of slender processes (barbs) which unite in a bladelike structure (web) on each side. **2.** kind or character: *birds of a feather flock together.* **3.** something very light, weak, or small. **4.** *Rowing* the act of feathering. *–v.t.* **5.** to provide with feathers, as an arrow. **6.** to clothe or cover with, or as with, feathers. **7.** *Rowing* to turn (an oar) after a stroke so that the blade becomes nearly horizontal, and hold it thus as it is moved back into position for the next stroke. **8.** to touch the controls of (a machine) lightly so as to cause it to respond gently and evenly. *–v.i.* **9.** (of a wave off the shore) to break very slowly, developing a white cap. **10.** *Rowing* to feather an oar. *–phr.* **11. a feather in one's cap**, a mark of distinction; an honour. **12. feather one's nest**, to provide for or enrich oneself. **13. in fine feather**, in excellent health and spirits. **14. in full feather**, **a.** (of a bird) with all its adult plumage. **b.** decked out in one's best clothes, formal uniform, etc. **15. in high feather**, in a state of great excitement. **16. make the feathers fly**, to cause confusion; create disharmony. **17. show the white feather**, to show cowardice. **–feathered**, *adj.* **–featherless**, *adj.* **–featherlike**, *adj.*

featherweight /'fɛðəweit/ *n.* **1.** a light weight division in boxing. **2.** a boxer of this weight class. **3.** a very light or insignificant person or thing.

feature /'fitʃə/ *n.* **1.** any part of the face: *his eyes are his worst feature.* **2.** an outstanding part or quality: *good surfing beaches are a feature of the Australian coast.* **3.** the main film in a cinema program. **4.** a special article, column, cartoon, etc., in a newspaper or magazine. **5.** a nonfiction radio or television program designed to entertain and inform. *–v.t.* **6.** to present or give prominence to: *to feature a new series of plays; to feature a special range of goods.* *–v.i.* **7.** to be a feature or distinctive mark of: *fine lines feature very largely in Aboriginal painting.* **8.** (fol. by *in*) to be prominent: *the Minister features often in the news.* **–featureless**, *adj.*

febri- a word element meaning 'fever', as in *febrifuge.*

febrile /'fɛbraɪl, fi-/ *adj.* relating to or marked by fever; feverish.

February /'fɛbruəri, 'fɛbjuri, -jəri/, *Orig. US* /'fɛbjəwɛri/ *n.* the second month of the year, containing ordinarily 28 days, in leap years 29.

feckless /'fɛkləs/ *adj.* inconsistent and shifting in resolve; irresponsible. **–fecklessly**, *adv.* **–fecklessness**, *n.*

fecund /'fɛkənd, 'fik-/ *adj.* capable of producing offspring, or fruit, vegetation, etc., in abundance; prolific; fruitful; productive. **–fecundity**, *n.*

fed /fɛd/ *v.* **1.** past tense and past participle of **feed**. *–phr.* **2. fed up (to the back teeth)**, *Colloq.* (sometimes fol. by *with*) annoyed; frustrated.

Fed /fɛd/ *n. Colloq.* (*also lower case*) a federal police officer.

federal /'fɛdərəl, 'fɛdrəl/ *adj.* **1.** of or relating to a compact or a league, especially a league between nations or states. **2. a.** of or relating to a union of states under a central government distinct from the individual governments of the separate states: *the federal government of Australia.* **b.** favouring a strong central government in such a union. **c.** relating to such a central government: *federal offices.* *–n.* **3.** an advocate of federation or federalism. **–federalism**, *n.* **–federalist**, *n.* **–federally**, *adv.*

federate *v.t.* /'fɛdəreɪt/ **1.** to join or bring together in a league or federation. **2.** to organise on a federal basis. *–v.i.* /'fɛdəreɪt/ **3.** to unite in a federation. *–adj.* /'fɛdərət, 'fɛdrət/ **4.** allied; federated: *federate nations.* **–federator**, *n.*

federation /fɛdə'reɪʃən/ *n.* **1.** the formation of a political unity with a central government, from a number of separate states, etc., each of which keeps control of its own internal affairs. **2.** the political unity so formed. *–adj.* **3.** of the style of architecture, etc., common at the time of the federation of the six Australian states: *a federation house.*

fee /fi/ *n.* **1.** a payment for services: *a doctor's fee.* **2.** a sum paid for a privilege: *an admission fee.* **3.** a charge allowed by law for the service of a public officer. **–feeless**, *adj.*

feeble /'fibəl/ *adj.* **1.** physically weak, as from age, sickness, etc. **2.** weak intellectually or morally: *a feeble mind.* **3.** lacking in force, strength, or effectiveness. **–feebleness**, *n.* **–feeblish**, *adj.* **–feebly**, *adv.*

feed /fid/ *verb* (**fed**, **feeding**) *–v.t.* **1.** to give food to; supply with nourishment. **2.** → **breastfeed**. **3.** to provide with the requisite materials for development, maintenance, or operation. **4.** to yield, or serve as, food for. **5.** to furnish for consumption. **6.** to satisfy; minister to; gratify. **7.** to supply for maintenance or to be operated upon, as to a machine. **8.** to use (land) as pasture. **9.** *Colloq.* to provide cues to (an actor, especially a comedian). **10.** *Media* **a.** to supply (data) to a broadcaster: *we'll be feeding footage live to air.* **b.** to supply (a broadcaster) with data: *we'll be feeding CNN with live footage.* *–v.i.* **11.** to take food; eat; graze. **12.** to be nourished or gratified; subsist. *–n.* **13.** food, especially for cattle, etc. **14. a.** milk, or other liquid preparations, for an unweaned baby. **b.** the act of feeding such a baby. **15.** *Colloq.* a meal. **16.** an act of feeding. **17.** a feeding mechanism. **18.** the rate of advance of a cutting mechanism, as a drill or cutting tool. **19.** *Media* data supplied to a media outlet: *a live feed.* *–phr.* **20. feed into**, to enter, so as to form part of a larger mass or collection. **21. feed up**, to give food to (a person or animal) with the object of making them larger, healthier, etc.: *we'll have to feed you up.* **–feeder**, *n.*

feedback /'fidbæk/ *n.* **1.** the returning of a part of the output of any system, especially a mechanical, electronic, or biological one, as input, especially for correction or control purposes, to alter the characteristic sound of conventional musical instruments, etc. **2.** an indication of the reaction of the recipient, as of an audience. **3.** the input of a signal into a microphone from the output of the same system, usually causing a high-pitched screech.

feel /fiːl/ *verb* (**felt**, **feeling**) –*v.t.* **1.** to perceive or examine by touch. **2.** to have a sensation (other than sight, hearing, taste, and smell) of. **3.** to find or pursue (one's way) by touching, groping, or cautious moves. **4.** to be or become conscious of. **5.** to form an impression; believe: *I felt it was going to rain; I felt the presence of a stranger in the room.* **6.** to be emotionally affected by: *to feel one's disgrace keenly.* **7.** to experience the effects of: *the whole region felt the storm.* **8.** to have a specified sensation or impression: *to feel oneself slighted.* **9.** to have a general or thorough conviction of. –*v.i.* **10.** to have perception by touch or by any nerves of sensation other than those of sight, hearing, taste, and smell: *the blind develop an ability to feel.* **11.** to make examination by touch; grope: *he felt for her hand; I felt in the bag.* **12.** to have mental sensations or emotions: *I was too exhausted to feel.* –*v.* (*copular*) **13.** to be consciously, in emotion, opinion, etc.: *to feel happy; to feel angry; to feel sure.* **14.** to have a sensation of being: *to feel warm; to feel free.* **15.** to seem (in the impression produced): *that feels strange to me; how does it feel to be rich?* –*n.* **16.** a quality of an object that is perceived by feeling or touching: *a soapy feel.* **17.** an act of feeling. **18.** a sensation of something felt; a vague mental impression or feeling. **19.** the sense of touch: *soft to the feel.* **20.** *Colloq.* the precise manner of doing, using, etc.: *you'll soon get the feel of it.* –*phr.* **21.** **feel for** (or **with**), to have sympathy or compassion for. **22.** **feel like**, to have a desire or inclination for. **23.** **feel like death warmed up**, *Colloq.* to feel extremely ill. **24.** **feel oneself**, **a.** to be in one's usual mental or physical state. **b.** to masturbate **25.** **feel out**, to make exploratory moves in order to assess possible reaction: *we felt out the opposition; we felt out the situation.* **26.** **feel up to**, *Colloq.* to be well enough to be capable of; to be able to cope with.

feeler /ˈfiːlə/ *n.* **1.** a proposal, remark, hint, etc., designed to bring out the opinions or purposes of others. **2.** *Zool.* an organ of touch, such as an antenna or a tentacle.

feel-good factor *n.* **1.** a quality of a film, book, etc., which leaves people feeling positive and optimistic. **2.** personal satisfaction; a feeling of optimism or well-being. Also, **feelgood factor.**

feeling /ˈfiːlɪŋ/ *n.* **1.** the sense of touch. **2.** a particular sensation, emotion or impression: *a feeling of warmth; a feeling of joy; a feeling of inferiority.* **3.** *Psychol.* consciousness itself. **4.** an intuition; premonition: *a feeling that something is going to happen.* **5.** capacity for emotion; pity: *she has no feeling.* **6.** sentiment; opinion: *the general feeling was in favour of the proposal.* **7.** Also, **bad feeling, ill feeling.** bitterness; collective or mutual hostility or ill will: *there was bad feeling over his promotion.* **8.** (*pl.*) sensibilities: *to hurt one's feelings.* **9.** fine emotional endowment: *a person of feeling.* **10.** *Music, etc.* **a.** emotional or sympathetic perception shown by an artist in his work. **b.** the general impression given by a work. **c.** sympathetic appreciation: *to play with feeling.* –*adj.* **11.** that feels; sentient; sensitive; as nerves. **12.** open to emotion; sympathetic: *a feeling person.* **13.** showing emotion: *a feeling look.* –**feelingly**, *adv.*

feet /fiːt/ *n.* **1.** plural of **foot.** –*phr.* **2.** **at someone's feet**, **a.** captive; at someone's mercy. **b.** utterly devoted to someone. **3.** **carry someone out feet first**, *Colloq.* **a.** to carry someone out dead. **b.** to carry someone out in a state of incapacitation, as by being drunk, unconscious, etc. **4.** **fall** (or **land**) **on one's feet**, to be lucky. **5.** **feet first**, *Colloq.* **a.** dead. **b.** thoughtlessly; impetuously.

6. **feet of clay**, an imperfection or blemish in the character of someone which mars the image of perfection. **7.** **get one's feet wet**, *Colloq.* to obtain firsthand and practical experience. **8.** **keep one's feet**, to keep one's balance. **9.** **keep one's feet on the ground**, to retain a sensible and practical outlook. **10.** **put one's feet up**, *Colloq.* to relax or rest, especially by lying down. **11.** **put** (or **set**) **someone on their feet**, **a.** to enable someone to act without help from others; make someone financially independent. **b.** to restore someone to a former position or condition. **12.** **six feet under**, *Colloq.* dead. **13.** **stand on one's own** (**two**) **feet**, to be self-sufficient. **14.** **sweep someone off their feet**, **a.** to cause someone to lose a footing, as a wave, etc. **b.** to impress or overwhelm someone romantically. See **foot.**

feign /feɪn/ *v.t.* **1.** to invent fictitiously or deceptively, as a story or an excuse. **2.** to represent fictitiously; put on an appearance of: *to feign sickness.* **3.** to imitate deceptively. –**feigner**, *n.* –**feigningly**, *adv.*

feijoa /fiˈdʒoʊə/ *n.* a South American bushy evergreen shrub, *Feijoa sellowiana*, with a green fruit similar to guava in texture and taste.

feint¹ /feɪnt/ *n.* **1.** a movement made with the object of deceiving an adversary; appearance of aiming at one part or point when another is the real object of attack. **2.** a feigned or assumed appearance. –*v.i.* **3.** to make a feint. –**feinting**, *n.*

feint² /feɪnt/ *n.* **1.** the lightest weight of line used in printing ruled paper. –*adj.* **2.** ruled with a line of such weight.

feisty /ˈfaɪsti/ *adj.* (**-tier, -tiest**) **1.** excitable; quarrelsome. **2.** showing courage and independence.

feldspar /ˈfɛldspɑː, ˈfɛlspɑː/ *n.* any of a group of minerals, principally aluminosilicates of potassium, sodium, and calcium, and characterised by two cleavages at nearly right angles. They are among the most important constituents of igneous rocks. Also, **felspar.** –**feldspathic** /fɛldˈspæθɪk/, *adj.*

felicitate /fəˈlɪsɪteɪt/ *v.t.* to compliment upon a happy event; congratulate: *to felicitate someone on their good fortune.* –**felicitation** /fəˌlɪsəˈteɪʃən/, *n.* –**felicitator**, *n.*

felicity /fəˈlɪsəti/ *n.* (*pl.* **-ties**) **1.** the state of being happy, especially in a high degree. **2.** an instance of this. **3.** a source of happiness. **4.** a skilful faculty: *felicity of expression.* –**felicitous**, *adj.*

feline /ˈfiːlaɪn/ *adj.* **1.** belonging or relating to the cat family, Felidae, which includes, besides the domestic cat, the lions, tigers, leopards, lynxes, jaguars, etc. **2.** catlike; characteristic of animals of the cat family: *feline softness of step.* **3.** sly; spiteful; stealthy; treacherous. –*n.* **4.** an animal of the cat family. –**felinely**, *adv.* –**felineness**, **felinity** /fəˈlɪnəti/, *n.*

feline agranulocytosis /ˈfiːlaɪn əˌgrænjəloʊsaɪˈtoʊsəs/ *n.* → **feline infectious enteritis.**

feline distemper *n.* → **feline infectious enteritis.**

feline infectious enteritis *n.* an often fatal, highly contagious viral disease of domestic cats, caused by a parvovirus and characterised by fever, somnolence, and diarrhoea; cat fever. *Abbrev.*: FIE Also, **feline agranulocytosis, feline distemper.**

fell¹ /fɛl/ *v.* past tense of **fall.**

fell² /fɛl/ *v.t.* **1.** to cause to fall; knock, strike, or cut down: *to fell an animal; to fell a tree.* **2.** *Sewing* to finish (a seam) by sewing the edge down flat. –**feller**, *n.*

fell³ /fɛl/ *adj. Archaic* **1.** fierce; cruel; dreadful. **2.** destructive; deadly: *fell poison; fell disease.* –*phr.* **3.** **at** (or **in**) **one fell swoop**, in a single action or coordinated series of actions. –**fellness**, *n.*

fell⁴ /fɛl/ *n.* the skin or hide of an animal; a pelt.

fellatio /fəˈleɪʃioʊ/ *n.* oral stimulation of the male genitals. Also, **fellation** /fəˈleɪʃən/.

fellow /ˈfɛloʊ, ˈfɛlə/ *n.* **1.** *Colloq.* a man or boy. **2.** a friend; companion; comrade: *my dear fellow.*

3. someone belonging to the same class; equal; peer: *the equal of his fellows.* **4.** one of a pair; mate or match: *put the glove with its fellow.* **5.** (*usu. upper case*) a member of a learned or professional society: *a Fellow of the Royal Australian College of Surgeons.* **6.** *Educ.* a scholar or postgraduate student in a college or university, who is engaged in research rather than teaching. –*adj.* **7.** having the same position, work, condition, etc.: *fellow students.*

fellowship /ˈfɛloʊʃɪp, ˈfɛlə-/ *n.* **1.** a sharing or unity of interest, feeling, etc.: *He feels fellowship with other workers.* **2.** companionship, especially between members of the same church. **3.** an association of people with similar tastes, interests, etc. **4. a.** the position or salary of a fellow of a university, etc. **b.** a foundation for the support of a fellow in a college or university.

felon /ˈfɛlən/ *n. Law* someone who has committed a felony.

felony /ˈfɛləni/ *n.* (*pl.* **-nies**) *Law* any of various indictable offences, such as murder, burglary, etc., of graver character than those called misdemeanours.

felspar /ˈfɛldspa, ˈfɛlspa/ *n.* → **feldspar.**

felt[1] /fɛlt/ *v.* past tense and past participle of **feel.**

felt[2] /fɛlt/ *n.* **1.** a non-woven fabric of wool, fur, or hair, matted together by pressure. **2.** any matted fabric or material. –*adj.* **3.** relating to or made of felt.

female /ˈfimeɪl/ *adj.* **1.** belonging to the sex which brings forth young, or any division or group corresponding to it. **2.** relating to this sex; feminine. **3.** made up of females: *a female cricket team.* **4.** *Bot.* **a.** indicating or relating to a plant or its reproductive structure which produces or contains elements that need fertilisation. **b.** (of seed plants) pistillate. **5.** *Mechanics* indicating some part, etc., into which a corresponding part fits: *a female outlet*; *a female plug.* –*n.* **6.** a human being of the sex which conceives and brings forth young; a woman or girl. **7.** any animal of corresponding sex. **8.** *Bot.* a pistillate plant. –**femalely**, *adv.* –**femaleness**, *n.*

feminine /ˈfɛmənən/ *adj.* **1.** relating to a woman. **2.** belonging to the female sex. **3.** marked by qualities thought to be possessed by women, as sympathy, gentleness, etc. **4.** effeminate. **5.** *Gram.* indicating or relating to one of the three genders of Latin, German, etc., or one of the two of French, Spanish, etc. **6.** *Poetry* **a.** (of a line) ending with an extra unaccented syllable. **b.** (of rhyming words) having a stressed first syllable followed by one or more unaccented syllables, as in *motion*, *notion.* –*n.* **7.** *Gram.* **a.** the feminine gender. **b.** a noun of that gender. –**femininely**, *adv.* –**femininity** /fɛməˈnɪnəti/, **feminineness**, *n.*

feminism /ˈfɛmənɪzəm/ *n.* advocacy of equal rights and opportunities for women, especially the extension of their activities in social and political life. –**feminist**, *n.*, *adj.*

femto- a prefix denoting 10^{-15} of a given unit, as in *femtogram.* Symbol: f

femur /ˈfima/ *n.* (*pl.* **femurs** or **femora** /ˈfɛmərə/) *Anat.* a bone in the limb of an animal extending from the pelvis to the knee; the thighbone.

fence /fɛns/ *n.* **1.** an enclosure or barrier, usually of wire or wood, as around or along a field, garden, etc. **2.** *Colloq.* **a.** a person who receives and disposes of stolen goods. **b.** the place of business of such a person. **3.** an obstacle to be jumped in show-jumping or steeplechasing. –*verb* (**fenced**, **fencing**) –*v.t.* **4.** to provide (a plot of land, etc.) with a fence or fences: *to fence the garden.* –*v.i.* **5.** to use a sword, foil, etc., in defence and attack or in exercise or exhibition of skill in that art. **6.** to parry arguments; strive to evade giving direct answers. **7.** *Colloq.* to receive stolen goods. –*phr.* **8. be on the fence**, to be undecided. **9. fence in**, to enclose by surrounding with a fence or fences.

10. fence off, to shut out by means of a fence. **11. over the fence**, *Aust.* immoderate; objectionable; unacceptable: *her behaviour was quite over the fence.* **12. rush one's fences**, to act precipitately. **13. sit on the fence**, to remain neutral; to avoid a conflict. –**fenceless**, *adj.* –**fencing**, *n.*

fend /fɛnd/ *v.t.* Also, **fend off. 1. a.** to ward off: *to fend off blows.* **b.** to parry: *he fended the questions skilfully.* –*phr.* **2. fend for**, to provide for: *to fend for oneself.*

fender /ˈfɛndə/ *n.* **1.** a device on the front of a railway engine, or the like, for clearing the track of obstructions. **2.** *US* a mudguard of a motor vehicle. **3.** a low metal guard in front of an open fireplace, to keep back falling coals.

feng shui /fɛŋ ˈʃweɪ, fʌŋ, ˈʃwi/ *n.* **1.** the balancing of Yin and Yang in one's physical surroundings in accordance with Chinese tradition achieved by following rules in relation to the architecture and location of buildings, the position of objects and furniture in a room, etc. –*adj.* **2.** of or relating to feng shui: *a feng shui expert.*

fennel /ˈfɛnəl/ *n.* **1.** an umbelliferous plant, *Foeniculum vulgare*, having yellow flowers, and bearing aromatic fruits, which, as well as the leaves and stem, are used in cookery and medicine. **2.** the fruits (**fennel seed**) of this plant. **3.** any of various more or less similar plants, as *Ferula communis* (**giant fennel**), a tall ornamental herb.

-fer a noun suffix meaning 'bearing', 'producing', 'yielding', 'containing', 'conveying', with a corresponding adjective in *-ferous*, as *conifer* (a coniferous tree).

feral /ˈfɛrəl/ *adj.* **1.** wild, or existing in a state of nature, as animals (or, sometimes, plants). **2.** having reverted to the wild state, as from domestication. **3.** of or characteristic of wild animals: *the feral state.* **4.** *Aust. Colloq.* living as or looking like a feral (def. 8). **5.** *Aust. Colloq.* disgusting; gross. **6.** *Aust. Colloq.* excellent; admirable. –*n.* **7.** a domesticated animal which has reverted to the wild state. **8.** *Aust.* a person who espouses environmentalism to the point of living close to nature in more or less primitive conditions and who deliberately shuns the normal code of society with regard to dress, habitat, hygiene, etc. –*phr.* **9. go feral**, **a.** (of domesticated animals) to revert to the wild state: *cats that had gone feral.* **b.** *Aust. Colloq.* to lose all self-control in an unrestrained verbal or physical attack on someone.

ferment *n.* /ˈfɜmɛnt/ **1.** any of various agents or substances which cause fermentation, especially: **a.** any of various living organisms (**organised ferments**), as yeasts, moulds, certain bacteria, etc. **b.** any of certain complex substances derived from living cells (**unorganised ferments** or **enzymes**) as pepsin, etc. **2.** agitation; excitement; tumult. –*v.t.* /fəˈmɛnt, fɜ-/ **3.** to cause to undergo fermentation. **4.** to inflame; foment. –*v.i.* /fəˈmɛnt, fɜ-/ **5.** to be fermented; undergo fermentation. **6.** to seethe with agitation or excitement. –**fermentable**, *adj.* –**fermentative**, *adj.*

fermentation /fɜmɛnˈteɪʃən/ *n.* **1.** *Biochem.* the breakdown of complex molecules brought about by a ferment, as in the changing of grape sugar into ethyl alcohol by yeast enzymes. **2.** the act or process of undergoing such a change. **3.** agitation; excitement.

fern /fɜn/ *n.* any of the pteridophytes constituting the order Filicales, distinguished from other pteridophytes in having few leaves, large in proportion to the stems, and bearing sporangia on the undersurface or margin. –**fernlike**, *adj.*

fernbird /ˈfɜnbɜd/ *n.* a small brown and white New Zealand bird, *Bowdleria punctata*, with loosely-barbed tail feathers; matata.

fern land n. NZ land covered or originally covered with bracken.

ferocious /fə'rouʃəs/ adj. savagely fierce, as a wild beast, person, action, aspect, etc.; violently cruel. **–ferocity**, n. **–ferociously**, adv. **–ferociousness**, n.

-ferous an adjective suffix meaning 'bearing', 'producing', 'yielding', 'containing', 'conveying', as in auriferous, balsamiferous, coniferous, pestiferous.

ferret /'fɛrət/ n. 1. a domesticated, albinistic, red-eyed form of the polecat, used for hunting rabbits and rats in their burrows. 2. Cricket Colloq. a person with very poor batting skills (one who goes in after the rabbits). Compare **rabbit**[1] (def. 2). –v.i. 3. to search about. –phr. 4. **ferret out**, to search out or bring to light: to ferret out the facts. **–ferreter**, n. **–ferrety**, adj.

ferri- a word element meaning 'iron', implying especially combination with ferric iron or ferrites.

ferric /'fɛrɪk/ adj. of or containing iron, especially in the trivalent state.

ferro- a word element meaning 'iron'. In chemistry, ferro- implies especially combination with ferrous iron as opposed to ferric iron. Also, **ferri-**.

ferrous /'fɛrəs/ adj. of or containing iron, especially in the divalent state.

ferrule /'fɛrul, -rəl/ n. 1. a metal ring or cap put round the end of a post, stick, handle, etc., for strength or protection. 2. (in steam boilers) a bush for expanding the end of a flue. Also, **ferrel**.

ferry /'fɛri/ n. (pl. **-ries**) 1. a service with terminals and floating equipment, for transport from shore to shore across a body of water, usually narrow, such as a river, harbour, or strait. 2. a ferryboat. 3. a vessel used in such a service. –v.t. (**-ried, -rying**) 4. to carry or convey over water in a boat or plane. 5. to transport to and from a place, especially on a regular basis: he ferried the children to and from school.

fertile /'fɜtaɪl/ adj. 1. bearing or capable of bearing vegetation, crops, etc., abundantly, as land or soil. 2. bearing offspring freely; prolific. 3. abundantly productive or inventive: a fertile imagination. 4. able to produce offspring. 5. conducive to productiveness: fertile showers. **–fertilely**, adv. **–fertileness**, n.

fertilisation /fɜtəlaɪ'zeɪʃən/ n. 1. the act or process of fertilising. 2. the state of being fertilised. 3. Biol. a. the union of male and female gametic nuclei. b. fecundation or impregnation of animals or plants. 4. the enrichment of soil for the production of crops, etc. Also, **fertilization**.

fertilise /'fɜtəlaɪz/ v.t. 1. Biol. a. to render (an egg, ovum, or female cell) capable of development by union with the male element, or sperm. b. to fecundate or impregnate (an animal or plant). 2. to make fertile; enrich (soil, etc.) for crops, etc. 3. to make productive. Also, **fertilize**. **–fertilisable**, adj.

fertiliser /'fɜtəlaɪzə/ n. any material used to fertilise the soil, especially a commercial or chemical manure. Also, **fertilizer**.

fertility /fɜ'tɪləti/ n. 1. the state or quality of being fertile. 2. Biol. the ability to produce offspring; power of reproduction. 3. (of soil) the quality of supplying nutrients in proper amounts for plant growth when other factors are favourable.

fertility clinic n. a medical centre which specialises in problems relating to human fertility and in treatments such as IVF.

fervent /'fɜvənt/ adj. having or showing great warmth and earnestness of feeling: a fervent admirer; a fervent plea. **–fervently**, adv. **–fervour, fervor**, n.

fescue /'fɛskju/ n. 1. any grass of the genus Festuca, some species of which, especially **Chewings fescue** and **creeping red fescue**, are cultivated for pasture or lawns. 2. any of several grasses belonging to other related genera, as Vulpia, **rat's-tail fescue**.

fess /fɛs/ phr. **fess up**, Colloq. to own up, especially reluctantly.

-fest a suffix indicating a period of festive or enthusiastic activity in the thing named: lovefest, musicfest, talkfest.

fester /'fɛstə/ v.i. 1. to generate purulent matter; suppurate. 2. to cause ulceration, or rankle, as a foreign body in the flesh. 3. to putrefy or rot. 4. to rankle, as a feeling of resentment. **–festering**, adj.

festival /'fɛstəvəl/ n. 1. a periodic religious or other feast: the festival of Christmas. 2. any time of feasting; an anniversary for festive celebration. 3. a public festivity, with performances of music, processions, exhibitions, etc., often timed to coincide with some natural event, such as spring, the blossoming of certain trees, etc.: Moomba festival. 4. a series of musical, dramatic, or other performances. –adj. 5. of, relating to, or befitting a feast or holiday; festal.

festive /'fɛstɪv/ adj. joyful; merry. **–festively**, adv. **–festiveness**, n.

festivity /fɛs'tɪvəti/ n. (pl. **-ties**) 1. a festive celebration or occasion. 2. (pl.) festive proceedings. 3. festive character; festive gaiety or pleasure.

festoon /fɛs'tun/ n. 1. a string or chain of flowers, foliage, ribbon, etc., suspended in a curve between two points. 2. a decorative representation of this, as in architectural work or on pottery. –v.t. 3. to adorn with, or as with, festoons.

fetch /fɛtʃ/ v.t. 1. to go and return with, or bring to or from a particular place: to fetch a book from another room. 2. to cause to come to a particular place or condition; succeed in bringing: to fetch a doctor. 3. to realise or bring in (a price, etc.). 4. to take (a breath). 5. to utter (a sigh, groan, etc.). 6. to deal or deliver (a stroke, blow, etc.). –v.i. 7. Hunting to retrieve game. –phr. 8. **fetch and carry**, to do minor menial jobs. 9. **fetch up**, Colloq. a. to reach a goal or final state; end up: you'll fetch up in prison. b. to vomit. c. to come to a sudden stop, as a ship running aground, or a walker suddenly pausing. d. to bring to a sudden stop. e. US to bring up (a child, etc.). **–fetcher**, n.

fetching /'fɛtʃɪŋ/ adj. charming; captivating. **–fetchingly**, adv.

fete /feɪt/ n. 1. a function to raise money for charity, church, school, etc., frequently outdoor and combining the activities of bazaar and fair. 2. a feast or festival. 3. a festal day; a holiday. –v.t. 4. to give a hospitable public reception to (someone); lionise. Also, **fête**.

fetid /'fɛtəd, 'fitəd/ adj. having a strong, offensive smell; stinking. Also, **foetid**. **–fetidly**, adv. **–fetidness, fetidity** /fə'tɪdəti/, n.

fetish /'fɛtɪʃ, 'fit-/ n. 1. a material, commonly an inanimate object, regarded with awe as being the embodiment or habitation of a potent spirit, or as having magical potency because of the materials and methods used in compounding it. 2. any object of blind reverence. 3. an obsession or fixation, usually expressed in ritualistic behaviour. **–fetishism**, n. **–fetishist**, n. **–fetishlike**, adj.

fetlock /'fɛtlɒk/ n. a part of a horse's leg situated behind the joint between the cannon bone and the great pastern bone, and bearing a tuft of hair.

fetta /'fɛtə/ n. a soft, ripened, white cheese cured in brine, originally from Greece, and made traditionally from goats' or ewes' milk, but now also from cows' milk. Also, **feta**.

fetter /'fɛtə/ n. 1. a chain or shackle placed on the feet. 2. (usu. pl.) anything that confines or restrains. –v.t. 3. to put fetters upon. 4. to confine; restrain.

fettle /'fɛtl/ phr. **in fine fettle**, 1. in good condition. 2. in good health or spirits.

fettuccine /fɛtəˈtʃiːni/ *n.* pasta cut into long narrow strips.

fetus /ˈfiːtəs/ *n.* the young of an animal in the womb or in the egg, especially in its later stages. Also, **foetus**. –**fetal, foetal**, *adj.*

feud /fjuːd/ *n.* **1.** a bitter, continuous hostility, especially between two families, clans, etc. **2.** a quarrel or contention. –*v.i.* **3.** to conduct a feud.

feudal /ˈfjuːdl/ *adj.* **1.** of or relating to a feoff or fee: *a feudal estate.* **2.** of or relating to the holding of land in a feoff or fee. **3.** of or relating to the feudal system: *feudal law.* –**feudalism**, *n.* –**feudality** /fjuˈdælɪti/, *n.* –**feudally**, *adv.*

fever /ˈfiːvə/ *n.* **1.** a morbid condition of the body characterised by undue rise of temperature, quickening of the pulse, and disturbance of various bodily functions. **2.** any of a group of diseases in which high temperature is a prominent symptom: *scarlet fever.* **3.** intense nervous excitement. –*phr.* **4. fever pitch**, the height of excitement (especially of crowds). –**fevered, feverish**, *adj.* –**feverless**, *adj.*

few /fjuː/ *adj.* **1.** not many; a small number: *few clouds in the sky.* –*pron.* **2.** a small number of people or things: *few would agree.* –*phr.* **3. a few, a.** a small number. **b.** (*ironic*) (especially with reference to alcoholic drink) a not small number: *he had sunk a few by then.* **4. few and far between**, rare; infrequent. **5. quite a few** or **a fair few** or **a good few** or **some few**, a fairly large number. **6. the few**, the minority. –**fewness**, *n.*

fey /feɪ/ *adj.* **1.** as if enchanted, under a spell, aware of supernatural influences. **2.** light-headed; eccentric; slightly crazy. **3.** dying; in the state of heightened awareness formerly supposed to presage death. –**feyly**, *adv.* –**feyness**, *n.*

fez /fɛz/ *n.* (*pl.* **fezzes**) a man's felt cap, usually of a red colour, having the shape of a truncated cone, and ornamented with a long black tassel, especially as worn by some Muslim men in the Middle East; formerly the national headdress of the Turks during the Ottoman period.

fiancée /fiˈɒnseɪ/ *n.* a woman engaged to be married. Also, **fiancee**. –**fiancé, fiance**, *masc. n.*

fiasco /fiˈæskoʊ/ *n.* (*pl.* **-cos**) an ignominious failure.

fiat /ˈfiːæt, ˈfiət/ *n.* an authoritative decree, sanction, or order.

fib /fɪb/ *Colloq.* –*n.* **1.** a trivial falsehood. –*v.i.* (**fibbed, fibbing**) **2.** to tell a fib.

fibr- a word element meaning 'fibre', as in *fibrin*. Also, **fibri-, fibro-**.

fibre /ˈfaɪbə/ *n.* **1.** a fine threadlike piece, as of cotton, or asbestos; filament. **2.** filaments collectively. **3.** matter made from such threads either natural or artificial: *muscle fibre*; *cloth fibre.* **4. a.** fibrous matter from plants, used in industry, etc. **b.** this matter as an essential part of the diet; roughage. –*phr.* **5. moral fibre**, strength of character. Also, *US*, **fiber**. –**fibrous, fibred**, *adj.* –**fibreless**, *adj.*

fibreglass /ˈfaɪbəɡlɑs/ *n.* (*from trademark*) a material consisting of extremely fine filaments of glass which are combined in yarn and woven into fabrics, or are used in masses as an insulator or used embedded in plastic as a construction material for boat hulls, light car bodies, etc.; glass fibre. Also, *Chiefly US*, **fiberglass, fiberglas**.

fibre optics *n. Telecommunications* **1.** the process of passing light along bundles of very fine fibres by internal reflection, used in medicine to transmit images, and in communication (in the form of light pulses) to transmit information. **2.** the study of this process.

fibro /ˈfaɪbroʊ/ (*from trademark*) *Aust.* –*n.* **1.** compressed asbestos and cement used for building materials such as wallboard, corrugated roofing, pipes, etc. –*adj.* **2.** made of this material: *a fibro house.* Also, **fibrocement**.

fibromyalgia /faɪbroʊmaɪˈældʒə/ *n. Med.* a musculoskeletal disorder, the cause of which is unknown, which has symptoms such as widespread pain and fatigue in the muscle ligaments and tendons. Also, **fibromyalgia syndrome**.

fibrositis /faɪbrəˈsaɪtəs/ *n. Pathol.* an inflammatory change in fibrous tissue, such as muscle sheaths, ligament tendons, fasciae, and the like, causing pain and difficulty in movement.

fibula /ˈfɪbjələ/ *n.* (*pl.* **-las** *or* **-lae** /-liː/) **1.** *Anat.* the outer and thinner of the two bones of the lower leg, extending from the knee to the ankle. **2.** *Archaeology* a clasp or brooch, usually more or less ornamented. –**fibular**, *adj.*

-fic an adjective suffix meaning 'making', 'producing', 'causing', as in *colorific, frigorific, horrific, pacific, prolific, soporific.*

-fication a suffix of nouns of action or state corresponding to verbs ending in *-fy*, as in *deification, pacification.*

fickle /ˈfɪkl/ *adj.* likely to change; capricious; irresolute. –**fickleness**, *n.* –**fickly**, *adv.*

fiction /ˈfɪkʃən/ *n.* **1.** the branch of literature comprising works of imaginative narration, especially in prose form. **2.** works of this class, such as novels or short stories. **3.** something feigned, invented, or imagined; a made-up story. –**fictional**, *adj.* –**fictionist**, *n.*

fictionalise /ˈfɪkʃənəlaɪz/ *v.t.* to turn (a real person, place, event, etc.) into a piece of fiction by altering details, motivations, sequence of events, etc. Also, **fictionalize**. –**fictionalisation**, *n.*

fictitious /fɪkˈtɪʃəs/ *adj.* **1.** counterfeit; false; not genuine: *fictitious names.* **2.** relating to or consisting of fiction; imaginatively produced or set forth; created by the imagination: *a fictitious hero.* –**fictitiously**, *adv.* –**fictitiousness**, *n.*

fictive /ˈfɪktɪv/ *adj.* invented or imagined; not real.

-fid an adjective suffix meaning 'divided', 'lobed', as in *bifid, trifid, multifid, pinnatifid.*

fiddle /ˈfɪdl/ *v.i.* **1.** to make aimless movements, as with the hands. **2.** to play on the fiddle. **3.** to trifle. **4.** *Colloq.* to profit or gain by surreptitious crookedness. –*v.t.* **5.** to play (a tune) on a fiddle. **6.** *Colloq.* to contrive by illegal or underhand means. **7.** *Colloq.* to falsify: *he was caught fiddling the accounts.* –*n.* **8.** a violin. **9.** any stringed musical instrument of the viol class. **10.** *Colloq.* a manipulation of the laws, rules etc., to execute an underhand transaction. –*phr.* **11. fit as a fiddle**, in excellent health. **12. have a face as long as a fiddle**, *Colloq.* to look dismal. **13. on the fiddle**, manipulating or covering up illicit money-making schemes. **14. play second fiddle**, to take a minor or secondary part. –**fiddler**, *n.*

fiddly /ˈfɪdli/ *adj.* (**-lier, -liest**) *Colloq.* difficult or exacting, as something small done with the hands.

fidelity /fəˈdɛləti/ *n.* (*pl.* **-ties**) **1.** the strict observance of promises, duties, etc. **2.** loyalty. **3.** conjugal faithfulness. **4.** strict adherence to truth or fact; (of persons) honesty, truthfulness; (of descriptions, copies, etc.) correspondence with the original. **5.** the ability of an electronic system, such as an amplifier, transmitter, etc., to reproduce accurately in its output the desired characteristics of its input.

fidget /ˈfɪdʒət/ *v.i.* **1.** to move about restlessly or impatiently; be uneasy. –*v.t.* **2.** to cause to fidget; make uneasy. –*n.* **3.** (*oft. pl.*) condition of restlessness or uneasiness. **4.** someone who fidgets. –**fidgety**, *adj.*

fiduciary /fɪˈdjuːʃəri/ *n.* (*pl.* **-ries**) **1.** *Law* a person to whom property is entrusted to hold, control, or manage for another. –*adj.* **2.** *Law* of or relating to the relation between a fiduciary and his or her principal: *a fiduciary capacity*; *a fiduciary duty.* **3.** depending on public confidence for value or currency.

fiefdom /'fifdəm/ *n.* **1.** a feudal lord's estate. **2.** a powerful person's area of control.

field /fild/ *n.* **1.** a piece of open or cleared ground, especially one suitable for raising animals or growing crops. **2.** a piece of ground used for sports or contests. **3.** *Sport* **a.** all those in a competition, especially a race. **b.** the runners in a race other than the leaders. **c.** those players who are fielding. **4.** *Mil.* a battlefield. **5.** any region characterised by a certain feature or product: *a gold field; a field of ice.* **6.** the background of a painting, shield, flag, etc. **7.** a range of activity, interest, study, etc.: *my field of work is law.* **8.** a place of study, work, etc., away from the office, laboratory, etc., especially one where basic material is gathered for later study. **9.** *Physics* an area or space influenced by some force or thing: *electric field; magnetic field; gravitation field.* **10.** *Physics* the whole area which can be seen through or projected by an optical instrument at one time. **11.** *Elect.* **a.** the main magnetic field of an electric motor or generator. **b.** the structure in a dynamo designed to establish magnetic lines of force in an armature. **12.** *Computers* a specified area of a record. *–v.t.* **13.** *Cricket, etc.* to place (a player) into the field to play. **14.** to deal with: *he fielded difficult questions. –v.i.* **15.** to act as a fielder. *–adj.* **16.** *Sport, etc.* of, or happening on, a field rather than a track: *pole vault and long jump are field events.* **17.** of, or conducted in, open air: *we'll have a field study.*

field day *n.* **1.** a day devoted to outdoor activities or sports. **2.** a day on which a hunt meets. **3. a.** a day on which military or civil security operations in the field are practised. **b.** a day of display of manoeuvres, techniques, etc. **4.** a day or occasion of unrestricted enjoyment, amusement, success, etc.

fielder /'fildə/ *n. Cricket, etc.* any member of the team which is fielding, as opposed to the one which is batting.

field glasses *pl. n.* a compact binocular telescope for use outdoors. See **binocular**.

field goal *n.* (in Rugby Football, etc.) a goal scored by drop-kicking the ball over the opponents' goal during play; drop goal.

fiend /find/ *n.* **1.** a devil or evil spirit. **2.** a diabolically cruel or wicked person. **3.** *Colloq.* a person or thing that causes mischief or annoyance. **4.** *Colloq.* someone who is devoted or addicted to some game, sport, etc.: *a bridge fiend; a drug fiend.* **–fiendish,** *adj.*

fierce /fiəs/ *adj.* (**fiercer, fiercest**) **1.** wild or vehement in temper, appearance, or action: *fierce animals, fierce looks.* **2.** violent in force, intensity, etc.: *fierce winds.* **3.** furiously eager or intense: *fierce competition.* **4.** *Colloq.* extreme; unreasonable: *the prices are fierce.* **–fiercely,** *adv.* **–fierceness,** *n.*

fiery /'faiəri/ *adj.* (**-rier, -riest**) **1.** consisting of, with, or containing fire: *a fiery furnace.* **2.** like or suggestive of fire: *a fiery heat; a fiery red colour.* **3.** having strong feelings; passionate: *a fiery speech.* **–fierily,** *adv.* **–fieriness,** *n.*

fiesta /fi'estə/ *n.* **1.** a religious celebration; a saint's day. **2.** a holiday or festival.

fife /faif/ *n.* **1.** a high-pitched flute much used in military music. *–v.i.* **2.** to play on a fife. **–fifer,** *n.*

fifteen /fif'tin/ *n.* **1.** a cardinal number, ten plus five. **2.** a symbol for this number, as 15 or XV. **3.** a set or group of fifteen, as a rugby union team. *–adj.* **4.** amounting to fifteen in number. *–pron.* **5.** fifteen people or things. **–fifteenth,** *adj.*

fifth /fifθ/ *adj.* **1.** next after the fourth. **2.** being one of five equal parts. *–n.* **3.** a fifth part, especially of one (⅕). **4.** the fifth member of a series. **5.** *Music* **a.** a note on the fifth degree from another note (counted as the first). **b.** the interval between such notes. **–fifthly,** *adv.*

fifth column *n.* a body of persons residing in a country who are in sympathy with its enemies, and who are serving enemy interests or are ready to assist an enemy attack. **–fifth columnist,** *n.*

fifth generation *n.* a theoretical stage of computer development, in which computers would have certain desirable capabilities, such as the ability to learn from past experiences, to make inferences, to understand natural language, and perform other functions in a way that resembles human thought.

fifty /'fifti/ *n.* (*pl.* **-ties**) **1.** a cardinal number, ten times five (10×5). **2.** a symbol for this number, as 50 or L. **3.** a set of fifty persons or things. **4.** (*pl.*) the numbers from 50 to 59 of a series, especially years of person's age or the years of a century. *–adj.* **5.** amounting to fifty in number: *fifty apples. –pron.* **6.** fifty people or things: *fifty came to the party.* **–fiftieth,** *adj., n.*

fifty-fifty *Colloq. –adv.* **1.** with profits, responsibilities, etc., equally shared. *–adj.* **2.** in equal quantities: *a fifty-fifty mixture.* **3.** of or relating to an arrangement by which profits, responsibilities, etc., are shared equally between two parties.

fig /fig/ *n.* Also, **fig tree.** any tree or shrub of the moraceous genus *Ficus*, especially a small tree, *F. carica*, native to south-western Asia, bearing a turbinate or pear-shaped fruit which is eaten fresh or preserved or dried. **2.** the fruit of such a tree or shrub, or of any related species. **3.** a gesture of contempt. *–phr.* **4. not to give a fig,** to have no concerns, anxieties or scruples.

fight /fait/ *n.* **1.** a battle or combat. **2.** any quarrel, contest, or struggle. **3.** ability or inclination to fight: *there was no fight left in him; to show fight. –verb* (**fought, fighting**) *–v.i.* **4.** to engage in battle or in single combat; attempt to defeat, subdue, or destroy an adversary. **5.** to contend in any manner; strive vigorously for or against something: *to fight to the death. –v.t.* **6.** to contend with in battle or combat; war against. **7.** to contend with or against in any manner. **8.** to carry on (a battle, duel, etc.). **9.** to maintain (a cause, quarrel, etc.) by fighting or contending. **10.** to make (one's way) by fighting or striving. *–phr.* **11. fight down,** to repress or overcome. **12. fight it out,** to struggle till a decisive result is obtained. **13. fight like Kilkenny cats,** to fight ferociously. **14. fight off,** to struggle against; drive away. **15. fight shy of,** to keep carefully aloof from (a person, affair, etc.). **–fightable,** *adj.* **–fighter,** *n.* **–fighting,** *n.*

figment /'figmənt/ *n.* **1.** a mere product of the imagination; a pure invention. **2.** a feigned, invented, or imagined story, theory, etc.

fig tree *n.* → **fig** (def. 1).

figurative /'figjərətiv, 'figə-/ *adj.* **1.** of or relating to a figure of speech, especially a metaphor; metaphorical; not literal: *a figurative expression.* **2.** metaphorically so called: *this remark was a figurative boomerang.* **3.** using or characterised by figures of speech. **4.** representing by means of a figure or likeness, as in drawing or sculpture. **5.** representing by a figure or emblem; emblematic. **–figuratively,** *adv.* **–figurativeness,** *n.*

figure /'figə/ *n.* **1.** a written symbol other than a letter. **2.** a numerical symbol, especially an Arabic numeral. **3.** an amount or value expressed in numbers. **4.** (*pl.*) the use of numbers in calculating: *poor at figures.* **5.** form or shape, as determined by outlines or exterior surfaces: *round in figure; bulky in figure.* **6.** the bodily form or frame: *a slender figure; a graceful figure.* **7.** an individual bodily form, or a person with reference to form or appearance: *a tall figure stood in the doorway.* **8.** a person as he or she appears, or as presented before the eyes of the world: *political figures.* **9.** a character or personage, especially one of distinction: *a figure in society.* **10.** the appearance or impression made by a person, or sometimes a thing: *the figure presented to the world.* **11.** a diagram or pictorial representation in a book, especially a textbook. **12.** a representation, pictorial or sculptured, of something, especially of the human form. **13.** an emblem or type: *the dove is a figure of peace.* **14.** *Rhetoric* a figure of speech. **15.** a device or pattern, as in cloth. **16.** a movement, pattern, or series of movements in skating. **17.** a distinct movement or division of a dance. **18.** *Geom.* a combination of geometrical elements disposed in a particular form or shape: *the circle, square, and polygon are plane figures; the sphere, cube, and polyhedron are solid figures.* –*v.t.* **19.** to compute or calculate. **20.** to express in figures. **21.** to mark or adorn with figures, or with a pattern or design. **22.** to represent by a pictorial or sculptured figure, a diagram, or the like; picture or depict; trace (an outline, etc.). **23.** to judge, reason, reflect. –*v.i.* **24.** to compute or work with numerical figures. **25.** to make a figure or appearance; be conspicuous: *his name figures in the report.* **26.** *Colloq.* to be in accordance with expectations or reasonable likelihood. –*phr.* **27. cut a (fine) figure**, to create a brilliant impression, especially with regard to clothes and manner. **28. figure on**, *Colloq.* **a.** to count or rely on. **b.** to take into consideration. **29. figure out**, to solve; understand; make out. **30. go figure**, *Chiefly US Colloq.* an expression used after a statement to indicate that the listener should try to make sense of it because the speaker cannot. –**figurer**, *n.*

figurehead /'fɪgəhɛd/ *n.* **1.** someone who is nominally the head of a society, community, etc., but has no real authority or responsibility. **2.** *Naut.* an ornamental figure, such as a statue or bust, placed over the cutwater of a ship.

figure of speech *n.* a literary mode of expression, such as a metaphor, simile, personification, antithesis, etc., in which words are used out of their literal sense, or out of ordinary locutions, to suggest a picture or image, or for other special effect; a trope.

figure-skating *n.* skating in which particular preselected patterns are traced out on the ice by the skater. –**figure-skater**, *n.*

figurine /fɪgəˈrin, fɪgjə-, ˈfɪgjurin/ *n.* a small ornamental figure of pottery, metalwork, etc.; statuette.

filament /'fɪləmənt/ *n.* **1.** a very fine thread or threadlike structure; a fibre or fibril. **2.** a single element of textile fibre (such as silk), or mechanically produced fibre (such as rayon or nylon). **3.** *Elect.* (in an incandescent lamp) the threadlike conductor in the bulb which is raised to incandescence by the passage of current.

filch /fɪltʃ/ *v.t.* to steal (especially something of small value); pilfer. –**filcher**, *n.*

file¹ /faɪl/ *n.* **1.** any device, as a cabinet, in which papers, etc., are arranged or classified for convenient reference. **2.** a collection of papers so arranged or classified; any orderly collection of papers, etc. **3.** *Computers* a collection of data with a unique name, held on a storage device such as a magnetic disk. **4.** a line of persons or things arranged one behind another, especially a group of soldiers moving in formation; single file. **5.** one of the vertical lines of squares on a chessboard. –*v.t.* **6.** to place in a file. **7.** to arrange (papers, records, official documents, etc.) methodically for preservation and convenient reference. **8.** to place on record, register (a petition, etc.). **9.** *Law* to bring (a suit) before a court of law. **10.** *Journalism* to send (a report, article, blog, etc.) for publication. –*v.i.* **11.** to march in a file or line, one after another, as soldiers. –*phr.* **12. on file**, on or in a file, or in an orderly arrangement for convenient reference, as papers. –**filer**, *n.*

file² /faɪl/ *n.* **1.** a metal (usually steel) tool of varying size and form, with numerous small cutting ridges or teeth on its surface, for smoothing or cutting metal and other substances. –*v.t.* **2.** to reduce, smooth, cut, or remove with or as with a file. –**filer**, *n.*

file extension *n. Computers* (in some operating systems) the final part of a filename, following a full stop or other separator and often identifying the file type.

file transfer protocol *n.* → FTP (def. 1).

filial /'fɪliəl, -jəl/ *adj.* **1.** relating to or befitting a son or daughter: *filial obedience.* **2.** bearing the relation of a child to a parent. –**filially**, *adv.* –**filialness**, *n.*

filibuster /'fɪləbʌstə/ *n.* **1.** the use of obstructive tactics, such as making prolonged speeches or using irrelevant material, in order to delay legislative action. **2.** someone who engages in an unlawful military expedition into a foreign country to inaugurate or to aid a revolution. –*v.i.* **3.** to impede legislation by using obstructive tactics, especially by making long speeches. **4.** to act as a freebooter, buccaneer, or irregular military adventurer. –**filibusterer** /fɪləˈbʌstərə/, *n.* –**filibusterism** /fɪləˈbʌstərɪzəm/, *n.* –**filibusterous** /fɪləˈbʌstərəs/, *adj.*

filigree /'fɪləgri/ *n.* **1.** ornamental work of fine wires, especially lacy jewellers' work of scrolls and arabesques. **2.** anything very delicate or fanciful. –*adj.* **3.** composed of or resembling filigree. –*v.t.* (**-greed**, **-greeing**) **4.** to adorn with or form into filigree. Also, **filagree, fillagree.**

fill /fɪl/ *v.t.* **1.** to make full; put as much as can be held into. **2.** to occupy to the full capacity: *water filled the basin; the crowd filled the hall.* **3.** to supply to fullness or plentifully: *to fill a house with furniture; to fill the heart with joy.* **4.** to satisfy, as food does. **5.** to be plentiful throughout: *fish filled the rivers.* **6.** to extend throughout; pervade completely: *the perfume filled the room.* **7.** to furnish (a vacancy or office) with an occupant or incumbent. **8.** to occupy and perform the duties of (a position, post, etc.): *to fill the position of salesman.* **9.** to execute (a business order). **10.** to supply (a blank space) with written matter, decorative work, etc. **11.** to meet (requirements, etc.) satisfactorily: *the book fills a long-felt want.* **12.** to make up or compound (a medical prescription). **13.** to stop up or close: *to fill a tooth; to fill a crevice.* –*v.i.* **14.** to become full: *the hall filled rapidly; her eyes filled with tears.* **15.** to become distended, as sails fill with the wind. –*n.* **16.** a full supply; enough to satisfy want or desire: *to eat one's fill.* **17.** an amount of something sufficient for filling; a charge. **18.** a mass of earth, stones, etc., used to fill a hollow, etc. –*phr.* **19. fill in**, **a.** to fill (a hole, hollow, blank, etc.) with something put in. **b.** to complete (a document, design, etc.) by filling blank spaces. **c.** to put in or insert so as to fill: *to fill in omitted names.* **d.** to occupy, spend (time). **e.** to act as a substitute. **20. fill out**, **a.** to distend (sails, etc.). **b.** to become larger or fuller, as the figure, etc. **c.** to complete the details of (a plan, design, etc.). **21. fill someone in**, to provide someone with all relevant information. **22. fill someone's shoes**, to replace someone effectively, usually in some specified capacity: *can you fill her shoes as an administrator?* **23. fill the bill**, *Colloq.* to satisfy the requirements of the case; be or do what is wanted. **24. fill up**, to fill completely. **25. one's fill**, *Colloq.* *I've had my fill of murder mysteries for a while.* –**filler**, *n.*

fillet /'fɪlət/ *n.* **1.** a narrow strip, as of ribbon, wood, or metal. **2.** a strip of any material used for binding. **3.** *Cookery* **a.** a strip or long (flat or thick) boned piece of fish or chicken. **b.** a standard cut of beef or pork, containing little fat and no bone. –*v.t.* **4.** *Cookery* to cut or prepare (meat or fish) as a fillet.

filling /'fɪlɪŋ/ *n.* **1.** something that is put in to fill something: *the filling of a pie.* **2.** a substance in plastic form, as cement, amalgam, or gold foil, used to close a cavity in a tooth.

fillip /ˈfɪləp/ *n.* anything that tends to rouse, excite, or revive; a stimulus.

filly /ˈfɪli/ *n.* (*pl.* **-lies**) **1.** a female horse not past its fourth birthday; a young mare. **2.** *Colloq.* (*dated*) a young woman.

film /fɪlm/ *n.* **1.** a thin layer or coating. **2.** a thin sheet of any material. **3.** *Photography* **a.** a sensitive coating, as of gelatine and silver bromide, used on photographic plate or film (def. 3b). **b.** a strip of cellulose material covered with this substance, used in cameras. **4.** *Film* **a.** a film strip containing an ordered set of pictures or photographs of objects in motion projected on to a screen so rapidly as to give the appearance that the objects or actors are moving. **b.** a story, event, etc., recorded in such a way and shown in a cinema, on television or video, etc. **c.** films in general: *the history of Australian film.* **d.** the creative art of filmmaking: *this director is one of the icons of film.* *–v.t.* **5.** to cover with a film, or thin skin. **6.** *Film* **a.** to photograph with a film camera. **b.** to reproduce in the form of a film or films: *to film a novel.* *–v.i.* **7.** to become covered by a film. **8.** to be reproduced in a film: *this story films easily.*

film clip *n.* **1.** a short extract from a film, usually shown as part of promotional material. **2.** → **video clip.**

film noir /fɪlm ˈnwɑ/ *n.* **1.** a black-and-white film genre, especially of the 1940s, concerned with the darker side of human nature, and typified by sombre, shadowy photography and an overall feeling of depression or pessimism. **2.** any later film style emulating this genre. **3.** a film of this genre or emulating it. *–adj.* **4.** of or relating to this genre: *a famous film noir actor.*

filmography /fɪlmˈɒɡrəfi/ *n.* (*pl.* **-phies**) a listing of films selected on the basis of containing the work of a particular actor, director, etc., or of dealing with a particular subject. *–***filmographic, filmographical,** *adj.* *–***filmographer,** *n.*

filmy /ˈfɪlmi/ *adj.* (**-mier, -miest**) being, resembling, or covered with a thin layer or film. *–***filmily,** *adv.* *–***filminess,** *n.*

filo pastry /ˈfiloʊ peɪstri, ˈfaɪloʊ peɪstri/ *n.* a paper-thin pastry made from flour and water, often used in Greek cookery. Also, **fillo pastry.**

filter /ˈfɪltə/ *n.* **1.** any device through which liquids are strained to remove unwanted particles or to recover solids. **2.** any of various similar devices, used for removing dust from air, unwanted elements from tobacco smoke, or blocking certain kinds of light rays. **3.** *Colloq.* a filter tip on a cigarette. **4.** *Physics* a device for picking out waves or currents of certain frequencies. *–v.t.* **5.** to remove by the action of a filter. **6.** to act as a filter for. **7.** to pass through a filter. *–v.i.* **8.** to pass through, or as through, a filter. *–***filterer,** *n.* *–***filterable,** *adj.*

filth /fɪlθ/ *n.* **1.** foul matter; offensive or disgusting dirt. **2.** foul condition: *the filth of the bathroom.* **3.** moral impurity, corruption, or obscenity. **4.** foul language. **5.** *Colloq.* people one does not approve of; annoying or disgusting people: *filth like you shouldn't be allowed on the streets.* **6.** *Colloq.* something excellent: *the waves were absolute filth.*

filthy /ˈfɪlθi/ *adj.* (**-thier, -thiest**) **1.** foul with, characterised by, or having the nature of filth; disgustingly dirty. **2.** vile; obscene. **3.** (as a general epithet of strong condemnation) highly offensive or objectionable: *filthy lucre.* **4.** *Colloq.* very unpleasant: *filthy weather.* **5.** *Colloq.* upset; annoyed. *–phr. Colloq.* **6. be filthy on,** to be angry with. **7. filthy rich,** very rich. *–***filthily,** *adv.* *–***filthiness,** *n.*

filtrate /ˈfɪltreɪt/ *v.t., v.i.* **1.** → **filter.** *–n.* **2.** liquid which has been passed through a filter. *–***filtration** /fɪlˈtreɪʃən/, *n.*

fin /fɪn/ *n.* **1.** any of several wing- or paddle-like organs on the body of a fish, used for propelling, steering or balancing. **2.** *Naut.* a fin-shaped plane on a submarine or boat. **3.** a small, fin-shaped attachment underneath the rear of a surfboard. **4.** → **flipper. 5.** any part, of a machine, etc., like a fin. *–***finless,** *adj.* *–***finlike,** *adj.*

final /ˈfaɪnəl/ *adj.* **1.** relating to or coming at the end; last in place, order, or time. **2.** bringing something to an end; conclusive or decisive: *a final argument.* *–n.* **3.** that which is last; that which forms an end of a series. **4.** (*oft. pl.*) something final, as a last game or contest in a series. **5.** (*pl.*) *Chiefly Brit., US* an examination at the end of a course. *–***finality,** *n.*

finale /fəˈnɑli, -ˈnɑleɪ/ *n.* **1.** the last piece, division, or movement of a concert, opera, or musical composition. **2.** Also, **the grand finale.** the concluding part of any performance, course of proceedings, etc.

finalise /ˈfaɪnəlaɪz/ *v.t.* to put into final form; conclude, settle. Also, **finalize.** *–***finalisation** /faɪnəlaɪˈzeɪʃən/, *n.*

finalist /ˈfaɪnəlɪst/ *n.* someone who is entitled to take part in the final trial or round, as of an athletic contest.

finance /ˈfaɪnæns, fəˈnæns/ *n.* **1.** the management of public revenues; the conduct or transaction of money matters generally, especially such as affect the public, as in the fields of banking and investment. **2.** (*pl.*) pecuniary resources, as of a sovereign, state, company, or an individual; revenue. *–verb* (**-anced, -ancing**) *–v.t.* **3.** to supply with means of payment; provide capital for; to obtain or furnish credit for. **4.** to manage financially. *–v.i.* **5.** to conduct financial operations; manage finances. *–***financial,** *adj.* *–***financier,** *n.*

financial institution *n.* an organisation offering financial services, as a bank, building society, finance company, or credit union.

financial institutions duty *n.* a tax on receipts by financial institutions, such as banks, credit unions, etc.; abolished on introduction of the GST. *Abbrev.*: FID

financial year *n.* any twelve-monthly period at the end of which a government, company, etc., balances its accounts and determines its financial condition. Also, **fiscal year.**

finch /fɪntʃ/ *n.* **1.** any of numerous small, often strikingly coloured, birds of the family Passeridae, including grassfinches, firetails and mannikins, as the **red-browed finch,** *Neochmia temporalis,* of eastern Australia; Australian finch. **2.** any of various small birds of the family Fringillidae, including the buntings, linnets, etc., many having heavy, conical, seed-cracking bills and some of which, as the goldfinch and the greenfinch, have been introduced into Australia.

find /faɪnd/ *verb* (**found, finding**) *–v.t.* **1.** to come upon by chance; meet: *to find a dollar in the street.* **2.** to learn, attain, or obtain by search or effort: *to find wisdom.* **3.** to discover: *to find gold.* **4.** to recover (something lost): *to find your keys under the couch.* **5.** to gain or regain the use of: *to find one's tongue.* **6.** to succeed in attaining; gain by effort: *to find safety in flight*; *to find occasion for revenge.* **7.** to provide or furnish. **8.** to discover by experience or to perceive: *to find something to be true*; *to find something new to be developing.* **9.** to ascertain by study or calculation: *to find the sum of several numbers.* **10.** *Law* **a.** to determine after judicial inquiry: *to find a person guilty.* **b.** to pronounce as an official act (an indictment, verdict, or judgement). *–v.i.* **11.** to determine an issue after judicial inquiry: *the jury found for the plaintiff.* *–n.* **12.** the act of finding: *his find was widely reported.* **13. a.** a thing found, especially one of great monetary or other value, such as a gold deposit, an archaeological site, etc. **b.** a thing or person found and then discovered to be unexpectedly pleasing or valuable: *the new cook was a real find.* *–phr.* **14. find fault,** (sometimes fol. by *with*) to find cause of blame or complaint; express dissatisfaction. **15. find oneself,** to discover one's true vocation; learn one's abilities and how to use them. **16. find one's feet, a.** to be able to stand and walk. **b.** to be able to act independently without the help of others. **17. find out, a.** to discover in the course of time or experience; discover by search or inquiry; ascertain by study. **b.** to detect, as in an offence; discover the actions or character of; discover or detect (a fraud, imposture, etc.). **c.** to discover the identity of (a person). –**findable,** *adj.*

fine[1] /faɪn/ *adj.* **1.** of the highest or of very high grade or quality. **2.** free from imperfections or impurities. **3.** (of weather) **a.** sunny. **b.** *Meteorol.* without rain. **4.** choice, excellent, or admirable: *a fine sermon.* **5.** consisting of minute particles: *fine sand.* **6.** very thin or slender: *fine thread.* **7.** keen or sharp, as a tool. **8.** delicate in texture: *fine linen.* **9.** delicately fashioned. **10.** highly skilled or accomplished: *a fine musician.* **11.** characterised by or affecting refinement or elegance: *a fine lady.* **12.** polished or refined: *fine manners.* **13.** ornate or elegant: *fine writing.* **14.** delicate or subtle: *a fine distinction.* **15.** showy or smart; smartly dressed. **16.** good-looking or handsome. **17.** (of gold, silver, etc.) having a high proportion of pure metal, or having the proportion as specified. **18.** *Cricket* towards fine leg. **19.** in good health; well: *I'm feeling fine.* **20.** acceptable; satisfactory: *if you haven't got any butter, margarine will be fine.* –*adv.* **21.** *Colloq.* in a fine manner; excellently or very well; elegantly; delicately; with nicety. –*v.i.* **22.** to become fine or finer. **23.** Also, **fine down**. to become fine or clear; clarify: *the cider will fine if it is left to stand.* –*v.t.* **24.** to make fine or finer. **25.** to clarify (wines or spirits) by fining. –*phr.* **26. fine down,** to become more elegantly slim: *her figure will fine down as she gets older.* **27. fine up,** (of weather) to become fine. –**fineness,** *n.*

fine[2] /faɪn/ *n.* **1.** a sum of money exacted as a penalty for an offence or dereliction. –*v.t.* **2.** to subject to a fine, or pecuniary penalty; punish by a fine. –*phr.* **3. in fine,** finally; in short. –**fineable, finable,** *adj.*

fine arts *pl. n.* the arts which seek expression through beautiful or significant modes, such as architecture, sculpture, painting, ceramics, engraving, and music.

fine leg *n. Cricket* **1.** a leg-side fielding position almost directly behind the wicket. **2.** a fielder in this position.

fine motor skills *pl. n.* those physical skills required for coordinated small muscle movements, such as picking up small items between the thumb and a finger. Compare **gross motor skills**.

finery /ˈfaɪnəri/ *n.* fine or showy dress, ornaments, etc.

finesse /fəˈnɛs/ *n.* **1.** delicacy of execution; subtlety of discrimination. **2.** artful management; craft; strategy. **3.** *Bridge, etc.* an attempt to win a trick by bluffing the opposition into withholding their winning card, allowing a low card to win. **4.** (of wine) fineness of character; elegance. –*v.t.* (**-nessed, -nessing**) **5.** to accomplish by finesse or artifice.

finger /ˈfɪŋgə/ *n.* **1.** any of the terminal members of the hand, especially one other than the thumb. **2.** a part of a glove made to receive a finger. **3.** the breadth of a finger as a unit of length; digit. **4.** the length of a finger, 12 cm, or approximately that. **5.** something like or likened to a finger: *a finger of toast; a finger of land; fish fingers.* –*v.t.* **6.** to touch with the fingers; handle; toy or meddle with. **7.** to pilfer; filch. **8.** *Colloq.* to point out; accuse. **9.** *Music* **a.** to play on (an instrument) with the fingers. **b.** to perform or mark (a passage of music) with a certain fingering (**fingering** def. 2). –*phr.* **10. burn one's fingers,** to get hurt or suffer loss from meddling with or engaging in anything. **11. give someone the finger,** to make an offensive gesture at someone by holding up the index finger. **12. have a**

finger in the pie, to have a share in the doing of something. **13. keep** (or **have**) **one's fingers crossed,** to wish for good luck, or success in a particular enterprise. **14. lay a finger on,** to touch or assault in the mildest degree: *if you lay so much as a finger on him I'll kill you.* **15. not lift a finger,** to do nothing; make no attempt. **16. point the finger,** (sometimes fol. by *at*) to suspect or accuse. **17. pull one's finger out,** *Colloq.* to become active; hurry. **18. put the finger on,** *Colloq.* **a.** to inform against or identify (a criminal) to the police. **b.** to designate as a victim, as of murder or other crime. **19. slip through someone's fingers,** to elude someone, as a missed opportunity. **20. snap one's fingers at,** to show disdain or contempt for. **21. twist round one's little finger,** to dominate; influence easily. –**fingerer,** *n.* –**fingerless,** *adj.*

fingering /ˈfɪŋgərɪŋ/ *n. Music* **1.** the action or method of using the fingers in playing an instrument. **2.** the indication of the way the fingers are to be used in performing a piece of music.

finger lime *n.* **1.** a shrub, *Citrus australasica*, with white flowers and cylindrical fruit containing edible vesicles; found in subtropical rainforest of coastal northern New South Wales and southern Queensland. **2.** the fruit of this shrub.

fingernail /ˈfɪŋgəneɪl/ *n.* the nail at the end of a finger.

fingerprint /ˈfɪŋgəprɪnt/ *n.* **1.** an impression of the markings of the inner surface of the last joint of the thumb or a finger. **2.** such an impression made with ink for purposes of identification. –*v.t.* **3.** to take the fingerprints of.

fingertip /ˈfɪŋgətɪp/ *n.* **1.** the tip of a finger. **2.** a covering used to protect the end of a finger. –*phr.* **3. at one's fingertips, a.** close at hand, within easy reach. **b.** readily at one's disposal, as a result of complete familiarity with the subject.

finicky /ˈfɪnɪki/ *adj.* **1.** excessively fastidious; too particular or fussy. **2.** (of things) overelaborate; containing too much unimportant detail. Also, **finikin, finicking.**

fining /ˈfaɪnɪŋ/ *n.* **1.** the process by which fused glass becomes free from undissolved gases. **2.** the process of clarifying a wine or spirit by adding an agent which binds with unwanted substances such as tannins, forming insoluble deposits which settle out of the liquid as a sediment. **3.** (*pl.*) a substance used in this process.

finish /ˈfɪnɪʃ/ *v.t.* **1.** to bring (action, speech, work, affairs, etc.) to an end or to completion. **2.** to come to the end of (a course, period of time, etc.). **3.** Also, **finish up, finish off.** to use up or consume completely: *to finish your dinner.* **4.** to complete and perfect in detail; put the final touches on. **5.** to put the last treatment or coating on (wood, metal, etc.). –*v.i.* **6.** to come to an end. **7.** to complete a course, etc. –*n.* **8.** the end or conclusion; the last stage. **9.** the end of a hunt, race, etc. **10.** a decisive ending: *a fight to the finish.* **11.** the quality of being finished or completed with smoothness, elegance, etc. **12.** (of wine) the lingering aftertaste. **13.** educational or social polish: *to give a young woman some finish.* **14.** the manner in which a thing is finished in preparation, or an effect imparted in finishing: *a soft finish; a dull finish.* **15.** the surface coating or texture of wood, metal, etc. **16.** something used or serving to finish, complete, or perfect a thing. **17.** woodwork, etc., especially in the interior of a building, not essential to the structure but used for purposes of ornament, neatness, etc. **18.** a final coat of plaster or paint. **19.** a material for application in finishing. **20.** *Football* the conversion of an attacking movement into a goal. –*phr.* **21. finish off,** to overcome completely; destroy or kill. **22. finish up,** *Colloq.* to reach a final condition, circumstance, or goal. –**finisher,** *n.*

finite /ˈfaɪnaɪt/ *adj.* **1.** having bounds or limits; not too great or too small to be measurable. **2.** subject to limitations or conditions, as of space, time, circumstances, or the laws of nature: *finite existence.* –**finitely,** *adv.* –**finiteness,** *n.*

finite verb *n. Gram.* a verb limited by person, number, tense, mood, and aspect (opposed to the infinite forms, participle, infinitive, and gerund, which have only a few limitations).

fink /fɪŋk/ *n. Colloq.* a contemptible or undesirable person, especially one who reneges on an undertaking.

fiord /ˈfiɔd/ *n.* → **fjord.**

fir /fɜ/ *n.* **1.** any of the pyramidal coniferous trees constituting the genus *Abies*, such as *A. balsamea*, the balsam fir. **2.** the wood of such a tree.

fire /ˈfaɪə/ *n.* **1.** the active principle of burning or combustion, manifested by the evolution of light and heat. **2.** a burning mass of material, as on a hearth or in a furnace. **3.** the destructive burning of a building, town, forest, etc.; a conflagration. **4.** flashing light; luminous appearance. **5.** brilliance, as of a gem. **6.** burning passion; ardour; enthusiasm. **7.** vigour; energy. **8.** liveliness of imagination. **9.** heating quality, as of strong drink. **10.** a spark or sparks. **11.** the discharge of firearms: *enemy fire.* **12.** the effect of firing military weapons: *to rain fire on the enemy.* –*v.t.* **13.** to set (something) on fire, usually for a specific purpose: *Aboriginal people used to fire the bush when hunting.* **14.** to supply (a furnace, etc.) with fuel; attend to the fire of (a boiler, etc.). **15.** to expose to the action of fire; subject to heat. **16.** to apply heat to in a kiln for baking or glazing; burn. **17.** to inflame, as with passion; fill with ardour. **18.** Also, **fire up.** to inspire: *the music fired his imagination*; *the news has really fired her up.* **19.** to discharge, as a gun. **20.** to project (a missile) by discharging from a gun, etc. **21.** to dismiss from a job. –*v.i.* **22.** to go off, as a gun. **23.** to discharge a gun, etc. **24.** to hurl a missile. **25.** (of an internal-combustion engine) to cause ignition of the air-fuel mixture in the cylinder or cylinders. **26.** to perform extremely well, successfully, and vigorously: *the team really fired in the second half.* –*phr.* **27. between two fires,** being attacked from both sides. **28. catch fire,** to become ignited. **29. fire away,** (*usu. in the imperative*) *Colloq.* to begin speaking: *fire away – I'm listening.* **30. fire up, a.** to start up (an internal-combustion engine). **b.** to start up (any device with an engine or motor, as a computer, blender, etc.). **c.** to inspire. **31. go through fire and water,** to face any hardship or danger. **32. hang fire,** to delay taking an action or accepting something. **33. lay a fire,** to arrange fuel to be lit. **34. on fire, a.** ignited; burning. **b.** eager; ardent; zealous. **35. play with fire,** to meddle carelessly or lightly with a dangerous matter. **36. set on fire** or **set fire to, a.** to cause to burn. **b.** to excite violently; inflame. **37. take fire, a.** to become ignited. **b.** to become filled with enthusiasm or zeal. **38. under fire, a.** exposed to enemy fire. **b.** under criticism or attack. –**fireable,** *adj.*

fire ant *n.* a small red ant, *Solenopsis invicta*, with a painful burning sting, native to South America, and introduced into the southern United States in the 1930s; in 2001 established in Australia in the Brisbane region; a serious environmental pest.

firearm /ˈfaɪəram/ *n.* a small arms weapon from which a projectile is discharged by the burning of a propellant.

firebreak /ˈfaɪəbreɪk/ *n.* a strip of ploughed or cleared land made to check the spread of fire.

fire brigade *n.* **1.** an organisation set up to fight fires. **2.** a unit of such an organisation.

firebug /ˈfaɪəbʌg/ *n. Colloq.* a person who deliberately starts fires, especially in the bush, gaining gratification from the drama that this creates. Also, **fire bug.**

fire cam *n.* a camera mounted on an observation tower which registers the smoke and flames from a bushfire and triggers an alert, while also providing a record of activity in the area, as for identifying arsonists.

fire-engine *n.* a motor vehicle equipped for fire fighting, now usually having a motor-driven pump for shooting water from fire hydrants, etc., or chemical solutions at high pressure.

fire-escape *n.* a fireproof staircase, or some other apparatus or structure, used to escape from a burning building.

firefighter /ˈfaɪəfaɪtə/ *n.* **1.** someone whose activity or employment is to extinguish fires, especially bushfires. **2.** *Colloq.* → **troubleshooter.** –**firefighting,** *adj.*, *n.*

firefly /ˈfaɪəflaɪ/ *n.* (*pl.* **-flies**) **1.** any of the soft-bodied, nocturnal beetles of the family Lampyridae, which possess abdominal light-producing organs; lightning bug. The luminous larvae or wingless females are called glow-worms. **2.** a fly (**fly¹** def. 17) designed to protect a camp fire.

fire front *n.* the part of a bushfire within which continuous flaming combustion is taking place. Also, **firefront.**

fireground /ˈfaɪəɡraʊnd/ *n.* the area where a wildfire is actively burning. Also, **fire ground.**

fire hazard reduction *n.* → **hazard reduction** (def. 2).

fireman /ˈfaɪəmən/ *n.* (*pl.* **-men**) **1.** a male firefighter. **2.** a man employed to tend fires; a stoker. **3.** *Railways* **a.** a man who tends the fire of a steam locomotive and assists the driver. **b.** the assistant to the driver on a diesel or electric locomotive.

fireplace /ˈfaɪəpleɪs/ *n.* **1.** the part of a chimney which opens into a room and in which fuel is burnt. **2.** any open structure, usually of masonry, for containing fire, as at a camp site.

firepower /ˈfaɪəpaʊə/ *n.* the capacity of a military unit, weapon, etc., to deliver fire.

fire station *n.* a building housing a unit of a fire brigade and its equipment.

firestorm /ˈfaɪəstɔm/ *n.* **1.** an atmospheric phenomenon caused by a large fire, as after the mass bombing of a city, in which a rising column of air above the fire draws in strong winds creating an inferno. **2.** a huge and uncontrollable bushfire, of such magnitude that it creates and sustains its own wind system. Also, **fire storm.**

fire trail *n.* a permanent track cleared through bush to provide firefighters with access to bushfires.

firetrap /ˈfaɪətræp/ *n.* a building which, because of the material or arrangement of the structure, is especially dangerous in case of fire.

firework /ˈfaɪəwɜk/ *n.* **1.** (*usu. pl.*) a combustible or explosive device for producing a striking display of light or a loud noise, often also used in signalling at night, etc. **2.** (*pl.*) **a.** a pyrotechnic display. **b.** a display of anger or bad temper. **c.** an exciting spectacle or performance.

firey /ˈfaɪəri, ˈfaɪri/ *n. Colloq.* a firefighter. Also, **firie.**

firing line *n.* **1.** the positions at which troops are stationed to fire upon the enemy or targets. –*phr.* **2. in the firing line, a.** in the thick of the action. **b.** subjected to vigorous analysis and criticism: *tax issues in the firing line.*

firing squad *n.* a military detachment assigned to execute a condemned person by shooting.

firm¹ /fɜm/ *adj.* **1.** relatively solid, hard or stiff: *firm ground*; *firm texture.* **2.** securely fixed in place. **3.** steady; not shaking or trembling: *a firm hand*; *a firm voice.* **4.** indicating firmness or determination: *a firm look*; *a firm tone.* **5.** (of a belief, decree, agreement, etc.) fixed, settled, or unchangeable. **6.** steadfast or unwavering: *a firm leader.* **7.** not subject to change: *a firm offer.* –*v.t.* **8.** to make firm. –*v.i.* **9.** to become firm.

–adv. **10.** in a firm manner: *stand firm.* **–firmly,** *adv.* **–firmness,** *n.*

firm² /fɜm/ *n.* **1.** a business organisation or partnership. **2.** the name or title under which associated parties transact business: *the firm of Jones & Co.*

firmament /ˈfɜməmənt/ *n.* the vault of heaven; the sky. **–firmamental,** *adj.*

first /fɜst/ *adj.* **1.** being before all others with respect to time, order, rank, importance, etc. (the ordinal of *one*). **2.** *Music* highest or chief among several voices or instruments of the same class: *first alto; first horn.* **3.** *Motor Vehicles* being or relating to a low transmission gear ratio. *–adv.* **4.** before all others or anything else in time, order, rank, etc. **5.** before some other thing, event, etc. **6.** for the first time. **7.** in preference to something else; rather; sooner. **8.** in the first place; firstly. *–n.* **9.** that which is first in time, order, rank, etc. **10.** the beginning. **11.** the first part; the first member of a series. **12.** *Motor Vehicles* first gear. **13.** the first place in a race, etc. **14.** a first-class degree. **15.** (*pl.*) the best quality of certain articles of commerce. *–phr.* **16. at first blush,** at the first view; on first consideration. **17. at first hand,** from the first or original source. **18. at (the) first,** at the beginning or outset. **19. be a first,** to be the first experience of something, or first attempt at doing something: *this tour is a first for me.* **20. draw first blood, a.** (in physical combat) to inflict the first injury. **b.** (in non-physical competition) to gain the initial advantage. **21. first and last,** altogether; in all. **22. first bash,** *Colloq.* the first go: *you can have first bash at this.* **23. first in, best dressed,** *Aust.* an expression meaning that the first person to arrive has an advantage over others in a group. **24. first thing,** before anything else; at once; early. **25. first up, a.** *Aust.* at the first attempt. **b.** before all others: *to race first up.* **26. from the first,** from the beginning or outset. **–firstly,** *adv.*

first aid *n.* emergency aid or treatment given to persons suffering from accident, etc., until the services of a doctor can be obtained.

first-class *adj.* **1.** of the highest or best class or quality. **2.** best-equipped and most expensive: *a first-class carriage.* **3.** denoting a degree bearing the highest class of honours in a university examination. *–adv.* **4.** by first-class conveyance: *to travel first-class.*

first-day cover *n.* an envelope bearing a newly-issued stamp, posted and cancelled on the day of issue.

first-degree *adj.* of a degree which is at the extreme end of a scale, either as the lowest (*first-degree burn*) or the highest (*first-degree murder*).

First Fleeter /fɜst ˈflitə/ *n.* a person whose family can be traced back to someone who came to Australia with the First Fleet in 1788.

firsthand *adv.* /fɜstˈhænd/ **1.** from or at the first or original source; directly. *–adj.* /ˈfɜstˈhænd/ **2.** of or relating to the first or original source. **3.** direct from the original source. Also, **first-hand.**

first language *n.* the language first used by a person for oral communication and often identified with one's nationality; mother tongue. Also, **native language.**

first officer *n.* **1.** → **mate¹** (def. 6). **2.** (in an aircrew) the officer next in seniority to the captain.

first-past-the-post *adj.* of or relating to a voting system in which the candidate who gains the largest number of votes wins. *Abbrev.*: FPP Compare **preferential voting.**

first person *n.* See **person** (def. 10).

first-person shooter *n.* a type of shooter game in which the scene of the action is depicted as the shooter would see it and the screen shows the virtual firearm being used and the player's virtual arm supporting it. *Abbrev.*: FPS Compare **third-person shooter.**

first principle *n.* any law, axiom, or concept which represents the highest degree of generalisation and which depends on fundamental principles.

first refusal *n.* the right of a customer to buy or refuse goods before they can be sold to anyone else.

First World problem *n.* a problem that relates to the affluent lifestyle associated with the First World, that would never arise in the poverty-stricken circumstances of the Third World, as having to settle for plunger coffee when one's espresso machine is not functioning.

fiscal /ˈfɪskəl/ *adj.* **1.** of or relating to the public treasury or revenues. **2.** of or relating to financial matters in general. *–n.* **3.** (in some countries) an official having the function of public prosecutor. **–fiscally,** *adv.*

fiscal policy *n.* the part of a government's economic policy which is involved with revenue raising through taxation and with setting the level and types of expenditure. Compare **monetary policy.**

fiscal year *n.* → **financial year.**

fish /fɪʃ/ *n.* (*pl.* **fishes** *or, especially collectively,* **fish**) **1.** any of various cold-blooded, completely aquatic vertebrates, having gills, fins, and typically an elongated body usually covered with scales. **2.** any of various other aquatic animals. **3.** the flesh of fish used as food. *–v.t.* **4.** to catch or attempt to catch (fish or the like). **5.** to try to catch fish in (a stream, etc.). **6.** to draw (*up, out,* etc.) as by fishing: *to fish a pin out of a crack.* **7.** to search through as by fishing. *–v.i.* **8.** to catch or attempt to catch fish, as by angling or drawing a net. **9.** to search for or attempt to catch on to something under water, in mud, etc., by the use of a dredge, rake, hook, or the like. **10.** to seek to obtain something by artifice or indirectly: *to fish for compliments; to fish for information. –phr.* **11. a poor fish,** *Colloq.* an ineffectual and characterless person. **12. a queer fish,** *Colloq.* an unusual or eccentric person. **13. drink like a fish,** to drink alcoholic liquor to excess. **14. feed the fishes, a.** to vomit over the side of a boat or ship as a result of seasickness. **b.** to drown. **15. fish in troubled waters,** to take advantage of uncertain conditions; profit from the difficulties of others. **16. fish out, a.** to exhaust of fish by fishing. **b.** to obtain by careful search or by artifice. **17. kettle of fish, a.** a mess, muddle, or awkward state of affairs (often preceded ironically by *pretty, fine,* etc.). **b.** any situation or state of affairs: *this is a different kettle of fish altogether.* **18. like a fish out of water,** out of one's proper environment; ill at ease in unfamiliar surroundings. **19. neither fish nor fowl,** Also, **neither fish, flesh, fowl, nor good red herring.** neither one thing nor the other. **20. other fish to fry,** other matters requiring attention. **21. what's that got to do with the price of fish,** *Colloq.* a phrase used to question the relevance of a piece of information. **–fishable,** *adj.* **–fishless,** *adj.* **–fishlike,** *adj.*

fisherman /ˈfɪʃəmən/ *n.* (*pl.* **-men**) **1.** a man engaged in fishing, whether for profit or pleasure. **2.** a vessel used in fishing. **–fisherwoman,** *n.* **–fisherperson,** *n.*

fishery /ˈfɪʃəri/ *n.* (*pl.* **-ries**) **1.** the occupation or industry of catching fish or taking other products of the sea or streams from the water. **2.** a place where such an industry is regularly carried on. **3.** a fishing establishment.

fishmonger /ˈfɪʃmʌŋgə/ *n.* a dealer in fish.

fishwife /ˈfɪʃwaɪf/ *n.* (*pl.* **-wives**) **1.** *Obs.* a woman who sells fish. **2.** a coarse-mannered woman who uses abusive language.

fishy /ˈfɪʃi/ *adj.* (**fishier, fishiest**) **1.** fishlike in smell, taste, etc. **2.** *Colloq.* odd or questionable. **3.** dull and expressionless: *fishy eyes.* **–fishily,** *adv.* **–fishiness,** *n.*

fissi- a word element meaning 'cleft'.

fissile /ˈfɪsaɪl/ *adj.* **1.** capable of being split or divided; cleavable. **2.** *Physics* (of an atom, isotope, or nucleus) capable of undergoing nuclear fission, especially of an isotope which is capable of undergoing fission upon impact with a slow neutron. Also, *US*, **fissionable** /ˈfɪʃənəbəl/.

fission /ˈfɪʃən/ *n.* **1.** the act of cleaving or splitting into parts. **2.** *Biol.* the division of an organism into new organisms as a process of reproduction. **3.** *Physics* the splitting of the nucleus of a heavy atom, such as uranium, to form the nuclei of lighter atoms.

fissure /ˈfɪʃə/ *n.* **1.** a crack or split; cleft. **2.** a breaking or dividing. –*v.t.* **3.** to crack or split. –*v.i.* **4.** to become split.

fist /fɪst/ *n.* **1.** the hand closed tightly, with the fingers doubled into the palm. **2.** *Colloq.* the hand. **3.** *Colloq.* a person's handwriting. –*phr.* **4. make a good fist of**, to perform (a task) well. **5. make a poor fist of**, to perform (a task) badly.

fistula /ˈfɪstʃələ/ *n.* (*pl.* **-tulas** *or* **-tulae** /-li/) **1.** a narrow passage or duct formed by congenital abnormality or by disease or injury, as one leading from an abscess to a free surface, or from one cavity to another. **2.** *Med.* such a passage surgically created for such procedures as dialysis or drip transfusions. **3.** *Vet. Science* any of various suppurative inflammations, such as in the withers of a horse, characterised by the formation of passages or sinuses through the tissues and to the surface of the skin.

fit[1] /fɪt/ *adj.* (**fitter, fittest**) **1.** well adapted or suited: *a fit choice*. **2.** proper or becoming. **3.** qualified or competent, as for an office or function: *a person fit for the job*. **4.** worthy or deserving: *not fit to be seen*. **5.** prepared or ready: *crops fit for gathering*. **6.** in good physical condition, as an athlete, a race horse, military troops, etc. **7.** in good health: *a fit person*. –*verb* (**fitted, fitting**) –*v.t.* **8.** to be adapted to or suitable for (a purpose, object, occasion, etc.). **9.** to be proper or becoming for. **10.** to be of the right size or shape for. **11.** to conform or adjust to something: *to fit a ring to the finger*. **12.** to make qualified or competent: *qualities that fit someone for leadership*. **13.** to prepare. **14.** to put (*in, into, on, together*, etc.) with precise adjustment. **15.** to provide; furnish; equip: *fit a door with a new handle*. **16.** *Colloq.* to bring (someone) before the law on a trivial or trumped-up charge while really intending to victimise them: *he had been trying to fit Chilla for years*. –*v.i.* **17.** to be suitable or proper. **18.** to be of the right size or shape, as a garment for the wearer, or any object or part for a thing to which it is applied. –*n.* **19.** the manner in which a thing fits: *a perfect fit*. **20.** something that fits: *that coat is a poor fit*. **21.** the process or a process of fitting. **22.** an instance of fitting together well. **23.** *Colloq.* the equipment used to prepare and inject drugs. –*phr.* **24. fit as a flea**, *Colloq.* very fit. **25. fit in**, to be well adapted. **26. fit like a glove**, to be a perfect fit. **27. fit out** (or **up**), to furnish with clothing, equipment, furniture, fixtures, or other requisites. **28. fit the bill**, to suit; be what is required. **29. fit to be tied**, *Colloq.* very angry. **30. fit up**, *Colloq.* to construct a false case against (someone). **31. not fit to be seen**, **a.** in an untidy or dirty state. **b.** dressed in a fashion not appropriate to the occasion. –**fitness**, *n.*

fit[2] /fɪt/ *n.* **1.** a sudden, acute attack or manifestation of a disease: *fit of epilepsy*. **2.** a spell or period of emotion or feeling, inclination, activity, idleness, etc. **3.** a convulsion. –*v.i.* (**fitted, fitting**) **4.** *Med.* to suffer a fit. –*phr.* **5. by** (or **in**) **fits** (**and starts**), by irregular spells; fitfully; intermittently. **6. in fits**, *Colloq.* laughing uncontrollably. **7. throw a fit**, to become very excited or angry.

fitful /ˈfɪtfəl/ *adj.* coming, appearing, acting, etc., in fits or by spells; irregularly intermittent. –**fitfully**, *adv.* –**fitfulness**, *n.*

fitter /ˈfɪtə/ *n.* **1.** someone who fits garments. **2.** someone who fits together or adjusts the parts of machinery. **3.** someone who supplies and installs fittings or fixtures. **4.** someone who furnishes or equips with whatever is necessary for some purpose.

fitting /ˈfɪtɪŋ/ *adj.* **1.** suitable or appropriate; proper or becoming. –*n.* **2.** an act or instance of trying on clothes which are being made to determine proper fit. **3.** (of clothes) size. **4.** anything provided as equipment, parts, accessories, etc. **5.** (*pl.*) furnishings, fixtures, etc. –**fittingly**, *adv.* –**fittingness**, *n.*

five /faɪv/ *n.* **1.** a cardinal number, four plus one. **2.** a symbol for this number, as 5 or V. **3.** a set of five persons or things. **4.** a playing card, etc., with five pips. –*adj.* **5.** amounting to five in number: *five apples*. –*pron.* **6.** five people or things: *sleeps five; give me five*. –*phr.* **7. take five**, *Colloq.* (especially of a performing group in rehearsal) to take a break, originally of five minutes, for rest or refreshment.

five-eighth /faɪv-ˈeɪtθ/ *n. Rugby Football* **1.** the back who is stationed between the halfback and the centre three-quarters; fly-half; stand-off half. **2.** *NZ* either of the two players positioned outside the halfback, either the five-eighth (def. 1) or the inside-centre. Also, **five-eight**.

fix /fɪks/ *verb* (**fixed, fixing**) –*v.t.* **1.** to make fast, firm, or stable. **2.** to place definitely and more or less permanently. **3.** to settle definitely; determine: *to fix a price*. **4.** to direct (the eyes, the attention, etc.) steadily. **5.** to attract and hold (the eye, the attention, etc.). **6.** to make set or rigid. **7.** to put into permanent form. **8.** to put or place (responsibility, blame, etc.) on a person. **9.** to assign or refer to a definite place, time, etc. **10.** to repair. **11.** to put in order or in good condition; adjust or arrange. **12.** *Colloq.* to arrange matters with, or with respect to, especially privately or dishonestly, so as to secure favourable action: *to fix a jury; to fix a game*. **13.** *US* to get (a meal); prepare (food). **14.** *Colloq.* to put in a condition or position to make no further trouble. **15.** *Colloq.* to get even with; get revenge upon. **16.** *Chem.* **a.** to make stable in consistency or condition; reduce from fluidity or volatility to a more permanent state. **b.** to convert atmospheric nitrogen into an ammonia for use as fertilisers. –*v.i.* **17.** to become fixed. **18.** to become set; assume a rigid or solid form. –*n.* **19.** *Colloq.* a position from which it is difficult to escape; a predicament. **20.** the determining of a position, as of an aeroplane by mathematical, electronic, or other means. **21.** *Colloq.* a shot of heroin or other drug. **22.** *Colloq.* a dose of something habitually consumed, viewed, etc., as food, entertainment, etc., especially when conceived of as addictive. **23.** a method of fixing some problem. –*phr.* **24. fix on** (or **upon**), to decide on, single out, or choose. **25. fix up**, **a.** to arrange, organise, or decide on. **b.** *Aust.*, *NZ* to put right; solve. **c.** *Aust.*, *NZ* to renovate. **d.** *Aust.*, *NZ* to attend to the needs of (someone). –**fixable**, *adj.* –**fixer**, *n.* –**fixity**, *n.*

fixation /fɪkˈseɪʃən/ *n.* **1.** the act of fixing. **2.** the state of being fixed. **3.** *Psychol.* a partial arrest of emotional and instinctual development at an early point in life, due to a severe traumatic experience or an overwhelming gratification. –**fixated**, *adj.*

fixed interest *n.* an interest rate which is payable on a loan and which is fixed for the entire period of the loan.

fixed line *n.* → landline.

fixture /ˈfɪkstʃə/ *n.* **1.** something securely fixed in position; a permanently attached part or appendage of a house, etc.: *an electric-light fixture*. **2.** a person or thing long established in the same place or position. **3.** a sporting event to be held on a date arranged in advance, as a football match. **4.** an act of fixing. –**fixtureless**, *adj.*

fizz /fɪz/ *v.i.* **1.** to make a hissing or sputtering sound. **2.** (of carbonated drinks) to give off bubbles of gas. *–n.* **3.** a hissing sound; effervescence. **4.** soda water or other effervescent water. **–fizzy**, *adj.*

fizzer /ˈfɪzə/ *n. Aust., NZ Colloq.* **1.** a firecracker which fails to explode. **2.** a failure; fiasco.

fizzle /ˈfɪzəl/ *v.i.* **1.** to make a hissing or sputtering sound, especially one that dies out weakly. *–n.* **2.** a fizzling, hissing, or sputtering. **3.** *Colloq.* a fiasco; a failure. *–phr.* **4. fizzle out**, *Colloq.* to fail ignominiously after a good start. **–fizzler**, *n.*

fjord /ˈfiɔd/ *n.* a long, relatively narrow arm of the sea, bordered by steep cliffs, as on the coast of Norway. Also, **fiord**.

flab /flæb/ *n. Colloq.* bodily fat; flabbiness.

flabbergast /ˈflæbəgæst, -gast/ *v.t.* to overcome with surprise and bewilderment; astound.

flabby /ˈflæbi/ *adj.* **(-bier, -biest) 1.** hanging loosely or limply, as flesh, muscles, etc. **2.** having such flesh. **3.** lacking firmness, as character, persons, principles, utterances, etc.; feeble. **–flabbily**, *adv.* **–flabbiness**, *n.*

flaccid /ˈflæsəd, ˈflæksəd/ *adj.* soft and drooping; flabby; limp; not firm: *flaccid muscles.* **–flaccidity** /fləˈsɪdəti/, **flaccidness**, *n.* **–flaccidly**, *adv.*

flag¹ /flæg/ *n.* **1.** a piece of cloth, commonly bunting, of varying size, shape, colour, and device, usually attached by one edge to a staff or cord, and used as an ensign, standard, symbol, signal, decoration, display, etc. **2.** a pennant awarded to a winning team. **3.** any signal or indicator. **4.** *Computers* a marker assigned to an item of stored data. **5.** a slip of paper used as a bookmark. **6.** an attachment to the meter of a taxi showing whether the taxi is engaged or not. *–v.t.* **(flagged, flagging) 7.** to place a flag or flags over or on; decorate with flags. **8.** *Computers* to mark with a flag: *all additions to the file will be flagged.* **9.** to identify in some way as marked for future reference: *she flagged her interest in the proposal very early in the meeting.* *–phr.* **10. flag down**, to signal (a driver of a motor vehicle) to stop. **11. flag of convenience**, the flag of a country in which a ship has been registered only to gain some financial or legal advantage. **12. flag of distress**, a flag displayed as a signal of distress, generally at half-mast or upside down. **13. flag of truce**, a white flag displayed as an invitation to the enemy to confer, or carried as a sign of peaceful intention by one sent to deal with the enemy. **14. have the flags out**, *Colloq.* **a.** to celebrate or welcome. **b.** to be menstruating. **15. keep the flag flying**, to appear courageous and cheerful in the face of difficulty. **16. show the flag, a.** to assert one's claim or interest, especially by the physical presence of troops, etc. **b.** *Colloq.* to put in an appearance. **17. strike** (or **lower**) **the flag, a.** to relinquish command, as of a ship. **b.** to submit or surrender. **–flagless**, *adj.*

flag² /flæg/ *v.i.* **1.** to hang loosely or limply; droop. **2.** to fall off in vigour, energy, activity, interest, etc.

flag³ /flæg/ *n.* **1.** a flat slab of stone used for paving, etc. **2.** (*pl.*) a walk paved with such slabs. *–v.t.* **(flagged, flagging) 3.** to pave with flags. **–flagless**, *adj.*

flagellate *v.t.* /ˈflædʒəleɪt/ **1.** to whip; scourge; flog; lash. *–n.* /ˈflædʒələt/ **2.** *Zool.* any of the Flagellata, a class of protists distinguished by having one or more long mobile filaments as locomotive organs. **–flagellation** /flædʒəˈleɪʃən/, *n.* **–flagellator**, *n.*

flag fall *n.* an initial fee for hiring a taxi, registered automatically on its meter.

flagon /ˈflægən/ *n.* **1.** a large bottle for wine, etc., especially one which is squat and of large circumference. **2.** a vessel for holding liquids, as for use at table, especially one with a handle, a spout, and usually a cover.

flagpole /ˈflægpoʊl/ *n.* Also, **flagstaff** /ˈflægstaf/ **1.** a staff or pole on which a flag is displayed. *–phr.* **2. run (something) up the flagpole**, *Colloq.* to test (an idea, proposal, etc.) by making it widely known.

flagrant /ˈfleɪgrənt/ *adj.* glaring; notorious; scandalous: *a flagrant crime, a flagrant offender.* **–flagrance, flagrancy**, *n.* **–flagrantly**, *adv.*

flagship /ˈflægʃɪp/ *n.* **1.** a ship which carries a flag officer of a fleet, squadron, or the like, and displays this officer's flag. **2.** the leading or most impressive element or product in an enterprise or organisation. *–adj.* **3.** relating to the finest example of some commercial item or enterprise.

flagship species *n.* a species which attracts attention and sympathy for its plight, as the dolphin, whale, frog, koala, etc., and thus more readily attracts funds for the conservation or protection of a whole ecosystem or group of creatures than do other lesser-known species.

flagstone /ˈflægstoʊn/ *n.* a flat slab of stone used for paving, etc.

flail /fleɪl/ *n.* **1.** an instrument for threshing grain by hand, consisting of a staff or handle to one end of which is attached a freely swinging stick or bar. *–v.t.* **2.** to strike with, or as if with, a flail. *–v.i.* **3.** to move as a flail, in a thrashing or erratic manner.

flair /fleə/ *n.* **1.** talent; aptitude; keen perception. **2.** elegance; stylishness: *to dress with flair.*

flak /flæk/ *n.* **1. a.** anti-aircraft fire, especially as experienced by the crews of military aircraft at which the fire is directed. **b.** the shrapnel from such fire. **2.** *Colloq.* heavy criticism; abuse.

flake¹ /fleɪk/ *n.* **1.** a small, flat, thin piece of anything. **2.** a small piece split off something. **3.** *Colloq.* a strange or bizarre person; an unconventional person. **4.** *Colloq.* a person who lacks substance; lightweight. **5.** *Colloq.* crack cocaine, especially in the form of shavings from a solid rock. *–v.i.* **6.** to peel off or separate in flakes. **7.** to fall in flakes, as snow. **8.** Also, **flake out**. *Colloq.* to collapse, faint, or fall asleep, especially as a result of complete exhaustion, or influence of alcohol, drugs, etc. *–v.t.* **9.** to remove in flakes. **10.** to break flakes or chips from. **11.** to cover with or as with flakes. **12.** to form into flakes. **–flaky**, *adj.*

flake² /fleɪk/ *n.* the flesh of various sharks and rays, often the flaps of the skate, commonly sold in fish shops.

flambé /flɒmˈbeɪ/ *adj.* **1.** (of food) dressed or served in flaming spirits, especially brandy. *–v.t.* **(-béed, -béing) 2.** to dress or serve in flaming spirits.

flamboyant /flæmˈbɔɪənt/ *adj.* **1.** extroverted and consciously theatrical: *a flamboyant personality.* **2.** flaming; gorgeous: *flamboyant colours.* **3.** florid; ornate; showy: *flamboyant rhetoric.* **–flamboyance, flamboyancy**, *n.* **–flamboyantly**, *adv.*

flame /fleɪm/ *n.* **1.** burning gas or vapour, as from wood, etc., undergoing combustion; a portion of ignited gas or vapour. **2.** (*oft. pl.*) state or condition of blazing combustion: *to burst into flames.* **3.** any flame-like condition; glow; inflamed condition. **4.** brilliant light; scintillating lustre. **5.** bright colouring; a streak or patch of colour. **6.** heat or ardour, as of zeal or passion. **7.** *Colloq.* an object of the passion of love; sweetheart. *–v.i.* **8.** to burn with a flame or flames; burst into flames; blaze. **9.** to glow like flame; shine brilliantly; flash. **10.** to burn as with flame, as passion; break into open anger, indignation, etc. *–v.t.* **11.** to subject to the action of flame or fire. **12.** *Internet* to express in emails, chat rooms, etc., one's strongly felt opinions, especially one's hostile reactions to others' opinions, with great intensity and frequency. *–phr.* **13. flame up**, to blush violently. **–flameless**, *adj.* **–flamy**, *adj.*

flame gum   *n.* a small tree, *Corymbia ficifolia*, of western Australia, widely cultivated for its bright red flowers. Also, **red flowering gum**.

flame mail   *n. Internet* a stream of persistent abusive emails to the subject of a flaming campaign.

flamenco /fləˈmɛŋkoʊ/ *n.* (*pl.* **-cos**) a type of Spanish music or dance, especially of the Romani style.

flame tree   *n.* an ornamental tree, *Brachychiton acerifolius*, of Australia, with scarlet, bell-shaped flowers.

flaming /ˈfleɪmɪŋ/ *adj.* **1.** emitting flames; blazing; fiery. **2.** glowing; brilliant. **3.** violent; vehement; passionate. **4.** *Colloq.* a euphemism for various expletives: *stone the flaming crows*. –*adv.* **5.** *Colloq.* an intensifier: *a flaming bore*. –*n.* **6.** *Internet* the intense and frequent expression of hostility towards a person, institution, etc., via email, chat rooms, websites, etc. –**flamingly**, *adv.*

flamingo /fləˈmɪŋgoʊ/ *n.* (*pl.* **-gos** *or* **-goes**) **1.** any of the aquatic birds constituting the family Phoenicopteridae, with very long neck and legs, webbed feet, bills bent downwards, and pinkish to scarlet plumage. **2.** a dark shade of pinkish orange.

flammable /ˈflæməbəl/ *adj.* easily set on fire; combustible (opposed to *nonflammable*). –**flammability** /flæməˈbɪləti/, *n.*

flan /flæn/ *n.* **1.** an open tart containing cheese, cream, or fruit. **2.** a piece of metal shaped ready to form a coin, but not yet stamped by the die. **3.** the metal of which a coin is made, as distinguished from its design.

flange /flændʒ/ *n.* a projecting rim, collar, edge, ridge, or the like, on an object, for keeping it in place, attaching it to another object, strengthening it, etc. –**flangeless**, *adj.*

flank /flæŋk/ *n.* **1.** the side of an animal between its ribs and hip. **2.** the thin piece of flesh of flank. **3.** the side of anything. **4.** *Mil.*, *Navy* the far right or left side of an army or fleet. **5.** *Aust. Rules* an outside position, as halfforward flank. –*v.t.* **6.** to be at the side of. **7.** to defend or guard at a flank. **8.** to pass round the flank of.

flannel /ˈflænəl/ *n.* **1.** a warm, soft fabric of wool or blends of wool and cotton, wool and rayon, or cotton warp with wool filling. **2.** → **face washer**. **3.** (*pl.*) an outer garment, especially trousers, made of flannel. **4.** (*pl.*) *Obs.* woollen undergarments. –*v.t.* (**-elled** *or*, *Chiefly US*, **-eled**, **-elling** *or*, *Chiefly US*, **-eling**) **5.** to cover or clothe with flannel. –**flannelly**, *adj.*

flannelette /flænəˈlɛt/ *n.* a cotton fabric, plain or printed, napped on one side to imitate flannel.

flannel flower   *n.* an Australian plant, *Actinotus helianthi*, having white, flannel-like bracts below the flowers, so that the whole has the appearance of a composite flower.

flap /flæp/ *verb* (**flapped**, **flapping**) –*v.i.* **1.** to swing about loosely, especially with a noise: *a curtain flaps in the wind*. **2.** to move up and down like wings. **3.** *Colloq.* to become nervous or excited; panic. –*v.t.* **4.** to move (arms, wings, etc.) up and down. **5.** to cause to swing loosely, especially with a noise. **6.** to slap. –*n.* **7.** a flapping movement. **8.** a flapping noise. **9.** a slap. **10.** something broad and bendable, or flat and thin, that hangs loosely, joined at one side only. **11.** *Aeronautics* a hinged part of a wing, that can be lifted in flight to change lift and drag. **12.** *Colloq.* an instance or state of panic or excitement: *her announcement caused quite a flap*; *she arrived in a terrible flap*. –**flapless**, *adj.*

flapper /ˈflæpə/ *n.* **1.** something broad and flat for striking with, or for making a noise by striking. **2.** a young bird just learning to fly. **3.** a young woman during the 1920s, especially one freed from the traditional social and moral restraints.

flare /flɛə/ *verb* (**flared**, **flaring**) –*v.i.* **1.** to burn with an unsteady, swaying flame, as a torch or candle in the wind. **2.** Also, **flare up**. to blaze with a sudden burst of flame. **3.** to shine or glow. **4.** to spread gradually outwards as the end of a trumpet, or a ship's sides or bows. **5.** Also, **flare out**. (of a skirt) to extend outwards gradually from top to bottom. –*v.t.* **6.** to cause (a candle, etc.) to burn with a swaying flame. **7.** to display conspicuously or ostentatiously. **8.** to signal by flares of fire or light. **9.** to cause (something) to spread gradually outwards in form. –*n.* **10.** a flaring or swaying flame or light as of torches in the wind. **11.** a sudden blaze or burst of flame. **12.** a sudden blaze of fire or light used as a signal or for illumination or guidance, etc. **13.** a device or substance used to produce such a blaze of fire or light. **14.** a sudden burst, as of zeal or of temper. **15.** a gradual spread outwards in form; outward curvature: *the flare of a skirt*. **16.** something that spreads out. **17.** *Optics* light reflected by the surfaces of an optical system. **18.** (*pl.*) trousers having the lower parts of the legs flared. –*phr.* **19. flare up**, to start up or burst out in sudden fierce passion, anger, etc.

flash /flæʃ/ *n.* **1.** a sudden, transitory outburst of flame or light: *a flash of lightning*. **2.** a sudden, brief outburst or display of joy, wit, etc. **3.** the time occupied by a flash of light; an instant: *to do something in a flash*. **4.** a distinctive mark or emblem, as on a soldier's uniform to identify his or her unit. **5.** *Journalism* → **newsflash**. **6.** *Photography* → **flashgun**. **7.** *Mining* an opal reflecting a single flash in a large patch of colour. –*v.i.* **8.** to break forth into sudden flame or light, especially transiently or intermittently; to gleam. **9.** to speak or behave with sudden anger. **10.** to burst suddenly into view or perception: *the answer flashed into his mind*. **11.** to move like a flash. **12.** *Colloq.* to make a sudden display. **13.** to expose oneself (see **expose** def. 10) briefly and unexpectedly. –*v.t.* **14.** to emit or send forth (fire or light) in sudden flashes. **15.** to communicate instantaneously, as by telegraph. **16.** *Colloq.* to make a sudden or ostentatious display of: *to flash one's diamonds*. –*adj. Colloq.* **17.** showy or ostentatious. **18.** smart and attractive: *that's a very flash shirt*. –*adv.* **19.** in a showy or ostentatious manner: *to act flash*. –*phr.* **20. flash in the pan**, something which begins promisingly but has no lasting significance. –**flasher**, *n.*

flashback /ˈflæʃbæk/ *n.* **1.** a representation, during the course of a novel, film, etc., of some event or scene which occurred at a previous time. **2.** a sudden remembering of someone or something from the past. **3.** an unexpected re-occurrence of psychedelic phenomena previously induced by drugs.

flashbulb /ˈflæʃbʌlb/ *n.* a glass bulb filled with oxygen and a thin sheet of magnesium or aluminium, giving a momentary bright light when fired, used as a light source, in photography.

flash drive   *n.* → **USB drive**.

flash flood   *n.* a sudden flood of water in a watercourse, storm channel, etc., usually due to heavy rain. –**flash flooding**, *n.*

flashforward /flæʃˈfɔwəd/ *n.* a representation, during the course of a film, etc., of an event or scene from some future time.

flashgun /ˈflæʃgʌn/ *n.* a device which discharges a flashbulb in synchronisation with a camera shutter, or which produces a flash by electronic means.

flash memory   *n. Computers* a type of EEPROM which can be erased and reprogrammed without the necessity of removing it from the computer.

flashpacker /ˈflæʃpækə/ *n. Colloq.* a backpacker who travels in relative luxury. –**flashpacking**, *n.*

flashpoint /ˈflæʃpɔɪnt/ *n.* **1.** the lowest temperature at which a volatile oil will give off explosive or ignitable vapours. **2.** the point or moment at which an explosion takes place or control is lost: *tempers reached flash-point after the chairman's speech.*

flashy /ˈflæʃi/ *adj.* (**-shier, -shiest**) **1.** sparkling or brilliant, especially in a superficial way or for the moment. **2.** pretentiously smart; showy; gaudy. **–flashily,** *adv.* **–flashiness,** *n.*

flask /flask/ *n.* a bottle-shaped container made of glass, metal, etc.: *a flask of oil, a brandy flask.*

flat¹ /flæt/ *adj.* (**flatter, flattest**) **1.** level, even, or without inequalities of surface, as land, etc. **2.** horizontally level: *a flat roof.* **3.** comparatively lacking in projection or depression of surface: *a broad flat face.* **4.** (of a sea, harbour, etc.) unbroken by waves; with little or no swell. **5.** lying at full length, as a person. **6.** lying wholly on or against something: *a ladder flat against a wall.* **7.** thrown down, laid low, or level with the ground, as fallen trees or buildings. **8.** (of a race) run on a level course or track, without obstacles to be jumped. **9.** having a generally level shape or appearance; not deep or thick: *a flat plate.* **10.** (of the heel of a shoe) low and broad. **11.** (of feet) having little or no arch. **12.** spread out, as an unrolled map, the open hand, etc. **13.** collapsed; deflated: *a flat tyre.* **14.** without qualification; unqualified, downright, or positive: *a flat denial*; *flat broke.* **15.** without modification: *a flat rate*; *a flat price.* **16.** uninteresting, dull, or tedious. **17.** (of wine) lacking substance and body; low in acidity. **18.** stale; tasteless or insipid, as food. **19.** (of beer, etc.) having lost its effervescence. **20.** pointless, as a remark, joke, etc. **21.** commercially dull, as trade or the market. **22.** lacking relief, contrast, or shading, as a painting. **23.** not giving the effect of perspective: *the flat quality of medieval painting.* **24.** *Painting* without gloss; matt. **25.** not clear, sharp, or ringing, as sound, a voice, etc. **26.** *Music* **a.** (of a note) lowered a semitone in pitch: *B flat.* **b.** below an intended pitch, as a note; too low (opposed to *sharp*). **c.** (of an interval) diminished. **27.** *Naut.* (of a sail) **a.** cut with little or no fullness. **b.** trimmed as nearly fore-and-aft as possible, for sailing to windward. **–** *adv.* **28.** in a flat position; horizontally; levelly. **29.** Also, **flatly.** positively; absolutely. **30.** exactly. **31.** Also, **flatly.** *Music* below the true pitch. **–** *n.* **32.** something flat. **33.** a flat surface, side or part of anything: *the flat of a blade; the flat of the hand.* **34.** flat or level ground; a flat area. **35.** (*oft. pl.*) low-lying land, especially when swampy or prone to flooding. **36.** *Music* **a.** (in musical notation) the character ♭, which, when attached to a note or a stave degree, lowers its pitch one chromatic semitone. **b.** a note one chromatic semitone below another. **c.** (on keyboard instruments, with reference to any given key) the key next below or to the left. **37.** a flat-heeled shoe. **38.** *Theatre* a piece of scenery consisting of a wooden frame, usually rectangular, covered with lightweight board or fabric. **–** *v.t.* **39.** *Music* to lower (a pitch) especially one semitone. **–** *phr.* **40. and that's flat,** *Colloq.* a phrase expressing resolution or determination: *well I'm going and that's flat.* **41. fall flat,** to fail to have a desired effect: *his jokes fell flat.* **42. flat out,** *Colloq.* **a.** as fast as possible. **b.** very busy, e. exhausted; unable to proceed. **43. flat out like a lizard drinking,** *Aust. Colloq.* **a.** exerting oneself to the utmost. **b.** lying prone. **44. flat to the boards,** *Colloq.* **a.** travelling at maximum speed. **b.** extremely busy. **–flatness,** *n.*

flat² /flæt/ *n.* **1.** a suite of rooms, usually on one floor only, forming a complete residence, and usually rented. **–** *v.i.* (**flatted, flatting**) **2.** *Aust., NZ* to live in a flat.

flatbread /ˈflætbrɛd/ *n.* any of various unleavened breads, baked in thin sheets.

flatfish /ˈflætfɪʃ/ *n.* (*pl.* **-fishes** *or, especially collectively,* **-fish**) any of a group of fishes (often considered as constituting the suborder Heterosomata), including the halibut, flounder, sole, etc., living near the seabed, having a greatly compressed body, swimming on one side, and having both eyes on the upper side.

flatfoot /ˈflætfʊt/ *n.* a condition in which the arch of the foot is flattened so that the entire sole rests upon the ground.

flat-footed /flæt-ˈfʊtəd/ *adj.* **1.** having flat feet. **2.** *Colloq.* clumsy and tactless. **3.** *Colloq.* unprepared, unable to react quickly. **–flat-footedly,** *adv.* **–flat-footedness,** *n.*

flathead /ˈflæthɛd/ *n.* any of numerous species of elongate, bottom-dwelling fishes with depressed, ridged heads, belonging especially to the family Platycephalidae, found in the Indian and Pacific Oceans and commercially important as food fishes.

flat-leaf parsley *n.* a variety of parsley with a broad flat leaf and a stronger flavour than curly-leaf parsley. Also, **continental parsley. Italian parsley.**

flatline /ˈflætlaɪn/ *v.i. Colloq.* **1.** to die. **2.** (of a project) to fail completely.

flat pack *n.* **1.** a product, especially an item of furniture, which is sold and delivered in its constituent pieces packed in a flat box for later assembly. **–** *adj.* **2.** of or relating to such a product: *a flat pack kitchen.* Also, **flatpack.**

flatten /ˈflætn/ *v.t.* **1.** to make flat. **2.** *Colloq.* to knock (someone) out. **3.** *Colloq.* to crush or disconcert. **–flattener,** *n.*

flattened management *n.* a management structure having fewer levels than the traditional pyramid or hierarchical structure.

flatter /ˈflætə/ *v.t.* **1.** to seek to please by complimentary speech or attentions; compliment or praise, especially insincerely. **2.** to represent too favourably, as in portrayal. **3.** to show to advantage. **4.** to play upon the vanity or susceptibilities of; cajole, wheedle, or beguile. **5.** to gratify by compliments or attentions, or as a compliment does: *to feel flattered by an invitation.* **–** *phr.* **6. flatter oneself,** to beguile oneself; please oneself with a thought or belief: *he flattered himself that he was creating just the impression he wanted.* **–flatterer,** *n.* **–flatteringly,** *adv.* **–flattery,** *n.*

flatulent /ˈflætʃələnt/ *adj.* **1.** generating gas in the alimentary canal. **2.** pretentious; empty. **–flatulence, flatulency,** *n.* **–flatulently,** *adv.*

flatworm /ˈflætwɜːm/ *n.* → **platyhelminth.**

flaunt /flɔnt/ *v.i.* **1.** to parade or display oneself conspicuously or boldly. **2.** to wave conspicuously in the air. **–flaunter,** *n.* **–flauntingly,** *adv.* **–flaunty,** *adj.*

flautist /ˈflɔtəst/ *n.* a flute player. Also, *US,* **flutist.**

flavo- a word element meaning 'yellow', as in *flavoprotein.* Also, (*before vowels*), **flav-.**

flavour /ˈfleɪvə/ *n.* **1.** taste, especially a characteristic taste, or a noticeable element in the taste, of a thing. **2.** a flavouring substance or extract. **3.** the characteristic quality of a thing: *a book which catches the flavour of the sea.* **4.** a particular quality noticeable in a thing: *language with a strong nautical flavour.* **–** *v.t.* **5.** to give flavour to. **–** *phr.* **6. flavour of the month,** someone or something that is currently popular. Also, **flavor. –flavourer,** *n.* **–flavourful,** *adj.* **–flavourless,** *adj.*

flaw /flɔ/ *n.* **1.** a marring feature; a defect; a fault. **2.** a defect impairing legal soundness or validity: *a flaw in a lease; a flaw in a will.* **3.** a crack, break, breach, imperfection, or rent. **–flawless,** *adj.* **–flawlessly,** *adv.* **–flawlessness,** *n.*

flax /flæks/ *n.* **1.** any plant of the genus *Linum,* especially *L. usitatissimum,* a slender, erect annual plant with narrow, lance-shaped leaves and blue flowers, much cultivated for its fibre and seeds. **2.** the fibre of this plant, manufactured into linen yarn for thread or woven fabrics. **3.** any of various plants or fibres resembling flax, as *Phormium tenax,* New Zealand flax.

flaxen /ˈflæksən/ *adj.* **1.** made of flax. **2.** resembling flax. **3.** of the pale yellowish colour of dressed flax. Also, **flaxy.**

flay /fleɪ/ *v.t.* **1.** to strip off the skin or outer covering of. **2.** to criticise or reprove with scathing severity. **3.** to strip of money or property; fleece. **–flayer,** *n.*

flea /fli/ *n.* any of numerous small, wingless, blood-sucking insects of the order Siphonaptera, parasitic upon mammals and birds, and noted for their powers of leaping.

flea market *n.* a market where usually second-hand or cheap articles are sold.

fleck /flɛk/ *n.* **1.** any spot or patch of colour, light, etc. *–v.t.* **2.** to mark with a fleck or flecks; spot; dapple.

fled /flɛd/ *v.* past tense and past participle of **flee.**

fledge /flɛdʒ/ *v.t.* (**fledged, fledging**) **1.** to bring up (a young bird) until it is able to fly. **2.** to furnish with or as with feathers or plumage; feather (an arrow).

fledgling /ˈflɛdʒlɪŋ/ *n.* **1.** a young bird just fledged. **2.** an inexperienced person. *–adj.* **3. a.** new and inexperienced: *a fledgling player.* **b.** newly established: *a fledgling business.* Also, *Rare,* **fledgeling.**

flee /fli/ *verb* (**fled, fleeing**) *–v.i.* **1.** to run away, as from danger, pursuers, etc.; take flight. **2.** to move swiftly; fly; speed. *–v.t.* **3.** to run away from (a place, person, etc.).

fleece /flis/ *n.* **1.** the coat of wool that covers a sheep or some similar animal. **2.** the wool shorn from a sheep at one time. **3.** a fabric with a soft, silky pile, used for warmth, as for lining garments. *–v.t.* (**fleeced, fleecing**) **4.** to strip of money or belongings; plunder; swindle. **–fleecy,** *adj.* **–fleeceable,** *adj.*

fleet[1] /flit/ *n.* **1.** the largest organised unit of naval ships grouped for tactical or other purposes. **2.** the vessels, aeroplanes, or vehicles collectively of a single transport company or undertaking. **3.** a number of aeroplanes, motor vehicles, etc., moving or operating in company.

fleet[2] /flit/ *adj.* **1.** swift; rapid: *fleet of foot; a fleet horse.* *–v.i.* **2.** *Naut.* to change the position of a ship, cable, etc., especially in a fore-and-aft direction. **–fleetly,** *adv.* **–fleetness,** *n.*

fleeting /ˈflitɪŋ/ *adj.* gliding swiftly away; passing swiftly; transient; transitory. **–fleetingly,** *adv.* **–fleetingness,** *n.*

flesh /flɛʃ/ *n.* **1.** the soft substance of an animal body, consisting of muscle and fat. **2.** muscular tissue. **3.** fatness; weight: *to put on flesh.* **4.** such substance of animals as an article of food, usually excluding fish and sometimes fowl; meat. **5.** the body, especially as distinguished from the spirit or soul. **6.** the physical or animal nature of humankind: *sins of the flesh.* **7.** one's kindred or family, or a member of it. **8.** the soft pulpy portion of a fruit, vegetable, etc., as distinguished from the core, skin, shell, etc. **9.** the surface of the body, especially with respect to colour. **10.** the colour of the skin of a white person; pinkish white with a tinge of yellow; pinkish cream. *–phr.* **11. flesh and blood, a.** offspring or relatives: *one's own flesh and blood.* **b.** human nature: *more than flesh and blood can endure.* **12. flesh out, a.** to make (a character in a story, film, etc.) come alive by adding details of appearance and behaviour. **b.** to explain; amplify. **13. in the flesh, a.** alive. **b.** in bodily form; in person. **14. pound of flesh,** a person's right or due, insisted on mercilessly with a total disregard for others. **15. press the flesh,** *Colloq.* (usually of politicians) to shake hands and talk with members of the public, as when campaigning for election, etc. **–fleshy,** *adj.* **–fleshless,** *adj.*

fleur-de-lis /flɜ-də-ˈli/ *n.* (*pl.* **fleurs-de-lis** /flɜ-də-ˈliz/) a heraldic device somewhat resembling three petals or floral segments of an iris tied by an encircling band.

flew /flu/ *v.* past tense of **fly**[1].

flex[1] /flɛks/ *v.t.* **1.** to bend (something pliant or jointed, as a part of the body). *–n.* **2.** a small, flexible insulated electric cable or wire, especially for supplying power to movable domestic appliances.

flex[2] /flɛks/ *v.i.* Also, **flex off, flex out. 1.** to absent oneself from work under a flexitime scheme. *–n.* Also, **flexi. 2.** a day off awarded under the flexitime system.

flexible /ˈflɛksəbəl/ *adj.* **1.** capable of being bent; easily bent. **2.** susceptible of modification or adaptation; adaptable. **3.** willing or disposed to yield. **–flexibility** /flɛksəˈbɪləti/, **flexibleness,** *n.* **–flexibly,** *adv.*

flexiday /ˈflɛksideɪ/ *n.* a day taken off from work under a flexitime scheme.

flexitime /ˈflɛksitaɪm/ *n.* an arrangement of ordinary hours of work in which employees may elect to vary their commencing, ceasing, and meal-break times while still maintaining the total number of hours worked.

flexor /ˈflɛksə/ *n. Anat.* a muscle which serves to flex or bend a part of the body (opposed to *extensor*).

flick /flɪk/ *n.* **1.** a sudden light blow or stroke, as with a whip or the finger. **2.** the sound thus made. **3.** something thrown off with or as with a jerk: *a flick of spray.* *–v.t.* **4.** to strike lightly with a whip, the finger, etc. **5.** to remove with such a stroke: *to flick dust from one's coat, to flick away a crumb.* **6.** to pass on (a message, request, etc.) immediately to someone else: *to flick the proposal to IT.* **7.** to turn on or off (a switch). **8.** to reject or dismiss (someone). *–phr.* **9. give someone** (or **something) the flick,** *Colloq.* to reject or dismiss someone or something.

flicker /ˈflɪkə/ *v.i.* **1.** to burn unsteadily. **2.** to move quickly to and fro; vibrate. *–n.* **3.** an unsteady flame or light. **4.** a flickering movement. **5.** a thing passing quickly: *a flicker of hope.* **–flickeringly,** *adv.*

flick-knife *n.* a knife the blade of which springs out at the press of a button on the handle; switchblade.

flier /ˈflaɪə/ *n.* → **flyer.**

flight[1] /flaɪt/ *n.* **1.** the act, manner, or power of flying. **2.** the distance covered or the course pursued by a flying object. **3.** a number of beings or things flying or passing through the air together: *a flight of swallows.* **4.** a journey by air, especially by aeroplane. **5.** a scheduled trip on an airline. **6.** the basic tactical unit of military air forces, consisting of two or more aircraft. **7.** the act, principles, or art of flying an aeroplane. **8.** the progress of a spacecraft into space and, sometimes, back. **9.** swift movement in general. **10.** a soaring above or transcending ordinary bounds: *a flight of fancy.* **11.** *Athletics* a specific number, usually ten, of hurdles in a race. **12.** the real or artificial feathers at the back of an arrow, dart, etc., designed to make it fly straight. **13.** *Archit.* **a.** the series of steps or stairs between two adjacent landings. **b.** a series of steps, etc., ascending without change of direction. *–v.t.* **14.** to deliver (a cricket ball, dart, etc.) in a certain manner, especially so that it flies comparatively slowly. *–phr.* **15. flight of fancy,** an elaborate daydream. **16. in flight,** in the act of flying. **17. in full flight, a.** at top speed. **b.** at the peak of performance: *a voice in full flight.* **18. in the first flight,** excellent; one of the best. **19. take flight, a.** (of a bird) to fly away. **b.** to flee.

flight[2] /flaɪt/ *n.* **1.** the act of fleeing; hasty departure. *–phr.* **2. put to flight,** to force to flee; rout. **3. take** (**to**) **flight,** to flee.

flight attendant *n.* someone whose job is to attend to passengers and to their safety on an aircraft, serving meals, giving information, etc.

flight lieutenant *n. Air Force* **1.** a commissioned officer in the Royal Australian Air Force ranking below squadron leader and above flying officer. **2.** the rank. *Abbrev.:* FLTLT.

flight log *n.* → **log** (def. 4).

flight recorder *n.* a box containing recording equipment which collects information about an aircraft's flight, used especially to determine the cause of a crash; black box.

flight sergeant *n. Air Force* **1.** a senior non-commissioned officer in the Royal Australian Air Force ranking below warrant officer and above sergeant. **2.** the rank. *Abbrev.*: FSGT

flighty /ˈflaiti/ *adj.* **(-tier, -tiest) 1.** given to flights or sallies of fancy, caprice, etc.; volatile; frivolous. **2.** slightly delirious; light-headed; mildly crazy. **3.** emotionally unreliable; flirtatious. **–flightily,** *adv.* **–flightiness,** *n.*

flimsy /ˈflimzi/ *adj.* **(-sier, -siest) 1.** without material strength or solidity: *a flimsy material*; *a flimsy structure.* **2.** weak; inadequate; not carefully thought out: *a flimsy excuse*; *a flimsy argument.* **–flimsily,** *adv.* **–flimsiness,** *n.*

flinch /flintʃ/ *v.i.* **1.** to draw back or shrink from what is dangerous, difficult, or unpleasant. **2.** to shrink under pain; wince. **–flincher,** *n.* **–flinchingly,** *adv.*

fling /fliŋ/ *verb* **(flung, flinging)** *–v.t.* **1.** to throw, cast, or hurl; throw with force or violence; throw with impatience, disdain, etc. **2.** to put suddenly or violently: *to fling someone into jail.* **3.** to send forth suddenly and rapidly: *to fling fresh troops into a battle.* **4.** to throw aside or off. **5.** Also, **fling out.** to utter (harsh or abusive language). **6.** to throw to the ground, as in wrestling or from horseback. *–v.i.* **7.** to move with haste or violence; rush; dash. **8.** to fly into violent and irregular motions, as a horse; throw the body about, as a person. *–n.* **9.** the act of flinging. **10.** a spell of unrestrained indulgence of one's impulses: *to have one's fling.* **11.** *Colloq.* a brief sexual affair. *–phr.* **12. (at) full fling,** at full speed; with reckless abandon. **13. fling aside,** to remove forcefully from out of one's way. **–flinger,** *n.*

flint /flint/ *n.* **1.** a hard kind of stone, a form of silica resembling chalcedony but more opaque, less pure, and less lustrous. **2.** a piece of this, especially as used for striking fire. **3.** something very hard or obdurate.

flip /flip/ *v.t.* **(flipped, flipping) 1.** to toss or put in motion with a snap of a finger and thumb; flick. **2.** to move (something) with a jerk or jerks. *–n.* **3.** a smart tap or strike. **4.** a somersault. *–phr.* **5. flip one's lid,** *Colloq.* to become angry. **6. the flip side (of the coin),** the necessary but unpleasant concomitant: *the flip side of going swimming is that I have to get up early.*

flip-flop *n.* **1.** an electronic circuit which alternates polarity. **2.** *Computers* a simple electronic circuit that changes from one stable state to another as it receives a pulse and then back again; used to store binary digits, and used in integrated circuits to build computers. *–v.i.* **(-flopped, -flopping) 3.** to reverse one's opinion, policy, etc.

flippant /ˈflipənt/ *adj.* **1.** clever or pert in speech. **2.** characterised by a shallow or disrespectful levity. **–flippancy, flippantness,** *n.* **–flippantly,** *adv.*

flipper /ˈflipə/ *n.* **1.** a broad, flat limb, as of a seal, whale, etc., especially adapted for swimming. **2.** a device resembling in form an animal's flipper, usually made of rubber, used as an aid in swimming. **3.** *Cricket* a delivery in which the ball kicks forward rapidly upon striking the pitch and comes through faster and lower than anticipated by the person batting. **4.** a small movable arm used to manoeuvre the ball in a pinball machine or similar device.

flirt /flɜt/ *v.i.* **1.** to trifle in love; play at love; coquet. **2.** to trifle or toy (with an idea, etc.). *–n.* **3.** a person given to flirting. **–flirtation,** *n.* **–flirtatious,** *adj.* **–flirter,** *n.* **–flirtingly,** *adv.*

flit /flit/ *v.i.* **(flitted, flitting) 1.** to move lightly and swiftly; fly, dart, or skim along. **2.** to pass away quickly, as time. *–phr.* **3. do a moonlight flit,** *Colloq.* to make a surreptitious departure at night.

float /flout/ *v.i.* **1.** to rest or move gently on the surface of a liquid. **2.** to rest or move as if in a liquid or gas: *the idea floated through my mind.* **3.** to move or drift about free from attachment. *–v.t.* **4.** to cause to float. **5.** to set going (a company, etc.). **6.** to sell (stocks, bonds, etc.) on the market. **7.** *Econ.* to allow the rate of exchange of (a currency) to find its own level in a foreign exchange market. *–n.* **8.** something that floats as **a.** the hollow ball used to control the liquid level in a tank, cistern, etc. **b.** the hollow, boat-like part under an aeroplane allowing it to float on water. **c.** the cork on a fishing line. **d.** the air-filled organ supporting an animal in the water. **9.** a platform on wheels, bearing a display, and drawn in a procession. **10.** Also, **horse float.** a van or trailer for transporting horses. **11.** a quantity of money used by shopkeepers, etc., to provide change. **–floatable,** *adj.* **–floaty,** *adj.*

floater /ˈfloutə/ *n.* **1.** a spot that appears to drift in front of the eye, caused by vitreous debris within the fluid of the eyeball casting a shadow on the retina. **2.** a loose piece of rock which can be moved by a bulldozer, as opposed to a large rock formation which must be drilled and blasted out. **3.** *Aust.* a meat pie served in pea soup. **4.** *Colloq.* someone who often changes their job; a temporary employee; one of the floating population. **5.** *Colloq.* a dead body found in the water.

float tank *n.* a tank used in flotation therapy. Also, **flotation tank.**

flocculent /ˈflɒkjələnt/ *adj.* consisting of or containing loose woolly masses, as certain chemical precipitates. **–flocculence,** *n.* **–flocculently,** *adv.*

flock[1] /flɒk/ *n.* **1.** a number of animals of one kind keeping, feeding, or herded together, now especially of sheep or goats, or of birds. **2.** a crowd; large number of people. **3.** (in New Testament and ecclesiastical use) **a.** the Christian church in relation to Christ. **b.** a single congregation in relation to its pastor. *–v.i.* Also, **flock together. 4.** to gather or go in a flock, company, or crowd. **–flockless,** *adj.*

flock[2] /flɒk/ *n.* **1.** a lock or tuft of wool, hair, etc. **2.** (*construed as pl. or sing.*) wool refuse, shearings of cloth, old cloth torn to pieces, etc., used for stuffing mattresses, upholstering furniture, etc. **3.** (*construed as sing. or pl.*) finely powdered wool, cloth, etc., used in making wallpaper.

floe /flou/ *n.* **1.** a field of floating ice formed on the surface of the sea, etc. **2.** a detached floating portion of such a field.

flog /flɒg/ *v.t.* **(flogged, flogging) 1.** to beat hard with a whip, stick, etc.; whip. **2.** *Colloq.* to sell or attempt to sell. **3.** *Colloq.* to steal. **4.** *Colloq.* to defeat (an opponent) overwhelmingly. *–phr.* **5. flog a dead horse,** to make useless efforts, as in attempting to raise interest in a dead issue. **6. flog to death,** to use over and over again. **–flogger,** *n.*

flood /flʌd/ *n.* **1.** a great flowing or overflowing of water, especially over land not usually beneath water. **2.** any great outpouring or stream: *a flood of words*; *a flood of light.* **3.** the flowing in of the tide (opposed to *ebb*). *–v.t.* **4.** to cover with a flood. **5.** to oversupply: *they flooded us with gifts.* *–v.i.* **6.** to flow or pour in, or as if in, a flood: *The water flooded into the house.* **7.** to rise in a flood; overflow: *the river flooded.* **–floodable,** *adj.* **–floodless,** *adj.* **–flooder,** *n.*

floodgate /ˈflʌdgeit/ *n.* **1.** a gate designed to regulate the flow of water. **2.** anything serving to control indiscriminate flow or passage. **3.** *NZ* a free-hanging fence across a gully or creek which floats above an occasional flood.

floodlight /ˈflʌdlaɪt/ *n.* **1.** an artificial light so directed or diffused as to give a comparatively uniform illumination over a given area. **2.** a floodlight lamp or projector. *–v.t.* (**-lit, -lighting**) **3.** to illuminate with or as with a floodlight. **–floodlit**, *adj.* **–floodlighting**, *n.*

flood-proof *v.t.* **1.** to protect from flooding, as by levees, walls, etc. *–adj.* **2.** of or relating to a location protected in such a way.

floor /flɔ/ *n.* **1.** that part of a room or the like which forms its lower enclosing surface, and upon which one walks. **2.** a storey of a building. **3.** a level supporting surface in any structure: *the floor of a bridge.* **4.** a platform or prepared level area for a particular use: *a threshing floor.* **5.** the flat bottom of any more or less hollow place: *the floor of a cave.* **6.** any more or less flat extent or surface. **7.** *Colloq.* the ground. **8.** the part of a legislative chamber, etc., where the members sit, and from which they speak. **9.** the right of one member to speak from such a place in preference to other members: *the member for Wentworth has the floor.* **10.** the main part of a stock exchange or the like, as distinct from galleries, etc. **11.** *Mining* **a.** the bottom of a horizontal passageway. **b.** an underlying stratum, as of ore, usually flat. **12.** the bottom, base, or minimum charged or paid: *a price floor; a wage floor.* *–v.t.* **13.** to cover or furnish with a floor. **14.** to bring down to the floor or ground; knock down. **15.** *Colloq.* to beat or defeat. **16.** *Colloq.* to confound or nonplus: *to be floored by a problem.* *–phr.* **17. take the floor,** to begin speaking in a public gathering. **18. wipe the floor with,** *Colloq.* to overcome or vanquish totally. **–floorer**, *n.* **–floorless**, *adj.*

floor show *n.* an entertainment given in a nightclub or cabaret, usually consisting of a series of singing, dancing, or comic episodes.

flop /flɒp/ *v.i.* (**flopped, flopping**) **1.** to fall or plump down suddenly, especially with noise; drop or turn with a sudden bump or thud. **2.** to fall flat on the surface of water. **3.** *Colloq.* to yield or break down suddenly; fail. *–n.* **4.** *Colloq.* a failure. **–flopper**, *n.* **–floppy**, *adj.*

floppy disk *n.* a flexible magnetic disk used for storing data; diskette.

flora /ˈflɔrə/ *n.* (*pl.* **floras** or **florae** /ˈflɔri/) **1.** the plants of a particular region or period, listed by species. **2.** a work systematically describing such plants. **3.** microorganisms normally inhabiting the surface of a human or animal body, or an internal body passage.

floral /ˈflɔrəl, ˈflɔrəl/ *adj.* relating to or consisting of flowers. **–florally**, *adv.*

florid /ˈflɒrəd/ *adj.* **1.** highly coloured or ruddy, as complexion, cheeks, etc. **2.** flowery; excessively ornate; showy: *a florid prose style, florid music.* **–floridity** /flɒˈrɪdəti/, **floridness**, *n.* **–floridly**, *adv.*

florin /ˈflɒrən/ *n.* a silver coin worth two shillings; a former unit of currency.

florist /ˈflɒrəst/ *n.* **1.** a retailer of flowers, ornamental plants, etc. **2.** a person who works in floristry.

floristry /ˈflɒrəstri/ *n.* the art of arranging flowers, especially for sale.

-florous an adjectival suffix meaning 'flowered', as in *uniflorous.*

floss /flɒs/ *n.* **1.** the cottony fibre yielded by the silkcotton trees. **2.** silk filaments with little or no twist, used in weaving as brocade or in embroidery. **3.** any silky filamentous matter, as the silk of maize. **4.** → **dental floss**. Also (for defs 1–3), **floss silk**.

flotation /floʊˈteɪʃən/ *n.* **1.** the act or state of floating. **2.** the floating or launching of a commercial venture, a loan, etc. **3.** *Metallurgy* a process for separating the different crystalline phases in a mass of powdered ore based on their ability to sink in, or float on, a

given liquid. **4.** the science of floating bodies. Also, **floatation**.

flotation therapy *n.* a method of relaxation in which a person floats in a specially designed tank that is sealed to eliminate external stimuli.

flotilla /fləˈtɪlə/ *n.* **1.** number of small naval vessels; a subdivision of a fleet. **2.** a small fleet.

flotsam /ˈflɒtsəm/ *n.* such part of the wreckage of a ship and its cargo as is found floating on the water. Compare **jetsam**.

flotsam and jetsam *n.* **1.** the wreckage of a ship and its cargo found either floating upon the sea or washed ashore. **2.** odds and ends.

flounce¹ /flaʊns/ *v.i.* (**flounced, flouncing**) **1.** to go (*away, off, out,* etc.) with an impatient or angry fling of the body: *to flounce out of a room in a rage.* **2.** to throw the body about, as in floundering or struggling; twist; turn; jerk. *–n.* **3.** action of flouncing; a flouncing movement.

flounce² /flaʊns/ *n.* **1.** a strip of material, wider than a ruffle, gathered and attached at one edge and with the other edge left hanging, used for trimming, especially on women's skirts. *–v.t.* (**flounced, flouncing**) **2.** to trim with a flounce or flounces.

flounder¹ /ˈflaʊndə/ *v.i.* **1.** to struggle (*along, on, through,* etc.) with stumbling or plunging movements, in or as in mud or water. **2.** to struggle clumsily or helplessly in embarrassment or confusion.

flounder² /ˈflaʊndə/ *n.* **1.** any of numerous species of flatfishes, belonging to the families Bothidae and Pleuronectidae, found in coastal Australian and New Zealand waters. **2.** a European marine flatfish, *Platichthys flesus,* widely caught for food.

flour /ˈflaʊə/ *n.* **1.** the finely ground meal of wheat or other grain, especially the finer meal separated by bolting. **2.** any fine, soft powder: *flour of emery.* *–v.t.* **3.** to sprinkle or dredge with flour, as food or utensils in cookery. **–floury**, *adj.* **–flourless**, *adj.*

flourish /ˈflʌrɪʃ/ *v.i.* **1.** to be in a strong, healthy state; thrive; prosper: *During this period art flourished.* **2.** to be at the height of fame or excellence. *–v.t.* **3.** to wave showily (a sword, a stick, the limbs, etc.) about in the air. *–n.* **4.** waving, as of a sword, a stick, or the like. **5.** anything used for display, as a decoration in writing or an elaborate passage in music. **6.** a trumpet call or fanfare. **–flourishing**, *adj.* **–flourisher**, *n.*

flout /flaʊt/ *v.t.* to mock; scoff at; treat with disdain or contempt: *to flout the rules.* **–flouter**, *n.* **–floutingly**, *adv.*

flow /floʊ/ *v.i.* **1.** to move along in or as in a stream. **2.** to stream or pour forth. **3.** to proceed continuously and smoothly, like a stream, as thought, speech, etc. **4.** to fall or hang loosely: *flowing hair.* **5.** to overflow with something: *a land flowing with milk and honey.* **6.** to rise and advance, as the tide (opposed to *ebb*). *–n.* **7.** the act, rate or amount of flowing. **8.** any continuous movement, as of thought, speech, trade, etc., like that of a stream of water. **9.** something that flows; stream. **10.** an outpouring of something, as in a stream: *a flow of blood.* **11.** the rise of the tide; flood (opposed to *ebb*). **12.** *Colloq.* the sustained rhythm which an individual achieves in performing, speaking, etc. *–phr.* **13. go with the flow,** to take advantage of the momentum provided by a general trend in order to achieve one's goals.

flow chart *n.* a diagram showing the step-by-step operation of a system. Also, **flow diagram, flow sheet.**

flowchart /ˈfloʊtʃat/ *v.t.* to provide a flow chart for: *to flowchart the work processes.* **–flowcharting**, *n.*

flower /ˈflaʊə/ *n.* **1.** the coloured and decorative part of a plant. **2.** *Bot.* the sexual reproductive structure of an angiosperm (a plant whose seeds are enclosed in an ovary). **3.** a plant grown for the beauty of its flower.

4. the state of bloom: *plants in flower.* **5.** the finest or choicest part or example. **6.** (*pl.*) *Chem.* a substance in the form of a fine powder, especially as obtained by sublimation: *flowers of sulphur.* *−v.i.* **7.** (of a plant) to produce flowers. **8.** to reach the stage of full development. *−***flowerless**, *adj.* *−***flower-like**, *adj.*

flower girl *n.* a very young girl attending a bride.

flowery /ˈflauəri/ *adj.* (**-rier, -riest**) **1.** full of or covered with flowers. **2.** containing highly ornate language: *a flowery style.* **3.** decorated with floral designs. *−***flowerily**, *adv.* *−***floweriness**, *n.*

flown /floun/ *v.* past participle of **fly¹**.

flow-on *n.* the wider application of changes in wages, costs, etc., which have arisen in one part of the community.

flu /flu/ *n.* → **influenza**. *−***fluey**, *adj.*

fluctuate /ˈflʌktʃueit/ *v.i.* to change continually, as by turns, from one course, position, condition, amount, etc., to another, as the mind, opinion, policy, prices, temperature, etc.; vary irregularly; be unstable. *−***fluctuation**, *n.* *−***fluctuant**, *adj.*

flue /flu/ *n.* **1.** the smoke passage in a chimney. **2.** any duct or passage for air, gases, or the like.

fluent /ˈfluənt/ *adj.* **1.** flowing smoothly and easily: *to speak fluent French.* **2.** able to speak or write readily: *a fluent speaker.* **3.** easy; graceful: *fluent motion; fluent curves.* *−***fluency, fluentness**, *n.* *−***fluently**, *adv.*

fluff /flʌf/ *n.* **1.** light, downy particles, as of cotton. **2.** a downy mass; something downy or fluffy. **3.** *Colloq.* a blunder or error in execution, performance, etc. *−v.t.* **4.** to make into fluff; shake or puff out (feathers, hair, etc.) into a fluffy mass. **5.** *Colloq.* to fail to perform properly: *to fluff a golf stroke; to fluff an examination; to fluff one's lines in a play.* *−v.i.* **6.** to become fluffy; move, float, or settle down like fluff. **7.** *Colloq.* to blunder; fail in performance or execution. **8.** to lie; bluff. *−phr.* **9.** (**a**) **bit of fluff**, *Colloq.* an attractive but unintelligent young woman. *−***fluffy**, *adj.*

fluid /ˈfluəd/ *n.* **1.** a substance which is capable of flowing and offers no permanent resistance to changes of shape; a liquid or a gas. *−adj.* **2.** capable of flowing; liquid or gaseous. **3.** changing readily; shifting, not fixed, stable, or rigid. *−***fluidal, fluidic** /fluˈidik/, *adj.* *−***fluidity**, /fluˈidəti/, **fluidness**, *n.* *−***fluidly**, *adv.*

fluid ounce *n.* a unit of volume in the imperial system, equal to $\frac{1}{20}$ of a pint ($28.413\,062\,5 \times 10^{-3}$ litres) or, in the US, $\frac{1}{6}$ of a pint ($29.573\,529\,562\,5 \times 10^{-3}$ litres).

fluke¹ /fluk/ *n.* **1.** the flat triangular piece at the end of each arm of an anchor, which catches in the ground. **2.** a barb, or the barbed head, of a harpoon, etc. **3.** either half of the triangular tail of a whale.

fluke² /fluk/ *n.* **1.** any accidental advantage; a lucky chance. **2.** an accidentally successful stroke in billiards or other sports. *−***fluky**, *adj.*

fluke³ /fluk/ *n.* **1.** the flounder, *Platichtys flesus.* **2.** → **trematode.**

flummox /ˈflʌməks/ *v.t. Colloq.* to bewilder; confuse.

flung /flʌŋ/ *v.* past tense and past participle of **fling.**

flunk /flʌŋk/ *Colloq.* *−v.i.* **1.** to fail, as a student in an examination. *−v.t.* **2.** to remove (a student) as unqualified from a school, course, etc.

flunkey /ˈflʌŋki/ *n.* (*pl.* **-keys**) **1.** a male servant in livery; a lackey. **2.** a servile follower; a toady. *−***flunkeydom, flunkeyism**, *n.* *−***flunkeyish**, *adj.*

fluor-¹ a word element indicating the presence of fluorine.

fluor-² a word element indicating fluorescence.

fluorescence /fluəˈrɛsəns, flɔ-, flu-/ *n.* **1.** the property possessed by certain substances of emitting light upon exposure to external radiation or bombardment by a stream of particles. **2.** the light or luminosity so produced. *−***fluoresce**, *v.* *−***fluorescent**, *adj.*

fluorescent light *n.* a light which relies on a fluorescent tube as the light source.

fluorescent tube *n.* an electric discharge tube in which light is produced when electricity excites mercury vapour in argon or neon gas, resulting in ultraviolet light which causes the phosphor coating on the inside of the tube to glow.

fluoridation /fluərəˈdeiʃən, ˈflu-/ *n.* the addition to toothpaste, public water supplies, etc., of fluoride compounds to prevent tooth decay in the populace.

fluoride /ˈfluəraid, ˈflu-/ *n.* **1.** a salt of hydrofluoric acid. **2.** an organic compound with one or more hydrogen atoms substituted by fluorine atoms, as methyl fluoride. *−adj.* **3.** of or relating to a substance containing fluoride, as toothpaste.

fluorine /ˈfluərin, ˈflu-/ *n.* a nonmetallic element, a pale yellow corrosive gas, occurring combined, especially in fluorspar, cryolite, phosphate rock, and other minerals. *Symbol:* F; *relative atomic mass:* 18.9984; *atomic number:* 9. See **halogen.**

fluorspar /ˈfluəspɑ/ *n.* a common mineral, calcium fluoride, CaF_2, occurring in colourless, green, blue, purple, and yellow crystals, usually in cubes. It is the principal source of fluorine, and is also used as a flux in metallurgy and for ornamental purposes. Also, **fluor**; *Chiefly US,* **fluorite.** *−***fluoric**, *adj.*

flurry /ˈflʌri/ *n.* (*pl.* **-ries**) **1.** a sudden gust of wind. **2.** commotion; sudden excitement or confusion; nervous hurry.

flush¹ /flʌʃ/ *n.* **1.** a blush; rosy glow. **2.** a rushing, as of water. **3.** a rush of emotion; elation: *the first flush of success.* **4.** a glowing freshness or energy: *the flush of youth.* **5.** a wave of heat experienced in fever, menopause, etc. *−v.t.* **6.** to flood with water, especially for cleaning purposes. *−v.i.* **7.** to blush; redden. *−***flusher**, *n.*

flush² /flʌʃ/ *adj.* **1.** even or level, as with a surface; in one plane. **2.** well-supplied, as with money; affluent. **3.** quite full; full to overflowing. *−adv.* **4.** so as to be flush or even. **5.** squarely; full on: *I hit him flush on the face.* *−n.* **6.** fresh growth, as of shoots and leaves.

flush³ /flʌʃ/ *adj.* consisting entirely of cards of one suit: *a flush hand.*

fluster /ˈflʌstə/ *v.t.* **1.** to confuse; make nervous. **2.** to excite and confuse with drink.

flute /flut/ *n.* **1.** a musical wind instrument consisting of a tube with a series of finger holes or keys in which the air is blown across a hole at the end or side of the tube. **2.** *Archit., etc.* a groove, as along the length of a pillar. *−v.i.* **3.** to produce flutelike sounds. **4.** to play a flute. *−v.t.* **5.** to utter in flutelike tones. **6.** to form lengthwise grooves in. *−***flutelike**, *adj.* *−***fluting**, *n.*

fluted /ˈflutəd/ *adj.* **1.** having flutes or grooves, as a pillar. **2.** fine, clear and mellow; flute-like: *fluted notes.*

flutter /ˈflʌtə/ *v.i.* **1.** to flap or wave lightly in the air: *the flags were fluttering.* **2.** (of birds, etc.) to flap the wings, or fly with flapping movements. **3.** to move with quick, uneven movements. **4.** (of the heart, etc.) to beat fast and unevenly. **5.** to tremble; be agitated. **6.** *Swimming* (of the feet) to kick up and down in turn, as in freestyle and backstroke. *−v.t.* **7.** to cause to flutter; vibrate; agitate. *−n.* **8.** a fluttering movement. **9.** a state of nervous excitement or confusion. **10.** *Colloq.* a small bet. *−***fluttery**, *adj.* *−***flutterer**, *n.* *−***flutteringly**, *adv.*

fluvial /ˈfluviəl/ *adj.* of, relating to, or produced by a river.

flux /flʌks/ *n.* **1.** a flowing or flow. **2.** the flowing in of the tide. **3.** continuous passage; continuous change: *to be in a state of flux.* **4.** *Pathol.* an abnormal or morbid discharge of blood or other matter from the body. **5.** a substance applied when soldering, which cleans the metal surfaces being joined and promotes adhesion of the solder to them.

fly[1] /flaɪ/ *verb* (**flew, flown, flying**) −*v.i.* **1.** to move through the air on wings, as a bird. **2.** to be borne through the air by the wind or any other force or agency. **3.** to float or flutter in the air, as a flag, the hair, etc. **4.** to travel through the air in an aircraft: *she flew to Brisbane.* **5.** to move or pass swiftly; move with a start or rush: *she flew to answer the door.* **6.** to change rapidly and unexpectedly from one state to another: *to fly open.* **7.** to flee. −*v.t.* **8.** to cause to fly: *to fly a model aeroplane*; *to fly a kite*; *to fly a hawk.* **9.** to operate (an aircraft or spacecraft). **10.** to hoist aloft or bear aloft: *to fly a flag.* **11.** to travel over by flying. **12.** to transport by flying. **13.** to avoid; flee from. −*n.* (*pl.* **flies**) **14.** a strip sewn along one edge of a garment, to aid in concealing the buttons or other fasteners. **15.** such a strip used to hide the opening on a pair of trousers, or the fastening itself. **16.** a flap forming the door of a tent. **17.** a piece of canvas extending over the ridgepole of a tent and forming an outer roof. **18.** a light tent. **19.** *US* the course of a flying object, as a ball. **20.** *Machinery* → **flywheel.** **21.** (*pl.*) *Theatre* the space and apparatus above the stage. **22.** *Colloq.* an attempt: *give it a fly.* −*phr.* **23. fly a kite,** to attempt to obtain reactions to a proposed course of action by allowing it to be circulated as a rumour or unconfirmed report. **24. fly at,** to attack. **25. fly high, a.** to be ambitious. **b.** *Colloq.* to be in a state of euphoria, as induced by drugs. **26. fly in the face of,** to be at variance with. **27. fly off,** to move away quickly by or as by flying. **28. fly off the handle,** *Colloq.* to lose one's temper, especially unexpectedly. **29. fly out,** *Aust. Colloq.* to lose one's temper; become suddenly violently angry. **30. go fly a kite,** *Colloq.* (a phrase used to rebuff someone); get lost. **31. let fly, a.** to make an attack. **b.** to throw or propel. **c.** to give free rein to, especially in attacking: *he let fly his pent-up anger.* **32. on the fly,** *US* **a.** while still in flight; on the volley. **b.** hurriedly.

fly[2] /flaɪ/ *n.* (*pl.* **flies**) **1.** any of the two-winged insects constituting the order Diptera (**true flies**), especially one of the family Muscidae, as the common housefly, *Musca domestica.* **2.** any of a number of other winged insects, as the mayfly or firefly. **3.** *Angling* a fishhook dressed with silk, tinsel, fur, etc., to resemble an insect. −*phr. Colloq.* **4. fly in the ointment,** a slight flaw that greatly diminishes the value or pleasure of something. **5. like to be a fly on the wall,** to wish to be in a position to observe secretly. −**flyless,** *adj.*

fly-by-night *Colloq. adj.* **1.** irresponsible; unreliable. −*n.* **2.** someone who leaves secretly at night, as in order to avoid paying debts. **3.** someone who leads an active and entertaining night-life. −**fly-by-nighter,** *n.*

flycatcher /ˈflaɪkætʃə/ *n.* any of numerous small, insectivorous birds.

flyer /ˈflaɪə/ *n.* **1.** something that flies, such as a bird or insect. **2.** an aviator or a passenger in a plane. **3.** a person or thing that moves at great speed. **4.** some part of a machine having a rapid motion. **5.** a newspaper placard advertising headline news. **6.** a single sheet of printed material circulated to announce an event, promote a cause or advertise a product: *an election flyer.* Also, **flier.**

flying buttress *n.* a segmental arch which carries the thrust of a wall over a space to a solid pier buttress.

flying fox *n.* **1.** any of various large bats of the suborder Megachiroptera, especially of the genus *Pteropus*, of Australia, tropical Asia, and Africa, having a foxlike head and feeding on fruit and blossom. **2.** *Aust., NZ* a cable-operated carrier over watercourses or difficult terrain.

flying officer *n. Air Force* **1.** a commissioned officer in the Royal Australian Air Force ranking below flight lieutenant and above pilot officer. **2.** the rank. *Abbrev.*: FLGOFF

flying phalanger *n.* → **glider** (def. 3).

flying saucer *n.* any of various disc-shaped objects allegedly seen flying at high speeds and altitudes and supposed to be alien spacecraft.

flyleaf /ˈflaɪlif/ *n.* (*pl.* **-leaves** /-livz/) a blank leaf in the front or at the back of a book.

flystrike /ˈflaɪstraɪk/ *n.* an infestation of the flesh of a living sheep by the maggots of a blowfly, especially the green blowfly. Also, **blowfly strike, sheep strike.**

flytrap /ˈflaɪtræp/ *n.* **1.** a trap for flies. **2.** any of various plants which entrap insects, especially the Venus flytrap.

flyweight /ˈflaɪweɪt/ *n.* **1.** a very light weight division in boxing. **2.** a boxer of this weight class.

flywheel /ˈflaɪwil/ *n.* **1.** a heavy wheel which by its momentum tends to equalise the speed of machinery with which it is connected. **2.** a wheel used to carry the piston over dead centre.

f number *n.* the ratio of the focal length of a lens system to its effective diameter, used to number aperture openings in a camera. Also, **f-stop.**

foal /foʊl/ *n.* **1.** a young horse or other equine animal. **2.** a horse not yet past its first birthday. −*v.i.* **3.** to give birth to a foal.

foam /foʊm/ *n.* **1.** an aggregation of minute gas bubbles formed in a liquid by agitation, fermentation, etc.; froth. **2.** the froth of perspiration formed on the skin of a horse or other animal from great exertion. **3.** froth formed in the mouth, as in epilepsy and rabies. **4.** a substance which on being discharged from an aerosol container forms a layer of small stable bubbles, as that from a fire-extinguisher. **5.** a light material, in either spongy or rigid form, produced by foaming. −*v.i.* **6.** to form or gather foam; emit foam. −*v.t.* **7.** to cause to foam. −*phr.* **8. foam at the mouth,** to be speechless with some emotion, especially with rage. −**foamy,** *adj.* −**foamingly,** *adv.* −**foamless,** *adj.*

fob[1] /fɒb/ *n.* **1.** Also, **fob pocket.** a small pocket just below the waistline in trousers or breeches (formerly in the waistband) to hold a watch, etc. **2.** a short chain or ribbon with a seal or the like, attached to a watch and worn hanging from the pocket.

fob[2] /fɒb/ *phr.* (**fobbed, fobbing**) **fob off, 1.** (sometimes fol. by *on*) to palm off: *to fob off an inferior watch on a person.* **2.** to put off.

fob watch *n.* a small watch, usually round and with a lid, designed to sit in the fob pocket and often attached to the button of a waistcoat by a chain.

focaccia /fəˈkatʃiə, fəˈkatʃə/ *n.* flat Italian bread which can be eaten with various fillings or toppings.

focal length *n. Optics* **1.** (of a mirror or lens) the distance from the optical centre to the focal point. **2.** (of a telescope) the distance between the object lens and its corresponding focal plane.

focal point *n.* **1.** *Optics* the focus for a beam of light rays parallel to the principal axis of a lens or mirror; principal focus. **2.** the main point of interest, agreement, disagreement, etc.

focus /ˈfoʊkəs/ *n.* (*pl.* **-ci** /-kaɪ, -saɪ/ *or* **-cuses**) **1.** *Physics* a point at which rays of light, heat, or other radiation, meet after being refracted or reflected. **2.** *Optics* **a.** a point from which diverging rays appear to proceed, or a point at which converging rays would meet if they could be prolonged in the same direction (**virtual focus**). **b.** clear and sharply defined condition of an image. **c.** the position of a viewed object, or the adjustment of an optical device, necessary to produce a clear image: *in focus, out of focus.* **3.** a central point, as of attraction, attention, or activity. **4.** *Geom.* one of the points from which the distances to any point of a given curve are in a linear relation. −*v.t.* (**-cused** *or* **-cussed, -cusing** *or* **-cussing**) **5.** to bring to a focus or into focus.

6. to concentrate; to focus one's attention. –**focal**, *adj.* –**focusable**, *adj.* –**focuser**, *n.*

fodder /ˈfɒdə/ *n.* **1.** food for livestock, especially dried food, such as hay, straw, etc. –*v.t.* **2.** to feed with or as with fodder.

foe /foʊ/ *n.* **1.** someone who entertains enmity, hatred, or malice against another; an enemy. **2.** an enemy in war; hostile army. **3.** an opponent in a game, or contest.

foetus /ˈfiːtəs/ *n.* → **fetus.**

fog /fɒg/ *n.* **1.** a cloudlike mass or layer of minute globules of water in the air near the earth's surface; thick mist. **2.** any darkened state of the atmosphere, or the diffused substance which causes it. **3.** a state of mental confusion or obscurity: *a fog of doubt.* –*v.t.* (**fogged, fogging**) **4.** to envelop with, or as with fog. –**foggy**, *adj.* –**fogless**, *adj.*

fogey /ˈfoʊgi/ *n.* (*pl.* **-gies** *or* **-geys**) (usu. preceded by *old*) an old-fashioned or excessively conservative person. Also, **fogy.**

foghorn /ˈfɒghɔːn/ *n.* **1.** *Naut.* a horn for sounding warning signals, as to vessels, in foggy weather. **2.** *Colloq.* a deep, loud voice.

foible /ˈfɔɪbəl/ *n.* a weakness or failing in an otherwise sound character.

foil[1] /fɔɪl/ *v.t.* to frustrate (a person, an attempt, a purpose); baffle; baulk.

foil[2] /fɔɪl/ *n.* **1.** a metallic substance formed into very thin sheets by rolling and hammering: *gold, tin, aluminium, or lead foil.* **2.** the metallic backing applied to glass to form a mirror. **3.** a thin layer of metal placed under a gem in a closed setting, to improve its colour or brilliance. **4.** anything that serves to set off another thing distinctly or to advantage by contrast. **5.** *Colloq.* a quantity of marijuana wrapped in aluminium foil. **6.** *Hairdressing* **a.** a quantity of dye applied to a section of hair which is then wrapped in a piece of aluminium foil. **b.** such a piece of foil.

foil[3] /fɔɪl/ *n.* **1.** a flexible, thin sword with a button at the point, for use in fencing. **2.** (*pl.*) the art of exercise or fencing with such swords.

foist /fɔɪst/ *phr.* **foist on** (or **upon**), to palm off or impose fraudulently or unwarrantably on.

fold[1] /foʊld/ *v.t.* **1.** to double or bend (cloth, paper, etc.) over upon itself. **2.** to bring together (the arms, hands, legs, etc.) with one round another: *to fold one's arms on one's chest.* **3.** to bring (the wings) close to the body, as a bird on alighting. **4.** to enclose; wrap: *to fold something in paper.* **5.** to clasp or embrace: *to fold someone in one's arms.* –*v.i.* **6.** to be folded or be capable of folding: *the doors fold back.* **7.** to be closed or brought to an end, usually with financial loss, as a business enterprise or theatrical production. –*n.* **8.** a part that is folded; pleat; layer: *to wrap something in folds of cloth.* **9.** a hollow made by folding: *to carry something in the fold of one's dress.* **10.** a crease made by folding. **11.** *Internet* the point in a web page where the user has to scroll down to read the bottom of the page. **12.** a hollow place in undulating ground: *a fold of the hills; a fold of the mountains.* **13.** *Geol.* a portion of strata which is folded or bent (as an anticline or syncline), or which connects two horizontal or parallel portions of strata of different levels (as a monocline). **14.** an act of folding or doubling over. –*phr.* **15. fold about** (or **around**), to bend or wind around: *to fold one's arms about a person's neck.* **16. fold in**, *Cookery* to mix in, as beaten egg whites added to a batter or the like, by gently turning one part over another with a spoon, etc. **17. fold up, a.** to bring into a compact form, or shut, by bending and laying parts together: *to fold up a map.* **b.** to collapse. **c.** to fail in business.

fold[2] /foʊld/ *n.* **1.** an enclosure for domestic animals, especially sheep. **2.** the sheep contained in it. **3.** a flock of sheep. **4.** a church or congregation. –*phr.* **5. the fold**, any community of like-minded people adhering to an established belief or point of view.

-fold a suffix attached to numerals and other quantitative words or stems to denote multiplication by or division into a certain number, as in *twofold, manifold.*

folder /ˈfoʊldə/ *n.* **1.** an outer cover, usually a folded sheet of light cardboard, for papers. **2.** Also, (*in some operating systems*), **directory.** *Computers* a defined area on a computer disk used to store files; directory.

Foley /ˈfoʊli/ *n.* sound effects created in a Foley studio: *our Foley has a very solid realistic sound.* Also, **foley.**

Foley artist *n.* (*also lower case*) a person who specialises in making the sounds to be recorded as sound effects for film or television.

Foley studio *n.* (*also lower case*) a studio which specialises in the production of sound effects for films or videos.

foliage /ˈfoʊliɪdʒ/ *n.* **1.** the leaves of a plant, collectively; leafage. **2.** leaves in general. **3.** the representation of leaves, flowers, and branches in architectural ornament, etc. –**foliaged**, *adj.*

folio /ˈfoʊlioʊ/ *n.* (*pl.* **-lios**) **1.** a sheet of paper folded once to make two leaves (four pages) of a book. **2.** a volume having pages of the largest size. **3.** a leaf of a manuscript or book numbered only on the front side. **4.** *Printing* the page number of a book.

folivore /ˈfoʊlivɔː/ *n.* an animal that subsists largely on leaves, as the koala.

folk /foʊk/ *n.* (*pl.* **folk** *or* **folks**) **1.** people in general, especially the common people. **2.** people of a specified class or group: *poor folk; clever folk.* **3.** (*pl.*) *Colloq.* the persons of one's own family; one's relatives. **4.** (*pl.*) *Colloq.* a form of address for everyone present: *that's all folks.* –*adj.* **5.** originating among the common people. **6.** performing in the folk music genre. –**folkish**, *adj.* –**folksy**, *adj.* –**folkishness**, *n.*

folk dance *n.* **1.** a traditional dance performed and passed down from generation to generation by the common people of a particular community, country, etc. **2.** a piece of music for such a dance. –**folk dancing**, *n.*

folk hero *n.* a person who is remembered with respect and affection by the general populace.

folklore /ˈfoʊklɔː/ *n.* **1.** the lore of the common people; the traditional beliefs, legends, customs, etc., of a people. **2.** the study of such lore. –**folkloric**, *adj.* –**folklorist**, *n.* –**folkloristic** /foʊklɔˈrɪstɪk/, *adj.*

folk music *n.* **1.** music, usually of simple character, originating and handed down among the common people. **2.** music originating in the urban American beat generation of the 1940s and 1950s which concentrates on lyrics of social comment. Also, **folk.**

follicle /ˈfɒlɪkəl/ *n.* **1.** *Bot.* a dry one-celled seed vessel consisting of a single carpel, and dehiscent only along the ventral suture, such as the fruit of larkspur. **2.** *Anat.* a small cavity, sac, or gland, especially the tube-shaped sheath surrounding the root of a hair.

follow /ˈfɒloʊ/ *v.t.* **1.** to come after in natural sequence, order of time, etc.; succeed. **2.** to go or come after; move behind in the same direction: *go on ahead and I'll follow you.* **3.** to accept as a guide or leader; accept the authority or example of, or adhere to, as a person. **4.** to conform to, comply with, or act in accordance with: *to follow a person's advice.* **5.** to imitate or copy. **6.** to move forward along (a path, etc.). **7.** to come after as a result or consequence; result from: *the effects that followed this decision.* **8.** to go after or along with (a person, etc.) as a companion. **9.** to go in pursuit of: *to follow an enemy.* **10.** to endeavour to obtain or to attain to. **11.** to watch the movements, progress, or course of. **12.** to keep up to date with; observe the development of: *to follow the news; to follow the cricket.* **13.** to support or barrack for (a sporting team). **14.** to keep up with and understand (an argument, etc.): *do you follow me?* **15.** *Internet* to link oneself to (a site on a social network). –*v.i.* **16.** to come next after something else in natural sequence, order of time, etc. **17.** to happen or occur after something else; come next as an event. **18.** to go or come after a person or thing in motion: *go on ahead and I'll follow.* **19.** to result as an effect; occur as a consequence. –*phr.* **20. follow out,** to execute; carry out to a conclusion. **21. follow suit, a.** *Cards* to play a card of the same suit as that first played. **b.** to follow the example of another. **22. follow through, a.** to carry out completely, as a stroke in tennis or golf. **b.** to pursue an endeavour to its conclusion. **23. follow up, a.** to pursue closely. **b.** to pursue to a conclusion. **c.** to increase the effect of by further action. **d.** to take further action, investigation, etc., after the elapse of an interval of time. –**follower,** *n.*

following /ˈfɒloʊɪŋ/ *n.* **1.** a body of followers, attendants, adherents, etc. **2. the following,** things, lines, pages, etc., that follow. –*adj.* **3.** that follows. **4.** that comes after or next in order or time: *the following day.* **5.** that is now to follow; now to be mentioned, described, related, or the like.

folly /ˈfɒli/ *n.* (*pl.* **-lies**) **1.** the state or quality of being foolish; lack of understanding or sense. **2.** a foolish action, practice, idea, etc.; an absurdity. **3.** *Archit.* a useless but costly structure, often in the form of a sham Gothic or classical ruin; especially popular in 18th-century England. **4.** (*pl.*) a theatrical revue.

foment /fəˈmɛnt/ *v.t.* **1.** to promote the growth or development of; instigate or foster (discord, rebellion, etc.). **2.** to apply warm water or medicated liquid, cloths dipped in such liquid, or the like, to (the surface of the body). –**fomentation,** *n.* –**fomenter,** *n.*

fond /fɒnd/ *adj.* **1.** loving: *give someone a fond look.* **2.** foolishly tender; over-affectionate; doting: *a fond parent.* **3.** cherished with strong or unreasoning affection: *nourish fond hopes.* **4.** *Archaic* foolish or silly. –*phr.* **5. fond of,** liking: *fond of children; fond of drink.* –**fondly,** *adj.* –**fondness,** *n.*

fondle /ˈfɒndl/ *v.t.* to handle or touch fondly; caress. –**fondler,** *n.*

fondue /ˈfɒndu, ˈfɒndju/ *n.* **1.** a dish of melted cheese and white wine, heated over a small burner at the table, into which pieces of bread are dipped before being eaten. **2.** any similar dish of oil or flavoured stock (def. 25) in which pieces of fish, meat, vegetable, or fruit are cooked at the table on individual skewers before being eaten.

font¹ /fɒnt/ *n.* **1.** a receptacle, usually of stone, as in a baptistery or church, for the water used in baptism. **2.** a receptacle for holy water; stoup. **3.** the reservoir for oil in a lamp.

font² /fɒnt/ *n.* a complete assortment of printing type of one style and size. Also, **fount.**

fontanelle /fɒntəˈnɛl/ *n. Anat.* one of the spaces, closed by membrane, between the bones of the fetal or young skull. Also, *Chiefly US,* **fontanel.**

Foo /fu/ *n.* a line drawing in a cartoon style of a character looking over a fence with just the nose, eyes and bald head visible.

food /fud/ *n.* **1.** what is eaten, or taken into the body, for nourishment. **2.** more or less solid nourishment (as opposed to *drink*). **3.** a particular kind of solid nourishment: *a breakfast food.* **4.** whatever supplies nourishment to organic bodies: *plant food.* **5.** anything serving as material for consumption or use: *food for thought.* –**foodless,** *adj.*

food additive *n.* a substance added to food to enhance its appearance or taste, to increase its nutritional value, or to maintain its freshness.

food irradiation *n.* a technique of preserving food by exposing it to gamma rays from cobalt-60 or caesium-137 which destroys the microorganisms which make food go bad, prevents insect attack, stops food such as potatoes or onions from sprouting, and extends the shelf life of many foods.

foodstuff /ˈfudstʌf/ *n.* a substance or material suitable for food.

fool¹ /ful/ *n.* **1.** someone who lacks sense; a silly or stupid person. **2.** a professional jester, formerly kept by a person of rank for amusement. **3.** a weak-minded or idiotic person. –*v.t.* **4.** to make a fool of; impose on; trick; deceive. –*v.i.* **5.** to act like a fool; joke; play. **6.** to jest; make believe: *I was only fooling.* –*phr.* **7. be a fool to oneself,** to unwittingly disadvantage oneself. **8. fool around** (or **about**), **a.** to behave foolishly; be silly. **b.** to potter aimlessly; waste time. **9. fool around with, a.** to waste time on: *to fool around with trivial details.* **b.** to philander or trifle with. **c.** to engage in sexual activities with. **10. fool with,** to play or meddle foolishly with: *to fool with a loaded gun.* **11. make a fool of,** to make appear foolish, often by deceiving or imposing on others. **12. more fool ...,** an expression declaring an action, often a well-intentioned one, performed by the person specified, was foolish.

fool² /ful/ *n.* a dish made of fruit stewed, made into a puree, and mixed with thick cream or custard: *gooseberry fool.*

foolhardy /ˈfulhadi/ *adj.* (**-dier, -diest**) bold without judgement; foolishly rash or venturesome. –**foolhardily,** *adv.* –**foolhardiness,** *n.*

foolish /ˈfulɪʃ/ *adj.* **1.** silly; without sense: *a foolish person.* **2.** resulting from or evidencing folly; ill-considered; unwise: *a foolish action; foolish speech.* –**foolishly,** *adv.* –**foolishness,** *n.*

foolproof /ˈfulpruf/ *adj.* **1.** involving no risk or harm, even when tampered with. **2.** never-failing: *a foolproof method.*

foolscap /ˈfulzkæp/ *n.* a printing paper size, $13\frac{1}{2} \times 17$ inches, most commonly in use before metrication.

foot /fut/ *n.* (*pl.* **feet**) **1.** (in vertebrates) the terminal part of the leg, below the ankle joint, on which the body stands and moves. **2.** (in invertebrates) any part similar in position or function. **3.** such a part considered as the organ of locomotion. **4.** a unit of length in the imperial system, derived from the length of the human foot. It is divided into 12 inches and equal to 0.3048 m. **5.** walking or running motion. **6.** (of furniture) a shaped or ornamented part terminating the leg. **7.** the flaring base or rim of a glass, teapot, etc. **8.** the part of a stocking, etc., covering the foot. **9.** an attachment to a sewing machine which guides the material under the needle: *a sewing foot; a hemming foot.* **10.** the lowest part, or bottom, as of a hill, ladder, page, sail, etc. **11.** the part of anything opposite the top or head. **12.** the end of a bed, grave, etc., towards which the feet are placed. **13.** *Prosody* a group of syllables constituting a metrical unit of a verse. –*phr.* **14. foot it, a.** to walk; go on foot. **b.** to move the feet to measure or music, or dance. **15. foot the bill,** to meet all expenses. **16. get off on the right foot,** to have a good start. **17. get off on the wrong foot,** to have a bad start. **18. have one foot in the grave,** to be near death. **19. my foot,** an exclamation of disbelief. **20. on foot, a.** on one's feet, rather than riding or sitting. **b.** in motion; astir. **c.** in active existence or operation. **21. put one's best foot forward, a.** to make as good an impression as possible. **b.** to do one's very best. **c.** to walk as fast as possible. **22. put one's (big) foot in it** or **put one's foot in one's mouth,** *Colloq.* to say something that causes embarrassment to oneself or anger to another. **23. put one's foot down, a.** to take a firm stand. **b.** to accelerate in a motor vehicle. **24. set**

foot in, to enter; go into. **25. set on foot**, to start (something) going; originate. **26. the foot**, *Obs.* infantry: *regiments of the foot.* See **feet**.

footage /ˈfʊtɪdʒ/ *n.* **1.** length or extent in feet: *the footage of timber.* **2. a.** material recorded on a film or video camera, either on film, tape or digitally. **b.** a length of cinematographic film; used for a scene or scenes. **c.** Also, **raw footage**. unedited recorded material.

foot-and-mouth disease *n.* *Vet. Science* a contagious virus disease of cattle and other cloven-hoofed animals, characterised by a vesicular eruption about the hoofs and mouth. The disease very rarely affects humans.

football /ˈfʊtbɔl/ *n.* **1.** any game in which the kicking of a ball has a large part, as Australian Rules, Rugby Union, Rugby League, soccer, American football, etc. **2.** the ball used in any of these games. Also, *Colloq.*, **footy**. –**footballer**, *n.*

footer /ˈfʊtə/ *n.* **1.** (with a numeral prefixed) a person or thing of the height or length in feet indicated: *a six-footer.* **2.** (with a numeral prefixed) a racing yacht with an unenclosed hull of the length in feet indicated: *that yacht is a sixteen-footer.* **3.** *Colloq.* → **football**. **4.** (in computer typesetting) an item programmed to appear regularly at the foot of a page. Compare **header** (def. 4).

foothill /ˈfʊthɪl/ *n.* a minor elevation at the base of a mountain or mountain range.

foothold /ˈfʊthoʊld/ *n.* **1.** a hold or support for the feet; a place where one may stand or tread securely. **2.** an initial or tenuous position in a project or enterprise, making further advancement in it possible.

footie /ˈfʊti/ *n.* → **footy**.

footing /ˈfʊtɪŋ/ *n.* **1.** a firm position; foothold. **2.** a foundation on which anything is established. **3.** a secure place or support for the feet. **4.** a firm placing of the feet. **5.** the condition of a relationship: *he is on a friendly footing with her.*

footlights /ˈfʊtlaɪts/ *pl. n.* **1.** *Theatre* a row of lights at the front of the stage, nearly on a level with the feet of the performers. **2.** *Colloq.* the stage; the acting profession.

footloose /ˈfʊtlus/ *adj.* free to go or travel about; not confined by responsibilities, etc.: *footloose and fancy-free.*

footloose industry *n.* an industry with low establishment costs that can take advantage of cheap labour and is prepared to move to find it.

footman /ˈfʊtmən/ *n.* (*pl.* **-men**) a male servant in livery who attends the door or the carriage, waits at table, etc.

footnote /ˈfʊtnoʊt/ *n.* **1.** a note or comment at the foot of a page, referring to a specific part of the text on the page. **2.** an added comment, of less importance than the main text. –*v.t.* **3.** to add footnotes to (a text).

footpath /ˈfʊtpaθ/ *n.* a path for pedestrians only, especially one at the side of a road or street.

footprint /ˈfʊtprɪnt/ *n.* **1.** a mark left by the foot **2.** the area of the earth's surface covered by a satellite transmission. **3.** the area of land which is overshadowed by something else, as a building. **4.** the area reached by a radio station's transmission. **5.** → **ecological footprint**.

footstep /ˈfʊtstɛp/ *n.* **1.** a step or tread of the foot, or the sound produced by it; footfall. –*phr.* **2. follow in someone's footsteps**, to succeed or imitate.

footsy /ˈfʊtsi/ *Colloq.* –*n.* (*pl.* **-sies**) **1.** a foot. –*phr.* **2. play footsies**, (sometimes fol. by *with*) to touch in secret a person's feet, knees, etc., with one's feet, especially as part of amorous play.

footy /ˈfʊti/ *n.* *Aust., NZ Colloq.* → **football**. Also, **footie**.

fop /fɒp/ *n.* a man who is excessively concerned about his manners and appearance. –**foppish**, *adj.*

for /fɔ/, *weak form* /fə/ *prep.* **1.** with the object or purpose of: *to go for a walk.* **2.** intended to belong to, suit the purposes or needs of, or be used in connection with: *a book for children; a box for gloves.* **3.** in order to obtain: *a suit for damages.* **4.** with inclination or tendency towards: *to long for a thing; to have an eye for beauty.* **5.** expressing a wish or desire for something to be obtained: *O for the wings of a dove.* **6.** in consideration of, or in return for: *three for a dollar; to be thanked for one's efforts.* **7.** appropriate or adapted to: *a subject for speculation.* **8.** with regard or respect to: *pressed for time; too warm for April.* **9.** during the continuance of: *for a long time.* **10.** in favour of, or on the side of: *to stand for honest government.* **11.** in place of, or instead of: *a substitute for butter.* **12.** in the interest of: *to act for a client.* **13.** as an offset to: *blow for blow.* **14.** in honour of: *to give a dinner for a person.* **15.** in punishment of: *fined for stealing.* **16.** with the purpose of reaching: *to start for Perth.* **17.** conducive to: *for the advantage of everybody.* **18.** in order to save: *to flee for one's life.* **19.** in order to become: *to go for a soldier.* **20.** in assignment or attribution to: *an engagement for this evening; it is for you to decide.* **21.** to allow of; to require: *too many for separate mention.* **22.** such as results in: *his reason for going.* **23.** as affecting the interests or circumstances of: *bad for one's health.* **24.** in proportion or with reference to: *tall for his age.* **25.** in the character of, or as being: *to know a thing for a fact.* **26.** by reason of, or because of: *to shout for joy; famed for its beauty.* **27.** in spite of: *for all that.* **28.** to the extent or amount of: *to walk for a mile.* **29.** sometimes used to govern a noun or pronoun followed by an infinitive, in a construction equivalent to a clause with *that* and *should*, etc., as in *it is time for him to go*, meaning *it is time that he should go.* –*conj.* **30.** seeing that; since. **31.** because. –*phr.* **32. be for it**, *Colloq.* to be about to suffer some punishment, injury, setback, or the like.

for- a prefix meaning 'away', 'off', 'to the uttermost', 'extremely', 'wrongly', or imparting a negative or privative force, occurring in words of Old or Middle English origin, many of which are now obsolete or archaic, as in *forswear, forbid.*

forage /ˈfɒrɪdʒ/ *n.* **1.** food for horses and cattle; fodder; provender. **2.** the act of searching for provisions of any kind. **3.** a raid. –*v.i.* (**-raged, -raging**) **4.** to wander in search of supplies. **5.** to hunt or search about. –*adj.* **6.** grown as a crop for forage: *forage cereals.* –**forager**, *n.*

foray /ˈfɔreɪ, ˈfɒ-/ *n.* **1.** a raid for the purpose of taking plunder. **2.** a trip made for a particular purpose: *to make a foray into town to do the shopping.* **3.** a first attempt at a new activity: *her foray into the fashion industry.* –**forayer**, *n.*

forbade /fəˈbeɪd/ *v.* past tense of **forbid**. Also, **forbad** /fəˈbæd/.

forbear /fɔˈbɛə/ *verb* (**-bore, -borne, -bearing**) –*v.t.* **1.** to refrain from; desist from; cease. **2.** to refrain from using, etc.; keep back; withhold. –*v.i.* **3.** to be patient; show forbearance. –**forbearer**, *n.* –**forbearingly**, *adv.*

forbearance /fɔˈbɛərəns/ *n.* **1.** the act of forbearing; a refraining from something. **2.** an abstaining from the enforcement of a right.

forbid /fəˈbɪd/ *v.t.* (**-bade** *or* **-bad, -bidden** *or* **-bid, -bidding**) **1.** to command (a person, etc.) not to do, have, use, etc., something, or not to enter some place. **2.** to put an interdiction against (something); prohibit. **3.** to hinder or prevent; make impossible. **4.** to exclude; repel. –**forbidder**, *n.*

forbidding /fəˈbɪdɪŋ/ *adj.* **1.** causing dislike or fear: *a forbidding countenance.* **2.** repellent; dangerous-looking: *forbidding cliffs; forbidding clouds.* –**forbiddingly**, *adv.* –**forbiddingness**, *n.*

force /fɔs/ *n.* **1.** strength; intensity of effect: *the force of a blow; the force of an argument; the force of* *circumstances.* **2.** power, as of a ruler or nation; might. **3.** strength or power used upon a thing or person; violence: *to use force in order to do something*; *to use force on a person.* **4.** *Agric.* the ability of a dog to control sheep, etc. **5.** mental or moral strength; power of effective action. **6.** (*oft. pl.*) the army, navy and air force of a country. **7.** any body of people combined for joint action: *the police force.* **8.** *Physics* **a.** an influence which produces or tends to produce motion or change of motion. **b.** the strength of this influence. **c.** a push, pull or twist. **9.** any strong influence: *the changes in the law were brought about by social forces.* **10.** the binding power of an agreement, etc. –*v.t.* (**forced, forcing**) **11.** to make (oneself or someone) do something; compel: *she forced him to confess.* **12.** to drive by force; overcome the resistance of. **13.** to bring about or effect by force or as a necessary result: *to force a passage*; *to force a confession.* **14.** to put or impose (something) by force on or upon a person. **15.** to enter or take by force; overpower. **16.** to break open (a door, lock, etc.). **17.** Also, **force-ripen.** to cause (plants, fruits, etc.) to grow or ripen at an increased rate by artificial methods. **18.** *Agric.* to keep (sheep, etc.) moving through a race or yard, usually using a dog. –*phr.* **19. in force, a.** in operation, effect, etc.: *a law now in force.* **b.** in full strength: *her friends came to see her in force.* –**forceless,** *adj.* –**forcer,** *n.*

forceful /'fɔsfəl/ *adj.* **1.** full of force; powerful; vigorous; effective. **2.** acting or driven with force. –**forcefully,** *adv.* –**forcefulness,** *n.*

forceps /'fɔsəps/ *n.* (*pl.* -**ceps** *or* -**cipes** /-səpiz/) an instrument, as pincers or tongs, for seizing and holding objects, as in surgical operations. –**forcepslike,** *adj.*

forceps delivery *n.* a delivery of a baby in which the emerging head is grasped with forceps.

forcible /'fɔsəbəl/ *adj.* **1.** effected by force. **2.** having force; producing a powerful effect; effective. **3.** convincing, as reasoning. **4.** characterised by the use of force or violence. –**forcibleness, forcibility** /fɔsə'bɪləti/, *n.* –**forcibly,** *adv.*

ford /fɔd/ *n.* **1.** a place where a river or other body of water may be crossed by wading. –*v.t.* **2.** to cross (a river, etc.) by a ford. –**fordable,** *adj.* –**fordless,** *adj.*

fore /fɔ/ *adj.* **1.** situated at or towards the front, as compared with something else. **2.** first in place, time, order, rank, etc.; forward; earlier. –*adv.* **3.** *Naut.* at or towards the bow. –*n.* **4.** the forepart of anything; the front. **5.** *Naut.* the foremast. –*phr.* **6. to the fore, a.** to or at the front; to or in a conspicuous place or position. **b.** ready at hand. **c.** still alive.

fore- a prefix form of **before** meaning 'front', (*forehead, forecastle*), 'ahead of time' (*forecast, foretell*), 'superior' (*foreman*), etc.

forearm[1] /'fɔram/ *n.* the part of the arm between the elbow and the wrist.

forearm[2] /fɔr'am/ *v.t.* to arm beforehand.

forebear /'fɔbɛə/ *n.* (*usu. pl.*) an ancestor; forefather.

forebode /fɔ'boʊd/ *v.t.* (-**boded,** -**boding**) **1.** to foretell or predict; portend; be an omen of; indicate beforehand: *clouds that forebode a storm.* **2.** to have a presentiment of (especially evil). –**foreboding,** *n.,* *adj.*

forecast /'fɔkast/ *v.t.* (-**cast** *or* -**casted,** -**casting**) **1.** to conjecture beforehand; predict. **2.** to make a forecast of (the weather, etc.). **3.** to serve as, a forecast of; foreshadow. **4.** to cast, contrive, or plan beforehand; prearrange. –*n.* **5.** a prediction, especially as to the weather. –**forecaster,** *n.*

forecastle /'foʊksəl/ *n.* the sailors' quarters in the forward part of a merchant vessel. Also, **fo'c's'le.**

foreclose /fɔ'kloʊz/ *v.t.* **1.** *Law* **a.** to deprive (a mortgagor or pledgor) of the right to redeem his or her property. **b.** to take away the right to redeem (a mortgage or pledge). **2.** to shut out; exclude or bar. **3.** to hinder or prevent, as from doing something. **4.** to close, settle, or answer beforehand. –*v.i.* **5.** to foreclose a mortgage or pledge. –**foreclosure,** *n.* –**foreclosable,** *adj.*

forefather /'fɔfaðə/ *n.* an ancestor.

forefinger /'fɔfɪŋgə/ *n.* the first finger, next to the thumb; the index finger.

forego /fɔ'goʊ/ *verb* (**forewent, foregone, foregoing**) –*v.i.* **1.** to go before. –*v.t.* **2.** to precede. –**foregoer,** *n.*

foreground /'fɔgraʊnd/ *n.* **1.** the ground or parts situated, or represented as situated, in the front; the nearer portion of a scene (opposed to *background*). –*v.t.* **2.** to emphasise; give importance or priority to. –**foregrounding,** *n.*

forehand /'fɔhænd/ *adj.* **1.** made to the right side of the body (when the player is right-handed). **2.** done beforehand; anticipative; given or made in advance, as a payment.

forehead /'fɔrəd, 'fɔhɛd/ *n.* **1.** the fore or front upper part of the head; the part of the face above the eyes; the brow. **2.** the fore or front part of anything.

foreign /'fɔrən/ *adj.* **1.** relating to, like, or coming from another country or nation. **2.** relating to dealings with other countries. **3.** outside one's own country, society, etc. **4.** *Law* outside the legal power of the state; alien. **5.** not belonging: *a foreign substance in the eye*; *foreign to our discussion.* **6.** strange; unfamiliar. –**foreignness,** *n.*

foreign affairs *pl. n.* international relations; activities of a nation arising from its dealings with other nations. Also, **external affairs.**

foreigner /'fɔrənə/ *n.* **1.** a person not native or naturalised in the country or jurisdiction under consideration; an alien. **2.** a thing produced in or coming from a foreign country.

foreign exchange *n.* **1.** the buying and selling of the money of other countries. **2.** the money of other countries.

forelock /'fɔlɒk/ *n.* **1.** the lock of hair that grows from the forepart of the head. –*phr.* **2. touch** (or **tug**) (or **pull**) **one's forelock,** to touch or tug one's forelock as a gesture of servility.

foreman /'fɔmən/ *n.* (*pl.* -**men**) **1.** a man in charge of a group of workers. **2.** the spokesman of a jury. –**foremanship,** *n.*

foremost /'fɔmoʊst/ *adj.* **1.** first in place, order, rank, etc. –*adv.* **2.** first.

forename /'fɔneɪm/ *n.* a name that precedes the family name or surname; a first name.

forensic /fə'rɛnzɪk, -sɪk/ *adj.* **1.** of or relating to courts of law or legal proceedings. **2.** applied to the process of collecting evidence for a legal case: *forensic accounting*; *forensic archaeology*; *forensic linguistics.* –**forensically,** *adv.*

forensic medicine *n.* the science of the application of medical knowledge to the law.

forensics /fə'rɛnzɪks/ *n.* (*construed as sing. or pl.*) **1.** the application of the investigative and analytical techniques used in scientific and technological disciplines to the collection of evidence, especially of evidence for presentation in a legal matter. **2.** → **forensic medicine.**

foreplay /'fɔpleɪ/ *n.* stimulation preceding sexual intercourse.

forerunner /'fɔrʌnə/ *n.* **1.** a predecessor; ancestor. **2.** a herald or harbinger. **3.** a prognostic or portent.

foresee /fɔ'si/ *verb* (-**saw,** -**seen,** -**seeing**) –*v.t.* **1.** to see beforehand; have prescience of; foreknow. –*v.i.* **2.** to exercise foresight. –**foreseeable,** *adj.* –**foreseer,** *n.*

foreshadow /fɔ'ʃædoʊ/ *v.t.* to show or indicate beforehand; prefigure. –**foreshadower,** *n.*

foreshore /'fɔʃɔ/ n. **1.** the forepart of the shore; the part of the shore between the ordinary high-water mark and low-water mark. **2.** the ground between the water's edge and the land cultivated or built upon.

foresight /'fɔsaɪt/ n. **1.** care or provision for the future; provident care. **2.** the act or power of foreseeing; prevision; prescience. **3.** perception gained by or as by looking forward; prospect; a view into the future. –**foresighted**, adj. –**foresightedness**, n.

foreskin /'fɔskɪn/ n. → **prepuce**.

forest /'fɒrəst/ n. **1.** an area of bushland dominated by trees, the type of tree often being specified: *paperbark forest*; *gum forest*. **2.** the trees alone: *to cut down a forest*. **3.** a thick cluster of many things. –v.t. **4.** to cover with trees; convert into a forest. –**forested**, adj. –**forestless**, adj.

forestall /fɔ'stɔl/ v.t. **1.** to prevent, hinder, or thwart by action in advance; take measures concerning or deal with (a thing) in advance. **2.** to deal with, meet, or realise in advance of the natural or proper time; be beforehand with or get ahead of (a person, etc.) in action. –**forestaller**, n. –**forestalment**, n.

forester /'fɒrəstə/ n. **1.** someone who practises or has expert knowledge of forestry. **2.** an officer having charge of a forest.

forestry /'fɒrəstri/ n. the science and practice of planting and taking care of forests.

foretell /fɔ'tɛl/ v.t. (-**told**, -**telling**) to tell of beforehand; predict or prophesy.

forever /fər'ɛvə/ adv. **1.** eternally; without ever ending: *to last forever*. **2.** continually; incessantly: *he's forever complaining*. **3.** finally and permanently: *to go away forever*. Also, **for ever**.

foreword /'fɔwɜd/ n. a preface or introductory statement in a book, etc.

forfaiting /'fɔfeɪtɪŋ/ n. the purchase of receivables such as promissory notes, bills of exchange, letters of credit, etc., from an exporter, usually at a discount, the advantage to the seller being that it converts credit to cash. –**forfaiter**, n.

forfeit /'fɔfət/ n. **1.** a fine; penalty. **2.** the act of forfeiting. **3.** something lost because of crime, carelessness, neglect, etc. –v.t. **4.** to lose, or become liable to lose (something) because of a crime, fault, etc. –adj. **5.** lost in this way. –**forfeiture**, n. –**forfeiter**, n.

forgave /fɔ'geɪv/ v. past tense of **forgive**.

forge[1] /fɔdʒ/ n. **1.** the special fireplace or furnace in which metal is heated before shaping. **2.** → **smithy**. –verb (**forged**, **forging**) –v.t. **3.** to form by heating and hammering. **4.** to form or make in any way. **5.** to invent (a lie, etc.). **6.** to copy (a signature, etc.) in order to deceive. –v.i. **7.** to commit forgery. **8.** to work at a forge. –**forgeable**, adj. –**forger**, n.

forge[2] /fɔdʒ/ phr. (**forged**, **forging**) **forge ahead**, **1.** to progress with increased speed: *the runner in second place forged ahead at the turn*. **2.** to progress because of vigorous effort or special circumstances, especially from a condition of difficulty: *the firm forged ahead after the restructuring of management*.

forgery /'fɔdʒəri/ n. (pl. -**ries**) **1.** the making of a fraudulent imitation of a thing, or of something spurious which is put forth as genuine, as a coin, a work of art, a literary production, etc. **2.** something, as a coin, a work of art, a writing, etc., produced by forgery. **3.** the act of fabricating or producing falsely.

forget /fə'gɛt/ verb (-**got**, -**gotten**, -**getting**) –v.t. **1.** to cease to remember; fail to remember; be unable to recall. **2.** to omit or neglect unintentionally (to do something). **3.** to omit to take; leave behind inadvertently: *to forget one's keys*. **4.** to omit to mention; leave unnoticed. **5.** to omit to think of; take no note of. **6.** to neglect wilfully; overlook, disregard, or slight. –v.i.

7. to cease or omit to think of something. –phr. **8. forget it**, to drop the subject or come to another view of it. **9. forget oneself**, **a.** to say or do something improper. **b.** to fail to remember one's station, position, or character. **c.** to become absent-minded. **d.** to lose consciousness, as in sleep. –**forgettable**, adj. –**forgetter**, n.

forgetful /fə'gɛtfəl/ adj. **1.** apt to forget; that forgets: *a forgetful person*. –phr. **2. forgetful of**, heedless or neglectful of: *to be forgetful of others*. –**forgetfully**, adv. –**forgetfulness**, n.

forget-me-not n. any small plant of the family Boraginaceae, especially of the genera *Myosotis* and *Cynoglossum*, a light blue flower, regarded as an emblem of constancy.

forgive /fə'gɪv/ verb (-**gave**, -**given**, -**giving**) –v.t. **1.** to grant free pardon for or remission of (an offence, debt, etc.); pardon. **2.** to give up all claim on account of; remit (a debt, etc.). **3.** to grant free pardon to (a person). **4.** to cease to feel resentment against: *to forgive one's enemies*. –v.i. **5.** to pardon an offence or an offender. –**forgiveness**, n. –**forgiving**, adj. –**forgivable**, adj. –**forgivably**, adv.

forgo /fɔ'goʊ/ v.t. (**forwent**, **forgone**, **forgoing**) to abstain or refrain from; do without; give up, renounce, or resign. –**forgoer**, n.

forgot /fə'gɒt/ v. past tense of **forget**.

forgotten /fə'gɒtn/ v. past participle of **forget**.

fork /fɔk/ n. **1.** an instrument having two or more prongs or tines, for holding, lifting, etc., as any of various agricultural tools, or an implement for handling food at table or in cooking. **2.** something resembling or suggesting this in form. **3.** the point or part at which a thing, as a river or a road, divides into branches. **4.** each of the branches into which a thing forks. –v.t. **5.** to pierce, raise, pitch, dig, etc., with a fork. –v.i. **6.** to form a fork; divide into branches. –phr. *Colloq.* **7. fork out**, to pay, usually grudgingly. **8. fork over**, to hand over. –**forkful**, n. –**forkless**, adj.

forklift /'fɔklɪft/ n. two power-operated, parallel, horizontal arms for lifting and carrying goods, fitted to a truck or other vehicle, especially in a warehouse or factory.

forlorn /fə'lɔn/ adj. **1.** abandoned, deserted, or forsaken. **2.** desolate or dreary; unhappy or miserable, as in feeling, condition, or appearance. **3.** desperate or hopeless. –phr. **4. forlorn of**, bereft of: *forlorn of hope*. –**forlornly**, adv. –**forlornness**, n.

form /fɔm/ n. **1.** definite shape; external shape or appearance considered apart from colour or material; configuration. **2.** the shape of a thing or person. **3.** a body, especially that of a human being. **4.** something that gives or determines shape; a mould. **5.** a particular structural condition, character, or mode of being exhibited by a thing: *water in the form of ice*. **6.** the manner or style of arranging and coordinating parts for a pleasing or effective result, as in literary or musical composition. **7.** the formal structure of a work of art; the organisation and relationship of lines or colours in a painting or volumes and voids in a sculpture so as to create a coherent image. **8.** due or proper shape; orderly arrangement of parts; good order. **9.** a set, prescribed, or customary order or method of doing something. **10.** a set order of words, as for use in religious ritual or in a legal document. **11.** a document with blank spaces to be filled in with particulars: *a tax form*. **12.** a typical document to be used as a guide in framing others for like cases: *a form for a deed*. **13.** a conventional method of procedure or behaviour. **14.** a formality or ceremony, often with implication of absence of real meaning. **15.** procedure, according to a set order or method. **16.** formality; ceremony; conformity to the usages of society. **17.** mere outward formality or ceremony;

conventional observance of social usages. **18.** conduct, as judged by social standards: *good form; bad form.* **19.** manner or method of performing something. **20.** condition, especially good condition, with reference to fitness for performing. **21.** *Gram.* **a.** any word, part of a word, or group of words arranged in a construction, which recurs in various contexts in a language with relatively constant meaning. **b.** a particular shape of a form (def. 21a) when it occurs in several ways: *in 'I'm', 'm' is a form of 'am'.* **c.** a word with a particular inflectional ending or other modification, as *goes* which is a form of *go*. **22.** → **year** (def. 11). **23.** a bench or long seat. **24.** *Horseracing, etc.* the record of an entrant's past performance by which chances of success in a race are assessed. **25.** *Colloq.* a person's record or reputation. *–v.t.* **26.** to give form or shape to; shape; fashion. **27.** to make or produce; to serve to make up, or compose; serve for, or constitute. **28.** to place in order; arrange; organise. **29.** to frame (ideas, opinions, etc.) in the mind. **30.** to contract (habits, friendships, etc.). **31.** to construct or frame. **32.** to give a particular form to, or fashion in a particular manner. **33.** to mould by discipline or instruction. **34.** *Gram.* to stand in relation to (a particular derivative or other form) by virtue of the absence or presence of an affix or other grammatical element or change: *'man' forms its plural by the change of -a- to -e-. –v.i.* **35.** to take or assume form. **36.** to be formed or produced. **37.** to take a particular form or arrangement. *–phr.* **38. a matter of form**, a routine activity, especially a procedural matter. **39. form up**, *Mil.* to draw up in lines or in formation. **40. have form**, *Colloq.* **a.** to have a criminal record. **b.** to have a record of misbehaviour, as in a school, office, etc. **41. in good form**, **a.** in good health. **b.** performing at one's peak: *a batsman in good form.* **c.** entertaining by being lively and amusing: *in good form at the party.* **42. in** (or **on**) **form**, performing at one's best. *–***formless**, *adj.*

-form a suffix meaning 'having the form of', as in *cruciform.*

formal /ˈfɔməl/ *adj.* **1.** being in accordance with custom; conventional. **2.** marked by form or ceremony: *a formal occasion.* **3.** (of a person) excessively ceremonious. **4.** being a matter of form only; perfunctory. **5.** following official method: *a formal vote; a formal complaint.* **6.** *Educ.* gained in a recognised place of learning: *a formal education.* **7.** relating to the form or shape of a thing, rather than the content or meaning. *–n.* **8.** *Aust., NZ* a dance or ball at which evening dress is to be worn. *–***formally**, *adv.* *–***formalness**, *n.*

formaldehyde /fɔˈmældəhaɪd/ *n.* a gas, HCHO, used most often in the form of a 40 per cent aqueous solution, as a disinfectant and preservative, and in the manufacture of various resins and plastics; methanal.

formalin /ˈfɔmələn/ *n.* (*from trademark*) an aqueous solution of formaldehyde used as a sterilising solution for non-boilable material, in the treatment of warts, and as a preservative for biological specimens.

formality /fɔˈmæləti/ *n.* (*pl.* **-ties**) **1.** the quality of being formal; obedience to rules and customs; conventionality. **2.** too great an attention to rules; stiffness. **3.** an official or formal act; ceremony. **4.** something done only to obey outward form or custom.

format /ˈfɔmæt/ *n.* **1.** the general physical appearance of a book, newspaper, or magazine, etc., such as the size, typeface, binding, quality of paper, margins, etc. **2.** the plan or style of something: *the format of a television series.* **3.** *Computers* an orderly arrangement of data elements to form a larger entity, as a list, table, file, etc. *–v.t.* (**-matted, -matting**) **4.** to organise (a book, data, etc.) into a particular format.

formation /fɔˈmeɪʃən/ *n.* **1.** the manner in which a thing is formed; disposition of parts; formal structure or

arrangement. **2.** *Mil.* a particular disposition of troops. **3.** a group of two or more aircraft flying as a unit according to a fixed plan. **4.** a team of ballroom dancers, gymnasts, etc., performing according to a previously arranged sequence. **5.** something formed.

formative /ˈfɔmətɪv/ *adj.* **1.** giving form or shape; forming; shaping; fashioning; moulding. **2.** relating to formation or development: *the formative period of a nation.* **3.** *Biol.* capable of developing new cells or tissue by cell division and differentiation: *formative tissue.* *–***formatively**, *adv.* *–***formativeness**, *n.*

former /ˈfɔmə/ *adj.* **1.** preceding in time; prior or earlier. **2.** past, long past, or ancient. **3.** preceding in order; being the first of two. **4.** being the first mentioned of two. **5.** having held a particular office in the past: *a former president.* *–phr.* **6. the former**, the item or person (out of two) previously mentioned (opposed to the *latter*).

formerly /ˈfɔməli/ *adv.* in time past; heretofore; of old.

form guide *n.* a guide containing information about the fitness and performance history of racing horses and dogs, and other material useful to punters. Also, **formguide**.

formica /fɔˈmaɪkə/ *n.* (*from trademark*) a thermosetting plastic usually used in transparent or printed sheets as a chemical-proof and heat-resistant covering for furniture, wall panels, etc.

formidable /ˈfɔmədəbəl, fɔˈmɪdəbəl/ *adj.* **1.** that is to be feared or dreaded, especially in encounters or dealings. **2.** of alarming strength, size, difficulty, etc. **3.** such as to inspire apprehension of defeat or failure. **4.** inspiring respect; powerful: *a formidable intellect.* *–***formidableness, formidability** /fɔmɪdəˈbɪləti/, *n.* *–***formidably**, *adv.*

formula /ˈfɔmjələ/ *n.* (*pl.* **-las** or **-lae** /-li/) **1.** a set form of words, as for stating or declaring something definitely or authoritatively, for indicating procedure to be followed, or for prescribed use on some ceremonial occasion. **2.** *Maths* a rule or principle frequently expressed in algebraic symbols. **3.** a fixed and successful method of doing something: *his book followed the usual formula of sex, sadism, and spying.* **4.** *Chem.* an expression of the constituents of a compound by symbols and figures, as an **empirical formula**, which merely indicates the proportions of each kind of atom in the molecule, as H_2O, a **molecular formula**, which indicates the actual numbers of atoms, or a **structural formula**, which represents diagrammatically the linkage of each atom in the molecule, as H–O–H. **5.** a recipe or prescription. **6. a.** a powdered substance to which water is added to produce a liquid food for young babies, especially as an alternative to breast milk: *could you please pick up some formula on your way home.* **b.** the liquid food so prepared. **7.** a formal statement of religious doctrine. **8.** one of the sets of specifications to which racing cars or motorcycles must conform to classify for particular races.

formulate /ˈfɔmjəleɪt/ *v.t.* **1.** to express in precise form; state definitely or systematically. **2.** to reduce to or express in a formula. *–***formulation** /fɔmjəˈleɪʃən/, *n.* *–***formulator**, *n.*

formwork /ˈfɔmwɜk/ *n.* (in building) the temporary structure into which concrete is poured which defines its shape once it has cured. Also, **forms**.

fornication /fɔnəˈkeɪʃən/ *n.* **1.** voluntary sexual intercourse between unmarried persons. **2.** *Bible* **a.** adultery. **b.** idolatry. *–***fornicate**, *v.*

forsake /fəˈseɪk/ *v.t.* (**forsook, forsaken, forsaking**) **1.** to desert or abandon: *forsake one's friends.* **2.** to give up or renounce (a habit, way of life, etc.).

forswear /fɔˈswɛə/ *verb* (**-swore, -sworn, -swearing**) *–v.t.* **1.** to reject or renounce upon oath or with protestations. **2.** to deny upon oath or with strong asseveration. **3.** to perjure (oneself). *–v.i.* **4.** to swear falsely; commit perjury. **–forswearer,** *n.*

fort /fɔt/ *n.* **1.** a strong or fortified place; any armed place surrounded by defensive works and occupied by troops; a fortification; a fortress. **2.** *Aust. Hist.* a stockade erected by settlers in unexplored territory: *Fort Bourke.* *–phr.* **3. hold the fort,** to look after an establishment or situation, especially in the absence of those who normally do it.

forte¹ *n.* /ˈfɔteɪ/ **1.** a strong point, as of a person; that in which one excels. *–adj.* /fɔt, ˈfɔteɪ/ **2.** *Pharmaceutical* (*following the name of a medication*) indicating a stronger version of the specified medication.

forte² /ˈfɔteɪ/ *adv.* *Music* loudly (opposed to *piano*).

forth /fɔθ/ *adv.* **1.** forwards; onwards or outwards in place or space. **2.** onwards in time, in order, or in a series: *from that day forth.* **3.** out, as from concealment or inaction; into view or consideration. **4.** away, as from a place or country; abroad. *–phr.* **5. and so forth,** and so on; et cetera.

forthcoming /ˈfɔθkʌmɪŋ/ *adj.* **1.** coming forth, or about to come forth; about to appear; approaching in time. **2.** ready or available when required or expected. **3.** ready to provide information; open. *–n.* **4.** a coming forth; appearance.

forthright /ˈfɔθraɪt/ *adj.* **1.** going straight to the point; outspoken. **2.** proceeding in a straight course; direct; straightforward. **–forthrightness,** *n.* **–forthrightly,** *adv.*

forthwith /fɔθˈwɪθ, -ˈwɪð/ *adv.* **1.** immediately; at once; without delay. **2.** as soon as can reasonably be expected.

fortification /fɔtəfəˈkeɪʃən/ *n.* **1.** the act of fortifying or strengthening. **2.** something that fortifies or protects. **3.** the art or science of constructing defensive military works. **4.** (*oft. pl.*) a military work constructed for the purpose of strengthening a position; fortified place; fort; castle.

fortify /ˈfɔtəfaɪ/ *v.t.* (**-fied, -fying**) **1.** to strengthen against attack; surround with defences; provide with defensive military works; protect with fortifications. **2.** to furnish with a means of resisting force or standing strain, wear, etc. **3.** to make strong; impart strength or vigour to, as the body. **4.** to enrich and increase the effectiveness, as of food, by adding further ingredients. **5.** to add alcohol to (wines, etc.) to stop fermentation or to increase the strength. **–fortified,** *adj.* **–fortifiable,** *adj.* **–fortifier,** *n.*

fortitude /ˈfɔtətjud/ *n.* patient courage under affliction, privation, or temptation; moral strength or endurance.

fortnight /ˈfɔtnaɪt/ *n.* the space of fourteen nights and days; two weeks.

fortress /ˈfɔtrəs/ *n.* **1.** a large fortified place; a fort or group of forts, often including a town. **2.** any place of security.

fortuitous /fɔˈtjuətəs/ *adj.* happening or produced by chance; accidental. **–fortuitously,** *adv.* **–fortuitousness,** *n.*

fortunate /ˈfɔtʃənət/ *adj.* **1.** having good fortune; receiving good from uncertain or unexpected sources; lucky. **2.** bringing or presaging good fortune; resulting favourably; auspicious. **–fortunately,** *adv.* **–fortunateness,** *n.*

fortune /ˈfɔtʃən, ˈfɔtʃun/ *n.* **1.** position in life as determined by wealth: *to make one's fortune; a man of fortune.* **2.** amount or stock of wealth. **3.** great wealth; ample stock of wealth. **4.** chance; luck. **5.** (*oft. pl.*) that which happens or is to happen to someone during their life. **6.** lot; destiny. **7.** (*oft. upper case*) chance personified, commonly regarded as a goddess distributing arbitrarily or capriciously the lots of life. **8.** good luck; success; prosperity. *–phr.* **9. tell someone's fortune,** to foretell coming events in a person's life. **–fortuneless,** *adj.*

fortune teller *n.* someone who professes to tell people what will happen in the future. **–fortune-telling,** *adj.*, *n.*

forty /ˈfɔti/ *n.* (*pl.* **-ties**) **1.** a cardinal number, ten times four. **2.** a symbol for this number, as 40 or XL or XXXX. **3.** (*pl.*) the numbers from 40 to 49 of a series, usually with reference to the years of a person's age, or the years of a century, especially the 20th. *–adj.* **4.** amounting to forty in number. *–pron.* **5.** forty people or things. **–fortieth,** *adj.*

forum /ˈfɔrəm/ *n.* (*pl.* **forums** or **fora** /ˈfɔrə/) **1.** the marketplace or public square of an ancient Roman city, the centre of judicial and other business and a place of assembly for the people. **2.** a court or tribunal. **3.** an assembly for the discussion of questions of public interest. **4.** a vehicle for public discussion, as a publication, radio program, website, etc. **5.** *Internet* an online discussion website, essentially a message board devoted to a particular topic.

forward /ˈfɔwəd/, *also for def. 10* /ˈfɔrəd/ *adj.* **1.** directed towards a point in advance, moving ahead; onward: *a forward step.* **2.** at the front: *the forward section of the plane.* **3.** well-advanced. **4.** ready, or eager; prompt. **5.** bold; presumptuous. **6.** of or relating to the future: *forward buying.* **7.** (of people or opinions) extreme; radical; progressive. *–n.* **8.** *Soccer, Hockey, etc.* a player placed in front of other members of the team. **9. a.** *Aust. Rules* one of six players who make up the forward line, the main attacking force of the team. **b.** *Rugby Union* one of the eight players in a team who form the scrum and act as a pack in rushing the ball forward and getting it to the three-quarters. **c.** *Rugby League* one of the six players with similar functions. *–adv.* **10.** towards the front of a ship or aeroplane. **11. → forwards. 12. a.** at or to a time which is earlier than before: *to move an event forward from Friday to the preceding Monday.* **b.** at or to a time which is later than before: *to move an event forward from Friday to the following Monday.* *–v.t.* **13.** to send forward; transmit, especially to a new address: *to forward a letter.* **14.** to advance or help onwards; hasten.

forward contract *n.* *Commerce* a contract in which a seller agrees to deliver to a buyer a given quantity of assets on an agreed date in the future at an agreed price.

forwards /ˈfɔwədz/ *adv.* **1.** towards or at a place, point, or time in advance; onwards; ahead: *to move forwards, from this day forwards, to look forwards.* **2.** towards the front. **3.** out; forth; into view or consideration. Also, **forward.**

forward short leg *n.* *Cricket* **1.** a fielding position in front of the wicket on the leg side close to the person batting. **2.** a fielder in this position.

forward slash *n.* **→ solidus** (def. 2).

fossick /ˈfɒsɪk/ *v.i.* Aust., NZ **1.** to search unsystematically or in a small way for mineral deposits, usually over ground previously worked by others. **2.** to search similarly for small items: *to fossick through a drawer for scissors.* **–fossicker,** *n.* **–fossicking,** *n.*

fossil /ˈfɒsəl/ *n.* **1.** any remains, impression, or trace of an animal or plant of a former geological age, such as a skeleton or a footprint. **2.** *Colloq.* an outdated or old-fashioned person or thing. *–adj.* **3.** being a fossil: *fossil insects.* **4.** obtained from below the earth's surface: *fossil salt.* **–fossiliferous** /fɒsəˈlɪfərəs/, *adj.* **–fossil-like,** *adj.*

fossil fuel *n.* a hydrocarbon-based energy source derived from the remains of living organisms (or their products) and formed deep within the earth, such as coal, petroleum, or natural gas.

fossil record *n.* the account of the history of living things derived by tracking species preserved as fossils in particular geological times, with regard to their evolutionary relationships.

foster /'fɒstə/ *v.t.* **1.** to promote the growth or development of; further; encourage: *to foster foreign trade.* **2.** to bring up or rear, as a foster-child. **3.** to care for or cherish. **4.** to place (a child) in a foster home. **–fosterer,** *n.*

fought /fɔt/ *v.* past tense and past participle of **fight**.

foul /faʊl/ *adj.* **1.** grossly offensive to the senses; disgustingly loathsome; noisome: *a foul smell.* **2.** charged with or characterised by offensive or noisome matter: *foul air.* **3.** filthy or dirty, as places, vessels, or clothes. **4.** clogged or obstructed with foreign matter: *a foul chimney.* **5.** unfavourable or stormy, as weather. **6.** contrary, as the wind. **7.** grossly offensive in a moral sense. **8.** abominable, wicked, or vile, as deeds, crime, slander, etc. **9.** scurrilous, profane, or obscene, as language. **10.** contrary to the rules or established usages, as of a sport or game; unfair. **11.** in collision or obstructing contact: *a ship foul of a rock.* **12.** entangled, caught, or jammed: *a foul anchor. –adv.* **13.** in a foul manner; foully; unfairly. *–n.* **14.** that which is foul. **15.** a collision or entanglement, especially in sailing or fishing. **16.** a violation of the rules of a sport or game. *–v.t.* **17.** to make foul; defile; soil. **18.** to clog or obstruct, as a chimney or the bore of a gun. **19.** to collide with. **20.** to cause to become entangled or caught, as a rope. **21.** to defile; dishonour; disgrace. **22.** *Naut.* to encumber (a ship's bottom) with seaweed, barnacles, etc. *–v.i.* **23.** to become foul. **24.** *Naut.* to come into collision, as two boats. **25.** to become entangled or clogged: *the rope fouled.* **26.** *Sport* to make a foul play; give a foul blow. *–phr.* **27. fall** (or **run**) **foul of, a.** (of ships) to collide with. **b.** to come into conflict with. **28. foul one's own nest,** to allow scandal or disgrace to enter one's own affairs. **29. foul up,** *Colloq.* **a.** to bungle or spoil **b.** to cause confusion. **–foulness,** *n.* **–foully,** *adv.*

found[1] /faʊnd/ *v.* **1.** past tense and past participle of **find**. *–phr.* **2. all found,** inclusive of necessary provisions, etc.; with everything provided.

found[2] /faʊnd/ *v.t.* **1.** to set up or establish on a firm basis or for enduring existence: *to found a dynasty.* **2.** to lay the lowest part of, fix, or build (a structure) on a firm base or ground: *a house founded upon a rock.* **3.** to afford a basis or ground for. *–phr.* **4. found on,** to base on or ground in: *a story founded on fact.*

foundation /faʊn'deɪʃən/ *n.* **1.** the basis of anything. **2.** the natural or prepared base on which some structure rests. **3.** *Building Trades* the lowest part of a building, wall, etc., usually of masonry, and partly or totally below the surface of the ground. **4.** the act of founding, setting up, establishing, etc. **5.** (a donation for the support of) an institution. **6.** Also, *Obsolesc.,* **foundation cream.** a cosmetic preparation, usually in the form of a cream or liquid, which is spread over the face to hide or minimise blemishes and to improve the colour and texture of the skin; make-up. *–adj.* **7.** of or relating to someone associated with the beginning: *a foundation member.*

founder[1] /'faʊndə/ *n.* someone who founds or establishes.

founder[2] /'faʊndə/ *v.i.* **1.** to fill with water and sink, as a ship. **2.** to fall or sink down, as buildings, ground, etc. **3.** to suffer wreck, or fail utterly. **4.** to stumble, break down, or go lame, as a horse.

foundling /'faʊndlɪŋ/ *n.* an infant found abandoned; a child without a parent or guardian.

foundry /'faʊndri/ *n.* (*pl.* **-ries**) an establishment for the production of castings, in which molten metal is poured into moulds to shape the castings.

fount[1] /faʊnt/ *n.* **1.** a spring of water; fountain. **2.** a source or origin.

fount[2] /fɒnt/ *n.* → **font**[2].

fountain /'faʊntn/ *n.* **1.** a spring or source of water; the source or head of a stream. **2.** the source or origin of anything. **3.** a jet or stream of water (or other liquid) made by mechanical means to spout or rise from an opening or structure, as to afford water for use, or to cool the air, or to serve for ornament. **4.** a structure for discharging such a jet or a number of jets, often an elaborate or artistic work with basins, sculptures, etc. **5.** a reservoir for a liquid to be supplied gradually or continuously. **6.** → **drinking fountain.** **–fountainless,** *adj.*

fountain pen *n.* a pen with a reservoir for supplying ink to the point of the nib.

four /fɔ/ *n.* **1.** a cardinal number, three plus one. **2.** a symbol of this number, as 4 or IV or IIII. **3.** a set of this many persons or things. **4.** a playing card, etc., with four pips. **5.** *Rowing* **a.** a crew of four rowers. **b.** a racing boat for a crew of four and sometimes a cox. **6.** *Cricket* a hit scoring four runs, when the ball is hit to the boundary, but first touches the ground inside the boundary. *–adj.* **7.** amounting to four in number: *four apples. –pron.* **8.** four people or things: *sleeps four; give me four. –phr.* **9. on all fours,** on the hands and feet (or knees). **10. on all fours with,** corresponding exactly to. **–fourth,** *adj.*

4GL /fɔ dʒi 'ɛl/ *n.* → **fourth-generation language.**

Fourier analysis /'fʊriər ə'næləsəs/ *n.* the decomposition of any periodic function such as a complex sound or electromagnetic waveform into the sum of a number of sine and cosine functions.

fourteen /fɔ'tin/ *n.* **1.** a cardinal number, ten plus four. **2.** a symbol for this number, as 14 or XIV or XIIII. *–adj.* **3.** amounting to fourteen in number. *–pron.* **4.** fourteen people or things. **–fourteenth,** *adj.*

fourth dimension *n.* the dimension of time, which is required in addition to the three dimensions of space, in order to locate a point in space-time. **–fourth-dimensional,** *adj.*

fourth estate *n.* the public press, the newspapers, or journalists collectively.

fourth-generation language *n.* a computer language in which the instructions are made in simple English statements by the user and interpreted by the computer into lower level languages. *Abbrev.:* 4GL Also, **fourth-generation query language.**

four-wheel drive *n.* **1.** the system which connects all four wheels of a motor vehicle to the source of power. **2.** a motor vehicle which has such a system. *Abbrev.:* 4WD *–adj.* **3.** (of a vehicle) having such a system. **4.** suitable for, or involving, four-wheel drive vehicles: *a four-wheel drive track; a four-wheel drive trip.* **–four-wheel driving,** *n.*

fowl /faʊl/ *n.* (*pl.* **fowls** *or, especially collectively,* **fowl**) **1.** → **chicken** (def. 1). **2.** any of various other gallinaceous or similar birds, as the turkey or duck. **3.** (in market and household use) a full-grown domestic fowl for food purposes (as distinguished from a chicken, or young fowl). **4.** the flesh or meat of a domestic fowl. **5.** any bird (now chiefly in combination): *waterfowl; wildfowl. –v.i.* **6.** to hunt or take wildfowl.

fox /fɒks/ *n.* **1.** any of certain carnivores of the dog family, Canidae, especially those constituting the genus *Vulpes,* smaller than the wolves, characterised by pointed muzzle, erect ears, and long, bushy tail. **2.** the fur of this animal. **3.** a cunning or crafty person. *–v.t.* **4.** *Colloq.* to deceive or trick. **–foxlike,** *adj.*

fox terrier *n.* one of a breed of small, active terriers, formerly used to drive foxes from their holes, having a coat which is either smooth and dense or harsh and wiry, according to variety, and is usually white with dark markings.

foxtrot /ˈfɒkstrɒt/ *n.* a ballroom dance, in 4/4 time, characterised by various combinations of short, quick steps.

foxy /ˈfɒksi/ *adj.* (**foxier, foxiest**) **1.** foxlike; cunning or crafty. **2.** yellowish or reddish brown; of the colour of the common red fox. **3.** impaired or defective in quality. **4.** *Colloq.* sexually attractive: *a foxy lady.* *–n.* Also, **foxie. 5.** *Colloq.* a fox terrier.

foyer /ˈfɔɪə, ˈfɔɪjə/ *n.* **1.** (in theatres and cinemas) the area between the outer lobby and the auditorium. **2.** a hall or anteroom, especially in a hotel.

fracas /ˈfræka, -kəs/ *n.* (*pl.* **fracas** /ˈfræka/ *or* **fracases** /ˈfrækəsəz/) a disorderly noise, disturbance, or fight; uproar.

fracking /ˈfrækɪŋ/ *n.* → **hydraulic fracturing.** Also, **fracing, fraccing.**

fractal /ˈfræktəl/ *n.* **1.** a geometric structure having an irregular or fragmented appearance which is of a similar character at all magnifications. *–adj.* **2.** of or relating to a fractal or fractals.

fraction /ˈfrækʃən/ *n.* **1.** *Maths* one or more parts of a unit or whole number; the ratio between any two numbers. **2.** a part as distinguished from the whole of anything: *only a fraction of the population is literate.* **3.** a piece broken off; fragment or bit. **–fractional,** *adj.*

fractious /ˈfrækʃəs/ *adj.* **1.** cross, fretful, or peevish. **2.** refractory or unruly. **–fractiously,** *adv.* **–fractiousness,** *n.*

fracto- a word element meaning 'broken'.

fracture /ˈfræktʃə/ *n.* **1.** the breaking of a bone, cartilage, etc., or the resulting condition (in a bone, called a **simple fracture** when the broken bone does not pierce the skin and a **compound fracture** when either the broken bone pierces the skin or protrudes into an open wound). See **compound fracture, greenstick fracture, hairline fracture, stress fracture. 2.** the characteristic manner of breaking. **3.** the characteristic appearance of a broken surface, as of a mineral. **4.** the act of breaking. **5.** the state of being broken. **6.** a break, breach, or split. *–v.t.* **7.** to break or crack. **8.** to cause or to suffer a fracture in (a bone, etc.). *–v.i.* **9.** to undergo fracture; break. **–fractural,** *adj.*

fragile /ˈfrædʒaɪl/ *adj.* easily broken, shattered, or damaged; delicate; brittle; frail: *fragile porcelain*; *a fragile ceasefire.* **–fragilely,** *adv.* **–fragility** /frəˈdʒɪləti/, **fragileness,** *n.*

fragile X syndrome *n.* a hereditary condition in which the X chromosome is easily damaged, causing a wide range of intellectual impairments.

fragment *n.* /ˈfrægmənt/ **1.** a part broken off or detached: *scattered fragments of rock.* **2.** a portion that is unfinished or incomplete: *fragments of a letter.* **3.** an odd piece, bit, or scrap. *–v.i.* /frægˈmɛnt/ **4.** to break into fragments: *this kind of rock fragments easily.* **–fragmentary,** *adj.* **–fragmented** /frægˈmɛntəd/, *adj.*

fragmentation /frægmənˈteɪʃən/ *n.* **1.** the act or process of fragmenting. **2.** the disintegration or breakdown of norms of thought, behaviour, or social relationship. **3.** *Computers* the process by which data is broken into parts and scattered throughout a disk, so as to be stored in spaces left vacant by previously deleted files.

fragrant /ˈfreɪɡrənt/ *adj.* **1.** having a pleasant odour; sweet-smelling. **2.** delightful; pleasant: *fragrant memories.* **–fragrance, fragrancy,** *n.* **–fragrantly,** *adv.*

frail /freɪl/ *adj.* **1.** weak; not robust; having delicate health. **2.** easily broken or destroyed; fragile. **3.** morally weak; not strong against temptation. **–frailly,** *adv.* **–frailness,** *n.* **–frailty,** *n.*

frame /freɪm/ *n.* **1.** an enclosing border or case: *a picture frame*; *a door frame*; *a frame of trees round a house.* **2.** anything composed of parts fitted and joined together; a structure. **3.** the sustaining parts of such a

structure: *the frame of a pair of spectacles*; *a house with a wooden frame.* **4.** body structure; build: *a heavy frame.* **5.** any of various machines operating on or within a framework. **6.** a machine or part of a machine used in textile production. **7.** the rigid part of a bicycle. **8.** a particular state, as of the mind: *an unhappy frame of mind.* **9.** form or structure in general; system; order. **10.** *Shipbuilding* one of the transverse structural members of a ship's hull, extending from the gunwale to the bilge or to the keel. **11.** a structure placed in a beehive on which bees build a honeycomb. **12.** *Colloq.* (in baseball) an inning. **13.** one of the successive small pictures on a strip of film. **14.** *Colloq.* (of livestock) a very thin animal. **15.** *Colloq.* → **frame-up.** *–v.t.* **16.** (of a boat, plan, poem, excuse, etc.) to form or make, put together; shape. **17.** to conceive or imagine, as ideas, etc. **18.** to shape or to prearrange falsely, as a plot, a race, etc. **19.** *Colloq.* to make someone appear guilty by a plot; incriminate. **20.** (of a picture) to provide with or put into a frame. **21.** to surround or act as a setting: *ivy framed the window*; *curly hair framed her face.* **–frameless,** *adj.* **–framer,** *n.*

frame of reference *n.* **1.** *Maths* a system of coordinates within which a particular set of conditions can be defined. **2.** a context, a set of considerations, factors, etc., in the light of which a present concern is to be considered.

frame-up *n. Colloq.* a situation created to make an innocent person appear to be guilty of a crime.

framework /ˈfreɪmwɜk/ *n.* **1.** a structure composed of parts fitted and united together. **2.** a structure designed to support or enclose something; frame or skeleton. **3.** frames collectively. **4.** work done in, on, or with a frame.

franc /fræŋk/ *n.* the principal monetary unit of various countries, including Switzerland and some African countries, and formerly (until the introduction of the euro in 2002), of France, most French dependencies, Belgium and Luxembourg, of varying value from country to country; in most cases divided into 100 centimes.

franchise /ˈfræntʃaɪz/ *n.* **1.** the rights of a citizen, especially the right to vote. **2.** a privilege arising from the grant of a sovereign or government, or from prescription, which presupposes a grant. **3.** permission granted by a manufacturer to a distributor or retailer to sell the manufacturer's products. **–franchisor,** *n.* **–franchising,** *n.*

Franco- a word element meaning 'French' or 'France', as in *Franco-German.*

frangible /ˈfrændʒəbəl/ *adj.* **1.** capable of being broken; breakable. **2.** (of telegraph poles, etc.) designed to detach from a solid base at ground level upon the impact of a motor vehicle. **–frangibility** /frændʒəˈbɪləti/, *n.*

frangipani /frændʒəˈpæni/ *n.* (*pl.* **-nis**) a shrub or tree, of the genus *Plumeria*, with thick, fleshy branches, cultivated for its strongly scented yellow and white, occasionally pink, flowers. Also, **frangipanni.**

frank /fræŋk/ *adj.* **1.** open or unreserved in speech; candid or outspoken; sincere. **2.** undisguised; avowed; downright: *frank mutiny.* *–v.t.* **3.** to mark (a letter, parcel, etc.) to indicate that postage has been paid or that it does not need to be paid. **4.** *Commerce* to indicate (a dividend) as having had tax paid on it by the company. **–frankly,** *adv.* **–frankness,** *n.* **–frankable,** *adj.* **–franker,** *n.*

franked /fræŋkt/ *adj.* **1.** (of a dividend) registered as having had tax paid at the corporate rate. **2. fully franked,** with tax paid at the corporate rate on the entire sum. **3. partly franked,** with tax paid at the corporate rate on some part, the rest being unfranked and therefore fully taxable.

franked dividend *n.* a dividend paid out of company profits on which the full corporate tax has been paid.

frankfurt /'fræŋkfət/ *n.* a reddish pre-cooked sausage made of beef or pork, commonly re-heated by steaming or boiling. Also, **frankfurter, frank**.

franking /'fræŋkɪŋ/ *n.* a system of giving taxation credits to shareholders in a company when the company has already paid corporate tax on the dividends being paid to the shareholders.

franking credit *n.* → **imputation credit**.

frantic /'fræntɪk/ *adj.* wild with excitement, passion, fear, pain, etc.; frenzied; characterised by or relating to frenzy. –**frantically**, *adv.* –**franticness**, *n.*

fraternal /frə'tɜnəl/ *adj.* **1.** of or befitting a brother or brothers; brotherly. **2.** of or being a society of men associated in brotherly union, as for mutual aid or benefit: *a fraternal society.* –**fraternalism**, *n.* –**fraternally**, *adv.*

fraternise /'frætənaɪz/ *v.i.* **1.** to associate in a fraternal or friendly way. **2.** to associate intimately with citizens of an enemy or conquered country. Also, **fraternize**. –**fraternisation** /ˌfrætənaɪ'zeɪʃən/, *n.* –**fraterniser**, *n.*

fraternity /frə'tɜnəti/ *n.* (*pl.* -**ties**) **1.** a body of persons associated as by ties of brotherhood. **2.** any body or class of persons having common purposes, interest, etc.: *the medical fraternity.* **3.** the relation of persons associated on the same footing as brothers: *liberty, equality, and fraternity.*

fraud /frɔd/ *n.* **1.** deceit, trickery, sharp practice, or breach of confidence, by which it is sought to gain some unfair or dishonest advantage. **2.** someone who makes deceitful pretences; impostor. –**fraudster**, *n.* –**fraudulent**, *adj.* –**fraudulence**, *n.*

fraught /frɔt/ *adj.* **1.** *Colloq.* upset; anxious; tense. –*phr.* **2. fraught with**, involving; full of (something undesirable): *an undertaking fraught with danger; a heart fraught with grief.*

fray¹ /freɪ/ *n.* a noisy quarrel; contest; brawl; fight, skirmish, or battle.

fray² /freɪ/ *v.t.* **1.** to wear (cloth, rope, etc.) to loose threads or fibres at the edge or end; cause to unravel. **2.** (sometimes fol. by *through*) to wear by rubbing. **3.** to strain (a person's temper); exasperate; upset. –*v.i.* **4.** (of cloth, temper, etc.) to become worn through, or unravelled.

frazzle /'fræzəl/ *v.t.* **1.** to cause to fray; wear to threads or shreds. **2.** to make weary; tire out. –*v.i.* **3.** to fray. **4.** to become weary. –*n.* **5.** a state of being frazzled or worn out. **6.** a remnant; shred. –**frazzled**, *adj.*

freak /frik/ *n.* **1.** a sudden and apparently causeless change or turn of events, the mind, etc.; a capricious notion, occurrence, etc. **2.** any abnormal product or curiously unusual object; monstrosity. **3.** a person or animal on exhibition as an example of some strange deviation from nature. **4.** someone who does not conform to orthodox, conservative forms of behaviour, as by taking illicit drugs, by wearing unconventional dress, etc. **5.** *Colloq.* someone who is enthused about a particular thing: *a Jesus freak, a drug freak.* –*adj.* **6.** unusual; odd; irregular: *a freak copy of a book.* –*v.i.* Also, **freak out. 7.** *Colloq.* **a.** (sometimes fol. by *on*) to have an extreme reaction, either favourable or adverse, to something, especially a drug-induced experience. **b.** to panic. –*v.t.* **8.** to terrify, as an experience produced by hallucinogenic drugs. –*phr.* **9. freak out**, *Colloq.* to fill with dread or terror: *the thought of the exams freaks me out.* –**freakish, freaky**, *adj.*

freckle /'frɛkəl/ *n.* **1.** a small brownish spot in the skin, especially on the face, neck, or arms. **2.** any small spot or discolouration. –*v.i.* **3.** to become freckled. –**freckled**, *adj.*

free /fri/ *adj.* (**freer, freest**) **1.** enjoying personal rights or liberty, as one not in slavery. **2.** relating to or reserved for those who enjoy personal liberty. **3.** *Aust. Hist.* **a.** relating to a convict who had been released or freed. **b.** relating to a settler, immigrant, etc., who had never been a convict (used in opposition to *freed*): *a threefold society of free, freed, and bond.* **4.** possessed of, characterised by, or existing under civil liberty as opposed to arbitrary or despotic government, as a country or state, or its citizens, institutions, etc. **5.** enjoying political liberty or independence, as a people or country not under foreign rule. **6.** exempt from external authority, interference, restriction, etc., as a person, the will, thought, choice, action, etc.; independent; unfettered. **7.** at liberty, permitted, or able at will (to do something): *free to choose.* **8.** not subject to special regulation or restrictions, as trade: *free trade.* **9.** not literal, as a translation. **10.** not subject to rules, set forms, etc.: *the free song of a bird; free verse.* **11.** clear of obstructions or obstacles, as a corridor. **12.** available; unoccupied; not in use: *the managing director is now free.* **13.** uncombined chemically: *free oxygen.* **14.** able to be used by or open to all: *a free port; a free market.* **15.** general: *a free fight.* **16.** unimpeded, as motion or movements; easy, firm, or swift in movement: *a free gait.* **17.** loose, or not held fast or attached: *to get one's arm free.* **18.** not joined to or in contact with something else: *a free surface.* **19.** acting without self-restraint or reserve: *too free with one's tongue.* **20.** frank and open; unconstrained, unceremonious, or familiar. **21.** unrestrained by decency; loose or licentious. **22.** ready in giving, liberal, or lavish: *to be free with one's advice.* **23.** given readily or in profusion, or unstinted. **24.** given without consideration of a return, as a gift. **25.** provided without, or not subject to, a charge or payment: *free milk.* –*adv.* **26.** in a free manner; freely. **27.** without cost or charge. **28.** *Naut.* farther from the wind than when close-hauled: *to sail free.* –*v.t.* (**freed, freeing**) **29.** make free; set at liberty; release from bondage, imprisonment, or restraint. –*phr.* **30. for free**, for nothing; gratis. **31. free and easy**, informal; casual; without restraint. **32. free from** (or **of**), **a.** to disengage or release from: *his captors freed him of his bonds.* **b.** to exempt or deliver from: *to free someone from their oath.* **c.** to release from (something that controls, restrains, burdens, etc.): *alcohol freed her of all inhibition.* **33. free, gratis** (**and for nothing**), a formula emphasising that something is not charged for. **34. make free with**, to treat or use too familiarly; take liberties with. –**freely**, *adv.*

free alongside ship *adj.* a term of sale meaning that the seller agrees to deliver the merchandise alongside ship without extra charge to the buyer. *Abbrev.*: FAS, f.a.s.

freebie /'fribi/ *n.* *Colloq.* a service or item provided without charge.

freeconomics /frikə'nɒmɪks/ *n.* a business model, especially on the internet, where much of the material is free but the income is derived from advertising, from sales of additional products or services, etc.

freecycle /'frisaɪkəl/ *v.t.* (**-cycled, -cycling**) to give away (items) so that they can be used again by others, by placing them in a public area so that people can take them away as they wish. –**freecycling**, *n.*

freedom /'fridəm/ *n.* **1.** the power to act or speak at will without fear of government oppression; civil liberty. **2.** political or national independence. **3.** a privilege enjoyed by a city or corporation. **4.** personal liberty, as opposed to bondage or slavery. **5.** the state of being unconfined: *to escape into freedom.* **6.** exemption from outside control, interference, regulation, etc.: *the freedom to do it in his own way.* **7.** an absence of or release from ties, obligations, etc. **8.** (fol. by *from*) an exemption from something unpleasant or burdensome: *freedom from fear.* **9.** ease of movement or action. **10.** frankness of manner or speech. **11. a.** absence of ceremony or reserve; familiarity; impertinence: *freedom of behaviour.* **b.** an instance of such behaviour; a liberty; an impertinence. **12.** the right of enjoying all the privileges or rights of citizenship, membership, etc.: *freedom of the city.*

freedom of speech *n.* → **free speech**.

free enterprise *n.* an economic system in which private business enterprises compete with each other with a minimum amount of government control.

freefall /ˈfriːfɔl/ *n.* **1.** the motion of any unpowered body travelling in a gravitational field. **2.** the part of a parachute descent before the parachute opens where acceleration is due to gravity. **3.** an unrestrained and uncontrollable fall in commodity prices, monetary units, etc.; a sharp reduction in prices. *–adj.* **4.** of or relating to a freefall. *–v.i.* (**-fell**, **-fallen**, **-falling**) **5.** to fall swiftly and without check, as or as if in a freefall. **6.** (of prices, monetary values, etc.) to fall sharply and unrestrainedly. Also, **free-fall**. **–freefalling**, *n.* **–freefalling**, *adj.*

free hand *n.* unrestricted freedom or authority.

freehand /ˈfriːhænd/ *adj.* done by the hand without guiding instruments, measurements, or other aids: *a freehand drawing.*

freehold /ˈfriːhoʊld/ *n.* **1.** a tenure of real property by which an estate of inheritance in fee simple or fee tail or for life is held. **2.** an estate held by such tenure. Compare **leasehold**.

freelance /ˈfriːlæns/ *n.* **1.** a journalist, commercial artist, editor, etc., who does not work on a regular salaried basis for any one employer. *–v.i.* (**-lanced**, **-lancing**) **2.** to act or work as a freelance. *–adj.* **3.** of or relating to a freelance. *–adv.* **4.** in the manner of a freelance. **–freelancer**, *n.*

freeload /ˈfriːloʊd/ *v.i. Colloq.* to contrive to take food, benefits, etc., without paying or contributing; cadge. **–freeloader**, *n.*

free love *n.* the doctrine or practice of free choice in sexual relations, without restraint of legal marriage or of any continuing obligations independent of one's will.

free market *n. Econ.* an economic system that allows unrestricted supply and demand, thus intended to be self-regulating in terms of prices, wages, etc., rather than government regulated. **–free marketeer**, *n.*

freemason /ˈfriːmeɪsən/ *n.* **1.** (in medieval Europe) one of a class of skilled stoneworkers. **2.** a member of a society or lodge composed of such workers, later (17th century) including honorary members (known as *accepted masons*) who were not connected with the building trades and were generally luminaries of some kind. **–freemasonic** /friːməˈsɒnɪk/, *adj.*

Freemason /ˈfriːmeɪsən/ *n.* a member of a widespread and once secret order of men (**Free and Accepted Masons**), having for its object mutual help, the fostering of brotherly love among its members, and universal charity and tolerance. Also, **Mason**. **–Freemasonry**, *n.*

free port *n.* **1.** a port open under equal conditions to all traders. **2.** a part or all of a port included in customs territory so as to expedite transhipment of what is not to be imported.

free radical *n.* a molecule or ion with one or more unpaired electrons and thus being highly reactive, which exists independently for short periods during the course of a chemical reaction, or for longer periods under special conditions.

free-range *adj.* **1.** of or relating to chickens reared in an open or free environment, rather than in a battery. **2.** of or relating to the eggs of such chickens.

free selection *Aust. Hist.* land selected, especially for agricultural use and taken up by lease or licence under various land acts, or after crown auction, as opposed to land granted by the Crown or taken by squatting. **–free selector**, *n.*

freesia /ˈfriːʒə/ *n.* any plant of the genus *Freesia*, native to southern Africa, cultivated for its fragrant white, yellow, or sometimes coloured, tubular flowers.

free speech *n.* the right to express oneself and impart one's opinions in speech or writing or any form of public media. Also, **freedom of speech**.

freestyle /ˈfriːstaɪl/ *n.* **1.** Also, **crawl**, **Australian crawl**. a swimming stroke in prone position characterised by alternate overarm movements and a continuous up-and-down kick. **2. a.** a swimming race in which the competitors may use any stroke they choose, usually the freestyle (def. 1) because it is the fastest. **b.** the style of swimming used in such a race. **3.** a style of BMX or skateboard riding consisting of complicated tricks and manoeuvres. **4.** (in sports such as skiing, skating, gymnastics, skydiving, etc.) a style which allows the performer scope to demonstrate skill, as by featuring unrestricted movement, aerobatics, etc. **5.** *Wrestling* a style of wrestling in which almost every kind of hold is permitted; all-in wrestling.

free-to-air *adj.* (of television programs) supplied at no cost to the consumer.

free trade *n.* **1.** trade between different countries, free from governmental restrictions, such as protective duties, import quotas, etc. **2.** the system, principles, or maintenance of such trade.

free verse *n.* verse unhampered by fixed metrical forms, in extreme instances consisting of little more than rhythmic prose in lines of irregular length.

free vote *n. Parliamentary Procedure* (in a house of parliament) a vote on a motion in which members are free to vote according to their own judgement without being bound by any party policy or decision, especially one involving considerable moral and ethical issues; conscience vote.

freeware /ˈfriːwɛə/ *n.* computer software which is available online for free.

freeway /ˈfriːweɪ/ *n.* a main road, usually divided and free of intersections, with entries and exits designed so as not to interrupt the flow of traffic. Also, **expressway**.

freewheel /ˈfriːwiːl/ *n.* **1.** an overrunning clutch device connected to the transmission gearbox of a motor vehicle which automatically disengages the drive shaft whenever it tends to rotate more rapidly than the shaft driving it. *–v.i.* **2.** to coast in a car, bicycle, etc., with the wheels disengaged from the driving mechanism. **3.** *Colloq.* to act independently, particularly in personal, social matters. **4.** *Colloq.* to discuss matters or to act in a wideranging, uninhibited manner, as a politician. **–freewheeling**, *adj.*

free will *n.* **1.** free choice; voluntary decision. **2.** *Philos.* the doctrine that the conduct of human beings expresses personal choice and is not simply determined by physical or divine forces. **–free-will**, *adj.*

freeze /friːz/ *verb* (**froze**, **frozen**, **freezing**) *–v.i.* **1.** to become hardened into ice or into a solid body; to change from the liquid to the solid state by loss of heat. **2.** to become hard or rigid because of loss of heat, as objects containing moisture. **3.** to become obstructed by the formation of ice, as pipes. **4.** to become fixed to something by or as by the action of frost. **5.** to be of the degree of cold at which water freezes. **6.** to be extremely cold: *the weather is freezing.* **7.** to suffer the effects of intense cold; have the sensation of extreme cold. **8.** to die of frost or cold. **9.** to lose warmth of feeling; be chilled with fear, etc. **10.** to stop suddenly; become immobilised, as through fear, shock, etc.

11. (of a computer) to stop outputting or accepting input due to some fault. –*v.t.* **12.** to congeal; harden into ice; change from a fluid to a solid state by loss of heat. **13.** to form ice on the surface of, as a river or pond. **14.** Also, **freeze up.** to obstruct or close by the formation of ice, as pipes. **15.** to fix fast in ice. **16.** to harden or stiffen by cold, as objects containing moisture. **17.** to subject (something) to a freezing temperature, as in a refrigerator. **18.** to cause to suffer the effects of intense cold; produce the sensation of extreme cold in. **19.** to kill by frost or cold. **20.** to congeal as if by cold; chill with fear; dampen the enthusiasm of. **21.** to cause (someone) to become immobilised, as through fear, shock, etc. **22.** *Finance* to render impossible of liquidation or collection: *bank loans are frozen in business depressions.* **23.** to fix (wages, prices, etc.) at a specific level, usually by government order. **24.** to make insensitive (a part of the body) by artificial freezing, as for surgery. –*n.* **25.** the act of freezing. **26.** the state of being frozen. **27.** *Meteorol.* a period during which temperatures remain constantly below 0°C. **28.** a frost. **29.** legislative action by a government to fix wages, prices, etc., at a specific level. **30.** (in films) an arresting of the motion by printing one frame many times. –*phr.* **31. freeze out,** to exclude, or compel to withdraw, from society, business, etc., as by chilling behaviour, severe competition, etc. **32. freeze over, a.** to become coated with ice. **b.** (of an expanse of water) to have a surface of ice. –**freezable,** *adj.*

freeze-dry *v.t.* (**-dried, -drying**) to dry (food, blood, serum, etc.) while frozen and under high vacuum, as for prolonged storage. –**freeze-drying,** *n.*

freezer /ˈfrizə/ *n.* a refrigerated cabinet held at or below 0°C.

freezing point *n.* the temperature at which a liquid freezes: *the freezing point of water is 0°C.*

freight /freɪt/ *n.* **1.** cargo or lading carried for pay either by land, water, or air. **2.** the charge made for transporting goods. –*v.t.* **3.** to transport as freight; send by freight. –**freighter,** *n.* –**freightless,** *adj.*

French bean *n.* a small twining or bushy annual herb, *Phaseolus vulgaris,* often cultivated for its slender green edible pods; haricot.

French cricket *n.* a game played with a ball and a cricket bat, in which the players when batting hold the bat in front of their legs, and can only be dismissed if the ball hits their legs or they are caught.

French fries *pl. n.* thin strips of potatoes fried in deep fat; chips. Also, **fries, French fried potatoes.**

French horn *n.* a mellow-toned brass wind instrument derived from the hunting horn and consisting of a long, coiled tube ending in a flaring bell.

French kiss *n.* → **tongue kiss.**

French-kiss *v.t., v.i.* → **tongue-kiss.** –**French-kisser,** *n.* –**French-kissing,** *n.*

French manicure *n.* a style of manicure in which the tips of the nails are painted white.

French polish *n.* **1.** a solution of shellac in methylated spirits with or without the addition of some colouring material; used as a high-quality furniture finish. **2.** a French manicure on acrylic or artificial nails.

frenemy /ˈfrɛnəmi/ *n.* (*pl.* **-mies**) a person who appears to be one's friend but acts in ways that are injurious to one's wellbeing or interests.

frenetic /frəˈnɛtɪk/ *adj.* frantic; frenzied. –**frenetically,** *adv.*

frenzy /ˈfrɛnzi/ *n.* (*pl.* **-zies**) **1.** violent mental agitation; wild excitement or enthusiasm. **2.** the violent excitement of a paroxysm of mania; mental derangement; delirium. –*v.t.* (**-zied, -zying**) **3.** to drive to frenzy; make frantic.

frequency /ˈfrikwənsi/ *n.* (*pl.* **-cies**) **1.** Also, **frequence.** the state or fact of being frequent; frequent occurrence. **2.** rate of recurrence. **3.** *Physics* the number of cycles, oscillations, or vibrations of a wave motion or oscillation in unit time; the derived SI unit of frequency is the hertz. **4.** *Statistics* the number of items occurring in a given category. See **relative frequency. 5.** *Bot.* a quantitative character of a plant community; an expression of the percentage of sample plots in which a particular species occurs.

frequency modulation *n.* *Radio* a broadcasting system, relatively free from static, in which the frequency of the transmitted wave is modulated or varied in accordance with the amplitude and pitch of the signal (distinguished from *amplitude modulation*). *Abbrev.:* FM

frequent *adj.* /ˈfrikwənt/ **1.** happening or occurring at short intervals: *to make frequent trips to a place.* **2.** constant, habitual, or regular: *a frequent guest.* **3.** at short distances apart: *a coast with frequent lighthouses.* –*v.t.* /frəˈkwɛnt/ **4.** to visit often; go often to; be often in. –**frequently,** *adv.* –**frequenter,** *n.*

frequent flyer *n.* **1.** a person who is part of an incentive scheme in which discounted or free flights are awarded after certain distances have been travelled with a particular airline or group of airlines, or after a certain number of points have been collected by spending on a credit or debit card which is linked to such a scheme. –*adj.* **2.** of or relating to such a scheme.

fresco /ˈfrɛskoʊ/ *n.* **1.** the art of painting on fresh lime plaster, as on a wall or ceiling, so that the pigments are absorbed (**true fresco**), or, less properly, on dried plaster (**dry fresco**). **2.** a picture or design so painted. –*v.t.* (*pl.* **-coes** *or* **-cos**) **3.** to paint in fresco. –**frescoer,** *n.*

fresh /frɛʃ/ *adj.* **1.** newly made or obtained, etc.: *fresh footprints.* **2.** newly arrived: *fresh from school.* **3.** additional or further: *fresh supplies.* **4.** not salt: *fresh water.* **5.** (of meat, etc.) in good natural condition; unspoiled. **6.** not canned, frozen or preserved: *fresh food.* **7.** not tired; brisk; vigorous. **8.** not faded or worn. **9.** looking youthful and healthy. **10.** pure, cool, or refreshing, as air. **11.** inexperienced: *fresh to the job.* **12.** forward or presumptuous; cheeky. –*n.* **13.** the fresh part or time. –**freshen,** *v.* –**freshly,** *adv.* –**freshness,** *n.*

freshwater /ˈfrɛʃwɔtə/ *adj.* of or living in water that is fresh, or not salt.

freshwater crocodile *n.* a small crocodile, *Crocodylus johnstoni,* inhabiting permanent freshwater areas such as lakes, billabongs and swamps, and less saline upstream areas of rivers and creeks in northern Australia; Johnstone's crocodile.

fret[1] /frɛt/ *v.i.* (**fretted, fretting**) **1.** to give oneself up to feelings of irritation, resentful discontent, regret, worry, or the like. **2.** to cause corrosion; gnaw. –**fretful,** *adj.* –**fretfully,** *adv.* –**fretfulness,** *n.*

fret[2] /frɛt/ *n.* **1.** an interlaced, angular design; fretwork. **2.** an angular design of bands within a border. –*v.t.* (**fretted, fretting**) **3.** to ornament with a fret or fretwork.

fret[3] /frɛt/ *n.* any of the ridges of wood, metal, or string, set across the fingerboard of a guitar or similar instrument which help the fingers to stop the strings at the correct points. –**fretting,** *n.*

fretwork /ˈfrɛtwɜk/ *n.* **1.** ornamental work consisting of interlacing parts, especially work in which the design is formed by perforation. **2.** any pattern of dark and light, such as that of perforated fretwork.

Freudian slip /frɔɪdiən ˈslɪp/ *n.* a slip of the tongue by which the speaker actually says something apposite or revealing, which was not primarily intended, but is taken to reveal the speaker's true or subconscious thoughts.

friable /ˈfraɪəbəl/ *adj.* easily crumbled or reduced to powder; crumbly: *friable rock.* –**friability** /fraɪəˈbɪləti/, **friableness,** *n.*

friand /ˈfriɒnd/ *n.* a small cake containing almond meal, which is usually oval or round in shape and sometimes flavoured with fruit, chocolate chips, etc.

friar /ˈfraɪə/ *n.* a brother or member of one of certain Christian religious orders, especially the mendicant orders of Franciscans (**Grey Friars**), Dominicans (**Black Friars**), Carmelites (**White Friars**), and Augustinians (**Austin Friars**).

friarbird /ˈfraɪəbɜd/ *n.* any of various honeyeaters of the genus *Philemon* of Australia, New Guinea and nearby islands, having the head partly naked like a friar.

friction /ˈfrɪkʃən/ *n.* **1.** clashing or conflict, as of opinions, etc. **2.** *Mechanics, Physics* the resistance to the relative motion (sliding or rolling) of surfaces of bodies in contact. **3.** the rubbing of the surface of one body against that of another. –**frictional,** *adj.* –**frictionless,** *adj.* –**frictionlessly,** *adv.* –**frictionlessness,** *n.*

Friday /ˈfraɪdeɪ, -di/ *n.* the sixth day of the week, following Thursday.

fridge /frɪdʒ/ *n. Colloq.* → **refrigerator.**

fried /fraɪd/ *v.* **1.** past tense and past participle of **fry**[1]. –*adj.* **2.** cooked in fat or oil.

friend /frɛnd/ *n.* **1.** someone attached to another by feelings of affection or personal regard. **2.** a wellwisher, patron, or supporter. **3.** someone who is on good terms with another; one not hostile. **4.** a member of the same nation, party, etc. **5.** (*upper case*) someone who supports an institution, charity, etc., with money or honorary services. –**friendship,** *n.* –**friendless,** *adj.* –**friendlessness,** *n.*

friendly /ˈfrɛndli/ *adj.* (**-lier, -liest**) **1.** characteristic of or befitting a friend; showing friendship: *a friendly greeting.* **2.** favourably disposed; inclined to approve, help, or support. **3.** *Sport* of a match which does not entail points in a competition. –**friendlily,** *adv.* –**friendliness,** *n.*

-friendly a combining element indicating ease of use with, suitability to, helpfulness to, acceptance of, etc., as *environment-friendly, user-friendly, pet-friendly.*

friendly fire *n.* fire (def. 12) originating with one's own or allied units.

fries /fraɪz/ *pl. n.* → **French fries.**

Friesian /ˈfriʒən/ *n.* one of a breed of dairy cattle, usually black and white in colouring.

frieze /friz/ *n.* any decorative band or similar feature, as on a wall. –**friezing,** *n.*

frig /frɪɡ/ *phr.* (**frigged, frigging**) **1. frig around** (or **about**), to behave in a stupid or aimless manner. **2. frig up,** to make a mess of; ruin: *the advertising department is always frigging up the layout.*

frigate /ˈfrɪɡət/ *n.* a general-purpose warship of about 2700 tonnes, used as an escort vessel.

frigatebird /ˈfrɪɡətbɜd/ *n.* any of several species of large, rapacious, tropical seabirds with huge wings, forked tails and small legs and feet, noted for their powers of flight, such as the **greater frigatebird,** *Fregata minor.*

fright /fraɪt/ *n.* **1.** sudden and extreme fear; a sudden terror. **2.** a person or thing of shocking, grotesque, or ridiculous appearance: *she looked a fright.*

frighten /ˈfraɪtn/ *v.t.* **1.** to throw into a fright; terrify; scare. **2.** to drive (*away, off,* etc.) by scaring. –**frightener,** *n.* –**frighteningly,** *adv.*

frightful /ˈfraɪtfəl/ *adj.* **1.** such as to cause fright; dreadful, terrible, or alarming. **2.** horrible, shocking, or revolting. **3.** unpleasant; disagreeable: *we had a frightful time.* **4.** *Colloq.* an intensifier: *a frightful lot.* –**frightfully,** *adv.* –**frightfulness,** *n.*

frigid /ˈfrɪdʒəd/ *adj.* **1.** very cold in temperature: *a frigid climate.* **2.** without warmth of feeling; without ardour or enthusiasm. **3.** stiff or formal. **4.** (of a woman) **a.** disinclined to sexual intercourse. **b.** unable to achieve orgasm during intercourse. –**frigidity** /frɪˈdʒɪdəti/, **frigidness,** *n.* –**frigidly,** *adv.*

Frigid Zone *n.* either of the two regions between the poles and the polar circles.

frill /frɪl/ *n.* **1.** a trimming consisting of a strip of material or lace, gathered at one edge and left loose at the other; a ruffle. **2.** something resembling such a trimming, such as the fringe of hair on the chest of some dogs. **3.** *Colloq.* an affectation of manner, style, etc. **4.** something superfluous or useless. –*v.t.* **5.** to trim or ornament with a frill or frills. –**frilly,** *adj.*

frill-necked lizard *n.* an agamid or dragon lizard, *Chlamydosaurus kingi,* of northern Australia possessing a large, ruff-like, erectable frill behind the head and using hind legs for propulsion.

fringe /frɪndʒ/ *n.* **1.** an ornamental border of cords or threads, loose or tied in bunches, as on a rug. **2.** anything like this: *a fringe of trees about a field.* **3.** hair falling over the forehead. **4.** a border; margin; outer part or extremity: *the fringes of society; the fringe of town.* –*v.t.* **5.** to give a fringe to. **6.** to serve as a fringe for: *trees fringe the field.* –*adj.* **7.** extra; on the side: *fringe benefits.* **8.** not socially acceptable. –**fringeless,** *adj.* –**fringy,** *adj.*

fringe benefit *n.* a reward received in addition to one's wage, such as a car, travel allowance, etc.

fringe benefits tax *n.* a tax on fringe benefits. *Abbrev.*: FBT

frisk /frɪsk/ *v.i.* **1.** to dance, leap, skip, or gambol, as in frolic. –*v.t.* **2.** *Colloq.* to search (a person) for concealed weapons, etc., by feeling their clothing. –**frisker,** *n.*

frisky /ˈfrɪski/ *adj.* (**-kier, -kiest**) lively; frolicsome; playful. –**friskily,** *adv.* –**friskiness,** *n.*

frisson /ˈfrɪsɒn/ *n.* a shiver; thrill.

fritter[1] /ˈfrɪtə/ *phr.* **fritter away,** to disperse or squander piecemeal, or waste little by little: *to fritter away one's money.* –**fritterer,** *n.*

fritter[2] /ˈfrɪtə/ *n.* a small cake of batter, sometimes containing fruit or some other ingredient, fried in deep fat or sautéed in a frying pan.

fritz /frɪts/ *n. Aust.* a large, mild-flavoured, precooked sausage, usually sliced thinly and eaten cold; devon; luncheon sausage; polony; Strasburg.

frivolous /ˈfrɪvələs/ *adj.* **1.** of little or no weight, worth, or importance; not worthy of serious notice: *a frivolous objection.* **2.** characterised by lack of seriousness or sense: *frivolous conduct.* **3.** given to trifling or levity, as persons. –**frivolity,** *n.* –**frivolously,** *adv.* –**frivolousness,** *n.*

frizz /frɪz/ *v.t.* (**frizzed, frizzing**) **1.** to make into small, crisp curls or little tufts. –*n.* (*pl.* **frizzes**) **2.** something frizzed; frizzed hair. Also, **friz.** –**frizzy,** *adj.*

frizzle[1] /ˈfrɪzəl/ *v.t.* **1.** to frizz. –*n.* **2.** a short, crisp curl. –**frizzler,** *n.*

frizzle[2] /ˈfrɪzəl/ *v.i.* **1.** to make a sizzling or sputtering noise in frying or the like. –*v.t.* **2.** to crisp (meat, etc.) by frying.

fro /froʊ/ *phr.* **to and fro,** back and forth.

frock /frɒk/ *n.* **1.** a dress. **2.** a loose outer garment worn by peasants and workmen; smock. **3.** a coarse outer garment with large sleeves, worn by members of some religious orders. –*v.t.* **4.** to provide with or clothe in a frock. **5.** to invest with priestly or clerical office. –**frockless,** *adj.*

frog[1] /frɒɡ/ *n.* **1.** any of various tailless amphibians, order Salientia, some of the web-footed aquatic species, typically having a smooth skin and long hind legs adapted for leaping. **2.** any of various frog-like amphibians. **3.** a small, heavy holder placed in a bowl or vase to hold flower stems in position. *–phr.* **4. a frog in one's throat**, a slight hoarseness due to mucus on the vocal cords.

frog² /frɒg/ *n.* **1.** an ornamental fastening for the front of a coat, consisting of a button and a loop through which it passes. **2.** a device at the intersection of two railway tracks, to permit the wheels and flanges on one track to cross or branch from the other, or a similar device on a system of overhead wires as on a tramway or electric railway.

frogman /ˈfrɒgmən/ *n. (pl.* **-men**) a swimmer specially equipped for swimming underwater, especially with wetsuit, flippers, aqualung, etc.

frogmouth /ˈfrɒgmaʊθ/ *n.* **1.** any of various species of nocturnal birds of the family Podargidae, with wide bills, soft wings, cryptic plumage and silent flight, found throughout Australasia and New Guinea. **2.** any of various similar species of nocturnal birds of the family Batrachostomidae, found in various parts of Asia.

frolic /ˈfrɒlɪk/ *n.* **1.** merry play; gaiety; fun. *–v.i.* **(-icked, -icking) 2.** to play merrily; have fun; play merry pranks. *–frolicsome, adj. –frolicker, n.*

from /frɒm/, *weak form* /frəm/ *prep.* a particle specifying a starting point, and hence used to express: **1. a.** removal or separation in space: *a train running west from Sydney.* **b.** in time: *from that time to the present.* **2.** discrimination or distinction: *from low to high.* **3.** source or origin: *sketches drawn from nature.* **4.** cause or reason: *to suffer from the heat.* **5.** (*with the gerund*) abstention: *to refrain from laughing.*

frond /frɒnd/ *n.* **1.** a finely divided leaf, often large (properly applied to the ferns and some of the palms). **2.** a leaf-like expansion not differentiated into stem and foliage, as in lichens. *–fronded, adj. –frondless, adj.*

front /frʌnt/ *n.* **1.** the foremost part or surface of anything. **2.** the part or side of anything, as a house, which seems to look out or be directed forwards. **3.** any side or face, as of a house. **4.** a place or position directly in front of anything. **5.** *Mil.* **a.** the foremost line or part of an army, etc. **b.** a line of battle. **c.** any location at which opposing military forces are engaged in combat. **6.** → **fire front**. **7.** land facing a road, river, etc. **8.** a seaside promenade. **9.** someone or something that serves as a cover for another activity, especially an illegal or disreputable one. **10.** outward impression of rank, position, or wealth. **11.** bearing or demeanour in confronting anything: *a calm front.* **12.** *Colloq.* cool assurance, or impudence. **13.** something attached or worn at the forepart, as a shirt front, a dicky, etc. **14.** *Meteorol.* a surface of discontinuity separating two dissimilar air masses. *–adj.* **15.** of or relating to the front. **16.** situated in or at the front. **17.** *Phonetics* pronounced with the tongue relatively far forward in the mouth: *the vowels of 'beet' and 'bat' are front vowels. –v.t.* **18.** to have the front towards; face. **19.** to meet face to face; confront. **20.** to face in opposition, hostility, or defiance. **21.** to furnish or supply with a front. **22.** to serve as a front to. *–v.i.* **23.** to have or turn the front in some specified direction: *our house fronts on to the lake.* **24.** *Colloq.* to appear before a court on a charge. **25.** Also, **front up**. *Colloq.* to arrive, turn up. **26.** to be the lead singer or musician of (a band). *–phr.* **27. up front, a.** in advance: *they paid a thousand dollars up front.* **b.** in the public eye: *the company needs to develop an image up front. –frontless, adj.*

frontage /ˈfrʌntɪdʒ/ *n.* **1.** the front of a building or plot of land. **2.** the lineal extent of this front. **3.** the direction it faces. **4.** land abutting on a river, street, etc. **5.** the space lying between a building and the street, etc.

frontal /ˈfrʌntl/ *adj.* **1.** of, in, or at the front: *a frontal attack.* **2.** *Anat.* denoting or relating to the bone (or pair of bones) forming the forehead, or to the forehead in general. **3.** *Meteorol.* of or relating to the division between dissimilar air masses. **4.** viewed from the front: *a frontal nude. –phr.* **5. full frontal**, a view of a naked body from the front. *–frontally, adv.*

front bench *n.* the government ministers and members of the opposition shadow cabinet, who by tradition sit on the front seats to the right and left of the presiding officer of the legislature. Also, **frontbench**. *–front-bencher, n. –frontbench, adj.*

frontier /frʌnˈtɪə, -ˈtɪə/, *Chiefly Brit.* /ˈfrʌntɪə/ *n.* **1.** the part of a country which borders another country; boundary; border; extreme limit. **2.** (*oft. pl.*) the current limits of a particular field of knowledge in which research is still being carried out: *the frontiers of women's health research.*

frontispiece /ˈfrʌntəspis/ *n.* **1.** an illustrated leaf preceding the titlepage of a book. **2.** *Archit.* **a.** the most richly decorated and usually central portion of the principal face of a building. **b.** the pediment over a door, gate, etc.

frost /frɒst/ *n.* **1.** the atmospheric condition which causes the freezing of water. **2.** a covering of minute ice needles, formed from the atmosphere at night on cold surfaces when the dewpoint is below freezing point (**white frost** or **hoarfrost**). **3.** the act or process of freezing. **4.** crushed glass of paper thickness, used for decorative purposes. **5.** a coolness between persons; an icy manner. **6.** *Colloq.* something which is received coldly; a failure. **7.** *Colloq.* a swindle. *–v.t.* **8.** to cover with frost. **9.** to give a frostlike surface to (glass, etc.). **10.** to ice (a cake, etc.). *–v.i.* Also, **frost up**. **11.** to freeze or become hardened with frost. *–frostless, adj. –frosty, adj.*

frostbite /ˈfrɒstbaɪt/ *n. Pathol.* the inflamed, sometimes gangrenous effect on a part of the body, especially the extremities, due to excessive exposure to extreme cold. *–frostbitten, adj.*

frosting /ˈfrɒstɪŋ/ *n.* **1.** a fluffy icing used to cover and decorate cakes. **2.** a decoration of granules of sugar, usually stuck on with egg whites, around the rim of a glass as for certain cocktails. **3.** a lustreless finish, as of metal or glass. **4.** a material used for decorative work, as signs, etc., made from coarse, powdered glass flakes.

froth /frɒθ/ *n.* **1.** an aggregation of bubbles, as on a fermented liquid; foam. **2.** the foamy top which forms on milk when it is whipped or agitated or heated with steam. **3.** any similar foamy surface, as on water stirred up by a surf. **4.** a foam of saliva at the mouth of a hard-driven horse. **5.** something unsubstantial or evanescent, as idle talk; trivial ideas. *–v.t.* **6.** to cause to foam. **7.** to emit like froth. *–v.i.* **8.** to give out froth; foam. *–phr.* **9. be all froth and bubble**, to be without substance. *–frothy, adj.*

frown /fraʊn/ *v.i.* **1.** to contract the brow as in displeasure or deep thought; scowl. **2.** to look displeased; have an angry look. *–n.* **3.** a frowning look; scowl. *–phr.* **4. frown on** (or **upon**), to regard disapprovingly: *making personal calls at work is frowned on. –frowner, n. –frowningly, adv.*

frowzy /ˈfraʊzi/ *adj.* **(-zier, -ziest) 1.** dirty and untidy; slovenly. **2.** ill-smelling; musty. Also, **frowsy, frouzy**. *–frowzily, adv. –frowziness, n.*

froze /frəʊz/ *v.* past tense of **freeze**.

frozen /ˈfrəʊzən/ *v.* **1.** past participle of **freeze**. *–adj.* **2.** made solid by cold. **3.** covered with ice. **4.** hurt or killed by cold. **5.** (of food) kept below 0°C for preservation. **6.** unfeeling or cold in manner. **7.** made unusable or not available: *a frozen bank account.* **8.** stopped, fixed or unmoving. *–frozenly, adv. –frozenness, n.*

fructify /'frʌktəfaɪ, frʊk-/ *verb* (**-fied**, **-fying**) *−v.i.* **1.** to bear fruit. *−v.t.* **2.** to make fruitful or productive; fertilise.

fructivorous /frʌk'tɪvərəs, frʊk-/ *adj.* → **frugivorous**.

fructose /'frʊktoʊz, -toʊs, 'frʌk-/ *n.* a white, crystalline, very sweet sugar found in honey and fruit, $C_6H_{12}O_6$; fruit sugar.

frugal /'frugəl/ *adj.* **1.** economical in use or expenditure; prudently saving or sparing. **2.** entailing little expense; costing little; scanty; meagre. −**frugality** /fru'gælɪti/, **frugalness**, *n.* −**frugally**, *adv.*

frugging /'frʌgɪŋ/ *n.* fundraising under the guise of market research where a survey is merely the introduction to an approach for a donation.

frugivore /'frudʒəvɔ/ *n.* an animal that feeds primarily on fruit, as the flying fox.

frugivorous /fru'dʒɪvərəs/ *adj.* feeding on fruit; fructivorous.

fruit /frut/ *n.* **1.** any product of vegetable growth useful to humans or animals. **2.** *Bot.* **a.** the developed ovary of a seed plant with its contents and accessory parts, as the pea pod, nut, tomato, pineapple, etc. **b.** the edible part of a plant developed from a flower, with any accessory tissues, as the peach, mulberry, banana, etc. **3.** anything produced or accruing; product, result or effect; return or profit. **4.** *Colloq.* a male homosexual. *−v.i.* **5.** to bear fruit. *−phr.* **6. fruit for** (or **on**) **the sideboard**, **a.** something extra; a luxury item. **b.** an additional source of income. −**fruitlike**, *adj.*

fruitful /'frutfəl/ *adj.* **1.** bearing fruit abundantly, as trees or other plants. **2.** producing an abundant growth, as of fruit. **3.** productive of results; profitable: *fruitful investigations.* −**fruitfully**, *adv.* −**fruitfulness**, *n.*

fruition /fru'ɪʃən/ *n.* **1.** attainment of anything desired; attainment of maturity; realisation of results: *the fruition of one's labours.* **2.** the state of bearing fruit.

fruitless /'frutləs/ *adj.* **1.** useless; unproductive; vain; without results. **2.** without fruit; barren. −**fruitlessly**, *adv.* −**fruitlessness**, *n.*

fruity /'fruti/ *adj.* (**-tier**, **-tiest**) **1.** resembling fruit; having the taste or flavour of fruit. **2.** (of wine) having body and fullness of flavour. **3.** (of a voice) mellow, florid. **4.** *Colloq.* sexually suggestive; salacious. **5.** *Colloq.* smelly.

frump /frʌmp/ *n.* a dowdy, drably dressed woman.

frustrate /frʌs'treɪt/ *v.t.* **1.** to make (plans, efforts, etc.) of no avail; defeat; baffle; nullify. **2.** to disappoint or thwart (a person). −**frustrating**, *adj.* −**frustration**, *n.*

fry[1] /fraɪ/ *v.t.* (**fried**, **frying**) **1.** to cook in fat, oil, etc., usually over direct heat. *−n.* (*pl.* **fries**) **2.** a dish of something fried.

fry[2] /fraɪ/ *n.* (*pl.* **fry**) Also, **fish fry**. **1.** the young of fishes, or of some other animals, as frogs. *−phr.* **2. small fry**, **a.** unimportant or insignificant people. **b.** young children.

f-stop /'ɛf-stɒp/ *n.* → **f number**.

FTP /ɛf ti 'pi/ *n.* **1.** a protocol for the transfer of files from one computer to another via a communications network. **2.** *Computers* a computer program which uses this protocol to transfer files. *−v.t.* (**FTPed**, **FTPing**) **3.** to transfer (data) by this means. *−adj.* **4.** *Computers* of or relating to this protocol: *an FTP server.* Also, **ftp**.

fuchsia /'fjuʃə/ *n.* **1.** any plant of the genus *Fuchsia*, which includes many varieties cultivated for their handsome drooping flowers. **2.** any of various unrelated species with flowers thought to resemble those of the fuchsia, as *Eremophila maculata*. **3.** a vivid reddish or pinkish purple colour, characteristic of the fuchsia flower.

fuck /fʌk/ *Colloq.* (*taboo*) *−v.t.* **1.** to have sexual intercourse with. **2.** Also, **fuck up**. to make a mess of; to ruin or break: *this doesn't work any more − you've fucked it.*

−v.i. **3.** to have sexual intercourse. *−n.* **4.** an act of sexual intercourse. **5.** a sexual partner (especially in contexts where performance, willingness, etc., is evaluated): *a good fuck; an easy fuck.* *−interj.* **6. a.** an exclamation of disgust or annoyance. **b.** an exclamation of wonder or delight. *−phr.* **7. fuck around** (or **about**), **a.** to behave stupidly or inanely. **b.** to be sexually unfaithful or promiscuous. **8. fuck off**, **a.** to go away; depart: *after that, we fucked off; just fuck off!* **b.** (*used imperatively*) (a harsh expression of abuse or dismissal). **9. fuck someone around** (or **about**), to treat someone unfairly; deceive, or cause inconvenience, distress, etc., to someone. **10. fuck someone off**, to annoy someone greatly. **11. fuck someone over**, to treat someone unfairly with calculated malice. **12. fuck someone up**, to destroy someone's emotional well-being and stability. **13. fuck up**, **a.** to make a mistake. **b.** to ruin; make a mess of: *I've fucked up this cake − we'll have to buy one.* **14. fuck you**, an exclamation of dismissal. **15. go fuck yourself**, an expression of rejection, dismissal, etc. **16. not give a (flying) fuck**, not to care at all. **17. the fuck**, an intensifier: *who the fuck are you?* **18. what the fuck**, an exclamation of astonishment combined with dismay or annoyance.

fuddle /'fʌdl/ *v.t.* **1.** to intoxicate. **2.** to muddle or confuse.

fuddy-duddy /'fʌdi-dʌdi/ *n.* (*pl.* **-duddies**) a fussy, stuffy, or old-fashioned person.

fudge[1] /fʌdʒ/ *n.* a kind of soft sweet composed of sugar, butter, cream, chocolate, or the like.

fudge[2] /fʌdʒ/ *verb* (**fudged**, **fudging**) *−v.t.* **1.** to put together in a makeshift, clumsy, or dishonest way; fake. *−v.i.* **2.** (in games and contests) to gain advantage improperly.

fuel /'fjuəl, fjul/ *n.* **1.** combustible matter used to maintain fire, as coal, wood, oil, etc. **2.** material used to feed an engine, as petrol, diesel, etc. **3.** a source of energy for operating machines, appliances, etc., as gas or electricity. **4.** a fissile material used in a nuclear reactor to produce energy. **5.** accumulated deadwood and vegetation which could feed a bushfire. **6.** the means of sustaining or increasing passion, ardour, etc. **7.** food; those elements in food which enable the body to produce energy. *−verb* (**-elled** *or*, *US*, **-eled**, **-elling** *or*, *US*, **-eling**) *−v.t.* **8. a.** to supply with fuel. **b.** to deliberately increase (a reaction) as if by adding fuel. *−v.i.* Also, **fuel up**. **9.** to procure or take in fuel. *−phr.* **10. add fuel to the fire**, to aggravate a situation.

fuel cell *n.* a continuously fed battery in which a chemical reaction is used directly to produce electricity, the fuel being on the anode side and the oxidant on the cathode side.

fuel-injection *n.* a method of spraying liquid fuel directly into the cylinders of an internal-combustion engine instead of using a carburettor. −**fuel-injector**, *n.* −**fuel-injected**, *adj.*

-fuge a word element referring to 'flight', as in *refuge*.

fugitive /'fjudʒətɪv, -əv/ *n.* **1.** someone who is fleeing; a runaway. *−adj.* **2.** having taken flight, or run away: *a fugitive slave.* **3.** fleeting; transitory. −**fugitively**, *adv.* −**fugitiveness**, *n.*

fugue /fjug/ *n.* **1.** *Music* a polyphonic composition based upon one, two, or even more themes, which are enunciated by the several voices or parts in turn, subjected to contrapuntal treatment, and gradually built up into a complex form having somewhat distinct divisions or stages of development and a marked climax at the end. **2.** *Psychol.* a state of dissociation from one's past identity, involving loss of memory, during which an individual often disappears from his or her usual haunts. −**fuguelike**, *adj.*

-ful a suffix meaning: **1.** full of or characterised by: *shameful, beautiful, careful, thoughtful.* **2.** tending or able to: *wakeful, harmful.* **3.** as much as will fill: *spoonful, handful.*

fulcrum /ˈfʊlkrəm/ *n.* (*pl.* **-crums** *or* **-cra** /-krə/) **1.** the support, or point of rest, on which a lever turns in moving a load. **2.** a prop.

fulfil /fʊlˈfɪl/ *v.t.* (**-filled, -filling**) **1.** to carry out, or bring to consummation, as a prophecy, promise, etc. **2.** to perform or do, as duty; obey or follow, as commands. **3.** to satisfy (requirements, etc.) **4.** to bring to an end, finish, or complete, as a period of time. –**fulfilment**, *n.* –**fulfiller**, *n.* –**fulfilled**, *adj.* –**fulfilling**, *adj.*

full /fʊl/ *adj.* **1.** filled; containing all that can be held; filled to utmost capacity: *a full cup; a full theatre.* **2.** complete; entire; maximum: *a full supply.* **3.** of unmixed ancestry: *a full Aborigine.* **4.** of the maximum size, amount, extent, volume, etc.: *a full kilometre; full pay; the full moon.* **5.** (of garments, etc.) wide, ample, or having ample folds. **6.** filled or rounded out, as in form. **7.** *Music* ample and complete in volume or richness of sound. **8.** (of wines) having considerable body. **9.** being fully or entirely such: *a full brother.* **10.** *Aust., NZ Colloq.* intoxicated. –*adv.* **11.** exactly or directly: *the blow struck him full in the face.* **12.** *Obs.* completely or entirely. –*n.* **13.** (of the moon) the stage of complete illumination. –*phr.* **14. be full of it**, *Colloq.* **a.** to habitually express opinions which are outrageous or incorrect. **b.** to put on airs. **15. full and by**, *Naut.* with the sails full and sailing close to the wind. **16. full as a boot** (or **goog**) (or **tick**) (or **fart**), *Aust., NZ Colloq.* **a.** very drunk. **b.** unable to eat any more. **17. full of**, **a.** engrossed with or absorbed in. **b.** *Colloq.* exasperated by: *I'm getting full of this job.* **18. full of oneself**, conceited; egoistic. **19. full up**, *Colloq.* **a.** filled to capacity. **b.** having all places taken: *the car park is full up.* **c.** (of a person) replete; having eaten enough. **d.** exasperated; disgruntled. **20. in full**, **a.** without reduction; to or for the full amount: *a receipt in full.* **b.** without abbreviation or contraction. **21. in full cry**, in hot pursuit, as dogs in the chase. **22. in full force**, with no-one missing. **23. on the full**, (of a ball) in flight before bouncing. **24. to the full**, in full measure; to the utmost extent. –**fullness**, *n.* –**fully**, *adv.*

full age *n. Law* the age at which one becomes an adult, in Australia the age of 18.

fullback /ˈfʊlbæk/ *n.* **1.** *Aust. Rules* **a.** the central position on the back line nearest to the defenders' goal. **b.** someone who plays in this position. **2.** *Soccer, Rugby Football, Hockey, etc.* a player whose main purpose is to defend their own goal.

full-blood *adj.* **1.** (especially of horses) purebred. **2.** (*usually derog.*) (*racist*) (of Aborigines, Melanesians, etc.) of unmixed ancestry (opposed to *half-caste*, etc.)

full bore *n.* **1.** the maximum production (of oil or gas from a drill hole). –*adv.* **2.** *Colloq.* with maximum effort; with the greatest possible speed or productivity. –*phr.* **3. the full bore**, *Colloq.* the maximum: *give it the full bore.*

full-cream *adj.* of or relating to milk containing the naturally occurring proportion of cream.

full monty *Colloq.* –*n.* **1.** everything; the full extent: *we don't want half the story – give us the full monty.* **2.** a striptease ending in complete nudity. **3.** a state of complete nudity. –*phr.* **4. go** (or **do**) **the full monty**, **a.** to do something to the fullest possible extent. **b.** to perform a striptease ending in complete nudity.

full moon *n.* → moon (def. 2c).

full preferential voting *n.* a form of preferential voting in which voters must indicate their order of preference for all the candidates. Compare **partial preferential voting, optional preferential voting**.

full stop *n.* the point or character (.) used to mark the end of a complete declarative sentence, indicate an abbreviation, etc.; a period. Also, **full point**.

full-time *adj.* **1.** taking all the normal working hours (opposed to *part-time*). **2.** of or relating to something that occupies someone all the time. **3.** *Sport* of or relating to the time at which play is to end: *the full-time whistle.* –*adv.* **4.** during all normal working hours. –*n.* **5.** *Sport* the time at which play is to end. Also, **fulltime**.

fully-fledged /ˈfʊli-flɛdʒd/ *adj.* **1.** able to fly. **2.** fully developed. **3.** of full rank or standing. **4.** fully qualified or established: *a fully-fledged professor.* Also, **full-fledged**.

fully-paid /ˈfʊli-peɪd/ *adj.* of or relating to shares or stock on which the face value of the capital represented has been paid in full.

fulmar /ˈfʊlmə/ *n.* any of certain oceanic birds of the petrel family, as the **southern fulmar**, *Fulmarus glacialoides*, a gull-like Antarctic species.

fulminate /ˈfʊlməneɪt, ˈfʌl-/ *v.i.* **1.** to explode with a loud noise; detonate. –*n.* **2.** *Chem.* one of a group of unstable explosive compounds derived from fulminic acid, $HONC$, found only in its salts, especially the mercury salt of fulminic acid which is a powerful detonating agent. –*phr.* **3. fulminate against**, to issue denunciations or the like against. –**fulmination**, *n.* –**fulminator**, *n.* –**fulminatory**, *adj.*

fulsome /ˈfʊlsəm/ *adj.* **1.** offensive to good taste, especially as being excessive; gushing; insincere: *fulsome praise.* **2.** (*not considered standard by some*) comprehensive; expansive: *in fulsome detail.* **3.** lavish; unstinted. **4.** *Obs.* copious; abundant. –**fulsomely**, *adv.* –**fulsomeness**, *n.*

fumble /ˈfʌmbəl/ *v.i.* **1.** to feel about clumsily: *he fumbled for his shoes in the dark; he just fumbles about all day wasting time.* –*v.t.* **2.** to handle clumsily: *to fumble a ball.* –*n.* **3.** the act of fumbling. –**fumbler**, *n.* –**fumbling**, *adj., n.* –**fumblingly**, *adv.*

fume /fjuːm/ *n.* **1.** (*oft. pl.*) any smoke-like or vaporous exhalation from matter or substances. –*v.i.* **2.** to show irritation or anger. **3.** to give off fumes. –**fumeless**, *adj.* –**fumelike**, *adj.* –**fumingly**, *adv.* –**fumy**, *adj.*

fumigate /ˈfjuːməɡeɪt/ *v.t.* to expose to smoke or fumes, as in disinfecting. –**fumigator**, *n.* –**fumigation** /fjuːməˈɡeɪʃən/, *n.*

fun /fʌn/ *n.* **1.** enjoyment or amusement. –*v.i.* (**funned, funning**) **2.** *Colloq.* to act in a joking way. –*adj. Colloq.* **3.** providing enjoyment or entertainment: *a fun place to be.* **4.** lively and entertaining: *a fun person.* **5.** enjoyable; entertaining: *a party that was so fun.* –*phr.* **6. for fun**, purely for amusement: *just for fun, we ran down the hill.* **7. in fun**, as a joke, playfully; not seriously: *I'm sorry you're offended – it was said in fun.* **8. like fun**, *Colloq.* not at all: *like fun I'll give you breakfast in bed.* **9. make fun of** or **poke fun at**, to ridicule.

function /ˈfʌŋkʃən, ˈfʌŋʃən/ *n.* **1.** the kind of action or activity proper to a person, thing, or institution. **2.** any ceremonious public or social gathering or occasion. **3.** any basic computer operation. –*v.i.* **4.** to perform a function; act; serve; operate. **5.** to carry out normal work, activity, or processes. –**functionless**, *adj.*

functional /ˈfʌŋkʃənəl/ *adj.* **1.** of or relating to a function or functions. **2.** designed or adapted primarily to perform some operation or duty: *a functional building.* –**functionally**, *adv.*

functional grammar *n.* a grammar in which the analysis begins with the functions of language and words rather than their forms.

functionality /fʌŋkʃəˈnæləti/ *n.* **1.** the purpose designed to be fulfilled by a device, tool, machine, etc. **2.** *Computers* the range of functions which an application has.

function key *n.* any of a numbered set of keys (usually 10 or 12) on a computer keyboard, which can be programmed, either by a piece of software, or by a user, to perform certain functions, often used to reduce the number of necessary keystrokes.

fund /fʌnd/ *n.* **1.** a stock of money. **2.** a store or stock of something: *a fund of knowledge.* **3.** an organisation which manages money invested for a particular purpose, such as superannuation **4.** (*pl.*) ready money. *–v.t.* **5.** to put into a fund. **6.** to change (a short-term debt or debts) into a long-term debt or loan, represented by interest-bearing bonds. **7.** to provide a fund or funds for. **–funding**, *n.*

fundamental /fʌndəˈmɛntl/ *adj.* **1.** serving as, or being a component part of, a foundation or basis; basic; underlying: *fundamental principles.* **2.** of or affecting the foundation or basis: *a fundamental change.* **3.** essential; primary; original. **4.** *Music* (of a chord) having its root as its lowest note. *–n.* **5.** a leading or primary principle, rule, law, or the like, which serves as the groundwork of a system; essential part. **–fundamentality** /fʌndəmɛnˈtæləti/, *n.* **–fundamentally**, *adv.*

fundamentalism /fʌndəˈmɛntəlɪzəm/ *n.* a religious movement which stresses the authority and literal application of its founding tenets: *Islamic fundamentalism.* **–fundamentalist**, *adj.* **–fundamentalist**, *n.*

fund manager *n.* **1.** a commercial organisation that manages investors' money for a fee. **2.** someone who manages an investment portfolio for a superannuation fund, pension fund, etc.

funeral /ˈfjunrəl, ˈfjunərəl/ *n.* **1.** the ceremonies connected with the disposition of the body of a dead person; obsequies. **2.** a funeral procession. **3.** *Colloq.* business; worry; concern: *that's his funeral.* *–adj.* **4.** of or relating to a funeral. *–phr.* **5. it's your (his, her,** etc.) **funeral**, *Colloq.* a phrase implying that the consequences of a particular action, or lack of it, are no one's fault but yours, his, hers, etc.: *if she doesn't apply on time, it's her funeral.* **–funerary**, *adj.*

funeral parlour *n.* an undertaker's place of business, sometimes containing a small chapel as well as the rooms where the dead are prepared for burial or cremation. Also, **funeral parlor**.

funereal /fjuˈnɪəriəl/ *adj.* **1.** of or relating to a funeral. **2.** mournful; gloomy; dismal. **–funereally**, *adv.*

fungi /ˈfʌŋgi, ˈfʌŋgaɪ/ *n.* a plural of **fungus**.

fung shui /fʊŋ ˈʃweɪ, fʌŋ, ˈʃwi/ *n.* → **feng shui**.

fungus /ˈfʌŋgəs/ *n.* (*pl.* **fungi** /ˈfʌŋgi, ˈfʌŋgaɪ, ˈfʌndʒaɪ** *or* **funguses**) **1.** any of the Fungi, a group of thallophytes including the mushrooms, moulds, mildews, rusts, smuts, etc., characterised chiefly by absence of chlorophyll and which subsist upon dead or living organic matter. **2.** *Pathol.* a spongy morbid growth, as proud flesh formed in a wound. **–fungous**, *adj.*

funicular railway /fəˌnɪkjələ ˈreɪlweɪ/ *n.* a railway system of short length operating up steep gradients, in which cable-linked cars or trains move up and down simultaneously, thus minimising the pull of gravity.

funk¹ /fʌŋk/ *Colloq.* *–n.* **1.** fear or a condition of terror: *he was in a funk about his exams.* **2.** a coward. *–v.t.* **3.** to be afraid of. **4.** to fear and try to avoid. *–v.i.* **5.** to be in a funk.

funk² /fʌŋk/ *n.* *US* a strong smell or stink.

funk³ /fʌŋk/ *n.* an up-tempo style of soul music originating on the west coast of America and distinguished by much syncopation.

funky /ˈfʌŋki/ *adj.* (**-kier, -kiest**) **1.** exciting, satisfying, or pleasurable. **2.** fashionable: *funky shoes.* **3.** *Music* relating to or in the style of funk. **4.** of or relating to a style of dress reminiscent of the period identified by the emergence of jazz. **5.** *US* having an unpleasant smell.

funnel /ˈfʌnəl/ *n.* **1.** a cone-shaped utensil with a tube at the apex, for conducting liquid, etc., through a small opening, as into a bottle. **2.** a metal chimney, especially of a ship or a steam engine. **3.** a flue, tube, or shaft, as for ventilation. *–v.t.* (**-nelled** *or, Chiefly US,* **-neled, -nelling** *or, Chiefly US,* **-neling**) **4.** to converge or concentrate: *to funnel all one's energies into a job.*

funnel-web spider *n.* **1.** either of three genera of spiders of the subfamily Atracinae of the family Hexathelidae, found along the eastern coast of Australia; found in moist, sheltered environments, typically under rocks or logs. **2.** any of various burrowing spiders of the family Hexathelidae, of Australasia, Eurasia, South America, and Africa, which line their tubelike lair with web. Also, **funnel-web**.

funny /ˈfʌni/ *adj.* (**-nier, -niest**) **1.** affording fun; amusing; comical. **2.** curious; strange; odd. **3.** *Colloq.* insolent. *–n.* (*pl.* **-nies**) **4.** *Colloq.* a joke. **–funnily**, *adv.* **–funniness**, *n.*

funny bone *n.* the part of the elbow where the ulnar nerve passes by the internal condyle of the humerus, which when struck causes a peculiar tingling sensation in the arm and hand. Also, *US,* **crazy bone**.

funny money *n.* *Colloq.* money which is nominally exchanged between different sections of the one organisation for bookkeeping purposes but which has no physical existence.

fur /fɜ/ *n.* **1.** the skin of certain animals (such as the cat, rabbit, seal, mink, etc.), covered with a fine, soft, thick, hairy coating. **2.** the cured and treated skin of certain of these animals used for lining or trimming garments or for entire garments. **3.** an article of dress made of or with such material, as a fur coat or stole. **4.** any coating resembling or suggesting fur, such as one of morbid matter on the tongue. *–v.t.* (**furred, furring**) **5.** to coat with foul or deposited matter. *–phr.* **6. make the fur fly**, *Colloq.* to quarrel noisily; make a scene or disturbance. **–furry**, *adj.* **–furless**, *adj.*

furbish /ˈfɜbɪʃ/ *v.t.* **1.** Also, **furbish up**. to restore to freshness of appearance or condition. **2.** to remove ust from (armour, weapons, etc.); polish; burnish. **–furbisher**, *n.*

furious /ˈfjuriəs/ *adj.* **1.** full of fury, violent passion, or rage. **2.** intensely violent, as wind, storms, etc. **3.** of unrestrained energy, speed, etc.: *furious activity.* **–furiously**, *adv.* **–furiousness**, *n.*

furl /fɜl/ *v.t.* to draw into a compact roll, as a sail against a spar or a flag against its staff.

furlong /ˈfɜloŋ/ *n.* a unit of distance, in the imperial system, equal to 220 yards or 201.168 m. *Symbol:* fur

furlough /ˈfɜloʊ/ *n.* leave of absence from official duty, usually for a longish period.

furnace /ˈfɜnəs/ *n.* **1.** a structure or apparatus in which to generate heat, as for heating buildings, smelting ores, producing steam, etc. **2.** a place of burning heat.

furnish /ˈfɜnɪʃ/ *v.t.* **1.** to provide or supply. **2.** to fit up (a house, room, etc.) with necessary appliances, especially furniture. **–furnisher**, *n.*

furniture /ˈfɜnɪtʃə/ *n.* **1.** the movable articles, as tables, chairs, beds, desks, cabinets, etc., required for use or ornament in a house, office, or the like. **2.** fittings, apparatus, or necessary accessories for something.

furore /ˈfjurɔ, fjuˈrɔri/ *n.* **1.** a public reaction of anger, disapproval, etc. **2.** an angry outburst; noisy hubbub. Also, **furor**.

furphy /ˈfɜfi/ *n.* (*pl.* **-phies**) *Aust.* a rumour; a false story.

furrier /ˈfʌriə/ *n.* a dealer in or dresser of furs.

furrow /ˈfʌroʊ/ *n.* **1.** a narrow trench made in the ground, especially by a plough. **2.** a narrow, trench-like depression in any surface. **3.** a groove, as in the skin of the forehead, etc. –*v.t.* **4.** to make a furrow or furrows in; plough (land, etc.). **5.** to make wrinkles in (the face, etc.). –**furrower**, *n.*

further /'fɜðə/ *adv. (comparative of far)* **1.** at or to a greater distance. **2.** to a greater degree. **3.** in addition. –*adj. (comparative of far)* **4.** more distant; farther. **5.** longer. **6.** more. –*v.t.* **7.** to encourage; promote; help: *to further a cause.* –**furtherer**, *n.*

furthermore /fɜðə'mɔ/ *adv.* moreover; in addition.

furtive /'fɜtɪv/ *adj.* **1.** taken, done, used, etc., by stealth; secret: *a furtive glance.* **2.** sly; shifty: *a furtive manner.* –**furtively**, *adv.* –**furtiveness**, *n.*

fury /'fjuri/ *n. (pl. -ries)* **1.** frenzied or unrestrained violent passion, especially anger. **2.** violence; vehemence; fierceness. **3.** a fierce and violent person, especially a woman. –*phr.* **4. like fury**, *Colloq.* furiously; violently.

fuse¹ /fjuz/ *n.* **1.** *Elect.* a device for preventing an excessive current from passing through a circuit, consisting of a piece of wire which breaks the circuit by melting if the current exceeds a specified value. **2.** a tube, ribbon, or the like, filled or saturated with combustible matter, for igniting an explosive. **3.** a mechanical or electronic device to detonate an explosive charge. –*v.i.* **4. a.** (of an electrical appliance) to fail because of an internal short circuit: *the toaster fused.* **b.** (of an electrical circuit) to cause, perhaps because of a short or overloading, the fuse governing it to burn out: *the power circuit has fused.* –*phr. Colloq.* **5. blow a fuse**, to lose one's temper. **6. have a short fuse**, to tend to become angry quickly.

fuse² /fjuz/ *v.t.* **1.** to combine or blend by melting together; melt. **2.** to unite or blend into a whole, as if by melting together. –*v.i.* **3.** to become liquid under the action of heat; melt. **4.** to become united or blended, as if by melting together. –**fusible**, *adj.*

fuselage /'fjuzəlaʒ, -lɪdʒ/ *n.* the body of an aircraft.

fusillade /'fjuzəleɪd, -lad/ *n.* **1.** a simultaneous or continuous discharge of firearms. **2.** an execution carried out by this means. **3.** a general discharge or outpouring of anything: *a fusillade of questions.* –*v.t.* **4.** to attack or shoot down by a fusillade.

fusilli /fju'zɪli/ *n.* a kind of pasta in the form of short strips in a spiral shape.

fusion /'fjuʒən/ *n.* **1.** the act or process of fusing. **2.** something that is fused. **3.** *Physics* a thermonuclear reaction in which nuclei of light atoms join to form nuclei of heavier atoms, such as the combination of deuterium atoms to form helium atoms, usually with the release of large amounts of energy.

fusion food *n.* a cuisine characterised by the blending of two or more different styles, cultures, etc.

fusion music *n.* a style of music blending two or more other styles, originally including jazz.

fuss /fʌs/ *n.* **1.** an excessive display of anxious activity; needless or useless bustle. **2.** a commotion, argument, or dispute. **3.** a person given to fussing. –*v.i.* **4.** to make a fuss; make much ado about unimportant things; to move fussily about. –*v.t.* **5.** to put into a fuss; disturb with unimportant things; bother. –*phr.* **6. fuss over**, to pay excessive attention to. **7. make a fuss about**, to draw attention forcefully to. **8. make a fuss of**, to treat with special care and affection. –**fusser**, *n.*

fusspot /'fʌspɒt/ *n. Colloq.* a fussy person; someone who is over-particular.

fussy /'fʌsi/ *adj. (-sier, -siest)* **1.** excessively busy with unimportant things; anxious or particular about petty details. **2.** (of clothes, etc.) elaborately made or trimmed. **3.** full of excessive detail: *a fussy cover on a book.* –**fussily**, *adv.* –**fussiness**, *n.*

fusty /'fʌsti/ *adj. (-tier, -tiest)* **1.** mouldy; musty; having a stale smell; stuffy. **2.** old-fashioned. **3.** stubbornly old-fashioned and out-of-date. –**fustily**, *adv.* –**fustiness**, *n.*

futile /'fjutaɪl/ *adj.* incapable of producing any result; ineffective; useless; not successful. –**futilely**, *adv.* –**futility** /fju'tɪləti/, **futileness**, *n.*

futon /'futɒn/ *n.* a Japanese-style bed consisting of an unsprung mattress on a support of wooden slats.

future /'fjutʃə/ *n.* **1.** a time that is going to be or come, after the present time: *things will be better in the future.* **2.** what will exist or happen in future time: *to tell the future.* **3.** future condition: *his future looks bright.* –*adj.* **4.** coming in, or relating to the future.

futureproof /'fjutʃəpruf/ *adj.* **1.** secure, whatever might happen in the future: *a futureproof power supply.* –*v.t.* **2.** to make secure, whatever might happen in the future: *to futureproof the city's water supply.*

futures contract *n.* a contract to buy or sell a fixed amount of a commodity, security or currency at a specified price on a specified future date.

futuristic /fjutʃə'rɪstɪk/ *adj.* **1.** of or relating to futurism. **2.** (of a work of art or the like) in a modern style; without reference to traditional forms, etc. **3.** (of design in clothes, furniture, etc.) expressing a vision of the future; avant-garde.

fuzz /fʌz/ *n.* **1.** loose, light, fibrous, or fluffy matter. **2.** a mass or coating of such matter. **3.** *Colloq.* a blur. **4.** *Colloq.* frizzy hair. **5.** *Colloq.* the police force or a police officer. –**fuzzy**, *adj.*

fuzzy logic *n. Computers* a method of decision-making that makes evaluations of data which does not lend itself to clear-cut decisions.

-fy a suffix meaning: **1.** to make; cause to be; render: *simplify, beautify.* **2.** to become; be made: *liquefy.* Also, **-ify**.

G g

G, g /dʒi/ *n.* **1.** the seventh letter of the English alphabet. **2.** the seventh in order of a series. **3.** *Music* the fifth note in the scale of C major.

gab /gæb/ *Colloq.* *–v.i.* (**gabbed, gabbing**) **1.** to talk idly; chatter. *–n.* **2.** idle talk; chatter. *–phr.* **3. the gift of the gab,** the ability to speak eloquently and persuasively. **–gabber,** *n.*

gabble /ˈgæbəl/ *v.i.* **1.** to talk rapidly and unintelligibly; jabber. **2.** (of geese, etc.) to cackle. **–gabbler,** *n.*

gaberdine /gæbəˈdin, ˈgæbədin/ *n.* **1.** a closely woven twill fabric of worsted, cotton, or spun rayon. **2.** a man's long, loose cloak or frock, worn in the Middle Ages. Also, **gabardine.**

gable /ˈgeɪbəl/ *n.* **1.** the triangular wall enclosed by the two slopes of a roof and a horizontal line across the eaves. **2.** any architectural feature shaped like a gable. *–v.t.* **3.** to build with a gable or gables; form as a gable. **–gabled,** *adj.*

gad /gæd/ *phr.* **gad about** (or **around**), to move restlessly or idly from place to place, especially in search of pleasure.

gadabout /ˈgædəbaʊt/ *n.* *Colloq.* a restless person, especially one who leads an active social life.

gadget /ˈgædʒət/ *n.* a mechanical contrivance or device; any ingenious article.

gado gado /gadoʊ ˈgadoʊ/ *n.* an Indonesian dish consisting of lightly steamed vegetables with boiled egg or strips of omelette, topped with a peanut sauce.

gaff /gæf/ *n.* **1.** a strong hook with a handle, used for landing large fish. *–v.t.* **2.** to hook or land with a gaff.

gaffe /gæf/ *n.* a social blunder.

gaffer /ˈgæfə/ *n.* *Film, TV* the chief lighting electrician.

gaffer tape *n.* a strong adhesive cloth tape for electrical and other purposes.

gag¹ /gæg/ *verb* (**gagged, gagging**) *–v.t.* **1.** to stop up the mouth of (someone) so as to prevent sound or speech. **2.** to use force or official power to prevent (someone) from using free speech, etc. **3.** (in parliament) to close (a debate) when some members still wish to speak. *–v.i.* **4.** to be unable to swallow, and to heave as though vomiting. *–n.* **5.** something pushed into or tied around the mouth to prevent speech. **6.** forceful discouragement of freedom of speech. **7.** a closing of parliamentary debate when some members still wish to speak. *–phr.* **8. gag for,** *Colloq.* to have a great desire for. **–gagger,** *n.*

gag² /gæg/ *Colloq.* *–v.i.* (**gagged, gagging**) **1.** to make jokes. *–n.* **2.** a joke. **3.** an interpolation introduced by an actor into his or her part. **–gagger, gagster,** *n.*

gaga /ˈgaga/ *adj.* *Colloq.* **1.** mad; fatuously eccentric. **2.** senile. **3.** besotted: *he is gaga about his new car.*

gage /geɪdʒ/ *n., v.t.* (**gaged, gaging**) → **gauge. –gager,** *n.*

gaggle /ˈgægəl/ *n.* **1.** a flock of geese. **2.** any disorderly group.

gaiety /ˈgeɪəti/ *n.* (*pl.* **-ties**) **1.** the state of being cheerful or gay (def. 6). **2.** (*oft. pl.*) merrymaking or festivity: *the gaieties of the New Year season.* **3.** showiness; finery: *gaiety of dress.*

gai lan /gaɪ ˈlan/ *n.* **1.** a green leafy plant of the genus *Brassica,* bearing small white clusters of flowers resembling miniature broccoli; Chinese broccoli; Chinese kale. **2.** the leaves of this plant, eaten as a vegetable. Also, **kai lan.**

gaily /ˈgeɪli/ *adv.* **1.** merrily. **2.** showily. **3.** unconcernedly.

gain /geɪn/ *v.t.* **1.** to obtain; secure (something desired); acquire: *gain time.* **2.** to win; get in competition: *gain the prize.* **3.** to acquire as an increase or addition: *to gain weight; to gain speed.* **4.** to obtain as a profit: *he gained ten dollars by that transaction.* **5.** to reach by effort; get to; arrive at: *to gain a good harbour.* *–v.i.* **6.** to improve; make progress; advance. **7.** (sometimes fol. by *on* or *upon*) to get nearer, as in pursuit. **8.** (of clocks, watches, etc.) to run too quickly. *–n.* **9.** profit; advantage. **10.** (*pl.*) profits; winnings. **11.** an increase or advance. **12.** the act of gaining; acquisition. **13.** *Electronics* an increase in a signal parameter, as voltage, current, or power, expressed as the ratio of the output to the input. **14.** (of an amplifier) volume. *–phr.* **15. gain ground, a.** to make an advance, as in the face of opposition. **b.** to obtain an advantage. **16. gain time, a.** (of a clock) to run too quickly. **b.** to delay; achieve a postponement.

gainful /ˈgeɪnfəl/ *adj.* profitable; lucrative. **–gainfully,** *adv.* **–gainfulness,** *n.*

gainsay /geɪnˈseɪ/ *v.t.* (**-said, -saying**) **1.** to deny. **2.** to speak or act against. **–gainsayer,** *n.*

gait /geɪt/ *n.* **1.** a particular manner of walking. **2.** any of the characteristic rhythms of locomotion of a horse, as the walk, trot, canter, or gallop.

gaiter /ˈgeɪtə/ *n.* (*oft. pl.*) a covering for the ankle and instep, and sometimes also the lower leg, made of cloth or leather and worn over the shoe, formerly part of male attire.

gala /ˈgalə/ *adj.* **1.** festive; festal; showy: *his visits were always gala occasions.* *–n.* **2.** a celebration; festive occasion.

galactic /gəˈlæktɪk/ *adj.* **1.** *Astron.* relating to a galaxy, especially the Milky Way. **2.** *Physiol.* relating to or stimulating the secretion of milk.

galah /gəˈla/ *n.* **1.** a common small cockatoo, *Cacatua* (or *Eolophus*) *roseicapilla,* pale grey above and deep pink below, found in open areas in most parts of Australia. **2.** *Aust. Colloq.* an empty-headed person; fool.

galaxy /ˈgæləksi/ *n.* (*pl.* **-xies**) **1.** *Astron.* any large system of stars held together by gravitation and separated from any other similar system by great areas of space. **2.** a gathering of famous people.

gale /geɪl/ *n.* **1.** a strong wind. **2.** a noisy outburst: *a gale of laughter.*

gall¹ /gɔl/ *n.* **1.** bile. **2.** something very bitter or severe. **3.** bitterness of spirit; rancour. **4.** impudence; effrontery.

gall² /gɔl/ *v.t.* to irritate or infuriate.

gall³ /gɔl/ *n.* any abnormal vegetable growth or excrescence on plants, caused by various agents, including insects, nematodes, fungi, bacteria, viruses, chemicals, and mechanical injuries.

gallant /ˈgælənt, gəˈlænt/ *adj.* **1.** brave and dashing: *gallant young men.* **2.** (of a man) noticeably polite and attentive to women. **3.** generous or sporting: *a gallant gesture.* **4.** amorous. **–gallantry,** *n.* **–gallantly,** *adv.* **–gallantness,** *n.*

gall bladder *n.* a vesicle attached to the liver which receives bile from the hepatic ducts, concentrates it, and discharges it after meals.

galleon /ˈgælian, ˈgæljən/ *n.* a kind of large sailing vessel formerly used by Spain and other countries, both as warships and as merchant ships.

gallery /ˈgæləri/ *n.* (*pl.* **-ries**) **1.** a long, narrow, covered walk, open at one or both sides. **2.** a corridor, usually large and with ornate walls and ceiling. **3.** a raised platform or passageway along the outside or inside of the wall of a building; balcony. **4.** a platform projecting from the interior walls of a church, theatre, etc., to provide seats or room for a part of the audience. **5.** the highest of such platforms in a theatre, usually containing the cheapest seats. **6.** the occupants of such a platform in a theatre. **7.** any body of spectators or auditors. **8.** a room, series of rooms, or building devoted to the exhibition of works of art. **9.** a collection of art for exhibition. **10.** a room or building in which to take pictures, practise shooting, etc. **11.** any of various tunnels or passages, as an underground passage in a fortification, a tunnel within the body of a dam, etc. **12.** *Mining* a level or drift. –*phr.* **13. play to the gallery**, to seek applause by playing to popular taste rather than considered judgement. –**galleried**, *adj.*

galley /ˈgæli/ *n.* (*pl.* **-leys**) **1.** an early seagoing vessel propelled by oars or by oars and sails. **2.** a large rowing boat, formerly used in England. **3.** the kitchen of a ship or airliner. **4.** *Printing* **a.** a long, narrow tray, usually of metal, for holding type which has been set. **b.** galley proof.

gallinaceous /gælə'neɪʃəs/ *adj.* **1.** relating to or resembling the domestic fowls. **2.** belonging to the group or order Galliformes, which includes the domestic fowls, pheasants, grouse, partridges, etc. Also, **gallinacean**.

galling /ˈgɔlɪŋ/ *adj.* chafing; irritating; exasperating. –**gallingly**, *adv.*

gallivant /ˈgælavænt/ *v.i.* to go from place to place in a rollicking, frivolous, or flirtatious manner. Also, **galavant**.

gallon /ˈgælən/ *n.* **1.** a unit of capacity in the imperial system, for the measurement of liquids and dry goods, defined as the volume occupied by 10 lbs of distilled water under specified conditions; equal to $4.546\,09 \times 10^{-3}$ m^3 (4.546 09 litres); imperial gallon. **2.** a US measure of liquid commodities only, defined in the US as 231 cubic inches; equal to 3.785 litres. One imperial gallon equals 1.200 94 US gallons.

gallop /ˈgæləp/ *v.i.* **1.** to ride a horse at a gallop; ride at full speed. **2.** to run rapidly by leaps, as a horse; go at a gallop. **3.** to go fast, race, or hurry, as a person, the tongue, time, etc. –*v.t.* **4.** to cause (a horse, etc.) to gallop. –*n.* **5.** a fast gait of the horse (or other quadruped) in which in the course of each stride all four feet are off the ground at once. **6.** a run or ride at this gait. **7.** a rapid rate of going, or a course of going at this rate. –*phr.* **8. the gallops**, *Colloq.* horseracing (distinguished from *the trots, the dogs*). –**galloper**, *n.*

gallows /ˈgælouz/ *n.* (*pl.* **-lows** *or* **-lowses**) **1.** a wooden frame, consisting of a crossbeam on two uprights, on which condemned persons were, and in certain countries still are, executed by hanging. **2.** a similar structure, as for suspending something or for gymnastic exercise. **3.** a device on which slaughtered animals, such as cattle, are hung. –*phr.* **4. the gallows**, execution by hanging.

gallstone /ˈgɔlstoʊn/ *n. Pathol.* a calculus or stone formed in the bile ducts or gall bladder.

gallup poll /ˈgæləp poʊl/ *n.* → **opinion poll**.

galoot /gəˈlut/ *n. Colloq.* an awkward, silly person: *silly galoot*. Also, **galloot**.

galore /gəˈlɔ/ *adj.* (*used only after nouns*) in abundance: *there was food galore.*

galoshes /gəˈlɒʃəz/ *pl. n.* a pair of boots made of rubber or other waterproof substance, worn over the shoes to protect them from water, snow, etc.

galvanise /ˈgælvənaɪz/ *v.t.* **1.** to stimulate by or as by electricity. **2.** to startle into sudden activity. **3.** to coat (iron or steel) with zinc. Also, **galvanize**. –**galvanisation** /gælvənaɪˈzeɪʃən/, *n.* –**galvaniser**, *n.*

galvanised iron *n.* **1.** iron coated with zinc to prevent rust. **2.** such iron formed into corrugated sheets, and used for roofing, etc., especially in rural buildings or outhouses. Also, **galvanized iron**.

gambit /ˈgæmbət/ *n.* **1.** an opening in chess, in which the player seeks by sacrificing a pawn or other piece to obtain some advantage. **2.** any act or course of action by which one seeks to obtain some advantage.

gamble /ˈgæmbəl/ *v.i.* **1.** to play at any game of chance for stakes. **2.** to stake or risk money, or anything of value, on the outcome of something involving chance. **3.** to act on favourable hopes or assessment: *in calling the general election, the prime minister is gambling on public acceptance of his policies to date.* –*v.t.* **4.** to risk or venture. –*n.* **5.** any matter or thing involving risk or uncertainty. **6.** a venture in or as in gambling. –*phr.* **7. gamble away**, to lose or squander by betting. –**gambler**, *n.* –**gambling**, *n.*

gambol /ˈgæmbəl/ *v.i.* (**-bolled** *or*, *Chiefly US*, **-boled**, **-bolling** *or*, *Chiefly US*, **-boling**) to skip about, as in dancing or playing; frolic.

game^1 /geɪm/ *n.* **1.** an amusement or pastime: *children's games.* **2.** the apparatus employed in playing any of certain games: *a shop selling toys and games.* **3.** a contest for amusement in the form of a trial of chance, skill, or endurance, according to set rules; a match: *a game of football; a game of chess.* **4.** a single contest of play, or a definite portion of play in a particular game: *a rubber of three games in bridge.* **5.** the number of points required to win a game. **6.** a particular manner or style of playing a game. **7.** a proceeding carried on according to set rules as in a game: *the game of diplomacy.* **8.** *Colloq.* business or profession. **9.** a trick; strategy: *to see through someone's game.* **10.** sport of any kind; joke: *to make game of a person.* **11.** wild animals, including birds and fishes, such as are hunted or taken for sport or profit. **12.** the flesh of wild animals or game, used for food. **13.** any object of pursuit or attack; prey. **14.** fighting spirit; pluck. –*adj.* **15.** relating to animals hunted or taken as game. **16.** with fighting spirit; plucky; resolute: *as game as a fighting cock.* **17.** *Colloq.* (sometimes fol. by *for* or by an infinitive) willing to undertake something hazardous or challenging: *I'm game to go bushwalking; I'm game for a swim.* –*v.i.* **18.** to play games of chance for stakes; gamble. –*phr.* **19. game, set, and match**, (sometimes fol. by *to*) a convincing victory; complete triumph. **20. give the game away**, **a.** to reject or abandon a pursuit or activity previously followed. **b.** *Aust., NZ* to reveal some strategy or secret. **21. have the game sewn up** (or **by the throat**), to be in control of the situation. **22. lift one's game**, to improve one's performance. **23. off one's game**, not giving one's best performance; out of form. **24. on one's game**, giving one's best performance; in form. **25. on the game**, *Colloq.* working as a prostitute. **26. play the game**, to act fairly or justly, or in accordance with recognised rules. **27. throw the game away**, to lose a contest as a result of ineptitude or blunders. **28. two can play at that game**, an expression hinting at intended retaliation. –**gamely**, *adv.* –**gameness**, *n.*

game^2 /geɪm/ *adj. Colloq.* → **gammy**.

game changer *n.* an event of such significance that it causes a complete change of plans.

game plan *n.* **1.** *Sport* a strategy to take into a game, designed to defeat a particular opponent. **2.** an overall strategy or long-term plan, as in politics, business, etc. Also, **gameplan**.

gameplay /ˈɡeɪmpleɪ/ *n.* the amount of time that it takes to complete a computer game.

gamer /ˈɡeɪmə/ *n.* a person who plays a game, especially a computer game.

games cafe *n.* commercial premises which offer for a fee a number of computers for the playing of computer games, sometimes also selling coffee and light refreshments.

gamesmanship /ˈɡeɪmzmənʃɪp/ *n.* the art or practice of winning games, or gaining advantages without actually cheating, by disconcerting the opponent.

gamete /ˈɡæmiːt, ɡəˈmiːt/ *n.* *Biol.* either of the two germ cells which unite to form a new organism; a mature reproductive cell. —**gametal** /ɡəˈmiːtl/, **gametic** /ɡəˈmetɪk/, *adj.*

gamete intrafallopian transfer *n.* → GIFT.

gamify /ˈɡeɪməfaɪ/ *v.t.* (**-fied, -fying**) *Computers* to convert (a task or learning activity) into a computer game, often in an attempt to make it more appealing. —**gamification** /ɡeɪməfəˈkeɪʃən/, *n.*

gamin /ˈɡæmən/ *n.* **1.** a neglected child left to run about the streets. **2.** a mischievous child. —*adj.* **3.** having the characteristics of a gamin; waiflike. **4.** (of a person's appearance, or hairstyle) elfin.

gamma rays /ˈɡæmə reɪz/ *pl. n.* rays similar to X-rays, but of higher frequency and penetrating power, forming part of the radiation of radioactive substance. —**gamma-ray**, *adj.*

gammon /ˈɡæmən/ *n.* **1.** a smoked or cured ham. **2.** the lower end of a side of bacon.

gammy /ˈɡæmi/ *adj. Colloq.* lame: *a gammy leg.*

gamo- a word element meaning 'sexual union'.

-gamous an adjectival word element corresponding to the noun element **-gamy**, as in *polygamous.*

gamut /ˈɡæmət/ *n.* **1.** the whole scale or range. —*phr.* **2. run the gamut**, to cover the full range of possibilities.

-gamy **1.** a word element meaning 'marriage', as in *polygamy.* **2.** *Biol.* a word element meaning 'sexual union', as in *allogamy.*

ganache /ɡəˈnaʃ/ *n.* a rich chocolate confection made from semisweet chocolate and cream, often used as a cake icing.

gander /ˈɡændə/ *n.* **1.** the male of the goose. —*phr.* **2. take** (or **have**) **a gander at**, *Colloq.* to take a look at.

gang /ɡæŋ/ *n.* **1.** a band or group: *a gang of boys.* **2. a.** a group of persons working together; squad; shift: *a gang of labourers.* **b.** *Aust. Hist.* a party of convicts labouring under the control of an overseer on public works: *a road gang; a wood-cutting gang.* **3.** a group of persons, usually considered disreputable, violent or criminal, associated for a particular purpose: *a gang of thieves.* **4.** an urban group of adolescent to young men who congregate together and who are, or are viewed as being, antisocial, and possibly involved in criminal activities; often adopting a characteristic style of dress. **5.** a set of tools, etc., arranged to work together or simultaneously. —*v.t.* **6.** to arrange in gangs; form into a gang. —*v.i.* **7.** *Colloq.* to form or act as a gang. —*phr. Colloq.* **8. gang up**, to form into a gang, usually in opposition to another person or group. **9. gang up on**, to attack in a gang; combine against.

gang-gang /ˈɡæŋ-ɡæŋ/ *n.* a greyish cockatoo, *Callocephalon fimbriatum*, endemic to south-eastern Australia, the male of which has a red head and crest. Also, **gang-gang cockatoo**.

gangling /ˈɡæŋɡlɪŋ/ *adj.* → **gangly**.

ganglion /ˈɡæŋɡliən/ *n.* (*pl.* **ganglia** /-gliə/ *or* **ganglions**) **1.** *Anat.* a bundle of nerve cells outside the brain and spinal cord. **2.** *Pathol.* a cyst or enlargement in connection with the sheath of a tendon, usually at the wrist. **3.** a centre of intellectual or industrial force, activity, etc. —**ganglionic** /ˌɡæŋɡliˈɒnɪk/, *adj.*

gangly /ˈɡæŋɡli/ *adj.* tall and thin, and awkward in movements as a consequence. Also, **gangling**. —**gangliness**, *n.*

gangplank /ˈɡæŋplæŋk/ *n.* a plank, often having cleats, used as a temporary bridge in passing into and out of a ship, etc.

gang rape *n.* **1.** rape committed by a group of men. **2.** an instance of such rape.

gang-rape *v.t.* to commit gang rape against.

gangrene /ˈɡæŋɡriːn/ *n.* *Pathol.* the dying of tissue, as from interruption of circulation; mortification. —**gangrenous** /ˈɡæŋɡrənəs/, *adj.*

gangster /ˈɡæŋstə/ *n.* a member of a gang of criminals. —**gangsterism**, *n.*

gangway /ˈɡæŋweɪ/ *n.* **1.** a passageway, often on a ship. **2.** (an opening or removable section of a ship's rail for) a gangplank. **3.** an aisle in a theatre. —*interj.* **4.** clear the way!

gannet /ˈɡænət/ *n.* any of several large pelagic birds of the family Sulidae, such as the **Australasian gannet**, *Morus serrator.*

gantry /ˈɡæntri/ *n.* (*pl.* **-tries**) **1.** a spanning framework, such as a bridge-like portion of certain cranes, a structure holding railway signals above the tracks, etc. **2.** a frame supporting something, such as a missile, standing vertical before blast-off. **3.** a simple frame holding a barrel or cask. Also, **gauntry**.

gaol /dʒeɪl/ *n., v.* → **jail**.

gap /ɡæp/ *n.* **1.** a break or opening, as in a fence, etc.; breach. **2.** a vacant space or interval. **3.** a wide divergence. **4.** a deep, sloping cut in a mountain range. **5.** (in Australia) the difference between the standard fee for a medical service and the refund payable by Medicare. **6.** a divergence, contradiction, disparity, or imbalance: *credibility gap; generation gap.* —*adj.* **7.** of or relating to a gap year: *a gap student.* —**gapless**, *adj.*

gape /ɡeɪp/ *v.i.* **1.** to stare with open mouth, as in wonder. **2.** to open as a gap; split or become open wide. —*n.* **3.** a breach or rent; wide opening. —**gaping**, *adj.* —**gapingly**, *adv.* —**gaper**, *n.*

gap year *n.* a period of one academic year taken off from study, usually between finishing secondary school and commencing tertiary studies.

garage /ˈɡæraʒ, -radʒ, ɡəˈraʒ, -ˈradʒ/ *n.* **1.** a building for sheltering a motor vehicle or vehicles. **2.** an establishment where motor vehicles are repaired, fuel is sold, etc. —*v.t.* (**-raged, -raging**) **3.** to put or keep in a garage.

garb /ɡab/ *n.* **1.** fashion or mode of dress, especially of a distinctive kind. **2.** clothes. **3.** covering, semblance, or form. —*v.t.* **4.** to dress; clothe.

garbage /ˈɡabɪdʒ/ *n.* **1.** refuse animal and vegetable matter. **2.** household, especially kitchen, waste; rubbish; refuse. **3.** anything worthless, undesirable, or unnecessary.

garbage bin *n.* → **rubbish bin**. Also, **garbage tin**.

garbage collector *n.* someone employed to collect garbage.

garble /ˈɡabəl/ *v.t.* **1.** to make unfair or misleading selections from (facts, statements, writings, etc.); corrupt. **2.** to make incomprehensible. —*n.* **3.** the process of garbling. —**garbler**, *n.*

garbo /ˈɡaboʊ/ *n. Aust. Colloq.* a garbage collector.

garden /ˈɡadn/ *n.* **1.** a plot of ground devoted to the cultivation of useful or ornamental plants. **2.** a piece of ground, or other space, commonly with ornamental plants, trees, etc., used as a place of recreation: *a botanical garden*; *a roof garden*. **3.** a fertile and delightful spot or region. –*adj.* **4.** relating to or produced in a garden. **5.** (of recent urban developments) deliberately planned so as to have many garden-like open spaces: *a garden city*. –*v.i.* **6.** to lay out or cultivate a garden. –*v.t.* **7.** to cultivate as a garden. –*phr.* **8. lead up the garden path**, *Colloq.* to mislead, hoax, or delude. –**gardener**, *n.* –**gardening**, *n.* –**gardenless**, *adj.* –**gardenlike**, *adj.*

gardenia /gɑˈdiniə, -dinjə/ *n.* any of the evergreen trees and shrubs of the genus *Gardenia*, native to the warmer parts of the eastern hemisphere, including species cultivated for their fragrant, waxlike, white flowers.

garfish /ˈgɑfɪʃ/ *n.* any of numerous fishes found in Australian marine and estuarine waters, having a slender body and the lower jaw produced as a needle-like point, as the widely distributed sea garfish *Hemirhamphus australis*.

gargantuan /gɑˈgæntʃuən/ *adj.* gigantic; prodigious.

gargle /ˈgɑgəl/ *v.t.* **1.** to wash or rinse (the throat or mouth) with a liquid held in the throat and kept in motion by a stream of air from the lungs. –*v.i.* **2.** to gargle the throat or mouth. –*n.* **3.** any liquid used for gargling. **4.** *Colloq.* a drink, usually alcoholic.

gargoyle /ˈgɑgɔɪl/ *n.* a spout, often terminating in a grotesque head (animal or human) with open mouth, projecting from the gutter of a building for carrying off rainwater.

garish /ˈgɛərɪʃ, ˈgɑr-/ *adj.* **1.** glaring, or excessively bright. **2.** crudely colourful or showy, as dress, etc. **3.** excessively ornate, as structures, writings, etc. –**garishly**, *adv.* –**garishness**, *n.*

garland /ˈgɑlənd/ *n.* **1.** a wreath or string of flowers, leaves, or other material, worn for ornament or as an honour, or hung on something as a decoration. **2.** a collection of short literary pieces, usually poems and ballads; a miscellany. –*v.t.* **3.** to crown with a garland; deck with garlands.

garlic /ˈgɑlɪk/ *n.* **1.** a hardy plant, *Allium sativum*, whose strong-scented pungent bulb is used in cookery and medicine. **2.** any of various other species of the same genus. **3.** the bulb of any such plant. –*adj.* **4.** seasoned with or containing garlic.

garment /ˈgɑmənt/ *n.* **1.** any article of clothing. –*v.t.* **2.** to clothe. –**garmentless**, *adj.*

garnet /ˈgɑnət/ *n.* **1.** any of a group of hard, vitreous minerals, silicates of calcium, magnesium, iron, or manganese with aluminium or iron, varying in colour. A deep red transparent variety is used as a gem and as an abrasive (**garnet paper**). **2.** deep red, as of a garnet. –**garnet-like**, *adj.*

garnish /ˈgɑnɪʃ/ *v.t.* **1.** to fit out with something that adorns or decorates. **2.** to decorate (a dish) for the table. **3.** *Law* to warn; give notice. –*n.* **4.** adornment or decoration. –**garnisher**, *n.*

garnishee /gɑnɪˈʃi/ *Law* –*v.t.* (**-sheed, -sheeing**) **1.** to attach (money or property) by garnishment. **2.** to make (a person) a garnishee. –*n.* **3.** a person served with a garnishment.

garnishment /ˈgɑnɪʃmənt/ *n. Law* a warning served on a person, at the suit of a credit or plaintiff, to hold, subject to the court's direction, money or property of the defendant in his or her possession.

garret /ˈgærət/ *n.* → **attic** (def. 1).

garrison /ˈgærəsən/ *n.* **1.** a body of troops stationed in a fortified place. **2.** the place where they are stationed. –*v.t.* **3.** to provide (a fort, town, etc.) with a garrison. **4.** to occupy (a fort, post, station, etc.).

garrotte /gəˈrɒt/ *n.* **1.** a method of killing, originally by means of an instrument causing death by strangulation,

later by one injuring the spinal column at the base of the brain, formerly used as a mode of capital punishment in Spain. **2.** the instrument used. **3.** strangulation or throttling, especially for the purpose of robbery. –*v.t.* (**-rotted, -rotting**) **4.** to execute by the garrotte. **5.** to throttle, especially for the purpose of robbery. Also, **garrote, garrote**. –**garrotter**, *n.*

garrulous /ˈgærələs/ *adj.* **1.** given to much talking, especially about trivial matters. **2.** wordy or diffuse, as speech. –**garrulousness, garrulity**, *n.* –**garrulously**, *adv.*

garter /ˈgɑtə/ *n.* a fastening, often in the form of a band passing round the leg, to keep up stockings or long socks.

gas¹ /gæs/ *n.* (*pl.* **gases**) **1.** *Physics* a substance consisting of atoms or molecules which move about freely so that it takes up the whole of the space in which it is contained. **2.** any such substance used as a fuel, especially coal gas or natural gas. **3.** a mist-like mass of fine particles, used in warfare to poison or otherwise harm the enemy. **4.** *Colloq.* empty talk. –*adj.* **5.** coming from, produced by, or involving gas: *a gas stove*. **6.** *Colloq.* great, wonderful: *a gas idea*. –*verb* (**gassed, gassing**) –*v.t.* **7.** to affect, overcome, or asphyxiate with gas or fumes. –*v.i.* **8.** *Colloq.* to spend time in empty talk. –**gaseous**, *adj.* –**gasify**, *v.* –**gassy**, *adj.* –**gasless**, *adj.*

gas² /gæs/ *n.* **1.** *Chiefly US Colloq.* petrol. –*phr.* **2. step on the gas**, to hurry.

gasbag /ˈgæsbæg/ *n.* **1.** a bag for holding gas, as in a balloon or airship. **2.** *Colloq.* an empty, voluble talker; a windbag. –*v.i.* (**-bagged, -bagging**) **3.** *Colloq.* to talk volubly; chatter.

gash /gæʃ/ *n.* a long, deep wound or cut, especially in the flesh; a slash.

gasket /ˈgæskət/ *n.* **1.** anything used as a packing or jointing material for making joints fluid-tight. **2.** a suitably punched asbestos sheet, usually sandwiched between thin sheets of copper, for making a gastight joint, especially between the cylinder block and the cylinder head of an internal-combustion engine. –*phr.* **3. blow a gasket, a.** *Motor Vehicles* to break the gasket seal. **b.** *Colloq.* to lose one's temper.

gas mantle *n.* a chemically prepared, incombustible network hood for a gas jet which, when the jet is lit, becomes incandescent and gives a brilliant light.

gasmask /ˈgæsmɑsk/ *n.* a mask-like device worn to protect against noxious gases, fumes, etc., as in warfare or in certain industries, the air inhaled by the wearer being filtered through charcoal and chemicals.

gasoline /ˈgæsəlin/ *n. Chiefly US* → **petrol**. Also, **gasolene**.

gasometer /gæˈsɒmətə, gə-/ *n.* **1.** a large tank or reservoir for storing gas, especially at a gasworks. **2.** a laboratory apparatus for measuring or storing gas. –**gasometric** /gæsəˈmɛtrɪk/, **gasometrical** /gæsə-ˈmɛtrɪkəl/, *adj.*

gasp /gæsp, gasp/ *n.* **1.** a sudden, short breath; convulsive effort to breathe. **2.** a short, convulsive utterance, especially as a result of fear or surprise. –*v.i.* **3.** to catch the breath, or struggle for breath, with open mouth, as from exhaustion; breathe convulsively. –*phr.* **4. be gasping for** (or **after**), to long for with breathless eagerness; desire; crave. **5. gasp for air** (or **breath**), to struggle to breathe. **6. gasp out**, to utter with gasps.

gastric /ˈgæstrɪk/ *adj.* of or relating to the stomach.

gastric brooding frog *n.* either of two species of aquatic frog of the genus *Rheobatrachus*, found in eastern Qld, which is distinguished by its habit of swallowing its fertilised eggs, incubating its eggs in its stomach, and finally giving birth to fully-formed young through its mouth.

gastric bypass *n.* a surgical procedure for the treatment of obesity in which the stomach is stapled to make it smaller.

gastric reflux *n.* → **gastro-oesophageal reflux**.

gastro- a word element meaning 'stomach', as in *gastropod, gastrology*. Also, **gastero-**, **gastr-**.

gastroenteritis /ˌgæstrouɛntəˈraɪtəs/ *n. Pathol.* inflammation of the stomach and intestines.

gastroenterology /ˌgæstrouɛntəˈrɒlədʒi/ *n.* the branch of medical science dealing with the structure and diseases of digestive organs. –**gastroenterologist**, *n.*

gastronome /ˈgæstrənoum/ *n.* a gourmet; epicure. Also, **gastronomer** /gæsˈtrɒnəmə/.

gastronomy /gæsˈtrɒnəmi/ *n.* the art or science of good eating. –**gastronomic** /gæstrəˈnɒmɪk/, **gastronomical** /gæstrəˈnɒmɪkəl/, *adj.* –**gastronomically** /gæstrəˈnɒmɪkli/, *adv.* –**gastronomist**, *n.*

gastro-oesophageal reflux /ˌgæstrou-əsɒfədʒiəl ˈriflʌks/ *n.* a flow of the acidic contents of the stomach back up into the oesophagus, caused by malfunctioning of the oesophageal sphincter. Also, **gastric reflux**, **reflux**.

gastro-oesophageal reflux disease *n.* any of various forms of damage caused to the oesophagus by gastric reflux. *Abbrev.*: GORD Also, **reflux disease**, **reflux oesophagitis**.

gastropod /ˈgæstrəpɒd/ *n.* any of the Gastropoda, a class of molluscs comprising the snails, having a shell of a single valve, usually spirally coiled, and a ventral muscular foot on which they glide about. Also, **gasteropod**.

gate /geɪt/ *n.* 1. a movable frame, in a fence or wall, or across a passageway. 2. an opening for passage into an enclosed area. 3. any narrow means of entrance. 4. a device for controlling the passage of water, steam, etc., as in a dam, pipe, etc.; valve. 5. the number of persons who pay for admission to a sporting event. 6. Also, **gate money**. the money taken for entrance to a sporting event. 7. *Motor Vehicles* the H-shaped arrangement controlling the gearstick movement. 8. *Elect.* an electronic circuit which controls the passage of information signals. –**gateman** /ˈgeɪtmən/, *n.*

gateau /ˈgætou/ *n.* (*pl.* **gateaux** /-touz, -tou/) an elaborate cake or dessert having a base of sponge, biscuit, or pastry, on top of which fruit, jelly, cream, etc., are added as garnish. Also, **gâteau**.

gatecrash /ˈgeɪtkræʃ/ *v.t.* to attend (a party) uninvited, or to attend (a public entertainment, etc.) without a ticket. –**gatecrasher**, *n.*

gateway /ˈgeɪtweɪ/ *n.* 1. a passage or entrance which is closed by a gate. 2. a frame or arch in which a gate is hung; structure built at or over a gate. 3. any means of entering or leaving a place. 4. a location through which one has access to an area: *this harbour is the gateway to the city*. 5. *Computers* a piece of software or hardware which acts as a translator between dissimilar networks or protocols.

gather /ˈgæðə/ *v.t.* 1. to bring (persons, animals, or things) together into one company or aggregate. 2. to get together from various places or sources; collect gradually. 3. to learn or infer from observation: *I gather that he'll be leaving*. 4. to pick (any crop or natural yield) from its place of growth or formation: *to gather grain; to gather fruit; to gather flowers*. 5. to wrap or draw around or close to someone or something: *to gather a person into one's arms*. 6. to pick up piece by piece. 7. to attract: *to gather a crowd*. 8. to take by selection from among other things; sort out; cull. 9. Also, **gather up**. to assemble or collect (one's energies or oneself) as for an effort. 10. to contract (the brow) into wrinkles. 11. to draw up (cloth) on a thread in fine folds or puckers by running a thread through.

12. *Bookbinding* to assemble (the printed sheets of a book) in their proper sequence to be bound. 13. to increase (speed, etc.), as a moving vehicle. –*v.i.* 14. Also, **gather together**. to come together or assemble: *to gather round a fir; to gather in crowds*. 15. to collect or accumulate. 16. to grow as by accretion; increase. 17. to come to a head, as a sore in suppurating. –*n.* 18. a drawing together; contraction. 19. (*usu. pl.*) a fold or pucker in gathered cloth, etc. –*phr.* 20. be **gathered to one's fathers**, to die. 21. **gather dust**, to lie unused or untouched. –**gathering**, *n.* –**gatherable**, *adj.* –**gatherer**, *n.*

gauche /gouʃ/ *adj.* awkward; clumsy; tactless: *her apology was as gauche as if she was a schoolgirl*. –**gaucheness**, *n.*

gaudy /ˈgɔdi/ *adj.* (**-dier**, **-diest**) 1. brilliant; excessively showy. 2. showy without taste; vulgarly showy; flashy. –**gaudily**, *adv.* –**gaudiness**, *n.*

gauge /geɪdʒ/ *v.t.* (**gauged**, **gauging**) 1. to appraise, estimate, or judge. 2. to determine the dimensions, capacity, quantity, or force of; measure, as with a gauge. 3. to make conformable to a standard. –*n.* 4. a standard of measure; standard dimension or quantity. 5. a means of estimating or judging; criterion; test. 6. extent; scope; capacity. 7. any instrument for measuring pressure, volume, or dimensions, as a pressure gauge, micrometer gauge, etc. 8. *Ordnance* the internal diameter of a gun bore. 9. the distance between the rails in a railway system; **standard gauge** is 1435 mm; **broad gauge** is wider, and **narrow gauge** narrower, than this. Also, **gage**. –**gaugeable**, *adj.* –**gauger**, *n.*

gaunt /gɔnt/ *adj.* 1. abnormally thin; emaciated; haggard. 2. bleak, desolate, or grim, as places or things. –**gauntly**, *adv.* –**gauntness**, *n.*

gauntlet¹ /ˈgɔntlət/ *n.* 1. a medieval glove, as of mail or plate, to protect the hand. 2. a glove with a cuff-like extension for the wrist. –*phr.* 3. **take up the gauntlet**, to accept a challenge, originally to a duel. 4. **throw down the gauntlet**, to extend a challenge, originally to a duel.

gauntlet² /ˈgɔntlət/ *phr.* **run the gauntlet**, 1. (of a person) to be forced to run between two rows of soldiers who strike at them with switches or other weapons as they pass (formerly a common military punishment). 2. to expose oneself to possible attack in order to achieve a goal. Also, *US*, **gantlet**.

gauss /gaos/ *n. Elect.* a unit of magnetic induction in the centimetre-gram-second system, equal to 0.1×10^{-3} teslas.

Gaussian blur /gaosiən ˈblɜ/ *n.* a type of blur filter applied to a digital image that uses a mathematical formula to create the effect of looking through a lens that is out of focus.

gauze /gɔz/ *n.* 1. any thin transparent fabric made from any fibre in a plain weave, used as a fabric for clothing, or for medical dressings. 2. something similar with a fine open weave, but made from a different material, such as wire. 3. a thin haze. –*v.t.* 4. to cover with gauze. –*v.i.* 5. to become misty. –**gauzy**, *adj.*

gave /geɪv/ *v.* past tense of **give**.

gavel /ˈgævəl/ *n.* 1. a small mallet used by a presiding officer to signal for attention or order. –*v.i.* (**-elled** *or, US*, **-eled**, **-elling** *or, US*, **-eling**) 2. to hammer, as with a gavel.

gawk /gɔk/ *n.* 1. an awkward, foolish person. –*v.i.* 2. *Colloq.* to act like a gawk; stare stupidly. –**gawker**, *n.*

gawky /ˈgɔki/ *adj.* (**-kier**, **-kiest**) awkward; ungainly; clumsy. –**gawkily**, *adv.* –**gawkiness**, *n.*

gay /geɪ/ *adj.* (**gayer**, **gayest**) 1. (especially of a male) homosexual. 2. of, relating to, or for homosexuals: *gay rights; a gay bar*. 3. *Colloq.* (*mildly derog.*) odd; eccentric. 4. *Colloq.* unfashionable; unstylish: *that bag is really gay; don't be so gay!* 5. *Colloq.* irritating;

annoying: *his fooling around is so gay.* **6.** having or showing a joyous mood: *gay spirits, music, scenes, etc.* **7.** bright or showy: *gay colours, flowers, ornaments, etc.* **8.** characterised by social or other pleasures: *a gay social season.* –*n.* **9.** a homosexual, especially male. –**gayness,** *n.*

gaze /geɪz/ *v.i.* **1.** to look steadily or intently; look with curiosity, wonder, etc. –*n.* **2.** a steady or intent look. –**gazer,** *n.*

gazebo /gəˈziboʊ/ *n.* (*pl.* **-bos** *or* **-boes**) a structure commanding an extensive prospect, especially a turret, pavilion, or summerhouse.

gazelle /gəˈzɛl/ *n.* (*pl.* **gazelles** *or, especially collectively,* **gazelle**) any of various small antelopes of the genus *Gazella* and allied genera, noted for their graceful movements and lustrous eyes.

gazette /gəˈzɛt/ *n.* **1.** a newspaper (now common only in newspaper titles). **2.** an official government journal, containing lists of government appointments and promotions, bankruptcies, etc. –*v.t.* (**-zetted, -zetting**) **3.** to publish, announce, or list in a gazette.

gazetteer /gæzəˈtɪə/ *n.* **1.** a geographical dictionary. **2.** *Archaic* a journalist, especially one appointed and paid by the government.

gazump /gəˈzʌmp/ *v.t.* **1.** to bypass (a buyer of real estate with whom a price has been agreed) by selling at a higher price to another. **2.** to force (a buyer) to accept a price higher than that previously agreed upon. –**gazumper,** *n.* –**gazumping,** *n.*

gear /gɪə/ *n.* **1.** *Mechanics* a device for passing on or changing movement, as by toothed wheels. **2.** tools or apparatus, especially as used for a particular operation. **3.** personal possessions; goods. **4.** *Colloq.* clothes. –*v.t.* **5.** to provide with or connect by gearing. **6.** to prepare or fit (someone or something) for a particular situation: *he gears his cooking to his family's tastes.*

gearbox /ˈgɪəbɒks/ *n.* the casing in which gears are enclosed, especially in a motor vehicle.

gearing /ˈgɪərɪŋ/ *n.* **1.** the parts collectively by which motion is transmitted in machinery, especially a train of toothed wheels. **2.** the installation of such gears.

gearstick /ˈgɪəstɪk/ *n.* a device for selecting or connecting gears for transmitting power, especially in a motor vehicle. Also, **gearlever** /ˈgɪəliːvə/.

gecko /ˈgɛkoʊ/ *n.* (*pl.* **-kos** *or* **-koes**) a lizard of the family Gekkonidae, mostly nocturnal, many with adhesive pads on the toes.

gee[1] /dʒi/ *interj.* a mild exclamation of surprise or delight.

gee[2] /dʒi/ *phr. Colloq.* **1. gee someone up,** to encourage someone; fire someone up. **2. gee up,** a command to horses, etc., directing them to go faster.

geek[1] /gik/ *n. Aust. Colloq.* a look: *have a geek at this.* Also, **geez, gig, gink.**

geek[2] /gik/ *Colloq.* –*n.* **1.** a social misfit, especially one who is overly preoccupied with some interest or pursuit that is seen as unfashionable. **2.** Also, **computer geek.** a person who is totally preoccupied with activities involving computers and other digital devices, especially in playing computer games. **3.** *US* a person who makes a spectacle of himself or herself by performing bizarre or grotesque acts for the entertainment of others, as in a circus or carnival. **4.** any eccentric person. –*adj.* **5.** *Computers* of, relating to, or for computer geeks: *geek magazine.* –**geeky,** *adj.*

geese /gis/ *n.* plural of **goose**[1].

gee-whiz /ˈdʒi-wɪz/ *adj. Colloq.* astonishing, especially by virtue of technological innovation: *gee-whiz gadgetry.* Also, **gee-whizz.**

geezer /ˈgizə/ *n. Colloq.* an odd character. Also, **geeser.**

Geiger counter /ˈgaɪgə kaʊntə/ *n.* an instrument for detecting and counting ionising particles, consisting of a tube which conducts electricity when the gas within is

ionised by such a particle. It is used in measuring the degree of radioactivity in an area left by the explosion of an atom bomb, in investigations of cosmic rays, etc. Also, **Geiger-Müller counter.**

geisha /ˈgeɪʃə/ *n.* (*pl.* **-sha** *or* **-shas**) (in Japan) a woman trained to entertain men with singing, dancing, and conversation.

gel /dʒɛl/ *n.* **1.** *Physical Chem.* a semirigid colloidal dispersion of a solid with a liquid or gas, such as jelly, glue, or silica gel. **2.** a clear, liquid jelly, sometimes tinted, used for cosmetic purposes. –*v.i.* (**gelled, gelling**) **3.** to form or become a gel. **4.** to unite to form a cohesive whole: *all the musical elements gelled to make a strong sound.* **5.** (of an idea, etc.) to become clearer or more fixed: *gradually, the notion that a more sinister motive was involved began to gel.* –*phr.* **6. gel with,** to agree with: *an account that gels with mine.*

gelatine /ˈdʒɛlətɪn, dʒɛləˈtin/ *n.* **1.** a brittle, nearly transparent, faintly yellow, odourless, and almost tasteless organic substance, obtained by boiling in water the ligaments, bones, skin, etc., of animals, and forming the basis of jellies, glues, and the like. **2.** any of various similar substances, such as vegetable gelatine. **3.** a preparation or product in which gelatine is the essential constituent. Also, **gelatin** /ˈdʒɛlətən/.

gelatinous /dʒəˈlætənəs/ *adj.* having the nature of jelly; jelly-like.

gelato /dʒəˈlatoʊ/ *n.* (*pl.* **-latos** *or* **-lati**) an iced confection made from cream, milk, or water in any combination, with fruit or nut flavouring, and whipped at a very low temperature.

geld /gɛld/ *v.t.* to castrate (especially animals).

gelding /ˈgɛldɪŋ/ *n.* a castrated animal, especially a horse.

gelignite /ˈdʒɛlɪgnaɪt/ *n.* an explosive consisting of nitroglycerine, nitrocellulose, potassium nitrate, and wood pulp which is used for blasting.

gem /dʒɛm/ *n.* **1.** a stone used in jewellery, fashioned to bring out its beauty. **2.** something likened to or prized as a gem because of its beauty or worth, especially something small: *the gem of the collection.* –**gemmy,** *adj.*

gemfish /ˈdʒɛmfɪʃ/ *n.* a heavy, thick-set food fish with delicate flavour, *Rexea solandri,* plentiful in waters of south-eastern Australia; hake.

Gemini /ˈdʒɛmɪnaɪ/ *n.* **1.** the third sign of the zodiac, which the sun enters about 21 May; the Twins. **2.** a person born under the sign of Gemini. –*adj.* **3.** of or relating to Gemini.

gemma /ˈdʒɛmə/ *n.* (*pl.* **gemmae** /ˈdʒɛmi/) **1.** *Bot.* a cell or cluster of cells, or a leaf- or budlike body, which separates from the parent plant and forms a new plant, as in mosses, liverworts, etc. **2.** *Zool.* an asexually produced mass of cells that will develop into an animal. Also, **gemmule.**

gen /dʒɛn/ *Colloq.* –*n.* **1.** general information. –*phr.* (*v.* **genned, genning**) **2. gen up,** (sometimes fol. by *on*) to become informed, to learn or read up. **3. the gen,** all the necessary information about a subject.

-gen a suffix meaning: **1.** something produced, or growing: *acrogen, endogen, exogen.* **2.** something that produces: *hydrogen, oxygen.*

gen C /dʒɛn ˈsi/ *n.* → **generation C.**

gender /ˈdʒɛndə/ *n.* **1.** *Gram.* **a.** (in many languages) a set of classes, such as masculine, feminine and neuter, which together include all nouns. Often the classification correlates in part with sex (**natural gender**) or animateness. **b.** one class of such a set. **2. a.** a sexual identity, such as heterosexuality, homosexuality, bisexuality, etc.; often distinguished from physiological determination as male or female. **b.** sex (def. 1). –**genderless,** *adj.*

gender fluid *adj.* **1.** of or relating to a person whose gender (def. 2a) varies over time, ranging from male to female or any combination of both; genderqueer. *–n.* **2.** such a person.

gender gap *n.* the difference in attitudes, opinions, social customs, etc., which exists between males and females.

gender identity disorder *n.* a psychiatric disorder affecting people whose sense of their own gender contradicts their biological sex, giving rise to depression, low self-esteem, etc. *Abbrev.*: GID Also, **gender dysphoria**

genderqueer /'dʒɛndəkwɪə/ *adj.* **1.** of or relating to, or designating a person who does not identify as either male or female or who feels that they are a little bit of both, and therefore not fully the stereotype of either gender. *–n.* **2.** such a person. Compare **transgender**, **cisgender**. *Abbrev.*: GQ

gender role *n.* a role such as breadwinner, nurturer, etc., which is assigned to a person on the basis of their gender.

gene /dʒin/ *n.* the unit of inheritance, associated with deoxyribonucleic acid, which is situated on and transmitted by the chromosome, and which develops into a hereditary character as it reacts with the environment and with the other genes. **–genic**, *adj.*

genealogy /dʒini'ælədʒi/ *n.* (*pl.* **-gies**) **1.** an account of the descent of a person or family through an ancestral line. **2.** the investigation of pedigrees as a department of knowledge. **–genealogical** /dʒiniə'lɒdʒɪkəl/, **genealogic** /dʒiniə'lɒdʒɪk/, *adj.* **–genealogically** /dʒiniə'lɒdʒɪkli/, *adv.* **–genealogist**, *n.*

gene gun *n.* a device for impelling genetic material into a living cell, the payload being a tungsten particle coated with plasmid DNA; biolistic particle delivery system.

gene mapping *n.* the identification of the place on one of the twenty-three pairs of human chromosomes where a particular gene lies.

gene pool *n.* the total amount of genetic information, and thus of possibilities for future evolutionary development, held by all the individuals in a specified population.

genera /'dʒɛnərə/ *n.* plural of **genus**.

general /'dʒɛnrəl/ *adj.* **1.** relating to, affecting, including, or participated in by all members of a class or group; not partial or particular: *a general election.* **2.** common to many or most of a community; prevalent; usual: *the general practice.* **3.** not restricted to one class or field; miscellaneous: *the general public*; *general knowledge.* **4.** not limited to a detail of application; not specific or special: *general instructions.* **5.** indefinite or vague: *to refer to a matter in a general way.* **6.** having extended command, or superior or chief rank (often follows noun): *a general officer*; *governor-general.* *–n.* **7.** *Mil.* **a.** an officer next in rank above a lieutenant general and below a field marshal. **b.** someone who fulfils the function of a general officer; a military commander: *Julius Caesar was a great general.* *–phr.* **8. in general**, **a.** with respect to the whole class referred to. **b.** as a general rule; commonly. **–generalness**, *n.*

general anaesthesia *n.* **1.** drug-induced insensibility to pain and other sensation throughout the whole body, involving a state of unconsciousness. **2.** the administration of a drug to produce this effect. Also, **general anesthesia**.

general anaesthetic *n.* **1.** a substance which anaesthetises the entire body and produces loss of consciousness. **2.** the procedure for this. Also, **general anesthetic**.

general election *n.* a parliamentary election, not a by-election, in which all seats in the house are thrown open, as a Federal or State election for the Lower House.

generalise /'dʒɛnrəlaɪz/ *v.t.* **1.** to give a general (rather than specific or special) character to. **2.** to form (a general principle, etc.) from studying facts, etc. **3.** to bring into general use or knowledge. *–v.i.* **4.** to form general ideas or principles. **5.** to talk generally or vaguely. Also, **generalize**. **–generalisation**, *n.*

generality /dʒɛnə'ræləti/ *n.* (*pl.* **-ties**) **1.** a general or vague statement: *to speak in vague generalities.* **2.** general principle; general rule or law. **3.** the greater part or majority: *the generality of people.* **4.** state or quality of being general.

generally /'dʒɛnrəli/ *adv.* **1.** with respect to the larger part, or for the most part: *a claim generally recognised.* **2.** usually; commonly; ordinarily: *he generally comes at noon.* **3.** without reference to particular persons or things: *generally speaking.*

general practitioner *n.* a doctor who does not specialise in any particular branch of medicine; a doctor in general practice. *Abbrev.*: GP

general strike *n.* a mass strike in all or many trades and industries in a section or in all parts of a country.

generate /'dʒɛnəreɪt/ *v.t.* **1.** to bring into existence; give rise to; produce; cause to be: *to generate electricity.* **2.** to beget, to procreate. **3.** *Maths* **a.** to specify (a set) by applying rules or operations to given quantities. **b.** to trace out (a figure) by the motion of another figure. **4.** *Ling.* to produce (sentences, etc.) from a limited inventory of linguistic items by applying a series of grammatical rules.

generation /dʒɛnə'reɪʃən/ *n.* **1.** the whole body of individuals born about the same time: *the rising generation.* **2.** the age or average lifetime of a generation; term of years (commonly thirty) accepted as the average difference of age between one generation of a family and the next. **3.** a single step in natural descent, as of human beings, animals, or plants. **4.** the act or process of generating; procreation. **5.** production by natural or artificial processes; evolution, as of heat or sound. **–generational**, *adj.*

generation alpha *n.* the generation growing up after 2010 when communications technology was focused on the smart phone, interactivity was assumed and social media gained great power alongside traditional media. Also, **gen alpha**.

generation C *n.* the generation which reached maturity in the early 2000s, typified by their facility with the internet as a means of communication, being familiar with the creation of individual content for general consumption as blogs, videos, text, etc., using multimedia tools. Also, **C generation**, **gen C**.

generation text *n.* the generation that has grown up using mobile phones, viewed as adept in texting.

generation X *n.* the generation born in the late 1960s and 1970s, portrayed as being cynical about traditional authority and pragmatic in their approach to life. Also, **X generation**. **–generation Xer**, *n.*

generation Y *n.* the generation born in the 1980s and 1990s, following generation X, portrayed as giving personal satisfaction in life a priority, being more visually-oriented than previous generations and less deferential to authority, and as being the first of the digital natives.

generation Z *n.* the generation born in the early 2000s, characterised as being at ease with computer technology, online and mobile phone communication, and multi-tasking, and active consumers influencing their parents' purchasing decisions, but brought up in the world where both parents work and where a sedentary lifestyle is the norm.

generator /ˈdʒɛnəreɪtə/ n. **1.** Elect. a machine which converts mechanical energy into electrical energy; dynamo. **2.** Chem. an apparatus for producing a gas or vapour.

generic /dʒəˈnɛrɪk/ adj. **1.** relating to a genus. **2.** applicable or referring to all the members of a genus or class. **3.** of or relating to a class of commodities marketed under the brand name of a retailing chain with the implication of greater cheapness than if they appeared under the brand name of the producer. **4.** identified by the name of the product itself, not by a particular brand name. –n. **5.** a generic commodity. Also, **generical**. –**generically**, adv.

generous /ˈdʒɛnərəs, ˈdʒɛnrəs/ adj. **1.** munificent or bountiful; unselfish: a generous giver; a generous gift. **2.** free from meanness or smallness of mind or character. **3.** provided liberally; abundant: a generous portion. **4.** rich or strong, as wine. **5.** fertile, as soil. –**generosity** /dʒɛnəˈrɒsəti/, **generousness**, n.

gene shears pl. n. molecules developed to target and destroy specific RNA within plant and animal cells and so to prevent an undesirable gene from carrying out its work.

genesis /ˈdʒɛnəsəs/ n. (pl. **-ses** /-siz/) origin; production; creation.

gene therapy n. a procedure in which defective genes are replaced or mutated in order to correct a genetic defect.

genetic /dʒəˈnɛtɪk/ adj. **1.** Biol. relating or according to genetics. **2.** relating to genesis or origin. –**genetically**, adv.

genetically-modified /dʒəˌnɛtɪkli-ˈmɒdəfaɪd/ adj. **1.** (of an animal or plant) having had its genetic material altered by technological means, usually with the intention of changing certain characteristics and thereby altering the organism to fulfil a specific purpose. **2.** (of a food) containing such raw material. Also, **GM**. –**genetic modification**, n.

genetic engineering n. the modification of an organism's genes through the direct isolation and transference of DNA material from one organism to another. –**genetically engineered**, adj.

genetic fingerprinting n. a process by which the genetic code of the DNA in human organic material such as skin, hair, blood, semen, etc., found at the scene of a crime is matched against the DNA of a suspect, thus, because of the uniqueness of each person's genetic code, establishing whether the suspect was or was not present. Also, **DNA fingerprinting**.

genetics /dʒəˈnɛtɪks/ n. the science of heredity, dealing with resemblances and differences of related organisms flowing from the interaction of their genes and the environment. –**geneticist**, n.

genetic screening n. genetic testing performed on an individual, group, or population, usually in order detect or exclude a genetic disease at an early stage, or to determine genetic predisposition or resistance to a disease, or to determine whether a person carries a gene variant which may produce disease in their children. Also, **genomic screening**.

genial /ˈdʒiniəl/ adj. **1.** sympathetically cheerful; cordial: a genial disposition, a genial host. **2.** enlivening; supporting life; pleasantly warm, or mild. –**geniality**, n. –**genially**, adv. –**genialness**, n.

genie /ˈdʒini/ n. a spirit of Arabian mythology. See **jinn**.

genital /ˈdʒɛnətl/ adj. relating to generation or the organs of generation.

genital herpes n. Pathol. a sexually transmitted disease caused by the herpes simplex virus type 2.

genitalia /dʒɛnəˈteɪliə/ pl. n. the genitals.

genitals /ˈdʒɛnətlz/ pl. n. the reproductive organs, especially the external organs.

genitive /ˈdʒɛnətɪv/ Gram. –adj. **1.** (in some inflected languages) denoting the case of nouns generally used to modify other nouns, often indicating possession, but used also in expressions of measure, origin, characteristic, as John's hat, week's holiday, duty's call. **2.** denoting the affix or other element characteristic of this case, or a word containing such an element. **3.** similar to such a case form in function or meaning. –n. **4.** the genitive case. **5.** a word in that case. **6.** a construction of similar meaning. –**genitival** /dʒɛnəˈtaɪvəl/, adj. –**genitivally** /dʒɛnəˈtaɪvəli/, adv.

genius /ˈdʒiniəs/ n. (pl. **geniuses** for defs 1–4 and 7, **genii** /ˈdʒiniaɪ/ for defs 5, 6 and 8) **1.** great natural ability for original ideas; highest level of mental ability. **2.** a person having such ability. **3.** natural ability: he has a genius for fixing cars. **4.** special character or spirit of a nation, period, language, etc. **5.** the spirit which attends and guards a place, etc. **6.** either of two mutually opposed spirits, one good and the other evil, supposedly attending someone throughout their life. **7.** a person who strongly influences the life of another: she is my evil genius. **8.** (pl.) any demon or spirit, especially genie or jinn.

genocide /ˈdʒɛnəsaɪd/ n. extermination of a national or racial group as a planned move. –**genocidal** /dʒɛnəˈsaɪdl/, adj.

genome /ˈdʒinoʊm, ˈdʒɛnoʊm/ n. the complete genetic material encoded in the DNA of an organism and the RNA of some viruses. –**genomic** /dʒəˈnoʊmɪk/, adj. –**genomically** /dʒəˈnoʊmɪkli/, adv.

genomics /dʒəˈnoʊmɪks/ n. the branch of genetics concerned with the study of genomes, especially the identification and sequencing of constituent genes.

genotype /ˈdʒɛnətaɪp/ n. **1.** the fundamental hereditary constitution of an organism. **2.** a group of organisms with a common heredity. –**genotypic** /dʒɛnəˈtɪpɪk/, adj. –**genotypically** /dʒɛnəˈtɪpɪkli/, adv.

genotyping /ˈdʒɛnətaɪpɪŋ/ n. the identification of genotypes for the purpose of medical research and diagnosis, usually on the basis of single nucleotide polymorphisms.

-genous an adjective suffix derived from nouns in **-gen** and **-geny**.

genre /ˈʒɒnrə/ n. **1.** kind; sort; genus. **2.** Art paintings, etc., which represent scenes from ordinary life (as opposed to landscapes, etc.). **3.** a conventional literary form or format, such as the novel, drama or letter. **4.** a type of discourse such as dialogue, email, etc.

genteel /dʒɛnˈtil/ adj. **1.** belonging or suited to polite society. **2.** well-bred or refined; polite; elegant; stylish. **3.** affectedly proper in manners and speech. –**genteelly**, adv. –**genteelness**, n.

gentile /ˈdʒɛntaɪl/ adj. **1.** of or relating to any person or people not Jewish. **2.** Christian, as opposed to Jewish. –n. **3.** someone who is not Jewish, especially a Christian. Also, **Gentile**.

gentility /dʒɛnˈtɪləti/ n. (pl. **-ties**) **1.** superior refinement or elegance, possessed or affected. **2.** gentle birth.

gentle /ˈdʒɛntl/ adj. **1.** kindly; amiable: gentle words. **2.** not severe, rough, or violent: a gentle wind; a gentle tap. **3.** gradual: a gentle slope. **4.** of upper class birth or family. **5.** easily handled: a gentle animal. **6.** soft or low: a gentle sound. **7.** Archaic polite; refined: a gentle lady. **8.** Archaic noble; chivalrous: a gentle knight. –**gentleness**, n. –**gently**, adv.

gentleman /ˈdʒɛntlmən/ n. (pl. **-men**) **1.** a man of good breeding, education, and manners. **2.** (as a polite form of speech) any man. –**gentlemanlike**, **gentlemanly**, adj.

gentrification /dʒɛntrəfəˈkeɪʃən/ n. the renewal of inner urban areas by young professional people, artists, etc., who find it convenient to live in them.

gentrify /'dʒɛntrəfaɪ/ v.t. (**-fied**, **-fying**) to subject to the process of gentrification. **–gentrified**, adj. **–gentrifier**, n.

gentry /'dʒɛntri/ n. **1.** people of good social standing. **2.** Brit. the class below the nobility.

genuflect /'dʒɛnjəflɛkt/ v.i. to bend the knee or knees, especially in reverence. **–genuflection**, n. **–genuflector**, n.

genuine /'dʒɛnjuən/ adj. **1.** being truly such; real; authentic: genuine regret; genuine worth. **2.** properly so called: genuine leprosy. **3.** sincere; free from pretence or affectation: a genuine person. **–genuinely**, adv. **–genuineness**, n.

genus /'dʒinəs/ n. (pl. **genera** /'dʒɛnərə/) **1.** a kind; sort; class. **2.** Biol. the usual major subdivision of a family or subfamily, usually consisting of more than one species, essentially very similar to one another and regarded as phylogenetically very closely related. The genus designation is the first part of the scientific name of a species, as in Lynx canadensis, the Canadian lynx. **3.** Logic a class or group of individuals including subordinate groups called species.

gen X /dʒɛn 'ɛks/ n. → **generation X**.

-geny a suffix meaning 'origin', as in phylogeny.

gen Y /dʒɛn 'waɪ/ n. → **generation Y**.

gen Z /dʒɛn 'zɛd/ n. → **generation Z**.

geo- a word element meaning 'the earth', as in geocentric.

geoblock /'dʒioʊblɒk/ v.t. **1.** to place access restrictions on (a digital transmission) according to geographical location. **–n. 2.** such a restriction. **–geoblocking**, n.

geocaching /dʒioʊ'kæʃɪŋ/ n. a game in which one player hides something in a location for which the latitude and longitude is then published on the internet while others try to find it using their GPS navigation devices.

geocentric /dʒioʊ'sɛntrɪk/ adj. **1.** Astron. as viewed or measured from the centre of the earth: the geocentric altitude of a star. **2.** having or representing the earth as a centre: a geocentric theory of the universe. Also, **geocentrical**. **–geocentrically**, adv.

geography /dʒi'ɒgrəfi/ n. (pl. **-phies**) **1.** the study of the areal differentiation of the earth's surface, as shown in the character, arrangement, and interrelations over the world of elements such as climate, relief, soil, vegetation, population, land use, industries, or states, and of the unit areas formed by the complex of these individual elements. **2.** the topographical features of a region, usually of the earth, but sometimes of Mars, the moon, etc. **–geographical**, **geographic**, adj. **–geographically**, adv.

geological time n. the time covering the development of the planet earth to the present; about 5000 million years.

geology /dʒi'ɒlədʒi/ n. (pl. **-gies**) **1.** the science that deals with the earth, the rocks of which it is composed, and the changes which it has undergone or is undergoing. **2.** the geological features of a locality. **–geological** /dʒiə'lɒdʒəkəl/, adj. **–geologist**, n.

geometric /dʒiə'mɛtrɪk/ adj. **1.** of or relating to geometry; according to the principles of geometry. **2.** of or relating to painting, sculpture, or ornamentation with predominantly geometric characteristics or figures. **3.** → **geometrical**.

geometrical /dʒiə'mɛtrɪkəl/ adj. **1.** resembling or using the lines or figures of geometry. **2.** → **geometric**. **–geometrically**, adv.

geometric progression n. Maths a sequence of terms in which the ratio of any term to its predecessor is a constant, as 1, 3, 9, 27, 81, and 243, and 144, 12, 1, and ⅟₁₂.

geometry /dʒi'ɒmətri/ n. **1.** the branch of mathematics that deals with the properties of figures in space. **2.** the

shape of a surface or solid. **3.** the spatial configuration of the elements of a system: the geometry of the apparatus.

geophysics /dʒioʊ'fɪzɪks/ n. the physics of the earth, dealing especially with the study of inaccessible portions of the earth by instruments and apparatus such as the torsion balance, seismograph, and magnetometer. **–geophysical**, adj. **–geophysicist**, n.

georgette /dʒɔ'dʒɛt/ n. sheer silk or rayon crepe of dull texture. Also, **georgette crepe**.

geotropic /dʒioʊ'trɒpɪk/ adj. **1.** of or relating to geotropism. **2.** taking a particular direction with reference to the earth. **–geotropically**, adv.

geranium /dʒə'reɪniəm/ n. **1.** any of the plants of the genus Geranium, most of which have pink or purple flowers, and some of which, such as G. maculatum, have an astringent root used in medicine; cranesbill. **2.** a plant of the allied genus Pelargonium, of which many species are commonly cultivated for their showy flowers (as the **scarlet geranium**) or their fragrant leaves (as the **rose geranium**).

geriatric /dʒɛri'ætrɪk/ adj. **1.** of or relating to geriatrics or with aged persons. **2.** Colloq. marked by debilitation by or as by old age: a geriatric performance. **–n. 3.** an aged person, especially one incapacitated or invalided by old age.

geriatrics /dʒɛri'ætrɪks/ n. the science of the medical and hygienic care of, or the diseases of, aged persons. Compare **gerontology**. **–geriatrician** /dʒɛriə'trɪʃən/, **geriatrist**, n.

germ /dʒɜm/ n. **1.** a microorganism, especially when disease-producing; microbe. **2.** that from which anything springs as if from a seed. **3.** Embryology **a.** a bud, offshoot, or seed. **b.** the rudiment of a living organism; an embryo in its early stages. **4.** Biol. the initial stage in development or evolution, as a germ cell or ancestral form. **–germless**, adj.

german /'dʒɜmən/ adj. **1.** having the same father and mother (always placed after the noun): a brother-german. **2.** being the child of the brother or sister of one's father or mother: a cousin-german.

germane /dʒɜ'meɪn/ adj. closely related; pertinent: a remark germane to the question.

German measles /dʒɜmən 'mizəlz/ n. → **rubella**.

German shepherd n. one of a highly intelligent wolf-like breed of dog, much used for police work, or as guide dogs, etc.; Alsatian.

germinal /'dʒɜmənəl/ adj. **1.** of or relating to a germ or germs. **2.** being a germ or germ cell. **3.** in the earliest stage of development: germinal ideas.

germinate /'dʒɜmɪneɪt/ v.i. **1.** to begin to grow or develop. **2.** Bot. **a.** to develop into a plant or individual, as a seed, or as a spore, bulb, or the like. **b.** to sprout; put forth shoots. **–v.t. 3.** to cause to develop; produce. **–germination** /dʒɜmə'neɪʃən/, n. **–germinator**, n.

gerontic /dʒə'rɒntɪk/ adj. of or relating to old age: gerontic nursing.

gerontology /dʒɛrən'tɒlədʒi/ n. the study of old age, its diseases and phenomena. Compare **geriatrics**. **–gerontologist**, n.

geroscience /dʒɛroʊ'saɪəns/ n. the study of disease in the context of normal ageing to develop an understanding of age-related disease and its treatments. **–geroscientist**, n.

-gerous a combining form meaning 'bearing' or 'producing', as in setigerous.

gerrymander /'dʒɛrimændə/ n. **1.** Politics an arbitrary arrangement of the political divisions of an electorate, etc., made so as to give one party an unfair advantage in elections. **–v.t. 2.** Politics to subject (an electorate, etc.) to a gerrymander. **3.** to manipulate unfairly.

gerund /ˈdʒɛrənd/ *n. Gram.* **1.** (in Latin and some other languages) a noun form derived from a verb, having all case forms but the nominative. **2.** the English *-ing* form of a verb when in nominal function. *Walking* and *writing* are gerunds in the sentences 'walking is good exercise' and 'writing is easy'. –**gerundial** /dʒəˈrʌndiəl/, *adj.*

gerygone /dʒəˈrɪɡəni/ *n.* any of various birds of the genus *Gerygone*, family Pardalotidae, of Australia, New Guinea, New Zealand, some Pacific islands and parts of Asia, as the **dusky gerygone**, *G. tenebrosa*, endemic to coastal north-western Australia; formerly known as warblers.

gestate /ˈdʒɛsteɪt/ *v.t.* to carry in the womb during the period from conception to delivery. –**gestation**, *n.*

gesticulate /dʒɛsˈtɪkjəleɪt/ *v.i.* **1.** to make or use gestures, especially in an animated or excited manner with or instead of speech. –*v.t.* **2.** to express by gesturing. –**gesticulator**, *n.*

gesture /ˈdʒɛstʃə/ *n.* **1.** movement of the body, head, hands, arms, or face expressive of an idea or an emotion: *the gestures of an orator, a gesture of impatience.* **2.** any action or proceeding intended for effect or as a formality; demonstration: *a gesture of friendship.* –*v.i.* **3.** to make or use gestures. –*v.t.* **4.** to express by gestures. –**gestural**, *adj.* –**gesturer**, *n.*

get /ɡɛt/ *verb* (**got**, **got** *or, Chiefly US,* **gotten**, *Archaic,* **gat**, **getting**) –*v.t.* **1.** to obtain, gain, or acquire by any means: *to get favour by service*; *get a good price.* **2.** to fetch or bring: *I will go and get it.* **3.** to receive or be awarded: *I got a present*; *they got five years for theft.* **4.** to obtain by working; earn: *to get one's living.* **5.** to acquire a mental grasp or command of; learn: *to get a lesson by heart.* **6.** to hear or understand: *I didn't get the last word.* **7.** to be afflicted with (an illness, etc.): *to be getting the flu.* **8.** to reach or communicate with (someone): *to get him on the phone.* **9.** to cause to be or do: *to get a friend appointed*; *get one's hair cut*; *get the fire to burn.* **10.** to manage; succeed in accomplishing: *I didn't get to see her.* **11.** to prevail on: *to get her to speak.* **12.** to prepare; make ready: *to get dinner.* **13.** *Colloq.* to hit: *the bullet got her in the leg.* **14.** *Colloq.* to have revenge on, especially by physical assault: *I'll get you for that.* **15.** *Colloq.* to grasp or understand the meaning or intention of (a person). **16.** *Colloq.* to look at; perceive: *get that hairdo!* **17.** *Colloq.* to baffle; reveal the ignorance of: *you've got me there, mate!* **18.** *Colloq.* to have a strong effect upon, as irritation, anger, amusement: *her behaviour really gets me.* **19.** *Colloq.* to trick or deceive. **20.** *Colloq.* to kill. **21.** *Colloq.* to answer: *who'll get the phone?* –*v.i.* **22.** to come to or arrive: *to get home.* **23.** to succeed in coming or going (*away, in, into, out, over, through,* etc.). –*v.* (*copular*) **24.** to become; grow: *to get tired.* –*v.* (*aux.*) **25.** used to form a passive verb: *to get married.* –*phr.* **26. be getting on,** to be advanced in years. **27. do a get,** *Colloq.* to escape; run away. **28. get about, a.** to move about. **b.** (of rumours, etc.) to become known. **29. get across, a.** to make understood. **b.** *Theatre* to communicate successfully (to an audience). **c.** *Colloq.* to irritate or annoy. **30. get ahead,** to be successful; make progress. **31. get along,** to go away. **32. get along** (or **on**), **a.** to advance one's cause; prosper. **b.** to make progress; proceed; advance. **c.** (sometimes fol. by *with*) to agree or be friendly. **33. get along with you,** an exclamation of disbelief. **34. get any,** *Colloq.* to have sexual intercourse: *are you getting any?* **35. get around, a.** to move about. **b.** (of rumours, etc.) to become known. **c.** to overcome (a difficulty). **36. get at, a.** to reach; make contact with: *I can't get at it.* **b.** *Colloq.* to hint at or imply: *what's she getting at?* **c.** *Colloq.* to tamper with, as by corruption or bribery. **d.** *Colloq.* to nag or find fault with:

why are you always getting at me? **37. get away, a.** to escape. **b.** to depart. **c.** to start in a race: *the horses got away cleanly.* **d.** to go away, especially on holiday: *we'll get away this evening.* **e.** *Colloq.* an exclamation of surprise or disbelief. **f.** (of grass or feed grains) to grow sufficiently to provide useful fodder for stock. **38. get away from, a.** to escape. **b.** to avoid. **39. get away from it all,** to leave business, work, worries, etc., for a holiday. **40. get away with,** to avoid punishment or blame for. **41. get away with you,** *Colloq.* an exclamation indicating good-humoured disbelief or dismissal. **42. get back, a.** to return: *we should get back before sunset.* **b.** to recover or make as a profit on: *they got back twice the amount they invested.* **43. get back on** (or **at**), *Colloq.* to get revenge on (someone). **44. get back to, a.** (of information intended to be suppressed or withheld) to reach the ears of: *the rumour will get back to him eventually.* **b.** to contact (someone) for a second time. **45. get by,** to manage; carry on in spite of difficulties. **46. get cracking,** *Colloq.* to begin vigorously; hurry. **47. get down, a.** to bring down. **b.** to come down. **c.** *Colloq.* to respond euphorically to music: *get down and boogie.* **d.** *Colloq.* to depress or discourage (someone). **48. get down to,** to begin to concentrate on or give one's attention to. **49. get even with,** to square accounts with. **50. get going,** to begin; make haste. **51. get his** (or **hers**, etc.), *Colloq.* **a.** to get a just reward. **b.** to be killed. **52. get in,** to order or stock up (provisions, etc.). **53. get in for one's chop,** *Aust., NZ Colloq.* to attempt to obtain a fair share. **54. get inside, a.** to make a way into. **b.** *Colloq.* to achieve deep understanding of. **55. get into, a.** to become involved or immersed in (an activity): *I was just getting into reading when the phone rang.* **b.** *Colloq.* to attack (someone) vigorously, either physically or verbally. **c.** *Colloq.* to set about (a task) vigorously. **d.** *Colloq.* to consume regularly in large quantities: *to get into the booze.* **56. get into** (or **in**) **bed with,** *Colloq.* **a.** to have sexual intercourse with. **b.** to enter into a close business arrangement with. **57. get in touch with, a.** to contact; exchange words with. **b.** to become familiar with; come to grips with. **58. get it in the neck,** *Colloq.* to be rebuked or punished. **59. get it on,** *Colloq.* (sometimes fol. by *with*) to have sexual intercourse. **60. get it together,** *Colloq.* to achieve harmony or success. **61. get it up,** *Colloq.* to achieve an erection. **62. get lost,** *Colloq.* to go away; desist: *get lost, will you!* **63. get off, a.** to escape; evade consequences. **b.** to start a journey; leave. **c.** to dismount from (a horse or train, etc.). **d.** *Colloq.* to cease to interfere. **e.** *Colloq.* to experience orgasm. **64. get off on,** *Colloq.* to enjoy thoroughly: *she really gets off on punk rock.* **65. get off one's bike,** *Colloq.* to become angry. **66. get on,** to age. **67. get on** (or **along**), **a.** to advance one's cause; prosper. **b.** to make progress; proceed; advance. **c.** (sometimes fol. by *with*) to agree or be friendly. **68. get oneself up,** to dress elaborately. **69. get one's jollies,** *Colloq.* to get pleasurable excitement, especially from or as from doing something forbidden or improper. **70. get one's own back,** to be revenged. **71. get on someone's nerves,** to annoy or irritate someone. **72. get on the telephone,** to initiate a telephone call. **73. get on to** (or **onto**), **a.** to discover. **b.** to contact; get in touch with (someone). **c.** (*usu. imperative*) *Colloq.* to look at: *get on to that outfit!* **d.** *Colloq.* to obtain: *to get on to some good bargains.* **74. get on top of,** *Colloq.* **a.** to become adept in or knowledgeable about (a subject, job, etc.); master. **b.** to dominate. **c.** to weigh down emotionally. **75. get out, a.** to escape. **b.** (of information) to become publicly known. **c.** to alight from a vehicle. **d.** to succeed in solving (a puzzle, mystery, etc.). **76. get out from under,** to escape from (a difficult or threatening situation); abandon (one's responsibilities). **77. get outside of,** *Colloq.* to eat. **78. get over, a.** to overcome (a difficulty, etc.). **b.** to recover from: *to get over a shock*; *to get over an illness.* **79. get real,** *Colloq.* to become sensible or realistic. **80. get round, a.** to outwit. **b.** to cajole or ingratiate oneself with (someone). **c.** to overcome (difficulties, etc.). **81. get round to,** to come at length to (doing something). **82. get set, a.** (as a command at the start of a running race) be ready. **b.** *Two-up, etc.* to place a wager. **83. get someone going,** *Colloq.* to arouse someone to anger, excitement, interest, etc. **84. get someone wrong,** *Colloq.* to misunderstand someone: *don't get me wrong!* **85. get (stuck) into,** *Colloq.* **a.** to attack (someone) vigorously either physically or verbally. **b.** to set about (a task) vigorously. **c.** to eat hungrily. **86. get the axe** (or **chop**) (or **spear**), *Colloq.* to be dismissed from a job. **87. get this,** *Colloq.* an exclamation calling for attention, especially to information about to be imparted. **88. get through to, a.** to make a telephone connection with. **b.** *Colloq.* to make understand. **89. get to, a.** to arouse deep feeling in. **b.** to annoy or irritate. **90. get together, a.** to confer. **b.** to meet informally. **91. get under someone's skin,** to arouse someone's irritation or embarrassment. **92. get up, a.** to arise; sit up or stand. **b.** to rise from bed. **c.** to ascend or mount. **d.** (of wind, sea, etc.) to increase in force. **e.** to make ready: *to get up wool for sale.* **f.** to prepare, arrange, or organise. **g.** to produce in a specified style, as a book. **h.** to work up (a feeling, etc.). **i.** to be acquitted. **j.** to win (an election, court case, contest, etc.). **93. get up to,** to be involved in (especially mischief, etc.). **94. get with,** to have intercourse with. **95. get with child,** *Archaic* to make pregnant. **96. get with it,** *Colloq.* to adopt the current fashion. –**getting,** *n.* –**gettable,** *adj.*

getaway /ˈgɛtəweɪ/ *n.* **1.** a getting away; an escape. **2.** a holiday, usually of short duration. **3.** the start of a race. –*adj.* **4.** relating to a getaway: *the getaway car was found.*

get-out *phr.* **as ... as all get-out,** *Colloq.* in the extreme: *he's as silly as all get-out.*

get-together *n. Colloq.* **1.** a meeting. **2.** a small and informal social gathering.

geyser *n.* **1.** /ˈgizə, ˈgaɪzə/ a hot spring which intermittently sends up fountain-like jets of water and steam into the air. **2.** /ˈgizə/ a hot-water heater.

g-force /ˈdʒiː-fɔːs/ *n.* an effect of acceleration on an object, perceived as weight and informally expressed as units of weight per unit mass; 1 g is the force of the earth's gravity, and at 2 gs the force experienced is twice the object's weight, so an object weighing 10 kilograms is, at 2 gs, 20 kilograms.

ghastly /ˈgastli/ *adj.* (**-lier, -liest**) **1.** frightful; dreadful; horrible: *a ghastly murder.* **2.** deathly pale: *a ghastly look.* **3.** bad; unpleasant; shocking: *a ghastly failure.* –**ghastliness,** *n.*

GHB /dʒiː eɪtʃ ˈbiː/ *n.* an anaesthetic drug, gamma hydroxybutyric acid, used recreationally as a stimulant; fantasy.

ghee /gi/ *n.* clarified butter, used especially in Indian cookery.

gherkin /ˈgɜːkən/ *n.* the small, immature fruit of some common varieties of cucumber, used in pickling.

ghetto /ˈgɛtoʊ/ *n.* (*pl.* **-tos** *or* **-toes**) a quarter in a city in which any minority group lives.

ghetto-blaster /ˈgɛtoʊ-blastə/ *n.* a large, powerful, portable stereo radio-cassette or CD player. Also, **ghetto blaster.**

ghost /goʊst/ *n.* **1.** the disembodied spirit of a dead person imagined as wandering among or haunting living persons. **2.** a mere shadow or semblance: *ghost of a chance.* **3.** (*upper case*) a spiritual being: *Holy Ghost.*

4. *Colloq.* → **ghostwriter. 5.** *Optics* a bright spot or secondary image caused by a defect in an optical instrument or system. **6.** *Electronics* an unwanted double or secondary image on the screen of a television or radar set caused by reflection of the received signals from an adjacent object. –*v.t.* **7.** to write for someone else who is publicly known as the author. –*phr.* **8. give up the ghost, a.** to die. **b.** to despair. **c.** (of a piece of machinery) to break down completely. –**ghostly,** **ghostlike,** *adj.*

ghost gum *n.* **1.** an inland Australian species of eucalypt, *Corymbia paracolpica*, with a mid-green crown and smooth white bark on the branches and upper trunk. **2.** → **snow gum.**

ghost town *n.* a deserted or semi-deserted town, such as a formerly prosperous goldmining town.

ghostwriter /ˈgoʊstraɪtə/ *n.* someone who does literary work for someone else who takes the credit.

ghoul /gul/ *n.* **1.** an evil demon of Islamic legend, supposedly feeding on human beings, and especially robbing graves, preying on corpses, etc. **2.** someone who revels in what is revolting. –**ghoulish,** *adj.* –**ghoulishly,** *adv.* –**ghoulishness,** *n.*

GI /dʒi ˈaɪ/ *n. Colloq.* a soldier, usually other than an officer, in any of the US armed forces.

giant /ˈdʒaɪənt/ *n.* **1.** an imaginary being of human form but superhuman size, strength, etc. **2.** one of a race of beings in Greek mythology, of more than human size and strength, who were subdued by the Olympian gods. **3.** a person or thing of unusually great size, endowments, importance, etc.: *an intellectual giant.* –*adj.* **4.** gigantic; huge: *the giant cactus.* **5.** great or eminent above others. –**giantess** /ˈdʒaɪəntɛs/, *n.*

giant kelp *n.* a variety of fast-growing kelp, *Macrocystis pyrifera*, which can grow to twenty metres in height, the fronds of the plant being held on the surface by air-filled floats.

giant kingfisher *n.* → **kookaburra** (def. 1).

giant perch *n.* → **barramundi.**

giardia /dʒiˈadiə, giˈadiə/ *n.* any flagellate of the genus *Giardia*, parasitic to the intestines of vertebrates.

gibber¹ /ˈdʒɪbə/ *v.i.* **1.** to speak inarticulately; chatter. –*n.* **2.** gibbering utterance.

gibber² /ˈgɪbə/ *n. Aust.* a pebble or stone found in parts of the arid Australian inland.

gibberish /ˈdʒɪbərɪʃ/ *n.* **1.** rapid, unintelligible talk. **2.** incomprehensible writing.

gibbon /ˈgɪbən/ *n.* any of the small, slender, long-armed anthropoid apes, genus *Hylobates*, of arboreal habits, found in southern Asia.

gibe /dʒaɪb/ *v.i.* **1.** to utter mocking words; scoff; jeer. –*v.t.* **2.** to taunt; deride; flout. –*n.* **3.** a taunting or sarcastic remark. Also, **jibe.** –**giber,** *n.* –**gibingly,** *adj.*

giblet /ˈdʒɪblət/ *n.* (*usu. pl.*) the heart, liver, or gizzard from a fowl, often cooked separately.

giddy /ˈgɪdi/ *adj.* (**-dier, -diest**) **1.** frivolously light; impulsive; flighty: *a giddy mind, a giddy girl.* **2.** affected with vertigo; dizzy. **3.** attended with or causing dizziness: *a giddy climb.* –**giddily,** *adv.* –**giddiness,** *n.*

gidgee¹ /ˈgɪdʒi/ *n.* **1.** a small gregarious Australian tree, *Acacia cambagei*, which gives off an unpleasant odour at the approach of rain; stinking wattle. **2.** any of certain other species of wattle, such as the poisonous **Georgina gidgee,** *Acacia georginae.*

gidgee² /ˈgɪdʒi/ *n.* an Aboriginal spear.

gift /gɪft/ *n.* **1.** something given; a present. **2.** the act of giving. **3.** a special ability or talent: *he has the gift of song.* **4.** *Colloq.* anything very easily obtained or understood: *the exam question was a gift.* –*phr.* **5. God's gift,** (*often ironic*) someone or something ideally suited to the needs of another or others: *he* *thinks he is God's gift to women.* **6. look a gift horse in the mouth,** to accept a gift ungratefully or critically.

GIFT /gɪft/ *n.* a technique of assisted reproduction in which a harvested egg and sperm are placed into one of the woman's fallopian tubes with the aim of fertilisation taking place there; gamete intrafallopian transfer.

gifted /ˈgɪftəd/ *adj.* endowed with natural gifts; talented: *a gifted artist.* –**giftedness,** *n.*

gift-horse *phr.* **look a gift-horse in the mouth,** to criticise a gift; accept a gift ungratefully.

gig¹ /gɪg/ *n.* **1.** *Naut.* **a.** a long, fast-pulling boat used especially for racing. **b.** the boat reserved for a ship's captain. **2.** a light, two-wheeled one-horse carriage. –*v.i.* (**gigged, gigging**) **3.** to ride in a gig.

gig² /gɪg/ *n. Colloq.* **1.** a booking for a musician, co-median, etc., to perform at a venue. **2.** the performance itself. **3.** any job or occupation, especially one that is intended to be of a short duration.

gig³ /gɪg/ *n.* (*pl.* **gigs** *or* **gig**) *Computers Colloq.* → **gigabyte.**

gigabyte /ˈgɪgəbaɪt/ *n.* a unit of measurement of computer memory equal to 2^{30} (approximately 10^9) bytes. *Symbol:* **G, GB**

gigajoule /ˈgɪgədʒul/ *n.* a metric unit of energy equal to 10^9 joules.

gigantic /dʒaɪˈgæntɪk/ *adj.* **1.** very large; huge. **2.** of, like, or befitting a giant. –**gigantically,** *adv.* –**giganticness,** *n.*

giggle /ˈgɪgəl/ *v.i.* **1.** to laugh in a silly, undignified way, as from youthful spirits or ill-controlled amusement; titter. –*n.* **2.** a silly, spasmodic laugh; a titter. **3.** *Colloq.* an amusing occasion: *a bit of a giggle.* –*phr.* **4. get the giggles,** *Colloq.* to giggle repeatedly, and sometimes helplessly, often at the one thing repeatedly brought to mind. –**giggly,** *adj.* –**giggler,** *n.*

gigolo /ˈʒɪgəloʊ/ *n.* (*pl.* **-los**) **1.** a man who is kept by a woman, especially a young man kept by an older woman, with the implication that there is a sexual relationship. **2.** a male professional dancing partner. **3.** a male prostitute.

gild /gɪld/ *v.t.* (**gilded** *or* **gilt, gilding**) **1.** to coat with gold, gold leaf, or gold-coloured substance. **2.** to give a bright, pleasing, or specious aspect to. –*phr.* **3. gild the lily,** to spoil beauty by overembellishment.

gill¹ /gɪl/ *n.* **1.** an aquatic respiratory organ, either external or internal, usually feathery, plate-like, or filamentous. **2.** one of the radiating vertical plates on the underside of the cap of a fungus such as the mushroom. **3.** the ground ivy. –*phr. Colloq.* **4. fed up to the gills,** thoroughly exasperated. **5. loaded to the gills, a.** carrying as much as can be carried **b.** drunk. **6. white** (or **green**) **at the gills,** pale-faced through fear, exhaustion, nausea, etc. –**gilled,** *adj.*

gill² /gɪl, dʒɪl/ *n.* a unit of liquid measure in the imperial system, equal to one quarter of a pint, or $0.142\,065\,3125 \times 10^{-3}$ m³ (approximately one seventh of a litre).

gilt /gɪlt/ *v.* **1.** a past tense and past participle of **gild.** –*adj.* **2.** gilded; golden in colour. –*n.* **3.** the gold or other material applied in gilding; gilding.

gilt-edged *adj.* **1.** having the edges gilded: *gilt-edged paper.* **2.** of the highest order or quality: *gilt-edged securities.*

gimchi /ˈgɪmtʃi/ *n.* → **kimchi.**

gimlet /ˈgɪmlət/ *n.* **1.** a small tool for boring holes, consisting of a shaft with a pointed screw at one end and a handle at the other. **2.** a tree, *Eucalyptus saluleris,* of western Australia, the bole of which is characteristically twisted and furrowed. –*v.t.* **3.** to pierce with or as with a gimlet. –*adj.* **4.** able to bore through, or penetrate. **5.** deeply penetrating, or thought to be deeply penetrating: *gimlet eyes.*

gimmick /ˈgɪmɪk/ *n. Colloq.* a pronounced eccentricity of dress, manner, voice, etc., or an eccentric action or device, especially one exploited to gain publicity. –**gimmicky,** *adj.*

gimp /gɪmp/ *n.* **1.** *US* (*derog.*) a physically handicapped person, especially one who is lame. **2.** a sexual fetishist in a submissive role, who dons a rubber suit and hood. **3.** (*derog.*) an incompetent or weak person. –**gimpy,** *adj.*

gin¹ /dʒɪn/ *n.* an alcoholic beverage obtained by redistilling spirits with flavouring agents, especially juniper berries, orange peel, angelica root, etc.

gin² /dʒɪn/ *n.* **1.** a machine for separating cotton from its seeds. **2.** a trap or snare for game, etc. –*v.t.* (**ginned, ginning**) **3.** to clear (cotton) of seeds with a gin. **4.** to catch (game, etc.) in a gin. –**ginner,** *n.*

gin³ /dʒɪn/ *n.* a card game similar to rummy in which a player with a total of 10 unmatched points or less may end the game. Also, **gin rummy.**

ginger /ˈdʒɪndʒə/ *n.* **1.** the pungent, spicy rhizome of any of the reed-like plants of the genus *Zingiber,* especially of *Z. officinale,* variously used in cookery and medicine. **2.** any of these plants, native to South-East Asia, but now cultivated in most tropical countries. **3.** a reddish brown or tawny colour. **4.** (of hair) red. **5.** *Colloq.* piquancy; animation. –*phr.* **6. ginger up,** *Colloq.* **a.** to impart spiciness or piquancy to. **b.** to increase the energy, gaiety, etc., of (a group, an activity, etc.).

ginger ale *n.* a soft drink, flavoured with ginger, used for mixing with spirits, especially brandy.

ginger beer *n.* a non-alcoholic carbonated drink of water, sugar, yeast, etc., flavoured with ginger.

gingerbread /ˈdʒɪndʒəbred/ *n.* **1.** a kind of cake flavoured with ginger and treacle or golden syrup. **2.** something showy but unsubstantial and inartistic. –*adj.* **3.** showy but unsubstantial and inartistic.

gingerly /ˈdʒɪndʒəli/ *adv.* with extreme care or caution; warily. –**gingerliness,** *n.*

gingham /ˈgɪŋəm/ *n.* a yarn-dyed, plain-weave cotton fabric, usually striped or checked.

gingivitis /dʒɪndʒəˈvaɪtəs/ *n. Pathol.* inflammation of the gums.

gingko /ˈgɪŋkoʊ/ *n.* → **ginkgo.**

ginkgo /ˈgɪŋkoʊ/ *n.* (*pl.* **-goes**) **1.** Also, **gingko biloba.** a large, ornamental, gymnospermous tree, *Ginkgo biloba,* with fan-shaped leaves, fleshy fruit with a foul-smelling outer covering, and edible nuts; originally of China (where it is the sole survivor of the family Ginkgoaceae, which flourished in the Jurassic period) but now frequently grown in Japan, Korea, and elsewhere. **2.** an extract drawn from the leaves of this tree, used traditionally in Chinese herbal medicine as a general restorative. Also, **gingko.**

ginormous /dʒaɪˈnɔməs/ *adj. Colloq.* very large.

ginseng /ˈdʒɪnsɛŋ/ *n.* **1.** either of two plants, *Panax ginseng* of China, Korea, etc., and *P. quinquefolium* of North America, yielding an aromatic root which is extensively used in medicine by the Chinese. **2.** the root itself. **3.** a preparation made from it.

gipsy /ˈdʒɪpsi/ *n.* (*pl.* **-sies**) → **gypsy.**

giraffe /dʒəˈraf/ *n.* a tall, long-necked, spotted ruminant, *Giraffa camelopardalis,* of Africa, the tallest of existing quadrupeds.

gird /gɜd/ *v.t.* (**girt** *or* **girded, girding**) **1.** Also, **gird up.** to encircle with a belt or girdle. **2.** to surround; hem in. –*phr.* **3. gird oneself** (**up**) **for,** to prepare oneself mentally for **4. gird one's loins,** to make ready or prepare oneself for action of some kind.

girder /ˈgɜdə/ *n.* **1.** (in structural work) any main horizontal supporting member or beam, as of steel, reinforced concrete, or wood. **2.** one of the principal horizontal timbers which support the joists in certain floors.

girdle /ˈɡɜdl/ n. 1. a belt, cord, or the like, worn around the waist. 2. a lightweight undergarment which supports the abdominal region of the body. 3. any encircling band; compass; limit. 4. *Gems* the edge around a brilliant or other cut stone at the junction of the upper and lower faces. 5. *Anat.* the bony framework which unites the upper or lower extremities to the axial skeleton. –v.t. 6. to encompass; enclose; encircle. 7. to cut away the bark in a ring around (a tree, branch, etc.), thus causing death. –**girdler**, n.

girl /ɡɜl/ n. 1. a female child or young person. 2. a young woman. 3. *Colloq.* a girlfriend (def. 1). 4. a female servant, especially (in India, Africa, and elsewhere) an indigenous female servant.

girlfriend /ˈɡɜlfrɛnd/ n. 1. a female companion with whom one has a steady romantic relationship. 2. a close female friend of a woman.

Girl Guide n. (*sometimes lower case*) → Guide.

girlie /ˈɡɜli/ *Colloq.* –n. 1. a girl. –adj. 2. illustrating or featuring nude or nearly nude women: *a girlie magazine*. 3. considered to be suitable for or befitting a girl: *a girlie throw in cricket*. 4. excessively feminine in behaviour, dress, speech, speech, etc., in a way that reflects a female stereotype. Compare **boysie**.

girth /ɡɜθ/ n. 1. the measure around anything; circumference. 2. a band passed under the belly of a horse, etc., to secure a saddle or pack on its back. 3. a band or girdle.

GIS /dʒi aɪ ˈɛs/ n. geographical information systems; a computer system that can capture, store, analyse, and present in various ways data that locates places on the earth's surface.

gist /dʒɪst/ n. 1. the substance or pith of a matter; essential part: *the gist of an argument*. 2. the ground on which a legal action rests.

give /ɡɪv/ *verb* (**gave**, **given**, **giving**) –v.t. 1. to deliver freely; bestow; hand over: *to give someone a present.* 2. to deliver to another in exchange for something; pay. 3. to grant permission or opportunity to; enable; assign; award. 4. to set forth or show; present; offer. 5. to present to, or as to an audience: *ladies and gentleman, I give you the Lord Mayor of Sydney*. 6. to propose as the subject of a toast: *I give you the bride*. 7. to assign as a basis of calculation or reasoning; suppose; assume: *given these facts*. 8. to assign to someone as their right, lot, etc.: *to give a child a name; to give someone their due*. 9. *Colloq.* to tell; offer as explanation: *don't give me that*. 10. to be prepared to assign: *I don't give a damn for your views*. 11. to set aside for a specified purpose: *he gives great attention to detail*. 12. concede to (someone); admit: *I'll give you that*. 13. to furnish or provide: *give aid; give evidence*. 14. to afford or yield; produce: *give satisfaction; give good results*. 15. to make, do or perform: *give a start; give a lurch*. 16. to issue; put forth, emit, or utter: *give a cry; give a command*. 17. to cause: *I was given to understand*. 18. to impart or communicate: *give advice; give someone a cold*. 19. to deal or administer: *give someone a blow; give someone medicine; give someone the sacrament*. 20. to relinquish or surrender: *to give ground*. 21. to produce; present: *to give a play*. 22. to act as host at (a social function, etc.): *to give a party*. 23. to pledge: *to give one's word of honour*. –v.i. 24. to make a gift or gifts. 25. to yield, as to pressure or strain; draw back; relax. 26. to break down; fail. 27. to be situated facing a specified direction: *the house gives on to the seafront*. 28. *Colloq.* to be happening: *hey man, what gives?* –n. 29. the act or fact of yielding to pressure; elasticity. –phr. 30. **give and take, a.** a method of dealing by compromise or mutual concession; cooperation.

b. good-humoured exchange of talk, ideas, etc. 31. **give away, a.** to give as a present. **b.** to hand over (the bride) to the bridegroom at a wedding. **c.** to let (a secret) be known. **d.** to betray (a person). **e.** *Aust., NZ* to abandon; give up: *times were hard so I gave farming away*. 32. **give birth to, a.** to bear. **b.** to be the origin of. 33. **give in, a.** to yield; acknowledge defeat. **b.** to hand in. **c.** to include additionally: *the cushions were given in with the lounge*. 34. **give in to**, to allow (someone) to have their way. 35. **give it a go** (or **whirl**), *Colloq.* to make an attempt. 36. **give it away**, *Aust.* to cease to do something, usually in exasperation. 37. **give it up for** ..., *Colloq.* an encouragement to others to cheer or applaud .... 38. **give of**, to devote; contribute largely. 39. **give off**, to put forth; emit. 40. **give oneself away**, to reveal something about oneself accidentally. 41. **give oneself up to**, to surrender or devote oneself to. 42. **give or take, a.** approximately: *there were 200 people, give or take*. **b.** allowing for: *there were 200 people, give or take the late arrivals*. 43. **give out, a.** to become worn out or used up. **b.** to send out; emit. **c.** to distribute; issue. **d.** to announce publicly. **e.** *Cricket* (of an umpire) to declare (the person batting) to be out. 44. **give over, a.** to transfer. **b.** to assign for a specific purpose: *the evening was given over to feasting.* **c.** *Brit. Colloq.* to desist. 45. **give rise to**, to be the origin of; cause; result in. 46. **give someone** (or **something**) **best**, to acknowledge the superiority of someone or something. 47. **give someone the benefit of the doubt**, to decide in someone's favour for lack of evidence to support a contrary ruling. 48. **give up, a.** to lose all hope. **b.** to abandon as hopeless. **c.** to desist from; forsake: *give up a task*. **d.** to surrender. **e.** to devote entirely. **f.** to inform against. 49. **give way, a.** to withdraw. **b.** to yield to pressure. **c.** to break down; collapse. **d.** (of traffic) to allow another vehicle to move into the lane. 50. **give way to, a.** to yield to. **b.** to succumb to (an emotion). **c.** to be replaced by: *to give way to the younger generation*. **d.** (of traffic) to allow (a vehicle) to move into the lane. –**givable**, *adj.* –**giver**, *n.*

giveaway /ˈɡɪvəweɪ/ *Colloq.* –n. 1. a disclosure or revelation, usually unintentional: *a dead giveaway*. 2. anything given away with an item for sale as a promotion. –adj. 3. (of a television program, etc.) characterised by the awarding of prizes, money, etc., to recipients chosen, usually through a question-and-answer contest.

given /ˈɡɪvən/ v. 1. past participle of **give**. –adj. 2. stated, fixed, or specified: *at a given time*. 3. assigned as a basis of calculation, reasoning, etc.: *given A and B, C follows*. 4. (on official documents) executed and delivered as of the date specified. –phr. 5. **given to**, addicted or disposed to: *given to drink*.

given name n. a name borne by an individual, often assigned by his or her parents shortly after birth, as opposed to the inherited surname; first name; forename. Compare **Christian name**.

gizzard /ˈɡɪzəd/ n. 1. the grinding or muscular stomach of birds, the organ in which food is triturated after leaving the glandular stomach. –phr. 2. **in one's gizzards**, *Colloq.* deep within one's being.

glacé /ˈɡlæseɪ, ˈɡlɑ-/ adj. 1. iced or sugared, as cake. 2. crystallised, as fruits. 3. finished with a gloss, as kid or silk.

glacial /ˈɡleɪʃəl, ˈɡleɪsiəl/ adj. 1. characterised by the presence of ice in extensive masses or glaciers. 2. due to or associated with the action of ice or glaciers. 3. of or relating to glaciers or ice sheets. 4. cold as ice; icy. 5. *Chem.* of or tending to assume an ice-like form, as certain acids. –**glacially**, *adv.*

glacial epoch n. 1. any of the glaciations or ice ages of past geological periods as in Australia during the

Permian. *–phr.* **2. the glacial epoch**, the geologically recent Pleistocene epoch, during which much of the Northern Hemisphere was covered by great ice sheets; ice age.

glacier /'gleɪsɪə, 'glæsɪə/ *n.* an extended mass of ice formed from snow falling and accumulating over the years and moving very slowly, either descending from high mountains, as in valley glaciers, or moving outwards from centres of accumulation, as in continental glaciers. **–glaciered**, *adj.*

glad /glæd/ *adj.* **1.** (sometimes fol. by *of*, *at*, etc., or an infinitive or clause) delighted or pleased: *to be glad at the news; glad to go; glad that one has come.* **2.** characterised by or showing cheerfulness, joy, or pleasure, as looks, utterances, etc. **3.** attended with or causing joy or pleasure: *a glad occasion; glad tidings.* **4.** willing. *–phr. Colloq.* **5. the glad eye**, an inviting or flirtatious look: *she gave him the glad eye.* **6. the glad hand**, (*usually ironic*) a welcome; greeting: *they gave her the glad hand.* **–gladden**, *v.* **–gladly**, *adv.* **–gladness**, *n.*

glade /gleɪd/ *n.* an open space in a forest.

gladiator /'glædɪeɪtə/ *n.* **1.** *Roman Hist.* a person, often a slave or captive, who fought in public with a sword or other weapon to entertain the people. **2.** someone who takes up a cause or right; a controversialist.

gladiolus /glædi'oʊləs/ *n.* (*pl.* **-lus** *or* **-li** /laɪ/ *or* **-luses**) any plant of the genus *Gladiolus*, native mainly to South Africa, with erect leaves, and spikes of variously coloured flowers; sword lily.

glamour /'glæmə/ *n.* **1.** alluring and often illusory charm; fascination. **2.** *Obs.* magic or enchantment; spell; witchery. Also, **glamor**. **–glamorous**, *adj.*

glamping /'glæmpɪŋ/ *n.* camping out with luxurious surrounds, fine cuisine, and comforts such as electricity, heating, etc. **–glamper**, *n.*

glance /glæns, glans/ *v.i.* (**glanced**, **glancing**) **1.** to look quickly. **2.** to flash; gleam. **3.** to hit and go off at an angle: *the blow glanced off the man's chest.* **4.** to make a brief reference to, in passing: *we'll just glance at the history of the subject.* *–n.* **5.** the act of glancing.

gland /glænd/ *n.* *Anat.* **a.** an organ or tissue which elaborates and discharges a substance which is used elsewhere in the body (*secretion*), or eliminated (*excretion*). **b.** any of various organs or structures likened to true glands. **2.** *Bot.* a secreting organ or structure, especially one on or near a surface. **–glandless**, *adj.* **–glandular**, *adj.*

glandular fever /glændʒələ 'fivə/ *n.* *Pathol.* an acute infectious disease characterised by sudden fever, a benign swelling of lymph nodes, and increase in leukocytes having only one nucleus in the bloodstream; infectious mononucleosis.

glare /glɛə/ *n.* **1.** a strong, bright light; brilliant or dazzling light: *the glare of oncoming car lights; the glare of ice.* **2.** showy appearance; dazzle. **3.** a fierce look: *she gave him a glare for his bad manners.* *–v.i.* (**glared**, **glaring**) **4.** to shine with a strong, dazzling light. **5.** to be too brightly decorated. **6.** to be very bright in colour. **7.** to be very noticeable. **8.** to give a (long) fierce look.

glaring /'glɛərɪŋ/ *adj.* **1.** that glares; brilliant; dazzling. **2.** excessively bright; garish. **3.** very conspicuous: *glaring defects.* **4.** staring fiercely. **–glaringly**, *adv.* **–glaringness**, *n.*

glass /glas/ *n.* **1.** a hard more or less transparent substance produced by the melting of silica and silicates. The type used for windows, bottles, etc., contains silica, soda, and lime. **2.** any substance similar to glass, e.g. fused borax, obsidian, etc. **3.** something made of glass, e.g. a mirror, barometer, etc. **4.** household articles ornaments, etc., made of glass; glassware. **5.** a glass container for drinking fluids. **6.** the quantity contained in a drinking glass. **7.** *Colloq.* methamphetamine

powder. *–adj.* **8.** made of glass. **9.** fitted with panes of glass; glazed. *–v.t.* **10.** to fit with panes of glass; cover with or put in glass. **11.** *Colloq.* to attack (someone) in the face with a glass or broken bottle. **–glassless**, *adj.* **–glassy**, *adj.* **–glassing**, *n.*

glass ceiling *n.* a barrier to the progress of something, especially to the promotion of women above a certain level of executive status in an organisation in spite of their being qualified for such positions.

glasses /'glasəz/ *pl. n.* a device to aid defective vision, consisting usually of two glass lenses set in a frame which rests on the nose and is held in place by pieces passing over the ears.

glaucoma /glɔ'koʊmə/ *n.* *Pathol.* a disease of the eye, characterised by increased pressure within the eyeball with progressive loss of vision. **–glaucomatous** /glɔ-'koʊmətəs, -'kɒmə-/, *adj.*

glaze /gleɪz/ *v.t.* **1.** to fit with glass; cover with or as if with glass. **2.** *Pottery* **a.** to produce a vitreous waterproof surface (either shiny or matt) on (pots). **b.** to cover with a glaze, before firing. **3.** *Cookery* to cover (food) with a glaze (def. 9). **4.** *Painting* to cover a painted surface, etc.) with a thin coat of transparent colour in order to change the tone slightly. *–v.i.* **5.** to become glazed or glassy: *his eyes glazed over as he remembered the past. –n.* **6.** a smooth shiny surface on certain materials. **7.** *Pottery* (a substance used to produce) this surface on glazed pottery. **8.** *Painting* a thin coat of transparent colour, over a painted surface. **9.** *Cookery* something used to coat food, as: **a.** egg white on pastry, or syrup on a cooked tart. **b.** stock cooked down to a thin paste, used on meats. **–glazer**, *n.* **–glazy**, *adj.*

glazier /'gleɪzɪə/ *n.* someone who fits windows, etc., with glass.

gleam /glim/ *n.* **1.** a flash or beam of light. **2.** dim or subdued light. **3.** a brief or slight manifestation: *a gleam of hope. –v.i.* **4.** to send forth a gleam or gleams. **5.** to appear suddenly and clearly, like a flash of light. *–phr.* **6. gleam in one's eye**, a look betokening humour or unstated intentions.

glean /glin/ *v.t.* **1.** to gather slowly and laboriously in bits. **2.** to gather (grain, etc.) after the reapers or regular gatherers. **3.** to discover or find out. *–v.i.* **4.** to collect or gather anything little by little or slowly. **–gleaner**, *n.*

glee /gli/ *n.* **1.** demonstrative joy; exultation. **2.** a kind of unaccompanied part-song, grave or joyful, for three or more voices.

glen /glɛn/ *n.* a small, narrow, secluded valley.

glib /glɪb/ *adj.* (**glibber**, **glibbest**) **1.** ready and fluent, often thoughtlessly or insincerely so: *glib speakers, a glib tongue.* **2.** easy, as action or manner. **–glibly**, *adv.* **–glibness**, *n.*

glide /glaɪd/ *v.i.* **1.** to move smoothly along, as if without effort, as a flying bird, a boat, a skater, etc. **2.** (fol. by *in, out*, etc.) to go quietly or unnoticed; slip. **3.** *Aeronautics* to move in the air, especially at an easy angle downwards, by the action of gravity, air-currents, etc., without use of an engine. **4.** *Music* to pass from note to note without a break; slur. *–v.t.* **5.** to cause to glide. *–n.* **6.** a gliding movement, as in dancing. **7.** *Ling.* → **semivowel**. **–glidingly**, *adv.*

glider /'glaɪdə/ *n.* **1.** a small cup-shaped mould in which the legs of chairs, etc., are stood to prevent them marking the floor. **2.** *Aeronautics* a motorless aeroplane for gliding from a higher to a lower level by the action of gravity, or from a lower to a higher level by the action of air currents. **3.** any of the arboreal marsupials of Australia and New Guinea, having a parachute-like membrane along the side of the body by which they are able to glide; flying phalanger.

glimmer /'glɪmə/ n. **1.** a faint or unsteady light; gleam. **2.** a dim perception; inkling. **3.** a faint appearance or indication: *a glimmer of hope.* –v.i. **4.** to shine faintly or unsteadily; twinkle; flicker. **5.** to appear faintly or dimly.

glimpse /glɪmps/ n. **1.** a momentary sight or view. **2.** a vague idea; inkling. –v.t. (**glimpsed, glimpsing**) **3.** to catch a glimpse of. –**glimpser,** n.

glint /glɪnt/ n. **1.** a gleam or glimmer; flash. **2.** gleaming brightness; lustre. –v.i. **3.** to gleam or flash.

glissando /glɪˈsændoʊ/ n. (*pl.* **glissandi** /glɪˈsændi/) *Music* any sliding effect performed on a musical instrument especially by sliding one finger rapidly over the keys of a piano or strings of a harp.

glisten /'glɪsən/ v.i. **1.** to shine with a sparkling light, especially as a result of being wet. –n. **2.** a glistening; sparkle. –**glisteningly,** adv.

glitch /glɪtʃ/ n. **1.** an extraneous electric current or signal, especially one that interferes in some way with the functioning of a system. **2.** *Computers* an intermittent or minor error in the hardware or software, especially when the source is unknown. **3.** a hitch; snag; malfunction.

glitter /'glɪtə/ v.i. **1.** to shine with a brilliant, sparkling light or lustre. **2.** to make a brilliant show: *glittering scenes of a court.* –n. **3.** glittering light or lustre. **4.** shiny ornamental metallic fragments, usually coloured, designed to be sprinkled onto some form of adhesive. –**glitteringly,** adv.

glitz /glɪts/ n. *Colloq.* conspicuous luxury of dubious taste. –**glitzy,** adj.

gloat /gloʊt/ v.i. **1.** to gaze with exultation; dwell mentally upon something with intense (and often evil) satisfaction: *to gloat over another's misfortunes.* **2.** to smile smugly or scornfully; to display complacency. –n. **3.** the act of gloating. –**gloater,** n. –**gloatingly,** adv.

glob /glɒb/ n. *Colloq.* a rounded lump of some soft but pliable substance: *a glob of cream.*

global /'gloʊbəl/ adj. **1.** spherical; globe-shaped. **2.** relating to or covering the whole world; international. **3.** all-embracing; comprehensive. **4.** (of a computer command) operating over an entire database, set of records, etc. –n. **5.** a computer operation performed on an entire document, database, etc. –**globally,** adv.

global commons *pl. n.* parts of the world which no individual or state may own, as the oceans, the atmosphere, outer space, and Antarctica (the last-named subject to the Antarctic Treaty, 1959).

globalisation /ˌgloʊbəlaɪˈzeɪʃən/ n. **1.** the process of becoming international in scope, application or influence: *the globalisation of the mining industry; the globalisation of the English language.* **2.** the perceived development of a single worldwide economy and culture, brought about by the removal of restrictions to international trade, travel and mass communication, seen by some as leading to a more equitable distribution of wealth and resources among nations, and by others to their more unequal distribution in favour of already wealthy industrialised nations, and to the loss of cultural diversity. Also, **globalization.**

globalise /'gloʊbəlaɪz/ v.t. **1.** to cause to become international in scope, application or influence: *the company plans to globalise its operations.* –v.i. **2.** to become international in scope, application or influence: *the industry has globalised rapidly.* Also, **globalize.**

globalism /'gloʊbəlɪzəm/ n. **1.** the pursuit of globalisation. **2.** the worldwide integration of economies with subsequent threats to national cultural and political independence. –**globalist,** n., adj.

global positioning system *n.* → GPS.

global warming *n.* a long-term gradual increase in the average global surface temperature, particularly one associated with the increase in greenhouse gases.

globe /gloʊb/ n. **1.** (usu. preceded by *the*) the earth. **2.** a planet or other celestial body. **3.** a sphere on which is depicted a map of the earth (terrestrial globe) or of the heavens (celestial globe). **4.** anything more or less spherical, such as a lampshade or a glass fishbowl. **5.** *Aust., NZ* → **bulb** (def. 3).

globetrotter /'gloʊbtrɒtə/ n. *Colloq.* someone who travels widely, especially for sightseeing. –**globetrotting,** n., adj.

globule /'glɒbjul/ n. a small spherical body. –**globular,** adj.

glocal /'gloʊkəl/ adj. able to operate at a local level within a global framework.

glockenspiel /'glɒkənspil, -kənʃpil/ n. *Music* a set of steel bars mounted in a frame and struck with hammers, used in military bands.

gloom[1] /glum/ n. darkness; dimness.

gloom[2] /glum/ n. **1.** a state of melancholy or depression; low spirits. **2.** a despondent look or expression. –**gloomy,** adj.

glorify /'glɔrəfaɪ/ v.t. (**-fied, -fying**) **1.** to magnify with praise; extol. **2.** to transform into something more splendid. **3.** to make glorious; invest with glory. **4.** to promote the glory of (God); ascribe glory and praise in adoration to (God). –**glorification** /ˌglɔrəfəˈkeɪʃən/, n. –**glorifiable,** adj. –**glorifier,** n. –**glorified,** adj.

glorious /'glɔriəs/ adj. **1.** admirable; delightful: *we had a glorious time.* **2.** conferring glory: *a glorious victory.* **3.** full of glory; entitled to great renown: *a glorious hero.* **4.** brilliantly beautiful: *the glorious heavens.* –**gloriously,** adv. –**gloriousness,** n.

glory /'glɔri/ n. (*pl.* **glories**) **1.** exalted praise, honour, or distinction, accorded by common consent: *paths of glory.* **2.** something that makes honoured or illustrious; a distinguished ornament; an object of pride. **3.** adoring praise or thanksgiving: *give glory to God.* **4.** resplendent beauty or magnificence: *the glory of God.* **5.** a state of splendour, magnificence, or greatest prosperity. **6.** a state of contentment, as one resulting from a triumphant achievement. **7.** the splendour and bliss of heaven; heaven. **8.** a ring, circle, or surrounding radiance of light represented about the head or the whole figure of a sacred person, as Christ, a saint, etc.; a halo, nimbus, or aureole. –v.i. (**gloried, glorying**) **9.** to exult with triumph; rejoice proudly. –*interj.* Also, **Glory be!. 10.** (*upper case*) a mild expression of surprise, elation, or exultation. –*phr.* **11. glory in,** to be boastful about; exult arrogantly in.

glory box *n.* a chest in which young women store clothes, linen, etc., in expectation of being married; bottom drawer; hope chest.

gloss[1] /glɒs/ n. **1.** a superficial lustre: *gloss of satin.* **2.** an external show; specious appearance. –v.t. **3.** to put a gloss upon; explain away. –*phr.* **4. gloss over,** to give a specious interpretation of; explain away: *to gloss over a mistake.* –**glosser,** n. –**glossless,** adj. –**glossy,** adj.

gloss[2] /glɒs/ n. **1.** an explanation in a foot-note of a technical or unusual expression in a text. **2.** a glossary. **3.** a cleverly misleading explanation. –v.t. **4.** to put glosses on; annotate. **5.** (oft. fol. by *over*) to cover up; explain away: *to gloss over a mistake.* –**glosser,** n.

glossary /'glɒsəri/ n. (*pl.* **-ries**) a list of technical, dialectal, and difficult terms in a subject or field, or in a particular text, with definitions. –**glossarial** /glɒˈsɛəriəl/, adj. –**glossarist,** n.

-glot a suffix indicating proficiency in language, as in *polyglot.*

glottis /'glɒtəs/ n. *Anat.* the opening at the upper part of the larynx, between the vocal cords.

glove /glʌv/ *n.* **1.** a covering for the hand, made with a separate sheath for each finger and for the thumb. **2.** → **boxing glove**. *–v.t.* **3.** to cover with or as with a glove; provide with gloves. **4.** to serve as a glove for. **5.** *Cricket* **a.** (of the person batting) to play (a ball) off the batting glove. **b.** (of the wicketkeeper) to catch or stop (a ball). *–phr.* **6. take off the gloves**, to become overly aggressive. **7. take up the glove**, See **gauntlet**¹ (def. 3). **8. throw down the glove**, See **gauntlet**¹ (def. 4). **–gloveless**, *adj.*

glove box *n.* **1.** Also, **glove compartment**. a small compartment in a car, usually set into the dashboard, for the storage of small articles. **2.** a metal box used by workers who need to manipulate radioactive materials, or materials requiring a dust-free, sterile, or inert atmosphere; manipulation is carried out by means of gloves attached to ports in the walls of the box.

glow /gloʊ/ *n.* **1.** the light given out by an extremely hot substance; incandescence. **2.** brightness of colour. **3.** a state of bodily heat. **4.** warmth of feeling, etc.; ardour. *–v.i.* **5.** to give out bright light and heat without flame. **6.** to shine like something strongly heated. **7.** to show a strong, bright colour. **8.** to be extremely hot. **9.** to show strong feelings; show enthusiasm: *she was glowing with pride.*

glower /ˈgloʊə, ˈglaʊə/ *v.i.* **1.** to look angrily; stare with sullen dislike or discontent. *–n.* **2.** a glowering look; frown. **–gloweringly**, *adv.*

glowing /ˈgloʊɪŋ/ *adj.* **1.** incandescent. **2.** rich and warm in colouring: *glowing colours.* **3.** exhibiting the glow of health, excitement, etc. **4.** ardent or impassioned; enthusiastic: *a glowing account.* **–glowingly**, *adv.*

glow-worm *n.* **1.** a firefly, especially the wingless female or the luminous larva. **2.** the larva of certain fungus flies such as, in New Zealand, *Bolitophila luminosa.*

gluco- a prefix indicating the presence of glucose.

glucosamine /gluˈkoʊsəmɪn/ *n.* an amino sugar required as a basis for all nitrogen-containing sugars; used in the treatment of osteoarthritis.

glucose /ˈglukoʊz, -oʊs/ *n.* **1.** *Chem.* hexose, a sugar $C_6H_{12}O_6$, the D- form of which (dextrose) occurs in many fruits, animal tissues, and fluids, etc., and has a sweetness about one half that of ordinary sugar. **2.** a syrup containing dextrose, maltose, and dextrin, obtained by the incomplete hydrolysis of starch.

glue /glu/ *n.* **1.** any adhesive substance made from any natural or synthetic resin or material. *–v.t.* (**glued, gluing**) **2.** to join or fasten with glue. **3.** to fix or attach firmly, as if with glue; make adhere closely. **–gluer**, *n.* **–gluey**, *adj.*

gluggy /ˈglʌgi/ *adj.* (**-gier, -giest**) *Colloq.* sticky.

glum /glʌm/ *adj.* (**glummer, glummest**) gloomily sullen or silent; dejected. **–glumly**, *adv.* **–glumness**, *n.*

glut /glʌt/ *v.t.* (**glutted, glutting**) **1.** to feed or fill to satiety; sate: *to glut the appetite.* **2.** to feed or fill to excess; cloy. **3.** to choke up: *glut a channel.* *–n.* **4.** a full supply. **5.** a surfeit. *–phr.* **6. glut the market**, to overstock the market; furnish a supply of any article largely in excess of the demand, so that the price is unusually low.

gluten /ˈglutn/ *n.* **1.** the tough, viscid nitrogenous substance remaining when the flour of wheat or other grain is washed to remove the starch. **2.** glue, or some gluey substance.

gluten-free *adj.* **1.** of or relating to forms of wheat prepared so that they are without gluten, required for people with coeliac disease. **2.** of or relating to foods prepared with such wheat: *gluten-free bread.* *Abbrev.:* GF

glutinous /ˈglutənəs/ *adj.* resembling glue; gluey; viscid; sticky. **–glutinously**, *adv.* **–glutinousness, glutinosity** /glutəˈnɒsəti/, *n.*

glutton /ˈglʌtn/ *n.* **1.** someone who eats to excess; a gormandiser. **2.** someone who indulges in something excessively. *–phr.* **3. a glutton for punishment**, someone who is eager to undertake arduous tasks that one would normally avoid. **–gluttonous**, *adj.* **–gluttony**, *n.*

glyceride /ˈglɪsəraɪd/ *n. Chem.* one of a group of esters obtained from glycerol in combination with acids.

glycerine /glɪsəˈrin, ˈglɪsərən/ *n. Chem.* → **glycerol**. Also, **glycerin** /ˈglɪsərən/.

glycerol /ˈglɪsərɒl/ *n.* a colourless, odourless, liquid alcohol, $HOCH_2CHOHCH_2OH$, of syrupy consistency and sweet taste, obtained by the saponification of natural fats and oils, and used as a solvent, plasticiser, or sweetener.

glycogen /ˈglaɪkədʒən/ *n.* a form of sugar found in liver and muscle; readily converted into glucose, it provides the body with a carbohydrate store of energy. **–glycogenic** /glaɪkəˈdʒɛnɪk/, *adj.*

glycolysis /glaɪˈkɒləsəs/ *n. Physiol.* a metabolic process by which glucose (or another sugar) is converted into a simple form, during which process energy is released.

GM /dʒi ˈɛm/ *adj.* → **genetically-modified**.

gnarl /nal/ *n.* **1.** a knotty protuberance on a tree; knot. *–v.t.* **2.** to twist.

gnarled /nald/ *adj.* **1.** (of trees) full of or covered with gnarls. **2.** (of persons) **a.** having a rugged, weather-beaten appearance. **b.** cross-grained; perverse; cantankerous. Also, **gnarly**.

gnash /næʃ/ *v.t.* **1.** to grind (the teeth) together, especially in rage or pain. **2.** to bite with grinding teeth.

gnat /næt/ *n.* **1.** any of various small dipterous insects, such as a non-biting midge of the family Chironomidae. **2.** *Chiefly Brit.* a mosquito.

gnaw /nɔ/ *verb* (**gnawed, gnawed** *or* **gnawn, gnawing**) *–v.t.* **1.** to wear away little by little by persistent biting. **2.** to make by gnawing. **3.** to corrode; consume. **4.** to consume with passion; torment. *–v.i.* **5.** to bite persistently. **–gnawer**, *n.*

gneiss /ˈnaɪs/ *n.* a coarse-grained metamorphic rock, generally made up of bands which differ in colour and composition, some bands being rich in feldspar and quartz, others rich in hornblende or mica. **–gneissic**, *adj.*

gnocchi /ˈnjɒki, ˈnɒki/ *pl. n.* small dumplings made from potato and flour or semolina.

gnome /noʊm/ *n.* **1.** one of a species of diminutive beings said in stories to inhabit the interior of the earth and to act as guardians of its treasures, usually thought of as shrivelled little old men. **2.** Also, **garden gnome**. a small statue of a gnome, usually displayed as a garden decoration. **3.** a person thought to exercise some mysterious and sinister influence, especially on world economic affairs. **–gnomish**, *adj.*

gnomic /ˈnoʊmɪk, ˈnɒm-/ *adj.* like or containing gnomes or aphorisms. **–gnomically**, *adv.*

gnu /nu/ *n.* (*pl.* **gnus** *or, especially collectively,* **gnu**) → **wildebeest**.

go /goʊ/ *verb* (**went, gone, going**) *–v.i.* **1.** to move or pass (in a direction specified); proceed. **2.** to move away or out; depart (opposed to *come*). **3.** *Cricket* to be dismissed. **4.** to keep or be in motion; act, work, or run: *the clock's not going.* **5.** to act or perform so as to achieve a specified state or condition. **6.** to move towards a point or a given result or in a given manner; proceed; advance. **7.** to be known: *to go by a name.* **8.** to reach or extend: *this road goes to the city.* **9.** (of time) to pass; elapse. **10.** to be awarded, transferred, or applied to a particular recipient or purpose. **11.** to be sold: *the property went for a song.* **12.** to conduce or tend: *this only goes to prove the point.* **13.** to turn out: *how did the game go?* **14.** to belong; have a place: *this book goes on the top shelf.* **15.** (sometimes fol. by *with*) (of colours, etc.) to harmonise; be compatible; be suited. **16.** to fit into, round, etc. **17.** to be used up, finished or consumed. **18.** to develop, especially with reference to success, or failure: *we'll have to see how things go.* **19.** to be phrased: *how do the words go?* **20.** to resort; have recourse: *to go to court.* **21.** to be given up; be worn out; be lost or ended. **22.** to die. **23.** to fail; give way. **24.** to begin; come into action: *here goes!* **25.** to be acceptable: *anything goes.* **26.** to carry final authority: *what I say goes.* **27.** to contribute to a result: *the items which go to make up a total.* *–v. (copular)* **28.** to become; assume another state or condition: *the teacher went mad; the plan may go wrong.* **29.** to make (a sound, effect, etc.) when operated: *the gun went bang.* **30.** to continue; be habitually in a specified condition: *to go hungry.* *–v.t.* **31.** to proceed on: *he went his way.* **32.** *Cards* to bid. **33.** *Colloq.* **a.** to say: *So I go, 'What are you doing?', and he goes, 'Nothing.'* **b.** to think: *But then I went, 'Oh no, what have I done?'* **34.** *Colloq.* to attack, especially physically. *–n.* (pl. **goes**) **35.** the act of going: *the come and go of the seasons.* **36.** *Colloq.* energy, spirit, or animation: *to be full of go.* **37.** *Colloq.* one's turn to play or to make an attempt at something. **38.** *US Colloq.* a bargain. *–adj.* **39.** ready; functioning properly: *all instruments are go.* *–phr.* **40. a rum go**, *Colloq.* a strange or inexplicable situation. **41. as ... go**, as is the normal run of ...: *she's quite young as grandmothers go.* **42. as things go**, as is the usual way. **43. be (all) the go**, *Colloq.* to be fashionable. **44. could go a ...**, *Colloq.* to want (something specified, especially food or drink): *I could go a cool drink.* **45. fair go**, *NZ Colloq., Aust.* **a.** a fair or reasonable course of action: *do you think that's a fair go?* **b.** a chance to get on with something without interference or distraction. **c.** an appeal for fairness or reason: *fair go, mate!* **46. from go to whoa**, *Colloq.* from beginning to end. **47. from the word go**, *Colloq.* from the beginning. **48. get a go on**, *Colloq.* to move more quickly: *we'll have to get a go on.* **49. give it a go**, *Colloq.* to make an attempt. **50. go about**, *Naut.* to change course. **51. go ahead**, **a.** to proceed. **b.** to take the lead; be in the forefront: *the big horse went ahead soon after the start.* **52. go all out**, *Colloq.* to expend the utmost energy. **53. go all the way**, *Colloq.* to have full sexual intercourse. **54. go all the way with**, **a.** to support wholeheartedly; agree with absolutely. **b.** *Sport* to equal; match. **55. go a long way toward(s)**, to make largely possible. **56. go along with**, to agree with; accept. **57. go around**, **a.** to move about; circulate. **b.** to be enough for all: *enough food to go around.* **58. go around with**, *Colloq.* **a.** to keep the company of (someone in whom one has a romantic interest). **b.** to maintain a friendship with (a person or group of people). **59. go at**, **a.** to undertake with vigour. **b.** to attack. **60. go back on**, **a.** to fail (someone); let (someone) down. **b.** to fail to keep (one's word, promise, etc.). **61. go by**, **a.** to pass. **b.** to be guided by. **62. go down**, **a.** to descend. **b.** to slope down. **c.** to be defeated. **d.** to be remembered by posterity. **e.** (of the sun) to set. **f.** to fall ill: *he has gone down with the mumps.* **g.** to be received (as specified): *the play went down well with the critics; how did your suggestion go down?* **h.** *Colloq.* to be sent to prison. **i.** *Brit.* to leave university at the end of the term or permanently. **j.** *Bridge* to fail to make one's contract. **k.** *Mining* to sink a shaft on a claim. **l.** *Boxing* to be knocked to the canvas or to slip to the canvas. **m.** *Colloq.* to happen. **n.** *Colloq.* (taboo) to perform oral sex. **63. go down on**, *Colloq.* (taboo) to perform oral sex on. **64. go for**, **a.** to attack; set upon. **b.** *Colloq.* to be attracted to: *I go for music in a big way.* **c.** to aim for: *he's going for the chairmanship.* **d.** to apply to: *that goes for all of us.* **65. go for it**, *Colloq.* an exclamation of encouragement or

exhortation, especially to a sporting competitor. **66. go for one's life**, *Colloq.* **a.** to indulge in any activity to the maximum. **b.** to move very quickly, as in running away. **67. go for your life**, *Colloq.* an expression giving support, encouragement, etc., to someone about to undertake an energetic activity. **68. go halves**, to share equally between two. **69. go in for**, to make (something) one's particular interest. **70. go into**, **a.** to investigate or study thoroughly. **b.** *Maths* to be a divisor of: *how many times does 4 go into 12?* **c.** *Maths* to be a factor of: *4 goes into 12.* **71. go in with**, to enter a partnership or other agreement with. **72. go it alone**, *Colloq.* to act alone. **73. go missing**, **a.** to become lost. **b.** to absent oneself. **74. go native**, to turn one's back on the comforts of civilisation and adopt a primitive style of life in a natural environment. **75. go off**, **a.** to go away: *she went off without a word.* **b.** to discharge; explode. **c.** (of food, etc.) to become bad; deteriorate: *the meat's gone off.* **d.** to take place (in a specified manner): *the rehearsal went off well.* **e.** *Colloq.* to get married. **f.** *Aust. Colloq.* to be raided by the police: *that club hasn't gone off in six months.* **g.** *Aust. Colloq.* to be stolen: *when I returned to the room my camera had gone off.* **h.** *Aust. Colloq.* (of a racehorse) to be set to win in a fixed race: *tell me when your horse is going off.* **i.** *Colloq.* to come to dislike. **j.** *Colloq.* (of a venue) to be full of a lively crowd enjoying itself: *that place goes off on a Saturday night.* **k.** *Colloq.* (of a party, dinner, event, etc.) to achieve a level of excitement that makes it a success: *last night's party really went off!* **76. go off at**, *Colloq.* to reprimand; scold. **77. go off one's head**, *Colloq.* **a.** to become insane. **b.** to become very angry. **78. go off pop**, *Colloq.* to lose one's temper suddenly and explosively. **79. go off the bite**, (of fish) to cease taking the bait. **80. go off the deep end**, *Colloq.* to become violently agitated; lose control of one's emotions. **81. go on**, **a.** to go ahead; proceed; continue. **b.** to manage; do. **c.** to behave; act. **d.** to take place. **e.** to chatter continually. **f.** an exclamation of astonishment verging on disbelief. **g.** to use as evidence or material. **h.** *Colloq.* to get near (an age or a time): *he's going on seventy; it's going on midnight.* **82. go out**, **a.** to be extinguished: *the light went out.* **b.** to attend social functions, etc. **c.** *Cards* to dispose of the last card in one's hand. **d.** to be broadcast. **e.** *Colloq.* to lose consciousness: *he went out like a light.* **83. go out with**, to frequent the society of; date regularly. **84. go over**, **a.** to read or re-read. **b.** to repeat. **c.** to examine. **d.** to have an effect (as specified): *my proposal went over very badly.* **e.** *Rugby Football* to score a try. **f.** to change sides, political allegiance, etc. **85. go places**, *Colloq.* to achieve notable success. **86. go round to**, to make a visit to. **87. go soft**, **a.** to deteriorate intellectually, morally, or physically. **b.** to become less severe. **88. go spare**, *Colloq.* to lose one's temper; become exasperated. **89. go the ...**, *Colloq.* to perform using the action indicated: *go the knuckle.* **90. go there**, (*usu. in the negative*) *Colloq.* to touch on a subject matter considered sensitive: *he has some very strange habits, but let's not go there.* **91. go through**, **a.** to undergo; endure. **b.** to examine in order. **c.** to be accepted. **d.** to consume: *we go through three litres of milk a day.* **e.** to deal with quickly and thoroughly: *the shearer went through the mob in a day.* **92. go through with**, to complete; bring to a finish. **93. go to**, to be relevant to; address. **94. go to bed with**, *Colloq.* to have sexual intercourse with. **95. go to it**, to undertake any activity with gusto. **96. go to show**, to serve as evidence; to help to prove. **97. go under**, to be overwhelmed; be ruined. **98. go up**, **a.** to rise or ascend; advance. **b.** *Brit.* to go to university for the first time or at the beginning of term. **99. go wild**, **a.** to revert to an untamed or uncivilised state. **b.** to respond very demonstratively or with extreme emotion, usually pleasure: *the crowd went wild when the home team won*. **100. go with, a.** to harmonise with. **b.** *Colloq.* to frequent the society of: *he went with a rough group at school.* **c.** *Colloq.* to be in an amorous or sexual relationship with. **101. go without,** to manage without; get along in the absence of, usually something agreeable. **102. go without saying,** to be self-evident. **103. have a go,** *Colloq.* **a.** to make an attempt; try: *come on, have a go!* **b.** *Cricket* to hit out recklessly. **104. how are you going?,** *Aust.* a conventional greeting, not necessarily seeking an answer. **105. it's a go,** *Colloq.* it's possible; all's clear. **106. let go, a.** to release. **b.** to give free rein to (one's emotion, etc.), especially in making an attack. **107. let go of,** to release one's hold on. **108. let oneself go, a.** to cease to care for one's appearance. **b.** to become uninhibited. **109. make a go of,** *Colloq.* to turn (something) into a success. **110. no go,** *Colloq.* not possible; futile; vain. **111. not go much on,** *Colloq.* not to be attracted to or enthused by: *I don't go much on him.* **112. on the go,** *Colloq.* constantly going; very active. **113. open go,** *Colloq.* **a.** a situation in which fair play prevails and no unfair restraints or limiting conditions apply: *the election was an open go.* **b.** a situation in which normal restraints do not apply: *it was open go at the bar that night.* **114. ready, set** (or **steady**), **go,** a command to begin a race, contest, etc. **115. that's the way it goes,** *Colloq.* that's how things are. **116. the go,** *Aust. Colloq.* the recommended or best course of action: *the go is to be there early.*

goad /ɡoʊd/ *n.* **1.** a stick with a pointed end, for driving cattle, etc. **2.** anything that pricks or wounds like such a stick; a stimulus. –*v.t.* **3.** to prick or drive with or as with a goad; incite. –**goadlike,** *adj.*

go-ahead *adj.* **1.** going forward; advancing. **2.** progressive; active; enterprising. –*n.* **3.** permission to proceed.

goal /ɡoʊl/ *n.* **1.** that towards which effort is directed; aim or end. **2.** (in ball games) an area, basket, cage, object or structure towards which the players strive to advance the ball, etc. **3.** the act of throwing or kicking the ball through or over the goal, thus qualifying for a score. **4.** the score made by accomplishing this. –**goalless,** *adj.*

goalkeeper /ˈɡoʊlkipə/ *n.* *Soccer, Hockey, etc.* a player whose special duty is to prevent the ball from going through, into, or over the goal.

goanna /ɡoʊˈænə/ *n.* any of various large Australian varanid (monitor) lizards such as the common lace monitor, *Varanus varius*, which occurs generally throughout mainland Australia.

goat /ɡoʊt/ *n.* **1.** any bovid animal of the tribe Caprini, comprising various agile hollow-horned ruminants closely related to the sheep, found native in rocky and mountainous regions of Africa, Asia and Europe, and including domesticated forms common throughout the world. **2.** any of various allied animals, as *Oreamnos montanus* (**Rocky Mountain goat**), a ruminant of western North America. **3.** *Colloq.* a scapegoat; someone who is the butt of a joke. **4.** *Colloq.* a fool: *to make a goat of oneself.* **5.** *Colloq.* a lecher; a licentious man. **6.** (*pl.*) (in collocations with *sheep*) evil, bad, or inferior people or things: *to separate the sheep from the goats.* –*phr. Colloq.* **7. act the (giddy) goat,** to behave in a foolish or frivolous manner; fool around. **8. get (on) someone's goat,** to annoy or irritate someone. **9. hairy goat,** a racehorse which does not perform well. **10. run like a hairy goat, a.** to run very slowly. **b.** to run very fast.

goatee /ɡoʊˈti/ *n.* a man's beard trimmed to a tuft or a point on the chin.

go-away money *n.* *Colloq.* a financial settlement made by an employer to an employee who has been

dismissed to persuade them not to pursue claims of unfair dismissal.

gob[1] /ɡɒb/ *n.* a mass or lump.

gob[2] /ɡɒb/ *n.* *Colloq.* the mouth.

gobble[1] /ˈɡɒbəl/ *v.t.* **1.** to swallow hastily in large pieces; gulp. **2.** to seize upon greedily or eagerly. –*v.i.* **3.** to eat hastily. –**gobbler,** *n.*

gobble[2] /ˈɡɒbəl/ *v.i.* to make the characteristic throaty cry of a turkey cock.

gobbledegook /ˈɡɒbldiˌɡʊk, -ˌɡuk/ *n.* *Colloq.* language characterised by circumlocution and jargon: *the gobbledegook of government reports.* Also, **gobbledygook.**

go-between *n.* someone who acts as agent between persons or parties.

goblet /ˈɡɒblət/ *n.* a drinking vessel with a foot and stem.

goblin /ˈɡɒblən/ *n.* a grotesque mischievous sprite or elf.

gobsmacked /ˈɡɒbsmækt/ *adj.* *Colloq.* astonished; flabbergasted.

go-cart *n.* **1.** a small, wheeled vehicle for small children to ride in. **2.** → **go-kart.**

god /ɡɒd/ *n.* **1.** a supernatural being or entity which is worshipped, revered, propitiated, or entreated according to particular conventions, and is believed to control nature or human destiny, often being associated with a particular aspect or facet of these: *among Hawaiians the god of war was called Kukailimoko.* **2.** the image of such a being or entity; idol: *she refused to bow down to any god of stone.* **3.** (*upper case*) (according to Jewish, Christian, Islamic, and certain other theologies) the one Supreme Being, the creator and ruler of the universe: *in the beginning God created the heaven and the earth.* **4.** any person or practice to which excessive attention or devotion is given: *George made a god of horseracing.* –*phr.* **5. for God's sake,** Also, **for godsake(s),** **for Godsake(s).** an exclamation indicating surprise, vexation, indignation, etc.: *for God's sake, shut up!* **6. God,** Also, **Oh God, My God.** an oath or exclamation used to express weariness, annoyance, disappointment, etc.: *oh God! will it never end?* **7. God's gift to ...,** *Colloq.* (*often ironic*) a truly wonderful person in a specified sphere of interest: *God's gift to the business world*; *God's gift to women.* **8. God's own, a.** an intensifier: *God's own good health.* **b.** (of a country) the best; a paradise. **9. good God,** an exclamation indicating surprise, consternation, etc. **10. the gods,** the highest gallery in a theatre: *the crowd in the gods was becoming restless.*

godchild /ˈɡɒdtʃaɪld/ *n.* (*pl.* **-children**) someone for whom a person (godparent) stands sponsor at baptism.

goddaughter /ˈɡɒddɔtə/ *n.* a female godchild.

goddess /ˈɡɒdɛs, ˈɡɒdəs/ *n.* **1.** a female god or deity. **2.** a woman of extraordinary beauty. **3.** an adored woman. –**goddess-hood, goddess-ship,** *n.*

godfather /ˈɡɒdfaðə/ *n.* a man who stands sponsor for a child at baptism or confirmation.

godforsaken /ˈɡɒdfəseɪkən/ *adj.* desolate; remote.

Godhead /ˈɡɒdhɛd/ *n.* **1.** the essential being of God; the Supreme Being. **2.** (*lower case*) a deity; god or goddess.

godly /ˈɡɒdli/ *adj.* (**-lier, -liest**) conforming to God's laws; pious. –**godlily,** *adv.* –**godliness,** *n.*

godmother /ˈɡɒdmʌðə/ *n.* a woman who stands sponsor for a child at baptism or confirmation.

godparent /ˈɡɒdpɛərənt/ *n.* a godfather or godmother.

God particle *n.* *Colloq.* → **Higgs boson.**

godsend /ˈɡɒdsɛnd/ *n.* something unexpected but particularly welcome and timely, as if sent by God.

godson /ˈɡɒdsʌn/ *n.* a male godchild.

godspeed /ɡɒdˈspid/ *Archaic* –*interj.* **1.** an expression of good wishes to someone taking a journey. –*n.* **2.** a wish of success to someone setting out on a journey or undertaking.

godwit /ˈgɒdwɪt/ *n.* any of several large shorebirds of the genus *Limosa*, all with long, slightly up-curved bills, two species of which, the **bar-tailed godwit**, *L. lapponica*, and the **black-tailed godwit**, *L. limosa*, regularly migrate to coastal areas of Australia.

goer /ˈgoʊə/ *n. Colloq.* **1.** a person or thing that moves fast. **2.** a person who is characterised by great energy in all their activities. **3.** any activity, project, etc., having evident prospects of success.

-goer a word element indicating habitual attendance at whatever is specified in the combining element, as *churchgoer, filmgoer.*

goes /ˈɡoʊz/ *v.* **1.** 3rd person singular present of **go**. *–n.* **2.** plural of **go**.

goggle /ˈgɒgəl/ *n.* **1.** (*pl.*) → **goggles**. *–v.i.* **2.** to stare with bulging eyes. **3.** to roll the eyes.

goggles /ˈgɒgəlz/ *pl. n.* spectacles often with special rims, lenses, or sidepieces, so devised as to protect the eyes from wind, dust, water, or glare.

going-over /goʊɪŋ-ˈoʊvə/ *n.* (*pl.* **goings-over**) *Colloq.* **1.** a thorough examination. **2.** a severe beating or thrashing.

goings-on /ˌgoʊɪŋz-ˈɒn/ *pl. n. Colloq.* **1.** actions; conduct; behaviour (used chiefly with depreciative force): *we were shocked by the goings-on at the office party.* **2.** current events: *she only kept in touch with the goings-on at home through newspapers.*

goitre /ˈgɔɪtə/ *n. Pathol.* an enlargement of the thyroid gland, on the front and sides of the neck. Also, *US*, **goiter**.

go-kart /ˈgoʊ-kat/ *n.* a small light vehicle, especially one without bodywork, having a low-powered engine, used for relatively safe racing. Also, **go-cart, kart**.

gold /goʊld/ *n.* **1.** a precious yellow metal, non-rusting, and able to be moulded. *Symbol*: Au; *atomic number*: 79; *relative atomic mass*: 196.967. **2.** money; wealth. **3.** something compared to this metal in brightness, preciousness, etc.: *a heart of gold.* **4.** a bright metallic yellow colour, sometimes shading towards brown. *–adj.* **5.** consisting of, or like gold. **6.** *Colloq.* fantastic; wonderful: *that's a gold idea; that's gold.*

gold disc *n.* a musical recording that is certified as having sold a certain number of copies, a gold-covered disc, formerly a record (**gold record**), being produced as recognition of this and presented to artists and other people involved in its production and promotion; in Australia, awarded for 35 000 sales.

golden /ˈgoʊldən/ *adj.* **1.** of the colour of gold; yellow: *golden hair.* **2.** made of gold: *golden keys.* **3.** like gold in value; excellent: *a golden chance.* **4.** gifted; likely to succeed: *golden girl.* **5.** relating to the fiftieth event of a series, as a wedding anniversary. *–***goldenly**, *adv.* *–***goldenness**, *n.*

Golden Delicious *n.* a variety of large, yellow-skinned apple, first produced in the US.

golden goal *n.* (in soccer, hockey, etc.) a goal scored in extra time which wins the game for the team which scored it and ends the match.

golden handshake *n. Colloq.* a gratuity or benefit, given to employees as a recognition of their services on the occasion of their retirement or resignation, or as compensation when they are dismissed.

golden mean *n.* the happy medium between extremes; moderate course of action.

golden opportunity *n.* a chance to do something that is extremely rare and ideally suited to one's current circumstances.

golden point *n. Rugby League* a match-winning point produced from a try, penalty goal, or field goal in extra

time when the teams are drawn at the end of 80 minutes.

golden retriever *n.* one of a breed of retrievers with thick, wavy, golden coat.

golden staph /goʊldən ˈstæf/ *n.* a pathogenic species of staphylococcus, *Staphylococcus aureus*, which causes boils, septic infections, bacterial food poisoning, etc., and usually forms a golden pigment.

golden syrup *n.* a supersaturated solution of sucrose, glucose, and fructose, derived from sugar processing; used in cookery and as a sauce for porridge, desserts, etc.

golden wattle *n.* **1.** a broad-leafed Australian acacia, *Acacia pycnantha*, yielding useful gum and tanbark; floral emblem of the Commonwealth of Australia. **2.** any similar acacia, especially the Sydney golden wattle, *A. longifolia.*

goldfield /ˈgoʊldfild/ *n.* a district in which gold is mined.

goldfinch /ˈgoʊldfɪntʃ/ *n.* a small songbird, *Carduelis carduelis*, of Eurasia and northern Africa, having a crimson face and wings marked with yellow, introduced into south-eastern mainland Australia from where it has extended its territory to Tasmania.

goldfish /ˈgoʊldfɪʃ/ *n.* a small fish, *Carassius auratus*, of the carp family and originally native to China, prized for aquariums and pools because of its golden colouring and variable form (produced by artificial selection); introduced, feral, and now quite widespread in the southern half of Australia.

gold leaf *n.* gold beaten into a very thin sheet, used for gilding, etc.

goldmine /ˈgoʊldmaɪn/ *n.* **1.** a mine yielding gold. **2.** a source of great wealth. **3.** a source of anything required: *a goldmine of information.* –**goldminer**, *n.* –**goldmining**, *n.*

gold reserve *n. Econ.* the total gold coin and bullion held by a central authority either national or international. It is used to make international payments, and nationally to maintain the value of the token notes and coinage issued on behalf of the government.

gold rush *n.* a large-scale and rapid movement of people to a region where gold has been discovered, as that to Bendigo and Ballarat, Victoria, in the mid-19th century.

gold standard *n. Econ.* a monetary system in which there is a free mintage of gold into standard legal coins, free movement of gold into and out of the country, and in which the currency unit is based on gold of a fixed weight and fineness.

golf /gɒlf/ *n.* an outdoor game, in which a small resilient ball is driven with special clubs into a series of holes, distributed at various distances over a course having natural or artificial obstacles, the object being to get the ball into each hole in as few strokes as possible. –**golfer**, *n.*

golf ball *n.* a small white ball with a resilient core of rubber used in playing golf.

golf course *n.* the ground or course over which golf is played. Also, **golf links**.

Goliath /gəˈlaɪəθ/ *n.* (*oft. lower case*) a person of great strength or size; a giant.

golliwog /ˈgɒliwɒg/ *n.* a soft, black-faced doll. Also, **gollywog**.

golly /ˈgɒli/ *interj. Colloq.* a mild expletive expressing surprise, etc.

-gon a suffix denoting geometrical figures having a certain number or kind of angles, as in *polygon, pentagon.*

gonad /ˈgoʊnæd/ *n.* **1.** the sex gland, male or female, in which gametes develop and appropriate sex hormones are produced. **2.** (*pl.*) *Colloq.* the testicles. –**gonadal** /goʊˈnædəl/, **gonadial** /goʊˈneɪdiəl/, **gonadic** /goʊˈnædɪk/, *adj.*

gondola /ˈgɒndələ/ *n.* **1.** a long, narrow boat with a high peak at each end and often a small cabin near the middle, used on the Venetian canals and usually propelled at the stern by a single oar or pole. **2.** the car of a airship. **3.** the basket suspended beneath a balloon, for carrying passengers, instruments, etc. **4.** a free-standing tray on legs for displaying goods on a shop floor. –**gondolier**, *n.*

gone /gɒn/ *v.* **1.** past participle of **go**. –*adj.* **2.** departed; left. **3.** lost or hopeless. **4.** used up. **5.** that has departed or passed away; dead. **6.** depleted of stamina (in a specified part of the body): *gone in the legs*. **7.** weak and faint: *a gone feeling*. **8.** pregnant: *three months gone*. **9.** *Colloq.* exhilarated, in a state of excitement (as by the influence of drugs, etc.). **10.** *Colloq.* infatuated: *one look from Harold and she was gone*. **11.** *Colloq.* incapacitated through laughter, drugs, alcohol, over-excitement, etc. –*phr.* **12. far gone**, *Colloq.* out of one's senses with exhaustion, illness, intoxication, insanity, etc. **13. far gone in**, in an advanced state of: *far gone in a disease*. **14. gone a million**, *Aust.*, *NZ Colloq.* utterly defeated or ruined. **15. gone in the head** (or **scone**, etc.), *Colloq.* crazy; insane. **16. gone on**, *Colloq.* infatuated with.

goner /ˈgɒnə/ *n. Colloq.* a person, thing, or situation that is dead, lost, or past recovery or rescue.

gong /gɒŋ/ *n.* **1.** *Music* a musical instrument of Asian origin, comprising a bronze disc with the rim turned up, to be struck with a soft-headed stick. **2.** any saucer-shaped bell, especially one sounded by a hammer. **3.** *Colloq.* a medal. –*phr.* **4. get the gong**, *Colloq.* to receive a peremptory rejection or refusal.

-gonium a word element referring to reproductive cells.

gonna /ˈgʌnə/ *v.* (*in representations of speech*) going to. Also, **gunna**.

gono- a word element meaning 'sexual' or 'reproductive', as in *gonococcus*.

gonorrhoea /gɒnəˈriə/ *n. Pathol.* a contagious disease causing purulent inflammation mainly of the urethra and cervix, but occasionally also causing inflammation of the anus, eye, or pharynx. Also, **gonorrhea**. –**gonorrhoeal**, *adj.*

-gony a word element meaning 'production', 'genesis', 'origination', as in *cosmogony*, *theogony*.

goo /gu/ *n. Colloq.* sticky matter. –**gooey**, *adj.*

good /gʊd/ *adj.* (**better**, **best**) **1.** morally excellent; righteous; pious. **2.** satisfactory in quality, quantity, or degree; excellent: *good food, good health* **3.** right; proper; qualified; fit: *do whatever seems good to you, her credit is good.* **4.** well-behaved: *a good child.* **5.** restorative or beneficial: *this medicine is good for you.* **6.** fresh and palatable; not tainted. **7.** honourable or worthy; in good standing: *a good name.* **8.** refined; well-bred; educated. **9.** reliable; safe: *good securities.* **10.** genuine; sound or valid: *good judgement; good reasons.* **11.** loyal; close: *a good friend.* **12.** attractive; fine; beautiful: *she has a good figure.* **13.** (of the complexion) without blemish or flaw. **14.** agreeable; pleasant; genial: *have a good time.* **15.** pleasurable; exciting. **16.** satisfactory for the purpose; advantageous: *a good day for fishing.* **17.** sufficient or ample: *a good supply.* **18.** (of clothes) best or newest. **19.** full: *a good day's journey.* **20.** competent or skilful; clever: *a good manager; good at arithmetic.* **21.** fairly great: *a good deal.* **22.** *Colloq.* in good health; well: *how are you? I'm good, thanks.* –*n.* **23.** profit; worth; advantage; benefit: *to work for the common good.* **24.** excellence or merit; righteousness; kindness; virtue. **25.** (*sometimes upper case*) the force which governs and brings about righteousness and virtue: *to be a power for good.* **26.** a good, commendable, or desirable thing. **27.** (*pl.*) possessions, especially movable effects or personal chattels. **28.** (*pl.*) articles of trade; wares; merchandise, especially that which is transported by land. **29.** an item of merchandise. –*interj.* **30.** an expression of approval or satisfaction. –*phr.* **31. all to the good**, generally advantageous (often used to justify an unpleasant event). **32. (a) good press**, *Colloq.* a favourable reaction by newspapers and journals. **33. a good question**, a difficult or demanding question. **34. a good way**, *Colloq.* a considerable extent. **35. as good as**, in effect; practically: *he as good as said it.* **36. as good as gold**, *Colloq.* (especially of children) well behaved. **37. be up to no good**, *Colloq.* to be doing wrong; to be breaking the law in some undisclosed way; to be behaving in a suspicious manner. **38. do good**, to perform acts of charity; help the needy: *she spends her life doing good.* **39. feel good**, *Colloq.* to be happy or in good health. **40. for good (and all)**, finally and permanently; forever: *to leave a place for good.* **41. good and**, *Colloq.* an intensifier: *you can wait until we're good and ready.* **42. good enough**, *Colloq.* satisfactory. **43. good for**, **a.** valid throughout: *this ticket is good for six months.* **b.** entitling a person to: *that is good for a beer or two.* **c.** (of a person) willing or thought to be willing to provide: *you're always good for a loan.* **44. good for you**, *Colloq.* (*often patronising or ironic*) an expression of approval, encouragement, etc. **45. good grief**, *Colloq.* an expression of surprise, vexation, etc. **46. good iron**, *Colloq.* **a.** an exclamation of approval. **b.** a likeable person. **47. good luck**, an expression wishing a person well. **48. good on you**, *Colloq.* an expression of approval, encouragement, etc. **49. good one**, *Colloq.* an exclamation of praise, admiration, etc. **50. goods and chattels**, **a.** all movable properties. **b.** *Colloq.* all someone's possessions. **51. good show**, *Colloq.* an expression of approval. **52. good to go**, *Colloq.* ready; fully prepared. **53. I'm good**, an expression indicating that the speaker is not in need of what is offered. **54. in good with**, *Colloq.* enjoying the approval of. **55. it's all good**, *Colloq.* an expression of approval, agreement, delight, etc. **56. make good**, **a.** to make recompense for; pay for. **b.** to be successful. **c.** to prove the truth of; substantiate. **57. make good on**, to keep to (an agreement); fulfil (a promise). **58. no good to gundy**, *Colloq.* worthless. **59. one's good lady**, *Colloq.* one's wife. **60. that's a good one**, *Colloq.* an ironic expression of disbelief. **61. the goods**, *Colloq.* **a.** what has been promised or is expected: *to deliver the goods.* **b.** the genuine article. **c.** evidence of guilt, as stolen articles: *to catch them with the goods.* **d.** information; rundown: *did you get the goods on him?* **62. too good to be true**, so satisfactory as to be unbelievable. **63. too much of a good thing**, **a.** excessive. **b.** an excessive amount.

goodbye /gʊdˈbaɪ/ *interj.* **1.** farewell (a conventional expression used at parting). –*n.* (*pl.* **-byes**) **2.** a farewell. –*phr.* **3. kiss something goodbye**, to accept the loss of something. **4. say goodbye to**, to accept the ending or loss of. Also, *Chiefly US*, **goodby**.

good cholesterol *n.* high-density lipoprotein (HDL), seen as being beneficial in that it has a tendency to unclog blood vessels; a high level of this component of cholesterol in the blood is associated with a reduced risk of coronary artery disease. Compare **bad cholesterol**.

Good Friday *n.* the Friday before Easter, a holy day of the Christian church, observed as the anniversary of the crucifixion of Jesus.

goodly /ˈgʊdli/ *adj.* (**-lier**, **-liest**) **1.** of a good quality: *a goodly gift.* **2.** of good or fine appearance. **3.** of good size or amount: *a goodly sum.* –**goodliness**, *n.*

goodness /ˈgʊdnəs/ *n.* **1.** moral excellence; virtue. **2.** kindly feeling; kindness; generosity. **3.** excellence of quality: *goodness of workmanship.* **4.** the best part of anything; essence; strength. **5.** used in various exclamatory or emphatic expressions: *goodness me!; goodness gracious; my goodness; thank goodness! –interj.* **6.** an exclamation expressing mild surprise.

goodnight *interj.* /gʊd'naɪt/ **1.** a conventional expression used when parting during the evening or night. –*n.* /gʊd'naɪt/ **2.** a farewell; a leave-taking. –*adj.* /'gʊdnaɪt/ **3.** of or relating to a parting, especially final or at night: *a goodnight kiss.*

goods and services tax *n.* an indirect tax, usually imposed on the consumption of goods and services and most often calculated on the value that is added at each stage of the manufacturing and distribution process. *Abbrev.*: GST

goodwill /gʊd'wɪl/ *n.* **1.** friendly disposition; benevolence; favour. **2.** cheerful acquiescence. **3.** *Commerce* an intangible, saleable asset arising from the reputation of a business and its relations with its customers, distinct from the value of its stock, etc. –*adj.* **4.** exhibiting or attempting to foster goodwill: *a goodwill mission.* Also, **good will.**

goof /guf, gʊf/ *Colloq.* –*n.* **1.** a foolish or stupid person. –*v.i.* **2.** (sometimes fol. by *on*) to blunder; slip up. –*phr.* **3. goof around,** to act the comedian; clown around. **4. goof off,** to daydream; fritter away time. **5. goof up,** to bungle (something); botch. –**goofy,** *adj.* –**goofily,** *adv.* –**goofiness,** *n.*

goog /gʊg/ *Aust., NZ Colloq.* –*n.* **1.** an egg. –*phr.* **2. full as a goog, a.** extremely drunk. **b.** feeling replete.

google /'gugəl/ (*from trademark*) –*v.i.* **1.** to search for information on the internet, in particular using the Google search engine. –*v.t.* **2.** to search the internet for information about (something), in particular using the Google search engine: *to google the research topic.* –*n.* **3.** an instance of such a search: *to have a little google.*

googly /'gugli/ *n.* (*pl.* **-lies**) *Cricket* a delivery which looks as if it will break one way but in fact goes the other.

goolie /'guli/ *n. Colloq.* (*usu. pl.*) a testicle: *hit in the goolies.* Also, **gooly.**

goon /gun/ *n. Colloq.* **1.** a stupid person. **2.** a hooligan or tough.

goori /'guri/ *n.* → **kuri.** Also, **goorie.**

goose[1] /gus/ *n.* (*pl.* **geese**) **1.** any of numerous wild or domesticated web-footed birds of the family Anatidae, most of them larger and with a longer neck than the ducks; the principal genera are *Anser, Branta,* and *Chen.* **2.** the female of this bird, as distinguished from the male (or *gander*). **3.** the flesh of the goose. **4.** a silly or foolish person; simpleton. –*phr.* **5. cook someone's goose,** *Colloq.* to cause the downfall of someone.

goose[2] /gus/ *v.t. Colloq.* to poke (someone) in the genital and anal regions, usually in fun and unexpectedly.

gooseberry /'gʊzbəri, -bri/ *n.* (*pl.* **-ries**) **1.** the small, edible, acid, globular fruit or berry of certain prevailingly prickly shrubs of the genus *Ribes,* especially *R. grossularia.* **2.** the shrub itself. –*phr.* **3. play gooseberry,** to embarrass or restrict two people who might like to be alone by accompanying them.

goosebumps /'gusbʌmps/ *pl. n.* a rough condition of the skin resembling that of a plucked goose, caused by erection of the papillae and induced by cold, fear, or intense emotion. Also, **goose bumps, goose pimples, goose flesh.**

goose pimples *pl. n.* → **goosebumps.** –**goosepimply,** *adj.*

goosestep /'gusstɛp/ *n.* **1.** a military exercise in which the body is balanced on one foot (without advancing) while the other foot is swung forwards and back. **2.** an exaggerated marching step in which the legs are swung high with straight, stiff knees. –*v.i.* (**-stepped, -stepping**) **3.** to walk or march in a goosestep.

gopher[1] /'goʊfə/ *n.* any of various ground squirrels of western North America, such as *Citellus* (or *Spermophilus*) *tridecemlineatus.*

gopher[2] /'goʊfə/ *n. Colloq.* someone employed to run errands, give general assistance, etc. Also, **gofer.**

gore[1] /gɔ/ *n.* blood that is shed, especially when clotted.

gore[2] /gɔ/ *v.t.* (of an animal) to pierce with the horns or tusks.

gore[3] /gɔ/ *n.* **1.** a triangular piece of cloth, etc., inserted in a garment, a sail, etc., to give greater width or secure the desired shape or adjustment. **2.** one of the breadths (mostly tapering, or shaped) of a woman's skirt.

gorge /gɔdʒ/ *n.* **1.** a narrow valley with steep, rocky walls, especially one through which a stream runs. **2.** the contents of the stomach. **3.** the throat; gullet. –*v.t.* (**gorged, gorging**) **4.** (*mainly reflexive or passive*) to stuff with food: *he gorged himself.* –**gorger,** *n.*

gorgeous /'gɔdʒəs/ *adj.* **1.** sumptuous; magnificent; splendid in appearance or colouring: *she was wearing a gorgeous necklace.* **2.** *Colloq.* very good, pleasing, or enjoyable: *I had a gorgeous weekend.* –**gorgeously,** *adv.* –**gorgeousness,** *n.*

gorilla /gə'rɪlə/ *n.* **1.** either of two species of ground-living, vegetarian, anthropoid apes, the **western gorilla,** *Gorilla gorilla,* and the **eastern gorilla,** *G. beringei,* of equatorial Africa, both now critically endangered. **2.** an ugly, brutal man.

gormandise /'gɔməndaɪz/ *v.i.* to eat like a glutton. Also, **gormandize.** –**gormandiser,** *n.*

gormless /'gɔmləs/ *adj. Colloq.* (of a person) dull; stupid; senseless. –**gormlessness,** *n.*

gorse /gɔs/ *n.* any plant of the genus *Ulex,* especially *U. europaeus,* a low, much-branched, spiny shrub with yellow flowers, native to Europe and introduced into many countries; furze. –**gorsy,** *adj.*

gory /'gɔri/ *adj.* (**-rier, -riest**) **1.** covered or stained with gore; bloody. **2.** resembling gore. **3.** *Colloq.* distasteful or unpleasant: *he read the gory details of the accident.* –**gorily,** *adv.* –**goriness,** *n.*

gosh /gɒʃ/ *interj.* an exclamation or mild oath.

goshawk /'gɒshɔk/ *n.* any of various powerful, short-winged hawks, formerly much used in falconry, widely dispersed throughout the world.

gosling /'gɒzlɪŋ/ *n.* a young goose.

go-slow *n. Colloq.* a deliberate curtailment of output by workers as an industrial sanction; work-to-rule.

gospel /'gɒspəl/ *n.* **1.** (*oft. upper case*) the body of doctrine taught by Christ and the apostles; Christian revelation. **2.** the story of Christ's life and teachings, especially as contained in the first four books of the New Testament. **3.** (*usu. upper case*) one of these books. **4.** something regarded as true and implicitly believed: *to take as gospel.* –*adj.* **5.** in accordance with the gospel; evangelical.

gospel music *n.* a primarily vocal music, a precursor of the blues, but based on hymns.

gossamer /'gɒsəmə/ *n.* **1.** a fine filmy cobweb, seen on grass and bushes, or floating in the air in calm weather, especially in autumn. **2.** an extremely delicate variety of gauze. **3.** any finely spun, silken fabric. –*adj.* Also, **gossamery** /'gɒsəməri/ **4.** of or like gossamer; thin and light.

gossip /'gɒsəp/ *n.* **1.** idle talk, especially about the affairs of others. **2.** light, familiar talk or writing. **3.** someone given to tattling or idle talk. –*v.i.* (**-siped** *or* **-siped, -siping** *or* **-sipping**) **4.** to talk idly, especially about the affairs of others. –**gossiper,** *n.* –**gossiping,** *n.* –**gossipingly,** *adv.*

got /gɒt/ *v.* **1.** past tense and past participle of **get.** –*phr.* **2. have got,** to have; possess: *I've got a house in Tamworth.* **3. have got to,** to be under an obligation to; be obliged to: *I've got to go; you've got to be joking.*

4. what's got into someone?, *Colloq.* a query as to what is causing someone to behave in an uncharacteristic way, such as angrily, absent-mindedly, etc.

Goth /gɒθ/ *n.* **1.** one of a Teutonic people who, in the 3rd to 5th century AD, invaded and settled in parts of the Roman Empire. **2.** (*usu. lower case*) **a.** a type of pop music which typically features bleak imagery, and which is associated with a style of dress featuring black clothes, black hair, silver jewellery, and often dramatic black eye make-up and lipstick. **b.** a person who adopts this style of dress.

Gothic /ˈgɒθɪk/ *adj.* **1.** *Archit.* denoting or relating to a style originating in France and spreading over western Europe from the 12th to the 16th century, characterised by a design emphasising skeleton construction, the elimination of wall planes, the comparatively great height of the buildings, the pointed arch, rib vaulting, and the flying buttress. **2.** (especially in literature) stressing irregularity and details, usually of a grotesque or horrible nature: *a Gothic novel.* **3.** *Printing* (of a typeface) having elaborate pointed characters. **4.** (*usu. lower case*) of or relating to the goth music cult. See **Goth** (def. 2). **–***n.* **5.** (*usu. lower case*) a person who is an adherent of the goth music cult and who dresses in austere black. See **Goth** (def. 2). **–Gothically**, *adv.*

go-to man *n. Colloq.* the man to whom one turns as the one most likely to produce results.

gotten /ˈgɒtn/ *v.* a past participle of **get**.

gouache /guˈaʃ, -ˈæʃ/ *n.* a method of painting with opaque watercolours.

gouda /ˈgaʊdə, ˈguː-/ *n.* a semi-soft to hard, sweet-curd cheese, with a smooth, mellow taste, made in a traditional flat wheel shape with rounded edges and a yellow rind.

gouge /gaʊdʒ/ *n.* **1.** a chisel whose blade has a concavo-convex cross-section, the bevel being ground on either the inside or the outside of the cutting end of the tool. **2.** a groove or hole made by gouging. **–***v.t.* (**gouged**, **gouging**) **3.** to dig or force out with or as with a gouge: *to gouge out an eye.*

goulash /ˈgulæʃ/ *n.* a stew made of meat, usually beef or veal, flavoured with chopped onions and paprika.

Gouldian finch /ˌguldiən ˈfɪntʃ/ *n.* a strikingly multi-coloured finch, *Erythrura gouldiae*, endemic to tropical northern Australia; often kept caged in aviaries; the wild population is endangered.

gourd /gʊəd, gɔd/ *n.* the fruit of any of various plants of the family Cucurbitaceae, especially that of *Lagenaria siceraria* (**bottle gourd**), whose dried shell is used for bottles, bowls, etc., or that of certain forms of *Cucurbita pepo* sometimes cultivated for ornament. **–gourd-shaped**, *adj.*

gourmand /ˈgɔˈmɒnd, ˈgɔmənd/ *n.* someone fond of good eating. Also, **gormand**.

gourmet /ˈgɔmeɪ, ˈgʊə-/ *n.* **1.** a connoisseur in the delicacies of the table; an epicure. **–***adj.* **2.** of a standard required by a gourmet; first-rate: *a gourmet meal.* **3.** befitting or suitable for the use of a gourmet: *a gourmet kitchen.*

gout /gaʊt/ *n. Pathol.* a constitutional disease characterised by painful inflammation of the joints (chiefly those in the feet and hands, and especially in the big toe), and by excess of uric acid in the blood.

govern /ˈgʌvən/ *v.t.* **1.** to rule by right of authority: *to govern a state.* **2.** to have a directing influence over; guide: *anger governed his decision.* **3.** to hold in control: *to govern your temper.* **4.** to serve as a law for: *the principles governing a case.* **5.** *Gram.* to control (the case of a noun or the mood of a verb); for example, in '*They helped us*', the verb '*helped*' is said to govern the objective case of the pronoun. **–***v.i.* **6.** to have a

controlling influence. **–governing**, *adj.* **–governable**, *adj.* **–governance**, *n.*

governess /ˈgʌvənɛs/ *n.* a woman who directs the education of children, generally in their own homes.

government /ˈgʌvənmənt/ *n.* **1.** the authoritative direction and restraint exercised over the actions of people in communities, societies, and states; direction of the affairs of a state, etc.; political rule and administration: *government is necessary to the existence of society.* **2.** the form or system of rule by which a state, community, etc., is governed: *monarchical government*; *episcopal government.* **3.** (*sometimes upper case*) (*sometimes construed as pl.*) the governing body of persons in a state, community, etc.; the executive power; the administration: *the government was defeated in the last election.* **4.** direction; control; rule: *the government of the hospital was passed to a private company.* **–***adj.* **5.** of or relating to a government. **–governmental** /gʌvənˈmɛntl/, *adj.* **–governmentally** /gʌvənˈmɛntəli/, *adv.*

governor /ˈgʌvənə, ˈgʌvnə/ *n.* **1.** someone placed in control of an organisation, society, etc.: *governor of a bank.* **2. a.** the main representative of the sovereign in a state of the Commonwealth of Australia. **b.** the representative of the sovereign with powers given by law, in a British dependent territory. **3.** the executive head of a state in the US. **4.** *Machinery* a device for controlling a supply of fuel in an engine.

governor-general *n.* (*pl.* **governor-generals** *or* **governors-general**) the principal representative of the sovereign in certain independent Commonwealth countries.

gown /gaʊn/ *n.* **1.** a woman's dress, usually formal, comprising bodice and skirt, usually joined. **2.** a loose, flowing, outer garment in various forms, worn by men or women as distinctive of office, profession, or status: *a judge's gown, an academic gown.* **–***v.t.* **3.** to dress in a gown.

gozleme /ˈgɜzləmeɪ/ *n.* (in Turkish cookery) a dish comprising two layers of flatbread dough with a filling of spinach, fetta, etc., the whole being cooked on a griddle.

GPS /dʒi pi ˈɛs/ *n.* **1.** global positioning system; a navigational system which relies on information received from a network of satellites to provide the latitude and longitude of an object, as a ship at sea, etc. **2.** a device which uses this system to determine location.

grab /græb/ *v.t.* (**grabbed**, **grabbing**) **1.** to seize suddenly and eagerly; snatch. **2.** to take illegal possession of; seize forcibly or unscrupulously: *to grab land.* **3.** *Colloq.* to affect; impress: *how does that grab you?* **–***n.* **4.** a sudden, eager grasp or snatch. **5. a.** an attempt to seize or acquire by violent or unscrupulous means. **b.** an instance where such a seizure or acquisition has been made. **6.** that which is grabbed. **7.** a mechanical device for gripping objects. **–***phr.* **8. up for grabs**, *Colloq.* ready for the taking; available for anyone to claim. **–grabber**, *n.*

grace /greɪs/ *n.* **1.** elegance or beauty of form, manner, motion, or act. **2.** a pleasing or attractive quality or endowment. **3.** favour or goodwill. **4.** manifestation of favour, especially by a superior. **5.** mercy; clemency; pardon. **6.** favour shown in granting a delay or temporary immunity: *an act of grace.* **7.** (*pl.*) affected manner; manifestation of pride or vanity: *to put on airs and graces.* **8.** *Law* an allowance of time to a debtor before suit can be brought against him or her after the debt has by its terms become payable: *seven days' grace.* **9.** a short prayer before or after a meal, in which a blessing is asked and thanks are given. **10.** *Music* an embellishment consisting of a note or notes not essential to the harmony or melody, as an appoggiatura, an inverted mordent, etc. **11.** (*usu. upper case*) (preceded by *your*, *his* or *her*) a formal title used in addressing or mentioning a duke, duchess, or archbishop, and formerly also a sovereign. *–v.t.* (**graced**, **gracing**) **12.** to lend or add grace to; adorn. **13.** to favour or honour: *to grace an occasion with one's presence*. *–phr.* **14. fall from grace**, **a.** *Theology* to descend into sin or disfavour with God. **b.** to lose favour, especially with someone in authority. **15. have the grace to**, to be so kind as to (do something). **16. state of grace**, *Theology* **a.** the condition of being in God's favour. **b.** the condition of being one of the elect. **17. with (a) bad grace**, unwillingly; reluctantly: *he conceded defeat with bad grace*. **18. with (a) good grace**, willingly; ungrudgingly.

graceful /ˈɡreɪsfəl/ *adj.* characterised by grace of form, manner, movement, or speech; elegant; easy or effective. *–gracefully*, *adv.* *–gracefulness*, *n.*

gracious /ˈɡreɪʃəs/ *adj.* **1.** disposed to show grace or favour; kind; benevolent; courteous. **2.** indulgent or beneficent in a condescending or patronising way, especially to inferiors. *–phr.* **3. (goodness) gracious (me)**, an exclamation of surprise, etc. *–graciously*, *adv.* *–graciousness*, *graciosity* /ɡreɪʃiˈɒsəti/, *n.*

gradation /ɡrəˈdeɪʃən/ *n.* **1.** any process or change taking place through a series of stages, by degrees, or gradually. **2.** a stage, degree, or grade in such a series. **3.** the passing of one tint or shade of colour to another, or one surface to another, by very small degrees, as in painting, sculpture, etc. *–gradational*, *adj.* *–gradationally*, *adv.*

grade /ɡreɪd/ *n.* **1.** a degree in a scale, as of rank, advancement, quality, value, intensity, etc. **2.** a class of persons or things of the same relative rank, quality, etc. **3.** a step or stage in a course or process. **4.** a non-SI unit of plane angle, equal to the angle between two radii of a circle which cut off an arc equal to $\frac{1}{400}$ of that circumference (approximately 15.7×10^{-3} radians). **5.** → **year** (def. 11). **6.** a number, letter, etc., indicating the relative quality of a student's work in a course, examination, or special subject. **7.** inclination with the horizontal of a road, railway, etc., usually expressed by stating the vertical rise or fall as a percentage of the horizontal distance. *–v.t.* **8.** to arrange in a series of grades; class; sort. **9.** to determine the grade of. **10.** to cause to pass by degrees, as from one colour or shade to another. *–v.i.* **11.** to be graded. **12.** to be of a particular grade or quality. *–phr.* **13. make the grade**, to reach a desired minimum level of achievement; qualification.

-grade a word element meaning 'walking', 'moving', 'going', as in *retrograde*.

grader /ˈɡreɪdə/ *n.* a motor-driven vehicle, with a blade for pushing earth, used for grading roads and for shallow excavation.

gradient /ˈɡreɪdiənt/ *n.* **1.** the degree of inclination, or the rate of ascent or descent, in a railway, etc. **2.** an inclined surface; grade; ramp. **3.** *Physics* change in a variable quantity, such as temperature or pressure, per unit distance.

gradual /ˈɡrædʒuəl/ *adj.* **1.** taking place, changing, moving, etc., by degrees or little by little: *gradual improvement in health*. **2.** rising or descending at an even, moderate inclination: *a gradual slope*. *–gradualism*, *n.* *–gradually*, *adv.* *–gradualness*, *n.*

graduate *n.* /ˈɡrædʒuət/ **1.** someone who has received a degree on completing a course of study, as at a university or college. *–adj.* /ˈɡrædʒuət/ **2.** that has graduated: *a graduate student*. **3.** of or relating to graduates: *a graduate course*. *–v.i.* /ˈɡrædʒueɪt/ **4.** to receive a degree or diploma on completing a course of study. *–v.t.* /ˈɡrædʒueɪt/ **5.** to divide into or mark with degrees

or other divisions, as the scale of a thermometer. *–graduation*, *n.* *–graduator*, *n.*

graffiti /ɡrəˈfiti/ *pl. n.* (*sing.* **graffito** /ɡrəˈfitoʊ/) **1.** (*usu. construed as sing.*) drawings or words, sometimes obscene, sometimes political, etc., written on surfaces such as the walls of buildings, billboards, partitions in public toilets, etc. **2.** (*sing.*) *Archaeology* an ancient drawing or writing scratched on a wall or other surface.

graffiti art *n.* a popular art form, usually produced as a mural, which adopts a graffiti style.

graffitist /ɡrəˈfitəst/ *n.* an exponent of the popular art of graffiti.

graft[1] /ɡraft/ *n.* **1.** *Hort.* a shoot or part of a plant (the scion) placed in a groove or slit in another plant (the stock) so as to be fed by and united with it. **2.** *Surg.* a piece of living tissue cut from one part of a person and placed elsewhere on their body or on another person's body. *–v.t.* **3.** to insert (a graft) into a plant or tree. **4.** to cause (a plant) to grow through grafting. **5.** *Surg.* to transplant (a part of living tissue) as a graft. *–v.i.* **6.** to become grafted. *–grafter*, *n.* *–grafting*, *n.*

graft[2] /ɡraft/ *n.* **1.** work, especially hard work. *–v.i.* **2.** to work hard, toil (especially at physical tasks).

Grail /ɡreɪl/ *n.* → **Holy Grail**.

grain /ɡreɪn/ *n.* **1.** a small hard seed, especially a seed of one of the cereal plants: wheat, rye, oats, barley, maize, or millet. **2.** the gathered seeds of cereal plants in the mass. **3.** the plants themselves, whether standing or gathered. **4.** any small, hard particle, as of sand, gold, pepper, gunpowder, etc. **5.** the smallest unit of weight in most imperial systems, originally determined by the weight of a plump grain of wheat. In the British and US systems – avoirdupois, troy, and apothecaries' – the grain is identical and equal to $64.798\,918 \times 10^{-6}$ kg. In an avoirdupois ounce there are 437.5 grains; in the troy and apothecaries' ounces there are 480 grains. *Symbol*: gr. **6.** the smallest possible amount of anything: *a grain of truth*. **7.** the arrangement or direction of fibres in wood, or the resulting appearance or markings. **8.** the size of constituent particles of any substance; texture: *sugar of fine grain*. **9.** granular texture or appearance: *a stone of coarse grain*. **10.** *Photography* one of the particles which constitute a photographic emulsion of a film or plate, the size of which limits the possible magnification of the projected image. **11.** temper or natural character: *to go against the grain*. *–phr.* **12. take with a grain of salt**, to believe in part only; have reservations. *–grainer*, *n.* *–grainy*, *adj.*

gram /ɡræm/ *n.* a metric unit of mass, one thousandth of a kilogram. *Symbol*: g

-gram[1] a word element meaning 'something drawn or written', as in *diagram*, *epigram*, *telegram*, *monogram*.

-gram[2] a word element meaning 'grams', 'of or relating to a gram', as in *kilogram*.

graminivorous /ɡræmoˈnɪvərəs/ *adj.* feeding on grass.

gramma /ˈɡræmə/ *n.* a type of pumpkin, *Cucurbita moschata*, the fruit of which is elongated and has an orange flesh and skin.

grammar /ˈɡræmə/ *n.* **1.** (a description of) the parts of a language (sounds, words, formation and arrangement of words, etc.) regarded as a system or structure: *English grammar*. **2.** → **syntax**. **3.** speech or writing conforming to standard usage: *He knows his grammar*. **4.** a book containing a grammar. *–grammarian*, *n.* *–grammarless*, *adj.*

grammar checker *n.* a computer program which checks the grammar of wording in a text file for mistakes and suggests corrections.

grammatical /ɡrəˈmætɪkəl/ *adj.* **1.** of or relating to grammar: *grammatical analysis*. **2.** conforming to standard usage: *grammatical speech*. *–grammatically*, *adv.* *–grammaticalness*, *n.*

gramophone /'græməfoʊn/ n. → **record-player**. Also, *Chiefly US*, **phonograph**. –**gramophonic**, *adj.*

grampus /'græmpəs/ n. **1.** a cetacean, *Grampus griseus*, of the dolphin family, widely distributed in northern seas. **2.** any of various related cetaceans, such as the killer whale, *Orcinus orca*.

granary /'grænəri/ n. (*pl.* **-ries**) **1.** a storehouse or repository for grain, especially after it has been threshed or husked. **2.** a region producing a lot of grain.

grand /grænd/ *adj.* **1.** impressive in size, appearance or effect: *grand mountain scenery*. **2.** stately; majestic; dignified. **3.** splendid; magnificent: *a grand palace*. **4.** noble; fine: *a grand old man*. **5.** highest, or very high, in importance or official position: *a grand ruler*. **6.** main; principal; chief: *the grand staircase*. **7.** complete; comprehensive: *a grand total*. **8.** first-rate; very good: *grand weather*. **9.** younger or older by one generation than the specified relationship (used in compounds), as in *grandfather*, *grandchild*, etc. –*n.* (*pl.* **grands** *for def. 10*, **grand** *for def. 11*) **10.** → **piano**[1] (def. 2). **11.** *Colloq.* a thousand dollars. –**grandly**, *adv.* –**grandness**, *n.*

grandchild /'græntʃaɪld/ n. (*pl.* **-children**) a child of one's son or daughter.

grandeur /'grændʒə/ n. the state or quality of being grand; imposing greatness; exalted rank, dignity, or importance.

grandfather /'grænfaðə, 'grænd-/ n. the father of one's father or mother.

grand final n. (in a sporting competition, etc., where the winner is not decided on a simple knockout basis) the final game of a competition, between the two remaining teams or contestants, to determine who shall win the premiership.

grand finale n. **the** → **finale** (def. 2).

grandiloquent /græn'dɪləkwənt/ *adj.* speaking or expressed in a lofty or pompous style; bombastic. –**grandiloquently**, *adv.*

grandiose /'grændioʊs/ *adj.* **1.** grand in an imposing or impressive way. **2.** affectedly grand or stately; pompous. –**grandiosely**, *adv.* –**grandiosity** /grændi'ɒsɪti/, *n.*

grandmaster /grænd'mastə/ n. *Chess, Bridge, etc.* **1.** an outstandingly expert player, and winner of numerous competitions, tournaments, etc. **2.** (*upper case*) the highest title a chess player can attain.

grandmother /'grænmʌðə, 'grænd-/ n. **1.** the mother of one's father or mother. –*phr.* **2. tell that to your grandmother**, an exclamation expressing disbelief.

grandparent /'grænpɛərənt/ n. a parent of a parent.

grand piano n. → **piano**[1] (def. 2).

grandstand /'grænstænd, 'grænd-/ n. **1.** the principal stand for spectators at a racecourse, athletic field, etc. **2.** the people sitting in the grandstand. –*v.i.* **3.** to behave ostentatiously in order to impress or win approval. –*adj.* **4.** of or relating to a grandstand or the spectators in it. **5.** from a good vantage point, as a grandstand: *a grandstand view of the incident*.

grange /greɪndʒ/ n. **1.** a farm. **2.** a country dwelling house with its various farm buildings; dwelling of a yeoman or gentleman farmer.

granite /'grænət/ n. **1.** a granular igneous rock composed chiefly of feldspar (orthoclase) and quartz, usually with one or more other minerals, such as mica, hornblende, etc., much used in building, and for monuments, etc. **2.** great hardness or firmness. –**granitic** /grə'nɪtɪk/, *adj.*

granivore /'grænɪvɔ/ n. an animal that feeds predominantly on grain.

granivorous /grə'nɪvərəs/ *adj.* feeding on grain and seeds.

granny /'græni/ n. *Colloq.* **1.** (*pl.* **-nies**) → **grandmother**. **2.** an old woman. **3.** a fussy person.

granny flat n. a extension to a house or additional structure within the boundaries of an existing property, providing a self-contained living unit.

Granny Smith n. a variety of apple with a green skin and crisp juicy flesh, suitable for eating raw or cooking.

grant /grænt, grant/ v.t. **1.** to bestow or confer, especially by a formal act: *to grant a right*. **2.** to give or accord: *to grant permission*. **3.** to agree or accede to: *to grant a request*. **4.** to admit or concede; accept for the sake of argument: *I grant that point*. **5.** to transfer or convey, especially by deed or writing: *to grant property*. –*n.* **6.** that which is granted, as a privilege or right, a sum of money, as for a student's maintenance, or a tract of land. **7.** the act of granting. –*phr.* **8. granted**, a reply acceding to a request for permission or pardon. **9. take someone for granted**, to fail to appreciate someone's efforts. **10. take something for granted**, to assume something without verification. –**grantable**, *adj.* –**granter**, *n.*

granular /'grænjələ/ *adj.* **1.** containing or composed of granules. **2.** of or relating to grains. **3.** showing a granulated structure. –**granularity** /grænjə'lærəti/, *n.* –**granularly**, *adv.*

granulate /'grænjəleɪt/ v.t. **1.** to form into granules or grains. –*v.i.* **2.** to become granular. –**granulation** /grænjə'leɪʃən/, *n.* –**granulator**, *n.*

granule /'grænjul/ n. a small grain, pellet, or particle.

grape /greɪp/ n. **1.** the edible, pulpy, smooth-skinned berry or fruit which grows in clusters on vines of the genus *Vitis* and related plants, especially *V. vinifera* from which wine is made. **2.** any vine bearing this fruit. **3.** dull, dark purplish red.

grapefruit /'greɪpfrut/ n. **1.** a large roundish, yellow-skinned edible citrus fruit with a juicy, acid pulp. **2.** the tropical or subtropical tree, *Citrus paradisi*, from which the fruit is obtained.

grapevine /'greɪpvaɪn/ n. **1.** a vine that bears grapes. **2.** *Colloq.* the network of personal and other contacts through which information ranging from gossip to substantive information is passed informally.

graph /græf, graf/ n. **1.** a diagram representing a system of connections or inter-relations among two or more things by a number of distinctive dots, lines, bars, etc. **2.** *Maths* a curve as representing a given function. –*v.t.* **3.** to draw a graph of. **4.** to draw (a curve) as representing a given function.

graph- variant of **grapho-** before vowels.

-graph a word element meaning: **1.** drawn or written, as in *autograph*. **2.** something drawn or written, as in *lithograph*, *monograph*. **3.** an apparatus for drawing, writing, recording, etc., as in *barograph*.

graphic /'græfɪk/ *adj.* **1.** Also, **graphical**. relating to the use of diagrams, graphs, mathematical curves, or the like. **2.** Also, **graphical**. relating to writing: *graphic symbols*. **3.** lifelike; vivid: *a graphic description of a scene*. **4.** shockingly explicit: *graphic images of the war*. –*n.* **5.** a graphic image or icon: *computer graphics*. –**graphically**, *adv.*

graphical user interface n. *Computers* an interface which uses graphic displays, such as icons and pull-down menus. Also, **GUI**, **graphic interface**.

graphic arts *pl.* n. drawing, engraving, etching, and other arts involving the use of lines, strokes, colour, etc., to express or convey ideas. –**graphic artist**, *n.*

graphic designer n. a designer, as of advertisements, book and magazine covers and pages, etc., who uses print styles, other typographical symbols, images, page layout, etc., as design elements. –**graphic design**, *n.*

graphics /'græfɪks/ n. **1.** the art of drawing, especially as concerned with mathematics, engineering, etc. **2.** the science of calculating by diagrams. **3.** the production of patterns and diagrams by computer. **4.** design that incorporates typographical elements; the production of diagrams or pictures in conjunction with text.

graphite /'græfaɪt/ *n.* a very common mineral, soft native carbon, occurring in black to dark grey foliated masses with metallic lustre and greasy feel, used in so-called lead pencils, as a lubricant, for making crucibles and other refractories, etc.; plumbago; black lead. –**graphitic** /grə'fɪtɪk/, *adj.*

grapho- a word element meaning 'writing', as in *graphology*. Also, **graph-**.

-graphy a word element denoting some process or form of drawing, representing, writing, recording, describing, etc., or an art or science concerned with some such thing, as in *biography, choreography, geography, orthography, photography*.

grapnel /'græpnəl/ *n.* a device consisting essentially of one or more hooks or clamps, for grasping or holding something; a grapple; grappling iron.

grapple /'græpəl/ *n.* **1.** a hook or an iron instrument by which one thing, such as a ship, fastens on another; a grapnel. **2.** a seizing or gripping. **3.** a grip or close hold in wrestling or hand-to-hand fighting. –*v.t.* **4.** to seize, hold, or fasten with or as with a grapple. **5.** to engage in a struggle or close encounter with. –*v.i.* **6.** to hold or make fast to something as with a grapple. **7.** to use a grapple. **8.** to seize another, or each other, in a firm grip, as in wrestling; clinch. –*phr.* **9. grapple with,** to try to overcome or to deal with: *to grapple with a problem*. –**grappler,** *n.*

grasp /græsp, grasp/ *v.t.* **1.** to seize and hold by or as by clasping with the fingers. **2.** to seize upon; hold firmly. **3.** to lay hold of with the mind; comprehend; understand. –*v.i.* **4.** to make the motion of seizing; seize something firmly or eagerly. –*n.* **5.** a grasping or gripping; grip of the hand. **6.** power of seizing and holding; reach: *to have a thing within one's grasp.* **7.** hold, possession, or mastery: *to wrest power from the grasp of a usurper.* **8.** mental hold or comprehension: *a subject beyond one's grasp.* –*phr.* **9. grasp at,** to catch at; try to seize. –**graspable,** *adj.* –**grasper,** *n.*

grasping /'græspɪŋ, 'grasp-/ *v.* **1.** present participle of **grasp.** –*adj.* **2.** that grasps. **3.** greedy. –**graspingly,** *adv.* –**graspingness,** *n.*

grass¹ /gras/ *n.* **1.** any plant of the family Gramineae (or Poaceae), characterised by jointed stems, sheathing leaves, flower spikelets, and fruit consisting of a seed-like grain or caryopsis (true grasses). **2.** herbage in general, or the plants on which grazing animals pasture, or which are cut and dried as hay. **3.** *Colloq.* marijuana. **4.** grass-covered ground; lawn. **5.** pasture: *half of the farm is grass; to put the animals to grass.* **6.** *(pl.)* stalks or sprays of grass: *filled with dried grasses.* –*v.t.* **7.** to cover with grass or turf. **8.** to feed with growing grass; pasture. –*phr.* **9. let the grass grow under one's feet,** to be lax in one's efforts; miss an opportunity. **10. put out to grass,** **a.** to withdraw (a racehorse) from racing, etc., due to old age. **b.** *Colloq.* to retire (a person). –**grassy,** *adj.*

grass² *Colloq.* –*n.* /gras/ **1.** a police informer. –*phr.* /gras/ **2. grass on,** to inform on.

grass court *n.* *Tennis* a court with a grassy surface, designed to produce a faster ball speed but a weak bounce. Compare **clay court, composition court, hardcourt.**

grassfinch /'grasfɪntʃ/ *n.* any of numerous finch-like birds of the family Passeridae, living and moving in flocks, widely distributed in Australia, Asia, and Africa.

grasshopper /'grashɒpə/ *n.* **1.** any of numerous orthopterous insects which are terrestrial, herbivorous and have long hind legs for leaping, many of which are

destructive to vegetation, as the locusts, crickets, certain katydids, etc. –*phr.* **2. knee-high to a grasshopper,** small; young.

grassroots /gras'ruts, 'grasruts/ *pl. n.* **1.** the basic essentials or foundation. –*adj.* **2.** relating to, close to, or emerging spontaneously from the people. –**grassroot,** *adj.*

grass tree *n.* **1.** any species of plant belonging to the genera *Xanthorrhoea* and *Kingia* found in temperate Australia; black boy; yacca. **2.** any of various other plants or trees, having leaves thought to resemble grass, as the **giant grass tree,** *Richea pandanifolia*, a Tasmanian shrub. Also, **grasstree.**

grate¹ /greɪt/ *n.* **1.** a frame of metal bars for holding fuel when burning, as in a fireplace or furnace. **2.** a framework of parallel or crossed bars used as a partition, guard, cover, or the like. **3.** a fireplace.

grate² /greɪt/ *v.t.* **1.** to reduce to small particles by rubbing against a rough surface or a surface with many sharp-edged openings: *to grate a cheese.* **2.** to rub together with a harsh, jarring sound: *to grate the teeth.* –*v.i.* **3.** to have an irritating or unpleasant effect on the feelings. **4.** to make a sound as of rough scraping. **5.** to sound harshly; jar: *to grate on the ear.* –**grater,** *n.* –**grating,** *adj.* –**gratingly,** *adv.*

grateful /'greɪtfəl/ *adj.* **1.** warmly or deeply appreciative of kindness or benefits received; thankful: *I am grateful to you for your kindness.* **2.** actuated by or expressing gratitude: *a grateful letter.* **3.** pleasing to the mind or senses; agreeable or welcome; refreshing: *grateful slumber.* –**gratefully,** *adv.* –**gratefulness,** *n.*

gratify /'grætəfaɪ/ *v.t.* **(-fied, -fying) 1.** to give pleasure to (persons) by satisfying desires or humouring inclinations or feelings. **2.** to satisfy; indulge; humour: *to gratify desires; to gratify appetites.* –**gratifier,** *n.* –**gratification** /grætəfə'keɪʃən/, *n.*

grating /'greɪtɪŋ/ *n.* a partition or frame of parallel or crossing bars; open latticework of wood or metal serving as a cover or guard, but admitting light, air, etc.

gratis /'gratəs/ *adv.* **1.** for nothing; gratuitously. –*adj.* **2.** free of cost; gratuitous.

gratitude /'grætətjud/ *n.* the quality or feeling of being grateful or thankful.

gratuitous /grə'tjuətəs/ *adj.* **1.** freely bestowed or obtained; free. **2.** being without reason, cause, or justification: *a gratuitous insult.* –**gratuitously,** *adv.* –**gratuitousness,** *n.*

gratuity /grə'tjuəti/ *n.* *(pl.* **-ties) 1.** a gift, usually of money, over and above payment due for service; tip. **2.** something that is given without claim or demand. **3.** a bounty given to soldiers.

graunch /grɒntʃ/ *v.i.* *Chiefly NZ* to make a grinding or grating sound: *the ship graunched over the rocks.*

grave¹ /greɪv/ *n.* **1.** an excavation made in the earth to receive a dead body in burial. **2.** any place of interment; a tomb or sepulchre. **3.** any place that becomes the receptacle of what is dead, lost or past: *the grave of dead reputations.* –*phr.* **4. dig one's own grave,** to cause one's own downfall or ruin. **5. have one foot in the grave,** to be infirm, old, or near death. **6. turn in one's grave,** (of a dead person) to be likely to have been offended or horrified by a modern event or events.

grave² /greɪv/; /grav/ *for defs 4 and 5* –*adj.* **1.** dignified; sedate; serious; earnest; solemn: *a grave person, grave thoughts, grave ceremonies.* **2.** weighty, momentous, or important: *grave responsibilities.* **3.** important or critical; involving serious issues: *a grave situation.* **4.** *Phonetics* of an accent (`) which may in ancient Greek indicate a syllable or vowel of particular pitch pattern, in Italian and English a vowel irregularly stressed or pronounced, as in *libertà* or *belovèd*, in

French a vowel of particularly quality, *père*, father, etc. *–n.* **5.** the grave accent. **–gravely,** *adv.* **–graveness,** *n.*

grave[3] /greɪv/ *v.t. Archaic* **1.** to carve or engrave. **2.** to impress deeply: *graven on the mind.*

gravel /ˈɡrævəl/ *n.* small stones and pebbles, or a mixture of these with sand.

gravelly /ˈɡrævəli/ *adj.* **1.** consisting of, containing, or resembling gravel. **2.** (of a voice) harsh.

graven image /greɪvən ˈɪmɪdʒ/ *n.* an idol (def. 1) carved from wood, stone, etc.

gravitate /ˈɡrævəteɪt/ *v.i.* **1.** to move or tend to move under the influence of gravitational force. **2.** to tend towards the lowest level; sink; fall. *–phr.* **3. gravitate to** (or **towards**), to have a natural tendency towards or be strongly attracted to.

gravitation /ɡrævəˈteɪʃən/ *n.* **1.** *Physics* **a.** the force of attraction between all particles or bodies, or that acceleration of one towards another, of which the fall of bodies to the earth is an instance. **b.** an act or process caused by this force. **2.** natural tendency towards some point or object of influence: *the gravitation of people towards the suburbs.* **–gravitational,** *adj.* **–gravitationally,** *adv.*

gravitational field *n. Physics* the region in which a body with a finite mass exerts an appreciable force of attraction on another body of finite mass.

gravity /ˈɡrævəti/ *n.* (*pl.* **-ties**) **1.** gravitation, especially the force of attraction by which earthly bodies tend to fall towards the centre of the earth. **2.** heaviness or weight: *centre of gravity; specific gravity.* **3.** solemnity; dignity; seriousness. **4.** seriousness; critical quality: *the gravity of his illness.*

gravy /ˈɡreɪvi/ *n.* (*pl.* **-vies**) **1.** the fat and juices that drip from meat during cooking, often made into a dressing for meat, etc. **2.** *Colloq.* any perquisite; money easily acquired.

graze[1] /ɡreɪz/ *v.i.* **1.** to feed on growing herbage, as cattle, sheep, etc. *–v.t.* **2.** to feed on (growing grass). **3.** to put cattle, sheep, etc., to feed on (grass, pasture, etc.). **4.** to put (cattle, sheep, etc.) to feed on pasture. *–phr.* **5. graze back** (or **down**), to crop (growth on a paddock) by putting cattle, etc. to graze on it.

graze[2] /ɡreɪz/ *v.t.* **1.** to touch or rub lightly in passing. **2.** to scrape the skin from (the leg, arm, etc.); abrade. *–v.i.* **3.** to touch or rub something lightly, or so as to produce slight abrasion, in passing. *–n.* **4.** a grazing; a touching or rubbing lightly in passing. **5.** a slight scratch in passing; abrasion.

grazier /ˈɡreɪziə/ *n. Aust., NZ* the owner of a rural property on which sheep or cattle are grazed.

grease *n.* /ɡris/ **1.** the melted or rendered fat of animals, especially when in a soft state. **2.** fatty or oily matter in general; lubricant. *–v.t.* /ɡriz, ɡris/ (**greased, greasing**) **3.** to put grease on; lubricate. **4.** to smear with grease. **5.** to cause to run easily. *–phr.* **6. grease someone's palm,** *Colloq.* to bribe someone. **–greaseless,** *adj.* **–greaser,** *n.*

greasepaint /ˈɡrispeɪnt/ *n.* **1.** a mixture of tallow or hard grease and a pigment, used by actors for painting their faces. **2.** any theatrical make-up.

greasy /ˈɡrizi, -si/ *adj.* (**-sier, -siest**) **1.** smeared or soiled with grease. **2.** composed of or containing grease; oily: *greasy food.* **3.** grease-like in appearance or to the touch; slippery. **–greasily,** *adv.* **–greasiness,** *n.*

great /ɡreɪt/ *adj.* **1.** unusually or comparatively large in size or dimensions: *a great house; a great lake; a great fire.* **2.** large in number; numerous: *a great many.* **3.** unusual or considerable in degree: *great pain.* **4.** notable or remarkable: *a great occasion.* **5.** distinguished; famous: *the great men and women of history.* **6.** of much consequence; important: *great issues.* **7.** chief or principal: *the great seal.* **8.** of high rank,

official position, or social standing: *a great noble.* **9.** of noble or lofty character: *great thoughts.* **10.** much in use or favour: *'wit' was a great word with the 18th-century critics.* **11.** being such in an extreme degree: *great friends; a great talker.* **12.** of extraordinary powers; having unusual merit; very admirable: *a great writer; a great politician.* **13.** *Colloq.* first-rate; very good; fine: *we had a great time.* **14.** one degree more remote in direct ascent or descent than a specified relationship: *great-grandfather.* *–n.* **15.** *Colloq.* a great person; a person who has accomplished great achievements. *–adv.* **16.** an intensifier: *you great big baby!* **17.** *Colloq.* successfully; well: *rosemary goes great with lamb.* *–interj.* **18.** an expression of admiration, enthusiasm, etc. *–phr.* **19. a great many,** a very large number of. **20. be a great one for,** *Colloq.* to be enthusiastic about: *she's a great one for computers.* **21. great at,** *Colloq.* **a.** skilful or expert in: *great at skating.* **b.** persistent in: *he was great at bossing others around.* **–greatness,** *n.* **–greatly,** *adv.*

great circle *n.* **1.** a circle on a sphere the plane of which passes through the centre of the sphere. **2.** the line of shortest distance between two points on the surface of the earth.

greatcoat /ˈɡreɪtkoʊt/ *n.* a heavy overcoat.

great crested grebe *n.* a large waterbird, *Podiceps cristatus*, dark brown above and silky white below with a double-horned crest and chestnut frills, which nests on a raft of water plants moored to reeds, and is found in Eurasia, Africa, and most of Australia excluding the dry interior.

Great Dane /ɡreɪt ˈdeɪn/ *n.* one of a breed of large, powerful, short-haired dogs, somewhat resembling the mastiff.

great egret *n.* the widespread egret, *Ardea alba*, a large graceful white bird, found beside rivers, lakes, or dams, on all continents except Antarctica.

great white shark *n.* → white shark. Also, **great white.**

grebe /ɡrib/ *n.* any of various waterbirds which dive for fish, having lobed toes, and legs set well back and adapted for swimming, as the **Australasian grebe,** *Tachybaptus novaehollandiae*, or the **pied-billed grebe,** *Podilymbus podiceps* of the Americas.

greed /ɡrid/ *n.* inordinate or rapacious desire, especially for food or wealth. **–greedy,** *adj.* **–greedily,** *adv.*

green /ɡrin/ *adj.* **1.** of the colour of growing leaves, between yellow and blue in the spectrum. **2.** covered with plants, grass, leaves, etc.; verdant: *green fields.* **3.** consisting of green vegetables: *a green salad.* **4.** characterised by, or relating to, a concern for environmental issues: *green politics; green light globe.* **5.** unseasoned; not dried or cured: *green timber.* **6.** not fully developed or perfected in growth or condition; unripe: *green bananas.* **7.** immature in age or judgement; untrained; inexperienced: *a green recruit.* **8.** easily fooled; gullible. **9.** pale; sickly. **10.** (of prawns) uncooked or raw. **11.** not fired, as bricks or pottery. **12.** *Colloq.* jealous. *–n.* **13.** a green colour. **14.** grassy land; a plot of grassy ground: *the village green.* **15.** Also, **putting green.** *Golf* the area of lawn at the end of the fairway, which surrounds the hole. **16.** *Bowls* a level plot of smooth, green lawn used for playing bowls. **17.** (*pl.*) the leaves and stems of plants, e.g. lettuce, used for food: *salad greens.* *–v.t.* **18.** to make green. *–v.i.* **19.** to become green. **–greenish,** *adj.*

green ban *n. Aust.* **1.** a refusal by employees to work or to allow work to proceed on a building site that is situated in a green belt. **2.** a similar refusal with respect to any construction work which would necessitate destroying something of natural, historical, or social significance.

green belt *n.* an area of parkland, rural or uncultivated land, or native bush, near a town or a city on which building is either strictly controlled or not permitted.

green curry *n.* (in Thai cookery) a dish seasoned chiefly with green chilli, ground to a paste, and coconut milk.

green energy *n.* energy derived from environmentally friendly sources, such as wind power, solar power, etc.

greenery /ˈgriːnəri/ *n.* (*pl.* **-ries**) **1.** green foliage or vegetation; verdure. **2.** a place where green plants are reared or kept.

green-eyed *adj.* **1.** having green eyes. **2.** jealous.

greenfield /ˈgriːnfiːld/ *adj.* **1.** of or relating to a location for a business where there has not previously been any building: *a greenfield site.* **2.** of or relating to any enterprise which is becoming active in a market where there has been little or no previous activity: *a greenfield operation.* Also, **greenfields.**

greenfields /ˈgriːnfiːldz/ *pl. n.* **1.** parkland or agricultural land on the outskirts of a city. *–adj.* **2.** → **greenfield.**

greenfinch /ˈgriːnfɪntʃ/ *n.* any of various green-plumaged finches, especially the **European greenfinch**, *Carduelis chloris*, with green and yellow plumage, native to Europe, the Middle East and northern Africa, often kept as a pet, having been widely introduced into various countries as Australia and New Zealand.

green footprint *n.* an ecological footprint which is environmentally friendly. See **ecological footprint.**

greengage /ˈgriːngeɪdʒ/ *n.* one of several varieties of light green plums.

greengrocer /ˈgriːngroʊsə/ *n.* a retailer of fresh vegetables and fruit.

greenhouse /ˈgriːnhaʊs/ *n.* a building, chiefly of glass or plastic, for the cultivation or protection of plants.

greenhouse effect *n.* **1.** the increase in temperature in a greenhouse caused by the radiant heat from the sun passing through the glass, while heat within the greenhouse is trapped there by the glass. **2. a.** the same effect on the temperature of the earth caused by its atmosphere acting as the glass of a greenhouse does, this warming of the lower atmosphere maintaining temperatures suitable for life on earth. **b.** Also, **enhanced greenhouse effect.** an intensification of this effect caused by pollution adding more carbon dioxide and other gases to the atmosphere, associated with global warming.

greenhouse-friendly *adj.* reducing, or not producing, greenhouse gas emissions.

greenhouse gas *n.* one of a number of gases found in the atmosphere that contribute to the greenhouse effect. *Abbrev.*: GHG

greenhouse gas credit *n.* a credit in the calculation of allowable greenhouse gas emission acknowledged, generated by a process or activity which reduces greenhouse gases.

greenie /ˈgriːni/ *n. Colloq.* a conservationist.

green lung *n.* an area in or near to a city which is covered with vegetation which acts to draw in carbon dioxide and produce oxygen.

greenmail /ˈgriːnmeɪl/ *n.* the purchase of a large block of a company's shares, threatening a takeover, but actually in order to have the shares purchased at a much higher price by a group friendly to the company. *–***greenmailer,** *n.* *–***greenmailing,** *n.*

green pepper *n.* **1.** the fruit of the bell or sweet pepper, *Capsicum frutescens* var. *grossum.* **2.** the mild, unripe fruit of any of the garden peppers, *Capsicum frutescens*, used as a green vegetable.

green room *n.* a room set aside for use of artists in a theatre, opera house, television studio, etc., in which they can relax and entertain when they are not performing.

green screen *n.* an alternative to a blue screen where an actor is wearing something blue that would be misinterpreted by the computer as needing to have a replacement image. See **blue screen.**

greenstick /ˈgriːnstɪk/ *n.* a type of make-up with a slight green hue to it which covers up redness on the skin.

greenstick fracture *n.* a partial fracture of a bone of a young person or animal, in which only one side of a bone is broken.

green tape *n. Politics* (*derog.*) the bureaucratic regulations and associated paperwork deriving from environmental legislation.

green tax *n.* → **ecotax.**

green wall *n.* a wall, indoor or outdoor, which is covered by vegetation supported by a modular construction with a soil base in each module, the whole being irrigated from a central reservoir.

green water *n.* water taken directly from rainfall. Compare **blue water.**

Greenwich Mean Time /grɛnɪtʃ ˈmiːn taɪm/ *n.* mean solar time of the meridian through Greenwich, England; from 1884 to 1972 widely used throughout the world as a basis for calculating local time. *Abbrev.*: GMT See **Coordinated Universal Time.**

greet /griːt/ *v.t.* **1.** to address with some form of salutation; welcome. **2.** to receive with demonstrations of feeling. **3.** to manifest itself to: *music greets the ear.* *–v.i.* **4.** to give salutations on meeting. *–***greeter,** *n.*

greeting /ˈgriːtɪŋ/ *n.* **1.** the act or words of someone who greets. **2.** (*usu. pl.*) a friendly message: *send greetings.*

gregarious /grəˈgɛəriəs/ *adj.* **1.** living in flocks or herds, as animals. **2.** *Bot.* growing in open clusters; not matted together. **3.** fond of company; sociable. **4.** relating to a flock or crowd. *–***gregariously,** *adv.* *–***gregariousness,** *n.*

Gregorian calendar /grəˌgɔriən ˈkæləndə/ *n.* the calendar now in use, according to which the ordinary year consists of 365 days, and a leap year of 366 days occurs in every year whose number is exactly divisible by 4 except centenary years whose numbers are not exactly divisible by 400, as 1700, 1800, and 1900.

Gregorian chant *n.* → **plainsong.**

gremlin /ˈgrɛmlən/ *n.* **1.** an invisible being, said to cause disorder and confusion out of a sense of malicious mischief. **2.** a young and inexperienced surfboard rider.

gremolata /grɛməˈlatə/ *n.* (in Italian cookery) a mixture of chopped lemon rind, garlic and parsley which is sprinkled over meats, such as osso buco, to add zest.

grenade /grəˈneɪd/ *n.* **1.** a small explosive shell thrown by hand or fired from a rifle. **2.** a glass missile for scattering chemicals in order to put out fires, spread tear gas, etc.

grevillea /grəˈvɪliə, -jə/ *n.* any shrub or tree of the very large, mainly Australian, genus *Grevillea*, family Proteaceae, many of which are attractive ornamentals and a number, such as *G. robusta*, silky oak, useful timber trees.

grew /gruː/ *v.* past tense of **grow.**

grey /greɪ/ *adj.* **1.** of a colour between white and black, having no definite hue; ash-coloured. **2.** dark, overcast, dismal, gloomy: *the cloudy sky was grey.* **3.** relating to old age: *grey power.* *–n.* **4.** any achromatic colour. **5.** grey material or clothing: *to dress in grey.* *–v.t.* **6.** to make grey. *–v.i.* **7.** to become grey. *–***greyish,** *adj.* *–***greyly,** *adv.* *–***greyness,** *n.*

grey area *n.* **1.** an issue which is not clear-cut; a subject which is vague and ill-defined. **2.** the area midway between two extremes.

grey-crowned babbler *n.* See **babbler** (def. 2).

grey gum *n.* any of several species of the genus *Eucalyptus*, especially *E. punctata*, of eastern NSW, with dull grey bark often with patches of a pinkish or cream colour.

greyhound /ˈgreɪhaʊnd/ *n.* one of a breed of tall, slender dogs, notable for keen sight and for fleetness.

grey nurse shark *n.* a common shark, *Odontaspis arenarius*, of Australian waters, with a large stout body coloured grey on top and off-white underneath, and long thin ripping teeth; protected since 1984 in NSW. Also, **grey nurse**.

greywater /ˈgreɪwɔtə/ *n.* untreated domestic or industrial wastewater that can be used for watering lawns and gardens, or for other purposes, instead of being drained into the sewerage system.

grid /grɪd/ *n.* **1.** a grating of crossed bars; gridiron. **2.** a network of cables, pipes, etc., for the supply of electricity, gas, water, etc. **3.** a network of horizontal and vertical lines on a map, printer's layout, plan, etc.

griddle /ˈgrɪdl/ *n.* **1.** a flat, heated surface on top of a stove for cooking oatcakes, biscuits, etc. –*v.t.* **2.** to cook on a griddle.

gridiron /ˈgrɪdaɪən/ *n.* **1.** a utensil consisting of parallel metal bars on which to grill meat, etc. **2.** → **American football. 3.** *American Football* the field of play, so called on account of the transverse white lines crossing it every five yards. **4.** a structure above the stage of a theatre, from which hung scenery, etc., is manipulated.

grid north *n.* the northerly or zero direction indicated by a grid (def. 3). Compare **magnetic north, true north.**

grief /grif/ *n.* **1.** keen mental suffering or distress over affliction or loss; sharp sorrow; painful regret. **2.** a cause or occasion of keen distress or sorrow. –*phr.* **3. come to grief,** to come to a bad end; turn out badly. **4. good grief,** an exclamation indicating surprise or consternation. –**griefless,** *adj.*

grievance /ˈgrivəns/ *n.* **1.** a wrong, real or fancied, considered as grounds for complaint: *a popular grievance.* **2.** resentment or complaint, or the grounds for complaint, against an unjust act: *to have a grievance against someone.*

grieve /griv/ *v.i.* **1.** to feel grief; sorrow. –*v.t.* **2.** to distress mentally; cause to feel grief or sorrow. –**griever,** *n.* –**grievingly,** *adv.*

grievous /ˈgrivəs/ *adj.* **1.** causing grief or sorrow: *grievous news.* **2.** flagrant; atrocious: *a grievous fault.* –**grievously,** *adv.* –**grievousness,** *n.*

griffin /ˈgrɪfən/ *n.* a mythical monster, usually having the head and wings of an eagle and the body of a lion. Also, **griffon, gryphon.**

grill /grɪl/ *n.* **1.** → **griller. 2.** a barbecue (def. 1). **3.** a meal in which the meat component is grilled. –*v.t.* **4.** to cook under a griller. **5.** *Colloq.* to subject to severe cross-examination or questioning.

grille /grɪl/ *n.* **1.** a lattice or openwork screen, such as a window or gate, usually of metal and often of decorative design. **2.** a grating or screen in a ventilation system. **3.** an ornamental metal screen at the front of a car. –**grilled,** *adj.*

griller /ˈgrɪlə/ *n.* a cooking device, or the part of a stove, in which meat, etc., is cooked by exposure to direct radiant heat.

grim /grɪm/ *adj.* (**grimmer, grimmest**) **1.** stern; unrelenting; uncompromising: *grim necessity.* **2.** of a sinister or ghastly character; repellent: *a grim joke.* **3.** of a fierce or forbidding aspect: *a grim countenance.* **4.** fierce, savage, or cruel: *grim warrior.* **5.** *Colloq.* disagreeable; unpleasant. –**grimly,** *adv.* –**grimness,** *n.*

grimace /ˈgrɪməs, grəˈmeɪs/ *n.* **1.** a wry face; facial contortion; ugly facial expression. –*v.i.* (**-maced, -macing**) **2.** to make grimaces. –**grimacer,** *n.*

grime /graɪm/ *n.* **1.** dirt or foul matter, especially on or ingrained in a surface. –*v.t.* **2.** to cover with dirt; soil; make very dirty. –**grimy,** *adj.*

grin /grɪn/ *v.i.* (**grinned, grinning**) **1.** to smile broadly, or with a wide distension of the mouth. **2.** to draw back the lips so as to show the teeth, as a snarling dog or a person in pain. –*n.* **3.** the act of grinning; a broad smile. **4.** the act of withdrawing the lips and showing the teeth. –*phr.* **5. grin and bear it,** *Colloq.* to endure without complaint. **6. grin through,** (of paint) to show through a top coat because of poor opacity of the top layer. –**grinner,** *n.* –**grinningly,** *adv.*

grind /graɪnd/ *verb* (**ground, grinding**) –*v.t.* **1.** to wear, smooth, or sharpen by friction; whet: *to grind a lens; to grind an axe.* **2.** to reduce to fine particles as by pounding or crushing. **3.** to oppress or torment. **4.** to rub harshly or gratingly; grate together; grit: *to grind one's teeth.* **5.** to operate by turning a crank: *to grind a barrel organ.* **6.** to produce by pulverising, turning a crank, etc.: *to grind flour.* –*v.i.* **7.** to perform the operation of reducing to fine particles. **8.** to rub harshly; grate. **9.** to be or become ground. **10.** to be polished or sharpened by friction. **11.** *Colloq.* to work or study laboriously. **12.** *Colloq.* to rotate the pelvis in an erotic way while dancing. –*n.* **13.** the act of grinding. **14.** a grinding sound. **15.** *Colloq.* laborious or monotonous work; close or laborious study. **16.** *Colloq.* a diligent or laborious student. **17.** *NZ* a hard, tiring hike. **18.** *Colloq.* (*taboo*) an act of sexual intercourse. –*phr.* **19. grind down, a.** to wear down. **b.** to oppress. **20. grind to a halt, a.** (of a wheeled vehicle) to be brought to a stop, with noisy friction in the wheels. **b.** (of an enterprise, scheme, etc.) to arrive slowly at the point where no progress is being made. **21. the daily grind,** the daily routine of work. –**grindingly,** *adv.*

grindstone /ˈgraɪndstoʊn/ *n.* **1.** a rotating solid stone wheel used for sharpening, shaping, etc. **2.** → **millstone.** –*phr.* **3. keep one's nose to the grindstone,** to force oneself to work without respite.

grip /grɪp/ *n.* **1.** the act of grasping; a seizing and holding fast; firm grasp: *the grip of a vice.* **2.** the power of gripping. **3.** a grasp, hold or control. **4.** a handle or hilt. **5.** a special way of clasping hands. **6.** a special way of holding something, such as a golf club or tennis racquet. **7.** a travelling bag; holdall. **8.** mental or intellectual hold; competence. **9.** something which seizes and holds, as a clutching device on a cable car. **10.** a sudden, sharp pain; spasm of pain. **11.** *Film, TV* a person employed to carry equipment, shift scenery, props, etc. –*verb* (**gripped, gripping**) –*v.t.* **12.** to grasp or seize firmly; hold fast. **13.** to take hold on; hold the interest of: *to grip the mind.* **14.** to attach by a grip or clutch. –*v.i.* **15.** to take firm hold; hold fast. **16.** to take hold on the mind. –*phr.* **17. come** (or **get**) **to grips with, a.** to tackle (an assailant). **b.** to deal with effectively. **18. get a grip,** *Colloq.* to control oneself. –**gripper,** *n.* –**grippingly,** *adv.*

gripe /graɪp/ *v.i.* **1.** *Colloq.* to complain constantly; grumble. –*n.* **2.** *Colloq.* an objection; complaint. **3.** (*usu. pl.*) an intermittent spasmodic pain in the bowels. –**griper,** *n.* –**griping,** *adj.*

grisly /ˈgrɪzli/ *adj.* (**-lier, -liest**) **1.** such as to cause a shuddering horror; gruesome: *a grisly monster.* **2.** formidable; grim: *a grisly countenance.* –**grisliness,** *n.*

grist /grɪst/ *n.* **1.** corn to be ground. **2.** ground corn; meal produced from grinding. –*phr.* **3. grist to the mill,** something which is of advantage or relevance.

gristle /ˈgrɪsəl/ *n.* cartilage, especially when found as inedible matter in meat.

grit /grɪt/ *n.* **1.** fine, stony, or hard particles such as are deposited like dust from the air or occur as impurities in food, etc. **2.** *Geol.* a sandstone composed of coarse angular grains and very small pebbles. **3.** firmness of character; indomitable spirit; pluck. –*v.t.* (**gritted, gritting**) **4.** to clench or grind: *to grit the teeth.* –**gritty,** *adj.*

grits /grɪts/ *pl. n.* a grain, especially oats, hulled and often coarsely ground.

grizzle /ˈgrɪzəl/ *v.i.* **1.** to whimper; whine; complain fretfully. *–n.* **2.** a fretful complaint.

grizzly[1] /ˈgrɪzli/ *adj.* **(-lier, -liest) 1.** somewhat grey; greyish. **2.** grey-haired. *–n. (pl.* **-lies**) **3.** → **grizzly bear.**

grizzly[2] /ˈgrɪzli/ *adj.* **(-lier, -liest)** inclined to complain fretfully: *a grizzly child.*

grizzly bear *n.* the variety of brown bear, *Ursus arctos horribilis*, found in western North America, now chiefly in Canada and Alaska.

groan /groʊn/ *n.* **1.** a low, mournful sound uttered in pain or grief. **2.** a deep murmur uttered in derision, disapproval, etc. **3.** a deep grating or creaking noise, as of wood, etc. *–v.i.* **4.** to utter a deep inarticulate sound expressive of grief or pain; moan. **5.** to make a sound similar to a groan; creak; resound harshly. **6.** to be overburdened or overloaded. *–v.t.* **7.** to utter with groans. *–phr.* **8. groan beneath** (or **under**), to suffer lamentably as a result of. **–groaner,** *n.* **–groaning,** *n.*, *adj.* **–groaningly,** *adv.*

grocer /ˈgroʊsə/ *n.* a dealer in general supplies for the table, such as flour, sugar, coffee, etc., and in other articles of household use.

grocery /ˈgroʊsəri/ *n. (pl.* **-ries**) **1.** a grocer's store. **2.** (*usu. pl.*) a commodity sold by grocers. **3.** the business of a grocer.

grog /grɒg/ *Aust., NZ Colloq. –n.* **1.** alcoholic drink, particularly of a cheap variety. *–v.i.* **(grogged, grogging) 2.** to drink alcoholic drinks: *the boys had been grogging all day. –phr.* **3. grog on,** to indulge in a long session of drinking **4. grog up,** to drink, usually to excess. **5. on the grog,** drinking alcoholic beverages, especially to an intoxicating degree: *she's back on the grog again.*

groggy /ˈgrɒgi/ *adj.* **(-gier, -giest) 1.** staggering, as from exhaustion or blows. **2.** *Colloq.* drunk; intoxicated. **–groggily,** *adv.* **–grogginess,** *n.*

groin /grɔɪn/ *n.* **1.** *Anat.* the fold or hollow where the thigh joins the abdomen. **2.** *Colloq.* the area of the genitals: *she kicked him in the groin.* **3.** *Archit.* the curved line or edge formed by the intersection of two vaults. **4.** → **groyne.**

grommet[1] /ˈgrɒmət/ *n.* **1.** *Machinery* a ring or eyelet of metal, rubber, etc. **2.** *Naut.* an eyelet of rope, metal, or the like, as on the edge of a sail. **3.** *Med.* a small, plastic tube inserted through the eardrum into the middle ear to assist in preventing infection.

grommet[2] /ˈgrɒmət/ *n. Colloq.* **1.** a young surfie. **2.** a young snowboarder.

groom /grum/ *n.* **1.** a man or boy in charge of horses or the stable. **2.** a man newly married, or about to be married; bridegroom. *–v.t.* **3.** to tend carefully as to person and dress; make neat or tidy. **4.** to tend (horses). **5.** to prepare for a position, election, etc.: *groom a political candidate.* **6.** to establish a trusting relationship with (a child), as a preliminary to obtaining their compliance in sexual activities.

groomsman /ˈgrumzmən/ *n. (pl.* **-men**) a man who attends the bridegroom at a wedding.

groove /gruv/ *n.* **1.** a furrow or channel cut by a tool. **2.** a rut, furrow, or channel formed by any agency. **3.** a fixed routine: *to get into a groove.* **4.** the track of a gramophone record in which the needle or stylus rides. **5.** *Colloq.* an exciting or satisfying experience. **6.** a rhythm or beat: *a funky groove. –v.t.* **7.** to cut a groove in; furrow. **8.** to fix in a groove. *–v.i. Colloq.* **9.** to be in a state of euphoria. **10.** to dance or listen to music: *groove to some original tunes. –phr. Colloq.* **11. groove on,** to be delighted or pleased with. **12. in the groove, a.** giving one's best performance, as in music (especially jazz), sport, etc. **b.** competently or

steadily engaged in an activity: *my work was rough at the start but I'm in the groove now.*

groovy /ˈgruvi/ *adj.* **(-vier, -viest)** *Colloq.* **1.** exciting, satisfying, or pleasurable. **2.** fashionable; stylish. **3.** (of music) having a strong groove (def. 6).

grope /groʊp/ *v.i.* **1.** to feel about with the hands; feel one's way. **2.** to search blindly or uncertainly. *–v.t.* **3.** to seek by or as by feeling. **4.** *Colloq.* to fondle sexually. **–groper,** *n.* **–gropingly,** *adv.*

groper /ˈgroʊpə/ *n.* any of several species of large Australian or New Zealand marine fish, typically with enormous gape.

gross /groʊs/ *adj.* **1.** whole, entire, or total, especially without having been subjected to deduction, as for charges, loss, etc.: *gross profits.* **2.** glaring or flagrant: *gross injustice.* **3.** morally coarse; lacking refinement; indelicate or indecent: *gross tastes.* **4.** large, big, or bulky. **5.** thick; dense; heavy: *gross vegetation.* **6.** *Colloq.* repulsive; disagreeable; objectionable. *–n. (pl.* **grosses** *for def. 7,* **gross** *for def. 8)* **7.** the main body, bulk or mass. **8.** a unit consisting of twelve dozen, or 144. *–v.t.* **9.** to make a gross profit of; earn a total of. *–interj.* **10.** *Colloq.* an exclamation indicating disgust, revulsion, etc. *–phr.* **11. gross out,** *Colloq.* **a.** to feel disgust. **b.** to disgust (someone). **12. gross up,** to amplify; enlarge; fill out the details of. **–grossly,** *adv.* **–grossness,** *n.*

gross domestic product *n. Econ.* an estimate of the total value of all legal goods and services produced in a country in a specified time, usually a year. *Abbrev.*: GDP

gross motor skills *pl. n.* the physical skills considered basic to human activity, such as locomotion, balance, spatial orientation, etc. Compare **fine motor skills.**

gross national product *n. Econ.* gross domestic product plus income earned by domestic residents from overseas investments, minus income earned in the domestic market accruing to overseas (foreign) residents. *Abbrev.*: GNP

gross tonnage *n.* a measure of the enclosed internal volume of a ship and its superstructure, with certain spaces exempted.

grotesque /groʊˈtɛsk/ *adj.* **1.** fantastic in the shaping and combination of forms, as in decorative work combining incongruous human and animal figures with scrolls, foliage, etc. **2.** odd or unnatural in shape, appearance, or character; fantastically ugly or absurd; bizarre. *–n.* **3.** any grotesque object or thing. **–grotesquely,** *adv.* **–grotesqueness,** *n.*

grotto /ˈgrɒtoʊ/ *n. (pl.* **-toes** *or* **-tos**) **1.** a cave or cavern. **2.** an artificial cavern-like recess or structure.

grotty /ˈgrɒti/ *adj.* **(-tier, -tiest)** *Colloq.* **1.** dirty; filthy. **2.** useless; rubbishy. **–grottiness,** *n.*

grouch /graʊtʃ/ *Colloq. –v.i.* **1.** to be sulky or morose; show discontent; complain. *–n.* **2.** a sulky or morose person. **3.** a sulky or morose mood.

ground[1] /graʊnd/ *n.* **1.** the earth's solid surface; firm or dry land: *fall to the ground.* **2.** earth or soil: *stony ground.* **3.** land having a special character: *rising ground.* **4.** (*oft. pl.*) a tract of land occupied, or appropriated to a special use: *hospital grounds.* **5.** (*oft. pl.*) the foundation or basis on which a theory or action rests; motive; reason: *grounds for a statement.* **6.** a field of study; topic for discussion; subject of a discourse: *the inquiry covered a great deal of ground;* the *conversation touched on delicate ground.* **7.** the underlying or main surface or background, in painting, decorative work, lace, etc. **8.** (*pl.*) dregs or sediment: *coffee grounds.* **9.** *Elect.* → **earth** (def. 9). *–adj.* **10.** situated on or at, or adjacent to, the surface of the earth: *the ground floor.* **11.** relating to the ground. **12.** *Mil.* operating on land: *ground forces. –v.t.* **13.** to lay or set on the ground. **14.** to place on a foundation; found; fix firmly; settle or establish. **15.** to instruct in elements or first principles. **16.** to furnish with a ground or background on decorative work, etc. **17.** *Elect.* to establish an earth for (a circuit, device, etc.). **18.** *Naut.* to run aground. **19.** to prevent (an aircraft or a pilot) from flying. **20.** to restrict, or withdraw privileges from. *–v.i.* **21.** to come to or strike the ground. *–phr.* **22. break new ground**, to achieve what has not been achieved before. **23. common ground**, matters on which agreement exists. **24. cover the ground**, to deal with the main points if not the fine details of a subject, plan, etc. **25. cut the ground from under someone's feet** or **cut the ground from under someone**, to anticipate the arguments, plans, etc., of another, to his or her disadvantage. **26. down to the ground**, *Colloq.* completely, entirely. **27. gain ground**, to advance; make progress. **28. get off the ground**, to become a viable project. **29. give ground**, to give way. **30. go over old ground**, to repeat information that is already well known. **31. go to ground**, to withdraw from public attention and live quietly. **32. have one's feet on the ground**, to be sensible and level-headed. **33. hold** (or **stand**) **one's ground**, to maintain one's position. **34. lose ground**, **a.** to lose what one has gained; retreat; give way. **b.** to become less well known or accepted. **35. run into the ground**, *Colloq.* **a.** to drive (a vehicle), often without proper maintenance, until it is worn out and beyond repair. **b.** to exhaust (someone) by making them overly busy. **36. run to ground**, **a.** to hunt down; track down. **b.** to pursue (an animal) to its burrow or hole. **37. shift one's ground**, to take another position or defence in an argument or situation.

ground² /graʊnd/ *v.* **1.** past tense and past participle of **grind**. *–adj.* **2.** reduced to fine particles or dust by grinding: *finely ground pepper.* **3.** having the surface abraded or roughened by or as by grinding: *ground glass.* **4.** minced, as of meat.

grounding /ˈgraʊndɪŋ/ *n.* fundamental knowledge of a subject: *a good grounding in mathematics.*

groundless /ˈgraʊndləs/ *adj.* without basis or reason: *groundless fears.* *–groundlessly*, *adv.* *–groundlessness, n.*

ground penetrating radar *n.* a device which uses radio waves that penetrate the ground to produce images of structures beneath the ground; used particularly in archaeology. *Abbrev.*: GPR

ground plan *n.* **1.** the plan of a ground floor of a building. **2.** first or fundamental plan.

ground rent *n.* the rent at which land is leased to a tenant for a specified term, usually ninety-nine years.

ground rule *n.* (*usu. pl.*) a basic rule of a game, meeting, procedure, etc.

groundsheet /ˈgraʊndʃit/ *n.* a waterproof sheet spread on the ground to give protection against dampness.

groundwater /ˈgraʊndwɔtə/ *n.* the water beneath the surface of the ground, which consists largely of surface water that has seeped down, and which eventually drains into rivers, lakes or wetlands.

groundwork /ˈgraʊndwɜk/ *n.* the foundation, base, or basis of anything.

ground zero *n.* **1.** Also, **surface zero**. the point on the surface of the earth directly below the point at which a nuclear weapon explodes, or the centre of the crater if the weapon is exploded on the ground. **2.** the target of a missile, bomb, etc. **3.** a starting point or base: *when I began learning Italian again, I had to return to ground zero.*

group /grup/ *n.* **1.** a number of people or things gathered, or considered as being connected in some way. **2.** a number of businesses, etc., connected in organisation and finance. **3.** *Chem.* **a.** a number of atoms in a

molecule connected or arranged together in a particular manner that keeps its identity but cannot exist independently; a radical: *the hydroxyl group, -OH.* **b.** a vertical column of the periodic table containing elements with similar properties. **4.** *Geol.* a division of stratified rocks consisting of two or more formations. **5.** a collection of musicians who play together: *pop group; rock group.* **6.** → **blood group. 7.** a grouping of similar plants or animals but which are not related under a scientific classification. *–v.t.* **8.** to place in a group, as with others. **9.** to arrange in or form into a group or groups. *–v.i.* **10.** to form a group. **11.** to be part of a group.

group captain *n.* Air Force **1.** a commissioned officer in the Royal Australian Air Force ranking below air commodore and above wing commander. **2.** the rank. *Abbrev.*: GPCAPT

group certificate *n.* See **PAYG payment summary**.

grouper /ˈgrupə/ *n.* any of various often large fishes, of *Epinephelus* and related genera, found in warm seas.

group house *n.* a residential facility which gives the residents, who have a physical or mental disability, the opportunity to live relatively independently in the general community through mutual support and interaction with that community. Also, **community house, group home**.

group housing *n.* housing provided for people on low to moderate incomes, either owned by the government or rented in the private market, and offering a similar degree of security as public housing.

group therapy *n.* the treatment of a group of psychiatric patients in sessions where all attend and in which problems are shared and discussed.

grouse¹ /graʊs/ *n.* any of various gallinaceous birds of the family Tetraonidae, of the Northern Hemisphere, including important game species as the **red grouse**, *Lagopus lagopus scoticus*, of Britain and the **ruffed grouse**, *Bonasa umbellus*, of North America.

grouse² /graʊs/ *Colloq.* *–v.i.* **1.** to grumble; complain. *–n.* **2.** a complaint. *–grouser, n.*

grouse³ /graʊs/ *Aust., NZ Colloq.* *–adj.* **1.** very good. *–phr.* **2. extra grouse**, excellent.

grout /graʊt/ *n.* **1.** a thin coarse mortar poured into the joints of masonry and brickwork. **2.** a fine finishing plaster for walls and ceilings. *–v.t.* **3.** to fill up, form, or finish the spaces between (stones, etc.) with grout.

grove /groʊv/ *n.* a small wood or plantation of trees.

grovel /ˈgrɒvəl/ *v.i.* (**-elled** or, *Chiefly US*, **-eled**, **-elling** or, *Chiefly US*, **-eling**) **1.** to humble oneself or act in an abject manner, as in fear or in mean servility. **2.** to lie or move with the face downwards and the body prostrate, especially in abject humility, fear, etc. *–groveller, n.*

grow /groʊ/ *verb* (**grew**, **grown**, **growing**) *–v.i.* **1.** to increase by natural development, as any living organism or part by assimilation of nutriment; increase in size or substance. **2.** to arise or issue as from a germ, stock, or originating source. **3.** to increase gradually; become greater. *–v. (copular)* **4.** to come to be, or become, by degrees: *to grow old.* *–v.t.* **5.** to cause to grow: *to grow a hedge.* **6.** to cultivate as a crop: *he grows corn.* **7.** to allow to grow: *to grow a beard.* **8.** to cause to develop or expand: *to grow a business; to grow a career.* **9.** (*used in the passive*) to cover with a growth: *a field grown with corn.* *–phr.* **10. grow apart**, to become gradually separated or disunited by or as by growth. **11. grow like Topsy**, *Colloq.* to grow in an unplanned, random way. **12. grow on**, **a.** to obtain an increasing influence, effect, etc., on. **b.** to win the affection or admiration of by degrees. **13. grow out of**, **a.** to become too big or too mature for; outgrow. **b.** to develop from; originate in. **14. grow together**, to become gradually attached or united by or as by growth.

15. grow up, a. to increase in growth; attain maturity. **b.** to spring up; arise.

growl /graʊl/ *v.i.* **1.** to utter a deep guttural sound of anger or hostility: *a dog growls.* **2.** to murmur or complain angrily; grumble. **3.** to rumble. *–v.t.* **4.** to express by growling. *–n.* **5.** the act or sound of growling. **–growlingly,** *adv.* **–growler,** *n.*

grown-up /ˈɡroʊn-ʌp/ *adj.* **1.** having reached the age of maturity. **2.** characteristic of or suitable for adults. *–n.* **3.** a grown-up person; an adult.

growth /ɡroʊθ/ *n.* **1.** the act, process, or manner of growing; development; gradual increase. **2.** stage of development. **3.** something that has grown or developed by or as by a natural process; a product: *a growth of weeds.* **4.** *Pathol.* a morbid mass of tissue, as a tumour.

groyne /ɡrɔɪn/ *n.* a small jetty built out into the sea or a river in order to prevent erosion of the beach or bank. Also, **groin.**

grub¹ /ɡrʌb/ *n.* **1.** the bulky larva of certain insects, especially beetles. **2.** *Colloq.* food. **3.** *Colloq.* **a.** a person, especially a child, covered with dirt: *you little grub!* **b.** a person with poor personal hygiene: *he's a dirty grub, and never washes.*

grub² /ɡrʌb/ *verb* (**grubbed, grubbing**) *–v.t.* **1.** (oft. fol. by *up* or *out*) to dig up by the roots; uproot. *–v.i.* **2.** to dig; search by or as by digging. **3.** to lead a hard-working life; drudge.

grubby /ˈɡrʌbi/ *adj.* (**-bier, -biest**) **1.** dirty; grimy. **2.** morally dubious; sleazy: *a grubby little film.* **3.** infested with or affected by grubs or larvae. **–grubbily,** *adv.* **–grubbiness,** *n.*

grudge /ɡrʌdʒ/ *n.* **1.** a feeling of ill will or resentment excited by some special cause, such as a personal injury or insult, etc. *–verb* (**grudged, grudging**) *–v.t.* **2.** to give or permit with reluctance; submit to unwillingly. **3.** to be dissatisfied at seeing the good fortune of (another). *–v.i.* **4.** to feel dissatisfaction or ill will. **–grudgeless,** *adj.* **–grudger,** *n.* **–grudgingly,** *adv.*

gruel /ˈɡruəl/ *n.* **1.** a light, usually thin, cooked cereal made by boiling meal, especially oatmeal, in water or milk. **2.** any similar substance.

gruelling /ˈɡruəlɪŋ/ *adj.* exhausting; very tiring; severe. Also, *Chiefly US,* **grueling.**

Gruen transfer /ɡruən ˈtrænsfɜ/ *n.* the response that customers in a shopping mall make when they react unconsciously to the spatial design, ambient sound, decor, etc., which have been deliberately chosen to distract them briefly from thoughts of their original buying intention, and so to make them vulnerable to impulse buying.

gruesome /ˈɡrusəm/ *adj.* such as to make one shudder; inspiring horror; revolting. **–gruesomely,** *adv.* **–gruesomeness,** *n.*

gruff /ɡrʌf/ *adj.* **1.** low and harsh; hoarse: *a gruff voice.* **2.** rough; surly: *a gruff manner.* **–gruffly,** *adv.* **–gruffness,** *n.*

grumble /ˈɡrʌmbəl/ *v.i.* **1.** to murmur in discontent; complain ill-humouredly. **2.** to speak low, indistinct sounds; growl. *–v.t.* **3.** to express or utter with murmuring or complaining; rumble. *–n.* **4.** an ill-humoured complaining; murmur; growl. **–grumbler,** *n.* **–grumblingly,** *adv.*

grump /ɡrʌmp/ *n.* a surly or ill-tempered person.

grumpy /ˈɡrʌmpi/ *adj.* (**-pier, -piest**) *Colloq.* surly; ill-tempered. **–grumpily,** *adj.* **–grumpiness,** *n.*

grunge /ɡrʌndʒ/ *n.* **1.** a substance of an unpleasant nature, especially a dirty scum or slime. **2.** → **grunge music.** **3.** a fashion in which clothes are worn which are normally considered shabby or unfashionable, as those bought in second-hand shops. **–grungy,** *adj.*

grunge music *n.* a guitar-based form of heavy rock music using simple minor-chord progressions, on-the-beat rhythms, and often provocative lyrics. Also, **grunge.**

grunt /ɡrʌnt/ *v.i.* **1.** to utter the deep guttural sound characteristic of a pig. **2.** to grumble, as in discontent. *–v.t.* **3.** to express with a grunt. *–n.* **4.** the sound of grunting. **5.** *Colloq.* the power of an engine or mechanism: *a car with grunt.* **–gruntingly,** *adv.* **–grunty,** *adj.*

gruyere /ˈɡrujə, ɡruˈjɛə/ *n.* a firm pale yellow variety of Swiss cheese with some surface growth which gives added flavour. Also, **Gruyère, Gruyere.**

gryphon /ˈɡrɪfən/ *n.* → **griffin.**

G-string /ˈdʒi-strɪŋ/ *n.* an item of apparel for men or women, comprising a narrow strip of cloth passing between the legs and supported by a waistband, providing minimal cover for the genitalia and leaving the buttocks bare.

guacamole /ɡwɒkəˈmoʊli, ɡwɑkə-/ *n.* a dip consisting of mashed avocado, seasonings, and lemon or lime juice, sometimes mixed with sour cream, mayonnaise, etc.

guano /ˈɡwɑnoʊ/ *n.* (*pl.* **guanos**) **1.** a natural manure composed chiefly of the excrement of seabirds. **2.** Also, **bat guano.** the droppings of bats, used as a fertiliser.

guarantee /ɡærənˈti/ *n.* **1.** a pledge or promise accepting responsibility for someone else's debts, liabilities, obligations, etc. **2.** a promise or assurance (especially given in writing) that a manufacturer will make good any defects under certain conditions. **3.** someone who gives a guarantee; guarantor. **4.** someone to whom a guarantee is made. **5.** anything which is taken or presented as security. **6.** something that has the force or effect of a guarantee: *wealth is no guarantee of happiness.* *–v.t.* (**-teed, -teeing**) **7.** to secure, as by giving or taking security. **8.** to accept responsibility: *to guarantee the carrying out of a contract.* **9.** (fol. by *from, against,* or *in*) to (promise to) compensate: *to guarantee someone against loss.* **10.** to promise.

guarantor /ɡærənˈtɔ/ *n.* someone who makes or gives a guarantee or guaranty.

guaranty /ˈɡærənti/ *n.* (*pl.* **-ties, -tied, -tying**) → **guarantee.**

guard /ɡɑd/ *v.t.* **1.** to keep safe from harm; protect; watch over. **2.** to keep under close watch in order to prevent escape, outbreaks, etc.: *to guard a prisoner.* **3.** to keep in check, from caution or prudence: *to guard the tongue.* **4.** to provide with some safeguard or protective appliance, etc. *–v.i.* **5.** to give protection; keep watch; be watchful. *–n.* **6.** someone who guards, protects, or keeps a protecting or restraining watch. **7.** someone who keeps watch over prisoners or others under restraint. **8.** a body of people, especially soldiers, charged with guarding a place from disturbance, theft, fire, etc. **9.** restraining watch, as over a prisoner or other person under restraint: *to be kept under close guard.* **10.** a contrivance, appliance, or attachment designed for guarding against injury, loss, etc. **11.** something intended or serving to guard or protect; a safeguard. **12.** a posture of defence or readiness, as in fencing, boxing, bayonet drill, etc. **13.** *Basketball* one of the defensive players in a team, stationed at the back-court. **14.** an official in general charge of a railway train. *–phr.* **15. guard against,** to take precautions against: *to guard against errors.* **16. off (one's) guard,** unprepared to meet a sudden attack; unwary. **17. on (one's) guard,** watchful or vigilant against attack; cautious; wary. **–guardable,** *adj.* **–guarder,** *n.*

guarded /ˈɡɑdəd/ *adj.* **1.** cautious; careful: *to be guarded in one's speech.* **2.** protected or watched, as by a guard. **–guardedly,** *adv.* **–guardedness,** *n.*

guardian /ˈɡɑdiən/ *n.* **1.** someone who guards, protects, or preserves. **2.** *Law* someone who is entrusted by law with the care of the person or property, or both, of another, as of a minor or of some other person legally incapable of managing his or her own affairs. *–adj.* **3.** guarding; protecting: *a guardian angel.* **–guardianship,** *n.*

guava /ˈgwavə/ *n.* **1.** any of various trees and shrubs of the genus *Psidium*, especially *P. guajava* and the cherry guava *P. cattleianum*, native to tropical and subtropical America, with a fruit used for jelly, etc. **2.** the fruit, used for making jam, jelly, etc.

guerilla /gəˈrɪlə/ *n.* **1.** a member of an irregular, usually politically motivated armed force, which harasses the enemy, usually the regular army, by surprise raids, attacks on communication and supply lines, etc. *–adj.* **2.** relating to such fighters or their method of warfare. **3.** of or relating to the strategies of a consumer attempting to get the best of the retailers by avoiding marketing hype, brand names, etc.: *guerilla shopping*; *guerilla living.* Also, **guerrilla.**

guerilla gardener *n.* a person who plants gardens in areas controlled by councils or other organisations but neglected by them in terms of vegetation, as nature strips, roundabouts, council-maintained gardens, etc. Also, **guerrilla gardener.**

guernsey /ˈgɜnzi/ *n.* (*pl.* **-seys**) **1.** (*upper case*) one of a breed of dairy cattle. **2.** a close-fitting knitted jumper, worn by fishermen, etc. **3.** *Sport* a distinctively coloured or marked top worn by footballers, especially the sleeveless variety worn by AFL players. *–phr.* **4. get a guernsey,** *Aust.* **a.** to be selected for a football team. **b.** *Colloq.* to succeed, win approval.

guess /gɛs/ *v.t.* **1.** to form an opinion of at random or from evidence admittedly uncertain: *to guess someone's age.* **2.** to estimate or conjecture correctly: *to guess a riddle.* **3.** to think, believe, or suppose: *I guess I can get there in time.* *–phr.* **4. guess at,** to form an estimate of; conjecture: *to guess at the height of a building.* **–guessable,** *adj.* **–guesser,** *n.* **–guessingly,** *adv.*

guesswork /ˈgɛswɜk/ *n.* work or procedure based on guessing; conjecture.

guest /gɛst/ *n.* **1.** someone who is entertained at the house or table of another. **2.** someone who receives the hospitality of a club, a city, or the like. **3.** someone who pays for lodging, and sometimes food, at a hotel, etc. **4.** *Internet* an unregistered user of a website. *–adj.* **5.** (of a performer, speaker, etc.) specially invited to make an occasional appearance in one of a series of meetings, concerts, broadcasts, etc. **–guestless,** *adj.*

guff /gʌf/ *n. Colloq.* empty or foolish talk; humbug; nonsense.

guffaw /gʌˈfɔ, gə-/ *n.* **1.** a loud, coarse burst of laughter. *–v.i.* **2.** to laugh loudly and boisterously.

GUI /ˈgui/ *n. Computers* → **graphical user interface.**

guidance /ˈgaɪdns/ *n.* advice; leadership; instruction.

guide /gaɪd/ *v.t.* **1.** to lead as to a place; show the way to. **2.** to direct the movement or course of: *to guide a horse.* **3.** to lead, direct or advise in any course or action. *–n.* **4.** someone who guides, especially a person employed to guide travellers, tourists, mountaineers, etc. **5.** a book with information for travellers, tourists, etc. **6.** anything that guides, as a device for guiding forward movement in a machine. **7.** → **Guide.** **–guidable,** *adj.* **–guideless,** *adj.* **–guider,** *n.*

Guide /gaɪd/ *n.* (*sometimes lower case*) a member of a worldwide youth movement for girls which developed from an organisation founded in England in 1910 by Lady Agnes Baden-Powell; members participate in organised activities which have the aim of promoting outdoor adventure, community service, and care for the environment. Also, **Girl Guide, girl guide.**

guide dog *n.* a dog specially trained to lead or guide a vision-impaired person.

guideline /ˈgaɪdlaɪn/ *n.* **1.** a line drawn as a guide for further writing, drawing, etc. **2.** (*usu. pl.*) a statement which defines policy or the area in which a policy is operative.

guild /gɪld/ *n.* **1.** an organisation of persons with common professional or cultural interests formed for mutual aid and protection. **2.** one of the associations, numerous in the Middle Ages, formed for mutual aid and protection or for a common purpose, most frequently by persons associated in trade or industry. Also, **gild.**

guilder /ˈgɪldə/ *n.* (formerly, until the introduction of the euro in 2002) the principal monetary unit of the Netherlands. Also, **gilder, gulden.**

guile /gaɪl/ *n.* **1.** insidious cunning; deceitfulness; treachery. *–phr.* **2. without guile,** artless and ingenuous. **–guileless,** *adj.*

guillotine *n.* /ˈgɪlətin/ **1.** an instrument for beheading persons by means of a heavy blade falling between two grooved posts. **2.** a device with a long blade for trimming paper. **3.** a time limit on a parliamentary debate. *–v.t.* /gɪləˈtin/ **4.** *Parliament* to limit the time allowed for debate of (each section of a bill). **5.** to behead by the guillotine. **–guillotiner,** *n.*

guilt /gɪlt/ *n.* **1.** the fact or state of having committed an offence or crime; grave culpability, as for some conscious violation of moral or penal law. **2.** a feeling of responsibility or remorse for some crime, wrong, etc., either real or imagined. *–phr.* **3. guilt by association,** guilt imputed to someone because of their connection with others who are guilty. **4. the guilts,** *Colloq.* feelings of guilt, remorse, etc.: *an attack of the guilts.* **–guilty,** *adj.* **–guiltily,** *adv.*

guinea /ˈgɪni/ *n.* (in Australia until the introduction of decimal currency in 1966) the sum of 21 shillings.

guinea pig *n.* **1.** a short-eared, short-legged rodent, *Cavia procellus*, originally native to temperate regions of South America but now only found in domestication; commonly kept as a pet, much used in scientific experiments. **2.** a person used as the subject of any sort of experiment.

guise /gaɪz/ *n.* **1.** external appearance in general; aspect or semblance: *an old principle in a new guise.* **2.** assumed appearance or mere semblance: *under the guise of friendship.*

guitar /gəˈta/ *n.* a musical stringed instrument with a long fretted neck and a flat, somewhat violin-like body. The strings, usually six in number, are plucked or struck with a sweeping motion. **–guitarist,** *n.*

gulf /gʌlf/ *n.* **1.** a portion of an ocean or sea partly enclosed by land. **2.** a deep hollow; chasm or abyss. **3.** any wide separation, as in social class, education, etc. **4.** something that engulfs or swallows up.

gull /gʌl/ *n.* any of numerous long-winged, web-footed, aquatic birds constituting the subfamily Larinae, family Laridae, especially of the genus *Larus*, usually white with grey back and wings, generally inhabiting coastal regions worldwide, as the silver gull.

gullet /ˈgʌlət/ *n.* **1.** the oesophagus, or tube by which food and drink swallowed pass to the stomach. **2.** the throat or pharynx.

gullible /ˈgʌləbəl/ *adj.* easily deceived or cheated. **–gullibility** /gʌləˈbɪləti/, *n.* **–gullibly,** *adv.*

gully /ˈgʌli/ *n.* (*pl.* **-lies**) **1.** a fold in a mountain or hill with an intermittent watercourse running down it at its lowest point **2.** *Chiefly Brit.* a ditch or gutter. **3.** *Cricket* **a.** a fielding position between the slips and point. **b.** the fielder in this position. **4.** *Chiefly Brit.* a steep-sided ravine cut into the side of a mountain by the action of running water.

gully trap *n.* a trap (def. 5) with a section filled with water through which the house drainage is connected to the external drains, the water seal preventing sewer gases leaking back into the house. Also, **gulley trap**.

gulp /gʌlp/ *v.i.* **1.** to gasp or choke as when taking large draughts of liquids. –*v.t.* Also, **gulp down**. **2.** to swallow eagerly, or in large draughts or pieces. –*n.* **3.** the act of gulping. **4.** the amount swallowed at one time; mouthful. –*phr.* **5. gulp down**, to suppress or choke back: *to gulp down a sob.* –**gulper**, *n.*

gum¹ /gʌm/ *n.* **1.** any of various viscid, amorphous exudations from plants, hardening on exposure to air, and soluble in, or forming a viscid mass with, water. **2.** any of various similar exudations, such as resin. **3.** a preparation of such a substance, as for use in the arts, etc. **4.** → **gum tree** (def. 1). **5.** Also, **gumwood**. the wood of any such tree or shrub. **6.** mucilage; glue. **7.** → **chewing gum. 8.** → **gumdrop.** –*v.t.* (**gummed, gumming**) **9.** to smear, stiffen, or stick together with gum. –*phr.* **10. gum up,** to clog with or as with some gummy substance. **11. gum up the works,** to interfere with or spoil something.

gum² /gʌm/ *n.* (*oft. pl.*) the firm, fleshy tissue covering the alveolar parts of either jaw and enveloping the bases of the teeth.

gum arabic /gʌm ˈærəbɪk/ *n.* a gum obtained from *Acacia senegal* and other species of acacia, used in calico printing; in making mucilage, ink, and the like; in medicine, etc.

gumboot /ˈgʌmbut/ *n.* a waterproof boot made of rubber, sometimes reaching to the knee or thigh. Also, **wellington boot**.

gumdrop /ˈgʌmdrɒp/ *n.* a hard gelatinous sweet.

gumland /ˈgʌmlænd/ *n. NZ* poor quality land in which kauri gum may be found.

gumnut /ˈgʌmnʌt/ *n.* the woody, inedible, ripe capsule of the eucalyptus.

gumption /ˈgʌmpʃən/ *n. Colloq.* **1.** initiative; resourcefulness. **2.** shrewd, practical common sense.

gum tree *n.* **1.** Also, **gum.** any tree or shrub of the myrtaceous genus *Eucalyptus*, almost entirely Australian apart from very few tropical species in New Guinea and other nearby islands, some yielding eucalyptus oil and some hardwood timber, and bearing gumnuts as fruits; eucalyptus. **2.** any of various other gum-yielding trees, such as the sweet gum and the sapodilla. –*phr.* **3. up a gum tree,** *Colloq.* **a.** in difficulties; in a predicament. **b.** completely baffled.

gun /gʌn/ *n.* **1.** a weapon comprising a metallic tube, with its stock or carriage and attachments, from which heavy missiles are thrown by the force of an explosive; a piece of ordnance. **2.** any portable firearm, as a rifle, revolver, etc. **3.** any similar device for projecting something: *an airgun; a cement gun.* **4.** a member of a shooting party. **5.** *Aust., NZ Colloq.* a champion, especially in shearing. **6.** (*oft. in the pl.*) *Colloq.* a biceps, especially one developed, as in bodybuilding. –*verb* (**gunned, gunning**) –*v.i.* **7.** to hunt with a gun. **8.** to shoot with a gun. **9.** *Colloq.* (of a motor vehicle) to take off at great speed. –*v.t.* **10.** to feed fuel to (an engine), suddenly and quickly resulting in a sudden increase in speed. –*adj.* **11.** *Aust., NZ Colloq.* of or relating to someone who is expert: *gun shearer; gun drover.* –*phr.* **12. beat** (or **jump**) **the gun, a.** (of a competitor in a race) to begin before the starting gun has fired. **b.** *Colloq.* to begin prematurely; be overeager. **13. carry** (or **hold**) (**big**) **guns,** to be in a powerful or strong position. **14. go great guns,** *Colloq.* (sometimes fol. by *at* or *with*) to be successful. **15. gun down,** to shoot with a gun. **16. gun for,** *Colloq.* to seek (a person) with the intention to harm or kill. **17. in the gun,** *Colloq.* in trouble; the object of criticism. **18. stick to one's guns,** *Colloq.* to maintain one's position in an argument, etc., against opposition.

gunboat diplomacy /gʌnbout dəˈploʊməsi/ *n.* diplomacy or foreign affairs in conjunction with the use or threat of military force.

gung-ho /gʌŋˈhoʊ/ *adj.* intemperately and naively enthusiastic.

gunk /gʌŋk/ *n. Colloq.* **1.** material, especially of a dirty, slimy, or offensive nature. **2.** a food judged to be bad or inappropriate, especially oversweet and cloying. **3.** an unpleasing sticky substance coating something else. **4.** any viscous substance: *she smeared cosmetic gunk all over her face.*

gunna /ˈgʌnə/ *v.* **1.** → **gonna.** –*n.* **2.** *Colloq.* a person who says that they intend to do something but who never gets around to doing it.

gunner /ˈgʌnə/ *n. Mil.* an artilleryman.

gunnery /ˈgʌnəri/ *n.* **1.** the art and science of constructing and managing guns, especially large guns. **2.** the firing of guns. **3.** guns collectively.

gunny /ˈgʌni/ *n.* (*pl.* **-nies**) **1.** a strong, coarse material made commonly from jute, used for sacking, etc. **2.** Also, **gunnybag, gunnysack.** a bag or sack made of this material. **3.** *Mining* a mine cavity from which ore has been removed.

gunpowder /ˈgʌnpaʊdə/ *n.* **1.** an explosive mixture of saltpetre (potassium nitrate), sulphur, and charcoal, used especially in gunnery. **2.** a fine variety of green China tea, each leaf of which is rolled into a small ball.

gun running *n.* the smuggling of guns, etc., into a country. Also, **gun-running.** –**gun runner,** *n.*

gunwale /ˈgʌnəl/ *n.* the upper edge of a vessel's or boat's side. Also, **gunnel.**

gunyah /ˈgʌnjə/ *n.* **1.** a hut traditionally made by Aboriginal people of boughs and bark. **2.** a small rough hut or shelter in the bush. Also, **gunya.**

guppy /ˈgʌpi/ *n.* (*pl.* **-pies**) a small viviparous fish, *Poecilia reticulata*, of the family Poeciliidae, common in home aquariums.

gurgle /ˈgɜgəl/ *v.i.* **1.** to flow in a broken, irregular, noisy current: *water gurgles from a bottle.* **2.** to make a sound as of water doing this (often used of birds or of human beings). –*v.t.* **3.** to utter with a gurgling sound. –*n.* **4.** the act or noise of gurgling. –**gurglingly,** *adv.*

gurgler /ˈgɜglə/ *phr.* **down the gurgler,** *Colloq.* ruined; irretrievably lost or destroyed.

guru /ˈguru, ˈguru/ *n.* **1.** (in Hinduism) a preceptor and spiritual guide. **2.** an influential teacher or mentor. **3.** a person who is recognised as an expert in a given field: *fashion guru; sports guru.*

gush /gʌʃ/ *v.i.* **1.** to issue with force, as a fluid escaping from confinement; flow suddenly and copiously. **2.** to express oneself extravagantly or emotionally; talk effusively. **3.** to have a copious flow of something, as of blood, tears, etc. –**gushingly,** *adv.* –**gusher,** *n.* –**gushy,** *adj.*

gusset /ˈgʌsət/ *n.* **1.** an angular piece of material inserted in a garment to strengthen, enlarge, or give freedom of movement to some part of it. **2.** a metal bracket for strengthening a structure at a joint or angle.

gust /gʌst/ *n.* **1.** a sudden, strong blast of wind. **2.** a sudden rush or burst of water, fire, smoke, sound, etc. **3.** an outburst of passionate feeling. –*v.i.* **4.** to blow in gusts: *the wind gusted to 50 knots.* –**gusty,** *adj.*

gusto /ˈgʌstoʊ/ *n.* keen relish or hearty enjoyment, as in eating, drinking, or in action or speech generally: *to tell a story with gusto.*

gut /gʌt/ *n.* **1.** → **intestine** (def. 1). **2.** the tissue or fibre of the intestine: *sheep's gut.* **3.** the processed gut of an animal, used for violin strings, etc. –*v.t.* (**gutted, gutting**) **4.** to take out the guts of; disembowel. **5.** to remove all content or value from. **6.** to destroy the inside of: *fire gutted the building.* –*adj.* **7.** of or relating to feelings or intuition: *a gut response.* See **guts.**

gutless /'gʌtləs/ *Colloq.* –*adj.* **1.** cowardly. **2.** lacking in power, especially of a car, motor, etc. –*phr.* **3. gutless wonder, a.** a very cowardly person. **b.** a machine, especially a motor vehicle, that lacks power. –**gutlessness,** *n.*

guts /gʌts/ *Colloq.* –*pl. n.* (*oft. construed as sing.*) **1.** the bowels or entrails. **2.** the stomach or abdomen. **3.** courage; stamina; endurance: *to have guts.* **4.** essential information: *the guts of the matter.* **5.** essential parts or contents: *let me get to the guts of the motor.* **6.** Also, **greedy-guts.** someone greedy for food; a glutton. –*v.t.* **7.** to cram (oneself) with food. –*phr.* **8. hate someone's guts,** to loathe or detest someone. **9. have someone's guts for garters,** to exact revenge on someone. **10. rough as guts,** (of a person) coarse in manner and behaviour. **11. spill** (or **give**) **one's guts,** to give information, as to the police, without restraint: *they had broken him - he was about to spill his guts to them.* **12. the (good) guts,** (sometimes fol. by *on*) accurate information, especially when intended to be used against someone. **13. work one's guts out,** to work excessively hard. See **gut.**

gutsy /'gʌtsi/ *adj.* (**-sier, -siest**) *Colloq.* **1.** full of courage; full of guts. **2.** warmly wholehearted; unreserved. **3.** strong, full-bodied: *a gutsy wine.* **4.** greedy; gluttonous.

gutta-percha /gʌtə-'pɜtʃə/ *n.* the coagulated milky juice, nearly white when pure, of various Malaysian trees of the family Sapotaceae, especially *Palaquium gutta,* variously used in the arts, medicine, and manufacturing, as for insulating electric wires.

gutter /'gʌtə/ *n.* **1.** a channel at the side (or in the middle) of a road or street, for carrying away surface water. **2.** any similar channel, for carrying off fluid. **3.** a channel at the eaves or roof of a building, for carrying off rainwater. **4.** the lowest social conditions in the community: *the language of the gutter.* –*v.i.* **5.** to form gutters, as running water does. **6.** (of a lighted candle) to melt away quickly and irregularly. –**guttery,** *adj.*

guttural /'gʌtərəl/ *adj.* **1.** relating to the throat. **2.** harsh; throaty. –**gutturally,** *adv.* –**gutturalness,** *n.*

guy[1] /gaɪ/ *Colloq.* –*n.* **1.** a fellow or man: *guys and dolls.* **2.** a boyfriend. **3.** (*pl.*) people of either sex, regarded as members of a group: *are you guys ready?* –*phr.* **4. the bad guys,** the villains. **5. the good guys,** the heroes

guy[2] /gaɪ/ *n.* **1.** a rope, wire, etc., used to guide and steady something being hoisted or lowered, or to secure anything liable to shift its position. –*v.t.* (**guyed, guying**) **2.** to guide, steady, or secure with a guy or guys.

guzzle /'gʌzəl/ *v.t.* **1.** to drink (or sometimes eat) frequently and greedily: *they sat there all evening guzzling their beer.* –*v.i.* **2.** to drink (or eat) in such a manner. –**guzzler,** *n.*

gym /dʒɪm/ *n.* **1.** a centre providing fitness equipment and classes. **2.** → **gymnasium.** **3.** → **gymnastics.**

gymkhana /dʒɪm'kɑnə/ *n.* **1.** a horseriding event featuring games and novelty contests. **2.** a festival featuring gymnastics and athletic showmanship. **3.** Also, **motorkhana.** a series of motoring events designed to test the skill and judgement of drivers.

gymnasium /dʒɪm'neɪziəm/ *n.* (*pl.* **-siums** *or* **-sia** /-ziə/) a building or room equipped with facilities for gymnastics and sport.

gymnast /'dʒɪmnæst, -nəst/ *n.* someone trained and skilled in, or a teacher of, gymnastics.

gymnastic /dʒɪm'næstɪk/ *adj.* relating to exercises which develop flexibility, strength, and agility. –**gymnastically,** *adv.*

gymnastics /dʒɪm'næstɪks/ *n.* **1.** (*construed as pl.*) gymnastic exercises. **2.** (*construed as sing.*) the practice or art of gymnastic exercises.

gymnosperm /'dʒɪmnoʊ,spɜm/ *n. Bot.* a plant having its seeds exposed or naked, not enclosed in an ovary (opposed to *angiosperm*). –**gymnospermous** /dʒɪmnoʊ-'spɜməs/, *adj.*

gyn- variant of **gyno-,** occurring before vowels, as in *gynarchy.*

gynaecology /gaɪnə'kɒlədʒi/ *n.* the branch of medical science which deals with the anatomy, physiology, and diseases of women, especially those affecting the reproductive organs. Also, **gynecology.** –**gynaecological** /gaɪnəkə'lɒdʒɪkəl/, *adj.* –**gynaecologist,** *n.*

gyno- a word element meaning 'woman', 'female', as in *gynogenic.* Also, **gyn-.**

-gynous **1.** a word element forming an adjective termination referring to the female sex, as in *androgynous.* **2.** a suffix meaning 'woman.'

gyp /dʒɪp/ *Colloq.* –*v.t.* (**gypped, gypping**) **1.** to swindle; cheat; defraud or rob by some sharp practice. **2.** to obtain by swindling or cheating; steal. –*n.* **3.** a swindle. **4.** a swindler or cheat. –**gypper,** *n.*

gypsum /'dʒɪpsəm/ *n.* a very common mineral, hydrated calcium sulphate, $CaSO_4$. $2H_2O$, occurring in crystals and in masses, soft enough to be scratched by the fingernail, used to make plaster of Paris, as an ornamental material, as a fertiliser, etc.

gypsy /'dʒɪpsi/ *n.* (*pl.* **-sies**) someone who has an unconventional or nomadic lifestyle. Also, **gipsy.**

gyrate /dʒaɪ'reɪt/ *v.i.* to move in a circle or spiral, or round a fixed point; whirl.

gyre /'dʒaɪə/ *n.* **1.** a ring or circle. **2.** a circular course or motion. **3.** *Oceanography* a swirling anticlockwise basin-wide current, as within the Indian, Pacific and Atlantic Oceans, which affects ocean life and climate patterns.

gyro- a word element meaning: **1.** ring; circle. **2.** spiral.

gyrocompass /'dʒaɪroʊ,kʌmpəs/ *n.* a device used like the ordinary compass for determining directions, but using a continuously driven gyroscope instead of a magnetised needle or bar, the gyroscope being so mounted that its axis constantly maintains its position with reference to the geographical north, thus dealing with true geographical meridians used in navigation instead of magnetic meridians. Also, **gyroscopic compass.**

gyroscope /'dʒaɪrəskoʊp/ *n.* an apparatus consisting of a rotating wheel so mounted that its axis can turn freely in certain or all directions, and capable of maintaining the same absolute direction in space in spite of movements of the mountings and surrounding parts. It is based on the principle that a body rotating steadily about an axis will tend to resist changes in the direction of the axis, and is used to maintain equilibrium, as in a plane or ship, to determine direction, etc. –**gyroscopic** /dʒaɪrə'skɒpɪk/, *adj.* –**gyroscopically** /dʒaɪrə-'skɒpɪkli/, *adv.*

H h

H, h /eɪtʃ/, *sometimes considered non-standard* /heɪtʃ/ *n.*
1. a consonant, the 8th letter of the English alphabet.
2. (as a symbol) the eighth in a series.

habeas corpus /ˌheɪbɪəs ˈkɔpəs/ *n. Law* a prerogative
writ directed to someone who detains another in custody, commanding them to produce the other person
before the court. It is mainly used to test the legality of
an imprisonment.

haberdashery /hæbəˈdæʃəri, ˈhæbə-/ *n.* (*pl.* **-ries**) **1.** a
shop, counter, or section of a department store where
small wares such as buttons, needles, ribbons, etc., are
sold. **2.** the goods themselves. **–haberdasher,** *n.*

habit /ˈhæbət/ *n.* **1.** a constant tendency to act in a certain
way. **2.** a particular practice or custom: *it is my habit to
read before bed.* **3.** a behaviour or need that is difficult
to stop; addiction; compulsion: *smoking has become a
habit.* **4.** a customary practice or use: *to act from force
of habit.* **5.** a condition: *a habit of mind.* **6.** a characteristic appearance or form of growth of an animal
or plant: *a twisting habit.* **7.** *Chem.* the characteristic
crystalline form of a mineral. **8.** the dress of a particular
profession, religious order, etc.: *a monk's habit.* **9.** a
woman's riding dress. **–habitable,** *adj.* **–habitual,** *adj.*

habitat /ˈhæbətæt/ *n.* **1.** the native environment or kind of
place where a given animal or plant naturally lives or
grows, such as warm seas, mountain tops, fresh waters,
etc. **2.** place of abode; habitation.

habitation /hæbəˈteɪʃən/ *n.* **1.** a place of abode; dwelling.
2. the act of inhabiting; occupancy by inhabitants.

habituate /həˈbɪtʃueɪt/ *v.t.* **1.** to accustom (a person, the
mind, etc.) as to something; make used (*to*). **2.** to frequent. **–habituation** /həbɪtʃuˈeɪʃən/, *n.*

habitué /həˈbɪtʃueɪ, həˈbɪtʃueɪ/ *n.* a habitual frequenter of
a place.

háček /ˈhætʃɛk, ˈhatʃɛk/ *n.* a mark (ˇ) over a letter used
especially in the spelling of Slavic languages to represent particular phonetic qualities.

hacienda /hæsiˈɛndə/ *n.* (in Latin America) **1.** a landed
estate, ranch, or farm. **2.** the main house on such an
estate; a country house. **3.** a stock-raising, mining, or
manufacturing establishment in the country.

hack¹ /hæk/ *v.t.* **1.** to cut, notch, or chop irregularly, as
with heavy blows. **2.** to break up the surface of (the
ground). **3.** to clear (a path, etc.) by cutting down brush,
etc. **4.** to damage by cutting harshly or ruthlessly: *the
subeditor hacked the article to bits.* **5.** to kick the
shins of intentionally, as in Rugby football. *–v.i.* **6.** to
make rough cuts or notches; deal cutting blows. *–n.* **7.** a
tool, such as an axe, hoe, pick, etc., for hacking. **8.** an
act of hacking; a cutting blow. **9.** a short, broken cough.
10. *Computers* a solution to a programming problem.
11. *Computers* unauthorised access to a computer, a
computer network, or a digital device. **12.** *Computers* a
contrived method of achieving a programming goal that
takes advantage of opportunities that are provided by
software but were not intended by the original developer. *–phr.* **13. hack into,** to gain unauthorised access
to, as to the information stored on an organisation's
computer, or the computer itself, or the organisation
itself.

hack² /hæk/ *n.* **1.** a riding horse kept for hire to the public,
or used for ordinary riding. **2.** an old or worn-out horse.
3. someone who does routine or poor quality literary or

other work for a living; someone who does hackwork.
–v.t. **4.** *Colloq.* to put up with; endure. *–v.i.* **5.** to ride a
horse on the road at an ordinary pace. *–adj.* **6.** hired; of
a hired sort: *hack writer.* **7.** unoriginal; hackneyed; trite.

hacker /ˈhækə/ *n.* **1.** someone or something that hacks.
2. a. a person who is adept at manipulating computer
systems, especially someone who achieves unauthorised access to the computer system of a business
organisation, government department, etc., or who
achieves unauthorised access to a person's digital
device, as a phone or tablet computer; cracker. **b.** any
person who has an intimate understanding of computer
programs, systems and networks.

hackey sack /ˈhæki sæk/ *n.* → **hacky sack.**

hackneyed /ˈhæknid/ *adj.* made commonplace or trite;
stale.

hacksaw /ˈhæksɔ/ *n.* a saw used for cutting metal, consisting typically of a narrow, fine-toothed blade fixed in
a frame.

hackwork /ˈhækwɜk/ *n.* the routine aspects of a creative
or artistic occupation, considered as mundane, or of an
inferior quality, especially in the literary field.

hacky sack /ˈhæki sæk/ *n.* (*from trademark*) **1.** a game in
which one or more players use various parts of their
bodies to keep a small stuffed ball in the air without
touching the ball with their hands or arms, or allowing
it to touch the ground; footbag. **2.** the stuffed ball used
in this game. Also, **hackey sack.**

had /hæd/, *weak forms* /həd, əd, d/ *v.* **1.** past tense and
past participle of **have.** *–phr.* **2. been had,** *Colloq.* to
have been cheated or duped. **3. had better,** ought to:
you had better do as you are told. **4. had rather**
(or **sooner**), to consider as preferable: *I had rather you
came early.* **5. have had,** to be utterly exasperated with:
I have had this government. **6. have had it,** *Colloq.* **a.** to
be utterly exasperated: *I've had it! I'm going home; I've
had it with junk mail.* **b.** to be exhausted. **c.** to be on the
point of death or doomed to die. **d.** to become out of
fashion or no longer popular. **e.** (of a device, machine,
etc.) to be irreparably broken.

haddock /ˈhædək/ *n.* a food fish, *Melanogrammus
aeglefinus,* of the northern Atlantic, related to but
smaller than the cod.

hadj /hadʒ/ *n.* → **hajj.**

hadja /ˈhadʒə/ *n.* → **haja.**

hadji /ˈhadʒi/ *n.* (*pl.* **-jis**) → **hajji.**

haematology /himəˈtɒlədʒi/ *n.* the scientific study of the
nature, function, and diseases of the blood. Also,
hematology. –haematologist, *n.*

haematoma /himəˈtoʊmə, hɛm-/ *n.* (*pl.* **-tomas** *or*
-tomata /-toʊmətə/) a bruise or collection of blood in a
tissue. Also, **hematoma.**

haemo- a word element meaning 'blood' as in *hae-
molysis.* Also, **hemo-, h(a)em-, h(a)ema-, h(a)emat-,
h(a)emato-.**

haemoglobin /himəˈgloʊbən/ *n. Physiol.* a protein in
blood responsible for the red colour of blood which
carries oxygen to the tissues. Also, **hemoglobin.**

haemophilia /himəˈfɪliə, -ˈfil-, -jə/ *n. Pathol.* a blood
disorder of males in which clotting occurs abnormally
slowly, resulting in excessive bleeding from even
minor injuries. Also, **hemophilia. –haemophiliac,** *n.*

haemorrhage /'hɛmərɪdʒ/ *n*. **1.** a discharge of blood, as from a ruptured blood vessel. –*v.i.* (**haemorrhaged, haemorrhaging**) **2.** to bleed severely. Also, **hemorrhage**. –**haemorrhagic** /hɛmə'rædʒɪk/, *adj*.

haemorrhagic stroke /hɛmərædʒɪk 'stroʊk/ *n*. a stroke (**stroke**[1] def. 4) occurring as a result of the rupture of a blood vessel in the brain; the less common form of stroke. Compare **ischaemic stroke**. Also, **hemorrhagic stroke**.

haemorrhoid /'hɛmərɔɪd/ *n*. a dilatation of a superficial vein of the canal or margin of the anus; pile. Also, **hemorrhoid**. –**haemorrhoidal** /hɛmə'rɔɪdl/, *adj*.

haft /haft/ *n*. a handle, especially of a knife, sword, dagger, etc.

hag /hæg/ *n*. **1.** a repulsive, often vicious or malicious, old woman. **2.** a witch. –**haggy**, *adj*.

haggard /'hægəd/ *adj*. careworn; gaunt, as from prolonged suffering, anxiety, exertion, or ill health. –**haggardly**, *adv*. –**haggardness**, *n*.

haggis /'hægəs/ *n*. a dish, originally Scottish, made of the heart, liver, etc., of a sheep, etc., minced with suet and oatmeal, seasoned, and boiled in the stomach of the animal.

haggle /'hægəl/ *v.i.* **1.** to bargain in a petty and tedious manner. **2.** to wrangle, dispute, or cavil. –**haggler**, *n*.

hagiography /hægi'ɒgrəfi, heɪdʒi-/ *n*. (*pl*. **-phies**) **1.** the writing and critical study of the lives of the saints; hagiology. **2.** an adulatory biography which idealises its subject. –**hagiographic** /hægiə'græfɪk, heɪdʒi-/, **hagiographical** /hægiə'græfɪkəl, heɪdʒi-/, *adj*.

haiku /'haɪku, haɪ'ku/ *n*. (*pl*. **haikus** *or* **haiku**) **1.** a Japanese verse form, developed in the 16th century, usually containing seventeen syllables, and having an allusion to the seasons of the year. **2.** an English poem modelled on this Japanese form.

hail[1] /heɪl/ *v.t.* **1.** to salute or greet; welcome. **2.** to salute or name as: *to hail someone (as) victor*. **3.** to acclaim; to approve with enthusiasm. **4.** to attract the attention of, by calling out, waving the hand, etc.: *to hail a person; to hail a taxi*. –*v.i.* **5.** to call out in order to greet, attract attention, etc. –*n*. **6.** a shout or call to attract attention. **7.** the act of hailing. **8.** a salutation or greeting. –*interj*. **9.** *Poetic* an exclamation of salutation or greeting. –*phr*. **10. hail from**, to belong to as the place of residence, point of departure, etc. **11. within hail**, within reach of the voice. –**hailer**, *n*.

hail[2] /heɪl/ *n*. **1.** a (shower of) small balls or lumps of ice falling from the clouds. **2.** a shower of anything: *a hail of bullets*. –*v.i.* **3.** to pour down hail: *it is hailing*. **4.** to fall as if hail: *bullets hailed down*. –*v.t.* **5.** to pour down as if, or like, hail: *it was hailing bullets*.

hair /hɛə/ *n*. **1.** the natural covering of the human head. **2.** the aggregate of hairs which grow on an animal. **3.** one of the numerous fine, usually cylindrical filaments growing from the skin and forming the coat of most mammals. **4.** a similar fine, filamentous outgrowth from the body of insects, etc. **5.** *Bot*. a filamentous outgrowth of the epidermis. **6.** cloth made of hair from such animals as camel and alpaca. **7.** a very small magnitude, measure, degree, etc.: *he lost the race by a hair*. –*phr*. **8. get in someone's hair**, *Colloq*. to irritate or annoy someone. **9. hair of the dog (that bit you)**, *Colloq*. an alcoholic drink taken to relieve a hangover. **10. keep one's hair on**, *Colloq*. to keep calm; not get angry. **11. let one's hair down**, to behave in an informal, relaxed, or uninhibited manner. **12. make someone's hair stand on end**, to fill someone with terror or alarm. **13. put hair on someone's chest**, *Colloq*. (of food or drink consumed by a person) to make them feel fitter, more robust, etc. **14. split hairs**, to make fine or unnecessary distinctions. **15. tear one's hair out**, to show extreme emotion, as anger, anxiety, etc.

16. without turning a hair, showing no emotion; keeping placid and unmoved. –**hairlike**, *adj*. –**hairless**, *adj*.

hairdo /'hɛədu/ *n*. (*pl*. **-dos**) **1.** the style in which a person's hair is arranged, cut, tinted, etc. **2.** the hair so arranged.

hairdresser /'hɛədrɛsə/ *n*. someone who cuts, styles and generally tends customers' hair. –**hairdressing**, *n*.

hairline /'hɛəlaɪn/ *n*. **1.** the line formed at the junction of the hair with the forehead. **2.** a very slender line. –*adj*. **3.** of, relating to, or being a hairline.

hairline fracture *n*. a break or fault in a bone, metal casting, etc., which reveals itself as a very thin line on the surface.

hairpiece /'hɛəpis/ *n*. false or substitute hair, usually mounted on a canvas and wire frame attached to the real hair to enhance or glamorise a style, or to conceal baldness.

hair-raising *adj*. terrifying.

hair's-breadth /'hɛəz-brɛdθ, -brɛtθ/ *n*. **1.** a very small space or distance. –*adj*. **2.** extremely narrow or close. Also, **hairsbreadth**, **hairbreadth**.

hair-trigger *n*. a trigger that allows the firing mechanism of a firearm to be operated by very slight pressure.

hairy /'hɛəri/ *adj*. (**-rier**, **-riest**) **1.** covered with hair; having much hair. **2.** consisting of or resembling hair. **3.** *Colloq*. difficult: *that's a hairy problem*. **4.** *Colloq*. frightening: *a hairy drive*.

haja /'hadʒa/ *n*. a Muslim woman who has made the pilgrimage to Mecca. Also, **hadja**, **hajah**, **hajja**.

hajj /hadʒ/ *n*. (*also upper case*) the pilgrimage to Mecca, which every Muslim is expected to make at least once in a lifetime. Also, **hadj**, **hajj**.

hajji /'hadʒi/ *n*. (*pl*. **-jis**) a Muslim person who has made the pilgrimage to Mecca. Also, **hadji**, **haji**.

haka /'hakə/ *n*. **1.** a Maori ceremonial posture dance with vocal accompaniment. **2.** a version of the haka, modified for use by sporting teams, schools, etc., as aggressive showpieces.

hake /heɪk/ *n*. (*pl*. **hakes** *or, especially collectively*, **hake**) **1.** → **gemfish**. **2.** any of several marine gadoid fishes of the genus *Merluccius*, related to the cod, such as *M. merluccius* of European coasts. **3.** any of various related marine fishes, especially of the genus *Urophycis*, or allied genera, such as *U. tenius* (**white hake**) of the US New England coast.

hakea /'heɪkiə/ *n*. any shrub or tree of the Australian genus *Hakea*, family Proteaceae, characterised by hard woody fruit with winged seeds.

halal /hæ'læl/ *adj*. (of meat from animals), slaughtered in accordance with Muslim rites: *halal meat*.

halcyon /'hælsiən/ *n*. **1.** a bird, usually identified with the kingfisher, fabled by the ancients to breed about the time of the winter solstice in a nest floating on the sea, and to have the power of charming winds and waves into calmness. –*adj*. **2.** calm, tranquil, or peaceful. **3.** carefree; joyous.

hale[1] /heɪl/ *adj*. free from disease or infirmity; robust; vigorous. –**haleness**, *n*.

hale[2] /heɪl/ *v.t.* **1.** to haul, pull, or draw with force. **2.** to drag, or bring as by dragging: *to hale someone into court*. –**haler**, *n*.

half /haf/ *n*. (*pl*. **halves** /havz/) **1.** one of the two equal (or approximately equal) parts into which anything is or may be divided. **2.** *Sport* either of the two periods of a game. **3.** *Rugby Football* **a.** → **halfback** (def. 1). **b.** → **five-eighth** (def. 1). **4.** *Golf* an equal score (with the opponent) either on a hole or on a round. **5.** one of a pair. **6.** *Colloq*. a half-pint, especially of beer. –*adj*. **7.** being one of the two equal (or approximately equal) parts into which anything is or may be divided. **8.** being equal to only about half of the full capacity or capability: *half speed*. **9.** partial or incomplete: *a half job*.

–adv. **10.** to the extent or measure of half: *a bucket half full of water.* **11.** in part; partly. **12.** to some extent. *–phr.* **13. and a half,** of an exceptional nature: *it's a job and a half.* **14. by half,** by a great deal; by too much: *too clever by half.* **15. not half!,** *Colloq.* certainly; indeed. **16. not half bad,** *Colloq.* surprisingly good; quite good: *his first poems were not half bad.* **17. not the half of it,** the less significant part of something: *you think we're in trouble, but that's not the half of it.*

halfback /'hafbæk/ *n.* **1.** *Rugby Football* the player who puts the ball in the scrum, and tries to catch it as it emerges. **2.** *Aust. Rules* any of the three positions on the line between the centre-line and the fullback line. **3.** *Soccer* one of the three players in the next line behind the forward line.

half-baked *adj.* **1.** insufficiently cooked. **2.** *Colloq.* not completed: *a half-baked scheme.* **3.** *Colloq.* lacking or failing to exhibit mature judgement or experience: *half-baked theorists.*

half-breed *n.* **1.** an animal whose parents are of two different breeds or the like. **2.** (*derog.*) (*racist*) (*dated*) a person having parents of two different ethnic origins, especially with one parent belonging to a dark-skinned people and one parent belonging to a fair-skinned people. *–adj.* **3.** Also, **half-bred.** of or relating to an animal which is the offspring of parents of different breeds. **4.** (*derog.*) (*racist*) (*dated*) of or relating to the offspring of parents of two different ethnic origins.

half-brother *n.* a brother by one parent only.

half-caste (*usually derog., racist*) (*dated*) *–n.* **1.** a person of mixed ancestry, especially the offspring of one dark-skinned and one fair-skinned parent. *–adj.* **2.** of or relating to such a person.

half-cock *n.* the position of the hammer of a firearm when held halfway by a mechanism so that it will not operate.

half-hearted /'haf-hatəd/ *adj.* having or showing little enthusiasm: *a half-hearted response to the suggestion.* **–half-heartedly,** *adv.* **–half-heartedness,** *n.*

half-life *n.* the time required for one half of a sample of unstable material to undergo chemical change, as the disintegration of radioactive material, the chemical change of free radicals, etc.

half-mast *n.* **1.** a position which is lower than the normal position of a flag on a flagpole; the position where a flag is flown to indicate death or mourning, the tradition possibly based on the idea of allowing space for the non-existent flag of death to fly above it. *–v.t.* **2.** to place (a flag) at half-mast (as a mark of respect for the dead). *–phr.* **3. at half-mast, a.** (of a flag) flying at this position. **b.** (of trousers) not extending to the ankles. **c.** (of any item of clothing) sagging below where it should reach: *socks at half-mast.*

half-sister *n.* a sister by one parent only.

halfway *adv.* /haf'weɪ/ **1.** half over the way: *to go halfway to a place.* **2.** to or at half the distance: *the rope reaches only halfway. –adj.* /'hafweɪ/ **3.** midway, as between two places or points. **4.** going to or covering only half the full extent; partial: *halfway measures. –phr.* **5. meet someone halfway,** to reach a compromise with someone.

halfway house *n.* **1.** a place for people who have left an institution, such as a prison or hospital, to live in while undergoing rehabilitation and adjusting to independent living. **2.** (formerly) an inn or coaching station half the distance to one's destination. **3.** a position midway between two extremes, as in an argument, debate, etc.

halibut /'hæləbət/ *n.* either of two species of large flatfishes, *Hippoglossus hippoglossus* of the North Atlantic and *H. stenolepis* of the North Pacific, widely used for food.

halitosis /hælə'tousəs/ *n.* bad or offensive breath.

hall /hɔl/ *n.* **1.** the entrance hall or vestibule of a house or building. **2.** a corridor or passageway in a building. **3.** a large building or room for public assembly and other community uses. **4.** a large building for residence, instruction, or other purposes, as in a university or college.

hallelujah /hælə'lujə/ *interj.* a religious exclamation meaning 'Praise (ye) the Lord!'. Also, **halleluiah, alleluia.**

hallmark /'hɔlmak/ *n.* **1.** Also, **plate-mark.** an official mark or stamp indicating a standard of purity, used in marking gold and silver articles. **2.** any mark or special indication of genuineness, good quality, etc. **3.** any outstanding feature or characteristic.

halloumi /hə'lumi/ *n.* → **haloumi.**

hallow /'hælou/ *v.t.* **1.** to make holy; sanctify; consecrate. **2.** to honour as holy.

Halloween /hælə'win, hælou'in/ *n.* the evening of 31 October, the eve of All Saints' Day. Also, **Hallowe'en.**

hallucination /həlusə'neɪʃən/ *n.* **1.** subjective sense perceptions for which there is no appropriate external source, such as 'hearing voices'. When persistent it is characteristic of severe psychiatric disorder or brain disease. Compare **delusion** (def. 4), **illusion** (def. 4). **2.** a suffering from illusion or false notions. **–hallucinate,** *v.*

hallucinogen /hə'lusənədʒən/ *n.* a drug or chemical capable of producing hallucinations. **–hallucinogenic** /həlusənə'dʒɛnɪk/, *adj.*

halo /'heɪlou/ *n.* (*pl.* **-loes** or **-los**) **1.** a radiance surrounding the head in the representation of a sacred personage. **2.** an ideal glory investing an object viewed with feeling or sentiment: *the halo around Shakespeare's plays.* **3.** a circle of light, appearing round the sun or moon, caused by the refraction of light in suspended ice crystals. **–halo-like,** *adj.*

halo- a word element meaning 'salt', as in *halogen.*

halo effect *n.* the flow-on of consumer approval and purchasing from one successful product to others of the same brand.

halogen /'heɪlədʒən, 'hæl-/ *n. Chem.* any of the electronegative elements fluorine, chlorine, iodine, bromine, and astatine, which form binary salts by direct union with metals.

haloumi /hə'lumi/ *n.* a soft cheese, common in Greece and Cyprus, with a firm, putty-like texture and a slightly mint flavour, matured in brine. Also, **halloumi.**

halt /hɔlt, hɒlt/ *v.i.* **1.** to undertake a temporary or permanent cessation of some activity: *the bus halted for five minutes before resuming its journey. –v.t.* **2.** to stop or cause to stop: *we must halt the train. –n.* **3.** a temporary stop. *–interj.* **4.** a command to stop and stand motionless, especially as to troops. *–phr.* **5. call a halt,** (sometimes fol. by *to*) to bring to an end: *we must call a halt to corruption.*

halter /'hɔltə, 'hɒltə/ *n.* **1.** a rope or strap with a noose or headstall, for leading or fastening horses or cattle. **2.** a rope with a noose for hanging criminals.

halve /hav/ *v.t.* **1.** to divide in halves; share equally. **2.** to reduce to half.

halves /havz/ *n.* **1.** plural of **half.** *–phr.* **2. by halves, a.** incompletely. **b.** half-heartedly. **3. go halves,** to divide equally; share equally.

halyard /'hæljəd/ *n.* a rope or tackle used to hoist or lower a sail, yard, flag, etc. Also, **halliard.**

ham¹ /hæm/ *n.* **1.** one of the rear quarters of a pig, especially the heavy-muscled part, between hip and hock. **2.** the meat of this part. **3.** (*oft. pl.*) the back of the thigh or the thigh and the buttock together.

ham² /hæm/ *Colloq. –n.* Also, **ham actor. 1.** an actor who overacts. *–v.i.* (**hammed, hamming**) **2.** to act with

exaggerated expression of emotion; overact. –*phr.*
3. ham it up, to exaggerate one's feelings or responses.
hamburger /'hæmbɜɡə/ *n.* **1.** a flat round cake of minced
beef, seasoned and fried. **2.** a bread roll or soft bun
containing such meat and often including onion, salad,
etc.
hamlet /'hæmlət/ *n.* **1.** a small village. **2.** a small cluster
of houses in the country. **3.** a village without a church
of its own, but belonging to the parish of another
village or a town.
hammer /'hæmə/ *n.* **1.** an instrument consisting of a
solid head, usually of metal, set crosswise on a handle,
used for beating metals, driving in nails, etc. **2.** any of
various instruments or devices resembling a hammer in
form, action, or use. **3.** *Firearms* that part of the lock
which by its fall or action causes the discharge, as
by exploding the percussion cap; the cock. **4.** one of
the padded levers by which the strings of a piano are
struck. **5.** *Athletics* a metal ball attached to a long,
flexible handle, used in certain throwing contests. –*v.t.*
6. to beat, drive or impel with or as with a hammer.
7. to fasten by or as by using a hammer. **8.** to put together or build with a hammer and nails. **9.** to hit with
some force; pound. **10.** to state forcefully; present
(facts, etc.) aggressively. **11.** to subject forcibly and
relentlessly to interrogation, pressure, etc.: *the Minister
was hammered by the opposition at question time.*
12. *Stock Exchange* **a.** to announce (a defaulter) on the
Stock Exchange. **b.** to depress or beat down (the price
of a stock). –*v.i.* **13.** to strike blows with or as with a
hammer. **14.** to make persistent or laborious attempts.
–*phr.* **15. come** (or **go**) **under the hammer,** to be sold
by auction. **16. hammer and tongs,** *Colloq.* with great
noise, vigour, or force. **17. hammer out, a.** to form by
hammering. **b.** to contrive or work out laboriously: *they
hammered out an agreement.* –**hammerer,** *n.* –**ham-
merless,** *adj.*
hammer and sickle *n.* **1.** the emblem of the Soviet
Union, adopted in 1923. **2.** any similar emblem of
communism outside the Soviet Union.
hammerhead /'hæməhɛd/ *n.* **1.** the head of a hammer.
2. any of the sharks constituting the genus *Sphyrna*,
characterised by a head expanded laterally so as to
resemble a double-headed hammer.
hammering /'hæmərɪŋ/ *n.* **1.** the act of using a hammer:
the sound of hammering met my ears. **2.** *Colloq.* a
beating; hiding. –*phr.* **3. take a hammering,** *Colloq.*
a. to be beaten up. **b.** to be subjected to intense cross-
examination or criticism. **c.** to be defeated soundly.
d. to suffer a financial loss.
hammock /'hæmək/ *n.* a kind of hanging bed or couch
made of canvas, netting, or the like.
hamper[1] /'hæmpə/ *v.t.* to impede; hinder; hold back.
hamper[2] /'hæmpə/ *n.* **1.** a large basket or receptacle made
from cane, wickerwork, etc., usually with a cover.
2. such a basket or other container filled with food or
other items, and given as a gift, prize, etc.
hamster /'hæmstə/ *n.* any of a number of short-tailed,
stout-bodied, burrowing rodents, having large cheek
pouches, and inhabiting parts of Europe and Asia, such
as *Cricetus cricetus.*
hamstring /'hæmstrɪŋ/ *n.* **1.** (in humans) any of the tendons bounding the ham, or hollow of the knee. –*v.t.*
(**-strung, -stringing**) **2.** to cut the hamstring or ham-
strings of and thus disable. **3.** to cripple; render useless;
thwart.
hand /hænd/ *n.* **1.** (in humans) the terminal, prehensile
part of the arm, consisting of the palm and five digits.
2. the corresponding part of the forelimb in any of the
higher vertebrates. **3.** something resembling a hand in
shape or function: *the hands of a clock.* **4.** a symbol
used in writing or printing to draw attention to something. **5.** a person employed in manual labour; worker;

labourer: *a factory hand.* **6.** a person who does a
specified thing: *a book by several hands.* **7.** a member
of a ship's crew: *all hands on deck!* **8.** (*oft. pl.*) possession or power; control, custody, or care: *to have
someone's fate in one's hands.* **9.** agency; active cooperation in doing something: *a helping hand.* **10.** side:
on every hand. **11.** a side of a subject, question, etc.: *on
the other hand.* **12.** a source, as of information or of
supply: *at first hand.* **13.** style of handwriting. **14.** a
person's handwriting. **15.** skill; execution; touch: *a
painting that shows a master's hand.* **16.** a person, with
reference to action, ability, or skill: *a poor hand at
writing letters.* **17.** a pledge of marriage. **18.** a linear
measure in the imperial system, used in giving the
height of horses, etc., equal to four inches or 0.1016 m
(approximately 10 cm). **19.** *Cards* **a.** the cards dealt to
or held by each player at one time. **b.** the person
holding the cards. **c.** a single part of a game, in which
all the cards dealt at one time are played. **20.** a bundle
or bunch of various fruit, leaves, etc., as a cluster of
bananas or tobacco leaves tied together. **21.** a round or
outburst of applause for a performer: *to get a hand.*
22. what is left from a pork forequarter after the removal of the foreloin: *pork hand.* –*v.t.* **23.** to deliver or
pass with the hand. **24.** to help or conduct with the
hand. –*adj.* **25.** of or belonging to the hand. **26.** done or
made by hand. **27.** made to be carried in, or worn on,
the hand. **28.** operated by hand. –*phr.* **29. a firm hand,**
strict control. **30. a free hand,** freedom to act as desired.
31. a heavy hand, severity or oppression. **32. a high
hand,** dictatorial manner or arbitrary conduct. **33. at
hand, a.** within reach; nearby. **b.** near in time. **c.** ready
for use. **34. at the hand** (or **hands**) **of,** from the action or
agency of. **35. bear a hand,** to give assistance. **36. by
hand,** by the use of the hands (as opposed to any other
means): *to make pottery by hand.* **37. change hands,** to
pass from one owner to another. **38. come to hand,**
to be received; come within one's reach. **39. declare
one's hand,** to reveal one's intentions or circumstances.
40. eat out of someone's hand, to be uncritically
compliant and trusting of another, often in a servile
or sycophantic manner. **41. force someone's hand,** to
compel someone to act prematurely or against their
better judgement. **42. from hand to hand,** from one
person to another. **43. from hand to mouth, a.** eating at
once whatever one gets. **b.** with attention to immediate
wants only. **44. get one's hand in,** to develop a skill
through practice. **45. give a hand,** to help; assist.
46. give one's hand on, to vouch for. **47. hand
and glove,** on very intimate terms. **48. hand down, a.** to
deliver (the decision of a court). **b.** to transmit from the
higher to the lower, in space or time: *to hand a legend
down to posterity.* **49. hand in,** to present for acceptance. **50. hand in glove,** (sometimes fol. by *with*) on
very intimate terms; in league. **51. hand in hand, a.** with
hands mutually clasped. **b.** conjointly or concurrently.
52. hand it to, *Colloq.* to give due credit to. **53. hand
on,** to pass on; transmit. **54. hand off,** *Rugby Football*
to thrust off (an opponent who is tackling). **55. hand
over, a.** to deliver into another's keeping. **b.** to give
up or yield control of. **56. hand over fist, a.** easily. **b.** in
large quantities: *to make money hand over fist.* **57. hand
out,** to distribute. **58. hands down,** totally; completely;
easily. **59. hands off,** keep off; refrain from blows or
touching. **60. hands up,** raise the hands (as a sign of
surrender). **61. hand to hand,** in close combat; at close
quarters. **62. have a hand in,** to have a part or concern
in doing. **63. have one's hands full,** to be fully occupied. **64. have one's hand in,** to have achieved skill
through practice. **65. hold the hand out,** *Colloq.* **a.** to
exploit the benefits given out by the government and
other welfare organisations. **b.** to demand bribe money.
66. in good hands, in the care of someone trustworthy.

67. in hand, a. under control. **b.** in immediate possession: *cash in hand.* **c.** in process: *keep to the matter in hand.* **68. in** (or **into**) **the hands of,** in (or into) the care, control or supervision of. **69. keep one's hand in,** to keep in practice. **70. lay hands on, a.** to assault; to beat up. **b.** to lay one's hands on the head of (a person) as part of a ritual. **71. lay one's hands on,** *Colloq.* to obtain. **72. off one's hands,** out of one's responsible charge or care. **73. on every hand,** all around; everywhere. **74. on hand, a.** in immediate possession: *cash on hand.* **b.** before someone for attention. **c.** present. **75. on one's hands,** in one's care: *he was left with his sister's children on his hands.* **76. out of hand, a.** beyond control: *to let one's temper get out of hand.* **b.** at once; without delay. **77. out of one's hands,** out of one's control or care. **78. play into the hands of,** to act, without full realisation, against one's best interest and in the interest of (an enemy or potential opponent). **79. shake hands,** to clasp another's right hand as a salutation, in closing a bargain, etc. **80. show of hands,** a voting procedure by which a motion is passed or lost on the basis of an estimate of the number of hands raised. **81. show one's hand,** to reveal one's attitudes, plans, opinions, etc., intentionally or not. **82. take a hand in,** to have a part or concern in doing. **83. take in hand, a.** to assume responsibility for. **b.** to subject to vigorous discipline. **84. take off someone's hands,** to remove from someone's responsibility. **85. the upper hand,** a position of marked superiority; whip hand. **86. throw in one's hand,** to give up; stop doing something; surrender. **87. to hand, a.** within reach; at hand. **b.** into one's immediate possession. **88. try one's hand,** (sometimes fol. by *at*) to make an attempt, especially for the first time. **89. turn one's hand to,** to turn one's energies to; set to work at. **90. wait on someone hand and foot,** attend to someone's every need; shower attention upon someone. **91. wash one's hands of,** to have nothing more to do with.

handbag /ˈhændbæg/ *n.* **1.** a small bag, most commonly used by women, for carrying money, personal articles, etc., held in the hand or worn over the shoulder by means of a strap. **2.** *Colloq.* a person who attends a social function purely as the partner of someone else.

handball /ˈhændbɔl/ *n.* **1.** a ball game, usually played on an indoor court, in which two teams of seven players attempt to hit the ball with their hands into the opponents' goal. **2.** a game in which a small ball is batted against a wall with the (usually gloved) hand. **3.** a game, often played in school playgrounds, in which a tennis ball is batted with the hand to an opponent across a line, the ball bouncing before crossing the line within a court marked on the ground. **4.** the kind of ball used in handball (defs 1 and 2). **5.** (in soccer) the offence of a player other than the goalkeeper in the penalty area touching the ball with the hand. **6.** Also, **handpass.** *Aust. Rules* a pass in which a player attempts to deliver the ball to a team-mate by holding the ball in one hand and hitting it away with the other, usually clenched as a fist. –*v.t.* Also, **handpass. 7.** *Aust. Rules* to pass the ball thus. –**handballer,** *n.*

handbook /ˈhændbʊk/ *n.* a small book or treatise serving for guidance, as in an occupation or study: *handbook of car maintenance.*

handcuff /ˈhændkʌf/ *n.* a ring-shaped shackle for the wrist, usually one of a pair connected by a short chain or linked bar.

handed /ˈhændəd/ *adj.* **1.** having a hand or hands. **2.** of or relating to preference or necessity in the use of hands, specified in combination: *right-handed, one-handed.* **3.** done by a specified number of hands: *a double-handed game.*

hand, foot and mouth disease *n.* a usually mild viral illness caused by a coxsackie virus, causing blisters on the hands and feet, in the mouth and groin. *Abbrev.:* HFMD

handful /ˈhændfʊl/ *n.* (*pl.* **-fuls**) **1.** as much or as many as the hand can grasp or contain. **2.** a small quantity or number: *a handful of men.* **3.** *Colloq.* a thing or a person that is as much as one can manage to control.

handicap /ˈhændikæp/ *n.* **1.** a race, etc., in which certain disadvantages or advantages of weight, distance, time, past records, etc., are placed upon competitors to make their chances of winning equal. **2.** the disadvantage or advantage itself. **3.** any disadvantage that makes success more difficult; encumbrance. **4.** a physical disability. –*v.t.* (**-capped, -capping**) **5.** to be a handicap or disadvantage to: *his age handicaps him.* **6.** to assign handicaps to (competitors). –**handicapped,** *adj.* –**handicapper,** *n.*

handicraft /ˈhændikraft/ *n.* **1.** manual skill or dexterity. **2.** a particular manual art or occupation such as weaving. **3.** the product of such manual art or arts: *a market for handicrafts.*

handiwork /ˈhændiwɜk/ *n.* **1.** work done or a thing or things made by the hands. **2.** the labour or action of a particular doer or maker: *the handiwork of humans.* **3.** the result of someone's action or agency.

handkerchief /ˈhæŋkətʃif/ *n.* a small square piece of fabric, usually cotton, carried about the person for wiping the nose, face, etc., or as an accessory to one's attire.

handle /ˈhændl/ *n.* **1.** the part of a thing which is intended to be held by the hand in using or moving it. **2.** *Colloq.* something that may be taken advantage of in bringing about a result. **3.** *Colloq.* a title in front of a name. **4.** *Colloq.* a person's name. –*v.t.* **5.** to touch or feel with the hand. **6.** to employ, or use: *he can handle his fists well in a fight.* **7.** to manage, direct, or control: *the captain cannot handle his soldiers.* **8.** to deal with (as a matter or subject). **9.** to deal with or treat in a particular way: *you must handle old people with respect.* **10.** to deal or trade in (goods, etc.). –*v.i.* **11.** to respond to handling: *how does the car handle?* –*phr.* **12. get a handle on,** to comprehend; find a way of proceeding with or dealing with. –**handled,** *adj.*

handler /ˈhændlə/ *n.* **1.** *Boxing* someone who assists in the training of a fighter or acts as their second during the fight. **2.** someone who manages a dog, etc., in a contest, in the police force, army etc.

hand-me-down *n. Colloq.* a garment handed down or acquired second-hand. Also, **reach-me-down.**

handout /ˈhændaʊt/ *n.* **1.** written information distributed free of charge. **2.** a free sample given as for advertisement. **3.** food, money, etc., given as charity. –*phr.* **4. live on handouts,** *Colloq.* to subsist on the social benefits offered by charity, private and public. Also, **hand-out.**

handover /ˈhændoʊvə/ *n.* **1.** a transferral or surrendering of something or someone: *the handover of hostages went smoothly.* **2.** the transfer of an organisation, enterprise, etc., from one management team to another.

handpass /ˈhændpas/ *Aust. Rules* –*n.* **1.** → **handball** (def. 6). –*v.i.* **2.** → **handball** (def. 7). Also, **handball.**

hand-pick *v.t.* **1.** to pick (fruit, etc.) by hand. **2.** to select carefully. –**hand-picked,** *adj.*

handrail /ˈhændreɪl/ *n.* a rail serving as a support or guard at the side of a stairway, platform, etc.

handset /ˈhændsɛt/ *n.* **1.** a part of a telephone combining both the receiver and the transmitter, one at each end of a handle. –*v.t.* (**-set, -setting**) **2.** *Printing* to set (type) by hand.

hands-free *adj.* of or relating to a telephone which does not require the use of a handset.

handshake /ˈhænʃeɪk, ˈhænd-/ *n.* **1.** a clasping of another's right hand as in salutation, congratulation, agreement, etc. **2.** *Computers* a signal sent from one device to another, indicating readiness to receive transferred information.

handsome /ˈhænsəm/ *adj.* **1.** of fine or admirable appearance; comely; tastefully or elegantly fine: *a handsome person.* **2.** considerable, ample, or liberal in amount: *a handsome fortune.* **3.** gracious; generous: *a handsome gift.* –**handsomely**, *adv.* –**handsomeness**, *n.*

handspring /ˈhændsprɪŋ/ *n.* a kind of somersault in which the body is supported upon one or both hands while turning in the air.

handstand /ˈhænstænd, ˈhænd-/ *n.* the act, or an instance of balancing upside down on one's hands.

hand-to-mouth /hænd-tə-ˈmaʊθ/ *adj.* with only enough means to barely exist.

handwriting /ˈhændˌraɪtɪŋ/ *n.* **1.** writing done with the hand. **2.** a kind or style of writing.

handy /ˈhændi/ *adj.* (**-dier, -diest**) **1.** ready to hand; conveniently accessible: *to have aspirins handy.* **2.** ready or skilful with the hands; deft; dexterous. **3.** convenient to handle; easily manipulated or manoeuvred: *a handy ship.* **4.** convenient or useful: *a handy tool.* –*phr.* **5. come in handy**, to prove to be useful: *a list of a few things that may come in handy.* –**handily**, *adv.* –**handiness**, *n.*

handyman /ˈhændimæn/ *n.* (*pl.* **-men**) **1.** someone hired to do odd jobs. **2.** someone who enjoys or is skilled at doing small repairs, etc., especially around the house. –**handyperson**, *n.* –**handywoman**, *n.*

hang /hæŋ/ *verb* (**hung** *or, esp. for capital punishment and suicide,* **hanged, hanging**) –*v.t.* **1.** to fasten or attach (a thing) so that it is supported only from above; suspend. **2.** to suspend so as to allow free movement as on a hinge. **3.** to fasten or suspend (a person) on a gallows or the like, especially as a method of capital punishment. **4.** to suspend by the neck until dead. **5.** to let droop or bend downwards: *to hang one's head in shame.* **6.** to furnish or decorate with something suspended: *to hang a room with tapestries.* **7.** to attach (paper, etc.) to walls. **8. a.** to suspend (game) by the feet until it becomes high. See **high** (def. 29a). **b.** to suspend (meat such as bacon, beef, etc.) to allow it to mature or to dry for preservation. **9.** *Art* **a.** to exhibit (a picture or pictures). **b.** to exhibit the work of (a painter or the like). **10.** to hinge (a door, window, etc.) to its frame. **11.** to keep (a jury) from rendering a verdict, as one juror by refusing to agree with the others. **12.** to cause (a computer) to hang (def. 24). **13.** *Colloq.* used in maledictions and emphatic expressions: *hang the rain, I'm going anyway.* **14.** *Colloq.* to perform (a specified manoeuvre) in a motor vehicle: *to hang a left*; *to hang a U-ey.* –*v.i.* **15.** to be suspended; dangle. **16.** to swing freely, as on a hinge. **17.** to be suspended from a cross or gallows; suffer death in this way as punishment. **18.** to bend forwards or downwards; lean over; incline downwards. **19.** to remain in doubt or undecided; remain unfinished. **20.** to rest, float, or hover in the air. **21.** to remain in attention or consideration: *to hang upon a person's words.* **22.** *Art* **a.** to be exhibited, as in an art gallery. **b.** to have one's works exhibited. **23.** to fail to agree, as a jury. **24.** (of a computer or computer peripheral) to cease to respond to further commands either because it is occupied in performing a task or because of some software error. –*n.* **25.** the way in which a thing hangs: *the hang of a curtain.* **26.** the least degree of care, concern, etc. (in mild expletives): *not to give a hang.* –*phr.* **27. go hang,** *Colloq.* an impolite dismissive interjection implying the speaker has no further interest in what the person addressed does: *go hang for all I care!* **28. hang about,** *Colloq.* an exclamation intended to interrupt a proceeding, discussion, etc., so as to introduce a new consideration, idea, etc. **29. hang about** (or **around**), to loiter; wait.

30. hang (a)round like a bad smell, *Colloq.* **a.** to loiter in a place, causing annoyance. **b.** to be an unwanted companion. **31. hang (around) with someone,** to spend time in someone's company. **32. hang back,** to resist advancing; be reluctant to proceed. **33. hang, draw, and quarter, a.** (formerly) to punish (someone) for treason by hanging, disembowelling, and subsequently cutting them into four pieces for public display. **b.** to punish severely. **34. hang fire,** *Colloq.* to delay taking an action or accepting something. **35. hang five,** *Colloq.* to ride a surfboard standing on the nose of the board with the toes of one foot over the edge. **36. hang in, a.** *Horseracing* (of horses) to veer away from the most direct course, toward the fence. **b.** *Surfing* to ride close to the breaking part of the wave. **c.** *Colloq.* to persevere. **37. hang in the balance,** to be in doubt or suspense. **38. hang loose,** *Colloq.* to relax; fill in time. **39. hang of a,** Also, **hanguva.** *Colloq.* an intensive phrase: *in a hang of a hurry.* **40. hang off,** to delay; procrastinate. **41. hang on,** *Colloq.* **a.** to persevere, to maintain existing conditions with effort. **b.** Also, **hang upon.** to be conditioned or contingent on; be dependent on. **c.** to hold fast, cling, or adhere to; rest for support on. **d.** to linger: *corruption still hangs on in the city.* **e.** to wait: *hang on! I'm not quite ready.* **42. hang one on someone,** *Colloq.* to punch someone. **43. hang out, a.** to lean through an opening. **b.** *Colloq.* (sometimes fol. by *at* or *in*) to reside or regularly be found at (a particular place). **c.** to pass time in a relaxed or idle manner; take it easy. **d.** to suspend in open view; display: *to hang out a banner.* **e.** to remain functioning: *can the motor hang out?* **f.** (of creases) to disappear once the article of clothing is left to hang. **g.** *Horseracing* (of horses) to veer away from the most direct course, that is, away from the fence. **44. hang out for,** *Colloq.* **a.** to remain adamant in expectation of (a goal, reward, etc.): *to hang out for a higher price before selling.* **b.** to be in need of; crave: *he's hanging out for some dope.* **45. hang ten,** *Colloq.* to ride a surfboard or skateboard while standing on the nose of the board with all one's toes over the edge. **46. hang together, a.** to hold together; remain united. **b.** to be consistent: *statements that do not hang together.* **47. hang up, a.** to suspend on a hook or peg. **b.** to hold up. **c.** to break off a telephone call by putting down the receiver. **d.** to tether or horse. **e.** *Shearing* to stop work, as by hanging up shears. **48. let it all hang out,** *Colloq.* **a.** to allow oneself to speak one's mind or show emotion freely. **b.** to be uninhibited in manner, dress, etc. **49. the hang of,** *Colloq.* **a.** the correct way of (doing, using, etc., something): *to get the hang of a tool.* **b.** an understanding of (the way something operates, is structured, etc.): *to get the hang of the way the new database works.* **c.** meaning or significance of: *to get the hang of a passage of writing.* –**hanger,** *n.*

hangar /ˈhæŋə/ *n.* **1.** a shed or shelter. **2.** a shed for aircraft.

hanged /hæŋd/ *v.* **1.** a past tense of **hang.** –*adj.* **2.** subjected to the punishment of hanging: *the hanged man.* –*phr.* **3. be hanged,** *Colloq.* used in emphatic assertions: *be hanged if I care; I'll be hanged if I'll go.*

hanger-on /hæŋər-ˈɒn/ *n.* (*pl.* **hangers-on**) someone who clings to a service, place, or connection; follower.

hang-glider *n.* **1.** a simple kite-like glider without a fuselage but with a framework from which a person hangs in a harness, using a horizontal bar to control flight. **2.** a person operating such a glider.

hangi /ˈhʌŋi/ *n.* **1.** a Maori oven in which food is steamed over hot stones in the ground. **2.** a feast at which such food is served.

hanging /ˈhæŋɪŋ/ *n.* **1.** death by suspending on a rope, gallows, etc. **2.** (*oft. pl.*) something that hangs on the walls of a room. *–adj.* **3.** positioned at a height: *a hanging garden.*

hangman /ˈhæŋmən/ *n.* (*pl.* **hangmen**) **1.** a person who hangs those condemned to death; public executioner. **2.** *NZ Colloq.* a character; eccentric person. **3.** Also, **hangman's noose.** a word game in which one player is required to guess the letters making up a word which the other player has chosen, each incorrect guess being registered by a line in a simple drawing of a hanged figure; a winning player guesses the word before the picture is completed.

hangout /ˈhæŋaʊt/ *n. Colloq.* a place where one lives or frequently visits.

hangover /ˈhæŋoʊvə/ *n.* **1.** the after-effects of excessive indulgence in alcoholic drink. **2.** something remaining behind from a former period or state of affairs.

hang-up *n. Colloq.* something which occasions unease, inhibition, or conflict in an individual.

hank /hæŋk/ *n.* **1.** a skein, as of thread or yarn. **2.** a coil, knot, or loop: *a hank of hair.*

hanker /ˈhæŋkə/ *v.i.* **1.** to have a restless desire (to do something): *to hanker to go back home. –phr.* **2. hanker after** (or **for**), to have a restless or incessant longing for: *to hanker after freedom. –***hankering,** *n.* **–hankerer,** *n.*

hanky /ˈhæŋki/ *n. Colloq.* → **handkerchief.** Also, **hankie.**

hanky-panky /ˌhæŋki-ˈpæŋki/ *n. Colloq.* **1.** trickery; subterfuge or the like. **2.** sexual play.

Hansard /ˈhænsəd/ *n.* the official printed reports of the debates and proceedings of parliament, especially in Australia, New Zealand, Britain, and Canada.

Hanukkah /ˈhanəkə/ /ˈhanukə/ *n.* the Feast of Dedication, a Jewish festival in commemoration of the victory of the Maccabees, usually falling within November or December and lasting eight days.

haphazard /hæpˈhæzəd/ *adj.* **1.** determined by or dependent on mere chance: *a haphazard remark. –adv.* **2.** in a haphazard manner; at random; by chance. *–n.* **3.** mere chance; accident: *to proceed at haphazard.* **–haphazardly,** *adv.* **–haphazardness,** *n.*

hapless /ˈhæpləs/ *adj.* luckless; unfortunate; unlucky. **–haplessly,** *adv.* **–haplessness,** *n.*

haplo- a word element meaning 'single', 'simple'.

haploid /ˈhæplɔɪd/ *adj.* Also, **haploidic.** **1.** single; simple. **2.** *Biol.* (of gametes, etc.) having a single set of chromosomes. *–n.* **3.** *Biol.* an organism or cell having only one complete set of chromosomes, ordinarily half the normal diploid number.

happen /ˈhæpən/ *v.i.* **1.** to come to pass, take place, or occur. **2.** to come to pass by chance; occur without apparent reason or design; chance. **3.** to have the fortune or lot (to do or be as specified): *I happened to see him.* **4.** to befall, as to a person or thing. *–phr.* **5. happen on** (or **upon**), to come upon by chance.

happy /ˈhæpi/ *adj.* (**-pier, -piest**) **1.** characterised by or indicative of pleasure, content, or gladness: *a happy mood.* **2.** delighted, pleased, or glad, as over a particular thing: *to be happy to see a person.* **3.** favoured by fortune; fortunate or lucky: *a happy event.* **4.** apt or felicitous, as actions, utterances, ideas, etc. **5.** *Colloq.* showing an excessive liking for, or quick to use an item indicated (used in combination): *trigger-happy. –phr. Colloq.* **6. happy as Larry,** very happy. **7. happy days,** (*sometimes ironic*) an expression indicating satisfaction with life. **8. the happy day,** the day of a prospective wedding: *when's the happy day?*

happy-go-lucky *adj.* **1.** trusting cheerfully to luck. *–adv.* **2.** haphazard; by mere chance.

hapuku /ˈhapəkə, həˈpukə/ *n.* the groper, *Polyprion oxygeneios,* of New Zealand and eastern Australian waters. Also, **hapuka.**

harakiri /hærəˈkɪri/ *n.* ritual suicide by ripping open the abdomen with a dagger or knife; the national form of honourable suicide in Japan, formerly practised among the samurai classes when disgraced or sentenced to death. Also, **harakari** /hærəˈkari/, **harikari.**

harangue /həˈræŋ/ *n.* **1.** a passionate, vehement speech; noisy and intemperate address. **2.** any long, declamatory or pompous speech. *–v.t.* (**-rangued, -ranguing**) **3.** to address in a harangue. **–haranguer,** *n.*

harass /həˈræs, ˈhærəs/ *v.t.* **1.** to trouble by repeated attacks, incursions, etc., as in war or hostilities; harry; raid. **2.** to disturb persistently; torment. **–harasser,** *n.* **–harassingly,** *adv.* **–harassment,** *n.*

harbinger /ˈhabɪndʒə/ *n.* **1.** someone who goes before and makes known the approach of another. **2.** something that foreshadows a future event; an omen.

harbour /ˈhabə/ *n.* **1.** a portion of a body of water along the shore deep enough for ships, and so situated with respect to coastal features, whether natural or artificial, as to provide protection from winds, waves, and currents. **2.** any place of shelter or refuge. *–v.t.* **3.** to conceal; give a place to hide: *to harbour smuggled goods.* **4.** to entertain in the mind; indulge (usually unfavourable or evil feelings): *to harbour suspicion.* **5.** to shelter (a ship) in a harbour or haven. Also, **harbor.** **–harbourer,** *n.* **–harbourless,** *adj.*

hard /had/ *adj.* **1.** solid and firm to the touch; not soft. **2.** firmly formed; tight: *a hard knot.* **3.** difficult to do or accomplish; fatiguing; troublesome: *a hard task.* **4.** difficult or troublesome with respect to an action specified: *hard to please.* **5.** difficult to deal with, manage, control, overcome, or understand: *a hard problem.* **6.** involving or performed with great exertion, energy, or persistence: *hard work.* **7.** carrying on work in this manner: *a hard worker.* **8.** vigorous or violent; severe: *a hard rain.* **9.** oppressive; harsh; rough: *hard treatment.* **10.** unpleasant; unfair; bad: *hard luck.* **11.** austere; uncomfortable; causing pain, poverty, etc.: *hard times.* **12.** unfeeling; callous: *a hard heart.* **13.** harsh or severe in dealing with others: *a hard master.* **14.** incapable of being denied or explained away: *hard facts.* **15.** based on solid evidence; factual: *hard information.* **16.** harsh or unfriendly; not easily moved: *hard feelings.* **17.** confronting to the eye, ear, or aesthetic sense. **18.** severe or rigorous in terms: *a hard bargain.* **19.** not swayed by sentiment or sophistry; shrewd: *to have a hard head.* **20. a.** alcoholic or intoxicating: *hard liquor.* **b.** dangerously addictive: *hard drugs.* **21.** (of water) containing mineral salts which interfere with the action of the soap. **22.** *Physics* (of radiation) of short wavelength and high penetrating power. **23.** *Phonetics* (of *c* and *g*) pronounced as in *come* and *go.* **24.** of or relating to hard-core pornography. *–adv.* **25.** with great exertion; with vigour or violence: *to work hard.* **26.** earnestly or intently: *to look hard at a thing.* **27.** harshly or severely; badly; gallingly: *it goes hard.* **28.** so as to be solid or firm: *frozen hard.* **29.** *Naut.* closely, fully, or to the extreme limit: *hard aport. –n.* **30.** *Colloq.* an erect penis. *–phr.* **31. do it the hard way,** to choose a needlessly difficult way of doing something. **32. hard by** (or **against**), close to or nearby. **33. hard cash,** cash, as opposed to cheques, credit, etc. **34. hard cheese** (or **cheddar**) (or **luck**), *Colloq.* **a.** bad luck. **b.** an off-hand expression of sympathy. **c.** a rebuff to an appeal for sympathy. **35. hard done by,** *Colloq.* unfairly treated. **36. hard of hearing,** partly deaf. **37. hard put** (**to it**), in great difficulties. **38. hard up,** *Colloq.* urgently in need of something, especially money. **39. live hard, a.** to indulge in life's pleasures to excess. **b.** to live on a frugal and physically exacting regimen. **40. one's hardest,** to the best of one's ability. **41. put the hard word on,** *Aust., NZ Colloq.* **a.** to ask a favour of (someone). **b.** to ask (someone) for sexual intercourse. **42. the too hard basket**, *Colloq.* a fictitious filing allocation in which to place matters which are too difficult to handle. **–hardness**, *v.* **–hardness**, *n.*

hardback /ˈhɑdbæk/ *n.* **1.** a book bound in stiff board covers. *–adj.* **2.** of or relating to such books or the publishing of such books; casebound. Compare **paperback**.

hardball /ˈhɑdbɔl/ *n.* **1.** baseball. *–phr.* **2. play hardball**, *Colloq.* to use tough, uncompromising or ruthless tactics in business, politics, etc.

hard-bitten /ˈhɑd-bɪtn/ *adj.* tough; stubborn.

hardboard /ˈhɑdbɔd/ *n.* a material made from wood fibres compressed into sheets, having many household and industrial uses.

hard case *n.* **1.** a tough, cynical person. **2.** *Aust., NZ* a witty, consistently amusing person; hard doer. **3.** an incorrigible criminal. **4.** a person suffering from drug addiction, especially to alcohol. **–hard-case**, *adj.*

hard core *n.* **1.** the unyielding or intransigent members forming the nucleus of a group: *a hard core of dissidents.* **2.** untreatable or unyielding matter or material within something: *the hard core of the infection remained.*

hardcore /ˈhɑdˈkɔ/ *n.* **1.** solid pieces of rock, gravel, or broken brick which form a foundation base for other building materials. *–adj.* **2.** of or relating to an unadulterated form of something; classic: *hardcore skating.* **3.** entirely committed to an ideology, belief, cause, way of life, etc.: *a hardcore communist.* **4.** of or relating to a residual chronic social condition: *hardcore unemployment.* **5.** explicit; blunt; unequivocal: *hardcore pornography.* **6.** physically addictive: *hardcore drugs.* **7.** *Music* typified by a very fast beat: *hardcore techno; hardcore punk; hardcore hip-hop.*

hardcourt /ˈhɑdkɔt/ *n. Tennis* a court with a surface prepared from asphalt or concrete, finished with a latex paint mixed with sand, designed to produce a faster ball speed and a strong bounce. Compare **clay court**, **composition court**, **grass court**. Also, **hard court**.

hard-headed /ˈhɑd-hɛdəd/ *adj.* not easily moved or deceived; practical; shrewd. **–hard-headedly**, *adv.* **–hard-headedness**, *n.*

hard-hearted /ˈhɑd-hɑtəd/ *adj.* unfeeling; unmerciful; pitiless. **–hard-heartedly**, *adv.* **–hard-heartedness**, *n.*

hardline /ˈhɑdlaɪn/ *adj.* not deviating from a set doctrine, policy, etc.: *a hardline attitude to drugs.* Also, **hard-line**.

hardly /ˈhɑdli/ *adv.* **1.** barely; almost not at all: *hardly any; hardly ever; hardly had he started when the command came to stop.* **2.** not quite: *that is hardly true.* **3.** with little likelihood: *he will hardly come now.* **4.** with trouble or difficulty. **5.** harshly or severely.

hard news *n.* *TV, Radio* news about matters of serious interest which is informative and factual, rather than interpretive. Compare **soft news**.

hard-nosed *adj.* ruthless, especially in business.

hardpan /ˈhɑdpæn/ *n.* **1.** any layer of firm detrital matter, as of clay, underlying soft soil. **2.** hard, unbroken ground. **3.** solid foundation; hard underlying reality.

hard-pressed *adj.* under pressure created by natural conditions, a rival, an enemy, etc.: *we will be hard-pressed to beat the other team.*

hard sell *n.* a method of advertising or selling which is direct, forceful, and insistent; high-pressure salesmanship. See **soft sell**.

hardship /ˈhɑdʃɪp/ *n.* **1.** a condition that bears hard upon one; severe toil, trial, oppression, or need. **2.** an instance of this; something hard to bear.

hard stuff *n.* *Colloq.* **1.** strong alcoholic liquor; spirits. **2.** hard drugs, as heroin, etc.

hard-up *adj.* in financial difficulties; poor. Also, (*especially in predicative use*), **hard up**.

hardware /ˈhɑdwɛə/ *n.* **1.** building materials, tools, etc.; ironmongery. **2.** the mechanical equipment necessary for conducting an activity, usually distinguished from the theory and design which make the activity possible. **3.** *Computers* the physical components of a computer system, such as the circuitry, peripherals, etc. (opposed to *software*).

hardwire /hɑdˈwaɪə/ *v.t. Computers* to wire (a circuit) permanently into a computer. Also, **hard-wire**.

hardwired /hɑdˈwaɪəd/ *adj.* **1.** *Computers* **a.** (of a circuit) permanently wired into a computer. **b.** (of a function) determined by the hardware and therefore not programmable. **2.** (of people) inherently equipped to act in a certain way: *humans are hardwired for language.* **3.** not modifiable. Also, **hard-wired**.

hardy /ˈhɑdi/ *adj.* (**-dier, -diest**) **1.** capable of enduring fatigue, hardship, exposure, etc.: *hardy animals.* **2.** (of plants) able to withstand the cold of winter in the open air. **3.** requiring great physical endurance: *the hardiest sports.* **4.** bold or daring; courageous, as persons, actions, etc. **5.** unduly bold; presumptuous; foolhardy. **–hardiness, hardihood**, *n.*

hare /hɛə/ *n.* (*pl.* **hares** *or, especially collectively,* **hare**) **1.** any of various large lagomorphs of the genus *Lepus*, resembling but larger than rabbits, with long ears, divided upper lip, short tail, and lengthened hind limbs adapted for leaping. *–v.i.* (**hared, haring**) **2.** to run fast. *–phr.* **3. start a hare**, to bring an irrelevant point into an argument. **–harelike**, *adj.*

harelip /ˈhɛəlɪp/ *n.* a congenitally deformed lip, usually the upper one in which there is a vertical fissure causing it to resemble the cleft lip of a hare. **–hare-lipped**, *adj.*

harem /ˈhɛərəm, hɑˈrim/ *n.* **1.** the part of a Muslim palace or house reserved for the residence of women. **2.** the women in a Muslim household: mother, sisters, wives, concubines, daughters, entertainers, servants, etc.

harem pants *pl. n.* long loose trousers gathered at the ankle, worn by women.

haricot /ˈhærɪkoʊ/ *n.* **1. → French bean. 2. haricot vert**, the fresh pod of the French bean containing its green beans. **3.** the dried seed of the French bean. See **kidney bean**.

harissa /həˈrɪsə/ *n.* a hot sauce made from chillies, garlic, cumin, coriander, caraway and olive oil, often served with couscous.

hark /hɑk/ *v.i.* **1.** (*used chiefly in the imperative*) to listen; hearken. *–phr.* **2. hark back**, (sometimes fol. by *to*) to return to a previous point or subject, as in discourse or thought; revert.

harlequin /ˈhɑləkwən/ *adj.* fancifully varied in colour, decoration, etc.

harlot /ˈhɑlət/ *n.* a promiscuous woman; a female prostitute.

harm /hɑm/ *n.* **1.** injury; damage; hurt: *to do him bodily harm.* **2.** moral injury; evil; wrong. *–v.t.* **3.** to do harm to; injure; damage; hurt. **–harmful**, *adj.* **–harmless**, *adj.* **–harmer**, *n.*

harmonica /hɑˈmɒnɪkə/ *n.* **1.** a musical instrument having a set of small metallic reeds mounted in a case and played by the breath; a mouth organ. **2.** any of various percussion instruments which use graduated bars of metal or other hard material as sounding elements.

harmonics /hɑˈmɒnɪks/ *n.* the science of musical sounds.

harmonium /hɑˈmoʊniəm/ *n.* a reed organ, especially one in which the air is forced outwards through the reeds.

harmony /ˈhɑməni/ *n.* (*pl.* **-nies**) **1.** agreement; accord; harmonious relations. **2.** a consistent, orderly, or pleasing arrangement of parts; congruity. **3.** *Music* **a.** any simultaneous combination of notes. **b.** the science of the structure, relations, and practical combination of chords. –**harmonious** /ha'mouniǝs/, **harmonic** /ha-'mɒnɪk/, *adj.* –**harmonise, harmonize,** *v.*

harness /'hanǝs/ *n.* **1.** the combination of straps, bands, and other parts forming the working gear of a horse or other draught animal. **2.** a similar combination worn by persons for safety, protection, restraint, etc. –*v.t.* **3.** to put harness on (a horse, etc.); attach by a harness, as to a vehicle. **4.** to bring under conditions for working. –*phr.* **5. in harness, a.** side by side; together. **b.** working; at one's job. –**harnesser,** *n.* –**harnessless,** *adj.*

harp /hap/ *n.* **1.** a musical instrument consisting of a triangular frame (comprising a sounding-board, a pillar, and a curved neck) and strings stretched between sounding-board and neck and plucked with the fingers. –*v.i.* **2.** to play on a harp. –*phr.* **3. harp on** (or **upon**), to dwell on persistently or tediously in speaking or writing. –**harper, harpist,** *n.*

harpoon /ha'pun/ *n.* **1.** a barbed, spear-like missile attached to a rope, and thrown by hand or shot from a gun, used in catching whales and large fish. –*v.t.* **2.** to strike, catch, or kill with or as with a harpoon. –**harpooner,** *n.* –**harpoonlike,** *adj.*

harpsichord /'hapsǝkɔd/ *n.* a keyboard instrument, precursor of the piano, in common use from the 16th to the 18th century, and revived in the 20th, in which the strings are plucked by leather or quill points connected with the keys. –**harpsichordist,** *n.*

harpy /'hapi/ *n.* (*pl.* **-pies**) **1.** a greedy, snatching person. **2.** an unattractive, bad-tempered, old woman.

harridan /'hærǝdǝn/ *n.* (*derog.*) a disreputable violent woman.

harrier /'hæriǝ/ *n.* **1.** a person or thing that harries. **2.** any of several small birds of prey of the genus *Circus*, family Accipitridae, which course back and forth over pasture lands searching for the small birds and mammals on which they feed.

harrow /'hærou/ *n.* **1.** a wheelless agricultural implement set with teeth, upright discs, etc., usually of iron, drawn over ploughed land to level it, break clods, etc. –*v.t.* **2.** to draw a harrow over (land, etc.); break or tear with a harrow. **3.** to disturb keenly or painfully; distress the mind, feelings, etc. –**harrower,** *n.* –**harrowingly,** *adv.*

harrowing /'hærouɪŋ/ *adj.* disturbing or distressing to the mind, feelings, etc.

harry /'hæri/ *verb* (**-ried, -rying**) –*v.t.* **1.** to harass by forced exactions, rapacious demands, etc.; torment; worry. **2.** to ravage, as in war; devastate. –*v.i.* **3.** to make harassing incursions.

harsh /haʃ/ *adj.* **1.** ungentle and unpleasant in action or effect: *harsh treatment.* **2.** rough to the touch or to any of the senses: *a harsh surface, a harsh voice.* **3.** jarring upon the aesthetic senses; inartistic: *his painting was full of harsh lines and clashing colours.* –**harshly,** *adv.* –**harshness,** *n.*

hart /hat/ *n.* (*pl.* **harts** *or, especially collectively,* **hart**) a male of the deer, commonly the red deer, *Cervus elaphus*, especially after its fifth year.

hartebeest /'hatǝbist/ *n.* (*pl.* **-beests** *or, especially collectively,* **-beest**) a large antelope of southern Africa of the genus *Alcephalus*, such as *A. caama*, of a red colour, having a long face with naked muzzle.

harum-scarum /hɛǝrǝm-'skɛǝrǝm/ *adj.* **1.** reckless; rash. –*adv.* **2.** recklessly; wildly.

harvest /'havǝst/ *n.* **1.** (the season of) the gathering of crops. **2.** a crop or yield, as of grain. **3.** a supply of anything gathered and stored up: *a harvest of nuts.* **4.** the result of any process. –*v.t.* **5.** to gather (a crop). **6.** to gather the crop from: *he will harvest the fields.* **7.** to gather, as the product of a biological process, experiment, etc.: *to harvest eggs for fertilisation.* **8.** to collect electronically, as in the gathering of email

addresses. –*v.i.* **9.** to gather a crop; reap. –**harvesting,** *n.* –**harvestless,** *adj.*

harvester /'havǝstǝ/ *n.* **1.** someone who harvests; a reaper. **2.** any of various machines for harvesting field crops, such as grain, flax, potatoes, etc.

has /hæz/, *weak forms* /hǝz, ǝz/ *v.* 3rd person singular present indicative of **have.**

has-been *n.* *Colloq.* a person or thing that is no longer effective, successful, popular, etc.

hash¹ /hæʃ/ *n.* **1.** a mess, jumble, or muddle. **2.** a dish of chopped, cooked meat, reheated in a highly seasoned sauce. **3.** any preparation of old material worked over. –*v.t.* **4.** to chop into small pieces; mince; make into a hash. –*phr.* **5. make a hash of,** to spoil or make a mess of.

hash² /hæʃ/ *n.* *Colloq.* → **hashish.**

hash³ /hæʃ/ *n.* **1.** the symbol #, found on a computer keyboard, telephone keypad, etc.; hatch. **2.** this symbol, used, for example, in engineering to denote drill sizes, as in #60, #90.

hash brown *n.* a small patty made by mashing, grating or dicing potato and frying it until crisp.

hashish /hæˈʃiʃ, 'hæʃɪʃ/ *n.* **1.** a resin produced from the flowering tops, leaves, etc., of Indian hemp, smoked, chewed, or otherwise used as a narcotic and intoxicant. **2.** any of various preparations made from this plant.

hashtag /'hæʃtæg/ *n.* *Internet* a tag to a tweet (**tweet²** def. 3), which connects it to a common theme. –**hashtagging,** *n.*

hasp /hæsp, hasp/ *n.* a clasp for a door, lid, etc., especially one passing over a staple and fastened by a pin or a padlock.

hassle /'hæsǝl/ *Colloq.* –*n.* **1.** a quarrel; squabble. **2.** a struggle; period of unease: *today was a real hassle.* –*v.t.* **3.** worry; harass: *don't hassle me.* –**hassled,** *adj.*

hassock /'hæsǝk/ *n.* **1.** a thick, firm cushion used as a footstool or for kneeling. **2.** a rank tuft of coarse grass or sedge, as in a bog.

haste /heɪst/ *n.* **1.** energetic speed in motion or action. **2.** speed as a result of urgency. **3.** quickness without due reflection; thoughtless or rash speed: *haste makes waste.* –*v.t., v.i.* **4.** *Archaic* → **hasten.** –*phr.* **5. in haste,** with speed, quickly. **6. make haste, a.** to exert oneself to do something quickly. **b.** to go somewhere with haste. –**hasty,** *adj.* –**hastily,** *adv.* –**hastiness,** *n.*

hasten /'heɪsǝn/ *v.i.* **1.** to move or act with haste; proceed with haste; hurry: *to hasten to a place.* –*v.t.* **2.** to cause to hasten; accelerate. –**hastener,** *n.*

hat /hæt/ *n.* **1.** a shaped covering for the head, usually with a crown and a brim, worn outdoors. **2.** *Colloq.* a rank or office among many: *which hat is he wearing now?* **3.** *Computers* → **caret** (defs 2 and 3). –*phr.* **4. at the drop of a hat,** on the spur of the moment; without preliminaries. **5. bad hat,** *Colloq.* a bad or immoral person. **6. eat one's hat,** *Colloq.* to be very surprised (if a certain event happens): *if they win this game I'll eat my hat.* **7. my hat,** an exclamation of surprise and disbelief. **8. old hat,** *Colloq.* (of ideas, etc.) old-fashioned; out-of-date. **9. send** (or **pass**) **around the hat,** to make a collection, sometimes in a hat, for a needy person or cause. **10. take one's hat off to,** to express respect or admiration for. **11. talk through one's hat,** *Colloq.* to talk nonsense; speak without knowledge of the true facts. **12. throw one's hat in the door,** to test the warmth of one's reception in company, as when arriving late. **13. throw one's hat into the ring,** to join in a competition or contest. **14. under one's hat,** *Colloq.* secret; confidential: *keep this information under your hat.* **15. wear two hats,** *Colloq.* to act in two official capacities at the same time. –**hatless,** *adj.*

hatch¹ /hætʃ/ *v.t.* **1.** to bring forth (young) from the egg. **2.** to cause young to emerge from (the egg). **3.** to contrive; devise; concoct: *to hatch a plot. –v.i.* **4.** to be hatched. **–hatchment**, *n.*

hatch² /hætʃ/ *n.* **1.** a cover for an opening in a ship's deck, a floor, a roof, or the like. **2.** the opening itself. **3.** (*oft. pl.*) a hatchway. **4.** an opening in the wall between a kitchen and dining room, through which food is served. *–phr.* **5. down the hatch**, an interjection urging someone to drink up. **6. under hatches**, below the ship's deck.

hatch³ /hætʃ/ *v.t.* **1.** to mark with lines, especially closely set parallel lines, as for shading in drawing or engraving. *–n.* **2.** a shading line in drawing or engraving. **3.** → **hash³** (def. 1).

hatchback /ˈhætʃbæk/ *n.* a type of car fitted with a door at the rear which includes the rear window, and which has hinges at the top.

hatchet /ˈhætʃət/ *n.* **1.** a small, short-handled axe for use with one hand. **2.** a tomahawk. *–phr.* **3. bury the hatchet**, to make peace. **4. dig up** (or **take up**) **the hatchet**, to prepare for war.

hatchet man *n.* **1.** someone employed or delegated to perform unpleasant tasks, such as cutting costs, firing personnel, etc., for an employer. **2.** a hired assassin.

hate /heɪt/ *v.t.* **1.** to regard with a strong or passionate dislike; detest. **2.** to dislike; be unwilling: *I hate to do it. –v.i.* **3.** to feel hatred. *–n.* **4.** hatred; strong dislike. **5.** something that is hated. *–adj.* **6.** devoted to expressing resentment or dislike: *a hate session; hate mail. –phr.* **7. have a hate on** (or **against**), to feel strong antipathy to or dislike for. **8. pet hate**, *Colloq.* someone or something particularly disliked. **–hater**, *n.*

hate crime *n.* criminal violence enacted upon an individual or group perceived as belonging to a social or racial group hated by the attacker.

hateful /ˈheɪtfəl/ *adj.* exciting hate; detestable; odious. **–hatefully**, *adv.* **–hatefulness**, *n.*

hate speech *n.* any communication which vilifies a person or group on the basis of race, gender, religion, sexual orientation, etc., and which may incite violence against them.

hatred /ˈheɪtrəd/ *n.* the feeling of someone who hates; intense dislike; detestation.

hatter /ˈhætə/ *n.* **1.** a maker or seller of hats. *–phr.* **2. mad as a hatter**, very eccentric; crazy.

hat-trick *n.* **1.** *Cricket* the act by a bowler of taking three wickets with three successive balls. **2.** three goals, tries, etc., achieved by a player in a single game, etc., especially in a sport in which it is unusual to do so. **3.** a feat involving a set of three successes.

haughty /ˈhɔti/ *adj.* (**-tier, -tiest**) disdainfully proud; arrogant; supercilious. **–haughtily**, *adv.* **–haughtiness**, *n.*

haul /hɔl/ *v.t.* **1.** to pull or draw with force; move or transport by drawing. *–v.i.* **2.** to pull or tug. **3.** to change one's course of procedure or action; go in a given direction. **4.** *Naut.* to sail, as in a particular direction. *–n.* **5.** the act of hauling; a strong pull or tug. **6.** that which is hauled. **7.** the distance over which anything is hauled: *a short haul; a long haul.* **8.** *Fishing* **a.** the quantity of fish taken at one draught of the net. **b.** the draught of a fishing net. **9.** the acquisition of anything, or that which is acquired or won. **10.** the proceeds of a robbery: *the thieves made away with a haul of $25 000. –phr.* **11. haul off, a.** *Naut.* to change the course of a ship so as to get farther off from an object. **b.** to draw off or away. **c.** *US Colloq.* to draw the arm back preparatory to striking a blow. **12. haul over the coals,** *Colloq.* to rebuke; scold. **13. haul round** (or **to**), (of the wind) to change direction; shift; veer. **14. haul up, a.** *Colloq.* to bring up, as before a superior, for reprimand; call to account. **b.** *Naut.* to change the course of (a ship),

especially so as to sail closer to the wind. **15. in** (or **over**) **the long haul**, in the long term; in a long period of time. **16. in** (or **over**) **the short haul**, in the short term; in a short period of time. **–hauler**, *n.*

haulage /ˈhɔlɪdʒ/ *n.* **1.** the act or labour of hauling. **2.** transport, especially heavy road transport. **3.** a charge for hauling.

haulier /ˈhɔliə/ *n.* a person or company engaged in haulage (def. 2).

haunch /hɔntʃ/ *n.* **1.** the hip. **2.** the fleshy part of the body about the hip. **3.** a hindquarter of an animal. **4.** the leg and loin of an animal, as used for food.

haunt /hɔnt/ *v.t.* **1.** to reappear frequently to after death. **2.** to push in upon continually: *memories that haunt one.* **3.** to worry: *his guilt haunted him.* **4.** to visit frequently. **5.** to be often with. *–n.* **6.** (*oft. pl.*) a place visited often: *I will return to my old haunts.* **–haunter**, *n.* **–hauntingly**, *adv.*

haute cuisine /oʊt kwəˈzin/ *n.* cooking to a high standard.

have /hæv/ *v.t.* **1.** to possess; own; to hold for use: *to have property; to have a car.* **2.** to be made of or to contain: *this volume has an index.* **3.** to hold or possess in some other relation, as of kindred, friendship, association, etc.: *he has two brothers; she has twenty private pupils.* **4.** to hold or possess in a relative position: *to have someone under one's thumb.* **5.** to possess as a characteristic or a feature: *he has blue eyes; I have a shocking temper.* **6.** to get, receive, or take: *I had no news for six months.* **7.** to experience, enjoy or suffer: *to have a pleasant time.* **8.** to hold or stage (a social occasion, etc.): *to have a party.* **9.** to entertain; accept as a welcome visitor: *thank you for having me.* **10.** to eat, drink or partake of: *he had a meal.* **11.** to hold in mind, sight, etc.: *to have doubts.* **12.** to require or cause (to do something, to be done, or as specified): *have it ready at five.* **13.** to arrange, put or keep in a specific place: *why not have the bookshelves in the corner.* **14.** to engage in or perform: *to have a talk.* **15.** to be scheduled for: *I have two appointments tomorrow.* **16.** to show or exhibit in action: *to have a care; have mercy.* **17.** to permit or allow: *I will not have it.* **18.** to buy, accept or take: *I'll have this one, thanks.* **19.** to invite or expect visitors, etc.: *we have twenty people coming for dinner.* **20.** to assert or maintain: *rumour has it so.* **21.** to know or understand, especially for use: *to have neither Latin nor Greek; to have the necessary technique.* **22.** to give birth to: *to have a baby.* **23.** to possess sexually; to copulate with. **24.** *Colloq.* to hold at a disadvantage: *she has you there.* **25.** *Colloq.* to outwit, deceive, or cheat: *a person not easily had. –v.i.* **26.** to possess money, etc.; be well off: *those who have should help the poor. –v. (aux.)* **27.** used with the past participle of a verb to form the grammatical perfect: *they have gone. –n.* **28.** *Colloq.* a deception; trick: *it was a bit of a have. –phr.* **29. have at**, *Archaic* to attack. **30. have** (or **be**) **done**, (sometimes fol. by *with*) to cease or finish. **31. have done with**, to sever relations with (someone). **32. have had someone** (or **something**), *Colloq.* to be annoyed or exasperated with someone or something: *I've had you; I've had this job.* **33. have it away**, *Brit. Colloq.* to have sexual intercourse. **34. have it coming**, *Colloq.* to deserve an unpleasant fate. **35. have it in for**, *Colloq.* to hold a grudge against. **36. have it made**, *Colloq.* to be assured of success. **37. have it off**, *Colloq.* to have sexual intercourse. **38. have it out**, to have a candid argument; to discuss a matter extensively. **39. have nothing to do with, a.** to have no dealings with: *she will have nothing to do with him.* **b.** to be of no concern to: *that has nothing to do with you.* **40. have on, a.** to be wearing. **b.** to have arranged or planned: *what appointments do you have on tomorrow?* **41. have oneself on**, *Colloq.* to delude oneself, especially as a result of pandering to one's own ego. **42. have someone in** (or **over**), to invite or entertain someone at home. **43. have someone on,** *Colloq.* **a.** to tease or deceive someone. **b.** to accept a fight or competition with someone: *I'll have him on anytime.* **44. have to,** to be required, compelled, or under obligation to: *you have to throw a six to start*; *we had to keep stopping.* **45. have to do with,** to concern; be about: *the second lecture has to do with mining.* **46. have up,** *Colloq.* (sometimes fol. by *for*) to bring before the authorities, especially in court: *he was had up for theft.* **47. let someone have it,** *Colloq.* to launch a strong attack upon someone. **48. the haves and the have-nots,** the rich and the poor.

Usage: The different forms of the verb **have** are:

Present tense: I **have**, you **have**, he/she/it **has**, we **have**, they **have**

Past tense: I **had**, you **had**, he/she/it **had**, we **had**, they **had**

Past participle: **had**

Present participle: **having**

Some archaic forms are also retained:

Present tense: thou **hast**, he/she/it **hath**

haven /ˈheɪvən/ *n.* **1.** a harbour or port. **2.** an inlet of a sea or river mouth where ships can obtain good anchorage. **3.** any place of shelter and safety. **–havenless,** *adj.*

haversack /ˈhævəsæk/ *n.* **1.** a soldier's bag for rations. **2.** any bag carried on the back or shoulders, used for provisions and the like.

havoc /ˈhævək/ *n.* **1.** devastation; ruinous damage. *–phr.* **2. play havoc with,** to ruin; destroy. **3. wreak havoc,** to cause great damage. **–havocker,** *n.*

hawk[1] /hɔk/ *n.* **1.** any of numerous diurnal birds of prey of the family Accipitridae, especially those smaller than eagles, as the buzzards, kites, harriers, goshawks, etc., generally having squarish wings with rounded ends or splayed primary feathers, as opposed to the family Falconidae, which includes falcons, hobbies and kestrels. **2.** any of certain unrelated birds thought to resemble hawks, as the sea hawk (skua). **3.** a politician or political adviser who favours aggressive or intransigent military policies. Compare **dove**[1] (def. 3). *–v.i.* **4.** to fly, or hunt on the wing, like a hawk. **5.** to hunt with hawks trained to pursue game. **–hawkish,** *adj.*

hawk[2] /hɔk/ *v.t.* **1.** to offer for sale by outcry in a street or from door to door. *–v.i.* **2.** to carry wares about; peddle. *–phr.* **3. hawk about,** to spread, especially news, etc.

hawk[3] /hɔk/ *v.i.* to make an effort to raise phlegm from the throat; clear the throat noisily.

hawker /ˈhɔkə/ *n.* someone who travels from place to place or house to house selling goods.

hawser /ˈhɔzə/ *n.* a small cable or large rope used in warping, mooring, towing, etc.

hawthorn /ˈhɔθɔn/ *n.* any species of the genus *Crataegus*, usually small trees with thorns, cultivated for their white or pink blossoms and bright-coloured fruits.

hay /heɪ/ *n.* **1.** grass, clover, lucerne, etc., cut and dried for use as fodder. **2.** grass mowed or intended for mowing. *–phr.* **3. a roll in the hay,** *Colloq.* an instance of sexual intercourse, especially a casual one. **4. hit the hay,** *Colloq.* to go to bed. **5. make hay, a.** to cut grass for fodder. **b.** to scatter everything in disorder. **6. make hay while the sun shines,** to make the most of opportunity.

hay fever *n. Pathol.* a catarrhal affection of the mucous membranes of the eyes and respiratory tract, attacking susceptible persons usually during the summer, and due to the action of the pollen of certain plants.

haywire /ˈheɪwaɪə/ *n.* **1.** wire used to bind hay. *–adj.* **2.** in disorder; out of order. **3.** out of control; crazy.

hazard /ˈhæzəd/ *n.* **1.** a risk; exposure to danger or harm. **2.** the cause of such a risk; a potential source of harm, injury, difficulty, etc.: *the motor car has become a*

major hazard in modern life. **3.** chance; uncertainty. **4.** *Golf* an obstacle, as a bunker, road, bush, water, or the like, on the course. *–v.t.* **5.** to venture to offer (a statement, conjecture, etc.). **6.** to put to the risk of being lost; to expose to risk. **7.** to take or run the risk of (a misfortune, penalty, etc.). **8.** to venture upon (anything of doubtful issue). *–phr.* **9. at hazard, a.** at risk; staked. **b.** by chance: *we met at hazard.* **–hazardous,** *adj.* **–hazardable,** *adj.* **–hazardless,** *adj.* **–hazarder,** *n.*

hazard reduction *n.* **1.** measures taken to reduce the risk of damage or harm occurring in the case of a dangerous or emergency situation. **2.** Also, **fire hazard reduction, bushfire hazard reduction.** (in bushfire prevention) the reducing or removing of combustible material, as dead leaves, dry grass, etc., from an area, usually in a controlled burn, to minimise the threat of damage by bushfire.

haze /heɪz/ *n.* **1.** an aggregation of minute suspended particles of vapour, dust, etc., near the surface of the earth, causing an appearance of thin mist in the atmosphere. **2.** obscurity or vagueness of the mind, perception, feelings, etc. **–hazy,** *adj.* **–haziness,** *n.*

hazel /ˈheɪzəl/ *n.* **1.** any shrub or small tree of the genus *Corylus*, which bears edible nuts, such as *C. avellana* of Europe or *C. americana* and *C. cornuta* of America. **2.** the light yellowish-brown of a hazelnut.

H-bomb /ˈeɪtʃ-bɒm/ *n.* hydrogen bomb.

HDL /eɪtʃ di ˈɛl/ *n.* a high-density lipoprotein which forms the lesser part of the cholesterol in the blood and which is thought to carry cholesterol from the artery wall to the liver. See **good cholesterol**. Compare **LDL**.

HDTV /ˌeɪtʃ di ti ˈvi/ *n.* high definition TV; a type of digital TV that sends a greater volume of information than analog TV with the same amount of bandwidth, by digitising and compressing the signal before transmitting, resulting in higher quality picture and sound. Compare **SDTV**.

he /hi/, *weak form* /i/ *pron. (personal), third person, sing., subjective (objective* **him**) **1.** the male being in question or last mentioned. **2.** anyone; that person: *he who hesitates is lost.* *–n.* (*pl.* **hes**) **3.** a man or any male person or animal (correlative to *she*). *–adj.* **4.** male or masculine, especially of animals.

head /hed/ *n.* **1.** the upper part of the human body, joined to the trunk by the neck. **2.** the corresponding part of an animal's body. **3.** the head considered as the seat of thought, memory, understanding, etc.: *to have a head for mathematics.* **4.** the position of leadership; chief command; greatest authority. **5.** someone to whom others are subordinate; a leader or chief. **6.** that part of anything which forms or is regarded as forming the top, summit, or upper end: *head of a page.* **7.** the foremost part or end of anything; a projecting part: *head of a procession*; *head of a rock.* **8.** Also, **loose head.** *Rugby Football* in a scrum, the front-row forward who has only one shoulder in contact with an opposite player. **9.** a person considered with reference to their mind, disposition, attributes, etc.: *wise heads*; *crowned heads.* **10.** (*pl.* **head**) a person or animal considered merely as one of a number: *ten head of cattle*; *to charge $10 a head.* **11.** a measurement to show the difference in height between two people, or the distance between two horses in a race. **12.** culmination or crisis; conclusion: *to bring matters to a head.* **13.** the hair covering the head: *to comb someone's head.* **14.** a rounded or compact part of a plant, usually at the top of the stem, as of leaves (as in the cabbage or lettuce), leaf-stalks (as in the celery), flower buds (as in the cauliflower), sessile florets crowded together on a receptacle, etc. **15.** that part of a cereal plant, as wheat, barley, etc., which contains the flowers and hence the fruit, grains, and kernels. **16.** the striking part of an instrument, tool, weapon, or the like (opposed to the gripping part), as the part of a golf club which includes the face and with which the ball is hit. **17.** the maturated part of an abscess, boil, etc. **18.** a projecting point of a coast, especially when high, as a cape, headland, or promontory. **19.** the obverse of a coin, as bearing a head or other principal figure (opposed to *tail*). **20.** one of the chief points or divisions of a discourse; topic. **21.** the source of a river or stream. **22.** collar, froth, or foam, as that formed on beer when poured. **23.** the height of the free surface of a liquid above a given level. **24.** *Machinery* a device on turning and boring machines, especially lathes, holding one or more cutting tools to the work. **25.** the pressure of a confined body of steam, etc., per unit of area. **26.** the height of a column of fluid required for a certain pressure. **27.** the electromagnet in a machine such as a tape recorder, VCR, or computer, which converts electromagnetic impulses stored on the tape or disk into electrical pulses to be produced. –*adj.* **28.** situated at the top or front: *the head division of a parade.* **29.** being in the position of leadership or superiority. –*v.t.* **30.** to go at the head of or in front of; lead, precede: *to head a list.* **31.** to race ahead of (a mob of moving animals, such as sheep, stampeding cattle, etc.) so as to stop their progress. **32.** to be the head or chief of. **33.** to turn the head or front of in a specified direction: *to head one's boat for the shore.* **34.** to go round the head of (a stream, etc.). **35.** to furnish or fit with a head. **36.** *Agric.* to harvest (especially a grain crop) by removing the head. **37.** *Football* to propel (the ball) by action of the head. –*v.i.* **38.** (sometimes fol. by *for*) to move forwards towards a point specified; direct one's course; go in a certain direction. –*phr.* **39. come to a head,** to reach a crisis. **40. do someone's head in,** *Colloq.* to utterly confuse and frustrate someone by, or as by, playing mind games with them. **41. (down) by the head,** *Naut.* so loaded as to draw more water forward than aft. **42. get a big** (or **swelled**) (or **fat**) **head,** *Colloq.* to become conceited. **43. give someone** (or **something**) **their** (or **its**) **head, a.** to allow someone or something greater freedom: *if we gave him his head he'd be at the beach every day.* **b.** to allow a horse greater freedom in running. **44. go to someone's head, a.** to make someone confused or dizzy. **b.** to make someone conceited. **45. have a (good) head on one's shoulders,** to have a balanced and sensible outlook. **46. have heads over,** *Colloq.* to punish the people responsible for (a blunder). **47. have one's head screwed on (the right way),** *Colloq.* to demonstrate great common sense, judgement, etc. **48. have someone's head,** *Colloq.* to punish someone severely. **49. head and shoulders above,** by far superior to. **50. head off,** to intercept (something) and force it to change course. **51. head over heels,** completely; utterly: *head over heels in love.* **52. head over heels** (or **tail**), *Colloq.* upside down; headlong as after a somersault. **53. head them,** (in two-up) to make the coins land with heads upwards. **54. head up,** to act as the head of: *to head up the new committee.* **55. hit one's head against a brick wall,** to persist in trying to do the impossible. **56. keep one's head above water,** to remain in control of a difficult situation, especially a financial one. **57. keep one's head down, a.** to work hard and consistently. **b.** to stay out of view and hence out of trouble. **58. lay** (or **put**) **heads together,** to come together to scheme. **59. let one's head go,** to behave somewhat more freely or recklessly than usual. **60. lose one's head,** to panic, become flustered, especially in an emergency. **61. head or tail of,** (*usu. with a negative*) *Colloq.* not able to understand or work out: *I can't make head or tail of this question.* **62. need one's head read,** *Colloq.* (*humorous*) to be insane. **63. off one's head,** *Colloq.* mad; very excited; delirious. **64. off the top of one's head,** *Colloq.* extempore; impromptu. **65. ... one's head off,** *Colloq.*

to an extreme; excessively: *talk one's head off.* **66. on one's own head,** as one's own responsibility. **67. out of one's head,** out of one's mind; demented; delirious. **68. out of someone's head,** from someone's mind, memory, imagination, etc.: *that story has come completely out of my head.* **69. over someone's head, a.** passing over someone having a prior claim or a superior position. **b.** beyond someone's comprehension. **70. pull one's head in,** *Aust. Colloq.* to mind one's own business. **71. take it into one's head,** to conceive an idea, plan, or the like. **72. turn someone's head,** to make someone vain or conceited.

-head[1] a suffix denoting state, condition, character, etc., as in *godhead,* and other words, now mostly archaic or obsolete, many being superseded by forms in **-hood.**

-head[2] a suffixal use of **head** indicating a person typified by a particular predilection associated with the term specified, as in *petrolhead, waxhead.*

headache /ˈhɛdeɪk/ *n.* **1.** a pain situated in the head. **2.** *Colloq.* a troublesome or worrying problem. –**headachy,** *adj.*

headbanging /ˈhɛdbæŋɪŋ/ *n.* **1.** a style of dancing to heavy metal music in which the dancer shakes the head violently or actually bangs it against something. –*adj.* **2.** of or relating to a style of music suitable for headbanging.

headbutt /ˈhɛdbʌt/ *v.t.* **1.** to butt (someone) using one's head as a weapon. –*n.* **2.** an act of butting with the head. –**headbutter,** *n.* –**headbutting,** *n.*

head cold *n.* a form of the common cold that mainly involves inflammation or infection of the nasal passages. Compare **chest cold.** Also, **headcold.**

-headed a suffix meaning: **1.** having a specified kind of head: *long-headed, wrongheaded.* **2.** having a specified number of heads: *two-headed.*

header /ˈhɛdə/ *n.* **1.** someone who or an apparatus which removes or puts a head on something. **2.** a form of reaping machine which cuts off and gathers only the head of the grain. **3.** *Building Trades* a brick or stone laid with its length across the thickness of a wall. Compare **stretcher** (def. 4). **4.** (in computer typesetting) an item programmed to appear regularly at the top of a page. Compare **footer** (def. 4). **5.** *Soccer* a shot made with the head. –*phr.* **6. take a header,** *Colloq.* to dive.

headfirst /hɛdˈfɜst/ *adv.* **1.** with the head in front or bent forwards; headlong. **2.** rashly; precipitately. Also, **headforemost** /hɛdˈfɔmoʊst/.

head honcho *n. Colloq.* the person with the greatest authority or power.

headhunt /ˈhɛdhʌnt/ *v.t.* **1.** to recruit (staff) by approaching people in existing jobs to offer them a new one. –*v.i.* **2.** (formerly) to collect the heads of slain enemies as trophies.

headhunting /ˈhɛdhʌntɪŋ/ *n.* **1.** (among certain tribal peoples) the practice of severing the heads of enemies as trophies or for use in religious ceremonies. **2.** *Colloq.* the eliminating of political enemies. **3.** *Colloq.* the search for new executives, usually senior, through personal contacts rather than advertisements. –**headhunter,** *n.*

heading /ˈhɛdɪŋ/ *n.* **1.** something that serves as a head, top, or front. **2.** a title or caption of a page, chapter, etc. **3.** a section of a subject of discourse; a topic. **4.** a horizontal passage in the earth, as for an intended tunnel, for working a mine, for ventilation or drainage, etc.; a drift. **5.** navigational direction; bearing.

headkicker /ˈhɛdkɪkə/ *n. Colloq.* a person whose role is to enforce a disciplined approach to established policy, as in a political party.

headland /ˈhɛdlənd, -lænd/ *n.* a promontory extending into a large body of water, such as a sea or lake.

headlight /ˈhɛdlaɪt/ *n.* a light equipped with a reflector, on the front of any vehicle.

headline /'hɛdlaɪn/ n. **1.** a display line over an article, etc., as in a newspaper. **2.** (pl.) the few most important items of news briefly stated: *here again are the headlines.* **3.** (in palmistry) a line of the head. *–v.t.* **4.** to furnish with a headline. *–adj.* **5.** given as a summary or key item: *a headline indicator.*

headlong /'hɛdlɒŋ/ adv. **1.** headfirst: *to plunge headlong.* **2.** rashly; without thought. **3.** with great speed; precipitately. *–adj.* **4.** done or going with the head foremost. **5.** marked by haste; precipitate. **6.** rash; impetuous.

headmaster /'hɛdmastə, hɛd'mastə/ n. the male principal of a school. **–headmastership,** n.

headmistress /'hɛdmɪstrəs, hɛd'mɪstrəs/ n. the female principal of a school.

head-on adv. **1.** with the head or front pointing towards, striking, or opposed to something: *the boat was head-on to the beach; the cars met head-on.* *–adj.* **2.** of or relating to what has met head-on: *a head-on collision.* **3.** of or relating to a direct confrontation: *a head-on argument.* *–n.* **4.** a head-on collision.

headphone /'hɛdfoʊn/ n. (oft. pl.) a device consisting of one or two earphones with attachments for holding them over the ears.

headquarters /'hɛdkwɔtəz, hɛd'kwɔtəz/ pl. n. (oft. construed as sing.) **1.** any centre from which official orders are issued: *police headquarters.* **2.** any centre of operations. **3.** the offices of a military commander; the place where a commander customarily issues orders. **4.** a military unit consisting of the commander, his or her staff, and other assistants. **5.** the building occupied by a headquarters.

headstand /'hɛdstænd/ n. a position of the body in which it is balanced vertically, the head and hands on the ground.

head start n. an initial advantage in a race, competition, etc.

headstone /'hɛdstoʊn/ n. a stone set at the head of a grave.

headstrong /'hɛdstrɒŋ/ adj. **1.** bent on having one's own way; wilful. **2.** proceeding from wilfulness: *a headstrong course.* **–headstrongness,** n.

heads-up n. Colloq. a quick issuing of advance notice: *thanks for the heads-up that the boss was on her way.*

headwaters /'hɛdwɔtəz/ pl. n. the upper tributaries of a river.

headway /'hɛdweɪ/ n. **1.** motion forwards or ahead; advance. **2.** progress in general. **3.** rate of progress. *–phr.* **4. make headway,** to make progress, especially against difficulties.

headwind /'hɛdwɪnd/ n. a wind that blows directly against the direction of travel: *the flight to Perth takes a bit longer because of the prevailing headwind.*

heady /'hɛdi/ adj. (-dier, -diest) **1.** rashly impetuous. **2.** intoxicating. **–headily,** adv. **–headiness,** n.

heal /hil/ v.t. **1.** to make whole or sound; restore to health; free from ailment. **2.** to free from anything evil or distressing; amend: *to heal a quarrel.* **3.** to cleanse or purify. *–v.i.* **4.** to effect a cure. **5.** Also, **heal up, heal over.** to become whole or sound; get well. **–healer,** n.

health /hɛlθ/ n. **1.** soundness of body; freedom from disease or ailment. **2.** the general condition of the body or mind with reference to soundness and vigour: *good health.* **3.** a polite or complimentary wish for a person's health, happiness, etc., especially as a toast. *–phr.* **4. your health,** an expression of goodwill, especially as a toast.

health care n. medical and other services provided for the maintenance of health, prevention of disease, etc. Also, **healthcare.**

healthcare /'hɛlθkɛə/ n. **1.** → **health care.** *–adj.* **2.** of or relating to health care: *health care professionals.*

health care directive n. → **living will.** Also, **advance health directive, advance (health) care directive.**

health inspector n. an officer appointed to inspect working and living conditions, buildings, etc., in the area, to ensure that they conform to health regulations.

health tourism n. travel for the purpose of a medical treatment to a country which offers the service at a cheaper rate or higher standard than that available in the traveller's home country. Also, **health care tourism, medical tourism.**

healthy /'hɛlθi/ adj. (-thier, -thiest) **1.** possessing or enjoying health: *healthy body; healthy mind.* **2.** relating to or characteristic of health: *a healthy appearance.* **3.** conducive to health, or healthful: *healthy recreations.* **–healthily,** adv. **–healthiness,** n.

heap /hip/ n. **1.** an assemblage of things, lying one on another; a pile: *a heap of stones.* **2.** (sometimes pl.) Colloq. a great quantity or number; a multitude: *a heap better; heaps further.* **3.** Colloq. something very old and dilapidated, especially a motor car. *–v.t.* **4.** (sometimes fol. by *up, on, together,* etc.) to gather, put, or cast in a heap; pile. **5.** (sometimes fol. by *up*) to accumulate or amass: *to heap up riches.* **6.** to cast or bestow in great quantity: *to heap blessings or insults upon a person.* **7.** to load or supply abundantly with something: *to heap a person with favours.* *–v.i.* **8.** to become heaped or piled, as sand, snow, etc.; rise in a heap or heaps. *–adv.* **9.** (pl.) an intensifier: *Bill's unit is heaps bigger than mine.* *–phr.* **10. give it heaps,** Aust., NZ Colloq. to treat something with firmness, in order to exact good performance. **11. give someone heaps,** Aust., NZ Colloq. **a.** to express strong displeasure with someone; criticise someone severely. **b.** to tease someone; provoke someone to anger, annoyance, etc., by banter or mockery. **12. heap coals of fire on someone's head,** to mortify or make ashamed someone who has acted unkindly by being especially kind to them. **13. strike all of a heap,** Colloq. to dumbfound; amaze; overwhelm. **–heaper,** n.

hear /hɪə/ verb (heard /hɜd/, hearing) *–v.t.* **1.** to perceive by the ear. **2.** to listen to: *to refuse to hear a person.* **3.** to learn by the ear or by being told; be informed of: *to hear news.* **4.** to be among the audience at or of: *to hear a lecture.* **5.** to give a formal, official, or judicial hearing to, as a sovereign, a teacher, an assembly, or a judge does. **6.** to listen to with favour, assent, or compliance. *–v.i.* **7.** to have perception of sound by the ear; have the sense of hearing. **8.** to listen or take heed. **9.** to receive information by the ear or otherwise: *to hear from a friend.* **10.** to listen with favour or assent: *he would not hear of it.* *–phr.* **11. hear, hear,** an exclamation of agreement, support, assent, etc. **12. hear out,** to listen to (someone or something) until the end. **13. hear things,** to imagine noises; hallucinate. **–hearer,** n.

hearing /'hɪərɪŋ/ n. **1.** the faculty or sense by which sound is perceived. **2.** the act of perceiving sound. **3.** opportunity to be heard: *to grant a hearing.* **4.** Law the trial of an action. *–phr.* **5. within hearing** (or **earshot**), (sometimes fol. by *of*) close by, so as able to be heard: *to live within hearing of the lapping of the waves.* **6. out of hearing** (or **earshot**), (sometimes fol. by *of*) distant, so as not able to be heard.

hearing aid n. a compact, inconspicuous amplifier worn to improve one's hearing.

hearsay /'hɪəseɪ/ n. gossip; rumour.

hearse /hɜs/ n. a funeral vehicle for conveying a dead person to the place of burial.

heart /hat/ n. **1.** a hollow muscular organ which by rhythmic contraction and dilatation keeps the blood in circulation throughout the body. **2.** this organ considered as the seat of life, or vital powers, or of thought, feeling, or emotion: *to die of a broken heart; in his heart he yearned to see her again.* **3.** the seat of emotions and affections (often in contrast to the *head* as the seat of the intellect): *to win a person's heart.* **4.** feeling; sensibility; capacity for sympathy. **5.** spirit, courage, or enthusiasm: *to lose heart.* **6.** the innermost or middle part of anything. **7.** the vital or essential part; core: *the very heart of the matter.* **8.** the breast or bosom: *to clasp a person to one's heart.* **9.** a person, especially in expressions of praise or affection: *dear heart.* **10.** a figure or object with rounded sides meeting in an obtuse point at the bottom and curving inwards to a cusp at the top; a stylised representation of the shape of a heart. **11.** *Cards* **a.** a playing card of a suit marked with heart-shaped figures in red. **b.** (*pl.*) the suit of cards bearing this symbol. **c.** (*pl. construed as sing.*) a game in which the players try to avoid taking tricks containing hearts. **12.** *Bot.* the core of a tree; the solid central part without sap or albumen. **13.** good condition for production, growth, etc., as of land or crops. *–phr.* **14. after someone's own heart,** appealing to someone's taste or affection. **15. at heart,** in one's heart, thoughts, or feelings; in reality. **16. be all heart,** (*usually ironic*) to be full of consideration and kindness. **17. break the heart of, a.** to disappoint grievously in love. **b.** to crush with sorrow or grief. **18. (off) by heart,** from memory; committing to memory. **19. close to someone's heart,** deeply affecting someone's interests and affections. **20. cry one's heart out,** to cry bitterly or violently. **21. eat one's heart out,** to pine or fret, especially with envy. **22. from (the bottom of) one's heart,** sincerely. **23. have a change of heart,** to reverse a decision or opinion. **24. have a heart,** to be reasonable; show mercy. **25. have at heart,** to cherish as an object, aim, etc. **26. have no heart,** to be lacking in kindly or sympathetic feeling. **27. have one's heart in one's mouth** (or **throat**), to be very frightened. **28. have the heart, a.** to have enough courage. **b.** (in negative sentences) to be unfeeling enough. **29. heart and soul,** completely; wholly. **30. heart of oak,** a courageous and long-suffering spirit. **31. in one's heart of hearts,** at the depth of one's feelings: *he knew in his heart of hearts that he was wrong.* **32. lose one's heart,** to fall in love. **33. set someone's heart at rest,** to ease someone's anxieties: *the doctor was able to set the patient's heart at rest.* **34. set one's heart on,** to desire greatly; to resolve to obtain. **35. take heart,** to find new courage or strength; be reassured or encouraged. **36. take to heart, a.** to think seriously about. **b.** to be deeply affected by; grieve over. **37. the red heart (of Australia),** the remote interior of Australia, thought of as the central point of the country, and by association with the red soil typical of the region. **38. to one's heart's content,** as much as one wishes. **39. wear one's heart on one's sleeve,** to display openly one's emotions, intentions, etc. **40. with all one's heart,** with all willingness; heartily.

heartache /'hateɪk/ *n.* mental anguish; painful sorrow.

heart attack *n.* **1.** any sudden severe instance of heart malfunction. **2.** the blocking of an artery to the heart resulting in the death of part of the heart muscle; myocardial infarct. Compare **coronary thrombosis.**

heartburn /'hatbɜn/ *n.* **1.** a burning sensation in the epigastrium. **2.** envy; bitter jealousy.

hearten /'hatn/ *v.t.* to give courage to; cheer.

heartfelt /'hatfɛlt/ *adj.* deeply or sincerely felt; earnest; sincere: *heartfelt joy; heartfelt words.*

hearth /haθ/ *n.* **1.** the part of the floor of a room on which the fire is made or above which is a stove, fireplace, furnace, etc. **2.** the fireside; home.

heartless /'hatləs/ *adj.* without heart or feeling; unfeeling; cruel: *heartless words.* **–heartlessly,** *adv.* **–heartlessness,** *n.*

heart-rending *adj.* causing acute mental anguish. **–heart-rendingly,** *adv.*

heart-throb *n.* the object of an infatuation, such as a pop singer, film star, or the like. Also, **heartthrob.**

heart-to-heart *adj.* **1.** frank; sincere. *–n.* **2.** a frank and sincere conversation usually between two people.

heartwarming /'hatwɔmɪŋ/ *adj.* emotionally moving in a way which evokes a pleased and approving response.

hearty /'hati/ *adj.* (**-tier, -tiest**) **1.** warm-hearted; affectionate; cordial; friendly: *a hearty welcome.* **2.** heartfelt; genuine; sincere: *hearty approval.* **3.** enthusiastic; vigorous: *a hearty laugh.* **4.** physically vigorous; strong and well: *hale and hearty.* **5.** large or satisfying: *a hearty meal.* **6.** enjoying or needing abundant food: *a hearty appetite.* *–n.* (*pl.* **-ties**) **7.** *Colloq.* an ostentatiously hearty person. **8.** *Archaic* a comrade, especially a fellow sailor: *ahoy there, my hearties!* **–heartiness,** *n.*

heat /hit/ *n.* **1.** the quality or condition of being hot. **2.** the sensation of hotness or warmth; heated bodily condition. **3.** *Physics* energy that is transferred between two regions by virtue of a temperature difference only, now measured in joules, formerly measured in calories. **4.** *Physics* the amount of heat (def. 3) evolved or absorbed per unit amount of substance in a process as combustion. **5.** hot condition of the atmosphere or physical environment; hot season or weather. **6.** a sensation of burning on the tongue, skin, etc., as produced by chilli, mustard, etc. **7.** warmth or intensity of feeling: *the heat of an argument.* **8.** intense feeling, especially of excitement or anger: *the heat of rage; in the heat of the moment.* **9.** the height of greatest intensity of any action: *to do a thing at white heat.* **10.** *Colloq.* pressure of police, prison, or other investigation or activity: *the thieves went into hiding until the heat was off.* **11.** a single course in or division of a race or other contest. **12.** *Zool.* **a.** sexual excitement in animals, especially females; oestrus. **b.** the period or duration of such excitement. *–v.t.* **13.** to make hot or warm. **14.** to excite in mind or feeling; inflame with passion. *–v.i.* **15.** to become hot or warm. **16.** to become excited in mind or feeling. *–phr.* **17. on heat,** (of female animals) at a stage of sexual receptivity in the oestrus cycle; in season. **18. put the heat on,** *Colloq.* to put pressure on. **–heatless,** *adj.*

heated /'hitəd/ *adj.* **1.** warmed; having the temperature raised. **2.** inflamed; vehement; angry.

heater /'hitə/ *n.* **1.** an apparatus for heating, such as a furnace. **2.** *Electronics* the element of a radio valve which carries the current for heating a cathode. **3.** *US Colloq.* a pistol or revolver.

heath /hiθ/ *n.* **1.** a tract of open, uncultivated land covered by low, usually small-leaved, shrubs. **2.** any of various low evergreen shrubs of the family Ericaceae, common on waste land, such as *Calluna vulgaris,* the common heather of England and Scotland with small pinkish purple flowers. **3.** any plant of the genus *Erica,* or of the family Ericaceae. **4.** any other heath-like species, especially of the family Epacridaceae, such as species of the genera *Epacris* and *Leucopogon.*

heathen /'hiðən/ *n.* (*pl.* **-thens** *or* **-then**) **1.** an unconverted individual of a people which does not acknowledge the god of Christianity, Judaism, or Islam; pagan. **2.** an irreligious or unenlightened person. *–adj.* **3.** pagan; relating to the heathen. **4.** irreligious or unenlightened. **–heathendom, heathenry, heathenness, heathenism,** *n.* **–heathenish,** *adj.*

heather /'hɛðə/ *n.* any of various heaths, especially *Calluna vulgaris* (**Scotch heather**). See **heath** (def. 2).

heat island *n.* a dome of raised temperature discernible in a particular area, commonly above a city or town; caused by any of various factors such as non-reflective surfaces on building structures which absorb and then emit heat, lack of vegetation providing shade, etc.

heat stroke *n.* a condition resulting from prolonged exposure to excessive heat, with symptoms such as exhaustion, dizziness, headache, fever, etc., in severe cases progressing to hyperthermia with high fever and, if untreated, potentially coma and death. Also, **heatstroke**.

heatwave /ˈhiːtweɪv/ *n.* **1.** an air mass of high temperature, covering an extended area and moving relatively slowly. **2.** a prolonged period of excessively warm weather.

heave /hiːv/ *verb* (**heaved** *or, Chiefly Naut.*, **hove**, **heaving**) *–v.t.* **1.** to raise or lift with effort or force; hoist. **2.** to lift and throw, often with effort or force: *to heave an anchor overboard.* **3.** *Naut.* **a.** to haul, draw, or pull, as by a cable. **b.** to cause (a ship) to move in a certain direction. **4.** to utter laboriously or painfully: *to heave a sigh.* **5.** to cause to rise and fall with or as with a swelling motion. **6.** to raise or force up in a swelling movement; force to bulge. *–v.i.* **7.** to rise and fall with or as with a swelling motion. **8.** to breathe with effort; pant. **9.** to vomit; retch. **10.** to rise as if thrust up, as a hill; swell or bulge. **11.** *Naut.* **a.** to haul or pull, as at a cable; to push, as at the bar of a capstan. **b.** to move a ship, or move as a ship does, by such action. **c.** to move or go (*about, ahead,* etc.). *–n.* **12.** the act of heaving. **13.** (of the sea) the force exerted by the swell. *–phr.* **14. heave ho,** an exclamation used by sailors when heaving the anchor up, etc. **15. heave in sight,** to rise into view as from below the horizon, as a ship. **16. heave to,** *Naut.* **a.** to stop the headway of (a vessel), especially by bringing the head to the wind and trimming the sails so that they act against one another; to stop (a vessel). **b.** to stop a vessel in this manner: *we hove to at night for safety.* **c.** (of a vessel) to be stopped in this manner.

heave-ho /ˈhiːv-hoʊ, hiːv-ˈhoʊ/ *phr.* **the** (**old**) **heave-ho,** dismissal, especially from a job.

heaven /ˈhɛvən/ *n.* **1.** (*also upper case*) (in many religions and mythologies) a place or state of existence where people (often those who have lived righteously or those chosen by a god or gods) live on after death in happiness. Compare **hell** (def. 1). **2.** (*chiefly pl.*) the sky or firmament, or expanse of space surrounding the earth. **3.** a place or state of supreme bliss: *a heaven on earth. –phr.* **4. be in heaven,** *Colloq.* to be extremely happy. **5. for heaven's sake, a.** an exclamation indicating irritation or entreaty. **b.** a rhetorical tag to indicate surprise, indignation, etc. **6. good heavens,** an exclamation indicating surprise, consternation, indignation, etc. **7. heaven help ...,** an expression implying that the person or thing named will be beyond human help: *heaven help him if he goes down that path.* **8. heaven knows, a.** a phrase implying that neither the speaker, nor any other person, knows: *heaven knows where my wallet is now.* **b.** an impolite interjection: *heaven knows, I did all I could to help.* **9. heaven on a stick,** *Colloq.* something wonderfully pleasurable. **10. heavens** (**above**), an exclamation indicating surprise, vexation, indignation, etc. **11. move heaven and earth,** to do all that is possible. **12. thank heaven(s),** a phrase expressing gratitude for a good outcome: *thank heaven the police arrived in time.* **13. to high heaven,** to an extreme degree: *to complain to high heaven; to stink to high heaven.*

heavenly /ˈhɛvənli/ *adj.* **1.** resembling or befitting heaven; blissful; beautiful: *a heavenly spot.* **2.** of or in the heavens: *the heavenly bodies.* **3.** belonging to or coming from the heaven of God, the angels, etc. **4.** celestial or divine: *heavenly peace.* **–heavenliness,** *n.*

heavy /ˈhɛvi/ *adj.* (**-vier, -viest**) **1.** of great weight; hard to lift or carry: *a heavy load.* **2.** of great amount, force, intensity, etc.: *a heavy vote.* **3.** bearing hard upon; burdensome; harsh; distressing: *heavy taxes.* **4.** having much weight in proportion to bulk; being of high specific gravity: *a heavy metal.* **5.** broad, thick, or coarse; not delicate: *heavy lines.* **6.** of more than the usual, average, or specified weight: *heavy cargo.*

7. connected or concerned with the manufacture of goods of more than the usual weight: *heavy industry.* **8.** *Mil.* **a.** heavily armed or equipped. **b.** of the larger sizes: *heavy weapons.* **9.** serious; grave: *a heavy offence.* **10.** hard to deal with; trying; difficult: *a heavy task.* **11.** being such in an unusual degree: *a heavy smoker.* **12.** weighted or laden: *air heavy with moisture.* **13.** depressed with trouble or sorrow; showing sorrow: *a heavy heart.* **14.** overcast or cloudy: *heavy sky.* **15.** clumsy; slow in movement or action. **16.** without vivacity or interest; ponderous; dull: *a heavy style.* **17.** loud and deep: *a heavy sound.* **18.** exceptionally dense in substance; insufficiently raised or leavened; thick: *heavy bread.* **19.** not easily digested: *heavy food.* **20.** (of music, literature, etc.) intellectual or deep. **21.** important; serious; meaningful: *a heavy emotion.* **22.** *Theatre* sober, serious, or sombre: *a heavy part.* **23.** *Colloq.* coercive; threatening: *the cops were really heavy.* **24.** *Chem.* (of an isotope) of greater atomic weight: *heavy hydrogen. –n.* (*pl.* **-vies**) **25.** *Colloq.* **a.** a person who is eminent and influential in the sphere of his or her activities, as a senior student, someone important in business, etc. **b.** a person of some status who exercises authority unpleasantly or seeks to intimidate. **c.** a man who attempts to intimidate a woman into sexual submission. **26.** *Colloq.* a detective. **27.** *Theatre* **a.** a villainous part or character. **b.** an actor who plays villainous parts or characters. *–v.t.* (**-vied, -vying**) **28.** *Colloq.* to confront, put pressure on. *–adv.* **29.** heavily. *–phr. Colloq.* **30. be heavy on,** to consume in excessive quantities: *this car is heavy on petrol.* **31. come the heavy** or **do a heavy,** to exert authority; intimidate others.

heavy-handed *adj.* **1.** oppressive; harsh. **2.** clumsy. **–heavy-handedness,** *n.*

heavy metal *n.* **1.** a metal with a density greater than five times that of water, particularly cadmium, chromium, cobalt, gold, lead, mercury, silver, thallium and vanadium; such metals can accumulate to toxic levels in animal tissues. **2.** a style of rock music dominated by electric guitars played at high levels of amplification. **3.** large military weapons or ammunition. **–heavy-metal,** *adj.*

heavyweight /ˈhɛviweɪt/ *n.* **1.** one of more than average weight. **2. a.** the heaviest weight division in boxing or wrestling. **b.** a boxer or wrestler of this weight class. **3.** *Colloq.* a person of considerable power, influence, or forcefulness in a certain field, such as a writer, philosopher, or politician.

hebe /ˈhiːbi/ *n.* any of various evergreen shrubs native to New Zealand belonging to the genus *Hebe* of the Plantaginaceae family; commonly grown as a garden shrub.

Hebrew /ˈhiːbruː/ *n.* **1.** a member of that branch of the Semitic race descended from the line of Abraham; Israelite; Jew. *–adj.* **2.** of or relating to the Hebrews or their language.

heckle /ˈhɛkəl/ *v.t.* to badger or torment; harass, especially a public speaker, with questions and gibes. **–heckler,** *n.* **–heckling,** *n.*

hectare /ˈhɛktɛə/ *n.* a surface measure, the common unit of land measure in the metric system, equal to 100 ares, or 10 000 square metres (approximately 2.47 acres). *Symbol:* ha

hectic /ˈhɛktɪk/ *adj.* **1.** characterised by great excitement, passion, activity, confusion, haste: *hectic meeting, hectic day.* **2.** marking a particular habit or condition of body, such as the fever of phthisis (**hectic fever**) when this is attended by flushed cheeks (**hectic flush**), hot skin, and emaciation. **3.** relating to or affected with such fever; consumptive. **–hectically,** *adv.*

hecto- a prefix denoting 10^2 of a given unit, as in *hectogram. Symbol:* h Also, (*before vowels*), **hect-**.

hector /'hɛktə/ v.t. **1.** to treat with insolence; bully; torment. –v.i. **2.** to act in a blustering, domineering way; be a bully.

hedge /hɛdʒ/ n. **1.** a row of bushes or small trees planted close together, especially when forming a fence or boundary. **2.** any barrier or boundary. **3.** an act or a means of hedging a bet or the like. **4.** an investment, fiscal policy, etc., designed to offset losses caused by inflation or other business hazard. –verb (**hedged, hedging**) –v.t. **5.** to enclose with or separate by a hedge: *the garden was hedged with acacias.* **6.** to protect (a bet, etc.) by taking some offsetting risk. –v.i. **7.** to avoid taking an open or decisive course. **8.** to avoid giving a question a direct answer. **9.** *Finance* to enter transactions that will protect against loss through a compensatory price movement. –phr. **10. hedge about** (or **around**), to surround so as to prevent escape or hinder free movement; obstruct: *to be hedged about by difficulties.* **11. hedge against**, to protect a bet, speculation, etc., from (risk) by taking some offsetting risk. **12. hedge in**, to cut off passage from, as with a hedge; hem in.

hedge contract n. a contract between two parties with different currencies in which they agree to indemnify each other against any movement of the relative value of their currencies.

hedge fund n. a fund which invests in a hedge market.

hedgehog /'hɛdʒhɒg/ n. any of several nocturnal, insectivorous mammals of the family Erinaceidae, of the genus *Erinaceus* of Europe, Africa, and Asia having erectile spines on the upper part of the body and able to roll into a ball for protection.

hedge market n. a market based on hedge contracts.

hedonism /'hidənɪzəm, 'hɛ-/ n. **1.** the teaching that pleasure or happiness is the highest good. **2.** devotion to pleasure. –hedonist, n. –hedonistic, adj.

heed /hid/ v.t. **1.** to give attention to; regard; notice. –v.i. **2.** to give attention; have regard. –n. **3.** (usu. with *give* or *take*) careful attention; notice; observation. –heedful, adj. –heedless, adj. –heeder, n.

heel[1] /hil/ n. **1.** (in humans) the back part of the foot, below and behind the ankle. **2.** an analogous part in other vertebrates. **3.** either hind foot or hoof of some animals, as the horse. **4.** the part of a stocking, shoe, or the like, covering the heel. **5.** a solid part of wood, rubber, etc., attached to the sole of a shoe, under the heel. **6.** the part of the palm of a hand or glove nearest the wrist. **7.** something resembling the human heel in position, shape, etc.: *heel of bread.* **8.** *Colloq.* a despicable person; cad. –v.t. **9.** to furnish with heels, as shoes. **10.** to follow at the heels of. –v.i. **11.** to follow at one's heels. –phr. **12. at** (or **to**) **heel, a.** (of a dog) following a person with the nose close to their left heel. **b.** under control. **13. at someone's heels**, close behind someone. **14. cool** (or **kick**) **one's heels**, to be obliged to wait patiently, as for someone to arrive or something anticipated to happen. **15. dig one's heels in**, to maintain an immovable position in debate, etc.; be stubborn. **16. down at heel, a.** having the shoe heels worn down. **b.** shabby. **c.** slipshod or slovenly. **d.** in straitened circumstances; impoverished. **17. heel in**, to plant (cuttings or plants) temporarily before putting them in their permanent growing site. **18. kick up one's heels**, to enjoy oneself. **19. lay by the heels**, to capture; seize. **20. on the heels of**, closely following. **21. show a clean pair of heels**, to escape by outdistancing pursuers. **22. take to one's heels**, to run off or away. **23. turn on one's heel**, to change the direction one's body is facing, usually quickly and as part of moving away from a person or persons just spoken to, as in anger, sudden resolve, etc. –heelless, adj.

heel[2] /hil/ v.i. **1.** (of a ship, etc.) to lean to one side; cant; tilt. –v.t. **2.** to cause to lean or cant. –n. **3.** a heeling movement; a cant.

heeler /'hilə/ n. **1.** a dog which follows at one's heel. **2.** a cattle or sheep dog which rounds up stock by following at their heels.

heft /hɛft/ v.t. **1.** to try the weight of by lifting. **2.** to heave or lift.

hefty /'hɛfti/ adj. (**-tier, -tiest**) *Colloq.* **1.** heavy; weighty. **2.** big and strong; powerful; muscular. –heftily, adv. –heftiness, n.

hegemony /hə'gɛməni, hə'dʒɛməni, 'hɛgəməni, 'hɛdʒəməni/, *Orig. US* /'hɛgəmouni, 'hɛdʒəmouni/ n. (pl. **-monies**) **1.** leadership or predominant influence exercised by one state over others, as in a confederation. **2.** leadership; predominance. –hegemonic /hɛgə'mɒnɪk, hɛdʒ-/, adj.

heifer /'hɛfə/ n. **1.** a cow that has not produced a calf and is under three years of age. **2.** *Colloq.* a young woman. **3.** *Colloq.* a woman of solid build, especially one who lacks grace.

height /haɪt/ n. **1.** the distance from bottom to top: *the height of the tree is 20 metres.* **2.** extent upwards; altitude; stature; distance upwards; elevation: *height above sea level.* **3.** a high place or level; hill or mountain. **4.** the highest part; top; apex. **5.** the highest or central point; utmost degree: *the height of the season.*

Heimlich manoeuvre /'haɪmlɪk mənuvə/ n. a method of assisting someone who is choking by bringing sudden pressure to bear just below their rib cage, thus forcing air up through the trachea and removing the obstruction.

heinous /'heɪnəs, 'hi-/ adj. hateful; odious; gravely reprehensible: *a heinous offence.* –heinously, adv. –heinousness, n.

heir /ɛə/ n. **1.** *Law* someone who inherits the estate (def. 2b) of a deceased person, normally after it has been reduced by the payment of any debts, liabilities or charges which may pertain to it. **2.** someone to whom something falls or is due. **3.** a person, society, etc., considered as the continuer of a tradition, policy, or the like previously established. –heiress /'ɛərɛs, -əs/, fem. n. –heirdom, n. –heirship, n. –heirless, adj.

heir apparent n. (pl. **heirs apparent**) an heir whose right cannot be lost as long as he survives the ancestor.

heirloom /'ɛəlum/ n. **1.** any family possession transmitted from generation to generation. –adj. **2.** (of a plant variety) grown from older stock which is not hybridised, the fruit of which retains a distinctive shape, colour and flavour; heritage.

heir presumptive /ɛə prə'zʌmptɪv/ n. (pl. **heirs presumptive**) an heir whose expectation may be defeated by the birth of a nearer heir.

heist /haɪst/ v.t. **1.** to rob; steal. –n. **2.** a robbery; burglary. Also, **hoist**.

heist movie n. a film with a plot based on the planning and execution of an ambitious and complicated robbery.

held /hɛld/ v. past tense and past participle of **hold**[1].

helicopter /'hɛlikɒptə, 'hɛlə-/ n. **1.** any of a class of heavier-than-air craft which are lifted and sustained in the air by helicoid surfaces or propellers turning on vertical axes by virtue of power supplied from an engine. –v.t. **2.** to convey in or transport by helicopter.

helicopter parenting n. a style of child rearing in which parents are excessively attentive to and involved in the lives of their children. –helicopter parent, n.

helio- a word element meaning 'sun', as in *heliocentric*. Also, **heli-**.

heliotrope /'hɛliətroup, 'hiliə-, 'hɛljə-, 'hiljə-/ n. **1.** any herb or shrub of the genus *Heliotropium*, especially *H. arborescens*, a garden plant with small, fragrant purple flowers, and caterpillar weed, *H. europaeum*, a common noxious weed. **2.** a light tint of purple; reddish lavender.

helipad /ˈhɛlipæd/ *n.* an aerodrome or landing place for helicopters.

heliport /ˈhɛlipɔt/ *n.* a landing place for helicopters, often the roof of a building, with facilities for passenger handling.

helium /ˈhiliəm/ *n.* an inert gaseous element present in the sun's atmosphere, certain minerals, natural gas, etc., and also occurring as a radioactive decomposition product. *Symbol*: He; *relative atomic mass*: 4.0026; *atomic number*: 2; *density*: 0.1785 at 0°C and 760 mm pressure.

helix /ˈhiliks, ˈhɛl-/ *n.* (*pl.* **helices** /ˈhiləsiz, ˈhɛl-/ *or* **helixes**) **1.** a spiral. **2.** *Geom.* the curve assumed by a straight line drawn on a plane when that plane is wrapped round a cylindrical surface of any kind, especially a right circular cylinder, as the curve of a screw thread. −**helical, helicoid,** *adj.*

hell /hɛl/ *n.* **1.** (*also upper case*) (in many religions and mythologies) the abode of the spirits of the dead, often, as in Christianity, a place or state of existence where the wicked are punished after death. Compare **heaven** (def. 1). **2.** any place or state of torment or misery. **3.** the powers of evil. **4.** anything that causes torment; any severe or extremely unpleasant experience, either mental or physical. −*interj.* **5.** an exclamation of annoyance, disgust, etc. −*phr. Colloq.* **6. a hell** (or **heck**) **of a...,** Also, **helluva**. appallingly difficult, unpleasant, etc. **7.** (**all**) **hell breaks loose,** much trouble ensues, especially occasioning uproar. **8. a** (or **one**) **hell** (or **heck**) **of a...,** Also, **helluva**. notable; remarkable. **9. beat** (**the**) **hell** (or **heck**) **out of,** to physically assault (someone) in a violent manner. **10. blast** (**the**) **hell** (or **heck**) **out of,** to reprimand severely. **11. come hell or high water,** whatever happens. **12. for the hell** (or **heck**) **of it,** for no specific reason; for its own sake. **13. frighten** (or **scare**) **the hell** (or **heck**) **out of,** to frighten severely. **14. from hell,** exceptionally bad, unpleasant etc.: *she was the business partner from hell.* **15. get the hell** (or **heck**) **away,** (sometimes fol. by *from*) to distance oneself. **16. get the hell** (or **heck**) **out,** (sometimes fol. by *of*) to leave rapidly. **17. give someone hell,** to make things unpleasant for someone. **18. hell for leather,** at top speed; recklessly fast. **19. hell's bells,** a mild imprecation. **20. hell's teeth,** an exclamation of astonishment, indignation, etc. **21. hell to pay,** serious unwanted consequences. **22. like hell** (or **heck**), **a.** an intensifier with adverbial force: *run like hell.* **b.** an intensifier in expressions of ironic negation: *like hell I will; like hell it was.* **23. merry hell** (or **heck**), an upheaval; a severe reaction; severe pain. **24. not a hope in hell,** not the slightest possibility. **25. play hell** (or **heck**) **with, a.** to cause considerable damage, injury, or harm to. **b.** to reprimand severely; scold. **26. raise hell** (or **heck**), **a.** to cause a lot of commotion or trouble. **b.** to complain or protest vociferously. **27. the hell** (or **heck**) or **in the hell** (or **heck**) or **in hell** (or **heck**), an intensifier used with interrogatives: *how the hell am I going to do that?; who in the hell are you?; what in hell are you doing here?* **28. the hell** (or **heck**) **out of,** (to kick, beat, etc.) with great vigour: *to hit the hell out of the ball.* **29. the hell** (or **heck**) **with it,** an expression of disgust or rejection. **30. what the hell** (or **heck**), an exclamation of contempt, dismissal, or the like.

hell-bent *adj.* stubbornly or recklessly determined. Also, **hellbent**.

hellebore /ˈhɛləbɔ/ *n.* **1.** any plant of the genus *Helleborus*, especially *H. niger* (**black hellebore**), a European herb with showy flowers; Christmas rose; winter rose. **2.** any of the coarse herbs constituting the genus *Veratrum*, as *V. album* (**white hellebore**).

hellhole /ˈhɛlhoʊl/ *n. Colloq.* a highly unpleasant place.

hello /hʌˈloʊ, hə-/ *interj.* **1.** an exclamation to attract attention, answer a telephone, or express greeting. **2.** an exclamation of surprise, etc. −*n.* (*pl.* **-los**) **3.** the call 'hello'. −*v.i.* (**-loed, -loing**) **4.** to call 'hello'. Also, **hallo**, **hullo**.

helm /hɛlm/ *n.* **1.** the tiller or wheel by which the rudder of a vessel is controlled. **2.** the entire steering apparatus. **3.** a moving of the helm. **4.** the place or post of control: *the helm of affairs.* −*v.t.* **5.** to steer; direct. −*phr.* **6. at the helm,** in command: *the company has a new manager at the helm.* −**helmless,** *adj.*

helmet /ˈhɛlmət/ *n.* any of various defensive coverings for the head, such as those worn by soldiers, firefighters, divers, etc. −**helmeted,** *adj.*

helmet orchid *n.* any species of the orchid genus *Corybas*, tiny terrestrial herbs found from India to New Zealand.

helminth /ˈhɛlmɪnθ/ *n.* a worm, especially a parasitic worm. −**helminthic,** *adj.* −**helminthoid,** *adj.*

helot /ˈhɛlət/ *n.* a serf or slave; a bondman.

help /hɛlp/ *v.t.* **1.** to cooperate effectively with (a person); aid; assist. **2.** to furnish aid to; contribute strength or means to; assist in doing: *remedies that help digestion.* **3.** to succour; save; rescue. **4.** to relieve (someone) in need, sickness, pain, or distress. **5.** (with *can* or *cannot*) to refrain from; avoid: *he can help doing it; he can't help doing it.* **6.** to remedy, stop, or prevent. **7.** to contribute an improvement to: *the use of a little make-up would help her appearance.* −*v.i.* **8.** to give aid; be of service or advantage: *every little helps.* −*n.* **9.** the act of helping; aid or assistance; relief or succour. **10.** a person or thing that helps. **11.** a hired helper. **12.** a body of such helpers. **13.** a domestic servant or a farm labourer. **14.** means of remedying, stopping, or preventing: *the thing is done, and there is no help for it now.* **15.** *Computers* a file accessed as part of a program or application, which contains instructions for its use and solutions to common problems. −*interj.* **16.** a call for assistance. −*phr.* **17. help out,** to be of assistance; assist in or as in a crisis or difficulty. **18. help oneself,** (sometimes fol. by *to*) to take or appropriate something at will: *help yourself to the salad.* **19. help someone to,** to serve food to someone at table: *can I help you to some salad?* **20. not be able to help oneself,** to be unable to resist a risk or temptation: *when it comes to flirting he just can't help himself.* **21. so help me** (**God**), an exclamation giving assurance of the speaker's veracity. −**helpful,** *adj.* −**helpable,** *adj.* −**helper,** *n.*

help desk *n.* a service providing assistance or guidance within a company or organisation, especially in relation to the use of computers and other technical equipment. Also, **helpdesk**.

helping /ˈhɛlpɪŋ/ *n.* **1.** a portion served to a person at one time. −*adj.* **2.** giving assistance, support, etc.: *a helping hand.* −**helpingly,** *adv.*

helpless /ˈhɛlpləs/ *adj.* **1.** unable to help oneself; weak or dependent: *a helpless invalid.* **2.** without help, aid, or succour. **3.** incapable, inefficient, or shiftless. −**helplessly,** *adv.* −**helplessness,** *n.*

helpmate /ˈhɛlpmeɪt/ *n.* **1.** a companion and helper. **2.** a wife or husband.

help screen *n. Computers* a screen with additional information relating to a system or program to assist the user.

helter-skelter /hɛltəˈskɛltə/ *adv.* **1.** in headlong, disorderly haste: *to run helter-skelter.* −*n.* **2.** tumultuous haste or disorder. **3.** a helter-skelter flight, course, or performance. **4.** a tower with an external spiral slide, as at a fairground. −*adj.* **5.** confused; disorderly; carelessly hurried.

hem¹ /hɛm/ *v.t.* (**hemmed, hemming**) **1.** to fold back and sew down the edge of (cloth, a garment, etc.). **2.** to form an edge or border to or around. *–n.* **3.** the edge or border of a garment, etc., especially at the bottom. *–phr.* **4. hem in**, to enclose or confine: *hemmed in by enemies.*

hem² /hɛm/ *interj.* **1.** an utterance resembling a slight clearing of the throat, used to attract attention, express doubt, etc. *–n.* **2.** the utterance or sound of 'hem'. *–v.i.* (**hemmed, hemming**) **3.** to utter the sound 'hem'. **4.** to hesitate in speaking. *–phr.* **5. hem and haw** (or **ha**), to avoid giving a direct answer.

he-man *n. Colloq.* a tough or aggressively masculine man.

hemi- a prefix meaning 'half', as in *hemialgia*. Compare **semi-**.

hemisphere /ˈhɛməsfɪə/ *n.* **1.** half of the terrestrial globe or celestial sphere. **2.** a map or projection of either of these. **3.** the half of a sphere. **4.** *Anat.* either of the lateral halves of the cerebrum.

hemlock /ˈhɛmlɒk/ *n.* **1.** a poisonous umbelliferous herb, *Conium maculatum*, with spotted stems, finely divided leaves, and small white flowers, used medicinally as a powerful sedative. **2.** a poisonous drink made from this herb.

hemp /hɛmp/ *n.* **1.** a tall, annual herb, *Cannabis sativa*, native to Asia, but cultivated in many parts of the world, and yielding hashish, bhang, cannabin, etc. **2.** the tough fibre of this plant used for making coarse fabrics, ropes, etc. **3.** → **marijuana**.

hemstitch /ˈhɛmstɪtʃ/ *v.t.* **1.** to hem along a line from which threads have been drawn out, stitching the cross-threads into a series of small groups. *–n.* **2.** the stitch used or the needlework done in hemstitching.

hen /hɛn/ *n.* **1.** the female of the domestic fowl. **2.** the female of any bird, especially of a gallinaceous bird. **3.** *Colloq.* a woman, especially a fussy or foolish woman. *–phr.* **4. scarce** (or **rare**) **as hen's teeth**, *Colloq.* extremely rare.

hence /hɛns/ *adv.* **1.** as an inference from this fact; for this reason; therefore: *of the best quality and hence satisfactory.* **2.** *Archaic* from this time onwards; henceforth. **3.** *Archaic* from this place; away from here.

henceforth /hɛnsˈfɔθ/ *adv.* from this time forth; from now on. Also, **henceforwards** /hɛnsˈfɔwədz/, **henceforward**.

henchman /ˈhɛntʃmən/ *n.* (*pl.* **-men**) **1.** a trusty attendant or follower. **2.** a ruthless and unscrupulous follower.

Hendra virus /ˈhɛndrə vaɪrəs/ *n.* a paramyxovirus affecting horses and human beings, the natural host being the fruit bat.

henna /ˈhɛnə/ *n.* **1.** a shrub or small tree, *Lawsonia inermis*, of Asia and the eastern Mediterranean. **2.** a reddish orange dye or cosmetic made from the leaves of this plant. **3.** reddish or orange-brown. *–v.t.* (**-naed, -naing**) **4.** to tint or dye with henna.

hen party *n.* a party exclusively for women.

henpeck /ˈhɛnpɛk/ *v.t.* (of a wife) to domineer over (her husband). **–henpecked**, *adj.*

henry /ˈhɛnri/ *n.* (*pl.* **-rys**) the derived SI unit of inductance, equivalent to the inductance of a circuit in which an electromotive force of one volt is produced by a current in the circuit which varies at the rate of one ampere per second. *Symbol:* H

he-oak /ˈhi-oʊk/ *n.* any of various species of casuarina, especially *Casuarina stricta*.

hepatic /həˈpætɪk/ *adj.* **1.** of or relating to the liver. **2.** acting on the liver, as a medicine. **3.** liver-coloured; dark reddish brown.

hepatitis /hɛpəˈtaɪtəs/ *n.* a serious disease characterised by inflammation or enlargement of the liver, appearing in various forms caused by different viruses, each form being identified by a letter of the alphabet.

hepatitis A *n.* a form of hepatitis caused by the hepatitis A virus, occurring mainly in young children and spread by contaminated food or eating utensils.

hepatitis B *n.* a form of hepatitis caused by the hepatitis B virus, which enters the blood of the recipient from infected blood (or blood products) or other body fluids, and which can be transmitted through sexual contact and contaminated needles and instruments.

hepatitis C *n.* a form of hepatitis caused by the hepatitis C virus, which is transmitted by infected body fluids and occurs mainly in intravenous drug users.

hepta- a prefix meaning 'seven'. Also, (*before vowels*), **hept-**.

heptathlon /hɛpˈtæθlən/ *n.* an athletic contest comprising seven different events and won by the contestant having the highest total score. **–heptathlete**, *n.*

her /hɜ/, *weak forms* /hə, ə/ *pron. (personal)* **1.** the objective case of **she**. *–adj.* **2.** the possessive form of **she**: *her mother.*

herald /ˈhɛrəld/ *n.* **1.** someone, often an official, who carries messages or makes announcements. **2.** a person or thing that tells of the approach of somebody or something; harbinger: *a cloudy sky is the herald of rain.* **3.** an officer who arranged medieval tournaments, etc., later employed to keep records of the use of coats of arms. *–v.t.* **4.** to tell of the approach of. **–heraldic**, *adj.*

heraldry /ˈhɛrəldri/ *n.* (*pl.* **-dries**) **1.** the science of tracing and recording coats of arms, family histories, etc. **2.** the art of blazoning coats of arms, of settling the right of persons to bear arms or to use certain bearings, of tracing and recording genealogies, of recording honours, and of deciding questions of precedence. **3.** the office or duty of a herald. **4.** heraldic symbolism. **5.** heraldic pomp or ceremony.

herb /hɜb/, *US* /ɜb/ *n.* **1.** a flowering plant whose stem above ground does not become woody and persistent. **2.** such a plant when valued for its medicinal properties, flavour, scent, or the like. **3. the herb**, *Colloq.* marijuana. **–herbal**, *adj.* **–herbalist**, *n.* **–herbless**, *adj.* **–herby**, *adj.*

herbaceous /hɜˈbeɪʃəs/ *adj.* **1.** of, relating to, or resembling a herb; herblike. **2.** (of plants or plant parts) not woody. **3.** (of flowers, sepals, etc.) having the texture, colour, etc., of an ordinary foliage leaf.

herbivore /ˈhɜbəvɔ/ *n.* a herbivorous animal.

herbivorous /hɜˈbɪvərəs/ *adj.* feeding on plants.

herculean /hɜkjəˈliən, hɜˈkjuliən/ *adj.* (*sometimes upper case*) **1.** requiring the strength of a Hercules; very hard to perform: *a herculean task.* **2.** prodigious in strength, courage, or size.

herd /hɜd/ *n.* **1.** a number of animals, especially cattle, kept, feeding, or travelling together; drove; flock. **2.** (*derog.*) a large company of people. **3. the herd**, the common people; the rabble. *–v.i.* **4.** to unite or go in a herd; to assemble or associate as a herd. *–v.t.* **5.** to form into or as if a herd.

here /hɪə/ *adv.* **1.** in this place; in this spot or locality (opposed to *there*): *put it here.* **2.** to or towards this place; hither: *come here.* **3.** at this point; at this juncture: *here the speaker paused.* **4.** often used in pointing out or emphasising some person or thing present: *my friend here knows the facts.* **5.** present (used in answer to rollcall, etc.). **6.** in the present life or state. *–n.* **7.** this place. **8.** this world; this life. *–phr.* **9. here and now**, at this very moment; immediately. **10. here and there**, **a.** in various places; at intervals. **b.** hither and thither; to and fro. **11. here goes**, an exclamation to show one's resolution on beginning some bold or unpleasant act. **12. here's to**, a formula in offering a toast: *here's to* *you!* **13. here today and gone tomorrow,** (of someone or something) existing or staying in one place for only a short time. **14. here we** (or **you**) **are,** *Colloq.* here is what we (or you) want, or are looking for. **15. here we go again,** an exclamation indicating exasperation or resignation at a course of action about to occur yet once again. **16. neither here nor there,** irrelevant; unimportant. **17. the here and now, a.** the immediate present. **b.** this world; this life.

here- a word element meaning 'this (place)', 'this (time)', etc., used in combination with certain adverbs and prepositions.

hereafter /hɪərˈaftə/ *adv.* **1.** after this in time or order; at some future time. **2.** in the world to come. *–n.* **3.** a future life; the world to come. **4.** time to come; the future.

hereby /ˈhɪəbaɪ/ *adv.* by this; by means of this; as a result of this.

hereditary /həˈrɛdətri/ *adj.* **1.** passing, or capable of passing, naturally from parents to offspring: *hereditary traits.* **2.** relating to inheritance or heredity: *hereditary descent.* **3.** being such through feelings, etc., derived from predecessors: *a hereditary enemy.* **4.** *Law* descending by inheritance. **–hereditarily,** *adv.* **–hereditariness,** *n.*

heredity /həˈrɛdəti/ *n.* (*pl.* **-ties**) **1.** the transmission of genetic characteristics from parents to progeny; the factor which determines the extent to which an individual resembles its progenitors, dependent upon the separation and regrouping of genes during meiosis and fertilisation. **2.** the genetic characteristics transmitted to an individual by its parents.

Hereford /ˈhɛrəfəd/ *n.* one of a highly productive, hardy, early maturing breed of beef cattle, characterised by a red body, white face, and other white markings.

heresy /ˈhɛrəsi/ *n.* (*pl.* **-sies**) **1.** doctrine contrary to the orthodox or accepted doctrine of a church or religious system. **2.** the maintaining of such an opinion or doctrine. **–heretic,** *n.* **–heretical** /həˈrɛtɪkəl/, *adj.*

heritage /ˈhɛrətɪdʒ/ *n.* **1.** something that comes or belongs to one by reason of birth; an inherited lot or portion. **2.** the culture, traditions, and national assets preserved from one generation to another. **3.** something reserved for someone: *the heritage of the righteous.* **4.** *Law* something that has been or may be inherited by legal descent or succession. **5.** *Bible* God's chosen people; the Israelites. *–adj.* **6.** → **heirloom** (def. 2).

hermaphrodite /hɜˈmæfrədaɪt/ *n.* **1.** an animal or a flower having normally both the male and the female organs of generation. **2.** a person with male and female sexual organs and characteristics. **3.** a person or thing in which two opposite qualities are combined. **–hermaphroditic** /hɜmæfrəˈdɪtɪk/, **hermaphroditical** /hɜmæfrəˈdɪtɪkəl/, *adj.* **–hermaphroditically** /hɜmæfrə-ˈdɪtɪkli/, *adv.*

hermeneutic /hɜməˈnjutɪk/ *adj.* interpretative; explanatory. Also, **hermeneutical. –hermeneutically,** *adv.* **–hermeneutist,** *n.*

hermetic /hɜˈmɛtɪk/ *adj.* **1.** made airtight by fusion or sealing. **2.** unaffected by external influences. **3.** relating to occult sciences. **–hermetically,** *adv.*

hermit /ˈhɜmət/ *n.* **1.** someone who has retired to a solitary place for a life of religious seclusion. **2.** any person living in seclusion. **3.** *Zool.* an animal of solitary habits. **–hermitic, hermitical,** *adj.* **–hermitically,** *adv.*

hermit crab *n.* any of numerous decapod crustaceans of the families Paguridae and Coenobitidae, which protect their exposed soft parts by occupying the cast-off shell of a univalve mollusc.

hernia /ˈhɜniə/ *n.* (*pl.* **-nias**) the protrusion of an organ or tissue through an opening in its surrounding tissues,

especially in the abdominal region; a rupture. **–hernial,** *adj.*

hero /ˈhɪəroʊ/ *n.* (*pl.* **-roes**) **1.** a person of distinguished courage or performance. **2.** someone invested with heroic qualities in the opinion of others. **3.** the principal male character in a story, play, etc. **4.** (in mythology) a being of godlike prowess and beneficence, especially one who came to be honoured as a divinity. *–adj.* **5.** dominant: *hero brand; hero colour.* **6.** *Colloq.* large in scope; impressive: *a hero purchase.*

heroic /həˈroʊɪk/ *adj.* Also, **heroical. 1.** like a hero; daring; noble: *a heroic explorer.* **2.** dealing with heroes: *heroic poetry.* **3.** like heroic poetry in language or style; grand; exalted. *–n.* **4.** (*usu. pl.*) → **heroic verse. 5.** (*pl.*) language or behaviour that is unnaturally grand. **–heroically,** *adv.* **–heroicalness, heroicness,** *n.*

heroic verse *n.* a form of verse adapted to the treatment of heroic or exalted themes; in classical poetry, the hexameter; in English, German, and Italian, the iambic of ten syllables; and in French, the Alexandrine.

heroin /ˈhɛrəwən/ *n.* (*from trademark*) a derivative of morphine, diacetylmorphine, $C_{21}H_{23}NO_5$, formerly used as a sedative, etc., often used illicitly as a narcotic producing euphoria, and constituting a dangerous addictive drug; diamorphine.

heroine /ˈhɛrəwən/ *n.* **1.** a woman of heroic character; a female hero. **2.** the principal female character in a story, play, etc.

heroin injecting room *n.* → **safe injecting room.** Also, **heroin room.**

heron /ˈhɛrən/ *n.* any of the long-legged, long-necked, long-billed wading birds constituting the family Ardeidae, including the true herons, bitterns, egrets, etc.

herpes /ˈhɜpiz/ *n. Pathol.* any of certain inflammatory viral infections of the skin or mucous membrane, characterised by clusters of vesicles which tend to spread. **–herpetic** /hɜˈpɛtɪk/, *adj.*

herpetology /hɜpəˈtɒlədʒi/ *n.* the branch of zoology that deals with reptiles and amphibians. **–herpetological** /hɜpətəˈlɒdʒɪkəl/, *adj.* **–herpetologically** /hɜpətə-ˈlɒdʒəkli/, *adv.* **–herpetologist,** *n.*

herring /ˈhɛrɪŋ/ *n.* **1.** any of a number of marine and freshwater fishes belonging to various families such as the oxeye herring, freshwater herring, tommy ruff. **2.** any fish of the marine family Clupeidae, including *Clupea harengus,* an important food fish which occurs in enormous shoals in the North Sea and the North Atlantic.

herringbone /ˈhɛrɪŋboʊn/ *n.* **1.** a pattern consisting of adjoining rows of parallel lines so arranged that any two rows have the form of a V or inverted V; used in masonry, textiles, embroidery, etc. **2.** an embroidery stitch resembling cross-stitch. *–v.t.* **3.** *Skiing* to climb (a steep slope) step by step with the skis turned out to form a V and edged into the snow.

hers /hɜz/ *pron. (possessive)* the possessive form of **she,** used predicatively or absolutely: *the fault was hers; hers was the clearer answer; a book of hers.*

herself /həˈsɛlf/ *pron.* **1.** the reflexive form of *her: she cut herself.* **2.** an emphatic form of *her* or *she* used: **a.** as object: *she used it for herself.* **b.** in apposition to a subject or object: *she did it herself.* **3.** (used after *be, become,* or *come to*) her proper or normal self; her usual state of mind: *she is herself again.*

hertz /hɜts/ *n.* the derived SI unit of frequency, defined as the frequency of a periodic phenomenon of which the periodic time is one second; one cycle per second. *Symbol:* Hz

hesitant /ˈhɛzətənt/ *adj.* **1.** hesitating; undecided. **2.** lacking readiness of speech. **–hesitancy,** *n.* **–hesitantly,** *adv.*

hesitate /'hɛzəteɪt/ v.i. **1.** to hold back in doubt or indecision: *to hesitate to believe.* **2.** to have scrupulous doubts; be unwilling. **3.** to pause. **4.** to falter in speech; stammer. **–hesitation,** n. **–hesitater,** n. **–hesitatingly,** adv.

hessian /'hɛʃən/ n. a strong fabric made from jute, used for sacks, carpet backing, etc. Also, *US,* **burlap.**

hetero- a word element meaning 'other' or 'different', as in *heterocercal.* Also, (*before vowels*), **heter-.**

heterodox /'hɛtərədɒks, 'hɛtrə-/ adj. **1.** not in accordance with established or accepted doctrines or opinions, especially in theology. **2.** holding unorthodox doctrines or opinions.

heterogeneous /hɛtərou'dʒiniəs/ adj. **1.** different in kind; unlike; incongruous. **2.** composed of parts of different kinds; having widely unlike elements or constituents; not homogeneous. **–heterogeneously,** adv. **–heterogeneousness,** **–heterogeneity** /,hɛtəroudʒə'niəti/, n.

heterosexism /hɛtərou'sɛksɪzəm/ n. a prejudice against any non-heterosexual form of behaviour, identity, relationship, or community. **–heterosexist,** adj., n.

heterosexual /hɛtərou'sɛkʃuəl/ adj. **1.** *Biol.* relating to the other sex or to both sexes. **2.** exhibiting or relating to heterosexuality. *–n.* **3.** a heterosexual person.

heterosexuality /hɛtərou,sɛkʃu'æləti/ n. the condition of being sexually attracted to people of the opposite sex.

heterosphere /'hɛtərəsfɪə/ n. the earth's atmosphere above the altitude of 80 km, characterised by a composition that varies with altitude, with higher mass constituents such as oxygen and nitrogen diminishing quickly and leaving lighter gases such as helium and hydrogen in the outermost portion. Compare **homosphere.**

heterozygote /hɛtərou'zaɪgoʊt/ n. a hybrid containing genes for two unlike characteristics; an organism which will not breed true to type. **–heterozygous,** adj.

het-up /'hɛt-ʌp/ adj. *Colloq.* in a nervous, excited or angry state. Also, **het up.**

heuristic /hju'rɪstɪk/ adj. **1.** serving to find out; furthering investigation. **2.** (of a teaching method) encouraging the student to discover for himself or herself. **–heuristically,** adv.

heuristics /hju'rɪstɪks/ n. **1.** the study of heuristic processes in problem-solving, decision-making, etc. **2.** *Hist., Archaeology* **a.** the search for and collation of source materials. **b.** the rules for doing this.

hew /hju/ v.t. (**hewed, hewed** or **hewn, hewing**) **1.** to strike forcibly with an axe, sword, or the like; chop; hack. **2.** to make or shape with cutting blows: *to hew a passage.* **3.** to cut (*away, off, out, from,* etc.) from a whole by means of cutting leaves. **–hewer,** n.

hex /hɛks/ n. **1.** an evil spell or charm. **2.** an evil, dominating influence over someone or something. *–v.t.* **3.** to wish or bring misfortune, as if by an evil spell.

hexa- a prefix meaning 'six', as in *hexagon.* Also, (*before vowels*), **hex-.**

hexachlorophene /hɛksə'klɔrəfin/ n. an antiseptic agent, $C_{13}H_6Cl_6O_2$, often used as an ingredient in soaps and creams intended to sterilise the skin.

hexagon /'hɛksəgɒn, -gən/ n. a polygon having six angles and six sides. **–hexagonal** /hək'sægənəl/, adj. **–hexagonally,** adv.

hexose /'hɛksoʊz, -oʊs/ n. any of a class of sugars containing six carbon atoms, as glucose and fructose.

hey /heɪ/ interj. an exclamation used to call attention, give encouragement, etc. Also, **heigh, ha.**

heyday /'heɪdeɪ/ n. the stage or period of highest vigour or fullest strength.

hi[1] /haɪ/ interj. *Colloq.* an exclamation, especially of greeting.

hi[2] /haɪ/ adj. (*esp. in compounds*) high: *hi-fi; hi-carb diet.*

hiatus /haɪ'eɪtəs/ n. (*pl.* **-tuses** or **-tus**) **1.** a break, with a part missing; an interruption; lacuna: *a hiatus in a manuscript.* **2.** a gap or opening. **–hiatal** /haɪ'eɪtl/, adj.

hiatus hernia n. a hernia in a part of the stomach through the oesophageal hiatus, often causing heartburn.

hibernate /'haɪbəneɪt/ v.i. **1.** to spend the winter in close quarters in a dormant condition, as certain animals. **2.** to withdraw into or remain in seclusion. **3.** *Computers* (of a personal computer) to shut down while storing all the contents of its RAM in a file on a hard disk which needs to be reloaded when the computer is started again; used as a safety mechanism in case of loss of power, or as a power-saving strategy. **–hibernation** /haɪbə'neɪʃən/, n.

hibiscus /haɪ'bɪskəs/ n. any of the herbs, shrubs, or trees belonging to the genus *Hibiscus,* especially *H. rosa-sinensis,* with broad, showy, short-lived flowers.

hiccup /'hɪkʌp/ n. **1.** a quick, involuntary inspiration suddenly checked by closure of the glottis, producing a characteristic sound. **2.** (*usu. pl.*) the condition of having such spasms: *to have the hiccups.* **3.** a minor problem arising in the course of a planned operation. *–v.i.* (**hiccuped, hiccuping**) **4.** to make the sound of a hiccup. **5.** to have the hiccups. Also, **hiccough** /'hɪkʌp/.

hick /hɪk/ *Colloq.* *–n.* **1.** an unsophisticated person. **2.** a farmer. *–adj.* **3.** relating to or characteristic of hicks; provincial; unsophisticated.

hickory /'hɪkəri/ n. (*pl.* **-ries**) **1.** any of the North American trees of the genus *Carya,* certain of which, such as the pecan, *C. illinoensis* (*C. pecan*), bear sweet, edible nuts (hickory nuts), and others, such as the shagbark, *C. ovata,* yield valuable hard wood and edible nuts. **2.** a switch, stick, etc., of this wood.

hid /hɪd/ v. past tense and past participle of **hide**[1].

hidden /'hɪdn/ v. **1.** past participle of **hide**[1]. *–adj.* **2.** concealed; obscure; latent.

hidden agenda n. a purpose which is not fully revealed but which is to be accomplished alongside or through the ostensible aims.

hide[1] /haɪd/ verb (**hid, hidden** or **hid, hiding**) *–v.t.* **1.** to conceal from sight; prevent from being seen or discovered. **2.** to obstruct the view of; cover up: *the sun was hidden by clouds.* **3.** to conceal from knowledge; keep secret: *to hide one's feelings.* *–v.i.* **4.** to conceal oneself; lie concealed. *–n.* **5.** a covered place to hide in while shooting or observing wildlife. *–phr.* **6. hide one's head,** *Colloq.* to be ashamed. **–hider,** n.

hide[2] /haɪd/ n. **1.** the skin of an animal, especially of the larger animals, raw or dressed: *the hide of a calf.* **2.** *Colloq.* the human skin. **3.** *Aust. Colloq.* impudence: *he's got a hide!* *–phr.* **4. a thick hide,** *Colloq.* insensitivity to criticism. **5. have a hide like an elephant,** *Colloq.* to be particularly insensitive and crass. **6. have more hide than Jessie,** *Aust. Colloq.* to be particularly impudent. **7. neither hide nor hair,** not a vestige; no clue. **8. no hide no Christmas box,** *Aust. Colloq.* no reward is to be had without impudent initiative.

hide-and-seek n. a children's game in which some hide and others seek them. Also, **hidings**; *Esp. Tasmania,* **hide-and-go-seek**; *Esp. Qld, Victoria, SA and WA,* **hidey.**

hideaway /'haɪdəweɪ/ n. **1.** a place of concealment; a refuge. **2.** a retreat, as a holiday home, where it is difficult for others to interrupt one's relaxation.

hidebound /'haɪdbaʊnd/ adj. **1.** narrow and rigid in opinion: *a hidebound pedant.* **2.** (of a horse, etc.) having the back and ribs bound tightly by the hide.

hideous /'hɪdiəs/ adj. **1.** horrible or frightful to the senses; very ugly: *a hideous monster.* **2.** shocking or revolting to the moral sense: *a hideous crime.* **–hideously,** adv. **–hideousness,** n.

hide-out *n.* a safe retreat for those who are being pursued, especially by the law; a hiding place; refuge.

hiding[1] /ˈhaɪdɪŋ/ *n.* **1.** the act of concealing; concealment: *to remain in hiding.* **2.** a place or means of concealment.

hiding[2] /ˈhaɪdɪŋ/ *n.* **1.** a beating. **2.** a defeat.

hidings /ˈhaɪdɪŋz/ *pl. n.* (*construed as sing.*) → **hide-and-seek**.

hierarchy /ˈhaɪəraki/ *n.* (*pl.* **-archies**) **1.** any system of persons or things in a graded order, etc. **2.** a series of successive terms of different rank. In zoology, the terms *phylum*, *class*, *order*, *family*, *genus*, and *species* constitute a hierarchy. **3.** government by ecclesiastical rulers. **–hierarchical** /haɪəˈrakɪkəl/, *adj.* **–hierarchism**, *n.*

hieratic /haɪəˈrætɪk/ *adj.* **1.** of or relating to priests or the priesthood; priestly. **2.** of or relating to a form of ancient Egyptian writing consisting of abridged forms of hieroglyphics, used by the priests in their records. **3.** of or relating to certain styles in art whose types or methods are fixed by or as by religious tradition. Also, **hieratical**. **–hieratically**, *adv.*

hiero- a word element meaning 'sacred', as in *hierocracy*. Also, (*before a vowel*), **hier-**.

hieroglyphic /haɪərəˈglɪfɪk/ *adj.* Also, **hieroglyphical**. **1.** of or relating to a writing system, particularly that of the ancient Egyptians, in which many of the symbols are conventionalised pictures of the thing named by the words for which the symbols stand. *–n.* **2.** Also, **hieroglyph** /ˈhaɪərəglɪf/ a hieroglyphic symbol. **3.** (*usu. pl.*) hieroglyphic writing. **4.** (*pl.*) writing difficult to decipher. **–hieroglyphically**, *adv.*

hi-fi /ˈhaɪ-faɪ/ *adj.* **1.** → **high-fidelity**. *–n.* **2.** a high-fidelity sound system for listening to music in the home.

higgledy-piggledy /hɪgəldi-ˈpɪgəldi/ *Colloq. –adv.* **1.** in a jumbled confusion. *–adj.* **2.** confused; jumbled.

Higgs boson /hɪgz ˈboʊzɒn/ *n.* an elementary particle the existence of which would explain the appearance of massive particles of zero spin in the electroweak theory; its existence theoretical until near certain scientific confirmation in 2013. Also, **Higgs boson particle, Higgs particle.**

high /haɪ/ *adj.* **1.** having a great or considerable reach or extent upwards; lofty; tall. **2.** having a specified extent upwards. **3.** situated above the ground or some base; elevated. **4.** far above the horizon, as a heavenly body. **5.** lying or being above the general level: *high ground.* **6.** of more than average or normal height or depth: *the river was high after the rain.* **7.** intensified; exceeding the common degree or measure; strong; intense, energetic: *high speed.* **8.** assigning or attributing a great amount, value, or excellence: *high estimate.* **9.** expensive, costly, or dear. **10.** exalted in rank, station, estimation, etc.; of exalted character or quality: *a high official.* **11.** exalted in tone, sentiment, etc., and often intended for a formal context such as the court, church, performance hall, or exhibition venue, etc.: *high art.* **12.** advanced in development or complexity: *high finance.* **13.** *Music* **a.** of notes, lying in the upper range of a musical instrument or voice. **b.** a little sharp, or above the desired pitch. **14.** produced by relatively rapid vibrations; shrill: *high sounds.* **15.** extending to or from an elevation: *a high dive.* **16.** of great amount, degree, force, etc.: *a high temperature.* **17.** chief; principal; main: *the high altar of a church.* **18.** of great consequence; important; grave; serious: *high treason.* **19.** of a period of time, at its fullest point of development: *the High Renaissance.* **20.** advanced to the utmost extent, or to the culmination: *high tide.* **21.** elated; merry or hilarious: *high spirits.* **22.** *Colloq.* intoxicated or elated with alcohol or drugs. **23.** luxurious; extravagant: *high living.* **24.** remote: *high latitude*; *high antiquity.* **25.** extreme in opinion or doctrine, especially religious or political. **26.** designating or relating to highland or inland regions. **27.** *Biol.* having a relatively

complex structure: *the higher mammals.* **28.** *Phonetics* pronounced with the tongue relatively close to the roof of the mouth: *'feed'* and *'food'* have high vowels. **29. a.** (of meat, especially game) tending towards a desirable amount of decomposition; slightly tainted. **b.** smelly; bad. **30.** having a comparatively large amount of a particular constituent: *food high in protein.* **31.** *Cards* **a.** having greater value than another card. **b.** capable of taking a trick; being a winning card. *–adv.* **32.** at or to a high point, place, or level, or a high rank or estimate, a high amount or price, or a high degree. *–n.* **33.** a high level: *share prices reached a new high.* **34.** top gear. **35.** *Meteorol.* a pressure system characterised by relatively high pressure at its centre; an anticyclone. **36.** *Colloq.* a euphoric state induced by, or as if by, drugs. *–phr.* **37. high and dry, a.** (of a ship) wholly above water level at low tide. **b.** *Colloq.* abandoned; stranded; deserted. **38. high and low**, everywhere. **39. high and mighty**, overweeningly proud; overbearing. **40. high as a kite**, *Colloq.* **a.** under the influence of drugs or alcohol. **b.** in exuberant spirits. **41. on a high**, *Colloq.* experiencing a euphoric state induced by, or as if by, drugs. **42. on high, a.** at or to a height; above. **b.** in heaven. **–highly**, *adj.*

highbrow /ˈhaɪbraʊ/ *n.* **1.** someone who has pretensions to superior taste in artistic matters. *–adj.* **2.** of or relating to things that highbrows approve of: *highbrow music* Compare **lowbrow**.

highchair /ˈhaɪtʃɛə/ *n.* a chair with extended legs which allows a young child to sit at normal table level, as at mealtimes, etc.

high-class *adj.* of superior quality.

high commissioner *n.* the chief representative of a sovereign member of the Commonwealth of Nations in the country of another sovereign member, usually equivalent in rank to an ambassador, as the Australian High Commissioner in London.

high-fibre *adj.* of or relating to foods with a high proportion of plant fibre, that is, the indigestible parts of plant cell walls.

high-fidelity *adj.* (of an amplifier, radio receiver, etc.) reproducing the full audio range of the original sounds with relatively little distortion. Also, **hi-fi**.

high five *n.* a form of salutation in which two people slap the palms of their hands together, often to express solidarity in victory.

high-five *v.t.* **1.** to give a high five to (someone). *–v.i.* **2.** to perform a high five.

high-flown *adj.* **1.** extravagant in aims, pretensions, etc. **2.** pretentiously lofty; bombastic.

high frequency *n.* **1.** any radiofrequency between 3 and 30 megahertz. *Abbrev.*: HF **2.** any audible frequency which is high in pitch. **–high-frequency**, *adj.*

high-grade *adj.* of superior quality.

high-handed *adj.* overbearing; arbitrary: *a high-handed manner.* **–high-handedly**, *adv.* **–high-handedness**, *n.*

high jump *–n.* **1.** *Athletics* **a.** a vertical jump in which one attempts to go as high as possible. **b.** a contest for the highest such jump. *–phr.* **2. for the high jump**, *Colloq.* about to face an unpleasant experience, especially a punishment or reprimand.

highland /ˈhaɪlənd/ *n.* **1.** an elevated region; a plateau: *a jutting highland.* **2.** (*pl.*) a mountainous region or elevated part of a country. *–adj.* **3.** of, relating to, or characteristic of highlands.

high-level language *n. Computers* a language used for writing programs which is closer to human language or conventional mathematical notation than to machine language. Compare **low-level language**.

high level waste *n.* radioactive waste from spent reactor fuel, which contains the fission products and transuranic elements generated in the reactor core; the most dangerous form of radioactive waste. *Abbrev.*: HLW Compare **low level waste**.

highlight /ˈhaɪlaɪt/ *v.t.* (**-lighted**, **-lighting**) **1.** to make noticeable or prominent; emphasise. **2.** (in photography, painting, etc.) to show up (the areas of greatest brightness) with paint or by exposing lighter areas. **3.** to dye (part of hair) with a light colour. **4.** to use a highlighter (def. 1) to emphasise (written or printed text). –*n.* **5.** a noticeable or striking part: *the highlight of his talk*. **6.** *Art* the point of strongest light in a picture or form.

highlighter /ˈhaɪlaɪtə/ *n.* **1.** a pen which puts a translucent colour over parts of a printed or other page to draw the eye to these parts. **2.** a cosmetic, usually glossy, used to highlight the cheekbones, or make other features, such as eyelids, prominent.

highly strung *adj.* tense; in a state of (especially nervous) tension: *highly strung nerves, highly strung people*. Also, **high-strung**.

high-minded *adj.* **1.** having or showing high, exalted principles or feelings: *a high-minded ruler*. **2.** proud or arrogant. –**high-mindedly**, *adv.* –**high-mindedness**, *n.*

highness /ˈhaɪnəs/ *n.* **1.** the state of being high; loftiness; dignity. **2.** (*upper case*) (preceded by *His, Her, Your*, etc.) a title of honour given to royal or princely personages.

high-pitched *adj.* **1.** *Music* played or sung at a high pitch. **2.** (of a discussion, argument, etc.) marked by strong feeling; emotionally intense. **3.** (of a roof) nearly perpendicular; steep. **4.** aspiring; lofty; lofty in tone.

high-powered *adj.* **1.** (of an optical instrument) capable of giving a high magnification. **2.** energetic; vigorous; forceful: *a high-powered sales campaign*. **3.** having great power or efficiency: *a high-powered car*.

high-pressure *adj.* **1.** having or involving a pressure above the normal: *high-pressure steam*. **2.** vigorous; persistent: *high-pressure salesmanship*.

high pressure system *n.* See **pressure system**.

high profile *n.* the conspicuousness which is gained by a public figure. –**high-profile**, *adj.*

high-rise *adj.* → **multistorey**.

high school *n.* → **secondary school**. –**high-schooler**, *n.*

high sea *n.* **1.** sea or ocean beyond a country's territorial waters. **2.** (*usu. pl.*) the open, unenclosed waters of any sea or ocean.

high-speed *adj.* **1.** operating, or capable of operating, at a high speed. **2.** *Photography* (of film) usable with low illumination and short exposures. **3.** (of steel) especially hard and capable of retaining its hardness even at red heat, so that it can be used for lathe tools.

high-spirited *adj.* having a high, proud, or bold spirit; mettlesome.

hightail /ˈhaɪteɪl/ *phr.* **hightail it**, *Chiefly US Colloq.* to move away quickly: *he hightailed it out of town*.

high tech *n.* high technology.

high-tech /ˈhaɪ-tɛk/ *adj.* ultra-modern, especially using materials or styles associated with high technology. Also, **hi-tech**.

high technology *n.* highly sophisticated, innovative technology, especially electronic.

high-tension *adj.* *Elect.* (of a device, circuit, circuit component, etc.) subjected to, or capable of operating under, a relatively high voltage, usually 1000 volts or more. *Abbrev.*: HT

high time *n.* **1.** the right time; the time just before it is too late: *it's high time that was done.* **2.** *Colloq.* an enjoyable and lively time: *a high old time at the party*.

high treason *n.* treason against the sovereign or state.

high-vis /haɪ-ˈvɪz/ *adj.* → **high-visibility**. Also, **hi-vis**.

high-visibility *adj.* of or relating to personal protective equipment, especially clothing, which is of a colour that is easily seen, as very bright or fluorescent colours. Also, **high-vis**, **hi-vis**.

highway /ˈhaɪweɪ/ *n.* **1.** a main road, such as one between towns. **2.** any public passage, either a road or waterway. **3.** any main or ordinary route, track, or course.

highwayman /ˈhaɪweɪmən/ *n.* (*pl.* **-men**) (formerly) a robber on the highway, especially one on horseback.

hijab /həˈdʒab/ *n.* the traditional Islamic headscarf worn by women, which covers the hair, neck and shoulders. Also, **hejab**.

hijack /ˈhaɪdʒæk/ *v.t.* **1.** to steal (something) in transit, such as a lorry and the goods it carries. **2.** to seize by force or threat of force (a vehicle, especially a passenger-carrying vehicle, such as an aircraft), and attempt to divert it to a different destination. **3.** to seize control of (something) for one's own purposes: *clearly his ideas had been hijacked by Ted*. Also, **highjack**. –**hijacker**, *n.*

hike /haɪk/ *v.i.* **1.** to walk a long distance, especially through country districts or the bush, for pleasure. –*n.* **2.** a long walk. **3.** an increase in wages, fares, prices, etc. –*phr.* **4. hike up, a.** to pull or drag up. **b.** to increase (a fare, price, etc.). –**hiker**, *n.*

hilarious /həˈlɛəriəs/ *adj.* **1.** very funny; provoking mirth. **2.** boisterously merry. **3.** cheerful. –**hilariously**, *adv.* –**hilariousness**, *n.* –**hilarity**, *n.*

hill /hɪl/ *n.* **1.** a conspicuous natural elevation of the earth's surface, smaller than a mountain. **2.** an artificial heap or pile: *a hill of beans*. –*phr.* **3. as old as the hills**, *Colloq.* very old. **4. over the hill**, *Colloq.* past prime efficiency; past the peak of physical or other condition, etc. **5. take to the hills**, to run away and hide.

hillbilly /ˈhɪlbɪli/ *n.* (*pl.* **-lies**) *Chiefly US* a rustic or yokel living in the backwoods or mountains.

hillock /ˈhɪlək/ *n.* a small hill. –**hillocky**, *adj.*

hilly /ˈhɪli/ *adj.* (**-lier**, **-liest**) **1.** characterised by many hills: *hilly country*. **2.** elevated; steep. –**hilliness**, *n.*

hilt /hɪlt/ *n.* **1.** the handle of a sword or dagger. **2.** the handle of any weapon or tool. –*phr.* **3. to the hilt**, fully; completely: *armed to the hilt*. –**hilted**, *adj.*

him /hɪm/ *pron.* (personal) objective case of **he**.

himself /hɪmˈsɛlf/ *pron.* **1.** the reflexive form of **he**: *he cut himself*. **2.** an emphatic form of *him* or *he* used: **a.** as object: *he used it for himself*. **b.** in apposition to a subject or object: *he did it himself*. **3.** (used after such verbs as *be, become,* or *come to*) his proper or normal self; his usual state of mind: *he is himself again*.

hind¹ /haɪnd/ *adj.* (**hinder, hindmost** *or* **hindermost**) situated behind or at the back; posterior: *the hind legs of an animal*.

hind² /haɪnd/ *n.* (*pl.* **hinds** *or, especially collectively,* **hind**) the female of the deer, chiefly the red deer, *Cervus elaphus*, especially in and after the third year.

hinder¹ /ˈhɪndə/ *v.t.* **1.** to interrupt; check; retard: *to be hindered by storms*. **2.** to prevent from acting or taking place; stop: *to hinder someone from committing a crime*. –*v.i.* **3.** to be an obstacle or impediment. –**hinderer**, *n.* –**hinderingly**, *adv.*

hinder² /ˈhaɪndə/ *adj.* situated at the rear or back; posterior: *the hinder part of the ship*.

hindrance /ˈhɪndrəns/ *n.* **1.** an impeding, stopping, or preventing. **2.** a means or cause of hindering.

hindsight /ˈhaɪndsaɪt/ *n.* perception of the nature and exigencies of a case after the event: *hindsight is easier than foresight*.

Hinduism /ˈhɪnduɪzəm/ *n.* the main religion of India, with a complex body of religious, social, cultural, and philosophical beliefs, and a strict system of castes.

hinge /hɪndʒ/ *n.* **1.** a movable joint or device on which a door, gate, shutter, lid, etc., turns or moves. **2.** that on which something turns or depends; principle; central rule. **3.** a small strip of adhesive paper for affixing a stamp to a page for display in a collection. *–verb* (**hinged**, **hinging**) *–v.i.* **4.** to hang from or turn on a hinge. *–v.t.* **5.** to supply with or attach by a hinge or hinges. *–phr.* **6. hinge on** (or **upon**), to depend on: *everything hinges on his decision.* **–hinged**, *adj.*

hint /hɪnt/ *n.* **1.** an indirect or covert suggestion or implication; an intimation. **2.** a brief, helpful suggestion; a piece of advice. **3.** a very small or barely perceptible amount. *–v.t.* **4.** to give a hint of. *–phr.* **5. hint at**, to make indirect suggestion of or allusion to. **–hinter**, *n.*

hinterland /ˈhɪntəlænd/ *n.* **1.** an inland area supplying goods to a port. **2.** the land lying behind a coastal district. **3.** an area or sphere of influence in the unoccupied interior claimed by the state possessing the coast. **4.** the remote or less developed parts of a country.

hip[1] /hɪp/ *n.* **1.** the projecting part of each side of the body formed by the side of the pelvis and the upper part of the femur, with the flesh covering them; the haunch. **2.** the hip joint. **–hipless**, *adj.*

hip[2] /hɪp/ *n.* the ripe fruit of a rose, especially of a wild rose.

hip[3] /hɪp/ *interj.* an exclamation used in cheers or in signalling for cheers: *hip, hip, hooray!*

hippie /ˈhɪpi/ *n.* a person who rejects conventional social values in favour of principles of universal love, union with nature, etc., sometimes making use of hallucinogenic drugs; especially one taking part in the 1960s movement espousing such a lifestyle. Also, **hippy**.

hip-pocket *n.* **1.** a pocket on the back of a person's trousers in which their wallet might be kept. *–adj.* **2.** concerned with money: *a hip-pocket issue.*

Hippocratic oath /hɪpəˌkrætɪk ˈoʊθ/ *n.* an oath embodying the duties and obligations of physicians, sometimes taken by those about to enter upon the practice of medicine.

hippopotamus /hɪpəˈpɒtəməs/ *n.* (*pl.* **-muses** *or* **-mi** /-maɪ/) **1.** a large herbivorous mammal, *Hippopotamus amphibius*, having a thick hairless body, short legs, and large head and muzzle, found in and near the rivers and lakes of Africa, and able to remain under water for a considerable time. **2.** Also, **pygmy hippopotamus**. a similar but much smaller animal, *Hexaprotodon liberiensis*, of West Africa.

hire /ˈhaɪə/ *v.t.* **1.** to engage the services of for payment: *to hire a clerk.* **2.** to engage the temporary use of for payment: *to hire a car.* **3.** Also, **hire out**. to grant the temporary use of, or the services of, for a payment. *–n.* **4.** the price or compensation paid, or contracted to be paid, for the temporary use of something or for personal services or labour; pay. **5.** the act of hiring. **–hireable**, *adj.* **–hirer**, *n.*

hireling /ˈhaɪəlɪŋ/ *n.* **1.** (*derog.*) someone working only for payment. **2.** a mercenary. *–adj.* **3.** venal; mercenary.

hire purchase *n.* **1.** a system whereby a person pays for a commodity by regular instalments, while having full use of it after the first payment. *–adj.* **2.** relating to or bought with the aid of such a system. Also, **hire-purchase**.

hirsute /ˈhɜːsjut, hɜːˈsjut/ *adj.* hairy. **–hirsuteness**, *n.*

his /hɪz/, *weak form* /ɪz/ *adj.* **1.** the possessive form of **he**: *his mother.* *–pron.* (*possessive*) **2.** the possessive form of **he**, used predicatively or absolutely: *this book is his; himself and his; a book of his.*

Hispanic /hɪsˈpænɪk/ *adj.* **1.** of or relating to Spain or Spanish-speaking Latin America. **2.** of or relating to a Spanish-speaking people or culture.

hiss /hɪs/ *v.i.* **1.** to make a sharp sound like that of the letter 's' prolonged, as a goose or snake does. **2.** to express disapproval or hatred by making this sound. *–v.t.* **3.** to show disapproval or by hissing. **4.** to utter with a hiss. *–n.* **5.** a hissing sound, especially in disapproval. **–hisser**, *n.*

hissy fit /ˈhɪsi fɪt/ *n. Colloq.* an outburst of bad temper; tantrum.

histamine /ˈhɪstəmɪn/ *n.* an amine released by the tissues in allergic reactions; it is a powerful uterine stimulant and lowers the blood pressure. **–histaminic** /hɪstəˈmɪnɪk/, *adj.*

histo- a word element meaning 'tissue', as in *histogen*. Also, (*before vowels*), **hist-**.

histology /hɪsˈtɒlədʒi/ *n.* the science concerned with the study of the detailed structure of animal and plant tissues. **–histological** /hɪstəˈlɒdʒəkəl/, **histologic** /hɪstəˈlɒdʒɪk/, *adj.* **–histologist**, *n.*

historian /hɪsˈtɔriən/ *n.* **1.** a writer of history. **2.** an expert in history; an authority on history. **3.** a student of history.

historic /hɪsˈtɒrɪk/ *adj.* well-known or important in history: *historic scenes.* Also, **historical**.

historical /hɪsˈtɒrɪkəl/ *adj.* **1.** relating to or concerned with the study of history or past events: *historical methodology.* **2.** dealing with history or past events: *historical documents.* **3.** based on fact, as opposed to legend or fiction: *the historical King Arthur.* **4.** narrated or mentioned in history; belonging to the past: *a historical event.* **5.** → **historic**. **–historically**, *adv.* **–historicalness**, *n.*

history /ˈhɪstri, ˈhɪstəri/ *n.* (*pl.* **-ries**) **1.** the branch of knowledge dealing with past events. **2.** the record of past events, especially in connection with humankind. **3.** a continuous, systematic written narrative, in order of time, of past events as relating to a particular people, country, period, person, etc. **4.** the aggregate of past events. **5.** a past worthy of record or out of the ordinary: *a ship with a history.* **6.** a systematic account of any set of natural phenomena, without reference to time. **7.** a drama representing historical events. *–phr.* **8. be ancient history**, to be finished or gone irrevocably. **9. be history**, *Colloq.* **a.** to be dead. **b.** to be ruined or incapacitated. **c.** to be broken beyond repair. **10. go down in history**, (of an event or person) to be sufficiently significant to be always remembered. **11. make history**, to achieve lasting fame. **12. the rest is history**, the rest of the story is well known and authenticated (usually following an account of facts alleged or hitherto not known).

histrionics /hɪstriˈɒnɪks/ *pl. n.* **1.** dramatic representation; theatricals; acting. **2.** artificial or melodramatic behaviour, speech, etc., for effect. **–histrionic**, **histrionical**, *adj.*

hit /hɪt/ *verb* (**hit**, **hitting**) *–v.t.* **1.** to deal a blow or stroke; bring forcibly into collision. **2.** to come against with an impact or collision, as a missile, a flying fragment, a falling body, or the like does. **3.** to reach with a missile, a weapon, a blow, or the like (intentionally or otherwise) as one throwing, shooting or striking; succeed in striking. **4.** to drive or propel by a stroke. **5.** to have a marked effect on; affect severely. **6.** to assail effectively and sharply. **7.** to reach (a specified level or figure). **8.** to be published in or appear in (a newspaper). **9.** to come or light upon; meet; find: *to hit the right road.* **10.** to guess correctly. **11.** to succeed in representing or producing exactly: *to hit a likeness in a portrait.* **12.** *Colloq.* to arrive at: *to hit town.* **13.** *Colloq.* to begin to travel on: *to hit the trail.* **14.** *Colloq.* to demand or obtain money from: *the building company hit me for a thousand dollars.* **15.** *Colloq.* to inject (any form of drugs). *–v.i.* **16.** to deal a blow or blows. *–n.* **17.** an impact or collision, as of one thing against another. **18.** a stroke that reaches an object; blow. **19. a.** a successful performance or production: *the play is a hit.* **b.** anything popular or successful: *ice-cream is always a hit with the kids.* **20.** an effective or telling expression or saying; gibe; taunt. **21.** *Internet* a connection made to a website. **22.** *Colloq.* a shot of heroin or any drug; a fix. *–adj.* **23.** successful; achieving popularity: *a hit movie. –phr.* **24. hit for six, a.** *Cricket* (of the person batting) to strike (the ball) so that it lands outside the playing area, the stroke being worth six runs. **b.** *Colloq.* to confuse or disturb greatly: *the bad news hit him for six.* **25. hit home,** to make an impact or impression upon someone. **26. hit it off,** *Colloq.* to get on well together; agree. **27. hit off,** to make a beginning; commence. **28. hit on, a.** Also, **hit upon.** to come upon unexpectedly; find by chance. **b.** *Colloq.* to make sexual advances to. **29. hit out at, a.** to aim a blow at. **b.** to make an attack on in speech or writing: *the press is hitting out at the inaction of politicians.* **30. hit someone hard,** to have a severe and distressing effect upon someone. **31. hit the bottle** (or **booze**), *Colloq.* to drink heavily; become an alcoholic. **32. hit the ceiling** (or **roof**), *Colloq.* to display extreme anger or astonishment. **33. hit the deck,** *Colloq.* **a.** to prostrate oneself on the ground, usually in self-protection. **b.** to get out of bed. **34. hit the headlines,** to gain publicity; to achieve notoriety. **35. hit the nail on the head, a.** to sum up a situation with clarity and incisiveness. **b.** to give perfect satisfaction. **36. hit the road,** *Colloq.* to set out. **37. hit the sack** (or **hay**), *Colloq.* to go to bed. **38. hit the spot,** *Colloq.* to fulfil a need; satisfy. **39. hit up, a.** *Tennis* to warm up by hitting the ball back and forth across the net, disregarding the rules of play. **b.** *Colloq.* to take a drug, as heroin, usually by injecting it into the bloodstream. **40. not to know what hit one,** to be taken unawares; be thrown into confusion or dismay. **–hittable,** *adj.* **–hitter,** *n.*

hit-and-run *adj.* **1.** Also, **hit-run.** of or relating to the driver of a motor vehicle who leaves the scene of an accident in which he or she was involved without stopping to give assistance or fulfil any legal obligations. **2.** Also, **hit-run.** of or relating to such an accident. **3.** (of an air raid) lasting only a short time and marked by a rapid withdrawal from the area of attack. *–n.* **4.** *Colloq.* a hit-and-run accident.

hitch /hɪtʃ/ *v.t.* **1.** to make fast, especially temporarily, by a hook, rope, etc.; tether. **2.** (oft. fol. by *up*) to harness (an animal) to a vehicle. **3.** (usu. fol. by *up*) to tug or jerk: *to hitch one's trousers up.* **4.** *Colloq.* to obtain or seek to obtain (a ride) from a passing vehicle as a means of obtaining transport from one location to another. *–v.i.* **5.** *Colloq.* → **hitchhike.** *–n.* **6.** *Naut., etc.* a kind of knot. **7.** a halt; obstruction: *a hitch in the proceedings.* **8.** a hitching movement; a jerk or tug. **9.** *Colloq.* a ride from a passing vehicle. *–phr.* **10. go without a hitch,** *Colloq.* to proceed without any difficulty. **–hitcher,** *n.*

hitched /hɪtʃt/ *adj. Colloq.* married.

hitchhike /ˈhɪtʃhaɪk/ *v.i.* to travel by obtaining rides in passing vehicles. **–hitchhiker,** *n.*

hither /ˈhɪðə/ *adv.* **1.** to or towards this place; here: *to come hither. –phr.* **2. hither and thither,** this way and that; in various directions.

hitherto /hɪðəˈtuː/ *adv.* up to this point in time; until now: *a fact hitherto unknown.*

hit man *n. Colloq.* a man hired as an assassin.

hit parade *n.* a selection of the current most popular songs.

HIV /eɪtʃ aɪ ˈviː/ *n.* the retrovirus which causes AIDS.

hive /haɪv/ *n.* **1.** a shelter for honey bees; a beehive. **2.** the bees inhabiting a hive. **3.** something resembling a beehive in structure or use. **4.** a place swarming with busy occupants: *a hive of activity; a hive of industry.* **5.** a swarming or teeming multitude. *–phr.* **6. hive off, a.** *Commerce* (of shareholders in a company) to buy shares in (a new company being formed by the existing one). **b.** *Commerce* (of an organisation, business, etc.) to separate (one group or function) from the rest. **c.** to break away from a group. **–hiveless,** *adj.*

hives /haɪvz/ *n. Pathol.* (*construed as sing.*) any of various eruptive diseases of the skin, such as the weals of urticaria.

HIV-negative *adj.* not having developed antibodies to HIV.

HIV-positive *adj.* having antibodies to HIV in the blood.

hoard /hɔd/ *n.* **1.** an accumulation of something for preservation or future use: *a hoard of gold. –v.t.* **2.** to accumulate for preservation or future use, especially in a secluded place. *–v.i.* **3.** to accumulate money, food, or the like, especially in a secluded place. **–hoarder,** *n.*

hoarding /ˈhɔdɪŋ/ *n.* **1.** a temporary fence enclosing a building during erection. **2.** a large board on which advertisements or notices are displayed; billboard.

hoarfrost /ˈhɔfrɒst/ *n.* → **frost** (def. 2).

hoarse /hɔs/ *adj.* **1.** having a vocal tone characterised by weakness of intensity and excessive breathiness; husky. **2.** having a raucous voice. **3.** making a harsh, low sound. **–hoarsely,** *adv.* **–hoarseness,** *n.*

hoary /ˈhɔri/ *adj.* (**-rier, -riest**) **1.** grey or white with age. **2.** ancient or venerable. **3.** grey or white. **–hoariness,** *n.*

hoax /hoʊks/ *n.* **1.** a humorous or mischievous deception, especially a practical joke. *–v.t.* **2.** to deceive by a hoax. **–hoaxer,** *n.*

hobble /ˈhɒbəl/ *v.i.* **1.** to walk lamely; limp. **2.** to go unsteadily and irregularly: *hobbling verse. –v.t.* **3.** to cause to limp. **4.** to tie loosely together the legs of (a horse, etc.) so as to prevent free motion. *–n.* **5.** an uneven, halting walk; limp. **6.** a rope, strap, etc., used to hobble an animal. **–hobbler,** *n.* **–hobbling,** *adj.* **–hobblingly,** *adv.*

hobby¹ /ˈhɒbi/ *n.* (*pl.* **-bies**) a spare-time activity or pastime, etc., pursued for pleasure or recreation. **–hobbyist,** *n.*

hobby² /ˈhɒbi/ *n.* (*pl.* **-bies**) a child's hobbyhorse.

hobby farm *n.* a farm maintained for interest's sake, usually not the owner's chief source of income. **–hobby farmer,** *n.*

hobbyhorse /ˈhɒbihɔs/ *n.* **1.** a stick with a horse's head, or a rocking horse, ridden by children. **2.** a favourite topic; obsessive notion.

hobgoblin /ˈhɒbɡɒblən/ *n.* **1.** a mischievous goblin. **2.** anything causing superstitious fear; a bogy.

hobnail /ˈhɒbneɪl/ *n.* a large-headed nail for protecting the soles of heavy boots and shoes.

hobnob /ˈhɒbnɒb/ *v.i.* to associate on very friendly terms: *hobnobbing with the management got him his golden handshake.*

hobo /ˈhoʊboʊ/ *n.* (*pl.* **-bos** *or* **-boes**) **1.** a tramp or vagrant. **2.** a migratory worker. **–hoboism,** *n.*

hock¹ /hɒk/ *n.* **1.** the joint in the hind leg of the horse, etc., above the fetlock joint, corresponding to the ankle in humans but raised from the ground and protruding backwards when bent. **2.** a cut of pork through the joint of a leg or foreleg.

hock² /hɒk/ *n.* **1.** a dry white wine, grown along the Rhine River. **2.** (in unofficial use) any similar wine made elsewhere.

hock³ /hɒk/ *Colloq. –v.t.* **1.** → **pawn¹** (def. 1). **2.** to sell (especially illegally). *–phr.* **3. in hock,** pawned.

hockey /ˈhɒki/ *n.* a game in which opposing sides seek with sticks curved at one end to drive a ball (in **field hockey**) or puck (in **ice hockey**) into their opponents' goal.

hocus-pocus /hoʊkəs-ˈpoʊkəs/ *interj.* **1.** a formula used in conjuring or performing magic. *–n.* **2.** skilful use of the hands to confuse an audience. **3.** trickery. **4.** unnecessary elaboration to cover a deception or to make a basically simple thing appear more mysterious.

hod /hɒd/ *n.* a portable trough for carrying mortar, bricks, etc., fixed crosswise on top of a pole and carried on the shoulder.

hoe /hoʊ/ *n.* **1.** a long-handled implement with a thin, flat blade usually set transversely, used to break up the surface of the ground, destroy weeds, etc. *–verb* (**hoed, hoeing**) *–v.t.* **2.** to dig, scrape, weed, cultivate, etc., with a hoe. *–v.i.* **3.** to use a hoe. *–phr.* **4. hoe in, a.** to commence to eat heartily. **b.** to begin something energetically. **5. hoe into, a.** to begin to eat (food) heartily. **b.** to attack (a person) vigorously, usually verbally. **c.** to undertake (a job) with vigour. *–hoer, n.*

hog /hɒg/ *n.* **1.** a domesticated pig, especially a castrated boar, bred for slaughter. **2.** a mammal of the family Suidae; a pig. **3.** → **hogget**. **4.** *Colloq.* a selfish, gluttonous, or filthy person. *–v.t.* (**hogged, hogging**) **5.** *Colloq.* to appropriate selfishly; take more than one's share of. *–phr. Colloq.* **6. go the whole hog**, to do something completely and thoroughly; to commit oneself unreservedly to a course of action. **7. live high on the hog**, to live luxuriously or extravagantly.

hogget /'hɒgət/ *n.* **1.** a young sheep of either sex, older than a lamb, that has not yet been sheared. **2.** the meat of such a sheep. Also, **hog**.

Hogmanay /hɒgmə'neɪ, 'hɒgməneɪ/ *n. Scottish* (*sometimes lower case*) **1.** New Year's Eve. **2.** the celebrations held on this occasion.

hogshead /'hɒgzhɛd/ *n.* a unit of measurement of capacity in the imperial system, equal to 52.5 imperial gallons or 63 US gallons (238.7 litres) for wine, and 54 imperial gallons or 64 US gallons (245.5 litres) for beer.

hogwash /'hɒgwɒʃ/ *n.* **1.** any worthless stuff. **2.** meaningless or insincere talk; nonsense.

ho-hum /hoʊ-'hʌm/ *interj.* **1.** an expression of boredom, weariness, etc. *–adj.* **2.** boring; plain; lacking vitality or interest.

hoick /hɔɪk/ *v.t.* **1.** to hoist abruptly. **2.** to cause to rise sharply or abruptly, as an aeroplane. **3.** *Colloq.* to throw: *hoick the magazine over here, would you.*

hoi polloi /hɔɪ pə'lɔɪ/ *n.* **the**, the common people; the masses.

hoisin sauce /hɔɪsɪn 'sɒs/ *n.* (in Chinese cookery) a sweet, spicy red-brown sauce made from fermented soybeans and seasonings.

hoist /hɔɪst/ *v.t.* **1.** to raise or lift, especially by some mechanical appliance: *to hoist sail.* **2.** *Colloq.* to steal, especially to shoplift. **3.** *Colloq.* to throw. *–n.* **4.** an apparatus for hoisting, as a lift. **5.** → **clothes hoist**. **6.** the act of hoisting; a lift. *–hoister, n.*

hokey-pokey /hoʊki-'poʊki/ *n.* **1.** → **hocus-pocus**. **2.** *Chiefly NZ* a toffee-like sweet.

Hokkien noodles /hɒkjɛn 'nudəlz/ *pl. n.* **1.** medium thick round egg noodles in the Asian style. **2.** (*construed as sing.*) an Asian-style stir-fry dish with these noodles as accompaniment, often including vegetables and chicken or prawns.

hold¹ /hoʊld/ *verb* (**held, held** *or, Archaic*, **holden, holding**) *–v.t.* **1.** to have or keep in the hand; keep fast; grasp. **2.** to reserve; retain; set aside. **3.** to bear, sustain, or support with the hand, arms, etc., or by any means. **4.** to keep in a specified state, relation, etc.: *to hold the enemy in check.* **5.** to keep in custody; detain. **6.** to engage in; preside over; carry on; pursue; observe or celebrate: *to hold a meeting.* **7.** to have the ownership or use of; keep as one's own; occupy: *to hold office.* **8.** to contain or be capable of containing: *this bottle holds two litres.* **9.** to have or keep in the mind; think or believe; entertain: *to hold a belief.* **10.** to regard or consider: *to hold a person responsible.* **11.** *Law* (of a

court) to decide. **12.** to regard with a specified degree of affection or attachment: *to hold someone dear; to hold someone cheap.* **13.** to keep (territory, etc.) forcibly, as against an adversary. *–v. (copular)* **14.** to remain or continue in a specified state, relation, etc.: *to hold still.* *–v.i.* **15.** to remain fast; adhere; cling: *the anchor holds.* **16.** to keep or maintain a grasp on something. **17.** to maintain one's position against opposition; continue in resistance. **18.** to remain attached, faithful, or steadfast: *to hold to one's purpose.* **19.** to remain valid; be in force: *the rule does not hold.* **20.** (*usu. in the imperative*) *Archaic* to refrain or forbear. *–n.* **21.** the act of holding fast by a grasp of the hand or by some other physical means; grasp; grip: *take hold.* **22.** something to hold a thing by, as a handle; something to grasp for support. **23.** one of a set of ways of grasping an opponent in wrestling. **24.** a thing that holds fast or supports something else. **25.** a controlling force, or dominating influence: *to have a hold on a person.* *–phr.* **26. get a hold on oneself,** *Colloq.* to get control over oneself. **27. hold a catch,** *Cricket* to retain control of the ball after a catch so that the catch is considered valid. **28. hold back, a.** to restrain or check. **b.** to retain possession of; keep back; withhold. **29. hold down, a.** to maintain a grasp on (someone or something) while exerting a downward pressure. **b.** to continue to hold (a position, job, etc.), especially in spite of difficulties. **30. hold forth, a.** to propose as likely: *he held forth little prospect of improvement.* **b.** to speak pompously or at tedious length: *she held forth about her achievements.* **31. hold from** (or **to**), to hold (property) by grant of; derive title to. **32. hold good,** to be valid. **33. hold in,** to restrain, check, or curb: *he managed to hold in his anger.* **34. hold it,** a call to someone to stop, wait, etc. **35. hold off, a.** to keep aloof or at a distance. **b.** to refrain from action. **36. hold on, a.** to keep fast hold on something. **b.** to continue; persist. **c.** (*chiefly in the imperative*) *Colloq.* to stop or wait: *to tell someone to hold on; hold on!* **37. hold one's own,** to maintain one's position or condition. **38. hold one's tongue** (or **peace**), to keep silent; cease or refrain from speaking. **39. hold out, a.** to offer or present. **b.** to extend or stretch forth. **c.** to continue to exist; last. **d.** to refuse to yield or submit. **e.** *Colloq.* to keep back something expected or due. **40. hold out for,** to remain adamant in expectation of: *I'm going to hold out for a better offer.* **41. hold over, a.** to keep for future consideration or action; postpone. **b.** *Music* to prolong (a note) from one bar to the next. **42. hold someone's hand,** *Colloq.* to provide moral support for someone. **43. hold the ball,** *Aust. Rules* to retain possession of the ball when seized by another player, thereby incurring a penalty. **44. hold the line,** (of someone on the telephone) to wait. **45. hold the road,** (of tyres on a car) to grip the road. **46. hold to,** to abide by; keep to. **47. hold together, a.** to cause to remain in one piece: *only one bolt holds it together.* **b.** to cause to remain functioning as a unit: *the sergeant held the company together.* **c.** to remain whole or in one piece. **48. hold up, a.** to hold in an erect position. **b.** to present to notice; exhibit; display. **c.** to hinder; delay. **d.** to stop by force in order to rob. **e.** to remain intact: *her testimony held up under cross-examination.* **f.** to cope in distressing circumstances. **49. hold water, a.** to retain water; not let water run through. **b.** to prove sound, tenable, or valid: *Mr Black's claims will not hold water.* **50. hold with,** to agree with; approve of. **51. no holds barred, a.** *Wrestling* with no restrictions as to rules. **b.** without restraint or inhibition. **52. on hold, a.** temporarily in abeyance: *we've got that plan on hold.* **b.** (of a telephone caller) temporarily kept waiting, but not disconnected, while the recipient of the call attends to other business.

hold² /hoʊld/ *n. Naut.* the interior of a ship below the deck, especially where the cargo is stowed.

holder /ˈhoʊldə/ *n.* **1.** something to hold a thing with. **2.** someone who has the ownership, possession, or use of something; an owner; a tenant. **3.** the payee or endorsee in possession of a bill of exchange or promissory note. **4.** → **shareholder**. **5.** someone who wins and keeps a sports cup until the next contest or championship is held.

holding /ˈhoʊldɪŋ/ *n.* **1.** (*oft. pl.*) property owned, especially stocks and shares, and land. *–adj.* **2.** used as an interim measure: *a holding yard.*

holding company *n.* **1.** a company controlling, or able to control, other companies by virtue of share ownership in these companies. **2.** a company which owns stocks or securities of other companies, deriving income from them.

hold-up *n.* **1.** a forcible stopping and robbing of a person, bank, etc. **2.** a delay; stoppage.

hole /hoʊl/ *n.* **1.** an opening through anything; an aperture. **2.** a hollow place in a solid body or mass; a cavity: *a hole in the ground.* **3.** a waterhole. **4.** *Goldmining* a shaft sunk into the ground from the surface; a miner's excavation. **5.** the excavated habitation of an animal; a burrow. **6.** a small, mean abode or town. **7.** a dungeon; place of confinement. **8.** *Golf* **a.** the small cavity into which the ball is to be hit. **b.** any one of the eighteen stages of a round of golf, in each of which the player must hit the ball in a series of strokes from the tee to a small hole in the putting green. **9.** *US* a cove or small harbour. **10.** *Colloq.* an embarrassing position or predicament: *to find oneself in a hole.* **11.** *Colloq.* (*taboo*) any of certain apertures of the body, as the anus or vagina. *–v.t.* **12.** to make a hole or holes in. **13.** to put or drive into a hole. **14.** *Golf* to drive (the ball) into a hole. **15.** *Colloq.* to fire a bullet into. *–v.i.* **16.** to make a hole or holes. **17.** Also, **hole out**. *Golf* to drive the ball into a hole. *–phr.* **18. hole up, a.** to go into a hole; retire for the winter, as a hibernating animal. **b.** to hide (often from the police). **19. like a hole in the head**, *Colloq.* not at all: *right now I need a visit from him like a hole in the head.* **20. put a big hole in**, *Colloq.* to eat or drink a large proportion of: *well, I may not have finished it, but I put a big hole in it.* *–holey, adj.*

hole-and-corner *adj.* furtive; secretive; underhand.

holiday /ˈhɒlədeɪ/ *n.* **1.** a day on which ordinary business is stopped, often in memory of some event, person, religious feast, etc. **2.** (*oft. pl.*) a break from work often involving a trip away from home; vacation. *–adj.* **3.** relating to or suited to a holiday: *a holiday frame of mind.* *–v.i.* **4.** to take a holiday: *she will holiday on the Gold Coast.*

holiness /ˈhoʊlinəs/ *n.* **1.** the state or character of being holy; sanctity. **2.** (*upper case*) (preceded by *his* or *your*) **a.** *Christian Church* a title of the pope, and formerly also of other high ecclesiastical dignitaries, etc. **b.** a title used for some other religious leaders.

hollow /ˈhɒloʊ/ *adj.* **1.** having a hole or cavity within; not solid; empty: *a hollow ball.* **2.** having a depression or concavity: *a hollow surface.* **3.** sunken, as the cheeks or eyes. **4.** (of sound) not resonant; dull, muffled, or deep: *a hollow voice.* **5.** without substantial or real worth; vain: *a hollow victory.* **6.** insincere or false: *hollow compliments.* **7.** hungry. *–n.* **8.** an empty space within anything; a hole; a depression or cavity. **9.** a valley: *the hollow of a hill.* *–v.t.* **10.** to make hollow. *–v.i.* **11.** to become hollow. *–adv.* **12.** in a hollow manner. *–phr.* **13. beat hollow**, *Colloq.* to defeat utterly or completely. **14. feel hollow** (**inside**), to be lacking physical or emotional strength. **15. have hollow legs**, *Colloq.* to have a prodigious appetite. **16. hollow out, a.** to form by making something hollow: *to hollow out a*

depression. **b.** to form a cavity in: *to hollow out a tree trunk.* *–hollowly, adv. –hollowness, n.*

holly /ˈhɒli/ *n.* (*pl.* **-lies**) **1.** any of the trees or shrubs of the genus *Ilex*, especially those species having glossy, spiny-edged leaves and small, whitish flowers succeeded by bright red berries. **2.** the foliage and berries, much used for decoration, especially during the Christmas season.

holo- a word element meaning 'whole' or 'entire', as in *holocaust.*

holocaust /ˈhɒləkɔst, -kəst/ *n.* great or total destruction of life, especially by fire.

Holocene /ˈhɒləsin/ *adj.* **1.** *Geol.* of, relating to, or formed in the second and most recent epoch of the Quaternary period, which began 10 000 years ago at the end of the Pleistocene. *–n.* Also, **Recent Age**. **2. the**, the Holocene epoch or rock series.

hologram /ˈhɒləgræm/ *n.* a negative produced by holography.

holography /həˈlɒgrəfi/ *n.* a form of photography in which no lens is used and in which a photographic plate records the interference pattern between two parts of a laser beam. The result is a plate which when exposed to bright light seems to reproduce a three-dimensional image. *–holographic, adj.*

Holstein /ˈhɒlstaɪn/ *n.* one of a breed of large, black-and-white dairy cattle, originating in North Holland and Friesland, provinces of the Netherlands. Also, **Holstein-Friesian**.

holster /ˈhoʊlstə/ *n.* a leather case for a handgun, often attached to a belt. *–holstered, adj.*

holus-bolus /ˌhoʊləs-ˈboʊləs/ *adv. Colloq.* **1.** all at once. **2.** in its entirety. **3.** all together.

holy /ˈhoʊli/ *adj.* (**-lier**, **-liest**) **1.** specially recognised as set aside to a god; consecrated: *a holy day.* **2.** dedicated or devoted to the service of a deity or religion: *a holy man.* **3.** of religious character, purity, etc.: *a holy love.* **4.** deserving deep respect: *a holy shrine.* *–n.* (*pl.* **-lies**) **5.** a holy place or thing.

Holy Grail *n.* **1.** (in medieval legend) a cup or chalice used by Jesus at the Last Supper, and in which Joseph of Arimathaea received the last drops of Jesus' blood at the cross; subsequently sought by many knights. **2.** one's ultimate objective. Also, **Grail**.

holy war *n.* a war waged for a religious cause, as a crusade or jihad.

homage /ˈhɒmɪdʒ/ *also for def. 5* /oʊˈmaʒ, ɒmˈaʒ/ *n.* **1.** respect or reverence paid or rendered. **2.** the formal acknowledgement by which a feudal tenant or vassal declared himself to be the man of his lord, owing him faith and service. **3.** the relation thus established of a vassal to his lord. **4.** something done or given in acknowledgement or consideration of vassalage. **5.** *Art* a work or a collection of works designed to acknowledge and draw on the work of another artist.

home /hoʊm/ *n.* **1.** a house, or other shelter that is the fixed residence of a person, a family, or a household. **2.** a place of one's domestic affections. **3.** (*oft. upper case*) an institution for the homeless, sick, etc. **4.** the dwelling place or retreat of an animal. **5.** the place or region where something is native or most common. **6.** any place of existence or refuge: *a heavenly home.* **7.** one's native place or own country. **8.** (in games) the goal; finishing post; base. **9.** *Baseball* the plate at which the batter stands and which he or she must return to and touch after running round the bases, in order to score a run. **10.** *Aust., NZ, Obs.* Great Britain, especially England, viewed as the homeland. *–adj.* **11.** of, relating to, or connected with one's home, town, centre of operations, or country; domestic. **12.** done or located at home: *home banking; home office.* **13.** *Sport* **a.** of or relating to a game played on a team's or player's own ground: *a home match.* **b.** of or relating to a team, player, etc., participating in a game played on their own ground: *the home team.* **14.** close to, or relating to, the homestead or main group of buildings of a station: *the home paddock.* **15.** that strikes home, or to the mark aimed at; to the point: *a home thrust.* –*adv.* **16.** to, towards, or at home: *to go home.* **17.** deep; to the heart; effectively and completely. **18.** to the mark or point aimed at: *to strike home.* **19.** *Naut.* all the way; as far as possible: *to heave the anchor home.* –*v.i.* **20.** to go or return home. –*v.t.* **21.** to bring or send home. –*phr.* **22.** (a) **home away from home,** a place having the comforts of home. **23. at home, a.** in one's own house or country. **b.** (of a sporting team, etc.) in one's own town or one's own grounds. **c.** in a situation familiar to one; at ease. **d.** prepared to receive social visits. **e.** (sometimes fol. by *with*) familiar; accustomed; well-informed. **24. bring home to,** to cause (someone) to realise fully: *this will bring home to you the folly of what you have done.* **25. home and hosed,** *NZ, Aust.* **a.** finished successfully. **b.** now judged to be sure of success. **26. home in on, a.** (of guided missiles, aircraft, etc.) to proceed, especially under control of an automatic aiming mechanism towards (an airport, fixed or moving target, etc.). **b.** to proceed towards, as if guided by an external force. **27. nothing to write home about,** not remarkable; unexciting; inferior. –**homeless,** *adj.*

homebirth /ˈhoʊmˌbɜθ/ *n.* a birth in which the mother gives birth in her own home.

homebody /ˈhoʊmˌbɒdi/ *n.* (*pl.* **-dies**) *Colloq.* someone who likes being at home.

homeboy /ˈhoʊmˌbɔɪ/ *n.* **1.** a member of a youth gang. **2.** *Orig. US Colloq.* (*esp. Black English*) a boy from one's home district or town.

home economics *n.* the art and science of home-making, including the purchase, preparation, and service of food, the selection and making of clothing, the choice of furnishings, the care of children, etc. Also, **home science.**

homegrown terrorism /hoʊmgroʊn ˈtɛrərɪzəm/ *n.* terrorist activities undertaken within a country by people who have lived all or most of their lives in that country. –**homegrown terrorist,** *n.*

home invasion *n.* the holding up of a family in their home.

homeland /ˈhoʊmlænd/ *n.* **1.** one's native land. **2.** an independent or self-governing territory inhabited by a particular people.

homely /ˈhoʊmli/ *adj.* (**-lier, -liest**) **1.** proper or suited to the home or to ordinary domestic life; plain; unpretentious: *homely fare.* **2.** not good-looking; plain: *a homely girl.* –**homeliness,** *n.*

homeopath /ˈhoʊmiəpæθ/ *n.* a practitioner of homeopathy. Also, **homoeopath, homeopathist, homoeopathist.**

homeopathic /hoʊmiəˈpæθɪk/ *adj.* **1.** of, relating to, or according to the principles of homeopathy. **2.** practising or advocating homeopathy. Also, **homoeopathic.** –**homeopathically** /hoʊmiəˈpæθɪkli/, *adv.*

homeopathy /hoʊmiˈɒpəθi/ *n.* a method of treating disease by drugs, given in minute doses, which produce in a healthy person symptoms similar to those of the disease. Also, **homoeopathy.**

homeostasis /ˌhoʊmioʊˈsteɪsəs/ *n.* **1.** physiological equilibrium within living creatures involving a balance of functions and chemical composition. **2.** maintenance of social equilibrium. Also, **homoeostasis.**

home page *n.* *Internet* the introductory page for a website on the internet, containing information about the site, addresses, menus, etc. Also, **homepage.**

home rule *n.* self-government, especially in internal affairs, by the inhabitants of a dependent country, colony, province, etc.

home shopping *n.* the purchasing of goods from one's home by telephone, mail order or via the internet. –**home shopper,** *n.*

homesick /ˈhoʊmsɪk/ *adj.* ill or depressed from a longing for home. –**homesickness,** *n.*

homespun /ˈhoʊmspʌn/ *adj.* **1.** spun or made at home: *homespun cloth.* **2.** made of such cloth. **3.** plain; unpolished; simple. –*n.* **4.** cloth made at home, or of homespun yarn. **5.** cloth of similar appearance to that hand-spun and hand-woven.

homestead /ˈhoʊmstɛd/ *n.* the main residence on a sheep or cattle station or large farm.

home truth *n.* a disagreeable statement of fact that hurts the sensibilities.

home unit *n. Aust., NZ* → **unit** (def. 4).

homeward /ˈhoʊmwəd/ *adj.* **1.** directed towards home. –*adv.* **2.** homewards.

homework /ˈhoʊmwɜk/ *n.* **1.** the part of a lesson or lessons prepared outside school hours. –*phr.* **2. do one's homework,** *Colloq.* to undertake preparatory work for a meeting, interview, discussion, etc.

homey /ˈhoʊmi/ *Colloq.* –*adj.* (**-mier, -miest**) **1.** homelike; comfortable; friendly. –*n.* **2.** → **homeboy.** Also, **homy.**

homicide /ˈhɒməsaɪd/ *n.* **1.** the killing of one human being by another. **2.** a murderer. –**homicidal,** *adj.*

homily /ˈhɒməli/ *n.* (*pl.* **-lies**) **1.** a religious discourse addressed to a congregation to give moral guidance and direction rather than to develop a theme as in a sermon. **2.** an admonitory or moralising discourse.

homing pigeon *n.* a pigeon trained to fly home from a distance, used to carry messages.

hominid /ˈhɒmənɪd/ *n.* a member of the Hominidae, a family comprising all of the great apes.

hominin /ˈhɒmənɪn/ *n.* a member of the tribe Hominini, comprising chimpanzees and monkeys.

hominine /ˈhɒmənaɪn/ *n.* a member of the subfamily Homininae, comprising gorillas, chimpanzees and humans, but excluding orangutans.

hominoid /ˈhɒmənɔɪd/ *n.* **1.** an ape of the superfamily Hominoidea, comprising lesser apes and great apes. **2.** a human-like creature. –*adj.* **3.** human-like.

hommos /ˈhɒməs, ˈhʊməs/ *n.* → **hummus.**

homo- a word element meaning 'the same' (opposed to *hetero-*), as in *homocercal.*

homocysteine /hoʊmoʊˈsɪstɪn/ *n.* an amino acid, $HSCH_2CH_2CH(NH_2)COOH$, produced by the human body, which, in excessive quantities, can cause damage to blood vessels.

homoeo- a word element meaning 'similar' or 'like', as in *homoeomorphism.* Also, **homeo-, homoio-.**

homoeopath /ˈhoʊmiəpæθ/ *n.* → **homeopath.**

homoeopathic /hoʊmiəˈpæθɪk/ *adj.* → **homeopathic.** –**homoeopathically,** *adv.*

homoeopathy /hoʊmiˈɒpəθi/ *n.* → **homeopathy.**

homoeostasis /hoʊmioʊˈsteɪsəs/ *n.* → **homeostasis.**

homogeneous /hoʊməˈdʒiniəs, hɒmə-/ *adj.* **1.** composed of parts all of the same kind; not heterogeneous. **2.** of the same kind or nature; essentially alike. –**homogeneously,** *adv.* –**homogeneity** /hoʊmədʒəˈniəti, hɒmə-/, *n.*

homogenise /həˈmɒdʒənaɪz/ *v.t.* **1.** to make homogeneous; form by mixing and emulsifying. –*v.i.* **2.** to become homogeneous. Also, **homogenize.** –**homogenisation** /həˌmɒdʒənaɪˈzeɪʃən/, *n.* –**homogeniser,** *n.*

homogenous /həˈmɒdʒənəs/ *adj.* **1.** corresponding in structure because of a common origin. **2.** → **nomogeneous.**

homograph /ˈhɒməɡræf, -ɡrɑːf/ *n.* a word identical with another in spelling, but different in meaning or pronunciation or both, such as *fair*[1] and *fair*[2], and *lead*[1] and *lead*[2]. –**homographic** /hɒməˈɡræfɪk/, *adj.*

homologous /həˈmɒləɡəs/ *adj.* **1.** having the same or a similar relation; corresponding, as in relative position, structure, etc. **2.** *Biol.* corresponding in type of structure and in origin, but not necessarily in function: *the wing of a bird and the foreleg of a horse are homologous.* **3.** *Chem.* of the same chemical type, but differing by a fixed increment in certain constituents. **4.** *Med.*, *etc.* relating to the relation between bacteria and the immune serum prepared from them.

homonym /ˈhɒmənɪm/ *n.* a word identical with another in pronunciation or spelling or both, but different in meaning, such as *fair*[1] and *fair*[2], *heir* and *air*, or *lead*[1] and *lead*[2]. –**homonymous** /həˈmɒnəməs/, **homonymic**, *adj.* –**homonymy** /həˈmɒnəmi/, *n.*

homophobia /hoʊməˈfoʊbiə/ *n.* fear of homosexuals, usually linked with hostility towards them. –**homophobe**, *n.* –**homophobic**, *adj.*

homophone /ˈhɒməfoʊn, ˈhoʊmə-/ *n.* a word identical with another in pronunciation, but different in meaning and spelling, such as *heir* and *air*.

Homo sapiens /ˌhoʊmoʊ ˈsæpiɛnz, ˈsæpiənz, ˈseɪpiɛnz, ˈseɪpiənz/ *n.* **1.** the human species, being the single surviving species of the genus *Homo* and of the primate family, Hominidae, to which it belongs. **2.** Also, **homo sapiens.** (in general usage) modern human beings.

homosexual /hoʊməˈsɛkʃuəl, hɒmə-/ *adj.* **1.** relating to or exhibiting homosexuality. –*n.* **2.** a homosexual person, especially a male. –**homosexualism**, *n.* –**homosexually**, *adv.*

homosexuality /ˌhoʊməsɛkʃuˈæləti, ˌhɒmə-/ *n.* the condition of being sexually attracted to people of the same sex as oneself.

homosphere /ˈhoʊmoʊsfɪə/ *n.* the earth's atmosphere up to the altitude of about 80 km, consisting of the troposphere, stratosphere and mesosphere, and characterised by proportions of the gaseous constituents remaining more or less uniform throughout. Compare **heterosphere**.

homozygote /hoʊmoʊˈzaɪɡoʊt, hɒmə-/ *n.* an organism with identical pairs of genes with respect to any given pair of hereditary characters, and hence breeding true for those characteristics. –**homozygous**, *adj.*

hone /hoʊn/ *n.* **1.** a whetstone of fine, compact texture, especially one for sharpening razors. –*v.t.* **2.** to sharpen on or as on a hone: *to hone a razor.* **3.** to cut back, trim. **4.** to improve by careful attention or practice: *to hone one's skills.*

honest /ˈɒnəst/ *adj.* **1.** honourable in principles, intentions, and actions; upright: *an honest person.* **2.** showing uprightness and fairness: *honest methods.* **3.** acquired fairly: *honest money.* **4.** open; sincere: *an honest face.* **5.** truthful; creditable; candid. **6.** chaste or virtuous; respectable. –*phr.* **7. honest to God!**, *Colloq.* an expression indicating an emphatic assertion to follow. **8. make someone an honest woman** or **make an honest woman of someone**, (*humorous*) to marry a woman with whom one has been having a sexual relationship: *he finally made an honest woman of her.* –**honesty**, *n.*

honestly /ˈɒnəstli/ *adv.* **1.** with honesty; in an honest manner. –*interj.* **2.** an exclamation used to emphasise the honesty or integrity of one's intentions, statements, etc.: *I do think so. Honestly!* **3.** an expression of exasperation.

honey /ˈhʌni/ *n.* (*pl.* **honeys**) **1.** a sweet, sticky fluid produced by bees from the nectar collected from flowers. **2.** something sweet, delicious, or delightful.

3. sweet one; darling. –*adj.* **4.** of or like honey; sweet; dear. –**honeyed**, *adj.* –**honey-like**, *adj.*

honeycomb /ˈhʌnikoʊm/ *n.* **1.** a structure of wax containing rows of hexagonal cells, formed by bees for the reception of honey and pollen and of their eggs. **2.** any substance, such as a casting of iron, etc., having cells like those of a honeycomb. –*adj.* **3.** having the structure or appearance of a honeycomb: *honeycomb weave.* –*v.t.* **4.** to pierce with many holes or cavities: *the hills were honeycombed with caves.* –**honeycombed**, *adj.*

honeydew melon /ˈhʌnidju mɛlən/ *n.* a sweet-flavoured, white-fleshed melon with a smooth, pale green rind.

honeyeater /ˈhʌniˌitə/ *n.* any of numerous birds constituting the family Meliphagidae, chiefly of Australasia, with a bill and tongue adapted for extracting the nectar from flowers.

honeymoon /ˈhʌnimun/ *n.* **1.** a holiday spent by a newly married couple before settling down to normal domesticity. **2.** the first weeks immediately after marriage. **3.** the early period of any relationship, especially when characterised by happiness or harmony: *the new government's honeymoon with the public lasted several months.* –*v.i.* **4.** to spend one's honeymoon. –**honeymooner**, *n.*

honey-pot ant *n.* any of various ants of several genera, including *Melophorus* and *Camponotus*, which has the ability to store a sweet liquid (like honey) in its distended crop, traditionally prized by Aboriginal people as food.

honeysuckle /ˈhʌnisʌkəl/ *n.* **1.** any of the upright or climbing shrubs constituting the genus *Lonicera*, some species of which are cultivated for their fragrant white, yellow, or red tubular flowers. **2.** any of various other fragrant or ornamental plants. **3.** any of several Australian trees or shrubs of the genus *Banksia*.

hongi /ˈhɒŋi/ *n.* a Maori greeting, expressed by touching noses.

honk /hɒŋk/ *n.* **1.** the cry of the goose. **2.** any similar sound, as a car horn. –*v.i.* **3.** to emit a honk. –**honker**, *n.*

honor /ˈɒnə/ *n.*, *v.t.* → **honour**. –**honorable**, *adj.*

honorarium /ɒnəˈrɛəriəm/ *n.* (*pl.* **-ariums** *or* **-aria** /-ˈrɛəriə/) **1.** an honorary reward, as in recognition of professional services on which no price may be set. **2.** a fee for services rendered by a professional person.

honorary /ˈɒnərəri, *Orig. US* ˈɒnərɛri/ *adj.* **1.** given for honour only: *an honorary title.* **2.** holding a title or position given for honour only: *an honorary president.* **3.** (of a position, job, etc.) unpaid: *the honorary secretary of the committee.* **4.** given, made, or serving as a sign of honour: *an honorary gift.* –*n.* **5.** (formerly) a specialist working in a public hospital.

honorific /ɒnəˈrɪfɪk/ *adj.* Also, **honorifical. 1.** doing or conferring honour. **2.** having the quality of an honorific. –*n.* **3.** (in certain languages, such as Chinese and Japanese) a class of forms used to show respect, especially in direct address. **4.** a title or term of respect, such as *Doctor*, *Professor*, *Rt Hon.* –**honorifically**, *adv.*

honour /ˈɒnə/ *n.* **1.** high public esteem; fame; glory. **2.** credit or reputation for behaviour that is becoming or worthy. **3.** a source of credit or distinction: *to be an honour to one's family.* **4.** high respect, as for worth, merit, or rank: *to be held in honour.* **5.** such respect manifested: *to be received with honour.* **6.** (*usu. pl.*) a mark or observance of public respect: *he was buried with full military honours.* **7.** something conferred on someone as a mark of distinction, especially an official award for achievement, community service, or bravery which confers rank or membership of an order: *an honour for services to the Aboriginal community; there are several ranks of knighthood in the imperial system of honours.* **8.** a special privilege or favour: *I have the honour of acknowledging your letter.* **9.** (*usu. pl.*)

high rank, dignity, or distinction: *political honours.* **10.** (*upper case*) (preceded by *His, Her,* etc.) a deferential title, especially of certain judges. **11.** high-minded character or principles; fine sense of one's obligations: *a man of honour.* **12.** (*pl.*) (in universities) **a.** scholastic or academic achievement in a degree examination higher than that required for a pass degree. **b.** the grade of scholarship achieved: *first-class honours.* **c.** the course of study. **13.** chastity or purity in a woman. **14.** *Bridge* any one of the five highest ranking cards in each suit; for scoring purposes, any one of the highest cards of the trump suit or any one of the four aces at no trump. **15.** *Whist* any of the four highest trump cards. **16.** *Golf* the preference of teeing off before the other players or side, given after the first hole to the player or players who won the previous hole. *–v.t.* **17.** to hold in honour or high respect; revere. **18.** to treat with honour. **19.** to confer honour or distinction upon. **20.** to worship (the Supreme Being). **21.** to show a courteous regard for: *to honour an invitation.* **22.** to accept and pay (a cheque, etc.) when due. **23.** to accept the validity of (a document, etc.). *–phr.* **24. do honour to, a.** to show respect to. **b.** to be a credit to. **25. do the honours,** to act or preside as host. **26. on** (or **upon**) **one's honour, a.** an expression acknowledging personal responsibility for one's actions. **b.** an expression pledging one's reputation as to the truthfulness of a statement, etc. **c.** an expression promising obedience or good behaviour. Also, **honor. –honourer,** *n.* **–honourless,** *adj.*

honourable /ˈɒnərəbəl/ *adj.* **1.** in accordance with principles of honour; upright: *an honourable man.* **2.** of high rank, dignity, or distinction; noble, illustrious, or distinguished. **3.** (*upper case*) **a.** a title prefixed to the name of certain high officials, including members of parliament, especially when one member refers to another: *the honourable member, the honourable gentleman.* **b.** *Brit.* a title prefixed to the given name of younger sons of earls and all children of viscounts and barons. *Abbrev.:* Hon. Also, **honorable. –honourably,** *adv.*

honour killing *n.* (in some societies) the killing of a woman by a close male relative because she is deemed to have dishonoured the family name, as by committing adultery or engaging in premarital sexual relations. Also, **honor killing.**

hood[1] /hʊd/ *n.* **1.** a soft covering for the head and neck, sometimes joined to a garment. **2.** something looking like this, as a hood-shaped petal, etc. **3.** a piece of hood-shaped material, worn with an academic gown, the colour and material of the lining depending on the degree held and the university by which the degree was given. **4.** the folding roof of a convertible car. **–hoodless,** *adj.*

hood[2] /hʊd/ *n. Colloq.* a hoodlum.

-hood a suffix denoting state, condition, character, nature, etc., or a body of persons of a particular character or class, as *childhood, likelihood, priesthood, sisterhood.*

hoodie /ˈhʊdi/ *n. Colloq.* a jacket with a hood.

hoodlum /ˈhudləm/ *n.* **1.** a petty gangster; ruffian. **2.** a destructive, noisy, or rough child or young person. **–hoodlumism,** *n.*

hoodoo /ˈhudu/ *n.* (*pl.* **-doos**) **1.** voodoo. **2.** *Colloq.* a person or thing that brings bad luck.

hoodwink /ˈhʊdwɪŋk/ *v.t.* to deceive; humbug. **–hoodwinker,** *n.*

hoof /hʊf/ *n.* (*pl.* **hoofs** /hʊfs/ *or* **hooves** /hʊvz/) **1.** the horny covering protecting the ends of the digits or encasing the foot in certain animals, as the ox, horse, etc. **2.** the entire foot of a horse, donkey, etc. **3.** a hoofed animal; one of a herd. **4.** *Colloq.* (*humorous*) the human foot. *–phr.* **5. hoof it,** *Colloq.* **a.** to walk.

b. to dance. **6. on the hoof,** (of livestock) alive, not butchered.

hoo-ha /ˈhu-ha/ *n. Colloq.* **1.** a fuss; turmoil. **2.** noise, bustle, etc., especially associated with publicity. **3.** nonsense.

hook /hʊk/ *n.* **1.** a curved or angular piece of metal or other firm substance catching, pulling, or sustaining something. **2.** a fishhook. **3.** that which catches; a snare; a trap. **4.** something curved or bent like a hook, as a mark or symbol, etc. **5.** a sharp curve or angle in the length or course of anything. **6.** a curved spit of land. **7.** a recurved and pointed organ or appendage of an animal or plant. **8.** Also, **hook shot.** *Golf* a drive or other stroke which curves to the left of the player striking the ball. **9.** Also, **hook shot.** *Cricket* a curving stroke of the bat, whereby the ball is hit to the on side of the field. **10.** *Boxing* a curving blow made with the arm bent, and coming in to the opponent from the side: *right hook.* **11.** *Surfing* the top of a breaking wave. **12.** *Music* a stroke or line attached to the stem of a quaver, semiquaver, etc. **13.** (*pl.*) *Colloq.* fingers. **14. a.** (in advertising, entertainment, etc.) an inducement or feature which catches the attention of listeners or onlookers and draws them further in to the material to where the main item lies. **b.** (in writing, especially journalism) something which catches the attention of the reader, usually in the first paragraph. **15.** *Music* a catchy lyric or strain of music. *–v.t.* **16.** to seize, fasten, or catch hold of and draw in with or as with a hook. **17.** to catch (fish) with a fishhook. **18.** *Colloq.* to seize by stealth, pilfer, or steal. **19.** to catch by artifice. **20.** to catch on the horns, or attack with the horns. **21.** *Boxing* to deliver a hook. **22.** *Cricket, Golf* to hit (the ball) so as to produce a hooking stroke. **23.** *Colloq.* to catch and hold the attention of: *to hook a new client; he's managed to hook a rich woman. –v.i.* **24.** to become attached or fastened by or as by a hook; join on. **25.** to curve or bend like a hook. **26.** *Boxing* to deliver a hook. **27.** *Golf, Cricket* **a.** (of the player) to make a hooking stroke. **b.** (of the ball) to describe a course to the left or on side of the player after being hooked. **28.** *Colloq.* to depart; clear off. *–phr.* **29. by hook or by crook,** by any means, fair or foul. **30. hook it,** *Colloq.* to depart; clear off. **31. hook, line, and sinker,** completely. **32. hook up, a.** to fasten with a hook or hooks. **b.** to put together (mechanical apparatus) and connect to the source of power. **c.** to arrange a communications link between (users of a communications system). **d.** *Colloq.* to meet and spend time with: *let's hook up sometime next week.* **33. hook up with,** *Colloq.* to make contact with: *to hook up with fellow enthusiasts.* **34. let someone off the hook,** to allow someone to escape the consequence of their actions or to evade their responsibilities. **35. off the hook, a.** (of a garment) available for immediate use; ready-made. **b.** out of a predicament. **c.** (of a telephone) with the receiver lifted. **36. on one's own hook,** *Colloq.* on one's own responsibility. **37. on the hook, a.** waiting; being delayed. **b.** in a predicament. **38. put the hooks into,** *Colloq.* to borrow from; cadge from. **39. sling one's hook,** *Brit. Colloq.* to depart.

hookah /ˈhʊkə/ *n.* a pipe with a long, flexible tube by which the smoke of tobacco, marijuana, etc., is drawn through a vessel of water and thus cooled. Also, **hooka.**

hooked /hʊkt/ *adj.* **1.** bent like a hook; hook-shaped. **2.** made with or having a hook. **3.** caught, as a fish. **4.** *Colloq.* (usu. fol. by *on*) addicted; obsessed. **5.** *Colloq.* married.

hooker[1] /ˈhʊkə/ *n. Rugby Football* the central forward in the front row of the scrum, whose job is to pull back the ball with their foot.

hooker[2] /ˈhʊkə/ *n. Colloq.* a female prostitute.

hook shot *n.* **1.** *Golf* → **hook** (def. 8). **2.** *Cricket* → **hook** (def. 9).

hook turn *n.* a right-hand turn made from the far left lane at designated intersections in Melbourne which have tramlines running through them.

hookworm /ˈhʊkwɜːm/ *n.* any of certain bloodsucking nematode worms, such as *Ancylostoma duodenale* and *Necator americanus*, parasitic in the intestine of humans and other animals.

hooky /ˈhʊki/ *phr.* **play hooky**, *Colloq.* to stay away from school, work, etc., without a justifiable excuse.

hooligan /ˈhuːləgən/ *n.* 1. a hoodlum; young street rough. –*adj.* 2. of or like hooligans. –**hooliganism**, *n.*

hoon /huːn/ *Aust., NZ Colloq.* –*n.* 1. a loutish, aggressive, or surly youth. 2. a fast, reckless driver of a car, boat, etc. 3. a foolish or silly person, especially one who is a show-off. 4. a drive, especially a speedy one: *going out for a short hoon around the block.* –*v.i.* 5. to drive fast and recklessly.

hoop /huːp/ *n.* 1. a circular band or ring of metal, wood, or other stiff material. 2. such a band to hold together the staves of a cask, barrel, etc. 3. a large ring of wood or plastic for children's games. 4. one of the iron arches used in croquet. 5. a circular band of stiff material used to make a woman's skirt stand out. 6. a large ring, with paper stretched over it through which circus animals, etc., jump. 7. *Colloq.* jockey –*v.t.* 8. to bind or fasten with a hoop or hoops. 9. to encircle; embrace. –*phr.* 10. **go through the hoop**, go through a bad time; undergo an ordeal. 11. **jump through hoops**, to obey without question, in the manner of a trained dog. 12. **put someone through (the) hoops**, to subject someone to a series of (often unreasonable) tests or trials. –**hooped**, *adj.*

hoop pine *n.* a valuable softwood timber tree of northern Australia and New Guinea, *Araucaria cunninghamii.*

hooray /həˈreɪ, huˈreɪ/ *interj.* 1. an exclamation of joy, applause, or the like. –*v.i.* 2. to shout 'hooray'. –*n.* 3. the exclamation 'hooray'. Also, **hoorah, hurray**.

hoot /huːt/ *v.i.* 1. to cry out or shout, especially in disapproval or derision. 2. (of an owl) to utter its cry. 3. to utter a similar sound. 4. to blow a horn or factory hooter; honk. 5. to laugh. –*v.t.* 6. to assail with shouts of disapproval or derision. 7. to drive (*out, away, off,* etc.) by hooting. 8. to express in hoots. –*n.* 9. the cry of an owl. 10. any similar sound, as an inarticulate shout. 11. a cry or shout, especially of disapproval or derision. 12. *Colloq.* an enjoyable and amusing experience. 13. *Colloq.* an amusing or funny person. –*phr.* 14. **not to give a hoot**, *Colloq.* to be dismissive; not to care.

hooves /huːvz/ *n.* a plural of **hoof**.

hop¹ /hɒp/ *verb* (**hopped, hopping**) –*v.i.* 1. to leap; move by leaping with all feet off the ground. 2. to spring or leap on one foot. 3. to make a flight or trip. 4. Also, **hop off**. *US Colloq.* (of an aeroplane, etc.) to leave the ground in beginning a flight. 5. *Colloq.* to dance. 6. to limp. 7. *Colloq.* to go, come, move, etc.: *I'll just hop down to the shop; hop onto the computer and look it up; she hopped on a plane to visit her mother.* –*v.t.* *Colloq.* 8. to jump over (a fence, ditch, etc.). 9. (of an aeroplane, etc.) to cross by a flight. –*n.* 10. an act of hopping; short leap. 11. a leap on one foot. 12. *Colloq.* a flight of an aeroplane. 13. *Colloq.* a dance, or dancing party. –*phr.* 14. **hop into**, *Colloq.* **a.** to set about (something) energetically: *she hopped into the job at once.* **b.** to put (clothes) on briskly: *he hopped into his cossie.* 15. **hop into bed**, *Colloq.* (sometimes fol. by *with*) to have casual sex. 16. **hop it**, *Colloq.* to go away; leave. 17. **hop the twig**, *Colloq.* to die. 18. **hop to it**, *Colloq.* to set about something quickly. 19. **hop up and down**, *Colloq.* to express agitation or irritation. 20. **on the hop**, **a.** unprepared. **b.** busy, moving.

hop² /hɒp/ *n.* 1. one of the twining plants of three species of the genus *Humulus*. 2. (*pl.*) the dried ripe cones of the female flowers of the hop plant, used in brewing, medicine, etc. 3. (*pl.*) *Colloq.* beer.

hop bush *n.* an evergreen shrub of Australia and New Zealand, *Dodonaea viscosa*, which has papery, often reddish, winged seed capsules resembling hops.

hope /hoʊp/ *n.* 1. expectation of something desired; desire accompanied by expectation. 2. a particular instance of such expectation or desire: *a hope of success.* 3. confidence in a future event; ground for expecting something: *there is no hope of his recovery.* 4. a person or thing that expectations are centred in: *the hope of the family.* –*v.t.* 5. to look forward to with desire and, to a certain extent, confidence: *I hope to meet you again.* 6. to trust in the truth of a matter (with a clause): *I hope that you are satisfied.* –*v.i.* 7. to be in a state of hope. 8. to trust or rely. –*phr.* 9. **great white hope**, a person from whom or a thing from which exceptionally great successes or benefits are expected. 10. **hope against hope**, to continue to hope, although there are no apparent grounds for such hope. 11. **hope for**, to have an expectation of (something desired): *to hope for forgiveness.* 12. **some hope**, an expression of pessimism, resignation, or disbelief. –**hopingly**, *adv.*

hopeful /ˈhoʊpfəl/ *adj.* 1. full of hope; expressing hope: *hopeful words.* 2. exciting hope; promising advantage or success: *a hopeful prospect.* –*n.* 3. a promising young person. –**hopefulness**, *n.*

hopefully /ˈhoʊpfəli/ *adv.* 1. in a hopeful fashion. 2. it is hoped: *hopefully the drought will soon end.*

hopeless /ˈhoʊpləs/ *adj.* 1. affording no hope; desperate: *a hopeless case.* 2. without hope; despairing: *hopeless grief.* 3. not possible to resolve or solve: *a hopeless problem.* 4. not able to learn, perform, act, etc., incompetent: *a hopeless actor.* –**hopelessly**, *adv.* –**hopelessness**, *n.*

hopper /ˈhɒpə/ *n.* 1. someone or something that hops. 2. any of various jumping insects, such as grasshoppers, etc. 3. a funnel-shaped chamber in which materials are stored temporarily and later discharged through the bottom.

hopping mouse *n.* any of various Australian endemic rodents of the genus *Notomys*, which hop rapidly like a kangaroo.

hopsack /ˈhɒpsæk/ *n.* 1. a coarse, jute sacking material. 2. a fabric with coarse surface, used to make clothing. Also, **hopsacking**.

hopscotch /ˈhɒpskɒtʃ/ *n.* a children's game in which the player hops from one compartment to another of a diagram traced on the ground, without touching a line.

horde /hɔːd/ *n.* 1. a large group of people, especially attackers or invaders. 2. (*usu. pl.*) a large and dangerous or threatening group of animals: *hordes of locusts.* 3. (*usu. pl.*) *Colloq.* a very large number of people: *hordes of football fans; hungry hordes descending on the restaurants.* 4. *Anthrop. Obs.* a subdivision of a tribe, especially a group travelling and hunting together. –*v.i.* (**horded, hording**) 5. to gather in a horde.

horizon /həˈraɪzən/ *n.* 1. the line or circle which forms the apparent boundary between earth and sky. 2. the limit or range of perception, knowledge, or the like. 3. *Geol.* a plane in rock strata characterised by particular features, such as occurrence of distinctive fossil species.

horizontal /hɒrəˈzɒntəl/ *adj.* 1. at right angles to the upright (vertical). 2. lying down. 3. near, on, or parallel to the horizon. 4. measured or contained in a plane parallel to the horizon: *a horizontal distance.* –*n.* 5. a horizontal line, plane, position, etc. –**horizontality, horizontalness**, *n.* –**horizontally**, *adv.*

hormone /ˈhɔːmoʊn/ *n.* *Physiol.* 1. any of various substances which are formed in cells in one part of an organism and transported to another part of the organism where they have a specific effect, as the regulation of growth. **2.** a synthetic substance having the same effect. –**hormonal,** *adj.*

hormone patch *n.* an adhesive dressing which slowly dispenses hormones by absorption through the skin, used to supplement a deficiency or correct an imbalance.

hormone replacement therapy *n.* the administration of oestrogen and progesterone to postmenopausal women to reduce the risk of osteoporosis and ease the symptoms of the menopause; the occurrence of adverse side effects has seen a reduction in its use. *Abbrev.:* HRT

horn /hɔn/ *n.* **1.** a hard, projected, often curved and pointed, hollow and permanent growth (usually one of a pair, a right and a left) on the head of certain mammals, as cattle, sheep, goats, antelopes, etc. (**true horn**). **2.** each of the pair of solid, deciduous, usually branched bony growths, or antlers, on the head of a deer. **3.** some similar growth, as the tusk of a narwhal. **4.** a process projecting from the head of an animal and suggestive of a horn, as a feeler, tentacle, crest, etc. **5.** the substance, consisting largely of keratin, of which true horns are composed. **6.** any similar substance, as that of hoofs, nails, corns, etc. **7.** something formed from or resembling the hollow horn of an animal: *a drinking horn.* **8.** *Colloq.* (*taboo*) an erection (def. 4b). **9.** *Music* a wind instrument, originally formed from the hollow horn of an animal but now usually made of brass or other metal or material. **10.** an instrument for sounding a warning signal: *a car horn.* **11.** each of the alternatives of a dilemma. –*v.t.* **12.** to butt or gore with the horns. **13.** to furnish with horns. –*adj.* **14.** made of horn. –*phr.* **15. draw** (or **pull**) **one's horns in,** to economise; reduce one's activities; retreat. **16. horn in,** *Colloq.* (sometimes fol. by *on*) to thrust oneself forward obtrusively. –**horned,** *adj.* –**hornless,** *adj.*

hornblende /ˈhɔnblɛnd/ *n.* any of the common black or dark-coloured aluminous varieties of amphibole. –**hornblendic** /hɔnˈblɛndɪk/, *adj.*

hornet /ˈhɔnət/ *n.* **1.** any large, strong, social wasp of the family Vespidae having an exceptionally severe sting. –*phr.* **2. mad as a hornet,** *Colloq.* extremely angry.

hornet's nest *n.* a great deal of trouble, hostility.

hornpipe /ˈhɔnpaɪp/ *n.* **1.** an English folk clarinet with an ox horn to conceal the reed and another one to form the bell. **2.** a lively dance (originally to hornpipe music) usually by a single person, popular among sailors. **3.** a piece of music for or in the style of such a dance.

horny /ˈhɔni/ *adj.* (**-nier, -niest**) **1.** horn-like through hardening; callous: *horny hands.* **2.** consisting of a horn or a horn-like substance; corneous. **3.** more or less translucent, like horn. **4.** having a horn or horns or horn-like projections. **5.** *Colloq.* randy; sexually excited. –**horniness,** *n.*

horology /həˈrɒlədʒi/ *n.* the art or science of making timepieces or of measuring time. –**horologic** /hɒrəˈlɒdʒɪk/, **horological** /hɒrəˈlɒdʒɪkəl/, *adj.* –**horologist,** *n.*

horoscope /ˈhɒrəskoʊp/ *n.* **1.** a forecast of a person's future derived from a study of the relative positions of the sun, moon, planets, and zodiacal constellations at the time of the person's birth. **2.** a diagram of the heavens for use in calculating horoscopes. **3.** the art or practice of foretelling future events by observation of the stars and planets.

horrendous /hɒˈrɛndəs, hə-/ *adj.* dreadful; horrible. –**horrendously,** *adv.*

horrible /ˈhɒrəbəl/ *adj.* **1.** causing or tending to cause horror; dreadful: *a horrible sight.* **2.** extremely unpleasant; deplorable; excessive: *horrible conditions.* –**horribleness,** *n.* –**horribly,** *adv.*

horrid /ˈhɒrəd/ *adj.* **1.** such as to cause horror; dreadful; abominable. **2.** extremely unpleasant or disagreeable: *horrid weather.* –**horridly,** *adv.* –**horridness,** *n.*

horrific /hɒˈrɪfɪk, hə-/ *adj.* causing horror.

horrify /ˈhɒrəfaɪ/ *v.t.* (**-fied, -fying**) to cause to feel horror; strike with horror; shock intensely. –**horrification** /hɒrəfəˈkeɪʃən/, *n.*

horror /ˈhɒrə/ *n.* **1.** great fear or disgust: *to draw back in horror.* **2.** anything that creates such a feeling: *the horrors of war.* **3.** *Colloq.* something considered ugly or bad: *that hat is a horror.* **4.** a strong or painful dislike: *a horror of violence.* **5.** (*pl.*) *Colloq.* **a.** a great feeling of fear: *heights give me the horrors.* **b.** → **delirium tremens.**

hors d'oeuvre /ɔ ˈdɜv/ *n.* an appetiser, canapé, or savoury, served with cocktails, before a meal, etc.

horse /hɔs/ *n.* **1.** a large, solid-hoofed quadruped, *Equus caballus,* domesticated since prehistoric times, and employed as a beast of draught and burden and for carrying a rider. **2.** a male horse, fully-grown and past its fourth birthday. **3.** any animal of the family Equidae, which includes the ass, zebra, etc. **4.** (*as collective pl.* **horse**) soldiers serving on horseback; cavalry: *a thousand horse.* **5.** something on which a person rides, sits, or exercises as if on a horse's back: *rocking horse.* **6.** a leather-covered block, adjustable in height, used for vaulting and other gymnastic exercises. **7.** a frame, block, etc., with legs on which something is mounted or supported. **8.** *Colloq.* heroin. –*v.t.* **9.** to provide with a horse or horses. **10.** to set on horseback. –*adj.* **11.** of or relating to a horse or horses. **12.** mounted on horses. **13.** unusually large for one of its kind. –*phr.* **14. a horse of another** (or **a different**) **colour,** a different thing altogether. **15. back the wrong horse,** to support the wrong or losing contender. **16. eat like a horse,** to have a prodigious appetite. **17. flog a dead horse,** to make useless efforts, as in attempting to raise interest in a dead issue. **18. (straight) from the horse's mouth,** from an authoritative source. **19. hold one's horses,** *Colloq.* to restrain one's impulses; hold back. **20. horse about** (or **around**), *Colloq.* to act or play roughly or boisterously. **21. horses for courses,** *Colloq.* **a.** an expression referring to the theory that a horse which races well on one track or type of track should not be run on a different track to which it is not suited. **b.** an expression referring to the notion that someone should be matched with a position, task, etc., suited to their particular talents. **22. white horse,** the foamy crest of a wave. **23. willing horse,** a willing worker.

horse float *n.* a van or trailer for conveying horses by road, rail, etc. Also, **float.**

horse flu *n.* → **equine influenza.**

horseplay /ˈhɔspleɪ/ *n.* rough or boisterous play.

horsepower /ˈhɔspaʊə/ *n.* a unit of measurement of power, or rate of doing work, in the imperial system, defined as 550 foot-pounds per second (equal to 745.7 watts).

horseradish /ˈhɔsrædɪʃ/ *n.* **1.** a cultivated plant, *Armoracia rusticana.* **2.** its pungent root, ground and used as a condiment and in medicine.

horseride /ˈhɔsraɪd/ *v.i.* (**-rode, -riding**) to go for a ride on a horse. –**horseriding,** *n.* –**horserider,** *n.*

horse sense *n.* *Colloq.* **1.** plain, practical common sense. **2.** an ability to judge horseflesh, to ride well, etc.

horseshoe /ˈhɔsʃu/ *n.* **1.** a U-shaped iron plate nailed to a horse's hoof to protect it. **2.** something shaped like a horseshoe. **3.** a symbol of good luck usually when vertical with the open end uppermost.

horsetrading /ˈhɔstreɪdɪŋ/ *n.* shrewd and close bargaining. –**horsetrader,** *n.*

horsy /ˈhɔsi/ *adj.* (**-sier, -siest**) **1.** of or relating to a horse or horses: *horsy talk.* **2.** (of a person) dealing with,

interested in, or devoted to horses, horseracing, etc.
3. *Colloq.* (of a person) large and supposedly horse-like in appearance or manner. –**horsiness**, *n.*

hortatory /ˈhɔːtətəri, ˈhɔːtətri/ *adj.* encouraging; inciting; exhorting; urging to some course of conduct or action: *a hortatory address.* Also, **hortative**.

horticulture /ˈhɔːtəkʌltʃə/ *n.* **1.** commercial cultivation of fruit, vegetables, and flowers, including berries, grapes, vines, and nuts. **2.** the science or art of growing fruit, vegetables, flowers, or ornamental plants. **3.** the cultivation of a garden. –**horticultural** /hɔːtəˈkʌltʃərəl/, *adj.* –**horticulturist** /hɔːtəˈkʌltʃərəst/, **horticulturalist** /hɔːtəˈkʌltʃərələst/, *n.*

hose /houz/ *n.* **1.** a flexible tube for conveying water, etc., to a desired point: *a garden hose.* **2.** → **hosiery**. –*v.t.* **3.** to water, wash, or drench by means of a hose.

hosiery /ˈhouʒəri, ˈhouzəri/ *n.* socks or stockings of any kind. Also, **hose**. –**hosier**, *n.*

hospice /ˈhɒspəs/ *n.* **1.** (formerly) a house of shelter or rest for pilgrims, strangers, etc., especially one kept by a religious order. **2.** a hospital for terminally ill patients.

hospitable /hɒsˈpɪtəbəl/ *adj.* **1.** affording a generous welcome to guests or strangers: *a hospitable city.* **2.** inclined to or characterised by hospitality: *a hospitable reception.* –*phr.* **3.** **hospitable to**, favourably receptive or open to: *hospitable to new ideas.* –**hospitableness**, *n.* –**hospitably**, *adv.*

hospital /ˈhɒspɪtl/ *n.* **1.** an institution in which sick or injured persons are given medical or surgical treatment. **2.** a similar establishment for the care of animals. **3.** a shop for repairing specific things: *a dolls' hospital.*

hospitalise /ˈhɒspətəlaɪz/ *v.t.* to place for medical care, etc., in a hospital. Also, **hospitalize**. –**hospitalisation** /hɒspətəlaɪˈzeɪʃən/, *n.*

hospitality /hɒspəˈtæləti/ *n.* (*pl.* **-ties**) the reception and entertainment of guests or strangers with liberality and kindness.

host¹ /houst/ *n.* **1.** someone who receives guests in his or her own home or elsewhere: *the host at a party.* **2.** the compere of a television or radio show or other public entertainment. **3.** the landlord of an inn. **4.** an animal or plant from which a parasite gains food. –*v.t.* **5.** to act as a host (def. 1). **6.** to compere (a television show, etc.).

host² /houst/ *n.* a multitude or great number of persons or things: *a host of details.*

hostage /ˈhɒstɪdʒ/ *n.* **1.** a person given or held as a security for the performance of certain actions such as the payment of ransom, etc. **2.** a security or pledge.

host computer *n.* the key or central computer in a network on which a range of operations can be performed which are not available to the peripheral or dependent computers. Also, **host**.

hostel /ˈhɒstəl, hɒsˈtɛl/ *n.* **1.** a supervised place of accommodation, usually supplying board and lodging at a comparatively low cost, such as one for students, nurses, etc. **2.** → **youth hostel**.

hostess /ˈhoustɛs/ *n.* **1.** a female host; a woman who entertains guests. **2.** an air hostess. **3.** a paid dancing partner. **4.** a female innkeeper.

hostile /ˈhɒstaɪl/, *Orig. US* /-təl/ *adj.* **1.** opposed in feeling, action, or character; unfriendly; antagonistic: *hostile criticism.* **2.** of or characteristic of an enemy: *hostile ground.* –*phr.* **3.** **go hostile**, *NZ Colloq.* (sometimes fol. by *at*) to become angry. –**hostilely**, *adv.* –**hostility**, *n.*

hot /hɒt/ *adj.* (**hotter**, **hottest**) **1.** having or communicating heat; having a high temperature: *a hot stove.* **2.** having a sensation of great bodily heat; attended with or producing such a sensation. **3.** having an effect as of burning on the tongue, skin, etc., as pepper, mustard, a blister, etc. **4.** having or showing intense feeling; ardent or fervent; vehement; excited: *hot temper.* **5.** lustful. **6.** violent, furious, or intense: *the hottest battle.*

7. strong or fresh, as a scent or trail. **8.** new; recent; fresh: *hot news.* **9.** following very closely; close: *to be hot on someone's heels.* **10.** (of colours) with red predominating. **11.** *Games* close to the sought-for object or answer. **12.** *Colloq.* (of motor cars) tuned or modified for high speeds: *a hot rod.* **13.** radioactive, especially to a degree injurious to health. **14.** *Colloq.* recently stolen or otherwise illegally obtained; wanted by the police. **15.** *Colloq.* fashionable and exciting. **16.** *Colloq.* currently popular: *the hot favourite in a race; a hot sales item.* **17.** *Colloq.* sexually attractive; sexually stimulating. **18.** *Colloq.* performing well; peaking –*adv.* **19.** in a hot manner; hotly. –*phr.* (*v.* **hotted**, **hotting**) **20.** **a bit hot**, *Colloq.* **a.** unfair; dishonest. **b.** highly priced. **21.** **blow hot and cold**, to change attitudes frequently; vacillate. **22.** **go hot and cold all over** or **go all hot and cold**, to experience, or exhibit signs of, shock or embarrassment. **23.** **have the hots for**, *Colloq.* to experience a strong sexual attraction to. **24.** **hot and bothered**, upset; flustered; exasperated. **25.** **hot as Hades**, *Colloq.* very hot. **26.** **hot as Hay, Hell, and Booligal**, *Aust. Colloq.* very hot. **27.** **hot to trot**, *Colloq.* ready for an undertaking. **28.** **hot under the collar**, angry; annoyed. **29.** **hot up**, **a.** to heat: *to hot up the milk.* **b.** to escalate: *he hotted up his attack.* **c.** to stir up: *to hot things up a bit.* **d.** to tune or modify (a motor vehicle) for high speeds. **e.** to grow excited or wild: *the party began to hot up.* **30.** **in hot water**, *Colloq.* in trouble. **31.** **like a cat on a hot tin roof**, in a state of extreme agitation. **32.** **like a cat on hot bricks**, in a state of extreme agitation. **33.** **make it hot for**, *Colloq.* to make life unpleasant for. **34.** **not so** (or **too**) **hot**, *Colloq.* **a.** not very good; disappointing. **b.** unwell. –**hotly**, *adv.*

hot air *n.* *Colloq.* empty, pretentious talk or writing.

hotbed /ˈhɒtbed/ *n.* **1.** a bed of earth, heated by fermenting manure, etc., and usually covered with glass, for growing plants out of season. **2.** a place favouring rapid growth, especially of something bad: *a hotbed of vice.*

hot-blooded /ˈhɒt-blʌdəd/ *adj.* virile; adventurous; excitable; impetuous.

hot cake *n.* **1.** *US* a pancake. –*phr.* **2.** **go** (or **sell**) **like hot cakes**, to sell quickly, especially in large quantities. Also, **hotcake**.

hotchpotch /ˈhɒtʃpɒtʃ/ *n.* **1.** a heterogeneous mixture; a jumble. **2.** a thick soup or stew made from meat and vegetables. Also, **hodgepodge**.

hot dog *n.* **1.** a hot frankfurt or sausage, especially as served in a split roll with mustard or sauce. **2.** a short surfboard designed to turn quickly back and forth across the wave. Also, **hot-dog**, **hotdog**.

hot-dog *v.i.* (**-dogged**, **-dogging**) to perform rapid and difficult manoeuvres with quick changes of direction, while riding a surfboard, skateboard, ski, etc. Also, **hotdog**. –**hot-dogger**, *n.*

hotel /houˈtɛl/ *n.* **1.** a building in which accommodation and food, and sometimes other facilities, are available. **2.** a building which houses a business selling beer and other alcoholic drinks; pub. –**hotelier**, *n.*

hotfix /ˈhɒtfɪks/ *Computers* –*n.* **1.** → **patch** (def. 9). –*v.i.* **2.** → **patch** (def. 13).

hotfoot /ˈhɒtfut/ *v.i.* Also, **hotfoot it**. **1.** to move with great speed. –*adv.* **2.** with great speed.

hot-headed /ˈhɒt-hedəd/ *adj.* hot or fiery in spirit or temper; impetuous; rash. Also, **hotheaded**. –**hothead**, *n.* –**hot-headedly**, *adv.* –**hot-headedness**, *n.*

hothouse /ˈhɒthaus/ *n.* **1.** an artificially heated greenhouse for the cultivation of tender plants. –*adj.* **2.** of or relating to a delicate plant grown in a hothouse. **3.** *Colloq.* delicate; over-protected.

hotline /ˈhɒtlaɪn/ *n.* **1.** a direct telephone connection open to immediate communication in an emergency, as between the heads of state of Russia and the US, or for members of the public seeking help or information after an accident or natural disaster, etc. **2.** a telephone line which gives direct access to people who wish to ring up to ask advice (as of a government department), give an opinion (as of a radio station or TV channel), or give solicited information (as to a police investigation).

hotplate /'hɒtpleɪt/ *n.* **1.** a portable appliance for cooking or keeping food warm. **2.** a solid, electrically heated metal plate, usually on top of an electric stove, upon which food, etc., may be heated or cooked.

hotpot /'hɒtpɒt/ *n.* a meat and vegetable stew, cooked in a covered pot. Also, **hot pot**.

hot potato *n. Colloq.* a risky situation, difficult person, or any other thing which needs careful handling.

hot rod *n. Colloq.* a car (usually an old one) whose engine has been altered for increased speed.

hot seat *n. Colloq.* **1.** the electric chair. **2.** a position involving difficulties or danger.

hot shot *adj.* **1.** exceptionally proficient. *–n.* **2.** someone who is exceptionally proficient, often ostentatiously so.

hotspot /'hɒtspɒt/ *n.* **1.** an unpleasantly hot locality, town, etc. **2.** *Geol.* a place of high heat concentration near the earth's surface. **3.** a place where a dangerous political situation exists or may develop into revolution, war, etc. **4.** any location where a problem has emerged, as in a computer network, traffic system, etc. **5.** an area in which wi-fi is available to the general public as a wireless local area network, as in a coffee shop. Also, **hot spot**.

hot tub *n.* a tub large enough for at least one person to take a bath in, and which is equipped with devices to heat the water, aerate it, and circulate it under pressure.

hoummus /'hʊməs, 'hɒməs/ *n.* → **hummus**. Also, **hoummos**.

hound /haʊnd/ *n.* **1.** a dog of any of various breeds used in the chase and commonly hunting by scent. **2.** any dog. **3.** *Colloq.* a mean, despicable man. *–v.t.* **4.** to hunt or track with hounds, or as a hound does; pursue. **5.** to harass unceasingly. **6.** to incite (a hound, etc.) to pursuit or attack; urge on. *–phr.* **7. follow the hounds**, to follow a hunt, especially on foot. **8. ride to hounds**, to take part in fox-hunting.

houndstooth /'haʊndztuːθ/ *adj.* **1.** printed, decorated, or woven with a pattern of broken checks. *–n.* **2.** a pattern of contrasting jagged checks. Also, **hound's-tooth**.

hour /'aʊə/ *n.* **1.** a space of time equal to one 24th part of a mean solar day or civil day; 60 minutes. **2.** a short or limited period of time. **3.** a particular or appointed time: *her hour of triumph.* **4.** the present time: *the song of the hour.* **5.** (*pl.*) time spent in work, study, etc.: *after hours, office hours.* **6.** (*pl.*) customary time of going to bed and getting up: *to keep late hours.* **7.** a single period of class instruction. **8.** (*pl.*) *Eccles.* **a.** the seven stated times of the day for prayer and devotion, the canonical hours. **b.** the offices or services prescribed for these times. **c.** Also, **book of hours**. a book containing them. *–phr.* **9. one's hour**, **a.** death; the time to die. **b.** a crucial moment. **10. the small hours**, the hours immediately following midnight.

hourglass /'aʊəglas/ *n.* **1.** an instrument for measuring time, consisting of two bulbs of glass joined by a narrow passage through which a quantity of sand (or mercury) runs in just an hour. *–adj.* **2.** (of a woman's figure) resembling an hourglass; having a narrow waist.

hourly /'aʊəli/ *adj.* **1.** of, relating to, occurring, or done each successive hour. **2.** frequent; continual. *–adv.* **3.** every hour; hour by hour. **4.** frequently.

house¹ *n.* /haʊs/ (*pl.* **houses** /'haʊzəz/) **1.** a building for people to live in, usually one which is self-contained and designed for a single family. **2.** a place of lodgement, rest, etc., as of an animal. **3.** a household. **4.** a

building for any purpose: *a house of worship.* **5.** a place of entertainment; a theatre. **6.** the audience of a theatre, etc. **7.** an inn; a public house. **8.** a family regarded as consisting of ancestors and descendants: *the house of Habsburg.* **9. a.** the building in which a legislative or deliberative body meets. **b.** the body itself: *the House of Representatives.* **c.** a quorum of such a body. **10.** a firm or commercial establishment: *the house of Rothschild.* **11.** an advisory or deliberative group, especially in Church or university affairs. **12.** a residential hall for students as in some universities. **13.** a subdivision of a school, comprising children of all ages and classes, especially for extracurricular activities such as sport, charity work, etc. **14.** the management of a gambling casino or commercial establishment. **15.** *Astrology* one of the twelve divisions of the heavens. *–verb* /haʊz/ (**housed**, **housing**) *–v.t.* **16.** to put or receive into a house; provide with a house. **17.** to give shelter to; harbour; lodge. **18.** to remove from exposure; put in a safe place. *–v.i.* **19.** to take shelter; dwell. *–adj.* /haʊs/ **20.** for, or suitable for a house. **21.** of or relating to a house. *–phr.* **22. bring down the house**, to be extraordinarily well received or applauded. **23. in house**, within the confines and resources of an organisation, institution, etc.: *we'll do the project in house rather than hand it over to outside consultants.* **24. keep house**, to manage a house; look after a home. **25. keep open house**, to be very hospitable. **26. like a house on fire**, very well; with great rapidity. **27. on the house**, free; as a gift from the management. **28. put** (or **set**) **one's house in order**, to put one's affairs into good condition. **29. safe as houses**, completely safe. **30. the little house**, *Colloq.* an outside toilet. *–***houseless**, *adj.*

house² /haʊs/ *n.* **1.** a style of pop music intended for dancing, which originated in Chicago and which features electronically simulated or modified effects. *–adj.* **2.** of or relating to house. *–***housey** /'haʊsi/, *adj.*

housebreaker /'haʊsbreɪkə/ *n.* **1.** someone who breaks into and enters a house with felonious intent. **2.** someone who demolishes houses. *–***housebreaking**, *n.*

housebroken /'haʊsbroʊkən/ *adj.* (of a pet) housetrained and generally able to act in a manner suited to being indoors.

household /'haʊshoʊld/ *n.* **1.** the people of a house collectively; a family, including servants, etc.; a domestic establishment. *–adj.* **2.** of or relating to a household; domestic: *household furniture.* **3.** used for maintaining and keeping a house. **4.** of or relating to a royal or imperial household. **5.** very common. *–***householder**, *n.*

household word *n.* **1.** a byword; a well-known phrase or word. *–phr.* **2. be a household word**, (of a person) to be extremely well known.

househusband /'haʊshʌzbənd/ *n.* a husband who opts to stay at home and perform the duties which traditionally attach to the role of a housewife, such as cooking, cleaning, looking after children, etc. Also, **house husband**.

house journal *n.* an internal journal of a company, presenting its news to its employees. Also, **house magazine**.

housekeeper /'haʊskiːpə/ *n.* **1.** a paid employee who is hired to run a house, direct the domestic work, catering, etc. **2.** an employee of a hotel responsible for the cleaning staff.

houselights /'haʊslaɪts/ *pl. n.* the auditorium lights of a theatre, cinema, etc., which are lowered during a performance.

House of Representatives *n.* a chamber of parliament, in some countries (including Australia and the US) the lower legislative branch of the federal parliament, and in others (including New Zealand) the sole chamber.

houseproud /ˈhaʊspraʊd/ *adj.* overcareful about the cleaning of a house and the appearance of its contents.

house-sit /ˈhaʊs-sɪt/ *verb* (**-sat**, **-sitting**) *–v.i.* **1.** to occupy a house, apartment, etc., temporarily and without the payment of rent, for the purpose of providing security or daily maintenance during the absence of the regular occupant. *–v.t.* **2.** to occupy (a house, apartment, etc.) under such an arrangement. **–house-sitter**, *n.* **–house-sitting**, *n.*

house-train /ˈhaʊs-treɪn/ *v.t.* to train (an animal) so that it may be kept inside a house without inconvenience to other occupants; especially to train it to control its natural excretory functions. **–house-training**, *n.*

house union *n.* a union to which all employees, regardless of profession or trade, may belong by virtue of working for the one employer.

house-warming /ˈhaʊs-wɔːmɪŋ/ *n.* a party to celebrate beginning one's occupancy of a new house.

housewife *n.* (*pl.* **-wives**) **1.** /ˈhaʊswaɪf/ the woman in charge of a household, especially a wife who does no other job. **2.** /ˈhʌsəf/ Also, **hussif**. a small case for needles, thread, etc. **–housewifery** /ˈhaʊswɪfəri/, *n.*

house wine *n.* a bulk wine served by a club or restaurant, often bearing the establishment's label.

housework /ˈhaʊswɜːk/ *n.* the work of cleaning, cooking, etc., to be done in housekeeping.

housing /ˈhaʊzɪŋ/ *n.* **1.** something serving as a shelter, covering, or the like; a shelter; lodging. **2.** houses or other dwellings collectively. **3.** the act of someone who houses or puts under shelter. **4.** the provision of houses or other accommodation for the community: *the housing of immigrants.* **5.** *Machinery* a frame, plate or the like, that encloses a part of a machine, etc., such as a bearing housing.

hove /hoʊv/ *v.* a past tense and past participle of **heave**.

hovea /ˈhoʊviə/ *n.* any plant of the Australian genus *Hovea*, family Fabaceae, with clusters of small purple pea-shaped flowers.

hovel /ˈhɒvəl/ *n.* **1.** a small, mean dwelling house; a wretched hut. **2.** an open shed, as for sheltering cattle, tools, etc.

hover /ˈhɒvə, ˈhʌvə/ *v.i.* **1.** to hang fluttering or suspended in the air: *a hovering bird.* **2.** to keep lingering about; wait near at hand. **3.** to remain in an uncertain or irresolute state; waver: *hovering between life and death.* **–hoverer**, *n.* **–hoveringly**, *adv.*

hoverboard /ˈhɒvəbɔːd/ *n.* **1.** a powered personal transporter, consisting of a small wheeled platform on which the rider stands and steers by exerting pressure with the feet. **2.** *Science Fiction* a board resembling a skateboard which hovers above the ground, on which the rider balances in a standing position.

hovercraft /ˈhɒvəkrɑːft/ *n.* a vehicle able to travel in close proximity to the ground or water, on a cushion of air created by and contained within a curtain of air formed by one or more streams of air ejected downwards from the periphery of the vehicle.

how /haʊ/ *adv.* **1.** in what way or manner; by what means: *how did it happen?* **2.** to what extent, degree, etc.: *how much?* **3.** by what unit: *how do you sell these apples?* **4.** in what state or condition: *how are you?* **5.** for what reason; why. **6.** to what effect or with what meaning: *how do you mean?* **7.** what? **8.** used to add intensity: *how well I remember.* *–conj.* **9.** concerning the condition or state in which: *she wondered how she appeared to a stranger.* **10.** concerning the extent or degree to which: *I don't mind how long you take.* **11.** concerning the means or way in which: *it worried him how she got to work.* **12.** in whatever manner: *come how you like.* *–n.* **13.** a question beginning with 'how'. *–phr.* **14. and how**, *Colloq.* very much indeed; certainly. **15. how about ...**, (used to suggest an activity) what about ...:

how about a cup of tea? **16. how about that**, an exclamation of surprise, sometimes ironic, or of triumph. **17. how come?**, *Colloq.* how did this happen; why? **18. how do you do**, a polite and formal form of greeting. **19. hows and whys**, the details of the implementation of a proposal. **20. how's that?**, **a.** what is the explanation of that? **b.** Also, **howzat?**. *Cricket* an appeal by the fielding side to the umpire to declare the person batting to be out. **21. how's that for ...**, an exclamation used to highlight a specified characteristic: *how's that for stamina!* **22. how's things?**, a form of greeting. **23. how's tricks?**, a form of greeting.

however /haʊˈɛvə/ *conj.* **1.** by whatever means: *however you do it, get it done.* **2.** in whatever condition, state, or manner: *come however you like.* *–adv.* **3.** nevertheless; yet; in spite of that. **4.** to whatever extent or degree; no matter how (far, much, etc.): *I'll sing, however badly.* **5.** (used emphatically) how: *however did you manage?*

howl /haʊl/ *v.i.* **1.** to utter a loud, prolonged, mournful cry, such as that of a dog or wolf. **2.** to utter a similar cry in distress, pain, rage, etc.; wail. **3.** to make a sound like an animal howling: *the wind is howling.* *–v.t.* **4.** to utter with howls. *–n.* **5.** the cry of a dog, wolf, etc. **6.** a cry or wail, as of pain or rage. **7.** a sound like wailing: *the howl of the wind.* **8.** a loud scornful laugh or yell. *–phr.* **9. howl down**, **a.** to ridicule or abuse (a speaker). **b.** to protest (a suggestion) vociferously so that it is abandoned.

howler /ˈhaʊlə/ *n.* **1.** Also, **howling monkey**. any of the large, prehensile-tailed tropical American monkeys of the genus *Alouatta*, the males of which make a howling noise. **2.** an especially glaring and ludicrous blunder. **3.** *Elect.* a device for testing telephone apparatus which provides a suitable current by using acoustic feedback between the telephone transmitter and receiver.

howling /ˈhaʊlɪŋ/ *adj.* **1.** producing or uttering a howl. **2.** *Colloq.* enormous; very great: *his play was a howling success.* *–n.* **3.** unwanted feedback at audio frequencies in an amplifier.

howling jackass *n.* → **kookaburra** (def. 2).

hoyden /ˈhɔɪdən/ *n.* **1.** a rude or ill-bred girl; tomboy. *–adj.* **2.** hoydenish; boisterous. Also, **hoiden**. **–hoydenish**, *adj.* **–hoydenishness**, *n.*

HTML /eɪtʃ ti ɛm ˈɛl/ *n.* a computer markup language, similar to SGML, used primarily to create documents for the World Wide Web.

HTTP *n.* *Computers* hypertext transfer protocol; the protocol used for transferring files on the World Wide Web. Also, **http**.

hub /hʌb/ *n.* **1.** the central part of a wheel, as that part into which the spokes are inserted. **2.** the part in central position around which all else revolves: *the hub of the universe.* **3.** a central connection point in a computer or telecommunications network. **4.** a centre within a region for a specified activity: *a trading hub; a transport hub.*

hubbub /ˈhʌbʌb/ *n.* **1.** a loud, confused noise, as of many voices. **2.** tumult; uproar.

hubby /ˈhʌbi/ *n.* *Colloq.* husband.

hubris /ˈhjubrəs/ *n.* insolence stemming from excessive pride. Also, **hybris**. **–hubristic** /hjuˈbrɪstɪk/, *adj.* **–hubristically** /hjuˈbrɪstɪkli/, *adv.*

huckster /ˈhʌkstə/ *n.* Also, **hucksterer**. **1.** a retailer of small articles; a hawker. **2.** a street pedlar of fruit and vegetables. **3.** a cheaply mercenary person. *–v.i.* **4.** to deal in small articles or make petty bargains.

huddle /ˈhʌdl/ *v.t.* **1.** to heap or crowd together. **2.** (oft. fol. by *up*) to draw (oneself) closely together; nestle. **3.** (oft. fol. by *up*, *over*, or *together*) to do hastily and carelessly. *–v.i.* **4.** to gather or crowd together in a confused mass. *–n.* **5.** a confused heap, mass, or crowd; a jumble. **6.** confusion or disorder. *–phr.* **7. go into a**

huddle, *Colloq.* to gather round so as to confer privately. –**huddler**, *n.*

hue[1] /hju/ *n.* **1.** the property of colour by which the various regions of the spectrum are distinguished, as red, blue, etc. **2.** variety of a colour; a tint: *pale hues.*

hue[2] /hju/ *n.* outcry, as of pursuers; clamour.

huff /hʌf/ *n.* **1.** a sudden swell of anger; a fit of resentment: *to leave in a huff.* –*v.t.* **2.** *Draughts* to remove (a piece) from the board as a penalty for failing to make a compulsory capture. –*v.i.* **3.** to puff or blow. –*phr.* **4. huff and puff**, to make a display of indignation. **5. in a huff**, in a state of being offended or annoyed; chagrined.

hug /hʌg/ *v.t.* (**hugged, hugging**) **1.** to clasp tightly in the arms, especially with affection; embrace. **2.** to cling firmly or fondly to: *to hug an opinion.* **3.** to keep close to, as in sailing, horseracing or going along: *to hug the shore; to hug the rails.* –*n.* **4.** a tight clasp with the arms; a warm embrace. –*phr.* **5. hug oneself**, to congratulate oneself; be self-satisfied.

huge /hjudʒ/ *adj.* **1.** extraordinarily large in bulk, quantity, or extent: *a huge mountain.* **2.** large in scope, character, extent. –**hugeness**, *n.*

hugely /ˈhjudʒli/ *adv.* extremely; immoderately: *he laughed hugely.*

Hughie /ˈhjui/ *n. Aust., NZ Colloq.* a jocular name for the powers above used when encouraging a heavy rainfall or a good surf: *send her down; Hughie! whip 'em up, Hughie!*

hula /ˈhulə/ *n.* a traditional Hawaiian dance, with intricate arm movements, which tells a story in mime. Also, **hula-hula**.

hulk /hʌlk/ *n.* **1.** the body of an old or dismantled ship. **2.** a vessel specially built to serve as a storehouse, prison, etc., and not for sea service. **3.** a bulky or unwieldy person or mass of anything. **4.** a burnt-out or stripped vehicle, building, or the like.

hulking /ˈhʌlkɪŋ/ *adj.* bulky; heavy and clumsy. Also, **hulky**.

hull[1] /hʌl/ *n.* **1.** the husk, shell, or outer covering of a seed or fruit. **2.** the calyx of certain fruits, such as the strawberry and raspberry. **3.** any covering or envelope. –*v.t.* **4.** to remove the hull of. –**huller**, *n.*

hull[2] /hʌl/ *n.* the frame or body of a ship, exclusive of masts, yards, sails, and rigging.

hullabaloo /hʌləbəˈlu/ *n.* a clamorous noise or disturbance; an uproar.

hum /hʌm/ *verb* (**hummed, humming**) –*v.i.* **1.** to make a low, continuous, droning sound. **2.** to give forth an indistinct sound of mingled voices or noises. **3.** to utter an indistinct sound in hesitation, doubt, embarrassment, dissatisfaction, etc., or to attract attention; hem. **4.** to sing with closed lips and without words. **5.** to be busy and active: *the shop hummed all day.* –*v.t.* **6.** to sound or sing by humming. **7.** to bring, put, etc., by humming: *to hum a child to sleep.* –*n.* **8.** the act of humming, an indistinct murmur. –**hummer**, *n.*

human /ˈhjumən/ *adj.* **1.** of, relating to, or characteristic of people: *human nature; the human race.* **2.** characterised by the weaknesses and faults typical of ordinary people: *human error.* –*n.* **3.** a human being. –**humanly**, *adv.* –**humanness**, *n.* –**humankind**, *n.*

humane /hjuˈmeɪn/ *adj.* **1.** characterised by tenderness and compassion for the suffering or distressed: *humane feelings.* **2.** (of branches of learning or literature) tending to refine; civilising: *humane studies.* –**humanely**, *adv.* –**humaneness**, *n.*

human growth hormone *n.* **1.** a growth hormone produced in the pituitary gland of humans. **2.** a synthetic form of this hormone developed for use in the treatment of growth disorders or to combat the effects of old age. *Abbrev.*: HGH

human immunodeficiency virus *n.* → HIV.

humanism /ˈhjumənɪzm/ *n.* **1.** any system or mode of thought or action in which human rather than spiritual concerns predominate. **2.** devotion to or study of the humanities; literary culture.

humanist /ˈhjumənəst/ *n.* **1.** a student of human nature or affairs. **2.** someone who studies or has expert knowledge of the humanities. **3.** a classical scholar. **4.** (*sometimes upper case*) one of the scholars of the Renaissance who pursued and disseminated the study and understanding of the cultures of ancient Rome and Greece. **5.** (*sometimes upper case*) someone who favours the thought and practice of a philosophy based on humanism (def. 1). –**humanistic** /hjuməˈnɪstɪk/, *adj.*

humanitarian /hjumænəˈtɛəriən/ *adj.* **1.** having regard to the interests of all humankind; broadly philanthropic. **2.** relating to ethical or theological humanitarianism. –*n.* **3.** someone who professes ethical or theological humanitarianism. **4.** a philanthropist.

humanity /hjuˈmænəti/ *n.* (*pl.* **-ties**) **1.** the human race; humankind. **2.** the condition or quality of being human; human nature. **3.** the quality of being humane; kindness; benevolence. –*phr.* **4. the humanities**, **a.** the study of the Latin and Greek classics. **b.** the study of literature, philosophy, art, etc., as distinguished from the social and physical sciences.

human papillomavirus *n.* any of various sexually transmitted papillomaviruses in humans, some of which cause genital infections, with one obvious symptom being genital warts.

human resources *pl. n.* the human component of an organisation, institution, business, country, etc., seen as one of the elements requiring skilled management to achieve a productive output. *Abbrev.*: HR

human swine influenza *n.* → **pandemic influenza A (H1N1)**. Also, **human swine flu, swine flu**.

humble /ˈhʌmbəl/ *adj.* **1.** low in station, grade, or importance, etc.; lowly: *humble origin.* **2.** modest; meek; without pride. **3.** courteously respectful: *in my humble opinion.* –*v.t.* **4.** to lower in condition, importance, or dignity; abase. **5.** to cause to have a sense of one's own lack of insignificance or importance: *I've been humbled by the support.* **6.** to make meek: *to humble one's heart.* –**humbleness**, *n.* –**humbler**, *n.* –**humbling**, *adj.* –**humbly**, *adv.*

humble pie *phr.* **eat humble pie**, to be humiliated; forced to apologise humbly.

humbug /ˈhʌmbʌg/ *n.* **1.** a quality of falseness or deception. **2.** someone who seeks to impose deceitfully upon others; cheat; impostor. **3.** *Aboriginal English* an annoying action: *stop that humbug.* **4.** a kind of hard, peppermint sweet, usually having a striped pattern. –*verb* (**-bugged, -bugging**) –*v.t.* **5.** to impose upon by humbug or false pretence; delude. **6.** *Aboriginal English* **a.** to irritate or bother. **b.** to pester (relatives) for money to spend on drugs or alcohol. –*v.i.* **7.** to practise humbug. **8.** *Aboriginal English* to make a nuisance of oneself. –**humbugger**, *n.* –**humbugging**, *n.*

humdrum /ˈhʌmdrʌm/ *adj.* **1.** lacking variety; dull: *a humdrum existence.* –*n.* **2.** humdrum character or routine; monotony. **3.** monotonous or tedious talk. **4.** a dull boring person.

humerus /ˈhjumərəs/ *n.* (*pl.* **-meri** /-məraɪ/) **1.** (in humans) the single long bone in the arm which extends from the shoulder to the elbow. **2.** a corresponding bone in the forelimb of other animals or in the wings of birds.

humid /ˈhjuməd/ *adj.* moist or damp, with liquid or vapour: *humid air.* –**humidly**, *adv.* –**humidness**, *n.*

humidicrib /hjuˈmɪdɪkrɪb/ *n. Med.* an enclosed crib with carefully controlled temperature and humidity, in which premature babies are kept until able to survive outside.

humidifier /hjuˈmɪdəfaɪə/ n. a device for regulating air moisture content and temperature in an air-conditioned room or building.

humidity /hjuˈmɪdəti/ n. **1.** humid condition; dampness. **2.** *Meteorol.* the condition of the atmosphere with regard to its water-vapour content.

humiliate /hjuˈmɪlieɪt/ v.t. to lower the pride or self-respect of; cause a painful loss of dignity to; mortify. –**humiliating**, *adj.* –**humiliatingly**, *adv.* –**humiliation** /hjuˌmɪliˈeɪʃən/, n.

humility /hjuˈmɪləti/ n. (pl. -**ties**) the quality of being humble; modest sense of one's own significance.

hummingbird /ˈhʌmɪŋbɜːd/ n. any of numerous very small nectar-feeding American birds constituting the family Trochilidae, characterised by long, slender bills, brush-tipped tongues, and narrow wings the outer section of which can be rotated to produce a powered upstroke and thus enable hovering flight which produces a humming sound.

hummock /ˈhʌmək/ n. **1.** an elevated tract rising above the general level of a marshy region. **2.** a knoll or hillock. –**hummocky**, *adj.*

hummus /ˈhuməs, ˈhɒməs/ n. a Middle Eastern dish made from ground chickpeas and sesame paste, flavoured with lemon juice and garlic. Also, **hommus**, **hommos**.

humorous /ˈhjumərəs/ adj. **1.** characterised by humour; amusing; funny: *the humorous side of things.* **2.** having or showing the faculty of humour; droll: *a humorous person.* –**humorously**, *adv.* –**humorousness**, n.

humour /ˈhjumə/ n. **1.** the quality of being funny: *the humour of a situation.* **2.** the faculty of perceiving what is amusing or comical: *sense of humour.* **3.** the faculty of expressing the amusing or comical. **4.** speech or writing showing this faculty. **5.** mental disposition or tendency; frame of mind. **6.** capricious or freakish inclination; whim or caprice; odd traits. **7.** *Obs. Physiol.* one of the four chief bodily fluids, blood, choler or yellow bile, phlegm, and melancholy or black bile (**cardinal humours**), regarded as determining, by their relative proportions in the system, a person's physical and mental constitution. **8.** *Biol.* any animal or plant fluid, whether natural or morbid, such as the blood or lymph. –*v.t.* **9.** to comply with the wishes of; indulge: *to humour a child.* –*phr.* **10.** **out of humour**, displeased or dissatisfied; cross. Also, **humor**. –**humourless**, *adj.*

hump /hʌmp/ n. **1.** a rounded protuberance, especially on the back, as that due to abnormal curvature of the spine in humans, or that normally present in certain animals such as the camel and bison. **2.** a low, rounded rise of ground; hummock. **3.** → **road hump**. **4.** *Colloq.* a good surfing wave. **5.** *Colloq.* (*taboo*) an act of sexual intercourse. **6.** *Colloq.* (*taboo*) a person with whom one has sexual intercourse. –*v.t.* **7.** to raise (the back, etc.) in a hump. **8.** *Colloq.* **a.** to place or bear on the back or shoulder. **b.** to carry: *to hump the bluey.* **9.** *Colloq.* (*taboo*) to have sexual intercourse with. –*v.i.* **10.** to rise in a hump. **11.** *Colloq.* (*taboo*) to have sexual intercourse. –*phr.* **12.** **over the hump**, over the worst part or period of a difficult, dangerous, etc., time. **13.** **the hump**, *Colloq.* a fit of bad humour: *to get the hump.* –**humped**, *adj.*

humpy /ˈhʌmpi/ n. (pl. -**pies**) **1.** a temporary bush shelter traditionally used by Aboriginal people; gunyah. **2.** any rough or temporary dwelling; a bush hut.

humungous /hjuˈmʌŋgəs/ adj. *Colloq.* of huge size or extent. –**humungously**, *adv.*

humus /ˈhjuməs/ n. the dark organic material in soils, produced by the decomposition of vegetable or animal matter, essential to fertility and favourable moisture supply.

humvee /ˈhʌmˈvi/ n. *Mil.* an off-road vehicle designed for military use.

hunch /hʌntʃ/ v.t. **1.** to thrust out or up in a hump: *to hunch one's back.* –*v.i.* Also, **hunch up**. **2.** to walk, sit, or stand in a bent position. –*n.* **3.** a hump. **4.** *Colloq.* a premonition or suspicion. **5.** a lump or thick piece.

hundred /ˈhʌndrəd/ n. (pl. -**dreds**, *as after a numeral*, -**dred**) **1.** a cardinal number, ten times ten. **2.** a symbol for this number, as 100 or C. –*adj.* **3.** amounting to one hundred in number. –*pron.* **4.** one hundred people or things. –*phr.* **5.** **a hundred to one**, of remote possibility.

hundreds and thousands pl. n. very small, brightly coloured sugary balls, used in decorating cakes, sweets, etc.

hundredweight /ˈhʌndrədweɪt/ n. (pl. -**weights**, *as after a numeral*, -**weight**) a unit of weight in the imperial system, equal to 112 lb. approximately 50.8 kg) and, in the US, to 100 lb. (approximately 45.36 kg). *Symbol:* cwt

hung /hʌŋ/ v. **1.** past tense and past participle of **hang**. –*adj.* **2.** (of a jury) unable to agree on a verdict. **3.** (of a legislative body) with no party having a working majority: *a hung parliament.* **4.** (of a committee, etc.) unable to reach a decision.

hunger /ˈhʌŋgə/ n. **1.** the painful sensation or state of exhaustion caused by need of food: *to collapse from hunger.* **2.** a craving appetite; need for food. **3.** strong or eager desire: *hunger for praise.* –*v.i.* **4.** to feel hunger; be hungry. –*phr.* **5.** **hunger for**, to have a strong desire for.

hunger strike n. a persistent refusal to eat, as a protest against imprisonment, restraint, compulsion, etc.

hungover /hʌŋˈoʊvə/ adj. suffering the after-effects of drinking too much alcohol.

hungry /ˈhʌŋgri/ adj. (-**grier**, -**griest**) **1.** craving food; having a keen appetite. **2.** showing characteristics of hunger or meanness: *a lean and hungry look.* **3.** strongly or eagerly desirous: *she was hungry for learning.* **4.** marked by scarcity of food: *a hungry country.* –**hungrily**, *adv.* –**hungriness**, n.

hunk /hʌŋk/ n. **1.** a large piece or lump; a chunk. **2.** *Colloq.* a sexually attractive male. –**hunky**, *adj.*

hunt /hʌnt/ v.t. **1.** to chase (game or other wild animals) for the purpose of catching or killing. **2.** to scour (a region) in pursuit of game. **3.** to use or manage (a horse, etc.) in the chase. **4.** to pursue with force, hostility, etc. **5.** to search for; seek; endeavour to obtain or find. **6.** to search (a place) thoroughly. –*v.i.* **7.** to engage in the chase. **8.** (sometimes fol. by *for* or *after*) to make a search or quest. –*n.* **9.** the act of hunting game or other wild animals; the chase. **10.** a body of persons associated for the purpose of hunting; an association of hunters. **11.** a pack of hounds engaged in the chase. **12.** a district hunted with hounds. **13.** pursuit. **14.** a search. –*phr.* **15.** **hunt along**, to drive (a motor vehicle) at its maximum speed. **16.** **hunt away**, to drive (sheep) forward during mustering. **17.** **hunt down**, to pursue with intent to kill or capture. **18.** **hunt up**, to look for, especially with success: *hunt up a reference in a book.* –**hunter**, n. –**huntress**, *fem. n.*

Huntington's disease /ˈhʌntɪŋtənz dəˌziz/ n. a hereditary neurological disease, characterised by involuntary jerky movements (chorea) sometimes gradually replaced by spasms and twisting movements, impaired speech and progressive mental deterioration. Also, (*formerly*), **Huntington's chorea**.

huntsman spider /ˈhʌntsmən ˈspaɪdə/ n. any of numerous species of the family Sparassidae, especially the medium to large spiders of the genus *Isopoda*, with flattened, brown or grey, hairy bodies.

Huon pine /ˈhjuɒn ˈpaɪn/ *n.* a large coniferous tree of Tasmania, *Lagarostrobos franklinii*, which yields a high-quality pale yellow timber.

hurdle /ˈhɜːdl/ *n.* **1.** a barrier in a racetrack, to be leapt by the contestants. **2.** a difficult problem to be overcome; obstacle. **3.** a movable rectangular frame of interlaced twigs, crossed bars, or the like, as for a temporary fence. **4. the hurdles**, a race in which barriers are leapt. *–v.t.* **5.** to leap over (a hurdle, etc.) as in a race. **6.** to master (a difficulty, problem, etc.). **7.** to construct with hurdles; enclose with hurdles. *–v.i.* **8.** to leap over a hurdle or other barrier. **–hurdler**, *n.*

hurl /hɜːl/ *v.t.* **1.** to drive or throw with great force. **2.** to state with strong feelings. **–hurler**, *n.*

hurricane /ˈhʌrəkən/ *–keɪn/ *n.* **1.** a violent tropical cyclonic storm. **2.** a storm of the most intense severity. **3.** *Meteorol.* a wind of Beaufort scale force 12, i.e. with average wind speed of more than 63 knots, or more than 117 km/h. **4.** anything suggesting a violent storm. **5.** → **hurricane lamp**.

hurricane lamp *n.* **1.** a kerosene lamp the flame of which is protected by a glass chimney or other similar device. **2.** a candlestick with a chimney.

hurry /ˈhʌri/ *verb* **(-ried, -rying)** *–v.i.* **1.** to move, proceed, or act with haste, often undue haste. *–v.t.* **2.** to drive or move (someone or something) with speed, often with confused haste. **3.** (oft. fol. by *up*) to hasten; urge forwards. **4.** to force with undue haste to thoughtless action: *to be hurried into a decision. –n.* *(pl. **-ries**)* **5.** the need or desire for haste: *to be in a hurry to begin.* **6.** a hurried movement or action; haste. **–hurryingly**, *adv.*

hurt /hɜːt/ *verb* **(hurt, hurting)** *–v.t.* **1.** to cause bodily pain to or in: *the wound still hurts him.* **2.** to harm or damage (a material object, etc.) by rough use, or otherwise: *to hurt furniture.* **3.** to harm or cause mental pain to; grieve: *to hurt someone's feelings; to hurt someone's reputation. –v.i.* **4.** to cause pain (bodily or mental): *my finger still hurts.* **5.** to cause injury, damage, or harm. **6.** to suffer physical pain: *I hurt all over.* **7.** to suffer psychological pain. **8.** to suffer economic injury: *the farmers are hurting this year. –n.* **9.** a blow; bodily injury. **10.** damage or harm. **11.** wounded feelings.

hurtle /ˈhɜːtl/ *v.i.* **1.** to rush violently and noisily. **2.** to resound, as in collision or rapid motion. *–v.t.* **3.** to drive violently; fling; dash.

husband /ˈhʌzbənd/ *n.* **1.** a man joined in marriage to a woman. *–v.t.* **2.** to manage, especially with prudent economy; economise: *to husband one's resources.* **–husbandless**, *adj.*

husbandry /ˈhʌzbəndri/ *n.* **1.** the business of a farmer; agriculture; farming. **2.** careful or thrifty management; frugality; thrift. **3.** the management of domestic affairs, or of resources generally.

hush /hʌʃ/ *interj.* **1.** a command to be silent or quiet. *–v.i.* **2.** to become or be silent or quiet. *–v.t.* **3.** to make silent; silence. **4.** to suppress mention of; keep concealed. **5.** to calm or allay: *to hush someone's fears.*

hush-hush *adj. Colloq.* highly confidential.

hush money /ˈhʌʃ mʌni/ *n.* a bribe to keep silent about something.

husk /hʌsk/ *n.* **1.** the dry external covering of certain fruits or seeds, especially of an ear of maize. **2.** the enveloping or outer part of anything, especially when dry or worthless. *–v.t.* **3.** to remove the husk from. **–husker**, *n.* **–husklike**, *adj.*

husky¹ /ˈhʌski/ *adj.* **(-kier, -kiest)** **1.** *Colloq.* burly; big and strong. **2.** having a semi-whispered vocal tone; somewhat hoarse. **3.** containing or consisting of husks. *–n.* *(pl. **-kies**)* **4.** *US Colloq.* a big strong person. **–huskily**, *adv.* **–huskiness**, *n.*

husky² /ˈhʌski/ *n.* *(pl. **-kies**)* *(also upper case)* a strong dog used in a team to pull sledges over the snow.

hussy /ˈhʌsi, ˈhʌzi/ *n.* *(pl. **-sies**)* **1.** an ill-behaved girl. **2.** a lewd woman: *dressed like a hussy.*

hustings /ˈhʌstɪŋz/ *pl. n.* **1.** an electioneering platform. **2.** election proceedings.

hustle /ˈhʌsəl/ *verb* **(-tled, -tling)** *–v.i.* **1.** to work quickly with great energy. **2.** to push or force one's way. *–v.t.* **3.** to force roughly or hurriedly: *they hustled him out of the city.* **4.** to shake or push roughly. **5.** to urge to greater efforts; hurry along. *–n.* **6.** energetic activity, as in work. **7.** impolite shoving, pushing, etc. **–hustler**, *n.*

hut /hʌt/ *n.* **1.** a simple, small house such as a beach hut, bushwalker's hut. **2.** (in snow country) a large building for accommodating skiers. **3.** *Mil.* a wooden or metal structure for the temporary housing of troops. **4.** the house in which the employees on a sheep or cattle station live. **–hutlike**, *adj.*

hutch /hʌtʃ/ *n.* a coop for confining small animals: *rabbit hutch.*

hyacinth /ˈhaɪəsənθ/ *n.* **1.** any of the bulbous plants constituting the genus *Hyacinthus*, especially *H. orientalis*, widely cultivated for its spikes of fragrant, white or coloured, bell-shaped flowers. **2.** a hyacinth bulb or flower.

hyalo- a word element meaning 'glass'. Also, *(before vowels)*, **hyal-**.

hybrid /ˈhaɪbrəd/ *n.* **1.** the offspring of two animals or plants of different breeds, varieties, species, or genera. **2.** a half-breed; a mongrel. **3.** anything derived from heterogeneous sources, or composed of elements of different or incongruous kind. **4.** a word derived from elements of different languages. *–adj.* **5.** bred from two distinct races, breeds, varieties, species, or genera. **6.** composed of elements of different or incongruous kinds. **7.** (of a word) composed of elements originally drawn from different languages.

hybrid car *n.* a car which has both an electric and a petrol engine, the latter being required at higher speeds.

hybrid embryo *n.* an embryo which has a human cell nucleus inserted into an animal egg; developed to create stem cells to be used in medical treatments.

hydatid /haɪˈdætəd/ *n.* a cyst with watery contents, produced in humans and animals by a tapeworm in the larval state.

hydrangea /haɪˈdreɪndʒə/ *n.* any shrub of the genus *Hydrangea*, species of which are cultivated for their large showy white, pink, or blue flower clusters.

hydrant /ˈhaɪdrənt/ *n.* an upright pipe with a spout, nozzle, or other outlet, usually in the street, for drawing water from a main or service pipe.

hydrate /ˈhaɪdreɪt/ *Chem.* *–n.* **1.** any of a class of compounds containing chemically combined water, especially salts containing water of crystallisation. *–v.t.* **2.** to combine chemically with water. **–hydration** /haɪˈdreɪʃən/, *n.* **–hydrator**, *n.*

hydraulic /haɪˈdrɒlɪk/ *adj.* **1.** operated by or using water or other liquid. **2.** of or relating to hydraulics. **3.** hardening under water, as a cement. **–hydraulically**, *adv.*

hydraulic fracturing *n.* (in oil and gas mining) a process by which fractures are made in rock by the application under pressure of chemically treated water mixed with sand to natural or man-made openings in order to gain access to oil or gas supplies; considered by some to be associated with groundwater contamination; fracking.

hydraulic power *n.* power, as for operating machinery, transmitted by the controlled circulation of pressurised fluid, usually a mineral oil or water, to a motor which converts it into mechanical energy.

hydraulics /haɪˈdrɒlɪks/ *n.* the science that deals with the laws governing water or other liquids in motion and their applications in engineering; practical or applied hydrodynamics.

hydro-¹ a word element meaning 'water', as in *hydrogen*. Also, **hydr-**.

hydro-² *Chem.* a word element often indicating combination of hydrogen with a negative element or radical: *hydrobromic*. Also, **hydr-**.

hydrocarbon /ˌhaɪdroʊˈkabən/ *n. Chem.* any of a class of compounds containing only hydrogen and carbon, such as methane, CH_4, ethylene, C_2H_4, acetylene, C_2H_2, and benzene, C_6H_6.

hydrocephalus /ˌhaɪdroʊˈsɛfələs/ *n. Pathol.* an accumulation of serous fluid within the cranium, especially in infancy, often causing great enlargement of the skull, and compression of the brain. Also, **hydrocephaly** /ˌhaɪdroʊˈsɛfəli/. —**hydrocephalic** /ˌhaɪdroʊsəˈfælɪk/, **hydrocephalous**, *adj.*

hydrochloric acid /ˌhaɪdrəklɒrɪk ˈæsəd/ *n.* a colourless, poisonous fuming liquid formed by the solution of hydrogen chloride in water, used extensively in chemical and industrial processes; the commercial form is muriatic acid.

hydrochlorofluorocarbon /ˌhaɪdroʊklɒroʊˌfluəroʊˈkabən/ *n. Chem.* any of a class of inert compounds containing hydrogen, chlorine, fluorine, and carbon; used instead of the earlier chlorofluorocarbons as coolants in refrigerators and propellants in spray cans because, although containing chlorine, they deplete the ozone layer to a much lesser extent than chlorofluorocarbons. *Abbrev.*: HCFC

hydro-electric /ˌhaɪdroʊ-əˈlɛktrɪk/ *adj.* relating to the generation and distribution of electric energy derived from the energy of falling water. —**hydro-electricity** /ˌhaɪdroʊ-əlɛkˈtrɪsəti/, *n.*

hydrofluorocarbon /ˌhaɪdroʊfluəroʊˈkabən/ *n. Chem.* any of a class of compounds containing hydrogen, fluorine, and carbon; used instead of the earlier chlorofluorocarbons as a coolant in refrigerators and a propellant in spray cans because they do not deplete the ozone layer although some have a high global warming potential. *Abbrev.*: HFC

hydrofoil /ˈhaɪdrəfɔɪl/ *n.* **1.** one of two or more ski-like members, mounted at the ends of struts beneath a powered boat, supporting the hull above the surface of the water when a certain speed has been attained. **2.** a boat equipped with such members. **3.** ski-like members at the side of a boat, acting as stabilisers.

hydrogen /ˈhaɪdrədʒən/ *n.* a colourless, odourless, flammable gas, which combines chemically with oxygen to form water; the lightest of the known elements. *Symbol*: H; *relative atomic mass*: 1.00797; *atomic number*: 1.

hydrogenate /haɪˈdrɒdʒəneɪt/ *v.t.* to combine or treat with hydrogen: *to hydrogenate vegetable oil to fat.* —**hydrogenation** /haɪˌdrɒdʒəˈneɪʃən/, *n.*

hydrogen bomb *n.* a bomb whose potency is based on the release of nuclear energy resulting from the fusion of hydrogen isotopes in the formation of helium. It is many times more powerful than the atom bomb. Also, **fusion bomb**.

hydrogen peroxide *n.* a colourless, unstable, oily liquid, H_2O_2, the aqueous solution of which is used as an antiseptic and a bleaching agent.

hydrogen sulphide *n.* a colourless, flammable, cumulatively poisonous gas, H_2S, smelling like rotten eggs. Also, **hydrogen sulfide**.

hydrology /haɪˈdrɒlədʒi/ *n.* the science dealing with water on the land, or under the earth's surface, its properties, laws, geographical distribution, etc. —**hydrologic** /haɪdrəˈlɒdʒɪk/, **hydrological** /haɪdrəˈlɒdʒɪkəl/, *adj.* —**hydrologist**, *n.*

hydrolysis /haɪˈdrɒləsəs/ *n.* (*pl.* **-lyses** /-ləsiz/) *Chem.* chemical decomposition by which a compound is

resolved into other compounds by taking up the elements of water. —**hydrolytic** /haɪdrəˈlɪtɪk/, *adj.*

hydrophone /ˈhaɪdrəfoʊn/ *n.* **1.** an instrument using the principles of the microphone, used to detect the flow of water through a pipe. **2.** a device for locating sources of sound under water, as for detecting submarines by the noise of their engines, etc.

hydrophyte /ˈhaɪdrəfaɪt/ *n. Bot.* a plant growing in water or very moist ground. —**hydrophytic** /haɪdrəˈfɪtɪk/, *adj.*

hydroplane /ˈhaɪdrəpleɪn/ *n.* **1.** a plane surface designed to control or facilitate the movement of an aeroplane or boat on or in the water. **2.** a motorboat, with hydrofoils or a shaped bottom, designed to plane along the surface of the water at high speeds. —*v.i.* **3.** to skim over water in the manner of a hydroplane. **4.** → **aquaplane** (def. 3).

hydroponics /haɪdrəˈpɒnɪks/ *n.* the cultivation of plants by placing the roots in liquid nutrient solutions rather than in soil; soil-less growth of plants. —**hydroponic**, *adj.* —**hydroponically**, *adv.*

hydrosphere /ˈhaɪdrəsfɪə/ *n.* the water on the surface of the globe; the water of the oceans.

hydrotropic /haɪdrəˈtrɒpɪk/ *adj.* **1.** turning or tending towards moisture, as growing organs. **2.** taking a particular direction with reference to moisture.

hyena /haɪˈinə/ *n.* any of three mainly nocturnal carnivores of the family Hyaenidae, having massive jaws for crushing bones, as the **striped hyena**, *Hyaena hyaena*, of Africa and Asia, a solitary scavenger, the **brown hyena**, *H. brunnea*, of southern Africa, which scavenges and hunts small mammals and reptiles, and the **spotted hyena** or **laughing hyena**, *Crocuta crocuta*, of sub-Saharan Africa, which hunts large mammals in packs and also feeds on carrion. Also, **hyaena**.

hyeto- a word element meaning 'rain'.

hygiene /ˈhaɪdʒin/ *n.* **1.** the science which deals with the preservation of health. **2.** the practices, such as keeping oneself clean, which maintain good health. **3.** the maintenance of a required level of operational safety in various environments in relation to a specified area of possible danger: *email hygiene*; *data hygiene*. **4.** the practices which prevent the introduction of risk in day-to-day operations, as in the workplace: *industrial hygiene*. Also, **hygienics** /haɪˈdʒinɪks/. —**hygienist**, *n.*

hygienic /haɪˈdʒinɪk/ *adj.* **1.** sanitary; clean. **2.** relating to hygiene. —**hygienically**, *adv.*

hygro- a word element meaning 'wet', 'moist'. Also, (*before vowels*), **hygr-**.

hygrometer /haɪˈgrɒmətə/ *n.* an instrument for determining the humidity of the atmosphere.

hylo- a word element meaning 'wood', 'matter'.

hymen /ˈhaɪmən/ *n.* the membrane that usually partly covers the opening of the vagina until it is broken, often at first sexual intercourse.

hymn /hɪm/ *n.* **1.** a song or ode in praise or honour of God, a nation, a deity, etc. —*v.t.* **2.** to praise or celebrate in a hymn; express in a hymn.

hymnal /ˈhɪmnəl/ *n.* Also, **hymnbook**. **1.** a book of hymns for use in divine worship. —*adj.* **2.** of or relating to hymns.

hype¹ /haɪp/ *Colloq.* —*n.* **1.** an atmosphere of deliberately stimulated excitement and enthusiasm. **2.** something which deliberately stimulates such an atmosphere, such as extravagant promotion of a product, media publicity for a celebrity, etc.: *media hype*. —*v.t.* Also, **hype up**. **3.** to promote (a product) extravagantly.

hype² /haɪp/ *Colloq.* —*n.* **1.** a hypodermic needle. **2.** a drug addict. —*phr.* **3. hype up**. **a.** to stimulate; make excited. **b.** to increase the power, speed, etc., of (a car engine, etc.): *he hyped up his FJ*.

hyper- a prefix meaning 'over', and usually implying excess or exaggeration.

hyperactive /haɪpərˈæktɪv/ *adj.* active to excess; overactive. **–hyperactivity**, *n.*

hyperbola /haɪˈpɜbələ/ *n.* (*pl.* **-las**) *Geom.* a curve consisting of two distinct and similar branches, formed by the intersection of a plane with a right circular cone when the plane makes a greater angle with the base than does the generator of the cone.

hyperbole /haɪˈpɜbəli/ *n.* obvious exaggeration, for effect; an extravagant statement not intended to be taken literally. **–hyperbolism**, *n.*

hyperbolic /haɪpəˈbɒlɪk/ *adj.* **1.** of or relating to hyperbole; exaggerated. **2.** *Geom.* of or relating to a hyperbola. Also, **hyperbolical**. **–hyperbolically**, *adv.*

hyperbolic function *n.* *Maths* one of the six mathematical functions which express angles in terms of distances between points on a hyperbola; analogous to the trigonometrical ratios, they are written *sinh*, *cosh*, *tanh*, *cosech*, *sech*, *cotanh*.

hyperlink /ˈhaɪpəlɪŋk/ *Computers* *–n.* **1.** an element of a hypertext document which is connected to another document, or to another place in the same document. *–v.t.* **2.** to connect by such an element. **–hyperlinked**, *adj.* **–hyperlinking**, *n.*

hyperreality /haɪpəriˈælɪti/ *n.* a state of being in which things have an existence which simulates reality, being not distinguished from reality in the mind of the individual as, for example, in a theme park where imaginary places, people, animals, etc., are given a seemingly real existence.

hypertension /haɪpəˈtɛnʃən/ *n.* *Pathol.* **1.** elevation of the blood pressure, especially the diastolic pressure. **2.** an arterial disease of which this is the outstanding sign.

hypertext /ˈhaɪpətɛkst/ *n.* *Computers* text created in HTML which has highlighted links to other documents or other areas in the same document.

hypertext transfer protocol *n.* *Internet* the protocol used for transferring files on the World Wide Web. Also, **HTTP, http.**

hyperthermia /haɪpəˈθɜmiə/ *n.* an acute condition caused by the absorption of more heat into the body than it can dissipate, usually as a result of prolonged exposure to high temperatures, causing the temperature of the body to climb uncontrollably and leading to dehydration, dizziness, prostration, convulsions, etc., and if not treated to coma and death.

hyperventilation /ˌhaɪpəvɛntəˈleɪʃən/ *n.* *Med.* the excessive exposure of the lungs to oxygen resulting in a rapid loss of carbon dioxide from the blood; abnormally increased respiration.

hyphen /ˈhaɪfən/ *n.* a short stroke (-) used to connect the parts of a compound word or the parts of a word divided for any purpose.

hyphenate /ˈhaɪfəneɪt/ *v.t.* **1.** to join by a hyphen. **2.** to write with a hyphen. **–hyphenation** /haɪfəˈneɪʃən/, *n.*

hypno- a word element meaning 'sleep' or 'hypnosis', as in *hypnology*. Also, (*usually before vowels*), **hypn-**.

hypnosis /hɪpˈnoʊsəs/ *n.* (*pl.* **-noses** /-ˈnoʊsiz/) **1.** *Psychol.* a trance-like mental state induced in a cooperative subject by suggestion. **2.** a sleepy condition. **3.** → **hypnotism. –hypnotise, hypnotize,** *v.*

hypnotic /hɪpˈnɒtɪk/ *adj.* **1.** relating to hypnosis or hypnotism. **2.** susceptible to hypnotism, as a person. **3.** hypnotised. **4.** inducing sleep. *–n.* **5.** an agent or drug that produces sleep; a sedative. **6.** a person under the influence of hypnotism. **–hypnotically**, *adv.*

hypnotism /ˈhɪpnətɪzəm/ *n.* **1.** the science dealing with the induction of hypnosis. **2.** the induction of hypnosis. **–hypnotist**, *n.*

hypo[1] /ˈhaɪpoʊ/ *n.* sodium thiosulphate (sometimes called sodium hyposulphite), $Na_2S_2O_3.5H_2O$, a photographic fixing agent.

hypo[2] /ˈhaɪpoʊ/ *n.* *Colloq.* a hypodermic needle or injection.

hypo- a prefix meaning 'under', either in place or in degree ('less', 'less than').

hypo-allergenic /haɪpoʊ-æləˈdʒɛnɪk/ *adj.* relating to a substance having relatively low allergenic properties.

hypochondria /haɪpəˈkɒndriə/ *n.* *Psychol.* a condition characterised by depression and unfounded anxiety about one's health. Also, **hypochondriasis** /haɪpəkɒnˈdraɪəsəs/. **–hypochondriac**, *n.*, *adj.* **–hypochondriacal** /haɪpəkɒnˈdraɪəkəl/, *adj.*

hypocrisy /hɪˈpɒkrəsi/ *n.* (*pl.* **-sies**) **1.** the act of pretending to have a character or beliefs, principles, etc., that one does not possess. **2.** pretence of virtue or piety; false goodness.

hypocrite /ˈhɪpəkrɪt/ *n.* someone given to hypocrisy; someone who feigns virtue or piety; a pretender. **–hypocritical** /hɪpəˈkrɪtɪkəl/, *adj.* **–hypocritically** /hɪpəˈkrɪtɪkli/, *adv.*

hypodermic /haɪpəˈdɜmɪk/ *adj.* **1.** relating to the introduction of liquid medicine under the skin: *a hypodermic needle.* **2.** of the parts under the skin, as tissue. *–n.* **3.** a hypodermic injection or syringe. **–hypodermically**, *adv.*

hypotenuse /haɪˈpɒtənjuz/ *n.* *Geom.* the side of a right-angled triangle opposite the right angle.

hypothalamus /haɪpəˈθæləməs/ *n.* (*pl.* **-thalami**) *Anat.* the portion of the middle brain concerned with emotional expression and visceral responses.

hypothermia /haɪpəˈθɜmiə/ *n.* **1.** *Pathol.* subnormal body temperature. **2.** the artificial reduction of body temperature to slow metabolic processes, usually to facilitate heart surgery. **–hypothermal**, *adj.*

hypothesis /haɪˈpɒθəsəs/ *n.* (*pl.* **-theses** /-θəsiz/) **1.** a proposition (or set of propositions) suggested as an explanation for the occurrence of some specified group of phenomena, either asserted merely as a provisional conjecture to guide investigation (a **working hypothesis**), or accepted as highly probable in the light of established facts. **2.** *Logic* a proposition assumed as a premise in an argument. **3.** *Logic* the antecedent of a conditional proposition. **4.** a mere assumption or guess. **–hypothesise, hypothesize,** *v.*

hypothetical /haɪpəˈθɛtɪkəl/ *adj.* Also, **hypothetic.** **1.** assumed by hypothesis; supposed: *a hypothetical case.* **2.** involving or being a hypothesis: *hypothetical reasoning.* **3.** given to making hypotheses: *a hypothetical person.* **4.** *Logic* **a.** characterising propositions having the form *if A, then B*; conditional. **b.** (of a syllogism) having a premise which is a hypothetical proposition. **5.** (of a proposition) not well supported by evidence, and therefore of highly conjectural status. *–n.* **6.** a hypothetical or supposed situation: *to put up a hypothetical for debate.* **–hypothetically**, *adv.*

hysterectomy /hɪstəˈrɛktəmi/ *n.* (*pl.* **-mies**) the surgical excision of the uterus.

hysteria /hɪsˈtɪəriə/ *n.* **1.** morbid or senseless emotionalism; emotional frenzy. **2.** a psychoneurotic disorder characterised by violent emotional outbreaks, perversion of sensory and motor functions, and various morbid effects due to autosuggestion. **–hysterical**, *adj.*

hysteric /hɪsˈtɛrɪk/ *n.* **1.** (*pl.*) a fit of hysteria; hysteria. **2.** a person subject to hysteria.

hystero- a word element meaning 'uterus', as in *hysterotomy*. Also, **hyster-**.

I i

I, i /aɪ/ *n.* **1.** the ninth letter and third vowel of the English alphabet. **2.** the Roman numeral for one.

-i- an ending for the first element of many compounds, originally found in the combining forms of many Latin words, but often used in English as a connective irrespective of etymology, as in *cuneiform, Frenchify,* etc.

I /aɪ/ *pron. (personal) first person, sing., subjective (objective* **me**) **1.** used by a speaker to refer to himself or herself. **2.** (*by hypercorrection*) me: *between you and I.* –*n.* (*pl.* **I's**) **3.** Metaphysics the ego.

-ia a suffix of nouns, especially having restricted application in various fields, thus, in medicine (diseases: *malaria*), in geography (countries: *Romania*), in botany (genera: *Wisteria*), in names of Roman feasts (*Lupercalia*), in Latin or Latinising plurals (*Reptilia, bacteria*), and in collectives (*insignia, militia*).

-ial variant of **-al¹**, as in *judicial, imperial.*

iamb /ˈaɪæmb, ˈaɪæm/ *n. Prosody* a metrical foot of two syllables, a short followed by a long, or an unaccented by an accented (˘ ¯), as in *Come live with me and be my love,* which consists of four iambs. –**iambic,** *adj.*

-ian variant of **-an**, as in *amphibian, Grecian.*

-iasis a suffix of nouns denoting state or condition, especially a morbid condition or a form of disease, as in *candidiasis, psoriasis.*

-iatry a combining form meaning 'medical care', as in *psychiatry.*

ibidem /ˈɪbədɛm, ɪˈbaɪdəm/ *adv.* in the same book, chapter, page, etc.

ibis /ˈaɪbəs/ *n.* (*pl.* **ibis** *or* **ibises**) any of various wading birds of the family Threskiornithidae, of warm regions, having a long, thin, down-curved bill.

-ible variant of **-able**, occurring in words taken from the Latin, as in *credible, horrible, legible, visible,* or modelled on the Latin type as *addible* (for *addable*), *reducible.*

-ic **1.** a suffix forming adjectives from nouns or stems not used as words themselves, meaning 'relating or belonging to' (*poetic, metallic, Homeric*), found extensively in adjective nouns of a similar type (*public, magic*), and in nouns the adjectives of which end in *-ical,* (*music, critic*). **2.** *Chem.* a suffix showing that an element is present in a compound at a high valency; at least higher than when the suffix *-ous* is used.

-ical a compound suffix forming adjectives from nouns (*rhetorical*), providing synonyms to words ending in *-ic* (*poetical*), and providing an adjective with additional meanings to those in the *-ic* form (*economical*).

ice /aɪs/ *n.* **1.** the solid form of water, produced by freezing; frozen water. **2.** the frozen surface of a body of water. **3.** any substance resembling this: *camphor ice.* **4.** ice-cream. **5.** a frozen dessert made of sweetened water and fruit juice. **6.** reserve; formality. **7.** *Colloq.* a diamond or diamonds. **8.** *Colloq.* a crystallised, very pure form of methamphetamine hydrochloride which is smoked in the same way as crack cocaine. –*verb* (**iced, icing**) –*v.t.* **9.** to cover with ice. **10.** to change into ice; freeze. **11.** to cool with ice, as a drink. **12.** to refrigerate with ice. **13.** to make cold as if with ice. **14.** to apply ice to (an injury) so as to reduce swelling, bruising, etc. **15.** to cover (cakes, etc.) with icing. **16.** *Colloq.* to kill; murder. –*v.i.* **17.** to freeze. –*adj.* **18.** of ice. –*phr.* **19. break the ice,** *Colloq.* **a.** to

overcome initial formality and reserve at a social occasion (as with friendliness or humour). **b.** to be the first to undertake a particular action. **20. cut no ice,** *Colloq.* (sometimes fol. by *with*) to make no impression; be unconvincing: *his excuses cut no ice with me.* **21. ice up,** to become covered with ice. **22. on ice,** waiting or in readiness: *he kept the project on ice for some time.* **23. on thin ice,** in a risky or delicate situation. –**iceless,** *adj.*

-ice a suffix used in many nouns to indicate state or quality, as in *service, justice.*

ice age *n.* (*sometimes upper case*) the Pleistocene glacial epoch.

iceberg /ˈaɪsbɜg/ *n.* **1.** a large floating mass of ice, detached from a glacier and carried out to sea. **2.** *Colloq.* a regular winter swimmer. **3.** *Colloq.* a cold, reserved person. –*phr.* **4. tip of the iceberg,** a small part of a larger whole, usually a problem: *the leaking roof was only the tip of the iceberg.*

ice cap *n.* a mass of ice which typically feeds a number of glaciers at its edge. Also, **icecap.**

ice-cream *n.* **1.** a frozen food made of cream, rich milk, or evaporated milk, sweetened and variously flavoured. **2.** a food item consisting of ice-cream in a cone, on a stick, etc., often with flavouring, chocolate, etc.

ice hockey *n.* a form of hockey, played on an icerink by two teams of six players each, with a puck in place of a ball.

icepack /ˈaɪspæk/ *n.* **1.** a large area of floating ice, as in arctic seas. **2.** a cold compress consisting of a bag filled with crushed ice.

icepick /ˈaɪspɪk/ *n.* a pick or other tool for breaking ice.

ice sheet *n.* **1.** a broad, thick sheet of ice covering an extensive area for a long period of time. **2.** a glacier covering a large part of a continent. Also, **icesheet.**

ice shelf *n.* a thick floating platform of ice which forms where a glacier flows to a coastline and onto the ocean surface. Also, **iceshelf.**

ice skate *n.* **1.** a thin metal runner attached to the shoe, for skating on ice. **2.** a shoe fitted with such a runner.

ice-skate *v.i.* to skate on ice. –**ice-skater,** *n.*

ichthyo- a word element meaning 'fish', as in *ichthyology.* Also, (*before vowels*), **ichthy-.**

ichthyology /ɪkθiˈɒlədʒi/ *n.* the branch of zoology that deals with fishes. –**ichthyologic** /ɪkθiəˈlɒdʒɪk/, **ichthyological** /ɪkθiəˈlɒdʒɪkəl/, *adj.* –**ichthyologist,** *n.*

-ician a compound suffix especially applied to an expert in a field, as in *geometrician.*

icicle /ˈaɪsɪkəl/ *n.* a pendent tapering mass of ice formed by the freezing of dripping water. –**icicled,** *adj.*

icing /ˈaɪsɪŋ/ *n.* **1.** one of various sugared coatings or toppings for cakes, usually made from icing sugar with some combinations of fruit juice, egg white, colouring, etc. **2.** the forming of ice on the wings of a plane, rigging of a ship, etc., in conditions of extreme cold. –*phr.* **3. the icing on the cake,** the most enjoyable or advantageous aspects of a job, situation, etc.; the finishing touches.

icky /ˈɪki/ *adj.* (**-kier, -kiest**) *Colloq.* **1.** sticky; gooey. **2.** difficult to deal with; disagreeable; troublesome.

icon /ˈaɪkɒn/ *n.* **1.** *Eastern Church* a representation in painting, enamel, etc., of some sacred personage, such as Christ or a saint or angel. **2.** a sign or representation which stands for its object by virtue of a resemblance or analogy to it. **3.** a person who is seen by a community as being closest to an admired stereotype. **4.** an artefact, practice, etc., which is associated with a particular way of life so strongly that it comes to be seen as a symbol of it. **5.** *Computers* a picture on a video display unit screen representing an instruction or menu option. –**iconic**, *adj.*

icono- a word element meaning 'likeness' or 'image', as in *iconography*.

iconoclast /aɪˈkɒnəklæst/ *n.* **1.** a breaker or destroyer of images, especially those set up for religious veneration. **2.** someone who attacks cherished beliefs as based on error or superstition. –**iconoclasm**, *n.* –**iconoclastic** /aɪˌkɒnəˈklæstɪk/, *adj.* –**iconoclastically** /aɪˌkɒnəˈklæstɪkli/, *adv.*

-ics a suffix of nouns, originally plural as denoting things relating to a particular subject, but now mostly used as singular as denoting the body of matters, facts, knowledge, principles, etc., relating to a subject, and hence a science or art, as in *ethics, physics, politics, tactics*.

icy /ˈaɪsi/ *adj.* (**icier, iciest**) **1.** made of or covered with ice. **2.** resembling ice. **3.** cold: *icy wind*. –**iciness**, *n.*

id /ɪd/ *n. Psychoanalysis* the part of the psyche residing in the unconscious which is the source of instinctive energy.

-id[1] a suffix of nouns and adjectives indicating members of a zoological family, as in *cichlid*, or of some other group or division, as in *acarid, arachnid*.

-id[2] variant of **-ide**, as in *parotid*.

-id[3] a quasi-suffix common in adjectives, especially of states which appeal to the senses, as in *torrid, acid*.

ID /aɪˈdi/ *Colloq.* –*n.* **1.** documentation providing personal details, such as name, address, date of birth, etc., used to verify the identity, age, etc., of a person: *you need ID to open a bank account.* **2.** an identification of a person: *to get a positive ID.* –*v.t.* (**ID'd, ID'ing**) **3.** to identify (a person).

I'd /aɪd/ contraction of *I would* or *I had*.

-idae a suffix of the taxonomic names of families in zoology, as in *Canidae*.

-ide a noun suffix in names of chemical compounds, as in *bromide*. Also, **-id**.

idea /aɪˈdɪə/ *n.* **1.** any conception existing in the mind as the result of mental apprehension or activity. **2.** a thought, conception, or notion: *what an idea!* **3.** an impression: *a general idea of what it's like.* **4.** an opinion, view, or belief. **5.** a plan of action; an intention: *the idea of becoming an engineer.* –**idealess**, *adj.*

ideal /aɪˈdɪəl/ *n.* **1.** an idea of something at its most perfect. **2.** a standard of excellence: *to set high ideals.* **3.** a perfect example; something to be copied. **4.** an ultimate object or goal: *my ideal is to finish in six weeks.* **5.** something which exists only in idea: *an ideal of goodness.* –*adj.* **6.** perfect and seen as a standard: *ideal beauty; ideal behaviour.* **7.** seen as the best or most suitable: *that's the ideal car for us.* **8.** existing only in idea; imaginary. –**ideally**, *adv.* –**idealness**, *n.*

idealise /aɪˈdɪəlaɪz/ *v.t.* **1.** to make ideal; represent in an ideal form or character; exalt to an ideal perfection or excellence. –*v.i.* **2.** to represent something in an ideal form; imagine or form an ideal or ideals. Also, **idealize**. –**idealisation** /aɪˌdɪəlaɪˈzeɪʃən/, *n.* –**idealiser**, *n.*

idealism /aɪˈdɪəlɪzəm/ *n.* **1.** the cherishing or pursuit of ideals, as for attainment. **2.** the practice of idealising. **3.** *Philos.* **a.** any system or theory which maintains that the real is of the nature of thought, or that the object of external perception consists of ideas. **b.** the tendency to represent things in an ideal form, or as they ought to be rather than as they are, with emphasis on values. –**idealist**, *n.* –**idealistic** /aɪdɪəˈlɪstɪk/, *adj.*

ideate /aɪˈdieɪt/ *v.t.* to form in idea, thought, or imagination. –**ideation** /aɪdiˈeɪʃən/, *n.* –**ideational** /aɪdiˈeɪʃənəl/, *adj.* –**ideationally** /aɪdiˈeɪʃənli/, *adv.*

idem /ˈɪdɛm, ˈaɪdɛm/ *pron.* the same as previously given or mentioned.

identical /aɪˈdɛntɪkəl/ *adj.* **1.** (sometimes fol. by *to* or *with*) corresponding exactly in nature, appearance, manner, etc.: *this leaf is identical to that.* **2.** the very same: *I almost bought the identical dress you are wearing.* **3.** (of twins) born from the same ovum which divides into two after fertilisation –**identically**, *adv.* –**identicalness**, *n.*

identification /aɪˌdɛntəfəˈkeɪʃən/ *n.* **1.** the act of identifying. **2.** something that identifies one, such as a driver's licence, passport, etc.

identify /aɪˈdɛntəfaɪ/ *v.t.* (**-fied, -fying**) **1.** to recognise or establish as being a particular person or thing; attest or prove to be as purported or asserted: *to identify handwriting, identify the bearer of a cheque.* **2.** to serve as a means of identification for: *this card identifies the bearer as a member.* **3.** *Biol.* to determine to what group (a given specimen) belongs. **4.** *Psychol.* to make (oneself) one with another person by putting oneself in his or her place. –*phr.* **5. identify with**, **a.** to make, represent to be, or regard or treat as the same as or identical to: *to identify success with happiness.* **b.** to associate in feeling, interest, action, etc., with: *to identify with people of similar background.* –**identifiable**, *adj.* –**identifier**, *n.*

identikit /aɪˈdɛntɪkɪt/ (*from trademark*) –*n.* **1.** a set of pictures of typical facial characteristics which can be superimposed upon a frame to form a likeness, used by police to help in the identification of suspects. **2.** any picture so composed. –*adj.* **3.** relating to such a picture: *an identikit portrait.*

identity /aɪˈdɛntəti/ *n.* (*pl.* **-ties**) **1.** the condition or fact of being or remaining the same one: *the group kept its identity under different leaders.* **2.** the condition of being oneself or itself, and not another: *he doubted his own identity.* **3.** an odd, interesting or famous person; a character: *a local identity.* See **old identity.** **4.** sameness, likeness or association: *the two groups showed identity of function.* **5.** *Maths* an equation which is true for all values of its variables. –*adj.* **6.** serving to identify: *identity card.*

identity theft *n.* the appropriation of someone else's identification mechanisms, such as PINs, social security numbers, banking details, etc., to commit fraud or theft.

ideo- a word element meaning 'idea', as in *ideograph*.

ideology /aɪdiˈɒlədʒi/ *n.* (*pl.* **-gies**) **1.** the body of doctrine, myth, and symbols of a social movement, institution, class, or large group. **2.** such a body of doctrine, etc., with reference to some political and cultural plan, as that of fascism, together with the devices for putting it into operation. **3.** *Philos.* the systematic study of ideas. **4.** theorising of a visionary or unpractical nature. –**ideological** /aɪdiəˈlɒdʒəkəl/, *adj.* –**ideologist**, *n.*

id est /ɪd ˈɛst/ that is.

idio- a word element meaning 'peculiar' or 'proper to one', as in *idiosyncrasy*.

idiocy /ˈɪdiəsi/ *n.* (*pl.* **-cies**) **1.** silliness; stupidity; senselessness. **2.** *Psychiatry Obsolesc.* the condition of being an idiot; extreme degree of mental deficiency.

idiom /ˈɪdiəm/ *n.* **1.** a form of expression peculiar to a language, especially one having a significance other than its literal one. **2.** the peculiar character or genius of a language. **3.** a distinct style or character, as in music, art, etc.: *the idiom of Bach.* –**idiomatic**, *adj.*

idiosyncrasy /ˌɪdioʊˈsɪŋkrəsi/ *n.* (*pl.* **-sies**) any tendency, characteristic, mode of expression, or the like, peculiar to an individual. –**idiosyncratic** /ˌɪdiousɪŋˈkrætɪk/, *adj.* –**idiosyncratically** /ˌɪdiousɪŋˈkrætɪkli/, *adv.*

idiot /ˈɪdiət/ *n.* **1.** a very foolish or senseless person. **2.** *Psychiatry Obsolesc.* a person who is extremely mentally deficient, especially from birth. –**idiotic,** *adj.*

idiot-proof *adj.* **1.** (of a device, method, etc.) very simple, thus making errors extremely unlikely even by those who lack skill in or aptitude for its use. –*v.t.* **2.** to make secure against even careless or foolish misuse.

-idium a diminutive suffix (Latinisation of Greek *-idion* used in zoological, biological, botanical, anatomical, and chemical terms.

idle /ˈaɪdl/ *adj.* (**idler, idlest**) **1.** unemployed, or doing nothing: *idle workmen.* **2.** unoccupied, as time: *idle hours.* **3.** not in use: *idle machinery.* **4.** habitually doing nothing or avoiding work: *idle fellow.* **5.** worthless, meaningless or vain: *idle talk; idle pleasures.* **6.** unfounded: *idle fears.* **7.** futile or ineffective: *idle threats.* –*verb* (**idled, idling**) –*v.i.* **8.** to spend time doing nothing or in worthless activities. **9.** to move idly; loiter; saunter. **10.** (of an engine) to operate with the transmission disengaged at minimum speed. –*v.t.* **11.** to waste: *to idle the hours away.* –*phr.* **12. the idle rich,** people rich enough not to have to work. –**idler,** *n.* –**idleness,** *n.* –**idly,** *adv.*

idol /ˈaɪdl/ *n.* **1.** a statue, etc., worshipped as a god. **2.** *Bible* a false god, as of a heathen people. **3.** any person or thing blindly adored or revered. –**idolise, idolize,** *v.*

idolatry /aɪˈdɒlətri/ *n.* (*pl.* **-ries**) **1.** the worship of idols. **2.** excessive adoration, reverence, or devotion. –**idolater,** *n.* –**idolatrous,** *adj.*

idyll /ˈaɪdl, ˈɪdəl/ *n.* **1.** a poem or prose composition consisting of a 'little picture', usually describing pastoral scenes or events or any charmingly simple episode, appealing incident, or the like. **2.** an episode or scene of idyllic charm. Also, *US,* **idyl.** –**idyllic,** *adj.*

-ie a hypocoristic suffix used colloquially: **1.** (*with nouns*) as an endearment, or affectionately, especially with and among children: *doggie,* a dog; *littlie,* a child. **2.** (*with nouns*) as a familiar abbreviation: *budgie,* a budgerigar; *conchie,* a conscientious objector; *mozzie,* a mosquito; *goalie,* a goalkeeper. **3.** (*with adjectives*) as a nominalisation: *greenie,* a conservationist; *cheapie,* a cheap product. **4.** (*with adjectives*) as a familiar abbreviation: *indie, nudie, juvie.*

i.e. /aɪ ˈi/ that is: *apparel, i.e., clothing.*

-ier variant of **-eer,** as in *brigadier, halberdier,* etc.

-ies a word element representing the plural formation of nouns and third person singular of verbs for words ending in *-y, -ie,* and sometimes *-ey.*

if /ɪf/ *conj.* **1.** in case that; granting or supposing that; on condition that. **2.** even though. **3.** whether. –*n.* **4.** a condition; a supposition. –*phr.* **5. if only,** used to introduce a phrase expressing a wish, especially one that cannot now be fulfilled or is thought unlikely to be fulfilled: *if only I had known!; if only he would come!*

if-clause *n. Gram.* → **conditional clause.**

iftar /ˈɪftaː/ *n. Islam* a meal eaten after sunset during Ramadan.

-ify variant of **-fy,** used when the preceding stem or word element ends in a consonant, as in *intensify.*

igloo /ˈɪgluː/ *n.* (*pl.* **-loos**) a dome-shaped Inuit hut, built of blocks of hard snow.

igneous /ˈɪgniəs/ *adj.* **1.** of or relating to fire. **2.** *Geol.* formed by the action of heat, as rocks.

igneous rock *n.* rock formed from magma which has cooled and solidified either at the earth's surface (volcanic rock) or deep within the earth's crust (plutonic rock).

ignite /ɪgˈnaɪt/ *v.t.* **1.** to set on fire; kindle. –*v.i.* **2.** to take fire; begin to burn. –**ignitable, ignitible,** *adj.* –**ignitability, ignitibility** /ɪgˌnaɪtəˈbɪləti/, *n.*

ignition /ɪgˈnɪʃən/ *n.* **1.** the act of igniting. **2.** the state of being ignited. **3.** (in an internal-combustion engine) the process which ignites the fuel in the cylinder.

ignoble /ɪgˈnoʊbəl/ *adj.* **1.** of low character, aims, etc.; mean; base. **2.** of low grade or quality; inferior. –**ignobility** /ɪgnoʊˈbɪləti/, **ignobleness,** *n.* –**ignobly,** *adv.*

ignominy /ˈɪgnəməni/ *n.* (*pl.* **-nies**) **1.** disgrace; dishonour; public contempt. **2.** base quality or conduct; a cause of disgrace. –**ignominious,** *adj.*

ignoramus /ɪgnəˈreɪməs, ɪgnəˈraməs/ *n.* (*pl.* **-muses**) an ignorant person.

ignorant /ˈɪgnərənt/ *adj.* **1.** destitute of knowledge; unlearned. **2.** uninformed; unaware. **3.** due to or showing lack of knowledge: *an ignorant statement.* –**ignorance,** *n.* –**ignorantly,** *adv.*

ignore /ɪgˈnɔː/ *v.t.* **1.** to refrain from noticing or recognising: *ignore his remarks.* **2.** *US Law* (of the grand jury) to reject (a bill of indictment) as without sufficient evidence. –*phr.* **3. treat with ignore,** *Aust. Colloq.* to disregard entirely. –**ignorable,** *adj.* –**ignorer,** *n.*

iguana /ɪˈgwanə/ *n.* any of various large lizards of the family Iguanidae, especially *Iguana iguana,* of tropical America, often having spiny projections on the head and back.

ikebana /ɪkiˈbanə/ *n.* the art of Japanese flower arrangement in which flowers are displayed according to strict rules.

il-¹ variant of **in-²,** (by assimilation) before *l,* as in *illation.*

il-² variant of **in-³,** (by assimilation) before *l,* as in *illogical.*

-il variant of **-ile,** as in *civil.*

-ile a suffix of adjectives expressing capability, susceptibility, liability, aptitude, etc., as in *agile, docile, ductile, fragile, prehensile, tensile, volatile.* Also, **-il.**

-ility a compound suffix making abstract nouns from adjectives by replacing the adjective suffixes: *-il(e), -le,* as in *civility, sterility, ability.*

ilk /ɪlk/ *n.* family, class, or kind: *he and all his ilk.*

ill /ɪl/ *adj.* (**worse** *or, also for def. 1,* **iller; worst** *or, also for def. 1,* **illest**) **1.** sick or unwell. **2.** evil, wicked, or bad: *ill repute.* **3.** offensive or faulty: *ill manners.* **4.** unfriendly or hostile: *ill feeling.* **5.** unfavourable; adverse: *ill luck.* –*n.* **6.** evil. **7.** harm; injury. **8.** a disease; ailment. **9.** trouble; misfortune. –*adv.* **10.** wickedly. **11.** unsatisfactorily or poorly. **12.** in an unfriendly or hostile manner: *ill disposed.* **13.** unfavourably or unfortunately. **14.** with displeasure or offence: *to take it ill.* **15.** with trouble, difficulty, or inconvenience: *buying a new car is an expense we can ill afford.*

I'll /aɪl/ contraction of *I will* or *I shall.*

ill-advised *adj.* acting or done without due consideration; imprudent. –**ill-advisedly,** *adv.*

ill-bred *adj.* showing or due to lack of proper breeding; unmannerly; rude: *he remained serene in a houseful of ill-bred children.* –**ill-breeding,** *n.*

ill-conceived *adj.* badly thought out: *an ill-conceived strategy that backfired.*

illegal /ɪˈliːgəl/ *adj.* **1.** not legal; unauthorised. –*n.* **2.** *Colloq.* an illegal immigrant. –**illegally,** *adv.* –**illegality** /ɪliˈgæləti/, **illegalness,** *n.*

illegal immigrant *n.* an immigrant to a country who is deemed to be illegal because they have arrived without prior authority from the government of that country, as in the form of a visa, or because they have stayed beyond the time allowed by their visa.

illegible /ɪˈlɛdʒəbəl/ *adj.* not legible; impossible or hard to read or decipher: *this letter is completely illegible.* –**illegibility** /ɪˌlɛdʒəˈbɪləti/, **illegibleness,** *n.* –**illegibly,** *adv.*

illegitimate /ɪləˈdʒɪtəmət/ *adj.* **1.** against the law: *an illegitimate act.* **2.** born outside marriage: *an illegitimate* *child.* **3.** not allowed; irregular; not in good usage: *an illegitimate use of words.* –*n.* **4.** an illegitimate person; bastard. **5.** (formerly) a free settler (as opposed to a *legitimate*). –**illegitimacy,** *n.* –**illegitimately,** *adv.*

ill-fated *adj.* **1.** destined to an unhappy fate: *an ill-fated person.* **2.** bringing bad fortune.

ill-gotten *adj.* acquired by evil means: *ill-gotten gains.*

ill health *n.* an unsound or disordered condition of health. Also, **ill-health.**

illicit /ɪˈlɪsət/ *adj.* not permitted or authorised; unlicensed; unlawful. –**illicitly,** *adv.* –**illicitness,** *n.*

illiterate /ɪˈlɪtərət, ɪˈlɪtrət/ *adj.* **1.** unable to read and write. **2.** lacking education. **3.** showing lack of culture. –*n.* **4.** an illiterate person. –**illiterately,** *adv.* –**illiteracy, illiterateness,** *n.*

ill-mannered *adj.* having bad manners; impolite; rude. –**ill-manneredly,** *adv.*

ill-natured /ˈɪl-neɪtʃəd/ *adj.* **1.** having or showing an unkindly or unpleasant disposition. **2.** cross; peevish. –**ill-naturedly,** *adv.* –**ill-naturedness,** *n.*

illness /ˈɪlnəs/ *n.* a state of bad health; sickness.

illogical /ɪˈlɒdʒɪkəl/ *adj.* not logical; contrary to or disregardful of the rules of logic; unreasonable. –**illogicality** /ɪˌlɒdʒɪˈkælətɪ/, **illogicalness,** *n.* –**illogically,** *adv.*

ill-treat *v.t.* to treat badly; maltreat. –**ill-treatment,** *n.*

illuminate /əˈluməneɪt, ɪ-, -ˈljum-/ *v.t.* **1.** to supply with light; light up: *to illuminate a building.* **2.** to decorate with lights. **3.** to throw light on (a subject), make clear or lucid. **4.** to enlighten (someone), as with knowledge. **5.** to decorate (a letter, page, manuscript, etc.) with colour, gold, etc. –*v.i.* **6.** to display lights, as in celebration. –**illumination,** *n.* –**illuminator,** *n.* –**illuminating, illuminative,** *adj.* –**illuminatingly,** *adv.*

ill-use /ɪl-ˈjuz/ *v.t.* to treat badly, unjustly, or cruelly.

illusion /ɪˈluʒən/ *n.* **1.** something that deceives by producing a false impression. **2.** the act of deceiving; deception; delusion; mockery. **3.** the state of being deceived, or an instance of this; a false impression or belief. **4.** *Psychol.* normal misperception of some object or situation (e.g. optical illusions). Compare **delusion** (def. 4), **hallucination.** –**illusionary,** *adj.*

illusory /ɪˈluzərɪ/ *adj.* **1.** causing illusion; deceptive. **2.** being an illusion; unreal. Also, **illusive.** –**illusorily,** *adv.* –**illusoriness,** *n.*

illustrate /ˈɪləstreɪt/ *v.t.* **1.** to make clear or intelligible, as by examples; exemplify. **2.** to furnish (a book, etc.) with drawings or pictorial representations intended for elucidation or adornment. –**illustrated,** *adj.* –**illustration,** *n.* –**illustrator,** *n.* –**illustrative** /ˈɪləstreɪtɪv, ɪˈlʌstrətɪv/, *adj.*

illustrious /ɪˈlʌstriəs/ *adj.* **1.** highly distinguished; renowned; famous. **2.** glorious, as deeds, etc. –**illustriously,** *adv.* –**illustriousness,** *n.*

ill will *n.* hostile or unfriendly feeling. –**ill-willed,** *adj.*

im-[1] variant of **in-**[2] used before *b, m,* and *p,* as in *imbrute, immingle.*

im-[2] variant of **in-**[3] used before *b, m,* and *p,* as in *immoral, imparity, imperishable.*

im-[3] variant of **in-**[1], before *b, m,* and *p,* as in *imbed, impearl.* Also, **em-.**

I'm /aɪm/ contraction of *I am.*

image /ˈɪmɪdʒ/ *n.* **1.** a likeness of a person, animal, or thing. **2.** the optical counterpart or appearance of an object, produced by a mirror, lens, etc. **3.** a mental picture; idea; conception. **4.** the impression a public figure or group works to create for the public. **5.** form; appearance. **6.** Also, **spitting image.** a counterpart or copy: *the child is the image of its mother.* **7.** a symbol or emblem. **8.** a type or embodiment. **9.** a description of something in speech or writing. **10.** *Rhetoric* a figure of speech, especially a metaphor or a simile. –*v.t.* (**imaged, imaging**) **11.** to make an image of.

imagery /ˈɪmɪdʒrɪ/ *n.* (*pl.* **-geries** /-dʒəri/) **1.** the formation of images, figures, or likenesses of things, or such images collectively: *a dream's dim imagery.* **2.** figurative description or illustration; rhetorical images collectively.

imaginary /ɪˈmædʒənəri, -ənri/, *Orig. US* /-ənɛri/ *adj.* existing only in the imagination or fancy; not real; fancied: *an imaginary illness.* –**imaginarily,** *adv.* –**imaginariness,** *n.*

imaginary number *n.* the square root of a negative number; thus $\sqrt{-1}$ is an imaginary number, denoted by i, and so $i^2 = -1$.

imagination /ɪˌmædʒəˈneɪʃən/ *n.* **1.** the action of imagining, or of forming mental images or concepts of what is not actually present to the senses. **2.** the faculty of forming such images or concepts. **3.** *Psychol.* the power of reproducing images stored in the memory under the suggestion of associated images (**reproductive imagination**), or of recombining former experiences in the creation of new images different from any known by experience (**productive imagination** or **creative imagination**). –**imaginational,** *adj.*

imaginative /ɪˈmædʒənətɪv/ *adj.* **1.** characterised by or bearing evidence of imagination: *an imaginative tale.* **2.** relating to or concerned with imagination: *the imaginative faculty.* **3.** given to imagining, as persons. –**imaginatively,** *adv.* –**imaginativeness,** *n.*

imagine /ɪˈmædʒən/ *v.t.* (**-ined, -ining**) **1.** to form a mental image of (something not actually present to the senses). **2.** to think, believe, or fancy. **3.** to assume or suppose. **4.** to conjecture or guess: *I cannot imagine what you mean.* –**imaginable,** *adj.* –**imagined,** *adj.* –**imagining,** *n.* –**imaginer,** *n.*

imago /ɪˈmeɪɡoʊ/ *n.* (*pl.* **imagos** *or* **imagines** /ɪˈmeɪdʒəniz/) **1.** *Entomology* an adult insect. **2.** *Psychoanalysis* an idealised concept of a loved one, formed in childhood and retained uncorrected in adult life.

imam /ɪˈmam/ *n.* (in Islam) a Muslim religious leader or chief.

imbalance /ɪmˈbæləns/ *n.* the state or condition of lacking balance.

imbecile /ˈɪmbəsil, -saɪl/ *n.* **1.** a silly person; fool. **2.** *Psychiatry Obsolesc.* a person of defective mentality above the grade of idiocy. –**imbecility,** *n.* –**imbecilely,** *adv.* –**imbecilic** /ɪmbəˈsɪlɪk/, *adj.*

imbibe /ɪmˈbaɪb/ *v.t.* **1.** to drink in, or drink. **2.** to take or receive into the mind, as knowledge, ideas, etc. –*v.i.* **3.** to drink; absorb liquid or moisture. –**imbiber,** *n.* –**imbibition,** *n.*

imbroglio /ɪmˈbroʊlioʊ/ *n.* (*pl.* **-lios**) an intricate and perplexing state of affairs; a complicated or difficult situation.

imbue /ɪmˈbju/ *v.t.* (**-bued, -buing**) **1.** to impregnate or inspire, as with feelings, opinions, etc. **2.** to saturate with moisture, impregnate with colour, etc. –**imbuement,** *n.*

imitate /ˈɪmɪteɪt/ *v.t.* **1.** to follow or endeavour to follow in action or manner. **2.** to mimic or counterfeit. **3.** to make a copy of; reproduce closely. **4.** to have or assume the appearance of; simulate. –**imitable,** *adj.* –**imitation,** *n.* –**imitative,** *adj.* –**imitator,** *n.*

immaculate /ɪˈmækjulət, -kjə-/ *adj.* **1.** free from spot or stain; spotlessly clean, as linen. **2.** free from moral blemish or impurity; pure, or undefiled. **3.** free from fault or flaw; free from errors, as a text. –**immaculacy, immaculateness,** *n.* –**immaculately,** *adv.*

immanent /ˈɪmənənt/ *adj.* remaining within; indwelling; inherent. –**immanence, immanency,** *n.* –**immanently,** *adv.*

immaterial /ɪməˈtɪəriəl/ *adj.* **1.** of no essential consequence; unimportant. **2.** not material; incorporeal; spiritual.

–**immaterially**, *adv.* –**immaterialness, immateriality** /ˌɪmətɪəriˈæləti/, *n.*

immature /ɪməˈtjuə, -tjʊə/ *adj.* not mature, ripe, developed, or perfected. –**immaturely**, *adv.* –**immaturity, immatureness**, *n.*

immeasurable /ɪˈmɛʒərəbəl/ *adj.* incapable of being measured; limitless. –**immeasurably**, *adv.*

immediate /ɪˈmidiət/ *adj.* **1.** happening or done without delay; instant: *an immediate reply.* **2.** relating to the present time or moment: *our immediate plans.* **3.** with no time coming between; next in order: *the immediate future.* **4.** with no object or space coming between; nearest or next: *in the immediate vicinity.* **5.** with no medium or agent coming between; direct: *an immediate cause.* –**immediately**, *adv.* –**immediacy**, *n.*

immemorial /ɪməˈmɔriəl/ *adj.* extending back beyond memory, record, or knowledge: *from time immemorial.* –**immemorially**, *adv.*

immense /ɪˈmɛns/ *adj.* **1.** vast; huge; very great: *an immense territory.* **2.** immeasurable; boundless. **3.** *Colloq.* very good or fine. –**immensely**, *adv.* –**immensity, immenseness**, *n.*

immerse /ɪˈmɜs/ *v.t.* **1.** to plunge into or place under a liquid; dip; sink. **2.** to involve deeply; absorb. –**immersed**, *adj.* –**immersive**, *adj.* –**immersion**, *n.*

immigrate /ˈɪməgreɪt/ *v.i.* **1.** to pass or come into a new habitat or place of residence. **2.** to come into a country of which one is not a native for the purpose of permanent residence. –**immigration** /ɪməˈgreɪʃən/, *n.* –**immigrant**, *n.*, *adj.*

imminent /ˈɪmənənt/ *adj.* **1.** likely to occur at any moment; impending: *war is imminent.* **2.** projecting or leaning forward; overhanging. –**imminence**, *n.* –**imminently**, *adv.*

immobile /ɪˈmoʊbaɪl/ *adj.* **1.** not mobile; immovable. **2.** that does not move; motionless. –**immobilise, immobilize**, *v.*

immoderate /ɪˈmɒdərət, -drət/ *adj.* not moderate; exceeding just or reasonable limits; excessive; extreme. –**immoderately**, *adv.* –**immoderateness, immoderation** /ɪˌmɒdəˈreɪʃən/, *n.*

immodest /ɪˈmɒdəst/ *adj.* **1.** not modest in conduct, utterance, etc.; indecent; shameless. **2.** not modest in assertion or pretension; forward; impudent. –**immodestly**, *adv.* –**immodesty**, *n.*

immolate /ˈɪməleɪt/ *v.t.* **1.** to sacrifice. **2.** to kill as a sacrificial victim; offer in sacrifice. –*phr.* **3. immolate oneself**, to practise self-immolation. –**immolator**, *n.* –**immolation** /ɪməˈleɪʃən/, *n.*

immoral /ɪˈmɒrəl/ *adj.* not moral; not conforming to the moral law; not conforming to accepted patterns of conduct. –**immorality** /ɪməˈræləti/, *n.* –**immorally**, *adv.*

immortal /ɪˈmɔtl/ *adj.* **1.** undying: *immortal spirit.* **2.** celebrated in undying memory; imperishable: *immortal fame*; *immortal name*; *immortal songs.* **3.** lasting, perpetual, or constant: *an immortal memory.* –*n.* **4.** someone of lasting fame, as Shakespeare, Bach, etc. **5.** (*usu. pl.*) one of the gods of Greek and Roman mythology. –**immortalise, immortalize**, *v.* –**immortality**, *n.* –**immortally**, *adv.*

immovable /ɪˈmuvəbəl/ *adj.* **1.** incapable of being moved; fixed; stationary. **2.** not subject to change; unalterable. **3.** incapable of being affected with feeling; emotionless: *an immovable heart*; *an immovable face.* **4.** incapable of being moved from one's purpose, opinion, etc.; steadfast; unyielding. Also, **immoveable**. –**immovability** /ɪˌmuvəˈbɪləti/, **immovableness**, *n.* –**immovably**, *adv.*

immune /əˈmjun, ɪ-/ *adj.* **1.** protected from a disease or the like, as by inoculation. **2.** unaffected by: *immune to criticism.* **3.** exempt: *immune from taxation.* –**immunise, immunize**, *v.* –**immunisation**, *n.* –**immunity**, *n.*

immune system *n.* a complex network of interacting systems within the body which protect it from pathogens and other foreign substances, and which can destroy infected, malignant, or broken-down cells.

immunodeficiency /ɪmjənoʊdəˈfɪʃənsi/ *n. Med.* an impairment in the autoimmune system caused especially by a lack of white blood cells and resulting in reduced immunity to infection. –**immunodeficient**, *adj.*

immunology /ɪmjuˈnɒlədʒi/ *n.* the branch of medical science that deals with immunity from disease and the production of such immunity. –**immunologic** /ɪmjunəˈlɒdʒɪk/, **immunological** /ɪˌmjunəˈlɒdʒɪkəl/, *adj.* –**immunologist**, *n.*

immure /ɪˈmjuə/ *v.t.* **1.** to enclose within walls. **2.** to shut in; confine. **3.** to imprison. **4.** to build into or entomb in a wall. –**immurement**, *n.*

immutable /ɪˈmjutəbəl/ *adj.* not mutable; unchangeable; unalterable; changeless. –**immutability** /ɪˌmjutəˈbɪləti/, **immutableness**, *n.* –**immutably**, *adv.*

imp /ɪmp/ *n.* **1.** a little devil or demon; an evil spirit. **2.** a mischievous child. –**impish**, *adj.*

impact *n.* /ˈɪmpækt/ **1.** the striking of one body against another. **2.** an impinging: *the impact of light on the eye.* **3.** forcible contact or impinging: *the tremendous impact of the shot.* **4.** influence or effect exerted by a new idea, concept, ideology, etc. –*v.t.* /ɪmˈpækt/ **5.** to drive or press closely or firmly into something; pack in. –*phr.* **6. impact on**, to have an effect on: *this law impacts on all of us.* **7. make an impact on**, to impress. –**impactful**, *adj.*

impacted /ɪmˈpæktəd/ *adj.* **1.** wedged in. **2.** *Dentistry* (of a tooth) incapable of growing out or erupting, and remaining within the jawbone. **3.** driven together; tightly packed.

impair /ɪmˈpɛə/ *v.t.* **1.** to make worse. **2.** to alter for the worse; to damage: *the blow impaired his hearing.* –**impaired**, *adj.* –**impairer**, *n.* –**impairment**, *n.*

-impaired an adjectival suffix denoting that the human function specified or implied is damaged or reduced in capacity, as in *sight-impaired, mentally-impaired.*

impala /ɪmˈpalə/ *n.* (*pl.* **impalas** *or, especially collectively,* **impala**) an antelope, *Aepyceros melampus*, from southern and eastern Africa, which can leap up to nine metres.

impale /ɪmˈpeɪl/ *v.t.* **1.** to fix upon a sharpened stake or the like. **2.** to pierce with a sharpened stake thrust up through the body, as for torture or punishment. **3.** to fix upon, or pierce through with, anything pointed. –**impalement**, *n.*

impart /ɪmˈpat/ *v.t.* **1.** to make known, tell, or relate: *to impart a secret.* **2.** to give, bestow, or communicate. –**impartation** /ɪmpaˈteɪʃən/, **impartment**, *n.* –**imparter**, *n.*

impartial /ɪmˈpaʃəl/ *adj.* not partial; unbiased; just. –**impartiality** /ɪmpaʃiˈæləti/, **impartialness**, *n.* –**impartially**, *adv.*

impassable /ɪmˈpasəbəl/ *adj.* not passable; that cannot be passed over, through, or along: *muddy, impassable roads.* –**impassability** /ɪmˌpasəˈbɪləti/, **impassableness**, *n.* –**impassably**, *adv.*

impasse /ˈɪmpas/ *n.* a position from which there is no escape.

impassive /ɪmˈpæsɪv/ *adj.* **1.** without emotion; apathetic; unmoved. **2.** calm; serene. **3.** unconscious. **4.** not subject to suffering. –**impassively**, *adv.* –**impassiveness, impassivity** /ɪmpæˈsɪvəti/, *n.*

impatient /ɪmˈpeɪʃənt/ *adj.* **1.** not patient; not bearing pain, opposition, etc., with composure. **2.** indicating lack of patience: *an impatient answer.* **3.** restless in desire or expectation; eagerly desirous (to do something). –*phr.* **4. impatient of**, intolerant of: *impatient of any interruptions.* –**impatience**, *n.* –**impatiently**, *adv.*

impeach /ɪmˈpitʃ/ *v.t.* **1.** to challenge the credibility of: *to impeach a witness.* **2.** to call (a person, especially an elected official) before a competent tribunal to answer an accusation in respect of treason or some other grave criminal offence, with a view to their removal from office. **–impeachable**, *adj.* **–impeachment**, *n.* **–impeacher**, *n.*

impeccable /ɪmˈpɛkəbəl/ *adj.* **1.** faultless or irreproachable: *impeccable manners.* **2.** not liable to sin; exempt from the possibility of doing wrong. **–impeccability** /ɪmˌpɛkəˈbɪləti/, *n.* **–impeccably**, *adv.*

impecunious /ɪmpəˈkjuniəs/ *adj.* having no money; penniless; poor. **–impecuniously**, *adv.* **–impecuniousness, impecuniosity** /ˌɪmpəkjuniˈɒsəti/, *n.*

impedance /ɪmˈpidns/ *n. Elect.* the apparent resistance, or total opposition to current of an alternating current circuit, consisting of two components, reactance and true or ohmic resistance.

impede /ɪmˈpid/ *v.t.* (**-peded, -peding**) to retard in movement or progress by means of obstacles or hindrances; obstruct; hinder. **–impeder**, *n.* **–impedingly**, *adv.*

impediment /ɪmˈpɛdəmənt/ *n.* **1.** some physical defect, especially a speech disorder: *an impediment in speech.* **2.** obstruction or hindrance; obstacle. **–impedimental** /ɪmˌpɛdəˈmɛntl/, **impedimentary** /ɪmˌpɛdəˈmɛntəri/, *adj.*

impel /ɪmˈpɛl/ *v.t.* (**-pelled, -pelling**) to drive or urge forward; press on; incite or constrain to action in any way. **–impeller**, *n.* **–impellent**, *adj.*

impend /ɪmˈpɛnd/ *v.i.* **1.** to be imminent; be near at hand. **2.** to threaten. *–phr.* **3. impend over,** *Archaic* to hang or be suspended over; overhang. **–impending, impendent**, *adj.*

impenetrable /ɪmˈpɛnətrəbəl/ *adj.* **1.** not penetrable; that cannot be penetrated, pierced, or entered. **2.** inaccessible to ideas, influences, etc. **3.** incapable of being comprehended; unfathomable: *an impenetrable mystery.* **–impenetrability** /ɪmˌpɛnətrəˈbɪləti/, **impenetrableness**, *n.* **–impenetrably**, *adv.*

imperative /ɪmˈpɛrətɪv/ *adj.* **1.** not to be avoided or evaded: *an imperative duty.* **2.** being or expressing a command; commanding. **3.** *Gram.* designating or relating to the verb mood specialised for use in command, requests, and the like, or a verb inflected for this mode, as *listen! go! run!* etc. *–n.* **4.** a command. **5.** anything which must be done, had, etc.: *cost-cutting was made an imperative.* **–imperatival** /ɪmˌpɛrəˈtaɪvəl/, *adj.* **–imperatively**, *adv.* **–imperativeness**, *n.*

imperceptible /ɪmpəˈsɛptəbəl/ *adj.* **1.** very slight, gradual, or subtle: *imperceptible gradations.* **2.** not perceptible; not affecting the perceptive faculties. **–imperceptibility** /ˌɪmpəsɛptəˈbɪləti/, **imperceptibleness**, *n.* **–imperceptibly**, *adv.*

imperfect /ɪmˈpɜfəkt/ *adj.* **1.** characterised by or subject to defects. **2.** not perfect; lacking completeness: *imperfect vision.* **3.** *Gram.* designating a tense which denotes action going on but not completed, especially in the past. For example, in the sentence *He was building the wall when it happened, was building* is in the imperfect tense. Compare **perfect, pluperfect. –imperfectly**, *adv.* **–imperfection** /ɪmpəˈfɛkʃən/, *n.* **–imperfectness**, *n.*

imperial /ɪmˈpɪəriəl/ *adj.* **1.** of or relating to an empire, emperor or empress. **2.** typical of the power of a ruling state over those countries, etc., under its control. **3.** having the power of an emperor or ruler. **4.** having a commanding or domineering quality, manner, or appearance; imperious. **5.** very fine or grand; magnificent. **6.** (of weights and measures) of the system legally established in Britain. **7.** (*oft. upper case*) of or relating to the British Empire. *–n.* **8.** a small, pointed beard growing beneath the lower lip. **–imperially**, *adv.* **–imperialness**, *n.*

imperialism /ɪmˈpɪəriəlɪzəm/ *n.* **1. a.** the policy of extending the rule or authority of an empire or nation over

foreign countries, or of acquiring and holding colonies and dependencies. **b. cultural imperialism**, the extending of the cultural patterns of one country over many others. **2.** the policy of extending the rule or authority of an empire or nation over foreign countries, or of acquiring and holding colonies and dependencies. **3.** advocacy of imperial interests. **4.** the policy of so uniting the separate parts of an empire with separate governments as to secure for certain purposes a single state. **5.** imperial government. **–imperialist**, *n.*, *adj.* **–imperialistic** /ɪmˌpɪəriəˈlɪstɪk/, *adj.* **–imperialistically** /ɪmˌpɪəriəˈlɪstɪkli/, *adv.*

imperial system *n.* a system of non-metric weights and measures established in Great Britain in 1824, previously used throughout the British Empire and Commonwealth, including Australia, and still used for some measures in Britain and elsewhere.

imperil /ɪmˈpɛrəl/ *v.t.* (**-rilled** *or, Chiefly US,* **riled, -rilling** *or, Chiefly US,* **-riling**) to put in peril; endanger. **–imperilment**, *n.*

imperious /ɪmˈpɪəriəs/ *adj.* **1.** domineering, dictatorial, or overbearing: *an imperious tyrant, imperious temper.* **2.** urgent; imperative: *imperious need.* **–imperiously**, *adv.* **–imperiousness**, *n.*

impermeable /ɪmˈpɜmiəbəl/ *adj.* **1.** not permeable; impassable. **2.** (of substances) not permitting the passage of a fluid through the pores, interstices, etc. **–impermeability** /ɪmˌpɜmiəˈbɪləti/, **impermeableness**, *n.* **–impermeably**, *adv.*

impersonal /ɪmˈpɜsənəl/ *adj.* **1.** not personal; without personal reference or connection: *an impersonal remark.* **2.** not exhibiting a warmth of feeling flowing from a personal involvement or interest: *an impersonal greeting.* **3.** *Gram.* **a.** (of a verb) having only third person singular forms, rarely if ever accompanied by an expressed subject, as Latin *pluit* (it is raining), or accompanied regularly by a non-significant subject word, as English *it is raining.* **b.** (of a pronoun) indefinite, as French *on* (one). **–impersonally**, *adv.* **–impersonality** /ɪmˌpɜsəˈnæləti/, *n.*

impersonate /ɪmˈpɜsəneɪt/ *v.t.* **1.** to assume the character of; pretend to be. **2.** to represent in personal or bodily form; personify; typify. **3.** to act (a part), especially on the stage. *–adj.* **4.** embodied in a person; invested with personality. **–impersonation** /ɪmˌpɜsəˈneɪʃən/, *n.* **–impersonator**, *n.*

impertinent /ɪmˈpɜtənənt/ *adj.* **1.** intrusive or presumptuous, as persons or their actions: *an impertinent boy.* **2.** not pertinent or relevant; irrelevant: *any impertinent detail.* **3.** inappropriate or incongruous. **4.** trivial, silly, or absurd. **–impertinence**, *n.* **–impertinently**, *adv.*

imperturbable /ɪmpəˈtɜbəbəl/ *adj.* incapable of being perturbed or agitated; not easily excited; calm: *imperturbable composure.* **–imperturbability** /ˌɪmpətɜbəˈbɪləti/, **imperturbableness**, *n.* **–imperturbably**, *adv.*

impervious /ɪmˈpɜviəs/ *adj.* **1.** (sometimes fol. by *to*) not pervious; impermeable: *impervious to water.* **2.** (sometimes fol. by *to*) impenetrable: *impervious to reason.* **3.** not disposed to be influenced or affected. Also, **imperviable. –imperviously**, *adv.* **–imperviousness**, *n.*

impetigo /ɪmpəˈtaɪɡoʊ/ *n. Pathol.* a contagious skin disease, especially of children, marked by a superficial pustular eruption, particularly on the face. **–impetiginous** /ɪmpəˈtɪdʒənəs/, *adj.*

impetuous /ɪmˈpɛtʃuəs/ *adj.* acting with or characterised by a sudden or rash energy: *an impetuous girl.* **–impetuosity** /ɪmˌpɛtʃuˈɒsəti/, **impetuousness**, *n.* **–impetuously**, *adv.*

impetus /ˈɪmpətəs/ *n.* (*pl.* **-tuses**) **1.** moving force; impulse; stimulus: *a fresh impetus.* **2.** *Physics* the force with which a moving body tends to maintain its velocity and overcome resistance; energy of motion.

impinge /ɪm'pɪndʒ/ *v.i.* (**-pinged, -pinging**) **1.** to strike or dash (*on, upon,* or *against*): *rays of light impinging on the eye.* –*phr.* **2. impinge on,** to have an effect on. **3. impinge on** (or **upon**), to encroach or infringe on. –**impingent,** *adj.* –**impingement,** *n.*

impious /'ɪmpiəs, ɪm'paɪəs/ *adj.* **1.** not pious; lacking reverence for God; ungodly. **2.** not reverent towards parents; undutiful. –**impiously,** *adv.* –**impiety, impiousness,** *n.*

implacable /ɪm'plækəbəl/ *adj.* not placable; not to be appeased or pacified; inexorable: *an implacable enemy.* –**implacability** /ɪm,plækə'bɪləti/, **implacableness,** *n.* –**implacably,** *adv.*

implant *v.t.* /ɪm'plænt, -'plɑnt/ **1.** to instil or inculcate: *to implant sound principles.* **2.** to plant in something; infix: *implant living tissue.* –*n.* /'ɪmplænt, -plɑnt/ **3.** *Med.* **a.** tissue implanted into the body by grafting. **b.** a small tube containing a radioactive substance, such as radium, surgically implanted in tissue for the treatment of tumours, cancer, etc. –**implantation** /ɪmplæn'teɪʃən/, *n.* –**implanter,** *n.*

implausible /ɪm'plɔzəbəl/ *adj.* not plausible; not having the appearance of truth or credibility. –**implausibility** /ɪm,plɔzə'bɪləti/, *n.* –**implausibly,** *adv.*

implement *n.* /'ɪmpləmənt/ **1.** an instrument, tool, or utensil: *agricultural implements.* **2.** a means; agent. –*v.t.* /'ɪmpləmənt/ **3.** to put (a plan, proposal, etc.) into effect. –**implemental** /ɪmplə'mɛntl/, *adj.* –**implementation** /ɪmpləmɛn'teɪʃən/, *n.*

implicate /'ɪmpləkeɪt/ *v.t.* **1.** to involve as being concerned in a matter, affair, condition, etc.: *to be implicated in a crime.* **2.** to imply as a necessary circumstance, or as something to be inferred or understood. **3.** to affect, or cause to be affected. **4.** to fold or twist together; intertwine; interlace: *implicated leaves.* –**implicative,** *adj.*

implication /ɪmplə'keɪʃən/ *n.* **1.** something implied or suggested as naturally to be understood without being actually stated. **2.** the state of being involved in some matter: *implication in a conspiracy.* –**implicational,** *adj.* –**implicationally,** *adv.*

implicit /ɪm'plɪsət/ *adj.* **1.** (of belief, confidence, obedience, etc.) unquestioning, unreserved, or absolute. **2.** implied, rather than expressly stated: *an implicit consent.* –*phr.* **3. implicit in,** virtually contained in. –**implicitly,** *adv.* –**implicitness,** *n.*

implode /ɪm'ploʊd/ *v.i.* to burst inwards (opposed to *explode*). –**implosion,** *n.*

implore /ɪm'plɔ/ *v.t.* to call upon in urgent or piteous supplication, as for aid or mercy; beseech; entreat: *they implored him to go.* –**imploratory,** *adj.* –**imploringly,** *adv.*

imply /ɪm'plaɪ/ *v.t.* (**-plied, -plying**) **1.** to involve as a necessary circumstance: *speech implies a speaker.* **2.** (of words) to signify or mean. **3.** to indicate or suggest, as something naturally to be inferred, without express statement.

impolite /ɪmpə'laɪt/ *adj.* not polite or courteous; uncivil; rude. –**impolitely,** *adv.* –**impoliteness,** *n.*

impolitic /ɪm'pɒlətɪk/ *adj.* inexpedient; injudicious. –**impoliticly,** *adv.* –**impoliticness,** *n.*

imponderable /ɪm'pɒndərəbəl, -drəbəl/ *adj.* not ponderable; that cannot be weighed or assessed. –**imponderability** /ɪm,pɒndərə'bɪləti/, **imponderableness,** *n.* –**imponderably,** *adv.*

import *v.t.* /ɪm'pɔt, 'ɪmpɔt/ **1.** to bring in from a foreign country, as goods, etc., for sale, use, processing, or to sell again to another country. **2.** to make known or express, as a meaning with words, actions, etc. –*n.* /'ɪmpɔt/ **3.** something that is brought in from abroad; an imported commodity or article. **4.** the act of importing or bringing in, as of goods from abroad. **5.** meaning; implication; purport. **6.** importance; consequence.

–**importable,** *adj.* –**importation** /ɪmpɔ'teɪʃən/, *n.* –**importability** /ɪm,pɔtə'bɪləti/, *n.* –**importer,** *n.* –**imported,** *adj.*

important /ɪm'pɔtnt/ *adj.* **1.** of much significance or consequence: *an important event.* **2.** prominent: *an important part.* **3.** of considerable influence or authority, as a person, position, etc. **4.** pompous. –*phr.* **5. important to,** mattering much regarding: *details important to a fair decision.* –**importance,** *n.* –**importantly,** *adv.*

importune /ɪm'pɔtʃun, ɪmpɔ'tjun/ *v.t.* **1.** to beset with solicitations; beg urgently or persistently. **2.** to beg for (something) urgently or persistently. –**importunate,** *adj.* –**importunely,** *adv.* –**importunity** /ɪmpɔ'tjunəti/, *n.* –**importuner,** *n.*

impose /ɪm'poʊz/ *v.t.* **1.** to lay on or set as something to be paid, put up with, obeyed, fulfilled, etc.: *to impose taxes.* **2.** to push or force (oneself, one's company, etc.) upon others. **3.** to pass off dishonestly or deceptively. –*v.i.* **4.** to make a mark on the mind. **5.** to push or force oneself or one's needs: *to impose upon someone's kindness.* –**imposition** /ɪmpə'zɪʃən/, *n.* –**imposable,** *adj.* –**imposer,** *n.*

imposing /ɪm'poʊzɪŋ/ *adj.* making an impression on the mind, as by great size, stately appearance, etc. –**imposingly,** *adv.* –**imposingness,** *n.*

impossible /ɪm'pɒsəbəl/ *adj.* **1.** not possible; that cannot be, exist, or happen. **2.** not able to be done or effected: *it is impossible for my son to carry me.* **3.** not able to be true. **4.** not to be done, put up with, etc.: *an impossible situation.* **5.** hopelessly unsuitable; objectionable: *an impossible person.* –**impossibly,** *adv.* –**impossibility,** *n.*

impost /'ɪmpɒst/ *n.* **1.** a tax, tribute, or duty. **2.** imposition. **3.** a customs duty.

impostor /ɪm'pɒstə/ *n.* **1.** someone who imposes fraudulently upon others. **2.** someone who practises deception under an assumed character or name. –**imposture,** *n.*

impotent /'ɪmpətənt/ *adj.* **1.** not potent; lacking power or ability. **2.** utterly unable (to do something). **3.** without force or effectiveness. **4.** lacking bodily strength, or physically helpless, as an aged person or a cripple. **5.** (of a male) wholly lacking in sexual power. –**impotence, impotency,** *n.* –**impotently,** *adv.*

impound /ɪm'paʊnd/ *v.t.* **1.** to shut up in a pound, as a stray animal. **2.** to confine within an enclosure or within limits: *water impounded in a reservoir.* **3.** to seize, take, or appropriate summarily. **4.** to seize (a document, evidence, etc.) and retain in custody of the law. –**impoundable,** *adj.* –**impoundment, impoundage,** *n.* –**impounder,** *n.*

impoverish /ɪm'pɒvərɪʃ, -vrɪʃ/ *v.t.* **1.** to reduce to poverty: *a country impoverished by war.* **2.** to make poor in quality, productiveness, etc.; exhaust the strength or richness of: *to impoverish the soil.* –**impoverisher,** *n.* –**impoverishment,** *n.*

impracticable /ɪm'præktɪkəbəl/ *adj.* **1.** not practicable; that cannot be put into practice with the available means: *an impracticable plan.* **2.** unsuitable for practical use or purposes, as a device, material, etc. **3.** (of ground, places, etc.) impassable. –**impracticability** /ɪm,præktɪkə'bɪləti/, **impracticableness,** *n.* –**impracticably,** *adv.*

impractical /ɪm'præktɪkəl/ *adj.* not practical. –**impracticality** /ɪm,præktə'kæləti/, **impracticalness,** *n.* –**impractically,** *adv.*

imprecate /'ɪmprəkeɪt/ *v.t.* **1.** call down or invoke (especially evil or curses), as upon a person. –*v.i.* **2.** curse; swear. –**imprecation,** *n.* –**imprecator,** *n.* –**imprecatory** /'ɪmprəkeɪtəri, ɪmprə'keɪtəri/, *adj.*

imprecise /ɪmprə'saɪs/ *adj.* not precise; ill-defined. –**imprecisely,** *adv.* –**impreciseness, imprecision,** *n.*

impregnable /ɪmˈprɛgnəbəl/ *adj.* strong enough to resist attack; not to be taken by force: *an impregnable fort.* –**impregnability** /ɪmˌprɛgnəˈbɪləti/, *n.* –**impregnably**, *adv.*

impregnate /ˈɪmprɛgneɪt/ *v.t.* **1.** to make pregnant; get with child or young. **2.** to fertilise. **3.** to charge with something infused or permeating throughout; saturate. **4.** to fill the interstices of with a substance. –**impregnation** /ɪmprɛgˈneɪʃən/, *n.* –**impregnator**, *n.*

impresario /ɪmprəˈsarioʊ/ *n.* (*pl.* **-rios**) **1.** the organiser or manager of an opera, ballet, or theatre company or orchestra. **2.** a personal manager, teacher, or trainer of concert artists.

impress *v.t.* /ɪmˈprɛs/ **1.** to affect deeply or strongly in mind or feelings, especially favourably; influence in opinion. **2.** to urge, as something to be remembered or done. **3.** to press (a thing) into or on something. **4.** to produce (a mark, figure, etc.) by pressure; stamp; imprint. **5.** to subject to, or mark by, pressure with something. –*n.* /ˈɪmprɛs/ **6.** a mark made by or as by pressure; stamp; imprint. –*phr.* **7. impress on** (or **upon**), to fix deeply or firmly in the mind or memory of (someone), as ideas, facts, etc.: *I impressed the seriousness of his position upon him.* –**impresser**, *n.*

impression /ɪmˈprɛʃən/ *n.* **1.** a strong effect produced on the mind, feelings, etc. **2.** the first effect upon the mind in outward or inward sensation. **3.** an idea, belief, etc., that is often unclear. **4.** a mark, indentation, figure, etc., produced by pressure. **5.** *Printing, etc.* **a.** the process or result of printing from type, plates, etc. **b.** a printed copy from type, a plate, etc. **6.** a mould taken in plastic materials, plaster of Paris, etc. **7.** imitation, especially for entertainment, of the habits of some person or type. –**impressionable**, *adj.*

impressionism /ɪmˈprɛʃənɪzəm/ *n.* **1.** a style of painting concerned with the analysis of tone and colour and with the effects of light on surfaces, and whose adherents painted landscapes from life, catching the impression of light by applying paint in small, bright dabs of colour. **2.** a musical or literary style intended to convey an effect or overall impression of a subject. –**impressionist**, *n.* –**impressionistic**, *adj.*

impressive /ɪmˈprɛsɪv/ *adj.* such as to impress the mind; arousing solemn feelings: *an impressive ceremony.* –**impressively**, *adv.* –**impressiveness**, *n.*

imprint *n.* /ˈɪmprɪnt/ **1.** a mark made by pressure; a figure impressed or printed on something. **2.** any impression or impressed effect. **3.** *Bibliography* information printed at the foot or back of the titlepage of a book indicating the name of the publisher, usually supplemented with the place and date of publication. **4. a.** the printer's name and address as indicated on any printed matter. **b.** a name, title, colophon, or other designation by which all or a specific range of books are identified as to the publisher. –*v.t.* /ɪmˈprɪnt/ **5.** to impress (a quality, character, or distinguishing mark). **6.** to fix firmly on the mind, memory, etc. –**imprinter**, *n.* –**imprinting**, *n.*

imprison /ɪmˈprɪzən/ *v.t.* **1.** to put into or confine in a prison; detain in custody. **2.** to shut up as if in a prison; hold in restraint. –**imprisonment**, *n.*

impro /ˈɪmproʊ/ *n.* improvisation, especially in theatre or film, as in creating unscripted dialogue, or in music, as in composing or performing on the spur of the moment. Also, **improv**.

improbable /ɪmˈprɒbəbəl/ *adj.* not probable; unlikely to be true or to happen. –**improbability** /ɪmˌprɒbəˈbɪləti/, *n.* –**improbably**, *adv.*

impromptu /ɪmˈprɒmptju/ *adj.* **1.** made or done without previous preparation: *an impromptu address.* **2.** suddenly or hastily prepared, made, etc.: *an impromptu dinner.*

improper /ɪmˈprɒpə/ *adj.* **1.** not proper; not strictly belonging, applicable, or right: *an improper use for*

a thing. **2.** not in accordance with propriety of behaviour, manners, etc.: *improper conduct.* –**improperly**, *adv.* –**improperness**, *n.*

impropriety /ɪmprəˈpraɪəti/ *n.* (*pl.* **-ties**) **1.** the quality of being improper; incorrectness. **2.** inappropriateness. **3.** unseemliness.

improve *v.t.* /ɪmˈpruv/ **1.** to bring into a more desirable or excellent condition: *to improve one's health.* **2.** to make (land) more profitable or valuable by enclosure, cultivation, etc.; increase the value of (property) by betterments, as buildings. –*v.i.* /ɪmˈpruv/ **3.** to increase in value, excellence, etc.; become better: *the situation is improving.* –*phr.* **4.** /ɪmˈpruv/ **improve on** (or **upon**), to make improvements in; do better than: *to improve on one's earlier work.* **5.** /ˈɪmpruv/ **on the improve**, *Colloq.* getting better. –**improvable**, *adj.* –**improvability** /ɪmˌpruvəˈbɪləti/, **improvableness**, *n.* –**improvement**, *n.*

improvise /ˈɪmprəvaɪz/ *v.t.* **1.** to prepare or provide offhand or hastily; extemporise. **2.** to construct without having access to the material or components normally thought of as necessary. **3.** to compose (verse, music, etc.) on the spur of the moment. **4.** *Jazz* to perform a solo part extemporaneously on the basis of an established melody and rhythm. –*v.i.* **5.** to compose, utter, or execute anything extemporaneously: *without proper equipment we had to improvise.* –**improvisation** /ɪmprəvaɪˈzeɪʃən/, *n.* –**improviser**, *n.*

imprudent /ɪmˈprudnt/ *adj.* not prudent; lacking prudence or discretion. –**imprudence**, *n.* –**imprudently**, *adv.*

impudent /ˈɪmpjudnt, -pjə-/ *adj.* characterised by a shameless boldness, assurance, or effrontery: *impudent behaviour.* –**impudently**, *adv.* –**impudence**, *n.*

impugn /ɪmˈpjun/ *v.t.* to assail by words or arguments, as statements, motives, veracity, etc.; call in question; challenge as false. –**impugnable**, *adj.* –**impugnation** /ɪmpʌgˈneɪʃən/, **impugnment**, *n.* –**impugner**, *n.*

impulse /ˈɪmpʌls/ *n.* **1.** the inciting influence of a particular feeling, mental state, etc.: *to act under the impulse of pity.* **2.** sudden, involuntary inclination prompting to action, or a particular instance of it: *to be swayed by impulse.* **3.** an impelling action or force, driving onwards or inducing motion. **4.** the effect of an impelling force; motion induced; impetus given. **5.** *Physiol.* a stimulus conveyed by the nervous system, muscle fibres, etc., either exciting or limiting organic functioning. –**impulsion**, *n.*

impulsive /ɪmˈpʌlsɪv/ *adj.* **1.** actuated or swayed by emotional or involuntary impulses: *an impulsive child.* **2.** having the power or effect of impelling; characterised by impulsion: *impulsive forces.* –**impulsively**, *adv.* –**impulsiveness**, **impulsivity**, *n.*

impunity /ɪmˈpjunəti/ *n.* exemption from punishment or ill consequences.

impure /ɪmˈpjuə/ *adj.* **1.** not pure; mixed with extraneous matter, especially of an inferior or contaminating kind: *impure water.* **2.** modified by admixture, as colour. **3.** mixed or combined with something else: *an impure style of architecture.* **4.** not morally pure; unchaste: *impure language.* –**impurity**, **impureness**, *n.* –**impurely**, *adv.*

imputation credit *n.* a credit to a person owning shares for the tax that has already been paid by the issuing company on their dividends. Also, **franking credit**.

impute /ɪmˈpjut/ *v.t.* **1.** to attribute (something discreditable) to a person. **2.** to attribute or ascribe. **3.** *Law* to charge. –**imputation** /ɪmpjuˈteɪʃən/, *n.* –**imputative**, *adj.*

in /ɪn/ *prep.* a particle expressing: **1.** inclusion within space or limits, a whole, material or immaterial surroundings, etc.: *in the city; in the army; in politics.* **2.** inclusion within, or occurrence during the course of or at the expiry of, a period or limit of time: *in ancient times; to do a task in an hour; return in ten minutes.* **3.** situation, condition, occupation, action, manner, relation, means, etc.: *in darkness*; *in sickness*; *in service*; *in crossing the street*; *in confidence*; *in French*; *dressed in white.* **4.** object or purpose: *in honour of the event.* **5.** motion or direction from without to a point within, or transition from one state to another: *to put in operation*; *break in two.* **6.** (of livestock) pregnant with: *the mare's in foal again.* –*adv.* **7.** in or into some place, position, state, relation, etc. **8.** on the inside, or within. **9.** towards a town or centre of population: *the drover started in before noon.* –*adj.* **10.** in one's house or office. **11.** in office or power. **12.** (in a game) within a specified area: *the ball was in.* **13.** in possession or occupancy. **14.** having the turn to play, in a game. **15.** that is or gets in; internal; inward; incoming; inbound. **16.** *Colloq.* in favour; on friendly terms: *he's in with the managing director.* **17.** in fashion: *Mexican jewellery is in this year.* **18.** in season: *strawberries are in now.* –*n.* **19.** influence; pull; connection: *he has an in with the management – he married a director.* **20.** (*pl.*) those who are in, as the political party in power. –*phr.* **21. be in for it,** *Colloq.* to be about to be reprimanded or punished. **22. be in it,** to be part of a project or venture. **23. be in like Flynn,** *Aust. Colloq.* to seize an opportunity, especially a sexual one, with impetuous enthusiasm. **24. have it in one,** to have the ability (to do something). **25. in for, a.** about to undergo (especially something boring or disagreeable). **b.** entered for. **c.** involved to the limit of. **26. in it,** of advantage; profitable: *what's in it for me?* **27. in it up to one's neck,** *Colloq.* in serious trouble. **28. in on,** having a share in or a part of, especially something secret, or known to just a few people. **29. in place,** (of a program, policy, enterprise, etc.) operating or functional. **30. ins and outs, a.** nooks or recesses; windings and turnings. **b.** intricacies; details. **31. in that,** for the reason that. **32. nothing in it,** (in a competitive situation) no difference in performance, abilities, etc., between the contestants. **33. the in thing,** *Colloq.* the latest fashion or craze. **34. well in, a.** *Horseracing* (of a horse) given a light handicap. **b.** comfortably off. **35. well in with,** on good terms with.

in-[1] a prefix representing English *in*, as in *income*, *indwelling*, *inland*, but used also as a verb-formative with transitive, intensive, or sometimes little apparent force, as in *intrust*, *inweave*, etc. It often assumes the same forms as **in-**[2], as **en-**[1], **em-**[1], and **im-**[3].

in-[2] a prefix of Latin origin meaning primarily 'in', but used also as a verb-formative with the same force as **in-**[1], as in *incarcerate*, *incantation*. Compare **em-**[1], **en-**[1]. Also, **il-, im-, ir-**.

in-[3] a prefix of Latin origin corresponding to English *un-*, having a negative or privative force, freely used as an English formative, especially of adjectives and their derivatives and of nouns, as in *inattention*, *indefensible*, *inexpensive*, *inorganic*, *invariable*. This prefix assumes the same phonetic forms as **in-**[2], as in *impartial*, *immeasurable*, *illiterate*, *irregular*, etc. Also, **il-, im-, ir-**.

-in[1] a suffix used in adjectives of Greek or Latin origin meaning 'relating to' and (in nouns thence derived) also imitated in English, as in *coffin*, *cousin*, *lupin*, etc.; and occurring unfelt in abstract nouns formed as nouns in Latin, as *ruin*.

-in[2] a noun suffix used in chemical and mineralogical nomenclature without any formal significance, though it is usually restricted to certain neutral compounds, glycerides, glucosides, and proteins as *albumin*, *butyrin*. In some compounds, as *glycerine*, the spelling *-ine* is also used, although an attempt is made to restrict *-ine* to basic compounds.

-in[3] the second part of a compound, indicating a communal session of the activity named, as *sit-in*, *sleep-in*, *teach-in*.

inability /ɪnəˈbɪləti/ *n.* lack of ability; lack of power, capacity, or means.

inaccessible /ɪnækˈsɛsəbəl/ *adj.* not accessible; unapproachable. –**inaccessibility**, *n.* –**inaccessibly**, *adv.*

inaccurate /ɪnˈækjərət/ *adj.* not accurate. –**inaccuracy**, **inaccurateness**, *n.* –**inaccurately**, *adv.*

inactive /ɪnˈæktɪv/ *adj.* not active; inert. –**inactivity**, *n.*

inadequate /ɪnˈædəkwət/ *adj.* not adequate. –**inadequacy**, **inadequateness**, *n.* –**inadequately**, *adv.*

inadvertent /ɪnədˈvɜtnt/ *adj.* **1.** not attentive; heedless. **2.** characterised by lack of attention, as actions, etc. **3.** unintentional: *an inadvertent insult.* –**inadvertently**, *adv.*

inalienable /ɪnˈeɪliənəbəl/ *adj.* not alienable; that cannot be transferred to another: *inalienable rights.* –**inalienability** /ɪnˌeɪliənəˈbɪləti/, *n.* –**inalienably**, *adv.*

inane /ɪnˈeɪn/ *adj.* lacking sense or ideas; silly: *inane questions.* –**inanity** /ɪnˈænəti/, *n.* –**inanely**, *adv.*

inanimate /ɪnˈænəmət/ *adj.* **1.** not animate; lifeless. **2.** spiritless; sluggish; dull. –**inanimately**, *adv.* –**inanimateness**, *n.*

in-app *adj.* within the one app: *in-app purchases.*

inappropriate /ɪnəˈproʊpriət/ *adj.* not appropriate. –**inappropriately**, *adv.*

inarguable /ɪnˈagjuəbəl/ *adj.* → **unarguable.** –**inarguably**, *adv.*

inarticulate /ɪnaˈtɪkjələt/ *adj.* **1.** not articulate; not uttered or emitted with expressive or intelligible modulations: *inarticulate sounds.* **2.** unable to use articulate speech: *inarticulate with rage.* **3.** habitually unable to express oneself clearly and fluently in speech. **4.** *Anat., Zool.* not jointed; having no articulation or joint. –**inarticulately**, *adv.*

inasmuch as /ɪnəzˈmʌtʃ əz/ *conj.* **1.** in view of the fact that; seeing that; since. **2.** in so far as; to such a degree as. Also, **in as much as.**

inaugurate /ɪnˈɔgjəreɪt/ *v.t.* **1.** to make a formal beginning of; initiate; commence; begin. **2.** to induct into office with formal ceremonies; install. –**inaugural**, *adj.* –**inauguration** /ɪnˌɔgjəˈreɪʃən/, *n.* –**inaugurator**, *n.*

inauspicious /ɪnɔˈspɪʃəs/ *adj.* not auspicious; ill-omened; unfavourable; unlucky. –**inauspiciously**, *adv.* –**inauspiciousness**, *n.*

inborn /ˈɪnbɔn/ *adj.* implanted by nature; innate.

inbox /ˈɪnbɒks/ *n. Computers* a folder for receiving incoming emails.

inbreed /ɪnˈbrid/ *v.t.* (**-bred, -breeding**) to breed (animals) repeatedly within the same strain. –**inbred**, *adj.*

incalculable /ɪnˈkælkjuləbəl, -kjə-/ *adj.* **1.** that cannot be calculated; beyond calculation. **2.** that cannot be forecast. –**incalculability** /ɪnˌkælkjuləˈbɪləti, -kjə-/, **incalculableness**, *n.* –**incalculably**, *adv.*

in camera *adj.* **1.** *Law* (of a case) heard by a judge in his or her private room or in court with the public excluded. –*adv.* **2.** in private; in secret: *the meeting was held in camera.*

incandescence /ɪnkænˈdɛsəns/ *n.* the state of a body caused by approximately white heat, when it may be used as a source of artificial light.

incandescent /ɪnkænˈdɛsənt/ *adj.* **1.** (of light, etc.) produced by incandescence. **2.** glowing or white with heat. **3.** intensely bright; brilliant. –**incandescently**, *adv.*

incantation /ɪnkænˈteɪʃən/ *n.* **1.** the chanting or uttering of words purporting to have magical power. **2.** the formula used; a spell or charm.

incapable /ɪnˈkeɪpəbəl/ *adj.* **1.** not capable. **2.** without ordinary capability or ability; incompetent: *incapable workers.* –*phr.* **3. incapable of, a.** not having the capacity or power for (a specified act or function). **b.** not open to the influence of; not susceptible to or admitting of: *incapable of exact measurement.* **c.** without qualification for, especially legal qualification: *incapable of* *holding public office.* **—incapability** /ɪnˌkeɪpəˈbɪləti/, **incapableness**, *n.* **—incapably**, *adv.*

incapacitate /ɪnkəˈpæsəteɪt/ *v.t.* to deprive of capacity; make incapable or unfit; disqualify. **—incapacitation** /ɪnkəˌpæsəˈteɪʃən/, *n.*

incapacity /ɪnkəˈpæsəti/ *n.* lack of capacity; incapability.

incarcerate /ɪnˈkasəreɪt/ *v.t.* to imprison; confine. **—incarceration** /ɪnˌkasəˈreɪʃən/, *n.* **—incarcerator**, *n.*

incarnate *adj.* /ɪnˈkanət, -neɪt/ **1.** embodied in flesh; invested with a bodily, especially a human, form: *a devil incarnate.* **2.** personified or typified, as a quality or idea: *chivalry incarnate.* *—v.t.* /ɪnˈkaneɪt/ **3.** to be the embodiment or type of. **—incarnation**, *n.*

incendiary /ɪnˈsɛndʒəri/ *adj.* **1.** used or made for setting property on fire: *incendiary bombs.* **2.** of or relating to the criminal setting on fire of property. **3.** likely to cause trouble, discontent, etc.; inflammatory: *incendiary speeches.* *—n.* (*pl.* **-aries**) **4.** someone who unlawfully sets fire to buildings; arsonist. **5.** *Mil.* a shell, bomb, etc., containing phosphorus or similar material producing great heat. **6.** someone who stirs up trouble, discontent, etc.; an agitator. **—incendiarism**, *n.*

incense[1] /ˈɪnsɛns/ *n.* **1.** an aromatic gum or other substance producing a sweet smell when burnt, used especially in religious ceremonies. **2.** the perfume or smoke arising from such a substance when burnt.

incense[2] /ɪnˈsɛns/ *v.t.* (**-censed, -censing**) to inflame with wrath; make angry; enrage. **—incensement**, *n.*

incentive /ɪnˈsɛntɪv/ *n.* **1.** something that incites to action, etc. **2.** an inducement such as extra money, better conditions, etc., offered to employees to encourage better work. *—adj.* **3.** inciting, as to action; stimulating; provocative. **4.** of or relating to extra money, benefits, etc., given to employees, to encourage greater output, or output of higher quality.

inception /ɪnˈsɛpʃən/ *n.* beginning; start.

incessant /ɪnˈsɛsənt/ *adj.* continuing without interruption: *an incessant noise.* **—incessancy, incessantness**, *n.* **—incessantly**, *adv.*

incest /ˈɪnsɛst/ *n.* sexual intercourse between persons closely related by blood. **—incestuous**, *adj.*

inch /ɪntʃ/ *n.* **1.** a unit of length in the imperial system, $\frac{1}{12}$ foot or 25.4×10^{-3} m (25.4 mm). *Symbol:* " *Abbrev.:* in **2.** a very small amount of anything. *—v.i.* **3.** to move by inches or small degrees. *—v.t.* **4.** to move (someone or something) by inches or small degrees. *—phr.* **5. by inches, a.** by a narrow margin: *he escaped death by inches.* **b.** Also, **inch by inch.** by degrees; very gradually. **6. every inch,** in every respect: *every inch a king.* **7. within an inch of,** almost; very near: *she came within an inch of being knocked down by a car.*

inchoate /ˈɪnkoʊeɪt/ *adj.* **1.** just begun; incipient. **2.** immature; rudimentary. **3.** lacking organisation; unformed. **—inchoately**, *adv.* **—inchoateness**, *n.*

incidence /ˈɪnsədəns/ *n.* **1.** the range of occurrence or influence of a thing, or the extent of its effects: *the incidence of a disease.* **2.** the falling, or direction or manner of falling, of a ray of light, etc., on a surface. **3.** the fact or the manner of being incident.

incident /ˈɪnsədənt/ *n.* **1.** an occurrence or event. **2.** a distinct piece of action, or an episode, as in a story or play. **3.** something that occurs casually in connection with something else. **4.** something relating or attaching to something else. **5. a.** an occurrence, such as a clash between troops of countries whose relations are already strained, which is liable to have grave consequences. **b.** a disturbance, especially one of a serious nature such as a riot or rebellion, about which precise information is lacking. *—adj.* **6.** conjoined or attaching, especially as subordinate to a principal thing. **7.** falling or striking on something. *—phr.* **8. incident to, a.** likely or apt to happen as a result of. **b.** naturally related to or connected with: *hardships incident to the life of an explorer.*

incidental /ɪnsəˈdɛntl/ *adj.* **1.** happening or likely to happen in fortuitous or subordinate conjunction with something else. **2.** incurred casually and in addition to the regular or main amount: *incidental expenses.* *—n.* **3.** (*pl.*) minor expenses. *—phr.* **4. incidental to,** liable to happen in connection with; naturally appertaining to. **—incidentally**, *adv.*

incidental exercise *n.* exercise that is built into the routine of one's daily life, such as walking up and down stairs rather than taking the lift, cleaning the house rather than employing a cleaner, etc.

incinerate /ɪnˈsɪnəreɪt/ *v.t.* to reduce to ashes; cremate. **—incineration** /ɪnˌsɪnəˈreɪʃn/, *n.*

incinerator /ɪnˈsɪnəreɪtə/ *n.* a furnace or apparatus for incinerating.

incipient /ɪnˈsɪpiənt/ *adj.* beginning to exist or appear; in an initial stage. **—incipience, incipiency**, *n.* **—incipiently**, *adv.*

incise /ɪnˈsaɪz/ *v.t.* to cut into; cut marks, etc., upon. **—incised**, *adj.*

incision /ɪnˈsɪʒən/ *n.* **1.** a cut, gash, or notch. **2.** the act of incising.

incisive /ɪnˈsaɪsɪv/ *adj.* **1.** penetrating, trenchant, or sharp: *an incisive tone of voice.* **2.** adapted for cutting: *the incisive teeth.* **—incisively**, *adv.* **—incisiveness**, *n.*

incisor /ɪnˈsaɪzə/ *n.* a tooth in the anterior part of the jaw adapted for cutting.

incite /ɪnˈsaɪt/ *v.t.* to urge on; stimulate or prompt to action. **—incitement**, *n.* **—inciter**, *n.*

inclement /ɪnˈklɛmənt/ *adj.* (of the weather, etc.) not clement; severe or harsh. **—inclemency**, *n.* **—inclemently**, *adv.*

incline *v.i.* /ɪnˈklaɪn/ **1.** to have a mental tendency; be disposed. **2.** to deviate from the vertical or horizontal; slant. **3.** to tend, in a physical sense; approximate: *the leaves incline to a blue.* **4.** to tend in course or character. **5.** to lean; bend. *—v.t.* /ɪnˈklaɪn/ **6.** to bow (the head, etc.). **7.** to cause to lean or bend in a particular direction. **8.** to turn towards (to listen favourably): *incline one's ear.* *—n.* /ˈɪnklaɪn, ɪnˈklaɪn/ **9.** an inclined surface; a slope. *—phr.* **10. incline someone to,** to dispose a person in mind, habit, etc., to. **—inclination**, *n.* **—incliner**, *n.*

include /ɪnˈklud/ *v.t.* **1.** to contain, embrace, or comprise, as a whole does parts or any part or element. **2.** to place in an aggregate, class, category, or the like. **3.** to contain as a subordinate element; involve as a factor. **—inclusion**, *n.* **—included**, *adj.* **—includible, includable**, *adj.*

inclusive /ɪnˈklusɪv/ *adj.* **1.** including in consideration or account, as the stated limit or extremes: *from six to ten inclusive.* **2.** including a great deal, or including everything concerned; comprehensive. **3.** that includes; enclosing; embracing. *—phr.* **4. inclusive of,** including. **—inclusively**, *adv.* **—inclusiveness, inclusivity**, *n.*

inclusive language *n.* non-sexist language viewed as including women in a hitherto male-dominated society, the attitudes of which were embedded in the language.

incognito /ɪnkɒɡˈniːtoʊ/ *adj.* **1.** having one's identity concealed, as under an assumed name (especially to avoid notice or formal attentions). *—adv.* **2.** with the real identity concealed: *to travel incognito.*

incoherent /ɪnkoʊˈhɪərənt/ *adj.* **1.** without logical connection; disjointed; rambling: *an incoherent sentence.* **2.** characterised by such thought or language, as a person: *incoherent with rage.* **3.** without congruity of parts; uncoordinated. **4.** naturally different, or incompatible, as things. **—incoherence, incoherency**, *n.* **—incoherently**, *adv.*

income /ˈɪnkʌm, ˈɪŋ-/ *n.* **1.** the returns that come in periodically, especially annually, from one's work, property, business, etc.; revenue; receipts. **2.** something that comes in.

income group   *n.* a group of people having similar incomes.

income splitting   *n.* the notional splitting of income between married partners for the purpose of reducing tax liability.

income tax   *n.* an annual government tax on personal incomes, usually graduated and with certain deductions and exemptions.

incommode /ɪnkəˈmoʊd/ *v.t.* to inconvenience or discomfort.

incommodious /ɪnkəˈmoʊdiəs/ *adj.* **1.** not affording sufficient room. **2.** inconvenient. —**incommodiously,** *adv.* —**incommodiousness,** *n.*

incommunicado /ˌɪnkəmjunəˈkadoʊ/ *adj.* **1.** (especially of a prisoner) deprived of communication with others. **2.** forced by circumstances to be out of contact or communication with others.

incomparable /ɪnˈkɒmpərəbəl, -prəbəl/ *adj.* matchless or unequalled: *incomparable beauty.* —**incomparability** /ɪnˌkɒmpərəˈbɪləti, -prə-/, **incomparableness,** *n.* —**incomparably,** *adv.*

incompatible /ɪnkəmˈpætəbəl/ *adj.* **1.** not compatible; incapable of existing together in harmony. **2.** contrary or opposed in character; discordant. **3.** that cannot co-exist or be conjoined. **4.** *Logic* (of two or more propositions) that cannot be true simultaneously. **5.** *Pharmacology* relating to drugs or the like which interfere with one another chemically or physiologically and therefore cannot be prescribed together. —**incompatibleness, incompatibility** /ɪnkəmpætəˈbɪləti/, *n.* —**incompatibly,** *adv.*

incompetent /ɪnˈkɒmpətənt/ *adj.* **1.** not competent; lacking qualification or ability: *an incompetent candidate.* **2.** characterised by or showing incompetence. —**incompetence, incompetency,** *n.* —**incompetently,** *adv.*

incomplete /ɪnkəmˈplit/ *adj.* not complete; lacking some part. —**incompletely,** *adv.* —**incompleteness, incompletion,** *n.*

incomprehensible /ˌɪnkɒmprəˈhɛnsəbəl/ *adj.* not comprehensible; not understandable; unintelligible. —**incomprehensibility** /ˌɪnkɒmprəˌhɛnsəˈbɪləti/, **incomprehensibleness,** *n.* —**incomprehensibly,** *adv.*

inconceivable /ɪnkənˈsivəbəl/ *adj.* unimaginable; unthinkable; incredible. —**inconceivability** /ˌɪnkənsivəˈbɪləti/, **inconceivableness,** *n.* —**inconceivably,** *adv.*

inconclusive /ɪnkənˈklusɪv/ *adj.* **1.** not conclusive; not such as to settle a question: *inconclusive evidence.* **2.** without final results: *inconclusive experiments.* —**inconclusively,** *adv.* —**inconclusiveness,** *n.*

incongruous /ɪnˈkɒŋgruəs/ *adj.* **1.** out of keeping or place; inappropriate; unbecoming; absurd: *an incongruous effect.* **2.** not harmonious in character; inconsonant; lacking harmony of parts: *incongruous mixtures.* **3.** inconsistent: *acts incongruous with their principles.* —**incongruity** /ɪnkɒŋˈgruəti/, **incongruousness,** *n.* —**incongruously,** *adv.*

inconsequential /ˌɪnkɒnsəˈkwɛnʃəl/ *adj.* **1.** of no consequence; trivial. **2.** inconsequent; illogical; irrelevant. —**inconsequentiality** /ˌɪnkɒnsəˌkwɛnʃiˈæləti/, *n.* —**inconsequentially,** *adv.*

inconsiderate /ɪnkənˈsɪdərət, -drət/ *adj.* **1.** without due regard for the rights or feelings of others: *it was inconsiderate of him to forget.* **2.** done or acting without consideration; thoughtless. —**inconsiderately,** *adv.* —**inconsiderateness, inconsideration** /ˌɪnkənsɪdəˈreɪʃən/, *n.*

inconsistent /ɪnkənˈsɪstənt/ *adj.* **1.** lacking in harmony between the different parts or elements; self-contradictory. **2.** lacking agreement, as one thing with another, or two or more things in relation to each other; at variance. **3.** not consistent in principles, conduct, etc.

4. acting at variance with professed principles. —**inconsistently,** *adv.* —**inconsistency,** *n.*

inconspicuous /ɪnkənˈspɪkjuəs/ *adj.* not conspicuous, noticeable, or prominent. —**inconspicuously,** *adv.* —**inconspicuousness,** *n.*

incontinent /ɪnˈkɒntənənt/ *adj.* **1.** *Pathol.* lacking control over the normally voluntary excretory functions of the body. **2.** not continent; not holding or held in; unceasing or unrestrained: *an incontinent flow of talk.* **3.** lacking in restraint, especially over the sexual appetite. —**incontinence, incontinency,** *n.* —**incontinently,** *adv.*

incontrovertible /ˌɪnkɒntrəˈvɜtəbəl/ *adj.* not controvertible; indisputable. —**incontrovertibility** /ˌɪnkɒntrəˌvɜtəˈbɪləti/, **incontrovertibleness,** *n.* —**incontrovertibly,** *adv.*

inconvenient /ɪnkənˈviniənt/ *adj.* arranged or happening in such a way as to be awkward, inopportune, disadvantageous, or troublesome: *an inconvenient time for a visit.* —**inconvenience,** *n.* —**inconveniently,** *adv.*

incorporate /ɪnˈkɔpəreɪt/ *v.t.* **1.** to create or form into a legal association. **2.** to form into a society or organisation. **3.** to introduce into or include in, as a part within a whole. **4.** to form or combine into one body as ingredients. **5.** to collect in a body; organise. –*v.i.* **6.** to unite or combine so as to form one body. –*adj.* **7.** formed, as a company. —**incorporated,** *adj.* —**incorporation** /ɪnˌkɔpəˈreɪʃən/, *n.* —**incorporative** /ɪnˈkɔpərətɪv/, *adj.*

incorrect /ɪnkəˈrɛkt/ *adj.* **1.** not correct as to fact: *an incorrect statement.* **2.** improper: *incorrect behaviour.* **3.** not correct in form or manner: *an incorrect copy.* —**incorrectly,** *adv.* —**incorrectness,** *n.*

incorrigible /ɪnˈkɒrədʒəbəl/ *adj.* **1.** not corrigible; bad beyond correction or reform: *an incorrigible liar.* **2.** impervious to punishment; wilful; uncontrollable: *an incorrigible child.* **3.** firmly fixed; not easily changed: *an incorrigible habit.* —**incorrigibility** /ɪnˌkɒrədʒəˈbɪləti/, **incorrigibleness,** *n.* —**incorrigibly,** *adv.*

increase *v.t.* /ɪnˈkris/ **1.** to make greater; augment; add to. **2.** to make more in number. –*v.i.* /ɪnˈkris/ **3.** to become greater or more in number: *sales increased.* –*n.* /ˈɪnkris/ **4.** growth in amount or numbers: *the increase of crime.* **5.** the act or process of increasing. **6.** the amount by which something is increased. **7.** product; profit; interest. —**increased,** *adj.* —**increasing,** *adj.* —**increasingly,** *adv.* —**increasable,** *adj.* —**increaser,** *n.*

incredible /ɪnˈkrɛdəbəl/ *adj.* **1.** seeming too extraordinary to be possible: *an incredible act of heroism.* **2.** not credible; that cannot be believed. —**incredibility** /ɪnˌkrɛdəˈbɪləti/, **incredibleness,** *n.* —**incredibly,** *adv.*

incredulous /ɪnˈkrɛdʒələs/ *adj.* **1.** not credulous; indisposed to believe; sceptical. **2.** indicating unbelief: *an incredulous smile.* —**incredulity** /ɪnkrəˈdjuləti/, **incredulousness,** *n.* —**incredulously,** *adv.*

increment /ˈɪnkrəmənt, ˈɪŋ-/ *n.* **1.** something added or gained; an addition or increase. **2.** profit. **3.** the act or process of increasing; growth. **4.** an increase in salary resulting from progression within a graduated scale of salaries, designed to reward an employee for increases in skill or experience. —**incremental** /ɪnkrəˈmɛntl, ɪŋ-/, *adj.* —**incrementally,** *adv.*

incriminate /ɪnˈkrɪməneɪt/ *v.t.* **1.** to imply or provide evidence of the fault of (someone): *incriminating evidence; her statement incriminated them both.* **2.** to involve in an accusation; implicate. —**incrimination** /ɪnkrɪmɪˈneɪʃən/, *n.* —**incriminator,** *n.* —**incriminatory** /ɪnˈkrɪmənətri/, *adj.*

incubate /ˈɪnkjubeɪt, ˈɪŋ-/ *v.t.* **1.** to sit upon (eggs) for the purpose of hatching. **2.** to hatch (eggs), as by sitting upon them or by artificial heat. **3.** to keep (bacterial mixtures, etc.) at the best temperature for growth. **4.** to keep at even temperature, as babies born too early (prematurely). –*v.i.* **5.** to sit upon eggs. **6.** to grow; take shape. –**incubation** /ɪnkjuˈbeɪʃən/, *n.* –**incubative, incubatory,** *adj.*

incubator /ˈɪnkjubeɪtə, ˈɪŋ-/ *n.* **1.** an apparatus for hatching eggs artificially, consisting essentially of a case heated by a lamp or the like. **2.** a boxlike apparatus in which prematurely born infants are kept at a constant and suitable temperature. **3.** a device in which bacterial cultures, etc., are developed at a constant suitable temperature.

incubus /ˈɪnkjubəs, ˈɪŋ-/ *n.* (*pl.* -**bi** /-baɪ/ *or* -**buses**) **1.** an imaginary demon or evil spirit supposedly descending upon sleeping persons, especially one reputed to have sexual intercourse with sleeping women. **2.** something that weighs upon or oppresses one like a nightmare.

inculcate /ˈɪnkʌlkeɪt/ *v.t.* (sometimes fol. by *upon* or *in*) to impress by repeated statement or admonition; teach persistently and earnestly; instil. –**inculcation** /ɪnkʌlˈkeɪʃən/, *n.* –**inculcator,** *n.*

incumbent /ɪnˈkʌmbənt/ *adj.* **1.** resting on one; obligatory: *a duty incumbent upon me.* **2.** lying, leaning, or pressing on something: *incumbent posture.* –*n.* **3.** the holder of an office. –**incumbency,** *n.* –**incumbently,** *adv.*

incur /ɪnˈkɜ/ *v.t.* (-**curred,** -**curring**) **1.** to run or fall into (some consequence, usually undesirable or injurious). **2.** to become liable or subject to through one's own action; bring upon oneself: *to incur his displeasure.* –**incurrable,** *adj.*

incurable /ɪnˈkjurəbəl/ *adj.* not curable. –**incurability** /ɪn₁kjurəˈbɪləti/, **incurableness,** *n.* –**incurably,** *adv.*

incursion /ɪnˈkɜʒən/ *n.* **1.** a hostile entrance into or invasion of a place or territory, especially one of sudden character; raid; attack. **2.** a harmful inroad. **3.** a running in: *the incursion of sea water.*

ind- variant of **indo-** before vowels.

indebted /ɪnˈdɛtəd/ *adj.* **1.** owing money. **2.** being under an obligation for benefits, favours, assistance, etc., received. –**indebtedness,** *n.*

indecent /ɪnˈdisənt/ *adj.* **1.** offending against recognised standards of propriety or good taste; vulgar: *indecent language.* **2.** not decent; unbecoming or unseemly: *indecent conduct.* –**indecency,** *n.* –**indecently,** *adv.*

indecent assault *n. Law* an assault in which an individual is subjected to some form of sexual activity against his or her will.

indecision /ɪndəˈsɪʒən/ *n.* inability to decide. –**indecisive,** *adj.*

indeed /ɪnˈdid/ *adv.* **1.** in fact; in reality; in truth; truly (used for emphasis, to confirm and amplify a previous statement, to intensify, to indicate a concession or admission, or, interrogatively, to obtain confirmation). –*interj.* **2.** an expression of surprise, incredulity, irony, etc.

indefatigable /ɪndəˈfætɪgəbəl/ *adj.* incapable of being tired out; not yielding to fatigue. –**indefatigability** /₁ɪndəfætɪgəˈbɪləti/, **indefatigableness,** *n.* –**indefatigably,** *adv.*

indefeasible /ɪndəˈfizəbəl/ *adj. Law* not defeasible; not to be annulled or made void; not forfeitable. –**indefeasibility** /₁ɪndəfizəˈbɪləti/, *n.* –**indefeasibly,** *adv.*

indefensible /ɪndəˈfɛnsəbəl/ *adj.* **1.** that cannot be justified; inexcusable: *an indefensible remark.* **2.** that cannot be defended by force of arms: *an indefensible frontier.* –**indefensibility** /₁ɪndəfɛnsəˈbɪləti/, **indefensibleness,** *n.* –**indefensibly,** *adv.*

indefinable /ɪndəˈfaɪnəbəl/ *adj.* not definable; indescribable. –**indefinableness,** *n.* –**indefinably,** *adv.*

indefinite /ɪnˈdɛfənət/ *adj.* **1.** not definite; without fixed or specified limit; unlimited: *an indefinite number.* **2.** not clearly defined or determined; not precise. –**indefinitely,** *adv.* –**indefiniteness,** *n.*

indelible /ɪnˈdɛləbəl/ *adj.* incapable of being deleted or obliterated: *an indelible impression.* –**indelibility** /ɪn₁dɛləˈbɪləti/, **indelibleness,** *n.* –**indelibly,** *adv.*

indelicate /ɪnˈdɛləkət/ *adj.* **1.** not delicate; lacking delicacy. **2.** offensive to a sense of propriety, or modesty; unrefined. –**indelicacy,** *n.* –**indelicately,** *adv.*

indemnify /ɪnˈdɛmnəfaɪ/ *v.t.* (-**fied,** -**fying**) to compensate for damage or loss sustained, expense incurred, etc. –**demnification** /ɪn₁dɛmnəfəˈkeɪʃən/, *n.* –**indemnifier,** *n.*

indemnity /ɪnˈdɛmnəti/ *n.* **1.** protection or security against damage or loss. **2.** compensation for damage or loss sustained.

indent *v.t.* /ɪnˈdɛnt/ **1.** to make deep hollows or notches in: *the sea indents the coast.* **2.** to set in or back from the margin: *to indent the first line of a paragraph.* **3.** to make an order for goods, etc., upon (someone, a company, etc.). **4.** to order (goods, etc.). –*v.i.* **5.** to make out an order, etc., in two copies. –*n.* /ˈɪndɛnt/ **6.** an official order for goods. **7.** Also, **indentation.** a tooth-like hollow or notch. **8.** Also, **indentation, indention.** the setting of a line back from the margin. **9.** → **indenture.** –**indentation,** *n.* –**indenter,** *n.*

indenture /ɪnˈdɛntʃə/ *n.* **1.** a written agreement between two or more parties. **2.** an agreement by which a person, such as an apprentice, is bound to work for another. **3.** a formal agreement between a group of bondholders and the debtor concerning the debt. –*v.t.* **4.** to bind (an apprentice, etc.) by indenture.

independent /ɪndəˈpɛndənt/ *adj.* **1.** not influenced by opinions, actions, etc., of others: *an independent thinker; independent research.* **2.** not under another's control or authority; autonomous: *an independent nation.* **3.** not depending on someone or something else for existence, operation, help, support, etc. **4.** refusing to accept others' help or support. **5.** showing a spirit of independence; self-confident. **6.** (of a school) neither a government school nor one in the Catholic education system. **7.** *Maths* (of a quantity or variable) having a value which does not depend on the value of another quantity or variable. –*n.* **8.** an independent person or thing. **9.** *Politics* someone who does not belong to any organised party and therefore votes freely. –**independently,** *adv.* –**independence,** *n.*

independent means *n.* an income which does not depend on a salary or the like. Also, **private means.**

in-depth *adj.* with thorough coverage: *an in-depth discussion.*

indescribable /ɪndəˈskraɪbəbəl/ *adj.* not describable. –**indescribability** /₁ɪndəskraɪbəˈbɪləti/, *n.* –**indescribably,** *adv.*

indestructible /ɪndəˈstrʌktəbəl/ *adj.* not destructible. –**indestructibility** /₁ɪndəstrʌktəˈbɪləti/, **indestructibleness,** *n.* –**indestructibly,** *adv.*

indeterminate /ɪndəˈtɜmənət/ *adj.* **1.** not determinate; not fixed in extent; indefinite; uncertain. **2.** not settled or decided. **3.** *Maths* (of a quantity) having no fixed value. –**indeterminately,** *adv.* –**indeterminacy,** **indeterminateness,** *n.* –**indetermination** /₁ɪndətɜməˈneɪʃən/, *n.*

index /ˈɪndɛks/ *n.* (*pl.* -**dexes** *or* -**dices** /-dəsɪz/) **1.** an alphabetical list of names, places, or subjects in a book, showing their page number, etc. **2.** something used or serving to point out; a sign; indication: *a true index of his character.* **3.** a pointer or indicator in a scientific instrument. **4.** a piece of wood, metal, or the like, serving as a pointer or indicator. **5.** *Science* a number or formula indicating some property, ratio, etc., of a thing: *refractive index.* **6.** *Algebra* **a.** an exponent. **b.** the integer n in a radical $\sqrt[n]{}$ defining the nth root: $\sqrt[3]{7}$ *is a radical having index 3.* **7.** (*upper case*) a list of books which Roman Catholics were forbidden by the Church to read without special permission, or which were not to be read unless shortened or corrected. **8.** *Obs.* a preface. –*v.t.* **9.** to provide (a book, etc.) with an index. **10.** to enter (a word, etc.) in an index. **11.** to change (wages, taxes, etc.) regularly in accordance with changes in prices of goods, etc. –**indexer**, *n.* –**indexical** /ɪnˈdɛksɪkəl/, *adj.* –**indexless**, *adj.*

indexation /ɪndɛkˈseɪʃən/ *n.* the adjustment of one variable in the light of changes in another variable, especially the adjustment of wages to compensate for rises in the cost of living.

index finger *n.* → **forefinger**.

Indian file /ˈɪndiən faɪl/ *n.* single file, as of persons walking.

Indian giver *n.* someone who gives something as a gift to another and later takes or demands it back.

Indian hemp *n.* a tall, annual herb, *Cannabis indica*, native to Asia but cultivated in many parts of the world and yielding hashish, bhang, cannabin, etc.

Indian ink *n.* **1.** a black pigment consisting of lampblack mixed with glue. **2.** a liquid ink from this. Also, *US*, **India ink**.

Indian myna *n.* → **myna** (def. 1).

Indian summer *n.* a period of summer weather occurring after the proper summer season.

indicate /ˈɪndəkeɪt, -dɪkeɪt/ *v.t.* **1.** to be a sign of; betoken; imply: *his hesitation indicates unwillingness.* **2.** to point out or point to; direct attention to: *to indicate a place on a map.* **3.** to show, or make known: *the thermometer indicates temperature.* **4.** to state or express, especially briefly or in a general way: *to indicate one's intentions.* –**indicant**, *adj.* –**indication** /ɪndəˈkeɪʃən/, *n.* –**indicatory** /ɪnˈdɪkətri/, *adj.*

indicative /ɪnˈdɪkətɪv/ *adj.* **1.** (sometimes fol. by *of*) that indicates; pointing out; suggestive. **2.** *Gram.* designating or relating to the mood of the verb used in ordinary statements, questions, etc., in contrast to hypothetical statements or those made without reference to a specific actor or time of action. For example: in the sentence *Kim plays football*, the verb *plays* is in the indicative mood. –**indicatively**, *adv.*

indicator /ˈɪndəkeɪtə, ˈɪndɪ-/ *n.* **1.** a pointing or directing device, such as a pointer on an instrument or a flashing light on a car. **2.** a statistic or set of statistics which suggest the state of some aspect of society: *a market indicator*; *an economic indicator.* **3.** *Chem.* a substance used (especially in volumetric analysis) to indicate (as by a change in colour) the condition of a solution, the point at which a certain reaction ends and another begins, etc.

indices /ˈɪndəsiz/ *n.* a plural of **index**.

indict /ɪnˈdaɪt/ *v.t.* to charge with an offence or crime; accuse. –**indictable**, *adj.* –**indictment**, *n.* –**indicter**, *n.* –**indictee**, *n.*

indie /ˈɪndi/ *adj.* **1.** (of a music or film production company, etc.) independent; not affiliated with one of the major commercial companies or studios. **2.** (of a CD, film, etc.) produced independently or by an independent studio, rather than by a large commercial studio. **3.** *Film, Music* of or relating to a style of popular film or music considered individual and less commercially motivated than mainstream popular films or music. Also, **indy**.

indifferent /ɪnˈdɪfrənt/ *adj.* **1.** without interest or concern; not caring. **2.** having neither favourable nor unfavourable feelings towards some thing or person. **3.** neither good nor bad in character or quality: *an indifferent specimen.* **4.** not very good: *an indifferent play*; *indifferent health.* **5.** unimportant; immaterial. **6.** neutral in chemical, electrical, or magnetic quality. **7.** *Biol.* not differentiated or specialised, as cells or tissues. –**indifference**, *n.* –**indifferently**, *adv.*

indigenous /ɪnˈdɪdʒənəs/ *adj.* (sometimes fol. by *to*) originating in and characterising a particular region or country; native: *the plants indigenous to Canada.* –**indigenously**, *adv.* –**indigenousness**, *n.* –**indigeneity** /ɪndɪdʒəˈniəti, ɪndɪdʒəˈneɪəti/, *n.*

Indigenous /ɪnˈdɪdʒənəs/ *adj.* of or relating to Aboriginal and Torres Strait Islander people: *Indigenous issues.* –**Indigenousness**, *n.* –**Indigeneity** /ɪndɪdʒəˈniəti, ɪndɪdʒəˈneɪəti/, *n.*

indigent /ˈɪndədʒənt/ *adj.* lacking the necessities of life; needy; poor. –**indigence**, *n.* –**indigently**, *adv.*

indigestion /ɪndəˈdʒɛstʃən, ɪndaɪ-/ *n.* incapability of, or difficulty in, digesting food; dyspepsia. –**indigestible**, *adj.*

indignant /ɪnˈdɪɡnənt/ *adj.* affected with or characterised by indignation. –**indignantly**, *adv.*

indignation /ɪndɪɡˈneɪʃən/ *n.* strong displeasure at something deemed unworthy, unjust, or base; righteous anger.

indignity /ɪnˈdɪɡnəti/ *n.* (*pl.* **-ties**) injury to dignity; slighting or contemptuous treatment; a humiliating affront, insult, or injury.

indigo /ˈɪndɪɡoʊ/ *n.* (*pl.* **-gos**) **1.** a blue dye obtained from various plants, especially of the genus *Indigofera.* **2.** a deep violet blue between violet and blue in the spectrum.

indirect /ɪndəˈrɛkt, ɪndaɪˈrɛkt/ *adj.* **1.** not direct in space; not following a straight line: *They took an indirect course across the park.* **2.** coming or resulting otherwise than directly or immediately: *an indirect effect.* **3.** not direct in action; not straightforward: *indirect methods.* **4.** not direct in bearing, use, force, etc.: *indirect evidence.* **5.** *Gram.* not consisting exactly of the words originally used, as in *He said he was hungry* instead of the direct *He said, 'I am hungry'.* –**indirection**, *n.* –**indirectly**, *adv.* –**indirectness**, *n.*

indirect taxation *n.* the levying of a tax that is charged as an expense of production of a good or service, rather than being imposed on the income of the producers of the good or service (as in *direct taxation*).

indiscreet /ɪndəsˈkrit/ *adj.* not discreet; lacking prudence; lacking sound judgement: *indiscreet praise.* –**indiscreetly**, *adv.*

indiscretion /ɪndəsˈkrɛʃən/ *n.* **1.** lack of discretion; imprudence. **2.** an indiscreet act or step.

indiscriminate /ɪndəsˈkrɪmənət/ *adj.* not discriminating; making no distinction: *indiscriminate in one's friendships.* –**indiscriminately**, *adv.* –**indiscriminateness**, *n.*

indispensable /ɪndəsˈpɛnsəbəl/ *adj.* not dispensable; absolutely necessary or requisite: *an indispensable man.* **2.** that cannot be disregarded or neglected: *an indispensable obligation.* –**indispensability** /ˌɪndəspɛnsəˈbɪləti/, **indispensableness**, *n.* –**indispensably**, *adv.*

indisposed /ɪndəsˈpoʊzd/ *adj.* **1.** sick or ill, especially slightly: *indisposed with a cold.* **2.** disinclined or unwilling. –**indisposition** /ˌɪndɪspəˈzɪʃən/, *n.*

indisputable /ɪndəsˈpjutəbəl/ *adj.* not disputable; not open to question. –**indisputability** /ˌɪndəspjutəˈbɪləti/, **indisputableness**, *n.* –**indisputably**, *adv.*

indistinct /ɪndəsˈtɪŋkt/ *adj.* **1.** not distinct; not clearly marked off or defined. **2.** not clearly distinguishable or perceptible, as to the eye, ear, or mind. –**indistinctly**, *adv.* –**indistinctness**, *n.*

individual /ɪndəˈvɪdʒuəl/ *adj.* **1.** single; particular; separate: *the individual members of a club.* **2.** relating to or characteristic of a single person or thing: *individual tastes*; *an individual style.* **3.** intended for one person only: *individual servings*; *he needs individual attention.* –*n.* **4.** a single human being or thing. **5.** *Colloq.* a person: *a strange individual.* **6.** *Biol.* **a.** a single or simple organism able to exist independently. **b.** a member of a compound organism or colony. –**individually**, *adv.*

individualism /ɪndəˈvɪdʒuəlɪzəm/ *n.* **1.** a social theory advocating the liberty, rights, or independent action of the individual. **2.** the principle or habit of independent thought or action. **3.** the pursuit of individual rather than common or collective interests; egoism.

4. individual character; individuality. –**individualist**, *n.* –**individualistic** /ˌɪndəvɪdʒʊəˈlɪstɪk/, *adj.*

individuality /ˌɪndəvɪdʒʊˈælətɪ/ *n.* **1.** the particular character, or aggregate of qualities, which distinguishes one person or thing from others: *a person of marked individuality.* **2.** the state or quality of being individual; existence as a distinct individual.

indo- a combining form of **indigo**. Also, **ind-**.

indoctrinate /ɪnˈdɒktrəneɪt/ *v.t.* **1.** to instruct (someone) in some particular teaching or doctrine: *he was indoctrinated in the ways of the Buddha.* **2.** to so instruct (someone) in a manner which leads to their total and uncritical acceptance of the teaching; brainwash. –**indoctrination** /ɪnˌdɒktrəˈneɪʃən/, *n.* –**indoctrinator**, *n.* –**indoctrinatory**, *adj.*

indolent /ˈɪndələnt/ *adj.* having or showing a disposition to avoid exertion: *an indolent person.* –**indolence**, *n.* –**indolently**, *adv.*

indomitable /ɪnˈdɒmətəbəl/ *adj.* that cannot be subdued or overcome, as persons, pride, courage, etc. –**indomitableness**, *n.* –**indomitably**, *adv.*

indoor /ˈɪndɔ/ *adj.* **1.** occurring, used, etc., in a house or building, rather than outdoors: *indoor games.* **2.** (of a sport) redesigned with different rules for playing indoors, usually on a smaller playing area and with fewer players to a side.

indoors /ɪnˈdɔz/ *adv.* in or into a house or building.

indubitable /ɪnˈdjubətəbəl/ *adj.* that cannot be doubted; unquestionable; certain. –**indubitableness**, *n.* –**indubitably**, *adv.*

induce /ɪnˈdjus/ *v.t.* (**-duced, -ducing**) **1.** to lead or move by persuasion or influence, as to some action, state of mind, etc.: *to induce a person to go.* **2.** to bring about, produce, or cause: *opium induces sleep.* **3. a.** to initiate (labour) artificially in pregnancy. **b.** to initiate labour in (a pregnant woman). –**inducer**, *n.* –**inducible**, *adj.*

inducement /ɪnˈdjusmənt/ *n.* **1.** the act of inducing (defs 1 and 2). **2.** something that induces or persuades; an incentive.

induct /ɪnˈdʌkt/ *v.t.* **1.** to lead or bring in; introduce, especially formally, as into an office or position, etc. –*phr.* **2. induct to**, to introduce in knowledge or experience to. –**inductee**, *n.*

inductance /ɪnˈdʌktəns/ *n.* *Elect.* the property of a circuit by virtue of which electromagnetic induction takes place. *Symbol:* L

induction /ɪnˈdʌkʃən/ *n.* **1.** the act of inducting, bringing about, or causing. **2.** *Elect.* **a.** the process by which a body with electrical or magnetic properties produces such properties in a nearby body without touching it directly. **b.** the tendency of electric currents to resist change. **3.** *Electronics* the process by which an electrical conductor may be charged. **4.** the act of inducing; introduction or initiation. **5.** the artificial initiation of labour in pregnancy. **6.** *Logic* **a.** the process of discovering general explanations for a whole class of facts by reasoning from a set of particular facts known from evidence based on experience. **b.** the conclusion thus reached.

indulge /ɪnˈdʌldʒ/ *verb* (**-dulged, -dulging**) –*v.i.* **1.** (sometimes fol. by *in*) to allow oneself to yield to an inclination: *to indulge in one's favourite pastime.* **2.** to drink alcohol in excessive amounts. –*v.t.* **3.** to yield to, satisfy, or gratify (desires, feelings, etc.). **4.** to yield to the wishes or whims of: *to indulge a child.* **5.** (sometimes fol. by *in*) to allow (oneself) to follow one's own wishes: *indulge yourself! have a chocolate.* –**indulger**, *n.* –**indulgingly**, *adv.*

indulgence /ɪnˈdʌldʒəns/ *n.* **1.** the act or practice of indulging; gratification of desire. **2.** indulgent allowance or tolerance. **3.** something granted or taken in gratification of desire. **4.** *Roman Catholic Church* a remission

of the temporal punishment still due to sin after it has been forgiven. –**indulgent**, *adj.*

industrial /ɪnˈdʌstriəl/ *adj.* **1.** relating to, of the nature of, or resulting from industry: *the industrial arts.* **2.** having highly developed industries: *an industrial nation.* **3.** working in an industry or industries: *industrial employees.* **4.** relating to the workers in industries: *industrial training.* **5.** used in industry: *industrial diamonds.* –**industrially**, *adv.*

industrial action *n.* organised disruptive action, such as a strike or go-slow, taken by a group of workers, to promote what they conceive to be either their own interests or the general public good.

industrial court *n.* a court set up to hear trade and industrial disputes.

industrial design *n.* the designing of objects for manufacture. –**industrial designer**, *n.*

industrialise /ɪnˈdʌstriəlaɪz/ *v.t.* to introduce industry into (an area) on a large scale. Also, **industrialize**. –**industrialisation** /ɪnˌdʌstriəlaɪˈzeɪʃən/, *n.*

industrialist /ɪnˈdʌstriələst/ *n.* someone who conducts or owns an industrial enterprise.

industrial relations *pl. n.* **1.** the management or study of the relations between employers and employees. **2.** the relationship itself usually in a given industry, locality, etc. *Abbrev.:* IR

industrial union *n.* **1.** a union having the right to enrol as members all of the people employed in a particular industry. **2.** a trade union, or organisation of employees, registered under the appropriate industrial legislation to give it access to industrial tribunals, etc.

industrious /ɪnˈdʌstriəs/ *adj.* hardworking; diligent: *an industrious person.* –**industriously**, *adv.* –**industriousness**, *n.*

industry /ˈɪndəstri/ *n.* (*pl.* **-tries**) **1.** a particular branch of manufacture: *the steel industry.* **2.** any large-scale business activity: *the tourist industry.* **3.** manufacture as a whole: *the growth of industry in underdeveloped countries.* **4.** ownership and management of companies, factories, etc.: *disagreement between labour and industry.* **5.** hard or steady work: *he lacks industry.*

industry fund *n.* a not-for-profit superannuation fund run jointly by the unions and employers in an industry, but nevertheless open to people outside the industry.

industry standard *n.* a standard which everyone involved in a particular industry agrees to adopt.

-ine¹ an adjective suffix meaning 'relating to', 'resembling', 'made of', as in *equine, asinine, crystalline, marine.*

-ine² **1.** a noun suffix denoting some action, procedure, art, place, etc., as in *discipline, doctrine, medicine, latrine.* **2.** a suffix occurring in many nouns of later formation and various meanings, as in *famine, routine, grenadine, vaseline.* **3.** a noun suffix used particularly in chemical terms, as *bromine, chlorine*, and especially names of basic substances, as *amine, aniline, caffeine, quinine, quinoline.* Compare **-in²**.

inebriate *v.t.* /ɪnˈibrieɪt/ **1.** to make drunk; intoxicate. **2.** to intoxicate mentally or emotionally; exhilarate. –*n.* /ɪnˈibriət/ **3.** a habitual drunkard. –*adj.* /ɪnˈibriət/ Also, **inebriated**. **4.** drunk; intoxicated. –**inebriant**, *n., adj.* –**inebriation** /ɪnˌibriˈeɪʃən/, *n.*

inedible /ɪnˈɛdəbəl/ *adj.* not edible; unfit to be eaten. –**inedibility** /ɪnˌɛdəˈbɪləti/, *n.*

ineffable /ɪnˈɛfəbəl/ *adj.* that cannot be uttered or expressed; inexpressible; unspeakable: *ineffable joy.* –**ineffability** /ɪnˌɛfəˈbɪləti/, **ineffableness**, *n.* –**ineffably**, *adv.*

ineffective /ɪnəˈfɛktɪv/ *adj.* not effective; ineffectual, as efforts. **2.** inefficient, as a person. **3.** lacking in artistic effect, as a design or work. –**ineffectively**, *adv.* –**ineffectiveness**, *n.*

ineffectual /ɪnəˈfɛktʃuəl/ *adj.* not effectual; without satisfactory or decisive effect: *an ineffectual remedy.*

-**ineffectuality** /ˌɪnəˌfɛktʃuˈælətɪ/, **ineffectualness**, *n.* -**ineffectually**, *adv.*

inefficient /ɪnəˈfɪʃənt/ *adj.* not efficient; unable to effect or accomplish in a capable, economical way. -**inefficiency**, *n.* -**inefficiently**, *adv.*

ineligible /ɪnˈɛlədʒəbəl/ *adj.* **1.** not eligible; not proper or suitable for choice. **2.** legally disqualified to hold an office. -**ineligibility** /ɪnˌɛlədʒəˈbɪlətɪ/, *n.* -**ineligibly**, *adv.*

inept /ɪnˈɛpt/ *adj.* **1.** not apt, fitted, or suitable; unsuitable. **2.** absurd or foolish, as a proceeding, remark, etc. **3.** (of a person) ineffectual; useless. -**ineptly**, *adv.* -**ineptitude**, **ineptness**, *n.*

inequality /ɪnəˈkwɒlətɪ/ *n.* (*pl.* -**ties**) **1.** the condition of being unequal; lack of equality; disparity: *inequality of treatment.* **2.** social disparity: *the inequality between the rich and the poor.* **3.** injustice; partiality. **4.** unevenness, as of surface. **5.** *Maths* an expression of two unequal quantities connected by the sign > or <, as *a* > *b*, '*a* is greater than *b*'; *a* < *b*, '*a* is less than *b*'.

inequitable /ɪnˈɛkwətəbəl/ *adj.* not equitable; unfair. -**inequitably**, *adv.*

inert /ɪnˈɜt/ *adj.* **1.** having no inherent power of action, motion, or resistance: *inert matter.* **2.** still, and apparently incapable of movement: *he lay exhausted and inert.* **3.** without active properties, as a drug. **4.** of an inactive or sluggish habit or nature. -**inertly**, *adv.* -**inertness**, *n.*

inert gas *n.* → **rare gas.**

inertia /ɪnˈɜʃə/ *n.* **1.** inert condition; inactivity; sluggishness. **2.** *Physics* the tendency of matter to retain its state of rest or of uniform motion in a straight line. -**inertial**, *adj.*

inescapable /ɪnəsˈkeɪpəbəl/ *adj.* that cannot be escaped or ignored. -**inescapably**, *adv.*

inestimable /ɪnˈɛstəməbəl/ *adj.* that cannot be estimated, or too great to be estimated. -**inestimably**, *adv.*

inevitable /ɪnˈɛvətəbəl/ *adj.* that cannot be avoided, evaded, or escaped; certain or necessary: *an inevitable conclusion.* -**inevitability** /ɪnˌɛvətəˈbɪlətɪ/, **inevitableness**, *n.* -**inevitably**, *adv.*

inexact /ɪnəgˈzækt, ɪnɛg-/ *adj.* not exact; not strictly accurate. -**inexactly**, *adv.* -**inexactitude**, **inexactness**, *n.*

inexcusable /ɪnəkˈskjuzəbəl, ɪnɛk-/ *adj.* not excusable; incapable of being explained away or justified. -**inexcusability** /ɪnəkˌskjuzəˈbɪlətɪ/, **inexcusableness**, *n.* -**inexcusably**, *adv.*

inexhaustible /ɪnəgˈzɔstəbəl, ɪnɛg-/ *adj.* not exhaustible; incapable of being exhausted: *an inexhaustible supply.* -**inexhaustibility** /ɪnəgˌzɔstəˈbɪlətɪ/, **inexhaustibleness**, *n.* -**inexhaustibly**, *adv.*

inexorable /ɪnˈɛksərəbəl, ɪnˈɛgz-/ *adj.* **1.** unyielding or unalterable: *inexorable facts.* **2.** not to be persuaded, moved, or affected by prayers or entreaties. -**inexorability** /ɪnˌɛksərəˈbɪlətɪ, ɪnˌɛgz-/, **inexorableness**, *n.* -**inexorably**, *adv.*

inexpensive /ɪnəkˈspɛnsɪv, ɪnɛk-/ *adj.* not expensive; costing little. -**inexpensively**, *adv.*

inexperience /ɪnəkˈspɪəriəns, ɪnɛk-/ *n.* lack of experience, or of knowledge or skill gained from experience. -**inexperienced**, *adj.*

inexplicable /ɪnəkˈsplɪkəbəl, ɪnɛk-/ *adj.* not explicable; incapable of being explained. -**inexplicability** /ˌɪnəksplɪkəˈbɪlətɪ/, **inexplicableness**, *n.* -**inexplicably**, *adv.*

in extremis /ɪn ɛkˈstriməs/ *adv.* **1.** in extremity. **2.** near death.

inextricable /ˌɪnəksˈtrɪkəbəl, ɪnˈɛkstrəkəbəl/ *adj.* **1.** from which one cannot extricate oneself: *an inextricable maze.* **2.** that cannot be untangled or undone. **3.** hopelessly intricate or involved. -**inextricably**, *adv.*

infallible /ɪnˈfæləbəl/ *adj.* **1.** not fallible; exempt from liability to error, as persons, their judgement,

pronouncements, etc. **2.** absolutely trustworthy or sure: *an infallible rule.* **3.** unfailing in operation; certain: *an infallible remedy.* -**infallibility** /ɪnˌfæləˈbɪlətɪ/, **infallibleness**, *n.* -**infallibly**, *adv.*

infamous /ˈɪnfəməs/ *adj.* **1.** of ill fame; having an extremely bad reputation: *an infamous city.* **2.** such as to deserve or to cause evil repute; detestable; shamefully bad: *infamous conduct.* -**infamously**, *adv.* -**infamousness**, **infamy**, *n.*

infant /ˈɪnfənt/ *n.* **1.** a baby. **2.** a child during the earliest period of its life. **3.** *Law* a person who is not of full age, especially one who is not yet 18 years of age. **4.** anything in the first stage of existence. -*adj.* **5.** of or relating to infants or infancy: *infant years.* **6.** being in infancy: *an infant child; an infant industry.* -**infancy**, **infanthood**, *n.*

infanticide /ɪnˈfæntəsaɪd/ *n.* the killing of an infant.

infantile /ˈɪnfəntaɪl/ *adj.* **1.** characteristic of or befitting an infant; babyish; childish: *infantile behaviour.* **2.** of or relating to infants: *infantile disease.*

infantry /ˈɪnfəntrɪ/ *n.* soldiers or military units that fight on foot, with bayonets, rifles, machine guns, grenades, mortars, etc.

infatuate /ɪnˈfætʃueɪt/ *v.t.* **1.** to affect with folly; make fatuous. **2.** to inspire or possess with a foolish or unreasoning passion, as of love. -**infatuation** /ɪnfætʃuˈeɪʃən/, *n.* -**infatuated**, *adj.*

infect /ɪnˈfɛkt/ *v.t.* **1.** to impregnate (a person, organ, wound, etc.) with disease-producing germs. **2.** to affect with disease. **3.** to impregnate with something that affects quality, character, or condition, especially unfavourably: *to infect the air with poison gas.* **4.** to taint, contaminate, or affect morally: *infected with greed.* **5.** to affect so as to influence feeling or action: *his courage infected the others.* -**infective**, *adj.* -**infector**, *n.*

infection /ɪnˈfɛkʃən/ *n.* **1.** an infecting with germs of disease. **2.** something that infects. **3.** state of being infected. **4.** infectious disease. **5.** an infecting with a feeling, idea, etc.

infectious /ɪnˈfɛkʃəs/ *adj.* **1.** communicable by infection, as diseases. **2.** causing or communicating infection. **3.** tending to spread from one to another: *laughter is infectious.* -**infectiously**, *adv.* -**infectiousness**, *n.*

infer /ɪnˈfɜ/ *v.t.* (-**ferred**, -**ferring**) **1.** to derive by reasoning; conclude or judge from premises or evidence. **2.** (*not considered standard by some*) (of facts, circumstances, statements, etc.) to indicate or involve as a conclusion; imply. -**inferable**, *adj.* -**inferably**, *adv.*

inference /ˈɪnfərəns/ *n.* **1.** the act or process of inferring. **2.** something that is inferred. **3.** implication. -**inferential** /ɪnfəˈrɛnʃəl/, *adj.*

inferior /ɪnˈfɪəriə/ *adj.* **1.** (fol. by *to*) lower in position, rank, or degree. **2.** of comparatively low importance, value or quality: *an inferior brand; an inferior worker.* **3.** lower in place or position (now chiefly in scientific or technical use). -*n.* **4.** someone inferior to another or others. -**inferiority** /ɪnˌfɪəriˈɒrəti, ˌɪnfɪə-/, -**inferiorly**, *adv.*

inferiority complex *n.* **1.** *Psychiatry* a complex arising from intense feelings of inferiority, and resulting in either extreme reticence or aggressiveness due to overcompensation. **2.** a feeling of inferiority or inadequacy.

infernal /ɪnˈfɜnəl/ *adj.* **1.** hellish; fiendish; diabolical: *an infernal plot.* **2.** *Colloq.* irksome; irritating: *an infernal nuisance.* -**infernality** /ɪnfɜˈnælətɪ/, *n.* -**infernally**, *adv.*

inferno /ɪnˈfɜnoʊ/ *n.* (*pl.* -**nos**) **1.** hell; the infernal regions. **2.** an infernal or hell-like region. **3.** a place or state of intolerable heat, especially due to fire.

infertile /ɪnˈfɜtaɪl/ *adj.* not fertile; unfruitful; unproductive; barren: *infertile soil.* -**infertility** /ɪnfəˈtɪlətɪ/, *n.*

infest /ɪnˈfɛst/ *v.t.* **1.** to haunt or overrun in a troublesome manner, as predatory bands, destructive animals, vermin, etc., do. **2.** to be numerous in, as anything troublesome: *the cares that infest the day.* –**infestation** /ɪnfɛsˈteɪʃən/, *n.* –**infester**, *n.*

infidel /ˈɪnfədɛl/ *n.* **1.** an unbeliever. **2.** someone who does not accept a particular religious faith, especially: **a.** (among Christians) someone who does not accept the Christian faith (formerly applied especially to a Muslim). **b.** (among Muslims) someone who does not accept the Muslim faith. –*adj.* **3.** without religious faith. **4.** not accepting a particular faith, especially Christianity or Islam; heathen.

infidelity /ɪnfəˈdɛləti/ *n.* (*pl.* **-ties**) **1.** unfaithfulness. **2.** adultery. **3.** lack of religious faith. **4.** a breach of trust.

infighting /ˈɪnfaɪtɪŋ/ *n.* **1.** *Boxing* fighting at close quarters, so that blows using the full reach of the arm cannot be delivered. **2.** the secret and often ruthless struggle that takes place among members of the same organisation competing for power within it. –**infighter**, *n.*

infiltrate /ˈɪnfɪltreɪt/ *v.t.* **1.** to filter into or through; permeate. **2.** to cause to pass in by, or as by, filtering: *the troops infiltrated the enemy lines.* **3.** to join (an organisation) for the unstated purpose of influencing it; to subvert. –*v.i.* **4.** to pass in or through a substance, etc., by or as by filtering. –**infiltration** /ɪnfəlˈtreɪʃən/, *n.* –**infiltrative**, *adj.* –**infiltrator**, *n.*

infinite /ˈɪnfənət/ *adj.* **1.** immeasurably great: *a truth of infinite importance; infinite number.* **2.** without limits, absolute: *the infinite wisdom of God.* **3.** endless; inexhaustible. **4.** *Maths* not finite. –*n.* **5.** something which is infinite. **6.** boundless regions of space. –*phr.* **7. the Infinite** or **the Infinite Being**, God. –**infinitely**, *adv.* –**infiniteness**, *n.*

infinitesimal /ˌɪnfɪnəˈtɛzməl, -ˈtɛsəməl/ *adj.* **1.** indefinitely or exceedingly small: *the infinitesimal vessels of the nervous system.* **2.** immeasurably small; less than an assignable quantity: *to an infinitesimal degree.* **3.** relating to or involving infinitesimals. –*n.* **4.** an infinitesimal quantity. **5.** *Maths* a variable having zero as a limit. –**infinitesimally**, *adv.*

infinitive /ɪnˈfɪnətɪv/ *Gram.* –*n.* **1.** (in many languages) a noun form derived from verbs, which names the action or state without specifying the subject, as Latin *esse* to be, *fuisse* to have been. **2.** (in English) the simple form of the verb (*come, take, eat*) used after certain other verbs (I didn't *eat*), or this simple form preceded by *to* (the **marked infinitive**, I wanted *to come*). –*adj.* **3.** of or relating to the infinitive or its meaning. –**infinitively**, *adv.*

infinity /ɪnˈfɪnəti/ *n.* (*pl.* **-ties**) **1.** the state of being infinite: *the infinity of the universe.* **2.** infinite space, time, or quantity. **3.** an indefinitely great amount, number or extent. **4.** *Maths* the concept of increasing without bound.

infirm /ɪnˈfɜm/ *adj.* **1.** feeble in body or health. **2.** not steadfast, unfaltering, or resolute, as persons, the mind, etc.: *infirm of purpose.* **3.** not firm, solid, or strong: *an infirm support.* **4.** unsound or invalid, as an argument, a title, etc. –**infirmly**, *adv.* –**infirmness**, *n.*

infirmary /ɪnˈfɜməri/ *n.* (*pl.* **-ries**) a place for the care of the infirm, sick, or injured; a hospital.

inflame /ɪnˈfleɪm/ *v.t.* **1.** to set aflame or afire. **2.** to light or redden with or as with flames: *the setting sun inflames the sky.* **3.** to arouse to a high degree of passion or feeling. **4.** to cause to redden through anger, rage, or some other emotion. **5.** to bring up redness in: *crying had inflamed her eyes.* **6.** to raise (the blood, bodily tissue, etc.) to feverish heat. –**inflamer**, *n.* –**inflamingly**, *adv.*

inflammable /ɪnˈflæməbəl/ *adj.* **1.** capable of being set on fire; combustible. **2.** easily roused to passion; excitable. –*n.* **3.** something which is inflammable.

–**inflammability** /ɪnˌflæməˈbɪləti/, **inflammableness**, *n.* –**inflammably**, *adv.*

inflammation /ɪnfləˈmeɪʃən/ *n.* **1.** the act of inflaming. **2.** the state of being inflamed. **3.** *Pathol.* a reaction of the body to injurious agents, commonly characterised by heat, redness, swelling, pain, etc., and disturbed function.

inflammatory /ɪnˈflæmətəri, -tri/ *adj.* **1.** tending to inflame; kindling passion, anger, etc.: *inflammatory speeches.* **2.** *Pathol.* relating to or attended with inflammation. –**inflammatorily**, *adv.*

inflate /ɪnˈfleɪt/ *v.t.* **1.** to stretch; swell or puff out; dilate; distend. **2.** to swell with gas: *to inflate a balloon.* **3.** to puff up with pride, satisfaction, etc.: *winning the race inflated his ego.* **4.** to expand (currency, prices, etc.) too much; raise above the previous or proper amount or value. –*v.i.* **5.** to cause inflation. **6.** to become inflated. –**inflatable**, *adj.* –**inflator**, *n.*

inflation /ɪnˈfleɪʃən/ *n.* **1.** undue expansion or increase of the currency of a country, especially by the issuing of paper money not redeemable in specie. **2. a.** a substantial rise of prices caused by an undue expansion in paper money or bank credit. **b. demand-pull inflation**, inflation occurring when total demand increases beyond existing supply at the existing price level. **c. cost-push inflation**, inflation occurring when total supply falls below existing demand at the existing price level, usually as a result of increases in the cost of production for whatever reason. **3.** the act of inflating. **4.** the state of being inflated. –**inflationary**, *adj.*

inflationary spiral *n. Econ.* the situation in which increasing prices lead to increasing wages which lead to increasing prices, and so on.

inflationism /ɪnˈfleɪʃənɪzəm/ *n. Econ.* the policy or practice of inflation through expansion of currency or bank deposits.

inflection /ɪnˈflɛkʃən/ *n.* **1.** modulation of the voice; change in pitch or tone of voice. **2.** *Gram.* **a.** the existence in a language of sets of forms built normally on a single stem, having different syntactic functions and meanings, but all those of a single stem being members of the same fundamental part of speech and constituting forms of the same 'word'. **b.** a change in the form of a word, generally by affixation, by means of which a change of meaning or relationship to some other word or group of words is indicated. **c.** the affix added to the stem to produce this change. For example: the *-s* in *dogs* and *-ed* in *played* are inflections. **3.** a bend or angle. **4.** *Maths* a change of curvature from convex to concave or vice versa. Also, **inflexion.** –**inflect**, *v.* –**inflectional**, *adj.* –**inflectionally**, *adv.* –**inflectionless**, *adj.*

inflexible /ɪnˈflɛksəbəl/ *adj.* **1.** not flexible; rigid: *an inflexible rod.* **2.** unyielding in temper or purpose: *inflexible under threat.* **3.** unalterable; not permitting variation. –**inflexibility** /ɪnˌflɛksəˈbɪləti/, **inflexibleness**, *n.* –**inflexibly**, *adv.*

inflict /ɪnˈflɪkt/ *v.t.* **1.** to lay on: *to inflict a dozen lashes.* **2.** to impose as something that must be borne or suffered: *to inflict punishment.* **3.** to impose (anything unwelcome). –**infliction**, *n.* –**inflictor**, *n.* –**inflictive**, *adj.*

inflorescence /ɪnfləˈrɛsəns/ *n.* **1.** a flowering or blossoming. **2.** *Bot.* **a.** the arrangement of flowers on the axis. **b.** the flowering part of a plant. **c.** a flower cluster. **d.** flowers collectively. **e.** a single flower. –**inflorescent**, *adj.*

influence /ˈɪnfluəns/ *n.* **1.** force or power exerted (knowingly or unknowingly) by someone or something on another, and producing change in behaviour, opinion, etc. **2.** a thing or person that exerts such action or power. –*v.t.* (**-enced, -encing**) **3.** to exercise influence on; modify; affect, or sway. –**influencer**, *n.* –**influential**, *adj.*

influenza /ˌɪnfluˈɛnzə/ n. **1.** Pathol. an acute, extremely contagious, commonly epidemic disease characterised by general prostration, and occurring in several forms with varying symptoms, usually with nasal catarrh and bronchial inflammation, and due to a specific virus; grippe. **2.** Vet. Science an acute, contagious disease occurring in horses and swine, manifested by fever and catarrhal inflammations of the eyes, nasal passages, and bronchi. –**influenzal**, adj.

influx /ˈɪnflʌks/ n. **1.** the act of flowing in; an inflow. **2.** the place or point at which one stream flows into another or into the sea. **3.** the mouth of a stream. **4.** the arrival of people or things in large numbers or great quantity.

infomercial /ˌɪnfoʊˈmɜːʃəl/ n. TV an advertisement of some length, in which the content is overtly instructive.

inform /ɪnˈfɔːm/ v.t. **1.** to impart knowledge of a fact or circumstance to: I informed him of my arrival. **2.** to supply (oneself) with knowledge of a matter or subject: he informed himself of all the pertinent facts. **3.** to give character to; pervade with determining effect on the character. **4.** to animate or inspire. –v.i. **5.** to give information, especially to furnish incriminating evidence to a prosecuting officer. –**informant**, n. –**informative**, adj. –**informingly**, adv.

informal /ɪnˈfɔːməl/ adj. **1.** not according to prescribed or customary forms; irregular: informal proceedings. **2.** without formality; unceremonious: an informal visit. **3.** not requiring formal dress: an informal dinner. **4.** denoting speech characterised by colloquial usage, having the flexibility of grammar, syntax, and pronunciation allowable in conversation. **5.** characterising the second singular pronominal or verbal form, or its use, in certain languages: the informal 'tu' in French. **6.** Aust., NZ (of a vote) invalid. –phr. **7.** **vote informal**, Aust. to mark a ballot paper incorrectly thereby invalidating one's vote. –**informality** /ˌɪnfɔˈmælɪti/, n. –**informally**, adv.

information /ˌɪnfəˈmeɪʃən/ n. **1.** knowledge given or received concerning some fact or circumstance; news. **2.** knowledge on various subjects, however obtained. **3.** (in communication theory) a quantitative measure of the contents of a message. –**informational**, adj.

information portal n. a website which provides information about an organisation, such as contacts, organisational structure, etc. Also, **enterprise information portal**.

information report n. a written or spoken text type or form which presents facts about an entire class of people, animals or objects.

information technology n. the use of computers to produce, store and retrieve information. Also, **IT**.

informer /ɪnˈfɔːmə/ n. **1.** someone who furnishes incriminating evidence to a prosecuting officer. **2.** an informant.

infotainment /ˌɪnfoʊˈteɪnmənt/ n. a genre of entertainment comprising television programs, computer games, etc., which presents information of educational value in an entertaining format.

infovore /ˈɪnfoʊvɔː/ n. a person who craves information, especially one who takes advantage of their ready access to it on digital devices.

infra /ˈɪnfrə/ adv. (in a text) below. Compare **supra**.

infra- a prefix meaning 'below' or 'beneath', as in infra-axillary (below the axilla).

infra-red n. /ˌɪnfrəˈrɛd/ **1.** the part of the invisible spectrum contiguous to the red end of the visible spectrum, comprising radiation of greater wavelength than that of red light. –adj. /ˈɪnfrəˌrɛd/ **2.** of or relating to the infra-red or its component rays: infra-red radiation.

infrastructure /ˈɪnfrəˌstrʌktʃə/ n. **1.** the basic framework or underlying foundation (as of an organisation or a system). **2.** the roads, railways, schools, and other capital equipment which comprise such an underlying system within a country or region. **3.** the buildings or permanent installations associated with any organisation, operation, etc. –**infrastructural**, adj. –**infrastructurally**, adv.

infrequent /ɪnˈfriːkwənt/ adj. **1.** happening or occurring at long intervals or not often: infrequent visits. **2.** not constant, habitual, or regular: an infrequent visitor. **3.** not plentiful. –**infrequency**, n. –**infrequently**, adv.

infringe /ɪnˈfrɪndʒ/ v.t. (**-fringed, -fringing**) **1.** to commit a breach or infraction of; violate or transgress. –phr. **2.** **infringe on** (or **upon**), to encroach or trespass on: don't infringe on his privacy. –**infringer**, n.

infuriate /ɪnˈfjʊrieɪt/ v.t. **1.** to make furious; enrage. **2.** to annoy intensely. –**infuriatingly**, adv. –**infuriation** /ɪnˌfjʊriˈeɪʃən/, n.

infuse /ɪnˈfjuːz/ v.t. **1.** to steep or soak (a plant, etc.) in a liquid so as to extract its soluble properties or ingredients. **2.** Cookery to boil slowly in a solution. **3.** to pour in. –phr. **4.** **infuse into**, to introduce into as by pouring; cause to penetrate; instil into: to infuse new life into an enterprise. **5.** **infuse with**, to imbue or inspire with. –**infuser**, n. –**infusive** /ɪnˈfjuːsɪv/, adj.

infusion /ɪnˈfjuːʒən/ n. **1.** the act of infusing. **2.** something that is infused. **3.** a liquid extract obtained from a substance by steeping or soaking it in water. **4.** Med. **a.** the introduction of a saline or other solution into a vein, artery, or tissue. **b.** the solution used.

-ing[1] a suffix of nouns formed from verbs, expressing the action of the verb or its result, product, material, etc., as in the art of building, a new building, cotton wadding. It is also used to form nouns from words other than verbs, as in offing, shirting.

-ing[2] a suffix forming the present participle of verbs, such participles often being used as adjectives (participial adjectives), as in warring factions. Compare **-ing**[1].

ingenious /ɪnˈdʒiːniəs/ adj. **1.** (of things, actions, etc.) showing cleverness of invention or construction: an ingenious machine. **2.** having inventive faculty; skilful in contriving or constructing: an ingenious mechanic. –**ingeniously**, adv. –**ingeniousness, ingenuity**, n.

ingenuous /ɪnˈdʒɛnjuəs/ adj. **1.** free from reserve, restraint, or dissimulation. **2.** artless; innocent. –**ingenuously**, adv. –**ingenuousness**, n.

ingest /ɪnˈdʒɛst/ v.t. **1.** Physiol. to put or take (food, etc.) into the body. **2.** Aeronautics (of a jet engine) to draw in (foreign matter). –**ingestion**, n. –**ingestive**, adj.

ingot /ˈɪŋɡət/ n. the casting obtained when melted metal is poured into a mould (**ingot mould**) with the expectation that it be further processed.

ingrain v.t. /ɪnˈɡreɪn/ Also, **engrain**. **1.** to fix deeply and firmly, as in the nature or mind. –adj. /ˈɪnɡreɪn/ **2.** Also, **engrain**. deeply fixed; ingrained. **3.** (of carpets) made of yarn dyed before weaving, and so woven as to show the pattern on both sides. **4.** dyed in grain, or through the fibre. **5.** dyed in the yarn, or in a raw state, before manufacture. –n. /ˈɪnɡreɪn/ **6.** yarn, wool, etc., dyed before manufacture. **7.** an ingrain carpet.

ingrained /ˈɪnɡreɪnd/ adj. **1.** fixed firmly: ingrained dirt. **2.** deep-rooted: ingrained habits. **3.** inveterate; thorough.

ingrate /ˈɪnɡreɪt/ n. **1.** an ungrateful person. –adj. **2.** ungrateful.

ingratiate /ɪnˈɡreɪʃieɪt/ v.t. to establish (oneself) in the favour or good graces of others. –**ingratiatingly**, adv. –**ingratiation** /ɪnˌɡreɪʃiˈeɪʃən/, n. –**ingratiatory**, adj.

ingratitude /ɪnˈɡrætətjuːd, -tʃuːd/ n. the state of being ungrateful; unthankfulness.

ingredient /ɪnˈɡriːdiənt/ n. **1.** something that enters as an element into a mixture: the ingredients of a cake. **2.** a constituent element of anything.

ingress /'ɪŋgrɛs/ *n.* **1.** the act of going in or entering. **2.** the right of going in. **3.** a means or place of going in; an entrance. –**ingression** /ɪn'grɛʃən/, *n.* –**ingressive** /ɪn'grɛsɪv/, *adj.* –**ingressiveness** /ɪn'grɛsɪvnəs/, *n.*

inhabit /ɪn'hæbət/ *v.t.* **1.** to live or dwell in (a place), as persons or animals. **2.** to have its seat, or exist, in. –**inhabitable**, *adj.* –**inhabitability** /ɪn,hæbətə'bɪləti/, *n.* –**inhabitation** /ɪn,hæbə'teɪʃən/, *n.* –**inhabitant**, *n.*

inhabited /ɪn'hæbətəd/ *adj.* **1.** lived in: *an inhabited island.* **2.** *Internet* (of virtual reality environments) accessible to public participation: *inhabited digital spaces.*

inhale /ɪn'heɪl/ *v.t.* **1.** to breathe in; draw in by, or as by, breathing: *to inhale air.* –*v.i.* **2.** to draw something into the lungs, especially smoke of cigarettes, cigars, etc.: *do you inhale?* –**inhalation**, *n.*

inherent /ɪn'hɛrənt, ɪn'hɪərənt/ *adj.* existing in something as a permanent and inseparable element, quality, or attribute. –**inherently**, *adv.* –**inherence**, *n.*

inherit /ɪn'hɛrət/ *v.t.* **1.** to take or receive (property, a right, a title, etc.) as the heir of the former owner. **2.** to possess as a hereditary characteristic: *she inherited her mother's blue eyes.* –*v.i.* **3.** to take or receive property, etc., as being heir to it. –**inheritor**, *n.* –**inheritress, inheritrix**, *fem. n.* –**inheritable**, *adj.*

inheritance /ɪn'hɛrətəns/ *n.* **1.** something that is or may be inherited; any property passing at the owner's death to the heir or those entitled to succeed. **2.** a hereditary characteristic or characteristics collectively. **3.** anything received from progenitors or predecessors as if by succession: *an inheritance of family pride.* **4.** portion, peculiar possession, or heritage: *the inheritance of the saints.* **5.** the act or fact of inheriting: *to receive property by inheritance.*

inhesion /ɪn'hiʒən/ *n.* the state or fact of inhering; inherence.

inhibit /ɪn'hɪbət/ *v.t.* **1.** to restrain, hinder, arrest, or check (an action, impulse, etc.). **2.** *Electronics* to prevent the occurrence of (a signal) in a circuit. **3.** *Chem.* to decrease the rate of (a chemical reaction) or to stop (it) completely. **4.** *Eccles.* to prohibit; forbid. –**inhibiter**, *n.* –**inhibitory, inhibitive**, *adj.*

inhibition /ɪnə'bɪʃən, ɪnhɪ-/ *n.* **1.** the act of inhibiting. **2.** the state of being inhibited. **3.** *Psychol.* the blocking of any psychological process by another psychological process. **4.** *Physiol.* a restraining, arresting, or checking, as of action; the reduction of a reflex or other activity as the result of an antagonistic stimulation.

inhospitable /ɪnhɒs'pɪtəbəl/ *adj.* **1.** not inclined to or characterised by hospitality, as persons, actions, etc. **2.** (of a region, climate, etc.) not offering shelter, favourable conditions, etc. –**inhospitableness**, *n.* –**inhospitably**, *adv.* –**inhospitality** /ɪn,hɒspə'tæləti/, *n.*

inhuman /ɪn'hjumən/ *adj.* **1.** lacking natural human feeling or sympathy for others; brutal. **2.** not human. –**inhumanity, inhumanness**, *n.* –**inhumanly**, *adv.*

inhumane /ɪnhju'meɪn/ *adj.* not humane; lacking humanity or kindness. –**inhumanely**, *adv.* –**inhumanity**, *n.*

inhume /ɪn'hjum/ *v.t.* to bury; inter. –**inhumation** /ɪnhju'meɪʃən/, *n.*

inimical /ɪ'nɪmɪkəl/ *adj.* **1.** adverse in tendency or effect: *a climate inimical to health.* **2.** unfriendly or hostile. –**inimicality** /ɪ,nɪmɪ'kæləti/, *n.* –**inimically**, *adv.*

inimitable /ɪ'nɪmətəbəl/ *adj.* incapable of being imitated; surpassing imitation. –**inimitability** /ɪ,nɪmɪtə'bɪləti/, **inimitableness**, *n.* –**inimitably**, *adv.*

iniquity /ɪ'nɪkwəti/ *n.* (*pl.* **-ties**) **1.** gross injustice; wickedness. **2.** a violation of right or duty; wicked action; sin. –**iniquitous**, *adj.*

initial /ɪ'nɪʃəl/ *adj.* **1.** of or relating to the beginning; incipient: *the initial step in a process.* –*n.* **2.** an initial letter, as of a word. **3.** the first letter of a proper name. **4.** a letter of extra size, often decorated, used at the

beginning of a chapter or other division of a book, etc. –*v.t.* (**-ialled** *or, US,* **-ialed, -ialling** *or, US,* **-ialing**) **5.** to mark or sign with an initial or initials, especially as an indication of responsibility for or approval of contents. –**initially**, *adv.*

initialism /ɪ'nɪʃəlɪzm/ *n.* an abbreviation formed from the initial letters of a sequence of words, as *ACTU* (from *Australian Council of Trade Unions*) or *LPG* (from *liquefied petroleum gas*).

initial public offering *n. Commerce* the first offering of shares in a company to the public, often to raise capital to finance new ventures, expansion of operations, or a continuation of current activities. Also, **IPO.**

initiate /ɪ'nɪʃieɪt/ *v.t.* **1.** to begin, set going, or originate: *to initiate reforms.* **2.** to introduce into the knowledge of some art or subject. **3.** to admit with formal rites into secret knowledge, a society, etc. **4.** to propose (a measure) by initiative procedure: *to initiate a constitutional amendment.* –**initiation**, *n.* –**initiator**, *n.* –**initiatory**, *adj.*

initiative /ə'nɪʃiətɪv, ə'nɪʃətɪv, ə'nɪʃʃətɪv/ *n.* **1.** an introductory act or step; leading action: *to take the initiative.* **2.** readiness and ability in initiating action; enterprise: *to lack initiative.* **3.** *Govt* **a.** a procedure by which a specified number of voters may propose a statute, constitutional amendment, or ordinance, and compel a popular vote on its adoption. **b.** the general right or ability to present a new bill or measure, as in a legislature. –*adj.* **4.** serving to initiate; relating to initiation. –**initiatively**, *adv.*

inject /ɪn'dʒɛkt/ *v.t.* **1.** to force (a fluid) into a passage, cavity, or tissue. **2.** to force a fluid into (a person, tissue, etc.) especially for medical purposes. **3.** to introduce (something new or different) into a thing: *to inject comedy into a situation.* **4.** to interject (a remark, suggestion, etc.), as into conversation. –*v.i.* **5.** (of an illegal drug user) to use a syringe to introduce a drug intravenously: *he's been injecting again.* –**injectable**, *adj.*

injecting room *n.* → **safe injecting room.**

injection /ɪn'dʒɛkʃən/ *n.* **1.** the act of injecting. **2.** something that is injected. **3.** a liquid injected into the body, especially for medical purposes, as a hypodermic or an enema. **4.** → **fuel-injection.**

injunction /ɪn'dʒʌŋkʃən/ *n.* **1.** *Law* a judicial process or order requiring the person or persons to whom it is directed to do or (more commonly) not to do a particular thing. **2.** the act of enjoining. **3.** something that is enjoined; a command, order or admonition. –**injunctive**, *adj.*

injure /'ɪndʒə/ *v.t.* **1.** to do or cause harm of any kind to; damage; hurt; impair: *to injure the hand.* **2.** to do wrong or injustice to. –**injurer**, *n.* –**injury**, *n.*

injustice /ɪn'dʒʌstəs/ *n.* **1.** the quality or fact of being unjust. **2.** unjust action or treatment; violation of another's rights. **3.** an unjust act or circumstance.

ink /ɪŋk/ *n.* **1.** a fluid or viscous substance used for writing or printing. **2.** a dark, protective fluid ejected by the cuttlefish and other cephalopods. –*v.t.* **3.** to mark, stain, cover, or smear with ink. –**inker**, *n.* –**inkless**, *adj.* –**inky**, *adj.*

inkling /'ɪŋklɪŋ/ *n.* **1.** a hint, intimation, or slight suggestion. **2.** a vague idea or notion.

inland /'ɪnlænd/ *adj.* **1.** relating to or situated in the interior part of a country or region: *inland cities.* **2.** carried on within a country; domestic; not foreign: *inland trade.* **3.** confined to a country. –*adv.* **4.** in or towards the interior of a country. –*n.* **5.** the interior part of a country, away from the border.

in-law *n.* a relative by marriage.

-in-law a suffix meaning 'related by marriage', as *grandparents-in-law.*

inlay *v.t.* /ɪn'leɪ/ (**-laid, -laying**) **1.** to ornament (an object) with thin layers of fine materials set in its surface. **2.** to fix (layers of fine materials) in a surface of an object. –n. /'ınleı/ **3.** work or decoration made by inlaying. **4.** a layer of fine material set in something else. **5.** *Dentistry* a filling of metal, etc., which is fitted and fastened into a tooth as a solid mass. **–inlayer,** *n.*

inlet *n.* /'ınlət/ **1.** an indentation of a shoreline, usually long and narrow, or a narrow passage between islands. **2.** a place of admission; an entrance. **3.** something put in or inserted. –v.t. /ın'let/ (**-let, -letting**) **4.** to put in; insert.

inline skate *n.* → **rollerblade**.

inmate /'ınmeıt/ *n.* one of those confined in a hospital, prison, etc.

inmost /'ınmoʊst/ *adj.* **1.** situated farthest within: *the inmost recesses of the forest.* **2.** most intimate: *one's inmost thoughts.*

inn /ın/ *n.* a small hotel that provides lodging, food, etc., for travellers and others: *a country inn.* **–innless,** *adj.*

innards /'ınədz/ *pl. n.* **1.** the inward parts of the body; entrails; viscera. **2.** the inner parts of objects, not normally visible: *the innards of a computer.*

innate /ı'neıt/ *adj.* **1.** inborn; existing or as if existing in one from birth: *innate modesty.* **2.** inherent in the essential character of something. **3.** arising from the constitution of the mind, rather than acquired from experience: *innate ideas.* **–innately,** *adv.* **–innateness,** *n.*

inner /'ınə/ *adj.* **1.** situated further within; interior: *an inner door.* **2.** more private or secret: *the inner circle of his friends.* **3.** mental or spiritual: *the inner life.* **4.** not obvious; esoteric: *an inner meaning.* –n. **5.** (the shot striking) the ring nearest the bullseye of a target. **–innerness,** *n.*

innermost /'ınəmoʊst/ *adj.* **1.** farthest inwards; inmost. –n. **2.** innermost part.

innings /'ınıŋz/ *pl. n.* (*construed as sing.*) **1.** *Cricket* **a.** the turn of any one member of the batting team to bat. **b.** one of the major divisions of a match, consisting of the turns at batting of all the members of one team until they are all out or until the team declares. **c.** the runs scored during such a turn or such a division. **2.** a similar opportunity to score in certain other games. **3.** any opportunity for some activity; a turn. –*phr.* **4. have had a good innings,** *Colloq.* to have had a long life or long and successful career.

innocent /'ınəsənt/ *adj.* **1.** free from any moral wrong; not tainted with sin; pure: *innocent children.* **2.** free from legal or specific wrong; guiltless: *to be innocent of crime.* **3.** not involving evil intent or motive: *an innocent misrepresentation.* **4.** free from any quality that can cause physical or moral injury; harmless: *innocent fun.* **5.** having or showing the simplicity or naivety of an unworldly person: *she looks so innocent.* –n. **6.** an innocent person. **7.** a young child. **8.** a guileless person. –*phr.* **9. an innocent abroad,** a guileless person in a situation where they are likely to be deceived or taken in by others. **10. innocent of,** devoid of: *a law innocent of merit.* **–innocence,** *n.* **–innocently,** *adv.*

innocuous /ı'nɒkjuəs/ *adj.* not harmful or injurious; harmless. **–innocuously,** *adv.* **–innocuousness,** *n.*

innovate /'ınəveıt/ *v.i.* (sometimes fol. by *on* or *in*) to bring in something new; make changes in anything established. –*v.t.* **2.** to bring in (something new) for the first time. **–innovator,** *n.*

innovation /ınə'veıʃən/ *n.* **1.** something new or different introduced. **2.** the act of innovating; introducing of new things or methods. **–innovational,** *adj.* **–innovationist,** *n.*

innovative /'ınəvətıv/ *adj.* new and original. Also, **innovatory.** **–innovativeness,** *n.* **–innovatively,** *adv.*

innuendo /ınju'ɛndoʊ/ *n.* (*pl.* **-dos** *or* **-does**) an indirect intimation about a person or thing, especially of a derogatory nature.

innumerable /ı'njumərəbəl, ı'njumrəbəl/ *adj.* **1.** very numerous. **2.** incapable of being numbered or definitely counted. **–innumerableness, innumerability** /ı,njumərə-'bıləti/, *n.* **–innumerably,** *adv.*

inoculate /ı'nɒkjəleıt/ *v.t.* **1.** to implant (a disease) in a person or animal by the introduction of germs or virus, as through a puncture, in order to produce a mild form of the disease and thus secure immunity. **2.** to impregnate (a person or animal) thus. **3.** to introduce (microorganisms) into surroundings suited to their growth, especially into the body. **4.** to imbue (a person, etc.), as with ideas. **–inoculant,** *n.* **–inoculation,** *n.* **–inoculative,** *adj.* **–inoculator,** *n.*

inoffensive /ınə'fɛnsıv/ *adj.* **1.** doing no harm; harmless; unoffending: *a mild, inoffensive man.* **2.** not objectionable, or not being a cause of offence. **–inoffensively,** *adv.* **–inoffensiveness,** *n.*

inoperable /ın'ɒpərəbəl, -'ɒprə-/ *adj.* **1.** not operable. **2.** not admitting of a surgical operation without risk.

inoperative /ın'ɒpərətıv, -'ɒprə-/ *adj.* **1.** not operative; not in operation. **2.** without effect: *inoperative remedies.* **–inoperativeness,** *n.*

inopportune /ınɒpə'tjun, -'tʃun, ın'ɒpətjun, -tʃun/ *adj.* not opportune; inappropriate; (with regard to time) unseasonable: *an inopportune visit.* **–inopportunely,** *adv.* **–inopportuneness, inopportunity** /ınɒpə'tjunəti/, *n.*

inordinate /ın'ɔdənət/ *adj.* not within proper limits; excessive: *inordinate demands.* **–inordinacy, inordinateness,** *n.* **–inordinately,** *adv.*

inorganic /ınɔ'gænık/ *adj.* **1.** not having the organisation which characterises living bodies. **2.** not characterised by vital processes. **3.** *Chem.* of or relating to compounds not containing carbon, excepting cyanides and carbonates. Compare **organic** (def. 1). **4.** not fundamental; extraneous. **–inorganically,** *adv.*

inpatient /'ınpeıʃənt/ *n.* a patient who is accommodated in a hospital for the duration of their treatment. Also, **in-patient.**

input /'ınpʊt/ *n.* **1.** something that is put in. **2.** the current or voltage fed to an electrical machine, circuit, or device. **3.** *Computers* information which is fed into a computer before computation. **4.** a contribution of information, advice, etc.: *did you have any input into the design?* –v.t. (**-put, -putting**) **5.** to feed (information) into a computer.

input tax credit *n.* a tax credit for all GST paid on inputs involved in the production and sale of taxable goods and services.

inquest /'ınkwɛst/ *n.* **1.** a legal or judicial inquiry, especially before a jury. **2.** such an inquiry made by a coroner (**coroner's inquest**). **3.** the body of people appointed to hold such an inquiry, especially a coroner's jury. **4.** their decision or finding.

inquire /ın'kwaıə, ən-/ *v.i.* **1.** to seek information by questioning; ask. –*v.t.* **2.** to seek to learn by asking. Also, **enquire. –inquirer,** *n.*

inquiry /ın'kwaırı, ən-/ *n.* (*pl.* **-ries**) **1.** an investigation, or into a matter. **2.** the act of inquiring, or seeking information by questioning; interrogation. Also, **enquiry.**

inquisition /ınkwə'zıʃən/ *n.* **1.** an investigation or inquiry, as one conducted by judicial or non-judicial officers. **2.** (*upper case*) *Roman Catholic Church* a special court for the defence of Catholic teaching and the judgement of heresy. **–inquisitional,** *adj.* **–inquisitor,** *n.*

inquisitive /ın'kwızətıv/ *adj.* **1.** unduly curious; prying. **2.** inquiring; desirous of or eager for knowledge. **–inquisitively,** *adv.* **–inquisitiveness,** *n.*

inroad /'ınroʊd/ *n.* **1.** (*usu. pl.*) forcible or serious encroachment: *inroads on our savings.* **2.** a hostile or predatory incursion; a raid; a foray.

insane /ın'seın/ *adj.* **1.** not sane; not of sound mind; mentally deranged. **2.** characteristic of one mentally deranged. **3.** set apart for the care and confinement of mentally deranged persons: *an insane asylum.* **4.** utterly senseless: *an insane attempt.* **5.** *Colloq.* fantastic; wonderful. **–insanity** /ɪnˈsænəti/, *n.* **–insanely,** *adv.*

insatiable /ɪnˈseɪʃəbəl/ *adj.* not satiable; incapable of being satisfied: *insatiable desire.* **–insatiability** /ɪnˌseɪʃə-ˈbɪləti/, **insatiableness,** *n.* **–insatiably,** *adv.*

inscribe /ɪnˈskraɪb/ *v.t.* **1.** to write or engrave (words, characters, etc.). **2.** to mark (a surface) with words, characters, etc., especially in a durable or conspicuous way. **3.** to address or dedicate (a book, photograph, etc.) informally, especially by a handwritten note. **4.** to enrol, as on an official list. **5.** *Geom.* to draw or delineate (one figure) within another figure so that the inner lies in the boundary of the outer at as many points as possible. **–inscribable,** *adj.* **–inscriber,** *n.* **–inscription,** *n.*

inscrutable /ɪnˈskruːtəbəl/ *adj.* **1.** incapable of being searched into or scrutinised; impenetrable to investigation. **2.** not easily understood; mysterious; enigmatic. **3.** impenetrable or unfathomable physically. **–inscrutability** /ɪnˌskruːtəˈbɪləti/, **inscrutableness,** *n.* **–inscrutably,** *adv.*

insect /ˈɪnsɛkt/ *n.* **1.** *Zool.* any animal of the subphylum Hexapoda, a group of small, air-breathing arthropods characterised by a body clearly divided into three parts, head, thorax, and abdomen, and by having only three pairs of legs, and usually having two pairs of wings. **2.** any small, air-breathing arthropod, such as a spider, tick, or centipede, having superficial, general similarity to the Hexapoda. **3.** *Obs. Colloq.* a contemptible person. **–insect-like,** *adj.*

insecticide /ɪnˈsɛktəsaɪd/ *n.* a substance or preparation used for killing insects. **–insecticidal** /ɪnˌsɛktəˈsaɪdl/, *adj.*

insectivore /ɪnˈsɛktəvɔ/ *n.* **1.** an animal that eats insects, such as the numbat or the echidna. **2.** a bird that eats insects, such as swallows, magpies, ravens, etc.

insectivorous /ɪnsɛkˈtɪvərəs/ *adj.* adapted to feeding on insects, as shrews, moles, hedgehogs, or certain bats, birds, etc.

insecure /ɪnsəˈkjuə, -ˈkjʊə/ *adj.* **1.** exposed to danger; unsafe. **2.** not firm or safe: *insecure foundations.* **3.** not free from fear, doubt, etc. **–insecurely,** *adv.* **–insecurity,** *n.*

inseminate /ɪnˈsɛmətneɪt/ *v.t.* **1.** to sow; inject seed into. **2.** to introduce semen into (a female) to cause fertilisation; impregnate. **3.** to sow as seed in something; implant. **–insemination** /ɪnˌsɛməˈneɪʃən/, *n.*

insensate /ɪnˈsɛnseɪt, -sət/ *adj.* **1.** not endowed with sensation: *insensate stone.* **2.** without feeling; unfeeling. **3.** without sense, understanding, or judgement. **–insensately,** *adv.* **–insensateness,** *n.*

insensible /ɪnˈsɛnsəbəl/ *adj.* **1.** incapable of feeling or perceiving; deprived of sensation; unconscious, as a person after a violent blow. **2.** without, or not subject to, a particular feeling: *insensible to shame.* **3.** unconscious, unaware, or unappreciative: *we are not insensible of your kindness.* **4.** not perceptible by the senses: *insensible transitions.* **–insensibly,** *adv.* **–insensibility** /ɪnˌsɛnsəˈbɪləti/, *n.*

insensitive /ɪnˈsɛnsətɪv/ *adj.* **1.** not sensitive: *an insensitive skin.* **2.** not susceptible to agencies or influences: *insensitive to light.* **3.** deficient in sensibility or acuteness of feeling: *an insensitive nature.* **–insensitiveness, insensitivity** /ɪnˌsɛnsəˈtɪvəti/, *n.* **–insensitively,** *adv.*

inseparable /ɪnˈsɛpərəbəl, -prə-/ *adj.* incapable of being separated, parted, or disjoined: *inseparable companions.* **–inseparability** /ɪnˌsɛpərəˈbɪləti/, **inseparableness,** *n.* **–inseparably,** *adv.*

insert *v.t.* /ɪnˈsɜt/ **1.** to put or set in: *to insert a key in a lock.* **2.** to introduce into the body of something: *to insert an advertisement in a newspaper.* **–n.** /ˈɪnsɜt/

3. something inserted, or to be inserted. **4.** an extra leaf printed independently of the sheets comprising a book but included when the book is bound. **–inserter,** *n.* **–insertion,** *n.*

in-service *adj.* of or relating to any training undertaken in conjunction with the actual performance of the work involved, as courses in remedial reading techniques, creative drama, etc., for teachers.

inset *n.* /ˈɪnsɛt/ **1.** something put or set into or inside something else. **–v.t.** /ɪnˈsɛt/ **(-set, -setting) 2.** to set in; insert.

inside *prep.* /ɪnˈsaɪd/ **1.** on the inner side of; within: *inside the circle.* **2.** before the elapse of: *inside an hour.* **–adv.** /ɪnˈsaɪd/ **3. a.** in or into the inner part: *to go inside.* **b.** *Colloq.* in or towards a more densely settled part of the country: *inside, somewhere east of Cobar.* **4.** indoors: *he is working inside.* **5.** by nature; fundamentally: *inside, he's very kind.* **6.** *Colloq.* to or in prison. **–n.** /ˈɪnsaɪd/ **7.** the inner part; interior: *the inside of the house.* **8.** the inner side or surface: *the inside of the hand.* **9.** (*oft. pl.*) *Colloq.* the inward parts of the body, especially the stomach and intestines. **10.** the inward nature. **11.** the part of a curved track or course nearer to the centre of the curves; the inside lane: *a horse coming up fast on the inside*; *the inside of the bend.* **12.** an inner group of persons having private knowledge about a circumstance or case. **13.** Also, **inside forward.** *Soccer, etc.* an inside left or inside right. **14.** *Surfing* the inner part of a breaking wave closest to the white water. **–adj.** /ˈɪnsaɪd/ **15. a.** situated or being on or in the inside; interior: *an inside loo.* **b.** *Colloq.* relating to a more densely settled part of the country: *he only shears in inside areas.* **16.** acting, employed, done, or originating within a building or place: *the robbery was an inside job.* **17.** derived from the inner circle of those concerned in and having private knowledge of a case: *inside information.* **18.** running nearer to the centre and therefore shorter: *the inside lane of a track.* **–phr.** **19. inside out, a.** with the inner side reversed to face outwards. **b.** thoroughly; completely: *he knows his job inside out.*

insider /ɪnˈsaɪdə/ *n.* **1.** someone who is inside some place, society, etc. **2.** someone who is within a limited circle of persons who understand the actual facts of a case.

insider attack *n.* an attack from a person within your own troops, police force, etc., usually an enemy who has infiltrated.

insider trading *n.* (in company law) the statutory offence of dealing in a company's securities by someone who through some connection with the company has special information about them which would materially affect the price of the securities if it were generally known.

inside track *n.* **1.** the lane on a racecourse nearest the inside edge, and therefore shorter than the other lanes. **2.** a favoured position. **–phr.** **3. have an inside track to,** to have access to (influential people) thus gaining an advantage over one's competitors. **4. have the inside track,** to have an advantage over one's competitors.

insidious /ɪnˈsɪdiəs/ *adj.* **1.** intended to entrap or beguile: *an insidious plot.* **2.** stealthily treacherous or deceitful: *an insidious enemy.* **3.** operating or proceeding inconspicuously but with grave effect: *an insidious disease.* **–insidiously,** *adv.* **–insidiousness,** *n.*

insight /ˈɪnsaɪt/ *n.* **1.** an understanding gained or given of something: *this little insight into the life of the village.* **2.** penetrating mental vision or discernment; faculty of seeing into inner character or underlying truth: *a man of great insight.*

insignia /ɪnˈsɪgniə/ *n.* (*pl.* **insignia** *or* **insignias**) **1.** a badge or distinguishing mark of office or honour: *her insignia of office.* **2.** a distinguishing mark or sign of anything: *the insignia of mourning.*

insignificant /ˌɪnsɪɡˈnɪfɪkənt/ *adj.* **1.** unimportant, trifling, or petty, as things, matters, details, etc. **2.** too small to be important: *an insignificant sum.* **3.** of no consequence, influence, or distinction, as persons. **4.** without weight of character; contemptible: *an insignificant fellow.* **5.** without meaning; meaningless, as terms. **–insignificance**, *n.* **–insignificantly**, *adv.*

insincere /ˌɪnsənˈsɪə, -sɪn-/ *adj.* not sincere; not honest in the expression of actual feeling. **–insincerely**, *adv.* **–insincerity** /ˌɪnsənˈsɛrəti, -sɪn-/, *n.*

insinuate /ɪnˈsɪnjueɪt/ *v.t.* **1.** to suggest or hint slyly. **2.** instil or infuse subtly or artfully into the mind: *to insinuate doubt.* **3.** to bring or introduce into a position or relation by indirect or artful methods: *to insinuate oneself into the favour of another. –v.i.* **4.** to make insinuations. **–insinuatingly**, *adv.* **–insinuative**, *adj.* **–insinuator**, *n.*

insipid /ɪnˈsɪpəd/ *adj.* **1.** without distinctive, interesting, or attractive qualities: *an insipid tale.* **2.** without sufficient taste to be pleasing, as food or drink: *a rather insipid fruit.* **–insipidity** /ˌɪnsɪˈpɪdəti/, **insipidness**, *n.* **–insipidly**, *adv.*

insist /ɪnˈsɪst/ *v.i.* **1.** to assert or maintain positively. **2.** to demand; require: *to insist that the correct uniform is worn. –phr.* **3. insist on**, to be emphatically firm in regard to: *to insist on complete obedience.* **–insister**, *n.*

insistent /ɪnˈsɪstənt/ *adj.* **1.** insisting; earnest or emphatic in dwelling upon, maintaining, or demanding something; persistent. **2.** compelling attention or notice: *an insistent tone.* **–insistence, insistency**, *n.* **–insistently**, *adv.*

in situ /ɪn ˈsɪtʃu/ *adv.* in the original, actual or appropriate place.

insofar as /ɪnsoʊˈfar æz/ *conj.* to the extent that. Also, **in so far as**.

insolent /ˈɪnsələnt/ *adj.* boldly rude or disrespectful; contemptuously impertinent; insulting: *an insolent reply.* **–insolence**, *n.* **–insolently**, *adv.*

insoluble /ɪnˈsɒljubəl/ *adj.* **1.** incapable of being dissolved: *insoluble salts.* **2.** that cannot be solved: *an insoluble problem.* **–insolubility** /ɪnˌsɒljuˈbɪləti/, **insolubleness**, *n.* **–insolubly**, *adv.*

insolvent /ɪnˈsɒlvənt/ *adj.* not solvent; unable to satisfy creditors or discharge liabilities, either because liabilities exceed assets or because of inability to pay debts as they mature. **–insolvency**, *n.* **–insolvently**, *adv.*

insomnia /ɪnˈsɒmniə/ *n.* inability to sleep, especially when chronic; sleeplessness. **–insomniac**, *n.* **–insomnious**, *adj.*

insouciant /ɪnˈsusiənt, -sjənt/ *adj.* free from concern; without anxiety; carefree. **–insouciance**, *n.* **–insouciantly**, *adv.*

inspect /ɪnˈspɛkt/ *v.t.* **1.** to look carefully at or over; view closely and critically: *to inspect every part.* **2.** to view or examine formally or officially: *to inspect troops.* **–inspection**, *n.*

inspector /ɪnˈspɛktə/ *n.* **1.** someone who inspects. **2.** an officer appointed to inspect. **3.** someone who makes assessments for taxation purposes: *an inspector of taxes.* **4.** a police officer ranking above sergeant and below chief inspector. **5.** the rank of any of these. **–inspectoral, inspectorial** /ɪnspɛkˈtɔriəl/, *adj.* **–inspectorship**, *n.*

inspiration /ˌɪnspəˈreɪʃən/ *n.* **1.** an inspiring action or influence, person or thing, as a divine influence brought to bear on a person. **2.** something inspired, as a thought. **3.** the drawing of air into the lungs; inhalation. **4.** the act of inspiring. **5.** the state of being inspired. **–inspirational**, *adj.*

inspire /ɪnˈspaɪə/ *v.t.* **1.** to impart an enlivening, quickening, or exalting influence to: *his courage inspired his followers.* **2.** to produce or awaken (a feeling, thought, etc.): *she inspires confidence in others.* **3.** to affect with a particular feeling, thought, etc.: *inspire a person with distrust.* **4.** of an influence, feeling, etc.) to move to action: *hope inspired her to persevere.* **5.** to guide or communicate by a divine influence. **6.** to give rise to: *what inspired the quarrel?* **7.** to take (air, gases, etc.) into the lungs in breathing; inhale. *–v.i.* **8.** to give inspiration. **9.** to inhale. **–inspirer**, *n.* **–inspiringly**, *adv.* **–inspirable**, *adj.*

inspirit /ɪnˈspɪrət/ *v.t.* to infuse (new) spirit or life into. **–inspiritingly**, *adv.*

instability /ɪnstəˈbɪləti/ *n.* the state of being instable; lack of stability or firmness.

install /ɪnˈstɔl/ *v.t.* **1.** to place in position for service or use, as a system of electric lighting, etc. **2.** to establish in any office, position, or place. **3.** to induct into an office, etc., with ceremonies or formalities, as by seating in a stall or official seat. **4.** *Computers* to load (a software application) onto a digital device. **–installer**, *n.* **–installation**, *n.*

instalment /ɪnˈstɔlmənt/ *n.* **1.** any of several parts into which a debt or other sum payable is divided for payment at successive fixed times: *to pay for furniture by instalments.* **2.** a single portion of something provided or issued by parts at successive times: *a serial in six instalments.* Also, *US*, **installment**.

instance /ˈɪnstəns/ *n.* **1.** a case of anything: *fresh instances of oppression.* **2.** an example put forth in proof or illustration: *an instance of carelessness.* **3.** legal process (now chiefly in certain expressions): *a court of first instance. –v.t.* (**-stanced, -stancing**) **4.** to cite as an instance or example. *–phr.* **5. at the instance of**, at the urgency, solicitation, instigation, or suggestion of. **6. for instance**, for example; as an example. **7. give someone a for instance**, *Colloq.* to give someone an example.

instant /ˈɪnstənt/ *n.* **1.** a very short space of time; a moment: *not an instant too soon.* **2.** the point of time now present, or present with regard to some action or event. *–adj.* **3.** following without any interval of time; immediate: *instant relief.* **4.** present; current: *the 10th instant* (the tenth day of the present month). **5.** pressing or urgent: *instant need.* **6.** (of a foodstuff) processed for simple preparation: *instant coffee.* **–instantly**, *adv.*

instantaneous /ˌɪnstənˈteɪniəs/ *adj.* **1.** occurring, done, or completed in an instant: *an instantaneous explosion.* **2.** existing at or relating to a particular instant: *the instantaneous position of something.* **–instantaneously**, *adv.* **–instantaneousness, instantaneity** /ɪnˌstæntəˈniəti/, *n.*

instant coffee *n.* a coffee preparation made by reducing brewed coffee to a powdered or granulated form by freeze-drying or spray-drying so that, with the addition of boiling water, it can be reconstituted as a coffee drink.

instantiate /ɪnˈstænʃieɪt/ *v.t.* to form or provide a concrete instance of: *to instantiate a particular usage in real text.* **–instantiation**, *n.*

instant messaging *n.* text-based, real-time communication between individuals by means of a network of computers and the internet.

instead /ɪnˈstɛd/ *adv.* **1.** in one's (its, their, etc.) stead: *she sent the boy instead. –phr.* **2. instead of**, in the stead or place of; in lieu of: *come by plane instead of by train.*

instep /ˈɪnstɛp/ *n.* **1.** the curved inner surface of the human foot, between the big toe and the heel. **2.** the part of the foot between the ankle and the toes. **3.** the part of a shoe, stocking, etc., covering this area.

instigate /ˈɪnstəɡeɪt/ *v.t.* **1.** to spur on, set on, or incite to some action or course: *to instigate someone to commit a crime.* **2.** to bring about by incitement; foment: *to instigate a quarrel.* **–instigative**, *adj.* **–instigator**, *n.* **–instigation** /ɪnstəˈɡeɪʃən/, *n.*

instil /ɪnˈstɪl/ v.t. (-stilled, -stilling) 1. to infuse slowly or by degrees into the mind or feelings; insinuate; inject: *courtesy must be instilled in childhood.* 2. to put in drop by drop. Also, *Chiefly US*, **instill**. –**instiller**, n. –**instillation** /ɪnstɪˈleɪʃən/, **instilment**, n.

instinct /ˈɪnstɪŋkt/ n. 1. *Zool., Psychol., etc.* an inborn pattern of activity and response common to a given biological stock. 2. innate impulse or natural inclination, or a particular natural inclination or tendency. 3. a natural aptitude or gift for something: *an instinct for art.* 4. natural intuitive power.

institute /ˈɪnstətʃut/ v.t. 1. to set up or establish: *to institute a government.* 2. to inaugurate; initiate: *to institute a new course.* 3. to bring into use or practice: *to institute laws.* 4. to establish in an office or position. –n. 5. a society or organisation for carrying on literary, scientific or educational work. 6. the building occupied by such a society. 7. *Educ.* a. an institution, usually attended after high school level, which teaches technical subjects. b. a unit in a university for advanced instruction and research. 8. an established principle, law, custom, or organisation.

institution /ɪnstəˈtjuʃən/ n. 1. an organisation for the advancement of a particular purpose, usually educational, charitable, etc. 2. a building used for such work, as a college, school, hospital, etc. 3. a concern engaged in some activity, as an insurance company. 4. any established law, custom, etc., in a particular culture, such as slavery. 5. the act of setting up; establishment: *the institution of laws.* –**institutionary**, adj. –**institutive** /ˈɪnstətjutɪv/, adj. –**institutor, instituter**, n.

institutional /ɪnstəˈtjuʃənəl/ adj. 1. relating to or established by institution. 2. of or relating to organised societies or to the buildings used for their work. 3. being an institution. 4. characterised by uniformity and dullness. 5. of or relating to institutes or principles, especially of jurisprudence. –**institutionally**, adv.

institutionalise /ɪnstəˈtjuʃənəlaɪz/ v.t. 1. to make institutional. 2. to make into or treat as an institution. 3. to put (a person) into an institution. 4. to make (a person) dependent on an institution, such as a prison, mental hospital, etc., to the point where he or she cannot live successfully outside it. Also, **institutionalize**. –**institutionalisation** /ɪnstəˌtjuʃənəlaɪˈzeɪʃən/, n.

instruct /ɪnˈstrʌkt/ v.t. 1. to direct or command; furnish with orders or directions: *the doctor instructed me to diet.* 2. to furnish with knowledge, especially by a systematic method; teach; train; educate. 3. to furnish with information; inform or apprise. 4. *Law* a. to give instructions, as a client to a solicitor, or a solicitor to a barrister. b. (of a judge) to outline or explain the legal principles involved in a case, for the guidance of (the jury). –**instructive**, adj. –**instructor**, n.

instruction /ɪnˈstrʌkʃən/ n. 1. the act or practice of instructing or teaching; education. 2. knowledge or information imparted. 3. an item of such knowledge or information. 4. the act of furnishing with authoritative directions. 5. *Computers* a number or symbol which causes a computer to perform some specified action. –**instructional**, adj.

instrument /ˈɪnstrəmənt/ n. 1. a mechanical device; tool: *a doctor's instruments.* 2. something made to produce musical sounds: *a stringed instrument.* 3. a thing with or by which something is done; a means: *an instrument of government.* 4. a formal legal document, as a contract, deed or will. 5. someone who is used by another. 6. a device for measuring the present value of a quantity under observation. 7. *Elect.* an electrical device which displays information about the state of some part of a mechanical or electrical machine, device, etc., as in a motor vehicle, aircraft, etc.

instrumental /ɪnstrəˈmɛntl/ adj. 1. serving as an instrument or means. 2. of or relating to an instrument.

3. performed on or written for a musical instrument or musical instruments: *instrumental music.* 4. *Gram.* a. (in some inflected languages) denoting a case having as its chief function the indication of means or agency. b. denoting the affix or other element characteristic of this case, or a word containing such an element. c. similar to such a case form in function or meaning, as the Latin *instrumental ablative.*

instrumentalist /ɪnstrəˈmɛntələst/ n. someone who performs on a musical instrument.

instrumentation /ɪnstrəmənˈteɪʃən/ n. 1. the arranging of music for instruments, especially for an orchestra; orchestration. 2. the use of, or work done by, instruments. 3. instrumental agency; instrumentality.

insubordinate /ɪnsəˈbɔdənət/ adj. not submitting to authority; disobedient: *insubordinate crew.* –**insubordinately**, adv. –**insubordination** /ɪnsəbɔdəˈneɪʃən/, n.

insubstantial /ɪnsəbˈstænʃəl/ adj. 1. not substantial; slight. 2. without reality; unreal: *the insubstantial stuff of dreams.* –**insubstantiality** /ɪnsəbstænʃiˈæləti/, n.

insufferable /ɪnˈsʌfərəbəl, -frəbəl/ adj. not to be endured; intolerable; unbearable: *insufferable insolence.* –**insufferableness**, n. –**insufferably**, adv.

insufficient /ɪnsəˈfɪʃənt/ adj. 1. not sufficient; lacking in what is necessary or required: *an insufficient answer.* 2. deficient in force, quality, or amount; inadequate: *insufficient protection.* –**insufficiency**, n. –**insufficiently**, adv.

insular /ˈɪnsjulə, ˈɪnʃulə/ adj. 1. of or related to an island or islands. 2. narrow-minded. –**insularity** /ɪnsjuˈlærəti/, n. –**insularism**, n. –**insularly**, adv.

insular climate n. a type of climate characterised by little seasonal temperature change and associated with coastal areas and islands in temperate latitudes.

insulate /ˈɪnʃuleɪt/ v.t. 1. to cover or surround (an electric wire, etc.) with nonconducting material. 2. *Physics, etc.* to separate by the interposition of a nonconductor, in order to prevent or reduce the transfer of electricity, heat, or sound. 3. to place in an isolated situation or condition; segregate. 4. to install an insulating material in the roof of (a house), to retain warmth in winter and keep out heat in summer.

insulin /ˈɪnʃələn, -sjələn/ n. *Physiol.* a hormone produced in the pancreas and secreted in response to high blood glucose levels; it allows the transport of glucose across cell membranes. A deficiency of insulin results in inability to utilise glucose and produces diabetes.

insulin pen n. a device, similar in shape to a fountain pen, for injecting insulin, containing a replaceable cartridge of a measured dose of insulin.

insulin pump n. a device consisting of a reservoir filled with insulin, a small battery-operated pump, a computer-operated measuring device to control how much insulin the pump delivers, and a needle or soft cannula for delivery of the insulin.

insult v.t. /ɪnˈsʌlt/ 1. to treat insolently or with contemptuous rudeness; affront. –n. /ˈɪnsʌlt/ 2. an insolent or contemptuously rude action or speech; affront. 3. something having the effect of an affront. –phr. 4. **add insult to injury**, to compound a grievance. –**insulter**, n. –**insulting**, adj. –**insultingly**, adv.

insuperable /ɪnˈsupərəbəl, -prəbəl, -ˈsju-/ adj. incapable of being passed over, overcome, or surmounted: *an insuperable barrier.* –**insuperability** /ɪnsupərəˈbɪləti/, **insuperableness**, n. –**insuperably**, adv.

insupportable /ɪnsəˈpɒtəbəl/ adj. not endurable; insufferable. –**insupportableness**, n. –**insupportably**, adv.

insurance /ɪnˈʃɔrəns, -ˈʃʊə-/ n. 1. the act, system, or business of insuring property, life, the person, etc., against loss or harm arising in specified contingencies, as fire, accident, death, disablement, or the like, in consideration of a payment proportionate to the risk involved. 2. the contract thus made, set forth in a written or printed agreement (policy). **3.** the amount for which anything is insured. **4.** the premium paid for insuring a thing. **5.** *Colloq.* an alternative to fall back on if one's main objective is lost: *she already has a boyfriend, so this bloke is just insurance.* **6.** *Colloq.* protection money. *–adj.* **7.** relating to a company, agent, etc., dealing with insurance. *–phr.* **8. buy insurance**, to protect oneself against a possible future setback.

insure /ɪn'ʃɔ, -'ʃʊə/ *v.t.* **1.** to guarantee against risk of loss or harm. **2.** to secure indemnity to or on, in case of loss, damage, or death. **3.** to issue or procure an insurance policy on. *–v.i.* **4.** to issue or procure an insurance policy. **–insurable**, *adj.* **–insurability** /ɪnˌʃɔrə'bɪləti/, *n.*

insured /ɪn'ʃɔd, ɪn'ʃʊəd/ *n.* a person covered by an insurance policy.

insurer /ɪn'ʃɔrə, -'ʃʊə-/ *n.* **1.** someone or something that contracts to indemnify against losses, etc., such as an insurance company. **2.** a person who seeks some sort of protection by taking out insurance.

insurgent /ɪn'sɜdʒənt/ *n.* **1.** someone who rises in forcible opposition to lawful authority; someone who engages in armed resistance to a government or to the execution of laws. *–adj.* **2.** rising in revolt; rebellious. **–insurgence, insurgency**, *n.*

insurmountable /ɪnsə'maʊntəbəl/ *adj.* incapable of being surmounted, passed over, or overcome: *an insurmountable obstacle.* **–insurmountably**, *adv.*

insurrection /ɪnsə'rɛkʃən/ *n.* **1.** the act of rising in arms or open resistance against civil or established authority. **2.** an instance of such an uprising. **–insurrectional**, *adj.* **–insurrectionally**, *adv.* **–insurrectionary**, *adj.*, *n.* **–insurrectionism**, *n.* **–insurrectionist**, *n.*

intact /ɪn'tækt/ *adj.* remaining uninjured, unaltered, sound, or whole; unimpaired. **–intactness**, *n.*

intake /'ɪnteɪk/ *n.* **1.** a point at which a fluid is taken into a channel, pipe, etc. **2.** the act of taking in. **3.** (the quantity of) that which is taken in. **4.** a number of people admitted at a given time, as of students into an educational institution, patients into a hospital, or immigrants into a country.

intangible /ɪn'tændʒəbəl/ *adj.* **1.** incapable of being perceived by the sense of touch, as incorporeal or immaterial things. **2.** not definite or clear to the mind: *intangible arguments.* **3.** (of an asset) existing only in connection with something else, as the goodwill of a business. *–n.* **4.** something intangible. **–intangibility** /ɪnˌtændʒə'bɪləti/, **intangibleness**, *n.* **–intangibly**, *adv.*

intangible asset *n.* an asset, such as a patent, copyright, brand name, etc., which has no physical properties but which can be identified, given a monetary value, and therefore recorded on a balance sheet.

integer /'ɪntədʒə/ *n.* **1.** Also, **positive integer**. any of the numbers 1, 2, 3, etc. **2.** any of the numbers 0, 1, -1, 2, -2, etc. **3.** a whole number as distinguished from a fraction, or a mixed number.

integral /'ɪntəgrəl, ɪn'tɛgrəl/ *adj.* **1.** belonging as a part of the whole: *the integral parts of the human body.* **2.** necessary to the completeness of the whole. **3.** made up of parts which together form a whole. **4.** *Maths* relating to or being an integer (a whole number); not fractional. *–n.* **5.** an integral whole. **6.** *Maths* the result of integration (def. 2); an expression from which a given function, equation, or system of equations is derived by differentiation. **–integrality** /ɪntə'græləti/, *n.* **–integrally**, *adv.*

integrate /'ɪntəgreɪt/ *v.t.* **1.** to bring together (parts) into a whole. **2.** to make up or complete as a whole, as parts do. **3.** to show the total amount or value of. **4.** *Maths* to find the integral of. **–integrative**, *adj.* **–integrable** /'ɪntəgrəbəl/, *adj.* **–integrator**, *n.*

integrated circuit *n. Electronics* an array of interconnected circuit elements formed on a single piece of

silicon (**monolithic integrated circuit**) or several of them (**hybrid integrated circuit**). Also, **IC**.

integration /ɪntə'greɪʃən/ *n.* **1.** the act of integrating; combination into a whole. **2.** *Maths* the operation of finding the integral of a function or equation (the inverse of *differentiation*). **3.** the amalgamation of an ethnic or religious minority group with the rest of the community.

integrative medicine *n.* a range of treatments and procedures which combines Western medicine with alternative medicine.

integrity /ɪn'tɛgrəti/ *n.* **1.** soundness of moral principle and character; uprightness; honesty. **2.** the state of being whole, entire, or undiminished: *to preserve the integrity of the empire.* **3.** sound, unimpaired, or perfect condition: *the integrity of the text.*

integument /ɪn'tɛgjumənt/ *n.* **1.** a skin, shell, rind, or the like. **2.** a covering. **–integumentary**, *adj.*

intellect /'ɪntəlɛkt/ *n.* **1.** the power or faculty of the mind by which one knows, understands, or reasons, as distinguished from that by which one feels and that by which one wills; the understanding. **2.** understanding or mental capacity, especially of a high order. **3.** a particular mind or intelligence, especially of a high order. **4.** the person possessing it. **5.** minds collectively, as of a number of persons, or the persons themselves.

intellectual /ɪntə'lɛktʃuəl/ *adj.* **1.** of interest to the mind: *intellectual books.* **2.** of or relating to the mind: *intellectual powers.* **3.** directed towards things that need to use the mind: *intellectual tastes.* **4.** showing mental ability, especially to a high degree: *an intellectual writer.* *–n.* **5.** an intellectual person. **–intellectuality** /ɪntəˌlɛktʃu'æləti/, **intellectualness**, *n.* **–intellectually**, *adv.*

intellectually disabled *adj.* having learning and developmental deficiencies as a result of impaired or faulty development of the brain.

intelligence /ɪn'tɛlədʒəns/ *n.* **1.** the ability to understand, learn, and to control behaviour in any new event. **2.** good mental ability. **3.** (*oft. upper case*) an intelligent being, especially not in bodily form. **4.** knowledge of an event, circumstance, etc., received or given; news; information. **5.** the gathering or giving of information, especially secret or military information. **6.** a group of people working to obtain such information; secret service. **7.** → **artificial intelligence**. **–intelligent**, *adj.* **–intelligential** /ɪnˌtɛlə'dʒɛnʃəl/, *adj.*

intelligence quotient *n.* (according to a system of specially designed tests) a ratio of mental age to chronological age. A child with a mental age of 12 years and an actual age of 10 years has an intelligence quotient, or IQ, of 1.2 (usually expressed as 120).

intelligent design *n.* the theory that postulates that features of the universe can only be explained by the existence of a conscious intelligent cause rather than the undirected process of natural selection.

intelligentsia /ɪnˌtɛlə'dʒɛntsiə/ *pl. n.* a class or group of persons having or claiming special enlightenment in views or principles; the intellectuals.

intelligible /ɪn'tɛlədʒəbəl/ *adj.* capable of being understood; comprehensible. **–intelligibleness, intelligibility** /ɪnˌtɛlədʒə'bɪləti/, *n.* **–intelligibly**, *adv.*

intemperate /ɪn'tɛmpərət, -prət/ *adj.* **1.** given to or characterised by immoderate indulgence in intoxicating drink. **2.** immoderate as regards indulgence of appetite or passion. **3.** not temperate; unrestrained or unbridled. **4.** extreme in temperature, as climate, etc. **–intemperately**, *adv.* **–intemperance**, *n.*

intend /ɪn'tɛnd/ *v.t.* **1.** to have in mind as something to be done or brought about: *he intends to enlist.* **2.** to design or mean for a particular purpose, use, recipient, etc.: *a book intended for reference.* **3.** to design to express or indicate. *–v.i.* **4.** to have a purpose or design: *he may intend otherwise.* **–intender**, *n.*

intended /ɪnˈtɛndəd/ *adj.* **1.** purposed or designed: *to produce the intended effect.* **2.** prospective: *one's intended wife.* –*n.* **3.** an intended husband or wife.

intense /ɪnˈtɛns/ *adj.* **1.** existing or happening in a high degree: *intense heat.* **2.** strong, eager, as sensations, or emotions: *intense joy.* **3.** of an extreme kind; very great, etc.: *an intense wind.* **4.** *Photography* **a.** strong: *intense light.* **b.** → **dense** (def. 4). **5.** strenuous; earnest, as activity, thought, etc.: *an intense game.* **6.** having or showing great strength of feeling, as a person, the face, language, etc. –**intensely**, *adv.* –**intenseness**, *n.*

intensifier /ɪnˈtɛnsəfaɪə/ *n.* **1.** someone or something that brings about intensification. **2.** *Gram.* a linguistic element or word which increases the semantic effect of a word or phrase but has itself minimal semantic content, as *very.*

intensify /ɪnˈtɛnsəfaɪ/ *verb* (**-fied, -fying**) –*v.t.* **1.** to make intense or more intense. –*v.i.* **2.** to become intense or more intense. –**intensification** /ɪntɛnsəfəˈkeɪʃən/, *n.*

intensity /ɪnˈtɛnsəti/ *n.* (*pl.* **-ties**) **1.** the quality or condition of being intense. **2.** great energy, strength, etc., as of activity, thought, or feeling. **3.** high degree, as of cold. **4.** the degree or extent to which something is intense, as a voice tone, or a colour range. **5.** *Photography* **a.** strength, as of light. **b.** → **density** (def. 4). **6.** *Physics* **a.** the strength of an electric current in amperes. **b.** the strength of an electrical or magnetic field. **c.** the size or strength of force, per unit of area, volume, etc.

intensive /ɪnˈtɛnsɪv/ *adj.* **1.** of, relating to, or marked by intensity: *intensive fire from machine guns.* **2.** with a lot of attention or work: *intensive care of a seriously ill person.* **3.** *Econ.* of methods aimed to increase effectiveness, as, in agriculture, the use of fertilisers, etc., to improve the quality and quantity of crops (opposed to *extensive*). **4.** *Gram.* indicating increased emphasis or force. For example, *certainly* and *tremendously* are intensive adverbs. –*n.* **5.** something that intensifies. **6.** *Gram.* → **intensifier**. –**intensively**, *adv.* –**intensiveness**, *n.*

intensive care *n.* medical therapy for the critically ill, usually given under hospital supervision and for a short period of time.

intent[1] /ɪnˈtɛnt/ *n.* **1.** an intending or purposing, as to commit some act: *criminal intent.* **2.** that which is intended; purpose; aim; design; intention: *my intent was to buy.* **3.** *Law* the state of someone's mind which directs their actions towards a specific object. –*phr.* **4. to all intents and purposes, a.** for all practical purposes; practically. **b.** for all the ends and purposes in view.

intent[2] /ɪnˈtɛnt/ *adj.* **1.** firmly or steadfastly fixed or directed (upon something): *an intent gaze.* **2.** having the gaze or thoughts earnestly fixed on something: *intent on one's job.* **3.** bent, as on some purpose: *intent on revenge.* **4.** earnest: *an intent person.* –**intently**, *adv.* –**intentness**, *n.*

intention /ɪnˈtɛnʃən/ *n.* **1.** the act of determining mentally upon some action or result; a purpose or design. **2.** the end or object intended. **3.** (*pl.*) purposes with respect to a proposal of marriage. **4.** the act or fact of intending or purposing. **5.** *Logic* the mental act of initially directing attention to something. **6.** *Med.* a manner or process of healing, as in the healing of a lesion or fracture without granulation (**healing by first intention**) or the healing of a wound by granulation after suppuration (**healing by second intention**). **7.** meaning. –**intentional**, *adj.* –**intentionally**, *adv.*

inter[1] /ɪnˈtɜ/ *v.t.* (**-terred, -terring**) to deposit (a dead body, etc.) in a grave or tomb; bury, especially with ceremonies. –**interment**, *n.*

inter- a prefix meaning 'between', 'among', 'mutually', 'reciprocally', 'together', as in *intercellular, intercity, intermarry, interweave.*

interact /ɪntərˈækt/ *v.i.* to act on each other.

interactive /ɪntərˈæktɪv/ *adj.* **1.** of or relating to things or persons which act on each other. **2.** of or relating to an electronic device, such as a computer, television, etc., which allows for a reciprocal transfer of data, the user providing a stimulus to a responsive central source. –**interactively**, *adv.* –**interactiveness**, *n.*

inter alia /ɪntər ˈeɪliə/ *adv.* among other things.

intercede /ɪntəˈsid/ *v.i.* (**-ceded, -ceding**) to interpose on behalf of one in difficulty or trouble, as by pleading or petition: *to intercede with the governor for a condemned man.* –**interceder**, *n.*

intercept *v.t.* /ɪntəˈsɛpt/, ˈɪntəsɛpt/ **1.** to take or seize on the way from one place to another: *to intercept a letter.* **2.** to stop the natural course of (light, water, etc.). **3.** to take possession of (a ball, etc.) passed or thrown to an opponent. **4.** to prevent or cut off the operation or effect of: *to intercept the view.* **5.** *Chiefly Maths* to mark off or include, as between two points or lines. –*n.* /ˈɪntəsɛpt/ **6.** an act of intercepting. **7.** the taking possession of the ball from one's opposition. **8.** *Maths* an intercepted part of a line. –**interceptive**, *adj.* –**interceptor**, *n.*

intercession /ɪntəˈsɛʃən/ *n.* **1.** the act of interceding. **2.** an interposing or pleading on behalf of one in difficulty or trouble. **3.** *Eccles.* prayer, especially a pleading with God on behalf of another or others, as that of Christ or that of the saints on behalf of humankind. –**intercessional**, **intercessory**, *adj.* –**intercessor**, *n.*

interchange *verb* /ɪntəˈtʃeɪndʒ/ (**-changed, -changing**) –*v.t.* **1.** to put each of (two things) in the place of the other; transpose. **2.** to give and receive (things) one to another; exchange: *they interchanged gifts.* **3.** to cause to follow one after the other: *to interchange cares with pleasures.* –*v.i.* **4.** to happen by turns; alternate. **5.** to change places, as two persons or things. –*n.* /ˈɪntətʃeɪndʒ/ **6.** the act of interchanging. **7.** a changing of places, as between two persons or things. **8.** any major road junction, especially where motorways converge. **9.** a point, in a public transport system, at which passengers can change from one vehicle to another. –**interchangeable**, *adj.* –**interchangeability** /ˌɪntətʃeɪndʒəˈbɪləti/, *n.* –**interchanger**, *n.*

intercom /ˈɪntəkɒm/ *n.* → **intercommunication system**.

intercommunication system /ˌɪntəkəmjunəˈkeɪʃən sɪstəm/ *n.* an internal or closed audio system, as within an office complex, a school, a ship, etc.

intercontinental /ˌɪntəkɒntəˈnɛntl/ *adj.* between continents.

intercourse /ˈɪntəkɔs/ *n.* **1.** dealings or communication between individuals. **2.** interchange of thoughts, feelings, etc. **3.** sexual intercourse.

interdependent /ɪntədəˈpɛndənt/ *adj.* mutually dependent; dependent on each other. –**interdependence**, **interdependency**, *n.* –**interdependently**, *adv.*

interdict *n.* /ˈɪntədɪkt, -daɪt/ **1.** *Civil Law* any prohibitive act or decree of a court or an administrative officer. –*v.t.* /ɪntəˈdɪkt, -ˈdaɪt/ **2.** to forbid; prohibit. **3.** *Mil.* **a.** to deny the use of a route to: *patrols to interdict smugglers.* **b.** to impede by steady bombardment: *constant air attacks interdicted the enemy's advance.* –**interdictory**, *adj.* –**interdiction**, *n.*

interest /ˈɪntrəst, -tərəst/ *n.* **1.** the feeling of someone whose attention or curiosity is particularly engaged by something: *to have great interest in a subject.* **2.** a particular feeling of this kind: *a woman of varied intellectual interests.* **3.** the power of exciting such feeling; interesting quality: *questions of great interest.* **4.** concernment, importance, or moment: *a matter of primary interest.* **5.** a business, cause, or the like, in which a number of persons are interested. **6.** a share in the ownership of property, in a commercial or financial undertaking, or the like. **7.** any right of ownership in property, commercial undertakings, etc. **8.** a number or group of persons, or a party, having a common interest: *the banking interest.* **9.** something in which one has an interest, as of ownership, advantage, attention, etc. **10.** the relation of being affected by something in respect of advantage or detriment: *an arbitrator having no interest in the outcome.* **11.** benefit or advantage: *to have one's own interest in mind.* **12.** regard for one's own advantage or profit; self-interest: *rival interests.* **13.** *Commerce* **a.** payment, or a sum paid, for the use of money borrowed (the principal), or for the forbearance of a debt. **b.** the rate per cent per unit of time represented by such payment. *–v.t.* **14.** to engage or excite the attention or curiosity of: *a story which interested him greatly.* **15.** to concern (a person, etc.) in something; involve: *every citizen is interested in this law.* **16.** to cause to take a personal concern or share; induce to participate: *to interest a person in an enterprise.* *–phr.* **17. in the interest** (or **interests**) **of**, on the side of what is advantageous to; on behalf of: *in the interest of good government.* **–interesting,** *adj.*

interested /ˈɪntrəstəd/ *adj.* **1.** having an interest in something; concerned: *those interested should apply in person.* **2.** participating; having an interest or share; having money involved: *one interested in the funds.* **3.** having the attention or curiosity engaged: *an interested spectator.* **4.** characterised by a feeling of interest. **5.** influenced by personal or selfish motives: *an interested witness.* **–interestedly,** *adv.* **–interestedness,** *n.*

interface *n.* /ˈɪntəfeɪs/ **1.** a surface regarded as the common boundary to two bodies or spaces. **2.** *Chem.* the surface which separates two phases. **3.** *Computers* the point at which an interconnection is made between a computer and a peripheral device or other piece of equipment. **4.** a point or area at which any two systems act on each other. *–verb* /ˈɪntəˈfeɪs/ (**-faced, -facing**) *–v.t.* **5.** to bring (a computer, piece of equipment, etc.) into an interface: *to interface the computer with the printer.* **6.** *Sewing* to insert an interfacing into. *–v.i.* **7.** (of computer systems, equipment, etc.) to interact. **8.** (sometimes fol. by *with*) to communicate or exchange ideas.

interfere /ɪntəˈfɪə/ *v.i.* (**-fered, -fering**) **1.** to interpose or intervene for a particular purpose. **2.** to take a part in the affairs of others; meddle: *to interfere in others' disputes.* **3.** to come into opposition, as one thing with another, especially with the effect of hampering action or procedure: *these interruptions interfere with the work.* **4.** (of things) to strike against each other, or one against another, so as to hamper or hinder action; come into physical collision. **5.** to strike one foot or leg against the opposite foot or leg in going, as a horse. **6.** *Physics* to cause interference. *–phr.* **7. interfere with,** to molest sexually. **–interferer,** *n.* **–interferingly,** *adv.*

interference /ɪntəˈfɪərəns/ *n.* **1.** the act or fact of interfering. **2.** *Physics* the action of waves (as of light, sound, etc.), when meeting, by which they reinforce or cancel each other. **3.** *Radio* **a.** the jumbling of radio signals by receiving signals other than the desired ones. **b.** the signals which produce the incoherence. *–phr.* **4. run interference, a.** *American Football, Rugby, etc.* to come between a player running with the ball and a tackler in order to obstruct the tackler. **b.** to ward off criticism or obstruction. **–interferential** /ɪntəfəˈrɛnʃəl/, *adj.*

interferon /ɪntəˈfɪərɒn/ *n. Physiol.* a protein produced by animal cells in response to virus infection, that inhibits replication of virus particles.

interim /ˈɪntərəm/ *n.* **1.** an intervening time; the meantime: *in the interim.* **2.** a temporary or provisional arrangement. *–adj.* **3.** belonging to or connected with an intervening period of time: *an interim dividend.* **4.** temporary; provisional: *an interim order.*

interior /ɪnˈtɪəriə/ *adj.* **1.** being within; internal: *the interior parts of a house.* **2.** existing inside and at a distance from the coast or border; inland: *the interior parts of a country.* **3.** inside a country, etc.; domestic: *the interior trade.* **4.** inner, private, or secret: *an interior meeting.* **5.** mental or spiritual. **6.** *Geom.* (of an angle) inner, as an angle formed between two parallel lines when cut by a third line, or an angle formed by two adjacent sides of a closed polygon. *–n.* **7.** the internal part; the inside. **8.** *Art* **a.** the inside part of a building, considered as a whole from the point of view of artistic design, etc., or a single room or apartment so considered. **b.** a painting of the inside of a building, room, etc. **9.** the inland parts of a country, etc. **10.** the domestic affairs of a country as separate from its foreign affairs: *the Department of the Interior.* **11.** the inner nature of anything. **–interiority** /ɪnˌtɪəriˈɒrəti/, *n.* **–interiorly,** *adv.*

interject /ɪntəˈdʒɛkt/ *v.t.* **1.** to throw in abruptly between other things. **2.** to interpolate; interpose: *to interject a careless remark.* **3.** to interrupt a conversation or speech; heckle. **–interjector,** *n.* **–interjectory,** *adj.*

interjection /ɪntəˈdʒɛkʃən/ *n.* **1.** the act of throwing between; an interjecting. **2.** the utterance of ejaculations expressive of emotion; an ejaculation or exclamation. **3.** something, such as a remark, interjected. **4.** *Gram.* **a.** (in many languages) a form class, or 'part of speech', comprising words which constitute utterances or clauses in themselves, without grammatical connection. **b.** a grammatically independent word expressing pain, feeling, etc., such as *ouch!, never!* **c.** a similar word or phrase which is grammatically independent and used to express or stimulate a reaction to or from an interlocutor, such as *yes, goodness me, your health.* **–interjectional,** *adj.* **–interjectionally,** *adv.*

interlace /ɪntəˈleɪs/ *verb* (**-laced, -lacing**) *–v.i.* **1.** to cross one another as if woven together; intertwine: *interlacing branches.* *–v.t.* **2.** to place (threads, branches, etc.) so as to intercross one another. **3.** to connect; blend. **4.** to scatter through; intermingle. **–interlacement,** *n.*

interlock *v.i.* /ɪntəˈlɒk/ **1.** to connect with each other: *the pieces of a jigsaw interlock.* **2.** to fit into each other, as parts of machinery. *–v.t.* /ɪntəˈlɒk/ **3.** to lock one with another. **4.** to fit the parts of (something) together so that all must move together. *–n.* /ˈɪntəlɒk/ **5.** *Textiles* a smooth knitted fabric, especially one made of cotton thread. **–interlocker,** *n.*

interlocutor /ɪntəˈlɒkjətə/ *n.* **1.** someone who takes part in a conversation or dialogue. **2.** someone who enters into conversation with another. **–interlocutress** /ɪntəˈlɒkjətrəs/, **interlocutrix** /ɪntəˈlɒkjətrɪks/, *fem. n.* **–interlocution,** *n.* **–interlocutory,** *adj.*

interlope /ˈɪntəloʊp/ *v.i.* to intrude into some region or field of trade without a proper licence. **–interloper,** *n.*

interlude /ˈɪntəlud/ *n.* **1.** an intervening episode, period, space, etc. **2.** an intermediate performance or entertainment, as between the acts of a play. **3.** an instrumental passage or a piece of music rendered between the parts of a song, church service, drama, etc. **4.** a period of inactivity; lull.

intermarry /ɪntəˈmæri/ *v.i.* (**-ried, -rying**) **1.** to become connected by marriage, as two families, tribes, castes, peoples, etc. **2.** to marry within the limits of the family or of near relationship. **3.** to marry, one with another. **–intermarriage,** *n.*

intermediary /ɪntəˈmidiəri, -dʒəri, -dʒəri/ *adj.* **1.** being between; intermediate. **2.** acting between persons, parties, etc.; serving as an intermediate agent or agency: *an intermediary power.* *–n.* (*pl.* **-aries**) **3.** an intermediate agent or agency; a go-between. **4.** a medium or means. **5.** an intermediate form or stage.

intermediate[1] /ɪntəˈmidiət, -dʒət/ *adj.* being, situated, or acting between two points, stages, things, persons, etc.: *the intermediate links.* –**intermediately**, *adv.* –**intermediateness**, **intermediacy**, *n.*

intermediate² /ɪntəˈmidieɪt/ *v.i.* to act as an intermediary; intervene; mediate. –**intermediation** /ˌɪntəmidiˈeɪʃən/, *n.* –**intermediator**, *n.*

intermediate level waste *n.* radioactive waste which does not have the level of heat generation associated with high level waste but which is more dangerously radioactive than low level waste; typically materials which have been irradiated in a nuclear reactor. *Abbrev.:* ILW

interminable /ɪnˈtɜmənəbəl/ *adj.* 1. that cannot be terminated; unending: *interminable talk.* 2. endless; having no limits: *interminable sufferings.* –**interminably**, *adv.*

intermission /ɪntəˈmɪʃən/ *n.* 1. an interval, especially in the cinema. 2. the act of intermitting. 3. the state of being intermitted. –**intermissive**, *adj.*

intermit /ɪntəˈmɪt/ *verb* (**-mitted**, **-mitting**) –*v.t.* 1. to discontinue temporarily; suspend. –*v.i.* 2. to stop or pause at intervals, or be intermittent. 3. to cease, stop, or break off operations for a time. –**intermittingly**, *adv.*

intermittent /ɪntəˈmɪtnt/ *adj.* 1. that intermits, or ceases for a time: *an intermittent process.* 2. alternately ceasing and beginning again: *an intermittent fever.* 3. (of streams, lakes, or springs) recurrent; showing water only part of the time. –**intermittence**, **intermittency**, *n.* –**intermittently**, *adv.*

intern¹ /ɪnˈtɜn/ *v.t.* 1. to oblige to reside within prescribed limits under prohibition to leave them, as prisoners of war or enemy aliens, or as combatant troops who take refuge in a neutral country. 2. to hold within a country until the termination of a war, as a vessel of a belligerent which has put into a neutral port and remained beyond a limited period allowed. –*n.* /ˈɪntɜn/ 3. *Chiefly US* an internee. –**internment**, *n.*

intern² /ˈɪntɜn/ *n.* 1. Also, **interne**. a resident member of the medical staff of a hospital, usually a recent graduate of a university still in partial training. 2. a person who is receiving practical experience in the workplace as a first step in a career. –*v.i.* 3. to be or perform the duties of an intern. –**internship**, *n.*

internal /ɪnˈtɜnəl/ *adj.* 1. relating to or existing on the inside of something; interior: *internal organs.* 2. to be taken inwardly: *internal medicines.* 3. existing or found within the limits of something. 4. relating to or happening within a country; domestic: *internal affairs.* 5. of the mind or soul; mental or spiritual; subjective. –**internality** /ɪntɜˈnælɪti/, *n.* –**internally**, *adv.*

internal-combustion engine *n.* an engine of one or more working cylinders in which the process of combustion takes place within the cylinder.

internalise /ɪnˈtɜnəlaɪz/ *v.t.* 1. to suppress (an emotion). 2. to establish (information, values, attitudes) within oneself. Also, **internalize**.

international /ɪntəˈnæʃnəl/ *adj.* 1. between or among nations: *an international armament race.* 2. of or relating to different nations or their citizens: *a matter of international concern.* 3. of or relating to the relations between nations: *international law.* –*n.* 4. a sporting fixture between two countries: *rugby international.* 5. someone chosen to represent their country in international sporting events. –**internationality** /ɪntəˌnæʃəˈnælɪti/, *n.* –**internationally**, *adv.*

International Date Line *n.* → **date line** (def. 2).

international law *n.* the body of rules, established by either custom or treaty, generally recognised as binding nations in their conduct towards one another.

International Phonetic Alphabet *n.* an alphabet designed to provide a consistent and universally understood system of letters and other symbols for writing the speech sounds of all languages. *Abbrev.:* IPA

International System of Units *n.* an internationally recognised system of metric units, now adopted as the basis of Australia's metric system, in which the seven base units are the metre, kilogram, second, ampere, kelvin, mole and candela. *Abbrev.:* SI See **metric system**. Also, **Système International d'Unités**.

international waters *pl. n.* those broad sweeps of ocean which are outside any national jurisdiction; high seas.

internecine /ɪntəˈnisaɪn/ *adj.* 1. mutually destructive. 2. characterised by great slaughter.

internee /ˌɪntɜˈni/ *n.* someone interned as a prisoner of war, or as a citizen of a hostile country in time of war.

internet /ˈɪntənɛt/ *n.* Also, **the Net**. 1. **the**, the communications system created by the interconnecting networks of computers around the world. –*adj.* 2. of or relating to the internet. Also, **Internet**.

internet cafe *n.* an establishment which provides connection to the internet for a fee, sometimes also selling coffee and light refreshments.

internet meme *n.* a concept, especially one that is quirky or amusing, that spreads swiftly through the internet. Also, **meme**.

internet relay chat *n.* an online discussion forum available through the internet, in which multiple users can communicate in real-time by means of typing text. Compare **newsgroup**. Also, **IRC**.

internet roaming *n.* a facility which allows a user to access their email and internet services outside their own country.

internet service provider *n.* a company that provides access to the internet, usually for a fee. *Abbrev.:* ISP

internet stalking *n.* → **cyberstalking**. –**internet stalker**, *n.*

interoperable /ɪntərˈɒpərəbəl/ *adj.* (of computer systems or software) able to connect with each other for the exchange of data, programs, etc. –**interoperability**, *n.*

interpellation /ɪnˌtɜpəˈleɪʃən, ɪntəpəˈleɪʃən/ *n.* a procedure in some legislative bodies of asking a government official to explain an act or policy, usually leading in parliamentary government to a vote of confidence.

interpersonal /ɪntəˈpɜsənəl/ *adj.* of or relating to relations between persons. –**interpersonally**, *adv.*

interplay *n.* /ˈɪntəpleɪ/ 1. reciprocal play, action, or influence: *the interplay of plot and character.* –*v.i.* /ɪntəˈpleɪ/ 2. to exert influence on each other.

interpolate /ɪnˈtɜpəleɪt/ *v.t.* 1. to alter (a text, etc.) by the insertion of new matter, especially deceptively or without authorisation. 2. to insert (new or spurious matter) thus. 3. to introduce (something additional or extraneous) between other things or parts; interject; interpose; intercalate. 4. *Maths* to insert or find intermediate terms in (a sequence). –*v.i.* 5. to make interpolations. –**interpolator**, *n.* –**interpolative** /ɪnˈtɜpəleɪtɪv/, *adj.*

interpose /ɪntəˈpoʊz/ *v.t.* 1. to place between; cause to intervene: *to interpose oneself between two fighters.* 2. to put (something which blocks) between, or in the way. 3. to put in (a remark, etc.) in the midst of a conversation, etc. –*v.i.* 4. to come between other things. 5. to step in between opposing parties; mediate. 6. to make a remark by way of interruption. –**interposition** /ɪntəpəˈzɪʃən/, **interposal**, *n.* –**interposer**, *n.* –**interposingly**, *adv.*

interpret /ɪnˈtɜprət/ *v.t.* 1. to give the meaning of; explain: *to interpret dreams.* 2. to understand in a particular way; construe: *to interpret an action as being friendly.* 3. to bring out the meaning of (a dramatic work, music, etc.) by performance. 4. to translate. –*v.i.* 5. to translate what is said in a foreign language. 6. to give an explanation. –**interpretable**, *adj.* –**interpretability** /ɪnˌtɜprətəˈbɪlɪti/, *n.* –**interpretation**, *n.* –**interpreter**, *n.* –**interpretative**, **interpretive**, *adj.*

interracial /ɪntəˈreɪʃəl/ *adj.* existing between, involving, or relating to people of different races: *interracial tension.*

interreact /ɪntəriˈækt/ *v.i.* to generate a new reaction, as of chemicals, medicines, etc., which are administered simultaneously. –**interreaction**, *n.* –**interreactive**, *adj.*

interregnum /ɪntəˈrɛgnəm/ *n.* (*pl.* -**nums** *or* -**na** /-nə/) **1.** an interval of time between the close of a sovereign's reign and the accession of his or her normal or legitimate successor. **2.** any period during which a state has no ruler or only a temporary executive. **3.** any pause or interruption in continuity. –**interregnal**, *adj.*

interrogate /ɪnˈtɛrəgeɪt/ *v.t.* **1.** to ask a question or a series of questions of (a person), especially closely or formally. **2.** to examine by questions; question: *they were interrogated by the police.* **3.** *Computers* to run a search through (a database). –*v.i.* **4.** to ask questions. **5.** *Elect.* to send a signal to a transponder. –**interrogatingly**, *adv.* –**interrogation** /ɪnˌtɛrəˈgeɪʃən/, *n.* –**interrogator**, *n.*

interrogative /ɪntəˈrɒgətɪv/ *adj.* **1.** relating to or conveying a question. **2.** *Gram.* (of an element or construction) forming or constituting a question: *an interrogative pronoun, an interrogative sentence.* –*n.* **3.** *Gram.* an interrogative word, element, or construction, as '*who?*' and '*what?*' –**interrogatively**, *adv.*

interrogatory /ɪntəˈrɒgətri/ *adj.* **1.** interrogative; questioning. –*n.* (*pl.* -**tories**) **2.** *Law* a formal or written question. –**interrogatorily**, *adv.*

interrupt *v.t.* /ɪntəˈrʌpt/ **1.** to make a break in (an otherwise continuous course, process, condition, etc.). **2.** to break off or cause to cease, as in the midst or course: *he interrupted his work to answer the phone.* **3.** to stop (a person) in the midst of doing or saying something. –*v.i.* /ɪntəˈrʌpt/ **4.** to cause a break; interrupt action or speech: *Please don't interrupt.* –*n.* /ˈɪntərʌpt/ **5.** *Computers* a command causing the computer to change from one program, usually the background, to another, usually to perform a short exercise, after which it returns to where it left off. –**interruption**, *n.* –**interruptive**, *adj.* –**interruptible**, *adj.*

intersect /ɪntəˈsɛkt/ *v.t.* **1.** to cut or divide by passing through or lying across: *one road intersects another.* –*v.i.* **2.** to cross, as lines. **3.** *Geom.* to have one or more points in common: *intersecting lines.*

intersection /ɪntəˈsɛkʃən, ˈɪntəsɛkʃən/ *n.* **1.** the act, fact, or place of intersecting. **2.** a place where two or more roads meet or cross. –**intersectional**, *adj.*

intersperse /ɪntəˈspɜs/ *v.t.* **1.** to scatter here and there among other things: *to intersperse flowers among shrubs.* **2.** to diversify with something scattered or introduced here and there: *his speech was interspersed with long and boring quotations from the poets.* –**interspersion** /ɪntəˈspɜʒən/, *n.*

interstate *adj.* /ˈɪntəsteɪt/ **1.** between or jointly involving states: *interstate trade.* –*adv.* /ɪntəˈsteɪt/ *Aust.* **2.** temporarily in a state (def. 9) of which one is not a resident: *he's interstate; travelling interstate.* **3.** from another state: *he gets his raw materials interstate.* Compare **intrastate.** –**interstater**, *n.*

interstice /ɪnˈtɜstəs/ *n.* (*pl.* **interstices** /ɪnˈtɜstəsiz/) **1.** an intervening space. **2.** a small or narrow space between things or parts; small chink, crevice, or opening. –**interstitial** /ɪntəˈstɪʃəl/, *adj.*

interstitial cystitis /ˌɪntəstɪʃəl sɪsˈtaɪtəs/ *n.* a chronic pelvic pain disorder with symptoms of urgency and frequency, and sometimes pinpoint bleeding in the bladder wall caused by recurrent irritation. *Abbrev.:* IC

intertwine /ɪntəˈtwaɪn/ *v.i.* **1.** to twine together. –*v.t.* **2.** to interweave with one another. –**intertwinement**, *n.* –**intertwiningly**, *adv.*

interval /ˈɪntəvəl/ *n.* **1.** an intervening period of time: *an interval of fifty years.* **2.** a period of cessation; a pause: *intervals between attacks.* **3.** a period during which action temporarily ceases; a break, as between acts of a play in a theatre. **4.** a space intervening between things, points, limits, qualities, etc.: *an interval of three metres between columns.* **5.** *Music* the difference in pitch between two notes as, **a. harmonic interval**, an interval between two notes sounded simultaneously. **b. melodic interval**, an interval between two notes sounded successively. –*phr.* **6. at intervals**, at particular times or places with gaps in between.

intervene /ɪntəˈvin/ *v.i.* **1.** to come between in action; intercede: *to intervene in a dispute.* **2.** to come or be between, as in place, time, or a series. **3.** (of things) to happen without plan so as to change a result: *war intervened in my studies.* –**intervener**, *n.* –**intervenient**, *adj.* –**intervention**, *n.*

interview /ˈɪntəvju/ *n.* **1.** a meeting of persons usually face to face, especially for formal conference in business, etc., or for radio and television entertainment, etc. **2.** the conversation of a writer or reporter with a person or persons from whom material for a news or feature story or other writing is sought. **3.** the report of such conversation. –*v.t.* **4.** to have an interview with: *to interview the president.* –**interviewer**, *n.*

interweave /ɪntəˈwiv/ *verb* (**-wove** *or* **-weaved**, **-woven** *or* **-wove** *or* **-weaved**, **-weaving**) –*v.t.* **1.** to weave together, one with another, as threads, strands, branches, roots, etc. **2.** to intermingle or combine as if by weaving: *to interweave truth with fiction.* –*v.i.* **3.** to become woven together, interlaced, or intermingled. –**interweaver**, *n.*

intestate /ɪnˈtɛsteɪt, -tət/ *adj. Law* **1.** (of a person) dying without having made a valid will. **2.** (of things) not disposed of by will; not legally devised or bequeathed. –*n.* **3.** someone who dies intestate. –**intestacy**, *n.*

intestine /ɪnˈtɛstən, ɪnˈtɛstaɪn/ *n.* **1.** (*oft. pl.*) the lower part of the alimentary canal, extending from the pylorus to the anus. **2.** a definite portion of this part. The **small intestine** comprises the duodenum, jejunum, and ileum; the **large intestine** comprises the caecum, colon, and rectum. –*adj.* **3.** internal; domestic; civil: *intestine strife.* –**intestinal** /ɪnˈtɛstənəl, ɪntɛsˈtaɪnəl/, *adj.*

intimate[1] /ˈɪntəmət/ *adj.* **1.** associated in close personal relations: *an intimate friend.* **2.** involving personally close association: *an intimate group.* **3.** private; closely personal: *one's intimate affairs.* **4.** having sexual relations. **5.** aimed at establishing a feeling of friendliness (as in a restaurant, etc.). **6.** detailed; deep: *an intimate knowledge of a subject.* **7.** close union: *an intimate mixture.* **8.** inmost; deep within. **9.** relating to the inmost nature; intrinsic: *the intimate structure of an organism.* –*n.* **10.** an intimate friend. –**intimacy**, *n.* –**intimately**, *adv.* –**intimateness**, *n.*

intimate[2] /ˈɪntəmeɪt/ *v.t.* **1.** to make known indirectly; hint; suggest. **2.** to make known, especially formally; announce. –**intimation** /ɪntəˈmeɪʃən/, *n.*

intimidate /ɪnˈtɪmədeɪt/ *v.t.* **1.** to make timid, or inspire with fear; overawe; cow. **2.** to force into or deter from some action by inducing fear: *to intimidate a voter.* –**intimidation** /ɪnˌtɪməˈdeɪʃən/, *n.* –**intimidator**, *n.* –**intimidating**, **intimidatory**, *adj.*

into /ˈɪntu/, *before consonants* /ˈɪntə/ *prep.* **1.** in to; in and to (expressing motion or direction towards the inner part of a place or thing, and hence entrance or inclusion within limits, or change to new circumstances, relations, condition, form, etc.). **2.** *Maths* being the divisor of: *2 into 10 equals 5.* **3.** *Colloq.* devoted to the use or practice of; having an enthusiasm for: *I am into health foods.*

intolerable /ɪnˈtɒlrəbəl/ *adj.* not tolerable; unendurable; insufferable: *intolerable agony.* –**intolerability** /ɪnˌtɒlərəˈbɪləti/, **intolerableness**, *n.* –**intolerably**, *adv.*

intolerance /ɪnˈtɒlərəns/ n. **1.** lack of toleration; indisposition to tolerate contrary opinions or beliefs. **2.** incapacity or indisposition to bear or endure: *intolerance of heat.* **3.** an abnormal sensitivity or allergy to a food, drug, etc.: *a lactose intolerance.*

intolerant /ɪnˈtɒlərənt/ adj. **1.** not tolerating contrary opinions, especially in religious matters; bigoted: *an intolerant zealot. –phr.* **2. intolerant of,** unable or indisposed to tolerate or endure: *intolerant of excesses.* –**intolerantly,** adv.

intonation /ɪntəˈneɪʃən/ n. **1.** *Phonetics* the pattern or melody of pitch changes revealed in connected speech; especially the pitch pattern of a sentence, which distinguishes kinds of sentences and speakers of different nationalities. **2.** the manner of producing musical notes, specifically the relation in pitch of notes to their key or harmony.

intone /ɪnˈtoʊn/ v.t. **1.** to utter with a particular tone. **2.** to give tone or variety of tone to; vocalise. **3.** to utter in a singing voice (the first notes of a section in a liturgical service). –v.i. **4.** to speak or recite in a singing voice, especially in monotone. –**intoner,** n.

intoxicate /ɪnˈtɒksəkeɪt/ v.t. **1.** to affect temporarily with loss of control over the physical and mental powers, by means of alcoholic liquor, a drug, or other substance. **2.** to excite mentally beyond self-control or reason. –v.i. **3.** to cause or produce intoxication: *an intoxicating liquor.* –**intoxicant,** adj., n. –**intoxicatingly,** adv. –**intoxication,** n. –**intoxicative,** adj.

intoxicated /ɪnˈtɒksəkeɪtəd/ adj. **1.** drunk. **2.** excited mentally beyond reason or self-control.

intra- a prefix meaning 'within', freely used as an English formative, especially in scientific terms, sometimes in opposition to *extra-*.

intractable /ɪnˈtræktəbəl/ adj. **1.** not docile; stubborn: *an intractable disposition.* **2.** (of things) hard to deal with; unmanageable. –**intractability** /ɪnˌtræktəˈbɪləti/, **intractableness,** n. –**intractably,** adv.

intransigent /ɪnˈtrænsədʒənt/ adj. **1.** uncompromising, especially in politics; irreconcilable. –n. **2.** someone who is irreconcilable, especially in politics. –**intransigence, intransigency,** n. –**intransigently,** adv.

intransitive /ɪnˈtrænsətɪv/ adj. **1.** having the quality of an intransitive verb. –n. **2.** an intransitive verb. –**intransitively,** adv.

intransitive verb n. **1.** a verb that is never accompanied by a direct object, as *come, sit, lie,* etc. **2.** a verb occurring without a direct object, as *drinks* in the sentence *he drinks only when thirsty.* Compare **transitive verb.**

intrastate /ˈɪntrəsteɪt/ adj. within a state: *intrastate commerce.*

intra-uterine device /ɪntrə-ˈjutəraɪn dəvaɪs/ n. a contraceptive device, usually made of metal, inserted into the uterus. *Abbrev.*: IUD

intra-uterine system n. a contraceptive method involving the insertion of a device into the uterus where it slowly releases the hormone progestogen to prevent ovulation; can last up to five years. *Abbrev.*: IUS

intravenous /ɪntrəˈvinəs/ adj. **1.** within a vein or the veins. **2.** of or relating to an injection into a vein. –**intravenously,** adv.

intrepid /ɪnˈtrɛpəd/ adj. fearless; dauntless: *intrepid courage.* –**intrepidity** /ɪntrəˈpɪdəti/, n. –**intrepidly,** adv.

intricate /ˈɪntrɪkət/ adj. **1.** entangled or involved: *a maze of intricate paths.* **2.** complex; complicated; hard to understand: *an intricate machine.* –**intricacy, intricateness,** n. –**intricately,** adv.

intrigue verb /ɪnˈtrig/ (-**trigued, -triguing**) –v.t. **1.** to excite the curiosity or interest of by puzzling, novel, or otherwise arresting qualities. **2.** to take the fancy of: *her hat intrigued me.* **3.** to puzzle: *I am intrigued by this event.* –v.i. **4.** to use underhand machinations; plot craftily. **5.** to carry on a clandestine or illicit love affair.

–n. /ɪnˈtrig, ˈɪntrig/ **6.** the use of underhand machinations to accomplish designs. **7.** a plot or crafty dealing: *political intrigues.* **8.** a clandestine or illicit love affair. **9.** the series of complications forming the plot of a play. –phr. **10. intrigue into,** to beguile into by appeal to the curiosity, interest, or fancy. –**intriguer, intrigant, intriguant,** n. –**intriguingly,** adv.

intrinsic /ɪnˈtrɪnzɪk, -sɪk/ adj. **1.** belonging to a thing by its very nature: *intrinsic merit.* **2.** *Anat.* (of certain muscles, nerves, etc.) belonging to or lying within a given part. Also, **intrinsical.** –**intrinsically,** adv.

intro- a prefix meaning 'inwardly', 'within', occasionally used as an English formative. Compare **intra-.**

introduce /ɪntrəˈdjus/ v.t. (-**duced, -ducing**) **1.** to bring into notice, knowledge, use, vogue, etc.: *to introduce a fashion.* **2.** to bring forward for consideration, as a proposed bill in parliament, etc. **3.** to bring forward with preliminary or preparatory matter: *to introduce a subject with a long preface.* **4.** to lead, bring, or put into a place, position, surroundings, relations, etc.: *to introduce a figure into a design.* **5.** to cause or allow to be established in a new country or geographical region, an animal, a fish, plant, etc., which is native to a different country: *to introduce carp into Australian rivers.* **6.** to bring (a person) into the acquaintance of another: *he introduced his sister to us.* **7.** to present formally, as to a person, an audience, or society. –phr. **8. introduce someone to,** to bring a person to the knowledge or experience of: *to introduce a person to chess.* –**introducer,** n. –**introductory** /ɪntrəˈdʌktri, -təri/, adj.

introduction /ɪntrəˈdʌkʃən/ n. **1.** the act of introducing. **2.** a formal presentation of one person to another or others: *allow me to do the introductions.* **3.** something introduced. **4.** a preliminary part, as of a book, musical composition, or the like, leading up to the main part. **5.** an elementary treatise: *an introduction to botany.*

intromission /ɪntroʊˈmɪʃən/ n. insertion or admission, as of genital organs in animal copulation.

introspection /ɪntrəˈspɛkʃən/ n. observation or examination of one's own mental states or processes.

introvert n. /ˈɪntrəvɜt/ **1.** *Psychol.* someone characterised by introversion; a person concerned chiefly with his or her own thoughts. Compare **extrovert** (def. 1). –v.t. /ɪntrəˈvɜt/ **2.** to turn inwards. **3.** to direct (the mind, etc.) inwards or upon the self. –**introversion,** n.

intrude /ɪnˈtrud/ v.t. **1.** to thrust or bring in without reason, permission, or welcome. –v.i. **2.** to thrust oneself in; come uninvited: *to intrude on someone's privacy.* –**intruder,** n. –**intrudingly,** adv. –**intrusion** /ɪnˈtruʒən/, n. –**intrusive** /ɪnˈtrusɪv, -zɪv/, adj.

intuition /ɪntʃuˈɪʃən/ n. **1.** direct perception of truths, facts, etc., independently of any reasoning process. **2.** a truth or fact thus perceived. **3.** the ability to perceive in this way. –**intuitive,** adj. –**intuitively,** adv.

inundate /ˈɪnʌndeɪt/ v.t. **1.** to overspread with a flood; overflow; flood; deluge. **2.** to overspread as with or in a flood; overwhelm. –**inundation** /ɪnʌnˈdeɪʃən/, n. –**inundator,** n.

inure /ənˈjuə, ɪn-/ v.i. **1.** to come into use; take or have effect. –phr. **2. inure to,** to toughen or harden (someone) to by exercise; accustom to; habituate to: *to inure a person to danger.* Also, **enure.** –**inurement,** n.

invade /ɪnˈveɪd/ v.t. **1.** to enter as or like an enemy: *Caesar invaded Britain; locusts invaded the fields.* **2.** to enter or penetrate: *the poison invaded his system; cooking smells invaded the bedroom.* **3.** to intrude upon; violate: *to invade privacy; to invade rights.* –v.i. **4.** to make an invasion. –**invader,** n.

invalid[1] /ˈɪnvəlɪd, -lid/ n. **1.** a weak or sick person. **2.** a member of the armed forces disabled for active service. –adj. **3.** weak or sick: *his invalid sister.* **4.** of or for invalids: *invalid food.* –v.t. **5.** to affect with disease;

make an invalid: *invalided for life.* **6.** to class, or remove from active service, as an invalid. —**invalidism**, *n.*

invalid² /ɪnˈvælɪd/ *adj.* **1.** not valid; of no force, weight, or cogency; weak: *invalid arguments.* **2.** without legal force, or void, as a contract. —**invalidity** /ˌɪnvəˈlɪdəti/, *n.* —**invalidly**, *adv.*

invalidate /ɪnˈvælədeɪt/ *v.t.* **1.** to render invalid. **2.** to deprive of legal force or efficacy. —**invalidation** /ɪnˌvælə-ˈdeɪʃən/, *n.* —**invalidator**, *n.*

invaluable /ɪnˈvæljəbəl/ *adj.* that cannot be valued or appraised; of inestimable value. —**invaluableness**, *n.* —**invaluably**, *adv.*

invariable /ɪnˈvɛəriəbəl/ *adj.* **1.** not variable or not capable of being varied; not changing or not capable of being changed; always the same. —*n.* **2.** an invariable quantity; a constant. —**invariability** /ɪnˌvɛəriəˈbɪləti/, **invariableness**, *n.* —**invariably**, *adv.*

invasion /ɪnˈveɪʒən/ *n.* **1.** the act of invading or entering as an enemy. **2.** the entrance or advent of anything troublesome or harmful, as disease. **3.** entrance as if to take possession or overrun. **4.** infringement by intrusion: *invasion of privacy.*

invective /ɪnˈvɛktɪv/ *n.* **1.** vehement denunciation; an utterance of violent censure or reproach. **2.** a railing accusation; vituperation. —*adj.* **3.** censoriously abusive; vituperative; denunciatory. —**invectively**, *adv.* —**invectiveness**, *n.*

inveigh /ɪnˈveɪ/ *v.i.* to attack vehemently in words; rail: *to inveigh against democracy.* —**inveigher**, *n.*

inveigle /ɪnˈveɪgəl/ *v.t.* (**-gled**, **-gling**) **1.** to draw (*into*, sometimes *from*, *away*, etc.) by beguiling or artful inducements: *to inveigle a person into playing bridge.* **2.** to allure, win, or seduce by beguiling. —**inveiglement**, *n.* —**inveigler**, *n.*

invent /ɪnˈvɛnt/ *v.t.* **1.** to originate as a product of one's own contrivance: *to invent a machine.* **2.** to produce or create with the imagination: *to invent a story.* **3.** to make up or fabricate as something merely fictitious or false: *to invent excuses.* —*v.i.* **4.** to devise something new, as by ingenuity. —**inventible**, *adj.* —**inventor**, *n.*

invention /ɪnˈvɛnʃən/ *n.* **1.** the act of inventing or creating. **2.** anything invented or devised. **3.** (the use of) imaginative or creative power in literature or art. **4.** the power or faculty of inventing, devising, or originating. **5.** something made up falsely; fabrication. **6.** *Music* a short piece, contrapuntal in nature, generally based on one subject.

inventive /ɪnˈvɛntɪv/ *adj.* **1.** apt at inventing, devising, or contriving. **2.** having the function of inventing. **3.** relating to, involving, or showing invention. —**inventively**, *adv.* —**inventiveness**, *n.*

inventory /ˈɪnvəntri, ɪnˈvɛntəri/, *Orig. US* /ˈɪnvəntɔri/ *n.* (*pl.* **-tories**) **1.** a detailed list of articles, goods, etc., kept by merchants, etc. **2.** (the items in) a complete listing of work, materials, goods, etc., in a business. **3.** the value of a stock of goods. —*v.t.* (**-toried**, **-torying**) **4.** to make an inventory of; enter in an inventory. —**inventorial** /ˌɪnvənˈtɔriəl/, *adj.* —**inventorially** /ˌɪnvənˈtɔriəli/, *adv.*

inverse /ɪnˈvɜs, ˈɪnvɜs/ *adj.* **1.** reversed in position, direction, or tendency: *inverse order.* **2.** opposite to in nature or effect, as a mathematical relation or operation: *subtraction is the inverse operation to addition.* **3.** inverted, or turned upside down. —*n.* **4.** an inverted state or condition. **5.** something that is inverse; the direct opposite. —**inversely**, *adv.*

invert /ɪnˈvɜt/ *v.t.* **1.** to turn upside down, inside out, or inwards. **2.** to reverse in position, direction, or order. **3.** to turn or change to the opposite or contrary, as in nature, bearing, or effect: *to invert a process.* —**inversion**, *n.* —**invertible**, *adj.* —**inverter**, *n.*

invertebrate /ɪnˈvɜtəbrət, -breɪt/ *adj.* **1.** *Zool.* not vertebrate; without a backbone. **2.** of or relating to animals without backbones. —*n.* **3.** an invertebrate animal.

4. someone who lacks strength of character. —**invertebracy** /ɪnˈvɜtəbrəsi/, **invertebrateness**, *n.*

inverted comma *n.* See **quotation mark**.

invest /ɪnˈvɛst/ *v.t.* **1.** to put (money) to use, by purchase or expenditure, in something offering profitable returns, especially interest or income. **2.** to spend: *to invest large sums in books.* **3.** to clothe. **4.** to cover or adorn as an article of attire does. **5.** to cover or surround as if with a garment, or like a garment: *spring invests the trees with leaves.* **6.** to surround (a place) with military forces or works so as to prevent approach or escape; besiege. **7.** to endue or endow: *to invest a friend with every virtue.* **8.** to install in an office or position; furnish with power, authority, rank, etc. —*v.i.* **9.** to invest money; make an investment. —*phr.* **10. invest in**, (*humorous*) to spend money on, as by gambling, purchasing, etc. —**investor**, *n.*

investigate /ɪnˈvɛstəgeɪt/ *v.t.* **1.** to search or inquire into; search or examine into the particulars of; examine in detail. **2.** to examine in order to obtain the true facts: *to investigate a murder.* —*v.i.* **3.** to make inquiry, examination, or investigation. —**investigation**, *n.* —**investigator**, *n.* —**investigable** /ɪnˈvɛstəgəbəl/, *adj.* —**investigative** /ɪnˈvɛstəgətɪv/, **investigatory** /ɪnˈvɛstəgeɪtəri/, *adj.*

investigative journalism *n.* journalism which does not just report news, but actively investigates a situation with the aim of exposing serious wrongdoing in the community, miscarriage of justice, etc.

investiture /ɪnˈvɛstɪtʃə/ *n.* **1.** the act of investing. See **invest** (def. 8). **2.** the ceremony in which a person is invested with an office or rank, usually by the putting on of the relevant insignia: *an investiture at Government House.* **3.** the state of being invested, as with a garment, quality, etc.

investment /ɪnˈvɛstmənt/ *n.* **1.** the investing of money in order to make a profit. **2.** a particular example or way of investing: *their investments are all in gold.* **3.** something in which money is invested, as housing, minerals, etc. **4.** the spending of anything for some purpose: *the investment of time in that program is huge.* **5.** the act of investing or the state of being invested, as with a garment or quality. **6.** *Biol.* any covering or outer layer.

investment bank *n.* → **merchant bank**.

inveterate /ɪnˈvɛtərət/ *adj.* **1.** confirmed in a habit, practice, feeling, or the like: *an inveterate gambler.* **2.** firmly established by long continuance, as a disease or sore, a habit or practice (often bad), or a feeling (often hostile); chronic. —**inveteracy, inveterateness**, *n.* —**inveterately**, *adv.*

invidious /ɪnˈvɪdiəs/ *adj.* **1.** such as to bring odium, unpopularity, or envious dislike: *an invidious honour.* **2.** calculated to excite ill will or resentment or give offence: *invidious remarks.* **3.** offensively or unfairly discriminating: *invidious comparisons.* —**invidiously**, *adv.* —**invidiousness**, *n.*

invigorate /ɪnˈvɪgəreɪt/ *v.t.* to give vigour to; fill with life and energy: *to invigorate the body.* —**invigoratingly**, *adv.* —**invigoration** /ɪnˌvɪgəˈreɪʃən/, *n.* —**invigorative** /ɪnˈvɪgərətɪv/, *adj.* —**invigoratively**, *adv.* —**invigorator**, *n.*

invincible /ɪnˈvɪnsəbəl/ *adj.* **1.** that cannot be conquered or vanquished: *an invincible force.* **2.** insuperable; insurmountable: *invincible difficulties.* —**invincibility** /ɪnˌvɪnsəˈbɪləti/, **invincibleness**, *n.* —**invincibly**, *adv.*

inviolable /ɪnˈvaɪələbəl/ *adj.* **1.** that must not be violated; that is to be kept free from violence or violation of any kind, or treated as if sacred: *an inviolable sanctuary.* **2.** that cannot be violated, subjected to violence, or injured. —**inviolability** /ɪnˌvaɪələˈbɪləti/, **inviolableness**, *n.* —**inviolably**, *adv.*

inviolate /ɪnˈvaɪələt, -leɪt/ *adj.* **1.** free from violation, injury, desecration, or outrage. **2.** undisturbed. **3.** unbroken. **4.** not infringed. —**inviolacy** /ɪnˈvaɪələsi/, **inviolateness**, *n.* —**inviolately**, *adv.*

invisible /ɪnˈvɪzəbəl/ adj. 1. not visible; not perceptible by the eye: *invisible agents of the Devil.* 2. withdrawn from or out of sight. 3. not perceptible or discernible by the mind: *invisible differences.* 4. concealed from public knowledge; clandestine. 5. not ordinarily found in financial statements: *goodwill is an invisible asset.* –n. 6. an invisible thing or being. 7. an invisible export or import. –phr. 8. **the invisible, a.** the unseen or spiritual world. **b.** (*upper case*) (*upper case*) God. –**invisibility** /ɪnˌvɪzəˈbɪləti/, **invisibleness,** n. –**invisibly,** adv.

invitation /ɪnvəˈteɪʃən/ n. 1. the act of inviting. 2. the written or spoken form with which a person is invited. 3. attraction or allurement. –adj. 4. restricted to invited individuals or teams: *an invitation golf match.* –**invitational,** adj.

invite /ɪnˈvaɪt/ v.t. 1. to ask in a kindly, courteous, or complimentary way, to come or go to some place, gathering, entertainment, etc., or to do something: *to invite friends to dinner.* 2. to request politely or formally: *to invite donations.* 3. to act so as to bring on or render probable: *to invite danger.* 4. to give occasion for. 5. to attract, allure, or tempt. –**inviter,** n. –**invitee,** n. –**invitatory** /ɪnˈvaɪtətri/, adj.

inviting /ɪnˈvaɪtɪŋ/ adj. that invites; especially attractive, alluring, or tempting: *an inviting offer.* –**invitingly,** adv. –**invitingness,** n.

in vitro /ɪn ˈvɪtroʊ/ adv. in an artificial environment, as a test tube. –**in-vitro,** adj.

in-vitro fertilisation n. the fertilisation of an egg, especially a human ovum, by a sperm in a test tube, the resulting embryo to be implanted in a uterus. *Abbrev.*: IVF Also, **in-vitro fertilization.**

invocation /ɪnvəˈkeɪʃən/ n. the act of invoking; calling upon a deity, etc., for aid, protection, inspiration, etc. –**invocatory,** adj.

invoice /ˈɪnvɔɪs/ n. 1. a written list of merchandise, with prices, delivered or sent to a buyer. 2. an itemised bill containing the prices which comprise the total charge. –v.t. (**-voiced, -voicing**) 3. to present an invoice to (a customer, or the like). 4. to make an invoice of. 5. to enter in an invoice.

invoke /ɪnˈvoʊk/ v.t. 1. to call for with earnest desire; make supplication or prayer for: *to invoke God's mercy.* 2. to call on (a divine being, etc.), as in prayer. 3. to appeal to, as for confirmation. 4. to call forth (a spirit) by incantation; conjure. –**invoker,** n.

involuntary /ɪnˈvɒləntri/, *Orig. US* /ɪnˈvɒləntɛri/ adj. 1. not voluntary; acting, or done or made without one's own volition, or otherwise than by one's own will or choice: *an involuntary listener.* 2. unintentional. 3. *Physiol.* acting independently of, or done or occurring without, conscious control: *involuntary muscles.* –**involuntarily,** adv. –**involuntariness,** n.

involve /ɪnˈvɒlv/ v.t. 1. to include as a necessary circumstance, condition, or consequence; imply; entail. 2. to affect, as something within the scope of operation. 3. to include, contain, or comprehend within itself or its scope. 4. to bring into an intricate or complicated form or condition. 5. to cause to be inextricably associated or concerned, as in something embarrassing or unfavourable. 6. to implicate, as in guilt or crime, or in any matter or affair. 7. to evoke great or excessive interest in: *the play really involved us.* 8. to roll, wrap, or shroud, as in something that surrounds. 9. *Archaic* to envelop or engulf, as the surrounding thing does. 10. *Archaic* to roll up on itself; wind spirally, coil, or wreathe. –phr. 11. **involve in** (or **with**), (*usu. in the passive*) to cause to have a concern in or an association with: *they were involved in several shaky businesses.* –**involvement,** n. –**involver,** n.

involved /ɪnˈvɒlvd/ adj. 1. complicated; difficult to follow: *his statistical procedures were very involved.*

2. sincerely concerned: *she is a caring and involved social worker.* 3. (*oft. placed after its noun*) implicated (in a crime): *one of the soldiers involved shot himself.* –phr. 4. **be involved,** *Colloq.* to have a close personal, especially sexual, relationship: *to be involved with an older man; how long have you and Harry been involved?*

invulnerable /ɪnˈvʌlnrəbəl/ adj. 1. incapable of being wounded, hurt, or damaged. 2. proof against attack: *invulnerable arguments.* –**invulnerability** /ɪnˌvʌlnrəˈbɪləti/, **invulnerableness,** n. –**invulnerably,** adv.

inward /ˈɪnwəd/ adj. 1. going or directed towards the inside or interior: *an inward glance.* 2. situated within; inner; interior; internal: *an inward room.* 3. essential; intrinsic; inherent: *the inward nature of a thing.* 4. mental, or spiritual: *inward peace.* –adv. 5. inwards. –n. 6. an inward or internal part; the inside.

inwardly /ˈɪnwədli/ adv. 1. towards or within the inside or inner part. 2. within one's thoughts or feelings; privately: *but inwardly he was pleased.* 3. not aloud or openly: *inwardly she was laughing wildly.*

inwards /ˈɪnwədz/ adv. 1. towards the inside or interior, as of a place, a space, or a body. 2. into the mind or soul. 3. in the mind or soul, or mentally or spiritually; inwardly. Also, **inward.**

in-your-face adj. *Colloq.* confronting or provocative. Also, **in your face.**

iod- variant of **iodo-**, usually before vowels, as in *iodic.*

iodine /ˈaɪədin, ˈaɪədaɪn/ n. a nonmetallic element occurring, at ordinary temperatures, as a greyish black crystalline solid, which sublimes to a dense violet vapour when heated. *Symbol*: I; *relative atomic mass*: 126.9044; *atomic number*: 53; *density*: (solid) 4.93 at 20°C. See **halogen.** Also, **iodin** /ˈaɪədən/.

iodo- a word element meaning 'iodine', as in *iodometry.* Also, **iod-.**

ion /ˈaɪən/ n. *Chem.* 1. an electrically charged atom, group, or molecule, formed by the loss or gain of one or more electrons, or by the dissolving of an electrolyte in a solvent of high dielectric constant. **Positive ions,** created by electron loss, are called *cations* and are attracted to the cathode in electrolysis. **Negative ions,** created by electron gain, are called *anions* and are attracted to the anode. The valency of an ion is equal to the number of electrons lost or gained and is indicated by a plus sign for cations and minus for anions, thus: Na^+, Cl^-, Ca^{++}, $S^=$. 2. one of the electrically charged particles formed in a gas by the action of an electric discharge, etc. –**ionic** /aɪˈɒnɪk/, adj.

-ion a suffix of nouns denoting action or process, state or condition, or sometimes things or persons, as in *allusion, communion, flexion, fusion, legion, opinion, suspicion, union.* Compare **-cion, -xion.** Also, **-tion, -ation.**

ionise /ˈaɪənaɪz/ v.t. 1. to separate or change into ions. 2. to produce ions in. –v.i. 3. to become changed into ions, as by dissolving. Also, **ionize.** –**ionisation** /aɪənaɪˈzeɪʃən/, n. –**ioniser,** n. –**ionised,** adj.

ionosphere /aɪˈɒnəsfɪə/ n. the succession of ionised layers that constitute the outer regions of the earth's atmosphere, having the highest concentrations of ions and free electrons; beyond the stratosphere and between about 60 and 1000 km above the earth.

iota /aɪˈoʊtə/ n. 1. the ninth letter (I, ι, = English I, i) of the Greek alphabet. 2. a very small quantity; a tittle; a jot.

IOU /aɪ oʊ ˈju/ n. a written acknowledgement of a debt, containing the expression 'IOU' (I owe you).

-ious a termination consisting of the suffix **-ous** with a preceding original or euphonic vowel *i.* Compare **-eous.**

IP address /aɪ ˈpi ˌædrɛs/ n. *Internet* a unique numerical identifier for a computer connected to the internet. Also, **IP number.**

ipso facto /ɪpsoʊ ˈfæktoʊ/ *adv.* by the fact itself; by that very fact: *it is condemned ipso facto.*

IQ /aɪ ˈkjuː/ *n.* intelligence quotient.

ir-[1] variant of **in-**[2], before *r*, as in *irradiate.*

ir-[2] variant of **in-**[3], before *r*, as in *irreducible.*

irascible /ɪˈræsəbəl/ *adj.* 1. easily provoked to anger: *an irascible old man.* 2. characterised by, excited by, or arising from anger: *an irascible nature.* –**irascibility** /ɪˌræsəˈbɪləti/, **irascibleness**, *n.* –**irascibly**, *adv.*

irate /aɪˈreɪt/ *adj.* angry; enraged: *the irate colonel.* –**irately**, *adv.*

ire /ˈaɪə/ *n.* anger; wrath. –**ireless**, *adj.*

iridescent /ɪrəˈdɛsənt/ *adj.* displaying colours like those of the rainbow. –**iridescently**, *adv.*

iridology /ɪrəˈdɒlədʒi/ *n.* a technique based on the belief that examination of the iris of the eye provides evidence of pathological changes in the body. –**iridologist**, *n.*

iris /ˈaɪrəs/ *n.* (*pl.* **irises** *or* **irides** /ˈaɪrədiz/) 1. *Anat.* the round coloured part of the eye surrounding the opening or pupil. 2. a type of perennial plant with handsome flowers and sword-shaped leaves; fleur-de-lis.

iris code *n.* a digital image of the iris of a customer, passenger, etc., matched against an image stored by the provider of a service, as a means of identification, such as for bank customers at automatic teller machines, airline passengers, etc.

iris scanning *n.* the digital scanning of the iris to obtain the iris code, as a means of identification of a customer, passenger, etc.

irk /ɜːk/ *v.t.* to weary, annoy, or trouble: *it irked him to wait.*

iron /ˈaɪən/ *n.* 1. *Chem.* a ductile, malleable, silver-white metallic element, scarcely known in a pure condition, but abundantly used in its crude or impure forms containing carbon for making tools, implements, machinery, etc. *Symbol:* Fe; *relative atomic mass:* 55.847; *atomic number:* 26; *density:* 7.86 at 20°C. 2. something hard, strong, rigid, unyielding, or the like: *hearts of iron.* 3. an instrument, utensil, weapon, etc., made of iron. 4. an iron or steel implement used heated for smoothing or pressing cloth, etc. 5. any golf club with a metal head, the face of which is sloped to achieve particular effects of drive or loft in a stroke: *a driving iron.* 6. a branding iron. 7. (*pl.*) a. an iron shackle or fetter: *body irons; leg irons.* b. iron supports to correct leg malformations, etc. 8. → **stirrup** (def. 1). –*adj.* 9. made of iron. 10. made of corrugated iron: *iron roofs.* 11. resembling iron in colour, firmness, etc.: *iron grey; an iron will.* 12. stern, harsh, or cruel. 13. not to be broken. 14. capable of great endurance; extremely robust or hardy. 15. firmly binding or clasping. –*v.t.* 16. to smooth or press with a heated iron, as clothes, etc. 17. to furnish, mount, or arm with iron. –*v.i.* 18. to press clothes, etc., with a heated iron. –*phr.* 19. **have an iron in the fire**, to have an interest in or a commitment to a particular enterprise: *I have too many irons in the fire.* 20. **iron out**, a. to press (a garment, etc.) b. to smooth and remove (problems and difficulties, etc.). c. to flatten; knock down: *he threatened to iron him out.* 21. **strike while the iron is hot**, to take immediate action while the opportunity is still available. –**ironless**, *adj.* –**ironer**, *n.*

Iron Age *n.* 1. *Archaeology* the time following the Stone and Bronze Ages, when early humans lived and made tools of iron. 2. (*lower case*) See **age** (def. 11).

ironbark /ˈaɪənbak/ *n.* any of a group of species of *Eucalyptus*, with a characteristic dark deeply fissured bark, as *E. paniculata*, **grey ironbark**.

iron fist *n.* severe control; strictness: *to rule with an iron fist.* Also, **iron hand**. –**iron-fisted**, *adj.*

iron gum *n.* any of several species of *Eucalyptus* which have particularly strong wood.

iron hand *n.* → **iron fist**.

ironic /aɪˈrɒnɪk/ *adj.* 1. characterised by or containing irony: *an ironic compliment.* 2. using or addicted to irony: *an ironic speaker.* Also, **ironical** /aɪˈrɒnɪkəl/. –**ironically**, *adv.* –**ironicalness**, *n.*

iron lung *n.* a chamber in which alternate pulsations of high and low pressure can be used to force normal lung movements, used especially in some cases of poliomyelitis.

iron man *n.* 1. a man of exceptional physical strength. 2. → **ironman**.

ironman /ˈaɪənmæn/ *n.* (*pl.* **-men**) 1. a contestant in a sporting event in which male competitors swim, cycle and run in succession. –*adj.* 2. of or relating to such an event. Also, **iron man**. –**ironwoman**, *n.*

ironwood /ˈaɪənwʊd/ *n.* any of various trees with hard heavy wood.

irony /ˈaɪrəni/ *n.* (*pl.* **-nies**) 1. a figure of speech or literary device in which the literal meaning is the opposite of that intended, especially, as in the Greek sense, when the locution understates the effect intended, used in ridicule or merely playfully. 2. an ironic utterance or expression. 3. simulated ignorance in discussion (**Socratic irony**). 4. the quality or effect, or implication of a speech or situation in a play or the like understood by the audience but not grasped by the characters of the piece (**dramatic irony**). 5. an outcome of events contrary to what was, or might have been, expected. 6. an ironic quality. –**ironist**, *n.*

irradiate /ɪˈreɪdieɪt/ *v.t.* 1. to cure or treat by exposure to radiation, as of ultraviolet light. 2. to expose to radiation. –**irradiative** /ɪˈreɪdiətɪv/, *adj.* –**irradiation**, *n.* –**irradiator**, *n.*

irrational /ɪˈræʃənəl/ *adj.* 1. without the faculty of, or not endowed with, reason: *irrational animals.* 2. without, or deprived of, sound judgement. 3. not in accordance with reason; utterly illogical: *irrational fear.* 4. *Maths* a. (of a number) not expressible as a ratio of two integers. b. (of a function) not expressible as a ratio of two polynomials. –*n.* 5. an irrational number or quantity. –**irrationally**, *adv.* –**irrationality** /ɪˌræʃəˈnæləti/, **irrationalness**, *n.*

irreconcilable /ɪˌrɛkənˈsaɪləbəl, ɪˈrɛkənsaɪləbəl/ *adj.* 1. that cannot be harmonised or adjusted; incompatible: *two irreconcilable statements.* 2. that cannot be brought to acquiescence or content; implacably opposed: *irreconcilable enemies.* –*n.* 3. a person or thing that is irreconcilable. 4. someone who remains opposed to agreement or compromise. –**irreconcilability** /ɪˌrɛkənsaɪləˈbɪləti/, **irreconcilableness**, *n.* –**irreconcilably**, *adv.*

irredeemable /ɪrəˈdiməbəl/ *adj.* 1. not redeemable; incapable of being bought back or paid off. 2. not convertible into specie, as paper money. 3. beyond redemption; irreclaimable. 4. irremediable, irreparable, or hopeless. –**irredeemableness**, *n.* –**irredeemably**, *adv.*

irrefutable /ɪˈrɛfjətəbəl, ɪrəˈfjutəbəl/ *adj.* not refutable; incontrovertible: *irrefutable logic.* –**irrefutability** /ɪrəfjutəˈbɪləti/, *n.* –**irrefutably**, *adv.*

irregular /ɪˈrɛgjələ/ *adj.* 1. without symmetry, even shape, formal arrangement, etc.: *an irregular pattern.* 2. not characterised by any fixed principle, method, or rate: *irregular intervals.* 3. not according to rule, or to the accepted principle, method, course, order, etc. 4. not conformed or conforming to rules of justice or morality, as conduct, transactions, mode of life, etc., or persons. 5. *Gram.* not conforming to the most prevalent pattern of formation, inflection, construction, etc.: *the verbs 'keep' and 'see' are irregular in their inflection.* –**irregularity** /ɪˌrɛgjəˈlærəti/, *n.* –**irregularly**, *adv.*

irrelevant /ɪˈrɛləvənt/ *adj.* not relevant; not applicable or pertinent: *irrelevant remarks.* –**irrelevantly**, *adv.* –**irrelevance, irrelevancy**, *n.*

irreligious /ɪrə'lɪdʒəs/ *adj.* **1.** not religious; impious; ungodly. **2.** showing disregard for or hostility to religion. –**irreligiously,** *adv.* –**irreligiousness,** *n.*

irreparable /ɪ'rɛpərəbəl, ɪ'rɛprəbəl, ɪrə'pɛərəbəl/ *adj.* not reparable; incapable of being rectified, remedied, or made good: *an irreparable loss.* –**irreparability** /ɪ,rɛpərə'bɪləti, -rɛprə-/, **irreparableness,** *n.* –**irreparably,** *adv.*

irreplaceable /ɪrə'pleɪsəbəl/ *adj.* that cannot be replaced: *an irreplaceable souvenir.*

irrepressible /ɪrə'prɛsəbəl/ *adj.* not repressible. –**irrepressibility** /,ɪrəprɛsə'bɪləti/, **irrepressibleness,** *n.* –**irrepressibly,** *adv.*

irreproachable /ɪrə'proʊtʃəbəl/ *adj.* not reproachable; free from blame. –**irreproachability** /,ɪrəproʊtʃə'bɪləti/, **irreproachableness,** *n.* –**irreproachably,** *adv.*

irresistible /ɪrə'zɪstəbəl/ *adj.* not resistible; that cannot be resisted or withstood; tempting: *an irresistible impulse.* –**irresistibility** /,ɪrəzɪstə'bɪləti/, **irresistibleness,** *n.* –**irresistibly,** *adv.*

irresolute /ɪ'rɛzəlut/ *adj.* not resolute; doubtful or undecided; infirm of purpose; vacillating. –**irresolutely,** *adv.* –**irresoluteness,** *n.*

irrespective /ɪrə'spɛktɪv/ *phr.* **irrespective of,** without regard to; independent of: *irrespective of all rights.* –**irrespectively,** *adv.*

irresponsible /ɪrə'spɒnsəbəl/ *adj.* **1.** not responsible; not answerable or accountable: *an irresponsible ruler.* **2.** not capable of responsibility; done without a sense of responsibility: *mentally irresponsible.* –*n.* **3.** an irresponsible person. –**irresponsibility** /,ɪrəspɒnsə'bɪləti/, **irresponsibleness,** *n.* –**irresponsibly,** *adv.*

irretrievable /ɪrə'trivəbəl/ *adj.* not retrievable; irrecoverable; irreparable. –**irretrievability** /,ɪrətrivə'bɪləti/, **irretrievableness,** *n.* –**irretrievably,** *adv.*

irreverence /ɪ'rɛvrəns, ɪ'rɛvərəns/ *n.* **1.** the quality of being irreverent; lack of reverence or respect. **2.** the condition of not being reverenced: *to be held in irreverence.*

irreverent /ɪ'rɛvrənt, ɪ'rɛvərənt/ *adj.* not reverent; manifesting or characterised by irreverence; deficient in veneration or respect: *an irreverent reply.* –**irreverently,** *adv.*

irreversible /ɪrə'vɜsəbəl/ *adj.* not reversible; that cannot be reversed. –**irreversibility** /,ɪrəvɜsə'bɪləti/, **irreversibleness,** *n.* –**irreversibly,** *adv.*

irrevocable /ə'rɛvəkəbəl, ɪrə'voʊkəbəl/ *adj.* not to be revoked or recalled; that cannot be repealed or annulled: *an irrevocable decree.* –**irrevocability** /ə,rɛvəkə'bɪləti, ,ɪrəvoʊkə'bɪləti/, **irrevocableness,** *n.* –**irrevocably,** *adv.*

irrigate /'ɪrəgeɪt/ *v.t.* **1.** to supply (land) with water and thereby promote vegetation by means of canals, especially artificially made ones, passing through it. **2.** *Med.* to supply (a wound, etc.) with a constant flow of some liquid. –**irrigable,** *adj.* –**irrigative,** *adj.* –**irrigator,** *n.* –**irrigation,** *n.*

irritable /'ɪrətəbəl/ *adj.* **1.** easily irritated; readily excited to impatience or anger. **2.** *Pathol.* susceptible to physical irritation; liable to shrink, become inflamed, etc., when stimulated: *an irritable wound.* –**irritability,** *n.* –**irritableness,** *n.* –**irritably,** *adv.*

irritable bowel syndrome *n.* a common intestinal disorder of unknown cause, the symptoms of which may include diarrhoea, constipation, cramping, abdominal pain and bloating. Also, **IBS.**

irritant /'ɪrətənt/ *adj.* **1.** irritating. –*n.* **2.** anything that irritates. **3.** *Pathol., Med.* something, such as a poison or a therapeutic agent, producing irritation. –**irritancy,** *n.*

irritate /'ɪrəteɪt/ *v.t.* **1.** to excite to impatience or anger. **2.** *Physiol., Biol.* to excite (a living system) to some characteristic action or function. **3.** *Pathol.* to bring (a bodily part, etc.) to an abnormally excited or sensitive condition. –**irritating,** *adj.* –**irritator,** *n.* –**irritation** /ɪrə-'teɪʃən/, *n.*

irrupt /ɪ'rʌpt/ *v.i.* to burst in or intrude suddenly.

Irukandji jellyfish /ɪrəkændʒi 'dʒɛlɪfɪʃ/ *n.* a small jellyfish, *Carukia barnesi,* the sting of which results in the Irukandji syndrome.

Irukandji syndrome *n.* a potentially fatal syndrome which results from being stung by the Irukandji jellyfish; characterised by severe backache and headache, shooting pains in the chest and abdomen, and, in some cases, pulmonary oedema which can be a cause of death.

is /ɪz/, *weak forms* /z, s/ *v.* 3rd person singular present indicative of **be.**

is- variant of **iso-,** before some vowels, as in *isallobar.*

-isation a noun suffix, combination of **-ise**[1] with **-ation.** Also, **-ization.**

ischaemic stroke /ɪskimɪk 'stroʊk/ *n.* a stroke (def. 4) occurring as a result of the blood supply to part of the brain being blocked; the most common form of stroke. Compare **haemorrhagic stroke.** Also, **ischemic stroke.**

ISDN /aɪ ɛs di 'ɛn/ *n.* a fully-integrated digital communications network which can transmit voice, data, text, and image.

-ise[1] a suffix of verbs having the following senses: **1.** intransitively, of following some line of action, practice, policy, etc., as in *apologise, economise, theorise,* or of becoming (as indicated), as *crystallise* and *oxidise* (intr.). **2.** transitively, of acting towards or upon, treating, or affecting in a particular way, as in *baptise, colonise,* or of making or rendering (as indicated), as in *civilise, legalise.* Compare **-ism, -ist.** Also, **-ize.**

-ise[2] a noun suffix indicating quality, condition, or function, as in *merchandise, franchise.*

-ish[1] **1.** a suffix used to form adjectives from nouns, with the sense of: **a.** 'belonging to' (a people, country, etc.), as in *British, Danish, English, Spanish.* **b.** 'after the manner of', 'having the characteristics of', 'like', as in *babyish, girlish, mulish* (such words being now often depreciatory). **c.** 'addicted to', 'inclined or tending to', as in *bookish, freakish.* **2.** a suffix used to form adjectives from other adjectives, with the sense of 'somewhat', 'rather', as in *oldish, reddish, sweetish.*

-ish[2] a suffix of verbs of French origin, as *cherish, finish,* etc.

Islam /'ɪzlæm, 'ɪs-, -lam/ *n.* **1.** the Muslim religion, based on the teachings of Mohammed as set down in the Koran, the fundamental principle being absolute submission to a unique and personal God, referred to as Allah. **2.** all Muslim believers, their civilisation, and their lands. –**Islamic,** *adj.* –**Islamism,** *n.* –**Islamite,** *n.*

Islamicist /ɪz'læməsəst/ *n.* **1.** someone who specialises in the study of Islam. **2.** a believer in Islam, especially a supporter of an Islamic revival movement; Islamist.

island /'aɪlənd/ *n.* **1.** an area of land completely surrounded by water, and not large enough to be called a continent. **2.** something like an island in that it is alone, or isolated or cut off: *traffic island.*

islander /'aɪləndə/ *n.* a native or inhabitant of an island.

isle /aɪl/ *n.* a small island: *the Scilly Isles.*

ism /'ɪzəm/ *n.* a distinctive doctrine, theory, system, or practice: *this is the age of isms.*

-ism a suffix of nouns denoting action or practice, state or condition, principles, doctrines, a usage or characteristic, etc., as in *baptism, barbarism, criticism, Darwinism, plagiarism, realism, Australianism.*

isn't /'ɪzənt/ *v.* contraction of *is not.*

iso- **1.** a prefix meaning 'equal'. **2.** *Chem.* a prefix added to the name of a compound to denote an isomer of that compound. Also, **is-.**

isobar /ˈaɪsəbɑ/ *n.* **1.** *Meteorol., etc.* a line drawn on a weather map, etc., connecting all points having the same barometric pressure (reduced to sea level), measured in hectopascals, at a specified time or over a certain period. **2.** Also, **isobare** /ˈaɪsəbɛə/ *Physics, Chem.* one of two or more atoms of different atomic number, but having the same atomic weight. –**isobaric**, *adj.*

isoclinal /aɪsoʊˈklaɪnəl/ *adj.* **1.** of or relating to a line on the earth's surface connecting points of equal dip or inclination of the earth's magnetic field. **2.** *Geol.* of or relating to a fold of strata which is an isocline. –*n.* **3.** an isoclinal line. Also, **isoclinic** /aɪsoʊˈklɪnɪk/.

isolate /ˈaɪsəleɪt/ *v.t.* **1.** to set or place apart; detach or separate so as to be alone. **2.** *Med.* to keep (an infected person) from contact with non-infected ones. **3.** *Chem.* to obtain (a substance) in an uncombined or pure state. **4.** *Elect.* to insulate. **5.** to track down; discover: *they isolated the fault.* –**isolation**, *n.* –**isolator**, *n.* –**isolated**, *adj.* –**isolative**, *adj.* –**isolable** /ˈaɪsələbəl/, *adj.*

isolationism /aɪsəˈleɪʃənɪzəm/ *n.* the policy of seeking political or national isolation.

isomer /ˈaɪsəmə/ *n.* **1.** *Chem.* a compound which is isomeric with one or more other compounds. **2.** *Physics* a nuclide which is isomeric with one or more other nuclides.

isomeric /aɪsoʊˈmɛrɪk/ *adj.* **1.** *Chem.* (of compounds) composed of the same kinds and numbers of atoms which differ from each other in the arrangement of the atoms and, therefore, in one or more properties. **2.** *Physics* (of nuclides) having the same atomic number and mass but a different energy state. –**isomerism** /aɪˈsɒmərɪzəm/, *n.*

isometric /aɪsəˈmɛtrɪk/ *adj.* Also, **isometrical. 1.** relating to or having equality of measure. **2.** (of a projection, drawing, etc., representing a solid object) having three mutually perpendicular axes represented as being equally inclined to the plane of projection, all lines being drawn to scale. –*n.* **3.** (*pl.*) a system of physical exercises in which muscles are pitted against each other or against a fixed object. –**isometrically**, *adv.*

isomorphic /aɪsəˈmɔfɪk/ *adj. Biol.* being of the same or of like form; different in ancestry, but alike in appearance.

ISO rating /ˌaɪ ɛs ˈoʊ reɪtɪŋ/ *n. Photography* **1.** (in film cameras) a classification of the film which relates to its sensitivity to light; the more sensitive it is, the better suited to high-speed photography and to low-light environments but the more grainy the resulting image; the numerically higher the ISO rating, the more sensitive the film. **2.** (in digital cameras) an indication of the light sensitivity of the camera's CCD (its image capturing device).

isosceles /aɪˈsɒsəliz/ *adj.* (of a triangle) having two sides equal.

ISO setting *n. Photography* a setting of digital cameras that allows adjustments to the sensitivity of the CCD.

isotherm /ˈaɪsəθ3m/ *n.* **1.** *Meteorol.* a line connecting points on the earth's surface having the same (mean) temperature. **2.** *Physics, Chem.* an isothermal line.

isothermal /aɪsəˈθ3məl/ –*adj.* **1.** *Physics, Chem.* of or relating to equality of temperature. **2.** *Meteorol.* of or relating to an isotherm. –*n.* **3.** *Meteorol.* → **isotherm.** –**isothermally**, *adv.*

isothermal line *n. Chem., Physics* a line or graph showing relations of variables under conditions of uniform temperature.

isotope /ˈaɪsətoʊp/ *n. Chem.* any of two or more forms of a chemical element, having the same number of protons in the nucleus and, hence, the same atomic number, but having different numbers of neutrons in the nucleus and, hence, different atomic weights. –**isotopic** /aɪsəˈtɒpɪk/, *adj.* –**isotopy** /aɪˈsɒtəpi/, *n.*

issue /ˈɪʃu, ˈɪʃju, ˈɪsju/ *n.* **1.** the act of sending, or promulgation; delivery; emission. **2.** that which is issued. **3.** a quantity issued at one time: *the latest issue of a periodical.* **4.** *Bibliography* the printing of copies of a work from the original setting of type, but with some slight changes in the preliminary or appended matter. **5.** a point in question or dispute, as between contending parties in an action at law. **6.** a point or matter the decision of which is of special or public importance: *the political issues.* **7.** a point the decision of which determines a matter: *the real issue.* **8.** a point at which a matter is ready for decision: *to bring a case to an issue.* **9.** a complaint; objection: *do you have an issue with this decision?* **10.** (*pl.*) unresolved psychological problems: *she has issues which she needs to work through.* **11.** something proceeding from any source, as a product, effect, result, or consequence. **12.** the ultimate result, event, or outcome of a proceeding, affair, etc.: *the issue of a contest.* **13.** a distribution of food (rations), clothing, equipment, or ammunition to a number of officers or service personnel, or to a military unit. **14.** offspring or progeny: *to die without issue.* **15.** a going, coming, passing, or flowing out: *free issue and entry.* **16.** a place or means of egress; an outlet or vent. **17.** that which comes out, as an outflowing stream. **18.** *Pathol.* **a.** a discharge of blood, pus, or the like. **b.** an incision, ulcer, or the like emitting such a discharge. **19.** *Chiefly Law* the yield or profit from land or other property. –*verb* (**issued, issuing**) –*v.t.* **20.** to put out; deliver for use, sale, etc.; put into circulation. **21.** to print (a publication) for sale or distribution. **22.** to distribute (food, clothing, etc.) to one or more officers or service personnel or to a military unit. **23.** to send out; discharge; emit. –*v.i.* **24.** to be sent or put forth authoritatively or publicly, as a writ, money, etc. **25.** to come or proceed from any source. **26.** to arise as a result or consequence; result. **27.** to be the outcome. –*phr.* **28. at issue, a.** in controversy: *a point at issue.* **b.** in disagreement. **c.** (sometimes fol. by *with*) inconsistent; inharmonious. **29. have issues,** to have unresolved personal difficulties and conflicts. **30. have issues with** (or **about**), to have concerns with regard to. **31. issue forth,** to go, pass, or flow out; come forth; emerge: *to issue forth to battle.* **32. issue in,** to end in; terminate in. **33. the** (**whole**) **issue,** everything; the lot. **34. join issue, a.** to join in controversy. **b.** to submit an issue jointly for legal decision. **35. take issue with,** to disagree with. –**issueless**, *adj.* –**issuer**, *n.*

-ist a suffix of nouns, often accompanying verbs ending in *-ise* or nouns ending in *-ism*, denoting someone who does, practises, or is concerned with something, or holds certain principles, doctrines, etc., as in *apologist, dramatist, machinist, plagiarist, realist, socialist, theorist.*

isthmus /ˈɪsməs, ˈɪsθməs/ *n.* (*pl.* **-muses**) **1.** a narrow strip of land, bordered on both sides by water, connecting two larger bodies of land. **2.** *Anat., etc.* a connecting part, organ, or passage, especially when narrow or joining structures or cavities larger than itself.

-istic a suffix of adjectives (and in the plural of nouns from adjectives) formed from nouns ending in *-ist*, and having reference to such nouns, or to associated nouns ending in *-ism*, as in *deistic, euphuistic, puristic*, etc. In nouns it has usually a plural form, as in *linguistics.*

it /ɪt/, *weak form* /ət/ *pron.* (*impersonal*), *third person, sing., neuter, subjective and objective* the pronoun which corresponds to *he* and *she*, used: **1.** as a substitute for a neuter noun or a noun representing something possessing sex when sex is not particularised or considered: *the baby laughs when it is tickled.* **2.** to refer to some matter expressed or understood, or some thing or notion not definitely conceived: *how goes it?* **3.** to refer to the subject of inquiry or attention, whether impersonal or personal, in sentences asking or stating what or who this is: *who is it?*; *it is I*. **4.** as the grammatical subject of a clause of which the logical subject is a phrase or clause following: *it is hard to believe that*. **5.** in impersonal constructions: *it is snowing*. **6.** as the grammatical object after certain verbs, as *to foot it*, (to go on foot). *–n.* **7.** *Colloq.* sex appeal. *–phr.* **8. with it**, *Colloq.* **a.** in accordance with current trends and fashions; fashionable. **b.** well-informed and quick-witted.

IT /aɪ ˈti/ *n.* → **information technology.**

Italian parsley /ɪtælʲən ˈpasli/ *n.* → **flat-leaf parsley.**

italic /ɪˈtælɪk, aɪ-/ *adj.* **1.** designating or relating to a style of printing types in which the letters usually slope to the right (thus, *italic*), patterned upon a compact manuscript hand, and used for emphasis, etc. *–n.* **2.** (*oft. pl.*) italic type.

itch /ɪtʃ/ *v.i.* **1.** to have or feel a peculiar irritation of the skin which causes a desire to scratch the part affected. **2.** to have a desire to do or to get something: *itch after fame. –n.* **3.** the sensation of itching. **4.** an uneasy or restless desire or longing: *an itch for authorship. –phr.* **5. the itch**, a contagious disease caused by the itch mite which burrows into the skin; scabies.

itchy /ˈɪtʃi/ *adj.* (**itchier, itchiest**) **1.** having an itching sensation. *–phr.* **2. have an itchy palm**, *Colloq.* to be expecting to receive a sum of money. **3. have itchy feet**, to have the desire to travel. *–***itchiness**, *n.*

-ite[1] a suffix of nouns meaning especially **1.** people connected with a place, tribe, leader, belief, system, etc., as in *Israelite, Laborite.* **2.** minerals and fossils, as in *ammonite, anthracite.* **3.** explosives, as in *cordite, dynamite.* **4.** chemical compounds, especially salts of acids whose names end in *-ous*, as in *phosphite, sulphites.* **5.** commercial products, as in *vulcanite.*

-ite[2] a suffix forming adjectives and nouns from adjectives, and some verbs, as in *composite, opposite, requisite, erudite*, etc.

item /ˈaɪtəm/ *n.* **1.** a separate article or particular: *fifty items on the list.* **2.** a separate piece of information or news, as in a newspaper. *–v.t.* **3.** to set down or enter as an item, or by or in items.

itemise /ˈaɪtəmaɪz/ *v.t.* to state by items; give the particulars of: *to itemise an account.* Also, **itemize.** *–***itemisation** /aɪtəmaɪˈzeɪʃən/, *n.* *–***itemiser**, *n.* *–***itemised**, *adj.*

iterate /ˈɪtəreɪt/ *v.t.* **1.** to utter again or repeatedly. **2.** to do (something) over again or repeatedly. *–***iteration**, *n.*

itinerant /aɪˈtɪnərənt/ *adj.* **1. a.** journeying; travelling from place to place. **b.** moving on a circuit, as a preacher, judge, or pedlar. *–n.* **2.** someone who travels from place to place, especially for duty or business. *–***itinerantly**, *adv.* *–***itinerancy**, *n.*

itinerary /aɪˈtɪnəri, aɪˈtɪnərəri/, *Orig. US* /aɪˈtɪnərɛri/ *n.* (*pl.* **-ries**) **1.** a plan of travel, often including details of accommodation, flights, etc. **2.** a line of travel; a route. **3.** an account of a journey; a record of travel. **4.** a book describing a route or routes of travel, with information for travellers.

-ition a noun suffix, as in *expedition, extradition*, etc., being *-tion* with a preceding original or formative vowel, or, in other words, **-ite**[2] + **-ion.**

-itious an adjective suffix occurring in adjectives associated with nouns in *-ition*, as *expeditious*, etc.

-itis a noun suffix used in pathological terms denoting inflammation of some part or organ, as in *bronchitis, gastritis, neuritis.*

-itive a suffix of adjectives and nouns of adjectival origin, as in *definitive, fugitive.*

it'll /ˈɪtl/ *v.* contraction of *it will* or *shall.*

its /ɪts/ *adj.* **1.** the possessive form of **it**: *its height is twenty metres; its bark is worse than its bite. –pron.* (*possessive*) **2.** the possessive form of **it**, used predicatively or absolutely: *the voice was its; its was the contribution that mattered.*

it's /ɪts/ contraction of *it is.*

itself /ɪtˈsɛlf/ *pron.* **1.** the reflexive form of *it*: *a thermostatically controlled electric heater switches itself off.* **2.** an emphatic form of *it* used: **a.** as object: *the earth gathers its fruits to itself.* **b.** in apposition to a subject or object: *the moon itself is dead.* **3.** in its normal or usual state: *the dog is itself again.*

-ity a suffix forming abstract nouns of condition, characteristics, etc., as in *jollity, civility, Latinity.*

IUD /aɪ ju ˈdi/ *n.* → **intra-uterine device.**

-ium a suffix representing Latin neuter suffix, used especially to form names of metallic elements.

IV[1] /aɪ ˈvi/ *adj.* → **in vitro.**

IV[2] /aɪ ˈvi/ *adj.* → **intravenous.**

IV drug user *n.* an intravenous drug user. Also, **IVDU.**

-ive a suffix of adjectives (and nouns of adjectival origin) expressing tendency, disposition, function, connection, etc., as in *active, corrective, destructive, detective, passive, sportive.* Compare **-ative.**

I've /aɪv/ *v.* contraction of *I have.*

ivory /ˈaɪvəri, ˈaɪvri/ *n.* (*pl.* **-ries**) **1.** the hard white substance, a variety of dentine, composing the main part of the tusks of the elephant, walrus, etc. **2.** a tusk, as of an elephant. **3.** *Colloq.* a tooth, or the teeth. **4.** an article made of ivory, as a carving or a billiard ball. **5.** (*pl.*) *Colloq.* **a.** the keys of a piano, accordion, etc. **b.** dice. **6.** creamy white. *–adj.* **7.** consisting or made of ivory. **8.** of the colour ivory. *–phr.* **9. tickle the ivories**, *Colloq.* to play the piano. *–***ivory-like**, *adj.*

ivory tower *n.* **1.** a place withdrawn from the world and worldly acts and attitudes. **2.** an attitude of aloofness from or contempt for worldly matters or behaviour.

ivy /ˈaɪvi/ *n.* (*pl.* **ivies**) **1.** a climbing vine, *Hedera helix*, with smooth, shiny, evergreen leaves, yellowish inconspicuous flowers, and black berries, widely grown as an ornamental. **2.** any of various other climbing or trailing plants, such as *Parthenocissus tricuspidata* (**Japanese ivy**), *Glechoma hederacea* (**ground ivy**), etc.

-ize → **-ise**[1].

izzat /ˈɪzæt/ *n.* (in India and Pakistan) one's honour. Compare **sharam.**

J j

J, j /dʒeɪ/ *n.* a consonant, the 10th letter of the English alphabet.

jab /dʒæb/ *verb* (**jabbed, jabbing**) −*v.i.* **1.** to thrust smartly or sharply, as with the end or point of something. −*v.t.* **2.** to poke (something) smartly or sharply. −*n.* **3.** a poke with the end or point of something; a smart or sharp thrust. **4.** *Colloq.* an injection with a hypodermic needle.

jabber /'dʒæbə/ *v.i.* **1.** to speak rapidly, indistinctly, imperfectly, or nonsensically; chatter. −*v.t.* **2.** to utter (words) in a confused, indistinct fashion. −*n.* **3.** rapid or nonsensical talk or utterance; gibberish. −**jabberer**, *n.* −**jabberingly**, *adv.*

jabiru /dʒæbə'ru/ *n.* **1.** Also, **jabiroo.** (in nonscientific use) the Australian subspecies of the black-necked stork, *Ephippiorhynchus asiaticus australis*, white with glossy green-black head, neck and tail, and a black band across upper and lower wing surfaces; found along the north and east coast; policeman bird. **2.** a rare and endangered stork, *Jabiru mycteria*, of Central and South America.

jacana /dʒə'kanə/ *n.* any of various birds of the family Jacanidae, having lengthened toes and a long, sharp hind claw, adapted for running on floating vegetation.

jacaranda /dʒækə'rændə/ *n.* **1.** any of the tall tropical American trees constituting the genus *Jacaranda*, especially *J. mimosifolia* cultivated in many warm countries for its lavender-blue flowers. **2.** their fragrant ornamental wood. **3.** any of various related or similar trees.

jack /dʒæk/ *n.* **1.** a man or fellow. **2.** (*upper case or lower case*) a sailor. **3.** any of various mechanical contrivances or devices, such as a contrivance for raising heavy weights short distances. **4.** a device for turning a spit, etc. **5.** any of the four knaves in playing cards. **6. a.** a knucklebone or plastic imitation, a set of which is used in a children's game where they are thrown into the air and caught on the back of the hand. **b.** (*pl.*) the game itself. **7.** a small bowl used as a mark for the players to aim at, in the game of bowls. **8.** a small union or ensign used by a ship or vessel as a signal, etc., and flown from the jackstaff as an indication of nationality. −*v.t.* Also, **jack up. 9.** to lift or move with or as with a jack, or contrivance for raising. −*phr.* **10. every man jack** or **every manjack**, *Colloq.* everyone without exception. **11. I'm all right Jack,** an expression of selfish complacency on the part of the speaker. **12. jack of,** *Aust. Colloq.* fed up with. **13. jack up,** *Colloq.* **a.** to raise (prices, wages, etc.) **b.** *Aust.* (*taboo*) (of a man) to have sexual intercourse with. **c.** *Aust.* to be obstinate in refusal; resist. **d.** *Aust.* to inject drugs intravenously. **e.** *NZ* to arrange; prepare: *to jack up a meal; to jack up a party.* **f.** *NZ* to fix up; renovate.

jackal /'dʒækəl/ *n.* **1.** any of several species of wild dog of the genus *Canis*, especially the **golden jackal,** *Canis aureus*, of Eurasia and Africa, which hunt in packs at night, feeding on small animals and carrion; formerly supposed to hunt prey for the lion. **2.** someone who does drudgery or performs base acts for another.

jackaroo /dʒækə'ru/ *n.* **1.** a young man gaining practical experience on a sheep or cattle station, in order to acquire skills needed to become an owner, overseer, manager, etc. Compare **jillaroo.** −*v.i.* (**-rooed, -rooing**) **2.** to work as a jackaroo. Also, **jackeroo.**

jackass /'dʒækæs/ *n.* **1.** a male donkey. **2.** a very stupid or foolish person.

jackboot /'dʒækbut/ *n.* a large leather boot reaching up to and sometimes over the knee, originally one serving as armour, now frequently associated with the exercise of force or oppression.

jacket /'dʒækət/ *n.* **1.** a short coat, in various forms, worn by both men and women. **2.** Also, **dust jacket.** a removable (usually paper) cover for protecting the binding of a book; dust cover. **3.** the skin of a potato. **4.** the outer covering of a boiler, pipe, tank, etc. **5.** the natural coat of certain animals. −**jacketed**, *adj.* −**jacketless**, *adj.*

jackhammer /'dʒækhæmə/ *n.* **1.** a handheld machine used for drilling rocks, road surfaces, etc., driven by compressed air. −*v.t.* **2.** to drill (a hole, etc.) using a jackhammer. −*v.i.* **3.** to use a jackhammer.

jack-in-the-box *n.* **1.** a toy consisting of a figure, enclosed in a box, which springs out when the lid is unfastened. **2.** a seashore tree, *Hernandia peltata*, widely spread from Asia to northern Australia and the western Pacific. Also, **jack-in-a-box.**

jackknife /'dʒæknaɪf/ *n.* (*pl.* **-knives**) **1.** a large knife with a blade that folds into the handle. **2.** Also, **jackknife dive.** a dive in the process of which the body bends so that the hands briefly touch or nearly touch the toes; pike dive. −*v.i.* (**-knifed, -knifing**) **3.** to bend or fold up, like a jackknife. **4.** (of a horse) to buck bringing all four feet to a point. **5.** (of a semitrailer or a car pulling a caravan, etc.) to go out of control in such a way that the trailer swings round towards the driver's cab.

jack-of-all-trades *n.* someone who can turn their hand to anything but who has no one special skill.

jackpot /'dʒækpɒt/ *n.* **1.** the chief prize to be won on a gambling machine, as a poker machine, or in a lottery, a game or contest such as bingo, a quiz, etc. **2.** *Poker* a pool that accumulates until a player opens the betting with a pair of jacks or better. −*v.i.* (**-potted, -potting**) **3.** to accumulate by the amount of the previous unclaimed prize. −*phr.* **4. hit the jackpot, a.** to win chief prize on a gambling machine. **b.** to achieve great success; be very lucky.

Jacky Winter /dʒæki 'wɪntə/ *n.* a small grey-brown flycatcher, *Microeca fascinans*, found in many parts of Australia and New Guinea.

jacuzzi /dʒə'kuzi/ *n.* (*from trademark*) a type of spa pool, usually not attached to a larger pool.

jade[1] /dʒeɪd/ *n.* **1.** either of two minerals, jadeite or nephrite, sometimes green, highly esteemed as an ornamental stone for carvings, jewellery, etc. **2.** Also, **jade green.** green; varying from bluish green to yellowish green. −**jadelike**, *adj.*

jade[2] /dʒeɪd/ *n.* **1.** a horse, especially one of inferior breed, or worn out, or vicious. **2.** (*derog.*) a woman. −*v.t.* **3.** to make exhausted by working hard; to weary or fatigue; tire. −*v.i.* **4.** to become exhausted by working hard. −**jadish**, *adj.* −**jadishly**, *adv.* −**jadishness**, *n.*

jaded /'dʒeɪdəd/ *adj.* **1.** worn out; tired; fatigued. **2.** dispirited; losing enthusiasm. **3.** sated: *a jaded appetite.* −**jadedly**, *adv.* −**jadedness**, *n.*

jaffle /ˈdʒæfəl/ n. Aust. (from trademark) a sealed toasted sandwich with a savoury or sweet filling, cooked in a buttered jaffle iron.

jag¹ /dʒæg/ n. **1.** a sharp projection on an edge or surface. −v.t. (**jagged, jagging**) **2.** to cut or slash, especially in points or pendants along the edge; form notches, teeth, or ragged points in.

jag² /dʒæg/ n. **1.** a drinking bout. **2.** any sustained single activity, often carried to excess: an eating jag, a fishing jag.

jagged /ˈdʒægəd/ adj. having notches, teeth, or ragged edges. −**jaggedly**, adv. −**jaggedness**, n.

jaguar /ˈdʒægjuə/ n. a large wild cat, Panthera onca, of tropical America, having a tawny coat with large broken-edged spots.

jail /dʒeɪl/ n. **1.** a prison. −v.t. **2.** to take into or hold in custody; imprison. Also, **gaol.**

jake /dʒeɪk/ adj. Aust., NZ Colloq. all right: she'll be jake. Also, **jakerloo.**

jalopy /dʒəˈlɒpi/ n. (pl. **-pies**) Colloq. an old, decrepit, or unpretentious car.

jam¹ /dʒæm/ verb (**jammed, jamming**) −v.t. **1.** to press or squeeze tightly between bodies or surfaces, so that motion or extrication is made difficult or impossible. **2.** to bruise or crush by squeezing. **3.** to press, push, or thrust violently, as into a confined space or against some object. **4.** to fill or block up by crowding: crowds jam the doors. **5.** to cause to become wedged, caught, or displaced, so that it cannot work, as a machine, part, etc. **6.** Radio **a.** to interfere with (signals, etc.) by sending out others of approximately the same frequency. **b.** (of signals, etc.) to interfere with (other signals, etc.). −v.i. **7.** to become wedged or fixed; stick fast. **8.** to press or push violently, as into a confined space or against one another. **9.** (of a machine, etc.) to become unworkable as through the wedging or displacement of a part. −n. **10.** the act of jamming. **11.** the state of being jammed. **12.** a mass of vehicles, people, or objects jammed together: a traffic jam. **13.** Colloq. a difficult or awkward situation; a fix. −phr. **14. jam on,** to apply (brakes) forcibly.

jam² /dʒæm/ n. **1.** a preserve of whole fruit, boiled with sugar and sometimes pectin, especially one in which the fruit is reduced to a thick pulpy consistency. Compare **conserve** (def. 2). **2.** a similar preserve used as a condiment: onion jam. −**jammy,** adj.

jam³ /dʒæm/ n. Also, **jam session. 1.** Music a meeting of musicians for the spontaneous and improvisatory performance of music, especially jazz, usually for their own enjoyment. −v.i. (**jammed, jamming**) **2.** to take part in a jam.

jamb /dʒæm/ n. the side of an opening; a vertical piece forming the side of a doorway, window, or the like. Also, **jambe.**

jamboree /dʒæmbəˈri/ n. **1.** a large gathering or rally of Scouts, usually national or international. **2.** a carousal; any noisy merrymaking.

jangle /ˈdʒæŋgəl/ v.i. **1.** to sound harshly or discordantly: a jangling noise. −v.t. **2.** to cause to sound harshly or discordantly. **3.** to cause to become upset or irritated. −n. **4.** a harsh or discordant sound. **5.** an altercation; quarrel. −**jangler,** n.

janitor /ˈdʒænətə/ n. **1.** a caretaker, especially one who does basic cleaning maintenance. **2.** a doorkeeper or porter. −**janitorial** /dʒænəˈtɔriəl/, adj. −**janitress** /ˈdʒænətrəs/, fem. n.

January /ˈdʒænjuəri, ˈdʒænjuri, -jəri/, Orig. US /ˈdʒænjueri/ n. the first month of the year, containing 31 days.

jape /dʒeɪp/ n. a joke; jest; gibe. −**japer,** n.

japonica /dʒəˈpɒnɪkə/ n. **1.** any of several garden shrubs with white, pink, or red flowers belonging to the genus Chaenomeles, such as C. speciosa and C. japonica. **2.** the most widely known type of camellia, Camellia japonica, which can have double blooms ranging in colour from white to pink to red.

jar¹ /dʒɑ/ n. **1.** a broad-mouthed earthen or glass vessel, commonly cylindrical in form. **2.** Colloq. a glass of beer.

jar² /dʒɑ/ verb (**jarred, jarring**) −v.i. **1.** to produce a harsh, grating sound; sound discordantly. **2.** to have a harshly unpleasant effect upon the nerves, feelings, etc. **3.** to vibrate audibly; rattle. **4.** to vibrate or shake (without reference to sound). **5.** to be at variance; conflict; clash. −v.t. **6.** to cause to sound harshly or discordantly. **7.** to cause to rattle or shake. −n. **8.** a harsh, grating sound. **9.** a discordant sound or combination of sounds. **10.** a vibrating movement, as from concussion. **11.** a harshly unpleasant effect upon the mind or feelings due to physical or other shock. **12.** Aboriginal English a quarrel. −phr. **13. jar on,** to have a harshly unpleasant effect on (the feelings, nerves, etc.). −**jarring,** adj. −**jarringly,** adj.

jargon /ˈdʒagən/ n. **1.** the language peculiar to a trade, profession, or other group: medical jargon. **2.** pretentious language characterised by the use of uncommon or unfamiliar words. **3.** unintelligible or meaningless talk or writing; gibberish.

jarrah /ˈdʒærə/ n. a large tree of western Australia, Eucalyptus marginata, with durable dark red timber.

jasmine /ˈdʒæzmən/ n. **1.** any of the shrubs or climbing plants of the genus Jasminum, often cultivated for their fragrant flowers. **2.** any of various plants of other genera as Carolina jasmine. Also, **jessamine.**

jasmine rice n. a variety of long-grained fragrant rice from Thailand.

jasper /ˈdʒæspə/ n. a compact, opaque, often highly coloured variety of quartz commonly used in decorative carvings.

jaundice /ˈdʒɔndəs/ n. **1.** Pathol. a morbid bodily condition due to the presence of increased amounts of bile pigments in the blood, characterised by yellowness of the skin, the whites of the eyes, etc., by lassitude, and by loss of appetite. **2.** a state of feeling in which views are coloured or judgement is distorted by envy or jealousy. −v.t. (**-diced, -dicing**) **3.** to affect with jaundice. **4.** to distort or prejudice, as with pessimism, jealousy, resentment, etc.

jaunt /dʒɔnt/ v.i. **1.** to make a short journey, especially for pleasure. −n. **2.** such a journey.

jaunty /ˈdʒɔnti/ adj. (**-tier, -tiest**) **1.** easy and sprightly in manner or bearing. **2.** smartly trim or effective, as clothing. −**jauntily,** adv. −**jauntiness,** n.

javelin /ˈdʒævələn/ n. **1.** a spear to be thrown by hand. **2.** (in athletics) a metal or wooden shaft, with a metal point, thrown for distance. −v.t. **3.** to strike or pierce with or as with a javelin.

jaw /dʒɔ/ n. **1.** one of the two bones or structures (upper and lower) which form the framework of the mouth. **2.** Dentistry either of these containing all its teeth and covered by the soft tissues. **3.** anything likened to these: the jaws of death; jaws of a valley. **4.** one of two or more parts of a machine, etc., which crush or hold something: the jaws of a vice. **5.** Colloq. continual talk, especially of moralising nature. −v.t. **6.** Colloq. to talk disapprovingly to; admonish. −**jawless,** adj.

jay /dʒeɪ/ n. **1.** one of a number of Australian birds such as certain currawongs, cuckoo-shrikes, or the white-winged chough. **2.** any of several birds of the subfamily Corvinae, several having erectile crests, all of them robust, noisy, and active, such as the **common jay** or **Eurasian jay**, Garrulus glandarius, of Europe and Asia, and the **blue jay**, Cyanocitta cristata, of North America. **3.** a simple-minded or gullible person; a simpleton.

jaywalk /'dʒeɪwɔk/ v.i. to cross a street otherwise than by a pedestrian crossing or in a heedless manner, as against traffic lights. –**jaywalker**, n. –**jaywalking**, n.

jazz /dʒæz/ n. **1.** a type of popular music in the African American tradition, which sprang up in and around New Orleans and is marked by frequent improvisation and syncopated rhythms. **2.** a piece of such music. **3.** dancing or a dance performed to such music, as with violent bodily motions and gestures. **4.** Colloq. liveliness; noisiness; spirit. **5.** Colloq. pretentious or insincere talk. –adj. **6.** of the nature of or relating to jazz. –v.t. **7.** to play (music) in the manner of jazz. –v.i. **8.** to dance to jazz music. **9.** to play or perform jazz music. **10.** Colloq. to act or proceed with great energy or liveliness. –phr. Colloq. **11. and all that jazz**, and all that sort of thing; et cetera. **12. jazz up**, to put vigour or liveliness into.

jazzy /'dʒæzi/ adj. (-zier, -ziest) **1.** relating to or suggestive of jazz music. **2.** Colloq. bright and lively in a modern way.

J-curve /'dʒeɪ-kɜv/ n. Econ. a curve representing the theoretical effects of currency devaluation on a country's balance of trade, namely an initial fall followed by a continuing improvement.

jealous /'dʒeləs/ adj. **1.** (sometimes fol. by of) feeling resentment against a successful rival or at success, advantages, etc. **2.** characterised by or proceeding from suspicious fears or envious resentment: jealous intrigues. **3.** inclined to or troubled by suspicions or fears of rivalry, as in love or aims: a jealous husband. **4.** solicitous or vigilant in maintaining or guarding something. –**jealousy, jealousness**, n. –**jealously**, adv.

jeans /dʒinz/ pl. n. casual trousers, especially those made of denim.

jeep /dʒip/ n. a small (usually ¼ tonne capacity) military motor vehicle.

jeer /dʒɪə/ v.i. **1.** to speak or shout derisively; gibe or scoff rudely. –v.t. **2.** to treat with derision; make a mock of. –n. **3.** a jeering utterance; a derisive or rude gibe. –phr. **4. jeer at**, to deride or mock. –**jeerer**, n. –**jeeringly**, adv.

Jehovah /dʒə'hoʊvə/ n. **1.** a name of God in the Old Testament **2.** (in modern Christian use) God.

jelly /'dʒeli/ n. (pl. -lies) **1.** a food preparation of a soft, elastic consistency due to the presence of gelatine, pectin, etc., as fruit juice boiled down with sugar. **2.** US jam, especially a thin jam. **3.** anything of the consistency of jelly. **4.** Colloq. → **gelignite**. –verb (-lied, -lying) –v.t. **5.** to bring to the consistency of jelly. –v.i. **6.** to come to the consistency of jelly. –phr. **7. turn to jelly**, to become weak with fear. –**jelly-like**, adj.

jellyfish /'dʒelifɪʃ/ n. any of various free-swimming marine coelenterates of a soft, gelatinous structure, especially one with an umbrella-like body and long, trailing tentacles; a medusa.

jemmy /'dʒemi/ n. a short crowbar. Also, US, **jimmy**.

jeopardise /'dʒepədaɪz/ v.t. to put in jeopardy; risk. Also, **jeopardize**.

jeopardy /'dʒepədi/ n. **1.** hazard or risk of loss or harm. **2.** peril or danger: for a moment his life was in jeopardy.

jerboa /dʒɜ'boʊə/ n. **1.** a small carnivorous marsupial Antechinomys laniger, which inhabits the central desert of Australia and resembles the jerboa (def. 2), although it does not hop. **2.** any of various mouse-like rodents of the family Dipodidae of North Africa and Asia, with long hind legs used for jumping, and a long tail.

jerk¹ /dʒɜk/ n. **1.** a quick, sharp thrust, pull, throw, or the like; a sudden start. **2.** Physiol. a sudden movement of an organ or a part. **3.** Weightlifting a lift in which the barbell is raised first to the shoulders, then jerked above the head with the arms held straight. **4.** Colloq. a stupid or naive person. –v.t. **5.** to give a sudden thrust, pull, or

twist to; move or throw with a quick, suddenly arrested motion. –v.i. **6.** to make a sudden or spasmodic movement. –phr. **7. jerk off**, Colloq. **a.** (taboo) (of a man) to masturbate. **b.** to waste time; procrastinate. **8. jerk out**, to utter in a broken, spasmodic way. **9. jerk someone around**, Colloq. to waste someone's time with folly or stupidity.

jerk² /dʒɜk/ v.t. **1.** to preserve meat, especially beef (**jerked beef**) by cutting in strips and curing by drying in the sun. –n. **2.** jerked meat, especially beef.

jerky¹ /'dʒɜki/ adj. (-kier, -kiest) characterised by jerks or sudden starts; spasmodic. –**jerkily**, adv. –**jerkiness**, n.

jerky² /'dʒɜki/ n. jerked beef. See **jerk**².

jerry-build /'dʒeri-bɪld/ v.t. (-built, -building) to build cheaply, shoddily, and flimsily. –**jerry-built**, adj. –**jerry-builder**, n.

jerry can /'dʒeri kæn/ n. a flat can for transporting fluids, especially motor fuel, and containing between 20 and 23 litres.

jersey /'dʒɜzi/ n. **1.** (upper case) one of a breed of dairy cattle whose milk contains a high proportion of butterfat. **2.** a close-fitting, usually woollen, outer garment for the upper part of the body; jumper. **3.** a similar garment worn by members of a sporting team as a uniform. **4.** Also, **jersey cloth**. a machine-knitted fabric of wool, silk, or artificial fibre, used for making garments, etc. **5.** (originally) a close-fitting, heavy woollen garment as worn by seamen.

Jerusalem artichoke /dʒə,rusələm 'atətʃoʊk/ n. **1.** a species of sunflower, Helianthus tuberosus, having edible tuberous underground stems or rootstocks. **2.** the tuber itself.

jest /dʒest/ n. **1.** a witticism, joke, or pleasantry. **2.** a piece of raillery or banter. **3.** sport or fun: to speak half in jest, half in earnest. **4.** the object of laughter, sport, or mockery; a laughing-stock. –v.i. **5.** to speak in a playful, humorous, or facetious way; joke.

jester /'dʒestə/ n. **1.** someone who is given to witticisms, jokes, and pranks. **2.** a professional fool or clown, kept by a prince or noble, especially during the Middle Ages.

jet¹ /dʒet/ n. **1.** a stream of liquid or gas flowing from a small opening, such as a spout. **2.** the opening used: a gas jet. **3.** → **jet plane**. –v.i. (**jetted, jetting**) **4.** to rush out in a stream; spout. **5.** to travel by jet plane.

jet² /dʒet/ n. **1.** a compact black coal, able to take a high polish, used for making beads, jewellery, buttons, etc. **2.** a deep, glossy black.

jet boat n. **1.** a powerboat that is propelled by a jet of pressurised water at the rear. –adj. **2.** of or relating to a jet boat. –v.i. **3.** to travel in a jet boat. Also, **jetboat**.

jet engine n. any engine in which a jet, especially of gaseous combustion products, provides the propulsive force.

jet lag n. bodily discomfort caused by the disturbance of normal patterns of eating and sleeping, as on a long journey by plane.

jet plane n. an aeroplane operated by jet propulsion.

jet propulsion n. a method of producing a propelling force upon an air or water craft through the reaction of a high-velocity jet, usually of heated gases, discharged towards the rear. Also, **reaction propulsion**. –**jet-propelled**, adj.

jetsam /'dʒetsəm/ n. goods thrown overboard to lighten a vessel in distress, which sink or are washed ashore. See **flotsam**.

jet set n. a rich and fashionable social set whose means enable them to travel from resort to resort by jet plane in the pursuit of pleasure.

jet ski n. (from trademark) a small powered vehicle that skims the water like a motorised water ski, with the driver standing, kneeling, or sitting on the ski and steering by means of handles similar to motorbike handles.

jettison /'dʒɛtəsən, -zən/ n. **1.** the act of casting cargo, etc., overboard to lighten a vessel or aircraft. **2.** → **jetsam.** –v.t. **3.** to throw (cargo, etc.) overboard, especially to lighten a vessel or aircraft in distress. **4.** to throw off, as an obstacle or burden.

jetty /'dʒɛti/ n. (pl. **-ties**) **1.** a wharf or landing pier. **2.** the piles or wooden structure protecting a pier.

Jew /dʒu/ n. **1.** one of the Hebrew or Jewish people; a Hebrew; an Israelite. **2.** someone whose religion is Judaism.

jewel /'dʒuəl/ n. **1.** a cut and polished precious stone; gem. **2.** an article for personal ornament, usually set with precious stones. **3.** a thing or person of great worth. **4.** a precious stone used as a bearing in a watch or delicate instrument. –v.t. (**-elled** or, Chiefly US, **-eled**, **-elling** or, Chiefly US, **-eling**) **5.** to set or ornament with jewels. –**jewel-like**, adj.

jewellery /'dʒuəlri/ n. articles for personal adornment, made of gold, silver, precious metals, etc., often ornamented with jewels. Also, US, **jewelry.**

jib¹ /dʒɪb/ n. Naut. a triangular sail (or either of two triangular sails, **inner jib** (and) **outer jib**) set in front of the forward (or single) mast.

jib² /dʒɪb/ v.i., v.t. (**jibbed, jibbing**) Naut. → **jibe¹.**

jib³ /dʒɪb/ v.i. (**jibbed, jibbing**) **1.** to move restively sideways or backwards instead of forwards, as an animal in harness; baulk. **2.** to hold back or baulk at doing something. –n. **3.** an animal that jibs. –phr. **4. jib at**, be reluctant to; show unwillingness to. –**jibber**, n.

jibe¹ /dʒaɪb/ Naut. –v.i. **1.** to shift from one side to the other when running before the wind, as a fore-and-aft sail or its boom. **2.** to alter the course so that the sail shifts in this manner. –v.t. **3.** to cause (a sail, etc.) to jibe. –n. **4.** the act of jibing. Also, **gybe, jib.**

jibe² /dʒaɪb/ v.i. → **gibe.** –**jiber**, n.

jiffy /'dʒɪfi/ n. (pl. **-fies**) Colloq. a very short time: to do something in a jiffy. Also, **jiff.**

jig¹ /dʒɪg/ n. **1.** a device for holding the work in a machine tool, especially one for accurately guiding a drill or group of drills so as to ensure uniformity in successive pieces machined. **2.** an apparatus for separating ore from gangue, etc., by shaking in or treating with water. –verb (**jigged, jigging**) –v.t. **3.** to treat, cut, or produce by using any of the mechanical contrivances called jigs. –v.i. **4.** to use a jig (mechanical contrivance).

jig² /dʒɪg/ n. **1.** a rapid, lively, springy dance for one or more persons, usually in triple time, which developed in England in the 16th century. **2.** a piece of music for, or in the time of, such a dance. –verb (**jigged, jigging**) –v.t. **3.** to dance (a jig or any lively dance). **4.** to move with a jerky or bobbing motion; jerk up and down or to and fro. –v.i. **5.** to dance or play a jig. **6.** to move with a quick, jerky motion; hop; bob. –phr. **7. the jig is up**, the game is up; there is no further chance.

jig³ /dʒɪg/ Aust. Colloq. –v.i. (**jigged, jigging**) **1.** to play truant. –phr. **2. jig it**, to play truant. **3. jig school**, to play truant from school.

jigger¹ /'dʒɪgə/ n. **1.** Naut. the lowest square sail on a fourth mast. **2.** any of various mechanical devices, many of which have a jerky or jolting motion. **3.** a name for any mechanical device, the correct name of which one does not know. **4. a.** a measure for alcohol used in cocktails. **b.** a small measure of whisky.

jigger² /'dʒɪgə/ v.t. to break or destroy.

jiggle /'dʒɪgəl/ v.i. **1.** to move up and down or to and fro with short, quick jerks. –v.t. **2.** to cause to jiggle. –n. **3.** a jiggling movement.

jigsaw /'dʒɪgsɔ/ n. **1.** a narrow saw mounted vertically in a frame, used for cutting curves, etc. **2.** a jigsaw puzzle.

jigsaw puzzle n. small, irregularly shaped pieces of wood or cardboard, which, when correctly fitted together, form a picture.

jihad /'dʒihæd, 'dʒihad/ n. **1.** Islam spiritual struggle; efforts made in the cause of God: **a.** at the personal level, the struggle to be righteous and follow God's path. **b.** at the communal level, a struggle or holy war in support of Islam against unbelievers. **2.** any vigorous campaign on behalf of a principle, etc.: the health promotion became a jihad against smokers. Also, **jehad.**

jillaroo /dʒɪlə'ru/ n. a young woman working on a sheep or cattle station to gain practical experience in the skills needed to become an owner, overseer, manager, etc. Compare **jackaroo.** Also, **jilleroo.**

jilt /dʒɪlt/ v.t. **1.** to cast off (a lover or sweetheart) after encouragement or engagement. –n. **2.** a woman who jilts a lover. –**jilter**, n.

jingle /'dʒɪŋgəl/ v.i. **1.** to make clinking or tinkling sounds, as coins, keys, etc. **2.** to move with such sounds. **3.** to sound in a manner like this, as verse or any pattern of words: a jingling ballad. –v.t. **4.** to cause to jingle. –n. **5.** a ringing or tinkling sound, as of small bells. **6.** a musical pattern of like sounds, as in rhyme; jingling verse. **7.** a simple, bright rhyme often set to music, used especially for advertising. –**jinglingly**, adv. –**jingly**, adj.

jingoism /'dʒɪŋgoʊɪzəm/ n. fervent and excessive patriotism. –**jingoist**, n., adj. –**jingoistic** /dʒɪŋgoʊ'ɪstɪk/, adj. –**jingoistically** /dʒɪŋgoʊ'ɪstɪkli/, adv.

jinn /dʒɪn/ pl. n. (sing. **jinnee**) (pl. **jinns** or **jinnee**) Islamic Myth. **1.** a class of spirits lower than the angels, capable of appearing in human and animal forms, and influencing humankind for good and evil. **2.** (construed as sing.) a spirit of this class. Also, **djinn.**

jinx /dʒɪŋks/ Colloq. –n. **1.** a person, thing, or influence supposedly bringing bad luck. –v.t. **2.** to bring bad luck to someone; hex.

jive /dʒaɪv/ n. **1.** jargon used by jazz musicians. **2.** a dance performed to beat music. –v.i. **3.** to dance to beat music.

jizz /dʒɪz/ n. the impression that a birdwatcher forms of the characteristics of a bird in the wild, in terms of its shape, movements and style of flying, that facilitate recognition

job¹ /dʒɒb/ n. **1.** a piece of work; an individual piece of work done in the routine of one's occupation or trade. **2.** a piece of work of defined character undertaken for a fixed price. **3.** the unit or material being worked upon. **4.** the product or result. **5.** anything one has to do. **6.** a post of employment. **7.** an affair, matter, occurrence, or state of affairs: to make the best of a bad job. **8.** Colloq. a difficult task. **9.** Colloq. a theft or robbery, or any criminal deed. –verb (**jobbed, jobbing**) –v.i. **10.** to work at jobs, or odd pieces of work; do piecework. **11.** to do business as a jobber (def. 2). **12.** to turn public business, etc., improperly to private gain. –v.t. **13.** to buy in large quantities and sell to dealers in small lots. **14.** Also, **job out.** to let out (work) in separate portions, as among different contractors or labourers. –adj. **15.** of or for a particular job or transaction. –phr. **16. a good job**, Colloq. a lucky state of affairs. **17. a job lot**, a group of miscellaneous items lumped together. **18. get on with the job**, to pursue a specific task with vigour and determination. **19. give up as a bad job**, to abandon as unprofitable (an undertaking already begun). **20. jobs for the boys**, Colloq. appointments of friends or supporters to office made by those in power. **21. just the job**, Colloq. exactly what is required. **22. make a good job of**, to complete satisfactorily. **23. on the job**, Colloq. **a.** busy; hard at work. **b.** engaged in sexual intercourse. **24. the devil's own job**, an extremely difficult or frustrating experience. –**jobless**, adj. –**joblessness**, n.

job² /dʒɒb/ *v.t.* (**jobbed, jobbing**) *Aust. Colloq.* jab; hit; punch: *shut up or I'll job you.*

jobber /ˈdʒɒbə/ *n.* **1.** a wholesale merchant, especially one selling to retailers. **2.** a dealer in stock exchange securities. Compare **broker**. **3.** a pieceworker. **4.** someone who practises jobbery.

jobbery /ˈdʒɒbəri/ *n.* the practice of making improper private gains from public or official business.

job lot *n.* **1.** any large lot of goods handled by a jobber. **2.** a miscellaneous quantity of goods.

job share *n.* an arrangement whereby one job is shared between two or more employees.

job-share *v.i.* (**-shared, -sharing**) (of an employee) to participate in a job share. –**job-sharing,** *n.*

jockey /ˈdʒɒki/ *n.* (*pl.* **-eys**) **1.** someone who professionally rides horses in races. **2.** someone who acts as an assistant to a driver as in a taxi, delivery vehicle, truck, etc. –*verb* (**-eyed, -eying**) –*v.t.* **3.** to ride (a horse) as a jockey. **4.** to bring, put, etc., by skilful manoeuvring: *to jockey the parcels into the boot.* –*v.i.* **5.** to perform skilful manoeuvres: *to jockey with cars and pedestrians.* –*phr.* **6. jockey for,** to try for by skilful manoeuvring. **7. jockey for position,** to attempt to gain an advantageous position (in a race, contest, etc.). –**jockeyship,** *n.*

jockstrap /ˈdʒɒkstræp/ *n. Colloq.* a support for the genitals; usually of elastic cotton webbing, and worn by male athletes, dancers, etc.

jocose /dʒəˈkoʊs/ *adj.* given to or characterised by joking; jesting; humorous; playful. –**jocosely,** *adv.* –**jocosity** /dʒəˈkɒsəti/, **jocoseness,** *n.*

jocular /ˈdʒɒkjələ/ *adj.* given to, characterised by, intended for, or suited to joking or jesting; waggish; facetious. –**jocularity** /dʒɒkjəˈlærəti/, *n.* –**jocularly,** *adv.*

jocund /ˈdʒɒkənd/ *adj. Poetic* cheerful; merry; blithe; glad. –**jocundity** /dʒəˈkʌndəti/, *n.* –**jocundly,** *adv.*

jodhpurs /ˈdʒɒdpəz/ *pl. n.* riding breeches reaching to the ankle, fitting closely from the knee down, worn also in sports, etc.

Joe Blow /dʒoʊ ˈbloʊ/ *n. Colloq.* the man in the street; the average citizen. Also, **Joe Bloggs.**

joey /ˈdʒoʊi/ *n.* (*pl.* **-eys**) *Aust.* **1.** any young animal, especially a kangaroo. **2.** *Colloq.* a young child. **3.** (*sometimes upper case*) → **Joey Scout.**

Joey Scout *n.* (*sometimes lower case*) (in Australia) a member of the youngest division (ages 6–7) of the Scout Association.

jog /dʒɒg/ *verb* (**jogged, jogging**) –*v.t.* **1.** to move or shake with a push or jerk. **2.** to give a slight push to, as to arouse the attention; nudge. **3.** to stir up by hint or reminder: *to jog a person's memory.* –*v.i.* **4.** to move with a jolt or jerk. **5.** to run at a jogtrot. **6.** to go or travel with a jolting pace or motion. –*n.* **7.** a shake; a slight push; a nudge. **8.** a slow, steady trot, etc. **9.** the act of jogging. –*phr.* **10. jog along,** to proceed in a steady or humdrum fashion.

jogger /ˈdʒɒgə/ *n.* **1.** a person who jogs for sport or exercise. **2.** Also, **jogging shoe.** a type of shoe suitable for jogging; runner. **3.** (*pl.*) loose trousers, usually elasticised at the waist and ankles, suitable for wearing for exercise such as jogging.

joggle /ˈdʒɒgəl/ *v.t.* **1.** to shake slightly; move to and fro as by repeated jerks. **2.** to join or fasten by a joggle or joggles. –*v.i.* **3.** to move irregularly; have a jogging or jolting motion; shake. –*n.* **4.** the act of joggling. **5.** a slight shake; a jolt. **6.** a moving with jolts or jerks. **7.** a projection on one of two joining surfaces, or a notch on the other, to prevent slipping.

john¹ /dʒɒn/ *n. Aust., NZ Colloq.* → **John Hop.**

john² /dʒɒn/ *n. Colloq.* a toilet.

John Dory *n.* (*pl.* **Dory** *or* **Dories**) **1.** Also, **dory.** a thin, deep-bodied, highly esteemed food fish of Australian waters, *Zeus australis.* **2.** See **dory²** (def. 3).

John Hop *n. Aust., NZ Colloq.* a police officer.

johnnycake /ˈdʒɒnikeɪk/ *n.* a small flat damper of wheatmeal or flour about as big as the palm of the hand, cooked on both sides often on top of the embers of a campfire or in a camp oven.

Johnstone's crocodile /dʒɒnstənz ˈkrɒkədaɪl/ *n.* → **freshwater crocodile.**

join /dʒɔɪn/ *v.t.* **1.** to bring or put together, in contact or connection. **2.** to come into contact, connection, or union with: *the brook joins the river.* **3.** to bring together in relation, purpose, action, coexistence, etc.: *to join forces.* **4.** to become a member of (a society, party, etc.); enlist in (one of the armed forces). **5.** to come into the company of: *I'll join you later.* **6.** to unite in marriage. **7.** to meet or engage in (battle, conflict, etc.). **8.** to adjoin: *his land joins mine.* **9.** *Geom.* to draw a curve or straight line between. **10.** (of animals) to mate with. –*v.i.* **11.** to come into or be in contact or connection, or form a junction. **12.** to be contiguous or close; lie or come together; form a junction. –*n.* **13.** joining. **14.** a place or line of joining; a seam. –*phr.* **15. join in,** to take part with others. **16. join up, a.** to enlist in one of the armed forces. **b.** to meet; come together: *I joined up with the stragglers; let's join up later for dinner.* **c.** to bring or put together, in contact or connection. **17. join with,** to become united, associated, or combined with; associate or ally oneself to. –**joinable,** *adj.*

joiner /ˈdʒɔɪnə/ *n.* a craftsman who works in wood already cut and shaped; a worker in wood who constructs the fittings of a house, furniture, etc. –**joinery,** *n.*

joint /dʒɔɪnt/ *n.* **1.** the place or part in which two things, or parts of one thing, are joined or united, either rigidly or so as to allow for motion; an articulation. **2.** (in an animal body) **a.** the movable place or part where two bones or two segments join. **b.** the hinge-like or other arrangement of such a part. **3.** *Biol.* **a.** a portion, especially of an animal or plant body, connected with another portion by an articulation, node, or the like. **b.** a portion between two articulations, nodes, or the like. **4.** *Bot.* the part of a stem from which a branch or a leaf grows; a node. **5.** one of the portions into which a carcase is divided by a butcher, especially one ready for cooking. **6.** *Colloq.* one's house, unit, office, etc.: *come round to my joint.* **7.** *Colloq.* a disreputable bar, restaurant, or nightclub; a dive. **8.** *Colloq.* a marijuana cigarette. –*adj.* **9.** shared by or common to two or more. **10.** sharing or acting in common. **11.** joined or associated, as in relation, interest, or action: *joint owners.* **12.** held, done, etc., by two or more in conjunction or in common: *a joint effort.* **13.** *Law* joined together in obligation or ownership. **14.** *Parliamentary Procedure* of or relating to both branches of a bicameral legislature. **15.** (of a diplomatic action) in which two or more governments are formally united. –*v.t.* **16.** to unite by a joint or joints. **17.** to form or provide with a joint or joints. **18.** to divide at a joint, or separate into pieces. **19.** to fill up (the joints of stone, interstices in brickwork, etc.) with mortar. –*phr.* **20. out of joint, a.** dislocated. **b.** out of order; in a bad state.

jointly /ˈdʒɔɪntli/ *adv.* together; in common.

joint sitting *n.* both the houses of parliament sitting together, as the House of Representatives and the Senate in Federal Parliament, to resolve a deadlock after a double dissolution.

joint-stock company *n.* a company whose ownership is divided into shares, the object usually being that the division of profits among the members be made in proportion to the number of shares held by each.

joint venture *n.* a business enterprise for which two or more parties join forces (not necessarily in partnership or by the formation of a company). —**joint venturer**, *n.*

joist /dʒɔɪst/ *n.* **1.** any of the parallel lengths of timber, steel, etc., used for supporting floors, ceilings, etc. —*v.t.* **2.** to furnish with or fix on joists. —**joistless**, *adj.*

jojoba /həˈhoʊbə, hoʊˈhoʊbə/ *n.* an evergreen shrub, *Simmondsia chinensis*, or *S. californica*, native to Mexico and south-western US, having edible seeds containing a liquid wax with many uses, as in high temperature and pressure lubrication, manufacture of cosmetics, soaps, plastics, etc.

joke /dʒoʊk/ *n.* **1.** something said or done to excite laughter or amusement; a playful or mischievous trick or remark. **2.** an amusing or ridiculous circumstance. **3.** an object of joking or jesting; a thing or person laughed at rather than taken seriously. **4.** a matter for joking about; trifling matter: *the loss was no joke.* **5.** *Colloq.* something extremely bad, pathetic, etc.: *their defensive play is a joke.* —*v.i.* **6.** to speak or act in a playful or merry way. **7.** to say something in mere sport, rather than in earnest. —*phr.* **8. the joke is on ...,** *Colloq.* said of a person who has become the object of laughter or ridicule, usually after a reversal of fortune. —**jokeless**, *adj.* —**jokingly**, *adv.*

joker /ˈdʒoʊkə/ *n.* **1.** someone who jokes. **2.** an extra playing card in a pack, used in some games, often counting as the highest card or to represent a card of any denomination or suit the holder wishes. **3.** *Aust., NZ Colloq.* a man; bloke: *a funny sort of joker.* **4.** *Colloq.* a hidden clause in any paper, document, etc., which largely changes its apparent nature. —*phr.* **5. the joker in the pack,** a person whose behaviour is unpredictable.

jollity /ˈdʒɒləti/ *n.* (*pl.* **-ties**) **1.** jolly state, mood, or proceedings. **2.** (*pl.*) jolly festivities.

jolly /ˈdʒɒli/ *adj.* (**-lier**, **-liest**) **1.** in good spirits; cheerful: *in a moment he was as jolly as ever.* **2.** cheerfully festive or convivial. **3.** amusing; pleasant. **4.** joyous, glad. —*v.t.* (**-lied**, **-lying**) **5.** (sometimes fol. by *into*) to humour; cajole; flatter. —*adv.* **6.** *Colloq.* extremely; very: *I was jolly glad to see her.* —*phr.* **7. get one's jollies,** *Colloq.* to derive pleasure or gratification: *is that how you get your jollies?* **8. jolly someone along,** to attempt to maintain the good spirits of someone by cheerful talk and encouragement. —**jollily**, *adv.* —**jolliness**, *n.*

jolt /dʒoʊlt/ *v.t.* **1.** to jar or shake as by a sudden rough thrust. —*v.i.* **2.** to proceed in an irregular or bumpy manner. —*n.* **3.** a jolting shock or movement. —**jolter**, *n.* —**jolty**, *adj.*

jonah /ˈdʒoʊnə/ *n.* a person regarded as bringing bad luck.

jonathan /ˈdʒɒnəθən/ *n.* (*sometimes upper case*) a variety of apple with a bright red skin and a crisp, juicy yellowish flesh. Also, **jonathon**.

jonquil /ˈdʒɒŋkwɪl/ *n.* **1.** a species of narcissus, *Narcissus jonquilla*, with long, narrow rush-like leaves and fragrant yellow or white flowers. **2.** any of certain species of *Narcissus* other than *N. jonquilla* which have a number of small flowers in the inflorescence and strap-shaped leaves.

jorts /dʒɔːts/ *pl. n. Colloq.* shorts made from denim.

jostle /ˈdʒɒsəl/ *verb* (**-tled**, **-tling**) —*v.t.* **1.** to strike or push roughly or rudely against; elbow roughly; hustle. **2.** to drive or force by or as by pushing or shoving. —*v.i.* **3.** to collide with, or strike others as in passing or in a crowd; push or elbow one's way rudely. **4.** to strive as with collisions, rough pushing, etc., for room, place, or any advantage. —*n.* **5.** a collision, shock, or push. —**jostlement**, *n.* —**jostler**, *n.*

jot /dʒɒt/ *n.* **1.** the least part of something; a little bit: *I don't care a jot.* —*phr.* (**jotted**, **jotting**) **2. jot down,** to write or mark down briefly.

jotter /ˈdʒɒtə/ *n.* a small notebook.

joule /dʒul/ *n.* the derived SI unit of work or energy, defined as the work done when the point of application of a force of one newton is displaced through a distance of one metre in the direction of the force. *Symbol*: J

journal /ˈdʒɜːnəl/ *n.* **1.** a daily record, as of experiences, or thoughts; diary. **2.** a record of the daily business of a public or governing body. **3.** a newspaper. **4.** any magazine, especially one published by a learned society. **5.** *Bookkeeping* **a.** a daybook. **b.** (in double entry) a book in which all transactions are entered (from the daybook). **6.** *Mechanics* the part of a shaft or axle in actual contact with a bearing.

journalese /dʒɜːnəˈliz/ *n.* a style of writing said to be common in journalism, characterised by superficiality and the use of clichés.

journalism /ˈdʒɜːnəlɪzəm/ *n.* **1.** the business or occupation of writing, editing, and producing photographic images for print media and the production or news and news analysis for broadcast media. **2.** such productions viewed collectively. —**journalist**, *n.* —**journalistic** /dʒɜːnəˈlɪstɪk/, *adj.*

journey /ˈdʒɜːni/ *n.* (*pl.* **-neys**) **1.** a course of travel from one place to another, especially by land. **2.** a distance travelled, or suitable for travelling, in a specified time: *a day's journey.* —*v.i.* (**-neyed**, **-neying**) **3.** to make a journey; travel. —**journeyer**, *n.*

joust /dʒaʊst/ *n.* **1.** a combat in which two armoured knights or men-at-arms on horseback opposed each other with lances. **2.** a public struggle or dispute between individuals. —*v.i.* **3.** to contend in a joust or tournament. **4.** to contend publicly over some issue. —**jouster**, *n.*

Jove /dʒoʊv/ *phr.* **by Jove**, a cry of surprise, an exclamation, etc.

jovial /ˈdʒoʊviəl/ *adj.* endowed with or characterised by a hearty, joyous humour or a spirit of good fellowship. —**jovially**, *adv.* —**joviality** /dʒoʊviˈæləti/, **jovialness**, *n.*

jowl[1] /dʒaʊl/ *n.* **1.** a jaw, especially the lower jaw. **2.** the cheek.

jowl[2] /dʒaʊl/ *n.* a fold of flesh hanging from the jaw, as of a fat person.

joy /dʒɔɪ/ *n.* **1.** an emotion of keen or lively pleasure arising from present or expected good; exultant satisfaction; great gladness; delight. **2.** a source or cause of gladness or delight: *a thing of beauty is a joy forever.* **3.** a state of happiness or felicity. **4.** the manifestation of glad feeling; outward rejoicing; festive gaiety. —*phr.* **5. not to have any joy,** (sometimes fol. by *of*) to be unsuccessful. —**joyful**, *adj.* —**joyfully**, *adv.* —**joyless**, *adj.*

joyous /ˈdʒɔɪəs/ *adj.* joyful. —**joyously**, *adv.* —**joyousness**, *n.*

joy ride *n.* **1.** a ride, as in a motor car, boat, etc., undertaken for pleasure. **2.** such a ride involving reckless driving in a motor vehicle, especially one that is stolen. **3.** a junket (def. 3).

joy-ride *v.i.* (**-rode**, **-riding**) to take a joy ride. —**joy-rider**, *n.* —**joy-riding**, *n., adj.*

joystick /ˈdʒɔɪstɪk/ *n.* **1.** the control stick of an aeroplane. **2.** a lever used to control the movement of the cursor and other images in computer games, or the arrangement of graphics on a computer screen.

jube /dʒub/ *n.* a fruit flavoured, chewy lolly made of gelatine or gum arabic, sugar, and flavourings. Also, **jujube**.

jubilant /ˈdʒubələnt/ *adj.* **1.** jubilating; rejoicing; exultant. **2.** expressing or exciting joy; manifesting exultation or gladness. —**jubilance**, **jubilancy**, *n.* —**jubilantly**, *adv.*

jubilate /ˈdʒubəleɪt/ *v.i.* **1.** to manifest or feel great joy; rejoice; exult. **2.** to celebrate a jubilee or joyful occasion. **–jubilation** /dʒubəˈleɪʃən/, *n.* **–jubilatory** /ˈdʒubəleɪtəri/, *adj.*

jubilee /dʒubəˈli/ *n.* **1.** the celebration of any of certain anniversaries, such as the 25th (**silver jubilee**), 50th (**golden jubilee**), or 60th or 75th (**diamond jubilee**). **2.** the completion of the 50th year of any continuous course or period, as of existence or activity, or its celebration. **3.** any season or occasion of rejoicing or festivity. **4.** rejoicing or jubilation.

Judaism /ˈdʒudeɪˌɪzəm/ *n.* the Jewish religion, deriving its authority from the precepts of the Old Testament and the teaching of the rabbis as expounded in the Talmud. It is founded on belief in the one and only God, who is transcendent, the creator of all things, and the source of all righteousness, and in the duty of all Jewish people to bear witness to this belief.

judder /ˈdʒʌdə/ *v.i.* **1.** to vibrate; shake. *–n.* **2.** a shaking; vibration.

judge /dʒʌdʒ/ *n.* **1.** a public officer having the power to hear and decide cases in a court of law. **2.** a person appointed to decide in any competition or contest. **3.** someone having the knowledge to pass judgement: *a judge of horses. –verb* (**judged, judging**) *–v.t.* **4.** to try (a person or a case) as a judge does. **5.** to form a judgement or opinion of or upon. **6.** to decide lawfully or authoritatively. *–v.i.* **7.** to act as a judge. **8.** to form an opinion. **–judger**, *n.* **–judgeless**, *adj.* **–judgeship**, *n.*

judgement /ˈdʒʌdʒmənt/ *n.* **1.** the act of judging. **2.** *Law* **a.** the judicial decision of a cause in court. **b.** the obligation, especially a debt, arising from a judicial decision. **c.** the certificate embodying such a decision. **3.** ability to judge justly or wisely, especially in matters affecting action; good sense; discretion. **4.** the forming of an opinion, estimate, notion, or conclusion, as from circumstances presented to the mind. **5.** the opinion formed. **6.** a misfortune regarded as inflicted by divine sentence, as for sin. **7.** (*oft. upper case*) the final trial of all human beings, both the living and the dead, at the end of the world (often, **Last Judgement**). Also, **judgment**.

judicature /ˈdʒudəkətʃə/ *n.* **1.** the administration of justice, as by judges or courts. **2.** the office, function, or authority of a judge. **3.** the extent of jurisdiction of a judge or court. **4.** a body of judges. **5.** the power of administering justice by legal trial and determination.

judicial /dʒuˈdɪʃəl/ *adj.* **1.** relating to judgement in courts of justice or to the carrying out of justice: *a judicial inquiry.* **2.** relating to courts of law or to judges: *judicial functions.* **3.** likely to make or give judgements; critical. **4.** relating to judgement in a fight or contest. **–judicially**, *adv.*

judiciary /dʒuˈdɪʃəri/ *adj.* **1.** relating to judgement in courts of justice, or to courts or judges; judicial. *–n.* (*pl.* **-aries**) **2.** the judicial arm of government. **3.** the system of courts of justice in a country. **4.** the judges collectively.

judicious /dʒuˈdɪʃəs/ *adj.* **1.** using or showing judgement as to action or practical expediency; discreet, prudent, or politic. **2.** having, exercising, or showing good judgement; wise, sensible, or well-advised: *a judicious selection.* **–judiciously**, *adv.* **–judiciousness**, *n.*

judo /ˈdʒudoʊ/ *n.* a Japanese martial art and sport developed from jujitsu, emphasising grappling, throws, and holds.

jug /dʒʌg/ *n.* **1.** a vessel in various forms for holding liquids, commonly having a handle, often a spout or lip, and sometimes a lid. **2.** the contents of any such vessel. **3.** *Colloq.* prison or jail. **–jugful**, *n.*

juggernaut /ˈdʒʌgənɔt/ *n.* **1.** anything requiring blind devotion or extreme sacrifice. **2.** any large, relentless, destructive force. **3.** *Brit.* a large truck used in long-distance road haulage.

juggle /ˈdʒʌgəl/ *v.t.* **1.** to keep (several objects, such as balls, plates, knives) in continuous motion in the air at the same time by tossing and catching. **2.** to manipulate or alter by artifice or trickery: *to juggle accounts. –v.i.* **3.** to perform feats of manual or bodily dexterity, such as tossing up and keeping in continuous motion a number of balls, plates, knives, etc. **4.** to use artifice or trickery. *–n.* **5.** the act of juggling; a trick; a deception.

jugular /ˈdʒʌgjulə/ *–adj.* **1.** *Anat.* **a.** of or relating to the throat or neck. **b.** denoting or relating to any of certain large veins of the neck, especially one (**external jugular vein**) collecting blood from the superficial parts of the head, or one (**internal jugular vein**) receiving blood from within the skull. *–n.* **2.** *Anat.* a jugular vein. *–phr.* **3.** go for the jugular, *Colloq.* to take ruthless action in order to secure a desired result.

juice /dʒus/ *n.* **1.** the liquid part of a plant or animal substance. **2.** any natural fluid coming from an animal body. **3.** liquid, as from a fruit. **4.** strength; essence. **5.** *Colloq.* **a.** electric power. **b.** petrol, oil, etc., used to run an engine. **6.** *Colloq.* any alcoholic drink. **–juiceless**, *adj.*

juicy /ˈdʒusi/ *adj.* (**-cier, -ciest**) **1.** full of juice; succulent. **2.** interesting; vivacious; colourful; spicy. **–juicily**, *adv.* **–juiciness**, *n.*

jujitsu /dʒuˈdʒɪtsu/ *n.* a Japanese method of self-defence without weapons, in which one overcomes or disables one's opponent applying certain techniques and holds which use the opponent's own strength and weight against them. Also, **jiujitsu, jiujutsu, jujutsu.**

jukebox /ˈdʒukbɒks/ *n.* a coin-operated machine which plays a selected musical item or items.

Juliet balcony /ˈdʒuliɛt bælkəni/ *n.* a small upper-storey balcony, especially one off a bedroom.

July /dʒəˈlaɪ/ *n.* the seventh month of the year, containing 31 days.

jumble /ˈdʒʌmbəl/ *v.t.* **1.** to mix in a confused mass; put or throw together without order. **2.** to muddle or confuse mentally. *–v.i.* **3.** to meet or come together confusedly; be mixed up. *–n.* **4.** a confused mixture; a medley. **5.** a state of confusion or disorder. **–jumbler**, *n.*

jumbo /ˈdʒʌmboʊ/ *n.* (*pl.* **-bos**) **1.** *Colloq.* an elephant. **2.** any very large intercontinental jet plane, especially the Boeing 747. **3.** anything bigger than usual. *–adj.* **4.** very large: *a jumbo sale.*

jumbuck /ˈdʒʌmbʌk/ *n. Aust., NZ Colloq.* a sheep.

jump /dʒʌmp/ *v.i.* **1.** to spring clear of the ground or other support by a sudden muscular effort; propel oneself forwards, backwards, upwards, or downwards; leap. **2.** to move or go quickly: *she jumped into a taxi.* **3.** to rise suddenly or quickly: *he jumped from his chair.* **4.** to move suddenly or abruptly, as from surprise or shock; start: *the sudden noise made him jump.* **5.** to rise suddenly in amount, price, etc. **6.** to pass abruptly, ignoring intervening stages: *to jump to a conclusion.* **7.** to change suddenly: *the traffic lights jumped from green to red.* **8.** to move or change suddenly, haphazardly, or aimlessly: *she kept jumping from one thing to another without being able to concentrate.* **9.** *Colloq.* (of a wound, etc.) to hurt; throb. **10.** (of a computer) to leave the sequence of instructions in a program and start obeying a different sequence elsewhere in the program. **11.** *Colloq.* (of a room, bar, club, etc.) to be full of excited activity: *the joint was really jumping. –v.t.* **12.** to leap or spring over: *to jump a stream.* **13.** to cause to jump or leap. **14.** to skip or pass over; bypass. **15.** to abscond from or evade by absconding. **16. a.** to seize or occupy (a mining claim, etc.) on the ground of some flaw in the holder's title. **b.** to encroach on the rights of (another). **17.** (of a train) to spring off or leave (the track). **18.** *Colloq.* to attack suddenly without warning. **19.** *Colloq.* (*taboo*) to have sexual intercourse with. *–n.* **20.** the act of jumping; a leap. **21.** a space or obstacle or apparatus cleared in a leap. **22.** a descent by parachute from an aeroplane. **23.** a sudden rise in amount, price, etc. **24.** a sudden upward or other movement of an inanimate object. **25.** an abrupt transition from one point or thing to another, with omission of what intervenes. **26.** *Colloq.* a head start in time or space; advantageous beginning. **27.** *Sport* any of several athletic games which feature a leap or jump. **28.** *Film* a break in the continuity of action due to a failure to match action between a long shot and a closer shot of the same scene. **29. a.** a sudden start, as from nervous excitement. **b.** (*pl.*) a physical condition characterised by such starts; restlessness; anxiety. **30.** *Colloq.* (*taboo*) an act of sexual intercourse. *–phr.* **31. for** (or **on**) **the** (**high**) **jump(s)**, *Colloq.* up for trial. **32. get the jump on**, *Colloq.* to take by surprise; get an advantage over. **33. go jump** (**in the lake**), *Colloq.* an expression of annoyance or dismissal. **34. jump at**, to accept eagerly; seize: *he jumped at the chance of a new job.* **35. jump bail**, *Colloq.* to abscond when at liberty following the payment of bail money. **36. jump down someone's throat**, *Colloq.* to speak suddenly and sharply to someone. **37. jump on** (or **upon**), *Colloq.* to scold; rebuke; reprimand. **38. jump out of one's skin**, *Colloq.* to be frightened suddenly. **39. jump ship**, to leave a ship, especially one on which one, as a passenger or as a crew member, is expected or contracted to remain. **40. jump the gun**, **a.** (of a competitor in a race) to begin before the starting gun has fired. **b.** *Colloq.* to begin prematurely; be overeager. **41. jump the lights**, *Colloq.* (of a motor vehicle or driver) to take off at a set of traffic lights before they have turned green. **42. jump the queue**, to overtake a queue; obtain something out of one's proper turn. **43. jump to it**, *Colloq.* to move quickly; hurry. **44. jump up and down**, *Colloq.* **a.** to show anxiety or impatience by constant movement. **b.** (sometimes fol. by *about*) to make a fuss: *you won't get any results unless you jump up and down about it.* **45. one jump ahead**, in a position of advantage. **46. take a** (**running**) **jump** (**at yourself**), *Colloq.* **a.** an impolite dismissal indicating the speaker's wish to end the conversation. **b.** an impolite instruction to someone to reconsider their attitude or performance.

jumper¹ /ˈdʒʌmpə/ *n.* **1.** a person or animal that jumps. **2.** a boring tool or device worked with a jumping motion. **3.** Also, **jumper lead**. *Elect.* a short length of conductor used to make a connection, usually temporary, between terminals, around a break in a circuit, or around an instrument.

jumper² /ˈdʒʌmpə/ *n.* **1.** an outer garment, usually of wool, for the upper part of the body; pullover; sweater; jersey; guernsey. **2.** *US* a pinafore frock.

jumper leads *pl. n.* a pair of heavy jumpers used in starting a motor vehicle with a flat battery, by connecting this battery to a charged one. Also, **jump leads**.

jumps race *n.* a horserace over a course which has artificial ditches, hedges, and other obstacles built into it; steeplechase. *–jumps racing*, *n. –jumps racer*, *n.*

jumpsuit /ˈdʒʌmpsut/ *n.* **1.** a close-fitting outer garment covering all of the body and the legs. **2.** a one-piece loose outer garment for a small child, combining a sleeved top and short or long trousers; all-in-one.

jumpy /ˈdʒʌmpi/ *adj.* (**-pier, -piest**) **1.** characterised by or inclined to sudden, involuntary starts, especially from nervousness, fear, excitement, etc. **2.** causing to jump or start. *–jumpiness*, *n.*

junction /ˈdʒʌŋkʃən/ *n.* **1.** the act of joining; combination. **2.** the state of being joined; union. **3.** a place or station where railway lines meet or cross. **4.** a place of joining or meeting.

juncture /ˈdʒʌŋktʃə/ *n.* **1.** a point of time, especially one made critical or important by a concurrence of circumstances. **2.** the line or point at which two bodies are joined; a joint or articulation; a seam.

June /dʒun/ *n.* the sixth month of the year, containing 30 days.

jungle /ˈdʒʌŋgəl/ *n.* **1.** wild land overgrown with dense, rank vegetation, often nearly impenetrable, as in tropical countries. **2.** a tract of such land. **3.** a tropical rainforest with thick, impenetrable undergrowth. **4.** anything confusing, perplexing, or in disorder. **5.** any place or situation characterised by a struggle for survival, ruthless competition, etc. *–jungly*, *adj.*

jungle juice *n. Colloq.* **1.** a rough alcoholic drink especially made by Europeans in the tropics as a substitute for commercially produced beverages. **2.** any drink considered to be as rough.

junior /ˈdʒunjə/ *adj.* **1.** younger, often shortened to *Jr* or *Jun* after a family name. **2.** of something made for young people: *a junior textbook.* **3.** of lower rank or standing. *–n.* **4.** a person who is younger than another. **5.** any child, especially a male. **6.** someone who is of more recent entrance into, or of lower standing in, an office, class, etc. **7.** *Law* any barrister who is not a Senior Counsel or Queen's Counsel.

juniper /ˈdʒunəpə/ *n.* any of the coniferous evergreen shrubs or trees constituting the genus *Juniperus*, especially *J. communis*, whose cones form purple berries used in making gin and in medicine as a diuretic, or *J. virginiana*, a North American species.

junk¹ /dʒʌŋk/ *n.* **1.** any old or discarded material, as metal, paper, rags, etc. **2.** anything that is regarded as worthless or mere trash. *–v.t.* **3.** *Colloq.* to cast aside as junk, discard as no longer of use.

junk² /dʒʌŋk/ *n.* a kind of seagoing ship used in Chinese and other waters, having square sails spread by battens, a high stern, and usually a flat bottom.

junk bond *n. Finance* a high-yield security, especially one issued to finance a takeover, and often involving high risk.

junket /ˈdʒʌŋkət/ *n.* **1.** a sweet custard-like food of flavoured milk curded with rennet. **2.** a feast or merrymaking; a picnic; a pleasure excursion. **3.** a trip, as by a legislative committee, official body, or individual politician at public expense and ostensibly to obtain information. *–v.i.* **4.** to feast; picnic; go on a junket or pleasure excursion. **5.** to go on a junket (def. 3). *–junketer*, *n.*

junketeer /dʒʌŋkəˈtɪə/ *n.* a person, especially a public official, who makes a practice of going on junkets (def. 3).

junkie /ˈdʒʌŋki/ *n. Colloq.* **1.** a drug addict. **2.** a person who is enthusiastic about something specified: *a sci-fi junkie.* Also, **junky**.

junk mail *n.* unsolicited mail, usually advertisements or prospectuses.

junta /ˈdʒʌntə/, *US* /ˈhʊntə/ *n.* a small ruling group in a country, either elected or self-chosen, especially one which has come to power after a revolution.

juridical /dʒuˈrɪdɪkəl/ *adj.* **1.** of or relating to the administration of justice. **2.** of or relating to law or jurisprudence; legal. *–juridically*, *adv.*

jurisdiction /dʒurəsˈdɪkʃən/ *n.* **1.** the right, power, or authority to administer justice by hearing and determining controversies. **2.** power; authority; control. **3.** the extent or range of judicial or other authority. **4.** the territory over which authority is exercised. *–jurisdictional*, *adj. –jurisdictionally*, *adv.*

jurisprudence /dʒurəs'pruːdns/ *n.* **1.** the science or philosophy of law. **2.** a body or system of laws. **3.** a department of law: *medical jurisprudence.* **4.** *Civil Law* decisions of courts of appeal or other higher tribunals. –**jurisprudential** /ˌdʒurəspruː'dɛnʃəl/, *adj.*

jurist /'dʒurəst, 'dʒuə-/ *n.* **1.** someone with expert knowledge of the law. **2.** someone who writes on the subject of law.

juror /'dʒuərə, 'dʒurə/ *n.* **1.** one of a body of persons sworn to deliver a verdict in a case submitted to them; a member of any jury. **2.** one of the panel from which a jury is selected.

jury[1] /'dʒuəri, 'dʒuri/ *n. (pl.* **juries**) **1.** a body of persons chosen at random from the community, who are engaged for a trial and sworn to deliver a verdict on questions of fact presented to them. **2.** a body of persons chosen to adjudge prizes, etc., as in a competition. –*phr.* **3. the jury is (still) out,** a general opinion has not yet been formed: *the jury is still out on the health effects of the new device.* –**juryless,** *adj.*

jury[2] /'dʒuəri, 'dʒuri/ *adj. Naut.* makeshift, temporary, as for an emergency.

just /dʒʌst/ *adj.* **1.** actuated by truth, justice, and lack of bias: *to be just in one's dealings.* **2.** in accordance with true principles; equitable; even-handed: *a just award.* **3.** based on right; rightful; lawful: *a just claim.* **4.** agreeable to truth or fact; true; correct: *a just statement.* **5.** given or awarded rightly, or deserved, as a sentence, punishment, reward, etc. **6.** in accordance with standards, or requirements; proper, or right: *just proportions.* **7.** (especially in biblical use) righteous. **8.** actual, real, or genuine. –*adv.* **9.** within a brief preceding time, or but a moment before: *they have just gone.* **10.** exactly or precisely: *that is just the point.* **11.** by a narrow margin; barely: *it just missed the mark.* **12.** only or merely: *he is just an ordinary man.* **13.** actually; truly; positively: *the weather is just glorious.* –*phr.* **14. just about, a.** almost: *to be just about time to go.* **b.** on the point of: *I am just about to go.* **15. just so, a.** carefully and exactly in place. **b.** an expression of affirmation or agreement. –**justly,** *adv.* –**justness,** *n.*

justice /'dʒʌstəs/ *n.* **1.** the quality of being just; righteousness, equitableness, or moral rightness: *to uphold the justice of a cause.* **2.** rightfulness or lawfulness, as of a claim or title; justness of ground or reason: *to complain with justice.* **3.** the moral principle determining just conduct. **4.** conformity to this principle as

manifested in conduct; just conduct, dealing, or treatment. **5.** the requital of desert as by punishment or reward. **6.** the maintenance or administration of law, as by judicial or other proceedings: *a court of justice.* **7.** judgement of persons or causes by judicial process: *to administer justice in a community.* **8.** a judicial officer; a judge or magistrate. **9.** (*upper case*) the title of the judges in the superior state courts and in the federal courts of Australia. –*phr.* **10. do justice to, a.** to render or concede what is due to (a person or thing, merits, intentions, etc.); treat or judge fairly. **b.** to exhibit (oneself) in a just light, as in doing something. **c.** to show just appreciation of (something) by action.

justice of the peace *n.* (in Australia) a person authorised to administer oaths, take declarations, and attest instruments. *Abbrev.:* JP

justify /'dʒʌstəfaɪ/ *v.t.* **1.** to show (an act, claim, statement, etc.) to be just, right, or warranted: *the end justifies the means.* **2.** to declare guiltless; absolve; acquit. **3.** *Typesetting* to adjust exactly; make (lines) of the proper length by spacing. –**justifiable,** *adj.* –**justifiably,** *adv.* –**justification,** *n.*

just-in-time *adj.* of or relating to a system of manufacturing in which materials are supplied within a short time of being needed in the manufacturing process, rather than being stored in advance.

jut /dʒʌt/ *v.i.* (**jutted, jutting**) Also, **jut out. 1.** to extend beyond the main body or line; project; protrude. –*n.* **2.** something that juts out; a projection or protruding point.

jute /dʒuːt/ *n.* **1.** a strong fibre used for making fabrics, cordage, etc., obtained from two tropical Asian plants of the family Malvaceae, *Corchorus capsularis* and *C. olitorius.* **2.** the coarse fabric woven from jute fibres; gunny. –**jutelike,** *adj.*

juvenile /'dʒuvənaɪl/ *adj.* **1.** of, relating to, or suitable for young people: *juvenile behaviour; juvenile books; a juvenile court.* **2.** young. **3.** like the behaviour or thoughts of a young person; frivolous. –*n.* **4.** a young person; a youth. –**juvenilely,** *adv.* –**juvenileness, juvenility,** *n.*

juvie /'dʒuvi/ *Colloq.* –*adj.* **1.** juvenile: *juvie justice.* –*n.* **2.** juvenile detention: *in juvie.* Also, **juvey, juvy.**

juxta- a word element meaning 'near', 'close to', 'beside'.

juxtapose /dʒʌkstə'pouz, 'dʒʌkstəpouz/ to place in close proximity or side by side. –**juxtaposition** /dʒʌkstəpə'zɪʃən/, *n.*

K k

K, k /keɪ/ *n.* a consonant, the 11th letter of the English alphabet.

K /keɪ/ *n.* **1.** *Computers* kilobytes: *how many K of memory have you got?* **2.** thousand (dollars, etc.): *we got the house for 800K.*

kabbalah /kəˈbalə/ *n.* **1.** (among certain Jewish rabbis and medieval Christians) a system of esoteric theosophy, based on a mystical interpretation of the Scriptures. **2.** any occult or secret doctrine or science. Also, **kabbala, kabala, qabala, cabbala, cabala.** –**kabbalism**, *n.*

kadaitja man /kəˈdaɪtʃə mæn/ *n.* (in some traditional Aboriginal cultures) a man who sets out to take vengeance, either at the request of his community or on his own initiative, on someone accused of injuring or killing another by magic. Also, **kurdaitcha man, kadaicha man, kaditcha man, goditcha man.**

Kaffir lime /kæfə ˈlaɪm/ *n.* → **lime²** (def. 2). Also, **kaffir lime.**

kaftan /ˈkæftæn/ *n.* → **caftan.**

kafuffle /kəˈfʌfəl, -ˈfʊfəl/ *n. Colloq.* → **kerfuffle.**

kai lan /gaɪ ˈlan/ *n.* → **gai lan.**

kaka /ˈkakə/ *n.* a New Zealand parrot, *Nestor meridionalis*, chiefly greenish or olive brown in colour.

kakapo /ˈkakəpoʊ/ *n.* a large, almost flightless, and now rare, nocturnal parrot, *Strigops habroptilus*, of New Zealand.

kalamata olive /kæləˌmatə ˈɒləv/ *n.* an almond-shaped Greek olive of a dark purple colour. Also, **calamata olive.**

kale /keɪl/ *n.* a kind of cabbage, *Brassica oleracea*, var. *acephala*, with wrinkled leaves; does not form a head.

kaleidoscope /kəˈlaɪdəskoʊp/ *n.* **1.** an optical instrument in which pieces of coloured glass, etc., in a rotating tube are shown by reflection in continually changing symmetrical forms. **2.** any highly-coloured, rapidly changing pattern: *the kaleidoscope of fashion.* **3.** a pattern of things or events which is complex and constantly changing: *Australian politics is a kaleidoscope.*

kamikaze /kæməˈkazi/ *adj. Colloq.* (*often humorous*) dangerous; suicidal: *his kamikaze driving.*

Kanaka /kəˈnækə/ *n. Hist.* a Pacific islander, especially one brought forcibly to Australia during the 19th century as a labourer.
Usage: The use of this term to refer to a Pacific islander in a contemporary, non-historical context is considered offensive.

kanga cricket /kæŋgə ˈkrɪkət/ *n.* a modified form of cricket, suitable for children, played with a softer ball and a plastic bat. Also, **Kanga, kanga.**

kangaroo /kæŋgəˈru/ *n.* **1.** any of the largest members of the family Macropodidae, herbivorous marsupials of the Australian region, with powerful hind legs developed for leaping, a sturdy tail serving as a support and balance, a small head, and very short forelimbs. –*v.i. Colloq.* **2.** (of a car) to move forward in a jerky manner. **3.** to squat over a toilet seat, while avoiding contact with it. –*phr.* **4. have kangaroos (loose) in the top paddock,** *Aust. Colloq.* to be crazy.

kangaroo bar *n.* a heavy metal bar in front of the radiator of a motor vehicle which protects the vehicle if it strikes kangaroos or stock. Also, **roo bar.**

kangaroo court *n.* an unauthorised or irregular court conducted with disregard for or perversion of legal procedure, such as a mock court by prisoners in a jail, or by trade unionists in judging workers who do not follow union decisions.

kangaroo grass *n.* **1.** a tall grass, *Themeda australis*, widespread in forest and grassland in Australia and providing useful fodder. **2.** any of several other similar Australian grasses.

kangaroo-paw *n.* any of several plants of the western Australian genus *Anigozanthos*, having an inflorescence bearing a resemblance to the paw of a kangaroo, especially *A. manglesii*, red and green kangaroo-paw, the floral emblem of WA.

kangaroo rat *n.* any of various small jumping rodents of the family Heteromyidae, of Mexico and the western United States, such as those of the genus *Dipodomys.*

kanooka /kæˈnukə/ *n.* → **water gum** (def. 1).

kaolin /ˈkeɪələn/ *n.* **1.** a rock composed essentially of clay minerals of the kaolinite group. **2.** a fine white clay used in the manufacture of porcelain and used medically as an absorbent; china clay.

kapok /ˈkeɪpɒk/ *n.* **1.** the silky down covering the seeds of several trees in the family Bombacaceae, as *Ceiba pentandra* of South-East Asia, Africa, and tropical America, which is used for stuffing pillows, etc., and for sound insulation. **2.** a tree bearing this or similar down.

kaput /kæˈpʊt, kə-/ *adj. Colloq.* **1.** smashed; ruined. **2.** broken, not working.

karabiner /kærəˈbinə/ *n.* → **carabiner.**

karaoke /kæriˈoʊki/ *n.* **1.** the entertainment of singing to a karaoke machine: *that restaurant offers karaoke.* –*adj.* **2.** (of bars, restaurants, etc.) equipped with a karaoke machine.

karaoke machine *n.* a music system which plays simultaneously a video clip of a song with subtitled lyrics and the backing tape of the song, and which is equipped with microphones for the use of a singer. Also, **karaoke unit.**

karate /kəˈrati/ *n.* a method of defensive fighting in which hands, elbows, feet, and knees are the only weapons used.

karma /ˈkamə/ *n.* **1.** *Hinduism, Buddhism, etc.* the cosmic operation of retributive justice, according to which a person's status in life is determined by their own deeds in a previous incarnation. **2.** fate; destiny. **3.** *Colloq.* the quality, mood, or atmosphere of a person or place. –**karmic**, *adj.* –**karmically**, *adv.*

karo /ˈkaroʊ/ *n.* (*pl.* **karos**) an evergreen shrub or small tree of New Zealand, *Pittosporum crassifolium*, family Pittosporaceae, having red flowers and hairy fruit and leaves.

karri /ˈkæri/ *n.* (*pl.* **-ris**) a rapidly growing western Australian tree valued for its hard, durable timber.

karst /kast/ *n.* a barren region composed of limestone or dolomite and characterised by underground drainage systems, sinkholes, gorges, etc. –**karstic**, *adj.*

karyo- a word element meaning 'nucleus of a cell'.

kata- variant of **cata-.** Also, **kat-, kath-.**

kauri /ˈkaʊri/ *n.* (*pl.* **-ris**) **1.** a tall coniferous tree, *Agathis australis*, of New Zealand, yielding a valuable timber and a resin. **2.** any of various other trees of the genus *Agathis*, such as Qld kauri, *A. robusta*.

kava /'kavə/ *n.* **1.** a Polynesian shrub, *Piper methysticum*, of the pepper family. Its root has aromatic and pungent qualities. **2.** an intoxicating beverage made from the roots of the kava.

kayak /'kaıæk/ *n.* **1.** an Inuit hunting craft with a skin cover on a light framework, made watertight by flexible closure round the waist of the occupant. **2.** any of various light canoes in imitation of this. –*v.i.* **3.** to travel in a kayak. –**kayaker**, *n.* –**kayaking**, *n.*

kazoo /kə'zu/ *n.* a short plastic or metal tube with a membrane-covered side hole, into which a person sings or hums.

kea /'kiə/ *n.* a large, greenish New Zealand parrot, *Nestor notabilis*.

kebab /kə'bæb/ *n.* **1.** → **shish kebab. 2.** → **doner kebab.**

keel /kil/ *n.* **1.** the main longitudinal structural member of a ship's hull, to which the frames are fastened and which lies in the middle of the bottom of the hull and runs along the whole length; the keel may project somewhat from the bottom of the vessel to improve its stability. **2.** a ship. **3.** a part corresponding to a ship's keel in some other structure, as in an aircraft fuselage. **4.** *Bot., Zool.* a longitudinal ridge, as on a leaf or bone; a carina. –*v.t.* **5.** to upset (a boat) so as to bring the wrong side or part uppermost. –*phr.* **6. keel over, a.** (of a boat) to turn or roll on the keel. **b.** *Colloq.* to collapse suddenly. **7. on an even keel,** in a steady or balanced state or manner.

keen¹ /kin/ *adj.* **1.** sharp, or so shaped as to cut or pierce substances readily: *a keen blade.* **2.** sharp, piercing, or biting: *a keen wind, keen satire.* **3.** characterised by strength and distinctness of perception, as the ear or hearing, the eye, sight, etc. **4.** having or showing great mental penetration or acumen: *keen reasoning.* **5.** animated by or showing competitiveness: *keen prices.* **6.** intense, as feeling, desire, etc. **7.** (sometimes fol. by *about, for,* etc., or an infinitive) ardent; eager. –*phr.* **8. keen as mustard,** extremely enthusiastic. **9. keen on,** having a fondness or devotion for. –**keenly,** *adv.* –**keenness,** *n.*

keen² /kin/ *n.* **1.** a wailing lament for the dead. –*v.i.* **2.** to wail in lamentation for the dead. –**keener,** *n.*

keep /kip/ *verb* (**kept, keeping**) –*v.t.* **1.** to maintain in one's action or conduct: *to keep watch; to keep step; to keep silence.* **2.** to cause to continue in some place, position, state, course, or action specified: *to keep a light burning.* **3.** to maintain in condition or order, as by care and labour. **4.** to hold in custody or under guard, as a prisoner; detain; prevent from coming or going. **5.** to have habitually in stock or for sale. **6.** to maintain in one's service or for one's use or enjoyment. **7.** to associate with: *to keep bad company.* **8.** to have the charge or custody of. **9.** to withhold from the knowledge of others: *to keep a secret.* **10.** to withhold from use; reserve. **11.** to restrain: *to keep someone from escaping.* **12.** to maintain by writing, as entries, etc.: *to keep a diary.* **13.** to record (business transactions, etc.) regularly: *to keep records.* **14.** to observe; pay obedient regard to (a law, rule, promise, etc.). **15.** to conform to; follow; fulfil: *to keep one's word.* **16.** to observe (a season, festival, etc.) with formalities or rites: *to keep Christmas.* **17.** to maintain or carry on, as an establishment, business, etc.; manage: *to keep house.* **18.** to guard, protect. **19.** to maintain or support (a person, etc.). **20.** to take care of; tend: *to keep sheep.* **21.** to maintain in active existence, or hold, as an assembly, court, fair, etc. **22.** to maintain one's position in or on. **23.** to continue to hold or have: *to keep a thing in mind.* **24.** to save, hold, or retain in possession. –*v.i.* **25.** to

remain or stay in a place: *to keep indoors.* **26.** to continue unimpaired or without spoiling: *the milk will keep on ice.* **27.** to remain; stay (*away, back, off, out,* etc.): *to keep off the grass.* **28.** to restrain oneself: *to try to keep from smiling.* **29.** to be reserved for a future occasion, often in a context of threat: *I won't deal with him now. He'll keep.* –*v.* *(copular)* **30.** to remain, or continue to be as specified: *to keep cool.* –*n.* **31.** subsistence; board and lodging: *to work for one's keep.* **32.** the innermost and strongest structure or central tower of a medieval castle. –*phr.* **33. for keeps,** *Colloq.* **a.** for keeping as one's own permanently: *to play for keeps.* **b.** permanently; altogether. **34. keep at, a.** to persist in. **b.** to badger, hector, or bully. **35. keep at it,** to maintain one's effort to do something. **36. keep back, a.** to withhold. **b.** to restrain; hold in check. **c.** to stay away; not advance. **37. keep down, a.** to restrain; prevent from rising. **b.** to retain or continue in, as a job. **c.** to consume (food) without regurgitating it. **38. keep in, a.** to retract: *he kept his stomach in.* **b.** to remain indoors. **c.** to provide with: *they kept me in clothes.* **d.** *Colloq.* to detain (a child) after school. **39. keep in with,** *Colloq.* to keep oneself in favour with. **40. keep on,** to persist. **41. keep the home fires burning,** (*humorous*) to stay at home so as to be ready to provide comforts to those journeying out on their return. **42. keep time, a.** to record time, as a watch or clock does. **b.** to beat, mark, or observe the rhythmic accents of music, etc. **c.** to perform rhythmic movements in unison. **43. keep to, a.** to adhere to (an agreement, plan, facts, etc.). **b.** to confine oneself to: *to keep to one's bed.* **44. keep to oneself,** to hold aloof from the society of others. **45. keep track of** or **keep tabs on,** to keep account of. **46. keep under, a.** to dominate. **b.** to maintain in an anaesthetised state. **47. keep up, a.** to continue (a task or activity): *keep up the good work!; she kept up her swimming until she turned 60.* **b.** to maintain: *to keep up appearances.* **48. keep up with the Joneses,** to compete with one's neighbours in the accumulation of material possessions, especially as status symbols. **49. keep watch,** to maintain a vigil over something or someone. **50. keep wicket,** *Cricket* to act as wicketkeeper.

keeper /'kipə/ *n.* **1.** someone who keeps or guards. **2.** the person in charge of something valuable, as an attendant in a museum, zoo, etc. **3.** something that keeps, or serves to guard, hold in place, retain, etc. **4.** *Colloq.* something or someone that you wish to keep. –*phr.* **5. let** (or **allow to**) **go through to the keeper,** *Colloq.* to allow an opinion or remark to pass without comment. –**keeperless,** *adj.* –**keepership,** *n.*

keeping /'kipıŋ/ *n.* **1.** just conformity in things or elements associated together: *his deeds are not in keeping with his words.* **2.** observance, custody, or care. **3.** maintenance or keep. **4.** holding, reserving, or retaining. **5.** *Machinery* any of various devices for holding something in position. –*phr.* **6. in keeping with,** as befits: *in keeping with one's position in life.*

keepsake /'kipseık/ *n.* anything kept, or given to be kept, for the sake of the giver, as a token of remembrance, friendship, etc.

keg /kεg/ *n.* **1.** (in the imperial system) a barrel or container, usually holding 9 gallons (40.9 litres) or 18 gallons (81.8 litres). **2.** a barrel of beer.

kelp /kεlp/ *n.* **1.** any of the large brown seaweeds, such as *Macrocystis* or *Sarcophycus*. **2.** the ash of such seaweeds.

kelp forest *n.* an underwater stand of high-growing kelp, as the giant kelp; found mostly in temperate and arctic waters, including waters along the coast of the southern Australian mainland and Tasmania.

kelpie /'kɛlpi/ n. one of a breed of Australian sheepdogs developed from imported Scottish collies, having a smooth coat of variable colour and pricked ears.

kelvin /'kɛlvən/ n. the base SI unit of thermodynamic temperature, equal to the fraction 1/273.16 of the temperature of the triple point of water; as a unit of temperature interval, one kelvin is equivalent to one degree Celsius. *Symbol*: K See **Celsius**.

Kelvin scale /'kɛlvən skeɪl/ n. a scale of temperature (**Kelvin temperature**), based on thermodynamic principles, in which zero is equivalent to –273.15°C or –459.67°F.

ken /kɛn/ n. **1.** range of sight or vision. **2.** knowledge or cognisance; mental perception.

kennel /'kɛnəl/ n. **1.** a house for a dog or dogs. **2.** (*usu. pl.*, *construed as sing.*) an establishment where dogs are bred or boarded. **3.** a wretched abode. –*verb* (**-nelled** *or*, *Chiefly US*, **-neled**, **-nelling** *or*, *Chiefly US*, **-neling**) –*v.t.* **4.** to put into or keep in a kennel. –*v.i.* **5.** to take shelter in a kennel.

kentia palm /'kɛntiə pam/ n. a palm, *Howea forsteriana* (syn. *Gronophyllum forsteriana*), native to Lord Howe Island but widely cultivated as an ornamental.

kept /kɛpt/ v. past tense and past participle of **keep**.

keratin /'kɛrətən/ n. a fibrous protein found in the outer layer of human and animal skin, also in horn, feathers, hair, hoofs, nails, etc.

kerb /kɜb/ n. **1.** a line of joined stones, concrete, or the like at the edge of a street, wall, etc. **2.** the fender of a hearth. **3.** the framework round the top of a well. –*v.t.* **4.** to furnish with, or protect by a kerb. Also, *Chiefly US*, **curb**.

kerchief /'kɜtʃəf, kəˈtʃif/ n. **1.** a cloth worn or carried on the person. **2.** a cloth worn as a head covering, especially by women.

kerfuffle /kəˈfʌfəl, -ˈfʊfəl/ n. *Colloq.* commotion; rumpus. Also, **kerfoofle**, **kafuffle**, **kafoofle**.

kernel /'kɜnəl/ n. **1.** the softer, usually edible, part contained in the shell of a nut or the stone of a fruit. **2.** the body of a seed within its husk or integuments. **3.** a grain, as of wheat. **4.** the central part of anything; the nucleus; the core.

kero /'kɛroʊ/ n. *Aust.*, *NZ Colloq.* → **kerosene**.

kerosene /kɛrəˈsin, 'kɛrəsin/ n. a mixture of liquid hydrocarbons, obtained in the distillation of petroleum, with boiling points in the range 150°-300°C, used for lamps, engines, heaters. Also, **kerosine**.

kerosene grass n. any of various short-lived native perennials of the genus *Aristida*, especially bunched kerosene grass, *A. contorta*, having coarse, wiry stems, three awns, and sparse leaf growth; plentiful on sandy soils in low rainfall areas of Australia.

kestrel /'kɛstrəl/ n. **1.** → **nankeen kestrel**. **2.** any of several small falcons, as *Falco tinnunculus*, of northern parts of the Eastern Hemisphere, notable for hovering in the air with its head to the wind.

ketch /kɛtʃ/ n. *Naut.* a fore-and-aft rigged vessel with a large mainmast and a smaller mast aft, but forward of the rudder post.

ketchup /'kɛtʃəp/ n. any of several sauces or condiments for meat, fish, etc.: *tomato ketchup; mushroom ketchup*. Also, *Chiefly US*, **catsup**.

ketone /'kitoʊn/ n. *Chem.* any of a class of organic compounds, having the general formula, RCOR′, containing the carbonyl group, $C=O$, attached to two organic groups, as acetone, CH_3COCH_3. –**ketonic** /kəˈtɒnɪk/, *adj.*

kettle /'kɛtl/ n. **1.** a portable container with a cover, a spout, and a handle, in which to boil water for making tea and other uses; teakettle. **2.** an electrical appliance made of either metal or plastic for boiling water; electric kettle. **3.** any of various containers for cooking foods, melting glue, etc. –*phr.* **4. kettle of fish**, **a.** a mess, muddle, or awkward state of affairs (often preceded ironically by *pretty*, *fine*, etc.). **b.** any situation or state of affairs: *this is a different kettle of fish altogether*.

kettledrum /'kɛtldrʌm/ n. a drum consisting of a hollow hemisphere of brass or copper with a skin stretched over it, which can be accurately tuned. –**kettledrummer**, n.

Kevlar /'kɛvla/ n. (*from trademark*) an extruded synthetic fibre which is extremely strong and resistant to high temperatures. Also, **kevlar**.

key¹ /ki/ n. (*pl.* **keys**) **1.** an instrument for fastening or opening a lock by moving its bolt. **2.** a means of attaining, understanding, solving, etc.: *the key to a problem*. **3.** a book or the like containing the solutions or translations of material given elsewhere as exercises. **4.** the system or pattern used to decode a cryptogram, etc. **5.** a systematic explanation of abbreviations, symbols, etc., used in a dictionary, map, etc. **6.** something that secures or controls entrance to a place. **7.** a pin, bolt, wedge, or other piece inserted in a hole or space to lock or hold parts of a mechanism or structure together; a cotter. **8.** *Carpentry, etc.* a small piece of wood, etc., set across the grain to prevent warping. **9.** a contrivance for grasping and turning a bolt, nut, etc., as for winding a clockwork mechanism, for turning a valve or stopcock. **10.** one of a set of levers or parts pressed in operating a keyboard, typewriter, etc. **11.** *Music* **a.** the part of the lever mechanism of a piano, organ, or woodwind instrument, which a finger operates. **b.** the keynote or tonic of a scale. **c.** the relationship perceived between all notes in a given unit of music to a single note or a keynote; tonality. **d.** the principal tonality of a composition: *symphony in the key of C minor*. **12.** tone or pitch, as of voice: *to speak in a high key*. **13.** strain, or characteristic style, as of expression or thought. **14.** degree of intensity, as of feeling or action. **15.** *Elect.* **a.** a device for opening and closing electrical contacts. **b.** a hand-operated switching device ordinarily formed of concealed spring contacts with an exposed handle or push-button, capable of switching one or more parts of a circuit. **16.** *Bot., Zool.* a systematic tabular classification of the significant characteristics of the members of a group of organisms to facilitate identification and comparison. **17.** *Masonry* a keystone. **18.** *Building Trades* any grooving or roughness on a surface to improve bond. **19.** the average of the tone and colour values of a painting, being high if the tones are kept near white and the colours pale and bright, and low if the tones are kept near black and the colours dark and dull. –*adj.* **20.** chief; major; fundamental; indispensable: *the key industries of a nation*. **21.** (in advertising, journalism, etc.) identifying: *a key line, a key number*. –*v.t.* (**keyed**, **keying**) **22.** to adjust (one's speech, actions, etc.) as if to a particular key, in order to come into harmony with external factors, as the level of understanding of one's hearers. **23.** Also, **key in**. to enter (data) into a computer by means of a keyboard. **24.** *Music* to regulate the key or pitch of. **25.** to fasten, secure, or adjust with a key, wedge, or the like, as parts of a mechanism. **26.** to provide with a key or keys. **27.** to give (an advertisement) a letter or number to enable replies to it to be identified. **28.** to lock with, or as with, a key. **29.** *Masonry* to provide (an arch, etc.) with a keystone. **30.** *Building Trades* **a.** to prepare (a surface) by grooving, roughening, etc., to receive paint. **b.** to cause (paint, etc.) to adhere to a surface. –*phr.* **31. key up**, to bring to a particular degree of intensity of feeling, excitement, energy, etc. –**keyer**, n.

key² /ki/ n. (*pl.* **keys**) **1.** (in the Caribbean area) a reef or low island; cay. **2.** a long low peninsula artificially created in a low-lying marshy or estuarine area, on which houses are built, most of which have water frontages.

keyboard /'kibɔd/ n. 1. the row or set of keys on a piano, typewriter, computer, etc. 2. any of two or more sets of keys, as on large organs, or harpsichords. −v.t. 3. to enter (data) by means of a keyboard. −v.i. 4. to use a keyboard machine, especially a computer. **−keyboarder**, n.

keyhole surgery /'kihoʊl sɜdʒəri/ n. surgery performed using very small incisions and fibre optics to provide direct vision.

keynote /'kinoʊt/ n. 1. Music the note on which a key (system of notes) is founded; the tonic. 2. the main interest or determining principle of a conference, political campaign, advertising campaign, etc. −adj. 3. being or relating to the main interest or determining principle: keynote address, keynote speaker.

keypad /'kipæd/ n. a panel containing a set of keys for entering data or commands into an electronic machine, system, etc.

key performance indicator n. a criterion in a performance management system which is used as a measure of the success or efficiency of an operation. Abbrev.: KPI

key signature n. Music (in notation) the group of sharps or flats placed after the clef to indicate the tonality of the music following.

keystone /'kistoʊn/ n. 1. the wedge-shaped piece at the summit of an arch, regarded as holding the other pieces in place. 2. something on which associated things depend.

keystone species n. a species which has a disproportionate effect on an ecosystem in relation to its population size, its removal resulting in significant change and possibly the ultimate destruction of the ecosystem.

keystroke /'kistroʊk/ n. an instance of pressing down a key on a typewriter or computer keyboard.

khaki /'kaki, 'kaki/ n. (pl. **-kis**) 1. a. a dull yellowish brown colour. b. a dull green with a yellowish or brownish tinge. 2. stout twilled cotton uniform cloth of this colour, worn especially by soldiers. 3. a similar fabric of wool. −adj. 4. of the colour of khaki. 5. made of khaki.

khaki election n. Politics a general election in which an ongoing or proposed war is a factor influencing the voters.

kia-ora /kiə-'ɔrə/ interj. NZ an expression of greeting or good wishes.

kibbutz /kɪ'bʊts/ n. (pl. **kibbutzim** /kɪ'bʊtsɪm, kɪbʊt'sim/) (in Israel) a communal agricultural settlement.

kibosh /'kaɪbɒʃ/ phr. **put the kibosh on**, Colloq. to put a stop to. Also, **kybosh**.

kick /kɪk/ v.t. 1. to strike with the foot. 2. to drive, force, make, etc., by or as by kicks. 3. to strike in recoiling. 4. Football to score (a goal) by a kick. −v.i. 5. to strike out with the foot. 6. to have the habit of thus striking out, as a horse. 7. Colloq. to resist, object, or complain. 8. to recoil, as a firearm when fired. 9. Also, **kick up**. to rise sharply, as a ball after bouncing. −n. 10. the act of kicking; a blow or thrust with the foot. 11. Football a. the act of kicking a football. b. the kicked ball: his first kick hit the crossbar. c. the distance covered by a kicked ball: a long kick for goal. d. a person who kicks the ball: he's a good kick. 12. power or disposition to kick. 13. the right of or a turn at kicking. 14. a recoil, as of a gun. 15. Colloq. an objection or complaint. 16. Colloq. any thrill or excitement that gives pleasure; any act, sensation, etc., that gives satisfaction: Mozart really gives her a kick. 17. Colloq. an interest or line of behaviour, often temporary, which dominates the attention of the person following it: he's on a health

kick. 18. Colloq. a stimulating or intoxicating quality in alcoholic drink. 19. Colloq. energy or vigour. −phr. 20. **a kick in the arse**, Colloq. a. a setback. b. retribution. 21. **a kick in the guts** (or **teeth**), Colloq. a grave setback. 22. **a kick in the pants**, Colloq. a sharp reprimand. 23. **for kicks**, Colloq. for the sake of gaining some excitement or entertainment. 24. **get a kick out of**, Colloq. to derive feelings of pleasure, excitement, etc., from: to get a kick out of a new hobby. 25. **kick about** (or **around**), Colloq. a. to treat harshly or unfairly. b. to discuss or consider at length or in some detail (an idea, proposal, or the like). 26. **kick against the pricks**, to indulge in futile struggles against the harsh realities of life. 27. **kick arse** (or **butt**), Colloq. a. to assert authority by being violent and aggressive towards people. b. to defeat opponents soundly. 28. **kick back**, Colloq. to relax. 29. **kick in**, a. Colloq. to contribute, as to a collection for a presentation. b. Also, **kick out**. Aust. Rules to kick the ball back into play after a behind has been scored. c. to take effect: drugs that kick in quickly. 30. **kick off**, a. Rugby Football, Soccer to kick the ball from the half-way line at the start of the game and of the second half, and after each score has been made. b. Colloq. to start, commence. c. Surfing to get off a wave by kicking the surfboard out of the wave. d. US Colloq. to die. 31. **kick on**, Aust. Colloq. a. to carry on or continue, especially with just adequate resources: we'll kick on until the fresh supplies get here. b. to continue a party or other festivity: we kicked on until the early hours. 32. **kick oneself**, to reproach oneself. 33. **kick out**, Colloq. to dismiss; get rid of. 34. **kick someone's butt**, Colloq. a. to defeat someone soundly. b. to reprimand someone severely. 35. **kick someone's head** (or **teeth**) **in**, Colloq. to assault someone violently. 36. **kick someone upstairs**, a. to promote someone to a position which has status but no real power. b. to remove someone, especially a potential rival, by appointing them to a higher position elsewhere. 37. **kick the bucket**, Colloq. to die. 38. **kick the habit**, Colloq. a. to give up cigarettes, alcohol, etc., to which one has become addicted. b. to forgo any pleasure. 39. **kick the tin**, Aust. Colloq. to give money; contribute. 40. **kick up**, Colloq. to stir up; to cause (disturbance, trouble, noise, etc.): to kick up a fuss. 41. **kick up one's heels**, to enjoy oneself in an exuberant manner. **−kickable**, adj. **−kicker**, n.

kick-arse adj. Colloq. (taboo) exciting; stimulating: kick-arse music. Also, **kickarse**.

kickback /'kɪkbæk/ n. Colloq. 1. a response, usually vigorous. 2. any sum paid for favours received or hoped for.

kickboxing /'kɪkbɒksɪŋ/ n. a form of boxing popular in Asian countries, in which the opponent can be kicked with the bare feet. **−kickboxer**, n.

kick-off n. 1. the act of kicking off. 2. Colloq. the beginning or initial stage of something.

kid¹ /kɪd/ n. 1. a young goat. 2. leather made from the skin of a young goat. 3. Colloq. a child or young person. 4. Colloq. a son or daughter. −v.i. (**kidded**, **kidding**) 5. (of a goat) to give birth to young. −adj. 6. Colloq. young; younger: my kid brother.

kid² /kɪd/ Colloq. −verb (**kidded**, **kidding**) −v.t. 1. to tease; banter; jest with. 2. to humbug or fool. −v.i. 3. to speak or act deceptively, in jest. −phr. 4. **... has got to** (or **must**) (or **has to**) **be kidding**, an exclamation of incredulity, disbelief, etc. 5. **I kid you not**, an assertion that one is speaking the truth. **−kidder**, n.

kidnap /'kɪdnæp/ v.t. (**-napped, -napping**) to steal or abduct (a child or other person); carry off (a person) against their will by unlawful force or by fraud, often with a demand for ransom. **−kidnapper**, n.

kidney /'kɪdni/ n. (pl. **-neys**) **1.** either of a pair of bean-shaped glandular organs, in humans and other animals about 10 cm in length, in the back part of the abdominal cavity, which get rid of waste from the blood. **2.** the meat of an animal's kidney used as a food.

kidney bean n. **1.** → **French bean**. **2.** the dried, somewhat kidney-shaped seed of the French bean, especially if dark in colour.

kikuyu /kaɪ'kuju/ n. a perennial grass, *Pennisetum clandestinum*, suitable to a wide variety of soil types and producing a thick growth of runners; widely used as a lawn grass.

kill /kɪl/ v.t. **1.** to deprive (any living creature or thing) of life in any manner; cause the death of; slay. **2.** to destroy; to do away with; extinguish: *kill hope.* **3.** to destroy or neutralise the active qualities of. **4.** to spoil the effect of. **5.** to pass (the time) idly while waiting for something to come, happen, or the like: *he killed time waiting for the bus to come.* **6.** to overcome completely or with irresistible effect. **7.** to cancel (a word, paragraph, item, etc.). **8.** to defeat or veto (a legislative bill, etc.). **9.** *Elect.* to render (a circuit) dead. **10.** *Tennis* to hit (a ball) with such force that its return is impossible. **11.** (in computer games) to eliminate (an opponent) by killing the persona which represents them in the game. **12.** *Colloq.* to put a stop to; terminate: *to kill a project.* –v.i. **13.** to inflict or cause death. **14.** to commit murder. **15.** to have an irresistible effect: *dressed to kill.* –n. **16.** the act of killing (game, etc.). **17.** an animal or animals killed. –phr. **18. kill off**, to destroy completely and often indiscriminately. **19. kill two birds with one stone**, to achieve two (or more) objectives by one action. –**killer**, n.

killer app n. *Computers Colloq.* a computing application which has widespread usefulness and thus generates big sales.

killing /'kɪlɪŋ/ n. **1.** the act of a person or thing that kills. **2.** *Colloq.* a stroke of extraordinary success, as in a successful speculation in stocks. –adj. **3.** that kills. **4.** exhausting. **5.** *Colloq.* irresistibly funny. –**killingly**, adv.

killing field n. a place where many people have been killed in warfare, civil massacres, etc.

killjoy /'kɪldʒɔɪ/ n. a person or thing that spoils the joy or enjoyment of others.

kiln /kɪln/ n. **1.** a furnace or oven for burning, baking, or drying something, especially one for calcining limestone or one for baking bricks. –v.t. **2.** to burn, bake, or treat in a kiln.

kilo /'kiloʊ/ n. → **kilogram**.

kilo- **1.** a prefix denoting 10^3 of a given unit, as in *kilogram. Symbol*: k **2.** *Computers* a prefix denoting 2^{10} (1024) of a given unit, as in *kilobyte. Symbol*: k

kilobit /'kɪləbɪt/ n. *Computers* a unit of measurement of computer storage equal to 2^{10} (1024) bits. *Abbrev.*: Kb

kilobyte /'kɪləbaɪt/ n. a unit of measurement of computer memory equal to 2^{10} (1024) bytes. *Symbol*: KB, kbyte

kilogram /'kɪləgræm/ n. **1.** a unit of mass equal to 1000 grams. **2.** *Physics* the SI unit of mass, based on the international prototype kept at Sèvres, France. *Symbol*: kg

kilohertz /'kɪləhɜts/ n. a unit of frequency equal to 1000 hertz; commonly used to express radiofrequency. *Symbol*: kHz

kilojoule /'kɪlədʒul/ n. one thousand joules; the unit used to express the fuel or energy value of food; the quantity of a food capable of producing such a unit of energy. *Symbol*: kJ

kilometre /'kɪləmitə, kə'lɒmətə/ n. a unit of length, the common measure of distances equal to 1000 metres. *Symbol*: km Also, *US*, **kilometer**. –**kilometric** /kɪlə-'mɛtrɪk/, **kilometrical** /kɪlə'mɛtrɪkəl/, adj.

kilopascal /'kɪləpæskəl/ n. a unit of pressure equal to 1000 pascals, used to express the amount of pressure in tyres, pumps, etc. *Symbol*: kPa

kilowatt /'kɪləwɒt/ n. one thousand watts. *Symbol*: kW

kilt /kɪlt/ n. any short, pleated skirt, especially one worn by men in the Scottish Highlands.

kilter /'kɪltə/ phr. **out of kilter**, not functioning properly; not in good working order.

kimchi /'kɪmtʃi/ n. (in Korean cookery) a vegetable pickle, especially one using cabbage, with various seasonings; sometimes served fresh and sometimes left to ferment. Also, **gimchi**.

kimono /'kɪmənoʊ, kə'moʊnoʊ/ n. (pl. **-nos**) a wide-sleeved robe characteristic of Japanese costume.

kin /kɪn/ n. **1.** one's relatives collectively, or kinsfolk. **2.** family relationship or kinship. **3.** a group of persons descended from a common ancestor, or constituting a family, clan, tribe, or people. –adj. **4.** of kin; related; akin. **5.** of the same kind or nature; having affinity. –phr. **6. of kin**, of the same family; related; akin. –**kinless**, adj.

-kin a diminutive suffix, attached to nouns to signify a little object of the kind mentioned: *lambkin, catkin.*

kina[1] /kinə/ n. a green-coloured sea urchin, *Evichinus chloroticus*, commonly eaten in New Zealand.

kina[2] /'kinə/ n. the unit of currency in Papua New Guinea.

kind[1] /kaɪnd/ adj. **1.** of a good or benevolent nature or disposition, as a person. **2.** having, showing, or proceeding from benevolence: *kind words.* **3.** cordial; well-meant: *kind regards.* **4.** (sometimes fol. by *to*) indulgent, considerate, or helpful: *to be kind to animals.* –**kindness**, n.

kind[2] /kaɪnd/ n. **1.** a class or group of individuals of the same nature or character, especially a natural group of animals or plants. **2.** nature or character as determining likeness or difference between things: *things differing in degree rather than in kind.* **3.** a person or thing as being of a particular character or class: *he is a strange kind of hero.* **4.** a more or less adequate or inadequate example, or a sort, of something: *the vines formed a kind of roof.* –phr. **5. in kind, a.** in something of the same kind; in the same way: *to retaliate in kind.* **b.** in goods or natural produce, instead of money. **6. kind of**, *Colloq.* after a fashion; to some extent; somewhat; rather: *the room was kind of dark.*

kindergarten /'kɪndəgatn/ n. **1.** → **preschool** (def. 2). **2.** any childcare centre. **3.** the first year in primary school in some Australian states.

kindle /'kɪndəl/ v.t. **1.** to set (a fire, flame, etc.) burning or blazing. **2.** to set fire to, or ignite (fuel or any combustible matter). **3.** to excite; stir up or set going; animate, rouse, or inflame. **4.** to light up, illuminate, or make bright. –v.i. **5.** (of fuel, a fire or flame) to begin to burn. **6.** to become excited, inflamed; become ardent. **7.** to become lit up, bright, or glowing, as the sky at dawn or the eyes with enthusiasm. –**kindler**, n.

kindling /'kɪndlɪŋ/ n. material for starting a fire.

kindly /'kaɪndli/ adj. (**-lier, -liest**) **1.** having, showing, or coming from a kind nature or spirit; kind-hearted; good-natured; sympathetic. **2.** pleasant; genial; benign. **3.** favourable, as soil for crops. –adv. **4.** in a kind manner. **5.** heartily; cordially: *we thank you kindly.* **6.** with liking; favourably: *to take kindly to an idea.* **7.** obligingly; please: *kindly go away.* –**kindliness**, n.

kindred /'kɪndrəd/ n. **1.** a body of people related to one another, or a family, tribe, or people. **2.** one's relatives as a group; kinsfolk; kin. –adj. **3.** associated by origin, nature, qualities, etc.: *kindred languages.* **4.** related by birth or descent, or having kinship: *kindred tribes.*

kinetic /kəˈnɛtɪk, kaɪ-/ *adj.* **1.** relating to motion. **2.** caused by motion.

kinetic energy *n. Physics* the energy which a body possesses by virtue of its motion; the energy which any system possesses by virtue of the motion of its components.

kinetics /kəˈnɛtɪks, kaɪ-/ *n.* the branch of mechanics that deals with the action of forces in producing or changing the motion of masses.

king /kɪŋ/ *n.* **1.** a man who has chief authority over a country and people, usually for life and by hereditary right; monarch; sovereign. **2.** (*upper case*) a title of God or Christ: *King of Heaven.* **3.** a person or thing outstanding in its class: *the lion is the king of beasts.* **4.** a playing card bearing the formalised picture of a king. **5.** the chief piece in a game of chess, moving one square at a time in any direction. **6.** a man who has grown wealthy and powerful from a specified industry: *a cattle king. –adj.* **7.** especially large: *king size*; *king prawn. –kingship, n. –kingly, adj.*

kingdom /ˈkɪŋdəm/ *n.* **1.** a state or government having a king or queen as its head. **2.** anything conceived as constituting a realm or sphere of independent action or control: *the kingdom of thought.* **3.** a realm or province of nature, especially one of the three great divisions of natural objects: *the animal, vegetable, and mineral kingdoms.* **4.** the spiritual sovereignty of God or Christ.

kingfisher /ˈkɪŋfɪʃə/ *n.* any of numerous birds of the families Alcedinidae, Halcyonidae or Cerylidae, which feed on fish or insects, are stout-billed and small-footed, and many of which are crested or brilliantly coloured.

king hit *n.* **1.** a savage blow, usually to the head and often delivered without warning, which fells the opponent. **2.** *Colloq.* any sudden, serious misfortune.

king parrot *n.* a large endemic parrot, *Alisterus scapularis*, of eastern Australia, the male having a scarlet head, neck and underparts, the female having a light green head and neck.

kingpin /ˈkɪŋpɪn/ *n.* **1.** the pin by which a stub axle is articulated to an axle beam or steering head in a car; a swivel pin. **2.** *Bowling* **a.** the pin in the centre when the pins are in place. **b.** the pin at the front apex. **3.** *Colloq.* the principal person or element in a company or system, etc.

king prawn *n.* a large, edible prawn of eastern Australian waters, *Penaeus plebejus*, brownish in colour with a blue tail; red when cooked.

kink /kɪŋk/ *n.* **1.** a twist, as in a thread, rope, or hair, caused by its doubling or bending upon itself. **2.** a mental twist; an odd idea; a whim. **3.** a turning away from normal, especially normal sexual, behaviour. *–v.i.* **4.** to form a twist or twists, as a rope. *–v.t.* **5.** to cause to form a twist or twists, as a rope. *–kinky, adj.*

kinship /ˈkɪnʃɪp/ *n.* **1.** the state or fact of being of kin; family relationship. **2.** relationship by nature, qualities, etc.; affinity.

kinship name *n.* → **skin name.**

kiosk /ˈkiɒsk/ *n.* **1.** a small, light structure for the sale of newspapers, cigarettes, etc. **2.** a building, or part of a building, for the sale of light refreshments as at a hospital, railway station, park, etc. **3.** → **canteen** (def. 2). **4.** a small booth, as in a shopping mall, for the distribution of information, advertising, etc. **5.** a kind of open pavilion or summerhouse common in Turkey and Iran.

kip¹ /kɪp/ *Colloq. –n.* **1.** a sleep or nap. *–phr.* (**kipped, kipping**) **2. kip down,** to go to bed; sleep.

kip² /kɪp/ *n.* a small thin piece of wood used for spinning coins in two-up; bat.

kipper /ˈkɪpə/ *n.* **1.** a kippered fish, especially a herring. *–v.t.* **2.** to cure (herring, salmon, etc.) by cleaning, salting, etc., and drying in the air or in smoke.

kirk /k3k/ *n. Scottish* a church.

kismet /ˈkɪzmət, ˈkɪs-/ *n.* fate; destiny.

kiss /kɪs/ *v.t.* **1.** to touch or press with the lips, while compressing and then separating them, in token of greeting, affection, etc. **2.** to join the lips together with (another person) in an expression of erotic love. **3.** to touch gently or lightly. *–v.i.* **4.** to kiss someone, something, or each other. *–n.* **5.** the act of kissing. **6.** a slight touch or contact. *–phr.* **7. kiss something goodbye** (or **kiss goodbye to something**), *Colloq.* to accept that something is certainly lost or impossible. **8. kiss something better,** (*esp. with children*) to kiss a part of the body as a gesture of removing pain or injury there. **9. kiss the dust, a.** to be killed. **b.** to be humiliated. *–kissable, adj.*

kiss of life *n.* **1.** mouth-to-mouth resuscitation. **2.** any action, event, etc., which offers new hopes of success to an enterprise previously considered destined to fail.

kit¹ /kɪt/ *n.* **1.** a set or collection of tools, supplies, etc., for a specific purpose: *a first-aid kit.* **2.** a set or collection of parts to be assembled: *a model aircraft kit.* **3.** → **toolkit. 4.** *Chiefly Mil.* a set of clothing or personal equipment for a specific purpose: *the soldiers were issued with a complete kit. –v.t.* (**kitted, kitting**) Also, **kit out. 5.** to provide with kit. *–phr.* **6. the whole kit and caboodle,** *Colloq.* **a.** the whole thing; an item with all its parts. **b.** the whole group.

kit² /kɪt/ *n. NZ* a woven flax basket.

kitchen /ˈkɪtʃən/ *n.* **1.** a room or place equipped for or appropriated to cooking. *–phr.* **2. the rounds of the kitchen,** *Aust. Colloq.* a severe scolding.

kitchen bench *n.* a flat surface in a kitchen, usually above built-in cupboards, designed for the preparation of food.

kitchen tea *n. Aust., NZ* → **bridal shower.**

kite /kaɪt/ *n.* **1.** a light frame covered with some thin material, to be flown in the wind at the end of a long string. **2.** any of various medium-sized hawks of the family Accipitridae with long wings and tail as the **black kite,** *Milvus migrans,* of Eurasia, Africa, and northern Australia, or the endemic Australian **black-shouldered kite,** *Elanus axillaris.* **3.** *Colloq.* a cheque, especially one forged or stolen. **4.** *Obs.* a person who preys on others; a sharper. *–phr.* **5. fly a kite,** *Colloq.* **a.** to pass off a forged cheque. **b.** to test public opinion by spreading rumours, etc. **c.** to give an idea a public airing.

kiteboard /ˈkaɪtbɔd/ *n.* **1.** a small surfboard used in kitesurfing. *–v.i.* **2.** to engage in the sport of kitesurfing. *–kiteboarder, n.*

kitesurfing /ˈkaɪtsɜfɪŋ/ *n.* the sport of riding a kiteboard whilst being propelled by a large controllable kite. Also, **kiteboarding.**

kith /kɪθ/ *phr.* **kith and kin,** friends and relatives.

kitsch /kɪtʃ/ *n.* **1.** showy and shallowly sentimental art, etc., considered to be in bad taste. *–adj.* **2.** of or relating to kitsch. *–kitschy, adj.*

kitten /ˈkɪtn/ *n.* **1.** a young cat. **2.** the young of any of various species of small mammal, as the rabbit. **3.** a playful or skittish girl. *–phr.* **4. have kittens,** *Colloq.* to be extremely anxious or alarmed. *–kittenish, adj.*

kitty¹ /ˈkɪti/ *n.* (*pl.* **-ties**) **1.** a kitten. **2.** a pet name for a cat.

kitty² /ˈkɪti/ *n.* (*pl.* **-ties**) **1.** a jointly held fund or collection, usually of small amounts of money; savings; accumulation. **2.** a pool into which each player in a card game places a certain sum of money as a stake. **3.** *Bowls* the jack.

kitty litter *n.* (*from trademark*) a granular, absorbent, and deodorised preparation designed for cat excreta.

kiwi /'kiwi/ *n.* **1.** any of several flightless birds of New Zealand, constituting the genus *Apteryx*, having vestigial wings, stout legs, and a long slender bill. **2.** *Finance Colloq.* the New Zealand dollar.

Kiwi /'kiwi/ *Colloq.* –*n.* **1.** a New Zealander. –*adj.* **2.** of or relating to New Zealand.

kiwi berry *n.* a small smooth-skinned kiwifruit.

kiwifruit /'kiwifrut/ *n.* **1.** a (vine bearing) round, hairy fruit about 7 cm long with a gooseberry-like flavour; Chinese gooseberry. **2.** the fruit. Also, **Kiwi fruit**.

klaxon /'klæksən/ *n.* (*from trademark*) a type of warning hooter with a strident tone, originally used in motor vehicles.

kleptomania /klɛptə'meɪniə/ *n.* *Psychol.* an irresistible desire to steal, without regard to personal needs. Also, **cleptomania**.

kludge /klʌdʒ/ *n.* a computer system or program which is improvised in a clumsy and inelegant fashion but which nevertheless succeeds in performing the required task.

klutz /klʌts/ *n.* *Colloq.* a clumsy, awkward person; an idiot. –**klutzy**, *adj.*

knack /næk/ *n.* a faculty or power of doing something with ease as from special skill; aptitude.

knacker /'nækə/ *n.* **1.** someone who buys old or useless horses for slaughter. **2.** someone who buys old houses, ships, etc., to break them up for scrap. –**knackery**, *n.*

knackered /'nækəd/ *adj.* *Colloq.* exhausted; worn out.

knapsack /'næpsæk/ *n.* a backpack, originally one of leather or canvas. Also, **rucksack**.

knave /neɪv/ *n.* **1.** an unprincipled or dishonest fellow. **2.** *Cards* a playing card bearing the formalised picture of a prince, in most games counting as next below the queen in its suit; jack. **3.** *Archaic* a male servant or man of humble position. –**knavery**, *n.* –**knavish**, *adj.*

knead /nid/ *v.t.* **1.** to work (dough, etc.) into a uniform mixture by pressing, folding, and stretching. **2.** to manipulate by similar movements, as the body in massage. **3.** to make by kneading. **4.** to make kneading motions with. –**kneader**, *n.*

knee /ni/ *n.* **1.** the joint or region in humans between the thigh and the lower part of the leg. **2.** the joint or region of other vertebrates homologous or analogous to the human knee, as in the leg of a bird, the hind limb of a horse, etc. **3.** a joint or region likened to this but not homologous with it, as the tarsal joint of a bird, or the carpal joint in the forelimb of a horse, cow, etc. **4.** the part of a garment covering the knee. **5.** something resembling a knee joint, especially when bent, as a fabricated support or brace with a leg running at an angle to the main member. –*v.t.* (**kneed, kneeing**) **6.** to strike or touch with the knee. –*phr.* **7. bring someone to their knees**, to compel someone to submit.

kneecap /'nikæp/ *n.* *Anat.* the patella, the flat, movable bone at the front of the knee.

knee jerk *n.* *Physiol.* a brisk reflex lifting of the leg induced by tapping the tendon below the kneecap.

kneejerk /'nidʒɜk/ *adj.* **1.** responsive in a way that is swift but unthinking: *a kneejerk announcement*. **2.** typically unthinking: *a kneejerk politician*. –*phr.* **3. kneejerk reaction**, an instinctive response to an event, situation, etc.

kneel /nil/ *v.i.* (**knelt** *or* **kneeled, kneeling**) **1.** to fall or rest on the knees or a knee. –*n.* **2.** the action or position of kneeling. –*phr.* **3. kneel on**, *Colloq.* to oppress; force into submission. –**kneeler**, *n.*

knell /nɛl/ *n.* **1.** the sound made by a bell rung slowly for a death or a funeral. **2.** any sound announcing the death of a person or the extinction, failure, etc., of something. **3.** any mournful sound.

knelt /nɛlt/ *v.* past tense and past participle of **kneel**.

knew /nju/ *v.* past tense of **know**.

knickerbockers /'nɪkəbɒkəz/ *pl. n.* **1.** loosely fitting short breeches gathered in at the knee. **2.** a similar garment worn as decorative underpants.

knickers /'nɪkəz/ *pl. n.* **1.** → **panties**. **2.** → **knickerbockers**. Also, **knicks**.

knick-knack /'nɪk-næk/ *n.* **1.** a pleasing trinket. **2.** a bit of bric-a-brac. Also, **nick-nack**.

knife /naɪf/ *n.* (*pl.* **knives** /naɪvz/) **1.** a cutting instrument consisting essentially of a thin blade (usually of steel and with a sharp edge) attached to a handle. **2.** a knifelike weapon; a dagger; a short sword. **3.** any blade for cutting, as in a tool or machine. –*v.t.* (**knifed, knifing**) **4.** to cut, stab, etc., with a knife. **5.** to endeavour to defeat in a secret or underhand way. –*phr.* **6. a knife in the back**, a surreptitious act of betrayal. **7. have one's knife into**, to bear a grudge against; desire to hurt. **8. knife someone in the back**, to betray someone, especially to destroy their reputation or career in their absence. **9. night of the long knives**, a time of savage attack or retribution. **10. not the sharpest knife in the drawer**, *Colloq.* not the most intelligent person. **11. put the knife into**, to destroy the reputation of (someone) maliciously. **12. under the knife**, *Colloq.* undergoing surgery. **13. war to the knife**, war without mercy. –**knifeless**, *adj.*

knifepoint /'naɪfpɔɪnt/ *adj.* **1.** involving a threat from a knife attack: *a knifepoint kidnapping.* –*phr.* **2. at knifepoint**, under threat from a knife attack.

knight /naɪt/ *n.* **1.** (in medieval Europe) **a.** (originally) a mounted soldier serving under a feudal superior. **b.** (later) a man, usually of noble birth, who, after an apprenticeship as page and squire, was raised to honourable military rank and bound to chivalrous conduct. **2.** a man upon whom a certain dignity, and with it the honorific *Sir*, is conferred by a sovereign for life, because of personal merit or for services rendered to the country. **3.** *Chess* a piece shaped like a horse's head, which moves two squares horizontally and then one square vertically, or two squares vertically and one horizontally. –*v.t.* **4.** to dub or create (a person) a knight. –*phr.* **5. knight in shining armour**, a man thought to be the embodiment of knightly virtue. –**knightly**, *adj.*

knit /nɪt/ *verb* (**knitted** *or* **knit, knitting**) –*v.t.* **1.** to make (a garment, etc.) by crossing together loops of yarn either by hand using long straight needles or by machine. **2.** to join (parts, members, etc.) closely and firmly together. **3.** to contract into folds or wrinkles: *to knit your brow.* –*v.i.* **4.** to perform the action of knitting (def. 1), especially by hand: *can you knit?* **5.** to grow or become closely and firmly joined together, as broken bones do. –*phr.* **6. knit together**, to form a closely bound unit. –**knitter**, *n.*

knitting /'nɪtɪŋ/ *n.* **1.** the act of a person or thing that knits. **2.** the act of forming a fabric by looping a continuous yarn. **3.** knitted work.

knives /naɪvz/ *n.* plural of **knife**.

knob /nɒb/ *n.* **1.** a projecting part, usually rounded, forming the handle of a door, drawer, or the like. **2.** a rounded lump or protuberance on the surface or at the end of something, such as a knot on a tree trunk, a pimple on the skin, etc. **3.** *Archit.* an ornamental boss, as of carved work. **4.** a rounded hill or mountain, especially an isolated one. –*phr.* **5. with knobs on**, *Colloq.* a rejoinder expressing strong affirmation. –**knobbed**, *adj.*

knobby /'nɒbi/ *adj.* (**-bier, -biest**) **1.** having many knobs. **2.** knob-like. –**knobbiness**, *n.*

knock /nɒk/ *v.i.* **1.** to strike a sounding blow with the fist, knuckles, or anything hard, especially on a door, window, or the like, as in seeking admittance, calling attention, giving a signal, etc. **2.** (of an internal-combustion engine) to make a metallic noise as a result of faulty combustion. *–v.t.* **3.** to give a sounding or forcible blow to; hit; strike; beat. **4.** to drive, force, or render by a blow or blows: *to knock a man senseless.* **5.** to strike (a thing) against something else. **6.** *Colloq.* to criticise; find fault with. *–n.* **7.** the act or sound of knocking. **8.** a rap, as at a door. **9.** a blow or thump. **10.** the noise resulting from faulty combustion or from incorrect functioning of some part of an internal-combustion engine. **11.** *Cricket* an innings. **12.** *Colloq.* adverse criticism. *–phr.* **13. knock about** (or **around**) (or **round**), **a.** to wander in an aimless way; lead an irregular existence. **b.** to treat roughly; maltreat. **14. knock around** (or **about**) **with**, *Colloq.* to keep company with. **15. knock back**, *Colloq.* **a.** to consume, especially rapidly: *he knocked back two cans of beer.* **b.** *Aust., NZ* to refuse. **c.** to set back; impede. **d.** to cost (someone): *how much did that knock you back?* **16. knock down**, **a.** to strike to the ground with a blow. **b.** *NZ* to fell (a tree). **c.** (in auctions) to signify the sale of (the thing bid for) by a blow with a hammer or mallet; assign as sold to the highest bidder. **d.** to reduce the price of. **e.** to take apart (a motor vehicle, machine, etc.) to facilitate handling. **f.** *Aust., NZ* to spend freely: *to knock down one's cheque.* **g.** *NZ* to swallow (a drink). **17. knock endwise** (or **endways**), to lay flat with a blow. **18. knock for six**, **a.** to completely annihilate or overcome. **b.** to confuse or disturb greatly: *the bad news knocked him for six.* **19. knock into**, to collide with. **20. knock into a cocked hat**, *Colloq.* to defeat; get the better of. **21. knock it off**, *Colloq.* stop it (usually used in the imperative to put an end to an argument, fight, criticism, etc.). **22. knock off**, *Colloq.* **a.** to cease (an activity, especially work): *they knocked off shearing for the day.* **b.** to cease an activity, especially work: *I knock off at five.* **c.** to deduct. **d.** to steal. **e.** to compose (an article, poem, or the like) hurriedly. **f.** to defeat, put out of a competition. **g.** to kill. **h.** (*taboo*) (of a man) to have sexual intercourse with. **i.** to eat up; consume. **j.** (of police) to arrest (a person) or raid (a place). **23. knock on**, *Rugby Football* to knock (the ball) forwards in catching it (an infringement of the rules). **24. knock oneself out**, to exhaust oneself by excessive mental or physical work. **25. knock on the head**, to put an end to. **26. knock out**, **a.** to defeat (an opponent) in a boxing match by striking them down with a blow after which they do not rise within a prescribed time. **b.** to render senseless. **c.** to destroy; damage severely. **d.** *Aust., NZ* to earn. **e.** to overwhelm; impress greatly: *her act knocked me out.* **27. knock someone's eye out**, to cause someone to feel great admiration. **28. knock the bottom out of**, to refute (an argument); render invalid. **29. knock (the) spots off**, *Colloq.* **a.** to defeat; get the better of. **b.** to be vastly superior to. **30. knock together**, to assemble (something) hastily; put together roughly. **31. knock up**, **a.** to arouse; awaken. **b.** to prepare or put together (something) hastily or roughly. **c.** *Sport* to score (runs, tries, etc.). **d.** *Chiefly Brit. Tennis, Squash* to have a hit-up. **e.** to exhaust; wear out. **f.** to become exhausted. **g.** *Colloq.* to make pregnant. **32. take a knock**, to suffer a reverse, especially a financial one.

knockback /ˈnɒkbæk/ *n.* *Aust., NZ Colloq.* a refusal; rejection. Also, **knock-back**.

knocker /ˈnɒkə/ *n.* **1.** someone or something that knocks. **2.** a hinged knob, bar, etc., on a door, for use in knocking. **3.** *Colloq.* a persistently hostile critic or carping detractor. **4.** (*pl.*) *Colloq.* breasts. *–phr.* **5. on the knocker**, *Aust., NZ Colloq.* at the right time, punctually: *he was there at 4 o'clock on the knocker.*

knock-knee *n.* **1.** inward curvature of the legs, causing the knees to knock together in walking. **2.** (*pl.*) such knees. **–knock-kneed**, *adj.*

knockout /ˈnɒkaʊt/ *n.* **1.** the act of knocking out. **2.** a knockout blow. **3.** *Colloq.* a person or thing that excites admiration. **4.** *Colloq.* an extremely good-looking person. *–adj.* **5.** that knocks out.

knoll /nɒl/ *n.* a small, rounded hill or eminence; a hillock.

knot /nɒt/ *n.* **1.** an interlacement of a cord, rope, or the like, drawn tight into a lump or knob, as for fastening two cords, etc., together or to something else. **2.** a piece of ribbon or similar material tied or folded upon itself and used or worn as an ornament. **3.** a cluster of persons or things. **4.** *Bot.* a protuberance in the tissue of a plant; an excrescence on a stem, branch, or root; a node or joint in a stem, especially when of swollen form. **5.** *Zool.* a hard lump in an animal body such as a swelling or the like in a muscle, gland, etc. **6.** the hard, cross-grained mass of wood at the place where a branch joins the trunk of a tree. **7.** a part of this mass showing in a piece of timber, etc. **8.** a unit of speed, used in marine and aerial navigation, and in meteorology, of one international nautical mile per hour or 0.514 444 44 m/s (approximately 1.85 km/h). *–verb* (**knotted, knotting**) *–v.t.* **9.** to tie in a knot or knots; form a knot or knots in. **10.** to secure by a knot. **11.** to form protuberances, bosses, or knobs in; make knotty. *–v.i.* **12.** to become tied or tangled in a knot or knots. **13.** to form knots or joints. *–phr.* **14. at a rate of knots**, very fast. **–knotted**, *adj.* **–knotty**, *adj.*

know /noʊ/ *verb* (**knew, known, knowing**) *–v.t.* **1.** to perceive or understand as fact or truth, or apprehend with clearness and certainty. **2.** to have fixed in the mind or memory: *to know a poem by heart.* **3.** to be cognisant or aware of; to be acquainted with (a thing, place, person, etc.) as by sight, experience, or report. **4.** to be able to distinguish, as one from another. *–v.i.* **5.** to have knowledge, or clear and certain perception, as of fact or truth. **6.** to be cognisant or aware, as of some fact, circumstances, or occurrence; have information, as about something. *–phr.* **7. in the know**, having inside knowledge. **8. know by heart**, to know as from learning by rote. **9. know chalk from cheese**, to be able to note differences. **10. know how to**, to be able from experience or attainment to (do something). **11. know which side one's bread is buttered**, to know where the advantage lies. **12. not to know someone from Adam**, not to know or recognise someone. **–knowable**, *adj.* **–knower**, *n.*

know-all *n.* *Colloq.* someone who claims to know everything, or everything about a particular subject. Also, **know-it-all**.

knowing /ˈnoʊɪŋ/ *adj.* **1.** shrewd, sharp, or astute: *a knowing glance.* **2.** having knowledge or information; intelligent; wise. **3.** intentional; deliberate. **–knowingly**, *adv.*

knowledge /ˈnɒlɪdʒ/ *n.* **1.** familiarity with facts, truths, or principles, as gained from study, examination, research, experience or report. **2.** the body of truths or facts built up by humankind in the course of time. **3.** the fact or state of knowing. **4.** something that is known, or may be known. **5.** the sum of what is known. **6.** *Archaic* sexual intercourse, now preserved in the legal term *carnal knowledge.* *–phr.* **7. to one's knowledge**, **a.** according to what one knows for certain. **b.** (with a negative) so far as one knows: *I never saw him, to my knowledge.*

knowledgeable /ˈnɒlədʒəbəl/ *adj.* possessing knowledge or understanding; intelligent.

knowledge base *n.* **1.** a broad range of sound knowledge in one or several areas: *the job requires a good knowledge base but also practical skills.* **2.** Also,

knowledgebase. a computer database which handles the collection, storage and retrieval of information.

knowledge-based *adj.* of or relating to a system, the successful operation of which depends on a sizeable body of knowledge, or to an organisation operating such a system: *a knowledge-based economy.*

knowledge economy *n.* an economy in which knowledge is treated as a major commodity and in which there is generation of, access to, and use of technological development in all sectors.

knowledge worker *n.* a person who is employed to acquire, develop or transfer knowledge, such as a teacher, academic, programmer, researcher, etc.

known /noʊn/ *v.* past participle of **know**.

knuckle /'nʌkəl/ *n.* **1.** a joint of a finger, especially one of the joints at the roots of the fingers. **2.** the rounded prominence of such a joint when the finger is bent. **3.** a joint of meat, consisting of the parts about the carpal or tarsal joint of a quadruped. **4.** an angle between two members or surfaces of a vessel. **5.** a cylindrical projecting part on a hinge, through which an axis or pin passes; the joint of a hinge. **6.** (*pl.*) → **jack** (def. 6b). –*v.t.* **7.** to assault, with fists or knuckle-dusters. **8.** to press or touch with the knuckles: *to knuckle one's brow in respect.* –*phr.* **9. go the knuckle,** *Colloq.* to fight; punch. **10. knuckle down, a.** to hold the knuckles close to the ground in playing marbles. **b.** to apply oneself vigorously or earnestly, as to a task. **11. knuckle under,** to yield or submit. **12. near** (or **close to**) **the knuckle,** (of a remark, joke, etc.) near the limit of what is permitted or acceptable.

knurl /nɜl/ *n.* **1.** a small ridge or the like, especially one of a series, as on the edge of a thumbscrew to assist in obtaining a firm grip. –*v.t.* **2.** to make knurls or ridges on. –**knurled,** *adj.*

koala /koʊˈalə/ *n.* a tailless, grey, furry, arboreal marsupial, *Phascolarctos cinereus*, of eastern Australia, about 75 cm long.

Kobe beef /'koʊbi bif/ *n.* a special grade of Wagyu beef from Kobe in Japan, noted for its fine marbling of fat and its tenderness.

koel /'koʊəl/ *n.* a cuckoo, *Eudynamys scolopacea*, of Asia, New Guinea, and northern Australia, which migrates to eastern Australian coastal areas during summer; the male is glossy blue-black with a conspicuously long tail and a distinctive 'cooee' call.

kofta /'kɒftə/ *n.* an Indian dish of seasoned minced meat, shaped into small balls and cooked.

kohl /koʊl/ *n.* a powder, used to darken the eyelids, emphasise eyebrows, etc.

koi /kɔɪ/ *n.* any of various colourful cultivated forms of the common carp, *Cyprinus carpio*, as developed in Japan and other parts of eastern temperate Asia.

komodo dragon /kəˌmoʊdoʊ 'dræɡən/ *n.* a giant monitor, *Varanus komodoensis*, of the island of Komodo in Indonesia; up to 3.5 m long.

kon-tiki /kɒn-'tiki/ *n.* *NZ* a small raft used to float fishing lines offshore.

kook /kuk/ *n.* *Colloq.* a strange or eccentric person. –**kooky,** *adj.*

kookaburra /'kʊkəbʌrə/ *n.* **1.** a large brown and white kingfisher, the **laughing kookaburra**, *Dacelo novaeguineae*, noted for its loud call resembling human laughter; native to eastern mainland Australia and introduced into south-western WA and Tasmania; giant kingfisher; laughing jackass. **2.** a similar bird, the **blue-winged kookaburra**, *Dacelo leachii*, with a pale head streaked with brown, blue wing patches and a blue rump, found in tropical northern Australia and New Guinea; howling jackass.

Koori /'kʊri/ *n.* **1.** an Aboriginal person of southern NSW and Victoria. Compare **Anangu, Murri, Nunga, Nyungar, Yamatji, Yolngu. 2.** any Aboriginal person. Also, **Koorie.**

Koran /kɔˈran, kə-/ *n.* the sacred scripture of Islam, believed by Muslims to contain revelations made in Arabic by Allah directly to Mohammed. Also, **Qur'an.** –**Koranic** /kɔˈrænɪk/, *adj.*

koru /'kɔru/ *n.* a spiral design occurring frequently in Maori carving and tattooing, leading to a loop motif like the top of an uncurling fern frond.

kosher /'koʊʃə, 'kɒʃə/ *adj.* **1.** fit, lawful, or ritually permitted, according to the Jewish law; used of food and vessels for food ritually proper for use, especially of meat slaughtered in accordance with the law of Moses. **2.** (of shops, houses, etc.) selling or using food prepared according to the Jewish law. **3.** *Colloq.* genuine or proper. Also, **kasher.**

kowtow /kaʊ'taʊ/ *v.i.* **1.** to knock the forehead on the ground while kneeling, as an act of reverence, worship, apology, etc. **2.** to act in an obsequious manner; show servile deference. –*n.* **3.** the act of kowtowing. Also, **kotow.** –**kowtower,** *n.*

Krishna /'krɪʃnə/ *n.* a Hindu deity, an incarnation of Vishnu; the famous teacher in the Bhagavad-gita.

kudos /'kjudɒs/ *n.* **1.** glory; renown. **2.** status; prestige: *to give your business kudos.*

kumara /'kumərə/ *n.* a sweet potato with a yellow to dark orange flesh; widely grown throughout the Pacific Islands. Also, **kumera.**

kumquat /'kʌmkwɒt/ *n.* → **cumquat.**

kung-fu /kʊŋ-'fu, kʌŋ-'fu/ *n.* an ancient Chinese martial art with fluid hand and leg movements used for self-defence and resembling karate.

kuri /'kuri/ *n.* **1.** one of an extinct breed of New Zealand dogs. **2.** *NZ* a mongrel. Also, **goori, goorie.**

kurrajong /'kʌrədʒɒŋ/ *n.* **1.** a tree, *Brachychiton populneus*, widespread in eastern Australia where it is valued as fodder. **2.** any of a number of species, mostly in the family Malvaceae, as *Hibiscus heterophyllus*, **green kurrajong.** Also, **currajong.**

kurta /'kɜtə/ *n.* a loose-fitting shirt worn by South Asian women with a salwar or churidar and by men with a pyjama.

kylie /'kaɪli/ *n.* a boomerang having one side flat and the other convex.

L l

L, l /ɛl/ *n.* **1.** a consonant, the 12th letter of the English alphabet. **2.** the Roman numeral for 50.

lab /læb/ *n. Colloq.* a laboratory.

lab coat *n.* a protective, knee-length coat of strong material, usually white, worn by workers in laboratories.

label /ˈleɪbəl/ *n.* **1.** a slip of paper or other material for affixing to something to indicate its nature, ownership, destination, etc. **2.** a short word or phrase of description for a person, group, movement, etc. **3.** the trade name, especially of a recording company in the music industry. **4.** the trade name owned by a fashion house or fashion design company: *a label popular with teenager girls.* –*v.t.* (**-belled** *or*, *Chiefly US*, **-beled**, **-belling** *or*, *Chiefly US*, **-beling**) **5.** to affix a label to; mark with a label. **6.** to designate or describe by or on a label: *the bottle was labelled poison.* –**labeller**, *n.*

labium /ˈleɪbiəm/ *n.* (*pl.* **-bia** /-biə/) **1.** a lip or lip-like part. **2.** *Anat.* **a.** either lip, upper or under, of the mouth, respectively called **labium superiore** and **labium inferiore**. **b.** one of the four lip-like folds protecting the orifice of the vulva, including the two outer cutaneous folds (**labia majora**) and the two inner membranous folds (**labia minora**).

labor /ˈleɪbə/ *n.* → **labour**.

laboratory /ləˈbɒrətri/, *Orig. US* /ˈlæbrətɔri/ *n.* (*pl.* **-ries**) **1.** a building or part of a building fitted with apparatus for conducting scientific investigations, experiments, tests, etc., or for manufacturing chemicals, medicines, etc. **2.** any place where or in which similar processes are carried on by natural forces. –*adj.* **3.** serving a function in a laboratory. **4.** relating to techniques of work in a laboratory. –**laboratorial** /ləbɒrəˈtɔriəl/, *adj.*

laborious /ləˈbɔriəs/ *adj.* **1.** requiring much labour, exertion, or perseverance: *a laborious undertaking.* **2.** given to or diligent in labour. –**laboriously**, *adv.* –**laboriousness**, *n.*

labour /ˈleɪbə/ *n.* **1.** physical work done usually for money. **2.** those employed in such work considered as a class, especially as organised in trade unions and political parties. **3.** work, especially of a hard or tiring kind. **4.** a work or job done or to be done: *the 12 labours of Hercules.* **5.** the pains and efforts of childbirth. –*v.i.* **6.** to perform labour; use one's powers of body or mind; work; toil. **7.** to be burdened or troubled: *you are labouring under a misunderstanding.* **8.** (of a ship) to roll or pitch (**pitch**[1] def. 12) heavily. –*v.t.* **9.** to work hard and long at; elaborate: *don't labour the point.* Also, **labor**. –**labouringly, laboringly**, *adv.*

laboured /ˈleɪbəd/ *adj.* **1.** laboriously formed; made or done with laborious pains or care. **2.** not easy or natural. Also, **labored**.

labourer /ˈleɪbərə/ *n.* **1.** someone engaged in work which requires physical effort rather than skill or training: *a farm labourer.* **2.** someone who labours. Also, **laborer**.

labour-intensive *adj.* of or relating to an industry which, while not needing a very large capital investment in plant, etc., requires a comparatively large labour force (opposed to *capital-intensive*). Also, **labor-intensive**.

labrador /ˈlæbrədɔ/ *n.* one of a breed of dogs with black or golden coats, originating in Newfoundland, Canada.

labyrinth /ˈlæbərɪnθ, ˈlæbərənθ, ˈlæbrənθ/ *n.* **1.** a confusing and complicated network of passages in which it is difficult to find one's way or to reach the exit; maze. **2.** a complicated or twisting arrangement, of streets, ideas, etc. –**labyrinthine**, *adj.*

lace /leɪs/ *n.* **1.** a net-like ornamental fabric made of threads by hand or machine. **2.** a cord or string for holding or drawing together, as when passed through holes in opposite edges: *shoelaces.* –*v.t.* (**laced, lacing**) **3.** to fasten, draw together, or compress by means of a lace. **4.** to pass (a cord, etc.) as a lace, as through holes. **5.** to intermix, as coffee with spirits. –**lacy**, *adj.*

lace monitor *n.* a large, common, tree-climbing goanna, *Varanus varius*, black with bands of yellow spots, widely distributed throughout mainland Australia.

lacerate /ˈlæsəreɪt/ *v.t.* **1.** to tear roughly; mangle: *to lacerate the flesh.* **2.** to hurt: *to lacerate a person's feelings.* –**lacerated**, *adj.* –**laceration**, *n.* –**lacerable**, *adj.* –**lacerative**, *adj.*

lachrymose /ˈlækrəmoʊs/ *adj.* **1.** given to shedding tears; tearful. **2.** suggestive of or tending to cause tears; mournful. –**lachrymosely**, *adv.*

lack /læk/ *n.* **1.** deficiency or absence of something requisite, desirable, or customary: *lack of money; lack of skill.* **2.** something lacking or wanting: *skilled labour was the chief lack.* –*v.t.* **3.** to be deficient in, destitute of, or without: *to lack strength.* **4.** to fall short by the amount of: *the vote lacks three to be a majority.* –*v.i.* **5.** to be absent, as something requisite or desirable.

lackadaisical /lækəˈdeɪzɪkəl/ *adj.* **1.** careless and indifferent. **2.** lacking life and spirit; listless. –**lackadaisically**, *adv.* –**lackadaisicalness**, *n.*

lackey /ˈlæki/ *n.* (*pl.* **-eys**) **1.** a footman or liveried manservant. **2.** a servile follower.

lacklustre /ˈlæklʌstə, lækˈlʌstə/ *adj.* lacking lustre or brightness; dull. Also, *US*, **lackluster**.

laconic /ləˈkɒnɪk/ *adj.* using few words; expressing much in few words; concise. Also, **laconical**. –**laconism**, *n.* –**laconically**, *adv.*

lacquer /ˈlækə/ *n.* **1.** a protective coating consisting of a resin and/or a cellulose ester dissolved in a volatile solvent, sometimes with pigment added. **2.** any of various resinous varnishes, especially a natural varnish obtained from a Japanese tree, *Rhus verniciflua*, used to produce a highly polished, lustrous coating on wood, etc. **3.** hairspray. –**lacquerer**, *n.*

lacrosse /ləˈkrɒs/ *n.* a ball game of Native American origin played by two teams of ten players each, who strive to send a ball through a goal by means of long-handled racquets.

lact- a word element meaning 'milk'. Also, **lacto-**.

lactate /lækˈteɪt/ *v.i.* (of mammals) to produce milk. –**lactation**, *n.*

lactic /ˈlæktɪk/ *adj.* relating to or obtained from milk.

lactic acid *n.* **1.** *Chem.* hydroxy acid, $CH_3CHOHCOOH$, found in sour milk. **2.** *Biochem.* an end product of anaerobic glycolysis.

lacto- variant of **lact-**, before consonants.

lactose /ˈlæktoʊz, -oʊs/ *n.* a crystalline disaccharide, $C_{12}H_{22}O_{11}$, present in milk, used as a food and in medicine.

lacuna /lə'kjunə, -'ku-/ *n.* (*pl.* **-nae** /-ni/ *or* **-nas**) **1.** a pit or cavity; an interstitial or intercellular space as in plant or animal tissue. **2.** a gap or hiatus, as in a manuscript.

lad /læd/ *n.* **1.** a boy or youth. **2.** *Colloq.* a devil-may-care, dashing man; a libertine. **3.** *Colloq.* a young man typically wearing brand-name clothing and presenting an image of an aggressive troublemaker.

ladder /'lædə/ *n.* **1.** a structure of wood, metal, or rope, with two sidepieces joined by bars, allowing a person to climb up or down. **2.** a line in a stocking, etc., where stitches have come undone. **3.** a means of rising, as to greatness: *ladder of success.* **4.** a ranking in order: *low on the social ladder.* **5.** *Sport* a listing of teams in order of their present placing in a long-running competition: *this week Gordon heads the ladder. –v.t.* **6.** to cause a ladder in (a stocking). *–v.i.* **7.** (of a stocking) to develop a ladder.

lade /leɪd/ *v.t.* **1.** to put (something) on or in as a burden, load, or cargo; load. **2.** to load oppressively; burden: *laden with responsibilities.* **3.** to fill abundantly: *trees laden with fruit.* **4.** to lift or throw in or out, as a fluid, with a ladle or other utensil.

ladette /læ'det/ *n. Colloq.* a young female partner of a lad (def. 3), with similar dress style and behaviour.

ladle /'leɪdl/ *n.* **1.** a long-handled utensil with a dish-shaped or cup-shaped bowl for dipping or conveying liquids. **2.** *Metallurgy* a bucket-like container for transferring molten metal. *–v.t.* **3.** to dip or convey with or as with a ladle. **–ladleful,** *n.* **–ladler,** *n.*

lady /'leɪdi/ *n.* (*pl.* **-dies**) **1.** a woman of good family or social position, or of good breeding, refinement, etc. (correlative of *gentleman*). **2.** a polite term for any woman: *the ladies should go to the left.* **3.** (*upper case*) **a.** a less formal substitute, often used conversationally, for the specific title and rank of a countess, marchioness, viscountess or baroness, which title she may hold in her own right, by marriage, or by courtesy. **b.** the title, prefixed to the given name of daughters of a duke, marquess, or earl. **c.** the courtesy title of the wife of a knight or a baronet. **d.** a prefix to a title of honour or respect: *Lady Mayoress.* **4.** (*usu. upper case*) **a.** a prefix to the names of allegorical personages: *Lady Luck.* **b.** a prefix to the name of a goddess. **5.** a woman: *a prominent lady.* **6.** a wife. **7.** a woman who has proprietary rights or authority, as over a manor (correlative of *lord*). **8.** a woman who is the object of chivalrous devotion. *–adj.* **9.** being a woman: *a lady reporter. –phr.* **10. Our Lady,** the Virgin Mary. **11. the lady of the house,** the principal woman in a household (opposed to *the man of the house*).

ladybird /'leɪdibɜd/ *n.* a beetle of the family Coccinellidae, of graceful form and delicate colouration. The larvae feed upon plant lice and small insects. Also, **lady beetle;** *US,* **ladybug.**

lady-in-waiting *n.* (*pl.* **ladies-in-waiting**) a woman who is in attendance upon a queen or princess.

lag[1] /læg/ *v.i.* (**lagged, lagging**) **1.** to decrease, wane, or flag: *his interest in the project is lagging. –n.* **2.** *Mechanics* the amount of retardation of some movement. *–phr.* **3. lag behind,** to fall behind; hang back. **–lagger,** *n.*

lag[2] /læg/ *Colloq. –v.t.* (**lagged, lagging**) **1.** to send to prison. **2.** to arrest. **3.** to report the misdemeanours of (someone). *–n.* **4.** a convict, especially a habitual criminal: *an old lag.* **5.** a term of penal servitude.

lag[3] /læg/ *n.* **1.** one of the staves or strips which form the periphery of a wooden drum, the casing of a boiler, etc. *–v.t.* (**lagged, lagging**) **2.** to cover, as pipes, to prevent heat loss.

lager /'lagə/ *n.* a German type of beer brewed by the bottom-fermentation method and stored for up to several months. Also, **lager beer.**

laggard /'lægəd/ *adj.* **1.** lagging; backward; slow. *–n.* **2.** someone who lags; lingerer. **–laggardly,** *adv.* **–laggardness,** *n.*

lagoon /lə'gun/ *n.* any small, pond-like body of water, especially one communicating with a larger body of water, as the expanse of water inside a coral atoll. **–lagoonal,** *adj.*

laid /leɪd/ *v.* past tense and past participle of **lay**[1].

laid-back *adj.* relaxed; nonchalant; at ease. Also, **laidback.**

lain /leɪn/ *v.* past participle of **lie**[2].

lair[1] /lɛə/ *n.* **1.** the den or resting place of a wild beast. **2.** a place in which to lie or rest; a bed.

lair[2] /lɛə/ *n. Aust., NZ Colloq.* a flashily dressed young man of brash and vulgar behaviour.

laird /lɛəd/ *n.* (in Scotland) a landed proprietor. **–lairdship,** *n.*

lairy /'lɛəri/ *adj.* (**-rier, -riest**) *Colloq.* **1.** exhibitionistic; flashy. **2.** vulgar.

laissez faire /ˌleɪseɪ 'fɛə/ *n.* **1.** the theory or system of government that holds that economic systems best govern themselves and that governments should therefore intervene as little as possible in economic affairs. **2.** the doctrine of non-interference, especially in the conduct of others. Also, **laisser faire. –laissez-faire, laisser-faire,** *adj.*

laity /'leɪəti/ *n.* **1.** layperson, as distinguished from a member of the clergy. **2.** the people outside a particular profession, as distinguished from those belonging to it.

lake[1] /leɪk/ *n.* **1.** a body of water (fresh or salt) of considerable size, surrounded by land. **2.** some similar body of water or other liquid.

lake[2] /leɪk/ *n.* **1.** any of various pigments prepared from animal, vegetable, or coal-tar colouring matters by union (chemical or other) with metallic compounds. **2.** a red pigment prepared from lac or cochineal by combination with a metallic compound.

laksa /'lʌksə/ *n.* a spicy Malay dish consisting of fine rice vermicelli, vegetables, and often seafood, meat or tofu, served in a soup.

lama /'lamə/ *n.* a priest or monk of the form of Buddhism prevailing in the Xizang Autonomous Region (Tibet), Mongolia, etc.

lamb /læm/ *n.* **1.** a young sheep. **2.** the meat of a young sheep with no permanent teeth, about 12 months old. **3.** someone who is young, gentle, meek, innocent, etc. **4.** someone who is easily cheated, especially an inexperienced speculator. *–v.i.* **5.** to give birth to a lamb. *–phr.* **6. lamb down, a.** to tend (ewes) at lambing time. **b.** *Aust. Colloq.* to spend (money) in a reckless or lavish fashion, especially of shearers in a drinking spree at the end of the shearing season. **c.** *Aust., NZ Colloq.* to induce (someone) to spend in a reckless fashion. **d.** *Colloq.* to swindle; cheat; fleece.

lambaste /læm'beɪst/ *v.t.* **1.** to beat severely. **2.** to scold; berate. Also, **lambast** /læm'bæst/.

lambent /'læmbənt/ *adj.* **1.** running or moving lightly over a surface: *lambent tongues of flame.* **2.** playing lightly and brilliantly over a subject: *lambent wit.* **3.** softly bright: *a steady, lambent light.* **–lambency,** *n.* **–lambently,** *adv.*

lame /leɪm/ *adj.* **1.** crippled or physically disabled, as a person or animal, especially in the foot or leg so as to limp or walk with difficulty. **2.** defective in quality or quantity; insufficient: *a lame excuse.* **–lamely,** *adv.* **–lameness,** *n.*

lamé /'lameɪ/ *n.* an ornamental fabric in which metallic threads are woven with silk, wool, artificial fibres, or cotton.

lament /lə'mɛnt/ *v.t.* **1.** to feel or express sorrow or regret for; mourn for or over: *to lament someone's absence*; *to lament one's folly. –v.i.* **2.** (sometimes fol. by *over*) to

feel, show, or express grief, sorrow, or sad regret. –*n.*
3. an expression of grief or sorrow. **4.** a formal
expression of sorrow or mourning, especially in verse
or song; an elegy or dirge. –**lamentable**, *adj.* –**lamentation**, *n.* –**lamenter**, *n.*

lamina /ˈlæmənə/ *n.* (*pl.* **-nae** /-ni/ *or* **-nas**) **1.** a thin plate,
scale, or layer. **2.** a layer or coat lying over another,
applied to the plates of minerals, bones, etc.

laminate /ˈlæməneɪt/ *v.t.* **1.** to separate or split into thin
layers. **2.** to form (metal) into a lamina, as by beating
or rolling. **3.** to construct by placing layer upon layer.
4. to cover or overlay with laminae.

lamington /ˈlæmɪŋtən/ *n.* an Australian cake confection
made by covering a cube of sponge cake in chocolate
icing and shredded coconut.

lamp /læmp/ *n.* **1.** any of various devices for using an
illuminant, as gas or electricity, or for heating, as by
burning alcohol. **2.** a vessel for containing an flammable liquid, as oil, which is burnt at a wick as a means
of illumination. **3.** any source as of intellectual or
spiritual light.

lampoon /læmˈpun/ *n.* **1.** a malicious or virulent satire
upon a person, institution, government, etc., in either
prose or verse. –*v.t.* **2.** to assail in a lampoon. –**lam-
pooner, lampoonist**, *n.* –**lampoonery**, *n.*

lamprey /ˈlæmpri/ *n.* (*pl.* **-reys** *or* **-rey**) any of the eel-like
jawless fishes of the class Agnatha. Some species are
parasitic, attaching themselves to fishes and rasping a
hole in the flesh with their horny teeth so that they can
suck the blood of the host.

lance /læns, lans/ *n.* **1.** a long, shafted weapon with
a metal head, used by mounted soldiers in charging.
2. an implement resembling the weapon, as a spear for
killing a harpooned whale. **3.** a lancet. –*v.t.* (**lanced,
lancing**) **4.** to open with, or as if with, a lancet: *to lance
an abscess.* **5.** to pierce with a lance.

lance corporal *n. Army* **1.** a non-commissioned officer
in the Australian Army ranking below corporal; the
lowest non-commissioned officer rank. **2.** the rank.
Abbrev.: LCPL

lancet /ˈlænsət, ˈlans-/ *n.* a small surgical instrument,
usually sharp-pointed and two-edged, for opening
abscesses, etc.

lancewood /ˈlænswʊd, ˈlans-/ *n.* **1.** the tough, elastic
wood of any of various trees, as *Harpullia pendula* and
Albizia basaltica. **2.** *NZ* a tree, *Pseudopanax crassifolium,* an immature form of which has distinctive
lanceolate leaves.

land /lænd/ *n.* **1.** the solid substance of the earth's surface.
2. the exposed part of the earth's surface, as distinguished from the submerged part: *to travel by land.*
3. ground, especially with reference to quality, character, or use: *forest land.* **4.** *Law* an area of ground
together with any trees, crops or permanently attached
buildings and including the air above and the soil beneath. **5.** *Econ.* natural resources as a factor of production. **6.** a part of the earth's surface marked off by
natural or political boundaries or the like; a region or
country. **7.** a realm or domain. **8.** *Chiefly US Colloq.*
(*euphemistic*) Lord: *land's sake; my land.* –*v.t.* **9.** to
bring to or put on land or shore: *to land passengers or
goods from a vessel.* **10.** to bring into, or cause to arrive
in, any place, position, or condition. **11.** *Colloq.* to secure; make certain of; gain or obtain: *to land a job.*
12. *Angling* to bring (a fish) to land, or into a boat, etc.,
as with a hook or a net. –*v.i.* **13.** to come to land or
shore: *the boat lands at Devonport.* **14.** to go or come
ashore from a ship or boat. **15.** to alight upon the
ground as from an aeroplane, a train, or after a jump or
the like. **16.** to come to rest or arrive in any place,
position, or condition. **17.** to hit or strike and come to
rest on the surface of something: *the plane landed in*

water. –*phr.* **18. be on the land**, to own, manage, or
work on a farm, etc. **19. land on one's feet, a.** to have
good luck. **b.** to emerge successfully from an adverse
situation. **20. land someone with**, to give someone (an
unwanted or difficult task): *the principal landed him
with the job of reorganisation.* **21. make land**, to reach
the land after a sea voyage. **22. see how the land lies**, to
investigate a situation, circumstances, etc. **23. the land**,
agricultural areas as opposed to urban.

land claim *n.* **1.** a claim for ownership of land. **2.** a claim
by an Indigenous community for ownership of land
under native title.

landfall /ˈlændfɔl/ *n.* **1.** an approach to or sighting of
land. **2.** the land sighted or reached.

landfill /ˈlændfɪl/ *n.* **1.** material as garbage, building
refuse, etc., deposited under layers of earth to raise the
level of the site. **2.** the area raised in this fashion.

landform /ˈlændfɔm/ *n.* any of the numerous features
which make up the surface of the earth, as plain,
plateau, canyon.

landing /ˈlændɪŋ/ *n.* **1. a.** the act of arriving on land as by
a plane or jumper. Compare **take-off. b.** the act of
arriving on shore as by a sea traveller. **2.** a place where
persons or goods are landed, as from a ship. **3.** *Archit.*
a. the floor at the head or foot of a flight of stairs. **b.** a
platform between flights of stairs.

landlady /ˈlændleɪdi/ *n.* (*pl.* **-ladies**) **1.** a woman who
owns and leases land, buildings, etc. **2.** a woman who
owns or runs an inn, lodging house, or boarding house.

landline /ˈlændlaɪn/ *n.* **1.** a telecommunications line
running under or over the ground. **2.** Also, **landline
telephone.** a telephone using a landline Also, **land line,
fixed line.**

landlocked /ˈlændlɒkt/ *adj.* shut in more or less completely by land.

landlord /ˈlændlɔd/ *n.* **1.** someone who owns and leases
land, buildings, etc., to another. **2.** (formerly) the master
of an inn, lodging house, etc. **3.** a landowner.

landlubber /ˈlændlʌbə/ *n. Naut.* a landsman or raw
seaman. –**landlubberly**, *adj.*

landmark /ˈlændmak/ *n.* **1.** a conspicuous object on land
that serves as a guide, as to vessels at sea. **2.** a prominent or distinguishing feature, part, event, etc.: *the
Eureka rebellion was a landmark in Australian history.*
3. something used to mark the boundary of land. –*adj.*
4. of or relating to a decision, alteration to a law, etc.,
with important and long-lasting consequences.

landmass /ˈlændmæs/ *n.* a body of land, usually extensive, as a large island or continent, surrounded by
water. Also, **land mass.**

landmine /ˈlændmaɪn/ *n.* a device containing an explosive charge, placed in the ground and detonated by
pressure, as that of someone stepping on it or driving
over it.

land mullet *n.* the largest Australian skink, of genus
Egernia, having shiny, dark brown, or black scales;
found in the coastal border region of Qld and NSW.

land rights *pl. n.* rights to possess land, especially the
rights of the original inhabitants of a country to possess
their traditional land.

landscape /ˈlændskeɪp/ *n.* **1.** a view or prospect of rural
scenery, such as is comprehended within the scope or
range of vision from a single point of view. **2.** a piece of
such scenery. **3.** a picture representing natural inland or
coastal scenery. –*v.i.* **4.** to do landscape gardening as a
profession. –**landscaping**, *n.*

landslide /ˈlændslaɪd/ *n.* **1.** the sliding down of a mass of
soil, detritus, or rock on a steep slope. **2.** the mass itself.
3. an election in which a particular candidate or party
receives an overwhelming mass or majority of votes.
4. any overwhelming victory.

land tax *n.* a tax on land, the unimproved value of which exceeds a specified sum.

lane /leɪn/ *n.* **1.** a narrow way or passage between fences, walls, or houses. **2.** a strip of road marked out for a single line of vehicles. **3.** a fixed course followed by ocean-going ships, or by aircraft. **4.** (in racing) each of the spaces between the marked lines which indicate the courses of the competitors. **5.** the narrow alley on which the ball is bowled in tenpin bowling.

language /ˈlæŋgwɪdʒ, ˈlæŋwɪdʒ/ *n.* **1.** communication in the distinctively human manner, using a system of arbitrary symbols with conventionally assigned meanings, as by voice, writing, or sign language. **2.** any set or system of such symbols as used in a more or less uniform fashion by a number of people, who are thus enabled to communicate intelligibly with one another: *to speak the French language; to translate into the Auslan language.* **3.** the non-linguistic means of communication of animals: *the language of birds.* **4.** any basis of communication and understanding: *the language of flowers; the language of laughter transcends all barriers.* **5.** strong language: *no language please.* **6.** the speech or phraseology peculiar to a class, profession, etc. **7.** form or manner of expression: *in his own language.* **8.** speech or expression of a particular character: *flowery language.* **9.** diction or style of writing. *–phr.* **10. speak someone's language**, to be in sympathy with someone; have the same mode of thinking; share the same jargon. **11. speak a different language**, to be out of sympathy or accord, especially as a result of different background, education, etc. **12. speak the same language**, to be in sympathy or accord, especially as a result of shared background, education, etc.

languid /ˈlæŋgwəd/ *adj.* **1.** drooping or flagging from weakness or fatigue; faint. **2.** lacking in spirit or interest; indifferent. **3.** lacking in vigour or activity; slack; dull: *a languid market.* **4.** slow and graceful in movement; luxuriating or voluptuous in idleness. *–***languidly**, *adv.* *–***languidness**, *n.*

languish /ˈlæŋgwɪʃ/ *v.i.* **1.** to become or be weak or feeble; droop or fade. **2.** to lose activity and vigour. **3.** to pine or suffer under any unfavourable conditions: *to languish ten years in a dungeon.* **4.** to pine with desire or longing for. **5.** to assume an expression of tender, sentimental melancholy. *–***languishment**, *n.* *–***languisher**, *n.*

languor /ˈlæŋgə/ *n.* **1.** physical weakness or faintness. **2.** lack of energy; indolence. **3.** emotional softness or tenderness. **4.** lack of spirit. **5.** soothing or oppressive stillness. *–***languorous**, *adj.* *–***languorously**, *adv.*

lank /læŋk/ *adj.* **1.** meagrely slim; lean; gaunt: *a tall, lank man.* **2.** (of plants, etc.) unduly long and slender. **3.** (of hair) straight and limp; not resilient or wiry. *–***lankly**, *adv.* *–***lankness**, *n.*

lanky /ˈlæŋki/ *adj.* (**-kier**, **-kiest**) ungracefully tall and thin; rangy. *–***lankily**, *adv.* *–***lankiness**, *n.*

lanolin /ˈlænələn/ *n.* a fatty substance, extracted from wool, used in ointments. Also, **lanoline** /ˈlænəlin/.

lantana /lænˈtanə/ *n.* any plant of the mostly tropical genus *Lantana*, including species much cultivated for their aromatic yellow or orange flowers, as *L. camara*, which has become a troublesome weed in tropical and subtropical regions.

lantern /ˈlæntən/ *n.* **1.** a transparent or translucent case for enclosing a light and protecting it from the wind, rain, etc. **2.** the chamber at the top of a lighthouse, surrounding the light.

lanyard /ˈlænjəd/ *n.* **1.** *Naut.* a short rope or cord for securing or holding something, especially a rope rove through deadeyes to secure and tighten rigging. **2.** a loop of webbing worn round the neck with an often detachable extension fitted with a clip, split key ring or similar device for attaching an ID card, keys, etc. **3.** a woven coloured cord worn around the shoulder of military (or some other) uniforms. Colours denote the regiment, corps, etc. Also, **laniard**.

lap¹ /læp/ *n.* **1.** the part of the clothing that lies on the front portion of the body from the waist to the knees when one sits. **2.** this portion of the body, especially as the place in or on which something is held or a child is nursed, cherished, etc. **3.** that in which anything rests or reposes, or is nurtured or fostered. **4.** an area of control or responsibility: *the task was dropped in my lap.* **5.** a lap-like or hollow place, as a hollow among hills. **6.** the front part of a skirt, especially as held up to contain something. **7.** a loose border or fold. **8.** a part of a garment which projects or extends over another. *–phr.* **9. in the lap of luxury**, in affluent circumstances. **10. in the lap of the gods**, unpredictable; controlled by chance.

lap² /læp/ *verb* (**lapped**, **lapping**) *–v.t.* **1.** to lay (something) partly over something underneath. **2.** to lie partly over (something underneath); overlap. **3.** to get a lap or more ahead of (a competitor) in racing. **4.** to cut or polish (a gem, etc.) with a lap (def. 9). *–v.i.* **5.** to fold or wind round something. **6.** to lie upon and reach beyond a thing. *–n.* **7.** the act of lapping or of overlapping. **8.** a single round or circuit of the course in racing. **9.** a rotating wheel with a polishing powder on its surface, used for gems, cutlery, etc. See **lapidary**. *–***lapper**, *n.*

lap³ /læp/ *verb* (**lapped**, **lapping**) *–v.t.* **1.** (of water) to wash against or beat upon (something) with a lapping sound. **2.** Also, **lap up**. to take up (liquid) with the tongue; lick up. *–v.i.* **3.** (of water) to wash with a sound as of licking up a liquid. **4.** to take up liquid with the tongue; lick up a liquid. *–n.* **5.** the act of lapping liquid. **6.** the lapping of water against something. **7.** the sound of this. *–phr.* **8. lap up**, to receive and accept avidly. *–***lapper**, *n.*

lap band *n. Med.* a band to restrict the amount contained by the stomach, so as to reduce food intake as a measure to combat obesity.

lap dance *n.* an erotic dance or striptease performed while sitting on the lap of a customer. *–***lap dancer**, *n.* *–***lap dancing**, *n.*

lapel /ləˈpɛl/ *n.* part of a garment folded back on the breast, especially a continuation of a coat collar. *–***lapelled**, *adj.*

lapidary /ˈlæpədəri/ *n.* (*pl.* **-ries**) **1.** someone who cuts, polishes, and engraves stones, especially precious stones. **2.** an expert on gems. *–adj.* **3.** relating to the cutting or engraving of stones.

lapis lazuli /læpəs ˈlæzjəli, læpəs ˈlæzjəlai/ *n.* **1.** a deep blue stone containing sodium, aluminium, calcium, sulphur, and silicon, and consisting of a mixture of several minerals, used chiefly for ornamental purposes. **2.** sky blue; azure.

lapse /læps/ *n.* **1.** a slip or small mistake: *a lapse of concentration.* **2.** a failure through some fault or bad management: *a lapse of justice.* **3.** a passing away, especially of time: *a lapse of three years.* **4.** a slipping or sinking, often to a lower degree or moral condition: *a lapse into drunkenness.* **5.** a falling into disuse. *–v.i.* (**lapsed**, **lapsing**) **6.** to pass slowly, silently, or by degrees. **7.** *Law* (of an estate, right, etc.) to fall away, or pass on (to someone else) owing to certain conditions not being met. **8.** to fall or sink to a lower grade or condition. **9.** to fall into disuse. **10.** to make a slip or error. **11.** (of time) to pass away. *–***lapsable**, *adj.* *–***lapser**, *n.*

laptop /ˈlæptɒp/ *n.* **1.** a portable computer, small enough to be operated while held on one's knees. *–adj.* **2.** of or relating to a laptop: *laptop displays are becoming much clearer.*

lapwing /ˈlæpwɪŋ/ n. **1.** a common wading bird, *Vanellus vanellus*, of Europe, northern Africa and parts of the Middle East, having green wings and a long crest. **2.** any of various other birds of the genus *Vanellus*, family Charadriidae, as the **masked lapwing**, *V. miles*, of Australasia.

larapinta /læraˈpɪntə/ n. a dunnart, *Sminthopsis macrura*, of Australian central areas, having a long tail and a prominent facial stripe.

larceny /ˈlasəni/ n. (*pl.* **-nies**) *Law* the wrongful taking and carrying away of the personal goods of another with intent to deprive him or her of them permanently. –**larcenous**, *adj.*

lard /lad/ n. **1.** rendered pig fat, especially the internal fat of the abdomen. –*v.t.* **2.** to intersperse with something for improvement or ornamentation. –**lardaceous**, *adj.* –**lardy**, *adj.*

larder /ˈladə/ n. a room or place where food is kept; a pantry.

large /ladʒ/ adj. (**larger**, **largest**) **1.** being of more than common size, amount, or number. **2.** of great scope or range; extensive or broad: *large powers.* **3.** on a great scale: *a large producer.* **4.** grand or pompous. –*adv.* **5.** *Naut.* before the wind; with the wind free or on the quarter, or in such a direction that all sails will draw. –*phr.* **6. at large**, **a.** at liberty; free from restraint or confinement: *the murderer is at large.* **b.** at length; to a considerable length: *to discourse at large on a subject.* **c.** as a whole; in general: *the country at large.* **7. in (the) large**, on a large scale: *viewed in the large.* –**largish**, *adj.* –**largeness**, *n.*

largely /ˈladʒli/ adv. **1.** to a great extent; in great part. **2.** in great quantity; much.

largesse /laˈdʒɛs, -ˈʒɛs/ n. generous bestowal of gifts. Also, **largess**.

lark[1] /lak/ n. any of numerous singing birds, of the family Alaudidae, mostly of Eurasia and Africa, but also found in America and Australia, characterised by an unusually long, straight hind claw, especially the skylark, *Alauda arvensis*.

lark[2] /lak/ n. a merry or hilarious adventure; prank. –**larker**, *n.* –**larksome**, *adj.*

larrikin /ˈlærəkən/ n. *Aust.*, *NZ* **1.** *Obsolesc.* a lout, a hoodlum. **2.** a mischievous young person. –**larrikinism**, *n.* –**larrikinish**, *adj.*

larva /ˈlavə/ n. (*pl.* **larvae** /ˈlavi/ or **larvas**) **1.** *Entomology* the young of any insect which undergoes metamorphosis. **2.** any animal in an analogous immature form. **3.** the young of any invertebrate animal.

laryngitis /lærənˈdʒaɪtəs/ n. *Pathol.* inflammation of the larynx. –**laryngitic** /lærənˈdʒɪtɪk/, *adj.*

laryngo- a combining form of **larynx** as in *laryngoscope*. Also, (*before vowels*), **laryng-**.

larynx /ˈlærɪŋks/ n. (*pl.* **larynges** /ləˈrɪndʒiz/ or **larynxes**) *Zool.*, *Anat.* the cavity at the upper end of the trachea or windpipe containing the vocal cords.

lasagne /ləˈsanjə, ləˈzanjə/ n. **1.** a form of pasta cut into flat sheets. **2.** any of several dishes made with this, especially with minced meat, tomato, and cheese. Also, **lasagna**.

lascivious /ləˈsɪviəs/ adj. **1.** inclined to lust; wanton or lewd. **2.** inciting to lust or wantonness. –**lasciviously**, *adv.* –**lasciviousness**, *n.*

laser /ˈleɪzə/ n. a device for producing a coherent, monochromatic, high-intensity beam of radiation of a frequency within, or near to, the range of visible light; an optical maser.

laser disc n. → **optical disc**. Also, **laser disk**.

laser pointer n. a pen-shaped device which projects a point of light, used to direct the attention of an audience to material on a board, screen, etc.

laser printer n. a high-speed sophisticated printer that uses a laser to form dot-matrix patterns on paper which are then covered with fused metallic particles by an electronic process, a page at a time.

lash[1] /læʃ/ n. **1.** the flexible part of a whip; the piece of cord or the like forming the extremity of a whip. **2.** a swift stroke or blow, with a whip, etc., as a punishment: *sentenced to fifty lashes.* **3.** a sharp stroke given to the feelings, etc., as of censure or satire. **4.** a swift dashing or sweeping movement; a switch: *a lash of an animal's tail.* **5.** a violent beating or impact, as of waves, rain, etc., against something. **6.** an eyelash. **7.** *Colloq.* **a.** (*taboo*) an act of sexual intercourse. **b.** anything which thrills or pleases. –*v.t.* **8.** to strike or beat, now usually with a whip or something slender and flexible. **9.** to beat violently or sharply against. **10.** to drive by strokes of a whip or the like. **11.** to dash, fling, or switch suddenly and swiftly. **12.** to assail severely with words, as by censure or satire. –*v.i.* **13.** to move suddenly and swiftly; rush, dash, or flash. –*phr.* **14. have a lash at**, *Colloq.* to attempt. **15. lash out**, **a.** (sometimes fol. by *at*) to strike out vigorously, as with a weapon, whip, or the like. **b.** (sometimes fol. by *at*) to burst into violent action or speech. **c.** to spend money freely. –**lasher**, *n.*

lash[2] /læʃ/ v.t. to bind or fasten with a rope, cord, or the like. –**lasher**, *n.*

lashing[1] /ˈlæʃɪŋ/ n. **1.** a whipping. **2.** a severe scolding. **3.** (*pl.*) *Colloq.* (sometimes fol. by *of*) large quantities; plenty.

lashing[2] /ˈlæʃɪŋ/ n. a binding or fastening with a rope or the like. **2.** the rope or the like used.

lass /læs/ n. **1.** a girl or young woman. **2.** any woman. **3.** a female sweetheart.

lassi /ˈlasi/ n. a sweet or savoury Indian drink made from yoghurt or buttermilk, mixed with water.

lassitude /ˈlæsətjud, -tʃud/ n. weariness of body or mind from strain, oppressive climate, etc.; languor.

lasso /læˈsu/ n. (*pl.* **-sos** or **-soes**) a long rope or line of hide or other material, with a running noose at one end, used for catching horses, cattle, etc. –**lassoer**, *n.*

last[1] /last/ adj. **1.** occurring or coming latest, or after all others, as in time, order, or place: *the last three lines on the page.* **2.** latest; next before the present; most recent: *last week.* **3.** being the only remaining: *one's last dollar.* **4.** final: *in his last hours.* **5.** conclusive: *the last word in an argument.* **6.** utmost; extreme. **7.** coming after all others in importance, suitability, or likelihood. –*adv.* **8.** after all others. **9.** on the most recent occasion. **10.** in the end; finally; in conclusion. –*n.* **11.** that which is last. **12.** *Colloq.* the final mention or appearance: *to see the last of that woman.* **13.** the end or conclusion. –*phr.* **14. at (long) last**, after much has intervened. **15. breathe one's last**, to die. **16. on one's** (or **its**) **last legs**, on the verge of collapse.

last[2] /last/ v.i. **1.** to go on, or continue in progress, existence or life; endure: *so long as the world lasts.* **2.** to continue unexpended or unexhausted; be enough (*for*): *while our money lasts.* **3.** to continue in force, vigour, effectiveness, etc.: *to last in a race.* –**laster**, *n.*

last[3] /last/ n. **1.** a model of the human foot, of wood or other material, on which boots or shoes are shaped, as in the making, or repaired. –*v.t.* **2.** to shape on or fit to a last. –**laster**, *n.*

last-ditch adj. **1.** made in or as a final and desperate effort. **2.** fought with desperate and uncompromising spirit.

last post *n.* **1.** a signal on a bugle giving notice to retire for the night. **2.** a similar bugle call sounded at military funerals.

last sacraments *pl. n.* the sacraments of penance, the Eucharist and extreme unction, when administered to a dying person. Also, **last rites**.

latch /lætʃ/ *n.* **1.** a device for holding a door, gate, or the like closed, consisting basically of a bar falling or sliding into a catch, groove, hole, etc. –*v.t.* **2.** to close or fasten with a latch. –*v.i.* **3.** to fasten tightly so that the latch is in position. –*phr.* **4. latch on to**, *Colloq.* **a.** to fasten or attach (oneself) to. **b.** to understand; comprehend.

late /leɪt/ *adj.* **1.** occurring, coming, or being after the usual or proper time: *late frosts*. **2.** continued until after the usual time or hour; protracted: *a late session*. **3.** far advanced in time: *a late hour*. **4.** immediately preceding that which now exists: *his late residence*. **5.** recently deceased: *the late president*. **6.** occurring at an advanced stage in life: *a late marriage*. **7.** belonging to an advanced period or stage in the history or development of something: *Late Latin*. **8.** recent: *a late model car*. –*adv.* **9.** after the usual or proper time, or after delay: *to come late*. **10.** until after the usual time or hour; until a late hour at night: *to work late*. **11.** at or to an advanced time, period, or stage. **12.** recently but no longer. –*phr.* **13. of late**, recently. –**latish**, *adj.* –**lateness**, *n.*

lately /ˈleɪtli/ *adv.* of late; recently; not long since.

latent /ˈleɪtnt/ *adj.* **1.** hidden; concealed; present, but not visible or apparent: *latent ability*. **2.** *Pathol.* (of an infectious agent) remaining in a resting or hidden phase; dormant. **3.** *Psychol.* below the surface, but potentially able to achieve expression. **4.** *Bot.* (of buds which are not externally manifest) dormant or undeveloped. –**latency**, *n.* –**latently**, *adv.*

lateral /ˈlætərəl, ˈlætrəl/ *adj.* of or relating to the side; situated at, proceeding from, or directed to a side: *a lateral view*. –**laterally**, *adv.*

lateral thinking *n.* a way of thinking which seeks the solution to a problem by making associations with other apparently unrelated areas, rather than by pursuing one logical train of thought.

laterite /ˈlætəraɪt/ *n.* a reddish ferruginous soil formed in tropical regions by the decomposition of the underlying rock.

latex /ˈleɪtɛks/ *n.* (*pl.* **latices** /ˈlætəsiz/ *or* **latexes** /ˈleɪtɛksəz/) **1.** *Bot.* a milky liquid in certain plants, as milkweeds, poppies, the plants yielding indiarubber, etc., which coagulates on exposure to the air. **2.** any emulsion of particles of synthetic rubber or plastic in water.

lath /laθ/ *n.* (*pl.* **laths** /laðz, laθs/) a thin, narrow strip of wood used with others like it to form a groundwork for supporting the slates or other covering of a roof or the plastering of a wall or ceiling, to construct latticework, and for other purposes. –**lathing**, **lathwork**, *n.*

lathe /leɪð/ *n.* a machine for use in working metal, wood, etc., which holds the material and rotates it about a horizontal axis so that it can be shaped with a handheld tool.

lather /ˈlæðə/ *n.* **1.** foam or froth made from soap moistened with water, as by a brush for shaving. **2.** foam or froth formed in profuse sweating, as of a horse. –**lathery**, *adj.* –**latherer**, *n.*

latitude /ˈlætətjud, -tʃud/ *n.* **1.** *Geog.* **a.** the angular distance north or south from the equator of a point on the earth's surface, measured on the meridian of the point. **b.** a place or region as marked by this distance. **2.** freedom from narrow restrictions; permitted freedom of action, opinion, etc. **3.** *Photography* the range of

exposures over which proportional representation of subject brightness is obtained.

latrine /ləˈtrin/ *n.* a toilet, especially in a camp, barracks, factory, or the like.

latte /ˈlateɪ/ *n.* → **cafe latte**.

latte liberal *n. Chiefly US* → **chardonnay socialist**.

latter /ˈlætə/ *adj.* **1.** being the second mentioned of two (opposed to *former*): *I prefer the latter proposition to the former*. **2.** more advanced in time; later: *in these latter days of human progress*. **3.** nearer, or comparatively near, to the end or close: *the latter years of one's life*. –*phr.* **4. the latter**, the item or person (out of two) last mentioned.

latter-day *adj.* of a latter or more advanced day or period, or modern: *latter-day problems*.

lattice /ˈlætəs/ *n.* **1.** a structure of crossed wooden or metal strips with open spaces between, used as a screen, fence, etc. **2.** a window, gate, or the like, so constructed. –**latticework**, *n.*

laud /lɔd/ *v.t. Literary* to praise; extol. –**laudable**, *adj.* –**laudatory**, **laudative**, *adj.* –**laudation**, *n.* –**lauder**, *n.*

laudanum /ˈlɔdnəm, ˈlɔdənəm/ *n.* **1.** tincture of opium. **2.** (formerly) any preparation in which opium was the chief ingredient.

laugh /laf/ *v.i.* **1.** to express mirth, amusement, derision, etc., by an explosive, inarticulate sound of the voice, facial expressions, etc. **2.** to experience the emotion so expressed. **3.** to utter a cry or sound resembling the laughing of human beings, as some animals do. –*v.t.* **4.** to utter with laughter. **5.** to drive, put, bring, etc., by or with laughter: *he was laughed off the stage*. –*n.* **6.** the act or sound of laughing, or laughter. **7.** the cry of an animal, as the spotted hyena, or the call of a bird, as a kookaburra, that resembles human laughter. **8.** an expression of mirth, derision, etc. **9.** (*often ironic*) a cause for laughter: *that's a laugh*. –*phr.* **10. don't make me laugh**, an exclamation indicating disbelief. **11. have a good laugh**, (sometimes fol. by *about*) to experience amusement. **12. have the (last) laugh**, to prove ultimately successful; win after an earlier defeat. **13. laugh about** (or **over**), to consider with amusement. **14. laugh at**, **a.** to make fun of; deride; ridicule. **b.** to be sympathetically amused by: *she laughed at his fear of air travel*. **15. laugh fit to kill**, to laugh extremely heartily. **16. laugh in** (or **up**) **one's sleeve**, to laugh inwardly at something. **17. laugh like a drain**, *Colloq.* to laugh loudly. **18. laugh off** (or **away**), to dismiss (a situation, criticism, or the like) by treating lightly or with ridicule. **19. laugh on the other** (or **wrong**) **side of one's face** (or **mouth**), to experience sudden disappointment, chagrin, displeasure, etc., especially after assuming victory or success. **20. laugh out of court**, to dismiss by means of ridicule. –**laugher**, *n.*

laughable /ˈlafəbəl/ *adj.* such as to excite laughter; funny; amusing; ludicrous. –**laughableness**, *n.* –**laughably**, *adv.*

laughing jackass *n.* → **kookaburra** (def. 1).

laughing-stock *n.* a butt for laughter; an object of ridicule.

laugh line *n.* → **laughter line**.

laughter /ˈlaftə/ *n.* **1.** the action or sound of laughing. **2.** an experiencing of the emotion expressed by laughing: *inward laughter*. **3.** an expression or appearance of merriment or amusement.

laughter line *n.* one of the wrinkles found at the corners of the eyes or mouth supposedly formed by a well-established habit of laughter. Also, **laugh line**.

launch¹ /lɔntʃ/ *n.* **1.** a heavy open or half-decked boat. **2.** the largest boat carried by a warship.

launch² /lɔntʃ/ *v.t.* **1.** to set (a boat, newly built ship) afloat; lower or slide into the water. **2.** to begin (a career, course, etc.). **3.** to set going: *to launch a scheme*.

4. to send forth; throw or hurl: *to launch a spear*; *to launch a plane from an aircraft carrier.* **5.** to introduce (a new project, product, etc.) with publicity, etc. *–v.i.* **6.** to burst out or plunge boldly (into action, speech, etc.). **7.** to start out or forth; push out or put forth on the water. *–n.* **8.** the act of launching a boat, glider, etc. **9.** the act of launching a project, product, etc., especially the social occasion which marks this: *a book launch.* **–launcher,** *n.*

launching pad *n.* a base from which a rocket is launched. Also, **launch pad.**

launder /ˈlɔndə/ *v.t.* **1.** to wash and iron (clothes, etc.). **2.** to transfer (funds of suspect or illegal origin) usually to a foreign country, and then later to recover them from sources which give them the appearance of being legitimate. *–v.i.* **3.** to do or wash laundry. *–n.* **4.** (in ore dressing) a passage carrying products of intermediate grade, and residue, which are in water suspension. **–launderer,** *n.* **–laundress,** *n.*

laundry /ˈlɔndri/ *n.* (*pl.* **-dries**) **1.** articles of clothing, etc., to be washed. **2.** the room in a house set aside for the washing of clothes. **3.** the act of laundering.

laurel /ˈlɒrəl/ *n.* **1.** a small evergreen tree, *Laurus nobilis,* of Europe (the **true laurel**), having aromatic leaves used in cookery; sweet bay. **2.** any tree of the same genus (*Laurus*). **3.** Also, **mountain laurel.** any of various trees or shrubs similar to the true laurel belonging to the genus *Kalmia.* **4.** the foliage of the true laurel as an emblem of victory or distinction. **5.** a branch or wreath of it. **6.** (*usu. pl.*) honour won, as by achievement. *–v.t.* (**-relled,** **-relling**) **7.** to adorn or wreathe with laurel. **8.** to honour with marks of distinction. *–phr.* **9. look to one's laurels,** to be aware of the possibility of being excelled by one's rivals. **10. rest on one's laurels,** to be content with present achievements.

laurel wreath *n.* a wreath made from the foliage of the laurel or bay tree, seen as an emblem of distinction.

lava /ˈlavə/ *n.* **1.** the molten or fluid rock (magma), which issues from a volcanic vent. **2.** the igneous rock formed when this solidifies and loses its volatile constituents, occurring in many varieties differing greatly in structure and constitution.

lavash /ləˈvaʃ/ *n.* a type of Armenian flatbread, sometimes unleavened.

lavatory /ˈlævətri/ *n.* (*pl.* **-ries**) **1.** a room fitted with a toilet, and often with other bathroom fittings and furniture. **2.** a toilet or urinal.

lavender /ˈlævəndə/ *n.* **1.** a plant of the genus *Lavandula,* especially *L. augustifolia* (syn. *L. officinalis*), a small shrub, originally native to the Mediterranean region, with spikes of fragrant pale purple flowers, yielding an oil (**oil of lavender**) used in medicine and perfumery. **2.** the dried flowers or other parts of this plant, often placed among linen, etc., for scent or as a preservative. *–adj.* **3.** pale bluish-purple.

lavish /ˈlævɪʃ/ *adj.* **1.** (sometimes fol. by *in, with* or *of*) using or bestowing in great abundance or without stint: *lavish of time*; *lavish in his praise.* **2.** expended, bestowed, or occurring in profusion: *lavish gifts*; *lavish spending.* *–v.t.* **3.** to expend or bestow in great abundance or without stint: *to lavish favours on a person.* **–lavisher,** *n.* **–lavishness,** *n.* **–lavishly,** *adv.*

law /lɔ/ *n.* **1.** the principles and regulations emanating from a government and applicable to a people, whether in the form of legislation or of custom and policies recognised and enforced by judicial decision. **2.** any written or positive rule of conduct, or collection of rules, prescribed under the authority of the state or nation, whether by the people in its constitution, as the **organic law,** or by the legislature in its **statute law,** or by the treaty-making power, or by municipalities in their ordinances or **by-laws. 3.** the controlling influence

of such rules; the condition of society brought about by their observance: *to maintain law and order.* **4.** the institutions and persons collectively responsible for the administration of the legal rules, or an agent that helps maintain the rules. **5.** a system or collection of such rules. **6.** the department of knowledge concerned with these rules; jurisprudence: *to study law.* **7.** the body of rules and legal principles concerned with a particular subject or derived from a particular source: *commercial law*; *the law of torts.* **8.** an act of the supreme legislative body of a state or nation, as distinguished from the constitution. **9.** the principles applied in the courts of common law, as distinguished from equity. **10.** the profession which deals with law and legal procedure: *to practise law.* **11.** legal action; litigation. **12.** any rule or principle of proper conduct or collection of such rules. **13.** (in philosophical and scientific use) **a.** a statement of a relation or sequence of phenomena invariable under the same conditions. **b.** a mathematical rule. *–phr.* **14. be a law unto oneself,** to do what one wishes, without regard for established rules and modes of behaviour. **15. lay down the law,** to tell people authoritatively what to do, or state one's opinions authoritatively. **16. take the law into one's own hands,** to seek justice by one's own means, disregarding usual judicial procedures. **17. the law,** *Colloq.* the police. **18. the Law,** the Mosaic Law (often in contrast to *the Gospel*). **19. the long arm of the law, a.** the power of law-enforcing bodies to catch criminals, even after many years have elapsed. **b.** *Colloq.* the police; a police officer. **–lawless,** *adj.*

lawfare /ˈlɔfɛə/ *n.* the use of international law by a country to attack or criticise another country, especially a superior military power, on moral grounds, that is, by accusing it of having violated international law.

lawful /ˈlɔfəl/ *adj.* **1.** allowed or permitted by law; not contrary to law. **2.** legally qualified or entitled: *lawful king.* **–lawfully,** *adv.* **–lawfulness,** *n.*

lawn[1] /lɔn/ *n.* a stretch of grass-covered land, especially one closely mowed, as near a house, etc. **–lawny,** *adj.*

lawn[2] /lɔn/ *n.* a thin or sheer linen or cotton fabric, either plain or printed. **–lawny,** *adj.*

lawn bowls *n.* a game in which the players roll balls biased or weighted balls along a green in an effort to bring them as near as possible to a stationary ball called the jack.

lawsuit /ˈlɔsut/ *n.* a suit at law; a prosecution of a claim in a law court.

lawyer /ˈlɔijə, ˈlɔiə, ˈlɔjə/ *n.* someone whose profession is to conduct suits in court or to give legal advice and aid.

lax /læks/ *adj.* **1.** lacking in strictness or severity; careless or negligent: *lax morals.* **2.** not rigidly exact or precise; vague: *lax ideas on a subject.* **3.** loose or slack; not tense, rigid, or firm: *a lax cord.* **4.** open or not retentive, as the bowels. **–laxly,** *adv.* **–laxity, laxness,** *n.*

laxative /ˈlæksətɪv/ *Med. –adj.* **1.** mildly purgative. *–n.* **2.** a laxative medicine or agent.

lay[1] /leɪ/ *verb* (**laid,** **laying**) *–v.t.* **1.** to put or place in a position of rest or recumbency: *to lay a book on a desk.* **2.** to bring, throw, or beat down, as from an erect position: *to lay a person low.* **3.** to cause to subside: *to lay the dust.* **4.** to allay, appease, or suppress. **5.** to smooth down or make even: *to lay the nap of cloth.* **6.** to bring forth and deposit (an egg or eggs). **7.** to deposit as a wager; stake; bet: *I'll lay you ten to one.* **8.** to place, set, or cause to be in a particular situation, state, or condition: *she laid her hand on his cheek.* **9.** to place before a person, or bring to a person's notice or consideration: *he laid his case before the commission.* **10.** to put to; place in contiguity; apply: *to lay a hand on a child.* **11.** to set (a trap, etc.). **12.** to place or locate (a scene): *the second act is laid in France.* **13.** to present, bring forward, or prefer, as a claim, charge, etc.

14. to impute, attribute, or ascribe. **15.** to impose as a burden, duty, penalty, or the like: *to lay an embargo on shipments of oil.* **16.** to bring down (a stick, etc.), as on a person, in inflicting punishment. **17.** to dispose or place in proper position or in an orderly fashion: *to lay bricks.* **18.** to set (a table). **19.** to form by twisting strands together, as a rope. **20.** to place on or over a surface, as paint; cover or spread with something else. **21.** to devise or arrange, as a plan. **22.** *Colloq. (taboo)* to have sexual intercourse with. *–v.i.* **23.** to lay eggs. **24.** to wager or bet. **25.** *Naut.* to take a specified position. *–n.* **26.** the way or position in which a thing is laid or lies. **27.** a share of the profits or the catch of a whaling or fishing voyage, distributed to officers and crew. **28.** *Colloq. (taboo)* **a.** an act of sexual intercourse. **b.** a sexual partner (in contexts where performance, willingness, etc., is evaluated): *a good lay; an easy lay. –phr.* **29.** lay aboard, *Naut.* (of a boat) to come alongside a ship. **30.** lay about, to deal or aim blows at. **31.** lay an egg, *Colloq.* **a.** to drop a bomb. **b.** to defecate. **c.** *Theatre* to be a failure. **32.** lay bare, to expose. **33.** lay down, **a.** to put (something) down on the ground; to relinquish. **b.** to record (speech, a track of music, etc.) on a tape or disc. **34.** lay down one's arms, to surrender. **35.** lay hands on, **a.** to assault. **b.** to attempt to heal by placing one's hands on, so as to impart spiritual strength. **c.** to locate and obtain. **36.** lay hold of (or on), to grasp; seize; catch. **37.** lay in, **a.** to build up a store of (provisions, etc.). **b.** *Naut.* to move along a yard, towards the mast. **38.** lay in (there), *Colloq.* to maintain a course of action despite opposition, setbacks, etc. **39.** lay into, *Colloq.* **a.** to attack physically or verbally. **b.** to apply oneself vigorously to. **40.** lay it on, *Colloq.* to chastise someone. **41.** lay it on (with a trowel or a bit thick), *Colloq.* to exaggerate. **42.** lay off, **a.** to put aside. **b.** to dismiss, especially temporarily, as an employee. **c.** to mark or plot off. **d.** *Colloq.* to desist. **e.** *Colloq.* to cease to annoy (someone). **f.** *Racing* (of a bookmaker) to make a bet with another bookmaker to cover projected losses on a race. **g.** to protect a bet or speculation by taking some off-setting risk. **43.** lay on, to provide or supply. **44.** lay oneself open, to expose oneself (to adverse criticism or the like). **45.** lay one's hands on, to obtain; find: *I just can't lay my hands on it at the moment.* **46.** lay out, **a.** to extend at length. **b.** to spread out to the sight, air, etc.; spread out in order. **c.** to stretch out and prepare (a body) for burial. **d.** *Colloq.* to expend (money) for a particular purpose. **e.** to exert (oneself) for some purpose, effect, etc. **f.** to plot or plan out. **g.** *Naut.* to move along a yard, away from the mast. **h.** to strike down, especially to knock unconscious. **47.** lay siege to, to besiege. **48.** lay someone low, *Colloq.* to make someone ill; weaken someone: *the flu laid him low for three weeks.* **49.** lay to, *Naut.* **a.** to check the motion of (a ship). **b.** to put (a ship, etc.) in a dock or other place of safety. **50.** lay up, **a.** to put away, as for future use; store up. **b.** to cause to remain in bed or indoors through illness or injury. **51.** lay waste to, to devastate.

lay² /leɪ/ *v.* past tense of **lie²**.

lay³ /leɪ/ *adj.* **1.** belonging to, relating to, or performed by the people or laity, as distinguished from the clergy: *a lay sermon.* **2.** not belonging to, connected with, or proceeding from a profession, especially the law or medicine.

lay⁴ /leɪ/ *n.* a short narrative or other poem, especially one to be sung.

lay-by *n.* **1.** *Aust., NZ* **a.** the reservation of an article by payment of a cash deposit. **b.** an item so reserved or so purchased. **2.** Also, **lay by.** a part of a road or railway where vehicles may draw up out of the stream of traffic. *–v.t.* (**-byed, -bying**) **3.** *Aust., NZ* to put (something) on lay-by. Also, **layby.**

layer /ˈleɪə/ *n.* **1.** a thickness of some material laid on or spread over a surface; a stratum. **2.** *Hort.* a shoot or twig placed partly under the ground while still attached to the living stock, for the purpose of propagation.

layette /leɪˈɛt/ *n.* a complete outfit of clothing, toilet articles, etc., for a newborn child.

layman /ˈleɪmən/ *n.* (*pl.* **-men**) **1.** a male layperson. **2.** someone who is not a member of a particular profession: *to the layman, computer jargon is unintelligible.*

layout /ˈleɪaʊt/ *n.* **1.** a laying or spreading out. **2.** an arrangement or plan of a location, building, city, etc. **3.** the plan or sketch of a page, magazine, book, advertisement, or the like, indicating the arrangement of materials.

layperson /ˈleɪpɜsən/ *n.* (*pl.* **-people** or **-persons**) **1.** one of the laity; someone who is not a member of the clergy. **2.** someone who is not a member of a particular profession. Also, **lay person.**

Lazarus species /ˈlæzərəs spisiz/ *n.* an organism that is rediscovered alive after being considered to be extinct, as the noisy scrub-bird of south-western Australia.

laze /leɪz/ *v.i.* to be lazy; idle or lounge lazily.

lazy /ˈleɪzi/ *adj.* (**-zier, -ziest**) **1.** disinclined to exertion or work; idle. **2.** slow-moving; sluggish: *a lazy stream.* **–lazily,** *adv.* **–laziness,** *n.*

LCD /ɛl si ˈdi/ *n.* **1.** a method of displaying data continuously (on watches, televisions, computers, calculators, etc.) by means of a liquid-crystal film, sealed between glass plates, which changes its optical properties when a voltage is applied. *–adj.* **2.** of or relating to watches, televisions, calculators, electronic games, etc., which display readings by means of LCD. Also, **lcd.**

LDL /ɛl di ˈɛl/ *n.* a low-density lipoprotein, which forms the greater part of the cholesterol in the blood and which, in large amounts, can cause a build-up of cholesterol on the artery walls. See **bad cholesterol.** Compare **HDL.**

leach /litʃ/ *v.t.* **1.** to cause (water, etc.) to percolate through something. **2.** to remove soluble constituents from (ashes, soil, etc.) by percolation.

lead¹ /lid/ *verb* (**led, leading**) *–v.t.* **1.** to take or conduct on the way; go before or with to show the way. **2.** to conduct by holding and guiding: *to lead a horse by a rope.* **3.** to guide in direction, course, action, opinion, etc.; to influence or induce: *too easily led.* **4.** to conduct or bring (water, wire, etc.) in a particular course. **5.** (of a road, passage, etc.) to serve to bring (a person, etc.) to a place through a region, etc. **6.** to take or bring: *the prisoners were led in.* **7.** to be at the head of, command, or direct (an army, organisation, etc.). **8.** to go at the head of or in advance of (a procession, list, body, etc.); to be first in or go before. **9.** to have the directing or principal part in (a movement, proceedings, etc.). **10.** to begin or open, as a dance, discussion, etc. **11.** to act as leader of (an orchestra, etc.). **12.** to go through or pass (life, etc.): *to lead a dreary existence.* **13.** *Cards* to begin a round, with (a card or suit specified). *–v.i.* **14.** to act as a guide; show the way. **15.** to be led, or submit to being led, as an animal. **16.** to afford passage to a place, etc., as a road, stairway, or the like. **17.** to go first; be in advance. **18.** to take the directing or principal part. **19.** *Boxing* to take the offensive by striking at an opponent. *–n.* **20.** the first or foremost place; position in advance of others. **21.** the extent of advance. **22.** something that leads. **23.** the animals at the front of a moving mob. **24.** a thong or line for holding a dog or other animal in check. **25.** a guiding indication; clue. **26.** precedence. **27.** *Theatre* **a.** the principal part in a play. **b.** the person who plays it. **28.** *Journalism* a short summary serving as an introduction to a news story or article. **29.** *Elect.* a single conductor, often flexible and insulated, used in connections between pieces of electrical apparatus. **30.** *Boxing* the act of taking the offensive by striking at an opponent. **31.** a track or route, especially one followed by travelling stock. **32.** *Mining* **a.** → **lode.** **b.** an auriferous deposit in an old river bed. *–adj.* **33.** solo or dominating as in a musical structure: *lead singer; lead guitar; lead break. –phr.* **34. in the lead,** ahead of others; in advance of others. **35. lead nowhere,** to be an unprofitable and unproductive activity, course of action, etc. **36. lead off, a.** to take the initiative. **b.** *Cards* to make the first play. **37. lead someone a merry chase** (or **dance**), to cause someone unnecessary difficulty or trouble. **38. lead someone by the nose,** to enforce one's will on someone, especially unpleasantly. **39. lead someone on,** to induce or encourage someone to a detrimental or undesirable course of action. **40. lead the way,** to go in advance of others, especially as a guide. **41. lead to** (or **towards**), to afford a passage to (a place, etc.), as a road, stairway, or the like. **42. lead up to,** to prepare gradually for. **43. on the lead,** at the head of travelling stock. **44. take the lead,** to move out in front of others, either to show the way or to win a race.

lead² /lɛd/ *n.* **1.** *Chem.* a heavy, comparatively soft, malleable bluish-grey metal, sometimes found native, but usually combined as sulphide, in galena. *Symbol:* Pb; *relative atomic mass:* 207.19; *atomic number:* 82; *density:* 11.34 at 20°C. **2.** something made of this metal or one of its alloys. **3.** a plumb-bob or mass of lead suspended by a line, as for taking soundings. **4.** bullets; shot. **5.** black lead or graphite. **6.** a small stick of this as used in pencils. **7.** Also, **leading.** *Printing* a thin strip of type metal or brass, less than type high, for increasing the space between lines of type. **8.** frames of lead in which panes are fixed, as in windows of stained glass. **9.** (*pl.*) sheets or strips of lead used for covering roofs. *–v.t.* **10.** to cover, line, weight, treat, or impregnate with lead or one of its compounds. **11.** *Printing* to insert leads between the lines of. **12.** to fix (window glass) in position with leads. *–adj.* **13.** containing or made of lead. *–phr.* **14. fill someone full of lead,** *Colloq.* to shoot someone numerous times with a gun. **15. go down like a lead balloon,** *Colloq.* to fail dismally; fail to elicit the desired response. **16. have a lead foot,** *Colloq.* to be given to driving too fast. **17. heave the lead,** *Naut.* to take a sounding with a lead. **18. lead in one's pencil,** *Colloq.* (of a male) sexual vigour; virility. **19. swing the lead,** *Colloq.* to be idle when there is work to be done.

leaden /ˈlɛdn/ *adj.* **1.** consisting or made of lead. **2.** very heavy and hard to move: *leaden eyes; leaden limbs.* **3.** oppressive; burdensome: *leaden fear.* **4.** slow; sluggish: *leaden pace.* **5.** dull, spiritless, or gloomy: *leaden thoughts.* **6.** dull grey: *leaden skies.* **–leadenly,** *adv.* **–leadenness,** *n.*

leader /ˈlidə/ *n.* **1.** someone or something that leads. **2.** *Music* **a.** the main violinist, cornet-player, or singer in an orchestra, band, or chorus, to whom solos are usually given. **b.** → **concertmaster. c.** the musical director of a band: *our school band has a new leader.* **3.** → **editorial. –leaderless,** *adj.*

leading /ˈlidɪŋ/ *adj.* **1.** directing; guiding. **2.** chief; principal; most important; foremost.

leading aircraftman /lidɪŋ ˈɛəkraftmən/ *n.* (*pl.* **-men**) *Air Force* **1.** a man in the Royal Australian Air Force ranking below corporal and above aircraftman. **2.** the rank. *Abbrev.:* LAC

leading aircraftwoman /lidɪŋ ˈɛəkraftwʊmən/ *n.* (*pl.* **-women**) *Air Force* **1.** a woman in the Royal Australian Air Force ranking below corporal and above aircraftwoman. **2.** the rank. *Abbrev.:* LACW

leading light *n.* a person outstanding in a particular sphere.

leading question *n.* a question so worded as to suggest the proper or desired answer.

leading seaman /lidɪŋ ˈsimən/ *n. Navy* **1.** a sailor in the Royal Australian Navy ranking below petty officer and above able seaman. **2.** the rank. *Abbrev.:* LS

leadlight /ˈlɛdlaɪt/ *n.* **1.** a decorative assembly in which pieces of coloured or patterned glass are framed in lead to create a picture or an abstract design. *–adj.* **2.** of or relating to a door, window, etc., which features a leadlight.

leaf /lif/ *n.* (*pl.* **leaves** /livz/) **1.** one of the expanded, usually green, organs borne by the stem of a plant. **2.** any similar or corresponding lateral outgrowth of a stem. **3.** *Bibliography* any of the sheets of paper, usually printed on both sides, that make up the pages of a book. **4.** a thin sheet of metal, etc. **5.** a lamina or layer. **6.** a sliding, hinged, or detachable flat part, as of a door, tabletop, etc. *–v.i.* (**leafed** or **leafed, leaving** or **leafing**) **7.** to put forth leaves. *–phr.* **8. in leaf,** covered with foliage or leaves. **9. leaf through,** to turn the pages of quickly. **10. take a leaf out of someone's book,** to follow someone's example. **11. turn over a new leaf,** to begin a new and better course of conduct or action. **–leaf-like,** *adj.*

leaflet /ˈliflət/ *n.* **1.** one of the separate blades or divisions of a compound leaf. **2.** a small leaf-like part or structure. **3.** a small or young leaf. **4.** a small flat or folded sheet of printed matter, as for distribution. *–v.i.* **5.** to distribute leaflets, especially as part of a campaign.

leaf spring *n.* a long, narrow, multiple spring composed of several layers of spring metal bracketed together.

league¹ /lig/ *n.* **1.** a covenant or compact made between persons, parties, states, etc., for the maintenance or promotion of common interests or for mutual assistance or service. **2.** the aggregation of persons, parties, states, etc., associated in such a covenant; a confederacy. **3.** category or class: *they are not in the same league.* **4.** a society or association, especially one with a national or state-wide structure and local branches. **5.** an association of sporting clubs which arranges matches between teams of approximately similar standard. **6.** (*upper case*) → **Rugby League.** *–verb* (**leagued, leaguing**) *–v.t.* **7.** to unite in a league; combine. *–v.i.* **8.** to join in a league. *–adj.* **9.** of or belonging to a league. **10.** of or relating to Rugby League. *–phr.* **11. in league,** (sometimes fol. by *with*) united by or having a compact or agreement; allied. **12. out of one's league,** attempting to compete against others who have much superior skill.

league² /lig/ *n.* a former unit of distance, varying at different periods and in different countries, usually estimated roughly at 3 miles or 5 kilometres.

league table *n.* **1.** *Football* the table of scores, updated with each new game, for teams in a competition. **2.** the rankings given to individual people, organisations, etc., within a group: *the league table of CEOs.*

leak /lik/ *n.* **1.** an unintended hole, crack, or the like by which liquid, gas, etc., enters or escapes. **2.** any avenue or means of unintended entrance or escape, or the entrance or escape itself. **3.** *Elect.* a point where current escapes from a conductor, as because of poor insulation. **4.** the act of leaking. **5.** an accidental or apparently accidental disclosure of information, etc. **6.** *Colloq.* an act of passing water; urination. *–v.i.* **7.** to let a liquid, gas, etc. enter or escape, as through an unintended hole, crack, permeable material, or the like: *the roof is leaking.* **8.** to pass in or out in this manner, as water, etc.: *gas leaking from a pipe.* **9.** *Colloq.* to pass water; urinate. *–v.t.* **10.** to let (fluid, etc.) leak in or out. **11.** to disclose (information, especially of a confidential nature), especially to the media. *–phr.* **12. leak out,** to transpire or become known undesignedly. **–leakage,** *n.* **–leaky,** *adj.*

lean¹ /lin/ *verb* (**leaned** *or* **leant** /lɛnt/, **leaning**) *–v.i.* **1.** to incline or bend from a vertical position or in a particular direction. **2.** to incline in feeling, opinion, action, etc.: *to lean towards socialism.* **3.** to rest against or on something for support. **4.** to depend or rely: *to lean on empty promises. –v.t.* **5.** to incline or bend: *he leaned his head forward.* **6.** to cause to lean or rest (*against, on, upon,* etc.): *lean your arm against the railing. –n.* **7.** the act of leaning; inclination. *–phr.* **8. lean on,** *Colloq.* to intimidate; apply pressure to.

lean² /lin/ *adj.* **1.** (of persons or animals) scant of flesh; thin; not plump or fat: *lean cattle.* **2.** (of meat) containing little or no fat. **3.** lacking in richness, fullness, quantity, etc.: *a lean diet, lean years.* **4.** deficient in a particular ingredient, as clay which is not very plastic, or one which contains little valuable material. **–leanly,** *adv.* **–leanness,** *n.*

lean body mass *n.* the weight of one's bones, muscles and organs, excluding the weight of fat. *Abbrev.:* LBM

lean-to *n.* (*pl.* **-tos**) a shelter made of wood, galvanised iron, etc., propped against a building, wall, etc.

leap /lip/ *verb* (**leapt** /lɛpt/ *or* **leaped**, **leaping**) *–v.i.* **1.** to spring through the air from one point or position to another: *to leap over a ditch.* **2.** to move quickly and lightly: *to leap aside.* **3.** to pass, come, rise, etc., as if with a bound: *to leap to a conclusion. –v.t.* **4.** to jump over: *to leap a wall.* **5.** to pass over as if by a leap. **6.** to cause to leap. *–n.* **7.** a spring, jump, or bound; a light springing movement. **8.** the space cleared in a leap. **9.** a place leapt, or to be leapt, over or from. **10.** an abrupt transition, especially a rise. **11.** *Music* a melodic interval greater than a second. *–phr.* **12. a leap forward,** a sudden progressive development. **13. by leaps and bounds,** very rapidly. **14. leap in the dark,** an action taken without knowledge of the possible outcomes. **–leaper,** *n.*

leapfrog /'lipfrɒg/ *n.* **1.** a game in which one player leaps over another who is in a stooping posture. *–v.t.* (**-frogged, -frogging**) **2.** *Mil.* to advance (two military units) by engaging one with the enemy while moving the other forward.

leap year *n.* a year containing 366 days, or one day (29 February) more than the ordinary year, to offset the difference in length between the ordinary year and the astronomical year (being, in practice, every year whose number is exactly divisible by 4, as 1948, except centenary years not exactly divisible by 400, as 1900).

learn /lɜn/ *verb* (**learned** /lɜnd/ *or* **learnt**, **learning**) *–v.t.* **1.** to acquire knowledge of or skill in by study, instruction, or experience: *to learn French.* **2.** to memorise. **3.** to become informed of or acquainted with; ascertain: *to learn the truth.* **4.** to acquire (a habit or the like). *–v.i.* **5.** to acquire knowledge or skill: *to learn rapidly.* **–learner,** *n.*

learned /'lɜnəd/ *adj.* **1.** having much knowledge gained by study; scholarly: *a group of learned men.* **2.** of or showing learning. **3.** applied as a term of courtesy to a member of the legal profession: *my learned friend.* **–learnedly,** *adv.* **–learnedness,** *n.*

learning /'lɜnɪŋ/ *n.* **1.** knowledge acquired by systematic study in any field or fields of scholarly application. **2.** *Psychol.* the modification of behaviour through interaction with the environment.

learning curve *n.* **1.** the rate at which a person acquires new skills, particularly if it conforms to typical patterns for such acquisition. *–phr.* **2. a steep learning curve,** a pattern of learning in which there is a lot to learn at first, making progress initially slow, but gradually increasing in speed as more knowledge is retained.

lease /lis/ *n.* **1.** an instrument conveying property to another for a definite period, or at will, usually in consideration of rent or other periodical compensation. **2.** the period of time for which it is made. **3.** land which has been leased, as for goldmining, farming, etc. *–v.t.* **4.** to grant the temporary possession or use of (lands, tenements, vehicles, etc.) to another, usually for compensation at a fixed rate; let. **5.** to take or to hold by a lease, as a flat, house, etc. *–phr.* **6. a new lease of** (or **on**) **life,** a renewed zest for life. **–leaser,** *n.*

leasehold /'lishoʊld/ *n.* **1.** a land interest acquired under a lease. *–adj.* **2.** held by lease. **3.** of or relating to land owned by the Crown and which is leased out, usually for a specified time period.

leash /liʃ/ *n.* a lead for a dog.

least /list/ *adj.* **1.** smallest; slightest: *the least distance to come.* **2.** *Archaic* lowest in consideration or dignity. *–pron.* **3.** that which is least; the least amount, quantity, degree, etc. *–adv.* **4.** to the least extent, amount, or degree. *–phr.* **5. at least, a.** at the least or lowest estimate. **b.** at any rate; in any case. **6. in the least,** in the smallest degree.

leather /'lɛðə/ *n.* the skin of animals prepared for use by tanning or a similar process.

leatherjacket /'lɛðədʒækət/ *n.* any of numerous species of fish, especially of the family Aleuteridae, having a roughened skin which can be removed in one piece like a jacket, and a prominent, erectable dorsal spine.

leave¹ /liv/ *verb* (**left**, **leaving**) *–v.t.* **1.** to go away from, depart from, or quit, as a place, a person, or a thing. **2.** to let stay or be as specified: *to leave a door unlocked.* **3.** to let (a person, etc.) remain in a position to do something without interference: *leave him alone.* **4.** to let (a thing) remain for action or decision. **5.** to allow to remain in the same place, condition, etc. **6.** to let remain, or have remaining behind, after going, disappearing, ceasing, etc.: *the wound left a scar.* **7.** to have remaining after death: *he leaves a widow.* **8.** to give in charge; give for use after one's death or departure. **9.** to have as a remainder after subtraction: *2 from 4 leaves 2. –v.i.* **10.** to go away, depart, or set out: *we leave for Tasmania tomorrow. –phr.* **11. leave be,** to refrain from intruding on (someone) or interfering in their plans: *to leave them be to do their own thing.* **12. leave for dead,** to outclass or outstrip in a competition. **13. leave it at that,** to go no further; do or say nothing more. **14. leave it be,** to cease to remonstrate; to allow a situation to take its own course. **15. leave off, a.** not to put on (an item of clothing): *he left off his hat.* **b.** to exclude from: *they left her name off the list.* **c.** to cease doing (something): *leave off crying now.* **d.** to desist from, stop, or abandon. **16. leave out,** to omit or exclude. **17. leave someone be,** to cease interfering or taking an active interest in someone's affairs. **18. leave someone cold,** to make little or no impression on someone. **19. leave someone to it,** to leave someone alone to get on with something. **–leaver,** *n.*

leave² /liv/ *n.* **1.** permission to do something. **2.** permission to be absent, as from duty: *to be on leave.* **3.** the time this permission lasts: *30 days' leave.* **4.** a farewell: *to take leave of someone.*

leaven /'lɛvən/ *n.* **1.** a mass of fermenting dough reserved for producing fermentation in a new batch of dough. **2.** any substance which produces fermentation. **3.** an agency which works in a thing to produce a gradual change or modification. **–leavening,** *n.*

leaves /livz/ *n.* plural of **leaf.**

lecher /'lɛtʃə/ *n.* a man whose behaviour exhibits lustfulness and lewdness, especially one who preys on others. **–lechery,** *n.* **–lecherous,** *adj.*

lecithin /ˈlɛsəθən/ n. phosphatidyl choline, an ester important in membranes.

lectern /ˈlɛktɜn/ n. a reading desk, especially that in a church from which the lessons are read.

lecture /ˈlɛktʃə/ n. **1.** a discourse read or delivered before an audience, especially for instruction or to set forth some subject: *a lecture on Picasso*. **2.** a speech of warning or reproof as to conduct; a long, tedious reprimand. –*v.i.* **3.** to give a lecture. –*v.t.* **4.** to deliver a lecture to or before; instruct by lectures. –**lecturer,** *n.* –**lectureship,** *n.*

led /lɛd/ v. past tense and past participle of **lead**[1].

ledge /lɛdʒ/ n. **1.** any relatively narrow, horizontal projecting part, or any part affording a horizontal shelf-like surface. **2.** a more or less flat shelf of rock protruding from a cliff or slope. **3.** a reef, ridge, or line of rocks in the sea or other water bodies. –**ledged,** *adj.*

ledger /ˈlɛdʒə/ n. **1.** *Bookkeeping* an account book with columns for credits and debits. **2.** a horizontal timber fastened to the vertical uprights of a scaffold, to support the putlogs. **3.** a flat slab of stone laid over a grave or tomb.

lee[1] /li/ n. **1.** the side or part that is sheltered or turned away from the wind. **2.** *Chiefly Naut.* the quarter or region towards which the wind blows.

lee[2] /li/ n. (*usu. pl.*) that which settles from a liquid, especially from wine; sediment; dregs.

leech /litʃ/ n. **1.** any of the bloodsucking or carnivorous, usually aquatic, worms constituting the class Hirudinea, certain freshwater species of which were formerly much used by physicians for bloodletting and now occasionally used in eye surgery and the like for reducing bruising. **2.** an instrument used for drawing blood. **3.** someone who clings to another with a view to gain.

leek /lik/ n. a plant of the lily family, *Allium porrum,* allied to the onion, but having a cylindrical bulb, used in cookery and well-known as the national emblem of Wales.

leer /lɪə/ n. **1.** a side glance, especially of sly or insulting suggestion or significance. –*v.i.* **2.** to look with a leer. –**leeringly,** *adv.*

leery /ˈlɪəri/ adj. Colloq. **1.** doubtful; suspicious. **2.** knowing; sly.

leeward /ˈliwəd/, *Naut.* /ˈluəd/ adj. relating to, situated in, or moving towards the quarter towards which the wind blows (opposed to *windward*).

leeway /ˈliweɪ/ n. **1.** *Aeronautics* the amount an aeroplane is blown off its normal course by cross-winds. **2.** *Naut.* the distance a ship is forced sideways from its course by the wind. **3.** extra space, time, money, etc. –*phr.* **4. make up leeway,** Colloq. to catch up on a competitor, opponent, etc.

left[1] /lɛft/ adj. **1.** belonging or relating to the side of a person or thing which is turned towards the west when facing north (opposed to *right*). **2.** belonging or relating to the political left. –*n.* **3.** the left side, or what is on the left side. **4.** a punch with the left hand, as in boxing. –*phr.* **5. have two left feet,** Colloq. to be clumsy. **6. left and right,** everywhere about: *children fainting left and right.* **7. take a left turn,** to make a radical departure from the expected course: *a career that took a left turn.* **8. the left,** (*oft. upper case*) a body of persons, political party, etc., holding progressive, socialist or radical views.

left[2] /lɛft/ v. **1.** past tense and past participle of **leave**[1]. –*adj.* **2.** remaining: *only two left.*

left-handed adj. **1.** using the left hand more than the right. **2.** for use by or performed by the left hand. **3.** insincere or ambiguous: *a left-handed compliment.* **4.** awkward; clumsy. –**left-handedly,** *adv.* –**left-hander,** *n.* –**left-handedness,** *n.*

leftist /ˈlɛftəst/ n. a member of a socialist or radical party or a person sympathising with their views.

leftover /ˈlɛftouvə/ n. **1.** something left over or remaining. **2.** a remnant of food, as from a meal. **3.** (*pl.*) a meal put together from such remnants of food. –*adj.* **4.** not fully used up; remaining: *leftover pasta.*

left wing n. **1.** members of a socialist, progressive or radical political party or section of a party. **2.** *Sport* the part of the field of play which forms the left flank of the area being attacked by either team. **3.** *Sport* a player positioned on the left flank, as the outside left in soccer, the left or the wing three-quarters in Rugby football, etc. –**left-wing,** *adj.* –**left-winger,** *n.*

leg /lɛg/ n. **1.** one of the members or limbs which support and move the human or animal body. **2.** this part of an animal, especially lamb or veal, used as meat to roast, bake, etc. **3.** that part of the limb between the knee and the ankle. **4.** something resembling or suggesting a leg in use, position, or appearance. **5.** that part of a garment, such as a stocking, trousers, or the like, which covers the leg. **6.** one of the supports of a piece of furniture. **7.** one of the sides of a pair of dividers or compasses. **8.** one of the sides of a triangle other than the base or hypotenuse. **9.** a timber, bar, etc., serving to prop or shore up a structure. **10.** one of the distinct portions of any course: *the last leg of a trip.* **11.** *Naut.* **a.** one of the series of straight runs which make up the zigzag course of a sailing ship. **b.** one straight or nearly straight part of a multiple-sided course in a sailing race. **12.** *Sport* **a.** one of a number of parts of a contest, each of which must be completed in order to determine the winner. **b.** a stage or given distance in a relay race. **13.** *Cricket* the leg side. –*adj.* **14.** *Cricket* of or relating to the leg side: *leg slip; leg stump.* –*phr.* (v. **legged,** **legging**) **15. a leg up, a.** assistance in climbing or mounting. **b.** any assistance. **16. break a leg,** Colloq. **a.** an expression of good luck to someone about to go on stage. **b.** (*usu. negative*) to hurry excessively: *well, don't break a leg getting there.* **17. get a leg in,** Colloq. to make a start. **18. get one's leg over,** Colloq. (taboo) to have sexual intercourse. **19. get one's leg over someone,** Colloq. (taboo) to have sexual intercourse with someone. **20. leg it,** Colloq. **a.** to walk. **b.** to run, often as a means of escape: *to leg it with a policeman in hot pursuit.* **21. not have a leg to stand on,** not to have any good justification for one's beliefs, actions, etc. **22. pull someone's leg,** Colloq. to tease or make fun of someone. **23. pull the other leg,** Colloq. an exclamation of ironic disbelief. **24. shake a leg,** Colloq. to hurry up. **25. show a leg,** Colloq. **a.** to make an appearance. **b.** to get out of bed.

legacy /ˈlɛgəsi/ n. (*pl.* -**cies**) **1.** *Law* a gift of property or money made by will; a bequest. **2.** anything handed down by an ancestor, etc. **3.** a result: *this is a legacy of the war in Vietnam.* (*pl.* -**cies**) **4.** handed down from one person or group to another: *a legacy project.*

legacy costs pl. n. the costs which a company incurs as a result of its obligations to employees, both current and retired, in terms of benefits such as health care, superannuation, etc.

legacy data n. data which is held in a legacy software system.

legacy software n. *Computers* software developed at an earlier stage in the history of a company or organisation, which is often limited in terms of performance, difficult to maintain, and poorly documented.

legal /ˈligəl/ adj. **1.** appointed, established, or authorised by law; deriving authority from law. **2.** of or relating to law: connected with the law or its administration: *the legal profession.* –**legally,** *adv.* –**legality** /ləˈgæləti, li-/, *n.*

legalise /'liɡəlaɪz/ *v.t.* to make legal; authorise; sanction. Also, **legalize**. –**legalisation** /liɡəlaɪ'zeɪʃən/, *n.*

legal tender *n.* currency which may be lawfully tendered or offered in payment of money debts and which may not be refused by creditors.

legate /'lɛɡət/ *n.* **1.** an ecclesiastic delegated by the pope as his representative. **2.** *Roman Hist.* an assistant to a general or to a consul or magistrate, in the government of any army or a province; a commander of a legion. **3.** → **envoy.** –**legateship**, *n.* –**legatine**, *adj.*

legatee /lɛɡə'ti/ *n. Law* someone to whom a legacy is bequeathed.

legation /lə'ɡeɪʃən/ *n.* (formerly) a diplomatic mission of lesser rank than an embassy. –**legationary**, *adj.*

legato /lə'ɡatoʊ/ *Music* –*adv.* **1.** in a smooth, even style, without breaks between the successive notes. –*adj.* **2.** performed legato. Compare **staccato**.

leg before wicket *n.* (in cricket) the act of stopping with the leg, or some other part of the body, a bowled ball which would otherwise have hit the wicket, for which the person batting may be declared out. *Abbrev.*: l.b.w. Also, **leg before.**

legend /'lɛdʒənd/ *n.* **1.** a story handed down by tradition from earlier times and popularly accepted as being based on historical fact. **2.** something written on a coin, coat of arms, or under a picture, etc. **3.** notes that explain a table, map, drawing, etc. **4.** a famous or admirable person about whom legend-like stories are told. **5.** *Colloq.* a person who is well-regarded, especially for excellence in a particular field or activity: *mate, you're a legend!* –**legendary**, *adj.*

legerdemain /lɛdʒədə'meɪn/ *n.* **1.** sleight of hand. **2.** trickery; deception.

leggings /'lɛɡɪŋz/ *pl. n.* a close-fitting covering for the leg, made of stretch material, similar to tights but stopping at the ankle.

legible /'lɛdʒəbəl/ *adj.* **1.** able to be read or deciphered, especially with ease, as writing or printing. **2.** capable of being discerned or distinguished. –**legibility** /lɛdʒə-'bɪləti/, **legibleness**, *n.* –**legibly**, *adv.*

legion /'lidʒən/ *n.* **1.** an infantry brigade in the army of ancient Rome, numbering from 3000 to 6000 men, and usually combined with from 300 to 700 cavalry. **2.** one of certain military bodies of modern times, as the Foreign Legion. **3.** any large body of armed men. **4.** any great host or multitude, whether of persons or of things. –**legionary**, *adj.*, *n.*

leg-iron *n.* a fetter for the ankle, as to secure or restrain a prisoner.

legislate /'lɛdʒəsleɪt/ *v.i.* to exercise the function of legislation; make or enact laws. –**legislative**, *adj.* –**legislator**, *n.*

legislation /lɛdʒəs'leɪʃən/ *n.* **1.** the act of making or enacting laws. **2.** a law or a body of laws enacted. –**legislatorial** /lɛdʒəslə'tɔriəl/, *adj.*

Legislative Assembly *n.* the lower chamber of certain bicameral parliaments.

Legislative Council *n.* the upper chamber of certain bicameral parliaments.

legislature /'lɛdʒəsleɪtʃə, -lətʃə/ *n.* the arm of government whose function is to make, amend and repeal laws, as a parliament.

legitimate *adj.* /lə'dʒɪtəmət/ **1.** in accordance with the law, or any established rules. **2.** in accordance with the laws of reasoning; logical: *a legitimate conclusion.* **3.** reasonable; justifiable: *a legitimate demand.* **4.** born of parents legally married. **5.** ruling by the principle of hereditary right: *a legitimate sovereign.* **6.** *Theatre* relating to plays or acting with a serious and literary purpose. –*v.t.* /lə'dʒɪtəmeɪt/ **7.** to make or declare lawful. **8.** to show or declare to be just or proper. –*n.*

9. (formerly) a convict. –**legitimately**, *adv.* –**legitimacy**, *n.* –**legitimation** /lədʒɪtə'meɪʃən/, *n.*

legless /'lɛɡləs/ *adj. Colloq.* drunk.

leg side *n.* (in cricket) that half of the field which is behind the person batting as they stand ready to receive the bowling (opposed to *off side*).

leg slip *n.* (in cricket) the position of a fielder who stands close behind and to the leg side of the person batting.

legume /'lɛɡjum, 'leɪ-/ *n.* **1.** any plant of the family Leguminosae (including the Fabaceae), especially those used for feed, food, or soil-improving crop, such as beans, peas, lentils, etc. **2.** the pod, fruit, or seed vessel of such a plant, which is usually dehiscent by both sutures, thus dividing into two parts or valves. **3.** any table vegetable of the family Leguminosae, as beans, lentils, etc. –**leguminous** /lə'ɡjumənəs/, *adj.*

leisure /'lɛʒə/ *n.* **1.** the condition of having one's time free from the demands of work or duty; ease: *enjoying a life of leisure.* **2.** free or unoccupied time. –*adj.* **3.** free or unoccupied: *leisure hours.* **4.** relating to one's time or period of leisure. –*phr.* **5. at leisure, a.** with free or unrestricted time. **b.** without haste. **6. at one's leisure,** when one has leisure. **7. lady of leisure,** a woman who has no regular paid employment.

leisurely /'lɛʒəli/ *adj.* showing or suggesting ample leisure; unhurried: *a leisurely manner.* –**leisureliness**, *n.*

leitmotiv /'laɪtmoʊˌtif/ *n.* (in a music drama or literary work) a theme associated throughout the work with a particular person, situation, or idea. Also, **leitmotif**.

lemming /'lɛmɪŋ/ *n.* any of various small, mouse-like rodents of the genera *Lemmus*, *Myopus*, and *Dicrostonyx*, of far northern regions, as *L. lemmus*, of Norway, Sweden, and elsewhere, noted for its mass migrations in periods of population increase.

lemon /'lɛmən/ *n.* **1.** (a tree bearing) a yellowish acid citrus fruit. **2.** a clear, light yellow colour. **3.** *Colloq.* something disappointing or unpleasant. –*adj.* **4.** made or flavoured with lemons. **5.** of a lemon colour.

lemonade /lɛmə'neɪd/ *n.* **1.** a lemon-flavoured carbonated soft drink. **2.** lemon squash.

lemur /'limə/ *n.* any of various small, arboreal, chiefly nocturnal mammals, especially of the genus *Lemur*, allied to the monkeys, usually having a foxlike face and woolly fur, and found chiefly in Madagascar.

lend /lɛnd/ *verb* (**lent**, **lending**) –*v.t.* **1.** to give the temporary use of (money, etc.) for a consideration. **2.** to grant the use of (something) with the understanding that it (or its equivalent in kind) shall be returned. **3.** to furnish or impart: *distance lends enchantment to the view.* **4.** to give or contribute obligingly or helpfully: *to lend one's aid to a cause.* **5.** to adapt (oneself or itself) to something. –*v.i.* **6.** to make a loan or loans. –*n.* **7.** (*in non-standard use*) a loan: *give me a lend of your pen.* –*phr.* **8. have a lend of someone,** *Colloq.* to tease someone. **9. lend a hand,** to assist. **10. lend an ear,** *Archaic* to listen. **11. lend itself to,** to be suitable or appropriate for: *the property lends itself to a variety of uses.* –**lender**, *n.*

length /lɛŋθ/ *n.* **1.** the linear magnitude of anything as measured from end to end: *the length of a river.* **2.** extent from beginning to end of a series, enumeration, account, book, etc. **3.** extent in time; duration: *the length of a battle.* **4.** a distance determined by the length of something specified: *to hold a thing at arm's length.* **5.** (as the second element in a compound adjective) hanging down to: *ankle-length pantaloons; knee-length shorts.* **6.** a piece or portion of a certain or a known length: *a length of rope.* **7.** a stretch or extent of something, especially a long stretch. **8.** the extent, or an extent, of going, proceeding, etc. **9.** the quality or fact of being long rather than short: *a journey remarkable for its length.* **10.** the measure from end to end of a horse, boat, etc., as a unit of distance in racing: *a horse wins by two lengths.* **11.** *Prosody, Phonetics* the length (long or short) of a vowel or syllable. –*phr.* **12. at length, a.** to or in the full extent. **b.** after a time; in the end. **13. go to any length(s),** to do whatever is necessary, no matter how difficult, dangerous, etc., to achieve something. **14. slip someone a length,** *Colloq.* (*taboo*) (of a man) to have sexual intercourse with someone. –**lengthen,** *v.* –**lengthily,** *adv.* –**lengthy,** *adj.*

lenient /ˈliniənt/ *adj.* mild, clement, or merciful, as in treatment, attitude, or tendency; gentle. –**leniently,** *adv.* –**leniency,** *n.*

lens /lɛnz/ *n.* (*pl.* **lenses**) **1.** *Optics* a piece of transparent substance, usually glass, having two (or two main) opposite surfaces, either both curved or one curved and one plane, used for changing the convergence of light rays, as in magnifying, or in correcting errors of vision. **2.** *Optics* a combination of such pieces. **3.** some analogous device, as for affecting soundwaves, electromagnetic radiation, or streams of electrons. **4.** *Anat.* a part of the eye, a crystalline lens.

lent /lɛnt/ *v.* past tense and past participle of **lend.**

Lent /lɛnt/ *n.* an annual season of fasting and penitence observed in some Christian churches in preparation for Easter, beginning on Ash Wednesday and including the forty weekdays next before Easter.

lentil /ˈlɛntəl/ *n.* **1.** the seed of the widely cultivated leguminous annual plant *Lens culinaris,* occurring in many varieties, and constituting an important food. **2.** the plant itself.

Leo /ˈliou/ *n.* **1.** the fifth sign of the zodiac, which the sun enters about 23 July; the Lion. **2.** a person born under the sign of Leo. –*adj.* **3.** of or relating to Leo.

leonine /ˈliənaɪn/ *adj.* **1.** of or relating to the lion. **2.** lion-like.

leopard /ˈlɛpəd/ *n.* **1.** a large, ferocious, spotted Asiatic or African carnivore, *Panthera pardus,* of the cat family, usually tawny, with black markings; the African or Asian panther. **2.** any of various related animals, as the jaguar (**American leopard**), the cheetah (**hunting leopard**), and the ounce (**snow leopard**). **3.** *Heraldry* a lion pictured as walking with its head turned towards the spectator, one front paw usually raised. –**leopardess,** *n.*

leotard /ˈliətad/ *n.* a close-fitting one-piece garment, worn by acrobats, dancers, etc.

leper /ˈlɛpə/ *n.* **1.** a person affected with leprosy. **2.** a person ostracised by society

leprechaun /ˈlɛprəkɔn/ *n.* **1.** (in Irish folklore) a little sprite, or goblin. **2.** *Colloq.* an Irishman.

leprosy /ˈlɛprəsi/ *n.* a mildly infectious disease due to a microorganism, *Bacillus leprae,* and variously characterised by ulcerations, tubercular nodules, spots of pigmentary excess or deficit, loss of fingers and toes, anaesthesia in certain nerve regions, etc. –**leprous,** *adj.*

lesbian /ˈlɛzbiən/ *n.* **1.** a female homosexual. –*adj.* **2.** of or relating to female homosexuals.

lesion /ˈliʒən/ *n.* an injury; a hurt; a wound.

less /lɛs/ *adv.* **1.** to a smaller extent, amount, or degree: *less exact.* –*adj.* **2.** smaller in size, amount, degree, etc.; not so large, great, or much: *less speed.* **3.** (*not considered standard by some*) fewer in number: *less clouds in the sky.* –*pron.* **4.** a smaller amount or quantity: *she ate less than me.* –*prep.* **5.** minus; without: *a year less two days.* –*phr.* **6. no less a ... than,** not lower in consideration, dignity, or importance than: *no less a person than the manager.*

-less a suffix of adjectives meaning 'without', as in *childless, peerless.* In adjectives derived from verbs, it indicates failure or inability to perform or be performed, as in *resistless, countless.*

lessee /lɛˈsi/ *n.* *Law* someone to whom a lease is granted. –**lessee-ship,** *n.*

lessen /ˈlɛsən/ *v.i.* to become less.

lesser /ˈlɛsə/ *adj.* **1.** less; smaller, as in size, amount, importance, etc.: *a lesser evil.* **2.** being the smaller or less important of two.

lesser panda *n.* → **red panda.**

lesson /ˈlɛsən/ *n.* **1.** something to be learned or studied. **2.** a length of time during which a pupil or class studies one subject. **3.** something from which one learns or should learn, as an instructive or warning example: *this experience was a lesson to me.* **4.** a reproof or punishment intended to teach one better ways. **5.** a portion of Scripture or other sacred writing read, or appointed to be read, at divine service.

lessor /lɛˈsɔ, ˈlɛsə/ *n.* *Law* someone who grants a lease.

lest /lɛst/ *conj.* **1.** for fear that; that ... not; so that ... not. **2.** (after words expressing fear, danger, etc.) that: *there was danger lest the plan become known.*

let[1] /lɛt/ *verb* (**let, letting**) –*v.t.* **1.** to allow or permit. **2.** to allow to pass, go, or come. **3.** to cause or allow to escape. **4.** Also, **let out.** to grant the occupancy or use of (land, buildings, rooms, space, etc., or moveable property) for rent or hire. **5.** to contract for performance: *to let work to a carpenter.* **6.** to cause or make: *to let one know.* **7.** as an auxiliary used to propose or order: *let me see.* –*v.i.* **8.** to be rented or leased. –*n.* **9.** a lease. –*phr.* **10. let down,** to lower. **11. let fly, a.** to throw. **b.** to express one's anger without restraint. **12. let go, a.** to release one's hold. **b.** *Colloq.* to break wind; fart. **c.** to express one's anger without restraint. **d.** to cease to make claims which are no longer appropriate on people with whom one has had a close relationship. **13. let go of,** to release one's hold on. **14. let in,** to give access to. **15. let in for,** to oblige (someone) to do (something) without their prior consent or knowledge. **16. let it be,** to allow a situation to take its own course. **17. let loose,** to free from restraint. **18. let off, a.** to excuse; to exempt from (something arduous, as a punishment, or the like). **b.** to explode (a firework, or other explosive device). **c.** *Colloq.* to fart. **19. let off steam,** to release pent-up energy or repressed emotions, such as anger and frustration, often by indirect and harmless means. **20. let on, a.** to divulge information, especially indiscreetly. **b.** to pretend: *he let on that he was a detective.* **21. let oneself go,** to neglect oneself. **22. let one's hair down,** to abandon oneself to pleasure. **23. let out, a.** to release from, as from confinement. **b.** to divulge. **c.** to make (a garment, etc.) larger. **d.** to emit: *he let out a laugh.* **e.** to free from imputation of guilt: *that lets him out.* **24. let rip,** to perform with great enthusiasm and energy. **25. let slide,** to cease gradually to attend to, especially something which should be routine or habitual: *to let your piano practice slide.* **26. let slip** (or **drop**) (or **fall**), to divulge unintentionally. **27. let someone alone** (or **be**), to cease to remonstrate with or harass someone. **28. let someone down, a.** to omit to fulfil an obligation to someone. **b.** to fail someone by proving to be inadequate for their needs. **29. let someone in on something,** to share secret information with someone about something. **30. let up,** to slacken or stop. –**lettable,** *adj.*

let[2] /lɛt/ *n.* **1.** *Tennis, etc.* an interference with the course of the ball (of some kind specified in the rules) on account of which the stroke or point must be played over again. **2.** *Squash* a bodily movement of one player which impedes that of the other player as he or she attempts to play the ball, as a result of which the point must be replayed.

-let a diminutive suffix: **1.** used often for little objects, as in *frontlet, booklet, kinglet.* **2.** applied to a noun denoting a part of the body, and thus forming a term for a piece of jewellery worn there, as *armlet, anklet.*

let-down *n.* a disappointment. Also, **letdown.**

lethal /'liːθəl/ *adj.* of, relating to, or such as to cause death; deadly.

lethargy /'lɛθədʒi/ *n.* (*pl.* **-gies**) **1.** a state of drowsy dullness or suspension of the faculties and energies; apathetic or sluggish inactivity. **2.** *Pathol.* a morbid state or a disorder characterised by overpowering drowsiness or sleep. **–lethargic** /lə'θadʒɪk/, **lethargical** /lə'θadʒɪkəl/, *adj.* **–lethargically** /lə'θadʒɪkli/, *adv.*

letter /'lɛtə/ *n.* **1.** a communication in writing or printing addressed to a person or a number of persons. **2.** one of the marks or signs conventionally used in writing and printing to represent speech sounds; an alphabetic character. **3.** a printing type bearing such a mark or character. **4.** actual terms or wording, as distinct from general meaning or intent. **5.** *Genetics* a single element or base in a DNA sequence, represented by an alphabetic letter. –*v.t.* **6.** to mark or write with letters. –*phr.* **7. to the letter, a.** with close adherence to the actual wording or the literal meaning. **b.** to the fullest extent. **–letterer**, *n.*

letterbox /'lɛtəbɒks/ *n.* **1.** a receptacle with a slot for posting mail. **2.** a box or other shaped receptacle for incoming mail at the front gate of a house or on the inside of the front door. –*v.t.* **3.** to distribute pamphlets, etc., throughout (an area) by placing them in letterboxes: *I'm letterboxing the northern suburbs this election.*

lettered /'lɛtəd/ *adj.* **1.** educated or learned. **2.** relating to or characterised by polite learning or literary culture. **3.** marked with or as with letters.

letterhead /'lɛtəhɛd/ *n.* a printed heading on writing paper, especially one giving the name and address of a business concern, an institution, etc.

letter of credit *n.* *Finance* **1.** an order issued by a banker, allowing a person named to draw money to a specified amount from correspondents of the issuer. **2.** an instrument issued by a banker, authorising a person named to make drafts upon the issuer up to an amount specified.

letterpress /'lɛtəprɛs/ *n.* a method of relief printing in which the type or illustrations to be printed stand above the areas of the printing forme which are not to be printed.

lettuce /'lɛtəs/ *n.* a biennial plant, *Lactuca sativa*, with large leaves which are much used for salad.

leuco- a word element meaning 'white'. Also, **leuko-**; (*before vowels*), **leuc-**.

leukaemia /luˈkimiə/ *n.* *Pathol.* a disease, often fatal, characterised by excessive production of white blood cells, which are usually found in greatly increased numbers in the blood. Also, **leukemia, leuc(a)emia**.

leukocyte /'lukəsaɪt/ *n.* one of the white or colourless corpuscles of the blood, concerned in the destruction of disease-producing microorganisms, etc.; white blood cell. Also, **leucocyte**.

levee¹ /'lɛvi/ *n.* **1.** a raised riverside built up naturally by the river by deposition of silt during flooding. **2.** a man-made embankment for preventing the overflowing of a river.

levee² /'lɛvi, 'lɛveɪ/ *n.* **1.** *Hist.* a reception of visitors held on rising from bed, as formerly by a royal or other personage. **2.** a reception held at any time of day.

level /'lɛvəl/ *adj.* **1.** having no part higher than another; having an even surface. **2.** being in a plane parallel to the plane of the horizon; horizontal. **3.** on an equality, as one thing with another, or two or more things with one another. **4.** even, equable, or uniform. **5.** mentally well-balanced: *a level head.* –*n.* **6.** a device used for determining, or adjusting something to, a horizontal surface. **7.** such a device consisting of a glass tube containing alcohol or ether with a movable bubble which when in the centre indicates horizontalness. **8.** a surveying instrument combining such a device with a mounted telescope. **9.** a measuring of differences in elevation with such an instrument. **10.** an imaginary line or surface everywhere perpendicular to the plumbline. **11.** the horizontal line or plane in which anything is situated, with regard to its elevation. **12.** level position or condition. **13.** a level tract of land, or an extent of country approximately horizontal and unbroken by irregularities. **14.** a level or flat surface. **15.** one of various positions with respect to height; a height: *the water rose to a level of ten metres.* **16.** *Mining* a depth at which tunnelling for gold, opal, etc., might take place. **17.** a position or plane, high or low: *acting on the level of amateurs.* –*verb* (**-elled** *or*, *US*, **-eled**, **-elling** *or*, *US*, **-eling**) –*v.t.* **18.** to make (a surface) level or even: *to level ground before building.* **19.** to raise or lower to a particular level, or position. **20.** to bring (something) to the level of the ground: *the city was levelled by one atomic bomb.* **21.** to knock down, as a person. **22.** to bring (two or more things) to an equality of status, condition, etc. **23.** to make even or uniform, as colouring. **24.** to aim or point at a mark, as a weapon, criticism, etc. **25.** to turn (looks, etc.) in a particular direction. –*v.i.* **26.** Also, **level out.** to arrive at a common level; stabilise: *food prices levelled last quarter.* **27.** *Aeronautics* to fly at a constant height. –*adv.* **28.** in a level, direct, or even way or line. –*phr.* **29. find one's level,** to find the most suitable place for oneself, especially with regard to the people around: *she found her level among the older students.* **30. level with,** to be frank or honest with: *let me level with you.* **31. one's level best,** *Colloq.* one's very best; one's utmost. **32. on the level,** *Colloq.* sincere; honest. **–leveller**, *n.* **–levelly**, *adv.* **–levelness**, *n.*

level crossing *n.* a place where a road and railway intersect at the same level.

lever /'livə/ *n.* **1.** a bar or rigid piece acted upon at different points by two forces, as a voluntarily applied force (the *power*) and a resisting force (the *weight*), which generally tend to rotate it in opposite directions about a fixed axis or support (the *fulcrum*). **2.** any of various mechanical devices operating on this principle, as a crowbar.

leverage /'livərɪdʒ, 'lɛvərɪdʒ/ *for defs 1–3*, /'lɛvərɪdʒ/ *for def. 4 n.***1.** the action of a lever. **2.** the mechanical advantage or power gained by using a lever. **3.** power of action; means of influence. **4.** *Finance* the proportion of fixed-interest loan capital to share capital employed in financing a company or a specific venture, but now often used to describe partial reliance on any form of debt finance.

leveret /'lɛvərət/ *n.* a young hare.

leviathan /lə'vaɪəθən/ *n.* **1.** a sea-monster mentioned in the Old Testament **2.** any huge marine animal, as the whale. **3.** anything, especially a ship, of huge size.

levitate /'lɛvəteɪt/ *v.i.* **1.** to rise or float in the air, especially through some allegedly supernatural power that overcomes gravity. –*v.t.* **2.** to cause to rise or float in the air. **–levitator**, *n.* **–levitation** /lɛvə'teɪʃən/, *n.*

levity /'lɛvəti/ *n.* **1.** lightness of mind, character, or behaviour; lack of proper seriousness or earnestness: *she accused him of levity in his discussion of the divorce law.* **2.** lightness in weight.

levy /'lɛvi/ *n.* (*pl.* **levies**) **1.** a raising or collecting, as of money or troops, by authority or force. **2.** something that is raised, as a tax assessment or a body of troops. –*v.t.* (**levied, levying**) **3.** to impose (a tax): *to levy a duty on imported wines.* **4.** to start, or make (war, etc.). **–levier**, *n.* **–leviable**, *adj.*

lewd /lud, ljud/ *adj.* **1.** inclined to, characterised by, or inciting to lust or lechery. **2.** obscene or indecent, as language, songs, etc. **–lewdly**, *adv.* **–lewdness**, *n.*

lexicography /lɛksəˈkɒɡrəfi/ n. the writing or compiling of dictionaries. −**lexicographic** /lɛksəkəˈɡræfɪk/, **lexicographical** /lɛksəkəˈɡræfɪkəl/, adj. −**lexicographically** /lɛksəkəˈɡræfɪkli/, adv.

lexicon /ˈlɛksəkən/ n. **1.** the total stock of words in a given language or used by a particular person. **2.** the list or vocabulary of words belonging to a particular subject, field, or class. −**lexical**, adj.

liability /laɪəˈbɪləti/ n. (pl. **-ties**) **1.** an obligation, especially for payment; debt or pecuniary obligations (opposed to asset). **2.** something disadvantageous.

liable /ˈlaɪəbəl/ adj. **1.** subject, exposed, or open to something possible or likely, especially something undesirable. **2.** under legal obligation; responsible or answerable. −**liableness**, n.

liaise /liˈeɪz/ v.i. (**-aised**, **-aising**) (sometimes fol. by with) to maintain contact and act in concert.

liaison /liˈeɪzən, -zɒn/ n. **1.** Mil., etc. the contact maintained between units, in order to ensure concerted action. **2.** a similar connection or relation maintained between non-military units, bodies, etc. **3.** an illicit sexual relationship. **4.** Phonetics (especially in French) the articulation of a normally silent final consonant in a word as the initial sound of a following word that begins with a vowel or a silent h.

liana /liˈanə/ n. a climbing plant or vine. Also, **liane** /liˈan/.

liar /ˈlaɪə/ n. **1.** someone who lies, or tells lies. −phr. **2. make a liar of,** Colloq. to prove wrong.

libel /ˈlaɪbəl/ n. **1.** Law **a.** defamation by written or printed words, pictures, or in any form other than by spoken words or gestures. **b.** the crime of publishing it. **2.** anything defamatory, or that maliciously or damagingly misrepresents. −v.t. (**-belled** or, Chiefly US, **-beled**, **-belling** or, Chiefly US, **-beling**) **3.** to publish a malicious libel against. −**libellous**, adj. −**libeller**, n.

liberal /ˈlɪbrəl, ˈlɪbərəl/ adj. **1.** favourable to progress or reform, as in religious or political affairs. **2.** favourable to or in accord with the policy of leaving the individual as unrestricted as possible in the opportunities for self-expression or self-fulfilment. **3.** of representational forms of government rather than aristocracies and monarchies. **4.** free from prejudice or bigotry; tolerant. **5.** giving freely or in ample measure: a liberal donor. **6.** given freely or abundantly: a liberal donation. **7.** not strict or rigorous: a liberal interpretation of a rule. −n. **8.** a person of liberal principles or views, especially in religion or politics. −phr. **9. small 'l' liberal,** a person with progressive views, favourable to reform (often as opposed to a supporter of the politically conservative policies of a Liberal Party, such as the Liberal Party of Australia). −**liberalism**, n. −**liberally**, adv. −**liberalness**, **liberality**, n.

liberate /ˈlɪbəreɪt/ v.t. **1.** to set free, as a prisoner, occupied territory, etc.; release. **2.** to disengage; set free from combination, as a gas. **3.** to free from convention or from a repressive social order. −**liberation** /lɪbəˈreɪʃən/, n. −**liberator**, n.

libertine /ˈlɪbətin/ n. **1.** someone who is free from restraint or control, especially in moral or sexual matters; a dissolute or licentious person. **2.** a freethinker in religious matters.

liberty /ˈlɪbəti/ n. (pl. **-ties**) **1.** freedom from arbitrary or despotic government. **2.** freedom from external or foreign rule; independence. **3.** freedom from control, interference, obligation, restriction, hampering conditions, etc.; power or right of doing, thinking, speaking, etc., according to choice. **4.** freedom from captivity, confinement, or physical restraint: the prisoner soon regained his liberty. **5.** leave granted to a sailor, especially in the navy, to go ashore. **6.** the freedom of, or right of frequenting or using a place, etc. **7.** unwarranted or impertinent freedom in action or speech, or a form or instance of it: to take liberties. −phr. **8. at liberty, a.** free from bondage, captivity, confinement, or restraint. **b.** unoccupied or disengaged. **c.** free, permitted, or privileged to do or be as specified.

libidinous /ləˈbɪdənəs/ adj. full of lust; lustful; lewd. −**libidinously**, adv. −**libidinousness**, n.

libido /ləˈbidoʊ/ n. **1.** Psychol. all of the instinctive energies and desires which are derived from the id. **2.** the innate actuating or impelling force in living beings; the vital impulse or urge. **3.** the sexual instinct. −**libidinal** /ləˈbɪdənəl/, adj.

Libra /ˈlɪbrə, ˈlibrə/ n. the seventh sign of the zodiac, which the sun enters about 23 September; the Scales or the Balance. −**Libran**, n., adj.

library /ˈlaɪbri, -brəri/, Orig. US /-rɛri/ n. (pl. **-ries**) **1.** a room or building containing books and other material for reading, study, or reference. **2.** such a place from which the public may borrow books, etc. **3.** a collection of books, etc. **4.** a collection of films, records, music, etc. −**librarian**, n.

libretto /ləˈbrɛtoʊ/ n. (pl. **-tos** or **-ti** /-ti/) the text or words of an opera or other extended musical composition.

lice /laɪs/ n. plural of **louse**.

licence /ˈlaɪsəns/ n. **1.** formal permission to do something, as to carry on some business, sell alcoholic drinks, etc. **2.** such permission in written form; a certificate or permit. **3.** freedom from strict rules of action, speech, writing style, etc.: poetic licence. **4.** uncontrolled freedom of behaviour.

licence plate n. → **numberplate**.

license /ˈlaɪsəns/ v.t. (**-censed**, **-censing**) to grant authoritative permission or licence to; authorise. −**licensor**, **licenser**, n. −**licensee**, n. −**licensing**, n.

licensed /ˈlaɪsənst/ adj. (of a club, restaurant, etc.) authorised to sell alcoholic beverages for consumption on the premises.

licentious /laɪˈsɛnʃəs/ adj. **1.** sensually unbridled; libertine; lewd. **2.** unrestrained by law or morality; lawless; immoral. **3.** going beyond customary or proper bounds or limits. −**licentiously**, adv. −**licentiousness**, n.

lichen /ˈlaɪkən/ n. **1.** any of the group Lichenes, of the Thallophyta, compound plants (fungi in symbiotic union with algae) having a vegetative body (thallus) growing in greenish, grey, yellow, brown, or blackish crust-like patches or bush-like forms on rocks, trees, etc. **2.** Pathol. any of various eruptive skin diseases. −**lichenous**, adj.

licit /ˈlɪsət/ adj. permitted; lawful. −**licitly**, adv.

lick /lɪk/ v.t. **1.** (sometimes fol. by off, from, etc.) to pass the tongue over the surface of. **2.** to affect by strokes of the tongue: to lick the plate clean. **3.** to pass or play lightly over, as flames do. **4.** Colloq. to overcome in a fight, etc.; defeat. **5.** Colloq. to outdo; surpass. −n. **6.** a stroke of the tongue over something. **7.** a small quantity. **8.** → **salt lick**. **9.** Jazz a short instrumental decoration usually about one bar long which is played between the phrases of a song or melodic line: he played hot licks on the trumpet. **10.** Colloq. speed: it all happened at a tremendous lick. −phr. **11. a lick and a promise,** Colloq. **a.** a hasty tidy-up or wash. **b.** a perfunctory, or superficial attempt at doing something. **12. lick into shape,** to bring to a state of completion or perfection; make efficient. **13. lick one's chops** (or **lips**), **a.** to indicate one's appetite for or appreciation of food by, or as by, licking one's lips. **b.** to anticipate something with greedy pleasure. **14. lick one's wounds,** to retire and recover after a defeat. **15. lick someone's boots,** to act in a subservient manner to someone; fawn upon someone. **16. lick the dust,** Colloq. **a.** to be killed or wounded. **b.** to grovel; humble oneself abjectly. −**licker**, n.

licorice /ˈlɪkərɪʃ, ˈlɪkrɪʃ, -rəs/ *n.* **1.** a leguminous plant, *Glycyrrhiza glabra*, of Europe and Asia. **2.** the sweet-tasting dried root of this plant, or an extract made from it, used in medicine, confectionery, etc. **3.** any of various related or similar plants, such as *G. acanthocarpa*. Also, **liquorice**.

lid /lɪd/ *n.* **1.** a movable piece, whether separate or hinged, for closing the opening of a vessel, box, etc.; a movable cover. **2.** an eyelid. **3.** *Aust. Colloq.* a hat. –*phr.* **4. keep the lid on**, *Colloq.* to maintain as a clandestine activity (corruption or secret dealings). **5. lift the lid on**, to reveal or expose (corruption or secret dealings). **6. put the lid on, a.** to clamp down on or put an end to: *to put the lid on prostitution.* **b.** to remove as a possibility: *that puts the lid on our holiday.* **7. take** (or **blow**) **the lid off**, to reveal or expose (corruption or secret dealings). –**lidded**, *adj.*

lie¹ /laɪ/ *n.* **1.** a false statement made with intent to deceive; an intentional untruth; a falsehood. **2.** something intended or serving to convey a false impression. –*verb* (**lied**, **lying**) –*v.i.* **3.** to speak falsely or utter untruth knowingly, as with intent to deceive. **4.** to express what is false, or convey a false impression. –*v.t.* **5.** to bring to a specific state or effect by lying: *to lie oneself out of a difficulty.* –*phr.* **6. give the lie to, a.** to charge with lying; contradict flatly. **b.** to imply or show to be false; belie.

lie² /laɪ/ *v.i.* (**lay**, **lain**, **lying**) **1.** to be in a recumbent or prostrate position, as on a bed or the ground; recline. **2.** (sometimes fol. by *down*) to assume such a position: *to lie down on the ground.* **3.** to be buried (in a particular spot). **4.** to rest in a horizontal position; be stretched out or extended: *a book lying on the table.* **5.** to be or remain in a position or state of inactivity, subjection, restraint, concealment, etc.: *to lie in ambush.* **6.** to be found, occur, or be (where specified): *the fault lies here.* **7.** to be placed or situated: *land lying along the coast.* **8.** to be in or have a specified direction: *the trail from here lies to the west.* –*n.* **9.** manner of lying; the relative position or direction in which something lies: *lie of the land.* **10.** the place where a bird, beast, or fish is accustomed to lie or lurk. **11.** *Golf* the ground position of the golf ball. –*phr.* **12. as far as in me lies**, to the best of my ability. **13. let sleeping dogs lie**, to avoid any disturbance, or a controversial topic or action. **14. lie down under**, to accept (abuse, etc.) without protest. **15. lie in, a.** to be confined in childbed. **b.** to stay late in bed. **c.** to consist or be grounded in: *the real remedy lies in education.* **16. lie in state**, (of a corpse) to be honourably displayed, as in a church, etc. **17. lie low**, to be in hiding. **18. lie off**, (of a ship) to stand some distance away from the shore. **19. lie on** (or **upon**), **a.** to rest, press, or weigh on: *these things lie upon my mind.* **b.** to depend on. **20. lie over**, to be postponed or deferred. **21. lie to**, *Naut.* (of a ship) to lie comparatively stationary, usually with the head as near the wind as possible. **22. lie up, a.** to stay in bed. **b.** (of a ship) to go into dock. **23. lie with, a.** to be the function or responsibility of: *it lies with you to resolve the problem.* **b.** to have sexual intercourse with.

lied /lid/ *n.* (*pl.* **lieder** /ˈlidə/) a song, lyric, or ballad, especially one characteristic of the German Romantic period.

liege /lidʒ, liʒ/ *n.* **1.** a lord entitled to allegiance and service. **2.** a vassal or subject, as of a ruler.

lien /ˈliən/ *n. Law* the right to hold property or to have it sold or applied for payment of a claim.

lieu /lu, lju/ *n.* place; stead. –*phr.* **2. in lieu of**, instead of.

lieutenant /lɛfˈtɛnənt, luˈtɛnənt/, *Navy* /ləˈtɛnənt/ *n.* **1.** *Navy* **a.** a commissioned officer in the Royal Australian Navy ranking below lieutenant commander and above sub lieutenant. **b.** the rank. *Abbrev.*: LEUT **2.** *Army* **a.** a commissioned officer in the Australian Army ranking below captain and above second lieutenant. **b.** the rank. *Abbrev.*: LT **3.** someone who holds an office, civil or military, in subordination to a superior, for whom he or she acts.

lieutenant colonel /lɛfˌtɛnənt ˈkɜnəl/ *n. Army* **1.** a commissioned officer in the Australian Army ranking below colonel and above major. **2.** the rank. *Abbrev.*: LTCOL

lieutenant commander /lətɛnənt kəˈmændə/ *n. Navy* **1.** a commissioned officer in the Royal Australian Navy ranking below commander and above lieutenant. **2.** the rank. *Abbrev.*: LCDR

lieutenant general /lɛfˌtɛnənt ˈdʒɛnrəl/ *n. Army* **1.** a commissioned officer in the Australian Army ranking below general and above major general. **2.** the rank. *Abbrev.*: LTGEN

life /laɪf/ *n.* (*pl.* **lives**) **1.** the condition which distinguishes animals and plants from inorganic objects and dead organisms. The distinguishing manifestations of life are: growth through metabolism, reproduction, and the power of adaptation to environment through changes originating internally. **2.** the animate existence, or the term of animate existence, of an individual: *to risk one's life.* **3.** a corresponding state, existence, or principle of existence conceived as belonging to the soul: *eternal life.* **4.** a state or condition of existence as a human being: *life is not a bed of roses.* **5.** a period of existence from birth to death: *in later life she became more placid.* **6. a.** the term of existence, activity, or effectiveness of something inanimate, as a machine or a lease. **b.** Also, **lifetime**. *Physics* the average period between the appearance and disappearance of a particle. **7.** a living being: *several lives were lost.* **8.** (often used in combination) living things collectively, whether animals or plants: *insect life.* **9.** a course or mode of existence: *married life.* **10.** a biography: *a life of Menzies.* **11.** animation, liveliness: *a speech full of life.* **12.** that which makes or keeps alive; the vivifying or quickening principle. **13.** existence in the world of affairs, society, etc. **14.** someone or something that enlivens: *the life of the party.* **15.** effervescence or sparkle, as of wines. **16.** pungency or strong, sharp flavour, as of substances when fresh or in good condition. **17.** *Cricket* the quality in the pitch which causes the ball to rise abruptly or unevenly after leaving the ground. **18.** the living form or model as the subject in art. **19. a.** a prison sentence covering the rest of the convicted person's natural life. **b.** the maximum possible term of imprisonment that can be awarded by the laws of a state. –*phr.* **20. (a matter of) life and death**, a critical situation. **21. as large as life**, actually; in person. **22. come to life, a.** to recover consciousness. **b.** to display liveliness or vigour. **c.** to appear lifelike; be convincing or realistic. **23. for dear life**, urgently; desperately. **24. for the life of one**, with one's greatest effort: *for the life of me I can't understand her.* **25. from (the) life**, (of a drawing, painting, etc.) drawn from a living model. **26. get a life**, *Colloq.* an exclamation of derision at another person's outlook on life as expressed in some mean or petty behaviour. **27. go for one's life**, *Colloq.* to do something with one's utmost vigour. **28. have the time of one's life**, to enjoy oneself enormously. **29. life of Riley**, a life of ease and luxury: *after I won the pools it was just a life of Riley.* **30. life sucks (and then you die)** or **life's a bitch (and then you die)**, *Colloq.* a catchphrase expressing the notion that life is full of difficulty and ultimately pointless. **31. not on your (sweet) life**, *Colloq.* (*emphatic*) absolutely not. **32. such is life**, an exclamation indicating resignation or tolerance. **33. take one's life in one's hands**, to risk death. **34. take one's own life**, to commit suicide.

35. take someone's life, to kill someone. **36. that's life**, an exclamation indicating resignation or tolerance. **37. to the life**, being an exact imitation or copy. –**lifelike**, *adj.* –**lifeless**, *adj.*

life assurance *n.* → **life insurance**.

lifebelt /'laɪfbɛlt/ *n.* a belt of buoyant material to keep a person afloat in the water.

lifeboat /'laɪfboʊt/ *n.* a boat, provisioned and equipped for abandoning ship.

lifebuoy /'laɪfbɔɪ/ *n.* a buoyant device (in various forms) for throwing, as from a vessel, to persons in the water, to enable them to keep afloat until rescued.

life coach *n.* a person who offers training in dealing with life situations in a way that maximises the client's potential. –**life coaching**, *n.*

lifeguard /'laɪfgɑd/ *n.* **1.** someone employed at a place where people swim to rescue and give first aid to those in distress. **2.** *Brit.* one of a bodyguard of soldiers.

life hack *n.* a tool or technique that makes some aspect of one's life easier.

life insurance *n.* insurance providing payment of a specific sum of money to a named beneficiary upon the death of the assured, or to the assured or to a named beneficiary should the assured reach a specified age. Also, **life assurance**.

life jacket *n.* an inflatable or buoyant sleeveless jacket for keeping a person afloat in water. Also, **life vest**.

lifeline /'laɪflaɪn/ *n.* **1.** a line or rope for saving life, e.g. one attached to a lifeboat. **2.** a route over which supplies can be sent to an area otherwise cut off. **3.** anything supplying emergency help, communication, counselling, etc.

lifesaver /'laɪfseɪvə/ *n.* **1.** *Aust.* a person trained in rescue and resuscitation methods, who patrols beaches, pools, lakes and other places of aquatic recreation. **2.** → **surf lifesaver**. **3.** any person who restores another to good spirits with comfort, help, etc. **4.** anything restorative or beneficial rectifying: *that bank loan was a real life-saver.*

lifesaving /'laɪfseɪvɪŋ/ *n.* *Aust.* the techniques and practices, especially rescue and resuscitation methods, developed to deal with emergency situations in or near the water, as in swimming pools, lakes, beaches, etc.

life sciences *pl. n.* the sciences concerned with living things, such as biology, botany, physiology, etc.

life skill *n.* a skill which enables one to deal effectively with the practical day-to-day requirements of adult life.

lifestreaming /'laɪfstrimɪŋ/ *n.* the online recording of one's daily life, delivered either by means of a webcam, or aggregated from personal blogs, microblogs, etc.

lifestyle /'laɪfstaɪl/ *n.* a mode of life chosen by a person or group.

lifestyle drug *n.* a prescription medicine that is used not to cure illness but to enhance the wellbeing of the healthy by improving looks, sexual performance, etc.

lifetime /'laɪftaɪm/ *n.* **1.** the time that one's life continues; one's term of life: *peace within our lifetime.* **2.** → **life** (def. 6b). –*adj.* **3.** lasting a lifetime.

lift /lɪft/ *v.t.* **1.** to move or bring (something) upwards from the ground or other support to some higher position; hoist. **2.** to raise or direct upwards: *to lift the hand*; *to lift the eyes.* **3.** to raise in rank, condition, estimation, etc.; elevate or exalt. **4.** to make louder: *to lift the voice.* **5.** to bring to an end: *to lift a ban.* **6.** *Colloq.* **a.** to copy; plagiarise. **b.** to steal. –*v.i.* **7.** to go up; give to upward pressure: *the lid won't lift.* **8.** (of clouds, fog, etc.) to rise and gradually disappear. –*n.* **9.** the act of lifting, raising, or rising: *the lift of a hand.* **10.** the distance anything is raised. **11.** a lifting or raising force. **12.** a moving platform or cage for bringing goods, people, etc., from one level to another in a building. **13.** any device or apparatus for lifting. **14.** a free ride in a

vehicle. **15.** a raising of spirits or feelings; encouragement. **16.** an upward force of air acting on an aeroplane wing, etc. –**lifter**, *n.*

lift-off *n.* Also, **blast-off**. **1.** the start of a rocket's flight from its launching pad. –*adj.* **2.** removable by lifting: *a lift-off lid.*

ligament /'lɪgəmənt/ *n.* (*pl.* **ligaments** *or* **ligamenta** /lɪgə-'mɛntə/) **1.** *Anat.* a band of tissue, usually white and fibrous, serving to connect bones, hold organs in place, etc. **2.** a connecting link; bond. –**ligamentous** /lɪgə-'mɛntəs/, **ligamentary** /lɪgə'mɛntəri/, *adj.*

ligature /'lɪgətʃə/ *n.* **1.** the act of binding or tying up. **2.** anything that serves for binding or tying up, as a band, bandage, or cord. **3.** a tie or bond. **4.** *Printing, Writing* a stroke or bar connecting two letters. **5.** *Music* **a.** a slur. **b.** a group of notes connected by a slur.

light¹ /laɪt/ *n.* **1.** that which makes things visible, or affords illumination: *all colours depend on light.* **2.** *Physics* **a.** Also, **luminous energy**, **radiant energy**. electromagnetic radiation to which the organs of sight react, ranging in wavelength from about 4×10^{-7} to 7.4×10^{-7} metres and travelling at a speed defined to be 299 792 458 metres per second. **b.** the sensation produced by it on the organs of sight. **c.** a similar form of radiant energy which does not affect the retina, as ultraviolet or infra-red rays. **3.** an illuminating agent or source, as the sun, a lamp, or a beacon. **4.** the light, radiance, or illumination from a particular source: *the light of a candle.* **5.** the illumination from the sun, or daylight. **6.** daybreak or dawn. **7.** daytime. **8.** measure or supply of light; illumination: *the wall cuts off our light.* **9.** a particular light or illumination in which an object seen takes on a certain appearance: *viewing the portrait in various lights.* **10.** the aspect in which a thing appears or is regarded: *this shows up in a favourable light.* **11.** a gleam or sparkle, as in the eyes. **12.** a means of igniting, as a spark, flame, match, or the like: *could you give me a light?* **13.** a window, or a pane or compartment of a window. **14.** mental or spiritual illumination or enlightenment: *to throw light on a mystery.* **15.** (*pl.*) information, ideas, or mental capacities possessed: *to act according to one's lights.* **16.** a person who is an illuminating or shining example; a luminary. **17.** a lighthouse. **18.** a traffic light. –*adj.* **19.** having light or illumination, rather than dark: *the lightest room in the entire house.* **20.** pale, whitish, or not deep or dark in colour: *a light red.* –*verb* (**lit** *or* **lighted**, **lighting**) –*v.t.* **21.** to set burning (a candle, lamp, pipe for smoking, etc.); kindle (a fire); ignite (fuel, a match, etc.). **22.** to give light to; illuminate; furnish with light or illumination. **23.** to conduct with a light: *a candle to light you to bed.* –*v.i.* **24.** to take fire or become kindled. –*phr.* **25. bring to light**, to discover; reveal. **26. come to light**, to be discovered; become known. **27. in a bad light**, under unfavourable circumstances. **28. in a good light**, under favourable circumstances. **29. in the light of**, taking into account; considering. **30. light up, a.** to make bright as with light or colour: *a huge room lit up with candles.* **b.** to cause (the face, etc.) to brighten or become animated: *a smile lit up her face.* **c.** to become bright as with light or colour: *the sky lights up at sunset.* **d.** to brighten with animation or joy, as the face, eyes, etc. **e.** to apply a flame to a cigarette, cigar, pipe, etc., in order to smoke it. **31. out like a light**, *Colloq.* unconscious, especially after being struck, or receiving an anaesthetic. **32. see the light, a.** to come into existence. **b.** to be made public, or published, as a book. **c.** to accept or understand an idea; realise the truth of something. **d.** to be converted, especially to Christianity. **33. shed (or throw) light on**, to make clear; explain. **34. stand in someone's light**, (*esp. in the negative*) *Colloq.* to actively prevent someone from doing what they want to do. **35. the lights are on but nobody's home**, *Colloq.* a catchphrase implying that someone is failing to comprehend.

light² /laɪt/ *adj.* **1.** of little weight; not heavy: *a light load.* **2.** of little weight in proportion to bulk; of low specific gravity: *a light metal.* **3.** of less than the usual or average weight: *light clothing.* **4.** connected or concerned with the manufacture of goods less substantial than those produced by large-scale engineering: *light industry.* **5.** of small amount, force, intensity, etc.: *light rain; light sleep.* **6.** gentle; delicate; exerting only slight pressure. **7.** easy to endure, deal with, or perform: *light duties.* **8.** not profound, serious, or heavy: *light reading.* **9.** of little moment or importance; trivial: *the loss was no light matter.* **10.** easily digested. **11.** not heavy or strong, as wine, etc. **12.** having less of a normal standard ingredient: *light beer.* **13.** (of bread, cakes, etc.) spongy or well leavened. **14.** porous or friable, as soil. **15.** slender or delicate in form or appearance: *a light, graceful figure.* **16.** airy or buoyant in movement: *light as air.* **17.** nimble or agile: *light on one's feet.* **18.** free from any burden of sorrow or care: *a light heart.* **19.** cheerful: *a light laugh.* **20.** characterised by lack of proper seriousness; frivolous. **21.** wanton; immoral. **22.** dizzy, as from fever: *a light head.* **23.** *Mil.* lightly armed or equipped: *light infantry.* **24.** adapted by small weight or slight build for small loads or swift movement: *light vessels.* **25.** *Phonetics* **a.** having a less than normally strong pronunciation, as of a vowel or syllable. **b.** (of *l* sounds) resembling a front vowel in quality: *French l is lighter than English l.* –*adv.* **26.** lightly. **27.** with little or no luggage: *to travel light.* **28.** with little or no cargo: *a ship sailing light.* –*phr.* **29. light on**, *Colloq.* **a.** *Aust.* in short supply; scarce: *money was light on then.* **b.** (sometimes fol. by *for*) poorly supplied: *we're light on for flour.* **30. make light of**, to treat as of little importance.

light³ /laɪt/ *v.i.* (**lighted** *or* **lit**, **lighting**) **1.** to get down or descend, as from a horse or a vehicle. **2.** to come to rest, as on a spot or thing; land. **3.** to fall, as a stroke, weapon, vengeance, choice, etc., on a place or person. –*phr.* **4. light on** (or **upon**), to come on by chance; happen on; hit on: *to light on a clue.* **5. light out**, *Colloq.* to depart hastily.

light-emitting diode *n.* a semiconductor diode that emits light when a current flows through it. *Abbrev.*: LED

lighten¹ /ˈlaɪtn/ *v.i.* **1.** to become lighter or less dark; brighten. **2.** to shine, gleam, or be bright. **3.** to flash like lightning. **4.** (of the face, eyes, etc.) to brighten or light up. –*v.t.* **5.** to illuminate. **6.** to brighten (the eyes, features, etc.). **7.** to make lighter; make less dark. –**lightener**, *n.*

lighten² /ˈlaɪtn/ *v.t.* **1.** to make lighter; lessen the weight of (a load, etc.); reduce the load of (a ship, etc.). **2.** to make less burdensome; mitigate: *to lighten taxes.* **3.** to cheer or gladden. –*v.i.* **4.** to become less burdensome, oppressive, etc. –*phr.* **5. lighten up**, *Colloq.* to become more cheerful or lively.

lighter¹ /ˈlaɪtə/ *n.* a mechanical device for lighting cigarettes, cigars, etc.

lighter² /ˈlaɪtə/ *n.* a vessel, commonly a flat-bottomed unpowered barge, used in lightening or unloading and also in loading ships, or in transporting goods for short distances.

lighthouse /ˈlaɪthaʊs/ *n.* a tower or other structure displaying a light or lights for the guidance of vessels at sea.

light meter *n. Photography* an instrument which measures the light intensity and indicates the proper exposure for a given scene. Also, **exposure meter**.

lightning /ˈlaɪtnɪŋ/ *n.* a flashing of light, or a sudden illumination of the sky, caused by the discharge of atmospheric electricity.

lightning strike *n.* **1.** a hit from a bolt of lightning onto the ground, or onto an object on the ground or in the air. **2.** a stoppage of work by employees with little or no warning to employers.

light-pen *n.* a light sensitive device, made to look like a pen, which by moving the position of a point of light on a display screen, can interact with a computer.

lightweight /ˈlaɪtweɪt/ *adj.* **1.** light in weight. **2.** unimportant, not serious; trivial. –*n.* **3.** one of less than average weight. **4.** *Colloq.* a person of little mental force or of slight influence or importance. **5. a.** a light-to-medium weight division in boxing. **b.** a boxer of this weight class.

light-year *n. Astron.* the distance traversed by light in one year ($9.460\,55 \times 10^{15}$ metres), used as a unit in measuring stellar distances. *Symbol:* l.y.

ligneous /ˈlɪgniəs/ *adj.* relating to or resembling wood; woody.

lignite /ˈlɪgnaɪt/ *n.* an imperfectly formed coal, usually dark brown, and often having a distinct woody texture; brown coal; wood coal. –**lignitic** /lɪgˈnɪtɪk/, *adj.*

ligno- a word element meaning 'wood'.

lignum /ˈlɪgnəm/ *n.* a tall, almost leafless shrub, *Muehlenbeckia florulenta*, growing in tangled, impenetrable thickets; common on wet, low-lying ground in the interior of Australia.

like¹ /laɪk/ *prep.* **1.** similarly to; in a manner characteristic of: *they lived like kings.* **2.** typical or characteristic of: *an act of kindness just like him.* **3.** bearing resemblance to: *he is like his father.* **4.** for example; as; such as: *the basic necessities of life, like food and drink.* **5.** indicating a probability of: *it looks like being a fine day; that seems like a good idea.* **6.** desirous of; disposed to (after *feel*): *I feel like a double whisky.* **7.** introducing an intensive, sometimes factious, comparison: *like hell; like anything.* –*adj. Archaic* **8.** of the same form, appearance, kind, character, amount, etc.: *a like instance.* **9.** corresponding or agreeing in general or in some noticeable respect; similar; analogous: *drawing, painting, and like arts.* **10.** bearing resemblance. **11.** likely. –*adv. Colloq.* **12.** (used after a clause to weaken the force of a direct statement) so to speak; as it were: *it was a bit tough, like; they've gone bad, like.* **13.** used for emphasis: *this big guy, like really big, suddenly, like, rushed up to me.* –*conj.* **14.** just as, or as: *she did it like she wanted.* **15.** as if: *he acted like he was afraid.* –*n.* **16.** a like person or thing, or like persons or things; a counterpart, match, or equal: *no one has seen her like in a long time.* –*phr.* **17. like enough**, likely: *he is like enough to go.* **18. the like**, something of a similar nature: *oranges, lemons, and the like.* **19. the likes of**, anyone who bears a resemblance to: *we will not see the likes of her again.*

like² /laɪk/ *v.t.* **1.** to take pleasure in; find agreeable to one's taste. **2.** to regard with favour, or have a kindly or friendly feeling for (a person, etc.). **3.** (in social media) to indicate support, enthusiasm, etc., for (a post, image, etc.), as by activating a button, tapping on an image, etc. –*v.i.* **4.** to feel inclined, or wish: *come whenever you like.* –*n.* **5.** (*usu. pl.*) a favourable feeling; preference: *likes and dislikes.* **6.** (in social media) an instance of liking (def. 3): *to get hundreds of likes for a photo.* –**likeable**, **likable**, *adj.* –**liking**, *n.*

-like a suffix of adjectives, use of **like¹**, as in *childlike, lifelike, businesslike*, sometimes hyphenated.

likely /ˈlaɪkli/ *adj.* (**-lier**, **-liest**) **1.** probably or apparently going or destined (to do, be, etc.): *likely to happen.* **2.** seeming like truth, fact, or certainty, or reasonably to be believed or expected; probable: *a likely story.*

3. apparently suitable: *a likely spot to build on.* **4.** promising: *a fine likely boy.* –*adv.* **5.** probably. –**likelihood,** *n.*

liken /ˈlaɪkən/ *v.t.* to represent as like; compare.

likeness /ˈlaɪknəs/ *n.* **1.** a representation, picture, or image, especially a portrait. **2.** the semblance or appearance of something: *to assume the likeness of a swan.* **3.** the state or fact of being like.

likewise /ˈlaɪkwaɪz/ *adv.* **1.** moreover; also; too. **2.** in like manner.

lilac /ˈlaɪlək/ *n.* **1.** any of the shrubs constituting the genus *Syringa,* as *S. vulgaris,* the common garden lilac, with large clusters of fragrant purple or white flowers. **2.** pale reddish purple. **3.** the scent of lilac, especially in perfumes, etc. –*adj.* **4.** having the colour lilac.

Lilliputian /lɪləˈpjuʃən/ *adj.* **1.** tiny; diminutive. **2.** narrow-minded; petty. –*n.* **3.** a tiny being. **4.** a person of narrow outlook; a petty-minded person.

lilly pilly /ˈlɪli pɪli/ *n.* a tree, *Acmena smithii,* with purplish white fruits, common along streams and in rainforests of eastern Australia. Also, **lilli pilli.**

lilt /lɪlt/ *n.* **1.** rhythmic swing or cadence. **2.** a lilting song or tune. –*v.i.* **3.** to sing or play in a light, tripping, or rhythmic manner. –*v.t.* **4.** to sing or play (a tune) in a light, tripping, or rhythmic manner.

lily /ˈlɪli/ *n.* (*pl.* **lilies**) **1.** a plant with a scaly bulb and showy, funnel-shaped or bell-shaped flowers of various colours. **2.** → **fleur-de-lis.** –*adj.* **3.** delicate, fair or white as a lily. **4.** pure; unspoiled. –*phr.* **5. gild the lily,** to spoil beauty by overembellishment.

lily-livered /ˈlɪli-lɪvəd/ *adj.* weak; cowardly.

lily-of-the-valley *n.* a stemless herb, *Convallaria majalis,* with a raceme of drooping, bell-shaped, fragrant white flowers.

lima bean /ˈlaɪmə bin/ *n.* **1.** a kind of bean, including several varieties of *Phaseolus lunatus,* with a broad, flat, edible seed. **2.** its seed, green or white when small or white when larger, much used for food.

limb /lɪm/ *n.* **1.** a part or member of an animal body distinct from the head and trunk, as a leg, arm, or wing. **2.** a large or main branch of a tree. **3.** a projecting part or member: *the four limbs of a cross.* **4.** a person or thing regarded as a part, member, branch, offshoot, or scion of something. –*phr.* **5. out on a limb,** in a dangerous or exposed position. –**limbed** /lɪmd/, *adj.* –**limbless,** *adj.*

limber /ˈlɪmbə/ *adj.* **1.** bending readily; flexible; pliant. **2.** characterised by ease in bending the body; supple; lithe. –*v.t.* **3.** to make limber. –*phr.* **4. limber up,** to make oneself limber. –**limberly,** *adv.* –**limberness,** *n.*

limbo¹ /ˈlɪmboʊ/ *n.* (*pl.* **-bos**) **1.** *Roman Catholic Church* (*oft. upper case*) (formerly) a supposed region on the border of hell or heaven, the abode after death of unbaptised infants (**limbo of infants**), or one serving as the temporary abode of the righteous who died before the coming of Christ (**limbo of the fathers** or **limbo of the patriarchs**). **2.** (*oft. upper case*) a place to which persons or things are regarded as being relegated when cast aside, forgotten, past, or out of date. **3.** (*oft. upper case*) prison, jail, or confinement. –*phr.* **4. in limbo,** in a situation characterised by uncertainty, as when waiting for a decision to be made.

limbo² /ˈlɪmboʊ/ *n.* a type of dance where each dancer in turn bends backwards in order to pass underneath a horizontal bar which is gradually lowered.

lime¹ /laɪm/ *n.* **1.** the oxide of calcium, CaO, a white caustic solid (**quicklime** or **unslaked lime**) prepared by calcining limestone, etc., used in making mortar and cement. When treated with water it produces calcium hydroxide, $Ca(OH)_2$, or **slaked lime**. **2.** any calcium compounds for improving crops on lime-deficient soils. –*v.t.* **3.** to treat (soil, etc.) with lime or compounds of calcium. **4.** to catch with, or as with, birdlime. –**limy,** *adj.*

lime² /laɪm/ *n.* **1.** Also, **Tahitian lime, Persian lime. a.** the oval, acid fruit of the tree, *Citrus latifolia,* which is green when ripe but yellowing and more juicy with age. **b.** the tree itself. **2.** Also, **Kaffir lime. a.** the small, knobbly fruit of the Asian tree, *Citrus hystrix.* **b.** the tree itself, whose dark, glossy, double-lobed leaves are used in cooking. **3.** Also, **key lime, West Indian lime, Mexican lime. a.** the small, greenish-yellow, acid fruit of a tropical tree, *Citrus aurantiifolia,* which is stronger in flavour than the Tahitian lime. **b.** the tree itself. **4.** any of several trees of the *Citrus* genus bearing similar fruit, as the desert lemon. **5.** a greenish yellow colour. –*adj.* **6.** having a lime colour. **7.** consisting of, made with, or flavoured with limes: *lime pickle.*

lime³ /laɪm/ *n.* → **linden.**

limelight /ˈlaɪmlaɪt/ *n.* **1.** a strong light, made by heating a cylinder of lime in a flame of mixed gases, formerly thrown upon the stage to illuminate particular persons or objects. **2.** the glare of public interest or notoriety. –*phr.* **3. steal the limelight,** to make oneself the centre of attention.

limerick /ˈlɪmərɪk/ *n.* a type of humorous verse of five lines, in which the first and second lines rhyme with the fifth line, and the shorter third line rhymes with the shorter fourth.

limestone /ˈlaɪmstoʊn/ *n.* a rock consisting wholly or chiefly of calcium carbonate, originating principally from the calcareous remains of organisms, and when heated yielding quicklime.

limit /ˈlɪmət/ *n.* **1.** the end or furthest point of something: *the limit of vision.* **2.** a boundary or bound, as of a country, district, etc. **3.** *Maths* **a.** (of a function at a point) a number such that the value of the function can be made arbitrarily close to this number by restricting its argument to be sufficiently near the point. **b.** (of a sequence to infinity) a number such that the elements of the sequence eventually approach it in value. –*v.t.* **4.** (fol. by *to*) keep within fixed limits: *to limit answers to 25 words.* **5.** to confine or keep within limits: *to limit expenditures.* –*phr.* **6. the** (**dizzy**) **limit,** someone or something that annoys beyond endurance. –**limitable,** *adj.* –**limitative,** *adj.* –**limitary,** *adj.* –**limiter,** *n.*

limitation /lɪməˈteɪʃən/ *n.* **1.** something that limits; a limit or bound; a limited condition or circumstance; restriction. **2.** a limiting condition: *one should know one's limitations.* **3.** act of limiting. **4.** state of being limited.

limited /ˈlɪmətəd/ *adj.* **1.** confined within limits; restricted, circumscribed, or narrow: *a limited space.* **2.** restricted with reference to governing powers by limitations prescribed in a constitution: *a limited monarchy.* **3.** restricted as to amount of liability. **4.** *Aust.* (of a train) restricted as to places at which it stops, class of tickets available, number of passengers, etc. –*n.* **5.** *Aust., NZ* a limited train: *the Brisbane Limited.* –**limitedly,** *adv.* –**limitedness,** *n.*

limited company *n. Law* a company which can issue subscription and which may be listed on the stock exchange; there is a minimum number of shareholders but no maximum; on liquidation the liability of the shareholders for the company's debts is limited to any amounts unpaid on their shares. Also, **limited-liability company.**

limited liability *n.* the liability, either by law or contract, only to a limited amount for debts of a trading company or limited partnership.

limited-overs cricket *n.* → **one-day cricket.**

limousine /lɪməˈzin, ˈlɪməzin/ *n.* any large, luxurious car, especially a chauffeur-driven one, often with a glass division between the passengers and the driver.

limp[1] /lɪmp/ *v.i.* **1.** to walk with a laboured, jerky movement, as when lame; progress with great difficulty. **2.** to proceed in a lame or faltering manner: *his verse limps.* *–n.* **3.** a lame movement or gait. **–limper,** *n.*

limp[2] /lɪmp/ *adj.* **1.** lacking stiffness or firmness, as of substance, fibre, structure, or bodily frame: *a limp body.* **2.** tired; lacking vitality. **3.** without proper firmness, force, energy, etc., as of character. **–limply,** *adv.* **–limpness,** *n.*

limpet /'lɪmpət/ *n.* **1.** *Zool.* any of various marine gastropod molluscs with a low conical shell open beneath, found adhering to rocks, used for bait and sometimes for food. **2.** someone who is reluctant to give up a position or office.

limpid /'lɪmpəd/ *adj.* **1.** clear, transparent, or pellucid, as water, crystal, air, etc. **2.** free from obscurity; lucid: *a limpid style.* **–limpidity** /lɪm'pɪdəti/, **limpidness,** *n.* **–limpidly,** *adv.*

linchpin /'lɪntʃpɪn/ *n.* **1.** a pin inserted through the end of an axle to keep the wheel on. **2.** the key point of a plan, argument, etc. **3.** a key person or event, as in a play, etc. Also, **lynchpin.**

linden /'lɪndən/ *n.* any of the trees of the genus *Tilia,* which have yellowish or cream-coloured flowers and more or less heart-shaped leaves, as *T. europaea,* a common European species, and *T. americana,* a large American species often cultivated as a shade tree.

line[1] /laɪn/ *n.* **1.** a mark or stroke long in proportion to its breadth, made with a pen, pencil, tool, etc., on a surface. **2.** something resembling a traced line, as a band of colour, a seam, a furrow, etc.: *lines of stratification in rock.* **3.** a furrow or wrinkle on the face, etc. **4.** something arranged along a line, especially a straight line; a row or series: *a line of trees.* **5.** a row of people standing side by side or one behind another. **6.** a row of written or printed letters, words, etc.: *a page of thirty lines.* **7.** a verse of poetry. **8.** (*pl.*) the spoken words of a drama, etc., or of an actor's part: *the hero forgot his lines.* **9.** a ploy; deceit: *he gave me the old line about working late.* **10.** an opening conversational gambit employed to attract someone in whom one is romantically or sexually interested. **11.** a short written message: *a line from a friend.* **12.** an indication of demarcation; boundary; limit: *to draw a line between right and wrong.* **13.** a course of action, procedure, thought, etc.: *the Communist Party line.* **14.** a course of direction; route: *the line of march.* **15.** *Aust., NZ Colloq.* a bush road. **16.** a continuous series of persons or animals in chronological succession, especially in family descent: *a line of great kings.* **17.** (*pl.*) outline or contour: *a ship of fine lines.* **18.** (*pl.*) plan of construction, action, or procedure: *two books written on the same lines.* **19.** a kind of occupation or business: *what line is your father in?* **20. a.** any transport company or system. **b.** a system of public conveyances, as buses, steamers, etc., plying regularly between places. **21.** a strip of railway track, a railway, or a railway system. **22.** *Elect.* a wire circuit connecting two or more pieces of electrical apparatus. **23.** *TV* one scanning line. **24.** *Fine Arts* a mark from a crayon, pencil, brush, etc., in a work of graphic art, which defines the limits of the forms employed and is used either independently or in combination with modelling by means of shading. **25.** *Maths* a continuous extent of length, straight or curved, without breadth or thickness; the trace of a moving point. **26.** a supply of commercial goods of the same general class. **27.** *Music* one of the straight, horizontal, parallel strokes of the stave, or one above or below it. **28.** *Music* **a.** one of the parts, usually melodic, of a composition for many instruments or voices: *the vocal line; the violin line.* **b.** the line of music which is fundamental to the harmonies being played, often played in jazz or rock bands by the bass guitar. **29.** *Mil.* **a.** a defensive position: *the*

Brisbane line. **b.** a series of fortifications: *the Maginot line.* **30.** the line of arrangement of an army or of the ships of a fleet as drawn up ready for battle: *line of battle.* **31.** a body or formation of troops or ships drawn up abreast. **32.** a thread, string, thin wire, or the like. **33.** a length of cord, nylon, silk, or the like, bearing a hook or hooks, used in fishing. **34.** a strong cord or slender rope. **35.** → **clothes line. 36.** a cord, wire, or the like used for measuring or as a guide. **37.** *Naut.* a length of rope for any purpose. **38.** a pipe or hose: *a steam line.* **39.** a wire or cable used for communications, as in a telephone system or a computer network. **40.** a telephonic channel to a particular party: *I'm sorry, sir, that line is busy.* **41.** telephonic access to external channels from an internal system: *press 0 to get a line.* **42.** *Sport* a mark indicating the boundaries or divisions of a field or court. **43.** (*pl.*) a school punishment, usually consisting of writing out a phrase or sentence a specified number of times. **44.** a former unit of length equivalent to $\frac{1}{12}$ inch. **45.** *Colloq.* a measure of cocaine laid out for inhalation. *–v.t.* **46.** to draw or represent with a line or lines; delineate. **47.** to mark with a line or lines: *to line paper for writing.* **48.** to cover with lines or wrinkles: *a face lined with worry.* **49.** to arrange a line along. **50.** to form a line along: *people lined the streets.* *–phr.* **51. bring into line,** to cause or persuade to agree or conform. **52. come (or fall) into line,** to agree; conform. **53. do a line,** *Colloq.* to inhale a measure of cocaine. **54. do a line for,** *Colloq.* to flirt with. **55. do a line with,** *Colloq.* to enter into an amorous relationship with. **56. draw the line,** (sometimes fol. by *at*) to impose a limit; refuse to do something. **57. get a line on,** *Colloq.* to obtain information about. **58. get one's lines crossed,** *Colloq.* to misunderstand. **59. hard lines,** *Colloq.* bad luck. **60. in line, a.** (of three or more objects) arranged in a straight line; in alignment. **b.** in conformity or agreement. **c.** well-placed; with a good chance: *in line for promotion.* **61. in the line of duty,** as a part of one's responsibilities or obligations. **62. lay it on the line,** *Colloq.* to state the case openly and honestly. **63. line of least resistance,** the course of action requiring the minimum of effort or presenting the fewest difficulties. **64. line up, a.** to take a position in a line; range or queue. **b.** to bring into a line, or into line with others. **c.** to get hold of; make available: *we must line up a speaker for the conference.* **65. out of line,** not in accord with standard practice, agreement, etc.; deviant. **66. pay on the line,** to pay promptly. **67. put on the line,** *Colloq.* to expose to risk, usually to prove a point, endorse a principle, etc.: *in making this claim, she put her job on the line.* **68. read between the lines,** to find in something spoken or written more meaning than the words appear to express. **69. shoot a line,** *Colloq.* to boast. **70. stand in line,** to queue. **71. the line,** the equator. **72. toe the line,** to behave according to the rules; conform; obey. **–liny, liney,** *adj.*

line[2] /laɪn/ *v.t.* **1.** to cover or fit on the inner side with something: *to line drawers with paper.* **2.** to provide with a layer of material applied to the inner side: *to line a coat with silk.* **3.** to cover: *walls lined with bookcases.* **4.** to furnish or fill: *to line one's pockets with money.* **5.** to reinforce (the back of a book) with glued fabric, paper, vellum, etc. **–linage, lineage** /'laɪnɪdʒ/, *n.*

lineage /'lɪniɪdʒ/ *n.* **1.** lineal descent from an ancestor; ancestry or extraction. **2.** the line of descendants of a particular ancestor; a family or people.

lineal /'lɪniəl/ *adj.* **1.** being in the direct line, as a descendant, ancestor, etc., or descent, etc. **2.** of or transmitted by lineal descent. **3.** linear. **–lineally,** *adv.*

linear /'lɪniə/ *adj.* **1.** stretched in a line: *a linear series.* **2.** relating to length, measurement in one dimension only: *linear measure.* **3.** of or relating to a line or lines: *linear perspective.* **4.** of or relating to a work of art with strong outlines and edges of forms, or marked by having lines (rather than masses or areas): *a linear painting*; *a linear design*. **5.** looking like a line; narrow: *linear nebulae*; *a linear leaf*. **6.** *Maths* of a line that can be shown on a graph and described by such an equation as $x + y = 3$. **–linearly**, *adv.* **–linearity** /lɪniˈærəti/, *n.*

linedance /ˈlaɪndæns/ *n.* a form of synchronised dance, performed to country music, which consists of a repeated sequence of choreographed steps performed by a group of dancers facing the same direction in a line. **–linedancing**, *n.* **–linedancer**, *n.*

linen /ˈlɪnən/ *n.* **1.** fabric woven from flax yarns. **2.** household articles, as sheets, tablecloths, etc., made of linen or some substitute, as cotton. **3.** *Obs.* shirts and underwear, made of linen or a substitute. *–adj.* **4.** made of linen. *–phr.* **5. wash one's dirty linen in public**, to discuss disagreeable personal affairs in public.

line of credit *n. Finance* a borrowing facility, such as an option to draw bank bills, usually extended on an indefinite basis so that the borrower can draw on the funds when the need arises, or arranged pending a project for which the money is needed.

liner /ˈlaɪnə/ *n.* **1.** one of a commercial line of ships or aeroplanes. **2.** a cosmetic used to outline and highlight the eyes.

linesman /ˈlaɪnzmən/ *n.* (*pl.* **-men**) **1.** *Sport* a man on the sidelines who assists the referee or umpire in determining whether the ball is still in play. **2.** a man who erects or repairs telephone, electric power, or other overhead wires. **3.** *Aust.* the member of a surf-lifesaving team who handles the surf-line. Also, **lineman**. **–lineswoman**, *n.* **–linesperson**, *n.*

line-up *n.* **1.** a particular order or disposition of persons or things as lined up or drawn up for action, inspection, participation, as in a sporting team, a music band, etc. **2.** the persons or things themselves: *two suspects were included in the police line-up*. **3.** an organisation of people, companies, etc., for some common purpose. **4.** a sequence of programs or events: *tonight's TV line-up is a knockout*. **5.** *Surfing* the point where the waves are consistently starting to break.

ling /lɪŋ/ *n.* **1.** a common fish, *Lotella calaria*, belonging to the family Gadidae, reddish-brown in colour with a small barbel on the chin, found around the southern coast of Australia. **2.** an elongated marine gadoid food fish, *Molva molva*, of Greenland and northern Europe. **3.** any of certain other fishes, as the burbot.

-ling[1] a suffix found in some nouns, often pejorative, denoting one concerned with (*hireling, underling*); also diminutive (*princeling, duckling*).

-ling[2] an adverbial suffix expressing direction, position, state, etc., as in *darkling, sideling*.

linger /ˈlɪŋɡə/ *v.i.* **1.** to stay on in a place longer than is usual or expected, as if not wanting to leave it. **2.** to stay with something, as if interested or enjoying it: *he lingered over his book*; *to linger over a cup of coffee*. **3.** to be slow in action; delay; dawdle. **–lingerer**, *n.*

lingerie /ˈlɒnʒəreɪ/ *n.* underwear or other garments of cotton, silk, nylon, lace, etc., worn by women.

lingo /ˈlɪŋɡoʊ/ *n.* (*pl.* **-goes**) *Colloq.* **1.** language. **2.** peculiar or unintelligible language. **3.** language or terminology peculiar to a particular field, group, etc.; jargon.

lingua franca /lɪŋɡwə ˈfræŋkə/ *n.* any language widely used as a medium among speakers who have different primary languages.

lingual /ˈlɪŋɡwəl/ *adj.* **1.** of or relating to the tongue or some tongue-like part. **2.** of or relating to languages. **–lingually**, *adv.*

linguine /lɪŋˈɡwini/ *n.* (in Italian cookery) a style of pasta in long thin strips.

linguist /ˈlɪŋɡwəst/ *n.* **1.** someone who is skilled in foreign languages; polyglot. **2.** someone who specialises in linguistics.

linguistics /lɪŋˈɡwɪstɪks/ *n.* the science of language, including among its fields phonetics, phonemics, morphology, and syntax. **–linguistic**, *adj.*

liniment /ˈlɪnəmənt/ *n.* a liquid preparation, usually oily, for rubbing on or applying to the skin, as for sprains, bruises, etc.

lining /ˈlaɪnɪŋ/ *n.* **1.** that with which something is lined; a layer of material on the inner side of something. **2.** *Bookbinding* the material used to strengthen the back of a book after the sheets have been folded, backed, and sewn.

link /lɪŋk/ *n.* **1.** one of the rings or separate pieces of which a chain is composed. **2.** anything serving to connect one part or thing with another; a bond or tie. **3.** *Computers* a hypertext connection between two documents. **4.** one of a number of sausages in a chain. **5.** one of the 100 wire rods forming the divisions of a surveyor's chain of 66 ft (20.12 m). **6.** the set or effective length of one of these rods used as a measuring unit in the imperial system, equal to one hundredth of a chain, 7.92 in. or 0.201 168 m. **7.** *Machinery* a rigid movable piece or rod connected with other parts by means of pivots or the like, for the purpose of transmitting motion. *–v.t.* **8.** to join by or as by a link or links. *–v.i.* **9.** to join; unite. *–phr.* **10. link up**, (sometimes fol. by *with*) to make contact; communicate. **–linkage**, *n.*

linkbait /ˈlɪŋkbeɪt/ *Internet –v.t.* **1.** to create points of interest in (a website) so that other sites will link to it and increase traffic on the site, as by running competitions, featuring high-profile contributors, etc. *–n.* **2.** such an attractive feature of a site. **–linkbaiting**, *n.*

link rot *n. Internet* **1.** the process by which links on an internet site gradually become inoperative because of changes to the websites to which the links were originally attached. **2.** the effect on a website of the gradual accumulation of broken or out-of-date web pages.

links /lɪŋks/ *pl. n. Obs.* → **golf course**.

links course *n.* a golf course on open, naturally undulating ground, often near the sea.

linocut /ˈlaɪnoʊkʌt/ *n.* **1.** a design cut in relief on a block of linoleum. **2.** a print made from such a cut.

linoleum /ləˈnoʊliəm, laɪ-/ *n.* a floor covering formed by coating hessian or canvas with linseed oil, powdered cork, and rosin, and adding pigments of the desired colour. Also, **lino** /ˈlaɪnoʊ/.

linotype /ˈlaɪnətaɪp/ *n.* (*from trademark*) **1.** *Printing* a keyboard-operated composing machine which casts solid lines of type. **2.** printing produced by such a machine.

linseed /ˈlɪnsid/ *n.* the seed of flax.

lint /lɪnt/ *n.* **1.** a soft material for dressing wounds, etc., procured by scraping or otherwise treating linen cloth. **2.** bits of thread or fluff. **–linty**, *adj.*

lintel /ˈlɪntl/ *n.* a horizontal supporting member above an opening such as a window or a door.

lion /ˈlaɪən/ *n.* **1.** a large, greyish-tan cat, *Panthera leo*, native to Africa and southern Asia, the male of which usually has a mane. **2.** a person of great strength, courage, etc. **3.** a person of note or celebrity who is much sought after. *–phr.* **4. the lion's share**, the largest portion of anything.

lioness /ˈlaɪənɛs, laɪəˈnɛs/ *n.* a female lion.

lionise /ˈlaɪənaɪz/ *v.t.* to treat (a person) as a celebrity. Also, **lionize**. **–lionisation** /laɪənaɪˈzeɪʃən/, *n.*

lip /lɪp/ *n.* **1.** either of the two fleshy parts or folds forming the margins of the mouth and performing an important function in speech. **2.** (*pl.*) these parts as organs of speech. **3.** *Colloq.* impudent talk. **4.** a lip-like part or structure. **5.** *Bot.* either of the two parts (**upper lip** and **lower lip**) into which the corolla or calyx of certain plants (especially the mint family) is divided. **6.** *Zool.* **a.** → **labium. b.** the outer or the inner margin of the aperture of a gastropod's shell. **7.** any edge or rim. **8.** a projecting edge, as of a jug. **9.** the crest of a wave which is starting to break, but is not yet curling. **10.** the edge of an opening or cavity, as of a canyon or wound. –*adj.* **11.** relating to, characterised by, or made with the lips. –*phr.* **12. bite one's lip, a.** to show vexation. **b.** to stifle one's feelings, especially anger or irritability. **13. button** (**up**) **one's lips** or **button the lip**, to cease talking; keep quiet. **14. curl one's lip**, to show scorn. **15. give someone lip**, *Colloq.* to talk to someone, especially a superior, in a cheeky or insolent manner. **16. hang on the lips of**, to listen to very attentively or eagerly. **17. keep a stiff upper lip**, to face misfortune bravely, especially without outward show of perturbation. **18. lick** (or **smack**) **one's lips, a.** to indicate one's appetite for or appreciation of food by, or as by, licking one's lips. **b.** to anticipate or recall something with greedy pleasure.

lip- variant of **lipo-**, before vowels, as in *lipectomy.*

lip gloss *n.* a cosmetic applied to the lips to give them a glossy sheen, sometimes with a small amount of colour.

lipid /ˈlɪpɪd, ˈlaɪ-/ *n.* any of a large group of organic compounds including fats and oils, which are one of the structured components of living cells. They are insoluble in water, but soluble in alcohol and other organic solvents. Also, **lipide** /ˈlɪpaɪd, ˈlaɪ-/.

lipliner /ˈlɪplaɪnə/ *n.* a cosmetic used to give definition to the lip outline.

lipo- in chemistry a word element meaning 'fat', as in *lipochrome.* Also, **lip-.**

lipoprotein /lɪpəˈproʊtɪn/ *n.* any of a group of complex compounds of lipids and proteins, especially those occurring in the blood, used in the assessment of cardiac disease risk factors.

liposuction /ˈlaɪpoʊsʌkʃən/ *n.* the removal of unwanted subcutaneous fatty deposits from the body by means of vacuum suction.

lip-read /ˈlɪp-rid/ *verb* (**-read** /-rɛd/, **-reading**) –*v.t.* **1.** to understand (spoken words) by watching the movement of a speaker's lips. –*v.i.* **2.** to read lips.

lip-service *n.* service with words only; insincere profession of devotion or goodwill.

lipsmacking /ˈlɪpsmækɪŋ/ *adj.* **1.** delicious: *lipsmacking treats.* **2.** anticipated with great pleasure: *a lipsmacking deal.*

lipstick /ˈlɪpstɪk/ *n.* **1.** a dispenser of a cosmetic preparation for colouring the lips. **2.** the coloured preparation itself.

liquefied natural gas *n.* a natural gas consisting primarily of methane, liquefied to facilitate transport and storage; usually later regasified and used as a fuel, etc. *Abbrev.*: LNG

liquefied petroleum gas *n.* → **LPG.**

liquefy /ˈlɪkwəfaɪ/ *verb* (**-fied, -fying**) –*v.t.* **1.** to make liquid. –*v.i.* **2.** to become liquid. Also, **liquify.** –**liquefiable,** *adj.* –**liquefier,** *n.*

liqueur /ləˈkjuə, ləˈkɜ/ *n.* any of a class of alcoholic liquors, usually strong, sweet, and highly flavoured, as chartreuse, curaçao, etc.

liquid /ˈlɪkwəd/ *adj.* **1.** composed of molecules which move freely among themselves but do not tend to separate like those of gases; neither gaseous nor solid. **2.** of or relating to liquids: *liquid measure.* **3.** such as to flow like water; fluid. **4.** clear, transparent, or bright: *liquid eyes.* **5.** sounding smoothly or agreeably: *liquid tones.* **6.** *Phonetics* identified with or being either *r* or *l.* **7.** in cash or readily convertible into cash: *liquid assets.* –*n.* **8.** a liquid substance. **9.** *Phonetics* either *r* or

l. –*phr.* **10. go liquid**, to realise assets for cash. –**liquidly**, *adv.* –**liquidness**, *n.*

liquid assets *pl. n.* **1.** the part of a trading bank's assets which consist of its notes and coins, its cash with the Reserve Bank of Australia, and its Commonwealth Treasury bills. **2.** the cash and readily realisable assets of a company.

liquidate /ˈlɪkwədeɪt/ *v.t.* **1.** to get rid of (a debt, etc.); settle or pay: *to liquidate a claim.* **2.** to change into cash. **3.** to get rid of, especially by killing or other violent means. **4.** to break up or do away with; abolish. –*v.i.* **5.** (of a company) to pay off debts or accounts and finish up; wind up; go into liquidation. –**liquidation**, *n.*

liquidator /ˈlɪkwədeɪtə/ *n.* a person appointed to carry out the winding up of a company.

liquidity /ləˈkwɪdəti/ *n.* **1.** liquid state or quality. **2.** the state of having assets either in cash or readily convertible into cash.

liquid ratio *n.* the ratio of a company's liquid assets to its current liabilities. Also, **liquidity ratio.**

liquor /ˈlɪkə/ *n.* **1.** spirits (as brandy or whisky) as distinguished from fermented beverages (as wine or beer). **2.** a solution of a substance, especially a concentrated one used in an industrial process.

liquorice /ˈlɪkərɪʃ, ˈlɪkrɪʃ, -rəs/ *n.* → **licorice.**

lira /ˈlɪərə/ *n.* (*pl.* **lira** *or* **liras** *or* **lire** /ˈlɪəreɪ/) **1.** (formerly, until the introduction of the euro in 2002) the principal monetary unit of Italy. **2.** the principal monetary unit of Turkey.

lisp /lɪsp/ *n.* **1.** a speech defect consisting in pronouncing *s* and *z* like or nearly like the *th* sounds of *thin* and *this*, respectively. **2.** the act, habit, or sound of lisping. –*v.t.* **3.** to pronounce with a lisp. –*v.i.* **4.** to speak with a lisp. –**lisper**, *n.* –**lispingly**, *adv.*

lissom /ˈlɪsəm/ *adj.* **1.** lithe, especially of body; limber or supple. **2.** agile or active. Also, *Chiefly US*, **lissome.** –**lissomness**, *n.*

list[1] /lɪst/ *n.* **1.** a record consisting of a series of names, words, or the like; a number of names of persons or things set down one after another. –*v.t.* **2.** to set down together in a list; to make a list of. **3.** to enter in a list with others. **4.** to register (a security) on a stock exchange so that it may be traded there. –**listing**, *n.*

list[2] /lɪst/ *v.i.* (of a ship) to careen; incline to one side: *the ship listed to starboard.*

listen /ˈlɪsən/ *v.i.* **1.** to give attention with the ear; attend closely for the purpose of hearing; give ear. **2.** to give heed; yield to advice. –*phr.* **3. listen for**, to wait attentively to hear. **4. listen in, a.** to eavesdrop. **b.** to listen to a radio program. **5. listen up**, *Chiefly US* to pay attention: *now listen up everybody.* –**listener**, *n.*

listicle /ˈlɪstɪkəl/ *n.* a type of article in online journalism and blogging which is presented in the form of a list.

listless /ˈlɪstləs/ *adj.* **1.** feeling no inclination towards or interest in anything. **2.** characterised by or indicating such feeling: *a listless mood.* –**listlessness**, *n.* –**listlessly**, *adv.*

listserv /ˈlɪstsɜv/ *n.* *Computers* a mailing list server which automatically sends emails addressed to a mailing list to all addresses on the list, operating in a similar way to a newsgroup but with the messages being accessible only to those included on the mailing list.

lit /lɪt/ *v.* **1.** past tense and past participle of **light**[1] and **light**[3]. –*phr.* **2. lit up** (**like a Christmas tree**) (or **birthday cake**), **a.** illuminated. **b.** *Colloq.* intoxicated.

litany /ˈlɪtəni/ *n.* (*pl.* **-nies**) **1.** a ceremonial or liturgical form of prayer consisting of a series of invocations or supplications with responses which are the same for a number in succession. **2.** a prolonged recitation; monotonous account.

-lite a word element used in names of minerals, or fossils: *chrysolite, aerolite*.

literacy /ˈlɪtərəsi/ *n.* **1.** the ability to read and write. **2.** the ability to use a language effectively: *her literacy in French was growing.* **3.** an ability to use communications technology that is digitally based: *computer literacy.*

literal /ˈlɪtrəl, ˈlɪtərəl/ *adj.* **1.** following the exact words of the original: *a literal translation.* **2.** (of people) tending to understand words too strictly or unimaginatively; matter-of-fact; prosaic: *a literal mind.* **3.** being the natural, basic, or strict meaning of a word; not figurative or metaphorical. **4.** true to fact; not exaggerated: *a literal statement of conditions.* **5.** of or relating to the letters of the alphabet: *a literal mistake.* **–literalness**, *n.*

literally /ˈlɪtrəli, ˈlɪtərəli/ *adv.* **1.** in a literal manner; word for word: *to translate literally.* **2.** in the literal sense: *parachutists dropping in, literally.* **3.** (an intensifier) **a.** applied to a literal meaning: *literally screaming with excitement.* **b.** (*not considered standard by some*) applied to a figurative meaning: *we are literally bending over backwards to take into account the concerns raised by the public.*

literary /ˈlɪtərəri, ˈlɪtrəri/, *Orig. US* /ˈlɪtərɛri/ *adj.* **1.** relating to or of the nature of books and writings, especially those classed as literature: *literary history.* **2.** knowledgeable about or having a great interest in literature. **3.** engaged in writing books, etc., or in literature as a profession: *a literary man.* **4.** pedantic; excessively affected in displaying learning. **–literarily**, *adv.* **–literariness**, *n.*

literate /ˈlɪtərət/ *adj.* **1.** able to read and write. **2.** having an education; educated. **3.** literary. *–n.* **4.** someone who can read and write. **5.** a learned person.

literature /ˈlɪtrətʃə, ˈlɪtərətʃə/ *n.* **1.** writings in which expression and form, together with ideas of lasting and universal interest, are important features, as poetry, drama, history, biography, essays, etc. **2.** all the writings of a particular language, period, people, etc.: *the literature of Australia*; *Russian medieval literature.* **3.** writings dealing with a particular subject: *the literature on sailing ships.* **4.** the profession of a writer or author. **5.** *Colloq.* printed matter of any kind, as circulars or advertising matter.

lith- a combining form meaning 'stone'. Also, **litho-**.

-lith a word element forming a noun termination meaning 'stone', as in *acrolith, megalith, nephrolith, palaeolith*, sometimes occurring in words, as *batholith, laccolith*, that are variants of forms in *-lite*. Compare **-lite**.

lithe /laɪð/ *adj.* bending readily; pliant; limber; supple. Also, **lithesome** /ˈlaɪðsəm/. **–lithely**, *adv.* **–litheness**, *n.*

lithic /ˈlɪθɪk/ *adj.* relating to or consisting of stone.

-lithic an adjective suffix identical with **lithic**, used especially in archaeology, as, *palaeolithic*.

litho- variant of **lith-**, before consonants, as in *lithography*.

lithography /lɪˈθɒɡrəfi/ *n.* the art or process of printing a picture, writing, or the like, from a flat surface of aluminium, zinc, or stone, with some greasy or oily substance. **–lithographer**, *n.* **–lithographic** /lɪθəˈɡræfɪk/, **lithographical** /lɪθəˈɡræfɪkəl/, *adj.* **–lithographically** /lɪθəˈɡræfɪkli/, *adv.*

lithosphere /ˈlɪθəsfɪə/ *n.* the crust or solid part of the earth, in contrast to the hydrosphere and the atmosphere, comprising the continental crust, oceanic crust and the brittle part of the upper mantle. See **continental crust, oceanic crust**.

litigant /ˈlɪtəgənt/ *n.* **1.** someone engaged in a lawsuit. *–adj.* **2.** litigating; engaged in a lawsuit.

litigate /ˈlɪtəgeɪt/ *v.t.* **1.** to make the subject of a lawsuit; to contest at law. **2.** to dispute (a point, etc.). *–v.i.* **3.** to carry on a lawsuit. **–litigation** /lɪtəˈgeɪʃən/, *n.* **–litigator**, *n.* **–litigable**, *adj.*

litmus /ˈlɪtməs/ *n.* a colouring substance obtained from certain lichens, especially *Roccella tinctoria*. In alkaline solution litmus turns blue, in acid solution red; hence it is widely used as an indicator, especially in the form of strips of paper impregnated with a solution of the colouring matter (**litmus paper**).

litmus test *n.* **1.** a test of acidity or alkalinity using litmus paper. **2.** a decisive test of a person's loyalty, character, determination, etc.

litre /ˈlitə/ *n.* a unit of capacity in the metric system, formerly equal to the volume of one kilogram of water at its maximum density or approximately equal to $1.00028 \times 10^{-3} \text{m}^3$, now exactly equal to 10^{-3}m^3. It is commonly used to express volumes of liquids. *Symbol*: L, l Also, *US*, **liter**.

-litre a word element meaning 'litres' or 'of or relating to a litre', as in *centilitre*. Also, *US*, **-liter**.

litter /ˈlɪtə/ *n.* **1.** things scattered about; scattered rubbish. **2.** a condition of disorder or untidiness. **3.** a number of young brought forth at one birth. **4.** a framework of canvas stretched between two parallel bars, for the transportation of the sick and the wounded. **5.** a vehicle carried by people or animals, consisting of a bed or couch, often covered and curtained, suspended between shafts. **6.** *Agric.* **a.** a bed or stratum of various materials, especially a deep layer of straw and dung in an animal shed. **b.** straw, hay, etc., used as a protection for plants. **7.** the rubbish of dead leaves and twigs scattered upon the floor of the forest. **8.** → **kitty litter**. *–v.t.* **9.** to strew (a place) with scattered objects. **10.** to scatter (objects) in disorder. **11.** to give birth to (young), said chiefly of animals. **12.** to supply (an animal) with litter for a bed. **13.** to use (straw, hay, etc.) for litter. **14.** to cover (a floor, etc.) with litter, or straw, hay, etc. *–v.i.* **15.** to give birth to a litter. *–phr.* **16. litter up**, to be strewn about (a place) in disorder. **–litterer**, *n.*

litterbug /ˈlɪtəbʌg/ *n.* someone who drops rubbish, especially in public places.

little /ˈlɪtl/ *adj.* **1.** small in size; not big or large: *a little child.* **2.** small in extent or duration; short; brief: *a little while.* **3.** small in number: *a little army.* **4.** small in amount or degree; not much: *little hope.* **5.** being such on a small scale: *little farmers.* **6.** small in force; weak: *a little voice.* **7.** small in consideration, dignity, consequence, etc.: *little discomforts.* **8.** mean, narrow, or illiberal: *a little mind.* **9.** endearingly small or considered as such: *bless your little heart!* **10.** held dear through familiarity: *I understand his little ways.* *–pron.* **11.** a small amount: *she ate very little*; *I remember little of what he told me.* *–adv.* **12.** not at all: *he little knows what awaits him.* **13.** in only a small amount or degree; not much: *a zeal little tempered by humanity.* **14.** rarely; infrequently: *I see my mother very little.* *–phr.* **15. a little, a.** a small amount: *give me a little more; there is still a little left; would you like a little soup?* **b.** sufficient to have an effect; appreciable: *we're having a little trouble.* **c.** in a small degree; somewhat: *I feel a little better now.* **d.** a short distance: *move back a little, please.* **e.** a short time: *why don't you stay a little?* **16. little by little**, by degrees; gradually. **17. make little of, a.** to belittle; disparage. **b.** to understand only partially; grasp inadequately: *I can make little of your writing.* **18. not a little**, a very great deal; considerable. **–littleness**, *n.*

little penguin *n.* → **fairy penguin**.

little tern *n.* the smallest Australian tern, *Sterna albifrons*, grey, with white underparts, black-tipped flight feathers, black crown, and white on the forehead extending in thin lines over the eyes, found on the north and east coasts of Australia, and also in North America, Africa, Europe, central Asia, and Japan.

littoral /ˈlɪtərəl/ *adj.* relating to the shore of a lake, sea, or ocean.

liturgy /ˈlɪtədʒi/ *n.* (*pl.* **-gies**) **1.** a form of public worship; a ritual. **2.** a collection of formularies for public worship. **3.** a particular arrangement of services. **4.** a particular form or type of the Eucharistic service. **5.** the service of the Eucharist, especially in the Eastern Church. –**liturgist,** *n.* –**liturgical** /lɪˈtɜːdʒɪkəl/, *adj.*

live[1] /lɪv/ *verb* (**lived** /lɪvd/, **living**) –*v.i.* **1.** to have life, as an animal or plant; be alive; be capable of vital functions. **2.** to continue to live; remain alive: *to live long.* **3.** to continue in existence, operation, memory, etc.; last: *looks which lived in my memory.* **4.** to escape destruction or remain afloat, as at sea. **5.** to maintain life; rely for maintenance: *to live on one's income.* **6.** to dwell or reside: *to live in a cottage.* **7.** to pass life (as specified): *they lived happily ever after.* **8.** to direct or regulate one's life: *to live by the golden rule.* **9.** to experience or enjoy life to the full. –*v.t.* **10.** to pass (life): *to live a life of ease.* **11.** to carry out or exhibit in one's life. –*phr.* **12. live and learn,** to acquire new knowledge; learn through experience. **13. live and let live,** to be tolerant. **14. live apart,** (especially of a husband and wife) to live separately after the rupture of a close relationship. **15. live dangerously,** to take risks; live with little regard to one's personal safety. **16. live down,** to live so as to cause (something) to lose force or be forgotten: *to live down a mistake; he'll never live it down.* **17. live high,** to live at a high standard; live luxuriously. **18. live in,** to reside at the place of one's work or study. **19. live it up,** *Colloq.* to live wildly and exuberantly; go on a spree. **20. live off,** to subsist from: *live off the land.* **21. live on** (or **upon**), to feed or subsist on: *to live on rice.* **22. live on borrowed time,** (of someone close to death) to live a period of time longer than might be expected. **23. live out,** to reside away from the place of one's work or study. **24. live together,** to dwell together as lovers; cohabit. **25. live up to,** to accord with or maintain (expectations or standards). **26. live with,** to dwell together with, as a husband or wife or lover; to cohabit with. **27. live with oneself,** to come to terms with one's conscience; to retain one's self-respect.

live[2] /laɪv/ *adj.* **1.** living or alive: *live animals.* **2.** full of energy, activity or brilliance. **3.** still burning: *live coals.* **4.** flowing freely: *live water.* **5.** loaded or unexploded: *live cartridge.* **6.** charged with electricity: *live wire.* **7. a.** (of a radio or television program) broadcast or televised at the moment it is being presented in the studio or elsewhere: *a live telecast; live to air.* **b.** (of a performance) given in concert or in the theatre, etc., opposed to a filmed or broadcast performance. **c.** (of an audience) actually present, as when a radio or television program is being recorded. **8.** *Colloq.* of interest at the moment: *a live issue.* –*adv.* **9.** (of a radio or television program) not taped; broadcast at the time of its happening: *this race is brought to you live from the Olympic swimming pool.*

live feed /laɪv ˈfid/ *n.* a transmission by a media outlet of an event, sporting match, concert, etc., as it is happening.

livelihood /ˈlaɪvlihʊd/ *n.* means of maintaining life; maintenance: *to gain a livelihood.*

lively /ˈlaɪvli/ *adj.* (**-lier, -liest**) **1.** energetic; vigorous; animated: *a lively discussion.* **2.** spirited; vivacious: *a lively tune.* **3.** eventful or exciting: *a lively time.* **4.** vivid or keen: *a lively colour; a lively imagination.* –**livelily,** *adv.* –**liveliness,** *n.*

liven /ˈlaɪvən/ *phr.* **liven up, 1.** to put life into; rouse; cheer. **2.** to become more lively; brighten. –**livener,** *n.*

live pause /laɪv ˈpɔz/ *n.* a facility on a DVR by which it is possible to interrupt a television program during its telecast and start recording it, making it possible to return to watch it from the point at which it was stopped.

liver[1] /ˈlɪvə/ *n.* **1.** (in humans) a large, reddish brown glandular organ (divided by fissures into five lobes) in the upper right-hand side of the abdominal cavity, secreting bile and performing various metabolic functions, and formerly supposed to be the seat of love, desire, courage, etc. **2.** an organ in other animals similar to the human liver, often used as food. **3.** a disordered state of the liver. **4.** a reddish brown colour. –*adj.* **5.** the colour of liver.

liver fluke *n.* a ribbon-like platyhelminth parasitic worm, *Fasciola hepatica*, which lives in the bile ducts of sheep.

liverish /ˈlɪvərɪʃ/ *adj.* **1.** having one's liver out of order. **2.** disagreeable as to disposition. Also, **livery**.

liver spot *n.* a brownish patch on the skin, usually of an elderly person.

liverwurst /ˈlɪvəwɜst/ *n.* a sausage made with a large percentage of liver. Also, **liver sausage**.

livery /ˈlɪvəri/ *n.* (*pl.* **-ries**) **1.** a distinctive dress, badge, or device provided for retainers, as of a feudal lord. **2.** a kind of uniform worn by servants, now only menservants, of a person or household. **3.** a distinctive dress worn by an official, a member of a company or guild, etc.

livery stable *n.* a stable where horses and vehicles are cared for or let out for hire.

lives /laɪvz/ *n.* plural of **life**.

livestock /ˈlaɪvstɒk/ *n.* the horses, cattle, sheep, and other useful animals kept or bred on a farm or ranch.

live stream /laɪv ˈstrim/ *Telecommunications* –*v.t.* **1.** to deliver (media content) directly to the end user by a streaming process as the action is occurring. See **streaming** (def. 2). –*n.* **2.** such a content delivery. –**live streaming,** *n.*

live trade /laɪv ˈtreɪd/ *n.* the export of live animals destined to be slaughtered in another country.

liveware /ˈlaɪvwɛə/ *n.* the personnel involved with the use of a computer, as programmers, key punch operators, etc. See **software, hardware**.

live weight *n.* the weight of an animal while living.

livewire /ˈlaɪvwaɪə/ *n.* *Colloq.* an energetic, alert person.

livid /ˈlɪvəd/ *adj.* **1.** having a discoloured bluish appearance due to a bruise, to congestion of blood vessels, etc., as the flesh, face, hands, or nails. **2.** dull blue; dark greyish blue. **3.** angry; enraged. –**lividly,** *adv.* –**lividness, lividity** /lɪˈvɪdəti/, *n.*

living /ˈlɪvɪŋ/ *adj.* **1.** that lives; alive, or not dead. **2.** in actual existence or use: *living languages.* **3.** active; strong: *a living faith.* **4.** burning or glowing, as a coal. **5.** flowing freely, as water. **6.** (of rock or stone, etc.) in its natural state and place; native, as part of the earth's crust. **7.** lifelike, as a picture. **8.** of or relating to living beings: *within living memory.* **9.** relating to or sufficient for living: *living conditions.* **10.** absolute; entire (used as an intensifier): *to scare the living daylights out of someone.* –*n.* **11.** the act or condition of someone or something that lives: *living is very expensive these days.* **12.** manner or course of life: *good living.* **13.** means of maintaining life; livelihood: *to earn one's living.* **14.** the benefits and responsibilities of an appointment as an ecclesiastical minister. –*phr.* **15. a good living,** a style of life which is typified by a high standard of material goods. **16. for a living,** as a livelihood. **17. the living,** those alive at any one given time.

living fossil *n.* a plant or animal species which has continued to survive in its native habitat since prehistoric times, such as the Wollemi pine, or is almost identical to species only known from the fossil record, such as the platypus.

living national treasure *n.* → **national living treasure**.

living will *n.* an instruction as to the type and level of health care a person wishes to receive in the case of the person being no longer able to indicate his or her wishes, particularly used to instruct against the use of extraordinary measures such as life support systems to prolong their life in the case of terminal illness or injury; health care directive.

lizard /ˈlɪzəd/ *n.* any reptile of the order Lacertilia, including also larger forms, the monitors, geckos, chameleons, and various limbless forms.

'll a shortening of *will* or *shall*.

llama /ˈlɑːmə/ *n.* **1.** a domesticated South American ruminant, *Lama glama*, used as a beast of burden, thought to be descended from the guanaco. **2.** the fine, soft fleece of the llama, combined with the wool for coating.

lo¹ /loʊ/ *interj. Archaic* look! see! behold!

lo² /loʊ/ *adj.* (*esp. in compounds*) low: *lo-cal; lo-fat.*

load /loʊd/ *n.* **1.** that which is laid on or placed in anything for conveyance. **2.** (*oft. used to create compound nouns*) the quantity that can be or usually is carried, as in a cart; this quantity taken as a unit of measure or weight. **3.** anything upborne or sustained: *the load of fruit on a tree.* **4.** something that weighs down or oppresses like a burden. **5.** the amount of work required of a person, machine, organisation, etc. **6.** the charge of a firearm. **7.** (*pl.*) *Colloq.* a great quantity or number: *loads of people.* **8.** the weight supported by a structure or part. **9.** *Elect.* the power delivered by a generator, motor, power station, or transformer. **10.** *Elect., Physics* the resistance or impedance connected to a network containing a source or sources of electromotive force. **11.** *Mechanics* the external resistance overcome by an engine, dynamo, or the like, under a given condition, measured by the power required. **12.** *Colloq.* an infection of venereal disease, usually gonorrhoea. **13.** *Colloq.* a sufficient quantity of liquor drunk to intoxicate. –*v.i.* **14.** to put a load on or in: *to load a cart.* **15.** to supply abundantly or excessively with something: *to load a person with gifts.* **16.** to weigh down, burden, or oppress. **17.** to give bias to, especially by fraudulent means. **18.** to make (dice) heavier on one side than on the others by fraudulent means so as to cause them to fall with a particular face upwards. **19.** *Insurance* to increase (a net premium, etc.). See **loading** (def. 5). **20.** to take on as a load: *a vessel loading coal.* **21.** to charge (a firearm, camera, etc.). –*v.i.* **22.** to put on or take on a load. **23.** to load a firearm, camera, etc. **24.** to become loaded. **25.** to enter a means of conveyance: *the football fans loaded into special buses.* –*phr.* **26. get a load of,** *Colloq.* to take notice of: *Get a load of that, would you!* **27. load the dice,** to cause a situation to be especially favourable or unfavourable, often unfairly. **28. shoot one's load,** *Colloq.* (*taboo*) (of a man) to ejaculate (def. 1). **29. take a load off** (**one's feet**), *Colloq.* to sit down. –**loader,** *n.*

loaded /ˈloʊdəd/ *adj.* **1.** carrying a load: *a loaded ship.* **2.** charged: *a loaded gun.* **3.** (of a question, statement, etc.) unfair; weighted so as to produce a prejudicial effect. **4.** (of dice) dishonestly weighted. **5.** *Colloq.* very rich. **6.** *Colloq.* drunk or under drugs.

loading /ˈloʊdɪŋ/ *n.* **1.** that with which something is loaded; a load; a burden; a charge. **2.** an extra rate paid to employees in recognition of a particular aspect of their employment, as shift work. **3.** *Elect.* the process of adding inductances to a telephone circuit, radio aerial, etc. **4.** *Aviation* the ratio of the gross weight of an aeroplane to engine power (**power loading**), wing span (**span loading**), or wing area (**wing loading**).

5. *Insurance* an addition to the normal premium on the policy of a person whose life expectancy is considered to be less than the mortality tables would indicate.

loaf¹ /loʊf/ *n.* (*pl.* **loaves** /loʊvz/) **1.** a portion of bread or cake baked in a mass of definite form. **2.** a shaped or moulded mass of food, as of sugar, chopped meat, etc.: *a veal loaf.*

loaf² /loʊf/ *v.i.* **1.** to lounge or saunter lazily and idly. **2.** to idle away time. –*n.* **3.** an idle or relaxing time; rest. **4.** an easy job; sinecure. –*phr.* **5. loaf away,** to idle away: *to loaf one's life away.*

loaf³ /loʊf/ *n.* **1.** *Colloq.* head; intelligence; brains. –*phr.* **2. use one's loaf,** to think; apply one's intelligence.

loafer /ˈloʊfə/ *n.* (*from trademark*) a casual shoe.

loam /loʊm/ *n.* **1.** a loose soil composed of clay and sand, especially a kind containing organic matter and of great fertility. **2.** a mixture of clay, sand, straw, etc., used in making moulds for founding, and in plastering walls, stopping holes, etc. –*v.t.* **3.** to cover or stop with loam. **4.** *Mining* to sort through (a section or container of dirt) and separate out opal, gold, etc. –*v.i.* **5.** to search for a mineral, usually gold, by washing loam from the base of a hill to isolate the required mineral. –**loamy,** *adj.*

loan /loʊn/ *n.* **1.** the act of lending; a grant of the use of something temporarily: *the loan of a book.* **2.** something lent or provided on condition of being returned, especially a sum of money lent at interest. –*v.t.* **3.** to make a loan of; lend. **4.** to lend (money) at interest. –*v.i.* **5.** to make a loan or loans. –**loaner,** *n.*

loath /loʊθ/ *adj.* **1.** reluctant, averse, or unwilling. –*phr.* **2. nothing loath,** very willingly. Also, **loth.**

loathe /loʊð/ *v.t.* to feel hatred, disgust, or intense aversion for. –**loather,** *n.*

loathsome /ˈloʊðsəm/ *adj.* such as to excite loathing; hateful; disgusting. –**loathsomely,** *adv.* –**loathsomeness,** *n.*

loaves /loʊvz/ *n.* plural of **loaf¹.**

lob /lɒb/ *n.* **1.** *Tennis, Squash, etc.* a ball hit high into the opponent's court. –*verb* (**lobbed, lobbing**) –*v.t.* **2.** *Tennis, Squash, etc.* to send (a ball) high into the air. **3.** to throw in a careless or untidy fashion. –*v.i.* **4.** *Tennis, Squash, etc.* to lob a ball. **5.** to land, usually after a highly curved trajectory: *it circled round and lobbed on the beach.* **6.** (sometimes fol. by *in, into, at,* etc.) to arrive: *they lobbed in at about 3 o'clock.* –*phr.* **7. lob on** (or **onto**), *Colloq.* to land on by chance: *the request lobbed on my desk.*

lobby /ˈlɒbi/ *n.* (*pl.* **-bies**) **1.** a corridor, vestibule, or entrance hall, as in a public building, often serving as an anteroom. **2.** a group of persons who attempt to influence legislators or other public officials on behalf of some particular cause or interest; originally those who frequented legislative lobbies or chambers. **3.** a particular interest, cause, etc., supported by a group of people. –*verb* (**-bied, -bying**) –*v.i.* **4. a.** *US Hist.* to often visit the entrance hall of a legislative chamber to influence the members. **b.** to request the votes of members of a law-making body. –*v.t.* **5.** to influence (law-makers), or urge or obtain the passage of (a bill), by trying to enlist political support. –**lobbyism,** *n.* –**lobbyist,** *n.*

lobe /loʊb/ *n.* **1.** a roundish projection or division, as of an organ, a leaf, etc. **2.** *Anat.* the soft pendulous lower part of the external ear.

lobotomy /ləˈbɒtəmi/ *n.* (*pl.* **-tomies**) *Surg.* the cutting into or across a lobe of the brain, usually of the cerebrum, to alter brain function, especially in the treatment of mental disorders. Also, **leucotomy.**

lobster /ˈlɒbstə/ *n.* **1.** → **rock lobster. 2.** any of various edible, freshwater, stalk-eyed decapod crustaceans of the family Nephropidae, found in the Northern

Hemisphere, with large claws and a smooth carapace; crayfish.

local /'loʊkəl/ *adj.* **1.** relating to or marked by place, or position in space. **2.** typical of, or limited to, a particular place or places: *a local custom.* **3.** belonging to or made in a particular country rather than overseas: *local wine.* **4.** relating to a town or a small area rather than the whole state or country. **5.** relating to or affecting particular part or parts, as of a system or object: *a local disease.* **6.** (of anaesthesia or an anaesthetic) acting on only a section of the body, without causing loss of consciousness. *–n.* **7.** a local train, bus, etc. **8.** a suburban newspaper. **9.** the closest or preferred hotel in the neighbourhood of one's home or place of work. **10.** an inhabitant of a particular place. **11.** → **local anaesthetic.** **–locally,** *adv.*

local anaesthesia *n.* **1.** drug-induced loss of sensation in a part of the body. **2.** the administration of a drug to produce this effect. Also, **local anesthesia.**

local anaesthetic *n.* **1.** a drug, usually injected, which anaesthetises only part of the body. **2.** the procedure for this. Also, **local anesthetic.**

local area network *n.* a computer networking system which links computers within a limited geographical area to a central computer by means of landlines. *Abbrev.*: LAN Compare **wide area network**.

locale /loʊ'kal/ *n.* a place or locality, especially with reference to events or circumstances connected with it.

local government *n.* **1.** the administration of the affairs of a regional district, in Australia usually an area smaller than that of a state such as a shire, municipality, town, etc., by officers elected by the residents and ratepayers of that district. **2.** the decision-making officers in such a group: *the local governments could not agree.*

localise /'loʊkəlaɪz/ *v.t.* to make local; fix in, or assign or restrict to, a particular place or locality. Also, **localize.** **–localisable,** *adj.* **–localisation** /loʊkəlaɪ'zeɪʃən/, *n.*

locality /loʊ'kæləti/ *n.* (*pl.* **-ties**) **1.** a place, spot, or district, with or without reference to things or persons in it. **2.** the place in which a thing is or occurs. **3.** state or condition of being local or having place.

locate /loʊ'keɪt/ *v.t.* **1.** to discover the place or location of: *to locate a leak in a pipe.* **2.** to set, fix, or establish in a place, situation, or locality; place; settle: *they located their headquarters in Brisbane.* **3.** to refer (something), as by opinion or statement, to a particular place: *this study locates the garden of Eden in Babylonia.*

location /loʊ'keɪʃən/ *n.* **1.** a house or place of business: *a good location for a doctor.* **2.** a place or position: *a house in a fine location.* **3.** a piece of land in a particular place and with limits: *a mining location.* **4.** *Film, TV* a place, outside the studio, providing suitable surroundings for photographing plays, events, etc. **5.** the act of settling in a certain position or place.

locavore /'loʊkəvɔː/ *n.* a person who eats only food that is locally produced, from the conviction that fresh food is nutritionally better and tastes better, and often also in an effort to reduce greenhouse gas emissions produced in transporting foodstuffs.

loch /lɒk/ *n. Scottish* **1.** a lake. **2.** Also, **sea loch.** an arm of the sea, especially when partially landlocked.

loci /'lɒkɪ, 'loʊkɪ/ *n.* plural of **locus.**

lock¹ /lɒk/ *n.* **1.** a device for securing a door, gate, lid, drawer, or the like in position when closed, consisting of a bolt or system of bolts propelled and withdrawn by a mechanism operated by a key, dial, etc. **2. a.** a device to keep a wheel from rotating. **b.** steering lock. **3.** a contrivance for fastening or securing something. **4.** the mechanism in a firearm by means of which it can be kept from operating. **5.** an enclosed portion of a canal,

river, etc., with gates at each end, for raising or lowering vessels from one level to another. **6.** any of various grapples or holds in wrestling, especially any hold in which an arm or leg of one wrestler is held about the body of the opponent. **7.** the extent by which the steering mechanism of a vehicle is able to turn the front wheels from one extreme to the other. *–v.t.* **8. a.** to fasten or secure (a door, building, etc.) by the operation of a lock. **b.** → **latch** (def. 2). **9.** to make fast or immovable by or as by a lock: *to lock a wheel.* **10.** Also, **lock up.** to fasten or fix firmly, as by engaging parts. **11.** to join or unite firmly by interlinking or intertwining: *to lock arms. –v.i.* **12.** to become locked. **13.** to become fastened, fixed, or interlocked. *–phr.* **14. lock down,** **a.** to secure (a location) against a perceived threat by cutting off the access and halting movement of people in and around it. **b.** to secure (a communications system) against a perceived threat from hackers, by restricting access. **15. lock into,** to involve in a system or situation from which it is not possible to withdraw **16. lock out,** to exclude by or as by a lock. **17. lock, stock, and barrel,** altogether; completely. **18. lock up** (or **in**), to shut in a place fastened by a lock or locks, as for security or restraining: *they locked the dog up for the night.* **19. lock up the land,** *Aust. Hist.* to make the land unavailable to all but very few people (by giving out only large parcels of it by grant or to squatters).

lock² /lɒk/ *n.* **1.** a tress or portion of hair. **2.** (*pl.*) the hair of the head.

lock-and-key theory *n. Biochem.* the theory that cells specifically react with only one or very few similar compounds, the cell having the lock and a chemical such as an enzyme, drug, etc., being the key.

lockdown /'lɒkdaʊn/ *n.* **1.** *Prison* the confining of prisoners to the cells, usually as a security measure. **2.** a state of security alert in which access is cut off and movement of people in and around a location is brought to a halt. **3.** a state of alert in response to a natural phenomenon such as a cyclone, flood, etc., in which movement in an area is brought to a halt and people are confined to their homes or other safe locations. **4.** a state of restricted access to a communications system, designed as a security measure.

locker /'lɒkə/ *n.* a chest, drawer, compartment, closet, or the like, that may be locked.

locket /'lɒkət/ *n.* a small case for a miniature portrait, a lock of hair, or other keepsake, usually worn on a chain hung round the neck.

lockjaw /'lɒkdʒɔː/ *n. Pathol.* tetanus in which the jaws become firmly locked together.

locksmith /'lɒksmɪθ/ *n.* someone who makes or mends locks.

lockup /'lɒkʌp/ *n.* **1.** a jail, especially a local jail to which offenders are taken before their first court hearing. **2.** the act of locking up. **3.** a garage or other storage space, usually rented, capable of being locked up. **4.** *Stock Exchange* the period of time in which insiders cannot sell their shares in a company, especially immediately after the initial public offering. **5.** *Parliamentary Procedure* the state of seclusion in which the media are permitted to study the budget papers in advance of the treasurer delivering it. *–adj.* **6.** (of a room, garage, etc.) able to be locked up.

locomotion /loʊkə'moʊʃən/ *n.* the act or power of moving from place to place.

locomotive /loʊkə'moʊtɪv/ *n.* **1.** an engine which drives itself forward, running on a railway track, designed to pull railway carriages or trucks. **2.** any vehicle able to drive itself from place to place. *–adj.* **3.** moving or travelling by means of its own machinery or powers. **4.** of or relating to movement from place to place.

locum /ˈloʊkəm/ *n.* a temporary substitute for a doctor, lawyer, etc. Also, **locum tenens** /ˈloʊkəm ˈtɛnənz/.

locus /ˈlɒkəs, ˈloʊkəs/ *n.* (*pl.* **loci** /ˈlɒki, ˈloʊki, ˈloʊkaɪ/) **1.** a place; a locality. **2.** *Maths* a curve or other figure considered as generated by a point, line, or surface, which moves or is placed according to a definite law. **3.** *Genetics* the chromosomal position of a gene as determined by its linear order relative to the other genes on that chromosome.

locust /ˈloʊkəst/ *n.* **1.** any of the grasshoppers with short antennae which constitute the family Acrididae, including the notorious migratory species, such as *Pachytylus cinerascens*, which swarm in immense numbers and strip the vegetation from large areas; found in Europe, Africa and Asia. **2.** *Colloq.* → **cicada**. **3.** any of various trees, as the carob and the honey-locust.

locution /ləˈkjuʃən/ *n.* **1.** a particular form of expression; a phrase or expression. **2.** style of speech or verbal expression; phraseology.

lode /loʊd/ *n.* **1.** a veinlike deposit, usually metalliferous. **2.** any body of ore set off from adjacent rock formations.

lodge /lɒdʒ/ *n.* **1.** a small, slight, or rough shelter or place to live, made of branches, poles, skins, earth, rough boards, etc.; cabin or hut. **2.** a building used for temporary, usually holiday, housing: *fishing lodge*; *ski lodge*. **3.** a small house as in a park or on an estate, lived in by a caretaker, gardener, etc. **4.** the meeting place of a branch of a secret society. **5.** a cave or shelter of an animal or animals, especially of beavers. *–verb* (**lodged, lodging**) *–v.i.* **6.** to have a shelter or quarters, especially temporarily, as in a place or house. **7.** to be fixed or implanted, or be caught in a place or position. *–v.t.* **8.** to provide with a shelter or rooms, especially temporarily. **9.** to provide with a room or rooms in one's house for payment, or have as a lodger. **10.** to put (something) in a certain place for safety, storage or keeping. **11.** to put or send into a particular place: *to lodge a stake firmly in the ground*. **12.** to lay (information, a complaint, etc.) before a court, etc. *–***lodger**, *n.*

lodgement /ˈlɒdʒmənt/ *n.* **1.** act of lodging. **2.** state of being lodged. **3.** something lodged or deposited. **4.** *Mil.* a position or foothold gained from an enemy, or an entrenchment made upon it. Also, **lodgment**.

lodging /ˈlɒdʒɪŋ/ *n.* **1.** accommodation in a house, especially in rooms for hire: *to furnish board and lodging*. **2.** a place of abode, especially a temporary one. **3.** (*pl.*) a room or rooms hired for residence in another's house.

lo-fi /ˈloʊ-faɪ/ *adj.* **1.** of or relating to, or resulting in, sound reproduction of a lower quality than hi-fi. **2.** of or relating to a style of popular music recorded in a lo-fi way with a resultant fresh but unsophisticated sound: *experimental lo-fi funk*.

loft /lɒft/ *n.* **1.** the space between the underside of a roof and the ceiling of a room beneath it. **2.** a gallery or upper level in a church, hall, etc., designed for a special purpose: *a choir loft*. **3.** an apartment designed in a style that resembles a loft (def. 1). **4.** *Golf* **a.** the slope of the face of a club backwards from the vertical, tending to drive the ball upwards. **b.** a lofting stroke. *–v.t.* **5.** *Golf, Cricket, etc.* to hit (a ball) into the air or over an obstacle. **6.** to clear (an obstacle) thus.

lofty /ˈlɒfti/ *adj.* (**-tier, -tiest**) **1.** extending high in the air; of imposing height: *lofty mountains*. **2.** exalted in rank, dignity, or character. **3.** elevated in style or sentiment, as writings, etc. **4.** haughty; proud. *–n.* **5.** *Colloq.* (*upper case*) a term of address to a tall person. *–***loftily**, *adv.* *–***loftiness**, *n.*

log /lɒg/ *n.* **1.** an unhewn portion or length of the trunk or a large limb of a felled tree. **2.** something inert or heavy. **3. a.** the official record which a ship's master is obliged by law to keep, of particulars of a ship's voyage, as weather, crew, cargo, etc. **b.** the record which the engine-room and bridge officers keep of the particulars of each watch. **4.** Also, **flight log**. a listing of navigational, meteorological, and other significant data concerning an air journey. **5.** any similar record of a journey. **6.** the register of the operation of a machine. **7.** *Computers* → **log file**. **8.** *Aust.* a submission or listing: *the trade union's log of claims*. **9.** Also, **log of wood**. *Colloq.* a fool; a lazy person. **10.** a cake or confection in the shape of a log. *–verb* (**logged, logging**) *–v.t.* **11.** to cut (trees) into logs. **12.** to cut down trees of (an area, forest, etc.) for timber. **13.** to obtain (timber) by the felling of trees. **14. a.** to enter in a ship's log. **b.** to record in a ship's log a punishment given to (a sailor). **15.** to record in an aeroplane's log (the number of hours spent in the air). **16.** *Aust.* (of a trade union) to submit a set of claims to (an employer): *all publishers were logged whether or not they employed unionists*. *–v.i.* **17.** to cut down trees and get out logs from the forest for timber. *–phr.* **18. log in** (or **on**), *Computers* to begin a session on a computer, usually gaining access with a username and password. **19. log off** (or **out**), to end a session on a computer. **20. log on**, to record the commencement of work, etc., especially of computing. **21. log up**, to complete (a certain amount of work, distance travelled, etc.).

loganberry /ˈloʊgənbəri, -bri/ *n.* (*pl.* **-ries**) **1.** the large, dark red, acid fruit of the plant *Rubus loganobaccus*, with long prostrate canes. **2.** the plant itself.

logarithm /ˈlɒgərɪðəm/ *n.* *Maths* the exponent of that power to which a fixed number (called the *base*) must be raised in order to produce a given number (called the *antilogarithm*): *3 is the logarithm of 8 to the base 2*.

log file *n.* *Computers* a file comprising a record of computer transactions, as internet connections, email traffic, etc. Also, **log**.

logger /ˈlɒgə/ *n.* the person who cuts trees into suitable lengths after the trees have been felled.

loggerhead /ˈlɒgəhɛd/ *phr.* **at loggerheads**, engaged in dispute.

logging /ˈlɒgɪŋ/ *n.* the process, work, or business of cutting down trees and getting out logs from the forest for timber.

logic /ˈlɒdʒɪk/ *n.* **1.** the science which investigates the principles governing correct or reliable inference. **2.** reasoning or argumentation, or an instance of it. **3.** the system or principles of reasoning applicable to any branch of knowledge or study. **4.** reasons or sound sense, as in utterances or actions. **5.** convincing force: *the irresistible logic of facts*. *–***logical**, *adj.* *–***logically**, *adv.* *–***logician** /ləˈdʒɪʃən/, *n.*

login /ˈlɒgɪn/ *n.* *Computers* the act of beginning a computer session, usually by gaining access via a username and password. Also, **log-in, logon, log-on**.

logistics /ləˈdʒɪstɪks/ *n.* (*oft. construed as pl.*) **1.** the branch of military science that deals with transportation and supply, and the movement of bodies of troops. **2.** (in industry, etc.) the planning, implementation, and control of the details of an enterprise, especially the flow of goods, services, or information. **3.** the management of the practical details of any enterprise. *–***logistic, logistical**, *adj.* *–***logistically**, *adv.*

logo /ˈloʊgoʊ/ *n.* (*pl.* **-gos**) a trademark or symbol designed to identify a company, organisation, etc. Also, **logotype**.

logo- a word element denoting speech.

logon /ˈlɒgɒn/ *n.* *Computers* → **login**. Also, **log-on**.

logotype /ˈlɒgoʊtaɪp/ *n.* **1.** a single printing type bearing two or more distinct (not combined) letters, or a syllable or word. Compare **ligature. 2.** → **logo. –logo-typy,** *n.*

logout /ˈlɒɡaʊt/ *n. Computers* the act of discontinuing a computer session. Also, **log-out, logoff, log-off.**

-logy 1. a word element used in the naming of sciences or bodies of knowledge, as in *palaeontology, theology.* **2.** a word element forming a noun termination used in reference to writing genres or collections of work, as in *trilogy, martyrology.*

loin /lɔɪn/ *n.* **1.** (*usu. pl.*) the part or parts of the body of humans or quadruped animals on either side of the vertebral column, between the false ribs and hipbone. **2.** a standard cut of lamb, veal, or pork from the upper flank including the lower eight ribs. **3.** *Bible and Poetic* the part of the body which should be clothed and girded, or which is regarded as the seat of physical strength and generative power. –*phr.* **4. gird (up) one's loins,** to make ready or prepare oneself for action of some kind.

loincloth /ˈlɔɪnklɒθ/ *n.* a piece of cloth worn around the loins or hips.

loiter /ˈlɔɪtə/ *v.i.* **1.** to linger idly or aimlessly in or about a place. **2.** to move or go in a slow or lagging manner: *to loiter along.* **3.** to waste time or dawdle over work, etc. –**loiterer,** *n.* –**loiteringly,** *adv.*

loll /lɒl/ *v.i.* **1.** to recline or lean in a relaxed or indolent manner; lounge: *to loll on a sofa.* **2.** to hang loosely or droopingly. –**loller,** *n.*

lollipop /ˈlɒlipɒp/ *n.* **1.** a kind of boiled sweet or toffee, often a piece on the end of a stick. **2.** (of music, films etc.) an item in a series more trivial and more superficially enjoyable than the others.

lollop /ˈlɒləp/ *v.i.* to move with bounding, ungainly leaps.

lolly /ˈlɒli/ –*n.* (*pl.* **-lies**) **1.** *Aust., NZ* any sweet, especially a boiled one. **2.** *Cricket* an easy catch. **3.** *Colloq.* the head. **4.** *Colloq.* money. –*phr.* **5. do one's lolly,** *Colloq.* to lose one's temper.

lone /loʊn/ *adj.* **1.** being alone; unaccompanied; solitary: *a lone traveller.* **2.** standing apart, or isolated, as a house.

lonely /ˈloʊnli/ *adj.* (**-lier, -liest**) **1.** lone; solitary; without company. **2.** destitute of sympathetic or friendly companionship or relationships: *a lonely exile.* **3.** remote from people or from places of human activity: *a lonely road.* **4.** standing apart; isolated: *a lonely tower.* **5.** affected with, characterised by, or causing a depressing feeling of being alone; lonesome: *a lonely heart.* –**lonelily,** *adv.* –**loneliness,** *n.*

loner /ˈloʊnə/ *n.* someone who dislikes being in the company of other people.

lonesome /ˈloʊnsəm/ *adj. Chiefly US* **1.** lonely in feeling; depressed by solitude or by a sense of being alone: *to feel lonesome.* **2.** attended with or causing such a state of feeling: *a lonesome journey.* **3.** depressingly lonely in situation: *a lonesome road.*

long¹ /lɒŋ/ *adj.* (**longer** /ˈlɒŋɡə/, **longest** /ˈlɒŋɡəst/) **1.** having considerable or great extent from end to end; not short: *a long distance.* **2.** having considerable or great extent in duration: *a long visit.* **3.** having many items; of more than average number: *a long list.* **4.** having considerable or great extension from beginning to end, as a series, enumeration, account, book, etc.; not brief. **5.** having a specified extension in space, duration, etc.: *ten metres long.* **6.** continuing too long: *a long speech.* **7.** beyond the normal extension in space, duration, quantity, etc.: *a long match.* **8.** extending to a great distance in space or time: *a long memory.* **9.** not likely: *a long chance.* **10.** (of drinks) of considerable or great quantity; thirst-quenching rather than intoxicating, as a diluted alcoholic drink. **11.** relatively much extended: *a long reach.* **12.** *Phonetics* **a.** lasting a relatively long time: *'feed' has a longer vowel than*

'feet' or 'fit'. **b.** belonging to a class of sounds considered as usually longer in duration than another class. **13.** *Commerce* **a.** owning some commodity or stock. **b.** depending for profit on a rise in prices. **14.** *Gambling* **a.** of an exceptionally large difference in proportional amounts on an event: *long odds.* **b.** of or relating to the larger number in the odds in betting. **15.** *Cricket* in the field, near the boundary; deep. –*adv.* **16.** for or through a great extent of space or, especially, time: *a reform long advocated.* **17.** for or throughout a specified extent, especially of time: *how long did she stay?* **18.** (in elliptical expressions) gone, occupying, delaying, etc., a long or a specified time: *don't be long.* **19.** (for emphasis, after nouns denoting a period of time) throughout the whole length: *all summer long.* **20.** at a point of time far distant from the time indicated: *long before.* –*phr.* **21. before long,** in the near future; soon. **22. in the long run,** after a long course of experience; in the final result. **23. long in the tooth,** *Colloq.* elderly. **24. so** (or **as**) **long as,** provided that. **25. so long,** *Colloq.* goodbye. **26. the long and the short of,** the kernel of; substance of; gist of. –**longish,** *adj.*

long² /lɒŋ/ *v.i.* **1.** to have a prolonged or unceasing desire, as for something not immediately (if ever) attainable. **2.** to have an earnest or strong desire. –**longing,** *n.*

longboard /ˈlɒŋbɔd/ *n.* a surfboard, generally over 2.75 metres in length, offering more buoyancy than a shorter board so it can be ridden in smaller surf.

longevity /lɒnˈdʒɛvəti/ *n.* **1.** length or duration of life. **2.** long life; great duration of life.

longhand /ˈlɒŋhænd/ *n.* writing of the ordinary kind, in which the words are written out in full (distinguished from *shorthand*).

longitude /ˈlɒŋɡətjud, ˈlɒŋətjud, -tʃud/ *n.* **1.** *Geog.* angular distance east or west on the earth's surface, measured along the equator by the angle contained between the meridian of a particular place and some prime meridian, as that of Greenwich, or by the corresponding difference in time. **2.** *Astron.* **a.** the arc of the ecliptic measured eastwards from the vernal equinox to the foot of the great circle passing through the poles of the ecliptic and the point on the celestial sphere in question (**celestial longitude**). **b.** the arc on the galactic circle measured from its intersection with the celestial equator (**galactic longitude**).

longitudinal /lɒŋɡəˈtjudənəl/ *adj.* **1.** of or relating to longitude or length: *longitudinal distance.* **2.** *Zool.* of or relating to the long axis of the body, or the direction from front to back, or head to tail. **3.** extending in the direction of the length of a thing; running lengthways. **4.** (of a study, experiment, etc.) conducted over a long period of time, with repeated observations taken of the same subjects throughout the period, usually at regular intervals. –**longitudinally,** *adv.*

long jump *n.* **1.** a jump in which athletes aim to cover the greatest distance from a given mark. **2.** the athletic contest for the longest such jump.

long leg *n. Cricket* **1.** a leg side fielding position behind the person batting and close to the boundary. **2.** a fielder in this position.

long-life *adj.* **1.** → **UHT. 2.** of or relating to any product which has been treated to extend its utility beyond the normal length of time: *long-life brake pads.*

long-necked tortoise *n.* the common water tortoise, *Chelodina longicollis,* of eastern and southern Australia which, like all Australian tortoises, retracts its head to one side of the body and possesses clawed and webbed feet. Also, **snake-necked tortoise.**

long paddock *n.* a stock route or open road, especially regarded as a place where people, too poor to own their own paddocks or pay for agistment, can graze their horses, cattle, etc.

long service leave *n.* (in Australia) an extended period of leave from employment, earned through long service. *Abbrev.*: LSL

long shot *n.* **1.** an attempt which has little hope of success, but which if successful may offer great rewards. **2.** a photograph or a film or television shot taken from some distance.

long-sighted *adj.* **1.** far-sighted; hypermetropic. **2.** having great foresight; foreseeing remote results. Compare **far-sighted.** –**long-sightedness,** *n.*

longstanding /ˈlɒŋstændɪŋ/ *adj.* existing or occurring for a long time: *a longstanding feud.*

long-suffering *adj.* **1.** enduring injury or provocation long and patiently. –*n.* **2.** long and patient endurance of injury or provocation.

longwinded /ˈlɒŋwɪndəd/ *adj.* **1.** tediously wordy in speech or writing. **2.** writing or talking tediously and continuously. **3.** able to breathe deeply. –**longwindedly,** *adv.* –**longwindedness,** *n.*

loo[1] /luː/ *n.* a game of cards in which forfeits are paid into a pool.

loo[2] /luː/ *n. Colloq. (from trademark)* a toilet.

loofah /ˈluːfə/ *n.* **1.** a tropical, annual, climbing herb, *Luffa cylindrica.* **2.** the fibrous network of its fruit, used as a bath sponge.

look /lʊk/ *v.i.* **1.** to fix the eyes upon something or in some direction in order to see. **2.** to glance or gaze, in a manner specified: *to look questioningly at a person.* **3.** to use the sight in seeking, searching, examining, watching, etc.: *to look through the papers.* **4.** to tend, as in bearing or significance: *conditions look towards war.* **5.** to direct the mental regard or attention: *to look at the facts.* **6.** to have an outlook or afford a view: *the window looks upon the street.* **7.** to face or front: *the house looks east.* –*v. (copular)* **8.** to appear or seem (as specified) to the eye: *to look pale.* **9.** to seem to the mind: *the case looks promising.* –*v.t.* **10.** to express or suggest by looks: *she looked compassion.* **11.** to direct a look towards: *she looked him full in the face.* **12.** to have the aspect or appearance appropriate to: *look one's age*; *look an idiot.* –*n.* **13.** the act of looking. **14.** a visual search or examination. **15.** way of looking or appearing to the eye or mind; aspect: *the look of an honest man.* **16.** *(pl.)* general aspect; appearance: *to like the looks of a place*; *good looks.* –*phr.* **17. for the look of the thing,** for the sake of appearances. **18. have a good look (around),** *Colloq.* to inspect inquisitively. **19. it looks like it,** it seems likely. **20. look after, a.** to follow with the eye, as a person or thing moving away. **b.** to seek, as something desired. **c.** to take care of: *to look after a child.* **21. look ahead,** to anticipate future events, especially future difficulties. **22. look alive,** *Colloq.* an expression used to urge haste. **23. look at, a.** to turn one's gaze upon. **b.** *Colloq.* to expect to pay: *you'd be looking at $800 000 for a house in that area.* **c.** *Colloq.* to experience or face: *Australia might be looking at a score of about 300 this time tomorrow.* **24. look daggers at,** to scowl at; to express anger with by a look. **25. look down on,** to have contempt for; regard with disdain. **26. look down one's nose,** to have an air of barely concealed contempt. **27. look for, a.** to seek, as a person or thing. **b.** to anticipate; expect. **28. look forward to,** to anticipate with pleasure. **29. look here,** an exclamation used to attract attention, for emphasis, or the like. **30. look in, a.** to take a look into a place. **b.** to come in for a brief visit. **31. look into,** to investigate; examine. **32. look like,** to seem likely to; appear probable that. **33. look lively (or sharp),** to make haste; be alert. **34. look on,** to be a mere spectator. **35. look on the bright side,** to consider something with optimism. **36. look on the worst side,** to consider something with pessimism. **37. look out, a.** to look

forth, as from a window or a place of observation. **b.** to be on guard. **c.** an exclamation used to attract attention, especially to warn of danger. **38. look out for, a.** to take watchful care of or about: *to look out for oneself.* **b.** to be vigilant in the expectation of finding: *I'm looking out for a good winter coat.* **39. look over,** to view, inspect, or examine. **40. look someone up,** to visit or make contact with someone. **41. look something out,** to retrieve something. **42. look to, a.** to direct the glance or gaze to. **b.** to give attention to. **c.** to direct the expectations or hopes to, as for something desired. **d.** to look forward expectantly to. **43. look the part,** to have an appearance, especially in dressing, appropriate to some special function or situation: *in his uniform he looked the part.* **44. look up, a.** to direct the eyes upwards. **b.** *Colloq.* to rise in amount or value; improve: *things are looking up.* **c.** to try to find; seek: *to look a name up in a directory.* **d.** to make contact with (a person): *look me up when you come to town.* **45. look up to,** to regard with admiration, or esteem. **46. not know which way to look,** to feel embarrassed.

looking glass *n.* **1.** a mirror made of glass with a metallic or amalgam backing. **2.** such glass as a material.

lookout /ˈlʊkaʊt/ *n.* **1.** a watch kept for something that may come or happen. **2.** a person or group placed or employed to keep such a watch. **3.** a station or place from which a watch is kept. **4.** a view; prospect; outlook. **5.** a place on a high point, especially a mountain, from which one can admire the view. **6.** *Colloq.* the proper object of one's watchful care or concern: *that's his lookout.* **7.** *Colloq.* a matter which is of sole interest to the person concerned and not therefore the responsibility of any other.

loom[1] /luːm/ *n.* **1.** a machine or apparatus for weaving yarn or thread into a fabric. **2.** the art or process of weaving. **3.** the part of an oar between the blade and the handle.

loom[2] /luːm/ *v.i.* **1.** to appear indistinctly, or come into view in indistinct and enlarged form. **2.** to rise before the vision with an appearance of great or portentous size. –*n.* **3.** a looming appearance, as of something seen indistinctly at a distance or through a fog.

loon[1] /luːn/ *n.* any of several large, short-tailed web-footed, fish-eating diving birds of the Northern Hemisphere, constituting the genus *Gavia*; diver.

loon[2] /luːn/ *n.* a simple-minded or stupid person.

loony /ˈluːni/ *Colloq.* –*adj.* (**-nier, -niest**) **1.** insane; crazy. **2.** extremely or senselessly foolish. –*n.* (*pl.* **-nies**) **3.** a lunatic. Also, **looney, luny.** –**looniness,** *n.*

loop /luːp/ *n.* **1.** a folding or doubling of a part of a cord, lace, ribbon, etc., upon itself, so as to leave an opening between the parts. **2.** anything shaped more or less like a loop, as a line drawn on paper, a part of a letter, a part of a path, a line of movement, etc. **3.** a curved piece or a ring of metal, wood, etc., used for the putting in of something, or as a handle, or otherwise. **4.** *Aeronautics* an exercise carried out in such a manner that the aeroplane performs a closed curve in a vertical plane. **5.** *Med.* an intra-uterine contraceptive device, formerly made in metal, now in plastic. **6.** *Elect.* a closed electric or magnetic circuit. **7.** *Music* a length of magnetic tape whose ends have been joined together, creating a strip which may be played repeatedly. –*v.t.* **8.** to form into a loop or loops. **9.** to make a loop or loops in. **10.** to enfold or encircle in or with something arranged in a loop. **11.** to fasten by forming into a loop, or by means of something formed into a loop. **12.** to fly (an aeroplane) in a loop or series of loops. –*v.i.* **13.** to make or form a loop or loops. –*phr.* **14. in the loop,** in communication with the group of people to whom information is given: *keep me in the loop – I like to know what's going on.* **15. out of the loop,** excluded from communication with the group of people to whom information is given: *she's been out of the loop since her son left the school.*

loophole /ˈluphoʊl/ *n.* **1.** a small or narrow opening, as in a wall, for looking through, or for admitting light and air, or particularly, in a fortification, for the discharge of missiles against an enemy outside. **2.** an opening or aperture. **3.** an outlet, or means of escape or evasion.

loopy /ˈlupi/ *adj.* (**-pier, -piest**) **1.** full of loops. **2.** *Colloq.* slightly mad or eccentric.

loose /lus/ *adj.* **1.** free from bonds, fetters, or restraint: *to get one's hand loose.* **2.** free or released from fastening or attachment: *a loose end.* **3.** free from restraining conditions or factors: *a loose association of sovereign states.* **4.** uncombined, as a chemical element. **5.** not bound together, as papers or flowers. **6.** not put in a package or other container: *loose mushrooms.* **7.** unemployed or unappropriated: *loose funds.* **8.** wanting in retentiveness or power of restraint: *a loose tongue.* **9.** lax, as the bowels. **10.** free from moral restraint, or lax in principle or conduct: *loose behaviour.* **11.** wanton or unchaste: *a loose woman.* **12.** not firm or rigid: *a loose tooth*; *a loose rein.* **13.** not fitting closely, as garments. **14.** not close or compact in structure or arrangement; having spaces between the parts, or open: *a loose weave.* **15.** (of earth, soil, etc.) not cohering: *loose sand.* **16.** not strict, exact, or precise: *loose thinking.* –*adv.* **17.** in a loose manner; loosely. **18.** so as to become free from restraint, independent, etc.: *he cut loose from his family.* –*v.t.* **19.** to let loose, or free from bonds or restraint. **20.** to release, as from constraint, obligation, penalty, etc. **21.** *Chiefly Naut.* to set free from fastening or attachment: *loose a boat from its moorings.* **22.** to unfasten, undo, or untie, as a bond, fetter, or knot. **23.** to shoot, or let fly. **24.** to make less tight; slacken or relax. **25.** to render less firmly fixed, or loosen. –*phr.* **26. cut loose, a.** to dissociate oneself from one's previous friends, family ties, etc., usually in order to pursue a new activity. **b.** *Colloq.* to adopt an irresponsible lifestyle: *after uni she cut loose big-time.* **27. hang loose,** *Colloq.* to relax. **28. on the loose, a.** free from restraint **b.** on a spree. **29. play fast and loose,** (oft. fol. by *with*) to behave in an inconsiderate, inconstant, or irresponsible manner. –**loosely,** *adv.* –**looseness,** *n.*

loose end *n.* **1.** something left unsettled or incomplete. –*phr.* Also, **at loose ends. 1. at a loose end, a.** without a specific task to do or pastime to follow. **b.** in an unsettled or disorderly condition.

loosen /ˈlusən/ *v.t.* **1.** to make loose or looser. –*v.i.* **2.** to become loose or looser. –**loosener,** *n.*

loot /lut/ *n.* **1.** anything dishonestly and cruelly taken for oneself: *a burglar's loot; loot taken in war.* **2.** *Colloq.* money. –*v.t.* **3.** to plunder or rob (a city, house, etc.), especially in war. –*v.i.* **4.** to take loot; plunder. –**looter,** *n.* –**looting,** *n.*

lop /lɒp/ *verb* (**lopped, lopping**) –*v.t.* **1.** to cut off (branches, twigs, etc.) from a tree or other plant. **2.** to cut off (the head, limbs, etc.) from a person. **3.** to reduce by removing what is superfluous or excessive: *to lop our spending.* –*v.i.* **4.** to remove parts by or as by cutting. –*n.* **5.** parts or a part lopped off. **6.** the smaller branches and twigs of trees. –**lopper,** *n.*

lope /loʊp/ *v.i.* **1.** to move or run with bounding steps, as a quadruped, or with a long, easy stride, as a person. **2.** to canter leisurely with a rather long, easy stride, as a horse. –*n.* **3.** the act or the gait of loping. **4.** a long, easy stride. –**loper,** *n.*

lopsided /ˈlɒpsaɪdəd/ *adj.* lopping or inclining to one side. **2.** heavier, larger, or more developed on one side than on the other; asymmetrical. –**lopsidedly,** *adv.* –**lopsidedness,** *n.*

loquacious /ləˈkweɪʃəs/ *adj.* **1.** talking or disposed to talk much or freely; talkative. **2.** characterised by or showing a disposition to talk much: *a loquacious mood.* –**loquacity** /ləˈkwæsəti/, **loquaciousness,** *n.* –**loquaciously,** *adv.*

loquat /ˈloʊkwɒt, -kɒt, -kwɒt/ *n.* **1.** a small, evergreen tree, *Eriobotrya japonica*, native to China and Japan, but cultivated elsewhere for ornament and for its yellow plum-like fruit. **2.** the fruit.

lord /lɔd/ *n.* **1.** someone who has dominion over others; a master, chief, or ruler. **2.** someone who exercises authority from property rights; an owner or possessor of land, houses, etc. **3.** a feudal superior; the proprietor of a manor. **4.** a man who dominates in a particular sphere or profession: *lords of the bush*; *the lords of finance.* **5.** a titled nobleman, or peer. –*interj.* **6.** (*oft. upper case*) an exclamation of surprise, etc. –*phr.* **7. drunk as a lord,** *Colloq.* extremely drunk. **8. lord and master,** (*humorous*) husband. **9. lord it over someone,** to behave in a high-handed and dictatorial fashion towards someone. **10. lords of creation,** (*ironic*) men. **11. the lord of the manor,** *Colloq.* (*humorous*) the principal man of a household. –**lordly,** *adj.*

lore /lɔ/ *n.* **1.** the body of knowledge, especially of a traditional, anecdotal, or popular nature, on a particular subject: *the lore of herbs.* **2.** learning, knowledge, or erudition.

lorgnette /lɔˈnjɛt/ *n.* a pair of eyeglasses mounted on a long handle.

lorikeet /ˈlɒrəkit, lɒrəˈkit/ *n.* any of various small, brightly coloured, arboreal parrots found mainly in Australasia, especially of the genera *Trichoglossus* and *Glossopsitta*, having brush-like tongues specialised for feeding on nectar.

lorry /ˈlɒri/ *n.* (*pl.* **-ries**) **1.** *Chiefly Brit.* → **truck**[1] (def. 2). **2.** a kind of large dray, usually horse-drawn.

lory /ˈlɒri/ *n.* (*pl.* **-ries**) any of various lorikeets and parrots of the Malay Archipelago, Australasia, etc.

lose /luz/ *verb* (**lost, losing**) –*v.t.* **1.** to come to be without, by some chance, and not know the whereabouts of: *to lose a ring.* **2.** to suffer the loss or deprivation of: *to lose one's life.* **3.** to be bereaved of by death: *to lose a child.* **4.** to fail to keep, preserve, or maintain control of: *to lose one's balance.* **5.** to cease to have: *to lose all fear.* **6.** (*now chiefly in the passive*) to bring to destruction or ruin: *ship and crew were lost.* **7.** to have slip from sight, hearing, attention, etc.: *to lose a face in a crowd.* **8.** to become separated from and ignorant of (the way, etc.). **9.** to leave far behind in a pursuit, race, etc. **10.** to use to no purpose, or waste: *to lose time in waiting.* **11.** to fail to have, get, catch, etc.; miss: *to lose an opportunity.* **12.** to fail to win (a prize, stake, etc.). **13.** to be defeated in (a game, lawsuit, battle, etc.). **14.** to cause the loss of: *the delay lost the battle for them.* **15.** (*usu. used reflexively or in the passive*) to absorb or engross in something to the exclusion of knowledge or consciousness of all else: *to be lost in thought.* –*v.i.* **16.** to suffer loss: *to lose on a contract.* **17.** to lose ground, fall behind, or fail to hold one's own, as in a race or other contest. **18.** to fail to win, as in a contest; be defeated. –*phr.* **19. lose face,** to lose prestige or dignity by having an error or foolish action made public. **20. lose it,** *Colloq.* **a.** to no longer have that quality which made one specially able or talented. **b.** to lose control of one's temper. **c.** to lose control of a vehicle. **21. lose one's head,** to behave irrationally or out of character. **22. lose one's heart to,** to form a deep emotional attachment to. **23. lose one's life,** (*euphemistic*) to die. **24. lose one's marbles,** *Colloq.* to go insane. **25. lose one's nerve,** to become afraid to do something. **26. lose out,** *Colloq.* (sometimes fol. by *to*) to be defeated or bettered: *I lost out to my rival.*

27. lose out on, *Colloq.* to fail to achieve (a goal, etc.): *I lost out on that deal.* **28. lose sleep over,** to worry about excessively. **29. lose the plot,** *Colloq.* (of a person) to no longer understand fully what is going on in a certain situation, job, etc., and thus fail to act effectively. **30. lose to, a.** to be defeated by. **b.** to be deprived of (a person) by: *she lost her husband to cancer*; *they lost their son to the army.* –**losing,** *adj.*, *n.*

loss /lɒs/ *n.* **1.** detriment or disadvantage from failure to keep, have, or get: *to bear the loss of a robbery.* **2.** that which is lost. **3.** amount or number lost. **4.** a being deprived of or coming to be without something that one has had: *loss of friends.* **5.** a bereavement. **6.** the accidental or inadvertent losing of something dropped, misplaced, or of unknown whereabouts: *to discover the loss of a document.* **7.** a losing by defeat, or failure to win: *the loss of a bet.* **8.** a failure resulting in a waste of time, resources, etc.: *that meeting was a complete loss.* **9.** failure to preserve or maintain: *loss of speed.* **10.** destruction or ruin: *the loss of properties by bushfires.* **11.** *Commerce* failure to recover the costs of a transaction or the like, in the form of benefits derived. **12.** *Mil.* **a.** the losing of soldiers by death, capture, etc. **b.** (*oft. pl.*) the number of soldiers so lost. **13.** *Insurance* **a.** occurrence of a risk covered by a contract of insurance so as to result in insurer liability. **b.** that which causes such a loss. **c.** an example of such a loss. –*phr.* **14. a dead loss, a.** a complete failure. **b.** an utterly useless person or thing. **15. at a loss,** in a state of bewilderment or uncertainty. **16. at a loss for,** completely lacking: *to be at a loss for words.*

lost /lɒst/ *v.* **1.** past tense and past participle of **lose.** –*adj.* **2.** no longer possessed or retained: *lost friends.* **3.** no longer to be found: *lost articles.* **4.** having gone astray or lost the way; bewildered as to place, direction, etc. **5.** not used to good purpose, as opportunities, time, labour, etc.; wasted. **6.** that one has failed to win: *a lost prize.* **7.** attended with defeat: *a lost battle.* **8.** destroyed or ruined: *lost ships.* –*phr.* **9. get lost,** (*esp. used in the imperative*) *Colloq.* to go away. **10. lost to, a.** no longer belonging to. **b.** no longer possible or open to: *the opportunity was lost to him.* **c.** insensible to: *to be lost to all sense of duty.*

lot /lɒt/ *n.* **1.** one of a set of objects drawn from a receptacle, etc., to decide a question or choice by chance. **2.** the casting or drawing of such objects as a method of deciding something: *to choose a person by lot.* **3.** the decision or choice so made. **4.** allotted share or portion. **5.** the portion in life assigned by fate or providence, or one's fate, fortune, or destiny. **6.** a distinct portion or piece of land; plot: *a parking lot.* **7.** *Chiefly US* a piece of land forming a part of a district, city, or other community. **8.** *Film* the site used for filmmaking, as the studios, locations, etc. **9.** a distinct portion or parcel of anything, as of merchandise. **10.** a number of things or persons collectively: *to take the lot.* **11.** a person of a specified quality, usually negative: *a bad lot*; *a mean lot.* –*phr.* **12. a fat lot of ...,** *Colloq.* (*ironic*) a great deal of ... **13. a lot, a.** to a considerable degree; much: *that is a lot better.* **b.** a great many or a great deal: *a lot of books.* **14. the lot, a.** the entire amount or quantity. **b.** all the available ingredients: *a hamburger with the lot.* **15. throw in one's lot with,** to give one's entire support to.

LOTE /loʊt/ *n.* a language other than English; languages other than English.

lotion /ˈloʊʃən/ *n.* a liquid containing oils or medicines, to be applied externally to the skin for soothing, healing, or cleansing.

lottery /ˈlɒtəri, ˈlɒtri/ *n.* (*pl.* **-ries**) **1.** a scheme or arrangement for raising money, as for some public, charitable, or private purpose, by the sale of a large number of tickets, certain among which, as determined by chance after the sale, entitle the holders to prizes. **2.** any scheme for the distribution of prizes by chance. **3.** any affair of chance.

lotus /ˈloʊtəs/ *n.* **1.** a plant, commonly identified with a species of jujube or of elm tree, referred to in Greek legend as yielding a fruit which induced a state of dreamy and contented forgetfulness in those who ate it. **2.** any species of *Nelumbo*, including the sacred lotus of India which is similar to the waterlily. **3.** any of various waterlilies of the genus *Nymphaea*, including *N. lotus* of Egypt.

lotus bird *n.* a common jacana of northern and eastern Australia, New Guinea, Indonesia and Borneo, having a bright red comb on the forehead.

loud /laʊd/ *adj.* **1.** striking strongly upon the organs of hearing, as sound, noise, the voice, etc.; strongly audible. **2.** making, giving out, or speaking with strong and easily heard sounds: *loud knocking.* **3.** full of sound or noise. **4.** noisy or crying out loudly. **5.** definite or firm: *to be loud in praising someone.* **6.** (of colours, clothes, etc.) offensively or overly showy; garish. **7.** (of manners, people, etc.) very coarse; vulgar. –**loudly,** *adv.* –**loudness,** *n.* –**loudish,** *adj.*

loudhailer /laʊdˈheɪlə/ *n.* a megaphone with a built-in amplifier.

loudspeaker /laʊdˈspikə, ˈlaʊdspikə/ *n.* any of various devices by which speech, music, etc., can be made audible throughout a room, hall, or the like.

lounge /laʊndʒ/ *v.i.* (**lounged, lounging**) **1.** to pass time lazily and with nothing to do. **2.** to lie back lazily. **3.** to move or go (*about, along, off,* etc.) in an unhurried, lazy manner: *lounge about in the sun.* –*n.* **4.** Also, *Aust.,* **lounge room.** a room in a private house for relaxation and entertainment. **5.** a large room in a hotel, airport, etc., used by guests or passengers for relaxation purposes or while waiting for a flight, etc. **6.** Also, **lounge bar.** in a hotel, a bar providing tables and chairs and which formerly, in some parts of Australia, was reserved for the use of women and their partners. Compare **public bar, saloon** (def. 2). **7.** (in a cinema) the most comfortable seats which also cost the most. **8.** a sofa or couch. –**lounger,** *n.*

lour /ˈlaʊə/ *v.i.* **1.** to be dark and threatening, as the sky or the weather. **2.** to frown, scowl, or look sullen. –*n.* **3.** a dark, threatening appearance, as of the sky, weather, etc. **4.** a frown or scowl. Also, *Chiefly US,* **lower.**

louse /laʊs/ *n.* (*pl.* **lice** /laɪs/ *for defs 1 and 2,* **louses** *for def. 3*) **1.** any of the small, wingless, bloodsucking insects of the order Phthiraptera, including several species associated with humans. **2.** any of various other insects parasitic on animals or plants, as those of the order Mallophaga, or the homopterous family Aphididae. **3.** *Colloq.* a despicable person. –*v.t.* (**loused, lousing**) **4.** *Goldmining* to pick through (waste matter, as a dump of mining rubble) in search of something of value: *they loused the broken stones.* –*phr.* **5. louse up,** *Colloq.* to spoil.

lousy /ˈlaʊzi/ *adj.* (**-sier, -siest**) **1.** infested with lice. **2.** *Colloq.* mean or hateful. **3.** *Colloq.* of little value; trifling: *a lousy $2.* **4.** *Colloq.* unwell. –**lousily,** *adv.* –**lousiness,** *n.*

lout /laʊt/ *n.* **1.** *Colloq.* a rough, uncouth and sometimes violent young man. **2.** an awkward, stupid person; a boor. –**loutish,** *adj.* –**loutishly,** *adv.* –**loutishness,** *n.*

louvre /ˈluvə/ *n.* **1.** a turret or lantern on the roof of a medieval building, to supply ventilation or light. **2.** an arrangement of louvre-boards, glass slats or the like closing a window or other opening, or a single louvre-board. **3.** one of a number of slit-like openings in the bonnet or body of a motor vehicle for the escape of heated air from within. Also, *US,* **louver.**

louvre-board *n.* one of a series of overlapping, sloping boards, slats, or the like, in an opening, so arranged as to admit air but exclude rain.

lovable /ˈlʌvəbəl/ *adj.* of such a nature as to attract love. Also, **loveable.** –**lovability** /lʌvəˈbɪləti/, **lovableness,** *n.* –**lovably,** *adv.*

love /lʌv/ *n.* **1.** a strong or passionate affection for another person. **2.** sexual passion or desire, or its gratification. **3.** an object of love or affection; a sweetheart. **4.** a feeling of warm personal attachment or deep affection, as for a friend (or between friends), parent, child, etc. **5.** *Colloq.* an affectionate term of address. **6.** strong predilection or liking for anything: *love of books.* **7.** *Tennis, etc.* nothing; no score. –*verb* (**loved, loving**) –*v.t.* **8.** to have love or affection for. **9.** to have a strong liking for; take great pleasure in: *to love music.* –*v.i.* **10.** to have love or affection, especially to be or fall in love with another person. –*phr.* **11. be in love,** (sometimes fol. by *with*) to feel deep affection or passion. **12. fall in love,** (sometimes fol. by *with*) to be overcome with affectionate and passionate feelings. **13. for love, a.** out of affection. **b.** for nothing; without compensation. **14. for love or** (or **nor**) **money,** *Colloq.* (after a negative verb) for any inducement: *I wouldn't do that, not for love or money.* **15. for the love of,** for the sake of. **16. love at first sight,** an overwhelming experience of falling in love with someone or something not previously encountered. **17. make love,** (sometimes fol. by *to* or *with*) **a.** to have sex. **b.** *Obsolesc.* to pay amorous attentions; court. –**loving,** *adj.* –**lovingly,** *adv.*

lovebird /ˈlʌvbɜd/ *n.* **1.** any of various small African parrots of the genus *Agapornis,* many species of which are commonly kept caged as pets; remarkable for the fact that the members of each pair keep close together when perching. **2.** *Colloq.* → **budgerigar. 3.** (*pl.*) *Colloq.* a couple who attract attention by their overt loving behaviour: *what lovebirds they were!*

lovelorn /ˈlʌvlɔn/ *adj.* forsaken by one's love; forlorn or pining from love. –**lovelornness,** *n.*

lovely /ˈlʌvli/ *adj.* (**-lier, -liest**) **1.** charmingly or exquisitely beautiful: *a lovely flower.* **2.** having a beauty that appeals to the heart as well as to the eye, as a person, a face, etc. **3.** delightful, or highly pleasing: *to have a lovely time.* **4.** of a great moral or spiritual beauty: *lovely character.* –**loveliness,** *n.*

lover /ˈlʌvə/ *n.* **1.** someone who loves another. **2.** a sexual partner, especially one distinguished by attentiveness or sexual powers: *he's quite a lover.* **3.** (*pl.*) a couple in love with each other or having a love affair. **4.** someone who has a strong predilection or liking for something: *a lover of music.*

low¹ /loʊ/ *adj.* **1.** being or happening not far above the ground, floor, or base: *a low shelf.* **2.** (of a heavenly body) not far above the horizon. **3.** lying or being below the general level: *low ground.* **4.** relating to areas near the sea level or sea as opposed to highland or inland areas. **5.** (of a bow) deep. **6.** (of a garment) cut so as to leave neck and shoulders exposed. **7.** not high or tall: *low walls.* **8.** rising only slightly from a surface. **9.** (of a river, etc.) of less than average height or depth. **10.** reduced to the least height, depth, or the like: *low tide.* **11.** lacking in strength; feeble; weak. **12.** small in amount, degree, force, etc.: *a low number.* **13.** indicated by a small number: *a low latitude* (one near the equator). **14.** having no great amount, value, or excellence: *a low opinion of something.* **15.** unhappy: *low spirits.* **16.** of lesser rank or quality: *low birth.* **17.** (of thought or expression) lacking in worth. **18.** hidden; unnoticeable: *lie low.* **19.** mean or nasty: *a low trick.* **20.** coarse or rude: *low company.* **21.** *Biol.* having a relatively simple structure. **22.** *Music* (of sounds) produced by relatively slow vibrations, and therefore low in pitch.

23. not loud: *a low whisper.* **24.** (of a vowel) with the tongue held fairly low in the mouth. –*adv.* **25.** in or to a low position, point, degree, etc. **26.** near the ground, floor, or base; not aloft. **27.** at or to a low pitch. **28.** in a low tone; softly; quietly. –*n.* **29.** that which is low; a low level. **30.** *Weather* a pressure system with relatively low pressure at the centre. **31.** a point of least value, amount, etc.; nadir: *prices reached an all-time low.* –**lowness,** *n.*

low² /loʊ/ *v.i.* **1.** to utter the sound characteristic of cattle; moo. –*v.t.* **2.** to utter by or as by lowing. –*n.* **3.** the act or the sound of lowing.

lowboy /ˈloʊbɔɪ/ *n.* a piece of furniture for holding clothes, similar to a wardrobe, but not so tall.

lowbrow /ˈloʊbraʊ/ *n.* **1.** a person of low intellectual calibre or culture. –*adj.* **2.** relating or proper to lowbrows.

low-doc loan /loʊ-dɒk ˈloʊn/ *n. Colloq.* a loan from a lending institution, such as a bank, for which minimal documentation of the borrower's ability to service the loan is required. Compare **no-doc loan.** Also, **lo-doc loan.**

low-down *adj.* low; dishonourable; mean.

lowdown /ˈloʊdaʊn/ *n. Colloq.* the actual unadorned facts or truth on some subject.

low-emission vehicle *n.* a motor vehicle, as a hybrid car, designed to produce less air pollution than a conventional vehicle. *Abbrev.:* LEV

lower /ˈloʊə/ *adj.* **1.** comparative of **low¹. 2.** (*oft. upper case*) *Geol.* indicating an earlier division of a period, system, etc.: *the lower Palaeozoic.* –*v.t.* **3.** to reduce in amount, price, degree, force, etc. **4.** to make (the voice, etc.) less loud. **5.** to bring down in rank or estimation; humble; degrade. **6.** to let down or make lower. **7.** *Music* to make lower in pitch; flatten. –*v.i.* **8.** to become lower or less. **9.** to descend; sink.

lower case *n. Printing* the lower half of a pair of cases which contains the small letters of the alphabet. *Abbrev.:* l.c.

lower-case *adj.* **1.** (of a letter) small; minuscule (as opposed to *capital*). **2.** *Printing* relating to or belonging in the lower case.

lower house *n.* in a bicameral parliament, the lower legislative body, usually more numerous and more directly representative of the electorate than the upper house. Also, **lower chamber.**

lowering /ˈlaʊərɪŋ/ *adj.* **1.** dark and threatening, as the sky, clouds, weather, etc. **2.** frowning or sullen, as the face, gaze, etc. –**loweringly,** *adv.*

lowest common denominator *n.* **1.** *Maths* → **common denominator. 2.** the least worthy of the goals, values, opinions, etc., which are held in common by a group of people. **3.** the group of people who hold the least worthy of goals, values, opinions, etc., in a society.

low-fat *adj.* of, relating to, or designating a food product or recipe containing less than the usual quantity of fat: *low-fat milk.*

low frequency *n.* any radiofrequency between 30 and 300 kilohertz. *Abbrev.:* LF –**low-frequency,** *adj.*

low-joule *adj.* of or relating to food or beverages which, being low in kilojoules, are suitable for dieters.

low-key *adj.* **1.** underplayed; restrained. **2.** (of a person) not given to emotional display; quiet; unobtrusive.

lowland /ˈloʊlənd/ *n.* **1.** land low with respect to neighbouring country. –*adj.* **2.** of, relating to, or characteristic of lowland or lowlands.

low-level language *n. Computers* a language used for writing programs which is closer to machine language than human language. See **high-level language.**

low level waste *n.* radioactive waste in which there are low levels of radioactivity per mass or volume. *Abbrev.*: LLW Compare **high level waste**.

lowly /ˈloʊli/ *adj.* (**-lier**, **-liest**) **1.** humble in station, condition, or nature: *a lowly cottage*. **2.** low in growth or position. **3.** humble in spirit; meek. *–adv.* **4.** in a low position, manner, or degree. **5.** in a lowly manner; humbly. **–lowliness**, *n.*

low pressure system *n.* See **pressure system**.

low profile *n.* a lack of notice or recognition as a result of a deliberate avoidance of publicity or prominence. **–low-profile**, *adj.*

low relief *n.* → **bas-relief**.

loyal /ˈlɔɪəl/ *adj.* **1.** faithful to one's allegiance, as to the sovereign, government, or state: *a loyal subject*. **2.** faithful to one's oath, engagements or, obligations: *to be loyal to a vow*. **3.** faithful to any leader, party, or cause, or to any person or thing conceived as imposing obligations: *a loyal friend*. **–loyally**, *adv.* **–loyalty**, *n.* **–loyalist**, *n.*

loyalty program *n.* a marketing strategy designed to make customers continue to buy from a particular retailer, airline, website, etc., by offering rewards for purchasing.

lozenge /ˈlɒzəndʒ/ *n.* **1.** a small flavoured cake or confection of sugar, often medicated, originally diamond-shaped. **2.** *Geom.* → **diamond**.

LPG /ɛl pi ˈdʒi/ *n.* liquefied petroleum gas; a mixture of hydrocarbon gases, mainly propane and butane liquefied and stored under pressure for use as a fuel gas. Also, **LP gas**.

L-plate /ˈɛl-pleɪt/ *n.* the usually small square placard, on which appears the letter L, which is displayed on a vehicle being driven by someone who is learning to drive.

LSD /ɛl ɛs ˈdi/ *n.* lysergic acid diethylamide, a crystalline solid, $C_{15}H_{15}N_2CON$ ($C_2H_5)_2$, which produces temporary hallucinations and a schizophrenia-like psychotic state.

lubber /ˈlʌbə/ *n.* **1.** a big, clumsy, stupid person. **2.** (among sailors) an awkward or unskilled seaman; landlubber.

lubra /ˈlubrə/ *n.* (*derog.*) (*racist*) (*dated*) an Aboriginal woman.

lubricate /ˈlubrəkeɪt/ *v.t.* **1.** to apply some oily, greasy, or other substance to, in order to diminish friction; oil or grease, as parts of a mechanism. **2.** to make slippery or smooth. **–lubricant** /ˈlubrəkənt/, *n.* **–lubrication** /lubrəˈkeɪʃən/, *n.* **–lubricative**, *adj.*

lucerne /ˈlusən/ *n.* **1.** a forage plant of the family Fabaceae, with bluish purple flowers, *Medicago sativa*; alfalfa. **2.** any of various other fodder legumes, as Townsville lucerne, *Stylosanthes sundaica*, and tree lucerne, *Chamaecytisus prolifer*.

lucid /ˈlusəd/ *adj.* **1.** shining or bright. **2.** clear or transparent. **3.** easily understood: *a lucid explanation*. **4.** characterised by clear perception or understanding; rational or sane: *a lucid interval*. **–lucidity** /luˈsɪdəti/, **lucidness**, *n.* **–lucidly**, *adv.*

luck /lʌk/ *n.* **1.** that which happens to a person, either good or bad, as if by chance, in the course of events: *to have good luck*. **2.** good fortune; advantage or success considered as the result of chance: *to wish someone luck*. *–phr.* **3. bad** (or **tough**) **luck**, (*sometimes ironic*) an exclamation of sympathy to someone in misfortune. **4. be in luck**, to experience good fortune. **5. be out of luck**, to experience a frustration of one's wishes, expectations, or needs. **6. down on one's luck**, in poor or unfortunate circumstances. **7. good luck**, an exclamation conveying the good wishes of the speaker. **8. half your luck**, *Aust. Colloq.* an expression indicating envy at someone else's good fortune. **9. here's luck**, an expression of goodwill, especially as a toast. **10. just one's luck**, typical of one's luck, regarded as invariably bad. **11. luck out**, *Colloq.* **a.** to run out of luck; experience misfortune. **b.** to come into luck; experience good fortune. **12. no such luck**, (*usually ironic*) unfortunately not. **13. one's luck is in**, one is experiencing a continued run of good fortune. **14. push one's luck**, **a.** to try for some gain over and above what one has already achieved in the hope one's luck will hold good. **b.** to take a risk by doing something that is proscribed or considered improper, too difficult, etc. **15. the devil's own luck** or **the luck of the devil**, unusually good fortune. **16. the luck of the draw**, the outcome of chance. **17. try one's luck**, to make an attempt in the hope that success or good fortune will be the outcome.

lucky /ˈlʌki/ *adj.* (**-kier**, **-kiest**) **1.** having or attended with good luck; fortunate. **2.** happening fortunately: *a lucky accident*. **3.** bringing or presaging good luck, or supposed to do so: *a lucky penny*. **–luckiness**, *n.* **–luckily**, *adv.*

lucrative /ˈlukrətɪv/ *adj.* profitable; remunerative: *a lucrative business*. **–lucratively**, *adv.* **–lucrativeness**, *n.*

lucre /ˈlukə/ *phr.* **filthy lucre**, monetary gain viewed as a sordid motivation.

ludicrous /ˈludəkrəs/ *adj.* such as to cause laughter or derision; ridiculous; amusingly absurd: *a ludicrous incident*. **–ludicrously**, *adv.* **–ludicrousness**, *n.*

lug¹ /lʌg/ *verb* (**lugged**, **lugging**) *–v.t.* **1.** to pull along or carry with force or effort. *–v.i.* **2.** to pull; tug.

lug² /lʌg/ *n.* **1.** *Colloq.* an ear. **2.** one of the earflaps of a cap. **3.** a projecting piece by which anything is held or supported.

luge /luʒ/ *n.* a type of toboggan ridden while lying on one's back.

luggage /ˈlʌgɪdʒ/ *n.* trunks, suitcases, etc., used in travelling; baggage.

lugger /ˈlʌgə/ *n. Naut.* a small sailing vessel, frequently two masted, often associated with island trading, pearling.

lugubrious /ləˈgubriəs/ *adj.* mournful; doleful; dismal: *lugubrious tones*. **–lugubriously**, *adv.* **–lugubriousness**, *n.*

lukewarm /ˈlukwɔm/ *adj.* **1.** moderately warm; tepid. **2.** having or showing little ardour or zeal; indifferent: *lukewarm applause*. **–lukewarmly**, *adv.* **–lukewarmness**, *n.*

lull /lʌl/ *v.t.* **1.** to put to sleep or rest by singing, rocking, etc. **2.** to calm or quiet. **3.** to lead into a false sense of security. *–v.i.* **4.** to become lulled, quieted, or stilled. *–n.* **5.** a short time of quiet or stillness: *a lull in a storm*.

lullaby /ˈlʌləbaɪ/ *n.* (*pl.* **-bies**) **1.** the utterance 'lullaby' or a song containing it; a cradlesong. **2.** any lulling song. *–v.t.* (**-bied**, **-bying**) **3.** to lull with or as with a lullaby.

lumbago /lʌmˈbeɪgoʊ/ *n. Pathol.* myalgia in the lumbar region; rheumatic pain in the muscles of the small of the back.

lumbar /ˈlʌmbə/ *adj.* **1.** of or relating to the loin or loins. *–n.* **2.** a lumbar vertebra, artery, or the like.

lumber¹ /ˈlʌmbə/ *n.* **1.** timber sawn or split into planks, boards, etc. **2.** miscellaneous useless articles that are stored away. *–v.i.* **3.** to cut timber and prepare it for market. *–v.t.* **4.** to heap together in disorder. **5.** to fill up or obstruct with miscellaneous useless articles; encumber. **6.** *Colloq.* to foist off on or leave with, as with something or someone unwelcome or unpleasant. **7.** *Colloq.* to arrest (def. 1). **–lumberer**, *n.*

lumber² /ˈlʌmbə/ *v.i.* to move clumsily or heavily, especially from great or ponderous bulk.

lumberjack /ˈlʌmbədʒæk/ *n. Canadian*, *Chiefly US* someone who fells and removes trees.

lumen /ˈlumən/ *n.* (*pl.* **-mens** or **-mina** /-mənə/) **1.** *Optics* the derived SI unit of luminous flux; the light emitted in a unit solid angle of one steradian by a point source having a uniform intensity of one candela. *Symbol*: lm **2.** *Anat.* the canal, duct, or cavity of a tubular organ. **3.** *Bot.* (of a cell) the cavity which the cell walls enclose.

luminary /'luːmənəri, -mənri/, *Orig. US* /'luːmənɛri/ *n.* (*pl.* **-ries**) **1.** a celestial body, as the sun or moon. **2.** a body or thing that gives light. **3.** someone who enlightens humanity or makes some subject clear. **4.** a famous person; celebrity.

luminescence /luːmə'nɛsəns/ *n.* *Physics* an emission of light not due directly to incandescence and occurring at a temperature below that of incandescent bodies; a term including phosphorescence, fluorescence, etc. **–luminescent**, *adj.*

luminous /'luːmənəs/ *adj.* **1.** radiating or reflecting light; shining. **2.** lighted up or illuminated; well lighted. **3.** brilliant intellectually; enlightening, as a writer or his or her writings. **4.** clear; readily intelligible. **–luminously**, *adv.* **–luminousness**, *n.* **–luminosity** /luːmə'nɒsəti/, *n.*

lump¹ /lʌmp/ *n.* **1.** a piece or mass of solid matter without regular shape, or of no particular shape. **2.** a protuberance or swelling: *a lump on the head.* **3.** *Colloq.* a stupid, clumsy person. **–adj. 4.** in the form of a lump or lumps: *lump sugar.* **5.** including a number of items taken together or in the lump: *a lump sum.* **–v.t. 6.** to unite into one aggregation, collection, or mass. **7.** to deal with in the lump or mass. **–v.i. 8.** to form or raise a lump or lumps. **9.** to move heavily. **–phr. 10. have a lump in the throat**, to feel very emotional. **–lumpy**, *adj.*

lump² /lʌmp/ *v.t. Colloq.* **1.** to carry (usually something heavy or cumbersome). **2.** to endure or put up with (a disagreeable necessity): *if you don't like it, you can lump it.*

lunacy /'luːnəsi/ *n.* (*pl.* **-cies**) **1.** insanity; madness. **2.** extreme foolishness or an instance of it: *her decision to resign was sheer lunacy.* **3.** *Law* unsoundness of mind sufficient to incapacitate one for civil transactions.

lunar /'luːnə/ *adj.* **1.** of or relating to the moon: *the lunar orbit.* **2.** measured by the moon's revolutions: *a lunar month.* **3.** resembling the moon; round or crescent-shaped.

Lunar New Year *n.* → **Chinese New Year.**

lunatic /'luːnətɪk/ *n.* **1.** someone who is regarded as mad or crazy. **2.** *Obs.* an insane person. **–adj. 3.** insane or mad; crazy. **4.** indicating lunacy; characteristic of a lunatic. **5.** *Obs.* (of an institution, etc.) designated for or used by the insane: *a lunatic asylum.* **–lunatically**, *adv.*

lunch /lʌntʃ/ *n.* **1.** a meal taken at midday or shortly after; luncheon. **–v.i. 2.** to eat lunch. **–phr. Colloq. 3. do lunch**, to have lunch with someone, especially as a social or business occasion. **4. out to lunch**, eccentric; not in touch with reality.

luncheon /'lʌntʃən/ *n.* → **lunch.**

luncheon sausage *n.* *Aust.* a large, mild-flavoured, precooked sausage, usually sliced thinly and eaten cold; devon; fritz; polony; Strasburg.

lung /lʌŋ/ *n.* **1.** either of the two saclike respiratory organs in the thorax of humans and the higher vertebrates. **2.** an analogous organ in certain invertebrates, as arachnids, terrestrial gastropods, etc. **–lungful**, *n.*

lunge /lʌndʒ/ *n.* **1.** a thrust, as in fencing. **2.** any sudden forward movement; plunge. **–verb (lunged, lunging) –v.i. 3.** to make a lunge or thrust; move with a lunge. **–v.t. 4.** to thrust; cause to move with a lunge.

lungfish /'lʌŋfɪʃ/ *n.* any of several elongated tropical freshwater fishes of the order Dipnoi, that breathe by means of modified lung-like structures as well as gills.

luni- a word element meaning 'moon'.

lupine /'luːpaɪn/ *adj.* relating to or resembling a wolf.

lurch¹ /lɜːtʃ/ *n.* **1.** sudden leaning or roll to one side, as of a ship or a staggering person. **2.** a sudden swaying or staggering movement. **–v.i. 3.** to make a lurch; move with lurches; stagger: *the wounded man lurched across the room at his assailant.*

lurch² /lɜːtʃ/ *n.* **1.** a position of one discomfited or in a helpless plight: *to leave someone in the lurch.* **2.** a situation at the close of various games in which the loser scores nothing or is far behind his or her opponent.

lure /'luə, 'ljuə/ *n.* **1.** anything that attracts. **2.** a device used to attract fish. **–v.t. 3.** to attract; entice; allure. **–lurer**, *n.*

lurex /'luːrɛks, 'luə-/ *n.* (*from trademark*) **1.** a yarn incorporating metallic thread. **2.** the fabric made from this yarn.

lurid /'luːrəd/ *adj.* **1.** lit up or shining with an unnatural or wild (especially red or fiery) glare: *a lurid sky.* **2.** glaringly vivid or sensational: *lurid tales.* **3.** terrible in fiery intensity, fierce passion, or wild unrestraint: *lurid crimes.* **4.** wan, pallid, or ghastly in hue. **–luridly**, *adv.* **–luridness**, *n.*

lurk /lɜːk/ *v.i.* **1.** to lie in concealment, as in ambush; remain in or about a place secretly or furtively. **2.** to go furtively; slink; steal. **3.** to exist unperceived or unsuspected. **–n.** *Colloq.* **4.** a place of resort; hide-out. **5.** *Aust., NZ* a convenient, often unethical, method of performing a task, earning a living, etc. **–lurky**, *adj.*

luscious /'lʌʃəs/ *adj.* **1.** highly pleasing to the taste or smell: *luscious peaches.* **2.** sweet to the senses or the mind. **3.** very luxurious; extremely attractive. **4.** sweet to excess; cloying. **–lusciously**, *adv.* **–lusciousness**, *n.*

lush¹ /lʌʃ/ *adj.* **1.** tender and juicy, as plants or vegetation; succulent; luxuriant. **2.** characterised by luxuriant vegetation. **3.** *Colloq.* characterised by luxury and comfort. **4.** *Colloq.* sexually attractive. **–lushly**, *adv.* **–lushness**, *n.*

lush² /lʌʃ/ *n. Colloq.* a heavy drinker; alcoholic.

lust /lʌst/ *n.* **1.** (sometimes fol. by *for* or *of*) passionate or overmastering desire: *a lust for power.* **2.** sexual desire or appetite. **–phr. 3. lust after**, to want (someone) sexually. **4. lust for** (or **after**), to have strong or inordinate desire for.

lustre /'lʌstə/ *n.* **1.** the condition or quality of shining by reflecting light: *the lustre of satin.* **2.** radiant brightness; radiance. **3.** radiance of beauty, excellence, glory, etc.: *achievements that add lustre to her name.* **4.** the shiny, metallic surface of some pottery or porcelain. **5.** *Mineral.* the nature of the surface of a mineral with respect to its reflecting qualities. This is one of the properties by which minerals are defined. **–lustrous**, *adj.*

lusty /'lʌsti/ *adj.* (**-tier, -tiest**) **1.** full of or characterised by healthy vigour. **2.** hearty, as a meal or the like. **–lustily**, *adv.* **–lustiness**, *n.*

lute /luːt/ *n.* a stringed musical instrument formerly much used, having a long, fretted neck and a hollow, typically pear-shaped body with a vaulted back.

lux /lʌks/ *n. Optics* the derived SI unit of illumination, defined as an illumination of one lumen per square metre. *Symbol*: lx

luxe /lʌks/ *adj.* **1.** sumptuous; luxurious. **–phr. 2. luxe out** or **luxe up**, *Colloq.* to equip or fit out in a luxurious style.

luxuriant /lʌg'ʒuriənt/ *adj.* **1.** abundant or exuberant in growth, as vegetation. **2.** producing abundantly, as soil. **3.** richly abundant, profuse, or superabundant. **4.** florid, as imagery or ornamentation. **–luxuriance**, *n.* **–luxuriantly**, *adv.*

luxuriate /lʌg'ʒurieɪt/ *v.i.* **1.** to indulge in luxury; revel; enjoy oneself without stint. **2.** to take great delight. **–luxuriation** /lʌg,ʒuri'eɪʃən/, *n.*

luxury /'lʌkʃəri/ n. (pl. **-ries**) **1.** anything conducive to sumptuous living, usually a delicacy, elegance, or refinement of living rather than a necessity. **2.** any form or means of enjoyment. **3.** free indulgence in sumptuous living, costly food, clothing, comforts, etc. **4.** the means of luxurious enjoyment or sumptuous living. *–adj.* **5.** relating or conducive to luxury. **–luxurious**, *adj.*

-ly 1. the normal adverbial suffix, added to almost any descriptive adjective, as in *gladly, gradually*. **2.** the adverbial suffix applied to units of time, meaning 'per', as in *hourly*. **3.** adjective suffix meaning 'like', as in *saintly, manly*.

lychee /'laɪˌtʃi, laɪ'tʃi/ n. **1.** the fruit of a Chinese tree, *Litchi chinensis*, consisting of a thin brittle shell, enclosing a sweet jelly-like pulp and a single seed. **2.** the tree. Also, **lichee, lichi, litchi.**

lycra /'laɪkrə/ n. (*from trademark*) a synthetic knitted fabric with great elasticity.

lye /laɪ/ n. any solution resulting from leaching, percolation, or the like.

lying[1] /'laɪɪŋ/ v. **1.** present participle of **lie**[1]. *–n.* **2.** the telling of lies; untruthfulness. *–adj.* **3.** that lies; untruthful; false.

lying[2] /'laɪɪŋ/ v. present participle of **lie**[2].

Lyme disease /'laɪm dəziz/ n. a disease caused by a bacterium, *Borrelia burgdorferi*, transmitted by the bites of various ticks; early symptoms include a skin rash, painful joints, fever, fatigue, and meningitis, with late infection causing intermittent or chronic arthritis.

lymph /lɪmf/ n. *Physiol.* a clear, yellowish, slightly alkaline fluid derived from the tissues of the body and conveyed to the bloodstream by the lymphatic vessels. **–lymphatic, lymphoid,** *adj.*

lymphoma /lɪm'foʊmə/ n. (pl. **-phomas** *or* **-phomata** /-'foʊmətə/) any of various forms of cancer involving the lymph glands. **–lymphomatoid,** *adj.*

lynch /lɪntʃ/ v.t. to put (a person) to death (by hanging, burning, or otherwise) by some concerted action without authority or process of law, for some offence known or imputed. **–lyncher,** n. **–lynching,** n.

lynx /lɪŋks/ n. (pl. **lynxes** or, *especially collectively*, **lynx**) any of various wildcats of the genus *Lynx*, having long limbs and short tail, and usually with tufted ears, as the **Eurasian lynx**, *L. lynx*, the **bay lynx** or bobcat, *L. rufus*, a common North American species, and the **Canada**

lynx, *L. canadensis*, a large, densely furred species of Canada and the northern US.

lyo- a word element meaning 'dispersion', 'solution', 'dissolved', as in *lyophilic*.

lyre /'laɪə/ n. a musical instrument of ancient Greece, consisting of a soundbox, with two curving arms carrying a crossbar (yoke) from which strings are stretched to the body, used to accompany the voice in singing and recitation.

lyrebird /'laɪəbɜd/ n. either of two ground-dwelling birds of south-eastern Australia, the **superb lyrebird**, *Menura novaehollandiae*, and the **Albert's lyrebird**, *M. alberti*, noted for their fine loud voices, powers of mimicry and the spectacular displays of the males during which they spread their long, lyre-shaped tails.

lyric /'lɪrɪk/ adj. Also, **lyrical. 1.** (of poetry) having the form and musical quality of a song. **2.** relating to or writing such poetry: *a lyric poet.* **3.** of or enjoying a heart-felt expression of feeling. **4.** relating to or using singing. **5.** (of a voice) light in volume and tone. *–n.* **6.** a lyric poem. **7.** (*oft. pl.*) the words of a song. **–lyrically,** adv. **–lyricalness,** n.

lyricist /'lɪrəsəst/ n. **1.** a lyric poet. **2.** someone who writes the words for songs.

lyric theatre n. an often large theatre capable of staging lavish performances involving voices and musical instruments, especially grand opera, musicals, etc.

-lyse a word element making verbs of processes represented by nouns in *-lysis*, as in *catalyse*. Also, *Chiefly US,* **-lyze.**

lysergic acid /laɪˌsɜdʒɪk 'æsəd/ n. **1.** a crystalline tetracyclic acid which can be produced from ergot. **2. →** LSD.

-lysis a word element, especially in scientific terminology, meaning 'breaking down', 'decomposition', as in *analysis, electrolysis*.

lyso- a word element meaning 'decomposition'. Also, **lys-.**

-lyte a word element denoting something subjected to a certain process (indicated by a noun ending in *-lysis*), as in *electrolyte*.

-lytic a termination of adjectives corresponding to nouns ending in *-lysis*, as in *analytic (analysis), paralytic (paralysis)*.

M m

M, m /ɛm/ n. **1.** a consonant, the 13th letter of the English alphabet. **2.** the Roman numeral for 1000.

ma'am /mæm, mam/, *if unstressed* /məm/ n. **1.** madam. **2.** the term of address for a female royal person.

macabre /mə'kab, mə'kabə, -brə/ adj. **1.** gruesome; horrible; grim; ghastly. **2.** of or suggestive of the allegorical dance of death.

macadam /mə'kædəm/ n. **1.** a macadamised road or pavement. **2.** the broken stone used in making such a road.

macadamia /mækə'deɪmiə/ n. **1.** any tree of the genus *Macadamia*, of eastern Australia and South-East Asia, which bears edible though hard-shelled nuts and is grown commercially. **2.** Also, **macadamia nut**. the nut of this tree.

macadamise /mə'kædəmaɪz/ v.t. to construct (a road) by laying and rolling successive layers of broken stone, then usually binding it with asphalt or tar. Also, **macadamize**. –**macadamisation** /məˌkædəmaɪ'zeɪʃən/, n.

macaron /mækə'rɒn, mækə'rɒ̃/ n. a small cake consisting of two smooth, rounded, soft-centred almond meringues, sandwiched together with a filling.

macaroni /mækə'rouni/ n. (pl. **-nis** or **-nies**) a kind of pasta, prepared from wheat flour, in the form of dried, hollow tubes. Also, **maccaroni**.

macaroon /mækə'run/ n. a sweet cake or biscuit made of egg whites, sugar, little or no flour, and frequently almond paste, coconut, etc.

macaw /mə'kɔ/ n. any of various large, long-tailed parrots, chiefly of the genus *Ara*, of tropical and subtropical America, noted for their brilliant plumage and harsh voice.

mace¹ /meɪs/ n. **1.** (formerly) a club-like weapon of war, often with a flanged or spiked metal head. **2.** a staff borne before or by certain officials as a symbol of office. **3.** the bearer of such a staff.

mace² /meɪs/ n. a spice ground from the layer between a nutmeg shell and its outer husk, resembling nutmeg in flavour.

macerate /'mæsəreɪt/ v.t. **1.** to soften, or separate the parts of (a substance) by steeping in a liquid, with or without heat. **2.** to soften or break up (food) by action of a solvent. **3.** to cause to grow thin. –v.i. **4.** to undergo maceration. **5.** to become thin; waste away. –**macerater, macerator**, n. –**maceration** /mæsə'reɪʃən/, n.

mach /mæk/ n. the ratio of the speed of an object to the speed of sound in the medium, usually air; mach 1 in air is about 340 metres per second at sea level.

machete /mə'ʃɛti/ n. a large, heavy knife used especially in Latin-American countries as both a tool and a weapon.

machinate /'mæʃəneɪt, 'mækəneɪt/ v.i. to contrive or devise, especially artfully or with evil purpose. –**machination**, n. –**machinator**, n.

machine /mə'ʃin/ n. **1.** an apparatus consisting of interrelated parts with separate functions, which is used in the performance of some kind of work: *a sewing machine*. **2.** a mechanical apparatus or contrivance; a mechanism. **3.** something operated by a mechanical apparatus, as a motor vehicle, a bicycle, or a plane. **4.** *Mechanics* a device which transmits and modifies force or motion. **5.** any complex agency or operating system: *the machine of government*. **6.** the body of persons conducting and controlling the activities of a political party or other organisation. –v.t. **7.** to make, prepare, or finish with a machine. –phr. **8. the machine** *NZ* → **totalisator**.

machine gun n. a firearm which is able to deliver a rapid and continuous fire of bullets as long as the firer keeps pressure on the trigger.

machine-gun adj. **1.** of or relating to a machine gun. –v.t. (**-gunned, -gunning**) **2.** to shoot at, using a machine gun.

machine language n. *Computers* a low-level and therefore complex binary code which is a precise set of operating instructions for a computer, as opposed to a more symbolic, generalised code. Compare **executable code, source code**. Also, **machine code**.

machinery /mə'ʃinəri/ n. (pl. **-ries**) **1.** machines or mechanical apparatus. **2.** the parts of a machine, collectively: *the machinery of a watch*. **3.** contrivances for producing stage effects. **4.** personages, incidents, etc., introduced into a literary composition, as in developing a story or plot. **5.** any system by which action is maintained: *the machinery of government*.

machismo /mə'tʃɪzmoʊ, mə'kɪzmoʊ/ n. flamboyant virility; masculine display emphasising strength.

macho /'mætʃoʊ, 'mækoʊ/ n. **1.** a man who displays machismo. –adj. **2.** showily virile.

-machy a combining form meaning 'combat'.

mackerel /'mækərəl/ n. **1.** a common iridescent greenish fish with irregular darker markings on the back, *Scomber australasicus*, widely distributed in Australian and New Zealand waters and in various parts of the Pacific. **2.** an abundant food fish of the North Atlantic, *Scomber scombrus*, with wavy cross markings on the back and streamlined for swift swimming.

mackintosh /'mækɪntɒʃ/ n. **1.** a raincoat made of cloth rendered waterproof by rubber. **2.** such cloth. **3.** any raincoat. Also, **macintosh**.

McLeod tool /mə'klaʊd ˌtul/ n. a firefighting implement consisting of a tool with a hardened blade on one side and a rake on the other at the end of a long handle; used for lopping and clearing foliage to create a firebreak; rake-hoe.

McMansion /mək'mænʃən/ n. *Colloq.* a home viewed as large and opulent, but lacking any individual character or charm, and not blending with the other houses in the neighbourhood.

macramé /mə'krami/ n. a kind of lace or ornamental work made by knotting thread or cord in patterns. Also, **macrame**.

macro¹ /'mækroʊ/ adj. broad or overarching (opposed to *micro*): *at the macro level*.

macro² /'mækroʊ/ n. a single-word computer command which sets in train a number of other commands to perform a specific task.

macro- a prefix meaning 'long', 'large', 'great', 'excessive', used especially in scientific terminology, contrasting with *micro-*, as in *macrocosm, macropod*. Also, (*before vowels*), **macr-**.

macrobiotic /ˌmækroʊbaɪ'ɒtɪk/ adj. **1.** of or relating to the prolongation of life; tending to prolong life. **2.** of or relating to a largely vegetarian dietary system formulated as part of Zen Buddhism and intended to prolong life.

macroclimate /'mækroʊˌklaɪmət/ *n.* the climate affecting a large geographical region. Compare **microclimate**.

macrocosm /'mækrəkɒzəm/ *n.* the great world, or universe (opposed to *microcosm*). –**macrocosmic** /mækrə-'kɒzmɪk/, *adj.*

macro-economics /ˌmækroʊ-ekə'nɒmɪks, -ikə-/ *n.* (*construed as sing.*) study of the economic system as a whole. Compare **micro-economics**.

macrofauna /'mækroʊfɔːnə/ *n.* small animal organisms found in the soil or at the bottom of bodies of water, measuring at least 1 mm in length and measured in centimetres rather than in microscopic units. Compare **microfauna**.

macroscopic /mækrə'skɒpɪk/ *adj.* 1. visible to the naked eye (opposed to *microscopic*). 2. comprehensive; concerned with large units or issues. –**macular**, *adj.*

macula /'mækjələ/ *n.* (*pl.* **-lae** /-li/) 1. a spot as on the sun, in the skin, or the like. 2. Also, **macula lutea**. a small, circular, yellowish area at the centre of the retina, responsible for detailed, central vision; yellow spot. –**macular**, *adj.*

macular degeneration /ˌmækjələ dədʒɛnə'reɪʃən/ *n. Ophthalmology* a degenerative disease of the macula (def. 2), causing a progressive loss of central vision.

mad /mæd/ *adj.* 1. disordered in intellect; insane. 2. *Colloq.* angry. 3. (of wind, etc.) furious in violence. 4. (of animals) **a.** abnormally furious: *a mad bull.* **b.** affected with rabies; rabid: *a mad dog.* 5. wildly excited; frantic: *mad haste.* 6. senselessly foolish or imprudent: *a mad scheme.* 7. wildly merry or boisterous: *to have a mad time.* 8. *Colloq.* wild with eagerness or desire; infatuated: *to be mad about someone.* 9. *Colloq.* extremely good; excellent: *she's got a mad outfit.* –*adv.* 10. *Colloq.* extremely: *mad keen to go.* –*phr.* 11. **like mad**, **a.** with great haste, impetuosity, or enthusiasm. **b.** in great amounts: *to sweat like mad.* 12. **mad as a (cut) snake**, insane; eccentric. 13. **mad as a meat axe, a.** very angry. **b.** insane; eccentric. –**madden**, *v.* –**madly**, *adv.* –**madness**, *n.*

madam /'mædəm/ *n.* (*pl.* **mesdames** /meɪ'dæm, meɪ-'dam/ *or* **madams** *for def. 1*, **madams** *for def. 2*) 1. **a.** a polite term of address used originally to a woman of rank or authority, but now used to any woman. **b.** used, added to the name of a rank presently held by a woman, to form a polite term of address or reference: *Madam Chair.* 2. the woman in charge of a brothel.

madcap /'mædkæp/ *adj.* 1. wildly impulsive; lively: *a madcap girl.* –*n.* 2. a madcap person, especially a girl.

mad cow disease *n.* a fatal virus disease of cattle which attacks the nervous system, and which can cross-infect humans; bovine spongiform encephalopathy.

made /meɪd/ *v.* 1. past tense and past participle of **make**. –*adj.* 2. produced by making, preparing, etc. 3. artificially produced. 4. assured of success or fortune: *a made man.* –*phr.* 5. **have (got) it made**, to be assured of success. 6. **made for**, extremely well suited to: *they were made for each other.*

Madeira /mə'dɪərə/ *n.* (*sometimes lower case*) 1. a rich, strong, white wine resembling sherry. 2. (in unofficial use) any similar wine made elsewhere.

madhouse /'mædhaʊs/ *n.* 1. an asylum for the insane. 2. a place of commotion and confusion.

madrasah /mə'dræsə/ *n.* a Muslim school or college. Also, **madrasa**.

madrigal /'mædrɪɡəl/ *n.* a part-song without instrumental accompaniment, usually for five or six voices, and making abundant use of contrapuntal imitation.

maelstrom /'meɪlstrɒm/ *n.* 1. any great or violent whirlpool. 2. a restless confusion of affairs, influence, etc.

maestro /'maɪstroʊ/ *n.* (*pl.* **-tros** *or* **-tri** /-tri/) 1. an eminent musical composer, teacher, or conductor. 2. (*upper case*) a title of respect for addressing such a person.

mafia /'mafiə, 'mæfiə/ *n.* (*sometimes humorous*) any group seen as resembling the Mafia, a criminal secret society of Sicilians or other Italians, by having a close-knit organisation, in-group loyalties, etc.

mag /mæɡ/ *v.i.* (**magged**, **magging**) *Aust.*, *NZ Colloq.* to chatter; to talk rapidly and to little purpose. –**magger**, *n.*

magazine /mæɡə'zin/ *n.* 1. a paper-covered publication containing various stories, articles, advertisements, etc., appearing at regular intervals. 2. a program on radio or television, usually documentary, on a variety of subjects. 3. a place for keeping explosives in a fort or warship. 4. a military storehouse. 5. *Guns* a container for cartridges, which is attached to some types of automatic weapons and replaced when empty. 6. *Photography* a light-proof enclosure containing film. –*adj.* 7. of or relating to a magazine.

magenta /mə'dʒɛntə/ *n.* 1. reddish purple. 2. the red subtractive primary colour used in four-colour printing.

maggot /'mæɡət/ *n.* 1. the legless larva of a fly, as of the housefly. 2. a fly larva living in decaying matter. 3. an odd fancy; whim. –**maggoty**, *adj.*

magic /'mædʒɪk/ *n.* 1. (the exercise of) the art of producing effects or controlling events by supernatural powers or by command of occult forces in nature. 2. the effects produced. 3. a magical event. 4. any extraordinary influence or attraction: *the magic in a great name.* 5. a theatrical performance of tricks; legerdemain; conjuring. –*adj.* Also, **magical**. 6. done by magic: *magic spells.* 7. mysteriously attractive: *magic beauty.* 8. of, relating to, or due to magic: *magic rites.* –**magically**, *adv.*

magic bullet *n.* 1. *Colloq.* any drug or treatment which acts effectively against a disease and has no harmful or unpleasant side effects. 2. any remedy which is remarkably effective.

magician /mə'dʒɪʃən/ *n.* 1. someone skilled in magic arts. 2. a juggler; conjurer.

magic realism *n.* a genre of literature that deals in an accepting way with aspects of life usually represented as outside reality.

magisterial /mædʒəs'tɪəriəl/ *adj.* 1. of, relating to, or befitting a master; authoritative: *a magisterial pronouncement.* 2. imperious; domineering. 3. of or befitting a magistrate or a magistrate's office. 4. of the rank of a magistrate. –**magisterially**, *adv.*

magistrate /'mædʒəstreɪt, -trət/ *n.* 1. a person charged with executive functions. 2. Also, **stipendiary magistrate**. a paid judicial officer presiding over a court of the lowest tier, and sometimes also performing other legal duties, for example, acting as coroner.

maglev /'mæɡlɛv/ *n.* 1. → **magnetic levitation train**. –*adj.* 2. of or relating to such a train: *a maglev system.*

magma /'mæɡmə/ *n.* (*pl.* **-mata** /-mətə/ *or* **magmas**) 1. any crude mixture of finely divided mineral or organic matters. 2. *Geol.* molten material under conditions of intense heat and great pressure occurring beneath the solid crust of the earth, and from which igneous rocks are formed. 3. *Chem.*, *Pharmacology* a paste composed of solid and liquid matter. –**magmatic** /mæɡ'mætɪk/, *adj.*

magnanimous /mæɡ'nænəməs/ *adj.* 1. generous in forgiving an insult or injury; free from petty resentfulness or vindictiveness. 2. high-minded; noble. 3. proceeding from or revealing nobility of mind, etc. –**magnanimously**, *adv.* –**magnanimousness**, **magnanimity** /mæɡnə'nɪməti/, *n.*

magnate /'mæɡneɪt, 'mæɡnət/ *n.* 1. a great or dominant person in some field of business: *a property magnate.* 2. a person of eminence or distinction.

magnesia /mæg'niʃə, -'niʒə, -'niziə/ *n.* magnesium oxide, MgO, a white tasteless substance used in medicine as an antacid and laxative. –**magnesian**, **magnesic**, *adj.*

magnesium /mæg'niziəm/ *n.* a light, ductile, silver-white metallic element which burns with a dazzling white light, used in lightweight alloys. *Symbol*: Mg; *relative atomic mass*: 24.312; *atomic number*: 12; *density*: 1.74 at 20°C.

magnet /'mægnət/ *n.* **1.** a body (as a piece of iron or steel) which possesses the property of attracting certain substances, especially iron; any piece of metal with ferromagnetic properties. **2.** a thing or person that attracts, as by some inherent power or charm.

magnetar /'mægnətə/ *n.* a neutron star with a super-strong magnetic field which slows the star's rotation and causes starquakes.

magnetic /mæg'nɛtɪk/ *adj.* **1.** of or relating to a magnet or magnetism. **2.** having the properties of a magnet. **3.** capable of being magnetised or attracted by a magnet. **4.** relating to the earth's magnetism: *the magnetic equator.* **5.** exerting a strong attractive power or charm: *a magnetic personality.* –**magnetically**, *adv.*

magnetic field *n. Physics* a condition of space in the vicinity of a magnet or electric current which manifests itself as a force on magnetic objects within that space.

magnetic levitation train *n.* a train which, using electromagnetism, travels suspended above the track, moving at very high speed and with little noise or vibration. Also, **maglev.**

magnetic north *n.* the direction in which the needle of a compass points, differing in most places from true geographic north. Compare **grid north, true north.**

magnetic pole *n.* **1.** a pole of a magnet. **2.** either of the two points on the earth's surface where the dipping needle of a compass stands vertical, one in the Arctic, the other in the Antarctic.

magnetic resonance imaging *n.* a non-invasive imaging technique that produces an image of internal body organs by measurement of the radiofrequency emitted by hydrogen nuclei in all tissues after they have been disturbed by an extremely strong magnetic field. *Abbrev.*: MRI

magnetic storm *n.* a sudden disturbance in the earth's magnetic field associated with sunspot activity.

magnetic stripe reader *n.* a computerised device which interprets the information recorded on a stripe of magnetised material on a card such as a credit card.

magnetic tape *n. Electronics* a plastic tape coated with a ferromagnetic powder, especially iron oxide, used to record sound in a tape recorder, and video signals in a video recorder, to retain digital information in computing, and machine instructions in industrial and other control systems.

magnetise /'mægnətaɪz/ *v.t.* **1.** to communicate magnetic properties to. **2.** to exert an attracting or compelling influence upon. Also, **magnetize.** –**magnetiser**, *n.* –**magnetisation**, *n.*

magnetism /'mægnətɪzəm/ *n.* **1.** the characteristic properties possessed by magnets; the molecular properties common to magnets. **2.** the agency producing magnetic phenomena. **3.** the science dealing with magnetic phenomena. **4.** magnetic or attractive power or charm.

magneto /mæg'nitoʊ/ *n.* (*pl.* -**tos**) a small electric generator, the poles of which are permanent magnets, as a hand-operated generator for telephone signalling, or the generator producing sparks in an internal-combustion engine.

magneto- a combining form of **magnet** or **magnetic.**

magni- **1.** a word element meaning 'large', 'great', as in *magnify.* **2.** *Zool.* a word element denoting length.

magnification /mægnəfə'keɪʃən/ *n.* **1.** the act of magnifying. **2.** the state of being magnified. **3.** the power to magnify. **4.** a magnified copy or reproduction. **5.** (of an optical instrument) the ratio of the linear dimensions of the final image to that of the object.

magnificent /mæg'nɪfəsənt/ *adj.* **1.** making a splendid appearance or show: *a magnificent cathedral.* **2.** extraordinarily fine; superb: *a magnificent opportunity.* **3.** noble; sublime: *a magnificent poem.* –**magnificence**, *n.* –**magnificently**, *adv.*

magnify /'mægnəfaɪ/ *verb* (**-fied, -fying**) –*v.t.* **1.** to increase the apparent size of, as a lens does. **2.** to make greater in size; enlarge. **3.** to cause to seem greater or more important. –*v.i.* **4.** to increase or be able to increase the apparent size of an object, as a lens does. –**magnifier**, *n.*

magnitude /'mægnətjud, -tʃud/ *n.* **1.** size; extent: *to determine the magnitude of an angle.* **2.** great amount, importance, etc.: *affairs of magnitude.* **3.** moral greatness: *magnitude of mind.* **4.** *Astron.* the brightness of a star expressed according to an arbitrary numerical system (the brightest degree being the first magnitude). Stars brighter than the sixth magnitude are visible to the unaided eye.

magnolia /mæg'noʊliə, -jə/ *n.* **1.** a large tree, *Magnolia grandiflora*, with large, spectacular, scented, cream flowers. **2.** Also, **port wine magnolia.** a small tree, *Magnolia × soulangiana*, much cultivated in gardens because of its pink to dark red, tulip-shaped flowers. **3.** any plant of the genus *Magnolia*, comprising shrubs and trees, usually with fragrant flowers and an aromatic bark, much cultivated for ornament.

magnum /'mægnəm/ *n.* (*pl.* -**nums**) **1.** a bottle for wine or spirits, holding about 2 normal bottles, or 1.5 litres. –*adj.* **2.** (of firearms) having a larger bore than is standard for its calibre: *a .44 magnum pistol.*

magpie /'mægpaɪ/ *n.* **1.** Also, **Australian magpie.** a common black and white bird, *Cracticus tibicen*, with a solid body, strong legs, and a large pointed bill, found throughout Australia and in New Guinea, and noted for its beautiful song and vigorous defence of nesting sites. **2.** any of various currawongs. **3.** any of various superficially similar but unrelated birds of the genus *Pica* and other genera of the family Corvidae as the **black-billed magpie**, *P. pica*, of Europe and North America. **4.** a chattering person. **5.** *Colloq.* someone who collects useless objects; bowerbird.

magpie lark *n.* a common black and white bird, *Grallina cyanoleuca*, building a mud nest high in a tree, and having a loud piping song; found throughout Australia, New Guinea and nearby islands; peewee; peewit.

maharajah /mahə'radʒə/ *n.* one of the great ruling princes in India, ranking above a rajah. Also, **maharaja.**

maharani /mahə'rani/ *n.* **1.** the wife of a maharajah. **2.** a female sovereign in her own right. Also, **maharanee.**

maharishi /mahə'rɪʃi/ *n. Hinduism* **1.** a spiritual leader; a teacher of religion or mystical knowledge. **2.** (*upper case*) a respectful title for such a leader or teacher.

mahatma /mə'hatmə, -'hætmə/ *n. Hinduism* **1.** a highly esteemed wise and saintly leader. **2.** (*upper case*) a respectful title for such a leader. –**mahatmaism**, *n.*

mahjong /'ma,dʒɒŋ, -ʒɒŋ/ *n.* a game of Chinese origin, usually for four persons, with 136 (or sometimes 144) domino-like pieces or tiles (marked in suits), counters, and dice.

mahogany /mə'hɒgəni/ *n.* (*pl.* -**nies**) **1.** any of certain tropical American trees, especially *Swietenia mahogoni* and *S. macrophylla*, yielding a hard, reddish brown wood highly esteemed for making fine furniture, etc. **2.** any of various related or similar trees, as species of the genus *Dysoxylum*, and *Eucalyptus robusta*, swamp mahogany, or their timber. **3.** a reddish brown colour.

maid /meɪd/ n. 1. a girl; young unmarried woman. 2. a spinster (usu. in the expression old maid). 3. a woman employed for various light domestic duties in houses, hotels, etc.; housemaid.

maiden /'meɪdn/ n. 1. a maid; girl; young unmarried woman; virgin. –adj. 2. of, relating to, or befitting a girl or unmarried woman. 3. unmarried: a maiden lady. 4. made, tried, appearing, etc., for the first time: maiden voyage.

maidenhead /'meɪdnhɛd/ n. 1. maidenhood; virginity. 2. → hymen.

maiden name n. a woman's surname before marriage.

maiden over n. (in cricket) an over in which no runs are made.

mail¹ /meɪl/ n. 1. letters, packages, etc., arriving or sent by post. 2. the system of transmission of letters, etc., by post. 3. a train or boat by which postal matter is carried. –adj. 4. of or relating to mail: a mail bag. –v.t. 5. to send by mail; place in a post office or postbox for transmission.

mail² /meɪl/ n. flexible armour of interlinked rings, the ends riveted, butted, or soldered.

mail merge n. Computers a software function for linking a document to a spreadsheet of names and addresses to output a document to multiple recipients.

mail order n. the system of conducting a business by receiving orders and payment by mail for goods supplied to the buyers.

maim /meɪm/ v.t. 1. to deprive of the use of some bodily member; mutilate; cripple. 2. to impair; make essentially defective. –maimer, n.

main /meɪn/ adj. 1. chief; principal; leading: the main office. 2. sheer; utmost, as strength, force, etc.: by main force. 3. of or relating to a broad expanse: main sea. 4. Gram. See main clause. –n. 5. a. a principal pipe, wire, cable or duct in a system used to distribute water, gas, electricity, etc. b. the mains, the principal distribution system for water, gas, electricity, etc.: turn the water off at the mains. 6. (pl.) the main course of a meal. 7. the chief or principal part or point. 8. Poetic the open ocean; high seas. 9. → mainland. –phr. 10. in the main, for the most part. 11. with might and main, with utmost strength, vigour, force, or effort.

main clause n. Gram. (in a complex sentence) the clause which may stand syntactically as a sentence by itself. For example, in I was out when he came in, the main clause is I was out.

mainframe computer /ˌmeɪnfreɪm kəm'pjutə/ n. a powerful, general-purpose computer with large storage capacity, capable of carrying out several programs simultaneously, and designed for institutional rather than individual use. Also, **mainframe**.

mainland /'meɪnlænd, -lənd/ n. the principal landmass as distinguished from nearby islands. –mainlander, n.

mainline /'meɪnlaɪn/ v.i. Colloq. to inject a narcotic drug directly into the vein.

mainstay /'meɪnsteɪ/ n. 1. Naut. the stay which secures the mainmast forward. 2. a chief support.

mainstream /'meɪnstrim/ n. 1. the dominant trend; chief tendency: she was in the mainstream of fashion. –adj. 2. of or relating to the mainstream. 3. of or relating to jazz which lies between traditional and modern in its stage of development.

maintain /meɪn'teɪn, mən-/ v.t. 1. to keep in existence; keep up; preserve: to maintain good relations with NZ; to maintain life in the Antarctic. 2. to keep in good condition, operation, etc.: to maintain order; to maintain roads. 3. to keep; hold on to; retain: to maintain the lead in a race. 4. to keep or hold against attack: to maintain one's ground. 5. to hold; declare; assert: I maintain that it is right. 6. to provide with a living: he

maintained his parents in their old age. –maintainable, adj. –maintainer, n.

maintenance /'meɪntənəns/ n. 1. the act of maintaining. 2. the state of being maintained. 3. means of provision for maintaining; means of subsistence. 4. Law the money paid either in a lump sum or by way of periodical payments for the support of the other spouse or infant children, usually after divorce.

maize /meɪz/ n. 1. a widely cultivated cereal plant, Zea mays, occurring in many varieties, bearing a large yellow grain (corn or sweet corn) in large ears or spikes which is used as food, made into flour, or used for animal feed. 2. a pale yellow colour.

majesty /'mædʒəsti/ n. (pl. -ties) 1. regal, lofty, or stately dignity; imposing character; grandeur. 2. supreme greatness or authority; sovereignty. 3. a royal personage, or royal personages collectively. 4. (usu. upper case) (preceded by his, her, your, etc.) a title used when speaking of or to a sovereign. –majestic /mə'dʒɛstɪk/, adj.

major /'meɪdʒə/ n. 1. Army a. a commissioned officer in the Australian Army ranking below a lieutenant colonel and above a captain. b. the rank. Abbrev.: MAJ 2. one of superior rank in a specified class. 3. a person of full legal age. 4. Music a major interval, chord, scale, etc. 5. a subject or field of study chosen by a student to represent their principal interest and upon which they concentrate a large share of their efforts. –adj. 6. greater, as in size, amount, extent, importance, rank, etc.: the major part of the town. 7. of or relating to the majority. 8. of full legal age. 9. very important or significant: a major problem. 10. Logic broader or more extensive: a. major term, of a syllogism is the term that enters into the predicate of the conclusion. b. major premise, is that premise of a syllogism which contains the major term. 11. Music a. (of an interval) being between the tonic and the second, third, sixth, and seventh degrees of a major scale: a major third; a major sixth. b. (of a chord) having a major third between the root and the note next above it. –phr. 12. major in, to pursue as a major or principal subject or course of study.

major general n. Army 1. a commissioned officer in the Australian Army ranking below lieutenant general and above brigadier. 2. the rank. Abbrev.: MAJGEN –major-generalcy, major-generalship, n.

majority /mə'dʒɒrəti/ n. (pl. -ties) 1. the greater part or number: the majority of the population. 2. the number of votes, seats, etc., by which a candidate or government wins an election: a majority of 200 votes. 3. the party with the majority (def. 2). 4. → full age.

Major Mitchell /meɪdʒə 'mɪtʃəl/ n. a cockatoo, Cacatua leadbeateri, with white wings, pink underparts, neck and face, and white crown suffused with salmon pink and forward-curving scarlet crest, endemic to the arid and semi-arid regions of Australia.

majuscule /'mædʒəskjul/ adj. large, as letters (whether capital or uncial).

make /meɪk/ verb (made, making) –v.t. 1. to bring into existence by shaping material, combining parts, etc.: to make a dress. 2. to produce by any action or causative agency: to make trouble. 3. to cause to be or become; render: to make an old man young. 4. to constitute; appoint: to make someone a judge. 5. to put into proper condition for use: to make a bed. 6. to bring into a certain form or condition: to make bookcases out of orange boxes. 7. to cause, induce, or compel (to do something): to make a horse go. 8. to give rise to; occasion. 9. to produce, earn, or win for oneself: to make a fortune. 10. to draw up, as a legal document. 11. to do; effect: to make a bargain. 12. to fix; establish; enact: to make laws. 13. to become by development; prove to be: he will make a good lawyer. 14. to form in the mind, as a judgement, estimate, or plan. **15.** to judge or infer as to the truth, nature, meaning, etc.: *what do you make of it?* **16.** to estimate; reckon: *to make the distance ten metres.* **17.** (of material or parts) to compose; form: *two and two make four.* **18.** to bring to; bring up the total to: *to make a kilo.* **19.** to serve for or as: *to make good reading.* **20.** to be sufficient to constitute; be essential to. **21.** to assure the success, fortune, or mature character of. **22.** to put forth; deliver: *to make a speech.* **23.** *US* to accomplish by travelling, etc.: *to make one hundred kilometres an hour.* **24.** to arrive at or reach: *to make a port.* **25.** to arrive in time for: *to make the first show.* **26.** to achieve a position on or inclusion in (a team, a list of honours, place of honour, etc.). **27.** *Colloq.* to seduce or have sexual intercourse with. **28.** *Sport, Games* to earn as a score. **29.** to close (an electric circuit). –*v.i.* **30.** to cause oneself, or something understood, to be as specified: *to make sure.* **31.** to show oneself in action or behaviour: *to make merry.* **32.** to direct or pursue the course; go: *to make for home.* –*n.* **33.** style or manner of being made; form; build. **34.** production with reference to the maker: *our own make.* **35.** disposition; character; nature. **36.** the act or process of making. **37.** quantity made; output. –*phr.* **38. make a face,** to grimace. **39. make as if** (or **as though**), to act as if; feign. **40. make at,** to attack or lunge towards: *he made at me with a knife.* **41. make away with, a.** to get rid of. **b.** to kill or destroy. **c.** to steal or abduct. **42. make believe,** to pretend. **43. make do,** (sometimes fol. by *with*) to operate or carry on using minimal or improvised resources. **44. make eyes,** (sometimes fol. by *at*) to flirt. **45. make for, a.** to travel towards or attempt to reach. **b.** to help to promote or maintain: *to make for better international relations.* **46. make good, a.** to achieve (a goal). **b.** to become a success. **47. make heavy weather,** *Naut.* to roll and pitch in heavy seas. **48. make heavy weather of,** to have difficulty with; progress laboriously with: *to make heavy weather of a simple calculation.* **49. make it, a.** to achieve one's object. **b.** to arrive successfully. **50. make it with,** *Colloq.* to have sexual intercourse with. **51. make like,** *Colloq.* **a.** to imitate: *to make like a monkey.* **b.** to pretend: *make like you're happy.* **52. make love to** (or **with**), **a.** to have sexual intercourse with. **b.** *Obs.* to court; woo. **53. make off,** to run away. **54. make off with,** to steal. **55. make out, a.** to write out (a bill, a cheque, etc.). **b.** to prove; establish. **c.** to discern; decipher. **d.** to present as; impute to be: *he made me out a liar.* **e.** *Colloq.* to manage; cope successfully. **f.** *Colloq.* to have sexual intercourse: *I made out last night.* **g.** *Colloq.* to kiss, pet, and fondle sexually: *making out at the movies.* **56. make over, a.** to make anew; alter: *to make over a dress.* **b.** to hand over into the possession or charge of another. **c.** to transfer the title of (property); convey. **57. make public,** to reveal to the public. **58. make the most of,** to get the maximum pleasure out of, in anticipation of being without in the near future. **59. make time, a.** to move quickly, especially in an attempt to recover lost time. **b.** to find time for something in spite of a busy schedule. **c.** *Chiefly US* to flirt: *to make time with the hostess.* **60. make up, a.** (of parts) to constitute; form. **b.** to put together; construct; compile. **c.** to concoct; invent. **d.** to compensate for; make good. **e.** to complete. **f.** to prepare; put in order. **g.** to bring to a definite conclusion, as one's mind. **h.** to settle amicably, as differences. **i.** Also, **make it up.** to become reconciled after a quarrel. **j.** *Printing* to arrange, set type, etc., into columns or pages. **k.** to apply cosmetics to, as the face. **l.** to prepare for a part, as on the stage, by appropriate dress, cosmetics, etc. **m.** to adjust or balance, as accounts; to prepare, as statements. **n.** *Educ.* to repeat (a course or examination in which one has failed) or to

take (an examination from which one has been absent). **o.** to give or work in lieu for; compensate for (time or work lost, etc.). **61. make up to, a.** *Colloq.* to try to be on friendly terms with; fawn on. **b.** to make advances or pay court to. **62. on the make,** *Colloq.* **a.** intent on gain or one's own advantage. **b.** looking for a sexual partner.

makeshift /'meɪkʃɪft/ *n.* **1.** a temporary expedient; substitute. –*adj.* **2.** serving as a makeshift.

make-up *n.* **1.** (the putting on of) cosmetics. **2.** the costume, face-paint, wigs, etc., worn on the stage. **3.** → **foundation** (def. 6). **4.** the manner of being made up or put together; composition. **5.** bodily or mental constitution: *his emotional make-up.* **6.** *Printing* the arrangement of type, pictures, etc., into columns or pages. Also, **makeup.**

mal- a prefix having attributive relation to the second element, meaning 'bad', 'wrongful', 'ill', as in *maladjustment, malpractice.*

Malabar rat /mæləba 'ræt/ *n.* → **bandicoot** (def. 2).

malachite /'mæləkaɪt/ *n.* a green mineral basic copper carbonate, $Cu_2CO_3(OH)_2$, an ore of copper, also used for making ornamental articles.

maladaptive /mælə'dæptɪv/ *adj. Psychol.* showing faulty adaptation. –**maladaptation,** *n.*

maladjustment /mælə'dʒʌstmənt/ *n.* **1.** a faulty adjustment. **2.** *Psychol.* a failure to function successfully with regard to personal relationships and environment, often a symptom of mental disturbance. –**maladjusted,** *adj.*

malady /'mælədi/ *n.* (*pl.* **-dies**) **1.** any bodily disorder or disease, especially one that is chronic or deep-seated. **2.** any form of disorder: *social maladies.*

malaise /mæ'leɪz, mə-/ *n.* a condition of indefinite bodily weakness or discomfort, often marking the onset of a disease.

malapropism /'mæləprɒp,ɪzəm/ *n.* **1.** the act or habit of ridiculously misusing words. **2.** a word so misused.

malaria /mə'lɛəriə/ *n. Pathol.* **1.** any of a group of diseases, usually intermittent or remittent, and characterised by attacks of chills, fever, and sweating; caused by a species of parasitic protozoans which are transferred to the human blood by mosquitoes. **2.** *Obs.* unwholesome or poisonous air. –**malarial, malarian, malarious,** *adj.*

malcontent /'mælkəntɛnt/ *adj.* **1.** discontented; dissatisfied. **2.** dissatisfied with the existing administration; inclined to rebellion. –*n.* **3.** a malcontent person.

male /meɪl/ *adj.* **1.** (of people, animals and plants) belonging to the sex capable of fertilising female ova. **2.** relating to or typical of this sex; masculine. **3.** composed of men: *a male choir.* **4.** designed for men: *male cosmetics.* –*n.* **5.** a man or boy. **6.** any animal of the male sex. **7.** *Bot.* a plant which has stamens.

male chauvinist *n.* **1.** a man who discriminates against women by applying to them stereotyped ideas of incompetence, inferiority, passivity, etc. **2.** a chauvinist for the male sex. –*adj.* **3.** having the characteristics of a male chauvinist. –*phr.* **4. male chauvinist pig,** an extreme male chauvinist. –**male chauvinism,** *n.*

malediction /mælə'dɪkʃən/ *n.* **1.** a curse; the utterance of a curse. **2.** slander. –**maledictory** /mælə'dɪktri, -təri/, *adj.*

malefactor /'mæləfæktə/ *n.* **1.** an offender against the law; a criminal. **2.** someone who does evil. –**malefaction,** *n.* –**malefactress** /'mæləfæktrəs/, *fem. n.*

malevolent /mə'lɛvələnt/ *adj.* **1.** wishing evil to another or others; showing ill will: *his failure made him malevolent towards others.* **2.** *Astrology* evil or malign in influence. –**malevolence,** *n.* –**malevolently,** *adv.*

malformation /mælfɔ'meɪʃən, -fə-/ *n.* faulty or anomalous formation or structure, especially in a living body. –**malformed** /mæl'fɔmd/, *adj.*

malfunction /mælˈfʌŋkʃən/ *v.i.* **1.** to fail to function properly. –*n.* **2.** failure to function properly.

malibu /ˈmæləbu/ *n. Surfing* a long surfboard with a rounded nose, offering more stability than a short board. Also, **malibu board**.

malice /ˈmæləs/ *n.* **1.** desire to inflict injury or suffering on another. **2.** *Law* evil intent on the part of someone who commits a wrongful act injurious to others, technically called *malitia praecogitata*, or *malice prepense* or *malice aforethought*. –**malicious**, *adj.*

malign /məˈlaɪn/ *v.t.* **1.** to speak ill of; slander. –*adj.* **2.** evil in effect; pernicious; baleful. **3.** having or showing an evil disposition; malevolent. –**maligner**, *n.* –**malignity** /məˈlɪgnəti/, *n.* –**malignly**, *adv.*

malignant /məˈlɪgnənt/ *adj.* **1.** disposed to cause suffering or distress; malicious. **2.** very dangerous; harmful in influence or effect. **3.** *Pathol.* **a.** of or relating to a tumour that destroys the tissue in which it originates and has the potential to spread to other regions of the body by dissemination through the bloodstream and lymphatic system, thus being life-threatening. **b.** of or relating to any disease or condition that is life-threatening. –**malignance, malignancy**, *n.* –**malignantly**, *adv.*

malinger /məˈlɪŋgə/ *v.i.* to feign sickness or injury, especially in order to avoid duty, work, etc. –**malingerer**, *n.*

mall /mɔl, mæl/ *n.* **1.** Also, **shopping mall**. a shopping complex. **2.** a shaded walk, usually public.

mallard /ˈmælad/ *n.* (*pl.* -**lards** *or, especially collectively,* -**lard**) **1.** a common duck, *Anas platyrhynchos*, of Eurasia and the Americas, introduced into Australia and New Zealand; most domestic ducks are descended from Eurasian populations of this bird. **2.** a male of this species.

malleable /ˈmæliəbəl/ *adj.* **1.** capable of being extended or shaped by hammering or by pressure with rollers. **2.** adaptable or tractable. –**malleability** /mæliəˈbɪləti/, **malleableness**, *n.*

mallee /ˈmæli/ *n.* **1.** any of various Australian species of *Eucalyptus* having a number of almost unbranched stems arising from a large underground lignotuber, as *E. dumosa*. –*phr.* **2. fit as a mallee bull**, *Aust. Colloq.* extremely fit. **3. strong as a mallee bull**, *Aust. Colloq.* very strong. **4. the mallee**, Also, **the Mallee**. *Aust.* **a.** any of various semi-arid areas in NSW, SA, WA, and especially Victoria, where the predominant species is a mallee. **b.** *Colloq.* any remote, isolated, or unsettled area.

malleefowl /ˈmælifaʊl/ *n.* a greyish-brown, spotted, Australian bird, *Leipoa ocellata*, found in dry inland scrub areas and now threatened with extinction. Also, **mallee fowl, mallee bird, mallee hen**.

mallet[1] /ˈmælət/ *n.* **1.** a hammer-like tool with a head commonly of wood but occasionally of rawhide, plastic, etc., used for driving any tool with a wooden handle, as a chisel. **2.** the wooden implement used to strike the balls in croquet. **3.** the stick used to drive the ball in polo.

mallet[2] /ˈmælət/ *n.* **1.** any of several species of the genus *Eucalyptus* in western Australia, especially *E. occidentalis*. **2.** the wood of these trees.

malnutrition /mælnjuˈtrɪʃən/ *n.* imperfect nutrition; lack of proper nutrition resulting from deficiencies in the diet or the process of assimilation.

malpractice /mælˈpræktəs/ *n.* **1.** improper professional action, as treatment by a physician, from reprehensible ignorance or neglect or with criminal intent. **2.** any improper conduct. –**malpractitioner** /mælprækˈtɪʃənə/, *n.*

malt /mɔlt, mɒlt/ *n.* **1.** germinated grain (usually barley), used in brewing and distilling. **2.** a liquor produced from malt by fermentation, as beer or ale. **3.** malt extract. –*v.t.* **4.** to turn (grain) into malt. –*v.i.* **5.** to produce malt from grain.

maltose /ˈmɔltoʊz, -toʊs, ˈmɒl-/ *n.* a white crystalline disaccharide, $C_{12}H_{22}O_{11}$, containing two glucose units, formed by the action of beta-amylase on starch. Also, **maltobiose, malt sugar**.

maltreat /mælˈtrit/ *v.t.* to treat badly; handle roughly or cruelly; abuse. –**maltreatment**, *n.*

malware /ˈmælwɛə/ *n. Computers* software created with a destructive intent, such as a virus, trojan horse, worm, etc.

mama /məˈma/ *n.* mother; mamma.

mamilla /mæˈmɪlə/ *n.* (*pl.* -**millae** /-ˈmɪli/) **1.** the nipple of the mamma or breast. **2.** any nipple-like process or protuberance. Also, *Chiefly US*, **mammilla**. –**mamillary** /ˈmæmələri/, *adj.* –**mamillate** /ˈmæmələɪt, -ləɪt/, *adj.*

mamma[1] /ˈmʌmə, məˈma/ *n.* (*with children*) mother.

mamma[2] /ˈmæmə/ *n.* (*pl.* **mammae** /ˈmæmi/) the organ, characteristic of mammals, which in the female secretes milk; a breast or udder.

mammal /ˈmæməl/ *n.* a member of the Mammalia, a class of vertebrates whose young feed upon milk from the mother's breast. Most species (except cetaceans) are more or less hairy, all have a diaphragm, and all (except the monotremes) are viviparous. –**mammalian**, *adj.*, *n.*

mammary /ˈmæməri/ *adj.* of or relating to the mamma or breast; mamma-like.

mammon /ˈmæmən/ *n.* **1.** *New Testament* riches or material wealth. **2.** (*upper case*) a personification of riches as an evil spirit or deity. –**mammonish**, *adj.*

mammoth /ˈmæməθ/ *n.* **1.** a large, extinct species of elephant, *Mammuthus primigenius*, the **northern woolly mammoth**, which resembled the present Indian elephant but had a hairy coat and long, curved tusks. –*adj.* **2.** huge; gigantic: *a mammoth enterprise.*

man /mæn/ *n.* (*pl.* **men**) **1.** *Anthrop.* the human species (genus *Homo*, family Hominidae, class Mammalia) at the highest level of animal development, mainly characterised by exceptional mentality. **2. a.** the human race; humankind. **b.** the human creature or being as representative of its kind, and distinguished from other beings, animals, or things. **3.** a male human being (as distinguished from *woman*). **4.** an adult male person (as distinguished from *boy*). **5.** a husband: *man and wife.* **6.** *Colloq.* a male lover, partner in a marriage or de facto relationship: *her man came also.* **7.** a male follower, subordinate, or employee: *officers and men of the army.* **8. a.** a man involved in servicing or supplying some specified item: *laundry man; ice-man.* **b.** a figure made, or said to be made, of some substance: *snow man; straw man; iron man.* **9.** someone having traditionally manly qualities or virtues. **10.** someone's representative in a specified place, country, etc. **11.** a male servant; a valet. **12.** a word of condescending address to a man: *my good man.* **13.** *Colloq.* a term of address. **14.** one of the pieces used in playing certain games, as chess or draughts. –*interj.* **15.** *Colloq.* an exclamation indicating astonishment, pleasure, displeasure, etc.: *Man! You should have been there.* –*v.t.* (**manned, manning**) **16.** to furnish with personnel, as for service or defence. **17.** to take one's place at for service, as a gun, post, etc. **18.** to make manly; brace. –*phr.* **19. make a man (out) of someone**, to bring out in someone qualities of courage, perseverance, etc., thought to distinguish a man from a boy. **20. man alive!**, *Colloq.* an expression of surprise, astonishment, etc. **21. man and boy**, (of a male) from childhood. **22. man on man**, *Sport* one contestant directly against another on the opposing team. **23. the man**, *Colloq.* a male employer; male boss. **24. the man of the house**, the principal male of a household (as opposed to *the lady of the house*). **25. to a man**, all; to the last man. –**manly**, *adj.*

manacle /ˈmænəkəl/ *n.* (*usu. pl.*) **1.** a shackle for the hand; handcuff. **2.** a restraint. –*v.t.* (**-cled, -cling**) **3.** to handcuff; shackle. **4.** to hamper; restrain.

manage /ˈmænɪdʒ/ *verb* (**-aged, -aging**) –*v.t.* **1.** to bring about; succeed in accomplishing: *He managed to see the governor.* **2.** to take charge or care of: *to manage a business.* **3.** to handle or control: *to manage a horse*; *to manage a child.* **4.** to be able to use properly: *can you manage that knife?* –*v.i.* **5.** to be able to make do: *can you manage on $50 a week?* –**manageable**, *adj.* –**manageably**, *adv.* –**manageability** /ˌmænɪdʒəˈbɪləti/, *n.*

management /ˈmænɪdʒmənt/ *n.* **1.** the act or manner of managing; handling, direction, or control. **2.** skill in managing; executive ability. **3.** the person or persons managing an institution, business, etc.: *this shop is under new management.* **4.** executives collectively: *conflicts between labour and management.*

management buy-in *n.* the employment of an external management team to run a business or organisation.

management buyout *n.* the purchase of a company by its own company managers. Also, **management buy-out, MBO.**

management information system *n. Computers* a software package which is designed to provide information for decision-making, usually intended for senior management.

manager /ˈmænədʒə/ *n.* **1.** someone charged with the management, or direction of an institution, a business or the like. **2.** someone who manages resources and expenditures, as of a household. **3.** someone in charge of the business affairs of an entertainer or group of entertainers. **4.** someone in charge of the performance and training of a sporting individual or team. –**managerial**, *adj.* –**managership**, *n.*

manageress /mænədʒəˈrɛs, ˈmænədʒərəs/ *n.* a female manager.

manchester /ˈmæntʃəstə, -tʃɛstə/ *n. Aust., NZ* sheets, towels, etc., as sold in shops.

-mancy a word element meaning 'divination', as in *necromancy.*

mandala /mænˈdalə/ *n.* a mystic symbol of the universe, in the form of a circle enclosing a square; used chiefly by Hindus and Buddhists as an aid to meditation.

mandarin /ˈmændərən, mændəˈrɪn/ *n.* **1.** (formerly) a member of any of the nine ranks of public officials in the Chinese Empire. **2.** an official or bureaucrat, especially one who is in or makes himself or herself in a high or inaccessible position. **3.** (*upper case*) standard Chinese. **4.** (*upper case*) the language of north China, especially of Beijing. **5.** Also, **mandarine** /mændəˈrin, mændəˈrin/ **a.** a small, roundish citrus fruit of which the tangerine is one variety, native to south-western Asia, of a characteristic sweet and spicy flavour. **b.** the tree producing it, *Citrus reticulata*, and related species.

mandate /ˈmændeɪt/ *n.* **1.** (formerly) a commission given by the League of Nations to administer a territory. **2.** a mandated territory. **3.** a command; order. **4.** *Politics* an instruction or permission from the electorate for a certain policy: *the Government has no mandate for higher taxes.* –*v.t.* **5.** to give (a territory, etc.) to the charge of a particular nation under a mandate. –**mandator**, *n.*

mandatory /ˈmændətri, -təri/, *Orig. US* /ˈmændətɔri/ *adj.* **1.** relating to, of the nature of, or containing a mandate. **2.** obligatory. **3.** *Law* permitting no option. **4.** having received a mandate, as a nation.

mandatory detention *n.* incarceration of an offender or deemed offender which is obligatory rather than

resting with the judgement of a court or other official body.

mandatory sentencing *n. Law* sentencing which is set down in legislation rather than resting with the judgement of the court.

mandible /ˈmændəbəl/ *n.* **1.** the bone of the lower jaw. **2.** (in birds) **a.** the lower part of the beak; the lower jaw. **b.** (*pl.*) the upper and lower parts of the beak; the jaws. **3.** (in arthropods) one of the first pair of mouthpart appendages. –**mandibular** /mænˈdɪbjələ/, *adj.* –**mandibulate** /mænˈdɪbjələt, -leɪt/, *adj.*

mandolin /mændəˈlɪn/ *n.* a musical instrument with a pear-shaped wooden body (smaller than that of the lute) and a fretted neck, usually having metal strings plucked with a plectrum. Also, **mandoline**. –**mandolinist**, *n.*

mane /meɪn/ *n.* **1.** the long hair growing on the back of or around the neck and neighbouring parts of some animals, as the horse, lion, etc. **2.** a long, bushy, often untended head of hair. –**maned**, *adj.*

manga /ˈmæŋɡə/ *n.* the Japanese form of comic book, which has a wide variety of subject areas, catering for both children and adults.

manga movie *n.* a Japanese animated movie, made in the style of the Japanese comic books.

manganese /ˈmæŋɡəˈniz/ *n.* a hard, brittle, greyish white metallic element used as an alloying agent with steel and other metals to give them toughness. *Symbol*: Mn; *relative atomic mass*: 54.938; *atomic number*: 25; *density*: 7.2 at 20°C.

mange /meɪndʒ/ *n. Vet. Science* any of various skin diseases due to parasitic mites affecting animals and sometimes humans, characterised by loss of hair and scabby eruptions. –**mangy**, *adj.*

manger /ˈmeɪndʒə/ *n.* a box or trough, as in a stable, from which horses or cattle eat.

mangle[1] /ˈmæŋɡəl/ *v.t.* **1.** to cut, slash, or crush so as to disfigure: *a corpse mangled in battle.* **2.** to mar; spoil: *to mangle a text by poor typesetting.* –**mangler**, *n.*

mangle[2] /ˈmæŋɡəl/ *n.* **1.** a machine for smoothing, or pressing water, etc., out of cloth, household linen, etc., by means of rollers. –*v.t.* **2.** to smooth with a mangle. –*phr.* **3. put through the mangle**, *Colloq.* exhausted, especially emotionally.

mango /ˈmæŋɡoʊ/ *n.* (*pl.* **-goes** *or* **-gos**) **1.** the ovoid fruit of a tropical tree, *Mangifera indica*, which is eaten ripe, or preserved or pickled. **2.** the tree itself.

mangrove /ˈmæŋɡroʊv, ˈmæn-/ *n.* a type of tree found in subtropical and tropical countries on salt or brackish, especially estuarine, mudflats, and characterised by a strongly developed system of aerial roots, as in species of the genera *Aegiceras*, *Avicennia* and *Rhizophora*.

manhandle /ˈmænhændl/ *v.t.* **1.** to handle roughly. **2.** to move by human effort, without mechanical appliances.

manhole /ˈmænhoʊl/ *n.* a hole, usually with a cover, through which a person may enter a sewer, drain, steam boiler, etc.

man-hour *n.* an hour of work by one person, used as an industrial time unit.

mania /ˈmeɪniə/ *n.* **1.** great excitement or enthusiasm; craze. **2.** *Psychol.* a form of insanity characterised by great excitement, with or without delusions, and in its acute stage by great violence.

-mania a combining form of **mania** (as in *megalomania*), extended to mean exaggerated desire or love for, as *balletomania.*

maniac /ˈmeɪniæk/ *n.* **1.** *Colloq.* a person exhibiting wild or violent behaviour, especially one viewed as suffering mental illness. **2.** *Psychiatry Obs.* a person suffering from mania. **3.** *Colloq.* a person with a great passion or enthusiasm for something: *a cricket maniac.* –*adj.* **4.** raving with madness; mad. –**maniacal** /məˈnaɪəkəl/, *adj.*

manic /'mænɪk/ *adj.* **1.** relating to mania. **2.** relating to manic depression. See **bipolar disorder**. **3.** *Colloq.* frenziedly overactive; agitated.

manic depression *n.* → **bipolar disorder**. Also, **manic-depression**. –**manic depressive**, *adj., n.*

manicure /'mænəkjuə, -kjʊə/ *n.* **1. a.** professional care of the hands and fingernails. **b.** a session of such treatment. **2.** a manicurist. –*v.t.* **3.** to care for (the hands and fingernails). **4.** to trim neatly. **5.** to take any roughness or offensiveness out of. –**manicurist**, *n.*

manifest /'mænɪfəst, -fɛst/ *adj.* **1.** plain; apparent; obvious; evident: *a manifest error; dislike was manifest on his face*. –*v.t.* **2.** to show plainly: *his dislike manifested itself in rudeness.* –*n.* **3.** a list of cargo carried by land, sea or air. **4.** → **manifesto**. –**manifestable**, *adj.* –**manifestative**, *adj.* –**manifestly**, *adv.* –**manifestness**, *n.*

manifestation /mænəfɛs'teɪʃən/ *n.* **1.** the act of manifesting. **2.** the state of being manifested. **3.** a means of manifesting; indication. **4.** a public demonstration, as for political effect. **5.** *Spiritualism* a materialisation.

manifesto /mænə'fɛstoʊ/ *n.* (*pl.* **-tos** *or* **-toes**) a public declaration, as of a sovereign or government, or of any person or body of persons taking important action, making known intentions, objects, motives, etc.; a proclamation.

manifold /'mænəfoʊld/ *adj.* **1.** of many and various kinds: *manifold duties*. **2.** in many or various ways. –*n.* **3.** something having many different parts or features. **4.** a copy; facsimile. **5.** a pipe or chamber with several inlets or outlets. **6.** very fine typing paper. –*v.t.* **7.** to make copies of, as with carbon paper. –**manifoldly**, *adv.* –**manifoldness**, *n.*

manikin /'mænəkɪn, -ɪkən/ *n.* **1.** a little man; a male dwarf; male pygmy. **2.** a model of the human body for teaching anatomy, demonstrating surgical operations, etc.

manila paper /mənɪlə 'peɪpə/ *n.* strong light brown paper, derived originally from Manila hemp, but now also from wood pulp substitutes.

manipulate /mə'nɪpjəleɪt/ *v.t.* **1. a.** to handle, manage, or use, especially with skill, in order to achieve a desired effect. **b.** to handle or move (part of the body) as for therapeutic purposes. **2.** to manage or influence by artful skill, or deviousness: *to manipulate people; to manipulate prices*. **3.** to adapt or change (accounts, figures, etc.) to suit one's purpose or advantage. **4.** *Computers* to edit or otherwise alter (data). –**manipulative**, *adj.* –**manipulator**, *n.* –**manipulation**, *n.*

mankind *n.* **1.** /mæn'kaɪnd/ the human race; human beings collectively. **2.** /'mænkaɪnd/ men, as distinguished from women: *mankind and womankind.*

manna /'mænə/ *n.* **1.** *Bible* the food miraculously supplied to the children of Israel in the wilderness. **2.** an exudate of insects living on many Australian eucalypts, especially *Eucalyptus viminalis*, once forming an important part of Aboriginal diet for limited periods. **3.** an exudate obtained by making an incision into the bark of the flowering ash, *Fraxinus ornus*, of southern Europe, and used as a mild laxative. –*phr.* **4. manna from heaven**, a welcome surprise.

mannequin /'mænəkən, -kwən/ *n.* **1.** Also, **manikin**. a model of the human figure made of wood, wax, etc., used by tailors, dress designers, etc., for displaying or fitting clothes. **2.** → **model** (def. 5).

manner /'mænə/ *n.* **1.** way of doing, being done, or happening; mode of action, occurrence, etc. **2.** characteristic or customary way of doing: *houses built in the Mexican manner*. **3.** (*pl.*) the prevailing customs, modes of living, etc., of a people, class, period, etc. **4.** a person's outward bearing; way of addressing and treating others. **5.** (*pl.*) ways of behaving, especially with reference to polite standards: *bad manners*. **6.** (*pl.*) good

or polite ways of behaving: *have you no manners?* **7.** outward bearing; way of behaving towards others: *the police officer had rather an awkward manner*. **8.** air of distinction: *he had quite a manner*. **9.** kind; sort: *all manner of things*. **10.** characteristic style in art, literature, or the like: *verses in the manner of Spenser*. –*phr.* **11. all manner of means**, by all means; certainly. **12. in a manner**, after a fashion; so to speak; somewhat. **13. in a manner of speaking**, in a way; so to speak. **14. to the manner born**, **a.** accustomed or destined by birth (to a high position, etc.). **b.** naturally fitted for a position, duty, etc. –**mannerly**, *adj.* –**mannerliness**, *n.*

mannered /'mænəd/ *adj.* **1.** having (specified) manners: *ill-mannered*. **2.** having mannerisms; affected.

mannerism /'mænərɪzəm/ *n.* **1.** marked or excessive adherence to an unusual manner, especially in literary work. **2.** a habitual peculiarity of manner. **3.** (*usu. upper case*) a style of late 16th century European art, mainly current in Italy. –**mannerist**, *n.* –**manneristic** /mænə'rɪstɪk/, *adj.*

manning scale *n.* a schedule prescribing the number of operatives which an employer is required to employ on a particular machine or process.

manoeuvre /mə'nuvə/ *n.* **1.** the planned and regulated movement of soldiers, warships, etc. **2.** (*pl.*) a series of tactical military exercises. **3.** a clever or skilful move: *by that manoeuvre we have stopped them competing with us.* –*verb* (**-vred, -vring**) –*v.t.* **4.** to move (soldiers, etc.) in a tactical manner. **5.** to manipulate or move with skill: *to manoeuvre a car out of a tight parking spot*. –*v.i.* **6.** to perform a manoeuvre or manoeuvres. **7.** to scheme; intrigue. –**manoeuvrable**, *adj.* –**manoeuvrability** /mə,nuvrə'bɪləti/, *n.* –**manoeuvrer**, *n.*

man of straw *n.* → **straw man**.

manor /'mænə/ *n.* **1.** a landed estate or territorial unit, originally of the nature of a feudal lordship, consisting of a lord's demesne and of lands within which he has the right to exercise certain privileges and exact certain fees, etc. **2.** the mansion of a lord with the land relating to it. –**manorial** /mə'nɔriəl/, *adj.*

manpower /'mænpaʊə/ *n.* **1.** the power supplied by the physical exertions of a person or people. **2.** a unit of power assumed to be equal to the rate at which a man can do mechanical work, commonly taken as $\frac{1}{10}$ horsepower. **3.** rate of work in terms of this unit. **4.** power in terms of people available or required: *the manpower of an army.*

manse /mæns/ *n.* **1.** the house and land occupied by a minister or parson, usually of nonconformist churches, as Uniting, Presbyterian, etc. **2.** (originally) the dwelling of a landholder, with the land attached.

mansion /'mænʃən/ *n.* **1.** an imposing or stately residence. **2.** (*pl.*) *Brit.* a block of flats.

manslaughter /'mænslɔtə/ *n.* **1.** the killing of a human being by another human being; homicide. **2.** *Law* the killing of a human being unlawfully but without malice aforethought. See **malice** (def. 2). –**manslaughterer**, *n.*

mansplain /'mænspleɪn/ *v.t. Colloq.* (*humorous*) (of a man) to explain (something) to a woman, in a way that is patronising because it assumes that a woman will be ignorant of the subject matter. –**mansplaining**, *n.* *Usage:* Some people regard this as a sexist term directed against men, and therefore offensive.

mantelpiece /'mæntlpis/ *n.* the more or less ornamental structure above and around a fireplace, usually having a shelf or projecting ledge. Also, **mantelpiece**.

mantelshelf /'mæntlʃɛlf/ *n.* (*pl.* **-shelves**) **1.** the projecting part of a mantelpiece. **2.** *Mountaineering* a small ledge on the rock wall.

mantilla /mæn'tɪlə/ *n.* **1.** a silk or lace headscarf arranged over a high comb and falling over the back and shoulders, worn in Spain, Mexico, etc. **2.** a short mantle or light cape.

mantis /ˈmæntəs/ *n.* (*pl.* **-tises** *or* **-tes** /-tiz/) any of the carnivorous orthopterous insects constituting the order Mantodea, which have a long prothorax and which are remarkable for their manner of holding the forelegs doubled up as if in prayer. Also, **praying mantis**.

mantle /ˈmæntl/ *n.* **1.** Also, **mantua**. a loose, sleeveless cloak. **2.** something that covers, envelops, or conceals. **3.** *Zool.* a single or paired outgrowth of the body wall that lines the inner surface of the valves of the shell in molluscs and brachiopods. **4.** → **gas mantle**. **5.** *Ornith.* the back, scapular, and inner wing feathers taken together, especially when these are all of the same colour. **6.** *Geol.* a layer of the earth between crust and core, consisting of solid rock. **7.** → **mantelpiece**. *–v.t.* **8.** to cover with or as with a mantle; envelop; conceal. *–v.i.* **9.** to spread like a mantle, as a blush over the face. **10.** to flush; blush. **11.** (of a liquid) to be or become covered with a coating; foam. *–phr.* **12. assume the mantle**, to take on the leading role in an endeavour.

mantra /ˈmæntrə/ *n.* a word, phrase or verse intoned, often repetitively, as a sacred formula in Hinduism and Mahayana Buddhism, designed to focus the mind. Also, **mantram**. *–***mantric**, *adj.*

manual /ˈmænjuəl/ *adj.* **1.** of or done by the hand: *manual work*. **2.** using human energy, power, etc.: *a manual drill*. *–n.* **3.** a book giving information or instructions; handbook. **4.** *Music* a keyboard of an organ played with the hands. **5.** a car whose gears are changed by hand. *–***manually**, *adv.*

manufacture /mænjəˈfæktʃə, ˈmænjəfæktʃə/ *n.* **1.** the making of goods by hand or machinery, especially on a large scale. **2.** the making of anything. *–v.t.* **3.** to make or produce by hand or machinery, especially on a large scale. **4.** to make up; concoct: *to manufacture arguments*. **5.** to produce in a mechanical way. *–***manufacturing**, *n.* *–***manufacturer**, *n.*

manuka /məˈnukə, ˈmanəkə/ *n.* either of the New Zealand tea-trees, *Leptospermum scoparium* and *Leptospermum ericoides*, both valuable honey plants.

manure /məˈnjuə/ *n.* **1.** any natural or artificial substance for fertilising the soil. **2.** excrement, especially of animals used as fertiliser. *–v.t.* **3.** to treat (land) with fertilising matter; apply manure to. *–***manurer**, *n.* *–***manurey**, *adj.*

manuscript /ˈmænjəskrɪpt/ *n.* **1.** a book, document, letter, musical score, etc., written by hand. **2.** an author's copy of a work, written by hand or typewriter, which is used as the basis for typesetting. **3.** writing, as distinguished from print. *–adj.* **4.** written by hand or typed (not printed). *–***manuscriptal**, *adj.*

many /ˈmɛni/ *adj.* **1.** constituting or forming a large number: *many people*. **2.** relatively numerous: *six may be too many*; *as many as seven*; *how many cups?* *–pron.* **3.** a great or considerable number: *many of the chairs*; *some were bought, but many remain*; *many were disappointed by her performance*. *–phr.* **4. a good** (or **great**) **many**, a large number. **5. many a** (or **an**), being one of a large number of (specified items): *many a day*. **6. the many**, the majority: *for the good of the many*.

Maori /ˈmaʊri, ˈmaəri, ˈmauri/ *n.* **1.** the indigenous Polynesian people of New Zealand. **2.** (*pl.* **Maori**) a member of this people. **3.** a Polynesian language, the language of the Maori. *–adj.* **4.** of or relating to the Maori or their language. Also, **Māori**.

Maoritanga /ˈmaʊritʌŋə/ *n.* the qualities inherent in being a Maori, relating to heritage, culture, etc.

map /mæp/ *n.* **1.** a representation, on a flat surface, of a part or the whole of the earth's surface, the heavens, or a heavenly body. **2.** a map-like representation of anything. *–v.t.* (**mapped, mapping**) **3.** to represent or delineate in or as in a map. **4.** *Computers* to translate (information) from one layer of organisation to another, such as from a computer language to machine language or from an image stored in memory to an image displayed on a screen. *–phr.* **5. map out**, to sketch or plan. **6. off the map**, out of existence, into oblivion: *whole cities were wiped off the map*. **7. put on the map**, to make widely known; make famous.

maple /ˈmeɪpəl/ *n.* any tree of the genus *Acer*, of the north temperate zone, species of which are valued for shade and ornament, for their wood, or for their sap, from which a syrup (**maple syrup**) and a sugar (**maple sugar**) are obtained.

mar /ma/ *v.t.* **1.** to damage; impair; ruin. **2.** to disfigure; deface.

maraca /məˈrækə/ *n.* a gourd filled with pebbles, seeds, etc., and used as a percussion instrument in Latin-American bands.

marathon /ˈmærəθɒn, -θən/ *n.* **1.** any long-distance race. **2.** a footrace of 26 miles and 385 yards, or 42.195 kilometres. **3.** any long contest with endurance as the primary factor: *a dance marathon*. **4.** any activity or pursuit sustained for a long period of time: *a movie marathon*.

maraud /məˈrɔd/ *v.i.* **1.** to rove in quest of plunder; make a raid for booty. *–v.t.* **2.** to raid for plunder. *–***marauder**, *n.* *–***marauding**, *adj.*

marble /ˈmabəl/ *n.* **1.** limestone in a more or less crystalline state and capable of taking a polish, occurring in a wide range of colours and variegations, and much used in sculpture and architecture. **2.** a variety of this stone. **3.** a piece of this stone. **4.** a work of art carved in marble. **5.** a marbled appearance or pattern; marbling. **6.** something resembling marble in hardness, coldness, smoothness, etc. **7.** *Games* a little ball of stone, baked clay, glass, etc., used in the game of marbles. **8.** (*pl.* construed as *sing.*) the game in which marbles (def. 7) are rolled or thrown at each other in accordance with various rules. *–adj.* **9.** consisting of marble. **10.** like marble, as being hard, cold, unfeeling, etc. **11.** of variegated or mottled colour. *–v.t.* **12.** to colour or stain like a variegated marble. *–phr.* **13. lose one's marbles**, *Colloq.* to act irrationally; go mad. **14. make one's marble good**, *Aust. Colloq.* (sometimes fol. by *with*) to ingratiate oneself. **15. pass in one's marble**, *Aust. Colloq.* to die. *–***marbly**, *adj.*

march[1] /matʃ/ *v.i.* **1.** to walk with regular and measured tread, as soldiers; advance in step in an organised body. **2.** to walk in a stately or deliberate manner. **3.** to proceed; advance. *–v.t.* **4.** to cause to march. *–n.* **5.** the act or course of marching. **6.** the distance traversed in a single course of marching. **7.** advance; forward movement: *the march of progress*. **8.** a piece of music with a rhythm suited to accompany marching. *–phr.* **9. steal a march on**, to obtain an advantage over, especially by surreptitious or underhand means.

march[2] /matʃ/ *n.* **1.** a tract of land along a border of a country; frontier. *–phr.* **2. march on** (or **upon**), to touch at the border; border.

March /matʃ/ *n.* the third month of the year, containing 31 days.

marching orders *pl. n.* **1.** *Mil.* directions to soldiers to proceed in order to take position for battle, etc.: *the brigade received its marching orders shortly after the general's visit*. **2.** orders to leave; dismissal (from a job, etc.).

marchioness /maʃəˈnɛs/ *n.* **1.** the wife or widow of a marquess. **2.** a woman holding in her own right the rank equal to that of a marquess.

mare[1] /mɛə/ *n.* a female horse, fully grown and past its fourth birthday.

mare² /ˈmareɪ/ *n.* (*pl.* **maria** /ˈmariə/) any of several large, dark plains on the moon or the planet Mars.

margarine /madʒəˈrin, mag-, ˈmadʒərən/ *n.* a butter-like product made from refined vegetable or animal oils or various mixtures of both, and emulsifiers, colouring matter, etc.

margin /ˈmadʒən/ *n.* **1.** an edge; border. **2.** the space beside the writing on a page. **3.** a limit, or a condition, etc., beyond which something ceases to exist or be possible: *the margin of understanding.* **4.** an amount allowed beyond what is actually necessary: *a margin of error.* **5.** *Finance* an amount of money (security), left with a broker to provide against loss in business dealings. **6.** *Commerce* the difference between the cost of a product and the amount for which it is sold. **7.** *Econ.* the point at which the return barely covers the cost of production, and below which production is unprofitable. **8.** that part of a wage, additional to the basic wage, which is offered to recompense an employee for their particular skills. **9.** an allowance made as a safety precaution: *a margin of safety.*

marginal /ˈmadʒənəl/ *adj.* **1.** relating to a margin. **2.** situated on the edge or border. **3.** written in the margin of a page: *a marginal note.* **4.** barely enough; slight. **5.** *Econ.* **a.** supplying goods at a rate just covering the cost of production. **b.** of or relating to goods produced and marketed at margin: *marginal profits.* **6.** of or relating to an electoral division in which the outcome of voting is likely to result in victory only by a small amount. **7.** of or relating to the rate at which the margin (def. 8) is paid. –**marginally,** *adv.*

marginal seat *n. Politics* an electorate which was won by the current representative by only a small number of votes, and therefore requires only a small swing for it to change from one party to another at the next election.

margin lending *n. Finance* the provision of margin loans.

margin loan *n. Finance* a loan secured for investment purposes, as for the purchase of shares. See **margin** (def. 5).

marigold /ˈmærɪɡoʊld/ *n.* **1.** any of the various chiefly golden-flowered plants especially of the genus *Tagetes,* as *T. erecta,* with strong-scented foliage. **2.** any of various other plants, especially of the genus *Calendula,* as *C. officinalis,* a common garden plant of some use in dyeing and medicine.

marijuana /mærəˈwanə/ *n.* **1.** the Indian hemp, *Cannabis sativa.* **2.** its dried leaves and flowers, used in cigarettes and food as a narcotic and intoxicant. Also, **marihuana.**

marina /məˈrinə/ *n.* a facility offering docking and other services for small craft.

marinade *n.* /mærəˈneɪd/ **1.** a liquid, especially wine or vinegar with oil and seasonings, in which meat, fish, vegetables, etc., may be steeped before cooking. –*v.t.* /ˈmærəneɪd/ **2.** → **marinate.**

marinate /ˈmærəneɪt/ *v.t.* to let stand in a liquid before cooking or serving in order to impart flavour; marinade. –**marination** /mærəˈneɪʃən/, *n.*

marine /məˈrin/ *adj.* **1.** of or relating to the sea; existing in or produced by the sea. **2.** relating to navigation or shipping; nautical; naval; maritime. **3.** serving on shipboard, as soldiers. **4.** of or belonging to the marines. **5.** adapted for use at sea: *a marine barometer.* –*n.* **6.** seagoing vessels collectively, especially with reference to nationality or class; shipping in general. **7.** one of a class of naval troops serving both on shipboard and on land. –*phr.* **8. dead marine,** *Colloq.* an empty and discarded beer, wine, or spirits bottle. **9. tell it** (or **that**) **to the marines,** an expression of disbelief, especially at an unlikely story.

mariner /ˈmærənə/ *n.* a seaman; sailor.

marionette /mæriəˈnɛt/ *n.* a puppet moved by strings attached to its jointed limbs.

marital /ˈmærətəl/ *adj.* **1.** of or relating to marriage. **2.** of or relating to a husband. –**maritally,** *adv.*

maritime /ˈmærətaɪm/ *adj.* **1.** of or relating to shipping, navigation at sea, etc.: *maritime law.* **2.** of or relating to the sea. **3.** living near the sea.

maritime climate *n.* a type of climate characterised by little temperature change, high cloud cover, and precipitation, and associated with coastal areas.

marjoram /ˈmadʒərəm/ *n.* any plant of the mint family belonging to the genera *Origanum,* especially the species *O. majorana* (**sweet marjoram**) used in cookery, or *O. vulgare,* a wild species native to Europe and naturalised elsewhere.

mark¹ /mak/ *n.* **1.** a visible trace or impression upon anything, as a line, cut, dent, stain, bruise, etc. **2.** a badge, brand, or other visible sign assumed or imposed. **3.** a symbol used in writing or printing: *a punctuation mark.* **4.** a sign, usually a cross, made by an illiterate person by way of signature. **5.** an affixed or impressed device, symbol, inscription, etc., serving to give information, identify, indicate origin or ownership, attest to character or comparative merit, or the like. **6.** a sign, token, or indication. **7.** a symbol used in rating conduct, proficiency, attainment, etc., as of pupils in a school. **8.** something serving as an indication of position, as a bookmark. **9.** a recognised or required standard: *to be below the mark.* **10.** repute; note; importance, or distinction: *a student of mark.* **11.** a distinctive trait. **12.** (*usu. upper case*) a designation for a model of a weapon, an item of military equipment, a motor vehicle, or the like, generally used together with a numeral: *the Mark-4 weapon-carrier.* **13.** an object aimed at, as a target. **14.** *Colloq.* a person who is chosen to be the object of a swindle: *she was following her mark.* **15.** an object of derision, scorn, hostile schemes, etc. **16.** *Athletics* the starting point allotted to a contestant. **17.** *Aust. Rules* **a.** the action of catching the ball on the full, after it has travelled not less than nine metres directly from the kick of another player without it having been touched while in transit from kick to catch. **b.** the place on the field where the mark was made, or where an infringement resulting in a free kick took place, and from or behind which the player must then kick. **c.** the field umpire's decision that the catch has been fairly taken. **d.** the player who takes a mark: *to be a good mark.* –*v.t.* **18.** to be a distinguishing feature of: *a day marked by rain.* **19.** to put a mark or marks on. **20.** to attach or affix to (something) figures or signs indicating price, quality, brand name, etc. **21.** to judge and record the quality or correctness of (exam papers, etc.). **22.** to castrate (a lamb, calf, etc.); usually associated with other procedures such as docking, earmarking, drenching, etc. **23.** to indicate or designate by or as by marks. **24.** to give heed or attention to: *mark my words.* **25.** to notice or observe. **26.** *Sport* to observe and keep close to (an opponent) with the intention of obtaining advantage. –*v.i.* **27.** to take notice; give attention; consider. –*phr.* **28. be quick off the mark, a.** (of a competitor in a race) to start promptly. **b.** to be prompt in recognising and acting upon the possibilities of a situation. **29. be slow off the mark, a.** (of a competitor in a race) to start slowly. **b.** to be sluggish or slow to start something. **30. easy mark,** an object or target which can be easily achieved or exploited. **31. give full** (or **top**) **marks,** (sometimes fol. by *to*) to approve warmly. **32. give someone a bad mark,** to disapprove of someone. **33. give someone a good mark,** to approve of someone. **34. leave one's mark,** to effect lasting changes. **35. make one's mark,** to become famous or successful. **36. mark down,** to reduce the price of. **37. mark off,** to separate, as by a line or boundary. **38. mark out, a.** to trace or form by or as by marks. **b.** to single out; destine. **39. mark time, a.** to suspend advance or progress temporarily as while awaiting development. **b.** *Mil.* to move the feet alternately as in marching, but without advancing. **40. mark up, a.** to mark with notations or symbols. **b.** to increase the price of. **41. mark you,** used to foreground the adjacent sentence weakly: *mark you, it'll be over by Christmas.* **42. on your mark(s),** (addressed to competitors at the beginning of a race) take your places! **43. overshoot the mark,** to err by overestimating the requirements of a situation. **44. overstep the mark, a.** (of a competitor in a race) to break the rules by placing a foot over or beyond the mark before the start of the race. **b.** to transgress the accepted standards of behaviour. **45. up to the mark,** of the required standard. **46. wide of the mark,** inaccurate; irrelevant.

mark² /mak/ *n.* **1.** a former silver coin of Germany, until 1924 the monetary unit. **2. → deutschmark.**

marked /makt/ *adj.* **1.** strikingly noticeable; conspicuous: *with marked success.* **2.** *Ling.* (of a phonetic or syntactic unit) abnormal; more complex or more unexpected than an opposed unit. **3.** watched as an object for suspicion or vengeance: *a marked man.* **4.** having a mark or marks. **–markedly** /ˈmakədli/, *adv.* **–markedness,** *n.*

marker /ˈmakə/ *n.* **1.** something used as a mark or indication, as a bookmark, etc. **2.** Also, **marker pen.** an implement used for marking or writing, especially a felt pen. **3.** someone who records a score, as in a game, etc. **4.** a counter used in card-playing.

market /ˈmakət/ *n.* **1.** a meeting of people for selling and buying. **2.** the assemblage of people at such a meeting. **3.** an open space or a covered building where such meetings are held, especially for the sale of food, etc. **4.** a store for the sale of food. **5.** trade or traffic, especially as regards a particular commodity. **6.** a body of persons carrying on extensive transactions in a specified commodity: *the cotton market.* **7.** the field of trade or business: *the best shoes on the market.* **8.** demand for a commodity: *an unprecedented market for leather.* **9.** a region where anything is or may be sold: *the foreign market.* **10.** current price or value: *a rising market.* *–v.i.* **11.** to deal (buy or sell) in a market. *–v.t.* **12.** to carry or send to market for disposal. **13.** to dispose of in a market; sell. *–phr.* **14. at the market,** at the best obtainable price in the open market. **15. go to market,** *Aust., NZ Colloq.* to become angry, excited, or unmanageable. **16. in the market for,** ready to buy; seeking to buy. **17. on the market, a.** for sale; available. **b.** *Colloq.* available for a sexual partner. **18. play the market,** to speculate on the stock exchange. **–marketeer,** *n.*

marketable /ˈmakətəbəl/ *adj.* **1.** readily saleable. **2.** of or relating to selling or buying. **–marketability** /makətəˈbɪləti/, **marketableness,** *n.*

market economy *n.* an economic structure in which the allocation of resources is achieved by the interdependent decisions of persons supplying and demanding those resources rather than by the decisions of a centralised planning agency such as a bureaucracy.

market garden *n.* a garden or smallholding where vegetables and fruit are grown for sale. **–market gardener,** *n.* **–market gardening,** *n.*

marketing /ˈmakətɪŋ/ *n.* **1.** the total process whereby goods are put on to the market. **2.** the act of buying or selling in a market.

market research *n.* the gathering of information by a firm about the preferences, purchasing powers, etc., of consumers, especially as a preliminary to putting a product on the market.

marksman /ˈmaksmən/ *n.* (*pl.* **-men**) **1.** a man skilled in shooting at a mark; someone who shoots well. **2.** *Law* someone unable to write who signs with a mark, usually X. **–marksmanship,** *n.* **–markswoman,** *n.*

markup language /ˈmakʌp læŋgwɪdʒ/ *n. Computers* a computer language in which various elements of a document, database, etc., are marked with tags, providing a flexible means of arranging and retrieving data. See **HTML, SGML, XML.**

marl /mal/ *n.* **1.** a soil or earthy deposit consisting of clay and calcium carbonate, used especially as a fertiliser. **2.** compact, impure limestones. **3.** *Poetic* earth. *–v.t.* **4.** to fertilise with marl. **–marlaceous** /maˈleɪʃəs/, **marly,** *adj.*

marlin /ˈmalən/ *n.* any of various species of large, powerful, game fishes having the upper jaw elongated into a rounded spear, as the **striped marlin,** *Makaira audax,* which is found seasonally in coastal waters of eastern Australia.

marmalade /ˈmaməleɪd/ *n.* a jelly-like preserve with fruit (usually citrus) suspended in small pieces.

marmoreal /maˈmɔriəl/ *adj.* of or like marble. Also, **marmorean.**

marmot /ˈmamət/ *n.* **1.** any of the bushy-tailed, thickset rodents constituting the genus *Marmota,* as the common woodchuck. **2.** any of certain related animals, as the prairie dogs.

maroon¹ /məˈroʊn, məˈrun/ *n.* **1.** dark brownish red. **2.** a firework exploding with a loud report, especially one used as a warning or distress signal.

maroon² /məˈrun/ *v.t.* **1.** to put ashore and leave on a desolate island or coast by way of punishment, as was done by buccaneers, etc. **2.** to isolate as if on a desolate island.

marquee /maˈki/ *n.* a large tent or tentlike shelter, sometimes with open sides, especially one for temporary use providing refreshment, entertainment, etc.

marquess /ˈmakwəs/ *n.* a nobleman ranking next below a duke and above an earl or count. Also, **marquis.**

marquise /maˈkiz/ *n.* **1.** the wife or widow of a marquess. **2.** a woman holding in her own right the rank equal to that of a marquess. **3.** a common diamond shape, pointed oval, usually with normal brilliant facets. **4.** a roof-like shelter or canopy, as of glass, projecting above the outer door of a building and over a pavement or terrace. **5. → marquee.**

marriage /ˈmærɪdʒ/ *n.* **1.** the legal union of a man with a woman; state or condition of being married; the legal relation of spouses to each other; wedlock. **2.** a like union between two people of the same sex, made legal in some jurisdictions, but not in Australia. **3.** the legal or religious ceremony that sanctions or formalises such a union. **4.** any intimate union. **5.** *Econ.* the offsetting of a buying order and a selling order in a broker's office, both orders having been placed by the broker's clients.

marriage celebrant *n.* someone who performs a marriage, especially in a civil marriage service.

marriage equality *n.* the legal status of marriage as a union between same-sex couples just as it is between heterosexual couples.

married /ˈmærid/ *adj.* **1.** united in wedlock; wedded. **2.** relating to marriage or married persons.

marron¹ /ˈmærən/ *n.* a chestnut; especially as used in cookery, or candied or preserved in syrup.

marron² /ˈmærən/ *n.* (*pl.* **marrons** *or, especially collectively,* **marron**) a freshwater crayfish *Cherax tenuimanus,* native to south-western WA, inhabiting sandy areas of rivers and dams.

marrow /ˈmæroʊ/ *n.* **1.** a soft, fatty vascular tissue in the interior cavities of bones. **2.** the inmost or essential part. **3.** rich and nutritious food. **4.** the green-skinned elongated fruit of a cultivated variety of *Cucurbita* *pepo*, widely used as a cooked vegetable; vegetable marrow.

marrowbone /ˈmærouboun/ *n.* **1.** a bone containing edible marrow. **2.** (*pl.*) (*humorous*) the knees. **3.** (*pl.*) → **crossbones.**

marry /ˈmæri/ *verb* (**-ried, -rying**) −*v.t.* **1.** to take in marriage. **2.** to unite as husband and wife. **3.** to give in marriage. **4.** to unite closely. −*v.i.* **5.** to enter into the bond of marriage; wed. −**marrier,** *n.*

Marsala /məˈsalə, ma-/ *n.* (*sometimes lower case*) **1.** a sweet, dark, fortified wine. **2.** (in unofficial use) any similar sweet wine made elsewhere.

marsh /maʃ/ *n.* a tract of low, wet land; a swamp.

marshal /ˈmaʃəl/ *n.* **1.** an officer of the highest rank in the armed forces. **2.** any of various other officials having judicial or police duties. **3.** a high officer of a royal household. **4.** a person who arranges or runs cere- monies, races, etc. **5.** *Athletics* at a competition, the person in charge of the arena and of seeing that only officials and competitors enter it. −*v.t.* (**-shalled** *or, Chiefly US,* **-shaled, -shalling** *or, Chiefly US,* **-shaling**) **6.** to arrange in proper order. **7.** to organise for battle, etc. **8.** to lead. −**marshalcy, marshalship,** *n.* −**marshaller,** *n.*

marshmallow /ˈmaʃmælou, -mɛl-/ *n.* a confection with an elastic, spongy texture, sometimes tinted pink or other colours, usually containing gelatine, sugar, and flavouring.

marsupial /maˈsupiəl, -ˈsjup-/ *adj.* **1.** of or relating to a marsupium. **2.** of or relating to the marsupials. −*n.* **3.** any of the Marsupialia, the order which includes all of the viviparous but non-placental mammals such as kangaroos, wombats, possums and related animals, found chiefly in the Australian region and in South and Central America. The female of most species has a marsupium.

marsupial mouse *n.* any of various small Australian carnivorous marsupials superficially resembling mice or small rats.

marsupium /maˈsupiəm, -sjup-/ *n.* (*pl.* **-pia** /-piə/) **1.** the pouch or fold of skin on the abdomen of a female marsupial which contains the mammary glands and serves as a receptacle for the developing young. **2.** a structure in certain other animals for enclosing eggs or young.

mart /mat/ *n.* **1.** market; trading centre. **2.** a shop.

marten /ˈmatn/ *n.* (*pl.* **-tens** *or, especially collectively,* **-ten**) any of various slender, fur-bearing carnivores of the genus *Martes*, as the American **pine marten,** *M. americana*, of the northern US and Canada.

martial /ˈmaʃəl/ *adj.* **1.** inclined or disposed to war; warlike; brave. **2.** relating to or appropriate for war: *martial music.* **3.** characteristic of or befitting a warrior: *a martial stride.* −**martially,** *adv.* −**martialness,** *n.*

martial art *n.* **1.** any of various methods, codes or tra- ditions of training for combat, mostly originating in Asia, as judo, kung-fu, taekwondo, etc., now com- monly also practised as sports. **2.** (*pl.*) these practices considered as a whole.

martial law *n.* the law imposed upon an area by military forces when civil authority has broken down.

martin /ˈmatn/ *n.* any of various small, insectivorous birds, resembling and related to the swallows, which breed in colonies, as the **tree martin,** *Petrochelidon nigricans,* and the **fairy martin,** *P. ariel,* widely distri- buted in Australia, or the common **house martin,** *Delichon urbica,* of Eurasia and Africa.

martinet /matəˈnɛt/ *n.* a rigid disciplinarian, especially a military one. −**martinetish,** *adj.* −**martinetism,** *n.*

martini /maˈtini/ *n.* (*from trademark*) any of various cocktails made with gin and vermouth and sometimes other ingredients, classically a **dry martini**, made largely of gin with a quarter or less of dry vermouth.

martyr /ˈmatə/ *n.* **1.** someone who is put to death or en- dures great suffering on behalf of any belief, principle, or cause. **2.** someone undergoing severe or constant suffering. −*v.t.* **3.** to put to death as a martyr. **4.** to make a martyr of. **5.** to torment or torture.

marvel /ˈmavəl/ *n.* **1.** a wonderful thing; a wonder or prodigy; something or someone that arouses wonder or admiration. −*verb* (**-velled** *or, Chiefly US,* **-veled, -velling** *or, Chiefly US,* **-veling**) −*v.t.* **2.** to wonder at (usually followed by a clause as object). **3.** to wonder or be curious about (usually followed by a clause as object). −*v.i.* **4.** to be affected with wonder, as at something surprising or extraordinary.

marvellous /ˈmavələs/ *adj.* **1.** such as to excite wonder; surprising, extraordinary. **2.** excellent; superb. −**mar- vellously,** *adv.* −**marvellousness,** *n.*

Marxism /ˈmaksɪzəm/ *n.* the system of thought developed by Karl Marx, 1818–83, German-born writer and phi- losopher, together with Friedrich Engels, 1820–95, German-born writer, especially the doctrine that the state throughout history has been a device for the ex- ploitation of the masses by a dominant class, that class struggle has been the main agency of historical change, and that the capitalist state will inevitably be super- seded by a socialist order and a classless society.

Marxist-Leninist /maksəst-ˈlɛnənəst/ *adj.* **1.** of or relat- ing a rigid form of Marxism as advocated by Vladimir Lenin, (1870–1924, Russian revolutionary leader), with emphasis on the sovereignty of the proletariat. −*n.* **2.** an adherent of this philosophy.

marzipan /ˈmazəpæn/ *n.* a confection made of almonds reduced to a paste with sugar, etc., and moulded into various forms, usually imitative fruits and vegetables.

mascara /mæsˈkarə/ *n.* a substance used as a cosmetic to colour the eyelashes.

mascot /ˈmæskɒt/ *n.* a person, animal, or thing supposed to bring good luck.

masculine /ˈmæskjələn/ *adj.* **1.** having manlike qualities; manly: *a masculine voice.* **2.** relating to or characteristic of a man: *masculine clothes.* **3.** *Gram.* of or relating to the gender to which males, and things classified by convention as masculine, belong. **4.** (of rhyming words) having the final syllable stressed as in *defend, pretend.* **5.** (of a woman) mannish. −*n.* **6.** *Gram.* the masculine gender. **7.** a noun or another element marking that gender. −**masculinely,** *adv.* −**masculinity** /mæskjə- ˈlɪnəti/, **masculineness,** *n.*

mash /mæʃ/ *n.* **1.** a soft mass. **2.** a soft condition. **3.** a mixture of boiled grain, bran, etc., fed warm to horses and cattle. −*v.t.* **4.** to crush. **5.** to reduce to a soft mass, as by heating or pressure. **6.** to mix (crushed malt, etc.) with hot water.

mashup /ˈmæʃʌp/ *n.* **1.** a song created by blending two or more songs, usually by overlaying the vocal track of one song onto the music track of another. **2.** *Computers* an application that combines data and functionality, drawing on two or more separate sources for the data and the software. **3.** *Lit.* a blending of a classic text with an element of contemporary fiction genres, as by recontextualising *Jane Eyre* with a zombie theme. Also, **mash-up.** −**mashupper,** *n.*

mask /mask/ *n.* **1.** a covering for the face, especially one worn to change the appearance. **2.** anything that hides or alters; disguise; pretence. **3.** a likeness of a face, as one moulded in plaster after death. **4.** a likeness of a face or head, often ugly, used as an ornament. **5.** Also, **face mask.** a covering of wire, gauze, tinted glass, cloth, etc., to protect the face, as from dust, smoke, glare, etc. **6.** → **gasmask. 7.** any of various devices, used by skin-divers to protect the face. −*v.t.* **8.** to hide;

disguise. **9.** to cover with a mask. *–v.i.* **10.** to put on a mask; disguise oneself.

masking tape *n.* an adhesive tape used for defining edges and protecting surfaces not to be painted.

masochism /ˈmæsəkɪzəm/ *n.* **1.** the condition in which sexual gratification depends on suffering. **2.** a condition in which one compulsively seeks, and sometimes derives pleasure from, suffering, as humiliation, pain, etc. **–masochist,** *n.* **–masochistic** /mæsəˈkɪstɪk/, *adj.*

mason /ˈmeɪsən/ *n.* **1.** someone who builds or works with stone. **2.** (*oft. upper case*) → **Freemason.**

masonic /məˈsɒnɪk/ *adj.* (*oft. upper case*) relating to or characteristic of Freemasons or Freemasonry.

masonite /ˈmeɪsənaɪt/ *n.* (*from trademark*) → **hardboard.**

masonry /ˈmeɪsənri/ *n.* **1.** the art or occupation of a mason. **2.** work constructed by a mason.

masquerade /mæskəˈreɪd, mas-/ *n.* **1.** a gathering of persons wearing masks and often fantastic costumes, for dancing, etc. **2.** a false outward show; disguise. *–v.i.* **3.** to go about with a false character. **4.** to change oneself, as with a mask. **5.** to take part in a masquerade. **–masquerader,** *n.*

mass¹ /mæs/ *n.* **1.** a body of coherent matter, usually of indefinite shape and often of considerable size: *a mass of dough.* **2.** an aggregation of incoherent particles, parts, or objects regarded as forming one body: *a mass of sand.* **3.** a considerable assemblage, number, or quantity: *a mass of errors*; *a mass of troops.* **4.** an expanse, as of colour, light, or shade in a painting. **5.** the main body, bulk, or greater part of anything: *the great mass of Australian products.* **6.** bulk, size, or massiveness. **7.** *Physics* that property of a body, commonly but inadequately defined as the measure of the quantity of matter in it, to which its inertia is ascribed, and expressed as the weight of the body divided by the acceleration due to gravity. *–adj.* **8.** relating to or involving a large number of people: *a mass exodus*; *mass hysteria.* **9.** large-scale or wide-reaching: *mass destruction.* *–v.i.* **10.** to come together in or form a mass or masses: *the clouds are massing in the west.* *–v.t.* **11.** to gather into or dispose in a mass or masses; assemble: *the houses are massed in blocks*; *to mass troops.* *–phr.* **12. in the mass,** in the main; as a whole. **13. the masses,** the great body of the common people; the working classes or lower social orders. **–massless,** *adj.*

mass² /mæs/ *n.* **1.** (in Roman Catholic and certain other churches) a religious service celebrating the Eucharist. **2.** a musical setting of certain parts of this service (now chiefly as celebrated in the Roman Catholic Church), as the Kyrie eleison, Gloria, Credo, Sanctus, Benedictus and Agnus Dei. Also, **Mass.**

massacre /ˈmæsəkə/ *n.* **1.** the unnecessary, indiscriminate slaughter of human beings. *–v.t.* (**-cred, -cring**) **2.** to kill indiscriminately or in a massacre. **–massacrer,** *n.*

massage /ˈmæsaʒ, ˈmæsadʒ/ *n.* **1.** the act or art of treating the body by rubbing, kneading, or the like, to stimulate circulation, increase suppleness, etc. *–v.t.* (**-saged, -saging**) **2.** to treat by massage. **–massager, massagist,** *n.*

masseur /mæˈsɜ/ *n.* a man who practises massage. **–masseuse** /mæˈsɜz/, *fem. n.*

massif /ˈmæsif/ *n. Physical Geog.* a compact portion of a mountain range, containing one or more summits.

massive /ˈmæsɪv/ *adj.* **1.** consisting of or forming a large mass. **2.** large, in size or amount. **3.** solid; substantial; great. **4.** *Mineral.* without outward crystal form. **5.** *Geol.* → **homogeneous. –massively,** *adv.* **–massiveness,** *n.*

mass media *n.* → **media**¹ (def. 2). Also, **the media.**

mass-produce /mæs-prəˈdjus/ *v.t.* to manufacture in large quantities by standardised mechanical processes.

mast /mast/ *n.* **1.** a tall spar rising more or less vertically from the keel or deck of a vessel, which supports the yards, sails, etc. **2.** any upright pole, as a support for an aerial, etc. **–mastlike,** *adj.*

mast- variant of **masto-,** before vowels, as in *mastectomy.*

mastectomy /mæsˈtɛktəmi/ *n.* (*pl.* **-mies**) *Surg.* the operation of removing the breast or mamma.

master /ˈmastə/ *n.* **1.** someone who has the power of controlling, using, or disposing of something: *a master of several languages.* **2.** an employer of workers or servants. **3.** also, **master mariner.** the commander of a merchant vessel. **4.** the male head of a household. **5.** an owner of a slave, horse, dog, etc. **6.** a presiding officer. **7.** a male teacher, tutor, or schoolmaster. **8. a.** a person whose teachings one accepts or follows. **b.** the, (*upper case*) (in Christianity) Jesus Christ, particularly as seen as a teacher whose precepts Christians accept and follow. **9.** a victor. **10.** a tradesperson qualified to carry on their trade independently and to teach apprentices. **11.** a person eminently skilled in something, as an occupation, art, or science. **12.** a title given to a bridge or chess player who has won or been placed high in a certain number of officially recognised tournaments. **13.** *Law* a legally qualified officer of a Supreme Court, empowered to perform auxiliary judicial duties. **14.** someone who has been awarded a further degree, usually subsequent to a bachelor's degree, at a university (used only in titles or in certain other expressions relating to such a degree). **15.** a boy or young man (used chiefly as a term of address). **16.** the head of a college at certain universities. **17.** the head teacher in a particular subject department in a secondary school: *the history master.* **18.** an original matrix, especially the first pressing of a gramophone record. **19.** *Music* **a.** an original recording from which copies, remixes, etc., are made. **b.** the final mix of a multi-track recording. *–adj.* **20.** being master, or exercising mastery. **21.** chief or principal: *the master bedroom.* **22.** directing or controlling. **23.** dominating or predominant. **24.** being a master carrying on his trade independently, rather than a workman employed by another. **25.** being a master of some occupation, art, etc.; eminently skilled. **26.** characteristic of a master; showing mastery. *–v.t.* **27.** to conquer or subdue; reduce to subjection. **28.** to rule or direct as master. **29.** to make oneself master of; to become an adept in. *–phr.* **30. be master in one's own house,** to manage one's own affairs without interference. **31. be one's own master,** to be completely free and independent. **32. master and servant,** *Law* the relationship which exists when the master or employer has the right to direct the servant or employee what to do, and to control how it is done; a master is liable for a tort committed by the servant in the course of his or her employment. **–masterdom,** *n.* **–mastery,** *n.* **–masterless,** *adj.* **–masterly,** *adj.* **–masterful,** *adj.*

master key *n.* a key that will open a number of locks whose proper keys are not interchangeable. Also, **pass key.**

mastermind /ˈmastəmaɪnd/ *v.t.* **1.** to plan and direct activities skilfully: *the revolt was masterminded by two colonels.* *–n.* **2.** someone who originates or is mainly responsible for the carrying out of a particular project, scheme, etc.

master of ceremonies *n.* someone who directs the entertainment at a party, dinner, etc. Also, **emcee, MC.**

masterpiece /ˈmastəpis/ *n.* **1.** one's most excellent production, as in an art: *the masterpiece of a painter.* **2.** any production of masterly skill. **3.** a consummate example of skill or excellence of any kind.

masterstroke /ˈmastəstrouk/ *n.* a masterly action or achievement.

masthead /ˈmasthɛd/ *n.* **1.** *Naut.* the top or head of the mast of a ship or vessel; usually the top of the highest mast in one vertical line. **2.** a statement printed at the top of the front page in all issues of a newspaper, magazine, etc., giving the name, owner, staff, etc.

mastic /ˈmæstɪk/ *n.* **1.** an aromatic, astringent resin obtained from a small evergreen tree, *Pistacia lentiscus*, native to the Mediterranean region, used in making varnish. **2.** *Building Trades* **a.** any of various preparations used for sealing joints, window frames, etc. **b.** a pasty form of cement used for filling holes in masonry or plastered walls.

masticate /ˈmæstəkeɪt/ *v.t.* **1.** to chew. **2.** to reduce to a pulp by crushing or kneading, as rubber. **–mastication** /mæstəˈkeɪʃən/, *n.* **–masticator**, *n.*

mastiff /ˈmæstɪf/ *n.* one of a breed of large, powerful, short-haired dogs having an apricot, fawn, or brindled coat.

mastitis /mæsˈtaɪtəs/ *n. Pathol.* inflammation of the breast.

masto- a word element meaning 'breast' or 'mastoid'. Also, **mast-**.

masturbation /mæstəˈbeɪʃən/ *n.* the manual stimulation of the genital organs of oneself or another in order to achieve or provide orgasm. **–masturbate**, *v.*

mat[1] /mæt/ *n.* **1.** a piece of fabric made of plaited or woven rushes, straw, hemp, or other fibre, used to cover a floor, to wipe the shoes on, etc. **2.** a small piece of material, often ornamental, set under a dish of food, a lamp, vase, etc. **3. a.** a thick covering, as of padded canvas, laid on a floor on which wrestlers, etc., contend. **b.** *Athletics* a thick portable slab usually of covered foam used with others to build up a safe landing area for high jumpers, etc.; the set of such mats. **4.** a thickly growing or thick and tangled mass, as of hair or weeds. *–verb* (**matted, matting**) *–v.t.* **5.** to cover with or as with mats or matting. **6.** to form into a mat, as by interweaving. *–v.i.* **7.** to become entangled; form tangled masses. *–phr.* **8. put on the mat**, to reprimand.

mat[2] /mæt/ *n.* **1.** a piece of cardboard or other material placed round a photograph, painting, etc., to serve as a frame or border. *–v.t.* (**matted, matting**) **2.** to provide (a picture) with a mat.

matador /ˈmætədə/ *n.* the bullfighter who has the principal role and who kills the bull in a bullfight.

match[1] /mætʃ/ *n.* **1.** a short, slender piece of wood or other material tipped with a chemical substance which produces fire when rubbed on a rough or chemically prepared surface. **2.** a wick, cord, or the like, prepared to burn at an even rate, used to fire cannon, etc.

match[2] /mætʃ/ *n.* **1.** a person or thing that equals or looks like another in some way. **2.** a person or thing that is an exact copy of another; pair. **3.** someone able to handle another as an equal. **4.** a contest; game. **5.** a person suitable as a partner in marriage. **6.** a marriage arrangement. *–v.t.* **7.** to equal, or be equal to. **8.** to be the match of. **9.** to make similar to; adapt. **10.** to fit together. **11.** to produce an equal to: *I will match your offer.* **12.** to place in opposition. **13.** to provide with a competitor of equal power. **14.** to prove a match for. **15.** to unite in marriage. *–v.i.* **16.** to be equal. **17.** to be similar in size, shape, etc. **–matchable**, *adj.* **–matchless**, *adj.* **–matcher**, *n.*

matchmaker /ˈmætʃmeɪkə/ *n.* **1.** someone who brings about, or seeks to bring about, a marriage or a romantic relationship between two people. **2.** someone who arranges matches for athletic contests, etc.

match point *n. Sport* the final point needed to win a contest.

mate[1] /meɪt/ *n.* **1.** one joined with another in any pair. **2.** a counterpart. **3.** husband or wife. **4.** one of a pair of mated animals. **5. a.** a habitual associate; comrade; friend; intimate: *they've been good mates from way back.* **b.** *Aust., NZ* a form of address: *how are you going, mate?* **6.** an officer of a merchant vessel who ranks below the captain or master (called **first mate**, **second mate**, etc., when there are more than one on a ship). **7.** an assistant to a tradesperson. *–v.t.* **8.** to join as a mate or as mates. **9.** to match or marry. **10.** to pair, as animals. **11.** to join suitably, as two things. **12.** to treat as comparable, as one thing with another. *–v.i.* **13.** (of animals) to copulate. *–phr.* **14. be mates with**, to be good friends with.

mate[2] /meɪt/ *n., v.t.* → **checkmate**.

material /məˈtɪəriəl/ *n.* **1.** the substance or substances of which a thing is made or composed. **2.** any constituent element of a thing. **3.** anything serving as crude or raw matter for working upon or developing. **4.** a person demonstrating potential in a particular skill or occupation: *he's good foreman material.* **5.** information, ideas, or the like on which a report, thesis, etc., is based. **6.** a textile fabric. **7.** (*pl.*) articles of any kind requisite for making or doing something: *writing materials.* *–adj.* **8.** formed or consisting of matter; physical; corporeal: *the material world.* **9.** relating to, concerned with, or involving matter: *material force.* **10.** concerned or occupied unduly with corporeal things or interests. **11.** relating to the physical rather than the spiritual or intellectual aspect of things: *material civilisation.* **12.** of substantial import or much consequence. **13.** *Law* (of evidence, etc.) likely to influence the determination of a cause. *–phr.* **14. material to**, pertinent or essential to. **–materially**, *adv.* **–materialness**, *n.*

materialise /məˈtɪəriəlaɪz/ *v.t.* **1.** to give material form to. **2.** to take on material qualities. *–v.i.* **3.** to assume bodily form. **4.** to appear. Also, **materialize**. **–materialiser**, *n.* **–materialisation** /mətɪəriəlaɪˈzeɪʃən/, *n.*

materialism /məˈtɪəriəlɪzəm/ *n.* **1.** the philosophical theory which regards matter and its motions as constituting the universe, and all phenomena, including those of mind, as due to material agencies. **2.** *Ethics* the doctrine that the self-interest of the individual is or ought to be the first law of life. **3.** devotion to material rather than spiritual objects, needs, and considerations.

materialist /məˈtɪəriəlɪst/ *n.* **1.** an adherent of philosophical materialism. **2.** someone absorbed in material interests; someone who takes a material view of life. **–materialistic** /mətɪəriəˈlɪstɪk/, *adj.* **–materialistically** /mətɪəriəˈlɪstɪkli/, *adv.*

matériel /məˈtɪəriəl/ *n.* **1.** the aggregate of things used or needed in any business, undertaking, or operation (distinguished from *personnel*). **2.** *Mil.* arms, ammunition, and equipment in general.

maternal /məˈtɜnəl/ *adj.* **1.** of or relating to, befitting, having the qualities of, or being a mother. **2.** derived from a mother. **3.** related through a mother: *his maternal aunt.* **–maternally**, *adv.*

maternity /məˈtɜnəti/ *n.* **1.** the state of being a mother; motherhood. **2.** motherliness. *–adj.* **3.** belonging to or characteristic of motherhood or of the period of pregnancy.

maternity ward *n.* a hospital ward which provides care for women during and after childbirth, or during pregnancy, and also provides care for their newborn babies.

mateship /ˈmeɪtʃɪp/ *n.* **1.** the quality or state of being a mate. **2.** a code of conduct among men stressing equality and fellowship.

mates rates *pl. n. Aust., NZ Colloq.* specially cheap rates for friends.

matey /'meɪti/ *adj. Colloq.* comradely; friendly.

mathematics /mæθə'mætɪks/ *n.* the science that deals with the measurement, properties, and relations of quantities, including arithmetic, geometry, algebra, etc. –**mathematical,** *adj.*

maths /mæθs/ *n.* → **mathematics**.

matilda /mə'tɪldə/ *n. NZ Colloq., Aust.* a swag.

matinee /'mætəneɪ/ *n.* an entertainment, as a dramatic or musical performance, film, etc., held in the daytime, usually in the afternoon. Also, **matinée**.

matri- a word element meaning 'mother'.

matriarch /'meɪtriak, 'mæt-/ *n.* **1.** a woman holding a position of leadership in a family, clan, tribal society, etc. **2.** a woman who dominates any group or field of activity. –**matriarchal, matriarchic,** *adj.* –**matriarchy,** *n.*

matrices /'meɪtrəsiz/ *n.* plural form of **matrix**.

matriculate *v.i.* /mə'trɪkjəleɪt/ **1.** to be admitted to membership, especially of a university or other institution of tertiary education. **2.** to pass matriculation (def. 2). –*v.t.* /mə'trɪkjəleɪt/ **3.** to enrol or admit. –*n.* /mə'trɪkjələt/ **4.** someone who has matriculated. –**matriculator, matriculant,** *n.*

matriculation /mətrɪkjə'leɪʃən/ *n.* **1.** the process of being formally enrolled in or admitted to certain universities, or similar tertiary education institutions. **2.** a secondary-school examination in which a required level must be reached before qualification for admission to a tertiary education institution.

matrilineal /mætrə'lɪniəl/ *adj.* of, relating to, or founded on the recognition of kinship and descent through the female line. Also, **matrilinear**. –**matriline,** *n.*

matrimony /'mætrəməni/, *Orig. US* /-moʊni/ *n.* (*pl.* **-nies**) the rite, ceremony, or sacrament of marriage. –**matrimonial,** *adj.*

matrix /'meɪtrɪks/ *n.* (*pl.* **-trices** /-trəsiz/ *or* **-trixes**) **1.** that which gives origin or form to a thing. **2.** *Biol.* the intercellular substance of a tissue. **3.** *Maths, Computers* a rectangular array of numbers. **4.** *Computers* a rectangular array of logical elements acting as a selection system. **5.** a network of communities, organisations, or people, forming an interconnected whole: *the social matrix.* **6.** *Printing* a mould for casting. **7.** a positive or negative copy of an original disc recording, used in reproducing other copies. **8.** in a punching machine, a perforated block upon which the object to be punched is rested. **9.** the rock in which a crystallised mineral is embedded. **10.** *Geol.* the material of smaller grainsize in a sedimentary rock containing material of two separate grainsizes.

matron /'meɪtrən/ *n.* **1.** a married woman, especially one of ripe years and staid character or established position. **2.** a woman in charge of the sick bay, as in a school or workplace, on board a ship, etc. **3.** (no longer in official use) a woman in charge of nursing, etc., in a hospital. **4.** a brood mare. –**matronal,** *adj.* –**matronly,** *adj.* –**matronage,** *n.*

matt /mæt/ *adj.* **1.** lustreless and dull in surface. –*n.* **2.** a dull or dead surface, without lustre, produced on metals, etc.; a roughened or frosted surface. **3.** a tool, as a punch, for producing such a surface. –*v.t.* **4.** to finish with a matt surface. Also, **mat**; *US,* **matte**.

matted[1] /'mætəd/ *adj.* **1.** covered with a dense growth or a tangled mass. **2.** covered with mats or matting. **3.** formed into a mat; entangled in a thick mass. **4.** formed of mats, or of woven material.

matted[2] /'mætəd/ *adj.* having a dull finish.

matter /'mætə/ *n.* **1.** the substance or substances of which physical objects consist or are composed. **2.** physical or corporeal substance in general (whether solid, liquid, or gaseous), especially as distinguished from incorporeal substance (as spirit or mind), or from qualities, actions, etc. **3.** whatever occupies space. **4.** a particular kind of substance: *colouring matter.* **5.** some substance excreted by a living body, especially pus. **6.** the material or substance of a discourse, book, etc., often as distinguished from the form. **7.** things written or printed: *printed matter.* **8.** a thing, affair, or business: *a matter of life and death.* **9.** an amount or extent reckoned approximately: *a matter of ten kilometres.* **10.** something of consequence: *it is no matter.* **11.** importance or significance: *what matter?* **12.** *Printing* **a.** material for work; copy. **b.** type set up. **13.** (*pl.*) the situation of the moment: *matters had reached rock bottom.* –*v.i.* **14.** to be of importance; signify: *it matters little.* –*phr.* **15.** **a matter of course,** the logical and inevitable outcome of a sequence of events. **16. as a matter of fact,** actually; in reality. **17. be the matter,** to be wrong: *what's the matter.* **18. don't matter,** *Colloq.* (*humorous*) an exclamation indicating amused resignation. **19. for that matter,** as far as that is concerned.

matter-of-fact *adj.* adhering to actual facts; not imaginative; prosaic; commonplace. –**matter-of-factly,** *adv.*

matting /'mætɪŋ/ *n.* a coarse fabric of rushes, grass, straw, hemp, or the like, used for covering floors, wrapping, etc.

mattock /'mætək/ *n.* an instrument for loosening the soil in digging, shaped like a pickaxe, but having one end broad instead of pointed.

mattress /'mætrəs/ *n.* **1.** a case filled with soft material, as straw, cotton, etc., often reinforced with springs, and usually quilted or fastened together at intervals, used as or on a bed. **2.** a mat woven of brush, poles, or similar material used to prevent erosion of the surface of dykes, jetties, embankments, dams, etc.

mature /mə'tjuə/ *adj.* **1.** complete in natural growth or development. **2.** ripe, as fruit. **3.** relating to full mental and emotional development; sensible and reasonable. **4.** *Commerce* having reached the limit of its time, i.e. become due or payable. –*v.t.* **5.** to make mature; especially, to ripen. **6.** to bring to full development. –*v.i.* **7.** to become mature; especially, to ripen. **8.** to come to full development. –**maturely,** *adv.* –**matureness,** *n.* –**maturation** /mætʃə'reɪʃən, -tju-/, *n.*

maturity /mə'tjurəti/ *n.* **1.** the state of being mature; ripeness. **2.** full development; perfected condition. **3.** *Physiol.* the period following attainment of full development of bodily structure and reproductive faculty. **4.** *Commerce* **a.** the state of being due. **b.** the time when a note or bill of exchange becomes due.

maudlin /'mɔdlən/ *adj.* **1.** tearfully or weakly emotional or sentimental. **2.** tearfully or emotionally silly from drink. –**maudlinly,** *adv.* –**maudlinness,** *n.*

maul /mɔl/ *n.* **1.** a heavy hammer as for driving piles. **2.** *Rugby Union* a loose scrum around the ball carrier. –*v.t.* **3.** to handle roughly; to injure by rough treatment. **4.** (of animals) to attack savagely and tear the flesh of. **5.** to criticise severely: *the critics mauled the play.* –**mauler,** *n.*

mausoleum /mɔsə'liəm, mɔz-/ *n.* (*pl.* **-leums** *or* **-lea** /-'liə/) **1.** a stately and magnificent tomb. **2.** a large, old, gloomy building. –**mausolean,** *adj.*

mauve /moʊv/ *n.* **1.** pale bluish purple. **2.** a purple dye obtained from aniline, the first of the coal-tar dyes (discovered in 1856). –*adj.* **3.** of the colour of mauve: *a mauve dress.*

maverick /'mævərɪk/ *n.* **1.** *US* (in cattle-raising regions) **a.** an animal found without an owner's brand. **b.** a calf separated from its dam. **2.** a dissenter; loner.

maw /mɔ/ *n.* the mouth, throat, or gullet as concerned in devouring (now chiefly of animals or in figurative use).

mawkish /'mɔkɪʃ/ *adj.* **1.** sickly or slightly nauseating. **2.** characterised by sickly sentimentality. –**mawkishly,** *adv.* –**mawkishness,** *n.*

max /mæks/ *phr. Colloq.* **1. max out**, to reach the limit of credit, as on credit card: *she maxed out her credit card and was broke.* **2. to the max**, extremely; to the greatest extent possible: *working the wave to the max.*

maxi /'mæksi/ *n.* a full-length dress, coat, or skirt for day wear.

maxi- a prefix applied to nouns meaning 'large' as in *maxibike, maxiskirt, maxiyacht.*

maxilla /mæk'sɪlə/ *n.* (*pl.* **maxillae** /mæk'sɪli/) *Anat.* a jaw or jawbone, especially the upper.

maxim /'mæksəm/ *n.* **1.** an expression, especially an aphoristic or sententious one, of a general truth, especially as to conduct. **2.** a principle of conduct.

maxima /'mæksəmə/ *n.* a plural form of **maximum**.

maximise /'mæksəmaɪz/ *v.t.* to increase to the greatest possible amount or degree. Also, **maximize**. **–maximisation** /mæksəmaɪ'zeɪʃən/, *n.* **–maximiser**, *n.*

maximum /'mæksəməm/ *n.* (*pl.* **-mums** *or* **-ma** /-mə/) **1.** the greatest quantity or amount possible, assignable, allowable, etc.; the highest amount, value or degree, attained or recorded (opposed to *minimum*). **2.** *Maths* a value of a function at a certain point which is not exceeded in the immediate vicinity of that point. *–adj.* **3.** that is a maximum; greatest possible; highest. **4.** relating to a maximum or maximums. **–maximal**, *adj.*

may[1] /meɪ/ *v.* (modal) **1.** expressing uncertainty: *this may be the case; he may be angry when he finds out; as many as 300 people may have been killed; we leave on Friday, come what may.* **2.** to have permission to: *may we come in?; you may go now* **3.** to be possible: *this may be achieved in various ways.* **4.** used to concede a point: *she may be the boss, but she's not always right; be that as it may, she's not entirely in the wrong; that's as may be, but we have to look to the future.* **5.** indicating an intention: *she may attend, but could be prevented by her husband's illness.* **6.** expressing a hope: *may all your dreams come true* *–phr.* **7. may as well ...**, used to make a suggestion in the absence of a better alternative: *he won't turn up now – we may as well go home.*

may[2] /meɪ/ *n.* **1. →** **hawthorn**. **2.** any of several, usually white-flowered, species of the genus *Spiraea*.

May /meɪ/ *n.* the fifth month of the year, containing 31 days.

maybe /'meɪbi, meɪ'bi/ *adv.* perhaps.

mayday /'meɪdeɪ/ *n.* (according to international radio regulations) the radio telephonic distress signal used by ships or aircraft.

mayhem /'meɪhɛm/ *n.* **1.** confusion and chaos, especially when caused by violence. **2.** *Law* the crime of violently inflicting a bodily injury rendering someone less able to defend themselves or to annoy their adversary (now often extended by statute to include any wilful mutilation of another's body). Also, **maihem**.

mayonnaise /meɪə'neɪz/ *n.* a thick dressing of egg yolks, vinegar or lemon juice, seasonings, and oil, used for salads or vegetables.

mayor /mɛə/ *n.* the principal officer of a municipality; the chief magistrate of a city or borough. **–mayorship**, **mayoralty**, *n.*

mayoress /'mɛərɛs, -rəs, mɛə'rɛs/ *n.* **1.** the wife of the man who is mayor. **2.** a woman appointed to assist a male mayor as hostess at official functions. **3.** a woman mayor.

maze /meɪz/ *n.* **1.** a confusing network of intercommunicating paths or passages; a labyrinth. **2.** a state of bewilderment or confusion. **–mazement**, *n.*

m-business /'ɛm-bɪznəs/ *n.* **→** **m-commerce**.

m-commerce /ɛm-'kɒmɜs/ *n.* business which is conducted using mobile phone technology. Also, **m-business**.

me /mi/ *pron.* (personal) **1.** the objective case of I. **2.** used in place of I, as in the phrases *it's me* or, in non-standard use, *you and me'll go.*

mea culpa /meɪə 'kʊlpə/ *interj.* **1.** an expression acknowledging that the speaker is at fault, has made a mistake, etc. *–n.* **2.** an admission of fault: *a surprising mea culpa from the politician.*

mead /mid/ *n.* an alcoholic liquor made by fermenting honey and water.

meadow /'mɛdoʊ/ *n.* **1.** *Chiefly Brit.* a piece of grassland, whether used for raising of hay or for pasture. **2.** *US* a low, level tract of uncultivated ground, as along a river, producing coarse grass. **–meadowy**, *adj.*

meagre /'migə/ *adj.* **1.** deficient in quantity or quality, or without fullness or richness. **2.** having little flesh, lean, or thin. Also, *US*, **meager**. **–meagrely**, *adv.* **–meagreness**, *n.*

meal[1] /mil/ *n.* **1.** one of the regular repasts of the day, as breakfast, lunch, or dinner. **2.** the food eaten or served for a repast. *–phr.* **3. make a meal of, a.** to turn into a satisfactory meal: *to make a meal of the leftovers.* **b.** *Colloq.* to do (something) with more effort than is required, usually from incompetence or inexperience: *to make a meal of sorting the forms.* **c.** *Colloq.* to mess up completely as in performing a task: *to make a meal of the garden while doing the weeding.* **d.** *Colloq.* to demonstrate one's superiority over: *to make a meal of the opposition.*

meal[2] /mil/ *n.* **1.** the edible part of any grain (now usually excluding wheat) or pulse ground to a (coarse) powder and not sifted. **2.** any ground or powdery substance, as of nuts or seeds, resembling this.

meal ticket *n.* **1.** a ticket entitling the holder to a meal. **2.** *Colloq.* any means or source of financial support, as a pimp's prostitute, a spouse, a university degree, etc.

mealy-mouthed /'mili-maʊðd/ *adj.* **1.** avoiding the use of plain terms, as from timidity, excessive delicacy, or hypocrisy. **2.** using soft words.

mean[1] /min/ *verb* (**meant** /mɛnt/, **meaning**) *–v.t.* **1.** to have in the mind as in intention or purpose (often with an infinitive as object): *I mean to talk to him.* **2.** to intend for a particular purpose, destination, etc.: *they were meant for each other.* **3.** to intend to express or indicate: *by 'liberal' I mean ...* **4.** (of words, things, etc.) to have as the signification; signify. *–v.i.* **5.** to be minded or disposed; have intentions: *he means well.*

mean[2] /min/ *adj.* **1.** poor in grade, quality or character: *he is no mean performer.* **2.** low in station, rank, etc. **3.** of little importance. **4.** unimpressive; shabby: *a mean abode.* **5.** small-minded; ignoble: *mean motives.* **6.** unwilling to give; miserly: *he is mean about money.* **7.** small; ashamed: *I feel mean not having helped.* **8.** troublesome; vicious, as a horse. **9.** (of someone in a competitive activity) skilful; accomplished: *he's a mean bowler.* **10.** *Colloq.* powerful: *a big, mean motor.*

mean[3] /min/ *n.* **1.** something intermediate; something that is midway between two extremes. **2.** *Maths* **a.** a quantity having a value intermediate between the values of other quantities; an average, especially the arithmetic mean. **b.** either the second or third term in a proportion of four terms. *–adj.* **3.** occupying a middle position or an intermediate place. **4.** intermediate in kind, quality, degree, time, etc.

meander /mi'ændə/ *v.i.* **1.** to proceed by a winding course. **2.** to wander aimlessly. *–n.* **3.** (*usu. pl.*) a turning or winding; a winding; a winding path or course. **4.** a circuitous movement or journey. **5.** an intricate variety of fret or fretwork. **–meandering**, *adj.* **–meanderingly**, *adv.*

meaning /'minɪŋ/ *n.* **1.** that which is intended to be, or actually is, expressed or indicated; signification; import. *–adj.* **2.** intending: *he is very well-meaning.*

3. expressive or significant: *a meaning look.* –**meaningful**, *adj.* –**meaningless**, *adj.* –**meaningly**, *adv.*

means /minz/ *pl. n.* **1.** (*oft. construed as sing.*) an agency, instrumentality, method, etc., used to attain an end: *a means of communication.* **2.** disposable resources, especially pecuniary resources: *to live beyond one's means.* **3.** considerable pecuniary resources: *a man of means.* –*phr.* **4. by all means, a.** at any cost; without fail. **b.** (in emphasis) certainly: *go, by all means.* **5. by any means,** in any way; at all. **6. by means of,** employing the method of; by the use of. **7. by no means,** in no way; not at all; certainly not: *a practice by no means to be recommended.* **8. within one's means,** not too expensive in terms of one's financial resources; able to be afforded.

means test *n.* an evaluation of the income and resources of a person, or of those upon whom he or she is dependent, in order to determine eligibility for part or all of a pension, grant, allowance, etc. Also, **means-test.** –**means-testable**, *adj.*

mean time *n.* the time at a given place on earth based on a day of 24 hours; the interval between successive local noons on which local time is based varies and so an average day of 24 hours is used, giving mean time. Also, **mean solar time.**

meantime /'mintaɪm/ *n.* **1.** the intervening time: *in the meantime.* –*adv.* **2.** meanwhile.

meanwhile /'minwaɪl, min'waɪl/ *adv.* in the intervening time; during the interval; at the same time.

measles /'mizəlz/ *sing. n.* (*sometimes construed as pl.*) **1.** an acute infectious disease occurring mostly in children, characterised by catarrhal and febrile symptoms and an eruption of small red spots; rubeola: *a case of (the) measles; measles has (have) broken out at school.* **2.** any of certain other eruptive diseases, as rubella (**German measles**). **3.** a disease in swine and other animals caused by the larvae of certain tapeworms of the genus *Taenia.*

measly /'mizli/ *adj.* (**-lier, -liest**) *Colloq.* wretchedly poor or unsatisfactory; very small.

measure /'mɛʒə/ *n.* **1.** the act or process of ascertaining the extent, dimensions, quantity, etc., of something, especially by comparison with a standard. **2.** size, dimensions, quantity, etc., as thus ascertained. **3.** an instrument, as a graduated rod or a vessel of standard capacity, for measuring. **4.** a unit or standard of measurement. **5.** a definite or known quantity measured out. **6.** a system of measurement. **7.** *Printing* the width of a page or column, usually measured in ems or picas. **8.** any standard of comparison, estimation, or judgement. **9.** a quantity, degree, or proportion. **10.** a limit, or an extent or degree not to be exceeded: *to know no measure.* **11.** reasonable bounds or limits: *beyond measure.* **12.** a legislative bill or enactment. **13.** an action or procedure intended as a means to an end: *to take measures to avert suspicion.* **14.** a short rhythmical movement or arrangement, as in poetry or music. **15.** a particular kind of such arrangement. **16.** a metrical unit. **17.** *Poetic* an air or melody. **18.** *US Music* → **bar¹** (def. 9). **19.** (*pl.*) *Geol.* beds; strata. –*v.t.* **20.** to ascertain the extent, dimensions, quantity, capacity, etc., of, especially by comparison with a standard. **21.** to estimate the relative amount, value, etc., of, by comparison with some standard. **22.** to judge of or appraise by comparison with something else. **23.** to serve as the measure of. **24.** to adjust or proportion. **25.** to bring into comparison or competition. **26.** to travel over or traverse. –*v.i.* **27.** to take measurements. **28.** to admit of measurement. **29.** to be of a specified measure. –*phr.* **30. for good measure,** as an extra and probably unnecessary act, precaution, etc.: *he padlocked the door for good measure.* **31. get someone's measure** or **get the measure of someone,** to achieve equality with someone, especially a competitor. **32. measure one's length,** to fall flat on one's face. **33. measure out** (or **off**), to mark or lay off or out, or deal out, with reference to measure. **34. measure up,** (sometimes fol. by *to*) to be adequate. –**measurer**, *n.* –**measurable**, *adj.* –**measurably**, *adv.* –**measurability** /mɛʒərə'bɪləti/, *n.*

measurement /'mɛʒəmənt/ *n.* **1.** the act of measuring. **2.** an ascertained dimension. **3.** a system of measuring or of measures. **4.** *Surveying* the estimation by a quantity surveyor, civil engineer, or the like, of the work to be done and billed, and later the measuring on the site of the work done and to be paid for.

meat /mit/ *n.* **1.** the flesh of animals as used for food. **2.** food in general: *meat and drink.* **3.** the edible part of anything, as a fruit, nut, etc. **4.** the main substance of something, as an argument. **5.** *Colloq.* (*taboo*) male or female genitalia. –*phr.* **6. strong meat,** books, films, etc., which would shock anyone with a nervous or squeamish disposition, as those depicting violence. **7. the meat in the sandwich,** *Aust. Colloq.* the person innocently involved in a conflict of interests. –**meatless**, *adj.*

meaty /'miti/ *adj.* (**-tier, -tiest**) **1.** of, relating to or resembling meat. **2.** full of substance; pithy.

Mecca /'mɛkə/ *n.* (*also lower case*) **1.** a place regarded as a centre of interest or activity and visited by many people. **2.** any goal to which people aspire.

mechanic /mə'kænɪk/ *n.* **1.** someone who repairs machinery, motor vehicles, etc. **2.** a skilled worker with tools or machines.

mechanical /mə'kænɪkəl/ *adj.* **1.** of or relating to machinery or tools. **2.** of the nature of or produced by such means. **3.** acting or performed without originality, spirit, etc.; automatic. **4.** belonging or relating to the subject matter of mechanics. **5.** reducing the spiritual to the material; materialistic. **6.** relating to material objects or physical conditions: *prevented by mechanical difficulties.* –**mechanically**, *adv.* –**mechanicalness**, *n.*

mechanics /mə'kænɪks/ *n.* **1.** the branch of physical science that deals (both theoretically and practically) with machinery or mechanical appliances. **2.** the science that deals with the action of forces on bodies and with motion, and comprising kinematics, statics, and dynamics. **3.** (*construed as pl.*) the mechanical or technical part or aspect. **4.** (*construed as pl.*) methods of operation, procedures, and the like.

mechanise /'mɛkənaɪz/ *v.t.* **1.** to make mechanical. **2.** to operate or perform by or as if by machinery. **3.** to introduce machinery into (an industry, etc.). **4.** *Mil.* to equip with tanks and other armoured motor vehicles. Also, **mechanize.** –**mechanisation** /mɛkənaɪ'zeɪʃən/, *n.*

mechanism /'mɛkənɪzəm/ *n.* **1.** a piece of machinery. **2.** the machinery, or other physical means, by which something is performed. **3.** the structure, or arrangement of parts of a machine or of anything similar. **4.** such parts collectively. **5.** *Philos., Biol.* a natural process seen as being machine-like.

mechatronics /mɛkə'trɒnɪks/ *n.* (*from trademark*) a branch of engineering technology which integrates mechanical engineering with electronics, especially in the design and manufacture of products and processes controlled by intelligent computers, such as robots performing certain tasks, air conditioners, cruise control in motor vehicles, etc.

med /mɛd/ *Colloq.* –*n.* **1.** a medication: *to take a med.* –*phr.* **2. on meds,** on medication.

medal /'mɛdl/ *n.* **1.** a flat piece of metal, usually in the shape of a disc, star, cross, or the like, bearing an inscription, device, etc., issued to commemorate a person, action, or event, or given to serve as a reward for bravery, merit, or the like. –*verb* (**-alled** *or, Chiefly US,*

-aled, -alling or, *Chiefly US*, -aling) –*v.t.* 2. to decorate or honour with a medal. –*v.i.* 3. to win a medal in a sporting competition. –**medallic,** *adj.*

medallion /mə'dæljən/ *n.* 1. a large medal. 2. *Archit.* a. a tablet, usually rounded, often bearing objects represented in relief. b. a member in a decorative design resembling a panel.

meddle /'mɛdl/ *v.i.* to concern or busy oneself with or in something without warrant or necessity; interfere. –**meddler,** *n.* –**meddlesome,** *adj.*

medevac /'mɛdivæk/ *n.* 1. evacuation of seriously ill or wounded person, usually by aircraft. –*v.t.* (**medevaced** /'mɛdivækt/, **medevacing** /'mɛdivækɪŋ/) 2. to evacuate (such a seriously ill or wounded person). Also, **medivac.**

media[1] /'midiə/ *n.* 1. a plural of **medium.** 2. Also, **mass media.** the means of communication, as radio, television, newspapers, magazines, etc., that reach large numbers of people. 3. (*always used in a pl. context*) a member of the media: *a pop star facing 50 media*; *a lot of media in the lobby.* –*adj.* 4. of or relating to the mass media: *media attention.*

media[2] /'midiə/ *n.* (*pl.* **-diae** /-dii/) 1. (in various scientific uses) something medial. 2. *Anat.* the middle layer of an artery or lymphatic vessel.

medial /'midiəl/ *adj.* 1. situated in or relating to the middle; median; intermediate. 2. relating to a mean or average; average. 3. ordinary. 4. within a word or syllable; neither initial nor final. –**medially,** *adv.*

median /'midiən/ *adj.* 1. of or relating to a plane dividing something into two equal parts, especially one dividing an animal into right and left halves. 2. situated in or relating to the middle; medial. –*n.* 3. the middle number in a given sequence of numbers: *4 is the median of 1, 3, 4, 8, 9.* 4. a line through a vertex of a triangle bisecting the opposite side. –**medianly,** *adv.*

median strip *n.* a dividing area, often raised or landscaped, between opposing traffic lanes on a highway.

mediate /'midieɪt/ *v.i.* 1. to act between disagreeing parties to bring about an agreement, etc. –*v.t.* 2. to bring about (an agreement, peace, etc.) by acting between disagreeing parties. 3. to settle (disagreements, etc.) in this way. –**mediately,** *adv.* –**mediation** /midi'eɪʃən/, *n.* –**mediatory, mediative,** *adj.*

medical /'mɛdɪkəl/ *adj.* 1. of or relating to the science or practice of medicine. 2. curative; medicinal; therapeutic: *medical properties.* –*n.* 3. a medical examination. –**medically,** *adv.*

medical certificate *n.* a certificate made out by a doctor testifying to the state of a person's health.

medical imaging *n. Med.* the creation of images of internal organs or parts of the body, as by X-ray, ultrasound or CAT scan, to assist diagnosis and the performance of medical procedures.

medical procedure *n.* → **procedure** (def. 4).

medical tourism *n.* → **health tourism.**

medicament /mə'dɪkəmənt/ *n.* a curative or healing substance. –**medicamental** /mədɪkə'mɛntəl/, **medicamentary** /mədɪkə'mɛntəri/, *adj.*

medicate /'mɛdəkeɪt/ *v.t.* 1. to treat with medicine or medicaments. 2. to impregnate with a medicine.

medication /mɛdə'keɪʃən/ *n.* 1. the use or application of medicine. 2. a medicament; a medicinal agent.

medicine /'mɛdəsən, 'mɛdsən/ *n.* 1. any substance or substances used in treating disease; a medicament; a remedy. 2. the art or science of restoring or preserving health or due physical condition, as by means of drugs, surgical operations or appliances, manipulations, etc. (often divided into medicine proper, surgery, and obstetrics). 3. the art or science of treating disease with drugs or curative substances (distinguished from *surgery* and *obstetrics*). 4. the medical profession. 5. any

object or practice regarded by primitive peoples as of magical efficacy. 6. any unpleasant treatment or experience, especially one that is difficult to accept. –*phr.* 7. **a taste** (or **dose**) **of one's own medicine,** any unpleasant treatment meted out to someone who usually punishes, bullies, etc. –**medicinal, medicative,** *adj.*

medieval /mɛdi'ivəl/ *adj.* of or relating to the Middle Ages: *medieval architecture.* Also, **mediaeval.** –**medievalism,** *n.* –**medievalist,** *n.* –**medievally,** *adv.*

medifraud /'mɛdifrɒd/ *n.* the obtaining of monies from a national health service, usually by doctors, on the basis of fraudulent claims.

mediocre /midi'ouka, 'midiouka/ *adj.* of middling quality; of only moderate excellence; neither good nor bad; indifferent; ordinary: *a person of mediocre abilities.* –**mediocrity** /midi'ɒkrəti, mɛdi-/, *n.*

meditate /'mɛdəteɪt/ *v.t.* 1. *Archaic* to consider in the mind as something to be done or effected; to intend or purpose. –*v.i.* 2. to engage in thought or contemplation; reflect. 3. to discipline the mind so that it contemplates particular, often spiritual, matters or contemplates some particular way such as in becoming unaware of present conditions. –**meditation** /mɛdə'teɪʃən/, *n.* –**meditator,** *n.* –**meditative,** *adj.*

Mediterranean climate /mɛdətəreɪniən 'klaɪmət/ *n.* the type of climate experienced by the lands bordering the Mediterranean Sea and also by other regions in both hemispheres, characterised by sunny, hot summers, and warm winters with rainfall in the winter half of the year.

medium /'midiəm/ *n.* (*pl.* **-dia** /-diə/ or **-diums**) 1. a middle state or condition; mean. 2. something in between in nature or degree; something intermediate. 3. a substance, such as air, etc., through which a force acts or an effect is produced. 4. the natural surroundings of an organism. 5. any surrounding things, conditions, or influences; environment. 6. a means; agent: *newspapers are used as an advertising medium.* 7. *Biol.* a substance in which specimens are shown or preserved. 8. *Bacteriol.* a substance in or upon which microorganisms are grown for study. 9. *Painting* the material or method used by an artist. 10. a person serving or thought to serve as a means of communication between living people and the spirits of the dead. –*adj.* 11. middling in degree, quality, etc.: *a man of medium size.* –*phr.* 12. **a happy medium,** an agreeable balance or compromise between two extremes.

medivac /'mɛdivæk/ *n., v.t.* (**medivaced** /'mɛdivækt/, **medivacing** /'mɛdivækɪŋ/) → **medevac.**

medley /'mɛdli/ *n.* (*pl.* **-leys**) 1. a mixture, especially of heterogeneous elements; a jumble. 2. a piece of music combining airs or passages from various sources. 3. a swimming race in which a competitor swims butterfly stroke, backstroke, breaststroke and freestyle in that order. –*adj.* 4. mixed; mingled; motley.

medulla /mə'dʌlə/ *n.* (*pl.* **-dullae** /-'dʌli/) 1. *Anat.* a. the marrow of bones. b. the soft marrow-like centre of an organ, such as the kidney, suprarenal, etc. c. the medulla oblongata. 2. *Bot.* the pith of plants.

medusa /mə'djusə/ *n.* (*pl.* **-sas** or **-sae** /-si/) → **jellyfish.** –**medusoid,** *adj.*

meek /mik/ *adj.* humbly patient or submissive, as under provocation from others. –**meekly,** *adv.* –**meekness,** *n.*

meerkat /'mɪəkæt/ *n.* any of several small, burrowing, southern African carnivores, with dark bands across the back, related to the mongoose. Also, **suricate.**

meet /mit/ *verb* (**met, meeting**) –*v.t.* 1. to come into contact, junction, or connection with. 2. to come before or to (the eye, gaze, ear, etc.). 3. to come upon or encounter; come face to face with or into the presence of. 4. to go to the place of arrival of, as to welcome, speak with, accompany, etc.: *to meet one's guests at the door.*

5. to come into the company of (a person, etc.) in intercourse, dealings, conference, etc. **6.** to come into personal acquaintance with, as by formal presentation: *to meet the governor.* **7.** to face, eye, etc., directly or without avoidance. **8.** to encounter in opposition or conflict. **9.** to oppose: *to meet charges with counter-charges.* **10.** to cope or deal effectively with (an objection, difficulty, etc.). **11.** to satisfy (needs, obligations, demands, etc.): *to meet a cheque.* **12.** to come into conformity with (wishes, expectations, views, etc.). **13.** to encounter in experience: *to meet hostility.* *–v.i.* **14.** to come together, face to face, or into company: *we met in the street.* **15.** to assemble, as for action or conference as a committee, a legislature, a society, etc. **16.** to become personally acquainted. **17.** to come into contact or form a junction, as lines, planes, areas, etc. **18.** to be conjoined or united. **19.** to concur or agree. **20.** to come together in opposition or conflict, as adversaries, hostile forces, etc. *–n.* **21.** a meeting, especially for a sporting event: *a swim meet; a track meet.* *–phr.* **22. meet halfway,** to reach an agreed compromise. **23. meet up with,** to have an encounter with, especially by chance. **24. meet with, a.** to have a meeting with. **b.** to experience or receive (praise, blame, etc.).

meet and greet *n.* **1.** an official occasion to welcome visitors. **2.** an event at which a politician, celebrity, etc., spends time meeting and chatting with members of the public. *–v.t.* **3.** to welcome (someone) officially. *–v.i.* **4.** (of a politician, celebrity, etc.) to spend time meeting and chatting with members of the public, usually at a planned and structured event. **–meet-and-greet,** *adj.*

meeting /ˈmitɪŋ/ *n.* **1.** a coming face to face. **2.** a coming together; assembly. **3.** a series of races or other sporting events. **4.** an assembly for religious worship. **5.** a coming into or being in connection; junction or union.

meeting house *n.* **1.** a house or building for religious worship. **2.** a house of worship of Quakers. **3.** *NZ* the central community building on a Maori place of meeting.

mega /ˈmɛɡə/ *Colloq.* *–adj.* **1.** extremely great in size, importance, etc. **2.** excellent; great. *–adv.* **3.** an intensifier: *she seemed mega unhappy.*

mega- **1.** a prefix denoting 10^6 of a given unit, as in *megawatt.* *Symbol:* M **2.** *Physical Geog.* a prefix meaning 'great', 'huge', as in *megalith.* **3.** *Colloq.* a prefix meaning 'extremely', used as a combining form with adjectives, as in *megatrendy.*

megabit /ˈmɛɡəbɪt/ *n.* a unit of measurement of computer memory size equal to one million bits. *Symbol:* Mb

megabyte /ˈmɛɡəbaɪt/ *n.* a unit of measurement of computer memory equal to 2^{20} (approximately 10^6) bytes. *Symbol:* MB Also, **meg.**

megafauna /ˈmɛɡəfɔnə/ *n.* **1.** the group of large animals, generally taken to be over 500 kg, which are the largest existing in a particular region or in a particular geological period. **2.** a group of such animals that are now extinct, in particular those that lived in the Pleistocene epoch.

megahertz /ˈmɛɡəhɜts/ *n.* a unit of radiofrequency equal to 1×10^6 hertz. *Symbol:* MHz *Abbrev.:* meg

megalith /ˈmɛɡəlɪθ/ *n.* a stone of great size, especially in ancient constructive work or in primitive monumental remains (as menhirs, dolmens, cromlechs, etc.). **–megalithic** /mɛɡəˈlɪθɪk/, *adj.*

megalitre /ˈmɛɡəlitə/ *n.* a unit of capacity in the metric system, equal to 1×10^6 litres. *Symbol:* ML Also, *US,* **megaliter.**

megalo- a word element denoting bigness or exaggeration.

megalomania /mɛɡələˈmeɪniə/ *n.* **1.** a form of mental alienation marked by delusions of greatness, wealth, etc. **2.** a mania for big or great things.

megaphone /ˈmɛɡəfoʊn/ *n.* a device for magnifying sound, or for directing it in increased volume, as a large funnel-shaped instrument used in addressing a large audience outdoors or in calling to a distance. **–megaphonic** /mɛɡəˈfɒnɪk/, *adj.*

megapixel /ˈmɛɡəˈpɪksəl/ *n.* *Photography* one million pixels, usually in reference to the resolution of a digital camera.

megapode /ˈmɛɡəpoʊd/ *n.* any of various large-footed gallinaceous birds of the family Megapodiidae, of Australasia, Polynesia, and South-East Asia, which construct mounds of earth and vegetation in which eggs are incubated, as the brush turkey, the malleefowl and the scrubfowl.

megaton /ˈmɛɡətʌn/ *n.* **1.** one million tons. **2.** an explosive force equal to that of one million tons of TNT.

megawatt /ˈmɛɡəwɒt/ *n.* *Elect.* a unit of power, equal to one million watts. *Symbol:* MW

meh /mɛ/ *Colloq.* *–interj.* **1.** an expression of resigned acceptance, indifference, etc. *–adj.* **2.** boring; mediocre.

meiosis /maɪˈoʊsəs/ *n.* *Biol.* the maturation process of gametes, consisting of chromosome conjugation and two cell divisions, in the course of which the diploid chromosome number becomes reduced to the haploid. **–meiotic,** *adj.*

melaleuca /mɛləˈlukə/ *n.* any tree or shrub of the predominantly Australian genus *Melaleuca,* family Myrtaceae, many of which are found on river banks or in swamps; paperbark; tea-tree.

melancholia /mɛlənˈkoʊliə/ *n.* a mental disorder characterised by a profound lack of energy, especially in the morning, and loss of pleasure in one's usual interests and pursuits. Also, **melancholic depression.**

melancholy /ˈmɛlənkɒli/ *n.* **1.** a gloomy state of mind, especially when habitual or prolonged; depression. **2.** sober thoughtfulness; pensiveness. *–adj.* **3.** affected with, characterised by, or showing melancholy: *a melancholy mood.* **4.** attended with or inducing melancholy or sadness: *a melancholy occasion.* **–melancholic** /mɛlənˈkɒlɪk/, *adj.*

melange /meɪˈlɒnʒ/ *n.* a mixture; medley. Also, **mélange.**

melanin /ˈmɛlənən/ *n.* any of various dark pigments in the body of humans and certain animals, as $C_{17}H_{98}O_{33}N_{14}S$, occurring in the hair, epidermis, etc.

melano- a word element meaning 'black'.

melanoma /mɛləˈnoʊmə/ *n.* (*pl.* **-nomas** *or* **-nomata** /-ˈnoʊmətə/) *Pathol.* a malignant tumour derived from pigment-containing cells especially in skin.

melatonin /mɛləˈtoʊnən/ *n.* a hormone produced by the pineal gland during the night, which is concerned with brain arousal and the regulation of several biological functions.

Melba toast /mɛlbə ˈtoʊst/ *n.* very thinly sliced bread, baked in the oven until crisp.

meld[1] /mɛld/ *v.t. Cards* to announce and display (a counting combination of cards in the hand) for a score.

meld[2] /mɛld/ *v.t.* **1.** to cause to merge or blend. *–v.i.* **2.** to blend or combine.

melee /ˈmɛˈleɪ, -ˈli/ *n.* **1.** a confused general hand-to-hand fight. **2.** any noisy or confused situation.

mellifluous /məˈlɪfluəs/ *adj.* sweetly or smoothly flowing: *mellifluous tones.* **–mellifluously,** *adv.* **–mellifluousness,** *n.*

mellow /ˈmɛloʊ/ *adj.* **1.** soft and sweet from ripeness, as fruit. **2.** fully developed in flavour, as wines. **3.** softened, made kindly or genial by age or experience: *a mellow old man.* **4.** soft and rich, as sound, tones, colour, light, etc. **5.** soft or moist, as soil. *–v.t.* **6.** to make mellow. –*v.i.* **7.** to become mellow. –**mellowly**, *adv.* –**mellowness**, *n.*

melodic /mə'lɒdɪk/ *adj.* **1.** melodious. **2.** relating to melody as distinguished from harmony and rhythm. –**melodically**, *adv.*

melodrama /'mɛlədramə/ *n.* **1.** a play which does not observe the dramatic laws of cause and effect and which intensifies sentiment and exaggerates passion. **2.** any work of fiction, as a novel, television series, etc., which has a similar character. **3.** angry or emotional display in a non-theatrical setting: *there was much melodrama in the locker room after the champion's defeat.* –**melodramatise** /mɛlə'dræmətaɪz/, **melodramatize**, *v.* –**melodramatist** /mɛlə'dræmətəst/, *n.* –**melodramatic** /mɛlədrə'mætɪk/, *adj.*

melody /'mɛlədi/ *n.* (*pl.* **-dies**) **1.** musical sounds in agreeable succession or arrangement. **2.** *Music* the succession of single notes in musical compositions, as distinguished from harmony and rhythm. –**melodious**, *adj.* –**melodist**, *n.*

melon /'mɛlən/ *n.* the fruit of any of various members of the family Cucurbitaceae, as the paddy melon, *Cucumis myriocarpus.*

melt /mɛlt/ *verb* (**melted, melted** *or* **molten, melting**) –*v.i.* **1.** to become liquefied by heat, as ice, snow, butter, metal, etc. **2.** (not in scientific use) to become liquid; dissolve. **3.** to pass, dwindle, or fade gradually. **4.** to become softened in feeling by pity, sympathy, love, or the like. –*v.t.* **5.** to reduce to a liquid state by heat; fuse. **6.** to soften in feeling, as a person, the heart, etc. –*n.* **7.** the act or process of melting. **8.** the state of being melted. **9.** something that is melted. **10.** a quantity melted at one time. –*phr.* **11. melt away, a.** to pass or fade away. **b.** to cause something to pass or fade away. **12. melt into,** to pass, change, or blend gradually into. –**melter**, *n.* –**meltage**, *n.*

melting point *n. Physics* the equilibrium temperature of the solid and liquid phases of a substance in the presence of a specified gas at a specified pressure (usually air at a pressure of 101.325 kilopascals).

melting pot *n.* **1.** a pot in which metals or other substances are melted or fused. **2.** any situation in which a mixture of diverse elements or ideas occurs, as a multiracial community.

member /'mɛmbə/ *n.* **1.** each of the persons composing a society, party, community, or other body. **2.** each of the persons included in the membership of a legislative body, as parliament. **3.** a part or organ of an animal body; a limb, as a leg, arm, or wing. **4.** a constituent part of any structural or composite whole, as a subordinate architectural feature of a building or the like. **5.** *Maths* either side of an algebraic equation. **6.** *Internet* a contributor to a forum who is logged in and identified. –*adj.* **7.** being a member: *a member nation of the UN.* –**membership**, *n.*

membrane /'mɛmbreɪn/ *n.* **1.** a thin, pliable sheet or layer of animal or vegetable tissue, serving to line an organ, connect parts, etc. **2.** *Chem.* a thin sheet of material, natural or synthetic, which allows substances in solution to pass through it. **3.** a piece of parchment. **4.** any thin connecting layer. –**membranous**, *adj.*

meme /mim/ *n.* → **internet meme**.

memento /mə'mɛntoʊ/ *n.* (*pl.* **-tos** *or* **-toes**) **1.** something that serves as a reminder of what is past or gone. **2.** anything serving as a reminder or warning.

memo /'mɛmoʊ, 'mi-/ *n.* (*pl.* **memos**) → **memorandum**.

memoir /'mɛmwα/ *n.* **1.** → **biography**. **2.** (*pl.*) records of one's own life and experiences. –**memoirist**, *n.*

memorabilia /mɛmərə'bɪliə/ *pl. n.* **1.** matters or events worthy to be remembered. **2.** things saved or collected as souvenirs.

memorable /'mɛmrəbəl, -ərəbəl/ *adj.* **1.** worthy of being remembered; notable: *a memorable speech.* **2.** easy to be remembered. –**memorability** /mɛmərə'bɪləti/, **memorableness**, *n.* –**memorably**, *adv.*

memorandum /mɛmə'rændəm/ *n.* (*pl.* **-dums** *or* **-da** /-də/) **1.** a note made of something to be remembered. **2.** a short record or written statement of something. **3.** a note, as one sent from one member of a firm to another, regarding business matters. **4.** a written statement which includes the main terms of a shipment of unsold goods and allows their return within a particular time.

memorial /mə'mɔriəl/ *n.* **1.** something designed to preserve the memory of a person, event, etc., as a monument, a periodic observance, etc. **2.** a written statement of facts presented to a sovereign, a legislative body, etc., as the basis of, or expressed in the form of, a petition or remonstrance. –*adj.* **3.** preserving the memory of a person or thing; commemorative: *memorial services.* **4.** of or relating to the memory. –**memorially**, *adv.*

memorise /'mɛməraɪz/ *v.t.* to commit to memory, or learn by heart: *he finally memorised the poem.* Also, **memorize**. –**memorisable**, *adj.* –**memorisation** /mɛmərəɪ'zeɪʃən/, *n.* –**memoriser**, *n.*

memory /'mɛmri, 'mɛməri/ *n.* (*pl.* **-ries**) **1.** the mental capacity or faculty of retaining and reviving impressions, or of recalling or recognising previous experiences. **2.** this faculty as possessed by a particular individual: *to have a good memory.* **3.** the act or fact of retaining mental impressions; remembrance; recollection: *to draw from memory.* **4.** the length of time over which recollection extends: *a time within the memory of living men.* **5.** a mental impression retained; a recollection: *one's earliest memories.* **6.** the reputation of a person or thing, especially after death. **7.** the state or fact of being remembered. **8.** a person or thing remembered. **9.** commemorative remembrance; commemoration: *a monument in memory of Captain Cook.* **10.** *Computers* the part of a digital computer in which data and instructions are held until they are required. –*phr.* **11. a trip down memory lane**, an experience that calls to mind the past; a nostalgic occasion.

memory bank *n.* **1.** *Computers* a storage device for computer data. **2.** any collection of stored information: *a memory bank of multiple choice questions.* **3.** a personal store of memories.

memory dump *n. Computers* → **core dump**.

memory stick *n.* → **USB drive**.

men /mɛn/ *n.* **1.** plural of **man**. –*phr.* **2. the men in white coats**, *Colloq.* (*humorous*) the supposed employees of a mental institution who collect insane people for incarceration.

menace /'mɛnəs/ *n.* **1.** something that threatens to cause evil, harm, injury, etc.; a threat. **2.** *Colloq.* nuisance. –*v.t.* (**-aced, -acing**) **3.** to utter or direct a threat against; threaten. **4.** to serve as a probable cause of evil, etc., to. –**menacer**, *n.* –**menacingly**, *adv.*

menacing driving *n.* an offence punishable in law whereby one driver of a vehicle intimidates another by their aggressive driving.

ménage à trois /meɪ,naʒ ə 'trwa/ *n.* a household of three people, at least one of whom is having a sexual relationship with the other two.

menagerie /mə'nædʒəri/ *n.* **1.** a collection of wild or strange animals, especially for exhibition. **2.** a place where they are kept or exhibited.

menarche /'mɛnak/ *n. Physiol.* the onset of menstruation in a young woman. Compare **menopause**.

mend /mɛnd/ *v.t.* **1.** to make whole or sound by repairing, as something broken, worn, or otherwise damaged; repair: *to mend clothes*; *to mend a road.* **2.** to remove or correct defects or errors in. **3.** to remove or correct (a defect, etc.). **4.** to set right; make better; improve: *to mend matters.* *−v.i.* **5.** to progress towards recovery, as a sick person. **6.** (of conditions) to improve. *−n.* **7.** the act of mending; repair or improvement. **8.** a mended place. *−phr.* **9. on the mend, a.** recovering from sickness. **b.** improving in state of affairs. **−mendable,** *adj.* **−mender,** *n.*

mendacious /mɛnˈdeɪʃəs/ *adj.* **1.** false or untrue: *a mendacious report.* **2.** lying or untruthful. **−mendaciously,** *adv.* **−mendacity** /mɛnˈdæsəti/, **mendaciousness,** *n.*

mendicant /ˈmɛndəkənt/ *adj.* **1.** begging, practising begging, or living on alms. **2.** relating to or characteristic of a beggar. *−n.* **3.** someone who lives by begging; a beggar. **4.** a mendicant friar. **−mendicancy,** *n.* **−mendicity,** *n.*

menhir /ˈmɛnhɪə/ *n.* an upright monumental stone, standing either alone or with others, as in a cromlech, found in various parts of Europe, also in Africa and Asia.

menial /ˈminiəl/ *adj.* **1.** relating or proper to domestic servants. **2.** of lowly status. *−n.* **3.** a domestic servant. **4.** a person employed in a lowly position to do work of an unfulfilling nature. **−menially,** *adv.*

meninges /məˈnɪndʒiz/ *pl. n.* (*sing.* **meninx** /ˈmiːnɪŋks/) *Anat.* the three membranes (dura mater, arachnoid, and pia mater) enveloping the brain and spinal cord. **−meningeal,** *adj.*

meningitis /mɛnənˈdʒaɪtəs/ *n. Pathol.* inflammation of the meninges, especially of the pia mater and arachnoid. **−meningitic** /mɛnənˈdʒɪtɪk/, *adj.*

meningococcal disease /mənɪndʒəˈkɒkəl dəˌziz/ *n.* a serious form of meningitis, sometimes also involving septicaemia, caused by the meningococcal bacterium, *Neisseria meningitidis,* marked by its rapid onset from flu-like symptoms.

meniscus /məˈnɪskəs/ *n.* (*pl.* **-nisci** /-ˈnɪsaɪ/) **1.** a crescent or crescent-shaped body. **2.** *Optics* a lens with a crescent-shaped section. **3.** *Physics* the convex or concave upper surface of a column of liquid, the curvature of which is caused by capillarity. **4.** *Anat.* a disc of cartilage between the articulating ends of the bones in a joint. **−meniscoid,** *adj.*

meno- a word element meaning 'month'.

menopause /ˈmɛnəpɔz/ *n. Physiol.* **1.** the final cessation of menstruation, occurring usually between the ages of 45 and 55. **2.** the period of irregular menstrual cycles prior to the final cessation of menstruation; climacteric. **−menopausal,** *adj.*

men's business *n.* **1.** Also, **man's business.** (in Aboriginal societies) matters, especially cultural traditions, which are the exclusive preserve of men, especially ceremonies which are open only to men. **2.** subjects which men may prefer to discuss with other men rather than with women, especially medical matters relating to men, bodily functions, etc. **3.** *Colloq.* (*humorous*) activities seen to be especially favoured or understood by men. Also, **secret men's business.**

menses /ˈmɛnsiz/ *pl. n. Physiol.* the (approximately) monthly discharge of blood and mucosal tissue from the uterus.

menstrual cycle *n.* (in most primates) the approximately monthly cycle of ovulation and menstruation.

menstruate /ˈmɛnstrueɪt/ *v.i.* to discharge the menses. **−menstrual,** *adj.*

menstruation /mɛnstruˈeɪʃən/ *n.* **1.** the act of discharging the menses. **2.** the period of menstruating.

mensuration /mɛnʃəˈreɪʃən/ *n.* **1.** the branch of mathematics that deals with the determination of length, area, and volume. **2.** the act, art, or process of measuring. **−mensural** /ˈmɛnsərəl/, *adj.* **−mensurative** /ˈmɛnʃərətɪv/, *adj.*

-ment a suffix of nouns, often concrete, denoting an action or state resulting (*abridgement, refreshment*), a product (*fragment*), or means (*ornament*).

mental[1] /ˈmɛntl/ *adj.* **1.** of or relating to the mind. **2.** performed by or existing in the mind: *mental arithmetic.* **3.** of or relating to the intellect; intellectual. **4.** denoting a disorder of the mind. **5.** of or relating to the care of those with disordered minds: *mental hospital, mental nurse.* **6.** *Colloq.* foolish or mad. *−phr.* **7. chuck** (or **throw**) **a mental,** *Colloq.* **a.** to throw a tantrum. **b.** to pretend to be mentally ill for a particular purpose, as insurance fraud, etc. **−mentally,** *adv.*

mental[2] /ˈmɛntl/ *adj.* of or relating to the chin.

mental disease *n.* → **mental illness.**

mental health *n.* **1.** a condition in which mental functions are successfully performed and there is no mental illness. **2.** the branch of medicine or the health services that deal with people with mental illnesses.

mental illness *n.* any disorder of the mind which causes a person to behave, think or feel so abnormally as to cause suffering to themself or others. Also, **mental disease.**

mentality /mɛnˈtæləti/ *n.* (*pl.* **-ties**) **1.** mental capacity or endowment; intellectuality; mind: *she was of average mentality.* **2.** outlook; frame of mind: *of a vulgar mentality.*

menthol /ˈmɛnθɒl/ *n.* a colourless, crystalline alcohol, $C_{10}H_{20}O$, present in peppermint oil, used in perfume, cigarettes, and confectionery, and for colds and nasal disorders because of its cooling effect on mucous membranes. **−mentholated,** *adj.*

mention /ˈmɛnʃən/ *v.t.* **1.** to refer briefly to; refer to by name incidentally; name, specify, or speak of. **2.** to cite as for some meritorious act. *−n.* **3.** a speaking of or mentioning; a reference, direct or incidental. **4.** recognition, as for a meritorious act or achievement. *−phr.* **5. not to mention,** to say nothing of; in addition to. **−mentionable,** *adj.* **−mentioner,** *n.*

mentor /ˈmɛntɔ/ *n.* **1.** a wise and trusted counsellor. **2.** (especially in an organisation) a person who is considered to have sufficient experience or expertise to be able to assist others less experienced. *−v.t.* **3.** to act as a mentor towards: *in our school, the older students mentor the younger ones.* **−mentoring,** *n.*

menu /ˈmɛnju, ˈmɪnju/ *n.* **1.** a list of the dishes served at a meal; a bill of fare. **2.** the dishes served. **3.** *Computers* a range of optional procedures presented to an operator by a computer. **4.** any range of items listed for selection: *pillow menu; drinks menu.*

meow /miˈaʊ/ *n.* **1.** the sound a cat makes. *−v.i.* **2.** to make such a sound. Also, **miaow, miau.**

mercantile /ˈmɜkəntaɪl/ *adj.* **1.** of or relating to merchants or trade; commercial. **2.** engaged in trade or commerce.

mercenary /ˈmɜsənri, -sənəri/, *Orig. US* /ˈmɜsənɛri/ *adj.* **1.** working or acting merely for gain. **2.** hired (now only of soldiers serving in a foreign army). *−n.* (*pl.* **-naries**) **3.** a professional soldier serving in a foreign army. **4.** any hireling. **−mercenarily,** *adv.* **−mercenariness,** *n.*

mercer /ˈmɜsə/ *n.* a dealer in textile fabrics, especially silks, etc.

merchandise *n.* /ˈmɜtʃəndaɪs/ **1.** goods; commodities; especially manufactured goods. **2.** the stock of a store. *−v.i.* /ˈmɜtʃəndaɪz/ **3.** to trade. *−v.t.* /ˈmɜtʃəndaɪz/ **4.** to trade in; buy and sell. **−merchandiser,** *n.*

merchandising /ˈmɜtʃəndaɪzɪŋ/ *n.* the promotion, and planning of the sales of a product, by using all available techniques of display, advertising and marketing.

merchant /ˈmɜtʃənt/ *n.* **1.** someone who buys and sells commodities for profit; a wholesaler. **2.** *Colloq.* a person noted or notorious for the aspect of their behaviour specified: *a panic merchant; a standover merchant.*

–adj. **3.** relating to trade or commerce: *a merchant ship.* **4.** relating to the merchant navy.

merchant bank *n.* a private banking firm engaged chiefly in accepting and endorsing bills of exchange, underwriting new issues of securities, and advising on corporate strategy. Compare **retail bank**. Also, **investment bank**. –**merchant banker**, *n.* –**merchant banking**, *n.*

merchant navy *n.* the vessels of a nation engaged in commerce.

mercurial /mɜˈkjuriəl/ *adj.* **1.** relating to, consisting of or containing, or caused by the metal mercury. **2.** sprightly; volatile. **3.** flighty; fickle; changeable. *–n.* **4.** a preparation of mercury used as a drug. –**mercurially**, *adv.* –**mercurialness**, *n.*

mercury /ˈmɜkjəri/ *n.* (*pl.* **-ries**) **1.** *Chem.* a heavy, silver-white, liquid metallic element. *Symbol*: Hg; *atomic number*: 80; *relative atomic mass*: 200.59. **2. a.** mercury as used in a thermometer to measure temperature. **b.** the temperature as recorded by such a thermometer: *the mercury reached 40°C today.* **3.** a messenger, or carrier of news (sometimes used as name of a newspaper, etc.). –**mercuric**, *adj.*

mercy /ˈmɜsi/ *n.* (*pl.* **-cies**) **1.** compassionate or kindly forbearance shown towards an offender, an enemy, or other person in one's power; compassion, pity, or benevolence. **2.** disposition to be merciful: *an adversary wholly without mercy.* **3.** discretionary power as to clemency or severity, pardon or punishment, or the like: *be at the mercy of a conqueror. –phr.* **4. at the mercy of**, defenceless against; unprotected from. –**merciful**, *adj.* –**merciless**, *adj.*

mere¹ /mɪə/ *adj.* (**merest**) being nothing more nor better than what is specified; pure and simple.

mere² /mɪə/ *n.* a lake; a pond.

merely /ˈmɪəli/ *adv.* only as specified, and nothing more; simply: *merely as a matter of form.*

meretricious /mɛrəˈtrɪʃəs/ *adj.* **1.** alluring by a show of false attractions; showily attractive; tawdry. **2.** insincere. –**meretriciously**, *adv.* –**meretriciousness**, *n.*

merge /mɜdʒ/ *verb* (**merged**, **merging**) *–v.t.* **1.** to unite or combine. *–v.i.* **2.** to lose identity by absorption. *–phr.* **3. merge into**, to become swallowed up or absorbed by. **4. merge something in** (or **into**), to cause something to be swallowed up or absorbed in; to sink the identity of something by combination with. –**mergence** /ˈmɜdʒəns/, *n.*

merger /ˈmɜdʒə/ *n.* **1.** a statutory combination of two or more companies by the transfer of the properties to one surviving company. **2.** any combination of two or more business enterprises into a single enterprise. **3.** the act of merging.

meridian /məˈrɪdiən/ *n.* **1.** *Geog.* **a.** a great circle of the earth passing through the poles and any given point on the earth's surface and cutting the equator at right angles. **b.** the half of such a circle included between the poles. **2.** an imaginary line on the earth's surface which coincides with the horizontal component of the earth's magnetic field. **3.** the point or period of greatest development, power, etc.; zenith.

meringue /məˈræŋ/ *n.* **1.** a mixture of sugar and beaten egg whites formed into small cakes and baked, or spread over pastry, etc. **2.** a dish, cake, or shell made with it.

merino /məˈrinoʊ/ *n.* (*pl.* **-nos**) **1.** (*upper case*) one of a variety of sheep, originating in Spain, valued for its fine wool. **2.** wool from such sheep. **3.** a knitted fabric made of wool or wool and cotton. *–adj.* **4.** made of merino wool, yarn, or cloth. *–phr.* **5. pure Merino**, *Aust. Hist.* **a.** a free settler, especially one who opposed the social advancement of the emancipists. **b.** a member of an old

and established Australian family of free, not convict, descent.

merit /ˈmɛrət/ *n.* **1.** excellence; worth. **2.** something that deserves reward or praise; a commendable quality, act, etc.: *the merits of a book; the merits of a performance.* **3.** (*pl.*) the basic right and wrong of a matter: *the merits of a case.* **4.** something that is deserved, whether good or bad. **5.** (*sometimes pl.*) the state or fact of deserving: *to treat a person according to their merits. –v.t.* **6.** to be worthy of; deserve.

meritocracy /mɛrəˈtɒkrəsi/ *n.* **1.** persons collectively who have reached positions of authority by reason of real or supposed merit (contrasted with *aristocracy*, etc.). **2.** government or administration by such persons. –**meritocratic**, *adj.*

meritorious /mɛrəˈtɔriəs/ *adj.* deserving of reward or commendation; possessing merit. –**meritoriously**, *adv.* –**meritoriousness**, *n.*

merlot /ˈmɜloʊ/ *n.* (*sometimes upper case*) **1.** a dark blue grape variety used in winemaking. **2.** the red wine made from this grape variety.

mermaid /ˈmɜmeɪd/ *n.* an imaginary female marine creature typically having the head and trunk of a woman and the tail of a fish.

merry /ˈmɛri/ *adj.* (**-rier**, **-riest**) **1.** full of cheer or gaiety; festive; joyous in disposition or spirit. **2.** laughingly cheerful; mirthful; hilarious. **3.** *Archaic* pleasant or delightful: *merry England.* **4.** *Colloq.* slightly intoxicated. *–phr.* **5. make merry**, to be festive. –**merrily**, *adv.* –**merriness**, **merriment**, *n.*

merry-go-round *n.* **1.** a revolving machine, as a circular platform fitted with wooden horses, etc., on which persons, especially children, ride for amusement; carousel. **2.** any whirl or rapid round of events, social activities, etc.

mesa /ˈmeɪsə/ *n.* a land form having a relatively flat top and bounded wholly or in part with steep rock walls, common in arid and semi-arid parts of the south-western US but also occurring in areas of inland Australia.

mescal /mɛsˈkæl/ *n.* **1.** either of two species of cactus, *Lophophora williamsii* or *L. lewinii*, of the southern US and northern Mexico, whose button-like tops (**mescal buttons**) are dried and used as a stimulant, especially by the indigenous people of these areas. **2.** an intoxicating spirit distilled from the fermented juice of certain species of agave. **3.** any agave yielding this spirit.

mescaline /ˈmɛskəlin, -lən/ *n.* a white water-soluble crystalline powder, $C_{11}H_{17}NO_3$, obtained from mescal buttons, used to produce hallucinations. Also, **mescalin**.

mesh /mɛʃ/ *n.* **1.** one of the open spaces of network of a net. **2.** (*pl.*) the threads that bound such spaces. **3.** (*pl.*) means of catching or holding fast: *caught in the meshes of the law.* **4.** a network or net. **5.** a knitted, woven, or knotted fabric, with open spaces between the threads. **6.** light woven or welded interlocking links or wires, as used for reinforcement, for sieves, etc. **7.** *Machinery* **a.** the engagement of gear teeth. **b.** **in mesh**, with gears engaged. *–v.t.* **8.** to catch or entangle in or as in the meshes of a net; enmesh. **9.** to form with meshes, as a net. **10.** to cause to coordinate or interlock. **11.** *Machinery* to engage, as gear teeth. *–v.i.* **12.** to become enmeshed. **13.** to interlock or coordinate. **14.** *Machinery* to become or be engaged, as the teeth of one wheel with those of another. *–adj.* **15.** in the form of a mesh: *mesh stockings.* –**meshing**, *n.*

mesmerise /ˈmɛzməraɪz/ *v.t.* **1.** to hypnotise. **2.** to fascinate; dominate; spellbind. Also, **mesmerize**. –**mesmerisation** /mɛzməraɪˈzeɪʃən/, *n.* –**mesmeriser**, *n.*

mesne /min/ *adj. Law* intermediate or intervening.

meso- a word element meaning 'middle', used in combination, chiefly in scientific terms. Also, **mes-**.

Mesolithic /mɛsoʊˈlɪθɪk, miz-/ *adj.* (*sometimes lower case*) of, relating to, or characteristic of a period between the Palaeolithic and Neolithic periods of the Stone Age.

meson /ˈmizɒn/ *n. Physics* any of a group of elementary particles, all of which have rest masses between that of the electron and the proton. Also, **mesotron**.

mesopause /ˈmizoʊpɔz/ *n.* the outer boundary of the earth's mesosphere where it meets the thermosphere, at an altitude of about 80 km above the earth.

mesosphere /ˈmɛsoʊsfɪə, ˈmiz-/ *n.* one of the concentric layers of the earth's atmosphere between the stratosphere and the thermosphere; at an altitude between 50 and 80 km above the earth, in which the temperature decreases rapidly with height.

mesothelioma /mizəθiːliˈoʊmə, mɛzə-/ *n.* (*pl.* **-omas** *or* **-omata**) a tumour, usually malignant, of the covering of the lung or lining of the chest and abdominal cavities, associated with exposure to airborne asbestos fibres.

Mesozoic /mɛsəˈzoʊɪk, miz-/ *Geol.* –*adj.* **1.** relating to the geological era of rocks between the Palaeozoic and Cainozoic; era of reptiles. –*n.* Also, **Mesozoic era**. **2.** the era of rocks including the Triassic, Jurassic, and Cretaceous periods or systems.

mess /mɛs/ *n.* **1.** a dirty or untidy condition: *the room was in a mess.* **2.** a state of embarrassing confusion: *his affairs are in a mess.* **3.** an unpleasant or difficult situation: *to get into a mess.* **4.** a dirty or untidy mass, litter, or jumble: *a mess of papers.* **5.** excrement, especially of an animal. **6.** a place where service personnel, etc., eat together. **7.** a place used by officers and senior NCOs for eating, recreation, and entertaining. **8.** *Navy* the living quarters of the crew. **9.** a group regularly taking meals together. **10.** a sloppy or unappetising preparation of food. **11.** a dish or quantity of soft or liquid food. **12.** *Colloq.* a person whose life is confused or without coherent purpose, often due to psychological difficulties. –*v.t.* **13.** Also, **mess up**. to make dirty or untidy: *mess up a room.* **14.** to make a mess of, or muddle (affairs, etc.). –*v.i.* **15.** to eat in company, especially as a member of a mess. **16.** to make a dirty or untidy mess. –*phr.* **17. make a mess of**, to perform unsuccessfully; botch. **18. mess around** (or **about**), *Colloq.* **a.** to busy oneself in an untidy or confused way. **b.** to waste time. **c.** to play the fool. **19. mess around with**, to associate with, especially for immoral or illegal purposes. **20. mess in**, *Colloq.* to meddle officiously in: *to mess in politics.* **21. mess someone around** (or **about**), *Colloq.* to cause inconvenience to someone. **22. mess with**, *Colloq.* to associate with; have dealings with: *don't mess with him, he's trouble.* –**messy**, *adj.*

message /ˈmɛsɪdʒ/ *n.* **1.** a communication, as of information, advice, direction, or the like, transmitted through a messenger or other agency. **2.** an inspired communication of a prophet. **3.** the moral or meaning intended to be conveyed by a book, film, play, or the like. **4.** the persuasive meaning intended to be conveyed by a document, advertisement, etc. –*v.t.* **5.** to communicate with (someone) by text messaging. –*phr.* **6. do** (or **go**) **a message**, *Aust., NZ* to run an errand for someone: *I have to do a message for the teacher.* **7. do the messages**, *Aust., NZ Colloq.* to perform errands, especially to do the shopping. **8. get the message**, *Colloq.* to understand. **9. on message**, completely focused on an issue and not distracted by irrelevant matters.

message board *n.* **1.** a board, located in a public place, to which messages can be affixed. **2.** a location on a website for posting messages available to be read by all visitors to the site.

messaging /ˈmɛsədʒɪŋ/ *n.* communication by text messages.

messenger /ˈmɛsəndʒə/ *n.* **1.** someone who bears a message or goes on an errand, especially as a matter of duty or business. **2.** someone employed to convey official dispatches or to go on other official or special errands: *a bank messenger.* **3.** anything that conveys a message.

messenger RNA *n. Physiol.* the RNA containing the information to form specific proteins by the process of protein synthesis.

Messiah /məˈsaɪə/ *n.* **1.** (in Judaism) the expected deliverer from oppression, seen as a great military and religious leader. **2.** (in Christianity) Jesus, seen as a deliverer from the power of evil. **3.** a hoped-for liberator of a country or people. –**Messiahship**, *n.* –**Messianic** /mɛsiˈænɪk/, *adj.*

messmate /ˈmɛsmeɪt/ *n.* **1.** a fellow member of a mess. **2.** any of a number of Australian trees of the genus *Eucalyptus*, especially *E. obliqua*, a tall forest tree of south-eastern Australia.

met /mɛt/ *v.* past tense and past participle of **meet**.

meta- **1.** a prefix meaning 'among', 'together with', 'after', 'behind', 'along with', as in *metacarpus, metatarsus*. **2.** a prefix meaning 'operating at a higher level', as in *metalanguage, meta-theory, metalevels*. **3.** a prefix indicating transposition or change, as in *metachromatism, metasomatism*. **4.** *Chem.* **a.** a prefix meaning 'containing least water', used of acids and salts, as in *metaphosphoric acid*, HPO₃. **b.** a prefix indicating the presence of a benzene ring with two substituents in the 1,3 positions.

metabolism /məˈtæbəlɪzəm/ *n. Physiol.* the sum of the processes or chemical changes in an organism or a single cell by which food is built up (*anabolism*) into living protoplasm and by which protoplasm is broken down (*catabolism*) into simpler compounds with the exchange of energy. –**metabolic** /mɛtəˈbɒlɪk/, *adj.* –**metabolise, metabolize**, *v.*

metadata /ˈmɛtədeɪtə, ˈmɛtədatə/ *n.* information about data, especially in relation to its structure and organisation.

metal /ˈmɛtl/ *n.* **1.** any of a group of elements, e.g. gold, silver, copper, tin, etc., which are shiny in appearance, malleable, ductile, generally electropositive, and are good conductors of electricity. **2.** a mixture composed wholly or partly of these substances; alloy. **3.** See **mettle**. **4.** Also, **road metal**. broken stone used for stability and drainage on railway tracks or for surfacing roads or mixing with cement to make concrete; blue metal. –*v.t.* (**-alled** *or, Chiefly US*, **-aled, -alling** *or, Chiefly US*, **-aling**) **5.** to supply or cover with metal. –**metallic** /məˈtælɪk/, *adj.* –**metallically** /məˈtælɪkli/, *adv.*

metalanguage /ˈmɛtəlæŋgwɪdʒ/ *n.* a language or code used to discuss a given object language or some aspect of it, as the syntax.

metal fatigue *n.* the cumulative damage suffered by metal which is subjected to repeated stress causing it to suffer localised cracking or damage and ultimate failure under load.

metallurgy /ˈmɛtəlɜdʒi, məˈtælədʒi/ *n.* **1.** the science of metals and their structures and properties. **2.** the art or science of separating metals from their ores, compounding alloys, or working metals. –**metallurgic** /mɛtəˈlɜdʒɪk/, **metallurgical** /mɛtəˈlɜdʒɪkəl/, *adj.* –**metallurgically** /mɛtəˈlɜdʒɪkli/, *adv.* –**metallurgist** /məˈtælədʒəst, ˈmɛtələdʒəst/, *n.*

metalwork /ˈmɛtlwɜk/ *n.* **1.** the art or craft of working with metal. **2.** objects produced by metalwork. –**metalworking**, *n.* –**metalworker**, *n.*

metamorphosis /mɛtəˈmɔfəsəs/ *n.* (*pl.* **-phoses** /-fəsiz/) **1.** a change of form, structure, substance or character;

transformation. **2.** the form resulting from any such change. **3.** a change of form during the growth of an animal by which it is adapted to a special environment or way of living usually different from that of the stage before: *the metamorphosis of tadpoles into frogs.* –**metamorphic**, *adj.*

metaphor /'mɛtəfə, -fɔ/ *n.* **1.** a figure of speech in which a term or phrase is applied to something to which it is not literally applicable, in order to suggest a resemblance, as *A mighty fortress is our God. –phr.* **2. mixed metaphor**, a figurative expression in which two or more metaphors are employed, producing an incongruous assemblage of ideas, as *the king put the ship of state on its feet.* –**metaphorical** /mɛtə'fɔrɪkəl/, **metaphoric** /mɛtə'fɔrɪk/, *adj.* –**metaphorically** /mɛtə'fɔrɪkli/, *adv.*

metaphysical /mɛtə'fɪzɪkəl/ *adj.* **1.** *Philos.* **a.** concerned with abstract thought or subjects, as existence, causality, truth, etc. **b.** concerned with first principles and ultimate grounds, as being, time, substance. **2.** highly abstract or abstruse. **3.** of or relating to that school of early 17th century English poets of whom John Donne was the chief, whose characteristic style is highly intellectual, philosophical, and crowded with ingenious conceits and turns of wit. –**metaphysically**, *adv.*

metaphysics /mɛtə'fɪzɪks/ *n.* **1.** the branch of philosophy that deals with first principles, including the sciences of being (*ontology*) and of the origin and structure of the universe (*cosmology*). It is always intimately connected with a theory of knowledge (*epistemology*). **2.** philosophy, especially in its more abstruse branches. –**metaphysician** /mɛtəfə'zɪʃən/, *n.*

metastasise /mə'tæstəsaɪz/ *v.i.* (especially of cells of malignant tumours, or microorganisms) to spread to other regions by dissemination usually through the blood circulation or lymphatic systems. Also, **metastasize**. –**metastasis** /mə'tæstəsəs/, *n.* –**metastatic** /mɛtə'stætɪk/, *adj.*

mete /mit/ *phr.* **mete out**, to distribute or apportion by measure; allot: *to rely on the judiciary to mete out fit punishment.* –**metage**, *n.*

meteor /'mitiə, -tiə/ *n.* **1.** a transient fiery streak in the sky produced by a meteoroid passing through the earth's atmosphere; a bolide or shooting star. **2.** any meteoroid or meteorite. **3.** someone or something that has a brief, dazzling success; prodigy; marvel.

meteoric /miti'ɒrɪk/ *adj.* **1.** relating to or like a meteor. **2.** consisting of meteors: *a meteoric shower.* **3.** flashing like a meteor; transiently brilliant: *a meteoric career.* **4.** swift or rapid. –**meteorically**, *adv.*

meteorite /'mitiəraɪt/ *n.* **1.** a mass of stone or metal that has reached the earth from outer space; a fallen meteoroid. **2.** a meteor or a meteoroid. –**meteoritic** /mitiə'rɪtɪk/, *adj.*

meteoroid /'mitiərɔɪd/ *n.* any of the small bodies, often remnants of comets, travelling through space, which, when encountering the earth's atmosphere, are heated to luminosity, thus becoming meteors.

meteorology /mitiə'rɒlədʒi/ *n.* the science dealing with the atmosphere and its phenomena, especially as relating to weather. –**meteorological** /mitiərə'lɒdʒɪkəl/, *adj.* –**meteorologist**, *n.*

meteor shower *n.* a celestial event in which a group of meteoroids enter the earth's atmosphere at high speed, burning and incandescing from the friction, and appearing as streaks of light radiating from a particular area of the sky.

meter /'mitə/ *n.* **1.** an instrument that measures, especially one that automatically measures and records the quantity of gas, water, electricity, or the like, passing through it or actuating it. –*v.t.* **2.** to measure by means of a meter.

-meter[1] a word element used in names of instruments for measuring quantity, extent, degree, etc., as in *altimeter*, *barometer*.

-meter[2] (in words taken from Greek or Latin) a word element denoting a certain poetic measure or rhythmic pattern, depending on the number of feet constituting the verse, as in *pentameter*, *trimeter*.

methadone /'mɛθədoʊn/ *n.* a powerful analgesic drug used for the treatment of drug withdrawal symptoms.

methamphetamine /mɛθæm'fɛtəmin/ *n.* a synthetic drug which acts as a powerful central nervous system stimulant. See **ice** (def. 8), **speed** (def. 6), **ecstasy** (def. 3).

methane /'miθeɪn/ *n.* a colourless, odourless, flammable gas, CH_4, the main constituent of marsh gas and the firedamp of coal mines, and obtained commercially from natural gas; the first member of the methane or paraffin series of hydrocarbons.

methane converter *n.* a device which converts methane to hydrogen with the by-product carbon dioxide being disposed of through carbon sequestration.

methanol /'mɛθənɒl/ *n.* → **methyl alcohol**.

methinks /mi'θɪŋks/ *v.* (*impersonal*) (**methought**) *Archaic* it seems to me.

metho /'mɛθoʊ/ *n.* *Colloq.* **1.** methylated spirits. **2.** someone addicted to drinking methylated spirits.

method /'mɛθəd/ *n.* **1.** a mode of procedure, especially an orderly or systematic mode: *a method of instruction.* **2.** a way of doing something, especially in accordance with a definite plan. **3.** order or system in doing anything: *to work with method.* **4.** orderly or systematic arrangement. –*phr.* **5. method in one's madness**, reason or sense underlying one's apparent stupidity.

method acting *n.* an acting technique by which actors try to immerse themselves in the emotional world of the character they are portraying so that the responses required by the part have a feeling of authenticity because they draw on a deeper emotional base. –**method actor**, *n.*

methodical /mə'θɒdɪkəl/ *adj.* performed, disposed, or acting in a systematic way; systematic; orderly: *a methodical man.* Also, **methodic**. –**methodically**, *adv.* –**methodicalness**, *n.*

methodology /mɛθə'dɒlədʒi/ *n.* (*pl.* **-gies**) a systematic approach to scientific inquiry based on logical principle, employed in various sciences.

methyl /'mɛθəl/ *n.* a univalent hydrocarbon radical, CH_3, derived from methane.

methyl alcohol *n.* a colourless, flammable, poisonous liquid, CH_3OH, of the alcohol class, formerly obtained by the distillation of wood, but now produced synthetically from carbon monoxide and hydrogen, used as a fuel, solvent, etc.; wood alcohol. Also, **methanol**.

methylated spirits /mɛθəleɪtəd 'spɪrəts/ *n.* ethyl alcohol denatured with 5–10 per cent of methyl alcohol to prevent its use as a beverage; sometimes also contains pyridine and methyl violet dye although the industrial spirit is normally free of these additives.

methylene /'mɛθəlin/ *n.* a bivalent hydrocarbon radical, CH_2, derived from methane.

meticulous /mə'tɪkjələs/ *adj.* solicitous about minute details; minutely or finically careful: *he was meticulous about his personal appearance.* –**meticulousness**, *n.* –**meticulously**, *adv.*

metier /'mɛtieɪ/ *n.* **1.** trade; profession; line of work or activity. **2.** a skill, activity, etc., in which a person is especially proficient: *his metier was the solacing of rich widows.* Also, **métier**.

metonymy /mə'tɒnəmi/ *n.* *Rhetoric* the use of the name of one thing for that of another to which it has some logical relation, as 'sceptre' for 'sovereignty' or 'the bottle' for 'strong drink'. **–metonymic** /mɛtə'nɪmɪk/, *adj.*

metre[1] /'miːtə/ *n.* **1.** a metric unit of length, equal to approximately 1.094 yards. **2.** the SI base unit of measurement of length equal to the distance travelled by electromagnetic radiation through a vacuum in 1/299 792 458 second; until 1983, defined as the distance equal to 1/650 763.73 wavelengths in vacuum of the (orange-red) radiation corresponding to the transition between the levels $2p_{10}$ and $5d_5$ of the krypton-86 atom; originally intended to be one ten millionth of the distance from the north pole to the equator measured on a meridian and in 1889 defined as the distance between lines on a standard bar, kept at the International Bureau of Weights and Measures in Sèvres, France. *Symbol:* m Also, *US*, **meter**.

metre[2] /'miːtə/ *n.* a poetic measure; arrangement of words in regularly measured or patterned or rhythmic lines or verses. Also, *US*, **meter**.

-metre a word element meaning 'metres', 'of or relating to a metre', as in *kilometre*.

metric[1] /'mɛtrɪk/ *adj.* relating to the metre or to the system of measures and weights originally based upon it.

metric[2] /'mɛtrɪk/ *adj.* → **metrical**.

metrical /'mɛtrɪkəl/ *adj.* **1.** relating to metre or poetic measure. **2.** composed in metre or verse. **3.** relating to measurement. Also, **metric**. **–metrically**, *adv.*

metricate /'mɛtrəkeɪt/ *v.t.* to convert to metric units.

metrication /mɛtrə'keɪʃən/ *n.* the process of conversion from British or imperial units to the metric units.

metric system *n.* a decimal system of measurement, first adopted in France in 1795, and adopted internationally by the Metric Convention in 1875. The modern metric system, known as the International System of Units (SI), was adopted in 1960. It comprises seven *base units*, the metre (m), kilogram (kg), second (s), ampere (A), kelvin (K), mole (mol), and candela (cd), two *supplementary units*, the radian (rad) and the steradian (sr), and *derived units*, formed by combining base and supplementary units according to the algebraic relations linking the corresponding physical quantities. Special names have been given to some derived units; thus the unit of power, defined as a joule per second, is called a *watt* (W).

metric ton *n.* → **tonne**.

metronome /'mɛtrənoʊm/ *n.* a mechanical contrivance for marking time, as for music. **–metronomic** /mɛtrə-'nɒmɪk/, *adj.*

metropolis /mə'trɒpələs/ *n.* (*pl.* **-lises**) **1.** the chief city (not necessarily the capital) of a country, state, or region. **2.** a central or principal point, as of some activity. **3.** the chief see of an ecclesiastical province.

metropolitan /mɛtrə'pɒlətən/ *adj.* of, relating to, or characteristic of a metropolis or chief city, or of the people who live in it.

metrosexual /mɛtroʊ'sɛkʃuəl/ *n.* **1.** a heterosexual male who devotes such attention to his appearance and presentation as would conventionally be considered feminine, such as the use of cosmetics, hair colouring, etc. **–adj. 2.** of or relating to such a male. **–metrosexuality**, *n.*

-metry a word element denoting the process of measuring, abstract for *-meter*, as in *anthropometry, chronometry*.

mettle /'mɛtl/ *n.* **1.** the characteristic disposition or temper: *to try a person's mettle.* **2.** spirit; courage. *–phr.* **3. on one's mettle**, incited to one's best.

mew /mju/ *n.* **1.** the sound a cat makes. **–v.i. 2.** to make this sound.

mews /mjuz/ *n.* (*usu. construed as sing.*) **1.** a set of stables or garages, usually with living accommodation attached, around a yard, court, or alley. **2.** a street, yard,

or court lined by buildings originally used as stables and servants' quarters.

Mexican stand-off /mɛksɪkən 'stænd-ɒf/ *n. Colloq.* a situation in which two opponents threaten each other loudly but neither makes any attempt to resolve the conflict.

Mexican wave *n.* a wavelike motion among spectators at a sporting event, pop concert, etc., achieved by having sections of the crowd sequentially stand and raise their arms, and then sit down again.

mezzanine /'mɛzənin, mɛzə'nin/ *n.* **1.** a low storey between two other storeys of greater height, especially when the low storey and the one beneath it form part of one composition; entresol. *–adj.* **2.** of or relating to such a storey.

mezzo-soprano /mɛtsoʊ-sə'prɑnoʊ/ *n.* (*pl.* **-nos** or **-ni** /-ni/) *Music* a voice or voice part intermediate in compass between soprano and contralto. Also, **mezzo soprano**.

mia-mia /'maɪə-maɪə, 'miə-miə/ *n.* a temporary bush shelter traditionally used by Aboriginal people; gunyah; humpy.

miaow /mi'aʊ, mjaʊ/ *n.* **1.** → **meow**. *–v.i.* **2.** → **meow**.

miasma /mi'æzmə, maɪ-/ *n.* (*pl.* **-mas** or **-mata**) **1.** noxious exhalations from putrescent organic matter. **2.** an atmosphere damaging to one's state of mind. **–miasmic**, *adj.*

mica /'maɪkə/ *n.* any member of a group of minerals, hydrous disilicates of aluminium with other bases, chiefly potassium, magnesium, iron, and lithium, that separate readily (by cleavage) into thin, tough, often transparent, and usually elastic laminae. **–micaceous** /maɪ'keɪʃəs/, *adj.*

mice /maɪs/ *n.* plural of **mouse**.

Mick /mɪk/ *n. Colloq.* **1.** a Roman Catholic (especially of Irish extraction). **2.** an Irishman.

mickey finn /mɪki 'fɪn/ *n. Colloq.* a drink, usually alcoholic, which has been surreptitiously laced so as to cause to fall asleep, to discomfort, or in some way to incapacitate the person who drinks it. Also, **Mickey Finn**, **mickey**.

Mickey Mouse *adj. Colloq.* **1.** Also, **mickey mouse**. of or relating to something that is less in seriousness or value than its name would suggest: *a Mickey Mouse course of literature.* **2.** (of cross-bred dairy and beef cattle) part Friesian with white faces and mainly black bodies.

micky /'mɪki/ *phr.* **take the micky**, *Colloq.* (sometimes fol. by *out of*) to tease by mild ridicule.

micra /'maɪkrə/ *n.* a plural of **micron**.

MICR encoding /maɪkər ɒn'koʊdɪŋ/ *n.* a machine-reading system by which ferrous-impregnated ink characters encoded on documents, as cheques, are read by a magnetically-sensitive device.

micro /'maɪkroʊ/ *adj.* individual or particular (opposed to *macro*): *at the micro level.*

micro- **1.** a prefix meaning: **a.** 'very small', as in *microorganism, microcosm.* **b.** 'enlarging' or 'amplifying', as in *microphone, microscope, microbarograph.* **2.** a prefix denoting 10^{-6} of a given unit, as in *microvolt. Symbol:* μ Also, (*before vowels*), **micr-**.

microbe /'maɪkroʊb/ *n.* a microorganism, usually one of vegetable nature; a germ. **–microbial** /maɪ'kroʊbiəl/, **microbic** /maɪ'kroʊbɪk/, *adj.*

microbiology /ˌmaɪkroʊbaɪ'ɒlədʒi/ *n.* the science concerned with the occurrence, activities, and utilisation of the extremely small, microscopic and submicroscopic organisms. **–microbiological** /ˌmaɪkroʊbaɪə'lɒdʒɪkəl/, *adj.* **–microbiologist**, *n.*

microblog /'maɪkroʊblɒg/ *n.* **1.** an internet posting which is extremely short, usually up to 140 characters, designed to give a brief but immediate text update. *–v.i.*

(**-blogged**, **-blogging**) **2.** to issue such an internet posting. –**microblogging**, *n.* –**microblogger**, *n.*

microbusiness /'maɪkroʊbɪznəs/ *n.* a small business operated by one person.

microchip /'maɪkroʊtʃɪp/ *n.* **1.** a very small chip (**chip** def. 6). **2.** such a chip with identifying information, as a unique number, recorded on it. –*v.t.* (**-chipped**, **-chipping**) **3.** to insert a microchip in, as a means of identification.

microclimate /'maɪkroʊ,klaɪmət/ *n.* the climate affecting a localised region, often created by terrain or conditions which are not prevalent throughout the wider area, ranging from something as small as a garden bed to something as large as a valley. Compare **macroclimate**. –**microclimatic** /,maɪkroʊklaɪˈmætɪk/, *adj.* –**microclimatically** /,maɪkroʊklaɪˈmætɪkli/, *adv.*

microcomputer /'maɪkroʊkəm,pjutə/ *n.* a small computer which has its central processor functions contained on a single printed circuit board.

microcopy /'maɪkroʊ,kɒpi/ *n.* (*pl.* **-pies**) a greatly reduced photographic copy of a book, page, etc., usually read by enlargement on a ground-glass screen.

microcosm /'maɪkrəkɒzəm/ *n.* **1.** a little world (opposed to *macrocosm*). **2.** anything regarded as a world in miniature. **3.** a human being viewed as an epitome of the universe. –**microcosmic** /maɪkrəˈkɒzmɪk/, **microcosmical** /maɪkrəˈkɒzmɪkəl/, *adj.*

microdisk /'maɪkroʊ,dɪsk/ *n.* a small computer disk designed for recording digital data.

microdot /'maɪkroʊ,dɒt/ *n.* **1.** a microphotograph reduced to the size of a printed or typed dot. **2.** *Colloq.* LSD in tablet form.

micro-economics /,maɪkroʊ-ɛkəˈnɒmɪks/ *n.* (*construed as sing.*) study of the economic system in terms of its different sectors. Compare **macro-economics**.

microfauna /'maɪkroʊfɔnə/ *n.* very small animals, usually too small to be seen with the naked eye, as single-celled protozoans and small nematodes. Compare **macrofauna**.

microfibre /'maɪkroʊfaɪbə/ *n.* an extremely fine synthetic textile which is wrinkle-resistant and easy to care for.

microfiche /'maɪkroʊfiʃ/ *n.* a microfilmed transparency about the size and shape of a filing card which may have on it many pages of print.

microfilm /'maɪkroʊfɪlm/ *n.* **1.** a narrow film, especially of motion-picture stock, on which microcopies are made. **2.** a film reproduction of a large or bulky publication, as a file of newspapers, used to conserve space or to copy material which is difficult to obtain. –*v.t.* **3.** to record on microfilm.

microflora /'maɪkroʊflɔrə/ *n.* microscopic plants.

microlight aircraft /maɪkrəlaɪt 'ɛəkraft/ *n.* an ultralight aircraft with weight shift controls for stabilisation. Also, **microlight**.

micromanage /'maɪkroʊmænɪdʒ/ *v.t.* (**-managed**, **-managing**) to manage closely by frequently inspecting and controlling the work of (employees), usually to the detriment of efficiency and output. –**micromanager**, *n.* –**micromanagement**, *n.*

micrometer /maɪˈkrɒmətə/ *n.* **1.** any of various devices for measuring minute distances, angles, etc., as in connection with a telescope or microscope. **2.** a U-shaped gauge for measuring thicknesses or short lengths in which the gap between the measuring faces is adjusted by a finely threaded screw, the end of which forms one face; a micrometer gauge. –**micrometry**, *n.*

micron /'maɪkrɒn/ *n.* (*pl.* **-cra** /-krə/ *or* **-crons**) the millionth part of a metre; micrometre. *Symbol*: μ

microorganism /maɪkroʊˈɔgənɪzəm/ *n.* a microscopic (animal or vegetable) organism.

microphone /'maɪkrəfoʊn/ *n.* an instrument which is capable of transforming the air-pressure waves of

sound into changes in electric currents or voltages. Qualifying adjectives, as *capacitor*, *crystal*, *velocity*, etc., describe the method of developing the electric quantity. –**microphonic** /maɪkrəˈfɒnɪk/, *adj.*

microprocessor /maɪkroʊˈproʊsɛsə/ *n.* a small stand-alone computer, often dedicated to specific functions, as directing a quality-control inspection in a factory or regulating a domestic procedure such as the keeping of a record of engagements, etc.

microscope /'maɪkrəskoʊp/ *n.* an optical instrument having a magnifying lens or a combination of lenses for inspecting objects too small to be seen, or to be seen distinctly and in detail, by the naked eye. –**microscopy** /maɪˈkrɒskəpi/, *n.* –**microscopist** /maɪˈkrɒskəpəst/, *n.*

microscopic /maɪkrəˈskɒpɪk/ *adj.* **1.** so small as to be invisible or indistinct without the use of the microscope. **2.** very small; tiny. **3.** of or relating to the microscope or its use. **4.** performing the work of a microscope. **5.** suggestive of the use of the microscope: *microscopic exactness*. –**microscopically**, *adv.*

microsuede /'maɪkroʊsweɪd/ *n.* a fabric with a suede finish, made from microfibre.

microwave /'maɪkrəweɪv, 'maɪkroʊ-/ *n.* **1.** an electromagnetic wave of extremely high frequency, approximately comprising the wavelength range from 50 cm to 1 mm. **2.** → **microwave oven**. –*v.t.* **3.** to cook (food) by using a microwave oven.

microwave oven *n.* an oven which cooks with unusual rapidity, by passing microwaves through food and generating heat inside it.

mid[1] /mɪd/ *adj.* **1.** central; at or near the middle point: *in the mid nineties of the last century*. **2.** *Phonetics* having a tongue position intermediate between high and low: *beet*, *bet*, and *bat* have high, mid, and low vowels respectively.

mid[2] /mɪd/ *prep.* → **amid**. Also, **'mid**.

mid- a combining form of 'middle'.

midair /mɪdˈɛə/ *n.* **1.** any elevated position above the ground. –*adj.* **2.** occurring or existing in midair. –*adv.* **3.** in a state of suspension.

midday /'mɪdeɪ/ *n.* **1.** the middle of the day; noon. –*adj.* **2.** of or relating to the middle part of the day.

middie /'mɪdi/ *n.* (*pl.* **-dies**) → **middy**.

middle /'mɪdl/ *adj.* **1.** being the same distance from both ends: *the middle point of a line*. **2.** being neither of any two opposites, but between them; halfway; intermediate; medium: *middle size*; *middle distance*. **3.** (*upper case*) (in various studies, e.g. history of a language, geology, history) being of the period of time that comes between other periods that are called Old and New, Upper and Lower, etc.: *Middle English*; *Middle Kingdom*. –*n.* **4.** the point, part, etc., which is the same distance from both ends of something. **5.** the waist, or middle part of the human body. –*phr.* **6. middle of the road**, not too much one way or the other; mediocre.

middle-aged /'mɪdl-eɪdʒd/ *adj.* **1.** intermediate in age between youth and old age; commonly, from about 45 to 60 years old. **2.** characteristic of or suitable for middle-aged people.

Middle Ages *pl. n.* the time in European history between classical antiquity and the Italian Renaissance (from the late 5th century to about AD 1350); sometimes restricted to the later part of this period (after 1100); sometimes extended to 1450 or 1500.

middle class *n.* a social class intermediate between the upper and lower classes, as a fluid socio-economic grouping comprising especially business and professional people and public servants of middle income, who do not have an upper-class or establishment background. –**middle-class**, *adj.*

middleman /'mɪdlmæn/ *n.* (*pl.* **-men**) **1.** a trader who makes a profit by buying from producers and selling to retailers or consumers. **2.** someone who acts as an intermediary between others. Also, **middle man**.

middle-of-the-road *adj.* **1.** between extremes; moderate. **2.** middlebrow; noncommittal. **3.** Also, **MOR**. of or relating to light or sentimental music, written to appeal to a wide audience. –**middle-of-the-roader**, *n.*

middleweight /ˈmɪdlweɪt/ *n.* **1.** a medium-to-heavy weight division in boxing. **2.** a boxer of this weight class.

middling /ˈmɪdlɪŋ/ *adj.* **1.** medium in size, quality, grade, rank, etc.; moderately large, good, etc. **2.** *Colloq.* in fairly good health. **3.** *Colloq.* mediocre; second-rate. –*n.* **4.** (*pl.*) any of various products or commodities of intermediate quality, grade, etc., as the coarser particles of ground wheat mingled with bran. –*phr.* **5. fair to middling**, *Colloq.* reasonably good; so-so. –**middlingly**, *adv.*

middy /ˈmɪdi/ *n.* (*pl.* **-dies**) *Aust.* a medium-sized glass, primarily used for serving beer; pot.

midge /mɪdʒ/ *n.* any of various small dipterous insects especially the non-biting Chironomidae, or the biting midges of the family Ceratopogonidae. See **gnat**. **2.** *Colloq.* a small or diminutive person.

midget /ˈmɪdʒət/ *n.* **1.** a very small person. **2.** something very small of its kind.

midi /ˈmɪdi/ *adj.* **1.** of or relating to a dress, skirt, or coat, with a hemline midway between a maxi and mini, usually about mid-calf. –*n.* **2.** such a dress, skirt, or coat.

midnight /ˈmɪdnaɪt/ *n.* **1.** the middle of the night; 12 o'clock at night. –*adj.* **2.** of or relating to midnight. **3.** resembling midnight, as in darkness. –*phr.* **4. burn the midnight oil**, to study or work far into the night. –**midnightly**, *adj., adv.*

midnight sun *n.* the sun visible at midnight in mid-summer in arctic and antarctic regions.

mid-off *n.* (in cricket) a fielding position on the off side, near the bowler.

mid-on *n.* (in cricket) a fielding position on the on side near the bowler.

midriff /ˈmɪdrɪf/ *n.* **1.** the diaphragm (in the human body). **2.** the middle part of the body, between the chest and the waist. –*adj.* **3.** of a dress, blouse, etc., which exposes this part of the body.

midshipman /ˈmɪdʃɪpmən/ *n.* a probationary rank held by naval cadets before qualifying as officers.

midst /mɪdst/ *n.* **1.** the position of anything surrounded by other things or parts, or occurring in the middle of a period of time, course of action, etc. **2.** the middle point, part, or stage. –*phr.* **3. in our (your, their) midst**, in the midst of us (you, them).

midstream *n.* /ˈmɪdˈstrim/ **1.** the middle of a stream. –*adv.* /ˈmɪdˈstrim/ **2.** in the middle of a stream: *we canoed midstream.* –*adj.* /ˈmɪdstrim/ **3.** of or relating to the middle of a stream. –*phr.* **4. change horses in midstream**, to change from one policy or procedure to another at a critical point. **5. in midstream**, in the middle; at a critical point.

midway *adv.* /ˈmɪdˈweɪ/ **1.** to the middle of the way or distance; halfway. –*adj.* /ˈmɪdweɪ/ **2.** in the middle.

mid wicket *n.* (in cricket) an on-side fielding position between square leg and mid-on.

midwife /ˈmɪdwaɪf/ *n.* (*pl.* **-wives** /ˈmɪdwaɪvz/) a nurse who assists women in childbirth. –**midwifery** /mɪdˈwɪfəri/, *n.*

mien /min/ *n.* air, bearing, or aspect, as showing character, feeling, etc.: *a man of noble mien.*

miffed /mɪft/ *adj. Colloq.* annoyed; displeased.

might[1] /maɪt/ *v.* (*modal*) **1.** expressing strong uncertainty: *I suppose he might be angry when he finds out.* **2.** referring to an event or situation contrary to fact: *we*

might all have been killed. **3.** used in tentative suggestions: *we might have a meal afterwards*; *you might check the tyre pressure.* **4.** used in very polite requests: *might I borrow your pen for a moment?* **5.** expressing reproach: *you might share the chocolates*; *he might have warned me.* **6.** past tense of **may**[1]: *they agreed we might go*; *he died so that we might live.* –*phr.* **7. might as well ..., a.** used to make a suggestion in the absence of a better alternative: *he won't turn up now – we might as well go home.* **b.** used to emphasise the unsatisfactory nature of a situation: *she won't listen – I might as well talk to a brick wall.*

might[2] /maɪt/ *n.* **1.** power to do or accomplish; ability. **2.** effective power or force of any kind. **3.** superior power: *the doctrine that might makes right.* –*phr.* **4. with might and main**, with utmost strength, vigour, force, or effort. –**mighty**, *adj.*

migraine /ˈmaɪɡreɪn, ˈmiɡreɪn/ *n. Pathol.* a paroxysmal headache often confined to one side of the head and usually associated with nausea; hemicrania.

migrate /maɪˈɡreɪt/ *v.i.* **1.** to go from one country, region, or place of abode to settle in another. **2.** to pass periodically from one region to another, as certain birds, fishes, and other animals. **3.** to transfer one's custom to a new system, service, etc. –*v.t.* **4.** *Computers* to transfer (data) from one system to another: *to migrate files from an old PC to a new one.* **5.** to transfer (customers, clients, etc.) to a new system, service, etc. –**migrant**, *n., adj.* –**migrator**, *n.* –**migratory**, *adj.*

migration /maɪˈɡreɪʃən/ *n.* **1.** the action of migrating: *the right of migration.* **2.** a migratory movement: *preparations for the migration.* **3.** a number or body of persons or animals migrating together. **4.** *Chem.* a movement or change of place of atoms within a molecule. **5.** *Computers* the transfer of data from one system to another. **6.** the transfer of customers, clients, etc., from one system or service to another. –**migrational**, *adj.*

migration corridor *n.* a narrow passage on land or sea along which migratory animals regularly travel in moving from one location to another as part of their migration cycle. Also, **corridor**.

mikado /məˈkadoʊ/ *n.* (*pl.* **-dos**) *Hist.* (*oft. upper case*) the emperor of Japan.

mike /maɪk/ *n. Colloq.* → **microphone**.

mil /mɪl/ *n.* **1.** a millilitre (0.001 of a litre), or cubic centimetre. **2.** a unit of length equal to 0.001 of an inch, used in measuring the diameter of wires.

milch /mɪltʃ/ *adj.* (of a cow, goat, or other animal) producing milk; kept for milk-production.

mild /maɪld/ *adj.* **1.** gentle in feeling or behaviour towards others. **2.** (of manners, speech, etc.) showing such gentleness. **3.** (of air, weather, etc.) not cold, severe, or extreme. **4.** not sharp, pungent, or strong: *a mild flavour.* **5.** gentle or moderate in degree, character or intensity: *mild regret*; *mild pain.* –**mildly**, *adv.* –**mildness**, *n.*

mildew /ˈmɪldju/ *n.* **1.** a plant disease usually characterised by a whitish coating or a discolouration on the surface, caused by any of various parasitic fungi. **2.** any of these fungi. **3.** similar coating or discolouration, due to fungi, on cotton and linen fabrics, paper, leather, etc., when exposed to moisture. –*v.t.* **4.** to affect with mildew. –*v.i.* **5.** to become affected with mildew. –**mildewy**, *adj.*

mile /maɪl/ *n.* **1.** a unit of measurement of length in the imperial system, equal to 5280 feet (1609.34 m). **2.** → **nautical mile**. **3.** any of various other lengths ascribed to the mile in different periods and in different countries. **4.** (*oft. pl.*) a large distance or quantity: *miles further*; *miles better.*

mileage /'maɪlɪdʒ/ *n.* **1.** the total length or distance expressed in miles. **2.** an aggregate number of miles or kilometres. **3.** an allowance for travelling expenses, at a specified rate per mile or kilometre. **4.** a ratio based on distance and fuel consumption used to indicate the fuel efficiency of a motor vehicle, expressed as miles per gallon or litres per kilometre. –*phr.* **5. get (good) mileage out of**, **a.** to get good use from (a vehicle) in terms of the ratio of miles (or kilometres) travelled to fuel consumption. **b.** to get good use out of (something) in terms of durability: *I got good mileage out of my old fridge.* **c.** to use advantageously as specified: *to get political mileage out of local scandal.*

milestone /'maɪlstoʊn/ *n.* **1.** a stone set up to mark the distance to or from a town, as along a highway or other line of travel. **2.** a birthday or some event regarded as marking a significant point in one's life or career.

milfoil /'mɪlfɔɪl/ *n.* a herbaceous plant, *Achillea millefolium*, with finely divided leaves and small white to red flowers, sometimes used in medicine as a tonic and astringent.

milieu /mi'ljɜ, mɪl'jɜ/ *n.* (*pl.* **milieus** *or* **milieux**) medium or environment.

militant /'mɪlətənt/ *adj.* **1.** combative; aggressive: *a militant reformer.* **2.** engaged in warfare; warring. –*n.* **3.** someone engaged in warfare or strife. **4.** a militant person. –**militancy**, *n.* –**militantly**, *adv.*

militarism /'mɪlətərɪzəm/ *n.* **1.** military spirit or policy. **2.** the principle of keeping a large military establishment. **3.** the tendency to regard military efficiency as the supreme ideal of the state, and to subordinate all other interests to those of the military. –**militaristic**, *adj.*

military /'mɪlətri, -təri/, *Orig. US* /-teri/ *adj.* **1.** of or relating to the armed forces. –*n.* **2.** soldiers generally; the armed forces: *the military.* –**militarily**, *adv.* –**militarist**, *adj.*

military service *n.* a period of service in the armed forces.

militate /'mɪləteɪt/ *v.i.* to operate (*against* or *in favour of*); have effect or influence: *every fact militated against his argument.* –**militation** /mɪlə'teɪʃən/, *n.*

militia /mə'lɪʃə/ *n.* **1.** a body of people enrolled for military service, called out periodically for drill and exercise but for actual service only in emergencies. **2.** a body of citizen soldiers as distinguished from professional soldiers. **3.** a member of a militia.

milk /mɪlk/ *n.* **1.** an opaque white or bluish white liquid secreted by the mammary glands of female mammals, serving for the nourishment of their young, and, in the case of the cow and some other animals, used by humans for food or as a source of dairy products. **2.** any liquid resembling this, as the liquid within a coconut, the juice or sap (latex) of certain plants, or various pharmaceutical preparations. –*v.t.* **3.** to press or draw milk by hand or machine from the udder of (a cow or other animal). **4.** to draw venom from (a spider, snake, etc.). **5.** to extract (the sap) from certain plants. **6.** to extract something as if by milking; siphon. **7.** to produce as a response; elicit: *to milk applause from an audience; to milk a penalty.* **8.** to seek to gain advantage from; exploit: *to milk the situation for sympathy.* –*v.i.* **9.** to yield milk, as a cow. **10.** to milk a cow or other animal. –*phr.* **11. cry over spilt milk**, to lament something which cannot be changed. **12. milk of human kindness**, tender emotions, especially pity. **13. milk someone dry**, to take from someone all their money, ideas, etc., for one's own benefit. **14. milk the till**, *Colloq.* to steal money from a cash register. –**milky**, *adj.*

milk bar *n.* **1.** a shop, often with an open front, where milk drinks, ice-cream, sandwiches, etc., are sold. **2.** *Chiefly Victoria* → **corner store**.

milking shed *n.* → **dairy** (def. 2).

milkmaid /'mɪlkmeɪd/ *n.* **1.** a woman who milks cows or is employed in a dairy. **2.** (*pl.*) either of two species of the genus *Burchardia*, family Liliaceae, native to Australia.

milk of magnesia *n.* a liquid suspension of magnesium hydroxide, Mg(OH)$_2$, used medicinally as an antacid or laxative.

milkshake /'mɪlkʃeɪk/ *n.* a frothy drink made of milk, flavouring, and sometimes ice-cream, shaken together. Also, **milk shake**.

milksop /'mɪlksɒp/ *n.* **1.** a dish of bread, etc., soaked in milk, as given to children and invalids. **2.** an effeminate man or youth. –**milksopism**, *n.*

milk tooth *n.* one of the temporary teeth of a mammal which are replaced by the permanent teeth. Also, **baby tooth**.

mill /mɪl/ *n.* **1.** a building or establishment fitted with machinery, in which any of various mechanical operations or forms of manufacture is carried on, especially the spinning or weaving of cotton or wool. **2.** a mechanical appliance or a building or establishment equipped with appliances for grinding corn into flour. **3.** a machine for grinding, crushing, pulverising, or extracting liquid from, any solid substance: *a coffee mill; a cider mill.* **4.** any institution or machine that churns out mass produced goods: *college is a diploma mill.* –*v.t.* **5.** to grind, work, treat, or shape in or with a mill. **6.** to finish the edge of (a coin, etc.) with a series of fine notches or transverse grooves. –*v.i.* Also, **mill about.** **7.** to move confusedly in a circle, as a herd of cattle. –*phr.* **8. go through the mill**, to undergo a gruelling or difficult experience. **9. run of the mill**, conventional; commonplace.

millennium /mə'lɛniəm/ *n.* (*pl.* **-ennia** /-niə/ *or* **-enniums**) **1.** a period of a thousand years. **2.** a thousandth anniversary. **3.** the period of 'a thousand years' (a phrase variously interpreted) during which Christ is to reign on earth, according to the prophetic statement in the Bible (Revelation 20:1-7). **4.** a period of general righteousness and happiness, especially in the indefinite future. –**millennial**, *adj.*

millennium bug *n. Computers* the inability of computer systems to recognise the abbreviation of the year 2000 as the final two digits '00', in accordance with the convention that the year is reduced to the last two numbers adopted in the 1960s because of the small amount of data storage space available at that time. Also, **millennium problem, Y2K problem.**

miller /'mɪlə/ *n.* **1.** someone who keeps or operates a mill, especially a flour mill. **2.** a milling machine.

millet /'mɪlət/ *n.* **1.** a cereal grass, *Setaria italica*, extensively cultivated in Asia and in southern Europe for its small seed or grain (used as a food for humans and fowls), but in the US grown chiefly for fodder. **2.** any of various related or similar grasses, especially those cultivated as grain plants or forage plants, as durra, and pearl millet. **3.** the grain of any of these grasses. **4.** the straw of any of these grasses, used in thatching, brooms, etc.

milli- a prefix denoting 10^{-3} of a given unit, as in *milligram. Symbol:* m

millibar /'mɪlibɑ/ *n.* a unit of atmospheric pressure, equal to 0.001 bar or 100 pascals.

milligram /'mɪləgræm/ *n.* a unit of mass equal to 0.001 gram. *Symbol:* mg

millilitre /'mɪləlɪtə/ *n.* a unit of capacity equal to 0.001 litre. *Symbol:* mL, ml Also, *US,* **milliliter**.

millimetre /'mɪləmitə/ *n.* a unit of length equal to 0.001 metre. *Symbol:* mm Also, *US,* **millimeter**.

milliner /'mɪlənə/ *n.* someone who makes or sells hats for women.

million /ˈmɪljən/ *n.* (*pl.* **-lions**, *as after a numeral*, **-lion**) **1.** a cardinal number, one thousand times one thousand, or 10^6. **2.** the amount of a thousand thousand units of money, as dollars, pounds, or euros. **3.** *Colloq.* a very great number. –*adj.* **4.** amounting to one million in numbers. –*phr.* **5. gone a million**, *Aust., NZ Colloq.* utterly defeated or ruined. **6. one in a million**, someone or something of great rarity or worth. –**millionth**, *adj.*

millionaire /mɪljəˈnɛə/ *n.* **1.** a person worth a million or millions, as of pounds, dollars, or euros. **2.** a very rich person. –**millionairess**, *n.*

millipede /ˈmɪləpid/ *n.* any of the many arthropods belonging to the class Diplopoda. These are slow-moving, mostly herbivorous, myriapods having a cylindrical body of numerous segments, most of which bear two pairs of legs. Also, **millepede**.

millpond /ˈmɪlpɒnd/ *n.* **1.** a pond for supplying water to drive a millwheel. **2.** an area of very calm water.

millstone /ˈmɪlstoʊn/ *n.* **1.** either of a pair of circular stones between which grain or other substance is ground, as in a mill. **2.** something that grinds or crushes. –*phr.* **3. a millstone around someone's neck**, a heavy burden on someone.

mime /maɪm/ *n.* **1.** the art or technique of expressing emotion, character, action, etc., by mute gestures and bodily movements. **2.** a play or entertainment in which the performers express themselves by such gestures and movements. **3.** a comedian or clown, especially one who entertains by mute gesture, facial expression, bodily movement, etc. –*v.t.* **4.** → **mimic**. –*v.i.* **5.** to play a part by mimicry, especially without words. –**mimer**, *n.* –**mimetic**, *adj.*

mimeograph /ˈmɪmiəɡræf, -ɡraf/ *n.* **1.** a stencil device for duplicating letters, drawings, etc. –*v.t.* **2.** to make copies of, using a mimeograph.

mimic /ˈmɪmɪk/ *v.t.* (**-icked, -icking**) **1.** to imitate or copy in action, speech, etc., often playfully or derisively. **2.** to imitate unintelligently or servilely; ape. **3.** (of things) to be an imitation of; simulate. –*n.* **4.** someone apt at imitating or mimicking the characteristic voice or gesture of others. **5.** an imitator or imitation.

mimicry /ˈmɪməkri/ *n.* (*pl.* **-cries**) **1.** the act, practice, or art of mimicking. **2.** *Zool.* the close external resemblance, as if from imitation or simulation, of an animal to some different animal or to surrounding objects, especially as serving for protection or concealment. **3.** an instance, performance, or result of mimicking.

minaret /mɪnəˈrɛt, ˈmɪnərɛt/ *n.* a lofty, often slender, tower or turret attached to a Muslim mosque, surrounded by or furnished with one or more balconies, from which the muezzin calls the people to prayer.

mince /mɪns/ *verb* (**minced, mincing**) –*v.t.* **1.** to cut or chop into very small pieces. **2.** to divide (land, a subject, etc.) into small parts. **3.** to soften (one's words, etc.) to a milder form. –*v.i.* **4.** to speak, walk, or move with a show of daintiness. –*n.* **5.** minced meat.

mincemeat /ˈmɪnsmit/ *n.* **1.** a mixture composed of minced apples, suet (and sometimes meat), candied peel, etc., with raisins, currants, etc., for filling a pie (mince pie). **2.** minced meat. **3.** anything cut up very small. –*phr.* **4. make mincemeat of**, *Colloq.* **a.** to defeat utterly, as in sport, or in verbal or physical assault: *the Tigers made mincemeat of the opposition.* **b.** to damage or reduce to ruin: *she made mincemeat of his suggestions.*

mind /maɪnd/ *n.* **1.** that which thinks, feels, and wills, exercises perception, judgement, reflection, etc., as in a human or other conscious being: *the processes of the mind.* **2.** *Psychol.* the psyche; the totality of conscious and unconscious activities of the organism. **3.** the intellect or understanding, as distinguished from the faculties of feeling and willing; the intelligence. **4.** a

particular instance of the intellect or intelligence, as in a person. **5.** a person considered with reference to intellectual power: *the greatest minds of the time.* **6.** intellectual power or ability. **7.** reason, sanity, or sound mental condition: *to lose one's mind.* **8.** way of thinking and feeling, disposition, or temper: *many men, many minds.* **9.** opinion or sentiments: *to read someone's mind.* **10.** inclination or desire. **11.** purpose, intention, or will. **12.** psychic or spiritual being, as opposed to matter. **13.** a conscious or intelligent agency or being: *the doctrine of a mind pervading the universe.* **14.** remembrance or recollection: *to keep in mind.* –*v.t.* **15.** to pay attention to, heed, or obey (a person, advice, instructions, etc.). **16.** to apply oneself or attend to: *to mind one's own business.* **17.** to look after; take care of; tend: *to mind the baby.* **18.** to be careful, cautious, or wary concerning: *mind what you say.* **19.** to care for or feel concern at. **20.** (*in negative and interrogative expressions*) to feel disturbed or inconvenienced by; object to: *do you mind my smoking?* **21.** to regard as concerning oneself or as mattering: *never mind what she does.* **22.** to be careful about (something): *mind the step.* –*v.i.* **23.** (*chiefly in the imperative*) to take notice, observe, or understand: *mind you look after him.* **24.** to be careful or wary. **25.** (*oft. in negative and interrogative expressions*) to care, feel concern, or object: *come in – he won't mind.* **26.** to regard a thing as concerning oneself or as mattering: *never mind about them.* –*phr.* **27. a piece of one's mind**, **a.** an uncomplimentary opinion. **b.** a reprimand or browbeating. **28. have a good** (or **great**) **mind to**, to be inclined to. **29. have a mind of one's own**, to be unswayed by other people's opinions. **30. have** (**half**) **a mind to**, to be almost decided to. **31. in two minds**, unable to choose between two courses of action or opinions. **32. make up one's mind**, to come to a decision. **33. mind you**, used to foreground the adjacent sentence weakly: *mind you, she won't agree.* **34. of one mind**, in accord. **35. out of one's mind**, demented; delirious. **36. presence of mind**, alacrity in controlled reaction when faced with danger or difficulty. **37. put in mind**, (sometimes fol. by *of*) to cause to remember; remind. **38. to one's mind**, in one's opinion or judgement.

mind-boggling /ˈmaɪnd-bɒɡlɪŋ/ *adj.* overwhelming; stupendous; astonishing. –**mind-bogglingly**, *adv.*

minded /ˈmaɪndəd/ *adj.* **1.** (*usu. used in combination*) having a certain kind of mind: *strong-minded.* **2.** inclined or disposed.

mindful /ˈmaɪndfəl/ *adj.* (sometimes fol. by *of*) attentive; careful. –**mindfully**, *adv.* –**mindfulness**, *n.*

mind game *n.* **1.** a contest in which psychological pressure is critical in deciding the outcome: *golf is the ultimate mind game.* –*phr.* **2. play mind games**, to exert psychological pressure: *to play mind games with the opposition.*

mind map *n.* a visual representation of the way in which concepts are related around a central key word or idea, used as a tool for the initial exploration of that idea, as a preliminary to developing a strategy, arriving at a decision, etc.

mine¹ /maɪn/ *pron.* (*possessive*) **1.** (*used predicatively or absolutely*) the possessive form of **I**: *it was mine; mine was the first offer; a book of mine.* –*adj.* **2.** *Archaic* my (used before a noun beginning with a vowel or *h*, or after a noun): *mine eyes; mine host.*

mine² /maɪn/ *n.* **1.** an excavation made in the ground to remove ores, precious stones, coal, etc. **2.** a deposit of such minerals, either under the ground or at its surface. **3.** a store of anything: *this book is a mine of information.* **4.** an underground passage dug to reach under an enemy's position, usually for placing explosives. **5.** a device containing a large charge of explosive in a watertight casing placed in the sea for the purpose of blowing up an enemy vessel. **6.** → **landmine**. *–v.i.* **7.** to dig in the earth for the purpose of removing ores, coal, etc. **8.** to remove ores, etc., from mines. **9.** to dig or lay mines, as in military operations. *–v.t.* **10.** to dig in (the ground, etc.) to obtain ores, coal, etc. **11.** to remove (ores, coal, etc.) from a mine. **12.** to make underground passages in or under; burrow. **13.** to dig or lay military mines under. **14.** to subject (a text database) to analysis by a computer search: *to mine the data*.

minefield /'mamfild/ *n.* **1.** an area on land or water throughout which mines have been laid. **2.** any situation with hidden dangers.

miner[1] /'mamə/ *n.* **1.** someone who works in a mine. **2.** *Stock Exchange* **a.** a mining company. **b.** a share in a mining company.

miner[2] /'mamə/ *n.* any of various honeyeaters of the genus *Manorina*, having yellow beaks and yellow or yellow-brown legs, which live in colonies, as the noisy miner or bellbird.

mineral /'mmərəl, 'mmrəl/ *n.* **1.** a substance obtained by mining; ore. **2.** any of a class of substances occurring in nature, usually inorganic substances of definite chemical composition and definite crystal structure and also natural products of organic origin, as coal, etc. **3.** a substance neither animal nor vegetable. *–adj.* **4.** of the nature of or containing minerals. **5.** neither animal nor vegetable; inorganic: *the mineral kingdom*.

mineralogy /mmə'rælədʒi, -'rɒl-/ *n.* the science of minerals. *–***mineralogical** /mmərə'lɒdʒikəl/, *adj.* *–***mineralogically** /mmərə'lɒdʒəkli/, *adv.* *–***mineralogist**, *n.*

mineral rights *pl. n.* rights to remove minerals that may be on or below an area of land, as by mining, usually separate from other rights held in relation to the same land.

mineral water *n.* **1.** water containing dissolved mineral salts or gases. **2.** carbonated water.

minestrone /mmə'strəuni/ *n.* a soup containing vegetables, herbs, pasta, etc., in chicken or meat stock.

mingle /'mmgəl/ *v.i.* **1.** to become mixed or united. **2.** to take part with others; participate. *–v.t.* **3.** to mix or combine; blend. **4.** to unite or join: *joy mingled with pain*. *–***mingler**, *n.*

mingy /'mmdʒi/ *adj.* (**-gier**, **-giest**) *Colloq.* mean and stingy.

mini /'mmi/ *n.* **1.** something small in size or dimension, as a skirt or motor vehicle. *–adj.* **2.** small; miniature.

mini- a word element meaning 'small' or 'miniature', as in *miniskirt*.

miniature /'mmətʃə/ *n.* **1.** a representation or image of anything on a very small scale. **2.** greatly reduced or abridged form. **3.** a very small painting, especially a portrait, on ivory, vellum, or the like. **4.** an illumination, as in manuscripts. *–adj.* **5.** on a very small scale; reduced. *–***miniaturist**, *n.*

mini-budget *n.* a budget which seeks to implement government fiscal policies decided upon after the normal budget session.

minibus /'mmibʌs/ *n.* a motor vehicle for carrying between five and ten passengers.

minigolf /'mmigɒlf/ *n.* a form of golf played on a very small course with fancifully contrived obstacles and hazards.

minim /'mməm/ *n.* **1.** the smallest unit of liquid measure in the imperial system, equal to $59.193\,880 \times 10^{-6}$ litres. **2.** *Music* a note, equal in time value to one half of a semibreve. **3.** something very small or insignificant.

minimalism /'mmməlızəm/ *n.* a reductive approach or practice, especially in literature, design, the arts, etc., which favours simplicity or the use of minimal means to an end. *–***minimalist**, *adj.*, *n.*

minimise /'mmməmaiz/ *v.t.* **1.** to reduce to the smallest possible amount or degree. **2.** to represent at the lowest possible estimate; to belittle. Also, **minimize**. *–***minimisation** /mmməmar'zeɪʃən/, *n.* *–***minimiser**, *n.*

minimum /'mmməm/ *n.* (*pl.* **-mums** *or* **-ma** /-mə/) **1.** the least quantity or amount possible, allowable, etc. **2.** the lowest amount, value, or degree reached or recorded (opposed to *maximum*). **3.** *Maths* the value of a function at a certain point which is less than or equal to the value at nearby points. *–adj.* **4.** that is a minimum. **5.** least possible. **6.** lowest. *–***minimal**, *adj.*

minimum wage *n.* the lowest wage legally payable to any adult employee.

mining /'mamm/ *n.* **1.** the action, process, or industry of extracting ores, etc., from mines. **2.** the action of laying explosive mines.

minion /'mmjən/ *n.* a subordinate or employee, usually seen as favoured or servile.

Mini Rugby *n.* a form of Rugby Union modified for children. Also, **Walla Rugby**.

minister /'mməstə/ *n.* **1.** someone authorised to conduct religious worship, especially of the Protestant churches. **2.** (*oft. upper case*) a person appointed by the sovereign or leader of a government to be head of an administrative department: *the minister of Education*. **3.** a diplomatic representative sent by one government to another. **4.** a person acting as the agent or instrument of another. *–v.i.* **5.** to give service, care, or aid. *–***ministerial**, *adj.*

ministroke /'mmistrouk/ *n.* → **TIA**.

ministry /'mmistri/ *n.* (*pl.* **-ries**) **1.** the service, work, or profession of a minister of religion. **2.** the body of ministers of religion; the clergy. **3.** the service, work, department, or headquarters of a minister of state. **4.** ministers of state taken as a group. **5.** the act of ministering; ministration; service.

mink /mmk/ *n.* (*pl.* **minks** *or, especially collectively,* **mink**) **1.** a semi-aquatic weasel-like animal of the genus *Mustela*, especially the North American *M. vison*. **2.** the valuable fur of this animal, brownish with lustrous outside hairs and thick, soft undercoat.

min min /'mm mm/ *n.* a mirage light seen in the Channel Country of western Qld.

minnow /'mmou/ *n.* **1.** a small European cyprinoid fish, *Phoxinus phoxinus*. **2.** any of various other small silvery fishes. **3.** an unimportant, insignificant person or thing.

minor /'mamə/ *adj.* **1.** lesser, as in size, extent, or importance, or being the lesser of two: *a minor share*; *minor faults*. **2.** under legal age. **3.** of or relating to the minority. **4.** *Logic* less broad or extensive: **a. minor term**, (in a syllogism) the term that is the subject of the conclusion. **b. minor premise**, the premise that contains the minor term. **5.** *Music* **a.** (of an interval) smaller by a semitone than the corresponding major interval. **b.** (of a chord) having a minor third between the root and the note next above it. *–n.* **6.** a person under the age of 18, and lacking the full legal capacity of an adult. **7.** one of inferior rank or importance in a specified class. **8.** *Music* a minor interval, chord, scale, etc. **9.** *US* **a.** a subject or a course of study pursued by a student, especially a candidate for a degree, subordinately or supplementarily to a major or principal subject or course. **b.** a subject for which less credit than a major is granted in university or occasionally in high school. **10.** Also, **minor score**. *Aust. Rules* a behind. *–phr.* **11. minor in**, *US* to pursue as a minor or subordinate subject or course of study.

minority /mar'norəti, mə-/ *n.* (*pl.* **-ties**) **1.** the smaller part or number; a number forming less than half the whole. **2.** a smaller party or group opposed to a majority, as in voting or other action. **3.** a group having in common ethnic, religious, or other ties different from those of the majority of the inhabitants of a country. **4.** the state or period of being a minor or under legal age. –*adj.* **5.** of or relating to a minority.

minority government *n.* a government formed by a party without a majority in the lower house of parliament.

minstrel /'mɪnstrəl/ *n.* **1.** one of a class of medieval musicians who sang or recited to the accompaniment of instruments. **2.** *Poetic* any musician, singer, or poet. **3.** one of a troupe of comedians, usually white men made up as dark-skinned people, presenting songs, jokes, etc. –**minstrelsy**, *n.*

mint¹ /mɪnt/ *n.* **1.** any plant of the genus *Mentha*, comprising aromatic herbs with opposite leaves and small verticillate flowers, as spearmint, peppermint, and horsemint. **2.** a soft or hard confection flavoured with peppermint or other similar flavouring. –*adj.* **3.** flavoured with or containing mint: *mint sauce.*

mint² /mɪnt/ *n.* **1.** a place where money is made by public authority. **2.** *Colloq.* a great amount, especially of money. –*v.t.* **3.** to coin (money). **4.** to make as if by coining: *to mint words.* –*phr.* **5. in mint condition,** in new or perfect condition, as when first issued. –**minter**, *n.* –**mintage**, *n.*

minuet /mɪnju'ɛt/ *n.* **1.** a slow stately dance of French origin. **2.** a piece of music for such a dance or in its rhythm.

minus /'maɪnəs/ *prep.* **1.** decreased by: *10 minus 6.* **2.** lacking or without: *a party minus a leader.* –*adj.* **3.** involving or indicating subtraction: *the minus sign.* **4.** negative: *a minus quantity.* –*n.* **5.** the minus sign (−). **6.** a minus quantity. –*v.t.* (**-nused, -nusing**) **7.** to subtract: *to minus 5 from 8.*

minuscule /'mɪnəskjul/ *adj.* **1.** small, as letters not capital or uncial. **2.** written in such letters (opposed to *majuscule*). **3.** very small; tiny. –*n.* **4.** a minuscule letter. **5.** a small cursive script developed in the 7th century from the uncial, which it afterwards superseded. –**minuscular** /mə'nʌskjulə/, *adj.*

minute¹ /'mɪnət/ *n.* **1.** the sixtieth part of an hour; sixty seconds. **2.** an indefinitely short space of time: *wait a minute.* **3.** a point of time, an instant, or moment: *come here this minute!* **4.** a rough draft, as of a document. **5.** a written summary, note, or memorandum. **6.** (*pl.*) the official record of the proceedings at a meeting of a society, board, committee, council, or other body. **7.** *Geom., etc.* the sixtieth part of a degree, or sixty seconds, equivalent to $290.888\,21 \times 10^{-6}$ radians, often represented by the sign (′), as 12°10′ (twelve degrees and ten minutes). –*v.t.* **8.** to make a draft of (a document, etc.). **9.** to record (something) in a memorandum; note down. **10.** to enter in the minutes of a society or other body. –*adj.* **11.** prepared in a very short time: *minute steak.* –*phr.* **12. up to the minute,** very modern; latest; most up to date.

minute² /maɪ'njut/ *adj.* **1.** extremely small, as in size, amount, extent, or degree: *minute differences.* **2.** of very small scope or individual importance: *minute particulars of a case.* **3.** attentive to or concerned with even very small details or particulars: *a minute history; minute regulations.* –**minuteness**, *n.*

minutely /maɪ'njutli/ *adv.* in a minute manner, form, or degree; in minute detail.

minutia /maɪ'njuʃə, -tiə/ *n.* (*pl.* **-tiae** /-ʃii, -tii/) (*usu. pl.*) a small or trivial detail; a trifling circumstance or matter.

minx /mɪŋks/ *n.* a pert, impudent, or flirtatious young woman.

mips /mɪps/ *n. Computers* a unit of measurement of computer speed (a million instructions per second). Also, **MIPS**.

miracle /'mɪrəkəl/ *n.* **1.** an effect in the physical world which surpasses all known human or natural powers

and is therefore ascribed to supernatural agency. **2.** a wonderful thing; a marvel. **3.** a wonderful or surpassing example of some quality. **4.** Also, **miracle play.** a medieval dramatic form dealing with religious subjects such as biblical stories or saints' lives, usually presented in a series or cycle by the craft guilds. –**miraculous**, *adj.*

mirage /mə'raʒ/ *n.* **1.** an optical illusion, due to atmospheric conditions, by which reflected images of distant objects are seen, often inverted. **2.** something illusory or unreal.

mire /'maɪə/ *n.* **1.** a piece of wet, swampy ground. **2.** deep mud. –*v.t.* **3.** to cause to stick fast in mire. **4.** to soil with mire. –**miry**, *adj.*

mirin /'mɪrən/ *n.* a sweet Japanese rice wine; sweet sake. Also, **mirrin.**

miro /'mɪəroʊ/ *n.* a coniferous timber tree, *Podocarpus ferrugineus*, native to New Zealand.

mirror /'mɪrə/ *n.* **1.** a reflecting surface, originally polished metal, now usually glass with a metallic or amalgam backing; a looking glass. **2.** such a surface set into an ornamental frame, especially one that can be held. **3.** any reflecting surface, as that of calm water. **4.** *Optics* a surface (plane, concave, or convex) for reflecting rays of light; a speculum. **5.** something that gives a faithful reflection or true picture of something else. –*v.t.* **6.** to reflect in or as in a mirror, or as a mirror does. –*phr.* **7. all smoke and mirrors,** an illusion or subterfuge. **8. done with mirrors,** done by sleight of hand or subterfuge.

mirth /mɜθ/ *n.* **1.** rejoicing; joyous gaiety; festive jollity. **2.** humorous amusement, as at something ludicrous, or laughter excited by it. –**mirthful**, *adj.* –**mirthless**, *adj.*

mis- a prefix applied to various parts of speech, meaning 'ill', 'mistaken', 'wrong', or simply negating, as in *mistrial, misprint, mistrust.*

misadventure /mɪsəd'vɛntʃə/ *n.* **1.** a piece of ill fortune; a mishap. **2.** ill fortune. **3.** *Law* an accident, as where a person doing a lawful act, without any intention of hurt, kills another.

misalign /mɪsə'laɪn/ *v.t.* to position incorrectly so that one component does not line up against another. –**misalignment**, *n.*

misandry /mɪs'ændri/ *n.* **1.** the hatred of men. **2.** entrenched prejudice against men. Compare **misogyny.** –**misandrist**, *n.*, *adj.*

misanthropy /mə'zænθrəpi/ *n.* hatred, dislike, or distrust of humankind.

misapprehension /mɪsæprə'hɛnʃən/ *n.* misunderstanding.

misappropriate /mɪsə'proʊprieɪt/ *v.t.* **1.** to put to a wrong use. **2.** to apply wrongfully or dishonestly to one's own use, as funds entrusted to one. –**misappropriation** /mɪsəˌproʊpri'eɪʃən/, *n.*

miscarriage /mɪs'kærɪdʒ, 'mɪskærɪdʒ/ *n.* **1.** failure to attain the right or desired result: *a miscarriage of justice.* **2.** premature expulsion of a fetus from the uterus, especially before it is viable.

miscarry /mɪs'kæri/ *v.i.* (**-ried, -rying**) **1.** to fail to attain the right end; be unsuccessful. **2.** to go astray or be lost in transit, as a letter. **3.** to have a miscarriage.

miscegenation /mɪˈsɛdʒəneɪʃən, mɪsɛdʒə'neɪʃən/ *n.* the amalgamation of peoples by interbreeding, especially between dark-skinned and light-skinned peoples. –**miscegenetic** /mɪsɛdʒə'nɛtɪk/, *adj.*

miscellaneous /mɪsə'leɪniəs/ *adj.* **1.** consisting of members or elements of different kinds: *miscellaneous volumes.* **2.** of mixed character. **3.** having various qualities or aspects; dealing with various subjects. –**miscellaneously**, *adv.* –**miscellaneousness**, *n.*

miscellany /mə'sɛləni/ *n.* (*pl.* **-nies**) **1.** a miscellaneous collection of literary compositions or pieces by several authors, dealing with various topics, assembled in a volume or book. **2.** (*oft. pl.*) a miscellaneous collection of articles or entries, as in a book.

mischance /mɪsˈtʃæns, -ˈtʃɑns/ *n.* ill luck; a mishap or misfortune.

mischief /ˈmɪstʃəf/ *n.* **1.** conduct such as to tease or cause playfully petty annoyance. **2.** a tendency or disposition to tease or vex. **3.** harm or trouble, especially as due to an agent or cause. **4.** an injury caused by a person or other agent, or an evil due to some cause. **5.** a cause or source of harm, evil, or annoyance. –*phr.* **6. make mischief, a.** (sometimes fol. by *between*) to set out to cause ill feeling between others. **b.** (especially of children) to engage knowingly in behaviour that will be considered bad.

mischievous /ˈmɪstʃəvəs/ *adj.* **1.** fond of mischief, as children. **2.** roguishly or archly teasing, as speeches, glances, etc. **3.** maliciously or playfully annoying, as persons, actions, etc. **4.** harmful or injurious. –**mischievously,** *adv.* –**mischievousness,** *n.*

miscommunicate /mɪskəˈmjunəkeɪt/ *v.t.* **1.** to fail in communicating (a message, idea, etc.) so that there is no understanding or a wrong understanding on the part of the person receiving the message. –*v.i.* **2.** to fail in communicating in this way. –**miscommunication,** *n.*

misconceive /mɪskənˈsiv/ *verb* (**-ceived, -ceiving**) –*v.t.* **1.** to conceive wrongly; misunderstand. –*v.i.* **2.** to misunderstand something or someone. –**misconception,** *n.* –**misconceiver,** *n.*

misconduct /mɪsˈkɒndʌkt/ *n.* **1.** improper conduct; wrong behaviour. **2.** unlawful conduct by an official in regard to his or her office, or by a person in the administration of justice, such as a lawyer, witness, or juror.

misconstrue /mɪskənˈstru/ *v.t.* to construe wrongly; take in a wrong sense; misinterpret; misunderstand.

miscreant /ˈmɪskriənt/ *adj.* **1.** depraved, villainous, or base. –*n.* **2.** a vile wretch; villain.

misdeed /mɪsˈdid/ *n.* a bad deed; a wicked action.

misdemeanour /mɪsdəˈminə/ *n.* **1.** misbehaviour; a misdeed. **2.** *Law* (in common law) a less serious crime. Compare **felony.** Also, **misdemeanor.**

misdiagnose /mɪsˈdaɪəgnoʊz/ *v.t.* to diagnose incorrectly. –**misdiagnosis** /mɪsdaɪəgˈnoʊsəs/, *n.*

miser /ˈmaɪzə/ *n.* **1.** someone who lives in wretched circumstances in order to save and hoard money. **2.** a niggardly, avaricious person. –**miserly,** *adj.* –**miserliness,** *n.*

miserable /ˈmɪzrəbəl, -zərəbəl/ *adj.* **1.** totally unhappy, uneasy, or uncomfortable. **2.** completely poor; needy. **3.** of completely unattractive character or quality; contemptible. **4.** causing unhappiness: *a miserable existence.* **5.** worthy of pity; deplorable: *a miserable failure.* –**miserableness,** *n.* –**miserably,** *adv.*

misère /məˈzɛə/ *n. Cards* **1.** a hand which contains no winning card. **2.** a bid made by a player who has such a hand, declaring that he or she will take no tricks.

misery /ˈmɪzəri/ *n.* (*pl.* **-ries**) **1.** great distress of mind; extreme unhappiness. **2.** a cause or source of wretchedness. **3.** distress caused by privation or poverty. **4.** wretchedness of condition or circumstances. –*phr.* **5. put out of misery, a.** to relieve (someone) of a distressful circumstance. **b.** to kill or render unconscious (a person or animal) so as to end bodily suffering.

misfire *v.i.* /mɪsˈfaɪə/ **1.** (of a gun or projectile, etc.) to fail to fire or explode. **2.** (of an internal combustion engine) to fail to fire; to fire at the wrong time. **3.** to fail to have a desired effect; be unsuccessful. –*n.* /ˈmɪsfaɪə/ **4.** (of a gun or projectile, etc.) a failure to explode or fire, or to explode or fire properly.

misfit *v.i.* /mɪsˈfɪt/ (**-fitted, -fitting**) **1.** to fit badly. –*n.* /ˈmɪsfɪt/ **2.** a bad fit, as an ill-fitting garment, etc. **3. a.** a

badly adjusted person. **b.** someone who feels ill at ease or out of place in a given environment, as a family, a school, a job, or society as a whole.

misfortune /mɪsˈfɔtʃən, -tʃun/ *n.* **1.** ill or adverse fortune; ill luck. **2.** an instance of this; a mischance or mishap.

misgiving /mɪsˈgɪvɪŋ/ *n.* a feeling of doubt, distrust, or apprehension.

mishap /ˈmɪshæp/ *n.* an unfortunate accident.

mishmash /ˈmɪʃmæʃ/ *n.* a hotchpotch; jumble.

misinterpret /mɪsɪnˈtɜprət/ *v.t.* to interpret, explain, or understand incorrectly. –**misinterpretation** /mɪsɪnˌtɜprəˈteɪʃən/, *n.*

mislay /mɪsˈleɪ/ *v.t.* (**-laid, -laying**) **1.** to put in a place afterwards forgotten. **2.** to lay or place wrongly; misplace. –**mislayer,** *n.*

mislead /mɪsˈlid/ *v.t.* (**-led, -leading**) **1.** to lead or guide wrongly; lead astray. **2.** to lead into error of conduct, thought, or judgement. –**misleader,** *n.* –**misleading,** *adj.* –**misleadingly,** *adv.*

misnomer /mɪsˈnoʊmə/ *n.* **1.** a misapplied name or designation. **2.** an error in naming a person or thing.

miso- a word element referring to hate.

misogyny /məˈsɒdʒəni/ *n.* **1.** hatred of women. **2.** entrenched prejudice against women. Compare **misandry.** –**misogynist,** *n.* –**misogynistic, misogynous,** *adj.*

misperception /mɪspəˈsɛpʃən/ *n.* mistaken or wrong perception.

misprint *n.* /ˈmɪsprɪnt/ **1.** a mistake in printing. –*v.t.* /mɪsˈprɪnt/ **2.** to print incorrectly.

mispronounce /mɪsprəˈnaʊns/ *v.t.* (**-nounced, -nouncing**) to pronounce wrongly. –**mispronunciation** /ˌmɪsprənʌnsiˈeɪʃən/, *n.*

misrepresent /mɪsrɛprəˈzɛnt/ *v.t.* to represent incorrectly, improperly, or falsely. –**misrepresentation** /mɪsˌrɛprəzɛnˈteɪʃən/, *n.* –**misrepresenter,** *n.* –**misrepresentative,** *adj.*

miss¹ /mɪs/ *v.t.* **1.** to fail to hit, light upon, meet, catch, receive, obtain, attain, accomplish, see, hear, etc.: *to miss a train.* **2.** to fail to perform, attend to, be present at, etc.: *to miss an appointment.* **3.** to perceive the absence or loss of, often with regret. **4.** to escape or avoid: *he just missed being caught.* **5.** to fail to perceive or understand: *to miss the point of a remark.* –*v.i.* **6.** to fail to hit, light upon, receive, or attain something. **7.** to fail of effect or success; be unsuccessful. **8.** (of an internal combustion engine) to fail to fire in one or more cylinders. **9.** *Colloq.* to fail to menstruate at the usual time. –*n.* **10.** a failure to hit, meet, obtain, or accomplish something. –*phr.* **11. give something a miss,** *Colloq.* to choose not to attend (an occasion), take up (an offer), etc. **12. miss out,** (sometimes fol. by *on*) to fail to be present, as at a function, or to fail to receive something desired. **13. miss the boat** (or **bus**), *Colloq.* to be too late; fail to grasp an opportunity. **14. not** (or **never**) **miss a trick,** *Colloq.* **a.** never to fail to exploit an opportunity, press an advantage, etc. **b.** never to fail to notice what is going on around one; be sharp-minded or intelligent in an observant way.

miss² /mɪs/ *n.* (*pl.* **misses**) **1.** (*upper case*) the conventional title of respect for an unmarried woman, prefixed to the name. **2.** (*usu. upper case*) a term of address, without the name, to a married or unmarried woman, especially one in a position of authority, as a teacher. **3.** a young unmarried woman; a girl. **4.** the title of respect often retained with maiden names or the name assumed by married women in public life, as actresses, writers, etc.

missal /ˈmɪsəl/ *n. Roman Catholic Church* a book containing the prayers and responses etc. needed for the celebration of mass for a whole year.

misshapen /mɪsˈʃeɪpən/ *adj.* badly shaped; deformed. –**misshapenly,** *adv.* –**misshapenness,** *n.*

missile /ˈmɪsaɪl/, *Orig. US* /-səl/ *n.* **1.** an object or weapon that can be thrown, hurled, or shot, such as a stone, a lance, an arrow, or a bullet. **2.** a ballistic or guided missile. *–adj.* **3.** capable of being thrown, hurled, or shot, as from the hand, a gun, etc.: *a missile weapon.* **4.** that discharges missiles.

missing /ˈmɪsɪŋ/ *adj.* lacking; absent; not found.

mission /ˈmɪʃən/ *n.* **1.** a body of people sent to a foreign country to carry out discussions, establish relations, etc. **2.** the business of an agent, envoy, etc. **3.** *Mil.* an operation on land, sea, or in the air, carried out against an enemy. **4.** a group of people of a particular religious faith who travel, usually to another country or region, with the purpose of converting other people to their faith, sometimes also setting up facilities such as schools, hospitals, etc. **5.** missionary duty or work. **6.** a self-imposed or assigned duty. **7.** the goals of an organisation.

missionary /ˈmɪʃənri/, *Orig. US* /ˈmɪʃənɛri/ *n.* (*pl.* **-ries**) **1.** a person sent to spread their religious faith, usually among the people of another country or region in which that faith is not widely practised. **2.** someone sent on a mission. *–adj.* **3.** of or relating to religious missions.

mission creep *n.* the gradual shift away from the original objective of a mission (def. 7) to a new one, usually under the influence of circumstances.

mission statement *n.* a formal statement of the goals of an organisation.

missive /ˈmɪsɪv/ *n.* **1.** a written message; a letter. *–adj.* **2.** sent, especially from an official source.

mist /mɪst/ *n.* **1.** a cloud-like collection of water vapour hanging in the atmosphere at or near the earth's surface. **2.** *Meteorol.* (by international agreement) a very thin fog in which the horizontal visibility is greater than one kilometre. **3.** something which looks like or blurs vision like a mist. **4.** a hazy appearance before the eyes, as due to tears, etc. **5.** a suspension of a liquid in a gas. *–v.t.* **6.** to make misty. *–v.i.* **7.** to become misty. **–misty,** *adj.*

mistake /məˈsteɪk/ *n.* **1.** an error in action, opinion or judgement. **2.** something understood wrongly. *–verb* (**-took, -taken, -taking**) *–v.t.* **3.** to take or regard as something or somebody else: *it is possible to mistake margarine for butter.* **4.** to understand wrongly; misunderstand; misjudge. *–v.i.* **5.** to be in error. **–mistaken,** *adj.* **–mistakenly,** *adv.* **–mistakable, mistakeable,** *adj.*

mister /ˈmɪstə/ *n.* **1.** (*upper case*) the conventional title of respect for a man, prefixed to the name or to certain official designations and usually written *Mr.* **2.** *Colloq.* (in address, without the name) sir. **3.** *Mil.* not followed by a name, a form of address to a man.

mistletoe /ˈmɪsəltoʊ/ *n.* **1.** the European plant *Viscum album,* often used in Christmas decorations. **2.** any of various plants of the genus *Amyema* which grow parasitically on other plants.

mistletoebird /ˈmɪsəltoʊbɜːd/ *n.* a small bird, *Dicaeum hirundinaceum,* which builds a nest of plant down and spider web in treetops, and spreads the seeds of the mistletoe plant by eating and then excreting them; common in most parts of mainland Australia. Also, **mistletoe bird.**

mistreat /mɪsˈtriːt/ *v.t.* to treat badly or wrongly. **–mistreatment,** *n.*

mistress /ˈmɪstrəs/ *n.* **1.** a woman who has authority or control as over a house, servants, etc. **2.** a female owner, as of horse, dog, etc. **3.** *Aust.* a female head teacher in a particular subject department in a secondary school. **4.** a woman with whom a man has a continuing extramarital sexual relationship. **5.** *Archaic or Poetic* a sweetheart. **6.** *Archaic* a term of address for a woman. Also **Mrs, miss².**

mistrial /mɪsˈtraɪəl/ *n.* *Law* a trial terminated without conclusion on the merits because of some error.

mistrust /mɪsˈtrʌst/ *n.* **1.** lack of trust or confidence; distrust. *–v.t.* **2.** to regard with mistrust; distrust. *–v.i.* **3.** to be distrustful. **–mistruster,** *n.* **–mistrustful,** *adj.* **–mistrustingly,** *adv.*

misunderstand /ˌmɪsʌndəˈstænd, mɪsˌʌn-/ *verb* (**-stood, -standing**) *–v.t.* **1.** to fail to understand the correct sense or significance of (a word, something said or written, an action, etc.). **2.** to misinterpret the words, actions, or feelings of (a person). *–v.i.* **3.** to understand wrongly.

misunderstanding /ˌmɪsʌndəˈstændɪŋ, mɪsˌʌn-/ *n.* **1.** disagreement or dissension. **2.** failure to understand; mistake as to meaning.

misuse *n.* /mɪsˈjuːs/ **1.** wrong or improper use; misapplication. *–v.t.* /mɪsˈjuːz/ **2.** to ill-use; maltreat.

mite¹ /maɪt/ *n.* any of various small arachnids (order Acari) with a saclike body, many being parasitic on plants and animals, others living in cheese, flour, unrefined sugar, etc.

mite² /maɪt/ *n.* **1.** a small contribution, but all that one can afford (in allusion to Mark 12:41-44): *to contribute one's mite.* **2.** a very small thing or person. *–adv.* **3.** (preceded by *a*) to a limited extent; somewhat: *a mite stupid.*

mitigate /ˈmɪtəgeɪt/ *v.t.* **1.** to lessen in force or intensity (wrath, grief, harshness, pain, etc.). **2.** to moderate the severity of (anything distressing). *–v.i.* **3.** to become milder; moderate in severity. **–mitigatory** /ˈmɪtəgeɪtəri/, *adj.* **–mitigation,** *n.* **–mitigator,** *n.*

mitosis /maɪˈtoʊsəs, mə-/ *n.* *Biol.* the usual (indirect) method of cell division, characterised typically by the resolving of the chromatin of the nucleus into a threadlike form, which separates into segments or chromosomes, each of which separates longitudinally into two parts, one part of each chromosome being retained in each of two new cells resulting from the original cell. **–mitotic,** *adj.* **–mitotically,** *adv.*

mitre /ˈmaɪtə/ *n.* **1.** the ceremonial headdress of a bishop symbolising his apostolic authority. **2.** the office or rank of bishop; bishopric. **3.** the ceremonial cap of ancient Jewish high priest. **4.** the abutting surface or bevel on either of the pieces joined in a mitre joint. *–v.t.* (**-tred, -tring**) **5.** to make a mitre joint in; cut to a mitre. Also, *US,* **miter.**

mitt /mɪt/ *n.* **1.** a kind of glove extending only to, or slightly over, the fingers, especially as worn by women. **2.** *Baseball* a kind of glove having the side next to the palm of the hand protected by a large, thick mitten-like pad. **3.** a mitten. **4.** *Colloq.* a hand.

mitten /ˈmɪtn/ *n.* a kind of hand-covering enclosing the four fingers together and the thumb separately.

mix /mɪks/ *v.t.* **1.** to put together (substances or things, or one substance or thing with another) in one mass or assemblage with more or less thorough diffusion of the constituent elements among one another. **2.** Also, **mix up.** to put together indiscriminately or confusedly. **3.** to combine, unite, or join: *to mix business and pleasure.* **4.** to put in as an added element or ingredient: *to mix a little baking powder into the flour.* **5.** to form by combining ingredients: *to mix a cake; to mix mortar.* **6.** to crossbreed. **7.** *Music* to create (a piece of music) by mixing sound. *–v.i.* **8.** to become mixed: *oil and water will not mix.* **9.** to associate, as in company. **10.** *Music* to put together separate tracks, either live or prerecorded, to create the desired blend of musical sound. **11.** *Music* to overlap one recorded piece with another, as a DJ does. *–n.* **12.** a mixing, or a mixed condition; a mixture. **13.** a commercially prepared blend of ingredients to which it is only necessary to add liquid and stir, before baking, cooking, serving, etc. **14.** a recording made by combining tracks separately recorded in a mixer. *–phr.* **15. mix and match,** to interchange items of clothing with others to create new and pleasing combinations. **16. mix it up**, to continually vary techniques, styles, strategies, etc., especially so as to outwit an opponent. **17. mix it (up) with**, *Colloq.* to fight vigorously, as with the fists. **18. mix one's drinks**, to drink a range of alcoholic liquors indiscriminately, usually resulting in a hangover. **19. mix up**, to confuse completely. **20. mix up in**, to involve in. **21. mix with**, to associate socially with.

mixed /mɪkst/ *adj.* **1.** composed of different constituents or elements. **2.** composed of male and female together: *a mixed school; mixed doubles.* **3.** of different kinds combined: *mixed sweets.* **4.** comprising persons of different ethnic, religious or cultural origins. *–phr.* **5. mixed up**, *Colloq.* mentally confused.

mixed marriage *n.* a marriage between persons of different religious, ethnic or cultural origins.

mixed metaphor *n.* See **metaphor** (def. 2).

mixer /ˈmɪksə/ *n.* **1.** a device or part that mixes. **2.** a kitchen utensil or electrical appliance used for beating. **3.** an electrical system, as in a broadcasting studio, providing for the mixing, etc., of sounds from various sources, as from studio microphones, discs, tapes, etc. **4.** *Radio, TV* a technician who controls the sound mixer in a studio. **5.** a person considered with reference to their ability to socialise at a party, function, etc.: *a good mixer.*

mixture /ˈmɪkstʃə/ *n.* **1.** the product of mixing. **2.** any combination of differing elements, kinds, qualities, etc. **3.** *Chem., Physics* two or more substances not chemically united, and which are mixed in no fixed proportion to each other. **4.** the state of being mixed.

mix-up *n.* **1.** a confused state of things; a muddle; a tangle. **2.** *Colloq.* a fight.

mnemonic /nəˈmɒnɪk/ *adj.* **1.** assisting, or intended to assist, the memory. **2.** relating to mnemonics or to memory. *–n.* **3.** a verse or the like intended to assist the memory.

mo[1] /moʊ/ *n.* **1.** *Colloq.* a moment. *–phr.* **2. half a mo**, just a moment.

mo[2] /moʊ/ *Aust., NZ Colloq. –n.* **1.** a moustache. *–phr.* **2. curl the** (or **a**) **mo**, an exclamation of admiration, delight, etc.

moa /ˈmoʊə/ *n.* any of various extinct, wingless birds of New Zealand, constituting the family Dinornithidae, allied to the apteryx but resembling an ostrich.

moan /moʊn/ *n.* **1.** a long, low, sound made from or as if from physical or mental suffering. **2.** any similar sound: *the moan of the wind.* **3.** *Colloq.* a grumble. *–v.i.* **4.** to utter moans, as of pain or grief. **5.** (of the wind, sea, trees, etc.) to make any sound suggestive of such moans. **6.** to state in complaint. *–v.t.* **7.** to lament or bemoan: *to moan one's fate.* **–moaner**, *n.* **–moaning**, *adj.* **–moaningly**, *adv.*

moat /moʊt/ *n.* **1.** a deep, wide trench surrounding a fortified place, as a town or a castle, usually filled with water. *–v.t.* **2.** to surround with, or as with, a moat.

mob /mɒb/ *n.* **1. a.** a large number, especially of people: *there was a mob of people in the streets to see the procession.* **b.** *Colloq.* a group of people, as friends, not necessarily large: *we'll invite the mob over for Saturday night.* **2.** *Aust., NZ* a collection of animals: *a mob of sheep.* **3. a.** *Aboriginal English* an Aboriginal tribe or language group: *all my mob; the Big River mob.* **b.** a community, whether related by kinship, geography, special interest, etc.: *the Newcastle mob; the Music Society mob.* **4.** a disorderly, riotous or hostile group of people: *the mob packed the presidential palace.* **5.** the common mass of people; the populace or multitude. **6.** (in Australia) a group or unit of Joey Scouts in the Scout Association. *–adj.* **7.** of, relating to, characteristic of, or suitable for a mob: *mob violence; mob oratory.*

–v.t. (**mobbed, mobbing**) **8.** to crowd around tumultuously. **9.** to surround and attack with riotous violence. **10.** to muster (stock animals). *–phr.* **11. a big mob**, *Aust.* **a.** a large number. **b.** a great amount. **12. mobs of**, *Aust. Colloq.* lots of. **–mobber**, *n.* **–mobbish**, *adj.*

mobile /ˈmoʊbaɪl/ *adj.* **1.** moving readily; movable. **2.** *Mil.* permanently equipped with vehicles for transport. **3.** flowing freely, as a liquid. **4.** (of facial expression) changing easily. **5.** (of the mind) responding quickly; versatile. **6.** of or relating to a mobile phone: *mobile technology. –n.* **7.** an arrangement of delicately balanced movable parts (of metal, wood, etc.), usually hanging. **8.** a mobile phone. *–phr.* **9. upwardly mobile**, (of a person) moving to a higher social class, a better job or a more prestigious area. **–mobility**, *n.*

mobile phone *n.* a portable cellular telephone.

mobilise /ˈmoʊbəlaɪz/ *v.t.* **1.** to put (armed forces) into readiness for active service. **2.** to marshal, as for a task: *to mobilise one's energies.* **3.** to put into motion, circulation, or use: *mobilise the wealth of a country.* **4.** to make (something) movable or capable of movement: *to mobilise the patient's shoulderblade. –v.i.* **5.** to be assembled, organised, etc., for war. Also, **mobilize.** **–mobilisation** /moʊbəlaɪˈzeɪʃən/, *n.*

mobility aid *n.* **1.** any device which helps a disabled person to achieve greater mobility, as a wheelchair, walking frame, etc. **2.** an electronic device, usually employing ultrasound, used by visually-impaired people to detect obstacles in their path.

moccasin /ˈmɒkəsən/ *n.* a slip-on shoe made entirely of soft leather, usually with stitching around the front part of the upper, as worn originally by Native Americans.

mocha /ˈmɒkə/ *n.* **1.** a choice variety of coffee, originally coming from Mocha, a seaport in south-west Yemen, a republic in Arabia. **2.** a flavouring obtained from coffee infusion or combined chocolate and coffee infusion. **3.** a glove leather, finer and thinner than doeskin, the best grades of which are made from Arabian goatskins. **4.** a dark chocolate colour. Also, **mokha.**

mock /mɒk/ *v.t.* **1.** to assail or treat with ridicule or derision. **2.** to ridicule by mimicry of action or speech; mimic derisively. **3.** to mimic, imitate, or counterfeit. **4.** to defy; set at naught. **5.** to deceive, delude, or disappoint. *–v.i.* **6.** (sometimes fol. by *at*) to use ridicule or derision; scoff; jeer. *–n.* **7.** imitation. *–adj.* **8.** being an imitation or having merely the semblance of something: *a mock battle. –phr.* **9. mock up**, to build or construct, especially quickly, as a mock-up. **10. put the mock(s) on**, *Aust. Colloq.* to bring bad luck to; jinx. **–mocker**, *n.* **–mockingly**, *adv.*

mockbuster /ˈmɒkbʌstə/ *n.* a low-budget movie which is modelled on a blockbuster and usually seeks to trade on its fame or to be a send-up of it.

mocker /ˈmɒkə/ *phr.* **1. have the mocker(s) on**, to be fated not to succeed; be jinxed: *that project has the mockers on it.* **2. put the mocker(s) on**, to bring bad luck to; jinx.

mockery /ˈmɒkəri/ *n.* (*pl.* **-ries**) **1.** an action or speech that unkindly laughs at something of a serious nature. **2.** a subject or occasion of unkind laughter at something. **3.** a copy, especially of a ridiculous or unsatisfactory kind. **4.** something pretended that aims to belittle or show no respect; mocking pretence. **5.** something absurdly or offensively inadequate or unfitting.

mockingbird /ˈmɒkɪŋbɜd/ *n.* **1.** any of several grey, black, and white songbirds of the genus *Mimus*, remarkable for their imitative powers, especially the celebrated mocker, *M. polyglottos*, of the southern US and Mexico. **2.** in Australia, the small, elusive, rufous scrub bird, *Atrichornis rufescens*, noted for its ability as a mimic.

mockumentary /mɒkjuˈmɛntri/ *n.* (*pl.* **-ries**) a parody of the documentary genre, which chooses a fictitious subject and treats it with all the mannerisms of the documentary.

mock-up *n.* **1.** a model, built to scale, of a machine, apparatus, or weapon, used in testing, teaching, etc. **2.** a model of a finished book or magazine with the essential detail only sketched in.

mod /mɒd/ *Colloq.* *–adj.* **1.** modern. *–n.* **2.** a young person of the early 1960s, especially in Britain, who was neatly dressed, had ungreased hair, and who usually rode a motor scooter in preference to a motor bike. Compare **rocker** (def. 5).

modal /ˈmoʊdl/ *adj.* **1.** of or relating to mode. **2.** *Gram.* denoting or relating to mood. **–modally,** *adv.* **–modality,** *n.*

mod cons /mɒd ˈkɒnz/ *pl. n. Colloq.* modern conveniences.

mode[1] /moʊd/ *n.* **1.** a method; way. **2.** the natural manner of existence or action of anything. **3.** *Music* the arrangement of the diatonic tones of an octave. **4.** *Geol.* the actual mineral composition of a rock, given in percentages by weight.

mode[2] /moʊd/ *n.* **1.** customary or conventional usage in manners, dress, etc., especially as observed by persons of fashion. **2.** a prevailing style or fashion. **–modish,** *adj.*

model /ˈmɒdl/ *n.* **1.** a standard or example for copying or comparison. **2.** a representation, usually on a small scale: *a model of an aircraft.* **3.** an image in clay, wax, etc. **4.** a person, who poses for a painter, photographer, etc. **5.** someone employed to wear and show new clothes to customers; mannequin. **6.** a form or style. **7.** a computerised projection into the future of an anticipated outcome. *–adj.* **8.** serving as a model. **9.** worthy to serve as a model; exemplary. *–verb* (**-elled** *or*, *US*, **-eled**, **-elling** *or*, *US*, **-eling**) *–v.t.* **10.** to form or plan according to a model. **11.** to make a model of. **12.** to form in clay, wax, etc. **13.** to show, especially by wearing. **14.** to create a computerised projection into the future of: *to model possible scenarios.* *–v.i.* **15.** to make models. **16.** to produce designs in clay, wax, etc. **17.** to be employed as a model. **–modeller,** *n.* **–modelling,** *n.*

modem /ˈmoʊdɛm, ˈmoʊdəm/ *n. Telecommunications* an electronic device that facilitates the linking of one computer to another via the telephone system by changing the binary information in the computer into electrical signals which can travel along the telephone lines, then changing it back again into binary information at the receiving end.

moderate *adj.* /ˈmɒdrət, -ərət/ **1.** keeping within proper bounds; not extreme: *a moderate request.* **2.** of medium quantity, power, etc.: *a moderate income.* **3.** fair; mediocre: *moderate ability.* *–n.* /ˈmɒdrət, -ərət/ **4.** someone who is moderate in opinion or action. *–v.t.* /ˈmɒdəreɪt/ **5.** to make less extreme, severe, etc. **6.** to hold the place of authority, as at a public meeting; preside over. *–v.i.* /ˈmɒdəreɪt/ **7.** to become less extreme, severe, etc. **8.** to act as moderator. **–moderately,** *adv.* **–moderateness,** *n.*

moderation /mɒdəˈreɪʃən/ *n.* **1.** the quality of being moderate; restraint; avoidance of extremes; temperance. **2.** the act of moderating. *–phr.* **3. in moderation,** without excess; moderately.

moderator /ˈmɒdəreɪtə/ *n.* **1.** a presiding officer, as over a public forum, a legislative body, or an ecclesiastical body in the Presbyterian and Uniting Churches. **2.** *Physics* a substance, such as graphite or heavy water, which slows down neutrons from the high energies at which they are released in fission to speeds suitable for further fission. **3.** → **chairperson.** **4.** *Internet* a person

who oversees all the messages in a forum, deleting any unregistered messages and assisting members. **–moderatorship,** *n.*

modern /ˈmɒdn/ *adj.* **1.** of or relating to present and recent time. **2.** characteristic of present and recent time. **3.** of or relating to various styles of jazz, since the 1940s. *–n.* **4.** a person of modern times. **5.** someone whose views and tastes are modern. **–modernise, modernize,** *v.* **–modernly,** *adv.* **–modernism,** *n.* **–modernist,** *n.*

modest /ˈmɒdəst/ *adj.* **1.** having or showing a moderate or humble estimate of one's merits, importance, etc.; free from vanity, egotism, boastfulness, or great pretensions. **2.** free from ostentation or showy extravagance: *a modest house.* **3.** moderate. **4.** having or showing regard for the decencies of behaviour, speech, dress, etc.; decent. **–modestly,** *adv.* **–modesty,** *n.*

modicum /ˈmɒdəkəm/ *n.* a moderate or small quantity.

modification /mɒdəfəˈkeɪʃən/ *n.* **1.** the act of partly changing something. **2.** the state of being partly changed. **3.** a variety. **4.** *Biol.* a change in a living organism gained from its own activity or environment and not passed to its descendants. **5.** a limitation; qualification.

modifier /ˈmɒdəfaɪə/ *n. Gram.* a word, phrase, or sentence element which limits or qualifies the sense of another word, phrase, or element in the same construction: *adjectives are modifiers.*

modify /ˈmɒdəfaɪ/ *verb* (**-fied, -fying**) *–v.t.* **1.** to change somewhat the form or qualities of; alter somewhat. **2.** to be the modifier or attribute of. **3.** to change (a vowel) by umlaut. **4.** to reduce in degree; moderate; qualify. *–v.i.* **5.** to change; to become changed. **–modifiable,** *adj.* **–modificatory,** *adj.*

modular /ˈmɒdʒələ/ *adj.* **1.** of or relating to module or modulus. **2.** composed of standardised units or sections for easy construction or flexible arrangement: *a modular home, modular furniture.* **–modularity,** *n.*

modulate /ˈmɒdʒəleɪt/ *v.t.* **1.** to tone down; to regulate or adjust to a certain measure. **2.** to change (the voice) fittingly in speech. **3.** *Music* **a.** to tune to a certain pitch or key. **b.** to change the volume of (tone). **4.** *Radio* to cause the amplitude, frequency, etc., of (the carrier wave) to change in accordance with the soundwaves or other signals. **–modulative,** *adj.* **–modulation,** *n.* **–modulator,** *n.*

module /ˈmɒdʒul/ *n.* **1.** a standard or unit for measuring. **2.** a structural part used as a basic unit for do-it-yourself furniture. **3.** a self-contained unit within a course of study. **4.** *Archit.* the size of some part, taken as a unit of measure. **5.** *Electronics* a small, standard unit which can be used in the making of a piece of equipment. **6.** *Astronautics* a section of a space vehicle able to function as a separate unit: *command module.*

mogul /ˈmoʊgəl/ *n.* an important person.

mohair /ˈmoʊhɛə/ *n.* **1.** the coat or fleece of an Angora goat. **2.** a fabric made of yarn from this fleece, in a plain weave for draperies and in a pile weave for upholstery.

moiety /ˈmɔɪəti/ *n.* (*pl.* **-ties**) **1.** a half. **2.** *Anthrop.* **a.** one of two units into which a society is divided on the basis of descent through either the mother's or father's line only. **b.** one of the two units into which a society is divided on the basis that people in alternate generations are grouped together. **c.** (in Aboriginal culture) a similar division of the Dreaming for those societies with moieties.

moiré /ˈmwareɪ/ *n.* a watered fabric, as of silk or wool.

moist /mɔɪst/ *adj.* **1.** moderately or slightly wet; damp; humid. **2.** (of the eyes) tearful. **3.** accompanied by or connected with liquid or moisture. **–moistly,** *adv.* **–moistness,** *n.* **–moisten,** *v.*

moisture /ˈmɔɪstʃə/ n. water or other liquid rendering anything moist. —**moisturise, moisturize,** v. —**moisturiser,** n.

molar¹ /ˈmoʊlə/ n. **1.** a tooth adapted for grinding with a broad biting surface as in human dentition, which has twelve molar teeth, three in each quadrant. —adj. **2.** adapted for grinding, as teeth, especially those in humans, with a broad biting surface, situated behind the bicuspids. **3.** relating to such teeth.

molar² /ˈmoʊlə/ adj. Physics of or relating to a body of matter as a whole (contrasted with molecular and atomic). **2.** Chem. of or relating to a solution containing one mole of solute per litre of solution.

molasses /məˈlæsəz/ n. the thick brown bitter uncrystallised syrup drained from raw sugar.

mold¹ /moʊld/ n., v.t. US → **mould¹.**

mold² /moʊld/ n. US → **mould².**

mole¹ /moʊl/ n. **1.** a small congenital spot or blemish on the human skin, usually of a dark colour and slightly elevated, and often hairy. **2.** a pigmented naevus.

mole² /moʊl/ n. **1.** any of various small insectivorous mammals, of Europe, Asia, and North America, especially of the family Talpidae, living chiefly underground, and having velvety fur, very small eyes, and strong, fossorial forefeet. **2.** someone who establishes themself in the bureaucracy of the enemy so that they can act as a spy when required.

mole³ /moʊl/ n. **1.** a massive structure, especially of stone, set up in the water, as for a breakwater or a pier. **2.** an anchorage or harbour protected by such a structure.

mole⁴ /moʊl/ n. Physics the SI base unit of measurement of amount of substance equal to the amount of substance of a system which contains as many elementary entities as there are atoms in 0.012 kg of carbon-12. Symbol: mol

molecular weight n. the average weight of a molecule of an element or compound measured in units based on one twelfth of the weight of an atom of carbon-12; the sum of the atomic weights of all the atoms in a molecule.

molecule /ˈmɒləkjul/ n. **1.** Physics, Chem. **a.** the smallest physical unit of an element or compound, consisting of one or more like atoms in the first case, and two or more different atoms in the second case. **b.** a quantity of a substance, the weight of which, measured in any chosen unit, is numerically equal to the molecular weight; gram molecule. **2.** any very small particle. —**molecular,** adj.

molest /məˈlɛst/ v.t. **1.** to assault sexually. **2.** to interfere with annoyingly or injuriously. —**molestation** /mɒləsˈteɪʃən/, n. —**molester,** n.

moll /mɒl/ n. Colloq. **1.** the girlfriend or mistress of a gangster, thief, etc. **2.** the girlfriend or surfie, bikie, etc. **3.** a female prostitute.

mollify /ˈmɒləfaɪ/ v.t. (**-fied, -fying**) **1.** to soften in feeling or temper, as a person, the heart or mind, etc. **2.** to mitigate or appease, as rage. —**mollification** /mɒləfəˈkeɪʃən/, n. —**mollifier,** n. —**mollifyingly,** adv. —**mollifiable,** adj.

mollusc /ˈmɒləsk/ n. any invertebrate of the phylum Mollusca, characterised by a calcareous shell (sometimes lacking) of one, two, or more pieces that wholly or partly encloses the soft unsegmented body and including the chitons, snails, bivalves, squids, octopuses, etc. Also, US, **mollusk.** —**molluscan** /məˈlʌskən/, adj., n.

mollycoddle /ˈmɒlikɒdl/ v.t. to coddle; pamper. —**mollycoddler,** n.

moloch /ˈmoʊlɒk/ n. **1.** (upper case) Also, **Molech.** anything seen as demanding terrible sacrifice: the moloch of war. **2.** → **thorny devil.**

Molotov cocktail /mɒlətɒv ˈkɒkteɪl/ n. an incendiary bomb consisting of a bottle filled with an flammable liquid, usually petrol, and a saturated wick which is ignited before the bottle is thrown.

molten /ˈmoʊltn/ v. **1.** a past participle of **melt.** —adj. **2.** liquefied by heat; in a state of fusion. **3.** produced by melting and casting: a molten image.

moment /ˈmoʊmənt/ n. **1.** an indefinitely short space of time; an instant: wait a moment. **2.** the present or other particular instant: I cannot recall his name at the moment. **3.** a definite stage, as in a course of events. **4.** importance or consequence: of great moment. **5.** Also, **moment of force.** the measure of the tendency of a force to cause rotation about an axis; the product of the force and the perpendicular distance from an axis.

momentarily /ˈmoʊməntrəli/, Orig. US /moʊmənˈtɛrəli/ adv. **1.** for a moment: to hesitate momentarily. **2.** Orig. US in a moment; very shortly: I'll be with you momentarily.

momentary /ˈmoʊməntri/, Orig. US /-tɛri/ adj. **1.** lasting but a moment; very brief: a momentary glimpse. **2.** occurring at any moment: to live in fear of momentary exposure. **3.** constant; occurring at every moment. —**momentariness,** n.

momentous /moʊˈmɛntəs, mə-/ adj. of great importance or consequence; fraught with serious or far-reaching consequences, as events, decisions, etc. —**momentously,** adv. —**momentousness,** n.

momentum /məˈmɛntəm/ n. (pl. **-ta** /-tə/) **1.** Physics the quantity of motion of a moving body, equal to the product of its mass and velocity; linear momentum. **2.** impetus, as of a moving body.

mon- variant of **mono-,** before vowels.

monarch /ˈmɒnək, -ak/ n. **1.** a hereditary sovereign with more or less limited powers, as a king, queen, emperor, etc. **2.** a sole and absolute ruler of a state. **3.** a person or thing that holds a dominating or pre-eminent position. **4.** a large migratory reddish brown butterfly, Danaus plexippus, having black and white markings, whose larva feeds on milkweed; wanderer.

monarchy /ˈmɒnəki/ n. (pl. **-chies**) **1.** a government or state in which the supreme power is actually or nominally lodged in a monarch (known as an **absolute monarchy** or **despotic monarchy** when the monarch's authority is not limited by laws or a constitution, and as a **limited monarchy** or **constitutional monarchy** when the monarch's authority is so limited). **2.** supreme power or sovereignty wielded by a single person. —**monarchism,** n. —**monarchist,** n.

monastery /ˈmɒnəstri, -təri/ n. (pl. **-ries**) a house or place of residence occupied by a community of persons, especially monks, living in seclusion from the world under religious vows. —**monasterial** /mɒnəsˈtɪəriəl/, adj.

monastic /məˈnæstɪk/ adj. **1.** of or relating to monasteries: monastic architecture. **2.** of or relating to monks, or other persons living in seclusion from the world under religious vows: monastic vows of poverty, chastity, and obedience. Also, **monastical.** —**monastically,** adv. —**monasticism,** n.

Monday /ˈmʌndeɪ, -di/ n. the second day of the week, following Sunday.

mondo grass /ˈmɒndoʊ grɑs/ n. any of various rhizomatous grasses of the lily family, especially the dwarf variety, Ophipogon japonicus, with glossy, dark green leaves, popular as a border or ground cover; native to Japan and Korea.

moneran /məˈnɪərən/ n. Biol. a member of the genus Monera, typically reproducing by asexual budding or fission and gaining nutrition by absorption, photosynthesis or chemosynthesis.

monetarism /ˈmʌnətərɪzəm/ *n. Econ.* an economic theory which holds that a nation's economy is governed by changes in the money supply. –**monetarist**, *adj.*, *n.*

monetary /ˈmʌnətri, -təri/, *Orig. US* /-teri/ *adj.* of or relating to money, or pecuniary matters: *monetary consideration.* –**monetarily**, *adv.*

monetary policy *n.* the part of a government's economic policy that relates to the management of the money supply and the control of interest rates. Compare **fiscal policy**.

money /ˈmʌni/ *n.* (*pl.* **-neys** or **-nies**) **1.** gold, silver, or other metal in pieces of convenient form stamped by public authority and issued as a medium of exchange and measure of value. **2.** current coin. **3.** coin or certificate (as banknotes, etc.) generally accepted in payment of debts and current transactions. **4.** any article or substance similarly used. **5.** a particular form or denomination of currency. **6.** an amount or sum of money. **7.** wealth viewed in terms of money: *a family with plenty of money.* **8.** (*pl.*) *Law, Archaic* pecuniary sums. –*phr.* **9. for one's money**, as far as one's own choice or preference is concerned; in one's own opinion. **10. in the money**, *Colloq.* rich. **11. make money**, to become rich. **12. money for jam** (or **old rope**), *Colloq.* money which is obtained by very little effort. **13. money's worth**, full value; greatest possible advantage. **14. put money into**, to invest in. **15. put one's money where one's mouth is**, to give financial support to a cause, project, etc., which one has openly expressed belief in.

moneyed /ˈmʌnid/ *adj.* **1.** having money; wealthy. **2.** consisting of or representing money: *moneyed interests.* Also, **monied**.

money-grubber /ˈmʌni-grʌbə/ *n. Colloq.* an avaricious person; one devoted entirely to the making of money. –**money-grubbing**, *adj.*

money laundering *n.* the illegal practice of transferring funds of illegal origin, usually as cash, into legal enterprises in such a way that they appear to be legitimate. –**money launderer**, *n.*

money market *n. Finance* a market in which large amounts of money are borrowed and lent for short periods of time (usually less than a month).

money matters *pl. n.* financial aspects of one's life, business, etc.

money order *n.* an order for the payment of money, as one issued by one post office and payable at another, usually for a sum larger than ten dollars, and requiring proof of ownership before being cashed. Compare **postal note**.

money shot *n. Film, TV* **1.** the shot (**shot**[1] def. 16c) in a production that is the most expensive to produce. **2.** a shot in a production that will grab the viewer's attention and attract an audience.

money-spinner *n. Colloq.* a business enterprise or property which is very profitable. –**money-spinning**, *adj.*

monger /ˈmʌngə/ *n.* (*usu. in compounds*) **1.** a dealer in some commodity: *a fishmonger.* **2.** someone who busies himself or herself with something in a sordid or petty way: *a scandalmonger.* –**mongering**, *n.*, *adj.*

Mongoloid /ˈmɒŋgəlɔɪd/ –*adj.* **1.** *Ethnology* (in a system devised in the 19th century) of, relating to, or characteristic of the racial division of the human species which includes the Mongols, Chinese, Japanese, Thais, Burmese, etc. Compare **Australoid**, **Negroid**, **Caucasian**. **2.** (*oft. lower case*) *Pathol. Obs.* of, relating to, or characteristic of Down syndrome. –*n.* **3.** *Ethnology* someone belonging to the Mongoloid race. **4.** (*oft. lower case*) *Pathol. Obs.* someone with Down syndrome.

mongoose /ˈmɒŋgus/ *n.* (*pl.* **-gooses**) a slender ferret-like carnivore, typified by *Herpestes edwardsii*, of India, of the same genus as the common ichneumon, used for destroying rats, etc., and noted for its ability to kill certain venomous snakes.

mongrel /ˈmʌngrəl/ *n.* **1.** any plant or animal (especially a dog) resulting from the crossing of different breeds or varieties. **2.** any cross between different things. **3.** *Colloq.* a task, project, etc., that presents great difficulty: *a mongrel of a job.* –*adj.* **4.** of or like a mongrel. **5.** of little value. **6.** *Colloq.* despicable: *a mongrel act.* –**mongrelism, mongrelness**, *n.* –**mongrelly**, *adv.*

monied /ˈmʌnid/ *adj.* → **moneyed**.

monilia /məˈnɪliə/ *n.* a yeast-like fungus, *Candida albicans*, which occasionally causes a condition of infection, mainly in the mouth and vagina.

monition /məˈnɪʃən/ *n.* **1.** admonition; warning; caution. **2.** an official or legal notice.

monitor /ˈmɒnətə/ *n.* **1.** someone who keeps order, especially in school. **2.** (in schools) a pupil responsible for a particular task, as the supervision of study. **3.** something that serves to remind or give warning. **4. a.** a device used to check or record the operation of a machine or system. **b.** *TV* a screen used to check the quality of the signal being sent. **c.** *Computers* the component of a desktop computer which houses the screen; visual display unit. **5.** a large lizard found in Africa, South-East Asia and Australia, and supposed to warn of the presence of crocodiles. –*v.t.* **6.** to check, look at, or record the operation of (a machine, etc.), without interfering with the operation. **7.** to keep careful watch over. –**monitorship**, *n.* –**monitory**, *adj.*

monk /mʌŋk/ *n.* a man who has withdrawn from the world from religious motives, either as a hermit or, especially, as a member of an order living under vows of poverty, chastity, and obedience, according to a rule.

monkey /ˈmʌŋki/ *n.* (*pl.* **-keys**) **1.** any member of the mammalian order Primates, including the guenons, macaques, langurs, capuchins, etc., but excluding humans, the anthropoid apes, and the lemurs. **2.** a person likened to such an animal, as a mischievous child, a mimic, etc. **3.** the fur of certain species of long-haired monkeys. **4.** any of various mechanical devices, as the ram of a pile-driving apparatus, or of a wool press. –*phr.* (*v.* **-keyed**, **-keying**) **5. a monkey on one's back**, any obsession, compulsion, or addiction, seen as a burden. **6. make a monkey of**, to make a fool of. **7. monkey (about) with**, *Colloq.* to play or trifle idly with; fool about with. **8. monkey tricks** (or **business**), **a.** trickery; underhand dealing. **b.** mischief.

monkey wrench *n.* a wrench with one fixed and one adjustable jaw, for turning nuts of different sizes, etc.

mono- a word element: **1.** meaning 'alone', 'single', 'one'. **2.** denoting a monomolecular thickness, as in *monofil*, *monolayer*, etc. **3.** adapted in chemistry to apply to compounds containing one atom of a particular element. Also, **mon-**.

monochromatic /mɒnəkroʊˈmætɪk/ *adj.* of, producing, or relating to one colour or one wavelength. –**monochromatically**, *adv.*

monochrome /ˈmɒnəkroʊm/ *n.* **1.** a painting or drawing in different shades of a single colour. **2.** the state or condition of being painted, decorated, etc., in shades of a single colour. **3.** a black and white photograph. –**monochromic** /mɒnəˈkroʊmɪk/, **monochromical** /mɒnəˈkroʊmɪkəl/, *adj.* –**monochromist**, *n.*

monocle /ˈmɒnəkəl/ *n.* an eyeglass for one eye. –**monocled**, *adj.*

monody /ˈmɒnədi/ *n.* (*pl.* **-dies**) **1.** a poem in which one person laments another's death. **2.** *Music* a style of composition in which one part or melody predominates; homophony, as distinguished from polyphony. –**monodist**, *n.* –**monodic**, *adj.*

monogamy /məˈnɒɡəmi/ *n.* **1.** the practice or condition of having only one spouse at a time. **2.** the practice of remaining faithful to a single sexual partner. **3.** *Zool.* the habit of having only one mate. **4.** the practice of marrying only once during lifetime. **–monogamist,** *n.* **–monogamous,** *adj.*

monogram /ˈmɒnəɡræm/ *n.* a character consisting of two or more letters combined or interlaced, commonly one's initials, often printed on stationery, embroidered on clothing, handkerchiefs, etc. **–monogrammatic** /mɒnəɡrəˈmætɪk/, *adj.*

monograph /ˈmɒnəɡræf, -ɡrɑf/ *n.* **1.** a treatise on a particular subject. **2.** *Bot., Zool.* an account of a single thing or class of things, as of a species of animals or plants. **–monographer,** *n.* **–monographic** /mɒnəˈɡræfɪk/, *adj.* **–monographically** /mɒnəˈɡræfɪkli/, *adv.*

monolith /ˈmɒnəlɪθ/ *n.* **1.** a single block or piece of stone of considerable size, whether in the natural state, as Uluru, or fabricated, as in architecture or sculpture. **2.** an obelisk, column, statue, etc., formed of a single block of stone. **3.** something resembling a large block of stone, especially in having a massive, uniform, or unyielding quality or character. **–monolithic,** *adj.*

monologue /ˈmɒnəlɒɡ/ *n.* **1.** a prolonged talk or discourse by a single speaker. **2.** any composition, as a poem, in which a single person speaks alone. **3.** a form of dramatic entertainment by a single speaker. **–monologic** /mɒnəˈlɒdʒɪk/, **monological** /mɒnəˈlɒdʒɪkəl/, *adj.* **–monologist** /ˈmɒnəlɒɡəst, məˈnɒləɡəst/, *n.*

monomania /mɒnoʊˈmeɪniə/ *n.* **1.** insanity in which the patient is irrational on one subject only. **2.** an exaggerated zeal for, or interest in, some one thing; a craze. **–monomaniac** /mɒnoʊˈmeɪniæk/, *n.* **–monomaniacal** /mɒnoʊməˈnaɪəkəl/, *adj.*

monophonic /mɒnəˈfɒnɪk/ *adj.* **1.** of or relating to monophony. **2.** of or relating to a system of sound reproduction through only one loudspeaker. Compare **stereophonic.**

monoplane /ˈmɒnəpleɪn/ *n.* an aeroplane with only one pair of wings.

monopolise /məˈnɒpəlaɪz/ *v.t.* **1.** *Econ.* to acquire, have, or exercise a monopoly of (a market, commodity, etc.). **2.** to obtain exclusive possession of; keep entirely to oneself: *she tried to monopolise his time.* Also, **monopolize. –monopolisation** /mənɒpəlaɪˈzeɪʃən/, **–monopoliser,** *n.*

monopoly /məˈnɒpəli/ *n.* (*pl.* **-lies**) **1.** the total control of an article or service in a particular market. **2.** the exclusive right to carry on such a trade or service, given by a government, etc. **3.** the total ownership or control of something. **4.** an article, service, etc., over which there is total control. **5.** a company or the like having such control.

monorail /ˈmɒnəreɪl/ *n.* a railway with coaches running on a single (usually overhead) rail.

monosaccharide /mɒnoʊˈsækəraɪd, -rəd/ *n.* *Chem.* a simple sugar, such as glucose, fructose, arabinose, and ribose, occurring in nature or obtained by the hydrolysis of glucosides or polysaccharides.

monosodium glutamate /mɒnəˌsoʊdiəm ˈɡlutəmeɪt/ *n.* a sodium salt of glutamic acid used in cookery to enhance the natural flavour of a dish; ajinomoto; taste powder; Chinese salt. *Abbrev.:* MSG

monosyllabic /mɒnəsəˈlæbɪk/ *adj.* **1.** having only one syllable, as the word *no.* **2.** having a vocabulary composed exclusively of monosyllables; uncommunicative. **–monosyllabically,** *adv.*

monosyllable /ˈmɒnəsɪləbəl/ *n.* a word of one syllable, as *yes* and *no.*

monotheism /ˈmɒnoʊθiˌɪzəm, mɒnoʊˈθiɪzəm/ *n.* the doctrine or belief that there is only one god.

–monotheist, *n., adj.* **–monotheistic** /ˌmɒnoʊθiˈɪstɪk/, *adj.* **–monotheistically** /ˌmɒnoʊθiˈɪstɪkli/, *adv.*

monotone /ˈmɒnətoʊn/ *n.* **1.** a vocal utterance, or series of speech sounds, in a single unvaried tone. **2.** a single tone without harmony or variation in pitch. **3.** recitation or singing of words in such a tone. **4.** sameness of style, as in composition or writing.

monotonous /məˈnɒtənəs/ *adj.* **1.** unvarying in any respect, lacking in variety, or tiresomely uniform. **2.** characterising a sound continuing on one note. **3.** having very little inflection; limited to a narrow pitch range. **–monotonously,** *adv.* **–monotonousness,** *n.*

monotony /məˈnɒtəni/ *n.* **1.** lack of variety, or wearisome uniformity, as in occupation, scenery, etc. **2.** the continuance of an unvarying sound; monotone. **3.** sameness of tone or pitch, as in utterance.

monotreme /ˈmɒnətrim/ *n.* any of the Monotremata, an order of mammals restricted to the Australian region and comprising only the platypus and the echidnas, oviparous mammals in which the genital, urinary, and digestive organs have a common opening; the female does not have nipples but feeds her young with milk secreted from pores on her belly.

monounsaturated /ˌmɒnoʊʌnˈsætʃəreɪtəd/ *adj.* of or relating to a fat or oil based on fatty acids having only one double bond per chain, as oleic acid in olive oil. Also, **mono-unsaturated.**

monseigneur /mɒseɪˈnjɜ/ *n.* (*pl.* **messeigneurs** /meɪsɛn-ˈjɜ/) a French title of honour given to princes, bishops, and other persons of eminence.

monsoon /mɒnˈsun/ *n.* **1.** any major wind system which reverses in direction seasonally, usually creating a difference between dry and rainy seasons. **2.** a rainy season associated with a monsoon, as the wet season of northern Australia from December to March, or of south Asia from April to October. **–monsoonal,** *adj.*

monsoon forest *n.* a semi-deciduous tropical forest occurring in areas which experience a monsoon climate, marked by dry periods followed by torrential rain.

monster /ˈmɒnstə/ *n.* **1.** an imaginary animal of part animal and part human form, such as a centaur, griffin, etc. **2.** an animal or a plant of abnormal form or structure. **3.** a person who excites horror. **4.** any animal or thing of huge size. *–adj.* **5.** huge; monstrous.

monstrosity /mɒnˈstrɒsəti/ *n.* (*pl.* **-ties**) something monstrous.

monstrous /ˈmɒnstrəs/ *adj.* **1.** huge; extremely great: *a monstrous sum.* **2.** frightful or hideous; extremely ugly. **3.** revolting; outrageous; shocking: *a monstrous proposal.* **4.** deviating greatly from the natural or normal form or type. **5.** having the nature or appearance of a legendary monster. **–monstrously,** *adv.* **–monstrousness,** *n.*

montage /mɒnˈtaʒ, ˈmɒntaʒ/ *n.* **1.** the art or method of arranging in one composition pictorial elements borrowed from several sources so that the elements are both distinct and blended into a whole, through techniques such as superimposition. **2.** *Film, TV* a technique of film editing in which several shots are juxtaposed or partially superimposed to form a single image.

montane /ˈmɒnteɪn/ *adj.* **1.** mountainous: *a montane region.* **2.** *Biol.* (of a species) found in a mountainous habitat.

month /mʌnθ/ *n.* **1.** approximately one twelfth of a tropical or solar year (**solar month**). **2.** any of the twelve parts (January, February, etc.) into which the calendar year is divided (**calendar month**). **3.** the time from any day of one calendar month to the corresponding day of the next. *–phr. Colloq.* **4. a month of Sundays,** a very long time. **5. that time of the month,** the menstrual period.

monument /'mɒnjəmənt/ *n.* **1.** something erected in memory of a person, event, etc., as a pillar, statue, or the like. **2.** any building, megalith, etc., surviving from a past age, and regarded as of historical or archaeological importance. **3.** any work, writing, or the like by a person, regarded as a memorial of them after their death. **4.** any enduring evidence or notable example of something.

monumental /mɒnjə'mɛntl/ *adj.* **1.** resembling a monument; massive or imposing. **2.** of great importance or significance: *a monumental event in the nation's history* **3.** involving great effort and resources: *a monumental task.* **4.** (of a work of art) **a.** of great physical size. **b.** noble in conception and execution. **–monumentally,** *adv.*

-mony a noun suffix indicating result or condition, as in *parsimony*; but sometimes having the same function as **-ment**.

MOO /muː/ *n. Computer Games* a game on the internet, similar to a MUD, but in which the users are able to modify the conditions under which the game is being played.

mooch /muːtʃ/ *Colloq.* –*v.i.* **1.** to skulk or sneak. **2.** to hang or loiter about. **3.** to slouch or saunter along. –*v.t.* **4.** to get without paying or at another's expense; cadge. Also, **mouch.** **–moocher,** *n.*

mood[1] /muːd/ *n.* **1.** a frame of mind, or state of feeling, as at a particular time. **2.** (*pl.*) fits of uncertainty, gloominess, or sullenness.

mood[2] /muːd/ *n. Gram.* (in many languages) a set of categories of verb inflection, whose selection depends either on the syntactic relation of the verb to other verbs in the sentence, or on a difference in the speaker's attitude towards the action expressed by the verb (e.g., certainty as opposed to uncertainty; question as opposed to statement; wish as opposed to command; emphasis as opposed to hesitancy).

moody /'muːdi/ *adj.* (**-dier, -diest**) **1.** given to gloomy or sullen moods; ill-humoured. **2.** proceeding from or showing such a mood: *a moody silence.* **3.** exhibiting sharply varied moods; temperamental. **–moodily,** *adv.* **–moodiness,** *n.*

Moody rating *n.* a scaled evaluation, published by US company Moody's Investor Service, of the default risk of bonds issued by a borrower, be it a company or a country.

moon /muːn/ *n.* **1.** (*oft. upper case*) the body which revolves around the earth monthly at a mean distance of 384 403 km, accompanying the earth in its annual revolution about the sun. It is 3 476 km in diameter, and its mass is 0.0123 that of the earth. **2.** this heavenly body during a particular lunar month, or during a certain period of time, or at a certain point of time, regarded as a distinct object or entity. **a.** **new moon,** the moon when in conjunction with the sun and hence invisible, or the phase so represented, or the moon soon afterwards when visible as a slender crescent. **b.** **half-moon,** the moon when half its disc is illuminated, occurring when at either quadrature, or quarter. **c.** **full moon,** the moon when the whole of its disc is illuminated, occurring when in opposition to the sun, or the phase so represented. **d.** **old moon,** the waning moon. **e.** **waxing moon,** the moon at any time before it is full, so called because its illuminated area is increasing. **f.** **waning moon,** the moon at any time after it has been full, so called because its illuminated area is decreasing. **3.** any planetary satellite. –*v.i.* **4.** *Colloq.* to expose one's buttocks, especially as a gesture of derision or defiance. –*phr.* **5.** **moon about,** *Colloq.* to wander about or gaze idly, dreamily, or listlessly. **6.** **once in a blue moon,** seldom; very rarely. **7.** **over the moon,** *Colloq.* highly delighted.

moon boot *n.* an orthopaedic shoe, having a rigid sole and side walls and secured by velcro straps; designed to hold the foot rigid to protect an injured or broken ankle.

moonlight /'muːnlaɪt/ *n.* **1.** the light of the moon. –*adj.* **2.** relating to moonlight. **3.** lit by moonlight. **4.** happening by moonlight. –*v.i.* **5.** *Colloq.* to work at a second job, often at night.

moonshine /'muːnʃaɪn/ *n.* **1.** the light of the moon. **2.** empty or foolish talk, ideas, etc.; nonsense. **3.** *Colloq.* smuggled or illicitly distilled liquor.

moonstone /'muːnstoʊn/ *n.* a white translucent variety of feldspar with a bluish pearly lustre, used as a gem.

moonwalk /'muːnwɔːk/ *n.* **1.** a walk on the surface of the moon by an astronaut. **2.** a dance move in which the dancer raises one foot to the toe while gliding the other foot backwards, the move being shifted from one foot to the other in succession, the result being the illusion of a forward walking movement while the actual movement is a backwards slide. –*v.i.* **3.** to walk on the surface of the moon. **4.** to perform a moonwalk (def. 2). Also, **moon walk.** **–moonwalking,** *n.*

moor[1] /mʊə/ *n.* **1.** a tract of open, peaty, wasteland, often overgrown with heath, common in high latitudes and altitudes where drainage is poor; a heath. **2.** a tract of land preserved for shooting game.

moor[2] /mʊə/ *v.t.* **1.** to secure (a ship, etc.) in a particular place, as by cables and anchors (especially two or more) or by lines. **2.** to secure, or fix firmly.

moorhen /'mʊəhɛn/ *n.* → **dusky moorhen.**

moose /muːs/ *n.* (*pl.* **moose**) any of the four subspecies of the elk, *Alces alces,* found in North America.

moot /muːt/ *adj.* **1.** subject to argument or discussion; debatable; doubtful: *a moot proposition.* –*v.t.* **2.** to bring forward (any point, subject, project, etc.) for discussion. –*n.* **3.** an early English assembly of the people, exercising political, administrative, and judicial powers. **4.** an argument or discussion, especially of a hypothetical legal case. **–mooter,** *n.*

moot court *n.* a mock court for the conduct of hypothetical legal cases, as for practice for students of law.

moot point *n.* a matter which is uncertain and open to debate.

mop /mɒp/ *n.* **1.** a bundle of coarse yarn, a piece of cloth, or the like, fastened at the end of a stick or handle, used for washing floors, dishes, etc. **2.** a cleaning or wiping with a mop: *give it a good mop.* **3.** a thick mass, as of hair. –*v.t.* (**mopped, mopping**) **4.** to rub, wipe, clean, or remove with a mop. **5.** to wipe: *to mop the face with a handkerchief.* –*phr.* **6.** **mop up, a.** to clean up. **b.** *Mil.* to clear (ground, trenches, towns, etc.) of scattered or remaining enemy combatants, after attacking forces have gone beyond the place. **c.** to clear away remaining danger points of a disastrous incident, as fire, earthquake, etc., after the main threat has been faced.

mope /moʊp/ *v.i.* to be sunk in listless apathy or dull dejection. **–moper,** *n.* **–mopey, mopish,** *adj.* **–mopingly, mopishly,** *adv.*

moped /'moʊpɛd/ *n.* a light, low-powered motorcycle equipped with pedals for starting and assisting the motor.

mopoke /'moʊpoʊk/ *n.* **1.** → **boobook. 2.** → **tawny frogmouth.**

moraine /mɒ'reɪn/ *n.* a ridge, mound, or irregular mass of boulders, gravel, sand and clay, transported in or on a glacier. **–morainal, morainic,** *adj.*

moral /'mɒrəl/ *adj.* **1.** relating to or concerned with right conduct or the distinction between right or wrong: *moral considerations.* **2.** able to act according to the rules of right conduct. **3.** sexually virtuous; chaste. **4.** of, relating to, or producing an effect upon the mind, feelings, or on results generally: *moral support.* **5.** having definite possibilities: *a moral certainty.* –*n.*

6. the moral teaching or practical lesson contained in a fable, tale, etc. **7.** *Colloq.* a certainty: *it's a moral to win.*

morale /mə'ral/ *n.* moral or mental condition with respect to cheerfulness, confidence, zeal, etc.: *the morale of troops.*

moral hazard *n.* **1.** a situation in which one's morals are at risk. **2.** *Finance* a situation in which a person engaged in a financial transaction has an incentive to take unwarranted risks because of the existence of a mechanism for redressing any adverse effects of a bad transaction.

moralise /'mɒrəlaɪz/ *v.i.* **1.** to make moral reflections. *–v.t.* **2.** to improve the morals of. Also, **moralize**. **–moralisation** /mɒrəlaɪ'zeɪʃən/, *n.* **–moraliser**, *n.* **–moralisingly**, *adv.*

morality /mə'ræləti/ *n.* (*pl.* **-ties**) **1.** conformity to the rules of right conduct; moral or virtuous conduct. **2.** sexual virtue; chastity. **3.** moral quality or character. **4.** a system of morals; ethics. **5.** moral teaching.

morality play *n.* a type of allegorical drama employing personifications of virtues and vices, a form of which was in vogue in Europe from the 14th to the 16th centuries.

morality tale *n.* a story of the kind told in a morality play.

morals /'mɒrəlz/ *pl. n.* **1.** principles or habits with respect to right or wrong conduct; ethics. **2.** behaviour or habits in sexual matters.

morass /mə'ræs/ *n.* a tract of low, soft, wet ground; marsh.

moratorium /mɒrə'tɔriəm/ *n.* (*pl.* **-toria** /-'tɔriə/ *or* **-toriums**) **1.** a general suspension of some type of legal obligation. **2.** the period of such a suspension. **3. a.** an agreed or imposed respite; a temporary cessation: *a moratorium on arms sales.* **b.** a deferring of a decision or discussion on a particular matter, usually in politics.

moray /'mɒreɪ/ *n.* any of numerous eels of the family Muraenidae, often found lurking amongst rocks and weeds, as the **long-tailed eel**, *Evenchelys macrurus* of northern Australia, or *Muraena helena*, common in the Mediterranean and valued as a food fish.

morbid /'mɔbəd/ *adj.* **1.** suggesting an unhealthy mental state; unwholesomely gloomy, sensitive, extreme, etc. **2.** affected by, proceeding from, or characteristic of disease. **3.** relating to diseased parts: *morbid anatomy.* **–morbidly**, *adv.* **–morbidness**, *n.*

mordant /'mɔdnt/ *adj.* **1.** caustic or sarcastic, as wit, a speaker, etc. *–n.* **2.** a substance used in dyeing to fix the colouring matter, especially a metallic compound, as an oxide or hydroxide, which combines with the organic dye and forms an insoluble coloured compound or lake in the fibre. **3.** an acid or other corrosive substance used in etching to eat out the lines, etc. **–mordancy**, *n.* **–mordantly**, *adv.*

mordent /'mɔdnt/ *n. Music* a melodic embellishment consisting of a rapid alternation of a principal note with a supplementary note a semitone below it, called *single* or *short* when the supplementary note occurs only once, and *double* or *long* when this occurs twice or more often.

more /mɔ/ *adj.* **1.** in greater quantity, amount, measure, degree, or number: *more money.* **2.** additional or further: *do not lose any more time. –pron.* **3.** an additional quantity, amount, or number: *would you like more?* **4.** a greater quantity, amount, or degree: *she ate more than me.* **5.** something of greater importance: *she refused, and what is more, very rudely.* **6.** (*construed as pl.*) a greater number of a class specified, or the greater number of persons: *she believed him, but more were sceptical. –adv.* **7.** in or to a greater extent or degree: *more rapid.* **8.** in addition; further; longer; again. *–phr.*

9. more or less, to a certain extent; approximately. **10. no more, a.** (in the past but) not now: *that style is the rage no more.* **b.** (*euphemistic*) dead: *the prince is no more.*

more-ish /'mɔr-ɪʃ/ *adj.* of or relating to something of which one would like more; tempting; delicious: *that cake is very more-ish.*

moreover /mɔr'ouvə/ *adv.* beyond what has been said; further; besides.

mores /'mɔreɪz/ *pl. n.* customs or conventions accepted without question and embodying the fundamental moral views of a group.

Moreton Bay fig *n.* a massive shady tree, *Ficus macrophylla*, native to the east coast of Australia which bears small, purplish, non-edible fruit.

morganatic /mɔgə'nætɪk/ *adj.* designating or relating to a form of marriage in which a person of high rank marries a person of lower station with the stipulation that neither the spouse nor the issue (if any) shall have any claim to his or her rank or property. **–morganatically**, *adv.*

morgue /mɔg/ *n.* **1.** a place in which the bodies of persons found dead are exposed for identification. **2.** *Journalism Colloq.* the reference library of clippings, mats, books, etc., kept by a newspaper, etc.

moribund /'mɒrəbʌnd/ *adj.* **1.** in a dying state. **2.** on the verge of extinction or termination. **–moribundity** /mɒrə'bʌndəti/, *n.* **–moribundly**, *adv.*

Mormon /'mɔmən/ *n.* **1.** a member of a religious body founded in the US in 1830 by Joseph Smith and calling itself 'The Church of Jesus Christ of Latter-day Saints'. **2. The Book of**, a sacred book of the Mormon Church, supposed to have been an abridgement by a prophet (**Mormon**) of a record of certain ancient peoples in America, written on golden plates and discovered and translated (1827–30) by Joseph Smith. *–adj.* **3.** of or relating to the Mormons or their religious system. **–Mormonism**, *n.*

mornay /'mɔneɪ/ *adj.* covered with a thick white sauce which has grated cheese added to it.

morning /'mɔnɪŋ/ *n.* **1.** the beginning of day; the dawn. **2.** the first part or period of the day, extending from dawn, or from midnight, to noon. **3.** the first or early period of anything. *–adj.* **4.** of or relating to morning: *the morning hours.* **5.** occurring, appearing, coming, used, etc., in the morning: *the morning sun. –phr.* **6. morning, noon, and night**, continuously; with monotonous persistence: *that baby cries morning, noon, and night.*

morning dress *n.* formal dress used in daytime, as at weddings, etc., consisting for men typically of morning coat, light grey striped trousers, a light-coloured top-hat, etc.

morning sickness *n.* nausea occurring often in the early part of the day, as a characteristic symptom in the first months of pregnancy.

morning star *n.* a bright planet, seen in the east before sunrise.

morocco /mə'rɒkou/ *n.* **1.** a fine leather made from goatskins tanned with sumach, originally in Morocco. **2.** any leather made in imitation of this. Also, **morocco leather**.

moron /'mɔrɒn/ *n.* **1.** a very stupid person. **2.** *Psychiatry Obsolesc.* a person with severe mental deficiency, whose mentality is judged incapable of developing beyond that of a child. **–moronic** /mə'rɒnɪk/, *adj.* **–moronism, moronity** /mə'rɒnəti/, *n.*

morose /mə'rous/ *adj.* gloomily or sullenly ill-humoured as a person, mood, etc. **–morosely**, *adv.* **–moroseness**, *n.*

morph /mɔf/ *v.i.* **1.** to alter shape by morphing. *–phr.* **2. morph into**, to change into: *a nice person who morphs into a tyrant at the office.*

morph- variant of **morpho-** before vowels.

-morph a word element meaning 'form', 'shape', 'structure', as in *isomorph*.

morpheme /ˈmɔfim/ *n. Ling.* any of the minimum meaningful elements in a language, not further divisible into smaller meaningful elements, usually recurring in various contexts with relatively constant meaning: either a word, as *girl*, *world*, or part of a word, as *-ish* or *-ly* in *girlish* and *worldly*. —**morphemic** /mɔˈfimɪk/, *adj.*

-morphic a word element used as adjective termination corresponding to **-morph**, as in *anthropomorphic*.

morphine /ˈmɔfin/ *n.* a bitter crystalline alkaloid, $C_{17}H_{19}NO_3.H_2O$, the most important narcotic principle of opium, used in medicine (usually in the form of a sulphate or other salt) to dull pain, induce sleep, etc. Also, **morphia** /ˈmɔfiə/.

morphing /ˈmɔfɪŋ/ *n. Film*, *TV*, *Computers* the manipulation of digitised images using a computer, producing a sequence whereby one image changes into another.

morpho- initial word element corresponding to **-morph**.

morphology /mɔˈfɒlədʒi/ *n.* **1.** the systematic study of form, structure, and the like. **2.** the branch of biology that deals with the form and structure of animals and plants, without regard to functions. **3.** *Gram.* the patterns of word formation in a particular language, including inflection, derivation, and composition. **4.** *Geog.* the systematic study of the physical form of lands, regions, or towns. —**morphologic** /mɔfəˈlɒdʒɪk/, **morphological** /mɔfəˈlɒdʒɪkəl/, *adj.* —**morphologically** /mɔfəˈlɒdʒɪkli/, *adv.* —**morphologist**, *n.*

-morphous a word element used as adjective termination corresponding to **-morph**, as in *amorphous*.

morrell /məˈrɛl/ *n.* a tall tree, *Eucalyptus longicornis*, with pointed buds, found in south-western Australia.

morrow /ˈmɒroʊ/ *n.* the day next after this or after some other particular day or night.

morse code /mɔs ˈkoʊd/ *n.* a system of dots, dashes, and spaces, or the corresponding sounds or the like, used in telegraphy and signalling to represent the letters of the alphabet, numerals, etc. Also, **Morse code, morse alphabet**.

morsel /ˈmɔsəl/ *n.* **1.** a bite, mouthful, or small portion of food or the like. **2.** a small piece, quantity, or amount of anything; a scrap; a bit.

mortal /ˈmɔtl/ *adj.* **1.** subject to death: *we are all mortal*. **2.** human: *this mortal life*. **3.** belonging to this world. **4.** relating to death: *mortal throes*. **5.** (of a sin) serious enough to cause spiritual death (opposed to *venial*). **6.** causing death; fatal: *a mortal wound*. **7.** to the death: *mortal combat*. **8.** deadly: *mortal enemy*. **9.** dreadful: *in mortal fear*. **10.** very great; extreme: *in a mortal hurry*. **11.** possible: *of no mortal use*. –*n.* **12.** a human being. —**mortally**, *adv.*

mortality /mɔˈtæləti/ *n.* (*pl.* **-ties**) **1.** the condition of being mortal or subject to death; mortal character, nature, or existence. **2.** mortal beings collectively; humanity. **3.** relative frequency of death, or death rate, as in a district or community. **4.** death or destruction on a large scale, as from war, plague, famine, etc.

mortality table *n.* an actuarial table compiled by an insurance company from statistics on the life spans of an arbitrarily selected population group or of former policy-holders.

mortar¹ /ˈmɔtə/ *n.* **1.** a vessel of hard material, having a bowl-shaped cavity, in which drugs, spices, herbs, etc., are reduced to powder or paste with a pestle. **2.** any of various mechanical appliances in which substances are pounded or ground. **3.** a cannon very short in proportion to its bore, for throwing shells at high angles. **4.** some similar contrivance, as for throwing pyrotechnic bombs or a lifeline.

mortar² /ˈmɔtə/ *n.* a material which binds bricks, stones, etc., into a compact mass.

mortarboard /ˈmɔtəbɔd/ *n.* **1.** a board, commonly square, used by masons to hold mortar. **2.** a kind of cap with a close-fitting crown surmounted by a stiff, flat, cloth-covered, square piece, worn by university students, graduates, teachers, etc.

mortgage /ˈmɔgɪdʒ/ *n.* **1.** *Law* a security by way of conveyance or assignment of property securing the payment of a debt or the performance of an obligation where the property is redeemable upon payment or performance. –*v.t.* (**mortgaged, mortgaging**) **2.** to convey or place (property, especially houses or land) under a mortgage.

mortgagee /mɔgəˈdʒi/ *n. Law* someone to whom property is mortgaged.

mortgagor /ˈmɔgədʒə, mɔgəˈdʒɔ/ *n.* someone who mortgages property. Also, **mortgager**.

mortice /ˈmɔtəs/ *n.* **1.** a rectangular cavity of considerable depth in one piece of wood, etc., for receiving a corresponding projection (tenon) on another piece, so as to form a joint (**mortice and tenon joint**). **2.** *Printing* the portion cut away from a letterpress printing plate for the insertion of type or another plate. –*v.t.* (**-ticed, -ticing**) **3.** to fasten by, or as by, a mortice. Also, **mortise**.

mortify /ˈmɔtəfaɪ/ *v.t.* (**-fied, -fying**) **1.** to humiliate in feeling, as by a severe wound to the pride or self-complacency. **2.** to bring (the body, passions, etc.) into subjection by abstinence, ascetic discipline, or rigorous austerities. **3.** *Pathol.* to affect with gangrene or necrosis. —**mortification**, *n.* —**mortifier**, *n.* —**mortifyingly**, *adv.*

mortuary /ˈmɔtʃəri/ *n.* (*pl.* **-ries**) **1.** a place for the temporary reception of the dead. –*adj.* **2.** relating to or connected with death or the burial of the dead.

morwong /ˈmɔwɒŋ/ *n.* any of a number of species of marine food fishes of the family Cheilodactylidae, especially *Nemadactylus douglasii*, of southern Australian and New Zealand waters; black perch.

mosaic /moʊˈzeɪk, məˈzeɪk/ *n.* **1.** a picture or decoration made of small pieces of stone, glass, etc., of different colours, inlaid to form a design. **2.** the process of producing it. **3.** something resembling a mosaic in composition. **4.** *Aerial Surveying* an assembly of aerial photographs taken vertically and matched in such a way as to show a continuous photographic representation of an area (**mosaic map**). **5.** *Plant Pathol.* a symptom of various virus diseases, a patchy variation of colour. **6.** *Genetics* an organism, usually animal, composed of a mixture of genetically distinct tissues; chimera. –*adj.* **7.** relating to or resembling a mosaic or mosaic work. **8.** composed of diverse elements combined. —**mosaicist** /moʊˈzeɪəsəst/, *n.*

mosh /mɒʃ/ *v.i.* to move as one of a crush of spectators jostling each other to the music of a live band or act. —**moshing**, *n.*

mosh pit *n.* the area in front of the stage on which a band is performing where the audience moshes.

mosque /mɒsk/ *n.* a Muslim temple or place of worship.

mosquito /məsˈkitoʊ/ *n.* (*pl.* **-toes** *or* **-tos**) any of various dipterous insects of the family Culicidae (genera *Culex*, *Anopheles*, etc.), the females of which have a long proboscis, by means of which they puncture the skin of animals (including humans) and draw blood, some species transmitting certain diseases, as malaria and yellow fever.

moss /mɒs/ *n.* any of the cryptogamic plants which belong to the class Musci, of the bryophytes, comprising small leafy-stemmed plants growing in tufts, sods, or mats on moist ground, tree trunks, rocks, etc.

most /moʊst/ *adj.* **1.** in the greatest quantity, amount, degree, or number: *the most votes.* **2.** in the majority of instances: *most exercises are good.* **3.** greatest, as in size or range: *the most part.* *–pron.* **4.** the greatest quantity, amount, or degree: *Jane did the most to help.* **5.** the greatest part: *most of the work is finished.* **6.** (*treated as pl.*) the majority of persons: *most of us agreed.* *–adv.* **7.** in or to the greatest range or degree (in this sense much used before adjectives and adverbs): *most rapid.*

-most a suffixal use of *most* found in a series of superlatives, as in *utmost, foremost.*

mostly /ˈmoʊstli/ *adv.* **1.** for the most part; in the main: *the work is mostly done.* **2.** chiefly.

mote /moʊt/ *n.* a particle or speck, especially of dust.

motel /moʊˈtɛl/ *n.* **1.** a roadside hotel which provides accommodation for travellers in self-contained, serviced units, with parking for their vehicles. **2.** *NZ* such a unit.

motet /moʊˈtɛt/ *n.* a vocal composition in polyphonic style, on a biblical or similar prose text, intended for use in a church service.

moth /mɒθ/ *n.* (*pl.* **moths**) any of a very large group of lepidopterous insects, generally distinguished from the butterflies by not having their antennae clubbed and by their (mainly) nocturnal or crepuscular habits.

mothball /ˈmɒθbɒl/ *n.* **1.** a small ball of naphthalene or (sometimes) camphor, stored with clothes, etc., to repel moths. *–v.t.* **2.** to put out of use; place in reserve. *–phr.* **3. in mothballs, a.** no longer in use; in reserve. **b.** out of commission, as a ship.

mother /ˈmʌðə/ *n.* **1.** a female parent. **2.** a mother-in-law, step-mother, or adoptive mother. **3.** a familiar term for an old woman. **4.** the head of a female religious community. **5.** a woman looked upon as a mother, or exercising control like that of a mother. **6.** the qualities characteristic of a mother: *the mother in her prompted her to comfort the lost child.* *–adj.* **7.** that is a mother: *a mother bird.* **8.** relating to or characteristic of a mother: *mother love.* **9.** learned from one's mother: *her mother tongue is Italian.* **10.** having a relation like that of a mother: *a mother church.* *–v.t.* **11.** to be the mother of. **12.** to take as one's own. **13.** to care for as a mother does. *–motherly, adj.* *–motherless, adj.* *–motherliness, n.* *–motherhood, n.*

motherboard /ˈmʌðəbɔd/ *n.* *Computers* a printed circuit board plugged into the back of a computer into which other boards (**daughter boards**) can be slotted so that the computer can operate an optional range of peripherals. Also, **mother board.**

mother-in-law *n.* (*pl.* **mothers-in-law**) the mother of one's husband or wife.

motherland /ˈmʌðəlænd/ *n.* **1.** one's native country. **2.** the land of one's ancestors.

mother-of-pearl *n.* a hard, iridescent substance which forms the inner layer of certain shells, as that of the pearl oyster; nacre.

mothership /ˈmʌðəʃɪp/ *n.* **1.** a large ship which services the group of smaller ships with which it sails. **2.** a spacecraft which is the main vehicle providing resources and services to a fleet of smaller craft. Also, **mother ship.**

mother tongue *n.* **1.** the language first learned by a person; first language. **2.** → **parent language.**

motif /moʊˈtif, ˈmoʊtɪf/ *n.* **1.** a recurring subject or theme for development or treatment, as in art, literature, or music. **2.** a distinctive figure in a design, as of wallpaper. **3.** a dominant idea or feature.

motion /ˈmoʊʃən/ *n.* **1.** the process of moving, or changing place or position. **2.** a movement. **3.** power of movement, as of a living body. **4.** the action or manner of moving the body in walking, etc.; gait. **5.** a bodily movement or change of posture; gesture. **6.** a proposal formally made to a deliberative assembly: *to make a motion to adjourn.* **7.** *Law* an application made to a court or judge for an order, ruling, or the like. **8.** a suggestion or proposal. **9.** *Machinery* **a.** a piece of mechanism with a particular action or function. **b.** the action of such mechanism. **10.** → **stool** (def. 3). *–v.t.* **11.** to direct by a significant motion or gesture, as with the hand: *to motion a person to a seat.* *–v.i.* **12.** to make a significant motion; gesture, as with the hand for the purpose of directing: *to motion to a person.* *–phr.* **13. go through the motions,** to do what is required of one without any real expectation of an outcome from the performance. **14. in motion,** in active operation; moving.

motion capture *n.* the recording of the movements of people or objects, in particular for use in computer animation to give authentic movement to digital models.

motion picture *n.* → **film** (def. 4b).

motivate /ˈmoʊtəveɪt/ *v.t.* **1.** to provide with a motive or motives. **2.** to enthuse or inspire: *to motivate the staff.* *–motivation, n.*

motivated /ˈmoʊtəveɪtəd/ *adj.* ambitious; determined; energetic: *the prime minister is a highly motivated person.*

motive /ˈmoʊtɪv/ *n.* **1.** something that prompts a person to act in a certain way or that determines volition; an incentive. **2.** the goal or object of one's actions: *his motive was revenge.* **3.** (in art, literature, and music) a motif. *–adj.* **4.** causing, or tending to cause, motion.

motley /ˈmɒtli/ *adj.* **1.** exhibiting great diversity of elements; heterogeneous: *a motley crowd.* **2.** being of different colours combined; particoloured. *–n.* (*pl.* **-leys**) **3.** the motley or particoloured garment of the medieval professional fool or jester: *to wear the motley.* **4.** a heterogeneous assemblage.

motocross /ˈmoʊtəkrɒs/ *n.* a short distance motorcycle race of at least two laps on a circuit presenting a variety of surfaces and terrain.

motor /ˈmoʊtə/ *n.* **1.** a fairly small and powerful engine, especially an internal-combustion engine in a car, boat, etc. **2.** (now rare) a self-powered vehicle, as a car. **3.** someone or something that imparts motion, especially a contrivance (as a steam engine) which receives and modifies energy from some natural source in order to utilise it in driving machinery, etc. *–adj.* **4.** causing or imparting motion: *motor energy.* **5.** relating to, used for or operated by a motor: *motor oil; motor cycle.* **6.** *Physiol.* to do with movement: *the fall has damaged some of her motor nerves.* *–v.i.* **7.** (now rare) to travel by car; drive. *–motorise, motorize, v.*

motorcade /ˈmoʊtəkeɪd/ *n.* a procession or parade of motor cars. Also, *US,* **autocade.**

motor car *n.* → **car** (def. 1).

motorcycle /ˈmoʊtəsaɪkəl/ *n.* a motor vehicle resembling a bicycle, for one or two riders, sometimes with a sidecar attached. *–motorcyclist, n.*

motorist /ˈmoʊtərəst/ *n.* **1.** someone who drives a car. **2.** the user of a privately owned car.

motor scooter *n.* a low-built motorcycle having small wheels, footboards, and an enclosed engine. Also, **scooter.**

motor vehicle *n.* a road vehicle driven by a motor, usually an internal-combustion engine, as a car, motorcycle, or the like.

motorway /ˈmoʊtəweɪ/ *n.* a high-speed road which has limited direct access, usually a toll road. Compare **freeway.**

mottled /ˈmɒtld/ *adj.* spotted or blotched in colouring.

motto /ˈmɒtoʊ/ *n.* (*pl.* **-tos** *or* **-toes**) **1.** a maxim adopted as expressing one's guiding principle. **2.** a sentence, phrase, or word attached to or inscribed on anything as appropriate to it.

mould¹ /moʊld/ *n.* **1.** a hollow form used to shape melted or soft material: *pottery is sometimes made in a mould.* **2.** a frame, etc., on which something is made. **3.** a shape or form: *made in his father's mould.* *–v.t.* **4.** to work into a required shape or form; shape: *to mould a figure in clay; to mould someone's character.* **5.** *Foundry* to form a mould of or from, in order to make a casting. Also, *US*, **mold.** **–mouldable,** *adj.*

mould² /moʊld/ *n.* a growth of minute fungi forming on vegetable or animal matter, commonly as a downy or furry coating, and associated with decay. Also, *US*, **mold.**

moulder /'moʊldə/ *v.i.* to turn to dust by natural decay; crumble; waste away. Also, *US*, **molder.**

moulding /'moʊldɪŋ/ *n.* **1.** *Archit., etc.* **a.** a decorative variety of contour or outline given to cornices, jambs, strips of woodwork, etc. **b.** a shaped member introduced into a structure to afford such variety or decoration. **2.** shaped material in the form of a strip, used for supporting pictures, covering electric wires, etc. Also, *US*, **molding.**

moult /moʊlt/ *v.i.* (of birds, insects, reptiles, etc.) to cast or shed the feathers, skin, or the like, to be succeeded by a new growth. Also, **molt.** **–moulter,** *n.*

mound /maʊnd/ *n.* **1.** an elevation formed of earth or sand, debris, etc., overlying ruins, a grave, etc. **2.** a tumulus or other raised work of earth dating from a prehistoric or long-past period. **3.** a natural elevation of earth; a hillock or knoll. **4.** an artificial elevation of earth, as for a defence work, a dam or barrier, or any other purpose; an embankment. **5.** a heap or raised mass: *a mound of hay.*

mount¹ /maʊnt/ *v.t.* **1.** to go up; ascend: *to mount the stairs.* **2.** to get up on (a platform, a horse, etc.) **3.** (*usu. passive*) to set on horseback: *they were mounted on two handsome bays.* **4.** to raise or put (guns, etc.) into position for use. **5.** (of a fort or ship) to have (guns) in position for use. **6.** to go or put on (guard), as a sentry. **7.** (of a male animal) to climb up on (a female) for copulation. **8.** to fix on or in a setting: *to mount a photograph; to mount a jewel.* **9.** to put on (a play, exhibition, etc.). **10.** to prepare (a dead animal or skeleton) as a specimen. **11. a.** to prepare (a slide) for a microscope. **b.** to prepare (a specimen, etc.) by placing it on a slide. *–v.i.* **12.** to rise to a higher position, etc.; ascend. **13.** (oft. fol. by *up*) to rise in amount: *costs are steadily mounting.* **14.** to get up on a platform, horse, etc. *–n.* **15.** a horse for riding. **16.** a backing or setting: *the print looks fine with a grey mount.* **17.** *Microscopy* a prepared slide. **–mounter,** *n.*

mount² /maʊnt/ *n.* a mountain or hill (now chiefly poetic, except in proper names, as *Mount Wellington*).

mountain /'maʊntən/ *n.* **1.** a natural elevation of the earth's surface rising more or less abruptly to a summit, and attaining an altitude greater than that of a hill. **2.** something resembling this, as in size: *a mountain of ice.* **3.** a huge amount. *–adj.* **4.** of mountains: *mountain air.* **5.** living, growing, or found on mountains: *mountain people, mountain plants.* *–phr.* **6. make a mountain out of a molehill,** to make something insignificant into a major obstacle or difficulty.

mountain devil *n.* **1.** → **thorny devil. 2.** a woody shrub, *Lambertia formosa*, of sandstone areas of NSW. **3.** a small doll-like figure with a body usually of wool wound around pipe cleaners and a head formed from the woody fruit of *Lambertia formosa* which fancifully resembles the head of the Devil.

mountaineer /maʊntə'nɪə/ *n.* **1.** a climber of mountains. **2.** an inhabitant of a mountainous district. *–v.i.* **3.** to climb mountains. **–mountaineering,** *n.*

mountainous /'maʊntənəs/ *adj.* **1.** characterised by many mountains. **2.** of the nature of a mountain. **3.** resembling a mountain or mountains; large and high; huge: *mountainous waves.* **–mountainously,** *adv.*

Mount Cook lily *n.* a large white buttercup, *Ranunculus lyallii*, native to the South Island alpine districts of NZ.

mountebank /'maʊntəbæŋk/ *n.* **1.** someone who sells quack medicines from a platform in public places, appealing to the audience by tricks, storytelling, etc. **2.** any charlatan or quack. **–mountebankery** /maʊntə'bæŋkəri/, *n.*

mourn /mɔn/ *v.i.* **1.** to feel or express sorrow or grief. **2.** to grieve or express grief for the dead; lament. *–v.t.* **3.** to feel or express sorrow (over something lost or gone): *to mourn the loss of freedom.* **4.** to grieve or lament over (the dead).

mournful /'mɔnfəl/ *adj.* **1.** full of, expressing, or showing sorrow or grief, as persons, the tone, etc.; sorrowful; sad. **2.** expressing, or used in, mourning for the dead. **3.** causing, or attended with, sorrow or mourning: *a mournful occasion.* **4.** gloomy, sombre or dreary, as in appearance or character: *mournful shadows.* **–mournfully,** *adv.* **–mournfulness,** *n.*

mourning /'mɔnɪŋ/ *n.* **1.** the act of someone who mourns; sorrowing or lamentation. **2.** the conventional manifestation of sorrow for a person's death, especially by the wearing of black, the hanging of flags at half-mast, etc. **3.** the outward tokens of such sorrow, as black garments, etc. *–adj.* **4.** of, relating to, or used in mourning. *–phr.* **5. in mourning,** recently bereaved, especially if showing the traditional outward tokens of grief. **–mourningly,** *adv.*

mouse /maʊs/ *n.* (*pl.* **mice** /maɪs/ *or, for def. 3,* **mouses**) **1.** a small rodent that lives in the bush or infests houses. **2.** someone who is very quiet and shy, especially a girl or woman. **3.** a small handheld device attached to a computer for controlling the cursor, the movement of the mouse across the desk paralleling the movement of the cursor to items on a menu, commands being located by the cursor and activated by pressing a button on the mouse. *–v.i.* (**moused, mousing**) **4.** to hunt for or catch mice.

mousepad /'maʊspæd/ *n. Computers* a pad over which a mouse is moved, providing more traction than a smooth surface.

moussaka /mʊ'sakə/ *n.* a Balkan and Middle Eastern dish based on minced lamb, tomatoes, and eggplant, layered, topped with a thick white sauce and baked.

mousse /mus/ *n.* **1.** any of various preparations of whipped cream, beaten eggs, gelatine, etc., flavoured (sweet or savoury) and usually chilled. **2.** any of various cosmetic preparations of similar consistency, usually dispensed from a pressure pack, as one used to style or colour the hair, cleanse the skin, etc.: *shaving mousse; shower mousse.*

moustache /mə'staʃ, 'mʌstæʃ/ *n.* **1.** the hair growing on the upper lip, or on either half of the upper lip, of men. **2.** such hair when allowed to grow without shaving, and usually trimmed to a particular shape. **3.** hair or bristles growing near the mouth of an animal. Also, *US*, **mustache.** **–moustachioed** /mə'staʃioʊd/, *adj.*

mousy /'maʊsi/ *adj.* (**-sier, -siest**) **1.** resembling or suggesting a mouse, as in colour, smell, etc. **2.** drab and colourless. **3.** quiet as a mouse. **4.** infested with mice. Also, **mousey.**

mouth *n.* /maʊθ/ (*pl.* **mouths** /maʊðz/) **1.** the opening through which an animal takes in food, or the cavity containing or the parts including the masticating apparatus. **2.** the masticating and tasting apparatus. **3.** a person or other animal as requiring food. **4.** the oral opening or cavity considered as the source of vocal utterance. **5.** a grimace made with the lips. **6.** an opening leading out of or into any cavity or hollow place or thing: *the mouth of a cave.* **7.** a part of a river or the like where its waters are discharged into some other body of water: *the mouth of the Nile.* **8.** the opening between the jaws of a vice or the like. **9.** *Colloq.* someone who talks volubly and at great length. *–v.t.* /mauð/ **10.** to utter in a sonorous, oratorical, or pompous manner, or with unnecessarily noticeable use of the mouth or lips. **11.** to examine the teeth of (a sheep) to determine its age. **12.** to form (words) with the lips, uttering no sound. *–v.i.* /mauð/ **13.** to speak or declaim sonorously and oratorically, or with mouthing of the words. **14.** to grimace with the lips. *–phr.* **15. by word of mouth,** orally, as opposed to in writing. **16. down in the mouth,** depressed; unhappy. **17. give mouth to,** to utter; speak: *to give mouth to one's thoughts.* **18. keep one's mouth shut,** *Colloq.* **a.** to refrain from talking: *you can keep your mouth shut!* **b.** to keep information secret: *he knows how to keep his mouth shut.* **19. mouth off,** *Colloq.* to release pent-up emotions of anger or frustration by speaking wildly or abusively. **20. put one's money where one's mouth is,** *Colloq.* to give financial support to a cause, project, etc., which one has openly expressed belief in. **21. run off at the mouth,** *Colloq.* to talk loosely and unguardedly. **22. shut one's big mouth,** *Colloq.* to cease disclosing information. **23. shut one's mouth,** *Colloq.* to be quiet.

mouthful /ˈmauθfʊl/ *n.* (*pl.* **-fuls**) **1.** as much as a mouth can hold. **2.** as much as is taken into the mouth at one time. **3.** a small quantity. **4.** *Colloq.* something long or difficult to say: *his name is quite a mouthful.*

mouth organ *n.* → **harmonica** (def. 1).

mouthpiece /ˈmauθpis/ *n.* **1.** a part of a musical instrument, telephone, etc., held in or to the mouth. **2.** a part of a horse's bridle held in the mouth. **3.** *Sport* a guard for the teeth. **4.** someone or something that speaks for or represents another; spokesperson.

mouth-to-mouth /mauθ-tə-ˈmauθ/ *adj.* **1.** denoting a method of resuscitation in which air is breathed rhythmically into the mouth of the patient. *–n.* **2.** the method itself: *he gave her mouth-to-mouth.*

move /muv/ *v.i.* **1.** to change place or position; pass from one place or situation to another. **2.** to change one's abode; go from one place of residence to another. **3.** to advance, progress, or make progress. **4.** to have a regular motion, as an implement or a machine; turn; revolve. **5.** *Commerce* to be disposed of by sale, as goods in stock. **6.** *Colloq.* to start off, or depart: *it's time to be moving.* **7.** (of the bowels) to operate. **8.** to be active in a particular sphere: *to move in society.* **9.** to take action, or act, as in an affair. **10.** to make a formal request, application, or proposal: *to move for a new trial.* *–v.t.* **11.** to change the place or position of; take from one place, posture, or situation to another. **12.** to set or keep in motion; stir or shake. **13.** to prompt, actuate, or impel to some action: *what moved you to do this?* **14.** to cause (the bowels) to act or operate. **15.** to affect with tender or compassionate emotion; touch. **16.** to propose formally, as to a court or judge, or for consideration by a deliberative assembly. **17.** to submit a formal request or proposal to (a ruler, a court, etc.). *–n.* **18.** the act of moving; a movement. **19.** a change of abode or residence. **20.** an action towards an end; a step. **21.** *Games, etc.* the right or turn to move. *–phr.* **22. get a move on,** *Colloq.* hurry up. **23. move heaven and earth,** to do one's utmost. **24. move in,** to take up residence in a new home. **25. move in on,** to attack. **26. move out,** to leave a home. **27. move someone to ...,** to arouse in someone (the feeling specified): *to move him to pity.* **28. move with the times,** to alter one's own attitudes or ideas in conjunction with changes in

society. **29. on the move,** moving. *–movable,* **moveable,** *adj.* *–mover,* *n.*

movement /ˈmuvmənt/ *n.* **1.** the act, process or result of moving. **2.** a particular manner of moving: *the graceful movements of a dancer.* **3.** (*chiefly pl.*) (a set of) actions or activities: *can you trace your movements of the past week?* **4.** *Mil.* a change of position of soldiers or ships. **5.** the rapid progress of events; momentum. **6.** the movement of events in a story, play, etc. **7.** the suggestion of action in a painting, etc. **8.** a group or a number of groups of people working for a particular cause or purpose: *the conservation movement.* **9.** the course or tendency of affairs in a particular field; trend: *the movement towards shorter working hours.* **10.** an emptying (of the bowels). **11.** the mechanism of a clock. **12.** *Music* **a.** the main division or section of a sonata, symphony, etc. **b.** time; tempo; motion; rhythm.

mover and shaker *n.* *Colloq.* an important and influential person.

movie /ˈmuvi/ *n.* **1.** → **film** (def. 4b). *–phr.* **2. the movies a.** → **film** (def. 4c). **b.** a screening of a film at a cinema: *we are going to the movies tonight.*

moving /ˈmuvɪŋ/ *adj.* **1.** that moves. **2.** causing or producing motion. **3.** actuating, instigating, or impelling: *the moving cause of a dispute.* **4.** that excites the feelings or affects with emotion, especially touching or pathetic. *–movingly,* *adv.*

mow /mou/ *verb* (**mowed, mown** *or* **mowed, mowing**) *–v.t.* **1.** to cut down (grass, grain, etc.) with a scythe or a machine. **2.** to cut grass, grain, etc., from. *–v.i.* **3.** to cut down grass, grain, etc. *–phr.* **4. mow down,** to cut down, destroy, or kill indiscriminately or in great numbers, as soldiers in battle. *–mower,* *n.*

mozzarella /mɒtsəˈrɛlə/ *n.* a soft, white, ripened cheese, with a plastic curd, giving it a smooth, close texture.

mozzie /ˈmɒzi/ *n.* *Colloq.* a mosquito. Also, **mossie** /ˈmɒzi/.

MP3 /ɛm pi ˈθri/ *n.* **1.** a digital audio file in which the audio signal is compressed to a size smaller than the original WAV format while apparently maintaining audio quality. *–adj.* **2.** of or relating to such a file. Also, **mp3.**

MP3 player *n.* a device for downloading, storing, and playing MP3s.

Mr /ˈmɪstə/ *a* title prefixed to a man's name or position: *Mr Lawson, Mr Prime Minister.*

Mrs /ˈmɪsəz/ *n.* a title prefixed to the name of a married woman: *Mrs Jones.*

Ms /mɜz/ *a* title prefixed to the name of a woman, used to avoid reference to marital status: *Ms Smith.*

much /mʌtʃ/ *adj.* **1.** in great quantity, amount, measure, or degree: *much work.* *–n.* **2.** a great quantity or amount; a great deal: *much of this is true.* **3.** a great, important, or notable thing or matter: *the house is not much to look at.* *–adv.* **4.** to a great extent or degree; greatly; far: *much pleased; much better; much too fast.* **5.** nearly, approximately, or about: *this is much the same as the others.* *–phr.* **6. as much,** the same; precisely that. **7. make much of, a.** to treat, represent, or consider as of great importance: *the prosecution made much of this discrepancy.* **b.** to treat (a person) with great, flattering, or fond consideration. **8. much of a muchness,** (of two or more objects, concepts, etc.) very similar; having little to choose between them. **9. not go much on,** *Colloq.* to be unenthusiastic about.

mucilage /ˈmjusəlɪdʒ/ *n.* **1.** any of various preparations of gum, glue, or the like, for causing adhesion. **2.** any of various gummy secretions or gelatinous substances present in plants.

muck /mʌk/ *n.* **1.** farmyard dung, decaying vegetable matter, etc., in a moist state; manure. **2.** a highly organic soil, less than fifty per cent combustible, often used as manure. **3.** filth; dirt. **4.** *Colloq.* something of no value; trash. **5.** *Civil Eng.*, *Mining*, *etc.* earth, rock, or other useless matter to be removed in order to get out the mineral or other substances sought. *–v.t.* **6.** to manure. **7.** to make dirty; soil. **8.** *Colloq.* to spoil; make a mess of. *–phr.* **9. make a muck of**, *Colloq.* to spoil; impair; disrupt. **10. muck about** (or **around**), *Colloq.* to idle; potter; fool about. **11. muck in**, *Colloq.* **a.** to share, especially living accommodation. **b.** to join in. **12. muck out**, to remove muck from: *to muck out the stables.* **13. muck up**, *Colloq.* **a.** to spoil. **b.** *Aust.* to misbehave.

muckrake /ˈmʌkreɪk/ *v.i.* to attempt to uncover information that will discredit someone, particularly someone in public life for whom such revelations would be damaging. **–muckraker**, *n.* **–muckraking**, *n.*

muck-up *n. Colloq.* fiasco; muddle.

mucous /ˈmjukəs/ *adj. Physiol.* **1.** relating to, consisting of, or resembling mucus: *a mucous discharge.* **2.** containing or secreting mucus: *a mucous membrane.* **–mucosity** /mjuˈkɒsəti/, *n.*

mucous membrane *n. Anat.* the thin membrane or skin that lines the body cavities and produces mucus.

mucus /ˈmjukəs/ *n.* a viscid secretion of the mucous membranes.

mud /mʌd/ *n.* **1.** wet, soft earth or earthy matter, as on the ground after rain, at the bottom of a pond, or among the discharges from a volcano; mire. *–phr. Colloq.* **2. someone's name is mud**, someone is in disgrace. **3. throw** (or **sling**) **mud at**, to speak ill of; abuse; vilify.

MUD /mʌd/ *n. Computer Games* a game on the internet in which a user assumes an identity and interacts with other users.

mud crab *n.* a large edible crab, *Scylla serrata*, inhabiting mangrove regions of the coastline of northern WA, NT, Qld and NSW.

muddle /ˈmʌdl/ *v.t.* **1.** to mix up or jumble together in a confused or bungling way. **2.** to render confused mentally, or unable to think clearly. **3.** to render confused or stupid with drink, or as drink does. **4.** to make muddy or turbid, as water. **5.** *US* to mix or stir. *–n.* **6.** a muddled condition; a confused mental state. **7.** a confused, disordered, or embarrassing state of affairs, or a mess. *–phr.* **8. muddle through**, to come to a satisfactory conclusion without planned direction.

muddy /ˈmʌdi/ *adj.* (**-dier**, **-diest**) **1.** covered with mud. **2.** (of water) containing mud; turbid. **3.** (of colour) not clear or pure. **4.** (of the complexion) dull. **5.** not clear in mind. **6.** (of thought, expression, literary style, etc.) obscure or vague. *–verb* (**-died**, **-dying**) *–v.t.* **7.** to make muddy. **8.** to make turbid. **9.** to make confused or obscure. *–v.i.* **10.** to become muddy or turbid. **–muddily**, *adv.* **–muddiness**, *n.*

mudflat /ˈmʌdflæt/ *n.* (*oft. pl.*) an area of muddy ground covered by water at high tide. Also, **mud flat.**

mudguard /ˈmʌdgad/ *n.* a guard or shield shaped to fit over the wheels of a motor vehicle or a bicycle to prevent splashing of water, mud, etc.

mudlark /ˈmʌdlak/ *n.* **1.** *Chiefly Victoria, SA and WA* → **magpie lark**. **2.** Also, **mudrunner.** *Horseracing* a horse that performs very well on wet tracks.

mudskipper /ˈmʌdskɪpə/ *n.* any of several tropical marine fishes mainly of the family Periophthalmidae with bulging eyes, air-breathing gills and stiffened pectoral fins which enable them to skip over mudflats and climb over rocks and mangrove roots.

mudslinging /ˈmʌdslɪŋɪŋ/ *n.* the act of discrediting an opponent, especially one in public office, by hurling abusive accusations at them **–mudslinger**, *n.*

muesli /ˈmjuzli, ˈmuzli/ *n.* a breakfast cereal of various mixed products such as oats, wheatgerm, chopped fruit and nuts, etc.

muff /mʌf/ *n.* **1.** a kind of thick tubular case covered with fur or other material, in which the hands are placed for warmth. **2.** *Colloq.* any failure. *–v.t.* **3.** *Sports* to fail to play (a stroke) successfully, to catch (a ball) properly, etc. *–v.i.* **4.** *Colloq.* to bungle.

muffin /ˈmʌfən/ *n.* **1.** a type of small, cup-shaped cake, usually sweet, and often containing fruit, nuts, chocolate, etc. **2.** → **English muffin.**

muffin top *n. Colloq.* the fold of fat around the midriff which, on an overweight woman, spills out over the top of tight-fitting pants or skirts.

muffle /ˈmʌfəl/ *v.t.* **1.** Also, **muffle up.** to wrap or envelop in a cloak, shawl, scarf, or the like disposed about the person, especially about the face and neck. **2.** to wrap with something to deaden or prevent sound: *to muffle drums.* **3.** to deaden (sound) by wrappings or other means. *–v.i.* **4.** to muffle oneself (*up*) as in garments or other wrappings. *–n.* **5.** something that muffles. **6.** muffled sound. **7.** an oven or arched chamber in a furnace or kiln, used for heating substances without direct contact with the fire: *muffle furnace.* **8.** the thick, bare part of the upper lip and nose of ruminants and rodents. *–phr.* **9. muffle oneself up**, to wrap oneself up as in garments or other wrappings.

muffler /ˈmʌflə/ *n.* **1.** a heavy neck scarf used for warmth. **2.** any device that reduces noise, especially that on the exhaust of an internal combustion engine.

mufti[1] /ˈmʊfti, ˈmʌfti/ *n.* (*pl.* **-tis**) **1.** a Muslim legal adviser consulted in applying the religious law. **2.** (*also upper case*) the leader of a Muslim community with both civil and religious jurisdiction: *the Mufti of Australia and New Zealand.*

mufti[2] /ˈmʌfti/ *n.* civilian dress as opposed to military or other uniform, or plain clothes as worn by someone who usually wears a uniform.

mug /mʌg/ *n.* **1.** a drinking cup, usually cylindrical and commonly with a handle. **2.** the quantity it holds. **3.** *Colloq.* the face. **4.** *Colloq.* a fool; someone who is easily duped. *–v.t.* (**mugged, mugging**) *Colloq.* **5.** to assault by hitting in the face. **6.** to assault and rob. *–adj.* **7.** *Aust. Colloq.* stupid: *a mug copper; a mug alec.* *–phr.* **8. mug up**, (sometimes fol. by *on*) to study hard. **–mugger**, *n.*

muggy /ˈmʌgi/ *adj.* (**-gier**, **-giest**) (of the atmosphere, weather, etc.) damp and close; humid and oppressive. **–mugginess**, *n.*

mugshot /ˈmʌgʃɒt/ *n.* a photograph, usually of the head only, taken for police records. Also, **mug shot.**

mulatto /mjuˈlætoʊ, mə-/ *n.* (*pl.* **-tos** *or* **-toes**) **1.** the offspring of parents of whom one is white and the other black. *–adj.* **2.** having a light brown colour (similar to the skin of a mulatto).

mulberry /ˈmʌlbəri, -bri/ *n.* (*pl.* **-ries**) **1.** the edible, berry-like collective fruit of any tree of the genus *Morus.* **2.** a tree of this genus, as *M. rubra* (**red mulberry** or **American mulberry**), with dark purple fruit, *M. nigra* (**black mulberry**), with dark-coloured fruit, and *M. alba* (**white mulberry**), with fruit nearly white and with leaves especially valued as food for silkworms. **3.** a dull, dark, reddish purple colour.

mulch /mʌltʃ/ *n.* **1.** straw, leaves, loose earth, etc., spread on the ground or produced by tillage to protect the roots of newly planted trees, crops, etc. *–v.t.* **2.** to cover with mulch.

mule[1] /mjul/ *n.* **1.** the sterile offspring of a male donkey and a mare, used especially as a beast of burden because of its patience, sure-footedness, and hardiness. **2.** any hybrid between the donkey and the horse. **3.** *Colloq.* a stupid or stubborn person. **4.** an infertile hybrid of any genetic cross. **5.** a machine which spins cotton, etc., into yarn and winds it on spindles. **6.** *Colloq.* a courier of illegal drugs.

mule² /mjul/ *n.* a kind of slipper which leaves the heel exposed.

mulga /ˈmʌlgə/ *n.* **1.** any of several species of *Acacia*, especially *A. aneura*, found in drier parts of Australia. **2.** the wood of the tree. –*phr.* **3. the mulga, a.** Also, **mulga country.** remote districts where mulga is the predominant vegetation. **b.** remote country: *in from the mulga.* **4. up (in) the mulga,** in the bush.

mulga grass *n.* any of a number of species of small, native, Australian drought-tolerant grasses, of the species *Neurachne*, found typically in mulga country.

mulish /ˈmjulɪʃ/ *adj.* like a mule; characteristic of a mule; stubborn, obstinate, or intractable. –**mulishly,** *adv.* –**mulishness,** *n.*

mull¹ /mʌl/ *v.t.* **1.** to make a mess or failure of. –*phr.* **2. mull over,** to study or ruminate over, especially in an ineffective way; ponder upon.

mull² /mʌl/ *v.t.* to heat, sweeten, and spice for drinking, as ale, wine, etc.: *mulled cider.*

mull³ /mʌl/ *n. Scottish* a promontory or headland.

mullah /ˈmʌlə, ˈmʊlə/ *n. Islam* someone who is learned in, teaches, or expounds the sacred law. Also, **mulla.**

mullet /ˈmʌlət/ *n.* **1.** any fish of the family Mugilidae, which includes various marine and freshwater species with a nearly cylindrical body and generally greyish-silver colouration, as the sea mullet, *Mugil cephalus,* widely distributed in Australian waters. **2.** a type of hairstyle, long at the back and cut short on the top and sides.

mulligatawny /mʌləgəˈtɔni/ *n.* a soup of Anglo-Indian origin, flavoured with curry.

mullion /ˈmʌliən, ˈmʌljən/ *n.* **1.** a vertical member, as of stone or wood, between the lights of a window, the panels in wainscoting, or the like. –*v.t.* **2.** to furnish with, or to form into divisions by the use of, mullions.

mullock /ˈmʌlək/ *n. NZ, Aust.* mining refuse; muck.

mullygrubber /ˈmʌligrʌbə/ *n. Cricket, etc.* a ball delivered in such a manner that on contact with the ground it does not bounce. Also, **grubber.**

multi- a word element meaning 'many'.

multichannel /mʌltiˈtʃænəl/ *v.i.* (**-nelled** *or, Chiefly US,* **-neled, -nelling** *or, Chiefly US,* **-neling**) (of a broadcaster) to transmit more than one program at the same time. –**multichannelling,** *n.*

multicoloured /ˈmʌltikʌləd/ *adj.* of many colours. Also, **multicolored.**

multicultural /mʌltiˈkʌltʃərəl/ *adj.* of or relating to a society which embraces a number of different cultures and peoples. –**multiculturally,** *adv.* –**multiculturalism,** *n.*

multifarious /mʌltəˈfɛəriəs/ *adj.* **1.** having many different parts, elements, forms, etc. **2.** of many kinds, or numerous and varied; manifold (modifying a plural noun): *multifarious activities.* –**multifariously,** *adv.* –**multifariousness,** *n.*

multifocal /mʌltiˈfoukəl/ *adj.* **1.** having more than one focus: *a multifocal report.* **2.** having a range of focal lengths: *a multifocal lens.* **3.** (of a disease) arising from or affecting more than one part of the body. –*n.* **4.** (*pl.*) multifocal spectacles.

multigrade /ˈmʌltigreɪd/ *adj.* (of a motor oil) having a stable viscosity level over a wide range of temperatures.

multilateral /mʌltiˈlætərəl, -ˈlætrəl/ *adj.* **1.** having many sides; many-sided. **2.** involving many parties; multipartite. –**multilaterally,** *adv.* –**multilateralism,** *n.*

multilingual /mʌltiˈlɪŋgwəl/ *adj.* **1.** able to speak at least three languages with approximately equal facility. **2.** expressed or contained in three or more different languages. **3.** characterised by the use or presence of many languages. –**multilingualism,** *n.*

multimedia /mʌltiˈmidiə/ *adj.* **1.** of or relating to several types of media: *we will have a multimedia advertising campaign.* **2.** (*often humorous*) of or relating to a personality who is or claims to be well-known through several types of media: *Edna Everage, a multimedia megastar.* **3.** combining text, sound, and video: *a multimedia encyclopedia on CD.*

multimeter /ˈmʌltimitə/ *n.* a meter for measuring voltages, currents, and resistances.

multimillion /mʌltiˈmɪljən/ *adj.* of or relating to more than one million: *a multimillion dollar jackpot.* Also, **multi-million.**

multinational /mʌltiˈnæʃənəl/ *adj.* **1.** of, relating to, or spreading across many nations: *a multinational operation.* –*n.* **2.** a multinational company or corporation.

multipartite /mʌltiˈpataɪt/ *adj.* **1.** divided into many parts; having many divisions. **2.** → **multilateral** (def. 2).

multiple /ˈmʌltəpəl/ *adj.* **1.** consisting of, having, or involving many individuals, parts, elements, relations, etc.; manifold. **2.** *Elect.* denoting two or more circuits connected in parallel. **3.** *Bot.* (of a fruit) collective. –*n.* **4.** *Maths* a number which contains another number some number of times without a remainder: *12 is a multiple of 3.* **5.** *Elect.* **a.** a group of terminals arranged to make a circuit or group of circuits accessible at a number of points at any one of which connection can be made. **b. in multiple,** in parallel. See **parallel** (def. 8). **6.** a work of art produced by any of the printing processes, in any quantity and replaceable at any time whose value lies in the fact that it reaches a vast audience.

multiple-choice *adj.* **1.** offering a number of choices. **2.** composed of multiple-choice questions: *a multiple-choice exam.*

multiple personality disorder *n.* → **dissociative identity disorder.**

multiple sclerosis *n. Pathol.* a disease of the nervous system, usually progressive, characterised by remissions and exacerbations, and caused by plaques of demyelisation of the white matter of the nervous system. *Abbrev.*: MS Also, **disseminated sclerosis.**

multiplication /ˌmʌltəpləˈkeɪʃən/ *n.* **1.** the act or process of multiplying. **2.** the state of being multiplied. **3.** *Arithmetic* the process of finding the number (the product) resulting from the addition of a given number (the multiplicand) taken as many times as there are units in another given number (the multiplier). *Symbol*: × **4.** *Maths* any generalisation of this operation applicable to numbers other than integers, such as fractions, irrationals, vectors, etc. **5.** *Physics* the process by which additional neutrons are produced by a chain reaction in a nuclear reactor. –**multiplicational,** *adj.* –**multiplicative,** *adj.*

multiplicity /mʌltəˈplɪsəti/ *n.* (*pl.* **-ties**) **1.** a multitude or great number. **2.** the state of being multiplex or manifold; manifold variety.

multiplier /ˈmʌltəplaɪə/ *n.* **1.** *Maths* the number by which another is to be multiplied. **2.** *Physics* a device for intensifying some phenomenon. **3.** *Finance* an indicator of the relative sizes of a given initial increase in investment and the total ultimate increase in income.

multiply /ˈmʌltəplaɪ/ *verb* (**-plied, -plying**) –*v.t.* **1.** to make many; increase the number, quantity, etc., of. **2.** *Maths* to find the product of by multiplication. –*v.i.* **3.** to grow in number, quantity, etc.; increase. **4.** *Maths* to perform the process of multiplication. **5.** to increase in number by natural generation. –**multipliable,** *adj.*

multiracial /mʌltiˈreɪʃəl/ *adj.* of or relating to more than one race (**race²**). –**multiracialism,** *n.*

multistorey /mʌltiˈstɔri/ *adj.* (of a building) having a considerable number of storeys. Also, *Chiefly US,* **multistory.**

multi-tasking /'mʌlti-taskɪŋ/ n. **1.** *Computers* the execution by a computer of a number of different tasks simultaneously, as data processing, printing, etc. **2.** the execution of a number of different jobs by one person. –*adj.* **3.** of or relating to computer software which facilitates multi-tasking. **4.** (of a computer) performing more than one task at a time.

multitude /'mʌltətjud, -tʃud/ n. **1.** a great number; host: *a multitude of friends*. **2.** a great number of persons gathered together; a crowd or throng. **3.** the state or character of being many. –*phr.* **4. the multitude**, the common people.

multivitamin /mʌlti'vaɪtəmən/ *adj.* **1.** containing a number of different vitamins. –*n.* **2.** such a pill or tonic.

mum[1] /mʌm/ n. *Colloq.* **1.** a mother. **2.** a familiar form of address for a mother.

mum[2] /mʌm/ *adj.* **1.** silent; not saying a word: *to keep mum.* –*phr.* **2. mum's the word**, *Colloq.* an expression indicating that something is to be kept a secret.

mum-and-dad *adj.* of or relating to parental couples, especially as opposed to corporations, wealthy speculators, etc.: *mum-and-dad investors.*

mumble /'mʌmbəl/ v.i. **1.** to speak indistinctly or unintelligibly, as with partly closed lips; mutter low, indistinct words. **2.** to chew ineffectively, as from loss of teeth: *to mumble on a crust.* –v.t. **3.** to utter indistinctly, as with partly closed lips. **4.** to chew, or try to eat, with difficulty, as from loss of teeth. –*n.* **5.** a low, indistinct utterance or sound. –**mumbler**, *n.* –**mumblingly**, *adv.*

mumbo jumbo /,mʌmboʊ 'dʒʌmboʊ/ n. **1.** meaningless incantation or ritual. **2.** an object of superstitious awe or reverence. **3.** unintelligible speech or writing, often intended to be impressive; gibberish.

mummify /'mʌməfaɪ/ *verb* (**-fied, -fying**) –v.t. **1.** to make (a dead body) into a mummy, as by embalming and drying. **2.** to make like a mummy. –v.i. **3.** to dry or shrivel up. –**mummification** /mʌməfəˈkeɪʃən/, *n.*

mummy[1] /'mʌmi/ n. (pl. **-mies**) **1.** the dead body of a human being or animal preserved by the ancient Egyptian (or some similar) method of embalming. **2.** a dead body dried and preserved by the agencies of nature. **3.** a withered or shrunken living being.

mummy[2] /'mʌmi/ n. (pl. **-mies**) *Colloq.* **1.** (*with children*) a mother. **2.** a familiar form of address for a mother.

mumps /mʌmps/ n. *Pathol.* (*construed as sing.*) a specific infectious viral disease characterised by inflammatory swelling of the parotid and (usually) other salivary glands, and sometimes by inflammation of the testicles, ovaries, etc.: *a case of (the) mumps.*

munch /mʌntʃ/ v.t. **1.** to chew with steady or vigorous working of the jaws, and often audibly. –v.i. **2.** to chew steadily or vigorously, and often audibly. –**muncher**, *n.*

munchies /'mʌntʃiz/ *pl. n. Colloq.* **1.** anything to eat, especially snacks between meals. **2.** a craving for food, especially as resulting from smoking marijuana.

mundane /'mʌndeɪn, mʌn'deɪn/ *adj.* **1.** of or relating to the world, universe, or earth, especially as opposed to heaven; worldly; earthly: *mundane affairs.* **2.** ordinary; pedestrian; boring. –**mundanely**, *adv.* –**mundaneness**, *n.*

mung bean /'mʌŋ bin/ n. a bushy annual herb, *Vigna radiata*, family Fabaceae, probably originally from India, cultivated as a food crop, yielding a bean used in cookery and as the chief source of bean sprouts; green gram.

munge /mʌndʒ/ *Computers* –verb (**munged, munging**) –v.i. **1.** (*derog.*) to transform information imperfectly. **2.** to completely rewrite a routine, program, etc. –v.t. **3.** (*derog.*) to transform (information) imperfectly. **4.** to completely rewrite (a routine, program, etc.). **5.** to rewrite (an email address) so that a human being can decode it but an email harvester cannot. –*n.* **6.** such a rewrite. –*adj.* **7.** of or relating to munging: *a munge program.* –**munging**, *n.*

municipal /mju'nɪsəpəl, mjunə'sɪpəl/ *adj.* of or relating to a municipality, its government, facilities, etc.: *municipal library; municipal elections.* –**municipally**, *adv.*

municipal council *n.* a local administrative body which serves a municipality, predominantly in a rural town or city suburban area. Compare **city council**, **shire council**.

municipality /mjunəsə'pæləti/ n. (pl. **-ties**) **1.** an area of land delineated for the purposes of local government and which, when first defined in NSW in 1858, was to be no larger than ten square miles with a minimum population of 500; (in Victoria) borough. **2.** a community under municipal jurisdiction.

munificent /mju'nɪfəsənt/ *adj.* **1.** extremely liberal in giving or bestowing; very generous. **2.** (of a gift, or the like) characterised by great generosity. –**munificence**, *n.* –**munificently**, *adv.*

munition /mju'nɪʃən/ n. **1.** (*usu. pl.*) materials used in war, especially weapons and ammunition. **2.** material or equipment for carrying on any undertaking. –v.t. **3.** to provide with munitions.

muppet /'mʌpət/ n. *Colloq.* a foolish or incompetent person.

mural /'mjurəl/ *adj.* **1.** of or relating to a wall; resembling a wall. **2.** executed on or affixed to a wall (of a decoration, or the like). –*n.* **3.** a mural painting.

murder /'mɜdə/ n. **1.** *Law* the unlawful killing of a human being by an act done with intention to kill or to inflict grievous bodily harm, or with reckless indifference to human life. **2.** *Colloq.* an uncommonly laborious or difficult task: *gardening in the heat is murder.* –v.t. **3.** *Law* to kill by an act constituting murder. **4.** to kill or slaughter inhumanly or barbarously. **5.** to spoil or mar by bad execution, representation, pronunciation, etc. **6.** *Colloq.* to consume (food or drink) with gusto: *I could murder a sandwich now.* –v.i. **7.** to commit murder. –*phr.* **8. get away with murder**, to behave outrageously, illegally, etc., with impunity. **9. like blue murder**, *Colloq.* to a remarkable degree or extent: *I hate dairying like blue murder.* **10. scream** (or **yell**) (or **cry**, etc.) **blue murder**, *Colloq.* to make a commotion; complain vociferously. –**murderer**, *n.* –**murderess**, *n.* –**murderous**, *adj.* –**murderously**, *adv.*

murder mystery *n.* a novel, play, etc., dealing with a murder or murders and the detection of the criminal; whodunnit.

murex /'mjurɛks/ n. (pl. **murices** /'mjurəsiz/ or **murexes**) **1.** any of the marine gastropods, common in tropical seas, constituting the genus *Murex* or the family Muricidae, certain species of which yielded the celebrated purple dye of the ancients. **2.** purplish red.

murk /mɜk/ n. darkness.

murky /'mɜki/ *adj.* (**-kier, -kiest**) **1.** intensely dark, gloomy, and cheerless. **2.** obscure or thick with mist, haze, or the like, as the air, etc. –**murkily**, *adv.* –**murkiness**, *n.*

murmur /'mɜmə/ n. **1.** any low, continuous sound, as of a creek, the wind, trees, voices, etc. **2.** a mumbled or private complaint, one not made openly. **3.** *Med.* an abnormal sound from the heart. –v.i. **4.** to make a low or continuous sound. **5.** to speak softly or unclearly: *he murmured to himself all the time they were speaking.* **6.** to complain in private, not openly. –v.t. **7.** to say softly or unclearly: *he murmured the words into her ear.* –**murmurer**, *n.* –**murmuring**, *adj.*, *n.* –**murmuringly**, *adv.*

Murray cod /mʌri 'kɒd/ n. a large Australian freshwater fish, *Maccullochella peelii*, principally of the

Murray-Darling river system, related to the marine gropers of genus *Polyprion*.

Murri /'mʌri/ *n.* an Aboriginal person from parts of Qld and NSW. Compare **Anangu, Koori** (def. 1), **Nunga, Nyungar, Yamatji, Yolngu**.

muscat /'mʌskət/ *n.* (*also upper case*) **1.** a grape variety with pronounced pleasant sweet aroma and flavour, much used for making wine. **2.** the vine bearing this grape. **3.** a sweet wine made from this grape.

muscatel /mʌskə'tel/ *n.* **1.** the muscat grape, especially in the dried form as a raisin. **2.** → **muscat** (def. 3).

muscle /'mʌsəl/ *n.* **1.** a discrete bundle or sheet of contractile fibres having the function of producing movement in the animal body. **2.** the tissue of such an organ. **3.** muscular strength; brawn. **4.** political or financial strength, especially when exercised in a ruthless fashion. *–v.i.* (**-cled, -cling**) **5.** *Colloq.* to make or shove one's way by sheer brawn or force. *–phr.* **6. muscle in,** *Colloq.* (sometimes fol. by *on*) to force one's way in, especially by violent means, trickery, or in the face of hostility, in order to obtain a share of something. **–muscly,** *adj.*

musclebound /'mʌsəlbaʊnd/ *adj.* having muscles enlarged and inelastic, as from excessive exercise.

muscular /'mʌskjələ/ *adj.* **1.** of or relating to muscle or the muscles. **2.** dependent on or affected by the muscles. **3.** having well-developed muscles; brawny. **–muscularity** /mʌskjə'lærəti/, *n.* **–muscularly,** *adv.*

muscular dystrophy /mʌskjələ 'dɪstrəfi/ *n. Pathol.* a disease of unknown origin which produces a progressive muscular deterioration and wasting, robbing the muscles of all vitality until the patient is completely helpless.

musculature /'mʌskjələtʃə/ *n.* the muscular system of the body or of its parts.

muse¹ /mjuz/ *v.i.* **1.** to reflect or meditate in silence, as on some subject, often as in a reverie. **2.** to gaze meditatively or wonderingly. *–v.t.* **3.** to meditate on. **–muser,** *n.*

muse² /mjuz/ *n.* artistic inspiration, especially when identified as a person or object. Also, **Muse**.

museum /mju'ziəm/ *n.* a building or place for the keeping, exhibition, and study of objects of scientific, artistic, and historical interest.

mush¹ /mʌʃ/ *n.* **1.** meal, especially corn meal, boiled in water or milk until it forms a thick, soft mass. **2.** any thick, soft mass. **3.** anything unpleasantly lacking in firmness, force, dignity, etc. **4.** *Colloq.* weak or maudlin sentiment or sentimental language. **–mushy,** *adj.*

mush² /mʌʃ/ *v.t.* **1.** to go or travel on foot, especially over the snow with a dog team. *–interj.* **2.** an order to start or speed up a dog team. *–n.* **3.** a journey on foot, especially over the snow with a dog team. **–musher,** *n.*

mushroom /'mʌʃrum/ *n.* **1.** any of various fleshy fungi including the toadstools, puffballs, coral fungi, morels, etc. **2.** any of certain edible species belonging to the family Agaricaceae, usually of umbrella shape. Compare **toadstool**. **3.** the common field mushroom, *Agaricus campestris*, white on top with pinkish-brown gills. **4.** anything of similar shape or correspondingly rapid growth. **5.** *Colloq.* a person who is deliberately kept ignorant and misinformed. *–adj.* **6.** of, relating to, or made of mushrooms. **7.** resembling or suggesting a mushroom in shape. **8.** of rapid growth and, often, brief duration: *mushroom fame. –v.i.* **9.** to gather mushrooms. **10.** to have or assume the shape of a mushroom. **11.** to spread or grow quickly, as mushrooms.

music /'mjuzɪk/ *n.* **1.** an art of organising sound in significant forms to express ideas and emotions through the elements of rhythm, melody, harmony, and colour. **2.** the tones or sounds employed, occurring in single line (melody) or multiple lines (harmony). **3.** musical work or compositions for singing or playing. **4.** the written or printed score of a musical composition. **5.** such scores collectively. **6.** any sweet, pleasing, or harmonious sounds or sound: *the music of the waves. –phr.* **7. face the music,** to face the consequences, usually unpleasant, of one's actions; accept responsibility for what one has done.

musical /'mjuzɪkəl/ *adj.* **1.** of or relating to music: *a musical instrument*; *a musical composition*. **2.** resembling music; melodious; harmonious. **3.** fond of or skilled in music: *I'm not very musical*. **4.** set to or accompanied by music: *a musical melodrama. –n.* **5.** a play or film, often of a light romantic variety, in which songs, choruses, dances, etc., in a popular musical idiom, form a substantial and essential part. **–musically,** *adv.* **–musicality** /mjuzə'kæləti/, **musicalness,** *n.*

music hall *n.* a theatre or hall for variety entertainment.

musician /mju'zɪʃən/ *n.* **1.** someone who makes music a profession, especially as a performer on an instrument. **2.** someone skilled in playing a musical instrument. **–musicianly,** *adj.* **–musicianship,** *n.*

musicology /mjuzə'kɒlədʒi/ *n.* the systematic study of music, as in historical research, musical theory, ethnic music, the physical nature of sound, etc. **–musicological** /mjuzəkə'lɒdʒɪkəl/, *adj.* **–musicologist,** *n.*

musing /'mjuzɪŋ/ *adj.* **1.** absorbed in thought; meditative. *–n.* **2.** contemplation. **–musingly,** *adv.*

musk /mʌsk/ *n.* **1.** a substance secreted in a glandular sac under the skin of the abdomen of the male musk deer, having a strong smell, and used in perfumery. **2.** a synthetic imitation of the substance. **3.** a similar secretion of other animals, as the civet, muskrat, otter, etc. **4.** the smell, or some similar smell. **5.** *Bot.* any of several plants, having a musky fragrance.

musk deer *n.* any of various small, hornless deer of the family Moschidae, especially *Moschus moschiferus*, of mountainous regions of central Asia, the male of which secretes musk and has large canine teeth.

musket /'mʌskət/ *n.* a handgun for infantry soldiers, introduced in the 16th century, the predecessor of the modern rifle.

musketeer /mʌskə'tɪə/ *n.* a soldier armed with a musket.

Muslim /'muzləm, 'mʊs-, 'mʌz-/ *adj.* **1.** of or relating to the religion, law, or civilisation of Islam. *–n.* (*pl.* **-lims** *or* **-lim**) **2.** an adherent of Islam. Also, **Moslem**.

muslin /'mʌzlən/ *n.* a cotton fabric made in various degrees of fineness, and often printed, woven, or embroidered in patterns; especially, a cotton fabric of plain weave, used for curtains and other purposes.

mussel /'mʌsəl/ *n.* any bivalve mollusc, especially an edible marine bivalve of the family Mytilidae and a freshwater bivalve of the family Unionidae.

must¹ /mʌst, mʌs/, *weak forms* /məst, məs/ *v.* (*modal*) **1.** indicating obligation or necessity: *all residents must pay taxes*; *we must make a big effort*; *I must get my hair cut*; *we must do lunch sometime*. **2.** indicating inevitability: *we must all die*. **3.** expressing a conclusion: *the letter must be in that box*; *that must be him at the door*; *you must have been very proud*. **4.** expressing an insistence on doing something objectionable: *must you contradict me?*; *he must always have the last word. –n.* **5.** *Colloq.* something viewed as necessary or vital: *champagne is a must on this occasion*.

must² /mʌst/ *n.* new wine; the unfermented juice as pressed from the grape or other fruit.

must³ /mʌst/ *n.* mould; mustiness.

mustang /'mʌstæŋ/ *n.* the small, wild or half-wild horse of the American plains, descended from Spanish stock.

mustard /'mʌstəd/ *n.* **1.** a pungent powder or paste prepared from the seed of the mustard plant, much used as a food seasoning or condiment, and medicinally in plasters, poultices, etc. **2.** any of various species of

Brassica and allied genera, as *B. juncea*, **Indian mustard**, and *Sisymbrium officinale*, **hedge mustard**. *–phr.* **3. cut the mustard**, *Colloq.* to be adequate (for some specified task). **4. keen as mustard**, extremely keen or eager.

mustard gas *n.* a chemical-warfare agent, (ClCH₂CH₂)₂S, stored in liquid form, producing burns, blindness, and death, introduced by the Germans in World War I.

muster /ˈmʌstə/ *v.t.* **1.** to assemble (troops, a ship's crew, etc.), as for battle, display, inspection, orders, discharge, etc. **2.** to round up (livestock) for shearing, branding, etc. *–v.i.* **3.** to assemble for inspection, service, etc., as troops or forces. **4.** to come together, collect, or gather. *–n.* **5.** an assembling of troops for inspection or other purposes. **6.** an assemblage or collection. **7.** the act of mustering. *–phr.* **8. muster up**, to gather or summon: *he mustered up all his courage*. **9. pass muster**, to measure up to specified standards. *–***musterer**, *n.* *–***mustering**, *n.*

musty /ˈmʌsti/ *adj.* **(-tier, -tiest) 1.** having a smell or flavour suggestive of mould, as old buildings, long-closed rooms, food, etc. **2.** made stale by time, or antiquated: *musty laws*. **3.** dull; apathetic. *–***mustily**, *adv.* *–***mustiness**, *n.*

mutant /ˈmjutnt/ *adj.* **1.** undergoing mutation; resulting from mutation. *–n.* **2.** *Biol.* a new type of organism produced as the result of mutation.

mutate /mjuˈteɪt/ *v.t.* **1.** to change; alter. *–v.i.* **2.** to change; undergo mutation. *–***mutative** /ˈmjutətɪv, mjuˈteɪtɪv/, *adj.*

mutation /mjuˈteɪʃən/ *n.* **1.** the act or process of changing. **2.** a change or alteration, as in form, qualities, or nature. **3.** *Biol.* **a.** a sudden departure from the parent type, as when an individual differs from its parents in one or more heritable characteristics, caused by a change in a gene or a chromosome. **b.** an individual, species, or the like, resulting from such a departure. **4.** *Phonetics* → **umlaut**. *–***mutational**, *adj.*

mute /mjut/ *adj.* **1.** silent; refraining from speech or utterance. **2.** not emitting or having sound of any kind. **3.** incapable of speech: *mute with shock*. **4.** *Gram.* (of letters) silent; not pronounced. **5.** (of a hound in fox-hunting) not giving tongue while hunting. *–n.* **6.** *Rare* (*now likely to give offence*) someone unable to utter words. **7.** a mechanical device of various shapes and materials for muffling the tone of a musical instrument. **8.** Also, **mute button**. a button on a television or sound amplifier remote control unit which can be used to switch the sound off and on again. *–v.t.* **9.** to deaden or muffle the sound of (a musical instrument, etc.). **10.** to reduce, as in volume; soften. *–phr.* **11. stand mute**, *Law* (of a prisoner) to make no response when arraigned, now resulting in the entry of a plea of not guilty. *–***mutely**, *adv.* *–***muteness**, *n.*

mute button *n.* → **mute** (def. 8).

mutilate /ˈmjutəleɪt/ *v.t.* **1.** to deprive (a person or animal, the body, etc.) of a limb or other important part or parts. **2.** → **castrate**. **3.** to injure, disfigure, or make imperfect by removing or irreparably damaging parts. *–***mutilation** /mjutəˈleɪʃən/, *n.* *–***mutilator**, *n.*

mutiny /ˈmjutəni/ *n.* (*pl.* **-nies**) **1.** revolt, or a revolt or rebellion, against constituted authority, especially by soldiers or sailors against their officers. *–v.i.* (**-nied, -nying**) **2.** to commit the offence of mutiny; revolt against constituted authority. *–***mutineer**, *n.* *–***mutinous**, *adj.*

mutt /mʌt/ *n.* *Colloq.* **1.** a dog, especially a mongrel. **2.** a simpleton; a stupid person.

mutter /ˈmʌtə/ *v.i.* **1.** to utter words indistinctly or in a low tone, often in talking to oneself or in making obscure complaints, threats, etc.; murmur; grumble. **2.** to

make a low, rumbling sound. *–v.t.* **3.** to utter indistinctly or in a low tone. *–n.* **4.** the act or utterance of someone who mutters. *–***mutterer**, *n.* *–***mutteringly**, *adv.*

mutton /ˈmʌtn/ *n.* **1.** the flesh of sheep, used as food. **2.** the flesh of the well-grown or more mature sheep, as distinguished from lamb, and hogget. *–phr.* **3. mutton dressed (up) as lamb**, a woman who is trying, unsuccessfully, to look younger and more attractive than she is. *–***muttony**, *adj.*

mutton-bird *n.* any of various species of petrel, the chicks of which are commercially harvested for their oil, feathers and flesh, especially the short-tailed shearwater, *Puffinus tenuirostris*. Also, **mutton bird**.

mutton-chops *pl. n.* side-whiskers narrow at the top, and broad and trimmed short at the bottom, the chin being shaved both in front and beneath. Also, **mutton-chop whiskers**.

mutual /ˈmjutʃuəl/ *adj.* **1.** possessed, experienced, performed, etc., by each of two or more with respect to the other or others; reciprocal: *mutual aid*. **2.** having the same relation each towards the other or others: *mutual foes*. **3.** of or relating to each of two or more; common: *mutual acquaintance*. **4.** of or relating to mutual insurance: *a mutual company*. *–***mutually**, *adv.* *–***mutuality** /mjutʃuˈæləti/, *n.*

mutual fund *n.* *Finance* an investment trust which pools the money of a large number of investors and invests on their behalf.

mutual insurance *n.* insurance in which those insured become members of a company who reciprocally engage, by payment of certain amounts into a common fund, to indemnify one another against loss.

muzak /ˈmjuzæk/ *n.* (*from trademark*) recorded background music played, usually continuously, in places of work, hotels, restaurants, etc., designed to increase efficiency or create a feeling of wellbeing.

muzzle /ˈmʌzəl/ *n.* **1.** the mouth, or end for discharge, of the barrel of a gun, pistol, etc. **2.** the projecting part of the head of an animal, including jaws, mouth, and nose. **3.** a device, usually an arrangement of straps or wires, placed over an animal's mouth to prevent the animal from biting, eating, etc. *–v.t.* **4.** to put a muzzle on (an animal or its mouth) so as to prevent biting, eating, etc. **5.** to restrain (by physical, legal, or procedural means) from speech or the expression of opinion; gag: *they tried to muzzle him but he insisted on finishing his speech*. *–***muzzler**, *n.*

Mx /mʌks, mɪks/ *Chiefly Brit.* a title adopted by those who do not wish to reveal their gender or who do not identify as male or female.

my /maɪ/, *weak forms* /mi, mə/ *adj.* **1.** the possessive form of I: *my house*; *my family*. *–interj.* **2.** an exclamation of surprise: *oh my!*

my- a word element meaning 'muscle'. Also, **myo-**.

myall¹ /ˈmaɪɔl/ *Aust.* *–n.* **1.** an Aboriginal person living in a traditional manner, outside European society. *–adj.* **2.** (of an Aboriginal) living in a traditional manner and not accustomed to European society **3.** (of plants, animals, etc.) living or running wild

myall² /ˈmaɪɔl/ *n.* **1.** any of several wattle trees. **2.** the hard fine-grained wood of such a tree used for carving.

myc- a word element meaning 'fungus'. Also, **myco-**.

mycelium /maɪˈsiliəm/ *n.* (*pl.* **-lia** /-liə/) *Bot.* the vegetative part or thallus of the fungi, when composed of one or more filamentous elements, or hyphae. *–***myceloid** /ˈmaɪsəlɔɪd/, *adj.*

-mycetes a word element meaning 'fungus', as in *myxomycetes*.

myco- variant of **myc-**, before consonants, as in *mycology*.

myelin /ˈmaɪələn/ *n. Anat.* a soft, white, fatty substance encasing the axon of certain nerve fibres. Also, **myeline** /ˈmaɪəlin/.

myelin sheath *n.* the layer of myelin encasing the axon of a nerve fibre, serving to insulate the nerve and to facilitate nerve impulses.

myna /ˈmaɪnə/ *n.* **1.** Also, **Indian myna**. a common bird, *Acridotheres tristis*, of parts of eastern Eurasia, having a brown body, white lower underparts, a black head, and yellow beak, legs and eye patches; introduced into Australia in the 1860s and now common around large cities and cane-growing areas along the eastern coast. **2.** any of various Asian birds of the family Sturnidae, especially those of the genus *Acridotheres*, some of which are often kept caged as pets and can learn to talk. Also, **mynah**.

myo- variant of **my-**, before consonants.

myocardial infarct /ˌmaɪoʊkadiəl ˈɪnfakt/ *n.* → **heart attack** (def. 2). Also, **myocardial infarction**.

myocardiogram /maɪoʊˈkadiəgræm/ *n. Med.* a tracing representing cardiac muscular activity, made by a myocardiograph.

myocardiograph /maɪoʊˈkadiəgræf, -graf/ *n. Med.* an apparatus which records the movements of the heart muscle. –**myocardiographic** /maɪoʊˌkadiəˈgræfɪk/, *adj.* –**myocardiography** /maɪoʊˌkadiˈɒgrəfi/, *n.*

myopia /maɪˈoʊpiə/ *n.* **1.** a condition of the eye in which parallel rays are focused in front of the retina, so that only near objects are seen clearly; near-sightedness (opposed to *hypermetropia*). **2.** a disinclination to acknowledge the existence of something. –**myopic** /maɪˈɒpɪk/, *adj.*

myosotis /maɪəˈsoʊtəs/ *n.* any plant of the boraginaceous genus *Myosotis*, as the common forget-me-not. Also, **myosote** /ˈmaɪəsoʊt/.

myriad /ˈmɪriəd/ *n.* **1.** an indefinitely great number: *a myriad of stars.* –*adj.* **2.** amounting to an indefinitely great number. **3.** of an indefinitely great number; innumerable: *the myriad stars.* **4.** having innumerable phases, aspects, etc.: *the myriad mind of Shakespeare.*

myrmeco- a word element meaning 'ant'.

myrrh /mɜ/ *n.* an aromatic resinous exudation from certain plants of the genus *Commiphora*, especially *C. myrrha*, a spiny shrub, used for incense, perfume, etc.

myrtle /ˈmɜtl/ *n.* **1.** any plant of the genus *Myrtus*, especially *M. communis*, a shrub of southern Europe with evergreen leaves, fragrant white flowers, and aromatic berries, used as an emblem of love and held sacred to Venus. **2.** any of certain other plants as the **myrtle beech**, *Nothofagus cunninghamii.*

myself /maɪˈsɛlf, məˈsɛlf/ *pron.* **1.** the reflexive form of **I**: *I cut myself.* **2.** an emphatic form of *me* or *I*, used: **a.** as object: *I used it for myself.* **b.** in apposition to a subject or object: *I did it myself.* **3.** (used after, *be, become,* or *come to*) my proper or normal self; my usual state of mind: *I am myself again.*

mystery /ˈmɪstri, -təri/ *n.* (*pl.* **-ries**) **1.** anything that is kept secret or remains unexplained or unknown; puzzle: *the mysteries of nature*; *it's a mystery how I came to lose that money.* **2.** anything that makes people curious: *the mystery of the scream in the night.* **3.** the condition or character of being unexplained; obscurity: *conversations wrapped in mystery.* **4.** the truth unknowable except by divine revelation: *the mystery of the Trinity.* **5.** (*pl.*) ancient religions which admitted people by secret ceremonies whose meaning was known only to those specially introduced to them. **6.** (*pl.*) secret ceremonies: *the mysteries of freemasonry.* –**mysterious**, *adj.*

mystic /ˈmɪstɪk/ *adj.* **1.** → **mystical**. –*n.* **2.** someone who practises or believes in mysticism.

mystical /ˈmɪstɪkəl/ *adj.* **1.** of or relating to mystics or mysticism: *a mystical religion*; *a mystical experience.* **2.** of occult character, power, or significance: *a mystical formula.* **3.** spiritually significant or symbolic, as, in Christianity, the image of the dove used to symbolise the Holy Spirit. **4.** inspiring a sense of spiritual mystery or wonder: *the mystical power of nature.* **5.** of the nature of or relating to mysteries known only to the initiated; esoteric: *mystical rites.* **6.** of obscure or mysterious character or significance. Also, **mystic**. –**mystically**, *adv.* –**mysticalness**, *n.*

mysticism /ˈmɪstəsɪzəm/ *n.* **1.** belief in the possibility of attaining an immediate spiritual intuition of truths thought to transcend ordinary understanding, or of a direct, intimate union of the soul with a deity or universal soul through contemplation and love. **2.** contemplative practices aimed at achieving such intuition or union. **3.** obscure thought or speculation.

mystify /ˈmɪstəfaɪ/ *v.t.* (**-fied, -fying**) **1.** to impose upon (a person) by playing upon their credulity; bewilder purposely. **2.** to involve (a subject, etc.) in mystery or obscurity. **3.** to confuse or bewilder. –**mystification** /ˌmɪstəfəˈkeɪʃən/, *n.*

mystique /mɪsˈtik/ *n.* **1.** an air of mystery or mystical power surrounding a particular person, object, pursuit, belief, etc. **2.** an incommunicable or esoteric quality; a secret known only to the devotees of a cult, etc.

myth /mɪθ/ *n.* **1.** a traditional story, usually concerning some superhuman being or some alleged person or event, and which attempts to explain natural phenomena; especially a traditional story about deities or demigods and the creation of the world and its inhabitants. **2.** stories or matter of this kind: *in the realm of myth.* **3.** any invented story. **4.** an imaginary or fictitious thing or person. –**mythical**, *adj.*

mytho- a word element meaning 'myth.'

mythology /məˈθɒlədʒi/ *n.* (*pl.* **-gies**) **1.** a body of myths, as that of a particular people, or that relating to a particular person: *Greek mythology.* **2.** myths collectively. **3.** the science of myths. –**mythological** /mɪθəˈlɒdʒɪkəl/, *adj.* –**mythologist**, *n.*

myx- a word element meaning 'slimy'. Also, **myxo-**.

myxomatosis /mɪksəməˈtoʊsəs/ *n.* a highly infectious viral disease of rabbits, deliberately introduced into Australia and some other countries to reduce the rabbit population.

N n

N, n /ɛn/ *n.* **1.** the 14th letter of the English alphabet. **2.** *Maths* an indefinite constant whole number, especially the degree of a quantic or an equation, or the order of a curve.

n- *Chem.* normal (indicating an unbranched carbon chain in an organic molecule): *an n-butyl ester.* Compare **iso-** (def. 2).

naan /nɑn/ *n.* a slightly leavened Indian flatbread, usually round, often served with Indian food. Also, **nan.**

nab /næb/ *v.t.* (**nabbed, nabbing**) *Colloq.* **1.** to catch or seize, especially suddenly. **2.** to capture or arrest.

nacre /ˈneɪkə/ *n.* → **mother-of-pearl.** –**nacreous** /ˈneɪkriəs/, *adj.*

nadir /ˈneɪdɪə/ *n.* **1.** the point of the celestial sphere vertically beneath any place or observer and diametrically opposite to the zenith. **2.** the lowest point, as of adversity.

nag[1] /næg/ *verb* (**nagged, nagging**) –*v.t.* **1.** to torment by persistent fault-finding, complaints, or importunities. –*v.i.* **2.** (sometimes fol. by *at*) to keep up an irritating or wearisome fault-finding, complaining, or the like. **3.** to cause continual pain, discomfort, or depression, as a headache, feeling of guilt, etc. –**nagger,** *n.* –**naggingly,** *adv.*

nag[2] /næg/ *n.* **1.** a small horse, or pony, especially for riding. **2.** *Colloq.* a horse. **3.** an old or inferior horse.

nail /neɪl/ *n.* **1.** a slender piece of metal, usually with one end pointed and the other enlarged, for driving into or through wood, etc., as to hold separate pieces together. **2.** a thin, horny plate, consisting of modified epidermis, growing on the upper side of the end of a finger or toe. –*v.t.* **3.** to fasten with a nail or nails: *to nail the cover on a box.* **4.** to stud with or as with nails driven in. **5.** to make fast or keep firmly in one place or position: *fear nailed him to the spot.* **6.** *Colloq.* to secure by prompt action; catch or seize. **7.** *Colloq.* to catch (a person) in some difficulty, a lie, etc. **8.** *Colloq.* to detect and expose (a lie, error). **9.** *Colloq.* (*taboo*) (of a man) to have sexual intercourse with. –*phr.* **10. hard as nails,** (of a person) stern; tough. **11. hit the nail on the head,** to say or do exactly the right thing. **12. nail up,** to shut within something by driving nails: *to nail goods up in a box.* **13. on the nail,** *Colloq.* on the spot, or at once. –**nailer,** *n.*

nail art *n.* the decoration of nails on fingers and toes, as by painting designs, affixing adornments such as rhinestones, etc. –**nail artist,** *n.*

naive /naɪˈiv, na-/ *adj.* having or showing natural simplicity of nature; unsophisticated; ingenuous. Also, **naïve.** –**naively,** *n.* –**naively,** *adv.*

naked /ˈneɪkəd/ *adj.* **1.** without clothing or covering; nude: *a naked person.* **2.** bare of any covering, vegetation, leaves, etc.: *naked fields; naked trees.* **3.** without the usual covering: *a naked sword; a naked wall.* **4.** (of the eye, sight, etc.) without the help of glasses, microscope or other instrument. **5.** simple; unadorned: *the naked truth; a naked outline of facts.* **6.** open to view: *a naked vein of ore.* **7.** *Bot.* (of seeds) not enclosed in a pod. **8.** *Zool.* having no covering of hair, feathers, shell, etc. –**nakedly,** *adv.* –**nakedness,** *n.*

naltrexone /nælˈtrɛksoʊn/ *n.* a drug which acts as a blocking agent to the body's opiate receptors, used to treat drug addiction, especially to heroin.

name /neɪm/ *n.* **1.** a word or a combination of words by which a person, place, or thing, a body or class, or any object of thought, is designated or known. **2.** mere designation as distinguished from fact: *king in name only.* **3.** an appellation, title, or epithet, applied descriptively, in honour, abuse, etc.: *to call him bad names.* **4.** a reputation of a particular kind given by common report: *a bad name.* **5.** a distinguished, famous, or great reputation; fame: *to seek a name for oneself.* **6.** a widely known or famous person. **7.** a personal or family name as exercising influence or bringing distinction. –*v.t.* **8.** to give a name to: *name a baby.* **9.** to call by a specified name: *name a child Regina.* **10.** to specify or mention by name: *three persons were named in the report.* **11.** to designate for some duty or office; nominate or appoint: *I have named you for the position.* **12.** to specify: *to name a price.* **13.** to tell the name of: *name the capital of France.* **14.** (in sittings of parliament) to cite (a member) for contempt. –*phr.* **15. in the name of, a.** with appeal to: *in the name of mercy, stop screaming!* **b.** by the authority of: *open, in the name of the law!* **c.** on behalf of: *to vote in the name of others.* **d.** under the name of: *money deposited in the name of my son.* **e.** under the designation of; in the character of: *murder in the name of mercy.* **16. name after,** Also, *US,* **name for.** to give (someone or something) the same name as another to commemorate or honour that person, place, event, etc. **17. the name of the game,** *Colloq.* the central issue or the essential part of an operation, business, etc. **18. to one's name,** belonging to one: *not a cent to my name.* –**nameable, namable,** *adj.* –**namer,** *n.*

nameless /ˈneɪmləs/ *adj.* **1.** unknown to fame; obscure. **2.** having no name. **3.** left unnamed: *a certain person who shall be nameless.* **4.** anonymous: *a nameless writer.* **5.** that cannot be specified or described: *a nameless charm.* **6.** too shocking or vile to be specified. –**namelessly,** *adv.* –**namelessness,** *n.*

namely /ˈneɪmli/ *adv.* that is to say; to wit: *two cities, namely, Sydney and Melbourne.*

namesake /ˈneɪmseɪk/ *n.* **1.** someone having the same name as another. **2.** someone named after another.

naming ceremony *n.* (*pl.* **-nies**) **1.** a ceremony at which someone or something is officially named. **2.** an occasion, usually conducted by a civil celebrant, at which a child is named, guardians (or godparents) appointed, etc.

nan[1] /næn/ *n.* → **nanna.**

nan[2] /nɑn/ *n.* → **naan.**

nana[1] /ˈnɑnə/ *n.* *Colloq.* **1.** a banana. **2.** an idiot; fool. –*phr.* **3. do one's nana,** to lose one's temper. **4. off one's nana,** mentally unhinged, especially temporarily.

nana[2] /ˈnɑnə/ *n.* → **nanna.**

nankeen kestrel /nænkin ˈkɛstrəl/ *n.* a small falcon, *Falco cenchroides,* rufous above and white below, found in Australia and New Guinea; the most common of the smaller Australian raptorial birds; sparrowhawk.

nanna /ˈnænə/ *n.* *Colloq.* a grandmother. Also, **nana, nan.**

nanna nap *n.* *Colloq.* a short sleep taken, often in the afternoon, in order to re-energise oneself.

nanny /ˈnæni/ *n.* (*pl.* **-nies**) **1.** Also, *Brit. Obs.,* **nurse.** a female professional helper who has the general care of someone else's child or children. **2.** a grandmother. **3.** → **nanny goat**.

nanny goat *n.* a female goat. Also, **nanny-goat**.

nano- **1.** a prefix denoting 10^{-9} of a given unit, as in *nanometre*. Symbol: n **2.** a prefix indicating very small size, as *nanoplankton*.

nanomedicine /ˈnænoʊmɛdəsən/ *n.* medical treatments which employ nanotechnology in a range of different ways, such as the use of controllable micro-sized robots to perform medical procedures.

nanometre /ˈnænoʊmitə/ *n.* one billionth (10^{-9}) of a metre.

nanoparticle /ˈnænoʊpatɪkəl/ *n.* a microscopic particle whose size is measured in nanometres.

nanoscience /ˈnænoʊˌsaɪəns/ *n.* the science concerned with objects of the smallest dimensions, ranging from a few nanometres to less than 100 nanometres, in the fields of chemistry, physics, electrical engineering, biology and biochemistry.

nanotechnology /ˈnænoʊtɛknɒlədʒi/ *n.* technology generated from nanoscience, as in microelectronics and chemistry. **–nanotechnologist,** *n.*

nanotherapy /ˈnænoʊθɛrəpi/ *n. Med.* therapy which uses nanoparticles, as plasmonic nanobubble therapy. **–nanotherapeutic** /ˌnænoʊθɛrəˈpjutɪk/, *adj.*

nap¹ /næp/ *v.i.* (**napped, napping**) **1.** to have a short sleep; doze. *–n.* **2.** a short sleep; a doze. *–phr.* **3. catch someone napping,** to discover someone unprepared or off guard.

nap² /næp/ *n.* **1.** the short fuzzy ends of fibres on the surface of cloth. **2.** any downy coating, as on plants. *–v.t.* (**napped, napping**) **3.** to raise a nap on. **–napless,** *adj.*

napalm /ˈneɪpam, ˈnæpam/ *n.* an aluminium soap, in the form of a granular powder, which is a mixture of fatty acids; mixed with petrol it forms a sticky gel, stable from −40°C to 100°C, used in flame throwers and fire bombs.

nape /neɪp/ *n.* the back of the neck.

napery /ˈneɪpəri/ *n.* **1.** table linen; tablecloths, napkins, etc. **2.** linen for household use.

naphthalene /ˈnæfθəlin/ *n.* a white crystalline hydrocarbon, $C_{10}H_8$, usually prepared from coal tar, used in making dyes, as a moth repellent, etc. Also, **naphthaline, naphthalin** /ˈnæfθələn/.

napkin /ˈnæpkən/ *n.* **1.** → **serviette**. **2.** a square or oblong piece of linen, cotton cloth, or paper used for **a.** a towel. **b.** a baby's nappy.

nappy /ˈnæpi/ *n.* (*pl.* **-pies**) a piece of cotton towelling, or some disposable material, fastened round a baby to absorb and contain its excrement.

narcissism /ˈnasəsɪzəm/ *n.* **1.** extreme admiration for oneself or one's own attributes; egoism; self-love. **2.** *Psychol.* sexual excitement through admiration of oneself. Also, **narcism** /ˈnasɪzəm/. **–narcissist,** *n.* **–narcissistic** /nasəˈsɪstɪk/, *adj.*

narcissus /naˈsɪsəs/ *n.* (*pl.* **-cissuses** *or* **-cissi** /-ˈsɪsaɪ/) any plant of the genus *Narcissus*, which comprises bulbous plants bearing showy flowers with a cup-shaped corona, as the narcissus, *N. poeticus*, and the wild daffodil, *N. pseudonarcissus*.

narcosis /naˈkoʊsəs/ *n.* **1.** a state of sleep or drowsiness. **2.** a temporary state of stupor or unconsciousness, especially produced by a drug.

narcotic /naˈkɒtɪk/ *adj.* **1.** having the power to produce narcosis, as a drug. **2.** relating to or of the nature of narcosis. **3.** relating to narcotics or their use. **4.** for the use or treatment of narcotic addicts. *–n.* **5.** any of a class of substances that blunt the senses, relieve pain, induce sleep, etc., and in large quantities produce complete insensibility; often used habitually to satisfy addiction.

nark /nak/ *Colloq.* *–n.* **1.** an informer; a spy, especially for the police. **2.** a scolding, complaining person. **3.** someone who is always interfering and spoiling the pleasure of others; spoilsport. *–v.t.* **4.** to nag; irritate; annoy. *–v.i.* **5.** to act as an informer. **–narky,** *adj.*

narrate /nəˈreɪt/ *v.t.* **1.** to give an account of or tell the story of (events, experiences, etc.). *–v.i.* **2.** to relate or recount events, etc., in speech or writing. **–narratable,** *adj.* **–narration** /nəˈreɪʃən/, *n.* **–narrator,** *n.*

narrative /ˈnærətɪv/ *n.* **1.** a story of events, experiences, or the like, whether true or fictitious. **2.** narrative matter, as in literary work. **3.** the act or process of narrating. **4.** the rationale for a sequence of events, presented as the underlying explanation: *the narrative of recent events in politics. –adj.* **5.** that narrates: *a narrative poem.* **6.** of or relating to narration: *narrative skill.* **–narratively,** *adv.*

narrow /ˈnæroʊ/ *adj.* **1.** not broad or wide: *a narrow room.* **2.** limited in size, range, or amount: *narrow circumstances; narrow resources.* **3.** lacking breadth of view or sympathy: *a narrow person; a narrow mind.* **4.** only just succeeding: *a narrow escape.* **5.** careful; minute: *a narrow search. –v.t.* **6.** to make narrower in width, range, outlook, etc. *–v.i.* **7.** to become narrower in width, range, outlook, etc. *–n.* **8.** a narrow part, place or thing. **9.** (*pl.*) the narrow part of a strait, river, ocean current, etc. **–narrowly,** *adv.* **–narrowness,** *n.*

narrowcast /ˈnæroʊkast/ *v.t.* (**-cast** *or* **-casted, -casting**) **1.** to transmit (data) to a limited number of recipients as in cable television where only subscribers' receivers can take the signal. *–n.* **2.** an instance of narrowcasting. **–narrowcasting,** *n.* **–narrowcaster,** *n.*

narrow-minded *adj.* having or showing a prejudiced mind, as persons, opinions, etc. **–narrow-mindedly,** *adv.* **–narrow-mindedness,** *n.*

nasal /ˈneɪzəl/ *adj.* **1.** of or relating to the nose. **2.** *Phonetics* with the voice issuing through the nose, either partly (as in French nasal vowels) or entirely (as in *m, n,* or the *ng* of *song*). *–n.* **3.** *Phonetics* a nasal speech sound. **–nasality** /neɪˈzæləti/, *n.* **–nasally,** *adv.*

nascent /ˈneɪsənt, ˈnæsənt/ *adj.* **1.** beginning to exist or develop: *the nascent republic.* **2.** *Chem.* (of an element) being in the nascent state, in which it is set free from a combination in which it has previously existed. **–nascence, nascency,** *n.*

nashi pear /ˈnæʃi ˈpɛə/ *n.* **1.** an Asian pear tree, *Pyrus pyrifolia,* with white flowers and red leaves in spring. **2.** the fruit of this tree, having a crisp texture and yellow skin. Also, **Asian pear**.

nasi goreng /ˌnʌsi ˈɡɔrɛŋ/ *n.* a dish of Indonesian origin consisting of cooked rice, fried in seasoned oil, garnished with hot chillies, beef shreds or slices, fried onions and sliced omelette.

nasturtium /nəˈstɜʃəm/ *n.* any of the garden plants constituting the genus *Tropaeolum,* much cultivated for their showy flowers of yellow, red, and other colours, and for their fruit, which is picked and used like capers.

nasty /ˈnasti/ *adj.* (**-tier, -tiest**) **1.** unpleasant; disgusting: *a nasty mess; nasty weather.* **2.** offensive: *a nasty taste; a nasty smell; a nasty habit.* **3.** spiteful; vicious: *a nasty dog; a nasty mind.* **4.** painful; dangerous: *a nasty cut.* **–nastily,** *adv.* **–nastiness,** *n.*

-nasty a suffix indicating irregularity of cellular growth because of some pressure.

natal /ˈneɪtl/ *adj.* **1.** of or relating to birth. **2.** presiding over or affecting someone at birth: *natal influences.*

natant /ˈneɪtənt/ *adj.* **1.** swimming; floating. **2.** *Bot.* floating on water, as the leaf of an aquatic plant.

nation /ˈneɪʃən/ *n.* **1. a.** a relatively large body of people living in a particular territory and organised under a single, usually independent, government; country; state: *the leading industrialised nations of the world; the* *whole nation was shocked at the news.* **b.** the territory occupied by such a group of people: *to travel from one end of the nation to the other.* **c.** the government or representatives of such a people: *a forum attended by 20 nations.* **2.** an aggregation of persons who identify themselves as forming a group, as by common descent, customs, history, and language, whether or not occupying and controlling their own territory. —**nationhood,** *n.* —**nationless,** *adj.*

national /ˈnæʃnəl, ˈnæʃənəl/ *adj.* **1.** of, relating to, or maintained by a nation as an organised whole or independent political unit: *national affairs.* **2.** peculiar or common to the whole people of a country: *national customs.* —*n.* **3.** a citizen or subject of a particular nation, entitled to its protection. —**nationally,** *adv.*

nationalise /ˈnæʃnəlaɪz/ *v.t.* **1.** to bring under the control or ownership of a government as industries, land, etc. **2.** to make nationwide. **3.** → **naturalise** (def. 1). **4.** to make into a nation. Also, **nationalize.** —**nationalisation** /næʃnələˈzeɪʃən/, *n.* —**nationaliser,** *n.*

nationalism /ˈnæʃnəlɪzəm/ *n.* **1.** national spirit or aspirations. **2.** devotion to the interests of one's own nation. **3.** desire for national advancement or independence. **4.** the policy of asserting the interests of a nation, viewed as separate from the interests of other nations or the common interests of all nations. **5.** extreme, fanatical devotion to one's own nation. —**nationalist,** *n.,* *adj.* —**nationalistic,** *adj.*

nationality /næʃəˈnæləti, næʃˈnæl-/ *n.* (*pl.* **-ties**) **1.** the condition of being a member of a particular nation: *this form requires you to state your nationality.* **2.** the condition of belonging to a particular nation, or to one or more of its members: *the nationality of a ship.* **3.** a nation or people. **4.** national quality or character.

national living treasure *n.* a person who has achieved such a high standard of excellence in his or her field over a long period of time, especially in performing arts or traditional crafts, as to be of significance to the nation. Also, **living national treasure.**

national park *n.* an area protected by law because of its diversity of native plants and animals, undisturbed or unique ecosystem, unspoilt landscapes or significant cultural features; able to be visited by the general public.

national service *n.* (in many countries) compulsory service in the armed forces for a period of varying duration.

native /ˈneɪtɪv/ *adj.* **1.** being the place or environment in which one was born or a thing came into being: *his native land.* **2.** (sometimes fol. by *to*) belonging to a person or thing by birth or nature; inborn. **3.** (*now likely to give offence*) being or relating to those descended from the original inhabitants of a country, as distinguished from its colonisers: *native art in New Guinea; native bearers in Africa; a native village.* **4.** belonging or relating to one by reason of one's birthplace or nationality: *one's native language.* **5.** born in a particular place or country: *native Italians.* **6.** remaining in a natural state; unadorned; untouched by art: *native beauty.* **7.** (of flora and fauna) indigenous to a particular region or country: *these herbs are native to Provence; the native cats of America.* **8.** found in nature rather than artificial, as a mineral substance. —*n.* **9.** (*now likely to give offence*) someone inhabiting a place before the arrival of colonisers, etc., or a descendant of an original inhabitant; an indigenous person: *they offered gifts to the natives.* **10.** someone born in a particular place or country, whether or not continuing to reside there: *a native of Muswellbrook.* **11.** an animal or plant native to a particular area. —**natively,** *adv.* —**nativeness,** *n.*

native cat *n.* any of several cat-sized, predatory marsupials of the genus *Dasyurus,* having slender, white-spotted bodies and very pointed snouts; marsupial cat.

native language *n.* → **first language.**

native title *n.* in Australia, the right to land or water held by Indigenous people who have maintained their connection to the land or water and whose possession under their traditional law or customs is recognised by Australian law.

nativity /nəˈtɪvəti/ *n.* (*pl.* **-ties**) **1.** birth. **2.** (*upper case*) *Christianity* **a.** the birth of Christ. **b.** the church celebration of the birth of Christ; Christmas.

natter /ˈnætə/ *v.i.* **1.** *Colloq.* to chatter; gossip. —*n.* **2.** a chat; idle talk.

natty /ˈnæti/ *adj.* (**-tier, -tiest**) **1.** neatly smart in dress or appearance; spruce; trim: *a natty white uniform.* **2.** (of a device, vehicle, etc.) small, trim, and highly functional. —**nattily,** *adv.* —**nattiness,** *n.*

natural /ˈnætʃərəl, ˈnætʃrəl/ *adj.* **1.** existing in, formed or established by nature; not artificial: *a natural bridge; natural resources.* **2.** of or relating to nature: *natural science.* **3.** in a state of nature; uncultivated or wild. **4.** of, relating to, or based on nature; inborn; innate: *natural ability; a manner natural to an aristocrat.* **5.** free from pretence or affectation: *a natural manner.* **6.** in accordance with the nature of things; normal: *it was natural that he should hit back; a natural outcome.* **7.** based upon the inborn moral feeling of mankind: *natural justice.* **8.** in accordance with the ordinary course of nature; not unusual, exceptional or irregular: *a natural death.* **9.** by birth only, and not legally recognised; illegitimate: *a natural child.* **10.** true to nature; life-like. **11.** being such by nature; born such: *a natural fool.* **12.** *Maths* of or relating to a sine, tangent, etc., which is expressed as the actual value, not the logarithm. —*n.* **13.** *Colloq.* a thing or person that is by nature satisfactory or successful. **14.** *Music* **a.** a white key on the piano, etc. **b.** the sign ♮ placed before a note, stopping the effect of a previous sharp or flat. —**naturally,** *adv.* —**naturalness,** *n.*

natural gas *n.* combustible gas formed naturally in the earth, as in regions yielding petroleum, and consisting typically of methane with certain amounts of hydrogen and other gases; used as a fuel, etc.

naturalise /ˈnætʃrəlaɪz/ *v.t.* **1.** to give (a foreign person) the rights and privileges of citizenship. **2.** to introduce (animals or plants) into an area and cause to grow or live as if native. **3.** to introduce (foreign practices, words, etc.) into a country or into general use: *to naturalise a French phrase.* **4.** to accustom to a place or to new surroundings. —*v.i.* **5.** to become naturalised, or as if native. Also, **naturalize.** —**naturalisation** /nætʃrəlaɪˈzeɪʃən/, *n.*

naturalist /ˈnætʃrələst/ *n.* **1.** someone versed in or devoted to natural history, especially a zoologist or botanist. **2.** an adherent of naturalism.

natural language processing *n.* the analysis, interpretation and generation of human languages by computer. *Abbrev.:* NLP

natural selection *n.* *Biol.* the process by which a species adapts to a particular environment, in which the mechanism is the differential survival and reproductive success of organisms in response to environmental pressures.

nature /ˈneɪtʃə/ *n.* **1.** the particular combination of qualities belonging to a person or thing by birth or constitution; native or inherent character: *the nature of atomic energy.* **2.** the instincts or inherent tendencies directing conduct: *a child of good nature.* **3.** character, kind, or sort: *a book of the same nature.* **4.** the material world, especially as surrounding humankind and existing independently of their activities. **5.** the universe, with all its phenomena. **6.** the sum total of the forces at work throughout the universe. **7.** reality, as distinguished from any effect of art: *true to nature*. **8.** the physical being. **9.** a primitive, wild condition; an uncultivated state. –*phr.* **10. by nature**, as a result of inherent qualities. **11. call of nature**, *Colloq.* the need to urinate or defecate. **12. of** (or **in**) **the nature of**, having the qualities of.

naturopathy /næt∫ˈrɒpəθi/ *n.* **1.** a system of treating disease and disorders in humans based on promoting the body's own natural defences, especially by use of herbs, natural foods, massage, exercise and sunlight. **2.** a similar method of treating disease and disorders in animals: *canine naturopathy*; *small animals naturopathy*; *horse naturopathy*. **–naturopath** /ˈnæt∫ərəˌpæθ/, *n.* **–naturopathic** /ˌnæt∫ərəˈpæθɪk/, *adj.*

naught /nɔt/ *n.* **1.** *Archaic or Poetic* nothing. **2.** destruction, ruin, or complete failure: *to bring to naught*; *to come to naught*. **3.** *Chiefly US* → **nought**. –*phr.* **4. set at naught**, to regard or treat as of no importance. Also, **nought**.

naughty /ˈnɔti/ *adj.* (**-tier**, **-tiest**) **1.** disobedient; mischievous (especially in speaking to or about children). **2.** improper; obscene: *a naughty word*. **–naughtily**, *adv.* **–naughtiness**, *n.*

nausea /ˈnɔsiə, -ziə/ *n.* **1.** sickness at the stomach; a sensation of impending vomiting. **2.** extreme disgust. **–nauseate**, *v.* **–nauseous**, *adj.* **–nauseously**, *adv.*

nautical /ˈnɔtɪkəl/ *adj.* of or relating to sailors, ships, or navigation: *nautical terms*. **–nautically**, *adv.*

nautical mile *n.* a unit of measurement of length, used in marine and aeronautical navigation, originally defined as the length of one minute of arc of a great circle of the earth, now usually specified as 1852 m (**international nautical mile**), based on the average length of a minute of latitude, and corresponding to a latitude of 45°.

nautilus /ˈnɔtələs/ *n.* (*pl.* **-luses** *or* **-li** /-laɪ/) any of various molluscs with tentacles joined to the head and a spiral shell with many internal sections with pearly walls.

naval /ˈneɪvəl/ *adj.* **1.** of or relating to ships, now only ships of war: *a naval battle*. **2.** of or relating to a navy: *naval affairs*.

nave /neɪv/ *n.* the main body, or middle part, lengthwise, of a church, flanked by the aisles and extending typically from the entrance to the apse or chancel.

navel /ˈneɪvəl/ *n.* **1.** a pit or depression in the middle of the surface of the belly; the umbilicus. **2.** the central point or middle of any thing or place.

navel orange *n.* a kind of orange having at the apex a navel-like formation containing a small secondary fruit.

navigate /ˈnævəgeɪt/ *v.t.* **1.** to traverse (the sea, a river, etc.) in a vessel, on (the air) in an aircraft. **2.** to direct or manage (a ship, aircraft, etc.) on its course. **3.** *Internet* to find one's way around (a website). –*v.i.* **4.** to direct or manage a ship, aircraft, etc., on its course. **5.** to travel by using a ship or boat, as over the water; sail. **–navigation**, *n.* **–navigator**, *n.*

navigation bar *n.* *Computers* the bar running along the top, side or bottom of a web page which encloses buttons which take the user to various places on the site.

navvy /ˈnævi/ *n.* (*pl.* **-vies**) a labourer employed in making roads, railways, canals, etc.

navy /ˈneɪvi/ *n.* (*pl.* **-vies**) **1.** the whole body of warships and auxiliaries belonging to a country or ruler. **2.** such a body of warships together with their officers and crew, equipment, yards, etc. **3.** Also, **navy blue**. a dark blue, as of a naval uniform.

nay /neɪ/ *adv.* **1.** no (used in dissent, denial, or refusal). **2.** also; and not only so but: *many good, nay, noble qualities*. –*n.* **3.** a denial or refusal. **4.** a negative vote or voter.

Nazi /ˈnɑtsi/ *n.* (*pl.* **Nazis**) **1.** a member of the National Socialist German Workers' party, which was founded in 1919 and which in 1933, under Adolf Hitler, obtained political control of Germany; it consequently established a dictatorship on the principles of control over all cultural, economic, and political activities of the people, belief in the supremacy of Hitler as Führer, anti-Semitism, and the establishment of Germany as a dominant world power. **2.** (*oft. lower case*) someone who supports the fascist ideas characteristic of this party, especially racist nationalism. **3.** (*oft. lower case*) *Colloq.* **a.** someone who is extremely domineering and unwilling to compromise with others. **b.** (*with a modifier*) someone who displays a dictatorial attitude about how people should think or behave with regard to a particular topic or thing: *a kitchen Nazi*. **–Nazism**, *n.*

NCO /ɛn si ˈoʊ/ *n.* a non-commissioned officer.

neap /nip/ *adj.* designating those tides, midway between spring tides, which attain the least height.

near /nɪə/ *adv.* **1.** close: *near by*. **2.** nigh; at, within, or to a short distance: *to stand near*. **3.** close at hand in time: *New Year's Day is near*. **4.** close in relation; closely with respect to connection, similarity, etc. **5.** all but; almost: *a period of near thirty years*. **6.** *Naut.* close to the wind. –*adj.* **7.** being close by; not distant: *the near meadows*. **8.** less distant: *the near side*. **9.** close in time: *the near future*. **10.** closely related or connected: *our nearest relation*. **11.** narrow: *a near escape*. **12.** parsimonious or niggardly: *a near man*. **13. a.** being on the left side of an animal such as a horse: *the near hind leg*. **b.** (in a team of animals) being on the left: *the near bullock*. **c.** (in driving) being on the left of a vehicle in a country where traffic drives on the left. –*prep.* **14.** at, within, or to a short distance, or no great distance, from: *regions near the equator*. **15.** close upon in time: *near the beginning of the year*. **16.** close upon (a condition, etc.): *a task near completion*. **17.** close to in similarity, resemblance, etc.: *near beer*. **18.** close to (doing something): *this act came near spoiling his chances*. –*v.t.* **19.** to come or draw near (to); approach. –*phr.* **20. near at hand**, close by. **21. near enough**, (of a task, piece of work, etc., just completed) adequately but not perfectly done. **22. near enough is good enough**, (*used ironically, for instance in criticism of Australian work habits*) it is sufficient to perform to a minimum standard. **–nearness**, *n.*

nearby *adj.* /ˈnɪəbaɪ/ **1.** close at hand; not far off; adjacent; neighbouring: *a nearby village*. –*adv.* /nɪəˈbaɪ/ **2.** close at hand; not far off.

nearly /ˈnɪəli/ *adv.* **1.** all but; almost: *nearly dead with cold*. **2.** with close approximation. **3.** with close agreement or resemblance: *a case nearly approaching this one*. **4.** with close kinship, interest, or connection; intimately. **5.** with parsimony.

nearside /ˈnɪəsaɪd/ *adj.* **1.** of or relating to the side of vehicle nearer to the footpath, i.e. the left-hand side in a country where traffic drives on the left. Compare **offside** (def. 2). –*n.* **2.** the side of a vehicle nearer to the footpath, i.e. the left-hand side in a country where traffic drives on the left. Compare **offside** (def. 5).

near-sighted *adj.* seeing distinctly at a short distance only; myopic. **–nearsightedly**, *adv.* **–nearsightedness**, *n.*

neat /nit/ *adj.* **1.** in a pleasingly orderly condition; tidy: *a neat room*. **2.** tidy in appearance, habits, etc.: *a neat person*. **3.** of a simple, pleasing appearance: *a neat cottage*. **4.** clever in character or performance: *a neat plan*. **5.** (of alcoholic drinks) without any other drink added; undiluted. **–neatly**, *adv.* **–neatness**, *n.* **–neaten**, *v.*

neb /nɛb/ *n. Obs.* **1.** a bill or beak, as of a bird. **2.** the nose, especially of an animal. **3.** the tip or pointed end of anything. **4.** the nib of a pen.

nebula /ˈnɛbjələ/ *n.* (*pl.* **-las** *or* **-lae** /-liː/) **1.** *Astron.* **a.** an irregular, luminous, or dark patch in the sky consisting of interstellar gases and dust. **b.** a small regular disc resembling (under low magnification) a planet, consisting of a gaseous envelope enclosing a central star; a planetary nebula. **c.** (formerly) any cloud-like luminous patch in the sky, such as a galaxy, cluster, etc. **2.** *Pathol.* **a.** a faint opacity in the cornea. **b.** cloudiness in the urine. **–nebular**, *adj.*

nebulise /ˈnɛbjəlaɪz/ *v.t.* **1.** to reduce to fine spray; atomise. **2.** to administer medication to (someone) by means of a nebuliser. Also, **nebulize**.

nebuliser /ˈnɛbjəlaɪzə/ *n. Med.* a device which reduces a liquid medication to a fine mist which is then inhaled into the lungs. Also, **nebulizer**.

nebulous /ˈnɛbjələs/ *adj.* **1.** hazy, vague, indistinct, or confused: *a nebulous recollection.* **2.** cloudy or cloud-like. **3.** of or characteristic of a nebula. **–nebulously**, *adv.* **–nebulousness**, *n.*

necessary /ˈnɛsəsɛri, ˈnɛsəsri/ *adj.* **1.** unable to be done without or dispensed with: *regular meals are necessary for health*; *buy only the necessary things.* **2.** that must happen or exist; inevitable: *war was a necessary result of the arms race.* *–n.* (*pl.* **-ries**) **3.** (*usu. pl.*) something necessary. **–necessarily**, *adv.* **–necessitous**, *adj.* **–necessity**, *n.*

necessitate /nəˈsɛsəteɪt/ *v.t.* **1.** to make necessary: *the breakdown of the motor necessitated a halt.* **2.** to compel, oblige, or force: *the rise in prices necessitated greater thrift.* **–necessitation** /nəsɛsəˈteɪʃən/, *n.* **–necessitative**, *adj.*

neck /nɛk/ *n.* **1.** that part of the body of some animals which is between the head and the trunk and connects these parts. **2. a.** a standard cut of meat, especially lamb, from this area, used mainly for chops, stews, etc. **b. best neck**, the section between the upper cervical vertebrae. **3.** the part of a garment covering the neck or extending about it. **4.** the length of the neck of a horse or other animal as a measure in racing. **5.** the slender part of a bottle, retort, or any similar object. **6.** that part of a golf club head by which this joins the shaft. **7.** any narrow, connecting, or projecting part suggesting the neck of an animal. **8.** the longer slender part of a violin or the like, extending from the body to the head. **9.** (*usu. pl.*) skirtings of wool which are removed from the neck of a fleece in the process of wool rolling. **10.** *Archit.* the lowest part of the capital of a column, above the astragal at the head of the shaft. **11.** a narrow strip of land, as an isthmus or a cape. *–v.i.* **12.** *Colloq.* to kiss, cuddle, and pet. *–phr.* **13. get it in the neck**, *Colloq.* to be reprimanded or punished severely. **14. get** (or **go**) **under someone's neck**, *Aust.* to beat someone by outwitting or anticipating them by finding a vulnerable part. **15. neck and crop**, entirely; completely. **16. neck and neck**, just even. **17. neck of the woods**, *Colloq.* a specific area, particular place: *we don't often see you in this neck of the woods.* **18. stick one's neck out**, *Colloq.* to act, express an opinion, etc., so as to expose oneself to criticism, hostility, danger, etc. **19. win by a neck**, *Horseracing, etc.* to be first by a head and neck.

neckerchief /ˈnɛkətʃɪf/ *n.* a cloth worn round the neck by women or men.

necklace /ˈnɛkləs/ *n.* **1.** Also, **necklet**. an ornament of precious stones, beads, or the like, worn especially by women round the neck. **2.** (in South Africa) a car tyre used to necklace someone. *–v.t.* (**-laced**, **-lacing**) **3.** (in

South Africa) to put (a person) to death by means of a burning car tyre around the neck.

necromancy /ˈnɛkrəˌmænsi/ *n.* **1.** magic in general; enchantment; conjuration; the black art. **2.** the pretended art of divination through communication with the dead. **–necromancer**, *n.* **–necromantic** /nɛkrəˈmæntɪk/, *adj.*

necrophilia /nɛkrəˈfɪliə, -ˈfil-, -jə/ *n.* morbid attraction to corpses. Also, **necrophilism** /nəˈkrɒfəlɪzəm/. **–necrophiliac**, *n.* **–necrophilic**, *adj.*

necrosis /nəˈkrousəs/ *n. Pathol.* death of a circumscribed piece of tissue or of an organ. **–necrotic** /nəˈkrɒtɪk/, *adj.*

nectar /ˈnɛktə/ *n.* **1.** *Bot.* the saccharine secretion of a plant which attracts the insects or birds that pollinate the flower, collected by bees in whose body it is elaborated into honey. **2.** any delicious drink.

nectarine /ˈnɛktərən, nɛktəˈrin/ *n.* a form of the common peach, having a skin destitute of down.

nee /neɪ/ *adj.* born (placed after the name of a married woman to introduce her maiden name): *Mrs Smith nee Brown.* Also, **née** /neɪ/.

need /nid/ *n.* **1.** something necessary or wanted; requirement: *to meet the needs of the occasion.* **2.** an urgent want of something necessary: *he has no need of your kindness; the need for leadership.* **3.** a necessity arising from a particular situation: *There is no need to worry.* **4.** a situation or time of difficulty or want: *a friend in need.* *–v.t.* **5.** to have need of; require: *to need money.* **6.** (fol. by infinitive, sometimes without *to*) to be under a necessity: *he need not go; she needs to see her friend.* *–v.i.* **7.** to be in need or want. **–needer**, *n.*

needle /ˈnidl/ *n.* **1.** a small, thin, pointed instrument, now usually of steel, with a hole for thread, used in sewing. **2.** a thin, rod-like instrument for use in knitting, or one hooked at the end for use in crocheting, etc. **3.** *Med.* **a.** a thin, pointed, steel instrument used in sewing tissues, etc., during surgical operations. **b.** a hypodermic needle. **4.** any of various objects suggesting a needle in shape, such as a sharp-pointed mass of rock. **5.** the magnetic pointer in a compass which indicates the direction of north. **6.** a pointed instrument used in engraving, etc. **7.** *Bot.* a needle-shaped leaf of a pine tree, etc. **8.** *Zool.* a thin, sharp spike. *–v.t.* **9.** to sew or pierce with a needle. **10.** to urge to action by making sharp remarks; goad. **11.** to make fun of (someone); tease. **–needle-like**, *adj.*

needlepoint /ˈnidlpɔɪnt/ *n.* embroidery on canvas worked to cover the area completely with even stitches to resemble tapestry.

needlepoint lace *n.* a kind of lace in which a needle works out the design upon parchment or paper.

needless /ˈnidləs/ *adj.* not needed or wanted; unnecessary: *a needless waste of food.* **–needlessly**, *adv.* **–needlessness**, *n.*

needlestick injury *n.* an accidental penetrating injury caused by a hypodermic needle which has already been used by another person and hence contaminated with blood.

needlework /ˈnidlwɜk/ *n.* the process or the product of working with a needle as in sewing or embroidery.

needy /ˈnidi/ *adj.* (**-dier**, **-diest**) in, or characterised by, need or want; very poor: *a needy family.* **–neediness**, *n.*

ne'er-do-well /ˈnɛə-du-wɛl/ *n.* **1.** a worthless person. *–adj.* **2.** worthless; good-for-nothing.

nefarious /nəˈfɛəriəs/ *adj.* extremely wicked; iniquitous: *nefarious practices.* **–nefariously**, *adv.* **–nefariousness**, *n.*

negate /nəˈgeɪt/ *v.t.* to deny; nullify. **–negation**, *n.* **–negatory**, *adj.*

negative /ˈnɛgətɪv/ *adj.* **1.** expressing or containing a refusal or denial: *a negative statement; a negative answer.* **2.** marked by the absence of positive qualities: *a* *negative character.* **3.** *Physics, Maths* **a.** involving or indicating subtraction; minus. **b.** opposite to positive. **4.** *Med.* failing to show a positive result in a test for a particular disease caused by bacteria or viruses. **5.** *Photography* indicating an image in which the relation of light and shade are reversed. **6.** *Elect.* relating to the kind of electricity developed on resin, etc., when rubbed with flannel, or that present at the pole from which electrons leave an electric generator or battery; having an excess of electrons. **7.** relating to the south-seeking pole of a magnet. **8.** *Chem.* **a.** (of a radical) having more electrons than the neutral atom or molecule and so being negatively charged. **b.** → **electronegative.** *–n.* **9.** a negative statement, word, opinion, etc. **10.** the side of a question which opposes the positive side. **11.** *Maths* a negative quantity or symbol. **12.** *Photography* a negative image on film, plate, etc., used chiefly for printing positive pictures. **13.** *Elect.* the negative plate or element in a voltaic cell. *–v.t.* **14.** to negate. **15.** to disprove. **16.** to refuse consent to; veto. **–negatively,** *adv.* **–negativeness, negativity,** *n.*

negative gearing *n. Finance* a financial situation where an investor borrows against an investment or portfolio of investments, and the loan interest payments exceed the investor's income from the investment, resulting in a negative cash flow and thus taxation benefits.

negative ion generator *n.* a device which releases negative ions into the air, thought to alleviate a wide range of ailments such as asthma, hay fever, headaches, etc., to reduce pollution as from dust or cigarette smoke, and to promote a feeling of wellbeing.

neglect /nəˈglɛkt/ *v.t.* **1.** to pay no attention to; disregard: *he neglected her entreaties.* **2.** to fail to care for or treat properly: *they neglected their children.* **3.** to fail to (do something) through carelessness, etc.: *he neglected to count the money.* *–n.* **4.** the act or fact of neglecting. **5.** the fact or state of being neglected. **–neglecter,** *n.* **–neglectful,** *adj.*

negligee /ˈnɛgləʒeɪ/ *n.* a form of night attire for women, which can be knee-length or to the floor, often decorated with lace, bows, and other trimmings, and mul-tilayered using soft sheer fabrics. Also, **négligé.**

negligent /ˈnɛglədʒənt/ *adj.* guilty of or characterised by neglect, as of duty: *negligent officials.* **–negligence,** *n.* **–negligently,** *adv.*

negligible /ˈnɛglədʒəbəl/ *adj.* so small that it may be neglected or disregarded; very little. **–negligibility** /nɛglədʒəˈbɪləti/, **negligibleness,** *n.* **–negligibly,** *adv.*

negotiate /nəˈgoʊʃieɪt/ *v.i.* **1.** to deal with another or others in the preparation of some kind of agreement, such as an international treaty or business arrangement. *–v.t.* **2.** to arrange for or bring about by talking and settlement of terms: *to negotiate a loan.* **3.** to clear or pass through or around: *the car negotiated the twisting mountain road.* **4.** to transfer (a bill of exchange, etc.) by endorsement or delivery. **5.** to sell or transfer: *to negotiate securities.* **–negotiable,** *adj.* **–negotiation,** *n.* **–negotiator,** *n.* **–negotiant,** *n.*

Negro /ˈnigroʊ/ *n.* (*pl.* **-groes**) (*sometimes derog.*) a member of one of the dark-skinned peoples of Africa or a descendant of these peoples elsewhere. Also, **negro.** **–Negress** /ˈnigrəs/, *fem. n.*

Negroid /ˈnigrɔɪd/ *Ethnology –adj.* **1.** (in a system devised in the 19th century) relating to or denoting a division of humankind, consisting of the peoples of Africa south of the Sahara and some Melanesian peoples, characterised by dark skin and tightly curled dark hair. *–n.* **2.** a person belonging to this division. Compare **Australoid, Caucasian, Mongoloid.**

neigh /neɪ/ *n.* **1.** the sound a horse makes; a whinny. *–v.i.* **2.** to make such a sound; to whinny.

neighbour /ˈneɪbə/ *n.* **1.** someone who lives near another. **2.** a person or thing that is near another. **3.** a fellow being subject to the obligations of humanity. *–v.t.* **4.** to live or be situated near to; adjoin; border on. *–v.i.* **5.** to live or be situated nearby. Also, **neighbor.**

neighbourhood /ˈneɪbəhʊd/ *n.* **1.** the region near or about some place or thing; the vicinity. **2.** a district or locality, often with reference to its character or inhabitants: *a fashionable neighbourhood.* **3.** a number of persons living near one another or in a particular locality: *the whole neighbourhood was there.* *–phr.* **4. in the neighbourhood of,** nearly; about. Also, **neighborhood.**

neither /ˈnaɪðə, ˈniðə/ *adj.* **1.** not either; not the one or the other: *neither statement is true.* *–pron.* **2.** not either; not the one or the other: *neither of the statements is true.* *–conj.* **3.** not either (a disjunctive connective preceding a series of two or more alternative words, etc., connected by the correlative *nor*): *neither you nor I nor anybody else knows the answer.* **4.** nor yet: *ye shall not eat of it, neither shall ye touch it.*

nematode /ˈnɛmətoʊd/ *n.* any of the Nematoda, the roundworms, a group variously considered a phylum or class. They are elongated smooth worms of cylindroid shape, parasitic or free-living, as ascarids, trichinae, vinegar eels, etc.

nemesis /ˈnɛməsəs/ *n.* (*pl.* **nemeses** /ˈnɛməsis/) an agent of retribution or punishment.

neo- a word element meaning 'new', 'recent', used in combination, as in *Neo-Darwinism* (a new or modified form of Darwinism), *Neo-Gothic* (Gothic after a new or modern style), *Neo-Hebraic* (pertaining to Hebrew of the modern period).

neologism /niˈɒlədʒɪzəm/ *n.* **1.** a new word or phrase. **2.** the introduction or use of new words, or new senses of words. **3.** a new doctrine. **–neologist,** *n.* **–neologistic** /niˌɒləˈdʒɪstɪk/, **neological** /niˌɒləˈdʒɪstɪkəl/, *adj.*

neon /ˈniɒn/ *n.* a chemically inert gaseous element occurring in small amounts in the earth's atmosphere, and chiefly used in orange-red tubular electrical discharge lamps. *Symbol:* Ne; *relative atomic mass:* 20.183; *atomic number:* 10.

neonate /ˈniəneɪt/ *n.* a newborn child. **–neonatal,** *adj.*

Neo-Nazi /nioʊ-ˈnatsi/ *n.* **1.** an adherent of any form of Nazism founded or revived since World War II. *–adj.* **2.** of or relating to such a person or such a form of Nazism. **–Neo-Nazism,** *n.*

neophyte /ˈniəfaɪt/ *n.* **1.** a converted heathen, heretic, etc. **2.** a newly ordained Roman Catholic priest. **3.** a novice belonging to a religious order. **4.** a beginner. **–neophytic** /niəˈfɪtɪk, nioʊ-/, *adj.*

nephew /ˈnɛfju, ˈnɛvju/ *n.* **1.** a son of one's brother or sister. **2.** a son of one's husband's or wife's brother or sister.

nepho- a word element meaning 'cloud'.

nephr- variant of **nephro-,** before vowels.

nephritis /nəˈfraɪtəs/ *n. Pathol.* inflammation of the kidneys. **–nephritic** /nəˈfrɪtɪk/, *adj.*

nephro- a word element referring to the kidneys. Also, **nephr-.**

nepotism /ˈnɛpətɪzəm/ *n.* patronage bestowed in consideration of family relationship and not of merit. **–nepotic** /nəˈpɒtɪk/, *adj.* **–nepotist,** *n.*

nerd /nɜd/ *n. Colloq.* **1.** a person who is unpopular by reason of not participating in the social life of a school, college, etc., because of an obsession with study, computers, etc.: *a computer nerd.* **2.** an idiot; fool. Also, **nurd.**

nerf gun /ˈnɜf gʌn/ *n.* (*from trademark*) a toy gun which shoots foam bullets, darts, etc.

nerve /nɜv/ *n.* **1.** *Anat.* one or more bundles of fibres, forming part of a system which conveys impulses of sensation, motion, etc., between the brain or spinal cord and other parts of the body. **2.** *Dentistry* **a.** the nerve tissue in the pulp of a tooth. **b.** (popularly but incorrectly) the pulp tissue of a tooth. **3.** strength, vigour, or energy. **4.** firmness or courage in trying circumstances: *a position requiring nerve.* **5.** (*pl.*) nervousness: *a fit of nerves.* **6.** *Colloq.* impertinent assurance. –*v.t.* **7.** to give strength, vigour, or courage to. –*phr.* **8. get on someone's nerves,** to irritate someone. **9. hit a raw nerve,** to bring to attention a painful or sensitive matter.

nerve cell *n.* → **neuron.**

nerve centre *n.* **1.** *Anat., Physiol.* a group of nerve cells closely connected with one another and acting together in the performance of some function. **2.** (of a large company, movement, or organisation) the centre from which plans, policies, and movements are directed.

nerve-racking *adj.* extremely trying.

nervous /ˈnɜːvəs/ *adj.* **1.** of or relating to the nerves: *central nervous system.* **2.** very excited or uneasy, especially while waiting for something to happen; not confident; frightened. –**nervously,** *adv.* –**nervousness,** *n.*

nervous breakdown *n.* any of various psychiatric illnesses, especially those attended by nervous debility and exhaustion and undefined physical complaints.

nervous system *n.* the system of nerves and nerve centres in an animal, comprising two major parts, the central nervous system and the peripheral nervous system. See **central nervous system, peripheral nervous system, somatic nervous system, autonomic nervous system, sympathetic nervous system, parasympathetic nervous system.**

nervy /ˈnɜːvi/ *adj.* (**-vier, -viest**) **1.** nervous. **2.** excitable; irritable. **3.** requiring nerve. **4.** having or showing courage; courageous; bold. **5.** strong or vigorous.

-ness a suffix used to form, from adjectives and participles, nouns denoting quality or state (also often, by extension, something exemplifying a quality or state), as in *darkness, goodness, kindness, obligingness, preparedness.*

nest /nɛst/ *n.* **1.** a structure made or a place used by a bird for hatching its eggs and bringing up its young. **2.** a place used by insects, fishes, turtles, rabbits, etc., for putting their eggs or young in. **3.** a number of birds or animals living in such a place. **4.** a comfortable place to live or to go to sometimes; a snug retreat. **5.** a group of things of the same type or form but of different sizes, that fit within each other: *a nest of tables, trays, etc.* **6.** a place where something bad goes on: *a robbers' nest.* –*v.t.* **7.** to settle or place in a nest. –*v.i.* **8.** to build or have a nest: *the swallows nested under the eaves.* **9.** to search for nests: *to go nesting.*

nest egg *n.* **1.** an egg (usually artificial) left in a nest to induce a hen to continue laying eggs there. **2.** money saved as the basis of a fund or for emergencies.

nestle /ˈnɛsəl/ *verb* (**-tled, -tling**) –*v.i.* **1.** to lie close and snug, like a bird in a nest; snuggle or cuddle. **2.** to lie in a sheltered or pleasant situation. –*v.t.* **3.** to settle or ensconce snugly. **4.** to put or press confidingly or affectionately. –**nestler,** *n.*

net[1] /nɛt/ *n.* **1.** a lacelike fabric with a uniform mesh made by knotting or weaving threads together; netting. **2.** such a fabric made from fine threads for people to wear, or to keep off mosquitoes, flies, etc. **3.** such a fabric made from strong cord or rope with bigger spaces, for catching fish, birds, or other animals. **4.** anything used to catch or snare. **5.** → **network.** **6.** a piece of netting used in various sports, especially tennis, netball, soccer, etc. –*v.t.* **7.** to cover, screen, or enclose with a net or netting. **8.** to catch or snare with, or as with, a net: *to net fish.* –*adj.* **9.** made in the form of or like a net.

net[2] /nɛt/ *adj.* **1.** exclusive of deductions, as for charges, expenses, loss, discount, etc.: *net earnings.* **2.** sold at net prices. **3.** ultimate; final; after all calculations have been made, or all additions and subtractions have had their effect: *the net result of the weather changes was a flow of air into the region.* –*n.* **4.** net income, profits, or the like. –*v.t.* (**netted, netting**) **5.** to gain or produce as clear profit. Also, **nett.**

Net /nɛt/ *n.* **the** → **internet** (def. 1). Also, **the net.**

netball /ˈnɛtbɔːl/ *n.* **1.** a game played by two teams of seven players, in which the ball must be passed between the players who are not allowed to run when in possession, and in which points are scored by throwing the ball through a hoop attached to a pole at the opponents' end of a rectangular court. **2.** the ball used in this game. –**netballer,** *n.*

Net Gen /ˈnɛt dʒɛn/ *n.* **1.** → **Net Gener.** –*adj.* **2.** of, relating to, or characteristic of a Net Gener. Also, **net gen.**

Net Gener /ˈnɛt dʒɛnə/ *n.* a member of the Net Generation. Also, **net gener.**

Net Generation *n.* the generation born in the 1990s for whom computer use was a central part of life. Also, **net generation.**

nether /ˈnɛðə/ *adj.* **1.** lying, or conceived as lying, beneath the earth's surface; infernal: *the nether world.* **2.** lower or under: *his nether lip.*

netiquette /ˈnɛtɪkɛt/ *n. Internet* the code of good manners which has evolved for users of the internet.

netizen /ˈnɛtəzən/ *n. Internet Colloq.* a habitual user of the internet.

Netspeak /ˈnɛtspiːk/ *n.* the language style that has evolved in online communication, especially abbreviated words, use of lower-case letters, infrequent punctuation, etc.

netsurfing /ˈnɛtsɜːfɪŋ/ *n.* exploring the internet. –**netsurfer,** *n.*

nett /nɛt/ *adj., n., v.t.* → **net**[2].

nettle /ˈnɛtl/ *n.* **1.** Also, **stinging nettle.** any plant of the genus *Urtica,* comprising widely distributed herbs armed with stinging hairs. **2.** any of various allied or similar plants, as Gympie nettle. –*v.t.* **3.** to irritate, irk, provoke, or vex. –*phr.* **4. grasp the nettle,** to approach an unpleasant task with courage and resolution.

network /ˈnɛtwɜːk/ *n.* **1.** any net-like combination of lines, passages, filaments, etc.: *railway network.* **2.** netting or net. **3.** a group of connected radio or television stations, sometimes commonly owned, and from which the same programs may be broadcast. **4.** *Elect.* a system of interconnected electrical elements, units, or circuits. **5.** *Computers* a system of connecting computer systems or peripheral devices, each one remote from the others. **6.** an interconnected and open-ended circle of people linked by a shared interest, occupation, etc.: *a network of friends.* –*v.t.* **7.** to link (a number of separate computers) into a computer network. **8.** to link (a number of business offices) by means of a computer network. –*v.i.* **9.** to establish social contact with particular people so as to share ideas and information, establish useful contacts, etc.

neur- variant of **neuro-,** before vowels.

neural /ˈnjʊrəl/ *adj.* of or relating to a nerve or the nervous system. –**neurally,** *adv.*

neuralgia /njuˈrældʒə/ *n. Anat.* sharp and paroxysmal pain along the course of a nerve. –**neuralgic,** *adj.*

neural network *n. Computers* a software simulation of the interconnecting links of the brain, used in artificial intelligence systems and research.

neuro- a word element meaning 'tendon', 'nerve'. Also, **neur-.**

neurology /njuˈrɒlədʒi/ *n.* the branch of anatomy or physiology that deals with the nerves or the nervous system, especially the diseases thereof. **–neurological** /njuərə'lɒdʒɪkəl/, *adj.* **–neurologist**, *n.*

neuron /'njurɒn/ *n.* any of the cells in nerve tissue adapted to transmit nerve signals, each having dendrites leading to a cyton, or cell body, and an axon leading away; nerve cell. Also, **neurone** /'njuroʊn/. **–neuronal** /nju'roʊnəl/, *adj.* **–neuronic** /nju'rɒnɪk/, *adj.*

neuroplasticity /,njuroʊplæs'tɪsəti/ *n.* the ability of the brain to change, both in physical structure and in functional organisation, in response to experience, such that functions believed previously to be supported only by particular areas of the brain become supported instead by other areas. **–neuroplastic** /njuroʊ'plæstɪk/, *adj.*

neurosis /nju'roʊsəs/ *n.* (*pl.* **-roses** /-'roʊsiz/) **1.** a relatively mild mental illness in which feelings of anxiety, obsessional thoughts, compulsive acts, and physical complaints without objective evidence of disease, in various patterns, dominate the personality. Compare **psychosis. 2.** (*in non-technical use*) an emotional condition characterised by depression, anxiety, etc. **–neurotic** /nju'rɒtɪk/, *adj.* **–neurotically**, *adv.*

neurotoxin /'njuroʊtɒksən/ *n.* a chemical, often highly toxic, which inhibits the function of the nervous system.

neurotransmitter /njuroʊtrænz'mɪtə/ *n.* a chemical stored in the axon of a nerve cell that transmits information across a synapse.

neuter /'njutə/ *adj.* **1.** *Gram.* of or relating to the gender which is neither masculine nor feminine, referring to objects and abstractions, of no sex, and to animals of unknown sex. **2.** sexless, apparently sexless, or of indeterminate sex, as a hermaphrodite or castrated person. **3.** *Zool.* of the workers among bees and ants having imperfectly developed sexual organs. **4.** *Bot.* having neither stamens nor pistils; asexual. *–n.* **5.** *Gram.* the neuter gender. **6.** an animal or person made sterile by castration. **7.** a neuter insect. *–v.t.* **8.** to castrate.

neutral /'njutrəl/ *adj.* **1.** (of a person or nation) not taking part in a quarrel or war between others. **2.** of no particular kind, colour, characteristics, etc.; indefinite. **3.** grey; without hue; achromatic. **4.** *Ling.* relating to the vowel schwa (/ə/). **5.** *Biol.* neuter. **6.** *Chem.* **a.** neither acid nor alkaline; having a pH of 7: *a neutral solution.* **b.** of or relating to an atom, molecule, group, etc., which is neither positively or negatively charged (as opposed to an ion). **7.** *Elect.* neither positive nor negative; not electrified; not magnetised. *–n.* **8.** a person or a state that remains neutral in a war or quarrel. **9.** a citizen of a neutral nation. **10.** *Mechanics* the position of the gears in a vehicle where they are not engaged. **–neutrality**, *n.* **–neutrally**, *adv.*

neutralise /'njutrəlaɪz/ *v.t.* **1.** to make neutral. **2.** to make ineffective; counteract. **3.** to declare a country neutral; invest with neutrality. **4.** *Chem.* to make chemically neutral, as by adding acid to alkali. Also, **neutralize.** **–neutralisation** /njutrəlaɪ'zeɪʃən/, *n.* **–neutraliser**, *n.*

neutron /'njutrɒn/ *n.* *Physics* an elementary particle which is a constituent of all atomic nuclei except normal hydrogen. It has zero electric charge and approximately the same mass as the proton.

neutron bomb *n.* a nuclear weapon which releases a shower of neutrons but relatively little blast, thus killing people but causing relatively little damage to property. Also, **neutron bomb.**

never /'nɛvə/ *adv.* **1.** not ever; at no time. **2.** not at all; absolutely not; not even. **3.** to no extent or degree.

never-never *Colloq. –n.* **1.** (*sometimes upper case*) sparsely inhabited desert country; a remote and isolated region, especially that of inland Australia. **2.** the hire purchase system: *on the never-never. –adj.* **3.** imaginary: *never-never land.*

nevertheless /nɛvəðə'lɛs/ *adv.* nonetheless; notwithstanding; however.

new /nju/ *adj.* **1.** of recent origin or production, or having only lately come or been brought into being: *a new book.* **2.** of a kind now existing or appearing for the first time; novel. **3.** having only lately or only now come into knowledge: *a new chemical element.* **4.** recently arrived: *New Australians.* **5.** having only lately come to a position, status, etc.: *a new minister.* **6.** coming or occurring afresh; further; additional: *new gains.* **7.** fresh or unused: *a new sheet.* **8.** different and better, physically or morally: *the operation made a new man of him.* **9.** other than the former or the old: *a new era.* **10.** being the later or latest of two or more things of the same kind: *the New Testament* **11.** (of a language) in its latest known period, especially as a living language at the present time: *New Latin. –adv.* **12.** recently or lately. **13.** freshly; anew or afresh. *–n.* **14.** something new. **15.** *Colloq.* → **new beer.** *–phr.* **16. new to, a.** unfamiliar or strange to: *ideas new to us.* **b.** unaccustomed to: *people new to such work.* **–newness**, *n.*

New Age *n.* a social revolution which replaces traditional attitudes and mores with a new approach based on a loose mysticism, especially in health and medicine and attitudes to the environment. **–New Ager**, *n.*

new beer *n.* beer brewed by the bottom-fermentation method, usually light in colour.

newbie /'njubi/ *n.* *Colloq.* **1.** a newcomer to the internet. **2.** a newcomer to any activity.

new chum *n.* *Aust.*, *NZ* a novice; one inexperienced in some field: *a new chum on the job.*

newcomer /'njukʌmə/ *n.* someone who has newly come; a new arrival.

New Earth Time *n.* a global standard time proposed for use on the internet and in related technologies, which divides a day into 360 degrees and a degree into 60 minutes, resulting in the time being the same in all parts of the world. *Abbrev.*: NET

newfangled /'njufæŋɡəld/ *adj.* **1.** of a novel kind and uncertain worth: *newfangled ideas.* **2.** fond of novelty. Also, **new-fangled.**

news /njuz/ *pl. n.* (*construed as sing.*) **1.** a report of any recent event, situation, etc. **2.** the report of events published in a newspaper, journal, radio, television, or any other medium. **3.** information, events, etc., considered as suitable for reporting: *it's very interesting, but it's not news.* **4.** information not previously known: *that's news to me. –phr.* **5. bad news**, *Colloq.* someone or something from whom or which nothing good is to be expected.

news agency *n.* an organisation which collects news and supplies it to newspapers, television and radio stations, etc.

newsagency /'njuzeɪdʒənsi/ *n.* (*pl.* **-cies**) **1.** the franchise to sell newspapers. **2.** a shop which sells principally newspapers, magazines, stationery, and books. **–newsagent**, *n.*

newsflash /'njuzflæʃ/ *n.* an announcement of very recent news on radio or television, usually interrupting a scheduled program.

newsgroup /'njuzɡrup/ *n.* *Internet* an online discussion forum for a particular topic, in which users can write and post messages, and read messages posted by others.

newspaper /'njuzpeɪpə/ *n.* **1.** a publication issued at regular intervals, usually daily or weekly, and commonly containing news, comment, features, and advertisements; produced in print and digital form. **2.** the organisation publishing a newspaper. **3.** a single copy or issue of a newspaper.

newsprint /'njuzprɪnt/ *n.* paper used or made to print newspapers on.

newsradio /'njuzreɪdioʊ/ *n.* a style of radio broadcasting which makes continuous news reporting the basis of the programming.

newsreader /'njuzrɪdə/ *n.* **1.** someone who reads news bulletins on radio, television, etc. **2.** in computers, a program which allows a user to access, read and post messages in a newsgroup.

newsreel /'njuzril/ *n.* a short film presenting current news events.

newt /njut/ *n.* any of various small, semi-aquatic salamanders of the genus *Triturus* and related genera, of Europe, North America, and northern Asia.

New Testament *n.* those books in the Bible which were produced by the early Christian church, and were added to the Jewish scriptures (Old Testament). *Abbrev.*: NT

newton /'njutn/ *n.* the derived SI unit of force; the force required to give an acceleration of one metre per second per second to a mass of one kilogram. *Symbol*: N

Newton's laws /'njutnz lɔz/ *pl. n.* three laws of motion which form the basis of classical dynamics: **1.** all bodies continue in a state of rest or uniform linear motion unless they are acted upon by external forces to change that state. **2.** the rate of change of momentum of a body is proportional to the force applied to it. **3.** to every action there is an equal and opposite reaction.

new wave *n.* **1.** a movement or trend to break with traditional concepts in art, literature, politics, etc. **2.** a form of rock music of the 1970s in the style of punk rock, but characterised by greater imaginativeness and performance skills.

next /nɛkst/ *adj.* **1.** immediately following in time, order, importance, etc.: *the next day.* **2.** nearest in place or position: *the next room.* **3.** nearest in relationship or kinship. *–adv.* **4.** in the nearest place, time, importance, etc. **5.** on the first subsequent occasion: *when next we meet.*

next of kin *n.* **1.** a person's nearest relative or relatives. **2.** *Law* the nearest relative(s), to whom the personal property passes upon the death of an intestate.

nexus /'nɛksəs/ *n.* (*pl.* **nexus**) **1.** a tie or link; a means of connection. **2.** a connected series. **3.** *Parliamentary Procedure* a constitutional condition which requires (as nearly as practicable) the ratio of two House of Representative members to one Senate member, in order to safeguard the numerical strength and constitutional power of the Senate.

nib /nɪb/ *n.* **1.** the point of a pen, especially a small, tapering metallic device having a split tip for drawing up ink and for writing. **2.** a point of anything. **3.** any pointed extremity. **4.** (*pl.*) crushed cocoa beans. *–v.i.* (**nibbed, nibbing**) **5.** to furnish with a nib or point.

nibble /'nɪbəl/ *v.i.* **1.** to bite off small bits. **2.** to eat or feed by biting off small pieces. *–v.t.* **3.** to bite off small bits of (a thing). **4.** to eat by biting off small pieces. **5.** to bite (*off*, etc.) in small pieces. *–n.* **6.** a small morsel or bit: *each nibble was eaten with the air of an epicure.* **7.** the act or an instance of nibbling. **8. a.** *Angling* the slight pull on a fishing line which indicates that a fish is attempting to take the bait. **b.** *Colloq.* a slight expression of interest in a proposal. **9.** (*pl.*) *Colloq.* items of finger food. *–phr.* **10. nibble at, a.** to bite slightly or gently. **b.** to evince interest in without actually accepting. **–nibbler**, *n.*

nice /naɪs/ *adj.* (**nicer, nicest**) **1.** pleasing; agreeable; delightful: *a nice visit.* **2.** amiably pleasant; kind: *they are always nice to strangers.* **3.** characterised by or requiring great accuracy, precision, skill, or delicacy: *nice workmanship.* **4.** requiring or showing tact or care; delicate. **5.** showing minute differences; minutely accurate, as instruments. **6.** minute, fine, or subtle, as a distinction. **7.** having or showing delicate and accurate perception: *a nice sense of colour.* **8.** refined as to

manners, language, etc. **9.** suitable or proper: *not a nice song.* **10.** carefully neat as to dress, habits, etc. **11.** dainty or delicious, as food. *–phr. Colloq.* **12. nice one**, an exclamation indicating approval, admiration, etc. **13. no more Mr Nice Guy**, no more acting nicely, being kind, generous, etc. **–nicely**, *adv.* **–niceness**, *n.*

nicety /'naɪsəti/ *n.* (*pl.* **-ties**) **1.** a delicate or fine point. **2.** a fine distinction; subtlety. **3.** (*oft. pl.*) a refinement or elegance, as of manners or living. *–phr.* **4. to a nicety**, in great detail; with precision.

niche /nɪʃ, nɪtʃ/ *n.* **1.** an ornamental recess in a wall, etc., usually round in section and arched, as for a statue or other decorative object. **2.** a place or position suitable or appropriate for a person or thing. **3.** *Ecol.* the position or function of an organism in a community of plants and animals. **4.** → **niche market**. *–v.t.* (**niched, niching**) **5.** to place in a niche.

niche market *n.* a section of a market (def. 5), usually small, which can be highly profitable if the product supplied is specially designed to meet targeted needs.

nick¹ /nɪk/ *n.* **1.** a notch, groove, or the like, cut into or existing in a thing. **2.** a hollow place produced in an edge or surface, as of a dish, by breaking. **3.** *Cricket* → **snick** (def. 5). *–v.t.* **4.** to make a nick or nicks in; notch. **5.** to record by means of a notch or notches. **6.** to cut through or into. **7.** *Cricket* → **snick** (def. 3). *–phr.* **8. in good nick**, *Colloq.* in good condition. **9. in the nick (of time)**, at the vital or last possible moment.

nick² /nɪk/ *phr.* **in the nick**, *Colloq.* in the nude; naked.

nick³ /nɪk/ *Colloq. –v.t.* **1.** to steal. **2.** to capture or arrest. **3.** to trick, cheat, or defraud. *–v.i.* **4.** *Aust.* to go quickly (*down, across, over*, etc.): *I'll just nick across the street*; *nick into the butchers'. –n.* **5.** prison. *–phr.* **6. get nicked**, an exclamation of contempt, dismissal, etc. **7. nick off**, *Aust.* to leave, especially surreptitiously. **8. nick out**, *Aust., NZ* to go out, especially for a short time and without drawing attention to one's absence.

nickel /'nɪkəl/ *n.* **1.** *Chem.* a hard, silvery-white, ductile and malleable metallic element, allied to iron and cobalt, not readily oxidised, and used in electroplating, in making alloys, etc. *Symbol*: Ni; *relative atomic mass*: 58.71; *atomic number*: 28; *density*: 8.9 at 20°C. **2.** *US* a coin composed of or containing nickel, now a five-cent piece. *–v.t.* (**-elled** *or, Chiefly US,* **-eled, -elling** *or, Chiefly US,* **-eling**) **3.** to cover or coat with nickel.

nickname /'nɪkneɪm/ *n.* **1.** a name added to or substituted for the proper name of a person, place, etc., as in ridicule or familiarity. **2.** a familiar form of a proper name, as *Jim* for *James.* **3.** a short name for a digital file, account, etc., that is easy to remember and to key in: *a nickname for my bank accounts. –v.t.* **4.** to give a nickname to, or call by a specified nickname. **5.** to call by an incorrect or improper name.

nicotine /nɪkə'tin, 'nɪkətin/ *n.* a poisonous alkaloid, $C_{10}H_{14}N_2$, the active principle of tobacco, obtained as a colourless or nearly colourless, oily, acrid liquid. Also, **nicotin** /'nɪkətən/.

niece /nis/ *n.* **1.** a daughter of one's brother or sister. **2.** a daughter of one's husband's or wife's brother or sister.

nifty /'nɪfti/ *adj.* (**-tier, -tiest**) *Colloq.* smart; stylish; fine: *a nifty little car.*

niggard /'nɪgəd/ *n.* **1.** an excessively parsimonious or stingy person. *–adj.* **2.** niggardly. **–niggardly**, *adj., adv.*

nigger /'nɪgə/ *n.* (*highly offensive*) (*derog.*) (*racist*) **1.** a black person, especially of Africa or of African descent. **2.** an Aboriginal person. Also, **nigga**.

niggle /'nɪgəl/ *v.i.* **1.** to trifle; work ineffectively. **2.** to make constant petty criticisms. *–v.t.* **3.** to irritate; annoy. **–niggler**, *n.*

nigh /naɪ/ *adv.* **1.** *Archaic* near in space, time, or relation. **2.** *Archaic* nearly or almost: *it might be nigh impossible.*

3. See **well-nigh.** *–phr.* **4. nigh on,** nearly: *they've been friends for nigh on fifty years.*

night /naɪt/ *n.* **1.** the interval of darkness between sunset and sunrise. **2.** nightfall. **3.** the darkness of night; the dark. **4.** a state or time of obscurity, ignorance, misfortune, etc.

nightcap /ˈnaɪtkæp/ *n.* **1.** (formerly) a cap for the head, worn in bed. **2.** an alcoholic or other drink, especially a hot one, taken before going to bed.

nightclub /ˈnaɪtklʌb/ *n.* **1.** a place of entertainment, open until late, offering food, drink, cabaret, dancing, etc. **2.** a dance venue which opens from evening until early morning.

nightfall /ˈnaɪtfɔl/ *n.* the coming of night.

nightgown /ˈnaɪtgaʊn/ *n.* a nightdress or nightshirt.

nighthawk /ˈnaɪthɔk/ *n.* **1.** a small nightjar, *Eurostopodus mystacalis*, of eastern Australia and the Solomon Islands. **2.** any of various related birds, especially the **common nighthawk,** *Chordeiles minor*.

nightingale /ˈnaɪtɪŋgeɪl/ *n.* a small migratory Eurasian bird, *Luscinia megarhynchos*, of the family Muscicapidae, noted for the melodious song of the male.

nightjar /ˈnaɪtdʒə/ *n.* any of various nocturnal insect-eating birds of the widely distributed family Caprimulgidae, as the spotted nightjar, *Eurostopodus argus*, found throughout Australia.

nightly /ˈnaɪtli/ *adj.* **1.** coming, occurring, appearing, or active at night: *nightly revels.* **2.** coming or occurring each night. **3.** of, relating to, or characteristic of night. *–adv.* **4.** at or by night. **5.** on every night: *for one week only, performances will be given nightly.*

nightmare /ˈnaɪtmɛə/ *n.* **1.** a condition during sleep, or a dream, marked by a feeling of suffocation or distress, with acute fear, anxiety, or other painful emotion. **2.** a condition, thought, or experience suggestive of a nightmare in sleep. **3.** a monster or evil spirit formerly supposed to oppress persons during sleep. **–nightmarish,** *adj.*

nightshade /ˈnaɪtʃeɪd/ *n.* **1.** any of various plants of the genus *Solanum*, as black nightshade. **2.** any of various other plants, as deadly nightshade.

night terrors *pl. n.* recurring intense nightmares.

nihilism /ˈnaɪəlɪzəm, ˈniː-/ *n.* **1.** total disbelief in religion or moral principles and obligations, or in established laws and institutions. **2.** *Philos.* **a.** a belief that there is no objective basis of truth. **b.** an extreme form of scepticism, denying all real existence. **c.** nothingness or non-existence. **3.** terrorism or revolutionary activity. **–nihilist,** *n.* **–nihilistic** /naɪəˈlɪstɪk, niː-/, *adj.*

nil /nɪl/ *n.* nothing.

nimble /ˈnɪmbəl/ *adj.* **1.** quick and light in movement; moving with ease; agile; active; rapid: *nimble feet.* **2.** quick in apprehending, devising, etc.: *nimble wits.* **3.** cleverly contrived. **–nimbleness,** *n.* **–nimbly,** *adv.*

nimbus /ˈnɪmbəs/ *n.* (*pl.* **-buses** *or* **-bi** /-baɪ/) **1.** a bright cloud anciently conceived of as surrounding a deity of the classical mythology when appearing on earth. **2.** a cloud or atmosphere of some kind surrounding a person or thing. **3.** *Art* a disc or otherwise shaped figure representing a radiance around the head of a divine or sacred personage, a medieval sovereign, etc.; a halo.

nimby /ˈnɪmbi/ *n.* (*pl.* **-bies**) someone who selfishly protests against having necessary developments such as new prisons, hospitals, airports, military installations, homes for the disabled, etc., in the vicinity of their home, although they would support such developments if they were located elsewhere. Also, **Nimby.**

nincompoop /ˈnɪŋkəmpup/ *n.* a fool or simpleton.

nine /naɪn/ *n.* **1.** a cardinal number, eight plus one. **2.** a symbol for this number, as 9 or IX. **3.** a set of nine persons or things. **4.** a playing card, etc., with nine pips. *–adj.* **5.** amounting to nine in number: *nine apples.*

–pron. **6.** nine people or things: *sleeps nine; give me nine.* *–phr.* **7. dressed (up) to the nines,** *Colloq.* smartly dressed or overdressed. **–ninth,** *adj.*

nineteen /naɪnˈtin, ˈnaɪntin/ *n.* **1.** a cardinal number, ten plus nine. **2.** a symbol for this number, as 19 or XIX. *–adj.* **3.** amounting to nineteen in number. *–pron.* **4.** nineteen people or things. *–phr.* **5. talk nineteen to the dozen,** to talk very quickly or excitedly. **–nineteenth,** *adj., n.*

ninety /ˈnaɪnti/ *n.* (*pl.* **-ties**) **1.** a cardinal number, ten times nine. **2.** a symbol for this number, as 90 or XC. **3.** (*pl.*) the numbers from 90 to 99 of a series, especially with reference to the years of a person's age, or the years of a century, especially the nineteenth. *–adj.* **4.** amounting to ninety in number. *–pron.* **5.** ninety people or things. **–ninetieth,** *adj., n.*

ninny /ˈnɪni/ *n.* (*pl.* **-nies**) a fool; a simpleton.

nip¹ /nɪp/ *verb* (**nipped, nipping**) *–v.t.* **1.** to compress sharply between two surfaces or points; pinch or bite. **2.** to check in growth or development: *to nip a plot in the bud.* **3.** to affect sharply and painfully or injuriously, as cold does. **4.** *Colloq.* to snatch or take (*away, up,* etc.) suddenly or quickly. **5.** *Colloq.* to steal. *–v.i.* **6.** *Colloq.* to move or go (*away, off, up,* etc.) suddenly or quickly, or slip. *–n.* **7.** the act of nipping; a pinch. **8.** a biting quality, as in cold or frosty air. **9.** biting taste or tang, as in cheese. **10.** a small bit or quantity of anything. *–phr.* **11. nip off,** to take off by pinching, biting, or snipping. **–nipper,** *n.*

nip² /nɪp/ *n.* **1.** a small drink; a sip. **2.** a small measure of spirits. *–verb* (**nipped, nipping**) *–v.t.* **3.** to drink (spirits, etc.) in small sips. *–v.i.* **4.** to take a nip or nips, especially repeatedly.

nipple /ˈnɪpəl/ *n.* **1.** a protuberance of the mamma or breast where, in the female, the milk ducts discharge; a teat. **2.** something resembling it, such as the mouthpiece of a nursing bottle. **3.** a short piece of pipe with threads on each end, used for joining valves, etc. **4.** *Machinery* a small drilled bush containing a one-way valve through which a lubricant can be supplied to a bearing, especially by a grease gun.

nippy /ˈnɪpi/ *adj.* (**-pier, -piest**) **1.** apt to nip; sharp; biting. **2.** biting, as the cold. **3.** *Colloq.* nimble; active.

niqab /ˈnikæb/ *n.* a veil covering the face, worn by some Muslim women attached to the hijab, often as part of the burqa. Also, **niquab.**

nirvana /nɜˈvanə, nə-, nɪə-/ *n.* **1.** *Buddhism* the ultimate state achieved usually after a series of reincarnations, when all passions and self-delusions have been shed. **2.** *Hinduism* salvation achieved by absorption into Brahman. **3.** any place or state thought of as characterised by complete freedom from pain, worry and the external world. **4.** *Colloq.* a place which provides complete satisfaction of desires: *a shopper's nirvana.*

nisi /ˈnaɪsaɪ/ *conj.* **1.** unless. *–adj.* **2.** *Law* (of a court order, decree, etc.) conditional; not coming into effect unless a person or persons fail to show cause against it within a certain time (opposed to *absolute*).

nit /nɪt/ *n.* **1.** the egg of a parasitic insect attached to a hair, or fibre of clothing; particularly the egg of a louse. **2.** the insect while young. **3.** *Colloq.* a foolish or stupid person.

nitpick /ˈnɪtpɪk/ *v.i.* to be unduly critical, concerned with insignificant details. **–nitpicker,** *n.* **–nitpicking,** *n., adj.*

nitr- variant of **nitro-,** before vowels.

nitrate /ˈnaɪˌtreɪt/ *n.* **1.** *Chem.* a salt or ester of nitric acid, or any compound containing the -NO₃ group. **2.** fertiliser consisting of potassium nitrate or sodium nitrate. *–v.t.* **3.** to treat with nitric acid or a nitrate. **4.** to convert into a nitrate.

nitric /ˈnaɪtrɪk/ *adj.* **1.** *Chem.* containing nitrogen, usually in the pentavalent state. **2.** of or relating to nitre.

nitric acid *n.* a corrosive liquid, HNO_3, with powerful oxidising properties.

nitro- **1.** a word element indicating the group NO_2. **2.** a misnomer for the nitrate group (NO_3), as in *nitrocellulose*. Also, **nitr-**.

nitrogen /'naɪtrədʒən/ *n.* a colourless, odourless, gaseous element which forms about four-fifths of the volume of the atmosphere and is present (combined) in animal and vegetable tissues, chiefly in proteins. It is used in compounds, as fertiliser, in explosives, and in dyes. *Symbol*: N; *relative atomic mass*: 14.0067; *atomic number*: 7. –**nitrogenous** /naɪ'trɒdʒənəs/, *adj.*

nitrogen cycle *n.* the continuous circulation of nitrogen and nitrogen compounds in nature between the atmosphere, the soil, and the various organisms to which nitrogen is essential.

nitroglycerine /naɪtroʊ'glɪsərin/ *n.* a colourless, highly explosive oil, $C_3H_5(ONO_2)_3$, a principal constituent of dynamites and certain propellent and rocket powders; a nitration product of glycerine, sometimes used in medicine as a vasodilator. Also, **nitroglycerin** /naɪtroʊ-'glɪsərən/.

nitrous /'naɪtrəs/ *adj.* **1.** of or relating to compounds obtained from nitrogen, usually containing less oxygen than the corresponding nitric compounds. **2.** *Chem.* containing nitrogen, usually trivalent.

nitty-gritty /'nɪti-ˌgrɪti/ *n. Colloq.* the hard core of a matter: *let's get down to the nitty-gritty.*

nitwit /'nɪtwɪt/ *n. Colloq.* a slow-witted or foolish person.

nix /nɪks/ *Colloq.* –*n.* **1.** nothing. –*adv.* **2.** no.

no¹ /noʊ/ *interj.* **1.** a word used: **a.** to express denial, disagreement, or refusal, as in reply (opposed to *yes*). **b.** to add force to an earlier negative, or to change or limit an earlier statement: *we will not give in, no, never!*; *I have seen her twice, no, three times.* –*adv.* **2.** not in any degree; not at all (used with a comparative): *he is no better.* **3.** not: *whether or no.* –*n.* (*pl.* **noes**) **4.** an act of speaking of the word 'no'. **5.** a disagreement or refusal. **6.** a negative vote or voter (opposed to *aye*).

no² /noʊ/ *adj.* **1.** not any: *no money.* **2.** not at all; very far from being; not at all a: *he is no genius.*

nob¹ /nɒb/ *n.* **1.** *Colloq.* the head. **2.** (in cribbage) the knave of the same suit as the card turned up, counting one to the holder. **3.** a double-headed coin.

nob² /nɒb/ *n. Colloq.* a member of a social elite.

no ball *Cricket* –*n.* **1.** a ball bowled in a way disallowed by the rules and automatically giving the side batting a score of one run, counted as a sundry. –*interj.* **2.** a call by the umpire as the bowler bowls indicating that he or she has infringed the rules. –*v.t.* **3.** to deliver a no ball to (the person batting).

nobble /'nɒbəl/ *v.t. Colloq.* **1.** to disable (a horse), as by drugging it. **2.** to win (a person, etc.) over by underhand means. **3.** to swindle. **4.** to catch or seize. –*phr.* **5. nobble someone with,** to give someone (a task, etc., which they may be unwilling to perform): *the principal nobbled him with the task of reorganisation.*

noble /'noʊbəl/ *adj.* **1.** noted by birth, rank, or title. **2.** belonging to or making up a class (the nobility) possessing a social or political importance passed down from parents to children, in a country or state. **3.** of a high moral character: *a noble thought.* **4.** of an admirably high quality; superior. **5.** forceful in appearance; stately: *a noble monument.* **6.** *Chem.* inert; chemically inactive. **7.** (of some metals, as gold and platinum) not able to be corroded in air or water, and very valuable and scarce. –*n.* **8.** a person of noble birth or rank; nobleman. –**nobility,** *n.* –**nobleness,** *n.* –**nobly,** *adv.*

nobleman /'noʊbəlmən/ *n.* (*pl.* **-men**) a man of noble birth or rank; a noble. –**noblewoman,** *n.*

nobody /'noʊbɒdi, -bədi/ *pron.* **1.** no person. –*n.* (*pl.* **-bodies**) **2.** a person of no importance, especially socially. –*phr.* **3. like nobody's business,** energetically; intensively: *to work like nobody's business.*

no-claim bonus *n.* a reduction in premium payments for insurance offered to policy holders who have made no claim on the insurance company for a specified length of time.

nocti- a word element meaning 'night'. Also, (*before a vowel*), **noct-**.

nocturnal /nɒk'tɜnəl/ *adj.* **1.** of or relating to the night. **2.** done, occurring, or coming by night. **3.** *Zool.* active by night, as many animals. **4.** *Bot.* opening by night and closing by day, as certain flowers. –**nocturnally** /nɒk'tɜnəli/, *adv.*

nocturnal emission *n.* an involuntary ejaculation of semen during sleep. See **wet dream.**

nocturne /'nɒktɜn/ *n.* **1.** *Music* a piece appropriate to the night or evening. **2.** *Music* an instrumental composition of a dreamy or pensive character. **3.** *Painting* a night scene.

nod /nɒd/ *verb* (**nodded, nodding**) –*v.i.* **1.** to make a slight, quick inclination of the head, as in assent, greeting, command, etc. **2.** to let the head fall forwards with a sudden, involuntary movement when sleepy. **3.** to grow careless, inattentive, or dull. **4.** (of trees, flowers, plumes, etc.) to droop, bend, or incline with a swaying motion. –*v.t.* **5.** to incline (the head) in a short, quick movement, as of assent, greeting, etc. **6.** to express or signify by such a movement of the head: *to nod assent.* –*n.* **7.** a short, quick inclination of the head, as in assent, greeting, command, or drowsiness. **8.** a bending or swaying movement of anything. **9.** a nap. –*phr.* **10. get the nod, a.** to gain approval or permission. **b.** to get unofficial assurance of a job, position, etc. **11. give the nod to, a.** to permit. **b.** to make a signal to. **12. nod off,** to go to sleep. **13. on the nod,** on credit. –**nodder,** *n.*

node /noʊd/ *n.* **1.** a knot, protuberance, or knob. **2.** a complication; difficulty. **3.** a centring point of component parts. **4.** *Bot.* **a.** a joint in a stem. **b.** a part of a stem which normally bears a leaf. **5.** *Geom.* a point on a curve or surface, at which there can be more than one tangent line or plane. **6.** *Physics* a point, line, or region in a vibrating medium at which there is comparatively no variation of the disturbance which is being transmitted through the medium. **7.** *Astron.* either of the two points at which the orbit of a heavenly body cuts the plane of the ecliptic, equator, or other properly defined plane (that passed as the body goes to the north being called the **ascending node,** and that passed as it goes to the south being called the **descending node**). **8.** *Pathol.* a circumscribed swelling. **9.** *Gram.* the labelled intersection of two or more branches in a tree diagram. **10.** *Computers* an end point of a branch or junction of two or more branches in a network (def. 5). **11.** *Internet* a host or gateway on the internet. –**nodal,** *adj.*

no-doc loan /noʊ-dɒk 'loʊn/ *n. Colloq.* a loan from a lending institution, such as a bank, for which no evidence is required of the borrower's ability to service the loan, other than the borrower's warranty. Compare **low-doc loan.**

nodule /'nɒdʒul/ *n.* **1.** a small node, knot, or knob. **2.** a small rounded mass or lump. **3.** *Bot.* → **tubercle.** –**nodular,** *adj.*

Noel /noʊ'ɛl/ *n.* **1.** Christmas. **2.** (*lower case*) a Christmas song or carol.

no-fault *adj.* of or relating to legislation, insurance, etc., which does not depend on the assignation of guilt or blame to any of the parties involved.

no-fly zone *n.* an area over which all or specified aircraft are forbidden to fly.

no-frills *adj.* **1.** having few, if any, additional luxuries or benefits which impose extra cost: *a no-frills airline service.* **2.** frugal; parsimonious: *a no-frills budget.* **3.** simple; straightforward: *a no-frills win against the Blues.* Also, **no frills.**

noggin /ˈnɒgən/ *n.* **1.** a small cup or mug. **2.** a small measure of spirits. **3.** *Colloq.* the head.

no-hoper /nou-ˈhoupə/ *n. Colloq.* **1.** someone who displays marked incompetence: *he is a real no-hoper at tennis.* **2.** a social misfit. **3.** an unpromising animal, as a second-rate racehorse, greyhound, etc.

noise /nɔɪz/ *n.* **1.** sound, especially of a loud, harsh, or confused kind: *deafening noises.* **2.** a sound of any kind. **3.** loud shouting, outcry, or clamour. **4.** *Physics* a superposition of signals of random frequencies which have no harmony and contain no information. **5.** *Electronics* interference which degrades the useful information in a signal. *–v.t.* (**noised, noising**) **6.** to spread the report or rumour of. **7.** to spread (a report, rumour, etc.). *–phr.* **8. big noise,** *Colloq.* an important person. **9. noise off,** to talk much or publicly. **–noisy,** *adj.* **–noisiness,** *n.* **–noiseless,** *adj.*

noise pollution *n.* unwanted or offensive sounds which intrude unreasonably on one's surroundings, especially when causing a disturbance to one's normal activities.

noisome /ˈnɔɪsəm/ *adj.* **1.** offensive or disgusting, often as to smell. **2.** harmful, injurious, or noxious. **–noisomely,** *adv.* **–noisomeness,** *n.*

noisy miner *n.* a miner of eastern Australia with grey-white plumage, white forehead, black crown and yellow skin patches behind the eyes; noted for its loud aggressive call.

nomad /ˈnoumæd/ *n.* **1.** one of a people or tribe without fixed abode, but moving about from place to place according to the state of the pasturage or food supply. **2.** any wanderer. *–adj.* **3.** of, relating to, or characteristic of nomads. **–nomadism,** *n.* **–nomadic,** *adj.*

no-man's-land *n.* **1.** an area not possessed by any power, e.g. the area between opposing armies. **2.** any place which is to be avoided as dangerous. **3.** a condition or period of insecurity resulting from the loss or disturbance of culture or identity.

nom de plume /nɒm də ˈplum/ *n.* → **pen-name.**

nomenclature /nəˈmɛnklətʃə, ˈnoumənkleɪtʃə/ *n.* **1.** a set or system of names or terms, as those used in a particular science or art by an individual or community, etc. **2.** the names or terms forming a set or system. **–nomenclative, nomenclatorial** /nəmɛnkləˈtɔriəl/, **nomenclatural,** *adj.*

nominal /ˈnɒmənəl/ *adj.* **1.** being such in name only; so-called: *nominal peace.* **2.** (of a price, consideration, etc.) named as a mere matter of form, being trifling in comparison with the actual value. **3.** of, relating to, or consisting in a name or names. **4.** *Gram.* **a.** of, relating to, or producing a noun or nouns. **b.** used as or like a noun. **5.** assigned to a person by name: *nominal shares of stock.*

nominal wages *pl. n. Econ.* wages measured in terms of money and not by their ability to command goods and services. Compare **real wages.**

nominate *v.t.* /ˈnɒmɪneɪt/ **1.** to propose as a proper person for appointment or election to an office. **2.** to appoint for a duty or office. **3.** to enter (a horse, etc.) in a race. *–v.i.* /ˈnɒmɪneɪt/ **4.** to stand as a candidate: *I'll nominate for preselection if there's a chance of winning. –adj.* /ˈnɒmɪnət/ **5.** having a particular name. **–nomination** /nɒmɪˈneɪʃən/, *n.* **–nominator,** *n.*

nominative /ˈnɒmənətɪv, ˈnɒmnə-/ *adj.* **1.** *Gram.* **a.** denoting a case which by its form, position, or function indicates that it serves as the subject of a finite verb, as in 'we enjoyed the meal and the men washed up', where *we* and *men* are in the nominative case. **b.** similar to

such a case form in function or meaning. **2.** nominated; appointed by nomination. *–n.* **3.** *Gram.* the nominative case, a word in that case, or a form or construction of similar function or meaning.

nominee /nɒməˈni/ *n.* **1.** a person nominated, as to fill an office or stand for election. **2.** someone appointed by another to act as his or her agent.

-nomy a final word element meaning 'distribution', 'arrangement', 'management', or having reference to laws or government, as in *astronomy, economy, taxonomy.*

non- a prefix indicating: **1.** exclusion from a specified class or group: *non-Jew, non-passerine.* **2.** objective negation or opposition: *non-porous, non-recurrent.* **3.** spuriousness or failure to fulfil a claim: *non-event, non-hero.* **4.** the absence of activity or achievement in the area named: *non-arrival, non-publication.*

non-action verb *n. Gram.* → **stative verb.**

nonagenarian /nɒnədʒəˈnɛəriən, nou-/ *adj.* **1.** of the age of 90 years, or between 90 and 100 years old. *–n.* **2.** a nonagenarian person.

nonagon /ˈnɒnəgɒn, -gən/ *n.* → **enneagon. –nonagonal** /nɒnˈægənəl/, *adj.*

non-binary *adj.* **1.** designating a person who does not identify as male or female. **2.** *Computers* designating a system, code, etc., which is not based on a sequence of the digits 1 and 0.

nonce /nɒns/ *n.* **1.** the one or particular occasion or purpose. *–phr.* **2. for the nonce,** for this one occasion only; for the time being.

nonchalant /ˈnɒnʃələnt/ *adj.* coolly unconcerned, indifferent, or unexcited; casual. **–nonchalance,** *n.* **–nonchalantly,** *adv.*

non-combatant /nɒn-kəmˈbætənt, nɒn-ˈkɒmbətənt/ *n.* **1.** someone who is not a combatant; a civilian in time of war. **2.** someone connected with a military or naval force in some capacity other than that of a fighter, as a surgeon, a chaplain, etc. *–adj.* **3.** not involving combat: *pacifists were ordered to undertake non-combatant duties in the armed forces.*

noncommittal /nɒnkəˈmɪtl/ *adj.* not committing oneself, or not involving committal, to a particular view, course, or the like: *a noncommittal answer.*

nonconformist /nɒnkənˈfɒməst/ *n.* **1.** someone who refuses to conform, especially to an established Church **2.** someone who does not conform to accepted social standards of behaviour, etc. *–adj.* **3.** of or relating to a nonconformist, or to nonconformists as a group: *nonconformist beliefs.* **–nonconforming,** *adj.* **–nonconformity,** *n.*

nonda /ˈnɒndə/ *n.* a tree, *Parinari nonda,* with a yellow edible fruit which is astringent to taste, found in Qld and the NT.

nondescript /ˈnɒndəskrɪpt/ *adj.* **1.** of no recognised, definite, or particular type or kind: *a nondescript garment.* *–n.* **2.** a person or a thing of no particular type or kind.

none /nʌn/ *pron.* **1.** no one; not one: *there is none to help; I waited for an answer, but none came.* **2.** not any of something indicated: *there is none left.* **3.** no part; nothing: *that is none of your business.* **4.** (*construed as pl.*) no, or not any, persons or things: *none were suitable.* *–adv.* **5.** to no extent; in no way; not at all: *the supply is none too great.*

nonentity /nɒnˈɛntəti/ *n.* (*pl.* **-ties**) **1.** a person or thing of no importance. **2.** something which does not exist, or exists only in imagination. **3.** non-existence.

nonetheless /nʌnðəˈlɛs/ *adv.* however; nevertheless. Also, **none the less.**

nonfiction /nɒnˈfɪkʃən/ *n.* **1.** a class of writing comprising works dealing with facts and events, rather than imaginative narration: *we publish only nonfiction.* *–adj.*

Also, **nonfictional. 2.** of or relating to writing of this class.

nonflammable /nɒnˈflæməbəl/ *adj.* not easily set alight; slow-burning; not flammable.

nong /nɒŋ/ *n. Aust., NZ Colloq.* a fool; an idiot.

nonplus /nɒnˈplʌs/ *v.t.* (**-plussed** *or, Chiefly US,* **-plused, -plussing** *or, Chiefly US,* **-plusing**) **1.** to bring to a nonplus; puzzle completely. –*n.* **2.** a state of utter perplexity.

nonproductive /ˈnɒnprədʌktɪv/ *adj.* **1.** not producing goods directly, as employees in charge of personnel, inspectors, etc. **2.** unproductive. –**nonproductively,** *adv.* –**nonproductiveness, nonproductivity** /ˌnɒnprɒdʌkˈtɪvəti/, *n.*

nonproliferation /ˌnɒnprəlɪfəˈreɪʃən/ *n.* **1.** the attempt to prevent countries which do not possess nuclear weapons from acquiring them. –*adj.* **2.** of or relating to nonproliferation: *the nonproliferation treaty.*

non-renewable resource *n.* a natural resource which, once it is depleted, cannot be replaced or restored, such as fossil fuels. Compare **renewable resource.**

nonsense /ˈnɒnsəns/ *n.* **1.** something that makes no sense or is lacking in sense. **2.** words without sense or conveying absurd ideas. **3.** senseless or absurd action; foolish conduct, notions, etc.: *to stand no nonsense from a person.* **4.** an absurdity: *the nonsense of an idea.* **5.** stuff, trash, or anything useless. –**nonsensical** /nɒnˈsɛnsɪkəl/, *adj.* –**nonsensically** /nɒnˈsɛnsɪkli/, *adv.* –**nonsensicalness** /nɒnˈsɛnsɪkəlnəs/, **nonsensicality** /ˌnɒnsɛnsəˈkæləti/, *n.*

non sequitur /nɒn ˈsɛkwɪtə/ *n.* an inference or a conclusion which does not follow from the premises.

non-U /nɒn-ˈjuː/ *adj. Colloq.* not appropriate to or characteristic of the upper class.

noodle /ˈnudl/ *n.* a type of pasta, cut into long, narrow, flat strips and served in soups or, with a sauce, as a main dish.

nook /nʊk/ *n.* **1.** a corner, as in a room. **2.** any secluded or obscure corner. **3.** any small recess. **4.** a remote spot.

noon /nun/ *n.* **1.** midday; twelve o'clock in the daytime. **2.** the highest, brightest, or finest point or part.

no-one *pron.* nobody. Also, **no one.**

Noongar /ˈnʊŋa/ *n.* → **Nyungar.**

noose /nus/ *n.* **1.** a loop with a running knot, as in a snare, lasso, hangman's halter, etc., which tightens as the rope is pulled. **2.** a tie or bond; a snare. –*v.t.* **3.** to secure by or as by a noose. **4.** to make a noose with or in (a rope, etc.).

nor /nɔ/ *conj.* a negative conjunction used: **1.** as the correlative to a preceding *neither: He could neither read nor write.* **2.** to continue the force of a negative, such as *not, no, never,* etc., occurring in a preceding clause: *he left and I never saw him again, nor did I regret it.* **3.** after an affirmative clause, or as a continuative, in the sense of *and … not: they are happy; nor need we mourn.*

nor' /nɔ/ *n., adj., adv. Chiefly Naut.* north.

nori /ˈnɔri/ *n.* (in Japanese cookery) paper-thin sheets of dried seaweed, generally used for wrapping sushi or rice balls.

norm /nɔm/ *n.* **1.** a standard, model, or pattern. **2.** a mean or average. **3.** *Educ.* **a.** a designated standard of average performance of people of a given age, background, etc. **b.** a standard of average performance by a person. –**normative,** *adj.*

normal /ˈnɔməl/ *adj.* **1.** keeping to the standard or the common type; regular, usual, natural, or not abnormal: *the normal procedure.* **2.** serving to fix a standard. **3. a.** just about average in respect to intelligence, personality, emotional balance, etc. **b.** without any mental irregularities; sane. **4.** *Maths* (of a line, etc.) being at right angles; perpendicular. **5.** *Chem.* **a.** (of a solution) containing one equivalent weight of the chemical in question in one litre of solution. **b.** relating to an aliphatic hydrocarbon having a straight unbranched carbon chain, each carbon atom of which is joined to no more than two other carbon atoms. See **n-. c.** relating to a normal element. **6.** *Biol., Med., etc.* **a.** free from any infection. **b.** happening naturally. –*n.* **7.** the standard or type. **8.** the normal form or state; the average or mean. **9.** *Maths* a perpendicular line or plane, especially one perpendicular to a tangent line of a curve, or a tangent plane of a surface, at the point of contact. –**normally,** *adv.* –**normality,** *n.* –**normalise, normalize,** *v.* –**normalisation,** *n.*

normal curve *n. Maths* a bell-shaped curve giving the distribution of probability associated with the different values of a variable.

normal distribution *n. Statistics* a form of statistical distribution in which the highest frequency is at the mean score, or in which the mean, median and mode are equal. Also, **Gaussian distribution.**

normcore /ˈnɔmkɔ/ *n.* a unisex fashion characterised as being deliberately without a distinctive style or conscious attempt to impress.

norovirus /ˈnɒrəʊvaɪrəs/ *n.* a virus which causes severe, highly infectious gastroenteritis.

north /nɔθ/ *n.* **1.** a cardinal point of the compass to the right of a person facing the setting sun or west. **2.** the direction in which this point lies. **3.** → **magnetic north. 4.** → **grid north. 5.** → **true north. 6.** (*lower case or upper case*) an area or territory situated in this direction: *we came from the north.* –*adj.* **7.** lying towards or situated in the north. **8.** directed or proceeding towards the north. **9.** coming from the north, as a wind. **10.** (*also upper case*) designating the northern part of a region, nation, country, etc.: *North Atlantic.* –*adv.* **11.** towards or in the north: *she was travelling north.* **12.** (of the wind) from the north. –*phr.* **13. head** (or **go**) (or **move**) **north,** *Colloq.* (of prices, market values, etc.) to increase: *petrol prices are heading north.* Also, (*especially Nautical*), **nor'.** –**northerly,** *adj., adv.*

north-east *n.* the point or direction midway between north and east. Also, *esp. Naut.,* **nor'-east.** –**north-easterner,** *n.*

northern /ˈnɔðən/ *adj.* **1.** lying towards or situated in the north. **2.** directed or proceeding northwards. **3.** coming from the north, as a wind. **4.** (*upper case*) of or relating to the North. **5.** *Astron.* north of the celestial equator or of the zodiac: *a northern constellation.* –**northerner,** *n.*

Northern Hemisphere *n.* (*also lower case*) the half of the earth between the North Pole and the equator.

North Pole *n.* that end of the earth's axis of rotation marking the northernmost point on the earth.

north-west *n.* the point or direction midway between north and west. Also, *esp. Naut.,* **nor'-west.**

nos- variant of **noso-,** before vowels.

nose /noʊz/ *n.* **1.** the part of the face or head which contains the nostrils, affording passage for air in respiration, etc. **2.** this part as the organ of smell: *the aroma of coffee greeted his nose.* **3.** the sense of smell: *a dog with a good nose.* **4.** a faculty of perceiving or detecting; ability to search out or locate: *a nose for news; a good nose for bargains.* **5.** the quality of prying or interfering: *keep your nose out of it.* **6.** something regarded as resembling the nose of a person or animal, as a spout or nozzle. **7.** the prow of a ship. **8.** the forward end of an aircraft. **9.** a projecting part of anything. **10.** → **bouquet** (def. 2). **11.** the length of the nose of a horse or other animal as a measure in racing. –*v.t.* **12.** to perceive by or as by the nose or the sense of smell. **13.** to bring the nose close to, as in smelling or examining; sniff. **14.** to move or push forward. **15.** to touch or rub with the nose; nuzzle. –*v.i.* **16.** to move (*in, out,* forward, etc.), usually slowly or gently. **17.** to meddle or pry. *–phr.* **18. by a nose**, *Colloq.* by a very narrow margin. **19. cut off one's nose to spite one's face**, to damage one's own interests by a spiteful or vengeful action. **20. follow one's nose**, to find one's own way, as by instinct. **21. get up someone's nose**, *Colloq.* to irritate or annoy someone. **22. keep one's nose clean**, *Colloq.* to follow rules and regulations meticulously so as to avoid any blame. **23. lead by the nose**, to exercise complete control over. **24. look down one's nose at**, to despise; disdain. **25. nose after** (or **for**), to seek as if smelling or scent. **26. nose into**, to pry into or be inquisitive about. **24. look down one's nose at**, to despise; disdain. **27. on the nose**, *Aust.*, *NZ Colloq.* **a.** smelly; objectionable; decayed; stinking (especially of rotten organic matter, as food). **b.** unpleasant; distasteful. **28. pay through the nose**, to pay an excessive amount. **29. pick one's nose**, to remove congealed mucus from the nose with one's finger. **30. put someone's nose out of joint**, to cause someone to feel upset. **31. turn one's nose up**, to be contemptuous or ungrateful. **32. under someone's nose**, in an obvious place. **33. under the nose of**, within observation of: *under the nose of the police.*

nosedive /ˈnoʊzdaɪv/ *n.* **1.** a plunge of an aeroplane with the fore part of the craft vertically downwards. **2.** any sudden drop. *–v.i.* **3.** to execute a nosedive.

nosegay /ˈnoʊzɡeɪ/ *n.* a bunch of flowers, or herbs; a bouquet; a posy.

nosh /nɒʃ/ *Colloq.* *–v.i.* **1.** to eat; have a snack or a meal. *–n.* **2.** anything eaten, especially a snack.

noso- a word element meaning 'disease'. Also, **nos-**.

nostalgia /nɒsˈtældʒə/ *n.* a longing and desire for home, family and friends, or the past. **–nostalgic**, *adj.* **–nostalgically**, *adv.*

nostril /ˈnɒstrəl/ *n.* one of the external openings of the nose.

nostrum /ˈnɒstrəm/ *n.* **1.** a patent medicine. **2.** a quack medicine. **3.** a medicine made by the person who recommends it. **4.** a pet scheme or device for effecting something.

nosy /ˈnoʊzi/ *adj.* (**-sier**, **-siest**) *Colloq.* prying; inquisitive. Also, **nosey**. **–nosily**, *adv.* **–nosiness**, *n.*

not /nɒt/ *adv.* a word expressing negation, denial, refusal, or prohibition: *not far; you must not do that.*

nota bene /noʊtə ˈbɛni, noʊtə ˈbeɪne/ note well.

notable /ˈnoʊtəbəl/ *adj.* **1.** worthy of note or notice; noteworthy: *a notable success.* **2.** prominent, important, or distinguished, as persons. *–n.* **3.** a notable person; a prominent or important person. **–notableness**, *n.* **–notably**, *adv.*

notary public /noʊtəri ˈpʌblɪk/ *n.* (*pl.* **notaries public**) *Law* an official, usually a solicitor, authorised to certify contracts, acknowledge deeds, take affidavits, protest bills of exchange, take depositions, etc.

notation /noʊˈteɪʃən/ *n.* **1.** a system of graphic symbols for a specialised meaning, other than ordinary writing: *musical notation.* **2.** the process of noting or setting down by means of a special system of signs or symbols. **3.** the act of noting, marking, or setting down in writing. **4.** a note, jotting, or record. **–notational**, *adj.*

notch /nɒtʃ/ *n.* **1.** a more or less angular cut, indentation, or hollow in a narrow object or surface or an edge. **2.** a cut or nick made in a stick or other object for record, as in keeping a score. **3.** *Colloq.* a step or degree. *–v.t.* **4.** to cut or make a notch or notches in. **5.** to make notches in by way of record. **6.** to record by a notch or notches. *–phr.* **7. notch up**, to score, as in a game: *he notched up three more deals before Saturday.*

note /noʊt/ *n.* **1.** a short record of something set down to help the memory. **2.** (*pl.*) a record of a speech, lecture, etc., or of one's own thoughts on something. **3.** an explanation, opinion, or mention of other sources, added

by an editor or author to a passage in a book. **4.** a short written or printed statement giving particulars or information. **5.** a written communication from a child's parents to the child's school, as to give permissions, explanations, etc. **6.** a short informal letter. **7.** a formal diplomatic or official message or information in writing. **8.** *Finance* a paper recognising money owed and promising payment; promissory note. **9.** high rank; distinction: *a man of note.* **10.** importance; consequence: *no other thing of note this year.* **11.** notice; heed: *take careful note of this rule.* **12.** a characteristic feature. **13.** a sound (of musical quality) produced by a singer, instrument, bird, etc. **14.** *Music* a sign or character used to represent a sound, where its position shows its pitch, and its form shows its length. **15.** a signal, hint, suggestion, etc.: *a note of warning; a note of unhappiness in her voice.* *–v.t.* **16.** to mark down, usually in writing. **17.** to make particular mention of in a writing. **18.** to give attention or heed to. **19.** to take notice of; perceive. *–phr.* **20. on a high note**, with something spectacular, successful or especially appealing: *the evening ended on a high note with the entire dance company performing.* **21. strike the wrong** (or **a false**) **note**, to seem jarring: *to strike the wrong note with the voters.* **–noter**, *n.*

notebook /ˈnoʊtbʊk/ *n.* **1.** a book of or for notes. **2.** Also, **notebook computer**. *Computers* a small, lightweight, portable computer.

noted /ˈnoʊtəd/ *adj.* **1.** celebrated; famous. **2.** specially observed or noticed. **–notedly**, *adv.* **–notedness**, *n.*

noteworthy /ˈnoʊtwɜːði/ *adj.* worthy of note or notice; notable. **–noteworthily**, *adv.* **–noteworthiness**, *n.*

nothing /ˈnʌθɪŋ/ *pron.* **1.** no thing; not anything; naught: *say nothing.* **2.** that which is non-existent. *–n.* **3.** something or someone of no importance or value. **4.** a trivial matter or remark. *–adv.* **5.** in no way: *it was nothing like what we expected.* *–phr.* **6. come to nothing**, to fail to reach fruition. **7. for nothing**, free of charge. **8. in nothing flat**, *Colloq.* in no time at all; very quickly. **9. make nothing of**, **a.** to be unable to understand. **b.** to cope easily with; treat lightly. **10. next to nothing**, very little. **11. nothing doing**, *Colloq.* definitely no or not. **12. nothing for it**, no other course of action is open. **13. nothing of**, no part, share, or trace of: *the place shows nothing of its former magnificence.* **14. nothing to write home about**, not worthy of special mention; ordinary. **15. there's nothing in it**, *Colloq.* it's unprofitable. **16. there's nothing to it**, *Colloq.* it's very simple; it's easily done.

notice /ˈnoʊtəs/ *n.* **1.** information or intelligence: *to give notice of a thing.* **2.** an intimation or warning. **3.** a note, placard, or the like conveying information or warning. **4.** a notification of the termination, at a specified time, of an agreement, as for renting or employment, given by one of the parties to the agreement. **5.** observation, perception, attention, or heed: *worthy of notice.* **6.** interested or favourable attention. **7.** a single observation or perception. **8.** a brief written mention or account, as of a newly published book; a review. *–v.t.* (**-ticed**, **-ticing**) **9.** to pay attention to or take notice of. **10.** to perceive: *did you notice her hat?* **11.** to treat with attention, politeness, or favour. **12.** to acknowledge acquaintance with. **13.** to mention or refer to; point out, as to a person. **14.** *Chiefly US* to give notice to; serve with a notice. *–phr.* **15. give notice of**, to make known that (some procedure, event, etc.) is impending. **–noticeable**, *adj.* **–noticer**, *n.*

noticeboard /ˈnoʊtəsbɔːd/ *n.* a board, located centrally in a school, office, etc., designed for the display of notices and other information of general interest.

notify /ˈnoʊtəfaɪ/ *v.t.* (**-fied**, **-fying**) **1.** to give notice to, or inform, of something. **2.** to make known; give information of: *the sale was notified in the newspapers.* –**notifiable**, *adj.* –**notifier**, *n.* –**notification** /noʊtəfə-ˈkeɪʃən/, *n.*

notion /ˈnoʊʃən/ *n.* **1.** a more or less general, vague or imperfect conception or idea of something: *notions of beauty.* **2.** an opinion, view, or belief. **3.** conception or idea. **4.** a fanciful or foolish idea; whim. **5.** (*pl.*) small wares, especially pins, needles, thread, tapes, etc.; haberdashery.

notional /ˈnoʊʃənəl/ *adj.* **1.** relating to or expressing a notion or idea. **2.** of the nature of a notion. **3.** abstract or speculative, as reflective thought. **4.** ideal or imaginary; not real. **5.** *Gram.* **a.** relating to the meaning expressed by a linguistic form. **b.** having full lexical meaning, in contrast to relational. –**notionally**, *adv.*

not negotiable *adj. Finance* (of a cheque) having been crossed, indicating that the person to whom it is given has no better title to it than the person had from whom he received it; popularly and inaccurately held to mean that the cheque can be paid only into the account, the name of which appears on the cheque.

notorious /nəˈtɔriəs/ *adj.* **1.** widely but unfavourably known: *a notorious gambler.* **2.** *Obs.* publicly or generally known: *a statesman notorious for his wise judgement.* –**notoriously**, *adv.* –**notoriousness**, **notoriety** /noʊtəˈraɪəti/, *n.*

notwithstanding /ˌnɒtwɪθˈstændɪŋ/ *prep.* **1.** without being withstood or prevented by; in spite of. –*adv.* **2.** nevertheless; yet (used after the statement it modifies). –*conj.* **3.** in spite of the fact that; although.

nougat /ˈnugɑ/ *n.* a hard, paste-like sweet, usually white or pink, containing almonds or other nuts.

nought /nɔt/ *n.* a cipher (0); zero.

noun /naʊn/ *Gram.* –*n.* **1.** (in most languages) one of the major form classes, or 'parts of speech', comprising words denoting persons, places, things, and such other words as show similar grammatical behaviour, as English *friend, city, desk, whiteness, virtue.* **2.** any such word. –*adj.* Also, **nounal. 3.** of or relating to a noun.

nourish /ˈnʌrɪʃ/ *v.t.* **1.** to sustain with food or nutriment; supply with what is necessary for maintaining life. **2.** to foster or promote. –**nourishment**, *n.* –**nourishable**, *adj.* –**nourisher**, *n.* –**nourishingly**, *adv.*

nous /naʊs/ *n. Colloq.* common sense.

nouvelle cuisine /ˌnuvɛl kwəˈzin/ *n.* a style of French cooking which emphasises simplicity, dispensing with rich flour-thickened sauces in favour of reduced stocks and relying on the quality and freshness of the food, and the imaginativeness of the presentation.

nova /ˈnoʊvə/ *n.* (*pl.* **-vas** *or* **-vae** /-vi/) *Astron.* the sudden increase in the luminosity of a star arising from thermonuclear reactions occurring on the surface of a white dwarf star in a binary system.

novel[1] /ˈnɒvəl/ *n.* a fictitious prose narrative of considerable length, usually having a plot that is developed by the actions, thoughts, speech, etc., of the characters. –**novelist**, *n.* –**novelistic**, *adj.*

novel[2] /ˈnɒvəl/ *adj.* **1.** of a new kind, or different from anything seen or known before: *a novel idea.* **2.** interestingly fresh and innovative; unusual. **3.** *Science* demonstrating groundbreaking research: *a novel vaccine.* –**novelly**, *adv.*

novella /nɒˈvɛlə/ *n.* (*pl.* **-vellas** *or* **-velle** /-vɛli/) **1.** a tale or short story of the type of those contained in the *Decameron* of Boccaccio, etc. **2.** a short novel, more complex than a short story.

novelty /ˈnɒvəlti/ *n.* (*pl.* **-ties**) **1.** novel character, newness, or strangeness. **2.** a novel thing, experience, or proceeding. **3.** a new or novel article of trade; a variety of goods differing from the staple kinds. **4.** a decorative and usually worthless trinket. –*adj.* **5.** of or relating to a novel game, article, etc.: *a novelty toy.*

November /noʊˈvɛmbə, nə-/ *n.* the eleventh month of the year, containing 30 days.

novice /ˈnɒvəs/ *n.* **1.** someone who is new to the circumstances, work, etc., in which he or she is placed; a tyro: *a novice in politics.* **2.** someone who has been received into a religious order or congregation for a period of probation before taking vows. **3.** a recent convert to Christianity. **4.** *Sport* a player who has not qualified for junior or senior status, as a rower who has never been a member of a winning crew at an open regatta.

novitiate /noʊˈvɪʃət, -eɪt/ *n.* **1.** the state or period of being a novice of a religious order or congregation. **2.** the quarters occupied by religious novices during probation. **3.** the state or period of being a beginner in anything. Also, **noviciate.**

now /naʊ/ *adv.* **1.** at the present time or moment: *he is here now.* **2.** (more emphatically) immediately or at once: *now or never.* **3.** at this time or juncture in some period under consideration or in some course of proceedings described: *the case now passes to the jury.* **4.** at the time or moment only just past: *I saw her just now in the street.* **5.** in these present times; nowadays. **6.** in the present or existing circumstances; as matters stand. **7.** used as a preliminary word before some statement, question, or the like: *now, what does she mean?* **8.** used to strengthen a command, entreaty, or the like: *come, now, stop that!* –*conj.* **9.** now that; since, or seeing that. –*n.* **10.** the present time or moment: *the here and now.* –*adj.* **11.** *Colloq.* fashionable: *a very now dress.* –*phr.* **12. now and again** or **now and then,** occasionally. **13. now that,** inasmuch as. **14. now, now** or **now then,** an expression used to reprove or placate someone.

nowadays /ˈnaʊədeɪz/ *adv.* **1.** at the present day; in these times. –*n.* **2.** the present.

nowhere /ˈnoʊwɛə/ *adv.* **1.** in, at, or to no place; not anywhere. –*n.* **2.** a state of apparent non-existence; a place unknown: *he disappeared into nowhere.* –*phr.* **3. get** (or **go**) **nowhere,** to achieve nothing. **4. the middle of nowhere,** a place considered to be isolated from major centres of activity, and difficult to access as a result.

noxious /ˈnɒkʃəs/ *adj.* **1.** harmful or injurious to health or physical wellbeing: *noxious vapours.* **2.** morally harmful; pernicious. **3.** (of an animal, insect, plant, etc.) declared harmful by Australian statute law for compulsory eradication. –**noxiously**, *adv.* –**noxiousness**, *n.*

nozzle /ˈnɒzəl/ *n.* a projecting spout, terminal discharging pipe, or the like, as of a hose or rocket.

nth /ɛnθ/ *adj.* **1.** denoting the last in a series of infinitely decreasing or increasing values, amounts, etc. –*phr.* **2. the nth degree** (or **power**), **a.** a high (sometimes, any) degree or power. **b.** the utmost extent.

nuance /ˈnjuɒns, njuˈɑns/ *n.* a subtle shade of colour, expression, meaning, feeling, etc.

nub /nʌb/ *n.* **1.** a knob or protuberance. **2.** a lump or small piece. **3.** the point or gist of anything.

nubile /ˈnjubaɪl/ *adj.* **1.** (of a girl or young woman) marriageable, especially as to age or physical development. **2.** (of a girl or young woman) sexually attractive. –**nubility** /njuˈbɪləti/, *n.*

nuclear /ˈnjukliə/ *adj.* **1.** of, relating to, or forming a nucleus. **2.** relating to, involving, or powered by atomic energy: *nuclear war, nuclear submarine.* **3.** armed with nuclear weapons: *a nuclear power.*

nuclear accelerator *n. Physics* a device which accelerates charged particles to velocities which enable them to overcome the coulomb repulsion from the nucleus, thus initiating a nuclear reaction.

nuclear bomb *n.* → **atomic bomb.**

nuclear core *n.* the heart of a nuclear reactor, where the radioactive material is situated and where nuclear reactions take place.

nuclear disarmament *n.* the dismantling of nuclear weapons, especially those of major military powers, often coupled with attempts to prevent an increase in the number of nuclear-armed countries.

nuclear energy *n.* → **atomic energy.**

nuclear family *n.* **1.** the family as a unit of social organisation, comprising only parents and children, where the children are the responsibility of the parents alone. **2.** the stereotype of this unit, typically seen as husband, wife, and two children.

nuclear fission *n.* the breakdown of an atomic nucleus of an element of relatively high atomic number into two or more nuclei of lower atomic number, with conversion of part of its mass into energy.

nuclear-free zone *n.* an area, as a local government area, which is declared to be free of nuclear material, and, in particular, through which the transport of nuclear hazardous goods is prohibited.

nuclear fusion *n.* the coming together of two atomic nuclei to form a single nucleus with a consequent release of energy.

nuclear medicine *n.* a branch of medicine in which mildly radioactive isotopes are introduced into the body and subsequently tracked, largely for diagnostic purposes but also as a form of treatment. Also, **nuclear tracing.**

nuclear power *n.* → **atomic power.**

nuclear reaction *n.* any reaction which involves a change in the structure or energy state of the nuclei of the interacting atoms.

nuclear reactor *n.* any device in which a self-sustaining chain reaction is maintained and controlled for the production of nuclear energy, fissile material, or radioactive isotopes.

nuclear waste *n.* the radioactive by-products of nuclear fission.

nuclear weapon *n.* any weapon in which the explosive power is derived from nuclear fission, nuclear fusion, or a combination of both.

nuclear winter *n.* a period of freezing temperatures and widespread famine, lasting several months, predicted to follow a nuclear war as a result of the blocking of sunlight by fallout.

nuclei /'njukliaɪ/ *n.* plural of **nucleus.**

nucleonics /njukli'ɒnɪks/ *n.* the techniques of applying nuclear science to industry and to biology, physics, chemistry, and other sciences.

nucleus /'njukliəs/ *n.* (*pl.* **-clei** /-kliaɪ/ *or* **-cleuses**) **1.** a central part or thing about which other parts or things are grouped. **2.** anything making up a central part, foundation, or beginning. **3.** *Biol.* a mass (usually rounded) of protoplasm, encased in a delicate membrane, present inside nearly all living cells and forming a necessary element in their growth, metabolism and reproduction. **4.** *Anat.* a mass of grey matter in the brain and spinal cord in which incoming nerve fibres form connections with outgoing fibres. **5.** *Physics* the central core of an atom, made of protons and neutrons, with a net positive charge equal to the number of protons.

nude /njud/ *adj.* **1.** naked or unclothed, as a person, the body, etc. **2.** without the usual coverings, furnishings, etc.; bare. **3.** *Law* unsupported; made without a consideration: *a nude pact.* –*n.* **4.** a nude figure as represented in art. –*phr.* **5. in the nude,** without clothing; naked. –**nudely,** *adv.* –**nudeness,** *n.* –**nudity,** *n.*

nudge /nʌdʒ/ *v.t.* (**nudged, nudging**) **1.** to push slightly or jog, especially with the elbow, as in calling attention or giving a hint or with sly meaning. –*n.* **2.** a slight push or jog. –*phr.* **3. give it a nudge,** *Aust.* **a.** to indulge in alcohol, drugs, etc., to excess: *gave it a bit of a nudge last night, did you?* **b.** to make an attempt, have a try at something. **4. give someone** (or **something**) **a nudge,** to impart impetus to someone or something. **5. nudge the bottle** or **give the bottle a nudge,** *Aust.* to drink alcoholic liquor to excess.

nudism /'njudɪzəm/ *n.* the practice of going nude as a means of healthful living; naturism. –**nudist,** *n.*

nugget /'nʌgət/ *n.* **1.** a lump of something. **2.** a lump of native gold. **3.** *Aust., NZ Colloq.* a short muscular young man or animal. –**nuggety,** *adj.*

nuisance /'njusəns/ *n.* **1.** a highly obnoxious or annoying thing or person. **2.** *Law* something offensive or annoying to individuals or to the community, to the prejudice of their legal rights.

nuke /njuk/ *Colloq.* –*n.* **1.** *Colloq., Chiefly US* a nuclear device. –*v.t.* **2.** *Chiefly US* to destroy utterly by, or as if by, a nuclear weapon. **3.** to cook in a microwave oven.

null /nʌl/ *adj.* **1.** of no effect, consequence, or significance. **2.** being none, lacking, or non-existent. **3.** zero. –*phr.* **4. null and void,** having no legal force or effect.

nulla-nulla /'nʌlə-nʌlə/ *n.* an Aboriginal club or heavy weapon. Also, **nulla.**

nulli- a word element meaning 'none'.

nullify /'nʌləfaɪ/ *v.t.* (**-fied, -fying**) **1.** to make ineffective, futile, or of no consequence. **2.** to render or declare legally void or inoperative: *to nullify a contract.* –**nullifier,** *n.* –**nullification** /nʌləfə'keɪʃən/, *n.*

numb /nʌm/ *adj.* **1.** deprived of or deficient in the power of sensation and movement: *fingers numb with cold.* **2.** of the nature of numbness: *a numb sensation.* –*v.t.* **3.** to make numb. –**numbly,** *adv.* –**numbness,** *n.*

numbat /'nʌmbæt/ *n.* a small, slender, reddish-brown, diurnal marsupial, *Myrmecobius fasciatus,* with a long, bushy tail, a pointed snout, and conspicuous white stripes across the back, found in certain areas of southwestern Australia.

number /'nʌmbə/ *n.* **1.** the sum, total, count, or aggregate of a collection of units or any generalisation of this concept. **2.** → **integer.** **3.** → **numeral.** **4.** (*pl.*) → **arithmetic.** **5.** the particular numeral assigned to anything in order to fix its place in a series: *a house number.* **6.** a telephone number. **7.** a word or symbol, or a combination of words or symbols, used in counting or to denote a total. **8.** one of a series of things distinguished by numerals. **9.** a single part of a book published in parts. **10.** a single issue of a periodical. **11.** a single part of a program made up of a number of parts. **12.** the full count of a collection or company. **13.** a collection or company. **14.** a quantity (large or small) of individuals. **15.** a certain collection, company, or quantity not precisely reckoned, but usually considerable or large. **16.** (*pl.*) considerable collections or quantities. **17.** (*pl.*) numerical strength or superiority, as in a political party, organisation, etc. **18.** quantity as composed of units. **19.** *Gram.* (in many languages) a category of the inflection of nouns, verbs, and related word classes, usually expressing the number of persons or objects referred to, comprising as subcategories the *singular* and *plural* and in some languages one or two intermediate subcategories (the *dual,* referring to two, and the *trial,* referring to three). **20.** *Colloq.* an individual person, especially an attractive woman: *that blonde number who lives out of town.* **21.** *Colloq.* a theatrical piece; a routine. **22.** *Colloq.* a song. **23.** *Colloq.* anything viewed as part of presentation designed to impress, as a special outfit, a special dish, an amateur performance of some kind: *to wear the little black number; do the pesto number; put on the poetry number.* –*v.t.* **24.** to ascertain the number of. **25.** to mark with or distinguish by a number or numbers. **26.** to count over one by one. **27.** to mention one by one; enumerate. **28.** to fix the number of, limit in number, or make few in number. **29.** to reckon or include in a number. **30.** to have or comprise in number. **31.** to amount to in number: *a crew numbering fifty men.* *–v.i.* **32.** *Poetic* to make enumeration; count. **33.** to be numbered or included. *–phr.* **34. do a number, a.** to perform a theatrical piece or routine. **b.** *Colloq.* to behave in some way to gain a particular end: *when I told her she did a number about going to the boss.* **35. have someone's number,** to have the measure of someone. **36. one's number is up,** *Colloq.* **a.** one is in serious trouble. **b.** one is due to die. **37. the numbers are up, a.** *Horseracing* the winners' numbers have been posted. **b.** *Colloq.* the result is known: *we won't know how we did till the numbers are up.* **38. without number,** of which the number is unknown or too great to be counted: *stars without number.* **–numberer,** *n.*

numberless /ˈnʌmbələs/ *adj.* **1.** innumerable; countless; myriad. **2.** without a number or numbers.

numberplate /ˈnʌmbəpleɪt/ *n.* an identifying plate, carried by motor vehicles, bearing a registration number. Also, **licence plate, registration plate.**

numbskull /ˈnʌmskʌl/ *n. Colloq.* a dull-witted person; a dunce; a dolt. Also, **numskull.**

numeral /ˈnjumərəl/ *n.* **1.** a figure or letter, or a group of figures or letters, denoting a number: *the numeral for 'nine' is 9; the Roman numeral for seven is VII.* *–adj.* **2.** of or relating to number; consisting of numbers. **3.** expressing or denoting number.

numerate *v.t.* /ˈnjuməreɪt/ **1.** to number; count; enumerate. **2.** to read (an expression in numbers). *–adj.* /ˈnjumərət/ **3.** having a basic competency in mathematics; able to understand and work with numbers. **–numeracy** /ˈnjumərəsi/, *n.*

numerator /ˈnjuməreɪtə/ *n. Maths* the term (usually written above the line) of a fraction which shows how many parts of a unit are taken.

numerical /njuˈmɛrɪkəl/ *adj.* **1.** of or relating to number; of the nature of number. **2.** denoting number or a number: *numerical symbols.* **3.** bearing, or designated by, a number. **4.** expressed by a number or figure, or by figures, and not by a letter or letters. **5.** *Maths* denoting value or magnitude irrespective of sign: *the numerical value of -10 is greater than that of -5.* Also, **numeric.** **–numerically,** *adv.*

numerology /njumaˈrɒlədʒi/ *n.* a study which assumes, and professes to interpret, the influence of numbers (as one's birth year, etc.) on one's life and future. **–numerological** /njumərəˈlɒdʒɪkəl/, *adj.* **–numerologist,** *n.*

numerous /ˈnjumərəs/ *adj.* **1.** very many; forming a great number. **2.** consisting of or comprising a great number of units or individuals. **–numerously,** *adv.* **–numerousness,** *n.*

numismatics /njuməzˈmætɪks/ *n.* the study, and commonly also the collection, of coins and medals. **–numismatist** /njuˈmɪzmətəst/, *n.* **–numismatic,** *adj.*

nun /nʌn/ *n.* a woman who has joined a religious order and leads a life of religious observance and service either in a convent or in the wider community.

Nunga /ˈnʊŋə/ *n.* an Aboriginal person from southern SA. Compare **Anangu, Koori** (def. 1), **Murri, Nyungar, Yamatji, Yolngu.**

nunnery /ˈnʌnəri/ *n.* (*pl.* **-ries**) a religious house for nuns; a convent.

nuptial /ˈnʌpʃəl/ *adj.* **1.** of or relating to marriage or the marriage ceremony: *the nuptial day.* *–n.* **2.** (*usu. pl.*) marriage; wedding.

nurdle /ˈnɜdl/ *n.* a pellet of plastic resin used as a base for the manufacture of plastic products; spilt in production processes or during transportation, nurdles constitute a

significant marine polluter, being poisonous to marine life.

nurse /nɜs/ *n.* **1.** a person (woman or man) who has the care of the sick or infirm. **2.** → **nanny** (def. 1). **3.** a woman employed to breastfeed an infant; wet nurse. *–v.t.* **4.** to tend in sickness or infirmity. **5.** to seek to cure (a cold, etc.) by taking care of oneself. **6.** to look after carefully so as to aid growth, development, etc.; foster; cherish (a feeling, etc.). **7.** to treat or handle with care in order to further one's own interests. **8.** to bring up, train, or care for. **9.** to hold or handle, especially fondly or tenderly. **10.** to hold while travelling: *you can nurse this box.* **11.** to hold in the arms: *he nursed the baby until she fell asleep.* **12.** to breastfeed (an infant). **13.** to feed and tend when a child is very young. *–v.i.* **14.** to act as nurse; tend the sick or infirm. **15.** to breastfeed an infant. **16.** (of an infant) to take the breast. **–nurser,** *n.*

nursemaid /ˈnɜsmeɪd/ *n.* a maidservant employed to take care of children. Also, **nurserymaid.**

nurse practitioner *n.* a nurse who is legally qualified to take on some of the responsibilities of a doctor, particularly with regard to prescribing medicines.

nursery /ˈnɜsri/ *n.* (*pl.* **-ries**) **1.** a room or place set apart for young children. **2.** any place in which something is bred, nourished, or fostered. **3.** any situation, condition, circumstance, practice, etc., serving to foster something. **4.** *Hort.* a place where young trees or other plants are raised for transplanting or for sale.

nursery rhyme *n.* a short, simple poem or song for children.

nursing home *n.* a nursing residence equipped for the care of patients who have chronic or terminal diseases, or who are disabled in some way.

nurture /ˈnɜtʃə/ *v.t.* **1.** to feed, nourish, or support during the stages of growth, as children or young; rear. **2.** to bring up; train; educate. *–n.* **3.** upbringing or training. **4.** education; breeding. **5.** nourishment or food. **–nurturer,** *n.* **–nurturance,** *n.*

nut /nʌt/ *n.* **1.** a dry fruit consisting of an edible kernel or meat enclosed in a woody or leathery shell. **2.** the kernel itself. **3.** *Bot.* a hard, indehiscent, one-seeded fruit, as the chestnut or the acorn. **4.** any of various devices or parts supposed in some way to resemble a nut. **5.** a small lump of coal. **6.** *NZ* a small lump of kauri resin. **7.** *Colloq.* the head. **8.** *Colloq.* an enthusiast. **9.** *Colloq.* a foolish or eccentric person. **10.** *Colloq.* an insane person. **11.** a perforated block (usually of metal) with an internal thread or female screw, used to screw on the end of a bolt, etc. **12.** (*usu. pl.*) *Colloq.* a testicle. *–phr.* **13. a hard nut to crack, a.** a difficult question, undertaking, or problem. **b.** a person who is difficult to convince, understand, or know. **14. do one's nut,** *Colloq.* to be very angry, anxious, or upset. **15. do one's nuts over,** *Colloq.* to become infatuated with. **16. nut out,** *Colloq.* to think out; solve (a problem, a plan of action, etc.). **17. off one's nut,** *Colloq.* **a.** mad; insane. **b.** crazy; foolish. **–nutlike,** *adj.*

nutmeg /ˈnʌtmɛg/ *n.* the hard, aromatic seed of the fruit of a tropical Asian tree, *Myristica fragrans,* used as a spice.

nutraceutical /njutrəˈsjutɪkəl/ *n.* a food which has health-giving properties.

nutrient /ˈnjutriənt/ *adj.* **1.** containing or conveying nutriment, as solutions or vessels of the body. **2.** nourishing; affording nutriment. *–n.* **3.** a nutrient substance.

nutriment /ˈnjutrəmənt/ *n.* **1.** any matter that, taken into a living organism, serves to sustain it in its existence, promoting growth, replacing loss, and providing energy. **2.** something that nourishes; nourishment; food.

nutrition /njuˈtrɪʃən/ *n.* **1.** the act or process of nourishing or of being nourished. **2.** food; nutriment. **3.** the process by which the food material taken into an organism is converted into living tissue, etc. **–nutritional, nutritive,** *adj.* **–nutritionally,** *adv.* **–nutritionist,** *n.*

nutritious /njuˈtrɪʃəs/ *adj.* nourishing, especially in a high degree. **–nutritiously,** *adv.* **–nutritiousness,** *n.*

nuts /nʌts/ *Colloq.* *–interj.* **1.** an expression of defiance, disgust, etc. *–adj.* **2.** crazy; insane. *–phr.* **3. nuts about** (or **on**) (or **over**), overwhelmingly attracted to.

nutshell /ˈnʌtʃel/ *n.* **1.** the shell of a nut. *–phr.* **2. in a nutshell,** in very brief form; in a few words: *just tell me the story in a nutshell.*

nutty /ˈnʌti/ *adj.* **(-tier, -tiest) 1.** nutlike, especially in taste. **2.** *Colloq.* silly or stupid; crazy. *–phr.* *Colloq.* **3. nutty as a fruitcake,** completely mad. **4. nutty over** (or **about**), overwhelmingly attracted to. **–nuttiness,** *n.*

nuzzle /ˈnʌzəl/ *v.i.* **1.** (fol. by *against, in, up,* etc.) to push the nose forward: *the pup nuzzled up close to the sick child.* **2.** to cuddle up with someone. *–v.t.* **3.** to touch or rub with the nose. **4.** to push the nose against or into: *the pup nuzzled me.*

nylon /ˈnaɪlɒn/ *n.* **1.** a synthetic polyamide capable of extrusion when molten into fibres, sheets, etc., of extreme toughness, strength, and elasticity, used for yarn (as for hosiery), for bristles (as for brushes), etc. **2.** (*pl.*) stockings made of nylon.

nymph /nɪmf/ *n.* **1.** one of a numerous class of inferior divinities of mythology, conceived as beautiful maidens inhabiting the sea, rivers, woods, trees, mountains, meadows, etc., and frequently mentioned as attending a superior deity. **2.** a beautiful or graceful young woman. **3.** *Entomology* **a.** Also, **nympha.** the young of an insect without metamorphosis. **b.** → **pupa.** **–nymphal, nymphean,** *adj.*

nymphomania /nɪmfəˈmeɪniə/ *n.* uncontrollable sexual desire in women. **–nymphomaniac,** *n.*, *adj.*

Nyungar /ˈnjʊŋa/ *n.* an Aboriginal person from southwestern WA. Compare **Anangu, Koori** (def. 1), **Murri, Nunga, Yamatji, Yolngu.** Also, **Nyunga, Nyoongah, Noongar.**

O o

O, o /oʊ/ *n.* **1.** a vowel, the 15th letter of the English alphabet. **2.** something resembling the letter O in shape. **3.** the Arabic cipher; zero; nought (0). **4.** a mere nothing.

o' /ə/ *prep.* **1.** an abbreviated form of *of*, now chiefly dialectal or colloquial, except in *o'clock*, *will-o'-the-wisp*, etc. **2.** an abbreviated form of *on*.

-o- an ending for the first element of many compounds, originally found in the combining forms of many Greek words, but often used in English as a connective irrespective of etymology, as in *Franco-Italian*, *speedometer*, etc.

-o a suffix used: **1.** in colloquial abbreviations, as *arvo*, afternoon; *combo*, combination; *commo*, communist; *compo*, compensation; *demo*, demonstration; *kero*, kerosene; *metho*, methylated spirits. **2.** to refer to a person **a.** in a particular occupation, as *bottle-o*, bottle collector; *garbo*, garbage collector; *journo*, journalist; *milko*, milk vendor; *scripto*, scriptwriter. **b.** of particular habits, as *weirdo*, one whose behaviour borders on perversion or eccentricity; *wino*, a wine addict. **3.** in colloquial responses showing compliance or agreement, as *goodo*, *righto*.

oaf /oʊf/ *n.* **1.** a simpleton or blockhead. **2.** a lout. **–oafish**, *adj.* **–oafishly**, *adv.* **–oafishness**, *n.*

oak /oʊk/ *n.* **1.** any tree or shrub of the large genus *Quercus*, of the family Fagaceae, including many forest trees with hard, durable wood, bearing the acorn as fruit. **2.** the wood of an oak tree. **–oaken**, *adj.*

oar /ɔ/ *n.* **1.** an instrument for propelling a boat, sometimes used also for steering, consisting of a long shaft of wood with a blade at one end. **2.** something resembling this or used for a similar purpose. *–phr.* **3. put one's oar in**, to interfere; meddle. **4. rest on one's oars**, to relax; take things easily. **–oarless**, *adj.*

oasis /oʊˈeɪsəs/ *n.* (*pl.* **oases** /oʊˈeɪsiz/) **1.** a fertile place in a desert region where groundwater brought to the surface or surface water from other areas provides for humid vegetation. **2.** any place that provides a welcome relief from discomfort or distress.

oatcake /ˈoʊtkeɪk/ *n.* a cake, usually thin and brittle, made of oatmeal.

oatgrass /ˈoʊtɡrɑs/ *n.* **1.** any of certain native Australian oat-like grasses, as *Themeda avenacea*. **2.** any wild species of oat.

oath /oʊθ/ *n.* (*pl.* **oaths** /oʊðz/) **1.** a solemn appeal to God, or to some revered person or thing, in attestation of the truth of a statement or the binding character of a promise: *to testify upon oath*. **2.** a statement or promise strengthened by such an appeal. **3.** a formally affirmed statement or promise accepted as an equivalent. **4.** the form of words in which such a statement or promise is made: *the Hippocratic oath*. **5.** an irreverent or blasphemous use of the name of God or anything sacred. **6.** any profane expression; a curse. *–phr.* **7. bloody oath**, *Aust.*, *NZ* an emphatic expression of agreement. **8. my (bloody) oath**, *Aust.*, *NZ* an emphatic expression of agreement. **9. on** (or **under**) **oath**, *Law* having sworn to tell the truth.

oatmeal /ˈoʊtmil/ *n.* meal made from oats and used in porridge, oatcakes, etc.

oats /oʊts/ *n.* **1.** a cereal grass, *Avena sativa*, cultivated for its edible seed, which is used in making oatmeal and

as a food for horses, etc. **2.** the seeds. **3.** (*sing.*) any species of the same genus, as *A. fatua*, the common **wild oat**. *–phr.* **4. feel one's oats**, **a.** to feel exuberant or lively. **b.** to be aware of and use one's importance and power. **5. sow one's wild oats**, to indulge in the excesses or follies of youth, especially in sexual promiscuity.

ob- a prefix meaning 'towards', 'to', 'on', 'over', 'against', originally occurring in loan words from Latin, but now used also, with the sense of 'reversely' or 'inversely', to form New Latin and English scientific terms. Also, **o-**, **oc-**, **of-**, **op-**.

ob doc /ɒb ˈdɒk/ *n.* a documentary in which events unfold naturally rather than according to direction or a script, and are recorded by a camera observing what happens.

obdurate /ˈɒbdʒərət/ *adj.* **1.** hardened against persuasions or tender feelings; hard-hearted. **2.** hardened against moral influence; persistently impenitent: *an obdurate sinner.* **–obduracy** /ˈɒbdʒərəsi/, **obdurateness**, *n.* **–obdurately**, *adj.*

obedient /əˈbidiənt/ *adj.* obeying, or willing to obey; submissive to authority or constraint. **–obedience**, *n.* **–obediently**, *adv.*

obeisance /oʊˈbeɪsəns/ *n.* **1.** a movement of the body expressing deep respect or deferential courtesy, as before a superior; a bow or curtsy. **2.** deference or homage. **–obeisant**, *adj.*

obelisk /ˈɒbələsk/ *n.* **1.** a tapering, four-sided shaft of stone, usually monolithic and having a pyramidal apex, of which notable examples are seen among the monuments of ancient Egypt. **2.** something resembling such a shaft. **3.** *Printing* the dagger (†), used especially as a reference mark. **–obeliscal** /ɒbəˈlɪskəl/, *adj.*

obese /oʊˈbis/ *adj.* excessively fat, as a person or animal, the body, etc.; corpulent. **–obesely**, *adv.* **–obeseness** , *n.*

obesity /oʊˈbisəti/ *n.* a medical condition in which excess body fat affects the health of the individual, often leading to heart disease and diabetes.

obey /oʊˈbeɪ/ *v.t.* **1.** to comply with or fulfil the commands or instructions of: *obey your parents.* **2.** to comply with or fulfil (a command, etc.). **3.** (of things) to respond conformably in action to: *a ship obeys her helm.* **4.** to submit or conform in action to (some guiding principle, impulse, etc.). *–v.i.* **5.** to be obedient. **–obeyer**, *n.*

obfuscate /ˈɒbfəskeɪt/ *v.t.* **1.** to confuse or stupefy. **2.** to darken or obscure. **–obfuscation** /ɒbfəsˈkeɪʃən/, *n.*

obituary /əˈbɪtʃəri/ *n.* (*pl.* **-aries**) **1.** a notice of the death of a person, often with a brief biographical sketch, as in a newspaper. *–adj.* **2.** relating to or recording a death: *an obituary notice.*

object *n.* /ˈɒbdʒɛkt/ **1.** something that may be perceived by the senses, especially by sight or touch; a visible or tangible thing. **2.** a thing or person to which attention or action is directed: *an object of study.* **3.** anything that may be presented to the mind: *objects of thought.* **4.** a thing with reference to the impression it makes on the mind: *an object of curiosity.* **5.** the end towards which effort is directed: *the object of our visit.* **6.** a person treated in terms of meeting a specific need in others: *a love object; sex object.* **7.** a person or thing which arouses feelings of pity, disgust, etc. **8.** *Gram.* (in

English and many other languages) the noun or its substitute which represents the goal of an action (in English either *direct* or *indirect*) or the ending point of a relation (in English expressed by a preposition). **9.** *Metaphysics* that towards which a cognitive act is directed; the non-ego. **10.** (in computer programming) a self-contained identifiable unit of a piece of software. *–v.i.* /əbˈdʒɛkt/ **11.** to offer a reason or argument in opposition. **12.** to express or feel disapproval; be averse. *–v.t.* /əbˈdʒɛkt/ **13.** to bring as a charge; attribute as a fault. *–phr.* **14. be no object**, to present no obstacle or hindrance: *money is no object.* **–objector**, *n.* **–objectless**, *adj.*

objection /əbˈdʒɛkʃən/ *n.* **1.** something adduced or said in disagreement or disapproval; an adverse reason. **2.** the act of objecting. **3.** a ground or cause of objecting. **4.** a feeling of disapproval or dislike. **–objectionable**, *adj.*

objective /əbˈdʒɛktɪv/ *n.* **1.** something aimed at; a goal. *–adj.* **2.** belonging to the object of thought rather than to the thinking subject (opposed to *subjective*). **3.** free from personal feelings or bias; unbiased. **4.** (of a person, book, etc.) intent upon or dealing with things outside the mind rather than thoughts or feelings. **–objectively**, *adv.* **–objectiveness**, *n.* **–objectivity**, *n.*

object-oriented /ˈɒbdʒɛkt-ˈɒrɪɛntəd/ *adj.* *Computers* of or relating to programming which uses discrete units (objects) comprising defined groupings of data and procedures.

objet d'art /ɒbʒeɪ ˈdɑ/ *n.* (*pl.* **objets d'art** /ɒbʒeɪ ˈdɑ/) an article of artistic worth.

oblate /ˈɒbleɪt/ *adj.* flattened at the poles, as a spheroid generated by the revolution of an ellipse about its shorter axis (opposed to *prolate*). **–oblately**, *adv.*

oblation /ouˈbleɪʃən, ɒ-/ *n.* **1.** the offering to God of the elements of bread and wine in the Eucharist. **2.** any offering for religious or charitable uses. **–oblatory** /ˈɒblətəri, ɒbˈleɪtəri/, *adj.*

obligation /ɒbləˈgeɪʃən/ *n.* **1.** a binding requirement to act in a particular way; duty. **2.** the binding power or force of a promise, law, duty, agreement, etc. **3.** *Law* a legal relationship between two people in which one person's right is the other person's duty. **4.** a debt, especially a debt of gratitude owed for a benefit, favour, etc. **–obligatory**, *adj.*

oblige /əˈblaɪdʒ/ *verb* (**obliged, obliging**) *–v.t.* **1.** to require or constrain, as by law, command, conscience, or necessity. **2.** to bind (a person, etc.) morally or legally, as by a promise, contract, or the like. **3.** to make (an action, course, etc.) incumbent or obligatory. **4.** to place under a debt of gratitude for some benefit, favour, or service. *–v.i.* **5.** to do something as a favour: *he'll do anything to oblige.* *–phr.* **6. oblige with**, to favour or accommodate with: *he obliged us with a song.* **–obliger**, *n.*

obliging /əˈblaɪdʒɪŋ/ *adj.* disposed to do favours or services, as a person: *the clerk was most obliging.* **–obligingly**, *adv.* **–obligingness**, *n.*

oblique /əˈblik/ *adj.* **1.** neither parallel nor at 90° to a given line or surface; slanting; sloping. **2.** not straight or direct. **3.** *Gram.* indicating any case of a noun except nominative and vocative, or except these two and accusative. **–obliquely**, *adv.* **–obliqueness**, *n.*

obliterate /əˈblɪtəreɪt/ *v.t.* **1.** to remove all traces of; do away with; destroy. **2.** to blot out or render undecipherable (writing, marks, etc.); cancel; efface. **–obliteration** /əblɪtəˈreɪʃən/, *n.* **–obliterative** /əˈblɪtərətɪv/, *adj.*

oblivion /əˈblɪvɪən/ *n.* **1.** the state of being forgotten, as by the world. **2.** the forgetting, or forgetfulness, of something: *five minutes of oblivion.* **3.** *Law* disregard or overlooking: *oblivion of political offences.*

oblivious /əˈblɪvɪəs/ *adj.* **1.** forgetful; without remembrance: *oblivious of my former failure.* **2.** *Obs.* inducing forgetfulness. *–phr.* **3. oblivious of** (or **to**), unmindful of; unconscious of. **–obliviously**, *adv.* **–obliviousness**, *n.*

oblong /ˈɒblɒŋ/ *adj.* **1.** elongated, usually from the square or circular form. **2.** in the form of a rectangle of greater length than breadth.

obnoxious /ɒbˈnɒkʃəs, ɒb-/ *adj.* objectionable; offensive; odious: *obnoxious remarks.* **–obnoxiously**, *adv.* **–obnoxiousness**, *n.*

oboe /ˈouboʊ/ *n.* a woodwind instrument in the form of a slender conical tube, in which the tone is produced by a double reed.

obscene /ɒbˈsin, ɒb-/ *adj.* **1.** offensive to modesty or decency; indecent; inciting to lust or sexual depravity; lewd: *obscene pictures.* **2.** abominable; disgusting; repulsive. **–obscenely**, *adv.* **–obscenity** /əbˈsɛnəti, ɒb-/, *n.*

obscure /ɒbˈskjuə, -ˈskjʊə/ *adj.* **1.** (of meaning) not clear or plain; uncertain. **2.** little seen or noticed: *the obscure beginnings of a great movement.* **3.** not readily or easily seen. **4.** dark, as from lack of light; murky; dim. *–v.t.* **5.** to make obscure, dark, dim, etc. **–obscurely**, *adv.* **–obscureness**, *n.* **–obscuration** /ɒbskjuˈreɪʃən/, *n.*

obsequious /əbˈsikwiəs, ɒb-/ *adj.* excessively deferential or compliant: *obsequious servants.* **–obsequiously**, *adv.* **–obsequiousness**, *n.*

observance /əbˈzɜvəns/ *n.* **1.** the action of conforming to, obeying, or following: *observance of laws.* **2.** a procedure, ceremony, or rite, as for a particular occasion: *patriotic observances.* **3.** a rule or custom to be observed. **4.** observation.

observant /əbˈzɜvənt/ *adj.* **1.** observing or regarding attentively; watchful. **2.** quick to notice or perceive; alert. **3.** careful in the observing of a law, custom, or the like. **–observantly**, *adv.*

observatory /əbˈzɜvətri/ *n.* (*pl.* **-ries**) **1.** a place or building designed for making observations of astronomical, meteorological, or other natural phenomena, usually equipped with a powerful telescope. **2.** a place or structure affording an extensive view.

observe /əbˈzɜv/ *v.t.* **1.** to see, perceive, or notice. **2.** to regard with attention, so as to see or learn something. **3.** to make or take an observation; to watch, view, or note for some scientific, official, or other special purpose: *to observe an eclipse.* **4.** to remark; comment. **5.** to keep or maintain in one's action, conduct, etc.: *you must observe the formalities.* **6.** to obey; comply with; conform to: *to observe a law.* **7.** to show regard for by some appropriate procedure, ceremonies, etc.: *to observe a holiday.* **8.** to perform duly, or solemnise (ceremonies, rites, etc.). *–v.i.* **9.** to notice. **10.** to act as an observer. *–phr.* **11. observe on** (or **upon**), to remark or comment on. **–observation**, *n.* **–observingly**, *adv.*

obsess /əbˈsɛs, ɒb-/ *v.t.* to beset, trouble, or dominate the thoughts, feelings, etc.; haunt: *fear of cancer obsesses her.* **–obsession**, *n.* **–obsessive**, *adj.*

obsessive-compulsive disorder *n.* a disorder of the mind in which the sufferer has intrusive irrational thoughts and engages in repetitive rituals to find temporary relief.

obsidian /ɒbˈsɪdiən/ *n.* a volcanic glass, usually of a dark colour and with a conchoidal fracture.

obsolescent /ɒbsəˈlɛsənt/ *adj.* becoming obsolete; passing out of use, as a word. **–obsolescence**, *n.* **–obsolescently**, *adv.*

obsolete /ˈɒbsəlit/ *adj.* fallen into disuse, or no longer in use: *an obsolete word.* **–obsoletely**, *adv.* **–obsoleteness**, *n.*

obstacle /ˈɒbstəkəl/ *n.* something that stands in the way or obstructs progress.

obstetrics /ɒbˈstetrɪks, əb-/ *n.* the branch of medicine concerned with caring for and treating women in, before, and after childbirth; midwifery.

obstinate /ˈɒbstənət/ *adj.* **1.** firmly and often perversely adhering to one's purpose, opinion, etc.; not yielding to argument, persuasion, or entreaty. **2.** inflexibly persisted in or carried out: *obstinate resistance.* **3.** not easily controlled: *the obstinate growth of weeds.* **4.** not yielding readily to treatment, as a disease. **–obstinately,** *adv.* **–obstinateness,** *n.*

obstreperous /əbˈstrepərəs, ɒb-/ *adj.* resisting control in a noisy manner; unruly. **–obstreperously,** *adv.* **–obstreperousness,** *n.*

obstruct /əbˈstrʌkt/ *v.t.* **1.** to block or close up, or make difficult of passage, with obstacles, as a way, road, channel, or the like. **2.** to interrupt, make difficult, or oppose the passage, progress, course, etc., of. **3.** to come in the way of or shut out (a view, etc.). **–obstructer, obstructor,** *n.* **–obstructive,** *adj.* **–obstructively,** *adv.* **–obstructiveness,** *n.*

obstruction /əbˈstrʌkʃən/ *n.* **1.** something that obstructs; an obstacle or hindrance: *obstructions to navigation.* **2.** the act of obstructing. **3.** the retarding of business before a legislative group by parliamentary devices, or an attempt at such a retarding. **4.** the state of being obstructed. **5.** *Football, Hockey, etc.* a foul or infringement whereby a player interposes his or her body between an opponent and the ball so as to form an obstacle. **–obstructionist,** *n.* **–obstructionism,** *n.*

obtain /əbˈteɪn/ *v.t.* **1.** to come into possession of; get or acquire; procure, as by effort or request: *he obtained a knowledge of Greek.* **–v.i. 2.** to be prevalent, customary, or in vogue; hold good or be valid: *the morals that obtained in Rome.* **–obtainable,** *adj.* **–obtainability** /əbteɪnəˈbɪləti/, *n.* **–obtainer,** *n.* **–obtainment,** *n.*

obtrude /əbˈtrud/ *v.t.* **1.** to thrust forward or upon a person, especially without warrant or invitation: *to obtrude one's opinions upon others.* **2.** to thrust forth; push out. **–v.i. 3.** to thrust oneself or itself forward, especially unduly; intrude. **–obtruder,** *n.* **–obtrusion,** *n.*

obtrusive /əbˈtrusɪv, -zɪv/ *adj.* **1.** having or showing a disposition to obtrude. **2.** showy; undesirably obvious. **–obtrusively,** *adv.* **–obtrusiveness,** *n.*

obtuse /əbˈtjus, ɒb-/ *adj.* **1.** blunt in form; not sharp or acute. **2.** (of a leaf, petal, etc.) rounded at the extremity. **3.** not sensitive or observant; stupid; dull in perception, feeling, or intellect. **4.** indistinctly felt or perceived, as pain, sound, etc. **–obtusely,** *adv.* **–obtuseness,** *n.*

obverse /ˈɒbvɜs/ *n.* **1.** the side of a coin, medal, etc., which bears the head or principal design (opposed to *reverse*). **2.** the front or principal face of anything. **3.** a counterpart. **–adj. 4.** corresponding to something else as a counterpart. **5.** having the base narrower than the top, as a leaf. **–obversely** /ɒbˈvɜsli/, *adv.*

obviate /ˈɒbvieɪt/ *v.t.* to meet and dispose of or prevent (difficulties, objections, etc.) by effective measures: *to obviate the necessity of beginning again.* **–obviation** /ɒbviˈeɪʃən/, *n.*

obvious /ˈɒbviəs/ *adj.* clearly perceptible or evident; easily recognised or understood; open to view or knowledge: *an obvious advantage.* **–obviously,** *adv.* **–obviousness,** *n.*

oc- variant of **ob-** (by assimilation) before *c,* as in *Occident.*

occasion /əˈkeɪʒən/ *n.* **1.** a particular time, especially as marked by certain circumstances or occurrences: *on several occasions.* **2.** a special or important time, event, ceremony, function, etc. **3.** a convenient or favourable juncture or time; opportunity. **4.** the ground, reason, immediate or incidental cause of some action or result. **–v.t. 5.** to give occasion or cause for; bring about. **–phr.**

6. on occasion, now and then; occasionally. **7. rise to the occasion,** to show oneself equal to a task.

occasional /əˈkeɪʒənəl/ *adj.* **1.** occurring or appearing from time to time, not at regular intervals: *an occasional visitor.* **2.** intended for use whenever needed: *an occasional table.* **3.** relating to, arising out of, or intended for a special occasion, ceremony, etc.: *occasional verses; occasional decrees.* **–occasionally,** *adv.*

Occident /ˈɒksədənt/ *n.* **the 1.** countries in Europe and America (contrasted with the *Orient*). **2.** (*also lower case*) the Western Hemisphere. **–occidental** /ɒksəˈdɛntl/, *adj.*

occiput /ˈɒksɪpʊt/ *n.* (*pl.* **occipita** /ɒkˈsɪpətə/) *Anat.* the back part of the head or skull.

occlude /əˈklud/ *v.t.* **1.** to close, shut, or stop up (a passage, etc.). **2.** *Chem.* (of certain metals and other solids) to absorb and retain (gases or liquids), in minute pores. **–occlusion,** *n.* **–occlusive,** *adj.*

occult /ˈɒkʌlt, əˈkʌlt/ *adj.* **1.** beyond the bounds of ordinary knowledge; mysterious. **2.** not disclosed; secret; communicated only to the initiated. **3.** (in early science) **a.** not apparent on mere inspection but discoverable by experimentation. **b.** of a nature not understood, as physical qualities. **–n. 4.** the supernatural. **–occultism,** *n.* **–occultist,** *n.* **–occulter,** *n.*

occupant /ˈɒkjəpənt/ *n.* **1.** someone who occupies. **2.** a tenant of a house, estate, office, etc. **–occupancy,** *n.*

occupation /ɒkjəˈpeɪʃən/ *n.* **1.** someone's usual employment, business, etc. **2.** possession, as of a place. **3.** the act of occupying. **4.** the condition of being occupied. **5.** a period during which a country is under foreign military control.

occupational health and safety *n.* **1.** the maintaining of the health and safety of employees in the workplace. **2.** the procedures put in place to ensure this. **3.** the legislation requiring this. *Abbrev.:* OH&S

occupational therapy *n.* a method of therapy which uses self-care, work and play activities to increase development and independent function, and to prevent disability. **–occupational therapist,** *n.*

occupy /ˈɒkjəpaɪ/ *v.t.* **(-pied, -pying) 1.** to take up (space, time, etc.). **2.** to engage or employ (the mind, attention, etc., or a person). **3.** to take possession of (a place), as by invasion. **4.** to hold (a position, office, etc.). **5.** to be resident or established in (a place) as its tenant; to tenant.

occur /əˈkɜ/ *v.i.* **(-curred, -curring) 1.** to come to pass, take place, or happen. **2.** to be met with or found; present itself; appear. **–phr. 3. occur to,** to suggest itself in thought to: *an idea occurred to me.* **–occurrence,** *n.*

ocean /ˈoʊʃən/ *n.* **1.** the vast body of salt water which covers almost three quarters of the earth's surface. **2.** any of the geographical divisions of this body (commonly given as five: the Atlantic, Pacific, Indian, Arctic, and Antarctic oceans). **3.** a vast expanse or quantity: *an ocean of grass.* **–oceanic,** *adj.*

oceanic crust *n. Geol.* that portion of the earth's lithosphere which forms the floor of much of the oceans. Compare **continental crust**.

oceanic plate *n. Geol.* that part of a tectonic plate which lies underneath an ocean, thinner and denser than a continental plate.

oceanography /oʊʃənˈɒgrəfi/ *n.* the branch of physical geography that deals with the ocean. **–oceanographer,** *n.* **–oceanographic** /oʊʃənəˈgræfɪk/, **oceanographical** /oʊʃənəˈgræfɪkəl/, *adj.* **–oceanographically** /oʊʃənəˈgræfɪkli/, *adv.*

ocean perch *n.* → **sea perch**.

ocelot /ˈɒsəlɒt/ *n.* a small, nocturnal wild cat, *Leopardis pardalis,* ranging from the central southern US to central South America, with a tawny coat marked with rows of spots and ocellations.

ochre /'oʊkə/ *n.* **1.** any of a class of natural earths, mixtures of hydrated oxide of iron with various earthy materials, ranging in colour from pale yellow to orange and red, and used as pigments. **2.** the colour of this, ranging from pale yellow to an orange or reddish yellow. **–ochreous** /'oʊkriəs, 'oʊkərəs/, **ochrous** /'oʊkrəs/, **ochry** /'oʊkəri, 'oʊkri/, *adj.*

-ock a noun suffix used to make descriptive names, as in *ruddock* (literally, the red one); diminutives, as in *hillock*; etc.

ocker /'ɒkə/ *Colloq.* *–n.* **1.** the archetypal uncultivated Australian. **2.** a boorish, uncouth, chauvinistic Australian. *–adj.* **3.** of or relating to an ocker. **4.** distinctively Australian: *an ocker sense of humour.* Also, **occa**, **okker**. **–ockerish**, *adj.* **–ockerism**, *n.* **–ockerdom**, *n.*

o'clock /ə'klɒk/ *adv.* of or by the clock (used in specifying or inquiring the hour of the day): *it is now one o'clock.*

OCR /oʊ si 'a, 'oʊkə/ *n.* *Computers* a system of machine reading by a light-sensitive electrical cell of standard character sets encoded on documents such as gas bills, etc.

OC spray /oʊ 'si spreɪ/ *n.* → **pepper spray.**

oct- variant of **octa-** or **octo-**, before a vowel.

octa- a word element meaning 'eight'. Also, **oct-**, **octo-**.

octagon /'ɒktəgɒn, -gən/ *n.* a polygon having eight angles and eight sides. **–octagonal** /ɒk'tægənəl/, *adj.*

octane /'ɒkteɪn/ *n.* any of eighteen isomeric saturated hydrocarbons, C_8H_{18}, some of which are obtained in the distillation and cracking of petroleum.

octave /'ɒktɪv/ *n.* **1.** *Music* **a.** a note on the eighth degree from a given note (counted as the first). **b.** the interval between such notes. **2.** a series or group of eight. **3.** *Prosody* a group or a stanza of eight lines, as the first eight lines of a sonnet. **4.** the eighth of a series. **–octaval** /ɒk'teɪvəl, 'ɒktəvəl/, *adj.*

octavo /ɒk'tavoʊ, -'teɪv-/ *n.* a book size determined by printing on sheets folded to form eight leaves or sixteen pages. *Abbrev.:* 8vo, 8° Also, **eightvo.**

octet /ɒk'tɛt/ *n.* **1.** a company of eight singers or players. **2.** a musical composition for eight voices or instruments. **3.** *Prosody* a group of eight lines of verse, especially the first eight lines (octave) of a sonnet. **4.** *Chem.* a stable group of eight electrons which form a shell surrounding an atomic nucleus. **5.** any group of eight. Also, **octette.**

octo- variant of **octa-**.

October /ɒk'toʊbə/ *n.* the tenth month of the year, containing 31 days.

octogenarian /,ɒktoʊdʒə'nɛəriən/ *adj.* of the age of 80 years, or between 80 and 90 years old.

octopus /'ɒktəpəs, -pʊs/ *n.* (*pl.* **-puses** *or* **-pi** /-paɪ/) any animal of the genus *Octopus*, comprising octopods with a soft, oval body and eight sucker-bearing arms, and living mostly on the sea bottom.

octopus strap *n.* a stretchable rope with hooks on either end used for securing goods to roof racks, etc. Also, **ockie strap.**

ocular /'ɒkjələ/ *adj.* **1.** of or relating to the eye: *ocular movements.* *–n.* **2.** the eyepiece of an optical instrument. **–ocularly**, *adv.*

oculist /'ɒkjələst/ *n.* *Rare* a doctor of medicine skilled in the examination and treatment of the eye; an ophthalmologist.

OD /oʊ 'di/ *Colloq.* *–n.* **1.** an overdose, especially of an injected addictive drug, as heroin. *–v.i.* (**OD'd**, **OD'ing**) **2.** (sometimes fol. by *on*) to give oneself an overdose.

3. (*humorous*) (sometimes fol. by *on*) to consume to excess; have a surfeit: *I OD'd on ice-cream.*

odd /ɒd/ *adj.* **1.** differing in character from what is ordinary or usual: *an odd choice.* **2.** singular or peculiar in a freakish or eccentric way, as persons or their manners, etc. **3.** fantastic or bizarre, as things. **4.** (of a number) leaving a remainder of one when divided by two (opposed to *even*). **5.** additional to a whole mentioned in round numbers; being a surplus over a definite quantity; more or less: *she owed him fifty-odd dollars.* **6.** additional to what is taken into account: *ten dollars and a few odd cents.* **7.** being part of a pair, set, or series of which the rest is lacking: *an odd glove.* **8.** (of a pair) not matching: *he was wearing odd shoes.* **9.** remaining after a division into pairs, or into equal numbers or parts. **10.** left over after the rest have been consumed, used up, etc. **11.** occasional or casual: *the odd day of work.* **12.** not forming part of any particular group, set, or class: *odd bits of information.* *–phr.* **13. odd one out**, **a.** one left over when the rest have been arranged in pairs, or in convenient groups. **b.** one differing from the other member of a group in some respect. **–oddly**, *adv.* **–oddness**, *n.* **–oddish**, *adj.*

oddball /'ɒdbɔl/ *n.* *Colloq.* someone who is unusual or peculiar; an eccentric.

oddity /'ɒdəti/ *n.* (*pl.* **-ties**) **1.** the quality of being odd; singularity or strangeness. **2.** an odd characteristic or peculiarity. **3.** an odd person or thing.

odd jobs *pl. n.* work which encompasses a variety of different, usually small tasks.

oddment /'ɒdmənt/ *n.* **1.** a left-over article, bit, remnant, or the like. **2.** an article belonging to a broken or incomplete set.

odds /ɒdz/ *n.* (*usu. construed as pl.*) **1.** the ratio of the money to be paid to a better if successful, to the money invested by that better: *the bookmaker could only give me odds of three to two.* **2. a.** the likelihood of a certain event happening: *the odds are she'll marry young.* **b.** such a likelihood expressed as a ratio: *the odds on his becoming manager are ten thousand to one.* **3.** the greater chance of success that one team or contender is judged to have over another: *the odds were with the contender; the champion was fighting against odds.* *–phr.* **4. at odds**, (of two or more people) in disagreement; at variance. **5. long odds**, odds (def. 1) in which the ratio is large, as a hundred to one. **6. make no odds**, not to matter; be of no importance. **7. over the odds**, too much; more than can be tolerated: *their behaviour was quite over the odds.* **8. short odds**, odds (def. 1) in which the ratio is small, as five to four. **9. what's the odds?**, Also, **what odds?**. *Colloq.* what difference does it make?

odds-on *adj.* (of a chance) better than even; that is more likely to win, succeed, etc.

ode /oʊd/ *n.* **1.** a lyric poem typically of elaborate or irregular metrical form and expressive of exalted or enthusiastic emotion. **2.** (originally) a poem intended to be sung. **–odic**, *adj.*

-ode[1] a suffix of nouns denoting something having some resemblance to what is indicated by the preceding part of the word, as in *phyllode*.

-ode[2] a noun suffix meaning 'way', as in *anode*, *electrode.*

odious /'oʊdiəs/ *adj.* **1.** deserving of or exciting hatred; hateful or detestable. **2.** highly offensive; disgusting. **–odiously**, *adv.* **–odiousness**, *n.*

odium /'oʊdiəm/ *n.* the reproach, discredit, or opprobrium attaching to something hated or odious.

odometer /ɒ'dɒmətə, oʊ-/ *n.* an instrument for measuring distance passed over, as by a motor vehicle. **–odometry**, *n.*

odonto- a word element meaning 'tooth'. Also, **odont-**.

odour /ˈoʊdə/ *n.* **1.** the property of a substance which affects the sense of smell: *rank odours.* **2.** an agreeable scent; fragrance. **3.** a bad smell. **4.** a savour or quality characteristic or suggestive of something. **5.** repute or estimation: *in bad odour.* Also, **odor.** **–odourless,** *adj.* **–odorous,** *adj.*

odyssey /ˈɒdəsi/ *n.* any long series of wanderings. **–odyssean,** *adj.*

oedema /əˈdimə/ *n.* (*pl.* **-mata** /-mətə/) *Pathol.* effusion of serous fluid into the interstices of cells in tissue spaces or into body cavities. Also, **edema.** **–oedematous** /əˈdɛmətəs/, **oedematose** /əˈdɛmətoʊs/, *adj.*

Oedipus complex /ˈidəpəs ˌkɒmplɛks/ *n.* **1.** (in psychoanalysis) the unresolved desire of a child for sexual gratification through the parent of the opposite sex. This involves, first, identification with and, later, hatred for the parent of the same sex, who is considered by the child as a rival. **2.** sexual desire of a son for his mother. Compare **Electra complex.**

o'er /ɔ/ *prep.*, *adv. Poetic* over.

oesophagus /əˈsɒfəgəs/ *n.* (*pl.* **-gi** /-gaɪ/) *Anat.* a tube connecting the mouth or pharynx with the stomach in invertebrate and vertebrate animals; gullet. Also, **esophagus.** **–oesophageal** /əsɒfəˈdʒiəl/, *adj.*

oestrogen /ˈistrədʒən, ˈɛs-/ *n. Physiol.* any of a group of female sex hormones secreted by the ovaries and responsible for secondary female characteristics. Also, **estrogen.** **–oestrogenic** /istrəˈdʒɛnɪk, ɛs-/, *adj.*

oestrous cycle /ˈistrəs saɪkəl/ *n.* a recurrent series of physiological changes in sexual and other organs in female mammals, extending from one rutting period to the next. Also, **estrus cycle.**

oestrus /ˈistrəs, ˈɛs-/ *n. Physiol.* **1.** Also, **oestrum** /ˈistrəm, ˈɛs-/, **estrus.** a period of the oestrous cycle, usually lasting 1–2 days, during which ovulation occurs, and the animal can copulate; heat. **2.** passion or passionate impulse. **3.** a stimulus.

of /ɒv/, *weak form* /əv/ *prep.* a particle indicating: **1.** distance or direction from, separation, deprivation, riddance, etc.: *within a metre of.* **2.** origin or source: *of good family; the plays of Shakespeare.* **3.** concerning: *and what of Marie-Louise?* **4.** cause, occasion, or reason: *he will die of hunger.* **5.** material, substance, or contents: *a packet of sugar; a suit of wool.* **6.** a relation of identity: *the city of Sydney.* **7.** belonging to or possession, connection, or association: *the queen of England; the property of us.* **8.** inclusion in a number, class, or whole: *one of us.* **9.** objective relation: *the ringing of bells.* **10.** reference or respect: *talk of peace.* **11.** qualities: *a man of tact.* **12.** time: *of an evening.* **13.** attaching of a quality to: *it was good of you to come.* **14.** *Chiefly Archaic* the person by whom something is done: *beloved of all.*

of- variant of **ob-**, (by assimilation) before *f*, as in *offend.*

off /ɒf/ *adv.* **1.** away from a position occupied, or from contact, connection, or attachment: *take off one's hat; the handle has come off.* **2.** to or at a distance from, or away from, a place: *to run off.* **3.** away or out of association or relation: *to cast off.* **4.** deviating, especially from what is normal or regular. **5.** as a deduction: *10 per cent off on all cash purchases.* **6.** away; distant (in future time): *summer is only a week off.* **7.** out of operation or effective existence; disconnected. **8.** so as to interrupt continuity or cause discontinuance: *to break off negotiations.* **9.** away from employment or service: *we have four days off at Easter.* **10.** so as to exhaust, finish, or complete; completely: *to kill off vermin.* **11.** forthwith or immediately: *right off.* **12.** with prompt or ready performance: *to dash off a letter.* **13.** to fulfilment, or into execution or effect: *the contest came off on the day fixed.* **14.** so as to cause or undergo reduction or diminution: *to wear off.* **15.** on one's way or

journey, as from a place: *to see a friend off on a journey.* **16.** *Naut.* away from the land, a ship, the wind, etc. *–prep.* **17.** away from; so as no longer to be or rest on: *to fall off a horse.* **18.** deviating from (something normal or usual): *off one's balance.* **19.** not up to the usual standard of: *off his game.* **20.** from by subtraction or deduction: *25 per cent off the marked price.* **21.** away or disengaged from (duty, work, etc.). **22.** *Colloq.* refraining from (some food, activity, etc.): *to be off gambling.* **23.** distant from: *a waterhole a fair way off the track.* **24.** leading out of: *an alley off the main street.* **25.** *Colloq.* from (indicating source): *I bought it off him.* **26.** from (indicating material): *to make a meal off fish.* **27.** *Naut.* to seaward of. *–adj.* **28.** wide of the truth or fact; in error: *you are off on that point.* **29.** no longer in effect or operation: *the agreement is off.* **30.** (of time) on which work is suspended: *pastime for one's off hours.* **31.** not so good or satisfactory as usual: *an off year for apples; off day.* **32.** off-colour; unwell. **33.** below the normal or expected standard; inferior. **34.** in bad taste; deviating from normal or accepted behaviour. **35.** (of food) tainted. **36.** of less than the ordinary activity, liveliness, or lively interest: *an off season in the woollen trade.* **37.** (with reference to animals or vehicles) right (opposed to *near*). **38.** *Naut.* farther from the shore. **39.** *Cricket* relating to the off side. **40.** (of items in a menu) not available. **41.** *Theatre* off stage: *I sacked my dresser as soon as I was off.* **42.** as to condition, circumstances, supplies, etc.: *better off.* *–n.* **43.** the state or fact of being off. **44.** *Cricket* the off side. *–interj.* **45.** an exclamation urging someone to distance themselves or go away. *–phr.* **46. be off,** to depart; leave. **47. off and on,** a. Also, **on and off.** intermittently: *to work off and on.* b. *Naut.* on alternate tacks. **48. off like a bucket of prawns (in the midday sun),** *Aust. Colloq.* extremely rotten; stinking. **49. off one's food,** not hungry, usually because of illness. **50. off the air,** *Colloq.* crazy; insane. **51. off the wall,** *Colloq.* eccentric in an amusing way; irrational. **52. off with ...,** an exclamation calling for the removal of something specified: *off with his head!*

offal /ˈɒfəl/ *n.* **1.** the internal organs of animals used for food, including brains, heart, kidney, liver, tripe, etc. **2.** the parts of a meat carcass discarded after slaughter, excluding the skin. **3.** anything worthless or discarded; rubbish.

offbeat /ˈɒfbit/ *adj.* **1.** unusual; unconventional. *–n.* **2.** *Music* the unaccented or less strongly accented beat of a bar.

off-chance *n.* **1.** a remote chance or possibility. *–phr.* **2. do something on the off-chance,** to embark on a course of action casually setting aside the odds against its completion.

off-colour *adj.* **1.** defective in colour, as a gem. **2.** Also, **off.** *Colloq.* unwell. **3.** of doubtful propriety or taste: *an off-colour story.* Also, **off-color.**

offcourse /ˈɒfkɔs/ *adj.* of or relating to something that takes place away from a racecourse, usually betting.

offcut /ˈɒfkʌt/ *n.* **1.** something that is cut off, as from paper which has been reduced to a particular size. **2.** (*pl.*) small lengths of timber or other material, left over after special orders have been prepared in a hardware store, etc. *–adj.* **3.** not being of the usual or standard sizes.

offence /əˈfɛns/ *n.* **1.** a transgression; a wrong; a sin. **2.** any crime. **3.** a crime which is not indictable, but is punishable summarily (**summary offence**). **4.** something that offends. **5.** the act of offending or displeasing. **6.** the feeling of resentful displeasure caused: *to give offence.* **7.** the act of attacking; attack or assault: *weapons of offence.* **8.** the persons, side, etc., attacking. Also, *US,* **offense.**

offend /əˈfɛnd/ v.t. **1.** to irritate in mind or feelings; cause resentful displeasure in. **2.** to affect (the sense, taste, etc.) disagreeably. –v.i. **3.** to err in conduct; commit a sin, crime, or fault. **–offender,** n.

offensive /əˈfɛnsɪv/ adj. **1.** causing offence or displeasure; irritating; highly annoying. **2.** disagreeable to the sense: an offensive odour. **3.** unacceptable to one's sense of what is right or proper; insulting. **4.** (of a word) **a.** used purposely in order to insult the hearer. **b.** not acceptable in polite conversation. **5.** relating to offence or attack: offensive movements. –n. **6.** a position or attitude of offence or attack: The army took the offensive. **7.** an action or movement of offence or attack: the 1918 German offensive along the Western front. –phr. **8. take** (or **go on) the offensive,** to adopt a strategy of positive action. **–offensively,** adv. **–offensiveness,** n.

offer /ˈɒfə/ v.t. **1.** to present for acceptance or consideration. **2.** to show intention or willingness (to do something). **3.** to present solemnly as an act of worship, as to God, etc. **4.** to attempt to do or make: they will offer battle; do not offer resistance. **5.** to present for sale. **6.** to bid as a price: he will offer $50 for the radio. –v.i. **7.** to present itself; occur: whenever an occasion offered. –n. **8.** an act of offering or what is offered. **9.** a proposal of marriage. **10.** a proposal to give or accept something as a price for something else; a bid: an offer of $500 000 for a house. **–offerer, offeror,** n.

offering /ˈɒfərɪŋ/ n. **1.** something offered in worship or devotion, as to God, a deity, etc.; an oblation; a sacrifice. **2.** a contribution given to or through the Church for a particular purpose, as at a service. **3.** anything offered; gift. **4.** the act of someone who offers.

offertory /ˈɒfətəri, -tri/ n. (pl. **-ries) 1.** Eccles. **a.** the verses, anthem, or music said, sung, or played while the offerings of the people are received at a religious service. **b.** the part of a service at which offerings are made. **c.** the offerings themselves. **2.** (in the Roman Catholic Church) the oblation of the unconsecrated elements made by the celebrant in a Eucharistic service.

offhand adv. /ˈɒfˈhænd/ **1.** without previous thought or preparation; extempore: to decide offhand. –adj. /ˈɒfhænd/ Also, **offhanded. 2.** cavalier, curt, or brusque. **3.** informal or casual. Also, **off-hand.**

office /ˈɒfəs/ n. **1.** a room or place for the carrying-out of a business, etc. **2.** a place in which the clerical work of a business is done. **3.** a place where tickets, etc., are sold, information given, etc. **4.** a building or a set of rooms given to the business of a government organisation: the post office. **5.** a position of duty, trust, or authority, especially in the government or in some company, society, etc. **6.** a duty of a person or agency: the office of adviser. **7.** something (good, or occasionally, bad) done for another: it was through your good offices that I got the job. **8.** Chiefly Brit. a department of government: the Foreign Office.

officer /ˈɒfəsə/ n. **1.** someone who holds a position of rank or authority in an army, navy, air force, or any similar organisation, especially one who holds a commission in the armed services. **2.** a police officer or constable. **3.** the master or captain of a merchant vessel or pleasure vessel, or any of his or her chief assistants. **4.** a person appointed or elected to some position of responsibility and authority in the public service, or in some corporation, society, or the like.

official /əˈfɪʃəl/ n. **1.** someone who holds an office or is charged with some form of official duty. –adj. **2.** of or relating to an office or position of duty, trust, or authority: official powers. **3.** authorised or issued authoritatively: an official report. **4.** appointed or authorised to act in a special capacity: an official representative. **5.** formal or ceremonious: an official dinner. **–officially,** adv.

officialese /əfɪʃəˈliz/ n. a style of language found in official documents and characterised by pretentiousness, pedantry, obscurity, and the use of jargon.

officiate /əˈfɪʃieɪt/ v.i. **1.** to perform the duties of any office or position. **2.** to perform the office of a priest or minister, as at divine worship. **–officiation** /əfɪʃiˈeɪʃən/, n. **–officiator,** n.

officious /əˈfɪʃəs/ adj. **1.** forward in tendering or obtruding one's services upon others. **2.** marked by or proceeding from such forwardness: officious interference. **–officiously,** adv. **–officiousness,** n.

offing /ˈɒfɪŋ/ n. **1.** the more distant part of the sea as seen from the shore, beyond the anchoring ground. **2.** position at a distance from the shore. –phr. **3. in the offing, a.** not very distant. **b.** close enough to be seen. **c.** ready or likely to happen, appear, etc.

off limits adj. out of bounds.

offline /ˈɒflaɪn/ adj. **1.** not connected to a computer network: an offline branch of the bank. **2.** temporarily disconnected from a computer network. –phr. **3. talk offline,** to confer outside a general meeting. Also, **off-line.**

off-load v.t. **1.** to unload (goods, etc.). **2.** to get rid of. **3.** Rugby Football, Aust. Rules to pass (the ball). –v.i. **4.** to unload.

off-peak adj. **1.** of or relating to a period of time of less activity than at peak hour: off-peak train services. **2.** (of a hot-water or other electrical system) set to operate only during an off-peak period, normally during the night.

off-putting /ˈɒfˈpʊtɪŋ/ adj. Colloq. disconcerting; discouraging.

off-road adj. **1.** of or relating to the functioning, etc., of a motor vehicle when it is not being driven. **2.** of or relating to driving in rugged conditions away from sealed roads, as through bush, on sand, etc., usually with a four-wheel drive vehicle. **3.** of or relating to a motor vehicle, motorbike, or bicycle, designed to travel in such terrain. –adv. **4.** off made roads into natural terrain: this car will go off-road.

off-season adj. of or relating to a time of year other than the usual or most popular for a specific activity; out of season.

offset v.t. /ˈɒfsɛt, ɒfˈsɛt/ (**-set, -setting) 1.** to balance as by something else; counterbalance: the gains offset the losses. –n. /ˈɒfsɛt/ **2.** something that offsets or compensates. **3.** any offshoot; branch. **4.** Printing an impression from an inked design, etc., on a lithographic stone or metal plate, made on another surface, and then transferred to paper. –adj. /ˈɒfsɛt/ **5.** of, or relating to an offset.

offshoot /ˈɒfʃut/ n. **1.** a shoot from a main stem, as of a plant; a lateral shoot. **2.** a branch, or a descendant or scion, of a family or people. **3.** anything conceived as springing or proceeding from a main stock: an offshoot of a mountain range; an offshoot of a large company.

offshore adv. /ˈɒfˈʃɔ/ **1.** off or away from the shore. **2.** at a distance from the shore. **3.** in or to another country; abroad: to study offshore; to move operations offshore. –adj. /ˈɒfʃɔ, ɒfˈʃɔ/ **4.** moving or tending away from the shore: an offshore wind. **5.** based in an overseas location: offshore processing of asylum seekers. **6.** (of a business) based in a foreign location where the taxation system is not as burdensome as it is in the country where the business is owned.

off side n. (in cricket) that half of the field towards which the feet of the person batting point as he or she stands ready to receive the bowling (opposed to leg side). Also, **off.**

offside /ˈɒfˈsaɪd, ˈɒfsaɪd/ adj. **1.** Soccer, Rugby Football, etc. illegally between the ball and the opposing team's goal line, or beyond a prescribed line or area, when the ball is in play. **2.** of or relating to the side of a vehicle nearer to the oncoming traffic, i.e. the right-hand side in a country where traffic drives on the left. Compare **nearside** (def. 1). **3.** of or relating to the side of a road furthest away from the footpath. **4.** *Aust., NZ Colloq.* opposed; uncooperative: *I don't want him offside.* **5.** *Cricket* of or relating to the off side: *an offside shot.* *–n.* **6.** the side of a vehicle nearer to the oncoming traffic, i.e. the right-hand side in a country where traffic drives on the left. Compare **nearside** (def. 2). *–v.i.* **7.** *Aust., NZ Colloq.* to act as an offsider: *I need you to offside.* *–phr.* **8. be** (or **get**) **offside with**, *Aust., NZ Colloq.* to be (or become) out of favour with.

offsider /ˈɒfˌsaɪdə/ *n. Aust., NZ* a partner; friend; assistant: *the cook's offsider.*

offspring /ˈɒfsprɪŋ/ *n.* **1.** children or young of a particular parent or progenitor. **2.** a descendant. **3.** the product, result, or effect of something: *the offspring of delirium.*

off-the-record /ˈɒf-ðə-rɛkəd/ *adj.* unofficial; not intended for public quotation: *an off-the-record discussion with the prime minister.* Also, (*especially in predicative use*), **off the record**.

off-white *n.* a white colour with a slight touch of grey in it.

often /ˈɒfən, ˈɒftən/ *adv.* **1.** many times; frequently. **2.** in many cases.

ogle /ˈoʊɡəl/ *v.t.* (**ogled, ogling**) **1.** to eye with amorous, flirtatious, ingratiating, or impertinently familiar glances. **2.** to eye; look at. *–ogler, n.*

ogre /ˈoʊɡə/ *n.* **1.** a monster, commonly represented as a hideous giant, of fairytales and popular legends, supposed to live on human flesh. **2.** a person likened to such a monster. *–ogreish* /ˈoʊɡərɪʃ/, **ogrish** /ˈoʊɡrɪʃ/, *adj. –ogress* /ˈoʊɡrəs/, *fem. n.*

oh /oʊ/ *interj.* **1.** an expression denoting surprise, pain, disapprobation, etc., or for attracting attention. *–n.* (*pl.* **oh's** *or* **ohs**) **2.** the exclamation 'oh'. *–v.i.* **3.** to utter or exclaim 'oh'.

ohm /oʊm/ *n.* the SI derived unit of resistance; the resistance of a conductor in which one volt produces a current of one ampere. *Symbol*: Ω, Ο *–ohmic* /ˈoʊmɪk/, *adj.*

-oid a suffix used to form adjectives meaning 'like' or 'resembling', and nouns meaning 'something resembling' what is indicated by the preceding part of the word (and often implying an incomplete or imperfect resemblance), as in *alkaloid, anthropoid, cardioid, cuboid, lithoid, ovoid, planetoid.*

-oidea a suffix used in naming zoological classes or entomological superfamilies.

oil /ɔɪl/ *n.* **1.** any of a large class of hydrocarbons or esters typically unctuous, viscous, combustible, liquid at ordinary temperatures, and soluble in ether and other organic solvents, but not in water, which are used for anointing, perfuming, lubricating, illuminating, heating, etc. **2.** → **petroleum** (def. 1). **3.** some substance of oily consistency. **4.** *Painting* **a.** an oil colour. **b.** an oil painting. *–v.t.* **5.** to smear, lubricate, or supply with oil. *–adj.* **6.** using oil, especially as a fuel. *–phr.* **7. burn the midnight oil**, to stay up late at night to study, work, etc. **8. pour oil on troubled waters**, to reconcile people who might otherwise have had a clash of interests, points of view, etc. **9. the good** (or **straight**) (or **dinkum**) **oil**, *Aust., NZ Colloq.* correct (and usually profitable) information, often to be used in confidence; the drum. **10. the oil**, *NZ Colloq.* the truth; correct or significant information. *–oily, adj. –oiliness, n.*

oil colour *n.* a colour or paint made by grinding a pigment in oil, usually linseed oil. Also, **oil color**, **oil paint**.

oilskin /ˈɔɪlskɪn/ *n.* a cotton fabric made waterproof by treatment with oil and used for fishermen's clothing and rain wear.

ointment /ˈɔɪntmənt/ *n.* a soft, unctuous preparation, often medicated, for application to the skin; an unguent.

OK /oʊˈkeɪ/ (**OK'd, OK'ing** *or* **OK's**) *Colloq.* → **okay**. Also, **o.k.**, **ok**.

okay /oʊˈkeɪ/ *Colloq. –adj.* **1.** all right; correct. *–adv.* **2.** well; effectively; correctly; acceptably. *–v.t.* **3.** to put an 'okay' on (a proposal, etc.); endorse; approve; accept. *–n.* **4.** an approval, agreement or acceptance. *–interj.* **5.** an exclamation of approval, agreement, delight, etc. Also, **ok, OK**.

okra /ˈɒkrə, ˈoʊk-/ *n.* **1.** a tall plant of the mallow family, *Abelmoschus esculentus*, cultivated for its edible mucilaginous pods, used in soups, etc. **2.** soup or stew thickened with okra pods.

-ol[1] a noun suffix used in the names of chemical derivatives, pharmaceutical compounds, commercial products, etc., representing 'alcohol' or 'phenol', as in *glycerol, naphthol.*

-ol[2] variant of **-ole**.

old /oʊld/ *adj.* (**older** *or* **elder, oldest** *or* **eldest**) **1.** far advanced in years or life. **2.** of or relating to a long life. **3.** having the appearance or characteristics of advanced age: *prematurely old.* **4.** having reached a given age: *a man thirty years old.* **5.** having existed for a long time, or made long ago: *old wine.* **6.** long known or in use: *the same old excuse.* **7.** former, past, or ancient, as time, days, etc.: *old kingdom.* **8.** no longer modern or recent: *he exchanged his old car for a new one.* **9.** having been so formerly: *the old boys of a school.* **10.** worn; decayed; dilapidated. **11.** (*upper case*) (in the history of a language) of or belonging to the earliest stage of development: *Old English.* **12.** of long experience: *an old hand at the game.* **13.** *Colloq.* showing friendly feeling: *good old Henry. –n.* **14.** an old or former time: *in days of old.* **15.** old people collectively: *the old.* **16.** *Colloq.* → **old beer. 17.** (used in combination) a person or animal of a given age or age-group: *a class of five-year-olds. –oldness, n. –oldish, adj.*

old beer *n.* beer brewed by the top-fermentation method, usually dark in colour.

old boy *n.* **1.** a former pupil of a specific school. **2.** *Colloq.* a familiar or affectionate term of address to a man, or sometimes to a male animal.

olden /ˈoʊldən/ *adj.* of old; ancient: *olden days.*

olde-worlde /oʊldi-ˈwɜldi/ *adj.* excessively quaint or old-fashioned.

old-fashioned /ˈoʊld-fæʃənd/ *adj.* **1.** of an old fashion or a style or type formerly in vogue. **2.** favoured or prevalent in former times: *old-fashioned ideas.* **3.** (of persons) having the ways, ideas, or tastes of a former period; out of fashion.

old girl *n.* **1.** a former pupil of a specific school. **2.** *Colloq.* a familiar or affectionate term of address to a woman, or sometimes to a female animal.

old guard *n.* **1.** the ultra-conservative members of any group, country, etc. **2.** the members of a previous generation, or the supporters of a previous order, who survive to see their way of life or their cause go into decline.

old hand *n.* **1.** someone with a great deal of experience in a particular situation, location, workplace, etc. **2.** an ex-prisoner.

old identity *n.* anyone long identified with a place, institution, job, etc.

old maid *n.* **1.** an elderly or confirmed spinster. **2.** *Colloq.* a person with the alleged characteristics of an old maid, such as primness, prudery, fastidiousness, etc. **3.** a game of cards in which the players draw from one another's hands to match pairs. *–old-maidish, adj.*

old man *Colloq. –n.* **1.** a father, usually one's own. **2.** a husband, usually one's own. **3.** an affectionate term of address, usually from one adult male to another. *–phr.* **4.** the old man, someone in a position of authority, as an employer.

old-man *adj. Aust., NZ* strikingly large or remarkable of its kind: *old-man flood.* Also, **old man.**

old school *n.* **1.** one's former school. **2.** the, advocates or supporters of long-established, especially conservative policies and practices.

old school tie *n.* **1.** a specific tie worn by former members of a school. **2.** the network of influences and associations formed among former students of independent schools.

Old Testament *n.* the collection of biblical books comprising the Hebrew Scriptures of 'the old covenant', and being the first of the two main divisions of the Christian bible. *Abbrev.*: OT

old-timer /oʊld-ˈtaɪmə/ *n. Colloq.* **1.** someone whose residence, membership, or experience dates from a long time ago. **2.** an old person.

old wives' tale *n.* an erroneous idea, superstitious belief, etc., such as is traditionally ascribed to old women.

Old World *n.* **the, 1.** the world known to Europeans before their discovery of the Americas. **2.** the continents of the Eastern Hemisphere; Africa, Asia and Europe, and sometimes also Australia.

-ole a noun suffix meaning 'oil'.

oleaginous /oʊliˈædʒənəs/ *adj.* **1.** having the nature or qualities of oil. **2.** containing oil. **3.** producing oil. **4.** oily or unctuous. **–oleaginousness,** *n.*

oleander /oʊliˈændə, ɒli-/ *n.* any plant of the genus *Nerium,* especially *N. oleander,* a poisonous evergreen shrub with handsome rose-coloured or white flowers, or *N. odorum,* a species from India with fragrant flowers.

olearia /ɒliˈɛəriə/ *n.* any shrub or tree of the large genus *Olearia,* of Australia, New Guinea and New Zealand, with numerous, daisy-like, usually white flowers; daisy bush.

oleo- a word element meaning 'oil'.

olfactory /ɒlˈfæktəri/ *adj.* of or relating to the sense of smell.

oligarchy /ˈɒlɔgaki/ *n. (pl.* **-chies)** a form of government in which the power is vested in a few, or in a dominant class or clique. **–oligarchic** /ɒləˈgakɪk/, **oligarchical** /ɒlə-ˈgakɪkəl/, *adj.*

oligo- a word element meaning 'few', 'little'. Also, *(before a vowel),* **olig-.**

Oligocene /ˈɒlɪgoʊsiːn/ *adj., n. Geol.* (relating to) a division of the Tertiary that follows the Eocene and comes before the Miocene.

oligopoly /ɒləˈgɒpəli/ *n. Econ.* a market situation in which a product is supplied by a relatively small number of firms whose actions and policies are constrained by the expected reactions of each other.

olive /ˈɒlɪv, -lɪv/ *n.* **1.** a fruit-bearing evergreen tree, of Mediterranean and other warm regions. **2.** a small, oval fruit, valuable for eating and as a source of oil. **3.** the olive, or a branch of olive, seen as a symbol of peace. **4.** a shade of brownish or yellowish green. *–adj.* **5.** of, relating to, or made of olives. **6.** of the colour olive. **7.** (of the complexion or skin) brownish; darker than fair.

olive branch *n.* **1.** a branch of the olive tree (an emblem of peace). **2.** anything offered in token of peace.

olivine /ˈɒləˈviːn, ˈɒlɪvɪn/ *n.* a very common mineral, magnesium iron silicate, $(Mg, Fe)_2SiO_2$, occurring commonly in olive green to grey-green masses as an important constituent of basic igneous rocks; rarely, in one variety, transparent and used as a gem.

Olympian /əˈlɪmpiən/ *adj.* **1.** of or relating to the gods of ancient Greece, who lived on Mt Olympus. **2.** grand; imposing; superior. *–n.* **3.** someone who has competed in the Olympic games.

-oma a suffix of nouns denoting a morbid condition of growth (tumour), as in *carcinoma, glaucoma, sarcoma.*

ombudsman /ˈɒmbədzmən/ *n. (pl.* **-men)** an official appointed by parliament, or some other legislative body, as a city council, to investigate complaints by citizens against the government or its agencies.

omega /əˈmiːgə, ˈɒməgə, əˈmeɪgə/ *n.* **1.** the last letter (Ω, ω = English long O, o) of the Greek alphabet. **2.** the last of any series; the end.

omelette /ˈɒmlət/ *n.* a dish consisting of eggs beaten and fried, often served folded round other ingredients, as mushrooms. Also, **omelet.**

omen /ˈoʊmən/ *n.* **1.** anything perceived or happening that is regarded as portending good or evil or giving some indication as to the future; a prophetic sign. **2.** a prognostic. **3.** prophetic significance; presage: *a bird of ill omen. –v.t.* **4.** to be an omen of; portend.

ominous /ˈɒmənəs/ *adj.* **1.** portending evil; inauspicious; threatening: *a dull, ominous rumble.* **2.** having the significance of an omen. **–ominously,** *adv.* **–ominousness,** *n.*

omit /oʊˈmɪt, ə-/ *v.t.* **(omitted, omitting) 1.** to leave out: *to omit passages of a text.* **2.** to forbear or fail to do, make, use, send, etc.: *to omit a greeting.* **–omission,** *n.*

omni- a word element meaning 'all', used in combination as in *omniactive* (all-active, active everywhere), *omnibenevolent, omnicompetent, omnicredulous, omniprevalent,* and various other words.

omnibus /ˈɒmnɪbəs, -bʌs/ *n. (pl.* **-buses) 1.** → **bus** (def. 1). **2.** a volume of reprinted works by a single author or related in interest or nature.

omnipotent /ɒmˈnɪpətənt/ *adj.* **1.** almighty, or infinite in power, as God or a deity. **2.** having unlimited or very great authority. **–omnipotently,** *adv.* **–omnipotence,** *n.*

omnipresent /ɒmnəˈprɛzənt/ *adj.* present everywhere at the same time: *the omnipresent God.* **–omnipresence,** *n.*

omniscient /ɒmˈnɪsiənt, ɒmˈnɪʃənt/ *adj.* **1.** knowing all things, or having infinite knowledge. *–n.* **2.** an omniscient being. **–omnisciently,** *adv.* **–omniscience,** *n.*

omnivore /ˈɒmnəvɔː/ *n.* an omnivorous person or animal.

omnivorous /ɒmˈnɪvərəs/ *adj.* **1.** eating all kinds of foods indiscriminately. **2.** eating both animal and plant foods. **3.** taking in everything, as with the mind. **–omnivorously,** *adv.* **–omnivorousness,** *n.*

on /ɒn/ *prep.* a particle expressing: **1.** position above and in contact with a supporting surface: *on the table.* **2.** contact with any surface: *the picture on the wall; the shoes on my feet.* **3.** immediate proximity: *a house on the coast; to border on absurdity.* **4.** situation, place, location, etc.: *a scar on the face.* **5.** support, suspension, dependence, reliance, or means of conveyance: *on foot; on wheels.* **6.** state, condition, course, process, etc.: *on the way; on strike.* **7.** ground or basis: *on good authority; a story based on fact.* **8.** risk or liability: *on pain of death.* **9.** time or occasion: *on Sunday.* **10.** position with relation to something else: *on the left; on the other side.* **11.** direction or end of motion: *to march on the capital.* **12.** encounter: *to happen on a person.* **13.** object or end of action, thought, desire, etc.: *to gaze on a scene.* **14.** membership or association: *on the staff of a newspaper; to serve on a jury.* **15.** agency or means: *to speak on the telephone; we saw it on television.* **16.** manner: *on the cheap; on the sly.* **17.** subject, reference, or respect: *views on public matters.* **18.** *Colloq.* relation of someone to an event which affects them, especially where they are morally responsible: *I don't want him to die on me; the apples went bad on me.*

19. liability for expense: *drinks are on the house.* **20.** *Aust.* engagement in the mining of a specified resource: *on the tin.* **21.** *Colloq.* indulgence to excess: *he's on the bottle, on the turps.* **22.** direction of attention or emotion: *don't go crook on me.* –*adv.* **23.** on oneself or itself: *to put one's coat on.* **24.** fast to a thing, as for support: *to hold on.* **25.** towards a place, point, or object: *to look on.* **26.** forwards, onwards or along, as in any course or process: *further on.* **27.** with continuous procedure: *to work on.* **28.** into or in active operation or performance: *to turn the gas on.* –*adj.* **29.** operating or in use: *the heating is on*; *the handbrake is on.* **30.** taking place; occurring: *sport is on tomorrow.* **31.** *Cricket* → **leg side.** **32.** (of items in a menu) available. **33.** *Theatre* on stage: *you'll be on in five minutes.* –*n.* **34.** *Cricket* the on side. –*phr.* **35. be on,** *Colloq.* **a.** to be willing or in agreement. **b.** to have placed a bet. **c.** to be habitually taking (a drug): *on heroin.* **d.** to be currently under the effects of (a drug): *he was on eccy that night.* **36. be on about,** *Colloq.* **a.** to be primarily concerned with: *what is this article on about?* **b.** to be complaining about: *he's always on about the way he's treated.* **37. be on at,** *Colloq.* to nag. **38. be on for young and old,** *Aust. Colloq.* (with impersonal *it* as subject) to be a situation in which there is general licence, especially fighting and brawling. **39. be on to a good thing, a.** to have hit upon a successful, especially money-making, scheme, project, etc. **b.** to be optimistic of having sexual intercourse. **40. be on with,** *Aust. Colloq.* to be involved in a relationship with. **41. get on to,** *Colloq.* **a.** to follow up (a matter). **b.** to consult (a person); contact. **42. go on (and on) about,** to complain repeatedly or incessantly about **43. go on at,** *Colloq.* to berate; scold. **44. have oneself on,** *Aust. Colloq.* to think oneself better, more skilled, or more important than one really is. **45. have someone on,** *Colloq.* **a.** to tease or deceive someone. **b.** to accept a fight or competition with someone: *I'll have you on anytime.* **46. not on,** *Colloq.* not a possibility; not allowable: *to buy a car now is just not on.* **47. on and off,** intermittently. **48. on and on,** at great length; without interruption. **49. on the road, a.** travelling as a salesperson. **b.** droving cattle. **c.** on tour, as a theatrical company. **d.** advancing or progressing in an enterprise or activity. **50. on to,** *Colloq.* in a state of awareness about; knowing or realising the true meaning, nature, etc., of: *the police are already on to your little game.* **51. you're on,** *Colloq.* an exclamation indicating agreement to a request, offer, suggestion, etc.

onanism /ˈoʊnənɪzəm/ *n.* **1.** (in sexual intercourse) withdrawal before occurrence of the male orgasm. **2.** → **masturbation.** –**onanist,** *n.* –**onanistic** /oʊnə-ˈnɪstɪk/, *adj.*

once /wʌns/ *adv.* **1.** at one time in the past; formerly: *a once powerful nation.* **2.** a single time: *once a day.* **3.** even a single time; at any time; ever: *if the facts once become known.* **4.** by a single degree: *a cousin once removed.* –*conj.* **5.** if or when at any time; if ever. **6.** whenever. –*n.* **7.** a single occasion: *once is enough.* –*phr.* **8. all at once, a.** suddenly. **b.** at the same time. **9. at once, a.** immediately. **b.** at the same time: *don't both speak at once.* **10. once and for all,** finally and decisively. **11. once in a while,** occasionally. **12. once upon a time,** long ago (a favourite beginning of a children's story, etc.).

once-over *n. Colloq.* **1.** a quick or superficial examination, inspection, treatment, etc., especially of a person viewed as a sexual object. **2.** a beating-up; act of physical violence.

oncology /ɒŋˈkɒlədʒi/ *n.* the branch of medical science that is concerned with the study and treatment of tumours. –**oncologist,** *n.* –**oncological** /ɒŋkəˈlɒdʒɪkəl/, *adj.*

oncoming /ˈɒnkʌmɪŋ/ *adj.* approaching.

oncourse /ˈɒnkɔːs/ *adj.* of or relating to facilities or activities on a racecourse: *oncourse betting.*

one /wʌn/ *adj.* **1.** being a single unit or individual, rather than two or more; a single: *one apple.* **2.** being a person, thing, or individual instance of a number of kind indicated: *one member of the party.* **3.** some (day, etc.), in the future): *you will meet her one day.* **4.** single through union, agreement, or harmony: *all were of one mind.* **5.** a certain (often used in naming a person otherwise unknown or undescribed): *one Jane Smith was chosen.* **6.** a particular (day, night, time, etc., in the past): *one evening last week.* **7.** being a unique or specially remarkable person or thing: *the one man we can rely on.* –*n.* **8.** the first and lowest whole number, or a symbol, as 1, or I, representing it; unity. **9.** a unit; a single person or thing: *to come one at a time.* **10.** an unusual person; character: *he's a one.* –*pron.* **11.** a single person or thing: *serves one; I'll eat one now and one later.* **12.** a person or thing of number or kind indicated or understood: *one of the poets.* **13.** (*in certain pronominal combinations*) a person unless definitely specified otherwise: *every one.* **14.** (*with a defining clause or other qualifying words*) a person, or a personified being or agency: *the evil one.* **15.** a person indefinitely; anyone: *as good as one would desire.* **16.** a person of the speaker's kind: *to press one's own claims.* **17.** (to avoid repetition) a person or thing of the kind just mentioned: *the portraits are fine ones.* –*phr.* **18. all one,** (*used predicatively*) all the same, as in character, meaning, consequence, etc.: *it's all one to me.* **19. at one,** (sometimes fol. by *with*) in a state of unity, agreement, or accord: *hearts at one.* **20. be one with,** to be of a single kind, nature or character: *to be one with the rebels* **21. get** (or **guess**) (or **have**) **it in one,** *Colloq.* to hit on the correct answer, etc., at one's first attempt. **22. have one for the road** (or **bitumen**), *Colloq.* to have one or more alcoholic drinks before departing, ostensibly to sustain one through a journey. **23. one and all,** everybody. **24. one by one,** singly and in succession. **25. one of a kind,** unique; exceptional. **26. one to one** or **one on one,** (of two people) just between or involving each other: *to talk one to one.* **27. the one day of the year,** *Aust.* Anzac Day.

-one a noun suffix used in the names of chemical derivatives, especially ketones.

one-day cricket *n.* a form of cricket in which there are a limited number of overs to be completed in a specified amount of time, each side having one innings, so that the game can be completed in one day. Also, **limited-overs cricket.**

one-eyed *adj.* **1.** having only one eye. **2.** having a strong bias in favour of someone or something: *he's one-eyed about his local football team.*

one-off /ˈwʌn-ɒf/ *adj.* individual, unique: *an architect-designed, one-off house.*

onerous /ˈoʊnərəs/ *adj.* burdensome, oppressive, or troublesome: *onerous duties.* –**onerously,** *adv.* –**onerousness,** *n.*

oneself /wʌnˈsɛlf/ *pron.* **1.** a person's self (often used for emphasis or reflexively): *one hurts oneself by such methods.* **2.** (used after *be, become,* or *come to*) one's proper or normal self; one's normal state of mind.

onesie /ˈwʌnzi/ *n.* **1.** a loose-fitting one-piece suit, usually of a stretch fabric, gathered at the wrists and ankles and loose at the crotch. **2.** a one-piece stretch garment for an infant, with or without legs and sleeves, sometimes enclosing the feet.

one-time *adj.* having been (as specified) at one time; former; quondam: *his one-time partner.*

one-upmanship /wʌn-ˈʌpmənʃɪp/ *n.* the art or practice of achieving or demonstrating superiority over others by the acquisition of privileges, status symbols, etc. Also, **oneupmanship.**

ongoing /ˈɒngoʊɪŋ/ *adj.* progressing or evolving; continuous.

onion /ˈʌnjən/ *n.* **1.** a widely cultivated plant of the lily family *Allium cepa*, having an edible succulent bulb of pungent taste and smell. **2.** the bulb. **3.** any of the certain plants similar to the onion, as *A. fistulosum* (**Welsh onion**). **4.** *Colloq.* the head. –*phr.* **5. know one's onions,** *Colloq.* to know one's job thoroughly; be experienced.

on-lending *n. Finance* the act of lending money, at a slightly higher rate of interest, money which has just been borrowed.

online /ˈɒnlaɪn/ *Computers* –*adj.* **1.** of or relating to a computer-controlled device which is directly linked to a computer (opposed to *standalone*). **2.** having direct access to a computer database: *an online branch of the bank.* **3.** (of information, etc.) able to be accessed directly by connection to a computer database, the internet, etc.: *the newspapers are online.* –*adv.* **4.** on the internet: *to publish online.* **5.** while interactively connected to the internet, to a computer database, etc.: *to browse the data online.* Also, **on-line.**

onlooker /ˈɒnlʊkə/ *n.* a spectator.

only /ˈoʊnli/ *adv.* **1.** without others or anything further; alone; solely: *only she remained.* **2.** no more than; merely; but; just: *if you would only consent.* **3.** singly; as the only one: *the only begotten Son of God.* **4.** as recently as: *he was here only a moment ago.* **5.** exclusively: *I work here only.* –*adj.* **6.** being the single one or the relatively few of the kind, or sole: *an only son.* **7.** single in superiority or distinction. –*conj.* **8.** but (introducing a single restriction, restraining circumstance, or the like): *I would have gone, only you objected.* –*phr.* **9. only too,** very; extremely: *she was only too pleased to come.*

onomatopoeia /ˌɒnəmætəˈpiə/ *n.* the formation of a name or word by imitating the sound associated with the thing designated, as in *mopoke* and *whippoorwill* which probably originated in onomatopoeia. –**onomatopoeic, onomatopoetic** /ˌɒnəmætəpoʊˈɛtɪk/, *adj.* –**onomatopoeically, onomatopoetically** /ˌɒnəmætoʊˈɛtɪkli/, *adv.*

onsell /ɒnˈsɛl, ˈɒnsɛl/ *v.t.* (**-sold, -selling**) to sell (assets, securities, etc.) shortly after purchase. –**onselling,** *n.*

onset /ˈɒnsɛt/ *n.* **1.** an assault or attack: *a violent onset.* **2.** a beginning or start.

onshore *adj.* /ˈɒnʃɔ, ɒnˈʃɔ/ **1.** towards or located on the shore. –*adv.* /ɒnˈʃɔ/ **2.** towards the shore.

onside /ɒnˈsaɪd/ *adj.* **1.** not offside. **2.** *Aust., NZ* in agreement, acting favourably: *I'll be right now the boss is onside.*

onslaught /ˈɒnslɔt/ *n.* an onset, assault or attack, especially a vigorous or furious one.

onto /ˈɒntu/ *prep.* **1.** (*used esp. after verbs of movement*) to a place or position on; upon; on: *to get onto a box.* **2.** aware of (especially something improper or secret): *the police are onto that scheme.* **3.** in communication with: *she's onto the police now.*

ontogeny /ɒnˈtɒdʒəni/ *n. Biol.* the development of an individual organism (as contrasted with *phylogeny*). Also, **ontogenesis** /ɒntoʊˈdʒɛnəsəs/. –**ontogenetic** /ˌɒntoʊdʒəˈnɛtɪk/, *adj.* –**ontogenist,** *n.*

ontology /ɒnˈtɒlədʒi/ *n.* **1.** the branch of metaphysics that investigates the nature of being. **2.** *Computers* the structural framework for a database, in terms of the rules which govern the elements in the database and the classification system on which it relies. –**ontological** /ɒntəˈlɒdʒɪkəl/, *adj.*

onus /ˈoʊnəs/ *n.* a burden; a responsibility.

onward /ˈɒnwəd/ *adj.* directed or moving onwards or forwards.

onwards /ˈɒnwədz/ *adv.* **1.** towards a point ahead or in front; forwards, as in space or time. **2.** at a position or point in advance.

onyx /ˈɒnɪks/ *n.* **1.** a quartz consisting of straight layers or bands which differ in colour, used for ornament. **2.** *Anat.* a nail of a finger or toe.

oo- a word element meaning 'egg'.

oocyte /ˈoʊəsaɪt/ *n. Biol.* a female germ cell in the maturation stage. Also, **ovocyte.**

oodles /ˈudlz/ *pl. n. Colloq.* a large quantity: *oodles of money.*

oomph /ʊmf/ *n. Colloq.* **1.** vitality; energy. **2.** sex appeal. –**oomphy,** *adj.*

oondoroo /undəˈru/ *n.* an Australian native evergreen shrub, *Solanum simile*, with purple star-shaped flowers.

oops /ʊps, ups/ *interj.* an exclamation of surprise or shock, as on bumping someone or dropping something.

ooze¹ /uz/ *v.i.* **1.** (of moisture, air, etc.) to pass slowly, as through small openings. **2.** (of a substance) to give out moisture, etc. **3.** (of information, charm, etc.) to pass (*out*, etc.) slowly or unnoticeably. –*v.t.* **4.** to give out (moisture, charm, etc.). –*n.* **5.** something that oozes.

ooze² /uz/ *n.* **1.** a calcareous mud (chiefly the shells of small organisms) covering parts of the ocean bottom. **2.** soft mud, or slime. **3.** a marsh or bog.

op- variant of **ob-**, (by assimilation) before *p*, as in *oppose.*

opal /ˈoʊpəl/ *n.* a mineral, an amorphous form of silica (SiO_2 with some water of hydration), not as hard or as heavy as quartz, found in many varieties and colours (often a milky white), certain of which are iridescent and valued as gems. –**opaline,** *adj.*

opaque /oʊˈpeɪk/ *adj.* **1.** not allowing light to pass through. **2.** not able to give off radiation, sound, heat, etc. **3.** not shining or bright. **4.** hard to understand, as an argument or reason. **5.** unintelligent. –**opacity,** *n.* –**opaquely,** *adv.* –**opaqueness,** *n.*

open /ˈoʊpən/ *adj.* **1.** not shut, as a door, gate, etc. **2.** not closed, covered, or shut up, as a house, box, drawer, etc. **3.** not enclosed as by barriers, as a space. **4.** eligible to be entered, used, shared, competed for, etc., by all: *an open session; open competition.* **5.** relating to land in which there are only scattered trees with grass or very light vegetation between them, usually suitable for grazing or cultivation: *open country; open brigalow.* **6.** (of shops, etc.) ready to do business; ready to admit members of the public. **7.** (of a court hearing, etc.) able to be attended by members of the public or the press. **8.** (sometimes fol. by *to*) accessible or available: *the only course still open.* **9.** unfilled, as a position. **10.** not engaged, as time. **11.** without prohibition as to hunting or fishing: *open season.* **12.** *US* without legal restrictions, or not enforcing legal restrictions, as to saloons, gambling places, etc.: *an open town.* **13.** undecided, as a question. **14.** liable or subject: *open to question.* **15.** having no cover, roof, etc.: *an open boat.* **16.** not covered or protected; exposed or bare: *to lay open internal parts with a knife.* **17.** unobstructed, as a passage, stretch of water, view, etc.: *the river mouth lay open before them.* **18.** free from ice: *open water in arctic regions.* **19.** exposed to general view or knowledge; existing, carried on, etc., without concealment: *open disregard of rules.* **20.** acting publicly or without concealment, as a person. **21.** unreserved, candid, or frank, as persons or their speech, aspect, etc.: *an open face.* **22.** having openings or apertures: *open ranks.* **23.** perforated or porous: *an open texture.* **24.** expanded, extended, or spread out: *an open newspaper.* **25.** generous, liberal, or bounteous: *to give with an open hand.* **26.** (of a cheque) uncrossed. **27.** *Music*

a. (of an organ pipe) not closed at the far end. b. (of a string) not stopped by a finger. c. (of a note) produced by such a pipe or string or, on a wind instrument, without the aid of a slide, key, etc. 28. (of the bowels) not constipated. 29. *Phonetics* a. pronounced with a relatively large opening above the tongue: '*cot*' *has a more open vowel than* '*caught*'. b. (of a syllable) ending with its vowel. 30. *Football* of or relating to fast play in which the ball travels rapidly and over some distance from player to player. 31. of or relating to certain jails, as prison farms, etc., which have fewer restrictions and fewer fences than conventional jails. –*v.t.* 32. to move (a door, gate, etc.) from a shut or closed position so as to admit of passage. 33. Also, **open up**. to make (a house, box, drawer, etc.) open. 34. to render (any enclosed space) open to passage or access. 35. to give access to; make accessible or available, as for use. 36. to clear of obstructions, as a passage, etc. 37. to make (bodily passages) clear. 38. to uncover, lay bare, or expose to view. 39. to render accessible to knowledge, enlightenment, sympathy, etc. 40. to expand, extend, or spread out: *to open a map*. 41. to make less compact, less close together, or the like: *to open ranks*. 42. to establish for the entrance or use of the public, customers, etc.: *to open an office*. 43. to set in action, begin, start, or commence: *to open a campaign*. 44. to cut or break into. 45. to make an incision or opening in. 46. to make or produce (an opening) by cutting or breaking, or by pushing aside or removing obstructions: *to open a way through a crowd*. 47. *Law* to make the first statement of (a case) to the court or jury. –*v.i.* 48. to become open, as a door, building, box, enclosure, etc. 49. to afford access or have an outlet (*into, onto, towards, down to,* etc.). 50. (of a building, shop, etc.) to open its doors to the public. 51. to begin a session or term, as a school. 52. to begin a season or tour, as a theatrical company. 53. to come apart or asunder, or burst open, so as to admit of passage or display the interior. 54. to come into view, or become more visible or plain, as on nearer approach. 55. to become receptive to knowledge, sympathy, etc., as the mind. 56. to disclose or reveal one's knowledge, thoughts, feelings, etc. 57. to spread out or expand, as the hand or a fan. 58. to open a book, etc.: *open at page 32*. 59. to become less compact, less close together, or the like: *the ranks opened*. 60. to begin, start, or commence; start operations. 61. *Law* to make the first statement of a case to the court or jury. 62. *Cards* to make the first bet, bid, lead, etc. –*n.* 63. an open competition: *the Australian open*. –*phr.* 64. **open to**, accessible to (appeals, ideas, offers, etc.): *to be open to persuasion*. 65. **open up**, a. (especially of a government, explorer, etc.) to make available or accessible (land previously unsettled). b. to settle and develop (such land): *cattle owners first opened up the region*. c. (of guns) to begin firing. 66. **the open**, a. an open or clear space. b. the open air. c. the open water, as of the sea. d. a situation in which hitherto restricted knowledge is extended to all parties: *to bring a subject out into the open*. –**openness**, *n.*

open-and-shut *adj.* obvious; easily decided: *an open-and-shut case of fraud*.

open cut *n. Mining* a shallow open pit allowing excavation of near surface rock layers. Also, **strip mine**. –**open-cut**, *adj.*

open day *n.* a day on which certain institutions, as schools, are open to members of the public and special activities, exhibitions, etc., are arranged for their entertainment.

open door *n.* 1. the policy of admitting all nations to a country upon equal terms, especially for trade. 2. free admission or access; admission to all upon equal terms.

open-ended /'oupən-ɛndəd/ *adj.* organised or arranged so as to allow for various contingencies; without fixed limits.

opener /'oupnə, 'oupənə/ *n.* 1. someone or something that opens, especially a tin-opener or a bottle opener. 2. *Cricket* either of the two people batting who open their side's innings by batting first. –*phr.* 3. **for openers**, to begin with.

opening /'oupnɪŋ, 'oupənɪŋ/ *n.* 1. a making or becoming open. 2. a space or place, not in use. 3. a gap; hole. 4. the act of beginning. 5. the first part of anything. 6. a vacancy. 7. an opportunity. 8. an official beginning. 9. the first performance of a theatrical production, etc.

open letter *n.* a letter made public by radio, newspaper, or such, but written as though to a specific person.

open-minded *adj.* having or showing a mind open to new arguments or ideas; unprejudiced. –**open-mindedly**, *adv.* –**open-mindedness**, *n.*

open-mouthed /oupən-'mauðd/ *adj.* 1. having the mouth open. 2. gaping with surprise or astonishment. 3. greedy, ravenous, or rapacious. 4. clamouring at the sight of game or prey, as hounds. 5. vociferous or clamorous. 6. having a wide mouth, as a vessel.

open order *n.* 1. a military formation of troops on a ceremonial parade in which the rear rank steps back if in two ranks, or the ranks open if in three ranks, to allow more space for the inspecting officer, etc., to pass. 2. a prescribed distance between ships in convoy or vehicles proceeding under orders.

open-plan *adj.* (of the interior space of a dwelling, office, etc.) not having walls between areas designed for different uses; having few fixed partitions.

open slather *n. Aust., NZ Colloq.* a situation in which there are no restraints, often becoming chaotic or rowdy; free-for-all.

open source software *n. Computers* free software for which the source code is provided.

opera /'ɒprə, 'ɒpərə/ *n.* 1. an extended dramatic composition in which music is an essential and predominant factor, consisting of recitatives, arias, choruses, etc., with orchestral accompaniment, scenery, acting, and sometimes dancing; a musical drama. 2. the branch of musical and dramatic art represented by such compositions. 3. the score or the words of a musical drama. 4. → **Chinese opera**.

operable /'ɒpərəbəl, 'ɒprə-/ *adj.* 1. capable of being put into practice. 2. *Med.* admitting of a surgical operation.

operate /'ɒpəreɪt/ *v.i.* 1. to work or run, as a machine does. 2. to work or use a machine, apparatus, etc. 3. (oft. fol. by *on* or *upon*) to use force or influence. 4. to perform some process of work or treatment. 5. *Surg.* to perform an operation on a patient with instruments, so as to remedy deformity, injury, or disease. 6. *Mil., Navy* to give orders and carry out military acts, opposed to staff work. 7. to carry on buying and selling in shares, etc. –*v.t.* 8. to manage (a machine, etc.) at work: *to operate a switchboard*. 9. to keep (a machine, factory, etc.) working. 10. to bring about, as by action. –**operatable**, *adj.*

operating system *n. Computers* the essential program which enables all other programs to be run on a computer, and which establishes an interface between a user and the hardware of the computer.

operation /ɒpə'reɪʃən/ *n.* 1. the act, process, or manner of operating. 2. the condition of being in use or working order: *a rule no longer in operation*. 3. the power of operating. 4. a course of productive or industrial activity: *building operations*. 5. a particular course or process: *mental operations*. 6. a business transaction, especially one on a large scale: *operations in oil*. 7. *Surg.* a procedure of operating on the body of a patient. **8.** *Maths* a process such as addition. **9.** a military campaign.

operational /ɒpəˈreɪʃənəl/ *adj.* **1.** of or relating to an operation or operations. **2.** ready for use; in working order. **3.** *Mil.* of or relating to military operations. –**operationally**, *adv.*

operations research *n.* the analysis, usually involving mathematical treatment, of a process, problem, or operation to determine its purpose and effectiveness and to gain maximum efficacy. Also, **operational research**.

operative /ˈɒpərətɪv, ˈɒprə-/ *n.* **1.** a worker, especially someone skilled in productive or industrial work; artisan. –*adj.* **2.** operating, or exerting force or influence. **3.** having force, or being in operation: *laws operative in a community.* **4.** serving the purpose; effective. **5.** concerned with, or relating to work. –**operatively**, *adv.* –**operativeness**, *n.*

operator /ˈɒpəreɪtə/ *n.* **1.** a worker; someone employed or skilled in operating a machine, apparatus, or the like: *a wireless operator; a telephone operator.* **2.** someone who conducts some working or industrial establishment, enterprise, or system: *the operators of a mine.* **3.** *Finance* someone who deals in shares, currency, etc., especially speculatively or on a large scale. **4.** *Maths, Computers, etc.* a symbol, character, word, etc., used to represent a particular action or logical relation, as the word 'and', or the plus symbol ($+$). **5.** *Colloq.* someone who successfully manipulates people or situations: *he's a smooth operator.*

operetta /ɒpəˈrɛtə/ *n.* a short opera, commonly of a light character.

ophthalmic /ɒfˈθælmɪk/ *adj.* of or relating to the eye; ocular.

ophthalmo- a word element meaning 'eye'.

ophthalmology /ɒfθælˈmɒlədʒi/ *n.* the branch of medical science that deals with the anatomy, functions, and diseases of the eye. –**ophthalmologist**, *n.* –**ophthalmological** /ɒfˌθælməˈlɒdʒɪkəl/, *adj.*

-opia a word element of nouns denoting a condition of sight or of the visual organs, as in *amblyopia, diplopia, emmetropia, hemeralopia, myopia.*

opiate /ˈoʊpiət, -eɪt/ *n.* **1.** a drug produced from opium or any of its derivatives. **2.** anything that causes dullness or inaction, or that calms the feelings. –*adj.* **3.** mixed with opium. **4.** producing sleep; soporific.

opine /oʊˈpaɪn/ *v.t.* **1.** think; deem; hold or express as one's opinion. –*v.i.* **2.** to hold or express an opinion.

opinion /əˈpɪnjən/ *n.* **1.** a judgement or belief not held firmly enough to produce certainty. **2.** a personal view: *public opinion.* **3.** *Law* formal non-binding advice on the legal position of some matter, as given by counsel or by a court.

opinionated /əˈpɪnjəneɪtəd/ *adj.* obstinate or conceited with regard to one's opinions; conceitedly dogmatic. –**opinionatedness**, *n.*

opinion poll *n.* the questioning of a representative cross-section of the population in order to assess public opinion, as of voting intentions. Also, **gallup poll**.

opium /ˈoʊpiəm/ *n.* the dried juice of the opium poppy, containing morphine and other alkaloids, a stimulant narcotic (in sufficient quantities a powerful narcotic poison) of great value in medicine to relieve pain, induce sleep, etc.

opossum /əˈpɒsəm/ *n.* **1. a.** a prehensile-tailed marsupial, *Didelphis virginiana*, about the size of a large cat, common in the southern US, which feigns death when caught. **b.** any of many neotropical genera of the same family. **2.** *Obs.* → **possum** (def. 1).

opponent /əˈpoʊnənt/ *n.* **1.** someone who is on the opposite side in a contest, controversy or the like; an adversary. –*adj.* **2.** being opposite, as in position. **3.** opposing; adverse. **4.** *Anat.* bringing parts into

opposition, as the muscles which set the thumb and little finger against each other. –**opponency**, *n.*

opportune /ˈɒpətjun, -tʃun/ *adj.* **1.** appropriate or favourable: *an opportune moment.* **2.** occurring or coming at an appropriate time; timely: *an opportune warning.* –**opportunely**, *adv.* –**opportuneness**, *n.*

opportunism /ɒpəˈtjunɪzəm, ˈɒpətʃunɪzəm/ *n.* **1.** the policy or practice, in politics or otherwise, of adapting actions, etc., to expediency or circumstances (often with implication of sacrifice of principle). **2.** an action or proceeding resulting from this policy. –**opportunist**, *n.*, *adj.*

opportunistic /ɒpətʃuˈnɪstɪk/ *adj.* **1.** displaying opportunism. **2.** *Med.* (of an illness) developing as a result of a weakness in the immune system. –**opportunistically**, *adv.*

opportunity /ɒpəˈtjunəti/ *n.* (*pl.* **-ties**) an appropriate or favourable time or occasion: *an opportunity to make good; an opportunity for gaining a place; an opportunity of testing a discovery.*

opportunity shop *n. Aust., NZ* → **op shop**.

oppose /əˈpoʊz/ *v.t.* **1.** to act in opposition to; resist; combat. **2.** to stand in the way of; hinder. **3.** to use or to take as being opposite: *words opposed in meaning.* –*v.i.* **4.** to be or act in opposition. –**opposer**, *n.* –**opposable**, *adj.*

opposite /ˈɒpəsət/ *adj.* **1.** placed or lying against or facing something else: *They were seated at opposite ends of a room; opposite to our house.* **2.** completely different, as in nature, qualities, result, etc. –*n.* **3.** someone or something that is opposite or contrary: *my opinion is the opposite to his.* **4.** → **antonym**. –*prep.* **5.** facing: *she sat opposite me.* **6.** in a position creating a unity with some other position: *she played opposite a famous actor.* –*adv.* **7.** on opposite sides. –**oppositely**, *adv.* –**oppositeness**, *n.*

opposition /ɒpəˈzɪʃən/ *n.* **1.** the action of opposing. **2.** opposing feelings; antagonism. **3.** an opposing group or body. **4.** (*usu. upper case*) the major political party or coalition of parties opposed to the party in power. **5.** the condition or position of being placed opposite. **6.** *Astron.* the situation of two heavenly bodies when they differ by 180°.

oppress /əˈprɛs/ *v.t.* **1.** to lie heavily upon (the mind, a person, etc.), as care, sorrow, or any disturbing thought does. **2.** to burden with cruel or unjust impositions or restraints; to subject to a burdensome or harsh exercise of authority or power. **3.** to weigh down, as sleep or weariness does. **4.** to put down, subdue, or suppress. –**oppressive**, *adj.* –**oppression**, *n.* –**oppressor**, *n.*

opprobrium /əˈproʊbriəm/ *n.* **1.** the disgrace or the reproach incurred by conduct considered shameful; infamy. **2.** a cause or object of such reproach.

op shop /ˈɒp ʃɒp/ *n. Aust., NZ* a shop that sells second-hand goods, run by a charity. Also, **opportunity shop**.

-opsis a word element indicating apparent likeness, as in *coreopsis.*

opt /ɒpt/ *phr.* **1. opt for**, to decide in favour of; choose. **2. opt out**, **a.** (sometimes fol. by *of*) to decide not to participate. **b.** to decide to take no part in the accepted social institutions and conventions.

optic /ˈɒptɪk/ *adj.* **1.** relating to or connected with the eye as the organ of sight, or sight as a function of the brain. –*n.* **2.** *Colloq.* an eye. –**optical**, *adj.*

optical disc *n.* any disc storage medium in which digitally-encoded data is read by laser beam. Also, **laser disc**; *Chiefly US,* **optical disk**.

optical scanner *n. Computers* a photoelectric cell that scans printed data and converts it into the electric impulses fed into a computer or data-processing machine.

optician /ɒpˈtɪʃən/ *n.* **1.** someone who makes glasses for remedying defects of vision, in accordance with the prescriptions of oculists. **2.** a maker or seller of optical glasses and instruments.

optimise /ˈɒptəmaɪz/ *v.t.* **1.** to make the best of; make the most effective use of. **2.** to produce the maximum amount of: *to optimise the harvest.* **3. a.** *Computers* to edit or adapt (a program) to improve its design and performance. **b.** to edit (a graphics file) to make it smaller. Also, **optimize.** −**optimisation** /ɒptəmaɪˈzeɪʃən/, *n.*

optimism /ˈɒptəmɪzəm/ *n.* **1.** disposition to hope for the best; tendency to look on the bright side of things. **2.** the belief that good ultimately predominates over evil in the world. **3.** the doctrine that the existing world is the best of all possible worlds. **4.** the belief that goodness pervades reality. −**optimist,** *n.* −**optimistic** /ɒptəˈmɪstɪk/, *adj.*

optimum /ˈɒptəməm/ *n.* (*pl.* **-ma** /-mə/ *or* **-mums**) **1.** the best or most favourable point, degree, amount, etc., for the purpose, as of temperature, light, moisture, etc., for the growth or reproduction of an organism. −*adj.* **2.** best or most favourable: *optimum conditions.* −**optimal,** *adj.*

option /ˈɒpʃən/ *n.* **1.** power or liberty of choosing; right of freedom of choice. **2.** something which may be or is chosen; choice. **3.** the act of choosing. **4.** a privilege acquired, as by the payment of a premium or consideration, of buying (or declining to buy) a property within a specified time on stipulated terms: *Paramount Pictures took out an option on the book as soon as it was published.* **5.** *Commerce, Stock Exchange* the right, obtained by payment, to buy or sell a specified commodity, parcel of shares, foreign exchange, etc., at a set price on or before a specified date. See **call option, put option.** **6.** *Aust. Rules* the privilege of a second kick given to a player who has scored a behind, in a case of a breach of the rules by an opponent while the ball is in flight. −**optional,** *adj.*

optional preferential voting *n.* a form of preferential voting in which voters may vote for one candidate only, or may choose to indicate preferences for others. Compare **full preferential voting, partial preferential voting.**

optometry /ɒpˈtɒmətri/ *n.* the study of the workings of the eye and the visual system, including diagnosis, treatment, and management of eye diseases, in addition to the management of disorders of refraction with corrective lenses.

opulent /ˈɒpjələnt/ *adj.* **1.** wealthy, rich, or affluent, as persons or places. **2.** richly supplied; abundant or plentiful: *opulent sunshine.* −**opulently,** *adv.* −**opulence,** *n.*

opus /ˈoupəs/ *n.* (*pl.* **opera** /ˈɒpərə/) **1.** a work or composition. **2.** a musical composition. **3.** one of the compositions of a composer as numbered according to order of publication. *Abbrev.*: op.

or[1] /ɔ/ *conj.* a particle used to connect words, phrases, or clauses representing alternatives: *to be or not to be.* **2.** to connect alternative terms for the same thing, or different ways of expressing the same concept: *the Hawaiian or Sandwich islands.*

or[2] /ɔ/ *n. Heraldry* the tincture gold or yellow.

-or[1] **1.** a suffix of nouns denoting a state or condition, a quality or property, etc., as in *error, terror.* **2.** an alternative of **-our,** as in *color, odor,* etc.

-or[2] a suffix of nouns denoting someone or that which does something, or has some particular function or office, as in *actor, confessor, creditor, distributor, elevator, emperor, governor, juror, refractor, tailor, traitor.* This suffix occurs chiefly in nouns originally Latin, or formed from Latin stems. In some cases it is used as an alternative or a substitute for **-er**[1], especially in legal terms (often correlative with forms in **-ee**) or

with some other differentiation of use, as in *assignor, grantor, lessor, sailor, survivor, vendor.*

oracle /ˈɒrəkəl/ *n.* **1.** (especially in ancient Greece) a saying, often hard to understand, given by a priest or priestess as the response of a god to a question. **2.** the source of such a reply: *the oracle of Apollo at Delphi.* **3.** a divine communication or revelation. **4.** the holy of holies in the Jewish temple. See I Kings, 6:16, 19–23. **5.** any person or thing serving as a means for contact with godlike forces. **6.** any statement made or received as being unquestionably correct. **7.** a person who makes such statements.

oral /ˈɔrəl/ *adj.* **1.** spoken. **2.** employing speech, as teachers or methods of teaching. **3.** of or relating to the mouth. **4.** done or taken by the mouth: *an oral dose of medicine.* **5.** *Zool.* relating to that surface of polyps and sea animals which contains the mouth and tentacles. **6.** *Phonetics* spoken with none of the voice sounding through the nose; *b* and *v* are oral consonants, and the normal English vowels are oral. −*n.* **7.** an oral examination. −**orally,** *adv.*

orange /ˈɒrɪndʒ/ *n.* **1.** a globose, reddish-yellow, edible citrus fruit of which there are two principal kinds, the bitter and sweet, the latter comprising the most important of the citrus fruits. **2.** any of the white-flowered evergreen rutaceous trees yielding it, as *Citrus aurantium* (**bitter orange, Seville orange,** or **sour orange**) and *C. sinensis* (**sweet orange**), cultivated in warm countries. **3.** any of several other citrus trees, as *Poncirus trifoliata* (**trifoliate orange**), a hardy Chinese species grown for hedges in the US. **4.** any of certain trees of other genera, as *Maclura pomifera* (**Osage orange**), or the fruit. **5.** a colour between yellow and red in the spectrum; reddish yellow. −*adj.* **6.** of or relating to the orange. **7.** made with or prepared from oranges or having the flavour of orange. **8.** reddish yellow. −**orangey,** *adj.*

orange pekoe /ɒrɪndʒ ˈpikoʊ/ *n.* a black tea composed of only the smallest top leaves and grown in India and Sri Lanka.

orange stick *n.* a small stick with one pointed and one rounded end, used in manicure.

orang-outang /əˈræŋ-ətæŋ/ *n.* → orangutan.

orangutan /əˈræŋətæn/ *n.* a large, long-armed anthropoid ape, *Pongo pygmaeus*, of arboreal habits, found in Borneo and Sumatra. Also, **orang-outang, orang, orang-utan.**

oration /ɒˈreɪʃən/ *n.* a formal speech, especially one delivered on a special occasion, as on an anniversary, at a funeral, or at academic exercises. −**orate,** *v.*

orator /ˈɒrətə/ *n.* someone who delivers an oration; a public speaker, especially one of great eloquence. −**oratress** /ˈɒrətrəs/, **oratrix** /ˈɒrətrɪks/, *fem. n.*

oratorio /ɒrəˈtɔrioʊ/ *n.* (*pl.* **-rios**) an extended musical composition, with a text more or less dramatic in character and usually based upon a religious theme, for solo voices, chorus, and orchestra, and performed without action, costume, or scenery.

oratory /ˈɒrətri/ *n.* **1.** the exercise of eloquence; eloquent speaking. **2.** the art of an orator; the art of public speaking. −**oratorical** /ɒrəˈtɒrɪkəl/, *adj.*

orb /ɔb/ *n.* **1.** *Chiefly Poetic* any of the heavenly bodies: *the orb of day* (the sun). **2.** a sphere or globe. **3.** *Chiefly Poetic* the eyeball or eye. **4.** a globe bearing a cross; the mound, or emblem of sovereignty, especially as part of the regalia of England. **5.** *Astrology* the space within which the influence of a planet, etc., is supposed to act.

orbit /ˈɔbət/ *n.* **1.** the elliptical or curved path described by a celestial object or spacecraft, about a star or planet. **2.** one complete circuit of an orbital path. **3.** the path that one object takes in relation to a fixed point. **4.** a course regularly pursued as in life. **5.** *Anat.* the eye socket. **6.** *Zool.* the part surrounding the eye of a bird or insect. **7.** an orb or sphere. **8.** *Physics* the path of an electron around the nucleus of an atom. −*v.t.* **9.** to move or travel around (the sun, etc.) in an orbital path. −*v.i.* **10.** to describe an orbit. −**orbital**, *adj.*

orchard /ˈɔːtʃəd/ *n.* **1.** a piece of ground, usually enclosed, devoted to the cultivation of fruit trees. **2.** a collection of such trees. −**orchardist**, *n.*

orchestra /ˈɔːkəstrə/ *n.* **1.** any group of performers on various musical instruments chosen in accordance with the requirements of the music to be played, as a string orchestra, a gamelan orchestra, etc. **2.** such a group with instruments from the four main families (string, woodwind, brass, and percussion) for the playing of concert music, as symphonies, operas, and other compositions in the tradition of Western music. −**orchestral** /ɔːˈkɛstrəl/, *adj.*

orchestrate /ˈɔːkəstreɪt/ *v.t.* **1.** to compose or arrange (music) for performance by an orchestra. **2.** to put together cohesively: *to orchestrate a policy.* −**orchestration** /ɔːkəsˈtreɪʃən/, *n.*

orchid /ˈɔːkɪd/ *n.* **1.** any plant of the family Orchidaceae, comprising terrestrial and epiphytic perennial herbs of temperate and tropical regions, with flowers which are usually beautiful and often singular in form. **2.** purple, varying from bluish to reddish.

ordain /ɔːˈdeɪn/ *v.t. Eccles.* to invest with ministerial or sacerdotal functions; confer holy orders upon. **2.** to appoint authoritatively; decree; enact. **3.** (of God, fate, etc.) to destine or predestine. −**ordainer**, *n.* −**ordainment**, *n.*

ordeal /ɔːˈdil, ˈɔːdil/ *n.* **1.** any severe test or trial; a trying experience. **2.** (especially formerly) a primitive form of trial to determine guilt or innocence, as by the effect of fire, poison, or water upon the accused, the result being regarded as a divine or preternatural judgement.

order /ˈɔːdə/ *n.* **1.** an authoritative direction, injunction, command, or mandate. **2.** Also, **court order.** *Law* a direction given by a court, judge, or minister of the crown. **3.** *Mil.* a command or notice issued by a military commander to subordinate troops. **4.** the disposition of things following one after another, as in space, time, etc.; succession or sequence. **5.** a condition in which everything is in its proper place with reference to other things and to its purpose; methodical or harmonious arrangement. **6.** *Mil.* different dress, equipment, etc., for some special purpose or occasion: *full marching order.* **7.** proper or satisfactory condition: *my watch is out of order.* **8.** state or condition generally: *affairs are in good order.* **9.** *Gram.* **a.** the arrangement of the elements of a construction in a particular sequence, as the placing of *John* before and of *George* after the verb *saw* in the sentence *John saw George.* **b.** the feature of construction resulting from such an arrangement, as in the sentences *John saw George* and *George saw John* which differ only in order. **10.** any class, kind, or sort, as of persons or things, distinguished from others by nature or character: *talents of a high order.* **11.** the usual major subdivision of a class or subclass, commonly comprising a plurality of families, as the Hymenoptera (ants, bees, etc.). **12.** a rank, grade, or class of persons in the community. **13.** a body of persons of the same profession, occupation, or pursuits: *the clerical order.* **14.** a body or society of persons living by common consent under the same religious, moral, or social regulations. **15.** a body of people who all hold a specific honour (def. 7) conferred on them by a sovereign or government. **16.** any of the degrees or grades of the clerical office (the number of which varies in different Churches, the Roman Catholic Church, for example, having the **major orders** of bishop, priest, deacon, formerly also subdeacon, and the **minor orders**

of acolyte and lector, formerly also exorcist and ostiary, while the Anglican Church recognises only the three grades of bishop, priest, and deacon). **17.** any of the nine grades of angels in medieval angelology. See **angel** (def. 1). **18.** a monastic society or fraternity: *the Franciscan order.* **19.** (*usu. pl.*) the rank or status of an ordained Christian minister. **20.** (*usu. pl.*) the rite or sacrament of ordination. **21.** a modern organisation or society more or less resembling the knightly orders: *fraternal orders.* **22.** conformity to law or established authority; absence of revolt, disturbance, turbulence, unruliness, etc. **23.** customary mode of procedure, or established usage. **24.** the customary or prescribed mode of proceeding in debates or the like, or in the conduct of deliberative or legislative bodies, public meetings, etc. **25.** conformity to this. **26.** the natural, moral, or spiritual constitution of the world; the prevailing course of things; the established system or regime: *the old order changeth.* **27.** a direction or commission to make, provide or furnish something: *shoes made to order.* **28.** a quantity of goods purchased. **29.** a written direction to pay money or deliver goods. **30.** *Archit.* **a.** a series of columns with their entablature arranged in given proportions. **b.** any one of the typical variations of such an arrangement distinguished by proportion, capital types, etc., including the Doric, Ionic, Corinthian of the classical Greeks, adapted by the Romans, the Tuscan created by the Romans, and the Composite dating from the Renaissance. **31.** *Maths* **a.** degree, as in algebra. **b.** (of a derivative) the number of times a function has been differentiated. **c.** (of a differential equation) the order of the highest derivative in the equation. −*v.t.* **32.** to give an order, direction, or command to. **33.** to direct or command to go or come (as specified): *to order a person out of one's house.* **34.** to give an order for. **35.** to prescribe: *a doctor orders a medicine for a patient.* **36.** to direct to be made, supplied, or furnished: *we ordered two steaks.* **37.** to regulate, conduct, or manage. **38.** to arrange methodically or suitably. **39.** to ordain, as God or fate does. −*v.i.* **40.** to issue orders: *to order rather than obey.* **41.** to order food, etc. −*phr.* **42. a tall order,** *Colloq.* a difficult task or requirement. **43. call to order,** to establish or re-establish order at (a meeting). **44. in order, a.** in a proper state; correctly arranged; in a state of readiness; functioning correctly. **b.** appropriate; suitable. **c.** correct according to parliamentary procedure. **45. in order that,** to the end that. **46. in order to,** as a means to. **47. in short order,** speedily; promptly. **48. keep order,** (in a classroom, military group, etc.) to maintain discipline. **49. of the order of,** about; approximately. **50. on order,** ordered but not yet received. **51. order about,** to keep giving orders to; act in a domineering fashion towards. **52. out of order, a.** not functioning properly; broken. **b.** not in accordance with the recognised rules of a meeting, organisation, etc. **c.** socially unacceptable; inappropriate. **53. the lower orders,** those whose rank or status in society is not high. −**orderer**, *n.*

orderly /ˈɔːdəli/ *adj.* **1.** arranged in an approved order, or tidy manner. **2.** systematic; disciplined: *an orderly mind.* **3.** willing to obey rules or laws: *an orderly citizen.* −*n.* (*pl.* **-lies**) **4.** someone, especially a soldier or hospital employee, who performs general duties. −**orderliness**, *n.*

ordinal /ˈɔːdənəl/ *adj.* **1.** relating to an order, as of animals or plants. −*n.* **2.** an ordinal number or numeral.

ordinal number *n.* any of the numbers *first, second, third,* etc., which indicate the order in which things occur in a given set, and not the total number of things in the set (the latter is indicated by the cardinal numbers, *one, two, three,* etc.)

ordinance /'ɔdənəns/ *n.* **1.** an authoritative rule or law; a decree or command. **2.** a public injunction or regulation. **3.** *Eccles.* **a.** an established rite or ceremony. **b.** a sacrament. **c.** the communion.

ordinary /'ɔdənəri, 'ɔdənri/, *Orig. US* /-nɛri/ *adj.* **1.** such as is commonly met with; of the usual kind. **2.** below the average level of quality; somewhat inferior. **3.** customary; normal: *for all ordinary purposes.* **4.** *Colloq.* not very good; of a low standard: *after heavy rain the track was pretty ordinary.* –*n.* (*pl.* **-ries**) **5.** the ordinary condition, degree, run, or the like: *out of the ordinary.* **6.** something regular, customary, or usual. –*phr.* **7. out of the ordinary,** the ordinary condition, degree, run, or the like. –**ordinarily,** *adv.* –**ordinariness,** *n.*

ordinary share *n. Finance* one of the series of shares into which the capital of a company is divided, which rank for dividends after preference shares and before deferred shares, if any such are in issue; common share.

ordination /ɔdə'neɪʃən/ *n.* **1.** *Eccles.* the act or ceremony of ordaining. **2.** the fact of being ordained. **3.** a decreeing. **4.** the act of arranging. **5.** the resulting state.

ordnance /'ɔdnəns/ *n.* **1.** cannon or artillery. **2.** military weapons of all kinds with their equipment, ammunition, etc.

ordure /'ɔdʒʊə/ *n.* filth; dung; excrement.

ore /ɔ/ *n.* **1.** a metal-bearing mineral or rock, or a native metal, especially when valuable enough to be mined. **2.** a mineral or natural product serving as a source of some nonmetallic substance, as sulphur.

oregano /ɒrə'ganoʊ/ *n.* a plant of the mint family of the genus *Origanum*, in particular *O. vulgare*, having a spicy flavour and used in cookery.

organ /'ɔgən/ *n.* **1.** a musical instrument (**pipe organ**) consisting of one or more sets of pipes sounded by means of compressed air, played by means of keys arranged in one or more keyboards; in its full modern development, the largest and most complicated of musical instruments. **2.** a musical instrument (**electronic organ** or **electric organ**) resembling a pipe organ but sounded electrically. **3.** a reed organ or harmonium. **4.** a barrel organ or hand organ. **5.** (in an animal or a plant) a part or member, as the heart, having some specific function. **6.** an instrument or means, as of performance. **7.** a means or medium of communicating thoughts, opinions, etc., as a newspaper serving as the mouthpiece of a political party.

organdie /'ɔgəndi/ *n.* (*pl.* **-dies**) a fine, thin stiff cotton fabric usually having a durable crisp finish, and either white, dyed, or printed; used for dresses, curtains, etc. Also, *US,* **organdy.**

organelle /ɔgə'nɛl/ *n. Biol.* a structure within a cell or single-celled organism, having a specialised function analogous to that of an organ in a more complex organism.

organic /ɔ'gænɪk/ *adj.* **1.** *Chem.* relating to a class of compounds consisting of all compounds of carbon except for its oxides, sulphides, and metal carbonates. Compare **inorganic** (def. 3). **2.** typical of, relating to or coming from living organisms: *organic remains found in rocks; organic fertiliser.* **3.** relating to the organ(s) of an animal or plant. **4.** marked by the systematic arrangement of parts; organised. **5.** of or relating to the constitution or structure of a thing. **6.** of or relating to farming and the produce of such farming which does not use chemical fertilisers or pesticides. –**organically,** *adv.*

organisation /ɔgənaɪ'zeɪʃən/ *n.* **1.** the act or process of organising. **2.** a body of persons organised for some end. **3.** the administrative personnel or apparatus of a business. Also, **organization.** –**organisational,** *adj.*

organise /'ɔgənaɪz/ *v.t.* **1.** to form into a group especially for united action: *to organise a party; to organise a club.* **2.** to bring together in an orderly way: *to organise facts.* **3.** to arrange: *I have organised a holiday for us.* **4.** to build a trade union among: *to organise workers.* –*v.i.* **5.** to combine in an organised company, party, etc.: *workers organised into trade unions in the 19th century.* Also, **organize.** –**organisable,** *adj.* –**organiser,** *n.*

organism /'ɔgənɪzəm/ *n.* **1.** an individual composed of mutually dependent parts constituted for subserving vital processes. **2.** any form of animal or plant life: *microscopic organisms.* **3.** any organised body or system analogous to a living being. **4.** *Philos.* any structure the parts of which function not only in terms of one another, but also in terms of the whole.

organist /'ɔgənəst/ *n.* someone who plays an organ.

organo- a word element meaning 'organ' or 'organic'.

organophosphate /ɔgənoʊ'fɒsfeɪt/ *n.* a pesticide that contains phosphorus, generally poisonous to humans and animals.

organza /ɔ'gænzə/ *n.* a fabric made from a mixture of silk or nylon with cotton, similar to organdie but less fine.

orgasm /'ɔgæzəm/ *n.* **1.** *Physiol.* a complex series of responses of the genital organs and skin at the culmination of a sexual act. **2.** immoderate excitement. –*v.i.* **3.** to experience an orgasm. –**orgasmic, orgastic** /ɔ'gæstɪk/, *adj.*

orgy /'ɔdʒi/ *n.* (*pl.* **-gies**) **1.** a gathering where people engage in unbridled sexual activity. **2.** wild, drunken, or licentious festivities or revelry. **3.** any proceedings marked by unbridled indulgence of passions: *an orgy of killing.* –**orgiastic** /ɔdʒi'æstɪk/, *adj.*

orient /'ɔriənt, 'ɒ-/ for defs 1 and 2, /'ɔriɛnt, 'ɒ-/ for defs 3 and 4 –*n.* **1.** the **Orient,** the East; the countries to the east (and south-east) of the Mediterranean especially the countries of eastern Asia. –*adj.* **2.** *Poetic* eastern or oriental. –*v.t.* **3.** → **orientate.** –*v.i.* **4.** → **orientate.**

oriental /ɔri'ɛntl, ɒri-/ *adj.* **1.** (*sometimes upper case*) of, relating to, or characteristic of the Orient or East. –*n.* **2.** (*usu. upper case*) (*dated*) (*likely to give offence*) a native or inhabitant of the Orient, especially one belonging to an indigenous race.

orientate /'ɔriənteɪt, 'ɒri-/ *v.t.* **1.** to place so as to face the east, especially to build (a church) with the chief altar to the east and the chief entrance to the west. **2.** to place in any definite position with reference to the points of the compass or other points: *to orientate a building north and south.* **3.** to adjust with relation to, or bring into due relation to, surroundings, circumstances, facts, etc.: *to orientate one's ideas to new conditions.* **4.** *Surveying* to turn a map or plane table sheet so that the north direction on the map is parallel to the north direction on the ground. –*v.i.* **5.** to turn towards the east or in specified direction. –**orientation,** *n.*

orienteering /ɔriən'tɪərɪŋ/ *n.* a sport in which competitors race on foot, skis, bicycle, etc., over a course consisting of a number of checkpoints which must be located with the aid of maps, compasses, etc.

orifice /'ɒrəfəs/ *n.* a mouth or aperture, as of a tube or pipe; a mouth-like opening or hole; a vent.

origami /ɒrə'gami/ *n.* **1.** the art of folding paper into shapes of flowers, birds, etc. **2.** an object made this way.

origin /'ɒrədʒən/ *n.* **1.** a starting point, source or beginning: *the origin of a stream; the origin of a plan.* **2.** birth; parentage; extraction: *Scottish origin.* **3.** *Maths* the point of intersection of two or more axes in a system of Cartesian or polar coordinates; the point from which a measurement is taken.

original /ə'rɪdʒənəl/ *adj.* **1.** first; earliest: *the original binding of the book is very old.* **2.** new; fresh; novel: *an* *original way of advertising.* **3.** doing or done by oneself independently; not derived from another: *original thinking*; *original research.* **4.** being that from which a copy, translation, etc., is made: *the original letter is in the National Library.* *–n.* **5.** the primary form or type. **6.** an original work, writing, etc., as opposed to a copy. **7.** something represented by a picture, description, etc. **8.** someone who thinks or acts for himself or herself. **9.** someone who behaves in unusual or odd ways; eccentric. –**originally,** *adv.* –**originality** /ərɪdʒə'næləti/, *n.*

originate /ə'rɪdʒəneɪt/ *v.i.* **1.** to take its origin or rise; arise; spring. *–v.t.* **2.** to give origin or rise to; initiate; invent. –**origination** /ərɪdʒə'neɪʃən/, *n.* –**originator,** *n.*

oriole /'ɔːrioʊl/ *n.* any bird of the family Oriolidae, mostly bright yellow with black on the head, wings, and tail.

orlon /'ɔːlɒn/ *n.* (*from trademark*) a synthetic acrylic textile fibre of light weight and good crease resistance.

ornament *n.* /'ɔːnəmənt/ **1.** something added for beauty rather than to be useful: *architectural ornaments.* **2.** an object meant to be beautiful rather than useful: *china ornaments.* **3.** a person who adds importance, honour, etc., to surroundings, society, etc.: *an ornament to his profession.* **4.** outward show: *the white chairs outside their house are just for ornament.* **5.** *Music* a note or group of notes not part of the melody, as a trill. *–v.t.* /'ɔːnəmɛnt/ **6.** to furnish with ornaments. **7.** to be an ornament to. –**ornamentation,** *n.*

ornate /ɔː'neɪt/ *adj.* elaborately adorned; sumptuously or showily splendid or fine. –**ornately,** *adv.* –**ornateness,** *n.*

ornitho- a word element meaning 'bird'. Also, **ornith-.**

ornithology /ɔːnə'θɒlədʒi/ *n.* the branch of zoology that deals with birds. –**ornithological** /ɔːnəθə'lɒdʒɪkəl/, *adj.* –**ornithologist,** *n.*

ornithorhynchus /ɔːnəθə'rɪŋkəs/ *n.* → **platypus.**

oro- a word element meaning 'mountain', as in *orography.*

orotund /'ɒroʊtʌnd/ *adj.* **1.** (of the voice or utterance) characterised by strength, fullness, richness, and clearness. **2.** (of a style of utterance) pompous or bombastic. –**orotundity,** *n.*

orphan /'ɔːfən/ *n.* **1. a.** a person, usually a child, bereaved by death of both parents. **b.** (in less common use) a person, usually a child, bereaved by death of one parent. *–adj.* **2.** of or for orphans: *an orphan institution.* **3.** bereaved of parents. *–v.t.* **4.** to bereave of parents or a parent. –**orphanhood,** *n.*

orphanage /'ɔːfənɪdʒ/ *n.* **1.** an institution for orphans. **2.** the state of being an orphan.

ortho- **1.** a word element meaning 'straight', 'upright', 'right', 'correct', used in combination. **2.** *Chem.* **a.** a prefix indicating that acid of a series which contains most water. Compare **meta-, pyro-.** **b.** a prefix applied to a salt of one of these acids: if the acid ends in *-ic*, the corresponding salt ends in *-ate*, as *orthoboric acid* (H_3BO_3) and *potassium orthoborate* (K_3BO_3); if the acid ends in *-ous*, the corresponding salt ends in *-ite*, as *orthoantimonous acid* (H_3SbO_3) and *potassium orthoantimonite* (K_3SbO_3). **c.** a prefix indicating the presence of a benzene ring with two substituents in the 1, 2 positions.

orthoclase /'ɔːθoʊkleɪs, 'ɔːθəkleɪz/ *n.* a very common mineral of the feldspar group, potassium aluminium silicate, $KAlSi_3O_8$, occurring as an important constituent in many igneous rocks; used in the manufacture of porcelain.

orthodontics /ɔːθə'dɒntɪks/ *n.* the branch of dentistry that is concerned with the correction of irregularities of the teeth or jaw. Also, **orthodontia.** –**orthodontic,** *adj.* –**orthodontist,** *n.*

orthodox /'ɔːθədɒks/ *adj.* **1.** sound or correct in opinion or doctrine, especially theological or religious doctrine.

2. (*upper case*) of, relating to, or designating the Eastern Church. **3.** (*upper case*) of, relating to, or designating Orthodox Jews or Orthodox Judaism. **4.** approved; conventional. –**orthodoxy,** *n.* –**orthodoxly,** *adv.*

Orthodox Church *n.* the Christian church of the countries which formerly comprised the Eastern Roman Empire, and of countries evangelised from it, as Russia; the group in communion or doctrinal agreement with the Greek patriarchal see of Constantinople.

orthogonal /ɔː'ɒɡənəl/ *adj.* *Maths* relating to or involving right angles or perpendicular lines: *an orthogonal projection.*

orthography /ɔː'θɒɡrəfi/ *n.* (*pl.* **-phies**) **1.** the art of writing words with the proper letters, according to accepted usage; correct spelling. **2.** the branch of grammar that deals with letters and spelling. **3.** manner of spelling. –**orthographer, orthographist,** *n.* –**orthographic** /ɔːθə'ɡræfɪk/, *adj.*

orthopaedics /ɔːθə'pidɪks/ *n.* the correction or cure of deformities and diseases of the spine, bones, joints, muscles, or other parts of the skeletal system. Also, **orthopedics, orthopaedy, orthopedy.** –**orthopaedic,** *adj.* –**orthopaedist,** *n.*

orthoptics /ɔː'θɒptɪks/ *n.* the study and treatment of abnormality of eye muscle function and the ability to use the eyes together. –**orthoptic,** *adj.* –**orthoptist,** *n.*

orthosis /ɔː'θoʊsəs/ *n.* (*pl.* **orthoses** /ɔː'θoʊsiz/) a device applied to the body to modify position or motion, as a supporting collar, plaster cast, etc.

orthotic /ɔː'θɒtɪk/ *adj.* **1.** of or relating to an orthosis. *–n.* **2.** an orthotic device, especially one for the foot.

-ory¹ a suffix of adjectives meaning 'having the function or effect of', as in *compulsory, contributory, declaratory, illusory.*

-ory² a suffix of nouns denoting especially a place or an instrument or thing for some purpose, as in *directory, dormitory, purgatory.*

os /ɒs/ *n.* (*pl.* **ossa** /'ɒsə/) *Anat.* a bone.

oscillate /'ɒsəleɪt/ *v.i.* **1.** to swing or move to and fro, as a pendulum does; vibrate. **2.** to fluctuate between states, opinions, purposes, etc. **3.** to have, produce, or generate oscillations. –**oscillatory,** *adj.*

oscillation /ɒsə'leɪʃən/ *n.* **1.** the act or fact of oscillating. **2.** a single swing, or movement in one direction, of an oscillating body, etc. **3.** fluctuation between states, opinions, etc. **4.** *Physics* a repetitive to and fro motion of an object; a repetitive fluctuation in amplitude of an electrical signal or electric or magnetic field.

osculate /'ɒskjəleɪt/ *v.t.* **1.** to kiss (someone). **2.** to bring or come into close contact or union. –**osculation** /ɒskjə'leɪʃn/, *n.* –**osculatory** /'ɒskjələtri, -leɪtəri/, *adj.*

-ose¹ an adjective suffix meaning 'full of', 'abounding in', 'given to', 'like', as in *frondose, globose, jocose, otiose, verbose.*

-ose² a noun termination used to form chemical terms, especially names of sugars and other carbohydrates, as *amylose, fructose, hexose, lactose,* and (rarely) of protein derivatives, as *proteose.*

osier /'oʊʒə/ *n.* **1.** any of various willows, as *Salix viminalis* (the common **basket osier**) and *Salix purpurea* (**red osier**), with tough flexible twigs or branches which are used for wickerwork. **2.** a twig from such a willow.

-osis (*pl.* **-oses**) a noun suffix denoting action, process, state, condition, etc., as in *metamorphosis,* and in many pathological terms, as *tuberculosis.*

-osity a noun suffix equivalent to **-ose¹** (or **-ous**) plus **-ity.**

osmium /'ɒzmiəm/ *n.* a hard, heavy, metallic element used for electric-light filaments, etc., having the greatest density of any known material. *Symbol:* Os; *relative* *atomic mass*: 190.2; *atomic number*: 76; *density*: 22.48 at 20°C.

osmosis /ɒzˈmoʊsəs/ *n.* **1.** *Physics* the tendency of a fluid to pass through a semipermeable membrane into a solution where its concentration is lower, thus equalising the conditions on either side of the membrane. **2.** *Biol.* the diffusion of fluids through membranes or porous partitions. **3.** a gradual interchange or spreading of ideas, etc. **–osmotic** /ɒzˈmɒtɪk/, *adj.* **–osmotically** /ɒzˈmɒtɪkli/, *adv.*

osprey /ˈɒspri, ˈɒspreɪ/ *n.* (*pl.* **-reys**) **1.** a large hawk, *Pandion haliaetus*, which feeds on fish. **2.** (formerly) a kind of feather used to trim hats.

ossify /ˈɒsəfaɪ/ *verb* (**-fied, -fying**) *–v.t.* **1.** to convert into, or harden like, bone. **2.** to render (attitudes, opinions, etc.) rigid or inflexible. *–v.i.* **3.** to become bone or hard like bone. **4.** to become rigid or inflexible in attitudes, opinions, etc.

ostensible /ɒsˈtɛnsəbəl/ *adj.* given out or outwardly appearing as such; professed; pretended. **–ostensibly,** *adv.*

ostentation /ɒstɛnˈteɪʃən/ *n.* pretentious show; display intended to impress others. Also, **ostentatiousness.** **–ostentatious,** *adj.*

osteo- a word element meaning 'bone'. Also, (*before vowels*), **oste-**.

osteoarthritis /ˌɒstioʊɑˈθraɪtəs/ *n.* *Pathol.* a degenerative type of chronic arthritis. *Abbrev.:* OA

osteopathy /ɒstiˈɒpəθi/ *n.* *Med.* a theory of disease resting upon the supposition that the body is a mechanical organism which can better resist disease if its structure is correctly aligned, leading therefore to medical treatment involving some kind of physical manipulation. **–osteopath** /ˈɒstioʊˌpæθ/, *n.* **–osteopathic** /ˌɒstioʊˈpæθɪk/, *adj.*

osteoporosis /ˌɒstioʊpəˈroʊsəs/ *n.* *Pathol.* a condition in which bones become thin and brittle, common in old people, especially women past the menopause.

ostler /ˈɒslə/ *n.* (formerly) someone who takes care of horses, especially at an inn.

ostracise /ˈɒstrəsaɪz/ *v.t.* **1.** to banish (someone) from their native country; expatriate. **2.** to exclude by general consent from society, privileges, etc. Also, **ostracize.** **–ostracism** /ˈɒstrəsɪzəm/, *n.* **–ostracisable,** *adj.* **–ostraciser,** *n.*

ostrich /ˈɒstrɪtʃ/ *n.* a large two-toed, swift-footed, flightless bird, *Struthio camelus*, the largest of existing birds, native to Africa and formerly Arabia, now extensively reared for the plumage.

ot- variant of **oto-**, before vowels.

other /ˈʌðə/ *adj.* **1.** additional or further: *he and one other person.* **2.** different or distinct from the one or ones mentioned or implied: *in some other city.* **3.** being the remaining one of two or more: *the other hand.* **4.** (with plural nouns) being the remaining ones of a number: *the other men.* **5.** unlike most of the same type; unusual: *she was quite other.* *–pron.* **6.** the other one: *each praises the other.* **7.** another person or thing. **8.** some person or thing else: *some day or other.* *–phr.* **9. every other,** every alternate: *a meeting every other week.* **10. one's other half,** *Colloq.* one's spouse. **11. other than,** different from in nature or kind: *I would not have him other than he is.* **12. the other day** (**night,** etc.), in recent days (nights, etc.). **13. the other half,** either of the two classes into which society is divided, the rich or the poor (but especially the poor): *to see how the other half lives.* **14. the other side,** *Spiritualism* the place where the spirits of dead people reside. **–otherness,** *n.* **–otherly,** *adv.*

otherwise /ˈʌðəwaɪz/ *adv.* **1.** under other circumstances. **2.** in another manner; differently. **3.** in other respects: *an otherwise happy life.* *–adj.* **4.** other or different; of another nature or kind. *–conj.* **5.** or else: *you'd better do it, otherwise I'll tell.*

otic /ˈoʊtɪk, ˈɒtɪk/ *adj.* of or relating to the ear; auricular.

-otic an adjectival form for nouns ending in *-osis*, as *hypnotic* from *hypnosis*, *neurotic* from *neurosis*.

oto- a word element meaning 'ear'.

otter /ˈɒtə/ *n.* any of the various aquatic, furred, carnivorous, musteline mammals of the genus *Lutra*, and allied genera, with webbed feet adapted for swimming, and a long tail slightly flattened horizontally to act as a rudder, as *L. vulgaris*, of Europe, and *L. canadensis*, of the US and Canada, and the sea-otter.

ottoman /ˈɒtəmən/ *n.* (*pl.* **-mans**) **1.** a low cushioned seat like a sofa without back or arms. **2.** a low chest with a padded top. **3.** a cushioned footstool. **4.** a corded silk or rayon fabric with large cotton cord for filling.

ouch /aʊtʃ/ *interj.* an exclamation expressing sudden pain.

ought¹ /ɔt/ *v.i.* **1.** to be bound in duty or moral obligation: *every citizen ought to help.* **2.** to be required on any ground, as of justice, propriety, expediency, fitness, or the like: *he ought to be punished; you ought to add more milk.* **3.** to be likely: *this glue ought to hold it.*

ought² /ɔt/ *n.* → **aught.**

ouija /ˈwidʒə, -dʒi/ *n.* (*from trademark*) a device consisting of a small board on legs, which rests on a larger board marked with words, letters of the alphabet, etc., used during seances. Also, **ouija board.**

ounce¹ /aʊns/ *n.* **1.** a unit of mass in the imperial system, equal to $\frac{1}{16}$ lb avoirdupois or $28.349\,523\,125 \times 10^{-3}$ kg. **2. troy ounce** or **apothecaries ounce,** a unit of mass in the imperial system equal to 480 grains, or $31.103\,476\,8 \times 10^{-3}$ kg. **3.** → **fluid ounce. 4.** a small quantity or portion.

ounce² /aʊns/ *n.* a long-haired alpine cat, *Uncia uncia*, inhabiting the mountain ranges of India and South-East Asia, having a light grey coat with spots and ocellations; snow leopard.

our /ˈaʊə/ *adj.* the possessive form of **we**: *we took our time.* Compare **ours.**

-our a suffix of nouns denoting state or condition, a quality or property, etc., as in *ardour, colour, honour, labour.* Also, **-or.**

ours /ˈaʊəz/ *pron.* (*possessive*) the possessive form of **we**, used predicatively or absolutely: *those books are ours; ours was the first attempt; a friend of ours.*

ourself /aʊəˈsɛlf/ *pron.* a form corresponding to *ourselves*, used of a single person, especially (like *we* for *I*) in the regal or formal style.

ourselves /aʊəˈsɛlvz/ *pron.* **1.** the reflexive form of **we**: *we hurt ourselves.* **2.** an emphatic form of *us* or *we* used: **a.** as object: *we used it for ourselves.* **b.** in apposition to a subject or object: *we did it ourselves.*

-ous 1. an adjective suffix meaning 'full of', 'abounding in', 'given to', 'characterised by', 'having', 'of the nature of', 'like', etc., as in *glorious, joyous, mucous, nervous, sonorous, wondrous.* **2.** *Chem.* a suffix used to imply the lower of two possible valencies compared to the corresponding suffix *-ic*, as *stannous chloride,* $SnCl_2$, and *stannic chloride,* $SnCl_4$. Also, **-eous, -ious.**

oust /aʊst/ *v.t.* **1.** to expel from a place or position occupied. **2.** *Law* to eject; dispossess.

out /aʊt/ *adv.* **1.** forth from, away from, or not in a place, position, state, etc.: *out of order.* **2.** away from one's home, office, etc. **3.** into the open: *to go out for a walk.* **4.** to exhaustion, extinction, or conclusion; to the end; so as to finish or exhaust or be exhausted; so as to bring to naught or render useless: *to pump out a well.* **5.** to or at an end or conclusion: *to fight it out.* **6.** no longer or not burning or furnishing light; extinguished: *the lamp went out.* **7.** not in vogue or fashion: *that style has gone out.* **8.** released from jail. **9.** into or in society: *a young woman who came out last season.* **10.** not in present or personal possession or use; let for hire, or placed at interest: *let out for a year.* **11.** on strike: *the miners are coming out.* **12.** so as to project or extend: *to stretch out.* **13.** into or in existence, activity, or outward manifestation: *fever broke out.* **14.** from a state of composure, satisfaction, or harmony: *to feel put out.* **15.** in or into a state of confusion, vexation, dispute, variance, or unfriendliness: *to fall out about trifles.* **16.** from a number, stock, or store: *to pick out.* **17.** aloud or loudly: *to call out.* **18.** with completeness or effectiveness: *to fit out.* **19.** thoroughly; completely; entirely. **20.** so as to make illegible or indecipherable: *to paint out; ink out.* **21.** away from a main centre, especially from Britain with regard to Australia or New Zealand: *they had only been out for two weeks.* –*adj.* **22.** away from one's home, workplace, etc.: *I went to visit her but she was out.* **23.** torn or worn into holes, as clothing: *his trousers were out at the knees.* **24.** incorrect or inaccurate: *to be out in one's calculations.* **25.** at a pecuniary loss: *to be out by ten dollars.* **26.** having none left; lacking: *I went to the shops for milk but they were out.* **27.** unconscious; senseless: *the boxer was out for about five minutes.* **28.** finished; ended: *before the month is out.* **29.** *Tennis, etc.* beyond the boundary lines: *the umpire declared the ball out.* **30.** *Cricket, etc.* (of a person batting) removed from play as by being bowled, leg before wicket, stumped, caught, or run out, etc. **31.** in public notice or knowledge: *the news is out.* **32.** in bloom: *the wattle is out.* **33.** (of a homosexual) known publicly to be such. **34.** external; exterior; outer. **35.** outlying. –*prep.* **36.** forth from: *throw it out the window.* –*interj.* **37.** an exclamation of dismissal. –*n.* **38.** a means of escaping from a place, punishment, retribution, responsibility, etc. –*v.i.* **39.** to become known: *murder will out.* –*v.t.* **40.** to put out; expel; discharge. **41.** to expose someone, especially a public figure, as homosexual. –*phr.* **42. be out to,** to intend to: *he's out to ruin me.* **43. get out of here,** *Colloq.* an expression of disbelief. **44. go all out,** to extend oneself; pursue an interest, goal, etc., with the utmost energy. **45. ins and outs,** all the detail related to something, in particular the workings of a machine or device. **46. out and away,** in a pre-eminent degree; by far. **47. be out of here,** *Colloq.* to be leaving: *I'm out of here, see you tomorrow.* **48. out here, a.** in Australia or New Zealand. **b.** in a town or place thought of as being remote from the main centre. **49. out of, a.** from (a source, ground or cause, material, etc.): *made out of scraps.* **b.** so as to deprive or be deprived: *to cheat someone out of money.* **c.** having used the last of; lacking: *to be out of sugar.* **50. out of it,** *Colloq.* **a.** incapacitated as a result of taking drugs or alcohol. **b.** in a dreamy or vague state of mind, as if under the influence of drugs or alcohol. **c.** neglected; rejected: *he's feeling a bit out of it.* **51. out there, a.** in a town or place thought of as being remote from both a main centre and the speaker: *how can you stand it out there?* **b.** *Colloq.* radical or innovative in style: *her designs are really out there.* **52. out to it,** *Aust., NZ Colloq.* **a.** unconscious. **b.** asleep. **53. out west,** in or to the remote regions west of the eastern seaboard of Australia; outback. **54. out with, a.** to make known; tell; utter: *when will he out with the truth?* **b.** to take out; produce from hiding.

out- prefixal use of **out**, *adverb, preposition,* or *adjective,* occurring in various senses in compounds, as in *outcast, outcome, outside,* and serving also to form many transitive verbs denoting a going beyond, surpassing, or outdoing in the particular action indicated, as in *outbid, outdo, outgeneral, outlast, outstay, outrate,* and many other words in which the meaning is readily perceived, the more important of these being entered below.

out-and-out *adj.* thoroughgoing; thorough; complete; unqualified.

outback /'aʊtbæk/ *n.* **1.** (*sometimes upper case*) remote, sparsely inhabited back country, especially in Australia. –*adj.* **2.** of or relating to the back country. –*adv.* **3.** in or to the back country: *to live outback.*

outbreak /'aʊtbreɪk/ *n.* **1.** a breaking out; an outburst. **2.** a sudden and active manifestation. **3.** a public disturbance; a riot; an insurrection.

outbuilding /'aʊtbɪldɪŋ/ *n.* a detached building subordinate to a main building.

outburst /'aʊtbɜst/ *n.* **1.** a bursting forth. **2.** a sudden and violent outpouring: *an outburst of tears.*

outcast /'aʊtkast/ *n.* **1.** someone who is cast out, as from home or society. **2.** homeless wanderer. –*adj.* **3.** cast out, as from one's home or society. **4.** relating to or characteristic of an outcast: *outcast misery.* **5.** rejected or discarded.

outclass /aʊt'klas/ *v.t.* to surpass in class or quality; be distinctly ahead of (a competitor, etc.).

outcome /'aʊtkʌm/ *n.* that which results from something; the consequence or issue.

outcrop *n.* /'aʊtkrɒp/ **1.** a cropping out, as of a stratum or vein at the surface of the earth. **2.** the emerging part. **3.** something that occurs unexpectedly, suddenly, or violently: *an outcrop of labour unrest.* –*v.i.* /aʊt'krɒp/ (**-cropped, -cropping**) **4.** to crop out, as strata.

outcry /'aʊtkraɪ/ *n.* (*pl.* **-cries**) **1.** a crying out. **2.** a cry of distress, indignation, or the like. **3.** loud clamour. **4.** widespread protest or indignation.

outdated /'aʊtdeɪtəd/ *adj.* made out of date by the passage of time; old-fashioned.

outdistance /aʊt'dɪstəns/ *v.t.* (**-tanced, -tancing**) to distance completely; leave far behind; outstrip.

outdo /aʊt'du/ *v.t.* (**-did, -done, -doing**) to surpass in doing or performance; surpass.

outdoor /'aʊtdɔ/ *adj.* occurring or used out of doors.

outdoors /aʊt'dɔz/ *adv.* **1.** out of doors; in the open air. –*n.* **2. the outdoors,** the world outside buildings; the open air. –*phr.* **3. the great outdoors,** the natural environment, especially wilderness areas. –**outdoorsy,** *adj.*

outdoorsy /aʊt'dɔzi/ *adj.* **1.** of or relating to the outdoors: *an outdoorsy lifestyle.* **2.** fond of outdoor activities such as sport, camping, bushwalking, etc.: *an outdoorsy person.*

outer /'aʊtə/ *adj.* **1.** farther out; external; of or relating to the outside. –*n.* **2.** that part of a sportsground which is without shelter. **3.** *Archery, etc.* **a.** the outermost ring or part of a target. **b.** a shot which strikes this part. **c.** the score value of this part. –*phr.* **4. on the outer,** *Aust. Colloq.* excluded from the group; mildly ostracised.

outfield /'aʊtfild/ *n.* **1.** *Cricket* the part of the field farthest from the person batting. **2.** the outlying land of a farm, especially beyond the enclosed land. **3.** an outlying region.

outfit /'aʊtfɪt/ *n.* **1.** the equipment for some activity: *a skier's outfit; an explorer's outfit.* **2.** a set of articles for any purpose: *a model aircraft outfit.* **3.** a set of clothes, especially women's, worn together. **4. a.** a group of people working together: *military outfit.* **b.** *Colloq.* a shop or business with its equipment. –*v.t.* (**-fitted, -fitting**) **5.** to provide with an outfit; fit out; equip. –**outfitter,** *n.*

outflank /aʊt'flæŋk/ *v.t.* **1.** to go or extend beyond the flank of (an opposing army, etc.); outmanoeuvre by a flanking movement. **2.** to get the better of (a rival, opponent, etc.).

outflow /'aʊtfloʊ/ *n.* **1.** the act of flowing out. **2.** something that flows out. **3.** any outward movement. Also, **outflowing.**

outfox /aʊt'fɒks/ *v.t.* to outmanoeuvre.

outgoing /ˈaʊtɡoʊɪŋ/ *adj.* **1.** going out; departing: *outgoing trains*. **2.** interested in and responsive to others: *an outgoing personality*. *–n.* **3.** (*usu. pl.*) an amount of money expended; outlay; expenses. **4.** a going out. **5.** something that goes out; an effluence.

outgrow /aʊtˈɡroʊ/ *verb* (**-grew, -grown, -growing**) *–v.t.* **1.** to grow too large for. **2.** to leave behind or lose in the changes incident to development or the passage of time: *to outgrow a bad reputation*. **3.** to surpass in growing. *–v.i.* **4.** to grow out; protrude.

outgrowth /ˈaʊtɡroʊθ/ *n.* **1.** a natural development, product, or result. **2.** an additional, supplementary result. **3.** a growing out or forth. **4.** something that grows out; an offshoot; an excrescence.

outhouse /ˈaʊthaʊs/ *n.* **1.** an outside toilet. **2.** an outbuilding.

outing /ˈaʊtɪŋ/ *n.* **1.** an excursion or pleasure trip. **2.** the part of the sea out from the shore. **3.** an appearance in the public arena, as of a sportsperson taking part in a competition, an actor in a film, etc.

outlandish /aʊtˈlændɪʃ/ *adj.* **1.** freakishly or grotesquely strange or odd, as appearance, dress, objects, ideas, practices, etc. **2.** looking foreign or strange. **3.** out-of-the-way, as places. **–outlandishly**, *adv.* **–outlandishness**, *n.*

outlast /aʊtˈlast/ *v.t.* to last longer than.

outlaw /ˈaʊtlɔ/ *n.* **1.** a criminal, especially formerly, one who is cut off from the protection of the law. **2.** a wild or untameable animal. *–v.t.* **3.** to cut off from the protection of the law. **4.** to forbid with the strong agreement of society.

outlay *n.* /ˈaʊtleɪ/ **1.** an expending; an expenditure, as of money. **2.** an amount expended. *–v.t.* /aʊtˈleɪ/ (**-laid, -laying**) **3.** to expend, as money.

outlet /ˈaʊtlɛt, -lət/ *n.* **1.** an opening or passage by which anything is let out; a vent or exit. **2.** *Elect.* **a.** a point on a wiring system from which current is taken to supply electrical devices. **b.** **outlet box**, the metal box or receptacle designed to facilitate connections to a wiring system. **2.** *Commerce* **a.** a market for goods. **b.** (of a wholesaler or manufacturer) a shop, merchant, or agency selling one's goods: *he has many good outlets*. **4.** a means of expression; an occasion for releasing energies, etc. **5.** discharge.

outline /ˈaʊtlaɪn/ *n.* **1.** a line, drawn or imagined, which traces round the shape of an object; the contour. **2.** a drawing with such lines only. **3.** a general account giving only the main points. **4.** (*pl.*) the main points or necessary parts of a subject. *–v.t.* **5.** to draw the outline of, or draw in outline. **6.** to give the main points of (a subject, etc.).

outlive /aʊtˈlɪv/ *v.t.* **1.** to live longer than; survive (a person, etc.). **2.** to outlast; live or last through: *the ship outlived the storm*.

outlook /ˈaʊtlʊk/ *n.* **1.** the view from a place; prospect. **2.** a mental point of view. **3.** what is likely for the future: *political outlook*.

outlying /ˈaʊtlaɪɪŋ/ *adj.* **1.** lying at a distance from the centre or the main body; remote; out-of-the-way. **2.** lying outside the boundary or limit.

out-of-date *adj.* **1.** (of a previous style or fashion) obsolete. **2.** (of a ticket, etc.) no longer valid. Also, (*especially in predicative use*), **out of date**.

out-of-pocket *adj.* of or relating to what has been paid out in cash or outlay incurred: *out-of-pocket expenses*. Also, (*especially in predicative use*), **out of pocket**.

out-of-the-way *adj.* **1.** remote from much-travelled ways or frequented or populous regions; secluded. **2.** unusual. **3.** improper. Also, (*especially in predicative use*), **out of the way**.

outpatient /ˈaʊtpeɪʃənt/ *n.* a patient receiving treatment at a hospital but not being an inmate. Also, **out-patient**.

outpost /ˈaʊtpoʊst/ *n.* **1.** a station at a distance from the main body of an army to protect it from surprise attack. **2.** any remote settlement: *an outpost of civilisation*.

output /ˈaʊtpʊt/ *n.* **1.** the act of turning out; production. **2.** the quantity or amount produced, as in a given time. **3.** the product or yield, as of a mine. **4.** *Computers* information obtained from a computer on the completion of a calculation. *–v.t.* (**-put, -putting**) **5.** to supply from a computer database, file, etc.: *we can output the data; I'll output copies for the meeting.*

outrage /ˈaʊtreɪdʒ/ *n.* **1.** a very wrong act that goes beyond all accepted limits of behaviour, especially one of great cruelty or violence. **2.** a feeling of very strong anger. *–v.t.* (**-raged, -raging**) **3.** to subject to great violence or humiliation. **4.** to affect with a sense of offended right or decency; shock. **5.** to rape (a woman). **–outraged**, *adj.* **–outrageous**, *adj.* **–outrageously**, *adv.*

outré /ˈuːtreɪ/ *adj.* passing the bounds of what is usual and considered proper.

outreach *v.t.* /aʊtˈriːtʃ/ **1.** to reach beyond; exceed. **2.** to reach out; extend. *–v.i.* /aʊtˈriːtʃ/ **3.** to reach out. *–n.* /ˈaʊtriːtʃ/ **4.** a reaching out especially in the provision of programs aimed at achieving social or educational objectives. **5.** length of reach. *–adj.* /ˈaʊtriːtʃ/ **6.** of or relating to outreach: *the development of outreach secondary education*.

outrigger /ˈaʊtrɪɡə/ *n.* **1.** a framework extended outboard from the side of a boat, especially, as in South Pacific canoes, supporting a float which gives stability. **2.** a bracket extending outwards from the side of a racing shell, to support a rowlock. **3.** the shell itself. **4.** a spar rigged out from a ship's rail or the like, as for extending a sail. **5.** *Building Trades* a beam projecting from a building and wedged against a ceiling inside the building, used for supporting certain kinds of scaffolding.

outright /ˈaʊtraɪt/ *adj.* **1.** complete or total: *an outright loss*. **2.** downright or unqualified: *an outright refusal.* *–adv.* **3.** completely; entirely. **4.** without restraint, reserve, or concealment; openly. **5.** at once.

outset /ˈaʊtsɛt/ *n.* the beginning or start of something such as an undertaking, project, etc.

outside *n.* /ˈaʊtsaɪd/ **1.** the outer side, surface, or part; the exterior. **2.** the external aspect or appearance. **3.** something merely external. **4.** the space without or beyond an enclosure, boundary, etc. **5.** seaward, beyond the point where the waves break. **6.** *Colloq.* the world outside prison. *–adj.* /ˈaʊtsaɪd/ **7.** being, acting, done, or originating beyond an enclosure, boundary, etc.: *outside noises*. **8.** situated on or relating to the outside; exterior; external. **9.** *Aust. Obs.* situated at or relating to areas remote from human settlement. **10.** not belonging to or connected with an institution, society, etc.: *outside influences*. **11.** extremely unlikely or remote: *an outside chance*. *–adv.* /aʊtˈsaɪd/ **12.** on or to the outside, exterior, or space without. **13.** *Fishing* away from enclosed waters and the shoreline. *–prep.* /aʊtˈsaɪd/ **14.** on or towards the outside of. *–phr.* **15.** **at the outside**, at the utmost limit: *not more than ten at the outside*. **16.** **outside of**, with the exception of. **17.** **the outside**, *Aust. Hist.* the remote areas far from centres of European settlement.

outsider /aʊtˈsaɪdə/ *n.* **1.** someone not within an enclosure, boundary, etc. **2.** someone not belonging to a particular group, set, party, etc. **3.** someone unconnected or unacquainted with the matter in question. **4.** a racehorse, etc., not included among the favourites.

outsize /ˈaʊtsaɪz/ *n.* **1.** an uncommon or irregular size. **2.** a garment of such a size, especially when larger. *–adj.* Also, **outsized**. **3.** unusually or abnormally large; larger than average: *a display of outsize dresses*.

outskirts /ˈaʊtskɜːts/ *pl. n.* outer or bordering parts or districts, as of a city.

outsmart /aʊtˈsmɑːt/ *v.t.* to prove too clever for; outwit.

outsource /ˈaʊtsɔːs/ *v.t.* to contract (work) outside the company rather than employ more in-house staff. **–outsourcing,** *n.*

outspoken /ˈaʊtspoʊkən/ *adj.* 1. uttered or expressed with frankness or lack of reserve: *outspoken criticism.* 2. free or unreserved in speech: *outspoken people.* **–outspokenly,** *adv.* **–outspokenness,** *n.*

outstanding /aʊtˈstændɪŋ/ *adj.* 1. prominent; conspicuous; striking. 2. that continues in existence; that remains unsettled, unpaid, etc. 3. standing out; projecting; detached. 4. that resists or opposes.

outstation /ˈaʊtsteɪʃən/ *n.* 1. a stock-handling depot with accommodation away from the main homestead. 2. any remote post: *a diplomatic outstation; a military outstation.* 3. a small community of Aboriginal people living away from the more populated areas, often associated with one of the larger settlements from which its community has decentralised. Also, **out-station.**

outstretch /aʊtˈstrɛtʃ/ *v.t.* 1. to stretch forth; extend. 2. to stretch beyond (a limit, etc.). 3. to stretch out; expand.

outstrip /aʊtˈstrɪp/ *v.t.* (**-stripped, -stripping**) 1. to outdo; surpass; excel. 2. to outdo or pass in running.

out-tray *n.* a tray or other receptacle for outgoing letters, files, job assignments, etc., which have received attention.

outward /ˈaʊtwəd/ *adj.* 1. of or relating to what is seen or apparent, as opposed to the underlying nature; superficial: *only her outward looks were calm; the outward man.* 2. relating to the outside; outer. 3. directed towards the outside: *outward gaze.* *–adv.* 4. Also, **outwards.** towards the outside; out. 5. away from port: *outward bound.*

outwardly /ˈaʊtwədli/ *adv.* 1. as regards appearance or outward manifestation. 2. towards the outside. 3. on the outside or outer surface.

outwards /ˈaʊtwədz/ *adv.* towards the outside; out. Also, **outward.**

outweigh /aʊtˈweɪ/ *v.t.* 1. to exceed in value, importance, influence, etc.: *the advantages of the plan outweighed its defects.* 2. to be too heavy or burdensome for. 3. to exceed in weight.

outwit /aʊtˈwɪt/ *v.t.* (**-witted, -witting**) to get the better of by superior ingenuity or cleverness.

ouzo /ˈuːzoʊ/ *n.* an aniseed-flavoured liqueur of Greece.

ova /ˈoʊvə/ *n.* plural of **ovum.**

oval /ˈoʊvəl/ *adj.* 1. having the general form, shape, or outline of an egg; egg-shaped. 2. ellipsoidal or elliptical. *–n.* 3. any of various oval things. 4. a body or a plane figure oval in shape or outline. 5. *Aust.* a flat area (sometimes elliptical) on which sporting activities can take place. **–ovally,** *adv.* **–ovalness,** *n.*

ovary /ˈoʊvəri/ *n.* (*pl.* **-ries**) 1. *Anat., Zool.* the female gonad or reproductive gland, in which the ova, or eggs, develop and the hormones that regulate female secondary sex characteristics are produced. 2. *Bot.* the enlarged lower part of the carpel in angiospermous flowers enclosing the ovules. **–ovarian** /oʊˈvɛəriən/, *adj.*

ovate /ˈoʊveɪt/ *adj.* 1. egg-shaped. 2. *Bot.* **a.** having a plane figure like the longitudinal section of an egg. **b.** having such a figure with the broader end at the base, as a leaf.

ovation /oʊˈveɪʃən/ *n.* an enthusiastic public reception of a person; enthusiastic applause.

oven /ˈʌvən/ *n.* a chamber or receptacle for baking or heating, or for drying with the aid of heat.

over /ˈoʊvə/ *prep.* 1. above in place or position; higher up than: *the roof over one's head.* 2. above and to the other

side of: *to leap over a wall.* 3. above in authority, power, etc.; so as to govern, control, or conquer. 4. on or upon, so as to rest on or cover. 5. on or on top of: *to hit someone over the head.* 6. here and there on or in: *at various places over the country.* 7. through all parts of; all through: *to look over some papers.* 8. to and fro on or in: *to travel all over Australia.* 9. from side to side of; to the other side of: *to go over a bridge.* 10. on the other side of: *lands over the sea.* 11. reaching higher than, so as to submerge: *12.* in excess of, or more than: *over a kilometre.* 13. above in degree, etc. 14. in preference to. 15. throughout the extent or length of: *over a great distance.* 16. until after the end of: *to adjourn over the holidays.* 17. throughout the duration of: *over a long term of years.* 18. in reference to, concerning, or about: *to quarrel over a matter.* 19. while engaged in or concerned with: *to fall asleep over one's work.* 20. by the agency of: *she told me over the phone; we heard the news over the radio.* 21. recovered from: *he's over the measles now.* *–adv.* 22. over the top or upper surface, or edge of something. 23. so as to cover the surface, or affect the whole surface: *to paint a thing over.* 24. through a region, area, etc.: *to travel all over.* 25. at some distance, as in a direction indicated: *over by the hill.* 26. from side to side, or to the other side: *to sail over.* 27. across any intervening space: *when are you coming over to see us?* 28. from beginning to end, or all through: *to read a thing over.* 29. from one person, party, etc., to another: *to make property over to others.* 30. on the other side, as of a sea, a river, or any space: *over in Fiji.* 31. so as to bring the upper end or side down or under: *to knock a thing over.* 32. *US* once more; again: *to do a thing over.* 33. in repetition: *twenty times over.* 34. in excess or addition: *to pay the full sum and something over.* 35. remaining beyond a certain amount: *five goes into seven once, with two over.* 36. throughout or beyond a period of time: *to stay over till Monday.* *–adj.* 37. upper; higher up. 38. higher in authority, station, etc. 39. serving or intended, as an outer covering. 40. in excess or addition; surplus; extra. 41. too great; excessive. 42. at an end; done; past: *when the war was over.* *–n.* 43. an amount in excess or addition; an extra. 44. *Cricket* **a.** the number of balls (six in most countries) delivered between successive changes of bowlers. **b.** the part of the game played between such changes. *–phr.* 45. **all over,** **a.** everywhere. **b.** thoroughly; entirely. **c.** done with; finished. **d.** *Colloq.* characteristically or typically: *that's him all over.* 46. **all over with,** done with; finished. 47. **be all over,** *Colloq.* to show great affection towards; be excessively attentive to: *she was all over him as soon as he entered the room.* 48. **be over something,** *Colloq.* to be no longer obsessed by something: *he is finally over golf.* 49. **be so over something,** *Colloq.* to be fed up with something: *I'm so over his constant complaining.* 50. **over again,** once more; with repetition. 51. **over against,** **a.** opposite to; in front of. **b.** contrasted with or distinguished from: *to set truth over against falsehood.* 52. **over and above,** in addition to; besides. 53. **over and over** or **over and again,** repeatedly. 54. **over the fence,** *Aust., NZ Colloq.* unreasonable; unfair. 55. **over there,** *Aust.* (especially during WWI) in Europe, that is, on the other side of the world. 56. **over the top,** **a.** *Mil.* over the top of a parapet, as in charging the enemy. **b.** *Colloq.* extreme or excessive; beyond normal restraints or limits

over- prefixal use of **over,** *preposition, adverb,* or *adjective,* occurring in various senses in compounds, as in *overboard, overcoat, overhang, overlap, overlord, overrun, overthrow,* and especially used, with the sense of 'over the limit', 'to excess', 'too much', 'too', to form verbs, adjectives, adverbs, and nouns, such as *overact, overcapitalise, overcrowd, overfull, overmuch, oversupply, overweight,* and many others, mostly self-explanatory. A hyphen, commonly absent from old or well-established formations, is often used in new coinages, or in any words whose compound parts it may be desirable to set off distinctly.

overall /ˈouvərɔl/ *adj.* **1.** from one extreme limit of a thing to another: *the overall length of a bridge.* **2.** covering or including everything: *an overall estimate.* −*n.* /ˈouvərɔl/ **3.** a coverall. −*adv.* /ouvərˈɔl/ **4.** covering or including everything; altogether: *the position viewed overall.*

overalls /ˈouvərɔlz/ *pl. n.* loose trousers of strong material, usually with a bib and shoulder straps.

overarm /ˈouvəram/ *adj.* **1.** performed with the arm being raised above the shoulder, as bowling. **2.** of or relating to a style of swimming similar to freestyle (def. 1). −*adv.* **3.** in an overarm manner.

overawe /ouvərˈɔ/ *v.t.* (**-awed, -awing**) to restrain or subdue by inspiring awe; intimidate.

overbalance /ouvəˈbæləns/ *verb* (**-anced, -ancing**) −*v.t.* **1.** to outweigh. **2.** to cause (someone or something) to lose balance or to fall or turn over. −*v.i.* **3.** to lose one's balance. −*n.* **4.** an overbalancing weight or amount. **5.** something that more than balances.

overbearing /ouvəˈbɛərɪŋ/ *adj.* domineering; dictatorial; haughtily or rudely arrogant. −**overbearingly**, *adv.*

overboard /ˈouvəbɔd/ *adv.* **1.** over the side of a ship or boat, especially into or in the water: *to fall overboard.* −*phr.* **2. go overboard,** to be unrestrained or excessively enthusiastic.

overcapitalise /ouvəˈkæpətəlaɪz/ *v.t.* **1.** to fix the nominal capital (total amount of securities) of a company in excess of the limits set by law or by sound financial policy. **2.** to overestimate the capital value (of a business property or enterprise). **3.** to provide an excessive amount of capital (for a business enterprise). **4.** to put more capital into (an investment) than is warranted by its likely future worth. Also, **overcapitalize**. −**overcapitalisation** /ouvəkæpətəlaɪˈzeɪʃən/, *n.*

overcast /ˈouvəkast/ *adj.* **1.** (of the sky) overspread with clouds. **2.** dark; gloomy.

overcharge *verb* /ouvəˈtʃadʒ/ (**-charged, -charging**) −*v.t.* **1.** to charge (someone) too high a price. −*v.i.* **2.** to charge too much for something. −*n.* /ˈouvətʃadʒ/ **3.** a charge which is more than a fair price.

overclock /ouvəˈklɒk/ *v.t. Computers* to adjust (computer hardware) to make the central processing unit run at a higher clock rate than intended by the original manufacturer, in order to increase the speed at which it performs. −**overclocking**, *n.*, *adj.* −**overclocker**, *n.* −**overclockability**, *n.*

overcoat /ˈouvəkout/ *n.* **1.** a coat worn over the ordinary clothing, as in cold weather; greatcoat; topcoat. **2.** an additional coat of paint applied for protection.

overcome /ouvəˈkʌm/ *verb* (**-came, -come, -coming**) −*v.t.* **1.** to get the better of in a struggle; conquer; defeat. **2.** to win against (opposition, difficulties, etc.) or not give in to (temptation, etc.). **3.** (of liquor, drugs, emotion, etc.) to make (a person) weak, helpless, or unconscious; overpower. −*v.i.* **4.** to gain the victory; conquer.

overcook /ouvəˈkʊk/ *v.t.* **1.** to cook (a dish) too long so that it is no longer of a desirable consistency or texture. **2.** to impair the condition of (something) by giving it too much attention, stimulation, etc. −**overcooking**, *n.*

overdo /ouvəˈdu/ *v.t.* (**-did, -done, -doing**) **1.** to do to excess: *to overdo exercise.* **2.** to carry to excess or beyond the proper limit. **3.** to overact (a part); exaggerate. **4.** to cook too much; overcook. −*phr.* **5. overdo it,** to overtax one's strength; fatigue oneself; exhaust oneself. −**overdone** /ouvəˈdʌn/, *adj.*

overdose *n.* /ˈouvədous/ **1.** an excessive dose. −*v.t.* /ouvəˈdous/ **2.** to dose to excess. −*v.i.* /ouvəˈdous/ **3.** to take an overdose of a drug.

overdraft /ˈouvədraft/ *n.* **1.** *Finance* a draft in excess of one's credit balance, or the amount of the excess. **2.** an excess draft or demand made on anything.

overdraw /ouvəˈdrɔ/ *v.t.* (**-drew, -drawn, -drawing**) **1.** *Finance* to draw upon (an account, allowance, etc.) in excess of the balance standing to one's credit or at one's disposal. **2.** to draw too far; strain, as a bow, by drawing. **3.** to exaggerate in drawing, depicting, or describing.

overdress /ouvəˈdrɛs/ *v.i.* **1.** to dress oneself to excess or with too much display. −*v.t.* **2.** to dress (someone) excessively or too elaborately. −*n.* **3.** a dress worn over another dress.

overdrive /ouvəˈdraɪv/ *v.t.* (**-drove, -driven, -driving**) **1.** to overwork; push or carry to excess. **2.** to drive too hard. −*n.* **3.** *Machinery* a device containing gearing that provides an extra-high ratio for motor cars when continuous high speed and low fuel consumption are required. **4.** a very high level of activity or operation: *in overdrive to get everything ready for opening night.*

overdue /ˈouvədju/ *adj.* past due, as a belated train or a bill not paid by the assigned date; late; long awaited.

overestimate *v.t.* /ouvərˈɛstəmeɪt/ **1.** to estimate at too high a value, amount, ratio, or the like. −*n.* /ouvərˈɛstəmət/ **2.** an estimate that is too high. −**overestimation** /ouvərɛstəˈmeɪʃən/, *n.*

overflow *verb* /ouvəˈflou/ (**-flowed, -flown, -flowing**) −*v.i.* **1.** (of a river, water in a glass, etc.) to flow or run over (banks, etc.). **2.** to pass from one place to another because the first is too full: *the crowd overflowed into the street.* **3.** (fol. by *with*) to be filled or supplied plentifully: *a heart overflowing with gratitude.* −*v.t.* **4.** to flow over; flood; inundate. **5.** to flow over or beyond (the brim, banks, borders, etc.). −*n.* /ˈouvəflou/ **6.** an overflowing or flooding: *the yearly overflow of the Nile.* **7.** something that flows or runs over: *to carry off the overflow from a fountain.* **8.** an outlet for overflowing liquid. **9.** an area of land covered by water in time of floods. **10.** too much of anything; excess.

overgrow /ouvəˈgrou/ *verb* (**-grew, -grown, -growing**) −*v.t.* **1.** to grow over; cover with a growth of something. **2.** to outdo in growing; choke or supplant by a more exuberant growth. **3.** to grow beyond, grow too large for, or outgrow. −*v.i.* **4.** to grow to excess; grow too large. −**overgrowth**, *n.* −**overgrown**, *adj.*

overhand /ˈouvəhænd/ *adj.* Also, **overhanded**. **1.** done or delivered overhand. −*adv.* **2.** with the hand over the object. **3.** with the hand raised above the shoulder. **4.** *Sewing* with close, shallow stitches over two selvages. −*v.t.* **5.** to sew overhand.

overhang *verb* /ouvəˈhæŋ/ (**-hung, -hanging**) −*v.t.* **1.** to hang over: *a tree overhung the cliff.* **2.** to be spread over: *a dark sky overhangs the earth.* **3.** to threaten: *the sadness which overhung him.* −*v.i.* **4.** to hang over; project or jut out over something below. −*n.* /ˈouvəhæŋ/ **5.** an overhanging; projection: *an overhang of two metres.*

overhaul *v.t.* /ouvəˈhɔl/ **1.** to investigate or examine thoroughly, as for repair. **2.** to make necessary repairs to; restore to proper condition. **3.** to gain upon or overtake. **4.** *Naut.* to slacken (a rope) by hauling in the opposite direction to that in which it was drawn taut. −*n.* /ˈouvəhɔl/ **5.** a thorough examination.

overhead *adv.* /ouvəˈhɛd/ **1.** over one's head; aloft; up in the air or sky, especially near the zenith: *overhead was a cloud.* −*adj.* /ˈouvəhɛd/ **2.** situated, operating, or passing overhead, aloft, or above. **3.** applicable to one and all; general; average. −*n.* /ˈouvəhɛd/ **4.** (*pl.*) the general cost of running a business. **5.** (*pl.*) the general cost which cannot be assigned to particular products or orders.

overhear /oʊvə'hɪə/ *v.t.* (**-heard**, **-hearing**) to hear (speech, etc., or a speaker) without the speaker's intention or knowledge. –**overhearer**, *n.*

overjoyed /oʊvə'dʒɔɪd/ *adj.* overcome with joy; made exceedingly joyful.

overkill /'oʊvəkɪl/ *n.* **1.** the capacity of a nation to destroy, by nuclear weapons, more of an enemy than would be necessary for a military victory. **2.** an instance of such destruction. **3.** the use of more resources or energy than is necessary to achieve one's aim. **4.** the pursuit of a policy or campaign, as the vilification of a political opponent, to unnecessary lengths.

overland /'oʊvəlænd/ *adv.* **1.** over or across the land. **2.** by land. –*adj.* **3.** proceeding, performed, or carried on overland: *the overland route.* –*v.t.* **4.** to drive (stock) overland for long distances. –*v.i.* **5.** to go on a journey overland, especially one driving stock.

overlander /'oʊvəlændə/ *n.* a drover bringing stock overland, especially through remote areas, as from the NT or NSW to Adelaide.

overlap *v.t.* /oʊvə'læp/ (**-lapped**, **-lapping**) **1.** to stretch over and cover a part of (something else): *branches are overlapping the house* **2.** to coincide in part with; correspond partly with: *your job overlaps (with) mine.* –*n.* /'oʊvəlæp/ **3.** an overlapping. **4.** the amount of overlapping: *an overlap of two centimetres.* **5.** an overlapping part or place.

overleaf /oʊvə'lif/ *adv.* on the other side of the page or sheet: *continued overleaf.*

overload /oʊvə'loʊd/ *v.t.* to load to excess; overburden.

overlook /oʊvə'lʊk/ *v.t.* **1.** to fail to notice: *to overlook a misspelt word.* **2.** to disregard; ignore: *I will overlook your lateness this time.* **3.** to look over, as from a higher position: *to overlook the crowd.* **4.** to give a view down over: *a hill overlooking the sea.*

overly /'oʊvəli/ *adv.* overmuch; excessively; too: *a voyage not overly dangerous.*

overnight /oʊvə'naɪt/ *for defs 1–3,* /'oʊvənaɪt/ *for defs 4–9* –*adv.* **1.** during the night: *to stay overnight.* **2.** *Aust.* on the evening before: *preparations were made overnight.* **3.** suddenly; very quickly: *new towns sprang up overnight.* –*adj.* **4.** done, happening, or continuing during the night: *an overnight stop.* **5.** staying for one night: *overnight guests.* **6.** designed to be used one night or very few nights: *overnight bag.* **7.** happening suddenly or rapidly: *an overnight success.* –*n.* **8.** an overnight stopover during a plane journey, etc. –*v.i.* **9.** to stay overnight at a place while in transit: *we overnighted in Taipei.*

overpass *n.* /'oʊvəpas/ **1.** a bridge designed to take traffic on one road over an intersecting road. –*v.t.* /oʊvə-'pas/ (**-passed** *or* **-past**, **-passing**) **2.** to pass over or traverse (a region, space, etc.). **3.** to get over (obstacles, etc.). **4.** to go beyond, exceed, or surpass.

overplay /oʊvə'pleɪ/ *v.t.* **1.** to play (a part, etc.) in an exaggerated manner; overemphasise. **2.** to defeat in playing. –*v.i.* **3.** to exaggerate one's part; overact, etc. –*phr.* **4. overplay one's hand, a.** to overestimate the strength of one's cards in game play. **b.** to go too far, through misplaced confidence in the strength of one's position.

overpower /oʊvə'paʊə/ *v.t.* **1.** to overcome, master, or subdue by superior force: *to overpower a maniac.* **2.** to overcome or overwhelm in feeling, or affect or impress excessively. **3.** to overmaster the bodily powers or mental faculties of: *overpowered with wine.* **4.** to furnish or equip with excessive power.

overproof /'oʊvəpruf/ *adj.* containing a greater proportion of alcohol than proof spirit does.

overreach /oʊvə'ritʃ/ *v.t.* to defeat (oneself) by doing too much or being too clever.

overriding /'oʊvəraɪdɪŋ/ *adj.* prevailing over all other considerations.

overrule /oʊvə'rul/ *v.t.* **1.** to rule against or disallow the arguments of (a person). **2.** to rule or decide against (a plea, argument, etc.); disallow. **3.** to prevail over so as to change the purpose or action. **4.** to exercise rule or influence over.

overrun *verb* /oʊvə'rʌn/ (**-ran**, **-run**, **-running**) –*v.t.* **1.** to spread over quickly and occupy (a country): *in 1940 German armies overran the Low Countries.* **2.** to take possession of (an enemy position, etc.). **3.** (of vermin, etc.) to swarm over in great numbers. **4.** (of weeds, etc.) to spread or grow rapidly over. –*v.i.* **5.** to extend beyond the proper or desired limit. –*n.* /'oʊvərʌn/ **6.** an amount overrunning or carried over; excess.

overseas *adv.* /oʊvə'siz/ **1.** over, across, or beyond the sea; abroad. –*adj.* /'oʊvəsiz/ **2.** of or relating to passage over the sea: *overseas travel.* **3.** situated beyond the sea: *overseas lands.* **4.** of or relating to countries beyond the sea; foreign: *overseas military service.*

oversee /oʊvə'si/ *v.t.* (**-saw**, **-seen**, **-seeing**) **1.** to direct (work or workers); supervise; manage. **2.** to see or observe without being seen. –**overseer**, *n.*

overshadow /oʊvə'ʃædoʊ/ *v.t.* **1.** to diminish the importance of, or render insignificant in comparison. **2.** to tower over so as to cast a shadow over. **3.** to cast a shadow over. **4.** to make dark or gloomy. **5.** to shelter or protect.

overshoot /oʊvə'ʃut/ *v.t.* (**-shot**, **-shooting**) **1.** to shoot or go beyond (a point, limit, etc.): *to overshoot the mark.* **2.** (of an aircraft) to go further than the stopping point when landing. **3.** to go further in anything than is intended or proper, or to go too far.

oversight /'oʊvəsaɪt/ *n.* **1.** failure to notice or take into account. **2.** an omission or mistake due to inadvertence. **3.** supervision; watchful care.

overstate /oʊvə'steɪt/ *v.t.* to state too strongly; exaggerate in statement: *to overstate one's case.* –**overstatement**, *n.*

overstock *v.t.* /oʊvə'stɒk/ **1.** to stock to excess. **2.** to stock with cattle in excess of the capacity of the land to provide feed. –*n.* /'oʊvəstɒk/ **3.** a stock in excess of need.

oversubscribed /'oʊvəsəbskraɪbd/ *adj.* (of share issues) having applications to buy exceeding the number of shares available.

overt /oʊ'vɜt, 'oʊvɜt/ *adj.* open to view or knowledge; not concealed or secret: *overt hostility.*

overtake /oʊvə'teɪk/ *verb* (**-took**, **-taken**, **-taking**) –*v.t.* **1.** to catch up with in travelling or in pursuit. **2.** to come up with or pass in any course of action. **3.** to come upon suddenly or unexpectedly (said especially of night, storm, death, etc.). **4.** to pass (another vehicle). –*v.i.* **5.** to pass another vehicle.

over-the-top *adj. Colloq.* extreme or excessive; beyond normal restraints or limits: *her over-the-top ideas lost her the job.* Also, (*especially in predicative use*), **over the top.**

overthrow *v.t.* /oʊvə'θroʊ/ (**-threw**, **-thrown**, **-throwing**) **1.** to put down from a position of power; depose; overcome, defeat, or vanquish. **2.** to put an end to by force: *to overthrow the government.* **3.** to throw (something) too far: *to overthrow the ball so it goes past the line.* –*n.* /'oʊvəθroʊ/ **4.** an act of overthrowing: *the overthrow of the government.* **5.** *Cricket* **a.** a ball returned by a fielder which is not caught at the wicket. **b.** a run scored as a result of this.

overtime /'oʊvətaɪm/ *for defs 1–4,* /oʊvə'taɪm/ *for def. 5* –*n.* **1.** time during which one works before or after regularly scheduled working hours; extra time. **2.** pay for such time. *–adv.* **3.** during extra time: *to work overtime.* *–adj.* **4.** of or relating to overtime: *overtime pay.* *–v.t.* **5.** to give too much time to, as in photographic exposure.

overtone /ˈoʊvətoʊn/ *n.* **1.** *Acoustics, Music* any frequency emitted by an acoustical instrument that is higher in frequency than the fundamental. **2.** (*usu. pl.*) additional meaning or implication.

overture /ˈoʊvətʃʊə/ *n.* **1.** an opening of negotiations, or a formal proposal or offer. **2.** *Music* **a.** an orchestral composition forming the prelude or introduction to an opera, oratorio, etc. **b.** an independent piece of similar character. **3.** an introductory part, as of a poem. *–v.t.* **4.** to submit as an overture or proposal. **5.** to make an overture or proposal to.

overturn /oʊvəˈtɜn/ *v.t.* **1.** to put an end to by force; overthrow. **2.** to turn over on its side, face, or back; upset. **3.** to turn (a decision, judgement, etc.) the other way; reverse: *the ruling was overturned in the High Court.* *–v.i.* **4.** to turn over; be upset; capsize.

overview /ˈoʊvəvju/ *n.* a general survey which avoids getting down to details.

overweening /ˈoʊvəwinɪŋ/ *adj.* **1.** conceited, arrogant, self-opinionated: *an overweening person.* **2.** exaggerated, excessive: *overweening pride.* **—overweeningly,** *adv.*

overweight *n.* /ˈoʊvəweɪt/ **1.** extra weight; excess of weight. *–adj.* /ˈoʊvəweɪt/ **2.** weighing more than normally or necessarily required. *–v.t.* /oʊvəˈweɪt/ **3.** to overburden, overload.

overwhelm /oʊvəˈwɛlm/ *v.t.* **1.** to come, rest, or weigh upon overpoweringly; crush. **2.** to overcome completely in mind or feeling. **3.** to vanquish, defeat, especially by force of numbers. **4.** to load, heap, treat, or address with an overpowering or excessive amount of anything. **5.** to cover or bury beneath a mass of something, as a flood, or the like, or cover as a mass or flood does. **—overwhelmingly,** *adv.*

overwork *verb* /oʊvəˈwɜk/ (**-worked** *or* **-wrought, -working**) *–v.t.* **1.** (*oft. used before a verb*) to cause to work too hard or too long; weary or exhaust with work: *she has overworked herself this term.* **2.** (*usu. as past participle*) to use too much: *the word 'literally' is overworked and is losing its meaning.* *–v.i.* **3.** to work too hard; work to excess. *–n.* /ˈoʊvəwɜk/ **4.** work that is beyond one's strength or ability.

overwrought /oʊvəˈrɔt/ *adj.* **1.** wearied or exhausted by overwork. **2.** worked up or excited excessively. **3.** extremely worried; having highly strained nerves. **4.** overworked; elaborated to excess.

ovi- a word element meaning 'egg', as in *oviferous.*

ovine /ˈoʊvaɪn/ *adj.* relating to or resembling sheep.

oviparous /oʊˈvɪpərəs/ *adj.* producing ova or eggs which are matured or hatched after being expelled from the body, as birds, most reptiles and fishes, etc. **—oviparity** /oʊvəˈpærəti/, *n.* **—oviparously,** *adv.*

ovoid /ˈoʊvɔɪd/ *adj.* **1.** egg-shaped; having the solid form of an egg. **2.** → **ovate** (def. 2). *–n.* **3.** an ovoid body.

ovulate /ˈɒvjəleɪt/ *v.i. Physiol.* to shed eggs from an ovary or ovarian follicle. **—ovulation** /ɒvjəˈleɪʃən/, *n.*

ovum /ˈoʊvəm/ *n.* (*pl.* **ova** /ˈoʊvə/) *Biol.* **1.** the female reproductive cell of animals, which (usually only after fertilisation) is capable of developing into a new individual. **2.** the female reproductive cell or gamete of plants.

owe /oʊ/ *verb* (**owed, owing**) *–v.t.* **1.** (sometimes fol. by *to*) to be indebted or beholden for. **2.** to be under obligation to pay or repay, or to render: *to owe interest on a mortgage.* **3.** to be in debt to: *to owe someone for their generosity.* **4.** to have or cherish (a certain feeling) towards a person: *to owe someone a grudge.* *–v.i.* **5.** to be in debt.

owing /ˈoʊɪŋ/ *adj.* **1.** that owes. **2.** owed or due: *to pay what is owing.* *–phr.* **3. owing to, a.** on account of; because of. **b.** attributable to.

owl /aʊl/ *n.* **1.** any of numerous birds of prey of the families Tytonidae (**barn owls**) and Strigidae (**typical owls**), chiefly nocturnal, with a broad head and with large eyes which are usually surrounded by discs of modified feathers and directed forwards. They feed on mice, small birds and reptiles, etc. **2.** a person of nocturnal habits. **3.** a person of owl-like solemnity or appearance. **4.** a wise person, especially one whose knowledge is derived from book learning.

own /oʊn/ *adj.* **1.** belonging or relating to oneself or itself (usually used after a possessive to emphasise the idea of ownership, interest, or relation conveyed by the possessive): *his own money.* *–pron.* **2.** (*absolutely, with a possessive preceding*) own property, relatives, etc.: *to be among one's own.* *–v.t.* **3.** to have or hold as one's own; possess. **4.** to acknowledge or admit: *to own a fault.* **5.** to acknowledge as one's own. *–v.i.* **6.** to admit: *to own to being uncertain.* *–phr.* **7. be one's own master,** to be independent. **8. come into one's own, a.** to receive an inheritance. **b.** to be in a situation where particular skills or attributes are evident. **9. get one's own back,** to have revenge. **10. of one's own,** belonging to oneself. **11. on one's own,** (sometimes fol. by *to*) **a.** on one's own account, responsibility, resources, etc. **b.** by oneself; alone. **12. own up,** (sometimes fol. by *to*) to acknowledge one's guilt. **—owner,** *n.*

ox /ɒks/ *n.* (*pl.* **oxen**) **1.** a mature castrated male bovine, used as a draught animal and for food; bullock. **2.** any bovine mammal. **—oxlike,** *adj.*

oxalis /ɒkˈsaləs/ *n.* any plant belonging to one of the numerous species of the genus *Oxalis*, as wood sorrel and yellow-flowered oxalis.

oxen /ˈɒksən/ *n.* plural of **ox**.

oxidant /ˈɒksədənt/ *n.* the oxidising agent which supplies oxygen, or accepts electrons, in an oxidation reaction.

oxidate /ˈɒksədeɪt/ *v.t.* to oxidise. **—oxidative,** *adj.*

oxidation /ɒksəˈdeɪʃən/ *n.* **1.** the act or process of oxidising. *–adj.* **2.** of or relating to oxidation: *an oxidation potential.*

oxide /ˈɒksaɪd/ *n. Chem.* a compound, usually containing two elements only, one of which is oxygen, as *mercuric oxide.*

oxidise /ˈɒksədaɪz/ *v.t.* **1.** to change (an element) into its oxide; to combine with oxygen. **2.** to cover with a coating of oxide, or rust. **3.** to take away hydrogen from (a substance). **4.** to increase the valency of (an element) by removing electrons. **5.** (of a wine) to combine with oxygen, damaging colour, smell and taste. *–v.i.* **6.** to become oxidised. Also, **oxidize.** **—oxidisable,** *adj.* **—oxidisation** /ɒksədaɪˈzeɪʃən/, *n.* **—oxidiser,** *n.*

oxyacetylene /ɒksiəˈsetələn/ *adj.* of or relating to a mixture of oxygen and acetylene.

oxygen /ˈɒksədʒən/ *n.* a colourless, odourless gaseous element, constituting about one fifth of the volume of the atmosphere and present in a combined state throughout nature. It is the supporter of combustion in air and is vital for aerobic respiration. *Symbol:* O; *relative atomic mass:* 15.9994; *atomic number:* 8.

oxylobium /ɒksəˈloʊbiəm/ *n.* any shrub of the endemic Australian genus *Oxylobium*, family Fabaceae, several western Australian species of which are poisonous to stock.

oxymoron /ɒksiˈmɔrɒn/ *n.* (*pl.* **-morons** *or* **-mora** /-ˈmɔrə/) *Rhetoric* a figure of speech by which a locution produces an effect by a seeming self-contradiction, as in *cruel kindness* or *to make haste slowly.* **—oxymoronic** /ɒksiməˈrɒnɪk/, *adj.*

oxywelding /ˈɒksiˈwɛldɪŋ/ *n.* welding in which oxygen is mixed with another gas, as acetylene or LPG. **—oxywelder,** *n.*

oyez /oʊˈjɛs, oʊˈjɛz/ *interj.* hear! attend! (a cry uttered, usually thrice, by a public or court crier to command silence and attention before a proclamation, etc., is made). Also, **oyes**.

oyster /ˈɔɪstə/ *n.* **1.** any of various edible marine bivalve molluscs, family Ostreidae, with irregularly shaped shell, found on the bottom or adhering to rocks, etc., in shallow water, some species being extensively cultivated for the market. **2.** the oyster-shaped bit of dark meat in the front hollow of the side bone of a fowl. **3.** a close-mouthed person. **4.** something from which one may extract or derive advantage. *–v.i.* **5.** to dredge for or otherwise take oysters.

oystercatcher /ˈɔɪstəkætʃə/ *n.* any of several long-billed, maritime wading birds constituting the genus *Haematopus*, with a plumage chiefly of black and white, as the **pied oystercatcher**, *H. longirostris*, of Eurasia, southern Africa and Australasia.

oyster mushroom *n.* a type of edible mushroom, *Pleurotus ostreatus*, found on living or dead wood, whose shape and collective appearance is reminiscent of the oyster.

Oz /ɒz/ *Colloq. –adj.* **1.** Australian. *–n.* **2.** Australia. Also, **oz**.

ozone /ˈoʊzoʊn/ *n.* **1.** *Chem.* a form of oxygen, O_3, having three atoms to the molecule, with a peculiar smell suggesting that of weak chlorine, which is produced when an electric spark is passed through air, and in several other ways. It is found in the atmosphere in minute quantities, especially after a thunderstorm, and is a powerful oxidising agent, used for bleaching, sterilising water, etc. **2.** *Colloq.* clear, invigorating, fresh air. *–ozonic* /oʊˈzɒnɪk/, *adj.*

ozone depleting substance *n.* a chemical, used in fumigation, refrigeration, food treatment, etc., which, if it escapes into the atmosphere, has the ability to reduce the levels of ozone. *Abbrev.*: ODS

ozone depletion *n.* a decline in the amount of ozone in the earth's stratosphere.

ozone hole *n.* a loss in the concentration of ozone in some part of the ozone layer

ozone layer *n.* a region in the outer portion of the stratosphere, where atmospheric ozone (O_3) is concentrated. Also, **ozonosphere**.

P p

P, p /pi/ *n.* **1.** a consonant, the 16th letter of the English alphabet. *–phr.* **2. mind one's p's and q's**, to heed one's behaviour. **3. Ps** or **P's**, *Aust. Colloq.* the P-plates issued by the motor registry with a provisional driver's licence.

pa¹ /pa/ *n. Colloq.* papa; father.

pa² /pa/ *n.* a Maori stockaded village.

pace /peɪs/ *n.* **1.** rate of stepping, or of movement in general: *a pace of ten kilometres an hour.* **2.** rate or style of doing anything: *they live at a tremendous pace.* **3.** the distance covered in a step: *stand six paces inside the gates.* **4.** manner of stepping; gait. **5.** a gait of a horse, etc., in which the feet on the same side are lifted and put down together. **6.** a raised step or platform. *–verb* (**paced, pacing**) *–v.t.* **7.** to set the pace for, as in racing: *this horse always paces the favourite.* **8.** to traverse with paces or steps: *he paced the floor.* **9.** to measure by paces. **10.** to train to a certain pace; exercise in pacing: *to pace a horse.* **11.** (of a horse) to perform as a pacer. *–v.i.* **12.** to walk (*up and down, about* etc.), especially in a state of nervous excitement: *the anxious job applicant paced about the foyer.* **13.** to take slow, regular steps. **14.** (of horses) to go at a pace (def. 5), especially in racing; amble. *–phr.* **15. put someone through their paces**, to cause someone to perform or show ability.

pacemaker /ˈpeɪsmeɪkə/ *n.* **1.** someone who sets the pace, as in racing. **2.** a person or group which is followed or imitated on account of its success. **3.** *Med.* an instrument implanted beneath the skin to control the rate of the heartbeat. *–pacemaking, n.*

pacer /ˈpeɪsə/ *n.* **1.** a pacemaker. **2.** a horse that paces, or whose natural gait is a pace.

pachyderm /ˈpækɪdɜm/ *n.* any of the thick-skinned non-ruminant ungulates, as the elephant, hippopotamus, and rhinoceros. *–pachydermatous* /pækiˈdɜmətəs/, **pachydermous** /pækiˈdɜməs/, *adj.*

pacific /pəˈsɪfɪk/ *adj.* **1.** tending to make peace; conciliatory: *pacific propositions.* **2.** peaceable; not warlike: *a pacific disposition.* **3.** peaceful; at peace: *pacific state of things.* *–pacifically, adv.*

Pacific black duck *n.* a duck, *Anas superciliosa*, mottled brown in colour with a black crown, two black facial stripes, a lead-grey bill and an iridescent speculum on the upper wing, found in great numbers in deepwater swamps throughout Australia, Indonesia, and Pacific islands.

Pacific solution *n.* the Australian government policy of the 1990s and 2000s of placing unauthorised asylum seekers in compounds on a number of small Pacific nations while awaiting assessment of their status.

pacifism /ˈpæsəfɪzəm/ *n.* **1.** opposition to war or violence of any kind. **2.** the principle or policy of establishing and maintaining universal peace. *–pacifist, n.*

pacify /ˈpæsəfaɪ/ *v.t.* (**-fied, -fying**) **1.** to bring into a state of peace; quiet; calm: *pacify an angry man.* **2.** to appease: *pacify one's appetite.* *–pacifiable* /ˈpæsəfaɪəbəl/, *adj. –pacifier, n.*

pack¹ /pæk/ *n.* **1.** a quantity of anything wrapped or tied up; a parcel; a packet. **2.** a wrapped or otherwise contained load carried on the back by a person or by an animal. **3.** a backpack, especially as used by a soldier.

4. the method, design, materials, etc., used in making a pack or parcel: *a vacuum pack.* **5.** a set or gang (of people): *a pack of thieves.* **6.** a group or unit of Cub Scouts in the Scout Association or the equivalent role in the Girl Guides Association. **7.** *Rugby Football* **a.** the forwards of a team collectively, especially acting together in rushing the ball forward or as a scrum. **b.** the forwards of two opposing teams in a scrum. **8.** a company of certain animals of the same kind: *a pack of wolves.* **9.** *Hunting* a number of hounds used regularly for hunting together. **10.** a group of things, usually abstract: *a pack of lies.* **11.** a complete set, as of playing cards. **12.** a considerable area of pack ice. **13.** *Med.* **a.** a wrapping of the body in wet or dry cloths for therapeutic purposes. **b.** the cloths so used. **14.** *Med.* material inserted into a wound or orifice, usually to control bleeding. **15.** a paste or the like consisting of cosmetic materials applied to the skin, especially of the face, to improve the complexion. *–v.t.* **16.** to make into a pack or bundle. **17.** to make into a group or compact mass, as animals, ice, etc. **18.** to fill with anything compactly arranged: *pack a trunk.* **19.** to press or crowd together within; cram. **20.** to put or arrange in suitable form for the market: *pack fruit.* **21.** to make airtight, steamproof, or watertight by stuffing: *pack the piston of a steam engine.* **22.** to cover or envelop with something pressed closely around. **23.** to carry, especially as a load. **24.** to put a load upon (a horse, etc.). **25.** *Colloq.* to be capable of (forceful blows): *he packs a mighty punch.* *–v.i.* **26.** to pack goods, etc., in compact form, as for transportation or storage. **27.** to admit of being compactly stowed: *articles that pack well.* **28.** to crowd together, as persons, etc. **29.** to become compacted. *–adj.* **30.** transporting, or used in transporting, a pack: *pack camel; pack animals.* **31.** made up of pack animals. **32.** in the manner of a pack of wild animals: *pack rape.* *–phr.* **33. go to the pack**, *Aust.* **a.** to degenerate; collapse. **b.** to give up; admit defeat. **34. pack away**, to stow (belongings, goods, etc.), away. **35. pack death** (or **it**) (or **shit**), *Aust. Colloq.* to be afraid. **36. pack down**, *Rugby Football* to form a scrum. **37. pack it in**, *Colloq.* **a.** to cease or desist. **b.** (of a machine) to break down. **38. pack off**, to send off summarily: *the kids were packed off to school.* **39. pack the (whole) game in**, *Colloq.* to give up or abandon totally some project, enterprise, activity, etc. **40. pack up**, **a.** to pack (goods, etc.) in compact form, as for transportation or storage. **b.** to put back (items which have been taken out and used) in their proper place: *pack up your toys now.* **c.** *Colloq.* (of a machine) to cease to function.

pack² /pæk/ *v.t.* to collect, arrange, or manipulate (a deliberative body) so as to serve one's own purposes: *pack a jury.*

package /ˈpækɪdʒ/ *n.* **1.** a parcel; bundle. **2.** something in which articles are packed, as a box, crate, etc. **3.** the act of packing goods, etc. **4.** a group of things considered as a single unit. *–v.t.* **5.** to put into wrappings or a container. **6.** to combine as a single unit. **7.** to present (a person), usually a figure in public life, in a particular way, especially to the media. *–phr.* **8. the full** (or **complete**) **package**, **a.** a product or service which has all the add-ons and extras included. **b.** an extremely skilled and competent person. –**packaging**, *n.*

packet /'pækət/ *n.* **1.** a small pack or package. **2.** a definite quantity or measure of something wrapped and retailed: *a packet of biscuits.* **3.** Also, **data packet.** *Computers* one of several units of data, each including a destination address, into which a message may be divided before being sent over a network link, the components being reassembled at the receiving end to form the original message. **4.** Also, **packet boat.** a ship, especially one that carries mail, passengers, and goods regularly on a fixed route. **5.** *Colloq.* a large sum of money. **6.** *Colloq.* a heavy or forceful blow, injury, setback, or the like: *he's caught a packet.*

packet boat *n.* → **packet** (def. 4).

pack ice *n.* an area in polar seas of large blocks of ice driven together over a long period by winds, currents, etc.

packing /'pækɪŋ/ *n.* **1.** material placed around goods in the boxes, etc., in which they are sold to protect them from shock and damage in transit. **2.** any material used for packing or making watertight, steamproof, etc., as a fibrous substance closing a joint, a metallic ring round a piston, etc.

pact /pækt/ *n.* an agreement; a compact.

pad¹ /pæd/ *n.* **1.** a cushion-like mass of some soft material, for comfort, protection, or stuffing. **2.** a guard for the leg, containing padding and stiffeners, as worn by the people batting and wicketkeeper in cricket, the goalkeeper in hockey, etc. **3.** Also, **writing pad.** a number of sheets of paper glued together at one edge. **4.** a soft ink-soaked block of absorbent material for inking a rubber stamp. **5.** one of the cushion-like protuberances on the underside of the feet of dogs, foxes, and some other animals. **6.** the large floating leaf of the waterlily. **7. a.** *Aerospace* → **launching pad. b.** *Aeronautics* a smallish area set aside for helicopter use. **8.** *Colloq.* a dwelling, especially a single room. **9.** *Colloq.* a bed. –*v.t.* (**padded, padding**) **10.** to furnish, protect, fill out, or stuff with a pad or padding. **11.** Also, **pad out.** to expand (writing or speech) with unnecessary words or matter. –*phr.* **12. pad up,** to put on padding in preparation for a sporting position requiring such protection, as the wicketkeeper in cricket or the goalkeeper in hockey. –**padder**, *n.*

pad² /pæd/ *n.* **1.** a dull sound, as of footsteps on the ground. **2.** a path worn by animals, as by cattle through paddocks. –*verb* (**padded, padding**) –*v.t.* **3.** to travel along on foot. –*v.i.* **4.** to travel on foot. **5.** to go with the dull sound of footsteps. –**padder**, *n.*

paddle¹ /'pædl/ *n.* **1.** a short oar held in the hands (not resting in the rowlock) and used especially for propelling canoes. **2.** one of the broad boards on the circumference of a paddlewheel; float. **3.** a paddlewheel. **4.** one of the similar projecting blades by means of which a waterwheel is turned. **5.** an adjustable shutter that lets waters into or out of a lock, reservoir, or the like. **6.** a flipper or limb of a penguin, turtle, whale, etc. **7.** any of various implements used for beating, stirring, mixing, etc. **8.** the act of paddling. –*v.i.* **9.** to propel a canoe or the like by using a paddle. **10.** to row lightly or gently with oars. **11.** to move by means of paddlewheels, as a steamer. –*v.t.* **12.** to propel (a canoe, etc.) with a paddle. **13.** to stir. **14.** *US Colloq.* to beat with or as with a paddle; spank. **15.** to convey by paddling, as in a canoe. –*phr.* **16. paddle one's own canoe,** to act independently. –**paddler**, *n.*

paddle² /'pædl/ *v.i.* **1.** to dabble or play in or as in shallow water. **2.** to toy with the fingers. –**paddler**, *n.*

paddleboarding /'pædlbɔdɪŋ/ *n.* the activity or sport of riding a stand-up paddleboard. Also, **paddleboard surfing.**

paddle-steamer /'pædl-stimə/ *n.* a steam vessel propelled by paddlewheels. Also, **paddleboat.**

paddlewheel /'pædlwil/ *n.* a wheel with floats or paddles on its circumference, for propelling a vessel over the water.

paddock /'pædək, 'pædɪk/ *n.* **1.** *Aust., NZ* a large fenced area of land, usually used for grazing stock. **2.** *Brit.* a small field, especially for pasture, near a stable or house. **3.** Also, **saddling paddock.** *Horseracing* the area in which horses are saddled before a race and to which the winners are brought back for the presentation of prizes. **4.** *Motor Racing* the area near the pits, in which cars are prepared for a race. **5.** *Colloq.* a football field. –*v.t.* **6.** to enclose (animals) in a paddock.

paddy¹ /'pædi/ *n.* (*pl.* **-dies**) **1.** rice. **2.** rice in the husk, uncut or gathered. **3.** a paddy field.

paddy² /'pædi/ *n.* (*pl.* **-dies**) *Colloq.* an intense anger; a rage.

paddymelon¹ /'pædiməl∂n/ *n.* either of two southern African plants, now widely distributed in Australia: **1.** a trailing herb, *Cucumis myriocarpus*, which has small melon-like fruit, harmful to stock. **2.** a vine, *Colocynthis lanatus*, similar to that which yields the common jam melon.

paddymelon² /'pædiməlɑn/ *n.* → **pademelon.**

paddy wagon *n.* a closed police vehicle used for conveying prisoners; black maria.

paddywhack /'pædiwæk/ *n.* *Colloq.* **1.** Also, **paddy.** a rage. **2.** a spanking.

pademelon /'pædiməlɑn/ *n.* any of several species of small wallabies of the genus *Thylogale* found in areas of thick scrub or dense, moist undergrowth of eastern Australia and Tasmania. Also, **paddymelon.**

padlock /'pædlɑk/ *n.* **1.** a portable or detachable lock having a pivoted or sliding hasp which passes through a staple, ring, or the like and is then made fast. –*v.t.* **2.** to fasten with or as with a padlock.

padre /'padreɪ/ *n.* **1.** *Mil. Colloq.* a chaplain. **2.** (especially in Italy, Spain, Portugal, and Latin America) a Christian priest.

pad thai /pæd 'taɪ, pad 'taɪ/ *n.* (in Thai cookery) a dish consisting of stir-fried rice noodles with a variety of other ingredients, such as vegetables and beef or tofu.

paed- a word element meaning 'child'. Also, **paedi-, paedo-;** *Chiefly US,* **ped-.**

paediatrics /pidi'ætrɪks/ *n.* the study and treatment of the diseases of children. Also, **pediatrics.** –**paediatric,** *adj.* –**paediatrician** /pidiə'trɪʃən/, *n.*

paedophile /'pɛdəfaɪl, 'pid-/ *n.* an adult who engages in sexual activities with children. Also, **pedophile.** –**paedophilic,** *adj.*

paedophilia /pɛdə'fɪliə, pidə-, -'fil-, -jə/ *n.* sexual attraction in an adult towards children. Also, **pedophilia.**

pagan /'peɪgən/ *n.* **1.** a follower of an ancient polytheistic or pantheistic religion or set of beliefs. **2. a.** one of a people or community professing some other than the Christian religion (applied to the ancient Romans, Greeks, etc., and sometimes the Jews). **b.** (*derog.*) someone who is not an adherent of one of the world's major religions. **3.** an irreligious or heathenish person. **4.** a person who follows a contemporary set of beliefs modelled on the ancient pagan religions. –*adj.* **5.** of, relating to, or typical of pagans. –**paganism,** *n.* –**paganish,** *adj.*

page¹ /peɪdʒ/ *n.* **1.** one side of a leaf of a book, manuscript, letter, or the like. **2.** the entire leaf of a book, etc.: *write on both sides of the page.* **3.** *Computing* a fixed-length block of data displayed on a computer screen. **4.** any event or period regarded as an episode in history: *a glorious page in history.*

page² /peɪdʒ/ *n.* **1.** a boy servant or attendant. **2.** a young man in attendance on a person of rank. **3.** a young male attendant, usually in uniform, in a hotel, etc.; pageboy. –*v.t.* (**paged, paging**) **4.** to try to find (a person) by calling out their name, or using a public-address system or a pager, as in a hotel, hospital, business office, etc. –**pager,** *n.*

pageant /'pædʒənt/ *n.* **1.** an elaborate public spectacle, whether processional or at some fitting spot, illustrative of the history of a place, institution, or other subject. **2.** a splendid or stately procession; a showy display. **3.** a specious show. –**pageantry,** *n.*

pageboy /'peɪdʒbɔɪ/ *n.* **1.** *Brit.* → **bellboy. 2.** a small boy who acts as an attendant at weddings or social occasions. **3.** a woman's hairstyle in which the hair falls straight and is rolled under at the bottom.

pagoda /pə'goʊdə/ *n.* **1.** (in India, Myanmar, China, etc.) a temple or sacred building, usually more or less pyramidal or forming a tower of many storeys. **2.** a building imitative of a pagoda in design but which has a decorative rather than religious purpose.

paid /peɪd/ *v.* past tense and past participle of **pay.**

pail /peɪl/ *n.* a container of wood, metal, etc., nearly or quite cylindrical, with a semicircular handle, for holding liquids, etc.; a bucket. –**pailful** /'peɪlfʊl/, *n.*

pain /peɪn/ *n.* **1.** bodily or mental suffering or distress. **2.** a distressing sensation in a particular part of the body. **3.** (*pl.*) laborious or careful efforts; assiduous care: *great pains have been taken.* **4.** (*pl.*) (*dated*) the suffering of childbirth. **5.** Also, **pain in the neck, pain in the gut;** (*taboo*), **pain in the arse.** *Colloq.* an irritating, tedious, or unpleasant person or thing. –*v.t.* **6.** to inflict pain on; hurt; distress. –*v.i.* **7.** to cause pain or suffering. –*phr.* **8. be at pains to,** to be extremely careful to. **9. on pain of,** liable to the penalty of. –**painful,** *adj.*

painkiller /'peɪnkɪlə/ *n.* a drug which relieves pain. –**painkilling,** *adj.*

painstaking /'peɪnzteɪkɪŋ/ *adj.* assiduously careful: *painstaking work.* –**painstakingly,** *adv.*

paint /peɪnt/ *n.* **1.** a substance composed of solid colouring matter intimately mixed with a liquid vehicle or medium, and applied as a coating. **2.** the dried surface pigment. **3.** the solid colouring matter alone; a pigment. **4.** application of colour. **5.** *Colloq.* colour, as rouge, used on the face. –*v.t.* **6.** to represent (an object, etc.) in colours or pigment. **7.** to execute (a picture, design, etc.) in colours or pigment. **8.** to depict as if by painting; describe vividly in words. **9.** to describe or represent: *he's not as bad as he's painted.* **10.** to coat, cover, or decorate (something) with colour or pigment. **11.** to colour as if by painting; adorn or variegate. **12.** to apply like paint, as a liquid medicine, etc. –*v.i.* **13.** to coat or cover anything with paint. **14.** to practise painting. –*phr.* **15. paint the town red,** *Colloq.* to indulge in riotous entertainment. –**painting,** *n.*

painter[1] /'peɪntə/ *n.* **1.** an artist who paints pictures. **2.** someone whose occupation is coating surfaces with paint.

painter[2] /'peɪntə/ *n.* a rope, usually at the bow, for fastening a boat to a ship, stake, etc.

pair /pɛə/ *n.* (*pl.* **pairs** *or* **pair**) **1.** two things of a kind, matched for use together: *a pair of gloves.* **2.** a combination of two parts joined together: *a pair of scissors.* **3.** a married or engaged couple. **4.** two people, animals, etc., regarded as having a common characteristic: *a pair of fools.* **5.** two mated animals. **6.** a span or team. **7.** *Parliamentary Procedure* **a.** two members on opposite sides in a deliberative body who for convenience (as to permit absence) arrange together to forgo voting on a given occasion. **b.** the arrangement thus made. **8.** *Cards* **a.** two cards of the same denomination, without regard to suit or colour. **b.** (*pl.*) two players who are matched together against different contestants. **9.** *Rowing* a racing shell having two rowers, with one

oar each. **10.** *Mechanics* two parts or pieces so connected that they mutually constrain relative motion (**kinematic pair**). **11.** *Cricket* **a.** a failure by the person batting to score in either innings of a match. **b. king pair,** a failure by the person batting to score in either innings of a match as a result of a dismissal on the first ball bowled to them in each case. **12.** *Mining* a party of miners (usually six) working together; a gang. –*v.t.* **13.** to arrange in pairs. **14.** to join in a pair; mate; couple. **15.** to cause to mate. –*v.i.* **16.** Also, **pair off.** to separate into pairs. **17.** to form a pair or pairs. **18.** *Parliamentary Procedure* to form a pair to forgo voting. –*phr.* **19. cancel pairs,** *Parliamentary Procedure* to suspend pairing, ensuring that votes are counted strictly according to the actual number of members present.

paisley /'peɪzli/ *n.* (*pl.* **-leys**) **1.** a soft fabric made from wool and woven with a colourful and minutely detailed pattern. **2.** any pattern similar to that woven on paisley. –*adj.* **3.** made of paisley: *a paisley shawl.*

pakeha /'pakəha, 'pakiha, 'pakiə/ *NZ* –*n.* **1.** a European; white person. –*adj.* **2.** being or relating to a white person.

pal /pæl/ *Colloq.* –*n.* **1.** a comrade; a chum. **2.** an accomplice. –*v.i.* (**palled, palling**) **3.** to associate as pals. –*phr.* **4. be a pal,** an appeal to someone for friendly assistance. **5. pal up with,** to become associated or friendly with. –**pally,** *adj.*

palace /'pæləs/ *n.* **1.** the official residence of a sovereign, a bishop, or some other exalted personage. **2.** a stately mansion or building. **3.** a large place for exhibitions or entertainment.

palaeo- a prefix meaning 'old', 'ancient'. Also, **paleo-, palae-, pale-.**

palaeontology /ˌpæliɒn'tɒlədʒi, ˌpeɪ-/ *n.* the systematic study of the forms of life existing in former geological periods, as represented by fossil animals and plants. Also, **paleontology.** –**palaeontologist,** *n.* –**palaeontologic** /ˌpæliɒntə'lɒdʒɪk, ˌpeɪ-/, *adj.*

palatable /'pælətəbəl/ *adj.* **1.** agreeable to the palate or taste; savoury. **2.** agreeable to the mind or feelings. –**palatability** /pælətə'bɪləti/, **palatableness,** *n.* –**palatably,** *adv.*

palate /'pælət/ *n.* **1.** the roof of the mouth, consisting of bone (**hard palate**) in front and of a fleshy structure (**soft palate**) at the back. **2.** this part of the mouth considered (popularly but erroneously) as the organ of taste. **3.** the sense of taste. **4.** mental taste or liking. –**palatal,** *adj.*

palatial /pə'leɪʃəl/ *adj.* relating to, of the nature of, or befitting a palace: *palatial homes.* –**palatially,** *adv.*

palaver /pə'lavə/ *n.* **1.** idle, useless or foolish talk. **2.** any unnecessarily long business; bother: *the palaver of writing out new instructions.* –*v.i.* **3.** to talk for a long time to little purpose.

palazzo pants /pə'latsoʊ pænts/ *pl. n.* full-length pants with an elasticised waist and full legs.

pale[1] /peɪl/ *adj.* **1.** of a whitish appearance; without much colour: *a pale face.* **2.** of a low degree of colour: *pale yellow.* **3.** lacking in brightness; dim: *the pale moon.* **4.** faint; feeble: *a pale attempt.* –*v.i.* **5.** to become pale. **6.** (fol. by *before, beside,* etc.) to seem less in importance, strength, etc.: *her happiness paled beside that of her friend.* –**palely,** *adv.* –**paleness,** *n.*

pale[2] /peɪl/ *n.* **1.** a stake or picket, as of a fence. **2.** any enclosing or confining barrier. **3.** limits or bounds. **4.** the area enclosed by a paling; any enclosed area. **5.** a district or region within fixed bounds. **6.** *Heraldry* a broad vertical stripe in the middle of an escutcheon and one third its width. –*v.t.* **7.** to enclose with pales; fence. **8.** to encircle. –*phr.* **9. beyond the pale,** socially or morally unacceptable.

palette /'pælət/ *n.* **1.** a thin, usually oval or oblong, board or tablet with a thumb hole at one end, used by painters to lay and mix colours on. **2.** the range of colours used by a particular artist.

palindrome /'pæləndroʊm/ *n.* a word or phrase which reads exactly the same forwards and backwards, as *madam, I'm Adam.* –**palindromic** /pælən'drɒmɪk/, *adj.*

paling /'peɪlɪŋ/ *n.* **1.** a pale, as in a fence. **2.** pales collectively. –*adj.* **3.** made from palings: *paling hut.*

palisade /pælə'seɪd/ *n.* **1.** a fence of pales or stakes set firmly in the ground, as for enclosure or defence. **2.** one of such pales or stakes.

pall[1] /pɒl/ *n.* **1.** a cloth, often of velvet, for spreading over a coffin, bier, or tomb. **2.** something that covers, shrouds, or overspreads, especially with darkness or gloom.

pall[2] /pɒl/ *v.i.* **1.** to become insipid, distasteful, or wearisome. –*v.t.* **2.** to satiate or cloy. –*phr.* **3. pall on** (or **upon**), to have a wearying effect on.

palladium /pə'leɪdiəm/ *n.* (*pl.* **-dia** /-diə/) anything believed to afford effectual protection or safety.

pallbearer /'pɔlbɛərə/ *n.* one of those who carry or attend the coffin at a funeral.

pallet[1] /'pælət/ *n.* **1.** a bed or mattress of straw. **2.** a small or poor bed.

pallet[2] /'pælət/ *n.* **1.** an implement consisting of a flat blade with a handle, used for shaping by potters, etc. **2.** *Horology* a lever with three projections, two of which intermittently lock and receive impulses from the escape wheel, and one which transmits these impulses to the balance. **3.** a lip or projection on a pawl, that engages with the teeth of a ratchet wheel. **4.** a movable platform on which goods are placed for storage or transportation, especially one designed to be lifted by a forklift truck. **5.** a painter's palette.

palliate /'pælieɪt/ *v.t.* **1.** to cause (an offence, etc.) to appear less grave or heinous; extenuate; excuse. **2.** to mitigate or alleviate: *to palliate a disease.* –**palliation** /pæli'eɪʃən/, *n.* –**palliator** /'pælɪeɪtɪv/, *adj.*

palliative care *n. Med.* the total care of patients whose disease is not responsive to curative treatment, including attention to the needs of their family, etc.

pallid /'pæləd/ *adj.* pale; deficient in colour; wan. –**pallidly**, *adv.* –**pallidness**, *n.* –**pallor**, *n.*

pallid cuckoo *n.* a medium-sized greyish-brown Australian cuckoo, *Cuculus pallidus,* having a distinctive penetrating call resembling a rising chromatic scale; brain-fever bird.

palm[1] /pɑm/ *n.* **1.** that part of the inner surface of the hand which extends from the wrist to the bases of the fingers. **2.** the corresponding part of the forefoot of an animal. **3.** the part of a glove covering the palm. **4.** a linear measure based on either the breadth of the hand (7 to 10 cm) or its length from wrist to fingertips (18 to 25 cm). –*v.t.* **5.** to conceal in the palm, as in cheating at cards or dice or in juggling. **6.** to touch or stroke with the palm or hand. **7.** *Aust. Rules* at a ball-up or throw-in, to hit (the ball) with an open hand. –*phr.* **8. cross** (or **grease**) (or **oil**) **someone's palm,** to bribe someone. **9. palm off,** (sometimes fol. by *on* or *upon*) to impose (something) fraudulently: *he tried to palm off the broken watch on me.* –**palmar,** *adj.*

palm[2] /pɑm/ *n.* **1.** any of the plants constituting the large and important family Palmae, the majority of which are tall, unbranched trees surmounted by a crown of large pinnate or palmately cleft (fan-shaped) leaves. **2.** any of various other palms or shrubs which resemble the palm. **3.** a leaf or branch of a palm tree, especially as formerly borne as an emblem of victory or as used on festal occasions. **4.** a representation of such a leaf or branch, as on a decoration of honour. **5.** the victor's reward of honour. **6.** victory; triumph.

palmistry /'pɑməstri/ *n.* the art or practice of telling fortunes and interpreting character by the lines and configurations of the palm of the hand. –**palmist** /'pɑməst/, *n.*

palmtop /'pɑmtɒp/ *n.* Also, **palmtop computer.** **1.** a small handheld personal computer. –*adj.* **2.** of or relating to a palmtop computer: *palmtop features.*

palomino /pælə'minoʊ/ *n.* (*pl.* **-nos**) a tan or cream-coloured horse with a white mane and tail. Also, **palamino.**

palpable /'pælpəbəl/ *adj.* **1.** readily or plainly seen, heard, perceived, etc.; obvious: *a palpable lie.* **2.** able to be touched or felt; tangible. –**palpability** /pælpə'bɪləti/, *n.* –**palpably,** *adv.*

palpate /'pælpeɪt/ *v.t.* to examine by the sense of touch, especially in medicine. –**palpation** /pæl'peɪʃən/, *n.*

palpitate /'pælpəteɪt/ *v.i.* **1.** to pulsate with unnatural rapidity, as the heart, from exertion, emotion, disease, etc. **2.** to quiver or tremble. –**palpitant,** *adj.* –**palpitation** /pælpə'teɪʃən/, *n.*

palsy /'pɒlzi/ *n.* (*pl.* **-sies**) paralysis. –**palsied,** *adj.*

paltry /'pɒltri/ *adj.* (**-trier, -triest**) **1.** trifling; petty: *a paltry sum.* **2.** trashy or worthless: *paltry rags.* **3.** mean or contemptible: *a paltry coward.* –**paltrily,** *adv.* –**paltriness,** *n.*

pamper /'pæmpə/ *v.t.* **1.** to indulge (a person, etc.) to the full or to excess: *to pamper a child*; *to pamper one's appetite.* **2.** to indulge with rich food, comforts, etc. –**pamperer,** *n.*

pamphlet /'pæmflət/ *n.* **1.** a short treatise or essay, generally controversial, on some subject of temporary interest: *a political pamphlet.* **2.** a complete publication generally less than 80 pages, stitched or stapled and usually enclosed in paper covers. **3.** → **brochure.**

pan[1] /pæn/ *n.* **1.** a dish commonly of metal, usually broad, shallow and open, used for culinary and other domestic purposes: *a frying pan*; *cake pan.* **2.** any pot or saucepan. **3.** any dish-like receptacle or part. **4.** any of various open or closed vessels used in industrial or mechanical processes. **5.** a vessel, usually of cast iron, in which the ores of silver are ground and amalgamated. **6.** a vessel in which gold or other heavy, valuable metals are separated from gravel, etc., by agitation with water. **7.** a depression in the ground, as a natural one containing water, mud, or mineral salts, or an artificial one for evaporating salt water to make salt. Compare **salt pan. 8.** → **hardpan. 9.** (in old guns) the depressed part of the lock which holds the priming. –*verb* (**panned, panning**) –*v.t.* **10.** to wash (auriferous gravel, sand, etc.) in a pan, to separate the gold or other heavy valuable metal. **11.** to separate by such washing. **12.** *US* to cook (oysters, etc.) in a pan. **13.** *Colloq.* to criticise or speak disparagingly about. –*v.i.* **14.** to wash gravel, etc., in a pan, seeking for gold. **15.** to yield gold, as gravel washed in a pan. –*phr.* **16. pan out,** *Colloq.* to result; turn out.

pan[2] /pæn/ *v.i.* (**panned, panning**) *TV, Film, etc.* **1.** (of a camera) to move continuously while shooting in order to record on film a panorama, or to keep a moving person or object in view. **2.** to operate a camera in such a manner.

panacea /pænə'siə/ *n.* **1.** a remedy for all diseases; cure-all. **2.** a solution to all problems: *technology is not the panacea some thought it would be.* –**panacean,** *adj.*

panache /pə'næʃ, -'nɑʃ/ *n.* **1.** a grand or flamboyant manner; swagger; verve. **2.** an ornamental plume or tuft of feathers, especially one worn on a helmet or on a cap.

Panama hat /pænəmə 'hæt/ *n.* (*sometimes lower case*) a fine plaited hat made of the young leaves of a palmlike plant, *Carludovica palmata,* of Central and South America.

pancake /ˈpænkeɪk/ *n.* **1.** a thin flat cake made from a batter of eggs, flour, sugar, and milk, cooked in a frying pan. **2.** cosmetic foundation in a compressed form, either as a stick or flat cake, especially as used by actors or others to give a thick coverage to the face. –*v.i.* **3.** (of an aeroplane) to drop flat to the ground after levelling off a few feet above it.

pancetta /pænˈtʃetə/ *n.* an Italian bacon cured with salt and spices but not smoked, used to flavour sauces, pasta, etc.

pancreas /ˈpæŋkriəs/ *n. Anat.* a gland situated near the stomach, secreting an important digestive fluid (**pancreatic juice**), discharged into the intestine by one or more ducts. –**pancreatic** /pæŋkriˈætɪk/, *adj.*

panda /ˈpændə/ *n.* **1.** Also, **panda bear.** a shy and rare mammal of central China, *Ailuropoda melanoleuca*, related to the bear, boldly marked in black and white and feeding on bamboo; giant panda. **2.** See **red panda**.

pandanus /pænˈdænəs, -ˈdeɪnəs/ *n.* any plant of the genus *Pandanus*, comprising tropical and subtropical trees and shrubs, especially of the islands of the Malay Archipelago and the Indian and Pacific oceans, having a palmlike or branched stem, long, narrow, rigid, spirally arranged leaves and often aerial prop roots, the leaves being used for flavouring Asian cakes and desserts, and the fibre for rope. Also, **pandan**.

P & C /pi ən ˈsi/ *n.* Parents and Citizens Association; a parent body within a public school which concerns itself with specific issues and fundraising. Compare **school council**.

pandemic /pænˈdemɪk/ *adj.* **1.** (of a disease) prevalent throughout an entire country or continent, or the whole world. **2.** general; universal. –*n.* **3.** a pandemic disease.

pandemic influenza A (H1N1) *n.* an influenza virus affecting pigs, which can be transmitted from pigs to humans and then transmitted by human-to-human contact, especially the H1N1 subtype of the influenza A virus; symptoms include fever, a sore throat and coughing. Also, **pandemic (H1N1), human swine influenza**.

pandemonium /pændəˈmoʊniəm/ *n.* **1.** (*oft. upper case*) the abode of all the demons. **2.** hell. **3.** a place of riotous uproar or lawless confusion. **4.** wild lawlessness or uproar. –**pandemoniac, pandemonic** /pændəˈmɒnɪk/, *adj.*

pander /ˈpændə/ *n.* **1.** *Obs.* a go-between in intrigues of love. **2.** a procurer; pimp. **3.** someone who ministers to the weaknesses or baser passions of others. –*v.t.* **4.** to act as a pander for. –*v.i.* **5.** to act as a pander; cater basely. –*phr.* **6. pander to**, to indulge.

Pandora's box /pænˌdɔrəz ˈbɒks/ *n.* **1.** *Gk Legend* a box or jar containing all human ills, given by Zeus to Pandora who was forbidden to open it, but did so out of curiosity, thus releasing its contents. **2.** any source of extensive troubles, especially one expected at first to yield blessings.

pane /peɪn/ *n.* **1.** one of the divisions of a window, etc., consisting of a single plate of glass in a frame. **2.** a panel, as of a wainscot, ceiling, door, etc.

panegyric /pænəˈdʒɪrɪk/ *n.* an oration, discourse, or writing in praise of a person or thing; a eulogy. –**panegyrical**, *adj.* –**panegyrically**, *adv.*

panel /ˈpænəl/ *n.* **1.** a division of a ceiling, door, etc., or of any surface sunk below or raised above the general level, or enclosed by a frame. **2.** a thin, flat piece of wood, etc. **3.** a broad piece of the same or another material set in or on a woman's dress, etc., for ornament. **4.** *Elect.* a division of a switchboard containing a set of related cords, jacks, relays, etc. **5.** the section of a machine on which controls, dials, etc., are fixed: *the instrument panel of a car*. **6.** *Law* a list of people called for service in a jury. **7.** any list or group of people, as one gathered to answer questions, discuss matters,

judge a competition, etc. –*v.t.* (**-elled** *or*, *Chiefly US*, **-eled**, **-elling** *or*, *Chiefly US*, **-eling**) **8.** to arrange in, or provide or ornament with, a panel or panels. –**panellist**, *n.*

panelbeater /ˈpænəlbitə/ *n.* someone who beats sheet metal into required shapes as for the bodywork of motor vehicles, etc. –**panelbeating**, *n.*

pang /pæŋ/ *n.* **1.** a sudden feeling of mental distress. **2.** a sudden, brief, sharp pain, or a spasm or severe twinge of pain: *the pangs of hunger*.

panic¹ /ˈpænɪk/ *n.* **1.** a sudden demoralising terror, with or without clear cause, often as affecting a group of persons or animals. **2.** an instance, outbreak, or period of such fear. –*adj.* **3.** of (fear, terror, etc.) suddenly destroying the self-control and impelling to some frantic action. **4.** of the nature of, due to, or showing panic: *panic haste*. –*verb* (**-icked**, **-icking**) –*v.t.* **5.** to affect with panic. –*v.i.* **6.** to be stricken with panic. –*phr.* **7. be at panic stations**, to be in a situation requiring extreme measures; be chaotic. –**panicky**, *adj.* –**panic-stricken** /ˈpænɪk-strɪkən/, **panic-struck** /ˈpænɪk-strʌk/, *adj.*

panic² /ˈpænɪk/ *n.* any grass of the genus *Panicum*, many species of which bear edible grain as native millet or giant panic. Also, **panic grass**.

panic attack *n.* **1.** *Psychol.* an episode of panic disorder. **2.** a feeling of intense anxiety: *she had a panic attack when she realised she had lost her wallet*.

panic disorder *n. Psychol.* a disorder characterised by unexpected and repeated episodes of intense fear accompanied by physical symptoms such as laboured breathing, palpitations, etc.

pannier /ˈpæniə/ *n.* **1.** a basket, especially one of considerable size, for carrying provisions, etc. **2.** a basket for carrying on a person's back, or one of a pair to be slung across the back of a beast of burden. **3.** one of a pair of bags, containers, etc., attached to either side of the rear wheel of a motorcycle, used as carriers.

pannikin /ˈpænəkən/ *n.* **1.** a small pan or metal cup. –*adj.* **2.** being someone who acts as though their status and importance are large, when in reality they are not, as *pannikin boss, pannikin snob*, etc.

panoply /ˈpænəpli/ *n.* (*pl.* **-lies**) **1.** a complete suit of armour. **2.** a complete covering or array of something. –**panoplied** /ˈpænəplid/, *adj.*

panorama /pænəˈramə/ *n.* **1.** an unobstructed view or prospect over a wide area. **2.** an extended pictorial representation of a landscape or other scene, often exhibited a part at a time and made to pass continuously before the spectators. **3.** a continuously passing or changing scene. **4.** a comprehensive survey, as of a subject. –**panoramic** /pænəˈræmɪk/, *adj.* –**panoramically** /pænəˈræmɪkli/, *adv.*

panpipe /ˈpænpaɪp/ *n.* a wind instrument consisting of a series of pipes of graduated length, the notes being produced by blowing across the upper ends. Also, **Pan's pipes**.

pansy /ˈpænzi/ *n.* (*pl.* **-sies**) **1.** any of several species of herbaceous plants of the genus *Viola*. **2.** *Colloq.* (*derog.*) **a.** an effeminate man. **b.** a male homosexual.

pant /pænt/ *v.i.* **1.** to breathe hard and quickly because of effort, emotion, etc. **2.** to give out steam, etc., in loud puffs. **3.** to desire greatly: *he panted for revenge*. **4.** to move up and down violently or rapidly; throb: *his chest was panting*. –*v.t.* **5.** to speak (words) breathlessly. –*n.* **6.** a short, quick, difficult effort of breathing; a gasp. **7.** an up and down movement of the chest, etc.; throb. –**pantingly**, *adv.*

pantaloons /pæntəˈlunz, ˈpæntəlunz/ *pl. n.* (formerly) a man's closely fitting garment for the hips and legs, varying in form at different periods; trousers.

pantechnicon /pæn'tɛknɪkən/ n. 1. a large or medium-sized truck or van with an enclosed back section, especially one used for transporting furniture. 2. a storage warehouse, especially for furniture.

pantheism /'pænθiːɪzəm/ n. 1. the doctrine that God is the transcendent reality of which the material universe and human beings are only manifestations, thereby denying God's personality, and identifying God with nature. Compare **theism**, **deism**. 2. any religious belief or philosophical doctrine which identifies the universe with God. –**pantheist**, n. –**pantheistic** /pænθi-'ɪstɪk/, **pantheistical** /pænθi'ɪstɪkəl/, adj. –**pantheistically** /pænθi'ɪstɪkli/, adv.

pantheon /'pænθiən/ n. 1. a public building containing tombs or memorials of the illustrious dead of a nation. 2. a temple dedicated to all the gods. 3. the gods of a particular mythology considered collectively.

panther /'pænθə/ n. (pl. **-thers** or, especially collectively, **-ther**) the leopard, Panthera pardus, especially in its black form. –**pantheress**

panties /'pæntiz/ pl. n. underpants as worn by women and girls.

pantihose /'pæntihoʊz/ n. (construed as pl.) women's tights, usually made out of fine-mesh material, as for stockings. Also, **pantyhose**.

pantomime /'pæntəmaɪm/ n. 1. a form of theatrical entertainment, originally including a harlequinade, but now based loosely on one of several fairytales, and including stock character types; commonly staged during the Christmas season. 2. → **mime** (def. 2). 3. gesturing without speech to convey meaning. –v.t. 4. to represent or express by pantomime. –v.i. 5. to express oneself by pantomime. –**pantomimic** /pæntə-'mɪmɪk/, adj.

pantry /'pæntri/ n. (pl. **-ries**) a room or cupboard in which provisions, especially food, and other household items are kept.

pants /pænts/ pl. n. 1. trousers. 2. underpants, especially women's. –phr. Colloq. 3. **be caught with one's pants down**, to be caught unexpectedly and ill-prepared. 4. **by the seat of one's pants**, **a**. without the benefit of prior instruction. **b**. deprived of the technical aids usually available, as in the case of an aircraft pilot with faulty instruments. 5. **wear the pants**, to be the dominant partner in a relationship.

pantyhose /'pæntihoʊz/ n. → **pantihose**.

panzer /'pænzə/ adj. 1. armoured: a panzer division. –n. 2. a tank (def. 5).

pap[1] /pæp/ n. 1. soft food for infants or invalids, as bread soaked in water or milk. 2. books, ideas, talk, etc., considered as having no intellectual or permanent value; rubbish; tripe.

pap[2] /pæp/ n. 1. a teat or nipple. 2. something resembling a teat or nipple.

papa /pə'pa, 'pʌpə/ n. → **father**.

papacy /'peɪpəsi/ n. (pl. **-cies**) 1. the office, dignity, or jurisdiction of the pope. 2. the system of ecclesiastical government in which the pope is recognised as the supreme head. 3. the succession or line of popes.

papal /'peɪpəl/ adj. of or relating to the pope, the papacy, or the Roman Catholic Church.

Papanicolaou smear /pæpə'nɪkəlaʊ smɪə/ n. → **Pap smear**.

paparazzo /papə'ratsoʊ, pæpə-/ n. (pl. **-razzi**) a press photographer who persistently pursues celebrities in order to photograph them.

papaya /pə'paɪə/ n. the large melon-like fruit of the shrub or small tree, Carica papaya, of the family Caricaceae, originally from tropical America, especially the smaller, sweet, pink-fleshed variety. See **pawpaw** (def. 1).

paper /'peɪpə/ n. 1. a substance made from rags, straw, wood, or other fibrous material, usually in thin sheets,

for writing or printing on, wrapping things in, etc. 2. something resembling this substance, as papyrus. 3. a piece, sheet, or leaf of paper, especially one bearing writing. 4. a written or printed document or instrument. 5. → **wallpaper**. 6. negotiable notes, bills, etc., collectively: commercial paper. 7. a set of questions for an examination, or an individual set of written answers to them. 8. an essay, article, or dissertation on a particular topic. 9. a newspaper or journal. 10. (pl.) documents establishing identity, status, etc. 11. (pl.) Naut. the documents required to be carried by a ship as evidence of its ownership, nationality, destination, etc.; ship's papers. –v.t. 12. to decorate (a wall, room, etc.) with wallpaper. 13. to line with paper: to paper a shelf. –adj. 14. made or consisting of paper: a paper bag. 15. paper-like; thin; flimsy; frail. 16. relating to, or carried on by means of, letters, articles, books, etc.: a paper war. 17. written or printed on paper. 18. existing on paper only and not in reality: a paper empire. –phr. 19. **on paper**, **a**. confirmed in writing. **b**. in the planning or design stage. **c**. in theory rather than practice: it seems all right on paper, but will it work? 20. **paper over**, to try to hide (the faults, inadequacies, etc., of something). –**papery**, adj.

paperback /'peɪpəbæk/ n. 1. a book bound in a flexible paper cover, usually cheaper than a hardback of comparable length. –adj. 2. of or relating to such books or the publishing of such books.

paperbark /'peɪpəbak/ n. 1. a form of bark, consisting of numerous thin layers of corky material, some parts of which peel off irregularly. 2. a tree bearing such bark, especially the broadleaved tea-trees of the genus Melaleuca.

paperclip /'peɪpəklɪp/ n. a piece of wire bent into a clip designed to hold together papers, etc.

paperweight /'peɪpəweɪt/ n. a small, heavy object laid on papers to keep them from being scattered.

papier-mâché /peɪpə'mæʃeɪ, pæpieɪ-'mæʃeɪ/ n. a substance made of pulped paper or paper pulp mixed with glue and other materials, or of layers of paper glued and pressed together, moulded when moist to form various articles, and becoming hard and strong when dry. Also, **papier-mache**.

papilla /pə'pɪlə/ n. (pl. **-pillae** /-'pɪli/) 1. any small nipple-like process or projection. 2. one of certain small protuberances concerned with the senses of touch, taste, and smell: the papillae of the tongue. 3. a small vascular process at the root of a hair. 4. a pimple. –**papillary**, adj. –**papillose** /'pæpəloʊs/, adj.

papillomavirus /pæpə'loʊməvaɪrəs/ n. any of various small species-specific viruses causing warts.

papist /'peɪpəst/ n. 1. an adherent of the pope. 2. (usually derog.) a member of the Roman Catholic Church. –**papism**, **papistry**, n. –**papistical** /pə'pɪstɪkəl/, adj.

papoose /pə'pus/ n. 1. (now likely to give offence) a baby or young child of one of the Native American peoples of North America. 2. a soft, pouch-like carrier in which a baby is held.

pappardelle /papə'dɛlə/ n. a kind of pasta in flat, very wide strips.

paprika /'pæprɪkə, pə'prikə/ n. the dried fruit of a cultivated form of Capsicum frutescens, ground as a condiment, much less pungent than ordinary red pepper. See **capsicum**.

Pap smear n. Med. (also lower case) a medical test in which a smear of a bodily secretion, especially from the cervix or vagina, is used to detect cancer in an early stage or to evaluate hormonal condition; cervical smear. Also, **Papanicolaou smear**.

papyrus /pə'paɪrəs/ n. (pl. **-pyri** /-'paɪraɪ/) 1. a tall aquatic plant, Cyperus papyrus, of the sedge family, of the Nile valley, Egypt, and elsewhere. 2. a material for writing on, prepared from thin strips of the pith of this plant laid together, soaked, pressed, and dried, used by the ancient Egyptians, Greeks, and Romans. **3.** an ancient document or manuscript written on this material.

par /paː/ n. **1.** an equality in value or standing; a level of equality: *the gains and the losses are on a par.* **2.** an average or normal amount, degree, quality, condition, or the like: *above par; below par; on a par with.* **3.** *Commerce* the state of the shares of any business, undertaking, loan, etc., when they may be purchased at the original price (called **issue par**) or at their face value (called **nominal par**). Such shares or bonds are said to be at par. **4.** *Golf* the number of strokes allowed to a hole or course as representing a target standard. –*phr.* **5. par for the course**, likely to happen; usual; expected.

para-¹ **1.** a prefix meaning 'beside', 'near', 'beyond', 'aside', 'amiss', and sometimes implying alteration or modification, occurring originally in words from the Greek, but used also as a modern formative, chiefly in scientific words. **2.** a prefix meaning ancillary: *paramedical, paralegal.* **3.** *Chem.* a prefix indicating the presence of a benzene ring with substituents in the 1,4 positions. Also, (*before vowels*), **par-**.

para-² a prefix meaning 'guard against', as in *parachute.*

para-³ a prefix meaning 'parachute', as in *paratroops.*

parable /ˈpærəbəl/ n. **1.** a short allegorical story, designed to convey some truth or moral lesson. **2.** a discourse or saying conveying the intended meaning by a comparison or under the likeness of something comparable or analogous.

parabola /pəˈræbələ/ n. *Geom.* a plane curve formed by the intersection of a right circular cone with a plane parallel to a generator of the cone. –**parabolic** /pærəˈbɒlɪk/, *adj.*

paracetamol /pærəˈsitəmɒl/ n. *Pharm.* an analgesic, fever-reducing drug.

parachute /ˈpærəʃut/ n. **1.** an apparatus used in descending safely through the air, especially from an aircraft, being umbrella-like in form and rendered effective by the resistance of the air, which expands in during the descent and then reduces the velocity of its motion. –*v.i.* **2.** to descend by or as by parachute. –**parachutist**, n.

parade /pəˈreɪd/ n. **1.** a show, display: *to make a parade of one's emotions.* **2.** a gathering of troops, Scouts, etc., for inspection or display. **3.** a body of people marching in the street to celebrate some public event; procession: *a parade of bands and floats.* **4.** a walk for pleasure or display; promenade. –*v.t.* **5.** to show something off: *to parade opinions.* **6.** to show by making someone or something walk or move along: *to parade cattle.* –*v.i.* **7.** to march or go with display. **8.** to walk in a public place to show oneself.

paradigm /ˈpærədaɪm/ n. **1.** *Gram.* **a.** the set of all forms containing a particular element, especially the set of all inflected forms of a single root, stem, or theme. For example: *boy, boys, boy's, boys'* constitutes the paradigm of the noun *boy.* **b.** a display in fixed arrangement of such a set. **2.** a pattern; an example. **3.** an intellectual framework of shared preconceptions and governing ideas which shapes research and analysis. –**paradigmatic** /pærədɪgˈmætɪk/, **paradigmatical** /pærədɪgˈmætɪkəl/, *adj.* –**paradigmatically** /pærədɪgˈmætɪkli/, *adv.*

paradigm shift n. **1.** a complete change of the framework within which an idea is expounded, a situation viewed, etc. **2.** any major change.

paradise /ˈpærədaɪs/ n. **1.** *Christianity, Judaism* heaven, as the final abode of the righteous. **2.** *Islam* the blissful, perfectly fulfilled existence of the righteous after death. **3.** (according to some beliefs) an intermediate place for

the departed souls of the righteous awaiting resurrection. **4.** a place of extreme beauty or delight. **5.** supreme felicity. See **bird of paradise**.

paradox /ˈpærədɒks/ n. **1.** a statement or proposition seemingly self-contradictory or absurd, and yet explicable as expressing a truth. **2.** a self-contradictory and false proposition. **3.** any person or thing exhibiting apparent contradictions. –**paradoxical** /pærəˈdɒksɪkəl/, *adj.* –**paradoxically** /pærəˈdɒksɪkli/, *adv.* –**paradoxicalness** /pærəˈdɒksɪkəlnəs/, **paradoxicality** /pærəˌdɒksəˈkaləti/, *n.*

paraffin /ˈpærəfən/ n. **1.** *Chem.* any hydrocarbon of the alkane series having general formula C_NH_{2N+2}. **2.** → **paraffin oil** (def. 1).

paraffin oil n. **1.** Also, **liquid paraffin**. a thick colourless mixture of hydrocarbons obtained from petroleum used as a laxative. **2.** any oil containing hydrocarbons obtained from the distillation of petroleum; mineral oil.

paraffin wax n. a white translucent solid with a melting point in the range 50°–60°C, consisting of the higher members of the paraffin series; used for candles, waxed papers, polishes, etc.

paraglide /ˈpærəglaɪd/ v.i. (**-glided, -gliding**) to engage in the sport of paragliding.

paraglider /ˈpærəglaɪdə/ n. **1.** a type of hang-glider in which the harness is attached to a wing made from fabric which fills with air in flight. **2.** a person who operates a paraglider.

paragliding /ˈpærəglaɪdɪŋ/ n. a sport similar to hang-gliding, in which a person jumps from a cliff or out of an aeroplane and releases a parachute which is used to make a controlled descent.

paragon /ˈpærəgɒn, ˈpærəgən/ n. **1.** a model or pattern of excellence, or of a particular excellence. **2.** an unusually large round pearl. **3.** a perfect diamond weighing 100 carats or more.

paragraph /ˈpærəgræf, -graf/ n. **1.** a part of written or printed matter dealing with a particular subject or point, beginning on a new, often indented, line. **2.** a character (now usually the pilcrow: ¶) used to indicate the beginning of a distinct or separate portion of a text, or as a mark of reference. **3.** a small part or article in a newspaper. –*v.t.* **4.** to divide into paragraphs. –**paragrapher, paragraphist**, n. –**paragraphic** /pærəˈgræfɪk/, **paragraphical** /pærəˈgræfɪkəl/, *adj.*

parakeelya /pærəˈkiljə/ n. any of various species of succulent Australian herbs, as *Calandrinia balonensis*, with fleshy leaves and pinkish-purple flowers on long stems. Also, **parakeelia**.

parakeet /ˈpærəkit/ n. any of the numerous slender parrots, usually with a long, pointed, graduated tail, especially those of the genera *Aratinga, Pyrrhura*, and *Psittacula*, as the **rose-ringed parakeet**, *Psittacula krameri*, of Africa and Asia, or other small parrots commonly kept caged as pets, as the budgerigar, *Melopsittacus undulatus*. Also, *Colloq.,* **'keet**.

paralegal /pærəˈligəl/ *adj.* **1.** of, relating to, or designating a person who is employed by a barrister or a solicitor to conduct administrative and research duties in relation to a case. –*n.* **2.** a person who acts in this capacity.

parallax /ˈpærəlæks/ n. *Optics* the apparent displacement of an observed object due to a change or difference in position of the observer. –**parallactic** /pærəˈlæktɪk/, *adj.* –**parallactically** /pærəˈlæktɪkli/, *adv.*

parallel /ˈpærəlɛl/ *adj.* **1.** having the same direction, course, or tendency; corresponding; similar; analogous: *parallel forces.* **2.** *Geom.* **a.** (of straight lines) lying in the same plane but never meeting however far extended. **b.** (of planes) having common perpendiculars. **c.** (fol. by *to* or *with*) (of a single line, plane, etc.) equidistant from another or others, at all corresponding points. **3.** *Music* (of two voice parts) going along so that the interval between them remains the same. **4.** *Computers, etc.* meaning or relating to a system in which several activities are carried on at the same time. *–n.* **5.** anything parallel. **6.** *Geog.* a circle on the earth's surface formed by the intersection of a plane parallel to the plane of the equator, bearing east and west and shown in degrees of latitude north or south of the equator along the arc of any meridian. **7.** something the same; correspondence; analogy: *his musical ability is without parallel.* **8.** *Elect.* a connection of two or more circuits in which all ends having the same instantaneous polarity are electrically connected together and all ends having the opposite polarity are similarly connected. The element circuits are said to be **in parallel** (opposed to *in series*). *–v.t.* (**-leled, -leling**) **9.** to make parallel in any way.

parallelogram /pærə'leləgræm/ *n. Geom.* a quadrilateral the opposite sides of which are parallel, as a square, rectangle or rhombus.

parallel port *n. Computers* a port that enables several bits of data to be sent or received concurrently. Compare **serial port**.

parallel processing *n. Computers* the handling of large computational problems by means of a number of computer processors which work simultaneously, thus reducing overall processing time.

parallel processor *n. Computers* a computer which is capable of parallel processing.

parallel universe *n.* a postulated universe in another space-time continuum parallel to our own.

parallel verb *n. Gram.* a verb which expands the range of actions, processes, states, etc., but which is grammatically identical to the preceding verb, as in *He can read and write Italian.*

paralyse /'pærəlaız/ *v.t.* **1.** to affect with paralysis. **2.** to bring to a condition of helpless inactivity. Also, *Chiefly US*, **paralyze.** **–paralysation** /pærəlaı'zeıʃən/, *n.* **–paralyser**, *n.*

paralysis /pə'ræləsəs/ *n.* (*pl.* **-lyses** /-ləsiz/) **1.** *Pathol.* **a.** loss of power of a voluntary muscular contraction. **b.** a disease characterised by this; palsy. **2.** a more or less complete crippling, as of powers or activities: *a paralysis of trade.*

paralytic /pærə'lıtık/ *n.* **1.** someone affected with general paralysis. *–adj.* **2.** affected with or subject to paralysis. **3.** relating to or of the nature of paralysis. **4.** *Colloq.* completely intoxicated with alcoholic drink; very drunk.

paramedical /pærə'mɛdıkəl/ *adj.* related to the medical profession in a supplementary capacity, as an ambulance officer, etc. **–paramedic**, *n.*

parameter /pə'ræmətə/ *n.* **1.** any constituent variable quality: *the parameters of voice quality include breathiness and degree of nasality.* **2.** *Maths* a variable entering into the mathematical form of any distribution such that the possible values of the variable correspond to different distributions. **3.** *Maths* a variable which may be kept constant while the effect of other variables is investigated. **–parametric** /pærə'mɛtrık/, *adj.*

paramount /'pærəmaʊnt/ *adj.* **1.** above others in rank or authority; superior in power or jurisdiction. **2.** chief in importance; supreme; pre-eminent. **–paramountcy**, *n.*

Paramount Leader *n.* the political leader of China, this title being also used as a term of address.

paramour /'pærəmɔ/ *n.* **1.** an illicit lover, especially of a married person. **2.** any lover. **3.** a beloved one.

paramyxovirus /pærə'mıksoʊvaırəs/ *n.* any of a range of viruses, causing such illnesses as mumps, measles and para-influenza.

paranoia /pærə'nɔıə/ *n.* a psychotic disorder characterised by systematised delusions, usually persecutory or

grandiose in nature, outside of which personality functioning tends to be intact. **–paranoiac**, *adj.* **–paranoid**, *adj.*

parapet /'pærəpət/ *n.* **1.** *Fortifications* a defensive wall or elevation, as of earth or stone, in a fortification. **2.** any protective wall or barrier at the edge of a balcony, roof, bridge, or the like. **–parapeted**, *adj.*

paraphernalia /pærəfə'neıliə, -jə/ *pl. n.* **1.** personal belongings. **2.** *Law* the personal articles, apart from dower, reserved by law to a married woman. **3.** (*sometimes construed as sing.*) equipment; apparatus. **4.** (*sometimes construed as sing.*) any collection of miscellaneous articles.

paraphrase /'pærəfreız/ *n.* **1.** a restatement of the sense of a text or passage, as for clearness; a free rendering or translation, as of a passage. *–v.t.* **2.** to restate; render in a paraphrase. *–v.i.* **3.** to make a paraphrase. **–paraphrasable**, *adj.* **–paraphraser**, *n.* **–paraphrastic** /pærə'fræstık/, *adj.*

paraplegia /pærə'plidʒə/ *n.* paralysis of the lower part of the body. **–paraplegic**, *n.*, *adj.*

parasite /'pærəsaıt/ *n.* **1.** an animal or plant which lives on or in an organism of another species (the host), from the body of which it obtains nutriment. **2.** someone who lives on others or another without making any useful and fitting return, especially one who lives on the hospitality of others.

parasol /'pærəsɒl/ *n.* a woman's small or light sun umbrella; a sunshade.

parasympathetic /pærəsımpə'θɛtık/ *adj.* **1.** of or relating to the parasympathetic nervous system. *–n.* **2.** a nerve of the parasympathetic nervous system.

parasympathetic nervous system *n. Physiol., Anat.* that part of the autonomic nervous system which consists of nerves arising from the cranial and sacral regions, and which functions in opposition to the sympathetic nervous system, thus inhibiting heartbeat, contracting the pupil of the eye, etc.

parataxis /pærə'tæksəs/ *n. Gram.* the placing together of sentences, clauses, or phrases without a conjunctive word, as *hurry up, it is getting late*; *I came, I saw, I conquered.* **–paratactic, paratactical**, *adj.* **–paratactically**, *adv.*

paratrooper /'pærətrupə/ *n.* a soldier who reaches battle, especially behind enemy lines, by landing from a plane by parachute.

parboil /'pabɔıl/ *v.t.* to boil partially, or for a short time.

parcel /'pasəl/ *n.* **1.** a quantity of something wrapped or packaged together, a package or bundle. **2.** a quantity of something, as of a commodity for sale; a lot. **3.** any group or assemblage of persons or things. **4.** a separable, separate, or distinct part or portion or section, as of land. **5.** a part or portion of anything. *–v.t.* (**-celled** or, *Chiefly US*, **-celed, -celling** or, *Chiefly US*, **-celing**) **6.** to make into a parcel, or put up in parcels, as goods. *–phr.* **7. parcel out** (or **up**), to divide into or distribute in parcels or portions.

parch /patʃ/ *v.t.* **1.** to make dry, especially to excess, or dry up, as heat, the sun, or a hot wind does. **2.** *Cookery* to brown in a dry heat. *–v.i.* **3.** to become parched; undergo drying by heat.

parchment /'patʃmənt/ *n.* **1.** the skin of sheep, goats, etc., prepared for use as a writing material, etc. **2.** a manuscript or document on such material. **3.** a paper resembling this material.

pardalote /'padəloʊt/ *n.* any of several species of the genus *Pardalotus*, small finch-like birds conspicuously marked with brown or white diamonds, as the diamond bird.

pardon /'padn/ *n.* **1.** forgiveness or favourable attitude: *I beg your pardon.* **2.** *Law* **a.** a giving of pardon for a crime. **b.** the document or warrant by which such pardon is declared. *–v.t.* **3.** to withhold the penalty for (an offence): *He will pardon your crimes.* **4.** to excuse (an action or person); to make courteous allowance for: *Pardon me, madam. –interj.* **5.** a conventional form of apology. **6.** an asking for something to be repeated.: *pardon, what did you say?* **–pardonable,** *adj.* **–pardonably,** *adv.*

pare /pɛə/ *v.t.* **1.** to cut off the outer coating, layer, or part of: *to pare apples. –phr.* **2. pare down,** to reduce or remove by, or as if by, cutting; diminish little by little: *to pare down one's expenses* **3. pare off** (or **away**), to remove (an outer coating, layer, or part) by cutting.

parenchyma /pəˈrɛŋkɪmə/ *n.* **1.** *Bot.* the fundamental (soft) cellular tissue of plants, as in the softer parts of leaves, the pulp of fruits, the pith of stems, etc. **2.** *Anat., Zool.* the proper tissue of an animal organ as distinguished from its connective or supporting tissue. **3.** *Zool.* a kind of jelly-like connective tissue in some lower animals. **4.** *Pathol.* the functional tissue of a morbid growth. **–parenchymatous** /pærɛnˈkɪmətəs/, *adj.*

parent /ˈpɛərənt/ *n.* **1.** a father or a mother. **2.** an author or source. **3.** a protector or guardian. **4.** any organism that produces or generates another. **5.** an organisation that produces and controls a subsidiary organisation. **6.** *Physics, Chem.* a precursor, such as a nucleus, which gives rise to a derived entity. **7.** (in computer programming) an object (def. 10) which has a primary status in a set of objects, having attributes and functions which are retained by all the objects (see child def. 7) retained within it. **–parental,** *adj.* **–parenthood,** *n.* **–parentless,** *adj.*

parenthesis /pəˈrɛnθəsəs/ *n.* (*pl.* **-theses** /-θəsiz/) **1. a.** a set of the upright brackets ( ), used to mark off an interjected explanatory or qualifying remark, indicate groupings in mathematics, etc.: *the abbreviations are set in parenthesis.* **b.** either of these brackets ( ) individually; round bracket. **2. a.** *Gram.* a qualifying or explanatory word (as an appositive), phrase, clause (as a descriptive clause), sentence, or other sequence of forms which interrupts the syntactic construction without otherwise affecting it, having often a characteristic intonation, and shown in writing by commas, parentheses, or dashes. For example: *William Smith – so the story goes – was a pirate.* **b.** a phrase, sentence, comment, etc., which is inserted into a conversation or written passage, and which is not directly related to the main subject: *The son – he's married now – will be here today.* **3.** an interval; interlude. **–parenthetic** /pærənˈθɛtɪk/, **parenthetical** /pærənˈθɛtɪkəl/, *adj.*

parent language *n.* a language from which a later language or group of languages is derived.

parfait /paˈfeɪ/ *n.* a dessert, served in a tall glass, made from layers of ice-cream, fruit, jelly, syrup, nuts, etc.

pariah /pəˈraɪə/ *n.* any person, organisation or nation generally despised; an outcast.

parietal /pəˈraɪətl/ *adj.* **1.** *Anat.* **a.** of or relating to the side of the skull, or with any wall or wall-like structure. **b.** of or relating to the parietal bones. **2.** *Biol.* of or relating to parietes or structural walls. **3.** *Bot.* of or relating to a wall, usually applied to ovules when they proceed from or are borne on the walls or sides of the ovary.

parish /ˈpærɪʃ/ *n.* **1.** an ecclesiastical district having its own church and member of the clergy. **2.** a local church with its field of activity. **3.** the people of a parish. **–parishioner,** *n.*

parity /ˈpærəti/ *n.* **1.** equality in amount, status, or character. **2.** similarity; correspondence; analogy.

parity pricing *n.* *Commerce* the policy of basing the local price of a commodity on an agreed international price where such exists.

park /pak/ *n.* **1.** an area of land within a town, set aside for public use, often landscaped with trees and gardens, and with recreational and other facilities: *Hyde Park.* **2.** an area of land set apart by a city or a nation, to be kept in its natural state for the benefit of the public: *Kosciuszko National Park.* **3.** an enclosed area of land for wild animals: *a lion park. –v.t.* **4.** to put or leave (a car, etc.) for a time in a particular place, as at the side of the road. **5.** to assemble (artillery, etc.) in compact arrangement. *–v.i.* **6.** to park a car, bicycle, etc.

parka /ˈpakə/ *n.* **1.** a strong waterproof jacket with a hood, originally for use in polar regions, now commonly used for any outdoor activity; anorak. **2.** a fur coat, cut like a shirt, worn in north-eastern Asia and Alaska.

parking meter *n.* a device for registering and collecting payment for a length of time during which a vehicle may be parked, consisting of a mechanism activated by a coin, and mounted on a pole near a parking space.

Parkinson's disease /ˈpakənsənz dəziz/ *n.* *Pathol.* a form of paralysis marked by uncontrollable shaking, stiff muscles and weak movement. Also, **Parkinsonism.**

parlance /ˈpaləns/ *n.* way of speaking, or language; idiom; vocabulary: *legal parlance.*

parley /ˈpali/ *n.* (*pl.* **-leys**) **1.** a discussion; a conference. **2.** an informal conference between enemies under truce, to discuss terms, conditions of surrender, etc.

parliament /ˈpaləmənt/ *n.* **1.** (*usu. upper case*) an assembly of elected representatives, often comprising an upper and lower house, which forms the legislature of a nation or constituent state. **2.** a meeting or assembly for conference on public or national affairs. **–parliamentary,** *adj.*

parliamentarian /paləmənˈtɛəriən/ *n.* **1.** a Member of Parliament. **2.** someone skilled in parliamentary procedure or debate. **3.** someone who supports a parliamentary system.

parliamentary privilege *n.* the sum of the special rights enjoyed by each house of parliament collectively and by the members of each house individually, necessary for the discharge of the functions of parliament without hindrance and without fear of prosecution.

parlour /ˈpalə/ *n.* **1.** a room for the reception and entertainment of visitors; a living room. **2.** a semi-private room in a hotel, club, or the like for relaxation, conversation, etc.; a lounge. **3.** a room in a monastery or a nunnery where conversation is allowed and where visitors are received. **4.** a room fitted up for the reception of business patrons or customers: *a beauty parlour, a funeral parlour.* Also, **parlor.**

parlous /ˈpaləs/ *adj.* perilous; dangerous. **–parlously,** *adv.*

parmesan /ˈpaməzən/ *n.* a hard, dry pale yellow cheese, with a granular texture, and a range of flavours depending on maturity, often used grated.

parochial /pəˈrʊkiəl/ *adj.* **1.** of or relating to a parish or parishes. **2.** confined to or interested only in one's own parish, or some particular narrow district or field. **–parochially,** *adv.*

parody /ˈpærədi/ *n.* (*pl.* **-dies**) **1.** a humorous or satirical imitation of a serious piece of literature or writing. **2.** a poor imitation; a travesty. *–v.t.* (**-died, -dying**) **3.** to imitate (a composition, author, etc.) in such a way as to ridicule. **4.** to imitate poorly. **–parodist,** *n.*

parole /pəˈroʊl/ *n.* **1. a.** the liberation of a person from prison, conditional upon good behaviour, prior to the end of the maximum sentence imposed upon that person. **b.** the temporary release of a prisoner. **2.** a word of honour given or pledged. *–v.t.* **3.** to put on parole.

-parous a word element forming an adjective termination meaning 'bringing forth','bearing', 'producing', as in *oviparous, viviparous.*

paroxysm /'pærəksɪzəm/ *n.* **1.** any sudden, violent outburst; a fit of violent action or emotion: *paroxysms of rage.* **2.** *Pathol.* a severe attack, or increase in violence of a disease, usually recurring periodically. **–paroxysmal** /pærək'sɪzməl/, **paroxysmic** /pærək'sɪzmɪk/, *adj.*

parquet /'pakeɪ, 'paki/ *n.* **1.** flooring composed of parquetry. **–***adj.* **2.** composed of parquetry: *a parquet floor*; *a parquet table.* **–***v.t.* (**-queted** /-keɪd, -kid/, **-queting** /-keɪɪŋ, -kiŋ/) **3.** to construct (a flooring, etc.) of parquetry. **4.** to furnish with a floor, etc., of parquetry. **–parquetry,** *n.*

parrot /'pærət/ *n.* **1.** any of numerous hook-billed, fleshy-tongued, often brightly coloured birds which constitute the order Psittaciformes, as the cockatoo, lorikeet, lovebird, macaw, parakeet, rosella, etc., especially those of the family Psittacidae, some varieties having the ability to mimic speech, leading to them having been popular as caged pets. **2.** someone who unintelligently repeats the words or imitates the actions of another. **–***v.t.* **3.** to repeat or imitate like a parrot.

parry /'pæri/ *verb* (**-ried, -rying**) **–***v.t.* **1.** to ward off (a thrust, stroke, weapon, etc.), as in fencing. **2.** to turn aside, evade, or avoid. **–***v.i.* **3.** to parry a thrust, etc. **–***n.* (*pl.* **-ries**) **4.** an act or mode of parrying as in fencing. **5.** a defensive movement in fencing.

parse /paz/ *v.t.* **1.** *Ling.* to describe (a word or series of words) grammatically, telling the part of speech, inflectional form, syntactic relations, etc. **2.** *Computers* (of a compiler) to read (program code) so as to produce a correct output. **3.** to analyse (data). **–parser,** *n.*

parsimony /'pasəməni/, *Orig. US* /-mouni/ *n.* extreme or excessive economy or frugality; niggardliness. **–parsimonious** /pasə'mouniəs/, *adj.*

parsley /'pasli/ *n.* **1.** a garden herb, *Petroselinum crispum,* with aromatic leaves which are much used to garnish or season food. **2.** any of certain allied or similar plants.

parsnip /'pasnɪp/ *n.* **1.** a plant, *Pastinaca sativa,* cultivated varieties of which have a large, whitish, edible root. **2.** the root.

parson /'pasən/ *n.* **1.** a clergyman or minister. **2.** the holder or incumbent of a parochial benefice.

parsonage /'pasənɪdʒ/ *n.* the residence of a parson or clergyman, as provided by the parish or church.

part /pat/ *n.* **1.** a portion or division of a whole, separate in reality, or in thought only; a piece, fragment, fraction, or section; a constituent. **2.** an essential or integral attribute or quality. **3. a.** a section or major division of a work of literature. **b.** a volume. **4.** a portion, member, or organ of an animal body. **5.** each of a number of more or less equal portions composing a whole: *a third part.* **6.** *Maths* an aliquot part or exact divisor. **7.** an allotted portion; a share. **8.** (*usu. pl.*) a region, quarter, or district: *foreign parts.* **9.** one of the sides to a contest, question, agreement, etc. **10.** an extra piece for replacing worn out parts of a tool, machine, etc. **11.** *Music* **a.** a voice either vocal or instrumental. **b.** the written or printed matter extracted from the score which a single performer or section uses in the performance of concerted music: *a horn part.* **12.** participation, interest, or concern in something. **13.** one's share in some action; a duty, function, or office: *Mary didn't do her part.* **14.** a character sustained in a play or in real life; a role. **15.** the words or lines assigned to an actor. **16.** (*usu. pl.*) a personal or mental quality or endowment: *a man of parts.* **17.** (*pl.*) the genitals. **18.** a part of nature. **19.** a parting in the hair. **–***v.t.* **20.** to divide (a thing) into parts; break; cleave; divide. **21.** to comb (the hair) away from a dividing line. **22.** to dissolve (a connection, etc.)

by separation of the parts, persons, or things involved: *she parted company with her sisters.* **23.** to divide into shares; distribute in parts; apportion. **24.** to put or keep asunder (two or more parts, persons, etc., or one part, person, etc., from another); draw or hold apart; disunite; separate. **–***v.i.* **25.** to be or become divided into parts; break or cleave: *the frigate parted amidships.* **26.** to go or come apart or asunder, or separate, as two or more things. **27.** to go apart from each other or one another, as persons: *we'll part no more.* **28.** *Naut.* to break or rend, as a cable. **29.** to depart. **30.** to die. **–***adj.* **31.** in part; partial. **32. a.** descending in part from a specified racial or ethnic group: *her mother was part Maori.* **b.** (of an animal) descending in part from a specified kind or breed: *the dog was part Rottweiler.* **–***adv.* **33.** in part; partly. **–***phr.* **34. for my** (his, her, etc.) **part,** so far as concerns me (him, her, etc.). **35. for the most part,** with regard to the greatest part; mostly. **36. in good part,** with favour; without offence. **37. in part,** in some measure or degree; to some extent. **38. part and parcel,** an essential part. **39. part from,** to be or become separated from. **40. part up,** *Aust. Colloq.* (sometimes fol. by *with*) to hand over; pay out. **41. part with, a.** to give up; relinquish: *I parted with my gold.* **b.** to depart from. **42. play a part, a.** to be instrumental. **b.** to act deceitfully; dissemble or dissimulate. **43. take part,** to participate. **44. take someone's part,** to support or defend someone. **–partible,** *adj.* **–partly,** *adv.*

partake /pa'teɪk/ *v.i.* (**-took, -taken, -taking**) **1.** (sometimes fol. by *in*) to take or have a part or share in common with others; participate. **–***phr.* **2. partake of, a.** to receive, take, or have a share in. **b.** to have something of both the nature or character of: *feelings partaking of both joy and regret.* **–partaker,** *n.*

partheno- a word element meaning 'virgin', 'without fertilisation', as in *parthenogenesis.*

parthenogenesis /paθənou'dʒɛnəsəs/ *n. Biol.* a type of reproduction characterised by the development of an egg without fertilisation. **–parthenogenetic** /ˌpaθənoudʒə-'nɛtɪk/, *adj.* **–parthenogenetically** /ˌpaθənoudʒə'nɛtɪkli/, *adv.*

partial /'paʃəl/ *adj.* **1.** relating to or affecting a part. **2.** being such in part only; not total or general; incomplete: *partial blindness.* **3.** being a part; component or constituent. **4.** biased or prejudiced in favour of a person, group, side, etc., as in a controversy. **–partially,** *adv.* **–partiality** /paʃi'æləti/, *n.*

partial preferential voting *n.* a form of preferential voting in which voters must indicate their order of preference for a minimum number of candidates. Compare **full preferential voting, optional preferential voting.**

participate /pə'tɪsəpeɪt, pa-/ *v.i.* (sometimes fol. by *in*) to take or have a part or share, as with others; share: *to participate in profits.* **–participant,** *n., adj.* **–participator,** *n.* **–participation** /pa,tɪsə'peɪʃən/, *n.* **–participatory** /pə'tɪsəpatri/, *adj.* **–participative** /pə'tɪsəpatɪv/, *adj.*

participation sport *n.* a sport in which people take part for the pleasure of engaging in it and the physical benefits it brings, rather than from a desire to excel in the sport or an ambition to become a professional.

participle /'patəsɪpəl/ *n. Gram.* (in many languages) an adjective form derived from verbs, which ascribes to a noun participation in the action or state of the verb, in English without specifying person or number of the subject. For example: *burning* in *a burning candle* or *devoted* in *his devoted friend.*

particle /'patɪkəl/ *n.* **1.** a minute portion, piece, or amount; a very small bit: *a particle of dust.* **2.** *Physics* → **elementary particle.** **3.** a clause or article, as of a document. **4.** *Roman Catholic Church* **a.** a small piece of the Host. **b.** the small Host given to each lay communicant. **5.** *Gram.* **a.** (in some languages) one of the major form classes, or parts of speech, consisting of words which are neither nouns nor verbs, or of all uninflected words, or the like. **b.** such a word. **c.** a small word of functional or relational use, such as an article, preposition, or conjunction, whether of a separate form class or not.

particular /pə'tɪkjələ/ *adj.* **1.** relating to some one person, thing, group, class, occasion, etc., rather than to others or all; special, not general: *one's particular interests.* **2.** being a definite one, individual, or single, or considered separately: *each particular item.* **3.** distinguished or different from others or from the ordinary; noteworthy; marked; unusual. **4.** exceptional or especial: *to take particular pains.* **5.** being such in an exceptional degree: *a particular friend of mine.* **6.** dealing with or giving details, as an account, description, etc., of a person; detailed; minute; circumstantial. **7.** attentive to or exacting about details or small points: *to be particular about one's food.* **8.** *Philos.* partaking of the nature of an unspecified individual as opposed to the universal and to the singular. −*n.* **9.** an individual or distinct part, as an item of a list or enumeration. **10.** a point, detail, or circumstance: *a report complete in every particular.* **11.** (*pl.*) details of a person's identity, such as name, age, address, especially when listed. **12.** *Logic* an unspecified member of a class. −*phr.* **13. in particular,** particularly; especially: *one book in particular.* −**particularly,** *adv.*

partisan /'pɑtəzən, ˌpɑtə'zæn, pɑtə'zæn/ *n.* **1.** an adherent or supporter of a person, party, or cause. **2.** *Mil.* a member of a party of light or irregular troops, especially as forming the indigenous armed resistance to an invader or conqueror; a guerilla. −*adj.* **3.** relating to or carried on by military partisans. **4.** excessively dedicated to a cause or party. Also, **partizan.** −**partisanship,** *n.*

partition /pɑ'tɪʃən/ *n.* **1.** division (of one thing) into shares. **2.** separation of two or more things. **3.** something that separates, e.g. a wall or barrier. **4.** the date or period of the division of a country or state into two or more new countries, or states: *before partition.* −*v.t.* **5.** to divide into parts. **6.** to divide or separate by a partition. −**partitioner,** *n.* −**partitionist,** *n.* −**partitionment,** *n.*

partner /'pɑtnə/ *n.* **1.** a person who shares or takes part in something; an associate. **2.** *Law* someone who starts or joins a business with other people, usually sharing its risks and profits. **3.** See **silent partner. 4.** a husband or a wife. **5.** someone's companion in a dance. −*v.t.* **6.** to associate as a partner or partners. **7.** to be, or act as, the partner of. −**partnerless,** *adj.* −**partnership,** *n.*

part of speech *n. Gram.* any of the mutually exclusive major form classes of a language, which taken together include the entire vocabulary. For example, in Latin, a word is either a *noun, verb, pronoun, adjective, adverb, preposition, conjunction,* or *interjection.*

partridge /'pɑtrɪdʒ/ *n.* (*pl.* -tridges *or, especially collectively,* -tridge) any of various gallinaceous game birds of the subfamily Perdicinae, especially the **common partridge,** *Perdix perdix,* widespread throughout Eurasia, and introduced into North America.

part-time *adj.* **1.** of, relating to, or occupying less than all normal working hours. **2.** not being one's chief occupation. **3.** participating in an activity for less than the full timetable or program: *a part-time student.* −*adv.* **4.** during less than all normal working hours. −**part-timer,** *n.*

parturition /pɑtʃə'rɪʃən/ *n.* the act of bringing forth young; childbirth.

party /'pɑti/ *n.* (*pl.* -ties) **1.** a group gathered together for some purpose, as for amusement or entertainment. **2.** a

social gathering or entertainment, as of invited guests at a private house or elsewhere: *to give a party.* **3.** a detachment of troops assigned to perform some particular service. **4.** (*oft. upper case*) a number or body of persons ranged on one side, or united in purpose or opinion, in opposition to others, as in politics, etc.: *the Australian Labor Party.* **5.** the system or practice of taking sides on public questions or the like. **6.** attachment or devotion to a side or faction; partisanship. **7.** a person immediately concerned in some transaction or legal proceeding. **8.** *Mining* a group of men performing geophysical work of a specific project, ordinarily using a single method. **9.** someone who participates in some action or affair. **10.** the person under consideration. **11.** a person in general. −*adj.* **12.** of or relating to a party or faction; partisan: *a party issue.* **13.** of or for a social gathering: *a party dress.* **14.** given to partying: *a party girl*; *a party boy.* −*v.i.* (-tied, -tying) **15.** to take part in festivities at or as at a party. −*phr.* **16. be (a) party to,** to help, take part in, or be involved in: *he regretted that he had ever been a party to the scheme.* **17. come to the party,** *Aust., NZ* to assist, especially with money; fall in with someone's plans. **18. party on,** to continue a party. −**partying,** *n.*

party line *n.* **1.** a telephone line shared by two or more subscribers. **2.** the bounding line between adjoining premises. **3.** the authoritatively announced policies and practices of a group, usually followed without exception: *the Communist party line.*

party machine *n.* the organisation behind a political party which influences the choice of candidates, runs elections, and manages fundraising.

party plan *n.* a method of direct selling in which representatives display products for sale at a party organised for this purpose. −**party-plan,** *adj.*

parvenu /'pɑvənu, -nju/ *n.* **1.** someone who has risen above their class or to a position above their qualifications; an upstart. −*adj.* **2.** being or characteristic of a parvenu.

parvovirus /'pɑvouvaɪrəs/ *n.* **1.** any of a group of very small viruses with a single strand of DNA, some of which cause disease in mammals. **2.** a contagious infection of dogs, caused by a parvovirus, often fatal and usually characterised by haemorrhagic gastroenteritis. Also, **parvo.**

pascal /'pæskəl, pæs'kal/ *n.* the derived SI unit of pressure, equal to 1 newton per square metre. *Symbol:* Pa

paschal /'pæskəl/ *adj.* **1.** relating to the Passover or to Pesach. **2.** relating to Easter.

pashmina /pæʃ'minə/ *n.* **1.** a fine woollen fabric made from the underbelly fur of Himalayan goats, sometimes blended with silk. **2.** a shawl made from this fabric.

paspalum /pæs'peɪləm/ *n.* any grass of the genus *Paspalum* but especially *P. dilatatum,* native to southern America but now one of the most widespread grasses in the higher-rainfall areas of Australia.

pass /pɑs/ *v.t.* **1.** to go by or move past (something). **2.** to go by without acting upon or noticing; leave unmentioned. **3.** to omit payment of (a dividend, etc.). **4.** to go or get through (a channel, barrier, etc.). **5.** to go across or over (a stream, threshold, etc.); cross. **6.** to undergo successfully (an examination, etc.). **7.** to undergo or get through (an obstacle, experience, ordeal, etc.). **8.** to permit to complete successfully. **9.** to go beyond (a point, degree, stage, etc.); transcend; exceed; surpass. **10.** to cause to go or move onwards: *to pass a rope through a hole.* **11.** *US* to cause to go by or move past: *to pass troops in review.* **12.** to exist through; live during; spend: *to pass one's days.* **13.** to cause to go about or circulate; give currency to. **14.** to cause to be accepted or received. **15.** to convey, transfer, or transmit; deliver. **16.** to pronounce; utter: *to pass remarks.*

17. to pledge, as one's word. **18.** to cause or allow to go through something, as through a test, etc. **19.** to discharge or void, as excrement. **20.** to sanction or approve: *to pass a bill.* **21.** to obtain the approval or sanction of (a legislative body, etc.), as a bill. **22.** to express or pronounce, as an opinion or judgement. **23.** *Football, Hockey, etc.* to transmit (the ball, etc.) to another player. **24.** to overtake. *–v.i.* **25.** to go or move onwards; proceed; make one's, or its, way. **26.** to go away or depart. **27.** to elapse, as time. **28.** to come to an end, as a thing in time. **29.** to go on or take place; happen; occur: *to learn what has passed.* **30.** to go by or move past, as a procession. **31.** to go about or circulate; be current. **32.** (sometimes fol. by *for* or *as*) to be accepted or received: *material that passed for silk.* **33.** to be transferred or conveyed. **34.** to be interchanged, as between two persons: *sharp words passed between them.* **35.** to undergo transition or conversion: *to pass from a solid to a liquid state.* **36.** to go or get through something, such as a barrier, test, examination, etc., especially without honours. **37.** to go unheeded, uncensured, or unchallenged: *but let that pass.* **38.** to be voided, as excrement. **39.** to be ratified or enacted, as a bill or law. **40.** to make a pass, as in football. **41.** *Cards* **a.** to forgo one's opportunity to bid, play, etc. **b.** to throw up one's hand. *–n.* **42.** a narrow route across a relatively low notch or depression in a mountain barrier separating the headwaters of approaching valleys from either side. **43.** a way affording passage, as through an obstructed region. **44.** *US* a navigable channel, as at the mouth or delta of a river. **45.** a permission or licence to pass, go, come, or enter. **46.** *Mil.* **a.** a military document granting the right to cross lines, or to enter or leave a military or naval reservation or other area or building. **b.** written authority given to a soldier to leave a station or duty for a few hours or days. **47.** *Aust. Hist.* a written document authorising and regulating the movement of a convict around the colony. **48. a.** a free ticket. **b.** a pre-paid or free ticket which allows one to travel on public transport without paying on each occasion of travel: *a bus pass.* **49.** an examination score which is classified as passing, especially one which does not gain honours. **50.** the transference of a ball, etc., from one player to another, as in football. **51.** a thrust or lunge, as in fencing. **52.** *Cards* an act of not bidding or raising another bid. **53.** *Magic* **a.** a passing of the hand over, along, or in front of anything. **b.** the transference or changing of objects by or as by sleight of hand; a manipulation, as of a juggler; a trick. **54.** a stage in procedure or experience; a particular stage or state of affairs: *things have come to a pretty pass.* **55.** the act of passing. *–phr.* **56. bring to pass**, to cause to happen. **57. come to pass**, to occur. **58. let something pass**, to ignore or overlook something. **59. make a pass**, (sometimes fol. by *at*) to make an amorous overture or gesture. **60. pass away**, **a.** to cease to be. **b.** (*euphemistic*) to die. **61. pass in**, (*usu. passive*) to leave unsold at an auction, the reserve price not being reached: *many bales of wool were passed in.* **62. pass off**, **a.** to put into circulation, or dispose of, especially deceptively: *to pass off a counterfeit $50 note.* **b.** to cause to be accepted or received in a false character: *he passed himself off as my servant.* **c.** to produce in the style or format associated with another manufacturer's product so as to gain commercial advantage: *to pass a dictionary off as a Macquarie.* **d.** to end gradually; to cease. **e.** to take place; occur: *the introduction passed off without incident.* **63. pass on**, **a.** (*euphemistic*) to die. **b.** to move to another place. **c.** to proceed to another topic. **d.** to convey to someone: *she passed on the good news.* **64. pass out**, **a.** to distribute. **b.** to faint. **c.** to complete the course, as at a military academy. **65. pass over**, **a.** to disregard. **b.** to omit to notice.

66. pass the buck, to avoid responsibility by passing it to another. **67. pass up**, *Colloq.* to refuse; reject. **68. the pass**, (in a restaurant) the place where orders are received and plates are placed for waitstaff to collect and take to diners.

passable /ˈpasəbəl/ *adj.* **1.** able to be passed. **2.** able to be proceeded through or over, or traversed, penetrated, crossed, etc., as a road, forest, or stream. **3.** tolerable, fair, or moderate: *a passable knowledge of history.* **4.** valid as currency and able to be circulated as a coin. **5.** able to be ratified, or enacted. **–passableness**, *n.*

passage /ˈpæsɪdʒ/ *n.* **1.** a part of a writing or speech; a paragraph, verse, etc.: *a passage of Scripture.* **2.** *Music* **a.** a scale- or arpeggio-like series of notes introduced as an ornament; a run, roulade, or flourish. **b.** a phrase or other division of a piece. **3.** the act of passing: *the passage of time*; *the passage of events.* **4.** permission to pass: *to refuse passage through a territory.* **5.** a means of passing; a way, route, avenue, channel, corridor, etc. **6.** movement from one place or state to another; transit: *a rough passage.* *–v.i.* **7.** to make a passage; cross; pass; voyage.

passata /pəˈsatə/ *n.* a fine tomato sauce in the Italian style, made from sieved tomatoes. Compare **sugo**.

passbook /ˈpasbʊk/ *n.* **1.** a bankbook. **2.** a customer's book in which a merchant or trader makes entries of goods sold on credit. **3.** a record of payments made to a building society.

passé /paˈseɪ/ *adj.* **1.** antiquated, or out-of-date. **2.** passed. **3.** past the prime; aged.

passenger /ˈpæsəndʒə/ *n.* someone who travels by some form of conveyance: *the passengers of a ship.*

passerine /ˈpæsəraɪn/ *adj.* **1.** belonging or relating to the Passeriformes, an order of birds, typically insessorial (perching), embracing more than half of all birds, and including the finches, thrushes, warblers, swallows, crows, larks, etc. *–n.* **2.** any bird of the order Passeriformes.

passion /ˈpæʃən/ *n.* **1.** any strong feeling or emotion, such as hope, fear, joy, grief, anger, love, desire, etc. **2.** strong, emotional, sexual love. **3.** a person who is the object of such a feeling: *she was his passion.* **4.** a strong or extravagant fondness, enthusiasm, or desire for anything: *a passion for music.* **5.** (*oft. upper case*) *Christianity* the sufferings of Christ from the Last Supper to his death on the Cross. **–passionate**, *adj.*

passionflower /ˈpæʃənflauə/ *n.* any plant of the genus *Passiflora*, or related genera, which comprise climbing vines or shrubs, mainly American, bearing showy flowers and a pulpy berry or fruit which in some species is edible, especially the passionfruit.

passionfruit /ˈpæʃənfrut/ *n.* **1.** Also, **passionfruit vine**. a passionflower, *Passiflora edulis*. **2.** the fruit of this plant.

passive /ˈpæsɪv, -səv/ *adj.* **1.** not acting, or not attended with or manifested in open or positive action: *passive resistance.* **2.** inactive, quiescent, or inert. **3.** suffering action, acted upon, or being the object of action (opposed to *active*). **4.** receiving or characterised by the reception of impressions from without. **5.** produced by or due to external agency. **6.** suffering, receiving, or submitting without resistance. **7.** characterised by or involving doing this: *passive obedience.* **8.** *Gram.* denoting a voice of verb inflection in which the subject is represented as being acted on (opposed to *active*). For example, in the sentence *He was hit, was hit* is in the passive voice. **9.** *Electronics* (of an electronic component, or a complete circuit) unable to amplify or switch a signal, as a resistor or capacitor (opposed to an active circuit component, as a transistor or valve). **10.** *Chem.* inactive, especially under conditions in which chemical activity is to be expected. **11.** (of a metal) having a protective oxide film on the surface rendering it impervious to attack. **12.** (of a communications satellite) only able to reflect signals, and not retransmit them. **13.** *Med.* relating to certain unhealthy but insufficiently virulent conditions; inactive (opposed to *active* or *spontaneous*). *–n.* **14.** *Gram.* **a.** the passive voice. **b.** a form or construction therein. **–passively,** *adv.* **–passiveness, passivity** /pæsˈɪvəti/, *n.*

passive aggressive *adj.* **1.** deliberately uncooperative; employing methods that frustrate the objectives of others without confronting them with outright refusal. *–n.* **2.** a person who behaves in such a manner.

passive euthanasia *n.* the deliberate bringing about of the death of a person suffering from an incurable disease or condition, by withdrawing life-sustaining measures, especially where it is deemed that such measures are not in the best interests of the sufferer.

passive smoking *n.* the inhaling by a nonsmoker of the smoke produced by cigarette, cigar and pipe smokers. **–passive smoker,** *n.*

Passover /ˈpɑːsoʊvə/ *n.* → **Pesach.**

passport /ˈpɑːspɔt/ *n.* **1.** an official document granting permission to the person specified to visit foreign countries, and authenticating the holder's identity, citizenship, and right to protection while abroad. **2.** an authorisation to pass or go anywhere. **3.** a document issued to a ship, especially to neutral merchant vessels in time of war, granting or requesting permission to proceed without molestation in certain waters. **4.** anything that gives admission or acceptance.

password /ˈpɑːswɜd/ *n.* **1.** a secret word or expression used to gain access to a restricted area or to distinguish a friend from an enemy. **2.** *Computers* a private code, usually a word or expression, used to gain access to a computer system.

past /pɑːst/ *v.* **1.** *Rare* past participle and occasional past tense of **pass.** *–adj.* **2.** gone by in time: *past feelings.* **3.** belonging to, or having existed or occurred in time before this: *past ages.* **4.** gone by just before the present time; just passed: *the past year.* *–n.* **5.** the time gone by: *far back in the past.* **6.** the events of that time: *to forget the past.* **7.** a past history, life, career, etc.: *a glorious past.* **8.** a past career which is kept concealed: *a woman with a past.* **9.** → **past tense.** *–adv.* **10.** so as to pass by or beyond; by: *the troops marched past.* *–prep.* **11.** beyond in time; after: *past noon.* **12.** beyond in position; farther on than: *the house past the church.* **13.** beyond in amount, number, etc. **14.** beyond the reach, scope, influence, or power of: *past belief.* *–phr. Colloq.* **15. a colourful past,** (*euphemistic*) a private history full of disreputable incidents. **16. be past it,** to have reached an age at which one loses various capacities for performance.

pasta /ˈpæstə, ˈpɑs-/ *n.* any of the several preparations made from a dough or paste of wheat flour, salt, water, and sometimes egg, such as spaghetti, macaroni, tagliatelle, etc.

paste /peɪst/ *n.* **1.** a mixture of flour and water, used for sticking paper. **2.** any material or preparation in a soft mass: *a toothpaste.* **3.** dough, especially when prepared with shortening, for making pastry. **4.** a sweet confection-like dough: *almond paste.* **5.** food reduced to a smooth, soft mass, for spreading on bread or for seasoning. **6.** a mixture of clay, water, etc., for making earthenware, porcelain, etc. **7.** a brilliant, heavy glass, used for making artificial gems. *–v.t.* (**pasted, pasting**) **8.** to fasten or stick with paste. **9.** *Computers* to insert (data) from one application or document into another, or from one location in a document to another. **10.** *Colloq.* to beat or scold someone.

pastel /ˈpæstl/ *n.* **1.** a soft, subdued shade of colour. **2.** (a crayon made with) a kind of dried paste, made of

pigments ground with chalk and mixed with gum water. **3.** the art of drawing with such crayons. **4.** a drawing so made. *–adj.* **5.** having a soft, subdued shade. **6.** drawn with pastels. **–pastellist,** *n.*

pasteurise /ˈpɑstʃəraɪz/ *v.t.* to swiftly heat (milk, etc.) to a high temperature and then swiftly cool to a low temperature, in order to destroy certain microorganisms and prevent or arrest fermentation. Also, **pasteurize.** **–pasteurisation** /pɑstʃəraɪˈzeɪʃən/, *n.*

pastiche /pæsˈtiʃ/ *n.* **1.** any work of art, literature, or music consisting of motifs borrowed from one or more masters or works of art. **2.** the mixing within one artistic production of styles, colours, etc., especially in imitation of established styles.

pastie /ˈpæsti, ˈpɑsti/ *n.* (*pl.* **pasties**) a type of pie in which a circular piece of pastry is folded around a filling of vegetables, meat, etc. and baked. Also, **pasty, Cornish pastie.**

pastille /pæsˈtil, ˈpæstl/ *n.* **1.** a flavoured or a medicated lozenge. **2.** a roll or cone of paste containing aromatic substances, burnt as a disinfectant, etc. Also, **pastil** /ˈpæstl/.

pastime /ˈpɑstaɪm/ *n.* something that serves to make time pass agreeably; amusement, or sport: *to play cards for a pastime.*

pastor /ˈpɑstə/ *n.* **1.** a minister or member of the clergy with reference to his or her congregation. **2.** a person having spiritual care of a number of persons. **–pastorship,** *n.*

pastoral /ˈpɑstərəl, -trəl/ *adj.* **1.** of or relating to the raising of stock, especially sheep or cattle, on rural properties. **2.** (of land) used for pasture. **3.** having the simplicity or charm of such country: *pastoral scenery.* **4.** (of a work of art, music, literature) describing the life of shepherds or of the country. **5.** of or relating to a minister or member of the clergy, or to their duties, etc. **–pastoralism,** *n.* **–pastorally,** *adv.*

pastoral care *n.* **1.** the responsibility of a member of the clergy to attend to the needs of the congregation. **2.** (especially in non-government schools) the provisions made to advise students about personal wellbeing and their moral and ethical concerns.

pastoralism /ˈpɑstərəlɪzəm/ *n.* the process of developing land for pasture for the grazing of domesticated or partially domesticated animals, especially for meat or wool production. **–pastoralist,** *adj., n.*

pastrami /pəsˈtrɑmi/ *n.* a highly seasoned shoulder cut of smoked beef, usually sold sliced.

pastry /ˈpeɪstri/ *n.* (*pl.* **-tries**) **1.** food made of paste or dough, as the crust of pies, etc. **2.** articles of food of which such paste forms an essential part, as pies, tarts, etc.

past tense *n.* a verb form which refers to events that have already happened.

pasture /ˈpɑstʃə/ *n.* **1.** ground covered with grass, etc., used or suitable for the grazing of cattle, etc.; grassland. *–v.t.* **2.** to feed (cattle, etc.) by putting them to graze on pasture. *–v.i.* **3.** (of cattle, etc.) to graze upon pasture. **–pasturable,** *adj.*

pasty[1] /ˈpeɪsti/ *adj.* (**-tier, -tiest**) **1.** of or like paste in consistency, colour, etc. *–n.* (*pl.* **-ties**) **2.** a small piece of material, usually decorated, worn on the nipples by striptease dancers.

pasty[2] /ˈpæsti, ˈpɑsti/ *n.* (*pl.* **-ties**) → **pastie.**

PA system /pi ˈeɪ sɪstəm/ *n.* → **public-address system.** Also, **PA.**

pat[1] /pæt/ *verb* (**patted, patting**) *–v.t.* **1.** to strike lightly with something flat, as an implement, the palm of the hand, or the foot. **2.** to stroke gently with the palm or fingers as an expression of affection, approbation, etc. **3.** to flatten or smooth into a desired shape, as butter. *–v.i.* **4.** to strike lightly or gently. **5.** to walk or run with lightly sounding footsteps. –n. **6.** a light stroke or blow with something flat. **7.** the sound of a light stroke, or of light footsteps. **8.** a small mass of something, as butter, shaped by patting or other manipulation. **9.** → **cow pat.** –*phr. Colloq.* **10. a pat on the back,** a gesture or word of encouragement or congratulation. **11. pat someone on the back,** to congratulate or encourage someone with praise.

pat² /pæt/ *adj.* **1.** exactly to the point or purpose. **2.** apt; opportune; ready. **3.** fluently glib; readily facile. –*adv.* **4.** exactly or perfectly. **5.** aptly; opportunely. –*phr.* **6. off pat, a.** exactly or perfectly. **b.** unhesitatingly or without deliberation. **7. sit** (or **stand**) (or **stay**) **pat,** *Aust. Colloq.* to stick to one's decision, policy, etc. –**patness,** *n.* –**patter,** *n.*

pat³ /pæt/ *phr.* **on one's pat,** *Colloq.* alone. Also, **Pat.**

Patagonian toothfish /pætəgouniən 'tuθfɪʃ/ *n.* a sea bass, *Dissostichus eleginoides,* widely distributed from South America to Australia and in the sub-antarctic regions of the Indian and Atlantic oceans and the Southern Ocean; highly prized as a food fish.

patch /pætʃ/ *n.* **1.** a piece of material used to mend a hole or break, or strengthen a weak place: *a patch on a sail.* **2.** a piece of material used to cover or protect a wound, an injured part, etc.: *a patch over the eye.* **3.** any of the pieces of cloth sewn together to form patchwork. **4.** a small piece or scrap of anything. **5. a.** a small piece or tract of land, road, etc. **b.** *Goldmining Colloq.* a small claim, usually one which produces gold. **6.** *Colloq.* an area of responsibility: *stay off my patch!* **7.** a distinctive mark, an emblem, as on a soldier's uniform to identify his or her unit; flash. **8.** a period of time. **9.** *Computers* a correction (usually temporary) made by the user to a computer program supplied by a software publisher, allowing the program to be customised for special uses; hotfix. **10.** Also, **skin patch.** *Med.* an adhesive dressing which slowly dispenses medicine or other needed chemicals which are absorbed through the skin of the body. –*v.t.* **11.** to mend or strengthen with or as with a patch or patches. **12.** to make by joining patches or pieces together: *to patch a quilt.* –*v.i.* **13.** *Computers* to apply a patch (def. 9); hotfix. –*phr.* **14. hit** (or **strike**) **a bad patch,** to suffer a series of misfortunes, especially financial. **15. not a patch on,** *Colloq.* not comparable to; not nearly as good as. **16. patch in,** to join, especially to join (an electronic circuit) to an existing set of circuits, usually on a temporary basis. **17. patch up, a.** to repair or restore, especially in a hasty or makeshift way. **b.** to settle; smooth over: *they patched up their quarrel.* –**patcher,** *n.*

patchwork /'pætʃwɜk/ *n.* **1.** work made of pieces of cloth or leather of various colours or shapes sewn together, used especially for covering quilts, cushions, etc. **2.** something made up of various pieces or parts put together: *a patchwork of verses.*

patchy /'pætʃi/ *adj.* (**-chier, -chiest**) **1.** marked by patches. **2.** occurring in, forming, or like patches. **3.** of unequal quality; irregular; not uniform. –**patchily,** *adv.* –**patchiness,** *n.*

pate /peɪt/ *n.* **1.** the head. **2.** the crown or top of the head.

pâté /'pæteɪ, 'pɑ-/ *n.* **1.** a paste or spread made of finely minced liver, meat, fish, etc. **2.** a small pastie, filled with forcemeat, mixed with dices or strips of the main ingredient.

patella /pə'tɛlə/ *n.* (*pl.* **-las** *or* **-lae** /-li/) **1.** *Anat.* the kneecap. **2.** *Bot., Zool., etc.* a pan-like or cuplike formation. **3.** *Archaeology* a small pan or shallow vessel. –**patellar,** *adj.*

patent /'peɪtnt, 'pætnt/ *n.* **1.** a government grant to an inventor, giving the right to make, use and sell an invention without competition. **2.** an invention, process, etc., which has been patented. –*adj.* **3.** (of a product,

invention, etc.) specially protected by a patent: *a patent door.* **4.** open to view or knowledge; manifest; evident; plain. **5.** lying open, or not shut in. **6.** *Chiefly Bot.* expanded or spreading. –*v.t.* **7.** to take out a patent on; obtain the exclusive rights to (an invention) by a patent. –**patentable,** *adj.* –**patentability** /ˌpeɪtntə'bɪləti, pæt-/, *n.* –**patently,** *adv.* –**patentor,** *n.*

patent leather *n.* **1.** leather lacquered to produce a hard, glossy, smooth finish. **2.** any imitation of this. –**patent-leather,** *adj.*

paternal /pə'tɜnəl/ *adj.* **1.** characteristic of or befitting a father; fatherly. **2.** of or relating to a father. **3.** related on the father's side. **4.** derived or inherited from a father. –**paternally,** *adv.*

paternalism /pə'tɜnəlɪzəm/ *n.* the principle or practice, on the part of a government or of any body or person in authority, of managing or regulating the affairs of a country or community, or of individuals, in the manner of a father dealing with his children, especially to the extent that individual rights are abrogated, such as freedom of choice and individual responsibility. –**paternalistic** /pətɜnə'lɪstɪk/, *adj.* –**paternalistically** /pətɜnə-'lɪstɪkli/, *adv.*

paternity /pə'tɜnəti/ *n.* **1.** derivation from a father. **2.** the state of being a father; fatherhood. **3.** origin or authorship.

paternity suit *n.* a court case to establish that a man is or is not the father of a child, as claimed by the person bringing the suit.

paternity test *n.* a DNA analysis done to establish paternity.

path /paθ/ *n.* **1.** a way beaten or trodden by the feet of people or animals. **2.** a walk in a garden or through grounds. **3.** a route, course, or track in which something moves. **4.** a course of action, conduct, or procedure.

-path a suffix used to form nouns denoting: **1.** a person suffering from the specified disorder, as in *neuropath.* **2.** a person who treats disorders by a specified method, usually one which is regarded as an alternative medicine, as in *naturopath, osteopath.*

pathetic /pə'θɛtɪk/ *adj.* **1.** exciting pity or sympathetic sadness; full of pathos. **2.** affecting or moving the feelings. **3.** relating or due to the feelings. **4.** *Colloq.* miserably inadequate: *her vegetables made a pathetic showing at the annual produce fair.* **5.** *Colloq.* inviting scorn or pity because of patent shortcomings, pettiness, greed, rudeness, etc. –**pathetically,** *adv.*

-pathic a word element forming adjectives from nouns ending in *-pathy,* as *psychopathic.*

patho- a word element meaning 'suffering', 'disease', 'feeling'.

pathogen /'pæθədʒən/ *n.* a pathogenic or disease-producing organism. Also, **pathogene** /'pæθədʒin/. –**pathogenic** /pæθə'dʒɛnɪk/, *adj.*

pathology /pə'θɒlədʒi/ *n.* (*pl.* **-gies**) **1.** the branch of medical science dealing with the origin, nature, and course of diseases. **2.** the conditions and processes of a disease, especially changes in bodily tissues or organs occurring as a manifestation of the disease. **3.** Also, **clinical pathology.** the study of diseased body organs, tissues, or cells, using laboratory tests. **4.** any abnormal state: *social pathology.* –**pathological,** *adj.* –**pathologist,** *n.*

pathos /'peɪθɒs/ *n.* the quality or power, as in speech, music, etc., of evoking a feeling of pity or sympathetic sadness; touching or pathetic character or effect.

-pathy a word element meaning 'suffering', 'feeling', as in *antipathy, sympathy,* and often, especially in words of modern formation, 'morbid affection', 'disease', as in *psychopathy,* and hence used also in names of systems or methods of treating disease, as in *homeopathy, osteopathy.*

patience /ˈpeɪʃəns/ n. 1. calm and uncomplaining endurance, as under pain, provocation, etc. 2. calmness in waiting: *have patience a little longer.* 3. quiet perseverance: *to labour with patience.* 4. a card game, usually played by one person alone.

patient /ˈpeɪʃənt/ n. 1. someone who is under medical or surgical treatment. 2. a person or thing that undergoes action (opposed to *agent*). –adj. 3. enduring pain, trouble, affliction, hardship, etc., with fortitude, calmness, or quiet submission. 4. quietly enduring strain, annoyance, etc.: *patient in a traffic jam.* 5. enduring delay with calmness or equanimity, or marked by such endurance: *be patient.* 6. quietly persevering or diligent: *patient workers.* –phr. 7. patient of, a. having or showing the capacity for. b. susceptible to. –**patiently**, adv.

patient-controlled analgesia n. a system whereby a patient on an intravenous drip can administer their own painkilling medication by means of a machine which also monitors and limits the amount dispensed. Also, **PCA**.

patina /ˈpætənə, pəˈtinə/ n. 1. a film or encrustation, usually green, caused by oxidisation on the surface of old bronze, and esteemed as ornamental. 2. a similar film or colouring on some other substance. 3. a surface calcification of implements, usually indicating great age.

patio /ˈpætioʊ, ˈpeɪʃioʊ/ n. (pl. **-tios**) 1. a court, as of a house, especially an inner court open to the sky. 2. an area, usually paved, adjoining a house, used for outdoor living.

patois /ˈpætwɑ/ n. (pl. **patois** /ˈpætwɑz/) a regional dialect often differing markedly from the standard form of the language.

patri- a word element meaning 'father'.

patriarch /ˈpeɪtriak, ˈpæt-/ n. 1. any of the earlier biblical personages regarded as the fathers of the human race, comprising those from Adam to the birth of Abraham. 2. one of the three great progenitors of the Israelites, Abraham, Isaac, or Jacob. 3. one of the sons of Jacob (the **twelve patriarchs**), from whom the tribes of Israel were descended. 4. (in the early Christian church) a bishop of high rank, especially one with jurisdiction over metropolitans. 5. *Gk Orthodox Church* the bishop of any of the ancient sees of Alexandria, Antioch, Constantinople, and Jerusalem, and in recent years of Russia, Romania, and Serbia. 6. a bishop of the highest rank or authority in any of the various non-Orthodox churches in the East. 7. *Roman Catholic Church* a. the pope (**Patriarch of Rome**). b. a bishop of the highest rank next after the pope. 8. one of the elders or leading older members of a community. 9. a venerable old man. 10. the male head of a family or tribal line. 11. a person regarded as the father or founder of an order, class, etc. 12. *Colloq.* an authoritarian man. –**patriarchal** /peɪtriˈakəl, pæt-/, adj. –**patriarchally**, adv.

patriarchy /ˈpeɪtriaki, ˈpæt-/ n. (pl. **-archies**) 1. a form of social organisation in which the father is head of the family, and in which descent is reckoned in the male line, and the children belonging to the father's clan. 2. a community organised and run upon such a system.

patrician /pəˈtrɪʃən/ n. 1. a member of the original senatorial aristocracy in ancient Rome. 2. a title or dignity conferred by the emperor under the later Roman and Byzantine Empires. 3. any noble or aristocrat. –adj. 4. of or belonging to the patrician families of ancient Rome. 5. befitting an aristocrat: *patrician aloofness.* –**patricianly**, adv.

patricide /ˈpætrəsaɪd/ n. 1. someone who kills his or her father. 2. the act of killing one's father. –**patricidal** /pætrəˈsaɪdl/, adj.

patrifilial /pætriˈfiliəl/ adj. of or relating to a line of descent from father to son: *a patrifilial guardian totem.*

patrilineal /pætrəˈlɪniəl/ adj. of or relating to associations by descent or title traced through the male line.

patriot /ˈpeɪtriət, ˈpæt-/ n. someone who loves their country, zealously supporting and defending it and its interests. –**patriotism**, n. –**patriotic** /peɪtriˈɒtɪk, pæt-/, adj.

patrol /pəˈtroʊl/ verb (-trolled, -trolling) –v.i. 1. to walk or travel regularly around or through a place to counter any trouble and maintain security. –v.t. 2. to guard or protect (an area, building, etc.) by traversing it. –n. 3. a person or a body of people who patrol. 4. the act of patrolling. –**patroller**, n.

patron /ˈpeɪtrən/ n. 1. someone who supports a shop, hotel, etc., by spending money there. 2. a protector or supporter of a person, cause, institution, art, or enterprise: *the club's patron.* 3. *Roman Hist.* someone who protected and helped another (the client) in return for certain benefits, often the ex-master of a freed slave. –**patronage**, n. –**patronal**, adj. –**patroness** /ˈpeɪtrənes/, fem. n.

patronise /ˈpætrənaɪz/ v.t. 1. to favour (a shop, restaurant, etc.) with one's patronage; to trade with. 2. to treat in a condescending way. 3. to act as patron towards; support. Also, **patronize**. –**patroniser**, n. –**patronisingly**, adv.

patron saint n. a saint regarded as the special guardian of a person, trade, place, etc.

patter¹ /ˈpætə/ v.i. 1. to strike or move with a succession of slight tapping sounds. –v.t. 2. to cause to patter. 3. to spatter with something. –n. 4. a pattering sound: *the heavy patter of the rain.* 5. the act of pattering.

patter² /ˈpætə/ n. 1. the slick and fast speech used by a salesperson, a magician performing tricks, or comedian or other entertainer. 2. rapid speech; mere chatter; gabble. 3. the jargon of any class, group, etc.; cant. –v.i. 4. to talk fast, especially with little regard to content; chatter. –**patterer**, n.

pattern /ˈpætn/ n. 1. a decorative design, as for china, wallpaper, textile fabrics, etc. 2. such a design carried out on something. 3. a style of marking of natural or chance origin: *patterns of frost on the window.* 4. style or type in general. 5. anything fashioned or designed to serve as a model or guide for something to be made: *a paper pattern for a dress.* 6. an example or instance. 7. a sample or specimen. 8. the distribution of shot in a target at which a shotgun or the like is fired. –v.t. 9. to make after a pattern; model. 10. to cover or mark with a pattern. –phr. 11. pattern by (or after), to model one's conduct, etc., on. 12. pattern oneself on, to use as a model; imitate.

pattern bargaining n. a method by which a trade union pursues better conditions for its members, by targeting one employer for negotiation on an entitlement and, once successful, then presenting this result to other employers as a matter in which they should follow suit.

patty /ˈpæti/ n. (pl. **-ties**) 1. a small pie; a pastie: *oyster patties.* 2. a savoury mixture formed into a ball or shape and cooked on a griddle or deep-fried.

paua /ˈpaʊə/ n. a univalve mollusc of the abalone family, *Haliotis iris*, of New Zealand, having edible flesh and an iridescent shell used in ornaments and jewellery.

paucity /ˈpɔsəti/ n. smallness of quantity; fewness; scantiness: *paucity of material.*

paunch /pɔntʃ/ n. 1. the belly or abdomen. 2. a large, prominent belly. –**paunchy**, adj.

pauper /ˈpɔpə/ n. 1. a very poor person. 2. someone without means, who is supported by a community. –**pauperism**, n.

pause /pɔz/ n. 1. a temporary stop or rest, especially in speech or action. 2. a cessation proceeding from doubt or uncertainty. **3.** delay; hesitation; suspense. **4.** a break or rest in speaking or reading as depending on sense, grammatical relations, metrical divisions, etc., or in writing or printing as marked by punctuation. **5.** *Prosody* → **caesura**. **6.** *Music* a symbol, ⌢ or ⌣, placed over or under a note or rest to indicate that it is to be prolonged. –*v.i.* **7.** to make a pause; stop; wait; hesitate. –*v.t.* **8.** to temporarily halt (a computer game, DVD, etc.): *he paused the film while he answered the phone.* –*phr.* **9.** **give pause**, to cause to hesitate. –**pausal**, *adj.* –**pauser**, *n.* –**pausingly**, *adv.*

pav /pæv/ *n. Aust., NZ Colloq.* → **pavlova**.

pave /peɪv/ *v.t.* **1.** to cover or lay (a road, walk, etc.) with stones, bricks, tiles, wood, concrete, etc., so as to make a firm, level surface. **2.** to prepare (the way) for. **3.** to mark (a text) with a translation or other helpful notes. –**paver**, *n.*

pavement /ˈpeɪvmənt/ *n.* **1.** a walk or footway, especially a paved one, at the side of a street or road. **2.** a surface, ground covering, or floor made by paving. **3.** a material used for paving.

pavilion /pəˈvɪljən/ *n.* **1.** a light, open structure for shelter, pleasure, etc., in a park. **2.** a projecting part at the front or side of a building. **3.** a large tent on posts.

pavlova /pævˈloʊvə/ *n.* a dessert made of a large soft-centred meringue, usually roughly circular and having an indented top filled with whipped cream and often topped with fruit, especially passionfruit.

paw /pɔ/ *n.* **1.** the foot of an animal with nails or claws. **2.** the foot of any animal. **3.** *Colloq.* (*humorous*) the human hand. –*v.t.* **4.** to strike or scrape with the paws or feet. **5.** *Colloq.* to handle clumsily, rudely, or too familiarly. –*v.i.* **6.** to strike or scrape the ground, etc., with the paws or feet. **7.** *Colloq.* to use the hands clumsily, rudely, or too familiarly on something.

pawl /pɔl/ *n.* a pivoted bar adapted to engage with the teeth of a ratchet wheel or the like so as to prevent movement or to impart motion.

pawn[1] /pɒn/ *v.t.* **1.** to deposit as security, as for money borrowed: *to pawn a watch.* **2.** to pledge or stake: *I pawn my honour.* –*n.* **3.** state of being deposited or held as security: *jewels in pawn.* **4.** any thing or person serving as security. **5.** the act of pawning. –**pawner**, *n.*

pawn[2] /pɒn/ *n.* **1.** *Chess* one of the 16 pieces of lowest value, usually moving one square straight ahead, but capturing diagonally. **2.** an unimportant person used as the tool of another.

pawnbroker /ˈpɔnbroʊkə/ *n.* someone who lends money at interest on pledged personal property. –**pawnbroking**, *n.*

pawpaw /ˈpɔpɔ/ *n.* **1.** the large melon-like fruit of the shrub or small tree, *Carica papaya*, of the family Caricaceae, originally from tropical America, especially the larger orange- or yellow-fleshed variety. See **papaya**. **2.** *US* the small fleshy fruit of the temperate North American bush or small tree, *Asimina triloba*. Also, **papaw, paw-paw**.

pay /peɪ/ *verb* (**paid** *or, for def. 28*, **payed**, **paying**) –*v.t.* **1.** to discharge (a debt, obligation, etc.), as by giving or doing something. **2.** to give (money, etc.) as in discharge of a debt or obligation. **3.** to satisfy the claims of (a person, etc.) as by giving money due. **4.** to defray (cost or expense). **5.** to give compensation for. **6.** to yield a recompense or return to; be profitable to: *it pays me to be honest.* **7.** to yield as a return: *the stock pays four per cent.* **8.** to requite, as for good, harm, offence, etc. **9.** to give or render (attention, regard, court, compliments, etc.) as if due or fitting. **10.** to admit the truth of; acknowledge that one has been outwitted, especially in repartee or argument: *I'll pay that.* **11.** to make (a call, visit, etc.). –*v.i.* **12.** to give money, etc., due: *to pay for goods.* **13.** to discharge debt. **14.** to yield a

return or profit; be advantageous or worthwhile: *his mining patch had just begun to pay.* **15.** to give compensation, as for damage or loss sustained. **16.** to suffer, or be punished, as for something; make amends. –*n.* **17.** payment, as of wages. **18.** wages, salary, or stipend. **19.** paid employ: *in the pay of the enemy.* –*adj.* **20.** (of earth, etc.) containing a sufficient quantity of metal or other value to be profitably worked by the miner. **21.** having a mechanism for payment when used: *a pay telephone.* –*phr.* **22.** **give someone a pay**, to castigate or rebuke someone. **23.** **pay dividends**, to result in benefits. **24.** **pay its way**, (of an investment) to yield a profit. **25.** **pay off**, **a.** to retaliate upon or punish. **b.** to discharge (a debt) in full. **c.** to discharge from one's employ and pay any wages, etc., due. **d.** *Colloq.* to bribe. **e.** to yield a profitable return. **26.** **pay one's way**, **a.** to take responsibility for one's expenses. **b.** to meet one's obligations. **27.** **pay out**, **a.** to disburse; hand out (money). **b.** to retaliate upon for an injury or affront; punish in revenge. **c.** *Colloq.* to reprimand or criticise (someone): *He really paid me out for being late.* **d.** *Colloq.* to protest volubly. **28.** **pay out** (or **away**), *Naut., etc.* to let out (a rope, etc.) as by slackening. **29.** **pay out on**, *Colloq.* to criticise; speak disparagingly about. **30.** **pay up**, **a.** to pay upon demand, especially as when threatened. **b.** to pay fully or promptly. **31.** **put paid to**, put an end to; prevent. –**payment**, *n.* –**payable**, *adj.*

pay-and-display *adj.* **1.** of or relating to a ticket vending machine in a parking area, where the driver must purchase a ticket and display it on the dashboard of the vehicle. **2.** of, relating to, or using this system of payment for parking.

pay-as-you-go tax *n.* a form of withholding tax in which tax is deducted from income before it is paid to the recipient. Also, **PAYG tax**.

PAYG /pi eɪ waɪ ˈdʒi/ *adj.* pay-as-you-go: *PAYG employees*. See **pay-as-you-go tax**.

PAYG payment summary *n.* (in the Australian tax system) a certificate issued by an employer to an employee at the end of a financial year or on termination of employment, detailing gross income, tax paid, contributions to superannuation, etc.; formerly known as a group certificate.

payload /ˈpeɪloʊd/ *n.* **1.** the income-producing part of a cargo. **2.** the load which a vehicle is designed to transport. **3.** *Mil.* the warhead, its container, and activating devices in a missile. **4.** *Astronautics* the load carried in a rocket or satellite to obtain the results for which the vehicle has been launched.

payola /peɪˈoʊlə/ *n.* a bribe, especially for the promotion of a commercial product through the abuse of one's position or influence.

payout /ˈpeɪaʊt/ *n.* **1.** a disbursement of money. **2.** a sum of money paid out as a reward, gain, or gambling win. **3.** a sum of money paid by a firm to an employee on retirement or redundancy, or as compensation for an injury, etc.: *he received a large payout.*

pay-per-view *n.* **1.** a system by which one can view films, programs, etc., on television as one pays for them. –*adj.* **2.** of or relating to this system: *pay-per-view movies.*

pay TV *n.* a television service to viewers who pay a subscription either as a monthly charge or as a fee for a particular program. Also, **pay television**.

paywall /ˈpeɪwɔl/ *n. Internet* a system for blocking access to content on a website, requiring payment from the user for the content to be released. Also, **pay wall**.

p-book /ˈpi-bʊk/ *n.* a book printed on paper. Compare **ebook**.

PC[1] /pi ˈsi/ *n.* **1.** → **personal computer**. **2.** a personal computer which is IBM-compatible.

PC[2] /pi ˈsi/ *adj.* → **politically correct**.

PCB /pi si 'bi/ *n.* polychlorinated biphenyl; one of a group of highly toxic chemicals, used in making plastics and electrical insulators.

PDA /pi di 'eɪ/ *n.* personal digital assistant; a palmtop computer, originally one used to store a diary, organiser, address book, calender, etc.

PDF /pi di 'ɛf/ *Computers* –*n.* **1.** a format in which documents may be saved and sent to others for viewing. **2.** a document in this format. –*adj.* **3.** of or relating to this format or a file stored in this format. –*v.t.* (**PDFed, PDFing**) **4.** to save (an electronic document) in this format. Also, **pdf**; (*in filenames*), **.pdf**.

pea /pi/ *n.* **1.** the small, round, highly nutritious seed of *Pisum sativum*, widely used as a vegetable. **2.** the plant itself, a hardy plant in wide cultivation. **3.** any of various related or similar plants, or their seed, as the chickpea. **4.** something small as a pea.

peace /pis/ *n.* **1.** freedom from war or hostilities. **2.** an agreement between contending parties to abstain from further hostilities. **3.** freedom from strife or dissension. **4.** freedom from mental disturbance: *peace of mind.* **5.** ease of mind or conscience. **6.** a state of being tranquil or serene. **7.** a state conducive, due to, or characterised by tranquillity or calm. **8.** quiet; stillness; silence. –*phr.* **9. hold one's peace,** to remain quiet; to keep silent. **10. keep the peace,** to refrain from creating a disturbance. **11. make one's peace,** (sometimes fol. by *with*) to effect reconciliation for oneself. **12. make peace,** to arrange for a stop to hostilities; to end war. –**peaceful,** *adj.* –**peaceable,** *adj.*

peach /pitʃ/ *n.* **1.** (a tree bearing) round, juicy fruit enclosing a single stone, of many varieties, and widely cultivated in temperate climates. **2.** the colour of a peach, a light pinkish yellow. **3.** *Colloq.* a person or thing especially admired or liked. **4.** of the colour peach. **5.** flavoured or cooked with peaches.

peacock /'pikɒk/ *n.* **1.** the male of the **peafowl,** a pheasant native to India but now widely domesticated, known for the spectacular eye-like patterning of its richly coloured tail feathers. **2.** a vain person. –*v.i.* (*pl.* **peacocks** *or, especially collectively,* **peacock**) **3.** to walk proudly like a peacock; make a boastful display. –**peacockish, peacocky,** *adj.*

peafowl /'pifaʊl/ *n.* any of the gallinaceous birds constituting the genus *Pavo*; a peacock or peahen.

peak[1] /pik/ *n.* **1.** the pointed top of a mountain. **2.** a mountain with a pointed summit. **3.** the pointed top of anything. **4.** the highest point: *the peak of his career.* **5.** the maximum point or degree of anything. **6.** *Mechanics, Elect., etc.* **a.** the maximum value of a quantity during a specified time: *a voltage peak.* **b.** the maximum power consumed or produced by a unit or group of units in a stated period of time. **7.** a projecting point: *the peak of a man's beard.* **8.** → **widow's peak.** **9.** a projecting front piece, or visor, of a cap. **10.** *Naut.* **a.** a part of a ship's hold, as the **after peak** and **forepeak.** **b.** the upper after corner of a sail that is extended by a gaff. –*adj.* **11.** of highest quality: *in peak condition.* **12.** of or relating to an organisation which represents the interests of a number of other organisations with similar interests, especially in developing policy, lobbying, etc. –*v.t.* **13.** *Naut.* to raise the after-end of (a yard, gaff, etc.) to or towards an angle above the horizontal. –*v.i.* **14.** to project in a peak. **15.** to reach a highest point.

peak[2] /pik/ *v.i.* to become weak, thin, and sickly. –**peaky,** *adj.* –**peakily,** *adv.* –**peakiness,** *n.*

peak body *n.* an organisation which represents a group of enterprises engaged in similar activities: *the recreational fishing peak body.*

peak gas *n.* that point when the world's demand for gas outstrips dwindling supplies from depleted gas reserves.

peak hour *n.* the period at which city traffic is at its densest. Also, **peak period, rush hour.** –**peak-hour,** *adj.*

peak oil *n.* that point when the world's demand for oil outstrips dwindling supplies from depleted oil reserves.

peal /pil/ *n.* **1.** a loud, long, drawn-out sound of bells. **2.** any other loud, prolonged sound: *peal of cannon; a peal of thunder.* **3.** a set of bells tuned to one another. –*v.i.* **4.** to sound forth in a peal; resound: *to peal with laughter.*

peanut /'pinʌt/ *n.* **1.** Also, **groundnut.** the fruit (pod) or the edible seed of a leguminous plant native to Brazil, the pod of which is forced underground in growing, where it ripens. **2.** (*pl.*) *Colloq.* any small amount, especially of money. –*adj.* **3.** of or relating to the peanut or peanuts. **4.** made with or from peanuts.

peanut butter *n.* a smooth paste made from finely ground roasted peanuts, used as a spread, etc. Also, **peanut paste.**

pear /peə/ *n.* **1.** the edible fruit, typically rounded but elongated and growing smaller towards the stem, of a tree, *Pyrus communis*, familiar in cultivation. **2.** the tree itself.

pearl /pɜl/ *n.* **1.** a hard, smooth, usually white, shiny, round mass found in oysters and other molluscs, grown as a protective coating around a piece of grit, etc., inside the shell. **2.** an artificial substance that looks like a pearl. **3.** nacre, or mother-of-pearl. **4.** something precious or special; the finest example of anything. **5.** a very pale colour grey, almost white. –*v.i.* **6.** to look for pearls. –*adj.* **7.** of the colour or lustre of pearl; nacreous. **8.** relating to, or made with pearls or mother-of-pearl. –*phr.* **9. cast pearls before swine,** to offer something of excellence to people who are incapable of appreciating it.

peasant /'pɛzənt/ *n.* **1.** one of a class of persons, of inferior social rank, living in the country and engaged usually in agricultural labour. **2.** a rustic or country person. **3.** *Colloq.* an unsophisticated person; one unable to appreciate that which is cultured and tasteful; a boor. –*adj.* **4.** of or characteristic of peasants, their crafts, traditions, etc. –**peasantry,** *n.*

peat /pit/ *n.* **1.** a highly organic soil (more than fifty per cent combustible) of partially decomposed vegetable matter, in marshy or damp regions, drained and cultivated, cut out and dried for use as fuel. **2.** such vegetable matter as a substance or fuel. –**peaty,** *adj.*

pebble /'pɛbəl/ *n.* **1.** a small, rounded stone, especially one worn by the action of water. **2.** pebbled leather, or its granulated surface. **3.** a transparent, colourless rock crystal used for the lenses of spectacles. –*v.t.* **4.** to prepare (leather, etc.) so as to have a granulated surface. **5.** to pelt with or as with pebbles. –**pebbly,** *adj.*

pecan /'pikæn, pi'kæn/ *n.* **1.** a hickory tree, *Carya illinoinensis*, indigenous to the lower Mississippi valley, southern US, and grown for its oval, smooth-shelled nut with a sweet, oily, edible kernel. **2.** the nut of this tree.

peccadillo /pɛkə'dɪloʊ/ *n.* (*pl.* **-loes** *or* **-los**) a petty sin or offence; a trifling fault.

peck[1] /pɛk/ *n.* **1.** a dry measure in the imperial system, equal to 8 quarts or $9.092\,18 \times 10^{-3}$ m^3; the fourth part of a bushel. **2.** a container for measuring this quantity. **3.** a considerable quantity: *a peck of trouble.*

peck[2] /pɛk/ *v.t.* **1.** to strike or indent with the beak, as a bird does, or with some pointed instrument, especially with quick, repeated movements. **2.** to make (a hole, etc.) by such strokes. **3.** to take (food, etc.) bit by bit, with or as with the beak. **4.** to kiss in a hasty dabbing manner. –*v.i.* **5.** to make strokes with the beak or a pointed instrument. **6.** to pick or nibble at food. –*n.* **7.** a pecking stroke. **8.** a hole or mark made by or as by pecking. **9.** a hasty kiss. –*phr.* **10. peck at,** to carp at or nag.

pecking order *n.* **1.** the natural hierarchy observable in a flock of poultry or in any gregarious species of birds. **2.** any order of precedence. Also, **peck order.**

peckish /ˈpɛkɪʃ/ *adj. Colloq.* mildly hungry; desiring a snack or light repast.

pectin /ˈpɛktən/ *n.* any of the acidic polysaccharides which occur in ripe fruits, especially in apples, currants, etc., and which dissolve in boiling water, forming a jelly upon cooling. –**pectic,** *adj.*

pectoral /ˈpɛktərəl/ *adj.* **1.** of or relating to the breast or chest; thoracic. **2.** worn on the breast or chest: *the pectoral cross of a bishop.* **3.** proceeding from the heart or inner consciousness. –*n.* **4.** something worn on the breast for ornament, protection, etc., as a breastplate. **5.** a pectoral fin.

peculate /ˈpɛkjəleɪt/ *Law* –*v.t.* **1.** to embezzle (public money); appropriate dishonestly (money or goods entrusted to one's care). –*v.i.* **2.** to engage in embezzling. –**peculation** /pɛkjəˈleɪʃən/, *n.* –**peculator,** *n.*

peculiar /pəˈkjuliə, -ljə/ *adj.* **1.** strange, odd, or queer: *a peculiar old man.* **2.** uncommon; unusual: *a peculiar hobby.* **3.** distinguished in nature or character from others. **4.** belonging exclusively to a person or thing. –*phr.* **5. peculiar to,** belonging characteristically to: *an expression peculiar to Australians.* –**peculiarity,** *n.* –**peculiarly,** *adv.*

pecuniary /pəˈkjuniəri, -nəri/, *Orig. US* /pəˈkjunieri/ *adj.* **1.** consisting of or given or exacted in money: *pecuniary penalties.* **2.** of or relating to money: *pecuniary affairs.* **3.** (of an offence, etc.) entailing a money penalty. –**pecuniarily,** *adv.*

-ped a word element meaning 'foot', serving to form adjectives and nouns, as *aliped, biped, quadruped.* Compare **-pod.**

pedagogue /ˈpɛdəgɒg/ *n.* **1.** a teacher of children; a schoolteacher. **2.** someone who is pedantic, dogmatic, and formal. –**pedagogic,** *adj.* –**pedagogy,** *n.*

pedal /ˈpɛdl/ *n.* **1.** a lever worked by the foot, in various musical instruments, as the organ, piano, and harp, and having various functions. **2.** a keyboard attached to the organ, harpsichord, etc., operated by the feet. **3.** a lever-like part worked by the foot, in various mechanisms, such as the sewing machine, bicycle, car, etc.; a treadle. –*verb* (**-alled** *or, US,* **-aled, -alling** *or, US,* **-aling**) –*v.t.* **4.** to work or use the pedals of, as in playing an organ or propelling a bicycle. –*v.i.* **5.** to operate the pedals. –*adj.* **6.** of or relating to a pedal or pedals. **7.** consisting of pedals: *a pedal keyboard.* –*phr.* **8. put the pedal to the metal,** *Colloq.* to accelerate in a motor vehicle.

pedant /ˈpɛdnt/ *n.* **1.** someone who makes an excessive or tedious show of learning or exacting precision; someone who possesses mere book-learning without practical wisdom. **2.** someone who displays a slavish attention to rules, details, etc. –**pedantry,** *n.* –**pedantic** /pəˈdæntɪk/, *adj.* –**pedantically** /pəˈdæntɪkli/, *adv.*

peddle /ˈpɛdl/ *v.t.* **1.** to carry about for sale at retail; hawk. **2.** to trade in (something illicit or viewed as undesirable): *to peddle drugs; to peddle porn.* **3.** to advocate, as ideas, philosophy, etc.: *peddling the government's ideas for tax reform.*

peddler /ˈpɛdlə/ *n.* **1.** someone who trades in drugs or other illicit or socially undesirable goods. **2.** → **pedlar** (def. 1).

-pede a word element meaning 'foot', as in *centipede.*

pederasty /ˈpɛdəræsti/ *n.* sexual relations between a male adult and a boy. Also, **paederasty.** –**pederast,** *n.* –**pederastic** /pɛdəˈræstɪk/, *adj.* –**pederastically** /pɛdəˈræstɪkli/, *adv.*

pedestal /ˈpɛdəstl/ *n.* **1.** an architectural support for a column, statue, vase, or the like. **2.** a supporting structure or piece; a base. **3.** one of two supports of a desk with a space in the centre for the knees, consisting of a boxlike frame containing drawers. –*phr.* **4. put** (or **place**) (or **set**) **someone on a pedestal,** to hold someone in high esteem; idealise someone: *he put her on a pedestal until he discovered her true nature.*

pedestrian /pəˈdɛstriən/ *n.* **1.** someone who goes or travels on foot; a walker. –*adj.* **2.** going or performed on foot; walking. **3.** relating to walking. **4.** commonplace; prosaic; dull.

pedestrian crossing *n.* an area of roadway on which pedestrians have, within legally defined limits, right of way to cross the road. See **zebra crossing.**

pedicel /ˈpɛdəsɛl/ *n.* **1.** *Bot.* a small stalk. **2.** *Zool., Anat.* a small stalk or stalk-like part; a peduncle.

pedicure /ˈpɛdəkjuə, -kjʊə/ *n.* **1.** professional care or treatment of the feet. **2.** someone who makes a business of caring for the feet; a chiropodist.

pedigree /ˈpɛdəgri/ *n.* **1.** an ancestral line, or line of descent, especially as recorded; lineage. **2.** a genealogical table: *a family pedigree.* **3.** derivation, as from a source: *the pedigree of a word.*

pediment /ˈpɛdəmənt/ *n. Archit.* **1.** a low triangular gable crowned with a projecting cornice, in the Greek, Roman, or Renaissance style, especially over a portico or porch or at the ends of a gable-roofed building. **2.** any member of similar outline and position, as over an opening. –**pedimental** /pɛdəˈmɛntl/, *adj.*

pedlar /ˈpɛdlə/ *n.* **1.** (formerly) someone who travelled from place to place selling clothing and other domestic articles. **2.** → **peddler** (def. 1). Also, **pedler;** *US,* **peddler.**

pedometer /pəˈdɒmətə/ *n.* an instrument for recording the number of steps taken in walking, thus showing approximately the distance travelled.

pedosphere /ˈpɛdəsfɪə/ *n.* the earth's envelope where soil is naturally formed and soil-forming processes are active.

peduncle /pəˈdʌŋkəl/ *n.* **1.** *Bot.* **a.** a flower stalk, supporting either a cluster or a solitary flower. **b.** the stalk bearing the fructification in fungi, etc. **2.** *Zool.* a stalk or stem; a stalk-like part or structure. **3.** *Anat.* a stalk-like part composed of white matter connecting various regions of the brain. –**peduncled, peduncular** /pəˈdʌŋkjələ/, **pedunculate** /pəˈdʌŋkjələt, -leɪt/ *adj.*

pee /pi/ *Colloq.* –*v.i.* (**peed, peeing**) **1.** to urinate. –*n.* **2.** an act of urination.

peek /pik/ *v.i.* **1.** to peep; peer. –*n.* **2.** a peeking look; a peep.

peel /pil/ *v.t.* **1.** to strip the skin, rind, bark, etc., from. **2.** to strip off (skin, etc.) –*v.i.* **3.** (of skin, etc.) to come off. –*n.* **4.** the skin or rind of a fruit, etc. –*phr.* **5. keep one's eyes peeled,** *Colloq.* to keep a close watch.

peen /pin/ *n.* **1.** the sharp, spherical, or otherwise modified end of the head of a hammer, opposite to the face. –*v.t.* **2.** to treat by striking regularly all over with the peen of a hammer.

peep¹ /pip/ *v.i.* **1.** to look through a small opening, or from a hiding place. **2.** to look slyly, pryingly, or furtively. **3.** to come partially into view; begin to appear: *the sun is peeping over the horizon.* –*n.* **4.** a peeping look or glance.

peep² /pip/ *n.* **1.** a peeping cry or sound. –*v.i.* **2.** to utter the shrill little cry of a young bird, a mouse, etc.; cheep; squeak. **3.** to speak in a thin, weak voice.

peer¹ /pɪə/ *n.* **1.** a person of the same civil rank or standing; an equal before the law. **2.** someone who ranks with another in respect to endowments or other qualifications; an equal in any respect. **3.** a nobleman.

peer² /pɪə/ *v.i.* **1.** to look narrowly, as in the effort to discern clearly. **2.** to peep out or appear slightly.

peerage /ˈpɪərɪdʒ/ *n.* **1.** the rank or dignity of a peer. **2.** the body of peers of a country or state. **3.** a book giving a list of peers, with their genealogy, etc.

peer group *n.* **1.** a group of people of about the same age. **2.** a group of people of the same social background, occupation, or class.

peerless /ˈpɪələs/ *adj.* having no peer or equal; matchless.

peer-to-peer *adj. Computers* of or relating to a computer network that relies on the power of the computers in the network, rather than on the computer power provided by a server alone to a network of clients. Also, **p2p**.

peevish /ˈpiːvɪʃ/ *adj.* cross, querulous, or fretful, as from vexation or discontent. –**peevishly**, *adv.* –**peevishness**, *n.*

peewee /ˈpiwi/ *n.* → **magpie lark**.

peewit /ˈpiwɪt/ *n.* → **magpie lark**.

peg /pɛg/ *n.* **1.** a pin of wood or other material driven or fitted into something, as to fasten parts together, to hang things on, to make fast a rope or string on, to stop a hole, or to mark some point. **2.** *Colloq.* a leg, sometimes one of wood. **3.** an occasion; reason: *a peg to hang a grievance on.* **4.** a pin of wood or metal to which one end of a string of a musical instrument is fastened, and which may be turned in its socket to adjust the string's tension. **5.** a clothes peg. –*v.t.* (**pegged**, **pegging**) **6.** to drive or insert a peg into. **7.** to fasten with or as with pegs. **8.** to maintain (prices, wages, etc.) at a set level by laws or by manipulation. **9.** to strike or pierce with or as with a peg. **10.** *Colloq.* to identify as a particular type, having certain abilities, etc.: *I pegged him as a cricketer.* –*phr.* **11. off the peg**, *Colloq.* (of a garment) available for immediate use; ready-made. **12. peg away**, (sometimes fol. by *at*) to work persistently, or keep on energetically. **13. peg out**, **a.** *Colloq.* to die. **b.** to fix on a line, rail, etc., by means of pegs: *to peg out the washing.* **c.** to mark out, as a block of land, gold claim, etc. **14. square peg in a round hole**, *Colloq.* a misfit. **15. take down a peg (or two)**, to humble.

peignoir /ˈpeɪnwɑ/ *n.* **1.** a dressing-gown. **2.** a negligee.

pejorative /pəˈdʒɒrətɪv/ *adj.* **1.** deprecatory. **2.** having a disparaging force, as certain derivative word forms. –*n.* **3.** a pejorative form or word. –**pejoratively**, *adv.*

Peking duck /pikɪŋ ˈdʌk/ *n.* (in Chinese cookery) a dish consisting of small pancakes wrapped around pieces of crisp roast duck skin and spring onions, cucumber and hoisin sauce, the flesh of the duck being traditionally served separately.

pelican /ˈpɛləkən/ *n.* any of various large, web-footed birds of the family Pelecanidae, having a large fish-catching bill with distensible pouch beneath, into which the young stick their heads when feeding.

pelican crossing *n.* a pedestrian crossing at which the lights can be activated by the pedestrian, and which usually incorporates a flashing orange signal after the red signal to indicate that caution is required.

pellet /ˈpɛlət/ *n.* **1.** a small rounded piece, especially of food or medicine. **2.** one of the small non-explosive bullets fired from a shotgun.

pellicle /ˈpɛlɪkəl/ *n.* a thin skin or membrane; a film; a scum. –**pellicular** /pəˈlɪkjələ/, *adj.*

pell-mell /pɛl-ˈmɛl/ *adv.* **1.** in an indiscriminate medley; in a confused mass or crowd. **2.** in disorderly, headlong haste. –*adj.* **3.** indiscriminate; disorderly; tumultuous. –*n.* **4.** an indiscriminate medley. **5.** violent and confused disorder. Also, **pellmell**.

pellucid /pəˈlusəd/ *adj.* **1.** allowing the passage of light; translucent. **2.** clear or limpid, as water. **3.** clear in meaning. –**pellucidity** /pɛləˈsɪdəti/, **pellucidness**, *n.* –**pellucidly**, *adv.*

pelmet /ˈpɛlmət/ *n.* a short ornamental drapery or board, placed across the top of a window in order to hide the curtain rail.

pelt¹ /pɛlt/ *v.t.* **1.** to assail with repeated blows or with missiles; beat or rush against. **2.** to throw (missiles). **3.** to drive, put, etc., by blows or missiles. –*v.i.* **4.** to strike blows; beat with force or violence. **5.** (of rain) to fall very heavily. **6.** to hurry. –*n.* **7.** the act of pelting. **8.** a vigorous stroke. **9.** a blow with something thrown. –*phr.* **10. full pelt**, with the utmost energy or speed. –**pelter**, *n.*

pelt² /pɛlt/ *n.* the skin of an animal with or without the hair.

pelvis /ˈpɛlvəs/ *n.* (*pl.* **-vises** *or* **-ves** /-viz/) *Anat.* **1.** the basin-like cavity in the lower part of the trunk of many vertebrates, formed in humans by the innominate bones, sacrum, etc. and enclosing the bladder and bowel, and in women, the uterus. **2.** the bones forming this cavity. **3.** the cavity of the kidney which receives the urine before it is passed into the ureter.

pen¹ /pɛn/ *n.* **1.** any instrument for writing with ink, e.g. a biro, nib, fountain pen or quill. **2.** the pen as a symbol of writing or authorship: *the pen is mightier than the sword.* –*v.t.* (**penned**, **penning**) **3.** to write with a pen.

pen² /pɛn/ *n.* **1.** an enclosure for domestic animals or livestock. **2.** animals so enclosed. **3.** any place of confinement or safekeeping. –*v.t.* (**penned**, **penning**) **4.** to confine in or as in a pen.

pen³ /pɛn/ *n. Colloq.* prison.

penal /ˈpinəl/ *adj.* of or relating to punishment, as for offences or crimes.

penal colony *n.* (formerly) a colony founded to receive convicts and established in part through convict labour.

penalise /ˈpinəlaɪz/ *v.t.* **1.** to subject to a penalty, as a person. **2.** to declare penal, or punishable by law, as an action. **3.** to lay under a disadvantage. Also, **penalize**. –**penalisation** /pinəlaɪˈzeɪʃən/, *n.*

penalty /ˈpɛnəlti/ *n.* (*pl.* **-ties**) **1.** a punishment for breaking a law or rule. **2.** a loss or forfeiture which someone incurs by not fulfilling an obligation. **3.** the consequence of a wrongful or foolish action. **4.** *Sport* **a.** a free shot, kick, etc., allowed to one team or player, because the other has broken a rule. **b.** *Golf* a stroke added to a player's score after a ball lands out of bounds, in water, etc.

penalty corner *n. Hockey* a corner (def. 10) given as a penalty for an infringement by a player on the defending team.

penalty rate *n.* (in Australia) a rate of pay determined by an award, higher than the usual rate, in compensation for working outside the normal spread of hours.

penalty shootout /pɛnəlti ˈʃutaʊt/ *n. Hockey, etc., Soccer* a method of deciding a match after a tied game, in which each team is given equal opportunity to score penalty goals, the team scoring the greatest number being declared the winner.

penalty shot *n. Hockey, Soccer, etc.* a shot at goal awarded to one side as a penalty for an infringement by a player on the other side.

penance /ˈpɛnəns/ *n.* **1.** punishment undergone in token of penitence for sin. **2.** a penitential discipline imposed by church authority. **3.** *Roman Catholic Church* a sacrament ministered in consideration of a confession of sin with contrition and the purpose of amendment, followed by the forgiveness of sin.

pence /pɛns/ *n.* plural of **penny**, used especially when value is indicated: *he gave me twenty-one pence change out of a pound, all in pennies.*

penchant /ˈpɛntʃənt, ˈpɒʃɒ̃/ *n.* a strong inclination; a taste or liking for something.

pencil /ˈpɛnsəl/ n. 1. a thin, pointed tube of wood, etc., with a core of graphite, chalk, etc., used for drawing or writing. 2. a slender, pointed piece of some marking substance. 3. → **pencil skirt**. –v.t. (-cilled or, Chiefly US, -ciled, -cilling or, Chiefly US, -ciling) 4. to use a pencil on. 5. to draw or write with, or as with, a pencil.

pencil skirt n. a long fitted skirt.

pendant /ˈpɛndənt/ n. a hanging ornament, such as on a necklace or earring.

pendent /ˈpɛndənt/ adj. 1. hanging or suspended. 2. overhanging; jutting or leaning over. 3. impending. 4. pending or undecided. –**pendency**, n. –**pendently**, adv.

pending /ˈpɛndɪŋ/ prep. 1. while awaiting; until: pending his return. 2. in the period before the decision or conclusion of; during: pending the negotiations. –adj. 3. remaining undecided; awaiting decision. 4. hanging; impending.

pendulous /ˈpɛndʒələs/ adj. 1. hanging. 2. swinging freely. 3. vacillating. –**pendulously**, adv. –**pendulousness**, n.

pendulum /ˈpɛndʒələm/ n. 1. a body so suspended from a fixed point as to move to and fro by the action of gravity and acquired kinetic energy. 2. a swinging device used for controlling the movement of clockwork.

pene- a prefix meaning almost, as peneplain, peninsula. Also, (before a vowel), **pen-**.

penetrate /ˈpɛnətreɪt/ v.t. 1. to go into or through with a sharp instrument. 2. to enter the interior of. 3. to enter and spread through; permeate. 4. to affect deeply. 5. to reach (a wide number of buyers, customers, etc.): to penetrate a market. 6. to understand. –v.i. 7. to enter, reach, or pass through, as if by piercing. –**penetrable** /ˈpɛnətrəbəl/, adj. –**penetrative** /ˈpɛnətrətɪv/, adj. –**penetrating**, adj. –**penetration**, n.

penfriend /ˈpɛnfrɛnd/ n. a person, especially one in another country, with whom a correspondence is maintained through regular exchange of letters. Also, **pen-friend**, **pen friend**, **penpal**.

penguin /ˈpɛŋgwən, ˈpɛŋwən/ n. 1. any of various flightless aquatic birds of the family Spheniscidae of the Southern Hemisphere, with webbed feet, and wings reduced to flippers, as the **little penguin** and the **Adélie penguin**. 2. Aeronautics an aeroplane which merely rolls along the ground, enabling a beginner to make certain manipulations safely.

penicillin /pɛnəˈsɪlən/ n. 1. a powerful anti-bacterial substance produced by moulds of the genus Penicillium. 2. any of a group of antibacterial substances made synthetically from penicillin.

peninsula /pəˈnɪnsələ, pəˈnɪnsjələ/ n. a piece of land almost surrounded by water, especially one connected with the mainland by only a narrow neck or isthmus. –**peninsular**, adj. –**peninsularity** /pəˌnɪnsjəˈlærəti/, n.

penis /ˈpinəs/ n. (pl. **-nises** /-nəsəz/ or **-nes** /-niz/) the male organ of copulation and urination.

penitent /ˈpɛnətənt/ adj. 1. repentant; contrite; sorry for sin or fault and disposed to atonement and amendment. –n. 2. a penitent person. 3. Roman Catholic Church someone who confesses their sin and submits to a penance. –**penitence**, n. –**penitently**, adv.

penitentiary /pɛnəˈtɛnʃəri/ n. (pl. **-ries**) 1. a place for imprisonment and punishment taking the form of correction and training designed to change behaviour. –adj. 2. of or relating to punishment as a sign of being sorry for wrongdoing; penitential.

penknife /ˈpɛnˌnaɪf/ n. (pl. **-knives** /-naɪvz/) a small pocketknife.

pen-name n. a name assumed to write under; an author's pseudonym; nom de plume.

pennant /ˈpɛnənt/ n. 1. Also, **pendant**, **pennon**. a long triangular flag, widest next to the mast, and going

almost to a point, borne on naval or other vessels or used in signalling, etc. 2. any flag serving as an emblem, as of success in an athletic contest.

penniless /ˈpɛnələs/ adj. without a penny; destitute of money.

penny /ˈpɛni/ n. (pl. **pennies** or, especially collectively, **pence**) 1. (in Australia before the introduction of decimal currency in 1966) a bronze or copper coin equal to one twelfth of a shilling or $1/_{240}$ of a pound. Abbrev.: d 2. (formerly) a similar coin of Britain. 3. a similar coin of certain other countries. 4. a bronze coin of the United Kingdom equal to a 100th part of a pound; new penny. Abbrev.: p 5. a bronze coin of Canada, the 100th part of a dollar. 6. a bronze coin of the US, the 100th part of a dollar; cent. 7. an unspecified, usually minimal sum of money: I haven't got a penny. –adj. 8. of the price or value of a penny. –phr. 9. **a bad penny**, a bad or undesirable person or thing. 10. **a pretty penny**, a considerable amount of money. 11. **spend a penny**, to go to the toilet. 12. **the penny drops**, the explanation or remark is understood. 13. **turn an honest penny**, to earn an honest living; earn money honestly.

penny-farthing n. a high bicycle of an early type with one large wheel in front and one small wheel behind.

penpal /ˈpɛnpæl/ n. → **penfriend**. Also, **pen-pal**, **pen pal**.

pension¹ /ˈpɛnʃən/ n. 1. a fixed periodical payment made in consideration of past services, injury or loss sustained, merit, poverty, etc. 2. an allowance or annuity. –v.t. 3. to grant a pension to. –phr. 4. **pension off**, to cause to retire on a pension. –**pensionable**, adj.

pension² /pɒ̃ˈsjɔ̃, ˈpɒnsjɒn/ n. (in France and some other countries) 1. a boarding house or small hotel. 2. room and board. Compare **pensione**.

pensione /pɛnsiˈoʊneɪ/ n. (in Italy) 1. a boarding house or small hotel. 2. room and board. Compare **pension²**.

pensive /ˈpɛnsɪv/ adj. 1. deeply, seriously, or sadly thoughtful. 2. expressing thoughtfulness or sadness. –**pensively**, adv. –**pensiveness**, n.

pent /pɛnt/ adj. 1. shut in. 2. confined.

pent- a word element meaning 'five'. Also, (before consonants), **penta-**.

pentad /ˈpɛntæd/ n. 1. a period of five years. 2. Meteorol. a period of five days. 3. a group of five. 4. the number five.

pentagon /ˈpɛntəgɒn, -gən/ n. a closed plane figure having five angles and five sides. –**pentagonal** /pɛnˈtægənəl/, adj.

pentagram /ˈpɛntəgræm/ n. 1. a five-pointed, star-shaped figure made by extending the sides of a regular pentagon until they meet (a symbolical figure used by the Pythagoreans and later philosophers). 2. a magical or talismanic symbol. 3. a suit in the tarot pack, in later card packs stylised to diamonds. Also, **pentacle**, **pentangle**.

pentameter /pɛnˈtæmətə/ n. Prosody a line of poetry consisting of five feet.

pentathlon /pɛnˈtæθlən/ n. an athletic contest comprising five different exercises or events, and won by the contestant having the highest total score. –**pentathlete**, n.

Pentecost /ˈpɛntəkɒst/ n. 1. a Christian festival commemorating the descent of the Holy Spirit upon the Apostles on the day of the Jewish festival of Shavuot. 2. → **Shavuot**.

penthouse /ˈpɛnthaʊs/ n. (pl. **-houses** /-haʊzəz/) 1. a separate flat on the top floor or floors of a tall building. 2. a structure on a roof, for housing lift machinery, etc. 3. any roof-like shelter or overhanging part.

pent-up adj. confined; restrained: pent-up rage.

penultimate /pəˈnʌltəmət/ adj. next to the last.

penumbra /pəˈnʌmbrə/ *n.* (*pl.* **-brae** /-bri/ *or* **-bras**) **1.** *Optics* the partial or imperfect shadow outside the complete shadow (umbra) of an opaque body, as a planet, where the light from the source of illumination is only partly cut off. **2.** *Astron.* the greyish marginal portion of a sunspot. **–penumbral,** *adj.*

penury /ˈpɛnjəri/ *n.* **1.** extreme poverty; destitution. **2.** dearth or insufficiency. **–penurious** /pəˈnjuriəs/, *adj.*

peony /ˈpiəni/ *n.* (*pl.* **-nies**) any plant of the genus *Paeonia*, which comprises perennial herbs and a few shrubs with large showy flowers, familiar in gardens.

people /ˈpipəl/ *pl. n.* **1.** (*construed as sing., with pl.* **peoples**) the whole body of persons constituting a community, tribe, race, or nation: *this is a united people*; *they are a nomadic people*; *the peoples of Africa*. **2.** the persons of any particular group, company, or number: *the people of a parish*. **3.** persons in relation to a ruler, leader, etc.: *the king and his people.* **4.** one's family or relatives: *to visit one's people.* **5.** the members of any group or number to which one belongs. **6.** the body of enfranchised citizens of a state: *representatives chosen by the people.* **7.** the commonalty or populace: *a priest of the people.* **8.** persons indefinitely, whether men or women: *people may say what they please.* **9.** human beings as distinguished from animals. *–v.t.* **10.** to furnish with people; populate. **11.** to stock with animals, inanimate objects, etc. *–phr.* **12. give back to the people,** to return to public ownership or control: *to give back the foreshores to the people.* **13. go to the people,** to hold an election. **14. put something to the people,** to hold an election or referendum on (an issue). **–peopler,** *n.*

people smuggling *n.* the illegal business of transporting people to a country which they are not authorised to enter as immigrants. **–people smuggler,** *n.*

pep /pɛp/ *Colloq. –n.* **1.** spirit or animation; vigour; energy. *–phr.* **2. pep up,** to give spirit or vigour to.

peperoni /pɛpəˈrouni/ *n.* → **pepperoni**.

pepita /pəˈpitə/ *n.* a pumpkin seed which has been shelled, roasted and salted; eaten as a snack.

pepper /ˈpɛpə/ *n.* **1.** a pungent condiment obtained from various plants of the genus *Piper*, especially from the dried berries, either whole or ground, of *P. nigrum*, a tropical climbing shrub. **2.** any plant of the genus *Piper*, such as the rainforest vine, *P. novaehollandiae*, which has small berries resembling those of *P. nigrum*. **3.** cayenne (**red pepper**), prepared from species of *Capsicum*. **4.** any species of *Capsicum*, or its fruit (green or red, hot or sweet), as the capsicum or common pepper of the garden. **5.** (*also pl.*) (*with children*) fast skipping. *–v.t.* **6.** to season with or as with pepper. **7.** to sprinkle as with pepper; dot; stud. **8.** to sprinkle like pepper. **9.** to pelt with shot or missiles **10.** to bombard as with shot or missiles: *to pepper the candidate with questions.*

peppercorn /ˈpɛpəkɔn/ *n.* **1.** the berry of the pepper plant, *Piper nigrum*, often dried and used as a condiment. **2.** anything very small, insignificant, or trifling.

peppermint /ˈpɛpəmənt/ *n.* **1.** a herb, *Mentha piperita*, cultivated for its aromatic pungent oil. **2.** any of a group of species of *Eucalyptus* with pungent oils and characteristic bark. **3.** a lozenge or confection flavoured with peppermint.

pepperoni /pɛpəˈrouni/ *n.* a type of salami, much used on pizzas. Also, **peperoni**.

pepper spray *n.* → **capsicum spray**.

peppertree /ˈpɛpəˌtri/ *n.* **1.** any of several evergreen trees, members of the genus *Schinus*, mostly native of South America and cultivated in subtropical regions as ornamentals because of their evergreen foliage and bright red fruits. **2.** an aromatic shrub or tree of New Zealand *Macropiper excelsum*. **3.** any of certain erect aromatic shrubs of the endemic New Zealand genus *Pseudowintera*.

pep talk *n.* a vigorous talk to a person or group calculated to arouse support for a cause, increase determination to succeed, etc.

peptic /ˈpɛptɪk/ *adj.* **1.** relating to or concerned in digestion; digestive. **2.** promoting digestion. **3.** of pepsin. **4.** associated with the action of digestive substances: *peptic ulcer. –n.* **5.** a substance promoting digestion.

peptic ulcer *n. Pathol.* an ulcer of the mucous membrane of the stomach or duodenum, caused by the digestive action of gastric juices.

per /pɜ/, *weak form* /pə/ *prep.* through; by; for each: *per annum* (by the year), *per diem* (by the day), *per yard* (for each yard).

per- **1.** a prefix meaning 'through', 'thoroughly', 'utterly', 'very', as in *pervert, pervade, perfect.* **2.** *Chem.* a prefix applied: **a.** to inorganic acids to indicate they possess excess of the designated element, as *perboric* (HBO$_3$ or H$_2$B$_4$O$_8$), *percarbonic* (H$_2$C$_2$O$_5$), *permanganic* (HMnO$_4$), and *persulphuric* (H$_2$S$_2$O$_5$) *acids.* **b.** to salts of these acids (the name ending in *-ate*), as *potassium perborate* (K$_2$B$_2$O$_8$), *potassium permanganate* (KMnO$_4$), and *potassium persulphate* (K$_2$S$_2$O$_5$).

perambulate /pəˈræmbjəleɪt/ *v.t.* **1.** to walk through, about, or over; travel through; traverse. **2.** to traverse and examine or inspect. *–v.i.* **3.** to walk or travel about; stroll. **–perambulation** /pəræmbjəˈleɪʃən/, *n.* **–perambulatory** /pəˈræmbjəleɪtəri/, *adj.*

perambulator /pəˈræmbjəleɪtə/ *n.* → **pram**.

per annum /pɜr ˈænəm, pər ˈænəm/ *adv.* by the year; yearly.

per capita /pə ˈkæpətə/ *adv.* by the individual person, used as a proportional statistic.

perceive /pəˈsiv/ *v.t.* (**-ceived, -ceiving**) **1.** to gain knowledge of through one of the senses; discover by seeing, hearing, etc. **2.** to apprehend with the mind; understand. **–perceiver,** *n.* **–perceivable,** *adj.*

per cent *adv.* **1.** by the hundred; for or in every hundred (used in expressing proportions, rates of interest, etc.): *to get 3 per cent interest. Symbol:* % *–n.* **2.** a proportion; a percentage. **3.** a stock which bears a specified rate of interest. Also, **percent**.

percentage /pəˈsɛntɪdʒ/ *n.* **1.** a rate or proportion per hundred. **2.** an allowance, duty, commission, or rate of interest on a hundred. **3.** a proportion in general. **4.** *Colloq.* gain; advantage.

percentile /pəˈsɛntaɪl/ *n. Statistics* one of the values of a variable which divides the distribution of the variable into 100 groups having equal frequencies. Thus, there are 100 percentiles: *the first, second, etc., percentile.*

perceptible /pəˈsɛptəbəl/ *adj.* capable of being perceived; cognisable; appreciable: *quite a perceptible time.* **–perceptibility** /pəsɛptəˈbɪləti/, **perceptibleness**, *n.* **–perceptibly,** *adv.*

perception /pəˈsɛpʃən/ *n.* **1.** the action or faculty of perceiving; cognition; a taking cognisance, as of a sensible object. **2.** an immediate or intuitive recognition, as of a moral or aesthetic quality. **3.** the result or product of perceiving, as distinguished from the act of perceiving; a percept. **4.** *Psychol.* a single unified meaning obtained from sensory processes while a stimulus is present. **–perceptional,** *adj.* **–perceptive,** *adj.*

perch[1] /pɜtʃ/ *n.* **1.** a pole or rod usually fixed between two supports to serve as a roost for birds. **2.** any thing or place serving for a bird, or for anything else, to alight or rest upon. **3.** a position or station high above the ground. **4.** a measurement in the imperial system of length equal to 5.0292 m. *–v.i.* **5.** (of a bird) to land or rest upon a perch. **6.** to settle or rest in some high position, as if on a perch. *–v.t.* **7.** to set or place (something) on, or as if on, a perch: *I perched the vase on the highest shelf.*

perch² /pɜtʃ/ *n.* (*pl.* **perches** *or, especially collectively,* **perch**) **1.** any of a number of species of Australian food and sport fishes, mainly freshwater but some marine, belonging to several different families, as the **golden perch,** *Plectroplites ambiguus* (Serranidæ) and the **spangled perch,** *Madigania unicolor* (Theraponidæ). **2.** a spiny freshwater fish of the genus *Perca* as the European *P. fluviatilis,* or the closely related *P. flavescens* of the US. **3.** any of various other similar fishes either freshwater or marine.

perchance /pə'tʃæns, -'tʃɑns/ *adv. Archaic* **1.** maybe; possibly. **2.** by chance.

percipient /pə'sɪpiənt/ *adj.* **1.** perceiving. **2.** having perception. –*n.* **3.** someone who perceives something. –**percipience, percipiency,** *n.*

percolate /'pɜkəleɪt/ *v.t.* **1.** to cause (a liquid) to pass through something porous (with tiny openings); filter. **2.** (of a liquid) to filter through; permeate. **3.** to make (coffee) in a percolator. –*v.i.* **4.** to pass through a porous substance; filter; ooze. **5.** to become known gradually: *the news percolated through to our office.* –**percolation** /pɜkə'leɪʃən/, *n.*

percolator /'pɜkəleɪtə/ *n.* a kind of coffeepot in which boiling water is forced up a hollow stem, filters through ground coffee, and returns to the pot below.

percussion /pə'kʌʃən/ *n.* **1.** the striking of one body against another with some force; impact. **2.** the striking of musical instruments to produce notes. **3.** a sharp light blow, especially one for setting off a cap formerly used to discharge firearms. **4.** *Music* the group of instruments in an orchestra which are played by striking. –**percussionist,** *n.* –**percussive,** *adj.*

perdition /pə'dɪʃən/ *n.* **1.** a condition of final spiritual ruin or damnation. **2.** the future state of the wicked. **3.** hell. **4.** utter destruction or ruin.

peregrine falcon /perəgrən 'fælkən/ *n.* the common falcon, *Falco peregrinus,* with a dark hood and cheeks, found on all continents except Antarctica, and much used in falconry.

peremptory /pə'rɛmptri, -təri/ *adj.* **1.** leaving no opportunity for denial or refusal; imperative: *a peremptory command.* **2.** imperious or dictatorial. **3.** *Law* that precludes or does not allow debate, question, etc.: *a peremptory edict.* –**peremptorily,** *adv.* –**peremptoriness,** *n.*

perennial /pə'rɛniəl/ *adj.* **1.** lasting for a long time; enduring. **2.** *Bot.* having a life cycle lasting more than two years. **3.** (of a stream, etc.) lasting or continuing throughout the year. **4.** everlasting; continuing; recurrent; perpetual. –*n.* **5.** a perennial plant. **6.** something continuing or recurrent. –**perennially,** *adv.*

perentie /pə'rɛnti/ *n.* the largest Australian lizard, *Varanus giganteus,* dark in colour with large pale yellow spots; found in arid areas of northern and central Australia. Also, **perenti.**

perfect *adj.* /'pɜfəkt/ **1.** having all the necessary parts, characteristics, etc.; complete. **2.** without blemish or defect; faultless: *perfect skin; perfect beauty.* **3.** completely suited for a particular purpose or occasion. **4.** completely matching a type; exact: *a perfect circle.* **5.** correct in every detail: *a perfect copy.* **6.** pure or unmixed: *perfect yellow.* **7.** complete; unqualified; absolute: *a perfect mastery; a perfect stranger.* **8.** *Music* relating to the consonances produced by unison, octave, fifth and fourth intervals. –*n.* /'pɜfəkt/ **9.** *Gram.* → **perfect tense.** –*v.t.* /pɜ'fɛkt, pə'fɛkt/ **10.** to bring to completion; complete, or finish. **11.** to make perfect or faultless; bring to perfection. **12.** to bring nearer to perfection; improve. –**perfecter,** *n.* –**perfection,** *n.*

perfectionist /pə'fɛkʃənəst/ *n.* **1.** someone who adheres to some doctrine concerning perfection. **2.** someone who demands nothing less than perfection in any sphere of activity, behaviour, etc. –*adj.* **3.** of, relating to, or characterised by perfection or perfectionism.

perfect storm *n.* **1.** the simultaneous occurrence of weather events which lead to a catastrophic storm, such as a cyclone hitting a low-lying area at the peak of a high tide, creating a storm surge. **2.** any such concurrence of devastating events, as in the economy, business, etc.

perfect tense *n. Gram.* the tense marking an action or state which is completed.

perfidy /'pɜfədi/ *n.* (*pl.* **-dies**) a deliberate breach of faith or trust; faithlessness; treachery. –**perfidious** /pɜ'fɪdiəs/, *adj.*

perforate /'pɜfəreɪt/ *v.t.* **1.** to make a hole or holes through by boring, punching, or other process. **2.** to pierce through or to the interior of; penetrate. –*v.i.* **3.** to make its way through or into something; penetrate. –**perforative** /'pɜfərətɪv/, *adj.* –**perforator,** *n.*

perforce /pə'fɔs/ *adv.* of necessity.

perform /pə'fɔm/ *v.t.* **1.** to carry out; execute; do: *to perform miracles.* **2.** to go through in proper form: *to perform a ceremony.* **3.** to fulfil: *he performed his duty.* **4.** to act (a play, a part, etc.), as on the stage. **5.** to play or sing (music), especially before an audience. –*v.i.* **6.** to fulfil a command, promise, or undertaking. **7.** to carry out or do something. **8.** to act in a play. **9.** to perform music. **10.** to display anger. –**performable,** *adj.* –**performer,** *n.*

performance /pə'fɔməns/ *n.* **1.** a musical, dramatic, or other entertainment. **2.** the performing of ceremonies, or of music, or of a play, part, or the like. **3.** execution or doing, as of work, acts, or feats. **4.** an action or proceeding of a more or less unusual or spectacular kind. **5.** the act of performing. **6.** the way in which something reacts under certain conditions or fulfils the purpose for which it is intended.

performance-enhancing drug *n.* a drug taken by an athlete or other competitive sportsperson to improve performance. Also, **performance enhancing drug.**

perfume *n.* /'pɜfjum/ **1.** a substance, extract, or preparation for diffusing or imparting a fragrant or agreeable smell. **2.** the scent, odour, or volatile particles emitted by substances that have an agreeable smell. –*v.t.* /pə'fjum/ **3.** (of substances, flowers, etc.) to impart fragrance to. **4.** to impregnate with a sweet odour; scent.

perfunctory /pə'fʌŋktəri/ *adj.* performed merely as an uninteresting or routine duty; mechanical; indifferent, careless, or superficial: *perfunctory courtesy.* –**perfunctorily,** *adv.* –**perfunctoriness,** *n.*

pergola /pə'goulə, 'pɜgələ/ *n.* **1.** an arbour formed of horizontal trelliswork supported on columns or posts, over which vines or other plants are trained. **2.** an architectural construction resembling such an arbour.

perhaps /pə'hæps, præps/ *adv.* maybe; possibly.

peri- a prefix meaning 'around', 'about', 'beyond', or having an intensive force, occurring in words from the Greek, and used also as a modern formative, especially in scientific terms.

perigee /'pɛrədʒi/ *n.* **1.** *Astron.* the point in an orbit round the earth that is nearest to the earth (opposed to *apogee*). **2.** *Astronautics* the point at which a satellite orbit is the least distance from the centre of the gravitational field of the controlling body or bodies. –**perigeal** /pɛrə'dʒiəl/, **perigean** /pɛrə'dʒiən/, *adj.*

peril /'pɛrəl/ *n.* exposure to injury, loss, or destruction; risk; jeopardy; danger. –**perilous,** *adj.*

perimeter /pə'rɪmətə/ *n.* **1.** the circumference, border, or outer boundary of a two-dimensional figure. **2.** the length of such a boundary. **3.** any boundary.

4. *Ophthalmology* an instrument for determining the extent and defects of the visual field. –**perimetric** /pɛri-ˈmɛtrɪk/, **perimetrical** /pɛriˈmɛtrɪkəl/, *adj.* –**perimetrically** /pɛriˈmɛtrɪkli/, *adv.* –**perimetry,** *n.*

period /ˈpɪəriəd/ *n.* **1.** a part of time, history, life, etc., characterised by certain events or conditions. **2.** any stated division or part of time. **3.** *Educ.* a particular length of time in a school timetable set aside for a single subject. **4.** *Geol.* the main division of a geological era, represented in the earth's crust by systems of rocks laid down during it. It is divided into epochs. **5.** *Physics* the time of one complete cycle of a motion. **6.** *Astron.* the time in which a planet or satellite revolves about its controlling body. **7.** *Chem.* the group of elements forming a horizontal row in the periodic table. **8.** the point of completion or end of a round of time or course of action. **9.** an episode of menstruation. **10.** → **full stop. 11.** a complete sentence, especially one worked out with great care. –*adj.* **12.** relating to, marking, characteristic of, copying, or representing (the fashions of) a particular period of history: *period costumes.*

periodic /pɪəriˈɒdɪk/ *adj.* **1.** marked by periods or rounds that come back again and again. **2.** happening or appearing at regular intervals. **3.** ceasing and then beginning again, etc. **4.** *Physics* recurring after equal intervals of time. **5.** of or relating to a period, especially of the revolution of a heavenly body. –**periodically,** *adv.* –**periodicity** /pɪəriəˈdɪsəti/, *n.*

periodical /pɪəriˈɒdɪkəl/ *n.* **1.** a magazine, journal, etc., issued at regularly recurring intervals. –*adj.* **2.** issued at regularly recurring intervals. **3.** → **periodic.**

periodic table *n. Chem.* a table in which the chemical elements are arranged in rows and columns so that elements with similar chemical properties lie in the same column.

periodontics /ˌpɛrioʊˈdɒntɪks/ *n.* the study of the structures surrounding and supporting the teeth, such as the gums, bone, etc., and its diseases.

peripatetic /ˌpɛripəˈtɛtɪk/ *adj.* **1.** walking or travelling about; itinerant. –*n.* **2.** someone who walks or travels about.

peripheral /pəˈrɪfərəl/ *adj.* **1.** relating to, situated in, or constituting the periphery. **2.** of minor importance; not essential; superficial. **3.** *Anat.* outside of; external (as distinguished from *central*). –*n.* Also, **peripheral device. 4.** a device attached to a computer which transfers information into or out of the computer. –**peripherally,** *adv.*

peripheral nervous system *n. Physiol., Anat.* a system of nerves and ganglia leading from the spinal cord and brain (the central nervous system) to the organs of the body, conveying sensory information from within and outside the body to the central nervous system and motor instructions from it in response. See **autonomic nervous system, somatic nervous system.**

periphery /pəˈrɪfəri/ *n.* (*pl.* **-ries**) **1.** the external boundary of any surface or area. **2.** the external surface, or outside, of a body.

periphrastic /pɛriˈfræstɪk/ *adj.* **1.** circumlocutory; roundabout. **2.** *Gram.* **a.** denoting a construction of two or more words with a class meaning which in other languages or in other forms of the same language is expressed by inflectional modification of a single word. For example: *the son of Mr Smith* is periphrastic; *Mr Smith's son* is inflectional. **b.** denoting a class meaning expressed by a construction of two or more words. –**periphrastically,** *adv.*

periscope /ˈpɛrəskoʊp/ *n.* an optical instrument consisting essentially of a tube with an arrangement of prisms or mirrors by which a view at the surface of

water, the top of a parapet, etc., may be seen from below or behind.

perish /ˈpɛrɪʃ/ *v.i.* **1.** to suffer death, or lose life, through violence, privation, etc.: *to perish in battle.* **2.** to pass away; decay and disappear. **3.** to rot: *rubber perishes.* **4.** to suffer destruction: *whole cities perish in an earthquake.* **5.** to suffer spiritual death. –*v.t.* **6.** *Aust. Colloq.* to kill: *it would perish the crows.* –*n.* **7.** *Aust. Colloq.* a time of suffering as from unemployment, cold, or especially thirst. –*phr.* **8. do a perish,** *Aust. Colloq.* **a.** to die, especially of thirst. **b.** (*sometimes humorous*) to suffer from deprivation, cold, etc.: *hurry up with the door, we're doing a perish out here.*

perishable /ˈpɛrɪʃəbəl/ *adj.* **1.** liable to perish; subject to decay or destruction. –*n.* **2.** (*usu. pl.*) a perishable thing, as food. –**perishableness, perishability** /ˌpɛrɪʃəˈbɪləti/, *n.*

peristaltic /pɛrəˈstæltɪk/ *adj. Physiol.* of or relating to the alternate waves of constriction and dilation of a tubular muscle system or cylindrical structure, as the wavelike circular contractions of the alimentary canal.

peritoneum /pɛrətəˈniəm/ *n.* (*pl.* **-nea** /-ˈniə/) *Anat.* the membrane lining the abdominal cavity and wrapping around its viscera. Also, **peritonaeum.** –**peritoneal,** *adj.*

peritonitis /pɛrətəˈnaɪtəs/ *n. Pathol.* inflammation of the peritoneum.

periwinkle[1] /ˈpɛriwɪŋkəl/ *n.* **1.** any of various marine gastropods or sea snails, especially *Littorina littorea,* used for food. **2.** the shell of any of various other small univalves.

periwinkle[2] /ˈpɛriwɪŋkəl/ *n.* any plant of the genus *Vinca,* or the related genus *Catharanthus,* as the **blue periwinkle,** *V. major,* or the **pink periwinkle,** *C. roseus.*

perjure /ˈpɜdʒə/ *v.t.* to render (oneself) guilty of swearing falsely, or of wilfully making a false statement under oath or solemn affirmation. –**perjurer,** *n.* –**perjured,** *adj.* –**perjury,** *n.*

perk[1] /pɜk/ *v.i.* **1.** to carry oneself, lift the head, or act in a jaunty manner. –*phr.* **2. perk oneself up,** to brighten up; become more cheerful. **3. perk up, a.** to become lively or vigorous, as after depression or sickness. **b.** to raise smartly or briskly. –**perky,** *adj.*

perk[2] /pɜk/ *v.i., v.t. Colloq.* → **percolate.**

perk[3] /pɜk/ *n. Colloq.* any fringe benefit, bonus, or other income, in cash or in kind, that an employee receives in addition to his or her normal salary. Also, **perquisite.**

perm /pɜm/ *n.* Also, **permanent wave. 1.** a hairstyle in which the hair has waves or curls set into it by a special technique involving chemicals, heat, etc., the effect remaining for a number of months. –*v.t.* **2.** to give (the hair) a perm.

permafrost /ˈpɜməfrɒst/ *n.* ground that is permanently frozen, as in arctic regions.

permanent /ˈpɜmənənt/ *adj.* lasting or intended to last indefinitely; remaining unchanged; not temporary; enduring; abiding. –**permanently,** *adv.* –**permanence,** *n.*

permanent residence *n.* a visa status which gives holders the right to stay permanently in their chosen country. *Abbrev.:* PR Also, **permanent residency.** –**permanent resident,** *n.*

permanent wave *n.* → **perm** (def. 1).

permeable /ˈpɜmiəbəl/ *adj.* capable of being permeated. –**permeability** /ˌpɜmiəˈbɪləti/, *n.*

permeate /ˈpɜmieɪt/ *v.t.* **1.** to pass through the substance or mass of. **2.** to penetrate through the pores, interstices, etc., of. **3.** to be diffused through; pervade; saturate. –*v.i.* **4.** to penetrate; become diffused. –*n.* **5.** that which passes through a permeable membrane. **6.** (in milk) whey which can be mixed back into milk to standardise the level of components such as fat and protein. –**permeation** /pɜmiˈeɪʃən/, *n.* –**permeative,** *adj.*

permission /pə'mɪʃən/ n. **1.** the act of permitting; formal or express allowance or consent. **2.** liberty or licence granted to do something. **3.** *Computers* the authority to access data or software. –**permissible**, *adj.*

permissive /pə'mɪsɪv/ *adj.* **1.** granting permission. **2.** permitted or allowed; optional. **3.** tolerant. **4.** sexually and morally tolerant: *we are living in a permissive society.* –**permissively**, *adv.* –**permissiveness**, *n.*

permit *verb* /pə'mɪt/ (**-mitted**, **-mitting**) –*v.t.* **1.** to allow (a person, etc.) to do something: *permit me to explain.* **2.** to let (something) be done or occur: *the law permits the sale of such drugs.* **3.** to tolerate; agree to. **4.** to afford opportunity for; allow: *vents permitting the escape of gases.* –*v.i.* **5.** to grant permission; allow liberty to do something. **6.** to afford opportunity or possibility: *write when time permits.* –*n.* /'pɜːmɪt/ **7.** a written order granting leave to do something. **8.** an authoritative or official certificate of permission; a licence. **9.** permission. –*phr.* **10.** **permit of**, to allow or admit: *she would permit of no delay.* –**permitter**, *n.*

permutation /pɜːmjə'teɪʃən/ n. **1.** *Maths* **a.** the act of changing the order of elements arranged in a particular order (as, *abc* into *acb*, *bac*, etc.), or of arranging a number of elements in groups made up of equal numbers of the elements in different orders (as, *a* and *b* in *ab* and *ba*). **b.** any of the resulting arrangements or groups. **2.** the act of permuting; alteration.

pernicious /pə'nɪʃəs/ *adj.* **1.** ruinous; highly hurtful: *pernicious teachings.* **2.** deadly; fatal. **3.** evil or wicked. –**perniciously**, *adv.* –**perniciousness**, *n.*

pernickety /pə'nɪkəti/ *adj. Colloq.* **1.** fastidious; fussy. **2.** requiring painstaking care.

peroxide /pə'rɒksaɪd/ n. **1.** *Chem.* **a.** an oxide derived from hydrogen peroxide which contains the -O-O- group; generally that oxide of an element or radical which contains an unusually large amount of oxygen. **b.** hydrogen peroxide, H_2O_2. –*adj.* **2.** (of a person) having hair bleached with peroxide (def. 1b) to make it blond. –*v.t.* **3.** to use peroxide (def. 1b) on (the hair) as a bleach.

perpendicular /pɜːpən'dɪkjələ/ *adj.* **1.** upright; vertical. **2.** *Geom.* meeting a given line or surface at right angles. **3.** (*upper case*) *Archit.* marking or relating to a style of architecture, the last stage of English Gothic, marked by the vertical lines of its tracery. –*n.* **4.** a line or plane at right angles to another line. **5.** an instrument for showing the upright line from any point. **6.** an upright position. –**perpendicularity** /ˌpɜːpəndɪkjəˈlærəti/, *n.* –**perpendicularly**, *adv.*

perpetrate /'pɜːpətreɪt/ *v.t.* to perform, execute, or commit (a crime, deception, etc.). –**perpetration** /pɜːpə'treɪʃən/, *n.* –**perpetrator**, *n.*

perpetual /pə'pɛtʃuəl/ *adj.* **1.** continuing or enduring forever or indefinitely: *perpetual snows.* **2.** continuing or continued without intermission or interruption: *a perpetual stream of visitors.* **3.** *Hort.* blooming more or less continuously throughout the season or the year. –*n.* **4.** a hybrid rose that is perpetual. –**perpetuality** /pɜːpɛtʃuˈæləti/, *n.* –**perpetually**, *adv.*

perpetuate /pə'pɛtʃueɪt/ *v.t.* to make perpetual; preserve from oblivion. –**perpetuation** /pəˌpɛtʃuˈeɪʃən/, **perpetuance**, *n.* –**perpetuator**, *n.* –**perpetuity**, *n.*

perplex /pə'plɛks/ *v.t.* **1.** to cause to be puzzled over what is not understood or certain; bewilder; confuse mentally. **2.** to make complicated or confused, as a matter, question, etc. **3.** to hamper with complications, confusion, or uncertainty. –**perplexity**, *n.* –**perplexed**, *adj.* –**perplexing**, *adj.* –**perplexingly**, *adv.*

perquisite /'pɜːkwəzət/ n. **1.** an incidental emolument, fee, or profit over and above fixed income, salary, or wages. **2.** Also, **perk.** **a.** anything customarily supposed to be allowed or left to an employee or servant as an incidental advantage of the position held. **b.** → **perk**³. **3.** something regarded as due by right.

per se /pɜ 'seɪ/ *adv.* by or in itself; intrinsically.

persecute /'pɜːsəkjut/ *v.t.* **1.** to pursue with harassing or oppressive treatment; harass persistently. **2.** to oppress with injury or punishment for adherence to principles or religious faith. **3.** to annoy by persistent attentions, importunities, or the like. –**persecution** /pɜːsə'kjuʃən/, *n.* –**persecutive**, **persecutory** /pɜːsə'kjutəri/, *adj.* –**persecutor**, *n.*

persevere /pɜːsə'vɪə/ *v.i.* (**-vered**, **-vering**) to persist in anything undertaken; maintain a purpose in spite of difficulty or obstacles; continue steadfastly. –**perseverance**, *n.*

persimmon /'pɜːsəmən, pə'sɪmən/ n. **1.** any of various trees of the genus *Diospyros*, especially *D. virginiana* of North America, with astringent plum-like fruit becoming sweet and edible when thoroughly ripe, and *D. kaki* of Japan and China, with soft, rich yellow-orange to orange-red fruits. **2.** the fruit.

persist /pə'sɪst/ *v.i.* **1.** to continue steadily or firmly in some state, purpose, course of action, or the like, especially in spite of opposition, remonstrance, etc. **2.** to last or endure. **3.** to be insistent in a statement or question. –**persistent**, *adj.* –**persistence**, *n.*

person /'pɜːsən/ n. **1.** a human being, whether man, woman, or child: *the only person in sight.* **2.** a human being as distinguished from an animal or a thing. **3.** the actual self or individual personality of a human being: *to assume a duty in one's own person.* **4.** the living body of a human being, often including the clothes worn. **5.** the body in its external aspect. **6.** a character, part, or role, in a play, story, or in real life, etc. **7.** an individual of distinction or importance. **8.** *Colloq.* someone not entitled to social recognition or respect: *that person!* **9.** *Law* any human being or artificial body of people, having rights and duties before the law. **10.** *Gram.* **a.** (in some languages) a category of verb inflection and of pronoun classification, distinguishing between the speaker (**first person**), the one addressed (**second person**), and anyone or anything else (**third person**), as *I* and *we* (first person), *you* (second person), and *he, she, it* and *they* (third person). **b.** any of these three (or more) divisions. **11.** *Theology* any of the three hypostases or modes of being in the Trinity (Father, Son, and Holy Spirit). –*phr.* **12.** **in person**, with one's own bodily presence: *to apply in person.*

-person a noun suffix used to avoid the specification or implication of sex, as in *chairman*, *salesman*; hence *chairperson*, *salesperson*.

persona /pɜ'souna/ n. (*pl.* **-nae** /-ni/) **1.** a person. **2.** (in the psychology of CG Jung) the outer or public personality, which is presented to the world and does not represent the inner personality of the individual.

personable /'pɜːsənəbəl/ *adj.* of pleasing personal appearance and manner; comely; presentable.

personage /'pɜːsənɪdʒ/ n. **1.** a person of distinction or importance. **2.** any person. **3.** a character in a play, story, etc.

personal /'pɜːsənəl/ *adj.* **1.** of or relating to a particular person; individual; private: *a personal matter.* **2.** relating to, directed to, or aimed at, a particular person: *a personal favour.* **3. a.** relating to the physical presence or involvement of a person: *a personal appearance at the concert*; *personal service.* **b.** relating to what serves the advantage of a particular person: *personal gain.* **4.** referring or directed to a particular person in a disparaging or offensive sense or manner: *personal remarks.* **5.** of the nature of an individual rational being: *a personal God.* **6.** relating to the person, body, or bodily aspect: *personal cleanliness.* **7.** *Gram.* **a.** denoting grammatical person. For example, in Latin *portō* 'I carry', *portās* 'you carry', *portat* 'he, she, or it carries', *-ō*, *-ās* and *-at* are personal endings. **b.** denoting a class of pronouns classified as referring to the speaker, the one addressed, and anyone or anything else. **8.** *Law* denoting or relating to estate or property consisting of moveable chattels, money, securities, and choses in action (distinguished from *real*). –*n.* **9.** *US* **a.** a short news paragraph in a newspaper, concerning a particular person or particular persons. **b.** a short notice in a newspaper, often addressed to a particular individual. –*phr.* **10. be personal**, to make disparaging remarks about a person rather than directing oneself to an argument. **11. get personal**, to touch on intimate or private matters. –**personally**, *adv.*

personal best *n.* **1.** *Sport* (in timed or measured events) an athlete's best performance. **2.** one's greatest achievement in any field of activity. *Abbrev.*: PB

personal computer *n.* a microcomputer designed for individual use, as in the office, at home, etc., for such applications as word processing, accounting, etc. Also, **PC**.

personal digital assistant *n.* → PDA.

personal identification number *n.* → PIN.

personalise /ˈpɜːsənəlaɪz/ *v.t.* **1.** to make personal. **2.** to mark in some way so as to identify as the property of a particular person. **3.** to adapt to the needs of a particular person. **4.** to direct to a particular individual: *she did not personalise her attack.* Also, **personalize**. –**personalisation** /ˌpɜːsənəlaɪˈzeɪʃən/, *n.*

personality /pɜːsəˈnæləti/ *n.* (*pl.* **-ties**) **1.** a clearly marked or notable personal character: *a man with personality.* **2.** a person as a being formed of a grouping together of qualities. **3.** *Psychol.* (an organised pattern of) all the mental, emotional, social, etc., characteristics of a particular person. **4.** the quality of being a person; existence as a self-conscious being; personal identity. **5.** a well-known or outstanding person; celebrity.

personal organiser *n.* **1.** a folder or wallet containing a diary, address book, etc. **2.** a small electronic device used to record appointments, store telephone numbers, etc. **3.** a computer program comprising features such as a diary, address book, etc. Also, **personal organizer**.

personal pronoun *n. Gram.* any of the pronouns which indicate grammatical person (*I*, *we*, *thou*, *you*, *he*, *she*, *it*, *they*).

personification /pəsɒnəfəˈkeɪʃən/ *n.* **1.** the attribution of personal nature or character to inanimate objects or abstract notions, especially as a rhetorical figure. **2.** the representation of a thing or abstraction in the form of a person, as in art. **3.** the person or thing embodying a quality or the like; an embodiment. **4.** an imaginary person or creature conceived or figured to represent a thing or abstraction. **5.** the act of personifying.

personify /pəˈsɒnəfaɪ/ *v.t.* (**-fied**, **-fying**) **1.** to attribute personal nature or character to (an inanimate object or an abstraction), as in speech or writing. **2.** to represent (a thing or abstraction) in the form of a person, as in art. **3.** to embody (a quality, idea, etc.) in a real person or a concrete thing. **4.** to be an embodiment of; typify. –**personifier**, *n.*

personnel /pɜːsəˈnel/ *n.* **1.** the body of persons employed in any work, undertaking, or service. –*adj.* **2.** of or relating to personnel.

person of interest *n.* (*pl.* **persons of interest**) a person whom police have identified as being possibly significantly involved in a criminal activity and on whom their attention is focused although there is not enough evidence of such involvement to allow them to nominate the person as a suspect.

perspective /pəˈspɛktɪv/ *n.* **1.** the art of depicting on a flat surface, various objects, architecture, landscape, etc., in such a way as to express dimensions and spatial relations. **2.** the relation of parts to one another and to the whole, in a mental view or prospect. **3.** a visible scene, especially one extending to a distance; a vista. **4.** the appearance of objects with reference to relative position, distance, etc. **5.** a mental view or prospect. –*adj.* **6.** of or relating to the art of perspective, or represented according to its laws. –*phr.* **7. in perspective**, **a.** according to the laws of perspective. **b.** in true proportion. –**perspectively**, *adv.*

perspex /ˈpɜːspɛks/ *n.* (*from trademark*) an optically clear thermoplastic resin, polymethyl methacrylate, used as a substitute for glass in certain applications.

perspicacious /pɜːspəˈkeɪʃəs/ *adj.* having keen mental perception; discerning. –**perspicacity**, **perspicuity**, *n.* –**perspicaciously**, *adv.*

perspicuous /pəˈspɪkjuəs/ *adj.* **1.** clear to the understanding. **2.** clear in expression or statement; lucid. **3.** → **perspicacious**. –**perspicuously**, *adv.* –**perspicuousness**, *n.*

perspire /pəˈspaɪə/ *Physiol.* –*v.i.* **1.** to excrete watery fluid through the pores; sweat. –*v.t.* **2.** to emit through pores; exude. –**perspiration**, *n.* –**perspiratory** /pəˈspaɪrətri/, *adj.*

persuade /pəˈsweɪd/ *v.t.* **1.** to prevail on (a person, etc.), by advice, urging, reasons, inducements, etc., to do something: *we could not persuade him to wait.* **2.** to induce to believe; convince. –**persuasive**, *adj.* –**persuader**, *n.* –**persuasion**, *n.*

pert /pɜːt/ *adj.* **1.** bold; forward; impertinent; impudent; saucy. **2.** lively; sprightly; in good health. –**pertly**, *adv.* –**pertness**, *n.*

pertain /pəˈteɪn/ *v.i.* **1.** to have reference or relation; relate: *documents pertaining to the case.* **2.** to belong or be connected as a part, adjunct, possession, attribute, etc. **3.** to belong properly or fittingly; be appropriate.

pertinacious /pɜːtəˈneɪʃəs/ *adj.* **1.** holding tenaciously to a purpose, course of action, or opinion. **2.** extremely persistent: *pertinacious efforts.* –**pertinaciousness**, **pertinacity** /pɜːtəˈnæsəti/, *n.* –**pertinaciously**, *adv.*

pertinent /ˈpɜːtənənt/ *adj.* relating to the matter in hand; relevant; apposite: *pertinent details.* –**pertinence**, **pertinency**, *n.* –**pertinently**, *adv.*

perturb /pəˈtɜːb/ *v.t.* **1.** to disturb or disquiet greatly in mind; agitate. **2.** to disturb greatly; throw into disorder; derange. –**perturbation** /pɜːtəˈbeɪʃən/, *n.* –**perturbable**, *adj.*

perusal /pəˈruːzəl/ *n.* **1.** a reading. **2.** the act of perusing; survey or scrutiny.

peruse /pəˈruːz/ *v.t.* **1.** to read through, as with thoroughness or care. **2.** to read in a leisurely fashion, with little attention to detail. –**perusable**, *adj.* –**peruser**, *n.*

perv /pɜːv/ *Colloq.* –*n.* **1.** a sexual pervert; a person with socially disapproved sexual desires. **2.** an attractive person; someone who is worth perving at. –*adj.* **3.** pornographic: *perv photos; a perv magazine.* –*v.i.* **4.** (sometimes fol. by *on* or *at*) to look lustfully. **5.** to loiter in the hope of being able to observe objects of one's lust. –*phr.* **6. have a perv**, to look at something, with or as if with lustful appreciation. Also, **perve**.

pervade /pəˈveɪd/ *v.t.* **1.** to extend its presence, activities, influence, etc., throughout: *spring pervaded the air.* **2.** to go, pass, or spread through. –**pervader**, *n.* –**pervasion**, *n.* –**pervasive** /pəˈveɪsɪv, -zɪv/, *adj.* –**pervasively**, *adv.* –**pervasiveness**, *n.*

perverse /pəˈvɜːs/ *adj.* **1.** wilfully determined or disposed to go counter to what is expected or desired; contrary. **2.** characterised by or proceeding from such a determination: *a perverse mood.* **3.** wayward; cantankerous. **4.** persistent or obstinate in what is wrong. **5.** turned away from what is right, good, or proper; wicked. –**perversity**, **perverseness**, *n.* –**perversely**, *adv.* –**perversive**, *adj.*

perversion /pəˈvɜːʒən/ *n.* **1.** the act of perverting. **2.** the state of being perverted. **3.** a perverted form of something. **4.** *Psychol.* unnatural or abnormal condition of the sexual instincts (**sexual perversion**). **5.** *Pathol.* change to what is unnatural or abnormal: *a perversion of function*; *perversion of taste.*

pervert *v.t.* /pəˈvɜːt/ **1.** to turn or lead away from the right course, either in moral or mental matters, judgements, etc. **2.** to bring over to a religious belief regarded as false or wrong. **3.** to turn to an improper use. **4.** to change or twist out of shape; distort. **5.** to bring to a less excellent state; vitiate or debase. **6.** to affect with a perversion. –*n.* /ˈpɜːvɜːt/ **7.** *Psychol.*, *Pathol.* someone affected with perversion. **8.** someone who has been perverted. **–perverter**, *n.* **–pervertible**, *adj.*

perverted /pəˈvɜːtəd/ *adj.* **1.** *Pathol.* changed to or being of an unnatural or abnormal kind: *a perverted appetite.* **2.** turned from what is right; wicked; misguided; misapplied; distorted. **3.** affected with or due to perversion. **–pervertedly**, *adv.*

pervious /ˈpɜːviəs/ *adj.* **1.** admitting of passage or entrance; permeable: *pervious soil.* **2.** accessible to reason, feeling, etc. **–perviousness**, *n.*

Pesach /ˈpeɪsɑːk/ *n.* an annual Jewish feast, instituted to commemorate the passing over or sparing of the Israelites in Egypt when God struck down the firstborn of the Egyptians, but used in the general sense of the Feast of Unleavened Bread in commemoration of the deliverance from Egypt; starts on the 15th day of the month of Nissan (falling in either March or April). Also, **Pesah**, **Passover**.

peseta /pəˈseɪtə, -ˈseɪ-/ *n.* (formerly, until the introduction of the euro in 2002) the principal monetary unit of Spain. *Abbrev.*: pta

peso /ˈpeɪsoʊ/ *n.* **1.** the principal monetary unit of several countries including Argentina, Chile, Cuba, Mexico, the Dominican Republic, Uruguay, and the Philippines, of varying value from country to country. **2.** any of various monetary units or coins of Spanish America. *Abbrev.*: p

pessary /ˈpesəri/ *n.* (*pl.* **-ries**) *Med.* **1.** an instrument worn in the vagina to remedy uterine displacement. **2.** a vaginal suppository.

pessimism /ˈpesəmɪzəm, ˈpes-/ *n.* **1.** disposition to take the gloomiest possible view. **2.** the doctrine that the existing world is the worst of all possible worlds, or that all things naturally tend to evil. **3.** the belief that the evil and pain in the world are not compensated for by the good and happiness. **–pessimist**, *n.* **–pessimistic** /pezəˈmɪstɪk, ˌpes-/, *adj.*

pest /pest/ *n.* **1.** an organism considered harmful, as in agriculture, horticulture, buildings either domestic or commercial, etc. **2.** a troublesome thing or person; nuisance.

pester /ˈpestə/ *v.t.* to harass with petty annoyances, vexing importunities, or the like; torment.

pesticide /ˈpestəsaɪd/ *n.* a substance or preparation for destroying pests, such as mosquitoes, flies, etc.

pestilence /ˈpestələns/ *n.* **1.** a deadly epidemic disease. **2.** something that produces or tends to produce epidemic disease. **3.** → **bubonic plague**. **–pestilential** /pestəˈlenʃəl/, *adj.*

pestilent /ˈpestələnt/ *adj.* **1.** (of a disease) infectious. **2.** destructive to life; deadly; poisonous. **3.** hurtful to peace, morals, etc. **4.** troublesome or annoying. **5.** dangerous or harmful. **–pestilential**, *adj.* **–pestilently**, *adv.*

pestle /ˈpesəl/ *n.* **1.** a club-shaped implement to be held in the hand when it is being used to crush material in a mortar (**mortar**[1] def. 1). **2.** any of various appliances for pounding, stamping, etc. –*verb* (**-tled**, **-tling**) –*v.t.* **3.** to

pound or triturate with or as with a pestle. –*v.i.* **4.** to work with a pestle.

pesto /ˈpestoʊ/ *n.* a thick, uncooked sauce consisting of a puree of pine nuts, garlic, basil, and cheese, with oil.

pet[1] /pet/ *n.* **1.** any animal living with humans that is cared for with warmth and liking. **2.** a person treated as especially dear; a favourite. **3.** a thing treated as particularly dear. –*adj.* **4.** treated as a pet, as an animal. **5.** treated as especially dear, and favoured as a child or other person. **6.** favourite: *a pet theory.* **7.** most important; principal: *pet aversion.* **8.** showing affection: *a pet name.* –*v.t.* (**petted**, **petting**) **9.** to treat as a pet; fondle; indulge. **10.** to pat or stroke fondly, or kiss, hold or touch someone.

pet[2] /pet/ *n.* **1.** a fit of peevishness: *to be in a pet.* –*v.i.* (**petted**, **petting**) **2.** to be peevish; sulk.

petal /ˈpetl/ *n.* one of the members of a corolla, usually leaf-like and sometimes brightly coloured. **–petalled**, *adj.*

PET bottle /pi ˈti bɒtl, ˌpet bɒtl/ *n.* a soft-drink bottle made of plastic which can be recycled for other uses.

peter /ˈpitə/ *phr.* **peter out**, to diminish gradually and then disappear or cease.

pethidine /ˈpeθədin, -dən/ *n.* an analgesic similar to morphine, administered especially in childbirth.

petiole /ˈpetioʊl/ *n.* **1.** *Bot.* the stalk by which a leaf is attached to the stem; a leafstalk. **2.** *Zool.* a stalk or peduncle, as that connecting the abdomen and thorax in wasps, etc. **–petiolar**, **petiolate**, *adj.*

petite /pəˈtit/ *adj.* (of women) little; of small size; tiny.

petition /pəˈtɪʃən/ *n.* **1.** a formally drawn-up request addressed to a person or a body of people in power, desiring some favour, right, mercy, or other benefit. **2.** a request made for something desired, especially a respectful or humble request, usually to someone or those in power: *a petition for aid.* **3.** something that is sought by request, etc. **4.** *Law* an application for an order of a court or for some action relating to the law. **5.** a prayer, usually to God.; supplication. –*v.t.* **6.** to beg, usually for something desired; supplicate; entreat. **7.** to address a formal petition to (a ruler, a law-making body, etc.). **8.** (fol. by *that*) to ask by petition for (something). –*v.i.* **9.** to present a petition. **10.** to address a formal petition. **–petitioner**, *n.* **–petitionary** /pəˈtɪʃənəri/, *adj.*

pet milk *n.* unpasteurised milk produced for animal consumption; sometimes also intended for human consumption but sold as though for animals to avoid local legal restrictions on the sale of unpasteurised milk for human consumption.

petranol /ˈpetrənɒl/ *n.* → **E10**.

petrel /ˈpetrəl/ *n.* any of numerous seabirds of the family Procellariidae, as the mutton-bird.

petrify /ˈpetrəfaɪ/ *verb* (**-fied**, **-fying**) –*v.t.* **1.** to convert into stone or a stony substance. **2.** to make rigid, stiffen, or benumb; deaden; make inert. **3.** to stupefy or paralyse with astonishment, horror, fear, or other strong emotion. –*v.i.* **4.** to become petrified. **–petrifaction** /petrəˈfækʃən/, *n.*

petro- a word element meaning 'stone' or 'rock'.

petrodiesel /ˈpetroʊdizəl/ *n.* diesel obtained from petroleum. Compare **biodiesel**.

petrol /ˈpetrəl/ *n.* a mixture of volatile liquid hydrocarbons, as hexane, heptane, and octane, used as a solvent and extensively as a fuel in internal-combustion engines; gasoline.

petroleum /pəˈtroʊliəm/ *n.* **1.** an oily, usually dark-coloured liquid (a form of bitumen or mixture of various hydrocarbons), occurring naturally in various parts of the world, and commonly obtained by boring. It is used (in its natural state or after certain treatment) as a fuel, or separated by distillation into petrol, naphtha,

benzine, lubricating oil, paraffin oil, paraffin wax, etc.
2. → **petrol**.

petroleum jelly *n.* a soft or semisolid unctuous substance obtained from petroleum, used as a base for ointments and as a protective dressing. Also, **petrolatum**.

petticoat /ˈpɛtikoʊt/ *n.* **1.** a skirt, especially an underskirt, worn by women and girls; a slip. **2.** *Colloq.* a woman, especially considered as a sex object. –*adj.* **3.** female or feminine.

petty /ˈpɛti/ *adj.* (**-tier, -tiest**) **1.** of small importance; trifling; trivial: *petty grievances.* **2.** of lesser or secondary importance, merit, etc. **3.** having or showing narrow ideas, interests, etc.: *petty minds.* **4.** mean or ungenerous in small or trifling things: *a petty revenge.* –**pettily**, *adv.* –**pettiness**, *n.*

petty cash *n.* a small cash fund set aside to meet incidental expenses, as for office supplies.

petty officer *n. Navy* **1.** a non-commissioned officer in the Royal Australian Navy ranking below chief petty officer and above leading seaman. **2.** the rank. *Abbrev.*: PO

petulant /ˈpɛtʃələnt/ *adj.* moved to or showing sudden, impatient irritation, especially over some trifling annoyance: *a petulant toss of the head.* –**petulance**, *n.*

petunia /pəˈtjunjə, -tjuniə/ *n.* **1.** any of the herbs constituting the genus *Petunia*, native to tropical America but cultivated elsewhere, bearing funnel-shaped flowers of various colours. **2.** a deep reddish purple.

pew /pju/ *n.* **1.** (in a church) one of an assemblage of fixed bench-like seats (with backs), accessible by aisles, for the use of the congregation. **2.** an enclosed seat in a church, or an enclosure with seats, appropriated to the use of a family or other worshippers. **3.** *Colloq.* any chair; any place to sit down: *take a pew.*

pewter /ˈpjutə/ *n.* **1.** any of various alloys in which tin is the chief constituent, originally one of tin and lead. **2.** a vessel or utensil made of such an alloy. **3.** such utensils collectively. –*adj.* **4.** consisting or made of pewter: *a pewter mug.*

pH /pi ˈeɪtʃ/ *n. Chem.* a measure of acidity or alkalinity, as of soil, water, etc., on a scale, running from 1 (extreme acidity) to 14 (extreme alkalinity), numerically equal to the negative logarithm of the concentration of the hydrogen ion in gram atoms per litre.

phage /feɪdʒ/ *n. Biol.* a virus for which the natural host is a bacterial cell.

-phage a word element meaning 'eating', 'devouring', used in biology to refer to phagocytes, as in *bacteriophage*.

phage therapy *n.* the treatment of bacterial diseases with bacteria-destroying viruses, a medical practice that fell out of use with the advent of antibiotics but which has subsequently returned to favour because of the developing resistance of bacteria to antibiotics.

phago- a word element corresponding to **-phage**.

-phagous a word element forming an adjective termination meaning 'eating', 'feeding on', 'devouring'.

-phagy a word element forming a noun termination meaning 'eating', 'devouring', especially as a practice or habit, as in *anthropophagy*.

phalanger /fəˈlændʒə/ *n.* any of numerous arboreal marsupials constituting the family Phalangeridae, of the Australian region, especially those of the genus *Phalanger*, as *P. maculatus* (**spotted cuscus**). The group also includes the brush-tailed possums of the genus *Trichosurus*.

phalanx /ˈfælæŋks/ *n.* (*pl.* **phalanxes** /ˈfælæŋksəz/ *or* **phalanges** /fəˈlændʒiz/) **1.** (in ancient Greece) a body of heavily armed foot soldiers in close formation with shields joined and long spears overlapping. **2.** a closely

grouped body of people, animals, or things. **3.** a number of people, etc., united for a common purpose.

phallus /ˈfæləs/ *n.* (*pl.* **phalluses** *or* **phalli** /ˈfælaɪ/) **1.** an image of the erect male reproductive organ, symbolising in certain religious systems the generative power in nature. **2.** *Anat.* the penis, clitoris, or the sexually undifferentiated embryonic organ out of which each develops. –**phallic**, *adj.* –**phallicism** /ˈfæləsɪzəm/, *n.*

-phane a word element indicating apparent similarity to some particular substance.

phantasmagoria /fænˌtæzməˈgɔriə/ *n.* **1.** a shifting series of phantasms, illusions, or deceptive appearances, as in a dream or as created by the imagination. **2.** a changing scene made up of many elements. **3.** an exhibition of optical illusions produced by a magic lantern or the like, as one in which figures increase or diminish in size, dissolve, pass into each other, etc. –**phantasmagorial, phantasmagoric** /fæntæzməˈgɒrɪk/, **phantasmagorical** /fæntæzməˈgɒrɪkəl/, *adj.*

phantom /ˈfæntəm/ *n.* **1.** an image appearing in a dream or formed in the mind. **2.** an apparition or spectre. **3.** a thing or person that is little more than an appearance or show. **4.** an appearance without material substance. –*adj.* **5.** of the nature of a phantom; unreal; illusive; spectral.

-phany a word element forming a noun termination meaning 'appearance', 'manifestation', as of deity or a supernatural being, as in *epiphany*.

Pharaoh /ˈfɛəroʊ/ *n.* (*also lower case*) a ruler of ancient Egypt. –**Pharaonic** /fɛəˈrɒnɪk/, *adj.*

pharmaceutical /faməˈsjutɪkəl/ *adj.* relating to pharmacy. Also, **pharmaceutic**. –**pharmaceutically**, *adv.*

pharmaceutics /faməˈsjutɪks/ *n.* → **pharmacy** (def. 1).

pharmacology /faməˈkɒlədʒi/ *n.* the science of drugs, their preparation, uses, and effects. –**pharmacological** /faməkəˈlɒdʒɪkəl/, *adj.* –**pharmacologist**, *n.*

pharmacy /ˈfaməsi/ *n.* (*pl.* **-cies**) **1.** the art or practice of preparing and dispensing drugs and medicines. **2.** the occupation of a chemist or pharmacist. **3.** a dispensary; chemist's shop. –**pharmacist**, *n.*

pharyngitis /færənˈdʒaɪtəs/ *n. Pathol.* inflammation of the mucous membrane of the pharynx.

pharyngo- a word element meaning 'pharynx'.

pharynx /ˈfærɪŋks/ *n.* (*pl.* **pharynges** /fəˈrɪndʒiz/ *or* **pharynxes**) *Anat.* the tube or cavity, with its surrounding membrane and muscles, which connects the mouth with the oesophagus. –**pharyngeal** /færənˈdʒiəl, fəˈrɪndʒiəl/, *adj.*

phase /feɪz/ *n.* **1.** any of the appearances or aspects in which a thing of varying modes or conditions manifests itself to the eye or mind. **2.** a stage of change or development. **3.** *Astron.* **a.** the particular appearance presented by a planet, etc., at a given time. **b.** one of the recurring appearances or states of the moon or a planet in respect to the form, or the absence, of its illuminated disc: *the phases of the moon.* **4.** *Biol.* an aspect of or stage in meiosis or mitosis. **5.** *Zool.* any of the stages of development of certain animals which take on a different colour according to the breeding condition. **6.** *Chem., Physics* a mechanically separate, homogeneous part of a heterogeneous system: *the solid, liquid, and gaseous phases of a substance.* **7.** *Physics, Electronics* a particular stage or point of advancement in a cycle; the fractional part of the period through which the time has advanced, measured from some arbitrary origin. –*v.t.* **8.** to plan or order (services, materials, etc.) to be available when required. **9.** to introduce (into a system or the like) in stages. **10.** to adjust or synchronise (with another element in a system). –*phr.* **11. in phase**, (of two similar waveforms) having reached corresponding points in the wave motion at the same time. **12. out of phase**, (of two similar waveforms) not in phase. **13. phase in,** to introduce gradually into a system, or the like. **14. phase out,** to withdraw gradually from a system.

-phasia a word element referring to disordered speech, as in *aphasia*. Also, **-phasy**.

pheasant /ˈfɛzənt/ *n.* (*pl.* **pheasants** *or, especially collectively,* **pheasant**) any of various large, long-tailed, gallinaceous birds of the genus *Phasianus* and allied genera, originally native to Asia, especially the **ring-necked pheasant,** *P. colchicus,* widely introduced around the world as a game bird, and now established in a number of localities in Australia.

phen- a word element used in chemical terms to indicate derivation from benzene, sometimes used with particular reference to phenol. Also, (*before consonants*), **pheno-**.

phenomenal /fəˈnɒmənəl/ *adj.* **1.** extraordinary or prodigious: *phenomenal speed.* **2.** of or relating to a phenomenon or phenomena. **3.** of the nature of a phenomenon; cognisable by the senses. **4.** *Colloq.* excellent: *a phenomenal movie.* –**phenomenally,** *adv.*

phenomenon /fəˈnɒmənən/ *n.* (*pl.* **-na** /-nə/) **1.** a fact, occurrence, or circumstance observed or observable: *a natural phenomenon.* **2.** something that impresses the observer as extraordinary; a remarkable thing or person. **3.** a particular happening or effect.

phew /fju/ *interj.* an exclamation of disgust, impatience, exhaustion, surprise, relief, etc.

phial /ˈfaɪəl/ *n.* Also, **vial.** **1.** a small vessel as of glass, for liquids. –*v.t.* (**-alled, -alling**) **2.** to put into or keep in a phial.

phil- a word element meaning 'loving', as in *philanthropy.* Also, **philo-**.

-phil variant of **-phile**.

philander /fəˈlændə/ *v.i.* (of a man) to make love, especially without serious intentions; carry on a flirtation. –**philanderer,** *n.*

philanthropic /fɪlənˈθrɒpɪk/ *adj.* of, relating to, or characterised by philanthropy; benevolent. –**philanthropically,** *adv.*

philanthropy /fəˈlænθrəpi/ *n.* (*pl.* **-pies**) **1.** love of humankind, especially as manifested in deeds of practical beneficence. **2.** a philanthropic action, work, institution, or the like. –**philanthropist,** *n.*

philately /fəˈlætəli/ *n.* the collecting and study of postage stamps, impressed stamps, stamped envelopes, postmarks, postcards, covers and similar material. –**philatelist,** *n.* –**philatelic** /fɪləˈtɛlɪk/, **philatelical** /fɪləˈtɛlɪkəl/, *adj.* –**philatelically** /fɪləˈtɛlɪkli/, *adv.*

-phile a word element meaning 'loving', 'friendly', or 'lover', 'friend', serving to form adjectives and nouns, as *Anglophile, bibliophile.* Also, **-phil**.

philharmonic /fɪlhaˈmɒnɪk, ˌfɪləmɒnɪk/ *adj.* fond of music; music-loving, used especially in the name of certain musical societies (**Philharmonic Societies**) and hence applied to their concerts (**philharmonic concerts**).

-philia a word element forming a noun termination meaning 'fondness', 'craving' or 'affinity for'.

philistine /ˈfɪləstaɪn/ (*sometimes upper case*) –*n.* **1.** someone looked down upon as lacking in and indifferent to culture, aesthetic refinement, etc., or contentedly commonplace in ideas and tastes. –*adj.* **2.** lacking in culture; commonplace. –**philistinism,** *n.*

philo- variant of **phil-**, before consonants, as in *philosopher.*

philology /fəˈlɒlədʒi/ *n.* **1.** the systematic study of written records, the establishment of their authenticity and their original form, and the determination of their meaning. **2.** linguistics. –**philologist, philologer,** *n.* –**philologic** /fɪləˈlɒdʒɪk/, *adj.*

philosophical /fɪləˈsɒfɪkəl/ *adj.* **1.** of or relating to philosophy: *philosophical studies.* **2.** knowledgeable about or occupied with philosophy, as persons. **3.** proper to or befitting a philosopher. **4.** rationally or sensibly calm in trying circumstances: *a philosophical acceptance of necessity.* –**philosophically,** *adv.*

philosophy /fəˈlɒsəfi/ *n.* (*pl.* **-phies**) **1.** the study or science of the truths or principles underlying all knowledge and being, including natural, moral and metaphysical philosophy. **2.** any system of philosophical principles: *the philosophy of Spinoza.* **3.** the study or science of the principles of a particular branch or subject of knowledge: *the philosophy of history.* **4.** a system of principles for guidance in practical affairs. –**philosopher,** *n.* –**philosophism,** *n.*

-philous a word element forming an adjective termination meaning 'loving', 'fond of', 'having an affinity for', or 'attracted to'.

philtre /ˈfɪltə/ *n.* **1.** a potion, drug, or the like, supposed to induce love. **2.** a magic potion for any purpose. –*v.t.* (**-tred, -tring**) **3.** to charm with a philtre. Also, *Chiefly US,* **philter**.

phishing /ˈfɪʃɪŋ/ *n.* a form of internet fraud in which an email purporting to be from a legitimate sender, such as a bank, government institution, etc., encourages the recipient to provide personal information, passwords, etc., ostensibly to confirm or update information which the legitimate organisation already has. –**phisher,** *n.*

phlebo- a word element meaning 'vein', as in *phlebotomy.* Also, (*before a vowel*), **phleb-**.

phlegm /flɛm/ *n. Physiol.* the thick mucus secreted in the respiratory passages and discharged by coughing, etc., especially that occurring in the lungs and throat passages during a cold, etc. –**phlegmy,** *adj.*

phlegmatic /flɛgˈmætɪk/ *adj.* **1.** not easily excited to action or feeling; sluggish or apathetic. **2.** cool or self-possessed. **3.** of the nature of or abounding in phlegm. Also, **phlegmatical.** –**phlegmatically,** *adv.*

phloem /ˈfloʊəm/ *n. Bot.* that part of the cell tissue which carries food within the plant.

-phobe a word element forming a noun termination meaning 'someone who fears or dreads', and often implying aversion or hatred, as in *homophobe.*

phobia /ˈfoʊbiə/ *n.* any extreme or irrational fear or dread. –**phobic,** *adj., n.*

-phobia a word element forming a noun termination meaning 'fear' or 'dread', often morbid, or with implication of aversion or hatred, as in *agoraphobia, claustrophobia.*

phoenix /ˈfinɪks/ *n.* **1.** Also, **Phoenix.** a mythical bird of great beauty, the only one of its kind, fabled to live 500 or 600 years in the Arabian wilderness, to burn itself on a funeral pyre, and to rise from its ashes in the freshness of youth and live through another cycle of years (often an emblem of immortality). **2.** a person or thing that is restored after death or destruction. **3.** a person or thing of peerless beauty or excellence; a paragon. Also, *Chiefly US,* **phenix**.

phon- a word element meaning 'voice', 'sound'. Also, **phono-**.

phone¹ /foʊn/ *n., v.t., v.i.* → **telephone.**

phone² /foʊn/ *n.* an individual speech sound, being the smallest discrete segment of sound which can be identified as meaningful. –**phonal,** *adj.*

-phone a word element meaning 'sound', especially used in names of instruments, as in *xylophone, megaphone, telephone.*

phoneme /ˈfoʊnim/ *n. Ling.* the smallest distinctive group or class of phones in a language. The phonemes of a language contrast with one another; e.g., in English, *pip* differs from *nip, pin, tip, pit, bib,* etc., and *rumple* from *rumble,* by contrast of the phoneme

/p/ with other phonemes. In writing, the same symbol can be used for all the phones belonging to one phoneme without causing confusion between words, for example, the /r/ consonant phoneme includes the voiceless fricative *r* phone of *tree*, the voiced *r* phone of *red*, etc. –**phonemic**, *adj.*

phonetic /fə'nɛtɪk/ *adj.* 1. of or relating to speech sounds and their production. 2. agreeing with or corresponding to pronunciation: *phonetic transcription.* –**phonetically**, *adv.*

phonetics /fə'nɛtɪks/ *n.* 1. the science of speech sounds and their production. 2. the phonetic system, or the body of phonetic facts, of a particular language. –**phonetician** /foʊnə'tɪʃən/, *n.*

phoney /'foʊni/ *Colloq.* –*adj.* (**-nier, -niest**) 1. not genuine; spurious, counterfeit, or bogus; fraudulent. –*n.* (*pl.* **-neys** *or* **-nies**) 2. a counterfeit or fake. 3. a faker. Also, **phony.** –**phoniness**, *n.*

phono- variant of **phon-**, before consonants, as in *phonogram.*

phonology /fə'nɒlədʒi/ *n. Ling.* 1. phonetics or phonemics, or both together. 2. the phonetic and phonemic system, or the body of phonetic and phonemic facts, of a language. –**phonologic** /foʊnə'lɒdʒɪk/, **phonological** /foʊnə'lɒdʒɪkəl/, *adj.* –**phonologically** /foʊnə'lɒdʒɪkli/, *adv.*

-phony a word element used in abstract nouns related to **-phone**, as in *telephony.*

-phore a word element forming a noun termination meaning 'bearer', 'thing or part bearing (something)'.

-phorous a word element forming an adjective termination meaning 'bearing', 'having'.

phosph- variant of **phospho-**, before vowels, as in *phosphate.*

phosphate /'fosfeɪt/ *n.* 1. *Chem.* (loosely) a salt or ester of phosphoric acid. 2. *Agric.* a fertiliser containing compounds of phosphorus.

phospho- a word element representing **phosphorus**, as in *phosphoprotein.* Also, **phosph-.**

phosphor /'fosfə/ *n. Physics* a substance which is capable of storing energy imparted from ultraviolet or other ionising radiations, and releasing it later as light; any substance which exhibits luminescence.

phosphoresce /fosfə'rɛs/ *v.i.* to be luminous without sensible heat, as phosphorus.

phosphorescence /fosfə'rɛsəns/ *n. Physics* 1. the property of being luminous at temperatures below incandescence, as from slow oxidation, in the case of phosphorus, or after exposure to light or other radiation. 2. any radiation emitted by a substance after the removal of the exciting agent.

phosphorus /'fosfərəs/ *n.* (*pl.* **-ri** /-raɪ/) 1. *Chem.* a solid nonmetallic element existing in three main allotropic forms; white or yellow (poisonous, flammable, exhibits phosphorescence at room temperature); red (less reactive and less poisonous); black (electrically conducting, insoluble in most solvents). *Symbol*: P; *relative atomic mass*: 30.9738; *atomic number*: 15; *density*: (white) 1.82, (red) 2.20, (black) 2.25–2.69. The element is used in forming smokescreens; its compounds are used in matches and in phosphate fertilisers. It is a necessary constituent in plant and animal life, in bones, nerves, and embryos. 2. *Rare* any phosphorescent substance.

photo /'foʊtoʊ/ *n.* (*pl.* **photos**) a photograph.

photo- 1. a word element meaning 'light' as in *photosynthesis, photoelectron.* 2. a word element meaning 'photograph' or 'photographic' as in *photocopy.*

photobomb /'foʊtoʊbɒm/ *v.t.* 1. to upstage (the intended subject of a photograph) by appearing in it, usually in some theatrical or distracting way. 2. to ruin (a photograph) by such behaviour as a prank. –*n.* 3. a picture with such an unwanted inclusion. –**photobombing**, *n.*

photochemical /foʊtoʊ'kɛmɪkəl/ *adj.* of, relating to, or produced by the action of light triggering a chemical process: *photochemical pollutant.*

photochemical smog *n.* smog produced by the reaction of hydrocarbons with nitrogen oxide in sunlight; common in large urban areas where there are stable atmospheric conditions and a high level of hydrocarbons, as from vehicle exhausts.

photocopy /'foʊtoʊkɒpi/ *n.* (*pl.* **-copies**) 1. a photographic reproduction of written or printed material. –*v.t.* (**-copied, -copying**) 2. to make a photocopy of. –**photocopier**, *n.*

photoelectric cell /ˌfoʊtoʊə,lɛktrɪk 'sɛl/ *n.* a device used for the detection of light. Its operation depends on the emission of electrons by various substances after exposure to light or other electromagnetic radiation.

photo finish *n.* a close finish to a race in which the decision is made from a photograph of the contestants as they cross the finishing line.

photogenic /foʊtə'dʒɛnɪk, -'dʒinɪk/ *adj.* 1. a. (of a person) suitable for being photographed for artistic purposes, etc. b. having features that make one attractive in photographs. 2. *Biol.* producing or emitting light as certain bacteria; luminiferous; phosphorescent. –**photogenically**, *adv.*

photograph /'foʊtəgræf, -graf/ *n.* 1. a picture produced by photography. –*v.t.* 2. to take a photograph of. –*v.i.* 3. to practise photography.

photographic /foʊtə'græfɪk/ *adj.* 1. of or relating to photography. 2. suggestive of a photograph; extremely realistic and detailed: *photographic accuracy*; *photographic memory.* Also, **photographical.** –**photographically**, *adv.*

photography /fə'tɒgrəfi/ *n.* the process or art of producing images of objects on sensitised surfaces by the chemical action of light or of other forms of radiant energy, as X-rays, gamma rays, cosmic rays, etc. –**photographer** /fə'tɒgrəfə/, *n.*

photon /'foʊtɒn/ *n. Physics* a quantum of light energy, the energy being proportional to the frequency of the radiation.

photo opportunity *n.* an arranged event featuring a politician, actor, etc., which the media are invited to film or photograph.

photorealism /foʊtoʊ'rɪəlɪzəm/ *n.* a style of painting which achieves a degree of realistic representation which is suggestive of a photograph. –**photorealist**, *adj., n.* –**photorealistic**, *adj.*

photo shoot *n.* a session during which a professional photographer takes shots of fashion models, a location, etc., as for a magazine, advertisement, website, etc. Also, **photoshoot.**

photoshop /'foʊtoʊʃɒp/ *v.t.* (**-shopped, -shopping**) *Computers* (*from trademark*) to alter (a digital image) using software which facilitates graphic manipulation. –**photoshopping**, *n.*

photostat /'foʊtəstæt/ (*from trademark*) –*n.* 1. a special camera for making facsimile copies of maps, drawings, pages of books or manuscripts, etc., which photographs directly as a positive on sensitised paper. 2. a copy or photograph made with such a camera. –*v.t.* (**-statted, -statting**) 3. to make a photostatic copy or copies of. –*adj.* Also, **photostatic.** 4. of or relating to such a camera or copy.

photosynthesis /foʊtoʊ'sɪnθəsəs/ *n. Biol.* the synthesis of complex organic materials by plants from carbon dioxide, water, and inorganic salts using sunlight as the source of energy and with the aid of a catalyst such as chlorophyll; commonly used in the more restricted sense of the synthesis of carbohydrates. –**photosynthetic** /ˌfoʊtoʊsɪn'θɛtɪk/, *adj.*

photovoltaic /ˌfoʊtoʊvɒlˈteɪk/ *adj. Elect.* providing a source of electric current under the influence of light or similar radiation.

phrase /freɪz/ *n.* **1.** *Gram.* **a.** group of two or more words arranged in a grammatical construction. **b.** such a group without a finite verb and acting as a unit within a clause. **2.** a way of speaking. **3.** an expression, sometimes having special interest or importance. **4.** a short remark. **5.** *Music* a group of notes forming a recognisable pattern. –*v.t.* **6.** to express or word in a particular way. –**phrasal**, *adj.*

phraseology /freɪziˈɒlədʒi/ *n.* manner or style of verbal expression; characteristic language: *the phraseology of lawyers.* –**phraseological** /freɪziəˈlɒdʒɪkəl/, *adj.*

phrenology /frəˈnɒlədʒi/ *n.* the theory postulating that one's mental powers are indicated by the shape of the skull, in particular by the shape and size of those parts of the skull which overlie the parts of the brain thought to be responsible for particular faculties. –**phrenologic** /frɛnəˈlɒdʒɪk/, **phrenological** /frɛnəˈlɒdʒɪkəl/, *adj.* –**phrenologist**, *n.*

phwoar /fwɔ/ *interj. Colloq.* an exclamation indicating that one finds a particular person sexually attractive. Also, **phwoah.**

-phyll a word element forming a noun termination meaning 'leaf', as in *chlorophyll.* Also, **-phyl.**

phyllo- a word element meaning 'leaf'. Also, (*before vowels*), **phyll-.**

-phyllous a word element forming an adjective termination meaning 'having leaves', 'leaved', or implying some connection with a leaf.

phylo- a word element meaning 'tribe'.

phylogenetics /faɪloʊdʒəˈnɛtɪks/ *n.* the systematic study of phylogeny.

phylogeny /faɪˈlɒdʒəni/ *n.* (*pl.* **-nies**) *Biol.* the development or evolution of genetically related groups of organisms. Compare **ontogeny.** Also, **phylogenesis** /faɪloʊˈdʒɛnəsəs/. –**phylogenetic** /ˌfaɪloʊdʒəˈnɛtɪk/, **phylogenic** /faɪloʊˈdʒɛnɪk/, *adj.* –**phylogenetically** /ˌfaɪloʊdʒəˈnɛtɪkli/, *adv.*

phylum /ˈfaɪləm/ *n.* (*pl.* **-la** /-lə/) **1.** *Biol.* a primary division of the animal or vegetable kingdom, as the arthropods, the molluscs, the spermatophytes. **2.** (in the classification of languages) a group of linguistic stocks or families having no known congeners outside the group.

-phyre a word element used to form names of porphyritic rocks, as in *granophyre.*

physic /ˈfɪzɪk/ *n.* **1.** a medicine, especially one that purges; a cathartic. **2.** any medicine; a drug or medicament. –*v.t.* (**-icked, -icking**) **3.** to treat with physic or medicine. **4.** to treat with or to act upon as a cathartic; purge. **5.** to work upon as a medicine does; relieve or cure.

physical /ˈfɪzɪkəl, ˈfɪzɪkəl/ *adj.* **1.** of or relating to the body; bodily: *physical exercise.* **2.** of or relating to material nature; material. **3.** of or relating to the properties of matter and energy other than those that are chemical or peculiar to living matter; relating to physics. **4.** of or relating to the properties of matter and energy other than those peculiar to living matter; relating to physical science. **5.** *Sport* involving some degree of violence: *a physical match.* –*n.* Also, **physical examination.** **6.** an examination of the various parts of a person's body, to determine state of health, especially as made by a physician. –**physically**, *adv.* –**physicality** /fɪzəˈkæləti/, *n.*

physical education *n.* instruction given in exercises, gymnastics, sports, etc., for the development and health of the body, especially as part of a school program. *Abbrev.:* PE Also, **physical training.**

physician /fəˈzɪʃən/ *n.* **1.** a person legally qualified to practise medicine. **2.** someone engaged in general medical practice as distinguished from one specialising in surgery. **3.** someone who is skilled in the art of healing.

physics /ˈfɪzɪks/ *n.* the science dealing with natural laws and processes, and the states and properties of matter and energy, other than those restricted to living matter and to chemical changes. –**physicist**, *n.*

physio- a word element representing 'physical', 'physics'.

physiognomy /fɪziˈɒnəmi/ *n.* (*pl.* **-mies**) **1.** the face or countenance, especially as considered as an index to the character. **2.** the art of determining character or personal characteristics from the features of the face or the form of the body. **3.** the general or characteristic appearance of anything. –**physiognomic** /fɪziəˈnɒmɪk/, **physiognomical** /fɪziəˈnɒmɪkəl/, *adj.* –**physiognomically** /fɪziəˈnɒmɪkli/, *adv.* –**physiognomist**, *n.*

physiology /fɪziˈɒlədʒi/ *n.* the science dealing with the functioning of living organisms or their parts. –**physiologist**, *n.* –**physiological** /fɪziəˈlɒdʒɪkəl/, *adj.*

physiotherapy /ˌfɪzioʊˈθɛrəpi/ *n.* the treatment of disease or bodily weaknesses or defects by physical remedies, such as massage, gymnastics, etc. Also, **physio.** –**physiotherapist**, *n.*

physique /fəˈzik/ *n.* **1.** human bodily structure or type: *a good muscular physique.* **2.** the structure or type of a given geographic region.

-phyte a word element forming a noun termination meaning 'a growth', 'plant', as in *epiphyte.*

phyto- a word element meaning 'plant'. Also, (*before vowels*), **phyt-.**

pi /paɪ/ *n.* (*pl.* **pis**) **1.** the sixteenth letter (Π, π, = English P, p) of the Greek alphabet. **2.** *Maths* **a.** the letter π, used as the symbol for the ratio (3.141 592 +) of the circumference of a circle to its diameter. **b.** the ratio itself.

piano[1] /piˈænoʊ/ *n.* (*pl.* **-nos**) **1.** a musical instrument in which hammers, operated from a keyboard, strike upon metal strings. **2. grand piano**, a piano with a harp-shaped body supported horizontally, called **concert grand piano** in the largest size, and **baby grand** in the smallest. **3. upright piano**, a piano with a rectangular body placed vertically. **4. square piano**, a piano with a rectangular body supported horizontally. –**pianist** /ˈpiənəst/, *n.* –**pianistic** /piəˈnɪstɪk/, *adj.*

piano[2] /piˈanoʊ/ *adv. Music* softly (opposed to *forte*). *Abbrev.:* p

piano accordion *n.* an accordion having a piano-like keyboard for the right hand.

pianoforte /piænoʊˈfɔteɪ, pianoʊ-/ *n.* → **piano**[1].

pianola /piəˈnoʊlə/ *n.* a piano played by machinery controlled by two pedals which, when operated by the performer, pump a pneumatic mechanism that turns a paper roll provided with perforations which cause air pressure to move the piano keys in a predetermined order and combination. Also, **player piano.**

piazza /piˈætsə, -a-/ *n.* (*pl.* **-zas**) **1.** an open square or public place in a city or town. **2.** an arcade or covered walk or gallery, as around a public square or in front of a building.

pica[1] /ˈpaɪkə/ *n. Printing* **1.** a type (12 point) of a size between small pica and English. **2.** the depth of this type size (4.217 5176 mm) as a unit of linear measurement for type, etc.

pica[2] /ˈpaɪkə/ *n.* an eating disorder characterised by a desire to eat non-nutritive substances such as clay, chalk, dirt, glass, bricks, etc.

picador /ˈpɪkədɔ/ *n.* a person who open a bullfight by irritating and enraging the bull by pricking it with lances, without disabling it.

picaresque /pɪkəˈrɛsk/ *adj. Lit.* of or relating to rogues; applied to a type of episodic fiction, of Spanish origin, with a rogue or rogues for hero(es).

piccaninny /ˈpɪkənɪni/ *n.* (*pl.* **-nies**) (*now likely to give offence*) a small child, especially (formerly) a dark-skinned child, as one of African descent. Also, **pickaninny.**

piccolo /ˈpɪkəloʊ/ *n.* (*pl.* **-los**) a small flute, sounding an octave higher than the ordinary flute.

pick¹ /pɪk/ *v.t.* **1.** to choose or select carefully. **2.** to choose (one's way or steps), as over rough ground or through a crowd. **3.** to seek and find occasion for: *to pick a quarrel.* **4.** to seek or find (flaws) in a spirit of fault-finding. **5.** to steal the contents of (a person's pocket, purse, etc.). **6.** to open (a lock) with a pointed instrument, a wire, or the like, as for robbery. **7.** to pierce, indent, dig into, or break up (something) with a pointed instrument. **8.** to form (a hole, etc.) by such action. **9.** to use a pointed instrument, the fingers, the teeth, the beak, etc., on (a thing), in order to remove something. **10.** to clear (a thing) of something by such action: *to pick one's teeth.* **11.** to detach or remove with the fingers, the beak, or the like, as *to pluck or gather: to pick flowers*; *pick fruit.* **13.** to separate, pull apart, or pull to pieces (fibres, etc.). **14.** *Music* **a.** to pluck (the strings of an instrument). **b.** to play (a stringed instrument) by plucking. **15.** *Mining* to select good ore out of a heap. *–v.i.* **16.** to strike with or use a pointed instrument or the like on something. **17.** to eat with dainty bites. **18.** to choose; make careful or fastidious selection. *–n.* **19.** choice or selection. **20.** that which is selected. **21.** the choicest or most desirable part, example, or examples. **22.** the right of selection. **23.** an act of picking. **24.** the quantity of a crop picked at a particular time. **25.** (*pl.*) *Mining* steel cutting points used on a coal cutter chain. **26.** → **plectrum. 27.** *Colloq.* a hypodermic needle used for taking drugs. *–phr.* **28. pick and choose,** to choose with great care, especially fussily. **29. pick at,** *Colloq.* **a.** to find fault with, in a petty way. **b.** to eat very little of: *the child picked at her food.* **30. pick holes in,** *Colloq.* to criticise; find fault with. **31. pick off,** to single out and deal with individually, as by shooting. **32. pick on,** *Colloq.* **a.** to annoy; tease; bully. **b.** to single out (a person), often indiscriminately, for something unpleasant, as punishment or criticism. **33. pick out, a.** to choose. **b.** to distinguish (something) from surrounding or accompanying things. **c.** to make out (sense or meaning). **d.** to extract by picking. **34. pick to pieces,** *Colloq.* to criticise, especially in petty detail. **35. pick up,** **a.** to take up: *to pick up a stone.* **b.** to pluck up, recover, or regain (health, courage, etc.). **c.** to learn by occasional opportunity or without special teaching. **d.** to get casually. **e.** to become acquainted with informally or casually. **f.** to take (a person or thing) into a car, ship, etc., or along with one. **g.** to come upon within the range of reception, observation, etc.: *to pick up New Zealand on one's radio.* **h.** *Colloq.* to make oneself responsible for (a debt, expense, etc.): *you have to pay the first $100 and the insurance company will pick up the rest.* **i.** *Colloq.* to acquire (a partner) for a sexual encounter. **j.** *Colloq.* to arrest. **k.** to remove fleeces from the shearing floor. **l.** to increase in speed; accelerate. **m.** *Colloq.* to improve. **36. pick up the pieces,** *Colloq.* to assume responsibility for rectifying a difficult situation: *when she left the children it was her husband who picked up the pieces.*

pick² /pɪk/ *n.* **1.** a hand tool consisting of an iron bar, usually curved, tapering to a point at one or both ends, mounted on a wooden handle, and used for loosening and breaking up soil, rock, etc. **2.** any pointed or other tool or instrument for picking.

pickaxe /ˈpɪkæks/ *n.* **1.** a pick, especially a mattock. *–verb* (**-axed, -axing**) *–v.t.* **2.** to cut or clear away

with a pickaxe. *–v.i.* **3.** to use a pickaxe. Also, *US,* **pickax.**

picket /ˈpɪkət/ *n.* **1.** a pointed post, stake, pale, or peg, as for driving into the ground in making a stockade, for placing vertically to form the main part of a fence (**picket fence**), for driving into the ground to fasten something to, etc. **2.** a person or a body of persons stationed by a trade union or the like in front of a place of work and attempting to dissuade or prevent workers from entering the building during a strike. **3.** *Mil.* a small detached body of troops, posted out from a force to warn against an enemy's approach. *–v.t.* **4.** to enclose, fence, or make secure with pickets. **5.** to fasten or tether to a picket. **6.** to place pickets at, as during a strike. **7.** *Mil.* to guard, as a camp, by or as pickets. *–v.i.* **8.** to stand or march by a place of employment as a picket. **–picketer,** *n.*

pickle /ˈpɪkəl/ *n.* **1.** (*oft. pl.*) vegetables, as cucumbers, onions, cauliflowers, etc., preserved in vinegar, brine, etc., and eaten as a relish. **2.** anything preserved in a pickling liquid. **3.** a liquid or marinade prepared with salt or vinegar for the preservation of fish, meat, vegetables, etc., or for the hardening of wood, leather, etc. **4.** a pickled article of food, especially cucumber. **5.** *Colloq.* a predicament. **6.** *Colloq.* a mischievous child. *–v.t.* **7.** to preserve or steep in pickle. **8.** to clean or treat (objects) in a chemical pickle. *–phr.* **9. have a rod in pickle,** *Colloq.* have a punishment ready.

pickpocket /ˈpɪkpɒkət/ *n.* **1.** someone who steals from the pockets, handbags, etc., of people in public places. *–v.t.* **2.** to steal (something) from a pocket, handbag, etc., in a public place. *–v.i.* **3.** to act as a pickpocket; steal from a pocket, handbag, etc., in a public place.

picnic /ˈpɪknɪk/ *n.* **1.** an outing or excursion, typically one in which those taking part carry food with them and share a meal in the open air. **2.** the meal eaten on such an outing. **3.** *Colloq.* an enjoyable experience or time. **4.** *Colloq.* an easy undertaking. *–v.i.* (**-nicked, -nicking**) **5.** to hold, or take part in, a picnic. *–phr.* **6. be no picnic,** to be difficult or unpleasant: *looking after three children is no picnic.* **–picnicker,** *n.*

pictogram /ˈpɪktəɡræm/ *n.* Also, **pictograph.** a written symbol representing something by a stylised drawing of it or something associated with it and not by its name or the sound of its name, as, for example, the ancient Egyptian pictogram for an ox which shows its yoke (from which the modern capital letter A is derived). **2.** a chart on which data is represented by symbols, as when assessments are represented by rows of different numbers of stars.

pictorial /pɪkˈtɔriəl/ *adj.* **1.** of or relating to a picture or pictures: *pictorial writing.* **2.** illustrated by or containing pictures: *a pictorial history.* **3.** of or relating to a painter or maker of pictures. **4.** suggestive of, or representing as if by, a picture; graphic. *–n.* **5.** a periodical in which pictures are the leading feature. **–pictorially,** *adv.*

picture /ˈpɪktʃə/ *n.* **1.** a representation, upon a surface, usually flat, as a painting, drawing or photograph, etc. **2.** any visible image, however produced: *the pictures in the fire*; *the pictures made by reflections in a pool of water.* **3.** a mental image: *a picture of what would happen.* **4.** a verbal description intended to be or taken as informative: *Gibbon's picture of ancient Rome.* **5.** a tableau, as in theatrical representation. **6.** a very beautiful object, especially a person: *she looks a picture in her new dress.* **7.** → **film** (def. 4b). **8.** the image or counterpart (of someone else). **9.** an object or person possessing a quality in such a high degree as to seem to embody that quality: *she is a picture of health.* **10.** a situation or set of circumstances: *the employment* *picture*. **11.** Also, **clinical picture.** *Pathol.* the overall view of a case. *–v.t.* **12.** to form a mental image of: *he couldn't picture himself doing such a thing.* **13.** to describe, verbally and, usually, plausibly. *–phr.* **14. get the picture,** *Colloq.* to understand. **15. in the picture,** informed about what is going on. **16. the pictures,** a showing of a film in a cinema.

picturesque /pɪktʃəˈrɛsk/ *adj.* **1.** visually charming or quaint, as resembling or suitable for a picture. **2.** (of written or spoken language) strikingly vivid or graphic. **3.** having pleasing or interesting qualities; strikingly effective in appearance. **–picturesquely,** *adv.* **–picturesqueness,** *n.*

piddle /ˈpɪdl/ *Colloq. –v.i.* **1.** to urinate. *–n.* **2.** the passing or discharging of urine. **3.** urine.

pide /ˈpidei/ *n.* **1.** a Turkish flatbread. **2.** a dish consisting of a piece of this bread dough with the edges folded in slightly, topped with meat, spinach, cheese, egg, etc., and then baked; Turkish pizza.

pidgin /ˈpɪdʒən/ *n.* a language used for communication between groups having different first languages, as between European traders or colonisers and indigenous peoples, and which typically has features deriving from each of those languages. Compare **creole.** Also, **pigeon.**

pie /paɪ/ *n.* **1.** a baked dish consisting of a sweet (fruit, etc.) or savoury (meat, fish, etc.) filling, enclosed in or covered by pastry, or sometimes other topping as mashed potatoes. **2.** a group of bidders at an auction who secretly agree not to bid against each other. **3.** Also, **pie-heap.** (in a freezing works) a mass of sheepskin, flesh, etc., from which wool is plucked. *–phr.* **4. have a finger in every pie,** to have an interest in or play a part in many affairs. **5. pie in the sky,** the illusory prospect of future benefits.

piebald /ˈpaɪbɔld/ *adj.* **1.** having patches of black and white or of other colours; particoloured. **2.** (of a horse) white with black patches. *–n.* **3.** a piebald animal, especially a horse.

piece /pis/ *n.* **1.** a limited portion or quantity, of something: *a piece of land.* **2.** a quantity of some substance or material forming a mass or body. **3.** one of the more or less definite parts or portions into which something may be divided: *a piece of chocolate.* **4.** one of the parts, fragments, or shreds into which something may be divided or broken: *to tear a letter into pieces.* **5.** one of the parts which, when assembled, form a combined whole: *the pieces of a machine.* **6.** an individual article of a set or collection: *a dinner service of 36 pieces.* **7.** a single item, as counted: *shirts: three pieces.* **8.** (*pl.*) inferior wool from the skirtings but not containing necks, bellies, stains, or locks. **9.** any of the counters, discs, blocks, or the like, of wood, ivory, or other material, used in any of a number of board games, as draughts, backgammon, or chess. **10.** *Chess* **a.** a superior chessman, as distinguished from a pawn. **b.** (in popular usage) any chessman. **11.** a particular length, as of certain goods prepared for sale: *cloth sold by the piece.* **12.** an amount of work forming a single job: *to work by the piece.* **13.** a specimen of work, especially of artistic production, as a picture or statue. **14.** a literary composition, in prose or verse, usually short. **15.** a play; drama. **16.** a passage of verse, music, or the like, prepared for recitation or performance on a particular occasion. **17.** a musical composition, usually a short one. **18.** an individual musical instrument in an ensemble: *a three-piece band.* **19.** an individual thing of a particular class or kind: *a piece of furniture.* **20.** an example, instance, or specimen of something: *a fine piece of workmanship.* **21.** *Colloq.* a woman, considered as a sex object: *she's a nice little piece.* **22. a.** *Mil.* an item of ordnance. **b.** a firearm: *a fowling piece.* **c.** *Prison*

Colloq. a concealable firearm. **23.** a coin: *a five cent piece.* **24.** *US* a distance, especially a short one. *–v.t.* (**pieced, piecing**) **25.** to fit together, as pieces or parts. *–phr.* **26. a (nasty) piece of work,** *Colloq.* a detestable, usually malevolent, person. **27. a piece of cake,** *Colloq.* an easily achieved enterprise or undertaking. **28. a piece of one's mind,** outspoken criticism or reproach. **29. a piece of the action,** *Colloq.* a share in an enterprise or activity, especially a profitable one. **30. go to pieces,** to lose emotional or physical control of oneself. **31. of a piece,** of the same kind; consistent. **32. piece of work,** an example or instance of workmanship; something produced. **33. piece out,** to complete, enlarge, or extend by making additions. **34. piece something into** (or **onto**), to add something as a piece or part: *to piece new palings into a fence.* **35. piece together, a.** to mend (something broken); reassemble. **b.** to make up or form into a whole by or as if by joining pieces: *to piece together a picture of the situation.* **36. piece up,** to patch; mend (a garment, etc.) by applying a piece or pieces. **37. say one's piece,** to express an opinion; speak one's mind. **38. take a piece out of,** *Colloq.* to reprimand severely.

pièce de résistance /pi͵ɛs də rəˈzɪstəns/ *n.* **1.** the principal dish of a meal. **2.** the principal event, incident, article, etc., of a series.

piecemeal /ˈpismil/ *adv.* **1.** piece by piece; gradually. **2.** into pieces or fragments. *–adj.* **3.** done piece by piece; fragmentary.

piecework /ˈpiswɜk/ *n.* work done and paid for by the piece. **–pieceworker,** *n.*

pied /paɪd/ *adj.* **1.** having patches of two or more colours, as various birds and other animals. **2.** wearing particoloured clothes.

pier /pɪə/ *n.* **1.** a structure built out into the water as a landing place for ships or as a pleasure ground; breakwater; jetty. **2.** one of the supports of a span of a bridge.

pierce /pɪəs/ *v.t.* (**pierced, piercing**) **1.** to go or run into or through (something); puncture; penetrate: *the needle pierced his fingers*; *the beam of light pierced the darkness.* **2.** to make a hole or opening in; perforate: *to pierce ears.* **3.** (of the eye or mind) to see into or through. **4.** to affect sharply with some sensation or emotion, as of cold, pain, grief, etc. **5.** to sound sharply through (the air, etc.). *–piercer,* *n.* **–piercingly,** *adv.*

piety /ˈpaɪəti/ *n.* (*pl.* **-ties**) **1.** reverence for God, or regard for religious obligations. **2.** the quality or fact of being pious. **3.** dutiful respect or regard for parents or others. **4.** a pious act, remark, belief, or the like.

piezoelectricity /paɪ͵izoʊəlɛkˈtrɪsəti/ *n. Physics* electricity produced by pressure, as in a crystal subjected to compression along a certain axis. **–piezoelectric** /paɪ͵izoʊəˈlɛktrɪk/, *adj.* **–piezoelectrically** /paɪ͵izoʊə- ˈlɛktrɪkli/, *adv.*

piffle /ˈpɪfəl/ *Colloq. –n.* **1.** nonsense; idle talk. *–v.i.* **2.** to talk nonsense. **–piffler,** *n.*

pig /pɪg/ *n.* **1.** the common domesticated swine, *Sus scrofa*, descended from the wild boar, widely distributed with humans and bred into many varieties to provide meat and fat; feral populations in Australia cause great ecological damage. Compare **hog** (def. 1). **2.** a young swine, of either sex, bred for slaughter. **3.** the flesh of swine; pork. **4.** *Colloq.* a person or animal of piggish character or habit. **5.** *Colloq.* (*derog.*) a police officer. **6.** *Metallurgy* **a.** an oblong mass of metal that has been run while still molten into a mould of sand or the like, especially such a mass of iron from a blast furnace; an ingot. **b.** one of the moulds for such masses of metal. **c.** metal in the form of such masses. **7.** an object that is placed in a pipeline and is propelled through by liquid or gas pressure from behind to clean it out or check its internal working. *–phr.* **8. a pig in a poke,** something purchased without inspection. **9. home on the pig's back,** *Aust., NZ Colloq.* successful by an easy margin. **10. in a pig's eye,** *Aust., NZ Colloq.* an exclamation of contemptuous disbelief. **11. make a pig of oneself** or **pig oneself,** to over-indulge oneself, as by eating too much. **12. pig it,** *Colloq.* to live, lie, etc., as if in a pigsty; live in squalor. **13. pig out,** *Colloq.* (sometimes fol. by *on*) to eat a great deal, especially of very appetising food. **14. pigs** or **pig's arse** or **pig's bum,** *Aust. Colloq.* an exclamation of contempt, derision, denial, etc. **15. pigs might fly,** *Colloq.* an exclamation of contemptuous disbelief. **16. pigs to you,** *Aust. Colloq.* an exclamation of contemptuous rebuttal.

pigeon /ˈpɪdʒən/ *n.* **1.** any bird of the family Columbidae, having a compact body and short legs, of which there are several species distributed throughout the world; especially the larger varieties with square or rounded tails. Compare **dove**[1] (def. 1). **2.** any domesticated member of this family, as bred for racing, exhibiting, etc. **3.** *Colloq.* responsibility; concern: *that's his pigeon.*

pigeonhole /ˈpɪdʒənhoʊl/ *n.* **1.** one of a set of small compartments in a desk, cupboard, etc., used for papers, etc. *–v.t.* **2.** to put away for future use or notice. **3.** to give a definite place to in some orderly system. **4.** to put aside and do nothing about. **5.** to classify (a person or thing) too narrowly or hastily: *to pigeonhole someone as a figure of fun.*

pigeon-toed /ˈpɪdʒən-toʊd/ *adj.* having the toes or feet turned inwards.

piggyback /ˈpɪgibæk/ *adv.* **1.** sitting on the back or shoulders of another: *to ride piggyback.* *–n.* **2.** a piggyback ride. **3.** a method of transportation in which truck trailers are carried on trains, or cars on specially designed trucks. *–v.t.* **4.** to attach or join (something extra) to a basic piece of equipment, system, etc. **5.** *Aerospace* to transport (a space shuttle or similar) on the back of an aircraft.

piggy bank /ˈpɪgi bæŋk/ *n.* **1.** a moneybox shaped like a pig, usually made of china, in which a child might keep savings. **2.** any small money-box.

pig-headed /ˈpɪg-hɛdəd/ *adj.* stupidly obstinate.

pig iron *n.* **1.** iron produced in a blast furnace, poured into special moulds in preparation for making wrought iron, cast iron, or steel. **2.** iron in the unrefined state, before conversion into steel, alloys, etc. Also, **pig-iron.**

piglet /ˈpɪglət/ *n.* a little pig.

pigment /ˈpɪgmənt/ *n.* **1.** a colouring matter or substance. **2.** a dry substance, usually pulverised, which when mixed with a liquid vehicle in which it is insoluble becomes a paint, ink, etc. **3.** *Biol.* any substance whose presence in the tissues or cells of animals or plants colours them. *–***pigmentation,** *n.*

pigsty /ˈpɪgstaɪ/ *n.* (*pl.* **-sties**) **1.** a sty or pen for pigs. **2.** any dirty, messy, or untidy place: *this room is a real pigsty.* Also, **pig sty.**

pigtail /ˈpɪgteɪl/ *n.* **1.** a braid of hair hanging down the side or back of the head. **2.** tobacco in a thin twisted roll.

pike[1] /paɪk/ *n.* (*pl.* **pikes** or, *especially collectively,* **pike**) **1.** → **sea pike. 2.** any of various large, slender, fierce, voracious freshwater fishes of the Northern Hemisphere, of the genus *Esox,* having a long snout, especially the **northern pike,** *E. lucius.*

pike[2] /paɪk/ *n.* (formerly) an infantry weapon with a long shaft and comparatively small metal head.

pike[3] /paɪk/ *n.* **1.** a sharp point; a spike. **2.** the pointed end of anything, as of an arrow or a spear.

pike[4] /paɪk/ *phr.* (**piked, piking**) *Aust. Colloq.* **1. pike on,** to let down; abandon. **2. pike out,** (sometimes fol. by *on*) to go back on an arrangement; to opt out: *he piked out on the deal.*

pikelet /ˈpaɪklət/ *n.* a small thick, sweet pancake, cooked on a flat heated surface, as a frypan or griddle; drop scone.

piker /ˈpaɪkə/ *n. Aust. Colloq.* **1.** someone who opts out of an arrangement or challenge or does not do their fair share. **2.** someone who, from diffidence or lack of courage, does anything in a contemptibly small or cheap way.

pilaf /ˈpɪlæf/ *n.* a rice dish of Central Asian origin consisting of rice, pre-cooked or raw, fried in butter or other fat with stock, meats, vegetables, nuts, etc., depending on the particular recipe. Also, **pilaff, pilau.**

pilaster /pəˈlæstə/ *n.* a square or rectangular pillar, with capital and base, engaged in a wall from which it projects.

Pilates /pəˈlatɪz/ *n.* a fitness regimen that introduces comprehensive stretching and strengthening movements into an exercise routine. Also, **Pilates method.**

pilchard /ˈpɪltʃəd/ *n.* **1.** a small abundant fish, *Sardinops neopilchardus,* occurring in shoals around the southern half of the Australian coast. **2.** any of numerous similar fishes found elsewhere.

pilchers /ˈpɪltʃəz/ *pl. n. Aust., NZ* flannel or plastic pants or a plastic wrapper worn by an infant over a nappy.

pile[1] /paɪl/ *n.* **1.** an assemblage of things laid or lying one upon another in a more or less orderly fashion: *a pile of boxes.* **2.** a heap of wood on which a dead body, a living person, or a sacrifice is burnt. **3.** a lofty or large building or mass of buildings. **4.** *Colloq.* a large accumulation of money. **5.** *Metallurgy* a bundle of pieces of iron ready to be welded and drawn out into bars; faggot. **6.** *Physics* a latticework of uranium and various moderating substances used to produce plutonium in the original harnessing of atomic energy, essentially a means of controlling the nuclear chain reaction; atomic pile; nuclear reactor. **7.** *Mil.* arms arranged systematically. *–v.t.* **8.** to cover or load, with a pile or piles. *–v.i.* **9.** *Colloq.* to move (*in, into, out, off, down,* etc.) in a body and more or less confusedly. **10.** to gather or rise in a pile or piles, as snow, etc. *–phr.* **11. pile on,** to keep on accumulating in a pile; heap up. **12. pile up, a.** to lay or dispose in or as in a pile. **b.** to accumulate: *to pile up debts.* **c.** to mount up or accumulate, as money, debts, evidence, etc. **d.** *Colloq.* (of a vehicle, driver, etc.) to crash.

pile[2] /paɪl/ *n.* **1.** a heavy timber, stake or pole, sometimes pointed at the lower end, driven vertically into the ground or the bed of a river, etc., to support a superstructure or form part of a wall. **2.** any steel or concrete member similarly used. **3.** *Archery* the tip of an arrow.

pile[3] /paɪl/ *n.* **1.** hair, especially soft, fine hair or down. **2.** wool, especially of a carpet or fur. **3.** a raised surface on cloth, composed of upright cut or looped yarns, as velvet, Turkish towelling, etc. **4.** one of the strands in such a surface. *–***pileous,** *adj.*

pile[4] /paɪl/ *n.* (*usu. pl.*) → **haemorrhoid.**

pile-up *n. Colloq.* **1.** a crash involving multiple vehicles: *a six-car pile-up.* **2.** an accumulation; backlog.

pilfer /ˈpɪlfə/ *v.t.* **1.** to steal (a small amount or object). *–v.i.* **2.** to practise petty theft. *–***pilferer,** *n. –***pilfering,** *n.*

pilgrim /ˈpɪlgrəm/ *n.* someone who journeys, especially a long distance, as an act of devotion.

pilgrimage /ˈpɪlgrəmɪdʒ/ *n.* **1.** a journey, especially a long one, made to some sacred place, as an act of devotion. **2.** any long journey.

pill /pɪl/ *n.* **1.** a small globular or rounded mass of medicinal substance, to be swallowed whole; tablet. **2.** something unpleasant that has to be accepted or endured: *a bitter pill to swallow.* **3.** *Colloq.* a disagreeable, insipid person. **4.** *Textiles* a small ball of fibre formed by friction. *–v.i.* **5.** (of woollen, and other fabrics, especially knitted) to form into small balls of fibres because of rubbing. *–phr.* **6. sugar the pill**, to make bearable some unpleasant experience. **7. the pill**, *Colloq.* oral contraceptive.

pillage /'pɪlɪdʒ/ *verb* (**-laged, -laging**) *–v.t.* **1.** to strip of money or goods by open violence, as in war; plunder. **2.** to take as booty. *–v.i.* **3.** to rob with open violence; take booty. *–n.* **4.** the act of plundering, especially in war. **5.** booty or spoil. **–pillager**, *n.*

pillar /'pɪlə/ *n.* **1.** an upright shaft or structure, of stone, brick, or other material, relatively slender in proportion to its height, and of any shape in section, used as a support, or standing alone, as for a monument. **2.** an upright supporting part. **3.** a person who is a chief support of a state, institution, etc.: *a pillar of society.* *–phr.* **4. from pillar to post, a.** from one predicament or difficulty to another. **b.** aimlessly from place to place.

pillbox /'pɪlbɒks/ *n.* **1.** a box, usually shallow and often round, for holding pills. **2.** a small cylindrical hat of similar shape. **3.** a small, low structure of reinforced concrete, enclosing machine guns, and used as a minor fortress in warfare.

pillion /'pɪljən/ *n.* **1.** a pad or cushion attached behind a saddle, especially as a seat for a woman. **2.** an extra saddle behind the driver's seat on a motorcycle. *–adj.* **3.** riding on a pillion: *a pillion passenger.* *–adv.* **4.** on a pillion: *to ride pillion.*

pillory /'pɪləri/ *n.* (*pl.* **-ries**) **1.** a wooden framework erected on a post, with holes for securing the head and hands, used to expose an offender to public derision. *–v.t.* (**-ried, -rying**) **2.** to set in the pillory. **3.** to expose to public ridicule or abuse.

pillow /'pɪloʊ/ *n.* **1.** a bag filled with feathers, plastic foam, or other soft material, used as a support for the head during sleep. **2.** anything used to support the head; a headrest. *–v.t.* **3.** to rest on or as on a pillow: *he pillowed his head on his arm.*

pillow talk *n.* confidences exchanged in bed by two people who are lovers.

pilot /'paɪlət/ *n.* **1.** a person who guides or steers ships into or out of a harbour or through difficult waters. **2.** *Aeronautics* the person who controls an aeroplane. **3.** a guide or leader. *–v.t.* **4.** to guide or steer. **5.** to guide or lead, as through unknown places, difficult affairs, etc. **6.** to act as pilot on, in or over. *–adj.* **7.** experimental: *a pilot study*; *a pilot film.* **8.** of or relating to pilots. **9.** acting as a guide. **–pilotage**, *n.*

pilotbird /'paɪlətbɜd/ *n.* a mottled reddish-brown, terrestrial bird, *Pycnoptilus floccosus*, with a melodious call, endemic to damp forest areas of south-eastern Australia, often accompanying ('piloting') the lyrebird. Also, **pilot bird**.

pilot officer *n. Air Force* **1.** a commissioned officer of the most junior rank in the Royal Australian Air Force ranking below flying officer and above air cadet. **2.** the rank. *Abbrev.*: PLTOFF

pilsner /'pɪlsnə, 'pɪlsənə/ *n.* a light pale lager. Also, **pilsener**.

pimento /pə'mɛntoʊ/ *n.* (*pl.* **-tos**) **1.** the dried fruits of the tree *Pimenta dioica*; allspice. **2.** the tropical American tree yielding this.

pimp /pɪmp/ *n.* **1.** someone who solicits for a prostitute, or brothel; a procurer. **2.** a contemptible person. **3.** an informer; a tale-bearer. *–v.i.* **4.** to procure; pander. **5.** to inform; tell tales. *–phr.* **6. pimp out** (or **up**), *Colloq.* to decorate or style in an ostentatious fashion.

pimple /'pɪmpəl/ *n.* a small, usually inflammatory swelling or elevation of the skin; a papule or pustule. **–pimply**, *adj.*

pin¹ /pɪn/ *n.* **1.** a small, slender, sometimes tapered or pointed piece of wood, metal, etc., used to fasten or hold things together, to hang things upon, to stop up holes, or to convey or check motion; a bolt; peg. **2.** a

short, slender piece of wire with a point at one end and a head at the other, for fastening things together, as cloth or paper. **3.** any of various forms of fastening or ornament consisting essentially or in part of a pointed penetrating bar: *a safety pin.* **4.** a badge or brooch having a pointed bar or pin attached, by which it is fastened to the clothing. **5.** a linchpin, serving to keep a wheel on its axle. **6.** the part of the stem of a key which enters the lock. **7.** a peg, nail, or stud marking the centre of a target. **8.** one of the bottle-shaped pieces of wood knocked down in ninepins, tenpins, etc. **9.** *Golf* the flagpole which identifies a hole. **10.** *Music* a peg. **11.** *Naut.* any of various pegs, fixing devices and axles, as a belaying pin. **12.** *Carpentry* → **dovetail**. *–v.t.* (**pinned, pinning**) **13.** to fasten or attach with a pin or pins, or as if with a pin. **14.** to hold fast in a spot or position: *the debris pinned him down.* **15.** to transfix with a pin or the like. **16.** Also, **underpin**. *Building Trades* to support (masonry, etc.), as by wedges driven in over a beam. *–phr.* **17. not give** (or **care**) **a pin for**, to regard as inconsequential. **18. pin down**, to bind or hold to a course of action, a promise, etc. **19. pull the pin**, to make the decision to bring the operation of a piece of equipment, an organisation, etc., to a close.

pin² /pɪn/ *v.i.* → **PIN** (def. 2).

PIN /pɪn/ *n.* Also, **PIN number**, **Pin number**. **1.** personal identification number; a sequence of numbers and/or letters used as part of an identification procedure in electronic banking, etc., as in gaining access to a computerised bank account via an automatic teller machine or in an EFTPOS transaction. *–v.i.* Also, **pin**. **2.** to offer a PIN number as authorisation for an EFTPOS transaction: *do you PIN or sign?*

pinafore /'pɪnəfɔ/ *n.* **1.** an apron, usually one large enough to cover most of the dress, especially a child's. **2.** a loose dress worn over clothing to protect it during housework, etc. **3.** a dress, sleeveless with low neck, worn with a jumper particularly in winter. Also, **pinny**.

pinball /'pɪnbɔl/ *n.* a game played on a sloping board in which a ball, driven by a spring, hits pins or bumpers which electrically record the score.

pince-nez /'pæns-neɪ, 'pɪns-neɪ/ *n.* a pair of spectacles kept in place by a spring which pinches the nose.

pincers /'pɪnsəz/ *n.* (*pl.* or *sing.*) **1.** a gripping tool consisting of two pivoted limbs forming a pair of jaws and a pair of handles (often called a **pair of pincers**). **2.** *Zool.* a grasping organ or pair of organs resembling this.

pinch /pɪntʃ/ *v.t.* **1.** to compress between the finger and thumb, the jaws of an instrument, or any two opposed surfaces. **2.** to compress, constrict, or squeeze painfully, as a tight shoe does. **3.** to cramp within narrow bounds or quarters. **4.** to render (the face, etc.) unnaturally thin and drawn, as pain or distress does. **5.** to nip (plants) injuriously, as frost does. **6.** *Colloq.* to steal. **7.** *Colloq.* to arrest. *–v.i.* **8.** to exert a sharp or painful compressing force. **9.** to cause sharp discomfort or distress: *when hunger pinches.* **10.** *Mining* (of a vein of ore, etc.) to become narrower or smaller, or to give out altogether. *–n.* **11.** the act of pinching; nip; squeeze. **12.** as much of anything as can be taken up between the finger and thumb: *a pinch of salt.* **13.** a very small quantity of anything. **14.** sharp or painful stress, as of hunger, need, or any trying circumstances. **15.** a situation or time of special stress; an emergency: *any help is useful in a pinch.* **16.** *Colloq.* an arrest. **17.** *Colloq.* a theft. *–phr.* **18. at a pinch**, in an emergency, crisis, etc.; if necessary. **19. pinch off** (or **out**) (or **back**), *Hort.* to snip off (part of a shoot, bud, etc.) to improve the shape, quality, etc., of a plant. **20. take with a pinch of salt**, to believe in part only; have reservations.

pincushion /'pɪnkʊʃən/ *n.* a small cushion in which pins are stuck, in readiness for use.

pine[1] /paɪn/ *n.* **1.** any member of the genus *Pinus* of the Northern Hemisphere, comprising evergreen coniferous trees varying greatly in size, with long needle-shaped leaves, including many species of economic importance for their timber and as a source of turpentine, tar, pitch, etc. **2.** any of various more or less similar Australian coniferous trees such as the Norfolk Island pine, Huon pine, etc. **3.** the wood of the pine tree.

pine[2] /paɪn/ *v.i.* **1.** to languish, droop, or waste away. *–phr.* **2. pine away**, to fail gradually in health or vitality from grief, regret, or longing. **3. pine for**, to suffer with longing for; long painfully for.

pineal gland /'pɪniəl glænd/ *n. Anat.* an endocrine organ located in the midbrain, which secretes the hormone melatonin. Also, **pineal body**.

pineapple /'paɪnæpəl/ *n.* **1.** the edible juicy fruit (somewhat resembling a pine cone) of a tropical plant, *Ananas comosus*, being a large collective fruit developed from a spike or head of flowers, and surmounted by a crown of leaves. **2.** the plant itself, native to tropical South America and now widely cultivated throughout the tropics, having a short stem and rigid, spiny-margined, recurved leaves. **3.** *Mil. Colloq.* a bomb or hand grenade especially of the fragmentation type, resembling a pineapple in appearance. **4.** an opal cluster. *–phr.* **5. rough end of the pineapple**, *Aust. Colloq.* a raw deal; the worst part of a bargain.

ping[1] /pɪŋ/ *v.i.* **1.** to produce a sharp, ringing, high-pitched sound like that of a bullet striking an object, or of a small bell. **2.** *Motor Vehicles* → **knock** (def. 2). *–v.t.* **3.** to hit or strike (something) sharply, producing a ringing sound. **4.** *Colloq.* to penalise for an infringement of rules. *–n.* **5.** a pinging sound.

ping[2] /pɪŋ/ *Internet –n.* **1.** a program for testing the availability of an IP address by sending a packet (def. 3) to it. *–v.t.* **2.** to test (a network connection to a host) by using this program.

ping-pong /'pɪŋ-pɒŋ/ *n.* (*from trademark*) → **table tennis**.

pinion[1] /'pɪnjən/ *n. Machinery* **1.** a small cogwheel engaging with a larger cogwheel or with a rack. **2.** a shaft or spindle with teeth which engage with a cogwheel.

pinion[2] /'pɪnjən/ *n.* **1.** the long end joint of a bird's wing carrying the primary feathers. **2.** a bird's wing. **3.** a feather. *–v.t.* **4.** to cut off the pinion of (a wing) or bind (the wings), as in order to stop a bird flying. **5.** to restrain (a person) by tying the arms or hands.

pink[1] /pɪŋk/ *n.* **1.** a light tint of crimson; pale reddish purple. **2.** any plant of the genus *Dianthus*, as *D. plumarius* (the common **garden pink**), *D. sinensis* (**China pink**), or *D. caryophyllus* (**clove pink** or carnation). **3.** the flower of such a plant; a carnation. **4.** (*oft. upper case*) a person with moderately left-wing or radical political opinions. *–adj.* **5.** of the colour pink. **6.** pink in the face; flushed: *she turned pink with excitement.* **7.** having moderately left-wing or radical political opinions. *–v.t.* **8.** *Agric.* to shear (a sheep) so closely that its skin is exposed.

pink[2] /pɪŋk/ *v.t.* **1.** to pierce with a rapier or the like; stab. **2.** to finish at the edge with a scalloped, notched, or other ornamental pattern. **3.** to punch (cloth, leather, etc.) with small holes or figures for ornament.

pink heath *n.* the pink-flowered form of the common heath, *Epacris impressa*; the floral emblem of Victoria.

pinking shears *pl. n.* shears with notched blades, used for giving a scalloped or notched edge to fabrics to prevent them fraying.

pinnacle /'pɪnəkəl/ *n.* **1.** a tall thin mountain top or rock formation. **2.** the highest point of anything: *the pinnacle*

of fame. **3.** *Archit.* an upright pointed part on top of a building, usually conical in shape; turret; spire.

pinnate /'pɪneɪt, -ət/ *adj.* **1.** resembling a feather. **2.** having parts arranged on each side of a common axis. **3.** *Bot.* (of a leaf) having leaflets or primary divisions arranged on each side of a common petiole or rachis. Also, **pinnated**. *–pinnately, adv.*

PIN number /'pɪn nʌmbə/ *n.* → **PIN**.

pinot /'pinoʊ/ *n.* (*sometimes upper case*) any of various purple or white Burgundian grape varieties.

pinot grigio /pinoʊ 'grɪdʒoʊ/ *n.* (*sometimes upper case*) an Italian style of white wine made from the pinot grape.

pinot noir /pinoʊ 'nwa/ *n.* (*sometimes upper case*) a red wine made from pinot grapes.

pinpoint /'pɪnpɔɪnt/ *n.* **1.** the point of a pin. **2.** an insignificant or trivial thing. *–v.t.* **3.** to locate or describe exactly as on the ground or on a map. *–adj.* **4.** exact, precise.

pins and needles *pl. n.* a tingling sensation in the limbs, as that which accompanies the return of feeling after numbness; a form of paraesthesia.

pinstripe /'pɪnstraɪp/ *n. Textiles* **1.** a very narrow stripe. **2.** any material having a regular pattern of such stripes.

pint /paɪnt/ *n.* a liquid measure of capacity in the imperial system equal to ⅛ gallon, or 0.568 261 litres or, in the US, to 0.104 085 gallon, or 0.473 176 litres.

pintuck /'pɪntʌk/ *n.* a fine tuck used especially as a decorative feature on a garment.

pin-up *n. Colloq.* **1.** a picture, typically pinned to the wall by a personally unknown admirer, of an attractive personality especially a film star, or a nude or nearly nude person. **2.** the person depicted.

pioneer /paɪə'nɪə/ *n.* **1.** someone who first enters or settles a region. **2.** someone who is the first in any field of activity: *pioneers in cancer research.* **3.** *Ecol.* a plant or animal which successfully invades and becomes established in a bare area. **4.** (*upper case*) a series of unmanned US spacecraft with lunar, solar, interplanetary and planetary missions. *–v.i.* **5.** to act as a pioneer: *last century they were pioneering in Central Australia.* *–v.t.* **6.** to be a pioneer in: *to pioneer the western plains*; *to pioneer the development of a new process.*

pious /'paɪəs/ *adj.* **1.** having or showing religious devotion or dutiful respect. **2.** showing pretended or mistaken religious feeling; hypocritical; sanctimonious. **3.** belonging to religion; sacred not secular: *pious literature.* **4.** heartfelt; earnest. *–piously, adv. –piousness, n.*

pip[1] /pɪp/ *n.* **1.** one of the spots on dice, playing cards, or dominoes. **2.** each of the small segments into which the surface of a pineapple is divided. **3.** *Mil. Colloq.* a badge of rank worn on the shoulders of certain commissioned officers.

pip[2] /pɪp/ *n.* **1.** a contagious disease of birds, especially poultry, characterised by the secretion of a thick mucus in the mouth and throat. **2.** (*humorous*) any minor ailment in a person. *–v.t.* **3.** to annoy. *–phr. Colloq.* **4. get** (or **have**) **the pip**, to be out of sorts, irritable: *she's had the pip for days.* **5. give someone the pip**, to annoy or irritate someone, especially without intention: *his stupidity gives me the pip.*

pip[3] /pɪp/ *n.* a small seed, especially of a fleshy fruit, as an apple or orange.

pip[4] /pɪp/ *verb* (**pipped, pipping**) *–v.i.* **1.** to peep or chirp. *–v.t.* **2.** (of a young bird) to crack or chip a hole through (the shell).

pip[5] /pɪp/ *v.t.* (**pipped, pipping**) *Colloq.* **1.** to beat in a race, etc., especially by a small margin: *the favourite was pipped at the post.* **2.** to hit with a missile, as by shooting.

pipe[1] /paip/ *n.* **1.** a hollow cylinder of metal, wood, or other material, for the conveyance of water, gas, steam, etc., or for some other purpose; a tube. **2.** any of various tubular or cylindrical objects, parts, or formations. **3.** a naturally occurring cylindrical cavity in a tree. **4.** a tube of wood, clay, hard rubber, or other material, with a small bowl at one end, used for smoking tobacco, opium, crack cocaine, ice, etc. **5.** *Aust. Hist.* a paper critical of some public figure, rolled into a tube and left in a public place. **6.** *Music* **a.** one of the wooden or metal tubes from which the sounds of an organ are produced. **b.** (*usu. pl.*) → **bagpipes. c.** (*usu. pl.*) a set of flutes, as panpipes. **7.** *Naut.* **a.** a boatswain's whistle. **b.** the sounding of it as a call. **8.** the note or call of a bird, etc. **9.** (*pl.*) *Colloq.* the respiratory passages. **10.** *Mining* **a.** a cylindrical vein or body of ore. **b.** one of the vertical cylindrical masses of bluish rock, of eruption origin, found in southern Africa, in which diamonds are found embedded. **11.** *Computers* the keyboard symbol (|); vertical bar. *–v.i.* **12.** to play on a pipe. **13.** *Naut.* to announce orders, etc., by a boatswain's pipe or other signal. **14.** to speak shrilly. **15.** to make or utter a shrill sound like that of a pipe. **16.** *Mining* to carve forming a cylindrical cavity. *–v.t.* **17.** to convey by means of pipes. **18.** to supply with pipes. **19.** to summon, order, etc., by sounding the boatswain's pipe or whistle: *all hands were piped on deck.* **20.** to bring, lead, etc., by playing on a pipe. **21.** to utter in a shrill tone. **22.** to trim or finish (a garment, etc.) with piping. **23.** to shape (cream, mashed potatoes, icing, etc.) by forcing through an icing bag and nozzle. *–phr. Colloq.* **24. pipe down,** to become or keep quiet. **25. pipe up, a.** to begin to talk, especially unexpectedly. **b.** to make oneself heard. **c.** to speak up, as to assert oneself.

pipe[2] /paip/ *n.* **1.** a large cask, of varying capacity, for wine, etc. **2.** such a cask as a measure of capacity for wine, etc., equal to 4 barrels, and containing 126 wine gallons (105 imperial gallons or 477 litres). **3.** such a cask with its contents.

pipe bomb *n.* an improvised bomb made from a hollow tube packed with explosive and projectiles such as shotgun pellets or nails.

pipedream /'paipdrim/ *n.* a futile hope, far-fetched fancy, or fantastic story. Also, **pipe dream.**

pipe gun *n.* an improvised gun fashioned from a piece of piping attached to a wooden stick with a nail as trigger.

pipeline /'paiplain/ *n.* **1.** a pipe or several pipes together forming a conduit for the transportation of petroleum, petroleum products, natural gas, etc. **2.** a channel of information, usually confidential, direct, or privileged. *–phr.* **3. in the pipeline,** on the way; in preparation.

pipette /pɪ'pɛt/ *n.* a slender graduated tube for measuring and transferring liquids from one vessel to another. Also, **pipet.**

pipi /'pɪpi/ *n.* any of several edible, smooth-shelled, burrowing, bivalve molluscs.

piping /'paipɪŋ/ *n.* **1.** pipes collectively. **2.** material formed into a pipe or pipes. **3.** the act of someone or something that pipes. **4.** the sound of pipes. **5.** shrill sound. **6.** the music of pipes. **7.** a cordlike ornamentation made of icing, used on cakes, pastry, etc. **8.** a tubular band of material, sometimes containing a cord, for trimming garments, etc., as along edges and seams. *–adj.* **9.** playing on a musical pipe. **10.** that pipes. **11.** emitting a shrill sound: *a piping voice.* *–phr.* **12. piping hot, a.** very hot. **b.** freshly arrived; brand-new.

pipit /'pɪpɪt/ *n.* any of various small birds of the family Motacillidae, especially the genus *Anthus*, bearing a superficial resemblance to the larks, as the Australian pipit.

pipsqueak /'pɪpskwik/ *n. Colloq.* a small or insignificant person or thing.

piquant /'pikənt, pi'kɒnt/ *adj.* **1.** agreeably pungent or sharp in taste or flavour; biting; tart. **2.** agreeably stimulating, interesting, or attractive. **3.** of a smart, lively or provocative character: *piquant wit.* **–piquancy,** *n.* **–piquantly,** *adv.*

pique /pik/ *v.t.* (**piqued, piquing**) **1.** (*oft. in the passive*) to annoy by hurting one's pride or vanity: *to be piqued at a refusal.* **2.** to excite or affect with interest, curiosity, etc. *–n.* **3.** anger, resentment, or ill feeling over some slight offence or from hurt pride.

piranha /pə'ranə/ *n.* any small (hand-sized) South American fish of the subfamily Serrasalminae, noted for voracious habits, and despite their small size, dangerous even to humans and large animals.

pirate /'pairət/ *n.* **1.** someone who robs or does illegal violence at sea. **2.** a pirate ship. **3.** someone who takes and uses the work or idea of someone else without permission. **4.** Also, **pirate radio.** a radio station broadcasting on an unauthorised wavelength, and often operating outside territorial waters or in a foreign country to avoid payment of copyright fees, etc. *–v.t.* **5.** to appropriate and reproduce (a literary work, video, CD, computer program, etc.) without authorisation or legal right. *–v.i.* **6.** to commit or practise piracy. **–piratical** /pɪ'rætɪkəl/, *adj.* **–piratically,** *adv.* **–piracy,** *n.*

piroshki /pə'rɒʃki/ *n.* (in Russian cookery) a small turn-over consisting of a yeast-pastry wrapping filled with meat, seafood, vegetables, etc. Also, **pirozhki.**

pirouette /pɪru'ɛt/ *n.* **1.** a whirling about on one foot or on the points of the toes, as in dancing. *–v.i.* (**-etted, -etting**) **2.** to perform a pirouette, whirl as on the toes.

piscatorial /pɪskə'tɔriəl/ *adj.* of or relating to fishing or fishery. Also, **piscatory** /'pɪskətəri, -tri/.

Pisces /'paisiz/ *n.* the twelfth sign of the zodiac, which the sun enters about 19 February; the Fishes. **–Piscean,** *n., adj.*

pisci- a word element meaning 'fish'.

piscine /'pɪsin/ *adj.* of or relating to fish.

piscivorous /pə'sɪvərəs/ *adj.* fish-eating.

piss /pɪs/ *Colloq.* (*taboo*) *–v.i.* **1.** to urinate. *–n.* **2.** urine. **3.** an act of passing water; urination. **4.** beer. *–adv.* **5.** an intensifier: *piss awful; piss easy.* *–phr.* **6. all piss and wind** (or **piss-'n'-wind**), **a.** loquacious but insincere: *he's all piss and wind.* **b.** of little substance: *her speech was all piss and wind.* **7. a piece of piss,** an easy task. **8. on the piss,** on a drinking spree. **9. piss about** (or **around**), to mess about. **10. piss (all) over,** to beat or confound utterly. **11. piss down,** to rain heavily. **12. piss in someone's pocket,** *Aust., NZ* to behave obsequiously towards someone. **13. piss into the wind,** to embark on a futile course of action. **14. piss it in,** to do something with ease. **15. piss off,** (*oft. used impera-tively in dismissal*) to go away. **16. piss on, a.** to drink considerable quantities of liquor, especially beer. **b.** to beat convincingly. **17. piss someone off, a.** to send someone away. **b.** to annoy someone intensely. **18. take the piss,** (sometimes fol. by *out of*) to poke fun.

pissed /pɪst/ *Colloq.* (*taboo*) *–adj.* **1.** drunk. *–phr.* **2. pissed as a newt** (or **parrot**), extremely drunk. **3. pissed off,** disgruntled; irritated.

pisspot /'pɪspɒt/ *n. Colloq.* (*taboo*) a person who is a heavy drinker. Also, **pisshead.**

piss-up *n. Colloq.* (*taboo*) an occasion on which a large quantity of alcohol is consumed by a group of people, as at a party, etc.

piss-weak *adj. Colloq.* (*taboo*) **1.** inadequate; disap-pointing; not up to standard. **2.** of weak character; cowardly; irresolute. Also, **piss-poor.**

pistachio /pə'staʃiou, pə'stæʃiou/ *n.* (*pl.* **-chios**) **1.** the edible greenish kernel of the fruit of a small tree,

Pistacia vera, of southern Europe and western Asia. **2.** the tree itself. **3.** pistachio nut flavour. **4.** light yellowish green. Also, **pistache**.

pistil /ˈpɪstɪl/ *n. Bot.* the ovule-bearing or seed-bearing organ of a flower.

pistol /ˈpɪstɪl/ *n.* a short firearm intended to be held and fired with one hand.

piston /ˈpɪstən/ *n.* **1.** a movable disc or cylinder fitting closely within a tube or hollow cylinder, and capable of being driven alternately forwards and backwards in the tube by pressure, as in an internal-combustion engine. **2.** *Music* a pump-like valve used to change the pitch in a cornet or the like.

pit[1] /pɪt/ *n.* **1.** a hole or cavity in the ground. **2.** a covered or concealed excavation in the ground to serve as a trap; pitfall. **3.** *Mining* **a.** an excavation made in digging for some mineral deposit. **b.** the shaft of a coalmine. **c.** the mine itself. **4.** a sunken area in the floor of a garage used for the inspection of vehicles from below. **5.** a hole in the ground used for any of various purposes, as disposal of waste, burning charcoal, making silage, etc. **6.** a hollow or indentation in a surface. **7.** a natural hollow or depression in the body: *the pit of the stomach.* **8.** a small depressed scar such as one of those left on the skin after smallpox. **9.** an enclosure for combats, as of dogs or cocks. **10.** that part of the floor of an exchange devoted to a special kind of business: *the grain pit.* **11.** (in a theatre) **a.** the ground floor of the auditorium. **b.** the part of the ground floor behind the stalls. **c.** the persons occupying this section. **12.** *Athletics* an area, typically slightly sunken and filled with sand, which softens the fall of a long jumper, high jumper, etc. **13.** any of the stalls beside the motor-racing track in which competing cars undergo running repairs, are refuelled, etc., during a race. **14.** *Bot.* a thin place in a cell wall affording communication with another cell. *–verb* (**pitted, pitting**) *–v.t.* **15.** to mark with pits or depressions. *–v.i.* **16.** to become marked with pits or depressions. **17.** *Pathol.* to retain for a time the mark of pressure by the finger, etc., as the skin. *–phr.* **18. pit against,** to set in active opposition, as one against another: *to pit brother against brother.* **19. the pit, a.** the abode of evil spirits and lost souls; hell, or a part of it. **b.** *Surfing Colloq.* the hollow tube of a breaking wave. **20. the pits,** *Colloq.* the most unpleasant or most obnoxious place, circumstance, condition, etc.: *this flu is the pits.* *–pitted, adj.*

pit[2] /pɪt/ *n.* **1.** the stone of a fruit, as of a cherry, peach, or plum. *–v.t.* (**pitted, pitting**) **2.** to take out the stone from (a fruit, etc.). *–pitted, adj.*

pita /ˈpɪtə/ *n.* a small, flat, round, slightly leavened bread forming a pocket, which, when opened, can be filled with food. Also, **pita bread, pitta**.

pitch[1] /pɪtʃ/ *v.t.* **1.** to set up or erect (a tent, camp, etc.). **2.** to put, set, or plant in a fixed or definite place or position (as cricket stumps, etc.). **3.** to set or aim at a certain point, degree, level, etc.: *he pitched his hopes too high.* **4.** *Music* to set at a particular pitch, or determine the key or keynote of (a tune, etc.). **5.** to throw, fling or toss. **6.** *Baseball* to deliver (the ball) to the batter. **7.** *Golf* to hit (the ball) so that it rises steeply and rolls very little on landing. **8.** *Cards* **a.** to lead (a card of a particular suit), thereby fixing that suit as trumps. **b.** to determine (trumps) thus. **9.** *Building Trades* to dress, work, or place (masonry, etc.). **10.** *Archit.* to build a roof with a certain slope or steepness: *to pitch a roof steeply.* *–v.i.* **11.** to plunge or fall forward or headlong. **12.** to lurch. **13.** to throw, fling, or toss. **14.** to slope downwards; dip. **15.** to plunge with alternate fall and rise of bow and stern, as a ship, aeroplane, etc. (opposed to *roll*). **16.** *Aeronautics* to change the angle which the longitudinal axis makes relative to the horizontal. **17.** to fix a tent or temporary habitation; encamp. **18.** *Golf* to hit the ball so that it rises steeply and does not roll much on landing. **19.** *Baseball* **a.** to deliver the ball to the batter. **b.** to fill the position of pitcher. *–n.* **20.** relative point, position, or degree. **21.** *Acoustics, Music* the apparent predominant frequency of a sound from an acoustical source, musical instrument, etc. **22.** a particular tonal standard with which given notes may be compared in respect to their relative level. **23.** the act or manner of pitching. **24.** a throw or toss, especially in baseball, softball, etc. **25.** the pitching movement, or the plunge forward of a ship, aeroplane or the like. **26.** inclination or slope. **27.** degree of inclination or slope; angle. **28.** a sloping part or place. **29. a.** *Sport* the whole area of play, usually of grass, of cricket, football, hockey, etc. **b.** *Cricket* the area between the wickets. **30.** a spot where a person or thing is placed or stationed especially the established location of a stall in a street market or of a street pedlar, singer, etc. **31.** a sales talk. **32.** specific plan of action; way of approaching a problem. **33.** *Mining, Geol.* **a.** the angle that a line in the plane makes with a horizontal line in that plane. **b.** in ore deposits, the angle between the axis of the ore shoot and the strike of the vein. **34.** *Mining* **a.** the defined section of a lode assigned to a tributer. **b.** working place in a slope. **35.** *Archit.* the slope or steepness of a roof. **36.** *Machinery* **a.** the distance between corresponding surfaces of adjacent teeth of a gearwheel or the like. **b.** the distance between two things in a regular series, as between threads of a screw, rivets, etc. *–phr.* **37. cruel** (or **queer**) **someone's pitch,** *Colloq.* to spoil someone's opportunity or plan. **38. pitch a line,** to attempt to impress by boastful and sometimes untruthful speech, often as a means of persuading someone to engage in sexual activity. **39. pitch a tale** (or **yarn,** etc.), to tell a story, especially one that is exaggerated or untrue. **40. pitch in,** *Colloq.* **a.** to contribute or join in. **b.** to begin vigorously. **41. pitch into, a.** to attack verbally or physically. **b.** to begin to do or work on. **42. pitch on** (or **upon**), to fix or decide on, often casually or without particular consideration.

pitch[2] /pɪtʃ/ *n.* **1.** any of various dark-coloured tenacious or viscous substances used for covering the seams of vessels after caulking, for making pavements, etc., as the residuum left after the distillation of coal tar (coal-tar pitch), or a product derived similarly from wood tar (wood pitch). **2.** any of certain bitumens, as *mineral pitch* (asphaltum). **3.** any of various resins. **4.** the sap or crude turpentine which exudes from the bark of pines. *–v.t.* **5.** to smear or cover with pitch. *–pitchy, adj.*

pitch-black *adj.* very black or dark.

pitchblende /ˈpɪtʃblɛnd/ *n.* an impure uraninite, occurring in black pitchlike masses; the principal ore of uranium and radium.

pitcher[1] /ˈpɪtʃə/ *n.* **1.** a container, usually with a handle and spout or lip, for holding and pouring liquids. *–phr.* **2. little pitchers have big ears,** *Colloq.* an expression used to indicate that children are listening to adult conversation.

pitcher[2] /ˈpɪtʃə/ *n. Baseball* the player who delivers or throws the ball to the batter.

pitcher plant *n.* any of various, often insectivorous, plants with leaves modified into a pitcher-like receptacle, as in some species of *Nepenthes* and *Cephalotus*.

pitchfork /ˈpɪtʃfɔk/ *n.* **1.** a fork for lifting and pitching hay, etc. *–v.t.* **2.** to pitch or throw with or as with a pitchfork.

piteous /ˈpɪtɪəs/ *adj.* such as to excite or deserve pity, or appealing strongly for pity; pathetic. *–piteously, adv. –piteousness, n.*

pitfall /ˈpɪtfɔl/ *n.* **1.** a concealed pit prepared as a trap for animals or humans to fall into. **2.** any trap or danger for the unwary.

pith /pɪθ/ *n.* **1.** the soft, spongy lining of the rind of oranges and other citrus fruits. **2.** *Bot.* the central cylinder of parenchymatous tissue in the stems of dicotyledonous plants. **3.** any of various similar inner parts of substances, as the centre of a log, a feather, etc. **4.** the important part; essence. –*v.t.* **5.** to destroy the spinal cord or brain of.

Pithecanthropus /pɪθiˈkænθrəpəs/ *n.* (*pl.* **Pithecanthropi** /pɪθiˈkænθrəpaɪ/) an extinct genus of apelike human, now classified under the genus Homo, as *homo erectus*; first known fossils of this species, Java man, discovered 1891–93.

pith helmet *n.* a sunhat, usually domed with a sloping brim, made of pith, and formerly much worn by Europeans in tropical countries; topee.

pithy /ˈpɪθi/ *adj.* (**pithier, pithiest**) **1.** full of vigour, substance, or meaning; terse; forcible: *a pithy criticism.* **2.** of or like pith, or having much pith. –**pithily,** *adv.* –**pithiness,** *n.*

pitiable /ˈpɪtiəbəl/ *adj.* **1.** deserving to be pitied; such as justly to excite pity; lamentable; deplorable. **2.** such as to excite a contemptuous pity; miserable; contemptible. –**pitiableness,** *n.* –**pitiably,** *adv.*

pitiful /ˈpɪtɪfəl/ *adj.* **1.** such as to excite or deserve pity: *a pitiful fate.* **2.** such as to excite contempt by smallness, poor quality, etc.: *pitiful attempts.* **3.** full of pity or compassion; compassionate. –**pitifully,** *adv.* –**pitifulness,** *n.*

pitta[1] /ˈpɪtə/ *n.* any of several species of small, brightly coloured, ground-dwelling birds of the genus *Pitta* of northern and eastern Australia.

pitta[2] /ˈpɪtə/ *n.* → **pita.** Also, **pitta bread.**

pittance /ˈpɪtns/ *n.* **1.** a small allowance or sum for living expenses. **2.** a scanty income or remuneration. **3.** any small portion or amount.

pittosporum /pəˈtɒspərəm/ *n.* **1.** the sweet-scented *Pittosporum undulatum* of eastern Australia which has white bell-shaped flowers and orange fruit. **2.** any of various other trees or shrubs of the large genus *Pittosporum* of Asia, Africa, and Australasia.

pituitary /pəˈtjuətri, -təri/ *n.* (*pl.* **-ries**) *Anat.* → **pituitary gland.**

pituitary gland *n.* *Anat.* a small, oval, endocrine gland attached to the base of the brain and situated in a depression of the sphenoid bone, which secretes several hormones, and was formerly supposed to secrete mucus. Also, **pituitary body.**

pity /ˈpɪti/ *n.* (*pl.* **pities**) **1.** sympathetic or kindly sorrow excited by the suffering or misfortune of another, often leading one to give relief or aid or to show mercy: *to weep from pity, to take pity on a person.* **2.** a cause or reason for pity, sorrow, or regret: *what a pity you could not go!* –*v.t.* (**pitied, pitying**) **3.** to feel pity or compassion for; be sorry for; commiserate. –*phr.* **4. for pity's sake,** an exclamation used to express exasperation or anger. –**pityingly,** *adv.* –**pitiless,** *adj.*

pivot /ˈpɪvət/ *n.* **1.** a pin or shaft on the end of which something rests and turns. **2.** a thing or person on which something turns or depends. **3.** *Rugby Union* a halfback. –*v.i.* **4.** to turn on or as on a pivot. –*v.t.* **5.** to join by, or provide with, a pivot.

pixel /ˈpɪksəl/ *n.* any of the extremely small discrete elements, known as dots, which together make a graphic image as on a television or computer screen or as produced by a digital camera. Each pixel consists of red, green, and blue components which together represent a particular colour to the human eye. The more pixels there are in an image, the greater its resolution.

pixel blur *n.* **1.** → **Gaussian blur. 2.** the diffuse digital image created by a pixel blur.

pixie /ˈpɪksi/ *n.* **1.** a fairy or sprite. –*phr.* **2. away** (or **off**) **with the pixies,** *Aust. Colloq.* no longer in tune with reality. Also, **pixy.**

pixilation /pɪksəˈleɪʃən/ *n.* an animation technique in which the animator photographs real objects and people frame by frame to achieve unusual effects of motion.

pizza /ˈpitsə, ˈpɪtsə/ *n.* an Italian dish made from yeast dough formed into a flat, round shape, covered with any of a variety of foods, such as tomato, grated cheese, anchovies, ham, olives, etc., baked in an oven; usually cut into wedge-shaped pieces for serving.

pizzazz /pəˈzæz/ *n.* *Chiefly US* panache; zest; verve. Also, **pizazz.**

pizzicato /pɪtsəˈkatoʊ/ *adj.* **1.** *Music* played by plucking the strings with the finger instead of using the bow, as on a violin. –*n.* **2.** a note or passage so played.

placard /ˈplækad/ *n.* **1.** a written or printed notice to be posted in a public place or carried, as in a demonstration. –*v.t.* **2.** to post placards on or in. **3.** to give notice of by means of placards. **4.** to post as a placard. –**placarder,** *n.*

placate /pləˈkeɪt/ *v.t.* to appease; pacify. –**placation,** *n.* –**placable** /ˈplækəbəl/, *adj.* –**placability** /plækəˈbɪləti/, *n.*

place /pleɪs/ *n.* **1.** a particular portion of space, of definite or indefinite extent. **2.** space in general (chiefly in connection with *time*). **3.** the portion of space occupied by anything. **4.** a space or spot, set apart or used for a particular purpose: *a place of worship.* **5.** any part or spot in a body or surface: *a decayed place in a tooth.* **6.** a particular passage in a book or writing. **7.** a space or seat for a person, as in a theatre, train, etc. **8.** the space or position customarily or previously occupied by a person or thing. **9.** position, situation, or circumstances: *if I were in your place.* **10.** a proper or appropriate location or position: *try to keep everything in its place.* **11.** a short street, a court, etc.: *Martin Place.* **12.** a job, post, or office. **13.** a function or duty. **14.** position or standing in the social scale, or in any order of merit, estimation, etc. **15.** official employment or position. **16.** a region. **17.** an open space, or square, in a city or town. **18.** an area, especially one regarded as an entity and identifiable by name, used for habitation, as a city, town, or village. **19.** a building. **20.** a part of a building. **21. a.** a residence, dwelling, or house. **b.** a property (def. 3) comprising land, buildings, residence, etc. **22.** stead or lieu: *use water in place of milk.* **23.** a step or point in order of proceeding: *in the first place.* **24.** a fitting opportunity: *there is a place for creative thinkers in today's business world.* **25.** a reasonable ground or occasion: *a wedding is not the place for long speeches; this is neither the time nor the place.* **26.** *Arithmetic* **a.** the position of a figure in a series, as in decimal notation. **b.** (*pl.*) the figures of the series. **27.** *Sport* **a.** a position among the leading competitors, usually the first three, at the finish of a race. **b.** the position of the second or third (opposed to *win*). –*verb* (**placed, placing**) –*v.t.* **28.** to put in a particular place; set. **29.** to put in an appropriate position or order. **30.** to put into a suitable or desirable place for some purpose, as money for investment, an order or contract, etc. **31.** to fix (confidence, esteem, etc.) in a person or thing. **32.** to appoint (a person) to a post or office. **33.** to find a place, situation, etc., for (a person). **34.** to determine or indicate the place of. **35.** to assign a certain position or rank to. **36.** to direct or aim with precision. **37.** to assign a position to (a horse, etc.) among the leading competitors, usually the first three, at the finish of a race, competition, etc. **38.** to put or set in a particular place, position, situation, or relation. **39.** to identify by connecting with the proper place, circumstances, etc.: *to be unable to place a person.* –*v.i.* **40.** *Racing* to finish among the three placegetters, usually second; to be placed. –*phr.* **41. give place to, a.** to make room for. **b.** to be superseded by. **42. go places,** *Colloq.* to be successful in one's career. **43. in a good place,** contented and satisfied with life. **44. in place,** (of a program, policy, enterprise, etc.) operating or functional. **45. know one's place,** to recognise one's (low) social rank and behave accordingly. **46. out of place, a.** not in the proper position. **b.** inappropriate; unsuitable. **47. pride of place,** the highest or most important position. **48. put someone in their place,** to humble an arrogant person. **49. take one's place,** to sit down, or take up a position, as of right. **50. take place,** to happen. **51. take the place of,** to be a substitute for; oust. –**placer,** *n.* –**placement,** *n.*

placebo /pləˈsiboʊ/ *n.* (*pl.* **-bos** *or* **-boes**) **1.** *Med.* a medicine which performs no physiological function but may benefit the patient psychologically. **2.** *Roman Catholic Church* the vespers of the office for the dead, so called from the opening word, being Latin for 'I shall be pleasing'.

placenta /pləˈsɛntə/ *n.* (*pl.* **-tas** *or* **-tae** /-ti/) **1.** *Zool.,* *Anat.* the organ formed in the lining of the mammalian uterus by the union of the uterine mucous membrane with the membranes of the fetus to provide for the nourishment of the fetus and the elimination of its waste products. **2.** *Bot.* **a.** the part of the ovary of flowering plants which bears the ovules. **b.** (in ferns, etc.) the tissue giving rise to sporangia. –**placental,** **placentate,** *adj.*

placid /ˈplæsəd/ *adj.* pleasantly calm or peaceful; unruffled; tranquil; serene. –**placidity** /pləˈsɪdəti/, **placidness,** *n.* –**placidly,** *adv.*

placket /ˈplækət/ *n.* an opening at the top of a skirt, or in a dress, blouse, or shirt to facilitate putting it on and taking it off.

plagiarise /ˈpleɪdʒəraɪz/ *v.t.* **1.** to appropriate by plagiarism. **2.** to appropriate ideas, passages, etc., from by plagiarism. –*v.i.* **3.** to commit plagiarism. Also, **plagiarize.** –**plagiariser,** *n.*

plagiarism /ˈpleɪdʒərɪzəm/ *n.* **1.** the appropriation or imitation of another's ideas and manner of expressing them, as in art, literature, etc., to be passed off as one's own. **2.** a piece of writing, music, art, etc., appropriated or commissioned from another and passed off as one's own. –**plagiarist,** *n.* –**plagiaristic** /pleɪdʒəˈrɪstɪk/, *adj.*

plagioclase /ˈpleɪdʒioʊˌkleɪz, -ˌkleɪs/ *n.* any of the feldspar minerals varying in composition from $NaAlSi_3O_8$ to $CaAl_2Si_2O_8$, important constituents of many igneous rocks.

plague /pleɪg/ *n.* **1.** an epidemic disease of high mortality; a pestilence. **2.** Also, **the plague, bubonic plague.** an infectious, epidemic disease, caused by the bacterium *Yersinia pestis* and carried by fleas from rodents. Symptoms include fever, chills, prostration and swellings, especially in the groin and armpit areas. **3.** either of two other forms of this disease, affecting the lungs, or in which the bloodstream is invaded. **4.** an acute infestation of insects, rodents, etc.: *a plague of mice.* **5.** an affliction, calamity, or evil, especially one regarded as a visitation from God: *the ten plagues.* **6.** any cause of trouble or vexation. –*v.t.* **(plagued, plaguing)** **7.** to trouble or torment in any manner **8.** to annoy, bother, or pester. **9.** to smite with a plague. **10.** to infect with a plague. **11.** to afflict with any evil. –**plaguer,** *n.*

plaid /plæd/ *n.* **1.** any fabric woven of different coloured yarns in a cross-barred pattern. **2.** a pattern of this kind. **3.** a long, rectangular piece of cloth, usually with such a pattern, worn about the shoulders by Scottish Highlanders. –*adj.* **4.** having the pattern of a plaid.

plain /pleɪn/ *adj.* **1.** clear to the eye or ear. **2.** clear to the mind; evident, obvious. **3.** easily understood: *plain talk.* **4.** total; downright: *plain silliness.* **5.** direct; candid. **6.** without special rank, importance, etc.: *plain people.* **7.** not beautiful. **8.** ordinary; simple; unadorned. **9.** (of paper) unruled. **10.** (of food) not rich, or difficult to prepare. **11.** flat; level: *plain country.* **12.** (of knitting) made of plain stitches. –*adv.* **13.** simply; absolutely. **14.** clearly; intelligibly. –*n.* **15.** a large, flat area of land. **16.** the simplest stitch in knitting. –**plainly,** *adv.* –**plainness,** *n.*

plain-clothes *adj.* wearing civilian clothes rather than a uniform, as a detective. Also, **plainclothes.** –**plain-clothed,** *adj.*

plainsong /ˈpleɪnsɒŋ/ *n.* the unisonal liturgical music used in the Christian church from the earliest times; Gregorian chant. Also, **plainchant.**

plains-wanderer /ˈpleɪnz-wɒndərə/ *n.* a small, shy, brownish, superficially quail-like bird, *Pedionomus torquatus,* which prefers to run rather than fly, once common but now infrequently seen in open plains and grasslands of eastern and central Australia; turkey quail.

plaint /pleɪnt/ *n.* **1.** → **complaint. 2.** *Law* a statement of grievance made to a court for the purpose of asking redress.

plaintiff /ˈpleɪntəf, -tɪf/ *n.* *Law* someone who brings an action in a civil case.

plaintive /ˈpleɪntɪv/ *adj.* expressing sorrow or melancholy discontent; mournful: *plaintive music.* –**plaintively,** *adv.* –**plaintiveness,** *n.*

plain turkey *n.* → **bustard.**

plait /plæt/ *n.* **1.** a braid, as of hair or straw. **2.** a pleat or fold, as of cloth. –*v.t.* **3.** to braid (hair, etc.). **4.** to make (a mat, etc.) by braiding. **5.** to pleat (cloth, etc.).

plan /plæn/ *n.* **1.** a scheme or set of ideas for acting. **2.** a design or pattern of arrangement. **3.** a drawing made to scale to represent the top view or a horizontal cut of a building or machine, town, etc. **4.** a system of payment for a mobile phone or internet service which can be either prepaid at a fixed amount per month, or paid according to use. –*verb* **(planned, planning)** –*v.t.* **5.** to form or arrange a plan for (any work or action). **6.** to draw or make a plan of (a building, etc.). –*v.i.* **7.** to make plans. –*phr.* **8. off (the) plan,** from the architect's plan of a proposed building before it is built: *to buy a unit off plan.*

planar /ˈpleɪnə, ˈpleɪnɑ/ *adj.* **1.** of or relating to a plane (**plane¹** defs 1 and 2). **2.** lying in one plane; flat. –**planarity,** *n.*

Planck's constant /ˈplæŋks kɒnstənt/ *n.* *Physics* a universal constant (approximately 6.626×10^{-34} joule seconds) expressing the proportion of the energy of any form of wavelike radiation to its frequency. *Symbol:* h

plane¹ /pleɪn/ *n.* **1.** a flat or level surface. **2.** *Maths* a surface such that the straight line joining any two separate points in it lies completely within it. **3.** a level of character, existence, development, etc.: *a high moral plane.* **4.** an aeroplane or hydroplane. –*adj.* **5.** flat or level, as a surface. **6.** of plane figures: *plane geometry.* –**planeness,** *n.*

plane² /pleɪn/ *n.* **1.** a tool with an adjustable blade for paring, truing, smoothing, or finishing the surface of wood, etc. **2.** a tool resembling a trowel for smoothing the surface of the clay in a brick mould. –*v.t.* **3.** to smooth or dress with or as with a plane or a planer. –*v.i.* **4.** to work with a plane. **5.** to function as a plane. –*phr.* **6. plane away** (or **off**), to remove by or as by means of a plane.

plane angle *n.* an angle between two intersecting lines.

planet /ˈplænət/ *n.* **1.** *Astron.* **a.** a celestial body revolving around the sun and visible by its reflected light, large enough to exert sufficient gravity on itself to achieve a rounded shape, and to clear its orbit of all asteroids, comets, and other space debris. **b.** a similar celestial body revolving around a star other than the sun. **c.** *Obs.* a celestial body moving among the fixed stars, including the sun and moon. **2.** *Astrology* a heavenly body regarded as exerting influence on people and events. –**planetary**, *adj.*

plangent /ˈplændʒənt/ *adj.* **1.** beating or dashing, as waves. **2.** resounding loudly. –**plangency**, *n.*

planigale /ˈplænəgeɪl/ *n.* any of the very small, carnivorous, flat-skulled dasyurids of the genus *Planigale*, native to Australia and New Guinea, which includes the smallest known marsupials.

plank /plæŋk/ *n.* **1.** a long, flat piece of timber thicker than a board. **2.** timber in such pieces. **3.** something to stand on or to cling to for support. **4.** a policy which is a key part of a political party's platform. **5.** *Yoga, Pilates* a pose in which the person faces towards the floor, with the arms extended stiffly and the body in one line from head to toe. –*v.t.* **6.** to lay, cover, or furnish with planks. **7.** *US* to cook (and usually to serve) meat or fish on a special wooden board of well-seasoned hardwood, of long or oval shape. –*phr.* **8. plank down**, *Aust. Colloq.* **a.** to lay or put down. **b.** to pay out. **9. walk the plank**, to be compelled, as by pirates, to walk to one's death by stepping off a plank extending from a ship's side over the water.

planktivore /ˈplæŋktəvɔː/ *n.* an organism which feeds on plankton. –**planktivorous** /plæŋkˈtɪvərəs/, *adj.*

plankton /ˈplæŋktən/ *n.* the mass of very small animal and plant organisms that float or drift in the water, especially at or near the surface. –**planktonic** /plæŋkˈtɒnɪk/, *adj.*

plant /plænt, plant/ *n.* **1.** any member of the vegetable group of living organisms. **2.** a herb or other small vegetable growth, in contrast to a tree or a shrub. **3.** a seedling. **4.** the machinery, tools, etc., and often the buildings, needed to carry on any industrial business. **5.** *Colloq.* **a.** something or someone used to trap (criminals, etc.). **b.** a spy. **6.** *Billiards, etc.* a shot in which the ball struck with the cue is made to hit one of two balls (which are touching) so as to pot the other. –*v.t.* **7.** to put (seeds, trees, etc.) in the ground for growth. **8.** to fix (ideas, feelings, etc.) in someone's mind. **9.** to put or set firmly in place. **10.** *Colloq.* to deliver (a blow, etc.). **11.** to locate; situate. **12.** *Colloq.* to hide (stolen goods). **13.** to place (evidence) so that its discovery will make an innocent person appear guilty.

plantain /ˈplæntən, -teɪn/ *n.* **1.** a tropical herbaceous plant, *Musa paradisiaca*. **2.** Also, **plantain banana**. its green-skinned, banana-like fruit, which, when cooked, is a staple food in many tropical regions.

plantar /ˈplæntə/ *adj.* of or relating to the sole of the foot.

plantation /plænˈteɪʃən, planˈteɪʃən/ *n.* **1.** a farm or estate, especially in a tropical or subtropical country, on which cotton, tobacco, coffee, sugar, or the like is cultivated, usually by resident labourers. **2.** a group of planted trees or plants.

plaque /plak, plæk/ *n.* **1.** a plate or tablet of metal, porcelain, etc., as on a wall or set in a piece of furniture, for ornamentation or, if inscribed, commemoration. **2.** a plate-like brooch or ornament, especially one worn as the badge of an honorary order. **3.** *Zool., Anat.* **a.** a small, flat, rounded formation or area, as a deposit of fibrous matter in the wall of a blood vessel or around a cell. **b.** a localised patch of skin disease. **4.** *Dentistry* a film on teeth harbouring bacteria.

-plasia a word element meaning 'biological cellular growth', as in *hypoplasia*. Also, **-plasy**.

-plasm a word element forming a noun termination meaning 'something formed or moulded' in biological and other scientific terms, as in *protoplasm*.

plasma /ˈplæzmə/ *n.* **1.** *Physiol.* the liquid part of blood or lymph, as distinguished from the corpuscles. **2.** *Biol.* → **protoplasm**. **3.** → **whey**. **4.** a green, faintly translucent chalcedony. **5.** *Physics* a highly ionised gas which, because it contains an approximately equal number of electrons and positive ions, is electrically neutral and highly conducting; used in a plasma display panel. **6.** *Astrophysics* **a.** a system of charged particles large enough to behave collectively, as in the sun. **b.** the ionised region of the earth's upper atmosphere. Also, **plasm** /ˈplæzəm/. –**plasmatic** /plæzˈmætɪk/, **plasmic**, *adj.*

plasma display *n.* a system for illuminating tiny coloured fluorescent lights in a plasma display panel, each set of three having one red, one green and one blue, to produce a pixel and from many pixels to form an image; used for television screens, computer screens, etc., to replace the cathode-ray tube.

plasma display panel *n.* a panel with numerous cells filled with plasma (def. 5) which is activated by passing an electronic current through it to produce light photons which are then amplified by the phosphorus material on the inside wall of the cell. See **plasma display**.

plasma screen *n.* a screen for a television set, computer, etc., which uses plasma display.

plasma TV *n.* a television which has a plasma screen. Also, **plasma television**, **plasma**.

plasmid /ˈplæzməd/ *n.* a segment of DNA which is not part of a chromosome but which is nonetheless capable of replication, occurring in bacteria and yeast; used in biotechnology to transfer genetic material from one cell to another.

-plast a word element forming a noun termination meaning 'formed', 'moulded', especially in biological and botanical terms.

plaster /ˈplɑːstə/ *n.* **1.** a pasty composition, as of lime, sand, water, and often hair, used for covering walls, ceilings, etc., where it hardens in drying. **2.** gypsum powdered but not calcined. **3.** calcined gypsum (**plaster of Paris**), a white powdery material which swells when mixed with water and sets rapidly, used for making casts, moulds, etc. **4.** a solid or semisolid preparation for spreading upon cloth or the like and applying to the body for some remedial or other purpose. **5.** → **sticking plaster**. –*v.t.* **6.** to cover (walls, etc.) with plaster. **7.** to treat with gypsum or plaster of Paris. **8.** to lay flat like a layer of plaster. **9.** to daub or fill with plaster or something similar. **10.** to apply a plaster to (the body, etc.). **11.** to overspread with anything, especially thickly or to excess: *a wall plastered with posters*. **12.** *Colloq.* to hit hard and often. **13.** *Colloq.* to bomb heavily. –**plasterer**, *n.* –**plastering**, *n.* –**plastery**, *adj.*

plastic /ˈplæstɪk/ *adj.* **1.** concerned with or relating to moulding or modelling: *plastic arts*. **2.** able to be moulded or to receive form: *plastic substances*. **3.** Also, **anaplastic**. *Surg.* concerned with or relating to the fixing or changing of badly formed, injured, or lost parts: *plastic surgery*. **4.** able to be moulded; pliable: *the plastic mind of youth*. **5.** made of or containing plastic: *a plastic bag*. –*n.* **6.** any of a group of chemically-produced or natural materials which may be shaped when soft and then hardened, such as resins, polymers, etc. –**plasticity** /plæsˈtɪsəti/, *n.* –**plastically**, *adv.*

-plastic a word element forming adjectives related to **-plast**, **-plasty**, as in *protoplastic*.

plastic bomb *n.* a bomb, often home-made, consisting of a plastic putty-like explosive manually moulded around a detonator and used, either by direct adhesion (without a container) or in any rudimentary form of container, especially in guerilla warfare, by commandos, or in civil disturbances.

plastic explosive *n.* an explosive substance in the form of a malleable, dough-like material. See **plastic bomb**.

plasticine /ˈplæstəsin/ *n.* (*from trademark*) a plastic modelling compound, in various colours.

plastic money *n.* *Colloq.* credit cards collectively. Also, **plastic**.

plastic soup *n.* a floating mass of waste, mainly plastic, which accumulates at the point in the ocean where a gyre is located.

plastic surgery *n.* the reconstruction or repair by surgery of part of the body for restorative or cosmetic purposes. –**plastic surgeon**, *n.*

-plasty a word element forming a noun termination meaning 'formation', occurring in the names of processes of plastic surgery, as *rhinoplasty*, and occasionally in other words.

-plasy variant of **-plasia**.

plate /pleɪt/ *n.* **1.** a shallow, usually circular dish, now usually of earthenware or porcelain, from which food is eaten. **2.** a service of food for one person at the table. **3.** an entire course: *a cold plate*. **4.** *Aust.*, *NZ* a plate of sandwiches, cakes, etc., prepared and brought to a party or similar social occasion. **5.** domestic dishes, utensils, etc., of gold or silver. **6.** a dish, as of metal or wood, used for collecting offerings in a church, etc. **7.** a thin, flat sheet or piece of metal or other material, especially of uniform thickness. **8.** metal in such sheets. **9.** a flat, polished piece of metal on which something may be or is engraved. **10.** *Printing* a sheet of metal for printing from, formed by stereotyping or electrotyping a page of type, or metal or plastic formed by moulding, etching, or photographic development. **11.** a printed impression from such a piece, or from some similar piece, as a woodcut. **12.** a full-page inserted illustration forming part of a book. **13.** *Dentistry* a piece of metal, vulcanite, or plastic substance, with artificial teeth or a wire attached. **14.** → **plate glass**. **15.** *Photography* a sensitised sheet of glass, metal, film, etc., on which to take a photograph or make a reproduction by photography. **16.** *Anat.*, *Zool.*, *etc.* a plate-like part, structure, or organ. **17.** *Geol.* → **tectonic plate**. **18.** a gold or silver cup or the like, or guaranteed prize money, awarded as a prize in horseracing, etc. –*v.t.* **19.** to coat (metal) with a thin film of gold, silver, nickel, etc., by mechanical or chemical means. **20.** to cover or overlay with metal plates for protection, etc. **21.** *Printing* to make a stereotype or electrotype plate from (type). –*phr.* **22. on a plate**, (of something offered) capable of being taken without effort. **23. on one's plate**, waiting to be dealt with; pending.

plateau /ˈplætoʊ/ *n.* (*pl.* **-eaus** *or* **-eaux** /ˈplætoʊz/) **1.** a tabular surface of high elevation, often of considerable extent. **2.** *Psychol.* a period of little or no progress in an individual's learning, marked by temporary constancy in speed, number of errors committed, etc., and indicated by a flat stretch on a graph. **3.** any period of minimal growth or decline. –*v.i.* (**-eaued**, **-eauing**) **4.** (of prices, costs, etc.) to reach a plateau (def. 3).

plateau indexation *n.* a form of indexation in which wages below a certain value are increased on a proportional basis, and wages above that value by a fixed amount.

plate glass *n.* a soda-lime-silica glass formed by rolling the hot glass into a plate which is subsequently ground and polished; used in large windows, mirrors, etc.

platelet /ˈpleɪtlət/ *n.* *Physiol.* a microscopic disc occurring in profusion in the blood, and acting as an important aid in coagulation.

platform /ˈplætfɔm/ *n.* **1.** raised flooring, as in a hall, for use by public speakers, performers, etc. **2.** a raised area

alongside the tracks of a railway station. **3.** the open entrance area at the end of a bus, etc. **4.** a flat elevated piece of ground. **5. a.** a sole several centimetres thick on a shoe. **b.** Also, **platform shoe**. the shoe itself. **6.** the body of principles which a political party uses to appeal to the public. **7. a.** *Computers* an operating system. **b.** a telecommunications system: *an SMS platform*.

plating /ˈpleɪtɪŋ/ *n.* **1.** a thin coating of gold, silver, etc. **2.** an external layer of metal plates.

platinum /ˈplætənəm/ *n.* **1.** *Chem.* a heavy, greyish white, highly malleable and ductile metallic element, resistant to most chemicals, practically unoxidisable save in the presence of bases, and fusible only at extremely high temperatures, used especially for making chemical and scientific apparatus, as a catalyst in the oxidation of ammonia to nitric acid, and in jewellery. *Symbol*: Pt; *relative atomic mass*: 195.09; *atomic number*: 78; *density*: 21.5 at 20°C. **2.** a light metallic grey with very slight bluish tinge when compared with silver. –**platinic** /pləˈtɪnɪk/, *adj.*

platinum disc *n.* a musical recording that is certified as having sold a certain number of copies, a platinum-covered disc, formerly a record (**platinum record**), being designated as recognition of this and presented to artists and other people involved in its production and promotion; in Australia, awarded for 70 000 sales.

platitude /ˈplætətjud, -tʃud/ *n.* a flat, dull, or trite remark, especially one uttered as if it were fresh and profound. –**platitudinous** /plætəˈtjudənəs/, *adj.*

platonic /pləˈtɒnɪk/ *adj.* purely spiritual; free from sensual desire. –**platonically**, *adv.*

platoon /pləˈtun/ *n.* **1.** a military sub-unit consisting of two or more sections, being part of a company. **2.** a company or group of persons.

platter /ˈplætə/ *n.* **1.** a large, shallow dish, commonly oval, for holding or serving meat, etc. **2.** *Music Colloq.* a record (def. 17). –*phr.* **3. handed on a** (**silver**) **platter**, (of something offered) capable of being taken without effort.

platyhelminth /plætiˈhɛlmɪnθ/ *n.* a member of the Platyhelminthes, the phylum of flatworms, having bilateral symmetry and a soft, solid, usually flattened body, including the planarians, flukes, tapeworms, and others.

platypus /ˈplætəpəs/ *n.* (*pl.* **-puses** *or* **-pi** /-paɪ/ *or, especially collectively,* **-pus**) an amphibious, egg-laying monotreme, *Ornithorhynchus anatinus*, of eastern mainland Australia and Tasmania, 45–60 cm in total length, having webbed feet and a muzzle like the bill of a duck; duckbill.

plaudit /ˈplɔdət/ *n.* (*usu. pl.*) **1.** a demonstration or round of applause, as for some approved or admired performance. **2.** any enthusiastic expression of approval.

plausible /ˈplɔzəbəl/ *adj.* **1.** having an appearance of truth or reason; seemingly worthy of approval or acceptance: *a plausible story*. **2.** fair-spoken and apparently worthy of confidence: *a plausible adventurer*. –**plausibility** /plɔzəˈbɪləti/, **plausibleness**, *n.* –**plausibly**, *adv.*

play /pleɪ/ *n.* **1.** a dramatic composition or piece; a drama. **2.** a dramatic performance, as on the stage. **3.** exercise or action by way of amusement or recreation. **4.** fun, jest, or trifling, as opposed to earnest: *he said it merely in play*. **5.** the playing or carrying on, of a game. **6.** manner or style of playing. **7.** the state, as of a ball, of being played with or in use in the active playing of a game: *in play*; *out of play*. **8.** action, activity, or operation: *the play of fancy*. **9.** brisk movement or action: *a fountain with a leaping play of water*. **10.** elusive change, as of light or colours. **11.** a space in which a thing, as a piece of mechanism, can move. **12.** freedom of movement, as within a space, as of a part of a mechanism. **13.** freedom for action, or scope for activity: *full play of the mind.* **14.** an act or performance in playing: *a stupid play in a game of football.* **15.** turn to play: *it is your play.* *–v.t.* **16.** to act the part of (a character) in a dramatic performance: *to play Lady Macbeth.* **17.** to perform (a drama, etc.) on or as on the stage. **18.** to sustain the part or character of in real life: *to play the innocent.* **19.** to give performances in, as a theatrical company does: *to play the larger cities.* **20.** to engage in (a game, pastime, etc.). **21.** to contend against in a game. **22.** to employ (a player, etc.) in a game. **23.** to move or throw (an object) in a game: *he played the card reluctantly.* **24.** to use as if in playing a game, as for one's own advantage: *play off one person against another.* **25.** to stake or wager, as in playing. **26.** to lay a wager or wagers on (something). **27.** to represent or imitate in diversion or recreation: *to play school.* **28.** to perform on (a musical instrument). **29.** to perform (music) on an instrument or instruments. **30.** to cause (a record, cassette, CD, DVD, etc.) to produce the sound recorded on it. **31.** to cause (music or other sound) to be produced by a record, cassette, CD or DVD player. **32.** to do, perform, bring about, or execute: *to play tricks.* **33.** to cause to move or change lightly or quickly: *play coloured lights on a fountain.* **34.** to operate, or cause to operate, especially continuously or with repeated action: *to play a hose on a fire.* **35.** to allow (a hooked fish) to exhaust itself by pulling on the line. *–v.i.* **36.** to exercise or employ oneself in diversion, amusement, or recreation. **37.** to do something only in sport, which is not to be taken seriously. **38.** to take part or engage in a game. **39.** to take part in a game for stakes; gamble. **40.** to act, or conduct oneself, in a specified way: *to play fair.* **41.** to act on or as on the stage; perform. **42.** to perform on a musical instrument. **43.** (of the instrument or the music) to sound in performance. **44.** (of a record, cassette, CD, etc.) to reproduce recorded sound. **45.** (of recorded music) to be reproduced. **46.** to move freely, as within a space, as a part of a mechanism. **47.** to move about lightly or quickly. **48.** to present the effect of such motion, as light or the changing colours of an iridescent substance. **49.** to operate continuously or with repeated action, often on something: *the noise played on his nerves.* **50.** to function during play: *the wicket played well at first.* *–phr.* **51.** in play, for amusement; as a joke: *to argue in play.* **52.** play around, *Colloq.* **a.** to behave in a lighthearted or irresponsible manner. **b.** (oft. fol. by *with*) to experiment with something in order to solve a problem, familiarise oneself, or produce a different result. **c.** to be sexually unfaithful to one's partner. **d.** to be sexually promiscuous. **e.** to engage in sexual play or sexual intercourse. **53.** play at, to take part in (a game, hobby, etc.), often without serious attention. **54.** play back, to reproduce (sound, music, vision, etc.) which has just been recorded. **55.** play ball, to cooperate. **56.** play cat and mouse, **a.** to delay the inevitable defeat of an opponent so as to enjoy observing their struggles and discomfiture. **b.** (in racing) to speed up and slow down as a tactic to gain an advantage over the rest of the field. **57.** play down, to minimise the importance of. **58.** play for time, to gain time for one's own purposes by prolonging something unduly. **59.** play into the hands of, to act in such a way as to give an advantage to. **60.** play it by ear, to handle a situation as it arises and without a set plan. **61.** play it close to the chest, to act without confiding in others involved. **62.** play it cool, *Colloq.* to act cautiously. **63.** play off, to play an extra game or round in order to settle a tie. **64.** play on, **a.** *Sport* to continue play. **b.** *Cricket* to hit the ball onto one's own wicket and thus be dismissed. **c.** *Cricket* (of a team) to play a second innings immediately after a bad first innings. **d.** *Aust. Rules* to kick, handball, or run with the ball, without either waiting for the umpire's

decision or going back to take a free kick. **65.** play on (or upon), to work on (the feelings, weaknesses, etc., of another) for one's own purposes: *to play on someone's emotions.* **66.** play out, **a.** (in a game when no result appears possible or one side is convincingly ahead) to play throughout without attempting to score: *to play out time.* **b.** to bring to an end; use up. **67.** play silly buggers, *Colloq.* to act the fool. **68.** play the ball, *Rugby League* to restart the play after being tackled by tapping the ball back with one's foot to the dummy half. **69.** play the field, **a.** to have as many flirtations as possible. **b.** to keep oneself open to advantage from a number of sources. **70.** play the fool, to behave in a foolish or frivolous manner. **71.** play the game, *Colloq.* **a.** to play in accordance with the rules. **b.** to perform one's part. **72.** play through, *Golf* (of a group of players) to catch up to the group of players in front and with their permission pass them and play ahead. **73.** play up, **a.** to behave naughtily or annoyingly. **b.** *Colloq.* to philander. **c.** (of a machine) to malfunction intermittently. **d.** (of a part of the body) to malfunction or cause pain, especially as a result of chronic disease or permanent disability. **74.** play up to, to attempt to get into the favour of. **75.** play with, to amuse oneself or toy with; trifle with. **76.** play with oneself, to masturbate.

playback /ˈpleɪbæk/ *n.* **1.** the reproduction of sound, music, vision, etc., which has just been recorded. *–adj.* **2.** of or relating to a device used in reproducing such a recording: *a hi-fi playback system.*

playboy /ˈpleɪbɔɪ/ *n.* a wealthy, carefree man who spends most of his time at parties, nightclubs, etc.

playdough /ˈpleɪdoʊ/ *n.* (*from trademark*) a soft, non-toxic preparation of coloured dough, designed for children's modelling. Also, **play dough**.

player /ˈpleɪə/ *n.* **1.** someone or something that plays. **2.** someone who takes part or is skilled in some game. **3.** a person engaged in playing a game professionally. **4.** someone who plays parts on the stage; an actor. **5.** someone who plays a musical instrument. **6.** a gambler. **7.** a participant in a business deal, etc. **8.** *Colloq.* a person who is known to have a very active sex life with many different partners.

player piano *n.* → **pianola**.

playful /ˈpleɪfəl/ *adj.* **1.** full of play; sportive; frolicsome. **2.** pleasantly humorous: *a playful remark.* *–playfully, adv.* *–playfulness, n.*

playhouse /ˈpleɪhaʊs/ *n.* **1.** a theatre. **2.** a one-room imitation house built for children to play in.

playing card *n.* **1.** one of the conventional set of 52 cards, in 4 suits (diamonds, hearts, spades, and clubs), used in playing various games of chance and skill. **2.** one of any set or pack of cards used in playing games.

play-off *n. Sport* a game conducted to determine a winner when the normal game or series of games has resulted in a tie. Also, **playoff**.

plaything /ˈpleɪθɪŋ/ *n.* **1.** a thing to play with; a toy. **2.** a person used without consideration for the gratification of another.

playwright /ˈpleɪraɪt/ *n.* a writer of plays; a dramatist.

plaza /ˈplazə/ *n.* a public square or open space in a city or town.

plea /pli/ *n.* **1.** an appeal or entreaty: *a plea for mercy.* **2.** that which is alleged, urged, or pleaded in defence or justification. **3.** an excuse; a pretext. **4.** *Law* **a.** an allegation made by, or on behalf of, a party to a legal suit, in support of his or her claim or defence. **b.** (in courts of equity) a plea which admits the truth of the declaration, but alleges special or new matter in avoidance. **c.** a suit or action at law: *to hold pleas* (to try actions at law).

plea bargaining *n.* the negotiation for an agreement between the prosecution and the defence in a law suit that the accused will face only specified charges or reduced penalties if a plea of guilty is entered.

plead /plid/ *verb* (**pleaded** *or* **plead** /plɛd/ *or*, *Chiefly US*, **pled**, **pleading**) –*v.i.* **1.** to beg; make an appeal. **2.** to use arguments for or against something. **3.** *Law* to make any plea in an action at law. –*v.t.* **4.** to claim in defence or excuse: *to plead ignorance.* **5.** *Law* to present (a cause, etc.) by argument before a court. **–pleadable**, *adj.* **–pleader**, *n.*

pleasant /ˈplɛzənt/ *adj.* **1.** pleasing, agreeable, or affording enjoyment; pleasurable: *pleasant news.* **2.** (of persons, manners, disposition, etc.) agreeable socially. **3.** (of weather, etc.) fair. **4.** jocular or facetious. **–pleasantly**, *adv.* **–pleasantness**, *n.*

pleasantry /ˈplɛzəntri/ *n.* (*pl.* **-ries**) **1.** good-humoured raillery; pleasant humour in conversation. **2.** a humorous or jesting remark or action. **3.** a conventional, polite remark: *they exchanged pleasantries.*

please /pliz/ *v.t.* **1.** to act to the pleasure or satisfaction of: *to please the public.* **2.** to be the pleasure or will of; seem good to: *may it please God.* –*v.i.* **3.** to be agreeable; give pleasure or satisfaction. **4.** to find something agreeable; like, wish or choose: *go where you please.* –*interj.* **5.** (as a polite addition to requests, etc.) if you are willing: *please come here.* –*phr.* **6. if you please, a.** if you like; if it be your pleasure. **b.** an expression indicating surprise or disapproval: *in his pocket, if you please, was the letter.*

pleasurable /ˈplɛʒərəbəl/ *adj.* such as to give pleasure; agreeable; pleasant. **–pleasurableness**, *n.* **–pleasurably**, *adv.*

pleasure /ˈplɛʒə/ *n.* **1.** a condition or feeling of being pleased. **2.** satisfaction to the senses. **3.** a cause of enjoyment. **4.** worldly or silly enjoyment: *the pursuit of pleasure.* **5.** one's desire or choice: *what is your pleasure?* –*v.t.* **6.** to give pleasure, especially sexual or sensual pleasure, to; gratify.

pleat /plit/ *n.* **1.** a fold, usually of definite even width, made by doubling cloth or the like upon itself, and pressing, stitching, or otherwise fastening in place. –*v.t.* **2.** to fold or arrange in pleats. **–pleated**, *adj.*

pleb /plɛb/ *n.* **1.** one of the common people. **2.** *Colloq.* a commonplace or vulgar person. –*adj.* **3.** *Colloq.* vulgar, commonplace.

plebeian /pləˈbiən/ *adj.* **1.** belonging to or relating to the ancient Roman plebs. **2.** belonging to or relating to the common people. **3.** common, commonplace, or vulgar. –*n.* **4.** a member of the Roman plebs. **5.** a plebeian person. **–plebeianism**, *n.*

plebiscite /ˈplɛbəsaɪt, -sət/ *n.* **1.** a direct vote of all the qualified electors in regard to some important issue. **2.** such a vote conducted by a country or state; referendum.

plectrum /ˈplɛktrəm/ *n.* (*pl.* **-trums** *or* **-tra** /-trə/) a small piece of wood, metal, ivory, etc., for plucking strings of a lyre, mandolin, guitar, etc.

pledge /plɛdʒ/ *n.* **1.** a solemn promise; vow. **2.** a piece of personal property given as a security for the payment of a debt. **3.** the condition of being given or held as security: *to put a thing in pledge.* **4.** anything given or seen as a security of something. **5.** a statement of support shown by drinking a person's health; toast. –*v.t.* (**pledged, pledging**) **6.** to bind by or as if by a pledge. **7.** to promise solemnly to give, maintain, etc. **8.** to give or leave as a pledge; pawn. **9.** to vow, as one's honour, etc. **10.** to give a pledge for. **11.** to drink a pledge to. **–pledger**, *n.*

-plegia a word element forming a noun termination in pathological terms denoting forms of paralysis, as in *paraplegia*.

Pleistocene /ˈplaɪstoʊsin/ *adj.*, *n. Geol.* (relating to) the earlier division of the Quaternary period, following the Pliocene and before the Recent; ice age.

plenary /ˈplinəri/ *adj.* **1.** full; complete; entire; absolute; unqualified. **2.** attended by all qualified members, as a council; fully constituted. **3.** (of a conference session) scheduled without parallel sessions, and so likely to be attended by most of those registered as participants, usually to hear a prominent invited speaker. **–plenarily**, *adv.*

plenipotentiary /ˌplɛnəpəˈtɛnʃəri/ *n.* (*pl.* **-ries**) **1.** a person, especially a diplomatic agent, invested with full power or authority to transact business. –*adj.* **2.** invested with full power or authority, as a diplomatic agent. **3.** absolute or full, as power.

plenitude /ˈplɛnətjud, -tʃud/ *n.* fullness in quantity, measure, or degree; abundance.

plenteous /ˈplɛntiəs/ *adj.* **1.** plentiful; copious; abundant: *a plenteous supply of corn.* **2.** yielding abundantly. **–plenteously**, *adv.* **–plenteousness**, *n.*

plentiful /ˈplɛntəfəl/ *adj.* existing in great plenty; abundant. **–plentifully**, *adv.* **–plentifulness**, *n.*

plenty /ˈplɛnti/ *n.* **1.** a full or abundant supply: *there is plenty of time.* **2.** abundance: *resources in plenty.* **3.** a time of abundance. –*adj.* **4.** *Chiefly Colloq.* (*usu. in the predicate*) existing in ample quantity or number: *this is plenty.* –*adv.* **5.** *Colloq.* fully: *plenty good enough.*

plethora /ˈplɛθərə/ *n.* overfullness.

pleur- a word element meaning 'side', 'pleura', or sometimes 'rib'. Also, (*before consonants*), **pleuro-**.

pleura /ˈplʊrə/ *n.* (*pl.* **pleurae** /ˈplʊri/) *Anat.* a delicate membrane enveloping each lung in mammals and folded back as a lining of the corresponding side of the thorax. **–pleural**, *adj.*

pleurisy /ˈplʊrəsi/ *n. Pathol.* inflammation of the pleura, with or without a liquid effusion. **–pleuritic** /plʊˈrɪtɪk/, *adj.*

plexus /ˈplɛksəs/ *n.* (*pl.* **plexuses** *or* **plexus**) a network, as of nerves or blood vessels. **–plexal**, *adj.*

pliable /ˈplaɪəbəl/ *adj.* **1.** easily bent; flexible; supple. **2.** easily influenced; yielding; adaptable. **–pliability** /plaɪəˈbɪləti/, **pliableness**, *n.* **–pliably**, *adv.*

pliant /ˈplaɪənt/ *adj.* **1.** bending readily; flexible; supple. **2.** easily inclined or influenced; yielding; compliant. **–pliancy**, **pliantness**, *n.* **–pliantly**, *adv.*

pliers /ˈplaɪəz/ *pl. n.* small pincers with long jaws, for bending wire, holding small objects, etc.

plight[1] /plaɪt/ *n.* condition, state, or situation (usually bad).

plight[2] /plaɪt/ *v.t.* to give in pledge; pledge (one's honour, etc.). **–plighter**, *n.*

Plimsoll line /ˈplɪmsəl laɪn/ *n.* a line or mark required to be placed on the hull of all British merchant vessels, showing the depth to which they may be submerged through loading. Also, **Plimsoll mark**.

plinth /plɪnθ/ *n. Archit.* **1.** the lower square part of the base of a column. **2.** a square base or a lower block, as of a pedestal. **3.** a course of stones, as at the base of a wall, forming a continuous plinthlike projection. **–plinthlike**, *adj.*

Pliocene /ˈplaɪoʊsin/ *adj.*, *n. Geol.* (relating to) the latest principal division of the Tertiary period, coming after the Miocene, and before the Pleistocene. Also, **Pleiocene**.

plod /plɒd/ *v.i.* (**plodded, plodding**) **1.** to walk heavily; trudge; move laboriously. **2.** to work with dull perseverance; drudge. –*n.* **3.** a sound of or as of a heavy tread. **4.** *Colloq.* a police officer. **–plodder**, *n.* **–plodding**, *adj.* **–ploddingly**, *adv.*

plonk[1] /plɒŋk/ *v.t.* Also, **plonk down**. **1.** to place or drop heavily or suddenly. –*v.i.* Also, **plonk down**. **2.** to drop heavily or suddenly. *–n.* **3.** the act or sound of plonking. *–adv.* **4.** with a plonking sound.

plonk² /plɒŋk/ *n. Colloq.* any alcoholic liquor, especially cheap wine.

plop /plɒp/ *v.i.* (**plopped, plopping**) **1.** to make a sound like that of a flat object striking water without a splash. **2.** to fall plump with such a sound. *–n.* **3.** a plopping sound or fall. **4.** the act of plopping. *–adv.* **5.** with a plop.

plot¹ /plɒt/ *n.* **1.** a secret plan or scheme to act for some purpose, usually unlawful or evil. **2.** the plan, scheme, or main story of a play, novel, poem, etc. *–verb* (**plotted, plotting**) *–v.t.* **3.** to plan secretly (something harmful or evil): *to plot a bank robbery.* **4.** to mark on a plan or map, as a ship's course, etc. **5.** to make a plan or map of, as an area of land, a building, etc. **6.** to determine and mark (points or a curve), as on graph paper. *–v.i.* **7.** to form secret plots; conspire: *to plot behind closed doors.* *–phr.* **8. lose the plot,** *Colloq.* (of a person) to cease to understand fully what is going on in a certain situation, job, etc., and thus fail to act effectively. *–***plotter,** *n.*

plot² /plɒt/ *n.* **1.** a small piece or area of ground: *a garden plot.* *–v.t.* (**plotted, plotting**) **2.** to divide (land) into plots.

plough /plaʊ/ *n.* **1.** an agricultural implement for cutting and turning over the soil. **2.** any of various implements resembling this, as a plane for cutting grooves or a device for snow clearance. *–v.t.* **3.** to make furrows in or turn up (the soil) with a plough. **4.** to make (a furrow, etc.) with a plough. **5.** to furrow, remove, etc., or make (a furrow, groove, etc.) with or as with a plough. **6.** *Naut.* **a.** to cleave the surface of (the water). **b.** to make (a way) or follow (a course) thus. *–v.i.* **7.** to till the soil with a plough; work with a plough. *–phr.* **8. plough back,** to reinvest (profits of a business) in that business. **9. plough into,** to attack energetically; throw oneself into. **10. plough through, a.** to move through in the manner of a plough. **b.** to work at slowly and with perseverance. **c.** to move through (water) by cleaving the surface. **11. the Plough,** a group of seven stars in the constellation of the Great Bear. Also, *Chiefly US,* **plow.** *–***plougher,** *n.*

plover /ˈplʌvə/ *n.* any of various small to medium-sized birds of the family Charadriidae, with a short, straight bill characteristically thickened at the end, and frequenting shores and wet grasslands.

ploy /plɔɪ/ *n.* a manoeuvre or stratagem, as in conversation, to gain the advantage.

pluck /plʌk/ *v.t.* **1.** to pull off or out from the place of growth, as fruit, flowers, feathers, etc. **2.** to give a pull at. **3.** to pull with sudden force or with a jerk. **4.** (sometimes fol. by *away, off, out,* etc.) to pull by force. **5.** to pull off the feathers, hair, etc. from. **6.** *Colloq.* to rob, plunder, or fleece. **7.** to sound (the strings of a musical instrument) by pulling at them with the fingers or a plectrum. *–n.* **8.** the act of plucking; a pull, tug, or jerk. **9.** courage or resolution in the face of difficulties. *–phr.* **10. pluck at, a.** to pull sharply; tug at. **b.** to snatch at. **11. pluck up, a.** to pull up; uproot; eradicate. **b.** to rouse (courage, spirit, etc.). *–***plucker,** *n.*

plucky /ˈplʌki/ *adj.* (**-kier, -kiest**) having or showing pluck or courage; brave. *–***pluckily,** *adv.* *–***pluckiness,** *n.*

plug /plʌg/ *n.* **1.** a piece of rubber or plastic for stopping the flow of water from a basin, bath (def. 3), or sink (def. 29). **2.** a piece of wood or other material used to stop up a hole or aperture, to fill a gap, or to act as a wedge. **3.** *Elect.* **a.** a tapering piece of conducting material designed to be inserted between contact surfaces and so establish connection between elements of an electric current connected to the respective surfaces. **b.** a device, usually with three prongs, which by insertion in a socket establishes contact between an electrical appliance and a power supply. **4.** → **spark plug. 5.** a cake or piece of pressed tobacco. **6.** *Colloq.* the favourable mention of a product or the like on radio, television, etc.; an advertisement, especially unsolicited. *–v.t.* (**plugged, plugging**) **7.** to stop or fill with or as with a plug. **8.** to insert or drive a plug into: *to plug a wall for the hanging of a picture.* **9.** to secure by a plug. **10.** to insert (something) as a plug. **11.** *Colloq.* to mention (a publication, product or the like) favourably and, often, repetitively as in a lecture, radio show, etc. **12.** *Colloq.* to shoot. *–phr.* **13. plug away,** *Colloq.* to work steadily or doggedly. **14. plug in,** to connect (an electrical device) with an outlet. **15. plug on,** *Colloq.* to work steadily or doggedly. *–***plugger,** *n.*

plug-and-play *adj. Computers* of or relating to a computer system which automatically configures certain peripheral devices connected to it, so that they may be used immediately upon being plugged in.

plum /plʌm/ *n.* **1.** the drupaceous fruit of any of various trees of the rosaceous genus *Prunus,* closely related to the cherry but with an oblong stone. **2.** a tree bearing such fruit. **3.** a raisin as in a cake or pudding. **4.** a deep purple varying from bluish to reddish. **5.** a good or choice thing, as one of the best parts of anything, a fine situation or appointment, etc. *–adj.* **6.** *Colloq.* good; choice; excellent.

plumage /ˈpluːmɪdʒ/ *n.* **1.** the entire feathery covering of a bird. **2.** feathers collectively.

plumb /plʌm/ *n.* **1.** a small mass of lead or heavy material, used for various purposes. **2.** the position of a plumbline when freely suspended; the perpendicular. *–adj.* Also, **plum. 3.** true according to a plumbline; perpendicular. **4.** *Colloq.* downright or absolute. *–adv.* Also, **plum. 5.** in a perpendicular or vertical direction. **6.** exactly, precisely, or directly. **7.** *Colloq.* completely or absolutely. *–v.t.* **8.** to test or adjust by a plumbline. **9.** to make vertical. **10.** to sound (the ocean, etc.) with, or as with, a plumbline. **11.** to measure (depth) by sounding. **12.** to sound the depths of, or penetrate to the bottom of. *–v.i.* **13.** *Colloq.* to work as a plumber. *–phr.* **14. out of plumb, a.** not perpendicular. **b.** not functioning properly.

plumbago /plʌmˈbeɪɡoʊ/ *n.* a genus of annual or perennial plants from warm regions, with blue, white, or pink flowers, including the frequently cultivated southern African climbing shrub *Plumbago capensis.*

plumber /ˈplʌmə/ *n.* **1.** someone who installs and repairs piping, fixtures, appliances, and appurtenances in connection with the water supply, drainage systems, etc., both in and out of buildings. **2.** a worker in lead or similar metals.

plumbing /ˈplʌmɪŋ/ *n.* **1.** the system of pipes and other apparatus for conveying water, liquid wastes, etc., as in a building. **2.** the work or trade of a plumber. **3.** the act of someone who plumbs, as in ascertaining depth.

plumbline /ˈplʌmlaɪn/ *n.* a string to one end of which is attached a metal bob, used to determine perpendicularity, find the depth of water, etc.

plume /pluːm/ *n.* **1.** a feather. **2.** any plumose part or formation. **3.** a stream of smoke or vapour issuing from a stack and blown by the wind. **4.** a feather, a tuft of feathers, or some substitute, worn as an ornament on the hat, helmet, etc. **5.** an ornament; a token of honour or distinction. *–v.t.* **6.** to furnish, cover, or adorn with plumes or feathers. **7.** (of a bird) to preen (itself or its feathers). *–phr.* **8. plume oneself,** (sometimes fol. by *onor upon*) to display or feel satisfaction with or pride in oneself. *–***plumy,** *adj.*

plummet /ˈplʌmət/ *n.* **1.** Also, **plumb-bob.** a piece of lead or some other weight attached to a line, used for determining perpendicularity, for sounding, etc.; the bob of a plumbline. **2.** *Angling* an apparatus consisting of a weight attached to a line, used to determine the depth of water. **3.** something that weighs down or depresses. *–v.i.* **4.** to plunge.

plump¹ /plʌmp/ *adj.* **1.** well filled out or rounded in form; somewhat fleshy or fat; chubby. *–phr.* **2. plump up** (or **out**), **a.** to become plump. **b.** to make plump: *to plump the cushion up.* –**plumply,** *adv.* –**plumpness,** *n.*

plump² /plʌmp/ *v.i.* **1.** to fall heavily or suddenly and directly; drop, sink, or come abruptly, or with direct impact. *–v.t.* **2.** to drop or throw heavily or suddenly. *–n.* **3.** a heavy or sudden fall. *–adv.* **4.** with a heavy or sudden fall or drop. **5.** straight. **6.** with direct impact. *–adj.* **7.** direct; downright; blunt. *–phr.* **8. plump for,** to vote exclusively for or choose (one out of a number): *to plump for oil rather than gas heating.*

plunder /'plʌndə/ *v.t.* **1.** to rob by open force, as in war. *–v.i.* **2.** to take plunder. *–n.* **3.** the act of plundering; pillage. **4.** that which is taken in plundering; loot. –**plunderer,** *n.* –**plunderage,** *n.*

plunge /plʌndʒ/ *verb* (**plunged, plunging**) *–v.t.* **1.** to cast or thrust forcibly or suddenly into a liquid, a penetrable substance, a place, etc.; immerse; submerge: *to plunge a dagger into someone's heart.* **2.** to bring into some condition, situation, etc.: *to plunge a country into war.* **3.** to immerse mentally, as in thought. *–v.i.* **4.** to cast oneself, or fall as if cast, into water, a deep place, etc. **5.** to dive headfirst into the water. **6.** to rush or dash with headlong haste: *to plunge through a doorway.* **7.** *Colloq.* to bet or speculate recklessly. **8.** to throw oneself impetuously or abruptly into some condition, situation, matter, etc.: *to plunge into war.* **9.** to descend abruptly or precipitously, as a cliff, a road, etc. **10.** to pitch violently forward, especially with the head downwards, as a horse, ship, etc. *–n.* **11.** the act of plunging. **12.** a leap or dive into water or the like. **13.** a headlong or impetuous rush or dash. **14.** a sudden, violent pitching movement. **15.** *US* a place for plunging or diving, as a swimming pool. *–phr.* **16. take the plunge,** to resolve to do something (usually unpleasant) and to act straightaway.

plunger /'plʌndʒə/ *n.* **1.** *Machinery* a device or a part of a machine which acts with a plunging or thrusting motion; a piston; a ram. **2.** a diver. **3.** *Colloq.* a reckless punter or speculator.

plunk /plʌŋk/ *v.t.* **1.** to pluck (a stringed instrument); twang. **2.** to throw, push, put, etc., heavily or suddenly. **3.** *Colloq.* to shoot at. *–v.i.* **4.** to give forth a twanging sound. **5.** to drop down heavily or suddenly; plump. *–n.* **6.** the act or sound of plunking. **7.** a direct, forcible blow. Also (for defs 2 and 5–7), **plank.**

pluperfect /plu'pɜfəkt/ *Gram.* *–adj.* **1.** perfect with respect to a temporal point of reference in the past. Compare **perfect, imperfect. 2.** designating a tense with such meaning. *–n.* **3.** the pluperfect tense. **4.** a form therein.

plural /'plurəl/ *adj.* **1.** consisting of, containing, or relating to more than one. **2.** relating to or involving a number of people or things. *–n.* **3.** *Gram.* the plural number.

plurality /plu'ræləti/ *n.* (*pl.* **-ties**) **1.** the condition or fact of being plural. **2.** more than half of the whole; the majority. **3.** a number greater than unity or one.

pluri- a word element meaning 'several', 'many'.

plus /plʌs/ *prep.* **1.** more by the addition of: *ten plus two.* *–adj.* **2.** involving or showing addition. **3.** positive: *a plus quantity.* **4.** *Colloq.* with something in addition: *he has energy plus.* **5.** *Bot.* indicating one of the two strains in fungi which must unite in the sexual process. *–n.* (*pl.* **pluses** *or* **plusses**) **6.** the plus sign ($+$). **7.** something additional. **8.** an advantage, asset, or gain.

plush /plʌʃ/ *n.* **1.** a fabric of silk, cotton, wool, etc., having a longer pile than that of velvet. *–adj.* Also, **plushy. 2.** (of a room, furnishings, or the like) luxurious and costly: *a plush hotel suite.*

plush toy *n.* a soft toy made from a plush fabric.

plus size *n.* an extra large clothing size.

plutocracy /plu'tɒkrəsi/ *n.* (*pl.* **-cies**) the rule or power of wealth or of the wealthy. –**plutocrat** /'plutəkræt/, *n.* –**plutocratic** /plutə'krætɪk/, *n.*

plutonium /plu'touniəm/ *n.* *Chem.* a radioactive element, capable of self-maintained explosive fission, formed by deuteron bombardment of neptunium, which is a fissionable isotope of major importance. *Symbol*: Pu; *atomic number*: 94.

pluvial /'pluviəl/ *adj.* **1.** of or relating to rain; rainy. **2.** *Geol.* due to rain.

ply¹ /plaɪ/ *verb* (**plied, plying**) *–v.t.* **1.** to use: *to ply the needle.* **2.** to carry on; practise: *to ply a trade.* **3.** to supply continuously: *to ply a person with drink.* **4.** to cross (a river, etc.), especially regularly. *–v.i.* **5.** to travel regularly over a fixed course: *the ferry plies between the two ports.* **6.** to perform work busily: *to ply with the oars.* **7.** to direct the course, on water or otherwise. **8.** *Naut.* to make way windward by tacking.

ply² /plaɪ/ *n.* (*pl.* **plies**) **1.** a fold; a thickness. **2.** a strand of yarn: *single ply.* **3.** bent, bias, or inclination. *–v.t.* (**plied, plying**) **4.** to bend, fold, or mould.

plywood /'plaɪwʊd/ *n.* a material consisting of an odd number of thin sheets or strips of wood glued together with the grains (usually) at right angles, used in building and cabinetwork.

pneumatic /nju'mætɪk/ *adj.* **1.** of or relating to air, or gases in general. **2.** operated by air, or by pressure of air. –**pneumatically,** *adv.*

pneumo- a word element referring to the lungs or to respiration.

pneumonia /nju'mounjə, njə-/ *n.* inflammation of the lungs.

poach¹ /poʊtʃ/ *v.i.* to take game or fish illegally from another's land. –**poacher,** *n.*

poach² /poʊtʃ/ *v.t.* to simmer in liquid in a shallow pan.

pock /pɒk/ *n.* **1.** a pustule on the body in an eruptive disease, as smallpox. **2.** a mark or spot left by or resembling such a pustule. –**pocked,** *adj.*

pocket /'pɒkət/ *n.* **1.** a small bag inserted in a garment, for carrying a purse or other small articles. **2.** a bag or pouch. **3.** money, means, or financial resources. **4.** any pouch-like receptacle, hollow, or cavity. **5.** a small isolated area: *a pocket of resistance.* **6.** *Mining* **a.** a small body of ore. **b.** an enlargement of a lode or vein. **c.** an irregular cavity containing ore. **d.** a small ore body or mass of ore, frequently isolated. **7.** a cavity in the earth, especially one containing gold or other ore. **8.** *Mining* **a.** a bin for ore or rock storage. **b.** a raise or small stope fitted with chute gates. **9.** a small bag or net at the corner or side of a billiard table. **10.** *Racing* a position in which a contestant is hemmed in by others. **11.** *Aust. Rules* a position to the side of the goals: *the back pocket.* *–adj.* **12.** suitable for carrying in the pocket: *a pocket handkerchief.* **13.** small enough to go in the pocket; diminutive: *a pocket edition of a novel.* *–v.t.* **14.** to put into one's pocket. **15.** to take possession of as one's own, often dishonestly. **16.** to submit to or endure without protest or open resentment. **17.** to conceal or suppress: *to pocket one's anger.* **18.** to enclose or confine as in a pocket. **19.** to drive (a ball) into a pocket, as in billiards. **20.** *US* (of the president or a legislative executive) to retain (a bill) without action on it and thus prevent it from becoming a law. **21.** to hem in (a contestant) so as to impede progress, as in racing. *–phr.* **22. in each other's pockets,** *Colloq.* (of two people) constantly together. **23. in one's pocket,** under one's control. **24. in pocket**, having money or a profit, especially after some transaction. **25. line one's pockets**, to gain, especially financially, at the expense of others. **26. out of pocket, a.** having made a loss, especially after some transaction. **b.** having incurred personal expenditure while working for a company, employer, etc. **27. pocket one's pride** or **put one's pride in one's pocket**, to accept humiliation for the sake of attaining some goal.

pocket-dial *v.t.* (**-dialled** *or, esp. US,* **-dialed, -dialling** *or, esp. US,* **-dialing**) **1.** to unintentionally call (someone) from a mobile phone by accidentally activating the speed-dial function while the phone is in one's pocket, as by sitting down, bumping into something, etc. *n.* **2.** such an unintended call. –**pocket-dialling**, *n.*

pocket money *n.* **1.** a small weekly allowance of money, as given to a child by his or her parents. **2.** money for minor personal expenses or small luxuries.

pod[1] /pɒd/ *n.* **1.** a more or less elongated, two-valved seed vessel, as that of the pea or bean. **2.** a dehiscent fruit or pericarp with several seeds. **3.** *Aeronautics* a streamlined structure suspended under the wing of an aircraft for housing a jet engine, cargo, missiles, or other weapons. **4.** a protective housing for a nuclear reactor. –*verb* (**podded, podding**) –*v.i.* **5.** to produce pods. **6.** to swell out like a pod. –*v.t.* **7.** to remove the shell from.

pod[2] /pɒd/ *n.* a small herd or school, especially of seals or whales.

-pod a word element meaning 'footed', as in *cephalopod.* Compare **-poda**.

-poda plural of **-pod**, as in *Cephalopoda.*

podcast /ˈpɒdkast/ (*from trademark*) –*v.t.* (**-cast** *or* **-casted, -casting**) **1.** to deliver a (radio program) over the internet as a file to be stored and played as required on a computer or MP3 player. –*n.* **2.** such a program. –*adj.* **3.** of or relating to such a program. –**podcasting**, *n., adj.*

poddy /ˈpɒdi/ *n.* (*pl.* **-dies**) Also, **poddy-calf. 1.** a handfed calf. –*adj.* **2.** (of a small animal, especially a lamb or calf) requiring to be handfed.

podiatry /pɒˈdaɪətri/ *n.* the investigation and treatment of foot disorders. –**podiatrist**, *n.*

podium /ˈpoʊdiəm/ *n.* (*pl.* **-diums** *or* **-dia** /-diə/) **1.** a small platform for the conductor of an orchestra, for a public speaker, for the recipients of awards, medals, etc. **2.** *Archit.* **a.** a continuous projecting base of a building forming the front of the basement of the foundation behind it. **b.** a raised platform surrounding the arena of an ancient amphitheatre. **3.** *Zool., Anat.* a foot.

-podous a word element forming an adjective termination, corresponding to **-pod**.

pod slurping *n.* the downloading of large quantities of data to an MP3 player, memory stick, etc., from a computer, especially when done illegally after gaining unauthorised access to a computer. –**pod slurper**, *n.*

podzol /ˈpɒdzɒl/ *n.* a forest soil, notably acidic, infertile and difficult to cultivate, found over vast areas in northern North America and Eurasia and common in eastern Australia. Also, **podsol**. –**podzolic** /pɒdˈzɒlɪk/, *adj.*

poem /ˈpoʊəm/ *n.* **1.** a composition in verse, especially one characterised by artistic construction and imaginative or elevated thought: *a lyric poem.* **2.** a composition which, though not in verse, is characterised by beauty of language or thought: *a prose poem.* **3.** something having qualities suggestive of or likened to those of poetry.

poet /ˈpoʊət/ *n.* **1.** someone who composes poetry. **2.** someone having the gift of poetic thought, imagination, and creation, together with eloquence of expression. –**poetess**, *n.*

poetic /poʊˈɛtɪk/ *adj.* **1.** possessing the qualities or the charm of poetry: *poetic descriptions of nature.* **2.** of or relating to a poet or poets. **3.** endowed with the faculty or feeling of a poet, as a person. **4.** affording a subject for poetry. Also, **poetical**. –**poetically**, *adv.*

poetic licence *n.* licence or liberty taken by a poet in deviating from rule, conventional form, logic, or fact, in order to produce a desired effect.

poet laureate /poʊət ˈlɒriət/ *n.* (*pl.* **poets laureate**) (*sometimes upper case*) (in Britain) a highly esteemed poet, appointed as a lifetime officer of the royal household; formerly expected to write odes, etc., in celebration of court and national events, but now having no special duty.

poetry /ˈpoʊətri/ *n.* **1.** the art of rhythmical composition, written or spoken, for exciting pleasure by beautiful, imaginative, or elevated thoughts. **2.** literary work in metrical form; verse. **3.** something suggestive of or likened to poetry.

po-faced /ˈpoʊ-feɪst/ *adj. Colloq.* expressionless.

pogrom /ˈpɒgrəm/ *n.* an organised massacre, especially of Jews.

pohutukawa /poʊˌhutəˈkawə/ *n.* a small New Zealand tree, *Metrosideros excelsa*, having brilliant red flowers in summer; Christmas tree.

poignant /ˈpɔɪnjənt, ˈpɔɪnənt/ *adj.* **1.** keenly distressing to the mental or physical feelings: *poignant regret, poignant suffering.* **2.** keen or strong in mental appeal: *a subject of poignant interest.* –**poignancy**, *n.* –**poignantly**, *adv.*

poinciana /pɔɪnsiˈanə, -ˈænə/ *n.* **1.** a plant of the genus *Poinciana*, of the warmer parts of the world, comprising trees or shrubs with showy orange or scarlet flowers. **2.** a closely related tree, *Delonix regia*, native to Madagascar but now widely cultivated, remarkable for its showy scarlet flowers.

poinsettia /pɔɪnˈsɛtiə/ *n.* a perennial, *Euphorbia* (*Poinsettia*) *pulcherrima*, native to Mexico and Central America, with variously lobed leaves and brilliant, usually scarlet, bracts.

point /pɔɪnt/ *n.* **1.** a sharp or tapering end, as of a dagger. **2.** projecting part of anything. **3.** something having a sharp or tapering end. **4.** a pointed tool or instrument, as an etching needle. **5.** (*pl.*) *Shearing* the parts of a sheep's fleece which become its edges when shorn in one piece: *stained points should be cut off.* **6.** a mark of punctuation. **7.** → **full stop. 8.** a decimal point, etc. **9.** a diacritical mark indicating a modification of a sound. **10.** one of the embossed dots used in certain systems of writing and printing for the blind. **11.** something that has position but not extension, as the intersection of two lines. **12.** a place of which the position alone is considered; a spot. **13.** any definite position, as in a scale, course, etc.: *the boiling point.* **14. a.** each of the 32 positions indicating direction marked at the circumference of the card of a compass. **b.** the interval of 11°15′ between any two adjacent positions. **15.** a tapering extremity of land, as a cape. **16.** a degree or stage: *frankness to the point of insult.* **17.** a particular instant of time. **18.** critical position in a course of affairs. **19.** a decisive state of circumstances. **20.** the important or essential thing: *the point of the matter.* **21.** an individual argument, in a coherent assemblage of such arguments: *a forceful point.* **22.** the salient feature of a story, epigram, joke, etc. **23.** a particular aim, end, or purpose: *he carried his point.* **24.** (*pl.*) hints or suggestions: *points on getting a job.* **25.** a single or separate article or item, as in an extended whole; a detail or particular. **26.** an individual part or element of something: *noble points in her character.* **27.** the darker markings at the ears, legs and tails, especially of a Siamese cat but of some other breeds also: *red point*; *chocolate point*. **28.** a distinguishing mark or quality, especially one of an animal, used as a standard in stockbreeding, etc. **29.** → **blocked shoe**. **30.** a single unit, as in counting, measuring rations allowed, etc. **31.** a unit of count in the score of a game. **32.** *Cricket* **a.** the position of the fielder who stands a short distance in front and to the offside of the person batting. **b.** the player in this position. **33.** *Aust. Rules* → **behind** (def. 12). **34.** *Hunting* the position taken by a pointer or setter when it finds game. **35.** *Elect.* **a.** either of a pair of contacts tipped with tungsten or platinum that makes or breaks current flow in a distributor in a car. **b.** → **power point**. **36.** *Commerce* a unit of price quotation in share transactions on the stock exchange: *copper advanced two points yesterday.* **37.** *Mil.* **a.** the stroke in bayonet drill or battle. **b.** a patrol or reconnaissance unit that goes ahead of the advance party of an advance guard, or follows the rear party of the rearguard. **c.** a target which requires the accurate placement of bombs or fire. **38.** *Printing* a unit of measurement equal to 0.351×10^{-3} m, or $\frac{1}{72}$ inch, or 0.35 millimetres. **39.** a unit of measurement of rainfall in the imperial system, equal to one hundredth of an inch or 0.254×10^{-3} m. **40.** a weight of measurement for precious stones, equal to one hundredth of a carat. **41.** (*usu. pl.*) *Railways* a device for shifting moving trains, etc., from one track to another, commonly consisting of a pair of movable rails. **42.** the act of pointing. –*v.t.* **43.** to direct (the finger, a weapon, the attention, etc.) at, to, or upon something. **44. a.** to mark with one or more points, dots, or the like. **b.** to mark (psalms) with signs indicating how they are to be chanted. **45.** *Hunting* (of a pointer or setter) to indicate (game) by standing rigid, with the muzzle usually directed towards it. **46.** to fill the joints of (brickwork, etc.) with mortar or cement, smoothed with the point of the trowel. –*v.i.* **47.** to indicate position or direction, or direct attention, with or as with the finger. **48.** to direct the mind or thought in some direction: *everything points to his guilt.* **49.** to have a tendency, as towards something. **50.** to have a specified direction. **51.** to face in a particular direction, as a building. **52.** *Hunting* (of a pointer or setter) to point game. –*phr.* **53. beside the point**, not relevant. **54. give points to**, to acknowledge the value of; praise. **55. in point**, pertinent; relevant: *the case in point.* **56. in point of**, as regards: *in point of fact.* **57. make a point**, to express a personal opinion, or offer some particular item of information which supports a personal opinion or position. **58. make a point of**, to consider as important; insist upon; do expressly. **59. off the point**, not relevant. **60. on points**, (of a ballerina wearing blocked shoes) dancing on the toes. **61. on** (or **upon**) **the point of**, close to; on the verge of. **62. point out**, **a.** to indicate the presence or position of, as with the finger. **b.** to direct attention to. **63. point to**, (of a website) to link to (another online location). **64. point up**, to highlight. **65. stretch a point**, to go beyond the usual limits. **66. to the point**, pertinent; relevant. **67. up to a point**, not completely. –**pointless**, *adj.*

point-blank *adj.* **1.** aimed or fired straight at the mark at close range; direct. **2.** straightforward, plain, or explicit. –*adv.* **3.** with a direct aim at close range; directly; straight. **4.** bluntly.

pointed /'pɔɪntəd/ *adj.* **1.** having a point or points: *a pointed arch.* **2.** sharp or piercing: *pointed wit.* **3.** having point or force: *pointed comment.* **4.** directed; aimed. **5.** marked; emphasised. –**pointedly**, *adv.* –**pointedness**, *n.*

pointer /'pɔɪntə/ *n.* **1.** a long, tapering stick used by teachers, lecturers, etc., in pointing things out on a map, blackboard, or the like. **2.** the hand on a watch, machine, or instrument. **3.** one of a breed of short-haired

hunting dogs trained to point game. **4.** a hint or suggestion; piece of advice.

pointy /'pɔɪnti/ *adj.* (**-tier**, **-tiest**) **1.** being pointed at the end: *pointy shoes*; *a pointy nose.* –*phr.* **2. at the pointy end**, at the moment of engagement or crisis.

pointy-head *n. Colloq.* (*derog.*) an expert in some field, considered to be limited in broader understanding or vision; boffin; intellectual. –**pointy-headed**, *adj.*

poise /pɔɪz/ *n.* **1.** a state of balance, as from equality or equal spreading of weight. **2.** self-possession, confidence and grace of manner. –*verb* (**poised**, **poising**) –*v.t.* **3.** to balance evenly. **4.** to hold supported or raised in readiness: *to poise a spear.* –*v.i.* **5.** to be balanced.

poised /pɔɪzd/ *adj.* **1.** self-possessed; self-assured; confident; dignified. **2.** in a state of balance or equilibrium. **3.** wavering. **4.** hovering; suspended.

poison /'pɔɪzən/ *n.* **1.** any substance which causes death or illness. **2.** anything harmful to character, happiness, wellbeing, etc.: *her remarks spread poison.* –*v.t.* **3.** to give poison to. **4.** to influence as poison does: *jealousy poisoned her thoughts.* **5.** to put poison into or upon: *to poison food.* –*adj.* **6.** containing poison: *a poison dart.* –**poisonous**, *adj.* –**poisonously**, *adv.*

poisoned chalice *n.* a prized position, situation, award, etc., which immediately presents serious difficulties for the person or people who have attained it: *the poisoned chalice of a difficult health portfolio.*

poison-pen *adj.* of or relating to a letter, note, etc., usually anonymous, and sent with malicious intent.

poke[1] /poʊk/ *v.t.* **1.** to thrust against or into (something) with the finger or arm, a stick, etc.; prod: *to poke a person in the ribs.* **2.** to make (a hole, one's way, etc.) by or as by thrusting. **3.** to thrust or push: *she poked her head through the door.* **4.** to force or drive (*away*, *in*, *out*, etc.) by or as by thrusting or pushing. **5.** to thrust obtrusively. **6.** *Colloq.* (*taboo*) (of a man) to have sexual intercourse with. –*v.i.* **7.** to make a thrusting or pushing movement with the finger, a stick, etc. **8.** to thrust oneself obtrusively. –*n.* **9.** a thrust or push. **10.** *Colloq.* a blow with the fist. **11.** *Colloq. (taboo)* an act of sexual intercourse. –*phr.* **12. more than one can poke a stick at**, *Colloq.* a lot of; many; much. **13. poke about** (or **around**), to pry; search curiously. **14. poke fun at**, *Colloq.* to ridicule, laugh at: *she poked fun at his tie.* **15. poke one's nose into**, to interfere in; pry into; show too much curiosity about. **16. poke out**, to extend or project; protrude. **17. take a poke at**, *Colloq.* **a.** to aim a blow at. **b.** to make a joke at the expense of.

poke[2] /poʊk/ *n.* **1.** *Obs.* a bag or sack. **2.** *Archaic* a pocket. –*phr.* **3. a pig in a poke**, something purchased without inspection.

poker[1] /'poʊkə/ *n.* a metal rod for poking or stirring a fire.

poker[2] /'poʊkə/ *n.* a card game played by two or more persons, in which the players bet on the value of their hands, the winner taking the pool.

poker machine *n.* a coin-operated gambling machine, with images such as playing cards, pictures of fruit, etc., on a set of (usually three or four) wheels which are set in motion by pressing a button or pulling a lever, the score depending on the combination of symbols visible when the wheels come to rest. Also, **fruit machine**, **slot machine**.

pokey[1] /'poʊki/ *n. Colloq.* → **jail**.

pokey[2] /'poʊki/ *n.* → **pokie**.

pokey[3] /'poʊki/ *adj.* → **poky**.

pokie /'poʊkiz/ *n.* (*pl.* **-kies**) *Colloq.* a poker machine. Also, **pokey**.

poky /'poʊki/ *adj.* (**-kier**, **-kiest**) (of a place) small and cramped. Also, **pokey**.

polar /'poʊlə/ *adj.* **1.** of or relating to a pole, as of the earth, a magnet, an electric cell, etc. **2.** opposite in character or action. **3.** *Chem.* existing as ions; ionised, as the crystals of sodium chloride. **4.** central. **5.** analogous to the Pole Star as a guide; guiding.

polar bear *n.* a large white bear, *Ursus maritimus*, of the arctic regions.

polar circles *pl. n.* the Arctic and Antarctic circles.

polarisation /ˌpoʊləraɪˈzeɪʃən/ *n.* **1.** *Optics* a state, or the production of a state, in which rays of light, or similar radiation, exhibit different properties in different directions, as when they are passed through a crystal of tourmaline, which transmits rays in which the vibrations are confined to a single plane. **2.** *Elect.* the process by which gases produced during electrolysis are deposited on the electrodes of a cell. **3.** *Chem.* the separation of a molecule into positive and negative ions. **4.** the production or acquisition of polarity. Also, **polarization.**

polarise /ˈpoʊləraɪz/ *v.t.* **1.** to cause polarisation in. **2.** to give polarity to. –*v.i.* **3.** to become polarised. Also, **polarize.** –**polarisable,** *adj.* –**polariser,** *n.*

polarity /poʊˈlærəti/ *n.* (*pl.* -**ties**) **1.** *Physics* **a.** the possession of an axis with reference to which certain physical properties are determined; the possession of two poles. **b.** the power or tendency of a magnetised bar, etc., to orientate itself along the lines of force. **c.** positive or negative polar condition. **2.** the possession or exhibition of two opposite or contrasted principles or tendencies.

polaroid /ˈpoʊlərɔɪd/ *n.* (*from trademark*) a material which polarises light and allows only light polarised in a particular direction to pass.

polaroid camera *n.* (*from trademark*) a type of camera which takes instant, self-developing pictures.

pole[1] /poʊl/ *n.* **1.** a long, rounded, usually slender piece of wood, metal, etc. **2.** the long tapering piece of wood extending from the front axle of a vehicle, between the animals drawing it. **3.** *Naut.* a light spar. **4.** a unit of length in the imperial system equal to 16½ ft or 5.0292 m; a rod. **5.** a square rod, 30¼ sq. yds or 25.29 m². **6.** the lane of a race track nearest the inner boundary. **7.** → **ski pole** (def. 1). –*v.t.* **8.** to push, strike, propel, etc., with a pole. –*v.i.* **9.** to propel a boat, etc., with a pole. –*phr.* **10. pitch pole,** *Naut.* to turn over end on end. **11. pole on,** *Aust.*, *NZ Colloq.* to impose on by loafing or cadging. **12. under bare poles,** *Naut.* (of a sailing ship) having all sails furled. **13. up the pole,** *Colloq.* **a.** in a predicament. **b.** slightly mad. **c.** completely wrong.

pole[2] /poʊl/ *n.* **1.** each of the extremities of the axis of the earth or of any more or less spherical body. **2.** each of the two points in which the extended axis of the earth cuts the celestial sphere, about which the stars seem to revolve (**celestial pole**). **3.** *Physics* each of the two regions or parts of a magnet, electric battery, etc., at which certain opposite forces are manifested or appear to be concentrated. **4.** one of two completely opposed or contrasted principles, tendencies, etc. –*phr.* **5. poles apart,** having completely opposite or widely divergent views, interests, etc.

poleaxe /ˈpoʊlæks/ *n.* **1.** an axe, usually with a hammer opposite the cutting edge, used in felling or stunning animals. –*v.t.* (-**axed, -axing**) **2.** to fell with or as with a poleaxe. Also, *US,* **poleax.**

polecat /ˈpoʊlkæt/ *n.* **1.** a European mammal, *Mustela putorius*, of the weasel family, having blackish brown fur, and giving off an offensive smell. **2.** any of various North American skunks.

polemic /pəˈlɛmɪk/ *n.* **1.** a controversial argument; argumentation against some opinion, doctrine, etc. **2.** someone who argues in opposition to another; a controversialist. –*adj.* Also, **polemical. 3.** of or relating

to disputation or controversy; controversial. –**polemically,** *adv.* –**polemics,** *n.*

police /pəˈlis/ *n.* (*construed as pl.*) **1. the,** an organised civil force for maintaining order, preventing and detecting crime, and enforcing the laws. **2.** the members of such a force: *after the explosion police were everywhere.* **3.** a body of people employed privately to keep order, enforce regulations, etc.: *on his estates he had his own police.* –*v.t.* (-**liced, -licing**) **4.** to regulate, control, or keep in order by police. **5.** to oversee, checking correct adherence to regulations: *council officers will police the new building code.*

police state *n.* a country in which the police, especially the secret police, are used to detect and suppress any form of opposition to the government in power.

policy[1] /ˈpɒləsi/ *n.* (*pl.* -**cies**) **1.** a definite course of action adopted as expedient or from other considerations: *a business policy.* **2.** a course or line of action adopted and pursued by a government, ruler, political party, or the like: *the foreign policy of a country.* **3.** prudence, practical wisdom, or expediency.

policy[2] /ˈpɒləsi/ *n.* (*pl.* -**cies**) a document embodying a contract of insurance.

polio /ˈpoʊlioʊ/ *n.* → **poliomyelitis.**

poliomyelitis /ˌpoʊlioʊmaɪəˈlaɪtəs/ *n. Pathol.* an acute viral disease, most common in infants but often attacking older children and even adults, characterised by inflammation of the nerve cells, mainly of the anterior horns of the spinal cord, and resulting in motor paralysis, followed by muscular atrophy, and often by permanent deformities; infantile paralysis.

-polis a word element meaning 'city', as in *metropolis* (literally, mother city).

polish /ˈpɒlɪʃ/ *v.t.* **1.** to make smooth and glossy, especially by friction: *to polish metal.* **2.** to render finished, refined, or elegant: *his speech needs polishing.* –*v.i.* **3.** to become smooth and glossy; take on a polish. –*n.* **4.** a substance used to give smoothness or gloss: *shoe polish.* **5.** the act of polishing. **6.** the state of being polished. **7.** smoothness and gloss of surface. **8.** superior or elegant finish imparted; refinement; elegance: *the polish of literary style.* –*phr.* **9. polish off, a.** to finish, or dispose of quickly: *to polish off an opponent.* **b.** *Colloq.* to kill; eliminate. **10. polish up,** to improve. –**polisher,** *n.*

polite /pəˈlaɪt/ *adj.* **1.** showing good manners towards others, as in behaviour, speech, etc.; courteous; civil: *a polite reply.* **2.** refined or cultured: *polite society.* –**politely,** *adv.* –**politeness,** *n.*

politic /ˈpɒlətɪk/ *adj.* **1.** sagacious; prudent. **2.** shrewd; artful. –**politicly,** *adv.*

political /pəˈlɪtɪkəl/ *adj.* **1.** relating to or dealing with the science or art of politics: *political writers.* **2.** of or relating to the governing of a nation, state, municipality, etc.: *political measures.* **3.** exercising or seeking power in the governmental or public affairs of a nation, state, municipality, or the like: *a political party.* **4.** relating to or connected with a political party, or its principles, aims, activities, etc.: *a political campaign.* **5.** affecting or involving the state of government: *a political offence.* **6.** engaged in or connected with civil administration: *political office.* **7.** having a definite policy or system of government: *a political community.* **8.** *Colloq.* interested in politics: *Sheila is not political.* –**politically,** *adv.*

political asylum *n.* asylum (def. 3) provided by a foreign country for someone fleeing political persecution in their own country.

political correctness *n.* conformity to current beliefs about correctness in language and behaviour, especially with regard to policies on sexism, racism, ageism, etc.

politically correct *adj.* of, relating to or demonstrating political correctness. Also, **PC**.

politics /ˈpɒlətɪks/ *n.* (*treated as sing. or pl.*) **1.** the science or art of government. **2.** political affairs, activities, or methods. **3.** political principles or opinions. **4.** the methods used to gain power or advancement within any organisation. **5.** tactical manoeuvring to gain advancement or favour within the internal structure of an organisation. **–politician,** *n.*

polity /ˈpɒləti/ *n.* (*pl.* **-ties**) **1.** a particular form or system of government (civil, ecclesiastical, or other). **2.** the condition of being constituted as a state or other organised community or body. **3.** government or administrative regulation. **4.** a state or other organised community or body.

polka /ˈpɒlkə/ *n.* **1.** a lively round dance of Bohemian origin, with music in duple time. **2.** a piece of music for such a dance or in its rhythm. *–v.i.* (**-kaed, -kaing**) **3.** to dance the polka.

polka dot *n.* **1.** a dot or round spot (printed, woven, or embroidered) repeated to form a pattern on a textile fabric. **2.** a pattern of, or a fabric with such dots.

poll /poʊl/ *n.* **1.** the registering of votes, as at an election. **2.** the voting at an election. **3.** the number of votes cast. **4.** an enumeration or a list of individuals, as for purposes of taxing or voting. **5.** (*usu. pl.*) the place where votes are taken. **6.** an analysis of public opinion on a subject, usually by selective sampling. **7.** the head, especially the part of it on which the hair grows. *–v.t.* **8.** to receive at the polls, as votes. **9.** to enrol in a list or register, as for purposes of taxing or voting. **10.** to take or register the votes of, as persons. **11.** to deposit or cast at the polls, as a vote. **12.** to cut off or cut short the hair, etc., of (a person, etc.); crop; clip; shear. **13.** to cut off the top of (a tree, etc.); pollard. **14.** to cut off or cut short the horns of (cattle). *–v.i.* **15.** to vote at the polls; give one's vote. *–adj.* **16.** (of cattle) bred to have no horns. *–phr.* **17. go to the polls, a.** to call an election, especially as a means of resolving a political issue. **b.** to vote at an election. **–pollable,** *adj.*

pollard /ˈpɒləd/ *n.* **1.** a tree cut back nearly to the trunk, so as to produce a dense mass of branches. **2.** an animal, as a stag, ox, or sheep, without horns. **3.** a by-product of the process of the milling of wheat, used especially for feeding domestic fowls. *–v.t.* **4.** to convert into a pollard.

pollen /ˈpɒlən/ *n.* **1.** *Bot.* the fertilising element of flowering plants, consisting of fine, powdery, yellowish grains or spores, sometimes in masses. *–v.t.* **2.** to pollinate. **–polliniferous** /pɒləˈnɪfərəs/, *adj.*

pollen count *n.* a measure of pollen in the air published as a guide to sufferers from hay fever.

pollinate /ˈpɒləneɪt/ *v.t.* to convey pollen for fertilisation to; shed pollen on. **–pollinator,** *n.* **–pollination** /pɒləˈneɪʃən/, *n.*

polling booth *n.* **1.** a small cubicle with a writing bench provided for a voter at elections, especially to ensure privacy. **2.** a place, often a school, town hall, etc., where voters go to record their votes in an election. Also, **booth**.

pollute /pəˈlut/ *v.t.* **1.** to make foul or unclean; dirty. **2.** to make morally unclean; defile. **3.** to render ceremonially impure; desecrate. **–pollutant,** *n.* **–polluter,** *n.* **–pollution,** *n.*

polo /ˈpoʊloʊ/ *n.* **1.** a game resembling hockey, played on horseback with long-handled mallets and a wooden ball. **2.** some game more or less resembling this, as water polo. **–poloist,** *n.*

polony /pəˈloʊni/ *n. Aust.* a large, mild-flavoured, pre-cooked sausage, usually sliced thinly and eaten cold; devon; fritz; luncheon sausage; Strasburg.

polo shirt *n.* a short-sleeved top, similar to a T-shirt, but having a collar and buttoned placket.

poltergeist /ˈpɒltəɡaɪst/ *n.* a ghost or spirit which manifests its presence by noises, knockings, movement of physical objects, etc.

poltroon /pɒlˈtrun/ *n.* a wretched coward; a craven.

poly- a word element or prefix, meaning 'much', 'many', first occurring in words from the Greek (as *polyandrous*), but now used freely as a general formative, especially in scientific or technical words. Compare **mono-**.

polyandry /pɒliˈændri/ *n.* the practice or the condition of having more than one husband at one time.

polycarbonate /pɒliˈkabəneɪt/ *n.* a strong, transparent thermoplastic resin, used to make shatterproof glass, lightweight spectacle lenses, etc.

polyester /ˈpɒliɛstə/ *n.* a synthetic polymer in which the structural units are linked by ester groups, formed by condensing carboxylic acids with alcohols.

polygamy /pəˈlɪɡəmi/ *n.* the practice or condition of having more than one spouse at one time.

polyglot /ˈpɒliɡlɒt/ *adj.* **1.** (of a person) knowing many or several languages. **2.** (of a book) written in several languages. *–n.* **3.** a polyglot person. **4.** a book, especially a Bible, containing the same text in several languages.

polygon /ˈpɒliɡon, -ɡən/ *n. Geom.* a closed, plane figure having three or more sides and angles. **–polygonal** /pəˈlɪɡənəl/, *adj.* **–polygonally** /pəˈlɪɡənəli/, *adv.*

polygyny /pəˈlɪdʒəni/ *n.* **1.** the practice or the condition of having more than one wife at one time. **2.** *Zool.* the habit or condition of mating with more than one female.

polyhedron /pɒliˈhidrən/ *n.* (*pl.* **-drons** *or* **-dra** /-drə/) *Geom.* a solid figure having many faces.

polymath /ˈpɒlimæθ/ *n.* a person of great and varied learning. **–polymathic,** *adj.*

polymer /ˈpɒləmə/ *n. Chem.* a compound of high molecular weight derived either by the combination of many smaller molecules or by the condensation of many smaller molecules eliminating water, alcohol, etc. **–polymerise, polymerize,** *v.* **–polymerisation,** *n.*

polyp /ˈpɒləp/ *n.* **1.** *Zool.* **a.** a sedentary type of animal form characterised by a more or less fixed base, columnar body, and free end with mouth and tentacles, especially as applied to coelenterates. **b.** an individual zooid of a compound or colonial organism. **2.** *Pathol.* a projecting growth from a mucous surface, being either a tumour or a hypertrophy of the mucous membrane.

polyphonic ringtone /pɒlifɒnɪk ˈrɪŋtoʊn/ *n.* a ringtone for a mobile phone which has the capacity to play multiple tones and to emulate different musical instruments. Also, **polyphonic**.

polysaccharide /pɒliˈsækəraɪd, -rəd/ *n. Chem.* a carbohydrate, as starch, cellulose, etc., containing more than three monosaccharide units per molecule, the units being attached to each other, and therefore capable of hydrolysis by acids or enzymes to monosaccharides.

polysemy /pəˈlɪsəmi/ *n. Ling.* the acquisition and retention of many meanings by one word, as in the case of the word *tank* which referred to a receptacle for liquids and then additionally to a military vehicle. **–polysemous,** *adj.*

polystyrene /pɒliˈstaɪrin/ *n.* a clear, plastic polymer of styrene, easily coloured and moulded, and used as a foam for insulation and packing.

polysyllabic /ˌpɒlisəˈlæbɪk/ *adj.* **1.** consisting of many, or more than three, syllables, as a word. **2.** characterised by such words, as language, etc. Also, **polysyllabical**.

polytheism /ˈpɒliθiˌɪzəm/ *n.* the doctrine of, or belief in, many gods or more gods than one. **–polytheist,** *n.* **–polytheistic** /ˌpɒliθiˈɪstɪk/, *adj.*

polythene /'pɒlɪθiɪn/ n. a plastic polymer of ethylene used for containers, electrical insulation, packaging, etc. Also, **polyethylene**.

polyunsaturated /ˌpɒliʌn'sætʃəreɪtəd/ adj. **1.** Chem. of or relating to a fat or oil based on fatty acids which have two or more double bonds per molecule. **2.** of or relating to food based on polyunsaturated oil or fat, as safflower oil, etc., or margarine.

polyurethane /pɒli'jʊərəθeɪn/ n. a class of synthetic materials made from a polymer of urethane; used in foam form as lightweight insulation and packing, but also produced as fibres, coatings, and in a flexible form for diaphragms and seals.

polyvinyl chloride /pɒli.vaɪnəl 'klɔraɪd/ n. a colourless thermoplastic resin, produced by the polymerisation of vinyl chloride, with good resistance to water, acids, and alkalis, used in a wide variety of manufactured products, including rain wear, garden hoses, gramophone records, and floor tiles. Abbrev.: PVC

Pom /pɒm/ n. Aust., NZ Colloq. (sometimes derog., racist) (also lower case) a person who is resident in or has migrated from the British Isles, especially England. Also, **Pommy**.

pomander /pə'mændə/ n. **1.** a mixture of aromatic substances, often in the form of a ball, formerly carried on the person for perfume or as a guard against infection. **2.** the container in which it is carried.

pomegranate /'pɒməgrænət/ n. **1.** a several-chambered, many-seeded, globose fruit of medium size, with a tough rind (usually red) and surmounted by a crown of calyx lobes, the edible portion consisting of pleasantly acid flesh developed from the outer seed coat. **2.** the shrub or small tree, Punica granatum, which yields it, native to south-western Asia but widely cultivated in warm regions.

pommel /'pʌməl, 'pɒməl/ n. Also, **pummel. 1.** a terminating knob, as on the top of a tower, hilt of a sword, etc. **2.** the protuberant part at the front and top of a saddle. –v.t. (**pommelled** or, US, **pommeled, pommelling** or, US, **pommeling**) **3.** → **pummel**.

Pommy /'pɒmi/ (also lower case) Aust., NZ Colloq. (sometimes derog., racist) –adj. **1.** British, especially English. –n. (pl. **-mies**) **2.** → **Pom**. Also, **Pommie**.

pomp /pɒmp/ n. **1.** stately or splendid display; splendour; magnificence. **2.** ostentatious or vain display, especially of dignity or importance. –phr. **3. pomp and circumstance**, ceremonial show.

pompom /'pɒmpɒm/ n. **1.** an ornamental tuft or ball of feathers, wool, or the like, used in millinery, etc. **2.** a tuft of wool or the like worn on a shako, a sailor's cap, etc. **3.** Hort. a form of small, globe-shaped flower head that characterises a class or type of various flowering plants, especially chrysanthemums and dahlias. Also, **pompon**.

pompous /'pɒmpəs/ adj. **1.** characterised by an ostentatious parade of dignity or importance: a pompous bow. **2.** (of language, style, etc.) ostentatiously lofty. –**pompously**, adv. –**pomposity** /pɒm'pɒsəti/, **pompousness**, n.

ponce /pɒns/ Colloq. –n. **1.** → **pimp**. –v.i. (**ponced, poncing**) **2.** to act as a pimp. –phr. **3. all ponced up**, effeminately overdressed; dandified. **4. ponce about**, to flounce; behave in a foolishly effeminate fashion. –**poncy**, adj.

poncho /'pɒntʃoʊ/ n. (pl. **-chos**) a blanket-like cloak with a hole in the centre for the head.

pond /pɒnd/ n. a body of water smaller than a lake, often one artificially formed.

ponder /'pɒndə/ v.i. **1.** to consider deeply; meditate. –v.t. **2.** to weigh carefully in the mind, or consider carefully.

ponderable /'pɒndərəbəl/ adj. capable of being weighed; having appreciable weight. –**ponderability** /pɒndərə'bɪləti/, n.

ponderous /'pɒndərəs, -drəs/ adj. **1.** of great weight; heavy; massive: a ponderous mass of iron. **2.** without graceful lightness or ease; dull: a ponderous dissertation. –**ponderously**, adv. –**ponderousness, ponderosity** /pɒndə'rɒsəti/, n.

pondweed /'pɒndwid/ n. any of the aquatic plants constituting the genus Potamogeton, most of which grow in ponds and quiet streams.

pong /pɒŋ/ Colloq. –n. **1.** a stink; unpleasant smell. –v.i. **2.** to stink.

ponga /'pɒŋə/ n. → **silver fern** (def. 1).

pontiff /'pɒntɪf/ n. **1.** a high or chief priest. **2.** Eccles. **a.** bishop. **b.** the bishop of Rome (the pope).

pontificate n. /pɒn'tɪfəkət/ **1.** the office, or term of office, of a pontiff. –v.i. /pɒn'tɪfəkeɪt/ **2.** to speak in a pompous manner. **3.** to serve as a pontiff or bishop, especially in a Pontifical Mass. –**pontifical**, adj. –**pontification**, n.

pontoon¹ /pɒn'tun/ n. **1.** a boat, or some other floating structure, used as one of the supports for a temporary bridge over a river. **2.** a floating construction serving as a temporary dock or a floating bridge. **3.** a watertight box or cylinder used in raising a submerged vessel, etc. **4.** a seaplane float. Also, **ponton** /'pɒntən/.

pontoon² /pɒn'tun/ n. a gambling game, the object of which is to obtain from the dealer cards whose total values add up to, or nearly add up to, 21, but do not exceed it; twenty-one; blackjack.

pony /'poʊni/ n. (pl. **-nies**) **1.** a horse of a small type, usually not more than 13 or 14 hands high. **2.** a small glass for beer or spirits.

ponytail /'poʊniteɪl/ n. a hairstyle in which the hair is drawn back tightly and tied at the back of the head and then hangs loose.

poo /pu/ Colloq. –n. Also, **pooh. 1.** faeces –v.i. **2.** to defecate. –v.t. **3.** to soil with excrement: the baby has pooed his pants. –interj. **4.** → **pooh** (defs 1 and 2). –phr. **5. do a poo**, to defecate. **6. in the poo**, (sometimes fol. by with) in trouble or bad favour.

pooch /putʃ/ n. Colloq. a dog.

poodle /'pudl/ n. one of a breed of intelligent pet dogs, of several varieties, with thick curly hair often trimmed in an elaborate manner.

poofter /'puftə/ n. Colloq. (often derog.) a male homosexual. Also, **poof**.
Usage: This word is generally derogatory but can be used within the gay community without being offensive.

pooh /pu/ interj. **1.** an exclamation of disdain or contempt. **2.** an exclamation indicating revulsion, especially from an unpleasant smell. –n. **3.** Colloq. → **poo**.

pool¹ /pul/ n. **1.** a small body of standing water; pond. **2.** a puddle. **3.** any small collection of liquid on a surface: a pool of blood. **4.** a still, deep place in a stream. **5.** a swimming pool.

pool² /pul/ n. **1.** an association of competitors who agree to control the production, market, and price of a commodity for mutual benefit, although they appear to be rivals. **2.** Chiefly US Finance a combination of persons to manipulate one or more securities. **3.** a combination of interests, funds, etc., for common advantage. **4.** the combined interests or funds. **5.** a facility or service that is shared by a number of people: a typing pool. **6.** the persons or parties involved. **7.** the stakes in certain games. **8.** Also, **pocket billiards**. any of various games played on a billiard table in which the object is to drive all the balls into the pockets with the cue ball. **9.** the total amount staked by a combination of betters, as on a race, to be awarded to the successful better or betters.

10. the combination of such betters. *–v.t.* **11.** to put (interests, money, etc.) into a pool, or common stock or fund, as for a financial venture, according to agreement. **12.** to form a pool of. **13.** to make a common interest of. *–v.i.* **14.** to enter into or form a pool. *–phr.* **15. dirty pool**, *Colloq.* dishonest, unethical, or improper practices.

poop[1] /pup/ *n.* **1.** the enclosed space in the aftermost part of a ship, above the main deck. *–v.t.* **2.** (of a wave) to break over the stern of (a ship).

poop[2] /pup/ *v.t. Colloq.* to tire or exhaust.

poop[3] /pup/ *n. Colloq.* excrement.

poor /pɔ/ *adj.* **1.** having little or nothing in the way of wealth, goods, or means of subsistence. **2.** (of a country, institution, etc.) meagrely supplied or endowed with resources or funds. **3.** (of the circumstances, life, home, dress, etc.) characterised by or showing poverty. **4.** faulty or inferior, as in construction. **5.** deficient in desirable ingredients, qualities, or the like: *poor soil.* **6. a.** deficient or lacking in something specified: *poor in minerals.* **b.** (*placed after the noun*) lacking a specified item: *mineral poor; nutrient poor; information poor.* **7.** lean or emaciated, as cattle. **8.** of an inferior, inadequate, or unsatisfactory kind; not good: *poor health.* **9.** deficient in aptitude or ability: *a poor cook.* **10.** deficient in moral excellence; cowardly, abject, or mean. **11.** scanty, meagre, or paltry in amount or number: *a poor pittance.* **12.** humble: *deign to visit our poor house.* **13.** hapless; to be pitied: *oh! the poor devil!* *–phr.* **14. poor man's ...**, considered a cheaper or lower quality alternative: *poor man's champagne.* **15. the poor**, poor persons collectively. **–poorness**, *n.*

poorly /ˈpɔli/ *adv.* **1.** in a poor manner or way. *–adj.* **2.** in poor health; somewhat ill.

pop[1] /pɒp/ *verb* (**popped, popping**) *–v.i.* **1.** to make a short, quick, explosive sound or report: *the cork popped.* **2.** to burst open with such a sound, as chestnuts or corn in roasting. **3.** to come or go (*in, into, out,* etc.) quickly, suddenly or unexpectedly. **4.** (of the ears) to adjust to a sudden change in air pressure. *–v.t.* **5.** to cause to make a sudden, explosive sound. **6.** to cause to burst open with such a sound, as a blister, balloon, champagne bottle, etc. **7.** to put or thrust quickly, suddenly or unexpectedly. **8.** to force air into the Eustachian tubes so as to adjust the pressure on the eardrums of the ears). **9.** *Colloq.* to take (a pill or recreational drug) orally. **10.** *Colloq.* to fire (a gun, etc.). **11.** Also, **pop off.** *Colloq.* to shoot (a target). **12.** *Colloq.* to pawn. *–n.* **13.** a short, quick, explosive sound. **14.** a popping. **15.** *Colloq.* a shot with a firearm. **16.** *Colloq.* an attempt: *to have a pop at something.* **17.** an effervescent beverage, especially a non-alcoholic one. *–adv.* **18.** with a pop or explosive sound. **19.** quickly, suddenly, or unexpectedly. *–phr. Colloq.* **20. a pop**, each: *they cost five dollars a pop.* **21. pop off, a.** to depart, especially abruptly. **b.** to die, especially suddenly. **22. pop the question**, to propose marriage. **23. pop up**, to appear suddenly: *he disappeared for a while and then three years later popped up in Hong Kong.*

pop[2] /pɒp/ *adj.* **1.** denoting or relating to a type of commercial modern music with wide popular appeal, especially among the young, and usually being tuneful, repetitive and having an insistent rhythmic beat. **2.** denoting or relating to a singer or player of such music. *–n.* **3.** pop music.

pop[3] /pɒp/ *n. Colloq.* father, or grandfather.

pop art *n.* modern art, including painting, sculpture, serigraphy, and collage, which rejects any distinction between good and bad taste, and which draws images and materials from popular culture and industry, especially mass production. **–pop artist**, *n.*

popcorn /ˈpɒpkɔn/ *n.* any of several varieties of maize whose kernels burst open and puff out when subjected to dry heat.

pope /poʊp/ *n.* **1.** (*oft. upper case*) the bishop of Rome as head of the Roman Catholic Church. **2.** someone who is considered to have, or has assumed, a supreme position in some field.

poplar /ˈpɒplə/ *n.* **1.** any of various rapidly growing trees constituting the genus *Populus*, yielding a useful, light, soft wood, as *P. nivra* var. *italica* (**Lombardy poplar**), a tall tree of striking columnar or spire-shaped outline due to the fastigiate habit of its branches. **2.** the wood itself. **3.** the wood of any such tree.

poplin /ˈpɒplən/ *n.* a strong, finely ribbed, mercerised cotton material, used for dresses, blouses, children's wear, etc.

poppet /ˈpɒpət/ *n.* **1.** Also, **poppet valve**. a valve which in opening is lifted bodily from its seat instead of being hinged at one side. **2.** *Naut.* a piece of shaped wood fitted to close up the slot cut in a boat's gunwale and top strake for shipping an oar. **3.** a term of endearment for a girl or child.

poppy /ˈpɒpi/ *n.* (*pl.* **-pies**) any plant of the family Papaveraceae, especially species of the genus *Papaver*, comprising herbs with showy flowers of various colours, as *P. somniferum*, the source of opium.

poppycock /ˈpɒpikɒk/ *n. Colloq.* nonsense; bosh.

populace /ˈpɒpjələs/ *n.* the inhabitants of an area; population.

popular /ˈpɒpjələ/ *adj.* **1.** regarded with favour or approval by associates, acquaintances, the general public, etc.: *a popular preacher.* **2.** of, relating to, or representing the people, or the common people: *popular discontent.* **3.** adapted to the ordinary intelligence or taste: *popular lectures on science.* **4.** suited to the means of ordinary people: *popular prices.* **–popularly**, *adv.* **–popularity**, *n.*

popular culture *n.* **1.** the collective ideas and attitudes of a given community as reflected in mainstream art, film, internet memes, etc., of a popular nature. **2.** such ideas and attitudes evident in Western culture generally. Also, **pop culture**.

populate /ˈpɒpjəleɪt/ *v.t.* **1.** to inhabit. **2.** to furnish with inhabitants, as by colonisation; people. **3.** *Computers* to enter (data) into: *to populate the database with client details.*

population /pɒpjəˈleɪʃən/ *n.* **1.** (the total number of) people living in a country, town, or any area. **2.** the number or body of inhabitants of a particular people or class in a place. **3.** *Statistics* the sum total of a defined group of events, objects, etc.

populist /ˈpɒpjələst/ *n.* **1.** a political advocate of the needs of the common people. *–adj.* **2.** of or for the common people.

populous /ˈpɒpjələs/ *adj.* full of people or inhabitants, as a region; well populated.

pop-up *adj.* **1.** equipped with a pop-up mechanism: *a pop-up card.* **2.** (of a shop, restaurant, bar, etc.) operating for a brief period only, often for a specific short-term marketing or advertising purpose; guerilla.

pop-up menu *n. Computers* a computer menu which comes up on the screen to provide the user with a list of options, even while a program is still running. Compare **pull-down menu**.

porcelain /ˈpɔsələn, ˈpɔslən/ *n.* a vitreous, more or less translucent, ceramic material; china.

porch /pɔtʃ/ *n.* an exterior appendage to a building, forming a covered approach or vestibule to a doorway.

porcine /ˈpɔsaɪn/ *adj.* **1.** relating to or resembling swine. **2.** swinish, hoggish, or piggish.

porcini mushroom /pɔtʃini ˈmʌʃrum/ *n.* an Italian mushroom, usually dried, with an intense flavour.

porcupine /'pɔkjəpaɪn/ n. any of various rodents covered with stout, erectile spines or quills, as the **crested porcupine**, *Hystrix cristata*, of southern Europe and northern Africa, with long spines, and the common porcupine of North America, *Erethizon dorsatum*, with short spines or quills partially concealed by the fur.

pore¹ /pɔ/ phr. **1. pore on** (or **over**), to gaze earnestly or steadily at. **2. pore over**, to read or study with steady attention or application.

pore² /pɔ/ n. **1.** a minute opening or orifice, as in the skin or a leaf, for perspiration, absorption, etc. **2.** a minute interstice in a rock, etc. **–poriferous** /pɔ'rɪfərəs/, *adj.*

pork /pɔk/ n. the flesh of pigs used as food.

pork barrel n. *Colloq.* a government appropriation, bill, or policy which supplies funds for local improvements designed to ingratiate legislators with their constituents. **–pork-barrelling**, n.

pork belly n. a cut of meat from the belly of a pig, often boneless, cooked as a slab or sliced in various dishes.

pornography /pɔ'nɒɡrəfi/ n. obscene literature, art, or photography, designed to excite sexual desire. **–pornographic** /pɔnə'ɡræfɪk/, *adj.*

porous /'pɔrəs/ adj. **1.** full of pores. **2.** permeable by water, air, or the like. **3.** allowing easy passage in and out: *porous borders.* **–porosity** /pɔ'rɒsəti/, **porousness**, n.

porphyry /'pɔfəri/ n. (pl. **-ries**) **1.** any igneous rock containing conspicuous phenocrysts in a fine-grained or aphanitic groundmass. **2.** a very hard rock, quarried in ancient Egypt, having a dark, purplish red groundmass containing small crystals of feldspar. **–porphyritic** /pɔfə'rɪtɪk/, *adj.*

porpoise /'pɔpəs/ n. (pl. **-poises** or, especially collectively, **-poise**) **1.** any of several small, gregarious cetaceans of the genus *Phocoena*, usually blackish above and paler underneath, and with a blunt, rounded snout, esp. the common porpoise, *P. phocoena*, of the North Atlantic and the Pacific. **2. → dolphin** (def. 1).

porridge /'pɒrɪdʒ/ n. a breakfast dish, originating in Scotland, consisting of oatmeal or the like with water or milk.

port¹ /pɔt/ n. **1.** a town or place where ships load or unload. **2.** a place along the coast where ships may take refuge from storms. **3.** *Law* any place where persons and merchandise are allowed to pass (by water, land, or air) into and out of a country and where customs officers are stationed to inspect or appraise imported goods; port of entry.

port² /pɔt/ n. the left-hand side of a ship or aircraft facing forward (opposed to *starboard*); larboard.

port³ /pɔt/ n. **1.** any of a class of very sweet, fortified wines, mostly dark red, made in Portugal. **2.** (in unofficial use) a similar wine made elsewhere.

port⁴ /pɔt/ n. **1.** *Naut.* a porthole. **2.** a steel door in the side of a ship for loading and discharging cargo and baggage. **3.** *Machinery* an aperture in the surface of a cylinder, for the passage of steam, air, water, etc. **4.** *Elect.* a point in a circuit where an external connection is made. **5.** *Computers* an interface to which a peripheral device can be connected. **6.** the curved mouthpiece of certain bits (**bit¹** def. 1).

port⁵ /pɔt/ v.t. **1.** *Mil.* to carry (a rifle, etc.) with both hands, in a slanting direction across the front of the body with the barrel or like part near the left shoulder. **2.** to carry (something). –n. **3.** *Mil.* the position of a rifle or other weapon when ported. **4.** manner of bearing oneself; carriage or bearing.

port⁶ /pɔt/ n. *Aust.* a portmanteau; suitcase.

portable /'pɔtəbəl/ adj. **1.** capable of being transported or conveyed. **2.** easily carried or conveyed by hand. **3.** (of benefits, superannuation, etc.) capable of being transferred with a change in job, especially from one department of the public service to another. **4.** *Computers* (of a program or application) easily moved from one type of computer or operating system to another. –n. **5.** something that is portable. **–portability** /pɔtə-'bɪləti/, n.

portal /'pɔtl/ n. **1.** a door, gate, or entrance, especially one of imposing appearance, as in a palace. **2. → web portal**.

portal site n. **→ web portal**.

portcullis /pɔt'kʌləs/ n. a strong grating, as of iron, made to slide in vertical grooves at the sides of a gateway of a fortified place, and let down to prevent passage.

portend /pɔ'tɛnd/ v.t. to indicate beforehand, or presage, as an omen does.

portent /'pɔtɛnt/ n. **1.** an indication or omen of something about to happen, especially something momentous. **2.** ominous significance: *an occurrence of dire portent.* **3.** a prodigy or marvel.

porter¹ /'pɔtə/ n. someone employed to carry burdens or luggage, as at a railway station, hotel, etc.

porter² /'pɔtə/ n. someone who has charge of a door or gate; a doorkeeper; a janitor.

porter³ /'pɔtə/ n. a heavy, dark brown beer made with malt browned by drying at a high temperature.

portfolio /pɔt'fouliou/ n. (pl. **-lios**) **1.** a portable case for loose papers, prints, etc. **2.** such a case for carrying documents of a state department. **3.** *Govt* **a.** the office or post of a minister of state or member of a cabinet. **b.** the public service department or departments for which a minister is responsible. **4.** an itemised account or list of financial assets, as securities, shares, discount paper, etc., of an investment organisation, bank, or other investor. **5.** a collection of an artist's drawings, photographs, etc., which may be shown to prospective employers, etc., as examples of their work. **6.** the collection of a student's best work stored in a folder or the like, for them to look at throughout the year and for parents to look at throughout the year.

porthole /'pɔthoʊl/ n. *Naut.* a usually circular aperture in the side of a ship, for admitting light and air.

portico /'pɔtəkoʊ/ n. (pl. **-coes** or **-cos**) *Archit.* a structure consisting of a roof supported by columns or piers, forming the entrance to a temple, church, house, etc.

portion /'pɔʃən/ n. **1.** a part of any whole, whether actually separated from it or not: *a portion of the manuscript is illegible.* **2.** the part of a whole allotted to or belonging to a person or group; a share. **3.** a quantity of food served for one person. **4.** the part of an estate that goes to an heir or next of kin. **5.** the money, goods, or estate which a woman brings to her husband at marriage; a dowry. **6.** that which is allotted to a person by God or fate. –v.t. **7.** to furnish with a portion, inheritance, or dowry. **8.** to provide with a lot or fate. –phr. **9. portion out**, to divide into or distribute in portions or shares; parcel out. **–portionless**, *adj.*

portly /'pɔtli/ adj. (**-lier**, **-liest**) **1.** large in person; stout; corpulent. **2.** stately, dignified, or imposing. **–portliness**, n.

portmanteau /pɔt'mæntoʊ/ n. (pl. **-teaus** or **-teaux**) a case or bag to carry clothing, etc., while travelling, especially a leather case which opens into two halves.

portrait /'pɔtrət/, *Chiefly Brit.* /'pɔtreɪt/ n. **1.** a likeness of a person, especially of the face, usually made from life. **2.** a spoken or written description, usually of a person. **–portraitist**, n.

portray /pɔ'treɪ/ v.t. **1.** to represent by a drawing, painting, carving, or the like. **2.** to represent dramatically, as on the stage. **3.** to depict in words; describe graphically. **–portrayable**, adj. **–portrayer**, n. **–portrayal**, n.

Portuguese man-of-war /pɔtʃə,ɡiz mæn-əv-'wɔ/ n. **1.** *Brit.*, *US* a bluebottle (def. 1) **2. → jellyfish**.

port wine magnolia *n.* → **magnolia** (def. 2).

pose /poʊz/ *v.i.* **1.** to act as a particular character, usually with a view to the impression made on others. **2.** to pretend to be something or someone. **3.** (in modelling) to hold a position or attitude. *–v.t.* **4.** to place in a suitable position or attitude for a picture, etc.: *the photographer will pose the group.* **5.** to state or put forward for consideration: *the refugees pose a hard problem.* **6.** to present: *the fire poses a threat to nearby residents.* *–n.* **7.** a position held by the body. **8.** a position taken in thought or conduct. **9.** a pretence of being some character or having some quality or feeling which is completely false: *his generosity is a pose.* **–poser,** *n.*

poser /ˈpoʊzə/ *n.* **1.** someone who poses. **2.** → **poseur. 3.** a puzzling question or problem.

poseur /poʊˈzɜ/ *n.* someone who affects a particular **pose** (def. 8) to impress others.

posh /pɒʃ/ *Colloq.* *–adj.* **1.** elegant; luxurious; smart; first-class. **2.** having or affecting the speech, dress, and manners thought to be typical of an upper class. *–phr.* **3. posh up,** to make smart or elegant. **–poshly,** *adv.* **–poshness,** *n.*

posit /ˈpɒzət/ *v.t.* **1.** to place, put, or set. **2.** to lay down or assume as a fact or principle; affirm; postulate.

position /pəˈzɪʃən/ *n.* **1.** a place; location. **2.** proper place: *out of position.* **3.** condition, especially in some particular state; situation: *he is in an awkward position.* **4.** rank or standing. **5.** high standing in society. **6.** a post of employment: *a position in a bank.* **7.** the manner of being placed or arranged. **8.** a way of viewing a matter; stand: *our position on this question.* *–v.t.* **9.** to put in a particular position; place. **10.** to determine the position of; locate. **–positional,** *adj.*

positive /ˈpɒzətɪv/ *adj.* **1.** actually laid down or expressed: *a positive declaration.* **2.** admitting of no question: *positive proof.* **3.** stated; express; emphatic. **4.** (of a person) sure in opinion or statement. **5.** overconfident. **6.** without relation to or comparison with other things; absolute (opposed to *relative* and *comparative*). **7.** *Colloq.* downright; out-and-out. **8.** possessing an actual force, being, existence, etc. **9.** *Philos.* based on matters of experience: *positive philosophy.* **10.** practical; not theoretical. **11.** marked by hopefulness: *a positive attitude.* **12.** consisting in or marked by the presence of definite or marked qualities (opposed to *negative*): *light is positive, darkness negative.* **13.** proceeding in a direction assumed as that of increase, progress, or onward motion. **14.** *Elect.* relating to the kind of electricity developed on glass when rubbed with silk, or the kind of electricity present at that pole where electrons enter, or return to. **15.** *Chem.* (of a radical) having fewer electrons than the neutral atom or molecule and so being positively charged. **16.** *Chem.* → **electropositive. 17.** *Photography* (of a print from a negative) showing the lights and shades as seen in the original. **18.** *Gram.* relating to the first degree of the comparison of adjectives and adverbs, as English *smooth* in contrast to *smoother* and *smoothest.* **19.** *Maths* indicating a quantity greater than zero. **20.** *Biol.* moving towards the point of excitation: *a positive tropism.* **21.** (of blood, affected tissue, etc.) showing the presence of an organism which causes a disease. *–n.* **22.** something positive, as a quality, characteristic, quantity, etc. **23.** a positive quantity or symbol. **24.** *Photography* a positive picture. **25.** *Gram.* (a form in) the positive degree. **–positively,** *adv.* **–positiveness,** *n.* **–positivism,** *n.*

positive discrimination *n.* discrimination which works actively to favour a previously disadvantaged group in society, or to further the interests of one group of people as opposed to another.

positron /ˈpɒzətrɒn/ *n.* *Physics* an elementary particle with positive charge and mass equal to that of the electron; the antiparticle corresponding to the electron. **–positronic,** *adj.*

posse /ˈpɒsi/ *n.* *Chiefly US* → **posse comitatus.**

posse comitatus /pɒsi kɒməˈtatəs/ *n.* *Law* **1.** the body of citizens that a sheriff is empowered to call to assist in preserving the peace, making arrests, and serving writs. **2.** a body of citizens so called into service.

possess /pəˈzɛs/ *v.t.* **1.** to have belonging to oneself. **2.** to have, as a quality or the like: *to possess courage.* **3.** to keep control over (oneself, one's mind, etc.). **4.** (of a spirit, feeling or idea) to take over and control (a person). **5.** (of a man) to have sexual relations with. **6.** *Archaic* to seize or take. **–possessor,** *n.* **–possessorship,** *n.*

possessed /pəˈzɛst/ *adj.* **1.** (sometimes fol. by *by* or *with*) moved by a strong feeling, madness, or some supernatural agency; frenzied: *possessed by rage.* **2.** self-possessed; calm; poised. *–phr.* **3. possessed of,** having; possessing: *possessed of beauty; possessed of the facts.*

possession /pəˈzɛʃən/ *n.* **1.** the act of possessing or being possessed. **2.** ownership. **3.** *Law* actual holding or occupancy, either with or without rights of ownership. **4.** a thing possessed. **5.** (*pl.*) property or wealth. **6.** control over oneself, one's mind, etc. **7.** control by a feeling, idea, etc. **8.** (in certain ball sports) control of the ball by a player or team during play

possessive /pəˈzɛsɪv/ *adj.* **1.** of or relating to possession or ownership. **2.** exerting or seeking to exert excessive influence on the affections, behaviour, etc., of others: *a possessive wife.* **3.** *Gram.* **a.** indicating possession, ownership, origin, etc. **b.** denoting a case that indicates possession, ownership, origin, etc. *–n.* *Gram.* **4.** the possessive case. **5.** a form in the possessive. **–possessively,** *adv.* **–possessiveness,** *n.*

possessive adjective *n.* *Gram.* the adjectival form of a possessive pronoun, as *my, his, her, our,* etc.

possessive pronoun *n.* *Gram.* the possessive case of a personal pronoun, as *mine, his, hers, ours,* etc.

possible /ˈpɒsəbəl/ *adj.* **1.** capable of existing, happening, being done, being used, etc.: *no possible cure.* **2.** that may be true or a fact, or may perhaps be the case, as something concerning which one has no knowledge to the contrary: *it is possible that he went.* **–possibility,** *n.* **–possibly,** *adv.*

possie /ˈpɒzi/ *n.* *Colloq.* a place; position. Also, **possy, pozzie, pozzy.**

possum /ˈpɒsəm/ *n.* **1.** Also, *Obs.,* **opossum.** any of many herbivorous, largely arboreal, Australian marsupials of the superfamily Phalangeroidea, especially of the genera *Trichosurus, Pseudochirus* and *Petaurus,* ranging in size from the mouse-like **pygmy possum** to the cat-sized **brush-tailed possum,** having both pairs of limbs well-developed for climbing and grasping, and a long, often prehensile, tail. **2.** *Aust. Colloq.* a more or less affectionate term for a person: *come along, possums; what a cheeky possum.* *–v.i.* **3.** to go hunting possums: *possuming in the moonlight.* *–phr.* *Colloq.* **4. like a possum up a gum tree,** *Aust.* happy; content to be in an unassailable position: *you'll be like a possum up a gum tree when the money arrives.* **5. play possum,** to dissemble; feign illness or death. **6. stir the possum,** *Aust.* to instigate a debate on a controversial topic, especially in the public arena.

post¹ /poʊst/ *n.* **1.** a strong piece of timber, metal, or the like, set upright as a support, etc. **2.** *Horseracing* a pole on a racecourse marking the starting or finishing points for races. *–v.t.* **3.** to fix (a notice, etc.) to a post, wall, etc. **4.** to bring to public attention with a notice: *we must post a reward.* **5.** to enter (the name of) in a published list. **6.** *Sport* to achieve (an official score) in a game, competition, etc.

post² /poʊst/ *n.* **1.** a position of duty, employment, or trust to which one is assigned or appointed: *a diplomatic post.* **2.** the station, or round of a soldier, sentry, or other person on duty. **3.** a military station with permanent buildings. **4.** *Mil.* either of two bugle calls (**first post** and **last post**) giving notice of the hour for retiring, as for the night. –*v.t.* **5.** to station at a post or place as a sentry or for some other purpose. **6.** *Mil.* to transfer away to another unit or command.

post³ /poʊst/ *n.* **1.** a single delivery of letters, packages, etc. **2.** the letters, packages, etc., themselves; mail. **3.** an established service for the carrying of letters, etc., especially under government authority. **4.** → **post office**. **5.** *Internet* a single message in a forum or on a message board. –*v.t.* **6.** to place (a letter, etc.) in a post-box, post office, etc., for sending. **7.** *Bookkeeping* **a.** to transfer (an entry or item) to the ledger. **b.** to make all the necessary entries in (the ledger, etc.). **8.** to supply with up-to-date information; inform: *please keep me posted about any developments.* **9.** *Internet* to send (a message) electronically to a mailing list or newsgroup on the internet. –*phr.* **10. keep someone posted**, to keep someone informed by constant updates, especially of events which occur in a sequence. –**postal**, *adj.*

post⁴ /poʊst/ *n.* an examination held after the main examination for those who were absent from the first one or whose result in the first needs confirmation by a second.

post- a prefix meaning 'behind', 'after', occurring originally in words from the Latin, but now freely used as an English formative: *post-Elizabethan, postfix, postgraduate.* Compare **ante-, pre-**.

postage /ˈpoʊstɪdʒ/ *n.* the charge for the conveyance of a letter or other matter sent by post, usually prepaid by means of a stamp or stamps.

postal note *n.* an order for the payment of a small amount of money, bought from and generally cashed at a post office. Compare **money order**. Also, **postal order**.

postbox /ˈpoʊst-bɒks/ *n.* a letterbox (def. 1), especially one on a public thoroughfare.

postcard /ˈpoʊstkad/ *n.* a card of standard size, often having a photograph, picture, etc., on one side, on which a message may be written and sent by post.

postcode /ˈpoʊstkoʊd/ *n.* a group of numbers or letters added as part of the address and intended to facilitate the delivery of mail.

postcolonial /poʊstkəˈloʊniəl/ *adj.* **1.** of or relating to a period following colonialism: *postcolonial nationalism.* **2.** of or relating to postcolonialism: *postcolonial literature.*

postcolonialism /poʊstkəˈloʊniəlɪzəm/ *n.* **1.** an attitude of mind typical of those who have experienced colonial rule. **2.** a philosophical, literary, or artistic theory that frames subjects in the context of the cultural aftermath of colonial rule. –**postcolonialist**, *adj.*

postdate /poʊstˈdeɪt/ *v.t.* **1.** to date (a document, cheque, invoice, etc.) with a date later than the current date. **2.** to follow in time.

poster /ˈpoʊstə/ *n.* **1.** a large placard or bill, often incorporating photographs or illustrations, and posted for advertisement or publicity or for decorative purposes. **2.** Also, **newsposter**. a sheet of paper advertising the headlines of the day, used for display by vendors of newspapers. **3.** → **billposter**.

poster child *n.* (*pl.* **poster children**) **1.** a child who is regarded as a focus of some community sentiment or aspiration, especially one with appealing looks used for advertising for donations. **2.** any person, organisation,

or entity, regarded as representative of a cause, development, etc.

poste restante /poʊst rəsˈtɒnt/ *n.* a department in a post office where letters may be kept until they are called for.

posterior /pɒsˈtɪəriə/ *adj.* **1.** situated behind; hinder (opposed to *anterior*). **2.** (sometimes fol. by *to*) coming after in time; later; subsequent. **3.** *Zool.* of or relating to the caudal end of the body. **4.** *Anat.* of or relating to the dorsal side of humans. –*n.* the hinder parts of the body; the buttocks. –**posteriorly**, *adv.* –**posteriority**, *n.*

posterity /pɒˈstɛrəti/ *n.* succeeding generations collectively.

postern /ˈpɒstən/ *n.* a back door or gate.

postgraduate /poʊstˈɡrædʒuət/ *n.* **1.** someone studying at a university for a higher degree. –*adj.* **2.** of or relating to courses of study offered for a higher degree. Also, **post-graduate**.

posthaste /poʊstˈheɪst/ *adv.* with all possible speed or promptness: *to come posthaste.*

posthumous /ˈpɒstʃəməs/ *adj.* **1.** (of books, music, medals, etc.) published or awarded after a person's death. **2.** born after the death of the father. **3.** arising, existing, or continuing after one's death. –**posthumously**, *adv.*

posting /ˈpoʊstɪŋ/ *n.* an appointment to a new position, usually in another location, formerly especially in the armed services and to an overseas country.

postman /ˈpoʊstmən/ *n.* (*pl.* **-men**) a male postal employee who sorts and delivers letters and parcels, or collects letters from post-boxes.

postmark /ˈpoʊstmak/ *n.* an official mark stamped on letters or other mail, to cancel the postage stamp, indicate the place and date of sending or of receipt, etc. –*v.t.* to stamp with a postmark.

postmodern /poʊstˈmɒdn/ *adj.* of or relating to postmodernism. Also, **post-modern**.

postmodernism /poʊstˈmɒdənɪzəm/ *n.* any of a number of trends in art or literature which developed in the 1970s as a reaction to the idea of modernism with its emphasis on individual expression, progressing through a sequence of styles. Also, **Postmodernism, post-modernism**. –**postmodernist**, *adj., n.*

post-mortem /poʊst-ˈmɔtəm/ *adj.* **1.** subsequent to death: *post-mortem injuries.* –*n.* **2.** a post-mortem examination; autopsy. **3.** an examination of the causes of failure of a plan, project, or the like. **4.** an evaluation of a party, concert, holiday, etc., after the event. Also, **postmortem**.

postnatal /poʊstˈneɪtl/ *adj.* occurring after birth.

postnatal depression *n. Psychiatry* a severe depression, often long-lasting, sometimes experienced by women after childbirth. *Abbrev.*: PND

post-obit /poʊst-ˈoʊbət, -ˈbət/ *adj.* effective after a particular person's death.

post office *n.* **1.** the authority responsible for a country's postal and telecommunications services. **2.** a local office of this authority for receiving, distributing, and transmitting mail, selling postage stamps, providing telecommunications services, etc. –**post-office**, *adj.*

post-op /ˈpoʊst-ɒp/ *Med.* –*adj.* **1.** of or relating to the period or the procedures immediately following an operation. –*n.* **2.** → **recovery ward**.

postpone /poʊstˈpoʊn, poʊsˈpoʊn/ *v.t.* **1.** to put off to a later time; defer: *he postponed his departure an hour.* **2.** to place after in order of importance or estimation; subordinate: *to postpone private ambitions to the public welfare.* –**postponable**, *adj.* –**postponement**, *n.* –**postponer**, *n.*

postscript /ˈpoʊstskrɪpt/ *n.* **1.** a paragraph, sentence, etc., added to a letter which has already been concluded and signed by the writer. *Abbrev.*: PS **2.** any supplementary part.

postulant /'pɒstʃələnt/ *n.* **1.** someone who asks or applies for something. **2.** a candidate, especially for admission into a religious order. **–postulancy**, *n.*

postulate *v.t.* /'pɒstʃəleɪt/ **1.** to ask, demand, or claim. **2.** to claim or take for granted the existence or truth of, especially as a basis for reasoning. **3.** *Geom.* to take as an axiom. *–n.* /'pɒstʃələt/ **4.** something taken to be the case, without proof as a basis for reasoning, or as self-evident. **–postulation**, *n.*

posture /'pɒstʃə/ *n.* **1.** the position of the body and limbs as a whole: *a sitting posture.* **2.** an unnatural attitude or position of the body. **3.** mental or spiritual attitude. **4.** a position, condition, or state, especially of affairs. *–v.t.* **5.** to place in a particular posture or attitude. *–v.i.* **6.** to take on a particular posture, often for a special effect or for show. **–postural**, *adj.* **–posturer**, *n.*

postvention *n.* a mental health intervention designed to support the friends and family of a person who has committed suicide, since they themselves may be at risk as a consequence.

posy /'poʊzi/ *n.* (*pl.* **-sies**) a nosegay or bouquet.

pot /pɒt/ *n.* **1.** an earthen, metallic, or other container, usually round and deep, used for domestic or other purposes. **2.** such a vessel with its contents. **3.** a potful of liquor. **4.** a wicker vessel for trapping fish or crustaceans. **5.** *Colloq.* a large sum of money. **6.** the aggregate of bets at stake at one time, as in card games, especially poker. **7.** → **pot shot**. **8.** a medium sized beer glass; middy. **9.** *Colloq.* → **pot belly**. **10.** a chamberpot; potty. **11.** *Colloq.* a trophy or prize in a contest, especially a silver cup. **12.** (*pl.*) *Colloq.* a large quantity. **13.** *Colloq.* marijuana. *–verb* (**potted**, **potting**) *–v.t.* **14.** to put into a pot. **15.** to preserve (food) in a pot. **16.** to cook in a pot. **17.** to plant in a pot of soil. **18.** *Hunting* **a.** to shoot (game birds) on the ground or water, or (game animals) at rest, instead of in flight or running. **b.** to shoot for food, not for sport. **19.** *Colloq.* to capture, secure, or win. **20.** *Billiards* to pocket. *–phr.* **21.** to make pots, as a potter does. *–phr.* **22. go to pot**, to deteriorate.

potable /'poʊtəbəl/ *adj.* **1.** fit or suitable for drinking. *–n.* **2.** (*usu. pl.*) anything drinkable. **–potability**, *n.*

potash /'pɒtæʃ/ *n.* **1.** potassium carbonate, especially the crude impure form obtained from wood ashes. **2.** the oxide of potassium, K₂O. **3.** potassium: *carbonate of potash.*

potassium /pə'tæsiəm/ *n.* a silvery-white metallic element, which oxidises rapidly in the air, and whose compounds are used as fertiliser and in special hard glasses. *Symbol*: K; *relative atomic mass*: 39.102; *atomic number*: 19; *density*: 0.86 at 20°C. **–potassic**, *adj.*

potassium nitrate *n.* a crystalline compound, KNO₃, used in gunpowder, fertilisers, preservatives, etc., and produced by nitrification in soil; saltpetre.

potato /pə'teɪtoʊ/ *n.* (*pl.* **-toes**) **1.** the edible tuber (**white potato** or **Irish potato**) of a cultivated plant, *Solanum tuberosum.* **2.** the plant itself.

pot belly *n.* (*pl.* **-lies**) a distended or protuberant belly. **–pot-bellied**, *adj.*

potch /pɒtʃ/ *n.* an opal which may have colour, but lacks the fine play of colour which distinguishes gem-quality opal; it is commonly the matrix stone in which precious opal is found.

potent /'poʊtnt/ *adj.* **1.** powerful; mighty. **2.** (of reasons, etc.) forceful. **3.** (of a drug) producing powerful physical or chemical effects. **4.** possessed of great power or authority. **5.** exercising great influence on a person. **6.** having sexual power. **–potently**, *adv.* **–potency**, **potence**, **potentness**, *n.*

potentate /'poʊtnteɪt/ *n.* someone who possesses great power; a sovereign, monarch, or ruler.

potential /pə'tɛnʃəl/ *adj.* **1.** possible as opposed to actual. **2.** able to be or become; latent. *–n.* **3.** *Physics* → **potential energy**. **4.** possibility. **5.** Also, **electric potential**. a measure of the potential energy at a point of an electric charge relative to its potential energy at some other reference point, such as the earth (which is seen to have zero potential). **–potentially**, *adv.* **–potentiality** /pətɛnʃi'æləti/, *n.*

potential energy *n.* *Physics* energy which is due to position rather than motion, as a coiled spring or a raised weight (opposed to *kinetic energy*).

potentiate /pə'tɛnʃieɪt/ *v.t.* to increase the effect or potency of, especially by working in conjunction with: *a drug potentiated by alcohol.* **–potentiation**, *n.* **–potentiator**, *n.*

pothole /'pɒthoʊl/ *n.* **1.** a deep hole; a pit. **2.** a hole in the surface of a road. **3.** a more or less cylindrical hole formed in rock by the grinding action of the detrital material in eddying water. **4.** Also, **sinkhole**. a hole formed in soluble rock by the action of water, serving to conduct water to an underground passage. Also, **pot hole**.

potion /'poʊʃən/ *n.* a drink or draught, especially one of a medicinal, poisonous, or magical kind.

pot luck *n.* *Colloq.* **1.** whatever food happens to be at hand without special preparation or buying. **2.** an unpredictable situation. *–phr.* **3. take pot luck**, to accept whatever is on offer. Also, **potluck**, **pot-luck**.

potluck *adj.* /'pɒtlʌk/ **1.** improvised from available resources: *a potluck archive. –n.* /pɒt'lʌk/ **2.** → **pot luck**.

potoroo /pɒtə'ru/ *n.* any of several species of small macropods of the genus *Potorous*, having pointed heads and living in dense grass and low, thick scrub in various parts of Australia.

potpourri /pɒt'puəri, poʊpə'ri/ *n.* (*pl.* **-ris**) **1.** a mixture of dried petals of roses or other flowers with spices, etc., kept in a jar for the fragrance. **2.** a collection of miscellaneous literary extracts. **3.** any mixture of unrelated things.

pot shot *n.* **1.** a shot fired at game merely for food, with little regard to skill or the rules of sport. **2.** a shot at an animal or person within easy range, as from ambush. **3.** a random or aimless shot.

potter¹ /'pɒtə/ *n.* someone who makes earthen pots or other vessels.

potter² /'pɒtə/ *v.i.* **1.** to busy or occupy oneself in an ineffective manner. **2.** to move or go (*about*, *along*, etc.) with ineffective action or little energy or purpose. **3.** to move or go slowly or aimlessly; loiter. *–n.* **4.** pottering or ineffective action; dawdling. Also, *US*, **putter**. **–potterer**, *n.* **–potteringly**, *adv.*

pottery /'pɒtəri/ *n.* (*pl.* **-ries**) **1.** ware fashioned from clay or other earthy material and hardened by heat. **2.** a place where earthen pots or vessels are made. **3.** the art or business of a potter; ceramics.

potty¹ /'pɒti/ *adj.* (**-tier**, **-tiest**) *Colloq.* foolish; crazy.

potty² /'pɒti/ *n.* (*pl.* **-ties**) *Colloq.* a chamber-pot, especially one for a child. Also, **pottie**.

pouch /paʊtʃ/ *n.* **1.** a bag, sack, or similar container, especially one for small articles. **2.** a small moneybag. **3.** something shaped or looking like a bag or pocket. **4.** *Zool.* a bag-like or pocket-like part, as the one beneath the bill of a pelican, or (especially) the one in which the young of marsupials are carried. *–v.t.* **5.** to put into or enclose in a pouch, bag, or pocket; pocket. *–v.i.* **6.** to form a pouch or a cavity like a pouch. **–pouchy**, *adj.*

pouf /puf, poʊf/ *n.* a large firm cushion, often cylindrical, strong and high enough to serve as a seat or leg rest.

poultice /'poʊltəs/ *n.* **1.** a soft, moist mass of some substance, as bread, meal, linseed, etc., applied as a medicament to the body. *–v.t.* (**-ticed, -ticing**) **2.** to apply a poultice to.

poultry /'poʊltri/ *n.* domestic fowls collectively, as chickens, turkeys, guineafowls, ducks, and geese.

pounce /paʊns/ *v.i.* (**pounced, pouncing**) **1.** to swoop down suddenly and lay hold, as a bird does on its prey. **2.** to spring, dash, or come suddenly. *–n.* **3.** the claw or talon of a bird of prey. **4.** a sudden swoop, as on prey.

pound[1] /paʊnd/ *v.t.* **1.** to strike repeatedly and with great force, as with an instrument, the fist, heavy missiles, etc. **2.** to force (a way) by battering. **3.** to crush by beating, as with an instrument; pulverise. *–v.i.* **4.** to strike heavy blows repeatedly: *to pound on a door*. **5.** to beat or throb violently, as the heart. **6.** to give forth a sound of or as of thumps: *the drums pounded loudly*. **7.** to walk or go with heavy steps; move along with force or vigour. *–n.* **8.** the act of pounding. **9.** a heavy or forcible blow. **10.** a thump. *–phr.* **11. pound out**, to produce (sound) by striking or thumping, or with an effect of thumping: *to pound out a tune on a piano*.

pound[2] /paʊnd/ *n.* (*pl.* **pounds** *or, especially collectively,* **pound**) **1.** a unit of mass, varying in different periods and different countries. **2.** either of two units in imperial measure, the **pound avoirdupois** (of 7000 grains, divided into 16 ounces, and equal to 0.453 592 37 kg) used for ordinary commodities, or the **pound troy** (of 5760 grains, divided into 12 ounces, equal to 0.373 241 721 6 kg) used for gold, silver, etc., and also serving as the basis of apothecaries' weight. **3.** a British unit of currency (**pound sterling**) of the value of 100 new pence. **4.** a former unit of currency in Australia of the value of 240 pence. **5.** the monetary unit of various countries. **6.** a note or coin of any of these denominations.

pound[3] /paʊnd/ *n.* **1.** an enclosure maintained by public authorities for confining stray or homeless animals. **2.** an enclosure for sheltering, keeping, confining, or trapping animals. **3.** a place of confinement or imprisonment. *–v.t.* **4.** to shut up in or as in a pound; impound; imprison.

pour /pɔ/ *v.t.* **1.** to send (a fluid, or anything in loose particles) flowing or falling, as from a container or into, over, or on something. **2.** to emit or discharge, especially continuously or rapidly. *–v.i.* **3.** to issue, move, or proceed in great quantity or number. **4.** to flow forth or along. **5.** to rain heavily. *–n.* **6. a.** the act or process of pouring molten metal, concrete, etc., into a mould. **b.** the amount poured. **7.** an abundant or continuous flow or stream. **8.** a heavy fall of rain; downpour. *–phr.* **9. pour on**, *Colloq.* to overdo or supply in excess: *pour on the sob stuff*. **10. pour out** (or **forth**), to express (feelings, emotions, etc.) in a stream or flood of words. *–pourer, n. –pouringly, adv.*

pout /paʊt/ *v.i.* **1.** to thrust out the lips, especially in displeasure or sullenness. **2.** to look sullen. *–v.t.* **3.** to say with a pout. *–n.* **4.** a thrusting out of the lips, as in pouting.

pouter /'paʊtə/ *n.* **1.** someone who pouts. **2.** one of a breed of long-legged domestic pigeons characterised by the habit of puffing out the crop.

poverty /'pɒvəti/ *n.* **1.** the condition of being poor with respect to money, goods, or means of subsistence. **2.** deficiency or lack of something specified: *poverty of ideas*. **3.** deficiency of desirable ingredients, qualities, etc.: *poverty of soil*. **4.** scantiness; scanty amount.

poverty trap *n.* a state of poverty from which it is difficult to escape because any attempt to improve one's circumstances by seeking employment leaves one worse off than one was when totally dependent on social security.

powder /'paʊdə/ *n.* **1.** any solid substance in the state of fine, loose particles, as produced by crushing, grinding, or disintegration; dust. **2.** a preparation in this form for some special purpose, as gunpowder, a medicinal powder, a cosmetic or toilet powder, etc. *–v.t.* **3.** to reduce to powder; pulverise. **4.** to sprinkle or cover with powder. **5.** to apply powder to (the face, skin, etc.) as a cosmetic. **6.** to sprinkle or strew as with powder. **7.** to ornament with small objects scattered over a surface. *–v.i.* **8.** to use powder as a cosmetic. **9.** to become pulverised. *–phr.* **10. take a powder**, *Colloq.* to depart; disappear. *–powderer, n. –powdery, adj.*

powder puff *n.* a soft, feathery ball or pad, as of down, for applying powder to the skin.

power /'paʊə/ *n.* **1.** ability to do or act; capability of doing or effecting something. **2.** (*usu. pl.*) a particular faculty of body or mind. **3.** political or national strength: *the balance of power in Europe*. **4.** great or marked ability to do or act; strength; might; force. **5.** the possession of control or command over others; dominion; authority; ascendancy or influence. **6.** political ascendancy or control in the government of a country, etc.: *the party in power*. **7.** legal ability, capacity, or authority. **8.** delegated authority; authority vested in a person or persons in a particular capacity. **9.** a written statement, or document, conferring legal authority. **10.** someone or something that possesses or exercises authority or influence. **11.** a state or nation having international authority or influence: *the great powers of the world*. **12.** a military or naval force. **13.** (*oft. pl.*) a deity or divinity. **14.** *Theology* a member of the sixth order of angels. See **angel** (def. 1). **15.** *Colloq.* a large number or amount. **16.** *Physics, Elect.* the time rate of transferring or transforming energy; work done, or energy transferred, per unit of time. **17.** mechanical energy as distinguished from hand labour. **18.** a particular form of mechanical energy. **19.** *Maths* the product obtained by multiplying a quantity by itself one or more times: *4 is the second, 8 the third power of 2*. **20.** *Optics* the magnifying capacity of a microscope, telescope, etc., expressed as ratio of diameter of image to object. *–v.t.* **21.** to supply with electricity or other means of power. **22.** (of an engine, etc.) to provide the force or motive power to operate (a machine). *–v.i.* **23.** to move with a surge of power: *to power past an opponent*. *–adj.* **24.** associated with a managerial or executive style: *power dressing; power lunch*. *–phr.* **25. power down**, *Colloq.* to switch off a computer or peripheral device. **26. power one's way**, *Colloq.* to draw on reserves of strength and energy to gain a victory. **27. power up**, *Colloq.* to switch on a computer or peripheral device. **28. the powers that be**, those in authority. *–powerful, adj.*

power board *n.* a single moulded plastic unit comprising a number of power points. Also, **powerboard**.

power nap *n.* a short sleep taken during the day in order to restore one's energy.

power play *n.* tactics designed to intimidate an opposition. *–power player, n.*

power point *n.* a socket, connected to a power supply, usually made of plastic and set in a wall, into which the plug of an electrical appliance may be inserted.

power station *n.* a commercial facility for the generation of electricity, comprising one or more generators, which harvests energy sources, traditionally fossil fuels, falling water, or biofuels, and, more recently, sun, wind, and wave energy; sometimes with associated buildings, stacks, and necessary infrastructure.

power steering *n.* a steering mechanism in a motor vehicle that provides mechanical or hydraulic aid in turning the wheels.

power walking *n.* a purposeful fast-paced walking, intended as exercise to improve fitness.

powwow /ˈpaʊwaʊ/ *n.* **1.** (among northern Native Americans) a ceremony, especially one accompanied by magic, feasting, and dancing, performed for the cure of disease, success in a hunt, etc. **2.** a council or conference of or with Native Americans. **3.** *Colloq.* any conference or meeting.

pox /pɒks/ *n.* **1.** a disease characterised by multiple skin pustules, as smallpox. **2.** → **syphilis. 3.** *Colloq.* any venereal disease.

P-plate /ˈpi-pleɪt/ *n.* (in Australia) one of a pair of identification plates which by law must be displayed (at the front and rear) on any motor vehicle driven by a driver with a provisional licence. **–P-plater,** *n.*

practicable /ˈpræktɪkəbəl/ *adj.* **1.** capable of being put into practice, done, or effected, especially with the available means or with reason or prudence; feasible. **2.** capable of being used or traversed, or admitting of passage: *a practicable road.* **–practicability** /ˌpræktɪkəˈbɪləti/, **practicableness,** *n.* **–practicably,** *adv.*

practical /ˈpræktɪkəl/ *adj.* **1.** relating to practice or action: *practical mathematics.* **2.** consisting of, using, or resulting from practice or action: *a practical application of a rule.* **3.** relating to the ordinary business, or work of the world: *practical affairs.* **4.** adapted for actual use: *a practical method.* **5.** doing or experienced in actual practice or work: *a practical politician.* **6.** interested in or fitted for actual work: *a practical man.* **7.** mindful of the results, usefulness, possibilities, etc., of a certain action or method; sensible. **8.** matter-of-fact; prosaic. **9.** being so in effect; virtual: *a practical certainty.* **10.** of or relating to a practical (def. 11). **–n. 11.** that part of a course of study which is meant to develop practical skills or to show the practical basis of a theory: *a Chemistry practical.* **–practicality** /ˌpræktəˈkæləti/, **practicalness,** *n.*

practical joke *n.* a trick played upon a person, often involving some physical action. **–practical joker,** *n.*

practically /ˈpræktɪkli/ *adv.* **1.** in effect; virtually. **2.** in a practical manner. **3.** from a practical point of view. **4.** nearly; almost.

practice /ˈpræktəs/ *n.* **1.** habitual or customary performance: *normal business practice.* **2.** a habit or custom. **3.** repeated performance or systematic exercise for the purpose of acquiring skill or proficiency: *practice makes perfect.* **4.** skill gained by experience or exercise. **5.** the action or process of performing or doing something (opposed to *theory* or *speculation*). **6.** the exercise of a profession or occupation, especially law or medicine. **7.** the business of a professional person: *a doctor with a large practice.* **8.** *Law* the established method of conducting legal proceedings. *–v.t., v.i.* **9.** *US →* **practise.** *–adj.* **10.** of or relating to an attempt which is undertaken merely to develop skill, refresh one's memory, etc.: *a practice shot.* *–phr.* **11. make a practice of,** to do something habitually or usually. **12. sharp practice,** deceitful or dishonest dealing or procedure; trickery.

practician /prækˈtɪʃən/ *n.* someone who works at a profession or occupation; practitioner.

practicum /ˈpræktɪkəm/ *n.* that part of a course of study which is designed to develop practical skills or to demonstrate the practical foundation of a theory. Also, **practical;** *Colloq.*, **prac.**

practise /ˈpræktəs/ *verb* (**-tised, -tising**) *–v.t.* **1.** to carry out, follow, observe or use or do habitually or usually. **2.** to exercise or work as a profession, art, or occupation: *to practise law.* **3.** to perform or do repeatedly in order to acquire skill or proficiency. *–v.i.* **4.** to act habitually; do something habitually or as a practice. **5.** to work in a profession, especially law or medicine.

6. to do something in order to improve one's skill: *to practise shooting.* **–practiser,** *n.*

practising /ˈpræktəsɪŋ/ *adj.* **1.** actively pursuing a particular profession in which one is qualified to work: *a practising accountant.* **2.** actively observing or following a particular religion, philosophy, way of life, etc.: *a practising Catholic.*

practitioner /prækˈtɪʃənə/ *n.* **1.** someone engaged in the practice of a profession or the like: *a medical practitioner.* **2.** someone who practises something specified.

prae- variant of **pre-.**

pragmatic /prægˈmætɪk/ *adj.* **1.** treating historical phenomena with special reference to their causes, antecedent conditions, and results. **2.** concerned with practical consequences or values. **3.** *Philos.* of or relating to pragmatism. **–pragmatically,** *adv.* **–pragmatism,** *n.* **–pragmatist,** *n.*

pragmatics /prægˈmætɪks/ *n. Ling.* (*construed as sing.*) the study of those aspects of language which relate to the conventions which regulate its use in a language community.

prairie /ˈprɛəri/ *n.* **1.** an extensive or slightly undulating treeless tract of land, characterised by highly fertile soil and originally grassland, which occurs in the interior of continents in temperate latitudes, as that of the upper Mississippi valley, US, and in Canada. **2.** a meadow.

praise /preɪz/ *n.* **1.** the act of expressing approval or admiration; commendation; laudation. **2.** the offering of grateful homage in words or song, as an act of worship. **3.** state of being approved or admired. *–v.t.* (**praised, praising**) **4.** to express approval or admiration of; commend; extol. **5.** to offer grateful homage to (God or a deity), as in words or song. *–phr.* **6. sing someone's praises** or **sing the praises of someone,** to be highly complimentary to someone. **–praiser,** *n.* **–praiseworthy,** *adj.*

praline /ˈpralin/ *n.* a confection of nuts and caramelised sugar.

pram /præm/ *n.* a small, four-wheeled vehicle used for carrying a baby, wheeled by pushing.

prance /præns, prans/ *v.i.* (**pranced, prancing**) **1.** to spring, or move from the hind legs, as a horse. **2.** to move or go in a happy manner; swagger. **3.** to leap or dance. *–n.* **4.** the act of prancing. **–prancer,** *n.* **–prancingly,** *adv.*

prandial /ˈprændiəl/ *adj.* of or relating to a meal, especially dinner. **–prandially,** *adv.*

prang /præŋ/ *Colloq. –v.t.* **1.** to crash-land (an aircraft) with resultant damage to it. **2.** to crash (a car or the like). *–v.i.* **3.** to have a crash. *–n.* **4.** a crash in a motor vehicle or the like.

prank /præŋk/ *n.* **1.** a trick or practical joke, sometimes mischievous in nature. **2.** a call to a mobile phone that cuts out before it can be answered leaving a phone number listed for a return call. *–v.t.* **3.** to call (someone) on their mobile phone allowing only enough time for the number or some prearranged signal to register before hanging up. **–prankster,** *n.* **–prankish,** *adj.* **–prankery,** *n.* **–pranking,** *n.*

prat /præt/ *–n. Colloq.* **1.** the buttocks. **2.** an incompetent or foolish person. *–phr.* **3. prat oneself in,** *Aust.* to butt in: *I don't want to prat myself in where I'm not wanted.*

prate /preɪt/ *v.i.* **1.** to talk too much; talk foolishly or pointlessly; chatter; babble. *–v.t.* **2.** to utter in empty or foolish talk. *–n.* **3.** the act of prating. **4.** empty or foolish talk. **–prater,** *n.* **–pratingly,** *adv.*

prattle /ˈprætl/ *v.i.* **1.** to talk or chatter in a simple-minded or foolish way; babble. *–v.t.* **2.** to utter by chattering or babbling. *–n.* **3.** the act of prattling. **4.** chatter; babble. **5.** a babbling sound. **–prattler,** *n.* **–prattlingly,** *adv.*

prawn /prɔn/ *n.* **1.** any of various shrimp-like decapod crustaceans of the genera *Palaemon, Penaeus,* etc.

(suborder Macrura), certain of which are used as food. **2.** *Aust., NZ Colloq.* a weak, spiritless, insignificant person: *he's a bit of a prawn.* –*v.i.* **3.** to catch prawns, as for food. –*phr.* **4. come the raw prawn**, *Aust., NZ Colloq.* (sometimes fol. by *with*) to try to put over a deception. **–prawner,** *n.*

pray /preɪ/ *v.t.* **1.** to strongly urge (a person, etc.): *tell me, I pray you.* **2.** to make a sincere request to (God, etc.). **3.** to offer (a prayer). –*v.i.* **4.** to make a strong plea as to a person. **5.** to make a sincere request to God, etc. **6.** to enter into spiritual union with God through prayer.

prayer /prɛə/ *n.* **1.** a sincere and earnest petition to God, etc. **2.** the act or practice of praying to God, etc., as in thanks, praise or request. **3.** a form of words used in praying. **4.** something that is prayed for.

praying mantis *n.* → **mantis**.

pre- a prefix applied freely to mean 'prior to', 'in advance of' (*prewar*), also 'early', 'beforehand', 'before', 'in front of' (*preoral, prefrontal*), and in many figurative meanings, often attached to stems not used alone (*prevent, preclude, preference, precedent*).

preach /pritʃ/ *v.t.* **1.** to advocate or inculcate (religious or moral truth, right conduct, etc.) in speech or writing. **2.** to proclaim or make known by sermon (the gospel, good tidings, etc.). –*v.i.* **3.** to deliver a sermon. **4.** to give earnest advice, as on religious subjects. **5.** to do this in an obtrusive or tedious way. **–preacher,** *n.*

preamble /priˈæmbəl/ *n.* **1.** an introductory statement; a preface; an introduction. **2.** *Law* the introductory part of a statute, deed, or the like, stating the reasons and intent of what follows. **3.** a preliminary or introductory fact or circumstance.

prebiotic /pribaɪˈɒtɪk/ *adj.* **1.** of or relating to a food or nutrient added to the diet to encourage the increase of desirable microflora in the intestines. –*n.* **2.** such a food or nutrient.

Precambrian /ˌpriˈkæmbriən/ *adj., n.* (relating to) a geological period, age, or systems of rocks older than the Cambrian, characterised by almost complete lack of fossils. Also, **Pre-Cambrian**.

precarious /prəˈkɛəriəs/ *adj.* **1.** dependent on circumstances beyond one's control; uncertain; unstable; insecure: *a precarious livelihood.* **2.** dependent on the will or pleasure of another; liable to be withdrawn or lost at the will of another: *precarious tenure.* **3.** exposed to or involving danger; dangerous; perilous; risky: *a precarious life.* **4.** having insufficient, little, or no foundation: *a precarious assumption.* **–precariously,** *adv.* **–precariousness,** *n.*

precaution /prəˈkɔʃən/ *n.* **1.** a measure taken beforehand to ward off possible evil or secure good results. **2.** caution used beforehand; prudent foresight. **–precautionary,** *adj.* **–precautious,** *adj.*

precede /priˈsid/ *verb* (**-ceded, -ceding**) –*v.t.* **1.** to go before, as in place, order, rank, importance, or time. **2.** to introduce by something preliminary; preface. –*v.i.* **3.** to go or come before.

precedence /ˈprɛsədəns, priˈsidəns/ *n.* **1.** the act or fact of preceding. **2.** priority in order, rank, importance, etc. **3.** priority in time. **4.** the right to precede others in ceremonies or social formalities. **5.** the order to be observed ceremonially by persons of different ranks. Also, **precedency** /ˈprɛsədənsi, priˈsidənsi/.

precedent /ˈprisədnt, priˈsi-/ *n.* **1.** a preceding instance or case which may serve as an example for or a justification in subsequent cases. **2.** *Law* a legal decision or form of proceeding serving as an authoritative rule or pattern in future similar or analogous cases.

precentor /prəˈsɛntə/ *n.* **1.** someone who leads a church choir or congregation in singing. **2.** the member of a cathedral chapter in charge of the music. **–precentorial** /prisɛnˈtɔriəl/, *adj.* **–precentorship,** *n.*

precept /ˈprisɛpt/ *n.* **1.** a commandment or direction given as a rule of action or conduct. **2.** an injunction as to moral conduct; a maxim. **3.** a rule, as for the performance of some technical operation. **4.** *Law* a writ or warrant.

precession /priˈsɛʃən/ *n.* **1.** the act or fact of preceding; precedence. **2.** *Astron.* **a.** the precession of the equinoxes. **b.** the related motion of the earth's axis of rotation. **3.** the motion of a rotating body which, as a result of an applied couple whose axis is perpendicular to the axis of rotation, also involves rotation about a third mutually perpendicular axis. **–precessional,** *adj.*

precinct /ˈprisɪŋkt/ *n.* **1.** a place or space of definite limits. **2.** (*oft. pl.*) an enclosing boundary or limit. **3.** (*pl.*) the areas immediately about any place; environs: *the precincts of a town.*

precious /ˈprɛʃəs/ *adj.* **1.** of great price or value; valuable; costly: *precious metals.* **2.** of great moral or spiritual worth. **3.** dear; beloved. **4.** too delicate, refined, or nice. –*n.* **5.** precious one; darling. –*adv.* **6.** extremely; very: *precious few supporters.* **–preciously,** *adv.* **–preciousness,** *n.*

precipice /ˈprɛsəpəs/ *n.* **1.** a cliff with a vertical, or nearly vertical, or overhanging face. **2.** a situation of great peril.

precipitant /prəˈsɪpətənt/ *adj.* **1.** falling headlong. **2.** rushing headlong, rapidly, or hastily onwards. **3.** hasty; rash. **4.** unduly sudden or abrupt. –*n.* **5.** *Chem.* anything that causes precipitation. **–precipitantly,** *adv.* **–precipitancy, precipitance,** *n.*

precipitate *v.t.* /prəˈsɪpəteɪt/ **1.** to bring about quickly or suddenly: *to precipitate an argument.* **2.** *Chem.* to separate out (a dissolved substance) in solid form from a solution, as by means of a reagent. **3.** *Physics, Weather* to change (moisture) from vapour into rain, dew, etc. **4.** to cast down headlong. –*v.i.* /prəˈsɪpəteɪt/ **5.** to separate from a solution as a precipitate. **6.** *Physics, Weather* to be condensed as rain, dew, etc. –*adj.* /prəˈsɪpətət/ **7.** headlong. **8.** moving with great haste. **9.** very sudden; abrupt. **10.** overhasty; rash. –*n.* /prəˈsɪpətət/ **11.** *Chem.* a substance precipitated from a solution. **12.** *Physics, Weather* moisture condensed in the form of rain, dew, etc. **–precipitately,** *adv.* **–precipitateness,** *n.* **–precipitative,** *adj.* **–precipitator,** *n.*

precipitation /prəsɪpəˈteɪʃən/ *n.* **1.** the act or fact of precipitating. **2.** a casting down or falling headlong. **3.** sudden haste. **4.** unwise speed. **5.** *Chem., Physics* the precipitating of a substance from a solution. **6.** *Weather* **a.** falling products of condensation as rain, snow, hail. **b.** the amount of such within a given period.

precipitous /prəˈsɪpətəs/ *adj.* **1.** of the nature of a precipice, or characterised by precipices: *a precipitous wall of rock.* **2.** extremely or impassably steep. **3.** hasty; rash. **–precipitously,** *adv.* **–precipitousness,** *n.*

precis /ˈpreɪsi/ *n.* (pl. **-cis** /-siz/ or **-cises** /-siz/) **1.** an abstract or summary. –*v.t.* (**-cised** /-sid/, **-cising** /-siŋ/) **2.** to make a precis of. Also, **précis**.

precise /prəˈsaɪs/ *adj.* **1.** exact; definite. **2.** being just that, and neither more nor less: *the precise amount.* **3.** being just that, and not some other: *the precise date.* **4.** clear, distinct, as the voice. **5.** exact in measuring, recording, etc., as an instrument. **6.** very particular; puritanical. **–precisely,** *adv.* **–preciseness,** *n.* **–precision,** *n.*

preclude /priˈklud/ *v.t.* **1.** to shut out or exclude; prevent the presence, existence, or occurrence of; make impossible. **2.** to shut out, debar, or prevent (a person, etc.) from something. **–preclusion** /priˈkluʒən/, *n.* **–preclusive** /priˈklusɪv/, *adj.* **–preclusively,** *adv.*

precocious /prəˈkoʊʃəs/ *adj.* **1.** forward in development, especially mental development, as a child. **2.** prematurely developed, as the mind, faculties, etc. **3.** (of a child) cheeky; forward; impertinent. **4.** relating to or showing premature development. **5.** *Bot.* flowering, fruiting, or ripening early, as plants or fruit. **–precociously,** *adv.* **–precociousness, precocity** /prə'kɒsəti/, *n.*

precognition /,prikɒg'nɪʃən/ *n.* foreknowledge; knowledge of future events, especially through extrasensory means. **–precognitive** /pri'kɒgnətɪv/, *adj.*

preconceive /prikən'siv/ *v.t.* **(-ceived, -ceiving)** to conceive beforehand; form an idea of in advance.

preconception /prikən'sɛpʃən/ *n.* **1.** a conception or opinion formed beforehand. **2.** bias; predilection.

precursor /,pri'kɜsə/ *n.* **1.** a person or thing that precedes another; a predecessor. **2.** a person or thing that indicates the approach of another or something else. **3.** *Biochem.* a metabolite which can be converted into another metabolite by one or more enzymic reactions. **–precursory, precursive,** *adj.*

predate /,pri'deɪt/ *v.t.* **1.** to date before the actual time: *he predated the cheque by three days.* **2.** to precede in date.

predator /'prɛdətə/ *n.* a predatory person, organism, or thing.

predatory /'prɛdətəri, -tri/ *adj.* **1.** of, relating to, or characterised by plundering, pillaging, or robbery. **2.** *Zool.* habitually preying upon other animals. **–predatorily,** *adv.* **–predatoriness,** *n.*

predatory driving *n. Law* driving in deliberate pursuit of another person as a form of harassment.

predatory pricing *n.* the deliberate ploy of selling goods or services at an unsustainably low price so as to capture a market from less powerful competitors who could not themselves survive such a strategy.

predecessor /'pridəsɛsə/ *n.* **1.** someone who precedes another in an office, position, etc. **2.** anything succeeded or replaced by something else. **3.** an ancestor or forefather.

predestine /pri'dɛstən/ *v.t.* **(-tined, -tining)** to destine beforehand; foreordain; predetermine: *he seemed almost predestined for the ministry.*

predetermine /pridə'tɜmən/ *v.t.* **1.** to determine or decide beforehand. **2.** to ordain beforehand; predestine. **3.** to direct or impel beforehand to something. **–predetermination** /pridə,tɜmə'neɪʃən/, *n.* **–predeterminative,** *adj.* **–predeterminate,** *adj.*

predicament /prə'dɪkəmənt/ *n.* **1.** an unpleasant, trying, or dangerous situation. **2.** a particular state, condition, or situation. **3.** *Logic* one of the classes or categories of logical predications. **–predicamental** /prədɪkə'mɛntl/, *adj.*

predicate *v.t.* /'prɛdɪkeɪt/ **1.** to declare; proclaim. *–v.i.* /'prɛdɪkeɪt/ **2.** to make a declaration. *–n.* /'prɛdɪkət/ **3.** *Gram.* (in many languages) the active verb in a sentence or clause together with all the words it governs and those which modify it, as *is here* in *Jack is here.* **4.** *Logic* something that is said of the subject in a proposition. **–predication** /prɛdə'keɪʃən/, *n.* **–predicative** /prə'dɪkətɪv/, *adj.* **–predicatively** /prə'dɪkətɪvli/, *adv.*

predict /prə'dɪkt/ *v.t.* **1.** to foretell; prophesy. *–v.i.* **2.** to foretell the future. **–predictable,** *adj.* **–predictability,** *n.* **–predictably,** *adv.* **–prediction,** *n.* **–predictive,** *adj.*

predictive text /prədɪktɪv 'tɛkst/ *n.* a function of mobile phones or similar devices, used in texting, etc., where the pressing of one key or a few keys results in suggestions as to what the full word might be, thus saving time and keystrokes for the user.

predilection /pridə'lɛkʃən/ *n.* a predisposition of the mind in favour of something; a partiality; preference.

predispose /pridəs'pouz/ *v.t.* **1.** to give a previous inclination or tendency to. **2.** to render subject, susceptible, or liable: *poor health predisposed them to infection.* **3.** to dispose beforehand. *–v.i.* **4.** to give or furnish a tendency or inclination. **–predisposition** /,pridɪspə'zɪʃən/, *n.*

predominate /prə'dɒməneɪt/ *v.i.* **1.** to be the stronger or leading element; preponderate; prevail. **2.** (sometimes fol. by *over*) to have or exert controlling power. **3.** to surpass others in authority or influence. **4.** to be more noticeable or imposing than something else. *–v.t.* **5.** to dominate or prevail over. **–predominance, predomination** /prədɒmə'neɪʃən/, *n.* **–predominant,** *adj.* **–predominantly, predominatingly,** *adv.* **–predominator,** *n.*

pre-eminent /pri-'ɛmənənt/ *adj.* eminent before or above others; superior to or surpassing others; distinguished beyond others. **–pre-eminently,** *adv.*

pre-empt /pri-'ɛmpt/ *v.t.* **1.** to occupy (land) in order to establish a prior right to buy. **2.** to acquire or appropriate beforehand. **3.** to anticipate. *–v.i.* **4.** *Bridge* to make a pre-emptive bid. **–pre-emptory,** *adj.* **–pre-emptor,** *n.* **–pre-emption,** *n.*

pre-emptive /pri-'ɛmptɪv/ *adj.* **1.** of or relating to pre-emption. **2.** *Bridge* of or relating to an unnecessarily high bid, made to deter one's opponents from bidding. **3.** *Mil.* of or relating to an action undertaken to destroy or weaken an enemy force before it can launch an attack: *a pre-emptive strike.* **–pre-emptively,** *adv.*

preen /prin/ *v.t.* **1.** to trim or dress with the beak, as a bird does its feathers. **2.** to prepare, dress, or array (oneself) carefully in making one's toilet. **3.** to pride (oneself) on an achievement, etc. **–preener,** *n.*

prefabricate /pri'fæbrəkeɪt/ *v.t.* **1.** to fabricate or construct beforehand. **2.** to manufacture (houses, etc.) in standardised parts or sections ready for rapid assembly and erection. **–prefabricated,** *adj.* **–prefabrication** /pri,fæbrə'keɪʃən/, *n.*

preface /'prɛfəs/ *n.* **1.** a statement placed at the front of a book, explaining its purpose, etc. **2.** an introductory part, as of a speech. *–v.t.* **(-aced, -acing) 3.** to introduce by a preface. **4.** to serve as a preface to. **5.** to introduce by something preliminary: *he prefaced his remarks to the farmers with a reference to the recent welcome rain.* **–prefatory,** *adj.*

prefect /'prifɛkt/ *n.* **1.** a person appointed to any of various positions of command, authority, or superintendence, as a chief magistrate in ancient Rome, or the chief administrative official of a department of France and Italy. **2.** (in many schools) one of a body of senior pupils with authority for maintaining order and discipline. **3.** the dean in a Jesuit school or college.

prefer /prə'fɜ/ *v.t.* **(-ferred, -ferring) 1.** to set or hold before or above other persons or things in estimation; like better; choose rather: *to prefer films to books.* **2.** *Law* to give priority, as to one creditor over another. **3.** to put forward or present (a statement, suit, charge, etc.) for consideration or sanction. **4.** to put forward or advance, as in rank or office. **5.** to favour: *to prefer kicking with your right foot.* **–preferable,** *adj.* **–preferably,** *adv.* **–preferrer,** *n.*

preference /'prɛfərəns, 'prɛfrəns/ *n.* **1.** the act or fact of preferring. **2.** something that is preferred. **3.** a practical advantage given to one over others. **4.** a right or claim before anyone else, as to payment of dividends, etc. **5. a.** a vote, usually specified in rank, given to a candidate in a preferential voting system: *Smith got my first preference.* **b.** Also, **preference vote.** a vote other than a first preference vote, which, when all such votes are counted, may have a bearing on the election of a candidate who lacks sufficient first preferences to have a clear majority: *Smith was elected only on preferences.* **–preferential** /prɛfə'rɛnʃəl/, *adj.*

preference share *n. Stock Exchange* a share which ranks before ordinary shares in the entitlement to dividends, usually at a fixed rate of interest. Also, *US,* **preferred stock.**

preferential voting *n.* a system of voting which enables the voter to indicate his or her order of preference for candidates in the ballot. If no candidate achieves an absolute majority, the candidate with fewest first preferences is eliminated and the second preferences on the relevant ballot papers are distributed and so on until one candidate has an absolute majority. Compare **first-past-the-post**.

prefix *n.* /ˈpriːfɪks/ **1.** *Gram.* an affix which is put before a word, stem, or word element to add to or qualify its meaning. **2.** something prefixed, as a title before a person's name. –*v.t.* /priːˈfɪks, ˈpriːfɪks/ **3.** to fix or put before or in front. **4.** *Gram.* to add as a prefix. –**prefixal** /ˈpriːfɪksəl, priːˈfɪksəl/, *adj.* –**prefixally**, *adv.*

pregnant /ˈprɛgnənt/ *adj.* **1.** being with child or young, as a woman or female mammal; having a fetus in the womb. **2.** full of meaning; highly significant: *a pregnant utterance.* **3.** full of possibilities, involving important issues or results, or momentous. **4.** teeming with ideas or imagination: *a pregnant wit.* –*phr.* **5.** **pregnant with**, fraught, filled, or loaded with: *words pregnant with meaning.* **6.** abounding in, fertile or rich in: *a mind pregnant in ideas.* –**pregnancy**, *n.* –**pregnantly**, *adv.*

prehensile /priˈhɛnsaɪl/ *adj.* **1.** adapted for seizing, grasping, or laying hold of anything. **2.** fitted for grasping by folding or wrapping round an object. –**prehensility** /prihɛnˈsɪləti/, *n.*

prehistory /ˌpriːˈhɪstəri/ *n.* **1.** the period of time before recorded history, or the events occurring in this period. **2.** a history of events leading up to a particular incident, situation, etc. –**prehistoric**, *adj.*

prejudge /ˌpriːˈdʒʌdʒ/ *v.t.* **1.** to judge beforehand. **2.** to pass judgement on prematurely or in advance of due investigation. –**prejudger**, *n.* –**prejudgement**, *n.*

prejudice /ˈprɛdʒədəs/ *n.* **1.** an unfavourable opinion or feeling formed beforehand or without knowledge, thought, or reason. **2.** any preconceived opinion or feeling, favourable or unfavourable. **3.** disadvantage resulting from some judgement or action of another. **4.** resulting injury or detriment. –*v.t.* (**-diced, -dicing**) **5.** to affect with a prejudice, favourable or unfavourable: *these facts prejudiced us in his favour.* **6.** to affect disadvantageously or detrimentally. –*phr.* **7. without prejudice**, *Law* without dismissing, damaging, or otherwise affecting a legal interest or demand. –**prejudicial** /prɛdʒəˈdɪʃəl/, *adj.* –**prejudicially** /prɛdʒəˈdɪʃəli/, *adv.*

prelate /ˈprɛlət/ *n.* an ecclesiastic of a high order, as an archbishop, bishop, etc.; a church dignitary. –**prelature**, **prelateship**, *n.* –**prelatic** /prəˈlætɪk/, *adj.*

preliminary /prəˈlɪmənəri, prəˈlɪmənri/ *adj.* **1.** preceding and leading up to the main matter or business; introductory; preparatory. –*n.* (*pl.* **-naries**) **2.** something preliminary; introductory or preparatory step, measure, sporting contest, or the like. –**preliminarily**, *adv.*

prelude /ˈprɛljuːd/ *n.* **1.** a preliminary to an action, event, condition, etc. **2.** *Music* **a.** a rather short, independent instrumental composition. **b.** a piece which comes before a more important movement. –*v.t.* **3.** to serve as a prelude to. **4.** to introduce by a prelude. –**preluder**, *n.*

premarital /ˌpriːˈmærətəl/ *adj.* before marriage.

premature /ˈprɛmətʃə, prɛməˈtjuə/ *adj.* **1.** coming into existence or occurring too soon. **2.** mature or ripe before the proper time. **3.** overhasty, as in action. –**prematurely**, *adv.* –**prematureness, prematurity**, *n.*

premeditate /priˈmɛdəteɪt/ *v.t.* to meditate, consider, or plan beforehand. –**premeditatedly**, *adv.* –**premeditation**, *n.* –**premeditative**, *adj.* –**premeditator**, *n.*

premenstrual /priˈmɛnstruəl/ *adj.* **1.** of or relating to the time in the menstrual cycle immediately preceding menstruation. **2.** suffering from the symptoms of

premenstrual syndrome. **3.** *Colloq.* tense and irritable, as if from premenstrual syndrome.

premenstrual syndrome *n.* a syndrome which affects some women especially just before menstruation, exhibiting itself in a variety of symptoms such as tension, irritableness, headache, pelvic discomfort, and breast enlargement. *Abbrev.*: PMS

premenstrual tension *n.* the symptoms of tension, irritableness, etc., associated with premenstrual syndrome. *Abbrev.*: PMT

premier /ˈprɛmiə/ *n.* **1.** (in Australia) the leader of a state government. **2.** (elsewhere) a prime minister, or other head of government. **3.** (*pl.*) *Aust.* (in sport) the team which wins the season's competition. –*adj.* **4.** chief; leading. **5.** winning: *the premier team.* –**premiership**, *n.*

premiere /ˈprɛmiˈeə/ *n.* **1.** a first public performance of a play, etc. **2.** the leading woman, as in a drama. –*verb* (**premiered, premiering**) –*v.t.* **3.** to present to the public for the first time. –*v.i.* **4.** to have the first public showing of a film, play, etc.

premise /ˈprɛməs/ *n.* **1.** Also, **premiss**. a proposition (or one of several) from which a conclusion is drawn. **2.** (*pl.*) a house or building with the grounds, etc., belonging to it. **3.** a basis for reasoned argument.

premium /ˈpriːmiəm/ *n.* **1.** a prize to be won in a competition. **2.** a bonus, gift, or sum additional to price, wages, interest, or the like. **3.** a bonus, prize, or the like, offered as an inducement to buy a product. **4.** the amount paid or agreed to be paid, in one sum or periodically, as the consideration for a contract of insurance. **5.** *Econ.* the excess value of one form of money over another of the same nominal value. **6.** a sum above the nominal or par value of a thing. **7.** *Stock Exchange* the amount that a buyer is prepared to pay for the right to subscribe for a new or rights issue of stocks or shares in a company. **8.** a fee paid for instruction in a trade or profession. –*adj.* **9.** highly regarded, special. **10.** of highest quality; best. –*phr.* **11. at a premium**, **a.** in high esteem; in demand. **b.** at a high price.

premonition /ˌprɛməˈnɪʃən, priː-/ *n.* **1.** a forewarning. **2.** → **presentiment**. –**premonitory** /priˈmɒnətəri, -tri/, *adj.*

prenatal /ˌpriːˈneɪtəl/ *adj.* **1.** before birth; during pregnancy: *a prenatal clinic.* –*n.* **2.** an prenatal examination. Also, **antenatal**. –**prenatally**, *adv.*

prenuptial agreement /priːnʌptʃəl əˈgriːmənt/ *n.* a legal contract made by two people before their wedding, detailing various financial or domestic arrangements, in particular outlining a settlement in the event of a divorce. Also, *Colloq.*, **prenup**.

preoccupied /priˈɒkjəpaɪd/ *adj.* **1.** completely engrossed in thought; absorbed. **2.** occupied previously. **3.** *Biol.* already used as a name for some species, genus, etc., and not available as a designation for any other.

preoccupy /priˈɒkjəpaɪ/ *v.t.* (**-pied, -pying**) **1.** to absorb or engross to the exclusion of other things. **2.** to occupy or take possession of beforehand or before others. –**preoccupant, preoccupier**, *n.* –**preoccupation**, *n.*

prepaid /ˈpriːpeɪd/ *adj.* paid before incurring a cost, as for a service, such as mobile phone use.

preparation /prɛpəˈreɪʃən/ *n.* **1.** an action, measure, or arrangement by which a person prepares for something. **2.** homework. **3.** the act or fact of preparing. **4.** something made ready, manufactured, or formed.

preparatory school *n.* (in Australia and the UK) a private school, often boarding, for pupils under about 13 years of age, before entering a private secondary school. Also, **prep school**.

prepare /prəˈpeə/ *v.t.* **1.** to make ready, or put in due condition, for something. **2.** to get ready for eating, as a meal, by due assembling, dressing, or cooking. **3.** to manufacture, compound, or compose. **4.** *Music* to lead up to (a discord, an embellishment, etc.) by some preliminary note or notes. *−v.i.* **5.** to put things or oneself in readiness; get ready: *to prepare for war.* **−preparedly** /prəˈpɛərədli, -ˈpɛədli/, *adv.* **−preparer**, *n.* **−preparedness**, *n.* **−preparative** /prəˈpærətɪv/, *adj.* **−preparatory** /prəˈpærətri/, *adj.*

preponderant /prəˈpɒndərənt, pri-, -drənt/ *adj.* superior in weight, force, influence, number, etc.; preponderating; predominant. **−preponderantly**, *adv.* **−preponderance**, *n.*

preponderate /prəˈpɒndəreɪt, pri-/ *v.i.* **1.** to exceed something else in weight; be the heavier. **2.** to incline downwards or descend, as one scale or end of a balance, because of greater weight; be weighed down. **3.** to be superior in power, force, influence, number, amount, etc.; predominate. **−preponderating**, *adj.* **−preponderatingly**, *adv.* **−preponderation** /prəˌpɒndəˈreɪʃən/, *n.*

preposition /prɛpəˈzɪʃən/ *n. Gram.* **1.** (in some languages) one of the major parts of speech, comprising words placed before nouns to indicate their relation to other words or their function in the sentence. **2.** any such word, as *by*, *to*, *in*, *from*. **3.** any word or construction of similar function or meaning, as *on top of* (= *on*). **−prepositional**, *adj.* **−prepositionally**, *adv.*

prepossessing /pripəˈzɛsɪŋ/ *adj.* that prepossesses, especially favourably. **−prepossessingly**, *adv.*

preposterous /prəˈpɒstərəs/ *adj.* directly contrary to nature, reason, or common sense; absurd, senseless, or utterly foolish. **−preposterously**, *adv.* **−preposterousness**, *n.*

prepuce /ˈpripjus/ *n. Anat.* the fold of skin which covers the head of the penis or clitoris; foreskin. **−preputial** /priˈpjuʃəl/, *adj.*

prequel /ˈprikwəl/ *n.* a play, film, or literary work in which the narrative begins at a point which precedes events described in an existing work.

prerequisite /priˈrɛkwəzət/ *adj.* **1.** required beforehand; requisite as an antecedent condition. *−n.* **2.** something prerequisite: *a knowledge of French was the only prerequisite for admission to the course.*

prerogative /prəˈrɒgətɪv/ *n.* **1.** an exclusive right or privilege attaching to an office or position. **2.** royal prerogative. **3.** a prior, peculiar, or exclusive right or privilege. *−adj.* **4.** having or exercising a prerogative. **5.** relating to, characteristic of, or existing by virtue of a prerogative.

presage *n.* /ˈprɛsɪdʒ/ **1.** a feeling of something about to happen; presentiment. **2.** something that foreshadows a future event; omen. **3.** a forecast; prediction. *−v.t.* /ˈprɛsɪdʒ, prəˈseɪdʒ/ (**-saged**, **-saging**) **4.** to have a feeling that something is about to happen. **5.** to forecast or make a forecast. **−presager**, *n.*

presbyter /ˈprɛzbətə, ˈprɛspətə/ *n. Christian Church* **1.** (in the early Christian church) an office-bearer exercising teaching, priestly, and administrative functions; elder. **2.** (in hierarchical churches) a priest. **3.** (in certain Protestant churches, as the Presbyterian Church) a lay officer with governing, teaching, or administrative duties; elder. **−presbyteral** /prɛzˈbɪtərəl/, *adj.* **−presbyterate** /prɛzˈbɪtərət/, *n.*

presbyterian /prɛzbəˈtɪəriən, prɛspə-/ *adj.* **1.** of or relating to the principle of ecclesiastical government by an elected body of lay elders. **2.** (*upper case*) of or relating to various churches having this form of government and holding more or less modified forms of Calvinism. *−n.* **3.** (*upper case*) a member or adherent of a Presbyterian church. **−Presbyterianism**, *n.*

presbytery /ˈprɛzbətri, ˈprɛspə-/ *n.* (*pl.* **-ries**) **1.** a body of presbyters or elders. **2.** (in Presbyterian churches) a judicatory consisting of all the ministers (teaching elders) and representative lay or ruling elders from the congregations within a district. **3.** the churches under the jurisdiction of a presbytery. **4.** the part of a church,

east of the choir, in which the high altar is situated. **5.** (now only in Roman Catholic use) a clergyman's or priest's house. **−presbyterial** /prɛzbəˈtɪəriəl/, *adj.*

preschool /ˈpriskul/ *adj.* **1.** of or relating to the period prior to compulsory school age. *−n.* **2.** a school for furthering the development of very young children, usually children under the age of five, by means of games, activities, etc.; kindergarten. **−preschooler**, *n.*

prescience /ˈprɛsiəns/ *n.* knowledge of things before they exist or happen; foreknowledge; foresight. **−prescient**, *adj.* **−presciently**, *adv.*

prescribe /prəˈskraɪb/ *v.t.* **1.** to lay down, in writing or otherwise, as a rule or a course to be followed; appoint, ordain, or enjoin. **2.** *Med.* to designate or order for use, as a remedy or treatment. *−v.i.* **3.** to lay down rules, direct, or dictate. **4.** *Med.* to designate remedies or treatment to be used. **5.** *Law* (esp. with *for* or *to*) to claim a right or title by virtue of long use and enjoyment. **−prescriber**, *n.*

prescribed burning *n.* → **controlled burning**.

prescription /prəˈskrɪpʃən/ *n.* **1.** *Med.* **a.** Also, **script**, **scrip**. a direction (usually written) by the doctor to the pharmacist for the preparation and use of a medicine or remedy. **b.** the medicine prescribed. **2.** the act of prescribing. **3.** something that is prescribed. **4.** *Law* **a.** a long or immemorial use of some right with respect to a thing so as to give a right to continue such use. **b.** the process of acquiring rights by uninterrupted assertion of the right over a long period of time.

prescriptive /prəˈskrɪptɪv/ *adj.* **1.** that prescribes; giving directions or injunctions. **2.** *Law* depending on or arising from effective prescription, as a right or title. **−prescriptively**, *adv.* **−prescriptiveness**, *n.*

preseason *adj.* /priˈsizən/ **1.** of or relating to a period of time just before the commencement of a sporting competition, series of performances, etc. *−n.* /ˈprisizən/ **2. the preseason**, *Sport* the period of training, preparation, etc., before the main competition begins. Also, **pre-season**.

preselection /prisəˈlɛkʃən/ *n. Politics* the process within a political party of choosing candidates to stand for election.

presence /ˈprɛzəns/ *n.* **1.** the condition or fact of being present. **2.** attendance or company. **3.** close vicinity: *in the presence of friends.* **4.** personal appearance or style, especially of a grand, important kind: *a man of fine presence.* **5.** a divine or spiritual being.

present¹ /ˈprɛzənt/ *adj.* **1.** being, existing, or happening at this time; now. **2.** for the time being: *clothes for present use.* **3.** being in attendance (opposed to *absent*): *to be present at a wedding.* **4.** being in a given place. **5.** existing in a place, thing, combination, etc. *−n.* **6.** the present time. **7.** *Gram.* → **present tense**.

present² *v.t.* /prəˈzɛnt/ **1.** to furnish or endow with a gift or the like, especially by formal act: *to present someone with a gold watch.* **2.** to bring, offer, or give, often in a formal or ceremonious way: *to present a message; to present one's business card.* **3.** to afford or furnish (an opportunity, possibility, etc.). **4.** to hand or send in, as a bill or a cheque for payment. **5.** to bring (a person, etc.) before, or into the presence of another, especially a superior. **6.** to introduce (a person) to another. **7.** to bring before or introduce to the public: *to present a new play.* **8.** to come to show (oneself) before a person, in or at a place, etc. **9.** to show or exhibit. **10.** to bring before the mind; offer for consideration. **11.** to set forth in words: *to present arguments.* **12.** to represent, impersonate, or act, as on the stage. **13.** to direct, point, or turn to something or in a particular way. **14.** to level or aim (a weapon, especially a firearm). *−v.i.* /prəˈzɛnt/ **15.** to make an impression, as specified: *he presents well.* *−n.* /ˈprɛzənt/ **16.** a thing presented as a gift; a gift: *Christmas presents.* –*phr.* **17. present with,** (of a medical, dental, or veterinary patient) to exhibit or complain of (a disability, illness, symptom, etc.). –**presenter**, *n.*

presentable /prəˈzɛntəbəl/ *adj.* **1.** fit to be presented. **2.** suitable as in appearance, dress, manners, etc., for being introduced into society or company. **3.** of sufficiently good appearance, or fit to be seen. –**presentability** /prəˌzɛntəˈbɪləti/, **presentableness**, *n.* –**presentably**, *adv.*

presentation /prɛzənˈteɪʃən/ *n.* **1.** the act or fact of presenting. **2.** exhibition or representation, as of a play. **3.** an address or report on a particular topic, especially one supported by images, digital data, exhibits, etc. **4.** offering or delivering, as of a gift. **5.** a gift. –**presentational**, *adj.*

presentiment /prəˈzɛntəmənt/ *n.* a feeling or impression of something about to happen, especially something evil; a foreboding. –**presentimental** /prəzɛntəˈmɛntl/, *adj.*

presently /ˈprɛzəntli/ *adv.* **1.** in a little while or soon. **2.** at this time, currently.

presentment /prɪˈzɛntmənt/ *n.* **1.** the act of presenting; presentation. **2.** a representation, picture, or likeness. **3.** *Commerce* the presenting of a bill, note, or the like, as for acceptance or payment. **4.** *Law* the written statement of an offence by a jury, of their own knowledge or observation, when no indictment has been laid before them.

present tense *n. Gram.* a tense which indicates that the action or state is happening or exists at the moment of speaking.

preservative /prəˈzɜvətɪv/ *n.* **1.** something that preserves or tends to preserve. **2.** a chemical substance used to preserve foods, etc., from decomposition or fermentation. **3.** a medicine that preserves health or prevents disease. –*adj.* **4.** tending to preserve.

preserve /prəˈzɜv/ *v.t.* **1.** to keep alive or in existence. **2.** to keep safe; save. **3.** to keep up; maintain. **4.** to keep possession of; retain. **5.** to prepare (food, etc.) so as to prevent decay. **6.** to prepare (fruit, etc.) by cooking with sugar. **7.** to keep (accrued superannuation benefits) in a superannuation or rollover fund until retirement age has been reached. –*v.i.* **8.** to preserve fruit, etc. –*n.* **9.** something that preserves. **10.** something that is preserved. **11.** (*usu. pl.*) fruit, etc., cooked with sugar. –**preservable**, *adj.* –**preservation** /prɛzəˈveɪʃən/, *n.* –**preserver**, *n.*

preside /prəˈzaɪd/ *v.i.* **1.** to occupy the place of authority or control, as in an assembly; act as chairman or president. **2.** to exercise superintendence or control. –**presider**, *n.*

president /ˈprɛzədənt/ *n.* **1.** (*oft. upper case*) the highest official in a republic. **2.** an officer appointed or elected to preside over an organised body of persons, as a council, society, etc. **3.** the chief officer of a college or university, or the chairperson of a company, etc. **4.** someone who presides over a meeting, conference, or the like. –**presidency**, *n.* –**presidential** /prɛzəˈdɛnʃəl/, *adj.*

press[1] /prɛs/ *v.t.* **1.** to act upon with weight or force. **2.** to move by weight or force in a certain direction or into a certain position. **3.** to compress or squeeze, as to alter in shape or size. **4.** to weigh heavily upon; subject to pressure. **5.** *Shearing* to compress (wool) in a wool press so as to create bales: *he was sewing up the pressed wool.* **6.** to make flat by subjecting to weight: *she pressed the flowers between the pages of a book.* **7.** to hold closely, as in an embrace; clasp. **8.** to iron (clothes, etc.). **9.** to extract juice, etc., from by pressure. **10.** to squeeze out or express, as juice. **11.** to beset or harass. **12.** to oppress or trouble; to put to straits, as by lack of something: *they were pressed for time.* **13.** to urge or impel, as to a particular course; constrain or compel. **14.** to urge onwards; hurry; hasten. **15.** to urge (a person, etc.), importune, beseech, or entreat. **16.** to insist on: *to press the payment of a debt; to press one's theories.* **17.** to plead with insistence: *to press a claim.* –*v.i.* **18.** to exert weight, force, or pressure. **19.** to bear heavily, as upon the mind. **20.** to compel haste: *time presses.* **21.** to demand immediate attention. **22.** to use urgent entreaty: *to press for an answer.* **23.** to push forward with force, eagerness, or haste. **24.** to crowd or throng. –*n.* **25.** printed publications collectively, especially newspapers and periodicals. **26. a.** Also, **printed press.** the body or class of persons engaged in writing for or editing newspapers or periodicals. **b.** the news media generally, including the electronic media. **27.** comment in the newspapers, etc., on some matter of current public interest, either approving (**good press**) or disapproving (**bad press**). **28.** *Printing* a machine used for printing, as a **flat-bed cylinder press**, one in which a flat bed holding the printing forme moves against a revolving cylinder which carries the paper, or a **rotary press**, one in which the types or plates to be printed are fastened upon a rotating cylinder and are impressed on a continuous roll of paper. **29.** an establishment for printing books, etc. **30.** the process or art of printing. **31.** any of various instruments or machines for exerting pressure, as a wool press. **32.** the act of pressing; pressure. **33.** a pressing or pushing forward. **34.** a pressing together in a crowd, or a crowding or thronging. **35.** a crowd, throng, or multitude. **36.** pressure or urgency, as of affairs or business. **37.** an upright case, or piece of furniture, for holding clothes, books, etc. **38.** a framework secured by screws for holding tennis racquets, and the like, when not in use. **39.** *Weightlifting* a lift where the barbell is raised first to the shoulders, then slowly and smoothly above the head with the arms held straight. –*phr.* **40. bad press**, unfavourable coverage in the media. **41. good press**, favourable coverage in the media. **42. go to press**, to begin to be printed. **43. press the flesh**, *Colloq.* (usually of politicians) to shake hands and talk with members of the public, as when campaigning for election, etc. –**presser**, *n.*

press[2] /prɛs/ *v.t.* **1.** to force into service, especially naval or military service; to impress. **2.** to make use of in a manner different from that intended or desired. –*n.* **3.** impressment into service, especially naval or military service.

press conference *n.* an interview of a famous person, public official, etc., with the press, often to make an important announcement or to answer questions.

press gallery *n.* **1.** a gallery or area reserved for journalists, especially in the legislative chamber of a house of parliament. **2.** the group or corps of journalists eligible to enter such a gallery: *the Canberra press gallery.*

pressing /ˈprɛsɪŋ/ *adj.* **1.** urgent; demanding immediate attention: *a pressing need.* –*n.* **2. a.** a run of gramophone records produced at one time. **b.** → **record** (def. 17). **3.** a physical stamping of an entire dataset onto a master CD or DVD or optical disc. Compare **burn** (def. 13). –**pressingly**, *adv.*

press release *n.* an item of news prepared for and distributed to the press.

press-stud *n.* a fastener, used especially on clothing, in which two parts are pressed together.

pressure /ˈprɛʃə/ *n.* **1.** the application of force upon a body by another body in contact with it; compression. **2.** *Physics* the force per unit area exerted at a given point. The SI unit of pressure is the pascal. **3.** the act or fact of pressing. **4.** annoyance; harassment. **5.** a condition of trouble or worry. **6.** a driving force or influence. **7.** urgency, as of business.

pressure group *n.* a group, in politics, business, etc., which attempts to protect or advance its own interests.

pressure pack *n.* a container from which a liquid is dispersed as a gas or under pressure of a gas; aerosol.

pressure point *n. Med.* **1.** any of the points in the body at which pressure applied with the fingers, a tourniquet, etc., will control bleeding from an artery at a point further away from the heart. **2.** a healing point in the body, stimulated by acupressure.

pressure system *n. Meteorol.* **1.** an atmospheric circulation system which may be a low pressure system such as a cyclone or depression, or a high pressure system such as an anticyclone. **2.** the pattern of isobars representing such a system.

pressurise /ˈprɛʃəraɪz/ *v.t.* **1.** to maintain normal air pressure in (the cockpit or cabin of an aeroplane designed to fly at high altitudes). **2.** to compress (a gas or liquid) to a pressure greater than normal. Also, **pressurize**. –**pressurisation** /prɛʃəraɪˈzeɪʃən/, *n.*

prestige /prɛsˈtiːʒ/ *n.* **1.** reputation or influence arising from success, achievement, rank, or other circumstances. **2.** distinction or reputation attaching to a person or thing and dominating the mind of others or of the public. –*adj.* **3.** characteristic of someone who has attained success, wealth, etc. –**prestigious** /prɛsˈtɪdʒəs/, *adj.*

presume /prəˈzjuːm/ *v.t.* **1.** to take for granted; assume: *I presume you're tired.* **2.** *Law* to suppose as true in the absence of proof to the contrary. –*v.i.* **3.** to take something for granted; suppose. **4.** to act or proceed with inexcusable boldness. –**presumable**, *adj.* –**presumably**, *adv.* –**presumedly**, *adv.* –**presumer**, *n.* –**presumption**, *n.*

presumptuous /prəˈzʌmptʃuəs/ *adj.* **1.** full of, characterised by, or showing presumption or readiness to presume in conduct or thought. **2.** unwarrantedly or impertinently bold; forward. –**presumptuously**, *adv.* –**presumptuousness**, *n.*

presuppose /prisəˈpoʊz/ *v.t.* **1.** to suppose or assume beforehand; to take for granted in advance. **2.** (of a thing) to require or imply as an antecedent condition: *an effect presupposes a cause.* –**presupposition** /ˌprisʌpəˈzɪʃən/, *n.*

pret-a-porter /prɛt-a-pɔˈteɪ/ *adj.* → **ready-to-wear**. Also, **prêt à porter**.

pretence /prəˈtɛns/ *n.* **1.** pretending or feigning; make-believe: *my sleepiness was all pretence.* **2.** a false show of something: *a pretence of friendship.* **3.** a piece of make-believe. **4.** the act of pretending or alleging, now especially falsely. **5.** an alleged or pretended reason or excuse, or a pretext. **6.** insincere or false profession. **7.** the putting forth of a claim. **8.** the claim itself. **9.** pretentiousness. –*phr.* **10. pretence to**, claim to: *destitute of any pretence to wit.* Also, *US*, **pretense**.

pretend /prəˈtɛnd/ *v.t.* **1.** to put forward a false appearance of; feign: *to pretend illness.* **2.** to venture or attempt falsely (to do something). **3.** to allege or profess, especially insincerely or falsely. –*v.i.* **4.** to make believe. –*phr.* **5. pretend to**, **a.** to lay claim to. **b.** to make pretensions to. **c.** to aspire to, as a suitor or candidate.

pretender /prəˈtɛndə/ *n.* **1.** someone who pretends; someone who makes false professions. **2.** an aspirant or candidate. **3.** a claimant to a throne.

pretension /prəˈtɛnʃən/ *n.* **1.** a laying claim to something. **2.** (*oft. pl.*) a claim made, especially indirectly or by implication, or right to some quality, merit, or the like: *pretensions to superior judgement.* **3.** pretentiousness. **4.** the act of pretending or alleging.

pretentious /prəˈtɛnʃəs/ *adj.* **1.** full of pretension. **2.** characterised by assumption of dignity or importance. **3.** making an exaggerated outward show; ostentatious. –**pretentiously**, *adv.* –**pretentiousness**, *n.*

preter- a prefix meaning 'beyond', 'more than'.

preterite /ˈprɛtərət, ˈprɛtrət/ *adj. Gram.* designating a tense usually denoting an action or state which was completed in the past. For example, in the sentence *John hit Jack, hit* could be said to be in the preterite tense, though in English grammar such verbs are more commonly said to be in the past tense.

preterm /ˈpritɜm/ *adj.* **1.** (of a baby) born or occurring before a pregnancy has reached its full term. **2.** (of an election) held before the parliament or other body for which members are elected has reached its full term. Also, **pre-term**.

pretext /ˈpritɛkst/ *n.* **1.** something that is put forward to conceal a true purpose or object; an ostensible reason. **2.** an excuse; a pretence.

pretty /ˈprɪti/ *adj.* (**-tier**, **-tiest**) **1.** fair or attractive to the eye in a feminine or childish way: *a pretty face.* **2.** (of things, places, etc.) pleasing to the eye, especially without grandeur. **3.** pleasing to the ear: *a pretty tune.* **4.** pleasing to the mind or aesthetic taste: *some pretty little story.* **5.** (*ironic*) dreadful: *a pretty mess.* **6.** *Colloq.* considerable; fairly great. –*n.* (*pl.* **-ties**) **7.** (*usu. pl.*) a pretty thing, as a trinket or ornament. **8.** a pretty one (used especially in address). –*adv.* **9.** moderately: *her work was pretty good.* **10.** quite; very: *the wind blew pretty hard.* –*v.t.* (**-tied**, **-tying**) Also, **pretty up**. **11.** to make pretty: *they prettied up the room with some flowers.* –*phr.* **12. a pretty penny**, a considerable sum of money. **13. be sitting pretty**, *Colloq.* to be in a satisfactory and unchallenged position. **14. pretty much** (or **well**), **a.** to a large extent: *his account of events pretty much agrees with hers.* **b.** very nearly: *the exams are pretty much over now.* –**prettily**, *adv.* –**prettiness**, *n.* –**prettyish**, *adj.*

pretzel /ˈprɛtsəl/ *n.* a crisp, dry biscuit, usually in the form of a knot or stick, salted on the outside.

prevail /prəˈveɪl/ *v.i.* **1.** to be widespread or current; to exist everywhere or generally: *dead silence prevailed.* **2.** to appear or occur as the more important or frequent feature or element; predominate: *green tints prevail in the picture.* **3.** to be or prove superior in strength, power, or influence. **4.** to operate effectually; to be efficacious. –*phr.* **5. prevail on** (or **upon**) (or **with**), to use persuasion or inducement successfully on. –**prevailing**, *adj.*

prevalent /ˈprɛvələnt/ *adj.* widespread; of wide extent or occurrence; in general use or acceptance. –**prevalence**, *n.* –**prevalently**, *adv.*

prevaricate /prəˈværəkeɪt/ *v.i.* to act or speak evasively; equivocate; quibble. –**prevarication** /prəværəˈkeɪʃən/, *n.* –**prevaricator**, *n.* –**prevaricating**, *adj.* –**prevaricatingly**, *adv.*

prevent /prəˈvɛnt/ *v.t.* **1.** to keep from occurring; hinder. **2.** to hinder (a person, etc.), as from doing something: *there is nothing to prevent us from going.* –*v.i.* **3.** to interpose a hindrance: *he will come if nothing prevents.* –**preventable**, **preventible**, *adj.* –**preventer**, *n.* –**prevention**, *n.*

preventative /prəˈvɛntətɪv/ *adj.* → **preventive**.

preventative detention order *n.* an order to detain a person in police custody for a specified period of time to prevent suspected terrorist activity or to prevent the loss of vital evidence after an attack.

preventive /prəˈvɛntɪv/ *adj.* **1.** *Med.* warding off disease. **2.** serving to prevent or hinder. Also, **preventative**. –**preventively**, *adv.* –**preventiveness**, *n.*

preventive medicine *n.* medical strategies and practices designed to prevent the onset of disease.

preview /ˈprivju/ *n.* **1.** a view in advance, as of a film. –*v.t.* **2.** to view beforehand or in advance.

previous /ˈpriviəs/ *adj.* **1.** coming or occurring before something else; prior. **2.** *Colloq.* done, occurring, etc.,

before the proper time; premature. **–previously**, *adv.*
–previousness, *n.*

prey /preɪ/ *n.* **1.** an animal hunted or seized for food, especially by a flesh-eating animal. **2.** a person or thing that falls victim to an enemy, disease, etc. **3.** the action or habit of preying: *bird of prey.* *–v.i.* **4.** to seek for and seize prey, as an animal does. *–phr.* **5. prey on** (or **upon**), **a.** to make profit by activities on a victim. **b.** to exert a harmful or destructive influence. **–preyer**, *n.*

price /praɪs/ *n.* **1.** the sum or amount of money or its equivalent for which anything is bought, sold, or offered for sale. **2.** a sum offered for the capture of a person alive or dead: *a price on a man's head.* **3.** the sum of money, or other consideration, for which a person's support, consent, etc., may be obtained: *he has his price.* **4.** that which must be given, done, or undergone in order to obtain a thing: *to gain a victory at a heavy price.* **5.** betting odds. *–v.t.* (**priced, pricing**) **6.** to fix the price of. **7.** *Colloq.* to ask the price of. *–phr.* **8. at any price**, at any cost, no matter how great. **9. at a price**, at a somewhat high price. **10. beyond** (or **without**) **price**, of incalculable value; priceless. **11. what price ...**, *Colloq.* **a.** what is the chance of (something specified). **b.** what do you think of (something specified).

price-fixing *n.* the setting of a price, usually a high price, for a commodity or service by agreement between business competitors so as to increase their profits. **–price-fixer**, *n.*

price gouging *n.* a high price which is only possible because the market is in some way captive.

price index *n.* an indicator used to show the general level of prices.

priceless /ˈpraɪsləs/ *adj.* **1.** having a value beyond all price; invaluable: *she was a priceless help to him.* **2.** *Colloq.* delightfully amusing; absurd.

pricey /ˈpraɪsi/ *adj. Colloq.* expensive.

prick /prɪk/ *n.* **1.** a puncture made by a needle, thorn, or the like. **2.** the act of pricking: *the prick of a needle.* **3.** the state or sensation of being pricked. **4.** *Archaic* a goad for oxen. **5.** *Colloq.* (*taboo*) **a.** the penis. **b.** an unpleasant or despicable person. *–v.t.* **6.** to pierce with a sharp point; puncture. **7.** to affect with sharp pain, as from piercing. **8.** to cause sharp mental pain to; sting, as with remorse or sorrow: *his conscience pricked him suddenly.* **9.** to cause to stand erect or point upwards: *the dog pricked up its ears.* *–v.i.* **10.** to perform the action of piercing or puncturing something. **11.** to have a sensation of being pricked. **12.** Also, **prick up.** to rise erect or point upwards, as the ears of an animal. *–phr.* **13. kick against the pricks**, to indulge in futile struggles against the harsh realities of life. **14. prick out**, to transplant (seedlings, etc.) from their original beds to larger boxes. **15. prick up one's ears**, to listen, especially at something unexpected or of particular interest. **–prickingly**, *adv.*

prickle /ˈprɪkəl/ *n.* **1.** a sharp point. **2.** a small, pointed outgrowth from the bark of a plant; thorn. **3.** any spiny burr, fruit or seed, as a bindi-eye. *–v.t.* **4.** to prick. **5.** to cause a pricking feeling in. *–v.i.* **6.** to tingle as if pricked. **–prickly**, *adj.*

prickly /ˈprɪkli/ *adj.* (**-lier, -liest**) **1.** full of or armed with prickles. **2.** full of troublesome points. **3.** prickling; smarting. **4.** sensitive; easily angered.

prickly pear *n.* **1.** the pear-shaped or ovoid, often prickly, and sometimes edible fruit of any of certain species of cactus (genus *Opuntia*). **2.** any of a number of species of *Opuntia*, as *O. stricta*, native to Mexico, which has become a noxious weed in Australia.

pride /praɪd/ *n.* **1.** high or inordinate opinion of one's own dignity, importance, merit, or superiority, whether as cherished in the mind or as displayed in bearing,

conduct, etc. **2.** the state or feeling of being proud. **3.** becoming or dignified sense of what is due to oneself or one's position or character; self-respect; self-esteem. **4.** pleasure or satisfaction taken in something done by or belonging to oneself or conceived as reflecting credit upon oneself: *civic pride.* **5.** the best or most admired part of anything. **6.** the most flourishing period or period: *in the pride of manhood.* **7.** a company of lions. *–phr.* **8. pride of place**, the most conspicuous position. **9. pride oneself on** (or **upon**), to feel pride about, often with a sense of complacency: *she prides herself on her sense of humour.* **–prideful**, *adj.* **–pridefully**, *adv.*

priest /prist/ *n.* **1.** someone whose office is to perform religious rites, and especially to make sacrificial offerings. **2.** (in Christian use) **a.** a person ordained to the sacerdotal or pastoral office; a person of the clergy; a minister. **b.** (in hierarchal churches) a person of the clergy of the order next below that of bishop, authorised to carry out the Christian ministry. **c.** *Roman Catholic Church* a member of one of the three major orders in the hierarchy, the others being bishop and deacon. **3.** a minister of any religion. **–priesthood**, *n.* **–priestly**, *adj.* **–priestliness**, *n.*

prig /prɪg/ *n.* someone who is precise to an extreme in attention to principle or duty, especially in a self-righteous way.

prim /prɪm/ *adj.* (**primmer, primmest**) affectedly precise or proper, as persons, behaviour, etc.; stiffly neat. **–primly**, *adv.* **–primness**, *n.*

primacy /ˈpraɪməsi/ *n.* (*pl.* **-cies**) **1.** the state of being first in order, rank, importance, etc. **2.** *Eccles.* the office, rank, or dignity of a primate. **3.** *Roman Catholic Church* the jurisdiction of the pope as supreme bishop.

prima donna /primə ˈdɒnə, prɪmə ˈdɒnə/ *n.* (*pl.* **prima donnas**) **1.** a first or principal female singer of an operatic company. **2.** *Colloq.* a temperamental, petulant person. Also, **diva.**

prima facie /praɪmə ˈfeɪsi, praɪmə ˈfeɪʃi/ *adv.* at first appearance; at first view, before investigation.

prima-facie evidence /ˌpraɪmə-feɪʃi ˈɛvədəns/ *n. Law* evidence sufficient to establish a fact, or to raise a presumption of fact, unless rebutted.

primal /ˈpraɪməl/ *adj.* **1.** first; original; primeval. **2.** of first importance; fundamental.

primary /ˈpraɪməri, ˈpraɪmri/ *adj.* **1.** first or highest in rank or importance; chief; principal. **2.** first in order in any series, order, etc. **3.** making up or belonging to, the first stage in any process. **4.** original; not derived; basic. **5.** immediate or direct; not involving intermediate agency. **6.** relating to any of the set of flight feathers found on the end part of a bird's wing. **7.** *Elect.* of or relating to the inducing circuit, coil, or current in an induction coil, etc. **8.** *Chem.* involving, or obtained by replacement of one radical. *–n.* (*pl.* **-ries**) **9.** the first in order, rank, or importance. **10.** *US* a meeting of the voters of a political party in an election district for choosing candidates for office, etc. **11.** one of any set of primary colours. See **primary colour. 12.** a primary feather. **–primarily**, *adj.*

primary colour *n.* a colour belonging to a group of colours which is regarded as generating all colours. **Additive primary colours** are red, green, and blue since light of these wavelengths, properly selected and mixed, can produce any hue, even white. In mixing dyes and pigments the colours act subtractively; the **subtractive primary colours** are loosely named as red, yellow, and blue. Also, **primary color.**

primary forest *n. Ecol.* forest that has not been logged or cleared in the past (opposed to *secondary forest*).

primary industry *n.* any industry such as dairy farming, forestry, mining, etc., which is involved in the growing, producing, extracting, etc., of natural resources.

primary producer *n.* **1.** someone who works in a primary industry as a farmer, fishes, etc. **2.** a business or industry devoted to primary production.

primary school *n.* a school for full-time elementary instruction of children from the age of five or six to about twelve years, varying between Australian states.

primate *n.* **1.** /ˈpraɪmət/ *Eccles.* an archbishop or bishop ranking first among the bishops of a province, country, etc. **2.** /ˈpraɪmeɪt/ *Zool.* any mammal of the order Primates, that includes humans, the apes, the monkeys, the lemurs, characterised by having a hand with an opposable first digit, acute binocular vision, and a developed brain. **–primateship**, *n.* **–primatial** /praɪˈmeɪʃəl/, *adj.*

prime /praɪm/ *adj.* **1.** first in importance, excellence, or value: *prime time*; *prime beef.* **2.** first or highest in rank or authority; principal: *the prime minister.* **3.** first in time; earliest; primitive. **4.** original; fundamental: *prime mover.* **5.** typical: *a prime example.* **6.** *Maths* **a.** of a number which has itself and unity as its only factors. **b.** having no common divisor except unity: *2 is prime to 9.* **–n. 7.** the period or condition of greatest vigour: *prime of youth*; *prime of life.* **8.** *Maths* → **prime number. 9.** *Music* (in a scale) the tonic or keynote. **–v.t. 10.** to put gunpowder into (an old-fashioned gun). **11.** to lay a train of gunpowder to (a charge, mine, etc.). **12.** to pour water into (a pump) to prepare it for working. **13.** to cover (a surface) with a preparatory coat of paint, etc. **14.** to supply or prepare with information, words, etc., for use. **–primeness**, *n.*

prime minister *n.* the first or principal minister of certain governments; the chief of the cabinet or ministry. **–prime ministry**, *n.* **–prime ministership**, *n.*

prime mover *n.* **1.** *Mechanics* the initial agent which puts a machine in motion, as wind, electricity, etc. **2.** *Aust.* a powerful motor vehicle designed to draw a trailer. **3.** such an engine with the driver's cabin as in a semitrailer. **4.** someone who is the prime organiser or creative force in an enterprise.

prime number *n. Maths* a positive integer not exactly divisible by any integer except itself and unity: *5 is a prime number.*

primer[1] /ˈpraɪmə, ˈprɪmə/ *n.* **1.** an elementary book for teaching children to read. **2.** any, often small, book of elementary principles: *a primer of phonetics.*

primer[2] /ˈpraɪmə/ *n.* **1.** a cap, cylinder, etc., containing a compound which may be exploded by percussion or other means, used for firing a charge of powder. **2.** the first complete coat of paint applied to an unpainted surface. **3.** any preliminary coating or preparation applied before a final surface finish.

primeval /praɪˈmivəl/ *adj.* of or relating to the first age or ages, especially of the world: *primeval forms of life.* Also, **primaeval. –primevally**, *adv.*

primitive /ˈprɪmətɪv/ *adj.* **1.** being the first or earliest of the kind or in existence: *primitive forms of life.* **2.** typical of early ages or of an early state of human development: *primitive art.* **3.** simple; crude. **4.** *Biol.* rudimentary; primordial. **–n. 5.** (a painting by) an artist who paints in a simple or naive style. **–primitively**, *adv.* **–primitiveness**, *n.*

primogeniture /praɪmoʊˈdʒɛnətʃə/ *n.* **1.** the state or fact of being the firstborn among the children of the same parents. **2.** *Law* the principle of inheritance or succession by the firstborn, specifically the eldest son.

primordial /praɪˈmɔdiəl/ *adj.* **1.** constituting a beginning; giving origin to something derived or developed; original; elementary. **2.** *Biol.* primitive; initial; first. **3.** relating to or existing at or from the very beginning: *primordial matter.* **–primordially**, *adv.*

primrose /ˈprɪmroʊz/ *n.* **1.** any plant of the genus *Primula* (family Primulaceae), comprising perennial herbs with variously coloured flowers, especially *P. vulgaris*, a common yellow-flowered European species. **2.** pale yellow. **–adj. 3.** relating to the primrose. **4.** of a pale yellow. **–phr. 5. the primrose path**, a way of life that is self-indulgent and hedonistic: *to be led down the primrose path of pleasure.*

prince /prɪns/ *n.* **1.** a non-reigning male member of a royal family. **2.** a ruler of a small state, lower in rank than a king. **3.** someone or something that is important, or the best, in any class, group, etc.: *a merchant prince; a prince among poets.* **–princedom**, *n.* **–princely**, *adj.*

princedom /ˈprɪnsdəm/ *n.* **1.** the position, rank, or dignity of a prince. **2.** a state ruled by a prince. **3.** → **principality** (def. 4).

princess /ˈprɪnsɛs/ *n.* **1.** a daughter or near relative of a king or queen. **2.** the wife of a prince.

principal /ˈprɪnsəpəl/ *adj.* **1.** first or highest in rank, importance, value, etc.; chief; foremost. **–n. 2.** the head of a school or college. **3.** someone who takes a leading part in a play, ballet, action, etc. **4.** something of chief importance. **5.** *Law* **a.** a person authorising another (an agent) to represent him or her. **b.** a person directly responsible for a crime. See **accessory** (def. 3). **6.** someone who has a debt to pay back (opposed to an *endorser*). **7.** *Commerce* a sum of money on which interest is paid or profit gained. **–principally**, *adv.* **–principalship**, *n.*

principality /prɪnsəˈpælətɪ/ *n.* (*pl.* **-ties**) **1.** a state ruled by a prince, usually a relatively small state or a state that falls within a larger state such as an empire. **2.** the position or authority of a prince or chief ruler; sovereignty; supreme power. **3.** the rule of a prince of a small or subordinate state. **4.** *Theology* a member of the seventh order of angels. See **angel** (def. 1).

principle /ˈprɪnsəpəl/ *n.* **1.** an accepted or professed rule of action or conduct: *a man of good principles.* **2.** a fundamental, primary, or general truth, on which other truths depend: *the principles of government.* **3.** a fundamental doctrine or tenet; a distinctive ruling opinion: *the principles of the Stoics.* **4.** (*pl.*) right rules of conduct. **5.** guiding sense of the requirements and obligations of right conduct: *a man of principle.* **6.** fixed rule or adopted method as to action. **7.** a rule or law exemplified in natural phenomena, in the construction or operation of a machine, the working of a system, or the like: *the principle of capillary attraction.* **8.** the method of formation, operation, or procedure exhibited in a given case: *a community organised on the principle of one great family.* **9.** a determining characteristic of something; essential quality of character. **10.** an originating or actuating agency or force. **11.** an actuating agency in the mind or character, as an instinct, faculty, or natural tendency. **12.** *Chem.* a constituent of a substance, especially one giving to it some distinctive quality or effect. **–phr. 13. in principle**, **a.** according to the rule generally followed. **b.** as an expression of general intentions or beliefs, without consideration of real-life complications: *a decision taken in principle.* **14. on principle**, **a.** according to fixed rule, method, or practice. **b.** according to one's personal rule for right conduct; as a matter of moral principle.

print /prɪnt/ *v.t.* **1.** to produce (a text, a picture, etc.) by applying inked types, plates, blocks, or the like, with direct pressure to paper or other material. **2.** to cause (a manuscript, etc.) to be reproduced in print. **3.** to write in letters like those commonly used in print. **4.** to indent or mark (a surface, etc.) by pressing something into or on it. **5.** to produce or fix (an indentation, mark, etc.) as by pressure. **6.** to impress on the mind, memory, etc. **7.** to apply (a thing) with pressure so as to leave an indentation, mark, etc. **8.** *Photography* to produce a positive picture from (a negative) by the transmission of light. **9.** Also, **print out.** *Computers* to produce (a result, data, etc.) in a legible form on paper. *–v.i.* **10.** to take impressions from type, etc., as in a press. **11.** to produce books, etc., by means of a press. **12.** to give an impression on paper, etc., as types, plates, etc. **13.** to write in characters such as are used in print. **14.** to follow the craft of a printer. **15.** Also, **print out.** *Computers* to transfer data onto paper or into a file. *–n.* **16.** the state of being printed. **17.** printed lettering, especially with reference to character, style, or size. **18.** printed matter. **19.** a printed publication, as a newspaper. **20.** newsprint. **21.** a picture, design, or the like, printed from an engraved or otherwise prepared block, plate, etc. **22.** an indentation, mark, etc., made by the pressure of one body or thing on another. **23.** something with which an impression is made; a stamp or die. **24.** a design, usually in colour, pressed on woven cotton with engraved rollers. **25.** the cloth so treated. **26.** *Photography* a picture made from a negative. *–adj.* **27.** made of printed material, especially cotton. **28.** of or relating to printed publications: *the print media.* **29.** produced in print: *a print dictionary.* *–phr.* **30. in print, a.** in printed form; published. **b.** (of a book, etc.) still available for purchase from the publisher. **31. out of print,** (of a book, etc.) no longer available for purchase from the publisher; sold out by the publisher. **–printable,** *adj.* **–printery,** *n.*

printer /ˈprɪntə/ *n.* **1.** a person or firm engaged in the printing industry. **2.** *Computers* a machine that prints on paper information sent by means of electrical or mechanical signals.

printout /ˈprɪntaʊt/ *n. Computers* a document printed out from a computer. Also, **print-out.**

prion¹ /ˈpraɪɒn/ *n.* any of various seabirds of the genus *Pachyptila*, pale blue above and pure white underneath, with a slightly wedge-shaped tail, which feed by collecting planktonic organisms, especially crustaceans and squid, from the surface of the sea, and which migrate to Australia.

prion² /ˈpraɪɒn/ *n. Pathol.* an infectious particle which is composed solely of protein and which is like a virus but contains no genetic material, linked to degenerative neurological diseases such as mad cow disease.

prior¹ /ˈpraɪə/ *adj.* **1.** preceding in time, or in order; earlier or former; anterior or antecedent: *a prior agreement.* *–phr.* **2. prior to, a.** earlier than: *prior to that time.* **b.** before: *he did it prior to going to bed.*

prior² /ˈpraɪə/ *n. Eccles.* **1.** an officer in a monastic order or religious house, sometimes next in rank below an abbot. **2.** the superior of certain monastic orders and houses. **–priorate,** *n.* **–priorship,** *n.* **–priory,** *n.*

priority /praɪˈɒrəti/ *n.* (*pl.* **-ties**) **1.** the state of being earlier in time, or of preceding something else. **2.** precedence in order, rank, etc. **3.** the having of certain rights before another. **4.** *Computers* the position in rank of an interrupt system in gaining the attention of the computer when there is more than one interrupt system. **–prioritise, prioritize,** *v.*

priority-paid *adj. Aust.* of or relating to mail, the delivery of which is guaranteed within a specified time.

prise /praɪz/ *v.t.* **1.** to raise, move, or force with or as with a lever. *–n.* **2.** leverage. Also, *Chiefly US,* **prize, pry.**

prism /ˈprɪzəm/ *n.* **1.** *Optics* a transparent body (especially one with triangular bases) used for decomposing light into its spectrum or for reflecting light beams. **2.** *Geom.* a solid whose bases or ends are any congruent and parallel polygons, and whose sides are parallelograms. **3.** *Crystallography* **a.** a form consisting of faces which are parallel to the vertical axis and intersect the horizontal axes. **b.** a dome (**horizontal prism**). **–prismatic** /prɪzˈmatɪk/, *adj.*

prison /ˈprɪzən/ *n.* **1.** a public building for the confinement or safe custody of criminals and others committed by law. **2.** a place of confinement or involuntary restraint. **3.** imprisonment.

prisoner /ˈprɪzənə, ˈprɪznə/ *n.* **1.** someone who is confined in prison or kept in custody, especially as the result of legal process. **2.** a person or thing that is deprived of liberty or kept in restraint.

prisoner of war *n.* someone captured by an enemy in war. *Abbrev.:* POW

prison officer *n.* an official having charge of prisoners in a jail; warder.

prissy /ˈprɪsi/ *adj.* (**-sier, -siest**) *Colloq.* precise; prim; affectedly nice.

pristine /ˈprɪstin/ *adj.* **1.** so clean as to appear new: *pristine white sheets*; *the house was in pristine condition.* **2.** of or relating to the earliest period or state; original; primitive. **3.** having its original purity.

privacy /ˈpraɪvəsi, ˈprɪvəsi/ *n.* (*pl.* **-cies**) **1.** the state of being private; retirement or seclusion. **2.** secrecy.

private /ˈpraɪvət/ *adj.* **1.** belonging to some particular person or persons; belonging to oneself; being one's own: *private property.* **2.** relating to or affecting a particular person or a small group of persons; individual; personal: *for your private satisfaction.* **3.** confined to or intended only for the person or persons immediately concerned; confidential: *a private communication.* **4.** not holding public office employment, as a person. **5.** not of an official or public character. **6.** (of a school) non-government. **7.** (of a company) having the right to transfer its shares restricted, the number of its members limited to 50, and prohibited from using public subscription for its shares or debentures. **8.** removed from or out of public view of knowledge; secret. **9.** not open or accessible to people in general: *a private road.* **10.** without the presence of others; alone; secluded. **11.** (of a member of parliament) not holding a government post. **12.** of lowest military rank. *–n.* **13.** *Army* **a.** a soldier in the Australian Army of the lowest military rank. **b.** the rank. *Abbrev.:* PTE **14.** *US* a soldier of one of the three lowest ranks (**private 1, private 2, private first class**). *–phr.* **15. in private,** in secret; not publicly; alone **–privately,** *adv.* **–privateness,** *n.*

private bill *n. Govt* a parliamentary bill for the particular interest or benefit of some person or body of persons.

private enterprise *n. Econ.* **1.** business or commercial activities independent of state ownership or control. **2.** the principle of free enterprise or laissez-faire capitalism.

private eye *n. Colloq.* a private investigator.

private investigator *n.* a detective working under private contract, as opposed to one employed by a public police force.

private means *pl. n.* → **independent means.**

private practice *n.* **1.** medical practice involving care for the health of private patients, for which charges are made to the individual. **2.** self-employment.

private school *n.* a school which is privately financed and managed, and is outside the state system of education.

private sector *n. Econ.* **1.** the sector of an economy which is owned and operated by individuals and privately-owned companies (opposed to the *public sector*). **2.** the companies and individuals operating within this sector.

privation /praɪˈveɪʃən/ *n.* **1.** lack of the usual comforts or necessaries of life, or an instance of this: *to lead a life of privation.* **2.** a depriving. **3.** the state of being deprived.

privatise /'praɪvətaɪz/ *v.t.* to change the status of (land, industries, etc.) from that of state to private ownership. Also, **privatize**. **–privatisation**, *n.*

privative /'prɪvətɪv/ *adj.* **1.** having the quality of depriving. **2.** consisting in or characterised by the taking away of something, or the loss or lack of something properly present. **3.** *Gram.* indicating negation or absence. *–n.* **4.** *Gram.* a privative element, as *a-* in *asymmetric* (without symmetry). **–privatively**, *adv.*

privet /'prɪvət/ *n.* one of three shrubs, *Ligustrum sinese*, *L. lucidum* or *L. ovalifolium*, with evergreen leaves and small, heavily perfumed white flowers, now considered a noxious weed.

privilege /'prɪvəlɪdʒ/ *n.* **1.** a right or immunity enjoyed by a person or persons beyond the common advantages of others. **2.** a special right or immunity granted to persons in authority or office; a prerogative. **3.** a prerogative, advantage, or opportunity enjoyed by someone in a favoured position (as distinguished from a right). **4.** a grant to an individual, a company, etc., of a special right or immunity, sometimes in derogation of the common right. **5.** the principle or condition of enjoying special rights or immunities. **6.** any of the more sacred and vital rights common to all citizens under a modern constitution. *–v.t.* (**-leged**, **-leging**) **7.** to grant a privilege to. **8.** to authorise or to license (something otherwise forbidden). *–phr.* **9. privilege from**, to free or exempt from.

privy /'prɪvi/ *adj.* **1.** (sometimes fol. by *to*) participating in the knowledge of something private or secret: *many persons were privy to the plot.* **2.** belonging or relating to some particular person or persons, now especially with reference to a sovereign. *–n.* (*pl.* **privies**) **3.** an outbuilding housing a toilet. **4.** *Law* a person participating directly in a legal transaction, or claiming through or under such a one. **–privity**, *n.*

prize¹ /praɪz/ *n.* **1.** a reward of victory in a race, competition, etc. **2.** that which is won in a lottery, raffle, etc. **3.** anything that someone tries hard to win, or anything greatly valued. *–adj.* **4.** having gained a prize; prize-winning. **5.** worthy of a prize; very valuable: *a prize bull.* **6.** remarkable: *a prize fool.* **7.** given or awarded as a prize: *a prize tour of NZ.*

prize² /praɪz/ *v.t.* **1.** to value or esteem highly. **2.** to estimate the worth or value of.

pro¹ /proʊ/ *adv.* **1.** in favour of a proposition, opinion, etc. (opposed to *con*). *–n.* (*pl.* **pros**) **2.** an argument, consideration, vote, etc., for something (opposed to *con*).

pro² /proʊ/ *Colloq. –n.* (*pl.* **pros**) **1.** a professional. *–adj.* **2.** professional.

pro³ /proʊ/ *n.* (*pl.* **pros**) *Colloq.* a prostitute.

pro- **1.** a prefix indicating favour for some party, system, idea, etc., usually without identity with the group, as *pro-British*, *pro-communist*, *pro-slavery*, having *anti-* as its opposite. **2.** a prefix of priority in space or time having especially a meaning of advancing or projecting forwards or outwards, having also extended figurative meanings, including substitution, and attached widely to stems not used as words, as *provision*, *prologue*, *proceed*, *produce*, *protract*, *procathedral*, *proconsul*.

proactive /proʊˈæktɪv/ *adj.* taking the initiative in directing the course of events, rather than waiting until things happen and then reacting. **–proactively**, *adv.*

probability /prɒbəˈbɪləti/ *n.* (*pl.* **-ties**) **1.** the quality or fact of being probable. **2.** a likelihood or chance of something: *there is a probability of his coming.* **3.** a probable event, circumstance, etc.: *to regard a thing as a probability.* **4.** *Statistics* the relative frequency of the occurrence of an event as measured by the ratio of the number of cases or alternatives favourable to the event

to the total number of cases or alternatives. *–phr.* **5. in all probability**, with likelihood; very probably.

probable /'prɒbəbəl/ *adj.* **1.** likely to occur or prove true. **2.** having more evidence for than against, or evidence which inclines the mind to belief but leaves some room for doubt. **3.** affording ground for belief: *probable evidence*. **–probably**, *adv.*

probate /'proʊbeɪt/ *n.* **1.** *Law* the official proving of a will as authentic or valid. *–adj.* **2.** of or relating to probate or a court of probate.

probation /prəˈbeɪʃən/ *n.* **1.** the act of testing. **2.** the testing or trial of a person's conduct, character, qualifications, or the like. **3.** the state or period of such testing or trial. **4.** *Law* **a.** a method of dealing with offenders, especially young persons guilty of minor crimes or first offences, by allowing them to go at large conditionally under supervision, as that of a person (**probation officer**) appointed for such duty. **b.** the state of having been conditionally released. **5.** a trial period in which a person can redeem failures, misconduct, etc. **–probational, probationary**, *adj.* **–probationer**, *n.*

probation order *n. Law* a form of bond by which an offender is not imprisoned but must report on a regular basis to a probation officer.

probe /proʊb/ *v.t.* **1.** to search into or examine thoroughly; question closely. **2.** to examine or explore as with a probe. *–v.i.* **3.** to penetrate or examine with or as with a probe. *–n.* **4.** the act of probing. **5.** an official inquiry. **6.** a thin surgical instrument for exploring the depth or direction of a wound, sinus, etc. **7.** *Aeronautics* a spacecraft able to explore, examine and test conditions in space and radio back the results. **–prober**, *n.*

probiotic /proʊbaɪˈɒtɪk/ *adj.* **1.** of or relating to a food containing live bacteria which have health-promoting properties: *a probiotic yoghurt can colonise the intestines with beneficial bacteria.* *–n.* **2.** such a food: *probiotics have been found to improve immunity.*

probity /'proʊbəti/ *n.* integrity; uprightness; honesty.

problem /'prɒbləm/ *n.* **1.** any question or matter involving doubt, uncertainty, or difficulty. **2.** a question proposed for solution or discussion. *–adj.* **3.** difficult to train or guide; unruly: *a problem student.* **–problematic**, *adj.*

problematise /'prɒbləmətaɪz/ *v.t.* to expose and analyse problems in (something previously assumed to be without problems): *to problematise the current assumptions.* Also, **problematize**. **–problematisation**, *n.*

problem child *n.* a child whose behaviour is antisocial in some way.

pro bono /proʊ ˈboʊnoʊ/ *adj.* **1.** (especially of legal work) performed without charge for clients who cannot afford to pay the usual fee: *a proportion of her time is spent on pro bono work.* *–adv.* **2.** without charging a fee: *he is working pro bono for this client.*

proboscis /prəˈbɒskəs, prəˈboʊsəs/ *n.* (*pl.* **-boscises** /-ˈbɒskəsəz, -ˈbɒsəsəz/ *or* **-boscides** /-ˈbɒskədiz, -ˈbɒsədiz/) **1.** an elephant's trunk. **2.** any long flexible snout, as of the tapir. **3.** *Entomology* **a.** an elongate but not rigid feeding organ of certain insects formed of the mouthparts, as in the Lepidoptera and Diptera. **b.** any elongate or snout-like feeding organ. **4.** (*humorous*) the human nose.

procedural /prəˈsidʒərəl/ *adj.* **1.** of or relating to procedure. **2.** of or relating to a text type or form which shows how something can be done, as a recipe. **–procedurally**, *adv.*

procedure /prəˈsidʒə/ *n.* **1.** the act or manner of proceeding in any action or process; conduct. **2.** a particular course or mode of action. **3.** mode of conducting legal, parliamentary, or other business, especially litigation and judicial proceedings. **4.** Also, **medical procedure**. a surgical operation or other medical technique performed on part of the body for a diagnostic or therapeutic purpose.

proceed /prə'siːd/ *v.i.* **1.** to move or go forwards or onwards, especially after stopping. **2.** to go on with or carry on any action or process. **3.** to go on (to do something). **4.** to be carried on, as an action, process, etc. **5.** to go or come forth; issue. **6.** to arise, originate, or result. *–n.* /'prəʊsiːd/ **7.** (*usu. pl.*) the sum derived from a sale or other transaction. *–phr.* **8. proceed against,** *Law* to take legal action against.

proceeding /prə'siːdɪŋ/ *n.* **1.** a particular action or course of action. **2.** action, course of action, or conduct. **3.** (*pl.*) records of the doings of a society. **4.** *Law* **a.** the instituting or carrying on of an action at law. **b.** a legal step or measure: *to institute proceedings against a person.*

process /'prəʊsɛs/ *n.* **1.** a systematic series of actions directed to some end: *the process of making butter.* **2.** a continuous action, operation, or series of changes taking place in a definite manner: *the process of decay.* **3.** *Law* **a.** the summons, mandate, or writ by which a defendant or thing is brought before court for litigation. **b.** the total of such summoning writs. **c.** the whole course of the proceedings in an action at law. **4.** *Biol.* a natural outgrowth, projection, or appendage: *a process of a bone.* **5.** a prominence or protuberance. **6.** the action of going forward or on. **7.** the condition of being carried on. **8.** course or lapse, as of time. *–v.t.* **9.** to treat or prepare by some particular process, as in manufacturing. **10.** to convert (an agricultural commodity) into marketable form by some special process. **11.** to apply a process to: *to process an application.* **12.** *Computers* to manipulate (data) in order to abstract the required information. *–phr.* **13. in (the) process of,** during the course of; in the middle of. *–processor,* *n.*

procession /prə'sɛʃən/ *n.* **1.** an orderly line or group of people, cars, etc., moving along in a formal or ceremonious way, especially in religious or civic ceremonies. **2.** the act of coming forth from a source. *–processional, adj., n.*

process worker *n.* a person engaged in a production line in a manufacturing process who is not required to make adjustments to machinery or to exercise skills of fitting or adjustment.

proclaim /prə'kleɪm/ *v.t.* **1.** to announce or declare publicly or in a tiresome way: *to proclaim one's opinions.* **2.** to announce or declare, publicly and officially: *to proclaim war; to proclaim a law.* **3.** (of things) to show or make known: *his speech proclaimed his ignorance.* *–proclaimer, n. –proclamation, n.*

proclivity /prə'klɪvəti/ *n.* (*pl.* -ties) natural or habitual inclination or tendency; propensity; predisposition: *a proclivity to fault-finding.*

procrastinate /proʊ'kræstəneɪt/ *v.i.* **1.** to defer action; delay: *to procrastinate until an opportunity is lost.* *–v.t.* **2.** to put off till another day or time; defer; delay. *–procrastination* /prəkræstə'neɪʃən/, *n.* *–procrastinator, n.*

procreate /'proʊkrieɪt/ *v.t.* **1.** to beget or generate (offspring). **2.** to produce; bring into being. *–v.i.* **3.** to beget young; reproduce. *–procreant, procreative, adj.* *–procreation* /proʊkri'eɪʃən/, *n.* *–procreator, n.*

proctor /'prɒktə/ *n.* (in some universities) an official responsible for matters such as supervising examinations or investigating misconduct. *–proctorial* /prɒk'tɔːriəl/, *adj.* *–proctorship, n.*

procure /prə'kjʊə/ *v.t.* **1.** to obtain or get by care, effort, or the use of special means: *to procure evidence.* **2.** to effect; cause; bring about, especially by unscrupulous or indirect means: *to procure a person's death.* **3.** to obtain for the gratification of lust or purposes of prostitution. *–v.i.* **4.** to act as a procurer or pimp. *–procurable, adj. –procurement, n.*

prod /prɒd/ *v.t.* (**prodded, prodding**) **1.** to poke or jab with something pointed: *to prod an animal with a stick.* **2.** to seek to rouse or incite as if by poking: *to prod his memory.* *–n.* **3.** the act of prodding; a poke or jab. **4.** any of various pointed instruments, as a goad. *–prodder, n.*

prodigal /'prɒdɪɡəl/ *adj.* **1.** wastefully or recklessly extravagant: *prodigal expenditure.* **2.** lavishly abundant; profuse. *–n.* **3.** someone who spends, or has spent, their money or substance with wasteful extravagance; a spendthrift. *–phr.* **4. prodigal of,** giving or yielding profusely; lavish with: *prodigal of smiles.* *–prodigality* /prɒdə'ɡæləti/, *n.* *–prodigally, adv.*

prodigious /prə'dɪdʒəs/ *adj.* **1.** extraordinary in size, amount, extent, degree, force, etc.: *a prodigious noise.* **2.** wonderful or marvellous: *a prodigious feat.* **3.** abnormal; monstrous. *–prodigiously, adv. –prodigiousness, n.*

prodigy /'prɒdədʒi/ *n.* (*pl.* -gies) **1.** a person, especially a child, endowed with extraordinary gifts or powers: *a musical prodigy.* **2.** something wonderful or marvellous; a wonder.

produce *verb* /prə'djuːs/ (-duced, -ducing) *–v.t.* **1.** to bring into existence; give rise to; cause: *to produce steam.* **2.** to make by mental or physical work: *to produce a book; to produce a sculpture.* **3.** *Econ.* to make (something that can be bought or sold). **4.** to bring forth; bear; give birth to. **5.** to yield; provide, furnish, or supply: *a mine producing silver.* **6.** to bring forward; present: *when everyone had arrived, he produced his plan.* **7.** to bring (a play, film, etc.) before the public. **8.** *Geom.* to extend or prolong (a line). *–v.i.* **9.** to bring forth or yield offspring, products, etc. **10.** *Econ.* to create value; bring crops, goods, etc., into a state in which they will fetch a price. *–n.* /'prɒdjuːs/ **11.** something that is produced; yield; product. **12.** farm or natural products as a whole: *to take produce to market.* *–producer, n. –producible, adj.*

product /'prɒdʌkt/ *n.* **1.** a thing produced by any action or operation, or by labour; an effect or result. **2.** something produced; a thing produced by nature or by a natural process. **3.** *Chem.* a substance obtained from another substance through chemical change. **4.** *Maths* the result obtained by multiplying two or more quantities together.

product disclosure statement *n.* the document provided to investors considering a financial product, as insurance, superannuation, etc. *Abbrev.*: PDS

production /prə'dʌkʃən/ *n.* **1.** the act of producing; creation; manufacture. **2.** something that is produced; product. **3.** *Econ.* the creation of value; producing of articles able to be bought and sold. **4.** the total amount produced: *production from our farm is good this year.* **5.** the act of showing: *the production of the letter just at that moment created a sensation.* **6.** the staging of a play.

production values *pl. n. Film, TV, Theatre, etc.* the quality of the technical aspects of a production, as lighting, sound, etc., as well as set design, costumes, etc.

productive /prə'dʌktɪv/ *adj.* **1.** having the power of producing; generative; creative. **2.** producing readily or abundantly; fertile; prolific. **3.** *Econ.* producing or tending to produce goods and services having exchangeable value. *–productively, adv. –productiveness, n. –productivity, n.*

profane /prə'feɪn/ *adj.* **1.** marked by lack of respect for God or sacred things; irreligious, especially speaking or spoken in open or implied contempt for sacred things. **2.** not sacred, or not given to sacred purposes; worldly; secular: *profane history.* **3.** common; vulgar; socially shocking: *profane language.* *–v.t.* **4.** to misuse (anything that should be held in respect); defile; debase.

5. to treat (anything holy) without respect. **–profanation** /profə'neɪʃən/, *n.* **–profanatory** /prə'fænətri/, *adj.* **–profanely,** *adv.* **–profaneness,** *n.* **–profanity,** *n.*

profess /prə'fɛs/ *v.t.* **1.** to declare (a feeling, etc.), often insincerely; pretend to: *he professed great sorrow.* **2.** to declare openly; avow: *he professed his satisfaction*; *to profess faith in God.* **3.** to declare oneself skilled or expert in. **4.** to receive or admit into a religious order.

profession /prə'fɛʃən/ *n.* **1.** a vocation requiring knowledge of some department of learning or science, especially one of the three vocations of theology, law, and medicine (formerly known specifically as **the professions** or **the learned professions**): *a lawyer by profession.* **2.** any vocation, occupation, etc. **3.** the body of persons engaged in an occupation or calling: *to be respected by the medical profession.* **4.** the act of professing; avowal; a declaration, whether true or false: *professions of love.* **5.** a religion or faith professed.

professional /prə'fɛʃnəl, -fənəl/ *adj.* **1.** following an occupation to earn a living or make money by it: *a professional actor.* **2.** relating or suitable to, or engaged in a profession: *professional studies; a professional manner.* **3.** expert; competent: *the teachers at that school are very professional.* **4.** making a business of something not properly to be regarded as a business: *a professional politician.* **5.** done to earn a living or to make money: *professional football.* –*n.* **6.** someone belonging to one of the learned or skilled professions. **7.** someone who earns a living by a skill, sport, etc. (opposed to *amateur*). **8.** an expert in a game or sport, hired by a sports club to teach members. **–professionally,** *adv.* **–professionalism,** *n.*

professor /prə'fɛsə/ *n.* **1.** a teacher of the highest rank, usually holding a chair in a particular branch of learning, in a university or college. **2.** a teacher. **3.** an instructor in some popular art, as singing, etc. **4.** someone who professes their sentiments, beliefs, etc. **–professorial** /profə'sɔriəl/, *adj.* **–professorially,** *adv.* **–professoriate** /profə'sɔriət/, *n.* **–professorship,** *n.*

proffer /'profə/ *v.t.* **1.** to put before a person for acceptance; offer. **2.** the act of proffering. **3.** an offer.

proficient /prə'fɪʃənt/ *adj.* **1.** well advanced or expert in any art, science, or subject; skilled. –*n.* **2.** an expert. **–proficiency,** *n.* **–proficiently,** *adv.*

profile /'proʊfaɪl/ *n.* **1.** the outline or contour of the human face, especially as seen from the side. **2.** a drawing, painting, etc., of the side view of the head. **3.** the outline of something seen against a background. **4.** *Archit., Eng.* a drawing of a section, especially a vertical section, through something. **5.** a vivid and concise sketch of the biography and personality of an individual. **6.** an analysis of the traits and characteristics of a person from the facts available, as of a criminal to assist in their capture. **7.** a public identity, as specialising in a particular field or having particular skills, acquired by a business or a group of business organisations, usually as a result of an advertising campaign. –*v.t.* **8.** to draw a profile of. **9.** to compile a profile of. **10.** to shape as to profile. –*phr. Colloq.* **11. keep** (or **maintain**) **a high profile,** to act so as to be conspicuous; maintain a prominent level of activity. **12. keep** (or **maintain**) **a low profile,** to act so as to be inconspicuous; maintain an unobtrusive level of activity.

profit /'profət/ *n.* **1.** (*oft. pl.*) pecuniary gain resulting from the employment of capital in any transaction: **a. gross profit,** gross receipts less the immediate costs of production. **b. net profit,** amount remaining after deducting all costs from gross receipts. **c.** the ratio of such pecuniary gain to the amount of capital invested. **2.** (*oft. pl.*) returns, proceeds, or revenue, as from property or investments. **3.** *Econ.* the surplus left to the producer or employer after deducting wages, rent, cost

of raw materials, etc. **4.** (*usu. pl.*) such additional benefits as interest on capital, insurance, etc. **5.** advantage; benefit; gain. –*v.i.* **6.** to gain advantage or benefit. **7.** to make profit. **8.** to be of advantage or benefit. **9.** to take advantage. –*v.t.* **10.** to be of advantage or profit to. **–profitable,** *adj.* **–profitability,** *n.* **–profitless,** *adj.*

profiteer /profə'tɪə/ *n.* **1.** someone who seeks or exacts exorbitant profits, as by taking advantage of public necessity. –*v.i.* **2.** to act as a profiteer. **–profiteering,** *n.*

profiterole /prə'fɪtəroʊl/ *n.* a small ball of pastry with a sweet or savoury filling.

profligate /'profləgət/ *adj.* **1.** utterly and shamelessly immoral; thoroughly dissolute. **2.** recklessly prodigal or extravagant. –*n.* **3.** a profligate person. **–profligacy, profligateness,** *n.* **–profligately,** *adv.*

pro forma /proʊ 'fɔmə/ *adv.* according to form; as a matter of form. **–pro-forma,** *adj.*

profound /prə'faʊnd/ *adj.* **1.** deep. **2.** having or showing great knowledge or deep understanding: *a profound thinker; a profound mind.* **3.** intense: *profound sleep.* **4.** going beyond the surface; not superficial or obvious: *profound insight.* **5.** of deep meaning; serious or abstruse: *a profound book.* –*n.* **6.** something that is profound: *a mind directed towards the profound.* **–profoundly,** *adv.* **–profoundness,** *n.* **–profundity,** *n.*

profuse /prə'fjus/ *adj.* **1.** made or done freely and abundantly: *profuse apologies.* **2.** abundant; in great amount. –*phr.* **3. profuse in,** generous to the point of extravagance in the giving of. **–profusely,** *adv.* **–profuseness,** *n.* **–profusion** /prə'fjuʒən/, *n.*

progenitor /prə'dʒɛnətə/ *n.* **1.** a direct ancestor; forebear. **2.** an originator, as of an artistic movement. **–progenitress,** *fem. n.*

progeny /'prodʒəni/ *n.* offspring; issue; descendants.

progesterone /prə'dʒɛstəroʊn/ *n. Physiol.* a hormone of the corpus luteum of the ovary, which prepares the uterus for the fertilised ovum and helps to maintain pregnancy.

progestogen /proʊ'dʒɛstədʒən/ *n. Physiol.* any of a class of steroid hormones that have functions similar to those of progesterone. Also, **progestin.**

prognosis /prog'noʊsəs/ *n.* (*pl.* **-noses** /-'noʊsiz/) **1.** a forecasting of the probable course and termination of a disease. **2.** a particular forecast made. **–prognostic,** *adj.*

prognosticate /prog'nostəkeɪt/ *v.t.* **1.** to forecast or predict (something future) from present indications or signs; to prophesy. –*v.i.* **2.** to make a forecast; to prophesy. **–prognostication** /prog,nostə'keɪʃən/, *n.* **–prognosticative,** *adj.* **–prognosticator,** *n.*

program /'proʊgræm/ *n.* **1.** a plan to be followed: *a program of study.* **2.** a list of things to be done; agenda: *a program for the day.* **3.** a list of pieces, performers, etc., in a concert or play. **4.** the contents of an entertainment: *there's a good program tonight.* **5.** *Radio, TV* a particular item or production. **6.** *Computers* a set of instructions in a computer language which will cause a computer to perform a desired operation. See **computer language, artificial language** (def. 2). –*verb* (**-grammed, -gramming**) –*v.t.* **7.** to insert instructions into (a device) in order to make it perform a certain task: *to program the video.* –*v.i.* **8.** to plan a program: *if you program carefully you'll find you have time for everything.* **9.** to write a computer program. Also, **programme. –programmable, programable,** *adj.* **–programmer,** *n.*

programming language *n.* → **computer language.**

progress *n.* /'proʊgrɛs/ **1.** a proceeding to a further or higher stage, or through such stages successively: *the progress of a scholar in his studies.* **2.** advancement in general. **3.** growth or development; continuous improvement. **4.** *Sociology* the development of an individual or group in a direction considered as beneficial and to a degree greater than that yet attained. **5.** *Biol.* increasing differentiation and perfection in the course of ontogeny or phylogeny. **6.** forward or onward movement. **7.** course of action, of events, of time, etc. *–v.i.* /prəˈgrɛs/ **8.** to advance. **9.** to go forwards or onwards. *–phr.* **10. in progress**, taking place; under way; happening. **11. make progress**, to achieve some gains; advance.

progression /prəˈgrɛʃən/ *n.* **1.** the act of progressing; forward or onward movement. **2.** a passing successively from one member of a series to the next; succession; sequence. **3.** *Maths* a sequence of numbers in which there is a constant relation between each number and its successor. Compare **arithmetical progression**, **geometric progression**. **4.** *Music* the manner in which notes or chords follow one another. **–progressional**, *adj.*

progressive /prəˈgrɛsɪv/ *adj.* **1.** favouring or making change, improvement, or reform: *a progressive politician*; *a progressive school*. **2.** going forwards or onwards; proceeding step by step: *progressive improvement in maths*; *a progressive disease*. *–n.* **3.** someone who favours (especially political) progress or reform. **–progressively**, *adv.* **–progressiveness**, *n.*

prohibit /prəˈhɪbət/ *v.t.* **1.** to forbid (an action, a thing) by authority: *smoking is prohibited.* **2.** to prevent; to hinder. **–prohibition**, *n.*

prohibitive /prəˈhɪbətɪv/ *adj.* **1.** that prohibits or forbids something. **2.** serving to prevent the use, purchase, etc., of something: *the prohibitive price of meat.* Also, **prohibitory**. **–prohibitively**, *adv.*

project *n.* /ˈproʊdʒɛkt, ˈprɒ-/ **1.** something that is thought of or planned; plan; scheme; undertaking. **2.** a special piece of work, usually research, done by schoolchildren. *–v.t.* /prəˈdʒɛkt/ **3.** to throw. **4.** to set forth (a plan, future action); present. **5.** to make known (an idea, impression, etc.); communicate; convey. **6.** to throw upon a surface or into space: *to project a film*; *to project the voice.* **7.** to see (something in the mind) as real: *the child projected the monster from his imagination.* **8.** to cause to jut out or protrude: *to project the lips.* **9.** to transform the points of (one figure) into those of another by any correspondence between points. *–v.i.* /prəˈdʒɛkt/ **10.** to jut out; protrude. **11.** to communicate or send an idea or impression. **–projection**, *n.*

projectile /prəˈdʒɛktaɪl/ *n.* **1.** *Mil.* an object fired from a gun with an explosive propelling charge, such as a bullet, shell, or grenade. **2.** an object set in motion by an exterior force which then continues to move by virtue of its own inertia. *–adj.* **3.** impelling or driving forwards, as a force. **4.** caused by impulse, as motion. **5.** capable of being impelled forwards, as a missile.

projector /prəˈdʒɛktə/ *n.* **1.** an apparatus for throwing an image on a screen, as of a slide; a film projector, etc. **2.** a device for projecting a beam of light.

prokaryote /proʊˈkærioʊt/ *n.* any organism which has cells without a distinct nucleus but containing single-strand DNA, such as bacteria. Compare **eukaryote**. **–prokaryotic** /proʊkæriˈɒtɪk/, *adj.*

prolapse *–n.* /ˈproʊlæps/ Also, **prolapsus**. **1.** *Pathol.* a falling down of an organ or part, as the uterus, from its normal position. *–v.i.* /ˈproʊlæps, prəˈlæps/ (**-lapsed, -lapsing**) **2.** *Chiefly Pathol.* to fall or slip down or out of place.

prolate /ˈproʊleɪt/ *adj.* elongated along the polar diameter, as a spheroid generated by the revolution of an ellipse about its longer axis (opposed to *oblate*).

proletariat /proʊləˈtɛəriət/ *n.* **1.** the class in society that owns no large property, but has to work to live. **2.** the working class, or wage-earners in general. **–proletarian**, *adj.*

proliferate /prəˈlɪfəreɪt/ *v.i.* **1.** to grow or produce by multiplication of parts, as in budding or cell division. **2.** to rapidly spread or increase in number. *–v.t.* **3.** to cause to proliferate. **–proliferation** /prəlɪfəˈreɪʃən/, *n.*

prolific /prəˈlɪfɪk/ *adj.* **1.** producing offspring, young, fruit, etc., especially abundantly; fruitful. **2.** abundantly productive of or fruitful in something specified. **–prolificacy, prolificness**, *n.* **–prolifically**, *adv.*

prolix /ˈproʊlɪks/ *adj.* **1.** extended to great, unnecessary, or tedious length; long and wordy. **2.** speaking or writing at great or tedious length. **–prolixity** /prəˈlɪksəti/, **prolixness**, *n.* **–prolixly**, *adv.*

prologue /ˈproʊlɒg/ *n.* **1.** an introductory speech, often in verse, calling attention to the theme of a play. **2.** a preliminary discourse; a preface or introductory part of a discourse, poem, or novel. **3.** any introductory proceeding, event, etc. *–v.t.* (**-logued, -loguing**) **4.** to introduce with, or as with, a prologue.

prolong /prəˈlɒŋ/ *v.t.* **1.** to lengthen out in time; to extend the duration of; to cause to continue longer: *to prolong one's life.* **2.** to make longer in spatial extent: *to prolong a line.* **–prolongation** /proʊlɒŋˈgeɪʃən/, **prolongment**, *n.* **–prolonger**, *n.*

promenade /prɒməˈnad, prɒməˈneɪd, ˈprɒmənad, ˈprɒməneɪd/ *n.* **1.** an unhurried walk, especially in a public place, for pleasure or show. **2.** an area suitable for such walking, especially one along a seafront; esplanade. *–v.i.* **3.** to take a promenade. *–v.t.* **4.** to take or lead on or as on a promenade; parade. **–promenader**, *n.*

prominent /ˈprɒmənənt/ *adj.* **1.** standing out so as to be easily seen; conspicuous; very noticeable: *a prominent feature.* **2.** important; leading; well-known: *a prominent citizen.* **–prominence**, *n.* **–prominently**, *adv.*

promiscuous /prəˈmɪskjuəs/ *adj.* **1.** having many sexual partners. **2.** indiscriminate; without discrimination. **3.** consisting of parts, elements, or individuals of different kinds brought together without order. **–promiscuity** /prɒməsˈkjuəti/, **promiscuousness**, *n.* **–promiscuously**, *adv.*

promise /ˈprɒməs/ *n.* **1.** an express assurance on which expectation is to be based. **2.** something that has the effect of an express assurance; indication of what may be expected. **3.** indication of future excellence or achievement: *a writer that shows promise.* **4.** something that is promised. *–verb* (**-ised, -ising**) *–v.t.* **5.** to engage or undertake by promise (with an infinitive or clause): *to promise not to interfere.* **6.** to make a promise of: *to promise help.* **7.** to afford ground for expecting. **8.** to engage to join in marriage. **9.** to assure (used in emphatic declarations). *–v.i.* **10.** to make a promise. *–phr.* **11. promise well** (or **fair**), to afford ground for expectation of success. **–promiser**; *Law,* **promisor** /prɒməˈsɔ/, *n.*

promising /ˈprɒməsɪŋ/ *adj.* giving promise; likely to turn out well: *a promising young man.* **–promisingly**, *adv.*

promissory note /ˈprɒməsəri noʊt/ *n.* *Finance* a written promise to pay a specified sum of money to a person designated or to his or her order, or to the bearer, at a time fixed or on demand.

promontory /ˈprɒməntri/ *n.* (*pl.* **-ries**) **1.** a high point of land or rock projecting into the sea or other water beyond the line of coast; a headland. **2.** *Anat.* a prominent or protuberant part.

promote /prəˈmoʊt/ *v.t.* **1.** to advance in rank, dignity, position, etc. **2.** to further the growth, development, progress, etc., of; encourage. **3.** to help to found; originate; organise; launch (a financial undertaking, publicity campaign, etc.). **–promoter**, *n.* **–promotion**, *n.* **–promotive**, *adj.*

prompt /prɒmpt/ *adj.* **1.** done, performed, delivered, etc., at once or without delay: *a prompt reply.* **2.** ready in action; quick to act as occasion demands. **3.** ready and willing. –*v.t.* **4.** to move or incite to action. **5.** to suggest or induce (action, etc.); inspire or occasion. **6.** to assist (a person speaking) by suggesting something to be said. **7.** *Theatre* to supply (an actor or reciter) with a missed cue or a forgotten line. –*v.i.* **8.** *Theatre* to supply off-stage cues and effects. –*n.* **9.** *Commerce* **a.** a limit of time given for payment for merchandise purchased, the limit being stated on a note of reminder called a **prompt note. b.** the contract setting the time limit. **10.** the act of prompting. **11.** something that prompts. **12.** *Theatre* someone who prompts (def. 8). **13.** *Computers* a message from a computer, appearing as words or symbols on the screen, which indicates to the user that the computer is ready for further instructions. –**promptly,** *adv.* –**promptness, promptitude,** *n.*

promulgate /ˈprɒməlgeɪt/ *v.t.* **1.** to make known by open declaration; to publish; to proclaim formally or put into operation (a law or rule of court or decree). **2.** to set forth or teach publicly (a creed, doctrine, etc.). –**promulgation** /prɒmalˈgeɪʃən/, *n.* –**promulgator,** *n.*

prone /proʊn/ *adj.* **1.** having a natural inclination or tendency to something; disposed; liable: *to be prone to anger.* **2.** having the front or ventral part downwards; lying face downwards. **3.** lying flat; prostrate. –**pronely,** *adv.* –**proneness,** *n.*

prong /prɒŋ/ *n.* **1.** one of the pointed divisions or tines of a fork. **2.** any pointed projecting part, as of an antler. –*v.t.* **3.** to pierce or stab with a prong.

pronoun /ˈproʊnaʊn/ *n.* **1.** *Gram.* (in many languages) one of the major parts of speech, comprising words used as substitutes for nouns. **2.** any such word, as *I, you, he, this, who, what.*

pronounce /prəˈnaʊns/ *verb* (**pronounced, pronouncing**) –*v.t.* **1.** to enunciate or articulate (words, etc.). **2.** to utter or sound in a particular manner in speaking. **3.** to declare (a person or thing) to be as specified. **4.** to utter or deliver formally or solemnly. **5.** to announce authoritatively or officially. –*v.i.* **6.** to pronounce words, etc. –*phr.* **7. pronounce on, a.** to make a statement or assertion, especially an authoritative statement, with regard to. **b.** to give an opinion on or decision about. –**pronouncement,** *n.* –**pronounceable,** *adj.* –**pronouncer,** *n.*

pronounced /prəˈnaʊnst/ *adj.* **1.** strongly marked. **2.** clearly indicated. **3.** decided; definite: *to have very pronounced views.* –**pronouncedly** /prəˈnaʊnsədli/, *adv.*

pronunciation /prənʌnsiˈeɪʃən/ *n.* the act or the result of producing the sounds of speech including articulation, vowel and consonant formation, accent, inflection, and intonation, often with reference to the correctness or acceptability of the speech sounds. –**pronunciational,** *adj.*

proof /pruːf/ *n.* **1.** something that shows that a thing is either true or false. **2.** a test; a trial: *to put a thing to the proof.* **3.** the effect of evidence in making the mind certain: *it was proof enough for her that he hadn't done it.* **4.** the condition of having been tested and approved. **5.** the relative strength of alcoholic liquors. **6.** *Photography* a trial print from a negative. **7.** *Printing* a trial impression of composed type, taken to correct errors and make changes. –*adj.* **8.** strong enough to resist attack, danger, etc.: *proof against fire; proof against fear.* **9.** of standard strength, as alcoholic liquor. –*v.t.* **10.** to treat or coat (a material) in order to make it resistant to wear or damage.

-proof a suffix meaning 'insulated from', 'impervious to', 'not affected by', etc., as in *waterproof.*

proofread /ˈpruːfriːd/ *verb* (**-read** /ˈpruːfrɛd/, **-reading**) –*v.t.* **1.** to read (printers' proofs, etc.) in order to detect and mark errors to be corrected. –*v.i.* **2.** to carry out such a reading. –**proofreader,** *n.* –**proofreading,** *n.*

prop[1] /prɒp/ *verb* (**propped, propping**) –*v.t.* **1.** (oft. fol. by *up*) to support, or prevent from falling, with something that holds (a thing) up: *to prop a roof; they propped her up with cushions.* **2.** to rest (a thing) against a support: *he propped the ladder against the wall.* **3.** to support or keep going: *to prop up a failing business.* –*v.i.* **4.** (of horses) to stop suddenly with all four legs stiff, jolting the rider. –*n.* **5.** a stick, pole, beam, or other support. **6.** a person or thing serving as a support. **7.** (*pl.*) *Colloq.* the legs. **8.** Also, **prop-forward.** *Rugby Football* either of the two forwards outermost in the front row of the scrum. **9.** a sudden stop.

prop[2] /prɒp/ *n.* *Theatre* an item of furniture, ornament, or decoration in a stage setting; any object handled or used by an actor in performance.

prop[3] /prɒp/ *n.* *Colloq.* → **propeller.**

propaganda /prɒpəˈgændə/ *n.* **1.** the systematic propagation of a given doctrine. **2.** the particular doctrines or principles propagated by an organisation or movement. **3.** dissemination of ideas, information, or rumour for the purpose of injuring or helping an institution, a cause, or a person. **4.** doctrines, arguments, facts spread by deliberate effort through any medium in order to further one's cause or to damage an opposing cause. **5.** a public action or display aimed at furthering or hindering a cause. –**propagandist,** *n.*, *adj.*

propagate /ˈprɒpəgeɪt/ *v.t.* **1.** to breed (plants, animals); cause to reproduce. **2.** (of a plant, animal) to breed; reproduce. **3.** to carry (characteristics, qualities) through offspring. **4.** to spread (ideas, etc.); disseminate. **5.** to carry, send, or help move through space or a medium: *to propagate sound.* –*v.i.* **6.** to breed. –**propagation** /prɒpəˈgeɪʃən/, *n.* –**propagative,** *adj.* –**propagator,** *n.*

propane /ˈproʊpeɪn/ *n.* a gaseous hydrocarbon, C_3H_8, of the methane series, found in petroleum.

propel /prəˈpɛl/ *v.t.* (**-pelled, -pelling**) **1.** to drive, or cause to move, forwards: *a boat propelled by oars.* **2.** to impel or urge onwards.

propellant /prəˈpɛlənt/ *n.* **1.** a propelling agent. **2.** *Mil.* the charges of explosive used in a gun to fire the projectile. **3.** *Aeronautics* one or more substances used in rocket motors for the chemical generation of gas at the controlled rates required to provide thrust. **4.** the compressed gas used in a spray container to expel the liquid product through a fine jet, in the form of a spray. Also, **propellent.**

propellent /prəˈpɛlənt/ *adj.* **1.** propelling; driving forward. –*n.* **2.** → **propellant.**

propeller /prəˈpɛlə/ *n.* a device having a revolving hub with radiating blades, for propelling a ship, aircraft, etc. Also, **propellor.**

propensity /prəˈpɛnsəti/ *n.* (*pl.* **-ties**) natural or habitual inclination or tendency: *a propensity to find fault.*

proper /ˈprɒpə/ *adj.* **1.** suited to the purpose or circumstances; fit; suitable: *the proper time to plant.* **2.** doing or agreeing with what is thought to be good manners; correct; decorous. **3.** belonging or relating particularly to a person or thing: *noise is proper to small children.* **4.** real; genuine: *give me some proper facts this time and I'll believe you.* **5.** in the strict sense of the word (now usually following the noun): *shellfish do not belong to the fishes proper.* **6.** normal or regular: *that is not the proper way to do it.* **7.** *Colloq.* complete; thorough: *a proper thrashing.* **8.** *Rare* excellent; fine: *you're a proper friend!* **9.** *Archaic* belonging to oneself or itself; own. –**properly,** *adv.*

proper noun *n.* *Gram.* a noun that is not usually preceded by an article or other limiting modifier and, when written, is spelt with an initial capital, in meaning applicable only to a single person or thing, or to several persons or things which constitute a unique class only by virtue of having the same name as: *Whitlam, Perth* in contrast to *man*, *city*. Compare **common noun**. Also, **proper name**.

property /ˈprɒpəti/ *n.* (*pl.* **-ties**) **1.** something that one owns; the possession(s) of a particular owner. **2.** goods, lands, etc., owned: *a man of property*. **3.** a piece of land owned: *property near the beach*. **4.** Also, **country property**. *Aust.*, *NZ* a farm, station, orchard, etc. **5.** something used by or belonging to a person, a group of people, or the public: *the secret became common property*. **6.** a power or quality that something has naturally; an attribute: *the properties of oxygen*. **7.** → **prop**[2].

property trust *n.* *Law* a unit trust in which property (mainly real estate) is purchased by investors whose interest in the trust property and any income or capital gain therefrom is proportionate to the number of units held.

prophecy /ˈprɒfəsi/ *n.* (*pl.* **-cies**) **1.** foretelling or prediction (originally by divine inspiration) of what is to come. **2.** divinely inspired utterance or revelation.

prophesy /ˈprɒfəsaɪ/ *verb* (**-sied**, **-sying**) −*v.t.* **1.** to foretell or predict: *to prophesy a storm*. **2.** to declare or foretell by or as by divine inspiration. −*v.i.* **3.** to make predictions. −**prophesier**, *n.*

prophet /ˈprɒfət/ *n.* **1.** someone who speaks as the mouthpiece of God. **2.** someone regarded as, or claiming to be, a great teacher or leader. **3.** someone who foretells the future or future events: *a weather prophet*. −*phr.* **4. the Prophet**, Mohammed, the founder of Islam. **5. the Prophets**, the books which form the second of the three Jewish divisions of the Old Testament. −**prophetess**, *fem. n.* −**prophetic**, *adj.*

prophylactic /prɒfəˈlæktɪk/ *adj.* **1.** defending or protecting from disease, as a drug. **2.** preventive; preservative; protective. −*n.* **3.** a contraceptive, especially a condom. −**prophylaxis**, *n.*

propinquity /prəˈpɪŋkwəti/ *n.* **1.** nearness in place; proximity. **2.** nearness of relation; kinship. **3.** affinity of nature; similarity. **4.** nearness in time.

propitiate /prəˈpɪʃieɪt/ *v.t.* to make favourably inclined; appease; conciliate. −**propitiation** /prəpɪʃiˈeɪʃən/, *n.* −**propitiable**, *adj.* −**propitiative**, **propitiatory**, *adj.* −**propitiator**, *n.*

propitious /prəˈpɪʃəs/ *adj.* **1.** presenting favourable conditions; favourable: *propitious weather*. **2.** indicative of favour: *propitious omens*. **3.** favourably inclined; disposed to bestow favours or forgive. −**propitiously**, *adv.* −**propitiousness**, *n.*

proponent /prəˈpoʊnənt/ *n.* **1.** someone who puts forward a proposition or proposal. **2.** someone who supports a cause or doctrine.

proportion /prəˈpɔːʃən/ *n.* **1.** comparative relation between things as to size, quantity, number, etc.; ratio: *a house tall in proportion to its width*. **2.** proper relation between things or parts; balance: *you must see things in proportion*. **3.** (*pl.*) dimensions: *a rock of gigantic proportions*. **4.** a part in relation to the whole: *a large proportion of the total*. **5.** *Maths* the relation of four quantities such that the first divided by the second is equal to the third divided by the fourth; equality of ratios. −*v.t.* **6.** to put (the parts of) something into proper relationship: *to proportion a building*. −*phr.* **7. in proportion**, in due balance. **8. out of (all) proportion**, **a.** lacking the correct relation (to something else); disproportionate: *a punishment out of proportion to the crime*. **b.** not balanced or fitting; exaggerated: *a reaction out of all proportion*. −**proportional**, *adj.* −**proportionate**, *adj.* −**proportionally**, *adv.* −**proportionately**, *adv.*

proportional representation *n.* *Govt* a system of electing representatives to a legislative body in which there are a number of members representing any one electorate. The number of successful candidates from each party is directly proportional to the percentage of the total vote won by the party. Compare **first-past-the-post**, **preferential voting**.

proposal /prəˈpoʊzəl/ *n.* **1.** the act of proposing for acceptance, adoption, or performance. **2.** a plan or scheme proposed. **3.** an offer, especially of marriage.

propose /prəˈpoʊz/ *v.t.* **1.** to put forward (a matter, subject, case, etc.) for consideration, acceptance, or action: *to propose a new method; to propose a toast*. **2.** to put forward or suggest as something to be done: *he proposed that a messenger be sent*. **3.** to present (a person) for some position, office, membership, etc. **4.** to propound (a question, riddle, etc.). −*v.i.* **5.** to make a proposal, especially of marriage. −**proposer**, *n.*

proposition /prɒpəˈzɪʃən/ *n.* **1.** the act of proposing, or a proposal of something to be considered, accepted, or done. **2.** a plan or subject put forward for action or discussion. **3.** an offer of terms for a business deal. **4.** a thing or person considered as something to be dealt with or faced: *a tough proposition*. **5.** *Philos.* a statement in which something (a predicate) is affirmed or denied. **6.** a proposal to have sexual intercourse. −*v.t.* **7.** to propose a plan, deal, etc., to. **8.** to suggest sexual intercourse to. −**propositional**, *adj.* −**propositionally**, *adv.*

propound /prəˈpaʊnd/ *v.t.* to put forward for consideration, acceptance, or adoption. −**propounder**, *n.*

proprietary /prəˈpraɪətri/ *adj.* **1.** belonging to a proprietor or proprietors. **2.** being a proprietor or proprietors; holding property: *the proprietary class*. **3.** relating to property or ownership: *proprietary rights*. **4.** belonging or controlled as property. **5.** manufactured and sold only by the owner of the patent, formula, brand name, or trademark associated with the product: *proprietary medicine*.

proprietary limited company *n.* (in Australia) a company with a limit of fifty shareholders, which cannot issue shares for public subscription and which is not listed on the stock exchange; shareholders enjoy limited liability, on liquidation. Also, **proprietary company**.

proprietor /prəˈpraɪətə/ *n.* **1.** the owner of a business establishment, a hotel, newspaper, etc. **2.** someone who has the exclusive right or title to something; an owner, as of property. −**proprietorship**, *n.*

propriety /prəˈpraɪəti/ *n.* (*pl.* **-ties**) **1.** conformity to established standards of behaviour or manners. **2.** appropriateness to the purpose or circumstances; suitability. **3.** rightness or justness. −*phr.* **4. the proprieties**, the conventional standards or requirements of proper behaviour.

propulsion /prəˈpʌlʃən/ *n.* the act of propelling or driving forward or onward. −**propulsive**, *adj.*

pro rata *adv.* /proʊ ˈratə/ **1.** in proportion; according to a certain rate. −*adj.* /proʊ ˈratə/ **2.** proportionate.

prorogue /prəˈroʊg/ *v.t.* *Parliamentary Procedure* to discontinue meetings of (parliament or similar legislative body) until the next session.

prosaic /proʊˈzeɪk, prə-/ *adj.* **1.** commonplace or dull; matter-of-fact or unimaginative: *a prosaic mind*. **2.** having the character or spirit of prose as opposed to poetry, as verse or writing. Also, **prosaical**. −**prosaically**, *adv.* −**prosaicness**, *n.* −**prosaism** /ˈproʊzeɪɪzəm/, *n.*

proscenium /prəˈsiniəm/ *n.* (*pl.* **-nia** /-niə/) **1.** (in the ancient classical theatre) the area between the backdrop and the orchestra forming the stage. **2.** (in the modern theatre) the front part of the stage, especially the area in front of the curtain. Also, **proscenium arch**.

prosciutto /prəˈʃutoʊ/ *n.* a dry-cured, spiced ham, often sold very thinly sliced.

proscribe /proʊˈskraɪb/ *v.t.* **1.** to denounce or condemn (a thing) as dangerous; to prohibit. **2.** to banish or exile.

3. to announce the name of (a person) as condemned to death and subject to confiscation of property. **–proscriber**, *n.* **–proscription**, *n.*

prose /proʊz/ *n.* **1.** the ordinary form of spoken or written language, without metrical structure (as distinguished from poetry or verse). **2.** matter-of-fact, commonplace, or dull expression, quality, discourse, etc.

prosecute /ˈprɒsəkjut/ *v.t.* **1.** *Law* **a.** to institute legal proceedings against (a person, etc.). **b.** to seek to enforce or obtain by legal process. **c.** to conduct criminal proceedings in court against. **2.** to follow up or go on with something undertaken or begun: *to prosecute an inquiry.* **3.** to carry on or practise. **–prosecution**, *n.* **–prosecutor**, *n.*

proselyte /ˈprɒsəlaɪt/ *n.* someone who has come over or changed from one opinion, religious belief, sect, or the like to another; a convert.

prosody /ˈprɒsədi, ˈprɒz-/ *n.* **1.** the science or study of poetic metres and versification. **2.** a particular or distinctive system of metrics and versification: *Milton's prosody.*

prospect /ˈprɒspɛkt/ *n.* **1.** (*usu. pl.*) an apparent probability of advancement, success, profit, etc. **2.** (*usu. pl.*) the outlook for the future. **3.** something in view as a source of profit. **4.** a prospective customer, as in business. **5.** a mental looking forward, or contemplation of something future or expected. **6.** a view or scene presented to the eye, especially of scenery. **7.** outlook or view over a region or in a particular direction. **8.** a mental view or survey, as of a subject or situation. **9.** *Mining* **a.** an apparent indication of metal, etc. **b.** a spot giving such indications. **c.** excavation or workings in search of ore. **10.** *Sport* a new recruit to a club; a young player of whom much is expected. *–v.t.* **11.** to search or explore (a region), as for gold. **12.** to work (a mine or claim) experimentally in order to test its value. *–v.i.* **13.** to search or explore a region for gold or the like. *–phr.* **14. in prospect**, in view; under consideration.

prospective /prəˈspɛktɪv/ *adj.* **1.** of or in the future. **2.** potential; likely; expected. **–prospectively**, *adv.*

prospector /ˈprɒspɛktə/ *n.* someone who prospects for gold and other minerals.

prospectus /prəˈspɛktəs/ *n.* (*pl.* **-tuses**) **1.** a circular or advertisement inviting applications from the public to subscribe for securities of a corporation or proposed corporation. **2.** a statement which describes or advertises a forthcoming literary work, a new enterprise, or the like. **3.** a pamphlet issued by a school or other institution giving details about itself.

prosper /ˈprɒspə/ *v.i.* **1.** to be prosperous or successful; to thrive. *–v.t.* **2.** to make prosperous or successful. **–prosperity**, *n.*

prosperous /ˈprɒspərəs, -prəs/ *adj.* **1.** having or characterised by continued good fortune; flourishing; successful: *a prosperous business.* **2.** well-to-do or well-off: *a prosperous family.* **–prosperously**, *adv.* **–prosperousness**, *n.*

prostate gland /ˈprɒsteɪt glænd/ *n. Anat.* the composite gland which surrounds the urethra of males at the base of the bladder.

prostate-specific antigen *n.* → **PSA**.

prosthesis /prɒsˈθiːsəs, prəs-/ *n.* (*pl.* **-theses** /-ˈθiːsiz/) *Med.* an artificial part to supply a defect of the body, such as an artificial limb. **–prosthetic**, *adj.*

prostitute /ˈprɒstətjut/ *n.* **1.** a person, especially a woman, who engages in sexual intercourse for money as a livelihood. **2.** someone who debases themselves or allows their talents to be used in an unworthy way, usually for financial gain. *–v.t.* **3.** to submit to sexual intercourse for money as a livelihood. **4.** to put to a base or unworthy use. **–prostitution**, *n.* **–prostitutor**, *n.*

prostrate *v.t.* /prɒsˈtreɪt/ **1.** to throw (oneself) down in humility, worship, etc. **2.** to throw (something or someone) down level with the ground. **3.** to overcome, or make helpless or physically weak. *–adj.* /ˈprɒstreɪt/ **4.** lying flat or at full length on the ground, often as sign of humility, worship, etc. **5.** overcome, helpless, or physically weak: *prostrate from grief; prostrate from the heat.* **6.** *Bot.* (of a plant or stem) lying flat on the ground. **–prostration**, *n.*

protagonist /prəˈtægənəst/ *n.* **1.** the leading character in a play, novel, etc. **2.** any leading character or personage in a movement, cause, etc. **3.** a champion, or supporter of a movement, cause, idea, etc.; advocate; spokesperson.

protea /ˈproʊtiə/ *n.* any of the shrubs or trees of the southern African genus *Protea*, which exhibits a wide variety of forms, as the giant protea, *Protea cynaroides*, which has large showy flowers.

protean /prəˈtiən, ˈproʊtiən/ *adj.* readily assuming different forms or characters; exceedingly variable.

protect /prəˈtɛkt/ *v.t.* **1.** to defend or guard from attack, invasion, annoyance, insult, etc.; cover or shield from injury or danger. **2.** *Econ.* to guard (a country's industry) from foreign competition by imposing import duties. **–protective**, *adj.* **–protector**, *n.*

protection /prəˈtɛkʃən/ *n.* **1.** the act of protecting. **2.** the state of being protected. **3.** preservation from injury or harm. **4.** something that protects. **5.** *Insurance* coverage. **6.** *Colloq.* **a.** immunity from prosecution or harassment obtained by a person involved in illegal activities by means of bribes to appropriate officials, payment to gangsters, etc. **b.** money paid to criminals as a guarantee against threatened violence. **7.** *Econ.* the system or theory of fostering or developing home industries by protecting them from foreign competition through duties imposed on imports from foreign countries. **8.** a treaty, safe-conduct, passport, or other writing which secures from molestation the person, persons, or property specified in it. **9.** patronage. *–adj.* **10.** of or relating to protection (def. 6).

protection money *n.* money extorted by criminals from victims, ostensibly to buy protection for them from other criminals.

protection racket *n.* a criminal scheme based on the extortion of protection money.

protector /prəˈtɛktə/ *n.* **1.** a person or thing that protects; a defender; a guardian. **2.** (*oft. upper case*) *Hist.* a person in charge of a kingdom during the sovereign's minority, incapacity, or absence. **3.** (*also upper case*) *Aust. Hist.* an official appointed to have responsibility for the management and welfare of Aborigines. **4.** *Cricket, etc.* a lightweight padded shield worn to protect the genitals. **–protectoral**, *adj.* **–protectorship**, *n.*

protectorate /prəˈtɛktərət, -trət/ *n.* **1.** the relation of a strong state towards a weaker state or territory which it protects and partly controls. **2.** a state or territory so protected. **3.** the office or position, or the term of office, of a protector. **4.** the government of a protector.

protégé /ˈproʊtəʒeɪ/ *n.* someone who is under the protection or friendly patronage of another. **–protégée**, *fem.*

protein /ˈproʊtin/ *n. Biochem.* any of the polymers formed from amino acids, which are found in all cells and which include enzymes, plasma proteins, and structural proteins such as collagen. Also, **proteid** /ˈproʊtid/.

proteome /ˈproʊtioʊm/ *n.* the complete protein complement expressed by the genome of an organism.

Proterozoic /proʊtərəˈzoʊɪk/ *adj., n.* (of or relating to) the era or rocks between Archaeozoic and Palaeozoic, presumed to be characterised by relative prominence of sedimentary rocks in a few of which fossils of early primitive organisms are found. Also, **Proterzoic.**

protest *n.* /ˈprouːtɛst/ **1.** a formal expression or declaration of objection or disapproval, often in opposition to something which one is powerless to prevent or avoid. **2.** a demonstration or meeting of people protesting against something. **3.** *Sport* a formal expression of objection or complaint placed with an official. **4.** *Commerce* the written declaration of a notary public that a bill of exchange has been dishonoured. **5.** *Law* **a.** (upon one's payment of a sum of money) a formal statement disputing the legality of the demand. **b.** a written and attested declaration made by the master of a ship stating the circumstances in which some injury has happened to the ship or cargo, or other circumstances involving the liability of the officers, crew, etc. –*v.i.* /prəˈtɛst, ˈprou-/ **6.** (sometimes fol. by *against* or *at*) to give expression to one's objection or disapproval; remonstrate: *he protested against nuclear testing*; *she protested at the treatment she received.* **7.** to make solemn declaration. –*v.t.* /prəˈtɛst, ˈprou-/ **8.** to make a protest or remonstrance against. **9.** to say in protest or remonstrance: *'That's not fair', he protested.* **10.** to declare solemnly or formally; affirm; assert: *she protested her innocence.* **11.** to make a formal declaration of the non-acceptance or non-payment of (a bill of exchange or note). –*phr.* **12. under protest,** having registered opposition or dissent: *to submit under protest.* –**protester,** *n.* –**protestingly,** *adv.*

Protestant /ˈprɒtəstənt/ *n.* **1.** a member of any of those Christian groups which separated from the Church of Rome at the Reformation, or of any group descended from them. **2.** (*lower case*) someone who protests. –*adj.* **3.** relating to Protestants or their religion. –**Protestantism,** *n.*

protestation /prɒtəsˈteɪʃən, prou-/ *n.* **1.** the act of protesting or affirming. **2.** a solemn declaration or affirmation. **3.** the formal expression of objection or disapproval; protest.

protist /ˈprouːtəst/ *n. Biol.* one of a variety of eukaryotic organisms, including some algae, protozoans, and moulds. Also, **protistan.**

protistan /prouˈtɪstən/ *n.* **1.** → **protist.** –*adj.* **2.** of or relating to a protist.

proto- a word element meaning: **1.** first, earliest form of, as *prototype.* **2.** (*usu. upper case*) *Ling.* the reconstructed earliest form of a language: *Proto-Germanic.*

protocol /ˈprouːtəkɒl/ *n.* **1.** the customs and regulations dealing with the ceremonies and etiquette of the diplomatic corps and others at a court or capital. **2.** an original draft, minute, or record from which a document, especially a treaty, is prepared. **3.** a supplementary international agreement. **4.** an agreement between states. **5.** *Computers* a set of rules governing the format in which messages are sent from one computer to another, as in a network.

proton /ˈprouːtɒn/ *n. Physics* an elementary particle present in every atomic nucleus, the number of protons being different for each element, which has an electric charge equal in magnitude to that of the electron but of opposite sign and a mass of 1.7×10^{-27} kg; hydrogen ion.

protoplasm /ˈprouːtəplæzəm/ *n. Biol.* a complex substance (typically colourless and semifluid) regarded as the physical basis of life, having the power of spontaneous motion, reproduction, etc.; the living matter of all vegetable and animal cells and tissues. –**protoplasmic** /prouːtəˈplæzmɪk/, *adj.*

prototype /ˈprouːtətaɪp/ *n.* **1.** the original or model after which anything is formed. **2.** *Biol.* an archetype; a primitive form regarded as the basis of a group.

–**prototypal** /ˈprouːtətaɪpəl/, **prototypic** /prouːtəˈtɪpɪk/, *adj.* –**prototypical,** *adj.*

protozoan /prouːtəˈzouːən/ *n.* **1.** a member of the phylum Protozoa, comprising animals consisting of one cell or of a colony of like or similar cells. –*adj.* Also, **protozoic.** **2.** of or relating to any of the Protozoa.

protract /prəˈtrækt/ *v.t.* **1.** to draw out or lengthen in time; extend the duration of; prolong. **2.** *Anat.*, *etc.* to extend or protrude. **3.** *Surveying*, *etc.* to plot; to draw by means of a scale and protractor. –**protraction,** *n.* –**protracted,** *adj.* –**protractive,** *adj.*

protractor /prəˈtræktə/ *n.* a flat semicircular instrument, graduated around the circular edge, used to measure or mark off angles.

protrude /prəˈtrud/ *v.i.* to project. –**protrusion,** *n.* –**protrusive, protrudent,** *adj.* –**protrusible** /prəˈtruːzəbəl/, *adj.*

protuberant /prəˈtjubərənt, -brənt/ *adj.* bulging out beyond the surrounding surface. –**protuberance,** *n.* –**protuberantly,** *adv.*

proud /praʊd/ *adj.* **1.** feeling pleasure or satisfaction over something conceived as highly honourable or creditable to oneself: *proud of her achievements*; *proud to be Australian*; *proud that we reached the final.* **2.** having or cherishing, or proceeding from or showing, a high, especially an inordinately high, opinion of one's own dignity, importance, or superiority. **3.** having or showing self-respect or self-esteem. **4.** highly gratifying to the feelings or self-esteem. **5.** highly honourable or creditable: *a proud achievement.* **6.** (of things) stately, majestic, or magnificent: *proud cities.* **7.** of lofty dignity or distinction: *a proud name*; *proud nobles.* **8.** projecting beyond the surrounding elements or objects: *to stand proud.* –*phr.* **9. do someone proud, a.** to be a source of credit to someone. **b.** to entertain someone generously or lavishly. –**proudly,** *adv.*

prove /pruv/ *verb* (**proved, proved** or **proven** /ˈpruvən, ˈprouvən/, **proving**) –*v.t.* **1.** to establish as true or genuine by evidence, argument, etc.: *to prove a theory*; *prove the worth of an object.* **2.** *Law* to establish the validity of (a will, etc.). **3.** to put to the test; try out. **4.** to show (oneself) to have the character, ability, etc., expected of one. **5.** to determine the characteristics of by scientific tests: *to prove ore.* **6.** *Cookery* to cause (dough) to rise before baking, by placing it in a warm place. –*v.i.* **7.** to turn out: *the report proved to be false.* –**provable,** *adj.* –**prover,** *n.*

provenance /ˈprovənəns/ *n.* the place of origin, as of a work of art, etc.

provender /ˈprovəndə/ *n.* **1.** dry food for livestock, as hay; fodder. **2.** food or provisions.

proverb /ˈprovɜb/ *n.* **1.** a short, popular saying, that has been in use for a long time, expressing some familiar truth, as *A stitch in time saves nine.* **2.** a wise saying; precept. **3.** (*upper case*) (*pl.*) *Bible* one of the books of the Old Testament, made up of sayings of wise men of Israel, including Solomon.

proverbial /prəˈvɜbiəl/ *adj.* **1.** relating to or characteristic of a proverb: *proverbial brevity.* **2.** having become an object of common mention or reference: *clean and fresh as the proverbial daisy.* –**proverbially,** *adv.*

provide /prəˈvaɪd/ *v.t.* **1.** to furnish or supply. **2.** to afford or yield. **3.** *Law* to arrange for or stipulate beforehand, as by a provision or proviso. –*phr.* **4. provide for, a.** to make arrangements for supplying means of support, money, etc., to. **b.** to supply means of support, etc., to. **c.** to cover; be applicable to: *clause 7 provides for such an event.*

provided /prəˈvaɪdəd/ *conj.* it being stipulated or understood (that); on the condition or supposition (that): *to consent, provided (that) all the others agree.*

providence /ˈprɒvədəns/ n. **1.** the foreseeing care and guardianship of God over his creatures. **2.** (upper case) God. **3.** provident or prudent management of resources; economy. –phr. **4. tempt providence,** to embark on a course which involves danger.

provident /ˈprɒvədənt/ adj. **1.** having or showing foresight; careful in providing for the future. **2.** characterised by or proceeding from foresight: provident care. **3.** economical or frugal. –phr. **4. provident of,** mindful in making provision for. –**providential** /prɒvəˈdɛnʃəl/, adj. –**providently,** adv.

provider /prəˈvaɪdə/ n. **1.** someone who provides. **2.** a person who supplies a means of support, especially financial: the main provider in the family. **3.** a company which provides access to a service: mobile phone provider. **4.** → **internet service provider.**

provider number n. a number allocated by the government to a medical practitioner, which must appear on prescriptions, receipts, etc.

providing /prəˈvaɪdɪŋ/ conj. provided.

province /ˈprɒvəns/ n. **1.** an administrative division or unit of a country: the provinces of Spain. **2.** Aust. Hist. (before Federation) a designated region of Australia: the province of Australia Felix; the British province of South Australia. **3.** a country, territory, district, or region. **4.** (in Victoria) an electorate represented by two members of the Legislative Council. **5.** Geog. an area lower in rank than a region. **6.** a department or branch of learning or activity: the province of mathematics. **7.** the sphere or field of action of a person, etc.; one's office, function, or business. –phr. **8. the provinces,** the parts of a country outside the capital or the largest cities.

provincial /prəˈvɪnʃəl/ adj. **1.** of or relating to some particular province or provinces; local: provincial customs. **2.** of or relating to the provinces: the provincial press. **3.** having or showing the manners characteristic of inhabitants of a province or the provinces; countrified; rustic; unsophisticated; narrow or illiberal. –n. **4.** someone who lives in or comes from the provinces. **5.** a member of a religious order presiding over the order in a given district or province. –**provinciality,** n. –**provincialism,** n. –**provincially,** adv.

provision /prəˈvɪʒən/ n. **1.** a clause in a document, a law, etc., providing for a particular matter; stipulation; proviso. **2.** the providing or supplying of something, such as food or other necessities. **3.** an arrangement or preparation made beforehand. **4.** something provided. **5.** (pl.) supplies of food. –v.t. **6.** to supply with provisions. –**provisioner,** n.

provisional /prəˈvɪʒənəl/ adj. serving until permanently replaced; temporary; conditional: a provisional agreement. Also, **provisionary.**

provisional tax n. (formerly, in Australia) tax paid in advance on income to be earned in the next financial year from sources other than salary and wages.

proviso /prəˈvaɪzoʊ/ n. (pl. -sos or -soes) a stipulation or condition.

provocateur /prəvɒkəˈtɜ/ n. **1.** a person who has radical and unsettling ideas that disturb the status quo. **2.** → **agent provocateur.**

provoke /prəˈvoʊk/ v.t. **1.** to anger, enrage, exasperate, or vex. **2.** to stir up, arouse, or call forth. **3.** to incite or stimulate (a person, etc.) to action. **4.** to give rise to, induce, or bring about. –**provocation,** n. –**provocative,** adj. –**provoker,** n. –**provoking,** adj. –**provokingly,** adv.

provost /ˈprɒvəst/ n. a person appointed to superintend or preside. –**provostship,** n.

prow /praʊ/ n. the forepart of a ship or boat above the waterline; the bow.

prowess /ˈpraʊɛs, praʊˈɛs/ n. **1.** valour; bravery. **2.** outstanding ability: prowess at shooting.

prowl /praʊl/ v.i. to rove or go about stealthily in search of prey, plunder, etc. –phr. **2. on the prowl, a.** moving about in a stealthy fashion to find prey. **b.** moving about in society looking specifically for a sexual partner, a gullible investor, or some other person to be used or imposed upon. –**prowler,** n.

proximate /ˈprɒksəmət/ adj. **1.** next; nearest. **2.** fairly accurate; approximate. –**proximately,** adv.

proximity /prɒkˈsɪməti/ n. nearness in place, time, or relation.

proximo /ˈprɒksəmoʊ/ adv. in or of the next or coming month: on the 1st proximo. Abbrev.: prox. Compare **ultimo.**

proxy /ˈprɒksi/ n. (pl. -xies) **1.** the agency of a person deputed to act for another. **2.** → **proxy server.**

proxy server n. Internet a server which acts as a buffer between the user and the internet, performing a range of functions such as storing frequently used data in a cache to speed access, imposing restrictions on access to some users, or hiding IP addresses to ensure anonymity. Also, **proxy.**

prude /prud/ n. someone who affects extreme modesty or propriety. –**prudery,** n. –**prudish,** adj.

prudence /ˈprudns/ n. **1.** cautious practical wisdom; good judgement; discretion. **2.** regard for one's own interests. **3.** provident care in management; economy or frugality. –**prudential** /pruˈdɛnʃəl/, adj.

prudent /ˈprudnt/ adj. **1.** wise, judicious, or wisely cautious in practical affairs, as a person; sagacious or judicious; discreet or circumspect. **2.** careful of one's own interests; provident, or careful in providing for the future. –**prudently,** adv.

prune¹ /prun/ n. **1.** the purplish black dried fruit of any of several varieties of plum tree, used for eating, cooked or uncooked. **2.** such a fruit, whether dried or not. **3.** a variety of plum tree bearing such fruit.

prune² /prun/ v.t. **1.** to cut or lop superfluous or undesired twigs, branches, or roots from; to trim. **2.** to remove (superfluities, etc.). –**pruning,** n. –**pruner,** n.

prurient /ˈpruriənt/ adj. **1.** inclined to or characterised by lascivious thought. **2.** morbidly uneasy, as desire or longing. **3.** itching. **4.** Bot. causing itching. –**prurience,** **pruriency,** n. –**pruriently,** adv.

pry¹ /praɪ/ v.i. **(pried, prying) 1.** to look closely or curiously, peer, or peep. **2.** to search or inquire curiously or inquisitively into something: to pry into the affairs of others.

pry² /praɪ/ v.t. **(pried, prying)** Chiefly US → **prise.**

PSA /pi ɛs ˈeɪ/ n. prostate-specific antigen; a protein in the blood of men, an elevated count of which may indicate the presence of prostate hypertrophy and possibly prostate cancer.

psalm /sam/ n. **1.** a sacred song or hymn. **2.** a poem of similar character. –**psalmist,** n.

psalter /ˈsɒltə/ n. a book containing psalms for liturgical or devotional use.

PSA test n. a blood screening test for prostate cancer.

psephology /səˈfɒlədʒi/ n. the systematic study of elections by analysing their results, trends, etc. –**psephological** /sɛfəˈlɒdʒɪkəl/, adj. –**psephologically** /sɛfəˈlɒdʒɪkli/, adv. –**psephologist,** n.

pseudo- a word element meaning 'false', 'pretended', freely used as a formative; in scientific use, denoting close or deceptive resemblance to the following element, used sometimes in chemical names of isomers. Also, (before vowels), **pseud-.**

pseudoephedrine /sjudoʊˈɛfədrin/ n. a sympathomimetic agent used as a nasal decongestant, causing narrowing of the blood vessels in the nasal mucous membranes. Abbrev.: PSE

pseudonym /ˈsjudənɪm/ *n.* an assumed name adopted by an author to conceal his or her identity; pen-name. –**pseudonymous** /sjuˈdɒnəməs/, *adj.* –**pseudonymity** /sjudəˈnɪməti/, *n.*

pseudoscience /ˈsjudoʊsaɪəns/ *n.* an apparently scientific approach to the process or presentation of a theory, invention, product, etc., which on close analysis is shown to have no scientific validity. –**pseudoscientist**, *n.* –**pseudoscientific**, *adj.* –**pseudoscientifically**, *adv.*

psoriasis /səˈraɪəsəs/ *n. Pathol.* a common chronic skin disease characterised by scaly patches. –**psoriatic** /sɒriˈætɪk/, *adj.*

psych /saɪk/ *v.t. Colloq.* **1.** to persuade by the application of psychological knowledge and techniques rather than overtly by argument, especially when leading others to perform better in a race, competition, etc.: *the coach psyched them into a brilliant display of tennis.* **2.** to gain advantage over (an opponent) by undermining their confidence using psychological means. –*phr.* **3. psych someone out,** to disturb someone's equanimity; intimidate. **4. psych up,** to bring to a state of intense focus and keen motivation in preparation for a match, contest, test, etc.

psyche /ˈsaɪki/ *n.* the human soul, spirit, or mind.

psyched /saɪkt/ *adj. Colloq.* fully enthused and excited. Also, **psyched up.**

psychedelic /saɪkəˈdɛlɪk/ *adj.* **1.** of or relating to a mental state of enlarged consciousness, involving a sense of aesthetic joy and increased perception transcending verbal concepts. **2.** of or relating to any of a group of drugs inducing such a state, especially LSD. **3.** *Colloq.* intensely pleasurable or fashionable. **4.** *Colloq.* having bright colours and imaginative patterns, as materials. **5.** of or relating to music which is played very loud and accompanied by a lightshow.

psychiatry /səˈkaɪətri, saɪ-/ *n.* the practice or the science of treating mental diseases. –**psychiatric** /saɪkiˈætrɪk/, **psychiatrical** /saɪkiˈætrɪkəl/, *adj.* –**psychiatrically** /saɪkiˈætrɪkli/, *adv.* –**psychiatrist**, *n.*

psychic /ˈsaɪkɪk/ *adj.* Also, **psychical. 1.** of or relating to the human soul or mind; mental (opposed to *physical*). **2.** *Psychol.* having extra-sensory mental powers, such as clairvoyance, telepathy. **3.** done by, proceeding from or relating to non-physical forces. –*n.* **4.** a psychic person. –**psychically**, *adv.*

psycho- a word element representing 'psyche' (as in *psychology* and *psychoanalysis*). Also, **psych-**.

psychoanalyse /saɪkoʊˈænəlaɪz/ *v.t.* to investigate or treat by psychoanalysis. Also, *US,* **psychoanalyze**. –**psychoanalyser**, *n.*

psychoanalysis /ˌsaɪkoʊəˈnæləsəs/ *n.* **1.** a systematic structure of theories concerning the relation of conscious and unconscious psychological processes. **2.** a technical procedure for investigating unconscious mental processes, and for treating neuroses. –**psychoanalyse**, *v.* –**psychoanalyst** /saɪkoʊˈænələst/, *n.* –**psychoanalytic** /ˌsaɪkoʊænəˈlɪtɪk/, **psychoanalytical** /ˌsaɪkoʊænəˈlɪtɪkəl/, *adj.* –**psychoanalytically** /ˌsaɪkoʊænəˈlɪtɪkli/, *adv.*

psychological /saɪkəˈlɒdʒɪkəl/ *adj.* **1.** of or relating to psychology. **2.** of or relating to the mind or to mental phenomena, especially as the subject matter of psychology. –**psychologically**, *adv.*

psychology /saɪˈkɒlədʒi/ *n.* (*pl.* **-gies**) **1.** the systematic study of mind, or of mental states and processes; the science of human nature. **2.** the systematic study of human and animal behaviour. **3.** the mental states and processes of a person or of a number of persons, especially as determining action: *the psychology of the fighter pilot.* –**psychologist**, *n.*

psychopathic /saɪkəˈpæθɪk/ *adj.* denoting a personality outwardly normal but characterised by a diminished sense of social responsibility, inability to establish deep human relationships, and sometimes, a tendency to manipulate others, and a lack of remorse for the harm done to others. –**psychopath**, *n.*

psychopathy /saɪˈkɒpəθi/ *n.* **1.** mental disease or disorder. **2.** a psychopathic personality.

psychosis /saɪˈkoʊsəs/ *n.* (*pl.* **-choses** /-ˈkoʊsiz/) any major, severe form of mental illness, as one in which the sufferer loses connection with external reality leading to personality and behaviour changes. Compare **neurosis.** –**psychotic**, *adj.*, *n.*

psychosomatic /ˌsaɪkoʊsəˈmætɪk/ *adj.* denoting a physical disorder which is caused by or notably influenced by the emotional state of the patient.

psychotherapy /saɪkoʊˈθɛrəpi/ *n.* the science or art of curing psychological abnormalities and disorders by psychological techniques. –**psychotherapist**, *n.*

psyllium /ˈsɪliəm/ *n.* an annual plant of the plantain family *Plantago psyllium,* with dense spikes of small flowers; native to Europe and Asia.

pterodactyl /tɛrəˈdæktl/ *n.* any member of the Pterosauria, an order of extinct (Jurassic to Cretaceous) flying reptiles, having the outside digit of the forelimb greatly elongated and supporting a wing membrane.

ptomaine /təˈmeɪn/ *n. Biochem.* any of a class of basic nitrogenous substances, some of them very poisonous, produced during putrefaction of animal or plant proteins. Also, **ptomain.**

p2p /pi tə ˈpi/ *adj. Computers* → **peer-to-peer.**

pub /pʌb/ *n. Colloq.* a hotel, especially one that is primarily a provider of alcoholic drinks rather than accommodation.

puberty /ˈpjubəti/ *n.* sexual maturity; the earliest age at which a person is capable of procreating offspring.

pubes /ˈpjubiz/ *n.* (*pl.* **-bes** /-biz/) **1.** *Anat.* the lower part of the abdomen, especially the region between the right and left iliac regions. **2.** the hair appearing on the lower part of the abdomen at puberty.

pubescent /pjuˈbɛsənt/ *adj.* **1.** arriving or arrived at puberty. **2.** *Bot., Zool.* covered with down or fine short hair. –**pubescence**, *n.*

pubic /ˈpjubɪk/ *adj.* relating to the pubes or pubis.

public /ˈpʌblɪk/ *adj.* **1.** of, relating to, or affecting the people as a whole or the community, state, or nation: *public affairs.* **2.** done, made, acting, etc., for the people or community as a whole: *a public prosecutor.* **3.** open to all the people: *a public meeting.* **4.** relating to or engaged in the affairs or service of the community or nation: *a public official.* **5.** maintained at the public expense, under public control, and open to the public generally: *a public library.* **6.** open to the view or knowledge of all; existing, done, etc., in public: *the fact became public.* **7.** having relations with or being known to the public generally: *a public character.* –*n.* **8.** Also, **the general public.** the people constituting a community, state, or nation. **9.** a particular section of the people: *the novel-reading public.* **10.** public view or access: *in public.* –*phr.* **11. go public, a.** (of a proprietary limited company) to sell part or all of its capital to the public at large. **b.** (of a company) to seek listing on the stock exchange. **c.** *Colloq.* to allow something to be generally known.

public-address system *n.* an electronic system consisting of microphone, amplifier, and a loudspeaker, or a number of each of these units, which serves to amplify sound, as for use in a public hall, for speech or music. Also, **PA, PA system.**

publican /ˈpʌblɪkən/ *n.* the owner or manager of a pub or hotel.

publication /pʌbləˈkeɪʃən/ *n.* **1.** the publishing of a book, ebook, periodical, blog, images, sheet music, sound recordings, or the like. **2.** the act of publishing. **3.** the state or fact of being published. **4.** something that is published, as a book or the like.

public bar *n.* (in a pub or hotel) the bar which is least comfortably furnished and where drinks are cheaper than at other bars. Compare **lounge** (def. 6), **saloon** (def. 2).

public company *n.* a company with the capacity to invite the public to subscribe for shares or debentures, the share capital of which must not be less than a statutory minimum.

public domain software *n.* computer software which may be freely used and copied.

public housing *n.* housing owned by the government and made available to low-income earners, usually at a low rent.

publicise /ˈpʌbləsaɪz/ *v.t.* to give publicity to; bring to public notice; advertise: *they publicised the meeting as best they could.* Also, **publicize.** –**publicist,** *n.*

publicity /pʌbˈlɪsəti/ *n.* **1.** the measures, process, or business of securing public notice. **2.** advertising matter, as leaflets, films, etc., intended to attract public notice.

public-private partnership *n.* a partnership between a government and an organisation in the public sector for the delivery of infrastructure and associated services traditionally provided by the government, as railways, freeways, etc. *Abbrev.*: PPP

public relations *n.* (*functioning as sing. or pl.*) the practice of promoting goodwill among the public for a company, government body, individual, or the like; the practice of working to present a favourable image.

public school *n.* **1.** → **state school. 2.** one of a small grouping of prestigious secondary schools in Australia, mainly private. **3.** *Brit.* a private school of the type on which Australian private schools were modelled.

public sector *n. Econ.* **1.** the sector of an economy which is owned and operated by government and government authorities (opposed to the *private sector*). **2.** the organisations operating within this sector.

public service *n.* the structure of government departments and personnel responsible for the administration of policy and legislation. –**public servant,** *n.*

public-spirited *adj.* having or showing an unselfish desire for the public good: *a public-spirited citizen.*

public utility *n.* an organisation performing an essential public service, as supplying gas, electricity, or transport, and operated or regulated either by a company, the state, or local government.

publish /ˈpʌblɪʃ/ *v.t.* **1.** to issue, or cause to be issued, in print or digital formats, for sale or distribution to the public, as a book, ebook, blog, periodical, images, sheet music, sound recordings, or the like. **2.** to issue to the public the works of (an author). **3.** to announce publicly; make generally known. –*v.i.* **4.** to have one's writing published: *does he publish?* –**publishable,** *adj.* –**publisher,** *n.*

puce /pjus/ *adj.* **1.** of a dark or purplish brown. –*n.* **2.** dark or purplish brown.

puck /pʌk/ *n.* a flat rubber disc used in place of a ball in ice hockey.

pucker /ˈpʌkə/ *v.i.* **1.** to gather into wrinkles or irregular folds. –*v.t.* **2.** to draw into wrinkles or irregular folds. –*n.* **3.** a puckered part, as of cloth tightly or crookedly sewn.

pudding /ˈpʊdɪŋ/ *n.* **1.** a sweet or savoury dish made in many forms and of various ingredients, as flour (or rice, tapioca, or the like), milk, and eggs, with fruit, meat, or other ingredients. **2.** a course in a meal following the main or meat course; dessert; sweet. **3.** *Brit.* a skin filled with seasoned minced meat, oatmeal, blood, etc., and cooked; a kind of sausage. **4.** anything resembling a pudding (def. 1), as in texture, etc.

puddle /ˈpʌdl/ *n.* **1.** a small pool of water, especially dirty water, as in a road after rain. **2.** a small pool of any liquid. **3.** clay, or a similar material, which has been mixed with water and tempered, used as a watertight canal lining, etc. –*v.t.* **4.** to mark or fill with puddles. **5.** *Mining* to work together water and earth rich in clay so as to separate out any gold, opal, etc. **6.** to subject (pig iron) to the process by which it is converted into wrought iron, that is, by heating and stirring the molten metal in a reverberatory furnace, with an oxidising agent.

puerile /ˈpjʊəraɪl, ˈpjuraɪl/ *adj.* **1.** of or relating to a child or boy. **2.** childishly foolish, irrational, or trivial: *a piece of puerile writing.* –**puerility** /pjuˈrɪləti/, *n.* –**puerilely,** *adv.*

puerperal /pjuˈɜpərəl/ *adj. Med.* **1.** of or relating to a woman in childbirth. **2.** relating to or consequent on childbirth.

puff /pʌf/ *n.* **1.** a short, quick blast, as of wind or breath. **2.** an abrupt emission of air, vapour, etc. **3.** a single inhalation and exhalation, as of a cigarette. **4.** the sound of an abrupt emission of air, etc. **5.** a small quantity of vapour, smoke, etc., emitted at one blast. **6.** an inflated or distended part of a thing; a swelling; a protuberance. **7.** a commendation, especially an exaggerated one, of a book, an actor's performance, etc. **8.** inflated or exaggerated praise, especially as uttered or written from interested motives. **9.** → **powder puff. 10.** a form of light pastry with a filling of cream, jam, or the like. –*v.i.* **11.** to blow with short, quick blasts, as the wind. **12.** to be emitted in a puff. **13.** to emit a puff or puffs; to breathe quick and hard, as after violent exertion. **14.** to go with puffing or panting. **15.** to emit puffs or whiffs of vapour or smoke. **16.** to move with such puffs. **17.** to take puffs at a cigar, etc. –*v.t.* **18.** to send forth (air, vapour, etc.) in short quick blasts. **19.** to drive or impel by puffing, or with a short quick blast. **20.** to smoke (a cigar, etc.). **21.** to inflate or distend, especially with air. **22.** to inflate with pride, etc. **23.** to praise in exaggerated language. **24.** to advertise with exaggerated commendation. –*phr.* **25. out of puff,** *Colloq.* out of breath. **26. puff out,** to extinguish with a puff; blow out: *to puff out a light.* **27. puff up,** to become inflated or distended.

puffed /pʌft/ *adj. Colloq.* out of breath.

puffed-up *adj. Colloq.* **1.** self-important. **2.** grandiose or inflated.

puffin /ˈpʌfən/ *n.* any of various seabirds of the genus *Fratercula*, with a bill that, in the male, changes shape and size and becomes brightly coloured during the breeding season, as the **Atlantic puffin,** *F. arctica,* the common species, which abounds on the coasts of the northern Atlantic, nesting in holes in the ground.

puff pastry *n.* a rich, flaky pastry used for pies, tarts, etc.; rough puff pastry; flaky pastry. Also, *US,* **puff paste.**

puffy /ˈpʌfi/ *adj.* (**-fier, -fiest**) **1.** gusty. **2.** short-winded. **3.** inflated or distended. **4.** fat. **5.** conceited. **6.** bombastic. –**puffiness,** *n.*

pug¹ /pʌg/ *n.* one of a breed of dogs having a short, smooth coat of silver, fawn, or black, a deeply wrinkled face, and a tightly curled tail. Also, **pugdog.**

pug² /pʌg/ *v.t.* (**pugged, pugging**) **1.** to knead (clay, etc.) with water to make it plastic, as in brick-making. **2.** to stop or fill in with clay or the like. **3.** to pack or cover with mortar, etc., to deaden sound. –**puggy,** *adj.* –**pugging,** *n.*

pugilist /ˈpjudʒələst/ *n.* someone who fights with the fists; a boxer; usually a professional. –**pugilistic** /pjudʒə-ˈlɪstɪk/, *adj.* –**pugilistically** /pjudʒəˈlɪstɪkli/, *adv.*

pugnacious /pʌgˈneɪʃəs/ *adj.* given to fighting; quarrelsome; aggressive. –**pugnaciously,** *adv.* –**pugnacity** /pʌgˈnæsəti/, **pugnaciousness,** *n.*

PUK /pʌk/ *n.* personal (or PIN) unblocking key; a code that is required to unblock a mobile phone when the user has entered an incorrect PIN more than the set number of times. Also, **PUK code**.

puke /pjuk/ *v.i., v.t., n. Colloq.* → **vomit**.

pull /pʊl/ *v.t.* **1.** to draw or haul towards oneself or itself, in a particular direction, or into a particular position: *to pull a sledge up a hill.* **2.** to draw or tug at with force: *to pull a person's hair.* **3.** to draw, rend, or tear (apart, to pieces, etc.). **4.** to draw or pluck away from a place of growth, attachment, etc.: *to pull a tooth.* **5.** (in timber-getting) to haul (a tree) out by the roots. **6.** *Colloq.* to draw out for use, as a knife or a pistol. **7.** *Colloq.* to put or carry through (something attempted): *I wouldn't pull a stunt like that!* **8.** to cause to form, as a grimace: *to pull a face.* **9.** *Golf* to play (the ball) with a curve to the left (or, if a left-handed player, to the right). **10.** *Printing* to take (an impression or proof) from type, etc. **11.** to propel by rowing, as a boat. **12.** to strain, as a ligament. **13.** *Boxing* to deliver (a punch) without full force; check or restrain. **14.** *Cricket* to hit (a ball pitched on the wicket or on the off side) to the on side, usually off the back foot. **15.** *Colloq.* to attract (someone) with the aim of having sexual intercourse. **16.** *Colloq.* to attract (an audience): *the band pulls a good crowd at the pub.* **17.** *Colloq.* to withdraw: *to pull an ad.* –*v.i.* **18.** (sometimes fol. by *at*) to exert a drawing, tugging, or hauling force. **19.** to inhale through a pipe, cigarette, etc. **20.** to become or come as specified, by pulling: *a rope pulls apart.* **21.** to row. **22.** to proceed by rowing. **23.** *Cricket, Golf* to pull the ball. –*n.* **24.** the act of pulling or drawing. **25.** force used in pulling; pulling power. **26.** a drawing of a liquid into the mouth: *he took a long pull at his glass of beer.* **27.** an inhalation of smoke, as from a pipe or cigarette. **28.** a part or thing to be pulled, as a handle or the like. **29.** an instrument or device for pulling something. **30.** a stroke of an oar. **31.** a pulling of the ball in cricket or golf. **32.** *Colloq.* influence, as with persons able to grant favours **33.** *Colloq.* the ability to attract or draw audiences, followers, etc.: *an actor with box office pull.* **34.** *Colloq. (taboo)* an act of sexual intercourse. **35.** *Colloq. (taboo)* an act of male masturbation. –*phr.* **36. pull a beer**, *Colloq.* to pour a beer by tapping a barrel. **37. pull a fast one** (or **a swiftie**), *Colloq.* to practise a deception. **38. pull ahead**, **a.** to move towards the front. **b.** to begin to win in a race or other contest. **39. pull apart**, **a.** to rend in pieces. **b.** to analyse critically in detail. **40. pull dirt**, (in opal mining) to haul the material excavated by a miner to the surface. **41. pull down**, **a.** to lower; draw downwards: *to pull down the blinds.* **b.** to demolish. **c.** to reduce or make lower: *to pull down prices in a sale.* **42. pull in**, **a.** (of a vehicle, driver, etc.) to move to the side of the road in order to stop. **b.** to arrive at a destination, stopping place, etc.: *the train pulled in to Central.* **c.** *Colloq.* to arrest (a person). **d.** to earn (a wage or salary). **43. pull off**, *Colloq.* to succeed in achieving or performing. **44. pull oneself off**, *Colloq. (taboo)* (of a male) to masturbate. **45. pull oneself together**, to recover one's self-control. **46. pull one's finger out**, *Colloq.* to attack a job, task, etc., with energy after a period of inertia or laziness. **47. pull one's head in**, *Aust. Colloq.* to withdraw; to mind one's own business. **48. pull one's punches**, **a.** *Boxing* to deliberately deliver punches without full force. **b.** to act with more show than effect, as by failing to follow through an initial move. **49. pull one's weight**, to make a full and fair contribution to a task or undertaking, as in rowing or any other activity. **50. pull out**, **a.** to leave; depart: *a train pulling out of a station.* **b.** (of a vehicle, driver, etc.) to move out of a lane or stream of traffic, as in preparing to overtake. **c.** *Colloq.* to withdraw, as from an agreement or enterprise. **d.** (of an aircraft) to return to level flight after a dive. **51. pull out all** (**the**) **stops**, *Colloq.* to make every effort. **52. pull over**, **a.** (of a vehicle, driver, etc.) to move towards the side of the road, or in some other direction as specified. **b.** to cause (a vehicle or driver) to stop at the side of the road: *the cops pulled me over for a breath test.* **53. pull rank** (or **the braid**), to invoke the privileges or powers of seniority. **54. pull round**, *Colloq.* to recover, as from an illness, period of adversity, or the like. **55. pull someone's leg**, *Colloq.* to tease someone. **56. pull strings**, *Colloq.* to seek the advancement of oneself or another by using social contacts and other means not directly connected with ability or suitability. **57. pull the plug on**, to prevent (someone) from continuing their present activities, as by making some damning revelation, issuing an order, etc. **58. pull the rug from under someone's feet**, *Colloq.* to place someone in a position of disadvantage. **59. pull the wool over someone's eyes**, *Colloq.* to deceive or hoodwink someone. **60. pull through**, *Colloq.* **a.** to recover, as from an illness, a period of adversity, or the like. **b.** to make one's way through, as by a pull or effort. **61. pull together**, **a.** to cooperate, as in a team. **b.** to assemble from various sources. **62. pull to pieces**, **a.** to rend in pieces; destroy completely. **b.** to analyse critically in detail. **63. pull up**, **a.** to stop. **b.** to cause to stop. **c.** to correct or rebuke. **d.** to improve; bring to a higher or required standard. **e.** to uproot or pull out of the ground. **f.** *Colloq.* to gain ground, as a horse in a race. –**puller**, *n.*

pull-down menu *n. Computers* a computer menu which is instantly accessible and which leaves the screen exactly as it was once an option has been chosen. Also, **drop-down menu**.

pulled /pʊld/ *v.* **1.** past tense and past participle of **pull**. –*adj.* **2.** (of cooked meat) torn into small pieces or fragments.

pullet /ˈpʊlət/ *n.* a young hen, less than one year old.

pulley /ˈpʊli/ *n.* (*pl.* **-leys**) *Mechanics* **1.** a wheel with a grooved rim for carrying a line, turning in a frame or block and serving to change the direction of or transmit power, as in pulling at one end of the line to raise a weight at the other end. **2.** a combination of such wheels in a block, or of such wheels or blocks in a tackle, to increase the power applied. **3.** a wheel driven by or driving a belt or the like, as in the transmission of power.

pullover /ˈpʊloʊvə/ *n.* → **jumper²** (def. 1).

pulmonary /ˈpʌlmənri, ˈpʊl-/ *adj.* **1.** of or relating to the lungs. **2.** of the nature of a lung; lung-like. **3.** affecting the lungs. **4.** having lungs or lung-like organs.

pulp /pʌlp/ *n.* **1.** the soft, juicy part of a fruit. **2.** the pith of the stem of a plant. **3.** the soft or fleshy part of an animal body. **4.** any soft, moist mass, such as that into which linen, wood, etc., are made in the production of paper. **5.** anything worthless, as a magazine containing sensational and lurid stories, articles, etc.; trash. –*v.t.* **6.** to reduce to pulp. –*v.i.* **7.** to become reduced to pulp.

pulpit /ˈpʊlpət/ *n.* a platform or raised structure in a church, from which the priest, minister, etc., delivers a sermon, etc.

pulsate /pʌlˈseɪt/ *v.i.* **1.** to expand and contract rhythmically, as the heart; beat; throb. **2.** to vibrate; quiver. –**pulsation**, *n.* –**pulsatile, pulsatory**, *adj.* –**pulsator**, *n.*

pulse¹ /pʌls/ *n.* **1.** the regular beating in the arteries caused by the contractions of the heart, especially as felt in an artery at the wrist. **2.** a single beat or throb of the arteries or heart. **3.** any regular stroke, beat, or vibration. **4.** the underlying force of life, feeling, etc.: *the pulse of a nation.* **5.** a brief increase in the size of an electric current, voltage, etc. –*v.i.* **6.** to beat, throb or vibrate.

pulse[2] /pʌls/ *n.* the edible seeds of certain leguminous plants, as peas, beans, lentils, etc.

pulverise /ˈpʌlvəraɪz/ *v.t.* **1.** to reduce to dust or powder, as by pounding, grinding, etc. **2.** to demolish. **3.** *Colloq.* to defeat overwhelmingly, as a fighter. –*v.i.* **4.** to become reduced to dust. Also, **pulverize**. –**pulverisable**, *adj.* –**pulverisation** /pʌlvəraɪˈzeɪʃən/, *n.* –**pulveriser**, *n.*

puma /ˈpjumə/ *n.* a large tawny wild cat, *Felis concolor*, of North and South America; cougar; mountain lion.

pumice /ˈpʌmɪs/ *n.* a porous or spongy form of volcanic glass, used, especially when powdered, as an abrasive, etc. Also, **pumice stone**. –**pumiceous** /pjuˈmɪʃəs/, *adj.*

pummel /ˈpʌməl/ *v.t.* (**-melled** *or*, *Chiefly US*, **-meled**, **-melling** *or*, *Chiefly US*, **-meling**) to beat or thrash with rapid blows, as with the fists or, originally, a pommel. Also, *Chiefly US*, **pommel**.

pump[1] /pʌmp/ *n.* **1.** an apparatus or machine for raising, driving, exhausting, or compressing fluids, as by means of a piston, plunger, or rotating vanes. –*v.t.* **2.** to raise, drive, etc., with a pump. **3.** to operate by action like that on a pump handle. **4.** to supply with air, as an organ, by means of a pump-like device. **5.** to drive, force, etc., as if from a pump: *they pumped ten bullets into him.* **6.** to seek to elicit information from, as by artful questioning. **7.** to elicit (information) by questioning. **8.** to shake (someone's hand) vigorously. –*v.i.* **9.** to work a pump; raise or move water, etc., with a pump. **10.** to operate as a pump does. **11.** to gush out in spurts, as if driven by a pump: *blood pumping from a wound.* **12.** to move up and down like a pump-handle. **13.** to exert oneself in a manner likened to pumping. **14.** Also, **pump out**. **a.** (of dance music) to be at such a volume that the bass beat can be felt physically. **b.** (of a venue at which such music is played) to be playing music of this kind. –*phr.* **15. pump iron**, *Colloq.* to exercise with weights in order to build muscles. **16. pump out**, to free from water, etc., by means of a pump. **17. pump up**, to inflate by pumping: *to pump up a tyre.* –**pumpable**, *adj.* –**pumper**, *n.*

pump[2] /pʌmp/ *n.* **1.** a low, light, black, patent-leather shoe worn by men for ballroom dancing, with formal dress, etc. **2.** a low, slipper-like shoe worn by women, originally for dancing.

pumpernickel /ˈpʌmpənɪkəl/ *n.* a coarse, slightly sour bread made with wholemeal rye.

pumpkin /ˈpʌmpkən/ *n.* **1.** the large edible fruit of various species of coarse trailing plants of the gourd family, especially *Cucurbita maxima* in Europe and Australia, and *C. pepo* and its varieties in the US. **2.** any of the plants themselves.

pun /pʌn/ *n.* **1.** the humorous use of a word in such a manner as to bring out different meanings or applications, or of words alike or nearly alike in sound but different in meaning; a play on words. –*v.i.* (**punned**, **punning**) **2.** to make puns.

punch[1] /pʌntʃ/ *n.* **1.** a thrusting blow, especially with the fist. **2.** *Colloq.* a vigorous, telling effect or force. **3.** *Aust. Rules* → **handball** (def. 6). –*v.t.* **4.** to give a sharp thrust or blow to, especially with the fist. **5.** *NZ* to strip pelts from (carcasses) in freezing works. **6.** to drive (cattle). –*v.i.* **7.** to deliver blows: *he punches cleanly.* **8.** *Aust. Rules* → **handball** (def. 6). –*phr.* **9. pack a punch**, **a.** to be capable of delivering vigorous blows. **b.** to have an extreme effect upon someone: *these cocktails certainly pack a punch.* **10. punch one through**, *Colloq.* (*taboo*) (of a man) to have sexual intercourse with. **11. punch the bundy**, *Aust. Colloq.* to operate a time clock. –**puncher**, *n.*

punch[2] /pʌntʃ/ *n.* a tool or apparatus for piercing, or perforating tickets, leather, etc., or stamping materials, impressing a design, forcing nails beneath a surface, driving bolts out of holes, etc.

punch[3] /pʌntʃ/ *n.* **1.** a beverage consisting of wine or spirits mixed with water, fruit juice, etc., and flavoured with sugar, lemon, spices, etc. **2.** a beverage of two or more fruit juices, sugar, and water, often carbonated.

punch-drunk *adj.* **1.** having cerebral concussion so that one's movements resemble those of a drunken person, a condition sometimes found in boxers. **2.** *Colloq.* dull-witted; stupid or dazed.

punchline /ˈpʌntʃlaɪn/ *n.* the culminating sentence, line, phrase, or the like of a joke, especially that on which the whole joke depends.

punch-up *n.* *Colloq.* a fight.

punctilious /pʌŋkˈtɪliəs/ *adj.* attentive to punctilios; strict or exact in the observance of forms in conduct or actions. –**punctiliously**, *adv.* –**punctiliousness**, *n.*

punctual /ˈpʌŋktʃuəl/ *adj.* **1.** strictly observant of an appointed or regular time; not late. **2.** prompt, as an action; made at an appointed or regular time: *punctual payment.* **3.** of or relating to a point: *punctual coordinates* (the coordinates of a point). –**punctually**, *adv.* –**punctualness**, **punctuality** /pʌŋktʃuˈælətɪ/, *n.*

punctuate /ˈpʌŋktʃueɪt/ *v.t.* **1.** to mark or divide with punctuation marks, as a sentence, etc., in order to make the meaning clear. **2.** to interrupt at intervals, as a speech by cheers. **3.** to give point or emphasis to. –**punctuator**, *n.*

punctuation /pʌŋktʃuˈeɪʃən/ *n.* the practice, art, or system of inserting marks or points in writing or printing in order to make the meaning clear; the punctuating of written or printed matter with commas, semicolons, colons, full stops, etc. (**punctuation marks**).

puncture /ˈpʌŋktʃə/ *n.* **1.** the act of pricking or perforating as with a pointed instrument or object. **2.** a mark or hole so made. –*v.t.* **3.** to prick, pierce, or perforate: *to puncture the skin with a pin.* –**puncturable**, *adj.*

pundit /ˈpʌndət/ *n.* someone who sets up as an expert.

pungent /ˈpʌndʒənt/ *adj.* **1.** sharply affecting the organs of taste or smell, as if by a penetrating power; biting; acrid. **2.** acutely distressing to the feelings or mind; poignant. **3.** caustic, biting, or sharply expressive, as speech, etc. **4.** mentally stimulating or appealing. **5.** *Biol.* piercing or sharp-pointed. –**pungency**, *n.* –**pungently**, *adv.*

punish /ˈpʌnɪʃ/ *v.t.* **1.** to subject to a penalty, or to pain, loss, confinement, death, etc., for some offence, transgression, or fault: *to punish a criminal.* **2.** to inflict a penalty for (an offence, fault, etc.): *to punish theft.* **3.** to handle severely or roughly, as in a fight. **4.** to put to painful exertion, as a horse in racing. **5.** *Colloq.* to make a heavy inroad on (a supply, etc.). –**punishable**, *adj.* –**punisher**, *n.* –**punishment**, *n.*

punitive /ˈpjunətɪv/ *adj.* serving for, concerned with, or inflicting punishment: *punitive laws.* Also, **punitory** /ˈpjunətəri, -tri/.

punk /pʌŋk/ *Colloq.* –*n.* **1.** *Chiefly US* something or someone worthless, degraded, or bad. **2.** a follower of punk rock and an associated style of dress and behaviour. **3.** → **punk rock**. **4.** a petty criminal. –*adj.* **5.** of or relating to punk rock or punk fashions. –*v.t.* **6.** to humiliate (someone) by playing an elaborate practical joke on them.

punk rock *n.* a type of rock music usually with a fast, energetic beat reminiscent of early rock, which is associated with rebelliousness, great aggressiveness, violence, and sexuality.

punnet /ˈpʌnət/ *n.* **1.** a small, shallow container, as for strawberries. **2.** a shallow rectangular pot used for growing seedlings.

punt[1] /pʌnt/ *n.* **1.** *Football* a kick given to a ball dropped from the hands before it touches the ground. **2.** *Soccer* a light, rising shot. –*v.t.* **3.** *Football* to kick (a ball dropped from the hands) before it touches the ground. **4.** *Soccer* to kick the ball so that it rises. –**punter**, *n.*

punt² /pʌnt/ *n.* **1.** a shallow, flat-bottomed, square-ended boat, usually propelled by thrusting with a pole against the bottom of the river, etc. **2.** a ferry for carrying vehicles across rivers, etc. –*v.t.* **3.** to propel (a punt or other boat) by thrusting with a pole against the bottom. –**punter**, *n.*

punt³ /pʌnt/ *v.i.* **1.** (in gambling games, as faro, etc.) to lay a stake against the bank. **2.** to gamble; wager; lay bets. –*n.* **3.** a wager; bet: *to take a punt.* –*phr.* **4. take** (or **have**) **a punt**, *Colloq.* to make an attempt in the hope that one's luck is good. –**punter**, *n.*

puny /ˈpjuni/ *adj.* (**-nier**, **-niest**) **1.** of less than normal size and strength; weakly. **2.** petty; insignificant. –**punily**, *adv.* –**puniness**, *n.*

pup /pʌp/ *n.* **1.** a young dog, especially one less than one year old; a puppy. **2.** a young seal. **3.** a conceited or empty-headed boy or young man. –*v.i.* (**pupped**, **pupping**) **4.** to bring forth pups. –*phr.* **5. be a pup**, to be in the early stages of development: *the night's only a pup.* **6. be sold a pup**, *Colloq.* to be the victim of some deception.

pupa /ˈpjupə/ *n.* (*pl.* **pupae** /ˈpjupi/ *or* **pupas**) *Entomology* an insect in the non-feeding, usually immobile, transformation stage between the larva and the imago. –**pupal**, *adj.*

pupil¹ /ˈpjupəl/ *n.* **1.** someone who is under an instructor or teacher; a student. **2.** *Civil Law* a person under a specified age (in Roman law, under puberty), orphaned or emancipated, and under the care of a guardian. –**pupillary**, *adj.*

pupil² /ˈpjupəl/ *n. Anat.* the expanding and contracting opening in the iris of the eye, through which light passes to the retina.

puppet /ˈpʌpət/ *n.* **1.** a doll. **2.** *Theatre* an artificial figure of a person, animal, or object, usually in miniature and capable of articulated movement, controlled by a puppeteer. **3.** a person or group whose actions are prompted and controlled by another or others. –*adj.* **4.** of or relating to puppets: *a puppet theatre.* **5.** controlled by external forces: *a puppet government.* –**puppeteer**, *n.* –**puppetry**, *n.*

puppy /ˈpʌpi/ *n.* (*pl.* **-pies**) **1.** a young dog. **2.** the young of certain other animals, as the shark. **3.** a presuming, conceited, or empty-headed young man.

purchase /ˈpɜtʃəs/ *v.t.* (**-chased**, **-chasing**) **1.** to get by the payment of money; buy. **2.** to win over by a bribe. **3.** to haul, draw, or raise, especially by the aid of a mechanical power. –*n.* **4.** a buying. **5.** something which is purchased or bought. **6.** an effective hold or position for applying leverage. –**purchaser**, *n.*

purdah /ˈpɜdə/ *n.* **1.** (in Muslim and Hindu communities) **a.** a screen hiding women from view. **b.** the system of such seclusion. **2.** the costume worn by devout Muslim women, consisting of a black robe and a veil covering the face.

pure /ˈpjuə, pjʊə/ *adj.* **1.** free from outside matter, or from mixture with anything of a different, inferior, or spoiling kind: *pure gold; pure colour.* **2.** (of literary style) straightforward; unaffected. **3.** abstract or theoretical (opposed to *applied*): *pure science.* **4.** clear and true: *a pure voice.* **5.** absolute; utter; sheer: *pure ignorance.* **6.** being that and nothing else; mere: *a pure accident.* **7.** clean; spotless; unsullied: *pure hands; a pure complexion.* **8.** inexperienced or uninterested in sexual matters; virginal. **9.** *Biol.* homozygous. –**pureness**, *n.*

puree /ˈpjureɪ/ *n.* a cooked and sieved vegetable or fruit used for soups or other foods. Also, **purée**.

purgative /ˈpɜɡətɪv/ *adj.* **1.** purging; cleansing; specifically, causing evacuation of the bowels. –*n.* **2.** a purgative medicine or agent. –**purgatively**, *adv.*

purgatory /ˈpɜɡətri/ *n.* (*pl.* **-ries**) **1.** (*also upper case*) (in the belief of Roman Catholics and others) a condition or place in which the souls of those dying penitent are purified from venial sins, or undergo the temporal punishment from which, after the guilt of mortal sin has been remitted, still remains to be endured by the sinner. **2.** any condition, situation, or place of temporary suffering, expiation, or the like. –*adj.* **3.** serving to purge, cleanse, or purify; expiatory.

purge /pɜdʒ/ *v.t.* (**purged**, **purging**) **1.** to cleanse; rid of whatever is impure or undesirable; purify. **2.** to clear (a person, etc.) of imputed guilt. **3.** to clear away or wipe out legally (an offence, accusation, etc.) by atonement or other suitable action. **4.** Also, **purge away**, **purge out**. to remove by cleansing or purifying. **5.** to clear or empty (the bowels, etc.) by causing evacuation. –*n.* **6.** the elimination from political activity, as by killing, of political opponents and others. **7.** the period when such an elimination takes place: *he disappeared in Stalin's great purge of 1936–38.* –*phr.* **8. purge from**, to expel from: *to purge undesirables from a group.* **9. purge of**, to rid or clear of: *to purge a party of undesirable members.* –**purgation** /pɜˈɡeɪʃən/, *n.* –**purger**, *n.*

purify /ˈpjurəfaɪ/ *verb* (**-fied**, **-fying**) –*v.t.* **1.** to make pure; free from extraneous matter, or from anything that debases, pollutes, or contaminates: *to purify metals.* **2.** to free from foreign or objectionable elements: *to purify a language.* **3.** to free from whatever is evil or base. **4.** to make ceremonially clean. –*v.i.* **5.** to become pure. –*phr.* **6. purify of** (or **from**), to clear or purge of. –**purification** /pjurəfəˈkeɪʃən/, *n.* –**purificatory** /pjurəfəˈkeɪtəri/, *adj.* –**purifier**, *n.*

purism /ˈpjurɪzəm/ *n.* scrupulous or excessive observance of or insistence on purity in language, style, etc. –**purist**, *n.* –**puristic** /pjuˈrɪstɪk/, *adj.*

puritan /ˈpjurətən/ *n.* **1.** someone who tries to be very pure or strict in moral and religious matters. **2.** (*upper case*) one of a class of Protestants who arose in the 16th century within the Church of England, demanding further reforms in doctrine and worship, and greater strictness in religious discipline, and during part of the 17th century constituting a powerful political party. –*adj.* **3.** relating to puritans. –**puritanical**, *adj.* –**puritanism**, *n.*

purity /ˈpjurəti/ *n.* the condition or quality of being pure.

purl¹ /pɜl/ *v.i.* **1.** to flow with curling or rippling motions, as a shallow stream does over stones. **2.** to flow with a murmuring sound. –*n.* **3.** the action or sound of purling.

purl² /pɜl/ *v.i.* **1.** to knit with inversion of the stitch. **2.** to finish with loops or a looped edging. –*v.t.* **3.** to knit (a garment, etc.) with inversion of the stitch. **4.** to finish off (a piece of knitting) with loops or a looped edging. –*n.* **5.** a stitch used in hand knitting.

purloin /pɜˈlɔɪn/ *v.t.* **1.** to take dishonestly or steal. –*v.i.* **2.** to commit theft. –**purloiner**, *n.*

purple /ˈpɜpəl/ *n.* **1.** any colour having both red and blue, especially a dark shade of such a colour. **2.** cloth or clothing of this hue, especially as formerly worn by persons of imperial, royal, or other high rank: *born to the purple.* –*adj.* **3.** of the colour of purple. **4.** imperial or regal. **5.** brilliant or gorgeous. –*v.t.* **6.** to make purple. –*v.i.* **7.** to become purple.

purple patch *n.* a period of good fortune.

purple swamphen *n.* a common and widespread waterbird of the rail family, *Porphyrio porphyrio*, a large black bird with a rich purple breast and bright red beak and shield, which inhabits the margins of lakes, swamps and rivers throughout Australasia, Europe, Asia and Africa.

purport *v.t.* /pɜˈpɔt, ˈpɜpɔt/ **1.** to profess or claim: *a document purporting to be official.* **2.** to convey to the mind as the meaning or thing intended; express; imply. –*n.* /ˈpɜːpɒt, -pət/ **3.** tenor, import, or meaning. **4.** purpose or object.

purpose /ˈpɜːpəs/ *n.* **1.** the object for which anything exists or is done, made, used, etc. **2.** an intended or desired result; end or aim. **3.** intention or determination. **4.** that which one puts before oneself as something to be done or accomplished. **5.** the subject in hand; the point at issue: *to the purpose.* **6.** practical result, effect, or advantage: *to good purpose.* –*v.t.* **7.** to put before oneself as something to be done or accomplished; propose. **8.** to determine on the performance of; design; intend. –*phr.* **9. on purpose, a.** by design; intentionally. **b.** with the particular purpose specified. –**purposeful,** *adj.* –**purposefully,** *adv.* –**purposeless,** *adj.* –**purposelessly,** *adv.* –**purposelessness,** *n.*

purr /pɜ/ *v.i.* **1.** to utter a low, continuous murmuring sound expressive of satisfaction, as a cat does. **2.** (of things) to make a sound suggestive of the purring of a cat. –*v.t.* **3.** to express by, or as if by, purring. –*n.* **4.** the act of purring. **5.** the sound of purring.

purse /pɜs/ *n.* **1.** a small bag, pouch, or case for carrying money. **2.** a purse with its contents: *hand over your purse.* **3.** money, resources, or wealth: *the public purse.* **4.** any bag-like receptacle. –*v.t.* **5.** to contract into folds or wrinkles; pucker: *to purse the lips.*

purser /ˈpɜsə/ *n.* an officer, especially on board a ship, charged with keeping accounts, etc.

pursuance /pəˈsjuəns/ *n.* the following or carrying out of some plan, course, injunction, or the like.

pursuant /pəˈsjuənt/ *adj.* **1.** pursuing. –*phr.* **2. pursuant to, a.** proceeding conformably with. **b.** according to: *to act pursuant to an agreement.* **c.** in a manner conformable to.

pursue /pəˈsju/ *verb* (**-sued, -suing**) –*v.t.* **1.** to follow in order to catch; chase. **2.** to follow close upon; go with; attend: *bad luck pursued him.* **3.** to carry on: *to pursue a course of action*; *to pursue an idea*; *to pursue pleasure.* –*v.i.* **4.** to follow in pursuit. **5.** to continue. –**pursuable,** *adj.* –**pursuer,** *n.*

pursuit /pəˈsjut/ *n.* **1.** the act of pursuing: *in pursuit of the fox.* **2.** the effort to secure; quest: *the pursuit of happiness.* **3.** any occupation, pastime, or the like, regularly or customarily pursued: *literary pursuits.*

purulent /ˈpjurələnt/ *adj.* **1.** full of, containing, forming, or discharging pus; suppurating: *a purulent sore.* **2.** attended with suppuration: *purulent appendicitis.* **3.** of the nature of or like pus: *purulent matter.* –**purulence, purulency,** *n.* –**purulently,** *adv.*

purvey /pəˈveɪ/ *v.t.* to provide, furnish, or supply (especially food or provisions). –**purveyor,** *n.*

purview /ˈpɜvju/ *n.* **1.** range of operation, activity, concern, etc. **2.** range of vision; view. **3.** *Law* that which is provided or enacted in a statute, as distinguished from the preamble. **4.** the full scope or compass of a statute or law, or of any document, statement, book, subject, etc.

pus /pʌs/ *n.* *Pathol.* a yellow-white, more or less viscid substance produced by suppuration and found in abscesses, sores, etc., consisting of a liquid plasma in which leukocytes, etc., are suspended.

push /puʃ/ *v.t.* **1.** to exert force upon or against (a thing) in order to move it away. **2.** to move (*away, off,* etc.) by exerting force thus; shove; thrust; drive. **3.** to press or urge (a person, etc.) to some action or course. **4.** to press (an action, etc.) with energy and insistence. **5.** to carry (an action or thing) further, to a conclusion or extreme, too far, etc. **6.** to press the adoption, use, sale, etc., of. **7.** to peddle (narcotics). **8.** to press or bear hard upon (a person, etc.) as in dealings. **9.** *Colloq.* to place excessive or dangerous strain on: *you're pushing your luck.* –*v.i.* **10.** to exert a thrusting force upon something. **11.** to use steady force in moving a thing away; shove.

12. to make one's way with effort or persistence, as against difficulty or opposition. **13.** to put forth vigorous or persistent efforts. –*n.* **14.** the act of pushing; a shove or thrust. **15.** a contrivance or part to be pushed in order to operate a mechanism. **16.** a vigorous onset or effort. **17.** a determined pushing forward or advance. **18.** the pressure of circumstances. **19.** an emergency. **20.** *Colloq.* persevering energy; enterprise. **21.** *Aust. Colloq.* a group or set of people who have a common interest or background. **22.** *Colloq.* influence; power. –*phr.* **23. push it,** *Colloq.* **a.** to work harder than normal, as to meet a deadline. **b.** to be exorbitant in one's demands. **24. push off,** to move away from the shore, etc., as the result of a push. **25. push off** (or **along**), *Colloq.* to leave; go away. **26. push on,** to continue; proceed. **27. push one's way through,** to make a path through by thrusting obstacles aside: *to push one's way through the crowd.* **28. push the panic button,** *Colloq.* to panic. **29. push up daisies,** *Colloq.* to be dead and buried. **30. the push,** *Colloq.* **a.** dismissal; rejection; the sack: *she gave him the push.* **b.** *Aust., NZ* (formerly) a gang of vicious city hooligans: *the push from Woolloomooloo.*

pushbike /ˈpuʃbaɪk/ *n.* a bicycle.

pusher /ˈpuʃə/ *n.* **1.** *Aust.* → **stroller** (def. 3). **2.** a small child's table implement for pushing food on to a spoon. **3.** an aggressively ambitious person. **4.** a pedlar of narcotics or other drugs.

pushover /ˈpuʃouvə/ *n.* **1.** *Colloq.* anything done easily. **2.** *Colloq.* an easily defeated person or team. **3.** *Canoeing* a paddle stroke used to move the canoe sideways, away from the paddle.

pushy /ˈpuʃi/ *adj.* (**-shier, -shiest**) aggressive; presuming.

pusillanimous /pjusəˈlænəməs/ *adj.* **1.** lacking strength of mind or courage; faint-hearted; cowardly. **2.** proceeding from or indicating a cowardly spirit. –**pusillanimity,** *n.* –**pusillanimously,** *adv.*

puss[1] /pus/ *n.* **1.** a cat. **2.** a hare. **3.** *Colloq.* a girl or woman.

puss[2] /pus/ *n.* *Colloq.* **1.** the face. **2.** the mouth.

pussy[1] /ˈpusi/ *n.* (*pl.* **-sies**) a cat.

pussy[2] /ˈpʌsi/ *adj.* **1.** full of pus: *a pussy wound.* **2.** puslike. Also, **pusy.**

pussy[3] /ˈpusi/ *n.* (*pl.* **-sies**) *Colloq.* (*taboo*) the vagina and external female genitalia.

pussyfoot /ˈpusifut/ *v.i.* **1.** to go with a soft, stealthy tread like that of a cat. **2.** to act cautiously or timidly, as if afraid to commit oneself on a point at issue. –**pussyfooter,** *n.* –**pussyfooting,** *n.*

pustule /ˈpʌstjul/ *n.* **1.** *Pathol.* a small elevation of the skin containing pus. **2.** any pimple-like or blister-like swelling or elevation. –**pustular,** *adj.*

put /put/ *verb* (**put, putting**) –*v.t.* **1.** to move or place (anything) so as to get it into or out of some place or position: *to put money in one's purse.* **2.** to bring into some relation, state, etc.: *put everything in order.* **3.** to place in the charge or power of a person, etc.: *to put oneself under a doctor's care.* **4.** to subject to the endurance or suffering of something: *to put a person to death.* **5.** to set to a duty, task, action, etc.: *to put someone to work.* **6.** to force or drive to some course or action: *to put an army to flight.* **7.** to render or translate, as into another language. **8.** to assign or attribute: *to put a certain construction upon an action.* **9.** to set at a particular place, point, amount, etc., in a scale of estimation: *he puts the distance at ten metres.* **10.** to wager; bet. **11.** to express or state: *to put a thing in writing.* **12.** to apply, as to a use or purpose. **13.** to set, give, or make: *to put an end to a practice.* **14.** to propose or submit for answer, consideration, deliberation, etc.: *to put a question.* **15.** to impose, as a burden, charge, or the like: *to put a tax on an article.* **16.** to invest: *to put*

$1000 into Commonwealth Bonds. **17.** to throw or cast, especially with a forward motion of the hand when raised close to the shoulder: *to put the shot.* *–v.i.* **18.** to go, move, or proceed: *to put to sea.* **19.** *US Colloq.* to make off: *to put for home.* *–n.* **20.** a throw or cast, especially one made with a forward motion of the hand when raised close to the shoulder. **21.** *Finance* the privilege of delivering a certain amount of stock, at a specified price, within a specified time to the maker of the contract. *–phr.* **22. put about, a.** to propagate; disseminate (a rumour, etc.). **b.** to inconvenience; upset. **c.** *Naut.* to change direction, as on a course. **23. put across, a.** to communicate; cause to be understood; explain effectively. **b.** to perform (a song, monologue, etc.) effectively so as to involve and win the approval of members of the audience. **24. put aside** (or **away**) (or **by**), to save or store up. **25. put away, a.** *Colloq.* to consume (food or drink) voraciously. **b.** *Colloq.* to send (someone) to jail. **c.** *Colloq.* to institutionalise for reasons of mental illness: *he should be put away.* **d.** to destroy (an animal), usually mercifully, as for reasons of sickness, old age, etc. **26. put down, a.** to record in writing. **b.** to repress or suppress. **c.** to humiliate or rebuke. **d.** to pay as a lump sum, especially the down payment on an article to be bought by hire purchase. **e.** to land (an aircraft): *to put the plane down in a paddock.* **f.** to land in an aircraft: *to put down in Sydney.* **g.** to destroy (an animal), usually mercifully, as for reasons of old age, disease, etc. **27. put down to,** to ascribe or attribute to: *she put her success down to hard work.* **28. put forth, a.** to bring out or bear: *a plant puts forth new shoots.* **b.** to set out: *to put forth from the shore.* **29. put forward, a.** to suggest or propose. **b.** to nominate. **30. put in, a.** *Naut.* to enter a port or harbour, especially in turning aside from the regular course for shelter, repairs, provisions, etc. **b.** to interpose; say as an intervention. **c.** to devote, as time, work, etc.: *I have put in a great deal of work on this project.* **d.** *Aust. Colloq.* to betray, report (someone) as for a misdemeanour. **e.** *Aust. Colloq.* to nominate (someone absent) for an unpleasant task. **31. put in for,** to apply or seek permission for: *I've put in for a day's leave next week.* **32. put in place,** to set up or install (a policy, program, enterprise, etc.). **33. put in the boot,** *Colloq.* **a.** to attack savagely by kicking. **b.** to attack without restraint. **c.** to take unfair advantage. **34. put in the fangs** (or **hooks**) (or **nips**) (or **screws**), *Colloq.* to ask for the loan of something, especially money. **35. put it across someone,** *Colloq.* to deceive or outwit someone. **36. put it on someone,** *Colloq.* **a.** to bring influence to bear on someone in order to gain something. **b.** to confront someone directly on an issue. **c.** to have someone else blamed for one's own misdemeanour. **37. put it over someone,** *Colloq.* to con or cheat someone. **38. put off, a.** to postpone. **b.** to bid or cause to wait until later. **c.** to get rid of (a person, demand, etc.) by delay or evasive shifts. **d.** to lay aside. **e.** to set down, as from a bus. **f.** to disconcert or distract: *be quiet, you're putting me off.* **g.** to distract from: *the noise is putting me off my work.* **h.** to disgust: *the smell of garlic always puts me off.* **i.** to cause to dislike: *the smell puts me off curry.* **j.** *Naut.* to start out, as on a voyage. **39. put on, a.** to assume: *to put on airs.* **b.** to assume insincerely or falsely: *his sorrow is only put on.* **c.** to don; dress in (clothing). **d.** to impose on or take advantage of. **e.** to tease (someone) by leading them to believe something incorrect: *oh, you're just putting me on!* **f.** to produce; stage. **g.** to cause to speak on the telephone: *she asked them to put on the manager.* **40. put on an act,** to make a show of anger, etc., in order to impress someone. **41. put one over,** *Colloq.* (sometimes fol. by *on*) to deceive, outwit, or defraud someone. **42. put out, a.** to extinguish (fire, etc.). **b.** to

confuse or embarrass. **c.** to distract, disturb, or interrupt. **d.** to subject to inconvenience. **e.** to annoy, irritate, or vex. **f.** *Cricket* to dismiss (the person batting). **g.** *Baseball* to retire (a player). **h.** *Naut.* to go out to sea. **i.** *Colloq.* to agree to have sexual intercourse. **43. put over, a.** to convey in speech, manner, etc.; communicate. **b.** *US Colloq.* to postpone. **c.** *US* to accomplish. **44. put paid to,** to destroy finally: *bankruptcy put paid to her hopes of becoming a millionaire.* **45. put right,** to restore (a circumstance or set of circumstances) for the loss of which one feels responsible. **46. put someone right,** to correct someone who is mistaken in their knowledge or beliefs. **47. put someone up to,** to persuade someone to do. **48. put something on** (or **onto**) **someone,** to lay the blame for something on someone. **49. put the acid on,** *Aust., NZ Colloq.* to ask something of (someone) in such a manner that refusal is difficult; pressure (someone). **50. put the boot in, a.** *Colloq.* to attack savagely by kicking. **b.** to attack or harass without restraint. **c.** to take unfair advantage. **51. put the hard word on,** *Colloq.* to ask favours of, especially in a sexual context. **52. put through, a.** to connect by telephone: *I'll put you through now.* **b.** to arrange (a sale, business deal, etc.) successfully: *the new contract was put through in March.* **c.** to shear (sheep): *the men said 10 000 had been put through.* **53. put up, a.** to erect. **b.** to preserve (jam, etc.). **c.** to arrange (hair) in some style so that it does not hang down. **d.** to provide (money, etc.). **e.** *Colloq.* to buy (a drink) on credit: *put up a whisky for me, please.* **f.** to give lodging to (someone). **g.** (sometimes fol. by *at*) to lodge. **h.** to show: *they put up fierce resistance.* **i.** to nominate (someone) as a candidate. **j.** to stand as a candidate. **k.** *Archaic* to sheathe one's sword; stop fighting. **54. put upon,** to impose on or take advantage of. **55. put up or shut up,** *Colloq.* to be prepared to support what one says or else remain silent. **56. put up the shutters,** to fail in business. **57. put up with,** to endure; tolerate; bear.

putative /ˈpjutətɪv/ *adj.* commonly regarded as such; reputed; supposed. –**putatively,** *adv.*

putonghua /putɒŋˈhwa/ *n.* a variety of Chinese based mostly on northern dialects, especially Mandarin, now the standard spoken language of the People's Republic of China. Also, **p'ut'unghua.**

put option *n. Commerce, Stock Exchange* the right to sell a specified commodity, parcel of shares, foreign exchange, etc., at a set price on or before a specified date. Compare **call option.**

putrefy /ˈpjutrəfaɪ/ *verb* (**-fied, -fying**) *–v.t.* **1.** to render putrid; cause to rot or decay with an offensive smell. *–v.i.* **2.** to become putrid; rot. **3.** to become gangrenous. –**putrefaction** /pjutrəˈfækʃən/, *n.* –**putrescent,** *adj.* –**putrescence,** *n.*

putrid /ˈpjutrəd/ *adj.* **1.** in a state of foul decay or decomposition, as animal or vegetable matter; rotten. **2.** attended with or relating to putrefaction. **3.** having the smell of decaying flesh. **4.** thoroughly corrupt, depraved, or bad. **5.** offensively or disgustingly objectionable or bad. –**putridity** /pjuˈtrɪdəti/, **putridness,** *n.* –**putridly,** *adv.*

putt /pʌt/ *Golf* *–v.t.* **1.** to strike (the ball) gently and carefully so as to make it roll along the putting green into the hole. *–n.* **2.** a stroke made in putting.

putter¹ /ˈpʌtə/ *n. Golf* **1.** someone who putts. **2.** a club with a relatively short, stiff shaft and a wooden or iron head, used in putting.

putter² /ˈpʊtə/ *n.* an athlete who puts the shot; shot-putter.

putty /ˈpʌti/ *n.* (*pl.* **-ties**) **1.** a kind of cement, of doughlike consistency, made of whiting and linseed oil and used for securing panes of glass, stopping up holes in woodwork, etc. **2.** any of various more or less similar preparations, prepared from other ingredients and used for the same or other purposes. **3.** a substance consisting of linseed oil and various other materials (as ferric oxide and red and white lead), employed in sealing the joints of tubes, pipes, etc. **4.** *Plastering, etc.* a very fine cement made of lime only. **5.** any person or thing easily moulded, influenced, etc. **6.** light brownish or yellowish grey. *–adj.* **7.** of a yellowish or light brownish grey colour. *–v.t.* (**-tied, -tying**) **8.** to secure, cover, etc., with putty. *–phr.* **9. up to putty,** *Aust.* worthless.

put-upon *adj.* constantly taken advantage of or imposed upon: *she felt used and put-upon.*

puzzle /ˈpʌzəl/ *n.* **1.** a toy or other contrivance designed to amuse by presenting difficulties to be solved by ingenuity or patient effort. **2.** something puzzling; a puzzling matter or person. **3.** puzzled or perplexed condition. *–v.t.* **4.** to cause to be at a loss; bewilder; confuse. **5.** to perplex or confound, as the understanding. **6.** to exercise (oneself, one's brain, etc.) over some problem or matter. *–v.i.* **7.** to be in perplexity. **8.** to ponder or study over some perplexing problem or matter. *–phr.* **9. puzzle out,** to solve (a problem) or resolve (a difficulty) by careful study and reflection: *to puzzle out the meaning of a sentence.* **–puzzled,** *adj.* **–puzzling,** *adj.*

pycno- a word element meaning 'dense', 'close', 'thick', as in *pycnometer.* Also, **pykno-**; (*before vowels*), **pycn-**.

pygmy /ˈpɪgmi/ *n.* **1.** *Colloq.* (*chiefly derog.*) a small or dwarfish person. **2.** anything very small of its kind. **3.** one of a people from equatorial Africa, mostly under 1.5 m in height. *–adj.* **4.** relating to small or dwarfish people. **5.** of very small size, capacity, power, etc. Also, **pigmy.**

pyjama /pəˈdʒamə/ *n.* (especially in northern India) loose trousers with a drawstring at the waist, worn by men or women.

pyjamas /pəˈdʒaməz/ *n.* (*construed as pl.*) **1.** nightclothes consisting of loose trousers and jacket. **2.** → **pyjama.** Also, *US*, **pajamas.** **–pyjama,** *adj.*

pylon /ˈpaɪlon/ *n.* **1.** a steel tower or mast carrying high-tension, telephonic or other cables and lines. **2.** a relatively tall structure at either side of a gate, bridge, or avenue, marking an entrance or approach. **3.** an architectural form of a projecting nature which flanks an entrance. **4.** a marking post or tower for guiding pilots, frequently used in races. **5.** *Aeronautics* a structure supporting an engine or fuel tank.

pyo- a word element meaning 'pus'.

pyramid /ˈpɪrəmɪd/ *n.* **1.** *Archit.* a massive structure built of stone, with square (or polygonal) base, and sloping sides meeting at an apex, such as those built by the ancient Egyptians as royal tombs or by the Mayas as platforms for their sanctuaries. **2.** anything of such form. **3.** a number of things heaped up or arranged in this form. **4.** *Geom.* a solid having the shape of a pyramid. **5.** *Econ.* a multi-company structure in which one company controls two or more companies, each of which may itself control a number of companies, and so on. **–pyramidal,** *adj.*

pyramiding /ˈpɪrəmɪdɪŋ/ *n.* *Commerce* a method by which corporate managers gain control over a large number of other companies for a relatively small outlay

by buying a 51 per cent share in one company, which then buys a 51 per cent share in another and so on.

pyre /ˈpaɪə/ *n.* **1.** a pile or heap of wood or other combustible material. **2.** such a pile for burning a dead body.

pyrethrum /paɪˈriθrəm/ *n.* **1.** a name given by horticulturalists to certain species of the genus *Chrysanthemum,* especially *C. coccineum* and its many cultivated varieties. **2.** an insecticide prepared from the dried heads of *C. coccineum.*

pyrex /ˈpaɪrɛks/ *n.* (*from trademark*) a heat-resistant glassware for baking, frying, etc.

pyrite /ˈpaɪraɪt/ *n.* a very common brass-yellow mineral, iron disulphide (FeS_2), with a metallic lustre, burnt to sulphur dioxide in the manufacture of sulphuric acid; fool's gold. Also, **pyrites, iron pyrites.** **–pyritic** /paɪˈrɪtɪk/, **pyritical** /paɪˈrɪtɪkəl/, *adj.*

pyrites /paɪˈraɪtiz/ *n.* **1.** pyrite (sometimes called **iron pyrites**). **2.** any of various other sulphides, as of copper, tin, etc.

pyro- a word element used: **1.** *Chem.* **a.** before the name of an inorganic acid, indicating that its water content is intermediate between that of the corresponding ortho- (more water) and meta- (least water) acids, as in *pyroantimonic acid,* $H_4Sb_2O_7$, *pyroarsenic acid,* $H_4As_2O_7$, and *pyrosulphuric acid,* $H_2S_2O_7$. **b.** applied to salts of these acids. If the acid ends in *-ic,* the corresponding salt ends in *-ate,* as *pyroboric acid,* $H_3B_4O_7$ and *potassium pyroborate,* $K_2B_4O_7$. If the acid ends in *-ous,* the corresponding salt ends in *-ite: pyrophosphorous acid,* $H_4P_2O_5$, *potassium pyrophosphite,* $K_4P_2O_5$. **2.** *Geol.* in the names of minerals, rocks, etc., indicating a quality produced by the action of fire. **3.** to mean 'of, relating to, or concerned with fire'. Also, (*before vowels*), **pyr-.**

pyrogenic /paɪroʊˈdʒɛnɪk/ *adj.* **1.** producing heat or fever. **2.** produced by fire, as igneous rocks.

pyromania /paɪrəˈmeɪniə/ *n.* a mania for setting things on fire. **–pyromaniac,** *n.* **–pyromaniacal** /ˌpaɪroʊməˈnaɪəkəl/, *adj.*

pyrotechnics /paɪroʊˈtɛknɪks/ *n.* **1.** the art of making fireworks. **2.** the making and use of fireworks for display, military purposes, etc. **3.** a brilliant or sensational display, as of rhetoric, etc. Also (for defs 1 and 2), **pyrotechny** /ˈpaɪroʊtɛkni/. **–pyrotechnician,** *n.*

pyroxene /ˈpaɪrɒksin/ *n.* a very common group of minerals of many varieties, silicates of magnesium, iron, calcium, and other elements, occurring as important constituents of many kinds of rocks, chiefly igneous. **–pyroxenic** /paɪrɒkˈsɛnɪk/, *adj.*

Pyrrhic victory /pɪrɪk ˈvɪktəri/ *n.* a victory gained at too great a cost.

pyrrhotite /ˈpɪrətaɪt/ *n.* a common mineral, iron sulphide (nearly FeS), occurring in crystalline and massive forms, of a bronze colour and metallic lustre, and generally slightly magnetic. Also, **pyrrhotine** /ˈpɪrətaɪn/.

python /ˈpaɪθən/ *n.* any of various non-venomous snakes, generally large and with vestiges of hind limbs, which kill by constriction.

Q q

Q, q /kju/ *n.* a consonant, the 17th letter of the English alphabet.

QR code *n.* a quick response code; a data matrix bar code which, when scanned by a mobile phone, connects to a website for the downloading of information, as for example, a QR code at a transport terminal which connects the user to a timetable.

qua /kweɪ, kwɑ/ *adv.* as; as being; in the character or capacity of.

quack[1] /kwæk/ *v.i.* **1.** to utter the cry of a duck, or a sound resembling it. *–n.* **2.** the cry of a duck, or some similar sound.

quack[2] /kwæk/ *n.* **1.** an ignorant or deceitful person who pretends to have medical or other skill; charlatan. *–adj.* **2.** relating to a quack: *a quack doctor*; *quack methods.* –**quackery**, *n.*

quad[1] /kwɒd/ *n. Colloq.* a quadrangle, as in a school, college, etc.

quad[2] /kwɒd/ *n. Colloq.* → **quadruplet**.

quad bike *n.* a four-wheeled motorbike designed to travel over rough terrain.

quadr- variant of **quadri-**, before vowels, as in *quadrangle.*

quadrangle /ˈkwɒdræŋɡəl/ *n.* **1.** *Geom.* a plane figure having four angles and four sides, as a square. **2.** a quadrangular space or court wholly or nearly surrounded by a building or buildings, as in a school, college, etc. **3.** the building or buildings around such a space or court. –**quadrangular** /kwɒdˈræŋɡjələ/, *adj.*

quadrant /ˈkwɒdrənt/ *n.* **1.** the quarter of a circle; an arc of 90°. **2.** the area included between such an arc and two radii drawn one to each extremity. **3.** something shaped like a quarter of a circle, as a part of a machine. **4.** *Geom.* one of the four parts into which a plane is divided by two perpendicular lines. **5.** an instrument, usually containing a graduated arc of 90°, used in astronomy, navigation, etc., for measuring altitudes. –**quadrantal** /kwɒdˈræntl/, *adj.*

quadraphonic /kwɒdrəˈfɒnɪk/ *adj.* having to so with four-channel sound reproduction. Compare **stereophonic**. Also, **quadrasonic**.

quadrasonic /kwɒdrəˈsɒnɪk/ *adj.* → **quadraphonic**.

quadrate /ˈkwɒdrət/ *adj.* **1.** square; rectangular. *–n.* **2.** a square, or something square or rectangular. **3.** *Zool.* one of a pair of bones in the skulls of many lower vertebrates, to which the lower jaw is articulated.

quadratic /kwɒdˈrætɪk/ *adj.* **1.** square. **2.** *Algebra* involving the square and no higher power of the unknown quantity; the second degree: *a quadratic equation.* *–n.* **3.** *Algebra* a quadratic polynomial or equation.

quadrature /ˈkwɒdrətʃə/ *n.* **1.** the act of squaring. **2.** *Maths* the act or process of finding a square equal in area to a given surface, especially a surface bounded by a curve. **3.** *Astron.* **a.** the situation of two heavenly bodies when their longitudes differ by 90°. **b.** either of the two points in the orbit of a body, as the moon, midway between the syzygies. **c.** (of the moon) one of the points or moments at which a half-moon is visible. **4.** *Electronics* the relationship between two waves which are out of phase by 90°.

quadri- a word element meaning 'four'. Also, (*before vowels*), **quadr-**.

quadricep /ˈkwɒdrəsɛp/ *n.* → **quadriceps**.

quadriceps /ˈkwɒdrəsɛps/ *n. Anat.* the great muscle of the front of the thigh, which extends the leg and is considered as having four heads or origins. Also, **quads**.

quadrilateral /kwɒdrəˈlætərəl, -ˈlætərəl/ *adj.* **1.** having four sides. *–n.* **2.** *Geom.* a plane figure having four sides and four angles. **3.** something of this form. **4.** the space enclosed between and defended by four fortresses.

quadrille /kwəˈdrɪl/ *n.* **1.** a square dance for four couples, consisting of five parts or movements, each complete in itself. **2.** the music for such a dance.

quadriplegia /kwɒdrəˈplidʒə/ *n.* a condition in which the arms and legs are paralysed. –**quadriplegic**, *n., adj.*

quadruped /ˈkwɒdrəpɛd/ *adj.* **1.** four-footed. *–n.* **2.** an animal, especially a mammal, having four feet. –**quadrupedal** /kwɒˈdrupədəl, ˈkwɒdrəpidəl/, *adj.*

quadruple /kwɒˈdrupəl, ˈkwɒdrəpəl/ *adj.* **1.** fourfold; consisting of four parts: *a quadruple alliance.* **2.** four times as great. *–n.* **3.** a number, amount, etc., four times as great as another. *–verb* (**-pled, -pling**) *–v.t.* **4.** to make four times as great. *–v.i.* **5.** to become four times as great.

quadruplet /kwɒˈdruplət/ *n.* **1.** any group or combination of four. **2.** (*pl.*) four children born at one birth. **3.** one of four such children. **4.** *Music* a group of four notes of equal value, as four crotchets, which are to be played in the time of three notes of the same value, i.e. three crotchets.

quadruple time *n. Music* **1.** a measure consisting of four beats or pulses with accent on the first and third. **2.** the rhythm created by use of this measure.

quaff /kwɒf/ *v.i.* **1.** to drink a beverage, especially an alcoholic one in large draughts, as with hearty enjoyment. *–v.t.* **2.** to drink (a beverage, etc.), copiously and heartily. *–n.* **3.** a quaffing. –**quaffer**, *n.*

quagmire /ˈkwɒɡmaɪə, ˈkwæɡ-/ *n.* **1.** a piece of miry or boggy ground whose surface yields under the tread; a bog. **2.** a situation from which extrication is difficult.

quail[1] /kweɪl/ *n.* (*pl.* **quails** *or, especially collectively,* **quail**) **1.** in Australia, **a.** any of several small ground-dwelling birds of the family Phasianidae, heavy-bodied with small heads, short legs and rounded wings, as the **stubble quail**, *Coturnix pectoralis.* **b.** → **button quail**. **c.** → **plains-wanderer**. **2.** elsewhere, **a.** a small migratory gallinaceous game bird, *Coturnix coturnix.* **b.** any of several other birds of the genus *Coturnix* and allied genera.

quail[2] /kweɪl/ *v.i.* to lose heart or courage in difficulty or danger; shrink with fear.

quaint /kweɪnt/ *adj.* **1.** strange or odd in an interesting, pleasing, or amusing way: *the quaint streets of an old English village.* **2.** oddly picturesque; having an old-fashioned attractiveness or charm: *a quaint old house.* –**quaintly**, *adv.* –**quaintness**, *n.*

quake /kweɪk/ *v.i.* **1.** (of persons) to shake from cold, weakness, fear, anger, or the like. **2.** (of things) to shake or tremble, as from shock, internal convulsion, or instability. *–n.* **3.** an earthquake. **4.** a trembling or tremulous agitation. –**quaky**, *adj.*

qualification /kwɒləfə'keɪʃən/ *n*. **1.** a quality, accomplishment, etc., which fits for some function, office, etc. **2.** a required circumstance or condition for acquiring or exercising a right, holding an office, or the like. **3.** the act of qualifying. **4.** the state of being qualified. **5.** modification, limitation, or restriction; an instance of this: *to assert a thing without any qualification.*

qualify /'kwɒləfaɪ/ *verb* (**-fied**, **-fying**) *–v.t.* **1.** to fit with the proper or necessary qualities, skills, etc.; make competent. **2.** to attribute some quality or qualities to; characterise, call, or name. **3.** to modify in some way; limit; make less strong or positive: *to qualify a statement.* **4.** *Gram.* to modify or describe: *an adjective qualifies a noun.* *–v.i.* **5.** to make or show oneself fit or competent for something: *to qualify for a job.* **6.** to obtain authority, licence, power, etc., by fulfilling the necessary conditions. **–qualifier**, *n*.

qualitative /'kwɒlə,teɪtɪv, 'kwɒlətətɪv/ *adj.* relating to or concerned with quality or qualities. **–qualitatively**, *adv.*

quality /'kwɒləti/ *n*. (*pl.* **-ties**) **1.** a distinguishing feature; a characteristic, property, or attribute. **2.** degree of excellence, fineness, etc., or grade of excellence: *food of poor quality; silk of the finest quality.* **3.** high grade; superiority; excellence: *goods of quality.* **4.** good or high social position, education, etc.: *a man of quality.* *–adj.* **5.** of fine quality: *quality wine.*

quality assurance *n*. the practices adopted by a business, service provider, etc., to ensure the quality of the products or services provided.

qualm /kwam/ *n*. **1.** an uneasy feeling or a pang of conscience as to conduct. **2.** a sudden misgiving, or feeling of apprehensive uneasiness. **3.** a sudden sensation of faintness or illness, especially of nausea.

quandary /'kwɒndri/ *n*. (*pl.* **-ries**) a state of embarrassing perplexity or uncertainty, especially as to what to do; a dilemma.

quandong /'kwɒndɒŋ/ *n*. **1.** a tree, *Santalum acuminatum*, of semi-arid regions of Australia, yielding an edible drupaceous fruit whose seed (**quandong nut**) has an edible kernel. **2.** the fruit, or the seed or nut of this tree.

quantify /'kwɒntəfaɪ/ *v.t.* (**-fied**, **-fying**) **1.** to determine the quantity of; measure. **2.** *Logic* to make explicit the quantity of. **–quantifiable**, *adj.* **–quantification** /kwɒntəfə-'keɪʃən/, *n*.

quantitative /'kwɒntə,teɪtɪv, 'kwɒntətətɪv/ *adj.* of or relating to the describing or measuring of quantity. **–quantitatively**, *adv.* **–quantitativeness**, *n*.

quantity /'kwɒntəti/ *n*. (*pl.* **-ties**) **1.** a particular, indefinite, or considerable amount of anything: *a small quantity of water.* **2.** amount or measure: *to mix the ingredients in the right quantities.* **3.** considerable or great amount: *to extract ore in quantity.* **4.** *Logic* the character of a proposition as either universal, or particular, or (with Kant) singular.

quantum /'kwɒntəm/ *n*. (*pl.* **-ta**) **1.** quantity or amount. **2.** *Physics* one of the discrete quantities of energy or momentum of an atomic system which are characteristic of the quantum theory.

quantum bit *n*. the smallest unit of information in a computer operating within a quantum system in which it has three values, namely a state labelled 0, a state labelled 1, and a state which is a combination of the two.

quantum mechanics *n*. *Physics* the branch of mechanics which deals with the dynamics of atomic and subatomic systems which do not obey Newtonian laws. **–quantum mechanical**, *adj.*

quantum number *n*. one of a set of integers or half-integers which defines the energy state of a system, or its components, in quantum mechanics.

quantum physics *n*. the branch of physics that uses quantum theory.

quantum state *n*. *Physics* a state of a system which is described by a set of quantum numbers.

quantum statistics *pl. n.* *Physics* (*construed as sing.*) statistics relating to the distribution of a number of identical elementary particles, atoms, etc., among possible quantum states.

quantum system *n*. a physical or theoretical system which can only be described by quantum physics.

quantum theory *n*. a theory concerning the behaviour of physical systems which states that a system has certain properties, such as energy and momentum in discrete amounts (quanta).

quarantine /'kwɒrəntin/ *n*. **1.** strict isolation to prevent the spread of disease. **2.** a period, originally forty days, of isolation required of ships, people, etc., when suspected of bringing some infectious disease to a port or place. **3.** a system of measures carried out by a public authority at ports, etc., for preventing the spread of disease. **4.** a place or station at which such measures are carried out, or where ships, people, etc., are kept in isolation. *–v.t.* **5.** to put in or subject to quarantine. **–quarantinable**, *adj.*

quark /kwak/ *n*. *Physics* one of six hypothetical particles with corresponding antiparticles which have been postulated as the basis of all other particles in the universe.

quarrel /'kwɒrəl/ *n*. **1.** an angry dispute or altercation; a disagreement marked by a break in friendly relations. **2.** a cause of complaint or hostile feeling against a person, etc. *–v.i.* (**-relled** *or, Chiefly US*, **-reled**, **-relling** *or, Chiefly US*, **-reling**) **3.** to disagree angrily, squabble, or fall out. **4.** to dispute angrily; wrangle. **5.** to raise a complaint, or find fault. **–quarrelsome**, *adj.* **–quarreller**, *n*.

quarry¹ /'kwɒri/ *n*. (*pl.* **-ries**) **1.** an excavation or pit, usually open to the air, from which building stone, slate, or the like is obtained by cutting, blasting, etc. *–v.t.* (**-ried**, **-rying**) **2.** to obtain (stone, etc.) from, or as from, a quarry. **3.** to make a quarry in.

quarry² /'kwɒri/ *n*. (*pl.* **-ries**) **1.** an animal or bird hunted or pursued. **2.** game, especially game hunted with hounds or hawks. **3.** any object of pursuit or attack.

quart /kwɔt/ *n*. **1.** a liquid measure of capacity in the imperial system, equal to a quarter of a gallon, or 1.136 522 5 litres. **2.** a vessel or measure holding a quart.

quarter /'kwɔtə/ *n*. **1.** one of the four equal or equivalent parts into which anything is or may be divided: *a quarter of an apple.* **2.** *Colloq.* one of the segments into which a citrus fruit, as an orange or a mandarin, naturally divides. **3.** *US, Canadian* one fourth of a dollar (25 cents). **4.** a silver coin of this value. **5.** one fourth of an hour (15 minutes). **6.** the moment marking this period. **7.** one fourth of a year. **8.** *Sport* any one of the four periods that make up certain games, such as Australian Rules, etc. **9.** a unit of weight in the imperial system, the fourth part of a hundredweight, or approximately 12.7 kg. **10.** a measure in the imperial system of capacity of grain, etc., equal to 8 bushels, or approximately 0.3 m³. **11.** the region of any of the four principal points of the compass or divisions of the horizon. **12.** such a point or division. **13.** any point or direction of the compass. **14.** a region, district, or place. **15.** a particular district of a city or town, especially one appropriated to or occupied by a particular class or group of people. **16.** (*usu. pl.*) **a.** a place of stay; lodgings; residence. **b.** *Mil.* the buildings, houses, barracks, or rooms occupied by military personnel or their families. **17.** a part or member of a community, government, etc., which is not specified: *information from* *a high quarter.* **18.** mercy or indulgence, especially as shown by sparing the life and accepting the surrender of a defeated enemy. **19.** one of the four parts, each including a leg, of the body or carcass of a quadruped. **20.** *Football* the space between the quarter-line and the back-line: *the ball was in Manly's quarter. –adj.* **21.** being one of the four equal (or approximately equal) parts into which anything is or may be divided. **22.** being equal to only about one fourth of the full measure. *–v.t.* **23.** to divide into four equal or equivalent parts. **24.** to cut the body of (a person) into quarters, especially in executing for treason or the like. **25.** *Machinery* to make holes in, fix, etc., a quarter of a circle apart. **26.** to provide with lodgings in a particular place. **27.** to impose (soldiers) on persons, etc., to be lodged and fed. **28.** to assign to a particular position for living purposes, action, etc., as on a ship. **29.** to traverse (the ground) from left to right and right to left while advancing, as dogs in search of game. *–v.i.* **30.** to take up or be in quarters; lodge. **31.** to range to and fro, as dogs in search of game. *–phr.* **32. give no quarter**, to show no mercy.

quarterback /'kwɔtəbæk/ *n.* **1.** *American Football* a back (**back¹** def. 11) who lines up immediately behind the centre and directs the offensive play of the team. *–v.i.* **2.** to play in this position.

quarterdeck /'kwɔtədɛk/ *n.* the afterdeck of a naval vessel used for official and ceremonial occasions.

quarter horse *n.* a small horse with well-developed hind quarters and chest, bred for speed over short distances, originally a quarter of a mile, and used for roping and cutting out cattle.

quarterly /'kwɔtəli/ *adj.* **1.** occurring, done, etc., at the end of every quarter of a year. **2.** relating to or consisting of a quarter. *–n. (pl.* **-lies**) **3.** a periodical issued every three months. *–adv.* **4.** by quarters; once in a quarter of a year.

quartermaster /'kwɔtəmastə/ *n.* **1.** *Mil.* a regimental officer in charge of quarters, rations, clothing, equipment, and transport. **2.** *Navy* a petty officer having charge of signals, navigating apparatus, etc. *Abbrev.:* QM

quartet /kwɔ'tɛt/ *n.* **1.** any group of four persons or things. **2.** a group of four singers or players. **3.** a musical composition for four voices or instruments. Also, **quartette**.

quartile /'kwɔtaɪl/ *–adj.* **1.** *Astrology* of or relating to the aspect of two heavenly bodies when their longitudes differ by 90°. *–n.* **2.** *Astrology* a quartile aspect. **3.** *Statistics* (in a frequency distribution) one of the values of a variable which divides the distribution of the variable into four groups having equal frequencies.

quarto /'kwɔtoʊ/ *n. (pl.* **-tos**) **1.** *Printing* **a.** a book page size created by folding a sheet of paper in half and then in half again to make four leaves or eight pages. *Abbrev.:* 4 to or 4° **b.** a book printed in this size. **2.** a size of writing or computer paper, 254 × 203 mm (formerly, 10 × 8 inches).

quartz /kwɔts/ *n.* **1.** one of the commonest minerals, silicon dioxide, SiO_2, having many varieties which differ in colour, lustre, etc., occurring in crystals (rock crystal, amethyst, citrine, etc.) or massive (agate, bloodstone, chalcedony, jasper, etc.), an important constituent of many rocks. It is piezoelectric and is cut into wafers used to control the frequencies of radio transmitters. *–adj.* **2.** → **quartz-crystal**.

quartz crystal *n.* a piece of piezoelectric quartz ground so as to vibrate at a particular frequency.

quartz-crystal *adj.* (of a watch, clock, etc.) having the function of the hairspring of a traditional clock performed by a quartz crystal, which gives great accuracy. Also, **quartz**.

quartzite /'kwɔtsaɪt/ *n.* a granular rock consisting essentially of quartz in interlocking grains. *–***quartzitic** /kwɔt'sɪtɪk/, *adj.*

quasar /'kweɪsɑ/ *n. Astron.* one of many extremely luminous extragalactic objects lying close to the edge of the known universe, comprising a highly active galactic nucleus common when the universe was young.

quash¹ /kwɒʃ/ *v.t.* to put down or suppress completely; subdue.

quash² /kwɒʃ/ *v.t.* to make void, annul, or set aside (a law, indictment, decision, etc.).

quasi /'kwazi, 'kweɪzaɪ/ *adj.* **1.** resembling; as it were. *–adv.* **2.** seemingly, but not actually.

quasi- a prefix form of 'quasi', adjective and adverb, as in *quasi-official, quasi-deify*.

quaternary /kwɒ'tɜnəri/ *adj.* **1.** consisting of four. **2.** arranged in fours. **3.** (*upper case*) *Geol.* relating to the most recent geological period or succession of strata, which constitutes the last principal division of the Cainozoic era. *–n. (pl.* **-ries**) **4.** a group of four. **5.** the number four. **6.** (*upper case*) *Geol.* the epoch following the Tertiary.

quaver /'kweɪvə/ *v.i.* **1.** to shake or tremble (now said usually of the voice). **2.** to sound, speak, or sing in a shaking manner. *–v.t.* **3.** to express, say, or sing with a trembling voice. *–n.* **4.** a quavering shake or tone, especially in the voice. **5.** *Music* a note equal in length to half a crotchet. *–***quavery**, *adj.*

quay /ki/ *n.* an artificial landing place, as of masonry built along navigable water, for vessels unloading or loading cargo, etc.

queasy /'kwizi/ *adj.* (**-sier, -siest**) **1.** inclined to nausea, as the stomach, a person, etc. **2.** tending to cause nausea, as articles of food. **3.** uneasy or uncomfortable, as feelings, the conscience, etc. **4.** squeamish; excessively fastidious. *–***queasily**, *adv.* *–***queasiness**, *n.*

queen /kwin/ *n.* **1.** a female sovereign or monarch; a woman who holds by life tenure (and usually by hereditary right) the position of official ruler, sometimes titular only, of a country. **2.** the wife or consort of a king. **3.** a woman who is considered outstanding or preeminent in some specified respect: *you should be the one to break the news to her – you're the tact queen.* **4.** a young woman chosen as the most attractive in a competition or election: *rodeo queen; pageant queen.* **5.** a playing card bearing the formalised picture of a queen, in most games counting as next below the king in its suit. **6.** *Chess* the most powerful piece, moving any distance in any straight or diagonal line. **7.** a fertile female of ants, bees, wasps, or termites. **8.** *Colloq.* a male homosexual. **9.** *Colloq.* an effeminate man. *–adj.* **10.** (of a bed, mattress, etc.) slightly smaller than king-size. *–phr.* **11. queen it**, to behave in an overbearing or pretentious manner. **12. queen it up** or **queen around**, *Colloq.* to adopt effeminate dress or manner.

Queensberry rules /'kwinzbəri rulz, 'kwinzbri rulz/ *pl. n.* a set of rules followed in modern boxing.

Queen's Counsel *n.* (in some legal systems) a member of the senior of the two grades of barrister. *Abbrev.:* QC Compare **junior** (def. 7). Also, (*when the reigning monarch is a man*), **King's Counsel**.

queer /'kwɪə/ *adj.* **1.** strange from the normal point of view; singular or odd: *a queer idea.* **2.** of questionable character; suspicious; shady. **3.** unwell; not normal: *I feel queer.* **4.** *Colloq.* mentally unbalanced. **5.** *Colloq.* (*derog.*) homosexual. *–v.t.* **6.** *Colloq.* to spoil; jeopardise; ruin. *–n.* **7.** *Colloq.* a male homosexual. *–***queerly**, *adv.* *–***queerness**, *n.*

quell /kwɛl/ *v.t.* **1.** to suppress (disorder, mutiny, etc.); put an end to; extinguish. **2.** to vanquish; subdue. **3.** to quiet or allay (feelings, etc.). *–***queller**, *n.*

quench /kwɛntʃ/ *v.t.* **1.** to slake, as thirst; allay; satisfy. **2.** to put out or extinguish (fire, flames, etc.). **3.** to cool suddenly, as by plunging into water, as steel in tempering it. **4.** to suppress; stifle; subdue; overcome. –**quenchless**, *adj.* –**quenchable**, *adj.* –**quencher**, *n.*

querulous /ˈkwɛrələs/ *adj.* **1.** full of complaints; complaining. **2.** characterised by, or uttered in, complaint; peevish: *a querulous tone.* –**querulously**, *adv.* –**querulousness**, *n.*

query /ˈkwɪəri/ *n.* (*pl.* **-ries**) **1.** a question; an inquiry. **2.** doubt; uncertainty. **3.** *Printing* a question or interrogation mark (?), especially as added on a manuscript, proofs or the like, with reference to some point in the text. –*v.t.* (**-ried**, **-rying**) **4.** to ask or inquire about. **5.** to ask questions of. **6.** *Computers* to search for information in (a database). –**querist**, *n.*

query language *n. Computers* a database search language.

quest /kwɛst/ *n.* **1.** a search or pursuit made in order to find or obtain something: *a quest for gold.* –*phr.* **2. quest for** (or **after**), to search for; seek. –**quester**, *n.*

question /ˈkwɛstʃən/ *n.* **1.** a sentence in an interrogative form, addressed to someone in order to elicit information. **2.** a problem for discussion or under discussion; a matter for investigation. **3.** a subject of dispute or controversy. **4.** a proposal to be debated or voted on, as in a meeting or a deliberative assembly. **5.** *Law* **a.** a controversy which is submitted to a judicial tribunal or administrative agency for decision. **b.** the interrogation by which information is secured. **6.** the act of asking or inquiring; interrogation; query. **7.** inquiry into or discussion of some problem or doubtful matter. –*v.t.* **8.** to ask a question or questions of; interrogate. **9.** to ask or inquire. **10.** to make a question of; doubt. **11.** to challenge; dispute. –*v.i.* **12.** to ask a question or questions. –*phr.* **13. a question of …**, a matter or point of (something) which raises uncertainty or difficulty: *to be a question of time.* **14. beyond question**, beyond dispute; indisputably. **15. call in** (or **into**) **question**, **a.** to dispute; challenge. **b.** to cast doubt upon. **16. in question**, **a.** under consideration. **b.** in dispute. **17. open question**, a matter which is still undecided. **18. out of the question**, not to be considered; impossible. **19. without question**, undoubtedly; certainly. –**questioner**, *n.*

questionable /ˈkwɛstʃənəbəl/ *adj.* **1.** of doubtful propriety, honesty, morality, respectability, etc. **2.** open to question or dispute; doubtful or uncertain: *whether this is true is questionable.* **3.** open to question as being such: *a questionable privilege.*

question mark *n.* a mark indicating a question as, in English, the mark (?) placed after the question; interrogation mark.

questionnaire /kwɛstʃənˈɛə, kɛs-/ *n.* a list of questions, usually printed on a form as for statistical purposes, or to obtain opinions on some subject.

queue /kju/ *n.* **1.** a file or line of people, vehicles, etc., waiting in turn to obtain something, enter a place, proceed along a road, etc. **2.** a braid of hair worn hanging down behind. –*v.i.* (**queued**, **queuing** *or* **queueing**) Also, **queue up**. **3.** to form in a line while waiting; line up. –**queuer**, *n.*

quibble /ˈkwɪbəl/ *n.* **1.** a use of ambiguous, prevaricating, or irrelevant language or arguments to evade a point at issue. **2.** the use of such arguments. **3.** trivial, petty, or carping criticism. –*v.i.* **4.** to use a quibble or quibbles; evade the point or the truth by a quibble. –**quibbler**, *n.*

quiche /kiʃ/ *n.* a savoury custard tart, a specialty of Alsace and Lorraine, regions in north-eastern France.

quick /kwɪk/ *adj.* **1.** done, proceeding, or occurring with promptness or rapidity, as an action, process, etc.; prompt; immediate: *a quick answer.* **2.** that is over or completed within a short space of time. **3.** moving with speed. **4.** swift or rapid, as motion. **5.** hasty; impatient: *a quick temper.* **6.** lively or keen, as feelings. **7.** prompt in action; acting with swiftness or rapidity. **8.** prompt or swift (to do something): *quick to respond.* **9.** prompt to perceive: *a quick eye.* **10.** prompt to understand, learn, etc.; of ready intelligence. **11.** consisting of living plants: *a quick hedge.* **12.** brisk, as fire, flames, heat, etc. **13.** *Mining* containing ore, or productive, as veins. **14.** *Archaic* living, as persons, animals, plants, etc. –*n.* **15.** living persons: *the quick and the dead.* **16.** living plants (especially hawthorn) as set to form a hedge. **17. a.** the sensitive flesh under the nails of the human hand: *nails bitten down to the quick.* **b.** *Obs.* the tender sensitive flesh of the living body. **18.** the vital or most important part. –*adv.* **19.** quickly. –*phr.* **20. a quick fix**, a quick but ultimately unsatisfactory solution to a problem: *he did a quick fix on the tap.* **21. cut to the quick**, to hurt deeply. **22. quick sticks**, an exclamation exhorting others to act more quickly: *come along children, quick sticks!* –**quicken**, *v.* –**quickly**, *adv.* –**quickness**, *n.*

quicksand /ˈkwɪksænd/ *n.* an area of soft or loose wet sand of considerable depth, as on a coast or inland, yielding under weight and hence apt to engulf persons, animals, etc., coming upon it.

quicksilver /ˈkwɪksɪlvə/ *n.* **1.** the metallic element mercury. –*adj.* **2.** mercurial; changing rapidly.

quickstep /ˈkwɪkstɛp/ *n.* **1.** (formerly) a lively step used in marching. **2.** music adapted to such a march, or in a brisk march rhythm. **3.** a rapid ballroom dance step.

quick-tempered /ˈkwɪk-tɛmpəd/ *adj.* easily moved to anger.

quick-witted /ˈkwɪk-wɪtəd/ *adj.* having a nimble, alert mind. –**quick-wittedly**, *adv.* –**quick-wittedness**, *n.*

quid[1] /kwɪd/ *n.* a portion of something, especially tobacco, for holding in the mouth and chewing.

quid[2] /kwɪd/ *Colloq.* –*n.* (*pl.* **quid** *or* **quids**) **1.** (formerly) a pound in money, especially £1 as a pound note. **2.** (*pl.*) money, especially a large amount: *I'll bet that cost quids and quids.* –*phr.* **3. a quick quid**, money earned with little effort, often by dishonest means. **4. earn** (or **make**) **a quid**, to earn some money. **5. have a quid** (or **two**), to be wealthy. **6. not for quids**, never; for no inducement at all. **7. not get the full quid**, not to obtain the full value for one's money. **8. not the full quid**, mentally slow; intellectually impaired; dull-witted. **9. turn an honest quid**, to earn money by honest means.

quid pro quo /kwɪd proʊ ˈkwoʊ/ *n.* **1.** one thing in return for another. **2.** *Law* compensation, consideration.

quiescent /kwiˈɛsənt/ *adj.* being at rest, quiet, or still; inactive or motionless. –**quiescently**, *adv.* –**quiescence**, **quiescency**, *n.*

quiet /ˈkwaɪət/ *n.* **1.** freedom from disturbance or tumult; tranquillity; rest; repose: *to live in quiet.* **2.** peace; peaceful condition of affairs. –*adj.* **3.** making no disturbance or trouble; not turbulent; peaceable. **4.** free from disturbance or tumult; tranquil; peaceful: *a quiet life.* **5.** free from disturbing emotions, etc.; mentally peaceful. **6.** being at rest. **7.** refraining or free from activity, especially busy or vigorous activity: *a quiet evening at home.* **8.** motionless or still; moving gently: *quiet waters.* **9.** making no noise or sound, especially no disturbing sound: *quiet neighbours.* **10.** free, or comparatively free, from noise: *a quiet street.* **11.** silent: *be quiet!* **12.** restrained in speech, manner, etc.; saying little. **13.** said, expressed, done, etc., in a restrained or unobtrusive way. **14.** of an inconspicuous kind; not showy; subdued. **15.** *Commerce* commercially inactive. –*v.t.* **16.** to make quiet. **17.** to make tranquil or peaceful; pacify. **18.** to subdue. **19.** to allay, as tumult, doubt, fear, etc. **20.** to silence. –*v.i.* **21.** to become quiet. –*phr.* **22. on the quiet**, *Colloq.* secretly. –**quieten**, *v.* –**quieter**, *n.* –**quietly**, *adv.* –**quietness**, **quietude**, *n.*

quill /kwɪl/ *n.* **1.** one of the large feathers of the wing or tail of a bird. **2.** the hard, tubelike part of a feather of a bird, extending the body, extending to the superior umbilicus. **3.** a feather, as of a goose, formed into a pen for writing. **4.** one of the hollow spines on a porcupine or hedgehog. **5.** a device for plucking the strings of a musical instrument (as of a harpsichord), made from the quill of a feather. **6.** a roll of bark, as of cinnamon, as formed in drying. **7.** a reed or other hollow stem on which yarn is wound. **8.** *Machinery* any object that resembles the quill of a bird, as a **quill bit** for boring in wood or a **quill shaft**. –*v.i.* **9.** *Textiles* to form work into the shape of a quill.

quilt /kwɪlt/ *n.* **1.** a cover for a bed, made by stitching together, usually in patterns or lines, two thicknesses of fabric filled with wool, down, etc. –*v.t.* **2.** to stitch together (two pieces of cloth with a soft filling), usually in an ornamental pattern. –**quilted**, *adj.* –**quilter**, *n.*

quince /kwɪns/ *n.* **1.** the hard, yellowish, acid fruit of a small, hardy tree, *Cydonia oblonga*. **2.** the tree itself.

quinella /kwəˈnɛlə/ *n. Aust.*, *NZ* a form of betting where bets are laid on the first and second placegetters in any order in the one race.

quinine /kwɪˈniːn, kwəˈniːn/ *n.* **1.** a bitter colourless alkaloid, $C_{20}H_{24}N_2O_2.3H_2O$, having needle-like crystals, which is used in medicine as a stimulant and to treat malaria, and which was originally derived from the bark of species of the genus *Cinchona*. **2.** a salt of this alkaloid, especially the sulphate.

quinoa /ˈkiːnwaː, kwəˈnoʊə/ *n.* a plant of the goosefoot family, *Chenopodium quinoa*, cultivated for its seeds which are ground and eaten as a cereal.

quinque- a word element meaning 'five'.

quintal /ˈkwɪntl/ *n.* a unit of mass equal to 100 kg. *Symbol*: q

quintessence /kwɪnˈtɛsəns/ *n.* **1.** the pure and concentrated essence of a substance. **2.** the most perfect embodiment of something.

quintessential /kwɪntəˈsɛnʃəl/ *adj.* of, relating to, or embodying a quintessence. –**quintessentially**, *adv.*

quintet /kwɪnˈtɛt/ *n.* **1.** any set or group of five persons or things. **2.** a set of five singers or players. **3.** a musical composition for five voices or instruments. Also, **quintette**.

quintuple /ˈkwɪntəpəl, kwɪnˈtjuːpəl/ *adj.* **1.** fivefold; consisting of five parts. **2.** five times as great. –*n.* **3.** a number, amount, etc., five times as great as another. –*verb* (**-pled**, **-pling**) –*v.t.* **4.** to make five times as great. –*v.i.* **5.** to become five times as great.

quintuplet /kwɪnˈtʌplət/ *n.* **1.** any group or combination of five. **2.** one of five children born at one birth. **3.** *Music* a group of five notes of equal length in a beat of different tempo.

quip /kwɪp/ *n.* **1.** a sharp, sarcastic remark; a cutting jest. **2.** a clever or witty saying. **3.** a quibble. **4.** an odd or fantastic action or thing. –*v.i.* (**quipped**, **quipping**) **5.** to utter quips.

quire /ˈkwaɪə/ *n.* **1.** a set of 24 uniform sheets of paper. **2.** *Bookbinding* the section of leaves or pages in proper sequence after the printed sheet or sheets have been folded; a gathering.

quirk /kwɜːk/ *n.* **1.** a trick or peculiarity. **2.** a sudden twist, turn, or curve.

quirky /ˈkwɜːki/ *adj.* (**-kier**, **-kiest**) unconventional; slightly eccentric. –**quirkily**, *adv.* –**quirkiness**, *n.*

quisling /ˈkwɪzlɪŋ/ *n.* someone who betrays their own country by helping an occupying enemy force; a fifth columnist.

quit /kwɪt/ *verb* (**quit** *or* **quitted**, **quitting**) –*v.t.* **1.** to stop, cease, or discontinue. **2.** to depart from; leave. **3.** to give up; let go; relinquish. **4.** to let go one's hold of (something grasped). –*v.i.* **5.** to cease from doing something; stop. **6.** to depart or leave. **7.** to give up one's job or position; resign. –*phr.* **8. quit of**, released from (obligation, penalty, etc.); free, clear, or rid of.

quite /kwaɪt/ *adv.* **1.** completely, wholly, or entirely: *quite the reverse.* **2.** actually, really, or truly: *quite a sudden change.* **3.** *Colloq.* to a considerable extent or degree: *quite pretty.* –*interj.* **4.** an expression of agreement, etc.

quit rent *n. Law* rent paid by a freeholder or copyholder in lieu of services which might otherwise have been required of him or her. Also, **quit-rent**.

quits /kwɪts/ *adj.* **1.** on equal terms by repayment or retaliation. –*phr.* **2. bet double or quits**, to make a bet, usually to cover a preceding lost bet, so that if the bet is lost, the better forfeits twice the stake, but if it is won, the previous debt is discharged. **3. call it quits**, to abandon an activity, relationship, etc.

quiver¹ /ˈkwɪvə/ *v.i.* **1.** to shake with a slight but rapid motion; vibrate tremulously; tremble. –*n.* **2.** the act or state of quivering; a tremble; a tremor. –**quivery**, *adj.*

quiver² /ˈkwɪvə/ *n.* a case for holding arrows.

quixotic /kwɪkˈsɒtɪk/ *adj.* extravagantly chivalrous or romantic; visionary; impracticable. –**quixotically**, *adv.*

quiz /kwɪz/ *v.t.* (**quizzed**, **quizzing**) **1.** to question closely. **2.** to examine or test (a student or class) informally by questions. –*n.* (*pl.* **quizzes**) **3.** a general knowledge test, especially as an entertainment on radio, television, etc. **4.** a questioning. **5.** an informal examination or test of a student or class. –**quizzer**, *n.*

quizzical /ˈkwɪzɪkəl/ *adj.* **1.** quizzing, ridiculing, or chaffing: *a quizzical smile.* **2.** *Rare* odd, queer, or comical: *a quizzical hat.* –**quizzically**, *adv.*

quoin /kɔɪn/ *n.* **1.** an external solid angle of a wall or the like. **2.** one of the stones forming it; a cornerstone. **3.** a wedge-shaped piece of wood, stone, or other material used for any of various purposes. –*v.t.* **4.** to provide with quoins, as a corner of a wall. **5.** to secure or raise with a quoin or wedge.

quoit /kɔɪt/ *n.* Also, **deck quoit**. a flattish ring of iron or some other material thrown in play to encircle a peg stuck in the ground or to come as close to it as possible. **2.** (*pl. construed as sing.*) the game so played.

quokka /ˈkwɒkə/ *n.* a small wallaby, *Setonix brachyurus*, found in considerable numbers on Rottnest and Bald Islands, off WA, and as small colonies in south-western mainland WA.

quoll /kwɒl/ *n.* **1.** any of several cat-sized, predatory marsupials of the genus *Dasyurus*, having slender, white-spotted bodies and very pointed snouts. **2.** Also, **eastern quoll**. a carnivorous marsupial, *Dasyurus viverrinus*, from eastern Australia, having a spotted body but without spots on the tail.

quorum /ˈkwɔːrəm/ *n.* **1.** the number of members of a body required to be present to transact business legally. **2.** a particularly chosen group.

quota /ˈkwoʊtə/ *n.* **1.** the proportional part or share of a total which is due from, or is due or belongs to, a particular district, area, person, etc. **2.** a proportional part or share of a fixed total amount or quantity. **3.** the number of persons of a particular group allowed to immigrate to a country, join an institution, etc. **4.** the maximum amount of a commodity which one is allowed to produce in an orderly marketing system.

quotation /kwoʊˈteɪʃən/ *n.* **1.** something that is quoted; a passage quoted from a book, speech, etc. **2.** the act or practice of quoting. **3.** *Commerce* **a.** the statement of the current or market price of a commodity or security. **b.** the price so stated. **4.** the statement of the current odds being offered in betting.

quotation mark *n.* one of the marks used to indicate the beginning and end of a quotation, in English usually consisting of an inverted comma (') at the beginning and an apostrophe (') at the end, or, for a quotation within a quotation, of double marks of this kind: '*He said,* "*I will go*".' Double marks are still sometimes used instead of single, the latter then being used for a quotation within a quotation. Also, **speech mark**.

quote /kwoʊt/ *v.t.* **1.** to repeat (a passage, etc.) from a book, speech, etc. **2.** to repeat words from (a book, author, etc.). **3.** to bring forward or refer to. **4.** *Commerce* to state (a price). *–v.i.* **5.** to make a quotation or quotations, as from a book or author. *–n.* **6.** a quotation. **7.** → **quotation mark**. **–quotable**, *adj.* **–quoter**, *n.*

quotient /ˈkwoʊʃənt/ *n. Maths* the result of division; the number of times one quantity is contained in another.

Qur'an /kɔˈran, kə-/ *n.* → **Koran**. **–Qur'anic** /kɔˈrænɪk/, *adj.*

R r

R, r /a/ *n.* the 18th letter of the English alphabet. See **three R's**.

rabbi /ˈræbaɪ/ *n.* (*pl.* **-bis**) **1.** the principal religious official of a synagogue, equivalent to the Christian minister of religion; the spiritual leader of a Jewish community. **2.** a Jewish scholar; an expounder of the Jewish law.

rabbit¹ /ˈræbəl/ *n.* **1.** a small, long-eared, burrowing lagomorph, *Oryctolagus cuniculus*, native to Europe and northern Africa, widely domesticated and kept as a pet; introduced to Australia and elsewhere. **2.** *Cricket* a team member with poor batting skills. Compare **ferret** (def. 2). *–v.i.* (**-bited**, **-biting**) **3.** to hunt rabbits.

rabbit² /ˈræbəl/ *v.i.* (**-bited**, **-biting**) *Colloq.* (fol. by *on*) to talk nonsense, usually at length.

rabbit haemorrhagic disease virus *n.* a highly infectious calicivirus of the genus *Calicivirus* that is believed to be specific to rabbits, causing death in infected animals within 30 to 40 hours. Also, **rabbit calicivirus.**

rabbit warren *n.* → **warren.**

rabble /ˈræbəl/ *n.* **1.** a disorderly crowd; a mob. **2.** (*derog.*) (preceded by *the*) the lowest class of people.

rabble-rouser /ˈræbəl-raʊzə/ *n.* a troublemaker. Also, **rabblerouser.** **–rabble-rousing,** *adj.*, *n.*

rabid /ˈræbəd/ *adj.* **1.** irrationally extreme in opinion or practice: *a rabid isolationist.* **2.** furious or raging; violently intense: *rabid hunger.* **3.** affected with or relating to rabies; mad. **–rabidity** /rəˈbɪdəti/, **rabidness,** *n.* **–rabidly,** *adv.*

rabies /ˈreɪbiz/ *n. Pathol.* an infectious disease of the brain, fatal if untreated, which occurs in all warm-blooded animals including humans, and is due to a specific virus which occurs in saliva and is transmitted to new victims by the bite of an afflicted animal, generally a dog; hydrophobia.

raccoon /rəˈkun/ *n.* any of several small nocturnal carnivores of the genus *Procyon*, especially the North American *P. lotor*, arboreal in habit, and having a sharp snout and a bushy ringed tail.

race¹ /reɪs/ *n.* **1.** a contest of speed, as in running, riding, driving, sailing, etc. **2.** (*pl.*) a series of races, especially horseraces or greyhound races run at a set time over a regular course. **3.** any contest or competition: *an armaments race*; *the race for the presidency.* **4. a.** a strong or rapid current of water, as in the sea or a river. **b.** the channel or bed of such a current, or of any stream. **5.** an artificial channel, leading water to or from a place where its energy is utilised. **6.** the current of water in such a channel. **7. a.** a narrow passageway for livestock, as one leading to a sheep dip. **b.** any similar passageway, as through a cafeteria: *a food race.* **8.** *Machinery* a channel, groove, or the like, for a sliding or rolling part, as for ball bearings. *–verb* (**raced, racing**) *–v.i.* **9.** to engage in a contest of speed; run a race. **10.** to run horses in races; engage in or practise horseracing. **11.** to run, move, or go swiftly. **12.** (of an engine, wheel, etc.) to run with undue or uncontrolled speed when the load is diminished without corresponding reduction of fuel, power, etc. *–v.t.* **13.** to run a race with; try to beat in a contest of speed. **14.** to cause to run in a race or races. **15.** to cause to run, move, or go swiftly: *to race a motor.* *–phr.* **16. not in the race,** having no chance at all. **17. race off with,**

Aust. Colloq. **a.** to steal. **b.** to leave a place, party, etc., with (a person) for sexual intercourse. **c.** to elope with. **18. race someone off,** *Aust. Colloq.* to seduce someone.

race² /reɪs/ *n.* **1.** a group of people sharing genetically determined characteristics such as skin pigmentation or hair texture. **2.** the differentiation of people according to genetically determined characteristics: *genetic studies of race*; *discrimination on the grounds of race.* **3.** a large class of living beings: *the human race*; *the race of fishes.* **4.** a group of people sharing a language or culture or traditional beliefs or practices: *the Scottish race.* **5.** *Zool.* a distinctive group within a species; subspecies.

racecourse /ˈreɪskɔs/ *n.* a piece of ground on which horseraces are held for public entertainment.

race fixing *n.* dishonestly arranging the outcome of a race, especially a horserace.

racehorse /ˈreɪshɔs/ *n.* a horse bred or kept for racing.

raceme /rəˈsim, ˈreɪsim/ *n. Bot.* **1.** a simple indeterminate inflorescence in which the flowers are borne on short pedicels lying along a common axis, as in the lily-of-the-valley. **2.** a compound inflorescence in which the short pedicels with single flowers of the simple raceme are replaced by racemes (**compound raceme**). **–racemose,** *adj.* **–racemiferous** /ræsəˈmɪfərəs/, *adj.*

rachis /ˈreɪkəs/ *n.* (*pl.* **rachises** /ˈreɪkəsɪz/ *or* **rachides** /ˈrækədiz, ˈreɪkə-/) **1.** *Bot.* **a.** the axis of an inflorescence when somewhat elongated, as in a raceme. **b.** (in a pinnately compound leaf or frond) the prolongation of the petiole along which the leaflets are disposed. **c.** any of various axial structures. **2.** *Zool.* the shaft of a feather, especially that part, anterior to the superior umbilicus, bearing the web, as distinguished from the quill. **3.** *Anat.* the spinal column. Also, **rhachis.**

racial /ˈreɪʃəl/ *adj.* **1.** relating to or characteristic of race or extraction, or a race or races. **2.** relating to the relations between people of different races. **–racially,** *adv.*

racial discrimination *n.* discrimination against someone because of their race.

racial vilification *n.* the vilification of people, originally on the basis of race, but now, in general use, broadened to cover derogatory national stereotypes or any other such abuse.

racism /ˈreɪsɪzəm/ *n.* **1.** the belief that human races have distinctive characteristics which determine their respective cultures, usually involving the idea that one's own race is superior and has the right to rule or dominate others. **2.** a policy or system of government and society based upon such a belief. **3.** behaviour or language based on this kind of belief in relation to a person or persons of a particular race, colour, descent, or national or ethnic origin, either demonstrating an inherent prejudice without specific hostile intent or, alternatively, intended to offend, insult, humiliate, or intimidate. **4.** such behaviour or language used against people of a different nationality. Also, **racialism.** **–racist,** *n.*, *adj.*

rack¹ /ræk/ *n.* **1.** a framework of bars, wires, or pegs on which articles are arranged or deposited (used especially in composition): *a shoe rack*; *a wine rack.* **2.** a spreading framework, fixed or movable, for carrying hay, straw, or the like in large loads, especially for fodder. **3.** *Printing* an upright framework with side cleats or other supports for the storing of cases or galleys of type, etc. **4.** *Machinery* **a.** a bar with teeth on one of its sides, adapted to engage with the teeth of a pinion or the like, as for converting circular into rectilinear motion or vice versa. **b.** a similar bar with notches over which the projections of such devices as pawls operate. **5.** an apparatus or instrument formerly in use for torturing persons by stretching the body. **6.** a cause or state of intense suffering of body or mind. −*v.t.* **7.** to torture; distress acutely; torment. **8.** to strain in mental effort: *to rack one's brains.* **9.** to strain by physical force or violence; shake violently. **10.** to strain beyond what is normal or usual. **11.** to stretch the joints of (a person) in torture by means of a rack. **12.** to furnish with, or put on or in a rack. **13.** *Building Trades* to leave (a wall) with unfinished ends for later additions. −*phr.* **14. on the rack, a.** in great pain, distress, or anxiety. **b.** under the strain of great effort. **15. rack up,** to score, as in a game: *she had racked up many a conquest.*

rack² /ræk/ *n.* **1.** wreck; destruction. −*phr.* **2. go to rack and ruin,** to fall into a state of disrepair or collapse, especially owing to neglect; become dilapidated.

rack³ /ræk/ *n.* **1.** the gait of a horse in which the legs move in lateral pairs but not quite simultaneously. −*v.i.* **2.** (of a horse) to go with a gait, similar to a pace, in which the legs move in lateral pairs but not quite simultaneously.

rack⁴ /ræk/ *n.* flying, broken clouds; a mass of clouds driven by the wind.

rack⁵ /ræk/ *n.* **1.** the neck portion of mutton, pork, or veal. **2. rack of lamb,** trimmed ribs or cutlets prepared for roasting on one piece.

rack-and-pinion *n.* a system for the conversion of rotary to linear motion and vice versa, consisting of a pinion and a mated rack (**rack¹** def. 4).

racket¹ /'rækət/ *n.* **1.** a loud noise, especially of a disturbing or confusing kind; din; uproar; clamour or noisy fuss. **2.** social excitement, gaiety, or dissipation. **3.** *Colloq.* an organised illegal activity such as the extortion of money by threat or violence from legitimate businessmen: *the protection racket.* **4.** *Colloq.* a dishonest scheme, trick, etc. **5.** *Colloq.* one's legitimate business or occupation: *he's in the advertising racket.* −**rackety,** *adj.*

racket² /'rækət/ *n.* → **racquet.**

raconteur /rækɒn'tɜ/ *n.* a person skilled in relating stories and anecdotes.

racquet /'rækət/ *n.* **1.** a light bat having a network of cord, catgut, or nylon, stretched in a more or less elliptical frame, used in tennis, etc. **2.** (*pl. construed as sing.*) an early form of squash, originally played against one wall, in which such bats were used. **3.** a snowshoe made in the manner of a tennis racquet. Also, **racket.**

racy /'reɪsi/ *adj.* (**-cier, -ciest**) **1.** vigorous; lively; spirited. **2.** sprightly; piquant; pungent: *a racy style.* **3.** suggestive; risqué: *a racy story.* −**racily,** *adv.* −**raciness,** *n.*

radar /'reɪda/ *n.* **1.** a device to determine the presence and location of an object by measuring the time for the echo of a radio wave to return from it, and the direction from which it returns. −*phr.* **2. off the** (or **someone's**) **radar, a.** not anticipated as happening within the foreseeable future. **b.** not currently having a focus of interest, awareness, etc., to (someone). **3. on the** (or **someone's**) **radar, a.** anticipated as happening in the foreseeable future. **b.** being currently a focus of interest, awareness, etc., to (someone). **4. under the** (or **someone's**) **radar,** entirely escaping (someone's) attention: *his offensive article managed to get under the radar and be published*; *the appointment time somehow slipped under*

my radar; *her behaviour is so good that she falls under the radar and doesn't get enough attention.*

radar detector *n.* an illegal device which detects the presence of a police radar trap.

radar trap *n.* a place beside a road where police have set up radar equipment to detect speeding motorists.

radial /'reɪdiəl/ *adj.* **1.** arranged like rays or radii. **2.** having spokes, bars, lines, etc., arranged like radii, as a machine. **3.** *Zool.* relating to structures that radiate from a central point, as the arms of a starfish. **4.** of, like, or relating to a radius or a ray. −*n.* **5.** → **radial-ply tyre.** −**radially,** *adv.*

radial-ply tyre *n.* a pneumatic tyre with flexible walls achieved by having the casing cords running radially and with additional plies strengthening the tread only.

radian /'reɪdiən/ *n.* the supplementary SI unit of measurement of plane angle, being the plane angle between two radii of a circle which cut off on the circumference an arc equal to the length of the radius. *Symbol*: rad

radiant /'reɪdiənt/ *adj.* **1.** emitting rays of light; shining; bright: *the radiant sun, radiant colours.* **2.** bright with joy, hope, etc.: *radiant smiles.* **3.** *Physics* emitted in rays, or by radiation. −**radiance, radiancy,** *n.* −**radiantly,** *adv.*

radiata pine /ˌreɪdiɑtə 'paɪn/ *n.* a valuable softwood timber tree, *Pinus radiata,* native to California but widely cultivated in Australia and New Zealand.

radiate *v.i.* /'reɪdieɪt/ **1.** to spread or move like rays or radii from a centre. **2.** to emit rays, as of light or heat; irradiate. **3.** to issue or proceed in rays. −*v.t.* /'reɪdieɪt/ **4.** (of persons) to exhibit abundantly (good humour, benevolence, etc.). −*adj.* /'reɪdiət/ **5.** represented with rays proceeding from it, as a head on a coin, in art, etc. −**radiative,** *adj.*

radiation /reɪdi'eɪʃən/ *n.* **1.** *Physics* the emission and propagation of particles or waves such as by a radioactive substance, a source of electromagnetic waves, or a source of sound waves. **2.** the act or process of radiating. **3.** something that is radiated; a ray or rays. **4.** radial arrangement of parts. **5.** → **radiotherapy.**

radiator /'reɪdieɪtə/ *n.* **1.** a device for heating a room in which a cylindrical rod, heated red-hot electrically, radiates heat directly and sometimes via a reflector placed behind it. **2.** any of various heating devices, as a series or coil of pipes through which steam or hot water passes. **3.** a device constructed from thin-walled tubes and metal fins, used for cooling circulating water, as in the cooling system of a car engine, etc. **4.** *Radio* a type of aerial.

radical /'rædɪkəl/ *adj.* **1.** going to the root or origin; fundamental: *a radical change.* **2.** favouring extreme political, religious, social or other reforms. **3.** forming the basis or foundation. **4.** existing as though a permanent part of the character of a thing or person: *radical defects of character.* **5.** *Maths* relating to or forming a root. **6.** *Gram.* of or relating to a root (**root¹** def. 12). −*n.* **7.** someone who holds or follows principles which are far from the ordinary, especially left-wing political principles; an extremist. **8.** *Chem.* → **free radical. 9.** *Gram.* → **root¹** (def. 12). −**radically,** *adv.* −**radicalness,** *n.*

radicalise /'rædɪkəlaɪz/ *verb* (**-lised, -lising**) −*v.t.* **1.** to make radical (def. 2). −*v.i.* **2.** to become radical (def. 2). Also, **radicalize.** −**radicalisation** /ˌrædɪkəlaɪ'zeɪʃən/, *n.*

radicchio /ra'dikiou, ra'dɪkiou/ *n.* an Italian variety of chicory, having a compact head of reddish, white-streaked leaves which, along with the roots, may be cooked or eaten raw in a salad.

radicle /'rædɪkəl/ *n.* **1.** *Bot.* **a.** the lower part of the axis of an embryo; the primary root. **b.** a rudimentary root; a radicel or rootlet. **2.** *Anat.* a small root-like part, as the beginning of a nerve fibre.

radii /ˈreɪdiaɪ/ n. plural of **radius**.

radio /ˈreɪdioʊ/ n. (pl. **-dios**) **1.** the sending of electrical signals through the air by electromagnetic waves to a receiving set; wireless telegraphy or telephony: *speeches broadcast by radio.* **2.** an apparatus for receiving radio broadcasts; wireless. **3.** a message sent by radio. –*verb* (**-dioed, -dioing**) –*v.t.* **4.** to transmit (a message, etc.) by radio. **5.** to send a message to (a person) by radio. –*v.i.* **6.** to transmit a message, etc., by radio.

radio- a word element meaning: **1.** radio. **2.** radial. **3.** radium, radioactive, or radiant energy.

radioactive /ˌreɪdioʊˈæktɪv/ adj. possessing, relating to, or caused by radioactivity.

radioactive decay n. the process by which an unstable atomic nucleus loses energy by emitting radiation so as to achieve a stable atomic nucleus.

radioactive waste n. waste material containing radionuclides from processes such as nuclear fission but also from various industrial and medical processes involving radioactive material. See **high level waste, intermediate level waste, low level waste, very low level waste**.

radioactivity /ˌreɪdiouækˈtɪvəti/ n. *Physics* the property of spontaneous disintegration possessed by certain elements due to changes in their atomic nuclei. The disintegration is accompanied by the emission of alpha, beta, or gamma radiation.

radiocarbon dating /reɪdiouˌkabən ˈdeɪtɪŋ/ n. the determination of the age of objects of plant or animal origin by means of their content of radioactive carbon. Also, **carbon dating**.

radiography /reɪdiˈɒgrəfi/ n. the production of images or pictures produced by the action of X-rays, or other rays, (as from radioactive substances) on a photographic plate, especially as used in medicine; X-ray photography. –**radiographer**, n. –**radiographic** /ˌreɪdiouˈgræfɪk/, adj.

radiology /reɪdiˈɒlədʒi/ n. **1.** the science dealing with X-rays or rays from radioactive substances, especially for medical uses. **2.** the examining or photographing of organs, etc., with such rays. –**radiologist**, n.

radio station n. **1.** a combination of devices for radio transmitting and/or receiving. **2.** a complete installation for radio broadcasting, including transmitting apparatus, broadcasting studios, etc. **3.** an organisation engaged in broadcasting, on a fixed frequency or frequencies, programs of news, entertainment, propaganda, etc.

radiotelephone /ˌreɪdiouˈtɛləfoʊn/ n. a telephone in which the signal is transmitted by radio; wireless telephone. –**radiotelephony** /ˌreɪdioutəˈlɛfəni/, n. –**radiotelephonic** /ˌreɪdiouˌtɛləˈfɒnɪk/, adj.

radio telescope n. a large parabolic reflector, used to gather radio signals emitted by celestial bodies or spacecraft and focus them for reception by a receiver.

radiotherapy /ˌreɪdiouˈθɛrəpi/ n. *Med.* treatment of disease by means of X-rays or of radioactive substances. –**radiotherapist**, n.

radish /ˈrædɪʃ/ n. **1.** the crisp, pungent, edible root of a plant, *Raphanus sativus*. **2.** the plant.

radium /ˈreɪdiəm/ n. a naturally occurring radioactive metallic element with chemical properties resembling those of barium. *Symbol*: Ra; *relative atomic mass*: 226; *atomic number*: 88.

radius /ˈreɪdiəs/ n. (pl. **-dii** /-diaɪ/ or **-diuses**) **1.** a straight line going from the centre of a circle or sphere to the circumference or surface. **2.** the length of such a line. **3.** any radial or radiating part. **4.** a circular area round some point: *every house within a radius of 50 kilometres.* **5.** *Anat.* one of the two bones of the forearm on

the thumb side. **6.** *Zool.* a corresponding bone in the forelimb of other vertebrates.

Rafferty's rules /ˈræfətiz rulz/ pl. n. *Aust., NZ* no rules at all, as of a contest or organisation run in a slipshod fashion. Also, **Rafferty rules**.

raffia /ˈræfiə/ n. **1.** a species of palm, *Raphia farinifera*, of Madagascar, bearing long, plume-like, pinnate leaves, the leafstalks of which yield an important fibre. **2.** the fibre, much used for tying plants, cut flowers, small parcels, etc., and for making matting, baskets, hats, and the like.

raffish /ˈræfɪʃ/ adj. **1.** disreputable, rakish. **2.** vulgar, tawdry. –**raffishly**, adv. –**raffishness**, n.

raffle /ˈræfəl/ n. **1.** a lottery in which the prizes are usually goods rather than money. –*v.t.* Also, **raffle off**. **2.** to dispose of by a raffle: *to raffle off a watch*. –**raffler**, n.

raft¹ /raft/ n. **1.** a more or less rigid floating platform made of buoyant materials, assembled for ease of transport or for the conveyance of people, their possessions, etc. **2.** a slab of reinforced concrete extending entirely under a building used to spread the weight of the building over the whole area, especially on yielding soils.

raft² /raft/ n. a collection or set of items: *a whole raft of issues to consider*.

rafter /ˈraftə/ n. one of the sloping timbers or members sustaining the outer covering of a roof.

rafting /ˈraftɪŋ/ n. the sport of travelling along rivers by raft.

rag¹ /ræg/ n. **1.** a comparatively worthless fragment of cloth, especially one resulting from tearing or wear. **2.** (pl.) ragged or tattered clothing. **3.** a shred, scrap, or fragmentary bit of anything. **4.** *Colloq.* an article of cloth, paper, etc., such as a handkerchief, a theatre curtain, or a piece of paper money. **5.** *Colloq.* a newspaper or magazine, especially one considered as being of little value. **6.** *Colloq.* a song or a piece of instrumental music in ragtime. –*phr.* **7. chew the rag, a.** to argue or grumble. **b.** to brood or grieve. **c.** to gossip or chat. **8. from rags to riches**, from poverty to wealth. **9. glad rags**, *Colloq.* fine clothes. **10. on the rags**, *Colloq.* menstruating.

rag² /ræg/ *Colloq.* –*v.t.* (**ragged, ragging**) **1.** to scold. **2.** to tease; torment. –*n.* **3.** any disorderly or high-spirited conduct, especially by a group of young people.

ragamuffin /ˈrægəmʌfən/ n. **1.** a ragged, disreputable person. **2.** a ragged child.

rage /reɪdʒ/ n. **1.** violent anger: *to fall into a rage*. **2.** violence or intensity: *rage of wind*; *rage of thirst*. **3.** *Colloq.* an exciting or entertaining event: *that party was a rage*. –*v.i.* (**raged, raging**) **4.** to act or speak with fury; show or feel violent anger. **5.** to move or happen with great violence: *the sea raged against the beach*; *the battle raged ten days*. **6.** *Colloq.* to set about enjoying oneself: *let's go raging*. –*phr.* **7. all the rage**, fashionable: *long hair for men used to be all the rage*.

ragged /ˈrægəd/ adj. **1.** wearing old and torn clothes. **2.** torn or worn to rags; tattered: *ragged clothing*. **3.** uneven; jagged: *ragged stones*. **4.** wild or uncared for: *a ragged garden*. **5.** rough or faulty: *a ragged piece of work*. **6.** rough or harsh: *a ragged voice*. –**raggedly**, adv. –**raggedness**, n.

raglan /ˈræglən/ n. **1.** a loose overcoat the sleeves of which are cut so as to continue up to the collar. –*adj.* **2.** (of a coat or sleeve) tailored in such a manner.

ragout /ˈrægu/ n. a highly seasoned stew of poultry or meat and vegetables, usually flavoured with mushrooms, tomatoes, port wine, etc. Also, **ragoust, ragu**.

ragtime /ˈrægtaɪm/ n. *Music* rhythm marked by frequent syncopation, such as is common in early African American piano music.

rag trade *n. Colloq.* the business of clothes manufacturing.

rah-rah skirt *n.* → ra-ra skirt.

raid /reɪd/ *n.* **1.** a sudden onset or attack, as upon something to be seized or suppressed: *a police raid on a gambling house.* **2.** *Mil.* a sudden attack on the enemy, especially by air or by a small force. *–v.t.* **3.** to make a raid on. *–raider, n.*

rail¹ /reɪl/ *n.* **1.** a bar of wood or metal fixed more or less horizontally for any of various purposes, as for a support, barrier, fence, railing, etc. **2.** (*pl.*) a fence; a railing, especially at a racecourse. **3.** one of a pair of steel bars that provide a guide and running surface for the wheels of trains, railway carriages, etc. **4.** the railway, as a means of transportation: *to travel by rail.* **5.** (*pl.*) *Stock Exchange* stocks, shares, etc., of railways. **6.** *Naut.* the upper part of the bulwarks of a ship. **7.** the edge of a surfboard. **8.** a horizontal timber or piece in a framework or in panelling. *–v.t.* **9.** to furnish with a rail or rails. *–v.i.* **10.** (of horses, dogs, etc.) to run close to the rails. *–phr.* **11. off the rails,** in an abnormal condition; insane; out of control. **12. on the rails,** *Colloq.* **a.** *Horseracing* running on the inside of the field, against the inner railings. **b.** functioning in a normal manner. **13. rail in** (or **off**), to enclose with a fence, rail, or rails.

rail² /reɪl/ *v.i.* **1.** (sometimes fol. by *at* or *against*) to utter bitter complaint or vehement denunciation: *to rail at fate.* *–v.t.* **2.** to bring, force, etc., by railing. *–railer, n.*

rail³ /reɪl/ *n.* any of numerous wading birds constituting the subfamily Rallinae, family Rallidae, characterised by short wings, a narrow body, strong legs, long toes, and a harsh cry, and found commonly in marshes in most parts of the world, as the **buff-banded rail,** *Gallirallus philippensis,* of insular South-East Asia, New Guinea, Australia and Oceania.

railing /ˈreɪlɪŋ/ *n.* **1.** (*oft. pl.*) a barrier made of rails, rails and supports, etc. **2.** rails collectively.

raillery /ˈreɪləri/ *n.* (*pl.* **-ries**) good-humoured ridicule; banter.

railroad /ˈreɪlroʊd/ *–n.* **1.** *US* a railway. *–v.t. Colloq.* **2.** to send or push forward with great or undue speed: *to railroad a bill through parliament.* **3.** to coerce, especially by unfair means: *he was railroaded out of office.*

railway /ˈreɪlweɪ/ *n.* **1.** a permanent road or way, laid or provided with rails of steel, iron, etc., commonly in one or more pairs of continuous lines forming a track or tracks, on which vehicles run for the transporting of passengers, goods, and mail. **2.** such a road together with its rolling stock, buildings, etc.; the entire railway plant, including fixed and movable property. **3.** the company of persons owning or operating it. **4.** any line or lines of rails forming a track for flanged-wheel equipment.

railway station *n.* → station (def. 2).

raiment /ˈreɪmənt/ *n. Archaic* clothing; apparel; attire.

rain /reɪn/ *n.* **1.** water in drops falling from the sky to the earth, being condensed from the aqueous vapour in the atmosphere. **2.** a rainfall, rainstorm, or shower. **3.** (*pl.*) the seasonal rainfalls, or the rainy or wet season, in some regions, as India. **4.** a large quantity of anything falling thickly: *a rain of blows.* *–v.i.* **5.** (of rain) to fall: *it rained all night.* **6.** to fall like rain: *tears rained from his eyes.* **7.** to send down or let fall rain (said of God, the sky, the clouds, etc.). *–v.t.* **8.** to send down, scatter, or sprinkle (rain, etc.). **9.** to offer, bestow, or give abundantly: *to rain blows upon a person.* *–phr.* **10. rain cats and dogs,** to rain heavily. **11. right as rain,** perfectly all right. *–rainy, adj.*

rainbird /ˈreɪnbɜd/ *n.* any of various birds whose call is thought to presage rain.

rainbow /ˈreɪnboʊ/ *n.* **1.** a bow or arc of prismatic colours appearing in the sky opposite the sun, due to the refraction and reflection of the sun's rays in drops of rain. **2.** a similar bow of colours, especially one appearing in the spray of cataracts, etc. **3.** any array of many bright colours. **4.** the spectrum. *–adj.* **5.** multicoloured.

rainbow family *n.* a family in which the parents are same-sex.

rainbow lorikeet *n.* a brightly coloured, noisy, sociable parrot, *Trichoglossus haematodus,* orange and green with a bright blue head and a red beak, common in rainforests, woodlands, heaths, gardens and urban areas, found in New Guinea, the Lesser Sunda Islands (an island group in Indonesia), some Pacific islands, and eastern Australia from Cape York to southern Australia.

Rainbow Serpent *n.* (*sometimes lower case*) (in Aboriginal mythology) a spirit of creation which appeared as a great snake in the Dreaming, fashioned the earth, and then returned to a spot east of the Kimberley at a place where the rainbow meets the earth. Also, **Rainbow Snake, Rainbow Spirit.**

raincoat /ˈreɪnkoʊt/ *n.* a waterproof coat, worn as a protection from rain.

rainfall /ˈreɪnfɔl/ *n.* **1.** a fall or shower of rain. **2.** *Meteorol.* the amount of water falling as rain, snow, etc., within a given time and area, ordinarily expressed as a hypothetical depth of coverage: *a rainfall of 1210 mm a year.*

rainforest /ˈreɪnfɒrəst/ *n.* moist, closed, evergreen forest with a high annual rainfall found in tropical and temperate areas and characterised by soft-leaved trees and multiple crown layers supporting a wide variety of plant and animal life.

raintree /ˈreɪnˌtri/ *n.* an evergreen shade tree of tropical America, *Albizia saman,* with a spreading crown and globular heads of pinkish flowers; monkey pod tree.

raise /reɪz/ *v.t.* (**raised, raising**) **1.** to move to a higher position; lift up; elevate: *to raise one's hand.* **2.** to set upright; lift up. **3.** to cause to rise or stand up. **4.** to build; erect: *to raise a monument.* **5.** *US* to set up the framework of (a house, etc.). **6.** to cause to project; bring into relief. **7.** to cause to be or appear: *to raise a tempest.* **8.** to cultivate, produce, breed (crops, plants, animals, etc.). **9.** to bring up; rear (children, etc.). **10.** to give rise to; bring up or about (a question, issue, etc.); put forward (an objection, etc.). **11.** *Law* to institute (a lawsuit, etc.). **12.** to restore to life: *to raise the dead.* **13.** to stir up: *to raise a rebellion.* **14.** to give vigour to; animate (the mind, spirits, hopes). **15.** to advance in rank, dignity, etc.: *to raise someone to chief justice.* **16.** to gather together; collect: *to raise an army; raise funds.* **17.** to increase in height or thickness. **18.** to cause (dough, etc.) to rise and become light, as by the addition of yeast. **19.** to increase in degree, intensity, pitch, or force. **20.** to utter (a cry, etc.) especially in a loud voice. **21.** to make (the voice) louder. **22.** to express, as in protest, agreement, or the like. **23.** to increase in amount, as rent, prices, wages, etc. **24.** to increase the price of (a commodity, stock, etc.). **25.** *Poker, etc.* to bet more than (another player, or previous bet). Compare **see¹** (def. 20). **26.** *Mil.* to end (a siege or blockade), by withdrawing or repelling the besieging forces. **27.** to remove (a prohibition, etc.). **28.** *Maths* to multiply (a number) by itself for a stated number of times: *100 is 10 raised to the power of 2.* **29.** *Colloq.* to establish communication with, as by two-way radio: *we tried in vain to raise headquarters.* *–n.* **30.** a rise (in wages). **31.** the amount of such an increase. **32.** a raising, lifting, etc. *–phr.* **33. raise an eyebrow, a.** to express slightly shocked surprise. **b.** to cause a surprise: *it won't raise an eyebrow.* **34. raise**

Cain (or **the devil**) (or **hell**), **a.** to cause a commotion or trouble. **b.** to complain or protest vociferously. **35. raise the roof**, *Colloq.* to cause a great noise, excitement, etc. **–raiseable,** *adj.* **–raiser,** *n.*

raisin /ˈreɪzən/ *n.* **1.** a grape of any of various sweet varieties dried in the sun or artificially. **2.** dark bluish purple.

raison d'être /reɪzɒn ˈdetrə/ *n.* reason or justification for being or existence. Also, **raison d'etre.**

raita /ˈraɪtə, ˈreɪtə/ *n.* (in Indian cookery) a dish of finely chopped cucumber or other raw vegetables mixed with yoghurt.

rake[1] /reɪk/ *n.* **1.** a long-handled tool with teeth or tines for gathering together hay or the like, breaking and smoothing the surface of ground, etc. **2.** a similar implement used in agriculture, especially one drawn by a tractor. **3.** any of various implements having a similar form or function, as a croupier's implement for gathering in money on a gaming table. **4.** a long, forcible sweep or onset. **5.** *Colloq.* a comb. **–v.t. 6.** to gather together, draw, or remove with a rake: *to rake dead leaves from a lawn.* **7.** to clear, smooth, or prepare with a rake: *to rake a garden bed.* **8.** to clear (a fire, etc.) by stirring with a poker or the like. **9.** to search thoroughly through. **10.** to scrape; scratch; graze. **11.** to traverse with gunfire, the length of (a place, ship, a body of troops, etc.). **12.** to sweep with the eyes. **–v.i. 13.** to use a rake. **14.** to search as with a rake. **15.** to scrape or graze (*against, over, along*, etc.). **–phr. 16. rake in**, to gather or collect abundantly: *to rake in the money.* **17. rake up**, **a.** to collect, especially with difficulty. **b.** to reveal, as to discredit someone: *to rake up an old scandal.*

rake[2] /reɪk/ *n.* a profligate or dissolute man, especially one in fashionable society; a roué. **–rakish,** *adj.*

rake[3] /reɪk/ *v.i.* **1.** to incline from the vertical (as a mast, funnel, stem, or keel of a vessel) or from the horizontal (as a stage). **–n. 2.** inclination or slope away from the perpendicular or the horizontal, as of a ship's mast, funnel, stem, or keel. **3.** *Machinery* the angle between the cutting face of a tool and a plane perpendicular to the surface of the work at the cutting point.

rake-hoe *n.* → **McLeod tool.**

rally[1] /ˈræli/ *verb* (**-lied, -lying**) *–v.t.* **1.** to bring together or into order again: *to rally an army.* **2.** to draw or call (people) together for common action. **3.** to recover; revive: *he rallied his spirits –v.i.* **4.** to come together for common action. **5.** to come together or into order again. **6.** to recover a little or get fresh strength: *the stock market rallied today.* **–n.** (*pl.* **-lies**) **7.** recovery from disorder or illness. **8.** a public meeting for common action: *a nuclear disarmament rally.* **9.** *Tennis, etc.* a long exchange of strokes. **10.** Also, **car rally**, a car race, mainly over public roads, in which competitors are required to adhere to specified rules and schedules.

rally[2] /ˈræli/ *v.t.* (**-lied, -lying**) to ridicule (someone) good-humouredly; banter.

rally car *n.* a car that has been specially modified for use in a car rally.

ram /ræm/ *n.* **1.** an uncastrated male sheep. **2.** any of various devices for battering, crushing, driving, or forcing something: *battering ram.* **–v.t.** (**rammed, ramming**) **3.** to drive or force by heavy blows. **4.** to strike with great force; dash violently against. **5.** to cram; stuff.

RAM /ræm/ *n.* *Computers* a computer memory which is so structured that each item can be accessed equally quickly.

Ramadan /ˈræmədæn/ /rʌmədan/ *n.* the daily fast which is observed by Muslims from dawn until sunset during the month of Ramadan (the ninth month in the Islamic calendar), in commemoration of the 30 days the

Prophet Mohammed spent in the desert during which time God revealed the Koran to him.

ramble /ˈræmbəl/ *v.i.* **1.** to wander about in a leisurely manner, without definite aim or direction; walk for pleasure. **2.** to have an aimless or meandering course, as a stream or path. **3.** to grow or extend in an unsystematic fashion, as a plant or building. **4.** to talk or write discursively, without sequence of ideas, or incoherently. **–n. 5.** a walk without a definite route, taken for pleasure.

ramen /ˈramɛn/ *n.* (in Japanese cookery) Chinese-style wheat-flour noodles, often served in soup.

ramification /ræməfəˈkeɪʃən/ *n.* **1.** the act, process, or manner of ramifying. **2.** a branch: *the ramifications of a nerve.* **3.** a division or subdivision springing or derived from a main stem or source: *to pursue a subject in all its ramifications.* **4.** *Bot.* **a.** a structure formed of branches. **b.** a configuration of branching parts. **5.** one of a number of results or consequences, especially one which complicates an issue.

ramp /ræmp/ *n.* **1.** a sloping surface connecting two different levels. **2.** a short sloping track, road, etc. **3.** a short concave slope or bend, as one connecting the higher and lower parts of a banister at a landing or of the top of a wall. **4.** any extensive sloping walk or passageway. **5.** a swindle, especially one depending on a rise in prices. **6.** → **cattle grid.** **–v.i. 7.** to rise or stand on the hind legs, as a quadruped, especially a lion (often one represented in heraldry or sculpture). **8.** to rear as if to spring. **9.** to leap or dash (*about, around,* etc.) with fury. **10.** to act violently; rage; storm. **–phr. 11. ramp up**, to increase the scope or level of activity of (a business, etc.).

rampage *n.* /ˈræmpeɪdʒ/ **1.** violent or furious behaviour. **2.** an instance of this: *to go on the rampage.* **–v.i.** /ræmˈpeɪdʒ/ (**-paged, -paging**) **3.** to rush, move, or act furiously or violently. **–rampageous,** *adj.*

rampant /ˈræmpənt/ *adj.* **1.** violent in action, spirit, opinion, etc.; raging; furious. **2.** in full sway; unchecked: *the rampant growth of anarchy.* **3.** luxuriant, as a plant. **4.** lustful. **5.** standing on the hind legs; ramping. **–rampancy,** *n.* **–rampantly,** *adv.*

rampart /ˈræmpɑt/ *n.* *Fortifications* a broad elevation or mound of earth raised as a fortification around a place, and usually having a stone or earth parapet built upon it.

ram raid *n.* a robbery involving gaining access to a property, such as a shop, service station, etc., by driving a vehicle into the front window.

ramraid /ˈræmreɪd/ *v.t.* to gain access to (a property, as a shop, service station, etc.) as part of a ram raid.

ramrod /ˈræmrɒd/ *n.* **1.** a rod for ramming down the charge of a muzzle-loading firearm. **2.** a cleaning rod for the barrel of a rifle, etc. **3.** any person or thing considered as exemplifying or exercising stiffness or unyielding rigidity.

ramshackle /ˈræmʃækəl/ *adj.* loosely made or held together; rickety; shaky: *a ramshackle house.*

ran /ræn/ *v.* past tense of **run.**

ranch /ræntʃ, rantʃ/ *n.* **1.** a farm for cattle, horses, or the like, generally having extensive grazing land. **2.** the establishment, staff, buildings, etc., of such. **3.** *Colloq.* (*humorous*) one's own home or workplace: *OK, I'll mind the ranch. –v.i.* **4.** to own, manage, or work on, a ranch.

rancid /ˈrænsəd/ *adj.* **1.** having a rank, unpleasant, stale smell or taste: *rancid butter.* **2.** rank in this manner: *a rancid smell.* **–rancidity, rancidness,** *n.*

rancour /ˈræŋkə/ *n.* bitter, rankling resentment or ill will; hatred; malice. Also, **rancor.** **–rancorous,** *adj.*

rand /rænd/ *n.* (*pl.* **rand**) the principal monetary unit of the Republic of South Africa, divided into 100 cents.

R & B → rhythm and blues.

random /'rændəm/ *adj.* **1.** going, made, occurring, etc., without definite aim, purpose, or reason. **2.** not according to a pattern or method. **3.** *Building Trades* (of slates, blocks, paving stones, etc.) irregular in size or arrangement. **4.** *Colloq.* **a.** (of a person) eccentric; odd. **b.** (of an occurrence) strangely coincidental. **c.** (of a film, story line, etc.) strange, unpredictable, or confusing. **5.** *Colloq.* ordinary; uninteresting: *that party was pretty random.* **6.** *Colloq.* of or relating to someone or something unknown or unspecified, or about which the speaker only knows the detail specified: *this random Dave I met last night. –phr.* **7. at random**, in a haphazard way; without definite aim, purpose, or method. **–randomly**, *adv.* **–randomness**, *n.*

random-access memory *n.* → RAM.

random breath test *n.* a breath test to detect the presence of alcohol in the driver's system, applied to randomly selected motorists. *Abbrev.*: RBT

random drug test *n.* a test to detect the presence of drugs in someone's system, usually by saliva, blood or urine sampling, applied to randomly selected motorists, athletes, workers, etc. *Abbrev.*: RDT **–random drug testing,** *n.*

R and R *n.* **1.** *Mil.* time off from military duties, when troops are allowed to leave the combat area for rest and recreation. **2.** *Colloq.* time off from one's work, studies, etc., for the purpose of rest and recreation.

randy /'rændi/ *adj.* (**-dier, -diest**) *Colloq.* **1.** lecherous. **2.** sexually aroused.

rang /ræŋ/ *v.* past tense of **ring²**.

ranga /'ræŋə/ *n. Colloq.* (*mildly derog.*) a red-headed person.

rangatira /rʌŋə'tɪərə, ræŋə-/ *n.* **1.** a Maori noble leader. **2.** *NZ Colloq.* a chief, boss, or superior of any kind.

range /reɪndʒ/ *n.* **1.** limits within which there can be differences or variation: *range of prices.* **2.** limits within which something can be or work; scope: *within range of vision; an oboe has a different range from a flute.* **3.** the distance to which a bullet, rocket, etc., can travel. **4.** distance away: *at a range of 20 metres.* **5.** an area for shooting practice. **6.** the distance which a plane, ship, etc., can travel without refuelling. **7.** *Statistics* the difference between the smallest and largest varieties in a statistical distribution. **8.** a set or series: *we have a new range of goods in our shops.* **9.** *Chiefly US* a wide open area of land. **10.** an area over which something is found, or occurs: *the range of a plant.* **11.** a chain of mountains. **12.** a cooking stove. *–verb* (**ranged, ranging**) *–v.t.* **13.** to set in order, especially in a row or line; arrange. **14.** to place in a particular class; classify. **15.** to pass over or through (an area) in all directions: *the search party ranged the hills. –v.i.* **16.** to vary within certain limits: *prices ranging from $5 to $10.* **17.** to run or go in a certain direction; extend: *a boundary ranging east and west.* **18.** to wander; rove; roam: *the talk ranged over many subjects; to range through the bush.* **19.** to be found over an area: *a plant which ranges from Qld to NSW.*

rangefinder /'reɪndʒfaɪndə/ *n.* any of various instruments for determining the range or distance of an object, as in order that a gun may be accurately sighted when firing at it, or to focus a camera.

ranger /'reɪndʒə/ *n.* **1.** a wanderer. **2.** a person employed to look after a nature reserve, park, etc. **3.** (*sometimes upper case*) a member of the senior division of the Guides.

rangy /'reɪndʒi/ *adj.* (**-gier, -giest**) **1.** slender and long-limbed, as animals or persons. **2.** given to or fitted for ranging or moving about, as animals. **3.** having a mountain range; mountainous.

rank¹ /ræŋk/ *n.* **1.** a number of persons forming a separate class in the social scale or in any graded body: *people of every rank and station.* **2.** position or standing in the social scale or in any graded body: *the rank of colonel.* **3.** high position or station in the social or some similar scale: *pride of rank.* **4.** a class in any scale of comparison. **5.** relative position or standing: *a writer of the highest rank.* **6.** a row, line, or series of things or persons. **7.** (*pl.*) the lines or body of an army or other force or organisation. **8.** the general body of any party, society, or organisation apart from the officers or leaders. **9.** a line of persons, especially soldiers, standing abreast (distinguished from *file*). **10.** *Chess* one of the horizontal lines of squares on a chessboard. *–v.t.* **11.** to arrange in a rank or row, or in ranks, as things or persons. **12.** to dispose in suitable order; arrange; classify. **13.** to assign to a particular position, station, class, etc. *–v.i.* **14.** to form a rank or ranks. **15.** to stand in rank. **16.** to take up or occupy a place in a particular rank, class, etc. **17.** *US* to be the senior in rank: *the major ranks here. –phr.* **18. close ranks, a.** (of soldiers or people in a similar military formation) to come together so that there are no gaps or spaces between individuals. **b.** (of a group, organisation, etc.) to unite as one body in the face of opposition or threat. **19. pull rank**, (sometimes fol. by *on*) to resort to use of a position of authority, especially military authority, to compel some action or behaviour.

rank² /ræŋk/ *adj.* **1.** growing too tall or coarse: *rank grass.* **2.** smelling or tasting strongly and offensively: *a rank cigar.* **3.** utter; unmistakable: *a rank outsider; rank treachery.* **4.** very coarse or indecent. **–rankly,** *adv.* **–rankness,** *n.*

rank and file *n.* the body of an army, or any other organisation or group, apart from officers or leaders.

rankle /'ræŋkəl/ *v.i.* (of unpleasant feelings, experiences, etc.) to produce or continue to produce within the mind keen irritation or bitter resentment; fester; be painful.

ransack /'rænsæk/ *v.t.* **1.** to search thoroughly or vigorously through (a house, receptacle, etc.). **2.** to search (a place, etc.) for plunder; pillage. **–ransacker,** *n.*

ransom /'rænsəm/ *n.* **1.** the redemption of a prisoner, slave, kidnapped person, captured goods, etc., for a price. **2.** the sum or price paid or demanded. **3.** a means of delivering or rescuing, especially, in religious use, from sin and its consequences. *–v.t.* **4.** to redeem from captivity, bondage, detention, etc., by paying a price demanded. **5.** to release or restore on receipt of a ransom. **6.** to deliver or redeem from sin and its consequences. *–phr.* **7. hold to ransom, a.** to confine (a person or thing) until redeemed at a price. **b.** to attempt to compel (someone) to accede to one's demands. **8. king's ransom**, any very large sum of money or valuables. **–ransomer,** *n.*

rant /rænt/ *v.i.* **1.** to speak or declaim extravagantly or violently; talk in a wild or vehement way. *–v.t.* **2.** to utter or declaim in a ranting manner. *–n.* **3.** ranting, extravagant, or violent declamation. **4.** a ranting utterance. *–phr.* **5. rant and rave**, to express great anger, frustration, etc. **–ranter,** *n.* **–ranting,** *adj.*

ranunculus /rə'nʌŋkjələs/ *n.* (*pl.* **-luses** or **-li** /-laɪ/) any plant of the large and widely distributed genus *Ranunculus*, comprising herbs with leaves mostly divided, and flowers, commonly yellow, with five petals; crowfoot; buttercup.

rap¹ /ræp/ *verb* (**rapped, rapping**) *–v.t.* **1.** to strike, especially with a quick, smart, or light blow, as to attract attention, communicate in code, etc. **2.** *Colloq.* to accelerate (a motor vehicle). *–v.i.* **3.** to knock smartly or lightly, especially so as to make a noise: *to rap on a door. –n.* **4.** a quick, smart, or light blow. **5.** the sound so produced. **6.** *Colloq.* punishment or blame, especially of someone who accepts punishment for a crime they did not commit: *to take the rap for a friend*. **7.** *Colloq.* a criminal charge: *a murder rap*. **8.** Also, **wrap**. *Aust.*, *Colloq.* a review or appraisal: *she gave the movie a good rap*. **9.** Also, **wrap**. *Colloq.* an enthusiastic approval or recommendation: *his latest novel got quite a rap*. **10.** (in spiritualism) a sound as of knocking, ascribed to the agency of disembodied spirits. –*phr.* **11. give it a rap**, *Colloq.* to accelerate a motor vehicle and travel at full speed for a short period. **12. rap out, a.** to utter sharply or vigorously: *to rap out an oath*. **b.** to announce by raps (used especially of communications ascribed to spirits). **13. rap someone over (or on) the knuckles**, *Colloq.* to reprimand someone sharply. **14. rap up**, *Aust. Colloq.* to praise extravagantly; extol. –**rapper**, *n.*

rap² /ræp/ *n. Colloq.* the least bit: *not to care a rap*.

rap³ /ræp/ *Colloq.* –*n.* **1.** *Chiefly US* a discussion. **2.** *Orig. US* → **rap music**. **3.** *Orig. US Music* a fast rhythmic monologue, sometimes improvised, over an instrumental backing. –*v.i.* (**rapped**, **rapping**) **4.** to utter a sustained spiel or verbal improvisation, usually to distract the listener's attention from some sleight of hand or other activity, as part of breakdancing. –**rapper, rapster**, *n.*

rapacious /rə'peɪʃəs/ *adj.* **1.** given to seizing for plunder or the satisfaction of greed. **2.** inordinately greedy; predatory; extortionate: *a rapacious disposition*. **3.** (of animals) subsisting by the capture of living prey; predacious. –**rapaciously**, *adv.* –**rapacity** /rə'pæsəti/, **rapaciousness**, *n.*

rape¹ /reɪp/ *n.* **1.** the act of having sexual intercourse with a person against their will. **2.** any assault or act of aggression: *the rape of land*. –*v.t.* **3.** to commit the crime or act of rape on. –**rapist**, *n.*

rape² /reɪp/ *n.* a variable herb, *Brassica napus*, widely cultivated as a fodder plant and for the seeds, which yield rapeseed oil.

raphis palm /'reɪfəs pam/ *n.* a fan palm of the genus *Raphis* of China and South-East Asia, especially *R. excelsa*, with richly patterned leaves; a common indoor plant.

rapid /'ræpəd/ *adj.* **1.** occurring with speed; coming about within a short time: *rapid growth*. **2.** moving or acting with great speed; swift: *a rapid worker*. **3.** characterised by speed, as motion. –*n.* **4.** (*usu. pl.*) a part of a river where the current runs very swiftly, as over a steep slope in the bed. –**rapidity**, *n.* –**rapidly**, *adv.*

rapid-response *adj.* of or relating to a specially trained group of personnel which is always in a state of readiness to meet a sudden emergency: *a rapid-response team*. Also, **rapid-reaction**.

rapier /'reɪpiə/ *n.* **1.** a sword, with elaborate hilt, and long, slender, pointed blade, used only for thrusting. **2.** (originally) a long, narrow, two-edged sword, used chiefly for thrusting.

rapine /'ræpaɪn, 'ræpən/ *n.* the violent seizure and carrying off of property of others; plunder.

rap music *n. Orig. US* the music of pop songs in a funk style in which the lyrics are rhythmically spoken rather than sung and have a strong rhyme pattern. Also, **rap**.

rapping /'ræpɪŋ/ *n.* the improvisation of patter to the accompaniment of a rhythmic beat.

rapport /rə'pɔ/ *n.* relation; connection, especially harmonious or sympathetic relation.

rapt¹ /ræpt/ *adj.* **1.** deeply engrossed or absorbed: *rapt in thought*. **2.** transported with emotion; enraptured: *rapt with joy*. **3.** showing or proceeding from rapture: *a rapt smile*.

rapt² /ræpt/ *adj.* → **wrapped** (def. 1).

raptorial /ræp'tɔriəl/ *adj.* preying upon other animals; predatory.

rapture /'ræptʃə/ *n.* **1.** ecstatic joy or delight; joyful ecstasy. **2.** (*oft. pl.*) an utterance or expression of ecstatic delight. **3.** *Obs.* the carrying of a person to another place or sphere of existence, especially from earth to heaven. –*phr.* **4. in raptures**, delighted; full of enthusiasm. **5. the Rapture**, (in American fundamentalist doctrine) a future event when earthly existence ends and when the saved ascend from the earth to meet Jesus Christ. –**rapturous**, *adj.*

ra-ra skirt *n.* a short, full skirt, usually layered or with rows of frills. Also, **rah-rah skirt**.

rare¹ /reə/ *adj.* (**rarer, rarest**) **1.** coming or occurring far apart in space or time; unusual; uncommon: *rare occasions, a rare smile, a rare disease*. **2.** few in number. **3.** thinly distributed over an area, or few and widely separated: *rare lighthouses*. **4.** having the component parts not closely compacted; of low density or pressure: *rare mountain air*. **5.** remarkable or unusual, especially in excellence or greatness: *rare tact, a rare find; sympathetic to a rare degree*. –**rarely**, *adv.* –**rareness**, *n.*

rare² /reə/ *adj.* (**rarer, rarest**) (of meat) not thoroughly cooked; underdone.

rarefied /'reərəfaɪd/ *adj.* **1.** belonging to or reserved for a small group; esoteric. **2.** (of air) having only a small amount of oxygen present. **3.** (of language) arcane; lofty. Also, **rarified**.

rarefy /'reərəfaɪ/ *verb* (**-fied, -fying**) –*v.t.* **1.** to make rare, more rare, or less dense. **2.** to make less gross; refine. –*v.i.* **3.** to become rare or less dense; become thinned. –**rarefaction**, *n.*

rare gas *n. Chem.* any of the gases, helium, neon, argon, krypton, xenon, or radon; chemically inactive, although some compounds have been reported. Also, **inert gas**, **noble gas**.

raring /'reərɪŋ/ *adj.* ready; eager: *he was raring to go*.

rarity /'reərəti/ *n.* (*pl.* **-ties**) **1.** something rare, unusual, or uncommon. **2.** something esteemed or interesting being rare, uncommon, or curious. **3.** rare state or quality. **4.** rare occurrence; infrequency. **5.** unusual excellence.

rarrk /rak/ *n.* the thin multicoloured crosshatched lines which feature in western Arnhem Land bark paintings, and which represent human connections to an ancestral past.

rascal /'raskəl/, *Esp. Victoria and Qld* /'ræskəl/ *for defs 1 and 2*; /'ræskəl/ *for def. 3* –*n.* **1.** a base, dishonest person. **2.** (mildly or affectionately reproving) any child or young animal: *you little rascal*. **3.** Also, **raskol**. (in PNG) a member of an urban gang given to violent criminal activities. –**rascality**, *n.*

rash¹ /ræʃ/ *adj.* **1.** acting too hastily or without due consideration. **2.** characterised by or showing too great haste or lack of consideration: *rash promises*. –**rashly**, *adv.* –**rashness**, *n.*

rash² /ræʃ/ *n.* **1.** an eruption or efflorescence on the skin. **2.** a proliferation: *a rash of complaints*.

rasher /'ræʃə/ *n.* a thin slice of bacon.

rash shirt *n.* → **surf shirt** (def. 1). Also, *Colloq.*, **rashie**.

rasp /rasp, ræsp/ *v.t.* **1.** to scrape with a rough tool; abrade: *to rasp wood with a file*. **2.** to scrape or rub roughly: *the cat's tongue rasped my hand*. **3.** to grate upon or irritate (the nerves, feelings, etc.). **4.** to say with a grating sound. –*v.i.* **5.** to scrape or grate: *to rasp away at wood; rasp away at emotions*. **6.** to make a grating sound: *the door hinges rasped as he came in*; '*No!*' *he rasped*. –*n.* **7.** the act of rasping or a rasping sound. **8.** a coarse file, with separate point-like teeth. –**raspy**, *adj.*

raspberry¹ /'razbəri, -bri/ *n.* (*pl.* **-ries**) **1.** the fruit of several shrubs of the rosaceous genus *Rubus*, consisting of small juicy drupelets, red, black, or pale yellow, forming a detachable cap around a convex receptacle, being thus distinguished from the blackberry. **2.** one of these plants, as the **red raspberry**, *R. idaeus*, of Europe. **3.** dark reddish purple.

raspberry² /ˈrazbəri, -bri/ *Colloq. –n.* (*pl.* **-ries**) **1.** a sound expressing derision or contempt made with the tongue and lips. *–v.i.* (**-ried, -rying**) **2.** to make such a sound.

rat /ræt/ *n.* **1.** any of certain long-tailed rodents of the genus *Rattus* and allied genera (family Muridae), resembling but larger than the mouse, as the **brown rat**, *R. norvegicus*. **2.** any rodent of the same family, or any of various similar animals. **3.** *Colloq.* someone who abandons friends or associates, especially in time of trouble. **4.** *Colloq.* a person considered as wretched or despicable. *–interj.* **5.** *Colloq.* (*pl.*) an exclamation of annoyance, incredulity, denial, or disappointment. *–verb* (**ratted, ratting**) *–v.i.* **6.** to hunt or catch rats. **7.** *Colloq.* to work as a scab (def. 3). *–v.t.* **8.** to steal from; loot: *he was caught ratting the tin.* **9.** *Mining* **a.** to pilfer (opal, gold, etc.) from a miner's hiding place. **b.** to enter (someone's mine) and take out opal rock, gold, etc. *–phr. Colloq.* **10. like a rat up a drainpipe**, with great speed or enthusiasm. **11. not to give** (or **care**) **a rat's** (**arse**), not to care at all. **12. rat on**, **a.** to desert (one's party or associates), especially in time of trouble: *a man who would rat on his friends*. **b.** to inform on; betray. **c.** to go back on (a statement, agreement, etc.). **13. rat through**, to sort through in a careless or hasty manner. **14. smell a rat**, to be suspicious.

ratatouille /rætəˈtui/ *n.* a type of vegetable casserole or stew.

ratbag /ˈrætbæg/ *n. Colloq.* **1.** a rascal; rogue. **2.** *Aust., NZ* someone of eccentric or nonconforming ideas or behaviour. *–***ratbaggery**, *n.* *–***ratbaggy**, *adj.*

ratchet /ˈrætʃət/ *n.* **1.** a toothed bar with which a pawl engages. **2.** the pawl used with such a device. **3.** a mechanism consisting of such a bar or wheel with the pawl. **4.** a ratchet wheel. *–phr.* **5. ratchet up**, **a.** to increase in number, intensity, volume, etc.: *dirty tricks ratchet up.* **b.** to cause such an increase in: *to ratchet up the pressure.*

rate /reɪt/ *n.* **1.** a certain quantity or amount of one thing considered in relation to a unit of another thing, used as a standard or measure: *at the rate of 60 kilometres an hour.* **2.** a fixed charge per unit of quantity: *a rate of 10 cents in the dollar.* **3.** the amount of a charge or payment with reference to some basis of calculation: *the rate of interest.* **4.** price: *to cut rates.* **5.** degree of speed, of travelling, working, etc.: *to work at a rapid rate.* **6.** degree or relative amount of action or procedure: *the rate of increase.* **7.** relative condition or quality; grade, class, or sort. **8.** assigned position in any of a series of graded classes; rating. **9.** (*usu. pl.*) a tax on property, imposed by a local authority and used for the maintenance and supply of services, as garbage, sewerage, etc.: *municipal rates; water rates. –v.t.* **10.** to estimate the value or worth of; appraise. **11.** to esteem, consider, or account: *he was rated one of the rich men of the city.* **12.** to fix at a certain rate, as of charge or payment. **13.** to value for purposes of taxation, etc. **14.** to make subject to the payment of a certain rate or tax. **15.** to deserve. **16.** *Chiefly Naut.* to place in a certain class, etc., as a ship or a sailor; give a certain rating to. **17.** *US* to arrange for the conveyance of (goods) at a certain rate. *–v.i.* **18.** to have value, standing, etc. **19.** to have position in a certain class. *–phr.* **20. at any rate**, **a.** under any circumstances; in any case; at all events. **b.** at least. **21. at a** (or **the**) **rate of knots**, *Colloq.* very fast. **22. at this rate**, if the present circumstances continue.

rather /ˈraðə/, *also for def. 6* /raˈðɜː/ *adv.* **1.** somewhat; quite; to a certain extent: *rather good.* **2.** (with verbs) in some degree: *I rather thought you'd like it.* **3.** more

properly; with better reason: *the opposite is rather to be supposed.* **4.** sooner or more willingly: *I'd rather walk.* **5.** (fol. by *than*) in preference: *I would like the blue wool rather than the yellow.* **6.** (fol. by *than*) instead of: *he is a hindrance rather than a help.* **7.** on the contrary: *that useless cat won't hunt. Rather, he just watches the mice. –interj.* **8.** *Chiefly Brit.* certainly: *Is it worth going to? Rather! –phr.* **9. would** (or **had**) **rather**, would prefer: *I had rather you didn't go*; *I would rather not do it.*

ratify /ˈrætəfaɪ/ *v.t.* (**-fied, -fying**) **1.** to confirm by expressing consent, approval, or formal sanction. **2.** to confirm (something done or arranged by an agent or by representatives) by such action. *–***ratification**, *n.* *–***ratifier**, *n.*

rating /ˈreɪtɪŋ/ *n.* **1.** classification according to grade or rank. **2.** *Naut.* **a.** assigned position in a particular class or grade, or relative standing, as of a ship or a seaman. **b.** *Navy* a sailor who has no commissioned rank. **3.** a person's or firm's credit standing. **4.** an amount fixed as a municipal rate; the act of assessing this. **5.** a measure of success, as of a television program, based on an assessment of audience size.

ratio /ˈreɪʃioʊ/ *n.* (*pl.* **-tios**) *Maths* **1.** the relation between two similar magnitudes in respect to the number of times the first contains the second: *the ratio of 5 to 2, which may be written 5:2, or $^5/_2$.* **2.** proportional relation; rate; quotient of two numbers.

ration /ˈræʃən/ *n.* **1.** a fixed allowance of provisions or food: *rations of coal and coffee.* **2.** (*usu. pl.*) a fixed allowance of food, clothing, etc., supplied to a soldier, sailor, shearer, etc. *–v.t.* **3.** to apportion or distribute as rations or by some method of allowance. **4.** to put on, or restrict to, rations. **5.** to supply with rations, as of food: *to ration an army. –***rationing**, *n.*

rational /ˈræʃnəl, ˈræʃənəl/ *adj.* **1.** reasonable; sensible: *a rational decision.* **2.** in possession of one's reason; sane: *the patient appeared perfectly rational.* **3.** having the power of reason: *humans are rational animals.* **4.** of or based on reason: *the rational faculty; a rational explanation.* **5.** *Maths* expressible as the quotient of two integers. *–***rationality**, *n.* *–***rationally**, *adv.*

rationale /ræʃəˈnal/ *n.* **1.** a statement of reasons. **2.** a reasoned exposition of principles. **3.** the fundamental reasons serving to account for something.

rationalise /ˈræʃnəlaɪz/ *v.t.* **1.** *Psychol.* to invent a rational, acceptable explanation for (behaviour which has its origin in the unconscious); to justify (behaviour triggered by the unconscious). **2.** to make economical or efficient; organise. **3.** to make rational or in agreement with reason. **4.** *Maths* to remove radicals from (part of an expression), without altering its value. **5.** to reorganise (a business, etc.) to make it more efficient and economical. *–v.i.* **6.** to use reason; think in a rational way. **7.** to reorganise and integrate (the operations of a business), especially when this results in job losses. **8.** to justify one's behaviour by apparently sensible explanations which serve to deceive oneself or others. Also, **rationalize**. *–***rationalisation** /ræʃnəlaɪˈzeɪʃən/, *n.* *–***rationaliser**, *n.*

rationalism /ˈræʃnəlɪzəm/ *n.* **1.** the principle or habit of accepting reason as the supreme authority in matters of opinion, beliefs, or conduct. **2.** *Philos.* **a.** the theory that reason is in itself a source of knowledge independently of the senses (distinguished from *empiricism* def. 2). **b.** the theory that even sense experience is possible only because of a rational element supplied by reason (distinguished from *sensationalism* def. 4). **3.** *Theology* the doctrine that revelation and scriptural tradition are to be accepted only so far as, in principle, they conform with reason. *–***rationalistic** /ræʃnəˈlɪstɪk/, **rationalistical** /ræʃnəˈlɪstɪkəl/, *adj.* *–***rationalistically** /ræʃnəˈlɪstɪkli/, *adv.*

rat-race *n.* **1.** the struggle for success, especially in career, fiercely competitive and often unscrupulous. **2.** the frantic pace of city life.

rat run *n. Colloq.* a circuitous route through suburban streets, usually taken by a driver wishing to avoid major thoroughfares. –**rat-running**, *n.*

ratshit /ˈrætʃɪt/ *adj. Aust. Colloq. (taboo)* **1.** useless; broken. **2.** depressed or unwell. **3.** no good: *that exam was ratshit.* Also, **RS**.

rattan /rəˈtæn/ *n.* **1.** any of various climbing palms of the genus *Calamus*, or allied genera. **2.** the tough stems of such palms, used for wickerwork, canes, etc. **3.** a stick or switch of this material. *–adj.* **4.** made of or from rattan.

rattle /ˈrætl/ *v.i.* **1.** to make a series of short sharp sounds: *the windows rattled in their frames.* **2.** to be filled with such sounds: *the hall was rattling with excitement.* **3.** to move or go, especially quickly, with such sounds: *the old car rattled off up the street.* **4.** to talk quickly; chatter. *–v.t.* **5.** to cause to rattle: *he rattled the doorknob violently.* **6.** to say or perform in a quick or meaningless way: *to rattle off a speech.* **7.** *Colloq.* to confuse (a person); disconcert. *–n.* **8.** a series of short, sharp sounds, from hard things knocking against each other. **9.** something designed to make such sounds, as a child's toy or the wooden clacker used by football fans. **10.** a rattling sound in the throat of a dying person. –**rattly**, *adj.*

rattlesnake /ˈrætlsneɪk/ *n.* any of various venomous American snakes of the genera *Crotalus* and *Sistrurus*, having several loosely articulated horny pieces or rings at the end of the tail, which produce a rattling or whirring sound when shaken.

ratty /ˈræti/ *adj.* (**-tier**, **-tiest**) **1.** full of rats. **2.** of or characteristic of a rat. **3.** wretched; shabby. **4.** *Colloq.* annoyed; irritable.

raucous /ˈrɔkəs/ *adj.* hoarse; harsh-sounding, as a voice. –**raucously**, *adv.* –**raucousness**, **raucity** /ˈrɔsəti/, *n.*

raunchy /ˈrɔntʃi/ *adj.* (**-chier**, **-chiest**) **1.** stimulating sexual desire; bawdy; earthy **2.** sexually aroused. –**raunchiness**, *n.* –**raunchily**, *adv.*

ravage /ˈrævɪdʒ/ *n.* **1.** devastating or destructive action. **2.** havoc; ruinous damage: *the ravages of war. –verb* (**-aged**, **-aging**) *–v.t.* **3.** to work havoc upon; damage or mar by ravages: *a face ravaged by grief. –v.i.* **4.** to work havoc; do ruinous damage. –**ravager**, *n.*

rave /reɪv/ *v.i.* **1.** to talk wildly, as in sickness. **2.** (of wind, water, storms, etc.) to make a wild or furious sound; rage. **3.** *Colloq.* to talk or write excitedly. *–n.* **4.** the act of raving. **5.** overdone praise. **6.** Also, **rave party.** an entertainment event, generally lasting throughout the night, at which patrons dance to loud dance music in a large empty space (typically a warehouse or an outdoor clearing), and commonly consume amphetamines. *–adj.* **7.** praising eagerly: *a rave review.* –**raver**, *n.*

ravel /ˈrævəl/ *verb* (**-elled** *or, Chiefly US*, **-eled**, **-elling** *or, Chiefly US*, **-eling**) *–v.t.* **1.** to tangle or entangle. **2.** to involve; confuse; perplex. *–v.i.* **3.** to become disjoined thread by thread or fibre by fibre; fray. **4.** to become tangled. **5.** to become confused or perplexed. **6.** *Civil Eng.* (of a road surface) to lose aggregate because of wear. *–n.* **7.** a tangle or complication. *–phr.* **8.** ravel out, **a.** to disengage the threads or fibres of (a woven or knitted fabric, a rope, etc.). **b.** to make plain or clear. –**raveller**, *n.*

raven /ˈreɪvən/ *n.* **1.** any of three large, glossy black, omnivorous and somewhat predacious birds with loud harsh calls, the **Australian raven**, *Corvus coronoides*, the **little raven**, *C. mellori*, and the **forest raven**, *C. tasmanicus*. **2.** any of a number of similar birds of the family Corvidae found elsewhere, especially

C. corax, often considered a bird of ill-omen. *–adj.* **3.** lustrous black: *raven locks.*

ravenous /ˈrævənəs/ *adj.* **1.** extremely hungry. **2.** extremely rapacious. **3.** voracious or gluttonous. **4.** given to seizing prey in order to devour, as animals. –**ravenously**, *adv.* –**ravenousness**, *n.*

ravine /rəˈvin/ *n.* a long, deep, narrow valley, especially one worn by water.

ravioli /rævɪˈouli/ *pl. n.* **1.** small pieces of pasta, cut square or otherwise, with a filling as of meat or cheese. **2.** (*construed as sing.*) a dish consisting of such pieces boiled in water and then served with a sauce.

ravish /ˈrævɪʃ/ *v.t.* **1.** to fill with strong emotion, especially joy. **2.** to seize and carry off by force. **3.** to carry off (a woman) by force. **4.** to rape (a woman). –**ravishment**, *n.* –**ravisher**, *n.*

ravishing /ˈrævəʃɪŋ/ *adj.* entrancing; enchanting. –**ravishingly**, *adv.*

raw /rɔ/ *adj.* **1.** uncooked, as articles of food. **2.** (of foods, textiles, etc.) not having undergone processes of preparing, dressing, finishing, refining, or manufacture. **3.** untreated: *raw sewage.* **4.** (of numerical data) exactly as counted, before scaling, adjustment, etc. **5.** unnaturally or painfully exposed, as flesh, etc., by removal of the skin or natural integument. **6.** painfully open, as a sore, wound, etc. **7.** painfully exposed or sensitive: *raw nerves.* **8.** crude in quality or character; not tempered or refined by art or taste: *raw talent; raw energy.* **9.** ignorant, inexperienced, or untrained: *a raw recruit.* **10.** brutally or grossly frank: *a raw portrayal of human passions.* **11.** *Colloq.* harsh or unfair: *a raw deal.* **12.** disagreeably damp and chilly, as the weather, air, etc. **13.** not diluted, as spirits. *–phr.* **14. in the raw**, **a.** in a crude, uncultured state: *the play portrayed life in the raw.* **b.** *Colloq.* in a state of nakedness; nudity: *she sunbakes in the raw.* **15. on the raw**, at a point of emotional vulnerability: *her remark touched him on the raw.*

raw footage *n.* → **footage** (def. 2c).

rawlplug /ˈrɔlplʌg/ *n.* (*from trademark*) a small drilled plug inserted into a hole in a wall as a fixing for a nail or screw.

ray¹ /reɪ/ *n.* **1.** a narrow beam of light. **2.** a slight showing of anything: *a ray of hope.* **3.** *Physics* **a.** any of the lines or streams in which light or particles appear to flow, often from a luminous object. **b.** the straight line perpendicular to the wavefront of radiant energy. **4.** *Maths* one of a system of straight lines coming from a point. **5.** any of a system of parts radially arranged. **6.** *Zool.* **a.** one of the branches or arms of a starfish or other radiate animal. **b.** one of the jointed supports of the soft fins of fishes. **7.** *Astron.* one of the many long bright streaks radiating from the large craters of the moon.

ray² /reɪ/ *n.* a fish, related to the sharks with flat (depressed) body fitted for life on the sea bottom, distinguished by having the gill openings on the lower surface.

rayon /ˈreɪɒn/ *n.* **1.** any textile fibres made from cellulose by passing an appropriate solution of it through spinnerets to form filaments which are used in yarns for making cloth; artificial silk. **2.** fabric made with the product.

raze /reɪz/ *v.t.* to tear down, demolish, or level to the ground. Also, **rase**. –**razer**, *n.*

razoo /rəˈzu/ *Aust., NZ Colloq.* *–n.* **1.** a gambling chip. *–phr.* **2. not have a brass razoo,** to have no money at all. **3. not worth a brass razoo,** not worth anything. Also, **rahzoo**.

razor /ˈreɪzə/ *n.* **1.** a sharp-edged instrument used especially for shaving hair from the skin. **2.** an electrically powered device, as one having rotating or reciprocating blades behind a foil, used for the same purpose. −*v.t.* **3.** to apply a razor to. **4.** to shave.

razorback /ˈreɪzəbæk/ *n.* **1.** a ridge with jagged sharp peaks. **2.** a bullock, or cow, etc., in poor condition. **3.** a wild pig with long legs, sharp snout, and lean body.

razor wire *n.* coiled stainless-steel wire having pieces of protruding metal with razor-sharp points attached at intervals along the wire.

razz /ræz/ *Colloq.* −*v.t.* **1.** to deride; make fun of; chiack. −*n.* **2.** severe criticism; derision.

re /ri, reɪ/ *prep.* in the case of; with reference to.

re- a prefix indicating repetition, as in *reprint*, *rebirth*.

reach /ritʃ/ *v.t.* **1.** to get to, or get as far as, in moving, going, travelling, etc.: *the boat reached the shore.* **2.** to come to or arrive at in some course of progress, action, etc.: *his letter reached me.* **3.** to succeed in touching or seizing with an outstretched hand, a pole, etc.: *to reach a book on a high shelf.* **4.** to stretch or hold out; extend. **5.** to stretch or extend so as to touch or meet: *the bookcase reaches the ceiling.* **6.** to establish communication with. **7.** to amount to, as in the sum or total: *the cost will reach millions.* **8.** to penetrate to (a point, etc.). **9.** to succeed in striking or hitting, as with a weapon or missile. **10.** to succeed in influencing, impressing, interesting, convincing, etc. −*v.i.* **11.** to make a stretch, as with the hand or arm. **12.** to become outstretched, as the hand or arm. **13.** to make a movement or effort as if to touch or seize something: *to reach for a weapon.* **14.** to extend in operation or effect: *power that reaches throughout the land.* **15.** to stretch in space; extend in direction, length, distance, etc.: *a coat reaching to the knee.* **16.** to extend or continue in time. **17.** to penetrate. *Naut.* to sail with the wind from somewhere near abeam, i.e., neither ahead nor dead astern. −*n.* **19.** the act of reaching: *to make a reach for a weapon.* **20.** the extent or distance of reaching: *within reach of his voice.* **21.** range of effective action, power, or capacity. **22.** the capacity of a media outlet to display advertising, measured usually in terms of readership or viewer or listener ratings. **23.** the length of the arm from the armpit to the finger tips. **24.** a continuous stretch or extent of something: *a reach of woodland.* **25.** a portion of a river between bends. −*phr.* **26. reach someone down something**, *Colloq.* to fetch something for someone from a high location: *reach me down that book on the top shelf.* **27. reach to, a.** to get or come to (a specified place, person, condition, etc.). **b.** to amount to: *sums reaching to a considerable total.* −**reacher**, *n.* −**reachable**, *adj.*

react /riˈækt/ *v.i.* **1.** to act in return on an agent or influence; act reciprocally upon each other, as two things. **2.** to act in opposition, as against some force. **3.** *Physics* to exert an equal force in the opposite direction to an acting force. **4.** *Chem.* to undergo a chemical reaction. −**reactant**, *n.*

reaction /riˈækʃən/ *n.* **1.** a movement, tendency or action in an opposite direction. **2.** an action in response to a stimulus, influence, or some other event. **3.** a political tendency or movement back to former policies and against change: *conservatism is often a reaction to socialism or radicalism.* **4.** *Chem.* the chemical action of substances upon each other; chemical change. **5.** → **nuclear reaction**. **6.** *Physics* See **Newton's laws**. −**reactive**, *adj.*

reactionary /riˈækʃənəri, -ʃənri/, *Orig. US* /riˈækʃənɛri/ *adj.* **1.** of, relating to, marked by, or favouring reaction, as in politics. −*n.* (*pl.* **-aries**) **2.** someone who favours or inclines to reaction (def. 3). Also, **reactionist**.

reaction propulsion *n.* → **jet propulsion**.

reactor /riˈæktə/ *n.* **1.** *Chem.* a substance undergoing a reaction. **2.** *Elect.* a device, the primary purpose of which is to introduce reactance into a circuit. **3.** *Physics* → **nuclear reactor**.

read¹ /rid/ *verb* (**read** /rɛd/, **reading** /ˈridɪŋ/) −*v.t.* **1.** to observe, and apprehend the meaning of (something written, printed, etc.): *to read a book.* **2.** to utter aloud; render in speech (something written, printed, etc.). **3.** to have such knowledge of (a language) as to be able to understand things written in it: *to read French.* **4.** to apprehend the meaning of (signs, characters, etc.) otherwise than with the eyes, as by means of the fingers. **5.** to make out the significance of, by scrutiny or observation: *to read the sky.* **6.** to foresee, foretell, or predict: *to read a person's fortune.* **7.** to make out the character, etc., of (a person, etc.), as by the interpretation of outward signs. **8.** to understand or take (something read or observed) in a particular way. **9.** to introduce (something not expressed or directly indicated) into what is read or considered. **10.** to adopt or give as a reading in a particular passage: *for 'one thousand' another version reads 'ten thousand'.* **11.** to register or indicate, as a thermometer or other instrument. **12.** to study, as by perusing books: *to read law.* **13.** to learn by, or as if by, perusal: *to read a person's thoughts.* **14.** to bring, put, etc., by reading: *to read oneself to sleep.* **15.** to give someone (a lecture or lesson) by way of admonition or rebuke. **16.** to discover or explain the meaning of (a riddle, a dream, etc.). **17.** (of a computer) to copy (information) from a secondary device, such as a magnetic tape or disk, into its primary storage area. −*v.i.* **18.** to read or peruse writing, printing, etc., or papers, books, etc. **19.** to utter aloud, or render in speech, written or printed words that one is perusing: *to read to a person.* **20.** to give a public reading or recital. **21.** to inspect and apprehend the meaning of written or other signs or characters. **22.** to occupy oneself seriously with reading or study, especially in a specific course of study: *to read for holy orders.* **23.** to obtain knowledge or learn of something by reading. **24.** to be capable of being read, especially properly or well. **25.** to have a certain wording. **26.** to be capable of being read or interpreted (as stated): *a rule that reads two different ways.* **27.** (of a computer) to take in information. −*n.* **28.** the act or process of reading: *to just lie in bed and have a read.* −*phr.* **29. a good read**, a book, magazine, etc., that is enjoyable to read. **30. read between the lines**, to find in something spoken or written more meaning than the words appear to express. **31. you wouldn't read about it**, *Aust., NZ, Colloq.* an exclamation of astonishment, sometimes ironic. −**readable**, *adj.* −**readability**, *n.*

read² /rɛd/ *adj.* having knowledge gained by reading: *a widely read person.*

reader /ˈridə/ *n.* **1.** someone who reads. **2.** a book of instruction and practice in reading. **3.** someone employed to read and report on manuscripts, etc., sent in for publication. **4.** someone who reads or recites before an audience. **5.** a university teacher ranking next below a professor. **6.** a proofreader. −**readership**, *n.*

reading /ˈridɪŋ/ *n.* **1.** the action or practice of someone who reads. **2.** ability to read: *good reading comes with practice.* **3.** the way a part in a play, etc., is performed by a particular person. **4.** knowledge through books: *a man of wide reading.* **5.** matter read or for reading: *a novel that makes good reading; today's reading is from St John.* **6.** a particular understanding of something: *what is your reading of the situation?* **7.** a figure given by an instrument, as a thermometer. −*adj.* **8.** relating to, or used for, reading: *reading skill; reading glasses.* **9.** given to reading: *the reading public.*

read me *Computers* −*n.* **1.** a file accompanying a piece of software which explains its history, gives additional advice on its operation, etc. −*adj.* **2.** of or relating to such a file. Also, **readme**.

readout /'ridaʊt/ *n.* → **digital display**.

read-write /rid-'raɪt/ *adj.* of or relating to a computer, etc., which reads and then restores memory data.

ready /'rɛdi/ *adj.* (**-dier, -diest**) **1.** completely prepared or in the right condition for immediate action or use: *soldiers ready for battle; dinner is ready; are you ready to go out?* **2.** willing: *ready to forgive.* **3.** quick: *he's very ready to understand; a ready answer; a ready wit.* **4.** eager or likely; apt: *too ready to criticise others.* **5.** likely at any moment (to do something): *a tree ready to fall.* **6.** immediately available for use: *ready money.* −*v.t.* (**-died, -dying**) **7.** to prepare. −*n.* **8.** the condition or position of being ready: *to bring a rifle to the ready.* −**readily**, *adv.*

ready-to-wear *adj.* (of clothing) made in standard sizes to fit a large number of people.

reagent /ri'eɪdʒənt/ *n.* Chem. a substance which, on account of the reactions it causes, is used in chemical analysis.

real /ril/ *adj.* **1.** true (rather than merely ostensible, nominal, or apparent): *the real reason for an act.* **2.** existing or occurring as fact; actual (rather than imaginary, ideal, or fictitious): *a story taken from real life.* **3.** being an actual thing, with objective existence (rather than merely imaginary). **4.** being actually such (rather than merely so called): *a real victory.* **5.** genuine; not counterfeit, artificial, or imitation: *a real antique, a real diamond, real silk.* **6.** unfeigned or sincere: *real sympathy.* **7.** *Philos.* **a.** existent or relating to the existent as opposed to the non-existent. **b.** actual as opposed to possible or potential. **c.** independent of experience as opposed to phenomenal or apparent. **8.** *Law* denoting immoveable property of a freehold type, as lands and tenements excluding leaseholds (opposed to *personal*). **9.** *Optics* (of an image) formed by the actual convergence of rays, as the image produced in a camera (opposed to *virtual*). **10.** *Maths* of or relating to a real number. −*adv.* **11.** *Colloq.* very. −*phr.* **12. for real**, *Colloq.* **a.** actual; definite: *that overseas trip is for real.* **b.** in earnest: *she's trying for real now.* **c.** genuine; sincere: *she's for real when she says she loves you.* **13. get real**, *Colloq.* an interjection to desist from unrealistic or impractical notions. **14. the real**, **a.** that which is real or actually exists. **b.** reality in general. **15. the real McCoy** (or **thing**), the genuine article. −**realness**, *n.*

real estate *n.* **1.** Also, **real property**, tangible and immovable property such as land and houses, buildings or any such structures on the land, and any rights attached to the ownership of the land, such as mineral rights (but excluding leasehold interests). **2.** *Computers* the physical device by means of which content is viewed, as the screen on a PC, mobile phone, television, etc.

real estate agent *n.* someone who acts as an intermediary between the buyer and the vendor of real estate; real estate broker.

realise /'rɪəlaɪz/ *v.t.* **1.** to come to understand clearly: *he realised for the first time that he was alone.* **2.** (*oft. in passive*) to make real, or give reality to (a hope, fear, plan, etc.): *his worst fears were realised when the business collapsed.* **3.** to turn into cash: *to realise assets.* Also, **realize**. −**realisable**, *adj.* −**realisation**, *n.* −**realiser**, *n.*

realism /'rɪəlɪzəm/ *n.* **1.** the tendency to face facts and deal with things as they really are, rather than as they exist in some ideal world. **2.** the taking of a practical view in human problems rather than one based on principles of right and wrong. **3.** the treatment of subjects in literature or art with faithfulness to nature or to real life (opposed to *idealism*): *Hogarth is a master of realism.* −**realist**, *n.* −**realistic**, *adj.* −**realistically**, *adv.*

reality /ri'æləti/ *n.* (*pl.* **-ties**) **1.** the state or fact of being real. **2.** a real thing or fact. **3.** *Philos.* **a.** that which exists independently of ideas concerning it. **b.** that which exists independently of all other things; an ultimate thing which produces derivatives. −*phr.* **4. in reality**, really; actually; in fact or truth.

reality check *n.* *Colloq.* **1.** an appraisal of the facts of a situation, often providing a contrast with current expectations based on wishful thinking. **2.** any event which causes one's expectations, beliefs, etc., to more closely reflect actual circumstances.

reality TV *n.* a television program format which uses actual footage of events as they occur, often in a contrived situation and with some competitive element providing the motivation for people to interact. Also, **reality television**.

real-life *adj.* that actually occurs or has occurred; not fictional.

really /'rɪəli/ *adv.* **1.** in reality; actually: *to see things as they really are.* **2.** genuinely or truly: *a really honest man.* **3.** indeed: *really, this is too much.*

realm /rɛlm/ *n.* **1.** a royal domain; kingdom: *the realm of England.* **2.** the region, sphere, or domain within which anything rules or prevails: *the realm of dreams.* **3.** the special province or field of something: *the realm of physics.* −*phr.* **4. beyond the realm(s) of possibility**, utterly impossible. **5. within the realm(s) of possibility**, possible, especially remotely possible.

real number *n.* *Maths* **1.** one of the set of numbers which include all rational and irrational numbers. **2.** → **decimal number**.

real time *n.* **1.** the actual time in which a process occurs or an event takes place. **2.** *Film, TV* a depiction of an event or story which takes the same time as it would take in real life. −*phr.* **3. in real time**, happening at the rate that it would happen in real life. −**real-time**, *adj.*

real-time *adj.* **1.** of or relating to an analytical or computing device which processes information and outputs results at the same rate at which the original information is presented. **2.** of or relating to computer simulations which reproduce the speed of the event being simulated. −*n.* **3.** a method using real-time processing: *this machine processes in real-time.* Also, **realtime**.

realtor /'rɪəltə, -tɔ/ *n.* *Chiefly US* → **real estate agent**.

realty /'rɪəlti/ *n.* → **real estate** (def. 1).

real wages *pl. n.* *Econ.* the wages paid for work done, expressed in terms of buying power (opposed to *money wages*, the actual amount of money paid out for work done).

ream /rim/ *n.* **1.** Also, **printer's ream**. a standard quantity among paper dealers meaning 20 quires or 500 sheets (formerly 480 sheets). **2.** (*pl.*) *Colloq.* a large quantity: *to write reams and reams of poetry.*

reap /rip/ *v.t.* **1.** to cut (grain, etc.) with a sickle or other implement or a machine, as in harvest. **2.** to gather or take (a crop, harvest, etc.). **3.** to get as a return, recompense, or result: *to reap large profits.* −*v.i.* **4.** to reap grain, etc.

reaper /'ripə/ *n.* **1.** a machine for cutting standing grain; a reaping machine. **2.** someone who reaps. −*phr.* **3. the grim reaper**, Death personified.

rear¹ /rɪə/ *n.* **1.** the back of anything, as opposed to the front. **2.** the space or position behind anything. **3.** the behind; buttocks. **4.** the hindmost portion of an army, fleet, etc. −*adj.* **5.** situated at or relating to the rear: *the rear door.* −*phr.* **6. bring up the rear**, **a.** to be the hindmost in a group or string of walkers, riders, etc. **b.** to be the last in a field of contestants, etc.

rear² /rɪə, rɛə/ *v.t.* **1.** to care for and support until fully grown: *to rear a child.* **2.** to raise by building; erect. **3.** to lift, raise, or hold up; elevate. −*v.i.* Also, **rear up**.

4. a. to rise on the hind legs, as a horse. **b.** (of persons) to start up in angry excitement, etc.

rear admiral *n. Navy* **1.** a commissioned officer in the Royal Australian Navy ranking below vice admiral and above commodore. **2.** the rank. *Abbrev.*: RADM

reason /ˈriːzən/ *n.* **1.** a ground or cause, as for a belief, action, fact, event, etc.: *the reason for declaring war.* **2.** a statement in justification or explanation of belief or action. **3.** the mental powers concerned with drawing conclusions or inferences. **4.** sound judgement or good sense. **5.** normal or sound powers of mind; sanity. **6.** *Logic* a premise of an argument. **7.** *Philos.* intellect as opposed to sensibility. *–v.i.* **8.** to think or argue in a logical manner. *–phr.* **9. by reason of**, on account of; because of. **10. in** (or **within**) **reason**, in accordance with reason; to the extent justifiable or proper. **11. it stands to reason**, it is obvious or logical. **12. reason out**, to think out (a problem, etc.) logically. **13. reason that ...**, to conclude or infer as stated. **14. reason with**, to urge reasons on which should determine belief or action. *–***reasoner**, *n.*

reasonable /ˈriːzənəbəl/ *adj.* **1.** endowed with reason. **2.** agreeable to reason or sound judgement: *a reasonable choice.* **3.** not exceeding the limit prescribed by reason; not excessive: *reasonable terms.* **4.** moderate, or moderate in price: *the coat was reasonable but not cheap.* *–***reasonableness**, **reasonability** /riːzənəˈbɪləti/, *n.* *–***reasonably**, *adv.*

reasonable benefit limit *n.* the maximum superannuation benefits a person can receive at concessional or lower tax rates. Also, **RBL**.

reassure /riːəˈʃɔː/ *v.t.* **1.** to restore (a person, etc.) to assurance or confidence: *his remarks reassured me.* **2.** to assure again. *–***reassurance**, *n.* *–***reassurer**, *n.* *–***reassuring**, *adj.* *–***reassuringly**, *adv.*

rebate[1] /ˈriːbeɪt/ *n.* **1.** a return of part of an original amount paid for some service or merchandise; repayment, as of a part of charges. *–v.t.* **2.** to allow as a discount. **3.** to deduct (a certain amount), as from a total. *–***rebatable**, **rebateable**, *adj.*

rebate[2] /ˈriːbeɪt/ *n.* **1.** a cut, groove, or recess made on the edge or surface of a board or the like, as to receive the end or edge of another board or the like similarly shaped. *–v.t.* **2.** to cut or form a rebate in (a board, etc.).

rebel *n.* /ˈrɛbəl/ **1.** someone who resists, or rises in arms against, the established government. **2.** someone or something that resists any authority or control. *–adj.* /ˈrɛbəl/ **3.** fighting authority; rebellious. **4.** of or relating to rebels. *–v.i.* /rəˈbɛl/ (**-belled, -belling**) **5.** to rise in arms or active resistance against the government. **6.** to resist any authority. *–***rebeldom**, *n.*

rebellion /rəˈbɛljən/ *n.* **1.** open, organised, and armed resistance to one's government or ruler. **2.** resistance against or defiance of any authority or control. **3.** rejection of traditional or established customs, culture, etc. **4.** the act of rebelling. *–***rebellious**, *adj.*

rebirth /ˌriːˈbɜːθ, ˈriːbɜːθ/ *n.* **1.** being born again; a second birth. **2.** a renaissance; a new activity or growth.

reboot /riːˈbuːt/ *v.t. Computers* to take (a computer which is already switched on) through the procedure which loads the operating system.

rebound *v.i.* /rəˈbaʊnd, riːˈbaʊnd/ **1.** to bound or spring back from force of impact. *–v.t.* /rəˈbaʊnd, riːˈbaʊnd/ **2.** to cause to bound back; cast back. *–n.* /ˈriːbaʊnd, rəˈbaʊnd/ **3.** the act of rebounding; recoil. *–phr.* **4. on the rebound, a.** in the act of bouncing back. **b.** during a period of reaction, as after being rejected: *she married him on the rebound after an unhappy love affair.*

rebuff /rəˈbʌf/ *n.* **1.** a blunt or abrupt check, as to someone making advances. **2.** a peremptory refusal of a request, offer, etc.; a snub. **3.** a check to action or

progress. *–v.t.* **4.** to give a rebuff to; check; repel; refuse; drive away.

rebuke /rəˈbjuːk/ *v.t.* **1.** to reprove or reprimand. *–n.* **2.** a reproof; a reprimand. *–***rebukeable**, *adj.* *–***rebuker**, *n.*

rebus /ˈriːbəs/ *n.* a representation of a word or phrase by pictures, symbols, etc., suggesting the word elements or words, as by using a picture of two gates and a head to represent *Gateshead.*

rebut /rəˈbʌt/ *v.t.* (**-butted, -butting**) **1.** to refute by evidence or argument. **2.** to oppose by contrary proof. *–***rebuttable**, *adj.*

recalcitrant /rəˈkælsətrənt/ *adj.* **1.** resisting authority or control; not obedient or compliant; refractory. *–n.* **2.** a recalcitrant person. *–***recalcitrance**, **recalcitrancy**, *n.*

recall *v.t.* /rəˈkɔl/ **1.** to remember. **2.** to bring back in thought or attention. **3.** to take back or withdraw. **4.** to remove (a public official) from office. *–n.* /ˈriːkɔl/ **5.** the act of recalling. **6.** memory; recollection. *–***recallable**, *adj.*

recant /rəˈkænt/ *v.t.* **1.** to withdraw or disavow (a statement, etc.), especially formally; retract. *–v.i.* **2.** to disavow an opinion, etc., especially formally. *–***recantation** /riːkænˈteɪʃən/, *n.* *–***recanter**, *n.*

recap /ˈriːkæp/ *n.* **1.** a summarised review, as at the end of a speech, lecture, etc. *–v.i.* (**-capped, -capping**) **2.** to recapitulate.

recapitulate /riːkəˈpɪtʃəleɪt/ *v.t.* **1.** to review by way of an orderly summary, as at the end of a speech or discourse. *–v.i.* **2.** to sum up statements or matters. *–***recapitulation**, *n.*

recede /rəˈsiːd/ *v.i.* (**-ceded, -ceding**) **1.** to go or move back, to or towards a more distant point. **2.** to become more distant. **3.** to slope backwards: *a receding chin.* **4.** to draw back or withdraw from a position taken in a matter, or from an undertaking, promise, etc.

receipt /rəˈsiːt/ *n.* **1.** a written acknowledgement of having received money, goods, etc. **2.** (*pl.*) the amount or quantity received. **3.** the act or result of receiving. *–v.t.* **4.** to acknowledge in writing the payment of (a bill).

receivable /rəˈsiːvəbəl/ *adj.* **1.** fit for acceptance. **2.** awaiting receipt of payment: *accounts receivable.*

receive /rəˈsiːv/ *verb* (**-ceived, -ceiving**) *–v.t.* **1.** to take into one's hand or one's possession (something offered or delivered). **2.** to have (something) granted, etc.: *to receive an honorary degree.* **3.** to get or learn: *to receive news.* **4.** to take into the mind. **5.** to experience: *to receive attention.* **6.** to suffer or undergo: *to receive a broken arm.* **7.** to be at home to (visitors). **8.** to admit (a person) to a place. **9.** to admit to a condition, membership, etc.: *to receive someone into the Church.* **10.** to accept as authoritative, true, or approved: *a principle universally received.* *–v.i.* **11.** to receive something. **12.** *Radio* to convert incoming electromagnetic waves into the original signal, as soundwaves or light on a television screen. *–***receival**, *n.*

receiver /rəˈsiːvə/ *n.* **1.** someone or something that receives. **2. a.** a device which receives electrical signals, waves, etc., and changes them to sounds or pictures, as a radio or television receiving set. **b.** the part of a telephone held to the ear. **3.** *Law* a person appointed, usually by a court, to take charge of a business or property of others, pending a law suit. **4.** *Commerce* someone appointed to receive money due. **5.** someone who knowingly receives stolen goods. **6.** a device for receiving or holding something. **7.** *Tennis* the player who receives the ball from the server. *–***receiving**, *n.*

recent /ˈriːsənt/ *adj.* **1.** of late occurrence, appearance, or origin; lately happening, done, made, etc.: *recent events.* **2.** not long past, as a period. **3.** belonging to such a period; not remote or primitive. *–***recency**, **recentness**, *n.* *–***recently**, *adv.*

Recent Age *n.* the → **Holocene** (def. 2). Also, **the Recent.**

receptacle /rə'sɛptəkəl/ *n.* **1.** something that serves to receive or hold anything; a repository; a container. **2.** *Bot.* the modified or expanded portion of an axis, which bears the organs of a single flower or the florets of a flower head.

reception /rə'sɛpʃən/ *n.* **1.** the act or result of receiving. **2.** an occasion when people are formally received. **3.** an office, desk, etc., where callers are received. **4.** *Radio* the quality gained in receiving under given conditions.

receptionist /rə'sɛpʃənəst/ *n.* someone employed to receive and direct callers, as in an office or hotel.

receptive /rə'sɛptɪv/ *adj.* **1.** having the quality of receiving, taking in, or admitting. **2.** able or quick to receive ideas, etc.: *a receptive mind.* **3.** having, or characterised by, a disposition to receive a suggestion, offer, or the like with favour: *a receptive person.* **4.** of or relating to reception or receptors. **–receptively,** *adv.* **–receptivity** /risɛp'tɪvəti/, **receptiveness,** *n.*

receptor /rə'sɛptə/ *n. Physiol.* one of or a group of the end organs of sensory or afferent neurons, specialised to be sensitive to stimulating agents.

recess *n.* /rə'sɛs, 'risɛs/ **1.** a part or space that is set back, as an alcove in a room. **2.** (*usu. pl.*) a quiet, hidden inner area or part. **3.** a stopping for a time, from work, or some activity. *–v.t.* /rə'sɛs/ **4.** to place or set in a recess. **5.** to form as or like a recess.

recession /rə'sɛʃən/ *n.* **1.** the act of receding or withdrawing. **2.** a receding part of a wall, etc. **3.** *Eccles.* a procession at the end of a church service. **4.** a decline in business. **5.** *Econ.* a period of adverse economic circumstances, usually less severe than a depression. **–recessionary,** *adj.*

recessional /rə'sɛʃənəl/ *adj.* **1.** *Eccles.* of or relating to a recession of the clergy and choir after a church service. **2.** of or relating to a recess, as of a legislative body. *–n.* **3.** *Eccles.* a recessional hymn, or music for it.

recessive /rə'sɛsɪv/ *adj.* **1.** tending to recede; receding. **2.** *Biol.* relating to or exhibiting a recessive, as opposed to a dominant. **3.** *Phonetics* (of accent) showing a tendency to recede from the end towards the beginning of a word. *–n. Biol.* **4.** a hereditary character resulting from a gene which possesses less biochemical activity than another termed the dominant, and hence is suppressed more or less completely by it when in a heterozygous condition. **5.** an individual exhibiting such character. **–recessively,** *adv.* **–recessiveness,** *n.*

recherché /rə'ʃɛəʃeɪ/ *adj.* **1.** sought out with care. **2.** rare or choice. **3.** of studied refinement or elegance.

recidivism /rə'sɪdəvɪzəm/ *n.* repeated or habitual relapse into crime. **–recidivist,** *n.*, *adj.* **–recidivistic** /rəsɪdə'vɪstɪk/, **recidivous,** *adj.*

recipe /'rɛsəpi/ *n.* **1.** any formula, especially one for preparing a dish in cookery. **2.** a method to attain a desired end.

recipient /rə'sɪpiənt/ *n.* **1.** a person or thing that receives something. *–adj.* **2.** receiving or capable of receiving.

reciprocal /rə'sɪprəkəl/ *adj.* **1.** given, felt, etc., by each towards each; mutual: *reciprocal love.* **2.** given, performed, felt, etc., in return: *reciprocal aid.* *–n.* **3.** something that is reciprocal to something else; a counterpart. **4.** *Maths* the number by which a given quantity is multiplied to produce one. **–reciprocality** /rəsɪprə'kæləti/, *n.* **–reciprocally,** *adv.* **–reciprocity,** *n.*

reciprocate /rə'sɪprəkeɪt/ *v.t.* **1.** to give, feel, etc., in return. **2.** to give and receive reciprocally; interchange: *to reciprocate favours.* **3.** to cause to move alternately backwards and forwards. *–v.i.* **4.** to make return, as for something given. **5.** to make an interchange. **6.** to move alternately backwards and forwards. **–reciprocative,** *adj.* **–reciprocator,** *n.* **–reciprocation,** *n.*

recital /rə'saɪtl/ *n.* **1.** a musical or other entertainment given usually by a single performer, or consisting of selections from a single composer. **2.** the act of reciting. **3.** a detailed statement. **4.** an account, narrative, or description. **–recitalist,** *n.*

recitative /rə'saɪtətɪv, 'rɛsə,teɪtɪv/ *adj.* of or relating to recital, as of facts.

recite /rə'saɪt/ *v.t.* **1.** to repeat the words of, as from memory, especially in a formal manner: *to recite a lesson.* **2.** to repeat (a piece of poetry or prose) before an audience, as for entertainment. **3.** to give an account of: *to recite one's adventures.* **4.** to enumerate. *–v.i.* **5.** to recite or repeat something from memory. **–recitation,** *n.* **–reciter,** *n.*

reckless /'rɛkləs/ *adj.* **1.** utterly careless of the consequences of action; without caution: *a reckless driver.* **2.** characterised by or proceeding from such carelessness: *reckless extravagance.* *–phr.* **3. reckless of,** careless of the consequences to: *reckless of life and limb.* **–recklessly,** *adv.* **–recklessness,** *n.*

reckon /'rɛkən/ *v.t.* **1.** to count, compute, or calculate as to number or amount. **2.** to esteem or consider (as stated): *to be reckoned a wit.* **3.** *Colloq.* to think or suppose. *–v.i.* **4.** to count; make a computation or calculation. **5.** to think; suppose. *–phr.* **6. reckon on,** to count, depend, or rely on, as in expectation. **7. reckon up,** (sometimes fol. by *with*) to settle accounts, as with a person. **8. reckon with,** to deal with, as with something to be taken into account or entering into a case. **9. reckon without,** to fail to take into account.

reclaim /rə'kleɪm/ *v.t.* **1.** to claim or demand the return or restoration of (something or someone): *to reclaim baggage*; *to reclaim someone's affection.* **2.** to bring (wild, waste, or marshy land) into a condition for cultivation or other use. **3.** to recover (substances) in a pure or usable form from refuse matter, articles, etc. **4.** to bring back to more socially, morally, or religiously acceptable courses, living, principles, ideas, etc. *–n.* **5.** reclamation: *beyond reclaim.* **–reclaimable,** *adj.* **–reclaimant, reclaimer,** *n.*

recline /rə'klaɪn, ri-/ *v.i.* **1.** to lean or lie back; rest in a recumbent position. *–v.t.* **2.** to cause to lean back on something; place in a recumbent position. **–reclinable,** *adj.* **–recliner,** *n.* **–reclination** /rɛklə'neɪʃən/, *n.*

recluse /rə'klus/ *n.* **1.** someone who lives in seclusion or apart from society, often for religious meditation. **2.** a religious voluntarily immured or remaining for life within a cell. **–reclusion,** *n.* **–reclusive,** *adj.* **–reclusiveness,** *n.*

recognise /'rɛkəgnaɪz/ *v.t.* **1.** to know again: *I scarcely recognised him.* **2.** to identify from knowledge of appearance or character. **3.** to understand as existing or true; realise: *to be the first to recognise a fact.* **4.** to admit formally as existing: *one government recognises another.* **5.** to admit or treat as correct: *to recognise a claim.* **6.** to show acquaintance with (a person, etc.) as by a salute. **7.** to show approval of (kindness, merit, etc.) as by some reward. Also, **recognize.** **–recognisable,** *adj.* **–recognisably,** *adv.* **–recognition,** *n.*

recoil *v.i.* /rə'kɔɪl/ **1.** to draw back, as in fear or horror. **2.** to spring or fly back, as a result of force of impact or of a discharge, as a gun. **3.** (fol. by *on* or *upon*) to spring or come back; react. *–n.* /rə'kɔɪl, 'rikɔɪl/ **4.** the act of recoiling.

recollect /rɛkə'lɛkt/ *v.t.* **1.** to recall to mind, or recover knowledge of by an act or effort of memory; remember. **2.** to concentrate or absorb (the mind, etc.), as in preparation for mystical contemplation. *–v.i.* **3.** to have a recollection; remember. **–recollection,** *n.* **–recollective,** *adj.* **–recollectively,** *adv.*

recombinant DNA /ri,kɒmbənənt ,di ɛn 'eɪ/ *n.* an artificially produced form of DNA achieved by joining fragments of DNA molecules obtained from different organisms.

recommend /rɛkə'mɛnd/ *v.t.* **1.** to commend by favourable representations; present as worthy of confidence, acceptance, use, etc.: *to recommend a book.* **2.** to represent or urge as advisable or expedient: *to recommend caution.* **3.** to advise (a person, etc., to do something): *to recommend one to wait.* **4.** to make acceptable or pleasing: *a plan that has very little to recommend it.* –**recommendable**, *adj.* –**recommendatory**, *adj.* –**recommendation**, *n.*

recompense /'rɛkəmpɛns/ *v.t.* (**-pensed, -pensing**) **1.** to repay or reward, for service, aid, etc. **2.** to make a return or repayment for. –*n.* **3.** a repayment made, as for loss, injury, etc. **4.** reward; remuneration.

reconcile /'rɛkənsaɪl/ *v.t.* **1.** to bring into agreement or harmony; make compatible or consistent: *to reconcile differing statements.* **2.** to win over to friendliness: *to reconcile a hostile person.* **3.** to compose or settle (a quarrel, difference, etc.). –*phr.* **4. reconcile to,** to render no longer opposed to; bring to acquiescence in: *to reconcile someone to their fate.* –**reconcilable**, *adj.* –**reconcilement, reconciliation**, *n.* –**reconciliatory**, *adj.* –**reconciler**, *n.*

recondite /rə'kɒndaɪt, 'rɛkəndaɪt/ *adj.* **1.** dealing with abstruse or profound matters: *a recondite treatise.* **2.** removed from ordinary knowledge or understanding; abstruse; profound: *recondite principles.* **3.** little known; obscure. –**reconditely**, *adv.* –**reconditeness**, *n.*

recondition /rikən'dɪʃən/ *v.t.* to restore to a good or satisfactory condition; repair; overhaul. –**reconditioned**, *adj.* –**reconditioning**, *n.*

reconnaissance /rə'kɒnəsəns/ *n.* **1.** the act of reconnoitring. **2.** *Mil.* a search made for useful military information in the field, especially by examining the ground. **3.** *Civil Eng.* a preliminary examination of a region as to its general natural features, before a more exact survey for triangulation, etc.

reconnoitre /rɛkə'nɔɪtə/ *verb* (**-tred, -tring**) –*v.t.* **1.** to inspect, observe, or survey (the enemy, the enemy's strength or position, a region, etc.) in order to gain information for military purposes. **2.** to examine or survey (a region, etc.) for engineering, geological, or other purposes. –*v.i.* **3.** to make a reconnaissance. –*n.* **4.** the act of reconnoitring; a reconnaissance. Also, *US*, **reconnoiter**. –**reconnoitrer**, *n.*

reconsider /rikən'sɪdə/ *v.t.* **1.** to consider again. **2.** to consider again with a view to a change of decision or action: *to reconsider a refusal.* –*v.i.* **3.** to reconsider a matter. –**reconsideration** /ˌrikənsɪdə'reɪʃən/, *n.*

reconstitute /ri'kɒnstətjut/ *v.t.* to constitute again; reconstruct; recompose: *reconstituted milk; a reconstituted committee.* –**reconstitution**, *n.*

reconstruct /rikən'strʌkt/ *v.t.* **1.** to construct again; rebuild. **2.** to re-create or re-enact past events or another place: *to reconstruct a crime, the scene of a crime.* **3.** *Ling.* to suggest hypothetical forms for (a language, or parts of a language, for which no documentary evidence survives) by comparison of related languages or forms for which such evidence is available. –**reconstruction**, *n.*

record *v.t.* /rə'kɔd/ **1.** to set down in writing or the like, as for the purpose of preserving evidence. **2.** to cause to be set down or registered: *to record one's vote.* **3.** to indicate or state: *they recorded a protest by sitting down in the streets.* **4.** to serve to relate or to tell of, as a written statement. **5.** to set down or register in some permanent form, as instruments. **6.** to transfer (sound and/or images) onto a recording medium, such as magnetic tape, CD-ROM, etc., or by employing digital electronic devices, for the purpose of reproduction: *to record an opera; to record a television show.* **7.** to

perform for the purposes of making a recording: *the orchestra recorded a symphony.* –*v.i.* /rə'kɔd/ **8.** to record something. –*n.* /'rɛkɔd/ **9.** the act of recording. **10.** the state or fact of being recorded, as in writing. **11.** an account in writing or the like preserving the memory or knowledge of facts or events. **12.** information or knowledge preserved in writing or the like. **13.** a report, list, or aggregate of actions or achievements, as in the case of a person, an organisation, a horse, a ship, etc.: *to have a good record.* **14.** *Computers* a self-contained grouping of data. **15.** any thing or person serving as a memorial. **16.** the tracing, marking, or the like made by recording instrument. **17.** a disc or, formerly, a cylinder, or other device having characteristic markings for reproducing sound, especially for use with a record-player or a gramophone; gramophone record. **18.** the highest or farthest recorded degree attained; the best rate, amount, etc., attained, as in some form of sport: *to break the record in the high jump.* **19.** an official writing intended to be preserved. **20.** *Law* **a.** the commitment to writing, as authentic evidence, of something having legal importance, especially as evidence of the proceedings or verdict of a court. **b.** evidence preserved in this manner. **c.** an authentic or official written report of proceedings of a court of justice. –*adj.* /'rɛkɔd/ **21.** making or affording a record. **22.** notable in the degree of attainment; surpassing all others: *a record year for sales.* –*phr.* **23. off the record,** unofficially; without intending to be quoted. **24. on (the) record,** recorded in a publicly available document: *he is on record as saying that Australia should become a republic.*

recorder /rə'kɔdə/ *n.* **1.** someone who records, especially as an official duty. **2.** a recording or registering apparatus or device. **3.** a soft-toned flute with a plug in the mouthpiece, played in vertical position.

recording /rə'kɔdɪŋ/ *n.* **1.** the act or practice of making a record. **2.** *Electronics* a record of music, speech, or the like made on magnetic tape or similar medium for purposes of reproduction; a CD, DVD, record or tape.

record-player /'rɛkɔd-pleɪə/ *n.* a machine that reproduces sound from a record; gramophone; phonograph.

re-count *v.t.* /ˌri-'kaʊnt/ **1.** to count again. –*n.* /'ri-kaʊnt/ **2.** a second or additional count, as of votes in an election.

recount *v.t.* /rə'kaʊnt/ **1.** to relate or narrate; tell in detail; give the facts or particulars of. **2.** to narrate in order. **3.** to tell one by one; enumerate. –*n.* /'rikaʊnt/ **4.** a written or spoken text type or form which typically records events in the order in which they happened.

recoup *v.t.* /rə'kup, ri'kup/ **1.** to get an equivalent for; compensate for. **2.** to regain or recover. **3.** to pay back; indemnify. –*n.* /'rikup/ **4.** the act of recouping. –**recoupment**, *n.*

recourse /rə'kɔs/ *n.* **1.** resort or application to a person or thing for help or protection, as when in difficulty: *to have recourse to someone.* **2.** a person or thing resorted to for help or protection. **3.** *Commerce* the right to resort to a person for pecuniary compensation. An endorsement **without recourse** is one by which a payee or holder of a negotiable instrument, by writing 'without recourse' with his or her name, merely transfers the instrument without assuming any liability upon it.

recover /rə'kʌvə/ *v.t.* **1.** to get again, or regain (something lost or taken away). **2.** to make up for or make good (loss, damage, etc., to oneself). **3.** to regain the strength, balance, etc., of (oneself). **4.** *Law* **a.** to get by judgement in a court of law: *to recover damages for a wrong.* **b.** to gain title to through legal process: *to recover land.* **5.** to regain from a bad state, practice, etc. –*v.i.* **6.** (oft. fol. by *from*) to regain health after sickness, etc.: *to recover from an accident.* **7.** to regain a former (and better) state or condition. **8.** to regain one's self-control, balance, etc. **−recoverable,** *adj.* **−recoverer,** *n.* **−recovery,** *n.*

recovered memory *n. Psychol.* a formerly repressed memory, as of a traumatic incident, which has been restored to the conscious mind, often through hypnosis or psychoanalysis.

recovery position *n.* a position used in first aid for a person who is unconscious but breathing, the patient being placed on their side and supported by one bent leg and their arms.

recovery strap *n.* → snatch strap.

recovery ward *n.* a hospital ward or area in which patients are monitored immediately after surgery, as they recover from the effects of anaesthesia; post-op. Also, **recovery.**

recreant /ˈrɛkriənt/ *adj.* **1.** cowardly or craven. **2.** unfaithful, disloyal, or false. **−n.** **3.** a coward or craven. **4.** an apostate; a traitor. **−recreance, recreancy,** *n.* **−recreantly,** *adv.*

recreation /rɛkriˈeɪʃən/ *n.* **1.** refreshment by means of some pastime, agreeable exercise, or the like. **2.** a pastime, diversion, exercise, or other resource affording relaxation and enjoyment. **3.** the act of recreating. **4.** the state of being recreated. **−adj.** **5.** of or relating to an area, room, etc., set aside for recreation. **−recreational,** *adj.*

recreational drug *n.* a drug taken, often illegally, for relaxation and enjoyment.

recriminate /rəˈkrɪmɪneɪt/ *v.i.* **1.** to bring a countercharge against an accuser. **−v.t.** **2.** to accuse in return. **−recrimination** /rəkrɪmɪˈneɪʃən/, *n.* **−recriminative, recriminatory,** *adj.* **−recriminator,** *n.*

recruit /rəˈkrut/ *n.* **1.** *Mil.* a newly enlisted member of the armed forces. **2.** a newly created member of any body or class. **−v.t.** **3.** to enlist (someone) for service in the armed forces. **−v.i.** **4.** to enlist someone for service in the armed forces. **−recruitable,** *adj.* **−recruiter,** *n.* **−recruitment,** *n.*

rectangle /ˈrɛktæŋgəl/ *n. Geom.* a parallelogram with all its angles right angles, especially one in which adjacent sides are equal. **−rectangular,** *adj.*

recti- a word element meaning 'straight', 'right'. Also, *(before vowels),* **rect-.**

rectify /ˈrɛktəfaɪ/ *v.t.* **(-fied, -fying) 1.** to make, put, or set right; remedy; correct. **2.** to put right by adjustment or calculation, as an instrument or a course at sea. **3.** *Chem.* to purify (especially a spirit or liquor) by repeated distillation. **4.** *Elect.* to change (an alternating current) into a direct current. **5.** *Maths* to determine the length of (a curve). **−rectifiable,** *adj.* **−rectification** /rɛktəfəˈkeɪʃən/, *n.*

rectilinear /rɛktəˈlɪniə/ *adj.* **1.** forming a straight line. **2.** formed by straight lines. **3.** characterised by straight lines. **4.** moving in a straight line. Also, **rectilineal.** **−rectilinearly,** *adv.*

rectitude /ˈrɛktətjud/ *n.* **1.** rightness of principle or practice: *the rectitude of one's motives.* **2.** correctness: *rectitude of judgement.*

rector /ˈrɛktə/ *n.* **1.** (in some Anglican churches) a member of the clergy who has the charge of a parish; vicar. **2.** the head of a Roman Catholic seminary or religious house. **3.** the head in some universities, colleges, and schools. **−rectorate,** *n.* **−rectorial** /rɛkˈtɔriəl/, *adj.*

rectory /ˈrɛktəri/ *n.* (pl. **-ries**) a rector's house; parsonage.

rectum /ˈrɛktəm/ *n.* (pl. **-tums** or **-ta** /tə/) *Anat.* the comparatively straight terminal section of the intestine, ending in the anus. **−rectal,** *adj.*

recumbent /rəˈkʌmbənt/ *adj.* **1.** lying down; reclining; leaning. **2.** inactive; idle. **3.** *Zool., Bot.* denoting a part that leans or reposes upon anything. **−n.** **4.** a recumbent

person, animal, plant, etc. **−recumbency,** *n.* **−recumbently,** *adv.*

recuperate /rəˈkupəreɪt/ *v.i.* **1.** to recover from sickness or exhaustion; regain health or strength. **2.** to recover from pecuniary loss. **−v.t.** **3.** to restore to health, vigour, etc. **−recuperation** /rəkupəˈreɪʃən/, *n.*

recur /rɪˈkɜ, rə-/ *v.i.* **(-curred, -curring) 1.** to occur again, as an event, experience, etc. **2.** to return to the mind: *recurring ideas.* **3.** to come up again for consideration, as a question. **4.** to return in action, thought, etc.: *to recur to a subject.* **5.** *Maths* to repeat a fixed set of one or more digits in a decimal. **−recurrence,** *n.* **−recurrent,** *adj.*

recurring decimal *n. Maths* a rational number containing a set of indefinitely recurring digits after the decimal point.

recursion /rəˈkɜʒən/ *n.* the operation of a rule or formula to determine a succession of terms, the rule being derived by analysis of the preceding terms.

recursive /rəˈkɜsɪv/ *adj.* **1.** of or relating to recursion. **2.** permitting or relating to an operation that may be repeated indefinitely, as a rule in generative grammar.

recusant /ˈrɛkjəzənt/ *adj.* **1.** refusing to submit, comply, etc. **2.** obstinate in refusal. **−recusancy,** *n.*

recycle /riˈsaɪkəl/ *v.t.* to treat (waste, empty bottles, tins, etc.) so that new products can be manufactured from them. **−recyclable,** *adj.*

red /rɛd/ *adj.* (**redder, reddest**) **1.** of a spectral hue beyond orange in the spectrum. **2.** distinguished by being red, wearing red, having red clothing, etc. **3.** (of wines) made from dark grapes and thus red-coloured from their skins (as opposed to *white*). **4.** (*oft. upper case*) ultraradical politically, especially communist. **−n.** **5.** any of the hues adjacent to orange in the spectrum, such as scarlet, vermilion, cherry. **6.** something red. **7.** red wine. **8.** (*oft. upper case*) an ultraradical in politics, especially a communist. **−phr.** **9. paint the town red,** *Colloq.* to indulge in riotous entertainment. **10. see red,** *Colloq.* to become angry or infuriated. **11. the red, a.** red ink as used in bookkeeping and accounting practice for recording losses and deficits in financial statements. **b.** loss or deficit: *in the red*; *out of the red.* **−redden,** *v.* **−reddish,** *adj.*

-red a noun suffix denoting condition, as in *hatred, kindred.*

red-back *n.* a small, highly venomous, Australian spider, *Latrodectus hasseltii,* glossy dark brown to black, usually with a red or orange streak on the body.

red-bellied black snake *n.* a venomous snake of eastern Australian forests and scrubs, *Pseudechis porphyriacus,* glossy black above and pale pink to red below, growing to two metres or more in length.

redbill /ˈrɛdbɪl/ *n.* any of various birds having a red bill, as the purple swamphen and the sooty oystercatcher.

red blood cell *n.* → erythrocyte.

red-blooded /ˈrɛd-blʌdəd/ *adj.* vigorous; virile. **−red-bloodedness,** *n.*

redbreast /ˈrɛdbrɛst/ *n.* the European robin, *Erithacus rubecula,* so called from the colour of the breast feathers.

red card *n.* **1.** *Sport* a red card shown by a referee to a player who has committed a serious infringement of the rules as an indication that the player is to leave the field for the remainder of the game. Compare **yellow card.** **−phr.** **2. give someone the red card,** to dismiss or reject someone, as from a job, a relationship, etc.

red carpet *n.* **1.** a red strip of carpet laid for important persons to walk on when entering or leaving a building, etc. **2.** highly favoured or deferential treatment.

red cedar *n.* **1.** a deciduous rainforest tree, *Toona ciliata,* native to New Guinea and eastern Australia, with easily worked red timber valued for cabinet work.

2. any of several coniferous trees, especially a juniper, *Juniperus virginiana*, with a fragrant reddish wood, and an arbor vitae, the Western red cedar, *Thuja plicata*, both of North America. **3.** the wood of these trees.

red-collared lorikeet   *n.* a brightly coloured, noisy, sociable lorikeet, *Trichoglossus rubritorquis*, of northern Australia, with a blue head and a scarlet collar; often considered a subspecies of the rainbow lorikeet; blue bonnet.

red curry   *n.* (in Thai cookery) a dish seasoned chiefly with red chilli powder and coconut milk.

Red Delicious   *n.* a sweet, red-skinned variety of eating apple, originally cultivated in the US.

red dwarf   *n. Astron.* a type of small, relatively cool, very faint star.

redeem   /rəˈdiːm/ *v.t.* **1.** to buy or pay off: *to redeem a debt.* **2.** to recover (something pledged or mortgaged) by payment, etc.: *to redeem a pawned watch.* **3.** to convert (bonds, etc.) into cash. **4. a.** to claim (an item) by presenting a coupon, voucher, etc. **b.** to claim (a prize) by presenting a winning ticket. **5.** to carry out (a pledge, promise, etc.). **6.** to make up for: *he redeemed his lie by later telling the truth.* **7.** to cause to be saved from dishonour: *He redeemed himself; a redeeming feature.* **8.** to obtain the release of, as from captivity, by paying a ransom. –**redeemable**, *adj.* –**redeemer**, *n.* –**redemption**, *n.*

redeploy   /ridəˈplɔɪ/ *v.t.* **1.** to rearrange, reorganise, or transfer (a person, department, military unit, or the like), as in order to promote greater efficiency. –*v.i.* **2.** to carry out a reorganisation or rearrangement. –**redeployment**, *n.*

redevelop   /ridəˈvɛləp/ *v.t.* **1.** to develop (something) again. **2.** *Photography* to intensify or tone by a second developing process. –*v.i.* **3.** to develop again. –**redeveloper**, *n.* –**redevelopment**, *n.*

red firefish   *n.* a graceful, brilliantly coloured scorpaenid fish, *Pterois volitans*, common in Great Barrier Reef waters; butterfly cod. Also, **red lionfish**.

red goshawk   *n.* a large endemic Australian hawk, *Erythrotriorchis radiatus*, brown tinged with cream with cream head, throat, and red-brown underparts, found throughout northern and eastern Australia, and feeding on other birds and small ground animals.

red-handed   *phr.* **catch red-handed,** to discover in the very act of a crime or other deed: *catch a thief red-handed.*

red herring   *n.* **1.** something to divert attention; a false clue. **2.** a smoked herring.

red lead   *n.* a heavy, earthy substance, Pb₃O₄, orange to red in colour, used as a paint pigment and in the manufacture of glass and glazes; minium.

red-letter day   *n.* a memorable or especially happy occasion: *a red-letter day for someone.*

red light   *n.* **1.** a red lamp, used as a signal to mean 'stop'. **2.** an order to stop. **3.** a warning signal. **4.** the symbol of a brothel.

red-light camera   *n.* a camera positioned at an intersection with traffic lights to photograph the numberplate of any motor vehicle that goes through a red light.

redolent   /ˈrɛdələnt/ *adj.* **1.** having a pleasant smell; fragrant. –*phr.* **2. redolent of, a.** smelling of. **b.** suggestive or reminiscent of: *stories redolent of mystery.* –**redolence**, *n.* –**redolently**, *adv.*

redouble   /riˈdʌbəl/ *v.t.* **1.** to double or increase greatly: *to redouble one's efforts.* **2.** to repeat: *to redouble an attack.* –*v.i.* **3.** to be doubled.

redoubtable   /rəˈdaʊtəbəl/ *adj.* **1.** that is to be feared; formidable. **2.** commanding respect. –**redoubtableness**, *n.* –**redoubtably**, *adv.*

redound   /rəˈdaʊnd/ *v.i.* **1.** to have an effect or result, as to the advantage, disadvantage, credit, or discredit of a person or thing. **2.** to come back or recoil, as upon a person.

red panda   *n.* a small forest-dwelling mammal of the Himalayas and eastern Asia, *Ailurus fulgens*, classified as the only living species of the genus *Ailurus*, having a deep reddish coat, long tail and feeding mainly on bamboo; lesser panda.

red-pencil   *v.t.* (**-cilled** *or, Chiefly US,* **-ciled, -cilling** *or, Chiefly US,* **-ciling**) to correct or edit (manuscript or typescript) with or as with a red pencil.

red pepper   *n.* **1.** the condiment cayenne. **2.** any of the hot peppers, *Capsicum frutescens* and botanical varieties, the yellow or red pods of which are used for flavouring, sauces, etc.

redress   /rəˈdrɛs/ *n.* **1.** the setting right of what is wrong. **2.** relief from wrong or injury. –*v.t.* **3.** to set right or correct (wrongs, injuries, etc.). **4.** to adjust evenly again, as a balance. –**redresser, redressor**, *n.*

red shift   *n. Astron.* a shift of spectral lines toward the red end of the visible spectrum in the light emitted by a receding celestial body; thought to be a consequence of the Doppler effect. Compare **blue shift**.

red soil   *n.* soil formed from iron-rich sedimentary rock, usually low in nutrients.

red tape   *n.* **1.** tape of a reddish colour, much used for tying up official papers. **2.** excessive attention to formality and routine. **3.** official procedures. –**red-tape**, *adj.*

red tide   *n.* the red bloom of marine algae which produces neurotoxins that kill fish and contaminate shellfish, and which is carried in on the tide.

reduce   /rəˈdjuːs/ *verb* (**-duced, -ducing**) –*v.t.* **1.** to bring down to a smaller size, amount, number, etc. **2.** to lower in degree, strength, etc.: *to reduce speed.* **3.** to bring down to a lower rank, standing, etc. **4.** to lower in price. **5.** to bring to a certain state, condition, etc.: *to reduce glass to powder.* **6.** to bring under control; subdue. **7.** *Photography* to treat so as to make less dense, as a negative. **8.** *Chem.* **a.** to remove oxygen from. **b.** to add hydrogen to. **c.** to lower the valency of the positively-charged element by the addition of electrons. **9.** *Chem., Metallurgy* to bring into the metallic state by separating from nonmetallic constituents; smelt. **10.** *Biol.* to cause (a cell) to undergo meiotic (cell) division. **11.** *Cookery* to simmer (a sauce) so as to decrease the volume of liquid and increase the intensity of the flavour. –*v.i.* **12.** to become reduced. –**reducer**, *n.* –**reducible**, *adj.* –**reducibility** /rədjusəˈbɪləti/, *n.* –**reducibly**, *adv.*

reduction   /rəˈdʌkʃən/ *n.* **1.** the act or result of reducing. **2.** the amount by which something is reduced. **3.** a copy on a smaller scale. **4.** → **meiosis**. **5.** *Chem.* the opposite of oxidation. **6.** *Cookery* a sauce obtained by reducing a liquid. –**reductional**, *adj.* –**reductive**, *adj.*

redundant   /rəˈdʌndənt/ *adj.* **1.** being in excess; exceeding what is usual or natural: *a redundant part.* **2.** characterised by or using too many words to express ideas: *a redundant style.* **3.** denoting or relating to an employee who is or becomes superfluous to the needs of the employer. **4.** having some unusual or extra part or feature. **5.** characterised by superfluity. –**redundancy, redundance**, *n.* –**redundantly**, *adv.*

red wine   *n.* a wine made from red or dark-coloured grapes, having a predominantly red colour derived from the grape skins being left in contact with the juice for a short time. Compare **white wine**.

redwood   /ˈrɛdwʊd/ *n.* **1.** a coniferous tree, *Sequoia sempervirens*, of the south-western US, especially California, remarkable for its height. **2.** its valuable brownish red timber.

reed   /riːd/ *n.* **1.** the straight stalk of any of various tall grasses, especially of the genera *Phragmites* and

Arundo, growing in marshy places. **2.** any of the plants themselves. **3.** *Music* **a.** a pastoral or rustic musical pipe made from a reed or from the hollow stalk of some other plant. **b.** a small flexible piece of cane or metal which, attached to the mouths of some wind instruments, is set into vibration by a stream of air and, in turn, sets into vibration the air column enclosed in the tube of the instrument. **c.** Also, **reed instrument**. any instrument with such a device, especially a wind instrument as the oboe, clarinet, etc. **4.** *Archit., Carpentry, etc.* a small convex moulding. **5.** (in a loom) the series of parallel strips of wires which force the weft up to the web and separate the threads of the warp. *–phr.* **6. a broken reed**, someone who is too weak to be relied upon.

reed organ *n.* a musical keyboard instrument resembling the pipe organ, but having the notes produced by small metal reeds.

reed-warbler *n.* **1.** → **clamorous reed-warbler. 2.** any of various birds of the genus *Acrocephalus*, family Acrocephalidae, inhabiting freshwater reedy areas.

reef[1] /riːf/ *n.* **1.** a narrow ridge of rocks or sand, often of coral debris, at or near the surface of water. **2.** *Mining* a lode or vein.

reef[2] /riːf/ *n.* **1.** a part of a sail which is rolled and tied down to reduce the area exposed to the wind. *–v.t.* **2.** *Naut.* to shorten (sail) by tying in one or more reefs.

reef[3] /riːf/ *phr.* **reef out**, *Aust. Colloq.* to remove, usually by force.

reefer[1] /ˈriːfə/ *n.* **1.** *Naut.* someone who reefs. **2.** → **reefer jacket.**

reefer[2] /ˈriːfə/ *n. Colloq.* a marijuana cigarette.

reefer jacket *n.* a double-breasted, blazer-style jacket of thick cloth. Also, **reefer.**

reef knot *n.* a kind of double knot, which does not slip, formed by tying a left-handed overhand knot followed by a right-handed overhand knot, or vice-versa; often used by sailors.

reek /riːk/ *n.* **1.** a strong, unpleasant smell. **2.** steam; vapour. *–v.i.* **3.** to smell strongly and unpleasantly: *that pipe reeks; he reeks of garlic.* **4.** to be strongly and unpleasantly suggestive of: *that letter reeks of insincerity.* **5.** to give off steam, smoke, etc. *–v.t.* **6.** to treat with smoke. **7.** to give off (smoke, fumes, etc.). **–reeker,** *n.* **–reeky,** *adj.*

reel[1] /riːl/ *n.* **1.** a cylinder, frame, or other device, turning on an axis, on which to wind something. **2.** a rotatory device attached to a fishing rod at the butt, for winding up or letting out the line. **3.** a small cylinder of wood or other material, now typically expanded at each end and having a hole lengthwise through the centre, on which thread is wound; spool. **4.** a quantity of something wound on a reel. **5. a.** the spool, usually metal, on which film is wound. **b.** a roll of celluloid bearing a series of photographs to be exhibited with a film projector. **c.** the standard length of cinema film for projection (about 300 metres). **6.** a rotatory spool of line used by surf-lifesavers. *–v.t.* **7.** to wind on a reel, as thread, yarn, etc. **8.** to draw with a reel, or by winding: *to reel in a fish. –phr.* **9. reel off,** to say, write, or produce in an easy, continuous way. **–reeler,** *n.*

reel[2] /riːl/ *v.i.* **1.** to sway or rock from a blow, dizziness, etc.; stagger. **2.** to fall back. **3.** to turn round and round; whirl; spin.

reel[3] /riːl/ *n.* **1.** a lively dance popular in Scotland. **2.** music for this.

reel-to-reel *n.* a tape recorder which uses reels of tape rather than cassettes or cartridges. *–adj.* **2.** of or relating to such a system of recording.

re-enact /riː-ənˈækt/ *v.t.* to act out again (a past event). **–re-enactment,** *n.*

re-engineer /riː-ɛndʒəˈnɪə/ *v.t.* **1.** to engineer anew: *to re-engineer a machine to achieve greater performance.* **2.** to reorganise entirely, as a business, to achieve greater efficiency or profits. **–re-engineering,** *n.*

re-entrant angle /riː-ˈɛntrənt ˌæŋgəl/ *n.* an angle directed back inwards, rather than extending outwards, as an exterior angle of less than 180° in a closed polygon.

re-entry /riː-ˈɛntri/ *n.* (*pl.* **-ries**) **1.** the act of re-entering. **2.** *Aeronautics* the return of a spacecraft, rocket, etc., into the earth's atmosphere. **3.** a surfing action in which the surfer heads up into, and comes over with, the breaking part of the wave.

reeve[1] /riːv/ *n.* **1.** *Hist.* an administrative officer of a town or district. **2.** *Hist.* someone of high rank representing the Crown. **3.** a bailiff, steward, or overseer.

reeve[2] /riːv/ *v.t.* (**reeved** *or* **rove, reeving**) **1.** to pass (a rope, etc.) through a hole, ring, or the like. **2.** to fasten by placing through or around something. **3.** to pass a rope through (a block, etc.).

refectory /rəˈfɛktri/ *n.* (*pl.* **-ries**) a dining hall in a religious house, a university, or other institution.

refer /rəˈfɜː/ *verb* (**-ferred, -ferring**) *–v.t.* **1.** to direct the attention or thoughts of. **2.** to direct for information or for anything needed. **3.** (of a medical practitioner) to direct (a patient) to another doctor, usually a specialist, for further consultation or treatment. **4.** to hand over for information, consideration, etc. *–v.i.* **5.** to direct attention. **6.** to direct anyone for information, especially about one's character, abilities, etc.: *to refer to a former employer.* **7.** to have relation; apply: *this decision refers back to a 1927 court case.* **8.** to turn, as for aid or information: *to refer to one's notes.* **9.** to direct a remark or mention. **–referable,** *adj.* **–referral,** *n.* **–referrer,** *n.*

referee /rɛfəˈriː/ *n.* **1.** a person to whom something is directed, especially for decision or settlement; arbitrator; umpire. **2.** Also, **reference**. someone prepared to testify as to the character, qualities, etc., of a person, especially a job applicant. *–verb* (**-reed, -reeing**) *–v.t.* **3.** to preside over as referee; act as referee in. *–v.i.* **4.** to act as referee.

reference /ˈrɛfrəns/ *n.* **1.** the act or fact of referring. **2.** direction of the attention: *marks of reference.* **3.** a directing of attention; allusion. **4.** a direction in a book or writing to some book, passage, etc.: *to look up a reference.* **5.** a note indicating this. **6.** direction or a direction to some source of information: *a library for public reference.* **7.** use or recourse for purposes of information: *a library for public reference.* **8.** a written or verbal testimonial given as to the character, abilities, etc., of a person, especially a job applicant. **9.** a person who supplies such a testimony; referee. **10.** relation, regard, or respect: *all persons, without reference to age. –phr.* **11. terms of reference,** the scope allowed to an investigating body. **12. with reference to,** concerning; with regard to. **–referential,** *adj.* **–referentially,** *adv.*

referendum /rɛfəˈrɛndəm/ *n.* (*pl.* **-dums** *or* **-da** /-də/) **1.** the principle or procedure of referring or submitting measures proposed or passed by a legislative body to the vote of the electorate for approval or rejection. **2.** an instance of this procedure.

referent /ˈrɛfərənt/ *n.* **1.** *Semantics, Rhetoric* **a.** the object to which a term of discourse refers. **b.** the object of thought, alternatively as viewed by the thinker or by a supposedly all-knowing mind. **2.** *Logic* any related term from which the relation proceeds. For example, in 'John loves Mary', *John* is the referent.

refine /rəˈfaɪn/ *v.t.* **1.** to bring to a fine or a pure state; free from impurities: *to refine metal; to refine sugar; to refine petroleum.* **2.** to purify from what is coarse, vulgar, or debasing; make elegant or cultured. **3.** to bring by purifying, as to a finer state or form. **4.** to make more fine, nice, subtle, or minutely precise. –*v.i.* **5.** to become pure. **6.** to become more fine, elegant, or polished. –*phr.* **7. refine on** (or **upon**), to improve on by superior fineness, excellence, etc. –**refiner**, *n.*

refined /rə'faɪnd/ *adj.* **1.** imbued with or showing nice feeling, taste, etc.: *refined people.* **2.** freed or free from coarseness, vulgarity, etc.: *refined taste.* **3.** freed from impurities: *refined sugar.* **4.** subtle: *refined distinctions.* **5.** minutely precise; exact.

refinery /rə'faɪnəri/ *n.* (*pl.* **-ries**) an establishment for refining something, as metal, sugar, petroleum, etc.

reflect /rə'flɛkt/ *v.t.* **1.** to throw back (light, heat, sound, etc.). **2.** to give back or show an image of; mirror. **3.** to reproduce; show: *followers reflecting the views of the leader.* **4.** to serve to cast or bring (honour, credit, etc.). –*v.i.* **5.** to be turned back, as light. **6.** to cast back light, heat, etc. **7.** to give back or show an image. **8.** to tend to bring disfavour or blame. **9.** to think; ponder; meditate. –**reflective**, *adj.* –**reflectiveness**, *n.*

reflective glass *n.* a highly-reflective coated glass used in buildings, which allows people inside the building to see out, but which gives a mirror effect to people looking in.

reflector /rə'flɛktə/ *n.* **1.** a body, surface, or device that reflects light, heat, sound, or the like. **2.** a reflecting telescope. **3.** *Physics* a layer of material surrounding the core of a nuclear reactor which reflects back into the core some of the neutrons which would otherwise escape. **4.** a piece of red glass or metal attached to the rear of a cycle or motor vehicle, or used to mark the edge of a road near road hazards.

reflex /'riflɛks/ *adj.* **1.** of or relating to an involuntary muscular or other bodily response. **2.** happening in reaction; responsive. **3.** cast back; reflected, as light, etc. **4.** bent or turned back. –*n.* **5.** *Psychol.* an immediate, often unconscious response to a stimulus, as blinking, perspiring, etc. **6.** a reflection or image of an object. **7.** a copy; adaptation. –**reflexion**, *n.*

reflex angle *n.* *Geom.* an angle greater than 180° but less than 360°.

reflexive /rə'flɛksɪv/ *adj. Gram.* **1.** (of a verb) having identical subject and object, as *shave* in *he shaved himself.* **2.** (of a pronoun) indicating identity of object with subject, as *himself* in the example above. –*n.* **3.** a reflexive verb or pronoun, as *himself* in *he deceived himself.* –**reflexively**, *adv.* –**reflexiveness**, **reflexivity** /riflɛk'sɪvəti/, *n.*

reflux /'riflʌks/ *n.* **1.** a flowing back; ebb. **2.** → **gastro-oesophageal reflux**.

reflux disease *n.* → **gastro-oesophageal reflux disease**. Also, **reflux oesophagitis**.

reform /rə'fɔm/ *n.* **1.** improvement or correction of what is wrong, evil, etc. **2.** an instance of this. **3.** improvement of behaviour, etc. –*v.t.* **4.** to bring back to a former and better state. **5.** to cause (a person) to give up wrong or evil ways of life. **6.** to put an end to (disorders, etc.). –*v.i.* **7.** to give up evil behaviour, etc. –**reformable**, *adj.* –**reformative**, *adj.* –**reformer**, *n.*

reformat /ˌri'fɔmæt/ *v.t.* (**-matted**, **-matting**) to give a new format to.

reformation /rɛfə'meɪʃən/ *n.* **1.** the act of reforming. **2.** the state of being reformed. **3.** (*upper case*) the religious movement in the 16th century which had for its object the reform of the Roman Catholic Church, and which led to the establishment of the Protestant Churches. –**reformational**, *adj.*

reformatory /rə'fɔmətri/, *Orig. US* /rə'fɔmətɔri/ *adj.* **1.** serving or designed to reform: *reformatory schools.* –*n.* (*pl.* **-ries**) Also, **reform school**. **2.** a penal institution for the reformation of young offenders.

refract /rə'frækt/ *v.t.* **1.** *Physics* to subject to refraction. **2.** *Optics* to determine the refractive condition of (an eye, a lens). –**refractor**, *n.*

refraction /rə'frækʃən/ *n.* **1.** *Physics* the change of direction of a ray of light, heat, or the like, in passing obliquely from one medium into another in which its speed is different. **2.** *Optics* **a.** the ability of the eye to refract light which enters it so as to form an image on the retina. **b.** the determining of the refractive condition of the eye. –**refractional**, **refractive**, *adj.*

refractory /rə'fræktəri/ *adj.* **1.** stubborn; unmanageable: *a refractory child.* **2.** resisting ordinary methods of treatment. **3.** difficult to fuse, reduce, or work, as an ore or metal. –*n.* (*pl.* **-ries**) **4.** a material having the ability to retain its physical shape and chemical identity when subjected to high temperatures. **5.** (*pl.*) bricks of various shapes used in lining furnaces. –**refractorily**, *adv.* –**refractoriness**, *n.*

refrain[1] /rə'freɪn/ *v.i.* (sometimes fol. by *from*) to forbear; keep oneself back. –**refrainer**, *n.*

refrain[2] /rə'freɪn/ *n.* **1.** a phrase or verse recurring at intervals in a song or poem, especially at the end of each stanza; chorus. **2.** a musical setting for the refrain of a poem.

refrangible /rə'frændʒəbəl/ *adj.* capable of being refracted, as rays of light. –**refrangibleness**, **refrangibility** /rəfrændʒə'bɪləti/, *n.*

refresh /rə'frɛʃ/ *v.t.* **1.** (*oft. reflexive*) to make fresh and strong again, as by rest, food, etc. **2.** to stimulate (the memory). **3.** to make fresh again. **4.** to take refreshment, especially food or drink. **5.** *Computers* to update the image on (a computer screen). –*v.i.* **6.** to become fresh or strong again; revive. **7.** *Computers* to initiate a re-supply of the image on a computer screen with new data: *this site refreshes every two minutes.* –**refreshing**, *adj.*

refreshment /rə'frɛʃmənt/ *n.* **1.** something that refreshes, especially food or drink. **2.** (*pl.*) articles or portions of food or drink, especially for a light meal. **3.** the act of refreshing. **4.** the state of being refreshed.

refrigerant /rə'frɪdʒərənt/ *adj.* **1.** refrigerating; cooling. **2.** reducing bodily heat or fever. –*n.* **3.** a refrigerant agent, as in a drug. **4.** a liquid capable of vaporising at a low temperature, as ammonia, used in mechanical refrigeration. **5.** a cooling substance, as ice, solid carbon dioxide, ammonia, hydrofluorocarbon, hydrochlorofluorocarbon, etc., used in a refrigerator.

refrigerate /rə'frɪdʒəreɪt/ *v.t.* **1.** to make or keep cold or cool. **2.** to freeze (food, etc.) for preservation. –**refrigeration**, *n.* –**refrigerative**, **refrigeratory**, *adj.*

refrigerator /rə'frɪdʒəreɪtə/ *n.* **1.** a cabinet, compartment or room in which food, drink, etc., is kept cool, now usually by means of mechanical refrigeration. **2.** the element of a refrigerating system consisting of the space or medium to be cooled. Also, *Colloq.*, **fridge**.

refuel /ri'fjuəl/ *verb* (**-fuelled** *or*, *US*, **-fueled**, **-fuelling** *or*, *US*, **-fueling**) –*v.t.* **1.** to supply again with fuel: *to refuel an aeroplane.* –*v.i.* **2.** to take on a fresh supply of fuel: *they refuelled at Perth and flew on.* –**refueller**, *n.*

refuge /'rɛfjudʒ/ *n.* **1.** shelter or protection from danger, trouble, etc.: *to take refuge from a storm.* **2.** a place of shelter, protection, or safety. **3.** anything to which one has recourse for aid, relief, or escape. **4.** a platform in the centre of a street for the use of pedestrians in crossing.

refugee /rɛfju'dʒi/ *n.* someone who flees for refuge or safety, especially to a foreign country, as in time of political upheaval, war, etc.

refund *v.t.* /rə'fʌnd/, 'rifʌnd/ **1.** to give back or restore (especially money); repay. **2.** to make repayment to; reimburse. –*v.i.* /rə'fʌnd/, 'rifʌnd/ **3.** to make repayment. –*n.* /'rifʌnd/ **4.** a repayment. –**refundable**, *adj.*

refurbish /ri'fɜːbɪʃ/ *v.t.* to renovate; polish up again; brighten.

refusal /rə'fjuːzəl/ *n.* **1.** the act of refusing. **2.** priority in refusing or taking something; option.

refuse[1] /rə'fjuːz/ *v.t.* **1.** to decline to accept (something offered). **2.** to decline to give. **3.** to express a determination not (to do something). *–v.i.* **4.** to decline acceptance. **–refuser,** *n.*

refuse[2] /'rɛfjuːs/ *n.* **1.** that which is discarded as worthless or useless; rubbish. *–adj.* **2.** rejected as worthless; discarded: *refuse matter.*

refute /rə'fjuːt/ *v.t.* **1.** to prove to be false or erroneous, as an opinion, charge, etc. **2.** to prove (a person) to be in error. **3.** to deny: *to refute the allegations.* **–refutation, refutal,** *n.* **–refutable** /'rɛfjətəbəl, rə'fjuːtəbəl/, *adj.* **–refutably,** *adv.* **–refuter,** *n.*

regal /'riːgəl/ *adj.* **1.** of or relating to a king or queen; royal: *the regal power.* **2.** befitting or resembling a king or queen. **3.** stately; splendid. **4.** tall, dignified, and elegant. **–regally,** *adv.* **–regality,** *n.*

regale /rə'geɪl/ *v.t.* **1.** to entertain agreeably; delight. **2.** to entertain with choice food or drink. *–v.i.* **3.** to feast. **–regalement,** *n.*

regalia /rə'geɪljə/ *pl. n.* **1.** the rights and privileges of a king or queen. **2.** the ensigns or emblems of royalty, as the crown, sceptre, etc. **3.** the decorations or insignia of any office or order.

regard /rə'gad/ *v.t.* **1.** to look upon or think of with a particular feeling, opinion, etc.: *to regard a person with favour; to regard a price as excessive.* **2.** to have or show respect or concern for. **3.** to think highly of. **4.** to take into account; consider. **5.** to look at; observe. **6.** to relate to; concern. *–n.* **7.** reference; relation: *in regard to facts.* **8.** a point or particular: *quite satisfactory in this regard.* **9.** thought; attention; concern. **10.** look; gaze. **11.** respect; deference: *due regard to authority.* **12.** kindly feeling; liking. **13.** (*pl.*) sentiments of esteem or affection: *give them my regards. –phr.* **14. as regards,** in relation to. **15. in** (or **with**) **regard to,** concerning.

regarding /rə'gadɪŋ/ *prep.* with regard to; respecting; concerning: *he knew nothing regarding the lost watch.*

regardless /rə'gadləs/ *adj.* **1.** without regard to expense, danger, etc. *–adv.* **2.** anyway: *to carry on regardless. –phr.* **3. regardless of, a.** paying no attention to: *regardless of interruption she continued.* **b.** without consideration of: *this applies regardless of status.* **–regardlessly,** *adv.* **–regardlessness,** *n.*

regatta /rə'gætə/ *n.* **1.** a boat race, as of rowing boats, yachts, or other vessels. **2.** an organised series of such races.

regenerate *v.t.* /rə'dʒɛnəreɪt/ **1.** to bring about a change for the better in a person's character. **2.** to make over, especially in a better form or condition. **3.** to bring into existence again. *–v.i.* /rə'dʒɛnəreɪt/ **4.** to come into existence or be formed again. **5.** to become as though a new and better person. *–adj.* /rə'dʒɛnərət/ **6.** remade in a better form. **7.** changed for a better character. **–regeneration,** *n.* **–regenerative,** *adj.*

regent /'riːdʒənt/ *n.* **1.** someone who exercises the ruling power in a kingdom during the minority, absence, or disability of the sovereign. **2.** a ruler or governor. *–adj.* **3.** acting as regent of a country. **–regency,** *adj.,* *n.* **–regentship,** *n.*

reggae /'rɛgeɪ/ *n.* music of the Rastafarians of Jamaica which, in the 1970s, developed into a highly stylised and influential pop music idiom with international appeal.

regicide /'rɛdʒəsaɪd/ *n.* **1.** someone who kills a king; someone responsible for the death of a king. **2.** the killing of a king. **–regicidal** /rɛdʒə'saɪdl/, *adj.*

regift /ri'gɪft/ *v.t.* to present (something which one has received as a gift) to another person as a gift from oneself. **–regifting,** *n.* **–regifter,** *n.*

regime /reɪ'ʒim/ *n.* **1.** a mode or system of rule or government. **2.** a ruling or prevailing system. **3.** → **regimen. 4.** the seasonal pattern of a climate. Also, **régime.**

regime change *n.* the overthrow of a regime deemed by world leaders to have transgressed to such a degree that it is no longer possible to countenance it.

regimen /'rɛdʒəmən/ *n.* **1.** *Med.* a regulated course of diet, exercise, or manner of living, intended to preserve or restore health or to attain some result. **2.** rule or government. **3.** a particular form or system of government. **4.** a prevailing system.

regiment *n.* /'rɛdʒəmənt/ **1.** *Mil.* a unit of ground forces, commanded by a lieutenant colonel, consisting of two or more battalions, a headquarters unit, and certain supporting units. *–v.t.* /'rɛdʒəmɛnt/ **2.** to form into a regiment or regiments. **3.** to assign to a regiment or group. **4.** to form into an organised body or group; organise or systematise. **5.** to group together and treat in a uniform manner; subject to strict discipline. **–regimentation** /rɛdʒəmən'teɪʃən/, *n.* **–regimental,** *adj.*

region /'riːdʒən/ *n.* **1.** any more or less continuous part of a surface or space. **2.** a part of the earth's surface (land or sea) of considerable and usually indefinite extent: *tropical regions.* **3.** one of the divisions into which a territory or country, as Italy, is divided for governing, etc. **–regional,** *adj.*

register /'rɛdʒəstə/ *n.* **1.** a book in which records of acts, happenings, names are made. **2.** any list of such recordings. **3.** a recording in such a book or list. **4.** a mechanical device by which certain information is automatically recorded, as a cash register. **5.** *Music* **a.** the range of a voice or an instrument. **b.** (in an organ) a stop. **6.** *Printing, etc.* exact correspondence, as of lines, columns, etc., especially on the two sides of a leaf. *–v.t.* **7.** to enter or have entered formally in a register. **8.** to have a car, etc., which has been judged safe for the road and on which the necessary tax has been paid, entered in the register of motor vehicles kept by a public authority. **9.** to record or have recorded the posting of (a letter, parcel, etc.) at the post office on payment of a special fee. **10.** (of a scale, etc.) to indicate or show. **11.** to show (surprise, joy, anger, etc.), usually by facial expression or by actions. *–v.i.* **12.** to enter one's name in an electoral or other register; enrol. **13.** (of surprise, joy, etc.) to be obvious or to show. **–registerer, registrant,** *n.* **–registrable,** *adj.* **–registration,** *n.*

registered /'rɛdʒəstəd/ *adj.* **1.** recorded, as in a register or book; enrolled. **2.** *Commerce* officially listing the owner's name with the issuing company and suitably inscribing the certificate, as with bonds to evidence title. **3.** officially or legally certified by a government officer or board: *a registered patent.* **4.** (of cattle, horses, dogs, etc.) having pedigrees verified and filed by authorised associations of breeders.

registered nurse *n.* a nurse who holds a degree in nursing from a university, or who qualified under the former system of intensive hospital training. *Abbrev.:* RN Compare **enrolled nurse.**

register tonnage *n. Naut.* a measure of volume of earning space on a ship, consisting of the gross tonnage less the volume of the master's cabin, crew accommodation, wheelhouse, galley, etc., measured in gross tons.

registrar /'rɛdʒəstrɑ/ *n.* **1.** someone who keeps a record; an official recorder. **2.** the chief administrative official in a university. **3.** *Med.* a doctor in a hospital next below a consultant, who is training to be a specialist.

4. *Law* an official in a court, subordinate to a judge, who deals with interlocutory matters, but who may also hear certain cases.

registry /ˈrɛdʒəstri/ *n.* (*pl.* **-ries**) **1.** the act of registering; registration. **2.** a place where a register is kept; an office of registration. **3.** a list compiled as a register, as a bridal registry, birthday registry, etc.

registry office *n.* an office where births, marriages, and deaths are recorded, and civil marriages take place.

regnant /ˈrɛɡnənt/ *adj.* **1.** reigning; ruling: *a queen regnant.* **2.** exercising sway or influence; predominant. **3.** prevalent; widespread. **–regnancy,** *n.*

regress *v.i.* /riˈɡrɛs/ **1.** to move in a backward direction; go back. *–n.* /ˈriɡrɛs/ **2.** the act of going back; return. **3.** backward movement or course; retrogression. **–regression,** *n.* **–regressive,** *adj.*

regret /rəˈɡrɛt/ *v.t.* (**-gretted, -gretting**) **1.** to feel sorry about (anything disappointing, unpleasant, etc.). **2.** to think of with a sense of loss: *they regret their vanished youth. –n.* **3.** a sense of loss, disappointment, dissatisfaction, etc. **4.** a feeling of being sorry for some fault, act, etc., of one's own. **5.** (*pl.*) feelings of sorrow over what is lost, gone, done, etc. **6.** (*pl. or sing.*) a polite and formal expression of regretful feelings. **–regrettable,** *adj.* **–regrettably,** *adv.* **–regretter,** *n.*

regroup /riˈɡruːp/ *v.t.* **1.** to reorganise (forces, etc.), especially after an attack or battle. **2.** to put back into order (people, plans, etc.) after any kind of setback or disruption. *–v.i.* **3.** (of forces, etc.) to return to order after an attack or setback. **4.** (of a person) to get one's emotions, personal resources, etc., back into order after a setback: *she needed time to regroup after the marriage breakdown.*

regrowth /ˈriɡroʊθ/ *n.* **1.** a growing again: *this forest is undergoing regrowth.* **2.** new hair growth, especially that which contrasts in colour with previously dyed hair.

regrowth forest *n.* a forest the timbers of which have been harvested and which is in the process of growing again.

regular /ˈrɛɡjələ/ *adj.* **1.** usual; normal; customary: *put it in its regular place.* **2.** conforming in form or arrangement; symmetrical: *regular teeth.* **3.** even; steady: *regular breathing.* **4.** happening at fixed times; periodic: *regular meals.* **5.** following a rule or procedure: *be regular in your diet.* **6.** observing fixed times or habits: *a regular customer.* **7.** orderly; well-ordered: *a regular life.* **8.** properly fitted for an occupation. **9.** normal, adequate, acceptable, or average: *regular size; regular petrol.* **10.** *Colloq.* complete; thorough: *a regular thief.* **11.** *Gram.* following the most usual pattern of formation, construction, etc. **12.** *Geom.* having all its angles and sides equal: *a regular polygon.* **13.** *Mil.* indicating or belonging to the permanently organised or standing army of a state. *–n.* **14.** a soldier in a regular army. **15.** *Colloq.* a regular customer, player, guest, etc. **–regularly,** *adv.* **–regularity** /rɛɡjəˈlærəti/, *n.*

regular expression *n.* *Computers* a formula that describes sets of characters that conform to a certain order or pattern, such as [A–Z] which might stand for any upper-case letter.

regulate /ˈrɛɡjəleɪt/ *v.t.* **1.** to control or direct by rule, principle, method, etc. **2.** to adjust to some standard or requirement, as amount, degree, etc.: *to regulate the temperature.* **3.** to adjust so as to ensure accuracy of operation: *to regulate a watch.* **4.** to put in good order: *to regulate the digestion.* **–regulative, regulatory,** *adj.* **–regulator,** *n.*

regulation /rɛɡjəˈleɪʃən/ *n.* **1.** a rule or order, as for conduct, prescribed by authority; a governing direction or law. **2.** the act of regulating. **3.** the state of being regulated. *–adj.* **4.** according to or prescribed by regulation: *regulation shoes had to be worn.*

regurgitate /rəˈɡɜːdʒəteɪt/ *v.i.* **1.** to surge or rush back, as liquids, gases, undigested food, etc. *–v.t.* **2.** to cause to surge or rush back. **3.** to bring back (food), digested or partially digested, into the mouth, as of some birds when feeding their young. **4.** to repeat (information) without thought or independent analysis. **–regurgitant,** *n., adj.*

rehabilitate /rihəˈbɪləteɪt/ *v.t.* **1.** to restore to a good condition, especially in a medical sense, of persons; regenerate, or alter to an improved form. **2.** to train for the resumption of normal activities, as a person disabled by an accident or disease. **3.** to restore (an addicted person) to a life free of drugs or alcohol. **4.** to re-establish in good repute or accepted respectability, as a person or the character, name, etc., after disrepute. **5.** to restore formally to a former capacity or standing, or to rank, rights, or privileges lost or forfeited. **–rehabilitation,** *n.*

rehash *v.t.* /riˈhæʃ/ **1.** to work up (old material) in a new form. *–n.* /ˈrihæʃ/ **2.** the act of rehashing. **3.** something rehashed.

rehearse /rəˈhɜːs/ *v.t.* **1.** to perform (a play, part, piece of music, etc.) in private by way of practice, before a public performance. **2.** to drill or train (a person, etc.) by rehearsal, as for some performance or part. **3.** to relate the facts or particulars of; enumerate. *–v.i.* **4.** to rehearse a play, part, etc. **–rehearsal,** *n.* **–rehearser,** *n.*

rehydrate /riˈhaɪdreɪt/ *v.t.* **1.** to replenish the fluid in (dehydrated plants). **2.** to replenish the bodily fluids of. **3.** to reconstitute (dried food, etc.) by the addition of water. *–v.i.* **4.** to replenish one's bodily fluids, as by drinking.

reign /reɪn/ *n.* **1.** the period or term of ruling, as of a king or queen. **2.** royal rule or sway. **3.** controlling power or influence: *the reign of law. –v.i.* **4.** to possess or exercise sovereign power or authority. **5.** to have first place; predominate: *disorder reigned in the stricken country.*

reiki /ˈreɪki/ *n.* the treatment of illness, injury, stress, etc., by the supposed release of unpolarised energy through the hands of a trained practitioner.

reimburse /riɪmˈbɜːs/ *v.t.* **1.** to make repayment to for expense or loss incurred. **2.** to pay back; refund; repay. **–reimbursement,** *n.*

rein /reɪn/ *n.* **1.** a long, narrow strap or thong, fastened to the bridle or bit, by which a rider or driver restrains and guides a horse or other animal. **2.** any of certain other straps or thongs forming part of a harness, as a bearing rein. **3.** any means of curbing, controlling, or directing; a check; restraint. **4.** (*pl.*) the controlling influence or power. *–v.t.* **5.** to furnish with a rein or reins, as a horse. **6.** to curb; restrain; control. *–phr.* **7. free** (or **full**) **rein**, complete licence or scope. **8. rein in,** to restrict or restrain. **9. rein in** (or **back**), **a.** to check or guide (a horse, etc.) by pulling at the reins. **b.** to restrain a horse or pull it up.

reincarnation /ˌriɪnkaˈneɪʃən/ *n.* **1.** the belief that the soul, upon death of the body, moves to another body or form. **2.** rebirth of the soul in a new body. **3.** a new incarnation or embodiment, as of a person. **–reincarnationist,** *n.*

reindeer /ˈreɪndɪə/ *n.* (*pl.* **-deer** *or* **-deers**) a large deer of the genus *Rangifer* with branched antlers in both males and females, found in northern or arctic regions, and often domesticated. See **caribou.**

reinforce /riɪnˈfɔːs/ *v.t.* (**-forced, -forcing**) **1.** to strengthen with some added piece, support, or material: *to reinforce a wall.* **2.** to strengthen with additional troops or ships for military or naval purposes: *to reinforce a garrison.* **3.** to strengthen; make more forcible or effective: *to reinforce efforts.* **4.** to augment; increase: *to reinforce a supply.*

reinforcement /riːnˈfɔːsmənt/ *n.* **1.** something that reinforces or strengthens. **2.** (*oft. pl.*) an additional supply of people, ships, etc., for a military or naval force. **3.** *Psychol.* anything which increases the possibility of a particular response being made to a situation. **4.** (in popular use) any reward which encourages learning.

reinstate /riːmˈsteɪt/ *v.t.* to put back or establish again, as in a former position or state. –**reinstatement**, *n.*

reinvent /riːmˈvɛnt/ *v.t.* **1.** to produce (a device, solution, etc.), believing it to be original, when it has in fact been invented before. –*phr.* **2. reinvent oneself,** to create a new character, appearance, role, etc.; for oneself: *when she turned thirty she reinvented herself as an intellectual.* **3. reinvent the wheel,** to attempt to work out again a method, solution, procedure, etc., which is already known and widely adopted.

reissue /riˈɪʃʊ, riˈɪsju/ *v.t.* **1.** to issue again, especially in a different form, at a different price, etc. –*n.* **2.** something that is reissued.

reiterate /riˈɪtəreɪt/ *v.t.* to repeat; say or do again or repeatedly. –**reiteration** /riˌɪtəˈreɪʃən/, *n.* –**reiterative**, *adj.* –**reiterant**, *adj.*

reject *v.t.* /rəˈdʒɛkt/ **1.** to refuse to accept, recognise, grant, etc.: *to reject a person; to reject a demand; to reject an offer.* **2.** to throw away or refuse as useless or unsatisfactory. –*n.* /ˈriːdʒɛkt/ **3.** something rejected, such as an imperfect article. **4.** *Colloq.* (*derog.*) a person despised by a particular group. –**rejecter**, *n.*

rejoice /rəˈdʒɔɪs/ *verb* (**-joiced, -joicing**) –*v.i.* **1.** to be glad; take delight (*in*). –*v.t.* **2.** to make joyful; gladden. –**rejoicer**, *n.*

rejoin[1] /rəˈdʒɔɪn/ *v.t.* **1.** to come again into the company of: *to rejoin a party after a brief absence.* **2.** to join together again; reunite. –*v.i.* **3.** to become joined together again.

rejoin[2] /rəˈdʒɔɪn/ *v.t.* **1.** to say in answer. –*v.i.* **2.** to answer. **3.** *Law* to answer the plaintiff's replication.

rejoinder /rəˈdʒɔɪndə/ *n.* **1.** an answer to a reply; response. **2.** *Law* the defendant's answer to the plaintiff's replication. Compare **replication.**

rejuvenate /rəˈdʒuːvəneɪt/ *v.t.* **1.** to make young again; restore to youthful vigour, appearance, etc. **2.** *Physical Geog.* to renew the activity, erosive power, etc., of (a stream) by the uplifting of the region it drains, or by removal of a barrier in the bed of the stream. –**rejuvenation** /rədʒuːvəˈneɪʃən/, *n.* –**rejuvenator**, *n.*

-rel a noun suffix having a diminutive or pejorative force, as in *wastrel.*

relapse *v.i.* /rəˈlæps/ (**-lapsed, -lapsing**) **1.** to fall or slip back into a former state, practice, etc.: *to relapse into silence.* **2.** to fall back into illness after convalescence or apparent recovery. **3.** to fall back into wrongdoing or error; backslide. –*n.* /rəˈlæps, ˈrilæps/ **4.** the act of relapsing. **5.** a return of a disease or illness after partial recovery. –**relapser**, *n.*

relate /rəˈleɪt/ *v.t.* **1.** to tell. **2.** to bring into or establish association, connection, or relation. –*v.i.* **3.** to have reference (*to*). **4.** to have some relation (*to*). –*phr.* **5. relate to,** to understand and often identify with: *to relate to a character in a film.* –**relatable**, *adj.* –**relater**, *n.*

related /rəˈleɪtɪd/ *adj.* **1.** associated; connected. **2.** allied by nature, origin, kinship, marriage, etc. **3.** narrated. **4.** (in diatonic music) of notes belonging to keys which have several notes in common.

relation /rəˈleɪʃən/ *n.* **1.** a connection; particular way of being related: *the relation between cause and effect.* **2.** (*pl.*) the various connections between peoples, countries, etc.: *commercial relations; foreign relations.* **3.** the kind of connection between one person and

another or others: *the relation between husband and wife.* **4.** a relative (def. 1). **5.** reference; regard: *to plan with relation to the future.* **6.** the act of relating or telling; narration: *his relation of the story.* **7.** something which is related or told; narrative. –**relational**, *adj.*

relational database *n.* a computer database in which the data is so arranged that it can be accessed at several different points or by combining a number of different criteria for searching, thus allowing for greater flexibility in retrieving and manipulating the data.

relationship /rəˈleɪʃənʃɪp/ *n.* **1.** connection; a particular connection. **2.** connection by blood or marriage. **3.** an emotional connection between people, sometimes involving sexual relations.

relative /ˈrɛlətɪv/ *n.* **1.** someone who is connected with another or others by blood or marriage. **2.** something having, or standing in, some relation to something else; especially, in scientific usage (as opposed to *absolute*). **3.** *Gram.* a relative pronoun. –*adj.* **4.** considered in relation to something else; comparative: *the relative merits of a republic and a monarchy.* **5.** existing only by relation to something else; not absolute or independent. **6.** having relation or connection: *relative phenomena.* **7.** (of a term, name, etc.) depending for significance upon something else: *better is a relative term.* **8.** *Gram.* **a.** designating words which introduce subordinate clauses and refer to some element of the principal clause (the antecedent), as *who* in 'he's the man who saw you'. **b.** (of a clause) introduced by such a word. –*phr.* **9. relative to, a.** having reference or regard to: *numbers will rise relative to other factors.* **b.** relevant or pertinent to: *matters not relative to your case.* **c.** correspondent; proportionate: *value is relative to demand.* –**relatively**, *adv.* –**relativeness**, *n.*

relative atomic mass *n. Physics* the average mass of the atoms of an element in its naturally occurring state, relative to the mass of an atom of the carbon-12 isotope taken as exactly 12. Compare **atomic mass.** Also, **atomic weight.**

relative frequency *n. Statistics* the number of items of a certain type divided by the number of all the items considered.

relative pronoun *n. Gram.* a pronoun with a relative function. See **relative** (def. 8a).

relativity /rɛləˈtɪvəti/ *n.* **1.** the state or fact of being relative. **2. a. special theory of relativity,** the theory formed by Albert Einstein, 1879–1955, German-born physicist in the US, of how the observed motion of objects changes from one frame of reference to another moving at constant velocity relative to it, based on the hypothesis that the observed velocity of light remains the same in all such frames of reference. **b. general theory of relativity,** Einstein's geometrical theory of gravitation based on the principle of equivalence. **3.** (*pl.*) the relative differences in wages between groups of workers.

relax /rəˈlæks/ *v.t.* **1.** to make less tense, rigid, or firm: *to relax the muscles.* **2.** to make less strict or severe: *to relax discipline.* –*v.i.* **3.** to become less tense, rigid, or firm. **4.** to become less strict or severe. **5.** to stop mental or bodily effort, etc.; take relaxation. –**relaxation**, *n.* –**relaxer**, *n.*

relay *n.* /ˈriːleɪ/ **1.** a set of people or animals relieving others or taking turns; a shift: *to work in relays.* **2.** Also, **relay race.** race between two or more teams, each member running, swimming, etc., one of the lengths of the distance. **3.** *Elect.* **a.** a device by means of which a change of current or voltage in one circuit can be made to produce a change in the electrical condition of another circuit. **b.** a device that is able, by a variation in the conditions of one electric circuit, to effect the operation of other devices in the same or another electric circuit. *–v.t.* /rə'leɪ, 'riːleɪ/ **4.** to carry forward by or as by relays: *to relay a message.*

release /rə'liːs/ *v.t.* **1.** to free from imprisonment, responsibility, pain, etc.; set free. **2.** to allow to be made public: *to release a news story.* **3.** *Law* to give up or relinquish (a right, claim, etc.). *–n.* **4.** the act of releasing. **5.** an instrument for releasing. **6.** a statement, news story, etc., released to the public. **7.** *Mechanics* a device for starting or stopping a machine, especially by removing some restrictive apparatus.

relegate /'rɛləgeɪt/ *v.t.* **1.** to send or consign to some obscure position, place, or condition. **2.** to consign or commit (a matter, task, etc.), as to a person. **3.** to assign or refer (something) to a particular class or kind. **4.** to send into exile; banish. **5.** *Sport* to transfer (the lowest scoring team) to a lower division, as a team in a football league. **–relegation** /rɛlə'geɪʃən/, *n.*

relent /rə'lɛnt/ *v.i.* to soften in feeling, temper, or determination; become more mild, compassionate, or forgiving.

relentless /rə'lɛntləs/ *adj.* that does not relent; unrelenting: *a relentless enemy.* **–relentlessly,** *adv.* **–relentlessness,** *n.*

relevant /'rɛləvənt/ *adj.* bearing upon or connected with the matter in hand; to the purpose; pertinent: *a relevant remark.* **–relevance, relevancy,** *n.* **–relevantly,** *adv.*

reliable /rə'laɪəbəl/ *adj.* able to be relied on; trustworthy: *reliable sources of information.* **–reliability** /rəlaɪə'bɪləti/, **reliableness,** *n.* **–reliably,** *adv.*

reliant /rə'laɪənt/ *adj.* **1.** having or showing dependence or trust. **2.** confident; trustful. **–reliance,** *n.*

relic /'rɛlɪk/ *n.* **1.** an object surviving from the past and having interest because of this: *historical relics.* **2.** a surviving trace of something: *a custom which is a relic of paganism.* **3.** (*pl.*) remaining parts or fragments. **4.** *Eccles.* (especially in Roman Catholic and Orthodox churches) the body, a part of the body of, or other things related to, a saint or holy person, kept as worthy of reverence.

relict /'rɛlɪkt/ *n.* **1.** *Ecol.* a plant or animal species living in an environment which has changed from that which is typical for it. **2.** a survivor. **3.** (*pl.*) remains; remnants; residue.

relief /rə'liːf/ *n.* **1.** (sometimes fol. by *from*) deliverance, alleviation, or ease through the removal of pain, distress, oppression, etc. **2.** a means of relieving, or a thing that relieves pain, distress, anxiety, etc. **3.** help or assistance given, as to those in poverty or need. **4.** something affording a pleasing change, as from monotony. **5.** release from a post of duty, as by the coming of a substitute or replacement. **6.** the person or persons thus bringing release. **7.** the deliverance of a besieged town, etc., from an attacking force. **8.** prominence, distinctness, or vividness due to contrast. **9.** the projection of a figure or part from the ground or plane on which it is formed, in sculpture or similar work. **10.** a piece or work in such projection: *high relief.* **11.** an apparent projection of parts in a painting, drawing, etc., giving the appearance of the third dimension. **12.** *Physical Geog.* the departure of the land surface in any area from that of a level surface. **13.** *Engraving* any printing process by which the printing ink is transferred to paper, etc., from areas that are higher than the rest of the block, as letterpress printing. **14.** a receipt of some state or charitable financial assistance. *–phr.* **15. on relief,** in the situation of being a relief worker.

relief map *n.* a map showing the relief of an area, usually by generalised contour lines.

relieve /rə'liːv/ *v.t.* **1.** to ease or alleviate (pain, distress, anxiety, need, etc.). **2.** to free from anxiety, fear, pain, etc. **3.** to deliver from poverty, need, etc. **4.** to bring efficient aid to (a besieged town, etc.). **5.** to ease (a person) of any burden, wrong, or oppression, as by legal means. **6.** to make less tedious, unpleasant, or monotonous; break or vary the sameness of. **7.** to bring into relief or prominence; heighten the effect of. **8.** to release (one on duty) by coming as or providing a substitute. *–phr.* **9. relieve oneself,** to empty the bowels or bladder. **–relievable,** *adj.* **–reliever,** *n.*

religion /rə'lɪdʒən/ *n.* **1.** a belief in a supreme supernatural power or powers thought to control the universe and all living things. **2.** a particular formalised system in which this belief is embodied: *the Christian religion.* **3.** recognition on the part of human beings of a controlling superhuman power entitled to obedience, reverence, and worship. **4.** the feeling or the spiritual attitude of those recognising such a controlling power. **5.** a point or matter of conscience, especially when zealously or obsessively observed: *to make a religion of doing something.*

religious /rə'lɪdʒəs/ *adj.* **1.** of or relating to religion. **2.** believing in religion; pious; devout. **3.** very conscientious: *to do something with religious care.* *–n.* **4.** a member of a religious order, etc.; monk, friar, or nun. **–religiously,** *adv.* **–religiousness,** *n.*

religious cleansing *n.* the removal by force from the population of all those who are not of a particular religion.

relinquish /rə'lɪŋkwɪʃ/ *v.t.* **1.** to renounce or surrender (a possession, right, etc.). **2.** to give up; put aside or desist from: *to relinquish a plan.* **3.** to let go: *to relinquish one's hold.* **–relinquisher,** *n.* **–relinquishment,** *n.*

relish /'rɛlɪʃ/ *n.* **1.** liking for or enjoyment of something, especially something eaten. **2.** something tasty added to a meal, such as a sauce. **3.** a pleasing taste or flavour. *–v.t.* **4.** to take pleasure in; enjoy. **5.** to like the taste or flavour of. **–relishable,** *adj.*

relive /ˌriː'lɪv/ *v.t.* to repeat (former experiences) or rehearse the memory of them.

reload /riː'loʊd/ *v.t.* **1.** to load (a vehicle, weapon, machine, etc.) again. **2.** *Computers* to load (a database) onto a computer.

reluctant /rə'lʌktənt/ *adj.* unwilling; disinclined. **–reluctance,** *n.* **–reluctantly,** *adv.*

rely /rə'laɪ/ *phr.* **(-lied, -lying) rely on** (or **upon**), to depend confidently on; put trust in.

remain /rə'meɪn/ *v.i.* **1.** to continue in the same condition or place: *to remain at peace; to remain at home.* **2.** to be left after the removal, departure, loss, etc., of others or other parts. **3.** to be left to be done, told, etc.

remainder /rə'meɪndə/ *n.* **1.** that which remains or is left: *the remainder of the day.* **2.** *Maths* the quantity that remains after subtraction or division. **3.** a copy of a book remaining in the publisher's stock when the sale has almost finished, usually sold at a reduced price. **–remaindered,** *adj.*

remains /rə'meɪnz/ *pl. n.* **1.** that which remains or is left; a remnant. **2.** that which remains of a person or animal after death; a corpse. **3.** parts or substances remaining from animal or plant life, occurring in the earth's crust or strata: *fossil remains; organic remains.*

remand /rə'mænd, -'mɑːnd/ *v.t.* **1.** to send back, remit, or consign again. **2.** *Law* (of a court or magistrate) to send back (a prisoner or accused person) into custody, as to await further proceedings. *–n.* **3.** the act of remanding. **4.** the state of being remanded. **5.** a person remanded.

remandee /rəmæn'diː/ *n.* a person who is remanded into custody.

remark /rə'mɑːk/ *v.t.* **1.** to say casually, as in making a comment. **2.** to note; perceive. *–n.* **3.** the act of remarking; notice. **4.** comment: *to let a thing pass without remark.* **5.** a casual or brief expression of thought or opinion. *–phr.* **6. remark on** (or **upon**), to make a remark or observation about.

remarkable /rəˈmakəbəl/ *adj.* **1.** notably or conspicuously unusual, or extraordinary: *a remarkable change.* **2.** worthy of remark or notice. **–remarkableness**, *n.* **–remarkably**, *adv.*

rematch /ˈriːmætʃ/ *n.* **1.** a match played against a contestant whom one has played before. *–v.i.* **2.** to play such a match. *–v.t.* **3.** to match again: *to rematch the files.*

remedial /rəˈmidiəl/ *adj.* **1.** affording remedy; tending to remedy something. **2.** of or relating to the treatment of physical defects with exercises, etc., rather than by medical or surgical means. **3.** (of teaching) designed to meet the needs of children with general or specific learning difficulties or with particular learning problems as aphasia, dyslexia, etc. **–remedially**, *adv.*

remediation /rəmidiˈeɪʃən/ *n.* **1.** the act or process of remedying. **2.** *Ecol.* the restoration of an environment to its pristine state, as by the removal of pollutants, contaminants, etc.

remedy /ˈrɛmədi/ *n.* (*pl.* **-dies**) **1.** something that cures or relieves a disease or bodily disorder. **2.** something that corrects or removes an evil of any kind. **3.** *Law* the legal means by which a wrong is redressed; legal redress. *–v.t.* (**-died, -dying**) **4.** to cure or heal. **5.** to put right: *to remedy a matter.* **6.** to correct or remove: *to remedy an evil.* **–remediable** /rəˈmidiəbəl/, *adj.*

remember /rəˈmɛmbə/ *v.t.* **1.** to bring back to the mind by an act of memory. **2.** to keep in the memory. **3.** to have (something) come into the mind again. **4.** to keep (a person) in mind as deserving a gift, reward, tip, etc. **5.** to mention to another as sending greetings: *remember me to your mother.* *–v.i.* **6.** to possess or use the faculty or ability of memory. **–remembrance**, *n.* **–rememberer**, *n.*

remind /rəˈmaɪnd/ *v.t.* **1.** to cause (someone) to remember. *–phr.* **2. remind someone of, a.** to make someone think of. **b.** to resemble in someone's estimation. **–reminder**, *n.*

reminisce /rɛməˈnɪs/ *v.i.* to indulge in reminiscence; recall past experiences.

reminiscence /rɛməˈnɪsəns/ *n.* **1.** the act or process of remembering one's past. **2.** a mental impression retained and revived. **3.** (*oft. pl.*) a recollection narrated or told. **4.** something that recalls or suggests something else. **–reminiscent**, *adj.*

remiss /rəˈmɪs/ *adj.* **1.** not diligent, careful, or prompt in duty, business, etc. **2.** characterised by negligence or carelessness. **3.** lacking force or energy; languid; sluggish. **–remissness**, *n.*

remission /rəˈmɪʃən/ *n.* **1.** the act of remitting. **2.** forgiveness of sins, offences, etc.; pardon. **3.** a lessening or abatement, as of labour, the symptoms of a disease, etc. Also, **remittal.**

remit *verb* (**-mitted, -mitting**) *–v.t.* /rəˈmɪt/ **1.** to send (money, etc.) to a person or place. **2.** to decide not to enforce (a punishment, etc.) or demand (a payment of a debt, etc.). **3.** to pardon or forgive (a sin, offence, etc.). **4.** to lessen; abate: *to remit watchfulness.* *–v.i.* /rəˈmɪt/ **5.** to send money, etc., as payment. **6.** to become less; abate: *her fever has remitted.* *–n.* /ˈrɛmɪt/ **7.** a set of instructions outlining an area of responsibility; brief: *a task within one's remit.* **–remittable**, *adj.* **–remittent**, *adj.*

remittance /rəˈmɪtns/ *n.* **1.** the remitting of money, etc., to a recipient at a distance. **2.** money or its equivalent sent from one place to another.

remix *n.* /ˈriːmɪks/ **1.** *Music* a recorded version of a piece of music containing a mix of the original recording tracks which is different from that used for the earlier published version. *–v.t.* /riˈmɪks/ **2.** to mix again. **3.** *Music* to produce as a remix.

remnant /ˈrɛmnənt/ *n.* **1.** a part, quantity, or number (usually small) remaining. **2.** a fragment or scrap, especially an odd piece of cloth, lace, etc., unsold or unused. **3.** a trace; vestige: *remnants of former greatness.* *–adj.* **4.** remaining.

remonstrate /ˈrɛmənstreɪt/ *v.t.* **1.** to say in remonstrance; protest. *–phr.* **2. remonstrate with,** to present reasons in complaint to; plead with in protest. **–remonstrance**, *n.* **–remonstration** /rɛmənˈstreɪʃən/, *n.* **–remonstrative** /rəˈmɒnstrətɪv/, *adj.* **–remonstrator**, *n.*

remorse /rəˈmɔs/ *n.* deep and painful regret for wrongdoing; compunction. **–remorseful**, *adj.* **–remorseless**, *adj.*

remote /rəˈmoʊt/ *adj.* **1.** far away; far distant in space or time: *a remote village*; *the remote past.* **2.** distant in relationship or connection: *a remote ancestor.* **3.** far removed; alien: *remote from common experience.* **4.** slight: *I do not have the remotest idea of what to do.* **5.** distant in feeling; aloof: *she seemed very remote at their first meeting.* **–remotely**, *adv.* **–remoteness**, *n.*

remote control *n.* **1.** the control of a system by means of electrical, radio, or other signals from a point at a distance from the system. **2.** Also, **remote.** a usually handheld device for the control of domestic appliances such as televisions, VCRs, air conditioners, etc.

remote sensing *n.* the identification of data, usually about features of the earth or other bodies in space, from a satellite, aeroplane, etc. **–remote-sensing**, *adj.*

removalist /rəˈmuvələst/ *n. Aust.* a person or firm engaged in moving household and office furniture, etc.

remove /rəˈmuv/ *v.t.* **1.** to move from a place or position; take away; take off: *please remove that book from the table*; *he removed his tie.* **2.** to displace from a position or office. **3.** to do away with; put an end to: *to remove guilt.* *–v.i.* **4.** to move from one place to another, especially to another home. *–n.* **5.** the distance by which one person, place, or thing is separated from another. **–removal**, *n.* **–remover**, *n.*

removed /rəˈmuvd/ *adj.* **1.** remote; separate; not connected with; distinct from. **2.** distant, used in expressing degrees of relationship: *a first cousin twice removed is a cousin's grandchild.*

remunerate /rəˈmjunəreɪt/ *v.t.* **1.** to pay, recompense, or reward for work, trouble, etc. **2.** to yield a recompense for (work, services, etc.). **–remuneration**, *n.* **–remunerative**, *adj.*

renaissance /rəˈneɪsəns, rəˈnæsəns/ *n.* **1.** a new birth; a revival, especially one in the world of art or learning. *–adj.* **2.** (*upper case*) of or relating to the style of building and decoration succeeding the medieval, originating in Italy in the early 15th century and based upon clarity and mathematical relationship of plan and design, and using to this end the forms and ornaments of classical Roman art. Also, **renascence.**

renal /ˈrinəl/ *adj.* of or relating to the kidneys or the surrounding regions.

rend /rɛnd/ *v.t.* (**rent, rending**) **1.** to tear apart with force or violence. **2.** (fol. by *away, off, up*, etc.) to pull or tear violently.

rendang /ˈrɛndæŋ/ *adj.* (*placed after the noun*) (in Asian cookery) designating a meat curry with coconut and spices: *beef rendang.*

render /ˈrɛndə/ *v.t.* **1.** to make or cause (a person or thing) to be or become as specified: *to render someone helpless.* **2.** to do; perform: *to render a service.* **3.** to furnish: *to render aid.* **4.** to present for consideration, approval, payment, action, etc., as an account. **5.** to pay as due (a tax, tribute, etc.). **6.** to deliver officially, as judgement. **7.** to reproduce in another language; translate. **8.** to represent; depict, as in painting. **9.** to bring out the meaning of by performance or execution, or interpret, as a part in a drama, a piece of music, a subject in representational art, etc. **10.** to give in return or requital. **11.** to give up; surrender. **12.** to cover (brickwork, stone, etc.) with a first coat of plaster. **13.** to extract (fat, etc.) from meat trimmings by melting. –*n.* **14.** the mixture of sand, cement, etc., used to render (def. 12). –*phr.* **15. render back**, to give back; restore. –**renderable**, *adj.* –**renderer**, *n.*

rendezvous /ˈrɒndeɪvu, ˈrɒndeɪˈvuː/ *n.* (*pl.* -**vous** /-vuz/) **1.** an appointment or engagement made between two or more persons to meet at a fixed place and time. **2.** a place for meeting or assembling, especially of troops, ships, or spacecraft. –*v.i.* (-**voused** /-vuːd/, -**vousing** /-vuːŋ/) **3.** to assemble at a place previously appointed.

rendition /rɛnˈdɪʃən/ *n.* **1.** the act of rendering. **2.** translation. **3.** interpretation, as of a role or a piece of music. **4.** → **extraordinary rendition**.

renegade /ˈrɛnəɡeɪd/ *n.* **1.** someone who deserts a party or cause for another. **2.** an apostate from a religious faith. **3.** someone who does not quite conform to expected social patterns. –*adj.* **4.** of or like a renegade; traitorous. –*v.i.* **5.** to turn renegade.

renege /rəˈnɛɡ, -ˈnɪɡ/ *v.i.* **1.** *Cards* to revoke. **2.** *Colloq.* to go back on one's word. Also, *Rare,* **renegue**. –**reneger**, *n.*

renew /rəˈnjuː/ *v.t.* **1.** to begin or take up again: *to renew a friendship*; *to renew a lease.* **2.** to restore or replenish: *to renew a stock of goods.* **3.** to make, say, or do again: *she renewed her demands.* –**renewal**, *n.* –**renewable**, *adj.*

renewable energy *n.* energy from a renewable source, such as solar energy, wind energy, or biomass.

renewable resource *n.* a natural resource which is not finite but can be renewed, such as the sun, wind, or biomass. Compare **non-renewable resource**.

rennet /ˈrɛnət/ *n.* **1.** the lining membrane of the fourth stomach of a calf, or of the stomach of certain other young animals. **2.** *Biochem.* the substance from the stomach of the calf which contains rennin. **3.** a preparation or extract of the rennet membrane, used to curdle milk, as in making cheese, junket, etc.

renounce /rəˈnaʊns/ *verb* (**renounced**, **renouncing**) –*v.t.* **1.** to give up or put aside voluntarily. **2.** to give up by formal declaration: *to renounce a claim.* **3.** to repudiate; disown. –*v.i.* **4.** *Cards* to play a card of a different suit from that led. –**renouncement**, *n.*

renovate /ˈrɛnəveɪt/ *v.t.* **1.** to make new or as if new again; restore to good condition; repair. **2.** to reinvigorate; refresh; revive. –**renovation** /rɛnəˈveɪʃən/, *n.* –**renovator**, *n.*

renown /rəˈnaʊn/ *n.* widespread and high repute; fame. –**renowned**, *adj.*

rent¹ /rɛnt/ *n.* **1.** a payment made regularly for the use of land or building, or other property. **2.** the return gained from any business in excess of production costs. –*v.t.* **3.** to allow the possession and use of (property) in return for regular payments. –*v.i.* **4.** to be let for rent: *this flat rents for $100 a week.* –**rentable**, *adj.*

rent² /rɛnt/ *n.* **1.** an opening made by rending or tearing; slit; fissure. **2.** a breach of relations or union. –*v.* **3.** past tense and past participle of **rend**.

rental /ˈrɛntl/ *n.* **1.** an amount received or paid as rent. **2.** an income arising from rents received. –*adj.* **3.** relating to rent. **4.** available for rent: *rental accommodation.*

renunciation /rənʌnsiˈeɪʃən/ *n.* **1.** the formal abandoning of a right, title, etc. **2.** a voluntary giving up, especially as a sacrifice. –**renunciative** /rəˈnʌnsiətɪv/, **renunciatory** /rəˈnʌnsiətri/, *adj.*

rep /rɛp/ *n. Colloq.* **1.** a travelling salesman or saleswoman. **2.** someone who is selected to represent their area in sport: *a hockey rep.* **3.** a union representative.

repair¹ /rəˈpɛə/ *v.t.* **1.** to restore to a good or sound condition after decay or damage; mend. **2.** to put right; remedy: *to repair damage.* –*n.* **3.** the act, process, or work of repairing: *the repair of a building.* **4.** a part that has been repaired or an addition made in repairing: *the repairs to the table were badly done.* **5.** condition in relation to need for repairing: *in good repair*; *in bad repair.* –**repairable**, *adj.* –**repairer**, *n.*

repair² /rəˈpɛə/ *v.i.* **1.** to betake oneself or go, as to a place: *he soon repaired in person to Auckland.* **2.** to go frequently or customarily. –*n.* **3.** the act of repairing or going: *to make repair to Auckland.*

reparable /ˈrɛpərəbəl, ˈrɛprəbəl/ *adj.* capable of being repaired or remedied. Also, **repairable** /rəˈpɛərəbəl/. –**reparably**, *adv.*

reparation /rɛpəˈreɪʃən/ *n.* **1.** the making of amends for wrong or injury done: *a wrong which admits of no reparation.* **2.** (*usu. pl.*) compensation in money, material, labour, etc., paid by a defeated nation (as by Germany and its allies after World War I) for damage to civilian population and property during war. **3.** restoration to good condition.

repartee /rɛpaˈtiː/ *n.* **1.** a ready and witty reply. **2.** speech or talk characterised by quickness and wittiness of reply. **3.** skill in making witty replies.

repast /rəˈpast/ *n.* **1.** a quantity of food taken or provided for one occasion of eating: *to eat a light repast.* **2.** a taking of food; a meal: *the evening repast.*

repatriate *v.t.* /riˈpætrieɪt/ **1.** to bring or send back (a person) to his or her own country, especially (prisoners of war, refugees, etc.) to the land of citizenship. –*n.* /riˈpætriət/ **2.** someone who has been repatriated.

repatriation /ˌripætriˈeɪʃən/ *n.* **1.** the act of returning to one's native land. **2.** *Aust.* assistance given to ex-service personnel returning to a civilian life, in the form of pensions, medical care, allowances for dependants, etc.

repay /riˈpeɪ/ *verb* (-**paid**, -**paying**) –*v.t.* **1.** to pay back or refund (money, etc.). **2.** to make return for: *repaid with thanks.* **3.** to make return to in any way: *feel repaid for sacrifices made.* **4.** to return: *repay a visit.* –*v.i.* **5.** to make repayment or return. –**repayable**, *adj.* –**repayment**, *n.*

repeal /rəˈpiːl/ *v.t.* **1.** to revoke or withdraw formally or officially: *to repeal a grant.* **2.** to revoke or annul (a law, tax, duty, etc.) by express legislative enactment; abrogate. –*n.* **3.** the act of repealing; revocation; abrogation. –**repealable**, *adj.* –**repealer**, *n.*

repeat /rəˈpiːt/ *v.t.* **1.** to say again (something already spoken by oneself or another): *please repeat that sentence.* **2.** to do, make, perform, etc., again: *to repeat an action*; *to repeat a passage of music.* –*v.i.* **3.** to do or say something again. **4.** (of food eaten) to be tasted again when the eater belches: *the onions are repeating on me.* **5.** (of a firearm) to fire several times without reloading. –*n.* **6.** the act of repeating. **7.** something repeated. **8.** an order for goods the same as a previous order. **9.** a radio or television program that has been broadcast at least once before. –**repeatable**, *adj.*

repeater /rəˈpiːtə/ *n.* **1.** a repeating firearm. **2.** *Elect.* an amplifier used in telephone circuits to make good losses of power. **3.** → **recurring decimal**.

repel /rəˈpɛl/ *verb* (-**pelled**, -**pelling**) –*v.t.* **1.** to drive or force back (an attack, attacker, etc.). **2.** to keep off or out; fail to mix with: *water and oil repel each other.* **3.** to turn away; refuse to have to do with; reject: *to repel temptation.* **4.** to cause feelings of distaste or disgust: *her dirty appearance repels me.* –*v.i.* **5.** to act with a force that drives or keeps away something. **6.** to cause distaste or disgust. –**repellence**, **repellency**, *n.* –**repellent**, *adj., n.* –**repeller**, *n.*

repent /rəˈpɛnt/ *v.i.* **1.** (sometimes fol. by *of*) to feel self-reproach, compunction, or contrition for past conduct; change one's mind with regard to past action in consequence of dissatisfaction with it or its results. –*v.t.* **2.** to remember or regard with self-reproach or contrition: *to repent one's injustice to another.* **3.** to feel sorry for; regret: *to repent one's words.* –*phr.* **4. repent of**, to feel such sorrow for (sin or fault) as to be disposed to change one's life for the better; be penitent for. –**repenter**, *n.* –**repentant**, *adj.* –**repentance**, *n.*

repercussion /ripə'kʌʃən/ *n.* **1.** an after-effect, often an indirect result, of some event or action: *the repercussions of the wool marketing plan were very widely felt.* **2.** the state of being driven back by a resisting body. **3.** a rebounding or recoil of something after impact. **4.** reverberation; echo. **5.** *Music* (in a fugue) the point after the development of an episode at which the subject and answer appear again. –**repercussive**, *adj.*

repertoire /'rɛpətwɑ/ *n.* **1.** the list of dramas, operas, parts, pieces, etc., which a company, actor, singer, or the like, is prepared to perform. **2.** all the works of a particular kind considered collectively.

repertory /'rɛpətri/ *n.* (*pl.* **-ries**) **1.** → **repertoire**. **2.** a type of theatrical company, usually based on a particular theatre, which prepares several plays, operas, or the like, and produces them alternately or in succession, for a limited run only. **3.** a store or stock of things available. **4.** → **storehouse**.

répétiteur /rəpətə'tɜ/ *n.* someone who rehearses and prompts opera singers.

repetition /rɛpə'tɪʃən/ *n.* **1.** the act of repeating; repeated action, performance, production, or presentation. **2.** repeated utterance; reiteration. **3.** something made by or resulting from repeating. **4.** a reproduction, copy, or replica. **5.** *Civil Law* an action for recovery of a payment or delivery made by error or upon failure to fulfil a condition. –**repetitious**, **repetitive**, *adj.*

repetition strain injury *n.* → **RSI**. Also, **repetitive strain injury**, **repetitive stress injury**.

repine /rə'paɪn/ *v.i.* to be fretfully discontented; fret; complain.

replace /rə'pleɪs/ *v.t.* **1.** to fill or take the place of; substitute for (a person or thing): *electricity has replaced gas as a means of illumination.* **2.** to provide a substitute or equivalent in the place of: *to replace a broken vase or dish.* **3.** to restore; return; make good: *to replace a sum of money borrowed.* **4.** to restore to a former or the proper place: *the stolen paintings were replaced in the museum.* –**replaceable**, *adj.* –**replacement**, **replacer**, *n.*

replay *n.* /'riplei/ **1.** (in sport) a match, contest, etc., which is played again because of some difficulty or disagreement. **2.** (in television coverage of sport by the electronic media) the playing again of some highlight of a game, often immediately after it has happened. **3.** → **playback**. –*v.t.* /ˌri'plei/ **4.** to repeat (a sporting event, match, etc., or a sequence from it) on radio or television.

replenish /rə'plɛnɪʃ/ *v.t.* **1.** to bring back to a state of fullness or completeness, as by supplying what is lacking: *to replenish a stock of goods.* **2.** to supply (a fire, stove, etc.) with fresh fuel. **3.** to fill again or anew. –**replenisher**, *n.* –**replenishment**, *n.*

replete /rə'plit/ *adj.* **1.** stuffed or gorged with food and drink. –*phr.* **2. replete with**, abundantly supplied or provided with. –**repletion**, **repleteness**, *n.*

replica /'rɛplɪkə/ *n.* **1.** a copy or reproduction of a work of art by the maker of the original. **2.** any copy or reproduction.

replication /rɛplə'keɪʃən/ *n.* **1.** a reply. **2.** *Law* the reply of the plaintiff or complainant to the defendant's plea or answer. **3.** *Biochem.* the process whereby new DNA is synthesised, by the exact copying of DNA already

present within the cell. **4.** reverberation; echo. **5.** a reproduction, copy, or duplication. –**replicate**, *v.*

reply /rə'plaɪ/ *verb* (**-plied**, **-plying**) –*v.i.* **1.** to make answer in words or writing; respond. **2.** to respond by some action, performance, etc.: *to reply to the enemy's fire.* –*v.t.* **3.** to return as an answer: *he replied that nothing would make him accept.* –*n.* (*pl.* **-plies**) **4.** an answer or response. –**replier**, *n.*

répondez s'il vous plaît /rə'pɒndeɪ sɪl vu ˌpleɪ/ please reply. *Abbrev.*: RSVP

report /rə'pɔt/ *n.* **1.** an account brought back or presented, especially containing information that is the result of investigation. **2.** an account of a speech, meeting, etc., especially as taken down for publication. **3.** a written account of a school pupil's academic progress, behaviour, attendance, etc., sent home to his or her parents. **4.** a story or information generally known; rumour: *the surf here is very dangerous according to report.* **5.** a loud explosive noise, especially from a gun. –*v.t.* **6.** to carry and repeat as an answer or message. **7.** to tell what has been learned by examination or investigation. **8.** to give a formal account or statement of. **9.** to lay a charge against (a person): *to be reported to the police.* **10.** to present (oneself) to a person in authority. **11.** to take down (a speech, etc.) in writing, as for publication in a newspaper, etc. –*v.i.* **12.** to make a report. **13.** to act as a reporter for a newspaper, etc. **14.** to present or give an account of oneself to someone in authority: *to report to the boss; report sick.* **15.** to present oneself at an appointed place, etc. –**reportable**, *adj.*

reporter /rə'pɔtə/ *n.* **1.** someone who reports. **2.** someone employed to gather and report news for a newspaper, news agency, or broadcasting organisation. **3.** someone who prepares official reports, as of legal or legislative proceedings.

repose¹ /rə'pəʊz/ *n.* **1.** a condition of peaceful resting. **2.** calmness of behaviour, appearance, etc. –*v.i.* **3.** to lie at rest; be peaceful. **4.** to lie or rest: *to repose on a park bench.* –*v.t.* **5.** (*oft. used reflexively*) to lay to rest: *I will repose myself here.* –**reposeful**, *adj.*

repose² /rə'pəʊz/ *v.t.* to put (confidence, trust, etc.) in a person or thing.

repository /rə'pɒzətri/ *n.* (*pl.* **-ries**) **1.** a receptacle or place where things are deposited, stored, or offered for sale, as a warehouse. **2.** a place in which a dead body is deposited. **3.** a person to whom something is entrusted or confided.

repossess /ripə'zɛs/ *v.t.* **1.** to possess again; regain possession of. **2.** to put again in possession of something. –**repossession** /ripə'zɛʃən/, *n.*

reprehensible /rɛprə'hɛnsəbəl/ *adj.* deserving to be reprehended; blameworthy: *reprehensible conduct.* –**reprehensibility** /ˌrɛprəhɛnsə'bɪləti/, **reprehensibleness**, *n.* –**reprehensibly**, *adv.*

represent /rɛprə'zɛnt/ *v.t.* **1.** (of a word, symbol, etc.) to serve to express, show, stand for, or mark; symbolise: *C represents common time in music.* **2.** to express or show by some term, character, symbol, etc.: *to represent musical sounds by notes.* **3.** to stand, act or speak in the place of, as a substitute, proxy, or agent: *to represent his government in a foreign country.* **4.** to act for (a constituency, etc.) by elected right in parliament or government. **5.** (of a picture, image, etc.) to present the likeness or outward appearance of; portray; depict. **6.** to present in words; set forth; describe; state: *the novel represents life in 19th century England.* **7.** (fol. by *as*, *to be*, etc.) to describe as having a particular character: *Superman is represented as a man of steel.* **8.** to be an example or type of; exemplify. **9.** to be the equivalent of; correspond to. –**representation**, *n.* –**representable**, *adj.* –**representational**, *adj.*

representative /ˌrɛprəˈzɛntətɪv/ *adj.* **1.** serving to represent; representing. **2.** typical; exemplifying a class: *a representative selection of Australian verse.* **3.** representing a constituency or community or the people generally, in the making and passing of laws or in government: *a representative assembly.* **4.** marked by, founded on, or relating to representation of the people in government: *representative government.* **5.** *Sport* **a.** of or relating to or designating a player drawn from a club team representing a district. **b.** of or relating to a team of such people. –*n.* **6.** someone or something that represents another or others, especially an agent, travelling salesperson or elected member of parliament. **7.** an example; specimen; type. –**representatively**, *adv.* –**representativeness**, *n.*

repress /rəˈprɛs/ *v.t.* **1.** to keep under control, check, or suppress (desires, feelings, action, tears, etc.). **2.** to put down or quell (sedition, disorder, etc.). **3.** to reduce (persons) to subjection. **4.** *Psychol.* to reject from consciousness, as thoughts, feelings, memories, or impulses not acceptable to the ego. –**repression**, *n.* –**repressive**, *adj.* –**repressed**, *adj.* –**represser**, *n.* –**repressible**, *adj.*

repressed memory *n.* a memory which because of the trauma associated with it or because of its unacceptability in terms of current codes of behaviour, is pushed into the subconscious mind.

reprieve /rəˈpriv/ *v.t.* (**-prieved**, **-prieving**) **1.** to respite (a person) from impending punishment, especially to grant a delay of the execution of (a condemned person). **2.** to relieve temporarily from any evil. –*n.* **3.** respite from impending punishment, especially from execution of a sentence of death. **4.** a warrant authorising this. **5.** any respite or temporary relief.

reprimand /ˈrɛprəmand, -mænd/ *n.* **1.** a severe reproof, especially a formal one by a person in authority. –*v.t.* **2.** to reprove severely, especially in a formal way.

reprint *v.t.* /riˈprɪnt/ **1.** to print again; print a new impression of. –*n.* /ˈriprɪnt/ **2.** a reproduction in print of matter already printed. **3.** a new impression, without alteration, of any printed work. **4.** *Philately* an impression from the original plate after issue of the stamps has ceased and their use for postage voided. –**reprinter**, *n.*

reprisal /rəˈpraɪzəl/ *n.* **1.** the infliction of similar or greater injury on the enemy in warfare, in retaliation for some injury, as by the punishment or execution of prisoners of war. **2.** an instance of this. **3.** the act or practice of using force, short of war, against another nation, to secure redress of a grievance. **4.** retaliation, or an act of retaliation. **5.** (originally) the forcible seizing of property or subjects in retaliation.

reprise *n.* **1.** /rəˈpraɪz/ a renewal or resumption of an event, activity, experience, etc.: *a reprise of a fantasy from childhood.* **2.** /rəˈpraɪz/ (*usu. pl.*) *Law* an annual deduction, duty, or payment out of an estate, as an annuity or the like. **3.** /rəˈpraɪz, rəˈpriz/ *Music* a return to the first theme or subject. –*v.t.* /rəˈpraɪz, rəˈpriz/ **4.** to repeat (a role or character played previously) as in a film or television show.

reproach /rəˈproʊtʃ/ *v.t.* **1.** to find fault with (a person, etc.); blame; censure. **2.** *Archaic* to be a cause of blame or discredit to. –*n.* **3.** blame or censure conveyed by reproaching: *a term of reproach.* **4.** an expression of upbraiding, censure, or reproof. **5.** disgrace, discredit, or blame incurred: *to bring reproach on one's family.* **6.** a cause or occasion of disgrace or discredit. –*phr.* **7. reproach someone with something**, to attempt to make someone feel ashamed about something. –**reproachful**, *adj.* –**reproachable**, *adj.* –**reproachableness**, *n.* –**reproachably**, *adv.* –**reproacher**, *n.*

reprobate /ˈrɛprəbeɪt/ *n.* **1.** an unprincipled, immoral or wicked person. –*adj.* **2.** bad; morally depraved; unprincipled. –*v.t.* **3.** to disapprove of; condemn; censure.

reproduce /riprəˈdjus/ *verb* (**-duced**, **-ducing**) –*v.t.* **1.** to make a copy, representation, or strong likeness of. **2.** to produce again or anew by natural process: *to reproduce a broken claw.* **3.** to produce young or offspring. **4.** to produce again or anew in any manner. –*v.i.* **5.** to reproduce its kind, as an animal or plant; propagate. **6.** to turn out (well, etc.) when copied. –**reproductive**, *adj.* –**reproducible**, *adj.*

reproduction /riprəˈdʌkʃən/ *n.* **1.** the act or process of reproducing. **2.** the state of being reproduced. **3.** something that is made by reproducing; a copy or duplicate, especially of a picture or the like made by photoengraving or some similar process. **4.** the natural process among animals and plants by which new individuals are generated and the species perpetuated.

reproof /rəˈpruf/ *n.* **1.** the act of reproving, censuring, or rebuking. **2.** an expression of censure or rebuke.

reprove /rəˈpruv/ *verb* (**-proved**, **-proving**) –*v.t.* **1.** to address words of disapproval to (a person, etc.); rebuke; blame. **2.** to express disapproval of (actions, words, etc.). –*v.i.* **3.** to speak in reproof; administer a reproof. –**reprover**, *n.* –**reprovingly**, *adv.*

reptile /ˈrɛptaɪl/ *n.* **1.** any of the Reptilia, a class of cold-blooded vertebrates, including the lizards, snakes, turtles, alligators, and rhynchocephalians, together with various extinct types. **2.** any of various creeping or crawling animals, as the lizards, snakes, etc. **3.** a grovelling, mean, or despicable person. –*adj.* **4.** creeping or crawling. **5.** grovelling, mean, or malignant. –**reptilian**, *adj.*

republic /rəˈpʌblɪk/ *n.* **1.** a state in which the supreme power rests in the body of citizens entitled to vote and is exercised by representatives chosen directly or indirectly by them. **2.** any body of persons, etc., viewed as a commonwealth. **3.** a nation in which the head of the state is a president, usually either elected or nominated and so deemed a representative of the people, not a hereditary monarch. –**republican**, *n.*, *adj.* –**republicanism**, *n.*

repudiate /rəˈpjudieɪt/ *v.t.* **1.** to reject as having no authority or binding force, as a claim, etc. **2.** to cast off or disown: *to repudiate a son.* **3.** to reject with disapproval or condemnation, as a doctrine, etc. **4.** to reject with denial, as a charge, etc. **5.** to refuse to acknowledge and pay, as a debt (said specifically of a state, municipality, etc.). –**repudiation**, *n.*

repugnant /rəˈpʌgnənt/ *adj.* **1.** distasteful or objectionable. **2.** making opposition; objecting; averse. **3.** opposed or contrary, as in nature or character. –**repugnance**, *n.* –**repugnantly**, *adv.*

repulse /rəˈpʌls/ *v.t.* **1.** to drive back, or repel, as an assailant, etc. **2.** to repel with denial, discourtesy, or the like; refuse or reject. **3.** to produce a feeling of strong aversion in; disgust. –*n.* **4.** the act of repelling. **5.** the state of being repelled, as in hostile encounter. **6.** refusal or rejection. –**repulser**, *n.*

repulsion /rəˈpʌlʃən/ *n.* **1.** the act of repelling or driving back. **2.** the state of being repelled. **3.** the feeling of being repelled; distaste, repugnance, or aversion. **4.** *Physics* a situation in which bodies are repelled from each other.

repulsive /rəˈpʌlsɪv/ *adj.* **1.** causing repugnance or aversion. **2.** tending to repel by denial, discourtesy, or the like. **3.** *Physics* of the nature of or characterised by physical repulsion; tending to repel or drive back. –**repulsively**, *adv.* –**repulsiveness**, *n.*

repurpose /riˈpɜpəs/ *v.t.* to convert for use in another format, medium, or product. Also, **re-purpose**.

reputable /ˈrɛpjətəbəl/ adj. held in good repute; honourable; respectable; estimable. –**reputability** /ˌrɛpjətəˈbɪləti/, n. –**reputably**, adv.

reputation /rɛpjəˈteɪʃən/ n. **1.** the estimation in which a person or thing is held, especially by the community or the public generally; repute: *a man of good reputation*. **2.** favourable repute; good name: *to ruin one's reputation by misconduct*. **3.** a favourable and publicly recognised name or standing for merit, achievement, etc.: *to build up a reputation*. **4.** the estimation or name of being, having, having done, etc., something specified.

repute /rəˈpjut/ n. **1.** estimation in the view of others; reputation: *persons of good repute*. **2.** favourable reputation; good name; credit or note. –v.t. **3.** (*commonly in the passive*) to consider or esteem (a person or thing) to be as specified; account or regard: *he was reputed to be a millionaire*.

reputed /rəˈpjutəd/ adj. accounted or supposed to be such: *the reputed author of a book*. –**reputedly**, adv.

request /rəˈkwɛst/ n. **1.** the act of asking for something to be given or done, especially as a favour or kindness; solicitation or petition. **2.** something that is asked for: *to obtain one's request*. **3.** the condition of being asked for; demand: *to be in great request as an after-dinner speaker*. –v.t. **4.** to ask for (something), especially politely or formally. **5.** to ask or beg (used with a clause or an infinitive): *to request that he leave; to request to be excused*. **6.** to ask, or beg (a person, etc.), to do something: *he requested me to go*.

requiem /ˈrɛkwiəm, ˈreɪkwiəm/ n. (*oft. upper case*) **1.** *Roman Catholic Church* **a.** the mass celebrated for the repose of the souls of the dead. **b.** a celebration of this mass (**requiem mass**). **c.** a musical setting of this mass. **2. a.** any musical service, hymn, or dirge composed for the repose of the soul of, or in memory of, a dead person. **b.** any writing so titled, such as a poem, which has the same purpose or sombre tone.

requiescat /rɛkwiˈɛskæt/ n. a wish or prayer for the repose of the dead.

require /rəˈkwaɪə/ v.t. **1.** to have need of; need: *he requires medical care*. **2.** to call on from a position of power; order or enjoin (a person, etc.) to do something: *to require an agent to account for money spent*. **3.** to place under a sense of duty or necessity. –v.i. **4.** to make a demand; impose an obligation or need: *to do as the law requires*. –**requirement**, n.

requisite /ˈrɛkwəzət/ adj. **1.** required by the nature of things or by circumstances; indispensable: *he has the requisite qualifications*. –n. **2.** something requisite; a necessary thing. –**requisitely**, adv. –**requisiteness**, n.

requisition /rɛkwəˈzɪʃən/ n. **1.** the act of demanding, or the demand made. **2.** the demanding formally or from a position of power that something be done, given, etc. **3.** the form on which such a demand is written. –v.t. **4.** to demand or to take for official use; press into service, especially for military purposes, public needs, etc.: *to requisition supplies*.

requite /rəˈkwaɪt/ v.t. **1.** to make repayment or return for (service, benefits, etc.). **2.** to make retaliation for (a wrong, injury, etc.). **3.** to make return to (a person) for service, etc. **4.** to make retaliation on (a person) for a wrong, etc. **5.** to give or do in return. –**requitable**, adj. –**requital**, **requitement**, n. –**requiter**, n.

reroute /riˈrut/ Chiefly US and Computers /riˈraʊt/ v.t. (**-routed**, **-routeing** or **-routing**) **1.** to direct (a road, river, etc.) into a different course. **2.** Finance to send (funds) to a different location. **3.** Computers to alter the connections for (computer hardware): *to reroute a computer on a network*. **4.** Internet to redirect (traffic) by adjusting a browser, IP address, etc. Also, **re-route**.

rescind /rəˈsɪnd/ v.t. **1.** to abrogate; annul; revoke; repeal. **2.** to invalidate (an act, measure, etc.) by a later action

or a higher authority. –**rescission**, n. –**rescindable**, adj. –**rescinder**, n.

rescue /ˈrɛskju/ v.t. (**-cued**, **-cuing**) **1.** to free or deliver from confinement, violence, danger, or evil. **2.** Law to liberate or take by forcible or illegal means from lawful custody. –n. **3.** the act of rescuing. –**rescuer**, n.

research /rəˈsɜtʃ, ˈrisɜtʃ/ n. **1.** diligent and systematic inquiry or investigation into a subject in order to discover facts or principles: *research in nuclear physics*. –v.i. **2.** to make researches; investigate carefully. –v.t. **3.** to investigate carefully: *to research a subject exhaustively*. –adj. **4.** of or relating to research. –**researcher**, n.

resemble /rəˈzɛmbəl/ v.t. to be like or similar to. –**resemblance**, n. –**resembler**, n.

resent /rəˈzɛnt/ v.t. to feel or show displeasure or indignation at, from a sense of injury or insult. –**resentful**, adj.

reservation /rɛzəˈveɪʃən/ n. **1.** a keeping back, withholding, or setting apart. **2.** the making of some exception or qualification. **3.** a tract of public land set apart for a special purpose, as (in the US) for the use of a Native American tribe. **4.** the allotting or the securing of accommodation at a hotel, on a train or boat, etc., as for a traveller: *to make reservations*.

reserve /rəˈzɜv/ v.t. **1.** to keep back or save for future use, arrangement, treatment, etc. **2.** to set aside or book in advance, especially a place to stay, theatre seats, etc. **3.** to set apart for a particular use, purpose, service, etc.: *ground reserved for a garden*. **4.** Law to delay handing down (a judgement or decision), especially to give time for better consideration of the matters involved. –n. **5.** something reserved, usually for some purpose or in case of accident, etc.; a store or stock. **6.** Sport **a.** a player kept in readiness to take the place of a team member who may drop out through being hurt, etc. **b.** (*pl.*) a club's second team. **7.** a piece of public land set apart for recreation, etc., as a public reserve, or for a special purpose, as a nature reserve. **8.** an area of land set aside by a government for indigenous people, to allow them to pursue a traditional lifestyle or to concentrate them under supervision and control. **9.** a limitation; reservation, exception, or qualification. **10.** the act of reserving. **11.** the condition of being reserved, especially for future use or for some purpose or person: *money in reserve*. **12.** → **army reserve**. **13.** the quality or habit of avoiding close friendships and familiarity; self-restraint in action or speech; reticence. **14.** → **reserve price**. –adj. **15.** kept in reserve; forming a reserve: *a reserve fund; a reserve supply*.

reserve bank n. the national banking organisation of a country which administers the monetary policy of a government, receives revenue, pays government expenditure, and issues money, both paper and coin, as legal tender.

reserve champion n. the runner-up to the champion, especially in animal judging.

reserved /rəˈzɜvd/ adj. **1.** kept in reserve; set apart for a particular use or purpose. **2.** kept by special arrangement for some person or persons: *a reserved seat*. **3.** self-restrained in action or speech; disposed to keep one's feelings, thoughts, or affairs to oneself. **4.** characterised by reserve, as the disposition, manner, etc. **5.** denoting an occupation of national importance which carries exemption from service in the armed forces in times of conscription. –**reservedly** /rəˈzɜvədli/, adv. –**reservedness**, n.

reserve powers pl. n. **1.** rights, as those held by a government or an official, that may be exercised on a discretionary basis under certain conditions. **2.** Also, **prerogative powers**. (in Australia) discretionary powers of the Crown, recognised by unwritten convention as lying with the governor-general, to act with a small degree of personal discretion, and without ministerial advice.

reserve price *n.* the lowest price at which a person is willing that their property shall be sold at auction. Also, **reserve**.

reservoir /ˈrɛzəvwa, ˈrɛzəvɔ/ *n.* **1.** a natural or artificial place where water is collected and stored for use, especially water for supplying a community, irrigating land, furnishing power, etc. **2.** a receptacle or chamber for holding a liquid or fluid, as oil or gas. **3.** *Biol.* a cavity or part which holds some fluid or secretion. **4.** a place where anything is collected or accumulated in great amount. **5.** a great supply, store, or reserve of something.

reshuffle /ˌriˈʃʌfəl/ *v.t.* **1.** to shuffle again. **2.** to make a new allocation of jobs, especially within a government or cabinet. *–n.* **3.** a rearrangement or reorganisation; a shake-up.

reside /rəˈzaɪd/ *v.i.* **1.** to dwell permanently or for a considerable time; have one's abode for a time: *he resided in Box Hill. –phr.* **2. reside in, a.** (of things, qualities, etc.) to abide, lie, or be present habitually in; exist or be inherent in. **b.** to rest or be vested in, as powers, rights, etc. **–resident**, *n.* **–residential**, *adj.*

residence /ˈrɛzədəns/ *n.* **1.** the place, especially the house, in which one resides; dwelling place; dwelling. **2.** a large house. **3.** the act or fact of residing. **4.** the time during which one resides in a place.

residency /ˈrɛzədənsi/ *n.* (*pl.* **-cies**) **1. →** residence. **2.** the dwelling place of officials or diplomats representing the heads of state of foreign countries. **3.** the time during which one resides in a place. **4.** the right to live in a country despite not being a citizen: *refugees seeking residency.*

residual powers *pl. n.* those powers which are not specifically listed in Section 51 of the Australian Constitution as the legislative responsibility of the Commonwealth government, and which therefore become state government areas of legislation.

residue /ˈrɛzədʒu/ *n.* **1.** that which remains after a part is taken, disposed of, or gone; remainder; rest. **2.** *Chem.* **a.** a quantity of matter remaining after evaporation, combustion, or some other process; a residuum. **b.** an atom or group of atoms considered as a radical or part of a molecule. **c.** that part remaining as a solid on a filter paper after a liquid passes through in the filtration procedure. **3.** *Law* that which remains of a testator's or intestate's estate when all his or her liabilities have been discharged. **–residual**, *adj.*

resign /rəˈzaɪn/ *v.i.* **1.** (oft. fol. by *from*) to give up an office or position. **2.** to give in to; yield; submit. *–v.t.* **3.** to give up (an office, position, right, claim, etc.) formally; relinquish. **4.** to yield (oneself, one's mind, etc.) without resistance. **5.** to hand or sign over; surrender, as to the care or control of another: *to resign a child to foster-parents.* **–resignation**, *n.*

resigned /rəˈzaɪnd/ *adj.* **1.** submissive or acquiescent. **2.** characterised by or indicative of resignation. **–resignedly** /rəˈzaɪnədli/, *adv.* **–resignedness** /rəˈzaɪnədnəs/, *n.*

resilient /rəˈzɪliənt, -ˈzɪljənt/ *adj.* **1.** springing back; rebounding. **2.** returning to the original form or position after being bent, compressed, or stretched. **3.** readily recovering, as from sickness, depression, or the like; buoyant; cheerful. **–resilience, resiliency**, *n.* **–resiliently**, *adv.*

resin /ˈrɛzən/ *n.* **1.** any of a class of non-volatile, solid or semisolid organic substances (copal, mastic, etc.) obtained directly from certain plants as exudations, and used in medicine and in the making of varnishes. **2.** substances made synthetically by polymerisation and used in the making of plastics. **3.** (not in scientific

usage) a substance of this type obtained from certain pines; rosin. *–v.t.* **4.** to treat or rub with resin. **–resiny, resinous, resinoid**, *adj.*

resist /rəˈzɪst/ *v.t.* **1.** to withstand, strive against, or oppose: *to resist infection.* **2.** to withstand the action or effect of: *gold resists corrosion.* **3.** to refrain or abstain from: *to resist a smile. –v.i.* **4.** to make a stand or make efforts in opposition; act in opposition; offer resistance. *–n.* **5.** a substance applied to a surface to enable it to resist corrosion or the like. **–resistant**, *adj.*, *n.* **–resister**, *n.*

resistance /rəˈzɪstəns/ *n.* **1.** the act or power of resisting, opposing, or withstanding. **2.** *Elect.* **a.** that property of a device which opposes the flow of an electric current. **b.** a measure of the ability of a device to oppose the flow of an electric current. **3.** (*oft. upper case*) a secret organisation in an enemy-occupied country working to keep fighting unofficially after a formal surrender, especially that in France during World War II.

resistor /rəˈzɪstə/ *n. Elect.* a device, the primary purpose of which is to introduce resistance into an electric circuit.

resolute /ˈrɛzəlut/ *adj.* **1.** firmly resolved or determined; set in purpose or opinion. **2.** characterised by firmness and determination, as the temper, spirit, actions, etc. **–resolutely**, *adv.* **–resoluteness**, *n.*

resolution /rɛzəˈluʃən/ *n.* **1.** a formal determination, or expression of opinion, of a meeting or other body of people brought together to make decisions, etc. **2.** firmness of purpose or determination. **3.** the act of settling on or determining, as to action, etc. **4.** the mental state or quality of being determined or firm; firmness of purpose. **5.** the act or process of determining or separating into the basic or elementary parts; reduction to a simpler form; conversion. **6.** the resulting condition. **7.** a solution or explanation, especially of a problem, a doubtful point, etc. **8.** *Music* the progression of harmony from a dissonance (unfinished and harsh chord) to a consonance (sweet-sounding chord), especially the tonic chord, or sometimes to a less violent dissonance. **9.** (in a novel, drama, etc.) the concluding part, where any problems are resolved and harmony is restored. **10.** the degree of fineness in the reproduction of an image, as by a photograph, television screen, etc.

resolve /rəˈzɒlv/ *v.t.* **1.** to fix or settle on by deliberate choice and will; determine (to do something). **2.** *Physics* (of forces, velocities, etc.) to divide into components. **3.** to settle, determine, or state formally in a vote or resolution, as of a deliberative assembly. **4.** to deal with (a question, a matter of uncertainty, etc.) conclusively; explain; solve (a problem). **5.** to clear away or dispel (doubts, etc.), as by explanation. **6.** *Chem.* to separate (a racemic mixture) into its optically active components. **7.** *Music* to cause (a voice part or the harmony as a whole) to progress from a dissonance to a consonance. **8.** *Optics* to separate and make visible the individual parts of (an image); to distinguish between. **9.** *Med.* to cause (swellings, inflammation, etc.) to disappear without suppuration. *–v.i.* **10.** to break up or disintegrate. **11.** *Music* to progress from a dissonance to a consonance. *–n.* **12.** a resolution or determination made, as to follow some course of action. **13.** determination; firmness of purpose. *–phr.* **14. resolve into** (or **to**), **a.** to reduce or convert to by or as by breaking up or disintegration. **b.** to be reduced or changed into by breaking up or otherwise. **15. resolve itself**, to change or alter: *the grey shape resolved itself into the figure of a man.* **16. resolve on** (or **upon**), to come to a determination about; make up one's mind about. **–resolvable**, *adj.* **–resolver**, *n.*

resonance /ˈrɛzənəns/ *n.* **1.** the condition or quality of being resonant. **2.** the amplification of the voice by the bones of the head and upper chest, and by the air cavities of the pharynx, mouth, and nasal passages. **3.** a similarity between two or more objects, ideas, words, etc. **4.** *Physics* (in a mechanical or electrical system) the increase of the amplitude vibrations as the frequency of an external periodic stimulus approaches the natural frequency of the system. **5.** *Chem.* the condition shown by a molecule when the arrangement of its valency electrons is between two or more arrangements having nearly the same energy, as in a benzene ring.

resonant /ˈrɛzənənt/ *adj.* **1.** resounding or re-echoing, as sounds, places, etc. **2.** deep and full of resonance: *a resonant voice.* **3.** relating to resonance. **4.** having the property of increasing the intensity of sound by sympathetic vibration. –**resonantly**, *adv.*

resonate /ˈrɛzəneɪt/ *v.i.* **1.** to resound. **2.** to act as a resonator; exhibit resonance. **3.** *Electronics* to reinforce oscillations because the natural frequency of the device is the same as the frequency of the source. **4.** to amplify vocal sound by the sympathetic vibration of air in certain cavities and bony structures. –*v.t.* **5.** to cause to resound. –*phr.* **6. resonate with**, to arouse a sympathetic response in (someone) based on a shared experience with another. –**resonation** /rɛzəˈneɪʃən/, *n.* –**resonator**, *n.*

resort /rəˈzɔt/ *v.i.* **1.** to have recourse for use, service, or help: *to resort to war.* **2.** to go, especially frequently or customarily: *a beach to which many people resort.* –*n.* **3.** a place frequented, especially by the public generally: *a summer resort.* **4.** a large hotel with special facilities offered, as sporting activities, health and fitness equipment, gambling, etc. **5.** a habitual or general going, as to a place or person. **6.** a resorting to some person or thing for aid, service, etc.; recourse: *to have resort to force.* **7.** a person or thing resorted to for aid, service, etc. –*phr.* **8. last resort**, the expedient to which one turns when all others have failed.

resound /rəˈzaʊnd/ *v.i.* **1.** to re-echo or ring with sound. **2.** to make an echoing sound, or sound loudly. **3.** to be echoed, or ring. –*v.t.* **4.** to re-echo (a sound). **5.** to make known loudly (praises, etc.); proclaim. –**resoundingly**, *adv.*

resource /rəˈzɔs, rəˈsɔs, ˈrisɔs, ˈrizɔs/ *n.* **1.** a source of supply, support, or aid. **2.** a source of economic wealth available to a country, organisation, individual, etc. **3.** a source of information. **4.** (*oft. pl.*) the collective wealth and assets of a country, organisation, individual, etc. **5.** (*oft. pl.*) money, or any property which can be changed into money; assets. **6.** the means at hand afforded by the mind or personal abilities. **7.** any action or measure which one may turn to in an emergency; expedient. **8.** the ability to deal with a situation or difficulty.

resourceful /rəˈzɔsfəl, rəˈsɔsfəl/ *adj.* full of resource; ingenious; skilful in overcoming difficulties. –**resourcefully**, *adv.* –**resourcefulness**, *n.*

respect /rəˈspɛkt/ *n.* **1.** (in phrases preceded by *in*) a particular, detail, or point: *to be defective in some respect.* **2.** (preceded by *in* or *with*) relation or direction of the attention to: *inquiries with respect to a route.* **3.** high and respectful regard felt or shown; esteem; deference. **4.** the condition of being highly regarded or honoured. **5.** (*pl.*) respectful or friendly words of praise, as paid when making a call on a person: *to pay one's respects.* **6.** consideration or regard, as to something that might influence a choice. –*v.t.* **7.** to hold in high regard or honour: *to respect one's elders.* **8.** to show high regard, or consideration for: *to respect someone's wishes.* **9.** to treat with consideration; refrain from interfering with: *to respect a person's privacy.* –**respectful**, *adj.* –**respecter**, *n.* –**respected**, *adj.*

respectable /rəˈspɛktəbəl/ *adj.* **1.** worthy of respect or high regard; estimable; worthy: *a respectable citizen.* **2.** of good social standing, name, etc.: *a respectable neighbourhood.* **3.** having socially accepted standards of moral behaviour; virtuous: *a respectable girl.* **4.** of a presentable appearance; decently clothed. **5.** of a passable standard; fairly good; fair: *a respectable performance.* –**respectability**, **respectableness**, *n.* –**respectably**, *adv.*

respective /rəˈspɛktɪv/ *adj.* relating individually or severally to each of a number of persons, things, etc.; particular: *the respective merits of the candidates.*

respectively /rəˈspɛktɪvli/ *adv.* with respect to each of a number in the stated or corresponding order: *Janet and Lara were awarded an A and a B respectively.*

respiration /rɛspəˈreɪʃən/ *n. Biol.* **1.** the act of respiring; inhalation and exhalation of air; breathing. **2.** (in living organisms) the process by which oxygen and carbohydrates are assimilated into the system and the oxidation products (carbon dioxide and water) are given off. –**respiratory**, *adj.*

respirator /ˈrɛspəreɪtə/ *n.* **1.** a device worn over the mouth, or nose and mouth, to prevent the inhalation of noxious substances, etc., as a gasmask. **2.** an apparatus to induce artificial respiration.

respire /rəˈspaɪə/ *v.i.* **1.** to inhale and exhale air for the purpose of maintaining life; breathe. **2.** to breathe freely again, after anxiety, trouble, exertion, etc. –*v.t.* **3.** to breathe; inhale and exhale.

respite /ˈrɛspət, ˈrɛspaɪt, rəˈspaɪt/ *n.* **1.** a delay or cessation for a time, especially of anything distressing or trying; an interval of relief: *to toil without respite.* **2.** temporary suspension of the execution of a person condemned to death; a reprieve. –*v.t.* **3.** to relieve temporarily, especially from anything distressing or trying; give an interval of relief from. **4.** to grant delay in the carrying out of (a punishment, obligation, etc.).

resplendent /rəˈsplɛndənt/ *adj.* shining brilliantly; gleaming; splendid: *resplendent in white uniforms.* –**resplendence**, **resplendency**, *n.* –**resplendently**, *adv.*

respond /rəˈspɒnd/ *v.i.* **1.** to answer; give a reply in words: *to respond briefly to a question.* **2.** to make a return by some action as if in answer: *to respond generously to a charitable appeal.* **3.** *Biol.* to exhibit some action or effect as if in answer; react: *nerves respond to a stimulus.*

respondent /rəˈspɒndənt/ *n.* **1.** *Law* (in some civil proceedings) a defendant. **2.** someone who responds or makes reply.

response /rəˈspɒns/ *n.* **1.** answer or reply, whether in words, in some action, etc. **2.** *Biol.* any behaviour of a living organism which results from stimulation. **3.** *Elect.* the ratio of the output level to the input level of an electrical device or transmission line, at a given frequency. **4.** *Eccles.* a verse, sentence, phrase, or word said or sung by the choir or congregation in reply to the officiant during public worship.

responsibility /rəspɒnsəˈbɪləti/ *n.* (*pl.* **-ties**) **1.** the state or fact of being responsible. **2.** an instance of being responsible. **3.** a particular burden of obligation upon someone who is responsible: *to feel the responsibilities of one's position.* **4.** something for which one is responsible: *a child is a responsibility to its parents.* –*phr.* **5. on one's own responsibility**, on one's own initiative or authority.

responsible /rəˈspɒnsəbəl/ *adj.* **1.** involving accountability or responsibility: *a responsible position.* **2.** having a capacity for moral decisions and therefore accountable; capable of rational thought or action. **3.** able to discharge obligations or pay debts. **4.** reliable in business or other dealings; showing reliability. –*phr.* **5. responsible for, a.** having the responsibility of. **b.** chargeable with being the author, cause, or occasion of. **6. responsible to,** answerable or accountable to, as for something within one's power, control, or management. –**responsibleness,** *n.* –**responsibly,** *adv.*

responsive /rə'spɒnsɪv/ *adj.* **1.** making answer or reply, especially responding readily to influences, appeals, efforts, etc. **2.** *Biol.* acting in response, as to some stimulus. –**responsively,** *adv.* –**responsiveness,** *n.*

rest¹ /rɛst/ *n.* **1.** the refreshing quiet or repose of sleep: *a good night's rest.* **2.** refreshing ease or inactivity after exertion or labour: *to allow an hour for rest.* **3.** relief or freedom, especially from anything that wearies, troubles, or disturbs. **4.** mental or spiritual calm; tranquillity: *to set one's mind at rest.* **5.** the repose of death: *to lay the dead to rest.* **6.** cessation or absence of motion: *to bring a machine to rest.* **7.** a pause or interval. **8.** *Music* **a.** an interval of silence between notes. **b.** a mark or sign indicating this. **9.** *Prosody* a short pause in reading; a caesura. **10.** an establishment for providing shelter or lodging for some class of persons. **11.** a piece or thing for something to rest on: *an elbow rest.* **12.** a support, or supporting device. **13.** *Billiards* → **bridge¹** (def. 7). –*v.i.* **14.** to refresh oneself, as by sleeping, lying down, or relaxing. **15.** to relieve weariness by cessation of exertion or labour. **16.** to be at ease; have tranquillity or peace. **17.** to repose in death. **18.** to be quiet or still. **19.** to cease from motion, come to rest, or stop. **20.** to become or remain inactive. **21.** to remain without further action or notice: *to let a matter rest.* **22.** to lie, sit, lean, or be set (*in, on, against,* etc.): *his arm rested on the table.* **23.** *Agric.* to lie fallow or unworked: *to let land rest.* **24.** to be found or be (where specified): *the blame rests with them.* **25.** to be fixed or directed on something, as the gaze, eyes, etc. **26.** *Law* to terminate voluntarily the introduction of evidence in a case. **27.** *Theatre Colloq.* to be unemployed, as an actor. –*v.t.* **28.** to give vent to; refresh with rest: *to rest oneself.* **29.** to lay or place for rest, ease, or support: *to rest one's back against a tree.* **30.** to direct (the eyes, etc.): *to rest one's eyes on someone.* **31.** to base, or let depend, as on some ground of reliance. **32.** to bring to rest; halt; stop. **33.** *Law* to terminate voluntarily the introduction of evidence on: *to rest one's case.* –*phr.* **34. at rest, a.** dead. **b.** quiescent, inactive, or motionless, as something formerly in motion. **c.** tranquil; unworried. **d.** in a state of rest, as asleep. **35. rest in** (or **with**), to be a responsibility for (someone), as something to be done: *it rests with you to complete the job.* **36. rest on** (or **upon**), **a.** to be imposed as a burden or responsibility on. **b.** to rely on. **c.** to be based or founded on. **d.** to be present on; dwell on: *the moonlight rests upon the floor.* **37. rest on one's laurels,** to allow one's reputation to rely on past achievements, and make no further effort. **38. rest on one's oars, a.** *Rowing* to stop rowing. **b.** to suspend any activity for a time.

rest² /rɛst/ *n.* **1.** that which is left or remains; the remainder: *the rest of the money is his.* –*v.i.* **2.** to continue to be; remain (as specified): *rest assured.* –*phr.* **3. for the rest,** with regard to anything beyond what has been specifically mentioned.

restaurant /'rɛstərɒnt/ *n.* an establishment where meals are served to customers.

restaurateur /rɛstərə'tɜ/ *n.* the keeper of a restaurant.

restful /'rɛstfəl/ *adj.* **1.** full of, or giving, rest. **2.** being at rest; quiet; tranquil; peaceful. –**restfully,** *adv.* –**restfulness,** *n.*

restitution /rɛstə'tjuʃən/ *n.* **1.** reparation made by giving an equivalent or compensation for loss, damage, or injury caused; indemnification. **2.** the restoration of property or rights previously taken away, conveyed, or surrendered. **3.** restoration to the former or original state

or position. **4.** *Physics* the return of an elastic material to its original form when released from strain. –**restitutionary,** *adj.*

restive /'rɛstɪv/ *adj.* **1.** restless; uneasy; impatient of control, restraint, or delay, as persons. **2.** → **refractory**. **3.** refusing to go forward, as a horse. –**restively,** *adv.* –**restiveness,** *n.*

restless /'rɛstləs/ *adj.* **1.** characterised by or showing inability to remain at rest: *a restless mood.* **2.** unquiet or uneasy, as a person, the mind, heart, etc. **3.** never at rest, motionless, or still; never ceasing. **4.** without rest; without restful sleep: *a restless night.* **5.** characterised by unceasing activity; averse to quiet or inaction, as persons. –**restlessly,** *adv.* –**restlessness,** *n.*

Rest of World *n.* *Marketing* the rest of the world, as when one price is being quoted for an item being bought locally and another when bought from anywhere else in the world.

restore /rə'stɔ/ *v.t.* **1.** to bring back into existence, use, etc.; re-establish: *to restore order.* **2.** to bring back to a former, original, or normal condition, as a building, statue, or painting. **3.** to bring back to a condition of health, soundness, or life. **4.** to put back to a former place, or to a former position, rank, etc. **5.** to give back (anything taken away or lost). **6.** to reproduce, rebuild, or represent (an ancient building, extinct animal, etc.). –**restoration,** *n.* –**restorative,** *adj.* –**restorer,** *n.*

restrain /rə'streɪn/ *v.t.* **1.** to hold back from action; keep in check or under control; keep down; repress. **2.** to deprive of liberty, as a person. –*phr.* **3. restrain oneself,** to curb one's initial impulses, desires, etc. –**restrainable,** *adj.* –**restrainedly,** *adv.*

restraining order *n.* *Law* an injunction made by a court, as one to prevent one spouse from visiting the other during divorce proceedings.

restraint /rə'streɪnt/ *n.* **1.** restraining action or influence: *freedom from restraint.* **2.** a means of restraining. **3.** the act of restraining, controlling, or checking. **4.** the condition or fact of being restrained; deprivation of liberty; confinement. **5.** a holding back of feelings. **6.** the ability to keep one's emotions in check: *show some restraint.*

restrict /rə'strɪkt/ *v.t.* to confine or keep within limits, as of space, action, choice, quantity, etc. –**restricted,** *adj.* –**restriction,** *n.* –**restrictive,** *adj.*

restrictive practice *n.* **1.** a practice on the part of the members of an association such as a trade union, tending to limit the freedom of choice of their co-workers or employers. **2.** → **restrictive trade practice**.

restrictive trade practice *n.* an agreement between trading companies which is contrary to the public interest, as resale price maintenance, exclusive dealing, price discrimination, etc.

restructure /ri'strʌktʃə/ *v.t.* **1.** to change the organisation or structure of: *to restructure the hospital's committee system.* **2.** (in business, manufacturing, etc.) to change the pattern of employment, distribution, etc., especially when this results in job losses. **3.** to reformulate, as when redrafting a document, policy, award, etc. –*n.* **4.** the act or process of restructuring: *an award restructure.* –**restructuring,** *n.*

result /rə'zʌlt/ *n.* **1.** that which results; the outcome, consequence, or effect. **2.** *Maths* a quantity, value, etc., obtained by calculation. –*v.i.* **3.** to spring, arise, or proceed as a consequence from actions, circumstances, premises, etc.; be the outcome. **4.** to terminate or end in a specified manner or thing. **5.** *Law* → **revert** (def. 4). –**resultant,** *adj.*

resume /rə'zjum/ *v.t.* **1.** to take up or go on with again after interruption: *to resume a journey.* **2.** to go back to: *to resume one's seat.* **3.** to take, or take on, again: *she resumed her maiden name.* –*v.i.* **4.** to go on or continue after interruption. **5.** to begin again. –**resumption** /rɪˈzʌmpʃən/, n. –**resumable**, adj. –**resumer**, n.

résumé /ˈrɛzjəmeɪ/ n. **1.** a summing up; a summary. **2.** → curriculum vitae. Also, **resumé**.

resurge /rɪˈsɜːdʒ/ v.i. (-**surged**, -**surging**) to rise again, as from the dead. –**resurgence**, n. –**resurgent**, adj.

resurrect /rɛzəˈrɛkt/ v.t. **1.** to raise from the dead; bring to life again. **2.** to bring back into use, practice, etc.: *to resurrect an ancient custom.* –v.i. **3.** to rise from the dead. –**resurrection**, n.

resuscitate /rəˈsʌsəteɪt/ v.t. **1.** to revive (someone), especially from apparent death or from unconsciousness. –v.i. **2.** to return to life or consciousness; become revived. –**resuscitable**, adj. –**resuscitation** /rəsʌsə-ˈteɪʃən/, n. –**resuscitative**, adj. –**resuscitator**, n.

retail /ˈriːteɪl/ *for defs 1–4 and 6,* /riːˈteɪl/ *for def. 5* n.**1.** the sale of goods directly to the people who use them, usually in small quantities (opposed to *wholesale*). –adj. **2.** relating to, or taking part in, sale at retail: *the retail price.* –adv. **3.** at a retail price or in a retail quantity; at retail. –v.t. **4.** to sell directly to the user. **5.** to relate or repeat in detail to others: *to retail scandal.* –v.i. **6.** to be sold at retail: *it retails at a dollar.* –**retailer**, n.

retail bank n. a bank which deals with transactions made by individual customers rather than businesses or other banks. Compare **merchant bank**. –**retail banking**, n.

retail therapy n. Colloq. (*humorous*) shopping, as a way of raising one's spirits.

retain /rəˈteɪn/ v.t. **1.** to keep possession of. **2.** to continue to use, practise, etc.: *to retain an old custom.* **3.** to keep in mind; remember. **4.** to hold in place or position. **5.** to engage, especially by the payment of a preliminary fee, as a lawyer. –**retainable**, adj. –**retainment**, n.

retainer[1] /rəˈteɪnə/ n. **1.** Hist. a person attached to a noble household or owing it service. **2.** any servant, especially a personal or family servant of long standing. **3.** Machinery the groove or frame in which roller-bearings operate. **4.** Orthodontics a custom-made, removable appliance that helps keep teeth in their new, straightened position after braces have been removed.

retainer[2] /rəˈteɪnə/ n. **1.** the act of retaining in one's service. **2.** the fact of being so retained. **3.** a fee paid to secure services, as of a barrister. **4.** a reduced rent paid during absence for a flat or lodging as an indication of future requirement.

retaliate /rəˈtælieɪt/ v.i. **1.** to return like for like, especially evil for evil or requital (especially for an injury); take reprisals: *to retaliate for an injury.* –v.t. **2.** to make return for or requite (now usually wrong, injury, etc.) –**retaliation**, n. –**retaliatory**, adj.

retard v.t. /rəˈtad/ **1.** to make slow; delay the progress of (an action, process, etc.); hinder or impede. **2.** to delay or limit (a person's intellectual or emotional development). –n. /ˈritad/ Colloq. **3.** (*derog.*) a person with delayed or limited intellectual or emotional development. **4.** a fool. –**retardant**, n., adj. –**retardation**, n. –**retarder**, n.

retarded /rəˈtadəd/ adj. slow in mental development, especially having an IQ of 70–85; backward.

retch /rɛtʃ/ v.i. **1.** to make the sound and spasmodic movement associated with the impulse to vomit. –n. **2.** the act or an instance of retching.

retention /rəˈtɛnʃən/ n. **1.** the act of retaining. **2.** the state of being retained. **3.** power to retain; capacity for retaining. **4.** the act or power of remembering things; memory.

retentive /rəˈtɛntɪv/ adj. **1.** tending or serving to retain something. **2.** having power or capacity to retain. **3.** having power or ability to remember; having a good memory. –**retentiveness**, n. –**retentivity** /riːtɛnˈtɪvəti/, n.

reticent /ˈrɛtəsənt/ adj. disposed to be silent; not inclined to speak freely; reserved. –**reticence**, n. –**reticently**, adv.

reticulate adj. /rəˈtɪkjələt/ **1.** netted; covered with a network. **2.** like a network or net. –v.t. /rəˈtɪkjəleɪt/ **3.** to form into a network. –v.i. /rəˈtɪkjəleɪt/ **4.** to form a network. –**reticulation**, n. –**reticulately**, adv.

retina /ˈrɛtɪnə/ n. (pl. -**nas** or -**nae** /-niː/) Anat. the innermost coat of the posterior part of the eyeball, serving to receive images; consists of a layer of light-sensitive cells connecting with the optic nerve by way of a layer of nerve cells. –**retinal**, adj.

retinal detachment n. → **detached retina**.

retinal scanner n. a device which scans the retina of the eye, as a means of identification of a person. –**retinal scanning**, n.

retinue /ˈrɛtənjuː/ n. a body of retainers in attendance upon an important personage; a suite.

retire /rəˈtaɪə/ v.i. **1.** to go away from others, as to a place of shelter. **2.** to go to bed. **3.** to withdraw from office, business, or active life: *I will retire at the age of 60.* **4.** Sport to leave the field, ring, etc., before completion of the contest, usually because of injury. –v.t. **5.** to remove from active service or the usual field of activity. –**retirement**, n. –**retiree**, n.

retiring /rəˈtaɪərɪŋ/ adj. **1.** that retires. **2.** withdrawing from contact with others; reserved; shy.

retort /rəˈtɔːt/ v.t. **1.** to reply in retaliation; make a retort or retorts, often quickly and sharply; reply in kind to. **2.** to return (an accusation, epithet, etc.) upon the person uttering it. –n. **3.** a severe, incisive, or witty reply, especially one that counters a first speaker's statement, argument, etc.

retrace /rəˈtreɪs/ v.t. **1.** to trace back; go back over: *to retrace one's steps.* **2.** to go back over with the memory. **3.** to go over again with the sight or attention. –**retraceable**, adj.

retract[1] /rəˈtrækt/ v.t. to draw back or in. –**retractable**, adj. –**retractor**, n.

retract[2] /rəˈtrækt/ v.t. **1.** to withdraw (a statement, opinion, etc.) as unjustified. **2.** to withdraw or revoke (a decree, promise, etc.). –**retractable**, adj. –**retraction**, **retractation** /riːtrækˈteɪʃən/, n. –**retractor**, n.

retractile /rəˈtræktaɪl/ adj. capable of being drawn back or in, as the head of a tortoise; exhibiting the power of retraction. –**retractility** /ritrækˈtɪləti/, n.

retread v.t. /ˌriːˈtrɛd/ (-**treaded**, -**treading**) **1.** to recondition (a worn motor-vehicle tyre) by moulding a fresh tread on to it and vulcanising by subjecting to heat and pressure. –n. /ˈritrɛd/ **2.** a retreaded tyre.

retreat /rəˈtriːt/ n. **1.** the forced or planned withdrawal of an armed force before an enemy, or the withdrawing of a ship or fleet from action. **2.** the act of withdrawing, especially into safety or privacy; retirement; seclusion. **3.** a place of shelter, seclusion, or privacy. **4.** a withdrawal, or a period of withdrawal, for religious exercises and prayer. –v.i. **5.** to make a retreat.

retrench /rəˈtrɛntʃ/ v.t. **1.** to cut down, reduce, or diminish; curtail (expenses). **2.** to sack or dismiss, as part of an effort to economise. –v.i. **3.** to economise; reduce expenses: *they retrenched by cutting down staff.* –**retrenchment**, n.

retribution /rɛtrəˈbjuːʃən/ n. **1.** requital according to merits or deserts, especially for evil. **2.** something given or inflicted in such requital. **3.** Theology the distribution of rewards and punishments in a future life. –**retributive**, adj.

retrieve /rəˈtriːv/ v.t. **1.** to recover or regain. **2.** to bring back to a former and better condition; restore: *to retrieve one's fortunes.* **3.** to make good; repair (a loss, error, etc.). **4.** to find and bring back. **5.** to save. –n. **6.** the act of retrieving; recovery. –**retrievable**, adj. –**retrieval**, n.

retriever /rəˈtriːvə/ n. any of several breeds of dog for retrieving game, as the golden retriever.

retro /ˈrɛtroʊ/ adj. of or relating to fashion or popular music of previous times which has become fashionable again.

retro- 1. a prefix meaning 'backwards' in space or time, as *retrogression*, *retrospect*. 2. a prefix indicating a style of fashion, music, etc., which looks back to a previous style: *retro-rock*.

retroactive /rɛtroʊˈæktɪv/ adj. operative with respect to past occurrences, as a statute; retrospective. –**retroactively**, adv. –**retroactivity** /ˌrɛtroʊækˈtɪvəti/, n.

retrofit /ˈrɛtroʊfɪt/ v.t. (-**fitted**, -**fitting**) 1. to fit out anew as part of repairs or maintenance, especially by replacing old or worn parts or items with new and up-to-date ones. 2. to fit out at a later time as part of a secondary stage of development: *to retrofit the inner suburbs with green spaces*.

retroflex /ˈrɛtrəflɛks/ adj. bent backwards. –**retroflexion**, n.

retrograde /ˈrɛtrəɡreɪd/ adj. 1. moving backwards; having a backward motion or direction; retiring or retreating. 2. returning to an earlier and inferior state: *a retrograde step*. 3. inverse or reversed, as order. 4. *Chiefly Biol.* exhibiting degeneration or deterioration. 5. *Astron.* denoting an apparent or actual motion in a direction opposite to the order of the signs of the zodiac, or from east to west.

retrogress /rɛtrəˈɡrɛs/ v.i. 1. to go backwards into a worse or earlier condition. 2. to move backwards. –**retrogression**, n.

retrosexual /rɛtroʊˈsɛkʃuəl/ n. a man who maintains an adherence to the conservative male stereotype in both dress and manners, as in old-fashioned courtesies to women, etc.

retrospect /ˈrɛtrəspɛkt/ n. 1. contemplation of the past; a survey of past time, events, etc. –*phr.* 2. **in retrospect**, looking backwards in time. 3. **retrospect to**, to refer back to. –**retrospection**, n.

retrospective /rɛtrəˈspɛktɪv/ adj. 1. directed to the past; contemplative of past events, etc. 2. looking or directed backwards. 3. retroactive, as a statute. –n. 4. an exhibition of an entire phase or representative examples of an artist's lifework. –**retrospectively**, adv.

retrospectivity /ˌrɛtroʊspɛkˈtɪvəti/ n. 1. the quality of being retrospective. 2. (in union or other agreements) the dating of the effectiveness of the agreement to a time prior to the date of the discussion concerning the agreement.

retroussé /rəˈtruːseɪ/ adj. (especially of the nose) turned up.

retroversion /rɛtrəˈvɜːʒən/ n. 1. a looking or turning back. 2. the resulting state or condition. 3. *Pathol.* a tilting or turning backwards of an organ or part: *retroversion of the uterus*.

retrovirus /ˈrɛtroʊvaɪrəs/ n. any of a family of single-stranded RNA viruses, *Retroviridae*, including the AIDS virus and a number of oncogene-carrying viruses suspected of inducing cancer. –**retroviral**, adj.

return /rəˈtɜːn/ v.i. 1. to go or come back, as to a former place, position, state, etc. 2. to revert to a former owner. 3. to revert or recur in thought or discourse. 4. to make reply; retort. –v.t. 5. to put, bring, take, give, or send back: *return a book to its shelf*. 6. to send or give back in reciprocation, recompense, or requital: *return shot for shot*. 7. to reciprocate, repay, or requite (something sent, given, done, etc.) with something similar: *return the enemy's fire*. 8. to answer; retort. 9. *Law* to render (a verdict, etc.). 10. to yield (a profit, revenue, etc.), as in return for labour, expenditure, or investment. 11. to report or announce officially. 12. to elect, as to a legislative body. 13. to turn back or in the reverse direction. 14. *Chiefly Archit.* to turn away from, or at an angle to, the previous line of direction. –n. 15. the act or fact of returning; a going or coming back; a bringing, sending, or giving back. 16. a recurrence: *many happy returns of the day*. 17. reciprocation, repayment, or requital: *profits in return for outlay*. 18. response or reply. 19. someone or something that is returned. 20. a ticket which is returned to a theatre box office by the original purchaser for resale. 21. the gain realised on an exchange of goods. 22. (*oft. pl.*) a yield or profit, as from labour, land, business, investment, etc. 23. a report, especially a formal or official report: *tax returns*; *election returns*. 24. the report or statement of financial condition. 25. a return ticket. 26. *Archit.* **a.** the continuation of a moulding, projection, etc., in a different direction. **b.** a side or part which falls away from the front of any straight work. 27. *Sport* **a.** the process of returning a ball. **b.** the ball which is returned. 28. *Econ.* yield per unit as compared to the cost per unit involved in a specific industrial process. –adj. 29. of or relating to return or returning: *a return trip*. 30. sent, given, or done in return: *a return shot*. 31. done or occurring again: *a return engagement of the opera*. 32. (of a game) played so that the loser of a previous game played between the same two players or teams has a second chance to win. 33. denoting a person or thing which is returned or returning to a place: *return cargo*. 34. changing in direction; doubling or returning on itself: *return bend in the road*. –*phr.* 35. **by return**, by the next post.

returning officer n. an official who administers federal or state electoral laws at the electorate level.

return key n. *Computers* the key sometimes labelled with the word 'return' or with the word 'enter' or with an arrow, which, when pressed, activates a command keyed in on a keyboard or produces a carriage return. Also, **enter key**.

return ticket n. a ticket entitling the holder to travel to a destination and, within a specified period, to return to the point of departure.

reunion /riˈjuːnjən/ n. 1. the act of uniting again. 2. the state of being united again. 3. a gathering of relatives, friends, or associates after separation: *a family reunion*.

rev /rɛv/ n. 1. a revolution (in an engine or the like). –*verb* (**revved**, **revving**) –v.t. Also, **rev up**. 2. **a.** to increase the speed of (an engine) without the gears engaged: *to rev the motor*. **b.** to cause the engine of (a vehicle) to speed up without the gears engaged: *to rev a truck*. –v.i. 3. (of an engine) to speed up with gears disengaged.

revalue /riˈvæljuː/ v.t. 1. to value again, especially to raise the legal value of (a currency). 2. to reassess; review. See **devalue**. –**revaluation** /rivæljuˈeɪʃən/, n.

revamp v.t. /riˈvæmp/ 1. to rework or reconstruct; renovate. –n. /ˈriːvæmp/ 2. such a renovation.

reveal /rəˈviːl/ v.t. 1. to make known; disclose; divulge: *to reveal a secret*. 2. to lay open to view; display; exhibit. –**revealable**, adj. –**revealing**, adj. –**revealer**, n.

reveille /rəˈvæli/ n. a signal, as of a drum or bugle, sounded at a prescribed hour, to waken soldiers or sailors for the day's duties.

revel /ˈrɛvəl/ v.i. (-**elled** or, *Chiefly US*, -**eled**, -**elling** or, *Chiefly US*, -**eling**) 1. to make merry; indulge in boisterous festivities. –n. 2. (*oft. pl.*) an occasion of merrymaking or noisy festivity with dancing, etc. –*phr.* 3. **revel in**, to take great pleasure or delight in. –**reveller**, n. –**revelry**, n.

revelation /rɛvəˈleɪʃən/ n. 1. the act of revealing; disclosure. 2. something revealed, especially causing astonishment.

revenge /rəˈvɛndʒ/ n. 1. the act of revenging; retaliation for injuries or wrongs; vengeance. 2. the desire to revenge; vindictiveness. 3. an opportunity of retaliation or satisfaction. *–v.t.* (**-venged, -venging**) **4.** to take vengeance or exact expiation on behalf of (a person) or for (a wrong), especially in a resentful or vindictive spirit **–revenger,** *n.* **–revengeful,** *adj.*

revenue /ˈrɛvənju/ *n.* **1.** the income of a government from taxation, excise duties, customs, or other sources, appropriated to the payment of the public expenses. **2.** (*pl.*) the collective items or amounts of income of a person, a state, etc. **3.** the return or yield from any kind of property; income.

revenue-neutral *adj.* resulting in neither a gain nor a loss in revenue.

reverberate /rəˈvɜbəreɪt/ *v.i.* **1.** to re-echo or resound. **2.** *Physics* to be reflected many times, as soundwaves from the walls, etc., of a confined space. **3.** to rebound or recoil. **4.** to be deflected, as flame in a reverberatory furnace. **5.** to linger in the memory: *words that reverberate through our history.* **–reverberation** /rəvɜbəˈreɪʃən/, *n.* **–reverberant, reverberative,** *adj.* **–reverberator,** *n.*

reverberatory /rəˈvɜbərətri/ *adj.* denoting a furnace, kiln, or the like, in which the fuel is not in direct contact with the ore, metal, etc., to be heated, but furnishes a flame that plays over the material, especially by being deflected downwards from the roof.

revere /rəˈvɪə/ *v.t.* to regard with respect tinged with awe; venerate.

reverence /ˈrɛvərəns, ˈrɛvrəns/ *n.* **1.** a feeling or attitude of deep respect combined with a sense of wonder at someone's greatness and goodness; veneration. **2.** a gesture showing this feeling; an obeisance, bow, or curtsy. *–v.t.* (**-renced, -rencing**) **3.** to regard or treat with reverence; venerate. **–reverential,** *adj.* **–reverent,** *adj.*

reverend /ˈrɛvrənd, ˈrɛvərənd/ *adj.* **1.** (*oft. upper case*) an epithet of respect applied to, or prefixed to the name of, a member of the clergy. **2.** worthy to be revered; entitled to reverence. **3.** relating to or characteristic of the clergy. *–n.* **4.** *Colloq.* a member of the clergy.

reverie /ˈrɛvəri/ *n.* **1.** a state of dreamy meditation or fanciful musing: *lost in reverie.* **2.** *Music* an instrumental composition of a vague and dreamy character. Also, **revery.**

revers /rəˈvɪə/ *n.* (*pl.* **-vers** /-ˈvɪəz/) a part of a garment turned back to show the lining or facing, as a lapel.

reverse /rəˈvɜs/ *adj.* **1.** opposite or contrary in position, direction, order, or character: *an impression reverse to what was intended.* **2.** acting in a manner opposite or contrary to that which is usual, as an appliance or apparatus. **3.** of or relating to the back or rear: *iron this fabric on the reverse side.* **4.** producing a rearward motion: *reverse gear.* **5.** *Motor Vehicles* of or relating to reverse (gear ratio). **6.** *Printing* of or relating to type matter which appears white on a solid or screened background. *–n.* **7.** the opposite or contrary of something. **8.** the back or rear of anything. **9.** *Coining* that side of a coin, medal, etc., which does not bear the principal design (opposed to *obverse*). **10.** an adverse change of fortune; a misfortune, check, or defeat: *to meet with an unexpected reverse.* **11.** *Motor Vehicles* a transmission gear ratio driving a car backwards. **12.** *Machinery* a reversing mechanism, etc. **13.** *Printing* type matter produced in reverse printing. *–v.t.* **14.** to turn in an opposite position; transpose. **15.** to turn inside out or upside down. **16.** to turn in the opposite direction; send on the opposite course. **17.** to turn in the opposite order: *to reverse the usual order.* **18.** to alter to the opposite in character or tendency, or change completely. **19.** to revoke or annul (a decree, judgement, etc.). **20.** *Law* to overrule (a judgement) on appeal. **21.** *Machinery* to cause to revolve or act in an opposite or contrary direction or manner. **22.** to drive (a motor vehicle) backwards: *he reversed the car into a parking*

space. *–v.i.* **23.** to turn or move in the opposite or contrary direction, as in dancing. **24.** (of an engine) to reverse the action of the mechanism. **25.** to drive a vehicle backwards: *he reversed into the garage. –phr.* **26. reverse arms,** *Mil.* to carry out a drill manoeuvre in which the rifle is turned muzzle downwards. **27. reverse charges,** to make a telephone call for which the receiver pays. **28. reverse out,** *Printing* to produce in reverse printing. **29. reverse stick,** *Hockey* to strike the ball with the face of the stick on the left side of the body if a right-handed player, and on the right side of the body if a left-handed player. **–reversal,** *n.* **–reversely,** *adv.* **–reverser,** *n.*

reverse-cycle *adj.* of or relating to an air conditioner able to cool an area in summer and heat it in winter.

reverse-engineer *v.t.* to analyse the construction of (a product), especially as a preliminary to designing a similar product.

reverse-park *v.t.* **1.** to park (a vehicle) by reversing it into the allocated space. *–v.i.* **2.** to park a vehicle in this manner. *–n.* **3.** such a parking procedure.

reversible /rəˈvɜsəbəl/ *adj.* **1.** capable of being reversed or of reversing. **2.** capable of re-establishing the original condition after a change by the reversal of that change. **3.** (of a fabric, garment, etc.) woven or printed so that either side may be exposed. *–n.* **4.** a garment, especially a coat, that may be worn with either side exposed. **–reversibility** /rəvɜsəˈbɪləti, ri-/, **reversibleness,** *n.* **–reversibly,** *adv.*

re-version /riˈvɜʒən/ *v.t.* to produce a different version of (a work) for a different format, communication channel, etc.

revert /rəˈvɜt/ *v.i.* **1.** to return to a former habit, practice, belief, condition, etc. **2.** to go back in thought or discourse, as to a subject. **3.** *Biol.* to return to an earlier or primitive type. **4.** *Law* to go back or return to the former owner or his or her heirs. *–phr.* **5. revert to type,** to resume earlier characteristics, habits of behaviour, etc., thought to be underlying later developments or sophistication. **–revertible,** *adj.* **–reversion,** *n.*

review /rəˈvju/ *n.* **1.** a report in a newspaper or magazine of a book, concert, art exhibition, play, etc.; critique. **2.** a magazine, journal, etc., containing articles on current events or affairs, books, art, etc.: *a literary review.* **3.** a looking again; a second view of something. **4.** inspection, or examination by looking, especially a formal inspection of any military or naval force. **5.** a general report or account of something. *–v.t.* **6.** to look over again. **7.** to inspect, especially formally or officially. **8.** to discuss (a book, etc.) in a critical review. **9.** *Law* to re-examine judicially. *–v.i.* **10.** to write reviews; review books, etc.: *to review for a journal.* **–reviewable,** *adj.* **–reviewer,** *n.*

revile /rəˈvaɪl/ *v.t.* to assail with contemptuous or opprobrious language; address, or speak of, abusively. **–revilement,** *n.* **–reviler,** *n.* **–revilingly,** *adv.*

revise /rəˈvaɪz/ *v.t.* **1.** to amend or alter: *to revise one's opinion.* **2.** to alter after one or more drafts or editions: *to revise a manuscript; to revise a book.* **3.** to go over (a subject, book, etc.) again or study in order to fix it in the memory, as before an examination. **–revision** /rəˈvɪʒən/, **revisal,** *n.* **–reviser,** *n.*

revisit /riˈvɪzət/ *v.t.* **1.** to visit again. **2.** to re-examine (a plan, argument, etc.): *to revisit a proposal.*

revival /rəˈvaɪvəl/ *n.* **1.** restoration to life, consciousness, vigour, strength, etc. **2.** restoration to use, acceptance, or currency: *the revival of old customs.* **3.** something produced anew, as a new version of an old play or recorded song. **4.** an awakening, in a church or a community, of interest in and care for matters relating to personal religion. **5.** Also, **revival meeting, revivalist**

meeting. a service for the purpose of effecting a religious awakening: *to hold a revival.*

revive /rə'vaɪv/ *v.t.* **1.** to set going or in activity again: *to revive old feuds.* **2.** to bring back into notice or use: *to revive a subject of discussion.* **3.** to restore to life, energy or consciousness. *–v.i.* **4.** to return to life, consciousness, vigour. **5.** to return to notice or use. **–reviver,** *n.*

revocable /'rɛvəkəbəl/ *adj.* able to be revoked. Also, **revokable** /rə'voʊkəbəl/. **–revocability** /rɛvəkə'bɪləti/, *n.* **–revocably,** *adv.*

revoke /rə'voʊk/ *v.t.* **1.** to take back or withdraw; annul, cancel, or reverse; rescind or repeal: *to revoke a decree.* *–v.i.* **2.** *Cards* to fail to follow suit when one can and should do so; renege. **–revoker,** *n.*

revolt /rə'voʊlt/ *v.i.* **1.** to break away from or rise against constituted authority, as by open rebellion; cast off allegiance or subjection to those in authority; rebel; mutiny. *–v.t.* **2.** to affect with disgust or abhorrence. *–n.* **3.** the act of revolting; an insurrection or rebellion. **4.** the state of those revolting: *to be in revolt.* *–phr.* **5. revolt against,** to rebel in feeling against. **6. revolt at,** to feel disgust or horror at. **7. revolt from,** to turn away from in mental rebellion, utter disgust, or abhorrence. **–revolter,** *n.*

revolting /rə'voʊltɪŋ/ *adj.* **1.** rebellious. **2.** disgusting; repulsive. **–revoltingly,** *adv.*

revolution /rɛvə'luʃən/ *n.* **1.** the complete overthrow of an established government or political system. **2.** a complete or marked change in something. **3.** *Mechanics* **a.** a turning round or rotating on an axis, especially in a motor car engine. **b.** a single cycle in such a course. **4.** *Astron.* **a.** (of a heavenly body) the action or fact of going round in an orbit: *the earth's revolution around the sun.* **b.** a single course of such movement.

revolutionary /rɛvə'luʃənəri, -fənri/ *adj.* **1.** relating to, characterised by, or of the nature of a revolution, or complete or marked change. **2.** subversive to established procedure, principles, etc. **3.** revolving. *–n.* (*pl.* **-ries**) **4.** someone who advocates or takes part in a revolution; revolutionist.

revolutionise /rɛvə'luʃənaɪz/ *v.t.* **1.** to bring about a revolution in; effect a radical change in. **2.** to subject to a political revolution. Also, **revolutionize.**

revolve /rə'vɒlv/ *v.i.* **1.** to turn round or rotate on an axis. **2.** to move in an orbit. **3.** to go in a cycle: *the seasons revolve.* **4.** to turn over in the mind. *–v.t.* **5.** to cause to turn round on an axis. **6.** to cause to move in a curving course around a central point. **7.** to think about; consider. **–revolvable,** *adj.*

revolver /rə'vɒlvə/ *n.* a pistol having a revolving chambered cylinder for holding a number of cartridges which may be discharged in succession without reloading.

revue /rə'vju/ *n.* **1.** a form of theatrical entertainment in which recent events, popular fads, etc., are parodied. **2.** any group of skits, and dances, and songs.

revulsion /rə'vʌlʃən/ *n.* **1.** a sudden and violent change of feeling or reaction in sentiment. **2.** a violent dislike or aversion for something. **3.** *Med.* the diminution of morbid action in one part of the body by irritation in another. **4.** the act of drawing something back or away. **5.** the fact of being so drawn.

reward /rə'wɔd/ *n.* **1.** something given or received in return or recompense for service, merit, hardship, etc. **2.** a sum of money offered for the detection or capture of a criminal, the recovery of lost or stolen property, etc. *–v.t.* **3.** to recompense or requite (a person, etc.) for service, merit, achievement, etc. **–rewarder,** *n.*

rewarding /rə'wɔdɪŋ/ *adj.* giving satisfaction that the effort made was worthwhile: *teaching children can be very rewarding.*

-rhagia a word element meaning 'bursting forth'. Also, **-rhage, -rhagy, -rrhagia, -rrhage, -rrhagy.**

rhapsody /'ræpsədi/ *n.* (*pl.* **-dies**) **1.** an exalted or exaggerated expression of feeling or enthusiasm. **2.** an unusually intense or irregular poem or piece of prose. **3.** *Music* an instrumental composition irregular in form and suggestive of improvisation: *Liszt's Hungarian Rhapsodies.* **–rhapsodical** /ræp'sɒdɪkəl/, **rhapsodic** /ræp'sɒdɪk/, *adj.*

rheo- a word element meaning 'something flowing', 'a stream', 'current'.

rheostat /'riəstæt/ *n.* a variable electrical resistor. **–rheostatic** /riə'stætɪk/, *adj.*

Rhesus factor /'risəs fæktə/ *n.* → **Rh factor.**

rhesus monkey *n.* a monkey, *Macacus rhesus,* common in India, much used in medical research.

rhetoric /'rɛtərɪk/ *n.* **1.** the art or science of all specially literary uses of language in prose or verse, including the figures of speech. **2.** the art of prose in general as opposed to verse. **3.** (in prose or verse) the use of exaggeration or display, in an unfavourable sense. **4.** (originally) the art of oratory. **5.** (in classical oratory) the art of influencing the thought of one's hearers. **–rhetorical,** *adj.*

rhetorical question *n.* a question designed to produce an effect and not to draw an answer.

rheumatic fever *n.* *Pathol.* a disease usually afflicting children and marked by fever, inflammation of the joints, generalised muscle pains, and frequently associated with pathological changes in the heart and the different serous membranes.

rheumatism /'rumətɪzəm/ *n.* **1.** any of various ailments of the joints or muscles, as certain chronic disabilities of the joints (**chronic rheumatism**) and certain painful affections of the muscles (**muscular rheumatism**). **2.** (in a growing child) rheumatic fever. **–rheumatic** /ru'mætɪk/, *adj.*

rheumatoid arthritis /rumətɔɪd a'θraɪtəs/ *n.* a chronic autoimmune disease marked by inflammation of the lining of the joints, frequently accompanied by marked deformities, and causing damage to the bone and cartilage. *Abbrev.:* RA

Rh factor /ar'eɪtʃ fæktə/ *n.* an agglutinogen often present in human blood. Blood containing this factor (**Rh positive**) may cause haemolytic reactions, especially during pregnancy or after repeated transfusions with blood lacking in it (**Rh negative**). In infants it may cause haemolytic anaemias. Also, **Rhesus factor.**

rhinestone /'raɪnstoʊn/ *n.* an artificial gem made of paste.

rhino /'raɪnoʊ/ *n.* (*pl.* **rhinos**) *Colloq.* a rhinoceros.

rhino- a word element meaning 'nose'. Also, **rhin-.**

rhinoceros /raɪ'nɒsərəs, raɪ'nɒsrəs/ *n.* (*pl.* **-ceroses** *or, especially collectively,* **-ceros**) any of various large, ungainly, thick-skinned, perissodactyl mammals, found in Asia and Africa, family Rhinocerotidae, with one or two upright horns on the snout. **–rhinocerotic** /ˌraɪnoʊsə-'rɒtɪk/, *adj.*

rhinoplasty /'raɪnoʊˌplæsti/ *n.* plastic surgery of the nose. **–rhinoplastic** /raɪnoʊ'plæstɪk/, *adj.*

rhizo- a word element meaning 'root'.

rhizome /'raɪzoʊm/ *n.* *Bot.* a root-like subterranean stem, commonly horizontal in position, which usually produces roots below and sends up shoots progressively from the upper surface. **–rhizomatous** /raɪ'zɒmətəs, -'zoʊmə-/, *adj.*

rhodo- a word element meaning 'rose'. Also, **rhod-.**

rhododendron /roʊdə'dɛndrən/ *n.* any plant of the genus *Rhododendron,* comprising evergreen and deciduous shrubs and trees with handsome pink, purple, or white flowers, and oval or oblong leaves, as *R. ponticum,* much cultivated for ornament.

-rhoea a word element meaning 'flow', 'discharge', as in *gonorrhoea*. Also, **-rrhoea**; *Chiefly US*, **-rhea**.

rhomboid /'rɒmbɔɪd/ *n.* **1.** *Geom.* an oblique-angled parallelogram with the adjacent sides unequal. *–adj.* Also, **rhomboidal** /rɒm'bɔɪdl/ **2.** having a form like, or approaching that of, a rhombus; shaped like a rhomboid.

rhombus /'rɒmbəs/ *n.* (*pl.* **-buses** *or* **-bi** /-baɪ/) *Geom.* an oblique-angled parallelogram with all sides equal.

rhubarb /'rubab/ *n.* **1.** a garden plant with edible leaf-stalks, or a related plant with a medicinal rhizome. **2.** the edible fleshy leafstalks of any of the garden species, used in making desserts.

rhyme /raɪm/ *n.* **1.** agreement in the terminal sounds of lines of verse, or of words. **2.** a word agreeing with another in terminal sound. **3.** verse or poetry having correspondence in the terminal sounds of the line. **4.** a poem or piece of verse having such correspondence. *–verb* (**rhymed, rhyming**) *–v.t.* **5.** to use (a word) as a rhyme to another word; use (words) as rhymes. *–v.i.* **6.** to make rhyme or verse; versify. **7.** to use rhyme in writing verse. **8.** to form a rhyme, as one word or line with another. **9.** to be composed in metrical form with rhymes, as verse. *–phr.* **10. rhyme or reason**, logic; explanation; meaning: *there was no rhyme or reason for that behaviour.* **–rhymer**, *n.*

rhythm /'rɪðəm/ *n.* **1.** movement in a (regular) pattern of time, especially with beat, accent, etc. **2. a.** a pattern of regular or irregular pulses caused in music or speech by the occurrence of strong and weak beats. **b.** a particular form of this: *duple rhythm, triple rhythm.* **3.** *Art* the proper relation of parts to each other and to an artistic whole. **4.** a pattern of regularity in changing elements or conditions: *the rhythm of the seasons.* **–rhythmical**, *adj.* **–rhythmist**, *n.*

rhythm and blues *n.* a style of music which first became popular in the early 1960s, using both vocal and instrumental elements based on the guitar, and derived ultimately from the African-American blues style and but with a quicker tempo and more complex rhythms. *Abbrev.*: R & B

rhythm method *n.* a method of avoiding conception by confining sexual intercourse to the infertile phases of the menstrual cycle.

rib[1] /rɪb/ *n.* **1.** one of a series of long, slender, curved bones, occurring in pairs, partly enclosing the chest cavity, and fitting into the vertebrae. **2.** something like a rib in form, position, or use, as a supporting or strengthening part. **3.** the primary vein of a leaf. **4.** *Knitting, Sewing, etc.* a raised pattern or ridge. *–v.t.* (**ribbed, ribbing**) **5.** to strengthen or enclose with ribs. **6.** to mark with rib-like ridges or markings. **–ribbed**, *adj.*

rib[2] /rɪb/ *v.t.* (**ribbed, ribbing**) *Colloq.* to tease; ridicule; make fun of. **–ribbing**, *n.*

ribald /'rɪbəld, 'raɪ-, 'raɪbɔld/ *adj.* offensive or scurrilous in speech, language, etc.; coarsely mocking or abusive; wantonly irreverent. **–ribaldry**, *n.*

ribbon /'rɪbən/ *n.* **1.** a woven strip or band of fine material, used for ornament, tying hair, etc. **2.** anything like a ribbon. **3.** a band of material soaked with ink that the keys of a typewriter hit to make a mark. **4.** a badge of an order of knighthood or other distinction: *the red ribbon of the French Legion of Honour.* **5.** *Sport* an award for success in a competition.

ribbon gum *n.* a tall tree, *Eucalyptus viminalis*, of eastern Australia with white smooth bark tending to hang in ribbons as it is shed, and from which manna is collected.

riboflavin /raɪboʊ'fleɪvən/ *n.* vitamin B$_2$, one of the vitamins in the vitamin B complex found in green vegetables, fish, milk, etc. Also, **riboflavine** /raɪboʊ-'fleɪvɪn/.

ribonucleic acid /,raɪboʊnju,kliɪk 'æsəd, ,raɪboʊnju-,kleɪɪk 'æsəd/ *n.* → **RNA**.

rice /raɪs/ *n.* **1.** the starchy seeds or grain of a species of grass, *Oryza sativa*, cultivated in warm climates and constituting an important food. **2.** the plant itself.

rice paper *n.* **1.** a thin, edible paper made from the straw of rice. **2.** a Chinese paper consisting of the pith of certain plants cut and pressed into thin sheets.

rice vinegar *n.* a mild, delicately-flavoured vinegar used in Chinese cookery. Also, **rice wine vinegar**.

rice wine *n.* **1.** → **sake**[2]. **2.** → **mirin**. **3.** any wine produced by fermenting white rice.

rich /rɪtʃ/ *adj.* **1.** having wealth or great possessions; abundantly supplied with resources, means, or funds: *a rich woman; a rich nation.* **2.** having an abundance of natural resources: *a rich territory.* **3.** of great value or worth; valuable: *a rich harvest.* **4.** costly; expensively elegant or fine, as dress, jewels, etc. **5.** sumptuous, as a feast. **6.** of valuable materials or elaborate workmanship, as buildings, furniture, etc. **7.** having many desirable elements or qualities **8. a.** having a large quantity of something specified: *rich in minerals.* **b.** (*placed after the noun*) having a large quantity of a specified item: *mineral rich; information rich.* **9.** (of food) containing good, nutritious, or choice ingredients, as butter, cream, sugar, etc. **10.** (of wine, gravy, etc.) strong and full-flavoured. **11.** (of colour) deep, strong, or vivid. **12.** (of sound, the voice, etc.) full and mellow in tone. **13.** (of smell) strongly scented. **14.** producing or yielding abundantly: *a rich soil.* **15.** abundant, plentiful, or ample: *a rich supply.* **16.** *Colloq.* ridiculous, absurd, or preposterous. *–phr.* **17. rich in**, having (valuable resources) in abundance: *a tract rich in minerals.* **18. rich in** (or **with**), abounding in: *a country rich in traditions.* **19. the rich**, rich people collectively. **–richly**, *adv.* **–richness**, *n.*

riches /'rɪtʃəz/ *pl. n.* abundant and valuable possessions; wealth.

Richter scale /'rɪktə skeɪl/ *n.* an open ended logarithmic scale used to express the magnitude or total energy of a seismic disturbance (as an earthquake). In this scale an increase of 1 indicates a thirty-fold increase in energy.

rick[1] /rɪk/ *n.* a stack of hay, straw, or the like, especially one thatched or covered for protection.

rick[2] /rɪk/ *v.t.* to sprain or strain as one's neck, back, etc.

ricker /'rɪkə/ *n.* *NZ* a kauri sapling. Also, **rika**.

rickets /'rɪkəts/ *n.* **1.** *Pathol.* a disease of childhood, characterised by softening of the bones as a result of malnutrition (ordinarily lack of vitamin D), or insufficient ingestion of calcium, or both, and often resulting in deformities. **2.** *Vet. Science* an insidious and incurable disease of cattle caused by eating certain poisonous plants prevalent in Qld cattle country.

rickety /'rɪkəti/ *adj.* **1.** liable to fall or collapse; shaky: *a rickety chair.* **2.** feeble in the joints; tottering; infirm. **3.** irregular, as motion or action. **4.** affected with or suffering from rickets. **5.** relating to or of the nature of rickets.

rickshaw /'rɪkʃɔ/ *n.* a small two-wheeled hooded vehicle drawn by one or more people, used in Asia. Also, **ricksha**.

ricochet /'rɪkəʃeɪ/ *n.* **1.** the motion of an object or projectile which rebounds one or more times from the surface or surfaces it strikes. *–v.i.* (**-cheted, -cheting**) **2.** to move in this way, as a projectile.

ricotta /rə'kɒtə/ *n.* a soft cottage cheese with a fresh bland flavour, made from the whey obtained in the manufacture of other cheeses.

rid /rɪd/ *phr.* (*v.* **rid** *or* **ridded, ridding**) **1. be rid of**, to be free from (something objectionable): *anything to be rid of the pain.* **2. get rid of**, **a.** to get free or relieved of. **b.** to get (a thing or person) off one's hands. **c.** to do away with. **3. rid of, a.** to clear, disencumber, or free of (something objectionable). **b.** to disembarrass or relieve of: *ridding the mind of doubt.* –**ridder,** *n.*

riddance /ˈrɪdns/ *n.* **1.** a clearing away or out, as of anything undesirable. **2.** a relieving or deliverance from something. –*phr.* **3. good riddance,** (sometimes fol. by *to*) an exclamation of relief of being rid of someone or something.

ridden /ˈrɪdn/ *v.* **1.** past participle of **ride.** –*adj.* **2.** (as second element in a compound adjective) afflicted by: *disease-ridden; hag-ridden.*

riddle[1] /ˈrɪdl/ *n.* **1.** a question or statement so framed as to exercise one's ingenuity in answering it or discovering its meaning; conundrum. **2.** a puzzling question, problem, or matter. **3.** a puzzling thing or person. **4.** any enigmatic or dark saying or speech.

riddle[2] /ˈrɪdl/ *v.t.* **1.** to pierce with many holes suggesting those of a sieve. **2.** to sift through a riddle, as gravel. **3.** to fill with (especially something undesirable). –*n.* **4.** a coarse sieve, as one for sifting sand in the foundry.

ride /raɪd/ *verb* (**rode, ridden, riding**) –*v.i.* **1.** to sit on and manage a horse or other animal in motion; be carried on the back of an animal. **2.** to be carried on something as if on horseback. **3.** to be borne along on or in a vehicle or any kind of conveyance. **4.** to move along in any way; be carried or supported: *distress riding among the people.* **5.** to move or float on the water. **6.** to lie at anchor, as a ship. **7.** to appear to float in space, as a heavenly body. **8.** to turn or rest on something. **9.** to extend or project over something, as the edge of one thing over the edge of another thing. –*v.t.* **10.** to sit on and manage (a horse or other animal, or a bicycle or the like) so as to be carried along: *the vessel rode the waves well.* **11.** to sit or be mounted on (something) as if on horseback; be carried or borne along on. **12.** to rest on, especially by overlapping. **13.** to ride over, along, or through (a road, boundary, region, etc.) so as to make an inspection, repairs, etc.: *his job was to ride the fences.* **14.** to execute by riding: *to ride a race.* **15.** to keep (a vessel) at anchor or moored. –*n.* **16.** a journey or excursion on a horse, etc., or on or in a vehicle. **17.** a short journey in a vehicle driven by someone else. **18.** a way, road, etc., made especially for riding. –*phr.* **19. ride down, a.** to trample under a horse's hooves. **b.** to pursue and catch up with. **20. ride for a fall, a.** to ride a horse recklessly. **b.** to act in a way which will inevitably bring disaster. **21. ride out, a.** to sustain (a gale, etc.) without damage, as while riding at anchor. **b.** to sustain or endure successfully. **22. ride up,** to work or move up from the proper position, as a piece of clothing, etc. **23. take for a ride,** *Colloq.* **a.** to wilfully mislead; deceive. **b.** to kidnap and murder. –**rideable, ridable,** *adj.*

rider /ˈraɪdə/ *n.* **1.** someone who rides a horse or other animal, or a bicycle or the like. **2.** any of various objects or devices straddling, mounted on, or attached to something else. **3.** an addition or amendment to a document, etc. –**riderless,** *adj.*

rideshare /ˈraɪdʃɛə/ *v.i.* (**-shared, -sharing**) **1.** to make use of a ride-sharing service. –*adj.* **2.** of or relating to ride-sharing services: *the rideshare economy; a rideshare driver.* –*n.* **3.** ride-sharing services collectively: *to use rideshare.* Also, **ride-share.**

ride-sharing service *n.* a service which offers one-time shared rides on short notice for a fee. Also, **ride-sharing service.**

ridge /rɪdʒ/ *n.* **1.** a long, narrow, high part of land, or a chain of hills or mountains. **2.** a long and narrow high part or crest of something, as of an animal's back, a wave, etc. **3.** any raised narrow strip, as on cloth, etc. **4.** the horizontal line in which the tops of the rafters of a roof meet. **5.** *Weather* a band of relatively high

pressure usually joining two anticyclones. **6.** the earth thrown up by a plough between furrows. **7.** a strip of arable land, usually between furrows. –*verb* (**ridged, ridging**) –*v.t.* **8.** to provide with or form into a ridge or ridges. **9.** to mark with ridges. –*v.i.* **10.** to form ridges. –**ridgy,** *adj.*

ridicule /ˈrɪdəkjul/ *n.* **1.** words or actions intended to excite contemptuous laughter at a person or thing; derision. –*v.t.* **2.** to deride; make fun of. –**ridiculer,** *n.*

ridiculous /rəˈdɪkjələs/ *adj.* **1.** such as to excite ridicule or derision; absurd, preposterous, or laughable. –*n.* **2.** (preceded by *the*) that which is ridiculous. –**ridiculously,** *adv.* –**ridiculousness,** *n.*

riding[1] /ˈraɪdɪŋ/ *n.* **1.** the act of being carried on the back of a horse or other animal. –*adj.* **2.** relating to or used in riding: *riding lessons; riding hat.*

riding[2] /ˈraɪdɪŋ/ *n.* (*usu. upper case*) an area division within a shire.

riesling /ˈrizlɪŋ, ˈrɪslɪŋ/ *n.* (*sometimes upper case*) **1.** a wine grape of Alsace, the Rhine region, and elsewhere. **2.** the wine made from this.

rife /raɪf/ *adj.* **1.** of common or frequent occurrence; prevalent; in widespread existence, activity, or use. **2.** current in speech or report. **3.** abundant, plentiful, or numerous. –*phr.* **4. rife with,** full of; having an abundance of.

riff /rɪf/ *n.* (in jazz and rock music) a short repeated melodic phrase, usually for guitar or piano, which is intended to give a strong rhythmic impetus.

riffle /ˈrɪfəl/ *n.* **1.** *Mining* the lining at the bottom of a sluice or the like, made of blocks or slats of wood, or of stones, arranged in such a manner that grooves or openings are left between them for catching and collecting particles of gold. **2.** the method of riffling cards. –*v.t.* **3.** to flutter and shift, as pages. **4.** to shuffle (cards) by dividing the pack in two, raising the corners slightly, and allowing them to fall alternately together.

riffraff /ˈrɪfræf/ *n.* **1.** the worthless or disreputable element of society; the rabble: *the riffraff of the city.* **2.** worthless or low persons.

rifle[1] /ˈraɪfəl/ *n.* **1.** a shoulder firearm with spiral grooves cut in the inner surface of the gun barrel to give the bullet a rotatory motion and thus render its flight more accurate. **2.** one of the grooves. **3.** a cannon with such grooves. **4. the rifles,** certain military units or bodies equipped with rifles.

rifle[2] /ˈraɪfəl/ *v.t.* **1.** to ransack and rob (a place, receptacle, etc.). **2.** to search and rob (a person). **3.** to plunder or strip bare of. **4.** to steal or take away. –**rifler,** *n.*

riflebird /ˈraɪfəlbɜd/ *n.* any of various birds of paradise of the genus *Ptiloris*, of Australia and New Guinea.

rift /rɪft/ *n.* **1.** an opening made by riving or splitting; a fissure; a cleft; a chink. **2.** a break in the friendly relations between two people, countries, etc.

rift valley *n.* a portion of the earth's crust, bounded on at least two sides by faults, that has been moved downwards in relation to the adjacent portions; graben.

rig /rɪg/ *v.t.* (**rigged, rigging**) **1.** *Chiefly Naut.* to put in proper order for working or use. **2.** *Aeronautics* to obtain the correct relative positions of the different components of (an aircraft). **3.** Also, **rig up.** to prepare or put together, especially as a makeshift. **4.** to manipulate fraudulently: *to rig an election.* –*n.* **5.** the arrangement of the masts, spars, sails, etc., on a boat or ship. **6.** an apparatus for some purpose; equipment; outfit. **7.** an articulated vehicle, such as a semitrailer, etc. **8.** (formerly) a vehicle with a horse or horses. **9.** the equipment used in drilling an oil or gas well. **10.** Also, **rig-out.** *Colloq.* costume or dress, especially when odd or conspicuous. –*phr.* **11. rig out** (or **up**), **a.** to furnish or provide with equipment, etc.; fit out. **b.** *Colloq.* to fit or deck with clothes, etc.: *rigged out like a field marshal in full regalia.* –**rigged**, *adj.*

rigging /'rɪgɪŋ/ *n.* **1.** the ropes, chains, etc., used to support and work the masts, yards, sails, etc., on a ship. **2.** *Aeronautical* a system of wires used to obtain the correct angles of incidence and dihedral, or the relative positions, of different components in an aircraft. **3.** tackle in general.

right /raɪt/ *adj.* **1.** in accordance with what is just or good: *right conduct.* **2.** in conformity with fact, reason, or some standard or principle; correct: *the right solution.* **3.** correct in judgement, opinion, or action. **4.** sound or normal, as the mind, etc.; sane, as persons. **5.** in good health or spirits, as persons: *he is all right again.* **6.** *Colloq.* in a satisfactory state; having what is needed: *do you need anything or are you right?* **7.** principal, front, or upper: *the right side of the cloth.* **8.** most convenient, desirable, or favourable. **9.** fitting or appropriate: *to say the right thing.* **10.** genuine; legitimate: *the right owner.* **11.** belonging or relating to the side of a person or thing which is turned towards the east when the face is towards the north (opposed to *left*). **12.** belonging or relating to the political right. **13.** straight: *a right line.* **14.** formed by, or with reference to, a line or a plane extending to another line or a surface by the shortest course: *a right angle.* **15.** *Geom.* having the axis perpendicular to the base: *a right cone.* **16.** *Colloq.* an intensifier: *he's a right idiot.* –*n.* **17.** a just claim or title, whether legal, prescriptive, or moral. **18.** that which is due to anyone by just claim. **19.** *Finance* **a.** the privilege, usually pre-emptive, which accrues to the owners of the stock of a company to subscribe for additional stock or shares at an advantageous price. **b.** (*oft. pl.*) a privilege of subscribing for a stock or bond. **20.** that which is ethically good and proper and in conformity with the moral law. **21.** that which accords with fact, reason, or propriety. **22.** the right or proper way of thinking: *to be in the right.* **23.** the right side or what is on the right side: *to turn to the right.* **24.** a punch with the right hand, as in boxing. –*adv.* **25.** in a straight line; straight; directly (*to, into, through,* etc.): *right to the bottom.* **26.** quite or completely: *his hat was knocked right off.* **27.** immediately: *right after dinner.* **28.** exactly, precisely, or just: *right here.* **29.** uprightly or righteously. **30.** correctly or accurately: *to guess right.* **31.** properly or fittingly: *to behave right; it serves you right.* **32.** advantageously, favourably, or well: *to turn out right.* **33.** into a satisfactory state or proper order: *to put things right.* **34.** towards the right hand; to the right. **35.** very (used in certain titles): *the right reverend.* **36.** *Brit. Colloq.* very; really; extraordinarily: *he's right stupid.* –*v.t.* **37.** to bring or restore to an upright or the proper position. **38.** to set in order or put right. **39.** to redress (wrong, etc.). –*v.i.* **40.** to resume an upright or the proper position. –*interj.* **41.** an exclamation indicating assent, agreement, etc. –*phr.* **42. by rights,** in all fairness; rightfully. **43. make it (all) right with,** *Colloq.* **a.** to mollify: *I'll make it all right with Mum.* **b.** to persuade, or especially, bribe: *he made it right with the nightwatchman before the job.* **44. right around, a.** all the way around: *right around the country.* **b.** immediately round: *right around the corner.* **45. right around to,** all the way to. **46. right as rain,** *Colloq.* safe, okay, in good health. **47. right for,** adequately supplied with: *are we right for bread?* **48. right on!,** an expression of approval, confirmation, etc. **49. she'll be right,** Also, **she's right.** *Aust., NZ Colloq.* an expression of confidence that everything is in order. **50. the right,** (*oft. upper case*) **a.** that part of a legislative assembly in continental Europe which sits on the right of the president, a position customarily assigned to the conservatives. **b.** a body of persons, political party, etc., holding conservative views.

51. too right!, *Aust., NZ Colloq.* an emphatic expression of agreement. **52. to rights,** into proper condition: *to set a room to rights.* –**rightness,** *n.* –**rightly,** *adv.*

right angle *n.* **1.** *Geom.* an angle formed at the interception of two perpendicular lines, and equal to half a straight angle, or approximately 1.57 radians; an angle of 90°. –*phr.* **2. at right angles to,** perpendicular to. –**right-angled,** *adj.* –**right-angledness,** *n.*

right-angled triangle *n.* *Geom.* a triangle in which one of the angles is a right angle. Also, **right triangle**.

right-click *v.i.* to activate a computer function by pressing on the right-hand button on the mouse: *if you right-click on delete, the file will go.*

righteous /'raɪtʃəs/ *adj.* **1.** characterised by uprightness or morality: *a righteous act.* **2.** morally right or justifiable: *righteous indignation.* **3.** in accordance with right; upright or virtuous: *a righteous and godly man.* –*phr.* **4. the righteous,** righteous people collectively. –**righteously,** *adv.* –**righteousness,** *n.*

rightful /'raɪtfəl/ *adj.* **1.** having a right, or just claim, as to some possession or position: *the rightful owner.* **2.** belonging by right, or just claim: *one's rightful property.* **3.** equitable or just, as actions, etc.: *a rightful cause.* –**rightfully,** *adv.* –**rightfulness,** *n.*

right-hand drive *n.* **1.** the arrangement of a motor vehicle in which the steering wheel and other controls are fitted on the right-hand side. **2.** a vehicle with a right-hand drive.

right-handed *adj.* **1.** having the right hand or arm more serviceable than the left; preferring to use the right hand. **2.** adapted to or performed by the right hand. **3.** situated on the side of the right hand. **4.** moving or rotating from left to right, or in the same direction as the hands of a clock. **5.** (of a rope) having the strands forming a spiral to the right. **6. right-handed helix** or **right-handed spiral,** one that is turned in this way and runs upwards from left to right when viewed from the side with the axis vertical, as the thread of a right-handed screw. –**right-handedly,** *adv.* –**right-hander,** *n.* –**right-handedness,** *n.*

right-minded *adj.* holding opinions or principles which are generally held to be correct in the community at large or in a defined section of it: *he was a right-minded young man; no right-minded communist would agree.* Also, **right-thinking.** –**right-mindedness,** *n.*

right of way *n.* **1.** the legal or customary right of a person, motor car or vessel to go on ahead of another in particular circumstances. **2.** a path or route which may lawfully be used, especially over another's land.

right-thinking *adj.* → **right-minded.**

right wing *n.* **1.** the members of a conservative or reactionary political party or section of a party, generally those opposing extensive political reform. **2.** such a group, party, or a group of such parties. **3.** *Sport* the part of the field of play which forms the right flank of the area being attacked by either team. **4.** *Sport* a player positioned on the right flank, as the outside right in soccer, the right of the wing-three-quarters in rugby football, etc. –**right-wing,** *adj.* –**right-winger,** *n.*

rigid /'rɪdʒəd/ *adj.* **1.** stiff or unyielding; not pliant or flexible; hard. **2.** firmly fixed, set, or not moving. **3.** rigorously strict. –**rigidity** /rə'dʒɪdəti/, **rigidness,** *n.* –**rigidly,** *adv.*

rigmarole /'rɪgməroʊl/ *n.* **1.** a succession of confused or foolish statements; incoherent or rambling discourse. **2.** a long and complicated process.

rigor mortis /rɪgə 'mɔːtəs/ *n.* the stiffening of the body after death.

rigour /'rɪgə/ *n.* **1.** strictness. **2.** severity of life; hardship. **3.** severity of the weather or climate: *the rigours of winter.* Also, **rigor.** –**rigorous,** *adj.*

rile /raɪl/ *v.t.* to irritate or vex.

rill /rɪl/ *n.* a small rivulet or brook.

rim /rɪm/ *n.* **1.** the outer edge, border, or margin, especially of a circular object. **2.** any edge or margin, often a raised one. **3.** the circular part of a wheel, farthest from the axle. –**rimless**, *adj.*

rime /raɪm/ *n.* a rough, white icy covering deposited on trees, etc., somewhat resembling white frost, but formed only from fog or vapour-bearing air. –**rimy**, *adj.*

rimu /ˈriːmuː/ *n.* a tall conifer, *Dacrydium cupressinum*, of New Zealand, having awl-shaped leaves; red pine.

rind /raɪnd/ *n.* a thick and firm coat or covering, as of animals, plants, fruits, cheeses, etc.

ring¹ /rɪŋ/ *n.* **1.** a circular band of metal or other material, especially one of gold or other precious metal, often set with gems, for wearing on the finger as an ornament, a token of betrothal or marriage, etc. **2.** anything having the form of a circular band. **3.** a mob of restless cattle moving confusedly in a circle: *all cattlemen fear a ring.* **4.** a circular line or mark. **5.** a circular course: *to dance in a ring.* **6.** the outside edge of a circular body, as a wheel. **7.** a single turn in a spiral or helix or in a spiral course. **8.** *Geom.* the area or space between two concentric circles. **9.** one of the concentric layers of wood produced yearly in the trunks of exogenous trees. **10.** a circle of bark cut from around a tree. **11.** a number of persons or things placed in a circle. **12. a.** an enclosed circular or other area, as one in which some sport or exhibition takes place: *the ring of a circus.* **b.** the area in which a two-up game takes place. **13.** an enclosure in which boxing and wrestling matches take place (usually a square area marked off by stakes and ropes). **14.** the sport of boxing. **15.** a space devoted to betting at a racecourse, not necessarily circular in shape: *betting ring; ledger ring; paddock ring.* **16.** (*plural*) *Gymnastics* **a.** an apparatus comprising two rings hanging freely from a metal frame, the gymnast performing various movements while gripping one or both rings. **b.** the artistic gymnastics event in which the gymnast, usually male, performs in this way. **17.** competition; contest: *to toss one's hat in the ring.* **18.** a group of persons cooperating for selfish or illegal purposes, as to control a business, monopolise a particular market, etc. **19.** *Chem.* a number of atoms linked in a cyclic form. **20.** *Colloq.* the anus. –*verb* (**ringed, ringing**) –*v.t.* **21.** to surround with a ring; encircle. **22. a.** to form into a ring. **b.** to cause (a mob of cattle) to form into a circling herd. **23.** to put a ring in the nose of (an animal). **24.** to hem in (animals, especially cattle) by riding or circling about them. **25.** *Agric.* to remove (wool from around the prepuce of rams and wethers) to prevent fouling. **26.** to ringbark. **27.** (in ring toss games) to hurl a ring over (a stake or peg). –*v.i.* **28.** to form a ring or rings. **29.** to move in a ring or a constantly curving course. **30.** (of a mob of cattle) to form into a circling herd. **31.** to work with cattle: *when we were ringing we were up before dawn each day.* –*phr.* **32. ring the board** (or **shed**), *Aust., NZ* to shear more sheep than anyone else in the shearing shed. **33. run rings round**, *Colloq.* to be markedly superior to; easily surpass. –**ringlike**, *adj.*

ring² /rɪŋ/ *verb* (**rang** or **rung, ringing**) –*v.i.* **1.** to give forth a clear, resonant sound when set in sudden vibration by a blow or otherwise, as a bell, glass, etc. **2.** to seem (true, false, etc.) in the effect produced on the mind: *his words ring true.* **3.** to cause a bell or bells to sound, especially as a summons: *ring for a messenger.* **4.** to sound loudly; be loud or resonant; resound. **5.** to be filled with sound; re-echo with sound, as a place. **6.** (of the ears) to have the sensation of a continued humming sound. **7.** to telephone. –*v.t.* **8.** to cause to ring, as a bell, etc. **9.** to produce (sound) by or as if by ringing. **10.** to proclaim, usher in or out, summon, signal, etc., by or as by the sound of a bell. **11.** to telephone. –*n.* **12.** a ringing sound, as of a bell, etc.: *the*

ring of sleighbells. **13.** a resonant sound or note: *there was a ring in his voice.* **14.** any loud sound; sound continued, repeated, or reverberated. **15.** a telephone call: *give me a ring tomorrow.* **16.** an act of ringing a bell. **17.** a characteristic sound, as of a coin. **18.** a characteristic or inherent quality: *his words had the ring of truth.* –*phr.* **19. ring a bell,** to arouse a memory; sound familiar. **20. ring down the curtain,** to give a direction to lower a theatre curtain, as at the end of a performance. **21. ring down the curtain on,** to bring to an end. **22. ring for,** to summon by ringing a bell. **23. ring in, a.** to announce the arrival of by ringing bells. **b.** *Aust.* to insert or substitute dishonestly (one racehorse, greyhound, etc.) for another in a race, or (a double-headed coin) for a normal one in two-up. **c.** to telephone headquarters or one's central office. **24. ring off,** to end a telephone conversation. **25. ring out, a.** to make a loud, resounding noise. **b.** to announce the departure of by ringing. **26. ring the changes,** to vary the manner of performing an action, especially one that is often repeated; execute a number of manoeuvres or variations. **27. ring the tin,** *Aust.* to summon workers to a meeting to consider a dispute by ringing a tin. **28. ring the tin on,** *Aust.* to refuse to cooperate or communicate with (a supervisor, etc.). **29. ring true,** to appear to be true, sincere, genuine, etc. **30. ring up, a.** to telephone. **b.** to record (the cost of an item) on a cash register. **31. ring up the curtain,** to give a direction to raise a theatre curtain, as at the beginning of a performance. **32. ring up the curtain on,** to begin; inaugurate.

ringbark /ˈrɪŋbak/ *v.t.* to cut away the bark in a ring around a tree trunk or branch, in order to kill the tree or the affected part. Also, **bark.** –**ringbarked,** *adj.*

ringer¹ /ˈrɪŋə/ *n.* **1.** a quoit or horseshoe so thrown as to encircle a peg. **2.** *Aust.* a station hand, especially a stock worker or drover.

ringer² /ˈrɪŋə/ *n. Colloq.* **1.** an athlete, horse, etc., entered in a competition under false representations as to identity or ability. **2.** Also, **dead ringer, dead ring.** a person or thing that closely resembles another: *he was a dead ringer for the local policeman.*

ringer³ /ˈrɪŋə/ *n. Aust., NZ* **1.** the fastest shearer of a group. **2.** any person of outstanding competence.

ringgit /ˈrɪŋgət/ *n.* the principal monetary unit of Malaysia, divided into 100 sen.

ring-in *n. Aust., NZ Colloq.* **1.** a person or thing substituted for another at the last moment, as a horse fraudulently substituted for another in a race. **2.** someone from another place; an outsider.

ringleader /ˈrɪŋliːdə/ *n.* someone who leads others in opposition to authority, law, etc.

ringlet /ˈrɪŋlət/ *n.* **1.** a small ring or circle. **2.** a curled lock of hair. –**ringleted** /ˈrɪŋlətəd/, *adj.*

ringmaster /ˈrɪŋmastə/ *n.* **1.** the person in charge of the performances in the ring of a circus. **2.** the person in charge of the ring at equestrian events.

ringside /ˈrɪŋsaɪd/ *n.* **1.** the space immediately surrounding an arena, as the first row of seats round a boxing or wrestling ring. **2.** any place providing a close view.

ringtone /ˈrɪŋtoʊn/ *n. Telecommunications* **1.** a tone returned by receiving equipment that tells a caller that the called telephone is ringing. **2.** the sound produced by a mobile phone to indicate that a call is being received, originally a ringing sound, but now any of various recorded sounds, fragments of music, etc. Also, **ring tone, ringing tone.**

ringworm /ˈrɪŋwɜːm/ *n.* tinea, especially when it presents with a protruding outer ring of reddish, scaly, irritated skin.

rink /rɪŋk/ *n.* **1.** a sheet of ice for skating, often one artificially prepared and under cover. **2.** a smooth floor for rollerskating. **3.** an area of ice marked off for the game of curling. **4.** a section of a bowling green where a match can be played. **5.** a set of players on one side in bowling or curling.

rinse /rɪns/ *v.t.* (**rinsed, rinsing**) **1.** to wash lightly, as by pouring water into or over or by dipping in water. **2.** to put through clean water, as a final stage in cleansing. **3.** to remove (impurities, etc.) thus. *–n.* **4.** an act or instance of rinsing. **5.** any liquid preparation used for impermanently tinting the hair. **–rinser,** *n.*

riot /ˈraɪət/ *n.* **1.** any disturbance of the peace by an assembly of persons. **2.** *Law* a disturbance of the peace by at least three persons (or, in NZ, at least six) carrying out a common purpose in a violent manner so as to cause alarm and so as to discourage any opposition. **3.** violent or wild disorder or confusion. **4.** an unbridled outbreak, as of emotions, passions, etc. **5.** a brilliant display: *a riot of colour.* **6.** *Colloq.* someone or something that causes great amusement, enthusiasm, etc. *–adj.* **7.** of, relating to, or dealing with riots: *riot squad*; *riot shields. –v.i.* **8.** to take part in a riot or disorderly public outbreak. **9.** to indulge unrestrainedly; run riot. *–phr.* **10. run riot, a.** to act without control or restraint; disregard all limits. **b.** to grow luxuriantly or wildly. **–rioter,** *n.* **–riotous,** *adj.*

rip¹ /rɪp/ *verb* (**ripped, ripping**) *–v.t.* **1.** to cut or tear apart in a rough or vigorous manner; slash; slit. **2.** to cut or tear away in a rough or vigorous manner. **3.** to saw (wood) in the direction of the grain. **4.** Also, **rip up.** to scarify or scratch (the soil) without turning it over. **5.** *Computers* to copy (digital data) from a CD or DVD to the hard drive of a computer. *–v.i.* **6.** to become torn apart or split open. **7.** *Colloq.* to move along with violence or great speed. *–n.* **8.** a rent made by ripping; a tear. *–phr.* **9. let it** (or **her**) **rip,** to allow an engine, etc., to go as fast as possible by ceasing to check or control its speed. **10. let rip, a.** to give free rein to anger, passion, etc. **b.** to utter oaths; swear. **11. rip into,** *Colloq.* **a.** to begin rapidly, eagerly: *let's rip into the housework.* **b.** to scold; abuse: *she ripped into me for losing her book.* **12. rip off, a.** to tear off violently. **b.** *Colloq.* to overcharge; swindle. **13. rip out, a.** to remove forcibly or violently; wrench. **b.** to utter angrily; shout.

rip² /rɪp/ *n.* **1.** a disturbance in the sea caused by opposing currents or by a fast current passing over an uneven bottom. **2.** a fast current, especially one at a beach which can take swimmers out to sea. **3.** → **rip-tide.**

rip³ /rɪp/ *n. Colloq.* a dissolute or irresponsible person.

ripcord /ˈrɪpkɔd/ *n.* a cord or ring which opens a parachute during a descent.

ripe /raɪp/ *adj.* **1.** ready for reaping or gathering, as grain, fruits, etc.; complete in natural growth or development, as when arrived at the stage most fit for eating or use. **2.** resembling ripe fruit, as in ruddiness and fullness. **3.** fully grown or developed, as animals when ready to be killed and used for food. **4.** advanced to the point of being in the best condition for use, as cheese, beer, etc. **5.** malodorous: *a ripe old pipe.* **6.** arrived at the highest or a high point of development or excellence; mature. **7.** of mature judgement or knowledge. **8.** characterised by full development of body or mind: *of ripe years.* **9.** ready for action, execution, etc. **10.** fully prepared or ready to do or undergo something, or for some action, purpose, or end. **11.** ready for some operation or process: *a ripe abscess.* **12.** (of time) fully or sufficiently advanced. **13.** *Colloq.* drunk. **14.** *Colloq.* obscene or relating to obscenity. *–phr.* **15. a ripe old age,** old age, seen as the completion of human life and development. **–ripely,** *adv.* **–ripeness,** *n.*

ripen /ˈraɪpən/ *v.i.* **1.** to become ripe. **2.** to come to maturity, the proper condition, etc.; mature. *–v.t.* **3.** to

make ripe. **4.** to bring to maturity, the proper condition, etc. **–ripener,** *n.*

rip-off *n.* an excessive charge or exorbitant price; swindle.

riposte /rəˈpɒst/ *n.* **1.** *Fencing* a quick thrust given after parrying a lunge. **2.** a quick, sharp return in speech or action. Also, **ripost.**

ripper /ˈrɪpə/ *n.* **1.** an excavating device, usually on the back of a bulldozer, used for breaking up rock. **2.** *Computers* a software program that rips (**rip¹** def. 5). **3.** *Colloq.* a killer who violently murders and mutilates women. **4.** *Colloq.* a person or thing that excites extreme admiration. *–adj.* **5.** *Colloq.* absolutely excellent: *a ripper movie. –interj.* **6.** *Colloq.* an exclamation expressing approval.

ripping /ˈrɪpɪŋ/ *adj.* **1.** that rips. **2.** *Colloq.* excellent, splendid, or fine.

ripple /ˈrɪpəl/ *v.i.* **1.** to have or form small waves on the surface. **2.** (of sound) to go on or proceed with an effect like that of water flowing in ripples. *–v.t.* **3.** to form small waves on. *–n.* **4.** a small wave, as on water. **5.** any similar movement or appearance. **6.** a sound like water flowing in ripples: *a ripple of laughter.* **–ripplingly,** *adv.*

rip-tide *n.* a fast-flowing tide such as might be associated with the formation of a rip. Also, **rip-current.**

risc /rɪsk/ *n.* **1.** *Computers* a computer for which the instruction set, that is, the complete set of operating commands, has been reduced to the minimum by removing rarely used commands, thus facilitating faster processing. *–adj.* **2.** of or relating to such a computer. Also, **RISC.**

rise /raɪz/ *v.i.* (**rose, risen, rising**) **1.** to get up from a lying, sitting, or kneeling posture; assume a standing position. **2.** to get up from bed: *to rise early.* **3.** to become erect and stiff, as the hair. **4.** to get up after falling or being thrown down. **5.** to become active in opposition or resistance; revolt or rebel. **6.** to be built up, erected, or constructed. **7.** to spring up or grow, as plants. **8.** to become prominent on a surface, as a blister. **9.** to come into existence; appear. **10.** to come into action, as a wind, storm, etc. **11.** to occur: *a quarrel rose between them.* **12.** to originate, issue, or be derived; to have its spring or source. **13.** to move from a lower to a higher position; move upwards; ascend: *a bird rises in the air.* **14.** to come above the horizon, as a heavenly body. **15.** to extend directly upwards: *the tower rises to the height of 20 metres.* **16.** to have an upward slant or curve: *the path rises as it approaches the house.* **17.** *Angling* (of a fish) to come to the surface of the water to take bait, etc. **18.** to attain higher rank, importance, etc. **19.** to advance to a higher level of action, thought, feeling, expression, etc. **20.** to prove oneself equal to a demand, emergency, etc.: *to rise to the occasion.* **21.** to become animated or cheerful, as the spirits. **22.** to become stirred or roused: *to feel one's temper rising.* **23.** to increase in height, as water: *the river sometimes rose 10 metres in eight hours.* **24.** to swell or puff up, as dough from the action of yeast. **25.** to increase in amount, as prices, etc. **26.** to increase in price or value, as commodities. **27.** to increase in degree, intensity, or force, as colour, fever, etc. **28.** to become louder or of higher pitch, as the voice. **29.** to adjourn, or close a session, as a deliberative body or court. **30.** to return from the dead. *–n.* **31.** the act of rising; upward movement or ascent. **32.** appearance above the horizon, as of the sun or moon. **33.** elevation or advance in rank, position, fortune, etc.: *the rise and fall of ancient Rome.* **34.** an increase in height, as of water. **35.** the amount of such increase. **36.** an increase in amount, as of prices. **37.** an increase in price or value, as of commodities. **38.** an increase in amount, as of wages, salary, etc. **39.** the amount of such an increase. **40.** an increase in degree of intensity, as of temperature. **41.** an increase in loudness or in pitch, as of the voice. **42.** the vertical height of any of various things as a stair step, a flight of steps, a roof, an arch, the crown of a road, etc. **43.** origin, source, or beginning: *the rise of a stream in a mountain.* **44.** a coming into existence or notice. **45.** extension upwards. **46.** the amount of this. **47.** upward slope, as of ground or a road. **48.** a piece of rising or high ground. **49.** *Angling* the movement of a fish to the surface of the water to take a bait. –*phr.* **50. get** (or **take**) **a rise out of,** to provoke to anger, annoyance, etc., by banter, mockery, deception, etc. **51. give rise to,** to cause, produce.

rising /ˈraɪzɪŋ/ *adj.* **1.** that rises; advancing, ascending, or mounting. **2.** growing, or advancing to adult years: *the rising generation.* –*n.* **3.** an uprising; revolt.

risk /rɪsk/ *n.* **1.** exposure to the chance of injury or loss; a hazard or dangerous chance: *to run risks.* **2.** *Insurance* **a.** the hazard or chance of loss. **b.** the degree of probability of such loss. **c.** the amount which the insurance company may lose. **d.** a person or thing with reference to the risk involved in insuring them. **e.** the type of loss, as life, fire, theft, etc., against which insurance policies are drawn. –*v.t.* **3.** to expose to the chance of injury or loss, or hazard: *to risk one's life to save another.* **4.** to take or run the risk of: *to risk a fall in climbing.* **5.** to venture upon despite the hazards: *to risk a battle.* –*phr.* **6. at risk,** in a state or situation in which injury, loss, the onset of disease, etc., is likely; vulnerable: *homeless children are at risk.* **7. no risk,** an exclamation of reassurance or approval. **8. take risks,** to embark on a course of action that involves danger. –**risky,** *adj.*

risk-taking *n.* **1.** the adoption of practices which are inherently dangerous, as drug-taking, extreme sports, gambling, etc. –*adj.* **2.** of, relating to, or exhibiting an inclination towards risk-taking: *risk-taking behaviour.* –**risk-taker,** *n.*

risoni /rəˈsouni/ *n.* pasta shaped into small beads like rice, often cooked in soup.

risqué /ˈrɪskeɪ, rɪsˈkeɪ/ *adj.* daringly close to indelicacy or impropriety: *a risqué story.*

rissole /ˈrɪsoul/ *n.* a small fried ball, roll, or cake of minced meat or fish mixed with breadcrumbs, egg, etc., formerly enclosed in a thin envelope of pastry before frying.

ristretto /rɪsˈtrɛtou/ *n.* a highly concentrated espresso coffee drink, made with the same amount of coffee as a normal espresso, but with about half the usual amount of water.

ritardando /rɪtəˈdændou/ *adv. Music* gradually more slowly.

rite /raɪt/ *n.* **1.** a formal or ceremonial act or procedure prescribed or customary in religious or other solemn use: *rites of baptism, sacrificial rites.* **2.** any customary observance or practice.

ritual /ˈrɪtjuəl/ *n.* **1.** an established or set procedure, code, form, system, etc., for a religious or other rite. **2.** the following of set forms in public worship. **3.** a ritual service: *the ritual of the dead.* **4.** any solemn or customary action, code of behaviour, etc., determining social conduct. –**ritually,** *adv.* –**ritualistic,** *adj.*

rival /ˈraɪvəl/ *n.* **1.** someone who is in pursuit of the same object as another, or strives to equal or outdo another; a competitor. **2.** a person or thing that is in a position to dispute pre- eminence or superiority with another: *a theatre without a rival.* –*adj.* **3.** being a rival; competing or standing in rivalry: *rival suitors; rival business houses.* –*v.t.* **(-valled** or, *US,* **-valed, -valling** or, *US,* **-valing) 4.** to compete with in rivalry; strive to equal or outdo. –**rivalry,** *n.*

rive /raɪv/ *v.t.* **(rived, rived** or **riven, riving) 1.** to tear or rend apart. **2.** to strike asunder; split; cleave. **3.** to rend, harrow, or distress (the heart, etc.).

river /ˈrɪvə/ *n.* **1.** a defined watercourse of considerable size and length, whether flowing or dry according to the seasons, and whether a single channel or a number of diverging or converging channels. **2.** such a watercourse, especially when flowing. **3.** a similar stream of something other than water. **4.** any abundant stream or copious flow: *rivers of lava, blood, etc.* –*phr.* **5. sell down the river,** *Colloq.* to betray; deceive.

rivercat /ˈrɪvəkæt/ *n.* (*from trademark*) a powered catamaran used as a ferryboat on a river.

rivet /ˈrɪvət/ *n.* **1.** a metal pin or bolt for passing through holes in two or more plates or pieces to hold them together. –*v.t.* **(-eted, -eting) 2.** to fasten with a rivet or rivets. **3.** to fasten or fix firmly: *fear riveted me to the spot.* **4.** to hold (the eye, attention, etc.) firmly. –**riveter,** *n.*

rivulet /ˈrɪvjələt/ *n.* a small stream; a streamlet; a brook.

RNA /ar ɛn ˈeɪ/ *n. Biochem.* any of a group of nucleic acids found in all living cells and some viruses, the main function of which is the translation of the genetic code in protein synthesis; ribonucleic acid.

roach¹ /routʃ/ *n.* (*pl.* **roaches** or, *especially collectively,* **roach**) a European freshwater fish, *Rutilus rutilus*, of the carp family, introduced into Tasmania.

roach² /routʃ/ *n.* **1.** *Aust.,* *NZ* a cockroach. **2.** *Colloq.* the butt of a cigarette or joint (def. 8).

road /roud/ *n.* **1.** a way, usually open to the public for the passage of vehicles, persons, and animals. **2.** any street so called. **3.** the track on which vehicles, etc., pass, as opposed to the pavement. **4. a.** *US* → **railway. b.** *Railways* one of the tracks of a railway: *the train took the wrong road.* **5.** a way or course: *the road to peace.* **6.** (*oft. pl.*) a protected place near the shore where ships may ride at anchor. –*phr.* **7. hit the road,** *Colloq.* to begin a journey. **8. one for the road,** *Colloq.* a final alcoholic drink consumed before setting out on a journey, returning home from a hotel, etc. **9. on the road, a.** travelling, especially as a salesperson or drover. **b.** on tour, as a theatrical company: *to spend years on the road with a play.* **c.** (formerly of convicts) employed in road building. **10. take the road for,** to set out for. **11. take to the road, a.** to begin a journey. **b.** to become a tramp. **12. up** (or **down**) **the road,** *Aust. Colloq.* at or to the local shops: *to pop down the road for some milk.*

roadhog /ˈroudhɒg/ *n.* a motorist who drives without consideration for other road users.

roadhouse /ˈroudhaus/ *n.* an inn, hotel, restaurant, etc., on a main road, especially in a country district.

road hump *n.* a raised transverse section of road which assists in controlling the speed at which vehicles can safely and comfortably travel. Also, **speed bump, speed hump, hump.**

roadie /ˈroudi/ *n. Colloq.* a person associated with a musical act who arranges road transportation, sets up equipment, etc., for tours and concerts.

roadkill /ˈroudkɪl/ *n.* the remains of any animal or animals struck and killed by a motor vehicle and lying on or beside a road. Also, **road kill.** –**road-killed,** *adj.*

road movie *n.* a film in which a journey along a road is a principal component, along which the plot is driven and the characters developed.

road rage *n.* uncontrolled violent behaviour by a motorist, usually directed towards another motorist, resulting from the tensions and frustrations of driving.

roadrunner /ˈroudrʌnə/ *n.* a terrestrial cuckoo of the south western US, *Geococcyx californianus.*

road toll *n.* the tally of traffic accident deaths.

road train *n. Aust.* a group of articulated motor vehicles, used for transportation, especially of cattle, and consisting of a prime mover and one or more trailers.

roadway /ˈroʊdweɪ/ *n.* **1.** a way used as a road; a road. **2.** the part of a road used by vehicles, etc.

roadworthy /ˈroʊdwɜːði/ *adj.* (of a vehicle) fit for use on the roads. **–roadworthiness,** *n.*

roam /roʊm/ *v.i.* **1.** to walk, go, or travel about without fixed purpose or direction; ramble; wander; rove. –*v.t.* **2.** to wander over or through: *to roam the bush.* **–roamer,** *n.*

roan /roʊn/ *adj.* **1.** (chiefly of horses) of a sorrel, chestnut, or bay colour sprinkled with grey or white. –*n.* **2.** a soft, flexible sheepskin leather, used in bookbinding, often made in imitation of morocco.

roar /rɔː/ *v.i.* **1.** to utter a loud, deep sound, especially of excitement, distress, or anger. **2.** to laugh loudly or boisterously. **3.** to make a loud noise in breathing, as a horse. **4.** to make a loud noise or din, as thunder, cannon, waves, wind, etc. **5.** to function or move with a roar, as a vehicle: *the sports car roared away.* –*v.t.* **6.** to utter or express in a roar. **7.** to bring, put, make, etc., by roaring: *to roar oneself hoarse.* –*n.* **8.** the sound of roaring; a loud, deep sound, as of a person or persons, or of a lion or other large animal. **9.** a loud outburst of laughter. **10.** a loud noise, as of thunder, waves, etc.: *the roar of the surf.* –*phr.* **11. roar up,** *Colloq.* to scold or abuse (someone) angrily. **–roarer,** *n.*

roaring /ˈrɔːrɪŋ/ *n.* **1.** a loud, deep cry or sound. **2.** *Vet. Science* a disease of horses causing them to make a loud noise in breathing under exertion. –*adj.* **3.** *Colloq.* brisk or highly successful, as trade. **4.** characterised by noisy or boisterous behaviour; riotous.

roaring forties *pl. n.* **1.** (*construed as sing.*) the area of ocean between 40°S and 50°S in which strong winds blow. **2.** (loosely) the strong westerly winds of the ocean between 40°S and 50°S, especially useful to sailing ships.

roast /roʊst/ *v.t.* **1.** to bake (meat or other food) by dry heat, as in an oven. **2.** to prepare by exposure to heat, as coffee. **3.** to heat (any material) more or less violently. **4.** *Colloq.* to criticise, scold or make fun of severely. –*v.i.* **5.** to undergo the process of becoming roasted. –*n.* **6.** a piece of roasted meat. –*adj.* **7.** roasted: *roast beef.* **–roasting,** *n.* **–roasted,** *adj.*

rob /rɒb/ *verb* (**robbed, robbing**) –*v.t.* **1.** to deprive of something by unlawful force or threat of violence; steal from. **2.** to deprive of something legally belonging or due. **3.** to plunder or rifle (a house, etc.). **4.** to deprive of something unjustly or injuriously: *the shock robbed him of speech.* –*v.i.* **5.** to commit or practise robbery. –*phr.* **6. rob Peter to pay Paul,** to benefit one person or thing at the expense of another. **–robber,** *n.* **–robbery,** *n.*

robe¹ /roʊb/ *n.* a long, loose or flowing gown or outer garment worn by men or women, especially for formal occasions; an official vestment, as of a judge.

robe² /roʊb/ *n.* → **wardrobe.**

robin /ˈrɒbən/ *n.* **1.** any of various birds of the family Petroicidae, of Australasia and Papua New Guinea, the male of some species having a red breast, similar to, but much brighter than, the unrelated European robin. **2.** any of several small European birds having a red or reddish breast, especially *Erithacus rubecula.* **3.** a large American thrush, *Turdus migratorius,* with a chestnut-red breast and abdomen.

robot /ˈroʊbɒt/ *n.* **1.** a mechanical self-controlling apparatus designed to carry out a specific task, which would normally be performed by a human. **2.** someone who behaves in a mechanical way; automaton. **3.** *Computers* → **web crawler. –robotism,** *n.* **–robotic** /roʊˈbɒtɪk/, *adj.*

robust /ˈroʊbʌst, rəˈbʌst/ *adj.* **1.** strong and healthy, hardy, or vigorous. **2.** strongly or stoutly built: *his robust frame.* **3.** suited to or requiring bodily strength or endurance. **4.** rough, rude, or boisterous. **5.** able to withstand critical analysis: *a robust report; a robust argument.* **6.** *Computers* fault tolerant: *a robust program; a robust network.* **–robustly,** *adv.* **–robustness,** *n.* **–robustious,** *adj.*

roc /rɒk/ *n.* (in Arabian mythology) a bird of enormous size and strength.

rock¹ /rɒk/ *n.* **1.** *Geol.* **a.** mineral matter of various composition, consolidated or unconsolidated, assembled in masses or considerable quantities in nature, as by the action of heat (**igneous rock**), or of water, air, or ice (**sedimentary rock**), or by the structural alteration of either of these two types by natural agencies of pressure and heat (**metamorphic rock**). **b.** a particular kind of such matter. **2.** a large mass of stone forming an eminence, cliff, or the like. **3.** stone in the mass. **4.** a stone of any size. **5.** a hard sweet made in various flavours, usually long and cylindrical in shape. **6.** *Colloq.* a jewel, especially a diamond. **7.** *Colloq.* crack cocaine in crystalline lumps. –*phr.* **8. get one's rocks off,** to have an orgasm. **9. have rocks in one's head,** to be very stupid. **10. on the rocks, a.** on rocks, as a shipwrecked vessel. **b.** *Colloq.* into or in a state of disaster or ruin. **c.** (of spirits) neat with ice cubes: *scotch on the rocks.* **–rocklike,** *adj.*

rock² /rɒk/ *v.i.* **1.** to move or sway to and fro or from side to side. **2.** to be moved or swayed powerfully with emotion, etc. **3.** to dance to or play rock'n'roll music. **4.** *Colloq.* (fol. by *along, over,* etc.) to go: *we're going to rock along to the party later.; let's rock over to his place.* **5.** *Colloq.* **a.** (of a venue or event) to be well patronised with a lively crowd enjoying itself: *this place really rocks on a Saturday night.* **b.** (of a person or thing) to be highly approved of. –*v.t.* **6.** to move or sway to and fro or from side to side, especially gently and soothingly. **7.** to lull to security, hope, etc. **8.** to move or sway powerfully with emotion, etc. **9.** to shake or disturb violently. **10.** *Mining* to pan with a cradle: *to rock gravel for gold.* **11.** *Colloq.* to upset the equanimity of (someone) with a cutting remark, witty comeback, etc. –*n.* **12.** → **rock music. 13.** → **rock'n'roll.** –*adj.* **14.** of or relating to rock music. –*phr. Colloq.* **15. rock the boat,** to threaten the status quo, as by raising awkward questions, etc. **16. rock up,** to arrive: *to rock up at any time; What time did they rock up?*

rock-and-roll *n., adj., v.* → **rock'n'roll.**

rock art *n.* **1.** the art of creating pictures on rock surfaces by painting, drawing, or carving out sections of rock, traditionally practised by Australian Aboriginal peoples. **2.** a picture created on a rock surface.

rock bottom *n.* the lowest level, especially of fortune: *to touch rock bottom.* **–rock-bottom,** *adj.*

rock climbing *n.* the sport of climbing on steep rock faces, both sheer and uneven, using specialised ropes and equipment. Also, **rockclimbing. –rock climber,** *n.*

rocker /ˈrɒkə/ *n.* **1.** one of the curved pieces on which a cradle or a rocking chair rocks. **2.** a rocking chair. **3.** any of various devices that operate with a rocking motion. **4.** *Mining* → **cradle** (def. 4). **5.** *Colloq.* a young person of the early 1960s, characterised by rough, unruly behaviour, who usually wore leather clothing, had greased-back hair, and rode a motorcycle. Compare **mod** (def. 2). **6.** *Colloq.* a rock'n'roll musician or fan. –*phr.* **7. off one's rocker,** *Colloq.* crazy; mad; demented: *you must be off your rocker to suggest such a thing.*

rockery /ˈrɒkəri/ *n.* (*pl.* **-ries**) a garden, or part of a garden, featuring rocks and plants which favour a rocky soil and are suited to dry, sunny conditions.

rocket[1] /'rɒkət/ n. **1.** *Aeronautics* a structure propelled by a rocket engine, used for pyrotechnic effect, signalling, carrying a lifeline, propelling a warhead, launching spacecraft, etc. **2.** a type of firework which shoots into the air and explodes forming coloured stars of light. **3.** *Colloq.* a severe reprimand; reproof. –*v.i.* (**-eted, -eting**) **4.** to move like a rocket. **5.** (of game birds) to fly straight up rapidly when flushed. **6.** to increase rapidly as prices, rents, or the like. –*phr.* **7. go like a rocket, a.** to move fast. **b.** (of a machine) to function well. **8. put a rocket under,** to stir (someone) to action.

rocket[2] /'rɒkət/ n. **1.** a Mediterranean cruciferous plant, *Eruca sativa*, with yellowish-white flowers and leaves used as a salad. **2.** any of numerous plants of the family Cruciferae, especially those belonging to the genera *Barbarea* and *Sisymbrium*, now commonly used in green salads.

rock face n. the rock surface of the side of a cliff or mountain, especially nearly vertical rock.

rocking chair n. a chair mounted on rockers, or on springs, so as to permit a rocking back and forth.

rocking horse n. a toy horse, as of wood, mounted on rockers, on which children play.

rock lily n. a widely cultivated epiphytic or rock orchid, *Dendrobium speciosum*, of eastern Australia, with numerous many-flowered racemes. Also, **rock orchid**.

rock lobster n. any of various large, edible, marine, stalk-eyed, decapod crustaceans of the family Palinuridae, having a spiny carapace, found in Australia waters and widely harvested for local and export markets; crayfish. Also, **spiny lobster**.

rockmelon /'rɒkmɛlən/ n. *Aust.*, *NZ* **1.** the edible fruit of the melon *Cucumis melo* var. *cantalupensis*, having a hard, usually ribbed and netted rind, and orange-coloured flesh; cantaloupe. **2.** any of several similar melons.

rock music n. any contemporary music which has developed from 1950s rock'n'roll.

rock'n'roll /rɒkən'roʊl/ n. **1.** a form of pop music originating in the 1950s in America which has a twelve bar blues form, and a heavily accented rhythm. **2.** a dance or style of dance performed to this music. –*adj.* **3.** of or relating to this music. –*v.i.* **4.** to play or dance to rock'n'roll music. **5.** *Colloq.* to set out on a journey, begin a task, etc. Also, **rock-and-roll**, **rock-'n'-roll**. –**rock'n'roller**, n.

rock orchid n. → **rock lily**.

rock painting n. a form of art executed with naturally occurring pigments, such as ochre and charcoal, on rock faces.

rock pool n. **1.** a swimming pool beside the sea which may be either artificially constructed or naturally occurring but which is made entirely or almost entirely of rocks in the locality, and which is filled and freshened by the recurring tides. **2.** a natural water-filled depression formed in rock by the action of a river or the sea, sometimes containing aquatic plants and animals. Also, **rockpool**.

rock salt n. a common salt (sodium chloride), occurring in extensive, irregular beds in rocklike masses.

rock-solid adj. **1.** incontrovertible: *rock-solid evidence.* **2.** strongly holding a position; not easily swayed or overcome: *a rock-solid supporter.*

rock-steady adj. completely stable; fixed.

rocky /'rɒki/ adj. (**-kier, -kiest**) **1.** full of rocks; characterised by many rocks. **2.** consisting of rock. **3.** rock-like. **4.** firm as a rock. **5.** (of the heart, etc.) hard or unfeeling. –**rockiness**, n.

rococo /rə'koʊkoʊ/ n. **1.** a style of art, architecture, and decoration of the 18th century, popular especially in France, evolved from baroque types and distinguished by its ornate use of scrolls and curves. –*adj.* **2.** in the rococo style. **3.** tastelessly or clumsily florid.

rod /rɒd/ n. **1.** a stick or the like, of wood, metal, or other material. **2.** a pole used in fishing. **3.** a measure in the imperial system, of 5½ yards or 16½ feet, equal to 5.0292 m. **4.** a staff carried to stand for office, authority, power, etc. **5.** any microorganism which is shaped like a rod. **6.** *Anat.* one of the rodlike cells in the retina of the eye which responds to dim light. –**rodlike**, adj.

rode /roʊd/ v. past tense of **ride**.

rodent /'roʊdnt/ n. **1.** a member of the Rodentia, the order of gnawing or nibbling mammals, that includes the mice, squirrels, beavers, etc. –*adj.* **2.** of or relating to a rodent.

rodeo /roʊ'deɪoʊ, 'roʊdioʊ/ n. (*pl.* **-deos**) a public exhibition, sometimes competitive, showing the skills of riding horses or steers bareback, roping calves and other similar activities deriving from work on a cattle station.

roe /roʊ/ n. **1.** the mass of eggs, or spawn, within the ovarian membrane of the female fish (**hard roe**). **2.** the milt or sperm of the male fish (**soft roe**).

roentgen /'rɜntgən/ n. a non-SI unit of measurement of exposure to ionising radiation equal to 0.258×10^{-3} coulombs per kilogram. *Symbol:* R

roesti /'rɜsti/ n. → **rosti**.

rogan josh /roʊgən 'dʒɒʃ/ n. (in Indian cookery) a type of rich spicy lamb curry.

roger /'rɒdʒə/ *interj.* **1.** message received and understood (used in signalling and telecommunications). **2.** an expression of agreement, comprehension, etc.

rogue /roʊg/ n. **1.** a dishonest person. **2.** a person who carries out playful tricks; rascal; scamp. **3.** an animal, especially an elephant, which is dangerously unpredictable, and tends to live apart from its group. –**roguish**, adj.

rogue state n. a nation which refuses to abide by the treaties, conventions, etc., which other nations observe.

roister /'rɔɪstə/ v.i. to act in a swaggering, boisterous, or uproarious manner. –**roisterer**, n. –**roisterous**, adj.

role /roʊl/ n. **1.** the part or character which an actor presents in a play. **2.** proper or customary function: *the teacher's role in society.* Also, **rôle**.

role-playing game n. a game in which players take on personas, either invented or made available within the game. Also, **role-play game**.

role reversal n. the playing of a role which is in some way the opposite of a role usually or previously played, as when a leader acts as a follower, a supplicant as a benefactor, etc.

role-sharing n. the sharing of the tasks and responsibilities usually assigned to a particular gender role between people of opposite gender.

rolfing /'rɒlfɪŋ/ n. a system of soft-tissue manipulation to re-align body posture and structure in order to ease chronic pain and to improve performance.

roll /roʊl/ v.i. **1.** to move along a surface by turning over and over, as a ball or a wheel. **2.** to move or be moved on wheels, as a vehicle or its occupants. **3.** to move onwards or advance in a stream or with an undulating motion, as water, waves, or smoke. **4.** to extend in undulations, as land. **5.** to continue with or have a deep, prolonged sound, as thunder, etc. **6.** to turn over, or over and over, as a person or animal lying down. **7.** *Colloq.* to luxuriate or abound (in wealth, etc.). **8.** to turn round in different directions, as the eyes in their sockets. **9.** to sway or rock from side to side, as a ship (opposed to *pitch*). **10.** to sail with a rolling motion. **11.** to walk with a rolling or swaying gait. **12.** (of a rocket or guided missile) to rotate about its longitudinal axis in flight. **13.** to admit of being rolled up, as a material. **14.** to spread out as under a roller. **15.** to cast dice. *–v.t.* **16.** to cause to move along a surface by turning over and over, as a cask, a ball, or a hoop. **17.** to move along on wheels or rollers; to convey in a wheeled vehicle. **18.** to drive, impel, or cause to flow onwards with a sweeping motion. **19.** to utter or give forth with a full, flowing, continuous sound. **20.** to trill: *to roll one's r's.* **21.** to cause to turn over, or over and over. **22.** to cause to turn round in different directions, as the eyes. **23.** to cause to sway or rock from side to side, as a ship. **24.** to wrap round an axis, round upon itself, or into a roll, ball, or the like. **25.** to make by forming a roll: *to roll a cigarette.* **26.** to wrap, enfold, or envelop, as in some covering. **27.** Also, **roll out.** to operate upon so as to spread out, level, compact, or the like, as with a roller, rolling pin, etc. **28.** Also, **roll down.** to flatten (scrub) using a roller. **29.** to beat (a drum) with rapid, continuous strokes. **30.** to cast (dice). **31.** *Colloq.* to rob (a person), often with violence. **32.** *Colloq.* to defeat; overcome. **33.** *Colloq.* to upset the equanimity of (someone) with a cutting remark, witty come-back, etc. *–n.* **34.** anything rolled up in cylindrical form. **35.** a piece of parchment, paper, or the like, as for writing, etc., which is or may be rolled up; a scroll. **36.** a list, register, or catalogue. **37.** a list containing the names of the persons belonging to any company, class, society, etc. **38.** a number of papers or the like rolled up together. **39.** a quantity of cloth, wallpaper, or the like, rolled up in cylindrical form (often forming a definite measure). **40.** a cylindrical or rounded mass of something: *rolls of fat.* **41.** some article of cylindrical or rounded form, as a moulding. **42.** a cylindrical piece upon which something is rolled along to facilitate moving. **43.** a cylinder upon which something is rolled up, as plastic food wrap, etc. **44.** a roller with which something is spread out, levelled, crushed, compacted, or the like. **45.** thin sponge spread with jam, cream, or the like and rolled up. **46.** Also, **bread roll.** a small cake of bread, often rolled or doubled on itself before baking. **47.** pastry spread with apple, jam, etc., and doubled on itself before baking. **48.** food which is rolled up. **49.** meat rolled up and cooked. **50.** the act or an instance of rolling. **51.** undulation of surface: *the roll of a prairie.* **52.** sonorous or rhythmical flow of words. **53.** a deep, prolonged sound, as of thunder, etc.: *the deep roll of a breaking wave.* **54.** the trill of certain birds. **55.** the continuous sound of a drum rapidly beaten. **56.** a rolling motion, as of a ship. **57.** a rolling or swaying gait. **58.** *Aeronautics* a single complete rotation of an aeroplane around the axis of the fuselage with little loss of altitude or change of direction. **59.** the rotation of a rocket or guided missile or the like about its longitudinal axis. **60.** *Athletics* a style used by competitors in the high jump and pole vault where the body is rolled over the bar in a near horizontal position. **61.** a single throw of dice. **62.** *Colloq.* a wad of paper currency. **63.** *Colloq. (taboo)* an act of sexual intercourse. *–phr.* **64. be on a roll,** *Colloq.* to be experiencing a run of good fortune or success. **65. roll along,** *Colloq.* to arrive: *just roll along whenever you like.* **66. roll in, a.** *Colloq.* to arrive. **b.** to retire to bed. **67. roll on** (or **away**), to move on or pass, as time. **68. roll out, a.** to spread out from being rolled up; unroll. **b.** to initiate the supply of: *to roll out a new model.* **c.** to introduce: *the government rolled out a new tax package.* **69. roll over, a.** *Aust. Colloq.* (of a politician) to resign gracefully. **b.** *Aust. Colloq.* (of a witness in a court case who was previously hostile) to decide to provide evidence helpful to the interrogator. **c.** *Aust. Colloq.* (of an offender) to confess to wrongdoing in a way that implicates others in order to gain more favourable treatment. **d.** to invest (a lump sum received on termination of employment) in an approved deposit fund. **70. roll round,** to move round as in a cycle, as

seasons. **71. roll up, a.** to form into a roll, or curl up upon itself. **b.** *Colloq.* to arrive. **c.** *Colloq.* to gather round. **72. roll up one's sleeves,** to prepare for hard work. **73. roll with the punches,** to adapt to meet ill fortune or difficulties. *–rollable, adj.*

rolled gold *n.* metal covered with a thin coating of gold.

roller /'roʊlə/ *n.* **1.** a cylinder, wheel, or the like, upon which something is rolled along. **2.** a cylinder around which something is rolled: *a hair roller.* **3.** a cylindrical body for rolling over something to be spread out, levelled, crushed, linked, etc. **4.** any of various other revolving cylindrical bodies, as the barrel of a musical box. **5.** a long, swelling wave advancing steadily.

rollerball pen *n.* a type of ballpoint pen which uses a water base for the ink, giving greater freedom of movement and requiring less pressure from the user. Also, **rollerball.**

rollerblade /'roʊləbleɪd/ *(from trademark) –n.* **1.** one of a pair of rollerskates designed in imitation of an ice-skating shoe with a single row of rollers instead of a skate; inline skate. *–v.i.* **2.** to move on rollerblades. Also, **blade.** *–rollerblading, n.*

rollerskate /'roʊləskeɪt/ *n.* **1.** a form of skate running on small wheels or rollers, for use on a smooth floor, footpath, etc. *–v.i.* **2.** to move on rollerskates. *–rollerskater, n. –rollerskating, n.*

rollick /'rɒlɪk/ *v.i.* to move or act in a careless, frolicsome manner; behave in a free, hearty, merry, or jovial way.

rollicking /'rɒlɪkɪŋ/ *adj.* swaggering and jolly: *a pair of rollicking drunken sailors.* Also, **rollicksome** /'rɒlɪksəm/.

rolling stock *n.* the wheeled vehicles of a railway, including engines and carriages.

rolling strike *n.* industrial action by employees against their employer in which groups of employees go on strike consecutively.

rollmop /'roʊlmɒp/ *n.* a marinated fillet of herring wrapped around a gherkin, pickled cucumber, or onion, and served as an hors d'oeuvre.

rollout /'roʊlaʊt/ *n.* the launch of a new product, service, etc.: *the rollout of the new software was well publicised.* Also, **roll-out.**

rollover /'roʊloʊvə/ *adj. Aust.* of or relating to the investment of a superannuation payout with a government-approved institution that allows the deferral of lump sum tax. Also, **roll-over.**

roly-poly /ˌroʊli-'poʊli/ *adj.* **1.** plump and podgy, as a person, a young animal, etc. *–n. (pl. -lies)* **2.** a roly-poly person or thing. **3.** a strip of suet-crust pastry spread with jam, fruit, or the like, or sometimes with a savoury mixture, rolled up, wrapped in greaseproof paper, and steamed or boiled as a pudding. **4.** any of several bushy plants, as *Salsola kali,* which break loose and roll in the wind.

ROM /rɒm/ *n. Computers* a computer storage device which holds data that can be read, but not altered, by program instructions.

Roman /'roʊmən/ *adj.* **1.** of or relating to Rome, ancient or modern, or those living there. **2.** *(usu. lower case)* indicating or relating to the upright style of printing types most commonly used in modern books, etc. **3.** indicating or relating to Roman numerals. *–n.* **4.** someone born or living in ancient or modern Rome.

roman à clef /roʊˌmɒn a 'kleɪ/ *n. (pl. romans à clef* /roʊˌmɒn a 'kleɪ/) a novel in which actual persons and events are disguised as fiction.

Roman Catholic Church *n.* See **Catholic Church** (def. 2). Also, **Church of Rome.**

romance¹ /rə'mæns, 'roʊmæns/ *n.* **1.** a tale depicting heroic or marvellous achievements, colourful events or scenes, chivalrous devotion, unusual, even supernatural, experiences, or other matters of a kind to appeal to

the imagination. **2.** the world, life, or conditions depicted in such tales. **3.** a made-up story; fanciful or
extravagant invention or exaggeration. **4.** romantic
spirit or sentiment. **5.** romantic character or quality. **6.** a
romantic affair or experience; a love affair. **7.** a novel or
film in which romantic love, usually leading to happiness, is a prevailing element. *–v.i.* (**-manced, -mancing**)
8. to invent or relate romances; indulge in fanciful or
extravagant stories. **9.** to think or talk romantically.
–**romancer,** *n.*

romance² /rə'mæns/ *n. Music* a short, simple melody,
vocal or instrumental, of tender character.

Roman numerals *pl. n.* the numerals in the ancient
Roman system of notation, still used for certain limited
purposes. The common basic symbols are I (= 1),
V (= 5), X (= 10), L (= 50), C (= 100), D (= 500),
and M (= 1000). Integers are written according to these
two rules: if a letter is immediately followed by one of
equal or lesser value, the two values are added, thus,
XX equals 20, XV equals 15, VI equals 6; if a letter
is immediately followed by one of greater value,
however, the first is subtracted from the second, thus
IV equals 4, XL equals 40, CM equals 900.

romantic /rə'mæntɪk/ *adj.* **1.** of, relating to, or of the
nature of romance: *a romantic adventure.* **2.** suited to
romance rather than to real or practical life; fanciful;
unpractical; quixotic: *romantic ideas.* **3.** showing or
expressing love, strong affection, etc. **4.** (*sometimes
upper case*) of or relating to a style of literature, art, and
music of the late 18th and 19th centuries, characterised
by freedom of treatment, a viewing of form as less
important than matter, imagination, experimentation
with form, etc. **5.** imaginary or made-up. *–n.* **6.** a romantic person. –**romantically,** *adv.*

romanticise /rə'mæntəsaɪz/ *v.t.* **1.** to make romantic;
invest with a romantic character: *she romanticised her
work as an actor.* *–v.i.* **2.** to have romantic ideas; indulge in romance. Also, **romanticize.**

romp /rɒmp/ *v.i.* **1.** to play or frolic in a lively or boisterous manner. **2.** to rise up rapidly and without
effort, as in racing. *–n.* **3.** a romping frolic. **4.** a swift,
effortless pace. *–phr.* **5. romp home** (or **in**), to win
easily.

rompers /'rɒmpəz/ *pl. n.* a one-piece loose outer garment
for a baby combining a sleeveless top and short or long
trousers; crawlers. Also, **romper suit.**

rondo /'rɒndoʊ/ *n.* (*pl.* **-dos**) *Music* a musical work or
movement, often the last movement of a sonata, having
one principal subject which is stated at least three times
in the same key and to which return is made after the
introduction of each subordinate theme.

roo /ruː/ *n. Aust. Colloq.* a kangaroo.

Rooball /'ruːbɔːl/ *n.* (*from trademark*) a form of soccer
modified for small children, using small fields and
small goals.

roo bar *n.* → **kangaroo bar.**

rood /ruːd/ *n.* **1.** a crucifix, especially a large one at the
entrance to the choir or chancel of a medieval church,
often supported on a special beam or rood screen. **2.** a
unit of length in the imperial system varying locally
from 5½ to 8 yards. **3.** a unit of land measure in the
imperial system, equal to 40 square rods or ¼ acre
(approximately 1011.714 m²). *Symbol:* rd

roof /ruːf/ *n.* (*pl.* **roofs** /ruːfs, ruːvz/) **1.** the external upper
covering of a house or other building. **2.** a house. **3.** the
highest part or summit. **4.** something which in form or
position resembles the roof of a house, as the top of a
car, the upper part of the mouth, etc. *–v.t.* **5.** to provide
or cover with a roof. *–phr.* **6. go through the roof,**
Colloq. **a.** to become angry; lose one's temper. **b.** (of a
business, sales, etc.) to become suddenly successful; to
increase. **c.** (of prices, costs, etc.) to escalate markedly.

7. hit the roof, *Colloq.* to become very angry; lose one's
temper. **8. raise the roof, a.** to create a loud noise. **b.** to
make loud protests or complaints. **9. under one's roof,**
in one's family circle; in one's home. **10. without a roof,**
without shelter of any kind.

roof rack *n.* a system of bars attached to the roof of a
car and used for the carriage of luggage, etc. Also,
roof-rack.

rook¹ /rʊk/ *n.* **1.** a large black, white-beaked, gregarious
bird, *Corvus frugilegus*, like a crow, found throughout
Eurasia; nests in colonies (rookeries) in trees near
buildings. **2.** a sharper, as at cards or dice; a swindler.
–v.t. **3.** to cheat; fleece; swindle.

rook² /rʊk/ *n.* a chess piece having the power to move
any unobstructed distance in a straight line forwards,
backwards, or sideways; castle.

rookery /'rʊkəri/ *n.* (*pl.* **-ries**) **1.** a colony of rooks. **2.** a
place where rooks congregate to breed. **3.** a breeding
place or colony of other birds or animals, as penguins,
seals, etc. **4.** any instance of cheating, sharp practice,
exorbitant prices, etc.

rookie /'rʊki/ *n. Colloq.* a raw recruit, originally in the
army, and hence in any service, sporting team, etc.
Also, **rooky.**

room /ruːm/ *n.* **1.** a portion of space within a building or
other structure, separated by walls or partitions from
other parts: *a dining room.* **2.** (*pl.*) lodgings or quarters,
as in a house or building. **3.** the persons present in a
room: *the whole room laughed.* **4.** space, or extent of
space, occupied by or available for something: *the desk
takes up too much room.* **5.** opportunity or scope for or
to do something: *room for improvement.* *–v.i.* **6.** to
occupy a room or rooms; to share a room; lodge. *–phr.*
7. no room to swing a cat, *Colloq.* an expression indicating a confined, cramped, or cluttered place. **8. room
in,** (of a mother in a maternity hospital) to sleep in the
same room as her baby. **9. room to move,** scope to
manoeuvre; options or choices. **10. the smallest room,**
Colloq. a toilet or bathroom.

roomy /'ruːmi/ *adj.* (**-mier, -miest**) affording ample room;
spacious; large. –**roomily,** *adv.* –**roominess,** *n.*

roost /ruːst/ *n.* **1.** a perch upon which domestic fowls rest
at night. **2.** a house or place for fowls or birds to roost
in. **3.** a place for sitting, resting, or staying. *–v.i.* **4.** to sit
or rest on a roost, perch, etc. **5.** to settle or stay, especially for the night. *–phr.* **6. come home to roost,** to
come back upon the originator; recoil. **7. rule the roost,**
to be in charge; dominate.

rooster /'ruːstə/ *n.* the male of the domestic fowl; cock.

root¹ /ruːt/ *n.* **1.** a part of the body of a plant which,
typically, develops from the radicle, and grows downwards into the soil, fixing the plant and absorbing nutriment and moisture. **2.** a similar organ developed from
some other part of the plant, as one of those by which
ivy clings to its support. **3.** any underground part of a
plant, as a rhizome. **4.** the embedded or basal portion of
a hair, tooth, nail, etc. **5.** the fundamental or essential
part: *the root of a matter.* **6.** the source or origin of a
thing: *love of money is the root of all evil.* **7.** the base or
point of origin of something. **8.** a person or family as
the source of offspring or descendants. **9.** an offshoot or
scion. **10.** (*pl.*) **a.** a person's real home and environment: *though I've lived in the city for ten years my roots
are still in the country.* **b.** those elements, as personal
relationships, a liking for the area, customs, etc., which
make a place one's true home: *he lived in Darwin for
five years but never established any roots there.*
11. *Maths* **a.** a quantity which, when multiplied by itself
a certain number of times, produces a given quantity:
*2 is the square root of 4, the cube root of 8, and the
fourth root of 16.* **b.** a quantity which, when substituted
for the unknown quantity in an algebraic equation,

satisfies the equation. **12.** *Ling.* **a.** a morpheme which underlies an inflectional paradigm or is used itself as a word or element of a compound. Thus, *dance* is the root of *dancer, dancing.* In German, *seh* is the root of *gesehen.* **b.** such a morpheme as posited for a parent language, such as proto Indo-European, on the basis of comparison of extant forms in daughter languages. **13.** *Music* **a.** the fundamental note of a chord or of a series of harmonies. **b.** the lowest note of a chord when arranged as a series of thirds; the fundamental. **14.** *Machinery* that part of a screw thread which connects adjacent flanks at the bottom of the groove. **15.** *Aust., NZ Colloq.* (*taboo*) an act of sexual intercourse. **16.** *Aust., NZ Colloq.* (*taboo*) a sexual partner (especially in contexts where performance, willingness, etc., is evaluated): *a good root; an easy root.* –*v.i.* **17.** to send out roots and begin to grow. **18.** to become fixed or established. **19.** (of a horse, etc.) to pigroot. **20.** *Aust., NZ Colloq.* (*taboo*) to engage in sexual intercourse. –*v.t.* **21.** to fix by, or as if by, roots. **22.** to implant or establish deeply. **23.** *Aust., NZ Colloq.* (*taboo*) to have sexual intercourse with. **24.** *Aust., NZ Colloq.* (*taboo*) to frustrate. **25.** *Aust., NZ Colloq.* (*taboo*) to break; ruin: *I told you not to do that – you've rooted it now.* –*phr.* **26. root and branch,** entirely; completely: *to reform tax root and branch.* **27. root out,** to extirpate; exterminate. Compare **root²** (def. 3). **28. root up, a.** to pull up by the roots. **b.** to eradicate; remove utterly. Compare **root²** (defs 3 and 4). **29. take** (or **strike**) **root, a.** to send out roots and begin to grow. **b.** to become fixed or established. **30. wouldn't it root you,** *Aust. Colloq.* (*taboo*) an exclamation of exasperation. –**rootless,** *adj.* –**rootage,** *n.* –**rooty,** *adj.*

root² /rut/ *v.i.* **1.** to turn up the soil with the snout, as swine. –*phr.* **2. root around,** to poke, pry, or search, as if to find something. **3. root out** (or **up**), to unearth; bring to light. Compare **root¹** (defs 27 and 28). **4. root up,** to turn over with the snout. Compare **root¹** (def. 28). –**rooter,** *n.*

root³ /rut/ *phr.* **root for,** *US Colloq.* to give encouragement to, or applaud (a contestant, etc.). –**rooter,** *n.*

rooted /'rutəd/ *adj.* **1.** having roots: *rooted plant cuttings.* **2.** firmly implanted: *deeply rooted beliefs.* **3.** *Aust., NZ Colloq.* exhausted. **4.** *Aust., NZ Colloq.* frustrated; thwarted. **5.** *Aust., NZ Colloq.* broken; ruined. –**rootedness,** *n.*

rootstock /'rutstɒk/ *n.* **1.** *Hort.* a root used as a stock in plant propagation. **2.** *Bot.* the basal persistent part of the stems of erect herbaceous perennials from which new roots and aerial shoots arise in the next growing season. **3.** a source from which offshoots have originated; ancestral form.

rope /roup/ *n.* **1.** a strong, thick line or cord, commonly one composed of twisted or braided strands of hemp, flax, or the like, or of wire or other material. **2.** (*pl.*) the cords used to enclose a boxing ring or other space. **3.** a quantity of material or a number of things twisted or strung together in the form of a thick cord: *a rope of beads.* **4.** *US* → **lasso.** **5.** a stringy, viscid, or glutinous formation in a liquid. –*v.t.* **6.** to tie, bind, or fasten with a rope. **7.** to enclose or mark off with a rope. **8.** to catch with a lasso. –*phr.* **9. give someone enough rope to hang themself,** *Colloq.* to allow someone the freedom to prove their unworthiness or incompetence. **10. on the ropes, a.** *Boxing* driven against the ropes by one's opponent. **b.** *Colloq.* in a hopeless position; near to failure. **11. rope in,** *Colloq.* to draw, entice, or inveigle into something. **12. the end of one's rope,** *Colloq.* the limit of one's possibilities, patience or resources. **13. the ropes,** methods; procedure; operations of a business, etc.: *to learn the ropes; to show someone the ropes.*

ropeable /'roupəbəl/ *adj.* **1.** (of animals) wild; intractable. **2.** *Colloq.* extremely angry or bad-tempered. Also, **ropable.**

roquefort /'roukfət/ *n.* a semi-soft ripened cheese made from sheep's milk, with a strong flavour, veined with mould.

Rorschach test /'rɔʃak tɛst/ *n. Psychol.* a test devised for the analysis of personality, calling for responses to ink blots and drawings.

rort¹ /rɔt/ *Colloq.* –*n.* **1.** a scheme which manipulates the law or any set of regulations to gain a wrongful advantage. –*v.t.* **2.** to gain control over (an organisation, as a branch of a political party) especially by falsifying records. **3.** to take wrongful advantage of; pervert: *to rort the system.*

rort² /rɔt/ *Colloq.* –*n.* **1.** (*dated*) a wild party. **2.** *NZ* (*taboo*) an act of sexual intercourse. –*v.t.* **3.** *NZ* (*taboo*) to have sexual intercourse.

rosacea /rou'zeisiə/ *n.* a skin condition of the face characterised by redness caused by enlargement of the blood vessels under the skin, combined with acne-like eruptions. Also, **acne rosacea.**

rosary /'rouzəri/ *n.* (*pl.* **-ries**) **1.** *Roman Catholic Church* **a.** a series of prayers consisting (in the usual form) of fifteen or twenty decades of Ave Marias, with associated prayers and meditations. **b.** a string of beads used for counting these prayers in reciting them. **2.** (among other religious bodies) a string of beads similarly used in praying. **3.** a rose garden; a bed of roses.

rose¹ /rouz/ *n.* **1.** any of the wild or cultivated, usually prickly-stemmed, showy-flowered shrubs constituting the genus *Rosa*, having in the wild state a corolla of five roundish petals. **2.** any of various related or similar plants. **3.** the flower of any such shrubs, usually of a red, pink, white, or yellow colour, and often fragrant. **4.** an ornament shaped like or suggesting a rose; a rosette of ribbon or the like. **5.** the traditional reddish colour of the rose, varying from a purplish red through different shades to a pale pink. **6.** a pinkish red colour in the cheek. **7.** a rose window. **8.** an ornamental plate or socket which surrounds a doorknob on the face of a door, an electric or gas light fitting, on a ceiling, etc. **9.** the compass card of the mariner's compass as printed on charts. **10.** a form of cut gem formerly much used with a triangularly faceted top and flat underside: *a rose diamond.* **11.** a perforated cap or plate at the end of a water pipe or the spout of a watering-can, etc., to break a flow of water into a spray. –*adj.* **12.** of the colour rose. –*phr.* **13. bed of roses,** a situation of luxurious ease; an easy and highly agreeable position or activity. **14. under the rose,** secretly; privately.

rose² /rouz/ *v.* past tense of **rise.**

rosé /rou'zei/ *n.* a light wine of a translucent pale red colour.

rosehip /'rouzhip/ *n.* → **hip².**

rosella¹ /rou'zɛlə/ *n.* **1.** Also, **rosella bush.** an annual shrub, *Hibiscus sabdariffa,* with large lobed leaves and yellow hibiscus-like flowers producing a fruit consisting of a green seed surrounded by dark red fleshy leaves. **2.** the fruit, picked when young and used to make jam.

rosella² /rou'zɛlə/ *n.* any of a number of brilliantly coloured, endemic Australian parrots of the genus *Platycercus,* as the **eastern rosella,** *P. eximius,* a common bird of eastern Australia.

rosemary /'rouzməri/ *n.* (*pl.* **-ries**) an evergreen shrub, *Rosmarinus officinalis,* native to the Mediterranean region, used as a herb in cookery and yielding a fragrant essential oil. It is a traditional symbol of remembrance.

rosette /rou'zɛt/ *n.* **1.** any arrangement, part, object, or formation more or less resembling a rose. **2.** a rose-shaped arrangement of ribbon or other material, used as an ornament or badge.

rosewood /'rouzwʊd/ *n.* **1.** any of various reddish cabinet woods (sometimes with a rose-like odour) yielded by trees such as *Dysoxylum fraserianum* of Australia and tropical species of the genus *Dalbergia* of India and Brazil. **2.** a tree yielding such wood.

rosin /'rɒzən/ *n.* **1.** the hard, brittle resin left after distilling off the oil of turpentine from the crude oleoresin of the pine, used in making varnish, for rubbing on violin bows, etc. **2.** (not in scientific usage) resin.

Ross River fever *n.* a fever accompanying infection by Ross River virus.

Ross River virus *n.* a virus transmitted by mosquitoes from some native animals, especially macropods, producing symptoms of fever, headaches, rashes, and aching muscles and joints.

roster /'rɒstə/ *n.* **1.** a list of persons or groups with their turns or periods of duty. **2.** any list, roll, or register. *–v.t.* **3.** to put on a roster; to list. *–***rostered**, *adj.*

rosti /'rɒsti/ *n.* (in Swiss cookery) grated potato mixed with other ingredients, as cheese, bacon, egg, tomato, vegetables, and then fried on both sides. Also, **rösti**, **roesti** /'rɜsti/.

rostrum /'rɒstrəm/ *n.* (*pl.* **-trums** or **-tra** /-trə/) **1.** any platform, stage, or the like, for public speaking. **2.** a platform for musicians or their conductor, or the like.

rosy /'rouzi/ *adj.* (**-sier, -siest**) **1.** pink or pinkish red; roseate. **2.** (of persons, the cheeks, lips, etc.) having a fresh, healthy redness. **3.** bright or promising: *a rosy future.* **4.** cheerful or optimistic: *rosy anticipations.* **5.** made or consisting of roses. *–***rosily**, *adv.* *–***rosiness**, *n.*

rot /rɒt/ *verb* (**rotted, rotting**) *–v.i.* **1.** to undergo decomposition; decay. **2.** to become morally corrupt or offensive. *–v.t.* **3.** to cause to rot. *–n.* **4.** the process of rotting. **5.** the state of being rotten; decay; putrefaction. **6.** rotting or rotten matter. **7.** any of various diseases characterised by decomposition. **8.** any of various plant diseases or forms of decay produced by fungi or bacteria. **9.** *Colloq.* nonsense. *–interj.* **10.** an exclamation of dissent, distaste, or disgust. *–phr.* **11. rot away** (or **off**), to fall or become weak due to decay. **12. where the rot sets in**, the point at which deterioration really begins. *–***rotting**, *adj.*

rotary /'routəri/ *adj.* **1.** turning round as on an axis, as an object. **2.** taking place round an axis, as motion. **3.** having a part or parts that rotate, as a machine. **4.** of or relating to a rotary engine. **5.** *Agric.* (of various implements) having rotating blades, scrapers, or the like: *rotary hoe.*

rotary hoe *n. Agric.* an implement with wheels with many finger-like extensions, pulled over the ground for early crop cultivation and destruction of weeds.

rotate /rou'teɪt/ *v.t.* **1.** to cause to turn round like a wheel on its axis. **2.** to cause to go through a round of changes; cause to pass or follow in a fixed routine of succession: *to rotate crops.* *–v.i.* **3.** to turn round as on an axis. **4.** to proceed in a fixed routine of succession. *–***rotatable**, *adj.* *–***rotation**, *n.* *–***rotative**, *adj.* *–***rotatory**, *adj.*

rote /rout/ *phr.* **by rote**, in a mechanical way without thought of the meaning.

rotisserie /rou'tɪsəri/ *n.* **1.** Also, **roasting spit**. a spit, driven by clockwork mechanism or electricity, on which meat, poultry, and game can be cooked. **2.** a restaurant, cafe, etc., where such a spit is used.

rotor /'routə/ *n.* **1.** *Elect.* the rotating member of a machine (opposed to *stator*). **2.** *Aeronautics* a system of rotating aerofoils, usually horizontal, as those of a helicopter. **3.** *Machinery* the rotating assembly of blades in a turbine.

rotten /'rɒtn/ *adj.* **1.** in a condition of decomposition or decay; putrid; tainted, foul, or ill-smelling. **2.** dishonest or offensive morally, politically, or otherwise. **3.** *Colloq.* pitifully bad, unsatisfactory, or unpleasant: *to feel rotten; rotten work.* **4.** disgusting; vile; worthless: *a rotten little snob.* **5.** (of soil, rocks, etc.) soft, yielding, or easily broken up as the result of decomposition. **6.** *Colloq.* extremely drunk. *–***rottenly**, *adv.* *–***rottenness**, *n.*

rotten egg gas *n. Chem. Colloq.* → **hydrogen sulphide**.

rotund /rou'tʌnd/ *adj.* **1.** rounded; plump. **2.** full-toned or sonorous: *rotund speeches.* *–***rotundity, rotundness**, *n.* *–***rotundly**, *adv.*

rotunda /rə'tʌndə/ *n.* **1.** a round building, especially one with a dome. **2.** a large and high circular hall or room in a building, especially one surmounted by a dome. **3.** a circular bandstand, especially one with a dome.

rouble /'rubəl/ *n.* the principal monetary unit of Russia and Belarus and formerly of other member states of the former Soviet Union, of varying value from country to country; divided into 100 kopecks. Also, **ruble**.

rouge /ruʒ/ *n.* **1.** any of various red cosmetics for colouring the cheeks or lips. **2.** a reddish powder, chiefly ferric oxide, used for polishing metal, etc. *–verb* (**rouged, rouging**) *–v.t.* **3.** to colour with rouge. *–v.i.* **4.** to use rouge.

rough /rʌf/ *adj.* **1.** uneven from projections, irregularities, or breaks of surface; not smooth: *rough boards; a rough road.* **2.** (of ground) wild; broken; covered with scrub, boulders, etc. **3.** shaggy: *a dog with a rough coat.* **4.** acting with or characterised by violence. **5.** violently disturbed or agitated, as the sea, water, etc. **6.** violently irregular, as motion. **7.** stormy or tempestuous, as wind, weather, etc. **8.** sharp or harsh: *a rough temper.* **9.** unmannerly or rude. **10.** disorderly or riotous. **11.** *Colloq.* severe, hard, or unpleasant: *to have a rough time of it.* **12.** harsh to the ear, grating, or jarring, as sounds. **13.** harsh to the taste; sharp, or astringent, as wines: *rough cider.* **14.** coarse, as food, cloth, materials, etc. **15. a.** (of people or their behaviour) lacking culture or refinement: *rough as bags.* **b.** (of sheep) difficult to manage while being shorn. **16.** without refinements, luxuries, or ordinary comforts or conveniences. **17.** requiring exertion or strength rather than intelligence or skill, as work. **18.** unpolished, as language, verse, style, etc.; not elaborated, perfected, or corrected: *a rough draft.* **19.** made or done without any attempt at exactness, completeness, or thoroughness: *a rough guess.* **20.** crude, unwrought, undressed, or unprepared: *a rough diamond; rough rice.* *–n.* **21.** that which is rough; rough ground. **22.** any piece of work, especially a work of art, in an unfinished or preliminary condition. **23.** *Golf* any part of the course bordering the fairway on which the grass, weeds, etc., are not trimmed. **24.** the rough, hard, or unpleasant side or part of anything: *the rough and tumble of life.* **25.** *Colloq.* a rough person; rowdy. *–adv.* **26.** in a rough manner; roughly. *–v.t.* **27.** to make rough; roughen. *–phr.* **28. a bit rough**, *Colloq.* unfair, unreasonable. **29. a rough trot**, *Aust.* a period of one's life which is marked by difficulty, ill fortune, or hardship. **30. cut up rough**, to behave angrily or violently; be upset. **31. in the rough**, in a rough, crude, unwrought, or unfinished state. **32. live rough**, to live outdoors, as in the bush with primitive shelter and few conveniences: *there was a man living rough in the next valley.* **33. rough in** (or **out**), to cut, shape, or sketch roughly: *to rough out a plan; to rough in the outlines of a plan.* **34. rough it**, *Colloq.* to live without the usually expected comforts or conveniences: *I was roughing it in the army at that time.* **35. rough on**, **a.** severe towards. **b.** unfortunate for (someone). **36. rough someone up**, to treat someone roughly or harshly.

37. rough up (or **out**), to subject to some rough preliminary process of working or preparation. **38. take the rough with the smooth**, to accept bad fortune with as good grace as good fortune, in the knowledge that equal amounts of both are likely to occur. **–roughen**, *v.* **–roughness**, *n.*

roughage /ˈrʌfidʒ/ *n.* **1.** rough or coarse material. **2.** the coarser kinds or parts of fodder or food, of less nutritive value, especially those which assist digestion, as distinguished from those affording more concentrated nutriment.

roughcast /ˈrʌfkast/ *n.* **1.** a coarse plaster mixed with gravel, shells, or the like, for outside surfaces, usually thrown against the wall. *–adj.* **2.** made of or covered with roughcast; crudely formed. *–v.t.* (**-cast**, **-casting**) **3.** to make, shape, or prepare in a rough form: *to roughcast a story*. **–roughcaster**, *n.*

roughhouse /ˈrʌfhaʊs/ *Colloq.* *–n.* **1.** noisy, disorderly behaviour or play; rowdy conduct; a brawl. *–v.i.* **2.** to engage or take part in a roughhouse. *–adj.* **3.** resembling a roughhouse; boisterous; violent: *roughhouse tactics.*

roughly /ˈrʌfli/ *adv.* **1.** in a crude, harsh or violent manner. **2.** inexactly; without precision. **3.** approximately; about.

roughshod /ˈrʌfʃɒd/ *adj.* **1.** shod with horseshoes having projecting nails or points. **2.** high-handed and inconsiderate: *roughshod methods*. *–phr.* **3. ride roughshod over**, to override harshly or domineeringly; treat without consideration.

rouleau /ˈruloʊ/ *n.* (*pl.* **-leaux** *or* **-leaus** /-loʊz/) **1.** a cylindrical pile or roll of something. **2.** a number of coins put up in cylindrical form in a paper wrapping.

roulette /ruˈlɛt/ *n.* **1.** a game of chance played at a table, in which an unlimited number of players bet on which of the compartments of a revolving disc or wheel will be the resting place of a ball circling it in the opposite direction. **2.** the wheel or disc used in this game. **3.** a small wheel, especially one with sharp teeth, mounted in a handle, for making lines of marks, dots, or perforations: *engravers' roulettes*; *a roulette for perforating sheets of postage stamps*. *–v.t.* (**-letted**, **-letting**) **4.** to mark, impress, or perforate with a roulette.

round /raʊnd/ *adj.* **1.** circular, as a disc. **2.** ring-shaped, as a hoop. **3.** curved like part of a circle, as an outline. **4.** having a circular cross-section, as a cylinder. **5.** spherical or globular, as a ball. **6.** rounded more or less like a part of a sphere. **7.** free from angularity; curved, as parts of the body. **8.** executed with or involving circular motion: *a round dance*. **9.** completed by passing through a course which finally returns to the place of starting: *a round trip*. **10.** full, complete, or entire: *a round dozen*. **11.** forming, or expressed by, an integer or whole number (with no fraction). **12.** expressed in tens, hundreds, thousands, or the like: *in round numbers*. **13.** portrayed in depth, rather than in stylised or stereotyped fashion as a literary character. **14.** full and sonorous, as sound. **15.** candid or outspoken. *–n.* **16.** something round; a circle, ring, curve, etc.; a circular, ring-shaped, or curved object; a rounded form. **17.** a completed course of time, a series of events, operations, etc. **18.** any complete course, series, or succession. **19.** (*sometimes pl.*) a circuit of any place, series of places, etc., covered in a customary or predetermined way: *the postman on his rounds*. **20.** a series (of visits, etc.). **21.** a completed course or spell of activity, commonly one of a series, in some game, sport, competition, or the like. **22.** a recurring period or time, succession of events, duties, etc.: *the daily round*. **23.** a single discharge of shot by each of a number of guns, rifles, etc., or by a single piece. **24.** a charge of ammunition for a single shot. **25.** a distribution

of drink, etc., to all the members of a company. **26.** movement in a circle or about an axis. **27.** a form of sculpture in which figures are executed apart from any background (contrasted with *relief*). **28.** a standard cut of beef from the lower part of the butt, used for roasting or as steaks. **29. a.** (of bread) a slice. **b.** a sandwich. **30.** one of a series of periods (separated by rests) making up a boxing or wrestling match, etc. **31.** *Music* **a.** a part-song in which the several voices follow one another at equal intervals of time, and at the same pitch as the octave. **b.** (*pl.*) the order followed in ringing a peal of bells in diatonic sequence from the highest to the lowest. **32.** *Golf* a complete circuit of a prearranged series of holes, usually the whole course of eighteen holes. **33.** *Cards* a single turn of play by each player. *–adv.* **34.** in a circle, ring, or the like, or so as to surround something. **35.** on all sides, or about, whether circularly or otherwise. **36.** in all directions from a centre. **37.** *Chiefly US* in the region about a place: *the country round*. **38.** in circumference: *a tree 40 centimetres round*. **39.** in a circular or rounded course: *to fly round and round*. **40.** through a round, circuit, or series, as of places or persons: *to show a person round*. **41.** through a round, or recurring period, of time, especially to the present or a particular time: *when the time rolls round*. **42.** throughout, or from beginning to end of, a recurring period of time: *all the year round*. **43.** by a circuitous or roundabout course. **44.** to a place or point as by a circuit or circuitous course: *to get round into the navigable channel*. **45.** *Chiefly US* in circulation, action, etc.; about. **46.** with a rotating course or movement: *the wheels went round*. **47.** with change to another or opposite direction, course, opinion, etc.: *to sit still without looking round*. *–prep.* **48.** so as to encircle, surround, or envelop: *to tie paper round a parcel*. **49.** on the circuit, border, or outer part of it. **50.** around; about. **51.** in or from all or various directions from: *to look round one*. **52.** in the vicinity of: *the country round Geelong*. **53.** in a round, circuit, or course through. **54.** to all or various parts of: *to wander round the country*. **55.** throughout (a period of time): *a resort visited all round the year*. **56.** here and there in: *people standing round a room*. **57.** so as to make a turn or partial circuit about or to the other side of: *to sail round a cape*. **58.** reached by making a turn or partial circuit about (something): *the church round the corner*. **59.** so as to revolve or rotate about (a centre or axis): *the earth's motion round its axis*. *–v.t.* **60.** to make round. **61.** to free from angularity or flatness; fill out symmetrically; make plump. **62.** to frame or form neatly, as a sentence, etc. **63.** to make a turn or partial circuit about, as to get to the other side of: *to round a cape*. **64.** to cause to move in a circle or turn round. **65.** *Phonetics* to pronounce with the lips forming an approximately oval opening: *'boot' has a rounded vowel*. **66.** Also, **round off**. **a.** to increase or decrease (a number which has fractions or decimal points) to the nearest whole number: *to round 94.89 up to 95*; *to round 94.30 down to 94*. **b.** (in currency transactions) to increase or decrease (an amount) to the nearest amount for which there is a coin or note. *–v.i.* **67.** to become round. **68.** to become free from angularity; become plump. **69.** to make a turn or partial circuit about something. **70.** to turn round as on an axis: *to round on one's heels*. *–phr.* **71. go the rounds**, **a.** (of people) to make a series of visits. **b.** (of gossip, information, etc.) to become generally known. **72. in the round**, (of a play, concert, etc.) with the audience seated all around the stage. **73. round of applause**, a single outburst of cheering, clapping, etc. **74. round off**, **a.** to bring to completeness or perfection; finish. **b.** to increase or decrease (a number which has fractions or decimal points) to the nearest whole number. **c.** (in currency transactions) to increase or decrease (an amount) to the nearest amount for which there is a coin or note. **75. round on** (or **upon**), to attack, usually verbally, with sudden and often unexpected vigour. **76. round out**, add more detail to; give finishing touches to. **77. round the bend** (or **twist**), *Colloq.* insane. **78. round up**, to collect (cattle, people, etc.) in a particular place or for a particular purpose. –**roundish**, *adj.* –**roundness**, *n.*

roundabout /'raʊndəbaʊt/ *n.* **1.** → **merry-go-round.** **2. a.** a road junction at which the flow of traffic is facilitated by moving in one direction only round a circular arrangement. **b.** the circular structure in the middle of an intersection around which the traffic flows. –*adj.* **3.** circuitous or indirect, as a road, journey, method, statement, person, etc.

round bracket *n.* See **bracket** (def. 3).

roundelay /'raʊndəleɪ/ *n.* a song in which a phrase, line, or the like is continually repeated.

rounders /'raʊndəz/ *n.* (*construed as sing.*) a game played with bat and ball, in which points are scored by running between bases, as in baseball.

roundly /'raʊndli/ *adv.* **1.** in a round manner. **2.** vigorously or briskly; thoroughly. **3.** outspokenly, severely, or unsparingly.

round robin *n.* **1.** a petition, remonstrance, or other letter or paper, having the signatures arranged in circular form, so as to conceal the order of signing. **2.** a notice or memorandum addressed to a number of persons, each of whom note it and send it to the next on the list of addressees. **3.** a competition in which each player or team plays against all other participants. Compare **knockout.**

roundsman /'raʊndzmən/ *n.* (*pl.* **-men**) **1.** a man who makes rounds, calling on customers to make deliveries, as of milk, bread, etc., or to take orders. **2.** *Aust., NZ* a male newspaper reporter covering a specific area: *police roundsman; industrial roundsman.*

round table *n.* a meeting for discussion of some subject at which all the participants are considered to be on an equal footing.

round-up *n.* **1.** the driving together of cattle, etc., for inspection, branding, or the like. **2.** any similar driving or bringing together, as of people, facts, etc.

roundworm /'raʊndwɜm/ *n.* any nematode, especially *Ascaris lumbricoides,* infesting the human intestine, or other ascarids in other animals.

rouse[1] /raʊz/ *verb* (**roused, rousing**) –*v.t.* **1.** to bring out of a state of sleep, unconsciousness, inactivity, fancied security, apathy, depression, etc. **2.** to stir to strong indignation or anger. **3.** to cause (game) to start from a covert or lair. –*v.i.* **4.** to come out of a state of sleep, unconsciousness, inaction, apathy, depression, etc. –*n.* **5.** a rousing. **6.** *US* → **reveille.** –*phr.* **7. rouse away,** *Naut.* to pull heavily on a rope. –**rouser,** *n.*

rouse[2] /raʊs/ *phr.* (**roused, rousing**) **rouse on** (or **at**), *Aust., NZ* to scold; upbraid.

rouseabout /'raʊsəbaʊt/ *n. Aust., NZ* a general hand on a station, in a hotel, etc.; blue-tongue. Also, **roustabout.**

rout[1] /raʊt/ *n.* **1.** a defeat attended with disorderly flight; dispersal of a defeated force in complete disorder: *to put an army to rout.* **2.** a defeated and dispersing army. **3.** a tumultuous or disorderly crowd of persons. **4.** a clamour or fuss. –*v.t.* **5.** to disperse in defeat and disorderly flight: *to rout an army.* **6.** to defeat utterly.

rout[2] /raʊt/ *v.i.* **1.** to poke, search, or rummage. –*v.t.* **2.** to turn over or dig up with the snout, as swine. **3.** to force or drive out. **4.** to hollow out or furrow, as with a scoop, gouge, or machine. –*phr.* **5. rout someone out,** to force or drive someone out: *to rout the children out of bed.* **6. rout something out,** to bring or get something in poking about, searching, etc.

route /rut/, *Orig. US and Computers* /raʊt/ *n.* **1.** a way or road taken or planned for passage or travel. **2.** a customary or regular line of passage or travel. **3.** *Computers* any path, such as that between hosts in a computer network. **4.** *Med.* the area of the body through which a curative is introduced: *the digestive route.* –*v.t.* (**routed, routeing** *or* **routing**) **5.** to fix the route of. **6.** to send or forward by a particular route.

router /'raʊtə/ *n. Computers* a device used in connecting networks which configures the best route between hosts; gateway.

routine /ru'tin/ *n.* **1.** a regular course of action or conduct: *the routine of an office.* **2.** regular, unvarying, or mechanical way of doing something. **3.** rehearsed, habitual, persuasive talk: *a salesman's routine.* –*adj.* **4.** customary or regular: *routine investigation.* **5.** (of an activity) dull or boring due to its unvarying nature. –**routinely,** *adv.*

roux /ru/ *n.* (*pl.* **roux** /ruz/) a mixture of fat and flour which forms the foundation of most sauces.

rove[1] /roʊv/ *v.i.* **1.** to wander about without definite destination; move hither and thither at random, especially over a wide area. **2.** to wander, as the eyes, mind, etc. –*v.t.* **3.** to wander over or through; traverse: *to rove the woods.*

rove[2] /roʊv/ *v.* a past tense and past participle of **reeve**[2].

rover /'roʊvə/ *n.* **1.** someone who roves; a wanderer. **2.** *Aust. Rules Obs.* a player, usually small, who specialises in ground play, especially taking and clearing the ball after ruck duels. **3.** (*usu. upper case*) a member of the most senior division (ages 18–25) of the Scout Association.

row[1] /roʊ/ *n.* **1.** a number of persons or things arranged in a line, especially a straight line. **2.** a line of adjacent seats facing the same way, as in a theatre. **3.** a street, especially a narrow one, formed by two continuous lines of buildings.

row[2] /roʊ/ *v.i.* **1.** to use oars, etc., for moving a boat. –*v.t.* **2.** to move (a boat, etc.) as by the use of oars. **3.** to carry in a boat, etc., using oars. **4.** to row against in a race: *we row Easts next week.* –*n.* **5.** an act of rowing. **6.** a trip in a rowing boat: *to go for a row.* –**rower,** *n.*

row[3] /raʊ/ *n.* **1.** a noisy dispute or quarrel; commotion. **2.** *Colloq.* noise or clamour.

rowdy /'raʊdi/ *adj.* (**-dier, -diest**) **1.** noisy and disorderly. –*n.* (*pl.* **-dies**) **2.** a rough, disorderly person. –**rowdily,** *adv.* –**rowdiness,** *n.* –**rowdyism,** *n.* –**rowdyish,** *adj.*

rowel /'raʊəl/ *n.* a small wheel with radiating points, forming the extremity of a rider's spur.

rowlock /'rɒlək/ *n.* a device on or attached by a rigger to a boat's gunwale in or on which the oar rests and swings. Also, *Chiefly US*, **oarlock.**

royal /'rɔɪəl/ *adj.* **1.** of or relating to a king or queen, or their family. **2.** established or existing under the support of a king or queen: *a royal society.* **3.** beyond the usual in size, quality, etc. –*n.* **4.** a traditional size of paper in imperial systems. **5.** *Colloq.* a member of a royal family (especially British). –**royally,** *adv.*

royal assent *n.* the formal act of recognition by the sovereign or the sovereign's representative (in Australia, the governor-general in federal parliament, the governor in state parliaments) which transforms a parliamentary bill into an act of parliament.

royal bluebell *n.* a bluebell native to Australia, *Wahlenbergia gloriosa,* with violet-blue flowers; floral emblem of the ACT.

royal commission *n.* (*also upper case*) (in Australia and Britain) a person or persons, usually judicial, appointed by the government to inquire into and report on some aspect of public affairs.

royalist /'rɔɪələst/ *n.* **1.** a supporter or adherent of a monarch or a royal government, especially in times of rebellion or civil war. *–adj.* **2.** of or relating to royalists. **–royalism,** *n.* **–royalistic** /rɔɪəˈlɪstɪk/, *adj.*

royal jelly *n.* a substance, secreted from the pharyngeal glands of worker honey bees, and fed to very young larvae and to those selected as queens.

royalty /ˈrɔɪəlti/ *n.* (*pl.* **-ties**) **1.** royal people as a group. **2.** royal rank or power; sovereignty. **3.** character proper to a king or queen; nobility. **4.** a payment received by an author, composer, etc., usually a percentage of the sales of their work. **5.** (a payment made for) royal right, as over minerals, given by a sovereign to a person or company.

-rrhagia variant of **-rhagia**. Also, **-rrhage, -rrhagy.**

RSI /ɑr ɛs ˈaɪ/ *n. Pathol.* an injury resulting in inflammation of the tendon sheath of a muscle, caused by the excessive repetition of a movement over a period of time; repetition strain injury.

RSVP /ˌɑr ɛs vi ˈpi/ please reply.

rtf /ɑ ti ˈɛf/ *n.* → **rich text format.**

rub /rʌb/ *verb* (**rubbed, rubbing**) *–v.t.* **1.** to subject (an object) to pressure and friction, especially in order to clean, smooth, polish, etc. **2.** to move, spread, or apply (something) with pressure and friction over something else. **3.** to chafe or abrade. *–v.i.* **4.** to exert pressure and friction on something. **5.** to move with pressure along the surface of something. *–n.* **6.** the act of rubbing. **7.** a difficulty; source of doubt or difficulty: *there's the rub.* **8.** an ointment. **9.** a mixture of spices and herbs to be applied to meat before cooking. *–phr.* **10. rub along,** to proceed, continue in a course, or keep going, with a little effort or difficulty. **11. rub down, a.** to rub (the surface of something) as to smooth, reduce, clean, etc. **b.** to massage, dry, or clean (an animal, athlete, etc.) by rubbing, as with a towel after exercise, etc. **12. rub in** (or **into**), to force in by rubbing. **13. rub it in**, to remind someone repeatedly of their mistakes, failures, or shortcomings. **14. rub noses,** *NZ* to touch noses in the Maori welcoming act of hongi. **15. rub off, a.** to remove or erase by rubbing: *to rub off rust.* **b.** to admit of being rubbed off: *that stain will rub off.* **16. rub off on,** to be transferred to, especially as a result of repeated close contact: *his vulgarity rubbed off on her.* **17. rub of the green,** *Golf* an accidental influence on the ball which may or may not be in the player's favour. **18. rub out, a.** to erase. **b.** *Colloq.* to kill. **c.** *Colloq.* to disqualify or suspend (a sporting competitor): *the jockey was rubbed out for a week.* **19. rub shoulders** (or **elbows**) **with,** to come into social contact. **20. rub together,** to move (things) with pressure and friction over each other. **21. rub up,** to polish or smooth. **22. rub up on,** to refresh or revive one's memory about. **23. rub (up) the right way,** to please. **24. rub (up) the wrong way,** to annoy.

rubber[1] /ˈrʌbə/ *n.* **1.** an elastic material, derived from the latex of species of the genera *Hevea* and *Ficus* (**natural rubber**). **2.** any of a class of elastomers made from polymers or copolymers of simple molecules with properties resembling those of natural rubber (**synthetic rubber**). **3.** a piece of rubber used for erasing pencil marks, etc. **4.** an instrument, tool, etc., used for rubbing something. **5.** a coarse file. **6.** someone who rubs, as in order to smooth or polish something. **7.** a cloth, pad, or the like, used for polishing, buffing, etc. **8.** (*pl.*) *US* rubber or rubberised waterproof clothes or shoes, as wellington boots or a mackintosh. **9.** *Chiefly US Colloq.* → **condom. 10.** *Colloq.* → **thong** (def. 3). *–phr.* **11. burn rubber,** *Colloq.* to drive a motor vehicle extremely fast.

rubber[2] /ˈrʌbə/ *n.* **1.** *Bridge, Whist, etc.* a set of games, usually three or five, a majority of which decides the overall winner. **2.** a series of games on this pattern in various other sports, as cricket, bowls, croquet, etc.

rubberneck /ˈrʌbənɛk/ *n. Colloq.* an extremely or excessively curious person. Also, **rubbernecker.**

rubber plant *n.* a plant, *Ficus elastica*, with oblong, shining, leathery leaves, growing native as a tall tree in India, the Malay Archipelago, etc., and much cultivated as an ornamental house plant.

rubber stamp *n.* **1.** a device of rubber for printing dates, etc., by hand. **2.** *Colloq.* someone who gives approval without consideration, or without demur. **–rubber-stamp,** *v.*

rubbish /ˈrʌbɪʃ/ *n.* **1.** waste or refuse material; debris; litter. **2.** worthless stuff; trash. **3.** nonsense. *–v.t.* **4.** *Colloq.* to speak of scornfully; criticise; denigrate. **–rubbishy,** *adj.*

rubbish bin *n.* **1.** Also, **rubbish tin, garbage bin**. a container in which household rubbish is kept for disposal. **2.** a wastepaper basket.

rubble /ˈrʌbəl/ *n.* **1.** rough fragments of broken stone, formed by geological action, in quarrying, etc., and sometimes used in masonry. **2.** rough fragments of brick, concrete, or any other building material, especially when re-used for building or foundation. **3. a.** mass of broken building material at the site of a catastrophic destruction. **b.** masonry built of rough fragments of broken stone. **4.** any solid substance, as ice, in irregularly broken pieces. **–rubbly,** *adj.*

rubella /ruˈbɛlə/ *n. Pathol.* a contagious disease, usually mild, accompanied by fever, often some sore throat, and a rash resembling that of scarlet fever, teratogenic in the first trimester of pregnancy; German measles.

rubric /ˈrubrɪk/ *n.* **1.** a title, heading, direction, or the like, in a manuscript, book, etc., written or printed in red or otherwise distinguished from the rest of the text. **2.** the title or a heading of a statute, etc. (originally written in red). **3.** a direction for the conduct of divine service or the administration of the sacraments, inserted in liturgical books. **4.** the instructions to the candidate printed at the top of an examination paper. **5.** anything important or worthy of note.

ruby /ˈrubi/ *n.* (*pl.* **-bies**) **1.** a red variety of corundum, highly prized as a gem (**true ruby** or **oriental ruby**). **2.** a piece of this stone. **3.** any of various similar stones, as the spinel ruby, balas ruby, etc. **4.** deep red; carmine. **5.** a sweet, fortified wine made in Australia, which is a deep red colour and younger and fresher than a tawny (def. 3). *–adj.* **6.** ruby-coloured: *ruby lips.* **7.** made from or containing a ruby.

ruck[1] /rʌk/ *n.* **1.** the great mass of unimportant people or things. **2.** a crowd; throng. **3.** *Aust. Rules* the group of players directly engaged in the competition for the control of the ball at a ball-up or when it is thrown into play after it has crossed one of the boundary lines. **4.** *Rugby Union* a group of players struggling for the ball in no set pattern of play; scrimmage. *–v.i.* **5.** to play as a member of a ruck. **6.** to form a ruck (def. 4).

ruckman /ˈrʌkmæn, -mən/ *n.* (*pl.* **-men**) *Aust. Rules* a player, usually tall, whose main role is to obtain initial control of the ball in a ball-up or when it is thrown into play after it has crossed one of the boundary lines.

ruck-rover *n. Aust. Rules Obs.* a player assigned to following the ball. **–ruck-roving,** *n.*

rucksack /ˈrʌksæk/ *n.* → **knapsack.**

ruction /ˈrʌkʃən/ *n. Colloq.* a disturbance, quarrel, or row.

rudder /ˈrʌdə/ *n.* **1.** a board or plate of wood or metal hinged vertically at the stern of a boat or ship as a means of steering. **2.** a device like a ship's rudder for steering an aeroplane, etc., hinged vertically (for right-and-left steering). **–rudderless,** *adj.*

ruddy /ˈrʌdi/ *adj.* (**-dier, -diest**) **1.** of or having a fresh, healthy red colour: *a ruddy face.* **2.** reddish. **3.** *Colloq.* an intensifier signifying disapproval: *that ruddy dog* *barked all night. —adv.* **4.** *Colloq.* an intensifier: *ruddy difficult.* **—ruddiness,** *n.*

rude /rud/ *adj.* **1.** impolite: *a rude reply.* **2.** without learning, or good taste. **3.** rough; harsh. **4.** roughly built, or formed: *a crude house.* **—rudely,** *adv.* **—rudeness,** *n.*

rudimentary /rudə'mɛntəri, -tri/ *adj.* **1.** relating to rudiments or first principles; elementary. **2.** vestigial.

rudiments /'rudəmənts/ *pl. n.* the elements or first principles of a subject.

rue[1] /ru/ *verb* (**rued, ruing**) *–v.t.* **1.** to feel sorrow over; repent of; regret bitterly. **2.** to wish (that something might never have been done, taken place, etc.): *to rue the day one was born.* *–v.i.* **3.** to feel sorrow; be repentant. **4.** to feel regret. **—rueful,** *adj.*

rue[2] /ru/ *n.* any of the strongly scented plants constituting the genus *Ruta,* especially *R. graveolens,* a yellow-flowered herb with decompound leaves formerly much used in medicine.

ruff /rʌf/ *n.* **1.** a neckpiece or collar of lace, lawn, etc., gathered or drawn into deep, full, regular folds, much worn in the 16th century by both men and women. **2.** something resembling such a piece in form or position. **3.** *Zool.* a collar, or set of lengthened or specially marked hairs or feathers, on the neck of an animal. **—ruffed,** *adj.*

ruffian /'rʌfiən/ *n.* **1.** a violent, lawless man; a rough brute. *–adj.* Also, **ruffianly. 2.** relating to or characteristic of a ruffian; lawless; brutal. **—ruffianism,** *n.*

ruffle[1] /'rʌfəl/ *v.t.* **1.** to destroy the smoothness or evenness of: *the wind ruffled the sand.* **2.** (of a bird) to erect (the feathers), as in aggressive display. **3.** to annoy, disturb, discompose, or irritate. **4.** to turn over (the pages of a book) rapidly. **5.** to pass (cards) through the fingers rapidly. **6.** to draw up (cloth, lace, etc.) into a ruffle by gathering along one edge. *–v.i.* **7.** to be or become ruffled. *–n.* **8.** a break in the smoothness or evenness of some surface. **9.** a strip of cloth, lace, etc., drawn up by gathering along one edge, and used as a trimming on dress, etc. **10.** some object resembling this, as the ruff of a bird. **11.** a disturbing experience; an annoyance or vexation. **12.** a disturbed state of the mind; perturbation.

ruffle[2] /'rʌfəl/ *n.* **1.** a low, continuous beating of a drum, less loud than a roll. *–v.t.* **2.** to beat (a drum) in this manner.

rufous /'rufəs/ *adj.* reddish; tinged with red; brownish red.

rug /rʌg/ *n.* **1.** a small, often thick, carpet, used as a floor covering or a hanging, and made of woven or tufted wool, cotton, or the like, fur, etc. **2.** a thick, warm blanket used as a coverlet, etc., or wrap, to keep travellers warm. **3.** *Colloq.* → **toupee.** *–phr.* (*v.* **rugged, rugging**) **4. cut a rug,** *Chiefly US, Colloq.* to dance, especially with verve, as to jazz. **5. rug (oneself) up,** to make or keep oneself warm by wrapping oneself up in thick clothing or covering, as coats, scarves, socks, rugs, etc.

Rugby football /ˌrʌgbi 'futbɔl/ *n.* (*also lower case*) **1.** → **Rugby Union. 2.** → **Rugby League.**

Rugby League *n.* (*also lower case*) one of the two forms of Rugby football, played by teams of thirteen players each, differing from Rugby Union in certain details of the rules and, historically, in permitting professionalism. Also, **League.**

Rugby Union *n.* (*also lower case*) one of the two forms of Rugby football, played by teams of fifteen players each, differing from Rugby League in certain details of the rules, formerly restricted to amateurs. Also, **Union;** *Chiefly Qld and NSW,* **Rugby.**

rugged /'rʌgəd/ *adj.* **1.** roughly broken; rocky; hilly: *rugged ground.* **2.** roughly irregular, heavy, or hard in outline or form. **3.** rough, harsh, or severe. **4.** rude,

uncultivated, or unrefined: *rugged manners.* **5.** (of machines or devices) able to withstand less than optimal operating conditions. **6.** *Colloq.* unpleasant; unfair. **—ruggedly,** *adv.* **—ruggedness,** *n.*

ruin /'ruən/ *n.* **1.** (*pl.*) the remains of a fallen building, town, etc. **2.** a ruined building, town, etc. **3.** a fallen or decayed state: *a building falls to ruin.* **4.** the total loss of wealth, social position, etc. **5.** (something that causes) downfall, destruction, or decay: *gambling will be his ruin.* **6.** a person as the wreck of his or her former self. *–v.t.* **7.** to reduce (someone or something) to ruin; destroy. **—ruinous,** *adj.* **—ruined,** *adj.* **—ruiner,** *n.*

rule /rul/ *n.* **1.** a principle or regulation governing conduct, action, procedure, arrangement, etc. **2.** the code of regulations observed by a religious order or congregation. **3.** that which customarily or normally occurs or holds good: *the rule rather than the exception.* **4.** control, government, or dominion. **5.** tenure or conduct of reign or office. **6.** a prescribed mathematical method for performing a calculation or solving a problem. **7.** → **ruler** (def. 2). **8.** *Printing* **a.** a thin, type-high strip of metal, usually brass, for printing a line or lines. **b.** (in photocomposition) a black tape in various widths and designs. **c.** a printed line. **9.** *Law* **a.** a formal order or direction made by a court and limited in application to the case for which it is given (**special rule**). **b.** an order or regulation governing the procedure of a court (**general rule**). **c.** a proposition of law. *–v.t.* **10.** to control or direct; exercise dominating power or influence over. **11.** to exercise authority or dominion over; govern. **12.** to decide or declare judicially or authoritatively; decree. **13.** to mark with lines, especially parallel straight lines, with the aid of a ruler or the like. **14.** to mark out or form (a line) by this method. *–v.i.* **15.** to exercise dominating power or influence. **16.** to exercise authority, dominion, or sovereignty. **17.** to make a formal decision or ruling, as on a point at law. **18.** to prevail or be current, as prices. **19.** *Colloq.* to be the best; be in command: *the Blues rule! –phr.* **20. as a rule,** usually. **21. bend the rules,** *Colloq.* to make an exception to the rules. **22. rule off,** to mark the end of (something written) by ruling a line beneath. **23. rule out,** to exclude, refuse to admit, declare (something) out of the question.

rule of thumb *n.* **1.** a rule based on experience or practice rather than on scientific knowledge. **2.** a rough, practical method of procedure.

ruler /'rulə/ *n.* **1.** someone who rules or governs; a sovereign. **2.** a strip of wood, metal, or other material with a graduated straight edge, used in drawing lines, measuring, etc. **—rulership,** *n.*

rum[1] /rʌm/ *n.* an alcoholic spirit distilled from molasses or some other sugarcane product.

rum[2] /rʌm/ *adj.* **1.** *Colloq.* odd, strange, or queer. *–phr.* **2. rum go,** harsh or unfair treatment.

rumba /'rʌmbə/ *n.* a dance, Cuban in origin and complex in rhythm (in 8 time). Also, **rhumba.**

rumble /'rʌmbəl/ *v.i.* **1.** to make a deep, heavy, continuous, echoing sound, as thunder, etc. **2.** to move or travel with such a sound: *the train rumbled on.* *–n.* **3.** a rumbling sound, as of thunder or a heavy vehicle. **4.** a rear part of a carriage containing a seat. **5.** *Colloq.* a fight. **—rumbly,** *adj.*

rumbustious /rʌm'bʌstʃəs/ *adj.* boisterous, noisy.

ruminant /'rumənənt/ *n.* **1.** any animal of the suborder Ruminantia, which comprises the various cloven-hoofed and cud-chewing quadrupeds, as cattle, bison, buffalo, sheep, goats, chamois, deer, antelopes, giraffes, etc. **2.** any cud-chewing animal, such as the camel. *–adj.* **3.** ruminating; chewing the cud. **4.** given to or characterised by meditation; meditative.

ruminate /'ruːməneɪt/ *v.i.* **1.** to chew the cud, as a ruminant. **2.** to meditate or muse; ponder. –**ruminatingly,** *adv.* –**rumination** /ruːmə'neɪʃən/, *n.* –**ruminative** /'ruːmənətɪv/, *adj.* –**ruminator,** *n.*

rummage /'rʌmɪdʒ/ *verb* (**-maged, -maging**) –*v.t.* **1.** to search thoroughly or actively through (a place, receptacle, etc.), especially by moving about, turning over, or looking through contents. –*v.i.* **2.** to search actively, as in a place or receptacle, or among contents, etc. –*n.* **3.** miscellaneous articles; odds and ends. **4.** a rummaging search. –*phr.* **5. rummage around,** to make a search, usually with accompanying noise and confusion. **6. rummage out,** to find by searching. –**rummager,** *n.*

rummy /'rʌmi/ *n.* a card game in which the object is to match cards into sets and sequences.

rumour /'ruːmə/ *n.* **1.** a story or statement in general circulation without confirmation or certainty as to facts. **2.** unconfirmed gossip. –*v.t.* **3.** to circulate, report, or assert by a rumour. Also, **rumor.**

rump /rʌmp/ *n.* **1.** the hinder part of the body of an animal. **2.** a cut of beef from this part of the animal, behind the loin and above the round. **3.** the buttocks. **4.** any remnant; the last and unimportant or inferior part; fag end.

rumple /'rʌmpəl/ *v.t.* **1.** to draw or crush into wrinkles; crumple: *a rumpled sheet.* **2.** Also, **rumple up.** to ruffle; tousle. –*v.i.* **3.** to become wrinkled or crumpled. –*n.* **4.** a wrinkle or irregular fold; crease.

rumpus /'rʌmpəs/ *n. Colloq.* **1.** disturbing noise; uproar. **2.** a noisy or violent disturbance or commotion.

run /rʌn/ *verb* (**ran, run, running**) –*v.i.* **1.** to move quickly on foot, so as to go more rapidly than in walking (in bipedal locomotion, so that for an instant in each step neither foot is on the ground). **2.** to do this for exercise, as a sport, etc. **3.** to hurry; go quickly. **4.** to move swiftly by rolling on wheels or in various other ways: *the train ran along the track.* **5.** to make a quick succession of movements, as with the fingers: *the pianist ran up the scale.* **6.** to move easily or swiftly, as a vehicle, on wheels, a vessel, etc. **7.** to make off quickly, take to flight. **8.** to make a short, quick, or casual journey (*up, over, round,* etc.), as for a visit, etc. **9.** *Racing* **a.** to take part in a race. **b.** to finish a race in a certain (numerical) position: *he ran second.* **10.** to stand as a candidate for election: *he is running for president.* **11.** to migrate, as fish: *to run in huge shoals.* **12.** (of fish) to pass upstream or inshore from deep water to spawn. **13.** to sail or be driven (ashore, into a channel, etc.), as a vessel or those on board. **14.** *Naut.* to sail before the wind. **15.** to ply between places, as a vessel. **16.** to traverse a route, as a public conveyance: *the buses run every hour.* **17.** to have recourse to, as for consolation: *he's always running to his mother.* **18.** to move, revolve, slide, etc., especially easily, freely, or smoothly: *a rope runs in a pulley.* **19.** to flow, as a liquid or a body of liquid, or as sand, grain, or the like. **20.** to flow along, especially strongly, as a stream, the sea, etc.: *with a strong tide running.* **21.** to melt and flow, as solder, varnish, etc. **22.** to spread or diffuse when exposed to moisture, as dyestuffs: *the colours in this fabric run.* **23.** to flow, stream, or be wet with a liquid. **24.** to discharge or give passage to a liquid. **25.** to creep, trail, or climb, as vines, etc. **26.** to pass quickly: *a thought ran across his mind.* **27.** to continue in or return to the mind persistently: *a tune running through one's head.* **28.** to recur or be inherent: *madness runs in the family.* **29.** to come undone, as stitches or a fabric; ladder. **30.** to be in operation or continue operating, as a machine. **31.** *Commerce* **a.** to accumulate, or become payable in due course, as interest on a debt. **b.** to make many withdrawals in rapid succession.

32. *Law* **a.** to have legal force or effect, as a writ. **b.** to continue to operate. **33.** to pass or go by, as time. **34.** to continue to be performed, as a play, over a period. **35.** to be disseminated, spread rapidly, as news. **36.** to spread or pass quickly from point to point: *a shout ran through the crowd.* **37.** to be in a certain form or expression: *so the story runs.* **38.** to extend or stretch. **39.** (of stock) to graze: *a holding where three thousand sheep could run.* –*v.* *(copular)* **40.** to have or attain a specified quality, character, form, etc.: *the water ran cold.* **41.** to be or tend to be of a specified size or number: *the costs ran high.* **42.** to exist or occur within a specified range of variation: *your seat numbering runs from 43 to 48.* **43.** to pass into a certain state or condition; become: *to run wild.* –*v.t.* **44.** to cause (an animal, etc.) to move quickly on foot. **45.** to cause (a vehicle, etc.) to move: *I'll just run the car into the garage.* **46.** to traverse (a distance or course) in running: *he ran a kilometre.* **47.** to perform by or as by running: *to run a race; run an errand.* **48.** to enter (a horse, etc.) in a race. **49.** to run along: *to run the streets.* **50.** to run or get past or through: *to run a blockade.* **51.** to bring into a certain state by running: *to run oneself out of breath.* **52.** to pursue or hunt (game, etc.), especially those on pasture. **53.** to drive (livestock), especially to pasture. **54.** to keep (livestock), as on pasture. **55.** to cause to move, especially quickly or cursorily: *to run one's fingers through one's hair*; *to run one's eyes over a letter.* **56.** to cause to ply between places, as a vessel, conveyance, or system of transport: *to run a train service between two cities.* **57.** to convey or transport, as in a vessel or vehicle. **58.** to keep operating or in service, as a machine. **59.** to possess and use, as a car. **60.** to expose oneself to or be exposed to (a risk, etc.). **61.** to sew, especially with quick, even stitches in a line. **62.** (in some games, as billiards) to complete a series of successful strokes, shots, etc. **63.** to bring, lead, or force into some state, action, etc.: *to run oneself into debt.* **64.** to cause (a liquid) to flow. **65.** to give forth or flow with (a liquid). **66.** to pour forth or discharge. **67.** to cause (a bath, etc.) to contain water; fill. **68.** to cause to move easily, freely, or smoothly: *to run a sail up the mast.* **69.** to drive, force, or thrust. **70.** to extend or build, as in a particular direction: *to run a road through the forest.* **71.** to draw or trace, as a line. **72.** to conduct, administer, or manage, as a business, an experiment, or the like. **73.** (of a newspaper) to publish (a story). **74.** *US* to put up (a candidate) for election. **75.** to melt, fuse, or smelt, as ore. **76.** → **smuggle.** –*n.* **77.** an act, instance, or spell of running: *to go for a run.* **78.** a running pace. **79.** an act or instance of escaping, running away, etc. **80.** an act or spell of moving rapidly, as in a boat or vehicle. **81.** the distance covered. **82.** a period or act of travelling, especially a scheduled journey: *an uneventful run to Paris.* **83.** a quick, short trip. **84.** a spell of driving in a car, riding a horse, etc. **85.** a spell or period of causing something, as a machine, to run or continue operating. **86.** the amount of something produced in any uninterrupted period of operation. **87.** a continuous course of performances, as of a play. **88.** *Shearing* an uninterrupted period of shearing: *he had shorn over 500 sheep in one eight-hour run.* **89.** a line or place in knitted or sewn work where a series of stitches have slipped or come undone; a ladder. **90.** the direction of something fixed: *the run of the grain of a piece of timber.* **91.** *Mining* a direction of secondary or minor cleavage grain; rift. **92.** onward movement, progression, course, etc. **93.** the particular course or tendency of something: *in the normal run of events*; *the general run of the voting.* **94.** freedom to range over, go through, or use: *the run of the house.* **95.** any rapid or easy course or progress. **96.** a continuous course of some condition of affairs, etc.: *a run* of bad luck. **97.** a continuous extent of something, as a vein of ore. **98.** *Mining* a ribbon-like, irregular ore body, lying nearly flat and following the stratification. **99.** a continuous series of something. **100.** a set of things in regular order, as a sequence of cards. **101.** any continued or extensive demand, call, or the like. **102.** a spell of being in demand or favour with the public. **103.** a series of sudden and urgent demands for payment, as on a bank. **104.** a spell of causing some liquid to flow. **105.** a flow or rush of water, etc. **106.** a small stream; brook; rivulet. **107.** a kind or class, as of goods. **108.** the ordinary or average kind: *that's the run of them.* **109.** that in or on which something runs or may run. **110.** an enclosure within which domestic animals may range about. **111.** a way, track, or the like, along which something runs or moves. **112.** a course for a particular purpose or activity, as an inclined course for skiing. **113.** the area and habitual route covered by a vendor who delivers goods to houses, etc.: *milk run*; *paper run.* **114.** a large area of grazing land; a rural property: *a grazing run*; *a sheep run.* **115.** *Mil.* the movement in a straight line up to the point of the launching of a bomb, torpedo, or the like, by an aeroplane, submarine, etc. **116.** *Aeronautics* the period during which an aeroplane moves along the ground or water under its own power preceding take-off and following touchdown. **117.** a trough or pipe through which water, etc., runs. **118.** the movement of a number of fish upstream or inshore from deep water. **119.** large numbers of fish in motion, especially inshore from deep water or upstream for spawning. **120.** a number of animals moving together. **121.** *Music* a rapid succession of notes; a roulade. **122.** *Cricket* **a.** the score unit, made by the successful running of both people batting from one popping crease to the other. **b.** a performance of such a running. **123.** *Baseball* **a.** the score unit, made by successfully running round all the bases and reaching the home plate. **b.** a successful performance of this. *–adj.* **124.** melted or liquefied. **125.** poured in a melted state; run into a cast in a mould. *–phr.* **126. at a run,** (of some action) performed while running, or by means of running; without stopping. **127. cut and run,** to take to flight. **128. give someone a run for their money,** to offer someone strenuous and exacting opposition. **129. in the long run,** ultimately. **130. in the short run,** ignoring possible future developments; considering only immediate effects, etc. **131. on the run,** escaped or hiding from pursuit, especially by the police. **132. run a book,** *Colloq.* to accept bets. **133. run about,** to roam without restraint: *children running about in the park.* **134. run across,** to meet or find unexpectedly. **135. run after,** to seek to attract. **136. run around,** to behave promiscuously. **137. run (around) with,** to keep company with. **138. run a temperature,** to be feverish. **139. run at the mouth,** to dribble. **140. run away, a.** to take flight. **b.** to depart: *run away, I'm busy; he ran away to sea.* **141. run away with, a.** to elope with. **b.** to steal. **c.** to win easily: *he ran away with the election.* **d.** to use up (money, etc.) quickly. **e.** to get out of the control of, as a horse, a vehicle, one's emotions or ideas, etc. **f.** *Colloq.* to accept (an idea), especially erroneously or with insufficient justification: *don't run away with the idea that you can go on behaving so badly.* **142. run close,** to press severely, as a competitor. **143. run down, a.** to slow up before stopping, as a clock or other mechanism. **b.** to knock down and injure, as a vehicle or driver; run over. **c.** *Naut.* to collide with and cause to sink, as a smaller vessel. **d.** to denigrate; make adverse criticism of. **e.** to reduce, as stocks. **f.** to find, especially after extensive searching. **g.** to pass quickly over or review: *to run down a list of possibilities.* **144. run hard,** to press severely, as a competitor. **145. run in, a.** to cause (new machinery, especially

a motor vehicle) to run at reduced load and speed for an initial period, so that excessive friction, etc., is reduced gradually and the machine becomes ready for full operation without damage. **b.** to muster (cattle). **c.** *Printing* to add (new text matter) without indentation. **d.** *Aeronautics* to approach a landing. **e.** *Colloq.* to arrest; seize. **146. run into, a.** to encounter unexpectedly. **b.** to collide with. **c.** to amount to: *an income running into five figures.* **147. run into the ground,** to use until worn out: *he ran his old car into the ground before he bought a new one.* **148. run off, a.** to depart or retreat quickly. **b.** to produce by a reproduction process, as printing, photocopying, etc. **c.** to write or otherwise create quickly. **d.** to elope. **e.** to determine the result of (a tied contest, etc.) by a run-off. **149. run off at the mouth,** to talk indiscreetly or wildly. **150. run off with,** to steal. **151. run on, a.** to have as a topic: *the conversation ran on politics.* **b.** to continue, as talking, at length and without interruption. **c.** (of handwritten lettering) to be linked up. **d.** *Printing* to print as continuous unindented text. **152. run out, a.** to depart, as from a room, quickly. **b.** to be completely used up: *the food has run out; time is running out.* **c.** *Cricket* to put (the person batting) out by hitting the wicket with the ball while neither the person batting nor the bat is touching the ground within the popping crease. **d.** *Naut.* to pass or pay out (a rope). **e.** *Showjumping* (of a horse) to refuse by running outside the jump. **f.** *US* to drive out; expel. **153. run out on,** to desert; abandon. **154. run over, a.** to knock down and injure, as a vehicle or driver. **b.** to exceed (a time-limit or the like). **c.** to review, rehearse, or recapitulate. **d.** to overflow or leak, as a vessel. **155. run rings (a)round someone,** to perform with far greater success than another. **156. run short,** to become scarce or nearly used up. **157. runs on the board,** *Colloq.* successes; achievements. **158. run the track of,** to follow the track of (a person or animal) in pursuit: *to run the wild horses' track.* **159. run through, a.** to rehearse or review. **b.** to exhaust or use up (money, etc.). **c.** to pass a sword or the like through (somebody). **160. run to, a.** to be sufficient for: *the money doesn't run to caviar.* **b.** to include: *his books don't run to descriptions.* **c.** to become as specified: *to run to fat.* **161. run up, a.** to climb quickly: *a sailor ran up the mast.* **b.** to hoist (a sail, flag, etc.). **c.** to amass or incur, as a bill. **d.** to make, especially quickly, as something sewn. **162. run up against, a.** to meet unexpectedly. **b.** to be impeded by. **163. run upon, a.** to have as a topic, as thoughts or a conversation. **b.** (of a ship) to go aground upon. **164. run with,** *Law* to go along with or accompany: *the easement runs with the land.* **165. the runs,** *Colloq.* diarrhoea.

runabout /'rʌnəbaʊt/ *n.* **1.** a small car used to make short trips, usually around the city and suburbs. **2.** a small boat, usually with an outboard motor, used mainly for short trips and recreational purposes.

run-around *–n.* **1.** *Colloq.* equivocation; evasion. **2.** *Printing* an arrangement of type using a column width narrower than the body of the text, as around an illustration. *–phr.* **3. give someone the run-around,** *Colloq.* to fob someone off with evasions and subterfuges. Also, **runround.**

run-down *adj.* **1.** in a poor or deteriorated state of health; depressed, sick, or tired. **2.** fallen into disrepair. **3.** (of a spring-operated watch or clock) not running because not wound. *–n.* **4.** a cursory review or summary of points of information: *this brief run-down of past events will bring you up to date.*

rune /run/ *n.* **1.** any of the characters of an alphabet used by the ancient Germanic-speaking peoples, especially the Scandinavians. **2.** something written or inscribed in such characters.

rung¹ /rʌŋ/ *v.* past participle of **ring².**

rung[2] /rʌŋ/ *n.* **1.** one of the rounded crosspieces forming the steps of a ladder. **2.** a rounded or shaped piece fixed horizontally, for strengthening purposes, as between the legs of a chair. **3.** a stout stick, rod, or bar, especially one of rounded section, forming a piece in something framed or constructed: *the rungs of a wheel.* **4.** a stage in a progress or ascent: *the next rung of the ladder to success.*

run-in *n. Colloq.* a disagreement; argument; quarrel.

runnel /ˈrʌnəl/ *n.* **1.** a small stream or brook, or a rivulet. **2.** a small channel, as for water.

runner /ˈrʌnə/ *n.* **1.** a competitor in a race. **2.** a messenger. **3.** something in or on which something else moves, as the strips of wood that guide a drawer, etc. **4.** either of the long pieces of wood or metal on which a sledge, etc., slides. **5.** the blade of a skate. **6.** a long, narrow rug, used in a hall or staircase. **7.** a long, narrow strip of linen, lace, etc., for placing across a table. **8.** *Bot.* a slender stem lying flat on the ground, which sends out roots, thus producing new plants. **9.** → **jogger** (def. 2). **10.** *Cricket* a member of the batting side who runs for a team mate who is injured and unable to run, but who can still bat. **11.** *Aust. Rules* a person who is permitted to run onto the field of play to pass on instructions from the coach to a player, to take a drink to a player, etc. –*phr.* **12. do a runner,** *Colloq.* **a.** to run away, especially in anticipation of being caught out in some illegal activity. **b.** to run away without paying for goods or services, as in a restaurant, petrol station, etc.

runner-up *n.* (*pl.* **runners-up**) the competitor, player, or team finishing in second place.

running /ˈrʌnɪŋ/ *n.* **1.** the action of proceeding on foot at a rapid pace: *I took up running to get some exercise.* **2.** competition, as in a race: *to be out of the running.* **3.** smuggling: *gun running.* **4.** managing or directing: *the running of a business.* –*adj.* **5.** that runs; moving or passing rapidly. **6.** moving or proceeding easily or smoothly. **7.** slipping or sliding easily, as a knot or a noose. **8.** operating, as a machine. **9.** cursive, as handwriting. **10.** flowing, as a stream. **11.** liquid or fluid. **12.** going or carried on continuously; sustained: *a running commentary.* **13.** extending or repeated continuously, as a pattern. **14.** following in succession (placed after the noun): *for three nights running.* **15.** performed with, by means of, or during a run: *a running jump.* **16.** discharging matter, especially fluid, as a sore. **17.** of or relating to the activity of running: *running shoes; running program* –*phr.* **18. in the running,** having a chance of success. **19. make the running,** to set the pace, as of a competition. **20. running battle,** a battle between pursuer and pursued. **21. running fire, a.** sustained discharge of firearms. **b.** sustained criticism.

running account *n.* an account kept with a shop, business, etc., so that goods can be supplied as needed, the total debt being paid at agreed intervals.

running stitch *n.* a small, even stitch made by passing the thread up and down through the cloth at small intervals; used for seams, gathering, quilting, etc.

runny /ˈrʌni/ *adj.* **1.** (of matter) fluid or tending to flow. **2.** tending to flow with excess liquid: *runny icing.* **3.** tending to discharge liquid: *a runny nose.*

run-off *n.* **1.** a deciding final contest held after a principal one. **2.** something which runs off, as rain which flows off from the land in streams. **3.** *Politics* an election held to vote for either of the two candidates who emerge from a previous election with the greatest number of votes. **4.** *NZ* pasture not adjacent to the farm and used only intermittently for grazing stock.

run-of-the-mill *adj.* ordinary; mediocre; commonplace.

runout campaign /ˈrʌnaʊt kæmˌpeɪn/ *n. Commerce* a vigorous program to sell cars of previous models before the release of the latest model.

runt /rʌnt/ *n.* **1.** an undersized, stunted animal, person, or thing, especially one that is small as compared with others of its kind. **2.** the smallest in a litter, as of pigs. **3.** a short, contemptible person.

runway /ˈrʌnweɪ/ *n.* **1.** a way along which something runs. **2.** a paved or cleared strip on which aeroplanes land and take off; airstrip. **3.** the beaten track of deer or other animals. **4.** → **catwalk** (def. 2).

rupee /ruˈpi/ *n.* the standard monetary unit of several countries, as India, Pakistan, Sri Lanka, and Mauritius.

rupiah /ˈrupiə/ *n.* the principal monetary unit of Indonesia. divided into 100 sen.

rupture /ˈrʌptʃə/ *n.* **1.** the act or result of breaking or bursting. **2.** a loss of friendly or peaceful relations. **3.** *Med.* → **hernia.** –*v.t.* **4.** to break or burst (a blood vessel, etc.). **5.** to cause a loss of (good relations, etc.). –*v.i.* **6.** to suffer a break or rupture. –**rupturable,** *adj.*

rural /ˈrʊrəl/ *adj.* **1.** of, relating to, or characteristic of the country (as distinguished from towns or cities), country life, or country people; rustic. **2.** living in the country. **3.** of or relating to agriculture: *rural economy.* –**ruralism,** *n.* –**ruralist,** *n.* –**rurally,** *adv.*

ruse /ruz/ *n.* a trick, stratagem, or artifice.

rush[1] /rʌʃ/ *v.i.* **1.** to move or go with speed, impetuosity, or violence. –*v.t.* **2.** to send or drive with speed or violence. **3.** to carry or convey with haste: *to rush an injured person to the hospital.* **4.** to perform, complete, or organise (some process or activity) with special haste. **5.** to send, push, force, etc., with unusual speed or undue haste: *to rush a bill through Parliament.* **6.** to attack with a rush. **7.** to overcome or take (a person, force, place, etc.). **8.** put pressure on someone. **9.** *Rugby Football* (of a pack of forwards, etc.) to move (the ball) rapidly forwards by short kicks. –*n.* **10.** the act of rushing; a rapid, impetuous, or headlong onward movement. **11.** a hostile attack. **12. a.** a sudden concerted movement, especially of cattle, as in a particular direction; stampede. **b.** an eager rushing of numbers of persons to some region to be occupied or exploited, especially to a new goldfield. **13.** a sudden coming or access: *a rush of blood to his face.* **14.** hurried activity; busy haste: *the rush of city life.* **15.** a hurried state, as from pressure of affairs: *to be in a rush.* **16.** press of work, business, traffic, etc., requiring extraordinary effort or haste. **17.** a period of intense activity: *the Christmas rush.* **18.** *Rugby Football* the act by a pack of forwards, etc., of moving the ball rapidly forward by short kicks. **19.** (*pl.*) *Film* the first prints made after shooting a scene or scenes. –*adj.* **20.** requiring or performed with haste: *a rush order.* **21.** characterised by rush or press of work, traffic, etc. –*phr.* **22. a rush on ...,** a great demand for (a commodity): *there was a rush on gold.* **23. a (sudden) rush (of blood) to the head,** *Colloq.* often ill-considered enthusiasm, rage, etc. –**rusher,** *n.*

rush[2] /rʌʃ/ *n.* **1.** any plant of the genus *Juncus* (family Juncaceae), which comprises grass-like herbs with pithy or hollow stems, found in wet or marshy places. **2.** any of various similar plants of other families as, bog rush, or spike rush. **3.** a stem of such a plant, used for making chair bottoms, mats, baskets, etc. –**rushy,** *adj.*

rusk /rʌsk/ *n.* **1.** a type of sweetened tea biscuit. **2.** a piece of bread or cake crisped in the oven. **3.** a similar commercially made product, given especially to babies when teething, and invalids.

russet /ˈrʌsət/ *n.* **1.** reddish brown; light brown; yellowish brown. **2.** a winter apple with a rough brownish skin. *−adj.* **3.** reddish brown; light brown; yellowish brown.

Russian roulette /rʌʃən ruˈlɛt/ *n.* a macabre game of chance, as formerly played by Russian army officers, in which each player in turn spins the cylinder of a revolver containing only one bullet, points it at his or her head, and pulls the trigger.

rust /rʌst/ *n.* **1.** the red or orange coating which forms on the surface of iron when exposed to air and water, consisting chiefly of ferric hydroxide and ferric oxide. **2.** any film or coating on metal due to oxidation, etc. **3.** a stain like iron rust. **4.** *Bot.* any of the various plant diseases caused by fungi, in which the leaves and stems become spotted and turn a red to brown colour. **5.** a rust colour. *−v.i.* **6.** to grow or become rusty. *−v.t.* **7.** to affect with or as if with rust. **−rustable**, *adj.*

rust belt *n.* an area where heavy industry, such as car manufacturing, is in decline.

rustic /ˈrʌstɪk/ *adj.* **1.** of, relating to, or living in the country as distinguished from the city; rural. **2.** simple; unsophisticated. **3.** rude; uncouth. **4.** made of rough timber, as garden seats, etc. **5.** *Masonry* having the surface rough or irregular, or the joints deeply sunk. *−n.* **6.** a country person, especially of simple tastes. **−rustically**, *adv.* **−rusticity** /rʌsˈtɪsəti/, *n.*

rustle /ˈrʌsəl/ *verb* **(-tled, -tling)** *−v.i.* **1.** to make a succession of slight, soft sounds, as of parts rubbing gently one on another, as leaves, silks, papers, etc. **2.** to cause such sounds by moving or stirring something. *−v.t.* **3.** to move or stir so as to cause a rustling sound. **4.** to steal (cattle, etc.). *−n.* **5.** the sound made by anything that rustles. *−phr.* **6. rustle up**, *Colloq.* to seek out from what is to hand; provide: *rustle up breakfast.* **−rustlingly**, *adv.*

rusty /ˈrʌsti/ *adj.* **(-tier, -tiest) 1.** covered or affected with rust. **2.** consisting of or produced by rust. **3.** of the colour of rust. **4.** faded or shabby. **5.** faulty through disuse or neglect: *my Latin is rusty.* **−rustily**, *adv.* **−rustiness**, *n.*

rut¹ /rʌt/ *n.* **1.** a furrow or track in the ground, especially one made by the passage of a vehicle or vehicles. **2.** any furrow, groove, etc. **3.** a fixed or established way of life; a dull routine: *to get into a rut. −v.t.* **(rutted, rutting) 4.** to make a rut or ruts in; furrow. **−rutty**, *adj.*

rut² /rʌt/ *n.* **1.** the periodically recurring sexual excitement of the deer, goat, sheep, etc. *−v.i.* **(rutted, rutting) 2.** to be in the condition of rut.

ruthless /ˈruθləs/ *adj.* without pity or compassion; pitiless; merciless. **−ruthlessly**, *adv.* **−ruthlessness**, *n.*

rutile /ˈrutaɪl/ *n.* a common mineral, titanium dioxide, TiO_2, having a brilliant metallic-adamantine lustre and usually of a reddish brown colour. It occurs usually in crystals and is used to coat welding rods.

-ry a suffix of abstract nouns of condition, practice (*heraldry*, *husbandry*, *dentistry*), and of collectives (*peasantry*, *Jewry*).

rye /raɪ/ *n.* **1.** a widely cultivated cereal grass, *Secale cereale*, with one-nerved glumes (differing from wheat which is many-nerved) and two- or three-flowered spikelets. **2.** the seeds or grain of this plant, used for making wholemeal flour, for livestock feed, and for a type of whisky. **3.** an American whisky distilled from a mash containing 51 per cent or more rye grain.

S s

S, s /ɛs/ *n.* **1.** a consonant, the 19th letter of the English alphabet. **2.** something resembling the letter S in shape.

's¹ an ending which marks the possessive singular of nouns, as in *man's*.

's² an ending which marks the possessive plural of nouns, as in *men's*.

-s¹ an ending which marks the third person singular present indicative active of verbs, as in *hits*.

-s² **1.** an ending which marks the regular plural of nouns, as in *dogs*. **2.** a quasi-plural ending occurring in nouns for which there is no proper singular, as *trousers*, *shorts*, *scissors*. **3.** a plural ending used to indicate a subject of study, area of activity, etc.: *physics*; *draughts*.

Sabbath /ˈsæbəθ/ *n.* **1.** the seventh day of the week (Saturday) as the day of rest and religious observance among the Jews and certain Christian denominations. **2.** the first day of the week (Sunday), similarly observed by most Christians in commemoration of the resurrection of Christ. **3.** (*lower case*) Also, **sabbat**. a secret nocturnal meeting of witches.

sabbatical /səˈbætɪkəl/ *adj.* **1.** of or relating to the Sabbath. **2.** bringing a period of rest. **3.** of or relating to a sabbatical. *–n.* Also, **sabbatical leave**. **4.** a year, term, or other period, of freedom from duties granted to a university teacher, or someone in one of certain other professional areas, often after seven years of service, as for study or travel. **–sabbatically**, *adv.*

sable /ˈseɪbəl/ *n.* **1.** a small mammal, *Martes zibellina*, of the weasel family, Mustelidae, inhabiting cold regions of Europe and Asia; valued for its dark brown fur. **2.** a marten, especially *Martes americana*. **3.** the fur of the sable. **4.** *Heraldry* the colour black. *–adj.* **5.** made of the hair of the sable. **6.** *Poetic* black; very dark.

sabotage /ˈsæbətaʒ/ *n.* **1.** malicious injury to work, tools, machinery, etc., or any underhand interference with production or business, by enemy agents during wartime, by employees during a trade dispute, etc. **2.** any malicious attack on or undermining of a cause. *–v.t.* (**-taged**, **-taging**) **3.** to injure or attack by sabotage. **–saboteur** /sæbəˈtɜ/, *n.*

sabre /ˈseɪbə/ *n.* **1.** a heavy one-edged sword, usually slightly curved, used especially by cavalry. **2.** a soldier armed with such a sword. **3.** a light sword for fencing and duelling, with a tapering flexible blade and a semicircular guard. *–v.t.* (**-bred**, **-bring**) **4.** to strike, wound, or kill with a sabre. Also, *US*, **saber**.

sabre-rattling /ˈseɪbə-rætlɪŋ/ *n.* the threat of using force by the overt display of military power. **–sabre-rattler**, *n.*

sac /sæk/ *n. Biol.* a bag-like structure in an animal or plant, as one containing fluid. **–saclike**, *adj.*

saccharide /ˈsækəraɪd/ *n.* any sugar or other carbohydrate, especially a simple sugar.

saccharin /ˈsækərən, -krən/ *n.* a crystalline compound, $C_6H_4SO_2CONH$, obtained from toluene. It is some 400 times as sweet as cane sugar and is used as a sweetening agent in cases of diabetes and obesity. Also, **saccharine**.

saccharine /ˈsækərən, -krən/ *adj.* **1.** of a sugary sweetness: *a saccharine smile*. **2.** relating to, of the nature of, or containing sugar. *–n.* **3.** → **saccharin**. **–saccharinity** /sækəˈrɪnəti/, *n.*

sachertorte /ˈsæʃəˈtɔt/ *n.* a rich Viennese cake made with layers of chocolate cake filled with apricot jam and covered in a smooth chocolate glaze. Also, **sacher torte**.

sachet /ˈsæʃeɪ/ *n.* **1.** a small sealed bag used for packaging a variety of goods, as foodstuffs, cosmetics, etc. **2.** a small bag, case, pad, etc., containing perfumed powder or the like for placing among articles of clothing. **3.** the powder.

sack¹ /sæk/ *n.* **1.** a large bag of stout woven material, as for grain, potatoes, coal, etc. **2.** the amount which a sack will hold, a varying unit of measure. **3.** a woman's loose-fitting, unbelted dress. **4.** Also, **sacque**. a loose-fitting coat or jacket, especially for women and children. **5.** *Colloq.* the scrotum. *–v.t.* **6.** to put into a sack or sacks. **7.** *Colloq.* to dismiss or discharge, as from employment. *–phr. Colloq.* **8. hit the sack**, to go to bed. **9. in the sack**, in bed. **10. the sack**, dismissal or discharge, as from employment.

sack² /sæk/ *v.t.* **1.** to pillage or loot after capture; plunder: *to sack a city*. *–n.* **2.** the plundering of a captured place; pillage: *the sack of Troy*. **–sacker**, *n.*

sacrament /ˈsækrəmənt/ *n.* **1.** *Eccles.* a visible sign divinely instituted to confer grace or Divine Life on those who worthily receive it as baptism, confirmation, etc. **2.** (*oft. upper case*) the Eucharist, or Lord's Supper. **3.** the consecrated elements of the Eucharist, especially the bread (the **Blessed Sacrament**). **4.** something regarded as possessing a sacred character or a mysterious significance. **5.** a sign, token, or symbol. **6.** an oath; solemn pledge.

sacred /ˈseɪkrəd/ *adj.* **1.** set aside or dedicated to a god or to some religious purpose; consecrated. **2.** worthy of religious respect; holy. **3.** relating to or connected with religion (opposed to *profane* and *secular*): *sacred music*. **4.** respectfully dedicated to some person or object: *a monument sacred to her memory*. **5.** regarded with deep respect: *the sacred memory of a dead hero*. **6.** not to be broken, damaged, violated, etc.: *sacred promises*. **–sacredly**, *adv.* **–sacredness**, *n.*

sacred site *n.* **1.** (in Australia) a site that is sacred to Aboriginal people or is otherwise of significance according to Aboriginal tradition. **2.** a site or institution that has particular religious, cultural or historical significance: *Lourdes is a sacred site to many Catholics.* **3.** (*usually ironic*) a site or institution of significance to a particular group of people: *the Melbourne Cricket Ground is a sacred site to cricketers.*

sacrifice /ˈsækrəfaɪs/ *n.* **1.** the offering of life or some material possession, etc., to a god. **2.** the giving up or destroying of something prized for the sake of something considered as having a higher claim. **3.** something sacrificed. **4.** a loss suffered in selling something below its value. **5.** *Theology* Christ's offering of his death to God for the sins of humankind. *–verb* (**-ficed**, **-ficing**) *–v.t.* **6.** to make a sacrifice of. *–v.i.* **7.** to offer or make a sacrifice. **–sacrificer**, *n.* **–sacrificial** /sækrəˈfɪʃəl/, *adj.*

sacrilege /ˈsækrəlɪdʒ/ *n.* **1.** the violation or profanation of anything sacred or held sacred. **2.** an instance of this. **3.** the stealing of anything consecrated to the service of God.

sacristy /ˈsækrəsti/ *n.* (*pl.* **-ties**) *Eccles.* an apartment in or a building connected with a church or a religious house, in which the sacred vessels, vestments, etc., are kept.

sacro- a word element: **1.** meaning 'holy'. **2.** referring to the sacrum.

sacrosanct /'sækrəsæŋkt/ *adj.* especially or superlatively sacred or inviolable. **–sacrosanctity** /sækrə-'sæŋktəti/, *n.*

sacrum /'seikrəm/ *n.* (pl. **-cra** /-krə/) *Anat.* a bone resulting from the ankylosis of two or more vertebrae between the lumbar and the coccygeal regions, in humans composed (usually) of five fused vertebrae and forming the posterior wall of the pelvis. **–sacral**, *adj.*

sad /sæd/ *adj.* (**sadder, saddest**) **1.** sorrowful; mournful: *to feel sad.* **2.** expressing or showing sorrow: *sad looks.* **3.** causing sorrow: *a sad disappointment.* **4.** shocking; deplorable: *a sad state of affairs.* **–sadly**, *adv.* **–sadness**, *n.*

sadden /'sædn/ *v.t.* **1.** to make sad. *–v.i.* **2.** to become sad.

saddle /'sædl/ *n.* **1.** a seat for a rider on the back of a horse or other animal. **2.** a similar seat on a bicycle, machine, etc. **3.** a part of a harness laid across the back of an animal and girded under the belly. **4.** that part of an animal's back on which the saddle is placed. **5.** (of mutton, venison, etc.) a cut including part of the backbone and both loins. **6.** (of poultry) the posterior part of the back. **7.** the saddle of an animal prepared for food. **8.** a ridge connecting two higher elevations. **9.** *Naut.* a hollowed-out piece of wood which provides a resting place for the end of a spar. *–v.t.* **10.** to put a saddle upon (a horse, etc.). *–v.i.* Also, **saddle up**. **11.** to put a saddle on a horse. *–phr.* **12. in the saddle,** in a position of authority; in control. **13. saddle someone with,** to load or charge someone with (a burden or responsibility). **14. saddle up, a.** to put a saddle on (a horse), usually as a preparation for immediate work or departure. **b.** to make such preparations for riding. **c.** *Colloq.* (*humorous*) to prepare oneself for work, etc.: *I'll go and saddle up for dinner.*

saddler /'sædlə/ *n.* someone who makes or deals in saddlery. **–saddlery**, *n.*

sadism /'seidizəm, 'sei-/ *n.* **1.** sexual gratification gained through causing physical pain and humiliation. **2.** any morbid enjoyment in inflicting mental or physical pain. **–sadist**, *n.* **–sadistic** /sə'dıstık/, *adj.* **–sadistically** /sə'dıstıkli/, *adv.*

sadomasochism /seidou'mæsəkızəm, sædou-/ *n.* a disturbed condition of the mind marked by the presence of sadistic and masochistic tendencies. **–sadomasochist**, *n.* **–sadomasochistic** /seidoumæsə'kıstık, sædou-/, *adj.*

safari /sə'fari/ *n.* (pl. **-ris**) **1.** a journey; an expedition, especially for hunting. **2.** the persons, animals, etc., forming such an expedition.

safari jacket *n.* **1.** → **bush jacket** (def. 1). **2.** a jacket worn as part of a safari suit.

safari suit *n.* a suit consisting of trousers and jacket, usually made from white or light coloured cloth, and resembling the clothes originally worn on safari.

safe /seif/ *adj.* **1.** secure from liability to harm, injury, danger, or risk: *a safe place.* **2.** free from hurt, injury, danger, or risk: *to arrive safe and sound.* **3.** involving no risk of mishap, error, etc.: *a safe estimate.* **4.** dependable or trustworthy: *a safe guide.* **5.** cautious in avoiding danger: *a safe player.* **6.** placed beyond the power of doing harm; in secure custody: *a criminal safe in jail.* *–n.* **7.** a steel or iron box or repository for money, jewels, papers, etc. **8.** any receptacle or structure for the storage or preservation of articles: *a meat safe.* *–phr.* **9. a safe pair of hands, a.** *Cricket* a person who can be trusted to take a catch. **b.** a person who can be trusted in a leadership role. **10. be on the safe side,** *Colloq.* to take every precaution. **11. make safe,** *Mil.* to

change (a weapon) from a state of readiness to a safe condition. **12. play** (**it**) **safe,** to act cautiously. **–safely,** *adv.* **–safeness,** *n.*

safe-conduct /seif-'kɒndʌkt/ *n.* **1.** a document securing a safe passage through a region, especially in time of war. **2.** this privilege. **3.** a conducting in safety.

safe-deposit *n.* **1.** a building containing safes, strong-rooms, etc., where valuables may be stored. *–adj.* **2.** providing safekeeping for valuables: *a safe-deposit vault or box.*

safeguard /'seifgad/ *n.* **1.** something serving as a protection or defence, or ensuring safety. **2.** a permit for safe passage. **3.** a guard or convoy. **4.** a mechanical device for ensuring safety. *–v.t.* **5.** to guard; protect; secure.

safe injecting room *n.* a place where drug addicts can go to inject drugs under medical supervision. Also, **heroin injecting room, injecting room**.

safe sex *n.* any sexual practices in which precautions are taken to prevent the transmission of sexually transmitted diseases, especially AIDS.

safety /'seifti/ *n.* (pl. **-ties**) **1.** the state of being safe; freedom from injury or danger. **2.** the quality of insuring against hurt, injury, danger, or risk.

safety pin *n.* **1.** a pin bent back on itself to form a spring, with a guard to cover the point. **2.** a locking device on grenades, mines, etc., to keep them safe until required for use.

safflower /'sæflaʊə/ *n.* **1.** a thistlelike herb, *Carthamus tinctorius*, originally native to parts of Africa and Asia, bearing large orange-red flower heads, and cultivated for seed oil. **2.** its dried florets, used medicinally or as a dyestuff.

saffron /'sæfrɒn, 'sæfrən/ *n.* **1.** a crocus, *Crocus sativus*, having handsome purple flowers with orange stigmas. **2.** the dried stigmas of this flower, used to colour food and as a spice, especially in rice dishes. **3.** Also, **saffron yellow.** yellow-orange.

sag /sæg/ *v.i.* (**sagged, sagging**) **1.** to sink or bend downwards by weight or pressure, especially in the middle. **2.** to droop; hang loosely: *his shoulders sagged; his trousers sagged.* **3.** to drop or become less: *prices sagged.* *–n.* **4.** the act, degree or place of sagging: *the sag in that pipeline needs repairing.* **5.** a drop in prices. **–sagging,** *adj.*

saga /'sagə/ *n.* **1.** a medieval Icelandic or Norse prose narrative of achievements and events in the history of a personage, family, etc. **2.** a form of novel in which the members or generations of a family or social group are chronicled in a long and leisurely narrative. **3.** any narrative or legend of heroic exploits.

sagacious /sə'geiʃəs/ *adj.* having acute mental discernment and keen practical sense; shrewd: *a sagacious author.* **–sagaciously,** *adv.* **–sagacity** /sə'gæsəti/, **sagaciousness,** *n.*

sage[1] /seidʒ/ *n.* **1.** a profoundly wise person; someone famed for wisdom. *–adj.* (**sager, sagest**) **2.** wise, judicious, or prudent: *sage conduct.* **–sagely,** *adv.* **–sageness,** *n.*

sage[2] /seidʒ/ *n.* a perennial plant, *Salvia officinalis*, whose greenish grey leaves are used for seasoning in cookery.

Sagittarius /sædʒə'tɛəriəs/ *n.* the ninth sign of the zodiac, which the sun enters about 22 November; the Archer. **–Sagittarian,** *n., adj.*

sago /'seigoʊ/ *n.* **1.** a starchy foodstuff derived from the soft interior of the trunk of various palms and cycads, used in making puddings, and other dishes. **2.** any of various plants from which this foodstuff may be obtained.

sahib /sab, 'sa,ıb/ *n. Indian English* **1.** a respectful term of address to a European man. **2.** a term of address to any man, or a title placed after the man's name, as an indication of respect.

said /sɛd/ v. **1.** past tense and past participle of **say**. *–adj.* **2.** named or mentioned before: *the said witness; the said sum.*

sail /seɪl/ n. **1.** an expanse of canvas or similar material spread to the wind to make a vessel move through the water. **2.** some similar piece or apparatus, as the part of an arm of a windmill which catches the wind. **3.** a voyage or excursion, especially in a sailing vessel. **4.** a sailing vessel or ship, or sailing vessels collectively: *the fleet numbered thirty sail.* **5.** sails for a vessel or vessels, collectively. *–v.i.* **6.** to travel in a vessel conveyed by the action of wind, steam, etc. **7.** to move along or be conveyed by wind, steam, etc.: *steamships sailing to Fremantle.* **8.** to manage a boat, especially for sport. **9.** to begin a journey by water: *sailing at dawn.* **10.** to move along in a manner suggestive of a sailing vessel: *clouds sailing overhead.* **11.** to travel through the air, as a balloon. **12.** to move along with dignity: *to sail into a room.* *–v.t.* **13.** to sail upon, over, or through: *to sail the seven seas.* **14.** to navigate (a ship, etc.). **15.** to cause to sail (a toy boat or the like). *–phr.* **16. make sail**, *Naut.* **a.** to set the sail or sails of a boat, or increase the amount of sail already set. **b.** to set out on a voyage. **17. sail in**, *Colloq.* to initiate an action without prudent regard to possible consequences. **18. sail through**, to complete (a task, test, etc.) easily and successfully: *she sails through all her exams.* **19. set sail**, to start a voyage. **20. under sail**, with sails set. *–***sailable**, *adj.* *–***sailless**, *adj.*

sailboard /ˈseɪlbɔd/ n. **1.** a lightweight, polyurethane surfboard, equipped with a mast and sail, on which the rider stands to manoeuvre the sail. *–v.i.* **2.** to ride on a sailboard. *–***sailboarder**, *n.* *–***sailboarding**, *n.*

sailor /ˈseɪlə/ n. **1.** someone whose occupation is sailing or navigation; a mariner; a seafarer. **2.** marines below the rank of officer. **3.** a person, with reference to susceptibility to seasickness: *a bad sailor.* **4.** a sailor hat.

sailplane /ˈseɪlpleɪn/ n. **1.** a glider designed especially for sustained flight using ascending air currents. *–v.i.* **2.** to soar in a sailplane.

saint /seɪnt/ n. **1.** one of certain persons formally recognised by a Christian church, especially the Roman Catholic Church, as having attained an exalted position in heaven because of the exceptional holiness of their life, and as being entitled to veneration on earth; a canonised person. *Abbrev.:* S, (*pl.* SS), St **2.** (in certain religious bodies) a designation applied by the members to themselves. **3.** a person of great holiness. **4.** a sanctimonious person. *–***saintly**, *adj.* *–***saintliness**, *n.*

St Vitus dance /sənt vaɪtəs ˈdæns/ n. (*in non-technical use*) → **Sydenham's chorea**. Also, **St Vitus's dance**.

saith /sɛθ/ v. *Archaic or Poetic* third person singular present of **say**.

sake[1] /seɪk/ n. **1.** cause, account, or interest: *for my sake.* *–phr.* **2. for the sake of**, in order to uphold or maintain: *for the sake of appearances.*

sake[2] /ˈsaki/ n. a Japanese alcoholic drink made from fermented rice.

sal /sæl/ n. *Chiefly Pharm.* salt.

salaam /səˈlam/ n. **1.** a greeting exchanged between Muslims. **2.** (chiefly amongst Muslims) a very low bow or obeisance, especially with the palm of the right hand placed on the forehead. *–v.i.* **3.** to salute someone with a salaam. Also, **salam** /ˈsʌˈlʌm/.

salacious /səˈleɪʃəs/ adj. **1.** lustful or lecherous. **2.** (of writings, etc.) obscene; titillating. *–***salaciously**, *adv.* *–***salaciousness**, salacity /səˈlæsəti/, *n.*

salad /ˈsæləd/ n. **1.** a dish of uncooked vegetables, typically served with a savoury dressing. **2.** any of various raw or cooked foods served cold, usually cut up and mixed with a dressing: *fruit salad; potato salad.* **3.** any of various herbs used for such a dish or commonly eaten raw. *–adj.* **4.** of or relating to a salad.

salad days *pl. n.* days of youthful inexperience.

salamander /ˈsæləmændə/ n. **1.** any of various tailed amphibians, most of which have an aquatic larval stage but are terrestrial as adults, such as *Salamandra salamandra*, the **European salamander** or **fire salamander** of central and western Europe. **2.** a mythical lizard or other reptile, or a being supposedly able to live in fire. **3.** any person or thing able to survive great heat. **4. a.** any of various portable stoves or burners. **b.** a small portable stove used on building sites to keep materials dry. *–***salamandrine** /sæləˈmændrən/, *adj.*

salami /səˈlami/ n. a kind of sausage, originally Italian, often flavoured with garlic.

salary /ˈsæləri/ n. (*pl.* **-ries**) a fixed periodical payment paid to a person for regular work or services, especially work other than that of a manual, mechanical, or menial kind. *–***salaried**, *adj.*

salary sacrifice *n.* a before-tax payment made from one's salary directly into a nominated account, as a regulated superannuation fund. Compare **employee contribution**. *–***salary sacrificing**, *n.*

sale /seɪl/ n. **1.** the act of selling. **2.** the quantity sold. **3.** opportunity to sell; demand: *slow sale.* **4.** a special disposal of goods, as at reduced prices. **5.** transfer of property for money or credit. *–phr.* **6. for** (or **on**) **sale**, offered to be sold; offered to purchasers.

salesperson /ˈseɪlzpɜsən/ n. (*pl.* **-people** *or* **-persons**) someone employed to sell goods, as in a shop, etc. *–***salesman**, *n.* *–***saleswoman**, *n.*

sales tax *n.* a tax charged as a percentage of the sale price of goods, imposed on the seller of goods in respect of goods sold, but generally passed on to the ultimate consumer in the retail price.

salient /ˈseɪliənt/ adj. **1.** prominent or conspicuous: *salient features.* **2.** projecting or pointing outwards, as an angle. **3.** leaping or jumping. *–n.* **4.** *Fortifications* a salient angle or part, as the central outward projecting angle of a bastion or an outward projection in a battle line. *–***saliently**, *adv.* *–***salience**, **saliency**, *n.*

salient angle *n.* an outward-pointing angle; an interior angle of a polygon that is less than 180°.

saline /ˈseɪlaɪn, -lin/ adj. **1.** salty or salt-like; containing or tasting like common table salt: *a saline solution.* **2.** of or relating to a chemical salt, of sodium, potassium, magnesium, etc., as used as a cathartic. *–n.* **3.** a saline health drink or medicine.

salinity /səˈlɪnəti/ n. **1.** the degree of salt present in a substance. **2.** a level of salt rising from the substratum to the surface of the earth which turns surface fresh water into brackish water and reduces the value of the soil for agriculture.

saliva /səˈlaɪvə/ n. *Physiol.* a fluid consisting of the secretions produced by glands which discharge into the mouth, containing ptyalin in humans and certain other animals; spittle. *–***salivary**, *adj.*

salivate /ˈsæləveɪt/ v.i. *Physiol.* to produce saliva. *–***salivation** /sæləˈveɪʃən/, *n.*

sallow[1] /ˈsæloʊ/ adj. **1.** of a yellowish, sickly hue or complexion: *sallow cheeks.* *–v.t.* **2.** to make sallow. *–***sallowish**, *adj.* *–***sallowness**, *n.*

sallow[2] /ˈsæloʊ/ n. any of several tall shrubby willows with elliptical or ovate leaves, as the common sallow, *Salix cinerea*, of Europe, temperate western Asia, and northern Africa.

sally /ˈsæli/ n. (*pl.* **-lies**) **1.** a sudden rush of troops from a besieged place upon an enemy. **2.** any sudden rushing forth or activity. **3.** an excursion or expedition. **4.** an outburst or flight of passion, fancy, etc.: *sally of anger.* **5.** a sprightly or brilliant utterance or remark. *–v.i.*

(**-lied, -lying**) **6.** to make a sally, as a body of troops from a besieged place. **7.** to set out briskly or energetically. –*phr.* **8. sally forth,** to set out briskly or energetically. **9. sally up,** *NZ* to berate; scold.

salmon /'sæmən/ *n.* (*pl.* **-mons** *or, especially collectively,* **-mon**) **1.** a marine and freshwater food fish, introduced into Australia, *Salmo salar* (family Salmonidae), with pink flesh, common in the northern Atlantic Ocean near the mouths of large rivers, which it ascends to spawn. **2.** any of several important food fishes of the North Pacific salmonoid genus *Oncorhynchus.* **3.** Also, **salmon pink.** light yellowish-pink. –*adj.* Also, **salmon pink. 4.** of the colour salmon.

salmonella /sælmə'nelə/ *n.* (*pl.* **-nellae** /-'neli/) any of several anaerobic bacteria (genus *Salmonella*), pathogenic for humans and warm-blooded animals.

salon /'sælɒn/ *n.* **1.** a drawing room or reception room in a large house. **2.** an assembly of guests in such a room, especially such an assembly consisting of leaders in fashion, art, politics, etc. (common during the 17th and 18th centuries). **3.** a hall or place used for the exhibition of works of art. **4.** a fashionable business establishment or shop: *beauty salon, hairdressing salon.*

saloon /sə'lun/ *n.* **1.** a room or place for general use for a specific purpose: *a dining saloon on a ship.* **2.** Also, **saloon bar.** in a hotel, a bar with better appointments and higher prices than those in the public bar. Compare **lounge** (def. 6), **public bar.**

salsa /'sælsə/ *n.* **1.** a type of lively popular dance music originating in Latin America and blending Cuban rhythms with elements of jazz, rock, and soul music. **2.** a dance performed to this music. **3.** a hot Mexican sauce usually based on tomatoes and chilli.

salt /sɒlt, sɔlt/ *n.* **1.** a crystalline compound, sodium chloride, NaCl, occurring as a mineral, a constituent of sea water, etc., and used for seasoning food, as a preservative, etc. **2.** *Chem.* a compound which upon dissociation yields cations (positively charged), and anions (negatively charged). **3.** (*pl.*) any of various salts used as purgatives: *Epsom salts.* **4.** that which gives liveliness, piquancy, or pungency to anything. **5.** wit; pungency. **6.** *Colloq.* a sailor, especially an experienced one: *old salt.* –*v.t.* **7.** to season with salt. **8.** to cure, preserve, or treat with salt. **9.** *Chem.* **a.** to treat with common salt or with any chemical salt. **b. salt out,** to add common salt to (a solution) in order to separate a dissolved substance. **10.** to introduce rich ore or other valuable matter, information, etc., to create a false impression of value: *to salt a mine; to salt a sample.* –*adj.* **11.** containing salt; having the taste of salt: *a salt solution.* **12.** saltwater: *a salt lagoon.* **13.** cured or preserved with salt: *salt cod.* **14.** overflowed with or growing in salt water: *salt marsh.* –*phr.* **15. below the salt,** of an inferior status. **16. go through like a dose** (or **packet**) **of salts,** *Colloq.* **a.** to have the same effect as a purgative. **b.** to make a brief visit causing great disturbance. **17. rub salt into the wound,** to make things worse; add insult to injury. **18. salt away** (or **down**), **a.** to preserve by adding quantities of salt. **b.** *Colloq.* to lay or store away in reserve: *to salt a lot of money away.* **19. salt of the earth,** the best kind of people. **20. take with a grain** (or **pinch**) **of salt,** to believe in part only; have reservations. **21. worth one's salt,** capable; efficient; deserving one's pay. –**salty,** *adj.*

saltbush /'sɒltbʊʃ/ *n.* **1.** any of various drought-tolerant plants of the family Chenopodiaceae, especially the Australian and New Zealand genus *Rhagodia* and the widespread genus *Atriplex,* used as grazing plants in arid, saline, and alkaline parts of Australia, North America, and southern Africa. –*phr.* **2. the saltbush,** regions where saltbush is the predominant vegetation.

saltcellar /'sɒltsɛlə/ *n.* **1.** a shaker or vessel for salt. **2.** *Colloq.* either of the hollows above the collarbone of thin people.

saltie /'sɒlti/ *n.* *Colloq.* a saltwater crocodile.

salt lick *n.* **1.** a place to which wild animals resort to lick salt occurring naturally there. **2.** *Agric.* rock salt or compressed salt in blocks with or without minerals and other additives placed in the paddock for animals grazing there.

salt pan *n.* a flat expanse of land covered by natural deposits of salt on its surface, left by evaporation. Also, **saltpan.**

saltpetre /sɒlt'pitə/ *n.* → **potassium nitrate.** Also, *US,* **saltpeter.**

salubrious /sə'lubriəs/ *adj.* **1.** (especially of air, climate, etc.) favourable to health; promoting health. **2.** (of a locality) attractive and prosperous: *they live in one of the more salubrious suburbs.* –**salubriously,** *adv.* –**salubriousness, salubrity** /sə'lubrəti/, *n.*

salutary /'sæljətri/, *Orig. US* /'sæljətɛri/ *adj.* **1.** conducive to health; healthful. **2.** promoting or conducive to some beneficial purpose; wholesome. –**salutarily,** *adv.* –**salutariness,** *n.*

salutation /sæljə'teɪʃən/ *n.* **1.** the act of saluting. **2.** something uttered, written, or done by way of saluting. **3.** the opening of a letter or of a speech as 'Dear Sir', 'Ladies and Gentlemen'. –**salutatory,** *adj.*

salute /sə'lut/ *v.t.* **1.** to greet with words or movements of goodwill, respect, etc. **2.** *Mil., Navy* to pay respect to or honour by some formal act, as raising the right hand to the side of the head, presenting arms, firing cannon, dipping colours, etc. –*v.i.* **3.** *Mil., Navy* to give a salute. –*n.* **4.** the act of saluting; salutation; greeting. –**saluter,** *n.*

salvage /'sælvɪdʒ/ *n.* **1.** the act of saving property, such as a ship or aircraft or their cargo, from some peril. **2.** the saving of anything from loss or danger. **3.** property or a thing so saved. –*v.t.* (**-vaged, -vaging**) **4.** to save from shipwreck, fire, etc. **5.** to recover or save: *to salvage his self-respect.* –**salvager,** *n.*

salvation /sæl'veɪʃən/ *n.* **1.** the act of saving or delivering. **2.** the state of being saved or delivered. **3.** a source, cause, or means of deliverance: *to be the salvation of a friend.* **4.** *Theology* deliverance from the power and penalty of sin; redemption.

salve /sav, sælv/ *n.* **1.** a healing ointment to be applied to wounds and sores for relief or healing. **2.** anything that soothes or mollifies. –*v.t.* (**salved, salving**) **3.** to soothe as if with salve: *to salve one's conscience.*

salver /'sælvə/ *n.* a tray.

salvo /'sælvoʊ/ *n.* (*pl.* **-vos** *or* **-voes**) **1.** a discharge of artillery or other firearms, in regular succession, often intended as a salute. **2.** the more or less simultaneous discharge of numerous guns, as from an artillery battery or a naval vessel. **3.** a round of cheers, applause, etc.

sal volatile /sæl və'lætəli/ *n.* **1.** → **ammonium carbonate. 2.** an aromatic alcoholic solution of this salt used as a restorative for fainting, dizziness, etc., by inhalation.

salwar /sal'wa/ *n.* a pair of loose pleated trousers, tight at the ankles. Also, **shalwar, chalwar.**

salwar kameez /salwa kə'miz/ *n.* a South Asian set of matching garments comprising baggy pants, a long tunic, and scarf. Also, **shalwar kameez.**

samba /'sæmbə/ *n.* a ballroom dance of Brazilian (ultimately African) origin.

same /seɪm/ *adj.* **1.** identical with what is about to be or has just been mentioned: *the very same person.* **2.** being one or identical, though having different names, aspects, etc.: *these are one and the same thing.* **3.** agreeing in kind, amount, etc.; corresponding: *two boxes of the same dimensions.* **4.** unchanged in character, condition, etc. –*pron.* **5.** the same person or thing.

–phr. **6. all the same, a.** notwithstanding; nevertheless. **b.** immaterial; unimportant. **7. just the same, a.** in the same manner. **b.** nevertheless. **8. same** (here), an exclamation indicating that the speaker concurs with the last statement or feeling expressed, or is in a corresponding situation. **9. the same,** with the same manner (used adverbially): *she played it the same each time.* **–sameness,** *n.*

same-sex marriage *n.* the union of a man with a man or a woman with a woman, legally recognised under certain legislatures, with the implication that they will live intimately together and enjoy some or all of the legal benefits of traditional marriage.

samovar /ˈsæməvaː/ *n.* a metal urn, commonly of copper, used in Russia and elsewhere for heating the water for making tea.

sampan /ˈsæmpæn/ *n.* any of various small boats of China, etc., as one propelled by a single scull over the stern, and provided with a roofing of mats.

sample /ˈsæmpəl, ˈsampəl/ *n.* **1.** a small part of anything or one of a number, intended to show the quality, style, etc., of the whole; a specimen. *–adj.* **2.** serving as a specimen: *a sample copy. –v.t.* **3.** to take a sample or samples of; test or judge by a sample.

sampler /ˈsæmplə/ *n.* **1.** someone who samples something. **2.** a piece of cloth embroidered with various devices, serving to show a beginner's skill in needlework.

samurai /ˈsæmərai, ˈsæmjərai/ *n.* (*pl.* **-rai**) (in feudal Japan) a member of the military class.

sanatorium /sænəˈtɔːriəm/ *n.* (*pl.* **-toriums** or **-toria** /-ˈtɔːriə/) **1.** an establishment for the treatment of invalids, convalescents, etc., especially in a favourable climate: *a tuberculosis sanatorium.* **2.** a health resort. **3.** the part of a boarding school set apart for the treatment or isolation of sick pupils. Also, **sanitarium.**

sanctify /ˈsæŋktəfai/ *v.t.* (**-fied, -fying**) **1.** to make holy; set apart as sacred; consecrate. **2.** to purify or free from sin: *sanctify your hearts.* **3.** to impart religious sanction to; render legitimate or binding: *to sanctify a vow.* **–sanctification** /sæŋktəfəˈkeiʃən/, *n.* **–sanctifier,** *n.* **–sanctifiable,** *adj.*

sanctimonious /sæŋktəˈmouniəs/ *adj.* making a show of holiness; affecting sanctity. **–sanctimoniously,** *adv.* **–sanctimoniousness, sanctimony** /ˈsæŋktəməni/, *n.*

sanction /ˈsæŋkʃən/ *n.* **1.** acceptance or approval; authorisation; ratification: *the plans now have the sanction of the Council.* **2.** powerful feelings or agreement among people about what is right or wrong: *social sanctions against crime.* **3.** (*usu. pl.*) *International Law* punitive action by one or more countries towards another designed to force it to keep certain laws: *trade sanctions. –v.t.* **4.** to approve or authorise; ratify: *we will sanction its use.* **–sanctionable,** *adj.*

sanctity /ˈsæŋktəti/ *n.* (*pl.* **-ties**) **1.** holiness, saintliness, or godliness. **2.** sacred or hallowed character: *inviolable sanctity of the temple.*

sanctuary /ˈsæŋktʃəri, ˈsæŋktʃuəri/, *Orig. US* /ˈsæŋktʃuɛri/ *n.* (*pl.* **-ries**) **1.** a sacred or holy place. **2.** the part of a church around the altar; chancel. **3. a.** (formerly) a church or other holy place where people running away from the law or from oppression were safe from arrest; asylum. **b.** the protection given by this. **4.** a place protected by law where plants and animals are left in peace; reserve.

sanctum /ˈsæŋktəm/ *n.* (*pl.* **-tums** or **-ta** /-tə/) **1.** a sacred or holy place. **2.** an especially private place or retreat: *the inner sanctum.*

sand /sænd/ *n.* **1.** coarse or fine grains from rocks that have been broken up or worn away. **2.** (*usu. pl.*) a region made up mainly of sand. **3.** a dull reddish yellow colour. *–v.t.* **4.** to smooth or polish with sand or

sandpaper. **5.** to sprinkle, fill or mix with, or as with, sand. **–sandy,** *adj.*

sandal /ˈsændl/ *n.* **1.** a kind of shoe, consisting of a sole of leather or other material fastened to the foot by thongs or straps. **2.** any of various kinds of low shoes or slippers. **–sandalled,** *adj.*

sandalwood /ˈsændlwʊd/ *n.* any of certain Asian and Australian trees of the genus *Santalum* (family Santalaceae), especially *S. album* (**white sandalwood**), an evergreen of India.

sandbar /ˈsændbaː/ *n.* a bar of sand formed in a river or sea by the action of tides or currents.

sandblast /ˈsændblast/ *n.* **1.** a blast of air or steam laden with sand, used to clean, grind, cut, or decorate hard surfaces, as of glass, stone, or metal. *–v.t.* **2.** to clean, smooth, etc., with a sandblast. **–sandblasting,** *n.* **–sandblaster,** *n.*

sandbox /ˈsændbɒks/ *n.* **1.** Also, **sandpit.** a container for holding sand for children to play in, usually located in an outdoors area. **2.** *Computers* a controlled space where experimental code, downloads, etc., can be tested in safety without affecting the rest of the system. *–adj.* **3.** *Computers* of or relating to such controlled space: *sandbox software.* **4.** of or relating to a video game or a particular mode of a video game in which the game is open-ended and non-linear, without requiring the user to move through a hierarchical sequence of goals or to preserve what is done for future game-playing.

sandpaper /ˈsændpeipə/ *n.* **1.** strong paper coated with a layer of sand or the like, used for smoothing or polishing. *–v.t.* **2.** to smooth or polish with or as with sandpaper.

sandpiper /ˈsændpaipə/ *n.* any of a number of shorebirds of the family Scolopacidae that breed in the Northern Hemisphere and are seen in Australia as non-breeding migrants, as the **sharp-tailed sandpiper,** *Calidris acuminata,* common in Australasia.

sandpit /ˈsændpit/ *n.* → **sandbox** (def. 1).

sandshoe /ˈsænʃu, ˈsændʃu/ *n. Aust., NZ* a rubber-soled, plain-coloured, usually canvas shoe, laced to fit the foot, worn especially for gymnastics, sports, etc., and as part of informal fashion.

sandsoap /ˈsændsoup/ *n.* a soap with mildly abrasive power used especially for cleaning tables, boards, wooden floors, etc.

sandspit /ˈsændspit/ *n.* a long narrow stretch of sand extending from the land into a body of water, often covered at high tide. Also, **sand spit.**

sandstone /ˈsændstoun/ *n.* a rock formed by the consolidation of sand, the grains being held together by a cement of silica, lime, gypsum, or iron salts.

sand wedge *n.* a golf club used for playing a ball which has landed in a bunker. Also, **wedge.**

sandwich /ˈsænwitʃ, -widʒ/ *n.* **1. a.** two or more slices of bread or toast, plain or buttered, with a layer of meat, cheese, salad or the like between. **b.** a single portion of such a sandwich having been cut, usually into quarters or halves. **2.** something formed by a similar combination. *–v.t.* **3.** to insert or hem in between two other things. *–phr.* **4. the meat in the sandwich,** *Aust. Colloq.* the person innocently involved in a conflict of interests.

sandy blight *n.* → **trachoma.**

sane /sein/ *adj.* **1.** free from mental derangement: *a sane person.* **2.** having or showing reason, sound judgement, or good sense: *a sane approach to the problem.* **–sanely,** *adv.* **–saneness, sanity,** *n.*

sang /sæŋ/ *v.* past tense of **sing.**

sangfroid /sɒ̃ˈfrwa/ *n.* coolness of mind; calmness; composure.

sangria /ˈsæŋgriə/ *n.* a cold drink made of red or white wine, with brandy and sugar, and slices of orange and lemon.

sangrita /sæŋˈgritə/ *n.* a drink made from orange juice, and sometimes with tomato juice and lime juice or other additions, often drunk as a chaser to tequila.

sanguine /ˈsæŋgwən/ *adj.* **1.** naturally cheerful and hopeful: *a sanguine temperament.* **2.** hopeful or confident: *sanguine expectations.* **3.** ruddy: *a sanguine complexion.* –**sanguinely,** *adv.* –**sanguineness,** *n.* –**sanguineous,** *adj.*

sanitarium /sænəˈtɛəriəm/ *n.* (*pl.* **-tariums** *or* **-taria** /-ˈtɛəriə/) → **sanatorium.**

sanitary /ˈsænətri/ *adj.* **1.** of or relating to health or the conditions affecting health, especially with reference to cleanliness, precautions against disease, etc. **2.** favourable to health; free from dirt, germs, etc. –**sanitarily,** *adv.* –**sanitariness,** *n.*

sanitary napkin *n.* a soft, absorbent, disposable pad worn during menstruation to absorb the discharge from the uterus. Also, **sanitary pad.**

sanitation /sænəˈteɪʃən/ *n.* **1.** the study and practical application of sanitary measures. **2.** a drainage system.

sanitise /ˈsænətaɪz/ *v.t.* **1.** to make sanitary: *sanitised for your convenience.* **2.** to make more acceptable by removing offensive aspects: *the editors will sanitise the article.* Also, **sanitize.** –**sanitiser,** *n.*

sank /sæŋk/ *v.* past tense of **sink.**

Santa Claus /ˈsæntə klɔz/ *n.* the legendary patron saint of children, dispenser of gifts on Christmas Eve; Father Christmas; Saint Nicholas.

sap[1] /sæp/ *n.* **1.** the juice or vital circulating fluid, especially of a woody plant. **2.** *Colloq.* a fool or weak person.

sap[2] /sæp/ *n.* **1.** *Fortifications* a deep narrow trench constructed to approach a besieged place or an enemy's position. *–v.t.* (**sapped**, **sapping**) **2.** *Fortifications* to approach (a besieged place, etc.) with deep narrow trenches. **3.** to undermine; weaken or destroy insidiously.

sapient /ˈseɪpiənt/ *adj.* (*often ironic*) wise or sage. –**sapience, sapiency,** *n.* –**sapiently,** *adv.* –**sapiential,** *adj.*

sapling /ˈsæplɪŋ/ *n.* **1.** a young tree. **2.** a young person.

sapphire /ˈsæfaɪə/ *n.* **1.** a variety of corundum, especially a transparent blue kind valued as a gem. **2.** a gem of this kind. **3.** the colour of the gem, a deep blue. *–adj.* **4.** resembling sapphire; deep blue: *a sapphire sky.*

sapro- a word element meaning 'rotten', or 'saprophytic', as in *saprolite.* Also, (*before vowels*), **sapr-.**

saprophyte /ˈsæprəfaɪt/ *n.* any vegetable organism that lives on dead organic matter, as certain fungi and bacteria. –**saprophytic** /sæprəˈfɪtɪk/, *adj.*

saraband /ˈsærəbænd/ *n.* **1.** a popular and vigorous Spanish castanet dance. **2.** a slow, stately Spanish dance in triple rhythm derived from this. **3.** a piece of music for, or in the rhythm of, this dance, usually forming one of the movements in the classical suite, following the courante.

sarc- a word element meaning 'flesh', as in *sarcous.* Also, (*before consonants*), **sarco-.**

sarcasm /ˈsɑkæzəm/ *n.* **1.** harsh or bitter derision or irony. **2.** an ironical taunt or gibe; a sneering or cutting remark. –**sarcastic** /sɑˈkæstɪk/, *adj.* –**sarcastically** /sɑˈkæstɪkli/, *adv.*

sarcoma /sɑˈkoʊmə/ *n.* (*pl.* **-mas** *or* **-mata** /-mətə/) *Pathol.* any of various malignant tumours originating in the connective tissue, attacking especially the bones. –**sarcomatoid, sarcomatous,** *adj.*

sarcophagus /sɑˈkɒfəgəs/ *n.* (*pl.* **-gi** /-gaɪ/ *or* **-guses**) a stone coffin, especially one bearing sculpture or inscriptions, etc., often displayed as a monument.

sardine /sɑˈdin/ *n.* (*pl.* **-dines** *or, especially collectively,* **-dine**) **1.** the young of the common pilchard, often preserved in oil and canned for food. **2.** any of various allied or similar fishes used in this way, especially the **California sardine,** *Sardinops caeruleus.*

sardonic /sɑˈdɒnɪk/ *adj.* bitterly ironical; sarcastic; sneering: *a sardonic grin.* –**sardonically,** *adv.*

sari /ˈsɑri/ *n.* (*pl.* **-ris**) a long piece of cotton or silk, the principal outer garment of Hindu women, worn round the body with one end over the head or shoulder.

sarking /ˈsɑkɪŋ/ *n. Building Trades* **1.** a layer of boarding, sometimes used to cover the rafters of a house under the tiles. **2.** sheet material laid under tiles, shingles, or slates for reflective insulation or additional waterproofing.

sarong /səˈrɒŋ/ *n.* **1.** → **sarung. 2.** a women's garment consisting of a piece of material knotted around the waist or trunk, often worn casually as over a swimming costume.

sarsaparilla /saspəˈrɪlə/ *n.* **1.** any of various climbing or trailing plants of the widely distributed genus *Smilax,* having a root which has been much used in medicine as an alterant. **2.** any of several plants, especially *Smilax australis* (**Austral sarsaparilla**) and *S. glyciphylla* (**sweet sarsaparilla**), found in rainforests and wet eucalypt forests along the east coast of Australia. **3.** any similar species as **false sarsaparilla,** *Hardenbergia violacea.* **4.** a soft drink flavoured with the root of the American species of sarsaparilla.

sartorial /sɑˈtɔriəl/ *adj.* of or relating to clothes or dress, generally men's: *sartorial splendour.* –**sartorially,** *adv.*

sarung /sʌˈrʊŋ/ *n.* a long patterned cloth wrapped around the waist or trunk, worn by Malays of both sexes as a casual garment or on formal occasions.

sasanqua /səˈsæŋkwə/ *n.* a type of widely-planted, hardy camellia, *Camellia sasanqua,* with a looser more straggling habit than the japonica, and slightly fragrant, usually single, blooms.

sash[1] /sæʃ/ *n.* a long band or scarf of silk, etc., worn over one shoulder or round the waist.

sash[2] /sæʃ/ *n.* a movable framework in which panes of glass are set, as in a window or the like.

sashay /ˈsæʃeɪ/ *v.i. Colloq.* to strut, move exaggeratedly.

sashimi /səˈʃimi, sæ-/ *n.* a Japanese dish of fresh seafood fillets cut into bite-sized, oblong strips, and eaten raw with soy sauce and Japanese horseradish.

sassafras /ˈsæsəfræs/ *n.* **1.** an American tree, *Sassafras albidum.* **2.** the aromatic bark of its root, used medicinally and especially for flavouring beverages, confectionery, etc. **3.** any of several Australian trees with fragrant bark.

sassy /ˈsæsi/ *adj.* (**-sier, -siest**) *Colloq.* saucy.

sat /sæt/ *v.* past tense and past participle of **sit.**

Satan /ˈseɪtn/ *n.* (in many beliefs) the chief evil spirit; the great adversary of humanity; devil.

satanic /səˈtænɪk/ *adj.* **1.** of Satan. **2.** characteristic of or befitting Satan; extremely wicked; diabolical. Also, **satanical.** –**satanically,** *adv.*

satay /ˈsateɪ/ *n.* **1.** Also, **satay sauce.** a spicy peanut-based sauce used in South-East Asian cookery. **2.** a dish consisting of pieces of marinated meat, chicken or seafood grilled on a skewer and served with satay sauce or a similar hot, spicy sauce.

satchel /ˈsætʃəl/ *n.* a bag, made of leather, canvas, or the like, usually with a shoulder strap, used for carrying schoolbooks.

sate /seɪt/ *v.t.* **1.** to satisfy (any appetite or desire) to the full. **2.** to surfeit; glut.

satellite /ˈsætəlaɪt/ n. **1.** a small body which moves around a planet; moon. **2.** someone or something which depends on, or is dominated by, another. **3.** Also, **artificial satellite**. an object, usually containing recording and transmitting instruments, for launching into orbit round the earth or another planet, for purposes of communication, research, etc. **4.** produced by the use of a satellite in the transmission of signals: *satellite imaging*; *satellite broadcasting*. –v.t. **5.** to send (pictures, messages, etc.) by satellite.

satellite phone n. a type of cellular telephone that connects by radio signals to orbiting satellites instead of terrestrial cells (**cell** def. 7).

satellite TV n. a television service in which a signal is transmitted via an artificial satellite to a satellite dish and then to the television set of a householder.

satiate /ˈseɪʃieɪt/ v.t. **1.** to supply with too much of something, so as to disgust or weary. **2.** to satisfy to the full. –**satiation**, n. –**satiable**, adj.

satin /ˈsætn/ n. **1.** a very smooth, glossy fabric made in a warp-face weave, usually rayon or silk. –adj. **2.** of or like satin; smooth; glossy.

satire /ˈsætaɪə/ n. **1.** the use of irony, sarcasm, ridicule, etc., in exposing, denouncing, or deriding vice, folly, etc. **2.** a literary composition, in verse or prose, in which vices, abuses, follies, etc., are held up to scorn, derision, or ridicule. **3.** the species of literature constituted by such composition. –**satirical** /səˈtɪrɪkəl/, **satiric** /səˈtɪrɪk/, adj.

satirise /ˈsætəraɪz/ v.t. to make the object of satire. Also, **satirize**. –**satiriser**, **satirist**, n.

satisfaction /sætəsˈfækʃən/ n. **1.** the act of satisfying or condition of being satisfied. **2.** the cause of being satisfied. **3.** the making good of a wrong; reparation. **4.** payment as for a debt or the fulfilling of obligations.

satisfactory /sætəsˈfæktəri, -tri/ adj. affording satisfaction; fulfilling all demands or requirements: *a satisfactory answer*. –**satisfactorily**, adv. –**satisfactoriness**, n.

satisfy /ˈsætəsfaɪ/ verb (-fied, -fying) –v.t. **1.** to fulfil the desires, expectations or needs of (a person, etc.); gratify; content. **2.** to fulfil (a desire, expectation, need, etc.): *to satisfy hunger*. **3.** to convince; assure: *he satisfied himself that all had gone well*. **4.** to pay back (a debt, etc.). –v.i. **5.** to give satisfaction. –**satisfier**, n. –**satisfying**, adj. –**satisfyingly**, adv. –**satisfied**, adj.

saturate /ˈsætʃəreɪt/ v.t. **1.** to cause (a substance) to unite with the greatest combination, or the like. **2.** to charge to the utmost, as with magnetism. **3.** to soak, impregnate, or imbue thoroughly or completely. **4.** *Mil.* **a.** to bomb or shell (an enemy position) so thoroughly that the enemy defences are powerless. **b.** to send so many planes over (a target area) that the enemy electronic tracking equipment is neutralised. **5.** to supply (a market) so fully as to exceed demand. –**saturable** /ˈsætʃərəbəl/, adj. –**saturability** /sætʃərəˈbɪləti/, n. –**saturation**, n.

Saturday /ˈsætədeɪ, -di/ n. the seventh day of the week, following Friday.

saturnalia /sætəˈneɪliə/ pl. n. any period of unrestrained revelry. –**saturnalian**, adj.

saturnine /ˈsætənaɪn/ adj. having or showing a sluggish, gloomy temperament; gloomy; taciturn. –**saturninely**, adv.

satyr /ˈseɪtə, ˈsætə/ n. **1.** *Classical Myth.* one of a class of woodland deities attendant on the god of wine, Bacchus; represented in Greek art as human with a horse's ears and tail, and in Roman art as part human and part goat, and noted for riot and lasciviousness. **2.** a lascivious man. **3.** any of the rather sombre butterflies that constitute the family Satyridae. –**satyric** /səˈtɪrɪk/, adj.

sauce /sɔs/ n. **1.** a cooked thick liquid put on, or eaten with, food to make it taste better: *chocolate sauce*;

chilli sauce. **2.** something that adds sharpness or interest. **3.** *Colloq.* cheekiness; impertinence; impudence. –v.t. (**sauced, saucing**) **4.** to prepare with sauce; season: *she sauced the dish with chilli.* **5.** to give sharpness or interest to. **6.** *Colloq.* to speak cheekily to.

saucepan /ˈsɔspən/ n. a metal container of moderate depth, usually having a long handle and a lid, for boiling, stewing, etc.

saucer /ˈsɔsə/ n. **1.** a small, round, shallow dish to hold a cup. **2.** any similar dish, plate, or the like. **3.** any saucer-shaped thing: *a flying saucer.*

saucy /ˈsɔsi/ adj. (**-cier, -ciest**) **1.** impertinent; insolent: *a saucy remark*; *a saucy child.* **2.** piquantly pert; smart: *a saucy hat.* –**saucily**, adv. –**sauciness**, n.

sauerkraut /ˈsauəkraut/ n. cabbage cut fine, salted, and allowed to ferment until sour.

sauna /ˈsɔnə/ n. **1.** a type of bath, originally Finnish, in which the bather sits in a room or cabinet filled with hot air to induce perspiration, while creating steam by pouring water on heated stones; traditionally followed by immersion in cold water or a light beating with birch twigs. **2.** a room or device for taking such a bath.

saunter /ˈsɔntə/ v.i. **1.** to walk with a leisurely gait; stroll. –n. **2.** a leisurely walk or ramble; a stroll. **3.** a leisurely gait. –**saunterer**, n.

-saur a word element meaning 'lizard'.

saurian /ˈsɔriən/ adj. **1.** belonging or relating to the Sauria, a group of reptiles originally including the lizards, crocodiles, etc., but now technically restricted to the lizards and their allies. **2.** lizard-like. –n. **3.** a saurian animal, as a dinosaur or lizard.

sauro- a word element meaning 'lizard'.

-saurus Latinised variant of **-saur**.

sausage /ˈsɒsɪdʒ/ n. **1.** minced pork, beef, or other meats (often combined), with various added ingredients and seasonings, and packed into a special skin which was formerly prepared from the entrails of pigs or oxen, but is now often made from a synthetic product. **2.** *Colloq.* the penis. –phr. *Colloq.* **3. not a sausage**, absolutely nothing. **4. silly sausage**, an affectionate reprimand, as from a mother to a child who has made a mistake.

sauté /ˈsouteɪ/ adj. **1.** cooked or browned in a pan containing a little fat. –v.t. (**-téed, -téing**) **2.** to cook in a small amount of fat; pan fry.

Sauterne /souˈtɜn, sɔ-/ n. (*sometimes lower case*) **1.** a rich sweet white table wine, especially one produced near Bordeaux, France. **2.** (in unofficial use) any similar white wine made elsewhere. Also, **Sauternes**.

sauvignon blanc /ˌsouvɪnjɒ ˈblɒk/ n. (*sometimes upper case*) **1.** a highly regarded grape variety grown for the production of white wine. **2.** a white wine made from this grape.

savage /ˈsævɪdʒ/ adj. **1.** wild; rugged: *savage wilderness.* **2.** (*dated*) (*likely to cause offence*) uncivilised; barbarous: *savage tribes.* **3.** fierce or cruel; untamed: *savage beasts.* **4.** furiously angry. –n. **5.** (*dated*) (*likely to cause offence*) a member of a usually pre-literate society regarded as uncivilised. **6.** an uncivilised human being. **7.** a fierce or cruel person. **8.** a rude person. –v.t. (**savaged, savaging**) **9.** to attack violently; maul. –**savagely**, adv. –**savageness**, **savagery**, n.

savanna /səˈvænə/ n. grassland region with scattered trees, grading into either open plain or woodland, usually in subtropical or tropical regions. Also, **savannah**.

savant /ˈsævənt, səˈvɒnt/ n. a learned or erudite person.

save¹ /seɪv/ v.t. **1.** to rescue from danger, harm, or loss: *to save someone from drowning*; *to save the game.* **2.** to keep safe; safeguard: *God save the Queen.* **3.** (in soccer, etc.) to prevent (a goal) being scored by stopping the ball from entering the net. **4.** to avoid the spending, using up, or waste of: *to save money*; *to save electricity.*

5. (oft. fol. by *up*) to put aside for future use: *I have saved (up) $1000.* **6.** *Computers* to store (a file) in memory. **7.** to treat carefully in order to preserve: *to save her eyes, she doesn't sew much.* **8.** to prevent or make unnecessary; obviate: *a stitch in time saves nine.* **9.** *Theology* to deliver from sin: *to save humanity from hell.* –*v.i.* **10.** (oft. fol. by *up*) to put aside money: *to save up for a new car.* **11.** *Theology* to deliver from sin: *Jesus saves.* –*n.* **12.** the act of saving, especially in sports. –**savable**, *adj.* –**saver**, *n.*

save² /seɪv/ *prep.* **1.** except; but. –*conj.* **2.** except; but.

saveloy /ˈsævəlɔɪ/ *n.* **1.** → **frankfurt. 2.** a highly seasoned, smoked sausage, usually of pork.

saving /ˈseɪvɪŋ/ *adj.* **1.** that saves; rescuing; preserving. **2.** making acceptable in spite of other bad qualities; redeeming: *he's a coward, but he has a saving sense of humour.* **3.** making an exception: *a saving clause.* –*n.* **4.** a lessening of expense: *a saving of 10 per cent.* **5.** something that is saved. **6.** (*pl.*) sums of money saved and put aside. –*prep.* **7.** except: *everyone came, saving Mark.* **8.** with all due respect to or for: *saving your presence.* –*conj.* **9.** save; except; but. –**savingly**, *adv.*

savings account *n. Banking* an account with a savings bank or permanent building society on which a rate of interest is paid and money can be withdrawn at short notice.

savings bank *n.* a bank which mainly accepts deposits from individual customers and invests them, and lends money for housing, as opposed to offering cheque account and other trading facilities.

saviour /ˈseɪvjə/ *n.* **1.** someone who saves, rescues, or delivers: *the saviour of the country.* **2.** the, (*upper case*) (in Christianity) Jesus Christ, who is believed to have saved humankind from the consequences of its sins. Also, **savior.**

saviour sibling *n.* a child selected in embryo for genetic characteristics which can be of benefit to an existing brother or sister with an illness, especially for potentially curative stem cells to be used in medical treatments.

savoir faire /ˌsævwa ˈfɛə, ˌsʌvwa ˈfɛə/ *n.* knowledge of what to do in any situation; tact.

savory¹ /ˈseɪvəri/ *n.* (*pl.* **-ries**) any of the aromatic plants constituting the genus *Satureja,* especially *S. hortensis* (**summer savory**), a European herb used in cookery, or *S. montana* (**winter savory**).

savory² /ˈseɪvəri/ *adj., n.* → **savoury.**

savour /ˈseɪvə/ *n.* **1.** the quality in a substance which affects the sense of taste or smell. **2.** a particular taste or smell. **3.** distinctive quality or property. **4.** power to excite or interest. –*v.i.* **5.** to have savour, taste, or smell. –*v.t.* **6.** to give a savour to; season; flavour. **7.** to perceive by taste or smell, especially with relish. **8.** to give oneself to the enjoyment of. –*phr.* **9. savour of,** to exhibit the peculiar characteristics of; smack of. Also, **savor.** –**savourer**, *n.* –**savourless**, *adj.*

savoury /ˈseɪvəri/ *adj.* **1.** having savour; agreeable in taste or smell: *a savoury smell.* **2.** piquant, pungent, or salty to the taste; not sweet. –*n.* (*pl.* **-ries**) **3.** a non-sweet, usually salty, bite-sized morsel such as a smoked oyster, slice of egg topped with an anchovy, etc., on a small biscuit or crouton; canapé. Also, **savory.** –**savouriness**, *n.*

savvy¹ /ˈsævi/ *verb* (**-vied, -vying**) *Colloq.* –*v.t.* **1.** to know or understand (something). –*v.i.* **2.** to know; understand: *do you savvy?*

savvy² /ˈsævi/ *n.* **1.** understanding; intelligence; common sense. –*adj.* (**-vier, -viest**) **2.** well-informed or experienced.

saw¹ /sɔ/ *n.* **1.** a tool for cutting, typically a thin blade of metal with a series of sharp teeth. **2.** any similar tool, as a circular saw. –*verb* (**sawed, sawn** *or* **sawed, sawing**) –*v.t.* **3.** to cut or shape with a saw: *to saw logs.* **4.** to make movements as if using a saw: *to saw the air with one's hands.* –*v.i.* **5.** to use a saw: *he is out the back sawing.* **6.** to make sawing movements or sounds like a saw: *to saw away at a violin.* **7.** to cut as a saw does. –**sawer**, *n.*

saw² /sɔ/ *v.* past tense of **see¹.**

saw³ /sɔ/ *n.* a sententious saying; maxim; proverb: *he could muster an old saw for almost every occasion.*

sax¹ /sæks/ *n.* an axelike tool for cutting roofing slate.

sax² /sæks/ *n. Colloq.* a saxophone.

saxophone /ˈsæksəfoʊn/ *n.* a musical wind instrument consisting of a conical metal tube (usually brass) with keys and a clarinet mouthpiece. –**saxophonist** /sækˈsɒfənəst/, *n.*

say /seɪ/ *verb* (**said, saying**) –*v.t.* **1.** to utter or pronounce; speak. **2.** to express in words; state; declare. **3.** to state as an opinion, or with assurance. **4.** to recite or repeat: *to say one's prayers.* **5.** to assume as a hypothesis or an estimate: *to learn in, say, ten lessons.* **6.** to report or allege; maintain: *people say he will resign.* –*v.i.* **7.** to speak; declare; express an opinion. –*n.* **8.** what a person says or has to say. **9.** *Colloq.* the right or opportunity to say, speak or decide: *to have a say.* **10.** turn to say something: *it is now my say.* –*phr.* **11. have the last say,** to have the final authority: *the treasurer has the last say on a budget of this size.* **12. I say,** an exclamation to attract attention or to express surprise, protest, joy, etc. **13. that is to say,** in other words; otherwise. –**sayer**, *n.*

saying /ˈseɪɪŋ/ *n.* **1.** something said, especially a proverb or apophthegm. –*phr.* **2. go without saying,** to be completely self-evident.

scab /skæb/ *n.* **1.** a crust which forms over a sore during healing. **2.** *Vet. Science* a mangy disease in animals, especially sheep; scabies. **3.** someone who goes on working during a strike, takes a striker's place or refuses to join a union; blackleg. **4.** *Colloq.* a despicable person, especially one who is disloyal. **5.** *Colloq.* a person who is mean or stingy. **6.** *Colloq.* someone who cadges from others; cadger. –*verb* (**scabbed, scabbing**) –*v.i.* **7.** to become covered with a scab. **8.** to act or work as a scab. –*v.t.* **9.** *Colloq.* to cadge: *to scab a lift.* –*phr.* **10. scab it,** *Colloq.* to act or work as a scab. –**scabby**, *adj.*

scabbard /ˈskæbəd/ *n.* a sheath or cover for the blade of a sword, dagger, or the like.

scabies /ˈskeɪbiz, -biiz/ *n. Pathol., Vet. Science* any of several infectious skin diseases occurring in sheep and cattle, and in humans, caused by parasitic mites; itch. –**scabietic** /ˌskeɪbiˈɛtɪk/, *adj.*

scaffold /ˈskæfəld, -oʊld/ *n.* **1.** Also, **scaffolding**. a temporary structure for holding workers and materials during the erection, repair, cleaning, or decoration of a building. **2.** an elevated platform on which a criminal is executed. **3.** any raised framework or platform. **4.** *Bio-engineering* a matrix of cellular material used as scaffolding (def. 3). –*v.t.* **5.** to furnish with a scaffold or scaffolding. –**scaffolder**, *n.*

scaffolding /ˈskæfəldɪŋ/ *n.* **1.** → **scaffold** (def. 1). **2.** materials for scaffolds. **3.** *Bio-engineering* cellular material used as a matrix to support cultured cells in growing artificial tissues.

scald /skɔld/ *v.t.* **1.** to burn or hurt with, or as with, hot liquid or steam. **2.** to put quickly into boiling water: *to scald vegetables.* **3.** to heat to just below boiling point: *to scald milk.* –*v.i.* **4.** to be or become scalded. –*n.* **5.** a burn caused by hot liquid or steam. –**scalding**, *adj.*

scale¹ /skeɪl/ *n.* **1.** one of the thin, flat, horny or hard plates that form the covering of certain animals, such as fishes. **2.** any thin plate-like piece or flake that peels off from a surface. **3.** an encrustation caused in various ways: *the inside of the kettle is covered with scale.* –*v.t.* **4.** to remove the scales from: *to scale fish.* **5.** to remove in scales or thin layers: *to scale off paint.* –*v.i.* **6.** to come off in scales: *the burnt skin scaled off.* **7.** to become coated with scale, as the inside of a boiler. –**scaly,** *adj.*

scale² /skeɪl/ *n.* **1.** the pan, or either of the pans or dishes, of a balance. **2.** (*usu. pl.*) a balance, or any of various other more or less complicated devices for weighing. –*phr.* **3. tip** (or **turn**) **the scales,** to determine the outcome of something that has been in doubt. **4. tip the scale(s) at,** to weigh.

scale³ /skeɪl/ *n.* **1.** a succession or progression of steps or degrees; a graduated series. **2.** a point on such a scale. **3.** a series of marks laid down at determinate distances, as along a line, for purposes of measurement or computation: *the scale of a thermometer.* **4.** a graduated line, as on a map, representing proportionate size. **5.** a graduated table of prices, wages, etc. **6.** an instrument with graduated spaces, for measuring, etc. **7.** the proportion which the representation of an object bears to the object: *a model on a scale of one centimetre to a metre.* **8.** the ratio of distances (or, less commonly, of areas) on a map to the corresponding values on the earth. **9.** a certain relative or proportionate size or extent: *a residence on a yet more magnificent scale.* **10.** a standard of measurement or estimation. **11.** *Arithmetic* a system of numerical notation: *the decimal scale.* **12.** *Music* a succession of notes ascending or descending according to fixed intervals, especially such a series beginning on a particular note: *the major scale of C.* **13.** *Music* the compass or range of a voice or an instrument. –*v.t.* **14.** to climb by, or as by, a ladder; climb up or over. **15.** to make according to scale. –*v.i.* **16.** to climb; ascend; mount. **17.** to progress in a graduated series. –*phr.* **18. scale down,** to decrease, especially according to a fixed proportion. **19. scale up,** to increase, especially according to a fixed proportion. **20. to scale,** with the proportions of the original correctly maintained in the representation: *a map drawn to scale.*

scallop /ˈskɒləp/ *n.* **1.** a type of mollusc having two fluted shell valves that can be opened and shut in order to swim. **2.** the large muscle of certain kinds of such molluscs, valued as a food. **3.** Also, *Chiefly NSW,* **Tasmanian scallop.** an edible bivalve mollusc, especially *Notovola meridionalis,* found in Tasmania and marketed commercially there and on the mainland. **4.** one of a series of curves along the edge of pastry, a garment, cloth, etc. –*v.t.* **5.** to finish (an edge) with scallops (def. 4). –**scalloper,** *n.*

scallywag /ˈskæliwæg/ *n.* a scamp; rascal (often used indulgently of children).

scalp /skælp/ *n.* **1.** the skin of the upper part of the head, sometimes including the associated structures just beneath the skin. **2.** a part of this skin with the accompanying hair, taken from an enemy as a trophy, especially, formerly, by certain Native Americans. –*v.t.* **3.** to cut or tear the scalp from. **4.** *Colloq.* to buy (tickets) and resell them unofficially at a higher rate. –**scalper,** *n.*

scalpel /ˈskælpəl/ *n.* a small, light, usually straight knife used in surgical and anatomical operations and dissections.

scam /skæm/ *Colloq.* –*n.* **1.** a ruse or confidence trick. –*v.t.* (**scammed, scamming**) **2.** to practise a confidence trick on (someone). **3.** to get (something) from someone by plausible deceit rather than paying: *he scammed some cakes from the tuckshop.* –**scammer,** *n.*

scamp /skæmp/ *n.* a mischievous child. –**scampish,** *adj.*

scamper /ˈskæmpə/ *v.i.* **1.** to run or go hastily or quickly. –*n.* **2.** a scampering; a quick run.

scan /skæn/ *verb* (**scanned, scanning**) –*v.t.* **1.** to examine closely; scrutinise. **2.** to look through quickly: *to scan a page.* **3.** to analyse the metrical structure of (verse). **4.** *Electronics* to traverse (a surface or area) with a beam of light or electrons in order to obtain information, especially to reproduce or transmit an image. **5.** *Radar* to go over (an area) with a beam from a radar transmitter. **6.** *Med.* to examine (an area, organ, or system of the body) using a moving detector or moving beam of radiation to produce an image of that body part, sometimes after an injection of a radioactive substance which has the ability to enhance the image of a particular tissue. –*v.i.* **7.** (of verse) to be in accordance with the rules of metre. –*n.* **8.** the act of scanning. –**scannable,** *adj.* –**scannability,** *n.*

scandal /ˈskændl/ *n.* **1.** a disgraceful action, happening, etc.: *it was a scandal that the murderer was set free.* **2.** displeasure or offence caused by such an action. **3.** talk or gossip that does harm to someone's reputation. **4.** *Colloq.* gossip in general. **5.** a person whose behaviour brings disgrace or offence. –**scandalous,** *adj.*

scandalise /ˈskændəlaɪz/ *v.t.* to shock or horrify by something considered immoral or improper. Also, **scandalize.** –**scandaliser,** *n.*

scanner /ˈskænə/ *n.* **1.** someone or something that scans. **2.** *Med.* a machine used to scan (def. 6) an area, organ, or system of the body. **3.** *Computers* → **optical scanner. 4.** → **barcode reader.**

scansion /ˈskænʃən/ *n.* the metrical analysis of verse.

scant /skænt/ *adj.* **1.** barely sufficient in amount or quantity; not abundant; inadequate: *to do scant justice.* **2.** limited; not large: *a scant amount.* **3.** barely amounting to as much as indicated: *a scant two hours.* –*phr.* **4. scant of,** having an inadequate or limited supply of: *scant of breath.* –**scantly,** *adv.* –**scantness,** *n.*

scanty /ˈskænti/ *adj.* (**-tier, -tiest**) **1.** scant in amount, quantity, etc.; barely sufficient. **2.** meagre; not adequate. **3.** lacking amplitude in extent or compass. –**scantily,** *adv.* –**scantiness,** *n.*

-scape a suffix indicating a view or expanse of the particular location indicated: *streetscape, desertscape, sandscape, cityscape.*

scapegoat /ˈskeɪpɡoʊt/ *n.* someone who is made to bear the blame for others or to suffer in their place.

scapula /ˈskæpjələ/ *n.* (*pl.* **-las** or **-lae** /-li/) **1.** *Anat.* either of two flat, triangular bones, each forming the back part of a shoulder; a shoulderblade. **2.** *Zool.* a dorsal bone of the pectoral arch. –**scapular,** *adj.*

scar¹ /ska/ *n.* **1.** the mark left by a healed wound, sore, or burn. **2.** any blemish remaining as a trace or result: *scars upon one's good name.* **3.** *Bot.* a mark indicating a former point of attachment, as where a leaf has fallen from a stem. –*verb* (**scarred, scarring**) –*v.t.* **4.** to mark with a scar. –*v.i.* **5.** to heal with a resulting scar.

scar² /ska/ *n.* **1.** a precipitous rocky place; a cliff. **2.** a low or submerged rock in the sea.

scarab /ˈskærəb/ *n.* **1.** Also, **scarab beetle.** any scarabaeid beetle, especially *Scarabaeus sacer,* regarded as sacred by the ancient Egyptians. **2.** a representation or image of a beetle, much used among the ancient Egyptians as a symbol, seal, amulet, or the like. **3.** a gem (as of emerald, green feldspar, etc.) cut in the form of a beetle.

scarce /skɛəs/ *adj.* (**scarcer, scarcest**) **1.** insufficient for the need or demand; not abundant: *commodities scarce in wartime.* **2.** seldom met with; rare: *a scarce book.* –*adv.* **3.** *Obs.* scarcely. –*phr.* **4. make oneself scarce,** *Colloq.* to make off; keep out of the way. –**scarceness,** *n.*

scarcely /ˈskɛəsli/ *adv.* **1.** barely; hardly; not quite. **2.** (*usually ironic*) definitely not. **3.** no sooner.

scare /skɛə/ *verb* (**scared**, **scaring**) −*v.t.* **1.** to strike with sudden fear or terror. −*v.i.* **2.** to become frightened: *that horse scares easily.* −*n.* **3.** a sudden fright or alarm, especially with little or no ground. **4.** a time or state of widespread fear, worry, etc. −*phr.* **5. scare away** (or **off**), to drive off; frighten away. **6. scare up**, *Colloq.* to obtain or find: *to scare up support for a project.* −**scared**, *adj.* −**scarer**, *n.* −**scaringly**, *adv.*

scarecrow /ˈskɛəkroʊ/ *n.* **1.** an object, usually a figure of a man in old clothes, set up to frighten crows, etc., away from crops. **2.** a person having a ragged, untidy appearance. **3.** a very thin person. **4.** anything frightening but not really dangerous.

scarf[1] /skaf/ *n.* (*pl.* **scarfs** or **scarves** /skavz/) a long, broad strip of silk, wool, lace, etc., worn around the neck, shoulders, or head for ornament or warmth.

scarf[2] /skaf/ *n.* (*pl.* **scarfs**) **1.** either of the tapered or specially cut ends of the pieces forming a scarf-joint. **2.** a notch; groove. −*v.t.* **3.** to join by a scarf or overlapping joint. **4.** to form a scarf, chamfer, or the like on, for a scarf-joint. **5.** to cut a vee notch in (a tree) to direct its falling. −**scarfer**, *n.*

scarify /ˈskærəfaɪ, ˈskɛər-/ *v.t.* (**-fied**, **-fying**) **1.** to make scratches or superficial incisions in (the skin, a wound, etc.), as in surgery. **2.** to lacerate by severe criticism. **3.** to loosen (the soil) with a type of cultivator. **4.** to hasten the sprouting of (hard-covered seeds) by making incisions in the seedcoats. −**scarifier**, *n.* −**scarification**, *n.*

scarlet /ˈskalət/ *n.* **1.** a bright red colour inclining towards orange. **2.** cloth or garments of this colour. −*adj.* **3.** of the colour scarlet.

scarlet fever *n. Pathol.* a contagious febrile disease, now chiefly of children, caused by streptococci and characterised by a scarlet eruption.

scarp /skap/ *n.* **1.** a steep ridge extending from a mountain range; escarpment. **2.** *Fortifications* the side of a ditch next to a rampart; an escarp. −*v.t.* **3.** to form or cut into a scarp.

scarper /ˈskapə/ *v.i. Colloq.* to run away; depart suddenly, especially leaving behind debts or other commitments.

scat[1] /skæt/ *v.i.* (**scatted**, **scatting**) *Colloq.* (*usu. in the imperative*) to go off hastily.

scat[2] /skæt/ *n.* **1.** (in jazz) an improvised form of singing where the vocalist sings nonsense syllables to the tune. **2.** an instrumental equivalent or imitation of this. **3.** an act or instance of doing this. −*v.i.* (**scatted**, **scatting**) **4.** to sing scat.

scathing /ˈskeɪðɪŋ/ *adj.* intended to hurt the feelings; scornful; contemptuous, as a remark. −**scathingly**, *adv.*

scato- a word element indicating faeces or excrement, as in *scatology.*

scatology /skæˈtɒlədʒi/ *n.* **1.** the branch of medical science that deals with diagnosis by examination of the faeces. **2.** the branch of palaeontology dealing with fossil excrement. **3.** Also, **coprology.** the study of, or preoccupation with, images of excrement in literature. −**scatologic** /skætəˈlɒdʒɪk/, **scatological** /skætəˈlɒdʒɪkəl/, *adj.*

scatter /ˈskætə/ *v.t.* **1.** to throw loosely about. **2.** to separate and drive off in various directions; disperse. −*v.i.* **3.** to separate and go in different directions; disperse. −*n.* **4.** the act of scattering. **5.** something which is scattered. −**scatterer**, *n.* −**scatteringly**, *adv.*

scattergun /ˈskætəgʌn/ *n.* **1.** a gun, such as a shotgun, which does not shoot a single missile but many smaller missiles in a scatter. −*phr.* **2. scattergun approach**, an approach to a problem, argument, etc., which relies on a broad range of not necessarily well-directed counter measures as a tactic, rather than a single well-directed one.

scatty /ˈskæti/ *adj.* (**-tier**, **-tiest**) thoughtless; unreliable.

scavenge /ˈskævəndʒ/ *verb* (**-enged**, **-enging**) −*v.t.* **1.** to search for and take (anything usable) from rubbish or material that is no longer being used. −*v.i.* **2.** to search amongst rubbish or disused material for anything usable, such as food, clothing, etc.

scavenger /ˈskævəndʒə/ *n.* a person or animal that scavenges, as any of various animals feeding on dead organic matter.

scenario /səˈnarioʊ, səˈnɛərioʊ/ *n.* (*pl.* **-rios**) **1.** an outline of the plot of a dramatic work, giving particulars as to the scenes, characters, situations, etc. **2.** the outline or script of a film, giving the action in the order in which it takes place, the description of scenes and characters, the printed matter to be shown on the screen, etc. **3.** the outline of a general situation; a plan to be followed or observed. −*phr.* **4. best-case scenario**, the best possible outcome. **5. worst-case scenario**, the worst possible outcome.

scene /sin/ *n.* **1.** the place where any action occurs. **2.** any view or picture. **3.** an incident or situation in real life. **4.** an exhibition or outbreak of excited or violent feeling before others. **5.** a division of a play or of an act of a play, now commonly representing what passes between certain of the actors in one place. **6.** the place in which the action of a play or part of a play is supposed to occur. **7.** → **scenery** (def. 2). **8.** an episode, situation, or the like, as described in writing. **9.** the setting of a story or the like. **10.** the stage, especially of an ancient Greek or Roman theatre. **11.** any sphere or domain, especially that of contemporary culture: *the pop scene.* **12.** *Colloq.* an area or sphere of interest or involvement: *politics is her scene.* **13.** *Colloq.* a social environment: *I had to leave that scene.* −*phr.* **14. a bad scene**, *Colloq.* a situation which has a negative effect. **15. a good scene**, *Colloq.* a situation which has a positive effect. **16. behind the scenes**, **a.** out of sight of the audience; offstage. **b.** secretly; privately. **17. on the scene**, **a.** present: *the first person on the scene was a police officer.* **b.** in fashion. **18. the scene**, **a.** the contemporary fashionable world. **b.** *Colloq.* the world of homosexuals, where their sexual preference is openly displayed, as in gay bars, etc.

scene kid *n. Colloq.* a person who adopts an unconventional style of dress, such as coloured hair worn high on the head, dramatic eyeliner and straight jeans, and who prefers hip-hop, punk rock, and other offbeat genres of music.

scenery /ˈsinəri/ *n.* (*pl.* **-ries**) **1.** the general appearance of a place; the aggregate of features that give character to a landscape. **2.** *Theatre* hangings, draperies, structures, etc., on the stage to represent some place or furnish decorative background.

scenic /ˈsinɪk/ *adj.* **1.** of or relating to natural scenery; having fine scenery. **2.** of or relating to the stage or with stage scenery; dramatic; theatrical. **3.** representing a scene, action, or the like, as painting or sculpture. −**scenically**, *adv.*

scent /sɛnt/ *n.* **1.** a particular smell, especially when agreeable. **2.** a smell left in passing, by means of which an animal or person may be tracked. **3.** → **perfume**. **4.** the sense of smell. −*v.t.* **5.** to become aware of or recognise by the sense of smell. **6.** to become aware of or discover in any way: *to scent trouble.* **7.** to put perfume on or into. −**scentless**, *adj.*

sceptic /ˈskɛptɪk/ *n.* **1.** someone who questions the validity or authenticity of something purporting to be knowledge. **2.** someone who mistrusts and who maintains a doubting pessimistic attitude towards people, plans, ideas, etc. **3.** someone who doubts the truth of the Christian religion or of important elements of it. –*adj.* **4.** relating to sceptics or scepticism; sceptical. Also, *US*, **skeptic**. –**sceptical**, *adj.* –**scepticism**, *n.*

sceptre /ˈsɛptə/ *n.* **1.** a rod or wand borne in the hand as an emblem of regal or imperial power. **2.** royal or imperial power or authority; sovereignty. –*v.t.* **3.** to give a sceptre to; invest with authority. Also, *US*, **scepter**. –**sceptred**, *adj.*

schedule /ˈʃɛdʒul, ˈskɛdʒul/ *n.* **1.** a plan for a particular project setting out the order of operations, time given for each part, etc. **2.** a list of things needed to be dealt with or undertaken: *he has a full schedule tomorrow.* **3.** a written or printed statement of details, often attached to another document. –*v.t.* **4.** to make a schedule of; enter in a schedule. **5.** to plan for a certain date: *to schedule publication for June.* –**schedular**, *adj.*

scheelite /ˈʃilaɪt/ *n.* calcium tungstate, $CaWO_4$, an important ore of tungsten usually occurring in crystals.

schema /ˈskimə/ *n.* (*pl.* **-mata** /-mətə/) **1.** a diagram, plan, or scheme. **2.** *Philos.* (in Kantianism) a rule or principle whereby a category of the understanding is applied to experience. It mediates between the universality of the pure concept (which is opaque to sense) and the particularity of sense (which is opaque to the understanding).

schematic /skiˈmætɪk, skə-/ *adj.* **1.** relating to or of the nature of a schema, diagram, or scheme; diagrammatic. –*n.* **2.** a schematic drawing or diagram. –**schematically**, *adv.*

scheme /skim/ *n.* **1.** a plan or design; program of action; project. **2.** a secret plan; plot; intrigue. **3.** any system of connected things, parts, beliefs, etc., or the manner of its arrangement: *a colour scheme.* –*v.t.* **4.** to devise as a scheme; plan; plot. –*v.i.* **5.** to lay schemes; devise plans; plot. –**schemer**, *n.*

scheming /ˈskimɪŋ/ *adj.* given to forming plans, especially underhand ones; crafty.

scherzo /ˈskɜtsoʊ, ˈskɛət-/ *n.* (*pl.* **-zos** *or* **-zi** /-si/) *Music* (in music) a movement or passage of lively, playful character, especially as the second or third division of a sonata or a symphony.

schism /ˈskɪzəm, ˈʃɪzəm, ˈsɪzəm/ *n.* **1.** division or disunion, especially into mutually opposed parties. **2.** the parties so formed. **3.** *Eccles.* **a.** a formal division within, or separation from, a church or religious body over some doctrinal difference. **b.** a group or body formed by such a division. **c.** the offence of causing or seeking to cause such a division.

schist /ʃɪst/ *n.* *Geol.* any of a class of crystalline rocks whose constituent minerals have a more or less parallel or foliated arrangement, due mostly to metamorphic action.

schizo /ˈskɪtsoʊ/ *n.* *Colloq.* **1.** a schizophrenic. **2.** a person having an unpredictable character. –*adj.* **3.** schizophrenic. **4.** unpredictable in behaviour; liable to sudden changes in disposition.

schizo- a word element referring to cleavage. Also, (*before vowels*), **schiz-**.

schizoid /ˈskɪtsɔɪd/ *adj.* **1.** related to, predisposed to, or afflicted with schizophrenia. –*n.* **2.** someone who is afflicted with schizophrenia.

schizophrenia /skɪtsəˈfriniə/ *n.* *Psychol.* any of various psychotic disorders characterised by breakdown of integrated personality functioning, withdrawal from reality, emotional blunting and distortion, and disturbances in thought and behaviour. Compare **dissociative identity disorder**.

schizophrenic /skɪtsəˈfrɛnɪk, -ˈfrinɪk/ *n.* Also, **schizophrene**. **1.** a person who is suffering from schizophrenia. –*adj.* **2.** of or relating to schizophrenia. **3.** suffering from schizophrenia. **4.** (in popular but erroneous use) suffering from dissociative identity disorder. **5.** *Colloq.*

having an unpredictable or extremely changeable personality. **6.** *Colloq.* unable to choose between two courses of action.

schlep /ʃlɛp/ *Chiefly US Colloq.* –*v.t.* (**schlepped**, **schlepping**) **1.** to carry; cart or lug. –*phr.* **2. schlep around**, to traipse or trudge around. Also, **shlep**.

schmaltz /ʃmɒlts, ʃmɔlts/ *n.* *Colloq.* excessive sentimentality, especially in the arts. Also, **schmalz**. –**schmaltzy**, *adj.*

schnapps /ʃnæps/ *n.* a type of gin often flavoured with caraway or cumin. Also, **schnaps**.

scholar /ˈskɒlə/ *n.* **1.** a learned or erudite person. **2.** a student; pupil. **3.** a student who, because of merit, etc., is granted money or other aid to pursue his or her studies. –**scholarly**, *adj.*

scholarship /ˈskɒləʃɪp/ *n.* **1.** learning; knowledge acquired by study; the academic attainments of a scholar. **2.** the position of a student who, because of merit, etc., is granted money or other aid to pursue his or her studies. **3.** the sum of money or other aid granted to a scholar. **4.** a foundation to provide financial assistance to students.

scholastic /skəˈlæstɪk/ *adj.* **1.** Also, **scholastical**. of or relating to schools, students, or education: *scholastic attainments.* **2.** of or relating to scholasticism. –*n.* **3.** (*sometimes upper case*) a supporter of scholasticism. –**scholastically**, *adv.*

school[1] /skul/ *n.* **1.** a place or establishment where instruction is given, especially one for children. **2.** the body of students or pupils attending a school. **3.** a regular course of meetings of a teacher or teachers and students for instruction: *a school held during the summer months.* **4.** a session of such a course: *no school today.* **5.** a building, room, etc., in a university, set apart for the use of one of the faculties or for some particular purpose. **6.** a department or faculty in a university or similar educational institution. **7.** a group of departments or faculties in a university or similar institution associated through a common disciplinary or interdisciplinary interest, or through a common purpose. **8.** a body of scholars, artists, writers, etc., who have been taught by the same master, or who are united by a similarity of method, style, principles, etc.: *the Platonic school of philosophy.* **9.** any body of persons who agree. **10.** *Colloq.* a group of people settled (either on one occasion or habitually) into a session of drinking or gambling: *a two-up school.* –*adj.* **11.** of or connected with a school or schools. –*v.t.* **12.** to educate in or as in a school; teach; train. –*phr.* **13. school of thought**, **a.** a group of people all holding the same opinion or point of view. **b.** a point of view held by such a group.

school[2] /skul/ *n.* **1.** a large number of fish, porpoises, whales, or the like, feeding or migrating together. –*v.i.* **2.** to form into, or go in, a school, as fish.

school council *n.* a governing body within a public school with representatives from staff, students and parents, and concerned with matters of broad policy, but whose decisions can always be vetoed by the school principal. Compare **P & C**.

schoolyard /ˈskuljad/ *n.* the playground of a school.

school zone *n.* a section of road in close proximity to a school in which special speed restrictions apply, usually during times when children are likely to be arriving at or leaving the school grounds.

schooner /ˈskunə/ *n.* **1.** a sailing vessel with two or more masts and fore-and-aft rig. **2.** *Aust.*, *NZ* a large glass, usually a beer glass.

sciatic /saɪˈætɪk/ *adj.* **1.** of the ischium or back of the hip: *sciatic nerve.* **2.** affecting the hip or the sciatic nerves.

sciatica /saɪˈætɪkə/ *n.* *Pathol.* **1.** pain and tenderness at some points of the sciatic nerve; sciatic neuralgia.

2. any painful disorder extending from the hip down the back of the thigh and surrounding area.

science /ˈsaɪəns/ *n.* **1. a.** the systematic study of the nature and behaviour of the material and physical universe, based on observation, experiment, and measurement, often leading to the formulation of laws to describe the results of such procedures in general terms. **b.** the knowledge so obtained. **2.** a particular branch of this. **3.** systematised knowledge in general. **4.** *Obs.* skill; proficiency.

science fiction *n.* a form of fiction which draws imaginatively on scientific knowledge and speculation in its plot, setting, theme, etc.

scientific /saɪənˈtɪfɪk/ *adj.* **1.** of or relating to science or the sciences: *scientific studies.* **2.** occupied or concerned with science: *scientific men.* **3.** regulated by or conforming to the principles of exact science: *a scientific method.* **4.** systematic or accurate. **–scientifically,** *adv.*

scientific method *n.* a method of research in which the steps are identification of a problem, collection of relevant data, formulation of a hypothesis on the basis of this data, and, finally, empirical testing of the hypothesis to prove its validity.

scientist /ˈsaɪəntəst/ *n.* someone with an expert knowledge of science, especially someone professionally qualified in one of the physical or natural sciences.

sci-fi /ˈsaɪ-faɪ, saɪ-ˈfaɪ/ *Colloq.* *–n.* **1.** science fiction. *–adj.* **2.** of or relating to science fiction.

scilicet /ˈsɪləset, ˈsaɪl-/ *adv.* to wit; that is to say; namely.

scimitar /ˈsɪmətə/ *n.* a curved, single-edged sword of Middle Eastern origin. Also, **scimiter, simitar.**

scintillate /ˈsɪntəleɪt/ *v.i.* **1.** to give out sparks; flash. **2.** to twinkle, as the stars do. **3.** to be bright and amusing in conversation.

scion /ˈsaɪən/ *n.* **1.** a descendant. **2.** *Hort.* a shoot or twig, especially one cut for grafting or planting; a cutting.

scissors /ˈsɪzəz/ *pl. n.* a cutting instrument consisting of two blades (with handles) so joined together that their edges work against each other (often called *a pair of scissors*).

sclero- a word element meaning 'hard'. Also, (*before vowels*), **scler-.**

sclerophyll /ˈsklɛrəfɪl, ˈsklɪə-/ *n.* **1.** *Bot.* any of various plants, typically found in low rainfall areas, having tough leaves which help to reduce water loss. *–adj.* **2.** composed of or relating to such plants.

sclerophyll forest *n.* a forest comprising sclerophyll plants.

sclerosis /skləˈrousəs/ *n.* (*pl.* **-roses** /-ˈrousiz/) **1.** *Pathol.* a hardening or induration of a tissue or part; increase of connective tissue or the like at the expense of more active tissue. **2.** *Bot.* a hardening of a tissue or cell wall by thickening or lignification. **–sclerosal,** *adj.*

scoff[1] /skɒf/ *n.* **1.** an expression of mockery, derision, or derisive scorn; a jeer. **2.** an object of mockery or derision. *–v.i.* **3.** (sometimes fol. by *at*) to speak derisively; mock; jeer. **–scoffer,** *n.* **–scoffingly,** *adv.*

scoff[2] /skɒf/ *Colloq.* *–v.t.* Also, **scoff down. 1.** to eat (food) greedily and quickly: *scoffing a sandwich and a cup of tea.* *–n.* **2.** food.

scold /skould/ *v.t.* **1.** to find fault with; chide. *–v.i.* **2.** to find fault; reprove. **3.** to use abusive language. *–n.* **4.** a person, who is habitually abusive. **–scolder,** *n.* **–scolding,** *adj., n.* **–scoldingly,** *adv.*

scoliosis /skɒliˈousəs/ *n.* abnormal lateral curvature of the spine, more common in females than males, and developing at any age but often accelerating in puberty in periods of growth spurts.

scone /skɒn/ *n.* **1.** a light plain cake, quickly made, containing very little fat, either baked in a very hot oven or cooked on a hot plate or griddle (**drop scone**),

usually eaten split open and spread with butter, etc. **2.** *Aust., NZ Colloq.* the head. *–v.t.* **3.** *Aust., NZ Colloq.* to strike a person, especially on the head. *–phr. Aust., NZ Colloq.* **4. do one's scone,** to lose one's temper. **5. off one's scone,** mad; insane.

scoop /skup/ *n.* **1.** a ladle or ladle-like utensil, especially a small, deep shovel with a short handle, for taking up flour, sugar, etc. **2.** the bucket of a dredge, steam shovel, etc. **3.** *Surg.* a spoon-like apparatus used to remove substances or foreign objects. **4.** a place scooped out; a hollow. **5.** the act of scooping; a movement as of scooping. **6.** the quantity taken up. **7.** *Colloq.* a big haul, as of money. **8.** *Journalism* an item of news, etc., published or broadcast in advance of, or to the exclusion of, rival newspapers, broadcasting organisations, etc. *–v.t.* **9.** to take up or out with, or as with, a scoop. **10.** to empty with a scoop. **11.** to form a hollow or hollows in. **12.** to form with or as with a scoop. **13.** *Journalism Colloq.* to get the better of (a rival newspaper, broadcasting organisation, etc.) by publishing or broadcasting an item of news, etc., first. **14.** *Hockey* to hit under (the ball) so that it rises into the air. *–v.i.* **15.** to remove or gather something with, or as with, a scoop. *–phr.* **16. scoop the pool,** to win all the prizes on offer. **17. scoop up,** to gather together or appropriate with the arms or hands: *he scooped up the jewels and put them into his pocket.* **–scooper,** *n.*

scoot /skut/ *Colloq.* *–v.i.* **1.** to dart; go swiftly or hastily. **2. →** **scram.** *–v.t.* **3.** to send or impel at high speed. *–n.* **4.** a swift, darting movement or course.

scooter /ˈskutə/ *n.* **1.** a child's vehicle with two wheels, one in front of the other, and a tread between them, and sometimes with an additional back wheel ensuring stability, steered by a handlebar and propelled by pushing against the ground with one foot. **2. →** **motor scooter.** *–v.i.* **3.** to go, or travel in or on a scooter.

scope /skoup/ *n.* **1.** the extent or range of view, outlook, use, operation, effectiveness, etc.: *an investigation of wide scope; he gave his imagination full scope.* **2.** extent in space; area. **3.** shortened form of *microscope, telescope,* etc.

-scope a word element referring to instruments for viewing, as in *telescope.*

-scopy a word element for forming abstract action nouns related to *-scope,* as in *telescopy.*

scorbutic /skɔˈbjutɪk/ *adj.* relating to, of the nature of, or affected with scurvy. Also, **scorbutical.**

scorch /skɔtʃ/ *v.t.* **1.** to change the colour, taste, etc., of by burning slightly. **2.** to dry up with heat. **3.** to criticise severely. *–v.i.* **4.** to be or become scorched. *–n.* **5.** a slight burn.

scorcher /ˈskɔtʃə/ *n.* **1.** *Colloq.* a very hot day. **2.** anything caustic or severe.

score /skɔ/ *n.* **1.** the record of points made by the competitors in a game or match. **2.** the aggregate of points made by a side or individual. **3.** the scoring of a point or points. **4.** *Educ.* the performance of an individual, or sometimes of a group, in an examination or test, expressed by a letter, number, or other symbol. **5.** a notch or scratch; a stroke or line. **6.** a notch or mark for keeping an account or record. **7.** a reckoning or account so kept. **8.** any account showing indebtedness. **9.** (*pl.* **score**) a group or set of twenty: *five score years ago.* **10.** (*pl.*) a great many. **11.** account, reason, or ground: *to complain on the score of low pay.* **12.** a successful move, remark, etc. **13.** *Music* **a.** a written or printed piece of music with all the vocal and instrumental parts arranged on staves, one under the other. **b.** the background music to a film, play, etc. **14.** *Colloq.* latest news or state of progress: *what's the score on the Rogers file?* *–v.t.* **15.** to gain for addition to one's score in a game. **16.** to make a score of. **17.** to be worth (as points): *four aces score one hundred.* **18.** *Educ.* to evaluate the responses a person has made on (a test or an examination). **19.** *Music* **a.** to orchestrate. **b.** to write out in score. **c.** to compose the music for (a film, play, etc.). **20.** *Cookery* to cut with shallow slashes, as meat. **21.** to make notches, cuts, or lines in or on. **22.** Also, **score up.** to record by notches, marks, etc.; to reckon. **23.** to gain or win: *a comedy scoring a great success.* **24.** *US* to censure severely: *newspapers scored him severely for the announcement.* **25.** *Colloq.* to be successful in obtaining (a commodity, especially drugs): *we scored a deal of dope.* –*v.i.* **26.** to make notches, cuts, lines, etc. **27.** to make a point or points in a game or contest. **28.** to keep score, as of a game. **29.** to achieve an advantage or a success. **30.** *Colloq.* to be successful in obtaining a commodity, especially drugs. **31.** *Colloq.* to be successful in securing a partner for sexual intercourse. –*phr.* **32. know the score,** to be aware of what is required. **33. pay off** (or **settle**) **a score, a.** to avenge a wrong. **b.** to fulfil an obligation. **34. score off someone,** to gain an advantage over someone. –**scorer,** *n.* –**scoring,** *n.* –**scoreless,** *adj.*

scoria /ˈskɔːriə/ *n.* (*pl.* **scoriae** /ˈskɔːriiː/) **1.** *Metallurgy* the refuse, dross, or slag left after smelting or melting metals. **2.** *Geol.* a clinker-like cellular lava. –**scoriaceous** /skɔːriˈeɪʃəs/, *adj.*

scorn /skɔn/ *n.* **1.** open lack of respect; contempt; disdain. –*v.t.* **2.** to treat or regard with scorn. **3.** to reject or refuse with scorn. –**scorner,** *n.* –**scornful,** *adj.* –**scornfully,** *adv.*

Scorpio /ˈskɔːpioʊ/ *n.* **1.** the eighth sign of the zodiac, which the sun enters about 23 October; the Scorpion. **2.** a person born under the sign of Scorpio. –*adj.* **3.** of or relating to Scorpio.

scorpion /ˈskɔːpiən/ *n.* **1.** any of numerous arachnids belonging to the order Scorpiones (Scorpionida) from the warmer parts of the world, having a long narrow abdomen terminating in a venomous sting. **2.** an insect which stings or which superficially resembles a true scorpion. **3.** (*upper case*) the zodiacal constellation or sign Scorpio.

scotch /skɒtʃ/ *v.t.* **1.** to injure so as to make harmless. **2.** to put an end to: *her mother soon scotched her plans for going out.*

scot-free /skɒt-ˈfriː/ *adj.* free from penalty or payment; unhurt: *to get off scot-free.*

scoundrel /ˈskaʊndrəl/ *n.* an unprincipled, dishonourable person; villain.

scour¹ /ˈskaʊə/ *v.t.* **1.** to clean or polish by hard rubbing: *to scour pots and pans.* **2.** to clear out (a channel, drain, etc.). **3.** to clear or remove what is dirty or undesirable. –*v.i.* **4.** to rub a surface in order to clean or polish it. **5.** to remove dirt, etc. –*n.* **6.** the act of scouring. **7.** the place scoured.

scour² /ˈskaʊə/ *v.i.* **1.** to move rapidly or energetically. **2.** to range about, as in search of something. –*v.t.* **3.** to run or pass quickly over or along. **4.** to range over, as in search.

scourge /skɜːdʒ/ *n.* **1.** a whip or lash, especially for the infliction of punishment or torture. **2.** any means of punishment. **3.** a cause of affliction or calamity. –*v.t.* (**scourged, scourging**) **4.** to whip with a scourge; lash. **5.** to punish or chastise severely; afflict; torment. –**scourger,** *n.*

scout¹ /skaʊt/ *n.* **1.** a soldier, ship, plane, or the like, used in reconnoitring. **2.** a person sent out to obtain information. **3.** → **Scout. 4.** a talent scout. **5.** the act of scouting. **6.** *Colloq.* a person: *a good scout.* –*v.i.* **7.** to act as a scout; reconnoitre. –*phr.* **8. scout out** (or **around for**), *Colloq.* to search for; seek: *to scout out a substitute player; to scout around for an entertainer.* –**scouting,** *n.*

Scout /skaʊt/ *n.* (*sometimes lower case*) **1.** a member of a worldwide youth movement, originating in the Boy Scout movement founded in England in 1907 by Sir Robert Baden-Powell; members participate in organised activities which have the aim of promoting physical, personal, and spiritual development, with emphasis on qualities such as self-reliance and citizenship. **2.** a member of the central division (ages 11–14) of the Scout Association of Australia. See **Joey Scout, Cub Scout, Venturer, rover.**

scowl /skaʊl/ *v.i.* **1.** to draw down or contract the brows in a sullen or angry manner. **2.** to have a gloomy or threatening look. –*n.* **3.** a scowling expression, look, or aspect. –**scowler,** *n.* –**scowlingly,** *adv.*

scrabble /ˈskræbəl/ *v.i.* **1.** to scratch or scrape, with the claws, hands, etc. **2.** to scribble. **3.** to struggle to gain possession of something. –*n.* **4.** a scramble.

scrag /skræg/ *n.* **1.** a lean person or animal. **2.** the lean end of a neck of mutton, etc. **3.** *Colloq.* the neck of a human being. –*v.t.* (**scragged, scragging**) **4.** *Colloq.* to wring the neck of; hang; garrotte.

scraggly /ˈskrægli/ *adj.* (**-glier, -gliest**) irregular; ragged; straggling.

scraggy /ˈskrægi/ *adj.* (**-gier, -giest**) **1.** lean or thin. **2.** meagre: *a scraggy meal.* **3.** irregular; jagged. –**scraggily,** *adv.* –**scragginess,** *n.*

scram /skræm/ *v.i.* (**scrammed, scramming**) *Colloq.* to get out quickly; go away.

scramble /ˈskræmbəl/ *v.i.* **1.** to make one's way hurriedly by use of the hands and feet: *to scramble over rough ground.* **2.** to struggle with others for possession of something. **3.** *Mil., Navy, etc.* (of the crew of an aircraft, submarine, etc., or the craft itself) to prepare for immediate action. –*v.t.* **4.** (fol. by *up*, etc.) to collect in a hurried or disorderly manner. **5.** to mix together confusedly. **6.** to cook (eggs) by mixing whites and yolks with butter, milk, etc. **7.** *Elect.* to send (a radio signal) in a confused form, so that it can be made intelligible only by a special receiver, and not by a normal instrument. –*n.* **8.** a climb or progression over rough, irregular ground, etc. **9.** a form of motorcycle race over very rough, uneven ground. **10.** a disorderly struggle for possession. –**scrambler,** *n.*

scrap¹ /skræp/ *n.* **1.** a small piece; fragment: *scraps of paper; scraps of poetry.* **2.** (*pl.*) bits of food, such as those left over after a meal. **3.** → **scrap metal. 4.** anything put aside as useless, unwanted or worn-out. –*adj.* **5.** consisting of scraps: *scrap heap.* **6.** thrown away or left over. –*v.t.* (**scrapped, scrapping**) **7.** to make into scrap; break up. **8.** to put aside as useless or worthless. –**scrappy,** *adj.* –**scrapper,** *n.*

scrap² /skræp/ *Colloq.* –*n.* **1.** a disagreement or quarrel. **2.** a physical fight. –*v.i.* (**scrapped, scrapping**) **3.** to engage in an argument or quarrel.. **4.** to come to blows; fight.

scrapbook /ˈskræpbʊk/ *n.* **1.** a blank book in which photographs, newspaper cuttings, etc., are pasted. –*v.i.* **2.** to engage in the activity of scrapbooking. –*v.t.* **3.** to add (a piece of memorabilia) to a scrapbook.

scrapbooking /ˈskræpbʊkɪŋ/ *n.* the presentation of photographs, memorabilia, etc., in a scrapbook.

scrape /skreɪp/ *verb* (**scraped, scraping**) –*v.t.* **1.** to deprive of or free from an outer layer, adhering matter, etc., by drawing or rubbing something, especially a sharp or rough instrument, over the surface. **2.** to remove (an outer layer, adhering matter, etc.) in this way. **3.** to scratch; produce as by scratching. **4.** to rub harshly on or across (something). **5.** to draw or rub (a thing) roughly across something. **6.** *Colloq.* (of a man) to have intercourse with (a woman). –*v.i.* **7.** to scrape something. **8.** to rub against something gratingly. **9.** to produce a grating and unmusical tone from a string instrument. **10.** to draw back the foot in making a bow. **11.** to practise laborious economy or saving: *they scraped for years in order to buy a house.* –*n.* **12.** the act of scraping. **13.** a drawing back of the foot in making a bow. **14.** a scraping sound. **15.** a scraped place. **16.** *Med. Colloq.* curettage of the uterus. **17.** an embarrassing situation. **18.** a fight; struggle; scrap. **19.** *Colloq.* (*taboo*) an act of sexual intercourse. –*phr.* **20. scrape an acquaintance with somebody,** to force one's attentions upon somebody in order to get acquainted with them. **21. scrape through, a.** to manage to get through (an examination, etc.) with difficulty or barely succeeding: *I just scraped through the driving test.* **b.** to manage to get by with difficulty; succeed by a narrow margin: *it was difficult having no money, but somehow we managed to scrape through.* **22. scrape up** (or **together**), to collect by or as by scraping, or laboriously, or with difficulty.

scrap metal *n.* pieces of old metal that can be reworked, especially iron.

scratch /skrætʃ/ *v.t.* **1.** to break or mark slightly by rubbing, scraping, or tearing with something sharp or rough. **2.** to dig, scrape, or to tear (*out, off,* etc.) with the claws, the nails, etc. **3.** to rub or scrape lightly with the fingernails, etc., as to relieve itching. **4.** to rub gratingly, as a match, on something. **5.** to erase or strike out (writing, a name, etc.). **6.** to withdraw (a horse, etc.) from the list of entries in a race or competition. **7.** to write or draw by scraping or cutting into a surface. **8.** *Mining* to engage in surface mining of (an area). –*v.i.* **9.** to use the nails, claws, etc., for tearing, digging, etc. **10.** to relieve itching by rubbing with the nails, etc. **11.** to make a slight grating noise, as a pen. **12.** to manage with difficulty: *to scratch along on very little money.* **13.** to withdraw from a contest. –*n.* **14.** a mark produced by scratching, such as one on the skin. **15.** a rough mark of a pen, etc.; a scrawl. **16.** an act of scratching. **17.** the starting place, starting time, or status of a competitor in a handicap who has no allowance and no penalty. –*adj.* **18.** starting from scratch, or without allowance or penalty, as a competitor. **19.** *Golf* able to play the course in par figures: *a scratch player.* **20.** *Colloq.* done by or dependent on chance: *a scratch shot.* **21.** *Colloq.* gathered hastily and indiscriminately: *a scratch crew; a scratch meal.* –*phr.* **22. come up to scratch,** to meet a required standard. **23. from scratch,** from the beginning or from nothing. **24. not be able to scratch oneself,** *Colloq.* to be physically helpless. **25. scratch a living,** to make a poor living. **26. up to scratch, a.** conforming to a certain standard; satisfactory. **b.** *Boxing* (of a boxer) arriving at the fight by an agreed time. –**scratcher,** *n.*

scratch card *n.* → **scratchie.**

scratchie /ˈskrætʃi/ *n.* a type of instant lottery ticket from which the purchaser scratches off a film which conceals a number of pictures, symbols, etc., a prize being won if a certain set of these is revealed. Also, **scratch card, scratch ticket.**

scratch ticket *n.* **1.** (formerly) a tram, train or bus ticket from which the purchaser scratches away a coating to reveal the month, day, and (for some tickets) the hour, prior to boarding, thus making the ticket valid. **2.** → **scratchie.**

scrawl /skrɔl/ *v.i.* **1.** to write or draw in a sprawling awkward manner. –*v.t.* **2.** to execute (writing, drawing, etc.) in a sprawling awkward manner: *she scrawled her name.* –*n.* **3.** something scrawled, as a letter or a note. **4.** awkward or careless handwriting: *his scrawl is difficult to read.* –**scrawler,** *n.* –**scrawly,** *adj.*

scrawny /ˈskrɔni/ *adj.* (**-nier, -niest**) lean; thin; scraggy: *a long scrawny neck.* –**scrawniness,** *n.*

scream /skrim/ *v.i.* **1.** to utter a loud, sharp, piercing cry. **2.** to emit a shrill, piercing sound, as a whistle, etc. **3.** to laugh immoderately. **4.** to make something known by violent, startling words. **5.** to be startlingly conspicuous, used especially of colours. **6.** to protest volubly, especially to those in authority. **7.** *Colloq.* to travel at great speed, often with harsh, high-pitched sound: *the jet screamed overhead.* –*v.t.* **8.** to utter with a scream or screams. **9.** to make by screaming: *to scream oneself hoarse.* –*n.* **10.** a loud, sharp, piercing cry. **11.** a shrill, piercing sound. **12.** *Colloq.* someone or something that is very funny. –*phr.* **13. scream blue murder,** to complain vociferously. **14. scream for,** to want desperately, be in great need of. –**screamingly,** *adj.*

screamer /ˈskrimə/ *n.* **1.** someone or something that screams. **2.** *Colloq.* anything travelling at great speed. **3.** a newspaper poster incorporating blatant but not necessarily accurate headlines.

scree /skri/ *n.* a steep mass of detritus on the side of a mountain.

screech /skritʃ/ *v.i.* **1.** to utter a harsh, shrill cry. –*v.t.* **2.** to utter with a screech. –*n.* **3.** a harsh, shrill cry. –**screecher,** *n.* –**screechy,** *adj.*

screech owl *n.* any owl with a harsh cry, especially the barn owl, *Tyto alba.*

screed /skrid/ *n.* **1.** a long speech or piece of writing; harangue. **2.** *Plastering* a strip of plaster or wood of the proper thickness, applied to a wall as a guide or gauge for the rest of the work.

screen /skrin/ *n.* **1.** a covered frame or the like, movable or fixed, serving as a shelter, partition, etc. **2.** an ornamental partition of wood, stone, etc., as in a church. **3.** something affording a surface for displaying films, slides, etc. **4.** films collectively. **5.** the component of a television, computer monitor, etc., on which the visible image is displayed. **6.** → **sightscreen. 7.** anything that shelters, protects, or conceals: *a screen of secrecy.* **8.** a sheet of fine wire mesh, as one set in a frame and fitted to a door or window to keep out insects: *window screens.* **9.** *Mil.* a body of troops sent out to cover the movement of an army. **10.** *Navy* a protective formation of small vessels, as destroyers. **11.** *Physics* a shield designed to prevent interference between various effects: *electric screens.* –*v.t.* **12.** to shelter, protect, or conceal with, or as with, a screen. **13.** to project (pictures, etc.) on a screen. **14.** to check the loyalty, character, ability, etc., of (applicants, employees, or the like). –*v.i.* **15.** to be projected, or suitable for projection, on a screen. –*phr.* **16. screen off,** to conceal or shut off behind a screen. –**screenable,** *adj.* –**screener,** *n.*

screen capture *n.* the process of copying what is displayed on a computer screen to a computer file or printer.

screen grab *n.* an image taken from a computer screen and saved as a pdf file.

screenplay /ˈskrinpleɪ/ *n.* the script of a film, including details of camera positions and movement, action, dialogue, lighting, etc.

screen-print *v.t.* **1.** → **silk-screen.** –*n.* **2.** a silk-screen print.

screensaver /ˈskrinseɪvə/ *n. Computers* a program which is activated when the mouse or keyboard has not been used for a specified length of time, replacing the screen's contents with either a blank screen or an animated graphic; designed to save power and to entertain. Also, **screen saver.**

screenshot /ˈskrinʃɒt/ *n. Computers* an image replicating the contents of a screen at a particular time. Also, **screen shot.**

screw /skru/ *n.* **1.** a metal device having a slotted head and a tapering body with a helical ridge usually driven into wood with the aid of a screwdriver to assemble and secure parts of a building construction, furniture, etc. **2.** a mechanical device consisting of a cylinder or cone having a helical ridge winding round it (**external screw** or **male screw**). **3.** a corresponding part into which such a device fits when turned, consisting of a cylindrical socket in whose wall is cut a helical groove (**internal screw** or **female screw**). **4.** → **propeller**. **5.** a little tobacco, salt, etc., in a twisted paper. **6.** a twisting movement; a turn of a screw. **7.** *Colloq.* wages. **8.** *Colloq.* a prison warder. **9.** *Colloq.* (*taboo*) an act of sexual intercourse. **10.** *Colloq.* a hard bargainer; a miser. –*v.t.* **11.** to force, press, hold fast, stretch tight, etc., by or as by means of a screw. **12.** to operate or adjust by a screw, as a press. **13.** to attach with a screw or screws: *to screw a bracket to a wall.* **14.** to work (a screw, etc.) by turning. **15.** to twist; contort; distort. **16.** *Colloq.* to extract or extort. **17.** *Colloq.* (*taboo*) to have sexual intercourse with. **18.** *Colloq.* to treat unfairly or cause distress to (someone). **19.** *Colloq.* to ruin or wreck: *you've screwed it this time.* **20.** *Colloq.* to swindle or cheat: *to screw someone for ten bucks.* –*v.i.* **21.** to turn as or like a screw. **22.** to turn with a twisting motion. **23.** *Colloq.* (*taboo*) to have sexual intercourse. –*phr.* **24. have a screw loose**, *Colloq.* to be slightly eccentric; have crazy ideas. **25. put the screws on**, *Colloq.* to apply pressure to; intimidate. **26. screw around**, *Colloq.* (*taboo*) to be sexually promiscuous. **27. screw around on**, *Colloq.* (*taboo*) to be unfaithful to. **28. screw down**, *Colloq.* to put compulsion on; force (a seller) to lower a price. **29. screw on** (or **off**) (or **together**), to be adapted for being connected or taken apart by means of a screw or screws **30. screw up**, **a.** to crumple: *screw up a piece of paper.* **b.** *Colloq.* to make a mess of; impair; frustrate. **c.** *Colloq.* to cause (someone) to become mentally and emotionally disturbed. **d.** *Colloq.* to make a mistake. **31. screw up one's courage**, to summon up all one's determination in preparation for an ordeal or challenge.

screw cap *n.* a cap for a bottle which is screwed on and off.

screwdriver /ˈskruːdraɪvə/ *n.* a tool fitting into the slotted head of a screw for driving in or withdrawing it by turning.

screwy /ˈskruːi/ *adj.* (**-wier, -wiest**) *Colloq.* **1.** eccentric; crazy. **2.** strange; peculiar.

scribble /ˈskrɪbəl/ *v.t.* **1.** to write hastily or carelessly: *to scribble a letter.* –*v.i.* **2.** to write literary matter in a hasty, careless way. **3.** to make meaningless marks. –*n.* **4.** a hasty or careless piece of writing or drawing. –*phr.* **5. scribble over**, to cover with meaningless writing or marks. –**scribbly**, *adj.*

scribbly gum *n.* any species of the genus *Eucalyptus* with smooth bark marked by insects in a way that resembles scribbling, especially *E. haemastoma* of the Port Jackson district of NSW.

scribe¹ /skraɪb/ *n.* **1.** a penman or copyist, as someone who formerly made copies of manuscripts, etc. **2.** any of various officials of ancient or former times who performed clerical duties. **3.** *Jewish Hist.* one of a class of teachers who interpreted the Jewish law to the people. **4.** someone who writes or types something which another dictates: *he injured his arm and so needed a scribe for the exam.*

scribe² /skraɪb/ *v.t.* **1.** to mark or score (wood, etc.) with a pointed instrument. –*n.* **2.** a pointed instrument for so marking (wood, etc.).

scrim /skrɪm/ *n.* **1.** a cotton or linen fabric of open weave, used for curtains, etc. **2.** such a fabric, used for cleaning, polishing, etc. **3.** a piece of such fabric, used as a drop to give the effect of opacity, hazy translucency, etc., in theatrical use, or in camouflage.

scrimmage /ˈskrɪmɪdʒ/ *n.* **1.** a rough or vigorous struggle. **2.** *Aust. Rules, Rugby Football, Soccer* the action of a number of players struggling for the ball in no set pattern of play. **3.** *Rugby Football* → **scrum**. –*v.i.* (**-maged, -maging**) **4.** to engage in a scrimmage. **5.** to search rapidly and in a disorderly fashion as through a drawer. Also, **scrummage**. –**scrimmager**, *n.*

scrimp /skrɪmp/ *v.t.* to be sparing of or in; stint.

scrip /skrɪp/ *n.* **1.** a writing, especially a receipt or certificate. **2.** a scrap of paper. **3.** *Finance* a document with an identifying number which shows ownership of shares in a company. **4.** *Finance* shares or stock issued to existing shareholders in a scrip issue. **5.** → **prescription** (def. 1a).

script /skrɪpt/ *n.* **1.** handwriting; handwritten letters or lettering; the characters used in handwriting. **2.** the working text, manuscript, or the like, of a play, film, television program, etc., or the contents of such a document. **3.** a manuscript or document. **4.** → **prescription** (def. 1a). **5.** *Computers* a set of computer instructions in a high-level language that can be both read by a person and executed by a computer. –*v.t.* **6.** to write a script for: *to script a film.* **7.** to plan or devise: *to script the conference carefully.*

scrofula /ˈskrɒfjələ/ *n. Pathol.* a constitutional disorder of a tuberculous nature, characterised chiefly by swelling and degeneration of the lymphatic glands, especially of the neck, and by inflammation of the joints, etc.

scroll /skroʊl/ *n.* **1.** a roll of parchment or paper, especially one with writing on it. **2.** something, especially an ornament, resembling a partly unrolled sheet of paper or having a spiral or coiled form. **3.** the ornamental carving, resembling this, at the head of a violin or similar instrument. –*v.t.* **4.** *Computers* to move (text, images, etc.) up, down, left or right on a computer screen in order to view material which is outside the limits of the screen.

scrooge /skruːdʒ/ *n.* a miserly, ill-tempered person.

scrotum /ˈskroʊtəm/ *n.* (*pl.* **-ta** /-tə/ *or* **-tums**) *Anat.* the pouch of skin that contains the testicles and their coverings. –**scrotal**, *adj.*

scrounge /skraʊndʒ/ *v.t.* (**scrounged, scrounging**) *Colloq.* to obtain by borrowing or pilfering. –**scrounger**, *n.*

scrub¹ /skrʌb/ *verb* (**scrubbed, scrubbing**) –*v.t.* **1.** to rub hard with a brush, cloth, etc., or against a rough surface, in washing. **2.** to cleanse (a gas). **3.** *Colloq.* to cancel; get rid of. –*v.i.* **4.** to cleanse things by hard rubbing. –*n.* **5.** the act of scrubbing. –*phr.* **6. scrub up**, to wash with vigour, especially as surgeons before an operation. **7. scrub up well**, *Colloq.* to look surprisingly well-dressed and presentable when washed and changed into more formal clothes: *you scrub up well!*

scrub² /skrʌb/ *n.* **1.** low trees or shrubs, collectively, especially when stunted and of poor quality: *a valley covered with light scrub.* **2.** a tract of land covered with such vegetation: *a tea-tree scrub.* –*v.i.* (**scrubbed, scrubbing**) **3.** to remove the scrub from (a paddock, etc.). –*adj.* **4.** of or relating to or typical of scrub: *scrub timber.* –*phr.* **5. the scrub**, *Aust., NZ Colloq.* **a.** a patch of scrub. **b.** *Obs.* the country, as opposed to the city. –**scrubby**, *adj.*

scrubber /ˈskrʌbə/ *n.* **1.** an apparatus for purifying gases. **2.** *Colloq.* a coarse or vulgar woman. **3.** *Chiefly Brit. Colloq.* a promiscuous woman.

scrubfowl /ˈskrʌbfaʊl/ *n.* a chestnut-brown mound-building bird, with a prominent crest, *Megapodius reinwardt,* of coastal forested areas of northern Australia, many parts of Asia, and New Guinea.

scrub turkey *n.* → **brush turkey**.

scruff /skrʌf/ *n.* the nape or back of the neck.

scruffy /ˈskrʌfi/ *adj.* (**-fier, -fiest**) *Colloq.* unkempt or dirty; shabby. **–scruffily,** *adv.* **–scruffiness,** *n.*

scrum /skrʌm/ *Rugby Football* *–n.* **1.** a method of restarting play after a rule infringement, in which the opposing forwards pack together and push in formation, heads down, in an attempt to gain ground, while the ball is thrown in and the hookers attempt to kick it back to their teammates. It may be called for by the referee (**set scrum**), or it may form spontaneously (**loose scrum**). **2.** the formation. *–v.i.* (**scrummed, scrumming**) **3.** Also, **scrum down.** to form a scrum. **4.** to play as a member of a scrum.

scrummage /ˈskrʌmɪdʒ/ *n.,* *v.i.* (**-maged, -maging**) **1.** → **scrum. 2.** → **scrimmage.** **–scrummager,** *n.*

scrumptious /ˈskrʌmpʃəs/ *adj. Colloq.* deliciously tasty; superlatively fine or nice; splendid: *to have a scrumptious time.*

scruple /ˈskrupəl/ *n.* hesitation or reluctance from conscientious or other restraining reasons.

scrupulous /ˈskrupjələs/ *adj.* **1.** having scruples; having or showing a strict regard for what is right. **2.** punctiliously or minutely careful, precise, or exact. **–scrupulosity** /skrupjəˈlɒsəti/, **scrupulousness,** *n.* **–scrupulously,** *adv.*

scrutineer /skrutəˈnɪə/ *n.* **1.** someone who is authorised, especially by a candidate at an election, to inspect the counting of votes by electoral officers. **2.** an official in a race, contest, etc., who checks that the rules are observed. *–v.i.* **3.** to act as a scrutineer.

scrutinise /ˈskrutənaɪz/ *v.t.* to examine closely or critically. Also, **scrutinize.** **–scrutiniser,** *n.* **–scrutinisingly,** *adv.*

scrutiny /ˈskrutəni/ *n.* (*pl.* **-nies**) **1.** searching examination or investigation; minute inquiry. **2.** a searching look.

scuba /ˈskubə/ *n.* a portable breathing device for free-swimming divers, consisting of a mouthpiece joined by hoses to one or two tanks of compressed air which are strapped on the back.

scud /skʌd/ *v.i.* (**scudded, scudding**) **1.** to run or move quickly or hurriedly. **2.** *Naut.* to run before a gale with little or no sail set. *–n.* **3.** clouds, spray, or the like, driven by the wind; a driving shower; a gust of wind. **4.** low drifting clouds appearing beneath a cloud from which precipitation is falling.

scuff /skʌf/ *v.t.* **1.** to scrape with the feet. **2.** to mar by scraping or hard use, as shoes, furniture, etc. *–n.* **3.** the act or sound of scuffing. **4.** a type of slipper or sandal without a back.

scuffle /ˈskʌfəl/ *v.i.* **1.** to struggle or fight in a scrambling, confused manner. *–n.* **2.** a confused struggle or fight. **3.** a shuffling: *a scuffle of feet.*

scull[1] /skʌl/ *n.* **1. a.** an oar worked from side to side over the stern of a boat as a means of propulsion. **b.** one of a pair of oars operated, one on each side, by one person. **2.** a boat propelled by a scull or sculls, especially a light racing boat propelled by one rower with a pair of oars. *–v.t.* **3.** to propel or convey by means of a scull or sculls. *–v.i.* **4.** to propel a boat with a scull or sculls. **5.** to swim while floating on the front or the back, with the arms close to the body, using only a wrist movement. **–sculler,** *n.*

scull[2] /skʌl/ *v.t. Colloq.* to consume (a drink) at one draught. Also, **skol.**

scullery /ˈskʌləri/ *n.* (*pl.* **-ries**) a small room where the rough, dirty work of a kitchen is done.

sculpture /ˈskʌlptʃə/ *n.* **1.** the fine art of forming figures or designs in relief, in intaglio, or in the round by cutting marble, wood, granite, etc., by fashioning plastic materials, by modelling in clay, or by making moulds for casting in bronze or other metal. **2.** such work collectively. **3.** a piece of such work. *–v.t.* **4.** to

carve, make, or execute by sculpture, as a figure, design, etc.; represent in sculpture. **–sculpt,** *v.* **–sculptor,** *n.* **–sculptress,** *fem. n.* **–sculptural,** *adj.* **–sculpturally,** *adv.*

scum /skʌm/ *n.* **1.** a film of foul or extraneous matter on a liquid. **2.** low, worthless persons: *scum of the earth.* **–scummy,** *adj.*

scumbag /ˈskʌmbæg/ *n. Colloq.* a contemptible or despicable person.

scunge /skʌndʒ/ *n. Aust., NZ Colloq.* **1.** an unkempt, slovenly person. **2.** dirt, mess, slime, etc. **3.** messy, untidy objects: *I'll clear the scunge off this desk.* **–scungy,** *adj.*

scupper /ˈskʌpə/ *n.* **1.** *Naut.* an opening in the side of a ship at or just below the level of the deck, to allow water to run off. *–v.t.* **2.** to sink (a ship) deliberately.

scurf /skɜf/ *n.* **1.** the scales or small shreds of epidermis that are continually exfoliated from the skin; dandruff. **2.** any scaly matter or encrustation on a surface. **–scurfy,** *adj.*

scurrilous /ˈskʌrələs/ *adj.* **1.** grossly or indecently abusive: *a scurrilous attack.* **2.** characterised by or using low buffoonery; coarsely jocular or derisive: *a scurrilous jest.* **–scurrilously,** *adv.* **–scurrilousness,** *n.*

scurry /ˈskʌri/ *v.i.* (**-ried, -rying**) **1.** to go or move quickly or in haste. *–n.* (*pl.* **-ries**) **2.** a scurrying rush: *we heard the scurry of little feet down the stairs.*

scurvy /ˈskɜvi/ *n.* **1.** *Pathol.* a disease marked by swollen and bleeding gums, livid spots on the skin, prostration, etc., due to a diet lacking in vitamin C. *–adj.* (**-vier, -viest**) **2.** low, mean, or contemptible: *a scurvy trick.* **–scurvily,** *adv.* **–scurviness,** *n.*

scuttle[1] /ˈskʌtl/ *n.* **1.** a coalscuttle; a coal hod. **2.** a large basket.

scuttle[2] /ˈskʌtl/ *v.i.* **1.** to run (*off, away,* etc.) with quick, hasty steps; hurry. *–n.* **2.** an act of scuttling.

scuttle[3] /ˈskʌtl/ *n.* **1.** a small rectangular opening in a ship's deck, with a movable lid or cover. **2.** a similar opening in a ship's side. **3.** the part of a motor vehicle between the bonnet and the body. *–v.t.* **4.** to sink (a vessel) by cutting a hole below the waterline or opening the valves in its hull. **5.** to deliberately destroy the chances of success for (a project, deal, etc.): *to scuttle a proposed merger.*

scuttlebutt /ˈskʌtlbʌt/ *n.* **1.** *Naut.* a cask having a hole cut in it for the introduction of a cup or dipper, and used to hold drinking water. **2.** *Colloq.* rumour; gossip.

scythe /saɪð/ *n.* **1.** an agricultural implement consisting of a long, curved blade fastened at an angle to a handle, for mowing grass, etc., by hand. *–verb* (**scythed, scything**) *–v.t.* **2.** to cut or mow with a scythe. *–v.i.* **3.** to use a scythe.

SDTV /ɛs di ti ˈvi/ *n.* standard definition TV; a type of digital TV which produces picture and sound quality similar to that of analog TV. Compare **HDTV.**

sea /si/ *n.* **1.** the salt waters that cover the greater part of the earth's surface. **2.** a division of these waters, of considerable extent, more or less definitely marked off by land boundaries: *the Tasman Sea.* **3.** a large lake or landlocked body of water. **4.** the turbulence of the ocean or other body of water as caused by the wind; the waves. **5.** a large, heavy wave or swell: *heavy seas rocked the boat.* **6.** one of various more or less clearly defined areas on the surface of the moon, formerly thought to be areas of water. **7.** a widely extended, copious, or overwhelming quantity: *a sea of faces*; *a sea of troubles. –adj.* **8.** of, relating to, or adapted for the sea. *–phr.* **9. at sea,** **a.** sailing or on the ocean. **b.** Also, **all at sea.** bewildered or confused. **10. by sea,** on a ship. **11. follow the sea,** to follow a nautical career. **12. go to sea,** **a.** to set out upon a voyage. **b.** to take up a nautical career. **13. half seas over,** drunk. **14. put to**

sea, to set out from port. **15. the high seas**, the sea away from land, especially outside territorial waters.

sea anemone *n.* any of the common marine animals of the phylum Coelenterata, class Anthozoa, of sedentary habits, having a columnar body topped by a disc bearing one or more circles of tentacles.

seaboard /'sibɔd/ *n.* **1.** the line where land and sea meet; the seashore. **2.** a region of a country adjoining the coast. *–adj.* **3.** bordering on or adjoining the sea.

sea breeze *n.* a thermally produced wind blowing during the day from the cool ocean surface on to the adjoining warm land.

sea-dog *n. Colloq.* a sailor, especially one of long experience.

sea eagle *n.* any of various eagles of the genus *Haliaeetus* which feed on fish, as the **white-bellied sea eagle** of Australia and certain areas of Asia.

sea egg *n.* a large sea urchin with a spherical brown test and short white spines; found in the West Indies.

seafood /'sifud/ *n.* any saltwater fish or shellfish which is used for food.

seafront /'sifrʌnt/ *n.* **1.** the side or edge of land and buildings bordering on the sea. **2.** a road or promenade at a seaside town, running along the edge of the sea.

seagoing /'sigouɪŋ/ *adj.* designed or fit for going to sea, as a vessel.

seagrass /'sigras/ *n.* any of various marine plants of temperate seas, having long straplike leaves.

seagull /'sigʌl/ *n.* **1.** a gull, especially any of the marine species. See **gull**. **2.** *NZ Colloq.* a casual wharf labourer who is not a member of a trade union.

sea hawk *n.* → **skua**.

seahorse /'sihɔs/ *n.* **1.** any of a number of small fishes of the pipefish family, chiefly of the genus *Hippocampus*, with a prehensile tail and a beaked head that is turned at right angles to the body. **2.** a fabled marine animal with the foreparts of a horse and the hinder parts of a fish.

sea ice *n.* ice made of frozen sea water as waters in polar regions roughly of latitudes greater than 60° become colder with the approach to winter. See **pack ice**.

seal[1] /sil/ *n.* **1.** a device impressed on a piece of wax or the like, or an impression, wafer, etc., affixed to a document as evidence of authenticity or attestation. **2.** a stamp engraved with such a device. **3.** an impression made with such a stamp. **4.** *Law* a mark or symbol attached to a legal document and imparting a formal quality to it, originally defined as wax with an impression. **5.** a piece of wax or similar substance, affixed to a document, an envelope, a door, etc., which cannot be opened without breaking this. **6.** anything that effectively closes a thing. **7.** something for keeping a thing close or secret. **8.** a decorative stamp or small sticker: *a Christmas seal.* **9.** a mark or the like serving as visible evidence of something. **10.** *Plumbing* **a.** a small amount of water left standing in a trap to prevent the escape of foul air from below. **b.** the depth of the water between the dip and the overflow of a trap. **11.** a road surface of hard material, as tar, bitumen, etc.: *the tar seal. –v.t.* **12.** to affix a seal to an authorisation, confirmation, etc. **13.** to approve, authorise, or confirm: *to seal an agreement.* **14.** to impress a seal upon as an evidence of legal or standard exactness, measure, quality, etc. **15.** to fasten with a seal. **16.** to close by any form of fastening that must be broken before access can be had. **17.** to fasten or close as if by a seal. **18.** to decide irrevocably: *to seal someone's fate.* **19.** to surface (a road) with tar, bitumen, etc. *–phr.* **20. seal of approval**, complete approbation: *to be given the seal of approval by one's prospective in-laws.* **21. set one's seal on** (or **to**), to approve or endorse. **22. under seal**, (of a document) bearing a seal (def. 4). –**sealable**, *adj.*

seal[2] /sil/ *n.* (*pl.* **seals** *or, especially collectively,* **seal**) **1.** any of the marine carnivores of the suborder Pinnipedia, including the eared or fur seals, as the sea lion and fur seal of commerce, and the earless or hair seals, of which the **harbour seal**, *Phoca vitulina*, is best known. **2.** the skin of the seal. **3.** leather made from it. **4.** the fur of the fur seal; sealskin. *–v.i.* **5.** to hunt or take seals.

sea legs *pl. n. Colloq.* **1.** the ability to walk with steadiness or ease on a rolling ship. **2.** the ability to resist seasickness.

sea level *n.* the horizontal plane or level corresponding to the surface of the sea when halfway between mean high and low water, widely used as a base from which to indicate the height of locations on land.

sea lion *n.* **1.** the Australian white-naped hair seal, *Neophoca cinerea*. **2.** any of various eared seals of large size, as *Eumetopias jubata* of the northern Pacific, and *Zalophus californianus* of the Pacific coast of North America.

seam /sim/ *n.* **1.** the line formed by sewing together pieces of cloth, leather, etc. **2.** any line between two edges; crack or fissure; groove. **3.** *Geol.* a comparatively thin layer or stratum; a bed, as of coal. *–v.t.* **4.** to join with a seam; sew the seams of. **5.** to mark with wrinkles, scars, etc.; furrow. *–v.i.* **6.** to become cracked, scarred, or furrowed. –**seamer**, *n.* –**seamless**, *adj.* –**seamlessly**, *adv.*

seamstress /'simstrəs, 'semstrəs/ *n.* a woman whose occupation is sewing. Also, *Rare,* **sempstress**.

seamy /'simi/ *adj.* (**-mier**, **-miest**) **1.** disagreeable; vulgar; sordid: *the seamy side of life.* **2.** having or showing seams; of the nature of a seam. –**seaminess**, *n.*

seance /'seɪɒns/ *n.* a meeting of people seeking to communicate with spirits of the dead with the help of a medium (def. 10). Also, **séance**.

sea perch *n.* **1.** any of a number of Australian marine, usually tropical fishes, mostly of the genus *Lutjanus* as the **scarlet sea perch**, *L. malabaricus*, of northern reef waters. **2.** elsewhere, any fish of the viviparous, almost exclusively marine family Embiotocidae. Also, **ocean perch**.

sea pike *n.* → **barracuda**.

seaplane /'sipleɪn/ *n.* an aeroplane provided with floats, or with a boat-like underpart, enabling it to land on or take off from water.

sear[1] /sɪə/ *v.t.* **1.** to burn or char the surface of. **2.** to mark with a branding iron. **3.** to burn or scorch injuriously or painfully. **4.** to harden, or make callous or unfeeling. **5.** to dry up or wither. *–v.i.* **6.** to become dry or withered, as vegetation.

sear[2] /sɪə/ *n.* a pivoted piece in the firing mechanism of small arms which holds the hammer at full cock or half-cock.

search /sɜtʃ/ *v.t.* **1.** to go or look through carefully in seeking to find something. **2.** to examine (someone) for concealed objects by going through their pockets or the like. **3.** to scrutinise or question: *to search one's feelings, search someone's face.* **4.** to probe (a wound, etc.). *–v.i.* **5.** to seek; make examination or investigation. *–n.* **6.** the act of searching; careful examination or investigation. **7.** the search of a neutral vessel, or the examining of its papers, cargo, etc., as at sea, by officers of a belligerent state, in order to verify its nationality and ascertain whether it carries contraband, etc. **8.** *Law* examination by a purchaser of records and registers at the Land Titles Office to find encumbrances affecting title to property. **9.** *Internet* **a.** → **search function**. **b.** an instance of requesting information by means of a search function. *–phr.* **10. search me**, *Colloq.* I don't know. **11. search out**, to bring or find out by a search: *to search out all the facts.* **—searchable**, *adj.* **—searcher**, *n.*

search-and-destroy *adj.* of or relating to a military operation which aims to find and eliminate specifically targeted enemy personnel or equipment.

search-and-rescue *adj.* of or relating to a rescue mission which depends on first finding the person or persons to be rescued, as with a helicopter rescue of sailors washed overboard.

search engine *n. Computers* software which enables a user to find items on the internet.

search function *n. Internet* a facility provided on a website allowing a user to enter a term which will then be located wherever it may occur in the whole text stored on a site, or in a subsection of a site.

search warrant *n. Law* a court order authorising the searching of a house, etc., as for stolen goods or other evidence of a crime.

sea rights *pl. n.* **1.** the rights of the original inhabitants of a country to have possession of waters adjacent to their land, sometimes including offshore islands, reefs, etc. **2.** the legal recognition of such rights.

sea salt *n.* salt obtained by evaporating sea water, especially in rough crystalline form, suitable to be ground and added to food.

Sea Scout *n.* (*sometimes lower case*) a Scout receiving training in skills related to the sea, boats, etc.

seashell /ˈsiʃɛl/ *n.* the shell of any marine mollusc.

seashore /ˈsiʃɔ/ *n.* **1.** land along the sea or ocean. **2.** *Law* the ground between the ordinary high-water and low-water marks.

seasickness /ˈsisɪknəs/ *n.* nausea or other physical derangement caused by the motion of a vessel at sea.

sea snake *n.* any of the venomous marine snakes with a fin-like tail, constituting the family Hydrophiidae of tropical seas.

season /ˈsizən/ *n.* **1.** one of the four periods of the year (spring, summer, autumn, and winter), astronomically beginning each at an equinox or solstice, but geographically at different dates in different climates. **2.** a period of the year characterised by particular conditions of weather, temperature, etc. **3.** the period of the year when something is best or available: *the avocado season.* **4.** a period of the year marked by certain conditions, festivities, activities, etc.: *the cricket season, a dull season in trade.* **5.** any period of time. **6.** a suitable, proper, fitting, or right time. **7.** *Agric.* the oestrus period in female stock; time for mating. **8.** **→ season ticket.** *–v.t.* **9.** to heighten or improve the flavour of (food) by adding condiments, spices, herbs, or the like. **10.** to give relish or a certain character to: *conversation seasoned with wit.* **11.** to mature, ripen, or condition by exposure to suitable conditions or treatment. **12.** to prepare (timber) for use by drying and hardening it. **13.** to accustom or harden: *troops seasoned by battle.* **14.** to moderate, alleviate, or temper: *to season one's admiration.* *–v.i.* **15.** to become seasoned, matured, hardened, or the like. *–phr.* **16. declare open season on**, to mark out for attack by anybody: *the media declared open season on the hapless entrepreneur.* **17. in good season**, sufficiently early. **18. in season**, **a.** in the time or state for use, eating, hunting, etc. **b.** at the right time; opportunely. **c.** (of female animals) at a stage of sexual receptivity in the oestrous cycle; in heat. **19. out of season**, **a.** not in the time or state for use, eating, hunting, etc. **b.** not at the right time. **—seasoner**, *n.*

seasonable /ˈsizənəbəl/ *adj.* **1.** suitable to the season: *seasonable weather.* **2.** timely; opportune. **—seasonableness**, *n.* **—seasonably**, *adv.*

seasonal /ˈsizənəl/ *adj.* relating to or dependent on the seasons of the year or some particular season; periodical: *seasonal work.* **—seasonally**, *adv.*

seasonal adjustment *n. Econ.* a statistical adjustment to data, as unemployment figures, to remove the influence of regular periodic variations, with the aim of reporting the underlying trend in the data.

seasoning /ˈsizənɪŋ/ *n.* **1.** something that seasons, especially salt, spices, herbs, or other condiments. **2.** *Aust., NZ* **→ stuffing** (def. 3).

season ticket *n.* a ticket valid any number of times for a specified period, usually at a reduced rate.

sea stinger *n.* **→ sea wasp.**

sea swell *n.* a swell occurring in the sea as a result of wind and storm in another area.

seat /sit/ *n.* **1.** something for sitting on, as a chair or bench; the place on or in which one sits. **2.** the part of a chair or the like on which one sits. **3.** the part of the body on which one sits; the buttocks. **4.** the part of the garment covering it. **5.** manner of sitting, as on horseback. **6.** that on which the base of anything rests. **7.** the base itself. **8.** *Carpentry* any surface of intended contact, as the prepared bearing of a beam. **9.** a place in which something prevails or is established: *a seat of learning.* **10.** an established place or centre, as of government. **11.** a place for a spectator in a theatre or the like. **12.** right of admittance to such a place, especially as indicated by ticket. **13.** a right to sit as a member in a legislative or similar body as the House of Representatives. **14.** a right to the privileges of membership in a stock exchange or the like. **15.** a parliamentary constituency. **16.** a directorship of a limited company. *–v.t.* **17.** to place on a seat or seats; cause to sit down. **18.** to find seats for; accommodate with seats: *a hall that seats a thousand persons.* **19.** to fix firmly or accurately in a particular place. *–phr.* **20. take a seat**, to sit down.

seatbelt /ˈsitbɛlt/ *n.* a belt attached to the frame of a motor vehicle, plane, etc. for securing a driver, pilot, or passenger against sudden turns, stops, collision, etc. Compare **child restraint**. Also, **safety belt**.

sea urchin *n.* any echinoderm of the class Echinoidea, comprising marine animals having a more or less globular or discoid form, and a spine-bearing shell composed of many calcareous plates.

sea wasp *n.* any of certain box jellyfishes that have a highly venomous sting, as *Chironex fleckeri* of tropical Australian waters.

seaweed /ˈsiwid/ *n.* any plant or plants growing in the ocean, especially marine algae.

seaworthy /ˈsiwɜði/ *adj.* (of a ship) adequately and safely constructed and equipped to sail at sea. **—seaworthiness**, *n.*

sebaceous /səˈbeɪʃəs/ *adj.* **1.** being, resembling, or relating to tallow or fat; fatty; greasy. **2.** secreting a fatty substance.

sec¹ /sɛk/ *adj.* (of champagne) dry.

sec² /sɛk/ *n. Colloq.* a second: *wait just a sec, please.*

secant /ˈsikənt/ *Maths* *–n.* **1.** *Geom.* a straight line which cuts a circle or other curve. **2.** the ratio of the hypotenuse to the base in a right-angled triangle; the reciprocal of the cosine of an angle. *–adj.* **3.** cutting or intersecting, as one line or surface in relation to another.

secateurs /ˈsɛkətəz, ˌsɛkəˈtɜz, sɛkəˈtɜz/ *pl. n.* a scissor-like cutting instrument for pruning shrubs, etc., typically having a pair of crossed, short, curved blades, and a spring for returning them to the open position; pruning shears.

secede /səˈsid/ *v.i.* (**-ceded**, **-ceding**) to withdraw formally from an alliance or association, as from a political or religious organisation. **—seceder**, *n.* **—secession**, *n.*

sech /sɛʃ/ *n.* hyperbolic secant. See **hyperbolic function**.

seclude /səˈklud/ *v.t.* to shut off or keep apart; place in or withdraw into solitude. **—secluded**, *adj.* **—seclusion**, *n.*

second¹ /ˈsɛkənd/ *adj.* **1.** next after the first in order, place, time, rank, value, quality, etc.; the ordinal of two; 2nd. **2.** alternate: *every second Monday.* **3.** *Music* the lower of two parts for the same instrument or voice: *second alto.* **4.** additional; further: *to get a second chance.* –*n.* **5.** someone or something that comes next to or after the first, in order, quality, rank, etc.: *King Charles the Second.* **6.** *Music* **a.** the interval between two successive notes. **b.** → **alto**. **7.** a helper or assistant, especially to a boxer, duellist, etc. –*v.t.* **8.** to support; assist. **9.** to express support of (a motion, etc.) as a necessary step before further discussion of the motion or voting on it. –*adv.* **10.** in the second place, group, etc. –**seconder**, *n.* –**secondly**, *adv.*

second² /ˈsɛkənd/ *n.* **1.** a sixtieth part of a minute of time; the basic SI unit of time, now defined as the duration of 9 192 631 770 periods of the radiation corresponding to the transition between the two hyperfine levels of the ground state of the caesium-133 atom. **2.** *Geom., etc.* the sixtieth part of a minute of a degree equivalent to $4.848\,136\,8 \times 10^{-6}$ radians (often represented by the sign ″; thus, 12°10′30″ means 12 degrees, 10 minutes, and 30 seconds). **3.** a moment or instant.

second³ /səˈkɒnd/ *v.t.* to transfer (a military officer or other) temporarily to another post, organisation, or responsibility. –**secondment**, *n.*

secondary /ˈsɛkəndri/, *Orig. US* /-dɛri/ *adj.* **1.** next after the first in order, place, time, importance, etc. **2.** belonging or relating to a second order, division, stage, period, rank, etc. **3.** of or taken from something else; derived; not primary or original: *he used too many secondary sources in his essay.* **4.** of or relating to the processing of primary products: *a secondary industry.* **5.** of minor or lesser importance; subordinate; auxiliary. **6.** *Chem.* **a.** involving, or obtained from replacement of, two atoms or radicals. **b.** containing a carbon atom united to two other carbon atoms in a chain or ring molecule. **7.** *Elect.* relating to the induced circuit, coil, or current in an induction coil, etc. **8.** *Geol.* relating to a rock or mineral derived from another, by decay, alteration, etc. **9.** *Birds* relating to any of a set of flight feathers on the second segment of a bird's wing. –*n.* (*pl.* **-aries**) **10.** someone or something that is secondary. –**secondarily**, *adv.*

secondary colour *n.* a colour produced by mixing two or more primary colours, as orange, green, or violet. Also, **secondary color**.

secondary forest *n. Ecol.* forest that has regrown after logging or clearing activities (opposed to *primary forest*).

secondary school *n.* a school providing post-primary education; a high school.

second cousin *n.* See **cousin**.

second-hand *adj.* /ˈsɛkənd-hænd, ˌsɛkənd-ˈhænd/ **1.** obtained from another; not original: *second-hand knowledge.* **2.** previously used or owned: *second-hand clothes.* **3.** dealing in previously used goods: *a second-hand bookseller.* –*adv.* /ˌsɛkənd-ˈhænd/ **4.** after having been owned by another person: *to buy goods second-hand.*

second lieutenant /ˌsɛkənd lɛfˈtɛnənt/ *n. Army* **1.** an officer of the lowest commissioned rank in the Australian Army. **2.** the rank. *Abbrev.:* 2LT

second nature *n.* habit, tendency, etc., so long practised that it is inalterably fixed in one's character: *correcting the English of others is second nature to him.*

second person *n.* See **person** (def. 10).

seconds /ˈsɛkəndz/ *pl. n.* (at a meal) **1.** a second helping. **2.** a second course.

second sight *n.* a supposed faculty of seeing distant objects and future events; clairvoyance.

second wind *n.* **1.** the restoration of more comfortable breathing and the reduction of muscular strain in an ongoing energetic activity, after one has got over the initial stresses. –*phr.* **2. get one's second wind**, to experience a revival of interest, enthusiasm, etc., in a task in hand.

secret /ˈsikrət/ *adj.* **1.** done, made, or conducted without the knowledge of others: *secret negotiations.* **2.** kept from the knowledge of any but the initiated: *a secret sign.* **3.** *Aboriginal English* of or relating to a place or object that is culturally very important; sacred: *I'll take you to the secret spring.* **4.** designed to escape observation or knowledge: *a secret drawer.* **5.** retired or secluded, as a place. **6.** beyond ordinary human understanding. –*n.* **7.** something secret, hidden, or concealed. **8.** a mystery: *the secrets of nature.* **9.** the reason or explanation, not immediately or generally apparent: *the secret of his success.* **10.** a method or art known only to the initiated or the few: *the secret of happiness.* –*phr.* **11. in secret**, secretly. –**secrecy**, *n.* –**secretly**, *adv.*

secret agent *n.* a spy.

secretariat /sɛkrəˈtɛəriət/ *n.* the officials or office entrusted with maintaining records and performing secretarial duties, especially for an international organisation.

secretary /ˈsɛkrətri/, *Orig. US* /-tɛri/ *n.* (*pl.* **-ries**) someone who conducts correspondence, keeps records, etc., for an individual or an organisation. –**secretarial** /sɛkrəˈtɛəriəl/, *adj.* –**secretaryship**, *n.*

secretary-general *n.* (*pl.* **secretaries-general**) the head of a secretariat.

secrete /səˈkrit/ *v.t.* (**-creted, -creting**) **1.** *Physiol.* to separate off, prepare, or elaborate from the blood, as in the physiological process of secretion. **2.** to hide or conceal; keep secret. –**secretor**, *n.*

secretion /səˈkriʃən/ *n. Physiol.* **1.** the process of an animal body, executed in the glands, by which various substances, as bile, milk, etc., are separated and elaborated from the blood. **2.** the product secreted. –**secretory** /səˈkritəri/, *adj.* –**secretionary** /səˈkriʃənəri/, *adj.*

secretive /ˈsikrətɪv/ *adj.* having or showing a disposition to secrecy; reticent: *he seemed secretive about his new job.* –**secretively**, *adv.* –**secretiveness**, *n.*

secret service *n.* **1.** a department of government concerned with national security, particularly with espionage and counterespionage. **2.** official service of a secret nature; espionage.

sect /sɛkt/ *n.* **1.** a subdivision within a larger religious faith or group, characterised by some kind of deviation from the belief or practice of the larger group. **2.** (especially in Christianity) **a.** a religious group regarded as deviating from the general religious tradition to the extent of being heretical. **b.** (*often derog.*) a religious group characterised by strict adherence to its beliefs and by exclusivity, as in resistance to outside influences and insistence on strict qualifications for membership, as distinguished from the more inclusive groups such as those called denominations or churches. –**sectarian**, *adj.*

-sect a word element meaning 'cut', as in *intersect.*

section /ˈsɛkʃən/ *n.* **1.** a part cut off or separated. **2.** one of a number of parts that go together to make a whole: *sections of a fishing rod*; *a section in a book.* **3.** *Aust. Hist.* a tract or plot of crown land made available for use by farmers, builders, etc. **4.** *NZ* an area of land, frequently suburban, as for building a house, etc. **5.** the act of cutting; separation by cutting. **6.** a thin slice of a tissue, mineral, etc., especially for examination under a microscope. **7.** the representation of an object as it would appear if cut by a plane, showing the structure inside; cross-section. **8.** *Mil.* a small unit, which may consist of two or more squads. **9.** *Surg.* a type of operation in which it is necessary to cut open the skin, etc., especially a caesarean section. **10.** a division of a bus route, etc., with a fixed fare. **11.** Also, **section mark.** a mark (§) used to mark a section of a book, chapter, etc., or as a mark of reference to a footnote, etc. **12.** (in some Aboriginal tribes) one of four exogamous kinship and totemic groups, sometimes overlapping with a moiety system. Compare **moiety** (def. 2), **subsection** (def. 2). *–v.t.* **13.** to cut or divide into sections.

sector /ˈsɛktə/ *n.* **1.** *Geom.* a plane figure bounded by two radii and the included arc of a circle, ellipse, or the like. **2.** a mathematical instrument consisting of two flat rulers hinged together at one end and bearing various scales. **3.** *Mil.* one of the sections of a forward fighting area as divided for military operations, etc. **4.** any field or division of a field of activity. Compare **–sectoral**, *adj.*

secular /ˈsɛkjələ/ *adj.* **1.** of or relating to the world, or to things not religious, holy, or spiritual; temporal; worldly. **2.** (of literature, music, etc.) not relating to or connected with religion. **3.** (of education, etc.) dealing with non-religious subjects, or, especially, excluding religious instruction. **4.** happening or celebrated once in an age or century: *the secular games of Rome.* **5.** going on from age to age; continuing through long ages. *–n.* **6.** → **layman. 7.** one of the clergy not belonging to a religious order. **–secularly,** *adv.*

secularism /ˈsɛkjələrɪzəm/ *n.* secular spirit or tendencies, especially a system of political or social philosophy which rejects all forms of religious faith and worship. **–secularist,** *n.* **–secularistic** /sɛkjələˈrɪstɪk/, *adj.*

secure /səˈkjuə, səˈkjʊə/ *adj.* **1.** free from or not open to danger; safe. **2.** not likely to fall, give in, become displaced, etc. **3.** affording safety, usually of a place. **4.** in safe keeping. **5.** free from care; without anxiety. **6.** sure; certain: *to be secure of victory.* **7.** self-confident; poised. *–v.t.* **8.** to get hold or possession of; obtain. **9.** to make secure from danger or harm; make safe. **10.** to make secure or certain; ensure. **11.** to make firm or fast. **12.** to confine or close in. **13.** to make not able to be entered, or nearly so, as a military position. **14.** to make someone to whom money is owed certain of payment by the pledge or mortgaging of property. *–v.i.* **15.** to be safe; get security: *to secure against danger.* **–securely,** *adv.* **–secureness,** *n.* **–securer,** *n.*

secure server *n. Computers* a website which makes use of a security protocol to prevent information such as a purchaser's credit card number or a respondent's personal information being obtained by a third party.

security /səˈkjurəti/ *n.* (*pl.* **-ties**) **1.** freedom from danger, risk, etc.; safety. **2.** freedom from care, worry, or doubt; confidence. **3.** something that secures or makes safe; protection; defence. **4.** protection from or measures taken against the giving away of state secrets, theft, infiltration, damage, etc. **5.** an assurance; guarantee. **6.** *Law* something given or left as surety for the fulfilment of a promise, the payment of a debt, etc. **7.** (*usu. pl.*) stocks and shares, etc.

sedan /səˈdæn/ *n.* a four-door passenger car seating four to six people. Also, **saloon car.**

sedate /səˈdeɪt/ *Med. –adj.* **1.** calm, quiet, or composed; sober; undisturbed by passion or excitement. *–v.t.* **2.** to calm or put to sleep by means of sedatives. **–sedately,** *adv.* **–sedateness,** *n.* **–sedation,** *n.*

sedative /ˈsɛdətɪv/ *adj.* **1.** tending to calm or soothe. **2.** *Med.* allaying irritability or excitement; assuaging pain; lowering functional activity. *–n.* **3.** a sedative agent or remedy.

sedentary /ˈsɛdəntri/, *Orig. US* /-tɛri/ *adj.* **1.** characterised by or requiring a sitting posture: *a sedentary occupation.* **2.** accustomed to sit much or take little exercise. **3.** *Chiefly Zool.* **a.** abiding in one place; not migratory. **b.** denoting animals that seldom move about or are permanently attached to a stationary object. **–sedentarily,** *adv.* **–sedentariness,** *n.*

sediment /ˈsɛdəmənt/ *n.* **1.** matter which settles to the bottom of a liquid; lees; dregs. **2.** *Geol.* mineral or organic matter deposited by water, air, or ice. **–sedimentation** /sɛdəmənˈteɪʃən/, *n.* **–sedimentary,** *adj.*

sedition /səˈdɪʃən/ *n.* incitement of discontent or rebellion against the government; action or language promoting such discontent or rebellion. **–seditious,** *adj.*

seduce /səˈdjus/ *v.t.* (**-duced, -ducing**) **1.** to induce to have sexual intercourse. **2.** to lead astray; entice away from duty or rectitude; corrupt. **3.** to win over; entice. **–seducer,** *n.* **–seducible,** *adj.* **–seduction,** *n.* **–seductive,** *adj.* **–seductively,** *adv.*

sedulous /ˈsɛdʒələs/ *adj.* **1.** diligent in application or attention; persevering. **2.** persistently or carefully maintained: *sedulous flattery.* **–sedulously,** *adv.* **–sedulity** /səˈdjulɪti/, **sedulousness,** *n.*

see¹ /si/ *verb* (**saw, seen, seeing**) *–v.t.* **1.** to observe, be aware of, or perceive, with the eyes. **2.** to look at; make an effort to observe in this way. **3.** to imagine, remember, or retain a mental picture of: *I see the house as it used to be.* **4.** to perceive or be aware of with any or all of the senses: *I hate to see food being wasted like that.* **5.** to have experience or knowledge of: *to see life; to see a bit of variety.* **6.** to view, or visit or attend as a spectator: *have you seen the old part of town?* **7.** to discern with the intelligence; perceive mentally; understand: *do you see where you went wrong?* **8.** to be willing that; to allow: *I'll see you dead first; I can't see an animal suffer.* **9.** to recognise; appreciate: *I don't see the use of that.* **10.** to interpret; regard; consider: *I see the problem quite differently.* **11.** to accept as reasonable or likely; be able to conceive or believe without difficulty: *I just don't see him as prime minister.* **12.** to predict; foresee. **13.** to ascertain, find out, or learn, as by inquiry: *see who is knocking.* **14.** to meet socially; visit. **15.** to visit formally; consult: *to see a doctor.* **16.** to receive as a visitor or the like: *the Minister will see you now.* **17.** to spend time in the company of, especially romantically: *may I see you home?* **18.** to accompany or escort: *see that the work is done.* **20.** *Poker, etc.* to match (a bet) or match the bet of (another better) by making an equal bet. Compare **raise** (def. 25). *–v.i.* **21.** to have or use the power of sight. **22.** to understand; discern. **23.** to inquire or find out. **24.** to deliberate; consider; think. *–phr.* **25. see about,** to deal with or attend to. **26. see here,** an expression used to attract attention, for emphasis, or the like. **27. see in,** to greet; celebrate: *see in the new year.* **28. seeing as** or **seeing how,** since: *Seeing as you got a present, I want one too.*; *Seeing how you are going to the movies, I think I should come too.* **29. see into,** to investigate: *the manager must see into the circumstances of the dismissal of these workers.* **30. see off, a.** to attend the departure of, especially as a courtesy; send off. **b.** to turn away, especially forcibly; cause to leave. **31. see out, a.** to see off. **b.** to continue in (an undertaking) until it is finished. **c.** to live until the end of (a period) or outlive (a person). **32. see over,** to inspect. **33. see things,** to hallucinate. **34. see through, a.** to penetrate or detect: *to see through a disguise; to see through an imposture.* **b.** to remain until the completion of; work to ensure the successful outcome of: *to see a project through.* **c.** to help or support in the achievement or completion of: *her family saw her through university.* **35. see to,** to give attention or care to: *I'll go and see to it now.* **36. see you (later),** a conventional expression used when parting, but not necessarily implying a further meeting.

see[2] /si/ *n. Eccles.* the seat, centre of authority, office, or jurisdiction of a bishop.

seed /sid/ *n.* (*pl.* **seeds** *or* **seed**) **1.** the propagative part of a plant, especially as preserved for growing a new crop, including ovules, tubers, bulbs, etc. **2.** such parts collectively. **3.** *Bot.* a structure containing an embryo plant and food reserves, formed from an ovule after it has been fertilised. **4.** any small, seedlike part or fruit, as a grain of wheat. **5.** (*usu. pl.*) the germ or beginning of anything: *the seeds of discord.* **6.** offspring; progeny. **7.** semen or sperm. **8.** a player who has been seeded: *Jones is number three seed this year.* *–v.t.* **9.** to sow (land) with seed. **10.** to sow or scatter (seed). **11.** *Chem.* to add a small crystal to (a super-saturated solution, or a supercooled liquid), in order to initiate crystallisation. **12.** to sow or scatter (clouds) with crystals or particles of silver iodide, solid carbon dioxide, etc., to induce precipitation. **13.** to remove the seeds from (fruit). **14.** (especially in tennis) **a.** to modify (the ordinary drawing of lots for position in a tournament) by distributing certain outstanding players so that they will not meet in the early rounds of play. **b.** to assign a particular ranking to (a player) for this purpose *–v.i.* **15.** to sow seed. **16.** to produce or shed seed. *–phr.* **17. go** (or **run**) **to seed, a.** to pass to the stage of yielding seed. **b.** to approach the end of vigour, usefulness, prosperity, etc. **–seedless,** *adj.* **–seedlike,** *adj.* **–seeder,** *n.*

seed bank *n.* a store of seeds as a source for their future planting should they become extinct in the natural world.

seed capital *n.* money invested in the early stages of an enterprise or project in the expectation of returns in the medium or longer term.

seedling /ˈsidliŋ/ *n.* a young plant developed from the embryo after germination of a seed.

seedy /ˈsidi/ *adj.* (**-dier, -diest**) **1.** (of a plant) at the stage of yielding seed. **2.** rather disreputable or shabby. **3.** *Colloq.* out of sorts physically. **–seedily,** *adv.* **–seediness,** *n.*

seek /sik/ *verb* (**sought, seeking**) *–v.t.* **1.** to try to find: *to seek a solution.* **2.** to try to get: *to seek fame.* **3.** to try: *to seek to convince a person.* *–v.i.* **4.** to make search or inquiry. *–phr.* **5. be sought after,** to be desired or in demand: *he is much sought after as an entertainer.* **–seeker,** *n.*

seem /sim/ *v.* (*copular*) **1.** to appear to be: *he seemed angry.* *–v.i.* **2.** to appear (to be, feel, do, etc.): *she seemed to enjoy the experience.* **3.** to appear to oneself (to be, do, etc.): *I seem to hear someone calling.* **4.** to appear to exist: *there seems no need to go now.* **5.** to appear to be true or the case: *it seems likely to rain.* **–seemer,** *n.*

seemly /ˈsimli/ *adj.* **1.** fitting or becoming with respect to propriety or good taste; decent; decorous. **2.** of pleasing appearance; handsome. **–seemliness,** *n.*

seep /sip/ *v.i.* **1.** to pass gradually, as liquid, through a porous substance; ooze. **2.** to enter or infiltrate gradually, as ideas. **–seepage,** *n.*

seer /siə/ *n.* **1.** someone who foretells future events; a prophet. **2.** a magician, clairvoyant, or other person claiming to have occult powers; a palmist, crystal-gazer, or the like.

seersucker /ˈsiəsʌkə/ *n.* a fabric, usually striped cotton with alternate stripes crinkled in the weaving.

seesaw /ˈsi,sɔ/ *n.* **1.** a plank or beam balanced at the middle so that its ends may rise and fall alternately. **2.** a children's game in which participants ride up and down on the ends of such a plank. **3.** an up-and-down or a back-and-forth movement or procedure. *–v.i.* **4.** to

move in the manner of a seesaw. **5.** to undergo a reversal or repeated reversals.

seethe /sið/ *v.i.* (**seethed, seething**) **1.** to surge or foam, as a boiling liquid. **2.** to be in a state of physical or mental agitation; to be excited, discontented, or agitated. **–seething,** *adj.* **–seethingly,** *adv.*

segment *n.* /ˈsɛgmənt/ **1.** one of the parts into which anything naturally separates or is naturally divided; a division or section. **2.** *Geom.* **a.** a part cut off from a figure (especially a circular or a spherical one) by a line or a plane, as a part of a circular area contained by an arc and its chord, or by two parallel lines or planes. **b.** a finite section of a straight line or curve. **3.** *Zool.* any of the rings that compose the body of an arthropod, or other animal with a comparable structure, or one of the sections of a limb between the joints. *–v.t.* /sɛgˈmɛnt/ **4.** to separate or divide into segments. *–v.i.* /sɛgˈmɛnt/ **5.** to become separated or divided into segments. **–segmentary** /ˈsɛgməntəri, -tri/, **segmental** /sɛgˈmɛntl/, *adj.* **–segmentation** /sɛgmənˈteɪʃən/, *n.*

segregate *v.t.* /ˈsɛgrəgeɪt/ **1.** to separate from the others; isolate. **2.** to impose a policy of segregation on (a particular racial, religious, or other group). **3.** to impose a policy of segregation on (a place, community, or state). *–v.i.* /ˈsɛgrəgeɪt/ **4.** to separate or go apart. **5.** *Biol.* (of allelomorphic characters) to separate according to Mendel's laws. *–adj.* /ˈsɛgrəgət/ **6.** set apart. **–segregation,** *n.* **–segregative,** *adj.* **–segregator,** *n.*

segue /ˈsɛgweɪ/ *n.* **1.** *Music* a smooth transition from one piece of music to another. **2.** any smooth transition, as from one topic of discussion to another. *–phr.* (**segued, seguing**) **3. segue into,** a. *Music* to move smoothly from one piece of music into (another) without a break. **b.** to make an effortless change of subject. **c.** to move smoothly into (a new state, activity, etc.) without a break: *to segue into a new relationship.*

seismic /ˈsaɪzmɪk/ *adj.* relating to, of the nature of, or caused by an earthquake. Also, **seismal, seismical.** **–seismically,** *adv.*

seismo- a word element meaning 'seismic', as in *seismology.*

seismograph /ˈsaɪzməgræf, -graf/ *n.* an instrument for measuring and recording vibrations within the earth as earthquakes. **–seismographic** /saɪzməˈgræfɪk/, *adj.*

seismology /saɪzˈmɒlədʒi/ *n.* the branch of geology that deals with earthquakes and their phenomena. **–seismologic** /saɪzməˈlɒdʒɪk/, **seismological** /saɪzməˈlɒdʒɪkəl/, *adj.* **–seismologically,** /saɪzməˈlɒdʒɪkli/, *adv.* **–seismologist,** *n.*

seize /siz/ *verb* (**seized, seizing**) *–v.t.* **1.** to lay hold of suddenly or forcibly; grasp: *to seize a weapon.* **2.** to grasp with the mind: *to seize an idea.* **3.** to take possession of by force or at will: *to seize enemy ships.* **4.** to take possession or control of as if by suddenly laying hold: *panic seized the crowd.* **5.** to take possession of by legal authority; confiscate: *to seize smuggled goods.* **6.** to take advantage of promptly: *to seize an opportunity.* *–v.i.* Also, **seize up. 7.** to become jammed or stuck solid, as an engine through excessive heat. **–seizer;** *Law,* **seizor** /ˈsizə, -zɔ/, *n.*

seizure /ˈsiʒə/ *n.* **1.** the act of seizing. **2.** a taking possession, legally or by force. **3.** a sudden attack, as of disease.

seldom /ˈsɛldəm/ *adv.* rarely; infrequently; not often.

select /səˈlɛkt/ *v.t.* **1.** to choose in preference to another or others; pick out. **2.** *Computers* to click the mouse on (a target icon, link, etc.) to perform an operation, as to open a file, open a window, delete, etc. *–adj.* **3.** selected; chosen in preference to others. **4.** choice; of special value or excellence. **5.** carefully or fastidiously chosen; exclusive: *a select party.* **–selectness,** *n.* **–selector,** *n.*

selection /sə'lɛkʃən/ *n.* **1.** the act of selecting or the fact of being selected; choice: *his selection for the team pleased him.* **2.** the thing or things selected: *take your selection to the counter.* **3.** a range of goods, etc., to choose from: *a wide selection of hats.* **4.** *Aust., NZ Hist.* a block of land acquired under the system of free selection. **5.** *Aust.* a farm (usually small). **6.** *Biol.* the singling out of certain forms of animal and vegetable life for reproduction and continuing the species, either by natural causes, or by human intervention.

selective /sə'lɛktɪv/ *adj.* **1.** having the function or power of selecting; making selection. **2.** fastidious; discriminating. **3.** characterised by selection. **4.** biased: *selective reporting.* **5.** *Educ.* of or relating to a school to which entry is restricted to those applicants who successfully complete a prescribed test or series of tests. **–selectively,** *adv.*

seleno- **1.** a word element meaning 'moon', as in *selenology.* **2.** *Chem.* a combining form of *selenium.*

self /sɛlf/ *n.* (*pl.* **selves**) **1.** a person or thing referred to with respect to individuality; one's own person: *one's own self.* **2.** one's nature, character, etc.: *one's better self.* **3.** personal interest; selfishness. *–pron.* (*pl.* **selves**) **4.** myself, himself, etc.: *to make a cheque payable to self.*

self- prefixal use of *self,* appearing in various parts of speech, expressing principally reflexive action, e.g., subject identical with direct object, as in *self-control, self-government, self-help;* with indirect-object or adverbial-type relations, as in *self-conscious, self-centred, self-evident.*

self-assurance *n.* self-confidence. **–self-assured,** *adj.*

self-centred *adj.* **1.** engrossed in self; selfish. **2.** centred in oneself or itself. **3.** being itself fixed as a centre. **–self-centredness,** *n.*

self-confidence *n.* confidence in one's own judgement, ability, power, etc., sometimes to an excessive degree. **–self-confident,** *adj.* **–self-confidently,** *adj.*

self-conscious *adj.* **1.** excessively conscious of oneself as an object of observation to others. **2.** conscious of oneself or one's own thoughts, etc. **–self-consciously,** *adv.* **–self-consciousness,** *n.*

self-contained *adj.* **1.** containing in oneself or itself all that is necessary; independent. **2.** (of a flat or house) having its own kitchen, bathroom, and lavatory; not necessitating sharing. **3.** reserved or uncommunicative. **4.** self-possessed; calm.

self-control *n.* control of oneself or one's actions, feelings, etc.

self-defence *n.* **1.** the act of defending one's own person, reputation, etc. **2.** *Law* the use of reasonable force against an attacker, constituting a defence in criminal law and tort. **–self-defensive,** *adj.*

self-determination /sɛlf-də,tɜːmə'neɪʃən/ *n.* **1.** determination by oneself or itself, without outside influence. **2.** the determining by a people or nationality of the form of government it shall have, without reference to the wishes of any other nation. **–self-determined** /sɛlf-də'tɜːmənd/, *adj.* **–self-determining** /sɛlf-də'tɜːmənɪŋ/, *adj., n.*

self-esteem *n.* one's sense of one's own worth.

self-evident *adj.* evident in itself without proof; axiomatic. **–self-evidence,** *n.* **–self-evidently,** *adv.*

self-funded *adj.* **1.** paid for out of private resources as opposed to government funding, subsidy, etc.: *a self-funded trip.* **2.** deriving financial support from private resources: *a self-funded retiree.* **–self-funding,** *adj.*

self-government *n.* **1.** government of a state, community, or other body or persons by its members jointly; democratic government. **2.** political independence of a country, people, region, etc. **3.** the condition of being self-governed. **4.** self-control. **–self-governed, self-governing,** *adj.*

selfie /'sɛlfi/ *n. Colloq.* a photograph one has taken of oneself using a digital device, such as the smart phone, usually with the intention of posting it on a social network.

selfie stick *n.* a device which comprises an extendible rod with a flexible grip head for holding a camera, smart phone, etc., allowing the user to take a selfie from an appropriate distance and include more people in the frame, the camera being activated by a remote control or set to operate by a timer.

self-important *adj.* having or showing an exaggerated opinion of one's own importance; conceited or pompous. **–self-importance,** *n.* **–self-importantly,** *adv.*

self-interest *n.* **1.** regard for one's own interest or advantage, especially with disregard of others. **2.** personal interest or advantage. **–self-interested,** *adj.*

selfish /'sɛlfɪʃ/ *adj.* **1.** devoted to or caring only for oneself, one's welfare, interests, etc. **2.** characterised by caring only for oneself: *selfish motives.* **–selfishly,** *adv.* **–selfishness,** *n.*

selfless /'sɛlfləs/ *adj.* unselfish; unheeding of one's own advantage or need. **–selflessly,** *adv.* **–selflessness,** *n.*

self-made *adj.* **1.** having succeeded in life, unaided by inheritance, class background, or other people: *a self-made man.* **2.** made by oneself.

self-opinionated *adj.* **1.** conceited. **2.** obstinate in one's own opinion.

self-possessed *adj.* having or showing control of one's feelings, behaviour, etc. **–self-possession,** *n.*

self-raising flour *n.* wheat flour with baking powder already added. Also, *US,* **self-rising flour.**

self-regulate *v.i.* to operate in a self-regulating manner.

self-regulating *adj.* **1.** (of a machine) capable of automatically and appropriately adjusting itself: *a self-regulating defrost system.* **2.** (of an industry, profession, market, etc.) functioning correctly without externally imposed regulations. **3.** (of a profession, industry, etc.) regulating practices by means of a professional or trade association. Also, **self-regulatory.**

self-respect *n.* proper esteem or regard for the dignity of one's character. **–self-respecting,** *adj.*

self-righteous *adj.* righteous in one's own esteem; pharisaic. **–self-righteously,** *adv.* **–self-righteousness,** *n.*

self-sacrifice *n.* sacrifice of one's interests, desires, etc., as for duty or the good of another. **–self-sacrificing,** *adj.*

selfsame /'sɛlfseɪm/ *adj.* (the) very same; identical. **–selfsameness** /sɛlf'seɪmnəs/, *n.*

self-satisfaction *n.* satisfaction with oneself, one's achievements, etc.; smugness. **–self-satisfied,** *adj.*

self-seeking *n.* **1.** the seeking of one's own interest or selfish ends. *–adj.* **2.** given to or characterised by self-seeking; selfish. **–self-seeker,** *n.*

self-service *adj.* (of a service station, restaurant, shop, etc.) operating on the principle that the customers perform part or all of the service themselves. Also, **self-serve.**

self-serving *adj.* **1.** of or relating to a person who assiduously seeks their own advantage, often to the disadvantage of others: *a self-serving swine. –n.* **2.** the actions of such a person: *I am tired of his self-serving.*

self-starter *n.* **1.** a device which starts an internal combustion engine, other than a crank or an auxiliary turning engine. **2.** someone who acts on personal initiative and does not require external motivation as an encouragement to work.

self-sufficient *adj.* **1.** able to supply one's own needs. **2.** having undue confidence in one's own resources, powers, etc. Also, **self-sufficing. –self-sufficiency,** *n.*

self-worth *n.* a self-valuation that recognises the best of one's talents, attributes, etc.

sell /sɛl/ *verb* (**sold, selling**) −*v.t.* **1.** to give up or make over for a consideration; dispose of to a purchaser for a price. **2.** to deal in; keep for sale. **3.** to act as a dealer in or seller of: *he sells insurance.* **4.** to facilitate or induce the sale of: *the package sells the product.* **5.** to induce or attempt to induce purchasers for: *he used to be a good actor, but now he is selling soap on television.* **6.** to cause to be accepted: *to sell an idea to the public.* **7.** *Colloq.* to cheat or hoax. −*v.i.* **8.** to sell something; engage in selling. **9.** to be on sale; find purchasers. **10.** to win acceptance, approval, or adoption. −*n. Colloq.* **11.** an act of selling or salesmanship. Compare **hard sell, soft sell. 12.** a hoax or deception. **13.** a disappointment. −*phr.* **14. be sold on,** *Colloq.* to be very enthusiastic about. **15. sell dearly,** to part with after great and protracted resistance: *to sell one's life dearly.* **16. sell down the river,** *Colloq.* to betray; deceive. **17. sell off,** to sell at reduced prices, or with some other inducement for quick sale. **18. sell one's body,** to become a prostitute. **19. sell out, a.** to dispose of (goods or a particular product) entirely by selling; have none left of. **b.** *Colloq.* to abandon one's principles, beliefs, lifestyle, etc., motivated by self-interested or monetary considerations rather than idealistic concerns. **c.** *Colloq.* to betray. **20. sell up, a.** to liquidate by selling the assets of. **b.** to sell a business.

selldown /'sɛldaʊn/ *n.* a sale at a reduced price, often to be rid of an unpopular item or one oversupplied.

sellout /'sɛlaʊt/ *n. Colloq.* **1.** a betrayal. **2.** a play, show, etc., for which all seats are sold.

selvage /'sɛlvɪdʒ/ *n.* **1.** the edge of woven fabric finished to prevent fraying, often in a narrow tape effect, different from the body of the fabric. **2.** any similar strip or part of surplus material, as at the side of wallpaper. **3.** *Meat Industry* the fatty edge on a cut of meat. Also, **selvedge.**

selves /sɛlvz/ *n.* plural of **self.**

semantic /sə'mæntɪk/ *adj.* relating to signification or meaning.

semantics /sə'mæntɪks/ *n.* **1.** *Ling.* the systematic study of the meanings of words and changes thereof. **2.** *Logic* the branch of modern logic that deals with the relations between signs and what they denote or signify.

semaphore /'sɛməfɔ/ *n.* **1.** an apparatus for conveying information by means of signals. **2.** a system of signalling by hand, in which a flag is held in each hand at arm's length in various positions. −*v.t.* **3.** to signal by semaphore. −*v.i.* **4.** to use semaphore. −**semaphoric** /sɛmə'fɒrɪk/, *adj.*

semblance /'sɛmbləns/ *n.* **1.** an outward aspect or appearance. **2.** an assumed or unreal appearance; a mere show. **3.** a likeness, image, or copy.

semen /'simən/ *n.* the impregnating fluid produced by male reproductive organs; seed; sperm.

semester /sə'mɛstə/ *n.* (in educational institutions) one of two (or sometimes three) divisions of the academic year. See **term** (def. 5). −**semestral,** *adj.*

semi /'sɛmi/ *n.* (*pl.* **semis**) *Colloq.* **1.** a semidetached house. **2.** semitrailer. **3.** *Sport* a semifinal.

semi- a prefix modifying the latter element of the word, meaning 'half' in its precise and less precise meanings, as in *semicircle, semiannual, semidetached, semiaquatic.*

semibreve /'sɛmibriv/ *n. Music* a note having half the length of a breve, being the longest note in common use.

semicircle /'sɛmisɜkəl/ *n.* **1.** the half of a circle. **2.** anything having, or arranged in, the form of a half of a circle. −**semicircular** /sɛmi'sɜkjələ/, *adj.*

semicolon /sɛmi'koʊlən, 'sɛmikoʊlən/ *n.* a mark of punctuation (;) used to indicate a more distinct separation between parts of a sentence than that indicated by a comma.

semiconductor /ˌsɛmikən'dʌktə/ *n.* **1.** *Physics* a substance whose electrical conductivity at normal temperatures is intermediate between that of a metal and an insulator, and whose conductivity increases with a rise in temperature over a certain range, as germanium, silicon. **2.** *Electronics* a device, as a transistor, which is based on the electronic properties of such substances. −**semiconducting,** *adj.*

semidetached /ˌsɛmidə'tætʃt/ *adj.* partly detached (used especially of a pair of houses joined by a common wall but detached from other buildings).

semi-formal /sɛmi-'fɔməl/ *adj.* **1.** of or relating to a style of clothing which is well-presented but not strictly formal. **2.** of or relating to an occasion at which such clothing is deemed appropriate. −*n.* **3.** a formal dance, as at a school, college, etc., at which a strictly formal dress code is not enforced.

semifreddo /sɛmi'frɛdoʊ/ *n.* an Italian dessert similar to ice-cream but with sufficient aeration, as by the inclusion of whipped cream, whisked egg white, etc., to prevent it from fully freezing.

semillon /'sɛmələn, 'sɛmijon, 'sɛmijõ/ *n.* (*sometimes upper case*) a widely grown white grape variety used in the making of white wines.

seminal /'sɛmənəl/ *adj.* **1.** of or relating to semen. **2.** *Bot.* of or relating to seeds. **3.** highly original and influential. **4.** having possibilities of development. **5.** rudimentary; embryonic. −**seminally,** *adv.*

seminar /'sɛmənɑ/ *n.* **1.** a small group of students, as in a university, engaged in advanced study and original research under a professor or the like. **2.** a meeting organised to discuss a specific topic: *a public seminar on uranium mining.*

seminary /'sɛmənri/, *Orig. US* /'sɛmənɛri/ *n.* (*pl.* **-ries**) **1.** *Roman Catholic Church* a college for the education of men for the priesthood or ministry. **2.** a school, especially one of higher level. −**seminarian** /sɛmə-'nɛəriən/, *n.*

semiprecious /sɛmi'prɛʃəs/ *adj.* (of a gem) having value, but not classified as precious, as the amethyst, garnet, etc.

semiquaver /'sɛmikweɪvə/ *n. Music* a note equivalent to one-sixteenth of a semibreve; half a quaver.

semitone /'sɛmitoʊn/ *n. Music* the smallest interval in the chromatic scale of Western music. Also, *US*, **half-tone.**

semitrailer /sɛmi'treɪlə/ *n.* an articulated goods vehicle consisting of a prime mover and a detachable trailer, supported at the front by the prime mover and at the back by its own wheels; rig.

semivowel /'sɛmivaʊəl/ *n. Phonetics* a speech sound of vowel quality used as a consonant, such as *w* in *wet* or *y* in *yet.*

semolina /sɛmə'linə/ *n.* the large, hard parts of wheat grains retained in the bolting machine after the fine flour has passed through it, which are used for making puddings, etc.

sempstress /'sɛmpstrəs, 'sɛmstrəs/ *n.* → **seamstress.**

senate /'sɛnət/ *n.* (*sometimes upper case*) **1.** an assembly or council of citizens having the highest deliberative functions in the government; a legislative assembly of a state or nation. **2.** a governing, advisory, or disciplinary body, as in certain universities. −**senator,** *n.*

send /sɛnd/ *v.t.* (**sent, sending**) **1.** to cause to go; direct or order to go: *to send a messenger.* **2.** to cause to be conveyed or transmitted to a destination: *to send a letter.* **3.** to compel, order, or force to go: *to send someone away.* **4.** to impel, or throw: *he sent down a fast ball.* **5.** to cause to become: *to send somebody mad.* **6.** *Elect.* **a.** to transmit. **b.** to transmit (an electromagnetic wave, etc.) in the form of pulses. **7.** *Colloq.* to excite or inspire (as a jazz musician, listener, or other person). –*phr.* **8. send ahead,** to dispatch in advance. **9. send away,** to dismiss. **10. send away for,** to write away to have delivered: *to send away for tickets.* **11. send for,** to summon: *to send for a doctor.* **12. send forth** (or **out**), to give off, as light, smell, or sound. **13. send in,** to submit, as an application, request, competition entry, etc. **14. send off, a.** to cause to depart. **b.** to be present to express good wishes at the departure of (someone). **15. send on,** to dispatch some time after the owner has left, as mail, luggage, etc. **16. send packing,** *Colloq.* to dismiss; send away. **17. send someone about their business,** to send someone away, especially forcibly. **18. send up,** *Colloq.* **a.** to mock or ridicule; satirise. **b.** to imprison. **19. send up the river,** *Chiefly US Colloq.* to send to prison. **–sender,** *n.*

senile /'sɛnaɪl, 'sinaɪl/ *adj.* **1.** of, relating to, or characteristic of old age. **2.** mentally or physically infirm due to old age. **3.** *Colloq.* stupid, as if from the mental infirmity of old age. **–senility** /sə'nɪləti/, *n.*

senior /'sinjə/ *adj.* **1.** older or elder (often used after the name of the older of two persons bearing the same name). *Abbrev.*: Sr, Sen **2.** of higher rank or standing, especially by virtue of longer service. –*n.* **3.** someone who is older than another. **4.** a member of the senior class in a university, college, or school. **–seniority,** *n.*

Senior Counsel *n.* (in some legal systems) a member of the senior of the two ranks of barrister. *Abbrev.*: SC Compare **junior** (def. 7).

seniors card *n.* a card identifying the holder as aged 60 or above and therefore entitled to certain concessions.

senna /'sɛnə/ *n.* **1.** a cathartic drug consisting of the dried leaflets of various plants of the genus *Senna,* as **Alexandrian senna** from *S. alexandrina,* an erect shrub with racemes of tawny yellow flowers. **2.** any plant yielding this drug. **3.** any of various similar plants as *S. aciphylla,* **Australian senna** and *Sutherlandia frutescens,* **bladder senna.**

sensation /sɛn'seɪʃən/ *n.* **1.** the working of the senses. **2.** a mental condition produced through an organ of sense or a physical feeling: *a sensation of fear; a sensation of cold.* **3.** *Physiol.* the ability to pick up stimuli. **4.** a mental feeling, especially of excitement. **5.** a state of excited feeling among people, caused by some event, etc. **6.** a cause of such feeling or interest. **–sensational,** *adj.*

sensationalism /sɛn'seɪʃənəlɪzəm/ *n.* **1.** matter, language, or style producing or designed to produce startling or thrilling impressions, or to excite and please vulgar taste. **2.** the exploitation of cheap emotional excitement by popular newspapers, novels, etc. **3.** the tendency of a writer, artist, etc., to be obsessed with a desire to thrill. **4.** *Philos.* the doctrine that sensation is the sole origin of knowledge. **–sensationalist,** *n., adj.*

sense /sɛns/ *n.* **1.** each of the special faculties connected with bodily organs by which human beings and other animals perceive external objects and their own bodily changes (commonly reckoned as sight, hearing, smell, taste, and touch). **2.** these faculties collectively. **3.** their operation or function; sensation. **4.** a feeling or perception produced through the organs of touch, taste, etc., or resulting from a particular condition of some part of the body: *to have a sense of cold.* **5.** a faculty or function of the mind analogous to sensation: *the moral sense.* **6.** any special capacity for perception, estimation, appreciation, etc.: *a sense of humour.* **7.** (*usu. pl.*) clear or sound mental faculties; sanity. **8.** any more or less vague perception or impression: *a sense of security.* **9.** a mental discernment, realisation, or recognition: *a just sense of the worth of a thing.* **10.** the recognition of something as incumbent or fitting: *a*

sense of duty. **11.** sound practical intelligence; common sense: *he has no sense.* **12.** what is sensible or reasonable: *to talk sense.* **13.** the meaning, or one of the meanings, of a word, statement, or a passage. **14.** the approximate, or the general overall meaning of a speech, book, essay, etc. –*v.t.* (**sensed, sensing**) **15.** to perceive by or as by the senses; become aware of. **16.** to perceive without certainty; be aware of dimly, vaguely or without positive sensory confirmation. **17.** to comprehend or understand, especially instinctively rather than by rational means. –*phr.* **18. in a sense,** according to one interpretation; in a way; in one but not every way. **19. make sense,** to be intelligible or acceptable. **20. make sense of,** to understand. **–senseless,** *adj.*

sensibility /sɛnsə'bɪləti/ *n.* (*pl.* **-ties**) **1.** the ability to feel; responsiveness to sensory stimuli. **2.** sharpness of emotion and fine feeling.

sensible /'sɛnsəbəl/ *adj.* **1.** having, using, or showing good sense or sound judgement. **2.** appreciable; considerable: *a sensible reduction.* **3.** capable of being perceived by the senses: *the sensible universe.* **4.** capable of feeling or perceiving, as organs or parts of the body. **5.** perceptible to the mind. **–sensibleness,** *n.* **–sensibly,** *adv.*

sensitise /'sɛnsətaɪz/ *v.t.* **1.** to render sensitive. **2.** *Photography* to render (a plate, film, etc.) sensitive to light or other forms of radiant energy. Also, **sensitize.** **–sensitisation** /sɛnsətaɪ'zeɪʃən/, *n.* **–sensitiser,** *n.*

sensitive /'sɛnsətɪv/ *adj.* **1.** having sensation. **2.** easily influenced or affected. **3.** having sharp mental or emotional sensibility. **4.** arousing strong feelings or reaction: *a sensitive issue.* **5.** (of a body part, etc.) having a low threshold of feeling. **6.** highly affected by certain agents, as photographic plates, films, or paper are to light. **7.** *Radio* easily affected by outside influences, especially by radio waves. **–sensitively,** *adv.* **–sensitiveness, sensitivity** /sɛnsə'tɪvəti/, *n.*

sensor /'sɛnsə/ *n.* **1.** an electronic device in a spacesuit or the like which detects a change in some function of the wearer, especially a physiological change, and converts it into a signal for measuring, recording, or for the taking of some action. **2.** any similar device which detects a variable quantity and converts it into a signal.

sensor light *n.* a light controlled by a motion detector which switches on automatically in response to movement in its vicinity.

sensory /'sɛnsəri/ *adj.* **1.** relating to sensation: *sensory deprivation.* **2.** *Physiol.* denoting a structure that conveys an impulse which results or tends to result in sensation, as a nerve.

sensual /'sɛnʃuəl/ *adj.* **1.** excessively inclined to the gratification of the senses; voluptuous. **2.** of or relating to the gratification of the senses or the indulgence of appetite. **3.** of or relating to the senses or physical sensation. **4.** of or relating to the doctrine of sensationalism. **–sensually,** *adv.* **–sensuality,** *n.*

sensuous /'sɛnʃuəs/ *adj.* **1.** of or relating to the senses. **2.** perceived by or affecting the senses: *the sensuous qualities of music.* **3.** readily affected through the senses: *a sensuous temperament.* **–sensuously,** *adv.* **–sensuousness,** *n.*

sent /sɛnt/ *v.* past tense and past participle of **send.**

sentence /'sɛntəns/ *n.* **1.** *Gram.* a linguistic form (a word or a sequence of words arranged in a grammatical construction) which is not part of any larger construction, typically expressing an independent statement, inquiry, command, or the like, as, *Fire!* or *Summer is here* or *Who's there?* **2.** *Law* **a.** an authoritative decision; a judicial judgement or decree, especially the judicial determination of the punishment to be inflicted on a convicted criminal. **b.** the punishment itself. –*v.t.*

(**-tenced, -tencing**) **3.** to pronounce sentence upon; condemn to punishment. **–sentencer,** *n.*

sententious /sɛnˈtɛnʃəs/ *adj.* **1.** characterised by many pithy sayings or maxims: *sententious style.* **2.** affectedly judicial in utterance; moralising; self-righteous. **–sententiously,** *adv.* **–sententiousness,** *n.*

sentient /ˈsɛntiənt, ˈsɛnʃənt/ *adj.* **1.** that feels; having the power of perception by the senses. **2.** characterised by sensation. **–sentiently,** *adv.*

sentiment /ˈsɛntəmənt/ *n.* **1.** a mental attitude to something; opinion. **2.** a mental feeling; emotion: *a sentiment of pity.* **3.** refined or tender emotion. **4.** a showing of feeling or sensibility in literature, art, or music.

sentimental /sɛntəˈmɛntl/ *adj.* **1.** expressive of or appealing to sentiment or the tender emotions: *a sentimental song.* **2.** relating to or dependent on sentiment: *sentimental reasons.* **3.** weakly emotional; mawkishly susceptible or tender: *a sentimental schoolgirl.* **4.** characterised by or showing sentiment or refined feeling. **–sentimentalist,** *n.* **–sentimentalism,** *n.* **–sentimentally,** *adv.* **–sentimentality,** *n.*

sentimental value *n.* the value which something often of little or no monetary value has because of its ability to arouse sentiments.

sentinel /ˈsɛntənəl/ *n.* someone who watches or stands as if watching.

sentry /ˈsɛntri/ *n.* (*pl.* **-ries**) **1.** a soldier stationed at a place to keep guard and prevent the passage of unauthorised persons, watch for fires, etc.; a sentinel. **2.** a member of a guard or watch.

sepal /ˈsipəl/ *n. Bot.* any of the individual leaves or parts of the calyx of a flower.

separate *v.t.* /ˈsɛpəreɪt/ **1.** to keep apart or divide, as by an intervening barrier, space, etc. **2.** to put apart; part: *to separate persons fighting.* **3.** to disconnect; disunite: *to separate church and state.* **4.** to remove from personal association, as a married person. **5.** to part or divide (an assemblage, mass, compound, etc.) into individuals, components, or elements. **6.** Also, **separate out**. to take by such parting or dividing: *separate metal from ore.* –*v.i.* /ˈsɛpəreɪt/ **7.** to draw or come apart; become disconnected or disengaged. **8.** to become parted from a mass or compound, as crystals. **9.** (of a married couple) to stop living together but without becoming divorced. –*adj.* /ˈsɛprət/ **10.** separated, disconnected, or disjoined. **11.** unconnected or distinct: *two separate questions.* **12.** being or standing apart; cut off from access: *separate houses.* **13.** existing or maintained independently: *separate organisations.* **14.** individual or particular: *each separate item.* –*phr.* **15. separate from,** to part company with; withdraw from personal association with. **16. separate the sheep from the goats,** to distinguish the good, worthy, or superior people or things from the rest. **–separately,** *adv.* **–separateness,** *n.* **–separation** /sɛpəˈreɪʃən/, *n.*

separatist /ˈsɛprətəst, ˈsɛpərə-/ *n.* **1.** an advocate of separation, especially ecclesiastical or political separation. **2.** (formerly) someone who advocated the separation from England of the administrative and judicial functions of the colonies in Australia, and their independence of each other. **–separatism,** *n.*

sepia /ˈsipiə/ *n.* **1.** a brown colouring matter obtained from the ink-like substance produced by various cuttlefish, and used in drawing. **2.** a drawing made with sepia. **3.** a dark brown. **4.** *Photography* a photograph in sepia colours. –*adj.* **5.** of a brown like that of sepia ink.

sepsis /ˈsɛpsəs/ *n. Pathol.* local or generalised bacterial invasion of the body, especially by pyogenic organisms: *dental sepsis, wound sepsis.*

sept- a prefix meaning 'seven', as in *septet.*

September /sɛpˈtɛmbə/ *n.* the ninth month of the year, containing 30 days.

septennial /sɛpˈtɛniəl/ *adj.* **1.** occurring every seven years. **2.** of or for seven years. **–septennially,** *adv.*

septet /sɛpˈtɛt/ *n.* **1.** any group of seven persons or things. **2.** a company of seven singers or players. **3.** a musical composition for seven voices or instruments. Also, **septette.**

septic[1] /ˈsɛptɪk/ *adj.* **1.** infective, usually with a pus-forming microbe. **2.** of or relating to sepsis; infected. **–septicity** /sɛpˈtɪsəti/, *n.*

septic[2] /ˈsɛptɪk/ *n. Colloq.* (*sometimes derog.*) an American.

septicaemia /sɛptəˈsimiə/ *n. Pathol.* the invasion and persistence of pathogenic bacteria in the bloodstream. Also, **septicemia.** **–septicaemic,** *adj.*

septic tank *n.* a tank in which solid organic sewage is decomposed and purified by anaerobic bacteria.

septum /ˈsɛptəm/ *n.* (*pl.* **septa** /ˈsɛptə/) **1.** *Biol.* a dividing wall, membrane, or the like in a plant or animal structure; a dissepiment. **2.** an osmotic membrane.

sepulchre /ˈsɛpəlkə/ *n.* **1.** a tomb, grave, or burial place. **2.** *Eccles.* a structure or a recess in some churches of the Middle Ages in which the sacred elements, the cross, etc., were deposited with due ceremonies on Good Friday to be taken out at Easter, in commemoration of Christ's entombment and resurrection (often called **Easter sepulchre**). –*v.t.* (**-chred, -chring**) **3.** to place in a sepulchre; bury. Also, *US,* **sepulcher.** **–sepulchral,** *adj.*

sequel /ˈsikwəl/ *n.* **1.** a literary work, film, etc., complete in itself, but continuing a preceding work. **2.** an event or circumstance following something; subsequent course of affairs. **3.** a result, consequence, or inference.

sequence /ˈsikwəns/ *n.* **1.** the following of one thing after another; succession. **2.** the order of following one after the other: *a list of books in alphabetical sequence.* **3.** a collection of poems or songs related to a particular theme: *a sonnet sequence.* Compare **cycle** (def. 4). **4.** something that follows; result; consequence. **5.** *Music* a pattern of notes or chords repeated at different pitches. **6.** *Film* a part of a story set in the same place and time, and without breaks of any kind. **7.** *Maths* a finite or countable set of numbers, arranged in order. **8.** *Cards* a set of three or more cards following one another in order of value. –*v.t.* **9.** to order or place in a sequence: *they sequenced the proceedings so that the mayor could leave early.* **–sequential,** *adj.*

sequester /səˈkwɛstə, si-/ *v.t.* **1.** to remove or withdraw into solitude or retirement; seclude. **2.** to remove or separate. **3.** to remove (a gas) from the atmosphere and store it to mitigate the effects of greenhouse gases. **4.** Also, **sequestrate.** *Law* to remove (property) temporarily from the possession of the owner; seize and hold, as the property and income of a debtor, until legal claims are satisfied. **–sequestrator** /ˈsɛkwəstreɪtə, ˈsi-/, *n.* **–sequestration** /sɛkwəsˈtreɪʃən/, *n.*

sequestered /səˈkwɛstəd, si-/ *adj.* secluded or out-of-the-way: *a sequestered village.*

sequin /ˈsikwən/ *n.* a small shining disc or spangle used to ornament a dress, etc. **–sequined, sequinned,** *adj.*

seraph /ˈsɛrəf/ *n.* (*pl.* **-aphs** or **-aphim** /-əfɪm/) **1.** *Bible* one of the celestial beings hovering above God's throne in Isaiah's vision. Isaiah 6. **2.** *Theology* a member of the highest order of angels, often represented as a child's head with wings above, below, and on each side. See **angel** (def. 1). **–seraphic** /səˈræfɪk/, *adj.*

sere[1] /sɪə/ *adj.* dry; withered.

sere[2] /sɪə/ *n.* the series of stages in the development of a plant community on a particular site over a period of time. **–seral,** *adj.*

serenade /sɛrəˈneɪd/ *n.* **1.** a complimentary performance of vocal or instrumental music in the open air at night, as by a man under the window of his lover. **2.** a piece of music suitable for such performance. *–v.t.* **3.** to entertain with a serenade. **–serenader**, *n.*

serendipity /sɛrən'dɪpəti/ *n.* the faculty of making desirable but unsought-for discoveries.

serene /sə'rin/ *adj.* **1.** calm; peaceful; tranquil: *serene sea*; *a serene old age.* **2.** clear; fair: *serene weather.* **3.** (*oft. upper case*) an epithet used in titles of princes, etc.: *his Serene Highness.* **–serenely**, *adv.* **–sereneness**, *n.* **–serenity**, *n.*

serf /sɜf/ *n.* (in medieval times) a person in a condition of servitude, required to render services to his or her lord, and commonly attached to the lord's land and transferred with it from one owner to another. **–serfdom** /'sɜfdəm/, **serfhood**, *n.*

serge /sɜdʒ/ *n.* **1.** a twilled worsted or woollen fabric used especially for clothing. **2.** cotton, rayon, or silk in a twill weave.

sergeant /'sadʒənt/ *n.* **1.** *Army* **a.** a non-commissioned officer in the Australian Army ranking below staff sergeant and above corporal. **b.** the rank. *Abbrev.*: SGT **2.** *Air Force* **a.** a non-commissioned officer in the Royal Australian Air Force ranking below flight sergeant and above corporal. **b.** the rank. *Abbrev.*: SGT **3.** a police officer ranking between constable and inspector. **–sergeancy** /'sadʒənsi/, **sergeantship**, *n.*

serial /'sɪəriəl/ *n.* **1.** anything published, broadcast, etc., in many instalments at regular intervals, as a story appearing in successive issues of a magazine. *–adj.* **2.** published in instalments or successive parts: *a serial story.* **3.** of, relating to, or arranged in an ordered sequence. **4. a.** of or relating to someone who repeats an action, often an offence or misdemeanour, a number of times: *a serial adulterer.* **b.** of or relating to an event, often unpleasant, which occurs repeatedly: *a serial failure.* **–serially**, *adv.*

serial killer *n.* someone who murders a number of people over a period of time, following a similar pattern of behaviour in each case.

serial number *n.* an individual number given to a particular person, article, etc., for identification.

serial port *n. Computers* a port which enables data to be sent or received one bit at a time. Compare **parallel port**.

series /'sɪəriz/ *n.* (*pl.* **-ries**) **1.** a number of things, events, etc., ranged or occurring in spatial, temporal, or other succession; a sequence. **2.** a set of radio or television programs which comprise a number of episodes but involve the same basic characters. **3.** a set, as of coins, stamps, etc. **4.** a set of volumes, as of a periodical, or as issued in like form with similarity of subject or purpose. **5.** *Maths* the formal summation of the elements of a sequence. **6.** *Music* an arrangement of twelve notes in a particular order taken as the basis of a composition. **7.** *Geol.* a division of a system of rocks, marked by sedimentary deposits formed during a geological epoch. **8.** *Elect.* an arrangement of conductors or cells such that the same current flows through each. The components are said to be **in series** (opposed to *in parallel*). *–adj.* **9.** *Elect.* consisting of, or having, components in series.

serious /'sɪəriəs/ *adj.* **1.** of solemn manner or character; thoughtful. **2.** being sincere; earnest. **3.** demanding serious thought or action: *serious reading*; *serious music.* **4.** important; weighty: *a serious matter.* **5.** giving cause for concern; critical: *a serious illness.* **–seriously**, *adv.* **–seriousness**, *n.*

sermon /'sɜmən/ *n.* **1.** a discourse for the purpose of religious instruction or exhortation, especially one based on a text of Scripture and delivered from a pulpit. **2.** any similar serious discourse or exhortation. **3.** a long, tedious speech. **–sermonic** /sɜ'mɒnɪk/, *adj.*

sero- a word element representing **serum**, as in *serology.*

serotonin /sɛrə'toʊnən/ *n.* a hormone which induces muscular contraction, found in the brain, intestines, and platelets; deficiencies linked to mood disorders, anxiety, etc.

serpent /'sɜpənt/ *n.* **1.** a snake. **2.** a wily, treacherous, or malicious person.

serpentine[1] /'sɜpəntaɪn/ *adj.* **1.** of or relating to a serpent. **2.** moving in a winding course or having a winding form; tortuous; winding. **3.** having the qualities of a serpent; subtle, artful, or cunning.

serpentine[2] /'sɜpəntaɪn/ *n.* a common mineral, hydrous magnesium silicate, $H_4Mg_3Si_2O_9$, usually oily green and sometimes spotted, occurring in many varieties, and used for architectural and decorative purposes.

serrated /sə'reɪtəd/ *adj.* serrate; having a notched or grooved edge.

serum /'sɪərəm/ *n.* (*pl.* **sera** /'sɪərə/ or **serums**) **1.** *Physiol.* the clear, pale yellow liquid which separates from the clot in the coagulation of blood; blood serum. **2.** *Med.* a fluid of this kind obtained from the blood of an animal which has been rendered immune to some disease by inoculation, used as an antitoxic or therapeutic agent. **3.** any watery animal fluid. **4.** (of milk) **a.** the portion left after butterfat, casein, and albumin have been removed. **b.** the portion left after the manufacture of cheese. **–serous**, *adj.*

servant /'sɜvənt/ *n.* **1.** someone employed in domestic duties. **2.** someone in the service of another.

serve /sɜv/ *v.i.* **1.** to act as a servant. **2.** to wait at table; hand food to guests. **3.** to render assistance; help. **4.** to go through a term of service; do duty as a soldier, sailor, councillor, juror, etc. **5.** to have definite use; be of use. **6.** to answer the purpose: *that will serve to explain my actions.* **7.** to be favourable, suitable, or convenient, as weather, time, etc. **8.** *Tennis, etc.* to put the ball in play. *–v.t.* **9.** to be in the service of; work for. **10.** to render service to; help. **11.** to go through (a term of service, imprisonment, etc.). **12.** to render active service to (a ruler, commander, etc.). **13.** to render obedience or homage to (God, a sovereign, etc.). **14.** to perform the duties of (an office, etc.): *to serve his mayoralty.* **15.** to be useful or of service to. **16.** to answer the requirements; suffice. **17.** to contribute to; promote. **18.** to wait upon; set food before. **19.** to set (food) on a table. **20.** to act as a host or hostess in presenting (someone) with food or drink: *may I serve you with some savouries?* **21.** to act as a host or hostess in offering (food or drink) to someone: *we served cocktails to our guests.* **22.** to provide with a regular or continuous supply of something. **23.** to treat in a specified manner: *her car served her well.* **24.** (of a male animal) to mate with. **25.** *Tennis, etc.* to put (the ball) in play. **26.** *Law* **a.** to make legal delivery of (a process or writ). **b.** to present (a person) with a writ. *–n.* **27.** the act, manner, or right of serving, as in tennis. **28.** a portion of food; a serving. **29.** *Aust. Colloq.* a strong rebuke; a tongue lashing: *she gave him a real serve when he came home drunk.* *–phr.* **30. serve out**, to distribute. **31. serve someone right**, to be someone's merited deserts, especially for a damaging treatment of another.

server /'sɜvə/ *n.* **1.** someone who serves. **2.** that which serves or is used in serving, as a serving spoon or fork. **3.** *Eccles.* an attendant on the celebrant during the Mass, who arranges the altar, makes the responses, etc. **4.** *Tennis, etc.* the player who puts the ball in play. **5.** *Computers* **a.** a program which provides services to another computer via a network: *a web server.* **b.** the computer on which the program operates.

servery /'sɜvəri/ *n.* (*pl.* **-ries**) a room or an area near the kitchen in which food is set out on plates.

service /ˈsɜːvəs/ *n.* **1.** an act of helpful activity. **2.** the supplying or supplier of any articles, commodities, activities, etc., required or demanded. **3.** the providing of, or a provider of, a public need, such as communications, transport, etc. **4.** the organised system of apparatus, appliances, employees, etc., for supplying a public need. **5.** the supplying or a supplier of water, gas, or the like to the public. **6.** the performance of duties as a servant; occupation or employment as a servant. **7.** employment in any duties or work for another, a government, etc. **8.** a department of public employment, or the body of public servants in it: *the diplomatic service.* **9.** the duty or work of public servants. **10.** the serving of a sovereign, state, or government in some official capacity. **11.** *Mil.* **a.** (*pl.*) the armed forces: *in the services.* **b.** period or duration of active service. **c.** a branch of the armed forces, as the army or navy. **12.** the act of servicing a piece of machinery, especially a motor vehicle. **13.** public religious worship according to prescribed form and order: *divine service.* **14.** a ritual or form prescribed for public worship or for some particular occasion: *the marriage service.* **15.** a set of dishes, utensils, etc., for a particular use: *a dinner service.* **16.** *Law* the serving of a process or writ upon a person. **17.** *Tennis, etc.* **a.** the act or manner of putting the ball in play. **b.** the ball as put in play. **18.** the insemination of a female animal by the male. –*adj.* **19.** of, relating to, or used by, servants, tradespeople, etc.: *service stairs.* **20.** of or relating to the armed forces. –*v.t.* (**-viced, -vicing**) **21.** to make fit for service; restore to condition for service: *to service a car.* **22.** (of a male animal) to inseminate (a female animal). **23.** to meet interest and other payments on, as a government debt: *to service a debt.* **24.** to meet the needs of (a group of people or organisation) by providing a particular service: *the road safety officer services all the schools in this area.* –*phr.* **25. at someone's service,** ready to help someone; at someone's disposal: *my chauffeur will be at your service during your stay here.* **26. be of service,** to be helpful or useful: *if I can be of service to you please call me.*

serviceable /ˈsɜːvəsəbəl/ *adj.* **1.** being of service; useful. **2.** capable of doing good service. **3.** wearing well; durable: *serviceable cloth.* –**serviceability** /sɜːvəsəˈbɪləti/, **serviceableness**, *n.* –**serviceably**, *adv.*

serviced /ˈsɜːvəst/ *adj.* (of accommodation) provided with services such as cleaning and changing of towels and linen.

service lift *n.* a goods lift.

service station *n.* a commercial premises selling fuel, oil, etc., for motor vehicles, and sometimes offering mechanical repairs. Also, **gas station, petrol station.**

serviette /sɜːviˈɛt/ *n.* a rectangular piece of linen, cotton, or paper, used at table to wipe the lips and hands and to protect the clothes; napkin; dinner napkin; table napkin.

servile /ˈsɜːvaɪl/ *adj.* **1.** obsequious: *servile flatterers.* **2.** of or relating to slaves; proper to or customary for slaves; characteristic of a slave; abject: *servile obedience.* **3.** slavishly exact; without originality. –**servilely**, *adv.* –**servility** /sɜˈvɪləti/, **servileness**, *n.*

serving /ˈsɜːvɪŋ/ *n.* **1.** a portion of food or drink; a helping. –*adj.* **2.** used for dishing out and distributing food at the table: *serving spoon.* **3.** being still in office: *a serving vice-president.*

servitude /ˈsɜːvətjud, -tʃud/ *n.* **1.** slavery; bondage: *political servitude; intellectual servitude.* **2.** compulsory service or labour as a punishment for criminals: *penal servitude.* **3.** *Law* a right possessed by one person with respect to some other person's property, and consisting either of a right to use such property, or of power to prevent certain uses of the other property.

sesame /ˈsɛsəmi/ *n.* **1.** a tropical herbaceous plant, *Sesamum indicum,* whose small oval seeds are edible and yield an oil. **2.** the seeds themselves.

sesqui- **1.** a word element meaning 'one and a half', as in *sesquicentennial.* **2.** a prefix applied to compounds where the ratio of radicals is 2:3, as in *iron sesquichloride* (Fe$_2$Cl$_3$).

sesquipedalian /ˌsɛskwɪpəˈdeɪliən/ *adj.* **1.** (of words or expressions) very long. **2.** given to using long words.

sessile /ˈsɛsaɪl/ *adj. Biol.* **1.** (of flowers and leaves) attached by the base, or without any distinct projecting support, as a leaf issuing directly from the stem. **2.** (of animals) permanently fixed in one place, as a barnacle.

session /ˈsɛʃən/ *n.* **1.** the sitting together of a court, council, legislature, or the like, for conference or the transaction of business: *Parliament is now in session.* **2.** a single continuous sitting, or period of sitting, of persons so assembled. **3.** a single continuous course or period of lessons, study, etc., in the work of a day at school: *two afternoon sessions a week.* **4.** a portion of the year into which instruction is organised at a college or other educational institution. **5.** a period of time during which a person or group of persons performs an activity: *a dancing session, a cards session.* –**sessional**, *adj.*

sestet /sɛsˈtɛt/ *n.* → **sextet** (def. 2).

set /sɛt/ *verb* (**set, setting**) –*v.t.* **1.** to put in a particular place or position: *to set a vase on a table.* **2.** to put into some condition or relation: *to set a house on fire.* **3.** to apply: *to set fire to a house.* **4.** to cause to begin: *to set someone thinking.* **5.** to put (a price or value) upon something. **6.** to fix the value of at a certain amount or rate. **7.** to post, station, or appoint for the purpose of performing some duty: *to set a watch over a camp.* **8.** to incite or urge to attack: *to set the dogs on an intruder.* **9.** to fix, appoint, or ordain: *to set a limit.* **10.** to place or prescribe in an estimation: *to set an early date.* **11.** to present or fix for others to follow: *to set an example.* **12.** to prescribe or assign, as a task. **13.** to prescribe for study for examination: *the examiners have set 'King Lear' this year.* **14.** to compile and prescribe (an examination, etc.). **15.** to put in the proper position, order, or condition for use; adjust or arrange. **16.** to adjust the settings of (a device) for operation. **17.** to cover (a table) with a cloth or cloths and arrange cutlery, crockery, etc., on; lay. **18.** to adjust according to a standard: *to set a clock.* **19.** to fix or mount (a gem, etc.) in gold or the like; place in a frame or setting. **20.** to adorn with, or as with, precious stones. **21.** to fix at a given point or calibration: *to set a micrometer.* **22.** to put into a fixed, rigid, or settled state, as the countenance, the muscles, or the mind. **23.** to cause (something, as mortar) to become firm or hard. **24.** *US* to prove (dough). **25.** to change into a curd. **26.** to cause (hair, etc.) to assume a desired shape, style, or form, as by inserting clips, rollers, etc., when it is wet. **27.** to cause to take a particular direction. **28.** *Surg.* to put (a broken or dislocated bone) back in position. **29.** (of a hunting dog) to indicate the position of (game) by standing stiffly and pointing with the muzzle. **30.** to pitch, as a tune. **31.** *Music* **a.** to fit, as words to music. **b.** to arrange for musical performance. **c.** to arrange (music) for certain voices or instruments. **32.** to furnish (a stage) with the scenery and properties for an act or scene. **33.** to spread (a sail) so as to catch the wind. **34.** *Printing* **a.** to arrange (type) in the order required for printing. **b.** to put together types corresponding to (copy): *to set an article.* –*v.i.* **35.** to pass below the horizon; sink: *the sun sets every evening.* **36.** to decline; wane. **37.** to assume a fixed or rigid state, as the countenance, the muscles, etc. **38.** to become firm (as jelly) or solid (as mortar). **39.** to become a curd, as junket. **40.** (of hair) to assume a desired shape, style, form, etc., by the insertion of clips, rollers, etc., when it is wet. **41.** (of a hunting dog) to indicate the position of game. **42.** to have a certain direction or course, as a wind, current, etc. **43.** *Dancing* to face in a certain direction while moving backwards and forwards or in opposite directions, especially in country dancing and square-dancing: *set to your partners.* –*n.* **44.** the act or state of setting. **45.** a number of things customarily used together or forming a complete assortment, outfit, or collection: *a set of dishes.* **46.** a series of volumes by one author, about one subject, or the like. **47.** a number or group of persons associating or classed together: *the smart set.* **48.** the fit or hang of an article of clothing: *the set of his coat.* **49.** fixed direction or bent, as of the mind, etc. **50.** bearing or carriage: *the set of one's shoulder.* **51.** the indication by a hunting dog of the position of game. **52.** the assumption of a fixed, rigid or hard state, as by mortar, etc. **53.** a radio or television receiving apparatus. **54.** *Tennis* a group of games, considered as a unit in a match. **55.** *Surfing* **a.** the succession of waves, progressing from small ones to large ones to form one group, usually of about seven. **b.** a large wave, suitable for surfing. **56.** a construction representing a place in which action takes place in a film, television production, or the like. **57.** a number of pieces of stage scenery arranged together. **58.** *Hort.* a young plant, or a slip, tuber, or the like, suitable for setting out or planting. **59.** *Maths* any collection of numbers or objects which have some common property. **60.** *Weightlifting* a specified number of repetitions of a particular exercise: *do three sets of bench presses, fifteen reps.* –*adj.* **61.** fixed beforehand: *a set time.* **62.** prescribed beforehand: *set rules.* **63.** deliberately composed; customary: *set phrases.* **64.** fixed; rigid: *a set smile.* **65.** resolved or determined; habitually or stubbornly fixed: *to be set in one's opinions.* **66.** ready; prepared; organised: *all set to go.* **67.** formed, built, or made (as specified): *stockily set.* –*phr.* **68. a set against** (or **on**), *Aust., NZ Colloq.* a grudge against; a feeling of ill will towards. **69. have someone set**, *Aust., NZ Colloq.* to single out someone for dislike, attack, or destruction: *she had him set.* **70. set about, a.** to begin; start. **b.** to attack. **c.** to begin to fight: *he set about him with a club.* **71. set against**, to cause to be hostile or antagonistic to. **72. set aside, a.** to put to one side. **b.** to discard from use. **c.** to dismiss from the mind. **d.** to annul or quash: *to set aside a verdict.* **73. set back, a.** to hinder; stop; delay. **b.** *Colloq.* to cost: *it set him back $10.* **74. set down, a.** to put down in writing or print. **b.** to consider: *to set someone down as a fool.* **c.** to rebuke or snub. **d.** to ascribe or attribute. **e.** to allow (passengers) to alight from a bus, etc. **75. set eyes on**, to see. **76. set forth, a.** to give an account of; expound. **b.** to start. **77. set in, a.** to begin: *darkness set in.* **b.** (of wind, tide, or the like) to blow or flow towards the shore. **78. set off, a.** to explode. **b.** to cause to explode. **c.** to begin; start, as on a journey. **d.** to intensify or improve by contrast. **e.** *Banking* to hold a credit balance on (one account) against a debit balance on another account held by the same person, company, etc. **79. set on, a.** to attack: *three men suddenly set on him.* **b.** to urge or persuade: *to set someone on to cause trouble.* **c.** *Colloq.* having a fixed intention of: *she was set on going to England.* **80. set out, a.** to arrange. **b.** to state or explain methodically. **c.** to start, as on a journey. **d.** to have an intention or goal: *to set out to become prime minister.* **81. set sail**, to start a voyage. **82. set someone up, a.** *Colloq.* to arrange a situation in which a person appears in a bad light or is incriminated falsely. **b.** (sometimes fol. by *with*) to provide what is needed: *his parents set him up with books for university.* **83. set store by**, to consider worthy or important: *she sets no store by what he says.* **84. set the ball rolling**, *Colloq.* to begin a project, etc. **85. set the world on fire**, to achieve fame or notable success. **86. set to, a.** to apply oneself; start, as to work. **b.** to start to fight. **87. set up, a.** to erect. **b.** to start (a business, etc.). **c.** to raise (a cry, etc.). **88. set up as**, to claim expertise as: *to set up as an organiser.* **89. set upon**, to attack, especially suddenly.

seti- a word element meaning 'bristle'.

set square *n.* a flat piece of wood, plastic, or the like, in the shape of a right-angled triangle, used in mechanical drawing.

settee /sɛˈtiː, səˈtiː/ *n.* a seat for two or more persons with a back, sometimes with arms, and usually upholstered.

setter /ˈsɛtə/ *n.* one of a breed of long-haired hunting dogs which originally had the habit of crouching when game was scented, but which are now trained to stand stiffly and point the muzzle towards the scented game, the breed being made up of three distinct groups: Irish setters, English setters, and Gordon setters.

setting /ˈsɛtɪŋ/ *n.* **1.** the surroundings or environment of anything. **2.** that in which something, as a jewel, is set or mounted. **3.** a group of all the combined articles, as of cutlery, china, etc., required for setting a table, or a single place at a table. **4.** the period or locale in which the action of a play, film, etc., takes place. **5.** *Music* a piece of music composed for certain words. **6.** a position or valve to which a device is adjusted for a particular function: *the correct setting on the instrument; to adjust the settings on a television to improve reception.*

settle¹ /ˈsɛtl/ *v.t.* **1.** to appoint or fix definitely; agree upon (a time, price, conditions, etc.). **2.** to place in a desired position or in order. **3.** to pay (a bill, account due, or the like). **4.** to close (an account) by payment. **5. a.** to furnish (a place) with inhabitants or settlers: *the north side of the river was soon settled.* **b.** to provide with a place to live: *he settled two of his sons across the river.* **6.** to establish in a way of life, a business, etc. **7.** to bring to rest; quiet (the nerves, stomach, etc.). **8.** *Colloq.* to cause to cease from opposition or annoyance. **9.** to make stable; place on a permanent basis. **10.** to cause (a liquid) to deposit dregs. **11.** to cause (dregs, etc.) to sink. **12.** to cause to sink down gradually; make firm or compact. **13.** to close up; dispose of finally: *to settle an estate.* **14.** *Law* **a.** to secure (property, title, etc.) on or to a person by formal or legal process. **b.** to terminate (legal proceedings) by mutual consent of the parties. –*v.i.* **15.** Also, **settle up**. to make a financial arrangement; pay. **16.** to take up residence in a new country or place. **17.** to come to rest, as from flight: *a bird settled on a bough.* **18.** to come to rest in a particular place: *a cold settles in one's head.* **19.** to sink down gradually; subside. **20.** to become clear, by the sinking of particles, as a liquid. **21.** to sink to the bottom, as sediment. **22.** to become firm or compact, as the ground. **23.** *Law* (of the parties in a dispute) to come to a compromise before or during the course of a hearing: *to settle out of court.* –*phr.* **24. settle down, a.** to come to a rest; become calm or composed. **b.** to apply oneself to serious work. **c.** to set oneself to a regular way of life, especially upon marrying. **25. settle in**, to move into a new home, job, relationship, environment, etc., and adapt oneself to the new circumstances or surroundings. **26. settle on** (or **upon**), to decide on; arrange: *to settle on a plan of action.* **27. settle with, a.** to pay one's debts to. **b.** to come to an agreement with.

settle² /ˈsɛtl/ *n.* a long seat or bench, usually wooden and with arms and high back.

settlement /ˈsɛtlmənt/ *n.* **1.** the act or result of settling. **2.** arrangement; adjustment. **3.** a colony. **4.** a small village, especially in an area with few people.

settler /ˈsɛtlə/ n. **1.** someone who settles in a new country, especially one who is freeborn and who takes up portions of the land for agriculture. **2.** *Law* someone who disposes of property by creating a succession of interests in it.

set-top box n. a device, connected to a conventional television set, which receives and decodes digital television broadcasts, and which can provide an internet interface through the television. Also, **STB**.

set-up n. **1.** organisation; arrangement; general state of affairs. **2.** *Colloq.* a contest or undertaking which presents no real challenge or problems, as a fixed boxing match. **3.** *Colloq.* a trap; ambush.

seven /ˈsɛvən/ n. **1.** a cardinal number, six plus one $(6+1)$. **2.** the symbol for this number, as 7 or VII. *–adj.* **3.** amounting to seven in number: *seven apples. –pron.* **4.** seven people or things: *seven came to the party.* **–seventh,** adj.

seventeen /sɛvənˈtin/ n. **1.** a cardinal number, ten plus seven. **2.** a symbol for this number, as 17 or XVII. *–adj.* **3.** amounting to seventeen in number. *–pron.* **4.** seventeen people or things.

seventy /ˈsɛvənti/ n. *(pl.* **-ties)** **1.** a cardinal number, ten times seven. **2.** a symbol for this number, as 70 or LXX. **3.** *(pl.)* the numbers from 70 to 79 of a series, especially with reference to the years of a person's age, or the years of a century, especially the twentieth. *–adj.* **4.** amounting to seventy in number. *–pron.* **5.** seventy people or things. **–seventieth** /ˈsɛvəntiəθ/, adj., n.

sever /ˈsɛvə/ v.t. **1.** to put apart; separate. **2.** to divide into parts, especially forcibly; cut; cleave. **3.** to break off or dissolve (ties, relations, etc.). **–severance,** n.

several /ˈsɛvrəl/ adj. **1.** being more than two or three, but not many. **2.** respective; individual: *they went their several ways.* **3.** separate; different: *three several occasions. –pron.* **4.** several persons or things; a few; some. **–severalty,** n.

severance pay n. money paid by a firm to employees or directors in compensation for loss of employment.

severe /səˈvɪə/ adj. **(-verer, -verest) 1.** harsh; extreme: *severe punishment.* **2.** unsmiling; stern: *a severe face.* **3.** serious; grave: *a severe illness.* **4.** simple; plain: *she wears severe clothes.* **5.** hard to endure, perform, achieve, etc.: *a severe test.* **6.** extremely strict, accurate, or methodical: *he lives by severe standards.* **–severely,** adv. **–severeness, severity,** n.

sew /soʊ/ verb **(sewed, sewn** or **sewed, sewing)** *–v.t.* **1.** to join or attach by a thread or the like, as with a needle. **2.** to make, repair, etc., (a garment) by such means. *–v.i.* **3.** to work with a needle and thread, or with a sewing machine. *–phr.* **4. sew up, a.** to close (a hole, wound, etc.) by means of stitches. **b.** to manage (a negotiation, game, etc.) so that a satisfactory conclusion or victory is ensured.

sewage /ˈsuɪdʒ/ n. the waste matter that passes through sewers.

sewer /ˈsuə/ n. an artificial conduit, usually underground, for carrying off wastewater and refuse, as from a town or city.

sewerage /ˈsurɪdʒ, ˈsuərɪdʒ/ n. **1.** the removal of wastewater and refuse by means of sewers. **2.** a system of sewers. **3.** the pipes and fittings conveying sewage.

sex /sɛks/ n. **1.** the character of being either male or female: *persons of both sexes.* **2.** the sum of the anatomical and physiological differences with reference to which the male and the female are distinguished, or the phenomena depending on these differences. **3.** the sexual urge, or its manifestation in life and conduct. **4.** men collectively or women collectively: *the fair sex.* **5.** sexual intercourse. **6.** sexually stimulating or suggestive behaviour: *there is too much sex on TV. –v.t.* **7.** to ascertain the sex of. *–phr. Colloq.* **8. have sex,** to have sexual intercourse. **9. sex up, a.** to arouse sexually. **b.** to add interest, excitement, etc., to: *to sex up a report with an astonishing revelation.*

sex- a word element meaning 'six', as in *sexcentenary*.

sex change n. a change in physical appearance, aided by surgery and hormone therapy, which enables a person to live as a member of the opposite sex.

sexism /ˈsɛksɪzəm/ n. the upholding or propagation of sexist attitudes.

sexist /ˈsɛksəst/ adj. **1.** of an attitude which stereotypes a person according to gender, or sexual preference, rather than judging on individual merits. **2.** of or relating to sexual exploitation or discrimination, especially in advertising, language, job opportunities, etc. *–n.* **3.** someone who displays sexist attitudes.

sex life n. *(pl.* **sex lives)** the totality of the various sex-related activities of a human, an animal, certain plants, etc.: *his was a very active sex life.* Also, **sexlife**.

sex object n. a person regarded solely in terms of their sexual attraction or availability.

sextant /ˈsɛkstənt/ n. an astronomical instrument used in measuring angular distances, especially the altitudes of sun, moon, and stars at sea in determining latitude and longitude.

sextet /sɛksˈtɛt/ n. **1.** any group or set of six. **2.** Also, **sestet. a.** a company of six singers or players. **b.** a musical composition for six voices or instruments. Also, **sextette.**

sex therapy n. the treatment, especially by counselling, of psychological problems relating to sexual relationships. **–sex therapist,** n.

sexting /ˈsɛkstɪŋ/ n. *Colloq.* the receiving or sending of a sexually explicit photograph or video clip on a mobile phone.

sexton /ˈsɛkstən/ n. *Christian Church* a church officer and guardian who is charged with taking care of the church, its contents and the graveyard, ringing the bell, digging the graves, etc.

sexual /ˈsɛkʃuəl/ adj. **1.** of or relating to sex. **2.** arising from the fact or condition of biological sex: *a sexual stereotype.* **3.** having sex or sexual organs, or reproducing by processes involving both sexes, as animals or plants. **4.** having a strong sex drive or having the ability to arouse strong sexual interest. **–sexually,** adv.

sexual discrimination n. discrimination against someone because of their gender.

sexual harassment n. persistent unwelcome sexual advances, obscene remarks, etc., especially when made by superiors in the workplace and when employment status is dependent upon compliance.

sexual intercourse n. **1.** sexual contact involving the genitals of at least one of the individuals. **2.** sexual union between a male and a female by the vagina, usually resulting in ejaculation by the male; coitus; copulation.

sexualise /ˈsɛkʃuəlaɪz/ v.t. **1.** to make sexual in nature: *to sexualise a relationship.* **2.** to imbue with sexual character: *to sexualise a marketing campaign.* Also, **sexualize. –sexualisation,** n. **–sexualised,** adj.

sexuality /sɛkʃuˈæləti/ n. *(pl.* **-ties) 1.** sexual character; the physical fact of being either male or female. **2.** the state or fact of being heterosexual, homosexual or bisexual; sexual preference or orientation: *to make one's sexuality public.* **3.** one's capacity to experience and express sexual desires: *to repress one's sexuality.* **4.** the recognition or emphasising of sexual matters.

sexual politics n. the relationships between men and women influenced by their relative positions of power in society and the manipulation of that power.

sex worker n. someone who earns a livelihood from giving sexual gratification to clients; prostitute.

sexy /ˈsɛksi/ *adj.* (**sexier, sexiest**) **1.** sexually interesting or exciting; having sex appeal. **2.** having or involving a predominant or intense concern with sex: *a sexy novel.* **3.** *Colloq.* (of a project, design, product, etc.) exciting; daring; trendy. –**sexily**, *adv.* –**sexiness**, *n.*

sforzando /sfɔt'sændoʊ/ *adv. Music* with force (used to indicate that a note or chord is to be rendered with special emphasis). *Abbrev.*: sf., sfz. Also, **sforzato**.

SGML /ɛs dʒi ɛm ˈɛl/ *n.* a computer markup language, designed as a multi-platform standard, in which various elements of a document, database, etc., are given tags, providing flexible structure and data retrieval.

shabby /ˈʃæbi/ *adj.* (**-bier, -biest**) **1.** having the appearance impaired by wear, use, etc.: *shabby clothes.* **2.** making a poor appearance. **3.** meanly ungenerous or unfair; contemptible, as persons, actions, etc. –**shabbily**, *adv.* –**shabbiness**, *n.*

shack /ʃæk/ *n.* **1.** a very small, usually roughly built and poorly appointed house; cabin; hut. **2.** *Aust.* a holiday house. –*phr.* **3. shack up** (**with**), *Colloq.* **a.** to live at a place; reside: *you can come and shack up with us till your house is ready.* **b.** to live in sexual intimacy with another.

shackle /ˈʃækəl/ *n.* **1.** a ring or fastening of iron or the like for securing the wrist, ankle, etc.; a fetter. **2.** a hobble or fetter for a horse or other animal. **3.** any of various fastening or coupling devices, as the curved bar of a padlock which passes through the staple. **4.** anything that serves to prevent freedom of procedure, thought, etc. –*v.t.* **5.** to put a shackle or shackles on; confine or restrain. –**shackler**, *n.*

shade /ʃeɪd/ *n.* **1.** the comparative darkness caused by the interception of rays of light. **2.** an area of comparative darkness; a shady place. **3.** comparative obscurity. **4.** a spectre or ghost. **5.** a lampshade. **6.** anything used for protection against excessive light, heat, etc. **7.** a shadow. **8.** degree of darkening of a colour by adding black or by decreasing the illumination. **9.** comparative darkness as represented pictorially; the dark part, or a dark part, of a picture. **10.** a slight variation, amount, or degree: *there is not a shade of difference between them.* –*v.t.* **11.** to produce shade in or on. **12.** to obscure, dim, or darken. **13.** to screen or hide from view. **14.** to protect (something) from light, heat, etc., as by a screen; to cover or screen (a light, candle, etc.). **15.** to introduce degrees of darkness into (a drawing or painting) for effects of light and shade or different colours. **16.** to render the values of light and dark in (a painting or drawing). **17.** to change by imperceptible degrees into something else. –*v.i.* **18.** to pass or change by slight graduations, as one colour or one thing into another. –*adj.* **19.** providing shade: *a shade tree.* –*phr.* **20. cast** (or **put**) **in the shade**, to render insignificant by comparison; surpass. **21. shades of …**, a reminder of; an allusion to someone or something. –**shadeless**, *adj.*

shades /ʃeɪdz/ *pl. n. Colloq.* sunglasses.

shadow /ˈʃædoʊ/ *n.* **1.** a dark figure cast on the ground, etc., by a body blocking a light source. **2.** shade or slight darkness. **3.** a slight suggestion: *not a shadow of a doubt.* **4.** a ghost: *pursued by shadows.* **5.** a faint resemblance: *he is a shadow of his former self.* **6.** a reflected image. **7.** the dark part of a picture. **8.** a constant or powerful threat, influence, etc.: *under the shadow of the atomic bomb.* **9.** a constant companion. **10.** someone who keeps close watch upon another, as a spy, etc. –*v.t.* **11.** to shade. **12.** to cast a gloom over. **13.** to protect from light, heat, etc. **14.** to follow (a person) about secretly, in order to keep watch over their movements. –**shadower**, *n.* –**shadowy**, *adj.*

shadow cabinet *n. Govt* the group of members of the chief opposition party who speak on behalf of the party on major issues.

shady /ˈʃeɪdi/ *adj.* (**-dier, -diest**) **1.** having a lot of shade; shaded: *shady paths.* **2.** shadowy; indistinct; spectral. **3.** *Colloq.* uncertain; questionable; of dubious character or reputation. –**shadily**, *adv.* –**shadiness**, *n.*

shaft /ʃaft/ *n.* **1.** a long pole or rod forming the body of some weapons, as a spear, arrow, etc. **2.** something directed as in sharp attack: *shafts of criticism.* **3.** a ray; beam: *a shaft of sunlight.* **4.** the handle of a hammer, axe, golf club, etc. **5.** a revolving bar serving to transmit motion, as from an engine to various machines. **6.** the body of a column between the base and the top. **7.** either of the parallel bars between which an animal drawing a vehicle is placed. **8.** any well-like passage or vertical or sloping enclosed space, as in a building: *a lift shaft; mine shaft.* **9.** *Bot.* the trunk of a tree. **10.** *Zool.* the main stem of a feather. –*v.t. Colloq.* **11.** (*taboo*) (of a male) to have sexual intercourse with. **12.** to cheat, betray or defraud; treat unfairly.

shag[1] /ʃæg/ *n.* **1.** rough, matted hair, wool, or the like. **2.** a cloth, usually woollen, with a nap on one side. **3.** a coarse tobacco cut into fine shreds. –*adj.* **4.** of, relating to, or having, a shag pile: *shag carpet.*

shag[2] /ʃæg/ *n.* **1.** → **cormorant.** –*phr.* **2. like a shag on a rock**, *Aust., NZ Colloq.* alone; deserted; forlorn.

shag[3] /ʃæg/ *Colloq.* –*v.t.* (**shagged, shagging**) **1.** (*taboo*) to have sexual intercourse with. –*n.* **2.** (*taboo*) an act or instance of sexual intercourse. –*phr.* **3. shag out**, to tire; exhaust. –**shagger**, *n.*

shaggy /ˈʃægi/ *adj.* (**-gier, -giest**) **1.** covered with or having long, rough hair. **2.** unkempt. **3.** rough and matted; forming a bushy mass, as the hair, mane, etc. **4.** having a rough nap, as cloth. –**shaggily**, *adv.* –**shagginess**, *n.*

shag pile *n.* carpet pile which is long and thick.

shah /ʃa/ *n.* a king (especially used as a title of the former rulers of Iran).

shake /ʃeɪk/ *verb* (**shook, shaken, shaking**) –*v.i.* **1.** to move or sway with short, quick, irregular vibratory movements. **2.** to tremble with emotion, cold, etc. **3.** to clasp a person's hand in greeting, agreement, etc. –*v.t.* **4.** to move to and fro with short, quick, forcible movements. **5.** to brandish or flourish. **6.** to bring, throw, force, rouse, etc., by or as by some vigorous movement to and fro; cause to quiver or tremble: *leaves shaken by the breeze.* **7.** to cause to totter or waver: *to shake the very foundations of society.* **8.** to agitate or disturb profoundly in feeling. **9.** to unsettle; weaken: *to shake one's faith.* **10.** to mix (dice) before they are cast. –*n.* **11.** the act of shaking. **12.** tremulous motion. **13.** a tremor. **14.** *Colloq.* an earthquake. **15.** → **milkshake.** **16.** (*pl.*) *Colloq.* a state of trembling, especially that induced by alcoholism, drugs, or nervous disorder. **17.** a dance in which the body is shaken violently in time to music. **18.** *Colloq.* a moment, a short time: *I'll be with you in a shake.* –*phr.* **19. a brace of shakes**, a very short time; an instant. **20. give it a good** (or **fair**) **shake**, *Colloq.* to put one's best efforts into attempting to do something. **21. in two shakes** (**of a lamb's tail**) (or **of a dog's tail**), *Colloq.* in a very short time. **22. no great shakes**, *Colloq.* of no particular importance; unimpressive. **23. shake down, a.** to settle in or retire to a bed, especially a makeshift or temporary one. **b.** to settle comfortably in or adapt oneself to new surroundings, etc. **c.** to bring down. **d.** to cause to settle. **e.** to condition: *to shake down a vessel by a first voyage.* **f.** *Colloq.* to extort money from. **g.** *Colloq.* to search (someone); frisk. **24. shake hands**, to clasp hands in greeting, congratulation, agreement, etc. **25. shake hands on**, to mark a formal, although unwritten, agreement on (a deal, arrangement, etc.) by shaking hands. **26. shake off**, *Colloq.* **a.** to get rid of; free oneself from. **b.** to get away from; elude. **27. shake**

one's head, to turn the head from side to side to indicate reluctance, disapproval, disbelief, etc. **28. shake the dust from one's feet**, to make one's departure, especially with a determination not to return. **29. shake up, a.** to shake in order to mix, loosen, etc. **b.** to upset. **c.** to disturb or agitate mentally or physically. **–shaky**, *adj.*

shale /ʃeɪl/ *n.* a rock of fissile or laminated structure formed by the consolidation of clay or argillaceous material.

shall /ʃæl/, *weak form* /ʃəl/ *v.* (*modal*) **1.** indicating future likelihood: *all this shall be yours.* **2.** expressing intention or expectation, in the first person: *I shall take a taxi; without treatment I shall die; what shall we do?* **3.** expressing resolve, in the second and third person: *you shall do as I say; the owner shall notify the tenant of any proposed inspection.* **4.** used in suggestions: *shall we dance?; shall I open the window?*

shallot /ʃəˈlɒt/ *n.* a plant of the lily family, *Allium ascalonicum*, whose bulb forms smaller bulbs which are used for flavouring in cookery and as a vegetable.

shallow /ˈʃæloʊ/ *adj.* **1.** of little depth; not deep: *shallow water, a shallow dish.* **–n. 2.** (*usu. pl.*) a shallow part of a body of water; a shoal. **–shallowly**, *adv.* **–shallowness**, *n.*

shalwar /ˈʃalˈwɑ/ *n.* → **salwar**.

sham /ʃæm/ *n.* **1.** something that is not what it purports to be; a spurious imitation. **–adj. 2.** pretended; counterfeit: *sham attacks.* **–v.t. 3.** to assume the appearance of: *to sham illness.*

shamble /ˈʃæmbəl/ *v.i.* to walk or go awkwardly; shuffle.

shambles /ˈʃæmbəlz/ *pl. n.* (*oft. construed as sing.*) any place or thing in confusion or disorder.

shame /ʃeɪm/ *n.* **1.** the painful feeling arising from the consciousness of something dishonourable, improper, ridiculous, etc., done by oneself or another. **2.** susceptibility to this feeling: *to be without shame.* **3.** disgrace; ignominy. **4.** a fact or circumstances bringing disgrace or regret. **5.** an unfortunate situation or state of affairs: *it's a shame you had to wait in the rain.* **–v.t. 6.** to cause to feel shame; make ashamed. **7.** to drive, force, etc., through shame. **8.** to cover with ignominy or reproach; disgrace. **–phr. 9. for shame**, *Archaic* an expression of disapproval or reproach. **10. put to shame, a.** to disgrace. **b.** to outdo or surpass. **–shameful**, *adj.* **–shameless**, *adj.*

shammy /ˈʃæmi/ *n.* (*pl.* **-mies**) → **chamois** (defs 2 and 3).

shampoo /ʃæmˈpu/ *v.t.* (**-pooed, -pooing**) **1.** to wash (the head or hair), especially with a cleaning preparation. **2.** to clean (upholstery, carpets, etc.), with a special preparation. **–n. 3.** a preparation used for shampooing. **–shampooer**, *n.*

shamrock /ˈʃæmrɒk/ *n.* a plant with trifoliate leaflets believed to have been used by St Patrick to symbolise the Trinity, especially wood sorrel, *Oxalis acetosella*, white clover, *Trifolium repens*, or lesser yellow trefoil, *T. dubium*.

shandy /ˈʃændi/ *n.* (*pl.* **-dies**) a mixed drink of beer with ginger beer or lemonade.

shanghai¹ /ˈʃæŋhaɪ, ʃæŋˈhaɪ/ *v.t.* (**-haied, -haiing**) **1.** *Naut.* (formerly) to obtain (a man) for the crew of a ship by unscrupulous means, as by force, drugs, or fraud. **2.** *Colloq.* to involve (someone) in an activity, usually against their wishes. **3.** *Colloq.* to steal.

shanghai² /ˈʃæŋhaɪ/ *n. Aust., NZ* → **catapult** (def. 2).

shank /ʃæŋk/ *n.* **1.** that part of the leg in humans between the knee and the ankle. **2.** a part in certain animals corresponding or analogous to the human shank. **3.** the whole leg. **4.** a cut of meat from the top part of the front (**fore shank**) or back (**hind shank**) leg. **5.** that portion of an instrument, tool, etc., connecting the acting part with the handle or any like part. **6.** the long, straight, middle part of an anchor. **7.** *Printing* the body of a type, between the shoulder and the foot. **–v.i. 8.** (of a leaf, flower, fruit, etc.) to decay as a result of disease.

shanks's pony *n. Colloq.* one's own legs, especially as a means of travelling, as opposed to riding on horseback or in a conveyance. Also, **shanks's mare**.

shan't /ʃænt/ *v.* contraction of *shall not*.

shantung /ʃænˈtʌŋ/ *n.* **1.** a silk fabric, a heavy variety of pongee made of rough, spun wild silk. **2.** a fabric imitating this made of rayon or cotton.

shanty¹ /ˈʃænti/ *n.* (*pl.* **-ties**) a roughly built hut, cabin, or house.

shanty² /ˈʃænti/ *n.* (*pl.* **-ties**) a sailors' song, especially one sung in rhythm to work. Also, **chanty, chantey**.

shape /ʃeɪp/ *n.* **1.** the quality of a thing depending on its outline or external surface. **2.** the form of a particular thing, person, or being. **3.** something seen indistinctly, as in outline or silhouette. **4.** an imaginary form; phantom. **5.** an assumed appearance; guise. **6.** a particular or definite form or nature: *the shape of things to come.* **7.** proper form; orderly arrangement. **8.** condition: *affairs in bad shape.* **9.** something used to give form, as a mould or a pattern. **–v.t. 10.** to give definite form, shape, or character to; fashion or form. **–v.i. 11.** to develop; take shape; become (as specified): *shaping as the next top tourist destination.* **–phr. 12. shape up, a.** to stand ready to fight. **b.** to develop; take place in a specified manner; assume a definite form or character: *shaping up as the new CEO.* **13. shape up or ship out**, to perform as required or leave. **14. take shape**, to assume a definite or concrete form. **–shaper**, *n.*

shapely /ˈʃeɪpli/ *adj.* (**-lier, -liest**) having a pleasing shape; well-formed. **–shapeliness**, *n.*

sharam /ˈʃarəm/ *n.* shame brought by an insult to one's honour. Compare **izzat**.

shard /ʃad/ *n.* **1.** a fragment, especially of broken earthenware. **2.** *Zool.* **a.** a scale. **b.** a shell, as of an egg or snail. Also, **sherd**.

share /ʃeə/ *n.* **1.** the portion or part allotted or belonging to, or contributed or owed by, an individual or group. **2.** *Commerce* one of the equal fractional parts into which the capital stock of a limited company is divided, generally classed as either an **ordinary share** or a **preference share**. **–verb** (**shared, sharing**) **–v.t. 3.** to use, participate in, enjoy, etc., jointly. **–v.i. 4.** (sometimes fol. by *in*) to have a share or part; take part. **–sharer**, *n.*

sharebroker /ˈʃeəbroʊkə/ *n.* → **stockbroker**.

shareholder /ˈʃeəhoʊldə/ *n. Commerce* someone who holds or owns a share or shares, as in a company.

share plate *n.* a serving in a restaurant designed as multiple small portions so that several diners can share the same dish.

shareware /ˈʃeəwɛə/ *n. Computers* computer software which is made available free on trial and for which a small fee is paid optionally after the trial period.

sharia /ˈʃariə, ʃəˈriə/ *n.* Also, **sharia law**. **1.** the law based on the Koran, the Sunna, and Arabic tradition, upheld by Muslims. **–adj. 2.** of or relating to this system: *a sharia court.* Also, **shariah**.

sharing economy *n.* an economy in which consumers have shared access to goods and services, rather than having individual ownership, as in car sharing or peer-to-peer accommodation provision. Also, **collaborative economy**.

shark¹ /ʃak/ *n.* any of a group of elongate elasmobranch (mostly marine) fishes, certain species of which are large and ferocious, and destructive to other fishes and sometimes dangerous to humans.

shark² /ʃak/ *n.* **1.** someone who preys greedily on others, as by swindling, usury, etc. **–v.t. 2.** *Ball Games* to intercept (the ball). **–v.i. 3.** *Ball Games* to intercept the ball, especially as a means of winning more than one's share of play from one's own teammates.

shark biscuit *n. Surfing Colloq. (humorous) (derog.)* **1.** a cheap surfboard made from foam rather than fibreglass. **2.** a bodyboard. **3.** a person who is new to surfboard riding. **4.** a bodyboard rider.

sharp /ʃɑp/ *adj.* **1.** having a thin cutting edge or a fine point. **2.** ending in an edge or point. **3.** sudden; abrupt: *a sharp rise in the road*; *a sharp bend*. **4.** (of a person's features) composed of hard, angular lines. **5.** clearly outlined; distinct: *a sharp picture on TV*. **6.** marked; noticeable: *a sharp distinction*. **7.** strong or biting in taste. **8.** piercing or shrill in sound. **9.** very cold: *a sharp wind*. **10.** very painful; distressing. **11.** angry; harsh: *sharp words*. **12.** alert; vigilant: *a sharp watch*. **13.** mentally quick and alert: *a sharp mind*. **14.** wise; shrewd; astute. **15.** cunning to the point of dishonesty: *sharp practice*. **16.** *Music* **a.** above an intended pitch; too high. **b.** (of a note) raised a semitone in pitch: *F sharp*. *–adv.* **17.** precisely: *at one o'clock sharp*. **18.** watchfully; alertly: *look sharp!* **19.** quickly; briskly. **20.** *Music* above the true pitch. *–n.* **21.** *Music* **a.** a note one semitone above a given note. **b.** (in notation) the symbol (♯) showing this. **22.** an implement, utensil, tool, etc., with a sharp point, as a hypodermic needle. *–sharpen, v. –sharply, adv. –sharpness, n.*

sharper /ʃɑpə/ *n.* a shrewd swindler.

shashlik /ʃæʃlɪk/ *n.* → **shish kebab.**

shat /ʃæt/ *v.* past tense and past participle of **shit.**

shatter /ʃætə/ *v.t.* **1.** to break in pieces, as by a blow. **2.** to damage, as by breaking or crushing: *ships shattered by storms.* **3.** to impair; weaken; destroy (health, nerves, etc.). *–v.i.* **4.** to break suddenly into fragments.

shave /ʃeɪv/ *verb* (**shaved, shaved** *or* **shaven, shaving**) *–v.i.* **1.** to remove hair with a razor. *–v.t.* **2.** to remove hair from (the face, legs, etc.) by cutting it close to the skin. **3.** (oft. fol. by *off* or *away*) to cut off (hair, especially the beard) close to the skin: *he shaved his beard off.* **4.** to take thin slices from, especially in order to smooth: *to shave wood.* **5.** to come very near to; graze: *to shave a corner. –n.* **6.** the act or process of shaving. **7.** a narrow miss or escape: *a close shave.*

shaving /ʃeɪvɪŋ/ *n.* (*oft. pl.*) a very thin piece or slice, especially of wood.

Shavuot /ʃəˈvuɒt/ /ʃəˈvuəs/ *n.* a Jewish harvest festival observed on the fiftieth day from the second day of Pesach; Pentecost. Also, **Shabuoth.**

shawl /ʃɔl/ *n.* a piece of material, worn as a covering for the shoulders, head, etc., chiefly by women, in place of coat or hat, sometimes as a decoration.

she /ʃi/ *pron. (personal)*, third person, sing., subjective (*objective* **her**) **1.** the female being in question or last mentioned. **2.** used instead of *it* of things to which female gender is attributed, as a ship. **3.** used instead of *it* in phrases: *she'll be right*; *she's apples. –n.* (*pl.* **shes**) **4.** a woman or any female person or animal (correlative to *he*). *–adj.* **5.** female or feminine, especially of animals: *she-goat.*

sheaf /ʃif/ *n.* (*pl.* **sheaves**) **1.** one of the bundles in which cereal plants, as wheat, rye, etc., are bound after reaping. **2.** any bundle, cluster, or collection: *a sheaf of papers.*

shear /ʃɪə/ *verb* (**sheared** *or* **shore, shorn** *or* **sheared, shearing**) *–v.t.* **1.** to remove by or as by cutting with a sharp instrument: *to shear wool from sheep.* **2.** to cut the hair, fleece, wool, etc., from. *–v.i.* **3.** *Physics* to become fractured by a shear or shears. *–n.* **4.** (*pl.*) scissors of large size. **5.** (*pl.*) any of various other cutting implements or machines resembling or suggesting scissors. **6.** a shearing of sheep (used in stating the age of sheep): *a sheep of one shear* (one year old). **7.** a quantity of wool, grass, etc., cut off at one shearing.

8. any machine using an adaptation of the shearing principle, especially to cut metal sheets. **9.** *Physics* a type of stress applied to an object tending to cause fracture in the plane in which the stress lies. *–phr.* **10. off** (**the**) **shears,** (of sheep) recently shorn. **11. shear of,** to strip or deprive of: *the assembly was shorn of its legislative powers.*

shearer /ʃɪərə/ *n.* **1.** someone who shears sheep. **2.** someone who uses shears on metal, textiles, leather, or other materials.

shearwater /ʃɪəwɔtə/ *n.* any of various long-winged seabirds, especially of the genus *Puffinus*, allied to the petrels, appearing, when flying low, to cleave the water with their wings.

sheath /ʃiθ/ *n.* (*pl.* **sheaths** /ʃiðz, ʃiθs/) **1.** a covering for the blade of a sword, dagger, etc. **2.** any similar covering. **3.** *Biol.* a closely enveloping part or structure, as in an animal or plant. **4.** *Elect.* the covering of a cable. **5.** → **condom. 6.** a close-fitting dress which follows the shape of the body.

sheathe /ʃið/ *v.t.* (**sheathed, sheathing**) **1.** to put (a sword, etc.) into a sheath. **2.** to plunge (a sword, etc.) in something as if in a sheath. **3.** to enclose in or as in a casing or covering. **4.** to cover or provide with a protective layer or sheathing: *to sheathe a roof with copper. –sheather, n.*

sheave /ʃiv/ *v.t.* to gather, collect, or bind into a sheaf or sheaves.

sheaves /ʃivz/ *n.* plural of **sheaf.**

shebang /ʃəˈbæŋ/ *phr.* **the whole shebang,** *Colloq.* the totality of something; the lot; everything.

shed¹ /ʃɛd/ *n.* **1.** an outbuilding, usually for a specific purpose, as storage, work area, etc.: *a tool shed*; *a shearing shed.* **2.** such an outbuilding with a roof but no walls: *a hay shed.* **3.** a small building in the backyard of a family home, often of light construction, used for storage of tools, lawnmower, workbench, etc. *–v.t.* (**shedded, shedding**) **4.** to place or keep (animals) under cover.

shed² /ʃɛd/ *verb* (**shed, shedding**) *–v.t.* **1.** to pour forth (water, etc.) as a fountain. **2.** to emit and let fall (tears). **3.** to cast; give or send forth (light, sound, fragrance, etc.). **4.** to throw off readily: *cloth that sheds water.* **5.** to cast off or let fall by natural process (leaves, hair, feathers, skin, shell, etc.). *–v.i.* **6.** to fall off, as leaves, etc.; drop out, as seed, grain, etc. **7.** to cast off hair, feathers, skin, or other covering or parts by natural process. *–phr.* **8. shed blood, a.** to cause blood to flow. **b.** to kill by violence.

sheen /ʃin/ *n.* lustre; brightness; radiance. *–sheeny, adj.*

sheep /ʃip/ *n.* (*pl.* **sheep**) **1.** any of the ruminant mammals constituting the genus *Ovis* (family Bovidae), closely allied to the goats, especially *O. aries*, which has many domesticated varieties or breeds, valuable for their flesh, fleece, etc. **2.** a meek, timid, or stupid person. *–phr.* **3. on the sheep's back,** (of a country, especially Australia) dependent on sales of wool for national income. **4. separate the sheep from the goats,** to distinguish the good, worthy, or superior people or things from the rest. *–sheeplike, adj.*

sheep dip *n.* **1.** a lotion or wash applied to the fleece or skin of sheep to kill vermin. **2.** a deep trough containing such a liquid through which sheep are driven.

sheepish /ʃipɪʃ/ *adj.* **1.** awkwardly bashful or embarrassed. **2.** like sheep, as in meekness, timidity, etc. *–sheepishly, adv. –sheepishness, n.*

sheepshank /ʃipʃæŋk/ *n.* a kind of knot, hitch, or bend made on a rope to shorten it temporarily.

sheep strike *n.* → **flystrike.**

sheer¹ /ʃɪə/ *adj.* **1.** transparently thin; diaphanous, as fabrics, etc. **2.** unmixed with anything else. **3.** unqualified; utter: *a sheer waste of time.* **4.** extending down or up very steeply: *a sheer descent of rock.* –**sheerly**, *adv.* –**sheerness**, *n.*

sheer[2] /ʃɪə/ *v.i.* **1.** to deviate from a course, as a ship; swerve. –*n.* **2.** the upward longitudinal curve of a ship's deck or bulwarks. **3.** the position in which a ship at anchor is placed to keep it clear of the anchor.

sheet[1] /ʃit/ *n.* **1.** a large rectangular piece of linen, cotton, or other material, used as an article of bedding, commonly one of a pair spread immediately above and below the sleeper. **2.** a broad, thin mass, layer, or covering. **3.** a broad, relatively thin, piece of iron, glass, etc. **4.** an oblong or square piece of paper or parchment, especially one on which to write or print. **5.** a newspaper.

sheet[2] /ʃit/ *n.* **1.** a rope or chain fastened: **a.** to a lower after corner of a sail, or to the boom of a fore-and-aft sail, to control its trim. **b.** to both lower corners of a square sail to extend them to the yardarms below. **2.** (*pl.*) the spaces beyond the thwarts in the forward or the after end of an open boat. –*v.t.* **3.** *Naut.* to trim, extend, or secure by means of a sheet or sheets. –*phr.* **4. sheet home, a.** *Naut.* to extend (sails) to the utmost by hauling on the sheets. **b.** to attach (blame, responsibility, etc.). **5. three sheets in** (or **to**) **the wind,** *Colloq.* intoxicated.

sheet anchor *n.* **1.** a large anchor used only in cases of emergency. **2.** a final reliance or resource.

sheikh /ʃeɪk, ʃik/ *n.* (*oft. upper case*) (in Arab and other Muslim use) **1.** chief or head; the headman of a village or tribe. **2.** the head of a Muslim religious body. Also, **sheik**.

sheila /ˈʃilə/ *n. Aust., NZ Colloq.* (*dated*) **1.** a girl or woman: *a beaut sheila.* **2.** a girlfriend.

shekel /ˈʃɛkəl/ *n.* the principal monetary unit of Israel.

shelf /ʃɛlf/ *n.* (*pl.* **shelves**) **1.** a thin slab of wood or other material fixed horizontally to a wall, or in a frame, for supporting objects. **2.** the contents of such a shelf. **3.** a shelf-like surface or projection; a ledge. **4.** a sandbank or submerged extent of rock in the sea or a river. **5.** *Mining, etc.* bedrock, as under alluvial deposits. **6.** *Aust., NZ Colloq.* an informer. –*v.t.* **7.** *Aust., NZ Colloq.* to inform on (someone): *he threatened to shelf his accomplice.* –*phr.* **8. buy off the shelf,** to purchase as a commercial product from readily available stock. **9. on the shelf,** *Colloq.* (of a woman) unattached or unmarried, and without prospects of marriage.

shell /ʃɛl/ *n.* **1.** a hard outer covering of an animal, as the hard case of a mollusc, or either half of the case of a bivalve mollusc. **2.** the exterior surface of an egg. **3.** a more or less hard outer covering of a seed, fruit, or the like, as the hard outside portion of a nut, the pod of peas, etc. **4.** an enclosing case or cover suggesting a shell. **5.** a hollow projectile for a cannon, etc., filled with an explosive charge arranged to explode during flight or upon impact or after penetration. **6.** a metallic cartridge used in small arms and small artillery pieces. **7.** a cartridge-like pyrotechnic device which explodes in the air. **8.** *Physics* a class of electron orbits in an atom, with small differences in energy compared with the energy differences of electrons in other orbits. **9.** *Rowing* a light racing boat having a very thin, carvel-built hull. **10.** the walls, external structure, etc., of an unfinished building, ship, etc., or of someone whose interior has been destroyed: *after the fire only the shell of the factory remained.* –*v.t.* **11.** to take out of the shell, pod, etc. **12.** to remove the shell of. **13.** to separate (maize, etc.) from the ear or cob. **14.** to throw shells or explosive projectiles into, upon, or among; bombard. –*v.i.* **15.** to fall or come out of the shell, husk, etc. **16.** to come away or fall off, as a shell or outer coat. –*phr.* **17. come out of one's shell,** to emerge from a state of

shyness or reserve. **18. shell out,** *Colloq.* to hand over; pay up. –**shell-like,** *adj.*

shellac /ʃəˈlæk/ *n.* lac which has been purified and formed into thin plates, used for making varnish, polish, and sealing wax, and in electrical insulation. –**shellacker,** *n.*

shellfish /ˈʃɛlfɪʃ/ *n.* (*pl.* **-fishes** *or, especially collectively,* **-fish**) **1.** an edible marine mollusc with a shell, as the oyster, clam, pipi, etc. **2.** an edible marine crustacean, as the prawn, crab, or lobster.

shelter /ˈʃɛltə/ *n.* **1.** something which affords protection or refuge, as from bad weather, bombing, etc.; a place of refuge or safety. **2.** protection: *the rocks gave us shelter from the wind.* **3.** an institution for the care of destitute or delinquent children. –*v.t.* **4.** to be a shelter for; afford shelter to. –*v.i.* **5.** to take shelter; find a refuge. –**shelterer,** *n.* –**shelterless,** *adj.*

shelve[1] /ʃɛlv/ *v.t.* **1.** to place on a shelf or shelves. **2.** to lay or put aside from consideration: *to shelve the question.* **3.** to remove from active service; cease to use; dismiss. **4.** to furnish with shelves. **5.** *Aust., NZ* to betray (someone who has committed a misdemeanour) to the authorities.

shelve[2] /ʃɛlv/ *v.i.* to slope gradually.

shemozzle /ʃəˈmɒzl/ *n. Colloq.* **1.** a confused state of affairs; muddle. **2.** an uproar; row. Also, **schemozzle.**

she-oak *n.* any casuarina which has slender, grooved, green branches bearing whorls of scale leaves, and hard durable wood.

shepherd /ˈʃɛpəd/ *n.* **1.** a person who looks after sheep. **2.** a person who looks after a group of people: *the priest is the shepherd of his flock.* –*v.t.* **3.** to care for or guard as a shepherd. **4.** to move (a person or people) along: *the police shepherded the crowd away from the accident.* –**shepherdess** /ˈʃɛpədɛs/, *n.*

sherbet /ˈʃɜbət/ *n.* **1.** a powdered confection eaten dry or used to make effervescent drinks. **2.** → **sorbet.**

sheriff /ˈʃɛrəf/ *n.* **1.** *Law* an officer of the Supreme Court with duties relating to service and execution of processes, summoning of juries, etc. **2.** *Brit.* the chief officer of the Crown in a county, appointed annually. **3.** *US* the law enforcement officer of a county or other civil subdivision of a state.

sherry /ˈʃɛri/ *n.* (*pl.* **-ries**) **1.** a fortified and blended wine of southern Spain. **2.** (in unofficial use) any similar fortified wine made elsewhere. See **apera.**

sherwani /ʃɜˈwɑni/ *n.* a close-fitting coat buttoned at the front which extends to slightly below the knees; the national dress of Pakistani men but worn widely in South Asia for formal occasions.

Shetland pony /ʃɛtlənd ˈpouni/ *n.* a pony of a small, sturdy, rough-coated breed.

shiatsu /ʃiˈætsu/ *n.* → **acupressure.**

shibboleth /ˈʃɪbəlɛθ/ *n.* **1.** a belief which has been, and may still be, accepted as reflecting a true account of reality but which is false or is implied to be false by so describing it: *to say that milk is good for you is a shibboleth of modern times.* **2.** a peculiarity of pronunciation, or a habit, mode of dress, etc., which distinguishes a particular class or set of persons. **3.** a test word or pet phrase of a party, sect, etc.

shicer /ˈʃaɪsə/ *n. Colloq.* **1.** *Aust., NZ* an unproductive gold mine. **2.** *Aust.* a swindler; shyster.

shied /ʃaɪd/ *v.* past tense and past participle of **shy**[1] and **shy**[2].

shield /ʃild/ *n.* **1.** a flat piece of metal, leather, or wood, carried to protect the body in battle. **2.** something shaped like or used as a shield. **3.** *Physics* a screen used to prevent the escape of radiation especially from a reactor. **4.** *Zool.* a protective plate, etc., on the body of an animal. **5.** *Geol.* a large, exposed mass of rocks formed before the Cambrian period and comprising a stable part of the earth's crust. −*v.t.* **6.** to protect with or as with a shield. −*v.i.* **7.** to act or serve as a shield. −**shielder**, *n.* −**shieldlike**, *adj.*

shift /ʃɪft/ *v.i.* **1.** to move from one place, position, etc., to another. **2.** to manage to get along or succeed. **3.** to get along by indirect methods; employ shifts or evasions. **4.** to change gear in driving a motor vehicle. **5.** *Ling.* to undergo a systematic phonetic change. **6.** *Colloq.* to travel at great speed: *the car was really shifting.* −*v.t.* **7.** to put by and replace by another or others; change. **8.** to transfer from one place, position, person, etc., to another: *to shift the blame onto someone else.* −*n.* **9.** a shifting from one place, position, person, etc., to another; a transfer. **10. a.** the portion of the day scheduled as a day's work when a factory, etc., operates continuously during the 24 hours, or works both day and night: *night shift.* **b.** a group of workers so employed. **11.** *Mining* a fault, or the dislocation of a seam or stratum. **12.** *Ling.* a change, or system of parallel changes, which seriously affects the phonetic or phonemic structure of the language, as the change in English vowels from Middle English to Modern English. **13.** an expedient; ingenious device. **14.** an evasion, artifice, or trick. **15. a.** a woman's loose-fitting dress. **b.** *Archaic* a woman's chemise or undergarment. **16.** *Motor Vehicles* → **gearstick**. −*phr.* **17. make shift**, **a.** to manage to get along or succeed. **b.** to manage with effort or difficulty. **c.** to do one's best. **18. shift for oneself**, to be independent; manage on one's own, especially in one's domestic arrangements. **19. shift house**, *Aust.*, *NZ* to move to a new place of residence. −**shifter**, *n.*

shiftless /ˈʃɪftləs/ *adj.* lacking in resource or ambition; inefficient; lazy. −**shiftlessly**, *adv.* −**shiftlessness**, *n.*

shiftwork /ˈʃɪftwɜk/ *n.* **1.** a system of work which is regularly carried out at hours outside the normal spread of hours in addition to work within the spread, so that work performed by one employee or group of employees during a shift (usually of eight hours) is continued by another employee or group for the following shift, etc. **2.** an arrangement of an employee's working hours under which, over a period of time, the employee works on different shifts. −**shiftworker**, *n.* −**shiftworking**, *n.*

shifty /ˈʃɪfti/ *adj.* (**-tier**, **-tiest**) **1.** given to or full of evasions; deceitful; furtive. **2.** resourceful; fertile in expedients. −**shiftily**, *adv.* −**shiftiness**, *n.*

shiitake mushroom /ʃɪtaki ˈmʌʃrum/ *n.* an edible mushroom, *Lentinus edodes*, native to Japan and thought to have health-giving properties. Also, **shiitake**.

shilling /ˈʃɪlɪŋ/ *n.* **1.** (in Australia until the introduction of decimal currency in 1966) a fractional monetary unit equal to $^1/_{20}$ of a pound. *Abbrev.*: s., sh. **2.** (formerly) a similar coin of Britain. **3.** a similar coin of other countries. −*adj.* **4.** of the price or value of a shilling. −*phr.* **5. cut someone off with** (or **without**) **a shilling**, to cut an heir out of one's will.

shillyshally /ˈʃɪliˌʃæli/ *v.i.* (**-lied**, **-lying**) to be irresolute; vacillate.

shimmer /ˈʃɪmə/ *v.i.* **1.** to shine with a subdued, tremulous light; gleam faintly. −*n.* **2.** a subdued, tremulous light or gleam. −**shimmery**, *adj.*

shimmy /ˈʃɪmi/ *n.* (*pl.* **-mies**) **1.** a US ragtime dance, marked by shaking of the hips or shoulders. **2.** excessive wobbling in the front wheels of a motor vehicle. **3.** *Colloq.* → **chemise**. −*v.i.* (**-mied**, **-mying**) **4.** to vibrate; shake.

shin /ʃɪn/ *n.* **1.** the front part of the leg from the knee to the ankle. **2.** the lower part of the foreleg in cattle; the metacarpal bone. **3.** the shinbone or tibia, especially its sharp edge or front portion. **4.** a cut of beef, usually used for stewing. −*verb* (**shinned**, **shinning**) −*v.i.* **5.** to

climb by holding fast with the hands or arms and legs and drawing oneself up. −*v.t.* **6.** to climb by shinning: *she shinned the downpipe.*

shindig /ˈʃɪndɪg/ *n. Colloq.* **1.** a dance, party, or other festivity, especially a noisy one. **2.** a disturbance; quarrel; row.

shine /ʃaɪn/ *verb* (**shone** *or* **shined**, **shining**) −*v.i.* **1.** to give forth, or glow with, light; shed or cast light. **2.** to be bright with reflected light; glisten; sparkle. **3.** to be unusually bright, as the eyes or face. **4.** to appear with brightness or clearness, as feelings. **5.** to excel; be conspicuous: *to shine at sports.* −*v.t.* **6.** to cause to shine. **7.** to direct the light of (a lamp, etc.): *shine the torch over here.* **8.** to put a gloss or polish on (shoes, etc.). −*n.* **9.** radiance; light. **10.** lustre; polish. **11.** sunshine; fair weather: *come rain or shine.* **12.** a polish given to shoes. **13.** a giving of such a polish. −*phr.* **14. take a shine to**, *Colloq.* to develop a liking or fancy for (someone). **15. take the shine out of**, **a.** to remove or spoil the lustre or brilliance of. **b.** to surpass; excel; get the better of; humiliate. −**shiny**, *adj.*

shiner /ˈʃaɪnə/ *n. Colloq.* a black eye.

shingle¹ /ˈʃɪŋgəl/ *n.* **1.** a thin piece of wood, slate, etc., usually oblong and with one end thicker than the other, used in overlapping rows to cover the roofs and sides of houses. **2.** a woman's close-cropped haircut. **3.** *Colloq.* a small signboard, especially that of a professional person. −*v.t.* **4.** to cut (hair) close to the head. −*phr.* **5. be a shingle short**, *Aust.*, *NZ Colloq.* to be eccentric; be mentally disturbed. −**shingler**, *n.*

shingle² /ˈʃɪŋgəl/ *n.* **1.** small, water-worn stones or pebbles such as lie in loose banks or layers on the seashore. **2.** an extent of small, loose stones or pebbles.

shingles /ˈʃɪŋgəlz/ *n. Pathol.* (construed as *sing. or pl.*) a viral skin disease characterised by vesicles (small blisters) which sometimes form a girdle about the body; herpes zoster.

shining /ˈʃaɪnɪŋ/ *adj.* **1.** radiant; gleaming; bright. **2.** resplendent; brilliant: *shining talents.* **3.** conspicuously fine: *a shining example.* −**shiningly**, *adv.*

Shinto /ˈʃɪntoʊ/ *n.* the indigenous religion of Japan, primarily a system of nature and ancestor worship. Also, **Shintoism.** −**Shintoist**, *n.*, *adj.*

ship /ʃɪp/ *n.* **1.** any vessel intended or used for navigating the water, especially one of large size and not propelled by oars, paddles, or the like. −*verb* (**shipped**, **shipping**) −*v.t.* **2.** to put or take on board a ship or the like, for transportation; to send or transport by ship, rail, etc. **3.** *Naut.* to take in (water) over the side, as a vessel does when waves break over it. **4.** to fix (oars, etc.) in a ship or boat in the proper place for use. **5.** *Colloq.* to send away or get rid of. −*v.i.* **6.** to go on board a ship; embark. −*phr.* **7. jump ship**, **a.** (of a member of a ship's crew) to abscond while the ship is in port. **b.** to leave an organisation, enterprise, etc., especially when it is experiencing difficulties. **8. run a tight ship**, to maintain good discipline and control. **9. shape up or ship out**, to perform as required or leave. **10. take ship**, to embark. **11. when one's ship comes in** (or **home**), when one has become prosperous or acquired a fortune.

-ship a suffix of nouns denoting condition, character, office, skill, etc., as in *kingship*, *friendship*, *statesmanship*.

shipment /ˈʃɪpmənt/ *n.* **1.** the act of shipping goods, etc.; the delivery of goods, etc., for transporting. **2.** something that is shipped.

shipping /ˈʃɪpɪŋ/ *n.* **1.** the act of someone who ships goods, etc. **2.** the action or business of sending or transporting goods, etc., by ship, rail, etc. **3.** ships collectively, or their aggregate tonnage.

shipping agent *n.* the representative of a shipowner, who transacts business on the shipowner's behalf.

shipshape /ˈʃɪpʃeɪp/ *adj.* in good order; well arranged; neat; tidy.

shiralee /ˈʃɪrəˈli, ˈʃɪrəˌli/ *n. Aust.* **1.** a burden or bundle. **2. →** **swag** (def. 1).

shiraz /ʃəˈræz/ *n.* (*sometimes upper case*) **1.** a red grape variety grown in Australia for the making of dry red table wines as well as sweet red wines. **2.** a wine made from such grapes.

shire /ˈʃaɪə/ *n.* (in Australia) an area of land delineated for the purposes of local government, usually larger than that designated to be a town, municipality, or borough and, at least originally, more sparsely populated.

shire council *n.* the local administrative body which serves a shire. Compare **city council, municipal council**.

shirk /ʃɜk/ *v.t.* to evade (work, duty, etc.).

shirr /ʃɜ/ *v.t.* **1.** to draw up or gather (cloth) on parallel threads. **2.** to bake (food, usually eggs) in a small shallow container or ramekin dish.

shirt /ʃɜt/ *n.* **1.** a garment for the upper part of the body, usually with buttons down the front, a collar, and short sleeves, or long sleeves with cuffs. **2.** *US* an undershirt; vest; singlet. *–phr.* **3. in one's shirt sleeves,** not wearing a jacket. **4. keep one's shirt on,** *Colloq.* to refrain from losing one's temper or becoming impatient. **5. lose one's shirt,** *Colloq.* to lose everything. **6. put one's shirt on,** *Colloq.* to bet heavily or all one has on (a horse, etc.). **–shirtless,** *adj.*

shirt front *n.* **1.** the starched front of a white dress shirt. **2.** the front part of any shirt. Also, **shirtfront**.

shirtfront /ˈʃɜtfrʌnt/ *v.t.* **1.** to make an intimidating move towards (someone), grabbing the front of their shirt or their coat lapels and pulling them towards you, or moving directly in their way, chest to chest. **2.** to confront (someone) aggressively and indignantly with a complaint or grievance. **3.** *Aust. Rules* to make a shoulder charge at the chest of (an opponent) with the aim of knocking them to the ground. *–n.* **4.** *Aust. Rules* such a shoulder charge. **5. →** **shirt front. –shirtfronter,** *n.* **–shirtfronting,** *n.*

shirty /ˈʃɜti/ *adj. Colloq.* bad-tempered; annoyed.

shish kebab /ˈʃɪʃ kəbæb/ *n.* a dish consisting of cubes of meat, marinated, and grilled on a skewer, often with onion, tomato, green pepper, etc. Also, **kebab**.

shit /ʃɪt/ *Colloq.* (*taboo*) *–verb* (**shitted** *or* **shat** *or* **shit**, **shitted**, **shitting**) *–v.i.* **1.** to defecate. *–v.t.* **2.** to pass with faeces: *to shit blood.* **3.** to anger or disgust. *–n.* **4.** faeces; dung; excrement. **5.** the act of defecating. **6.** a contemptible or despicable person. **7. →** **bullshit** (def. 2). **8.** events or experiences which occasion deep dissatisfaction or disgust: *I don't have to take this shit from her.* **9.** marijuana or hashish. *–adj.* **10.** unpleasant: *I've had a shit day.* **11.** of poor quality: *that was a shit book. –interj.* **12.** an exclamation expressing anger, disgust, disappointment, disbelief, etc. *–phr.* **13. dump** (or **heap**) (or **pour**) **shit on,** to denigrate; criticise. **14. get the shits,** (sometimes fol. by *with*) to become exasperated or angry. **15. give someone the shits,** to arouse dislike, resentment, annoyance in someone. **16. have one's shit together,** to be in complete control of one's life, emotions, etc. **17. have shit for brains,** to be extremely stupid. **18. have shit on the** (or **one's**) **liver,** to be ill-tempered. **19. have the shits, a.** to have diarrhoea. **b.** to feel fed up or weary. **c.** to feel annoyed; to be in a bad mood. **20. have the shits with someone,** to feel fed up or angry with someone. **21. holy shit,** an exclamation of surprise. **22. in the shit,** in trouble. **23. not give a shit,** to not care in the slightest. **24. not worth a pinch of shit,** completely worthless. **25. piece of shit,** a despicable person. **26. push shit uphill (with a pointy stick),** to attempt the impossible. **27. put shit on,** to denigrate; criticise. **28. scare** (or **frighten**) (**the**) **shit out of someone,** to give someone an intense fright.

29. shit a brick, an exclamation of astonishment, wonder, dismay, etc. **30. shit happens,** a catchphrase expressing an acknowledgement that in life unpleasant and unfair things happen. **31. shit it in,** *Aust.* to win easily. **32. shit oneself, a.** to soil oneself with excrement. **b.** to be terrified. **33. sure as shit,** absolutely sure; positive. **34. the shit hits the fan,** the trouble begins. **35. tough** (or **stiff**) **shit,** an exclamation indicating a lack of sympathy for another's misfortune. **36. up shit creek (without a paddle)** (or **in a barbwire canoe**), in trouble; in difficulties. **37. up to shit,** worthless; useless.

shithouse /ˈʃɪthaʊs/ *Colloq.* (*taboo*) *–n.* **1.** a toilet. *–adj.* **2.** foul; wretchedly bad.

shitty /ˈʃɪti/ *adj.* (**-tier, -tiest**) *Colloq.* (*taboo*) **1.** containing or covered in excrement: *a shitty nappy.* **2.** annoyed; bad-tempered. **3.** unpleasant; disagreeable; of low quality.

Shiva /ˈʃivə/ *n.* one of the three chief divinities, the third member of the Hindu trinity, known also as 'the Destroyer'. Also, **Siva. –Shivaism,** *n.* **–Shivaist,** *n.* **–Shivaistic** /ʃɪvɛɪˈɪstɪk, ʃɪv-/, *adj.*

shiver[1] /ˈʃɪvə/ *v.i.* **1.** to shake or tremble with cold, fear, excitement, etc. **2.** (of a sail) to shake when too close to the wind. *–n.* **3.** a tremulous motion; a tremble or quiver. *–phr.* **4. cold shivers,** a sensation of fear, anxiety, or distaste. **5. the shivers,** a fit or attack of shivering. **–shivery,** *adj.*

shiver[2] /ˈʃɪvə/ *v.t.* **1.** to break or split into fragments. *–v.i.* **2.** to become broken or split into fragments.

shlep /ʃlɛp/ *v.t.* (**shlepped, shlepping**) **→** **schlep**.

shoal[1] /ʃoʊl/ *n.* **1.** a place where a body of water is shallow. **2.** a sandbank or sandbar in the bed of a body of water, especially one which shows at low water. *–v.t.* **3.** *Naut.* to proceed from a greater to a lesser depth of (water).

shoal[2] /ʃoʊl/ *n.* **1.** a group of fish crowded fairly close together. **2.** any large number of persons or things.

shock[1] /ʃɒk/ *n.* **1.** a sudden and violent upset or fright. **2.** *Med.* a sudden collapse of the nervous mechanism caused by physical injury or strong emotional upset: *to be in shock.* **3.** a sudden collision. **4.** the physiological effect produced by the passage of an electric current through the body. *–v.t.* **5.** to strike with intense surprise, horror, disgust, etc. **6.** to give an electric shock to. *–v.i.* **7.** to come into violent contact; collide. **–shockable,** *adj.* **–shocking,** *adj.*

shock[2] /ʃɒk/ *n.* a thick, bushy mass, as of hair.

shod /ʃɒd/ *v.* past tense and past participle of **shoe**.

shoddy /ˈʃɒdi/ *n.* (*pl.* **-dies**) **1.** a fibrous material obtained by shredding woollen rags or waste. *–adj.* (**-dier, -diest**) **2.** pretending to a superiority not possessed; sham. **3.** of poor quality or badly made: *shoddy workmanship*; *shoddy goods.* **–shoddily,** *adv.* **–shoddiness,** *n.*

shoe /ʃu/ *n.* **1.** an external covering, usually of leather, for the human foot, consisting of a more or less stiff or heavy sole and a lighter upper part. **2.** *US* **→** **boot**[1] (def. 1). **3.** a horseshoe, or a similar plate for the hoof of some other animal. **4.** a ferrule or the like, as of iron, for protecting the end of a staff, pole, etc. **5.** the part of a brake mechanism fitting into the drum and expanded outwardly to apply the friction lining to the drum or rim for stopping or slowing a car, etc. **6.** the outer casing of a pneumatic tyre. **7.** a drag or skid for a wheel of a vehicle. **8.** a part having a larger area than the end of an object on which it fits, serving to disperse or apply its thrust. **9.** the sliding contact by which an electric locomotive takes its current from the conductor rail. *–v.t.* (**shod, shoeing**) **10.** to provide or fit with a shoe or shoes. **11.** to protect or arm at the point, edge, or face with a ferrule, metal plate, or the like. *–phr.* **12. in someone's shoes,** in the position or situation of another: *I shouldn't like to be in his shoes.* **13. know**

where the shoe pinches, to know the cause or real meaning of trouble, misfortune, sorrow, etc., especially from personal experience.

shoe boot *n.* any of various styles of dress shoe which lace up like a boot.

shoehorn /ˈʃuhɔn/ *n.* a shaped piece of horn, metal, or the like, inserted in a shoe at the heel to make it slip on more easily.

shoelace /ˈʃuleɪs/ *n.* a string or lace for fastening a shoe.

shoestring /ˈʃustrɪŋ/ *n.* **1.** → **shoelace.** –*phr.* **2. on a shoestring**, with a very small amount of money.

shogun /ˈʃoʊɡən/ *n.* (in Japan) **1.** originally, a military chief, the title, originating in the 8th century, equivalent to commander-in-chief. **2.** (in later history) a member of a quasi-dynasty, holding real power while the imperial dynasty remained theoretically and ceremonially supreme.

shone /ʃɒn/ *v.* past tense and past participle of **shine.**

shonky /ˈʃɒŋki/ *adj.* (**-kier, -kiest**) *Aust., NZ Colloq.* **1.** of dubious integrity or honesty. **2.** mechanically unreliable. Also, **shonkie, shonkey.**

shoo /ʃu/ *interj.* **1.** an exclamation used to scare or drive away poultry, birds, etc. –*v.t.* (**shooed, shooing**) **2.** to drive away by calling 'shoo'.

shoosh /ʃʊʃ/ *Colloq.* –*interj.* **1.** an exclamation calling for quiet. –*n.* **2.** quiet: *let's have a bit of shoosh.* –*v.i.* **3.** to become quiet: *will you shoosh now!* –*v.t.* **4.** to make quiet: *you'll have to shoosh the children.* Also, **shush.**

shoot /ʃut/ *verb* (**shot** /ʃɒt/, **shooting**) –*v.t.* **1.** to hit, wound, or kill with a missile discharged from a weapon. **2.** to execute or put to death with a bullet. **3.** to send forth (arrows, bullets, etc.) from a bow, firearm, or the like. **4.** to discharge (a weapon): *to shoot a gun.* **5.** to send forth like an arrow or bullet: *to shoot questions at someone.* **6.** to fling; throw; propel; direct. **7.** to pass rapidly along with: *to shoot a rapid; to shoot a wave.* **8.** to emit (rays, etc.) swiftly. **9.** to variegate by threads, streaks, etc., of another colour. **10.** *Sport* to hit, throw, kick or drive (the ball, etc.) as at the goal. **11.** to accomplish by hitting, throwing, kicking or driving the ball, etc.: *to shoot a goal.* **12.** to propel (a marble or the like) from the thumb and forefinger. **13.** *Dice* to toss (the dice). **14.** *Photography* to photograph or film. **15.** to put forth (buds, branches, etc.), as a plant. **16.** to slide (a bolt, etc.) into or out of its fastening. **17.** *Colloq.* to inject intravenously (any form of drug). –*v.i.* **18.** to send forth missiles, from a bow, firearm, or the like. **19.** to send forth missiles, or be discharged, as a firearm. **20.** to move, start to move, or pass suddenly or swiftly (*ahead, away, into, off,* etc.). **21.** to come forth from the ground, as a stem, etc. **22.** to put forth buds or shoots, as a plant; germinate. **23.** *Photography* to photograph or film. **24.** *Film, TV* to engage in a session of filming. **25.** to propel a ball, etc., in a particular direction or way, as in games. **26.** (of pain) to move quickly through a part of the body: *pain shot through his arm.* **27.** to kill game with a gun for sport. –*n.* **28.** an act of shooting with a bow, firearm, etc. **29.** an expedition for shooting game. **30.** a match or contest at shooting. **31.** a new or young growth which shoots off from some portion of a plant. **32.** a young branch, stem, twig, sprout, or the like. **33.** a session of filming or photography. **34.** → **chute.** –*interj. Colloq.* **35.** an invitation or command to someone to begin, especially to begin speaking: *OK, shoot!* **36.** *Chiefly US* (*euphemistic*) shit. –*phr.* **37. shoot a line**, *Colloq.* to boast. **38. shoot along**, to move forward at great speed. **39. shoot down, a.** to kill or cause to fall by hitting with a shot. **b.** to bring down (an aircraft) by gunfire. **c.** to defeat decisively (an argument or person putting forward an argument): *his plan was so obviously impossible, he was shot down in flames.* **40. shoot from the**

hip, to make an instant verbal attack without pausing to consider one's words. **41. shoot off**, *Colloq.* to go away quickly. **42. shoot one's bolt**, *Colloq.* **a.** to do one's utmost. **b.** (*taboo*) to ejaculate prematurely. **43. shoot oneself in the foot**, to harm one's own cause through incompetence, carelessness, etc. **44. shoot (off) one's mouth** or **shoot one's mouth off** or **shoot off at the mouth**, *Colloq.* **a.** to talk indiscreetly, especially to reveal secrets, etc.; talk wildly or tactlessly. **b.** to exaggerate; boast. **45. shoot out**, to extend; jut: *a cape shooting out into the sea.* **46. shoot the breeze**, *Colloq.* to chat idly. **47. shoot the moon**, *Colloq.* to abscond. **48. shoot through**, *Aust., NZ Colloq.* **a.** to go away, usually absenting oneself improperly: *instead of going to the exam, she shot through.* **b.** to move away rapidly: *to shoot through like a Bondi tram.* **49. shoot up, a.** *Colloq.* to cause damage, confusion, etc., to by reckless or haphazard shooting. **b.** *Colloq.* to take drugs intravenously. **c.** to grow, especially rapidly. –**shooter**, *n.*

shooter game *n.* a genre of action computer games in which the main character defeats the enemy by shooting them. See **first-person shooter, third-person shooter.**

shooting star *n.* a falling star; a meteor.

shop /ʃɒp/ *n.* **1.** a building where goods are sold retail. **2.** a place for doing certain work; a workshop. **3.** an act of shopping for goods: *we do a big weekly shop.* –*verb* (**shopped, shopping**) –*v.i.* **4.** to visit shops for purchasing or examining goods. –*v.t.* **5.** *Chiefly Brit. Colloq.* to inform against, betray, to the police. –*phr.* **6. all over the shop**, *Colloq.* all over the place; in confusion. **7. set up shop**, to set oneself up in business. **8. shop around, a.** to visit a number of shops comparing quality and price before making a purchase. **b.** to make general and wideranging inquiries before making a decision. **9. shut up shop**, to close a business either temporarily or permanently. **10. talk shop**, to discuss one's trade, profession, or business, especially at a social occasion with the effect of excluding those not similarly employed.

shop floor *n.* **1.** the part of a factory where the machines, etc., are situated. **2.** workers collectively, especially factory workers. –**shopfloor**, *adj.*

shopfront /ˈʃɒpfrʌnt/ *n.* **1.** the part of a shop which fronts the street. **2.** the part of an organisation which deals directly with the public.

shoplift /ˈʃɒplɪft/ *v.t.* to steal (goods) from a shop while appearing to be a legitimate shopper. –**shoplifter**, *n.*

shoplifting /ˈʃɒplɪftɪŋ/ *n.* the crime of stealing goods from a shop while appearing to be a legitimate customer. Also, **shop stealing.**

shopping /ˈʃɒpɪŋ/ *n.* **1.** the act of someone who shops. **2.** the articles bought.

shopping trolley *n.* a basket-shaped metal trolley used by customers for carrying purchases in supermarkets.

shop stealing *n.* → **shoplifting.** –**shop stealer**, *n.*

shop steward *n.* a trade-union official representing workers in a factory, workshop, etc.

shore[1] /ʃɔ/ *n.* **1.** land along the edge of a sea, lake, large river, etc. **2.** some particular country: *my native shore.* **3.** land: *marines serving on shore.* **4.** *Law* the space between the ordinary high-water mark and low-water mark. –*adj.* **5.** of, relating to, or situated on land.

shore[2] /ʃɔ/ *n.* **1.** a supporting post or beam and auxiliary members, especially one placed obliquely against the side of a building, a ship in dock, or the like; a prop; a strut. –*phr.* **2. shore up**, to support by, or as by, a shore or shores; prop up.

shorn /ʃɔn/ *v.* past participle of **shear.**

short /ʃɔt/ *adj.* **1.** having little length; not long. **2.** having little height; not tall; low. **3.** extending or reaching only a little way. **4.** brief; not extensive: *a short speech.*

5. concise, as writing. **6.** rudely brief; curt; hurting: *short temper; she was short with him.* **7.** low in amount; scanty: *short rations.* **8.** not reaching a mark or the like, as a throw or a missile. **9.** below the standard in extent, quantity, duration, etc.: *short measure.* **10.** having a scanty or insufficient amount of (money, food, etc.): *we are short of bread.* **11.** breaking or crumbling readily, as pastry that contains a large proportion of butter or other shortening. **12.** *Commerce* **a.** not possessing at the time of sale commodities or stocks that one sells. **b.** denoting or relating to sales of commodities or stocks which the seller does not at that time possess, depending for profit on a decline in prices at the point where they need to purchase them to complete the sale. **13.** *Phonetics* **a.** lasting a relatively short time: *bit* has a shorter vowel than *bid* or *bead*. **b.** belonging to a class of sounds considered as usually shorter in duration than another class, such as the vowel of *hot* as compared to *bought;* conventionally, the vowels of *bat, bet, bit, hot, good,* and *but*. **14.** (of an alcoholic drink) small, usually with a comparatively high alcoholic content. **15.** *Cricket* of a ball which pitches well down the wicket from the person batting. *–adv.* **16.** abruptly or suddenly: *to stop short.* **17.** briefly; curtly. **18.** on the nearer side of an intended or particular point: *to fall short.* **19.** *Commerce* without possessing at the time the stocks, etc., sold: *to sell short.* **20.** *Cricket* pitching well down the wicket from the person batting. *–n.* **21.** something that is short. **22.** *Elect.* a short circuit. **23.** *Prosody* a short sound or syllable. **24.** *Film* **a.** (*usu. pl.*) *Aust.* a short film made up of excerpts from a feature film soon to be released; trailer. **b.** any short film. *–v.i.* **25.** *Colloq.* to short-circuit. *–v.t.* **26.** *Colloq.* to short-circuit. *–phr.* **27. be caught short**, *Colloq.* **a.** to discover an inconvenient lack of something, as money. **b.** to have an urgent need to urinate or defecate when no toilet facilities are available. **28. cut short**, to end abruptly; curtail; interrupt. **29. for short**, by way of abbreviation. **30. in short**, in a few words; in brief; briefly. **31. make short work of**, to finish or dispose of quickly. **32. nothing short of**, nothing less than. **33. sell oneself short**, *Colloq.* **a.** to underestimate one's abilities or achievements. **b.** to behave in a fashion considered to be unworthy of one. **34. short for**, being a shorter form of: *'phone' is short for 'telephone'.* **35. short of**, **a.** less than; inferior to: *little short of the best.* **b.** without going to the length of: *to stop short of actual crime.* **36. short on**, deficient in: *short on sense.* *–shortness, n.*

shortage /ˈʃɔtɪdʒ/ *n.* **1.** deficiency in quantity. **2.** an amount deficient.

shortbread /ˈʃɔtbrɛd/ *n.* a thick, crisp biscuit, rich in butter, often baked in one piece and cut into pieces when cool.

short-change *v.t. Colloq.* **1.** to give less than proper change to. **2.** to cheat. *–short-changer, n.*

short circuit *n. Elect.* an abnormal connection of relatively low resistance, whether made accidentally or intentionally, between two points of different potential in an electrical circuit.

shortcoming /ˈʃɔtkʌmɪŋ/ *n.* a failure or defect in conduct, condition, etc.

short cut *n.* a shorter or quicker way.

shorten /ˈʃɔtn/ *v.t.* **1.** to make shorter; curtail. **2.** to take in; reduce: *to shorten sail.* **3.** to make (pastry, etc.) short, as with butter or other fat. *–v.i.* **4.** to become shorter. **5.** (of odds) to decrease. *–shortener, n.*

shortening /ˈʃɔtnɪŋ/ *n.* butter, lard, or other fat, used to make pastry, etc., short.

shorthand /ˈʃɔthænd/ *n.* **1.** a method of rapid handwriting using extremely simple strokes in place of letters, often with other abbreviating devices. *–adj.* **2.** using shorthand. **3.** written in shorthand.

shorthanded /ʃɔtˈhændəd/ *adj.* not having the necessary number of workers, helpers, etc.

Shorthorn /ˈʃɔthɔn/ *n.* one of a breed of dairy or beef cattle, with white, red, or roan markings, having short horns.

short leg *n. Cricket* **1.** the on-side fielding position close to and more or less square of the person batting; bat-pad. **2.** a fielder in this position; bat-pad.

short list *n.* a list of especially favoured candidates for a position, promotion, etc., who have been selected from a larger group of applicants.

shortly /ˈʃɔtli/ *adv.* **1.** in a short time; soon. **2.** briefly; concisely. **3.** curtly; abruptly.

short-pitched *adj. Cricket* of or relating to a bowled ball which first strikes the pitch at a short distance from the bowler.

shorts /ʃɔts/ *pl. n.* short trousers, not extending beyond the knee.

short-sighted *adj.* **1.** unable to see far; near-sighted; myopic. **2.** lacking in foresight. *–short-sightedly, adv. –short-sightedness, n.*

short-staffed /ʃɔtˈstaft/ *adj.* not having the usual number of personnel present, especially as a result of sickness, understaffing, etc.

short-tailed shearwater *n.* a large, dark seabird, *Puffinus tenuirostris,* breeding on islands in Bass Strait and in coastal areas of Tasmania and south-eastern Australia, and migrating to the Northern Hemisphere in winter; mutton-bird.

short-tempered /ʃɔtˈtɛmpəd/ *adj.* having a hasty temper; inclined to become angry on little provocation.

short-term *adj.* **1.** covering a comparatively short period of time. **2.** having a maturity within a comparatively short time: *a short-term loan.*

short-winded /ʃɔtˈwɪndəd/ *adj.* **1.** short of breath; liable to difficulty in breathing. **2.** brief; succinct. **3.** choppy; disconnected.

shot[1] /ʃɒt/ *n.* (*pl.* **shots** *or, for def. 5,* **shot**) **1.** the discharge or a discharge of a firearm, bow, etc. **2.** the range of the discharge, or the distance covered by the missile in its flight. **3.** an attempt to hit with a projectile discharged from a gun or the like. **4.** the act of shooting. **5.** a small ball or pellet of lead, of which a number are used for one charge of a shooter's gun. **6.** such pellets collectively: *a charge of shot.* **7.** a person who shoots: *he was a good shot.* **8.** a heavy metal ball which competitors cast as far as possible in shot-put. **9.** an aimed stroke, throw, or the like, as in games, etc. **10.** an attempt or try. **11.** a remark aimed at some person or thing. **12.** a guess at something. **13.** *Colloq.* an injection of a drug, vaccine, etc. **14.** a small measure of alcoholic liquor: *a shot of tequila.* **15.** a small quantity of anything. **16.** *Film, Photography* **a.** the making of a photograph. **b.** a photograph. **c.** a length of film taken without stopping or cutting. **17.** *Mining, etc.* an explosive charge in place for detonation. *–phr.* **18. big shot**, *Colloq.* an important person. **19. call the shots**, *Colloq.* to exercise control over events, decisions, etc.; be in command. **20. have a shot at**, *Colloq.* to make an attempt at. **21. have a shot at someone**, *Colloq.* to criticise or ridicule someone. **22. like a shot**, *Colloq.* instantly; very quickly. **23. one's best shot**, one's greatest effort. **24. shot in the arm**, *Colloq.* something that gives renewed confidence, vigour, etc. **25. shot in the dark**, a wild or random guess. **26. that's the shot**, *Aust.* an exclamation of approval. **27. the shot**, *Aust. Colloq.* the best option: *SP betting's the shot.*

shot[2] /ʃɒt/ *v.* **1.** past tense and past participle of **shoot**. *–adj.* **2.** woven so as to present a play of colours, as silk. **3.** spread or streaked with colour. **4.** *Colloq.*

rendered useless; irreparable: *the motor's shot.* **5.** *Colloq.* drunk: *it was plain he was half shot.* –*phr. Colloq.* **6. be shot of,** to be rid of. **7. get shot of,** to get rid of.

shot glass *n.* **1.** a measure, glass or metal, of a shot of liquor. **2.** a small glass used for drinking liquor.

shotgun /ˈʃɒtɡʌn/ *n.* **1.** a smoothbore gun for firing small shot to kill small game, though often used with buckshot to kill larger animals. –*adj.* **2.** of, relating to, or used in a shotgun. –*phr.* **3. ride shotgun, a.** to travel as an armed guard in the front passenger seat of a vehicle. **b.** *Colloq.* to ride in the front passenger seat of a vehicle.

shot-put *n.* **1.** the athletic exercise of casting a heavy metal ball (the **shot**) as far as possible. **2.** the ball itself; shot. **3.** one throw of the shot in this exercise.

should /ʃʊd/ *v.* **1.** indicating obligation: *I should visit my parents; you should show more tolerance.* **2.** indicating advisability: *you should lock the car door when you get out; he should have checked before starting.* **3.** referring to a likely event or situation: *you should get there in three hours.* **4.** referring to a remote possibility: *should he mention it, pretend you don't know; the policy pays $100,000 if you should die within five years.* **5.** in polite phrases: *I should like to apply for the position advertised; it'll take about two hours, I should think.* **6.** used emphatically: *I should say so!; I should hope so too!*

shoulder /ˈʃoʊldə/ *n.* **1.** either of two corresponding parts of the human body, situated at the top of the trunk and extending respectively from the right side and left side of the neck to the upper joint of the corresponding arm. **2.** (*pl.*) these two parts together with the portion of the back joining them, forming a place where burdens are sometimes carried. **3.** a corresponding part in animals. **4.** the upper foreleg and adjoining parts of a sheep, etc. **5.** the joint connecting the arm or the foreleg with the trunk. **6.** a shoulder-like part or projection. **7.** a cut of meat including the upper joint of the foreleg. **8.** *Fortifications* the angle of a bastion between the face and the flank. **9.** *Printing* the flat surface on a type body extending beyond the base of the letter or character. **10.** that part of a garment which covers, or fits over the shoulder. **11.** either of two strips of land bordering a road, especially that part on which vehicles can be parked in an emergency. **12.** the unbroken, tapering part of the wave, away from the curl. –*v.t.* **13.** to push, as with the shoulder, especially roughly. **14.** to take onto or support with the shoulder: *he shouldered his swag and left.* **15.** to assume as a burden, or responsibility: *to shoulder the expense.* –*v.i.* **16.** to push with the shoulder. –*phr.* **17. have broad shoulders,** to be able to accept responsibility. **18. put one's shoulder to the wheel,** to work hard. **19. rub shoulders with,** to associate with; come into contact with. **20. shoulder arms,** *Mil.* to execute a movement in arms drill in which the rifle is brought into a vertical position, muzzle pointing upwards, on the right side of the body, and held by the right hand at the trigger guard. **21. shoulder to shoulder,** with united action and support. **22. straight from the shoulder,** without evasion. **23. the cold shoulder,** *Colloq.* a rebuff or rejection: *to get the cold shoulder.*

shoulderblade /ˈʃoʊldə-bleɪd/ *n.* → **scapula**.

shout¹ /ʃaʊt/ *v.i.* **1.** to call or cry out loudly and vigorously. **2.** to speak or laugh noisily or unrestrainedly. –*v.t.* **3.** to express by a shout or shouts. –*n.* **4.** a loud call or cry. **5.** a loud burst, as of laughter. –*phr.* **6. shout down,** to make it impossible to hear (someone) by shouting or talking loudly. –**shouter,** *n.* –**shouting,** *n.*

shout² /ʃaʊt/ *Aust., NZ Colloq.* –*v.t.* **1. a.** to pay for a round of drinks for (a group of people). **b.** to pay for something for (another person); treat: *I'll shout you to the pictures; I'll shout you a new dress.* –*n.* **2.** the act of

shouting, as by providing drinks. **3.** one's turn to shout (def. 1).

shove /ʃʌv/ *v.t.* **1.** to move along by force from behind. **2.** to push roughly or rudely; jostle. –*v.i.* **3.** to push. –*n.* **4.** an act of shoving. –*phr.* **5. shove it,** an expression of dismissal, contempt, etc. **6. shove off, a.** to push a boat off. **b.** *Colloq.* to leave; start. –**shover,** *n.*

shovel /ˈʃʌvəl/ *n.* **1.** a tool with a broad blade or scoop attached to a handle. **2.** a machine for shovelling, removing matter, etc. –*verb* (**-elled** *or,* *Chiefly US,* **-eled, -elling** *or,* *Chiefly US,* **-eling**) –*v.t.* **3.** to take up and throw or remove with a shovel. **4.** to push or put carelessly or quickly: *to shovel food into one's mouth.* **5.** to dig or clear with a shovel: *to shovel a path.* –*v.i.* **6.** to work with a shovel. –**shovelling,** *n.*

shoveler /ˈʃʌvələ/ *n.* **1.** a nomadic, freshwater duck, *Anas rhynchotis,* of Australia and New Zealand, having a broad, flat, olive-brown bill. **2.** a common and widespread Northern Hemisphere freshwater duck, *Anas clypeata.* Also, **shoveller.**

show /ʃoʊ/ *verb* (**showed, shown** *or* **showed, showing**) –*v.t.* **1.** to cause or allow to be seen; exhibit; display; present. **2.** to point out: *to show the way.* **3.** to guide; escort: *he showed me to my room.* **4.** to make clear; make known; explain. **5.** to prove; demonstrate. **6.** to indicate; register: *the thermometer showed ten degrees below zero.* **7.** to allege, as in a legal document; plead, as a reason or cause. **8.** to produce, as facts in an affidavit or at a hearing. **9.** to make evident by appearance, behaviour, etc.: *to show one's feelings.* **10.** to accord or grant (favour, etc.). –*v.i.* **11.** to be seen; be or become visible. **12.** to look or appear: *to show to advantage.* **13.** *Colloq.* to give an exhibition, display, or performance. **14.** *US, Brit.* to finish in third place in a horserace, etc. **15.** to appear pregnant: *she started to show in the fifth month.* –*n.* **16.** a display: *a show of freedom.* **17.** ostentatious display. **18.** any kind of public exhibition. **19.** appearance: *to make a sorry show.* **20.** an unreal or deceptive appearance. **21.** an indication; trace. **22.** a non-commercial quantity of oil or gas encountered in drilling. **23.** (in pregnancy) a discharge of blood and mucosal tissue, indicating the onset of labour. **24.** *Colloq.* a theatrical performance or company. **25.** *Aust., NZ Colloq.* a chance; opportunity: *a bloke can't get a fair show here.* **26.** a sight or spectacle. **27.** any undertaking, organisation, etc.; affair. **28.** a public collection of things on display; a competitive exhibition of farm produce, livestock, etc. **29.** *Mining* **a.** a small trace of precious mineral, as gold, opal, etc., taken as an indication of a greater deposit; colour: *a show of gold.* **b.** *Colloq.* a mine: *they worked a little show at Hill End.* **30.** *SA, Colloq.* a party. –*adj.* **31.** of or relating to an animal bred or trained to be entered into a show (def. 28). –*phr.* **32. a show of hands,** a voting procedure in which hands are raised to show assent for or dissent from a proposition. **33. give the show away,** to reveal all the details of a plan, scheme, etc. **34. have no show,** *Aust., NZ Colloq.* to have no chance whatsoever. **35. run the show,** to control or manage a business, etc. **36. show off, a.** to exhibit for approval or admiration, or ostentatiously: *she was showing off her new dress.* **b.** to display one's abilities, cleverness, etc., with the object of gaining attention. **37. show someone up,** to reveal the weaknesses, failings, etc., of someone: *the newspaper story showed him up as being a traitor.* **38. show up, a.** to stand out in a certain way; appear: *blue shows up well against that background.* **b.** to turn up; appear at a certain place. **c.** to expose (faults, etc.); reveal: *the emergency showed up his lack of courage.* **d.** to appear superior to (another); outdo. **39. steal the show,** to attract most attention; be the most popular person or item, in a theatrical performance, etc. **40. stop the show,** (in a theatrical performance, etc.) to be applauded so enthusiastically as to cause the performance to be temporarily interrupted. –**shower**, *n*.

show business *n*. the entertainment industry, especially that part concerned with variety. Also, **show biz**.

showdown /ˈʃoʊdaʊn/ *n*. **1.** the laying down of one's cards, face upwards, in a card game, especially poker. **2.** a confrontation of parties for the final settlement of a contested issue.

shower /ˈʃaʊə/ *n*. **1.** a brief fall of rain, hail, sleet, or snow. **2.** a similar fall, as of sparks or bullets. **3.** a large supply or quantity: *a shower of questions*. **4.** a party to which people bring presents for a specified recipient: *a baby shower*; *a bridal shower*. **5. a.** an apparatus for spraying water for bathing, usually set overhead above a bath or in a shower recess. **b.** a washing of the body in the water sprayed from such an apparatus. **6.** *Physics* a group of high-energy particles which originate from one fast particle, from cosmic radiation, or from an accelerator. –*v.t*. **7.** to wet with a shower. **8.** to pour (something) down in a shower. **9.** to bestow liberally or lavishly. –*v.i*. **10.** to rain in a shower. **11.** (of a person) to take a shower (def. 5b). –*phr*. **12. ... didn't come down in the last shower**, *Aust., NZ Colloq*. an expression used to indicate that someone is not naive or gullible. –**showery**, *adj*.

shower tea *n*. *Aust*. → **bridal shower**.

show-off *n*. *Colloq*. someone given to pretentious display or exhibitionism.

showroom /ˈʃoʊrum/ *n*. a room used for the display of goods or merchandise.

showrunner /ˈʃoʊrʌnə/ *n*. a person who has management responsibility for a television show, often being involved in the writing of the script, the selection of talent, and the overall creative direction.

showy /ˈʃoʊi/ *adj*. (**-wier, -wiest**) **1.** making an imposing display: *showy flowers*. **2.** ostentatious; gaudy. –**showily**, *adv*. –**showiness**, *n*.

shrank /ʃræŋk/ *v*. past tense of **shrink**.

shrapnel /ˈʃræpnəl/ *n*. **1.** a hollow projectile containing bullets or the like and a bursting charge, designed to explode before reaching its target, and to set free a shower of missiles. **2.** such projectiles collectively.

shred /ʃrɛd/ *n*. **1.** a piece cut or torn off, especially in a narrow strip. **2.** a bit; scrap. –*verb* (**shredded** *or* **shred, shredding**) –*v.t*. **3.** to cut or tear into small pieces, especially small strips; reduce to shreds. –*v.i*. **4.** to tear; be reduced to shreds.

shrew /ʃru/ *n*. **1.** any of various small, insectivorous mammals of the genus *Sorex* and allied genera, having a long, sharp snout and a mouse-like form, as the **water shrew**, *Neomys fodiens*, of Europe and the British Isles. **2.** a woman of violent temper and speech; a termagant.

shrewd /ʃrud/ *adj*. astute or sharp in practical matters: *a shrewd politician*. –**shrewdly**, *adv*. –**shrewdness**, *n*.

shriek /ʃrik/ *n*. **1.** a loud, sharp, shrill cry or other sound: *a shriek of fright*; *a shriek of laughter*; *the shriek of a whistle*. –*v.i*. **2.** to utter a loud, sharp, shrill cry. **3.** to make loud, high-pitched sounds in laughing. **4.** (of a musical instrument, a whistle, the wind, etc.) to give forth a loud, shrill sound. –*v.t*. **5.** to cry in a shriek: *to shriek defiance*. –**shrieker**, *n*.

shrift /ʃrɪft/ *phr*. **short shrift**, little consideration in dealing with someone or something; summary treatment.

shrike /ʃraɪk/ *n*. **1.** any of numerous predacious birds of the family Laniidae, of Eurasia and Africa, with a strong hooked and toothed bill, which feed on insects and sometimes on small birds and other animals. **2.** any of various other birds resembling shrikes but belonging to different families, as the Australian butcherbird of the genus *Cracticus*.

shrill /ʃrɪl/ *adj*. **1.** high-pitched and piercing: *a shrill cry*. –*v.i*. **2.** to cry shrilly. –*v.t*. **3.** to express in a shrill cry. –*n*. **4.** a shrill sound. –**shrillness**, *n*. –**shrilly**, *adv*.

shrimp /ʃrɪmp/ *n*. **1.** any of various small, long-tailed, chiefly marine, decapod crustaceans of the genus *Crangon* and allied genera (suborder Macrura), as the European *C. vulgaris*, esteemed as a table delicacy. **2.** *Colloq*. a diminutive person. **3.** *Colloq*. (*derog*.) an insignificant person. –*v.i*. **4.** to catch or attempt to catch shrimps. –**shrimper**, *n*.

shrine /ʃraɪn/ *n*. **1.** a receptacle for sacred relics; a reliquary. **2.** a structure, often of a stately or sumptuous character, enclosing the remains or relics of a saint or other holy objects and forming an object of religious veneration and pilgrimage. **3.** any structure or place consecrated or devoted to some saint or deity, as an altar, chapel, church, or temple. **4.** any place or object hallowed by its history or associations. –*v.t*. **5.** to enshrine.

shrink /ʃrɪŋk/ *verb* (**shrank** *or* **shrunk, shrunk** *or* **shrunken, shrinking**) –*v.i*. **1.** to draw back: *the frightened child shrank into a corner*. **2.** to become smaller with heat, cold, moisture, etc.; contract. **3.** to become less in extent or compass: *business is shrinking these days*. –*v.t*. **4.** to cause to shrink or contract. –*n*. **5.** a shrinking. **6.** a shrinking movement. **7.** Also, **headshrinker**. *Colloq*. a psychiatrist. –**shrinkable**, *adj*. –**shrinker**, *n*. –**shrinkingly**, *adv*. –**shrinkage**, *n*.

shrink-wrap *v.t*. (**-wrapped, -wrapping**) to enclose (an object) in a flexible plastic wrapping which shrinks to the shape of the object, sealing it in.

shrivel /ˈʃrɪvəl/ *verb* (**-elled** *or, Chiefly US*, **-eled, -elling** *or, Chiefly US*, **-eling**) –*v.i*. **1.** to contract and wrinkle, as from great heat or cold. **2.** to wither; become impotent. –*v.t*. **3.** (of heat or cold) to make (something) contract and wrinkle. **4.** to make impotent. –**shrivelled**, *adj*.

shroud /ʃraʊd/ *n*. **1.** a cloth in which a corpse is wrapped for burial. **2.** something which covers or hides like a garment: *a shroud of rain*. **3.** (*usu. pl*.) *Naut*. one of a set of strong ropes running from a masthead to the side of a ship to help support the mast. **4.** *Mechanics* **a.** circular webs used to stiffen the sides of gear teeth. **b.** a strip used to strengthen turbine blades. –*v.t*. **5.** to wrap or clothe for burial. **6.** to cover; hide from view. **7.** to veil; wrap in darkness or mystery. –**shroudless**, *adj*.

shrub /ʃrʌb/ *n*. a woody perennial plant smaller than a tree, usually having permanent stems branching from or near the ground. –**shrublike**, *adj*.

shrubbery /ˈʃrʌbəri/ *n*. (*pl*. **-ries**) **1.** shrubs collectively. **2.** a plantation or plot of shrubs.

shrug /ʃrʌg/ *verb* (**shrugged, shrugging**) –*v.t*. **1.** to raise and lower (the shoulders), expressing indifference, disdain, etc. –*v.i*. **2.** to raise and lower the shoulders, expressing indifference, disdain, etc. –*n*. **3.** this movement. –*phr*. **4. shrug off**, to disregard; take no notice of: *to shrug off an insult*.

shtum /ʃtʊm/ *phr*. **keep shtum**, *Colloq*. to keep quiet about something. Also, **shtoom**.

shudder /ˈʃʌdə/ *v.i*. **1.** to tremble with a sudden convulsive movement, as from horror, fear, or cold. –*n*. **2.** a convulsive movement of the body, as from horror, fear, or cold. –**shudderingly**, *adv*.

shuffle /ˈʃʌfəl/ *v.i*. **1.** to walk without lifting the feet or with clumsy steps and a shambling gait. **2.** to scrape the feet over the floor in dancing. **3.** to get (*into*, etc.) in a clumsy manner: *to shuffle into one's clothes*. **4.** to get (*into, out of*, etc.) in an underhand or evasive manner: *to shuffle out of responsibilities*. **5.** to mix cards in a pack so as to change their relative position. –*v.t*. **6.** to move (the feet, etc.) along the ground or floor without lifting them. **7.** to perform (a dance, etc.) with such movements. **8.** to move this way and that. **9.** to put, thrust, or bring (*in, out*, etc.) trickily, evasively, or haphazardly. **10.** to mix (cards in a pack) so as to change their relative position. **11.** to jumble together; mix in a disorderly heap. *–n.* **12.** a scraping movement; a dragging gait. **13.** an evasive trick; evasion. **14.** a shuffling of cards in a pack. **15.** right or turn to shuffle in card-playing. **16.** a dance in which the feet are shuffled along the floor. *–phr.* **17. shuffle off, a.** to thrust aside or get rid of. **b.** to go off with a shuffling gait. **–shuffler**, *n.*

shun /ʃʌn/ *v.t.* (**shunned, shunning**) to keep away from (a place, person, etc.), from dislike, caution, etc.; take pains to avoid. **–shunner**, *n.*

shunt /ʃʌnt/ *v.t.* **1.** to move or turn aside or out of the way. **2.** *Trains* to move from one line of rails to another or from the main track to a siding. *–v.i.* **3.** to move or turn aside or out of the way. *–n.* **4.** the act of shunting; a move. **5.** *Elect.* a conducting element bridged across (part of) a circuit, establishing a second current path. **6.** a railway siding. **–shunter**, *n.*

shush /ʃʊʃ/ *interj., n., v.* → **shoosh**.

shut /ʃʌt/ *verb* (**shut, shutting**) *–v.t.* **1.** to put (a door, cover, etc.) in position to close or obstruct. **2.** Also, **shut up.** to close the doors of: *shut up the shop.* **3.** to close by folding or bringing the parts together: *shut your eyes; shut the book; shut the fan.* **4.** to confine; enclose: *to shut a bird into a cage.* **5.** to bar; exclude: *to shut a person from one's house.* **6.** to close down; cease normal operation: *they decided to shut the office during redecoration.* *–v.i.* **7.** to become shut or closed; close. *–adj.* **8.** closed; fastened up. *–phr.* **9. keep one's mouth shut, a.** to remain silent. **b.** to keep a secret. **10. shut away,** to hide or confine. **11. shut down, a.** to close by lowering, as a lid. **b.** to cover or envelop, as fog. **c.** to close down, especially for a time, as a factory. **d.** to stop (a machine, engine, etc.). **12. shut down on** (or **upon**), *Colloq.* to put a stop or check to. **13. shut in,** to imprison; confine; enclose. **14. shut off, a.** to stop the flow of (water, electricity, etc.). **b.** to keep separate; isolate. **15. shut one's eyes to,** to refuse to notice; ignore. **16. shut out,** to exclude; keep out. **17. shut up, a.** to imprison; confine; hide from view. **b.** (*oft. used imperatively*) *Colloq.* to stop talking; become silent. **c.** *Colloq.* to stop (someone) from talking; silence.

shut-eye *n. Colloq.* sleep.

shutter /ˈʃʌtə/ *n.* **1.** a hinged or otherwise movable cover for a window. **2.** a movable cover, slide, etc., for an opening. **3.** *Photography* a mechanical device for opening and closing the aperture of a camera lens to expose a plate or film. *–v.t.* **4.** to close or provide with shutters.

shutter speed *n. Photography* the period of time between the opening and closing of the shutter; together with the aperture setting, this determines how much light is admitted per exposure.

shuttle /ˈʃʌtl/ *n.* **1.** a device in a loom for passing or shooting the weft thread through the shed from one side of the web to the other. **2.** the sliding container that carries the lower thread in a sewing machine. **3.** Also, **shuttle service.** a transport service, usually running at frequent intervals directly between two points. *–v.i., v.t.* **4.** to move quickly to and fro like a shuttle.

shuttlecock /ˈʃʌtlkɒk/ *n.* **1.** a piece of cork, or similar light material, with feathers stuck in one end, intended to be struck to and fro, as with a racquet in the game of badminton or with a battledore in the game of battledore, or with a wooden bat in the game of shuttlecock. **2.** the game of battledore. *–v.t.* **3.** to send, or bandy to and fro, like a shuttlecock. *–v.i.* **4.** to move to and fro like a shuttlecock.

shy¹ /ʃaɪ/ *adj.* (**shyer** *or* **shier, shyest** *or* **shiest**) **1.** bashful; retiring. **2.** easily frightened away; timid. **3.** suspicious; distrustful: *once bitten, twice shy.* **4.** reluctant; wary. **5.** *Colloq.* short of the required amount or sum: *shy of funds.* *–v.i.* (**shied, shying**) **6.** to start back or aside, as in fear, especially a horse. **7.** to draw back; recoil. *–n.* (*pl.* **shies**) **8.** a sudden start aside, as in fear. *–phr.* **9. fight shy of,** to avoid; keep away from. **10. shy away from,** to recoil from, as in fear or distaste. **–shyer,** *n.* **–shyly,** *adv.* **–shyness,** *n.*

shy² /ʃaɪ/ *v.t.* (**shied, shying**) **1.** to throw with a sudden swift movement: *to shy a stone.* *–n.* (*pl.* **shies**) **2.** a sudden swift throw.

shyster /ˈʃaɪstə/ *n. Colloq.* **1.** someone who gets along by petty, sharp practices. **2.** a lawyer who uses unprofessional or questionable methods.

Siamese cat /saɪəmiz ˈkæt/ *n.* one of a breed of slender, short-haired cats having blue eyes, a small head, and a fawn or grey colour with extremities of a darker shading. Also, **Siamese.**

Siamese twins *pl. n.* → **conjoined twins.**

sibilant /ˈsɪbələnt/ *adj.* **1.** hissing. **2.** *Phonetics* characterised by a hissing sound; denoting sounds like those spelt with *s* in *this, rose, pressure, pleasure.* **–sibilance, sibilancy,** *n.* **–sibilantly,** *adv.*

sibling /ˈsɪblɪŋ/ *n.* a brother or sister.

sibyl /ˈsɪbəl/ *n.* a prophetess or witch. **–sibylic** /səˈbɪlɪk/, **sibylline** /ˈsɪbəlaɪn, səˈbɪlaɪn/, *adj.*

sic¹ /sɪk/ *adv.* so; thus (often used parenthetically to show that something, especially an error, has been copied exactly from the original).

sic² /sɪk/ *v.t.* (**sicked, sicking**) **1.** to attack (especially of a dog). **2.** to incite (especially a dog) to attack.

sick /sɪk/ *adj.* **1.** affected with any disorder of health; ill, unwell, or ailing. **2.** affected with nausea; inclined to vomit, or vomiting. **3.** of or attended with sickness. **4.** of or appropriate to sick persons: *on sick leave.* **5.** deeply affected with some feeling comparable to physical disorder, as sorrow, longing, repugnance, weariness, etc.: *sick at heart.* **6.** morbid; macabre: *sick humour; a sick joke.* **7.** *Agric.* **a.** failing to sustain adequate harvests of some crop, usually specified: *a lucerne-sick soil.* **b.** containing harmful microorganisms: *a sick field.* **8.** *Colloq.* not in proper condition; impaired: *a sick engine.* **9.** *Colloq.* excellent; terrific. **10.** *Colloq.* disgusted; chagrined. *–n.* **11.** vomit. *–phr.* **12. be sick (and tired) of** *or* **be sick to death of,** to feel fed up with; have had enough of: *he was sick of his employer's complaints about his work.* **13. sick as a dog,** *Colloq.* very sick. **14. sick in the head,** *Colloq.* mentally deranged. **15. sick up,** to vomit. **16. the sick,** sick people. **–sicken,** *v.* **–sickness,** *n.*

sickie /ˈsɪki/ *n. Aust., NZ Colloq.* a day taken off work with pay, because of genuine or feigned illness.

sickle /ˈsɪkəl/ *n.* an implement for cutting grain, grass, etc., consisting of a curved, hooklike blade mounted in a short handle.

sick leave *n.* leave of absence granted because of illness.

sicklebill /ˈsɪkəlbɪl/ *n.* any of various birds with a curved bill, such as various birds-of-paradise of the genus *Epimachus*, or either of two hummingbirds of the genus *Eutoxeres*, or the white ibis, *Threskiornis molucca.*

sickly /ˈsɪkli/ *adj.* (**-lier, -liest**) **1.** not strong; unhealthy; ailing. **2.** of, connected with, or resulting from ill health: *a sickly complexion.* **3.** (of food) too sweet; rich. **4.** weak or nauseating: *sickly sentimentality.* **5.** (of light, colour, etc.) faint or feeble. **–sickliness,** *n.*

side /saɪd/ *n.* **1.** one of the surfaces or lines bounding a thing. **2.** either of the two surfaces of paper, cloth, etc. **3.** one of the two surfaces of an object other than the front, back, top, and bottom. **4.** either of the two lateral (right and left) parts of a thing. **5.** either lateral half of the body of a person or an animal, especially of the trunk. **6.** the space immediately beside someone or something: *the girl stood at his side.* **7.** an aspect; phase: *all sides of a question.* **8.** *Colloq.* the region of or near a specified town or natural feature: *I come from the Cowra side.* **9.** region, direction, or position with reference to a central line, space, or point: *the east side of a city.* **10.** a department or division, as of teaching in a school: *the science side; the arts side.* **11.** a slope, as of a hill. **12.** one of two or more parties concerned in a case, contest, etc. **13.** line of descent through either the father or the mother: *his maternal side.* **14.** *Colloq.* an affectedly superior manner; pretentious airs: *to put on side.* –*adj.* **15.** being at or on one side: *the side aisles of a theatre.* **16.** coming from one side: *side glance.* **17.** directed towards one side: *side blow.* **18.** subordinate: *a side issue.* –*phr.* (*v.* **sided, siding**) **19. on side**, likely to support another, as in an argument, application, etc.: *John thinks he has Diana on side.* **20. on the far side of**, on the more remote side of (some event, place, etc., seen as a point of divide): *on the far side of the grave.* **21. on the side, a.** separate from the main subject. **b.** *Colloq.* as a sideline; secretly. **22. on the … side**, tending towards the quality or condition specified: *this coffee is a little on the weak side.* **23. on this side of**, on the nearer side of (some event, place, etc., seen as a point of divide): *on this side of sleep.* **24. put on one side**, to leave for later consideration; shelve. **25. side against**, to place oneself against (a side or party) to support or oppose an issue. **26. side by side**, next to one another; together; in close proximity. **27. side with**, to place oneself with (a side or party) to support or oppose an issue. **28. take sides**, to support or show favour for one person or party in a dispute, contest, or the like. **29. this side of**, before: *this side of Christmas.*

-side a combining form used to indicate a locality which is specified: *beachside; harbourside; poolside.*

sidebar /ˈsaɪdba/ *n. Internet* a window shaped like a narrow column placed down the side of a web page, offering various options, information, etc.

sideboard /ˈsaɪdbɔd/ *n.* **1.** a piece of furniture, as in a dining room, often with shelves, drawers, etc., for holding articles of table service. **2.** (*oft. pl.*) → **sideburn**.

sideburn /ˈsaɪdbɜn/ *n.* (*oft. pl.*) a short amount of facial hair extending from the hairline to below the ear of a man, usually worn with an unbearded chin. Also, **sideboard, sidelever**.

sidecar /ˈsaɪdka/ *n.* **1.** a small car attached on one side to a motorcycle and supported on the other by a wheel of its own: used for a passenger, parcels, etc. –*adv.* **2.** in a sidecar: *he rode sidecar.*

side effect *n.* any effect produced, as of a drug, other than those originally intended, especially an unpleasant or harmful effect.

sidekick /ˈsaɪdkɪk/ *n. Colloq.* **1.** an assistant. **2.** a close friend.

sidelever /ˈsaɪdlivə/ *n.* (*oft. pl.*) → **sideburn**. –**sidelevered,** *adj.*

sideline /ˈsaɪdlaɪn/ *n.* **1.** a line at the side of something. **2.** an additional or auxiliary line of goods or of business. **3.** *Sport* **a.** a line or mark defining the limit of play on the side of the field in football, etc. **b.** (*pl.*) the area immediately beyond any of the sidelines. –*v.t.* **4.** *Sport* to cause (a player) to become a non-participant, an observer from the sidelines: *the accident sidelined him for eight months.* **5.** to put outside the group involved in the main activity of an enterprise, organisation, etc. –*phr.* **6. on the sidelines, a.** not playing in a contest or game. **b.** not involved in the main action.

sidelong /ˈsaɪdlɒŋ/ *adj.* **1.** directed to one side. –*adv.* **2.** towards the side; obliquely.

sidereal /saɪˈdɪəriəl/ *adj.* **1.** determined by the stars: *sidereal time.* **2.** of or relating to the stars.

sidero- a word element meaning 'iron', 'steel', as in *siderolite.* Also, (*before vowels*), **sider-**.

sideshow /ˈsaɪdʃoʊ/ *n.* **1.** a minor show or exhibition in connection with a principal one as at a fair, circus, live band performance, etc. **2.** any subordinate event or matter. Also, **side show**.

sidestep /ˈsaɪdstɛp/ *verb* (**-stepped, -stepping**) –*v.i.* **1.** to step to one side, as in avoidance. **2.** to try to avoid making a decision, solving a problem, etc. –*v.t.* **3.** to avoid by or as if by stepping to one side: *I sidestepped the puddle.* –**sidestepper,** *n.*

sidetrack /ˈsaɪdtræk/ *v.t.* **1.** to distract from the main subject or course. –*v.i.* **2.** to move from the main subject or course. –*n.* **3.** an act of sidetracking; a diversion; distraction. **4.** a temporary road constructed as a detour for the use of traffic while work is being done on the main road.

sideways /ˈsaɪdweɪz/ *adv.* **1.** with the side foremost. **2.** facing or inclining to the side. **3.** towards or from one side. –*adj.* **4.** moving from or towards one side. **5.** towards or from one side. Also, **sidewise** /ˈsaɪdwaɪz/.

siding /ˈsaɪdɪŋ/ *n.* **1.** a short branch off a railway track, often connected at both ends to the main-line track, and used for shunting or for loading, unloading, and storing goods trucks. **2.** the timber, metal, or composite material forming the cladding of a framed building.

sidle /ˈsaɪdl/ *v.i.* **1.** to move sideways or obliquely. **2.** *NZ* to negotiate a steep slope by moving across it at an angle. **3.** to edge along furtively. –*n.* **4.** a sidling movement.

SIDS /sɪdz/ *n.* → **sudden infant death syndrome**.

siege /sidʒ/ *n.* **1.** the operation of reducing and capturing a fortified place by surrounding it, cutting off supplies, undermining, bringing guns to bear, bombing, and other offensive operations. **2.** any prolonged or persistent endeavour to overcome resistance. –*phr.* **3. lay siege to**, to besiege. **4. under siege, a.** experiencing a siege imposed by an enemy. **b.** opposed by everyone.

siemens /ˈsimənz/ *n.* (*pl.* **-mens**) the SI unit of electrical conductance; the conductance of a conductor that has an electrical resistance of one ohm. *Symbol:* S

sierra /siˈɛərə, siˈɛrə/ *n.* a chain of hills or mountains, the peaks of which suggest the teeth of a saw.

siesta /siˈɛstə/ *n.* a midday or afternoon rest or nap, especially as taken in Spain and other hot countries.

sieve /sɪv/ *n.* **1.** an instrument, with a meshed or perforated bottom, used for separating coarse from fine parts of loose matter, for straining liquids, etc., especially one with a circular frame and fine meshes or perforations. –*v.t.* (**sieved, sieving**) **2.** to put or force through a sieve; sift. –*phr.* **3. have a head like a sieve**, *Colloq.* to be very forgetful.

sievert /ˈsivɜt/ *n.* the SI derived unit of dose equivalent. *Symbol:* Sv See **dose equivalent**.

sift /sɪft/ *v.t.* **1.** to separate the coarse parts of (flour, ashes, etc.) with a sieve. **2.** to scatter by means of a sieve: *to sift sugar onto cake.* **3.** to separate by or as if by a sieve. **4.** to examine or question closely. –*v.i.* **5.** to use a sieve. **6.** to pass through a sieve. –**sifter,** *n.*

sig file /ˈsɪg faɪl/ *n. Computers* a small text file identifying the sender of an email that can be automatically attached to returning email messages.

sigh /saɪ/ *v.i.* **1.** to let out one's breath slowly and with a drawn-out sound, as from sorrow, tiredness, relief, etc. **2.** (usu. fol. by *for*) to yearn or long. **3.** to make a sound like that of sighing: *the wind was sighing.* –*v.t.* **4.** to express with a sigh. –*n.* **5.** an act or sound of sighing. –**sigher,** *n.*

sight /saɪt/ *n.* **1.** the power or faculty of seeing; vision. **2.** the act or fact of seeing. **3.** range of vision: *in sight of* *land.* **4.** a view; glimpse. **5.** mental view or regard. **6.** something seen or to be seen; spectacle: *the sights of the town.* **7.** *Colloq.* something that looks odd or unsightly: *he looks a sight in his new suit.* **8.** an observation taken with a surveying or other instrument. **9.** a device on or used with a surveying instrument, a firearm, etc., serving to guide the eye. *–v.t.* **10.** to get sight of: *to sight a ship.* **11.** to take a sight or observation of, especially with an instrument. **12.** to direct by a sight or sights, as a firearm. **13.** to provide with sights, or adjust the sights of, as a gun. **14.** to view as part of an official procedure: *to sight the documents.* *–v.i.* **15.** to take a sight, as in shooting. *–phr.* **16. a sight,** *Colloq.* a great deal. **17. at sight,** on presentation: *a bill of exchange payable at sight.* **18. catch sight of,** to glimpse; see, especially briefly or momentarily. **19. have someone in one's sights,** to be intent on attacking some particular person. **20. know by sight,** to recognise (somebody or something) seen previously. **21. lower one's sights,** to adopt a less lofty ambition. **22. not by a long sight,** on no account; definitely not. **23. on sight,** as soon as one sees a thing. **24. out of sight,** beyond view; out of the line of one's vision. **25. raise one's sights,** to adopt a more lofty ambition. **26. set one's sights on,** to adopt as an ambition or goal: *he set his sights on the prime ministership.* **27. sight unseen, a.** without an examination of the goods before purchase. **b.** without an interview previous to employment.

sightscreen /'saɪtskrɪn/ *n.* (in cricket) a screen, often movable, set on the boundary behind the wicket, as an aid to the person batting in sighting the ball. Also, **sight screen, sightboard.**

sightseeing /'saɪtsiɪŋ/ *n.* the act of seeing objects or places of interest. **–sightseer,** *n.*

sign /saɪn/ *n.* **1.** a token; indication. **2.** a conventional mark, figure, or symbol used technically instead of the word or words which it represents, as an abbreviation. **3.** *Music* a signature. **4.** *Maths* the plus or minus sign. **5.** a motion or gesture intended to express or convey an idea. **6.** an inscribed board, space, etc., serving for information, advertisement, warning, etc., on a building, along a street, or the like. **7.** an omen; portent. **8.** *Astrology* any of the twelve divisions of the zodiac, each denoted by the name of a constellation or its symbol, and each (because of the precession of the equinoxes) now containing the constellation west of the one from which it took its name. *–v.t.* **9.** to affix a signature to. **10.** to write as a signature: *to sign one's name.* **11.** to engage by written agreement: *to sign a new player.* **12.** to communicate by a sign. *–v.i.* **13.** to write one's signature, as a token of agreement, obligation, receipt, etc. **14.** to make a sign or signal. **15.** to use sign language to communicate with deaf people. *–phr.* **16. sign away,** to dispose of by affixing one's signature to a document. **17. sign off, a.** to cease broadcasting a radio or television program, as at the end of the day. **b.** to withdraw from some responsibility, project, etc. **c.** to terminate a session on a computer. **18. sign off on,** to indicate one's agreement with (a statement, plan, budget, etc.) by one's signature on a document. **19. sign on, a.** to employ; hire. **b.** to commit oneself to employment, as by signing a contract. **c.** to commence a session on a computer. **20. sign up, a.** to enlist, as for the armed services. **b.** to commit (someone) to a contract by having them sign it.

signal /'sɪgnəl/ *n.* **1.** a gesture, act, light, etc., serving to warn, direct, command, etc. **2.** anything seen as the occasion for action: *her success was the signal for a party.* **3.** a token; indication. **4.** *Radio, etc.* **a.** the impulses, waves, sounds, etc., sent or received. **b.** the wave which controls and varies the carrier wave. *–adj.* **5.** serving as a sign: *a signal flag.* **6.** remarkable or notable: *a signal failure.* *–verb* **(-nalled** *or,* US, **-naled,**

-nalling *or,* US, **-naling)** *–v.t.* **7.** to make a signal to. **8.** to make known by a signal. *–v.i.* **9.** to exchange information by a signal or signals. **–signaller,** *n.* **–signalling,** *n.*

signature /'sɪgnətʃə/ *n.* **1.** a person's name, or a mark representing it, written by himself or herself. **2.** the act of signing a document. **3.** *Music* a sign or set of signs at the beginning of a stave to indicate the key or the time of a piece. *–adj.* **4.** typical of a style: *signature dish; signature building.* **–signatory,** *n.*

signet /'sɪgnət/ *n.* **1.** a small seal, as in a finger ring. **2.** a small official seal. **3.** an impression made by or as if by a signet. *–v.t.* **4.** to stamp or mark with a signet.

significant /sɪg'nɪfəkənt/ *adj.* **1.** important; of consequence. **2.** expressing a meaning; indicative. **3.** having a special or covert meaning; suggestive. **–significance,** *n.* **–significantly,** *adv.*

signify /'sɪgnəfaɪ/ *verb* **(-fied, -fying)** *–v.t.* **1.** to make known by signs, speech, or action. **2.** to be a sign of; mean; portend. *–v.i.* **3.** to be of importance or consequence. **–signifier,** *n.* **–signification** /sɪgnəfə'keɪʃən/, *n.*

sign language *n.* a communication system using gestures rather than speech or writing, as that used with the hearing-impaired.

silage /'saɪlɪdʒ/ *n.* green fodder preserved in a silo, silage pit, or mound.

silence /'saɪləns/ *n.* **1.** the absence of any sound or noise; stillness. **2.** the condition or fact of being silent; muteness. **3.** lack of mention: *to pass over a matter in silence.* **4.** secrecy. *–v.t.* **(-lenced, -lencing) 5.** to put or bring to silence; still. **6.** to put to rest (doubts, etc.); quieten. *–interj.* **7.** be silent! **–silent,** *adj.* **–silently,** *adv.*

silent majority *n.* the people within a community who are not active politically and who do not express their views publicly, presumed to be numerous and to support moderate or conservative policies.

silent partner *n.* a partner taking no active or public part in the conduct of a business. Also, **dormant partner, sleeping partner.**

silhouette /sɪlu'ɛt, sɪlə'weɪ/ *n.* **1.** an outline drawing, uniformly filled in with black, like a shadow. **2.** a dark image outlined against a lighter background. *–v.t.* **(-etted, -etting) 3.** to show in, or as in, a silhouette.

silic- a word element meaning 'flint', 'silica', 'silicon', as in *silicide.* Also, **silici-, silico-.**

silica /'sɪlɪkə/ *n.* silicon dioxide, SiO_2, appearing as quartz, sand, flint, and agate. **–siliceous,** *adj.*

silicate /'sɪləkət, -keɪt/ *n.* any salt derived from silica.

silicon /'sɪləkən/ *n.* a nonmetallic element, having amorphous and crystalline forms, occurring in the combined state in minerals and rocks and constituting more than one fourth of the earth's crust; used in steelmaking, etc.; widely used as a semiconductor in solid-state electronics. *Symbol:* Si; *relative atomic mass:* 28.086; *atomic number:* 14; *density:* 2.33 at 20°C.

silicosis /sɪlə'koʊsəs/ *n. Pathol.* a disease of the lungs due to inhaling siliceous particles, as by stonecutters.

silk /sɪlk/ *n.* **1.** the fine, soft, lustrous fibre obtained from the cocoon of the silkworm. **2.** thread made of this fibre. **3.** cloth made of this fibre. **4.** a garment of this cloth. **5.** the gown of such material, worn distinctively by a Queen's or King's Counsel at the bar. **6.** any fibre or filamentous matter resembling silk. **7.** the hair-like styles on an ear of maize. **8.** *Colloq.* a Queen's or King's Counsel. *–adj.* **9.** made of silk. **10.** resembling silk; silky. **11.** of or relating to silk. *–v.i.* **12.** *US* (of corn) to be in the course of forming silk. *–phr.* **13. take silk,** to become a Queen's or King's Counsel. **–silken,** *adj.* **–silky,** *adj.*

silk-screen *v.t.* to produce by silk-screen printing. Also, **screen-print.**

silk-screen printing *n.* a process of printing from stencils, which may be photographically made or cut by hand, through a fine mesh of silk, metal, or other material. **–silk-screen print,** *n.*

silkworm /ˈsɪlkwɜm/ *n.* the caterpillar of any moth of the families Bombycidae and Saturniidae, which spins a fine, soft filament (silk) to form a cocoon, in which it is enclosed while in the pupal stage, especially the **Chinese silkworm,** *Bombyx mori.*

sill /sɪl/ *n.* **1.** a horizontal timber, block, or the like, serving as a foundation of a wall, house, etc. **2.** the horizontal piece or member beneath a window, door, or other opening. **3.** *Geol.* a tabular body of intrusive igneous rock, ordinarily between beds of sedimentary rocks or matter ejected by a volcano.

silly /ˈsɪli/ *adj.* **(-lier, -liest) 1.** lacking good sense; foolish; stupid. **2.** absurd or ridiculous. **3.** *Colloq.* stunned. **4.** *Cricket* (of a fielding position) close in to the wicket of the person batting: *silly mid-off.* *–n.* (*pl.* **-lies) 5.** *Colloq.* a silly person. **–sillily,** *adv.* **–silliness,** *n.*

silo /ˈsaɪloʊ/ *n.* (*pl.* **-los) 1.** a tower-like structure, proofed against weather and vermin, for storing grain. **2.** a similar structure in which fermenting green fodder is preserved for future use as silage. **3.** a unit within an organisation that does not cooperate with other units but remains inward-looking.

silt /sɪlt/ *n.* **1.** earthy matter, fine sand, or the like, carried by moving or running water and deposited as a sediment. *–v.i.* Also, **silt up. 2.** to become filled or choked up with silt. **–silty,** *adj.* **–siltation,** *n.*

Silurian /saɪˈljʊriən/ *adj.* **1.** relating to an early Palaeozoic geological period or system of rocks. *–n.* **2.** the Silurian period or system of rocks.

silver /ˈsɪlvə/ *n.* **1.** *Chem.* a white ductile metallic element, used for making mirrors, coins, ornaments, table utensils, etc. *Symbol:* Ag; *atomic number:* 47; *relative atomic mass:* 107.87. **2.** coin made of silver or of a metal resembling silver; money. **3.** silverware; meal-table articles made of or plated with silver. **4.** something looking like this metal in colour, lustre, etc. **5.** a shiny whitish-grey colour. *–adj.* **6.** consisting or made of silver; plated with silver. **7.** of or relating to silver. **8.** (of coins) made of a metal or alloy resembling silver, as cupronickel. **9.** producing or yielding silver. **10.** having the colour silver, or tinted with silver: *a silver dress; silver blue.* **11.** clear and soft: *silver sounds.* **12.** persuasive; eloquent: *a silver tongue.* **13.** indicating the 25th event of a series, as a wedding anniversary. *–v.t.* **14.** to coat with silver or some silver-like substance. **15.** to give a silver colour to. *–v.i.* **16.** to become a silver colour. **–silverer,** *n.*

silverback /ˈsɪlvəbæk/ *n.* a fully mature male gorilla with white hair on its back.

silver beech *n.* a New Zealand forest tree, *Nothofagus menziesii,* with a silvery bark.

silverbeet /ˈsɪlvəbit/ *n.* a form of beet, *Beta vulgaris cicla,* with large, fleshy, strongly veined, green leaves and a long fleshy stalk, and used as a vegetable; spinach. Also, **silver beet.**

silver belly *n.* **1.** → **silver biddy. 2.** *NZ* a freshwater eel.

silver biddy *n.* any of various small, silvery fish of the family Gerreidae, found in tropical Australian coastal waters.

silver birch *n.* **1.** a widely distributed European tree, *Betula pendula,* having a whitish papery bark. **2.** any other member of the genus *Betula* with a similar bark. **3.** *NZ* → **silver beech.**

silver bullet *n.* a certain and effective remedy, as a drug, defence system, etc., usually seen as an unrealistic ideal.

silvereye /ˈsɪlvəraɪ/ *n.* a common, small, predominantly yellow-olive white-eye, *Zosterops lateralis,* of Australasia, feeding on insects, seed, nectar and fruit, and having numerous subspecies as the **Capricorn silvereye,** *Z. l. chlorocephalus* of Heron Island; the subspecies *Z. l. lateralis,* was self-introduced to New Zealand in the 1850s.

silver fern *n.* **1.** a handsome tree fern, *Cyathea dealbata,* of New Zealand characterised by the white undersurface of its fronds; ponga. **2.** a different New Zealand fern, *Paesia scaberula,* with a similar colouring.

silverfish /ˈsɪlvəfɪʃ/ *n.* (*pl.* **-fishes** *or, especially collectively,* **-fish) 1.** a white or silvery goldfish, *Carassius auratus.* **2.** any of various other silvery fishes. **3.** any of certain small, wingless, thysanuran insects (genus *Lepisma*) damaging to books, wallpaper, etc.

silver gull *n.* the common seagull of Australia, *Larus novaehollandiae,* having white plumage with a grey back, black-tipped flight feathers, and red eye-ring, bill, and legs.

silver plate *n.* **1.** a thin silver coating deposited on the surface of another metal, usually by electrolysis. **2.** silver-plated tableware. **–silver-plate,** *v.*

silverside /ˈsɪlvəsaɪd/ *n.* a cut of beef from the outside portion of a full butt, below the aitchbone and above the leg, usually boiled or pickled.

SIM card /ˈsɪm kad/ *n.* a circuit-bearing card inserted into a mobile phone which contains the subscriber's authorisation to use a certain mobile phone network. Also, **sim card.**

sim game *n.* a computer game that is based on the simulation of some real-world activity, the player taking on one or more personas of the characters involved.

simian /ˈsɪmiən/ *adj.* **1.** of or relating to an ape or monkey. **2.** characteristic of apes or monkeys. *–n.* **3.** an ape or monkey.

similar /ˈsɪmələ/ *adj.* **1.** having likeness or resemblance, especially in a general way. **2.** *Geom.* (of figures) having the same shape; having corresponding sides proportional and corresponding angles equal. **–similarly,** *adv.* **–similarity,** *n.*

simile /ˈsɪməli/ *n. Rhetoric* **1.** a figure of speech directly expressing a resemblance, in one or more points, of one thing to another, as *a man like an ox.* **2.** an instance of this figure, or a use of words exemplifying it.

similitude /səˈmɪlətjud, -tʃud/ *n.* **1.** likeness; resemblance. **2.** a person or thing that is the like, match, or counterpart of another. **3.** semblance; image. **4.** a likening or comparison; a parable or allegory.

simmer /ˈsɪmə/ *v.i.* **1.** (of food) to cook in a liquid just below the boiling point. **2.** to be in a state of subdued activity, excitement, etc. *–v.t.* **3.** to cook (food) in a liquid just below the boiling point. *–n.* **4.** the state or process of simmering. *–phr.* **5. simmer down,** *Colloq.* to become calm or calmer.

simper /ˈsɪmpə/ *v.i.* **1.** to smile in a silly, self-conscious way. *–v.t.* **2.** to say with a simper. *–n.* **3.** a silly, self-conscious smile. **–simperer,** *n.* **–simperingly,** *adv.*

simple /ˈsɪmpəl/ *adj.* **1.** easy to understand, deal with, use, etc.: *a simple matter; simple tools.* **2.** not having complicated or unnecessary elements: *a simple style.* **3.** not having or offering the best in comfort and luxury. **4.** plain and open in behaviour; unaffected. **5.** lacking mental acuteness or sense. **6.** considered alone; mere; bare: *the simple truth; a simple fact.* **7.** sincere; innocent. **8.** common or ordinary: *a simple soldier.* **9.** unlearned; ignorant. **10.** *Chem.* **a.** made of one substance or element: *a simple substance.* **b.** not mixed. **11.** *Zool.* not compound. **–simpleness,** *n.* **–simplicity,** *n.*

simple carbohydrate *n.* any monosaccharide or disaccharide such as sucrose, lactose or fructose, present in milk, fruits, some vegetables, processed foods, etc. Compare **complex carbohydrate.**

simple interest *n. Finance* interest which is not compounded, that is, interest calculated only on the original capital invested or the original amount of the loan.

simple past tense *n. Gram.* the form of the past tense which signifies an action which has occurred and has been completed in the past, as in *He cooked dinner* contrasted with *He has been cooking dinner.*

simple present tense *n. Gram.* the form of the present tense which signifies an action happening now with no indication as to whether it is continuing, as in *She goes to school* contrasted with the continuous form *She is going to school.*

simpleton /'sɪmpəltən/ *n.* a foolish, ignorant, or half-witted person; fool.

simplex /'sɪmplɛks/ *adj.* simple; consisting of or characterised by a single element, action, or the like: *a simplex circuit* (in which one telephone call and one telegraph message are transmitted simultaneously over a single pair of wires).

simplify /'sɪmpləfaɪ/ *v.t.* (**-fied, -fying**) to make less complex or complicated; make plainer or easier. –**simplification** /sɪmpləfə'keɪʃən/, *n.* –**simplifier**, *n.*

simplistic /sɪm'plɪstɪk/ *adj.* characterised by extreme simplification, especially if misleading; oversimplified. –**simplistically**, *adv.*

simply /'sɪmpli/ *adv.* **1.** in a simple manner. **2.** plainly; unaffectedly. **3.** not deceitfully or craftily. **4.** merely; only. **5.** unwisely; foolishly. **6.** absolutely: *simply irresistible.*

simulate /'sɪmjəleɪt/ *v.t.* **1.** to make a pretence of. **2.** to assume or have the appearance of. **3.** *Maths* to set up an analogue of (a system) in order to study its properties. –**simulative**, *adj.* –**simulatively**, *adv.*

simulation /sɪmjə'leɪʃən/ *n.* **1.** a pretending; a feigning. **2.** assumption of a particular appearance or form. **3.** *Computers* **a.** the technique of establishing a routine for one computer to make it function as nearly as possible like another computer. **b.** the representation of physical systems, phenomena, etc., by computers. **4.** the practice of constructing a model of a machine in order to test behaviour.

simulator /'sɪmjəleɪtə/ *n.* a training or experimental device that simulates movement, flight, or some other condition.

simulcast /'sɪməlkast, 'saɪ-/ *n.* simultaneous broadcast of the same program by two separate radio stations or by a radio and a television station.

simultaneous /sɪməl'teɪniəs/, *Orig. US* /saɪ-/ *adj.* existing, occurring, or operating at the same time: *simultaneous movements*; *simultaneous announcements.* –**simultaneously**, *adv.* –**simultaneousness, simultaneity** /sɪməltə'nɪəti/, *n.*

sin¹ /sɪn/ *n.* **1.** transgression of divine law. **2.** an act regarded as such transgression, or any violation, especially a wilful or deliberate one, of some religious or moral principle. **3.** any serious transgression or offence. –*v.i.* (**sinned, sinning**) **4.** to do a sinful act. **5.** to offend against a principle, standard, etc. –*phr.* **6. sin against**, to take advantage of; abuse or offend. –**sinner**, *n.* –**sinful**, *adj.*

sin² /saɪn/ *Maths* sine.

since /sɪns/ *adv.* **1.** (oft. preceded by *ever*) from then until now. **2.** between a particular past time and the present; subsequently: *he at first refused, but has since agreed.* **3.** ago; before now: *long since.* –*prep.* **4.** continuously from or counting from: *since noon.* **5.** between (a past time or event) and the present: *changes since the war.* –*conj.* **6.** in the period following the time when: *he has written once since he left.* **7.** continuously from or counting from the time when: *busy since he came.* **8.** because.

sincere /sɪn'sɪə, sən-/ *adj.* (**-cerer, -cerest**) free from any element of deceit, dissimulation, duplicity, or hypocrisy. –**sincerely**, *adv.* –**sincereness**, *n.* –**sincerity**, *n.*

sine¹ /saɪn/ *n. Maths* **1.** a trigonometric function defined for an acute angle in a right-angled triangle as the ratio of the side opposite the angle to the hypotenuse, and defined for angles of any size as the ordinate of a point P, a unit distance from the origin O and such that OP is inclined at the given angle to the x-axis. **2.** the function (of a real variable x) defined as the sine of an angle of radian measure x; any extension of this function. *Abbrev.*: sin

sine² /'saɪni, 'saɪneɪ/ *prep.* without.

sinecure /'sɪnəkjuə, 'saɪnəkjuə/ *n.* **1.** an office requiring little or no work, especially one yielding profitable returns. **2.** *Christian Church* a church benefice which does not entail spiritual or pastoral care or duties. –**sinecurist**, *n.*

sinew /'sɪnju/ *n.* **1.** a tendon. **2.** something that supplies strength. **3.** strength; vigour. –*v.t.* **4.** to furnish with sinews; strengthen as by sinews. –**sinewless**, *adj.*

sing /sɪŋ/ *verb* (**sang** *or, Obs.,* **sung, sung, singing**) –*v.i.* **1.** to utter words or sounds in succession with musical modulations of the voice. **2.** to execute a song or voice composition, as a professional singer. **3.** to produce melodious sounds, as certain birds, insects, etc. **4.** (of humpback whales) to produce a complex series of repeated vocal phases. **5.** to give out a continuous ringing, whistling, murmuring, or sound of musical quality, as a kettle coming to the boil, a brook, etc. **6.** to make a short ringing, whistling, or whizzing sound: *the bullet sang past his ear.* **7.** *Colloq.* to turn informer. –*v.t.* **8.** to utter with musical modulations of the voice, as a song. **9.** to escort or accompany with singing. **10.** to proclaim enthusiastically: *to sing a person's praises.* **11.** to bring, send, put, etc., with or by singing: *to sing a child to sleep.* **12.** to chant or intone. **13.** (in tribal Aboriginal culture) to direct a chant at (someone) with the intention of bringing about their death. –*n.* **14.** the act or performance of singing. **15.** a singing, ringing, or whistling sound, as of a bullet. –*phr.* **16. sing out, a.** *Colloq.* to call out in a loud voice; shout. **b.** to sing loudly: *ask the altos to sing out more.* –**singable**, *adj.* –**singer**, *n.*

Singapore noodles /sɪŋəpɔ 'nudəlz/ *pl. n.* **1.** thin round noodles in the Asian style. **2.** (*construed as sing.*) a dish based on these noodles in a style originating in Singapore, with a sauce, and including vegetables, prawns and chicken.

singe /sɪndʒ/ *v.t.* (**singed, singeing**) **1.** to burn slightly. **2.** to burn the ends of (hair, etc.). **3.** to subject to flame in order to remove hair, etc. –*n.* **4.** a slight burn. **5.** the act of singeing. –**singed**, *adj.* –**singeing**, *n.*

single /'sɪŋgəl/ *adj.* **1.** one only; separate; individual. **2.** of or relating to one person, family, etc.: *a single room.* **3.** alone; solitary. **4.** without a spouse or permanent partner. **5.** of one against one, as combat or fight. **6.** consisting of one part, element, or member. **7.** *Bot.* having but one set of petals, as a flower. **8.** (of the eye) seeing rightly. –*n.* **9.** something single or separate; a single one. **10.** a ticket for a train, bus, etc., valid for a one-way journey only. **11.** *Music* a record, usually a 45, with a single title on each side. **12.** *Music* a song title issued on such a record. **13.** *Music* a single title issued as a CD often packaged with one or two additional songs. **14.** *Music* a song title issued as an MP3 file usually available for purchase on the internet. **15.** *Colloq.* a person without a spouse or permanent partner. **16.** (*pl.*) *Tennis, etc.* a game or match played with one person on each side. **17.** *Cricket* a hit for which one run is scored. –*phr.* (**-gled, -gling**) **18. single out**, to pick or choose out from others: *to single out a fact for special mention.*

single-breasted /ˈsɪŋɡəl-brɛstəd/ *adj.* (of a coat, jacket, or the like) having a single row of buttons in the front for fastening. See **double-breasted**.

single desk *n.* (in international trade) a sole agency for the sale of a commodity: *a single desk for wheat*.

single file *n.* a line of persons or things arranged one behind the other.

single-handed *adj.* **1.** acting or working alone or unaided. **2.** having, using, or requiring the use of but one hand or one person. –*adv.* **3.** alone. –**single-handedly**, *adv.*

single-minded *adj.* **1.** having or showing undivided purpose. **2.** having or showing a sincere mind; steadfast. –**single-mindedly**, *adv.* –**single-mindedness**, *n.*

single nucleotide polymorphism /ˌsɪŋɡəl ˌnjukliˈətaɪd ˈpɒliˈmɔfɪzəm/ *n. Genetics* a single unit variation in a genome, occurring approximately once in every 1000 units.

singlet /ˈsɪŋlət, ˈsɪŋɡlət/ *n.* **1.** a short garment, with or without sleeves, usually worn next to the skin under a shirt, jumper, or dress. **2.** a similar garment worn to cover the torso by boxers, athletes, etc. **3.** *Chem.* a chemical bond consisting of one shared electron.

singly /ˈsɪŋli/ *adv.* **1.** apart from others; separately. **2.** one at a time; as single units. **3.** single-handed.

singsong /ˈsɪŋsɒŋ/ *n.* **1.** an informal gathering at which the company sing; community singing. –*adj.* **2.** characterised by a regular rising and falling intonation. **3.** monotonous in rhythm.

singular /ˈsɪŋɡjələ/ *adj.* **1.** out of the ordinary; remarkable: *singular success*. **2.** unusual or strange; odd; eccentric. **3.** being the only one of the kind; unique. **4.** *Gram.* indicating one person, thing, or collection, as English *man, thing, he, goes.* –*n.* **5.** *Gram.* the singular number, or a form of it. –**singularly**, *adv.* –**singularness, singularity** /sɪŋɡjəˈlærəti/, *n.*

sinh /ʃaɪn, saɪnˈeɪtʃ/ *n.* hyperbolic sine. See **hyperbolic function**.

sinister /ˈsɪnəstə/ *adj.* **1.** threatening or portending evil; ominous. **2.** bad; evil; base. **3.** unfortunate; disastrous; unfavourable. **4.** of or on the left side; left. –**sinisterly**, *adv.* –**sinisterness**, *n.* –**sinisterwise**, *adv.*

sink /sɪŋk/ *verb* (**sank** *or*, *Chiefly US*, **sunk**, **sunk** *or* **sunken, sinking**) –*v.i.* **1.** to descend gradually to a lower level, as water, flames, etc. **2.** to go down towards or below the horizon. **3.** to slope downwards, as ground. **4.** to go under or to the bottom; become submerged. **5.** to settle or fall gradually, as a heavy structure. **6.** to fall slowly from weakness, fatigue, etc. **7.** to pass gradually (into gumbum, silence, oblivion, etc.). **8.** to pass or fall into some lower state, as of fortune, estimation, etc. **9.** to degenerate; decline. **10.** to fail in physical strength. **11.** to decrease in amount, extent, degree, etc., as value, prices, rates, etc. **12.** to become lower in tone or pitch, as sound. **13.** to fall in; become hollow, as the cheeks. **14.** to drop or fall (on to a seat, bed, etc.) through weariness or fatigue: *she put down her books and sank thankfully into the nearest armchair*. **15.** to sit or lie down in a slow, luxurious manner: *he sank back into the soft cushions and dreamed*. –*v.t.* **16.** to cause to fall or descend. **17.** to cause to sink or become submerged. **18.** to depress (a part, area, etc.), as by excavating. **19.** to put down or lay (a pipe, post, etc.), as into the ground. **20.** *Golf, Billiards, etc.* to cause (the ball) to run into a hole. **21.** to bring to a worse state; lower. **22.** to bring to ruin or perdition. **23.** to reduce in amount, extent, etc., as value or prices. **24.** to lower (the voice, etc.). **25.** to invest (money), now especially unprofitably. **26.** to lose (money) in an unfortunate investment, etc. **27.** to make (a hole, shaft, well, etc.) by excavating or boring downwards; hollow out (any cavity): *to sink a dam*. **28.** *Colloq.* to drink: *let's sink a middy*. –*n.* **29.** a basin with a water supply and outlet, installed especially in a kitchen, used for washing dishes, etc. **30.** a low-lying area where waters collect or where they disappear by sinking down into the ground or by evaporation. **31.** a place of vice or corruption. **32.** a drain or sewer. **33.** *Physics* any device, place, or part of a system in which energy is consumed or drained from the system. –*phr.* **34. sink in**, to enter or permeate the mind; become understood. **35. sink into**, to be or become deeply absorbed in (a mental state): *he sank into a state of deep depression*. **36. sink or swim**, with two extreme possible outcomes, either complete success or failure. –**sinking**, *adj.* –**sinkable**, *adj.*

sinker /ˈsɪŋkə/ *n.* a weight of lead, etc., for sinking a fishing line, fishing net, or the like in the water.

sinking fund *n.* a fund into which regular payments are made, either for the purpose of liquidating a debt by degrees, or for meeting future commitments.

Sino- a word element meaning 'Chinese', as in *Sino-Tibetan, Sinology*.

sinter /ˈsɪntə/ *v.t. Metallurgy* to bring about the agglomeration of particles of a metal (or other substance as glass or carbides) by heating, usually under pressure, to just below the melting point of the substance, or in the case of a mixture, to the melting point of the lowest melting constituent.

sinuous /ˈsɪnjuəs/ *adj.* **1.** having many curves, bends, or turns; winding. **2.** indirect; devious. –**sinuousness**, *n.* –**sinuously**, *adv.*

sinus /ˈsaɪnəs/ *n.* (*pl.* **-nuses**) **1.** a curve; bend. **2.** a curving part or recess. **3.** *Anat.* **a.** any of various cavities, recesses, or passages, as a hollow in a bone, or a reservoir or channel for venous blood. **b.** one of the hollow cavities in the skull connecting with the nasal cavities. **c.** an expanded area in a canal or tube. **4.** *Pathol.* a narrow, elongated abscess with a small orifice; a narrow passage leading to an abscess or the like. **5.** *Bot.* a small, rounded depression between two projecting lobes, as of a leaf.

sinusitis /saɪnəˈsaɪtəs, saɪnjəˈsaɪtəs/ *n. Pathol.* inflammation of a sinus or sinuses.

-sion a suffix having the same function as **-tion**, as in *compulsion*.

sip /sɪp/ *verb* (**sipped**, **sipping**) –*v.t.* **1.** to drink a little at a time. –*v.i.* **2.** to drink by sips. –*n.* **3.** an act of sipping. **4.** a small quantity taken by sipping. –**sipper**, *n.*

siphon /ˈsaɪfən/ *n.* **1.** an enclosed tube or conduit through which a liquid is conveyed from a reservoir at one elevation to a lower elevation, the liquid being initially forced into the tube by suction or immersion and then, once the tube is raised with a short section to the higher end and a long section to the lower end, falling from the lower end in response to gravity, thus creating suction at the higher end which draws liquid through the tube. **2.** *Zool.* a projecting tubular part of some animals, through which water enters or leaves the body. –*v.t.* **3.** to convey or pass through or as if through a siphon. –*phr.* **4. siphon off**, to transfer (something) bit by bit. Also, **syphon**. –**siphonal, siphonic** /saɪˈfɒnɪk/, *adj.*

sir /sɜ/ *n.* **1.** a respectful term of address used to a man. **2.** (*upper case*) the distinctive title of a knight or baronet: *Sir Joh Bjelke-Petersen*. **3.** an ironic or humorous title of respect: *sir critic*.

sire /ˈsaɪə/ *n.* **1.** the male parent of an animal, especially a domesticated quadruped, as a horse. **2.** a respectful term of address, now used only to a sovereign. **3.** *Poetic* a father or forefather. –*v.t.* **4.** to beget.

siren /ˈsaɪrən/ *n.* **1.** *Classical Myth.* one of several sea nymphs, part woman and part bird, who supposedly lured mariners to destruction by their seductive singing. **2.** any alluring or seductive woman. **3.** an acoustic instrument for producing sounds, consisting essentially of a disc pierced with holes arranged equidistantly in a circle, rotated over a jet or stream of compressed air, steam, or the like, so that the stream is alternately interrupted and allowed to pass, the chopped jet of air producing a soundwave. **4.** a device of this kind used as a whistle, fog signal, warning sound on an ambulance, fire-engine, or the like, etc. *–adj.* **5.** of or like a siren.

sirloin /ˈsɜːlɔɪn/ *n.* the portion of the loin of beef in front of the rump, used whole as a roast or cut into steaks.

sisal /ˈsaɪsəl/ *n.* **1.** Also, **sisal hemp.** a fibre yielded by *Agave sisalana* of southern Mexico, used for making ropes, etc. **2.** a plant yielding such fibre.

sissy /ˈsɪsi/ *n.* (*pl.* **-sies**) *Colloq.* **1.** an effeminate man or boy. **2.** a timid or cowardly person. Also, **cissy.**

sister /ˈsɪstə/ *n.* **1.** a daughter of the same parents (**full sister** or **sister-german**). **2.** a daughter of only one of one's parents (**half-sister**). **3.** a female member of the same kinship group or nationality. **4.** a female associate in occupation or friendship. **5.** a term of solidarity used to refer to a female who shares a common political perspective and purpose, especially that which is feminist. **6.** a female member of a religious community, which observes the simple vows of poverty, chastity, and obedience: *a Sister of Charity.* **7.** *Aboriginal English* a term used to express solidarity with a woman rather than an actual kin relationship. **8.** → **registered nurse. 9.** a form of address, especially between African American women. *–adj.* **10.** made to the same design: *sister ships.* **11.** belonging to the same group, fleet, etc.: *Queensland lacked the enthusiasm of some of its sister states. –sisterhood, n.*

sister-in-law *n.* (*pl.* **sisters-in-law**) **1.** a husband's or wife's sister. **2.** a brother's wife. **3.** a husband's or wife's brother's wife.

sit /sɪt/ *verb* (**sat**, **sitting**) *–v.i.* **1.** to rest on the lower part of the body; be seated. **2.** to be situated; dwell. **3.** to rest or lie. **4.** to place oneself in position for an artist, photographer, etc.: *to sit for a portrait.* **5.** to act as a model. **6.** to remain quiet or inactive. **7.** (of a bird) to perch or roost. **8.** to cover eggs to hatch them. **9.** to fit or be adjusted, as a garment. **10.** to occupy a seat in an official capacity, as a judge or bishop. **11.** to have a seat, be an elected representative, as in parliament. **12.** to be convened or in session, as an assembly. **13.** to act as a babysitter. **14.** to be a candidate for an examination; take an examination. *–v.t.* **15.** Also, **sit down.** to cause to sit; seat. **16.** to provide seating room for; seat: *a table which sits eight people. –phr.* **17. be sitting pretty,** *Colloq.* to be comfortably established; be at an advantage. **18. sit across,** to stay in touch with, so as to be kept informed of developments: *this group sit across our website on a daily basis.* **19. sit down,** to take a seat; be seated. **20. sit in for,** to take the place of temporarily: *he'll be out for an hour so I'll sit in for him.* **21. sit in on,** take part in as a spectator, observer, or visitor: *we were allowed to sit in on the debate.* **22. sit on** (**one's**) **hands,** to be inactive, often in dereliction of duty: *the committee just sat on its hands for three months.* **23. sit on** (or **upon**), **a.** to have a place on a committee, etc.): *she has sat on several committees during the past few years.* **b.** to check; rebuke; repress. **c.** to prevent (a document) from becoming public knowledge so as to avoid the action demanded by it: *the government is sitting on the report.* **d.** to be close behind, especially in a race. **e.** to travel steadily at (a speed): *I sat on 60 all the way.* **24. sit out,** **a.** to stay till the end of: *though the film was boring we sat it out.* **b.** to take no part in; keep one's seat during (a dance, etc.): *she sat out the last few dances because she was tired.* **25. sit pat,** *Colloq.* to stick to one's decision, policy, etc., taking no further action. **26. sit tight,** to take no action; bide one's time: *I'll sit tight till I know what the decision is.* **27. sit up,** **a.** to raise oneself from a lying to a sitting position. **b.** to stay up later than usual; not go to bed. **c.** to sit upright or erect. **d.** to be startled; become interested or alert: *the speaker's next announcement made us sit up.*

sitar /ˈsɪta, ˈsita/ *n.* a guitar-like instrument of India, having a long neck and usually three strings. Also, **sittar. –sitarist, n.**

sitcom /ˈsɪtkɒm/ *n. Colloq.* → **situation comedy.**

sit-down strike *n.* a strike during which workers refuse either to leave their place of employment or to work or to allow others to work until the strike is settled. Also, **sit-down.**

site /saɪt/ *n.* **1.** the position of a town, building, etc., especially as to its environment. **2.** the area on which anything, as a building, is, has been, or is to be situated. **3.** → **website.** *–v.t.* **4.** to locate; place; provide with a site: *they sited the school next to the oval.*

site map *n.* **1.** a map of a building site showing the location of different buildings, areas of interest, etc. **2.** *Computers* a map of a website showing the various pages and links between them.

sito- a word element referring to food.

-sitter a suffix indicating a person who will look after someone or something specified: *a pet-sitter.*

sitting duck *n.* **1.** any particularly easy mark to shoot at. **2.** *Colloq.* a person, organisation, etc., vulnerable to attack, takeover, etc.

situate /ˈsɪtʃueɪt/ *v.t.* to give a site to; locate.

situated /ˈsɪtʃueɪtəd/ *adj.* **1.** located; placed. **2.** in certain circumstances: *well situated financially.*

situation /sɪtʃuˈeɪʃən/ *n.* **1.** manner of being situated; location or position with reference to environment. **2.** a place or locality. **3.** condition; case; plight. **4.** the state of affairs; combination of circumstances: *to meet the demands of the situation.* **5.** a position or post of employment. *–situational, adj.*

situation comedy *n.* **1.** comedy derived from the situations of ordinary life. **2.** a movie, show, series, etc., involving situation comedy. Also, **sitcom.**

SI unit /ɛs ˈaɪ junət/ *n.* a unit of the International System of Units (Système International d'Unités).

six /sɪks/ *n.* **1.** a cardinal number, five plus one. **2.** a symbol for this number, as 6 or VI. **3.** a set of this many persons or things. **4.** a playing card, die face, etc., with six pips. **5.** *Cricket* a hit scoring six runs, the ball clearing the boundary without touching the ground. *–adj.* **6.** amounting to six in number: *six apples. –pron.* **7.** six people or things: *sleeps six; give me six. –phr.* **8. at sixes and sevens,** in disorder or confusion. **9. go for six** (or **a sixer**), *Colloq.* **a.** to fall over heavily. **b.** to suffer a major setback. **10. hit for six,** **a.** *Cricket* (of the person batting) to strike (the ball) so that it lands outside the playing area, the stroke being worth six runs. **b.** Also, **knock for six,** to completely annihilate or overcome. **c.** to confuse or disturb greatly: *the bad news hit him for six. –sixth, adj.*

sixteen /sɪksˈtin/ *n.* **1.** a cardinal number, ten plus six. **2.** a symbol for this number, as 16 or XVI. *–adj.* **3.** amounting to sixteen in number. *–pron.* **4.** sixteen people or things. *–sixteenth, adj.*

sixth sense *n.* a power of perception beyond the five senses; intuition.

sixty /ˈsɪksti/ *n.* (*pl.* **-ties**) **1.** a cardinal number, ten times six. **2.** a symbol for this number, as 60 or LX. **3.** (*pl.*) the numbers from 60 to 69 of a series, especially with reference to the years of a person's age, or the years of a century. *–adj.* **4.** amounting to sixty in number. *–pron.* **5.** sixty people or things. *–sixtieth, adj.*

size[1] /saɪz/ *n.* **1.** the dimensions, proportions, or magnitude of anything: *the size of a city; the size of a problem.* **2.** considerable or great magnitude: *to seek* *size rather than quality.* **3.** one of a series of graduated measures for articles of manufacture or trade: *children's sizes of shoes.* **4.** *Colloq.* actual condition, circumstances, etc. –*v.t.* **5.** to separate or sort according to size. **6.** to make of a certain size. –*phr.* **7. size up, a.** to form an estimate of. **b.** to come up to a certain standard.

size² /saɪz/ *n.* **1.** any of various gelatinous or glutinous preparations made from glue, starch, etc., used for glazing or coating paper, cloth, etc. –*v.t.* **2.** to coat or treat with size.

-size a combining form indicating something of size specified, as in *king-size, bite-size.*

sizeable /ˈsaɪzəbəl/ *adj.* of considerable size; fairly large: *he inherited a sizeable fortune.* Also, **sizable.** –**size-ableness,** *n.* –**sizeably,** *adv.*

sizzle /ˈsɪzəl/ *v.i.* **1.** to make a hissing sound, as in frying or burning. **2.** *Colloq.* to be very hot. –*n.* **3.** a sizzling sound. –**sizzler,** *n.*

skank¹ /skæŋk/ *n. Colloq. (derog.)* a promiscuous woman.

skank² /skæŋk/ *v.i. Colloq.* to dance to punk music.

skanky /ˈskæŋki/ *adj.* (**-kier, -kiest**) *Colloq.* dirty; unattractive.

skate¹ /skeɪt/ *n.* **1.** a steel blade attached to the bottom of a shoe, enabling a person to glide on ice. **2.** a shoe with such a blade attached. **3.** → **rollerskate** (def. 1). **4.** *Elect.* the sliding contact which collects current in an electric traction system. –*v.i.* **5.** to glide over ice, the ground, etc., on skates. **6.** to glide or slide smoothly along. **7.** to ride a skateboard. –*phr.* **8. get one's skates on,** *Colloq.* to hurry. **9. skate round** (or **over**), to avoid, as in conversation. **10. skate on thin ice,** to place oneself in a delicate situation; touch on a contentious topic.

skate² /skeɪt/ *n.* (*pl.* **skates** *or, especially collectively,* **skate**) any of certain rays (genus *Raja*), usually having a pointed snout and spines down the back, but no serrated spine on the tail, as the common skate, *Raja australis* of Australian waters, or *Raja batis* of European coastal waters.

skateboard /ˈskeɪtbɔd/ *n.* a short plank on rollerskate wheels, ridden, usually standing up, as a recreation.

skatey /ˈskeɪti/ *n.* → **skatie.**

skatie /ˈskeɪti/ *n. Colloq.* **1.** a skateboard rider. **2.** a skateboard. Also, **skatey.**

skedaddle /skəˈdædl/ *Orig. US Colloq.* –*v.i.* **1.** to run away; disperse in flight. –*n.* **2.** a hasty flight. Also, **skidaddle.**

skein /skeɪn/ *n.* **1.** a length of thread or yarn wound in a coil. **2.** anything resembling this, as a coil of hair or the like. **3.** a flock of geese or similar birds in flight formation.

skeleton /ˈskɛlətn/ *n.* **1.** the bones of a human or other animal body considered together, or assembled or fitted together as a framework; the bony or cartilaginous framework of a vertebrate animal. **2.** *Colloq.* a very lean person or animal. **3.** a supporting framework, as of a leaf, building, or ship. **4.** mere lifeless, dry, or meagre remains. **5.** an outline, as of a literary work; basic essentials. –*adj.* **6.** of or relating to a skeleton. **7.** like a skeleton or mere framework. **8.** reduced to the essential minimum: *skeleton staff.* –*phr.* **9. skeleton in the cupboard** (or **closet**), some shameful or embarrassing fact in the history or lives of a family which is kept secret. –**skeletal** /ˈskɛlətl, skəˈliːtl/, *adj.*

skeleton key *n.* a key with nearly the whole substance of the bit filed away, so that it may open various locks. Also, **pass key.**

skerrick /ˈskɛrɪk/ *n. Aust., NZ* a very small quantity; a scrap: *not a skerrick left.*

sketch /skɛtʃ/ *n.* **1.** a simply or hastily done drawing or painting, giving the important features without the details. **2.** a rough design, plan, or outline. **3.** a short and

usually light literary work, as a story, essay or short play. –*v.t.* **4.** to make a sketch of. –*v.i.* **5.** to make a sketch or sketches. –**sketcher,** *n.* –**sketchy,** *adj.*

skew /skjuː/ *v.i.* **1.** to turn aside or twist. –*v.t.* **2.** to give a sloping direction to. **3.** to describe unfairly; distort. –*adj.* **4.** having a sloping direction or position; slanting. **5.** *Geom.* not lying in the same plane. –*n.* **6.** a twisting or sloping movement, direction, or position.

skewer /ˈskjuːə/ *n.* **1.** a long pin of wood or metal for putting through meat to hold it together or in place while being cooked. **2.** any similar pin for some other purpose. –*v.t.* **3.** to fasten with, or as with, skewers.

ski /skiː/ *n.* (*pl.* **skis**) **1.** one of a pair of long, slender pieces of hard wood, metal, or plastic, one fastened to each shoe, used for travelling or gliding over snow, and often (especially as a sport) down slopes. **2.** a water-ski. –*v.i.* (**ski'd** *or* **skied, skiing**) **3.** to travel on or use skis. **4.** to water-ski.

skid /skɪd/ *n.* **1.** a plank, bar, log, or the like, especially one of a pair, on which something heavy may be slid or rolled along. **2.** *US* one of a number of such logs or planks forming a skidway. **3.** a runner on the underpart of some aeroplanes, enabling the machine to slide along the ground when alighting. **4.** an act of skidding: *the car went into a skid on the icy road.* –*verb* (**skidded, skidding**) –*v.t.* **5.** to place on or slide along a skid or skids. –*v.i.* **6.** to slide along without rotating, as a wheel to which a brake has been applied. **7.** to slip or slide sideways relative to direction of wheel rotation, as a car in turning a corner rapidly. **8.** to slide forward under its own momentum, as a car when the wheels have been braked. –*phr.* **9. on the skids,** deteriorating fast. **10. put the skids under,** to place (someone) in a precarious position; to ensure the downfall of (someone).

skid row *n.* **1.** a disreputable district inhabited by derelicts. –*phr.* **2. on skid row,** destitute.

skiff /skɪf/ *n.* any of various types of small boat, usually propelled by oars or sails.

skilful /ˈskɪlfəl/ *adj.* **1.** having or exercising skill. **2.** showing or involving skill: *a skilful display of fancy diving.* Also, *Chiefly US,* **skillful.** –**skilfully,** *adv.* –**skilfulness,** *n.*

skill /skɪl/ *n.* **1.** the ability that comes from knowledge, practice, aptitude, etc., to do something well. **2.** competent excellence in performance; expertness; dexterity.

skilled /skɪld/ *adj.* **1.** having skill; trained or experienced. **2.** showing, involving, or requiring skill, as work. **3.** of or relating to workers performing a specific operation requiring apprenticeship or other special training or experience.

skillet /ˈskɪlət/ *n.* a small frying pan.

skillion /ˈskɪljən/ *n.* **1.** Also, **skillion room.** a lean-to or outhouse. **2.** a hill or bluff sloping in one direction, with a sheer fall on the other side.

skillshare /ˈskɪlfɛə/ *v.i.* (**-shared, -sharing**) **1.** to share one's acquired skills with other people, as between students. –*n.* **2.** the process of such sharing.

skim /skɪm/ *verb* (**skimmed, skimming**) –*v.t.* **1.** to take up or remove (floating matter) from a liquid with a spoon, ladle, etc.: *to skim cream.* **2.** to clear (liquid) thus: *to skim milk.* **3.** to move or glide lightly over or along the surface of (the ground, water, etc.). **4.** to cause (a thing) to fly over or near a surface, or in a smooth course: *to skim stones.* **5.** to go over in reading, treatment, etc., in a superficial manner. **6.** to cover (liquid, etc.) with a thin layer. **7.** *Colloq.* to take the details of (a plastic card) so as to steal money from the account of the owner. –*v.i.* **8.** to pass or glide lightly along over or near a surface. **9.** to become covered with a thin layer. –*n.* **10.** the act of skimming. **11.** that which is skimmed off, such as the cream from skim milk. –*phr.* **12. skim**

over, to go, pass, glance, etc., over in a superficial way. **–skimmer**, *n.*

skim milk *n.* milk from which the cream has been removed. Also, **skimmed milk**.

skimming /ˈskɪmɪŋ/ *n.* **1.** (*usu. pl.*) something that is removed by skimming. **2.** *Colloq.* the practice of taking the details of (a plastic card) so as to steal money from the account of the owner.

skimp /skɪmp/ *v.t.* **1.** to do hastily or inattentively; scamp. **2.** to be sparing with; scrimp. **–v.i. 3.** to be extremely thrifty. **–phr. 4. skimp on**, to provide in meagre quantities.

skimpy /ˈskɪmpi/ *adj.* (**-pier, -piest**) **1.** lacking in size, fullness, etc.; scanty. **2.** too thrifty; stingy: *a skimpy housekeeper.* **–skimpily**, *adv.* **–skimpiness**, *n.*

skin /skɪn/ *n.* **1.** the external covering or integument of an animal body, especially when soft and flexible. **2.** such an integument stripped from the body of an animal; pelt. **3.** any integumentary covering, outer coating, or surface layer, as a sheathing membrane, the rind or peel of fruit, or a film on liquid. **4.** (in Aboriginal culture) a section (def. 12) or subsection (def. 2). **5.** a sheathing or casing forming the outside surface of a structure, as an exterior wall of a building, etc. **6.** *Computers* the design of a web page as opposed to its functionality. **7.** a container made of animal skin, used for holding liquids. **8.** one's resistance or sensitivity to criticism, censure, etc.: *a thick skin; a thin skin.* **9.** *Colloq.* a condom. **–verb** (**skinned, skinning**) **–v.t. 10.** to strip or deprive of skin; flay; peel. **11.** to strip off, as or like skin. **12.** *Colloq.* to strip of money or belongings; fleece, as in gambling. **13.** *Computers* to create a skin (def. 6) for (a website). **–v.i. 14.** *US Colloq.* to slip off hastily. **–phr. 15. by the skin of one's teeth**, scarcely; just; barely. **16. get under someone's skin**, **a.** to irritate someone. **b.** to fascinate or attract someone. **17. jump out of one's skin**, to be very frightened, surprised, or the like. **18. save someone's skin**, to rescue someone from a dangerous or difficult situation.

skindiving /ˈskɪndaɪvɪŋ/ *n.* underwater swimming for which the diver is equipped with a lightweight mask, an aqualung or snorkel, and foot fins. **–skindiver**, *n.*

skinflint /ˈskɪnflɪnt/ *n.* a mean, niggardly person.

skinhead /ˈskɪnhɛd/ *n. Colloq.* a member of any group of young men identified by close-cropped hair and sometimes indulging in aggressive activities.

skink /skɪŋk/ *n.* any of the harmless, generally smooth-scaled lizards constituting the family Scincidae, as the land mullet *Egernia major bungana* of eastern Australia, or as *Scincus scincus* of northern Africa, formerly much used for medicinal purposes.

skin name *n.* a name which identifies an Aboriginal person to a particular section or subsection. See **section** (def. 12), **subsection** (def. 2). Also, **kinship name**.

skinny /ˈskɪni/ *adj.* (**-nier, -niest**) **1.** lean; emaciated. **2.** of or like skin. **3.** *Colloq.* having less than the usual fat content: *skinny milk; a skinny cappuccino.* **4.** reduced by being shorter or less complicated or having less functionality: *a skinny version of an operating system; a skinny memoir.* **–skinniness**, *n.*

skinny-dip *Colloq.* **–v.i.** (**-dipped, -dipping**) **1.** to swim in the nude. **–n. 2.** a nude swim. **–skinny-dipper**, *n.*

skin patch *n.* → **patch** (def. 10).

skint /skɪnt/ *adj. Colloq.* completely without money; broke.

skip¹ /skɪp/ *verb* (**skipped, skipping**) **–v.i. 1.** to spring, jump, or leap lightly; gambol. **2.** to pass from one point, thing, subject, etc., to another, taking no notice of or leaving out what is in between. **3.** *Colloq.* to leave hastily; abscond. **4.** to use a skipping-rope. **–v.t. 5.** to jump lightly over: *skip the puddle.* **6.** to miss out (one of a series). **7.** to pass over without reading, notice,

mention, action, etc. **8.** to send (a stone) ricocheting along a surface. **9.** *Colloq.* to leave (a place) hastily. **–n. 10.** a movement in which one foot jumps lightly and then the other.

skip² /skɪp/ *n.* **1.** a container designed to be attached to a crane or cable for transporting materials or refuse in building operations. **2.** a truck used in an underground railway system for transporting coal, minerals, etc.

ski pole *n.* **1.** Also, **pole**. one of two slender poles, metal-tipped and having a disc near the lower end to prevent it from sinking into the snow, used by a skier for balance and to increase speed; stock. **2.** one of a set of poles set at prescribed distances to mark out a snow-covered track for skiers.

skipper¹ /ˈskɪpə/ *n.* **1.** the master or captain of a ship, especially of a small trading or fishing vessel. **2.** a captain or leader, as of a team. **–v.t. 3.** to act as skipper of.

skipper² /ˈskɪpə/ *n.* **1.** any of various insects that hop or fly with jerky motions. **2.** any of the quick-flying lepidopterous insects constituting the family Hesperiidae, closely related to the true butterflies.

skirmish /ˈskɜmɪʃ/ *n.* **1.** *Mil.* a fight between small bodies of troops, especially advanced or outlying detachments of opposing armies. **2.** any brisk encounter. **–v.i. 3.** to engage in a skirmish. **–skirmisher**, *n.*

skirt /skɜt/ *n.* **1.** the lower part of a gown, coat, or the like, hanging from the waist. **2.** a separate garment (outer or under) worn by women and girls, extending from the waist downwards. **3.** some part resembling or suggesting the skirt of a garment. **4.** one of the flaps hanging from the sides of a saddle. **5.** a skirting board or bordering finish in building. **6.** (*usu. pl.*) the bordering, marginal, or outlying part of a place, group, etc. **7.** a cut of beef from the flank. **–v.t. 8.** to lie on or along the border of. **9.** to border or edge with something. **10.** to pass along or around the border or edge of: *to skirt a town.* **11.** to remove skirtings from (fleeces). **–v.i. 12.** to be, lie, live, etc., on or along the edge of something. **13.** to pass or go around the border of something. **–phr. 14. bit** (or **piece**) **of skirt**, *Colloq.* a woman, considered as a sex object.

skirting /ˈskɜtɪŋ/ *n.* **1.** material for making skirts. **2.** a skirting board. **3.** (*pl.*) the trimmings or inferior parts of fleece.

skirting board *n.* **1.** Also, **skirting**. a line of boarding protecting an interior wall next to the floor. **2.** Also, **skirting table**. the table on which a fleece is skirted.

skit /skɪt/ *n.* a slight parody, satire, or caricature, especially dramatic or literary.

skite /skaɪt/ *Aust., NZ Colloq.* **–v.i. 1.** to boast; brag. **–n. 2.** a boast; brag. **3.** Also, **skiter**. a boaster; braggart. **–skiting**, *n.*

skittish /ˈskɪtɪʃ/ *adj.* **1.** apt to start or shy. **2.** restlessly or excessively lively. **3.** fickle; uncertain. **4.** coy. **–skittishly**, *adv.* **–skittishness**, *n.*

skittle /ˈskɪtl/ *n.* **1.** (*pl.*) ninepins. **–v.t. 2.** to knock over or send flying, in the manner of skittles.

skive /skaɪv/ *phr.* (**skived, skiving**) **skive off**, *Colloq.* to depart so as to avoid work or responsibility.

skivvy¹ /ˈskɪvi/ *n.* (*pl.* **-vies**) *Aust., NZ* a close-fitting garment with long sleeves and a turtle neck, similar to a jumper, but usually made of machine-knitted cotton.

skivvy² /ˈskɪvi/ *n.* (*pl.* **-vies**) *Chiefly Brit. Colloq.* a female servant, especially one who does rough work.

skol /skɒl, skʌl/ *interj.* **1.** (used as a toast before drinking) to your health. **–v.t.** (**skolled, skolling**) **2.** → **scull**². Also, **skoal** /skoʊl/.

skort /skɔt/ *n.* a garment for women, comprising shorts with a loose leg designed to fold so as to appear to make a short skirt.

skua /ˈskjuə/ *n.* any of various seabirds of the genus *Stercorarius*, which pursue other seabirds, as petrels and shearwaters, in order to make them disgorge their prey; sea hawk.

skulduggery /skʌlˈdʌɡəri/ *n.* dishonourable proceedings; mean dishonesty or trickery. Also, **skullduggery**.

skulk /skʌlk/ *v.i.* **1.** to lie or keep in hiding, as for some evil or cowardly reason. **2.** to shirk duty; malinger. **3.** to move or go in a mean, stealthy manner; sneak; slink. **–skulker,** *n.*

skull /skʌl/ *n.* **1.** the bony framework of the head, enclosing the brain and supporting the face; the skeleton of the head. **2.** *Colloq.* the head as the seat of intelligence or knowledge.

skunk /skʌŋk/ *n.* **1.** a small, striped, fur-bearing, bushy-tailed, North American mammal, *Mephitis mephitis*, of the weasel family, Mustelidae, which ejects a fetid fluid when attacked. **2.** *Colloq.* a thoroughly contemptible person.

sky /skaɪ/ *n.* (*pl.* **skies**) **1.** (*oft. pl.*) the region of the clouds or the upper air. **2.** (*oft. pl.*) the heavens or firmament, appearing as a great arch or vault. **3.** climate. *–v.t.* (**skied** *or* **skyed, skying**) *Colloq.* **4.** to raise aloft; strike (a ball) high into the air. **5.** to hang (a picture, etc.) high on the wall of a gallery. *–phr.* **6. the sky's the limit,** *Colloq.* there is no limitation or obstacle. **7. to the skies,** highly; extravagantly.

skyboard /ˈskaɪbɔd/ *n.* **1.** a lightweight board similar to a snowboard, used for skysurfing. *–v.i.* **2.** to skydive on such a skyboard.

skydiving /ˈskaɪdaɪvɪŋ/ *n.* the sport of freefalling from an aeroplane for a great distance, controlling one's course by changes in body position, before releasing one's parachute. **–skydiver,** *n.*

skylark[1] /ˈskaɪlak/ *n.* **1.** a Eurasian lark, *Alauda arvensis*, noted for its singing in flight; introduced into Australia in 1857. **2.** any of several native Australian birds of similar habit.

skylark[2] /ˈskaɪlak/ *v.i.* to frolic, sport, or play about, especially boisterously or in high spirits; play tricks.

skylight /ˈskaɪlaɪt/ *n.* **1.** an opening in a roof or ceiling, fitted with glass or other such translucent material, for admitting daylight. **2.** the frame set with glass fitted to such an opening.

sky marshal *n.* a guard placed on an aeroplane to maintain security. Also, **air marshal.**

skyrocket /ˈskaɪrɒkət/ *n.* **1.** a firework that ascends into the air and explodes at a height. *–v.i.* **2.** to move like a skyrocket. **3.** to rise suddenly or rapidly in amount, position, reputation, etc.

skyscraper /ˈskaɪskreɪpə/ *n.* a tall building of many storeys, especially one for office or commercial use.

skysurf /ˈskaɪsɜf/ *v.i.* to skydive on a skyboard. Also, **skyboard. –skysurfer,** *n.*

skysurfing /ˈskaɪsɜfɪŋ/ *n.* a sport in which one skydives with a skyboard attached to the feet, performing surfing-like actions during freefall and then releasing a parachute for the final descent. *–adj.* **2.** of or relating to skysurfing.

slab /slæb/ *n.* **1.** a broad, flat, somewhat thick piece of stone, wood, or other solid material. **2.** a thick slice of anything: *a slab of bread.* **3.** a rough outside piece cut from a log, as in sawing it into boards. **4.** *Colloq.* a mortuary table. **5.** *Colloq.* a carton of 24 drink cans or small bottles.

slack[1] /slæk/ *adj.* **1.** not tense or taut; loose: *slack rope.* **2.** indolent; negligent; remiss. **3.** slow; sluggish. **4.** lacking in activity; dull; not brisk: *slack times for business.* **5.** sluggish, as the water, tide, or wind. **6.** *Colloq.* promiscuous. *–adv.* **7.** in a slack manner; slackly. *–n.* **8.** a slack condition, interval, or part. **9.** part of a rope, sail, or the like, that hangs loose, without

strain upon it. **10.** a decrease in activity, as in business, work, etc. **11.** a period of decreased activity. *–v.t.* **12.** to be remiss in respect to (some matter, duty, right, etc.); shirk; leave undone. **13.** to make or allow to become less active, vigorous, intense, etc.; relax or abate (efforts, labour, speed, etc.). **14.** to make loose, or less tense or taut, as a rope; loosen. **15.** to slake (lime). *–v.i.* **16.** to be remiss; shirk one's duty or part. **17.** to become less tense or taut, as a rope; to ease off. **–slacken,** *v.* **–slacker,** *n.* **–slackly,** *adv.* **–slackness,** *n.*

slack[2] /slæk/ *n.* the fine screenings of coal; small or refuse coal.

slacks /slæks/ *pl. n.* long trousers, worn by either men or women as informal wear.

slag[1] /slæɡ/ *n.* **1.** the more or less completely fused and vitrified matter separated during the reduction of a metal from its ore. **2.** the scoria from a volcano. **3.** *Colloq.* a woman who is unattractive, dirty, or promiscuous. *–verb* (**slagged, slagging**) *–v.t.* **4.** to convert into slag. *–v.i.* **5.** to form slag; become a slag-like mass. **–slaggy,** *adj.*

slag[2] /slæɡ/ *Colloq. –v.t.* (**slagged, slagging**) Also, **slag down. 1.** to criticise; denigrate. *–phr.* **2. slag off,** to speak disparagingly. **3. slag off at someone, a.** to talk disparagingly about someone. **b.** to speak disparagingly to someone.

slain /sleɪn/ *v.* past participle of **slay.**

slake /sleɪk/ *v.t.* **1.** to allay (thirst, desire, wrath, etc.) by satisfying. **2.** to combine (lime) with water or moist air, causing it to undergo a process of crumbling or disintegration resulting in the formation of a white powder (calcium hydroxide).

slalom /ˈsleɪləm, ˈslaləm/ *n.* **1.** a downhill skiing race over a winding course defined by artificial obstacles. **2.** a similar zigzag contest or exercise for canoes or cars.

slam[1] /slæm/ *verb* (**slammed, slamming**) *–v.t.* **1.** to shut with force and noise. **2.** to hit, throw, etc., with violent and noisy force. **3.** to criticise severely. *–v.i.* **4.** to shut so as to produce a loud noise. **5.** to hit or fall against something with force; crash. *–n.* **6.** a violent and noisy closing or hitting together. **7.** the noise made.

slam[2] /slæm/ *n. Cards* the winning of all the tricks in one deal, as at whist (in bridge, called **grand slam**), or of all but one (in bridge, called **little slam**).

slam dancing *n.* a style of dancing to heavy metal or similar forms of rock music in which the dancers deliberately crash into each other. **–slam dancer,** *n.* **–slamdance,** *v.*

slam dunk *n. Basketball* a particularly forceful shot in which a player jumps up at the basket and thrusts the ball down through it with one or both hands.

slander /ˈslændə, ˈslɑndə/ *n.* **1.** defamation; calumny. **2.** a malicious, false, and defamatory statement or report. **3.** *Law* defamation in a transient form, as speech. *–v.t.* **4.** to utter slander concerning; defame. *–v.i.* **5.** to utter or circulate slander. **–slanderer,** *n.* **–slanderous,** *adj.* **–slanderously,** *adv.* **–slanderousness,** *n.*

slang /slæŋ/ *n.* **1.** language differing from standard or written speech in vocabulary and construction, involving extensive metaphor, ellipsis, humorous usage, etc., less conservative and more informal than standard speech, and sometimes regarded as being in some way inferior. **2.** the jargon of a particular class, profession, etc.

slant /slænt, slant/ *v.i.* **1.** to slope. *–v.t.* **2.** to cause to slope. **3.** to present (a piece of writing, story, etc.) in such a way that it emphasises a particular point of view or attracts a particular class of people. *–n.* **4.** a slanting direction; slope: *the slant of a roof.* **5.** a slanting line, surface, etc. **6.** attitude or point of view, especially unusual or unfair; bias. **–slanting**, *adj.* **–slantingly**, **slantly**, *adv.*

slap /slæp/ *n.* **1.** a smart blow, especially with the open hand or with something flat. **2.** the sound of such a blow. **3.** a sarcastic or censuring hit or rebuke. *–v.t.* (**slapped, slapping**) **4.** to strike smartly, especially with the open hand or with something flat. **5.** to bring (the hands, etc.) against with a smart blow. **6. a.** to put or apply vigorously, haphazardly, or in large quantities. **b.** to dash or cast forcibly. *–adv.* **7.** smartly; suddenly. **8.** *Colloq.* directly; straight. *–phr.* **9. a slap in the face**, a rebuke or insult. **10. a slap on the wrist**, a mild rebuke. **11. slap down, a.** to put down forcibly. **b.** to rebuke or suppress the enthusiasm of. **12. slap up** (or **together**), *Colloq.* to make in a hurried or improvised way: *to slap up a breakfast.*

slapdash /ˈslæpdæʃ/ *adv.* **1.** in a hasty, haphazard manner. *–adj.* **2.** carelessly, hasty or offhand. *–n.* **3.** roughcast.

slaphappy /ˈslæphæpi/ *adj. Colloq.* **1.** cheerful. **2.** irresponsible; lackadaisical.

slapstick /ˈslæpstɪk/ *n.* broad comedy in which rough play and knockabout methods prevail.

slap-up *adj. Colloq.* first-rate; excellent.

slash /slæʃ/ *v.t.* **1.** to cut with a violent sweeping movement. **2.** to whip; lash. **3.** to reduce greatly; to slash prices. **4.** to make ornamental cuts in (a garment) to show an underlying material. **5.** to cut down weeds, old growth, etc., on (a piece of land) using a slasher (def. 4): *to slash the paddock rather than burn it.* *–v.i.* **6.** to make a sweeping, cutting stroke. *–n.* **7.** a sweeping stroke. **8.** a cut or wound made with such a stroke; gash. **9.** Also, **forward slash**. a short diagonal line (/), used in writing or typing to separate or enclose words or characters. See **solidus** (def. 2). Compare **backslash**.

slash-and-burn *adj.* of or relating to a method of cultivation of land, especially in developing countries, in which natural vegetation is cut down and burnt as a preliminary to sowing crops or pasture.

slasher /ˈslæʃə/ *n.* **1.** someone who uses a knife or other weapon on another. **2.** someone who cuts down timber in a wasteful or destructive manner. **3.** a machine used in timber-getting for sawing logs, etc., into pieces suitable for disposal as firewood, pulpwood, etc. **4.** a machine with a rotary cutting action used to control excess growth of weeds, etc.

slat /slæt/ *n.* **1.** a long, thin, narrow strip of wood, metal, etc., used as a support for a bed, as one of the horizontal laths of a venetian blind, etc. **2.** *Aeronautics* an auxiliary aerofoil constituting the forward part of a slotted aerofoil. **3.** (*pl.*) *Aust. Colloq.* **a.** bottom; buttocks. **b.** ribs. *–v.t.* (**slatted, slatting**) **4.** to furnish or make with slats.

slate[1] /sleɪt/ *n.* **1.** a fine-grained rock formed by the compression of mudstone, that tends to split along parallel cleavage planes, usually at an angle to the planes of stratification. **2.** a thin piece or plate of this rock or a similar material, used especially for roofing, or (when framed) for writing on. **3.** a dull, dark bluish grey. **4.** a tentative list of candidates, officers, etc., for acceptance by a nominating convention or the like. *–v.t.* **5.** to cover with or as with slate. **6.** to write or set down for nomination or appointment; to appoint, schedule. *–phr.* **7. a clean slate, a.** a good record. **b.** Also, **a blank slate**. a fresh beginning with all previous mistakes erased. **8. put on the slate**, to record (a debt), as on a slate; give credit for.

slate[2] /sleɪt/ *v.t.* **1.** to censure or reprimand severely. **2.** *Colloq.* to criticise or review adversely.

slater /ˈsleɪtə/ *n.* any of various small, terrestrial isopods, chiefly of the genera *Oniscus* and *Porcellio*, having a flattened elliptical, segmented body often able to roll

into a ball, commonly pale brown or greyish in colour and found under stones or logs; woodlouse.

slather /ˈslæðə/ *v.t.* **1.** to use in large quantities, to lavish. **2.** to spread thickly with or on. *–n.* **3.** a lot; a large quantity. **–slathering**, *n.*

slattern /ˈslætn/ *n.* a slovenly, untidy woman or girl; a slut. **–slatternly**, *adj.*

slaughter /ˈslɔtə/ *n.* **1.** the killing of cattle, sheep, etc., especially for food; butchering. **2.** the violent killing of a person. **3.** the killing by violence of great numbers of people. *–v.t.* **4.** to kill (animals), especially for food; butcher. **5.** to kill (a person) in a violent manner. **6.** to kill (people) in great numbers; massacre. **7.** *Colloq.* to defeat thoroughly. **–slaughterer**, *n.* **–slaughterman**, *n.*

slave /sleɪv/ *n.* **1.** someone who is the property of another. **2.** someone who works without payment and is the prisoner of another. **3.** someone who is completely under the influence of another person, a habit, etc.: *she is a slave to her child*; *a slave to smoking.* **4.** someone who works very hard; a drudge. *–v.i.* **5.** to work like a slave; drudge. *–adj.* **6.** of or relating to a computer, electronic device or other mechanism which is dependent on a main computer, electronic device, or mechanism. **–slavery**, *n.*

slaver[1] /ˈsleɪvə/ *n.* **1.** a dealer in or an owner of slaves. **2.** a vessel engaged in the traffic in slaves.

slaver[2] /ˈslævə/ *v.i.* **1.** to let saliva run from the mouth; slobber. **2.** to fawn. **3.** to express great desire by or as by slavering. *–v.t.* **4.** to wet or smear with saliva. *–n.* **5.** saliva coming from the mouth.

slavish /ˈsleɪvɪʃ/ *adj.* **1.** of or befitting a slave: *slavish submission.* **2.** painstakingly faithful, as a copy; lacking originality: *a slavish reproduction.*

slay /sleɪ/ *v.t.* (**slew** *or, in certain contexts*, **slayed, slain, slaying**) **1.** to kill by violence. **2.** *Colloq.* to amuse (someone) greatly: *that comedian really slays me.* **–slayer**, *n.*

sleazebag /ˈslizbæg/ *n. Colloq.* an objectionable person, especially a male, who constantly attempts seduction in an offensive manner. Also, **sleaze-bag**, **sleazeball**, **sleazebucket**.

sleaze-pit /ˈsliz-pɪt/ *n. Colloq.* a place inhabited or frequented by sleazy people.

sleazy /ˈslizi/ *adj.* (**-zier, -ziest**) *Colloq.* **1.** of dubious moral character, especially in relation to sexual matters. **2.** shabby, shoddy, untidy, or grubby. **–sleazily**, *adv.* **–sleaziness**, *n.*

sled /slɛd/ *n.* **1.** a vehicle mounted on runners for conveying loads over snow, ice, rough ground, etc. **2.** a small vehicle of this kind used in tobogganing, etc.; a toboggan. *–verb* (**sledded, sledding**) *–v.i.* **3.** to ride or be carried on a sled. *–v.t.* **4.** to convey on a sled.

sledge[1] /slɛdʒ/ *n.* **1.** any of various vehicles mounted on runners for travelling or conveying loads over snow, ice, rough ground, etc. **2.** a sled, especially a large one. **3.** → **toboggan**. *–verb* (**sledged, sledging**) *–v.t.* **4.** to convey by sledge. *–v.i.* **5.** to travel by sledge.

sledge[2] /slɛdʒ/ *n.* **1.** a sledge-hammer. *–v.t.* (**sledged, sledging**) **2.** to strike, beat with, or strike down with or as with a sledge-hammer. **3.** *Cricket* (of bowlers and fielders) to bait and taunt (the player batting) in order to break their concentration. **4.** *Colloq.* to ridicule or criticise.

sledgehammer /ˈslɛdʒhæmə/ *n.* **1.** a large heavy hammer, often held with both hands; sledge. *–adj.* **2.** like a sledgehammer; powerful or ruthless. **3.** crude; heavy-handed. *–v.t.* **4.** to strike or fell with, or as with, a sledgehammer.

sleek[1] /slik/ *adj.* **1.** smooth; glossy, as hair, an animal, etc. **2.** well-fed or well-groomed. **3.** smooth of manners, speech, etc. **4.** suave; insinuating. **–sleekly**, *adv.* **–sleekness**, *n.*

sleek² /slik/ *v.t.* to make sleek; smooth. –**sleeker**, *n.*

sleep /slip/ *verb* (**slept**, **sleeping**) –*v.i.* **1.** to take the repose or rest afforded by a suspension of the voluntary exercise of the bodily functions and the natural suspension, complete or partial, of consciousness. **2.** to be dormant, quiescent, or inactive, as faculties. **3.** to be unalert or inattentive. **4.** to lie in death. –*v.t.* **5.** to take rest in (sleep). **6.** to have beds or sleeping accommodation for: *a caravan that sleeps four.* –*n.* **7.** the state of a person or animal that sleeps. **8.** a period of sleeping: *a brief sleep.* **9.** (*with children*) a single night, used as a measurement of time: *only four sleeps until Christmas.* **10.** dormancy or inactivity. **11.** the repose of death. **12.** the mucus congealed in the corner of the eyes which has been secreted while sleeping. –*phr.* **13. go to sleep, a.** (of a person) to enter a sleeping state. **b.** (of a device, as a mobile phone, tablet computer, etc.) to go into sleep mode. **14. put to sleep**, (*euphemistic*) to kill (an animal) by giving a painless poison or lethal injection. **15. sleep around**, to be sexually promiscuous. **16. sleep away** (or **out**), to spend or pass (time, etc.) in sleep. **17. sleep in**, to sleep later than usual. **18. sleep like a top** (or **log**) (or **baby**), *Colloq.* to sleep very soundly. **19. sleep off**, to get rid of (a headache, hangover, etc.) by sleeping. **20. sleep on**, to postpone (a decision, etc.) overnight. **21. sleep out, a.** to sleep away from the place of one's work. **b.** to sleep in the open air. **22. sleep over**, to spend the night at another person's home. **23. sleep rough**, *Colloq.* **a.** to sleep without a bed or bedding. **b.** to sleep in public streets and parks, as a homeless person. **24. sleep with**, to have sexual intercourse with. –**sleepy**, *adj.*

sleep apnoea /slip ˈæpniə/ *n.* a temporary cessation of breathing during sleep, often caused by obstruction of the airway, as by enlarged tonsils, etc. Also, **sleep apnea**.

sleeper /ˈslipə/ *n.* **1.** a wooden, concrete, or steel beam forming part of a railway track, serving as a support for the rails. **2.** a bed in a sleeping car on a train. **3.** a small ring, bar, etc., worn in the ear after piercing to prevent the hole from closing. **4.** *Colloq.* someone or something that unexpectedly gains success or fame.

sleeper cell *n.* a small group of people, committed to a cause, who infiltrate a community waiting for an instruction to carry out sabotage, undertake a specific terrorist activity, etc.

sleeping partner *n.* **1.** → **silent partner**. **2.** a person with whom one has regular sexual intercourse.

sleep mode *n.* a low power mode for electronic devices as computers, radios, mobile phones, etc., which saves power consumption but avoids having to turn the device completely off.

sleepwalk /ˈslipwɔk/ *v.i.* to walk or perform other activities while asleep. –**sleepwalking**, *n.* –**sleepwalker**, *n.*

sleepwear /ˈslipwɛə/ *n.* clothing for sleeping in.

sleet /slit/ *n.* **1.** snow or hail and rain falling together. –*v.i.* **2.** to fall as or like sleet. –**sleety**, *adj.*

sleeve /sliv/ *n.* **1.** the part of a garment that covers the arm, varying in form and length but commonly tubular. **2.** *Machinery* a tubular piece, as of metal, fitting over a rod or the like. **3.** *Building Trades* a metal insert in a wall or floor to allow pipes, conduits, and ducts fitted within the sleeve to move independently of the structure. **4.** a cover or container for a CD, DVD, or gramophone record. –*phr.* **5. laugh up one's sleeve**, to be secretly or inwardly amused. **6. up one's sleeve**, secretly ready or at hand. **7. wear one's heart on one's sleeve**, to display openly one's emotions, intentions, etc. –**sleeveless**, *adj.*

sleigh /sleɪ/ *n.* **1.** a vehicle on runners, drawn by horses, dogs, etc., and used for transport on snow or ice.

2. → **toboggan**. –*v.i.* **3.** to travel or ride in a sleigh. –**sleigher**, *n.*

sleight /slaɪt/ *n.* skill; dexterity.

slender /ˈslɛndə/ *adj.* **1.** small in circumference in proportion to height or length: *slender column.* **2.** small in size, amount, extent, etc.: *a slender income.* **3.** having little value, force or justification: *slender prospects.* **4.** thin or weak, as sound. –**slenderly**, *adv.* –**slenderness**, *n.*

sleuth /sluθ/ *n.* **1.** *Colloq.* a detective. **2.** a bloodhound. –*v.t.* **3.** to track or trail as a detective does.

slew¹ /slu/ *v.* past tense of **slay**.

slew² /slu/ *v.t.* **1.** to turn or twist (something), especially upon its own axis or without moving it from its place. **2.** to cause to swing round. –*v.i.* **3.** to swerve awkwardly; swing round; twist. –*n.* **4.** a slewing movement. **5.** a position reached by slewing.

slew³ /slu/ *n. Colloq.* a large number: *a whole slew of kids.*

slice /slaɪs/ *n.* **1.** a thin, broad, flat piece cut from something: *a slice of bread.* **2.** a part; portion. **3.** any of various implements with a thin, broad blade or part, as for turning food in a frying pan, for serving fish at table, for taking up printing ink, etc. **4.** any of several cakes or biscuits cooked or formed as a thin slab and cut into rectangular pieces. **5.** *Sport* a slicing stroke, kick, hit, etc. –*verb* (**sliced**, **slicing**) –*v.t.* **6.** to cut into slices; divide into parts. **7.** to cut through or cleave like a knife: *the ship sliced the sea.* **8.** to cut (*off*, *away*, *from*, etc.) as or like a slice. **9.** *Sport* **a.** (in cricket, golf, soccer, etc.) to hit or kick the ball with the striking surface oblique, deliberately or accidentally, so that it does not travel along the line of force of the stroke. **b.** (in rowing) to put the blade slantwise into the water instead of square to the surface, so that it goes too deep. –*v.i.* **10.** *Sport* to slice the ball. –*phr.* **11. a slice of the cake**, *Colloq.* a share in the profits. –**sliceable**, *adj.* –**slicer**, *n.*

slick¹ /slɪk/ *adj.* **1.** sleek; glossy. **2.** smooth of manners, speech, etc. **3.** sly; shrewdly adroit. **4.** ingenious; cleverly devised. **5.** slippery, as though covered with oil. –*n.* **6.** a patch or film of oil or the like, as on the sea. –**slickly**, *adv.* –**slickness**, *n.*

slick² /slɪk/ *v.t.* to make sleek or smooth.

slide /slaɪd/ *verb* (**slid**, **slid** *or* **slidden**, **sliding**) –*v.i.* **1.** to move along in continuous contact with a smooth or slippery surface: *to slide down a snow-covered hill.* **2.** to slip, as one losing foothold or as a vehicle skidding. **3.** to glide or pass smoothly onwards. **4.** to slip (*in*, *out*, *away*, etc.) easily, quietly, or unobtrusively. **5.** to pass or fall gradually into a specified state, character, practice, etc. –*v.t.* **6.** to cause to slide, as over a surface or with a smooth, gliding motion. –*n.* **7.** the act of sliding. **8.** a smooth surface for sliding on. **9.** *Geol.* **a.** a landslide or the like. **b.** the mass of matter sliding down. **10.** a single image for projection in a projector; transparency. **11.** a plate of glass or other material on which objects are placed for microscopic examination. **12.** Also, **hair slide**. a clip for holding a woman's hair in place. **13.** something that slides, as a part of a machine. **14.** *Music* **a.** an embellishment or grace-note consisting of an upward or downward series of three or more notes, the last of which is the principal note. **b.** (in instruments of the trumpet class, especially the trombone) a section of the tube, usually U-shaped, which can be pushed in or out to alter the length of the air column and thus the pitch of the notes. **c.** any of various devices with a smooth surface as a bottle neck, a blunt knife, a copper or glass tube, etc., used for producing a gliding from one pitch to another from the strings of a guitar, rather than the regular pitches measured by the frets. –*phr.* **15. let slide**, to allow to become neglected: *to let the housework slide.* **16. slide in,** to slip (something) in easily or quietly. **–slider,** *n.*

slider /'slaɪdə/ *n.* **1.** someone who or something that slides. **2.** a small hamburger, often served as finger food. **3.** *Computers* a set of images on a website which can be activated to slide continuously across a screen.

slide rule *n.* a device for rapid calculation, consisting essentially of a rule having a sliding piece moving along it, both marked with graduated logarithmic scales.

sliding scale *n.* **1.** a variable scale, especially of industrial costs, as wages, raw materials, etc., which may be adapted to demand. **2.** a wage scale varying with the selling price of goods produced, the cost of living, or profits.

slight /slaɪt/ *adj.* **1.** small in amount, degree, etc.: *a slight increase; a slight sneer.* **2.** of little weight, or importance. **3.** slender; slim. **4.** lacking strength or solidity; frail; flimsy. *–v.t.* **5.** to treat as of slight importance; treat with indifference. *–n.* **6.** (an instance of) slighting treatment. **–slightly,** *adv.* **–slightness,** *n.*

slim /slɪm/ *adj.* (**slimmer, slimmest**) **1.** slender, as in girth or form; slight in build or structure. **2.** poor; insufficient; meagre: *a slim chance, a slim excuse. –v.i.* (**slimmed, slimming**) **3.** to make oneself slim, as by dieting, exercise, etc. **–slimly,** *adv.* **–slimness,** *n.*

slime /slaɪm/ *n.* **1.** thin, glutinous mud. **2.** any ropy or viscous liquid matter, especially of a foul or offensive kind. **3.** a viscous secretion of animal or vegetable origin. **4.** *Colloq.* servility; quality of being ingratiating.

slimline /'slɪmlaɪn/ *adj.* **1.** having a long, slender shape in structure, design, or appearance. **2.** trimmed down; thinned down; made smaller in size or bulk. Also, **slim-line, slim-lined.**

slimy /'slaɪmi/ *adj.* (**slimier, slimiest**) **1.** of or like slime. **2.** covered with slime. **3.** foul; vile. **4.** *Colloq.* servile; unpleasantly ingratiating. *–n.* **5.** a beachworm, *Australonuphis parateres,* found on the southern and eastern coast of Australia, commonly used for bait. Also, **slimey. –slimily,** *adv.* **–sliminess,** *n.*

sling¹ /slɪŋ/ *n.* **1.** an instrument for hurling stones, etc., by hand, consisting of a strap or piece for holding the missile, with two strings attached, the ends of which are held in the hand (or attached to a staff), the whole being whirled rapidly before discharging the missile. **2.** → **catapult** (def. 1). **3.** a bandage used to suspend an injured part of the body, as an arm or hand, by looping round the neck. **4.** a strap, band, or the like forming a loop by which something is suspended or carried, as a strap attached to a rifle and passed over the shoulder. **5.** *Naut.* **a.** a rope or chain supporting a yard. **b.** a rope, wire, or chain forming a loop, used for hoisting cargo, etc. **6.** *Colloq.* money given as a bribe; protection money. *–v.t.* (**slung, slinging**) **7.** to throw, cast, or hurl; fling, as from the hand. **8.** to place in or secure with a sling to raise or lower. **9.** to raise, lower, etc., by such means. **10.** to hang in a sling or so as to swing loosely: *to sling a rifle over one's shoulder.* **11.** *Colloq.* to give (money) as a tip. **12.** *Colloq.* to give or pass along: *sling me the tomato sauce. –phr.* **13. sling it in,** *Colloq.* to abandon an occupation, situation, etc. **14. sling off,** *Aust., NZ Colloq.* (sometimes fol. by *at*) to speak disparagingly: *he slings off at his teachers.* **15. sling the hook,** *Colloq.* to pass on the responsibility for a task, etc. **–slinger,** *n.*

sling² /slɪŋ/ *n.* an iced alcoholic drink, containing gin or the like, water, sugar, and lemon or lime juice.

slingshot /'slɪŋʃɒt/ *n.* **1.** → **catapult** (def. 2). **2.** → **sling¹** (def. 1).

slink /slɪŋk/ *verb* (**slunk, slinking**) *–v.i.* **1.** to go in a furtive, abject manner, as from fear, cowardice, or shame. **2.** to move stealthily, as to evade notice. *–v.t.*

3. (of cows, etc.) to bring forth (young) prematurely. *–n.* **4.** a prematurely born calf or other animal. **–slinkingly,** *adv.*

slinky /'slɪŋki/ *adj.* (**-kier, -kiest**) gracefully flowing; sinuous.

slip¹ /slɪp/ *verb* (**slipped, slipping**) *–v.i.* **1.** to pass or go smoothly or easily; glide; slide: *water slips off a smooth surface.* **2.** to slide suddenly and involuntarily, as on a smooth surface; to lose one's foothold. **3.** to move, slide, or start from a place, position, fastening, hold, etc. **4.** to go, come, get, etc., easily or quickly. **5.** to pass insensibly, as from the mind or by, etc., as time. **6.** to move quickly, smoothly and quietly: *she slipped into bed.* **7.** to go stealthily; steal: *he slipped out of the room without being noticed.* **8.** to pass superficially, carelessly, or without attention, as over a matter. **9.** *Colloq.* to become somewhat reduced in quantity or quality: *the market slipped today.* **10.** *Motor Vehicles* (of a clutch) to engage with difficulty as a result of wear. *–v.t.* **11.** to cause to slip, pass, etc., with a smooth, easy, or sliding motion: *to slip one's hand into a drawer.* **12.** to put or draw quickly or stealthily: *to slip a letter into a person's hand.* **13.** to let slip from fastenings, the hold, etc. **14.** to untie or undo (a knot). **15.** *Naut.* to let go entirely, as an anchor cable or an anchor. **16.** to escape (someone's memory, notice, knowledge, etc.). **17.** (of animals) to bring forth (offspring) prematurely. **18.** *Motor Vehicles* to operate (the clutch) gradually so that the drive to the wheels increases speed smoothly. *–n.* **19.** the act of slipping. **20.** a slipping of the feet, as on slippery ground. **21.** a mishap. **22.** a mistake, often inadvertent, as in speaking or writing: *a slip of the tongue.* **23.** an error in conduct; an indiscretion. **24.** something easily slipped on or off. **25.** a woman's sleeveless underdress. **26.** a pillowcase. **27.** → **slipway.** **28.** *NZ* → **landslide** (defs 1 and 2). **29.** *US* a space between two wharves or in a dock, for vessels to lie in. **30.** *Naut.* the difference between the theoretical speed at which a screw propeller or paddlewheel would move if it were working against a solid and the actual speed at which it advances through the water. **31.** *Mechanics* the difference between the actual volume of water or other liquid delivered by a pump during one complete stroke and the theoretical volume as determined by calculation of the displacement. **32.** *Elect.* the fraction by which the rotor speed of an induction motor is less than the speed of rotation of the stator field. **33.** *Cricket* **a.** the position of a fielder who stands behind and to the offside of the wicketkeeper. **b.** this fielder. **34.** *Geol.* **a.** → **fault** (def. 5). **b.** a smooth joint or crack where the strata have moved upon each other. **c.** the relative displacement of formerly adjacent points on opposite sides of a fault, measured in the fault plane. **35.** a form of landslide caused by the downhill movement of a mass of soil when saturated. **36.** *Metallurgy* the deformation of a metallic crystal caused by one part gliding over another part along a plane (**slip plane**). **37.** (*pl.*) *Theatre* **a.** the space on either side of the stage. **b.** corresponding parts of the auditorium. *–phr.* **38. be slipping,** to be losing one's acuteness, abilities, or the like. **39. give someone the slip,** to elude someone. **40. let slip, a.** to reveal unintentionally: *to let slip the surprise.* **b.** to say unintentionally: *to let slip a swearword.* **41. slip it to,** *Colloq.* (*taboo*) (of a male) to have sexual intercourse with. **42. slip off,** to take off (a garment, etc.) easily or quickly. **43. slip of the tongue,** an unintentional utterance, ranging from an accidental mispronunciation to a remark which one wishes, in hindsight, one had not made. **44. slip on,** to put on (a garment, etc.) easily or quickly. **45. slip up,** to make a slip, mistake, or error.

slip² /slɪp/ *n.* **1.** *Hort.* a piece suitable for propagation cut from a plant; a scion or cutting: *will this rose grow from a slip?* **2.** any long, narrow piece or strip, as of wood, paper, land, etc. **3.** a small paper form on which information is noted: *a withdrawal slip.* *–phr.* **4. a slip of a ...,** a young person, especially one of slender form.

slip[3] /slɪp/ *n.* potter's clay made semifluid with water, used for coating or decorating pottery.

slipped disc *n.* the displacement of a disc between two vertebrae, often responsible for pain in the back radiating down the back of the leg.

slipper /'slɪpə/ *n.* **1.** a light shoe into which the foot may be easily slipped for indoor wear. **2.** any similar shoe, as a woman's shoe for dancing. *–v.t.* **3.** to beat with a slipper. **–slippered,** *adj.* **slipper-like,** *adj.*

slippery /'slɪpəri, 'slɪpri/ *adj.* **(-rier, -riest) 1.** tending to cause slipping or sliding, as ground, surfaces, things, etc. **2.** tending to slip from the hold or grasp or from position: *a slippery rope.* **3.** likely to slip away or escape. **4.** not to be depended on; fickle; shifty, tricky, or deceitful. **–slipperiness,** *n.*

slippery dip *n. Aust.* a construction bearing an inclined smooth slope for children to slide down for amusement; slide. Also, **slippery slide.**

slipshod /'slɪpʃɒd/ *adj.* **1.** untidy, or slovenly; careless or negligent. **2.** wearing slippers or loose shoes, especially ones down at the heel.

slip-stitch *n.* **1.** one of a series of stitches used for dress hems, etc., in which only a few threads of material are caught up from the outer material, and the stitches which hold it are invisible from the outside. **2.** a stitch slipped, or not worked, in knitting, crocheting, etc.

slipstream /'slɪpstrim/ *n.* **1.** *Aeronautics* the air current forced back by an aircraft propeller or jet at speeds greater than the surrounding air. **2.** any similar air current behind any moving object.

slip-up *n. Colloq.* a mistake or blunder: *several minor slip-ups in spelling.*

slipway /'slɪpweɪ/ *n.* an inclined plane or ramp, especially one sloping to the water, serving as a landing place or a site on which vessels are built or repaired.

slit /slɪt/ *v.t.* **(slit, slitting) 1.** to cut apart or open along a line; make a long cut, fissure, or opening in. **2.** to cut or rend into strips; split. *–n.* **3.** a straight, narrow cut, opening, or aperture. **–slitter,** *n.* **–slitty,** *adj.*

slither /'slɪðə/ *v.i.* **1.** to slide down or along a surface, especially unsteadily or with more or less friction or noise. *–n.* **2.** a slithering movement; a slide. **–slithery,** *adj.*

sliver /'slɪvə/ *n.* **1.** a slender piece, as of wood, split, broken, or cut off, usually lengthwise or with the grain; splinter. **2.** a continuous strand or band of loose, untwisted wool, cotton, etc., ready for roving or slubbing. *–v.t.* **3.** to split or cut off, as a sliver; split or cut into slivers.

slob /slɒb/ *n. Colloq.* a stupid, clumsy, uncouth, or slovenly person.

slobber /'slɒbə/ *v.i.* **1.** to let saliva, etc., run from the mouth; slaver; dribble. **2.** to indulge in mawkish sentimentality. *–n.* **3.** saliva or liquid dribbling from the mouth; slaver. **4.** mawkishly sentimental speech or actions. **–slobberer,** *n.* **–slobbery,** *adj.*

slog /slɒg/ *Colloq.* *–verb* **(slogged, slogging)** *–v.t.* **1.** to hit hard. *–v.i.* **2.** to give heavy blows. **3.** to walk steadily and firmly; plod. **4.** to work hard. *–n.* **5.** a strong, rough blow. **6.** a period of hard work or walking. **–slogger,** *n.*

slogan /'slougən/ *n.* **1.** a distinctive cry or phrase of any party, class, body, or person; a catchword. **2.** a war cry or gathering cry, as formerly used among the Scottish clans.

sloop /slup/ *n.* a single-masted sailing vessel carrying fore-and-aft sails consisting of a mainsail and headsail.

slop[1] /slɒp/ *verb* **(slopped, slopping)** *–v.t.* **1.** to spill or splash (liquid). *–v.i.* **2.** Also, **slop about.** to spill or splash liquid. **3.** *Colloq.* (of persons, etc.) to be unduly

effusive; gush. **4.** to walk or go through mud, slush, or water. *–n.* **5.** a quantity of liquid carelessly spilled or splashed about. **6.** (*oft. pl.*) weak or unappetising liquid or semiliquid food. **7.** (*oft. pl.*) the dirty water, liquid refuse, etc., of a household or the like. **8.** swill, or the refuse of the kitchen, etc., often used as food for pigs or the like. **9.** liquid mud. **10.** (*pl.*) *Distilling* the mash remaining after distilling. **11.** (*pl.*) *Colloq.* beer. **12.** *Colloq.* a choppy sea. *–phr.* **13. slop over,** (of liquid) to run over in spilling.

slop[2] /slɒp/ *n.* (*oft. pl.*) **1.** clothing, bedding, tobacco, etc., supplied or sold to sailors from the ship's stores. **2.** cheap ready-made clothing in general.

slope[1] /sloup/ *v.i.* **1.** to take or have an inclined or slanting direction, especially downwards or upwards from the horizontal. **2.** to descend or ascend at a slant. *–v.t.* **3.** to direct at a slope or inclination; incline from the horizontal. **4.** to form with a slope or slant. *–n.* **5.** inclination or slant, especially downwards or upwards. **6.** deviation from the horizontal. **7.** an inclined surface. **8.** (*oft. pl.*) an area of sloping ground. **9.** *Mil.* the position of standing with the rifle resting at a slope on the shoulder. **10.** Also, **slopehead.** *Colloq.* (*derog.*) (*racist*) a member of certain Asian peoples, as Chinese, Vietnamese, etc. **–sloper,** *n.* **–sloping,** *adj.* **–slopingly,** *adv.* **–slopingness,** *n.*

slope[2] /sloup/ *Colloq.* *–v.i.* **1.** to move or go. *–phr.* **2. slope off,** to go away, especially furtively.

sloppy /'slɒpi/ *adj.* **(-pier, -piest) 1.** muddy, slushy, or very wet, as ground, walking, weather, etc. **2.** splashed or soiled with liquid. **3.** of the nature of slops, as food; watery and unappetising. **4.** *Colloq.* weak, silly, or maudlin: *sloppy sentiment.* **5.** *Colloq.* loose, careless, or slovenly: *to use sloppy English.* **–sloppily,** *adv.* **–sloppiness,** *n.*

sloppy joe /slɒpi 'dʒoʊ/ *n.* a loose, thick sweater.

slosh /slɒʃ/ *n.* **1.** → **slush. 2.** *Colloq.* a heavy blow. *–v.i.* **3.** to splash in slush, mud, or water. *–v.t.* **4.** to pour or spread (*in, on, round,* etc.) (a liquid or similar). **–sloshy,** *adj.*

sloshed /slɒʃt/ *adj. Colloq.* drunk.

slot /slɒt/ *n.* **1.** a narrow, elongated depression or aperture, especially one to receive or admit something. **2.** a position within a system. *–verb* **(slotted, slotting)** *–v.t.* **3.** to provide with a slot or slots; make a slot in. *–v.i.* **4.** (sometimes fol. by *into*) to fit: *your talk can slot into the morning program.* *–phr.* **5. slot in, a.** to insert into a slot. **b.** to settle in; adapt. **–slotter,** *n.*

slot car *n.* a powered miniature car which runs on a grooved track along which it is guided by a pin extending from the base of the car.

sloth /sloʊθ, sloʊð/ *n.* **1.** habitual disinclination to exertion; indolence; laziness. **2.** *Zool.* either of two genera of sluggish arboreal edentates of the family Bradypodidae of tropical America: the **two-toed sloth,** *Chloepus,* having two toes on the front foot, and the **three-toed sloth,** *Bradypus,* having three toes on the front foot.

slothful /'sloʊθfəl, 'slɒθfəl/ *adj.* sluggardly; indolent; lazy. **–slothfully,** *adv.* **–slothfulness,** *n.*

slouch /slaʊtʃ/ *v.i.* **1.** to sit or stand in an awkward, drooping posture. **2.** to move or walk with loosely drooping body and careless gait. *–v.t.* **3.** to cause to droop or bend down, as the shoulders or a hat. *–n.* **4.** a drooping or bending forward of the head and shoulders; an awkward, drooping carriage of a person. **5.** an awkward, ungainly, or slovenly person. **–slouchy,** *adj.* **–slouchily,** *adv.* **–slouchiness,** *n.*

slouch hat *n.* **1. a.** an army hat of soft felt, having a brim capable of being attached to the crown on one side to facilitate the carrying of rifles at the slope. **b.** such a hat regarded in Australia as a symbol of courage, past greatness, virtue, or national feeling. **2.** any soft hat, especially one with a broad, flexible brim.

slough[1] /slaʊ/ *n.* **1.** a piece of soft, muddy ground; a hole full of mire, as in a road; marsh; swamp. **2.** a condition of degradation, embarrassment, or helplessness. –**sloughy**, *adj.*

slough[2] /slʌf, slɒf/ *n.* **1.** the skin of a snake, especially the outer skin which is shed periodically. **2.** *Pathol.* a mass or layer of dead tissue which separates from the surrounding or underlying tissue. –*v.t.* **3.** to be shed or cast off, as the slough of a snake. **4.** *Pathol.* to separate from the sound flesh, as a slough. –*v.t.* **5.** to shed as or like a slough. –*phr.* **6. slough off**, to cast off. –**sloughy**, *adj.*

sloven /ˈslʌvən/ *n.* **1.** someone who is habitually negligent of neatness or cleanliness in dress, appearance, etc. **2.** someone who works, or does anything, in a negligent, slipshod manner. –**slovenly**, *adj.* –**slovenliness**, *n.*

slow /sloʊ/ *adj.* **1.** taking or requiring a comparatively long time for moving, going, acting, occurring, etc.; not fast, rapid, or swift. **2.** leisurely; gradual, as change, growth, etc. **3.** sluggish in nature, disposition, or function. **4.** dull of perception or understanding, as a person, the mind, etc. **5.** burning or heating with little speed or intensity, as a fire or an oven. **6.** slack, as trade. **7.** showing a time earlier than the correct time, as a clock. **8.** passing heavily, or dragging, as time. **9.** not progressive; behind the times. **10.** *Photography* (of film) requiring a long exposure. **11.** *Sport* (of a pitch, track, court, etc., or its surface) tending to slow down movement, as of a ball. –*adv.* **12.** in a slow manner; slowly. –*v.t.* **13.** to make slow or slower. **14.** Also, **slow up.** to retard; reduce the speed of. –*v.i.* Also, **slow down. 15.** to become slow or slower; slacken in speed. –*phr.* **16. slow to**, not prompt, readily disposed, or in haste to: *slow to anger*; *slow to take offence.* –**slowly**, *adv.* –**slowness**, *n.*

slowcoach /ˈsloʊkoʊtʃ/ *n. Colloq.* a slow or dull person.

slow food *n.* food which is the end product of a chain of local agriculture and processing, prepared in the context of a traditional cuisine.

slowmo /ˈsloʊmoʊ/ *n. Colloq.* (in film or television) slow motion. Also, **slow-mo, slomo.**

slow motion *n.* the process or technique used in film or television production in which images are made to move more slowly than their originals, due to having been photographed at a greater number of frames per second than normal, or being projected more slowly than normal.

slow-release *adj.* of or relating to a substance, such as a medicine or fertiliser, which is designed to release its contents over a period of time.

sludge /slʌdʒ/ *n.* **1.** mud, mire, or ooze; slush. **2.** a deposit of ooze at the bottom of bodies of water. **3.** any of various more or less mud-like deposits or mixtures. **4.** a later stage of sea freezing than frazil, in which the ice particles coagulate to form a thick, soupy surface layer having a matt appearance. **5.** sediment deposited during the treatment of sewage. –**sludgy**, *adj.*

slug[1] /slʌg/ *n.* **1.** any of various slimy, elongated terrestrial gastropods related to the terrestrial snails, but having no shell or only a rudimentary one. **2.** a slow-moving animal, vehicle, or the like. **3.** any heavy piece of crude metal. **4.** a piece of lead or other metal for firing from a gun. **5.** a metal disc used as a token in slot machines or as a counterfeit coin.

slug[2] /slʌg/ *v.t.* (**slugged, slugging**) **1.** to hit hard, especially with the fist. **2.** *Colloq.* to exact heavy payment from. –*n.* **3.** a heavy blow, especially with the fist. **4.** *Colloq.* a high price or tax.

sluggard /ˈslʌgəd/ *n.* **1.** someone who is habitually inactive or slothful. –*adj.* **2.** sluggardly.

sluggish /ˈslʌgɪʃ/ *adj.* **1.** indisposed to action or exertion, especially by nature; inactive, slow, or of little energy or vigour. **2.** not acting or working with full vigour, as bodily organs. **3.** slow, as motion. –**sluggishly**, *adv.* –**sluggishness**, *n.*

sluice /slus/ *n.* **1.** a channel built for carrying water, fitted with a gate for controlling the flow. **2.** a body of water held back or controlled by a sluicegate. **3.** any device for controlling a flow from or into a container. **4.** any channel, especially one carrying off extra water; drain. **5.** *Mining* a long, sloping trough into which water is directed to separate gold from gravel or sand. –*verb* (**sluiced, sluicing**) –*v.t.* **6.** to let out (water, etc.) or draw off the contents of (a pond, etc.) by, or as if by, the opening of a sluice. **7.** to wash with running water. –*v.i.* **8.** to flow or pour through or as if through a sluice.

slum /slʌm/ *n.* **1.** (*oft. pl.*) an overpopulated, squalid part of a city, inhabited by the poorest people. **2.** a squalid street, place, dwelling, or the like. –*adj.* **3.** of or relating to a slum: *slum area*; *slum dwellings.* –*verb* (**slummed, slumming**) –*v.i.* **4.** to visit slums, especially from curiosity. –*v.t.* **5.** to go about (a job, etc.) in a way that will result in work of inferior quality, as by using cheap materials, etc. –*phr.* **6. slum it**, *Colloq.* to live in circumstances below one's usual or expected standard of living. –**slummer**, *n.* –**slummy**, *adj.*

slumber /ˈslʌmbə/ *v.i.* **1.** to sleep, especially deeply. **2.** to be in a state of inactivity, negligence, quiescence, or calm. –*n.* **3.** (*oft. pl.*) sleep, especially deep sleep. **4.** a state of inactivity, quiescence, etc. –*phr.* **5. slumber away**, to spend (time) in slumbering. –**slumberer**, *n.* –**slumberous**, *adj.*

slump /slʌmp/ *v.i.* **1.** to drop heavily and loosely: *she slumped into a chair.* **2.** to sink heavily: *his spirits slumped at the bad news.* **3.** to slow down markedly in progress, growth, etc.: *the share market slumped.* –*n.* **4.** an act of slumping. **5.** a marked slowing down in the growth of the economy, market, prices, etc.

slur /slɜ/ *v.t.* (**slurred, slurring**) **1.** to pronounce (a syllable, word, etc.) indistinctly, as in hurried or careless utterance. **2.** *Music* to sing in a single breath, or play without a break (two or more notes of different pitch). **3.** to calumniate, disparage, or deprecate. –*n.* **4.** a slurred utterance or sound. **5.** *Music* **a.** the combination of two or more notes of different pitch, sung to a single syllable or played without a break. **b.** a curved mark indicating this. **6.** a disparaging remark; a slight. **7.** a blot or stain, as upon reputation; discredit. –*phr.* **8. slur over**, to pass over lightly, or without due mention or consideration.

slurp /slɜp/ *v.t.* **1.** to eat or drink (something) with a lot of noise. –*v.i.* **2.** to eat or drink noisily. –*n.* **3.** the noise produced by eating in such a manner.

slush /slʌʃ/ *n.* **1.** snow in a partly melted state. **2.** liquid mud; watery mire. **3.** fat, grease, etc. discarded from the galley of a ship. **4.** *Colloq.* silly, sentimental, or weakly emotional writing, talk, etc. –*v.t.* **5.** to splash with slush.

slush fund *n.* **1.** money collected unofficially, sometimes by secret or deceitful means, by an individual or an organisation for a special purpose. **2.** a fund from the sale of slush, refuse fat, etc., aboard ship, spent for any small luxuries.

slushie /ˈslʌʃi/ *n.* → **slushy** (def. 2).

slushy /ˈslʌʃi/ *adj.* (**-shier, -shiest**) **1.** of or relating to slush. –*n.* (*pl.* **-shies**) Also, **slushie. 2.** a semifrozen drink consisting of flavoured liquid to which finely crushed ice is added.

slut /slʌt/ *n.* **1.** (*derog.*) a woman who has many sexual partners. **2.** *Obs.* a dirty, slovenly woman. –**sluttish**, *adj.* –**slutty**, *adj.*

sly /slaɪ/ *adj.* (**slyer** *or* **slier, slyest** *or* **sliest**) **1.** cunning or wily, as persons or animals, or their actions, ways, etc. **2.** stealthy, insidious, or secret. **3.** playfully artful, mischievous, or roguish: *sly humour*. **4.** illicit; illegal: *sly gambling*; *sly watering*. *–phr.* **5. on the sly**, secretly. **–slyly,** *adv.* **–slyness,** *n.*

smack[1] /smæk/ *n.* **1.** a taste or flavour, especially a slight flavour distinctive or suggestive of something. **2.** a trace, touch, or suggestion of something. **3.** a taste, mouthful, or small quantity. *–phr.* **4. smack of**, to have a taste, flavour, trace, or suggestion of.

smack[2] /smæk/ *v.t.* to strike smartly, especially with the open hand or anything flat. **2.** to bring, put, throw, send, etc., with a sharp, resounding blow or a smart stroke. **3.** to separate (the lips) smartly so as to produce a sharp sound, often as a sign of relish, as in eating. *–v.i.* **4.** to smack together, as the lips. **5.** to come or strike smartly or forcibly, as against something. **6.** to make a sharp sound as of striking against something. *–n.* **7.** a smart, resounding blow, especially with something flat. **8.** a resounding or loud kiss. **9.** a smacking of the lips, as in relish. **10.** *Colloq.* heroin. *–adv. Colloq.* **11.** with a smack; suddenly and sharply. **12.** directly; straight. *–phr. Colloq.* **13. have a smack at**, to attempt. **14. smack in the eye, a.** a snub. **b.** a setback or disappointment.

smack[3] /smæk/ *n.* **1.** a sailing vessel, usually sloop-rigged, used especially in coasting and fishing. **2.** a fishing vessel with a well to keep fish alive.

small /smɔl/ *adj.* **1.** of limited size; of comparatively restricted dimensions; not big; little. **2.** slender, thin, or narrow. **3.** not large, as compared with other things of the same kind. **4.** not great in amount, degree, extent, duration, value, etc. **5.** not great numerically. **6.** of low numerical value; denoted by a low number. **7.** having only little land, capital, etc., or carrying on business on a limited scale: *a small investor*. **8.** of minor importance, moment, weight, or consequence. **9.** (of a letter) lower-case. **10.** humble, modest, or unpretentious. **11.** characterised by or indicative of littleness of mind or character; mean-spirited; ungenerous. **12.** ashamed or mortified: *to feel small*. **13.** of little strength or force. **14.** (of sound or the voice) gentle, soft, or low. **15.** (of a child) young. **16.** weak; diluted. *–adv.* **17.** in a small manner. **18.** into small pieces: *to slice small*. **19.** in low tones; softly. *–phr.* **20. small of the back**, the lower central part of the back.

small arms *pl. n.* firearms collectively which are small enough to be carried by a person, as rifles, revolvers, etc. **–small-arms,** *adj.*

small business *n.* **1.** a commercial enterprise conducted on a small scale. **2.** the people who operate small enterprises, considered collectively: *small business will resist the new tax.*

small fry *n.* **1.** small or young fish. **2.** young or unimportant persons or objects.

smallgoods /'smɔlgʊdz/ *pl. n. Aust., NZ* processed meats, as salami, frankfurts, etc.

smallpox /'smɔlpɒks/ *n. Pathol.* an acute, highly contagious, febrile disease caused by a virus and characterised by a pustular eruption which often leaves permanent pits or scars.

smart /smat/ *v.i.* **1.** to be a cause of sharp, surface pain, as a wound, blow, etc. **2.** to feel a sharp pain, as in a wounded surface. **3.** to suffer from keen emotion, such as hurt, anger, etc. *–adj.* **4.** sharp or keen: *a smart slap on the arm*. **5.** sharply active or vigorous: *a smart walk*. **6.** intelligent; clever. **7.** cleverly ready or effective: *a smart reply*. **8.** effectively neat in appearance. **9.** stylish; fashionable. **10.** (of a device or set of devices) controlled with computer software so that it performs some functions without the human input usually required. *–adv.* **11.** in a smart manner. *–n.* **12.** a feeling of smarting. **–smartly,** *adv.* **–smartness,** *n.*

smart alec /'smat ælɪk/ *n. Colloq.* someone who is ostentatious in the display of knowledge or skill, often despite basic ignorance or lack of ability. Also, **smart aleck**.

smart card *n.* a plastic card containing integrated circuits capable of storing digital information, used for performing financial transactions, accessing restricted areas, accessing secure computer records, etc. Also, **smartcard**.

smarten /'smatn/ *v.t.* **1.** to make more trim or spruce; improve in appearance. **2.** to make more brisk, as a pace. Also, **smarten up**.

smart phone *n.* a mobile phone with access to the internet and the functionality of a personal computer. Also, **smartphone**.

smash /smæʃ/ *v.t.* **1.** to break to pieces with violence and often with a crashing sound; shatter. **2.** to defeat, ruin or destroy. **3.** *Tennis* to hit (the ball) hard and fast with an overhead stroke. *–v.i.* **4.** to break to pieces. **5.** (fol. by *against, into, through*, etc.) to move with great violence; crash. *–n.* **6.** a smashing, or the sound of it. **7.** a violent and destructive collision. **8.** a process or condition of failure, ruin, or destruction, especially in financial affairs. **9.** Also, **smash-hit**. a play, film, etc., that is immediately very successful. **10.** *Tennis* a forceful overhead stroke. **–smasher,** *n.*

smashed /smæʃt/ *adj. Colloq.* incapacitated as a result of taking drugs, alcohol, etc.

smashing /'smæʃɪŋ/ *adj. Colloq.* excellent or extremely good; first-rate.

smattering /'smætərɪŋ/ *n.* a slight or superficial knowledge of something. **–smatteringly,** *adv.*

smear /smɪə/ *v.t.* **1.** to rub or spread with oil, grease, paint, dirt, etc. **2.** to spread (oil, grease, etc.) on or over something. **3.** to rub something over (a thing) so as to cause a blurred mark or smudge. **4.** to harm (someone's reputation); defame. *–n.* **5.** a mark or stain made by smearing. **6.** something smeared on a thing, as a glaze for pottery, or a substance put on a slide for microscopic examination. **7.** an act of defamation; slander.

smear test *n.* → **Pap smear**.

smell /smɛl/ *verb* (**smelt** *or* **smelled, smelling**) *–v.t.* **1.** to perceive through the nose, by means of the olfactory nerves; inhale the odour of. **2.** to test by the sense of smell. **3.** to perceive, detect, or discover by shrewdness or sagacity. *–v.i.* **4.** to have the sense of smell. **5.** to give out an odour. **6.** to give out an offensive odour. **7.** to seem or be unpleasant or bad. *–v. (copular)* **8.** to give out an odour as specified: *to smell sweet*. *–n.* **9.** the faculty or sense of smelling. **10.** that quality of a thing which is or may be smelled; odour. **11.** a trace or suggestion. **12.** the act of smelling. *–phr.* **13. on the smell of an oily** (or **oil**) **rag**, cheaply or parsimoniously: *they live on the smell of an oily rag*. **14. smell around** (or **about**), to search or investigate. **15. smell of, a.** to have the odour of. **b.** to have a trace or suggestion of. **16. smell out**, to search or find as if by smell.

smelt[1] /smɛlt/ *v.t.* **1.** to fuse or melt (ore) in order to separate the metal contained. **2.** to obtain or refine (metal) in this way.

smelt[2] /smɛlt/ *v.* a past tense and past participle of **smell**.

smidgen /'smɪdʒən/ *n.* a very small quantity; a bit. Also, **smidgin, smidgeon**.

smilax /'smaɪlæks/ *n.* **1.** any plant of the genus *Smilax*, of the tropical and temperate zones, consisting mostly of vines with woody stems. **2.** a delicate, twining plant, *Asparagus asparagoides*, with glossy, bright green leaves, often used in floral decoration; a noxious weed in Australia.

smile /smaɪl/ v.i. **1.** to assume a facial expression, characterised especially by a widening of the mouth, indicative of pleasure, favour, kindliness, amusement, derision, scorn, etc. **2.** to have a pleasant or agreeable aspect, as natural scenes, objects, etc. –v.t. **3.** to assume or give (a smile). **4.** to express by a smile: *to smile approval.* –n. **5.** the act of smiling; a smiling expression of the face. **6.** favouring look or regard: *fortune's smile.* **7.** pleasant or agreeable look or aspect. –phr. **8. smile at, a.** to look at with such an expression, especially in a pleasant or kindly way. **b.** to look at in amusement. **9. smile on** (or **upon**), to look on with favour, or support. –**smiler**, n. –**smilingly**, adv.

smirch /smɜtʃ/ v.t. **1.** to discolour or soil with some substance, as soot, dust, dirt, etc., or as the substance does. **2.** to sully or tarnish, as with disgrace. –n. **3.** a dirty mark or smear. **4.** a stain or blot, as on reputation.

smirk /smɜk/ v.i. **1.** to smile in a condescending or knowing way. –v.t. **2.** to utter with a smirk. –n. **3.** the smile or the facial expression of someone who smirks. –**smirker**, n. –**smirkingly**, adv.

smite /smaɪt/ v.t. (**smote, smitten** or **smit, smiting**) **1.** to strike or hit hard, as with the hand, a stick or weapon, etc., or as the hand or a weapon does. **2.** to render by, or as by, a blow: *to smite a person dead.* **3.** to fall upon or attack with deadly or disastrous effect, as lightning, blight, pestilence, etc., do. **4.** to affect suddenly and strongly with a specified feeling: *smitten with terror.* **5.** to impress favourably; charm; enamour. –**smiter**, n.

smith /smɪθ/ n. **1.** a worker in metal. **2.** → **blacksmith**. –v.t. **3.** to make by forging.

smithereens /smɪðəˈrinz/ pl. n. Colloq. small fragments.

smithy /ˈsmɪθi, ˈsmɪði/ n. (pl. **-thies**) **1.** the workshop of a smith, especially a blacksmith. **2.** a forge.

smitten /ˈsmɪtn/ v. **1.** past participle of **smite**. –adj. **2.** struck, as with a hard blow. **3.** stricken with affliction, etc. **4.** Colloq. very much in love.

smock /smɒk/ n. **1.** any loose overgarment, especially one worn to protect the clothing while at work: *an artist's smock.* –v.t. **2.** to draw (a fabric) by needlework into a honeycomb pattern with diamond-shaped recesses.

smog /smɒg/ n. a mixture of smoke and fog. –**smoggy**, adj.

smoke /smoʊk/ n. **1.** the visible exhalation given off by a burning or smouldering substance, especially the grey, brown, or blackish mixture of gases and suspended carbon particles resulting from the combustion of wood, peat, coal, or other organic matter. **2.** something resembling this, as vapour or mist, flying particles, etc. **3.** something unsubstantial, evanescent, or without result. **4.** an act or spell of smoking tobacco, or the like. **5.** that which is smoked, as a cigar or cigarette. **6.** *Physical Chem.* a dispersion of solid particles in a gaseous medium. –v.i. **7.** to give off or emit smoke. **8.** to give out smoke offensively or improperly, as a stove. **9.** to send forth steam or vapour, dust, or the like. **10.** to draw into the mouth and puff out the smoke of tobacco or the like, as from a pipe, cigar, or cigarette. –v.t. **11.** to draw into the mouth and puff out the smoke of (tobacco, etc.). **12.** to use (a pipe, cigarette, etc.) in this process. **13.** to expose to smoke. **14.** → **fumigate**. **15.** to colour or darken by smoke. **16.** to cure (meat, fish, etc.) by exposure to smoke. –phr. **17. go into smoke**, Colloq. to disappear, especially to go into hiding. **18. go** (or **end**) **up in smoke, a.** to be burnt up completely. **b.** to have no solid result; end or disappear without coming to anything. **19. smoke and mirrors**, a hoax or deception. **20. smoke out, a.** to drive out by means of smoke, as an animal from its hole or a person from a hiding place. **b.** to force into public view or

knowledge. **21. the big smoke**, Colloq. the city. –**smoker**, n. –**smoky**, adj.

smoke-free adj. free of tobacco smoke; of or relating to an office, restaurant, etc., in which smoking is not permitted: *a smoke-free dining room.* Also, **smokefree**.

smokescreen /ˈsmoʊkskrin/ n. **1.** a mass of dense smoke produced to conceal an area, vessel, or plane from the enemy. **2.** any device or artifice used for concealment of the truth, as a mass of verbiage.

smoking ceremony n. an Aboriginal cleansing ritual in which green leaves from local plants are burnt creating smoke which is said to cleanse and heal the area; often used to prepare a site for a new purpose, or after a death to remove spirits.

smoking gun n. **1.** a gun that has just been fired. **2.** a piece of incontrovertible evidence which points to the perpetrator of a crime, the cause of a disaster, etc.

smoko /ˈsmoʊkoʊ/ n. (pl. **-kos**) Aust., NZ Colloq. a rest from work; tea-break. Also, **smoke-o, smoke-oh**.

smooch /smutʃ/ v.i. Colloq. to kiss; cuddle; behave amorously.

smoodge /smudʒ/ v.i. (**smoodged, smoodging**) Colloq. **1.** to kiss; caress. **2.** to flatter; curry favour. Also, **smooge**. –**smoodger**, n. –**smoodging**, n.

smooth /smuð/ adj. **1.** free from projections or irregularities of surface such as would be perceived in touching or stroking. **2.** free from hairs or a hairy growth. **3.** free from inequalities of surface, ridges or hollows, obstructions, etc. **4.** generally flat or unruffled, as a calm sea. **5.** of uniform consistency; free from lumps, as a batter, a sauce, etc. **6.** free from or proceeding without breaks, abrupt bends, etc. **7.** free from unevenness or roughness: *smooth driving.* **8.** easy and uniform, as an outline, motion, the working of a machine, etc. **9.** having projections worn away: *a tyre worn smooth.* **10.** free from hindrances or difficulties. **11.** undisturbed, tranquil, or equable, as the feelings, temper, etc. **12.** easy, flowing, elegant, or polished, as speech, a speaker, etc. **13.** pleasant, agreeable, or ingratiatingly polite, as manner, persons, etc.; bland or suave. **14.** free from harshness or sharpness of taste, as wine. **15.** not harsh to the ear, as sound. **16.** *Phonetics* without aspiration. **17.** *Tennis* of or relating to the back of a racquet (from the texture of the strings on that side). –adv. **18.** in a smooth manner; smoothly. –v.t. **19.** Also, **smooth down**. to make smooth of surface, as by scraping, planing, pressing, stroking, etc. **20.** Also, **smooth away**. to remove (projections, etc.) in making something smooth. **21.** to tranquillise, calm, or soothe, as the feelings. –n. **22.** the act of smoothing. **23.** a smooth part or place. –phr. **24. smooth over**, to gloss over or palliate, as something unpleasant or wrong. –**smoother**, n. –**smoothly**, adv. –**smoothness**, n.

smoothie /ˈsmuði/ n. **1.** a man who attempts to ingratiate himself with a woman by assuming charming behaviour and manners. **2.** someone who is suave or has polished manners, especially one who is possibly insincere or dishonest. **3.** a drink made from fruit, honey, etc., blended with milk. Also, **smoothy**.

smooth muscle n. a type of muscle occurring in the digestive system, airways and blood vessels, which acts involuntarily.

smorgasbord /ˈsmɔgəzbɔd/ n. **1.** a buffet meal of various hot and cold hors d'oeuvres, salads, meat dishes, etc. **2.** a wide choice or variety.

smote /smoʊt/ v. past tense of **smite**.

smother /ˈsmʌðə/ v.t. **1.** to stifle or suffocate, especially by smoke or by cutting off the air necessary for life. **2.** to put out or deaden (fire, etc.) by covering so as to keep out air. **3.** (oft. fol. by *up, in*) to cover closely or thickly. **4.** to surround with love, kindness, etc., to such an extent that it prevents personal development. **5.** to repress, as feelings, impulses, etc.; stifle: *to smother laughter. –v.i.* **6.** to be prevented from breathing freely. *–n.* **7.** dense, stifling smoke. **–smothered,** *adj.* **–smothering,** *adj.* **–smothery,** *adj.*

smoulder /'smouldə/ *v.i.* **1.** to burn or smoke without flame. **2.** to exist or continue in a suppressed state or without outward demonstration. **3.** to display repressed feelings, especially of indignation: *his eyes smouldered. –n.* **4.** dense smoke resulting from slow or suppressed combustion. **5.** a smouldering fire. Also, *US,* **smolder.**

SMS /ɛs ɛm 'ɛs/ *n.* (*pl.* **SMSs** *or* **SMSes** *or* **SMS's**) **1.** short message service; a service which enables a user to key in the text of a message on a mobile phone and send it to another mobile phone where it can be read on the screen. **2.** → **text message.** *–verb* (**SMS'ed** *or* **SMSed, SMS'ing** *or* **SMSing**) *–v.t.* **3.** to send (a text message) especially in SMS. **4.** to send (a person) a text message especially in SMS. *–v.i.* **5.** to use SMS.

SMS code *n.* a code devised to reduce the length of words, in order to maximise communication within the SMS system.

SMS message *n.* → **text message.** Also, **SMS. –SMS messaging,** *n.*

smudge /smʌdʒ/ *n.* **1.** a dirty mark or smear. **2.** a blurred mass: *the house was a smudge on the horizon. –verb* (**smudged, smudging**) *–v.t.* **3.** to mark with dirty streaks or smears. *–v.i.* **4.** to be or become smudged.

smug /smʌg/ *adj.* (**smugger, smuggest**) complacently proper, righteous, clever, etc.; self-satisfied. **–smugly,** *adv.* **–smugness,** *n.*

smuggle /'smʌgəl/ *v.t.* **1.** to import or export (goods) secretly, without payment of legal duty or in violation of law. **2.** to bring, take, put, etc., surreptitiously: *she smuggled the gun into prison inside a cake. –v.i.* **3.** to smuggle goods. **–smuggler,** *n.*

smut /smʌt/ *n.* **1.** a tiny piece of soot; sooty matter. **2.** a black or dirty mark; a smudge. **3.** offensive talk or writing; obscenity. **4.** a fungous disease of plants, especially cereals, in which the affected parts are converted into a black powdery mass of spores. **5.** the fungus itself. *–v.i.* (**smutted, smutting**) **6.** to become affected with smut, as a plant.

snack /snæk/ *n.* **1.** a small portion of food or drink; a light meal. **2.** *Colloq.* anything easily done. *–v.i.* **3.** to eat small portions of food at times other than meal times.

snaffle[1] /'snæfəl/ *n.* a slender, jointed bit used on a bridle.

snaffle[2] /'snæfəl/ *v.t. Colloq.* **1.** to steal. **2.** to take away quickly before anyone else: *early shoppers snaffled the sales bargains.*

snag[1] /snæg/ *n.* **1.** a short, projecting stump, as of a branch broken or cut off. **2.** any sharp or rough projection. **3.** a tree or part of a tree held fast in the bottom of a river or other water which is a danger to navigation. **4.** any obstacle or impediment: *to strike a snag in carrying out plans.* **5.** a pulled thread in a stocking. *–v.t.* (**snagged, snagging**) **6.** to ladder (def. 6); catch upon, or damage by, a snag. **7.** to obstruct or impede, as a snag does. **–snaggy,** *adj.*

snag[2] /snæg/ *n. Aust., NZ Colloq.* a sausage.

snag[3] /snæg/ *n. Colloq.* a man who displays sensitivity in personal relationships. Also, **SNAG.**

snail /sneɪl/ *n.* **1.** a mollusc of the class Gastropoda, having a single, usually spirally coiled shell. **2.** a slow or lazy person; a sluggard.

snail mail *n.* (*humorous*) the ordinary post (as opposed to email).

snake /sneɪk/ *n.* **1.** a scaly, limbless, usually slender reptile, occurring in venomous and non-venomous forms, widely distributed in numerous genera and species and constituting the order (or suborder)

Serpentes. **2.** a treacherous person; an insidious enemy. **3.** any of various flexible coil springs used for clearing drains, threading wires, etc., through tubes, or the like. *–v.i.* **4.** to move, twist, or wind in the manner of a snake: *the path snakes through the field. –v.t.* **5.** to follow (a course) in the shape of a snake: *he snaked his way through the jungle. –phr.* **6. like a cut snake,** *Colloq.* in a frenzy of activity. **7. lower than a snake's belly,** *Colloq.* unprincipled; despicable. **8. mad** (or **silly**) **as a** (**cut**) **snake,** insane; eccentric. **9. snake in the grass,** a deceitful or treacherous person; a hidden enemy.

snaky /'sneɪki/ *adj.* (**-kier, -kiest**) **1.** of or relating to a snake or snakes. **2.** snake-like; twisting, winding, or sinuous. **3.** venomous; treacherous or insidious. **4.** *Aust., NZ Colloq.* annoyed; angry or spiteful. Also, **snakey.**

snap /snæp/ *verb* (**snapped, snapping**) *–v.i.* **1.** to make a sudden, sharp sound; crackle. **2.** to click, as a mechanism. **3.** to move, strike, shut, catch, etc., with a sharp sound, as a lid. **4.** to break suddenly, especially with a sharp, cracking sound, as something slender and brittle. **5.** to act or move with quick, neat motions of the body: *to snap to attention.* **6.** *Photography* to take snapshots. **7.** to make a quick or sudden bite or snatch. **8.** to utter a quick, sharp speech, reproof, retort, etc. **9.** *Football* to make a hurried shot at goal. *–v.t.* **10.** Also, **snap up.** to seize with, or as with, a quick bite or snatch. **11.** to cause to make a sudden, sharp sound: *to snap one's fingers.* **12.** to bring, strike, shut, open, operate, etc., with a sharp sound or movement: *to snap a lid down.* **13.** Also, **snap out.** to utter or say in a quick, sharp manner. **14.** to break suddenly, especially with a crackling sound. **15.** *Photography* to take a snapshot of. **16.** *Football* to kick (a goal or behind) under pressure. *–n.* **17.** a sharp, crackling or clicking sound, or a movement or action causing such a sound: *a snap of the fingers.* **18.** a catch or the like operating with such a sound. **19.** a sudden breaking, as of something brittle or tense, or a sharp crackling sound caused by it. **20.** a small, thin, brittle or crisp biscuit. **21.** *Colloq.* briskness, vigour, or energy, as of persons or actions. **22.** a quick or sudden bite or snatch, as at something. **23.** a short spell, as of cold weather. **24.** → **snapshot** (def. 1). **25.** a simple card game in which cards are thrown in turn on to a pile. When a card of equal value to the preceding card is put down, the first player to call 'snap' wins the pile. **26.** *Colloq.* an easy and profitable or agreeable position, piece of work, or the like. **27.** *Football* a hurried shot at goal. *–adj.* **28.** denoting devices closing by pressure on a spring catch, or articles using such devices. **29.** made, done, taken, etc., suddenly or offhand: *a snap judgement. –adv.* **30.** in a brisk, sudden manner. *–interj.* **31.** used in the game of snap to take cards from an opponent. *–phr.* **32. snap one's fingers at,** to disregard; scorn. **33. snap out of it,** to recover quickly from a mood, as anger, unhappiness, etc. **34. snap someone's head off,** to speak angrily and sharply to someone.

snapdragon /'snæpdrægən/ *n.* a plant of the genus *Antirrhinum,* especially *A. majus,* a plant long cultivated for its spikes of showy flowers, of various colours, with a corolla that supposedly looks like the mouth of a dragon.

snapper /'snæpə/ *n.* **1.** Also, **schnapper.** a marine food fish of the family Sparidae, *Chrysophrys auratus,* widely distributed in Australian and New Zealand coastal waters, and known as cockney bream when very young, then with increasing age as red bream, squire, and old man; wollomai. **2.** elsewhere, **a.** any of various large marine fishes of the family Lutjanidae of warm seas, as the **red snapper,** *Lutjanus blackfordii,* a food fish of the Gulf of Mexico. **b.** any of various other fishes, as the bluefish, *Pomatomus saltratix*. **3.** *Colloq.* a form of address to a thin person.

snappy /'snæpi/ *adj.* (**-pier, -piest**) **1.** snappish, as a dog, a person, the speech, etc. **2.** quick or sudden in action or performance. **3.** *Colloq.* crisp, smart, lively, brisk, etc. **4.** *Colloq.* stylish: *a snappy dresser.* –*phr.* **5. make it snappy**, *Colloq.* to hurry up. –**snappily**, *adv.* –**snappiness**, *n.*

snapshot /'snæpʃɒt/ *n.* **1.** Also, **snap**. a photograph taken quickly without any formal arrangement of the subject, mechanical adjustment of the camera, etc. **2.** a quick shot from a gun, taken without deliberate aim.

snare /snɛə/ *n.* **1.** a device, usually consisting of a noose, for capturing birds or small animals. **2.** anything serving to entrap, entangle, or catch unawares; a trap. **3.** *Surg.* a noose which removes tumours, etc., by the roots or the base. –*v.t.* (**snared, snaring**) **4.** to catch with a snare; entrap; entangle. **5.** to catch or involve by trickery or wile. –**snarer**, *n.*

snarl¹ /snal/ *v.i.* **1.** to growl angrily or viciously, as a dog. **2.** to speak in a savagely sharp, angry, or quarrelsome manner. –*v.t.* **3.** to utter or say with a snarl. –*n.* **4.** the act of snarling. **5.** a snarling sound or utterance. –**snarler**, *n.* –**snarling, snarly**, *adj.* –**snarlingly**, *adv.*

snarl² /snal/ *n.* **1.** a tangle, as of thread or hair. **2.** a complicated or confused condition or matter, as a traffic snarl. –*v.t.* **3.** to bring into a tangled condition, as thread, hair, etc.; tangle. **4.** to render complicated or confused.

snatch /snætʃ/ *v.i.* **1.** (usu. fol. by *at*) to make a sudden effort to seize something, as with the hand. –*v.t.* **2.** (oft. fol. by *up, from, out of, away,* etc.) to seize by a sudden or hasty grasp. **3.** to rescue or save by prompt action. –*n.* **4.** a sudden motion to seize something. **5.** a bit, scrap, or fragment of something: *snatches of conversation.* **6.** a brief spell of effort, activity, or any experience: *to work in snatches.* –**snatcher**, *n.*

snatch strap *n.* an elasticised strap designed to be attached at the ends to two vehicles, the first being used to haul out the second which has become bogged or stuck. Also, **recovery strap**.

snazzy /'snæzi/ *adj.* (**-zier, -ziest**) *Colloq.* very smart; strikingly fashionable; stylish.

sneak /snik/ *verb* (**sneaked** or, *Colloq.*, **snuck, sneaking**) –*v.i.* **1.** to go (*about, along, in, off, out,* etc.) in a stealthy or furtive manner; slink; skulk. **2.** to act in a furtive, underhand, or mean way. **3.** to let out secrets, especially deceitfully; tell tales. **4.** *Colloq.* to go (*out, off, away,* etc.) quickly and quietly in departure. –*v.t.* **5.** to move, put, pass, etc., in a stealthy or furtive manner. **6.** *Colloq.* to take surreptitiously, or steal. –*n.* **7.** someone who sneaks; a sneaking, underhand, or contemptible person. **8.** a telltale. –*phr.* **9. sneak up**, (sometimes fol. by *on*) to approach furtively. –**sneaky**, *adj.* –**sneakily**, *adv.*

sneaker /'snikə/ *n.* a shoe with a rubber or other soft sole, worn for sport or as part of casual fashion.

sneer /snɪə/ *v.i.* **1.** to smile or curl the lip in a manner that shows scorn, contempt, etc. **2.** to speak or write in a manner expressive of derision, scorn, or contempt. –*v.t.* **3.** to utter or say in a sneering manner. –*n.* **4.** an act of sneering. –**sneerer**, *n.* –**sneering**, *adj.* –**sneeringly**, *adv.*

sneeze /sniz/ *v.i.* **1.** to emit air or breath suddenly, forcibly, and audibly through the nose and mouth by involuntary, spasmodic action. –*n.* **2.** an act or sound of sneezing. –*phr.* **3. not to be sneezed at**, worth consideration. **4. sneeze at**, (*usu. with a negative*) *Colloq.* to show contempt for, or treat with contempt. –**sneezer**, *n.* –**sneezy**, *adj.*

sneezeweed /'snizwid/ *n.* any species of *Centipeda*, of Asia, Australia, and New Zealand, herbs with a pungent aroma irritating to the mucous membranes.

snib /snɪb/ *n.* **1.** a mechanism which is usually part of a lock and which can be operated from only one side of a door, holding the lock in position independently of the key. **2.** → **latch** (def. 1). –*v.t.* (**snibbed, snibbing**) **3.** to hold (a lock) by means of a snib.

snick /snɪk/ *v.t.* **1.** to cut, snip, or nick. **2.** to strike sharply. **3.** *Cricket* to hit (the ball), especially accidentally, with the edge of the bat. –*n.* **4.** a small cut; a nick. **5.** *Cricket* a glancing blow given to the ball.

snicker /'snɪkə/ *v.i.* **1.** (of a horse) to make a low snorting neigh. **2.** → **snigger**.

snide /snaɪd/ *adj.* derogatory in a nasty, insinuating manner: *snide remarks.*

sniff /snɪf/ *v.i.* **1.** to draw air through the nose in short, audible inhalation. **2.** to clear the nose by so doing; sniffle, as with emotion. **3.** to smell by short inhalations. –*v.t.* **4.** to draw in or up through the nose by sniffing, as air, smells, liquid, powder, etc.; inhale. **5.** to perceive by, or as if by, smelling. –*n.* **6.** an act of sniffing; a single short, audible inhalation. **7.** the sound made. **8.** a scent or smell perceived. –*phr.* **9. sniff around**, to make enquiries about someone or something. **10. sniff at**, to show disdain, contempt, etc., by, or as if by, a sniff. –**sniffable**, *adj.* –**sniffer**, *n.* –**sniffy**, *adj.*

sniffer dog *n.* a dog trained to detect by smell the presence of hidden illegal drugs, explosives, blood, etc.; detection dog.

sniffle /'snɪfəl/ *v.i.* **1.** to sniff repeatedly, as from a cold in the head or in repressing tearful emotion. –*n.* **2.** an act or sound of sniffling. –*phr.* **3. the sniffles**, a cold, or other condition marked by sniffling. –**sniffling**, *n.*

snigger /'snɪgə/ *v.i.* to laugh in a half-suppressed, often indecorous or disrespectful, manner.

snip /snɪp/ *verb* (**snipped, snipping**) –*v.t.* **1.** to cut with a small, quick stroke, or a number of such strokes, as with scissors, etc. –*v.i.* **2.** to cut with small, quick strokes. –*n.* **3.** a small cut, notch, slit, etc., made by snipping. **4.** the sound made by snipping. **5.** a small piece or amount snipped off.

snipe /snaɪp/ *n.* **1.** any of several shorebirds of the genus *Gallinago*, and related genera, having plump bodies, striped heads and long, straight bills, frequenting swamps and wet grasslands in many parts of the world; some, such as **Latham's snipe**, *G. hardwickii*, are seen in Australia as non-breeding migrants. **2.** a bird of genus *Rostratula*, rather similar in appearance but having a down-curved tip to its bill, as the **painted snipe**, *Rostratula beghalensis* of Australia, Africa, and southern Asia. –*v.i.* **3.** to shoot or hunt snipe. **4.** to shoot at individual soldiers, etc., as opportunity offers from a concealed or long-range position. –*phr.* **5. snipe at**, to make critical or damaging comments about (someone) without entering into open conflict. –**snipelike**, *adj.*

sniper /'snaɪpə/ *n.* **1.** someone or something that snipes. **2.** a marksman who shoots at other people from a concealed or long-range position.

snippet /'snɪpət/ *n.* **1.** a small piece snipped off; a small bit, scrap, or fragment. **2.** *Colloq.* a small or insignificant person.

snitch¹ /snɪtʃ/ *v.t. Colloq.* to snatch or steal.

snitch² /snɪtʃ/ *Colloq.* –*v.i.* **1.** to turn informer. –*n.* **2.** Also, **snitcher**. an informer. **3.** *Aust., NZ* a feeling of ill-will: *to have a snitch against someone.*

snivel /'snɪvəl/ *v.i.* (**-elled** or, *Chiefly US*, **-eled, -elling** or, *Chiefly US*, **-eling**) **1.** to weep or cry with sniffing. **2.** to put on or pretend a tearful state; whine. **3.** to draw up mucus noisily through the nose. –*n.* **4.** a light sniff, as in weeping. **5.** mucus running from the nose. **−sniveller**, *n.* **−snivelly**, *adj.*

snob /snɒb/ *n.* **1.** someone who admires, imitates, or seeks association with those with social rank, wealth, etc., and is condescending or overbearing to others. **2.** someone who has, or assumes, knowledge of a subject or subjects, and scorns anyone without this. **−snobbish, snobby**, *adj.* **−snobbery**, *n.*

snooker /ˈsnukə/ *n.* **1.** a game played on a billiard table with fifteen red balls and six balls of other colours, the object being to pocket them. **−v.t. 2.** *Colloq.* to obstruct or hinder (someone), especially from reaching some object, aim, etc. **−v.i. 3.** *Aust., NZ Colloq.* to hide.

snoop /snup/ *Colloq.* **−v.i. 1.** to prowl or pry; go about in a sneaking, prying way; pry in a mean, sly manner. **−n. 2.** an act or instance of snooping. **3.** someone who snoops. **−snooper**, *n.* **−snoopy**, *adj.*

snooty /ˈsnuti, ˈsnʊti/ *adj.* **(-tier, -tiest)** *Colloq.* **1.** snobbish. **2.** haughty; supercilious.

snooze /snuz/ *Colloq.* **−v.i. 1.** to sleep; slumber; doze; nap. **−n. 2.** a rest; nap. **3.** a setting of a radio, mobile phone, etc., in which an alarm is turned off but then reactivated after a short period of time.

snore /snɔ/ *v.i.* **1.** to breathe during sleep with hoarse or harsh sounds. **−n. 2.** an act of snoring, or the sound made. **−snorer**, *n.*

snorkel /ˈsnɔkəl/ *n.* **1.** a device on a submarine consisting of two vertical tubes for the intake and exhaust of air for diesel engines and general ventilation. **2.** a tube enabling a person swimming face downwards in the water to breathe, consisting of a tube, one end of which is put in the mouth while the other projects above the surface. **3.** *Motor Vehicles* an erect extension to an exhaust pipe to facilitate driving through water. **−v.i. (-kelled** *or,* *Chiefly US,* **-keled, -kelling** *or,* *Chiefly US,* **-keling) 4.** to swim using such a device, usually in order to look at the seabed, fish, etc. **−snorkeller**, *n.*

snort /snɔt/ *v.i.* **1.** to force the breath violently through the nostrils with a loud, harsh sound, as a horse, etc. **2.** to express contempt, indignation, etc., by such a sound. **−v.t. 3.** to utter with a snort. **−n. 4.** the act or sound of snorting.

snot /snɒt/ *n. Colloq.* mucus from the nose. **−snotty**, *adj.*

snout /snaʊt/ *n.* **1.** the part of an animal's head projecting forward and containing the nose and jaws; the muzzle. **2.** *Entomology* a prolongation of the head bearing the feeding organs. **3.** anything that resembles or suggests an animal's snout in shape, function, etc. **4.** *Colloq.* a person's nose, especially when large or prominent.

snow /snoʊ/ *n.* **1.** the aqueous vapour of the atmosphere precipitated in partially frozen crystalline form and falling to the earth in white flakes. **2.** these flakes as forming a layer on the ground, etc. **3.** the fall of these flakes. **4.** *Poetic* the white colour of snow. **5.** frozen carbon dioxide. **6.** *Colloq.* a powdered form of a drug, usually cocaine but sometimes heroin. **7.** white spots on a television screen caused by a weak signal. **−v.i. 8.** (of snow) to fall: *it snowed last night.* **9.** to descend like snow. **−v.t. 10.** to let fall as or like snow. **11.** to overwhelm (someone) with facts and information in an attempt to distract attention from some aspect of the situation. **−phr. 12. be snowed under**, to be overcome by something, as work. **13. it's snowing down south**, *Colloq.* a euphemistic expression pointing out that someone's underwear is showing. **14. snow in** (or **over**) (or **under**), to cover, obstruct, isolate, etc., with snow. **15. the snow**, *Aust.* snowfields, usually developed for recreational use: *are you going to the snow this year?* **−snowy**, *adj.*

snowberry /ˈsnoʊbɛri/ *n.* (*pl.* **-ries**) any of several species of the genus *Gaultheria* of Tasmania and New

Zealand which have white, red, or purple berries. Also, **waxberry**.

snowboard /ˈsnoʊbɔd/ *n.* **1.** a board for gliding over the snow, which resembles a surfboard in that the rider stands on it, the feet being strapped to it as with skis. **−v.i. 2.** to glide over the snow on a snowboard. **−snowboarder**, *n.* **−snowboarding**, *n.*

snow chains *pl. n.* chains placed around the driving wheels of a motor vehicle to give added traction in icy conditions, etc.

snow daisy *n.* any of a number of herbs of the Australasian, especially New Zealand, genus *Celmisia*.

snowdrop[1] /ˈsnoʊdrɒp/ *n.* a low spring-blooming herb, *Galanthus nivalis*, bearing drooping white flowers.

snowdrop[2] /ˈsnoʊdrɒp/ *v.i.* **(-dropped, -dropping)** *Colloq.* to steal laundry from clothes lines. **−snowdropper**, *n.*

snowgrass /ˈsnoʊɡras/ *n.* **1.** any of many species of the tussock grass *Poa*. **2.** *NZ* any of certain mountain grasses of the genus *Danthonia* which often form large tussocks at high altitudes.

snow gum *n.* any of several trees of the genus *Eucalyptus* found growing at high altitudes in Australia, especially *E. pauciflora niphophila*. Also, **ghost gum**.

snowmelt /ˈsnoʊmɛlt/ *n.* the surface water which runs off from melting snow, having a significant effect on river systems and vegetation in the region. Also, **snow melt**.

snub /snʌb/ *v.t.* **(snubbed, snubbing) 1.** to treat with disdain or contempt, especially by ignoring. **2.** to rebuke sharply. **−n. 3.** an act of snubbing; rebuke or slight. **−adj. 4.** (of the nose) short, and turned up at the tip. **−snubber**, *n.*

snuff[1] /snʌf/ *v.t.* **1.** to draw in through the nose by inhaling. **−v.i. 2.** to draw air, etc., into the nostrils by inhaling, as in order to smell something. **−n. 3.** an act of snuffing; an inhalation; a sniff. **4.** a preparation of powdered tobacco, usually taken into the nostrils by inhalation.

snuff[2] /snʌf/ *n.* **1.** the charred or partly consumed portion of a candlewick or the like. **−v.t. 2.** to cut off or remove the snuff of (a candle, etc.). **3.** *Colloq.* to kill. **−phr. 4. snuff it**, to die. **5. snuff out**, **a.** to extinguish. **b.** *Colloq.* to kill.

snuffle /ˈsnʌfəl/ *v.i.* **1.** to draw the breath or mucus through the nostrils in an audible or noisy manner. **2.** to sniff; snivel. **−v.t. 3.** to utter in a snuffling or nasal tone. **−n. 4.** an act of snuffling. **−phr. 5. the snuffles**, *Colloq.* a condition of the nose, as from a cold, causing snuffling. **−snuffler**, *n.*

snug /snʌɡ/ *adj.* **(snugger, snuggest) 1.** (of a place, etc.) comfortable or cosy. **2.** (of a ship, etc.) neat or compactly arranged, especially if limited in size. **3.** (of a garment) fitting closely, but comfortably. **4.** (of people, etc.) comfortably situated. **−adv. 5.** in a snug manner. **−snugly**, *adv.* **−snugness**, *n.*

snuggle /ˈsnʌɡəl/ *v.i.* Also, **snuggle up, snuggle in. 1.** to lie or press closely, as for warmth, comfort, or affection; nestle; cuddle. **−v.t. 2.** to draw or press closely, as for warmth or comfort, or from affection. **−n. 3.** a cuddle; embrace.

so /soʊ/ *adv.* **1.** in the way or manner indicated, described, or implied: *do it so.* **2.** as stated or reported: *is that so?* **3.** in the aforesaid state or condition: *it is broken, and has long been so.* **4.** to that extent; in that degree: *do not walk so fast.* **5.** (an intensifier) very or extremely: *you are so kind.* **6.** (an intensifier) very greatly: *my head aches so!* **7.** (*used emphatically*) indeed: *I did so do it!* **8.** (*used emphatically*) *Colloq.* completely: *you are so dumped!* **−conj. 9.** with the intention that: *I called my parents so they wouldn't worry.* **10.** consequently; with the result that: *he passed his exams so he felt elated.*

–pron. **11.** such as has been stated: *and I say so too.* *–interj.* Also, **so what!**. **12.** an interrogative expressing contempt, disdain, etc.: '*First you said you wanted to come, and now you are saying you don't.*' '*So!*' *–phr.* **13. and so, a.** used to confirm or emphasise a previous statement: *I said I would come, and so I will.* **b.** likewise or correspondingly: *he is going, and so am I.* **c.** consequently or accordingly: *she is ill, and so cannot come.* **d.** thereupon or thereafter: *and so they were married.* **14. and so forth, a.** continuing in the same way. **b.** et cetera. **15. and so on,** et cetera. **16. be** (or **have**) **so,** (*followed by a preposition or participle*) *Colloq.* to be emphatically as described: *I am so over your whining*; *you are so going to be in trouble*; *we have so missed our bus.* **17. just so,** in perfect order; carefully arranged: *her room was just so.* **18. or so,** about thus, or about that amount or number: *a day or so ago.* **19. quite so,** an expression of concurrence, agreement, etc. **20. so ... as,** to such a degree or extent: *so far as I know*; *not so tall as his brother.* **21. so as to,** with the result or purpose of. **22. so called, a.** called or designated thus. **b.** incorrectly called or styled thus. **23. so much,** an unspecified amount. **24. so much for,** there is no more to be said or done about: *so much for your childhood ideals.* **25. so that, a.** with the effect or result that. **b.** in order that: *he wrote so that they might expect him.* **26. so to speak** (or **say**), to use such manner of speaking.

soak /soʊk/ *v.i.* **1.** to lie in and become saturated or permeated with water or some other liquid. **2.** to pass (*in*, *through*, *out*, etc.), as a liquid, through pores or interstices. **3.** to be thoroughly wet. **4.** to become known slowly: *the facts soaked into his mind.* *–v.t.* **5.** to place and keep in liquid in order to saturate thoroughly; steep. **6.** to wet thoroughly, or drench. **7.** to permeate thoroughly, as liquid or moisture. *–n.* **8.** the act of soaking. **9.** the state of being soaked. **10.** the liquid in which anything is soaked. **11.** Also, **soak hole.** a shallow depression holding rainwater. **12.** *Colloq.* a heavy drinker. **13.** *Colloq.* a prolonged drinking bout. *–phr.* **14. soak it up,** *Colloq.* to drink alcoholic liquor in considerable quantities, especially without appearing to be affected by it. **15. soak out,** to draw out by or as by soaking. **16. soak up,** to take in or up by or as by absorption: *blotting paper soaks up ink.* **–soaker,** *n.*

so-and-so *n.* (*pl.* **so-and-sos**) **1.** someone or something not definitely named: *Mr So-and-so.* **2.** *Colloq.* a very unpleasant or unkind person: *he really is a so-and-so.*

soap /soʊp/ *n.* **1.** a substance used for washing and cleansing purposes, usually made by treating a fat with an alkali (as sodium or potassium hydroxide), and consisting chiefly of the sodium or potassium salts of the acids contained in the fat. **2.** *Chem.* any metallic salt of a fatty acid or fatty acid mixture. **3.** → **soap opera.** *–v.t.* **4.** to rub, cover, or treat with soap. *–phr.* **5. not to know someone from a bar of soap,** *Aust., NZ Colloq.* not to know or be able to recognise someone. **6. soap someone up,** to flatter someone. **–soapy,** *adj.*

soapbox /ˈsoʊpbɒks/ *n.* **1.** a box, usually wooden, in which soap has been packed, especially one used as a temporary platform by speakers addressing a street audience. **2.** any place, means, or the like, used by a person to make a speech, voice opinions, etc. **3.** *Esp. WA and SA* → **billycart.**

soap opera *n. Colloq.* a radio or television play presented serially in short regular programs, dealing usually with domestic problems, especially in a highly emotional manner. Also, **soap.** **–soap operatic,** *adj.*

soapstone /ˈsoʊpstoʊn/ *n.* a massive variety of talc with a soapy or greasy feel, used to make hearths, tabletops, carved ornaments, etc.; steatite.

soar /sɔ/ *v.i.* **1.** to fly upwards, as a bird. **2.** to fly at a great height, without visible wing movements, as a bird. **3.** *Aeronautics* to fly without engine power, especially in a glider. **4.** to rise to a height, as a mountain. **5.** to rise to a higher level, as hopes, spirits, etc. *–n.* **6.** the act of soaring. **–soarer,** *n.*

sob /sɒb/ *verb* (**sobbed**, **sobbing**) *–v.i.* **1.** to weep with a sound caused by sharp intakes of breath. **2.** to make a sound like this. *–v.t.* **3.** to utter with sobs. *–n.* **4.** the act or sound of sobbing. **–sobbingly,** *adv.*

sober /ˈsoʊbə/ *adj.* **1.** not intoxicated or drunk. **2.** habitually temperate, especially with alcoholic drink. **3.** quiet or sedate in demeanour, as persons. **4.** marked by seriousness, gravity, solemnity, etc., as demeanour, speech, etc. **5.** subdued in tone, as colour; not bright or showy, as clothes. **6.** free from excess, extravagance, or exaggeration: *sober facts.* **7.** showing self-control. **8.** sane or rational. *–v.i.* **9.** to become sober. *–v.t.* **10.** to make sober. *–phr.* **11. sober as a judge,** completely sober. **12. sober up, a.** to become sober: *to sober up before driving.* **b.** to make sober: *to sober someone up.* **–soberly,** *adv.* **–soberness,** *n.* **–sobriety,** *n.*

soccer /ˈsɒkə/ *n.* a form of football in which there are eleven players in a team, the ball is spherical, and the use of the hands and arms is prohibited except to the goalkeeper; association football.

sociable /ˈsoʊʃəbəl/ *adj.* **1.** inclined to associate with or be in the company of others. **2.** friendly or agreeable in company; companionable. **3.** characterised by or relating to companionship with others. **–sociableness,** *n.* **–sociably,** *adv.*

social /ˈsoʊʃəl/ *adj.* **1.** relating to or marked by friendly companionship or relations: *a social club*; *a social gathering.* **2.** (of people, disposition, etc.) friendly or sociable. **3.** relating to fashionable society: *a social column.* **4.** (of people or animals) tending to live with others, rather than alone. **5.** of or relating to human society, especially as being divided into classes according to status: *social rank.* **6.** of or relating to the life of people in a community: *social problems.* *–n.* **7.** a social gathering or party. **–socially,** *adv.* **–socialness,** *n.*

social capital *n.* the investment in the form of institutions, relationships, voluntary activity, and communications that shape the quality and quantity of social interaction within a community.

social engineering *n.* **1.** a strategy to produce a certain outcome for a community by influencing the behaviour pattern of all its members. **2.** the act of breaking into a computer network by interacting deceptively with the people operating the network to gain the necessary information, such as a password.

socialise /ˈsoʊʃəlaɪz/ *v.t.* **1.** to make social; educate to conform to society. **2.** to make socialistic; establish or regulate according to the theories of socialism. **3.** *Educ.* to alter (an individual activity) into one involving all or a group of pupils *–v.i.* **4.** to go into society; frequent social functions. **5.** to be sociable and mix freely, as at a social gathering. Also, **socialize.** **–socialisation** /soʊʃəlaɪˈzeɪʃən/, *n.*

socialism /ˈsoʊʃəlɪzəm/ *n.* **1.** a theory or system of social organisation which advocates the vesting of the ownership and control of the means of production, capital, land, etc., in the community as a whole. **2.** procedure or practice in accordance with this theory. **–socialist,** *n.*, *adj.*

socialite /ˈsoʊʃəlaɪt/ *n.* a member of the social elite, or someone who aspires to be such.

social media *n.* online social networks used to disseminate information through online social interaction.

social network *n.* **1.** a supportive group of friends and relatives or acquaintances with similar interests, etc., who are in turn interconnected with other such groups in complex arrangements. **2.** such a group whose point of contact is an online website, allowing for the sharing of conversations, information, film and television viewing, etc. –**social networker**, *n.* –**social networking**, *n.*

social security *n.* the provision by the state for the economic and social welfare of the public by means of old-age pensions, sickness and unemployment benefits.

social service *n.* organised welfare efforts carried on under professional rules by trained personnel.

social studies *pl. n.* social sciences, as taught in schools.

social welfare *n.* a system of services provided by a government or other organisation to meet the needs of the community in areas such as health, housing, pensions for the aged or unemployed, etc.

social work *n.* **1.** organised work directed towards the betterment of social conditions in the community, as by seeking to improve the condition of the poor, to promote the welfare of children, etc. **2.** the study of the methods by which this can be effected. –**social worker**, *n.*

society /sə'saɪəti/ *n.* (*pl.* **-ties**) **1.** people regarded collectively: *human society.* **2.** people seen as members of a culturally related community: *Western society.* **3.** the structure and organisation of the above as divided into classes, etc.: *the lower classes of society.* **4.** an organisation of people associated together because of common interests, employment, etc. **5.** companionship or company: *she enjoyed his society.* **6.** the wealthy and their social relations, activities, etc. **7.** *Ecol.* a group of organisms of the same species held together by mutual dependence, and showing division of labour. –*adj.* **8.** of or relating to society (def. 6): *a society party.*

socio- a word element representing 'social', 'sociological', as in *sociometry.*

sociology /sousi'ɒlədʒi/ *n.* the systematic study of the origin, development, organisation, and functioning of human society; the science of the fundamental laws of social relations, institutions, etc. –**sociological** /sousiə-'lɒdʒɪkəl/, *adj.* –**sociologist**, *n.*

sociopath /'sousioupæθ/ *n.* a person who has not developed a proper regard for society, and who behaves in an antisocial way, ignoring rules of normal moral behaviour. –**sociopathic**, *adj.*

sock[1] /sɒk/ *n.* (*pl.* **socks** *or* **sox**) **1.** a woven or knitted covering for the foot and lower leg, worn inside a shoe; of varying length, from below the ankle to just below the knee. –*phr. Colloq.* **2. bore the socks off**, to bore exceedingly. **3. pull one's socks up**, to make more effort. **4. put a sock in it**, to be quiet. **5. sock away**, **a.** to accumulate (a store of something), especially in secret. **b.** to consume large quantities of (something, especially alcohol).

sock[2] /sɒk/ *Colloq.* –*v.t.* **1.** to strike or hit hard. –*n.* **2.** a hard blow.

socket /'sɒkət/ *n.* **1.** a hollow part for holding some part or thing: *an eye socket.* **2.** one of a set of different-sized circular heads for use with a ratchet spanner. **3.** *Elect.* a device, usually on a wall, to plug electrical power leads into.

sockeye /'sɒkaɪ/ *n.* the red salmon, *Oncorhynchus nerka*, most highly valued of the Pacific salmons.

sod[1] /sɒd/ *n.* **1.** a piece (usually square or oblong) cut or torn from the surface of grassland, containing the roots of grass, etc. **2.** the surface of the ground, especially when covered with grass; turf; sward. –*v.t.* (**sodded**, **sodding**) **3.** to cover with sods.

sod[2] /sɒd/ *Colloq.* –*n.* **1.** a disagreeable person. –*phr.* **2. sod it**, a strong exclamation of annoyance, disgust,

etc. **3. sod off**, (*used in the imperative as an offensive dismissal*) to go away.

soda /'soudə/ *n.* **1.** sodium hydroxide, NaOH; caustic soda. **2.** oxide of sodium, Na$_2$O. **3.** sodium (in phrases): *carbonate of soda.* **4.** soda water. **5.** a drink made with soda water, and fruit or other syrups, ice-cream, etc.

soda water *n.* an effervescent beverage consisting of water charged with carbon dioxide.

sodden /'sɒdn/ *adj.* **1.** soaked with liquid or moisture. **2.** (of bread, cake, etc.) heavy, doughy, or soggy. **3.** intoxicated on a specified beverage: *beer-sodden; gin-sodden.* **4.** (of the face) **a.** bloated, as with crying. **b.** dulled with excessive drinking. –**soddenly**, *adv.* –**soddenness**, *n.*

sodium /'soudiəm/ *n.* a soft, silver-white metallic element which oxidises rapidly in moist air, occurring in nature only in the combined state. The metal is used in the synthesis of sodium peroxide, sodium cyanide, and lead tetraethyl. *Symbol:* Na; *relative atomic mass:* 22.9898; *atomic number:* 11; *density:* 0.97 at 20°C.

sodium bicarbonate *n.* a white, crystalline compound, NaHCO$_3$, used in cookery, medicine, etc. Also, **sodium hydrogen carbonate**.

sodium chloride *n.* common salt, NaCl.

sodomy /'sɒdəmi/ *n.* **1.** sexual intercourse using the anal orifice, especially of one man with another. **2.** → **bestiality** (def. 3). **3.** any sexual practice regarded as unnatural or perverted.

soever /sou'evə/ *adv. Archaic* at all; in any case; of any kind; in any way: *choose what person soever you please.*

sofa /'soufə/ *n.* a long upholstered seat, or couch, with a back, and two arms or raised ends.

sofa bed *n.* a couch or sofa with a foldaway mattress base, that allows for it to be turned into a bed.

soft /sɒft/ *adj.* **1.** yielding readily to touch or pressure; easily penetrated, divided, or altered in shape; not hard or stiff. **2.** relatively deficient in hardness, as metal. **3.** smooth and agreeable to the touch; not rough or coarse. **4.** low or subdued in sound; gentle and melodious. **5.** not harsh or unpleasant to the eye; not glaring, as light or colour. **6.** not hard or sharp, as outlines. **7.** gentle or mild, as wind, rain, etc.; genial or balmy. **8.** gentle, mild, lenient, or compassionate. **9.** smooth, soothing, or ingratiating, as words. **10.** not harsh or severe, as terms. **11.** yielding readily to the tender emotions, as persons; impressionable. **12.** sentimental, as language. **13.** not strong or robust; delicate; incapable of great endurance or exertion. **14.** *Colloq.* not hard, trying, or severe; involving little effort: *a soft job.* **15.** (of water) relatively free from mineral salts that interfere with the action of soap. **16.** *Physics* (of radiation) having a relatively long wavelength and low penetrating power. **17.** *Phonetics* **a.** (of consonants) lenis, especially lenis and voiced. **b.** (of *c* and *g*) pronounced as in *cent* and *gem.* **c.** (of consonants in Slavic languages) palatalised. **18.** (of drugs) non-addictive, as marijuana and LSD. **19.** with little or no publicity: *a soft launch.* **20.** *Colloq.* easily influenced or swayed, as a person, the mind, etc.; easily imposed upon. **21.** *Colloq.* foolish; feeble; weak. –*n.* **22.** that which is soft or yielding; the soft part; softness. –*adv.* **23.** in a soft manner. –*phr.* **24. a soft touch**, someone who yields too easily to requests for money, etc. **25. be soft on someone**, *Colloq.* **a.** to be sentimentally inclined towards someone. **b.** to act towards someone in a less harsh manner than expected. **26. have a soft spot for**, to be fond of. **27. soft in the head**, *Colloq.* stupid; insane. –**soften** /'sɒfən/, *v.* –**softly**, *adv.* –**softness**, *n.*

softball /'sɒftbɔl/ *n.* a form of baseball played with a larger and softer ball, in which the pitcher delivers the ball underarm. –**softballer**, *n.*

softcore /'sɒftkɔ/ adj. of or relating to pornography in which erotic activity is not explicitly presented (opposed to *hardcore*).

soft drink n. **1. a.** a carbonated, non-alcoholic, highly sweetened and flavoured drink. **b.** a glass, can, etc., of this drink. **2.** a non-alcoholic drink, as soda water, fruit juice, etc., especially when drunk instead of alcohol at a social occasion.

soft focus n. (in photography) a focus setting of the camera which produces a less than fully sharp image; thought to be flattering in portrait work.

soft goods pl. n. merchandise such as textiles, furnishings, etc.

softie /'sɒfti/ n. Colloq. **1.** a generous or soft-hearted person. **2.** someone who is easily duped. **3.** someone (especially a man) who is not as brave or hardy as others consider proper. Also, **softy**.

soft news n. TV, Radio news which is of an entertaining or lighthearted nature, often related to local events. Compare **hard news**.

soft pedal n. a pedal, as on a piano, for lessening the volume.

soft-pedal verb (**-alled** or, Chiefly US, **-aled**, **-alling** or, Chiefly US, **-aling**) −v.i. **1.** to use the soft pedal. **2.** Colloq. to make concessions or be conciliatory, as in an argument. −v.t. **3.** to soften the sound of by means of the soft pedal. **4.** Colloq. to tone down; make less strong, uncompromising, noticeable, or the like.

soft porn n. softcore pornography.

soft sell n. a method of advertising or selling which is quietly persuasive, subtle, and indirect. See **hard sell**.

soft serve n. a gelatine confection, similar to but softer than ice-cream, usually served in a cone. Also, **soft serve ice-cream**. −**soft-serve**, adj.

soft target n. an enemy target without military protection.

soft tissue n. the flesh of the body as distinct from bone and cartilage.

soft-top adj. **1.** of or relating to a motor vehicle with a roof which is made of fabric, polypropylene, etc., rather than metal, and which is usually removable. −n. **2.** such a car.

soft toy n. a toy animal such as a bear, dog, monster, etc., which is made from fabric stuffed with a soft filling.

software /'sɒftwɛə/ n. Computers programs which enable a computer to perform a desired operation or series of operations (opposed to *hardware*).

softwood /'sɒftwʊd/ n. **1.** Bot. any of the generally coniferous, gymnospermous trees with sieve cells for the conduction of nutrient solutions, which include pine, spruce, etc., and some trees with much harder wood. **2.** (in popular use) timber which is light and easily cut.

soggy /'sɒgi/ adj. (**-gier**, **-giest**) **1.** soaked; thoroughly wet. **2.** damp and heavy, as ill-baked bread. **3.** spiritless, dull, or stupid. −**soggily**, adv. −**sogginess**, n.

soignée /'swanjeɪ/ adj. **1.** carefully done. **2.** well groomed.

soil[1] /sɔɪl/ n. **1.** the portion of the earth's surface in which plants grow; a well-developed system of inorganic and organic material and of living organisms. **2.** a particular kind of earth: *sandy soil*. **3.** the ground as producing vegetation or cultivated for its crops: *fertile soil*. **4.** a country, land, or region: *on foreign soil*. **5.** the ground or earth.

soil[2] /sɔɪl/ v.t. **1.** to make dirty or stain, especially on the surface: *to soil one's clothes*. **2.** to tarnish or disgrace (someone or someone's reputation). **3.** to make foul with excrement: *to soil one's pants*. −v.i. **4.** to become soiled. −n. **5.** a spot, mark or stain due to soiling. **6.** manure; sewage.

soiree /swa'reɪ, 'swareɪ/ n. an evening party or social gathering, often for a particular purpose: *a musical soiree*. Also, **soirée**.

sojourn /'soʊdʒ3n, 'sɒdʒ3n, 'sʌdʒ-, -ən/ v.i. **1.** to dwell for a time in a place; make a temporary stay. −n. **2.** a temporary stay. −**sojourner**, n.

solace /'sɒləs/ n. **1.** comfort in sorrow or trouble; alleviation of distress or discomfort. **2.** something that gives comfort, consolation, or relief. −v.t. (**-aced**, **-acing**) **3.** to comfort, console, or cheer (a person, oneself, the heart, etc.). **4.** to alleviate or relieve (sorrow, distress, etc.). −**solacement**, n. −**solacer**, n.

solanum /soʊ'leɪnəm/ n. any plant of the genus *Solanum*, which comprises herbs, shrubs, and small trees, including the nightshades, eggplant, common potato, etc. −**solanaceous**, adj.

solar /'soʊlə/ adj. **1.** of or relating to the sun: *solar phenomena*. **2.** determined by the sun: *solar hour*. **3.** proceeding from the sun, as light or heat. **4.** operating by the light or heat of the sun, as a device or mechanism −**solarian**, adj.

solar energy n. energy derived from the sun, as for home heating, industrial use, etc.

solar heating n. the use of solar energy to provide heating for air or water in a building. −**solar-heated**, adj.

solarium /sə'lɛəriəm/ n. (pl. **-riums** or **-ria** /-riə/) **1.** a room, gallery, or the like, exposed to the sun's rays, as at a seaside hotel or, for convalescents, in a hospital. **2.** a place in which one exposes one's skin to concentrated ultraviolet radiation to achieve an immediate tan, being either a sun bed, or a booth in which the user stands in front of a panel or angles a sun lamp over their skin.

solar panel n. **1.** a glass sheet housing an interconnected assembly of solar cells which convert energy from the sun into electricity. **2.** Also, **solar heating panel**. a panel which is part of a solar heating system.

solar plexus n. **1.** Anat. a network of nerves situated at the upper part of the abdomen, behind the stomach and in front of the aorta. **2.** Colloq. a point on the stomach wall, just below the sternum, where a blow will affect this nerve centre.

solar pond n. a shallow body of saline water with salinity increasing with depth, in which the heat from solar radiation is stored in the lower layer and then available for industrial use.

solar system n. the sun together with all the planets, satellites, asteroids, etc., revolving around it.

sold /soʊld/ v. past tense and past participle of **sell**.

solder /'sɒldə/ n. **1.** any of various fusible alloys, some (**soft solders**) fusing readily, and others (**hard solders**) fusing only at red heat, applied in a melted state to metal surfaces, joints, etc., to unite them. **2.** anything that joins or unites. −v.t. **3.** to unite with solder or some other substance or device. **4.** to join closely and intimately. **5.** to mend; repair; patch up. −v.i. **6.** to unite things with solder. **7.** to become soldered or become united; grow together. −**solderer**, n.

soldier /'soʊldʒə/ n. **1.** someone who serves in an army for pay; someone engaged in military service. **2.** one of the rank and file in such service, sometimes including non-commissioned officers. **3.** Zool. (in certain ants and termites) one of a caste of individuals with powerful jaws or other devices for protecting the colony. **4.** Colloq. a strip or finger of bread or toast, especially for dipping into a soft-boiled egg. −v.i. **5.** to act or serve as a soldier. −phr. **6. soldier on**, to continue, persist. −**soldiership**, n. −**soldiering**, n.

sole[1] /soʊl/ adj. **1.** being the only one or ones; only. **2.** being the only one of the kind; unique. **3.** belonging or relating to one individual or group to the exclusion

of all others; exclusive: *the sole right to a thing.*
4. functioning automatically or with independent power. **–solely,** *adv.*

sole[2] /soʊl/ *n.* **1.** the bottom or under surface of the foot. **2.** the corresponding under part of a shoe, boot, or the like, or this part exclusive of the heel. **3.** the bottom, under surface, or lower part of anything. *–v.t.* **4.** to furnish with a sole, as a shoe. **–soled,** *adj.*

sole[3] /soʊl/ *n.* (*pl.* **soles** *or, especially collectively,* **sole**) any flatfish of the families Soleidae and Cynoglossidae, with a hooklike snout.

solecism /ˈsɒləsɪzəm/ *n.* **1.** a use of language regarded as substandard or non-standard. **2.** a breach of good manners or etiquette. **3.** any error, impropriety, or inconsistency. **–solecistic** /sɒləˈsɪstɪk/, *adj.*

solemn /ˈsɒləm/ *adj.* **1.** (of a person, face, mood, tone, etc.) humourless. **2.** causing serious thoughts or a grave mood: *solemn music.* **3.** serious or earnest: *solemn assurances.* **4.** marked by formality. **5.** marked or observed with ritual, especially of a religious nature. **–solemnly,** *adv.* **–solemnness, solemness,** *n.* **–solemnity** /səˈlɛmnəti/, *n.*

solemnise /ˈsɒləmnaɪz/ *v.t.* **1.** to observe or commemorate with rites or ceremonies. **2.** to hold or perform (ceremonies, etc.) in due manner. **3.** to perform the ceremony of (marriage). **4.** to go through with ceremony or formality. **5.** to render solemn, serious, or grave. Also, **solemnize. –solemnisation** /ˌsɒləmnaɪˈzeɪʃən/, *n.* **–solemniser,** *n.*

solenoid /ˈsoʊlənɔɪd, ˈsɒl-/ *n. Elect.* an electrical conductor wound as a helix with a small pitch, or as two or more coaxial helices, a current passing through which establishes a magnetic field usually so as to activate a metal bar within the helix and so perform some mechanical task. **–solenoidal** /soʊləˈnɔɪdl/, *adj.* **–solenoidally** /soʊləˈnɔɪdəli/, *adv.*

solfa /sɒlˈfa/ *Music –n.* Also, **tonic solfa. 1.** the set of syllables *doh, ray, me, fah, soh, lah,* and *te,* used to represent the notes of the scale. **2.** the system of singing notes to these syllables. *–verb* (**-faed, -faing**) *–v.i.* **3.** to use the solfa syllables in singing, or to sing these syllables. *–v.t.* **4.** to sing to the solfa syllables, as a tune. Compare **solfège. –solfaist,** *n.*

solfège /sɒlˈfeɪʒ, -ˈfɛʒ/ *n. Music* **1.** → **solmisation. 2.** a singing exercise of runs, scales, etc., sung on syllables as the solfa syllables. Compare **solfa.**

soli-[1] a word element meaning 'alone', 'solitary', as in *solifidian.*

soli-[2] a word element meaning 'sun'.

solicit /səˈlɪsət/ *v.t.* **1.** to seek seriously and respectfully: *to solicit funds.* **2.** (of a prostitute, etc.) to seek the custom of. **3.** to try to get (orders or trade) for business. *–v.i.* **4.** to solicit something or someone.

solicitor /səˈlɪsətə/ *n.* a member of the branch of the legal profession whose services consist of advising clients, representing them before the lower courts, and preparing cases for barristers to try in the higher courts.

solicitor-general *n.* (*pl.* **solicitors-general** *or* **solicitor-generals**) the second legal officer of the government whose principal functions are to appear on behalf of the government in litigation to which the government is a party and to offer such legal advice to the government as is requested by the attorney-general.

solicitous /səˈlɪsətəs/ *adj.* **1.** anxious or concerned: *solicitous about a person's health; solicitous for our comfort; solicitous that she should be happy.* **2.** anxiously desirous: *solicitous of the esteem of others.* **3.** eager: *solicitous to please.* **4.** careful or particular. **–solicitously,** *adv.* **–solicitousness, solicitude** /səˈlɪsətjud/, *n.*

solid /ˈsɒləd/ *adj.* **1.** (of a geometrical body or figure) having three dimensions (length, breadth, and thickness).

2. of or relating to figures of three dimensions: *solid geometry.* **3.** having the inside completely filled up: *a solid ball.* **4.** without gaps or breaks; continuous: *a solid wall.* **5.** firm, hard, or compact in substance or appearance: *solid ground; solid cloud.* **6.** of matter that is not liquid or gaseous, whose particles stick closely together: *solid particles floating in a liquid.* **7.** relating to such matter: *ice is water in a solid state.* **8.** having substance; not flimsy: *solid buildings; solid furniture.* **9.** whole or entire: *one solid hour.* **10.** forming the whole; being the only substance or material: *solid gold.* **11.** sound or good: *solid reasons; solid arguments.* **12.** full of common sense: *she is such a solid person.* **13.** financially sound or strong. **14.** *Obs.* cubic: *a solid foot contains 1728 solid inches.* **15.** thorough, vigorous, great, big, etc. (with emphatic force, often after *good*): *a good solid blow.* **16.** united in opinion, policy, etc.; unanimous. *–n.* **17.** a body or magnitude having three dimensions (length, breadth, and thickness). **18.** a solid substance or body. **19.** (*pl.*) food that is not in liquid form: *milk solids. –interj.* **20.** *Colloq.* an exclamation of approval or approbation: '*How was the movie?' 'Solid!'* **–solidify** /səˈlɪdəfaɪ/, *v.* **–solidity** /səˈlɪdəti/, *n.* **–solidly,** *adv.* **–solidness**

solidarity /sɒləˈdærəti/ *n.* (*pl.* **-ties**) **1.** union or fellowship arising from common responsibilities and interests, such as between members of a group or between classes, peoples, etc. **2.** community of interests, feelings, purposes, etc.

solid-state *adj.* **1.** *Physics* of or relating to the structure and properties of solids. **2.** *Electronics* of or relating to electronic devices which are composed of components in the solid state as transistors, semiconductor diodes, integrated circuits, etc.

solidus /ˈsɒlɪdəs/ *n.* (*pl.* **-di** /-daɪ/) **1.** a Roman gold coin introduced by Constantine. **2.** a short, sloping line (/) representing the old long form of the letter 's' (abbreviation of solidus) generally used as a dividing line, as in dates, fractions, etc.; forward slash; slash.

soliloquy /səˈlɪləkwi/ *n.* (*pl.* **-quies**) the act of talking when alone or as if alone; an utterance or discourse by someone who is talking to himself or herself, while alone or as if alone.

solipsism /ˈsɒləpsɪzəm/ *n.* the theory that the self is the only object of verifiable knowledge, or that nothing but the self exists. **–solipsist,** *n.* **–solipsistic,** *adj.*

solitaire /ˈsɒlətɛə/ *n.* **1.** a game played by one person alone, as a game played with marbles or pegs on a board having hollows or holes. **2.** *US* → **patience** (def. 4). **3.** a precious stone, especially a diamond, set by itself, as in a ring.

solitary /ˈsɒlətri/ *adj.* **1.** quite alone; without companions; unattended. **2.** being the only one or ones: *a solitary exception.* **3.** (of a place) marked by solitude; unfrequented, secluded, or lonely. **4.** *Zool.* (of certain wasps) not social. *–n.* (*pl.* **-ries**) **5.** someone who lives alone. **6.** *Colloq.* solitary confinement. **–solitarily,** *adv.* **–solitariness,** *n.*

solitary confinement *n.* a punishment in jails of locking a prisoner alone in a special cell. Also, **solitary.**

solitude /ˈsɒlətjud, -tʃud/ *n.* **1.** the state of being or living alone; seclusion. **2.** remoteness from habitations, as of a place; absence of human life or activity.

solmisation /sɒlməˈzeɪʃən/ *n. Music* the act, process, or system of using certain syllables, especially the solfa syllables, to represent the notes of the scale. Also, **solmization.**

solo /ˈsoʊloʊ/ *n.* (*pl.* **-los** *or* **-li** /-li/) **1.** a musical composition performed by or intended for one singer or player, with or without accompaniment. **2.** any performance, as a dance, by one person. **3.** a flight in an aeroplane during which the aviator is unaccompanied by an instructor or other person. *–adj.* **4.** *Music* performing alone, as an instrument or its player. **5.** performed alone; not combined with other parts of equal importance; not concerted. **6.** alone; without a companion or partner: *a solo flight in an aeroplane.* *–adv.* **7.** alone: *he made his first flight solo. –phr.* **8. go solo, a.** to undertake an enterprise, activity, etc., alone. **b.** to leave a group and embark upon a solo career. **–soloist**, *n.*

so long *interj. Colloq.* goodbye.

solstice /ˈsɒlstəs/ *n.* **1.** *Astron.* either of the two times in the year when the sun is at its greatest distance from the celestial equator, about June 21st and about December 22nd (called respectively, in the Southern Hemisphere, **winter solstice** and **summer solstice**). **2.** either of the two points in the ecliptic farthest from the equator. **3.** a farthest or culminating point; a turning point. **–solstitial** /sɒlˈstɪʃəl/, *adj.*

soluble /ˈsɒljəbəl/ *adj.* **1.** capable of being dissolved or liquefied. **2.** capable of being solved or explained. **–solubility**, *n.* **–solubleness**, *n.* **–solubly**, *adv.*

solution /səˈluʃən/ *n.* **1.** the act of solving a problem, etc., or the state of being solved. **2.** a particular instance or method of solving; explanation or answer. **3.** *Maths* **a.** the act of determining the answer to a problem. **b.** the answer. **4.** the act by which a gas, liquid, or solid is spread out evenly in a gas, liquid, or solid without chemical change. **5.** the fact of being dissolved; dissolved state: *salt in solution.* **6.** a mixture of two or more substances when the molecules are perfectly mixed.

solve /sɒlv/ *v.t.* **1.** to clear up or explain; find the answer to. **2.** to work out the answer or solution to (a mathematical problem). **–solver**, *n.*

solvent /ˈsɒlvənt/ *adj.* **1.** able to pay all just debts. **2.** having the power of dissolving; causing solution. *–n.* **3.** the component of a solution which dissolves the other component: *water is a solvent for sugar.* **4.** something that solves or explains. **–solvency**, *n.*

somatic /souˈmætɪk/ *adj.* **1.** *Anat., Zool.* relating to the body of an animal, or more especially to its walls, as distinguished from the viscera, limbs, and head. **2.** *Biol.* relating to the soma. **3.** of the body; bodily; physical.

somatic nervous system *n. Physiol., Anat.* the part of the peripheral nervous system involved with the voluntary control of body movements through the action of skeletal muscles, and with reception of external stimuli. Compare **autonomic nervous system**.

sombre /ˈsɒmbə/ *adj.* **1.** gloomily dark, shadowy, or dimly lit. **2.** dark and dull, as colour, or as things in respect to colour. **3.** gloomy, depressing, or dismal. Also, *US*, **somber**. **–sombrely**, *adv.* **–sombreness**, *n.*

sombrero /sɒmˈbrɛərou/ *n.* (*pl.* **-ros**) a broad-brimmed hat, usually of felt, worn in Spain, Mexico, the southwestern US, etc.

some /sʌm/, *weak form* /səm/ *adj.* **1.** being one thing or person not named: *some poor fellow.* **2.** certain (with plural nouns): *some friends of mine.* **3.** of a certain unspecified number, amount, degree, etc.: *some variation.* **4.** unspecified but fairly large in number, amount, degree, etc.: *he was here for some weeks.* **5.** used to show an approximate amount: *some four or five of us*; *some little value.* **6.** *Colloq.* great or important: *that was some storm! –pron.* **7.** certain people, instances, etc., not named: *some think he is dead.* **8.** an unstated number, amount, etc., as distinguished from the rest: *some of this is useful.*

-some¹ suffix found in some adjectives showing especially a tendency, as in *quarrelsome, burdensome.*

-some² collective suffix used with numerals, as in *twosome, threesome, foursome.*

-some³ a word element meaning 'body', as in *chromosome.*

somebody /ˈsʌmbɒdi, ˈsʌmbədi/ *pron.* **1.** some person. *–n.* (*pl.* **-bodies**) **2.** a person of some note or importance.

somehow /ˈsʌmhaʊ/ *adv.* **1.** in some way not specified, apparent, or known. *–phr.* **2. somehow or other**, in a way not as yet determined.

someone /ˈsʌmwʌn/ *pron., n.* somebody.

somersault /ˈsʌməsɔlt, -sɒlt/ *n.* **1.** an acrobatic movement of the body in which it describes a complete revolution, heels over head. **2.** a complete overturn or reversal, as of opinion. *–v.i.* **3.** to perform a somersault.

somewhat /ˈsʌmwɒt/ *adv.* **1.** in some measure or degree; to some extent. *–n.* **2.** some part, portion, amount, etc.

somewhere /ˈsʌmwɛə/ *adv.* **1.** in or at some place not specified, determined, or known. **2.** to some place not specified or known. **3.** at or to some point in amount, degree, etc., not precisely specified: *he is somewhere about 60.* **4.** at some point of time not precisely specified: *this happened somewhere between 3 o'clock and 5 o'clock. –n.* **5.** an unspecified or uncertain place.

somnambulism /sɒmˈnæmbjəlɪzəm/ *n.* the fact or habit of walking about, and often of performing various other acts, while asleep; sleepwalking. **–somnambulist** /sɒmˈnæmbjələst/, *n.* **–somnambulistic** /sɒmˌnæmbjəˈlɪstɪk/, *adj.*

somnolent /ˈsɒmnələnt/ *adj.* **1.** sleepy; drowsy. **2.** tending to cause sleep. **–somnolence, somnolency**, *n.* **–somnolently**, *adv.*

son /sʌn/ *n.* **1.** a male child or person in relation to his parents. **2.** someone adopted legally as a son. **3.** a male descendant. **4.** someone related as if by ties of sonship. **5.** a male person looked upon as the product or result of particular agencies, forces, influences, etc.: *sons of liberty.* **6.** a familiar term of address to a man or boy from an older person. *–phr.* **7. the Son**, the second person of the Trinity; Jesus, the Christ.

sonar /ˈsounɑ/ *n.* **1.** any device or method of echo ranging or echolocation involving underwater sonics. **2.** an echo sounder. Also, **SONAR**.

sonata /səˈnɑtə/ *n. Music* an extended instrumental composition usually in several (commonly three or four) movements in contrasted moods and keys, each movement being developed with a balanced form in mind.

sonatina /sɒnəˈtinə/ *n.* (*pl.* **-tinas** *or* **-tine** /-ˈtineɪ/) *Music* a short or simplified sonata.

song /sɒŋ/ *n.* **1.** a short metrical composition combining words and music; a ballad; a lyric. **2.** a piece adapted for singing or simulating a piece to be sung: *Mendelssohn's 'Songs without Words'.* **3.** the act or art of singing; vocal music. **4.** that which is sung. **5.** the musical or tuneful sounds produced by certain birds, insects, etc. **6.** the complex series of repeated vocal phrases made by a humpback whale. *–phr.* **7. for a song**, at a very low price. **8. make a song and dance about**, *Colloq.* to make a fuss about. **9. on song, a.** (of an engine) well-tuned; running smoothly. **b.** (especially of an athlete, sportsperson, etc.) performing well.

songlark /ˈsɒŋlɑk/ *n.* either of two endemic Australian larks of the genus *Cincloramphus*, found generally throughout Australia and noted for their song.

songline /ˈsɒŋlaɪn/ *n.* (in Aboriginal mythology) a path made by the ancestors in the Dreaming and recorded in the songs of the Aboriginal peoples living along its sometimes very great length; Dreaming track.

sonic /ˈsɒnɪk/ *adj.* **1.** of or relating to sound waves. **2.** of or relating to a speed approximating that of the propagation of sound.

son-in-law *n.* (*pl.* **sons-in-law**) the husband of one's daughter.

sonnet /'spnət/ *n. Prosody* a poem, properly expressive of a single complete thought, idea, or sentiment, of 14 lines (usually in 5-foot iambic metre) with rhymes arranged according to one of certain definite schemes. **–sonneteer** /spnə'tɪə/, *n.*

sonography /sp'nɒgrəfi/ *n.* the operation of ultrasound equipment to produce images for medical diagnostic purposes. **–sonographer**, *n.*

sonorous /'spnərəs/ *adj.* 1. giving out, or capable of giving out, a sound, especially a deep resonant sound, as a thing or a place. 2. loud, deep, or resonant, as a sound. 3. rich and full in sound, as language, verse, etc. 4. grandiloquent: *a sonorous address.* **–sonorously**, *adv.* **–sonorousness**, *n.*

-sonous a word element used in adjectives to refer to sounds, as in *unisonous.*

sook /sʊk/ *n. Aust., NZ Colloq.* (usually of children) a timid, shy, cowardly person; a crybaby. **–sooky**, *adj.*

sool /sul/ *Aust., NZ –v.t.* 1. to attack: *sool him! –phr.* 2. **sool off**, to chase away. 3. **sool on**, *Colloq.* a. to incite (a dog, etc.) to attack or chase an animal or person. b. to urge or incite (someone) to do something.

soon /sun/ *adv.* 1. within a short period after this (or that) time, event, etc.: *we shall soon know.* 2. before long; in the near future; at an early date. 3. promptly or quickly. 4. readily or willingly: *I would as soon walk as ride.*

soot /sʊt/ *n.* a black carbonaceous substance produced during the imperfect combustion of coal, wood, oil, etc., rising in fine particles and adhering to the sides of the chimney or pipe conveying the smoke.

soothe /suð/ *verb* (**soothed**, **soothing**) *–v.t.* 1. to tranquillise or calm, as a person, the feelings, etc.; relieve, comfort, or refresh. 2. to mitigate, assuage, or allay, as pain, sorrow, doubt, etc. *–v.i.* 3. to exert a soothing influence; bring tranquillity, calm, ease, or comfort. **–soother**, *n.* **–soothing**, *adj.* **–soothingly**, *adv.*

soothsayer /'suθseɪə/ *n.* someone who professes to foretell events.

sooty shearwater *n.* a brown bird with pale wing linings, *Puffinus griseus*, which ranges widely in the Atlantic, Pacific and Indian oceans, breeding in south-eastern Australia, New Zealand and some Southern Hemisphere islands.

sop /spp/ *n.* 1. piece of bread, etc., dipped in milk, soup, etc. 2. anything thoroughly soaked. 3. something given to pacify or quieten, or as a bribe. 4. *Colloq.* a weak or cowardly person. *–v.t.* (**sopped**, **sopping**) 5. to dip or soak. 6. (usu. fol. by *up*) to take or soak up (water, etc.): *The cloth will sop up the water.*

sophism /'spfɪzəm/ *n.* 1. a specious but fallacious argument, used to display ingenuity in reasoning or to deceive someone. 2. any false argument; a fallacy.

sophist /'spfəst/ *n.* 1. someone who reasons adroitly and speciously rather than soundly. 2. a person of learning. **–sophistic** /sə'fɪstɪk/, **sophistical** /sə'fɪstɪkəl/, *adj.* **–sophistry**, *n.*

sophisticated /sə'fɪstəkeɪtəd/ *adj.* 1. (of a person, the ideas, tastes, manners, etc.) altered by education, experience, etc., to be worldly-wise; changed from the natural character or simplicity; refined; artificial. 2. of intellectual complexity; reflecting a high degree of skill, intelligence, etc.; subtle: *sophisticated music.* 3. deceptive; misleading. 4. (of machinery, etc.) complex; intricate. **–sophisticate**, *v.* **–sophisticatedly**, *adv.*

sophistication /səfɪstə'keɪʃən/ *n.* 1. sophisticated character, ideas, tastes, or ways as the result of education, worldly experience, etc. 2. change from the natural character or simplicity, or the resulting condition. 3. impairment or debasement, as of purity or genuineness. 4. the use of sophistry; a sophism or quibble. 5. advanced refinement or complexity: *solid-state*

technology has advanced electronics to a new level of sophistication.

-sophy a word element referring to systems of thought, as in *theosophy.*

soporific /spp'rɪfɪk/ *adj.* 1. causing or tending to cause sleep. 2. relating to or characterised by sleep or sleepiness; sleepy; drowsy. *–n.* 3. something causing sleep, as a drug or medicine.

sopping /'spɪŋ/ *adj.* soaked; drenched: *his coat was sopping after the storm.*

soppy /'spi/ *adj.* (**-pier**, **-piest**) 1. soaked, drenched, or very wet, as ground. 2. rainy, as weather. 3. *Colloq.* excessively sentimental; mawkish; silly. **–soppily**, *adv.* **–soppiness**, *n.*

soprano /sə'pranoʊ/ *Music –n.* (*pl.* **-nos** *or* **-ni** /-ni/) 1. the uppermost part or voice. 2. the highest singing voice in women and boys. 3. a part for such a voice. 4. a singer with such a voice. *–adj.* 5. of or relating to the soprano; having the compass of a soprano.

sorbet /'sɔbeɪ, 'sɔbət/ *n.* a light frozen dish made with fruit, egg whites, etc., and sometimes flavoured with liqueur or wine, served between the courses of a meal to clear the palate or as a dessert. Also, **sherbet.**

sorcery /'sɔsəri/ *n.* (*pl.* **-ries**) the art, practices, or spells of a sorcerer; magic, especially black magic in which supernatural powers are exercised through the aid of evil spirits; witchcraft. **–sorcerer**, *n.* **–sorceress**, *fem. n.* **–sorcerous**, *adj.*

sordid /'sɔdəd/ *adj.* 1. dirty or filthy; squalid. 2. morally mean or ignoble: *sordid gains.* 3. meanly selfish, self-seeking, or mercenary. **–sordidly**, *adv.* **–sordidness**, *n.*

sore /sɔ/ *adj.* 1. physically painful or sensitive, as a wound, hurt, diseased part, etc. 2. suffering bodily pain from wounds, bruises, etc., as a person. 3. suffering mental pain; grieved, distressed, or sorrowful: *to be sore at heart.* 4. causing great mental pain, distress, or sorrow: *a sore bereavement.* 5. causing very great suffering, misery, hardship, etc.: *sore need.* 6. *Colloq.* irritated, offended, or feeling aggrieved: *what are you sore about?* 7. being an occasion of annoyance or irritation: *a sore subject. –n.* 8. a sore spot or place on the body, especially an ulceration. *–phr.* 9. **a sore point**, a matter about which a sense of grievance, disappointment, etc., is felt: *Martha's remarriage was a sore point with George.* 10. **done up like a sore finger** (or **toe**), *Aust. Colloq.* dressed up in one's best clothes. 11. **stand** (or **stick**) **out like a sore finger** (or **toe**) (or **thumb**), *Colloq.* to catch the eye by virtue of a contrast with surrounding people or objects. **–sorely**, *adv.* **–soreness**, *n.*

sorghum /'sɔgəm/ *n.* a cereal grass, *Sorghum bicolor*, of many varieties.

sorrel[1] /'sɒrəl/ *n.* 1. light reddish brown. 2. a horse of this colour. *–adj.* 3. having the colour sorrel.

sorrel[2] /'sɒrəl/ *n.* 1. any of various plants of the genus *Rumex* and related genera, having succulent acid leaves often used in salads, sauces, etc. 2. any of various similar plants.

sorrow /'sɒroʊ/ *n.* 1. distress caused by loss, affliction, disappointment, etc.; grief, sadness. 2. a cause or occasion of grief or regret. 3. an affliction, misfortune, or trouble. *–v.i.* 4. to feel sorrow; grieve. **–sorrower**, *n.* **–sorrowful**, *adj.* **–sorrowing**, *adj.*

sorry /'sɒri/ *adj.* (**-rier**, **-riest**) 1. feeling regret, compunction, sympathy, pity, etc.: *to be sorry for a remark.* 2. of a deplorable, pitiable, or miserable kind: *to come to a sorry end.* 3. sorrowful, grieved, or sad. 4. associated with sorrow; suggestive of grief or suffering; melancholy; dismal. 5. wretched, poor, mean, or pitiful: *a sorry horse.* 6. *Aboriginal English* (especially in relation to death or matters to do with country) grieving; sorrowful. *–interj.* 7. a conventional form of apology for injury or inconvenience caused. **8.** a request for the repetition of something not clearly heard. –**sorrily**, *adv.* –**sorriness**, *n.*

sort /sɔt/ *n.* **1.** a particular kind, species, variety, class, group, or description, as distinguished by the character or nature: *to discover a new sort of mineral.* **2.** character, quality, or nature. **3.** a more or less adequate or inadequate type or example of something: *he's some sort of friend.* **4.** manner, fashion, or way. **5.** (*usu. pl.*) *Printing* one of the kinds of characters of a font of type. **6.** *Colloq.* a person described in terms of attractiveness: *a good sort.* –*v.t.* **7.** to arrange according to sort, kind, or class; separate into sorts; classify. **8.** *Agric.* to prepare (wool) for processing by breaking up fleeces into bales of matching types according to quality, number, length, and colour. –*phr.* **9. a good sort**, *Colloq.* **a.** someone who is likeable, trustworthy, reliable. **b.** a sexually attractive woman or man. **10. of sorts**, **a.** of a mediocre or poor kind. **b.** of one sort or another; of an indefinite kind. **11. out of sorts**, not in a normal condition of good health, spirits, or temper. **12. sort of**, to a certain extent; in some way; as it were. **13. sort out**, **a.** to separate or take out from a miscellany. **b.** to deal with: *to sort the matter out.* **14. sort someone out**, **a.** to attend to someone's needs. **b.** to assert a point of view so as to override a conflicting view from someone else, sometimes with violence. **15. sort with**, to assign to (a particular class, group, or place). –**sortable**, *adj.* –**sorter**, *n.* –**sorting**, *n.*

sortie /ˈsɔti/ *n.* **1.** a sally of troops from a besieged place to attack the besiegers. **2.** a body of troops making such a sally. **3.** the flying of a military aircraft on a mission, as a bombing raid. –*v.i.* (**-tied**, **-tieing**) **4.** to go out on a sortie.

SOS /ɛs oʊ ˈɛs/ *n.* **1.** the letters represented by the radio telegraphic signal used, as by ships in distress, to call for help. **2.** any call for help.

so-so *adj.* **1.** indifferent; neither very good nor very bad. –*adv.* **2.** in an indifferent or passable manner; indifferently; tolerably.

sot /sɔt/ *n.* **1.** a confirmed drunkard. **2.** someone befuddled by alcoholic drink. –**sottish**, *adj.*

sotto voce /sɒtoʊ ˈvoʊtʃei/ *adv.* in a low tone intended not to be overheard.

soufflé /ˈsuflei/ *n.* **1.** a light baked dish made fluffy with beaten eggwhites combined with egg yolks, white sauce, and fish, cheese, or other ingredients. **2.** a similar sweet or savoury cold dish like a mousse. –*adj.* **3.** puffed-up; made light, as by beating and cooking.

sought /sɔt/ *v.* past tense and past participle of **seek**.

soul /soʊl/ *n.* **1.** the principle of life, feeling, thought, and action in humans, believed to be separate in existence from the body, and living after death; the spiritual part of humans as distinct from the physical. **2.** high-mindedness; noble warmth of feeling, spirit or courage, etc. **3.** a leader or inspirer of some movement, etc.; moving spirit: *he was the soul of the Resistance.* **4.** the spirit of a dead person. **5.** a human being; person: *she was a kindly soul.* **6.** → **soul music**. –**soulful**, *adj.*

soul music *n.* commercial African American blues music which combines gospel music with a blues style.

sound[1] /saʊnd/ *n.* **1.** the sensation produced in the organs of hearing when certain vibrations (**soundwaves**) are caused in the surrounding air or other elastic medium, as by a vibrating body. **2.** the vibrations in the air, or vibrational energy, producing this sensation; longitudinal vibrations are propagated at about 335 metres per second. **3.** the particular auditory effect produced by a given cause: *the sound of music.* **4.** any auditory effect, or vibrational disturbance such as to be heard. **5.** a noise, vocal utterance, musical note, or the like. **6.** the recorded music, dialogue, background noise, etc., for a

film or videotape (opposed to *vision*). **7.** *Phonetics* a segment of speech corresponding to a single articulation or to a combination of articulations constantly associated in the language; a phone. **8.** the quality of an event, letter, etc., as it affects a person: *this report has a bad sound.* –*v.i.* **9.** to make or emit a sound. **10.** to give forth a sound as a call or summons. **11.** to be heard, as a sound. –*v.* (*copular*) **12.** to convey a certain impression when heard or read: *to sound strange.* **13.** to emit sound as specified: *to sound loud.* **14.** to give the appearance of being: *his account sounds true.* –*v.t.* **15.** to cause (an instrument, etc.) to make or emit a sound. **16.** to give forth (a sound). **17.** to announce, order, or direct by a sound as of a trumpet: *to sound a retreat.* **18.** to utter audibly, pronounce, or express: *to sound each letter.* **19.** to examine by percussion or auscultation. –*adj.* **20.** of, relating to, or by the medium of radio broadcasting (as opposed to television broadcasting). –*phr.* **21. sound off**, *Colloq.* **a.** to speak or complain frankly. **b.** to speak angrily; lose one's temper. **c.** to boast; exaggerate. **d.** *US* to call one's name, sequence, number, etc. –**soundless**, *adj.* –**soundlessly**, *adv.* –**sounder**, *n.*

sound[2] /saʊnd/ *adj.* **1.** free from injury, damage, decay, defect, disease, etc.; in good condition; healthy; robust: *a sound heart.* **2.** financially strong, secure, or reliable: *a sound business.* **3.** reliable: *sound judgement.* **4.** without defect as to truth, justice, or reason: *sound advice.* **5.** of substantial or enduring character: *sound value.* **6.** without logical defect, as reasoning. **7.** without legal defect, as a title. **8.** free from moral defect or weakness; upright, honest, or good; honourable; loyal. **9.** unbroken and deep, as sleep. **10.** vigorous, hearty, or thorough, as a beating. –*phr.* **11. sound as a bell**, in perfect health or condition. **12. sound asleep**, deeply asleep. –**soundly**, *adv.* –**soundness**, *n.*

sound[3] /saʊnd/ *v.t.* **1.** to measure or try the depth of (water, a deep hole, etc.) by letting down a lead or plummet at the end of a line or by some equivalent means. **2.** to measure (depth) in such a manner, as at sea. **3.** to examine or test (the bottom of water, etc.) with a lead that brings up adhering bits of matter. –*v.i.* **4.** to use the lead and line, (or some other device) for measuring depth, etc., as at sea. **5.** to go down or touch bottom, as a lead. **6.** to plunge downwards or dive, as a whale. –*n.* **7.** *Surg.* a long, solid, slender instrument for sounding or exploring body cavities or canals. –*phr.* **8. sound someone out**, (sometimes fol. by *on*) to seek to elicit the views or sentiments of someone by indirect inquiries, etc.

sound[4] /saʊnd/ *n.* **1.** a relatively narrow passage of water, not a stream, between larger bodies or between the mainland and an island: *Marlborough Sounds.* **2.** an inlet, arm, or recessed portion of the sea. **3.** the air bladder of a fish.

soundbar /ˈsaʊndba/ *n.* a small, thin device, usually positioned under a television screen, providing multispeaker sound. Also, **sound bar**.

sound barrier *n.* a point near the speed of sound at which an aircraft or projectile meets a sudden increase in air resistance and creates a shock wave; a sonic barrier. This point is viewed as a barrier separating subsonic from supersonic speed.

sound bite *n.* *TV, Radio* a small segment of an audio interview, selected for its newsworthiness or interest. Also, **soundbite**.

sound effect *n.* (*usu. pl.*) any sound other than speech or music forming part of a radio or television program or a film and used to create an effect, as the noise of a train, storm, gunfire, etc.

soundtrack /ˈsaʊndtræk/ *n.* **1.** a strip at the side of a cinema film which carries the sound recording. **2.** such a recording, especially when transferred on to a gramophone record, cassette or CD.

soup /sup/ *n.* **1.** a liquid food made from meat, fish, or vegetables, with various added ingredients, by boiling or simmering. **2.** *Surfing, Colloq.* foaming water, caused by the breaking of a wave. *–phr. Colloq.* **3. in the soup,** in trouble. **4. soup up,** to modify (the engine of a motor vehicle) in order to increase its power: *to soup up a motorbike.*

soupçon /ˈsupsɒn/ *n.* **1.** a suspicion; a slight trace or flavour. **2.** a very small amount.

sour /ˈsaʊə/ *adj.* **1.** having an acid taste, such as that of vinegar, lemon juice, etc.; tart. **2.** acidified or affected by fermentation; fermented.: *sour milk.* **3.** harsh in spirit or temper; austere; morose; embittered; peevish. **4.** *Agric.* (of soil) having excessive acidity. *–v.i.* **5.** to become sour. *–v.t.* **6.** to make sour. *–phr.* **7. turn sour, a.** (of milk or cream) to become spoiled. **b.** (of a project, deal, etc.) to begin to fail or come unstuck. **c.** *Colloq.* to become angry. **–sourish,** *adj.* **–sourly,** *adv.* **–sourness,** *n.*

source /sɔs/ *n.* **1.** any thing or place from which something comes, arises, or is obtained; origin. **2.** a spring of water from the earth, etc., or the place of issue; a fountain; the beginning or place of origin of a stream or river. **3.** a book, statement, person, etc., supplying information. *–v.t.* (**sourced, sourcing**) **4.** to establish the source of or the authority for (a statement, document, etc.). **5.** to obtain (a product) from a particular producer.

source code *n.* *Computers* a high-level programming language version of a program. Compare **executable code, machine language.**

souse /saʊs/ *verb* (**soused, sousing**) *–v.t.* **1.** to plunge into water or other liquid. **2.** to soak with water, etc. *–v.i.* **3.** to plunge into water, etc.; fall with a splash. **4.** to become soaked with water, etc. *–n.* **5.** the act of sousing.

sous-vide /su-ˈvid/ *n.* **1.** a cooking technique in which food is sealed in airtight plastic bags and cooked in water at a low temperature for a long period of time. *–adj.* **2.** of or relating to this method of cooking.

south /saʊθ/ *n.* **1.** a cardinal point of the compass directly opposite to the north. **2.** the direction in which this point lies. *–adj.* **3.** lying towards or situated in the south. **4.** directed or proceeding towards the south. **5.** coming from the south, as a wind. **6.** (*also upper case*) designating the southern part of a region, nation, country, etc.: *South Pacific.* *–adv.* **7.** towards or in the south. **8.** from the south. *–phr.* **9. head** (or **go**) (or **move**) **south, a.** *Finance* to decrease in value: *the stock market is heading south.* **b.** to take a turn for the worse; decline or deteriorate. **10. the south,** (*also upper case*) a quarter or territory situated in a southern direction. Also, *esp. Naut.,* **sou'** /saʊ/.

south-east *n.* **1.** the point or direction midway between south and east. **2.** a region in this direction. *–adj.* **3.** situated in, proceeding towards, or coming from the south-east. *–adv.* **4.** towards, in, or from the south-east. Also, *esp. Naut.,* **sou'-east.** **–south-eastern,** *adj.* **–south-easterner,** *n.*

southerly /ˈsʌðəli/ *adj.* **1.** moving, directed, or situated towards the south. **2.** coming from the south, as a wind. *–adv.* **3.** towards the south. **4.** from the south. *–n.* (*pl.* **-lies**) **5.** a wind from the south. **–southerliness,** *n.*

southerly buster *n.* *Aust.* a strong, cool southerly wind which blows after a hot day on the south-eastern coast of Australia, often bringing rain.

southern /ˈsʌðən/ *adj.* **1.** lying towards or situated in the south. **2.** directed or proceeding southwards. **3.** coming from the south, as wind. **4.** (*upper case*) of or relating to the South. **5.** *Astron.* south of the celestial equator, or of the zodiac: *a southern constellation.*

Southern Hemisphere *n.* (*also lower case*) the half of the earth between the South Pole and the equator.

southern lights *pl. n.* the aurora of the Southern Hemisphere.

South Pole *n.* that end of the earth's axis of rotation marking the southernmost point of the earth.

south-west *n.* **1.** the point or direction midway between south and west. **2.** a region in this direction. *–adj.* **3.** situated in, proceeding towards, or coming from the south-west. *–adv.* **4.** towards, in or from the south-west. Also, *Chiefly Naut.,* **sou'-west** /saʊ-ˈwɛst/. **–south-western,** *adj.*

souvenir /suvəˈnɪə/ *n.* **1.** something given or kept for remembrance; a memento. **2.** a memory. *–v.t.* **3.** *Colloq.* to pilfer.

sou'-wester /saʊ-ˈwɛstə/ *n.* a waterproof hat, usually of oilskin, having the brim very broad behind, worn especially by seamen.

sovereign /ˈsɒvrən/ *n.* **1.** someone who has sovereign power or authority, especially a monarch. **2.** a group or body of persons or a state possessing sovereign authority. **3.** a former British gold coin. *–adj.* **4.** belonging to or characteristic of a sovereign or sovereignty. **5.** involving a nation: *a sovereign risk agreement.* **6.** supreme, as power, authority, etc.: *a sovereign land.* **7.** greatest in degree; pre-eminent: *a sovereign right.* **–sovereignty,** *n.* **–sovereignly,** *adv.*

soviet /ˈsoʊviət, ˈsɒv-/ *n.* **1.** (in Russia, before the 1917 revolution) a council of any kind, presumably elected by all. **2.** (in the Soviet Union, after the revolution) **a.** a local council, originally elected only by manual workers, with certain powers of local administration. **b.** a higher local council elected by a local council, part of a pyramid of soviets, culminating in the **Supreme Soviet. 3.** any similar assembly connected with a socialist governmental system elsewhere. *–adj.* **4.** of a soviet.

sow[1] /soʊ/ *verb* (**sowed, sown** or **sowed, sowing**) *–v.t.* **1.** to scatter (seed) over land, earth, etc., for growth; plant (seed, and hence a crop). **2.** to scatter seed over (land, earth, etc.) for the purpose of growth. **3.** to introduce for development; seek to propagate or extend; disseminate: *to sow distrust; to sow dissension.* **4.** to strew or sprinkle with anything. *–v.i.* **5.** to sow seed, as for the production of a crop. **–sower,** *n.*

sow[2] /saʊ/ *n.* **1.** an adult female pig. **2.** the adult female of various other animals. **3.** *Metallurgy* a mould of larger size than a pig (def. 6). **4. a.** *Metallurgy* a channel which conducts the molten metal to the rows of moulds in the pig bed. **b.** a mass of metal solidified in such a channel or mould. **5.** *Metallurgy* an accretion that frequently forms in the hearth or crucible of a furnace and which consists mainly of iron.

sox /sɒks/ *n.* a plural of **sock**[1].

soybean /ˈsɔɪbin/ *n.* **1.** a bushy, leguminous plant, *Glycine max,* of South-East Asia. **2.** the seed of this plant which is used as food, livestock feed, etc., and which yields an oil used as a food and in the manufacture of soap, candles, etc. Also, **soy, soya bean.**

soy sauce *n.* a salty dark brown sauce, made by fermenting soybeans in brine. Also, **soya sauce.**

spa /spa/ *n.* **1.** a mineral spring, or a locality in which such springs exist. **2.** → **spa bath. 3.** → **spa pool. 4.** a facility which offers mind and body treatments such as massage, beauty therapy, etc.

spa bath *n.* a bath equipped with submerged water jets which create water turbulence to massage the bather's muscles. Also, **spa.**

space /speɪs/ *n.* **1.** the unlimited or indefinitely great general receptacle of things, commonly conceived as an expanse extending in all directions (or having three dimensions), in which, or occupying portions of which, all material objects are located. **2.** the portion or extent of this in a given instance; extent or room in three dimensions: *the space occupied by a body.* **3.** the part of the universe which lies outside the earth's atmosphere in which the density of matter is very low; outer space. **4.** extent or area; a particular extent of surface: *to fill in blank spaces in a document.* **5.** the area or position for a person to stand, sit, etc.: *save me a space in the queue.* **6.** linear distance; a particular distance: *trees set at equal spaces apart.* **7.** extent, or a particular extent, of time: *a space of two hours.* **8.** *Music* one of the intervals between the lines of the stave. **9.** *Maths* a collection of points that have geometric properties in that they obey a specified set of axioms: *Euclidean space.* –*v.t.* (**spaced, spacing**) **10.** to fix the space or spaces of; divide into spaces. **11.** to set some distance apart. –*phr.* **12. space out, a.** to extend (a text, document, etc.) by inserting more space or spaces. **b.** to extend over a period of time: *to space out drinks over an evening.* **c.** to become relaxed and vague, by or as by the use of drugs.

space age *n.* the period in human history when exploration of and travel in space has been possible.

space-age *adj.* **1.** of or relating to the space age, especially with its advanced technology. **2.** ultra-modern; highly sophisticated: *a car with space-age styling.*

space blanket *n.* a light plastic blanket coated with aluminium foil on one or both sides, designed to reflect body heat back toward the body.

spacecraft /'speɪskrɑft/ *n.* a vehicle capable of travelling in space.

spaced-out *adj.* in a euphoric or dreamy state, under or as if under the influence of a hallucinogen. Also, (*especially in predicative use*), **spaced out.**

space shuttle *n.* a re-usable rocket-propelled spacecraft designed to transport equipment and personnel from earth into space and back.

space-time *n.* **1.** a four-dimensional continuum in which the coordinates are the three spatial coordinates and time. The events and objects of any spatial and temporal region may be conceived as part of this continuum. –*adj.* **2.** of or relating to any system with three spatial and one temporal coordinates. **3.** of or relating to both space and time.

spacious /'speɪʃəs/ *adj.* **1.** containing much space, as a house, room, court, street, etc.; amply large. **2.** occupying much space; vast. **3.** of a great extent or area; broad; large; great. **4.** broad in scope, range, inclusiveness, etc. –**spaciously,** *adv.* –**spaciousness,** *n.*

spade¹ /speɪd/ *n.* **1.** a tool for digging, having an iron blade adapted for pressing into the ground with the foot, and a long handle commonly with a grip or crosspiece at the top. –*v.t.* **2.** to dig, cut, or remove with a spade. –*phr.* **3. call a spade a spade,** to call a thing by its real name; speak plainly or bluntly. –**spadeful** /'speɪdfʊl/, *n.*

spade² /speɪd/ *n.* **1.** a black figure shaped like an inverted heart with a short stem at the cusp opposite the point, used on playing cards. **2.** *Colloq.* (*derog.*) (*racist*) someone of very dark skin, as an African, African American, Aboriginal person, etc.

spadework /'speɪdwɜk/ *n.* preliminary or initial work, especially of a laborious or tedious nature.

spag /spæg/ *n. Colloq.* **1.** spaghetti. **2.** (*sometimes upper case*) (*derog.*) (*racist*) **a.** an Italian. **b.** the Italian language.

spaghetti /spə'gɛti/ *n.* a kind of pasta made from wheat flour, in long, thin, solid strips or tubes.

spam /spæm/ *n.* (*from trademark*) –*n.* **1.** a type of ready-cooked tinned meat. **2.** unsolicited email, especially advertising material sent to many recipients. **3.** such an email. –*verb* (**spammed, spamming**) –*v.t.* **4.** to send

(someone) spam (def. 2). –*v.i.* **5.** to send spam (def. 2). –**spammer,** *n.* –**spamming,** *n.*

span /spæn/ *n.* **1.** the distance between the tip of the thumb and the tip of the little finger when the hand is fully stretched out. **2.** a unit of length corresponding to this distance, commonly taken as 9 inches or 23 cm. **3.** the distance or space between two supports of a bridge, beam, or arch. **4.** the full stretch of anything: *the span of memory.* –*v.t.* (**spanned, spanning**) **5.** to measure by the span of a hand. **6.** to extend over or across (a space, a river, etc.): *the bridge spans the river.*

spangle /'spæŋgəl/ *n.* **1.** a small, thin, often circular piece of glittering material, as metal, for decorating garments, etc. **2.** any small, bright drop, object, spot, or the like. –*v.t.* **3.** to decorate with spangles.

spaniel /'spænjəl/ *n.* a dog of any of various breeds of small or medium size, usually with a long, silky coat and drooping ears, used in hunting and as pets.

spank¹ /spæŋk/ *v.t.* **1.** to strike (a person, usually a child) with the open hand, a slipper, etc., especially on the buttocks, as in punishment. –*n.* **2.** a blow given in spanking; a smart or resounding slap.

spank² /spæŋk/ *v.i.* to move quickly, vigorously, or smartly.

spanking¹ /'spæŋkɪŋ/ *adj.* **1.** moving rapidly and smartly. **2.** quick and vigorous, as the pace. **3.** blowing briskly, as a breeze. **4.** *Colloq.* unusually fine, great, large, etc.

spanking² /'spæŋkɪŋ/ *n.* **1.** the act of someone who spanks. **2.** this act administered as a punishment.

spanner /'spænə/ *n.* **1.** a tool for catching upon or gripping and turning or twisting the head of a bolt, a nut, a pipe, or the like, commonly consisting of a bar of metal with fixed or adjustable jaws. –*phr.* **2. a spanner in the works,** *Colloq.* any cause of confusion or impediment.

spa pool *n.* a large spa bath, often part of a larger pool, as a swimming pool, in which heated water is agitated and aerated to massage the bather's muscles. Also, **spa.**

spar¹ /spɑ/ *n.* **1.** *Naut.* a stout pole such as those used for masts, etc.; a mast, yard, boom, gaff, or the like. **2.** *Aeronautics* a principal lateral member of the framework of a wing of an aeroplane. –*v.t.* (**sparred, sparring**) **3.** to provide or make with spars.

spar² /spɑ/ *v.i.* (**sparred, sparring**) **1.** *Boxing* to make the movements of attack and defence with the arms and fists. **2.** to argue vigorously but not very seriously. –*n.* **3.** a motion of sparring.

spar³ /spɑ/ *n.* any of various more or less lustrous, transparent or translucent, easily cleavable crystalline minerals, as fluorspar.

spare /spɛə/ *v.t.* (**spared, sparing**) **1.** to refrain from harming or destroying; leave uninjured; forbear to punish: *to spare a fallen adversary.* **2.** to deal gently or leniently with; show consideration for: *to spare a person's feelings.* **3.** to save from strain, discomfort, annoyance, or the like, or from a particular cause of it: *to spare oneself trouble.* **4.** to refrain from, forbear, omit, or withhold, as action or speech: *to spare someone the details.* **5.** to refrain from employing, as some instrument, means, aid, etc.: *to spare the rod.* **6.** to set aside for a particular purpose: *to spare land for a garden.* **7.** to part with or let go, as from a supply, especially without inconvenience or loss: *to spare a few cents.* **8.** to dispense with or do without. **9.** to use economically or frugally; refrain from using up or wasting. **10.** to have left over or unused: *we have room to spare.* –*adj.* (**sparer, sparest**) **11.** kept in reserve, as for possible use: *a spare tyre.* **12.** being in excess of present need; free for other use: *spare time.* **13.** frugally restricted; meagre, as living, diet, etc. **14.** lean or thin, as a person. **15.** scanty or scant, as in amount, fullness, etc. –*n.* **16.** a spare thing, part, etc., as an extra tyre for emergency use. **17.** *Tenpin Bowling* **a.** the knocking down of all the pins in two consecutive bowls. **b.** the score made by bowling a spare. **18.** *Colloq.* → **spare part. 19. go spare,** *Colloq.* to lose one's temper; become exasperated. –**sparely,** *adv.* –**spareness,** *n.* –**sparer,** *n.*

spare part *n.* a part which replaces a faulty, worn, or broken part of a machine, especially a motor vehicle. Also, **spare.**

sparing /'spɛərɪŋ/ *adj.* **1.** that spares; lenient; merciful. **2. sparing of,** frugally restricted in: *sparing of his praises.* –**sparingly,** *adv.* –**sparingness,** *n.*

spark /spak/ *n.* **1.** an ignited or fiery particle such as is thrown off by burning wood, etc., or produced by one hard body striking against another. **2.** *Elect.* **a.** the light produced by a sudden discontinuous discharge of electricity through air or another dielectric. **b.** the discharge itself. **c.** any electric arc of relatively small energy content. **d.** such a spark in the spark plug of an internal-combustion engine. **e.** the arrangement of devices producing and governing this spark. **3.** a small amount or trace of something. **4.** a trace of life or vitality. –*v.i.* **5.** to emit or produce sparks. **6.** (of the ignition in an internal-combustion engine) to function correctly in forming the sparks. –*v.t.* **7.** *Colloq.* to kindle or stimulate (interest, activity, etc.). –*phr.* **8. spark off,** *Colloq.* to bring about; cause; precipitate.

sparkle /'spakəl/ *v.i.* **1.** (of fire, light, etc.) to come out in or as if in little sparks. **2.** to shine with little gleams of light: *a diamond sparkles.* **3.** to have bubbles of air: *wine sparkling in the glass.* **4.** to be brilliant, lively, or vivacious: *his eyes sparkled.* –*n.* **5.** a little spark. **6.** sparkling appearance or shine: *the sparkle of a diamond.* **7.** brilliance; liveliness or vivacity: *the sparkle in your eyes.* –**sparkling, sparkly,** *adj.*

spark plug *n.* a device inserted in the cylinder of an internal-combustion engine, containing two terminals between which passes the electric spark for igniting the explosive gases. Also, **sparking plug.**

sparrow /'spærou/ *n.* a common small bird, *Passer domesticus,* inhabiting urban areas and farmland, native to Europe, Asia and North Africa, and widely introduced elsewhere.

sparrowhawk /'spærouhɔk/ *n.* **1.** a small, brownish, square-tailed hawk which preys on smaller birds, the **collared sparrowhawk,** *Accipiter cirrocephalus,* of mainland Australia, Tasmania, and New Guinea. **2.** → **nankeen kestrel. 3.** any of certain small hawks of the genus *Accipiter* which prey on birds, especially the **Eurasian sparrowhawk,** *A. nisus,* of Eurasia and Africa, used in falconry. **4.** an American falcon, *Falco sparverius,* which preys especially on grasshoppers and small mammals.

sparse /spas/ *adj.* **1.** thinly scattered or distributed: *a sparse population.* **2.** thin; not thick or dense: *sparse hair.* **3.** scanty; meagre. –**sparsely,** *adv.* –**sparseness, sparsity** /'spasəti/, *n.*

spartan /'spatn/ (*sometimes upper case*) –*adj.* **1.** rigorously simple, frugal, or austere; sternly disciplined. –*n.* **2.** a person of spartan characteristics. –**spartanism,** *n.*

spasm /'spæzəm/ *n.* **1.** *Pathol.* a sudden, abnormal, involuntary muscular contraction; an affection consisting of a continued muscular contraction (**tonic spasm**), or of a series of alternating muscular contractions and relaxations (**clonic spasm**). **2.** any sudden, brief spell of great energy, activity, feeling, etc.

spasmodic /spæz'mɒdɪk/ *adj.* **1.** of or relating to a spasm; characterised by spasms. **2.** resembling a spasm or spasms; sudden and violent, but brief; intermittent: *spasmodic efforts.* **3.** given to or characterised by bursts of excitement. Also, **spasmodical.** –**spasmodically,** *adv.*

spastic /'spæstɪk/ *adj.* **1.** relating to, of the nature of, or characterised by spasm, especially muscular spasm. **2.** *Colloq.* (*likely to give offence*) idiotic; clumsy. –*n.* **3.** *Obsolesc.* a person exhibiting such spasms, especially one who has cerebral palsy. **4.** *Colloq.* (*likely to give offence*) **a.** a fool. **b.** a clumsy person. –**spastically,** *adv.* –**spasticity,** *n.*

spat¹ /spæt/ *n.* **1.** a light blow; a slap; a smack. **2.** a petty quarrel. –*v.i.* (**spatted, spatting**) **3.** to slap. **4.** to engage in a petty quarrel or dispute.

spat² /spæt/ *v.* past tense and past participle of **spit¹.**

spat³ /spæt/ *n.* (*usu. pl.*) a short gaiter worn over the instep, usually fastened under the foot with a strap.

spate /speɪt/ *n.* **1.** a sudden, almost overwhelming, outpouring: *a spate of words.* **2.** a flood or inundation; a state of flood. **3.** a sudden heavy downpour of rain.

spatial /'speɪʃəl/ *adj.* **1.** of or relating to space. **2.** existing or occurring in space; having extension in space. –**spatiality** /speɪʃi'æləti/, *n.* –**spatially,** *adv.*

spatio- a word element meaning 'space'.

spatter /'spætə/ *v.t.* **1.** to scatter or splash in small particles or drops: *to spatter mud.* –*v.i.* **2.** to send out small particles or drops. –*n.* **3.** the act or sound of spattering: *the spatter of rain on a roof.* **4.** splash or spot of something spattered. –**spatteringly,** *adv.*

spatula /'spætʃələ/ *n.* an implement with a broad, flat, flexible blade, used for blending foods, mixing drugs, spreading plasters and paints, etc. –**spatular,** *adj.*

spawn /spɔn/ *n.* **1.** *Zool.* a mass of sex cells of fishes, amphibians, molluscs, crustaceans, etc., after being shed from the body. **2.** (*usually offensive*) a large number of children. –*v.i.* **3.** to shed eggs and sperm, especially into water. –*v.t.* **4.** to produce (spawn). **5.** to give birth to; give rise to. **6.** (*usually offensive*) to produce (children) in large numbers. –**spawner,** *n.*

spay /speɪ/ *v.t.* to remove the ovaries of (a female animal).

SP bookmaker /ɛs pi 'bʊkmeɪkə/ *n.* an unlicensed bookmaker operating off racetracks paying the starting price odds. Also, **SP bookie.** –**SP bookmaking,** *n.*

speak /spik/ *verb* (**spoke, spoken, speaking**) –*v.i.* **1.** to utter words or articulate sounds with the ordinary (talking) voice. **2.** to make oral communication or mention: *to speak to a person about various matters.* **3.** to converse. **4.** to deliver an address, discourse, etc. **5.** to make a statement in written or printed words. **6.** to make communication or disclosure by any means; convey significance. **7.** to emit a sound, as a musical instrument; make a noise or report. **8.** (of hunting dogs) to give tongue; bay. –*v.t.* **9.** to utter orally and articulately: *to speak words of praise.* **10.** to express or make known with the voice: *to speak the truth.* **11.** to declare in writing or printing, or by any means of communication. **12.** to make known, indicate, or reveal. **13.** to use, or be able to use, in oral utterance, as a language: *to speak French.* –*phr.* **14. so to speak,** to use a certain way of speaking; as one might say. **15. speak for, a.** to recommend; intercede for; to act as spokesperson for. **b.** to reserve; bespeak: *this dress is already spoken for.* **16. speak for itself,** to show itself to be self-evidently good without need for further support or argument: *her record speaks for itself.* **17. speak for oneself,** to express only one's own views. **18. speak for yourself,** an expression of disagreement. **19. speak one's mind,** to express one's opinion. **20. speak out,** to express one's views openly and without reserve. **21. speak up,** to speak loudly and clearly. **22. speak well for,** to be favourable evidence for. **23. to speak of,** worth mentioning: *he has no money to speak of.* –**speakable,** *adj.*

-speak a suffix denoting the peculiar jargon of a particular business, subculture, or other group, as in *adspeak, bureauspeak.*

speaker /'spikə/ *n.* **1.** someone who speaks formally before an audience; an orator. **2.** (*usu. upper case*) the presiding officer of the lower house of a parliament, as in the House of Representatives. **3.** a loudspeaker. –**speakership**, *n.*

speakerphone /'spikəfoʊn/ *n. Telecommunications* a telephone with a microphone and loudspeaker that is used without the handset.

speaker recognition *n.* → **voice recognition** (def. 1).

spear[1] /spɪə/ *n.* **1.** a weapon for thrusting or throwing, being a long staff with a sharp head, of iron or steel. –*v.t.* **2.** to pierce with a spear. –**spearer**, *n.*

spear[2] /spɪə/ *n.* **1.** a sprout or shoot of a plant; a blade of grass, grain, etc. –*v.i.* **2.** to sprout; shoot; send up or rise in a spear or spears.

spear grass *n.* **1.** a native, drought-tolerant grass of the genus *Stipa* with narrow leaves, twisted awns, and seeds which are spear-shaped and can cause damage to stock, as plains grass. **2.** either of two native, perennial grasses of the genus *Heteropogon*, found in northern Australia, which can cause damage to livestock with their sharp-pointed seeds. **3.** → **wire grass**. **4.** a New Zealand perennial, umbelliferous plant, *Aciphylla squarrosa*, having a large basal rosette of stiff, narrow leaves about 60 cm long and inflorescences up to three metres high.

spearhead /'spɪəhɛd/ *n.* **1.** the sharp-pointed head which forms the piercing end of a spear. **2.** any person or thing that leads an attack, undertaking, etc. –*v.t.* **3.** to act as a spearhead for.

spearmint /'spɪəmɪnt/ *n.* the common garden mint, *Mentha spicata*, an aromatic herb much used for flavouring.

spear phishing *n.* a targeted form of phishing which focuses on a specific organisation using emails disguised as messages from managers, colleagues, etc.

spear tackle *n. Rugby Football* an illegal tackle in which the player with the ball is lifted into the air, turned upside down, then thrust violently headfirst into the ground, and exposed to the possibility of serious injury.

spec /spɛk/ *Colloq.* –*n.* **1.** speculation. –*adj.* **2.** speculative. –*phr.* **3. on spec**, as a guess, risk, or gamble.

spec builder *n. Aust., NZ* someone who builds houses, etc., as a speculative enterprise, rather than under contract.

special /'spɛʃəl/ *adj.* **1.** of a distinct or particular character. **2.** being a particular one; particular, individual, or certain. **3.** relating or peculiar to a particular person, thing, instance, etc.: *the special features of a plan.* **4.** having a particular function, purpose, application, etc.: *a special messenger.* **5.** dealing with particulars, or specific, as a statement. **6.** distinguished or different from what is ordinary or usual: *a special occasion.* **7.** extraordinary; exceptional; exceptional in amount or degree; especial: *special importance.* **8.** especially beloved or favoured: *Myra was special to us.* –*n.* **9.** a special person or thing. **10.** a special train. **11.** an item sold at a special, usually bargain price. **12.** *Aust. Hist.* a convict receiving special indulgence because of ability or birth. **13.** a special edition of a newspaper. **14.** a special constable. –*verb* (**specialled, specialling**) –*v.t.* **15.** *Aust.* (of a nurse) to care for (a patient) as a special responsibility, especially in a private home. –*v.i.* **16.** *Aust.* (of a nurse) to special a patient. –*phr.* **17. on special**, *Colloq.* available at a bargain price. –**specially**, *adv.*

specialise /'spɛʃəlaɪz/ *v.i.* **1.** to concentrate on some special line of study, work, etc. **2.** *Biol.* to develop characteristics for special purposes. –*v.t.* **3.** *Biol.* to change (an organism or one of its organs) to fit it for a special function or environment. Also, **specialize**. –**specialisation** /spɛʃəlaɪ'zeɪʃən/, *n.*

specialist /'spɛʃəlɪst/ *n.* **1.** someone who is devoted to one subject, or to one particular branch of a subject or pursuit. **2.** a medical practitioner with advanced qualifications in a particular field of medicine, usually acting as a consultant. –**specialistic** /spɛʃə'lɪstɪk/, *adj.*

speciality /spɛʃi'æləti/ *n.* (*pl.* **-ties**) **1.** a special or particular character. **2.** an article of unusual or superior design or quality. **3.** → **specialty** (defs 1, 2 and 4).

specialty /'spɛʃəlti/ *n.* (*pl.* **-ties**) **1.** a special feature or characteristic. **2.** a special study, line of work, or the like. **3.** *Med.* a particular field of medicine, practitioners of which require advanced qualifications. **4.** an article particularly dealt in, manufactured, etc., or one to which the dealer or manufacturer professes to devote special care. **5.** *Law* a special agreement, contract, etc., expressed in an instrument under seal. **6.** → **speciality**. –*phr.* **7. specialty of the house**, a dish by which a restaurant claims to be distinguished from others.

speciation /spiʃi'eɪʃən/ *n.* (in biology) the development of a new species by evolutionary processes.

specie /'spiʃi/ *n.* **1.** coin; coined money. –*phr.* **2. in specie**, **a.** in kind. **b.** (of money) in actual coin.

species /'spisiz, -ʃiz/ *n.* (*pl.* **species**) **1.** a group of individuals having some common characteristics or qualities; distinct sort or kind. **2.** *Biol.* the basic category of biological classification, intended to designate a single kind of animal or plant, any variations existing among the individuals being regarded as not affecting the essential sameness which distinguishes them from all other organisms within the category. **3.** *Logic* **a.** any group contained in a next larger group (the genus). **b.** the sum of those qualities of such a contained group that are common to all members of the group and are sufficient to identify it, i.e. to specify its members. –*adj.* **4.** *Bot.* (of a plant) being a natural member of a species (opposed to *cultivar*): *a species grevillea.*

speciesism /'spisiziːzəm/ *n.* human discrimination against other animal species, especially in regard to the exploitation of certain animals for human benefit. –**speciesist**, *n., adj.*

specific /spə'sɪfɪk/ *adj.* **1.** being particular or definite, describing one type: *specific mention.* **2.** *Zool., Bot.* of or relating to a species: *specific characters.* **3.** *Physics* indicating a physical quantity which has been divided by mass, i.e. quantity per unit mass, as *specific activity, specific charge, specific heat*, etc. –*n.* **4.** something particular; an item; detail. –**specifically**, *adv.* –**specificity** /spɛsə'fɪsəti/, **specificness**, *n.*

specification /spɛsəfə'keɪʃən/ *n.* **1.** the act of specifying. **2.** a statement of particulars; a detailed description setting forth the dimensions, materials, etc., for a proposed building, engineering work, or the like. **3.** something specified, as in a bill of particulars; a specified particular, item, or article. **4.** the act of making specific. **5.** the state of having a specific character.

specific gravity *n. Physics* the ratio of the mass of a given volume of any substance to that of the same volume of some other substance taken as a standard, water being the standard for solids and liquids, and hydrogen or air for gases; relative density. *Abbrev.*: s.g.

specify /'spɛsəfaɪ/ *verb* (**-fied, -fying**) –*v.t.* **1.** to mention or name specifically or definitely; state in detail. **2.** to give a specific character to. **3.** to name or state as a condition. –*v.i.* **4.** to make a specific mention or statement.

specimen /'spɛsəmən/ *n.* **1.** a part or an individual taken as exemplifying a whole mass or number; a typical animal, plant, mineral, part, etc. **2.** *Med.* a sample of a substance to be examined or tested for a specific purpose. **3.** *Colloq.* a person as a specified kind, or in some respect a peculiar kind, of human being: *he's a poor specimen.*

specious /'spiʃəs/ *adj.* **1.** apparently good or right but without real merit; superficially pleasing: *specious arguments.* **2.** pleasing to the eye, but deceptive. –**speciously,** *adv.* –**speciousness,** *n.*

speck /spɛk/ *n.* **1.** a small spot, often different in quality, colour, etc., from its background. **2.** a very little bit or particle. **3.** something appearing small by comparison or distance. –*v.t.* **4.** to mark with, or as if with, a speck or specks.

speckle /'spɛkəl/ *n.* **1.** a small speck, spot, or mark, as on skin. **2.** speckled colouring or marking. –*v.t.* **3.** to mark with, or as with, speckles. –**speckled,** *adj.*

spectacle /'spɛktəkəl/ *n.* **1.** anything presented to the sight or view, especially something of a striking kind. **2.** a public show or display, especially on a large scale. **3.** (*pl.*) a device to aid defective vision or to protect the eyes from light, dust, etc., consisting usually of two glass lenses set in a frame which rests on the nose and is held in place by pieces passing over or around the ears (often called **a pair of spectacles**). –*phr.* **4. make a spectacle of oneself,** to draw attention to oneself by unseemly behaviour.

spectacular /spɛk'tækjələ/ *adj.* **1.** relating to or of the nature of a spectacle; marked by or given to great display. **2.** dramatic; thrilling. –*n.* **3.** a lavishly produced film, television show, etc. **4.** any lavish entertainment or sporting display, etc. –**spectacularly,** *adv.*

spectator /spɛk'teɪtə, 'spɛkteɪtə/ *n.* **1.** someone who looks on; an onlooker. **2.** someone who is present at and views a spectacle or the like. –**spectatorial** /spɛktə-'tɔriəl/, *adj.*

spectra /'spɛktrə/ *n.* plural of **spectrum.**

spectre /'spɛktə/ *n.* **1.** a visible incorporeal spirit, especially one of a terrifying nature; ghost; phantom; apparition. **2.** some object or source of terror or dread. Also, **specter.** –**spectral,** *adj.*

spectro- a word element representing **spectrum.**

spectroscope /'spɛktrəskoʊp/ *n.* an optical instrument for producing and examining the spectrum of the light or radiation from any source. –**spectroscopic** /spɛktrə'skɒpɪk/, **spectroscopical** /spɛktrə'skɒpɪkəl/, *adj.* –**spectroscopically** /spɛktrə'skɒpɪkli/, *adv.*

spectrum /'spɛktrəm/ *n.* (*pl.* **-tra** *or* **-trums**) **1.** *Optics* the band of colours (red, orange, yellow, green, blue, indigo, violet) produced when white light passes through a prism. **2.** *Physics* a continuous range of frequencies within which waves have some specified common characteristic (as in audio-frequency spectrum, radio-frequency spectrum, visible spectrum, etc.). **3.** a visual display, a photographic record, or a graph of the intensity of radiation as a function of wavelength, energy, or frequency, etc. **4.** a range of interrelated values, objects, opinions, etc.: *the spectrum of Australian English speech varieties.* –*phr.* **5. on the spectrum,** presenting some of the symptoms of autism spectrum disorder.

speculate /'spɛkjəleɪt/ *v.i.* **1.** (sometimes fol. by *on* or *upon*) to engage in thought or reflection, or meditate. **2.** to indulge in conjectural thought. **3.** *Commerce* to buy and sell commodities, shares, etc., in the expectation of profit through a change in their market value; engage in any business transaction involving considerable risk, or the chance of large gains. –**speculation,** *n.* –**speculator,** *n.* –**speculative,** *adj.*

sped /spɛd/ *v.* past tense and past participle of **speed.**

speech /spitʃ/ *n.* **1.** the ability or power of speaking; oral communication; expression of human thought and emotion by speech sounds. **2.** something that is spoken; utterance, remark, or declaration. **3.** a series of remarks or statements in spoken language, made by a speaker before an audience. **4.** the form of speech typical of a

particular people or area; language or dialect. **5.** manner of speaking, usually of a person. –**speechless,** *adj.*

speech recognition *n.* the decoding of human speech by a computer so that it may respond with appropriate information or action. Also, **voice recognition.**

speed /spid/ *n.* **1.** rapidity in moving, going, travelling, or any proceeding or performance; swiftness; celerity. **2.** *Physics* the ratio of the distance covered by a moving body to the time taken. **3.** *Motor Vehicles* a transmission gear-ratio. **4.** *Photography* a measure of the exposure required by an emulsion. **5.** *Archaic* success or prosperity. **6.** *Colloq.* amphetamines; pep pills. –*verb* (**sped** *or* **speeded, speeding**) –*v.t.* **7.** to promote the success of (an affair, undertaking, etc.); further, forward, or expedite. **8.** to cause to move, go, or proceed, with speed. **9.** to expedite the going of: *to speed the parting guest.* –*v.i.* **10.** to move, go, pass, or proceed with speed or rapidity. **11.** to drive a vehicle at a rate exceeding the maximum permitted by law. –*phr.* **12. at full speed,** as fast as possible. **13. get** (or **pick**) **up speed,** to accelerate. **14. get up to speed,** to bring oneself up to date. **15. speed up, a.** to increase the rate or progress of: *to speed up industrial production.* **b.** to increase in rate or progress. **16. up to speed,** to be functioning appropriately or be fully informed; adequately efficient: *we'll bring her up to speed with more training.* –**speeder,** *n.* –**speedster,** *n.* –**speedy,** *adj.*

speed camera *n.* a computerised camera positioned to monitor traffic and photograph the numberplate of any vehicle that exceeds the speed limit.

speed dial *n.* a feature of a phone in which telephone numbers are entered into the memory to be accessed and dialled by pressing one button on the phone.

speed-dial *adj.* **1.** of or relating to speed dial. –*v.t.* (**-dialled** *or, esp. US,* **-dialed, -dialling** *or, esp. US,* **-dialing**) **2.** to telephone (someone) using a speed-dial facility.

speedometer /spi'dɒmətə/ *n.* a device attached to a motor vehicle or the like to indicate the rate of travel. Also, **speedo.**

speedway /'spidweɪ/ *n.* **1.** a racing track for motor vehicles, especially motorcycles. **2.** a road or course for fast driving, motoring, or the like, or on which more than ordinary speed is allowed.

speleology /spili'ɒlədʒi/ *n.* **1.** the systematic study of caves, especially in relation to their geological structure, flora and fauna. **2.** the sport or recreation of exploring caves. Also, **spelaeology.** –**speleological** /spiliə'lɒdʒɪkəl/, *adj.* –**speleologist** /spili'ɒlədʒəst/, *n.*

spell[1] /spɛl/ *verb* (**spelt** *or* **spelled, spelling**) –*v.t.* **1.** to name, write, or otherwise give (as by signals), in order, the letters of (a word, syllable, etc.). **2.** (of letters) to form (a word, syllable, etc.). **3.** Also, **spell out.** to read letter by letter or with difficulty. **4.** to signify; amount to: *this delay spells disaster for us.* –*v.i.* **5.** to name, write, or give the letters of words, etc. **6.** to express words by letters, especially correctly. –*phr.* **7. spell out, a.** to discern or find, as if by reading or study. **b.** to make absolutely clear and understandable.

spell[2] /spɛl/ *n.* **1.** a form of words supposedly possessing magic power; a charm, incantation, or enchantment. **2.** any dominating or irresistible influence; fascination.

spell[3] /spɛl/ *n.* **1.** a period of work or other activity: *to take a spell at the wheel.* **2.** a turn, bout, fit, or period of anything: *a spell of coughing.* **3.** *Colloq.* (a short) interval or space of time. **4.** a period of weather of a particular kind: *a hot spell.* **5.** an interval or period of rest. –*v.t.* (**spelled, spelling**) **6.** to take the place of or relieve (a person, etc.) for a time while they rest.

spellbound /'spɛlbaʊnd/ *adj.* bound by, or as by, a spell; enchanted, entranced, or fascinated: *a spellbound audience.*

spellchecker /'spɛltʃɛkə/ *n.* a computer program which checks the spelling of words in a text file for mistakes and suggests correct spellings.

spelling /'spɛlɪŋ/ *n.* **1.** the manner in which words are spelt; orthography. **2.** a group of letters representing a word. **3.** the act of a speller. **4.** the ability to spell or degree of proficiency in spelling.

spelt /spɛlt/ *v.* a past tense and past participle of **spell**[1].

spencer /'spɛnsə/ *n.* **1.** a short coat or jacket, formerly worn by men. **2.** a jacket or bodice, formerly worn by women. **3.** *Aust., NZ* a kind of woman's vest, worn under clothes for extra warmth.

spend /spɛnd/ *verb* (**spent, spending**) –*v.t.* **1.** to pay out (money, wealth, resources, etc.); expend; disburse. **2.** to use (labour, thought, words, time, etc.) on some object, in some business, etc. **3.** to pass (time) in a particular manner, place, etc. **4.** to use up; consume; exhaust: *the storm had spent its fury.* **5.** to give (one's) blood, life, etc.) for some cause. –*v.i.* **6.** to spend money, etc. –**spendable**, *adj.* –**spender**, *n.*

spendthrift /'spɛndθrɪft/ *n.* **1.** someone who spends their possessions or money extravagantly or wastefully; a prodigal. –*adj.* **2.** wastefully extravagant; prodigal.

spent /spɛnt/ *v.* **1.** past tense and past participle of **spend**. –*adj.* **2.** used up, consumed, or exhausted.

spent fuel *n.* nuclear fuel that has been irradiated in a nuclear reactor to the point where it is no longer useful in sustaining a nuclear reaction.

sperm /spɜm/ *n.* **1.** → **semen**. **2.** a male reproductive cell; a spermatozoon.

-sperm a a suffixal use of **sperm**, as in *angiosperm*.

-spermal a word element used to form adjectives related to **sperm**.

spermatozoon /ˌspɜmətə'zoʊɒn/ *n.* (*pl.* **-zoa**) *Zool.* one of the minute, usually actively motile, gametes in semen, which serve to fertilise the ovum; a mature male reproductive cell. –**spermatozoal, spermatozoan, spermatozoic,** *adj.*

sperm bank *n.* a storage place for sperm which are to be used for artificial insemination.

sperm whale *n.* a large, square-headed whale, *Physeter macrocephalus*, valuable for oil and spermaceti, a whitish, waxy substance, used in making ointments, cosmetics, etc,.

spew /spju/ *v.i.* **1.** to discharge the contents of the stomach through the mouth; vomit. –*v.t.* **2.** to eject from the stomach through the mouth; vomit. **3.** to thrust forth or discharge violently. –*n.* **4.** that which is spewed; vomit. –**spewer**, *n.*

SPF /ɛs pi 'ɛf/ *n.* the effectiveness of a sunscreen preparation in protecting the skin from ultraviolet radiation, indicated on a scale, usually from 2 to 15. Compare **UPF**. Also, **sun protection factor**.

sphagnum /'sfægnəm/ *n.* any of the bog mosses constituting the genus *Sphagnum*, used by gardeners in potting and packing plants, and (formerly) in surgery for dressing wounds, etc.

sphalerite /'sfælərait, 'sfeilə-/ *n.* a very common mineral, zinc sulphide, ZnS, usually containing some iron and a little cadmium, occurring in yellow, brown, or black crystals or cleavable masses with resinous lustre, the principal ore of zinc and cadmium.

sphere /sfɪə/ *n.* **1.** a round body whose surface is at all points of equal distance from the centre. **2.** anything shaped like a sphere, as a tennis ball. **3.** a heavenly body; planet or star. **4.** (in ancient astronomy) any of the transparent, concentric, spherical shells, or 'heavens', in which the planets, fixed stars, etc., were supposedly set. **5.** the place or environment within which a person or thing exists: *He was out of his sphere.* **6.** a particular level of society or walk of life. **7.** a field of something particular: *a sphere of influence.* –**spherelike**, *adj.*

-sphere a word element representing **sphere**, as in *planisphere*; having a special use in the names of the layers of gases, etc., surrounding the earth and other celestial bodies, as in *ionosphere*.

spherical /'sfɛrɪkəl/ *adj.* **1.** having the form of a sphere; globular. **2.** formed in or on a sphere, as a figure. **3.** of or relating to a sphere or spheres: *spherical trigonometry.* Also, **spheric.** –**sphericality** /sfɛrə'kæləti/, *n.* –**spherically**, *adv.*

spherical angle *n.* an angle formed by arcs of great circles of a sphere.

sphincter /'sfɪŋktə/ *n. Anat.* a circular band of voluntary or involuntary muscle which encircles an orifice of the body or one of its hollow organs. –**sphincteral**, *adj.*

spice /spais/ *n.* **1.** any of a class of strongly or sweetly smelling substances of vegetable origin, such as pepper, cinnamon, cloves, etc., used as seasoning or preservatives. **2.** something that gives interest; a piquant element or quality. –*v.t.* (**spiced, spicing**) **3.** to prepare or season with a spice or spices. **4.** to give flavour or interest to by something added. –**spicy**, *adj.*

spick-and-span /spik-ən-'spæn/ *adj.* **1.** neat and clean. **2.** perfectly new; fresh. Also, **spick and span**.

spider /'spaidə/ *n.* **1.** any of the eight-legged wingless, insect-like arachnids, most of which spin webs that serve as nests and as traps for prey. **2.** any vehicle, apparatus, tool, etc., looking like or suggesting a spider.

spider flower *n.* **1.** any of several species of the Australian genus *Grevillea* with inflorescences resembling spiders, as the **grey spider flower**, *G. buxifolia.* **2.** any of certain species of the genus *Cleome*, as *C. spinosa* which has pinkish flowers with long protruding stamens. **3.** any of certain species of the genus *Strophanthus*.

spiel /spil, ʃpil/ *Colloq.* –*n.* **1.** glib or plausible talk, especially for the purpose of persuasion, swindling, seduction, etc. **2.** a salesman's, conjurer's, or swindler's patter. –*v.i.* **3.** to talk plausibly; deliver a patter or sales talk. –*v.t.* **4.** to attempt to lure, persuade, or deceive (someone) by glib talk.

spigot /'spigət/ *n.* **1.** a small peg or plug for stopping the vent of a cask, etc. **2.** a small peg which stops the passage in the tap of a cask, etc. **3.** the end of a pipe which enters the enlarged end of another pipe to form a joint.

spike[1] /spaik/ *n.* **1.** a large, strong nail or pin, especially made of iron. **2.** a stiff, sharp-pointed piece or part. **3. a.** a sharp metal projection on the bottom of a shoe, as that of a golf player, to prevent slipping. **b.** (*pl.*) running shoes having spikes. **4. a.** a peak on a graph. **b.** *Commerce* a sudden increase or rise in the supply of a commodity. –*v.t.* **5.** to fasten or make firm with a spike or spikes. **6.** to provide or set with a spike or spikes. **7.** to pierce with a spike. **8.** to make ineffective: *to spike a rumour.* **9.** *Colloq.* to add alcohol to (a drink). **10.** to increase the impact, interest or attractiveness of a speech, conversation, etc. –**spiky**, *adj.*

spike[2] /spaik/ *n.* **1.** an ear, as of wheat or other grain. **2.** *Bot.* an inflorescence in which the flowers are sessile (or apparently so) along an elongated, unbranched axis.

spill[1] /spil/ *verb* (**spilt** *or* **spilled, spilling**) –*v.t.* **1.** to cause or allow (liquid, or any matter in grains or loose pieces) to run or fall from a container, especially accidentally or wastefully. **2.** to shed (blood), especially in killing or wounding. **3.** to cause to fall from a horse, vehicle, etc. **4.** *Colloq.* to disclose, or tell (a secret, etc.). –*v.i.* **5.** (of a liquid, loose particles, etc.) to run or escape from a container. –*n.* **6.** Also, **spillage**. an act of spilling.

7. Also, **spillage**. the quantity spilt. **8.** a throw or fall from a horse, vehicle, etc. **9.** *Aust. Politics* the declaring vacant of a number of positions when one of them falls vacant.

spill[2] /spɪl/ *n.* **1.** a splinter. **2.** a slender piece of wood or twisted paper, for lighting candles, lamps, etc. **3.** a peg made of metal.

spillage /'spɪlɪdʒ/ *n.* **1.** an act of spilling. **2.** something that is spilled: *a great spillage of oil.*

spin /spɪn/ *verb* (**spun** *or, Archaic,* **span, spun, spinning**) *–v.t.* **1.** to make (yarn) by drawing out, twisting, and winding fibres. **2.** to form (any material) into thread. **3.** (of spiders, silkworms, etc.) to produce (a thread, cobweb, gossamer, silk, etc.) by extruding from the body a long, slender filament of a natural viscous matter that hardens in the air. **4.** to cause to turn round rapidly, as on an axis; twirl; whirl: *to spin a coin on a table.* **5.** (in sheet metalwork) to shape into hollow, rounded form, during rotation on a lathe or wheel, by pressure with a suitable tool. **6.** to produce, fabricate, or evolve in a manner suggestive of spinning thread, as a story. **7.** *Colloq.* to give a desired slant to (a story) in the media so as to ensure a good reception from the public. **8. a.** *Cricket* (of a bowler) to cause (the ball) to revolve on its axis so that on bouncing it changes direction or speed. **b.** *Tennis, etc.* to hit (the ball) so that it behaves thus. **9.** *Two-up* to toss (the coins). *–v.i.* **10.** to turn round rapidly, as on an axis, as the earth, a top, etc. **11.** to produce a thread from the body, as spiders, silkworms, etc. **12.** to move, go, run, ride, or travel rapidly. **13.** to be affected with a sensation of whirling, as the head. *–n.* **14.** the act of causing a spinning or whirling motion. **15.** a spinning motion given to a ball or the like when thrown or struck. **16.** *Aeronautics* a condition of stalled flight in which the aircraft is rotating about all its axes simultaneously. **17.** a rapid run, ride, drive, or the like, as for exercise or enjoyment. **18.** the exercise of pedalling on a stationary exercise bike. **19.** *Physics* the angular momentum of a molecule, atom, or particle, when it has no velocity of translation. **20.** *Colloq.* a state of confusion or excitement. **21.** *Colloq.* experience or chance generally: *a rough spin; a fair spin.* **22.** *Colloq.* the particular slant deliberately given to a media story so as to achieve the desired outcome in terms of public awareness and acceptance. *–phr.* **23. spin a yarn, a.** to tell a tale. **b.** to tell a false or improbable story or version of an event. **24. spin out, a.** to draw out, protract, or prolong: *to spin out a story tediously.* **b.** to spend (time, one's life, etc.). **c.** to make last, as money; eke out. **d.** *Colloq.* to lose control of a vehicle with the result that the vehicle spins off the road. **e.** *Colloq.* to react with extreme apprehension; freak out. **f.** *Two-up* to lose the right to continue spinning the coins by throwing a pair of tails. **25. spin someone out,** *Colloq.* to cause someone to feel extremely apprehensive.

spina bifida /spaɪnə 'bɪfədə/ *n. Pathol.* a congenital defect in the development of the vertebral column giving rise to a hernial protrusion of the meninges.

spinach /'spɪnɪtʃ/ *n.* **1.** Also, **English spinach**. an annual herb, *Spinacia oleracea*, cultivated for its succulent leaves. **2.** a form of beet, *Beta vulgaris cicla*, with large, firm, strongly veined green leaves and a long fleshy stalk, used as a vegetable; silverbeet.

spinal cord *n. Anat.* the cord of nervous tissue extending through the spinal column.

spin control *n.* a method of controlling the point of view presented in the media, especially in relation to politics.

spindle /'spɪndl/ *n.* **1.** a rod, usually of wood, used to twist or wind the thread in spinning by hand, wheel or machine. **2.** any rod or pin suggestive of a spindle used

in spinning, usually one which turns round or on which something turns; axle, axis, or shaft. **3.** either of the two shaft-like parts in a lathe which support the work to be turned, one (**live spindle**) turning and giving movement to the work, and the other (**dead spindle**) not turning. **4.** *Biol.* fine threads of material arranged within the cell, during mitosis (a method of cell division), in a spindle-shaped manner. **5.** a short turned or circular ornament, such as in a stair rail. *–adj.* **6.** of or looking like spindles. *–v.i.* **7.** to grow tall and slender.

spindly /'spɪndli/ *adj.* (**-lier, -liest**) long or tall and slender; attenuated; slender and fragile.

spin-dry *v.t.* (**-dried, -drying**) to dry (laundry) by spinning it in a tub so that the moisture is extracted by centrifugal force.

spine /spaɪn/ *n.* **1.** the vertebral or spinal column; backbone. **2.** any backbone-like part. **3.** a pointed process or projection, usually of a bone. **4.** a stiff, pointed process or part on an animal, such as a quill of a porcupine, or a sharp, bony ray in a fish's fin. **5.** a ridge, usually of ground, rock, etc. **6.** a sharp-pointed, hard or woody outgrowth on a plant; thorn. **7.** *Bookbinding* the part of a book's cover that holds the front and back together, and which usually shows title and author. *–spinal, adj.* *–spined, adj.* *–spinelike, adj.* *–spinous, adj.* *–spiny, adj.*

spinechilling /'spaɪntʃɪlɪŋ/ *adj.* terrifying, especially of a book, film, etc. *–spinechiller, n.*

spineless /'spaɪnləs/ *adj.* without moral force, resolution, or courage; feeble. *–spinelessly, adv. –spinelessness, n.*

spinet /'spɪnət/ *n.* **1.** a small keyboard instrument resembling the harpsichord, the main difference being that the strings run across the instrument more or less in the direction of the keyboard, not at right angles to it. **2.** an early small square piano.

spinifex /'spɪnəfɛks/ *n.* **1.** any of the spiny grasses of the genus *Spinifex*, chiefly of Australia, often useful for binding sand on the seashore. **2.** any species of the genus *Triodia*, spiny-leaved tussock-forming grasses of inland Australia.

spinnaker /'spɪnəkə/ *n.* a large triangular sail with a light boom (**spinnaker boom**), carried by yachts on the side opposite the mainsail when running before the wind, or with the wind abaft the beam.

spinner /'spɪnə/ *n.* **1.** someone or something that spins. **2.** *Cricket* **a.** a delivery in which the bowler imparts lateral spin to the ball, making it deviate upon pitching. **b.** a bowler specialising in such deliveries. **3.** *Two-up* the person who tosses the coins. *–phr.* **4. come in spinner, a.** *Two-up* an expression indicating to the spinner that play has reached the point where the coins should now be tossed. **b.** *Aust. Colloq.* an expression used to inform someone that they have just been successfully duped.

spinneret /'spɪnərɛt/ *n.* **1.** an organ or part by means of which a spider, insect larva, or the like spins a silky thread for its web or cocoon. **2.** a finely perforated tube or plate through which a viscous liquid passes into the solidifying medium during the course of manufacture of artificial fibres.

spinning wheel *n.* a device for spinning wool, flax, etc., into yarn or thread consisting essentially of a single spindle driven by a large wheel operated by hand or foot.

spin-off *n.* **1.** an object, product, or enterprise derived as an incidental or secondary development of a larger enterprise: *the non-stick frying pan is a commercially valuable spin-off of space research.* **2.** *Econ.* the formation of a new company by an already existing company, with shareholders in the existing company entitled to subscribe for shares in the new company.

spinster /ˈspɪnstə/ *n.* **1.** a woman still unmarried beyond the usual age of marrying. **2.** *Chiefly Law* a woman who has never married. **–spinsterhood,** *n.* **–spinsterish,** *adj.*

spiny anteater *n.* → echidna.

spiny lobster *n.* → rock lobster.

spiracle /ˈspaɪrəkəl, ˈspɪrəkəl/ *n.* **1.** a breathing hole; an opening by which a confined space has communication with the outer air; an air hole. **2.** *Zool.* **a.** an aperture or orifice through which air or water passes in the act of respiration, as the blowhole of a cetacean. **b.** an opening in the head of sharks and rays through which water is drawn and passed over gills. **c.** one of the external orifices of a tracheal respiratory system, usually on the sides of the body. **–spiracular** /spəˈrækjələ/, *adj.* **–spiraculate** /spəˈrækjələt/, *adj.*

spiral /ˈspaɪrəl/ *n.* **1.** a plane curve traced by a point which runs continuously round and round a fixed point or centre while constantly receding from or approaching it. **2.** a single circle or ring of a spiral or helical curve or object. **3.** a spiral or helical object, formation, or form. **4.** → helix. **5.** *Aeronautics* a manoeuvre in which an aeroplane descends in a helix of small pitch and large radius, with the angle of incidence within that of the normal flight range. **6.** *Econ.* a reciprocal interaction of price and cost changes forming an overall economic change upwards (**inflationary spiral**) or downwards (**deflationary spiral**). **–adj. 7.** resembling or arranged in a spiral or spirals. **8.** (of a curve) like a spiral. **9.** helical. **–verb** (**-ralled** *or*, *US*, **-raled**, **-ralling** *or*, *US*, **-raling**) **–v.i. 10.** to take a spiral form or course. **11.** *Aeronautics* to move an aeroplane through a spiral course. **–v.t. 12.** to cause to take a spiral form or course. **–spirally,** *adv.*

spire¹ /ˈspaɪə/ *n.* **1.** a tall, tapering structure, generally an elongated, upright cone or pyramid, erected on a tower, roof, etc. **2.** such a structure forming the upper part of the steeple, or the whole steeple. **3.** a tapering, pointed part of something; a tall, sharp-pointed summit, peak, or the like. **4.** the highest point or summit of something. **5.** a sprout or shoot of a plant; a blade or spear of grass, etc. **–v.i. 6.** to shoot or rise into spire-like form; rise or extend to a height in the manner of a spire. **–spiry,** *adj.*

spire² /ˈspaɪə/ *n.* **1.** a coil or spiral. **2.** one of the series of convolutions of a coil or spiral. **3.** *Zool.* the upper, convoluted part of a spiral shell, above the aperture. **–spiry,** *adj.*

spirit /ˈspɪrət/ *n.* **1.** the principle of conscious life, originally related to the breath; vital principle animating a person's life and actions. **2.** a vital, unseen part of a person: *present in spirit though absent in body.* **3.** the soul as separable from the body at death. **4.** any supernatural being. **5.** a life-giving principle: *a spirit of reform.* **6.** (*pl.*) feelings with respect to mood: *in low spirits*; *in high spirits.* **7.** temper or nature: *meek in spirit.* **8.** mental or moral attitude; mood: *take my advice in the right spirit.* **9.** the main tendency or character of anything: *the spirit of the age*; *team spirit.* **10.** *Chem.* **a.** a distilled aqueous solution of ethyl alcohol. **b.** a distilled liquid extract. **11.** (*oft. pl.*) strong distilled alcoholic liquor. **12.** *Pharmaceutical* an alcohol solution of an essential or volatile principle. **–adj. 13.** relating to something which works by burning alcoholic spirits: *a spirit lamp.* **14.** of or relating to spiritualist bodies or activities. **–v.t. 15.** to carry (*away, off*, etc.) mysteriously or secretly.

spirited /ˈspɪrətəd/ *adj.* **1.** having a spirit, or having spirits, as specified: *low-spirited.* **2.** having or showing mettle, courage, vigour, liveliness, etc. **–spiritedly,** *adv.* **–spiritedness,** *n.*

spiritual /ˈspɪrətʃuəl, -tʃəl/ *adj.* **1.** of or consisting of the spirit or soul. **2.** standing in a relationship of the spirit;

non-material: *a spiritual attitude*; *a spiritual father.* **3.** of or relating to the spirit as the centre of the moral or religious nature. **4.** of or relating to sacred things or matters of religion; religious; devotional; sacred. **–n. 5.** a traditional religious song, especially of African Americans. **–spiritually,** *adv.* **–spirituality, spiritualness,** *n.*

spiritualism /ˈspɪrətʃəlɪzəm/ *n.* **1.** a belief or doctrine that the spirits of the dead keep living after the mortal life, and communicate with the living, especially through a person (a medium) particularly open to their influence. **2.** the practices or phenomena associated with this belief. **3.** a belief that all or some reality is immaterial and therefore spiritual. **4.** *Metaphysics* any belief that claims the separate but related existence of God, human (or other thinking) beings, and physical nature. **5.** a spiritual quality or tendency. **6.** insistence on the spiritual aspect of a subject, as in philosophy or religion. **–spiritualist,** *n.* **–spiritualistic** /spɪrətʃəˈlɪstɪk/, *adj.*

spirituous /ˈspɪrətʃuəs/ *adj.* **1.** of or relating to alcohol; alcoholic. **2.** (of liquors) distilled, as opposed to fermented. **–spirituousness,** *n.*

spiro-¹ a word element referring to respiration, as in *spirograph.*

spiro-² a word element meaning 'coil', 'spiral', as in *spirochaete.*

spirochaete /ˈspaɪrəkit/ *n.* slender, corkscrew-like bacterial microorganisms constituting the genus *Spirochaeta*, and found on humans, animals, and plants, and in soil and water. Some cause disease, as the *Spirochaeta pallida* or *Treponema pallidum* (the causative agent of syphilis); most, however, are saprophytic. Also, **spirochete.**

spit¹ /spɪt/ *verb* (**spat** *or* **spit, spitting**) **–v.i. 1.** to eject saliva from the mouth; expectorate. **2.** to do this at or on a person, etc., to express hatred, contempt, etc. **3.** to sputter. **4.** to fall in scattered drops or flakes, as rain or snow. **5.** to make a noise as of spitting. **–v.t. 6.** to eject (saliva, etc.) from the mouth. **7.** to throw out or emit, especially violently. **8.** to utter vehemently. **–n. 9.** saliva, especially when ejected. **10.** the act of spitting. **11.** a frothy or spit-like secretion exuded by various insects; spittle. **12.** a light fall of rain or snow. **–phr. 13. dead spit** *Colloq.* → spitting image. **14. spit blood,** *Colloq.* to feel and express extreme annoyance, anger, etc. **15. spit chips,** *Colloq.* to be very annoyed. **16. spit it out,** *Colloq.* speak up. **17. spit the dummy,** *Aust. Colloq.* **a.** to give up or opt out of a contest or the like before there is reasonable cause to do so. **b.** to throw a tantrum. **18. the big spit,** *Colloq.* vomit. **–spitter,** *n.*

spit² /spɪt/ *n.* **1.** a sharply pointed, slender rod or bar for thrusting into meat to be roasted at a fire or grilled. **2.** a narrow point of land projecting into the water and attached at one end to land; cape. **–v.t.** (**spitted, spitting**) **3.** to pierce, stab, or hold, as if with a spit; impale on something sharp.

spite /spaɪt/ *n.* **1.** a keen, ill-natured desire to humiliate, annoy, or injure another; venomous ill will. **2.** a particular instance of such ill will; a grudge. **–v.t. 3.** to wreak one's spite or malice on. **4.** to annoy or thwart, out of spite. **–phr. 5. in spite of,** in disregard or defiance of; notwithstanding. **–spiteful,** *adj.*

spitfire /ˈspɪtfaɪə/ *n.* **1.** a person of fiery temper, easily provoked to outbursts, especially a girl or woman. **2.** (*upper case*) a British single-engined fighter aircraft much used in World War II.

spitting image *n. Colloq.* a person or thing that is an exact likeness of another: *she is the spitting image of her sister.* Also, **dead spit.**

spittle /ˈspɪtl/ *n.* **1.** saliva; spit. **2.** the frothy protective secretion exuded by certain insects.

spittoon /spɪˈtuːn/ *n.* a bowl, etc., for spitting into.

spiv /spɪv/ *n. Chiefly Brit. Colloq.* someone who lives by their wits, without working or by dubious business activity, and usually affecting ostentatious dress and tastes. **–spivvy,** *adj.*

splash /splæʃ/ *v.t.* **1.** to wet or soil by dashing masses or particles of water, mud, or the like; spatter. **2.** to fall upon (something) in scattered masses or particles, as a liquid does. **3.** to cause to appear spattered. **4.** to dash (water, etc.) about in scattered masses or particles. **5.** *Colloq.* to display or print very noticeably, as in a newspaper. *–v.i.* **6.** to dash a liquid or semiliquid substance about. **7.** to fall, move, or go with a splash or splashes. **8.** (of liquid) to dash or fall in scattered masses or particles. *–n.* **9.** the act of splashing. **10.** the sound of splashing. **11.** a quantity of some liquid or semiliquid substance splashed upon or in a thing. **12.** a spot caused by something splashed. **13.** a patch, as of colour or light. **14.** a striking show, or an ostentatious display; sensation or excitement. *–phr.* **15. make a splash,** to be noticed; make an impression on people. **16. splash out,** *Colloq.* to spend money freely.

splat /splæt/ *n.* **1.** a broad, flat piece of wood, as the central upright part of the back of a chair. **2.** a slapping sound as made with something wet.

splatter /ˈsplætə/ *v.t.* **1.** to splash: *to splatter paint on a canvas. –v.i.* **2.** to splash: *the paint splattered everywhere.*

splay /spleɪ/ *v.t.* **1.** to spread out, expand, or extend. **2.** to make slanting; bevel. *–v.i.* **3.** to have a sloping or slanting direction. **4.** to spread or flare. *–n.* Also, **reveal.** **5.** *Archit.* a surface which makes a slanting or sloping angle with another. *–adj.* **6.** spread out; wide and flat; turned outwards. **7.** slanted or twisted to one side.

spleen /spliːn/ *n.* **1.** *Anat.* a highly vascular, gland-like but ductless organ, situated in humans near the cardiac end of the stomach, in which the blood undergoes certain corpuscular changes. **2.** ill humour, peevish temper, or spite: *venting his spleen on his unfortunate wife.* **3.** *Archaic* melancholy. **–spleenish, spleeny,** *adj.*

splendid /ˈsplɛndəd/ *adj.* **1.** gorgeous; magnificent; sumptuous. **2.** grand; superb; as beauty. **3.** glorious, as a name, reputation, victory, etc. **4.** strikingly admirable or fine: *splendid talents.* **5.** excellent, fine, or very good: *to have a splendid time.* **–splendidly,** *adv.* **–splendidness,** *n.*

splendour /ˈsplɛndə/ *n.* **1.** brilliant or gorgeous appearance, colouring, etc.; magnificence, grandeur, or pomp, or display of it: *the splendour and pomp of his coronation.* **2.** brilliant distinction; glory: *the splendour of ancient Roman architecture.* **3.** great brightness; brilliant light or lustre. Also, **splendor.** **–splendorous,** *adj.*

splice /splaɪs/ *v.t.* **(spliced, splicing) 1.** to join together or unite, such as two ropes or parts of a rope, by the interweaving of strands. **2.** to join or unite, usually two pieces of timber, etc., by overlapping. *–n.* **3.** a joining of two ropes or parts of a rope by splicing. **4.** the union so effected. **5.** a joining or meeting of two pieces of timber, etc., by overlapping and fastening the ends. **–splicer,** *n.*

splint /splɪnt/ *n.* **1.** a thin piece of wood or other rigid material used to immobilise a fractured or dislocated bone, or to maintain any part of the body in a fixed position. **2.** one of a number of thin strips of wood woven together to make a chair seat, basket, etc. *–v.t.* **3.** to secure, hold in position, or support by means of a splint or splints, as a fractured bone. **4.** to support as if with splints.

splinter /ˈsplɪntə/ *n.* **1.** a rough piece of wood, bone, etc., usually fairly long, thin, and sharp, split or broken off from a main body. **2.** fragment or small piece of metal resulting from the explosion of a bomb or shell. *–v.t.*

3. to split or break into splinters. **4.** to break off in splinters. *–v.i.* **5.** to be split or broken into splinters. **6.** to break off in splinters. **–splintery,** *adj.*

split /splɪt/ *verb* **(split, splitting)** *–v.t.* **1.** to rend or cleave lengthwise; separate or part from end to end or between layers, often forcibly or by cutting, as when splitting a log with an axe to make rails, slabs, shingles, etc. **2.** to separate off by rending or cleaving lengthwise: *to split a piece from a block.* **3.** to tear or break asunder; rend or burst. **4.** to divide into distinct parts or portions. **5.** to separate (a part) by such division. **6.** to divide (persons) into different groups, factions, parties, etc., as by discord. **7.** to share between two or more persons, etc.: *to split a bottle of wine.* **8.** to separate into parts by interposing something: *to split an infinitive.* **9.** *Chem.* to divide (molecules or atoms) by cleavage into smaller parts. **10.** to make (a vote) less effective by offering more than one candidate with a similar policy: *Liberal intervention in the National Party seat split the anti-Labor vote and won Labor the seat. –v.i.* **11.** to break or part lengthways, or suffer longitudinal division. **12.** to part, divide, or separate in any way. **13.** to break asunder; part by striking on a rock, by the violence of a storm, etc., as a ship. **14.** to become separated off by such a division as a piece or part from a whole. **15.** (of stock animals) to break away from the main group. **16.** to break up or separate through disagreement, etc. **17.** *Colloq.* to commit a betrayal by divulging information. **18.** *Colloq.* to leave hurriedly. *–n.* **19.** the act of splitting. **20.** a crack, rent, or fissure caused by splitting. **21.** a breach or rupture in a party, etc., or between persons. **22.** *Colloq.* something combining different elements, as a drink composed of half spirits, half soda water. **23.** *Colloq.* a dish made from sliced fruit (usually banana) and ice-cream, and covered with syrup and nuts. **24.** *(usu. pl.)* the feat of separating the legs while sinking to the floor, until they extend at right angles to the body, as in stage performances, as in ballet, gymnastics, etc. **25.** *Tenpin Bowling* the arrangement of the remaining pins after the first bowl so that a spare is practically impossible. **26.** *Colloq.* an act or arrangement of splitting, as of a sum of money. *–adj.* **27.** that has undergone splitting; parted lengthwise; cleft. **28.** divided. *–phr.* **29. split on,** *Colloq.* to betray, denounce, or divulge secrets concerning. **30. split one's sides,** to laugh heartily. **31. split the difference,** to reach a compromise by which each side concedes an equal amount. **32. split up,** *Colloq.* to part; leave each other; become separated. **–splitter,** *n.*

split infinitive *n. Gram.* a simple infinitive with a word between the *to* and the verb, as *to readily understand.*

split-level *adj.* **1.** of or relating to a building having certain floors at other than main storey level, or a room with a floor at more than one level. *–n.* **2.** a house, etc., built like this.

split personality *n.* **1.** (in popular use) → **schizophrenia. 2.** (in popular use) → **multiple personality disorder. 3.** *Colloq.* an unpredictable or extremely changeable personality.

splotch /splɒtʃ/ *n.* **1.** a large, irregular spot; blot; stain. *–v.t.* **2.** to mark with splotches. Also, **splodge** /splɒdʒ/. **–splotchy,** *adj.*

splurge /splɜːdʒ/ *Colloq. –n.* **1.** an ostentatious display, especially of wealth. *–verb* **(splurged, splurging)** *–v.t.* **2.** to spend (money) extravagantly. *–v.i.* **3.** to be extravagant: *we splurged and bought champagne.*

splutter /ˈsplʌtə/ *v.i.* **1.** to talk hastily, confusedly or unintelligently, especially in excitement or embarrassment. **2.** to give out particles of something explosively, as something frying or a pen scattering ink: *the fat was spluttering in the pan.* **3.** to fly or fall in particles or drops; spatter, as a liquid. *–n.* **4.** spluttering speech or talk; dispute; noise or fuss. **5.** the sputtering or spattering of liquid, etc. –**splutterer,** *n.*

spoil /spɔɪl/ *verb* (**spoiled** *or* **spoilt, spoiling**) –*v.t.* **1.** to damage or impair (a thing) irreparably as to excellence, value, usefulness, etc.: *to spoil a sheet of paper.* **2.** to impair in character or disposition by unwise treatment, benefits, etc., especially by excessive indulgence. **3.** *Aust. Rules* to prevent (an opponent) from marking by punching the ball away. –*v.i.* **4.** to become spoiled, bad, or unfit for use, as food or other perishable substances; become tainted or putrid. –*n.* **5.** (*oft. pl.*) booty, loot, or plunder taken in war or robbery. **6.** (*usu. pl.*) emoluments and advantages associated with a powerful or prestigious position: *the spoils of office.* **7.** treasures won or accumulated. **8.** waste materials, as those cast up in mining, excavating, quarrying, etc. **9.** *Aust. Rules* an act of spoiling: *a good spoil.* –*phr.* **10. be spoiling for,** to be eager for (a fight, action, etc.)

spoilsport /'spɔɪlspɔt/ *n.* someone who interferes with the pleasure of others.

spoilt /spɔɪlt/ *v.* **1.** a past tense and past participle of **spoil**. –*adj.* **2.** selfish; used to getting one's own way because of being overindulged. Also, **spoiled**.

spoke[1] /spoʊk/ *v.* past tense of **speak**.

spoke[2] /spoʊk/ *n.* **1.** one of the bars, rods, or rungs radiating from the hub or nave of a wheel and supporting the rim. **2.** one of a number of pins or handles projecting from a cylinder or wheel, or joining hub and rim, especially on a steering wheel. –*phr.* **3. put a spoke in someone's wheel(s),** to interfere with someone's plans.

spoken /'spoʊkən/ *v.* **1.** past participle of **speak**. –*adj.* **2.** uttered or expressed by speaking; oral. **3.** (*in compounds*) speaking, or using speech, as specified: *fair-spoken, plain-spoken.*

spokesmodel /'spoʊksmɒdəl/ *n.* a person, usually famous, who brings recognition to a product by their association with it.

spokesperson /'spoʊkspɜsən/ *n.* (*pl.* -**persons** *or* -**people**) **1.** someone who speaks for another or others. **2.** the principal advocate or practitioner (of a movement, organisation, etc.), considered as speaking on its behalf. **3.** a public speaker. –**spokesman,** *n.* –**spokeswoman,** *n.*

spondee /'spɒndi/ *n. Prosody* a metrical foot consisting of two long syllables or two heavy beats.

sponge /spʌndʒ/ *n.* **1.** any of a group of aquatic (mostly marine) animals (phylum Porifera) which are characterised by a porous structure and (usually) a horny, siliceous, or calcareous skeleton or framework, and which, except in the larval state, are fixed, occurring in large, complex, often plant-like colonies. **2.** the light, yielding, porous, fibrous skeleton or framework of certain animals, or colonies of this group, from which the living matter has been removed, characterised by readily absorbing water, and becoming soft when wet while retaining toughness, used (especially formerly) in bathing, in wiping or cleaning surfaces, etc. **3.** any of various other spongelike substances. **4.** someone or something that absorbs something freely, as a sponge does water. **5.** someone who persistently lives at the expense of others; a parasite. **6.** *Cookery* **a.** dough raised with yeast, especially before kneading, as for bread. **b.** a light sweet pudding of spongy texture, made with gelatine, eggs, fruit juice or other flavouring material, etc. **c.** sponge cake. –*verb* (**sponged, sponging**) –*v.t.* **7.** to wipe or rub with a wet sponge, as in order to clean or moisten. **8.** *Colloq.* to get from another or at another's expense by indirect exactions, trading on generosity, etc.: *to sponge a dinner.* –*v.i.* **9.** to take in liquid by absorption. **10.** to gather sponges. **11.** *Colloq.* to live at the expense of others. –*phr.* **12. sponge off**

(or **away**), to remove with a wet sponge. **13. sponge on** (or **off**), *Colloq.* to live as a parasite of. **14. sponge out,** to wipe out or efface with or as with a sponge. **15. sponge up,** to take up or absorb with a sponge or the like: *to sponge up water.* **16. throw** (or **toss**) **in the sponge,** to admit defeat; give up. –**spongelike,** *adj.* –**spongy,** *adj.* –**sponger,** *n.*

sponsor /'spɒnsə/ *n.* **1.** someone who is responsible for a person or thing. **2.** someone who makes an engagement or promise on behalf of another; a surety. **3.** someone who answers for an infant at baptism, making the required professions and promises; a godfather or godmother. **4.** a person or organisation which **a.** finances a radio or television program in return for advertisement of a commercial product, service, etc. **b.** finances an entertainment or sporting event in return for advertising and marketing rights. **5.** *Parliamentary Procedure* a member of a legislative assembly responsible for the introduction of a particular bill (usually with reference only to private bills). –*v.t.* **6.** to act as sponsor for; promise, vouch, or answer for. –**sponsorial** /spɒn-'sɔriəl/, *adj.* –**sponsorship,** *n.*

spontaneous /spɒn'teɪniəs/ *adj.* **1.** proceeding from a natural personal impulse, without effort or premeditation; natural and unconstrained: *a spontaneous action; a spontaneous remark.* **2.** (of impulses, motion, activity, natural processes, etc.) arising from internal forces or causes, or independent of external agencies. **3.** growing naturally or without cultivation, as plants, fruits, etc. **4.** produced by natural process. –**spontaneously,** *adv.* –**spontaneity** /spɒntə'niəti, -'neɪəti/, **spontaneousness,** *n.*

spoof /spuf/ *Colloq.* –*n.* **1.** a humorous imitation of a serious piece of writing, performance, etc.; parody. –*v.t.* **2.** to imitate (a piece of writing, a style, a person, etc.) in a ridiculing manner; parody. –*adj.* **3.** being a parodying imitation. –**spoofer,** *n.*

spook /spuk/ *Colloq.* –*n.* **1.** a ghost; a spectre. **2.** an agent of an intelligence organisation; a spy. –*v.t.* **3.** to frighten.

spooked /spukt/ *adj.* frightened; on edge; nervous: *a horse spooked by moving shadows.*

spooky /'spuki/ *adj.* (-**kier, -kiest**) *Colloq.* like or suggestive of a spook or ghost; eerie. –**spookily,** *adv.* –**spookiness,** *n.*

spool /spul/ *n.* **1.** any cylindrical piece or appliance on which something is wound. **2.** such a device for holding film, magnetic tape, or the like, which is stopped from slipping off by a disc on each side. **3.** a small cylindrical piece of wood or other material on which yarn is wound in spinning, for use in weaving; bobbin. **4.** → **reel**[1] (def. 3). –*v.t.* **5.** to wind on a spool.

spoon /spun/ *n.* **1.** a utensil consisting of a bowl or concave part and a handle, for taking up or stirring liquid or other food, or other matter. **2.** any of various implements, objects, or parts resembling or suggesting this. –*v.t.* **3.** to take up or transfer in or as in a spoon. **4.** *Sport* **a.** to push or shove (the ball) with a lifting motion instead of striking it soundly, as in croquet or golf. **b.** to hit (the ball) up in the air as in cricket. –*v.i.* **5.** *Sport* to spoon the ball. **6.** *Colloq.* to show affection, especially in an openly sentimental manner. –*phr.* **7. be born with a silver spoon in one's mouth,** to inherit social or financial advantages and privileges. –**spooning,** *n.*

spoonbill /'spunbɪl/ *n.* any of several wading birds closely related to the ibis and having a long, flat bill with a spoon-like tip.

spoonerism /'spunərɪzəm/ *n.* a slip of the tongue whereby initial or other sounds of words are transposed, as in 'our queer old dean' for 'our dear old queen'.

spoor /spɔ/ *n.* **1.** a track or trail, especially that of a wild animal pursued as game. –*v.t.* **2.** to track by a spoor. –*v.i.* **3.** to follow a spoor. –**spoorer**, *n.*

sporadic /spə'rædɪk/ *adj.* **1.** appearing or happening at intervals in time; occasional: *only sporadic interest in the new website.* **2.** appearing in scattered or isolated instances, as a disease: *sporadic outbreaks.* **3.** occurring singly, or widely apart, in locality: *sporadic genera of plants.* Also, **sporadical.** –**sporadically**, *adv.* –**sporadicalness**, *n.*

spore /spɔ/ *n.* **1.** *Biol.* a walled body that contains or produces one or more uninucleate organisms that develop into an adult individual, especially: **a.** a reproductive body (**asexual spore**) produced asexually and capable of growth into a new individual, such individual often, as in ferns, etc., being one (a gametophyte) unlike that which produced the spore. **b.** a walled reproductive body (**sexual spore**) produced sexually (by the union of two gametes). **2.** a germ, germ cell, seed, or the like. –*v.i.* **3.** to bear or produce spores.

sporo- a word element meaning 'seed'. Also, **spor-.**

sporran /'spɒrən/ *n.* (in Scottish Highland costume) a large pouch, commonly of fur, worn hanging from the belt over the front of the kilt.

sport /spɔt/ *n.* **1.** an activity pursued for exercise or pleasure, usually requiring some degree of physical prowess, as racing, baseball, tennis, golf, bowling, wrestling, boxing, etc. **2.** a particular form of such activity. **3.** (*pl.*) a meeting for athletic competition. **4.** the pastime of hunting, shooting, or fishing with reference to the pleasure achieved: *we had good sport today.* **5.** diversion; recreation; pleasant pastime. **6.** playful trifling, jesting, or mirth: *to do or say a thing in sport.* **7.** derisive jesting; ridicule. **8.** an object of derision; a laughing-stock. **9.** something sported with or tossed about like a plaything: *to be the sport of circumstances.* **10.** *Aust., NZ Colloq.* a term of address, usually between males: *g'day, sport.* **11.** *Colloq.* someone who is interested in pursuits involving betting or gambling. **12.** *Biol.* an animal or a plant, or a part of a plant, that shows an unusual or singular deviation from the normal or parent type; a mutation. –*v.i.* **13.** to amuse oneself with some pleasant pastime or recreation. **14.** to play, frolic, or gambol, as a child or an animal. **15.** to deal lightly; trifle. –*v.t.* **16.** to have or wear, especially ostentatiously, proudly, etc. **17.** *Colloq.* to display freely or with ostentation: *to sport a roll of money.* –*phr.* **18. a bad sport**, **a.** a person who exhibits despised qualities in playing sport, such as cheating or the inability to lose graciously, etc. **b.** a person who is ill-natured and irritable. **19. a good sport**, **a.** a person who exhibits esteemed qualities in playing sport, such as fairness or the ability to lose graciously, etc. **b.** a person who is good-natured and easygoing. **20. be a sport**, **a.** to play fair. **b.** to accede to a request; be agreeable. –**sporter**, *n.* –**sportful**, *adj.* –**sportfully**, *adv.* –**sportfulness**, *n.*

sporting /'spɔtɪŋ/ *adj.* **1.** taking part in, given to, or interested in sport. **2.** concerned with or suitable for such sport: *a sporting glove.* **3.** exhibiting qualities especially esteemed in those who engage in sports, such as fairness, good humour when losing, etc. **4.** willing to take a chance: *a sporting fellow.* **5.** even or fair: *a sporting chance.* –**sportingly**, *adv.*

sportive /'spɔtɪv/ *adj.* **1.** playful or frolicsome; jesting, jocose, or merry. **2.** done in sport, rather than in earnest. **3.** relating to or of the nature of sport or sports. **4.** *Biol.* mutative. –**sportively**, *adv.* –**sportiveness**, *n.*

sports /spɔts/ *adj.* **1.** of, relating to, or used in conjunction with a sport or sports: *the sports department*; *sports headphones*; *sports cream.* **2.** concerned with sport: *the sports editor of a newspaper.* **3.** (of garments, etc.) suitable for use in open-air sports, or for outdoor or informal use.

sports car *n.* a high-powered car, usually a two-seater with a low body, built for speed and manoeuvrability.

sportsman /'spɔtsmən/ *n.* (*pl.* **-men**) **1.** a man who engages in sport, usually with a degree of expertise. **2.** someone who exhibits sporting (def. 3) qualities. –**sportsmanlike**, **sportsmanly**, *adj.* –**sportsmanship**, *n.*

sportsperson /'spɔtspɜsən/ *n.* (*pl.* **-people**) a person who engages in sport, usually with a degree of expertise.

sportswoman /'spɔtswʊmən/ *n.* (*pl.* **-women**) a woman who engages in sport, usually with a degree of expertise.

sporty /'spɔti/ *adj.* (**sportier, sportiest**) *Colloq.* **1.** flashy; vulgarly showy. **2.** stylish. **3.** like or befitting a sportsman. –**sportiness**, *n.*

spot /spɒt/ *n.* **1.** a mark made by foreign matter, as mud, blood, paint, ink, etc.; a stain, blot, or speck, as on a surface. **2.** a blemish of the skin, as a pimple. **3.** a relatively small, usually roundish, part of a surface differing from the rest in appearance or character. **4.** a place or locality: *a monument marks the spot.* **5.** a position or period of time in a program of entertainment assigned to a particular performer. **6.** a short period of advertising time on radio or television: *they booked ten twenty-second spots per week.* **7.** a spotlight. **8.** *Soccer* **a.** the centre spot. **b.** a penalty spot. **9.** *Colloq.* a small quantity of something: *a spot of tea.* **10.** *Colloq.* an alcoholic drink: *he stopped at the pub for a spot.* **11.** *Colloq.* a predicament: *he was in a bit of a spot when the crash came.* **12.** *US* an object bearing a specified device or numeral: *he gave the waiter a five-spot.* –*verb* (**spotted, spotting**) –*v.t.* **13.** to stain with spots. **14.** to sully; blemish. **15.** to mark or diversify with spots, as of colour. **16.** to see or perceive, especially suddenly, by chance, or when it is difficult to do so. **17.** *Colloq.* to detect or recognise. –*v.i.* **18.** to make a spot; cause a stain. **19.** to become or tend to become spotted, as some fabrics when spattered with water. **20.** (of fires, especially bushfires) to occur in small isolated sections ahead of the main fire as a result of flying sparks, debris, etc.: *fires were spotting 100 metres ahead of us.* –*adj.* **21.** *Commerce* made, paid, delivered, etc., at once: *a spot sale.* –*phr.* **22. change one's spots**, to alter one's fundamental character. **23. hit the spot**, *Colloq.* to fulfil a need; satisfy. **24. knock (the) spots off**, *Colloq.* **a.** to defeat; get the better of. **b.** to be vastly superior to. **25. on the spot**, **a.** instantly. **b.** at the place in question. **c.** without change of location. **d.** obliged to deal with a situation. **e.** in trouble, embarrassment, or danger. **26. soft spot**, a special sympathy or affection: *she has a soft spot for small animals.* **27. tight spot**, a serious predicament. **28. weak spot**, an aspect of a person's character which is liable to criticism or opposition. –**spotted**, *adj.* –**spotty**, *adj.*

spot check *n.* **1.** an inspection made without warning, as of motor vehicles, etc. **2.** a check made on a random sample, as of manufactured articles.

spotlight /'spɒtlaɪt/ *n.* **1.** *Theatre* a strong light with a narrow beam thrown upon a particular spot on the stage in order to render some object, person, or group especially conspicuous. **2.** the lamp producing such light. **3.** a similar lamp attached to a car, usually not able to be swivelled. **4.** conspicuous public attention. –*v.t.* (**-lighted** *or* **-lit, -lighting**) **5.** to direct a spotlight at. **6.** to focus attention on. –*phr.* **7. in the spotlight**, receiving a great deal of attention, as from the group one is with, the public in general, or the media.

spot-on *Colloq.* –*adj.* **1.** absolutely right or accurate; excellent. –*interj.* **2.** an exclamation of approbation, etc.

spot price *n.* (in commodities trading) the price agreed on for immediate delivery of the commodity.

spotted gum *n.* a tall tree with a spotted smooth bark, *Corymbia maculata*, which forms forests in coastal districts of eastern Australia.

spotting scope *n.* a portable telescope designed to be used by birdwatchers, spectators at sporting events, etc.

spouse /spaʊs, spaʊz/ *n.* either member of a married pair in relation to the other; one's husband or wife.

spout /spaʊt/ *v.t.* **1.** to discharge or emit (a liquid, etc.) in a stream with some force. **2.** *Colloq.* to utter or declaim in an oratorical manner. *−v.i.* **3.** to discharge a liquid, etc., in a jet or continuous stream. **4.** to issue with force, as liquid through a narrow orifice. **5.** *Colloq.* to talk or speak at some length or in an oratorical manner. *−n.* **6.** a pipe or tube, or a tubular or lip-like projection, by which a liquid is discharged or poured. **7.** a trough or chute for discharging or conveying grain, flour, etc. *−phr.* **8. up the spout**, *Colloq.* **a.** ruined; lost. **b.** pawned. **−spouter,** *n.* **−spoutless,** *adj.*

sprain /spreɪn/ *v.t.* **1.** to overstrain or wrench (the ankle, wrist, or other part of the body at a joint) so as to injure without fracture or dislocation. *−n.* **2.** a violent straining or wrenching of the parts around a joint, without dislocation. **3.** the condition of being sprained.

sprang /spræŋ/ *v.* past tense of **spring**.

sprat /spræt/ *n.* **1.** a small, herring-like marine fish, *Clupea sprattus*, of European waters. *−phr.* **2. a sprat to catch a mackerel**, something given in expectation of a larger return.

sprawl /sprɔl/ *v.i.* **1.** to be stretched out in ungraceful movements, as the limbs. **2.** to lie or sit with the limbs stretched out in a careless or ungraceful way. **3.** to fall in such a manner. **4.** to spread out in an untidy or irregular manner, as buildings, handwriting, etc. *−v.t.* **5.** to stretch out (the limbs) as in sprawling. *−n.* **6.** the act of sprawling. **7.** a scattered or irregular grouping of something. **−sprawler,** *n.* **−sprawly,** *adj.*

spray[1] /spreɪ/ *n.* **1.** water or other liquid broken up into small particles and blown or falling through the air: *the sea spray.* **2.** a jet or fine particles of liquid coming from an atomiser or other appliance. **3.** an appliance for sending out such a jet. **4.** a quantity of small objects, flying through the air: *a spray of bullets. −v.t.* **5.** to scatter in the form of fine particles. **6.** to apply as a spray: *to spray perfume on the wrist.* **7.** to direct a spray of particles, bullets, etc., upon. *−v.i.* **8.** to scatter spray. **9.** to come forth as spray. **−sprayer,** *n.*

spray[2] /spreɪ/ *n.* **1.** a single slender shoot, twig, or branch with its leaves, flowers, or berries, growing or detached. **2.** an ornament, decorative figure, etc., with a similar form. **3.** a single flower or small bouquet of flowers designed to be pinned to one's clothes as an adornment.

spray can *n.* a small metal container for storing under pressure, and subsequently dispensing as a spray, such products as insecticides, waxes, lacquers, etc.; aerosol can. Also, **spraycan.**

spread /sprɛd/ *verb* (**spread, spreading**) *−v.t.* **1.** Also, **spread out**, to draw or stretch out to the full width, as a cloth, a rolled or folded map, folded wings, etc. **2.** Also, **spread out**, to extend over a greater or a relatively great area, space, or period: *to spread out handwriting.* **3.** to force apart, as walls, rails, etc., under pressure. **4.** to flatten out: *to spread the end of a rivet by hammering.* **5.** to display the full extent of; set forth in full. **6.** to dispose or distribute in a sheet or layer: *to spread hay to dry.* **7.** to apply in a thin layer or coating. **8.** to extend or distribute over a region, place, etc. **9.** to set or prepare (a table, etc.), as for a meal. **10.** to send out in various directions, as light, sound, mist, etc. **11.** to shed or scatter abroad; diffuse or disseminate, as knowledge,

news, disease, etc. **12.** *Phonetics* to form a long, narrow opening between (the lips), as for the vowel /i/ in *me.* **13.** *Colloq.* to exert (oneself) to an unusual extent to produce a good effect or fine impression. *−v.i.* **14.** to become stretched out or extended, as a flag in the wind; expand, as in growth. **15.** to extend over a greater or a considerable area or period. **16.** to be or lie outspread or fully extended or displayed, as a landscape or scene. **17.** to be capable of being spread or applied in a thin layer, as a soft substance. **18.** to become extended or distributed over a region, as population, animals, plants, etc. **19.** to become diffused abroad, or disseminated, as light, influences, rumours, ideas, infection, etc. **20.** to be forced apart, as rails; go out of gauge. *−n.* **21.** expansion; extension; diffusion. **22.** the extent of spreading: *to measure the spread of branches.* **23.** the distribution of cards in a hand. **24.** capacity for spreading: *the spread of an elastic material.* **25.** widening of girth: *middle-age spread.* **26.** a stretch, expanse, or extent of something. **27.** *Chiefly US* a property; station; ranch. **28.** a cloth covering for a bed, table, or the like, especially a bedspread. **29.** any food preparation for spreading on bread, etc., as jam or peanut butter. **30.** *Colloq.* a meal set out, especially a feast. **31.** *Colloq.* a pretentious display made. **32.** *Aeronautics* the wingspan. **33.** *Stock Exchange* **a.** the difference between the highest and the lowest prices at which business has been done during one day. **b.** the difference between the prices quoted by a stockjobber for buying and selling. **c.** any difference between buying and selling rates. **34.** a pair of facing pages of a book, magazine, or the like, or any part of them. **35.** *Journalism* a balance in the coverage of a newspaper, in relation to news, entertainment, sports, pictures, etc. *−adj.* **36.** extended, especially fully. **37.** *Phonetics* (of the lips) forming a long, narrow opening, as for the vowel /i/ in *me. −phr.* **38. a good spread,** *Colloq.* a lot of publicity, especially in the various channels of the media. **39. be spread thin,** to be made available as a resource over a large area so as to be barely sufficient in each circumstance.

spread-eagle *adj.* **1.** having or suggesting the form of a spread eagle. *−v.t.* **2.** to stretch out in the manner of a spread eagle. **3.** *Colloq.* to knock (a person) out. *−v.i.* **4.** *Colloq.* to form a shape or take a position resembling a spread eagle. Also, **spreadeagle.**

spreadsheet /'sprɛdʃit/ *Computers −n.* **1.** a software product for organising large amounts of numerical data in tabular formats, allowing rapid calculations with changing variables. **2.** a table produced by such a software product. *−adj.* **3.** of or relating to a spreadsheet.

spree /spri/ *n.* **1.** *Obs.* a lively frolic. **2.** a bout or spell of drinking to intoxication. **3.** a session or period of excessive indulgence: *a spending spree.*

sprig /sprɪg/ *n.* **1.** a shoot, twig, or small branch: *sprig of holly.* **2.** an ornament having this form. **3.** (*humorous*) a person, especially young, as a descendant or offshoot of a family. **4.** → **spike**[1] (def. 3a). **5.** a stud on the sole of a boot, running shoe, etc., which gives the wearer greater purchase on the ground; cleat; stud. *−v.t.* (**sprigged, sprigging**) **6.** to decorate (cloth, pottery, etc.) with a design of sprigs. **−spriggy,** *adj.*

sprightly /'spraɪtli/ *adj.* (**-lier, -liest**) animated or vivacious; lively. **−sprightliness,** *n.*

spring /sprɪŋ/ *verb* (**sprang** *or* **sprung, sprung, springing**) *−v.i.* **1.** to rise or move suddenly and lightly as by some inherent power: *to spring into the air; a tiger about to spring.* **2.** to go or come suddenly as if with a leap: *blood springs to the face.* **3.** to fly back or away in escaping from a forced position, as by resilient or elastic force or from the action of a spring: *a trap springs.* **4.** to start or work out of place, as parts of a mechanism, structure, etc. **5.** Also, **spring forth, spring**

out, **spring up**. to issue suddenly, as water, blood, sparks, fire, etc. **6.** to arise by growth, as from a seed or germ, bulb, root, etc.; grow, as plants. **7.** to proceed or originate, as from a source or cause. **8.** to have one's birth, or be descended, as from a family, person, stock, etc. **9.** to rise or extend upwards, as a spire. **10.** to take an upward course or curve from a point of support, as an arch. **11.** to start or rise from cover, as partridges, pheasants, etc. **12.** to become bent or warped, as boards. **13.** to explode, as a mine. *–v.t.* **14.** to cause to spring. **15.** to cause to fly back, move, or act by elastic force, a spring, etc.: *to spring a lock.* **16.** to cause to start out of place or work loose. **17. a.** to undergo the splitting or cracking of: *the ship sprang a mast.* **b.** to cause or bring about the splitting or cracking of: *the last blow sprang the axe-handle.* **18.** to come to have by cracking, etc.: *to spring a leak.* **19.** to bend by force, or force (*in*) by bending, as a slat or bar. **20.** to explode (a mine). **21.** to bring out, disclose, produce, make, etc., suddenly: *to spring a surprise.* **22.** to equip or fit with springs. **23.** to leap over. **24.** to make a surprise attack on (someone). **25.** *Colloq.* to come upon (someone) unexpectedly doing something wrong; catch out. **26.** *Colloq.* to cause or enable (someone) to escape from prison. **27.** to obtain the release of a prisoner on bail. *–n.* **28.** a leap, jump, or bound. **29.** a springing or starting from place. **30.** a flying back from a forced position. **31.** an elastic or springy movement. **32.** elasticity or springiness. **33.** a split or crack, as in a mast; a bend or warp, as in a board. **34.** an issue of water from the earth, flowing away as a small stream or standing as a pool or small lake, or the place of such an issue: *mineral springs.* **35.** a source of something; a beginning or cause of origin. **36.** the rise of an arch, or the point or line at which an arch springs from its support. **37.** the season of the year between winter and summer. **38.** the first and freshest period: *the spring of life.* **39.** an elastic contrivance or body, as a strip or wire of steel coiled spirally, which recovers its shape after being compressed, bent, etc. **40.** any device or contrivance designed to impart resilience or elasticity. **41.** (of pork) the belly. *–adj.* **42.** of, relating to, characteristic of, or suitable for the season of spring: *spring flowers.* **43.** sown in the spring, as a cereal forming a second crop. **44.** young: *spring chicken.* **45.** resting on or containing springs: *a spring bed; spring mattress. –phr.* **46. spring up,** to come into being; rise or arise: *new industries springing up.* **–springy,** *adj.* **–springless,** *adj.*

springboard /'sprɪŋbɔd/ *n.* **1.** a semiflexible board projecting over water from which persons dive. **2.** a flexible board used as a take-off in vaulting, tumbling, etc., to increase the height of leaps. **3.** anything serving to assist departure, initiation of a project, or the like. **4.** the short plank on which the person wielding the axe stands when chopping a tree at a point above shoulder height; jiggerboard.

springbok /'sprɪŋbɒk/ *n.* (*pl.* **-boks** *or, especially collectively,* **-bok**) a gazelle, *Antidorcas marsupialis,* of southern Africa which has a habit of springing upwards in play or when alarmed. Also, **springbuck** /'sprɪŋbʌk/.

spring tide *n.* **1.** the large rise and fall of the tide at or soon after the new or the full moon. **2.** any great flood or swelling rush. Also, **king tide**.

sprinkle /'sprɪŋkəl/ *v.t.* **1.** to scatter, as a liquid or a powder, in drops or particles. **2.** to give or place here and there: *his speech was sprinkled with jokes. –v.i.* **3.** to scatter a liquid, powder, etc., in drops or particles. **4.** to be sprinkled. **5.** to rain slightly. *–n.* **6.** an act or result of sprinkling. **7.** light rain. **–sprinkler,** *n.* **–sprinkling,** *n.*

sprint /sprɪnt/ *v.i.* **1.** to race at full speed, especially for a short distance, as in running, rowing, etc. *–v.t.* **2.** to

cover by sprinting: *to sprint a hundred metres. –n.* **3.** a short race at full speed. **4.** a spell of running at full speed, as to the finish of a long race. **5.** a brief spell of great activity. **–sprinter,** *n.*

sprite /spraɪt/ *n.* **1.** an elf, fairy, or goblin. **2.** an icon which moves around a screen in computer graphics.

spritzer /'sprɪtsə/ *n.* a drink consisting of white wine topped up with soda water.

spritzig /'sprɪtsɪg/ *adj.* (of wine) showing a slight degree of gassiness or prickle caused by secondary fermentation in the bottle.

sprocket /'sprɒkət/ *n.* **1.** *Machinery* one of a set of projections on the rim of a wheel which engage the links of a chain. **2.** *Building Trades* a wedge-shaped piece fitted to the bottom of a rafter to flatten the slope at the eaves.

sprout /spraʊt/ *v.i.* **1.** to begin to grow, especially quickly. **2.** (of a seed, plant, the earth, etc.) to put forth buds or shoots. *–v.t.* **3.** to cause to sprout. *–n.* **4.** the shoot of a plant. **5.** new growth from a germinating seed, or from a tuber, bud, etc., often used in salads. **6.** Also, **brussels sprout.** a vegetable with small edible heads or sprouts which look like miniature cabbage heads.

spruce¹ /sprus/ *n.* **1.** any member of the coniferous genus *Picea,* consisting of evergreen trees with short angular needle-shaped leaves attached singly around twigs, as *P. abies* (**Norway spruce**), *P. glauca* (**white spruce** or **Canadian spruce**), and *P. mariana* (**black spruce**). **2.** any of various allied trees, as the Douglas fir and the hemlock spruce. **3.** the wood of any such tree. *–adj.* **4.** made of or containing such trees or such wood.

spruce² /sprus/ *adj.* (**sprucer**, **sprucest**) **1.** smart in dress or appearance; trim; neat; dapper. *–phr.* **2. spruce up**, **a.** to make spruce or smart. **b.** to make oneself spruce. **–sprucely,** *adv.* **–spruceness,** *n.*

spruik /spruːk/ *v.i. Aust. Colloq.* **1.** to harangue or address a meeting. **2.** to harangue prospective customers to entice them into a show, strip joint, etc. **–spruiker,** *n.*

sprung /sprʌŋ/ *v.* a past tense and past participle of **spring**.

spry /spraɪ/ *adj.* (**spryer** *or* **sprier**, **spryest** *or* **spriest**) active; nimble; brisk. **–spryly,** *adv.* **–spryness,** *n.*

spud /spʌd/ *n.* **1.** a spade-like instrument, used for digging up or cutting the roots of weeds. **2.** *Colloq.* a potato.

spume /spjum/ *n.* **1.** foam; froth; scum. *–v.i.* **2.** to foam; froth. *–v.t.* **3.** to send forth as or like foam or froth. **–spumous, spumy,** *adj.*

spun /spʌn/ *v.* **1.** past tense and past participle of **spin**. *–adj.* **2.** formed by or as by spinning: *spun rayon, spun silk.*

spun glass *n.* → **fibreglass**.

spunk /spʌŋk/ *n. Colloq.* **1.** pluck; spirit; mettle. **2.** (*taboo*) semen. **3.** *Aust.* a good-looking person.

spunky /'spʌŋki/ *adj.* (**-kier, -kiest**) *Colloq.* **1.** plucky; spirited. **2.** *Aust.* good-looking; attractive. **–spunkily,** *adv.* **–spunkiness,** *n.*

spur /spɜ/ *n.* **1.** a pointed device attached to a rider's boot heel, for goading a horse onwards, etc. **2.** anything that goads, impels, or urges to action or speed. **3.** something projecting, and resembling or suggesting a spur. **4.** a sharp piercing or cutting instrument fastened on the leg of a gamecock, for use in fighting. **5.** a stiff, usually sharp, horny process on the leg of various birds, especially the domestic cock. **6.** *Physical Geog.* a ridge or line of elevation projecting from or subordinate to the main body of a mountain or mountain range. **7.** a structure built to protect a river bank from a fast current; a river groyne. **8.** *Archit.* **a.** a short wooden brace, usually temporary, for strengthening a post or some other part. **b.** any offset from a wall, etc., as a buttress. **9.** *Railways* a siding. *–verb* (**spurred, spurring**) *–v.t.*

10. Also, **spur on.** to prick with, or as with, spurs or a spur, as in order to urge on. **11.** to furnish with spurs or a spur. –*v.i.* **12.** to prick one's horse with the spur; ride quickly. **13.** to proceed hurriedly; press forward. –*phr.* **14. on the spur of the moment,** suddenly; without premeditation. **15. win one's spurs,** to achieve one's first distinction or success. –**spurrer,** *n.*

spurge laurel /spɜdʒ ˈlɒrəl/ *n.* an evergreen shrub, *Daphne laureola,* of southern and western Europe and western Asia, with fragrant green axillary flowers.

spurious /ˈspjuriəs/ *adj.* **1.** not genuine or true; counterfeit; not from the reputed, pretended, or right source; not authentic. **2.** *Bot.* bearing superficial resemblances but having morphological differences. –**spuriously,** *adv.* –**spuriousness,** *n.*

spurn /spɜn/ *v.t.* to reject with disdain; treat with contempt; scorn; despise. –**spurner,** *n.*

spurt /spɜt/ *v.i.* **1.** to rush suddenly in a stream, as a liquid. **2.** to show marked energy or activity for a short period. –*v.t.* **3.** to throw out suddenly in a stream, as a liquid. –*n.* **4.** a forcible rush of water, etc.: *a spurt of water from the tap.* **5.** a sudden outburst, as of feeling: *a spurt of words.* **6.** a sudden, short increase of effort as in running, rowing, etc.

sputter /ˈspʌtə/ *v.i.* **1.** to give off particles of anything in an explosive manner, as a candle does in burning. **2.** to spit particles of saliva, food, etc., from the mouth in a similar manner. **3.** to utter words or sounds in an explosive, meaningless manner. –*n.* **4.** the act, process, or sound of sputtering. **5.** explosive, meaningless sound. –**sputterer,** *n.*

sputum /ˈspjutəm/ *n.* (*pl.* **-ta** /-tə/) **1.** spittle mixed with mucus, purulent matter, or the like. **2.** that which is expectorated; spittle.

spy /spaɪ/ *n.* (*pl.* **spies**) **1.** someone who keeps secret watch on the actions of others. **2.** someone employed by a government to obtain secret information or intelligence, especially with reference to military or naval affairs of other countries. **3.** the act of spying; a careful view. –*verb* (**spied, spying**) –*v.i.* **4.** to act as a spy. –*v.t.* **5.** to catch sight of; descry; see. –*phr.* **6. spy on,** to make secret observations of. **7. spy out, a.** to make secret observations in (a place) with hostile intent. **b.** to find out by observation or scrutiny.

spyglass /ˈspaɪglas/ *n.* a small telescope.

spyware /ˈspaɪwɛə/ *n. Computers* a piece of software that performs such tasks as monitoring the computer user's internet access, redirecting web browser activity, etc., without the user's knowledge or consent.

squabble /ˈskwɒbəl/ *v.i.* **1.** to engage in a petty quarrel. –*n.* **2.** a petty quarrel. –**squabbler,** *n.*

squad /skwɒd/ *n.* **1.** any small group of soldiers operating as a unit. **2.** any small group or party of persons engaged in a common enterprise, etc. **3.** a group of sportspeople, often selected for a tour, from whom teams for specific occasions are drawn.

squadron /ˈskwɒdrən/ *n.* **1.** a portion of a naval fleet, or a detachment of warships used on a particular service; a subdivision of a fleet. **2.** an armoured cavalry or cavalry unit consisting of two or more troops (companies), a headquarters, and certain supporting units. **3.** the basic administrative and tactical unit of an air force, smaller than a group and composed of two or more flights. **4.** a number of persons grouped or united together for some purpose; a group or body in general. –*v.t.* **5.** to form into a squadron or squadrons; marshal or array in or as in squadrons.

squadron leader *n. Air Force* **1.** a commissioned officer in the Royal Australian Air Force ranking below wing commander and above flight lieutenant. **2.** the rank. *Abbrev.:* SQNLDR

squalid /ˈskwɒləd/ *adj.* **1.** foul and repulsive, as from the want of care or cleanliness; dirty; filthy. **2.** wretched; miserable; degraded. –**squalidly,** *adv.* –**squalidity** /skwɒˈlɪdəti/, **squalidness,** *n.*

squall[1] /skwɔl/ *n.* **1.** *Meteorol.* a sudden strong wind which dies away rapidly after lasting only a few minutes, often associated with a temporary change of wind direction. **2.** *Colloq.* a disturbance or commotion. –*v.i.* **3.** to blow in a squall. –**squally,** *adj.*

squall[2] /skwɔl/ *v.i.* **1.** to cry out loudly; scream violently. –*v.t.* **2.** to utter in a screaming tone. –*n.* **3.** the act or sound of squalling. –**squaller,** *n.*

squalor /ˈskwɒlə/ *n.* filth and misery.

squamous cell carcinoma /ˈskweɪməs/ *n.* a malignant, epithelial tumour, metastatic in nature, primarily caused by excessive exposure to the sun and appearing as a thickened red, scaly spot on the skin. Compare **basal cell carcinoma.** Also, **SCC.**

squander /ˈskwɒndə/ *v.t.* Also, **squander away.** **1.** to spend (money, time, etc.) extravagantly or wastefully. –*n.* **2.** extravagant or wasteful expenditure. –**squanderer,** *n.*

square /skwɛə/ *n.* **1.** *Geom.* a four-sided plane figure, or rectangle, with four equal sides and four right angles. **2.** anything having this form or a form approximating it. **3.** one of the rectangular or otherwise shaped divisions of a game board, as a chess or draughts board. **4.** an open area in a city or town, as at the intersection of streets, often planted with grass, trees, etc. **5.** an L-shaped or T-shaped instrument for determining or testing right angles, and for other purposes. **6.** *Maths* the second power of a number or quantity: *the square of 4 is 4×4, or 16.* **7.** *Aust. Building Trades* a former unit of surface measurement equalling 100 square feet. **8.** *Colloq.* someone who is conservative in manner, dress or behaviour. –*v.t.* (**squared, squaring**) **9.** to reduce to square, rectangular, or cubic form. **10.** to mark out in squares or rectangles. **11.** to test for deviation from a right angle, straight line, or plane surface. **12.** *Maths* **a.** to multiply (a number or quantity) by itself. **b.** to describe or find a square which is equivalent to: *to square a circle.* **13.** to bring to the form of a right angle or right angles; set at right angles to something else. **14.** to make the score of (a contest, etc.) even. **15.** to set (the shoulders, arms, etc.) so as to present an approximately rectangular outline. **16.** Also, **square off.** to make straight, level, or even. **17.** to adjust harmoniously or satisfactorily; balance; settle: *to square a debt.* **18.** *Colloq.* to bribe. (**squarer, squarest**) **19.** of the form of a right angle; having some part or parts rectangular: *a square corner.* **20.** having four equal sides and four equal angles; cubical or approximately so: *a square box.* **21.** at right angles, or perpendicular: *one line square to another.* **22.** designating a unit representing an area in the form of a square: *a square metre.* **23.** relating to such units, or to surface measurement: *square measure.* **24.** of a specified length on each side of a square: *an area 2 metres square.* **25.** having a square section, or one that is merely rectangular: *a square file.* **26.** having a solid, sturdy form with rectilinear and angular outlines. **27.** straight, level, or even, as a surface or surfaces. **28.** leaving no balance of debt on either side; having all accounts settled: *to make accounts square.* **29.** just, fair, or honest. **30.** straightforward, direct, or unequivocal. **31.** *Colloq.* substantial or satisfying: *a square meal.* **32.** conservative in manners, dress, or behaviour. –*adv.* **33.** so as to be square; in square or rectangular form. **34.** at right angles. **35.** *Colloq.* solidly or directly: *to hit a nail square on the head.* **36.** *Colloq.* fairly, honestly or uprightly. –*phr.* **37. break square,** to have one's credits or profits equal one's debits or losses. **38. on the square,** *Colloq.* **a.** fair; fairly. **b.** abstaining from alcohol; teetotal. **39. out of square**, not at right angles. **40. square off**, to assume a posture of offence or defence, as in boxing. **41. square off with**, *Aust.* **a.** *NZ* to apologise to; make recompense to. **b.** to get revenge on; pay back. **42. square one's account**, **a.** *Accounting* to achieve a balance. **b.** (sometimes fol. by *with*) to secure reconciliation or forgiveness. **43. square the circle**, to attempt the impossible. **44. square up**, (sometimes fol. by *with*) to pay or settle a bill, debt, etc. **45. square up to**, to face, especially courageously; prepare to contest or resist. **46. square with**, to accord or agree with: *his theory does not square with the facts*. **47. think outside the square**, to take an unconventional approach. –**squarely**, *adv.* –**squareness**, *n.* –**squarer**, *n.*

square bracket *n.* See **bracket** (def. 3).

square dance *n.* a dance, as a quadrille, by couples arranged in a square or in some set form. –**square dancing**, *n.*

square leg *n. Cricket* a fielding position on the leg side at right angles to the pitch opposite the wicket of the person batting.

square root *n. Maths* the quantity of which a given quantity is the square: *4 is the square root of 16*.

squash[1] /skwɒʃ/ *v.t.* **1.** to press into a flat mass; crush. **2.** to put down; quash: *to squash an uprising*. **3.** *Colloq.* to silence, as with a crushing reply. –*v.i.* **4.** to be pressed into a flat mass. –*n.* **5.** the act or result of squashing. **6.** something squashed or crushed. **7.** a game for two players, played in a small walled court with light racquets and small rubber ball. **8.** a drink based on a fruit juice, with soda, etc., added. –**squasher**, *n.*

squash[2] /skwɒʃ/ *n.* any of various varieties of *Cucurbita pepo*, usually round in shape and having paler flesh and softer skin than the pumpkin, *Cucurbita maxima*.

squat /skwɒt/ *v.i.* (**squatted** *or* **squat**, **squatting**) **1.** to rest in a posture close to the ground with the knees bent and the back more or less straight, resting on the balls of the feet; crouch. **2.** *Aust., NZ Hist.* to settle on land without government permission. **3.** to occupy a building without title or right. –*adj.* **4.** short and thickset or thick: *a squat body*. –*n.* **5.** the act or fact of squatting. **6.** the position or posture in which one squats. –**squatly**, *adv.* –**squatness**, *n.* –**squatty**, *adj.*

squatter /ˈskwɒtə/ *n.* **1.** *Aust., NZ Hist.* someone who settled on crown land to run stock, especially sheep, initially without government permission, but later with a lease or licence. **2.** *Aust., NZ Hist.* one of a group of rich and influential rural landowners. **3.** someone who occupies a building without right or title.

squattocracy /skwɒˈtɒkrəsi/ *n.* (in Australia and NZ) the long-established and wealthy landowners who regard themselves as an aristocracy. –**squattocratic** /skwɒtəˈkrætik/, *adj.*

squaw /skwɔ/ *n.* (*derog.*) (*racist*) (*dated*) a Native American woman or wife.

squawk /skwɔk/ *v.i.* **1.** to utter a loud, harsh cry, as a duck or other fowl when frightened. **2.** *Colloq.* to complain loudly and vehemently. –*v.t.* **3.** to give forth with a squawk. –*n.* **4.** a loud, harsh cry or sound. **5.** *Colloq.* a loud, vehement complaint. –**squawker**, *n.*

squeak /skwik/ *n.* **1.** a short, sharp, shrill cry; a sharp, high-pitched sound. **2.** *Colloq.* a narrow escape. –*v.i.* **3.** to utter or emit a squeak or squeaky sound. **4.** *Colloq.* to confess or turn informer. –*v.t.* **5.** to utter or produce with a squeak or squeaks. –**squeaky**, *adj.*

squeal /skwil/ *n.* **1.** a sharp, high-pitched cry, as of pain, fear, etc. **2.** *Colloq.* a complaint; protest. –*v.i.* **3.** to utter a squealing sound. **4.** *Colloq.* to give information (to police, etc.) against another. **5.** *Colloq.* to complain; protest. –*v.t.* **6.** to utter or produce with a squeal. **7.** *Colloq.* to tell (something secret): *he squealed the information to the police*. –**squealer**, *n.*

squeamish /ˈskwimɪʃ/ *adj.* **1.** easily nauseated or sickened; qualmish. **2.** easily shocked by anything slightly immodest; prudish. **3.** excessively particular or scrupulous as to the moral aspect of things. **4.** fastidious or dainty. –**squeamishly**, *adv.* –**squeamishness**, *n.*

squeeze /skwiz/ *v.t.* **1.** to press forcibly together; compress. **2.** to apply pressure to in order to remove something: *to squeeze a lemon*. **3.** to force by pressure; cram: *to squeeze clothes into a suitcase*. **4.** (usu. fol. by *out* or *from*) to force out, by or as if by pressure: *to squeeze juice from an orange*; *he was squeezed out of business*. **5.** to hug; embrace. **6.** to press (someone's hand, arm, etc.) as an expression of friendship, concern, etc. –*v.i.* **7.** to apply a pressing force: *he squeezed hard*. **8.** to force a way through some narrow or crowded place. –*n.* **9.** the act or result of squeezing. **10.** *Colloq.* a difficult situation: *in a tight squeeze*. **11.** a crowded gathering. **12.** control or pressure, as enforced by a government: *a credit squeeze*. **13.** a small quantity of anything obtained by squeezing: *a squeeze of lemon*. **14.** Also, **main squeeze**. *Colloq.* a girlfriend or boyfriend. –*phr.* **15. put the squeeze on someone**, to apply pressure to someone to obtain something, as goods or favours. –**squeezer**, *n.*

squelch /skweltʃ/ *v.t.* **1.** to crush down; squash: *to squelch a strawberry between the teeth*. **2.** *Colloq.* to silence, as with a crushing reply. –*v.i.* **3.** to make a splashing sound: *water squelched in her shoes*. **4.** to tread heavily in water, mud, etc., with such a sound. –*n.* **5.** a squelched mass of anything. **6.** a squelching sound. **7.** *Elect.* a circuit which cuts off the output of a radio receiver until a signal begins. –**squelcher**, *n.*

squid /skwɪd/ *n.* (*pl.* **squids** *or, especially collectively,* **squid**) any of various decapod cephalopods, with two gills, especially any of certain small species (as of the genera *Loligo* and *Ommastrephes*) having slender bodies and caudal fins and much used for bait.

squint /skwɪnt/ *v.i.* **1.** to look with the eyes partly closed: *to squint at the sun*. **2.** to be cross-eyed. **3.** to look or glance sideways. –*v.t.* **4.** to close (the eyes) partly. –*n.* **5.** *Med.* a condition where the muscles of the eyes do not work in coordination. **6.** *Colloq.* a secret glance: *to take a quick squint at something*. –*adj.* **7.** looking with a side glance. **8.** affected with poor muscle coordination in the eyes. –**squinter**, *n.*

squire /ˈskwaɪə/ *n.* **1.** (in England) a country gentleman, especially the chief landowner in a district. **2.** *Hist.* a young man of noble birth who waits upon a knight. –*v.t.* **3.** to attend as or in the manner of a squire.

squirm /skwɜm/ *v.i.* **1.** to wriggle or writhe. **2.** to feel or display discomfort or disgust as from reproof, embarrassment, or repulsion. –*n.* **3.** a squirming or wriggling movement. –**squirmy**, *adj.*

squirrel /ˈskwɪrəl/ *n.* **1.** any of the arboreal, bushy-tailed rodents constituting the genus *Sciurus* (family Sciuridae), as the **red squirrel**, *S. vulgaris*, of Europe (including Britain) and Asia, and the **grey squirrel**, *S. carolinensis*, of North America and (by introduction) Britain. **2.** any of various other members of the family Sciuridae, as the chipmunks, flying squirrels, woodchucks, etc. **3.** the pelt or fur of such an animal. **4.** *Colloq.* a person who hoards objects of little value. –*v.i.* (**-relled** *or, Chiefly US,* **-reled**, **-relling** *or, Chiefly US,* **-reling**) **5.** to hoard or save, as money in times of economic depression: *people are squirrelling away funds in the savings banks*. –**squirrel-like**, *adj.*

squirt /skwɜt/ *v.i.* **1.** to force out liquid in a jet from a narrow opening. **2.** (of a liquid) to pour in a jet-like stream. –*v.t.* **3.** to force (liquid) in a jet from a narrow opening: *to squirt water from a hose*. **4.** to wet with a liquid so forced out: *to squirt someone with water*. –*n.* **5.** the act of squirting. **6.** a jet, as of water. **7.** an instrument for squirting, as a syringe. **8.** a small quantity of liquid squirted. **9.** *Colloq.* a. an insignificant, self-assertive person. **b.** a short person. –**squirter**, *n.*

squiz /skwɪz/ *n. Colloq.* a quick but close look.

stab /stæb/ *verb* (**stabbed, stabbing**) –*v.t.* **1.** to pierce or wound with, or as with, a pointed weapon. **2.** to thrust or plunge (a knife, etc.) into something. **3.** to penetrate sharply, like a knife. **4.** to make a thrusting or plunging motion at or in. –*v.i.* **5.** to thrust with or as with a knife or other pointed weapon: *to stab at an adversary.* **6.** to deliver a wound, as with a pointed weapon. –*n.* **7.** the act of stabbing. **8.** a thrust or blow with, or as with, a pointed weapon. **9.** a wound made by stabbing. **10.** a sudden, usually painful sensation. **11.** *Colloq.* an attempt; try. –*phr.* **12. stab someone in the back**, *Colloq.* to do harm to someone, especially someone defenceless or unsuspecting, as by making a treacherous attack upon their reputation. –**stabber**, *n.*

stable[1] /ˈsteɪbəl/ *n.* **1.** a building for the keeping and feeding of horses. **2.** a collection of animals belonging in such a building. **3.** *Racing* **a.** an establishment where racehorses are kept and trained. **b.** the horses belonging to, or people connected with, such an establishment. **4.** a group of people associated in some way with a centre of creative production, as a recording company, gallery, publishing house, etc. –*v.t.* **5.** to put or keep in or as in a stable. –**stabling**, *n.*

stable[2] /ˈsteɪbəl/ *adj.* **1.** not likely to fall or give way, as a structure, support, foundation, etc.; firm; steady. **2.** able or likely to continue or last; enduring or permanent: *a stable government.* **3.** steadfast; not wavering or changeable, as a person, the mind, etc. **4.** *Physics* having or showing an ability or tendency to maintain or re-establish position, form, etc.: *stable equilibrium.* **5.** *Chem.* not readily decomposing, as a compound; resisting molecular or chemical change. –**stabilise, stabilize,** *v.* –**stabiliser, stabilizer,** *n.* –**stabilisation, stabilization,** *n.* –**stability,** *n.* –**stably,** *adv.*

staccato /stəˈkatoʊ/ *Music* –*adj.* **1.** detached, disconnected, or abrupt. **2.** with breaks between the successive notes. –*adv.* **3.** in a staccato manner. Compare **legato.**

stack /stæk/ *n.* **1.** a large, usually circular or rectangular pile of hay, straw, or the like. **2.** any more or less orderly pile or heap. **3.** a number of chimneys or flues grouped together. **4.** a single chimney or funnel for smoke, or a vertical pipe inside or outside a building for passing waste products down, circulating heat, or expelling exhaust gases. **5.** *Geol.* a column or pillar of rock, isolated from the shore by the erosive action of waves. **6.** *Colloq.* a combination of amplifiers and speaker boxes. **7.** a measure for coal and wood, equal to 108 cubic feet or 3.06 cubic metres. **8.** *Aeronautics* a number of aircraft circling at different altitudes above an airport awaiting their signal to land. **9.** *Colloq.* a motor vehicle accident, especially one involving a number of vehicles. **10.** (*pl.*) that part of a library in which the main holdings are kept and to which the general user is often denied access. **11.** *Colloq.* a great quantity or number. **12.** (*pl.*) *Colloq.* a great amount. –*v.t.* **13.** to pile or arrange in a stack: *to stack hay.* **14.** to cover or load with something in stacks or piles. **15.** to arrange (playing cards in the pack) in an unfair manner. **16.** to bring a large number of one's own supporters to (a meeting) in order to outvote those of opposing views. **17.** *Aeronautics* to control the aircraft waiting to land at an airport, so that they form a stack. **18.** to crash (a motor vehicle, bicycle, etc.). –*phr.* **19. stack it on**, *Colloq.* to exaggerate one's concern, grief, anger, etc. **20. stack on**, *Colloq.* to start; instigate: *stack on a blue.* **21. stack up**, to accumulate; add up. –**stacker**, *n.*

stadium /ˈsteɪdiəm/ *n.* (*pl.* **-diums** *or* **-dia** /-diə/) **1.** a sporting facility, often, though not necessarily,

enclosed, comprising an arena, tiers or seats for spectators, parking, etc. **2.** an ancient Greek course for races, typically semicircular. **3.** a stage of development in a process, disease, etc.

staff[1] /staf/ *n.* (*pl.* **staffs** *or* **staves** /steɪvz/ *for defs 1–4 and 8*, **staffs** *for defs 5–7*) **1.** a stick, pole, rod, or wand for aid in walking or climbing, for use as a weapon, etc. **2.** a rod or wand serving as an ensign of office or authority, as a crozier, baton, truncheon, or mace. **3.** a pole on which a flag is hung or displayed. **4.** something which serves to support or sustain: *bread is the staff of life.* **5.** a body of assistants to a manager, superintendent, or executive head. **6.** a body of persons charged with carrying out the work of an establishment or executing some undertaking. **7.** the teaching personnel of a school, college, or the like. **8.** *Music* → **stave** (def. 5). –*adj.* **9.** of, or being a member of, a military or naval staff or unit: *staff officer.* –*v.t.* **10.** to provide with a staff.

staff[2] /staf/ *n.* a kind of plaster combined with fibrous material, used for temporary ornamental buildings, etc.

stag /stæg/ *n.* **1.** an adult male deer. **2.** the male of various other animals. **3.** *Colloq.* a man, especially one at a social gathering exclusively for men. **4.** an animal castrated after maturation of the sex organs. –*adj.* **5.** *Colloq.* for or of men only: *a stag party.*

stage /steɪdʒ/ *n.* **1.** a single step or degree in a process; a particular period in a process of development. **2.** a raised platform or floor, as for speakers, performers, etc. **3.** *Theatre* **a.** the platform in a theatre on which the actors perform. **b.** this platform with all the parts of the theatre, and all the apparatus behind the proscenium. **4.** the theatre, the drama, or the dramatic profession. **5.** the scene of any action. **6.** a stagecoach. **7.** Also, **staging post.** a regular stopping place of a stagecoach or the like, for the change of horses, etc. **8.** the distance between two places of rest on a journey; each of the portions of a journey. **9.** a portion or period of a course of action, of life, etc. **10.** *NZ* each year in the study of a university subject. **11.** *Zool.* **a.** any one of the major time periods in the development of an insect, as the embryonic, larval, pupal, and imaginal stages. **b.** any one of the periods of larval growth between moults. **12.** *Econ., Sociology* a major phase of the economic or sociological life of people or society: *the matriarchal stage.* **13.** *Geol.* a division of stratified rocks next in rank to series, representing deposits formed during the fraction of an epoch that is called an age. **14.** a powered section of a rocket which can be jettisoned after firing. –*v.t.* (**staged, staging**) **15.** to put, represent, or exhibit on or as on a stage. **16.** to write, direct, or produce (a play) as if the action were taking place in a specific place or period of time. **17.** to plan, organise, or carry out (an action) in which each participant has a specific task to perform. **18.** to arrange; set up, as for a particular event: *he staged a comeback.* –*phr.* **19. by easy stages,** without rushing; working or travelling with many stops. **20. go on the stage,** to take up acting as a career. **21. hold the stage,** to be the centre of attention. **22. on stage,** performing on a stage: *she was on stage at the time.* **23. take centre stage,** to behave so as to attract attention.

stagecoach /ˈsteɪdʒkoʊtʃ/ *n.* (formerly) a coach that ran regularly over a fixed route with passengers, parcels, etc.

stage dive *v.i.* to dive from the stage into the audience in a mosh pit. See **crowd-surfing.** –**stage diving,** *n.* –**stage diver,** *n.*

stagflation /stægˈfleɪʃən/ *n. Econ.* a situation in the economy in which stagnant economic growth is accompanied by high inflation.

stagger /ˈstægə/ v.i. **1.** to walk, move, or stand unsteadily; sway. –v.t. **2.** to cause to stagger. **3.** (usu. in passive) to shock: I was staggered by the price. **4.** to arrange a series so that the beginnings and ends of its component parts are at different positions, times, etc.: to stagger lunch hours. –n. **5.** the act of staggering. –**staggerer**, n. –**staggeringly**, adv.

staghorn fern /ˈstæghɔn fɜn/ n. any of various ferns of the tropical and subtropical genus Platycerium, family Polypodiaceae, having large fertile leaves resembling the horns of a stag, as P. superbum of Qld.

stagnant /ˈstægnənt/ adj. **1.** not running or flowing, as water, air, etc. **2.** foul from standing, as a pool of water. –**stagnancy**, n. –**stagnantly**, adv.

stagnate /ˈstægneɪt, stægˈneɪt/ v.i. **1.** to cease to run or flow, as water, air, etc. **2.** to become foul from standing, as a pool of water. **3.** to become inactive, sluggish, or dull. **4.** to make no progress; stop developing. –**stagnation** /stægˈneɪʃən/, n.

staid /steɪd/ adj. of settled or sedate character; not flighty or capricious. –**staidly**, adv. –**staidness**, n.

stain /steɪn/ n. **1.** a semipermanent discolouration; spot: the wine made a stain on his tie. **2.** a cause of dishonour; blemish: a stain on one's reputation. **3.** a mixture of colouring matter in water, spirit, or oil, used to colour but not hide a surface. **4.** a dye made into a mixture and used to colour cloth, biological specimens, etc. –v.t. **5.** to cause a stain in. **6.** to colour with stain. **7.** to treat (a microscopic specimen) with a reagent or dye in order to colour the whole or parts and so give distinctness, contrast of tissues, etc. –v.i. **8.** to produce a stain: red wine stains. **9.** to become stained: the wood stained easily. –**stainable**, adj. –**stainer**, n. –**stainless**, adj. –**stainlessly**, adv.

stair /stɛə/ n. **1.** one of a series or flight of steps forming a means of passage from one storey or level to another, as in a building. **2.** (pl.) such steps collectively, especially as forming a flight or a series of flights. **3.** a series or flight of steps; a stairway: a winding stair.

staircase /ˈstɛəkeɪs/ n. a flight of stairs with its framework, banisters, etc., or a series of such flights.

stairwell /ˈstɛəwɛl/ n. the vertical shaft or opening containing a stairway.

stake¹ /steɪk/ n. **1.** a stick or post pointed at one end for driving into the ground as a boundary mark, a part of a fence, a support for a plant, etc. **2.** a post, especially one to which a person is bound for execution, usually by burning. –v.t. **3.** Also, **stake off**, **stake out**. to mark with stakes. **4.** Also, **stake out**. to possess, lay claim to, or reserve a share of (land, profit, etc.): to stake a claim. **5.** to support with a stake or stakes, as a plant. **6.** to tether or secure to a stake, as an animal. –phr. **7.** **pull up stakes**, Colloq. to leave one's job, home, etc., and move away. **8.** **stake out**, to surround (a building, etc.) for the purposes of a raid, a siege, or keeping watch. **9.** **the stake**, the punishment of death by burning.

stake² /steɪk/ n. **1.** that which is wagered in a game, race, or contest. **2.** an interest held in something. **3.** Colloq. personal concern, involvement, etc. **4.** the funds with which a gambler operates. **5.** (oft. pl.) a prize in a race or contest. **6.** (pl. construed as sing.) a race in which equal amounts are contributed by the owners of each of the competing horses as prize money. **7.** (pl. construed as sing.) a fictitious race or contest in a specified field: she is way ahead of her sister in the beauty stakes. –v.t. **8.** to put at hazard upon the result of a game, the event of a contingency, etc.; wager; venture or hazard. **9.** to furnish with necessaries or resources, often by way of a business venture with a view to a possible return. –phr. **10.** **at stake**, involved; in a state of being staked or at hazard.

stalactite /ˈstæləktaɪt/ n. a deposit, usually of calcium carbonate, shaped like an icicle, hanging from the roof of a cave or the like, and formed by the dripping of percolating calcareous water. –**stalactitic** /stæləkˈtɪtɪk/, **stalactitical** /stæləkˈtɪtɪkəl/, adj.

stalagmite /ˈstæləgmaɪt/ n. a deposit, usually of calcium carbonate, more or less resembling an inverted stalactite, formed on the floor of a cave or the like by the dripping of percolating calcareous water. –**stalagmitic** /stæləgˈmɪtɪk/, **stalagmitical** /stæləgˈmɪtɪkəl/, adj.

stale¹ /steɪl/ adj. **1.** not fresh; vapid or flat, as beverages; dry or hardened, as bread. **2.** having lost novelty or interest; hackneyed; trite: a stale joke. **3.** having lost fresh vigour, quick intelligence, initiative, or the like, as from overstrain, boredom, etc. **4.** Law having lost force or effectiveness through absence of action, as a claim. –v.t. **5.** to make stale. –v.i. **6.** to become stale. –**stalely**, adv. –**staleness**, n.

stale² /steɪl/ n. **1.** urine, especially of horses and cattle. –v.i. **2.** (of livestock, especially horses and cattle) to urinate.

stalemate /ˈsteɪlmeɪt/ n. **1.** Chess a position of the pieces when no move can be made by a player without putting his or her own king in check, the result being a draw. **2.** any position in which no action can be taken; a deadlock. –v.t. **3.** to subject to a stalemate. **4.** to bring to a standstill.

stalk¹ /stɔk/ n. **1.** the stem or main axis of a plant. **2.** any slender supporting or connecting part of a plant, as the petiole of a leaf, the peduncle of a flower, or the funicle of an ovule. **3.** a similar structural part of an animal. **4.** a stem, shaft, or slender supporting part of anything. –**stalkless**, adj.

stalk² /stɔk/ v.i. **1.** to follow or approach game, etc., quietly and carefully. **2.** to walk in a slow, stiff, or proud manner. **3.** to go with a slow, relentless and often evil movement: hunger stalked through the land. –v.t. **4.** to follow (game, a person, etc.) quietly and carefully. **5.** to harass (someone) by persistently and obsessively following them, telephoning them, etc. **6.** to harass (someone) through the use of the internet, email, chat rooms, or other digital communications devices. –n. **7.** the act of stalking game, etc. **8.** a slow, stiff walk. –**stalker**, n.

stall¹ /stɔl/ n. **1.** an enclosed space in a stable or shed, for keeping one animal. **2.** a booth, bench, table, or stand on which goods are shown for sale. **3.** → **carrel**. **4.** a seat in a theatre, separated from others by armrests. **5.** (pl.) the front section on the ground floor of a theatre. **6.** the fact of an engine stopping, as through an incorrect fuel supply. –v.t. **7.** to put or keep in a stall, as animals. **8.** to bring (a vehicle) to a standstill, especially by mismanagement. –v.i. **9.** to come to a standstill. **10.** (of a vehicle or aeroplane engine) to stop.

stall² /stɔl/ v.i. **1.** to act evasively or deceptively. **2.** Sport to play below one's best in order to deceive for any reason. –v.t. Also, **stall off**. **3.** to put off, evade, or deceive. –phr. **4.** **stall for time**, to engage in a delaying tactic.

stallion /ˈstæljən/ n. a male horse not castrated, especially one kept for breeding.

stalwart /ˈstɔlwət/ adj. **1.** strongly and stoutly built; well-developed and robust. **2.** strong and brave; valiant. **3.** firm, steadfast, or uncompromising. –n. **4.** a physically stalwart person. **5.** a steadfast or uncompromising partisan. –**stalwartly**, adv. –**stalwartness**, n.

stamen /ˈsteɪmən/ n. (pl. **stamens** or **stamina** /ˈstæmənə/) Bot. the pollen-bearing organ of a flower, consisting of the filament and the anther. –**staminate**, adj.

stamina¹ /ˈstæmənə/ n. strength of physical constitution; power to endure disease, fatigue, privation, etc.

stamina² /ˈstæmənə/ n. a plural of **stamen**.

stammer /'stæmə/ v.i. **1.** to speak with involuntary breaks and pauses or with spasmodic repetitions of syllables or sounds. –v.t. Also, **stammer out**. **2.** to say with a stammer. –n. **3.** a stammering mode of utterance. **4.** a stammered utterance. –**stammerer**, n. –**stammeringly**, adv.

stamp /stæmp/ v.t. **1.** to strike or beat with a forcible downward thrust of the foot. **2.** to bring (the foot) down forcibly or smartly on the ground, floor, etc. **3.** to crush or pound with or as with a pestle. **4.** to impress with a particular mark or device, as to indicate genuineness, approval, ownership, etc. **5.** to impress with an official mark. **6.** to mark or impress with any characters, words, designs, etc. **7.** to impress (a design, figure, words, etc.) on something; imprint deeply or permanently on anything. **8.** to affix an adhesive paper stamp to (a letter, etc.). **9.** to characterise, distinguish, or reveal. –v.i. **10.** to bring the foot down forcibly or smartly, as in crushing something, expressing rage, etc. **11.** to walk with forcible or heavy, resounding steps: to stamp out of a room in anger. –n. **12.** the act or an instance of stamping. **13.** a die, engraved block, or the like, for impressing a design, characters, words, or marks. **14.** an impression, design, characters, words, etc., made with or as with a stamp. **15.** an official mark indicating genuineness, validity, etc., or payment of a duty or charge. **16.** the impression of a public seal required for revenue purposes, to be obtained from a government office, for a fee, on the paper or parchment on which deeds, bills, receipts, etc., are written. **17.** a peculiar or distinctive impress or mark: a story which bears the stamp of truth. **18.** character, kind, or type. **19.** a small adhesive piece of paper printed with a distinctive design, issued by a government for a fixed sum, for attaching to documents, goods subject to duty, letters, etc., to show that a charge has been paid: an excise stamp, a postage stamp. **20.** a similar piece of paper issued by a private organisation to show that the charges for postage have been paid: a local stamp. **21.** a similar piece of paper issued privately for various purposes: a trading stamp. **22.** an instrument for stamping, crushing, or pounding. **23.** a heavy piece of iron or the like, as in a stamp mill, for dropping on and crushing ore or other material. –phr. **24. stamp on**, to trample on by or as by beating down with the foot. **25. stamp out**, to destroy all vestige of by or as beating down with the foot: to stamp out a fire; to stamp out a rebellion.

stamp duty n. a duty imposed on a number of commercial and financial transactions, and certain legal instruments.

stampede /stæm'pid/ n. **1.** a sudden scattering or headlong flight of a body of cattle or horses in fright. **2.** any headlong general flight or rush. –v.i. **3.** to scatter or flee in a stampede. **4.** to make an unconcerted general rush. –v.t. **5.** to cause to stampede. –**stampeder**, n.

stamping ground n. Colloq. the habitual place of resort of an animal or person. Also, **stomping ground**.

stance /stæns, stans/ n. **1.** the position or bearing of the body while standing: a boxer's stance. **2.** emotional or intellectual attitude to something: a hostile stance towards important poetry.

stanchion /'stænʃən, 'stan-, -tʃən/ n. **1.** an upright bar, beam, post, or support, as in a window, stall, ship, etc. **2.** a post or posts, often with a crossbar, which supports the electric wiring of an electric railway. –v.t. **3.** to furnish with stanchions. **4.** to secure by or to a stanchion or stanchions.

stand /stænd/ verb (**stood**, **standing**) –v.i. **1.** to take or keep an upright position on the feet (opposed to sit, lie, etc.). **2.** to have a specified height when in this position: he stands two metres in his socks. **3.** to remain

motionless or steady on the feet. **4.** to cease moving; halt; stop: stand and deliver!; to stand and fight. **5.** to take a position or stand as indicated: to stand aside. **6.** to remain firm or steadfast, as in a cause. **7.** to take up or maintain a position or attitude with respect to a person, question, or the like: to stand sponsor for a person. **8.** to adopt a certain course or attitude, as of adherence, support, opposition, or resistance. **9.** (of things) to be in an upright position (opposed to lie); be set on end; rest on or as on a support; be set, placed, or fixed. **10.** to be located or situated. **11.** to be at a certain degree: the temperature stands at 25°C. **12.** (of an account, score, etc.) to show a specified position of the parties concerned: the account stands in my favour. **13.** to remain erect and entire; resist change, decay, or destruction. **14.** to continue in force or remain valid. **15.** to become or remain still or stationary. **16.** to be or become stagnant, as water. **17.** (of persons or things) to be or remain in a specified state, condition, relation, etc.: he stood alone in his opinion. **18.** to be likely or in a position as specified: to stand to lose. **19.** to become or be a candidate, as for parliament. –v.t. **20.** to cause to stand; set upright; set. **21.** to face or encounter: to stand an assault. **22.** to endure, undergo, or submit to: to stand trial. **23.** to endure or undergo without hurt or damage, or without giving way: he cannot stand the sun. **24.** to tolerate: I will stand no nonsense. **25.** Colloq. to bear the expense of; pay for. –n. **26.** the act of standing; an assuming of or a remaining in upright position. **27.** a coming to a position of rest; a halt or stop. **28.** a halt to give battle or repel an attack. **29.** a determined opposition to or support for some cause, circumstance, or the like. **30.** Cricket a period of batting and scoring, usually of some length, during which neither person batting is out: a ninth wicket stand of 44. **31.** the place where a person or thing stands; station. **32.** a shearer's place in a shed: a sixteen-stand shed. **33.** a witness box. **34.** a raised platform or other structure, as for spectators at a racecourse or a sports field, or along the route of a ceremonial parade, or for a band or the like. **35.** a place, usually under cover, from which a hunter shoots game. **36.** a framework on or in which articles are placed for support, exhibition, etc. **37.** a piece of furniture of various forms, on or in which to put articles. **38.** a stall where articles are displayed for sale or for some other purpose, especially at a show or exhibition. **39.** a place or station occupied by vehicles available for hire. **40.** the growing trees, or those of a particular species, in a given area. **41.** a standing growth, as of grass, wheat, etc. **42. a.** a halt of a theatrical company on tour, to give a performance or performances. **b.** the town at which a theatrical company gives a performance. –phr. **43. stand a chance**, to have a chance or possibility, especially of winning, surviving, or the like. **44. stand back**, to get out of the way, as by moving backwards. **45. stand by**, **a.** to wait in a state of readiness: stand by for further instructions. **b.** to aid, uphold, or sustain. **c.** to adhere to (an agreement, promise, etc.); abide by. **46. stand down**, **a.** to go off duty. **b.** to withdraw, as from a contest. **c.** Law to leave the witness box. **d.** to suspend (employees) without pay during periods in which they cannot be usefully employed. **47. stand for**, **a.** to endure or tolerate: I won't stand for any nonsense. **b.** to represent: the symbol x stands for an unknown quantity. **c.** to be an advocate of: he stands for racial equality. **d.** to be a candidate for: to stand for parliament. **48. stand in**, **a.** to act as a substitute or representative. **b.** to join in; take a part in. **49. stand off**, **a.** to keep at a distance. **b.** to suspend from employment, especially temporarily: owing to the drop in sales, the factory is standing workers off. **50. stand on**, **a.** to rest or depend on. **b.** to claim respect for (one's rights, dignity, etc.) **c.** Naut. to continue on the same course or tack. **51. stand on ceremony**, *Colloq.* to be excessively formal or polite. **52. stand one's ground**, to be unyielding; remain steadfast in the face of opposition or attack. **53. stand on one's (two) feet**, to be self-sufficient. **54. stand out**, **a.** to project or protrude. **b.** to be prominent or conspicuous. **c.** to hold aloof. **d.** to persist in opposition or resistance. **55. stand over**, to intimidate. **56. stand someone in good stead**, to be of use or advantage to someone: *his knowledge of Indonesian stood him in good stead in Jakarta.* **57. stand to**, (of military personnel) to assemble or take up assigned posts in readiness, as for inspection or awaiting orders. **58. stand to reason**, to be in accordance with reason. **59. stand up**, **a.** to assume a standing position, especially from sitting. **b.** to fail to keep an appointment with. **60. stand up for**, to defend the cause of; support. **61. stand up to**, **a.** to remain in good condition despite: *to stand up well to wear.* **b.** to retain credibility, authority, respect, etc., despite: *will this play stand up to the passage of time?* **c.** to resist or oppose, especially bravely. **62. stand with**, to ally oneself with.

standalone /'stændəloʊn/ *adj.* **1.** of or relating to a computerised device which does not need to be linked up to a larger computer system. –*n.* **2.** such a device. Also, **stand-alone**.

standard /'stændəd/ *n.* **1.** anything taken by general consent as a basis of comparison; an approved model. **2.** the authorised exemplar of a unit of weight or measure. **3.** a certain commodity in which the basic monetary unit is stated, historically usually either gold or silver (**gold standard**, **silver standard**, or **single standard**), or both gold and silver in a fixed proportion to each other (**bimetallic standard**). **4.** the legal rate of intrinsic value for coins. **5.** the prescribed degree of fineness for gold or silver. **6.** a grade or level of excellence, achievement, or advancement: *a high standard of living.* **7.** a level of quality which is regarded as normal, adequate, or acceptable. **8.** a fitting or size, as for clothes, which is regarded as normal or average. **9.** (*usu. pl.*) behaviour, beliefs, etc., regarded as socially desirable or acceptable. **10.** a class in certain schools. **11.** a flag, emblematic figure, or other object raised on a pole to indicate the rallying point of an army, fleet, etc. **12.** a flag indicating the presence of a sovereign. **13.** *Mil.* **a.** any of various military or naval flags. **b.** the colours of a mounted unit. **14.** *Heraldry* a long tapering flag or ensign, as of a king or a nation. **15.** something which stands or is placed upright. **16.** an upright support or supporting part. **17.** an upright timber, bar, or rod. **18.** *Hort.* a tree, shrub, or other plant having a tall, erect stem, and not grown in bush form or trained upon a trellis or other support. **19.** a piece of music or the like of lasting popularity, especially one often revived with new arrangements. **20.** standard petrol. –*adj.* **21.** serving as a basis of weight, measure, value, comparison, or judgement. **22.** of recognised excellence or established authority: *a standard author.* **23.** normal, adequate, acceptable, or average: *standard goods, a standard fitting.* **24.** (of a variety of a given language, or of usage in the language) characterised by preferred pronunciations, expressions, grammatical constructions, etc., the use of which may be helpful for maintaining or achieving social prestige. **25.** *Hort.* of or relating to, or in the shape of, a standard (def. 18): *a standard rose.* –**standardness**, *n.*

standard deviation *n. Statistics* the square root of the average of the squares of a set of deviations about an arithmetic mean; the root mean square of the deviations of a set of values.

standardise /'stændədaɪz/ *v.t.* **1.** to bring to or make of an established standard size, weight, quality, strength, or the like: *to standardise manufactured products.* **2.** to compare with or test by a standard. Also, **standardize**. –**standardisation** /ˌstændədaɪˈzeɪʃən/, *n.* –**standardiser**, *n.*

stand-by *n.* (*pl.* **-bys**) **1.** a staunch supporter or adherent; someone who can be relied upon. **2.** something upon which one can rely; a chief support. **3.** something kept in a state of readiness for use, as for an emergency. **4.** a recipe, piece of music, theme of discourse, etc., often simple and well-known, which one falls back on when disinclined to be adventurous. **5.** a person who is on stand-by. –*phr.* **6. on stand-by**, **a.** (of doctors, etc.) available for duty at short notice. **b.** in readiness, as of a person wishing to travel by plane, to take up a cancelled booking. Also, **standby**.

stand-in *n.* a substitute, especially for a film actor.

standing /'stændɪŋ/ *n.* **1.** position, as to rank, credit, reputation, etc.: *men of good standing.* **2.** length of existence, membership, experience, etc.: *a member of long standing.* –*adj.* **3.** that stands upright. **4.** performed in or from a stationary or upright position: *a standing start.* **5.** still; not flowing, as water. **6.** continuing without stopping or changing: *a standing rule.* **7.** out of use; idle: *a standing engine.*

standing committee *n.* **1.** a committee that may be appointed without a term, to oversee an aspect of the running of an institution. **2.** *Parliamentary Procedure* a parliamentary committee, the members of which are appointed at the beginning of each parliamentary session, which has a continuing responsibility for a general sphere of government activity.

standing order *n.* **1.** any of the rules ensuring continuity of procedure during the meetings of an assembly, especially the rules governing the conduct of business in parliament. **2.** *Mil.* (formerly) a general order that is always in force in a command and that establishes uniform procedures for it.

stand-out *Colloq.* –*n.* **1.** a person in a team, competition, etc., who impresses as having abilities greater than all the others. –*adj.* **2.** outstanding; obvious: *a standout choice.* **3.** brilliant, excellent: *a stand-out season.* Also, **standout**.

standpoint /'stændpɔɪnt/ *n.* **1.** the point at which one stands to view something. **2.** the mental position from which one views and judges things.

standstill /'stændstɪl/ *n.* a standing still; a state of cessation of movement or action; a halt; a pause; a stop.

stand-up paddleboard *n.* a surfboard designed so that the rider stands up on it and propels and steers it with a paddle. *Abbrev.*: SUP

stank /stæŋk/ *v.* a past tense of **stink**.

stannite /'stænaɪt/ *n.* a mineral, copper iron tin sulphide, Cu_2FeSnS_4, an ore of tin, iron-black to steel-grey in colour, with a metallic lustre.

stanza /'stænzə/ *n.* a group of lines of verse, commonly four or more in number, arranged and repeated according to a fixed plan as regards the number of lines, the metre, and the rhyme, and forming a regularly repeated metrical division of a poem. –**stanzaic** /stænˈzeɪɪk/, *adj.*

staphylococcus /ˌstæfələˈkɒkəs/ *n.* (*pl.* **staphylococci** /ˌstæfələˈkɒkaɪ, stæfələˈkɒki/) any bacterium of the genus *Staphylococcus* in which the individual organisms form irregular clusters, as *S. albus*, a skin commensal, or *S. aureus*, a chief agent, or *S. pyogenes*, which causes pus formation. –**staphylococcal** /ˌstæfələˈkɒkəl/, **staphylococcic** /ˌstæfələˈkɒksɪk/, *adj.*

staple[1] /'steɪpəl/ *n.* **1.** a bent piece of wire used to bind papers, sections of a book, etc., together. **2.** a U-shaped or other piece of metal with pointed ends for driving into a surface to hold a hasp, hook, pin, bolt, or the like. **3.** a similar device used in medical operations. –*v.t.*

4. to secure or fasten by a staple or staples: *to staple three sheets together.*

staple² /'steɪpəl/ *n.* **1.** an item, especially of food, which is used or needed continually: *all kitchens need staples such as flour, sugar, etc.* **2.** a main item, thing, feature, element, or part. **3.** the fibre of wool, cotton, etc., considered with reference to length and fineness. *–adj.* **4.** most important among the products exported or produced by a country or district. **5.** (of industries) chief or principal. **6.** principally used: *staple subjects of conversation.*

stapler /'steɪplə/ *n.* a stapling machine.

star /stɑ/ *n.* **1.** any of the heavenly bodies appearing as apparently fixed luminous points in the sky at night. **2.** *Astron.* any of the self-luminous bodies outside the solar system, as distinguished from planets, comets, and meteors. The sun is classed with the stars and appears to be a typical member of the galaxy. **3.** any heavenly body. **4.** *Astrology* **a.** a heavenly body, especially a planet that is considered as influencing humankind and events. **b.** (*pl.*) a horoscope, especially one in a magazine, etc. **5.** one's destiny, fortune, or luck, especially as regarded as influenced by the heavenly bodies. **6.** a conventional figure having rays (commonly five or six) proceeding from, or angular points disposed in a regular outline about, a central point, and considered as representing a star of the sky. **7.** an emblem in this shape, worn as a badge of rank, an award, etc.: *a four-star general.* **8.** a white mark on the forehead of an animal, especially a horse; a blaze. **9.** *Printing, etc.* an asterisk. **10.** a person who is preeminent or distinguished in some art, profession, or other field. **11.** a prominent actor, singer, or the like, especially one who plays the leading role in a performance. *–adj.* **12.** brilliant, prominent, or distinguished; chief. *–verb* (**starred, starring**) *–v.t.* **13.** to set with, or as with, stars; spangle. **14.** to present or feature (an actor, etc.) as a star. **15.** to mark with a star or asterisk, as for special notice. *–v.i.* **16.** to shine as a star; be brilliant or prominent. **17.** (of an actor, etc.) to appear as a star. *–phr.* **18. see stars,** to seem to see bright flashes of light, as after a heavy blow on the head. **19. under the stars,** exposed to the night sky: *we slept under the stars.* *–stardom, n. –starry, adj.*

starboard /'stɑbəd/ *Naut. –n.* **1.** the side of a ship to the right of a person looking towards the bow (opposed to *port*). *–v.t.* **2.** to turn (the helm) to starboard.

starch /stɑtʃ/ *n.* **1.** a white, tasteless solid, chemically a carbohydrate, $(C_6H_{10}O_5)_n$, occurring in the form of minute grains in the seeds, tubers, and other parts of plants, and forming an important constituent of rice, corn, wheat, beans, potatoes, and many other vegetable foods; amylum. **2.** a commercial preparation of this substance used (dissolved in water) to stiffen linen, etc., in laundering, and also for many industrial purposes. **3.** (*pl.*) foods rich in starch. **4.** stiffness or formality, as of manner. *–v.t.* **5.** to stiffen or treat with starch. *–phr.* **6. starch up,** to make stiff or rigidly formal. *–starcher, n. –starchless, adj. –starchy, adj.*

star-crossed /'stɑ-krɒst/ *adj.* characterised by consistent ill fortune; having much bad luck, as if brought about by the influence of the stars: *Romeo and Juliet were star-crossed lovers.*

stare /steə/ *verb* (**stared, staring**) *–v.i.* **1.** to gaze fixedly, especially with the eyes wide open. **2.** to stand out boldly or obtrusively to view. **3.** (of hair, feathers, etc.) to stand on end; bristle. *–v.t.* **4.** to put, bring, etc., by staring: *to stare one out of countenance.* *–n.* **5.** a staring gaze; a fixed look with the eyes wide open: *the banker greeted him with a glassy stare. –phr.* **6. stare someone down,** to gaze imperiously or angrily at a person with whom one is seeking an ascendancy, until they

look away in defeat or discomfort. **7. stare someone in the face, a.** to be inescapably obvious. **b.** to be impending and require immediate action. **8. stare someone out,** to gaze fixedly at someone until they look away. *–starer, n.*

starfish /'stɑfɪʃ/ *n.* (*pl.* **-fishes** *or, especially collectively,* **-fish**) any echinoderm of the class Asteroidea, comprising marine animals having the body radially arranged, usually in the form of a star, with five or more rays or arms radiating from a central disc; an asteroid.

star fruit *n.* → **carambola.** Also, **starfruit.**

stark /stɑk/ *adj.* **1.** sheer, utter, downright, or arrant: *stark madness.* **2.** harsh, grim, or desolate to the view, as places, etc. *–adv.* **3.** utterly, absolutely, or quite: *stark mad. –starkly, adv. –starkness, n.*

starkers /'stɑkəz/ *adj. Colloq.* **1.** stark-naked. **2.** absolutely mad; insane.

starling¹ /'stɑlɪŋ/ *n.* any of numerous birds constituting the family Sturnidae, especially the common European species, *Sturnus vulgaris*; introduced into and now widespread in eastern Australia.

starling² /'stɑlɪŋ/ *n.* a set of piles driven into a riverbed upstream of a bridge pier to protect it from floating debris, the force of the current, etc.

Star of David *n.* a figure which is star-shaped with six points, formed of two equilateral triangles interlaced, one being inverted, used as a symbol of Judaism.

start /stɑt/ *v.i.* **1.** to begin to move, go, or act: *to start on a journey.* **2.** to begin, etc.: *when did you start on your career? When did your career start?* **3.** to come suddenly into activity, life, view, etc. **4.** to spring or move suddenly from a position or place: *he started from his seat.* **5.** to move with a sudden jerk, as from a shock. **6.** to stick out: *eyes starting from their sockets.* **7.** (of timbers, etc.) to spring, slip, or work loose from place or fastenings. **8.** to be among the starters in a race, contest, etc. *–v.t.* **9.** to set moving, going, or acting: *he will start the engine.* **10.** to set in operation; establish: *the company will start another newspaper.* **11.** to enter upon or begin: *will you start the letter?* **12.** to cause or help (a person, etc.) to begin a journey, a career, etc.: *he started his son in business.* *–n.* **13.** a beginning. **14.** a signal to start, as on a course or in a race. **15.** the first part of anything. **16.** a sudden, involuntary jerking movement of the body: *I woke with a start.* **17.** a lead or advance of a certain amount, as over competitors, etc.: *I had a start of half a lap.* **18.** a chance or opportunity of starting on a course or career. **19.** a spurt of activity: *she works in fits and starts. –phr.* **20. in fits and starts,** intermittently. **21. start into,** *Colloq.* to begin to scold, reprimand, etc. **22. start off,** to leave on a journey: *they started off next morning.* **23. start on,** *Colloq.* to criticise, abuse: *now don't start on me.* **24. start out, a.** Also, **start off.** to leave on a journey. **b.** to begin one's working life: *he started out as a farmer.* **c.** to begin a sequence of events: *she started out wanting blue curtains.*

starter /'stɑtə/ *n.* **1.** someone who gives the signal for starting, as in a race. **2.** a self-starter (def. 1). **3.** any competitor who begins a race, contest, or the like. **4.** a bacterial culture used to start fermentation, as in the making of cheese, dough, etc. **5.** the first course of a large meal; entree. **6.** *Colloq.* a likely prospect, as a person willing to take part in some activity: *any starters for bingo? –phr.* **7. for starters, a.** at first: *for starters, he played a Mozart concerto.* **b.** in the first place: *well, for starters, he's a crook.*

starting gun *n.* a handgun, either specially made for the purpose, or of a usual type which has been modified, which does not shoot a projectile, but makes a loud noise when fired; used to start a race. Also, **starter gun.**

starting price *n.* 1. the betting odds on a horse, greyhound, etc., at the time when a race begins. 2. the price at which bidding for a commodity should reasonably start, this being taken as a benchmark for prices.

startle /ˈstatl/ *v.t.* 1. to disturb or agitate suddenly by a surprise, alarm, or the like. 2. to cause to start involuntarily, as under a sudden shock. –*v.i.* 3. to start involuntarily, as from a surprise or alarm. –*n.* 4. a sudden surprise, alarm, or the like. 5. something that startles. –**startler**, *n.* –**startling**, *adj.* –**startlingly**, *adv.*

starve /stav/ *v.i.* 1. to die or perish from hunger. 2. to be in process of perishing, or to suffer severely, from hunger. 3. *Colloq.* to be hungry. 4. to suffer from extreme poverty and need. –*v.t.* 5. to cause to starve; weaken or reduce by lack of food. 6. to subdue, or force to some condition or action, by hunger: *to starve a besieged garrison into surrender.* 7. to cause to suffer for lack of something needed or craved. –*phr.* 8. **starve for**, to pine or suffer for lack of. 9. **starve the lizards** (or **bardies**) (or **crows**), *Aust. Colloq.* an exclamation of surprise or disgust. –**starving**, *adj.* –**starvation**, *n.*

stash /stæʃ/ *Colloq.* –*v.t.* 1. to put away, as for safekeeping or in a prepared place. –*n.* 2. a hoard. 3. a cache of drugs for personal use.

stat- a prefix attached to the name of electrical units to indicate the corresponding electrostatic unit, as *statcoulomb.*

-stat a word element used to mean 'causing to remain stationary or constant', and thus in calibrating instruments, as in *thermostat.*

state /steɪt/ *n.* 1. the condition of a person or thing, as with respect to circumstances or attributes: *a state of disrepair.* 2. condition with respect to constitution, structure, form, phase, or the like: *a liquid state; the larval state.* 3. a mode or form of existence: *the future state.* 4. a person's condition or position in life, or estate, station, or rank. 5. the style of living befitting a person of high rank and great wealth; sumptuous, imposing, or ceremonious display of dignity; pomp: *a hall used on occasions of state.* 6. a particular condition of mind or feeling: *to be in an excited state.* 7. a particularly tense, nervous, or excited condition: *to be in quite a state over a matter.* 8. a body of people occupying a definite territory and organised under one, usually independent, government; nation; country. 9. (*sometimes upper case*) one of the divisions or regions of a country, each more or less independent as regards internal affairs, which together make up a federal union, as in the Commonwealth of Australia, the United States of America, or India. 10. the domain or the authority of a state. 11. (*sometimes upper case*) the body politic as organised for civil rule and government, often contrasted with the church. 12. the operations or activities of supreme civil government, or the sphere of supreme civil authority and administration: *affairs of state.* –*adj.* 13. of or relating to the supreme civil government or authority. 14. (*sometimes upper case*) of or relating to one of the territories which make up a federal union, as any of the states of Australia. 15. characterised by, attended with, or involving ceremony: *a state dinner.* 16. used on or reserved for occasions of ceremony. –*v.t.* 17. to declare definitely or specifically: *to state one's views.* 18. to set forth formally in speech or writing: *to state a case.* 19. to set forth in proper or definite form: *to state a problem.* 20. to say. 21. to fix or settle, as by authority. –*phr.* 22. **lie in state**, (of a body) to be publicly displayed in honour before burial. 23. **the state of play**, the current situation. –**statehood**, *n.* –**stateless**, *adj.*

stately /ˈsteɪtli/ *adj.* (**-lier, -liest**) 1. dignified or majestic; imposing in magnificence, elegance, etc.: *a stately palace.* –*adv.* 2. in a stately manner. –**stateliness**, *n.*

statement /ˈsteɪtmənt/ *n.* 1. something stated. 2. a communication or declaration in speech or writing setting forth facts, particulars, etc. 3. an expression of one's beliefs, principles, etc. 4. *Commerce* an abstract of an account, as one rendered to show the balance due. 5. the occurrence of a theme, subject, or motif in a piece of music. 6. the act or manner of stating something.

stateroom /ˈsteɪtrum/ *n.* 1. a private room or cabin on a ship. 2. *US* a private sleeping compartment on a train. 3. any magnificent room for use on state occasions.

state school *n.* a school maintained at public expense for the education of the children and youth of a community or district, as part of a system of public, free education.

statesman /ˈsteɪtsmən/ *n.* (*pl.* **-men**) 1. a man who is active in the affairs of government; a politician, especially one who is experienced or who holds a high position in government. 2. someone who exhibits ability of the highest kind in directing the affairs of a government or in dealing with important public issues. –**statesmanlike, statesmanly,** *adj.* –**stateswoman**, *n.* –**statesmanship**, *n.*

static /ˈstætɪk/ *adj.* Also, **statical.** 1. relating to or characterised by a fixed or non-changing condition. 2. of or relating to static electricity. 3. *Physics* acting by weight without producing motion: *static pressure.* –*n.* *Elect.* 4. static or atmospheric electricity. 5. *Radio* unwanted noises, crackling, etc., caused by electrical currents from storms, etc; atmospherics. –**statically**, *adv.*

static electricity *n.* 1. electricity at rest, as that produced by friction. 2. electricity in the atmosphere which interferes with the sending and receiving of radio messages, etc.

station /ˈsteɪʃən/ *n.* 1. the place in which anything stands. 2. (the buildings at) a place at which a train, etc., regularly stops. 3. the end of a bus or coach route; terminus. 4. *Aust., NZ* a large rural establishment for raising sheep or cattle; a sheep or cattle station. 5. a place equipped for some particular kind of work, service, etc.: *a power station; a police station.* 6. *TV, Radio* **a.** (an organisation which manages) studios, recording and transmitting equipment, buildings, etc., used for producing and sending out programs. **b.** the wavelength on which a radio or television program is broadcast. 7. (of people) social standing; rank. 8. place or position of duty. –*v.t.* 9. to place or post in a station or position.

stationary /ˈsteɪʃənri, ˈsteɪʃənəri/, *Orig. US* /ˈsteɪʃəneri/ *adj.* 1. standing still; not moving. 2. having a fixed position; not movable. 3. established in one place; not itinerant or migratory. 4. remaining in the same condition or state; not changing. –**stationarily**, *adv.* –**stationariness**, *n.*

stationery /ˈsteɪʃənri, ˈsteɪʃənəri/, *Orig. US* /ˈsteɪʃəneri/ *n.* 1. writing paper. 2. writing materials, as pens, pencils, paper, etc. –**stationer**, *n.*

station wagon *n.* a car with an extended interior, allowing extra space behind the rear seat, and a door or tailgate at the back.

statism /ˈsteɪtɪzəm/ *n.* the principle or policy of concentrating extensive economic, political, and related controls in the state at the cost of individual liberty. –**statist**, *n.*

statistic /stəˈtɪstɪk/ *n.* 1. a numerical fact: *she quoted an interesting statistic about home ownership.* 2. a person or event seen as one summarised in official statistics: *I'm a person, not a statistic; you nearly became an accident statistic.*

statistics /stəˈtɪstɪks/ *n.* 1. (*construed as sing.*) the science which deals with the collection, classification, and use of numerical facts or data, bearing on a subject or matter. **2.** (*construed as pl.*) the numerical facts or data themselves. **–statistical**, *adj.* **–statistically**, *adv.* **–statistician**, *n.*

stative verb /'steɪtɪv vɜb/ *n. Gram.* a verb which indicates a state or condition which is not changing, as in *I own a house*, or *I hate vegetables*. Compare **dynamic verb**. Also, **non-action verb**.

stator /'steɪtə/ *n. Elect.* the fixed part of an electrical machine (motor or generator) which contains the stationary magnetic circuits.

statue /'stætʃu/ *n.* a representation of a person or an animal carved in stone or wood, moulded in a plastic material, or cast in bronze or the like, especially one of some size, in the round.

statuesque /stætʃu'esk/ *adj.* like or suggesting a statue, as in formal dignity, grace, immobility, proportions, or beauty. **–statuesquely**, *adv.* **–statuesqueness**, *n.*

stature /'stætʃə/ *n.* **1.** the height of an animal body, especially of a human. **2.** the height of any object. **3.** degree of development or achievement attained. **4.** impressive achievement; moral greatness.

status /'steɪtəs, 'stætəs/ *n.* (*pl.* **-tuses**) **1.** condition, position, or standing socially, professionally, or otherwise. **2.** the relative rank or social position of an individual or group. **3.** the relative standing, position, or condition of anything. **4.** the state or condition of affairs. **5.** *Law* the standing of a person before the law.

status quo /steɪtəs 'kwoʊ/ *n.* the existing or previously existing state or condition. Also, **status in quo**.

statute /'stætʃut/ *n.* **1.** *Law* **a.** an enactment made by a legislature and expressed in a formal document. **b.** the document in which such an enactment is expressed. **2.** *International Law* an instrument annexed or subsidiary to an international agreement, as a treaty. **3.** a permanent rule established by an institution, corporation, etc., for the conduct of its internal affairs. **–statutory**, *adj.*

statutory declaration *n.* (in Australia) a written statement declared before, and witnessed by, an authorised official, as a justice of the peace, etc., but not sworn on oath and therefore not recognised as evidence in a court of law. Compare **affidavit**.

staunch[1] /stɔntʃ/ *v.t.* **1.** to stop the flow of or as of (a liquid, especially blood). **2.** to stop the flow of blood from (a wound). **–v.i.** **3.** to stop flowing, as blood; be staunched. **–n.** **4.** *Civil Eng.* a device on primitive river navigation systems in which changes of level are overcome by sending boats down in a rush of water. **–stauncher**, *n.*

staunch[2] /stɔntʃ/ *adj.* **1.** firm or steadfast in principle, adherence, loyalty, etc., as a person. **2.** characterised by firmness or steadfastness. **3.** strong; substantial. **4.** impervious to water or other liquids; watertight. **–staunchly**, *adv.* **–staunchness**, *n.*

stave /steɪv/ *n.* **1.** one of the thin, narrow, shaped pieces of wood which form the sides of a cask, tub, or similar vessel. **2.** a stick, rod, pole, or the like. **3.** a rung of a ladder, chair, etc. **4.** *Prosody* **a.** a verse or stanza of a poem or song. **b.** the alliterating sound in a line of verse, thus, *w* is the stave in *the way of the wind*. **5.** Also, **staff**. *Music* a set of horizontal lines, now five in number, with the corresponding four spaces between them, music being written on both the lines and spaces. **–phr.** **6. stave in**, to break a hole in; crush inwards. **7. stave off**, to put, ward, or keep off, as by force or evasion.

stay[1] /steɪ/ *v.i.* **1.** to remain in a place, situation, company, etc.: *the visitors stayed all afternoon.* **2.** to sojourn; reside temporarily: *we stayed at the Hilton*; *my sister is staying with me.* **3.** to stop or halt. **4.** to pause or wait, as for a moment, before proceeding or continuing; linger or tarry. **–v.** (*copular*) **5.** to continue to be

(as specified), as to condition, etc.: *to stay clean.* **–v.t.** **6.** to stop or halt. **7.** to hold back, detain, or restrain, as from going further. **8.** to suspend or delay (proceedings, etc.). **9.** to suppress or quell (violence, strife, etc.). **10.** to appease or satisfy temporarily the cravings of (the stomach, appetite, etc.). **11.** to remain through or during (a period of time, etc.). **12.** to remain to the end of; last out; endure. **–n.** **13.** a stop, halt, or pause; a standstill. **14.** a sojourn or temporary residence. **15.** *Law* a stoppage or arrest of action; a suspension of a judicial proceeding. **16.** *US Colloq.* staying power; endurance. **–phr.** **17. stay put**, to remain where placed; not to move from a position. **18. stay with**, to keep up with, as with a competitor in a race.

stay[2] /steɪ/ *n.* **1.** something used or serving to support or steady a thing. **2.** a flat strip of steel, plastic, etc., for stiffening corsets, etc. **3.** (*pl.*) a corset. **–v.t.** **4.** (sometimes fol. by *up*) to support or hold up.

stay[3] /steɪ/ *Chiefly Naut.* **–n.** **1.** a strong rope, now commonly of wire, used to support a mast. **2.** any rope similarly used; a guy. **–v.t.** **3.** to support or secure with a stay or stays: *to stay a mast.* **–phr.** **4. in stays**, heading into the wind while going about from one tack to the other.

stay-up *n.* (*usu. pl.*) a stocking that reaches to above the knee with an elasticised strip at the top to hold it up.

STD /es ti 'di/ *n.* sexually transmitted disease; any disease such as syphilis, gonorrhoea, AIDS, herpes, some forms of hepatitis, genital warts, etc., which is transmitted through sexual contact between people.

stead /sted/ *n.* **1.** the place of a person or thing as occupied by a successor or substitute: *since he could not come, his brother came in his stead.* **–phr.** **2. stand someone in good stead**, to be useful or advantageous to someone.

steadfast /'stedfast, -fɑst/ *adj.* **1.** fixed in direction; steadily directed: *a steadfast gaze.* **2.** firm in purpose, resolution, faith, attachment, etc., as a person. **3.** unwavering, as resolution, faith, adherence, etc. **4.** firmly established, as an institution or a state of affairs. **5.** firmly fixed in place or position. **–steadfastly**, *adv.* **–steadfastness**, *n.*

steady /'stedi/ *adj.* (**steadier**, **steadiest**) **1.** firmly placed or fixed; stable in position or equilibrium; even or regular in movement: *a steady ladder.* **2.** free from change, variation, or interruption; uniform; continuous: *a steady wind.* **3.** constant, regular, or habitual: *steady drinkers.* **4.** free from excitement or agitation: *steady nerves.* **5.** firm, unwavering, or steadfast, as persons or their principles, policy, etc. **6.** settled, staid, or sober, as a person, habits, etc. **7.** *Naut.* (of a vessel) keeping nearly upright, as in a heavy sea. **–interj.** **8.** Also, **steady on**. be calm! control yourself! **9.** *Naut.* a helm order to keep a vessel on a certain course. **–n.** (*pl.* **steadies**) **10.** *Colloq.* a regular boyfriend or girlfriend. **–verb** (**steadied**, **steadying**) **–v.t.** **11.** to make steady, as in position, movement, action, character, etc. **–v.i.** **12.** to become steady. **–adv.** **13.** in a firm or steady manner. **–phr.** **14. go steady**, *Colloq.* to go about regularly with the same boyfriend or girlfriend. **–steadier**, *n.* **–steadily**, *adv.* **–steadiness**, *n.*

steak /steɪk/ *n.* **1. a.** a slice of meat, beef unless indicated otherwise, as ham steak, usually cut thick and across the grain of the muscle. **b.** a thick slice of a large fish cut across the body and including part of the backbone. **2.** chopped or minced meat formed to resemble steak and cooked in the manner of steak.

steal /stil/ *verb* (**stole**, **stolen**, **stealing**) **–v.t.** **1.** to take or take away dishonestly or wrongfully, especially secretly. **2.** to appropriate (ideas, credit, words, etc.) without right or acknowledgement. **3.** to take, get, or win by insidious, surreptitious, or subtle means: *to steal* *a nap during a sermon.* **4.** to move, bring, convey, or put (*away, from, in, into,* etc.) secretly or quietly. **5.** (in various games) to gain (a point, etc.) by strategy, by chance, or by luck. **6.** to obtain more than one's share of; appropriate entirely to oneself: *the new baby stole everybody's attention.* –*v.i.* **7.** to commit or practise theft. **8.** to move, go, or come secretly, quietly, or un-observed. **9.** to pass, come, spread, etc., imperceptibly, gently or gradually: *the years steal by.* –*n.* **10.** *Colloq.* something acquired at very little cost or at a cost well below its true value. –*phr.* **11. steal a march on,** to obtain an advantage over, especially by surreptitious or underhand means. **12. steal the show,** to outshine other performers and achieve popular success, as an actor in a play, etc. –**stealer,** *n.* –**stealing,** *n.*

stealth /stɛlθ/ *n.* secret, clandestine, or surreptitious procedure. –**stealthy,** *adj.*

steam /stim/ *n.* **1.** water in the form of a gas or vapour. **2.** water changed to this form by boiling, and exten-sively used for the generation of mechanical power, for heating purposes, etc. **3.** the mist formed when the gas or vapour from boiling water condenses in the air. **4.** an exhalation. **5.** *Colloq.* power or energy. –*v.i.* **6.** to emit or give off steam or vapour. **7.** to rise or pass off in the form of steam, as vapour. **8.** to generate or produce steam, as in a boiler. **9.** to move or travel by the agency of steam. –*v.t.* **10.** to expose to or treat with steam, as in order to heat, cook, soften, renovate, or the like. **11.** to expose (an animal carcass) to steam in order to melt and separate out the tallow. **12.** to emit or exhale (steam or vapour); send out in the form of steam. –*adj.* **13.** heated by or heating with steam: *steam radiator.* **14.** propelled by or propelling with a steam engine: *a steam train.* **15.** operated by steam. **16.** (*humorous*) antiquated; old-fashioned; belonging to the age of steam. –*phr. Colloq.* **17. let off steam,** to release pent-up energy or repressed emotions, such as anger and frustration, often by indirect and harmless means. **18. under one's own steam,** without the assistance of others; independently.

steamroller /'stimroʊlə/ *n.* **1.** a heavy locomotive, or-iginally steam-powered, having a roller or rollers, for crushing or levelling materials in road-making. **2.** an overpowering force, especially one that crushes oppo-sition with ruthless disregard of rights. –*v.t.* Also, **steamroll. 3.** to go over or crush as with a steamroller or an overpowering force.

stearic /sti'ærɪk/ *adj.* **1.** of or relating to suet or fat. **2.** *Chem.* of or relating to stearic acid.

steed /stid/ *n.* **1.** a horse, especially one for riding. **2.** a high-spirited horse.

steel /stil/ *n.* **1.** iron in a modified form, artificially pro-duced, containing a certain amount of carbon (more than in wrought iron and less than in cast iron) and other constituents, and possessing a hardness, elasticity, strength, etc., which vary with the composition and the heat treatment. It is commonly made by removing a certain amount of the carbon from pig iron, and used in making tools, girders, etc. **2. high** (or **hard**) **steel,** steel with a comparatively high percentage of carbon. **3. low** (or **mild**) (or **soft**) **steel,** steel with a comparatively low percentage of carbon. **4. medium steel,** a tough-tempering steel having a medium carbon content. **5.** something made of steel, as a knife-sharpener, device for striking sparks from flints, etc. **6.** a sword. **7.** *Stock Exchange* **a.** the market quotation of a steel concern. **b.** stocks, shares, etc., of steel companies. –*adj.* **8.** re-lating to or made of steel. **9.** like steel in colour, hard-ness, or strength. –*v.t.* **10.** to fit with steel, as by pointing, edging, or overlaying. **11.** to render insen-sible, inflexible, unyielding, determined, etc. –*phr.* **12. steel oneself,** (sometimes fol. by *against*) to harden

oneself, especially in anticipation of something that must be endured.

steel wool *n.* fine threads or shavings of steel, tangled into a small pad, and used for scouring, polishing, etc.

steelyard /'stiljad, 'stɪljəd/ *n.* a portable balance with two unequal arms, the longer one having a movable counterpoise, and the shorter one bearing a hook or the like for holding the object to be weighed.

steep[1] /stip/ *adj.* **1.** having an almost perpendicular slope or pitch, or a relatively high gradient, as a hill, an as-cent, stairs, etc. **2.** *Colloq.* unduly high, or exorbitant, as a price or amount. **3.** *Colloq.* extreme or extravagant, as a statement. –*n.* **4.** a steep place; a declivity, as of a hill. –**steeply,** *adv.* –**steepness,** *n.*

steep[2] /stip/ *v.t.* **1.** to soak in water or other liquid, as for the purpose of softening, cleaning, or extracting something. **2.** to wet thoroughly in or with any liquid, or as a liquid does. **3.** to be filled with some absorbing influence: *a mind steeped in romance.* –*v.i.* **4.** to lie soaking in a liquid. –*n.* **5.** the act or process of steeping. **6.** a liquid in which something is steeped. –**steeper,** *n.*

steeple /'stipəl/ *n.* a lofty tower attached to a church, temple, or the like, and often containing bells.

steeplechase /'stipəltʃeɪs/ *n.* **1.** → **jumps race. 2.** a horserace across country; point-to-point. **3.** a race run on foot by persons across country or over a course having obstacles, as ditches, hurdles, etc. –*v.i.* **4.** to ride or run in a steeplechase. –**steeplechaser,** *n.*

steer[1] /stɪə/ *v.t.* **1.** to guide the course of (anything in motion) by a rudder, helm, wheel, etc.: *to steer a ship.* **2.** to follow or pursue (a particular course). **3.** *Colloq.* to direct the course of. –*v.i.* **4.** to direct the course of a vessel, vehicle, aeroplane, or the like by the use of a rudder or other means. **5.** to direct one's course, or pursue a course (as specified). **6.** (of a vessel, etc.) to be capable of being steered; be steered or guided in a particular direction. –*phr.* **7. bum steer,** a misleading idea or suggested course of action. **8. steer clear of,** to avoid. –**steerable,** *adj.* –**steerer,** *n.*

steer[2] /stɪə/ *n.* a young castrated male bovine, especially one raised for beef.

steerage /'stɪərɪdʒ/ *n.* **1.** a part or division of a ship, or-iginally that containing the steering apparatus, later varying in use. **2.** (in a passenger ship) the part allotted to the passengers who travel at the cheapest rate.

steering committee *n.* a committee, especially one of a legislative body, entrusted with the preparation of the agenda of a conference, session, etc.

stego- a word element meaning 'cover', as in *stegosaurus.*

stein /staɪn/ *n.* **1.** an earthenware mug, especially for beer. **2.** the quantity of beer held by this.

stellar /'stɛlə/ *adj.* **1.** of or relating to the stars; consisting of stars. **2.** starlike. **3.** relating to a leading actor, etc. **4.** *Colloq.* special; outstanding: *a stellar person*; *a stellar performance.*

stem[1] /stɛm/ *n.* **1.** the ascending axis of a plant, whether above or below ground, which ordinarily grows in an opposite direction to the root or descending axis. **2.** the stalk which supports a leaf, flower, or fruit. **3.** the main body of that portion of a tree, shrub, or other plant which is above ground; a trunk; a stalk. **4.** a petiole; a peduncle; a pedicel. **5.** a stalk of bananas. **6.** something resembling or suggesting the stem of a plant, flower, etc. **7.** a long, slender part: *the stem of a tobacco pipe.* **8.** the slender, upright part of a goblet, wineglass, etc. **9.** the cylindrical projection on a watch, having a knob at the end for winding. **10.** the circular rod of some locks around which the key fits and rotates. **11.** the stock, or line of descent, of a family; ancestry or pedigree. **12.** *Gram.* the element common to all the forms of an inflectional paradigm, or to some sub-set thereof, usually more than a root. Thus *ten-* or *tan-* would be the root of Latin *tendere* and *tend-* would be the stem. **13.** *Music* the vertical line forming part of a note. **14.** the main or relatively thick stroke of a letter in printing, etc. *–v.t.* (**stemmed, stemming**) **15.** to remove the stem from (a fruit, etc.). *–phr.* **16. stem from,** to originate out of. *–***stemless,** *adj.*

stem² /stɛm/ *v.t.* (**stemmed, stemming**) **1.** to stop or check. **2.** to dam up (a stream, etc.). **3.** to tamp, plug, or make tight, as a hole or a joint. **4.** to staunch (bleeding, etc.). *–***stemless,** *adj.*

stem³ /stɛm/ *v.t.* (**stemmed, stemming**) **1.** to make headway against (a tide, current, gale, etc.). **2.** to make progress against (any opposition).

stem⁴ /stɛm/ *n. Naut.* **1.** an upright at the bow of a ship into which the side timbers or plates are jointed. **2.** the forward part of a ship: *from stem to stern.*

stem cell *n.* an unspecialised form of cell (def. 4a), capable of dividing and giving rise to various specialised cells.

stench /stɛntʃ/ *n.* **1.** an offensive smell; stink. **2.** ill-smelling quality.

stencil /ˈstɛnsəl/ *n.* **1.** a thin sheet of paper, cardboard, or metal cut through so as to reproduce a design, letters, etc., when colour is rubbed through it. **2.** the letters, designs, etc., produced. *–v.t.* (**-cilled** *or, Chiefly US*, **-ciled, -cilling** *or, Chiefly US,* **-ciling**) **3.** to mark or paint (a surface) or produce (letters, etc.) by means of a stencil.

steno- a word element meaning 'little', 'narrow', referring especially to shorthand, as in *stenography.*

stenotype /ˈstɛnətaɪp/ *n.* (*from trademark*) **1.** a keyboard instrument resembling a typewriter, used in a system of phonetic shorthand. **2.** the symbols typed in one stroke on a stenotype machine.

stentorian /stɛnˈtɔriən/ *adj.* very loud or powerful in sound: *a stentorian voice.*

step /stɛp/ *n.* **1.** a movement made by lifting the foot and setting it down again in a new position, as in walking, running, marching, or dancing. **2.** the space passed over or measured by one movement of the foot in stepping. **3.** the sound made by the foot in stepping. **4.** a mark or impression made by the foot on the ground; footprint. **5.** the manner of walking; gait. **6.** a pace uniform with that of another or others, or in time with music: *to that step.* **7.** a repeated pattern or unit of movement in a dance formed by a combination of foot and body motions. **8.** (*pl.*) movements or course in stepping or walking: *to retrace one's steps.* **9.** a very short distance; a distance easily walked. **10.** a move or proceeding, as towards some end or in the general course of action: *the first step towards peace.* **11.** a degree on a notional scale: *one step up the hierarchy.* **12.** *Music* **a.** a degree of the scale. **b.** the interval between two adjacent scale degrees; a second. **13.** a support for the foot in ascending or descending: *a step of a ladder; a step of a staircase.* **14.** (*pl.*) a series of such supports, usually outside, as part of a pathway, the entrance to a house, etc. **15.** (*pl.*) a stepladder. **16.** *Machinery, etc.* a part or offset resembling a step of a stair. *–v.i.* (**stepped, stepping**) **17.** to move, go, etc., by lifting the foot and setting it down again in a new position, or by using the feet alternately in this manner: *to step forward.* **18.** to walk, or go on foot, especially for a few steps or a short distance: *please step this way.* **19.** to move with measured steps, as in a dance. **20.** to go briskly or fast, as a horse. **21.** to come easily as if by a step of the foot: *to step into a fortune.* **22.** to press with the foot, as on a lever, spring, or the like, in order to operate some mechanism. *–v.t.* **23.** to take (a step, pace, stride, etc.). **24.** to go through or perform the steps of (a dance). **25.** to make or arrange in the manner of a series of steps. *–phr.* **26. break step,** to stop marching or

walking in step. **27. in step, a.** moving in time with and on the same foot as others. **b.** in harmony or conformity. **28. out of step, a.** not moving in time with and on the same foot as others. **b.** not in harmony or conformity. **29. step by step,** by degrees; gradually. **30. step down, a.** to decrease. **b.** to resign; relinquish a position, etc. **31. step in,** to intervene; become involved. **32. step on** (or **upon**), to put the foot down on, as on the ground, a support, etc.; tread on by intention or accident: *to step on a worm.* **33. step on it,** *Colloq.* to hasten; hurry. **34. step out, a.** to leave a place, especially for a short time. **b.** to walk briskly. **c.** *US* to go out to a social gathering, etc.; walk out. **d.** to measure (a distance, ground, etc.) by steps. **35. step up,** to increase. **36. step up (to the mark), a.** (of a sportsperson) to accept the challenge of competing, often at a higher level than usual. **b.** to meet challenges, especially by taking on additional responsibility. **37. take steps,** to initiate a course of action. **38. watch one's step,** to go, behave, etc., with caution. *–***steplike,** *adj. –***stepper,** *n.*

step- a prefix indicating connection between members of a family by the remarriage of a parent, and not by blood.

stepfamily /ˈstɛpfæməli/ *n.* **1.** the family of one's stepparent. **2.** a family in which at least one of the parents has had children with a previous partner.

stepladder /ˈstɛplædə/ *n.* a ladder having flat steps or treads in place of rungs and a hinged support to keep it upright.

steppe /stɛp/ *n.* a large plain, especially one without trees.

stepping stone *n.* **1.** a stone, or one of a line of stones, in shallow water, a marshy place, or the like, used for stepping on in crossing. **2.** a stone for use in mounting or ascending. **3.** any means of advancing or rising.

-ster a suffix of personal nouns, often derogatory, referring especially to occupation or habit, as in *songster, gamester, trickster,* also having less apparent connotations, as in *youngster, roadster.*

stereo /ˈstɛriou, ˈstɪəriou/ *n.* (*pl.* **stereos**) **1.** (any system equipped for) stereophonic sound reproduction. **2.** a stereoscopic photograph or photography. *–adj.* **3.** relating to stereophonic sound, stereoscopic photography, etc.

stereo- a word element referring to hardness, solidity, three-dimensionality, as in *stereogram, stereoscope.* Also, (*before some vowels*), **stere-**.

stereophonic /stɛriəˈfɒnɪk, stɪə-/ *adj.* **1.** of or relating to a three-dimensional auditory perspective. **2.** of or relating to the multi-channel reproduction or broadcasting of sound which simulates three-dimensional auditory perspective. Most commonly two channels are used and reproduction is from two speakers or speaker systems placed apart in front of the listener. **3.** of or relating to the discs, tapes, equipment, etc., used in creating stereophonic effects. Compare **monophonic, quadraphonic.** *–***stereophonically,** *adv. –***stereophony** /stɛriˈɒfəni, stɪə-/, *n.*

stereotype /ˈstɛriətaɪp, ˈstɪə-/ *n.* **1.** a process of making metal plates to use in printing by taking a mould of composed type or the like in papier-mâché or other material and then taking from this mould a cast (plate) in type metal. **2.** a plate made by this process. **3.** a set form; convention; standardised idea or concept. *–v.t.* **4.** to make a stereotype of. **5.** to give a fixed form to. *–***stereotyper,** *n. –***stereotypic** /stɛriəˈtɪpɪk, stɪə-/, ***stereotypical** /stɛriəˈtɪpɪkəl, stɪə-/, *adj. –***stereotypically** /stɛriəˈtɪpɪkli, stɪə-/, *adv. –***stereotyped,** *adj.*

sterile /ˈstɛraɪl/ *adj.* **1.** free from living germs or microorganisms: *sterile bandage.* **2.** incapable of producing, or not producing, offspring. **3.** barren; unproductive of vegetation, as soil. **4.** *Bot.* **a.** denoting a plant in which reproductive structures fail to develop. **b.** bearing no stamens or pistils. **5.** unproductive of results; fruitless.

–**sterilely**, *adv.* –**sterilise**, **sterilize**, *v.* –**sterilisation**, **sterilization**, *n.* –**sterility** /stə'rɪləti/, *n.*

sterling /'stɜːlɪŋ/ *adj.* **1.** of or relating to British currency. **2.** (of silver) being of standard quality, 92½ per cent pure silver. **3.** made of sterling silver: *sterling cutlery.* **4.** thoroughly excellent: *a man of sterling worth.* **5.** *Aust. Hist.* born in Britain or Ireland (opposed to *currency*).

stern¹ /stɜːn/ *adj.* **1.** firm, strict, or uncompromising: *stern discipline.* **2.** hard, harsh, or severe: *a stern warning.* **3.** rigorous or austere; of an unpleasantly serious character: *stern times.* **4.** grim or forbidding in aspect: *a stern face.* –**sternly**, *adv.* –**sternness**, *n.*

stern² /stɜːn/ *n.* **1.** the hinder part of a ship or boat (often opposed to *stem*). **2.** the hinder part of anything.

sternum /'stɜːnəm/ *n.* (*pl.* **-nums** *or* **-na** /-nə/) *Anat.* a bone or series of bones extending along the middle line of the ventral portion of the body of most vertebrates, consisting in humans of a flat, narrow bone connected with the clavicles and the true ribs; the breastbone. –**sternal**, *adj.*

steroid /'stɛrɔɪd, 'stɪə-/ *n.* **1.** *Biochem.* any of a large group of lipids most of which have specific physiological action, as the sterols, bile acids, and many hormones. **2.** a hormone, used by some athletes for body building. –*phr.* **3. on steroids**, exhibiting hypernatural energy, power, etc. –**steroidal**, *adj.*

stertorous /'stɜːtərəs/ *adj.* **1.** characterised by heavy snoring. **2.** breathing heavily or noisily. –**stertorously**, *adv.* –**stertorousness**, *n.*

stet /stɛt/ *verb* (**stetted**, **stetting**) –*v.i.* **1.** let it stand (a direction on a printer's proof, a manuscript, or the like to retain cancelled matter, usually accompanied by a row of dots under or beside the matter). –*v.t.* **2.** to mark with the word 'stet' or with dots.

stetho- a word element meaning 'chest'. Also, (*before vowels*), **steth-**.

stethoscope /'stɛθəskoʊp/ *n.* an instrument used in auscultation to convey sounds in the chest or other parts of the body to the ear of the examiner. –**stethoscopy** /stə'θɒskəpi/, *n.* –**stethoscopic** /stɛθə'skɒpɪk/, *adj.*

stetson /'stɛtsən/ *n.* a man's hat having a broad brim and a wide crown, common in the western US.

stevedore /'stiːvədɔː/ *n.* a firm or individual engaged in the loading or unloading of a vessel.

stew /stjuː/ *v.t.* **1.** to cook (food) by simmering or slow boiling. –*v.i.* **2.** to undergo cooking by simmering or slow boiling. **3.** *Colloq.* to fret, worry, or fuss. –*n.* **4.** a preparation of meat, fish, or other food cooked by stewing. **5.** *Colloq.* a state of uneasiness, agitation, or worry. **6.** (*usu. pl.*) *Archaic* a brothel. –*phr.* **7. stew in one's own juice**, to suffer misfortunes or the consequences of one's own actions without help.

steward /'stjuːəd/ *n.* **1.** someone who manages another's property or financial affairs. **2.** someone who has charge of the household of another, providing for the table, directing the servants, etc. **3.** an employee who has charge of the table, the servants, etc., in a club or other establishment. **4.** any person on a ship or aircraft who waits on passengers. **5.** someone responsible for arranging the details and conduct of a public meeting, race meeting, public entertainment, etc. –**stewardship**, *n.*

-stichous *Bot.*, *Zool.* a word element referring to rows, as in *distichous.*

stick¹ /stɪk/ *n.* **1.** a branch or shoot of a tree or shrub cut or broken off. **2.** a relatively long and slender piece of wood. **3.** an elongated piece of wood for burning, for carpentry, or for any special purpose. **4.** a rod or wand; a baton. **5.** a walking stick or cane. **6.** a club or cudgel. **7.** an elongated, stick-like piece of some material: *a stick of rock.* **8.** *Sport* the stick or racquet used to hit the ball in hockey or lacrosse. **9.** (*pl.*) *Football* the goal posts. **10.** *Mil.* **a.** a group of bombs so arranged as to be released in a row across a target. **b.** the bombload. **c.** a group of parachutists jumping in sequence. **11.** (*usu. pl.*) a piece of furniture: *a few old sticks.* **12.** *Colloq.* a person: *a decent stick.* **13.** *US Colloq.* a marijuana cigarette. –*phr.* **14. in a cleft stick**, in a dilemma, awkward position, etc. **15. more than one can poke** (or **shake**) **a stick at**, *Colloq.* a lot of; many; much. **16. the sticks**, *Colloq.* **a.** an area or district regarded as lacking in the amenities of urban life. **b.** → **back country** (def. 1). **17. wrong end of the stick**, a complete misunderstanding of facts, a situation, etc.

stick² /stɪk/ *verb* (**stuck**, **sticking**) –*v.t.* **1.** to pierce or puncture with a pointed instrument, as a dagger, spear, or pin; stab. **2.** to kill by this means: *to stick a pig.* **3.** to thrust (something pointed) in, into, through, etc.: *to stick a pin into a balloon.* **4.** to fasten in position by thrusting the point or end into something: *to stick a nail in a wall.* **5.** to fasten in position by, or as by, something thrust through: *to stick a badge on one's coat.* **6.** to fix or impale upon something pointed: *to stick a potato on a fork.* **7.** to set with things piercing the surface: *to stick a cushion full of pins.* **8.** to thrust or poke into a place or position indicated: *to stick one's head out of the window.* **9.** to place in a specified position: *stick your books on the table.* **10.** to fasten or attach by causing to adhere: *to stick a stamp on a letter.* **11.** to bring to a standstill; render unable to proceed or go back: *to be stuck in the mud.* **12.** *Colloq.* to endure; tolerate. –*v.i.* **13.** to have the point piercing, or embedded in something. **14.** to remain attached by adhesion: *the mud sticks to one's shoes.* **15.** to hold, cleave, or cling: *to stick to a horse's back.* **16.** to remain persistently or permanently: *a fact that sticks in the mind.* **17.** to become fastened, hindered, checked, or stationary by some obstruction. **18.** to be at a standstill, as from difficulties. **19.** to be thrust or extend, project, or protrude: *a branch sticking up from the mud.* **20.** to remain or stay, usually for a considerable time: *I can't bear to stick indoors all day.* –*n.* **21.** a thrust with a pointed instrument; a stab. **22.** the quality of adhering or of causing things to adhere. **23.** something causing adhesion. –*phr.* **24. stick around**, *Colloq.* to stay nearby; linger. **25. stick at**, **a.** to keep steadily or unremittingly at (a task, undertaking, or the like): *to stick at a job.* **b.** to hesitate or scruple to do. **26. stick by**, to remain loyal or faithful to. **27. stick in someone's throat**, to be hard to accept. **28. stick it**, *Colloq.* an expression of contempt, dismissal, disgust, etc. **29. stick one's neck out**, *Colloq.* to expose oneself to blame, criticism, etc.; take a risk. **30. stick one's nose in**, *Colloq.* to pry; interfere. **31. stick out**, **a.** to protrude; thrust out. **b.** to be obvious, conspicuous, etc.: *to stick out a mile.* **c.** to endure; put up with something until the very end: *they were bored by the film but stuck it out for two hours.* **32. stick out for**, to continue to ask for; be persistent in demanding. **33. stick out like dogs' balls**, *Colloq.* to be extremely noticeable. **34. stick to**, to remain firm with regard to (an opinion, statement, resolution, promise, etc.): *he stuck to his view that the mayor was wrong.* **35. stick together**, to remain friendly, loyal, etc., to one another. **36. stick up**, **a.** to project or protrude upwards. **b.** *Colloq.* to rob, especially at gunpoint. **37. stick up for**, to speak or act in favour of; defend; support. **38. stick up to**, to confront boldly; resist strongly. **39. stick with**, to remain loyal or faithful to. **40. (you can) stick that for a joke** (or **lark**), *Colloq.* an expression indicating complete and often derisive rejection of a proposal, plan, etc.

sticker /'stɪkə/ *n.* **1.** an adhesive label, usually with an advertisement or other message printed on it. **2.** someone who, despite difficulties, keeps trying to succeed.

sticking plaster *n.* an adhesive cloth or other material for covering and closing superficial wounds, etc.

stick insect *n.* any of certain orthopterous insects of the order Phasmatodea, with long, slender, twig-like or leaf-like bodies.

stickleback /'stɪkəlbæk/ *n.* any of the small, pugnacious, spiny-backed fishes of the family Gasterosteidae, of fresh waters and sea inlets.

stickler /'stɪklə/ *phr.* **a stickler for ...**, a person who insists unyieldingly on (something specified): *a stickler for punctuality*.

stick-up *n. Colloq.* a hold-up or robbery.

sticky[1] /'stɪki/ *adj.* (**-kier, -kiest**) **1.** having the property of adhering, as glue; adhesive. **2.** covered with adhesive matter: *sticky hands*. **3.** (of the weather, etc.) humid: *an unbearably sticky day*. **4.** *Colloq.* difficult to deal with; awkward; troublesome. *–n.* (*pl.* **-kies**) **5.** a sweet dessert wine. **–stickily,** *adv.* **–stickiness,** *n.*

sticky[2] /'stɪki/ *Aust. Colloq. –n.* (*pl.* **-kies**) **1.** a look. *–phr.* **2. have a sticky** (**at**), to take a look (at).

stickybeak /'stɪkibik/ *Aust., NZ –v.i.* **1.** to pry; meddle. *–n.* **2.** someone who pries. **3.** an inquisitive inspection: *have a bit of a stickybeak*.

stiff /stɪf/ *adj.* **1.** rigid or firm in substance; not flexible, pliant, or easily bent: *a stiff collar*. **2.** not moving or working easily: *a stiff hinge*. **3.** (of the body or part of the body) unable to move without difficulty or causing pain, as from cold, age, exhaustion, etc. **4.** blowing violently, strongly, or with steady force: *stiff winds*. **5.** strong, as alcoholic beverages. **6.** stubbornly maintained, as a struggle, etc. **7.** firm against any lowering action, as prices, etc. **8.** rigidly formal, as persons, manners, proceedings, etc. **9.** lacking ease and grace; awkward: *a stiff style of writing*. **10.** excessively regular, as a design; not graceful in form or arrangement. **11.** laborious or difficult, as a task. **12.** severe, as a penalty. **13.** excessive; unusually high or great, as a price, demand, etc. **14.** firm from tension; taut: *to keep a stiff rein*. **15.** relatively firm in consistency, as semisolid matter: *a stiff jelly*. **16.** dense, compact, or tenacious: *stiff soil*. **17.** *Naut.* (of a ship) resistant to heeling; stable. **18.** *Aust., NZ Colloq.* unfortunate; unlucky: *if you want a job here, you'll be stiff*. **19.** *Aust. Colloq.* without money; hard-up. **20.** *Colloq.* drunk. *–n. Colloq.* **21.** a dead body; corpse. **22.** a drunk. **23.** Also, **stiffy, stiffie.** (*taboo*) an erect penis. *–adv.* **24.** in a rigid state: *the clothes were frozen stiff*. **25.** completely or utterly: *scared stiff*; *bored stiff*; *frozen stiff*. *–phr.* **26. stiff cheese** (or **cheddar**) (or **luck**) (or **shit**), **a.** bad luck. **b.** an off-hand expression of sympathy. **c.** a rebuff to an appeal for sympathy. **27. stiff with,** bristling with; full of: *the area was stiff with cops*. **–stiffen,** *v.* **–stiffish,** *adj.* **–stiffly,** *adv.* **–stiffness,** *n.*

stifle /'staɪfəl/ *v.t.* **1.** to kill by impeding respiration; smother. **2.** to keep back or repress: *to stifle a yawn*. **3.** to suppress, crush, or stop: *to stifle a revolt*. *–v.i.* **4.** to become stifled or suffocated. **5.** to suffer from difficulty in breathing, as in a close atmosphere. **–stifler,** *n.*

stigma /'stɪgmə/ *n.* (*pl.* **stigmas** or **stigmata** /'stɪgmətə/ for *defs 1–4*, /stɪg'matə/ for *def. 5*) **1.** a mark of shame; a stain, as on one's reputation. **2.** a characteristic mark or sign of a fault or imperfection, disease, etc. **3.** *Zool.* a small mark, spot, pore, or the like, on an animal or organ, as: **a.** the eyespot, usually red, of a protozoan. **b.** (in insects) the entrance into the respiratory system. **4.** *Bot.* that part of a pistil which receives the pollen. **5.** (*pl.*) *Roman Catholic Church* marks said to have been supernaturally produced upon certain persons in the likeness of the wounds on the crucified body of Christ. **–stigmatise, stigmatize,** *v.*

stile /staɪl/ *n.* **1.** a series of steps or the like for ascending and descending in getting over a fence, etc., which remains closed to cattle. **2.** → **turnstile**.

stiletto /stə'letoʊ/ *n.* (*pl.* **-tos**) **1.** a dagger having a narrow blade, thick in proportion to its width. **2. a.** Also, **stiletto heel,** a high heel on a woman's shoe that tapers to an extremely small base. **b.** a shoe with a stiletto heel. *–v.t.* (**-toed, -toing**) **3.** to stab or kill with a stiletto.

still[1] /stɪl/ *adj.* **1.** remaining in place or at rest; motionless; stationary: *to stand still*. **2.** free from sound or noise, as a place, time, etc.; silent: *a still night*. **3.** quiet or low in sound; hushed: *a still, small voice*. **4.** free from movement of any kind; quiet; tranquil; calm: *still water*. **5.** not bubbling or sparkling, as wine. **6.** *Photography* denoting or relating to a still (photograph). *–n.* **7.** *Poetic* stillness or silence: *in the still of the night*. **8.** a single photographic picture, especially a print of one of the frames of a moving film. *–adv.* **9.** up to or at this time; as previously: *points still unsettled; Is she still here?* **10.** even or yet (with comparatives, etc.): *still more complaints*. **11.** even then; yet; nevertheless: *to be rich and still crave for more*. **12.** without sound or movement. **13.** *Poetic* steadily; constantly; always. *–conj.* **14.** and yet; but yet; nevertheless: *it was futile, still they fought*. *–v.t.* **15.** to silence or hush (sounds, etc.). **16.** to calm, quieten; appease; allay. *–v.i.* **17.** to become still or quiet. **–stillness,** *n.*

still[2] /stɪl/ *n.* **1.** a distilling apparatus, consisting of a vessel, in which the substance is heated and vaporised, and a cooling device or coil for condensing the vapour. **2.** → **distillery**.

stillbirth /'stɪlbɜθ/ *n.* **1.** the birth of a dead child or organism. **2.** a fetus dead at birth. **–stillborn,** *adj.*

still life *n.* (*pl.* **still lifes**) a picture representing inanimate objects, such as fruit, flowers, etc. **–still-life,** *adj.*

stilt /stɪlt/ *n.* **1.** one of two poles, each with a support for the foot at some distance above the ground. **2.** one of several high posts underneath any structure built above land or over water. **3.** any of various shoreline wading birds of the family Recurvirostridae, with very long legs, long neck, and slender, recurved bill, found in temperate and subtropical regions worldwide, as the **black-winged stilt,** *Himantopus himantopus,* of Eurasia, Africa and Australia. *–v.t.* **4.** to raise on or as on stilts.

stilted /'stɪltəd/ *adj.* **1.** stiffly dignified or formal, as speech, literary style, etc.; pompous. **2.** *Archit.* raised on or as on stilts: *a stilted arch*. **–stiltedly,** *adv.* **–stiltedness,** *n.*

stilton /'stɪltən/ *n.* (*from trademark*) a rich, waxy, white cheese, veined with mould.

stimulant /'stɪmjələnt/ *n.* **1.** *Physiol., Med.* something that temporarily quickens some vital process or the functional activity of some organ or part. **2.** any beverage or food that stimulates. *–adj.* **3.** *Physiol., Med.* temporarily quickening some vital process or functional activity. **4.** stimulating.

stimulate /'stɪmjəleɪt/ *v.t.* **1.** to rouse to action or effort, as by pricking or goading; spur on; incite: *to stimulate production*. **2.** *Physiol., Med., etc.* to excite (an organ, etc.) to its functional activity. **3.** to invigorate by an alcoholic or other stimulant. *–v.i.* **4.** to act as a stimulus or stimulant. **–stimulator,** *n.* **–stimulation** /stɪmjə'leɪʃən/, *n.* **–stimulative,** *adj.*

stimulus /'stɪmjələs/ *n.* (*pl.* **-li** /-laɪ, -li/ or **-luses**) **1.** something that incites to action or exertion, or quickens action, feeling, thought, etc.; an incentive. **2.** *Physiol., etc.* something that excites an organism or part to functional activity.

sting /stɪŋ/ *verb* (**stung, stinging**) *–v.t.* **1.** to prick or wound with some sharp-pointed, often poison-bearing organ, which certain animals have: *a bee has stung me*. **2.** to affect painfully, especially as a result of contact with certain plants: *to be stung by nettles.* **3.** to cause (someone) mental or moral suffering: *to be stung with remorse*; *her unkind words stung me.* **4.** to drive or goad as by sharp irritation: *he stung me into answering back.* −*v.i.* **5.** (of bees, etc.) to use a sting. **6.** to cause a sharp, smarting physical or mental pain: *nettles sting*; *sarcasm aims to sting.* **7.** to feel sharp physical or mental pain or irritation. −*n.* **8.** the act or power of stinging or causing pain. **9.** a wound or pain caused by a sting. **10.** any sharp or smarting wound, hurt, or pain (physical or mental). **11.** *Bot.* a type of hair on certain plants, especially nettles, which gives off an irritating fluid. **12.** *Zool.* a sharp-pointed, often poison-bearing, organ of insects and other animals, able to cause painful or dangerous wounds. **13.** *Colloq.* an undercover operation set up by police to trap a criminal. **14.** *Colloq.* a short, usually dramatic, musical chord or series of chords, used to separate segments of a radio program, etc. −*phr.* **15. sting in the tail**, an unexpectedly unpleasant ending or outcome. −**stinging**, *adj.*

stinger /ˈstɪŋə/ *n.* **1.** an animal or plant that stings, especially the box jellyfish. **2.** the sting (def. 12) of an insect or the like.

stingray /ˈstɪŋreɪ/ *n.* any of the rays, especially the family Dasyatidae, having a long, flexible tail armed near the base with a strong, serrated bony spine with which they can inflict severe and very painful wounds.

stingy /ˈstɪndʒi/ *adj.* (**-gier, -giest**) **1.** reluctant to give or spend; niggardly. **2.** scanty or meagre. −**stingily**, *adv.* −**stinginess**, *n.*

stink /stɪŋk/ *v.i.* (**stank** *or* **stunk, stunk, stinking**) **1.** to emit a strong offensive smell. **2.** to be in extremely bad repute or disfavour. **3.** *Colloq.* to be very inferior in quality. −*n.* **4.** a strong offensive smell; stench. **5.** *Colloq.* a commotion; fuss; scandal: *kick up a stink.* −*phr.* **6. stink of, a.** to smell strongly and offensively of. **b.** *Colloq.* to have a large quantity of (something, especially money). **7. stink out, a.** to cause to stink. **b.** to repel, drive out, etc., by an offensive smell. −**stinking**, *adj.*

stinker /ˈstɪŋkə/ *n. Colloq.* **1.** a dishonourable, disgusting, or objectionable person. **2.** something objectionable, of poor quality, etc.: *that movie was an absolute stinker.* **3.** a very hot day.

stinking wattle *n.* → **gidgee**[1] (def. 1).

stint /stɪnt/ *v.t.* **1.** to limit to a certain amount, number, share, or allowance, often unduly; set limits to; restrict. −*v.i.* **2.** to be sparing or frugal; get along on a scanty allowance. −*n.* **3.** a limited or prescribed quantity, share, rate, etc.: *to exceed one's stint.* **4.** an allotted amount or piece of work: *to do one's daily stint.* **5.** a period of time, usually short, allotted to a particular activity. −*phr.* **6. without stint**, generously; freely: *to give without stint.* −**stinter**, *n.* −**stintingly**, *adv.*

stipend /ˈstaɪpɛnd/ *n.* fixed or regular pay; periodic payment; salary. −**stipendiary**, *adj.*, *n.*

stipendiary magistrate *n.* → **magistrate** (def. 2). *Abbrev.*: SM

stipple /ˈstɪpəl/ *v.t.* **1.** to paint, engrave, or draw by means of dots or small touches. −*n.* Also, **stippling**. **2.** the method of painting, engraving, etc., by stippling. **3.** stippled work; a painting, engraving, or the like, executed by means of dots or small spots. −**stippler**, *n.*

stipulate /ˈstɪpjəleɪt/ *v.i.* **1.** to make an express demand or arrangement (*for*), as a condition of agreement. −*v.t.* **2.** to arrange expressly or specify in terms of agreement: *to stipulate a price.* **3.** to require as an essential condition in making an agreement. **4.** to promise, in making an agreement. −**stipulation** /stɪpjəˈleɪʃən/, *n.* −**stipulator**, *n.* −**stipulatory**, *adj.*

stir[1] /stɜ/ *verb* (**stirred, stirring**) −*v.t.* **1.** to move or agitate (a liquid, or any matter in separate particles or pieces)

so as to change the relative position of component parts, as by passing an implement continuously or repeatedly through: *to stir one's coffee with a spoon.* **2.** to move, especially in some slight way: *the noise stirred the baby in her sleep.* **3.** to set in tremulous, fluttering, or irregular motion; shake: *leaves stirred by the wind.* **4.** to move briskly; bestir: *to stir oneself.* **5.** (sometimes fol. by *up*) to rouse from inactivity, quiet, contentment, indifference, etc.: *to stir a people to rebellion.* **6.** to affect strongly; excite: *to stir pity; to stir the heart.* −*v.i.* **7.** to move, especially slightly or lightly: *not a leaf stirred.* **8.** to move about, especially briskly. **9.** to be in circulation, current, or afoot: *is there any news stirring?* **10.** to become active, as from some rousing or quickening impulse. **11. a.** to touch on controversial topics in a deliberate attempt to incite a heated discussion. **b.** to cause trouble deliberately. −*n.* **12.** the act of stirring or moving, or the sound made. **13.** brisk or busy movement. **14.** a state or occasion of general excitement; a commotion. −*phr.* **15. for a stir**, *Colloq.* with the aim of causing trouble. **16. stir along**, *Colloq.* to make frequent use of the gears when driving a heavy vehicle. **17. stir the possum**, *Aust.* to instigate a debate on a controversial topic, especially in the public arena. **18. stir up**, to incite, instigate, or prompt: *to stir up a rebellion.* −**stirrer**, *n.*

stir[2] /stɜ/ *n. Colloq.* a prison.

stir-fry 1. to fry lightly in a little hot fat or oil, while stirring continually. −*n.* **2.** a dish prepared by stir-frying.

stirrup /ˈstɪrəp/ *n.* **1.** a loop, ring, or other contrivance of metal, wood, leather, etc., suspended from the saddle of a horse to support the rider's foot. **2.** any of various similar supports, or any of various clamps, etc., used for special purposes. **3.** one of a series of vertical steel loops used in a reinforced concrete beam to resist shear.

stitch /stɪtʃ/ *n.* **1.** one complete movement of a threaded needle through a fabric or material such as to leave behind it a single loop or portion of thread, as in sewing, embroidery, surgical closing of wounds, etc. **2.** a loop or portion of thread disposed in place by one movement in sewing: *to rip out stitches.* **3.** a particular mode of disposing the thread in sewing, or the style of work produced. **4.** one complete movement of the needle or other implement used in knitting, crocheting, netting, tatting, etc. **5.** the portion of work produced. **6.** a thread or bit of any fabric or of clothing, etc.: *every stitch she had on.* **7.** a sudden, sharp pain in the side, brought on by physical exertion. −*v.t.* **8.** to work upon, join, or fasten with stitches; sew; ornament with stitches. **9.** to put staples through for fastening. −*v.i.* **10.** to make stitches; sew (by hand or machine). −*phr.* **11. in stitches**, laughing unrestrainedly. **12. without a stitch on**, naked. −**stitcher**, *n.*

stoat /stoʊt/ *n.* the brown colour phase of *Mustela erminea*, a small carnivore of the weasel family found in Europe, Asia and North America; the white colour phase is called the ermine. Compare **ermine**.

stock /stɒk/ *n.* **1.** an aggregate of goods kept on hand by a merchant, business firm, manufacturer, etc., for the supply of customers. **2.** a quantity of something accumulated, as for future use: *a stock of provisions.* **3.** → **livestock**. **4.** *Hort.* **a.** a stem, tree, or plant that furnishes slips or cuttings; a stock plant. **b.** a stem in which a graft is inserted and which is its support. **5.** the trunk or main stem of a tree or other plant, as distinguished from roots and branches. **6.** → **rootstock**. **7.** the type from which a group of animals or plants has been derived. **8.** a breed, variety, or other related group of animals or plants. **9.** the person from whom a given line of descent is derived; the original progenitor. **10.** *Ethnology* a major division of humankind. **11.** a group of languages having certain features in common and considered to be ultimately related. **12.** the handle of a whip, etc. **13.** *Firearms* **a.** the wooden or metal piece to which the barrel and mechanism of a rifle or like firearm are attached. **b.** a part of an automatic weapon, as a machine gun, similar in position or function. **14.** the stump of a tree left standing. **15.** a log or block of wood. **16.** the main upright part of anything, especially a supporting structure. **17.** → **ski pole** (def. 1). **18.** (*pl.*) an instrument of punishment (no longer in use), consisting of a framework with holes for the ankles and (sometimes) the wrists of an offender exposed to public derision. **19.** (*pl.*) a frame in which a horse or other animal is secured in a standing position for shoeing or for a veterinary operation. **20.** (*pl.*) the frame onto which a boat rests while under construction. **21.** a tool for holding dies used in cutting screw threads on a rod. **22.** the piece of metal or wood which constitutes the body of a carpenter's plane. **23.** *Building Trades* the base plate of the timber mould on which bricks are formed. **24.** the raw material from which anything is made: *paper stock*. **25.** *Cookery* the liquor or broth prepared by boiling meat, fish, vegetables, etc., used especially as a foundation for soups and sauces. **26.** any of various widely cultivated plants of the genus *Matthiola*, especially *M. incana* and the **nightscented stock**, *M. bicornis*. **27.** a collar or cravat fitting like a band about the neck. **28.** *Cards* that portion of a pack of cards which, in certain games, is not dealt out to the players, but is left on the table, to be drawn from as occasion requires. **29.** *Theatre* the repertoire of pieces produced by a stock company. **30.** *Finance* **a.** the capital of a company converted from fully paid shares. **b.** the shares of a particular company. **c.** → **capital stock**. **31.** repute; standing. **32.** *Obs.* a stocking. –*adj.* **33.** kept regularly on hand, as for use or sale; staple; standard: *stock articles*. **34.** having as one's job the care of a concern's goods: *a stock clerk*. **35.** of the common or ordinary type; in common use: *a stock argument*. **36.** commonplace: *a stock remark*. **37.** designating or relating to livestock raising: *stock farming*. **38.** *Commerce* of or relating to the stock of a company. **39.** *Theatre* **a.** relating to repertory plays or pieces, or to a stock company. **b.** appearing together in a repertoire, as a company. **c.** forming part of a repertoire, as a play. –*v.t.* **40.** to furnish with a stock or supply. **41.** to furnish with stock, as a farm with horses, cattle, etc. **42.** to lay up in store, as for future use. –*phr.* **43. in stock**, available for use or sale. **44. on the stocks**, under construction; in preparation. **45. out of stock**, not available for use or sale. **46. stock up**, to lay in a stock of something. **47. take** (or **put**) **stock in**, *Chiefly US* to put confidence in; trust; believe. **48. take stock**, **a.** to make an inventory of stock on hand. **b.** to make an appraisal of resources, prospects, etc.

stockade /stɒˈkeɪd/ *n.* **1.** *Fortifications* a defensive barrier consisting of strong posts or timbers fixed upright in the ground. **2.** an enclosure or pen made with posts and stakes. **3.** (formerly) an enclosure in which convict labourers employed in road gangs, etc., were held at night. **4.** *US* a prison for military personnel. –*v.t.* **5.** to protect, fortify, or encompass with a stockade.

stock and station agent *n.* **1.** someone engaged in the business of buying and selling rural properties and stock. **2.** a firm which supplies provisions to rural properties. Also, **stock agent**.

stockbroker /ˈstɒkbroʊkə/ *n.* a broker who buys and sells stocks and shares for customers for a commission. –**stockbrokerage**, **stockbroking**, *n.*

stock car *n.* a production-model car modified for racing. –**stock-car**, *adj.*

stock certificate *n.* a certificate evidencing ownership of one or more shares of a company's stock.

stock exchange *n.* **1.** (*oft. upper case*) a building or place where stocks and shares are bought and sold.

2. an association of brokers, jobbers, and dealers in stocks and bonds, who meet to transact business according to fixed rules.

Stockholm syndrome /ˈstɒkhoʊm ˌsɪndroʊm/ *n.* the tendency of hostages to form a sympathetic bond with their captors.

stocking /ˈstɒkɪŋ/ *n.* **1.** a woman's garment consisting of a close-fitting covering for the foot and leg, usually made of finely knitted translucent nylon or silk, reaching to the thigh and held up by suspenders or an elasticised strip at the top. **2.** (formerly) a similar garment for women or men, made of wool, cotton, etc. **3.** something resembling a stocking, such as a medical support for the leg, or a stocking-shaped bag hung up by children to receive their Christmas presents. –**stockingless**, *adj.*

stock-in-trade *n.* **1.** goods, assets, etc., necessary for carrying on a business. **2.** the abilities, resources, etc., characteristic of or belonging to a particular group: *eloquence is part of a salesman's stock-in-trade*.

stockist /ˈstɒkəst/ *n.* a vendor, as a retailer or distributor, who keeps goods in stock.

stockjobber /ˈstɒkdʒɒbə/ *n.* a stock exchange dealer who acts as an intermediary between brokers and buyers but does not deal directly with the public. –**stockjobbery**, **stockjobbing**, *n.*

stockman /ˈstɒkmən/ *n.* (*pl.* **-men**) a man employed to tend livestock, especially cattle. –**stockwoman**, *n.*

stock market *n.* a market where stocks and shares are bought and sold; a stock exchange. Also, **stockmarket**.

stockpile /ˈstɒkpaɪl/ *n.* **1.** a supply of material, as a pile of gravel in road maintenance. **2.** a large supply of essential materials, held in reserve for use during a period of shortage, etc. **3.** a supply of munitions, weapons, etc., accumulated for possible future use. –*v.t.* **4.** to accumulate for future use. –*v.i.* **5.** to accumulate in a stockpile. –**stockpiler**, *n.*

stock-still *adj.* motionless.

stocktake /ˈstɒkteɪk/ *n.* **1.** an instance of stocktaking. –*v.i.* (**-taken**, **-taking**) **2.** to conduct a stocktaking. –**stocktaker**, *n.*

stocktaking /ˈstɒkteɪkɪŋ/ *n.* **1.** the examination and listing of goods, assets, etc., in a shop, business, etc. **2.** a reappraisal or reassessment of one's position, progress, prospects, etc.

stockworker /ˈstɒkwɜkə/ *n.* a person employed to tend livestock, especially cattle.

stocky /ˈstɒki/ *adj.* (**-kier**, **-kiest**) **1.** of solid and sturdy form or build; thickset, often short. **2.** having a strong, stout stem, as a plant. –**stockily**, *adv.* –**stockiness**, *n.*

stoke /stoʊk/ *v.t.* **1.** to poke, stir up, and feed (a fire). **2.** to tend the fire of (a furnace, especially one used with a boiler to generate steam for an engine); supply with fuel. –*v.i.* **3.** to shake up the coals of a fire. **4.** to tend a fire or furnace; act as a stoker: *to make a living by stoking*. –*phr.* **5. stoke up**, *Colloq.* to eat, especially a big meal.

stole[1] /stoʊl/ *v.* past tense of **steal**.

stole[2] /stoʊl/ *n.* **1.** an ecclesiastical vestment, a narrow strip of silk or other material worn over the shoulders and hanging down in front to the knee or below. **2.** a woman's scarf or similar garment of fur or cloth, usually worn with the ends hanging down in front.

stolen /ˈstoʊlən/ *v.* past participle of **steal**.

stolid /ˈstɒləd/ *adj.* not easily moved or stirred mentally; impassive; unemotional; dull; unenterprising or unimaginative. –**stolidity** /stɒˈlɪdəti/, **stolidness**, *n.* –**stolidly**, *adv.*

stomach /ˈstʌmək/ *n.* **1.** (in humans and other vertebrates) a sac-like enlargement of the alimentary canal, forming an organ of storage, dilution, and digestion. **2.** any similar digestive cavity or tract in invertebrates.

3. appetite for food. **4.** desire, inclination, or liking: *no stomach for fighting.* **5.** spirit or courage: *to have the stomach for dangerous enterprises.* −*v.t.* **6.** to take into or retain in the stomach. **7.** to endure or tolerate.

stomato- a word element referring to the mouth, as in *stomatoplasty.* Also, (*before vowels*), **stomat-**.

-stome a word element referring to the mouth, as in *cyclostome.*

stomp /stɒmp/ *n.* **1.** a form of jazz music. **2.** a dance, usually characterised by stamping of the feet, done to such music. −*v.i.* **3.** *Colloq.* to stamp. **4.** to perform the stomp. −*v.t.* **5.** *Colloq.* to stamp.

stomping ground *n.* → **stamping ground.**

-stomy a word element used in names of surgical operations for making an artificial opening, as in *colostomy.*

stone /stoʊn/ *n.* (*pl.* **stones** *or, for def. 7,* **stone**) **1.** the hard substance of which rocks consist. **2.** a particular kind of rock. **3.** *Mining* opal-bearing material. **4.** a piece of rock of definite size, shape, etc., for any particular purpose, e.g. a gravestone, building block, etc. **5.** a piece of rock of small or moderate size. **6.** a precious stone; gem. **7.** (*pl.* **stone**) a unit of mass in the imperial system, equal to 14 lb., or approximately 6.35 kg. **8.** any hard, stone-like mass, especially as produced abnormally in some bodily organs. **9.** *Bot.* the hard seed of a soft fruit, e.g. peach, cherry, etc. **10.** a light grey or beige colour. −*adj.* **11.** made of or relating to stone. **12.** made of stoneware: *a stone jug; an old stone bottle.* −*v.t.* **13.** to drive away by hitting with stones. **14.** to put to death by hitting with stones. **15.** to take the stone(s) out of (fruit). −*adv.* **16.** completely: *stone deaf; stone cold sober.* −*phr.* **17. stone the crows,** *Colloq.* an exclamation of astonishment, exasperation, or disgust. −**stoneless,** *adj.* −**stoner,** *n.*

Stone Age *n.* the time during which early humans lived and made implements of stone, chiefly of flint; it corresponds to the Pleistocene and Holocene epochs up to the beginning of the Bronze Age.

stoned /stoʊnd/ *adj. Colloq.* completely drunk or under the influence of drugs.

stonefish /ˈstoʊnfɪʃ/ *n.* any of several species of highly venomous, tropical Indo-Pacific fishes of *Synanceja* or a related genus, remarkably camouflaged to resemble weathered coral or rock.

stonemason /ˈstoʊnmeɪsən/ *n.* a dresser of or builder in stone. −**stonemasonry,** *n.*

stoneware /ˈstoʊnweə/ *n.* hard, glazed clay pottery which is not translucent, fired at a very high temperature.

stonkered /ˈstɒŋkəd/ *adj. Colloq.* **1.** defeated; destroyed; overthrown. **2.** exhausted. **3.** confounded; discomfited. **4.** drunk.

stony /ˈstoʊni/ *adj.* (**-nier, -niest**) **1.** full of or having many stones or rocks. **2.** relating to or typical of stone. **3.** like or suggesting stone, especially hard like stone. **4.** unfeeling; merciless; obdurate: *a stony heart.* **5.** unmoving or rigid; without expression: *a stony look.* −**stonily,** *adv.* −**stoniness,** *n.*

stood /stʊd/ *v.* past tense and past participle of **stand.**

stooge /studʒ/ *Colloq.* −*n.* **1.** an entertainer who feeds lines to a comedian and is often the object of his or her ridicule. **2.** someone who acts on behalf of another, especially in an obsequious, corrupt, or secretive fashion. −*v.i.* (**stooged, stooging**) **3.** to act as a stooge.

stool /stul/ *n.* **1.** a seat, usually without arms or a back, and for one person. **2.** a low support for resting the feet on, etc. **3.** (*pl.*) → **faeces.**

stool pigeon *n.* **1.** *Chiefly US* → **nark** (def. 1). **2.** *Colloq.* someone used as a decoy or secret confederate, as by gamblers.

stoop /stup/ *v.i.* **1.** to bend the head and shoulders, or the body generally, forwards and downwards from an

upright position: *to stoop over a desk.* **2.** to carry the head and shoulders habitually bowed forwards: *to stoop from age.* **3.** to descend from one's level of dignity; condescend; deign. **4.** to lower oneself by undignified or unworthy behaviour: *how could he stoop so low?* **5.** to swoop down, as a hawk at prey. −*v.t.* **6.** to bend (oneself, one's head, etc.) forwards and downwards. −*n.* **7.** the act of stooping; a stooping movement. **8.** a stooping position or carriage of body. **9.** a downward swoop, as of a hawk.

stop /stɒp/ *verb* (**stopped** *or, Poetic,* **stopt, stopping**) −*v.t.* **1.** to cease from, leave off, or discontinue: *to stop running.* **2.** to cause to cease; put an end to: *to stop noise in the street.* **3.** to interrupt, arrest, or check (a course, proceeding, process, etc.). **4.** to cut off, intercept, or withhold: *to stop supplies.* **5.** (sometimes fol. by *from*) to restrain, hinder, or prevent: *to stop a person from doing something.* **6.** to prevent from proceeding, acting, operating, continuing, etc.: *to stop a speaker; to stop a car.* **7.** Also, **stop up.** to block, obstruct, or close (a passageway, channel, opening, duct, etc.). **8.** to fill the hole or holes in (a wall, a decayed tooth, etc.). **9.** to close (a container, tube, etc.) with a cork, plug, bung, or the like. **10.** to close the external orifice of (the ears, nose, mouth, etc.). **11.** *Boxing, Fencing, etc.* **a.** to check (a stroke, blow, etc.); parry; ward off. **b.** to defeat by a knockout or the like: *the local boy stopped his opponent in the fourth round.* **12.** *Banking* to notify a banker not to honour (a cheque) on presentation. **13.** *Music* **a.** to close (a finger hole, etc.) in order to produce a particular note from a wind instrument. **b.** to press down (a string of a violin, etc.) in order to alter the pitch of the note produced from it. **c.** to insert the hand in (the bell of a horn) in order to alter the pitch and quality of the note. **d.** to produce (a particular note) by so doing. −*v.i.* **14.** to come to a stand, as in a course or journey; halt. **15.** to cease moving, proceeding, speaking, acting, operating, etc.; to pause; desist. **16.** to cease; come to an end. **17.** to stay temporarily: *I stopped there for dinner; come and stop with us for a few weeks.* −*n.* **18.** the act of stopping. **19.** a cessation or arrest of movement, action, operation, etc.; end. **20.** a stay or sojourn made at a place, as in the course of a journey. **21.** a place where buses or other transport vehicles stop to pick up and set down passengers. **22.** a closing or filling up, as of a hole. **23.** a blocking or obstructing, as of a passage or way. **24.** a plug or other stopper for an opening. **25.** an obstacle, impediment, or hindrance. **26.** any piece or device that serves to check or control movement or action in a mechanism. **27.** *Banking* a stop order. **28.** *Music* **a.** the act of closing a finger hole, etc., or of pressing down a string, of an instrument, in order to produce a particular note. **b.** a device or contrivance, as on an instrument, for accomplishing this. **c.** (in an organ) a graduated set of pipes of the same kind and giving tones of the same quality. **d.** a knob or handle which is drawn out or pushed back to permit or prevent the sounding of such a set of pipes or to control some other part of the organ. **e.** a similar group of reeds on a reed organ. **29.** *Phonetics* **a.** an articulation which interrupts the flow of air from the lungs. **b.** a consonant sound resulting from stop articulation: /p/, /b/, /t/, /d/, /k/, and /g/ are the English stops. **30.** *Photography* the aperture size of a lens, especially as indicated by an f number. **31.** → **full stop. 32.** the word 'stop' spelt out, and used instead of a full stop in telegraphic and cable messages. −*phr.* **33. pull out all (the) stops,** *Colloq.* **a.** to speak with extreme emotion. **b.** to push oneself or a machine to the utmost. **34. stop by,** to call somewhere briefly on the way to another destination. **35. stop down,** *Photography* to reduce the aperture size of (a camera). **36. stop off at** (or **in**), to interrupt (a journey) at or in: *they* *stopped off in Geraldton.* **37. stop one,** *Colloq.* **a.** to have an alcoholic drink. **b.** to receive an injury, as from a bullet, a fist, etc. **38. stop over,** to make a stopover. –**stoppage,** *n.*

stopcock /'stɒpkɒk/ *n.* a valve, with a tapered plug operated by a handle, used to control the flow of a liquid or gas from a receptacle or through a pipe.

stopgap /'stɒpgæp/ *n.* **1.** something that fills the place of something lacking; a temporary substitute; a makeshift. –*adj.* **2.** makeshift.

stopover /'stɒpoʊvə/ *n.* any brief stop in the course of a journey, especially one with the privilege of proceeding later on the ticket originally issued.

stop payment *n.* an order by the drawer of a cheque to a financial institution not to pay a specified cheque.

stopper /'stɒpə/ *n.* a plug or piece for closing a bottle, tube, or the like.

stop press *n.* news inserted in a newspaper after printing has begun.

stopwatch /'stɒpwɒtʃ/ *n.* a watch in which the timing mechanism can be stopped or started at any instant, and which is adapted for indicating fractions of a second (used for timing races, etc.).

stop-work meeting *n. Aust., NZ* a meeting of employees held during working time to consult with unions or management over conditions of work, etc.

storage /'stɔːrɪdʒ/ *n.* **1.** the act of storing or the state or fact of being stored. **2.** a space for storing. **3.** *Computers* the capacity to hold information. **4.** a place where something is stored. **5.** the price charged for storing goods.

store /stɔː/ *n.* **1.** a large shop with many departments or belonging to a chain with many branches: *a Myer store.* **2.** a small shop: *corner store; video store.* **3.** a supply or stock of something, especially one for future use. **4. a.** a place on a country property where supplies are held for sale or distribution to workers. **b.** (*pl.*) supplies of food, clothing, or other requisites, as for a household or other establishment, a ship, naval or military forces, or the like. **5.** a storehouse or warehouse. **6.** measure of esteem or regard: *to set little store by a thing.* **7.** quantity, especially great quantity; abundance, or plenty. **8.** a computer memory. –*adj.* **9.** of or relating to sheep, cattle, etc., bought to be fattened for market. –*v.t.* **10.** Also, **store up.** to lay up or put away, as a supply for future use. **11.** to deposit in a storehouse, warehouse, or other place, for keeping. –*phr.* **12. in store, a.** kept in readiness for future use. **b.** coming in the future: *I did not know what was in store for me.* **c.** deposited in a warehouse until needed. **13. set (great) store by,** to regard as important or valuable: *he sets great store by her opinion.* **14. the stores,** *Aust. Hist.* government rations. –**storable,** *adj.*

storehouse /'stɔːhaʊs/ *n.* **1.** a house or building in which things are stored. **2.** any repository or source of abundant supplies, as of facts or knowledge.

storey /'stɔːri/ *n.* (*pl.* **-reys** *or* **-ries**) **1.** a complete horizontal section of a building, having one continuous or approximately continuous floor. **2.** the set of rooms on the same floor or level of a building. **3.** each of the stages separated by floors, one above another, of which a building consists. Also, *Chiefly US,* **story.**

stork /stɔːk/ *n.* any of various long-legged, long-necked, long-billed wading birds, allied to the ibises and herons, which constitute the family Ciconiidae, especially *Ciconia ciconia* (white stork) of Europe, or, in Australia, the jabiru.

storm /stɔːm/ *n.* **1.** a disturbance of the normal condition of the atmosphere, manifesting itself by winds of unusual force or direction, often accompanied by rain, snow, hail, thunder and lightning, or flying sand or dust. **2.** a heavy fall of rain, snow, or hail, or a violent outbreak of thunder and lightning, unaccompanied by strong wind. **3.** *Meteorol.* a wind of Beaufort scale force 11, i.e., one with average wind speed of 56 to 63 knots, or 103 to 116 km/h. **4.** a violent assault on a fortified place, strong position, or the like. **5.** a heavy descent or discharge of missiles, blows, or the like. **6.** a violent disturbance of affairs, as a civil, political, social, or domestic commotion. **7.** a vigorous outburst or outbreak: *a storm of applause.* –*v.i.* **8.** (*used impersonally*) to blow with unusual force, or to rain, snow, hail, etc., especially with violence: *it stormed all day.* **9.** to rage or complain with violence or fury. **10.** to deliver a violent attack or fire, as with artillery. **11.** to rush to an assault or attack. **12.** to rush with angry violence: *to storm into the room.* **13.** to proceed with vigour, brushing opposition aside: *the country team stormed to victory.* –*v.t.* **14.** to utter or say with angry vehemence. **15.** to assault (a fortified place). –*phr.* **16. cook up a storm, a.** to engage in activities which will lead to a confrontation or quarrel. **b.** to cook a large amount of food, especially with enthusiasm. **17. storm in a teacup,** a great deal of fuss arising out of a very unimportant matter. **18. storm out,** to leave abruptly with angry violence. **19. take by storm, a.** to take by military assault. **b.** to captivate and overwhelm completely. **20. ... up a storm,** an expression indicating that a specified activity is performed with great intensity: *dance up a storm; laugh up a storm.* –**stormy,** *adj.*

stormwater /'stɔːmwɔːtə/ *n.* a sudden, excessive run-off of water following a storm.

story[1] /'stɔːri/ *n.* (*pl.* **-ries**) **1.** a narrative, either true or fictitious, in prose or verse, designed to interest, instruct, or amuse the hearer or reader; a tale. **2.** a fictitious tale, shorter and less elaborate than a novel. **3.** such narratives or tales as a branch of literature. **4.** the plot, or succession of incidents of a novel, poem, drama, etc. **5.** a narration of a series of events, or a series of events that are or may be narrated. **6.** a narration of the events in the life of a person or the existence of a thing, or such events as a subject for narration. **7.** a report or account of a matter; a statement. **8.** *Media* a news item; an account of an event or situation, as in a newspaper, on television, etc.: *we are having trouble with that film and will go on to the next story.* **9.** *Colloq.* a lie; a fib. –*v.t.* (**-ried, -rying**) **10.** to ornament with pictured scenes, as from history or legend.

story[2] /'stɔːri/ *n.* (*pl.* **-ries**) *Chiefly US →* **storey.**

storyboard /'stɔːribɔːd/ *n. Film, TV* a basic graphic realisation of a sequence of scenes in a film, advertisement, etc., as a visual aid in the planning or explanation of a visual narrative.

stout /staʊt/ *adj.* **1.** thick or bulky in figure; solidly built; thickset; corpulent. **2.** bold; fearless; dauntless: *a stout heart.* **3.** firm; stubborn: *stout resistance.* **4.** strong; sturdy: *a stout fence; stout fellows.* –*n.* **5.** a beer, darker and heavier than ale, getting its colour and taste from the roasted malt used in the brewing process. –**stoutly,** *adv.* –**stoutness,** *n.*

stove[1] /stoʊv/ *n.* **1.** an apparatus, portable or fixed, and in many forms, for furnishing heat, as for comfort, cooking, or mechanical purposes, commonly using coal, oil, gas, or electricity. **2.** a heated chamber or box for some special purpose, as a drying room, or a kiln for firing pottery. –*v.t.* **3.** to apply heat to (metalware, etc.) in a kiln to fuse paint to its surface.

stove[2] /stoʊv/ *v.* a past tense and past participle of **stave.**

stow /stoʊ/ *v.t.* **1.** *Naut.* to place (cargo, etc.) in the hold or some other part of a ship. **2.** to put in a place or receptacle as for storage or reserve; pack. **3.** *Colloq.* to desist from. –*phr.* **4. stow away, a.** to conceal oneself aboard a ship or other conveyance in order to get a free trip. **b.** to put away, as in a safe convenient place. **5. stow it,** (*oft. used imperatively*) *Colloq.* to stop talking or doing something. –**stowage**, *n.*

stowaway /ˈstoʊəweɪ/ *n.* someone who conceals himself or herself aboard a ship or other conveyance, as to get a free trip.

strabismus /strəˈbɪzməs/ *n.* a disorder of vision due to the turning of one eye or both eyes from the normal position so that both cannot be directed at the same point or object at the same time; squint; cross-eye. –**strabismal, strabismic, strabismical,** *adj.*

straddle /ˈstrædl/ *v.i.* **1.** to walk, stand, or sit with the legs wide apart; stand or sit astride. **2.** (of the legs) to stand wide apart. –*v.t.* **3.** to walk, stand, or sit with one leg on each side of; stand or sit astride of. **4.** to spread (the legs) wide apart. **5.** *Mil.* to cover (an area) with bombs. –*n.* **6.** the act of straddling. **7.** *Athletics* a style of high jumping in which the athlete crosses the bar horizontally and face down, rolling forward to land on the back. –**straddler**, *n.* –**straddlingly**, *adv.*

strafe /straf, streɪf/ *v.t.* **1.** to attack (ground troops or installations) by aircraft with machine-gun fire. **2.** to bombard heavily. –**strafer**, *n.*

straggle /ˈstrægəl/ *v.i.* **1.** to stray from the road, course, or line of march. **2.** to wander about in a scattered fashion; ramble. **3.** to go, come, or spread in a scattered, irregular fashion. **4.** to fail to keep up with one's companions in a journey, walk, etc.; drop behind.

straight /streɪt/ *adj.* **1.** without a bend, crook, or curve; not curved; direct: *a straight path.* **2.** flat; horizontal. **3.** *Cricket* **a.** (of a bat) held perpendicular to the ground. **b.** (of a stroke) playing the ball down the wicket past the bowler: *a straight drive.* **4.** (of a line) generated by a point moving constantly in the same direction. **5.** evenly formed or set: *straight shoulders.* **6.** delivered with arm extended straight from the shoulder, as a blow: *straight left.* **7.** without guile or prevarication: *a straight answer.* **8.** honest, honourable, or upright, as conduct, dealings, methods, persons, etc. **9.** *Colloq.* **a.** conforming to orthodox forms of behaviour, as avoidance of illegal drugs, etc. **b.** heterosexual. **10.** *Colloq.* reliable, as reports, information, etc. **11.** right or correct, as reasoning, thinking, a thinker, etc. **12.** continuous or unbroken: *in straight succession.* **13.** thoroughgoing or unreserved: *a straight lie.* **14.** undiluted, as an alcoholic beverage; neat. **15.** *Theatre* (of a play, acting style, etc.) serious; without music or dancing and not primarily comic in intent. **16.** *Cards* made up of cards in consecutive denominations, as the two, three, four, five, and six. –*adv.* **17.** in a straight line: *to walk straight.* **18.** in an even form or position: *pictures hung straight.* **19.** directly: *to go straight to a place.* **20.** Also, **straight out.** without circumlocution. **21.** honestly, honourably, or virtuously: *to live straight.* **22.** in a continuous course: *to keep straight on.* **23.** at once; immediately; without delay: *I'll come straight over.* **24.** in the proper order or condition, as a room: *he set the room straight after the meeting.* **25.** *US* without discount regardless of the quantity bought: *candy bars are seventy cents straight.* –*n.* **26.** the condition of being straight. **27.** a straight form or position. **28.** a straight line. **29.** a straight part, as of a racecourse or a railway. **30.** *Colloq.* **a.** a person who is straight (def. 9a). **b.** a heterosexual. **31.** *Poker* a sequence (def. 7) of five cards of various suits. –*phr.* **32. go straight,** to lead an honest life, especially after a prison sentence. **33. in straight sets,** *Tennis* in sets won successively. **34. keep a straight face,** to maintain a calm and unsmiling expression, despite an inclination to laugh. **35. set** (or **put**) **someone straight,** to point out an error to someone. **36. the straight and narrow,** a way of life governed by strict moral principles. –**straighten**, *v.* –**straightly**, *adv.* –**straightness**, *n.*

straightaway /streɪtəˈweɪ/ *adv.* immediately; at once; right away. Also, **straight away.**

straightforward /streɪtˈfɔwəd/ *adj.* **1.** going or directed straight forward: *a straightforward glance.* **2.** proceeding without circuity; direct. **3.** free from crookedness or deceit; honest: *straightforward in one's dealings.* **4.** without difficulty; uncomplicated: *the subject set was very straightforward.* –*adv.* Also, **straightforwards. 5.** *Chiefly US* straight ahead; directly or continuously forward. –**straightforwardly**, *adv.* –**straightforwardness**, *n.*

strain[1] /streɪn/ *v.t.* **1.** to pull tight or taut; stretch tightly: *to strain a rope.* **2.** to use to the utmost: *to strain one's ears to catch a sound.* **3.** to damage by overuse: *to strain a muscle.* **4.** to stretch beyond the proper limit: *to strain resources.* **5.** to pass (liquid matter) through a filter, sieve, etc. –*v.i.* **6.** to pull forcibly: *a dog straining at a leash.* **7.** to stretch one's muscles, nerves, etc., to the utmost. **8.** to ooze; filter; percolate. –*n.* **9.** any force or pressure that may alter shape, cause breakage, etc. **10.** any strong or great effort. **11.** damage to a muscle, tendon, etc., from overuse; a sprain. **12. a.** damage to any body or structure resulting from stress. **b.** *Physics* the amount of such deformation to a structure resulting from stress expressed as the ratio of the change to the original unstrained dimension (length, area, or volume). **13.** the condition of being strained or stretched: *the strain on the rope brought it near breaking point.* **14.** great pressure that wears down; stress: *the strain of hard work.* **15.** great demand on resources, feelings, a person, etc.: *a strain on hospitality.* **16.** (*sing. or pl., oft. collective pl.*) the sound of music or song: *the strains of a violin.* **17.** a passage or piece of poetry. **18.** tone, style, or spirit in expression: *a humorous strain.* –**strained**, *adj.*

strain[2] /streɪn/ *n.* **1.** stock; ancestry; lineage: *there are few people left now of her father's strain.* **2.** a variety of a species of domestic animal or cultivated plant. **3.** a variety of microorganism. **4.** a quality that tends to be passed down through generations: *a strain of madness in a family.*

strainer /ˈstreɪnə/ *n.* **1.** a filter, sieve, or the like for straining liquids. **2.** a stretcher or tightener, as on a wire fence. **3.** Also, **strainer post.** a solid post against which the wires in a post and wire fence are tightened or strained.

strait /streɪt/ *n.* **1.** (*oft. pl.*) a narrow passage of water connecting two large bodies of water. **2.** (*oft. pl.*) a position of difficulty, distress, or need. –**straitly**, *adv.*

straitjacket /ˈstreɪtdʒækət/ *n.* a kind of coat for confining the arms of violently insane persons, etc. Also, **straightjacket.**

straitlaced /ˈstreɪtleɪst/ *adj.* excessively strict in conduct or morality; puritanical; prudish.

strand[1] /strænd/ *v.t.* **1.** to drive aground on a shore, especially of the sea, as a ship, a fish, etc. **2.** (*usu. in the passive*) to bring into a helpless position. **3.** to leave without means of transport. –*v.i.* **4.** to be driven or run ashore, as a ship, etc.; run aground. –*n.* **5.** *Poetic* the land bordering the sea or ocean, or, formerly, a river; the shore. –**stranded**, *adj.* –**stranding**, *n.*

strand[2] /strænd/ *n.* **1.** each of a number of strings or yarns twisted together to form a rope, cord, wire, etc. **2.** a single thread in cloth. **3.** a lock of hair; tress. **4.** a string of pearls, beads, etc.

strange /streɪndʒ/ **1.** unusual, extraordinary, or curious; odd; queer; peculiar: *a strange remark to make.* **2.** distant, foreign: *to move to a strange place.* **3.** unfamiliar; so far unknown: *I saw a strange bird this morning.* **4.** unacquainted (with); unaccustomed (to) or inexperienced (at). **5.** *Colloq.* slightly mad: *she is a little strange.* –**strangely**, *adv.*

stranger /'streɪndʒə/ *n.* **1.** a person with whom one has, or has hitherto had, no personal acquaintance. **2.** an outsider. **3.** (in a group of animals) one which belongs to a neighbouring herd or flock. **4.** a visitor or guest. **5.** a newcomer in a place or locality. **6.** *Law* someone not privy or party to an act, proceeding, etc. *–phr.* **7. little stranger,** *Colloq.* an unborn or new-born infant. **8. no stranger to ...,** a person accustomed to (something specified): *he is no stranger to poverty.*

strangle /'stræŋgəl/ *v.t.* **1.** to kill by compression of the windpipe, as by a cord around the neck. **2.** to kill by stopping the breath in any manner; choke; stifle; suffocate. **3.** to prevent the continuance, growth, rise, or action of; suppress. *–v.i.* **4.** to be choked, stifled, or suffocated. *–n.* **5.** *Vet. Science* (*pl. construed as sing.*) an infectious febrile disease of equine animals, characterised by catarrh of the upper air passages and suppuration of the submaxillary and other lymphatic glands; distemper. **–strangler,** *n.* **–strangulation,** *n.*

strap /stræp/ *n.* **1.** a narrow strip of some material that will bend, especially leather, for tying or holding things together, etc. **2.** a strop for a razor. **3.** a straplike ornament, as a watchstrap. **4.** a beating with a leather strap. *–v.t.* (**strapped, strapping**) **5.** to fasten or secure with a strap or straps. **6.** to beat with a strap. **–straplike,** *adj.* **–strappy,** *adj.*

strapper /'stræpə/ *n.* **1.** *Colloq.* a tall, robust person. **2.** someone employed to attend and groom racehorses in the stables.

strapping /'stræpɪŋ/ *adj.* **1.** tall, robust, and strongly built. **2.** *Colloq.* very large of its kind; whopping. *–n.* **3.** straps collectively. **4.** *Colloq.* a thrashing.

Strasburg /'stræzbɜg/ *n. Aust.* a large, mild-flavoured, precooked sausage, usually sliced thinly and eaten cold; devon; fritz; luncheon sausage; polony. Also, **Strasburg.**

strata /'stratə/ *n.* **1.** a plural of **stratum.** *–adj.* **2.** of or relating to or sold under a strata title: *a strata unit*; *strata manager. –v.t.* (**strataed, strata-ing** *or* **strataing**) **3.** to develop (a building) into apartments or units under strata title.

stratagem /'strætədʒəm/ *n.* **1.** a plan, scheme, or trick for deceiving the enemy. **2.** any artifice, ruse, or trick.

strata title *n.* (in Australia) a system of registration of strata of air space in multistorey buildings, similar to the registration of titles under the Torrens System, to create a type of interest similar to the interest a person has in the land with a single storey building.

strategic /strə'tidʒɪk/ *adj.* **1.** relating to, characterised by, or of the nature of strategy: *strategic movements.* **2.** important in strategy: *a strategic point.* **3.** important; highly crucial to one's position. Also, **strategical.** **–strategically,** *adv.*

strategy /'strætədʒi/ *n.* (*pl.* **-gies**) **1.** Also, *Chiefly US,* **strategics** /strə'tidʒiks/ generalship; the science or art of combining and using the means of war in planning and directing large military movements and operations. **2.** the use, or a particular use, of this science or art. **3.** skilful management in getting the better of an adversary or attaining an end. **4.** the method of conducting operations, especially by the aid of manoeuvring or stratagem. **–strategist,** *n.*

strati- a word element representing **stratum,** as in *stratify.*

stratification /strætəfə'keɪʃən/ *n.* **1.** the act of stratifying. **2.** stratified state or appearance: *the stratification of medieval society.* **3.** *Geol.* **a.** formation of strata; deposition or occurrence in strata. **b.** → **stratum** (def. 3).

stratify /'strætəfaɪ/ *verb* (**-fied, -fying**) *–v.t.* **1.** to form in strata or layers. **2.** *Hort.* to preserve or germinate (seeds) by placing them between layers of earth. *–v.i.* **3.** to form strata. **4.** *Geol.* to lie in beds or layers.

5. *Sociology* to develop horizontal status groups in society.

stratigraphy /strə'tɪgrəfi/ *n.* the branch of geology that deals with the classification, nomenclature, correlation, and interpretation of stratified rocks. **–stratigrapher** /strə'tɪgrəfə/, **stratigraphist** /strə'tɪgrəfəst/, *n.* **–stratigraphic** /strætə'græfɪk/, **stratigraphical** /strætə'græfɪkəl/, *adj.*

strato- a word element meaning 'low and horizontal', as in *stratosphere.*

stratopause /'strætoʊpɔz/ *n.* the outer boundary of the earth's stratosphere where it meets the mesosphere; at an altitude of approximately 50 km above the earth.

stratosphere /'strætəsfɪə/ *n.* the region of the atmosphere outside the troposphere but below the mesosphere and ionosphere, at an altitude of about 20 to 50 km above the earth, characterised by relatively uniform temperature over considerable differences in altitude or by a markedly different lapse rate from that of the troposphere below. **–stratospheric** /strætəs'fɛrɪk/, *adj.*

stratum /'stratəm/ *n.* (*pl.* **-ta** /-tə/ *or* **-tums**) **1.** a horizontal layer of any material. **2.** one of a number of portions likened to layers or levels. **3.** *Geol.* a single bed of sedimentary rock. **4.** *Biol.* a layer of tissue; lamella. **5.** a layer of the ocean or atmosphere within natural or arbitrary limits. **6.** *Sociology* a level or grade of a people or population with reference to social position or education: *the lowest stratum of society.* **–stratal,** *adj.*

stratus /'streɪtəs/ *n.* (*pl.* **-ti** /-taɪ/) *Meteorol.* a continuous horizontal sheet of cloud, resembling fog but not resting on the ground, usually of uniform thickness and comparatively low altitude.

straw /strɔ/ *n.* **1.** a single stalk or stem, especially of certain species of grain, chiefly wheat, rye, oats, and barley. **2.** a mass of such stalks, especially after drying and threshing, used as fodder, as material for hats, etc. **3.** a hollow paper or plastic tube, plant stem, etc., used in drinking some beverages, etc. **4.** anything of trifling value or consequence: *not worth a straw.* **5.** a desperate and insubstantial expedient: *to clutch at a straw. –adj.* **6.** of, relating to, or made of straw. *–phr.* **7. a straw in the wind,** an indication of how things will turn out. **8. draw the short straw,** to get the worst of a deal; be most disadvantaged. **9. get the short end of the straw,** *Colloq.* to experience bad luck or hardship. **10. the last straw,** the final fact, circumstance, etc., which makes a situation unbearable. **–strawy,** *adj.*

strawberry /'strɔbəri, -bri/ *n.* (*pl.* **-ries**) **1.** the fruit of any of the stemless herbs constituting the genus *Fragaria,* consisting of an enlarged fleshy receptacle bearing achenes on its exterior. **2.** the plant bearing it. *–adj.* **3.** of the colour of a strawberry; reddish; strawberry blonde.

straw company *n.* a company set up not to produce anything but simply as a legal device to obtain some benefit, especially tax benefits.

straw man *n.* **1.** a figure of a man stuffed with straw, as for a scarecrow, target, etc. **2.** an argument deliberately put up so that it can be knocked down, usually as a distraction from other arguments which cannot be so easily countered: *to put up a straw man with regard to the proposal.* Also, *Brit.,* **man of straw.**

straw poll *n.* an unofficial vote taken, as at a casual gathering or in a particular district, to obtain some indication of the general drift of opinion. Also, **straw vote.**

stray /streɪ/ *v.i.* **1.** to wander from the proper course or place or beyond the proper limits, especially aimlessly; ramble; roam. **2.** to turn away from the right course; go astray; get lost. **3.** to turn aside from a subject of talk or writing; digress. –*n.* **4.** a domestic animal found wandering without an owner. **5.** any homeless or friendless creature or person. –*adj.* **6.** (of a domestic animal) straying, or having strayed. **7.** found apart from others, or as a single or casual instance. –**strayer**, *n.*

streak /strik/ *n.* **1.** a long, narrow mark, smear, band of colour, or the like: *streaks of mud*; *a streak of lightning*. **2.** a portion or layer of something, distinguished by colour or nature from the rest; a vein or stratum: *streaks of fat in meat*. **3.** a vein, strain, or admixture of anything: *a streak of humour*. **4.** *Colloq.* a run (of luck): *she's had a tough streak lately*. **5.** *Colloq.* a tall, thin person. **6.** *Mining* rock which shows good colour opal. **7.** *Mineral.* the line of powder obtained by scratching a mineral or rubbing it upon a hard, rough white surface, often differing in colour from the mineral in the mass, and forming an important distinguishing character. –*v.t.* **8.** to mark with a streak or streaks. **9.** to dye (hair) with streaks of colour. –*v.i.* **10.** to become streaked. **11.** to flash or go rapidly, like a streak of lightning. **12.** to run stark naked through a crowd of people in a street, at a cricket match, etc., for dramatic effect. –*phr.* **13. be on a streak**, *Mining* to come across rock showing good colour opal. **14. be on a winning streak**, *Colloq.* to experience a run of successes or wins. **15. streak of misery**, *Colloq.* a very tall, thin, morose person. –**streaky**, *adj.* –**streaker**, *n.*

stream /strim/ *n.* **1.** a body of water flowing in a channel or bed, as a river, rivulet, or brook. **2.** a steady current in water, as in a river or the ocean: *to row against the stream*. **3.** any flow of water or other liquid or fluid: *streams of blood*. **4.** a current of air, gas, or the like; a beam or trail of light. **5.** a continuous flow or succession of anything: *a stream of words*. **6.** prevailing direction; drift: *the stream of opinion*; *a stream of cars*. **7.** *Educ.* a division of children in a school to bring together those of similar age and ability in one class. –*v.i.* **8.** to flow, pass, or issue in a stream, as water, tears, blood, etc. **9.** (sometimes fol. by *with*) to send forth or throw off a stream; run or flow: *eyes streaming with tears*. **10.** to extend in a beam or trail, as light. **11.** to move or proceed continuously like a flowing stream, as a procession. **12.** to wave or float outwards, as a flag in the wind. **13.** to hang in a loose, flowing manner, as long hair. –*v.t.* **14.** to transmit a digitised form of (media content) by streaming (def. 2). **15.** to send forth or discharge in a stream. **16.** to cause to stream or float outwards, as a flag. **17.** *Educ.* to divide into streams. –*phr.* **18. come on stream**, to become operational or productive. **19. on stream**, (of a factory, etc.) productive; operating.

streamer /ˈstrimə/ *n.* **1.** a long, narrow flag; pennant. **2.** a long, narrow strip of coloured paper, thrown on special public occasions, or strung across streets or rooms.

streaming /ˈstrimɪŋ/ *n.* **1.** *Educ.* the process of dividing schoolchildren into groups, usually on the basis of ability. **2.** *Computers* the process of transmitting digital data in a continuous, steady flow, so that it may be processed and displayed as it is being received, rather than being stored and only displayed when the entire file has been received and processed.

streamline /ˈstrimlaɪn/ *n.* **1.** a teardrop line of contour, as of a car. **2.** *Physics* a line of motion in a fluid; the actual path of a particle in a flowing fluid mass whose motion is steady. –*v.t.* **3.** to make streamlined. **4.** to simplify, especially to improve efficiency: *to streamline the hospital's admission system*.

streamlined /ˈstrimlaɪnd/ *v.* **1.** past participle of **streamline**. –*adj.* **2.** having a shape designed to offer the least possible resistance: *a streamlined car*. **3.** simplified, especially to improve efficiency: *the new streamlined regulations*.

street /strit/ *n.* **1.** a public way or road, paved or unpaved, in a town or city, sometimes including a pavement or pavements, and having houses, shops, or the like, on one side or both sides. **2.** such a way or road together with the adjacent buildings. **3.** a main way or thoroughfare, as distinct from a lane, alley, or the like. **4.** the inhabitants of or the people in a street. –*adj.* **5.** relating to 'the street', viewed as the focal point of modern urban life and counterculture: *street cred*; *street culture*; *street fashions*; *street tough*. **6.** *Colloq.* relating to unregulated trading at the retail level: *heroin with a street value of $100 000*; *street prices for the new models start around $1000*. –*phr.* **7. on the streets**, **a.** earning one's living as a prostitute. **b.** destitute; homeless. **8. the man in the street**, the average person; a typical citizen. **9. streets ahead**, a long way ahead. **10. up one's street**, in the sphere that one knows or likes best. **11. up** (or **down**) **the street**, *Aust. Colloq.* at or to the local shops.

street kid *n.* a homeless child living in an urban or suburban area, especially one who is street smart.

street luge *n.* **1.** a sled with wheels, ridden in the style of a luge down a bitumen road. **2.** the sport of riding street luges.

street race *n.* a motor vehicle race conducted, often illegally, on ordinary streets as opposed to a purpose-built racing track. –**street racer**, *n.* –**street racing**, *n.*

street smart *adj.* used to dealing with the people on the street, especially in business transactions, and therefore keenly aware of and prepared for the sordid and underhand aspects of urban life. Also, **street-smart**.

streetwise /ˈstritwaɪz/ *adj.* skilled in living in an urban environment; knowing how to survive on the streets.

street worker *n.* **1.** a prostitute who solicits customers from the streets and other such public places. **2.** a social worker who works with clients on the street, as in outreach programs. Also, **streetworker**.

strength /strɛŋθ/ *n.* **1.** the quality or state of being strong; bodily or muscular power; vigour, as in robust health. **2.** mental power, force, or vigour. **3.** moral power, firmness, or courage. **4.** power by reason of influence, authority, resources, numbers, etc. **5.** number, as of troops or ships in a force or body: *a regiment of a strength of three thousand*. **6.** effective force, potency, or cogency, as of inducements or arguments. **7.** power of resisting force, strain, wear, etc. **8.** vigour of action, language, feeling, etc. **9.** large proportion of the effective or essential properties of a beverage, chemical, or the like. **10.** a particular proportion of these properties; intensity, as of light, colour, sound, flavour, or smell. –*phr.* **11. gain strength**, **a.** to improve in health. **b.** to achieve increased vigour, intensity, skill, etc. **12. get with the strength**, to side with the most powerful, influential person or group. **13. go from strength to strength**, to gain more and more success, power, etc. **14. on the strength of**, relying on; on the basis of. **15. the strength of**, *Aust.*, *NZ Colloq.* reliable information concerning. –**strengthen**, *v.*

strenuous /ˈstrɛnjuəs/ *adj.* **1.** vigorous, energetic, or zealously active, as a person, etc. **2.** characterised by vigorous exertion, as action, efforts, life, etc.: *a strenuous opposition*. –**strenuously**, *adv.* –**strenuousness**, **strenuosity** /strɛnjuˈɒsəti/, *n.*

streptococcus /strɛptəˈkɒkəs/ *n.* (*pl.* **-tococci** /-təˈkɒkaɪ, -təˈkɒki/)) one of a group of organisms of the genus *Streptococcus*, which divide in one plane only and remain attached to one another, forming long, short, or conglomerated chains. Some cause serious diseases such as scarlet fever, erysipelas, puerperal sepsis, sepsis, etc. –**streptococcic** /strɛptəˈkɒksɪk/, **streptococcal** /strɛptəˈkɒkəl/, *adj.*

streptomycin /ˌstrɛptəˈmaɪsən/ *n.* an antibiotic effective against diseases caused by bacteria, including several against which penicillin is ineffective, as tuberculosis.

stress /strɛs/ *v.t.* **1.** to give special importance to; emphasise: *to stress the need for safety.* **2.** *Ling.* to pronounce strongly: *you should stress the second syllable in 'pronounce'.* **3.** to put pressure or strain on, especially on a piece of machinery. –*v.i.* **4.** to work oneself into a state of nervousness or anxiety: *don't stress about it.* –*n.* **5.** importance; significance; emphasis: *to lay stress upon the need for safety.* **6.** an accent or emphasis on a syllable in speech, especially so as to form a metrical pattern. **7.** an emphasis in music, rhythm, etc. **8.** the physical pressure, pull, etc., of one thing on another. **9.** *Physics* **a.** the forces or system of forces, load, etc., on a body which produce a strain. **b.** a measure of the amount of stress, expressed as a force per unit area. **c.** the internal resistance or reaction of an elastic body to the external forces applied to it. **10.** the state of being under great mental or emotional pressure. –*phr.* **11. stress out**, *Colloq.* **a.** to subject to stress: *exams really stress me out.* **b.** to feel extreme stress: *don't stress out about it.*

-stress a feminine equivalent of **-ster**, as in *seamstress, songstress.*

stress fracture *n.* a fracture in a bone caused by constant repetitive pressure on the bone, as in the bones of the legs and feet in sports such as jogging, tennis, etc.

stressful /ˈstrɛsfəl/ *adj.* causing anxiety and tension: *teaching can be a very stressful job.*

stress test *n. Med.* a test which places the body under extreme stress while measurements of physiological reactions are taken, especially cardiovascular reaction, to gauge the efficiency of the heart.

stretch /strɛtʃ/ *v.t.* **1.** Also, **stretch out**. to draw out or extend (oneself, the body, limbs, wings, etc.) to the full length or extent: *to stretch oneself out on the ground.* **2.** to hold out, reach forth, or extend (the hand or something held, etc.). **3.** to extend, spread, or place so as to reach from one point or place to another: *to stretch a rope across a road.* **4.** to draw tight or taut: *to stretch the strings of a violin.* **5.** to lengthen, widen, distend, or enlarge by tension: *to stretch a rubber band.* **6.** to draw out, extend, or enlarge unduly: *a sweater stretched at the elbows.* **7.** to extend or force beyond the natural or proper limits; strain: *to stretch the facts.* **8.** to construct (the fuselage of a plane, the body of a car, etc.) so that it is longer than usual. –*v.i.* **9.** to extend the hand, or reach, as for something. **10.** to extend over a distance, area, period of time, or in a particular direction: *the forest stretches for as far as the eye can see.* **11.** to stretch oneself by extending the limbs, straining the muscles, etc. **12.** to become stretched, or admit of being stretched, to greater length, width, etc., as any elastic material. –*n.* **13.** the act of stretching. **14.** the state of being stretched. **15.** capacity for being stretched. **16.** a continuous length, distance, tract, or expanse: *a stretch of bush.* **17.** one of the two straight sides of a racecourse, as distinguished from the bend or curve at each end, especially that part of the course (**home stretch**) between the last turn and the winning post. **18.** an extent in time or duration: *a stretch of ten years.* **19.** *Colloq.* a term of imprisonment. –*adj.* **20.** made to stretch in order to fit different shapes and sizes, as clothing: *stretch stockings.* **21.** Also, **stretched**. (of a motor vehicle, aeroplane, etc.) constructed with a longer body than usual, usually by adding an extra section which increases the overall length but not the width or height: *a stretch hummer; a stretch A380.* –*phr.* **22. stretch a point**, to go beyond the usual limits. **23. stretch one's legs**, to take a walk. **24. stretch out,**

to recline at full length: *to stretch out on a couch.* –**stretchable**, *adj.*

stretched /strɛtʃt/ *adj.* **1.** *Colloq.* exhausted; nervously debilitated. **2. →** stretch (def. 21).

stretcher /ˈstrɛtʃə/ *n.* **1.** a light, folding bed; camp stretcher. **2.** a light frame covered with canvas, for carrying the sick or dead. **3.** any instrument for stretching. **4.** *Building Trades* a brick or stone laid horizontally, with its long side facing outward. Compare **header** (def. 3). –*v.t.* **5.** to carry (an ill or injured person) on a stretcher.

stretch mark *n.* a purplish scar that appears in overstretched skin, caused by a tearing of the dermis associated with rapid growth or rapid weight gain or pregnancy; stria.

strew /stru/ *v.t.* (**strewed**, **strewed** *or* **strewn**, **strewing**) **1.** to let fall in separate pieces or particles over a surface; scatter or sprinkle: *to strew seed in a garden bed.* **2.** to cover or overspread (a surface, place, etc.) with something scattered or sprinkled: *to strew a floor with rushes.* **3.** to be scattered or sprinkled over (a surface, etc.).

stria /ˈstraɪə/ *n.* (*pl.* **striae** /ˈstraɪiː/) **1.** a slight furrow or ridge; a narrow stripe or streak, especially one of a number in parallel arrangement. **2.** (*pl.*) *Geol.* scratches or tiny grooves on the surface of a rock, resulting from the action of moving ice, as of a glacier. **3.** (*pl.*) *Mineral.* parallel lines or tiny grooves on the surface of a crystal, or on a cleavage face of a crystal, due to its molecular organisation. **4.** *Pathol.* a linear mark on the abdomen which may appear in pregnancy or obesity or in some endocrine abnormalities. **5.** Also, **strix**. *Archit.* a fillet between the flutes of a column.

striate *v.t.* /ˈstraɪeɪt/ **1.** to mark with striae; furrow; stripe; streak. –*adj.* /ˈstraɪət/ Also, **striated**. **2.** marked with striae; furrowed; striped. –**striation**, *n.*

stricken /ˈstrɪkən/ *adj.* **1.** struck; hit or wounded by a weapon, missile, or the like. **2.** smitten or afflicted, as with disease, trouble, or sorrow. **3.** deeply affected, as with horror, fear, or other emotions. **4.** characterised by or showing the effects of affliction, trouble, misfortune, a mental blow, etc.

strict /strɪkt/ *adj.* **1.** severe; stringent: *a strict upbringing; strict laws.* **2.** exact; precise: *a strict statement of facts.* **3.** narrowly or carefully limited: *a strict interpretation.* **4.** complete; absolute: *told in strict confidence.* –**strictly**, *adv.* –**strictness**, *n.*

stricture /ˈstrɪktʃə/ *n.* **1.** a remark or comment, especially an adverse criticism. **2.** *Pathol.* a morbid contraction of any passage or duct of the body.

stride /straɪd/ *verb* (**strode**, **stridden**, **striding**) –*v.i.* **1.** to walk with long steps, as with vigour, haste, impatience, or arrogance. **2.** to take a long step. **3.** to straddle. –*v.t.* **4.** to walk with long steps along, on, through, over, etc.: *to stride the deck.* **5.** to pass over or across by one stride: *to stride a ditch.* **6.** to straddle. –*n.* **7.** a striding or a striding gait. **8.** a long step in walking. **9.** (in animal locomotion) an act of progressive movement, completed when all the feet are returned to the same relative position as at the beginning. **10.** the distance covered by such a movement. **11.** a regular or steady course, pace, etc.: *to take it in one's stride.* **12.** (*pl.*) *Colloq.* trousers. –*phr.* **13. make strides**, (sometimes fol. by *in*) to gain greater power, success, etc. –**strider**, *n.*

strident /ˈstraɪdnt/ *adj.* making or having a harsh sound; grating; creaking. –**stridence**, **stridency**, *n.* –**stridently**, *adv.*

stridulate /ˈstrɪdʒəleɪt/ *v.i.* to produce a shrill grating sound, as a cricket, by rubbing together certain parts of the body; shrill. –**stridulation** /ˌstrɪdʒəˈleɪʃən/, *n.* –**stridulator**, *n.* –**stridulatory** /ˈstrɪdʒəleɪtəri/, *adj.*

strife /straɪf/ *n.* **1.** conflict, discord, or variance: *to be at strife.* **2.** a quarrel, struggle, or clash. *–phr.* **3. in strife,** *Aust., NZ Colloq.* in trouble. **–strifeful,** *adj.* **–strifeless,** *adj.*

strike /straɪk/ *verb* (**struck, struck** *or, especially for defs* **25–28, stricken, striking**) *–v.t.* **1.** to deal a blow or stroke to (a person or thing), as with the fist, a weapon, or a hammer; hit: *he struck her and she fell to the floor.* **2.** to deliver a blow, stroke, or thrust with (the hand, a weapon, etc.): *she struck the dagger into his chest.* **3.** to deal or inflict (a blow, stroke, etc.). **4.** to drive or thrust forcibly: *to strike the hands together.* **5.** to produce (fire, sparks, light, etc.) by percussion, friction, etc. **6.** to cause (a match) to ignite by friction. **7.** to smite or blast with some natural or supernatural agency: *struck by lightning.* **8.** to come into forcible contact or collision with: *the ship struck a rock.* **9.** to fall upon (something), as light or sound. **10.** to enter the mind of; occur to: *a happy thought struck him.* **11.** to catch or arrest (the eyes, etc.): *the first object that strikes one's sight.* **12.** to impress strongly: *a picture which strikes one's fancy.* **13.** to impress in a particular manner: *how does it strike you?* **14.** to come across, meet with, or encounter suddenly or unexpectedly: *to strike the name of a friend in a newspaper.* **15.** to come upon or find (ore, oil, etc.) in prospecting, boring, or the like. **16.** to send down or put forth (a root, etc.), as a plant, cutting, etc. **17.** to remove from the stage (the scenery and properties of an act or scene). **18.** *Building Trades* to remove formwork from (concrete, etc.) after it has gained its initial set. **19.** *Naut.* **a.** to lower or take down (a sail, mast, etc.). **b.** to lower (a sail, flag, etc.) as a salute or as a sign of surrender. **c.** to lower into the hold of a vessel by means of a rope and tackle. **20.** to harpoon, spear, as in hunting. **21.** (in various technical uses) to make level or smooth. **22.** to stamp (a coin, medal, etc.) or impress (a device), by a stroke. **23.** *Rowing* to make (a specified number of strokes) in a given time: *the blues struck forty in the first minute.* **24.** to indicate (the hour of day) by a stroke or strokes, as a clock: *to strike twelve.* **25.** to afflict suddenly, as with disease, suffering, or death. **26.** to affect deeply or overwhelm, as with terror, fear, etc. **27.** to render (blind, dumb, etc.) suddenly, as if by a blow. **28.** to cause (a feeling) to enter suddenly: *to strike terror into a person.* **29.** to induce a favourable reaction in: *he was struck by her beauty.* **30.** to start suddenly into (vigorous movement): *the horse struck a gallop.* **31.** to assume (an attitude or posture). **32.** to cause (chill, warmth, etc.) to pass or penetrate quickly. **33.** to come upon or reach in travelling or in a course of procedure. **34.** to make, conclude, or ratify (an agreement, treaty, etc.). **35.** to reach by agreement, as a compromise: *to strike a rate of payment.* **36.** to estimate or determine (a mean or average). **37.** to break (camp). *–v.i.* **38.** to deal or aim a blow or stroke, as with the fist, a weapon, or a hammer; make an attack. **39.** to knock, rap, or tap. **40.** to hit or dash on or against something, as a moving body; come into forcible contact. **41.** to run upon a bank, rock, or other obstacle, as a ship. **42.** to make an impression on the mind, senses, etc., as something seen or heard. **43.** to sound by percussion: *the clock strikes.* **44.** to be indicated by such sounding: *the hour has struck.* **45.** to be ignited by friction, as a match. **46.** to make a stroke, as with the arms or legs in swimming or with an oar in rowing. **47.** to produce a sound, music, etc., by touching a string or playing upon an instrument. **48.** to take root, as a slip of a plant. **49.** to go, proceed, or advance, especially in a new direction. **50.** (of an employee or employees) to engage in a strike (def. 53). **51.** *Naut.* **a.** to lower the flag or colours, especially as a salute or as a sign of surrender. **b.** to run up the white flag of surrender. *–n.* **52.** an act of striking. **53.** a concerted stopping of work or withdrawal of workers' services in order to compel an employer to accede to demands or in protest against terms or conditions imposed by an employer. **54.** *Baseball* an unsuccessful attempt on the part of the batter to hit a pitched ball, or anything ruled to be equivalent to this. **55.** *Cricket* the obligation to face the bowling. **56.** *Tenpin Bowling* **a.** the knocking down of all the pins with the first bowl. **b.** the score made by bowling a strike. **57.** *Geol.* **a.** the direction of the line formed by the intersection of the bedding plane of a bed or stratum of sedimentary rock with a horizontal plane. **b.** the direction or trend of a structural feature, as an anticlinal axis or the lineation resulting from metamorphism. **58.** the discovery of a rich vein of ore in mining, of oil in drilling, etc. *–phr.* **59. on strike, a.** (of an employee or employees) engaged in a strike (def. 53). **b.** *Cricket* (of the person batting) facing the bowler and ready to receive the next delivery. **60. strike a light,** an expression of surprise, indignation, etc. **61. strike me lucky** (or **pink**) (or **blue**) (or **dead**) (or **handsome**), an exclamation of surprise, indignation, etc. **62. strike off, a.** to forbid (someone) to continue practising a profession because of unprofessional conduct, or the like: *the doctor was struck off for advertising.* **b.** to remove or separate with a cut. **63. strike on,** to come on suddenly or unexpectedly: *to strike on a new way of doing a thing.* **64. strike on** (or **upon**), to fall on or reach, as light or sound. **65. strike out, a.** to direct one's course boldly. **b.** *Baseball* (of a batter) to make three strikes and be declared out. **66. strike out** (or **off**), to efface or cancel with, or as with, the stroke of a pen. **67. strike up, a.** (of an orchestra or band) to begin to play. **b.** to enter upon or form (an acquaintance, etc.). **–striker,** *n.*

striking /ˈstraɪkɪŋ/ *adj.* **1.** that strikes. **2.** attractive; impressive. **3.** being on strike, as workers. **–strikingly,** *adv.*

Strine /straɪn/ *n. Colloq.* **1.** Australian English, humorously and affectionately regarded. **2.** the form of it which appeared in the books of Alastair Morrison, pen-name 'Afferbeck Lauder', where it was written in scrambled form to suggest excessive assimilation, ellipsis, etc., as in *Gloria Soame* for *glorious home*, *muncer go* for *months ago*, etc. Also, **strine**.

string /strɪŋ/ *n.* **1.** a line, cord, or thread, used for tying parcels, etc. **2.** a narrow strip of cloth, leather, etc., for tying parts together: *strings of a bonnet.* **3.** something resembling a string or thread. **4.** a number of objects, as beads or pearls, threaded or arranged on a cord. **5.** any series of things arranged or connected in a line or following closely one after another: *a string of islands*; *a string of vehicles*; *to ask a string of questions.* **6.** a set or number, as of animals: *a string of racehorses.* **7.** (in musical instruments) a tightly stretched cord or wire which produces a note when caused to vibrate, as by plucking, striking, or friction of a bow. **8.** (*pl.*) **a.** stringed musical instruments, especially such as are played with a bow. **b.** players on such instruments in an orchestra or band. **9.** a cord or fibre in a plant. **10.** the tough piece uniting the two parts of a pod: *the strings of beans.* **11.** *Archit.* **a.** a string-course. **b.** → **stringer** (def. 3). **12.** *Physics* a hypothetical elementary subatomic particle which is in the form of a one-dimensional line rather than a point-like object. **13.** (*pl.*) *Colloq.* limitations on any proposal: *an offer with no strings attached.* *–verb* (**strung, stringing**) *–v.t.* **14.** to furnish with or as with a string or strings. **15.** to extend or stretch (a cord, etc.) from one point to another. **16.** to thread on, or as on, a string: *to string beads.* **17.** to connect in, or as in, a line; arrange in a series or succession. **18.** to cause (stock) to move in a line. **19.** to provide or adorn with something suspended or slung: *a room strung with festoons.* **20.** to deprive of a string or strings; strip the strings from: *to string beans.* *–v.i.*

21. to form or move in a string, as a mob of animals stretched out in a line: *the sheep behind him stringing.* **22.** to form into a string or strings, as glutinous substances do when pulled. *–phr.* **23. keep on a string,** to have (someone) under one's control, especially emotionally: *she kept him on a string and then agreed to marry him.* **24. pull strings,** *Colloq.* to seek the advancement of oneself or another by using social contacts and other means not directly connected with ability or suitability. **25. string along** (or **on**), *Colloq.* to deceive (someone) in a progressive series of falsehoods; con. **26. string along with,** *Colloq.* **a.** to go along with; accompany. **b.** to cooperate with; agree with. **27. string out, a.** to extend or spread out at intervals. **b.** to extend over a period of time; prolong. **28. string up,** to kill by hanging. **–stringlike,** *adj.*

stringent /'strɪndʒənt/ *adj.* **1.** narrowly binding; rigorously exacting; strict; severe: *stringent laws.* **2.** compelling, constraining, or urgent: *stringent necessity.* **3.** convincing or forcible, as arguments, etc. **4.** (of the money market) tight; characterised by a shortage of loan money. **–stringency,** *n.* **–stringently,** *adv.*

stringer /'strɪŋə/ *n.* **1.** a longitudinal timber, metal rod, etc., which is fitted to frames or ribs in the construction of a boat, the fuselage or wing of an aeroplane, etc. **2.** *Building Trades* a long horizontal timber connecting upright posts, supporting a floor, etc. **3.** Also, **string.** *Archit.* one of the sloping sides of a stair, supporting the treads and risers.

string quartet *n. Music* a quartet, usually consisting of two violins, a viola, and a cello.

stringy /'strɪŋi/ *adj.* (**stringier, stringiest**) **1.** resembling a string; consisting of strings or stringlike pieces. **2.** coarsely or toughly fibrous, as meat. **3.** sinewy or wiry, as a person. **4.** ropy, as a glutinous liquid. **–stringiness,** *n.*

stringybark /'strɪŋibak/ *n.* **1.** any of a group of species of the genus *Eucalyptus* with a characteristic tough fibrous bark as the **red stringybark,** *E. Macrorhyncha.* *–adj.* **2.** rustic, uncultured: *stringybark settler.*

strip¹ /strɪp/ *verb* (**stripped, stripping**) *–v.t.* **1.** to deprive of covering: *to strip a fruit of its rind.* **2.** to deprive of clothing; make bare or naked. **3.** to take away or remove: *to strip pictures from a wall.* **4.** to deprive or divest: *to strip a tree of its fruit.* **5.** to clear out or empty: *to strip a house of its contents.* **6.** to deprive of equipment; dismantle: *to strip a ship of rigging.* **7.** to rob, plunder, or dispossess: *to strip someone of their possessions.* **8.** to separate the leaves from the stalks of (tobacco). **9.** to remove the midrib, etc., from (tobacco leaves). **10.** *Machinery* to tear off the thread of (a screw, bolt, etc.) or the teeth of (a gear, etc.), as by applying too much force. **11.** *Agric.* to harvest (part of a plant), using a specially constructed machine, as grains of wheat. **12.** to remove old paint, distemper, etc., from (a surface) prior to redecorating. **13.** *Chem.* to remove the most volatile components from a mixture by distillation or evaporation. **14.** to draw the last milk from (a cow), especially by a stroking and compressing movement. **15.** to draw out (milk) thus. *–v.i.* **16.** to strip something; especially, to strip oneself of clothes. **17.** to perform a striptease. **18.** to become stripped.

strip² /strɪp/ *n.* **1.** a narrow piece, comparatively long and usually of uniform width: *a strip of cloth*; *a strip of metal*; *a strip of land.* **2.** a continuous series of pictures, as in a newspaper, illustrating incidents, conversation, etc. See **comic strip. 3.** *Philately* three or more stamps joined in either a horizontal or vertical row. **4.** → **airstrip. 5.** a cluster or row of shops, businesses, etc., especially as specified, on one or both sides of a stretch of road: *the nightclub strip. –v.t.* (**stripped, stripping**)

6. to cut into strips. *–phr.* **7. tear** (or **take**) **strips off,** *Colloq.* to castigate mercilessly.

stripe¹ /straɪp/ *n.* **1.** a relatively long, narrow band of a different colour or appearance from the rest of a surface or thing: *the stripes of a zebra.* **2.** (*pl.*) a number or combination of strips of braid worn on a uniform as a badge of rank, etc. **3.** a long, narrow piece of anything. **4.** a streak or layer of a different nature within a substance. *–v.t.* **5.** to give a stripe or stripes to. *–adj.* **6.** having racing stripes: *stripe swimwear.*

stripe² /straɪp/ *n.* a stroke with a whip, rod, etc., as in punishment.

stripling /'strɪplɪŋ/ *n.* a youth just passing from boyhood to manhood.

strip mine *n.* → **open cut. –strip mining,** *n.*

stripper /'strɪpə/ *n.* **1.** a striptease dancer. **2.** something that strips, as an appliance, machine, or solvent for stripping.

striptease /'strɪptiz/ *n.* **1.** an act in which a person, usually a woman, disrobes garment by garment, usually to the accompaniment of music before an audience. *–adj.* **2.** of or relating to such an act.

strive /straɪv/ *v.i.* (**strove** or **strived, striven** /'strɪvən/ or **strived, striving**) **1.** to exert oneself vigorously; try hard. **2.** to make strenuous efforts towards any end: *to strive for success.* **3.** to contend in opposition, battle, or any conflict. **4.** to struggle vigorously, as in opposition or resistance: *to strive against fate.* **–striving,** *n.*, *adj.* **–striver,** *n.*

strobe /stroʊb/ *n.* a high-intensity flash device used in stroboscopic photography or an analogous electronic system.

strobe lighting *n.* **1.** flashing light of great intensity, as at a theatre, dance, etc., obtained by using a strobe. **2.** lighting designed to be similar in effect to that of a strobe.

stroboscope /'stroʊbəskoʊp/ *n.* an instrument used in studying the motion of a body (especially one in rapid revolution or vibration) by rendering it visible at frequent intervals, as by illuminating it with an electric spark or the like, or by viewing it through openings in a revolving disc. **–stroboscopic** /stroʊbə'skɒpɪk/, *adj.*

strode /stroʊd/ *v.* past tense of **stride.**

stroke¹ /stroʊk/ *n.* **1.** an act of striking; blow. **2.** (the sound made by) a striking of one thing upon another, as a clapper on a bell. **3.** an attack of apoplexy or paralysis. **4.** *Med.* a sudden interruption to the supply of blood to the brain, caused by haemorrhage, thrombosis or embolism. **5.** a sudden event, etc., befalling one: *a stroke of good luck.* **6.** a single complete, repeated, movement as in swimming, bowing a violin, etc. **7.** *Mechanics* one of a series of repeated back and forth movements. **8.** a style of swimming: *freestyle is the fastest stroke.* **9.** an act, feat or achievement: *a stroke of genius.* **10.** (a mark made by) the movement of a pen, pencil, etc. **11.** *Rowing* **a.** the manner or style of moving or pulling the oars. **b.** the oarsman nearest to the stern of the boat, to whose strokes those of the other oarsmen must conform. *–v.t.* **12.** to row as stroke oarsman of (a boat or crew). *–v.i.* **13.** to row as stroke in a race.

stroke² /stroʊk/ *v.t.* **1.** to pass the hand or an instrument over (something) lightly or with little pressure; rub gently, as in soothing or caressing. *–n.* **2.** the act or an instance of stroking; a stroking movement.

stroll /stroʊl/ *v.i.* **1.** to walk leisurely as inclination directs; ramble; saunter; take a walk. **2.** to wander or rove from place to place; roam: *strolling minstrels. –n.* **3.** a leisurely walk; a ramble; a saunter: *a short stroll before supper.*

stroller /'stroʊlə/ *n.* **1.** a person taking a walk or a stroll. **2.** an itinerant performer. **3.** Also, **pushchair, pusher.**

a light collapsible chair on wheels, used for carrying small children.

strong /strɒŋ/ *adj.* **1.** having, showing, or involving great bodily or muscular power; physically vigorous or robust. **2.** mentally powerful or vigorous: *a strong mind.* **3.** (sometimes fol. by *on* or *in*) especially powerful, able, or competent: *strong in maths.* **4.** of great moral power, firmness, or courage: *strong under temptation.* **5.** powerful in influence, authority, resources, or means of prevailing or succeeding: *a strong nation.* **6.** clear and firm; loud: *a strong voice.* **7.** well-supplied or rich in something: *a strong hand in a game of cards.* **8.** of great force, effectiveness, potency, or cogency: *strong arguments.* **9.** able to resist force or stand strain, wear, etc.: *strong walls*; *strong cloth.* **10.** firm or unfaltering under trial: *strong faith.* **11.** moving or acting with force or vigour: *strong wind.* **12.** containing alcohol, or much alcohol: *strong drink.* **13.** intense, as light or colour. **14.** distinct, as marks or impressions; marked, as a resemblance or contrast. **15.** strenuous or energetic; forceful or vigorous: *strong efforts.* **16.** (of language, speech, etc.) **a.** forceful; forthright. **b.** indecent; vulgar. **17.** hearty, fervent, or thoroughgoing: *strong prejudice.* **18.** having a large proportion of the effective or essential properties or ingredients: *strong tea.* **19.** having a high degree of flavour or smell: *strong perfume.* **20.** of an unpleasant or offensive flavour or smell: *strong butter.* **21.** *Commerce* characterised by steady or advancing prices: *a strong market.* **22.** *Gram.* **a.** (of Germanic verbs) indicating differentiation in tense by internal vowel change rather than by the addition of a common inflectional ending, as *sing, sang, sung*; *ride, rode, ridden.* **b.** (of Germanic nouns and adjectives) inflected with endings generally distinctive of case, number, and gender, as German *alter Mann* 'old man'. *–adv.* **23.** in a strong manner; powerfully; forcibly; vigorously. **24.** in number: *the army was twenty thousand strong. –phr.* **25. come on (a bit) strong,** to speak rather too forcefully. **26. going strong,** continuing vigorously, in good health: *he is nearly ninety but still going strong.* **–strongly,** *adv.*

strongarm /ˈstrɒŋam/ *adj. Colloq.* having, using, or involving the use of muscular or physical force: *strongarm methods.*

stronghold /ˈstrɒŋhoʊld/ *n.* **1.** a strong or well-fortified place; a fortress. **2.** a place where anything, as an ideology, opinion, etc., is strong.

strop /strɒp/ *n.* **1.** a strip of leather or other flexible material, or a long, narrow piece of wood having its faces covered with leather or an abrasive, or some similar device, used for sharpening razors. **2.** *Naut.* a ring of rope fitted round a block or spar, with an eye used for connecting. *–v.t.* (**stropped, stropping**) **3.** to sharpen on, or as on, a strop.

strophe /ˈstroʊfi/ *n.* (in modern poetry) any separate or extended section in a poem, opposed to the stanza, a group of lines which necessarily repeats a metrical pattern. **–strophic** /ˈstrɒfɪk/, *adj.*

stroppy /ˈstrɒpi/ *adj.* (**-pier, -piest**) *Colloq.* rebellious and difficult to control; awkward; complaining.

strove /stroʊv/ *v.* past tense of **strive.**

struck /strʌk/ *v.* **1.** past tense and a past participle of **strike.** *–phr.* **2. struck on,** *Colloq.* in love or infatuated with.

structure /ˈstrʌktʃə/ *n.* **1.** the arrangement of parts to make up a whole: *the structure of the atom.* **2.** something built, as a building, bridge, dam, etc. **3.** anything made up of parts arranged together in some way; an organisation. **4.** *Biol.* the construction and arrangement of tissues, parts, or organs: *bone structure.* **5.** *Geol.* **a.** the attitude of a bed or stratum of sedimentary rocks,

as indicated by the dip and strike. **b.** the coarser features of rocks as contrasted with their texture. **6.** *Chem.* the manner by which atoms in a molecule are joined to each other, especially in organic chemistry where it is represented by a diagram of the molecular arrangement; configuration. *–v.t.* **7.** to give form or organisation to. **–structural,** *adj.* **–structurally,** *adv.*

strudel /ˈstrudəl/ *n.* a very thin sheet of pastry, spread with a filling, such as apples, sour cherries, cottage cheese, etc., rolled up, brushed with butter and baked slowly.

struggle /ˈstrʌgəl/ *v.i.* **1.** to make violent movements or effort: *he struggled for an hour, but could not break his bonds.* **2.** to fight with an enemy, especially without weapons. **3.** to make a great effort for or against something: *to struggle for existence. –n.* **4.** a violent movement. **5.** a fight. **6.** a strong effort against any bad conditions. **–struggling,** *adj.* **–struggler,** *n.*

strum /strʌm/ *verb* (**strummed, strumming**) *–v.t.* **1.** to play on (a stringed musical instrument) unskilfully or carelessly. **2.** to produce (notes, etc.) by such playing: *to strum a tune.* **3.** to play (chords, etc., especially on a guitar) by sweeping across the strings with the fingers or with a plectrum. *–v.i.* **4.** to play chords on a stringed instrument unskilfully or as a simple accompaniment. *–n.* **5.** the act of strumming. **–strummer,** *n.*

strumpet /ˈstrʌmpət/ *n. Archaic* a female prostitute; a harlot.

strung /strʌŋ/ *v.* past tense and past participle of **string.**

strut¹ /strʌt/ *v.i.* (**strutted, strutting**) **1.** to walk with a vain, pompous bearing, as with head erect and chest thrown out, as if expecting to impress observers. *–n.* **2.** the act of strutting; a strutting walk or gait. **–strutter,** *n.*

strut² /strʌt/ *n.* **1.** a piece of wood or iron, or some other member of a structure, designed for the reception of pressure or weight in the direction of its length. *–v.t.* (**strutted, strutting**) **2.** to brace or support by a strut or struts.

strychnine /ˈstrɪknin, -nən/ *n.* a colourless crystalline poison, $C_{21}H_{22}N_2O_2$, derived from the nux vomica. It has a powerful stimulating effect on the central nervous system and can be used in small quantities to stimulate the appetite.

stub /stʌb/ *n.* **1.** a short projecting part. **2.** the end of a fallen tree, shrub, or plant left fixed in the ground; a stump. **3.** a short remaining piece, as of a pencil, a candle, a cigar, etc. **4.** something unusually short, as a short, thick nail or a short-pointed, blunt pen. **5.** the counterfoil of a chequebook, etc. *–v.t.* (**stubbed, stubbing**) **6.** to strike, as one's toe, against something projecting from a surface. **7.** to clear of stubs, as land. **8.** to dig up by the roots; grub up (roots). *–phr.* **9. stub out,** to extinguish (a cigarette) by pressing the lighted end against a hard surface.

stubbies /ˈstʌbiz/ *pl. n. Aust.* (*from trademark*) short shorts of tough material for informal wear.

stubble /ˈstʌbəl/ *n.* **1.** the stumps of grain stalks or the like, left in the ground when the crop is cut. **2.** such stumps collectively. **3.** any short, rough growth, as of beard. **–stubbled, stubbly,** *adj.*

stubborn /ˈstʌbən/ *adj.* **1.** unreasonably obstinate; obstinately perverse. **2.** fixed or set in purpose or opinion; resolute. **3.** obstinately maintained, as a course of action: *a stubborn resistance.* **4.** hard to deal with or manage. **5.** hard, tough, or stiff, as stone or wood. **–stubbornly,** *adv.* **–stubbornness,** *n.*

stubby /ˈstʌbi/ *adj.* (**-bier, -biest**) **1.** short and thick or broad; thickset. **2.** bristly, as the hair or beard. *–n.* (*pl.* **-bies**) Also, **stubbie. 3.** *NZ* **a.** a small squat beer bottle. **b.** the contents of such a bottle. **4.** a short surfboard. **–stubbiness,** *n.*

stubby holder *n.* a lightweight casing designed as insulation for a stubby (def. 3a) or can. Also, **stubby cooler**.

stucco /'stʌkoʊ/ *n.* (*pl.* **-coes** or **-cos**) **1.** a plaster (as of slaked lime, chalk, and pulverised white marble, or of plaster of Paris and glue) used for cornices and mouldings of rooms and for other decorations. **2.** a cement or concrete imitating stone, for coating exterior walls of houses, etc. **3.** any of various plasters, cements, etc. *–v.t.* (**-coed, -coing**) **4.** to cover or ornament with stucco. **–stuccoer,** *n.*

stuck /stʌk/ *v.* **1.** past tense and past participle of **stick**[2]. *–phr.* **2. get stuck into, a.** to set about (a task) vigorously. **b.** to attack (someone) vigorously either physically or verbally. **c.** to eat hungrily. **3. stuck on,** infatuated with. *–adj.* **4.** *Colloq.* at a loss; uncertain: *to be a bit stuck about what to do next.*

stuck-up *adj. Colloq.* conceited; haughty.

stud[1] /stʌd/ *n.* **1.** a small knob or boss sticking out from a surface, especially as an ornament. **2.** a nail-like metal piece fixed to the sole of a sporting shoe, to give better grip. **3.** an upright post in the frame of a building, to which panels of lining material are fixed. **4.** any pin, lug, etc., sticking out on a machine. **5.** a kind of small button or fastener on a shirt. *–v.t.* (**studded, studding**) **6.** to set with or as with studs, knobs, etc. **7.** to scatter or be scattered over with things set at intervals: *stars studded the sky.*

stud[2] /stʌd/ *n.* **1.** a number of horses, as for racing or hunting, belonging to one owner. **2.** an establishment in which horses, cattle, etc., are kept for breeding. **3.** a young man of obvious sexual power. *–adj.* **4.** of, associated with, or relating to a studhorse. **5.** retained for breeding purposes.

student /'stjudnt/ *n.* **1.** someone who is engaged in a course of study and instruction, as at a college, university, or professional or technical school. **2.** someone who studies a subject systematically or in detail. **–studentship,** *n.*

studied /'stʌdid/ *adj.* **1.** marked by or suggestive of effort, rather than spontaneous or natural: *studied simplicity.* **2.** carefully considered. **–studiedly,** *adv.* **–studiedness,** *n.*

studio /'stjudioʊ/ *n.* (*pl.* **-dios**) **1.** the workroom or atelier of an artist, as a painter or sculptor. **2.** a room or place in which some other form of art is pursued: *a music studio.* **3.** a room or set of rooms specially equipped for broadcasting radio or television programs or making recordings. **4.** (*oft. pl.*) all the buildings occupied by a company engaged in making films.

studio apartment *n.* an apartment with one main room; a bed-sitter, especially when up-market and having some saleable feature such as city views, ocean views, etc. Also, **studio unit**.

studious /'stjudiəs/ *adj.* **1.** disposed or given to study: *a studious boy.* **2.** concerned with, characterised by, or relating to study: *studious tastes.* **3.** zealous, assiduous, or painstaking: *studious care.* **4.** studied or carefully maintained. **–studiously,** *adv.* **–studiousness,** *n.*

study /'stʌdi/ *n.* (*pl.* **studies**) **1.** the putting of the mind to gaining knowledge, by reading, searching, and thinking. **2.** a branch of learning: *the study of law.* **3.** a subject or subjects studied: *to spend more time at his studies.* **4.** (a written account of) any thorough examination: *to publish a study of the NSW railways.* **5.** deep thought; reverie. **6.** a room set apart for private study, reading, writing, etc. **7.** *Music* a piece of music written to give a performer exercise in technical matters, but with artistic value also. **8.** *Art* something produced as an exercise, or as a record of observations, or as a guide for a finished work. *–verb* (**studied, studying**) *–v.i.* **9.** to give oneself to gaining knowledge, by reading,

searching, thinking, making notes, etc. *–v.t.* **10.** to give oneself to gaining a knowledge of a subject, especially systematically: *to study science.* **11.** to examine carefully and in detail: *to study the political situation.* **12.** to think deeply about.

stuff /stʌf/ *n.* **1.** the material of which anything is made. **2.** material to be worked upon, or to be used in making something. **3.** matter or material indefinitely: *cushions filled with some soft stuff.* **4.** woven material or fabric. **5.** inward character, qualities, or capabilities. **6.** worthless matter or things. **7.** worthless or foolish ideas, talk, or writing. **8.** *Colloq.* property, as personal belongings, equipment, etc. **9.** *Colloq.* actions, performances, talk, etc.: *to cut out the rough stuff.* **10.** *Colloq.* literary, artistic, or musical material, productions, compositions, etc. **11.** *Colloq.* one's own trade, profession, occupation, etc.: *to know one's stuff.* **12.** *Colloq.* money. *–v.t.* **13.** to fill (a receptacle), especially by packing the contents closely together; cram full. **14.** to fill (an aperture, cavity, etc.) by forcing something into it. **15.** to fill or line with some kind of material as a padding or packing. **16.** to fill or cram (oneself, one's stomach, etc.) with food. **17.** to fill (a chicken, turkey, piece of meat, etc.) with seasoned breadcrumbs or other savoury matter. **18.** to fill the skin of (a dead animal) with material, preserving the natural form and appearance. **19.** to thrust or cram (something) tightly into a receptacle, cavity, or the like. **20.** to pack tightly in a confined place; crowd together. **21.** to crowd (a vehicle, room, etc.) with persons. **22.** to fill (the mind) with details, facts, etc. **23.** *Colloq.* (*taboo*) (of males) to have sexual intercourse with. *–v.i.* **24.** to cram oneself with food; feed gluttonously. *–phr.* **25. do one's stuff,** to do what is expected of one; show what one can do. **26. not to give a stuff,** to be unconcerned. **27. stuff it,** an exclamation indicating anger, frustration, etc. **28. stuff up, a.** to stop up or plug; block or choke. **b.** *Colloq.* to cause to fail; render useless. **c.** *Colloq.* to fail; act incompetently: *trust him to stuff up.* **29. that's the stuff,** an exclamation of support, encouragement, approval, etc.

stuffed /stʌft/ *v.* **1.** past tense and past participle of **stuff**. *–adj.* **2.** *Colloq.* broken beyond repair; ruined. **3.** (of a person) **a.** exhausted. **b.** extremely full of food. **c.** in deep trouble; ruined: *if she catches you now, you're stuffed. –phr. Colloq.* **4. get stuffed,** an impolite expression of dismissal. **5. stuffed up,** having the nasal passages blocked with mucus, usually as a result of a cold.

stuffing /'stʌfɪŋ/ *n.* **1.** the act of someone or something that stuffs. **2.** that with which anything is or may be stuffed. **3.** seasoned breadcrumbs or other filling used to stuff a chicken, turkey, etc., before cooking. *–phr.* **4. knock** (or **beat**) **the stuffing out of,** *Colloq.* **a.** to defeat utterly. **b.** to destroy the self-confidence of.

stuffy /'stʌfi/ **1.** badly ventilated; close: *a stuffy room; a stuffy train.* **2.** self-important; conceited; pompous. **3.** easily shocked; straitlaced; prim. **4.** old-fashioned or dull. **–stuffily,** *adv.* **–stuffiness,** *n.*

stultify /'stʌltəfaɪ/ **1.** to make, or cause to appear, foolish or ridiculous. **2.** to render absurdly or wholly futile or ineffectual, as efforts. **3.** *Law* to allege or prove to be of unsound mind; allege (oneself) to be insane. **–stultification** /stʌltəfəˈkeɪʃən/, *n.* **–stultifier,** *n.*

stumble /'stʌmbəl/ *v.i.* **1.** to strike the foot against something in walking, running, etc., so as to stagger or fall; trip. **2.** to walk or go unsteadily. **3.** to make a mistake especially in words. **4.** to act or speak in a hesitating way. *–n.* **5.** the act of stumbling. **6.** a mistake; slip; blunder. *–phr.* **7. stumble on** (or **upon**) (or **across**), to find accidentally or unexpectedly. **–stumbler,** *n.* **–stumblingly,** *adv.*

stumblebum /'stʌmbəlbʌm/ *n. Colloq.* a stupid and ineffectual person.

stump /stʌmp/ *n.* **1.** the lower end of a tree or plant left after the main part falls or is cut off; a standing tree trunk from which the upper part and the branches have been removed. **2.** the part of a limb of the body remaining after the rest has been amputated or cut off. **3.** a part of a broken or decayed tooth left in the gum. **4.** a short remnant of a pencil, candle, cigar, etc. **5.** any basal part remaining after the main or more important part has been removed. **6.** a wooden post used as a pier for a house. **7.** *Qld, NT* one of the tall wooden supports by which a highset building is elevated above the ground. **8.** a wooden or artificial leg. **9.** *(usu. pl.) Colloq.* a leg: *to stir one's stumps.* **10.** *Chiefly US* the platform or place of political speech-making: *to go on the stump.* **11.** an instrument consisting of a short, thick, roll of paper or soft leather, or a bar of rubber or other soft material, usually cut to a blunt point at each end, used for rubbing the lights and shades in crayon drawing or charcoal drawing, or for otherwise altering the effect. **12.** *Cricket* each of the three upright sticks which, with the two bails laid on the top of them, form a wicket. **13.** *(pl.) Cricket* the end of a day's play. **14.** *Colloq.* union dues. *–v.t.* **15.** to reduce to a stump; truncate; lop. **16.** to clear of stumps, as land. **17.** *US Colloq.* to stub, as one's toe. **18.** to nonplus, embarrass, or render completely at a loss. **19.** *Chiefly US Colloq.* to make political speeches in or to. **20.** *Cricket* (of the wicketkeeper) to put (the person batting) out by knocking down a stump or by dislodging a bail with the ball held in the hand, at a moment when the person batting is out of his or her ground. **21.** to tone or modify (crayon drawings, etc.) by means of a stump (def. 11). **22.** *Qld, NT* to set (a house) on stumps. *–v.i.* **23.** to walk heavily or clumsily, as if with a wooden leg: *the sailor stumped across the deck.* **24.** *Chiefly US Colloq.* to make speeches in an election campaign. *–phr.* **25. draw** (or **pull**) **stumps**, *Cricket* to cease play. **26. get up on the stump**, to address a public meeting. **27. pull up stumps**, *Colloq.* to leave one's home or place of residence for good. **28. stump up**, *Colloq.* to pay up or hand over money required.

stump-jump plough *n.* a plough designed to rise and fall over roots and stumps in newly cleared ground.

stun /stʌn/ *v.t.* (**stunned**, **stunning**) **1.** to deprive of consciousness or strength by or as by a blow, fall, etc. **2.** to strike with astonishment; astound; amaze. **3.** to daze or bewilder by distracting noise. *–n.* **4.** the act of stunning. **5.** the condition of being stunned.

stung /stʌŋ/ *v.* **1.** past tense and past participle of **sting**. *–adj. Colloq.* **2.** *Aust.* drunk. **3.** tricked; cheated.

stun gun *n.* **1.** a weapon which administers a mild electric shock to a person, sufficient to temporarily stun them. **2.** (formerly) a long-barrelled gun that fires a small weighted bag containing sand, bird shot, etc., used for riot control.

stunning /'stʌnɪŋ/ *adj.* **1.** that stuns. **2.** *Colloq.* of striking excellence, beauty, etc. **–stunningly**, *adv.*

stunt¹ /stʌnt/ *v.t.* **1.** to check the growth or development of; dwarf; hinder the increase or progress of. *–n.* **2.** a check in growth or development. **3.** arrested development. **4.** a creature hindered from attaining its proper growth.

stunt² /stʌnt/ *n.* **1.** a performance serving as a display of strength, activity, skill, or the like, as in athletics, etc.; a feat. **2.** anything done to attract publicity. *–v.i.* **3.** to do a stunt or stunts.

stupefy /'stjupəfaɪ/ **1.** to put into a state of stupor; dull the faculties of. **2.** to stun as with a narcotic, a shock, strong emotion, etc. **3.** to overwhelm with amazement;

astound. **–stupefaction** /stjupə'fækʃən/, *n.* **–stupefacient** /stjupə'feɪʃənt/, *n.*, *adj.* **–stupefier**, *n.*

stupendous /stju'pendəs/ *adj.* **1.** such as to cause amazement; astounding; marvellous. **2.** amazingly large or great; immense: *a stupendous mass of information.* **–stupendously**, *adv.* **–stupendousness**, *n.*

stupid /'stjupəd/ *adj.* **1.** lacking ordinary activity and keenness of mind; dull. **2.** characterised by, indicative of, or proceeding from mental dullness: *a stupid act.* **3.** tediously dull or uninteresting: *a stupid book.* **4.** in a state of stupor; stupefied. **–stupidly**, *adv.* **–stupidness**, **stupidity** /stju'pɪdəti/, *n.*

stupor /'stjupə/ *n.* **1.** suspension or great diminution of sensibility, as in disease or as caused by narcotics, intoxicants, etc. **2.** a state of suspended or deadened sensibility. **3.** mental torpor, or apathy; stupefaction. **–stuporous**, *adj.*

sturdy /'stɜdi/ **1.** strongly built, stalwart, or robust. **2.** strong, as in substance, construction, texture, etc.: *sturdy walls.* **3.** firm, stout, or indomitable: *sturdy defenders.* **4.** of strong or hardy growth, as a plant. **–sturdily**, *adv.* **–sturdiness**, *n.*

sturgeon /'stɜdʒən/ *n.* any of various large ganoid fishes of the family Acipenseridae, found in fresh and salt waters of the northern temperate zone, and valued for their flesh and as a source of caviar.

Sturt's desert pea *n.* an Australian plant, *Swainsona formosa*, with brilliant scarlet and black flowers, found in inland desert country; the floral emblem of SA. Also, **Sturt's pea**.

Sturt's desert rose *n.* a shrub of inland Australia, *Gossypium sturtianum*, with attractive mauve flowers; the floral emblem of the NT.

stutter /'stʌtə/ *v.i.* **1.** to utter sounds in which the rhythm is interrupted by blocks or spasms, repetitions, or prolongation of sounds or syllables, sometimes accompanied by facial contortions. *–v.t.* **2.** to utter (words, etc.) in a stutter. *–n.* **3.** unrhythmical and distorted speech characterised principally by blocks or spasms interrupting the rhythm. **–stutterer**, *n.* **–stutteringly**, *adv.*

sty¹ /staɪ/ *n.* (*pl.* **sties**) **1.** a pen or enclosure for pigs. **2.** any filthy abode. **3.** a place of bestial debauchery. *–verb* (**stied**, **stying**) *–v.t.* **4.** to keep or lodge in or as in a sty. *–v.i.* **5.** to live in or as in a sty.

sty² /staɪ/ *n.* (*pl.* **sties**) → **stye**. Also, **stye**.

stye /staɪ/ *n.* a circumscribed inflammatory swelling, like a small boil, on the edge of the eyelid. Also, **sty**.

style /staɪl/ *n.* **1.** a particular kind, sort, or type, as relating to form, appearance, or character. **2.** a particular way of doing things: *a style of singing.* **3.** a way of living, as relating to expense, possessions, etc.: *they live in a simple style.* **4.** an elegant or fashionable way of living: *since winning the lottery, they live in style.* **5. a.** (good) design, as in dress; elegance. **b.** an admired and distinctive personal expression: *she writes letters with style.* **6.** a particular manner of writing or speaking, depending on historical period, literary form, personality, etc., rather than on content: *the style of Henry Lawson; the Baroque style.* **7.** a particular, distinctive, method or form of construction in any art or work. **8.** a legal, official, or business title: *a firm under the style of Smith, Jones and Co.* **9.** → **stylus** (def. 1). **10.** *Bot.* a narrow tube sometimes coming from the ovary, having the stigma at the top. *–v.t.* **11.** to call by a particular style or specific name. **12.** to design in a particular or new style: *to style an evening dress.* **–styler**, *n.* **–stylistic**, *adj.*

stylise /'staɪlaɪz/ to bring into conformity with a particular style, as of representation or treatment in art; conventionalise. Also, **stylize**. **–stylisation** /staɪlaɪ-'zeɪʃən/, *n.* **–styliser**, *n.*

stylish /ˈstaɪlɪʃ/ *adj.* characterised by style, or by conforming to the fashionable standard; modishly elegant; smart. –**stylishly**, *adv.* –**stylishness**, *n.*

stylus /ˈstaɪləs/ *n.* (*pl.* **-li** /-laɪ/ *or* **-luses**) **1.** Also, **style**. a pointed instrument for writing on wax or other suitable surfaces. **2.** *Computers* a pen-shaped instrument used to write, draw, etc., directly onto a touch-sensitive computer screen, the resultant text or image being digitised by the computer's software. **3.** a cutting tool, often needle-shaped, used to cut grooves in making gramophone records. **4.** a needle tipped with diamond, sapphire, etc., for reproducing the sound of a gramophone record. **5.** any of various pointed instruments used in drawing, tracing, stencilling, etc.

stymie /ˈstaɪmi/ *n.* **1.** *Golf* a position in which an opponent's ball is lying directly between the player's ball and the hole for which he or she is playing. **2.** any problem which is difficult to resolve. *–v.t.* (**-mied**, **-mieing**) **3.** to hinder or block, as with a stymie; thwart; frustrate.

styptic /ˈstɪptɪk/ *adj.* Also, **styptical. 1.** contracting organic tissue; astringent; binding. **2.** checking haemorrhage or bleeding, as a drug; haemostatic. *–n.* **3.** a styptic agent or substance. –**stypticity** /stɪpˈtɪsəti/, *n.*

suave /swɑv/ *adj.* (of persons or their manner, speech, etc.) smoothly agreeable or polite; agreeably or blandly urbane. –**suavity**, *n.* –**suavely**, *adv.*

sub¹ /sʌb/ *Colloq. –n.* **1.** a subeditor. *–v.t.* (**subbed**, **subbing**) **2.** to subedit.

sub² /sʌb/ *n. Colloq.* a subscription.

sub³ /sʌb/ *n. Colloq.* a submarine (def. 1).

sub⁴ /sʌb/ *Colloq. –n.* **1.** an advance against wages, etc. *–v.t.* (**subbed**, **subbing**) **2.** to pay or receive (an advance against wages, etc.).

sub- a prefix meaning 'under', freely used as a formative, as in *submerge*, *subsoil*.

subcommittee /ˈsʌbkəˌmɪti/ *n.* a secondary committee appointed out of a main committee.

subconscious /sʌbˈkɒnʃəs/ *adj.* **1.** existing or operating beneath or beyond consciousness: *the subconscious self.* **2.** imperfectly or not wholly conscious. *–n.* **3.** the totality of mental processes of which the individual is not aware; unreportable mental activities. –**subconsciously**, *adv.* –**subconsciousness**, *n.*

subcontract *Law –n.* /sʌbˈkɒntrækt/ **1.** a contract by which one agrees to render services or to provide materials necessary for the performance of another contract. *–v.t.* /sʌbkənˈtrækt/ **2.** to make a subcontract for. *–v.i.* /sʌbkənˈtrækt/ **3.** to make a subcontract.

subculture /ˈsʌbkʌltʃə/–*v.t.* **1.** *Bacteriol.* to cultivate (a bacterial strain) again on a new medium. *–n.* **2.** *Bacteriol.* a culture derived in this way. **3.** *Sociology* a distinct network of behaviour, beliefs, and attitudes existing within a larger culture. –**subcultural**, *adj.*

subcutaneous /sʌbkjuˈteɪniəs/ *adj.* **1.** situated or lying under the skin, as tissue. **2.** performed or introduced under the skin, as an injection by a syringe. **3.** living below the several layers of the skin, as certain parasites. –**subcutaneously**, *adv.*

subdivide /ˈsʌbdəvaɪd, sʌbdəˈvaɪd/ *v.t.* **1.** to divide (a part, or an already divided whole) into smaller parts; divide anew after a first division. **2.** to divide into parts. *–v.i.* **3.** to become separated into subdivisions. –**subdivider**, *n.*

subdivision /ˈsʌbdəvɪʒən/ *n.* **1.** the act or process of subdividing, or the fact of being subdivided. **2.** one of the parts into which something is subdivided. **3.** *Aust., NZ* an area of land divided into lots for specified development: *an urban subdivision*; *a rural subdivision*.

subdue /səbˈdju/ *v.t.* **1.** to win control over, usually by force; conquer; overcome. **2.** to put down or repress (feelings, etc.). **3.** to reduce the amount or force of

(sound, light, colour, etc.); soften. –**subduable**, *adj.* –**subduedly**, *adv.* –**subduedness**, *n.* –**subduer**, *n.*

subeditor /sʌbˈɛdətə/ *n.* **1.** *Journalism* someone who edits and corrects material written by others. **2.** an assistant or subordinate editor. –**subedit**, *v.* –**subeditorial** /ˌsʌbɛdəˈtɔriəl/, *adj.* –**subeditorship**, *n.*

subgenre /ˈsʌbʒɒnrə/ *n.* a subsection of a genre, as fantasy fiction within science fiction. Also, **sub-genre**.

subheading /ˈsʌbhɛdɪŋ/ *n.* **1.** a title or heading of a subdivision or subsection in a chapter, treatise, essay, newspaper article, etc. **2.** a subordinate division of a heading or title. Also, **subhead**.

subject *n.* /ˈsʌbdʒɛkt/ **1.** something that may become a matter of thought, discussion, investigation, etc.: *a subject of conversation.* **2.** a branch of knowledge organised as a course of study. **3.** a reason, or cause: *a subject for complaint.* **4.** the underlying idea of a sermon, book, story, etc.; theme. **5.** an object, scene, incident, etc., chosen by an artist or shown in a work of art. **6.** someone who is under the rule of a sovereign, state, or government: *a British subject.* **7.** *Gram.* (in English and other languages) the word or words of a sentence about which something is said. **8.** a person used for medical, surgical, or psychological treatment or experiment. *–adj.* /ˈsʌbdʒɛkt/ **9.** being under rule or authority; owing loyalty or obedience: *a subject people.* *–v.t.* /səbˈdʒɛkt/ **10.** (usu. fol. by *to*) to bring under control, rule, or influence. **11.** (fol. by *to*) to cause to undergo or experience something: *to subject metal to intense heat.* **12.** (fol. by *to*) to lay open, or expose: *he subjected himself to ridicule.* *–phr.* /ˈsʌbdʒɛkt/ **13. subject to, a.** open or exposed to: *subject to criticism.* **b.** dependent or conditional upon: *his consent is subject to your approval.* **c.** under control or influence of: *subject to colonial rule.* **d.** likely or sure to undergo something: *I am subject to headaches.*

subjective /səbˈdʒɛktɪv/ *adj.* **1.** existing in the mind; belonging to the thinker rather than to the object of thought (opposed to *objective*). **2.** relating to, caused by, or typical of a particular person's ideas, feelings and prejudices; personal; individual. **3.** *Philos.* of or relating to thought itself. –**subjectively**, *adv.* –**subjectivity** /sʌbdʒɛkˈtɪvəti/, **subjectiveness**, *n.*

sub judice /sʌb ˈdʒudəsi/ *adv.* before a judge or court of law; under judicial consideration.

subjugate /ˈsʌbdʒəgeɪt/ *v.t.* **1.** to bring under complete control or into subjection; subdue; conquer. **2.** to make submissive or subservient. –**subjugation** /sʌbdʒəˈgeɪʃən/, *n.* –**subjugator**, *n.*

subjunctive /səbˈdʒʌŋktɪv/ *Gram. –adj.* **1.** (in many languages) designating or relating to a verb mood having among its functions the expression of contingent or hypothetical action. For example, in the sentence *Were I but king, things would alter*, the verb *were* is in the subjunctive mood. Compare **indicative.** *–n.* **2.** the subjunctive mood. **3.** a verb in the subjunctive mood, as *be* in *if it be true.*

sublet /sʌbˈlɛt/ *v.t.* (**-let, -letting**) **1.** to let to another person, the party letting being himself or herself a lessee. **2.** to let (work, etc.) under a subcontract.

sub lieutenant /sʌb ləˈtɛnənt/ *n. Navy* **1.** a commissioned officer in the Royal Australian Navy ranking below lieutenant and above midshipman. **2.** the rank. *Abbrev.:* SBLT

sublimate *v.t.* /ˈsʌbləmeɪt/ **1.** *Psychol.* to redirect (sexual energies, etc.) into socially constructive or creative activities. **2.** *Chem., etc.* ➝ **sublime** (def. 7). **3.** to make nobler. *–n.* /ˈsʌbləmət/ **4.** *Chem.* the crystals, deposit, etc., obtained when a substance is sublimated. –**sublimation** /sʌbləˈmeɪʃən/, *n.*

sublime /səˈblaɪm/ *adj.* **1.** elevated or lofty in thought, language, bearing, etc.: *sublime poetry.* **2.** impressing the mind with a sense of greatness or power; awe-inspiring: *sublime scenery*. **3.** perfect or supreme: *a sublime moment*. **4.** *Poetic* haughty or proud. –*n.* **5.** that which is sublime: *from the sublime to the ridiculous*. –*v.t.* **6.** to make higher, nobler, or purer. **7.** *Chem., etc.* to change (a solid) by heat directly into a vapour, which on cooling condenses back to solid form, without becoming liquid first. –*v.i.* **8.** *Chem., etc.* to change from solid state to a gas, and then condense as a solid without becoming liquid. –**sublimely**, *adv.* –**sublimeness**, **sublimity** /sə'blɪməti/, *n.*

subliminal /sə'blɪmənəl/ *adj. Psychol.* (of stimuli, etc.) being or operating below the threshold of consciousness or perception; subconscious: *subliminal advertising*. –**subliminally**, *adv.*

submarine /'sʌbmərin, sʌbmə'rin/ *n.* **1.** a type of vessel that can be submerged and navigated under water, especially one used in warfare for the discharge of torpedoes, guided missiles, etc. **2.** something submarine, as a plant, animal, etc. –*adj.* **3.** situated, occurring, operating, or living under the surface of the sea or any large body of water. **4.** of, relating to, or carried on by submarine ships: *submarine warfare*. –**submariner** /sʌb'mærənə/, *n.*

submerge /səb'mɜdʒ/ *verb* (-**merged**, -**merging**) –*v.t.* **1.** to put under water; plunge below the surface of water or any enveloping medium. **2.** to cover with or as with water; immerse. –*v.i.* **3.** to sink or plunge under water, or beneath the surface of any enveloping medium. –**submergence**, *n.*

submission /səb'mɪʃən/ *n.* **1.** the act or result of submitting. **2.** submissive behaviour. **3.** anything which is submitted, e.g. an official report, application for funds, etc.

submissive /səb'mɪsɪv/ *adj.* **1.** inclined or ready to submit; unresistingly or humbly obedient. **2.** marked by or indicating submission: *a submissive reply*. –**submissively**, *adv.* –**submissiveness**, *n.*

submit /səb'mɪt/ *verb* (-**mitted**, -**mitting**) –*v.t.* **1.** to yield in surrender, compliance, or obedience. **2.** to subject (especially oneself) to conditions imposed, treatment, etc. **3.** to refer (something) to the decision or judgement of another or others. **4.** to hand over for assessment, valuation, etc.: *to submit an essay on contemporary art*. **5.** to state or urge with deference: *I submit that full proof should be required*. –*v.i.* **6.** (sometimes fol. by *to*) to yield in surrender, compliance, or obedience: *to submit to a conqueror*. –*phr.* **7. submit to, a.** to allow oneself to be subjected to (something imposed or to be undergone): *to submit to punishment*. **b.** to defer to the opinion, judgement, etc., of (another). –**submittable**, **submissible** /səb'mɪsəbəl/, *adj.* –**submittal**, *n.* –**submitter**, *n.*

subordinate *adj.* /sə'bɔdənət/ **1.** placed in or belonging to a lower order or rank. **2.** of lesser importance; secondary. **3.** subject to or under the authority of a superior. **4.** dependent. **5.** *Gram.* denoting or relating to a subordinate clause or other dependent phrase. **b.** denoting or relating to a subordinating conjunction. –*n.* /sə'bɔdənət/ **6.** a subordinate person or thing. –*v.t.* /sə'bɔdəneɪt/ **7.** to place in a lower secondary to rank. –*phr.* **8. subordinate to, a.** to make secondary to. **b.** to make subject or subservient to. –**subordination** /səbɔdə-'neɪʃən/, *n.* –**subordinately**, *adv.* –**subordinative**, *adj.*

subordinate clause *n. Gram.* a clause that modifies and is dependent upon a main clause, as *when I came* in the sentence *They were glad when I came*.

suborn /sə'bɔn/ *v.t.* to bribe or procure (a person) to commit some unlawful or wrongful act, usually perjury. –**subornation** /ˌsʌbɔ'neɪʃən/, *n.* –**subornative**, *adj.* –**suborner**, *n.*

subpoena /sə'pinə/ *Law* –*n.* **1.** the usual writ process for the summoning of witnesses. –*v.t.* (-**naed**, -**naing**) **2.** to serve with a subpoena.

subprime /sʌb'praɪm/ *adj. US* of, relating to, or designating a loan, usually a housing loan, which is risky because the borrower is less than ideal or has an ability to repay which has not been accurately assessed.

subroutine /'sʌbrutin/ *n. Computers* a section of a program which can be called up as required from various points in the main program, returning the user to the point at which it was called up.

subscribe /səb'skraɪb/ *v.t.* **1.** to promise (usually by signature) to give or pay (a sum of money) as a contribution, payment, share, etc. **2.** to give or pay (money) in fulfilment of such a promise. **3.** to express agreement to (a contract, etc.) by signing one's name. **4.** to write (something) beneath or at the end of a thing; sign (one's name) to a document, etc. –*v.i.* **5.** to promise to give or pay money for some special purpose. **6.** to obtain a subscription to a magazine, newspaper, etc.: *I subscribe to several magazines*. **7.** to give or pay money. **8.** to sign one's name to something. **9.** to agree, especially by signing one's name. –**subscriber**, *n.*

subscriber trunk dialling *n.* a system for making long-distance calls in which the subscriber dials the required number direct, rather than going through an operator. *Abbrev.*: STD

subscript /'sʌbskrɪpt/ *n.* **1.** a character written or set slightly below and immediately to one side of another, as 'x' in 'B$_x$'. –*adj.* **2.** lower than the main line of type, as the '2' in 'H$_2$O'.

subscription /səb'skrɪpʃən/ *n.* **1.** a contribution of money towards some object or a payment for shares, a periodical, club membership, etc. **2.** a sum of money given. **3.** agreement, assent, or approval expressed by, or as if by, signing one's name. –**subscriptive** /səb-'skrɪptɪv/, *adj.* –**subscriptively**, *adv.*

subsection /'sʌbsɛkʃən/ *n.* **1.** a part or division of a section. **2.** one of eight exogamous kinship groups within some Aboriginal tribes having a kinship system with sections; equivalent to half a section. Compare **moiety** (def. 2), **section** (def. 12).

subsequent /'sʌbsəkwənt/ *adj.* **1.** occurring or coming later or after: *subsequent events*. **2.** following in order or succession: *a subsequent section in a treaty*. –**subsequently**, *adv.*

subservient /səb'sɜviənt/ *adj.* **1.** serving or acting in a subordinate capacity; subordinate. **2.** (of persons, their conduct, etc.) servile; excessively submissive; obsequious. **3.** of use as a means to promote a purpose or end. –**subservience**, **subserviency**, *n.* –**subserviently**, *adv.*

subside /səb'saɪd/ *v.i.* **1.** to sink to a low or lower level. **2.** to become quiet, less violent, or less active; abate: *the laughter subsided*. **3.** to sink or fall to the bottom; settle, as lees; precipitate. –**subsider**, *n.*

subsidence /səb'saɪdəns/ *n.* **1.** the act or process of subsiding. **2.** the collapse of a section of the surface of the ground to create a hole, as a result of mining, or by the water saturation of the soil, or by groundwater extraction from an aquifer.

subsidiary /səb'sɪdʒəri/ *adj.* **1.** serving to assist or supplement; auxiliary; supplementary; tributary, as a stream. **2.** subordinate or secondary. –*n.* (*pl.* -**ries**) **3.** a subsidiary thing or person. **4.** Also, **subsidiary company.** a company whose controlling interest is owned by another company. **5.** *Music* a subordinate theme or subject. –**subsidiarily**, *adv.*

subsidise /'sʌbsədaɪz/ *v.t.* **1.** to furnish or aid with a subsidy. **2.** to purchase the assistance of by the payment of a subsidy. **3.** to secure the cooperation of by bribery;

buy over. Also, **subsidize**. **–subsidisation** /sʌbsədaɪ-ˈzeɪʃən/, *n*. **–subsidiser**, *n*.

subsidy /ˈsʌbsədi/ *n*. (*pl*. **-dies**) **1**. a grant by a government to a company, organisation or individual, for which it receives nothing in return. **2**. a sum paid, often in accordance with a treaty, by one government to another, to secure some service in return. **3**. any grant or contribution of money towards the cost of some purchase or endeavour.

subsist /səbˈsɪst/ *v.i*. **1**. to exist, or continue in existence. **2**. to continue alive; live, as on food, resources, etc., especially when these are limited. **3**. to have existence in, or by reason of, something. *–v.t*. **4**. to provide sustenance or support for; maintain. *–phr*. **5**. **subsist in**, to reside, lie, or consist in.

subsistence /səbˈsɪstəns/ *n*. **1**. the state or fact of subsisting; continuance. **2**. the state or fact of existing. **3**. the providing of sustenance or support. **4**. means of supporting life; a living or livelihood.

subsistence farming *n*. farming in which the produce is consumed by the farmer's family leaving little or no surplus for marketing. Also, **subsistence agriculture**.

subsoil /ˈsʌbsɔɪl/ *n*. the bed or stratum of earth or earthy material immediately under the surface soil.

substance /ˈsʌbstəns/ *n*. **1**. that of which a thing consists; matter or material. **2**. a species of matter of definite chemical composition. **3**. the matter with which thought, discourse, study, or the like, is occupied; subject matter. **4**. the actual matter of a thing, as opposed to the appearance or shadow; reality. **5**. substantial or solid character or quality: *claims lacking in substance*. **6**. body: *soup without much substance*. **7**. the meaning or gist, as of speech or writing. **8**. something that has separate or independent existence. **9**. possessions, means, or wealth: *to squander one's substance*. *–phr*. **10**. **in substance**, **a**. substantially. **b**. actually; really.

substance abuse *n*. the detrimental and addictive use of drugs, legal or illegal.

substantial /səbˈstænʃəl/ *adj*. **1**. of a bodily or material nature; real or actual. **2**. of a considerable amount, size, etc.: *a substantial sum of money*. **3**. of a solid nature; firm, stout, or strong. **4**. being such with respect to basic parts: *two stories in substantial agreement*. **5**. wealthy: *one of the substantial men of the town*. **6**. relating to the substance, or essence of a matter. **7**. being a substance; having independent existence. **–substantiality** /səbstænʃiˈæləti/, **substantialness**, *n*. **–substantially**, *adv*.

substantiate /səbˈstænʃieɪt/ *v.t*. **1**. to establish by proof or competent evidence: *to substantiate a charge*. **2**. to give substantial existence to. **3**. to present as having substance. **–substantiation** /səbstænʃiˈeɪʃən/, *n*. **–substantiative** /səbˈstænʃiətɪv/, *adj*.

substantive /ˈsʌbstəntɪv, ˈsʌbstəntɪv/ *n*. **1**. *Gram*. a noun, pronoun, or other word or phrase which acts like a noun. *–adj*. **2**. having independent existence; independent. **3**. real or actual. **4**. of considerable amount or quantity. **–substantival** /sʌbstənˈtaɪvəl/, *adj*. **–substantively** /sʌbˈstæntɪvli/, *adv*. **–substantiveness** /sʌbˈstæntɪvnəs/, *n*.

substitute /ˈsʌbstətjut/ *n*. **1**. a person or thing acting or serving in place of another. **2**. *Gram*. a word which under given conditions replaces any of a class of other words or constructions, as English *do* replacing verbs (I *know* but he *doesn't*). *–v.t*. **3**. to put (one person or thing) in the place of another. **4**. to take the place of; replace. *–v.i*. **5**. to act as substitute. **–substitution** /sʌbstəˈtjuʃən/, *n*. **–substitutional** /sʌbstəˈtjuʃənəl/, **substitutionary** /sʌbstəˈtjuʃənəri/, *adj*. **–substitutive** /ˈsʌbstətjutɪv/, **substitutable** /sʌbstəˈtjutəbəl/, *adj*. **–substitutionally** /sʌbstəˈtjuʃənli/, *adv*.

subsume /səbˈsjum/ *v.t*. **1**. to consider (an idea, term, proposition, etc.) as part of a more comprehensive one. **2**. bring (a case, instance, etc.) under a rule. **3**. to take up into or include in a larger or higher class or a more inclusive classification. **–subsumption** /sʌbˈsʌmpʃən/, *n*. **–subsumptive** /sʌbˈsʌmptɪv/, *adj*.

subter- a prefix meaning 'position underneath', with figurative applications, as in *subterfuge*.

subterfuge /ˈsʌbtəfjudʒ/ *n*. an artifice or expedient used to escape the force of an argument, to evade unfavourable consequences, hide something, etc.

subterranean /sʌbtəˈreiniən/ *adj*. **1**. existing, situated, or operating below the surface of the earth; underground. **2**. existing or operating out of sight or secretly; hidden or secret. Also, **subterraneous**.

subtext /ˈsʌbtɛkst/ *n*. the underlying idea or motivation behind what is said, done, or written. Also, **sub-text**. **–subtextual**, *adj*.

subtitle /ˈsʌbtaɪtl/ *n*. **1**. a secondary or subordinate title of a literary work, usually of explanatory character. **2**. a repetition of the leading words in the full title of a book at the head of the first page of text. **3**. *Film* **a**. one of a series of captions projected on to the lower part of the screen which translate and summarise the dialogue of foreign language films. **b**. (in silent films) a title or caption usually giving an explanation to a following scene. *–v.t*. **4**. to provide with a subtitle or subtitles.

subtle /ˈsʌtl/ *adj*. **1**. fine or delicate, often when likely to escape perception or understanding: *subtle irony*. **2**. delicate or faint and mysterious: *a subtle smile*. **3**. needing mental sharpness: *a subtle point*. **4**. characterised by mental acuteness or penetration: *a subtle understanding*. **5**. cunning; crafty. **6**. not easily noticed, as poison, etc. **7**. skilful, clever; ingenious. **–subtlety**, **subtleness**, *n*. **–subtly** /ˈsʌtli/, *adv*.

subtract /səbˈtrækt/ *v.t*. **1**. to withdraw or take away, as a part from a whole. **2**. *Maths* to take (one number or quantity) from another; deduct. *–v.i*. **3**. to take away something or a part, as from a whole. **–subtraction** /sʌbˈtrækʃən/, *n*. **–subtracter**, *n*.

subtropical /sʌbˈtrɒpɪkəl/ *adj*. **1**. bordering on the tropics; nearly tropical. **2**. relating to or occurring in a region intermediate between tropical and temperate.

suburb /ˈsʌbɜb/ *n*. **1**. a district, usually residential and to some degree remote from the business or administrative centre of a city or large town and enjoying its own facilities, as schools, shopping centres, railway stations. **2**. an outlying part.

suburban /səˈbɜbən/ *adj*. **1**. relating to, inhabiting, or being in a suburb or the suburbs of a city or town. **2**. characteristic of a suburb or suburbs. **3**. narrowminded; conventional in outlook.

suburbia /səˈbɜbiə/ *n*. **1**. the suburbs collectively especially as they embody the middle range of community standards and values. **2**. suburban inhabitants collectively. **3**. the characteristic life of people in suburbs.

subvert /səbˈvɜt/ *v.t*. **1**. to overthrow (something established or existing). **2**. to cause the downfall, ruin, or destruction of. **3**. to undermine the principles of; corrupt. **–subversion** /səbˈvɜʒən/, *n*. **–subverter**, *n*.

subway /ˈsʌbweɪ/ *n*. an underground passage or tunnel enabling pedestrians to cross beneath a street, railway line, etc.

succeed /səkˈsid/ *v.i*. **1**. to have the desired result. **2**. to do or accomplish what is attempted. **3**. to have success in a particular field. **4**. (oft. fol. by *to*) to follow or replace another by descent, election, appointment, etc.: *he succeeded to the throne*. **5**. to come next after something else. *–v.t*. **6**. to come after and take the place of: *I succeeded my father in the family business*. **7**. to come next after in a series or in the course of events; follow. **–succeeder**, *n*.

success /sək'sɛs/ n. **1.** the favourable or prosperous termination of attempts or endeavours. **2.** the gaining of wealth, position, or the like. **3.** a successful performance or achievement. **4.** a thing or a person that is successful. –**successful**, adj.

succession /sək'sɛʃən/ n. **1.** the coming of one after another in order, or in the course of events; sequence. **2.** a number of people or things following one another in order. **3.** the right, act or process, by which one person succeeds to the office, rank, estate, etc., of another. **4.** the order or line of those entitled to succeed. **5.** Ecol. the gradual replacement of one community by another in development towards a stable community of vegetation. –**successional**, adj. –**successionally**, adv.

successive /sək'sɛsɪv/ adj. **1.** following in order or in uninterrupted course: three successive days. **2.** following another in a regular sequence: the second successive day. **3.** characterised by or involving succession. –**successively**, adv. –**successiveness**, n.

successor /sək'sɛsə/ n. **1.** a person or thing that succeeds or follows another. **2.** someone who succeeds another in an office, position, or the like.

succinct /sək'sɪŋkt/ adj. **1.** characterised by conciseness or verbal brevity. **2.** compressed into a small area or compass. –**succinctly**, adv. –**succinctness**, n.

succour /'sʌkə/ n. **1.** help; relief; aid; assistance. **2.** a person or thing that gives help, relief, aid, etc. –v.t. **3.** to help or relieve in difficulty, need, or distress; aid; assist. Also, **succor**. –**succourer**, n.

succulent /'sʌkjələnt/ adj. **1.** full of juice; juicy. **2.** rich in desirable qualities. **3.** affording mental nourishment; not dry. **4.** (of plants, etc.) having fleshy and juicy tissues. –n. **5.** a fleshy or juicy plant, as a cactus. –**succulence, succulency**, n. –**succulently**, adv.

succumb /sə'kʌm/ v.i. **1.** to give way to superior force; yield. **2.** to yield to disease, wounds, old age, etc.; die.

such /sʌtʃ/ adj. **1.** of the kind, character, degree, extent, etc., of that or those indicated or implied: such a man is dangerous. **2.** of that particular kind or character: the food, such as it was, was plentiful. **3.** like or similar: tea, coffee, and such commodities. **4.** in such a manner or degree: such terrible deeds. **5.** an intensifier: he is such a nice man. **6.** being the person or thing, or the persons or things, indicated: if any member be behind in his or her payments, such member shall be suspended. **7.** Also, **such and such**. being definite or particular, but not named or specified: it happened at such a time in such a town. –pron. **8.** being as stated or indicated: such is the case. **9.** such a person or thing, or such persons or things. **10.** the person or thing, or the persons or things, indicated: he claims to be a friend but is not such. –phr. **11. as such, a.** as being what is indicated; in that capacity: the leader, as such, is entitled to respect. **b.** in itself or themselves: wealth, as such, does not appeal to him. **12. such as, a.** of the kind specified: people such as these are not to be trusted. **b.** for example: she likes outdoor sports such as tennis and football.

suck /sʌk/ v.t. **1.** to draw into the mouth by action of the lips and tongue which produces a partial vacuum: to suck lemonade through a straw. **2.** to draw (water, moisture, air, etc.) by any process resembling this: plants suck up moisture from the earth. **3.** to apply the lips or mouth to, and draw upon by producing a partial vacuum, especially for extracting fluid contents: to suck an orange. **4.** to apply the mouth to, or hold in the mouth, and draw upon similarly, for some other purpose: to suck one's thumb. **5.** to hold in the mouth and dissolve in the saliva, assisted by the action of the tongue, etc.: to suck a piece of toffee. **6.** to render or bring (as specified) by or as by sucking: they sucked him dry. –v.i. **7.** to draw something in by producing a

partial vacuum in the mouth, especially to draw milk from the breast. **8.** to draw or be drawn by, or as by, suction. **9.** (of a pump) to draw air instead of water, as when the water is low or a valve is defective. **10.** Colloq. to be contemptible, bad, despicable, disgusting, boring, etc.: housework sucks! –n. **11.** the act or instance of sucking with the mouth or otherwise. **12.** a sucking force. **13.** the sound produced by sucking. –phr. Colloq. **14. suck face**, to tongue-kiss. **15. suck in**, to cheat; swindle; deceive; defraud. **16. suck it up**, to tolerate or endure something unpleasant or undesirable without complaint. **17. suck off**, (taboo) to bring to orgasm by oral stimulation of the genitalia. **18. suck up to**, to flatter; toady to; fawn upon.

sucker /'sʌkə/ n. **1.** someone or something that sucks. **2.** a baby or a young animal that is suckled. **3.** a part or organ of an animal adapted for sucking nourishment, or for sticking to or adjacent by suction. **4.** Bot. a shoot rising from an underground stem or a root. **5.** Colloq. a person easily deceived or taken advantage of; dupe.

suckle /'sʌkəl/ v.t. **1.** to nurse at the breast. **2.** to nourish or bring up. **3.** to put to suck. –v.i. **4.** to suck at the breast.

suckling /'sʌklɪŋ/ n. an infant or a young animal that is not yet weaned.

sucrose /'sukrouz, -ous/ n. a crystalline disaccharide, $C_{12}H_{22}O_{11}$, the sugar obtained from the sugar cane, the sugar beet, and sorghum, and forming the greater part of maple sugar. Also, **saccharose**.

suction /'sʌkʃən/ n. **1.** the act, process, or condition of sucking. **2.** the tendency to suck a substance into an interior space when the atmospheric pressure is reduced in the space. **3.** the reduction of pressure in order to cause such a sucking. **4.** the act or process of sucking a gas or liquid by such means.

sudden /'sʌdn/ adj. **1.** happening, coming, made, or done quickly, without warning or unexpectedly: a sudden attack. **2.** sharp; abrupt: a sudden turn. –phr. **3. all of a sudden**, suddenly; without warning; quite unexpectedly. **4. on a sudden**, Archaic unexpectedly; suddenly. –**suddenly**, adv. –**suddenness**, n.

sudden infant death syndrome n. the sudden unexplained death of an apparently healthy baby, usually while asleep; cot death. Also, **SIDS**.

sudoku /sə'douku/ n. (pl. **-dokus** or **-doku**) a logic puzzle in which the solution depends on correctly inserting digits from 1 to 9 in a grid so that each row and each column and each marked subset within the grid has only one occurrence of each digit.

suds /sʌdz/ pl. n. soapy water; foam; lather. –**sudsy**, adj.

sue /su/ verb (**sued, suing**) –v.t. **1.** to institute process in law against, or bring a civil action against. **2.** to make petition or appeal to. –v.i. **3.** to institute legal proceedings, or bring suit. **4.** to make petition or appeal. –**suer** /'suə/, n. –**suable**, adj.

suede /sweɪd/ n. kid or other leather finished on the flesh side with a soft, napped surface, or on the outer side after removal of a thin outer layer. Also, **suède**. –**sueded**, adj.

suet /'suət/ n. the hard fatty tissue about the loins and kidneys of cattle, sheep, etc., used in cookery, etc., and prepared as tallow. –**suety**, adj.

suffer /'sʌfə/ v.i. **1.** to experience or feel pain or distress. **2.** to experience injury, disadvantage or loss. **3.** to endure patiently or bravely. –v.t. **4.** to undergo, experience, or be forced to experience (pain, distress, injury, loss, or anything unpleasant). **5.** to undergo (any action, process, etc.): to suffer change. **6.** to allow; tolerate. –**sufferable**, adj. –**sufferableness**, n. –**sufferably**, adv. –**sufferer**, n.

sufferance /'sʌfərəns, 'sʌfrəns/ n. **1.** tolerance, as of a person or thing; tacit permission. **2.** capacity to endure pain, hardship, etc. –*phr.* **3. on sufferance**, reluctantly tolerated.

suffering /ˈsʌfərɪŋ, ˈsʌfrɪŋ/ *n.* **1.** the act of someone who suffers. **2.** a particular instance of this.

suffice /səˈfaɪs/ *verb* (**-ficed, -ficing**) –*v.i.* **1.** to be enough or adequate, as for needs, purposes, etc. –*v.t.* **2.** to be enough or adequate for; satisfy. –*phr.* **3. suffice (it) to say**, let it be enough to say. –**sufficer**, *n.*

sufficient /səˈfɪʃənt/ *adj.* that suffices; enough or adequate: *sufficient proof; sufficient protection.* –**sufficiently**, *adv.* –**sufficiency**, *n.*

suffix /ˈsʌfɪks/ *n.* **1.** *Gram.* an affix added to the end of a word, e.g. *-ly* in *kindly*, and *-er* in *heater*. **2.** something added to the end. –*v.t.* **3.** to attach at the end of something. –**suffixal** /ˈsʌfɪksəl/, *adj.* –**suffixion** /sʌˈfɪkʃən/, *n.*

suffocate /ˈsʌfəkeɪt/ *v.t.* **1.** to kill by preventing air entering the lungs or gills. **2.** to restrict the free breathing of. **3.** to cause discomfort to through lack of cool or fresh air. **4.** to overcome; suppress. –*v.i.* **5.** to die from lack of air; smother. **6.** to feel uncomfortable through lack of cool or fresh air. –**suffocating**, *adj.* –**suffocatingly**, *adv.* –**suffocation** /sʌfəˈkeɪʃən/, *n.* –**suffocative**, *adj.*

suffrage /ˈsʌfrɪdʒ/ *n.* **1.** the right of voting, especially in political elections. **2.** a vote given in favour of a proposed measure, a candidate, or the like. **3.** *Eccles.* a prayer, especially a short intercessory prayer or petition.

suffragette /sʌfrəˈdʒɛt/ *n.* one of an association of women in the early 20th century who advocated women's suffrage. –**suffragettism**, *n.*

suffuse /səˈfjuz/ *v.t.* to overspread with or as with a liquid, colour, etc. –**suffusion** /səˈfjuʒən/, *n.* –**suffusive** /səˈfjusɪv/, *adj.*

sugar /ˈʃʊgə/ *n.* **1.** a sweet crystalline substance, sucrose, $C_{12}H_{22}O_{11}$, obtained chiefly from sugar cane or sugar beet, used to sweeten food. **2.** a member of the same class of carbohydrates. –*v.t.* **3.** to cover, sprinkle, mix, or sweeten with sugar. **4.** to make more agreeable. –**sugary**, *adj.*

sugar beet *n.* a variety of beet, *Beta vulgaris*, with a white root, cultivated for the sugar it yields.

sugar cane *n.* a tall grass, *Saccharum officinarum*, of tropical and warm regions, having a stout, jointed stalk, and constituting the chief source of sugar. Also, **sugarcane**.

sugar-coat *v.t.* **1.** to encase (a food, medicine, etc.) in a coating of sugar. **2.** to make (something unpleasant) seem more agreeable, pleasant or acceptable. Also, **sugarcoat**.

suggest /səˈdʒɛst/ *v.t.* **1.** to place or bring (an idea, proposition, plan, etc.) before a person's mind for consideration or possible action. **2.** to propose (a person or thing) as suitable or possible. **3.** (of things) to prompt the consideration, making, doing, etc., of. **4.** to bring before a person's mind indirectly or without plain expression. **5.** (of a thing) to call up in the mind (another thing) through association or natural connection of ideas. –**suggester**, *n.* –**suggestion**, *n.*

suggestible /səˈdʒɛstəbəl/ *adj.* **1.** able to be suggested. **2.** open to influence by suggestion. –**suggestibility** /sədʒɛstəˈbɪləti/, *n.*

suggestive /səˈdʒɛstɪv/ *adj.* **1.** that suggests; tending to suggest thoughts, ideas, etc. **2.** relating to hypnotic suggestion. **3.** such as to suggest something improper or indecent. –**suggestively**, *adv.* –**suggestiveness**, *n.*

sugo /ˈsugoʊ/ *n.* a tomato sauce in the Italian style, made from coarsely chopped tomatoes. Compare **passata**.

suicide /ˈsuəsaɪd/ *n.* **1.** the intentional taking of one's own life. **2.** deliberate destruction of one's own interests or prospects. **3.** someone who intentionally takes their own life. –*v.i.* **4.** to commit suicide. –*phr.* **5. commit suicide, a.** to kill oneself intentionally. **b.** to embark on a course which is disastrous to oneself, especially financially.

suit /sut/ *n.* **1.** a set of garments, vestments, or armour, intended to be worn together. **2.** a set of outer garments of the same material, worn by men, consisting of trousers, jacket, and sometimes a waistcoat. **3.** a set of outer garments worn by women, usually consisting of skirt and jacket, and sometimes a blouse. **4.** *Colloq.* a businessperson, especially an executive, seen as typically wearing a business suit. **5.** *Cards* **a.** one of the sets or classes (usually four: spades, clubs, hearts, and diamonds) into which playing cards are divided. **b.** the aggregate of cards belonging to one of these sets held in a player's hand at one time. **6.** a number of things of the same kind or purpose forming a series or set. **7.** the wooing or courting of a woman. **8.** the act of making petition or appeal. **9.** the act or process of suing in a court of law; legal prosecution. **10.** a petition, as to a person of exalted station. –*v.t.* **11.** to provide with a suit of clothes; clothe; array. **12.** to make appropriate, adapt, or accommodate, as one thing to another. **13.** to be appropriate or becoming to. **14.** to be or prove satisfactory, agreeable, or acceptable to; satisfy or please. –*v.i.* **15.** to be appropriate or suitable; accord. **16.** to be satisfactory, agreeable, or acceptable. –*phr.* **17. follow suit, a.** to play a card of the suit led. **b.** to follow another's example. **18. one's strong suit**, one's particular talent or skill. **19. suit oneself**, to do what one chooses, regardless of the interests or advice of others.

suitable /ˈsutəbəl/ *adj.* such as to suit; appropriate; fitting; becoming. –**suitability** /sutəˈbɪləti/, **suitableness**, *n.* –**suitably**, *adv.*

suitcase /ˈsutkeɪs/ *n.* a portable rectangular travelling bag, usually with stiffened frame, for carrying clothes, etc.

suite /swit/ *n.* **1.** a company of followers or attendants; a train or retinue. **2.** a number of things forming a series or set: *a suite of computer programs.* **3.** a connected series of rooms to be used together by one person or a number of persons. **4.** a set of furniture of similar design and complementary in function: *a three-piece suite consists of a settee and two armchairs.* **5.** *Music* **a.** an ordered series of instrumental dances, in the same or related keys, commonly preceded by a prelude. **b.** an ordered series of instrumental movements of any character.

suitor /ˈsutə/ *n.* **1.** someone who courts or woos a woman. **2.** *Law* a petitioner or plaintiff. **3.** someone who sues or petitions for anything.

sulfur /ˈsʌlfə/ *n.*, *v.t.* → **sulphur**.

sulk /sʌlk/ *v.i.* **1.** to hold aloof in a sullen, morose, ill-humoured, or offended mood. –*n.* **2.** a state or fit of sulking. **3.** (*pl.*) ill humour shown by sulking: *to have the sulks.* **4.** Also, **sulker**. someone who sulks.

sulky /ˈsʌlki/ *adj.* (**sulkier, sulkiest**) **1.** sullenly ill-humoured or resentful; marked by ill-humoured aloofness. **2.** (of weather, etc.) gloomy. –*n.* (*pl.* **sulkies**) **3.** a light two-wheeled one-horse carriage. –**sulkily**, *adv.* –**sulkiness**, *n.*

sullage /ˈsʌlɪdʒ/ *n.* **1.** refuse, scum, or filth. **2.** *Building Trades* dirty water, as from bathrooms, laundries, kitchens, etc., excluding sewage. **3.** scoria. **4.** silt.

sullen /ˈsʌlən/ *adj.* **1.** showing ill humour by a gloomy silence or reserve. **2.** silently and persistently ill-humoured; morose. **3.** indicative of gloomy ill humour: *sullen silence.* **4.** gloomy or dismal, as weather, sounds, etc.: *a sullen sky.* **5.** sluggish, as a stream. –**sullenly**, *adv.* –**sullenness**, *n.*

sully /'sʌli/ *verb* (**-lied, -lying**) *–v.t.* **1.** to soil, stain, or tarnish. **2.** to mar the purity or lustre of; defile. *–v.i.* **3.** to become sullied, soiled, or tarnished.

sulphate /'sʌlfeɪt/ *n. Chem.* a salt of sulphuric acid. Also, **sulfate**. **–sulphatic** /sʌl'fætɪk/, *adj.*

sulphide /'sʌlfaɪd/ *n.* a compound formed of sulphur and another chemical element or radical, usually one more electropositive than sulphur. Also, **sulfide**. **–sulphidic** /sʌl'fɪdɪk/ , *adj.*

sulphur /'sʌlfə/ *n.* **1.** *Chem.* a nonmetallic element which exists in several forms, the ordinary one being a yellow crystalline solid, and which burns with a blue flame and a suffocating odour; used especially in making gunpowder and matches, in vulcanising rubber, in medicine, etc. *Symbol:* S; *relative atomic mass:* 32.064; *atomic number:* 16; *density:* 2.07 at 20°C. **2.** a pale yellow colour with a greenish tinge. **3.** any of various yellow or orange butterflies of the family Pieridae. *–v.t.* **4.** to treat or fumigate with sulphur. Also, **sulfur**. **–sulphurous**, *adj.* **–sulphuric**, *adj.*

sulphur-crested cockatoo *n.* a large common Australian parrot, *Cacatua galerita*, predominantly white, with yellow on the undersides of wings and tail and a forward curving yellow crest, found in Australia, New Guinea and nearby islands; white cockatoo. Also, **sulfur-crested cockatoo**.

sulphur dioxide /sʌlfə daɪˈɒksaɪd/ *n.* a colourless gas or liquid with a strong pungent odour which is noncombustible and is soluble in water, ether, and alcohol; it is used as an oxidising and reducing agent and for various industrial uses. Also, **sulfur dioxide**.

sulphuric acid *n.* the dibasic acid of sulphur, H_2SO_4, a colourless, corrosive, oily liquid, made from sulphur trioxide and used in many industrial processes; oil of vitriol. Also, **sulfuric acid**.

sultan /'sʌltən/ *n.* (*upper case*) the sovereign of a Muslim kingdom. **–sultanate** /'sʌltənət/, **sultanship**, *n.* **–sultanic** /sʌl'tænɪk/, *adj.*

sultana /sʌl'tanə, səl-/ *n.* **1.** a wife or concubine of a sultan. **2.** any close female relative of a sultan. **3.** a small, green, seedless grape. **4.** a raisin made from such a grape.

sultry /'sʌltri/ *adj.* (**-trier, -triest**) **1.** oppressively hot and close or moist; sweltering. **2.** oppressively hot, as the weather, etc. **3.** characterised by or associated with sweltering heat. **4.** characterised by or arousing temper or passion. **–sultrily**, *adv.* **–sultriness**, *n.*

sum /sʌm/ *n.* **1.** the aggregate of two or more numbers, magnitudes, quantities, or particulars as determined by mathematical process: *the sum of 5 and 7 is 12.* **2.** a particular aggregate or total, especially with reference to money: *the expenses came to an enormous sum.* **3.** a quantity or amount, especially of money: *to lend small sums.* **4. a.** an arithmetical calculation: *it was a hard sum to do.* **b.** (*pl.*) arithmetic: *I was never good at sums.* **5.** the total amount, or the whole. **6.** the substance or gist of a matter, comprehensively viewed or expressed: *the letter contains the sum and substance of his opinions.* **7.** concise or brief form: *in sum.* *–v.t.* (**summed, summing**) **8.** to combine into an aggregate or total. **9.** to ascertain the sum of, as by addition. *–adj.* **10.** denoting or relating to a sum: *sum total.* *–phr.* **11. sum up, a.** to reckon: *to sum up advantages and disadvantages.* **b.** to bring into or contain in a brief and comprehensive statement: *the article sums up the work of the year.* **c.** to form a quick estimate of: *to sum someone up.* **d.** to give a brief and comprehensive statement or summary.

sum- occasional variant of **sub-** (by assimilation) before *m*.

summary /'sʌməri/ *n.* (*pl.* **-ries**) **1.** a brief and comprehensive presentation of facts or statements; an abstract, compendium, or epitome. *–adj.* **2.** brief and comprehensive; concise. **3.** direct and prompt; unceremoniously fast. **4.** (of legal proceedings, jurisdiction, etc.) conducted without or exempt from the various steps and delays of full proceedings. **–summarily** /'sʌmərəli/, *adv.* **–summarise, summarize**, *v.*

summer /'sʌmə/ *n.* **1.** the warmest season of the year, between spring and autumn. **2.** a whole year as represented by this season: *a child of eight summers.* **3.** the period of finest development, perfection, or beauty previous to any decline: *the summer of life.* *–adj.* **4.** of, relating to, or characteristic of summer: *summer resorts.* *–v.i.* **5.** to spend or pass the summer.

summit /'sʌmɪt/ *n.* **1.** the highest point or part, as of a hill, a line of travel, or any object; the top; the apex. **2.** the highest point of attainment or aspiration. **3.** a meeting or conference between heads of state or the heads of any other organisation. *–adj.* **4.** (in diplomacy) between heads of state: *summit conference.*

summon /'sʌmən/ *v.t.* **1.** to call as with authority to some duty, task, or performance; call upon (to do something). **2.** to call for the presence of, as by command, message, or signal; call. **3.** to call upon to surrender. *–phr.* **4. summon up,** to call into action; rouse; call forth: *to summon up all one's courage.* **–summonable**, *adj.* **–summoner**, *n.*

summons /'sʌmənz/ *n.* (*pl.* **-monses**) **1.** a command, message, or signal by which one's presence is called for. **2.** a call to do something: *a summons to surrender.* **3.** an order to appear at a particular place, especially before a court of law, or the document by which the order is made. **4.** an order for the meeting of an assembly or parliament. *–v.t.* **5.** to serve with a summons; summon.

sump /sʌmp/ *n.* **1.** a pit, well, or the like in which water or other liquid is collected. **2.** *Machinery* a container situated at the lowest point in a circulating system, especially the crankcase of an internal-combustion engine, which acts as an oil reservoir. **3.** *Mining* **a.** a space at the bottom of a shaft or below a passageway where water is allowed to collect. **b.** a pilot shaft or tunnel pushed out in front of a main bore.

sumptuous /'sʌmptʃuəs/ *adj.* **1.** entailing great expense, as from fine workmanship, choice materials, etc.; costly: *a sumptuous residence.* **2.** luxuriously fine; splendid or superb. **–sumptuously**, *adv.* **–sumptuousness**, *n.*

sun /sʌn/ *n.* **1.** (*oft. upper case*) the star which is the central body of the solar system and around which the planets revolve, and from which they receive light and heat. **2.** the sun considered with reference to its position in the sky, its visibility, the season of the year, the time at which or the place where it is seen, etc. **3.** a self-luminous heavenly body. **4.** sunshine: *to be exposed to the sun.* **5.** a figure or representation of the sun, as a heraldic bearing usually surrounded with rays and charged with the features of a human face. *–verb* (**sunned, sunning**) *–v.t.* **6.** to expose to the sun's rays. **7.** to warm, dry, etc., in the sunshine. *–v.i.* **8.** to expose oneself to the sun's rays. *–phr.* **9. a place in the sun,** a pleasant or advantageous situation. **10. one's time in the sun,** the moment when one is at the peak of one's chosen profession or pursuit, winning acclaim from others. **11. sun up,** (of weather) to clear and become sunny. **12. under the sun,** on earth: *the most beautiful girl under the sun.*

sunbake /'sʌnbeɪk/ *v.i. Aust.* to expose one's body to the sun in order to acquire a suntan or as a relaxation. **–sunbaking**, *n.* **–sunbaker**, *n.*

sunburn /'sʌnbɜn/ *n.* **1.** superficial inflammation of the skin, caused by excessive or too sudden exposure to the sun's rays. *–verb* (**-burnt** *or* **-burned, -burning**) *–v.t.*

2. to affect with sunburn. *–v.i.* **3.** to become affected with sunburn.

suncream /ˈsʌnkrim/ *n.* → **sunscreen** (def. 2).

sundae /ˈsʌndeɪ/ *n.* a portion of ice-cream with fruit or other syrup poured over it, and often whipped cream, chopped nuts, or other additions.

Sunday /ˈsʌndeɪ, -di/ *n.* **1.** the first day of the week, the day of worship for most Christian denominations, observed in commemoration of the resurrection of Christ. *–adj.* **2.** of, relating to, occurring on, or suitable for Sunday: *the Sunday newspapers; Sunday clothes.* *–phr.* **3. a month of Sundays**, an extremely long time.

sunder /ˈsʌndə/ *v.t.* **1.** to separate; part; divide; sever. *–v.i.* **2.** to become separated; part. **–sunderance** /ˈsʌndərəns, -drəns/, *n.* **–sunderer**, *n.*

sundew /ˈsʌndju/ *n.* any of a group of small bog plants, species of the genus *Drosera*, with sticky hairs which capture insects.

sundial /ˈsʌndaɪəl/ *n.* an instrument for indicating the time of day by the position of a shadow (as of a vertical shaft) cast by the sun on a graduated plate or surface.

sundowner /ˈsʌndaʊnə/ *n.* **1.** *Aust., NZ* a swagman who arrives at a homestead at nightfall, too late for work, but obtains shelter for the night. **2.** an alcoholic drink taken in the evening, traditionally at sundown.

sundries /ˈsʌndriz/ *pl. n.* sundry things or items.

sundry /ˈsʌndri/ *adj.* **1.** various or divers: *sundry persons.* *–n.* (*pl.* **-dries**) **2.** *Cricket* (*usu. pl.*) a score or run not made by hitting the ball with the bat, as a bye or a wide; an extra. *–phr.* **3. all and sundry**, everyone collectively and individually.

sunfish /ˈsʌnfɪʃ/ *n.* (*pl.* **-fishes** *or, especially collectively,* **-fish**) **1.** a huge fish, the **ocean sunfish**, *Mola mola*, found in Australian waters and elsewhere, having a deep body abbreviated behind, seeming to consist of little more than the head. **2.** any fish of the same family, Molidae. **3.** any of the small freshwater fishes of the family Centrarchidae, of North America, closely related to the perch.

sunflower /ˈsʌnflaʊə/ *n.* any plant of the genus *Helianthus*, characterised by yellow-rayed flowers, as *H. annuus*, the common species of North America, a tall plant grown for its showy flowers, and for its seeds which are valued as food for poultry and as the source of an oil.

sung /sʌŋ/ *v.* a past tense and past participle of **sing**.

sunglasses /ˈsʌnglasəz/ *pl. n.* spectacles having tinted, darkened, or polaroid lenses to protect the eyes from the glare of the sun.

sunk /sʌŋk/ *v.* **1.** past participle of **sink**. **2.** *Chiefly US* a past tense of **sink**.

sunken /ˈsʌŋkən/ *v.* **1.** a past participle of **sink**. *–adj.* **2.** having sunk or having been sunk beneath the surface; submerged. **3.** having settled down to a lower level, as walls. **4.** depressed or lying below the general level, as a garden. **5.** hollow: *sunken cheeks.*

Sunna /ˈsʌnə/ *n.* the traditional part of Muslim law, claimed to be based on the words and acts of Mohammed, although not attributed verbatim to him.

sunny /ˈsʌni/ *adj.* (**-nier, -niest**) **1.** having a lot of sunshine: *a sunny day.* **2.** exposed to, lit or warmed by the direct rays of the sun: *a sunny room.* **3.** cheery, cheerful, or joyous: *a sunny disposition.* **–sunnily**, *adv.* **–sunniness**, *n.*

sun protection factor *n.* → **SPF**.

sunrise /ˈsʌnraɪz/ *n.* **1.** the rise or ascent of the sun above the horizon in the morning. **2.** the atmospheric phenomena accompanying this.

sunrise industry *n.* industry based upon innovative, local technology, especially electronic.

sunscreen /ˈsʌnskrin/ *n.* **1.** a device, as an awning, which acts as a screen against the rays of the sun. **2.** Also, **sunblock, suncream, blockout**. a lotion or cream which, when applied to the skin, protects it against damage from the rays of the sun.

sunset /ˈsʌnsɛt/ *n.* **1.** the setting or descent of the sun below the horizon in the evening. **2.** the atmospheric phenomena accompanying this. **3.** the close or final stage of any period.

sunshine /ˈsʌnʃaɪn/ *n.* **1.** the shining of the sun; direct light of the sun. **2.** brightness; cheerfulness or happiness. **–sunshiny**, *adj.*

sunspot /ˈsʌnspɒt/ *n.* **1.** one of the relatively dark patches which appear periodically on the surface of the sun, and which have a certain effect on terrestrial magnetism and other terrestrial phenomena. Their appearance is spasmodic but their number reaches a maximum approximately every eleven years (the **sunspot cycle**). **2.** a discolouration and roughening of part of the skin, usually as a result of exposure to the sun.

sunstroke /ˈsʌnstroʊk/ *n.* a condition caused by excessive exposure to the sun, marked by prostration, which may lead to convulsions, coma, and death. **–sunstruck**, *adj.*

suntan /ˈsʌntæn/ *n.* brownness of the skin induced by exposure to the sun, cultivated by some as a mark of health or beauty. Also, **tan**. **–sun-tanned**, *adj.*

sup[1] /sʌp/ *v.i.* (**supped, supping**) to eat the evening meal; take supper.

sup[2] /sʌp/ *verb* (**supped, supping**) *–v.t.* **1.** to take (liquid food, or any liquid) into the mouth in small quantities, as from a spoon or a cup. *–v.i.* **2.** to take liquid into the mouth in small quantities, as by spoonfuls or sips. *–n.* **3.** a mouthful or small portion of liquid food or of drink.

sup- variant of **sub-** (by assimilation) before *p*.

super /ˈsupə/ *n.* *Colloq.* **1.** high-octane petrol. **2.** *Aust., NZ* → **superannuation**. **3.** → **superintendent**. **4.** → **supernumerary**. **5.** *Aust., NZ* → **superphosphate**. *–adj.* **6.** of a superior quality, grade, size, etc. **7.** extremely good, pleasing, etc.

super- **1.** a prefix meaning 'superior to' or 'over-', applied variously, as of quality (*superman*), size (*superdreadnought*), degree (*superheat, supersensitive*), space (*superstructure*), and other meanings (*supersede, supernatural*). **2.** *Chem.* a prefix having the same sense as 'per-'.

superannuate /supərˈænjueɪt/ *v.t.* **1.** to allow to retire from service or office on a pension, on account of age or infirmity. **2.** to set aside as out of date; remove as too old. **–superannuant**, *n.* **–superannuated**, *adj.*

superannuation /ˌsupərænjuˈeɪʃən/ *n.* **1.** the act of superannuating. **2.** the state of being superannuated. **3.** *Aust., NZ* a pension or allowance to a superannuated person. **4.** *Aust., NZ* a sum paid periodically as contribution to a superannuation fund.

superannuation fund *n.* *NZ, Aust.* a retirement fund to which an employee (and usually also the employer) contributes during the period of employment, and which provides benefits after retirement. Also, **provident fund**.

superb /səˈpɜb, su-/ *adj.* **1.** stately, majestic, or grand: *superb jewels.* **2.** admirably fine or excellent: *a superb performance.* **3.** of a proudly imposing appearance or kind: *superb beauty.* **–superbly**, *adv.* **–superbness**, *n.*

superb fairy-wren *n.* a small bird, *Malurus cyaneus*, the adult male in breeding plumage having bright blue feathers on the crown and upper back, while the female is brown; widely distributed throughout south-eastern coastal areas of Australia. Also, **superb blue wren**.

superbug /ˈsupəbʌg/ *n.* a bacterium which has adapted so that it has become resistant to all existing antibiotics.

supercharge /ˈsupətʃɑdʒ/ *v.t.* **1.** to supply air to (an internal-combustion engine) at greater than atmospheric pressure; boost. **2.** to charge with an excessive amount of emotion, tension, energy, or the like. **3.** to pressurise (a gas or liquid). **–supercharger,** *n.*

supercilious /supəˈsɪliəs/ *adj.* haughtily disdainful or contemptuous, as persons, their expression, bearing, etc. **–superciliously,** *adv.* **–superciliousness,** *n.*

supercomputer /ˈsupəkəmpjutə/ *n.* the fastest type of computer, particularly suited to carrying out complex mathematical calculations very quickly, and used for specialised applications such as meteorological research. **–supercomputing,** *n.*

supercontinent /supəˈkɒntənənt/ *n.* any great landmass that existed in the geological past and split into smaller landmasses.

superego /supərˈigoʊ/ *n.* (*pl.* **-egos**) *Psychoanalysis* a personification of the development of the ego in the direction of social ideals, etc., so that distress is felt when the ego is unduly influenced by primitive impulses; similar to 'conscience', but is largely unconscious.

superficial /supəˈfɪʃəl/ *adj.* **1.** of or relating to the surface: *superficial measurement.* **2.** being at, on, or near the surface: *a superficial wound.* **3.** on the surface only; apparent, rather than real or deep: *a superficial resemblance; superficial piety.* **4.** concerned with only what is on the surface or obviously shallow; not profound: *a superficial observer; a superficial writer.* **–superficiality** /ˌsupəfɪʃiˈæləti/, **superficialness,** *n.* **–superficially,** *adv.*

superfluity /supəˈfluəti/ *n.* (*pl.* **-ties**) **1.** the state of being superfluous. **2.** an excessive amount. **3.** something superfluous, as a luxury.

superfluous /suˈpɜfluəs/ *adj.* **1.** being over and above what is sufficient or required. **2.** unnecessary or needless. **–superfluously,** *adv.* **–superfluousness,** *n.*

supergene /ˈsupədʒin/ *n.* a group of genes on a chromosome which are viewed collectively because they are inherited together and have related functions.

superglue /ˈsupəglu/ (*from trademark*) **–n. 1.** a fast-acting and powerful glue. **–v.t.** (**-glued, -gluing**) **2.** to glue together by means of such a glue.

supergrass /ˈsupəgras/ *n.* an informer whose information concerns terrorism or large-scale corruption and crime.

superhuman /ˈsupəhjumən/ *adj.* **1.** above or beyond what is human; having a higher nature or greater powers than human beings. **2.** exceeding ordinary human power, achievement, experience, etc.: *a superhuman effort.* **–superhumanity** /supəhjuˈmænəti/, *n.* **–superhumanly,** *adv.*

superimpose /supərɪmˈpoʊz/ *v.t.* **1.** to impose, place, or set on something else. **2.** to put or join as an addition to (something). **–superimposition** /ˌsupərɪmpəˈzɪʃən/, *n.*

superintend /supərɪnˈtɛnd, suprɪn-/ *v.t.* **1.** to oversee and direct (work, processes, affairs, etc.); exercise supervision over (an institution, place, etc.). **–v.i. 2.** to exercise supervision. **–superintendence,** *n.*

superintendent /supərɪnˈtɛndənt, suprɪn-/ *n.* **1.** someone who has the oversight or direction of some work, enterprise, establishment, institution, house, etc. **2.** a police officer ranking above chief inspector and below chief superintendent. **–superintendentship,** *n.*

superior /səˈpɪəriə, su-/ *adj.* **1.** higher in station, rank, degree, or grade: *a superior officer.* **2.** above the average in excellence, merit, intelligence, etc. **3.** of higher grade or quality. **4.** greater in quantity or amount: *superior numbers.* **5.** showing a consciousness or feeling of being above others in such respects: *superior airs.* **6.** *Bot.* **a.** situated above some other organ. **b.** (of a calyx) seeming to originate from the top of the ovary.

c. (of an ovary) free from the calyx. **7.** *Printing* higher than the main line of type, as algebraic exponents, reference figures, etc.; superscript. **8.** *Astron.* (of a planet) having an orbit outside that of the earth. **–n. 9.** someone superior to another or others. **10.** *Eccles.* the head of a monastery, convent, or the like. **–phr. 11. superior to,** not yielding or susceptible to: *to be superior to temptation.* **–superiorly,** *adv.*

superlative /suˈpɜlətɪv/ *adj.* **1.** of the highest kind or order; supreme: *superlative wisdom.* **2.** being more than is proper or normal; exaggerated: *a superlative style of writing.* **3.** *Gram.* indicating the highest degree of the comparison of adjectives and adverbs, as English *smoothest* in contrast to *smooth* and *smoother.* **–n. 4.** the highest degree. **5.** *Gram.* the superlative degree, or a form or word in this degree. **–superlatively,** *adv.* **–superlativeness,** *n.*

supermarket /ˈsupəmakət/ *n.* a large, usually self-service, retail store or market selling food and other domestic goods.

supermodel /ˈsupəmɒdl/ *n.* one of the very few most highly paid fashion models, each with a worldwide reputation.

supernatural /supəˈnætʃrəl, -ˈnætʃərəl/ *adj.* **1.** being above or beyond what is natural; not explicable in terms of natural laws or phenomena. **2.** of or relating to supernatural beings, as ghosts, spirits, etc. **3.** abnormal; extraordinary; unprecedented: *a man of supernatural intelligence.* **–n. 4.** supernatural forces, effects, and beings collectively. **–supernaturalism,** *n.* **–supernaturally,** *adv.*

supernova /ˈsupənoʊvə/ *n.* (*pl.* **-vas** *or* **-vae** /-vi/) *Astron.* the sudden gravitational collapse of a giant star resulting in an explosion of stellar matter and energy into space and leaving a black hole or neutron star as a remnant.

supernumerary /supəˈnjumərəri/ *adj.* **1.** being in excess of the usual, proper, or prescribed number; additional; extra. **–n.** (*pl.* **-aries**) **2.** a supernumerary or extra person or thing. **3.** *Theatre* someone not belonging to the regular company, who appears on the stage but has no lines to speak.

superordinate /supərˈɔdənət/ *adj.* **1.** higher in rank, degree, etc. **2.** *Logic* of superior order or generality, as genus to species or as universal to particular. **–n. 3.** a person or thing that is superordinate.

superphosphate /supəˈfɒsfeɪt/ *n.* **1.** an artificial fertiliser consisting of a mixture of calcium sulphate and calcium dihydrogen phosphate, $Ca(H_2PO_4)_2$, made by treating phosphate rock with sulphuric acid. **2.** any fertiliser containing this mixture.

superpower /ˈsupəpaʊə/ *n.* an extremely powerful and influential nation.

superscript /ˈsupəskrɪpt/ *n.* **1.** a character written or set slightly above and immediately to one side of another, as 'x' in 'B^x'. **–adj. 2.** written above, as a diacritical mark or a correction of a word.

supersede /supəˈsid/ *v.t.* **1.** to replace in power, authority, effectiveness, acceptance, use, etc., as by another person or thing. **2.** to set aside, as void, useless, or obsolete, now usually in favour of something mentioned. **3.** to displace in office or promotion by another. **4.** to succeed to the position, function, office, etc., of; supplant. **–supercession** /supəˈsɛʃən/, *n.* **–superseder,** *n.*

supersize /ˈsupəsaɪz/ *v.t.* **1.** to increase in magnitude to an unusual degree: *to supersize one's income.* **–adj. 2.** unusually large: *supersize ice-creams.*

supersonic /supəˈsɒnɪk/ *adj.* **1.** (of sound frequencies) above the audible limit; ultrasonic. **2.** (of velocities) above the velocity of sound in the medium.

superstar /ˈsupəstɑ/ *n.* a singer, actor, or show-business personality who is very famous.

superstition /supəˈstɪʃən/ *n.* **1.** a belief or notion entertained, regardless of reason or knowledge, of the ominous significance of a particular thing, circumstance, occurrence, proceeding, or the like. **2.** any blindly accepted belief or notion. **3.** a system or collection of superstitious beliefs and customs. **4.** irrational fear of what is unknown or mysterious, especially in connection with religion. –**superstitious**, *adj.*

superstructure /ˈsupəstrʌktʃə/ *n.* **1.** all of an edifice above the basement or foundation. **2.** any structure built on something else.

supertax /ˈsupətæks/ *n.* **1.** a tax in addition to a normal tax, as one upon income above a certain amount. **2.** → **surtax**.

supervene /supəˈvin/ *v.i.* **1.** (sometimes fol. by *on* or *upon*) to come as something additional or extraneous. **2.** to ensue. –**supervenience**, **supervention** /supəˈvɛnʃən/, *n.* –**supervenient**, *adj.*

supervise /ˈsupəvaɪz/ *v.t.* to oversee (a process, work, workers, etc.) during execution or performance; superintend; have the oversight and direction of. –**supervision** /supəˈvɪʒən/, *n.* –**supervisor**, *n.*

supine /ˈsupaɪn/ *adj.* **1.** lying on the back, or with the face or front upwards. **2.** having the palm upwards, as the hand. **3.** inactive; passive; inert; especially, inactive or passive from indolence or indifference. –**supinely**, *adv.* –**supineness**, *n.*

supper /ˈsʌpə/ *n.* **1.** a very light meal, as of a biscuit and a cup of tea taken at night, which is the last meal of the day. **2.** *Chiefly Brit. and US* the evening meal; the last major meal of the day, taken in the evening. **3.** any evening meal, often one forming part of a social entertainment.

supplant /səˈplænt, -ˈplant/ *v.t.* to take the place of (another), as in office or favour, through scheming, strategy, or the like. –**supplantation** /sʌplænˈteɪʃən/, *n.* –**supplanter**, *n.*

supple /ˈsʌpl/ *adj.* **1.** bending readily without breaking or suffering harm; pliant: *a supple rod*; *a supple body*. **2.** marked by ease in bending; lithe: *supple movements*. **3.** adapting or yielding easily: *a supple mind*. –**suppleness**, *n.*

supplement *n.* /ˈsʌpləmənt/ **1.** something added to extend a thing, supply a lack, or correct mistakes, etc.: *a supplement to a book*. **2.** a special feature of a newspaper, etc., put out as an additional part: *an educational supplement*. **3.** *Maths* the quantity by which an angle or an arc falls short of 180° or a semicircle. –*v.t.* /ˈsʌpləmənt/ **4.** to add to, or extend by a supplement; form a supplement or addition to. –**supplementary**, *adj.* –**supplementation** /sʌpləmɛnˈteɪʃən/, *n.* –**supplementer**, *n.*

suppliant /ˈsʌpliənt/ *n.* someone who supplicates; a humble petitioner. –**suppliance**, *n.*

supplicate /ˈsʌpləkeɪt/ *v.i.* **1.** to pray humbly; make humble and earnest entreaty or petition. –*v.t.* **2.** to pray humbly to; entreat or petition humbly. **3.** to seek by humble entreaty. –**supplicant**, *n.* –**supplication** /sʌpləˈkeɪʃən/, *n.*

supply¹ /səˈplaɪ/ *verb* (**-plied**, **-plying**) –*v.t.* **1.** to furnish (a person, establishment, place, etc.) with what is lacking or requisite. **2.** to furnish or provide (something wanting or requisite): *to supply electricity to a community*. **3.** to make up (a deficiency); make up for (a loss, lack, absence, etc.); satisfy (a need, demand, etc.). **4.** to fill (a place, vacancy, etc.); occupy as a substitute. –*v.i.* **5.** to fill the place of another, temporarily, or as a substitute. –*n.* (*pl.* **-plies**) **6.** the act of supplying, furnishing, providing, satisfying, etc. **7.** a quantity of something provided or on hand, as for use; a stock or

store. **8.** (*usu. pl.*) a provision, stock, or store of food or other things necessary for maintenance. **9.** *Govt* a parliamentary grant or provision of money for the expenses of government, especially those not covered by other revenue. **10.** *Econ.* **a.** the quantity of a commodity, etc., that is in the market and available for purchase, or that is available for purchase at a particular price. **b.** the willingness of sellers to offer various quantities of a good or service at specific prices. See **demand** (def. 9). **11.** *Elect.* a source of electrical energy. **12.** (*pl.*) *Mil.* articles and materials used by an army or navy of types rapidly used up, such as food, clothing, equipment, and fuel. –*phr.* **13. be in short supply**, to be scarce. –**supplier**, *n.*

supply² /ˈsʌpli/ *adv.* in a supple manner. Also, **supplely**.

supply bill *n. Parliamentary Procedure* a bill to secure the money which the government needs to carry out its business.

supply-side economics *n.* a method of managing the national economy which seeks to overcome a recession by stimulating the production of goods and the supply of services.

support /səˈpɔt/ *v.t.* **1.** to bear or hold up (a weight, load, structure, part, etc.). **2.** to bear, especially with patience or humility; endure; tolerate. **3.** to give help, strength, courage, etc., to: *his kindness supported her in her grief*. **4.** to supply (a person, family, establishment, etc.) with things necessary to existence; provide for. **5.** to help to show the truth or validity of (a statement, argument, etc.). **6.** to act in a secondary part with (a leading actor). **7.** to form a secondary part of a program with: *the main film will be supported by two documentaries*. –*n.* **8.** the act of supporting. **9.** the state of being supported. **10.** the provision of necessities, money, etc., to a person, family, etc. **11.** advocacy or endorsement. **12.** a thing or a person that supports. **13.** the part of a structure that carries its weight. **14.** Also, **supporter**. a device, usually of elastic material, for holding up some part of the body. **15.** practical or emotional assistance: *she was a great source of support after his break-up*; *the company provides customer support to all its clients*. **16.** an organisation or a person that gives aid or assistance. **17.** an actor or group of actors, who play secondary roles. –**supporter**, *n.* –**supportive**, *adj.*

suppose /səˈpoʊz/ *v.t.* **1.** to take as a fact, for the sake of argument, etc.: *suppose the distance to be one kilometre*. **2.** to consider as a possibility or idea suggested: *suppose we wait till tomorrow*. **3.** to think or believe, in the absence of positive knowledge: *I supposed that it was an accident*; *what do you suppose he will do?* **4.** → **presuppose**. **5.** (*used in the passive*) to expect: *you are supposed to be at work on time*. –*n.* –**supposition** /sʌpəˈzɪʃən/, *n.* –**supposer**, *n.* –**supposable**, *adj.* –**supposably**, *adv.*

supposed /səˈpoʊzd, səˈpoʊzəd/ *adj.* **1.** assumed as true, regardless of fact; hypothetical: *a supposed case*. **2.** accepted or received as true, without positive knowledge and perhaps erroneously: *the supposed site of an ancient temple*. **3.** merely thought to be such: *to sacrifice real for supposed gains*. –**supposedly** /səˈpoʊzədli/, *adv.*

suppository /səˈpɒzətri/ *n.* (*pl.* **-ries**) a solid or encapsulated medicinal substance inserted into the rectum or vagina to be dissolved therein.

suppress /səˈprɛs/ *v.t.* **1.** to put an end to the activities of (a person, group of people, etc.). **2.** to put an end to (a practice, etc.), abolish; prohibit. **3.** to keep in or repress (a feeling, smile, groan, etc.). **4.** to keep (truth, evidence, a book, names, etc.) from being known or published. **5.** to stop (a flow of blood, etc.). **6.** to put an end to (a revolt, etc.) by force; quell; subdue.

–**suppression** /sə'prɛʃən/, *n.* –**suppressor**, *n.* –**suppressible**, *adj.* –**suppressive**, *adj.*

suppurate /'sʌpjəreɪt/ *v.i.* to produce or discharge pus, as a wound; maturate. –**suppuration** /sʌpjə'reɪʃən/, *n.* –**suppurative** /'sʌpjərətɪv/, *adj.*

supra /'suprə/ *adv.* (especially used in making reference to parts of a text) above.

supra- a prefix meaning 'above', equivalent to **super-**, but emphasising situation or position, as in *supraorbital*, *suprarenal*.

suprarenal /suprə'rinəl/ *adj.* **1.** situated above or on the kidney. **2.** relating to or connected with a suprarenal. –*n.* **3.** a suprarenal body, capsule, or gland.

supreme /su'prim, sə-/ *adj.* **1.** highest in rank or authority; paramount; sovereign; chief. **2.** of the highest quality, character, importance, etc.: *supreme courage.* **3.** greatest, utmost, or extreme: *supreme disgust.* **4.** last (with reference to the end of life): *the supreme moment.* –**supremacy**, *n.* –**supremely**, *adv.* –**supremeness**, *n.*

sur-¹ a prefix corresponding to **super-** but mainly attached to stems not used as words and having figurative applications (*survive*, *surname*), used especially in legal terms (*surrebuttal*).

sur-² occasional variant of **sub-** (by assimilation) before *r*.

surcharge *n.* /'sɜtʃadʒ/ **1.** an additional charge for payment, tax, etc. **2.** an excessive sum or price charged. **3.** *Philately* a mark printed over a stamp which alters or restates its face value. –*v.t.* /'sɜtʃadʒ, sɜ'tʃadʒ/ (**-charged**, **-charging**) **4.** to charge an additional sum (for payment). **5.** to over-charge. **6.** to overload. –**surcharger**, *n.*

sure /ʃɔ/ *adj.* **1.** (sometimes fol. by *of*) free from apprehension or doubt as to the reliability, character, action, etc., of something: *to be sure of one's data.* **2.** confident, as of something expected: *sure of ultimate success.* **3.** convinced, fully persuaded, or positive, as of something firmly believed: *sure of a person's guilt.* **4.** assured or certain beyond question: *we are all sure of death.* **5.** worthy of confidence; reliable: *a sure messenger.* **6.** firm or stable: *to stand on sure ground.* **7.** unfailing; never disappointing expectations: *a sure cure.* **8.** unerring; never missing, slipping, etc.: *a sure aim.* **9.** admitting of no doubt or question: *sure proof.* **10.** inevitable: *death is sure.* **11.** destined; bound inevitably; certain: *he is sure to come.* **12.** *Colloq.* surely, undoubtedly, or certainly. **13.** *US Colloq.* inevitably or without fail. –*phr.* **14. a sure thing**, *Colloq.* a certainty; something assured beyond any doubt. **15. be sure**, be certain or careful (to do as specified): *be sure to close the windows*; *you must be sure and visit us.* **16. be sure of**, to be confident in the support or possession of. **17. for sure**, as a certainty; surely. **18. make sure**, to ensure (that something happens). **19. make sure of**, to secure the support or possession of. **20. sure thing**, *Colloq.* an expression of assurance. **21. to be sure**, surely; certainly; without doubt. –**sureness**, *n.*

sure-fire *adj. Colloq.* certain to succeed; assured: *a sure-fire winner for tomorrow's race.*

surely /'ʃɔli/ *adv.* **1.** firmly; unerringly; without missing, slipping, etc. **2.** undoubtedly, assuredly, or certainly: *the results are surely encouraging.* **3.** (in emphatic utterances that are not necessarily sustained by fact) assuredly: *surely you are mistaken.* **4.** inevitably or without fail: *slowly but surely the end approached.*

surety /'ʃɔrəti, 'ʃurəti/ *n.* (*pl.* **-ties**) **1.** security against loss or damage; security for the fulfilment of an obligation, the payment of a debt, etc.; a pledge, guaranty, or bond. **2.** certainty. **3.** something that makes sure; a ground for confidence or safety. **4.** someone who is legally answerable for the debt, default, or miscarriage of another.

surf /sɜf/ *n.* **1.** the swell of the sea which breaks upon a shore or upon shoals. **2.** the mass or line of foamy water caused by the breaking of the sea upon a shore, etc. **3.** the beach, especially when used for recreation in the surf: *they spent the day at the surf.* **4.** a time spent in the surf, standing, swimming, bodysurfing, etc.: *let's go for a surf.* –*v.i.* **5.** to engage in surfing. –*v.t.* **6.** to explore (an information network): *to surf the internet.*

surface /'sɜfəs/ *n.* **1.** the outer face, or outside, of a thing. **2.** the area of such a face. **3.** any face or side of a thing: *the six surfaces of a cube.* **4.** outward appearance, especially as opposed to inner nature: *to look below the surface of a matter.* **5.** *Geom.* any figure having only two dimensions; part or all of the boundary of a solid. –*adj.* **6.** of, on, or relating to the surface. **7.** apparent, rather than real; superficial. **8.** of, on, or relating to land or sea: *surface travel*; *surface mail.* –*verb* (**-faced**, **-facing**) **9.** to give a particular kind of surface to; make even or smooth. –*v.i.* **10.** to rise to the surface. **11.** *Colloq.* to appear in public, as by arriving at one's job, rising from sleep, etc. –**surfacer**, *n.*

surfboard /'sɜfbɔd/ *n.* a long, narrow board, slightly rounded and usually longer than body-length, used by surfers in riding waves towards the shore.

surfeit /'sɜfət/ *n.* **1.** excess; an excessive amount. **2.** oppression or disorder of the system due to excessive eating or drinking. **3.** general disgust caused by excess or satiety. –**surfeiter**, *n.*

surfie /'sɜfi/ *n. Aust. Colloq.* a devotee of surfing, especially of surfboard riding.

surfing /'sɜfɪŋ/ *n.* **1.** the sport in which one paddles a surfboard out over the surf, and then, usually standing on the board, attempts to ride on or with a wave towards the shore; surfboard riding. **2.** → **bodysurfing**.

surf lifesaver *n. Aust., NZ* a lifesaver on a surf beach. Also, **surf life saver**.

surf lifesaving *n. Aust., NZ* lifesaving which is appropriate for emergency situations occurring on surf beaches. Also, **surf life saving**.

surf shirt *n.* **1.** a garment worn with a swimming costume to protect the upper body from sunburn, usually made from a light synthetic fabric and having short or long sleeves; rash shirt. **2.** a loose, short-sleeved, men's casual shirt, usually brightly patterned.

surge /sɜdʒ/ *n.* **1.** a strong forward or upward movement, like that of swelling or rolling waves: *the onward surge of an angry crowd.* **2.** a wave-like rush of something: *a surge of anger*; *a surge of energy.* **3.** the rolling swell of the sea. **4.** a large swelling or sudden wave. **5.** *Mechanics* unevenness of action in an engine. –*v.i.* (**surged, surging**) **6.** to rise and fall, or move along, on the waves: *The ship surged at anchor.* **7.** to rise or roll in waves, or like waves: *the crowd surged around the mounted policeman*; *blood surged to his face.*

surgeon /'sɜdʒən/ *n.* **1.** a medical practitioner who has undertaken postgraduate studies to specialise in surgery. **2.** any medical practitioner qualified to practise surgery. **3.** an army or naval medical officer. –**surgeoncy**, *n.*

surgeonfish /'sɜdʒənfɪʃ/ *n.* (*pl.* **-fishes** *or, especially collectively,* **-fish**) any tropical coral-reef fish of the family Acanthuridae, with one or more spines near the base of the tail fin; tang.

surgery /'sɜdʒəri/ *n.* (*pl.* **-ries**) **1.** the art, practice, or work of treating diseases, injuries, or deformities by manual operation or instrumental appliances, especially by incision into the body. **2.** the branch of medicine concerned with such treatment. **3.** treatment, operations, etc., performed by a surgeon. **4.** a room or place for surgical operations. **5.** the consulting room of a medical practitioner, dentist, or the like. –**surgical**, *adj.* –**surgically**, *adv.*

surgical appliance *n.* any device designed to be worn to support a damaged or deformed part of the body.

surly /ˈsɜːli/ *adj.* (**-lier, -liest**) **1.** churlishly rude or ill-humoured, as a person or the manner, tone, expression, etc. **2.** (of an animal) ill-tempered and unfriendly. –**surlily**, *adv.* –**surliness**, *n.*

surmise *v.t.* /sɜˈmaɪz/ **1.** to think or infer without certain or strong evidence; conjecture; guess. –*n.* /sɜˈmaɪz, ˈsɜmaɪz/ Also, **surmisal. 2.** a matter of conjecture. –**surmisable**, *adj.* –**surmiser**, *n.*

surmount /sɜˈmaʊnt/ *v.t.* **1.** to mount upon; get on the top of; mount upon and cross over: *to surmount a hill.* **2.** to get over or across (barriers, obstacles, etc.). **3.** to prevail over. **4.** to be on top of or above: *a statue surmounting a pillar.* **5.** to furnish with something placed on top or above: *to surmount a tower with a spire.* –**surmountable**, *adj.* –**surmounter**, *n.*

surname /ˈsɜneɪm/ *n.* **1.** the name which a person has in common with the other members of his or her family, as distinguished from a Christian or first name; family name; last name. **2.** a name added to a person's name or names, as from birth or abode or from some characteristic or achievement.

surpass /sɜˈpas/ *v.t.* **1.** to go beyond in amount, extent, or degree; be greater than; exceed. **2.** to go beyond in excellence or achievement; be superior to; excel. **3.** to be beyond the range or capacity of; transcend: *misery that surpasses description.* –**surpassing**, *adj.* –**surpassable**, *adj.*

surplice /ˈsɜplɪs/ *n.* **1.** a loose-fitting, broad-sleeved white vestment properly of linen, worn over the cassock by certain members of the clergy and choristers. **2.** a garment in which the fronts cross each other diagonally. –**surpliced**, *adj.*

surplus /ˈsɜpləs/ *n.* **1.** that which remains above what is used or needed. **2.** an amount of assets in excess of what is requisite to meet liabilities. –*adj.* **3.** being a surplus; being in excess of what is required: *the surplus wheat of Australia.*

surprise /səˈpraɪz/ *v.t.* **1.** to come upon suddenly and unexpectedly; catch (a person, etc.) in the act of doing something; discover (a thing) suddenly. **2.** to assail, attack, or capture suddenly or without warning, as an army, fort, or person that is unprepared. **3.** to strike with a sudden feeling of wonder that arrests the thoughts, as at something unexpected or extraordinary. **4.** to lead or bring (a person, etc.) unawares, as into doing something not intended. –*n.* **5.** an act of surprising. **6.** a sudden assault, attack, or capture. **7.** a sudden and unexpected event, action, or the like. **8.** the state or feeling of being surprised as by something unexpected. –*adj.* **9.** sudden and unexpected: *a surprise attack.* –*phr.* **10. take by surprise, a.** to come upon unawares or without visible preparation. **b.** to catch unprepared. **c.** to amaze; astonish. –**surprisal**, *n.* –**surpriser**, *n.* –**surprising**, *adj.*

surreal /səˈril/ *adj.* **1.** of or relating to the dreamlike experiences, etc., dealt with by surrealism. –*phr.* **2. the surreal**, the world of these experiences.

surrealism /səˈriəlɪzəm/ *n.* a movement in literature and art from about 1919, based on the expression of imagination uncontrolled by reason, and seeking to suggest the activities of the subconscious mind. –**surrealist**, *n.*, *adj.* –**surrealistic** /səˌriəˈlɪstɪk/, *adj.* –**surrealistically** /səˌriəˈlɪstɪkli/, *adv.*

surrender /səˈrɛndə/ *v.t.* **1.** to yield (something) to the possession or power of another: *to surrender weapons; to surrender office.* **2.** to give (oneself) up, especially as a prisoner or to some emotion, course of action, etc. **3.** to give up (comfort, hope, etc.); relinquish. –*v.i.* **4.** to

give oneself up, especially as a prisoner or to an emotion, course of action, etc. –*n.* **5.** the act of surrendering. **6.** *Insurance* the voluntary termination of a life insurance policy by the policyholder prior to the policy running its full term, the amount receivable (**surrender value**) depending on the number of years elapsed from the commencement of the policy.

surreptitious /sʌrəpˈtɪʃəs/ *adj.* **1.** obtained, done, made, etc., by stealth; secret and unauthorised; clandestine: *a surreptitious glance.* **2.** acting in a stealthy way. –**surreptitiously**, *adv.* –**surreptitiousness**, *n.*

surrogate *n.* /ˈsʌrəgət/ **1.** someone appointed to act for another; a deputy. **2.** a substitute. –*v.t.* /ˈsʌrəgeɪt/ **3.** to put into the place of another as a successor, substitute, or deputy; substitute for another. –**surrogateship**, *n.* –**surrogation** /sʌrəˈgeɪʃən/, *n.*

surrogate mother *n.* a woman who, usually for a fee, performs a service for a couple who wish to have a child, either of being impregnated by the male partner and bringing the child to term, or of having an embryo conceived by the couple transplanted into her uterus and bringing the child to term, or of transplanting an embryo conceived by herself and the male to the female partner who brings it to term. –**surrogate motherhood**, *n.*

surround /səˈraʊnd/ *v.t.* **1.** to enclose on all sides, or encompass. **2.** to form an enclosure round; encircle. **3.** to enclose (a body of troops, fortification, or the like) so as to cut off communication or retreat. –*n.* **4.** a border which surrounds, as of uncovered floor around a carpet. **5.** (*pl.*) surroundings.

surrounding /səˈraʊndɪŋ/ *n.* **1.** something that surrounds. **2.** (*pl.*) environing circumstances, conditions, etc.; environment. **3.** the act of encircling or enclosing. –*adj.* **4.** that encloses or encircles. **5.** neighbouring; nearby; in the environment of.

surtax /ˈsɜtæks/ *n.* **1.** one of a graded series of additional taxes levied on incomes exceeding a certain amount. **2.** an additional or extra tax on something already taxed.

surveillance /səˈveɪləns, sɜˈveɪləns/ *n.* **1.** watch kept over a person, etc., especially over a suspect, a prisoner, or the like. **2.** supervision or superintendence.

survey *v.t.* /sɜˈveɪ, ˈsɜveɪ/ **1.** to take a general or overall view of. **2.** to view in detail, especially in order to determine the overall situation, condition, value, etc., for official reasons. **3.** to determine the form, boundaries, position, extent, etc., of (an area of land) by measurements and the use of the principles of geometry and trigonometry. –*v.i.* /sɜˈveɪ, ˈsɜveɪ/ **4.** to survey land, etc. –*n.* /ˈsɜveɪ/ (*pl.* **-veys**) **5.** the act of surveying; an overall view. **6.** a formal or official examination of the particulars of something made in order to determine an overall situation, condition, character, etc. **7.** the act of surveying land. **8.** a plan or description resulting from this. –**surveyable**, *adj.* –**surveyor**, *n.*

survive /səˈvaɪv/ *verb* (**-vived, -viving**) –*v.i.* **1.** to remain alive after the death of someone or after the cessation of something or the occurrence of some event; continue to live. **2.** to remain in existence after some person, thing, or event; continue to exist. **3.** *Colloq.* to remain unaffected or nearly so: *she doesn't love me, but I'll survive.* –*v.t.* **4.** to continue to live or exist after the death, cessation, or occurrence of; outlive. **5.** *Colloq.* to remain unaffected or nearly unaffected by. –**survival**, *n.* –**survivor**, *n.* –**surviving**, *adj.*

susceptible /səˈsɛptəbəl/ *adj.* **1.** capable of being affected, especially easily; readily impressed; impressionable. **2.** accessible or especially liable: *susceptible to a disease; susceptible to flattery.* –*phr.* **3. susceptible of** (or **to**), capable of receiving, admitting, undergoing, or being affected by: *susceptible of a high* *polish*; *susceptible to various interpretations.* **–susceptibleness**, *n.* **–susceptibly**, *adv.*

sushi /ˈsuʃi, ˈsuʃi/ *n.* (in Japanese cookery) any of various preparations of boiled Japanese rice flavoured with a sweetened rice vinegar and combined with toppings or fillings of raw seafood, vegetables, etc., and wrapped in nori.

suspect *v.t.* /səˈspɛkt/ **1.** to think to be guilty, false, bad, etc., with little or no proof: *they suspected him of being a thief.* **2.** to think to be likely; surmise: *I suspect his knowledge did not amount to much.* *–n.* /ˈsʌspɛkt/ **3.** a person suspected, especially of a crime, offence, etc. *–adj.* /ˈsʌspɛkt/ **4.** open to suspicion. **–suspecter** /səˈspɛktə/, *n.*

suspend /səˈspɛnd/ *v.t.* **1.** to hang by being joined to something above or to something that allows free movement, as a hinge. **2.** to keep from falling or sinking, as if by hanging: *solid particles suspended in a liquid.* **3.** to put off until a later time; defer or postpone, as sentence on a convicted person, judgement, etc. **4.** to cause to stop happening or being effective for a time: *to suspend payment; to suspend a rule.* **5.** to remove for a time from office, position, membership, etc.: *the headmaster suspended the pupil for bad behaviour.* **–suspensible** /səˈspɛnsəbəl/, *adj.*

suspender /səˈspɛndə/ *n.* **1.** a strap, usually elastic, with fastenings to support women's stockings, attached to a corset, step-ins, or belt. **2.** a similar device attached to a garter below the knee to support men's socks. **3.** (in a suspension bridge) one of the cables or chains which support the deck from the main suspension cables. **4.** (*pl.*) *US* brace (def. 7).

suspense /səˈspɛns/ *n.* **1.** a state of mental uncertainty, as in awaiting a decision or outcome, usually with more or less apprehension or anxiety. **2.** a state of mental indecision. **3.** undecided or doubtful condition, as of affairs: *for a few days matters hung in suspense.* **4.** the state or condition of being suspended; suspension. **–suspenseful**, *adj.* **–suspensefully**, *adv.*

suspension /səˈspɛnʃən/ *n.* **1.** the act of suspending. **2.** the condition of being suspended. **3.** *Chem.* the state in which particles of a solid are mixed in a liquid but are undissolved. **4.** *Chem.* a substance in such a state. **5.** *Physical Chem.* a system consisting of small particles kept dispersed by shaking (in **mechanical suspension**), or by molecular motion in liquid (in **colloidal suspension**). **6.** something on or by which something else is hung. **7.** the arrangement of springs, etc., that support the body of a motor vehicle, railway carriage, etc., and protect it from shock from the movement of the wheels. **8.** *Music* the continuing of a note in one chord into the following chord, usually producing a temporary dissonance.

suspicion /səˈspɪʃən/ *n.* **1.** the act of suspecting; imagination of the existence of guilt, fault, falsity, defect, or the like, on slight evidence or without evidence. **2.** imagination of anything to be the case or to be likely; a vague notion of something. **3.** a slight trace: *a suspicion of a smile.* **–suspicious**, *adj.* **–suspiciously**, *adv.*

suss /sʌs/ *Colloq.* *–adj.* **1.** suspect; dubious; unreliable: *her story sounded pretty suss to me.* **2.** suspicious: *to be suss about the offer.* *–v.i.* **3.** to realise: *to suss that you are not welcome.* *–phr.* **4.** **suss out**, to investigate directly, especially in a situation involving a particular challenge or presenting probable difficulties: *before the minister proposed his bill, he sussed out the likely reaction of the opposition.*

sustain /səˈsteɪn/ *v.t.* **1.** to hold up from below; bear the weight of; be the support of. **2.** to bear (a burden, charge, etc.). **3.** to undergo, experience, or suffer (injury, loss, etc.); endure without giving way. **4.** to keep

up or keep going an action or process: *to sustain a conversation.* **5.** to supply (a person) with food and drink, or the necessities of life. **6.** to confirm or support; uphold. **–sustainment**, *n.*

sustainable /səˈsteɪnəbəl/ *adj.* **1.** able to be sustained. **2.** designed or developed to have the capacity to continue operating perpetually, by avoiding adverse effects on the natural environment and depletion of natural resources: *a sustainable transport system; sustainable forestry.* **–sustainability**, *n.* **–sustainably**, *adv.*

sustainable development *n.* economic development designed to meet present needs while also taking into account future costs, particularly impacts on the environment and depletion of natural resources.

sustenance /ˈsʌstənəns/ *n.* **1.** means of sustaining life; nourishment. **2.** means of livelihood.

sutra /ˈsutrə/ *n.* a set of concise rules or teachings, chiefly in Hindu or Buddhist literature. Also, **sutta** /ˈsutə/.

suture /ˈsutʃə/ *n.* **1.** *Surg.* **a.** joining of the edges of a wound, etc., by stitching or some similar process. **b.** one of the stitches used. **2.** *Anat.* the line where two bones meet, especially in the skull. *–v.t.* **3.** to join by or as if by a suture. **–sutural**, *adj.* **–suturally**, *adv.*

SUV /ɛs ju ˈvi/ *n.* a car of a large or medium size, similar to a station wagon in having an extended interior to provide room for both passengers and cargo and a door or tailgate at the back, but with a design that sets the body of the car at a higher level above the road; usually with a 4-wheel drive capacity.

svelte /svɛlt, sfɛlt/ *adj.* slender, especially gracefully slender in figure; lithe.

swab /swɒb/ *n.* **1.** a large mop used on shipboard for cleaning decks, etc. **2.** *Med.*, *Vet. Science* a piece of sponge, cloth, cottonwool, or the like, often mounted on a stick, for cleansing the mouth of a sick person, or for applying medicaments, taking specimens of discharges and secretions, etc. *–v.t.* (**swabbed**, **swabbing**) **3.** to clean with or as with a swab. **4.** to test (a racehorse) for possible drugging by taking a saliva sample with a swab. **–swabber**, *n.*

swaddle /ˈswɒdl/ *v.t.* **1.** to bind (an infant, especially a newborn infant) with long, narrow strips of cloth to prevent free movement; wrap tightly with clothes. **2.** to wrap (anything) round with bandages.

swag /swæg/ *n.* **1.** *Aust.*, *NZ* a bundle or roll carried across the shoulders or otherwise, and containing the bedding and personal belongings of a traveller through the bush, a miner, etc.; shiralee; bluey. **2.** a form of portable bedding consisting of a waterproof bag with a tent-like frame, the whole able to be dismantled and rolled up. **3.** a decorative curtain drape. **4.** a wreath, garland, festoon of fruit, etc., especially as used as an ornament in carving, plaster, etc. **5.** *Obs. Colloq.* stolen goods; booty. **6.** *Colloq.* an unspecified but large number or quantity: *a swag of people.*

swagger /ˈswægə/ *v.i.* **1.** to walk or strut with a defiant or insolent air. **2.** to boast or brag noisily. *–v.t.* **3.** to bring, drive, force, etc., by blustering. **–swaggerer**, *n.*

swagman /ˈswægmən/ *n.* (*pl.* **-men**) *Aust.*, *NZ* (formerly) a man who travelled about the country on foot, living on earnings from occasional jobs, or gifts of money or food.

swain /sweɪn/ *n. Chiefly Poetic* **1.** a country lad or gallant. **2.** a lover. **–swainish**, *adj.* **–swainishness**, *n.*

swallow[1] /ˈswɒloʊ/ *v.t.* **1.** to take into the stomach through the throat or gullet (oesophagus), as food, drink, or other substances. **2.** *Colloq.* to accept without question or suspicion. **3.** to accept without opposition; put up with: *to swallow an insult.* **4.** to suppress (emotion, a laugh, sob, etc.) as if by drawing it down one's throat. **5.** to take back or retract (one's words, etc.). *–v.i.* **6.** to perform the act of swallowing. *–n.*

7. the act of swallowing. **8.** a quantity swallowed at one time; a mouthful. *–phr.* **9. swallow up,** to take in so as to envelop; withdraw from sight; assimilate; consume. **–swallowable,** *adj.* **–swallower,** *n.*

swallow² /ˈswɒloʊ/ *n.* any of numerous small, long-winged birds constituting the family Hirundinidae, notable for their swift, graceful flight and for the extent and regularity of their migrations.

swam /swæm/ *v.* past tense of **swim.**

swami /ˈswɑmi/ *n.* (*pl.* **-mis**) **1.** a Hindu religious teacher. **2.** (*upper case*) a respectful title for such a teacher.

swamp /swɒmp/ *n.* **1.** an area of wet, spongy land; marsh. *–v.t.* **2.** to flood with water, etc. **3.** to flood over; cover; overwhelm: *to be swamped with work. –v.i.* **4.** (of a boat) to fill with water and sink.

swamp gum *n.* any of various eucalypts, especially *Eucalyptus ovata,* found growing in swampy areas.

swamphen /ˈswɒmphɛn/ *n.* See **purple swamphen.**

swamp oak *n.* a tree, *Casuarina glauca,* found on the east coast of Australia especially along tidal rivers and on brackish soil.

swan /swɒn/ *n.* **1.** any large, stately swimming bird of the subfamily Anserinae, having a long, slender neck, such as the **mute swan,** *Cygnus olor,* of Europe and Asia, introduced to parks and gardens throughout the world, and the **black swan.** *–phr.* **2. swan about** (or **around**), to walk, travel around, etc., while aware of the favourable visual impression being created.

swank /swæŋk/ *Colloq. –n.* **1.** dashing smartness, as in bearing, appearance, etc.; style. **2.** swagger. *–adj.* **3.** pretentiously stylish. *–v.i.* **4.** to swagger in behaviour; show off. **–swanky,** *adj.*

swan song *n.* a final speech, performance, public appearance, etc., before one gives up a position, project, activity, etc.

swap /swɒp/ *verb* (**swapped, swapping**) *–v.t.* **1.** to exchange, barter, or trade, as one thing for another. *–v.i.* **2.** to make an exchange. *–n.* **3.** an exchange. Also, **swop. –swapper,** *n.*

sward /swɔd/ *n.* **1.** the grassy surface of land; turf. **2.** a stretch of turf; a growth of grass.

swarm¹ /swɔm/ *n.* **1.** a body of honey bees which emigrate from a hive and fly off together under the direction of a queen, to start a new colony. **2.** a body of bees settled together, as in a hive. **3.** a great number of things or persons, especially in motion. **4.** *Biol.* a group of aggregation of free-floating or free-swimming cells or organisms. *–v.i.* **5.** to fly off together in a body from a hive to start a new colony, as bees. **6.** to move about, along, forth, etc., in great numbers, as things or persons. *–v.t.* **7.** to swarm about, over, or in; throng; overrun. *–phr.* **8. swarm with,** (of a place) to be thronged or overrun by; abound or teem with: *a pond swarming with tadpoles.*

swarm² /swɔm/ *phr.* **swarm up,** to climb (a tree, pole, or the like) by clasping it with the hands or arms and legs and drawing oneself up; shin up.

swarthy /ˈswɔði/ *adj.* (**-thier, -thiest**) dark-coloured, now especially as the skin, complexion, etc., of a person. **–swarthily,** *adv.* **–swarthiness,** *n.*

swashbuckler /ˈswɒʃbʌklə/ *n.* a swaggering swordsman or bully. Also, **swasher. –swashbuckling,** *adj.,* *n.*

swastika /ˈswɒstɪkə/ *n.* **1.** a figure used as a symbol or an ornament since prehistoric times, consisting of a cross with arms of equal length, each arm having a continuation at right angles, and all four continuations turning the same way. **2.** this figure with clockwise arms as the official emblem of the Nazi Party and the Third Reich.

swat /swɒt/ *v.t.* (**swatted, swatting**) *Colloq.* to hit with a smart or violent blow. Also, *US,* **swot. –swatter,** *n.*

swath /swɔθ/ *n.* → **swathe².**

swathe¹ /sweɪð/ *v.t.* (**swathed, swathing**) **1.** to wrap, bind, or swaddle with bands of some material; wrap up closely or fully. **2.** to enfold or envelop, as wrappings do. *–n.* **3.** a band of linen or the like in which something is wrapped; a wrapping; a bandage. **–swather,** *n.*

swathe² /sweɪð/ *n.* **1.** the space covered by the stroke of a scythe or the cut of a mowing machine. **2.** a strip, belt, or long and relatively narrow extent of anything. Also, **swath.**

sway /sweɪ/ *v.i.* **1.** to move, usually gently, from side to side. **2.** to move or incline to one side or in a particular direction. **3.** to incline in opinion, sympathy, tendency, etc.: *to sway towards radicalism. –v.t.* **4.** to cause to sway. **5.** to cause (the mind, etc., or a person) to turn in a particular way: *to sway the voters towards another point of view.* **6.** to cause to turn aside: *I swayed him from his idea. –n.* **7.** the act of swaying; a swaying movement. **8.** control; rule; dominion. **–swayer,** *n.* **–swayingly,** *adv.*

swear /swɛə/ *verb* (**swore, sworn, swearing**) *–v.i.* **1.** to make a solemn declaration with an appeal to God or some superhuman being in confirmation of what is declared; make affirmation in a solemn manner by some sacred being or object, as the deity or the Bible. **2.** to engage or promise on oath or in a solemn manner (to do something); vow; bind oneself by oath: *to swear to uphold the law.* **3.** (sometimes fol. by *to*) to give evidence or make any statement on oath or by solemn declaration. **4.** to use profane or taboo oaths or language, as in imprecation or anger or for mere emphasis. *–v.t.* **5.** to declare or affirm by swearing by a deity, some sacred object, etc. **6.** to affirm or say with solemn earnestness or great emphasis. **7.** to promise or undertake on oath or in a solemn manner; vow. **8.** to testify or state on oath or by solemn declaration; make oath to (something stated or alleged). **9.** to take (an oath), as in order to give solemnity or force to a declaration, promise, etc. **10.** (sometimes fol. by *to*) to administer an oath to; bind by an oath: *to swear someone to secrecy.* *–phr.* **11. swear at,** to speak to with curses or blasphemies; abuse. **12. swear by, a.** to name (some sacred being or thing, etc.) as one's witness or guarantee in swearing. **b.** to rely on; have confidence in. **13. swear in,** to admit to office or service by administering an oath. **14. swear off,** *Colloq.* to promise to give up (something, especially intoxicating drink). **–swearer,** *n.*

sweat /swɛt/ *verb* (**sweat** or **sweated, sweating**) *–v.i.* **1.** to excrete watery fluid through the pores of the skin, as from heat, exertion, etc.; perspire, especially freely or profusely. **2.** to exude moisture, as green plants piled in a heap. **3.** to gather moisture from the surrounding air by condensation. **4.** *Colloq.* to exert oneself strenuously; work hard. **5.** *Colloq.* to feel distress, as from anxiety, impatience, vexation, etc. *–v.t.* **6.** to emit (watery fluid, etc.) through the pores of the skin. **7.** to exude (moisture, etc.) in drops or small particles. **8.** to cause (a person, a horse, etc.) to sweat. **9.** to cause (substances, etc.) to exude moisture, especially as a step in some industrial process of treating or preparing. **10.** to cause (persons, etc.) to work hard. **11.** to employ (workers) at low wages, for long hours, or under other unfavourable conditions. **12.** *Colloq.* to deprive (a person) of money, etc., as by exaction. **13.** *Colloq.* to subject (a person) to severe questioning in order to extract information. **14.** *Metallurgy* **a.** to heat (metal) to partial fusion in order to remove an easily fusible constituent. **b.** to heat (solder or the like) until it melts. **c.** to join (metal objects) by heating and pressing together, usually with solder. *–n.* **15.** the process of sweating or perspiring, as from heat, exertion, perturbation, disease, etc. **16.** the secretions of sweat glands; the product of sweating. **17.** a state or period of sweating. **18.** moisture or liquid matter exuded from something or gathered on a surface in drops or small particles. **19.** an exuding of moisture by a substance, etc., or an inducing of such exudation, as in some industrial process. **20.** *Colloq.* a state of perturbation, anxiety, or impatience. **21.** *Colloq.* hard work. –*phr.* **22. no sweat,** *Colloq.* an expression of reassurance. **23. sweat blood,** *Colloq.* to be under a strain; be anxious; worry. **24. sweat it out,** *Colloq.* to hold out; endure until the end. **25. sweat on,** *Colloq.* to await anxiously. **26. sweat out** (or **off**), to get rid of by sweating. –**sweatless,** *adj.*

sweated /'swetəd/ *adj.* **1.** made by underpaid workers. **2.** underpaid and overworked. **3.** having poor working conditions.

sweater /'swetə/ *n.* a knitted jumper, usually of wool.

sweatshirt /'swetʃɜt/ *n.* a loose pullover worn especially by athletes to prevent chill or to induce sweating.

sweatshop /'swetʃɒp/ *n.* a workshop, or the like, employing workers at low wages during overlong hours, under insanitary or otherwise unfavourable conditions.

swede /swid/ *n.* **1.** a cultivated variety of turnip, *Brassica napus*, frequently grown for its edible, swollen taproot. **2.** the root itself.

sweep /swip/ *verb* (**swept, sweeping**) –*v.t.* **1.** to move, drive, or bring, by passing a broom, brush, or the like over the surface occupied, or as the broom or other object does: *to sweep dust away.* **2.** to move, bring, take, etc., by or as by a steady, driving stroke or with continuous, forcible actions: *the wind sweeps the snow into drifts.* **3.** *Cricket* to strike (the ball) with a cross bat close to the ground, on the leg side, usually backward of square leg. **4.** to pass or draw (something) over a surface, or about, along, etc., with a steady, continuous stroke or movement: *to sweep a brush over a table.* **5.** to clear or clean (a floor, room, chimney, etc.) of dirt, litter, etc., by means of a broom or the like. **6.** to make (a path, etc.) by clearing a space with a broom or the like. **7.** to clear (a surface, place, etc.) of something on or in it: *to sweep the sea of enemy ships.* **8.** to pass over (a surface, region, etc.) with a steady, driving movement or unimpeded course, as winds, floods, or fire. **9.** to direct the gaze over (a region, etc.) with the unaided eye or with a telescope; survey with a continuous view over the whole extent. **10.** to win an overwhelming victory, as in an election: *the Labor Party swept the polls in the 1972 election.* **11.** *Electronics* to scan (a band of frequency) when receiving a signal, or to generate a signal which moves across (a band of frequency). –*v.i.* **12.** to sweep a floor, room, etc., as with a broom, or as a broom does: *a new broom sweeps clean.* **13.** to move (*down, over*, etc.) steadily and strongly or swiftly. **14.** to pass in a swift but stately manner, as a person, a procession, etc. **15.** to trail, as garments, etc. **16.** to move or pass in a continuous course, especially a wide curve or circuit: *his glance swept about the room.* **17.** to extend in a continuous or curving stretch, as a road, a shore, fields, etc. **18.** to conduct an underwater search by towing a drag under the surface of the water, as for mines, a lost anchor, or the like. **19.** *Cricket* to execute a sweep. –*n.* **20.** the act of sweeping, especially a moving, removing, clearing, etc., by or as by the use of a broom: *to abolish all class distinctions at one sweep.* **21.** the steady, driving motion or swift onward course of something moving with force or unimpeded: *the sweep of the wind; the sweep of the waves.* **22.** a trailing movement, as of garments. **23.** *Cricket* the action of a person batting who sweeps (def. 3) **24.** a swinging or curving movement or stroke, as of the arm or a weapon, oar, etc. **25.** reach, range or compass, as of something swept about: *the sweep of a road about a marsh.* **26.** a continuous extent or stretch: *a broad sweep of sand.* **27.** *Navy* a wire or rope dragged

beneath the surface of the water by two mine-sweeping ships to cut mines loose. **28.** a curving, especially widely or gently curving, line, form, part, or mass. **29.** a large oar used in small vessels, sometimes to assist the rudder in turning the vessel but usually to propel the craft. **30.** (in a lifesaving boat) the person who steers by means of a sweep (def. 29) at the stern. **31.** someone who sweeps, especially a chimneysweep. **32.** *Cards* **a.** (in whist) the winning of all the tricks in a hand. Compare **slam**[2]. **b.** (in a casino) a pairing or combining, and hence taking, of all the cards on the board. **33.** *Physics* **a.** an irreversible process tending towards thermal equilibrium. **b.** the motion of the spot across the screen of a cathode-ray tube. **34.** → **sweepstake.** –*phr.* **35. make a clean sweep, a.** to have a complete victory or success. **b.** to get rid of something completely. **36. sweep under the carpet,** to remove (inconvenient things) from consideration.

sweepstake /'swipsteik/ *n.* **1.** a race or other contest in which the prize consists of the stakes contributed by the various competitors. **2.** the prize itself. **3.** a method of gambling, as on the outcome of a horserace, in which each participant contributes a stake, usually by buying a numbered ticket entitling the holder to draw the name of a competitor, the winnings being provided from the stake money. Also, **sweepstakes.**

sweet /swit/ *adj.* **1.** pleasing to the taste, especially having the pleasant taste or flavour characteristic of sugar, honey, etc. **2.** not rancid, or stale; fresh. **3.** fresh as opposed to salt, as water. **4.** pleasing to the ear; making a pleasant or agreeable sound; musical. **5.** pleasing to the smell; fragrant; perfumed. **6.** pleasing or agreeable; yielding pleasure or enjoyment; delightful. **7.** pleasant in disposition or manners; amiable; kind or gracious as a person, action, etc. **8.** dear; beloved; precious. **9.** financially profitable and personally beneficial: *a sweet deal.* **10.** (of wine) sweet-tasting (opposed to *dry*). **11.** free from sourness or acidity, as soil. **12.** *Chem.* **a.** devoid of corrosive or acidic substances. **b.** (of substances such as petrol) containing no sulphur compounds. **13.** *Aust., NZ Colloq.* all right; satisfactory as arranged: *everything will be sweet for the party.* –*adv.* **14.** in a sweet manner; sweetly. –*interj.* **15.** an exclamation of delight, reassurance, approval, etc. –*n.* **16.** sweet taste or flavour; sweet smell; sweetness. **17.** that which is sweet. **18.** Also, **sweetie.** any of various small confections made wholly or partly from sugar. **19.** (*oft. pl.*) any sweet dish, as a pudding, tart, etc., served at the end of a meal. **20.** something pleasant to the mind or feelings. **21.** a beloved person; darling; sweetheart. –*phr. Colloq.* **22. sweet (as)!,** an exclamation of approval, delight, admiration, etc. **23. sweet as a nut,** very satisfactory. **24. sweet on,** in love with; fond of. –**sweeten,** *v.* –**sweetly,** *adv.* –**sweetness,** *n.*

sweetbread /'switbrɛd/ *n.* **1.** the pancreas (**stomach sweetbread**) of an animal, especially a calf or a lamb, used for food. **2.** the thymus gland (**neck sweetbread** or **throat sweetbread**), used for food.

sweet corn *n.* **1.** any maize of a sweetish flavour and suitable for eating, especially a particularly sweet variety, *Zea mays* var. *saccharata.* **2.** the unripe and tender ears of maize, especially when used as a table vegetable and when the kernels have been removed from the cob. Also, **sweetcorn.**

sweetheart /'swithat/ *n.* **1.** one of a pair of lovers with relation to the other, sometimes especially the girl or woman. **2.** a beloved person (often used in affectionate address).

sweetheart deal *n.* a private agreement reached between two parties, as an employer and a trade union, to their mutual advantage, often made without proper regard for other parties affected or society as a whole. Also, **sweetheart agreement.**

sweetmeat /'switmit/ *n.* **1.** a sweet delicacy, prepared with sugar, honey, or the like, as preserves, sweets, or (formerly) cakes or pastry. **2.** (*usu. pl.*) any sweet delicacy of the confectionery kind, as crystallised fruit, sugar-covered nuts, sweets, bonbons, etc.

sweet potato *n.* **1.** a plant of central America, *Ipomaea batatas*, widely cultivated in the tropics for its edible root. **2.** the edible root itself.

sweet tooth *n. Colloq.* a strong liking for sweets, sweet dishes, etc.

swell /swɛl/ *verb* (**swelled, swollen** *or* **swelled, swelling**) –*v.i.* **1.** to grow in size, by taking in water or air or by addition of material in growth. **2.** (of the sea) to rise in waves. **3.** (of tears, etc.) to rise or well up. **4.** (of a sail, sides of a cask, etc.) to bulge out. **5.** to grow in amount, degree, force: *the music swelled and then died away.* **6.** to become proud. –*v.t.* **7.** to make (someone or something) swell. –*n.* **8.** the act of swelling: *the swell of the waves.* **9.** increase in size, amount, degree, etc.; inflation. **10.** a part that bulges out. **11.** a wave, especially when long and unbroken, or such waves collectively. **12.** *Music* **a.** a gradual increase (crescendo) followed by a gradual decrease (diminuendo) in the loudness or force of a musical sound. **b.** the sign (< >) for indicating this. **13.** *Chiefly US Colloq.* **a.** a fashionably dressed person. **b.** a person of high social standing. –*adj.* **14.** *Chiefly US Colloq.* (of things) stylish; elegant; grand: *a swell hotel.*

swelling /'swɛlɪŋ/ *n.* **1.** the act of one that swells. **2.** the condition of being swollen. **3.** a swollen part; a protuberance or prominence.

swelter /'swɛltə/ *v.i.* to suffer or languish with oppressive heat; perspire profusely from heat.

swept /swɛpt/ *v.* past tense and past participle of **sweep**.

swerve /swɜv/ *v.i.* **1.** to turn aside abruptly in movement or direction; deviate suddenly or sharply from the straight or direct course. –*n.* **2.** the act of swerving; a turning aside; a deviation. **3.** *Cricket* deviation of a ball in mid-air, usually as a result of spin rather than swing. –**swerver**, *n.*

swift /swɪft/ *adj.* **1.** moving with great speed or velocity; fleet; rapid: *a swift ship.* **2.** coming, happening, or performed quickly or without delay. –*n.* **3.** any of the rapidly flying birds of the families Apodidae and Hemiprocnidae, found throughout the world, as the **fork-tailed swift**, *Apus pacificus*, which migrates from Asia to the Australian mainland and Tasmania. –**swiftly**, *adv.* –**swiftness**, *n.*

swiftie /'swɪfti/ *n.* **1.** *Aust., NZ Colloq.* an unfair act; a deceitful practice. –*phr.* **2.** **pull** (or **put over**) **a swiftie**, to hoodwink; practise deception. Also, **swifty**.

swig /swɪg/ *Colloq.* –*n.* **1.** a large or deep drink, especially of alcoholic liquor, taken in one swallow; draught. –*verb* (**swigged, swigging**) –*v.t.* **2.** to drink (liquid) heartily or greedily. –*v.i.* **3.** to drink heartily or greedily. –**swigger**, *n.*

swill /swɪl/ *n.* **1.** liquid or partly liquid food for animals, especially kitchen waste given to pigs. **2.** any liquid matter; slops. –*v.i.* **3.** to drink greedily or too much. –*v.t.* **4.** to drink (something) greedily or too much; guzzle. **5.** to wash or clean by flooding with water. –**swiller**, *n.*

swim /swɪm/ *verb* (**swam, swum, swimming**) –*v.i.* **1.** to move along or in water by movements of the limbs, fins, tail, etc.; move on or in water or other liquid in any way, especially on the surface. **2.** to float on the surface of water or other liquid. **3.** to move, rest, or be suspended in air or the like, as if swimming in water. **4.** to move, glide, or go smoothly over a surface. **5.** to be immersed or steeped in, or overflowed or flooded with, a liquid. **6.** to be dizzy or giddy; have a whirling sensation; seem to whirl. –*v.t.* **7.** to move along on or in by

swimming; float on or in; cross by swimming, as a stream. **8.** to cause to swim; cause to float, as on a stream. **9.** to furnish with sufficient water to swim or float. **10.** to perform (a particular stroke) in swimming. –*n.* **11.** an act, instance, or period of swimming. **12.** a motion as of swimming; a smooth gliding movement. –*adj.* **13.** of or relating to swimming: *a swim school.* –*phr.* **14.** **in the swim**, actively engaged in current affairs, social activities, etc. –**swimmer**, *n.*

swimming costume *n.* a garment or garments worn for swimming.

swimmingly /'swɪmɪŋli/ *adv.* without difficulty; with great success.

swimsuit /'swɪmsut/ *n.* a woman's swimming costume.

swindle /'swɪndl/ *v.t.* **1.** to cheat (a person) out of money, etc. **2.** to obtain by fraud or deceit. –*n.* **3.** the act of swindling; a fraudulent transaction or scheme. –**swindler**, *n.*

swine /swaɪn/ *n.* (*pl.* **swine**) **1.** the domestic pig. **2.** any animal of the same family, Suidae, omnivorous non-ruminant mammals, with a two-chambered stomach and muscular snout and forelegs adapted to rooting for food, as the giant forest hog, *Hylochoerus meinertzhageni*. **3.** a coarse, gross, or brutish person. **4.** a contemptible person.

swine flu *n.* → **human swine influenza**.

swing /swɪŋ/ *verb* (**swung, swinging**) –*v.t.* **1.** to cause to move to and fro, sway, or oscillate, as something suspended from above: *ladies swinging their parasols.* **2.** to cause to move in alternate directions, or in either direction, about a fixed point or line of support, as a door on its hinges. **3.** *Cricket* (of a bowler) to cause (the ball) to deviate to the left or right in its flight towards the wicket, as a result of the action of air on the seam of a shiny ball. **4.** to move (something held or grasped) with an oscillating or rotary movement: *swing a club about one's head.* **5.** to cause to move in a curve as if about a central point. **6.** to sway, influence, or manage as desired: *to swing the voting in an election.* –*v.i.* **7.** to move to and fro, as something suspended from above, as a pendulum. **8.** to move to and fro on a swing, as for amusement. **9.** to move in alternate directions, or in either direction, about a point or line of support, as a gate on its hinges. **10. a.** to move in a curve as if about a central point, as around a corner. **b.** *Cricket* (of a ball) to deviate to the left or right in its flight toward the wicket, through atmospheric action on the seam. **11.** to move with a free, swaying motion, as soldiers on the march. **12.** (of music and musicians) to evince the characteristics of swing (def. 25). **13.** to be suspended so as to hang freely, as a bell, etc. **14.** *Colloq.* to suffer death by hanging. **15.** to change or shift one's attention, opinion, interest, etc.; fluctuate. **16.** to aim at or hit something with a sweeping movement of the arm. **17.** *Colloq.* (of a place) to have a lively atmosphere. **18.** *Colloq.* (of two people) to be in mental or spiritual harmony; be in accord in outlook or feeling. **19.** *Colloq.* to change sexual partners frequently, especially to be a member of a group agreeing to exchange sexual partners on a casual basis. –*n.* **20.** the act or the manner of swinging; movement in alternate directions, or in a particular direction. **21.** the amount of such movement. **22.** a curving movement or course. **23.** a moving of the body with a free, swaying motion, as in walking. **24.** a steady, marked rhythm or movement, as of verse or music. **25.** Also, **swing music**. a smooth, orchestral type of jazz popular in the 1930s, often arranged for big bands. **26.** the rhythmic element that excites dancers and listeners to move in time to jazz music. **27.** *US* freedom of action: *have free swing.* **28.** active operation: *to get into the swing of things.* **29.** something that is swung or that swings. **30.** a seat suspended from above as in a loop of rope or between ropes or rods, in which one may sit and swing to and fro for amusement. **31.** *Cricket* deviation of a ball in mid-air, as a result of atmospheric action on the seam. **32.** *Politics* the measure of the electoral support transferred from one party to another, as expressed in percentage points, between a party's vote at one election and its vote at the next. *–phr.* **33. in full swing,** fully active; operating at maximum speed or with maximum efficiency. **34. swing into action,** to commence.

swinging voter *n. Aust.* someone who changes their political allegiance at different elections.

swipe /swaɪp/ *n.* **1.** *Colloq.* a sweeping stroke; a stroke with a full swing of the arms, as in cricket or golf. *–v.t.* **2.** *Colloq.* to strike with a sweeping blow. **3.** *Colloq.* to steal. **4.** to move (a card with a magnetic strip) through the slot of an electronic device. *–v.i.* **5.** *Colloq.* to make a sweeping stroke. *–phr.* **6. swipe in,** to gain access using a swipe card. **7. swipe out,** to exit using a swipe card.

swirl /swɜl/ *v.i.* **1.** to move about or along with a whirling motion; whirl; eddy. **2.** to be dizzy or giddy, or swim, as the head. *–v.t.* **3.** to cause to swirl or whirl; twist. *–n.* **4.** a swirling movement; a whirl; an eddy. **5.** a twist, of hair about the head or of trimming on a hat. **6.** a pattern created by a whirling movement, as in icing, painting, etc.

swish /swɪʃ/ *v.i.* **1.** to move with or make a hissing sound: *the slender rod swished through the air. –v.t.* **2.** to cause to move with a swishing movement or sound: *the horse swished its tail.* **3.** to bring, take, etc., with such a movement or sound: *to swish the tops off plants with a cane. –n.* **4.** a swishing movement or sound. **5.** a cane or rod for whipping, or a stroke with this.

switch /swɪtʃ/ *n.* **1.** a slender, flexible shoot, rod, etc., used especially in whipping, beating, etc. **2.** the act of switching; a stroke, lash, or whisking movement. **3.** a slender growing shoot, as of a plant. **4.** a separate bunch or tress of long hair (or some substitute) fastened together at one end, worn by women to supplement their hair. **5.** *Elect.* a device for turning on or off or directing an electric current, or making or breaking a circuit. **6.** *Chiefly US* → **point** (def. 41). **7.** a turning, shifting, or changing: *a switch of votes to another candidate.* **8.** *Bridge* a change to a suit other than the one played or bid previously. **9.** *Aust. Colloq.* → **switchboard** (def. 2). *–v.t.* **10.** to whip or beat with a switch or the like; lash: *he switched the lad with a cane.* **11.** to move, swing, or whisk (a cane, a fishing line, etc.) like a switch or with a swift, lashing stroke. **12.** to exchange; shift. **13.** to turn, shift, or divert: *to switch conversation from a painful subject.* **14.** *Chiefly US* → **shunt** (def. 2). *–v.i.* **15.** to strike with or as with a switch. **16.** to change direction or course; turn, shift, or change. **17.** to be shifted, turned, etc., by means of a switch. *–phr.* **18. switch off, a.** to turn off (an electric current or appliance). **b.** (of electric lights, appliances, etc.) to cease to operate. **c.** *Colloq.* (of a person) to lose interest or become oblivious. **19. switch on, a.** to cause (an electric current) to flow or (an electrical appliance) to operate. **b.** (of electric lights, appliances, etc.) to begin to operate. **c.** *Colloq.* to cause (someone) to be interested and enthused: *Bach really switches him on.* **d.** *Colloq.* (of a person) to become interested and enthused. *–switcher, n.*

switchblade /'swɪtʃbleɪd/ *n.* → **flick-knife.**

switchboard /'swɪtʃbɔd/ *n.* **1.** *Elect.* a structural unit mounting switches, instruments, and/or meters necessary for the control of electrical energy. **2.** *Telecommunications* an arrangement of switches, plugs, and jacks mounted on a board or frame enabling an operator

to make temporary connections between telephone users.

swivel /'swɪvəl/ *n.* **1.** a fastening device which allows the thing fastened to turn round freely upon it. **2.** such a device consisting of two parts, each of which turns round independently. **3.** a pivoted support for allowing a gun to turn round in a horizontal plane. *–v.i.* (**-elled** *or, Chiefly US,* **-eled, -elling** *or, Chiefly US,* **-eling**) **4.** to turn on a swivel, pivot, or the like.

swollen /'swoʊlən/ *v.* **1.** past participle of **swell.** *–adj.* **2.** swelled; enlarged by or as by swelling; puffed up; tumid. **3.** turgid or bombastic. **–swollenly,** *adv.* **–swollenness,** *n.*

swoon /swun/ *v.i.* **1.** to faint; lose consciousness. **2.** to become enraptured; enter a state of ecstasy. **–swooningly,** *adv.*

swoop /swup/ *v.i.* **1.** to sweep through the air, as a bird or a bat, especially down upon prey. *–n.* **2.** the act of swooping; a sudden, swift descent. *–phr.* **3. at** (or **in**) **one fell swoop,** in a single action or coordinated series of actions. **4. swoop down,** (sometimes fol. by *on* or *upon*) to come down in a sudden swift attack: *the enemy troops swooped down on the town.* **5. swoop up,** to take, lift, or remove, with, or as with, a sweeping motion.

sword /sɔd/ *n.* **1.** a weapon having various forms but consisting typically of a long, straight or slightly curved blade, sharp-edged on one side or both sides, with one end pointed and the other fixed in a hilt or handle. **2.** (*pl.*) *Shearing Colloq.* hand shears. *–phr.* **3. a two-edged** (or **double-edged**) **sword,** any circumstance, ruling, policy, etc., which brings both advantages and disadvantages. **4. cross swords, a.** to join in combat. **b.** to argue; disagree violently. **c.** *Colloq.* (of men) to urinate at the same time, in the same toilet or urinal. **5. give something the sword,** *Colloq.* to discard something as broken or no longer useful. **6. have had the sword,** *Aust. Colloq.* to be finished or ruined. **7. put to the sword,** to massacre; slaughter. **–swordless,** *adj.*

swordfish /'sɔdfɪʃ/ *n.* a large marine sport fish of the genus *Xiphias,* with the upper jaw elongated into a swordlike weapon.

swore /swɔ/ *v.* past tense of **swear.**

sworn /swɔn/ *v.* **1.** past participle of **swear.** *–adj.* **2.** having taken an oath; bound by or as by an oath. **3.** confirmed; inveterate; avowed.

swot¹ /swɒt/ *v.t.* (**swotted, swotting**) *US* → **swat.**

swot² /swɒt/ *Colloq. –v.i.* (**swotted, swotting**) **1.** to study hard. *–n.* **2.** someone who studies hard. *–phr.* **3. swot up,** to study hard.

SWOT analysis /'swɒt ənæləsəs/ *n.* an analysis of a business under the headings of strengths, weaknesses, opportunities and threats.

swum /swʌm/ *v.* past participle of **swim.**

swung /swʌŋ/ *v.* past tense and past participle of **swing.**

swy /swaɪ/ *n. Aust., NZ Colloq.* → **two-up.** Also, **swy-game.**

sy- variant of **syn-,** before *s* followed by a consonant, and before *z,* as in *systaltic.*

sybarite /'sɪbəraɪt/ *n.* someone devoted to luxury and pleasure; an effeminate voluptuary. **–sybaritic** /sɪbə-'rɪtɪk/, *adj.* **–sybaritically** /sɪbə'rɪtɪkli/, *adv.*

sycamore /'sɪkəmɔ/ *n.* **1.** (in Europe) a maple, *Acer pseudoplatanus,* grown as a shady ornamental tree and for its wood. **2.** (in the US) the plane tree or buttonwood, *Platanus occidentalis.* **3.** a tree, *Ficus sycomorus,* of the Near East, allied to the common fig and bearing an edible fruit. **4.** any of various trees resembling the sycamore, as the sandalwood.

sycophant /'sɪkəfænt, -fənt, 'saɪ-/ *n.* a self-seeking flatterer; a fawning, servile parasite. **–sycophancy,** *n.*

–**sycophantic** /sɪkəˈfæntɪk/, **sycophantical** /sɪkə-ˈfæntɪkəl/, *adj.* –**sycophantically** /sɪkəˈfæntɪkli/, *adv.*

syl- variant of **syn-** (by assimilation) before *l*, as in *syllepsis*.

syllable /ˈsɪləbəl/ *n.* **1.** *Phonetics* a segment of speech uttered with a single impulse of air pressure from the lungs. **2.** (in writing systems) a character or a set of characters representing (more or less exactly) such an element of speech. **3.** the least portion or amount of speech or writing; the least mention: *do not breathe a syllable of all this.* –**syllabic**, *adj.*

syllabus /ˈsɪləbəs/ *n.* (*pl.* **-buses** *or* **-bi** /-baɪ/) **1.** an outline or summary of a course of studies, lectures, etc. **2.** subjects to be studied on a particular course, as at a school, university, etc. **3.** a list: *the syllabus of errors.*

syllogism /ˈsɪlədʒɪzəm/ *n.* **1.** *Logic* an argument with two premises and a conclusion. **2.** deductive reasoning. –**syllogistic** /sɪləˈdʒɪstɪk/, *adj.* –**syllogistically** /sɪləˈdʒɪstɪkli/, *adv.*

sylph /sɪlf/ *n.* **1.** a slender, graceful, lightly moving woman or girl. **2.** one of a race of imaginary beings, supposedly inhabiting the air. –**sylphic**, *adj.*

sylvan /ˈsɪlvən/ *adj.* **1.** of, relating to, or inhabiting the woods. **2.** consisting of or covered with woods or trees; wooded; woody. –*n.* **3.** a fabled deity or spirit of the woods. Also, **silvan**.

sym- variant of **syn-**, before *b*, *p*, and *m*, as in *sympathy*.

symbiosis /sɪmbaɪˈoʊsəs, -bi-/ *n. Biol.* the living together of two species of organisms, a term usually restricted to cases in which the union of the two animals or plants is advantageous or necessary to both, as the case of the fungus and alga which together make up the lichen; mutualism. –**symbiotic** /sɪmbaɪˈɒtɪk/, **symbiotical** /sɪmbaɪˈɒtɪkəl/, *adj.* –**symbiotically** /sɪmbaɪˈɒtɪkli/, *adv.*

symbol /ˈsɪmbəl/ *n.* **1.** something used or regarded as standing for or representing something else; a material object representing something immaterial; an emblem, token, or sign. **2.** a letter, figure, or other character or mark, or a combination of letters or the like, used to represent something: *the algebraic symbol, x; the chemical symbol, Au.* **3.** something which expresses, through suggestion, an idea or mood which would otherwise remain inexpressible or incomprehensible; the meeting point of many analogies. –*v.t.* (**-bolled** *or*, *Chiefly US*, **-boled, -bolling** *or*, *Chiefly US*, **-boling**) **4.** to symbolise. –**symbolic** /sɪmˈbɒlɪk/, *adj.* –**symbolically**, *adv.*

symbolise /ˈsɪmbəlaɪz/ *v.t.* **1.** to be a symbol of; stand for, or represent, as a symbol does. **2.** to represent by a symbol or symbols. **3.** to regard or treat as symbolic. –*v.i.* **4.** to use symbols. Also, **symbolize**. –**symbolisation** /ˌsɪmbəlaɪˈzeɪʃən/, *n.*

symbolism /ˈsɪmbəlɪzəm/ *n.* **1.** the practice of representing things by symbols, or of investing things with a symbolic meaning or character. **2.** a set or system of symbols. **3.** the principles and practice of symbolists in art or literature. –**symbolist**, *n.*

symmetry /ˈsɪmətri/ *n.* (*pl.* **-ries**) **1.** the correspondence, in size, form, and arrangement, of parts on opposite sides of a plane, line, or point; regularity of form or arrangement with reference to corresponding parts. **2.** the proper or due proportion of the parts of a body or whole to one another with regard to size and form; excellence of proportion. –**symmetrical, symmetric**, *adj.*

sympathetic /sɪmpəˈθɛtɪk/ *adj.* **1.** characterised by, proceeding from, exhibiting, or feeling sympathy; sympathising; compassionate. **2.** characterised by a special natural affinity; congenial. **3.** of or relating to the sympathetic nervous system. –*phr.* **4. sympathetic to**

(or **towards**), looking with favour or liking upon: *he is sympathetic to the project.* –**sympathetically**, *adv.*

sympathetic nervous system *n. Anat., Physiol.* that portion of the autonomic nervous system which is made up of a system of nerves and ganglia which arise from the thoracic and lumbar regions of the spinal cord, and which supply the walls of the vascular system and the various viscera and glands where they function in opposition to the parasympathetic nervous system, as in accelerating heartbeat, dilating the pupil of the eye, etc.

sympathise /ˈsɪmpəθaɪz/ *v.i.* **1.** (sometimes fol. by *with*) to be in sympathy, or agreement of feeling; share in a feeling or feelings. **2.** (sometimes fol. by *with*) to feel a compassionate sympathy, as for suffering or trouble. **3.** (sometimes fol. by *with*) to express sympathy or condole. **4.** (sometimes fol. by *with*) to be in approving accord, as with a person, cause, etc.: *sympathise with a person's aims.* **5.** to agree, correspond, or accord. Also, **sympathize**. –**sympathiser**, *n.* –**sympathisingly**, *adv.*

sympathomimetic /sɪmpæθoʊməˈmɛtɪk/ *n.* **1.** one of a class of drugs whose effects mimic those of a stimulated sympathetic nervous system, increasing cardiac output, dilating bronchioles and constricting blood vessels. –*adj.* **2.** of or relating to such a drug.

sympathy /ˈsɪmpəθi/ *n.* (*pl.* **-thies**) **1.** a feeling shared between people. **2.** the shared feeling naturally existing between people of similar tastes or opinion, etc. **3.** the fact or power of entering into the feelings of another, especially in sorrow or trouble; fellow feeling, compassion, or commiseration. **4.** favourable or approving agreement.

symphony /ˈsɪmfəni/ *n.* (*pl.* **-nies**) **1.** *Music* **a.** an elaborate instrumental composition, usually in several (traditionally three or four) movements, similar in form to a sonata but written for an orchestra, and usually of far grander proportions and more varied elements. **b.** an instrumental passage occurring in a vocal composition, or between vocal movements in a composition. **c.** an instrumental piece, often in several movements, forming the overture to an opera or the like. **2.** anything characterised by a harmonious combination of elements and especially an effective combination of colours.

symposium /sɪmˈpoʊziəm/ *n.* (*pl.* **-siums** *or* **-sia** /-ziə/) **1.** a meeting or conference for discussion of some subject. **2.** a collection of opinions expressed, or articles contributed, by several persons on a given subject or topic.

symptom /ˈsɪmptəm/ *n.* **1.** a sign or indication of something. **2.** *Pathol.* a phenomenon which arises from and accompanies a particular disease or disorder and serves as an indication of it. –**symptomless**, *adj.*

symptomatic /sɪmptəˈmætɪk/ *adj.* **1.** relating to a symptom or symptoms. **2.** (sometimes fol. by *of*) of the nature of or constituting a symptom; indicative. **3.** according to symptoms: *a symptomatic classification of disease.* –**symptomatically**, *adv.*

syn- a prefix having the same function as **co-** (def. 1), as in *synthesis, synoptic*. Also, **sy-, syl-, sym-, sys-**.

synagogue /ˈsɪnəgɒg/ *n.* **1.** a Jewish house of worship, usually also providing religious instruction. **2.** an assembly or congregation of the Jews for the purposes of worship. –**synagogical** /sɪnəˈgɒdʒɪkəl/, **synagogal** /ˈsɪnəgɒgəl/, *adj.*

synapse /ˈsaɪnæps/ *n.* the region of contact between processes of two or more nerve cells, across which an impulse passes. –**synaptic**, *adj.*

synchromesh /ˈsɪŋkroʊmɛʃ/ *Motor Vehicles* –*adj.* **1.** of, relating to, or fitted with a system consisting of small friction clutches, by means of which the speeds of the driven and driving gears in a gearbox are automatically synchronised before they engage, to assist gear changing and reduce wear. –*n.* **2.** such a system.

synchronise /ˈsɪŋkrənaɪz/ *v.i.* **1.** to occur at the same time, or coincide or agree in time. **2.** to go on at the same rate and exactly together; recur together. *–v.t.* **3.** to cause to indicate the same time, as one clock with another. **4.** to cause to go on at the same rate and exactly together. Also, **synchronize.** **–synchronisation** /ˌsɪŋkrənaɪˈzeɪʃən/, *n.* **–synchroniser,** *n.* **–synchronous,** *adj.*

synclinal /sɪŋˈklaɪnəl/ *adj.* **1.** sloping downwards in opposite directions so as to meet in a common point or line. **2.** *Geol.* **a.** inclining upwards on both sides from a median line or axis, as a downward fold of rock strata. **b.** relating to such a fold. **–syncline,** *n.*

syncopate /ˈsɪŋkəpeɪt/ *v.t.* *Music* **a.** to place (the accents) on beats which are normally unaccented. **b.** to use notes so affected in (a passage, piece, etc.). **2.** *Ling.* to contract (a word) by omitting one or more sounds from the middle, as in reducing the pronunciation of *Gloucester* from /ˈglɒsəstə/ to /ˈglɒstə/. **–syncopation** /sɪŋkəˈpeɪʃən/, *n.* **–syncopator,** *n.*

syndical /ˈsɪndɪkəl/ *adj.* **1.** of or relating to a union of persons engaged in a particular trade. **2.** of or relating to syndicalism.

syndicate *n.* /ˈsɪndɪkət, ˈsɪndəkət/ **1.** a combination of persons, as business associates, commercial firms, etc., formed for the purpose of carrying out some project, especially one requiring large resources of capital. **2.** *Journalism* any agency which buys and supplies articles, stories, etc., for simultaneous publication in a number of newspapers or other periodicals in different places. *–v.t.* /ˈsɪndəkeɪt/ **3.** to combine into a syndicate. **4.** *Journalism* to publish simultaneously, or supply for simultaneous publication, in a number of newspapers or other periodicals in different places. **–syndication** /sɪndəˈkeɪʃən/, *n.*

syndrome /ˈsɪndroʊm/ *n.* *Pathol.* the pattern of symptoms in a disease or the like; a number of characteristic symptoms occurring together. **–syndromic** /sɪnˈdrɒmɪk/, *adj.*

synergy /ˈsɪnədʒi/ *n.* (*pl.* **-gies**) combined action. **–synergetic,** *adj.*

synod /ˈsɪnəd/ *n.* **1.** *Christian Church* an assembly of ecclesiastics or other church delegates duly convoked, pursuant to the law of the church, for the discussion and decision of ecclesiastical affairs; an ecclesiastical council. **2.** any council. **–synodal,** *adj.*

synonym /ˈsɪnənɪm/ *n.* **1.** a word having the same, or nearly the same, meaning as another in the language, as *joyful, elated, glad.* **2.** a word or expression accepted as another name for something, as *Arcadia* for *pastoral simplicity.* **–synonymic** /sɪnəˈnɪmɪk/, **synonymical** /sɪnəˈnɪməkəl/, *adj.* **–synonymity** /sɪnəˈnɪməti/, *n.* **–synonymous,** *adj.*

synopsis /səˈnɒpsəs/ *n.* (*pl.* **-nopses** /-ˈnɒpsiz/) **1.** a brief or condensed statement giving a general view of some subject. **2.** a compendium of headings or short paragraphs giving a view of the whole. **3.** the outline of the plot of a novel, play, film, etc.

synoptic /səˈnɒptɪk/ *adj.* **1.** relating to or constituting a synopsis; affording or taking a general view of the whole or of the principal parts of a subject. **2.** (*oft. upper case*) taking a common view (applied to the first three Gospels, Matthew, Mark, and Luke, from their similarity in contents, order, and statement). **3.** (*oft. upper case*) relating to the synoptic Gospels. **–synoptically,** *adv.*

synoptic chart *n.* *Meteorol.* a chart showing distribution of meteorological conditions over a region at a given moment.

syntax /ˈsɪntæks/ *n.* **1.** *Gram.* **a.** the patterns of formation of sentences and phrases from words in a particular language. **b.** the study and description thereof. **2.** *Logic*

the branch of modern logic that deals with the various kinds of signs that occur in a system and the possible arrangements of those signs, complete abstraction being made of the meaning of the signs. **–syntactic,** *adj.*

synthesis /ˈsɪnθəsəs/ *n.* (*pl.* **-theses** /-θəsiz/) **1.** the combination of parts or elements, as material substances or objects of thought, into a complex whole (opposed to *analysis*). **2.** a complex whole made up of parts or elements combined. **3.** *Chem.* the forming or building up of a more complex substance or compound by the union of elements or the combination of simpler compounds or radicals. **–synthesist,** *n.*

synthesise /ˈsɪnθəsaɪz/ *v.t.* **1.** to make up by combining parts or elements. **2.** to combine into a complex whole. **3.** to treat synthetically. **4.** *Chem.* to manufacture (a complex product, especially a product resembling one of natural origin) by combining simple substances. Also, **synthesize.** **–synthesisation** /ˌsɪnθəsaɪˈzeɪʃən/, *n.*

synthesiser /ˈsɪnθəsaɪzə/ *n.* **1.** a person or thing that synthesises something. **2.** a machine which creates speech or music by generating electrical signals of different frequencies which are played through an amplifier as single or combined sounds. Also, **synthesizer.**

synthetic /sɪnˈθɛtɪk/ *adj.* Also, **synthetical. 1.** of, relating to, proceeding by, or involving synthesis (opposed to *analytic*). **2.** of or relating to chemical compounds, resins, rubbers, etc., formed by chemical reaction in a laboratory or chemical plant, as opposed to those of natural origin. **3.** (of languages) characterised by the use of affixes (bound forms) to express relationships between words, as in Latin; as opposed to *analytic*, as in English. **4.** denoting or relating to a chemical compound which mimics the effects of a recreational drug: *synthetic cannabis.* *–n.* **5.** something made by a synthetic (chemical) process. **–synthetically,** *adv.*

synthetic drug *n.* **1.** a drug which is made in a laboratory rather than extracted from a natural source. **2.** such a drug which mimics the effects of an illegal drug such as cocaine or marijuana.

syphilis /ˈsɪfələs/ *n.* *Pathol.* a chronic, infectious venereal disease, caused by the microorganism *Spirochaeta pallida*, or *Treponema pallidum* (see **spirochaete**), and transmitted sexually or sometimes from a syphilitic woman to her unborn child. **–syphilitic,** *adj.*

syphon /ˈsaɪfən/ *n., v.t., v.i.* → **siphon.**

syringe /səˈrɪndʒ, ˈsɪrɪndʒ/ *n.* **1.** *Med.* a small device consisting of a glass, metal, rubber, or plastic tube, narrowed at its outlet, and fitted with either a piston or a rubber bulb for drawing in a quantity of fluid and ejecting it in a stream, injecting fluids into the body, etc. **2.** any similar device for pumping and spraying liquids through a small aperture. *–v.t.* (**-ringed, -ringing**) **3.** to cleanse, wash, inject, etc., by means of a syringe.

syrup /ˈsɪrəp/ *n.* **1.** any of various sweet, more or less viscid liquids, consisting of fruit, juices, water, etc., boiled with sugar. **2.** any of various solutions of sugar used in pharmacy. **3.** any of various thick sweet liquids for use in cookery, prepared from molasses, glucose, etc., water, and often with a flavouring agent. Also, *US*, **sirup.**

sys- variant of **syn-**, before *s*, as in *syssarcosis.*

systaltic /sɪsˈtæltɪk/ *adj.* **1.** rhythmically contracting. **2.** of the nature of contraction. **3.** characterised by alternate contraction (systole) and dilatation (diastole), as the action of the heart.

system /ˈsɪstəm/ *n.* **1.** a combination of things or parts forming a complex whole: *a mountain system*; *a railway system.* **2.** any set of correlated members: *a system of currency*; *a system of shorthand characters.* **3.** an ordered and wide grouping of facts, principles, doctrines, etc., in a particular field of knowledge or thought: *a system of philosophy.* **4.** an ordered body of methods; scheme or plan: *a system of marking*; *a system of numbering*; *a measuring system.* **5.** an orderly way of doing something: *to have system in one's work.* **6.** *Biol.* **a.** a grouping of parts of organs of the same or similar tissues, or with the same function: *the nervous system*; *the digestive system.* **b.** the entire human or animal body: *to get rid of poison from the system.* **7.** (*also pl.*) *Computers* (in data-processing) the working together of personnel, procedure, hardware, and software. **8.** *Geol.* a major division of rocks comprising sedimentary deposits and igneous masses formed during a geological period. **9.** society generally or an organisation within it: *to buck the system.* **–systemless**, *adj.*

system administrator *n.* a person responsible for maintaining a multi-user computer system.

systematic /ˌsɪstə'mætɪk/ *adj.* **1.** having, showing, or involving a system, method, or plan: *a systematic course of reading, systematic efforts.* **2.** characterised by system or method; methodical: *a systematic person, systematic habits.* **3.** arranged in or comprising an ordered system: *systematic theology.* **4.** concerned with classification: *systematic botany.* **5.** relating to, based on, or in accordance with a system of classification: *the systematic names of plants.* Also, **systematical. –systematically**, *adv.*

systematise /'sɪstəmətaɪz/ *v.t.* to arrange in or according to a system; reduce to a system; make systematic. Also, **systematize. –systematisation** /ˌsɪstəmətaɪ'zeɪʃən/, *n.* **–systematiser**, *n.*

systemic /sɪs'tɛmɪk, sɪs'timɪk/ *adj.* **1.** of or relating to a system. **2.** *Pathol., Physiol.* **a.** of or relating to the entire bodily system, or the body as a whole. **b.** of or relating to a particular system of parts or organs of the body. **–systemically**, *adv.*

system operator *n.* a person who assists in the maintenance of a computer system.

systems analysis *n.* the analysis of an activity or project, usually with the aid of a computer, to determine its aims, methods, and effectiveness. **–systems analyst**, *n.*

systems engineer *n.* an engineer who is concerned with the design of systems in the light of systems analysis and information theory. **–systems engineering**, *n.*

systole /'sɪstəli/ *n. Physiol.* the normal rhythmical contraction of the heart, especially that of the ventricles, which drives the blood into the aorta and the pulmonary artery. Compare **diastole. –systolic** /sɪs'tɒlɪk/, *adj.*

T t

T, t /ti/ *n.* **1.** a consonant, the 20th letter of the English alphabet. **2.** something shaped like the letter T. –*phr.* **3. to a T**, exactly: *to suit to a T; to fit to a T.*

-t 1. a suffix forming the regular past tense or past participle of certain verbs, as in *built, spent.* **2.** a suffix which alternates with **-ed**[1] and **-ed**[2] in forming the past tense or past participle of certain verbs such as *dreamt, spelt,* and is regularly used for the participial adjective, as in *burnt toast, spilt milk.*

tab[1] /tæb/ *n.* **1.** a small flap, strap, loop, or similar appendage, as on a garment, etc. **2.** a tag or label. **3. a.** a stiffened projection from a file, document, or the like, for ready identification; tag. **b.** a graphic representation of this on a computer screen, which, when clicked, opens the document to which it is linked. –*v.t.* (**tabbed, tabbing**) **4.** to furnish or ornament with a tab or tabs. –*phr. Colloq.* **5. keep tabs on**, to keep account of or a check on: *keep tabs on your expenses.* **6. pick up the tab**, to pay the bill.

tab[2] /tæb/ *n.* → **tab key.**

tabby /ˈtæbi/ *n.* (*pl.* **-bies**) **1.** a cat with a striped or brindled coat. –*adj.* **2.** striped or brindled. Also, **tabbie.**

tabernacle /ˈtæbənækəl/ *n.* **1.** (in the Old Testament) a tent used by the Israelites as a portable sanctuary before their final settlement in Palestine. **2.** any place of worship, especially one for a large congregation. **3.** *Church* an ornamental container for the reserved Eucharist. –**tabernacular** /tæbəˈnækjələ/, *adj.*

tab key *n.* a key on a typewriter or computer keyboard which is depressed to set the point at which the line or section of the line of type begins. Also, **tab.**

table /ˈteɪbəl/ *n.* **1.** an article of furniture consisting of a flat top resting on legs or on a pillar. **2.** such an article of furniture designed for the playing of any of various games: *a billiard table.* **3.** the board at or round which persons sit at meals. **4.** a company of persons at a table, as for a meal, game, or business transaction. **5.** a flat or plane surface; a level area. **6.** a flat and relatively thin piece of wood, stone, metal, or other hard substance, especially one artificially shaped for a particular purpose. **7.** *Archit.* a flat, vertical, usually rectangular surface forming a distinct feature in a wall, and often ornamental. **8.** a smooth, flat board or slab on which inscriptions, etc., may be put. **9.** an arrangement of words, numbers, or signs, or combinations of them, as the multiplication table, to exhibit a set of facts or relations in a definite, compact, and comprehensive form; a synopsis or scheme. –*v.t.* **10.** to place (a proposal, etc.) on the table of an assembly for discussion. –*phr.* **11. keep a good table**, to provide plentiful, high-quality food. **12. on the table**, under discussion; put forward for discussion. **13. turn the tables**, to cause a complete reversal of circumstances. **14. under the table, a.** *Colloq.* drunk to the extent of being incapable. **b.** given as a bribe. –**tableless**, *adj.*

tableau /ˈtæbloʊ/ *n.* (*pl.* **-leaux** /-loʊz, -loʊ/ *or* **-leaus**) **1.** a picture, as of a scene. **2.** a picturesque grouping of persons or objects; a striking scene.

tableland /ˈteɪbəllænd/ *n.* an elevated and generally level region of considerable extent; a plateau.

tablespoon /ˈteɪbəlspun/ *n.* **1.** a spoon larger than a teaspoon and a dessertspoon, used in the service of the table and as a standard measuring unit in recipes. **2.** a

unit of capacity, equal to four household teaspoons. **3.** the quantity a tablespoon holds; tablespoonful.

tablet /ˈtæblət/ *n.* **1.** a small, flat or flattish piece of some solid substance, such as a drug, chemical, soap, etc. **2.** *US* a writing pad. **3.** a small, flat slab or surface, especially one that can be carved or written on. **4.** Also, **tablet computer.** a small, portable computer which has one side as a touch screen, and an on-screen virtual keyboard.

table tennis *n.* a miniature tennis game usually played indoors on a table, with small bats and a hollow celluloid or plastic ball; ping-pong.

tablet PC *n.* a tablet computer with a PC operating system, having a touch screen attached by a swivel or slide joint so that the touch screen can be moved out of use to expose the keyboard.

tabloid /ˈtæblɔɪd/ *n.* **1.** a newspaper, with pages about half the size of a broadsheet. **2.** such a newspaper, characterised as favouring pictorial presentations and short articles, and adopting a sensationalised editorial approach. –*adj.* **3.** compressed in or as in a tabloid: *a tabloid newspaper.*

taboo /təˈbu, tæ-/ *adj.* **1.** forbidden to general use; placed under a prohibition or ban. **2.** (among the Polynesians and other peoples of the southern Pacific) separated or set apart as sacred or unclean. –*n.* (*pl.* **-boos**) **3.** a prohibiting from use or practice. **4.** (among Polynesians, etc.) a system, practice, or act, whereby things are set apart as holy, forbidden to general use, or placed under a ban. –*v.t.* (**-booed, -booing**) **5.** to put under a taboo; prohibit; forbid. Also, **tabu.**

tabular /ˈtæbjələ/ *adj.* **1.** relating to or of the nature of a table or tabulated arrangement. **2.** ascertained from or computed by the use of tables. **3.** having the form of a table, tablet, or tablature. **4.** flat and expansive. –**tabularly**, *adv.*

tabulate *v.t.* /ˈtæbjəleɪt/ **1.** to put or form into a table, scheme, or synopsis; formulate tabularly. –*v.i.* /ˈtæbjəleɪt/ **2.** to operate or set the tab on a typewriter. –*adj.* /ˈtæbjələt, -leɪt/ **3.** shaped like a table or tablet; tabular. **4.** having transverse septa, as certain corals. –**tabulation** /tæbjəˈleɪʃən/, *n.*

tacheometer /tækiˈɒmətə/ *n.* → **tachometer** (def. 3). –**tacheometric** /ˌtækiəˈmɛtrɪk/, **tacheometrical** /ˌtækiə-ˈmɛtrɪkəl/, *adj.* –**tacheometrically** /ˌtækiəˈmɛtrɪkli/, *adv.* –**tacheometry**, *n.*

tacho- a word element meaning 'swift'.

tachometer /tæˈkɒmətə/ *n.* **1.** an instrument for measuring the number of revolutions per minute made by a revolving shaft, as that in a motor vehicle which indicates the revolutions per minute of the engine. **2.** an instrument for determining the speed of blood in the vessels. **3.** Also, **tacheometer, tachymeter.** an instrument used in surveying to measure the distance from the point of observation to another point at which a staff is held. The length of the staff seen between two reference hairs in the telescope of the instrument is multiplied by a factor to give the distance. **4.** any of various other instruments for measuring speed. –**tachometric** /tækəˈmɛtrɪk/, **tachometrical** /tækə-ˈmɛtrɪkəl/, *adj.* –**tachometrically** /tækəˈmɛtrɪkli/, *adv.* –**tachometry**, *n.*

tachy- a word element meaning swift, as in *tachygraphy.*

tachymeter /tæˈkɪmətə/ *n.* → **tachometer** (def. 3). –**tachymetric** /tækəˈmɛtrɪk/, **tachymetrical** /tækəˈmɛtrɪkəl/, *adj.* –**tachymetrically** /tækəˈmɛtrɪkli/, *adv.* –**tachymetry,** *n.*

tacit /ˈtæsət/ *adj.* **1.** silent; saying nothing. **2.** not openly expressed, but implied; understood or inferred. **3.** unspoken: *tacit consent.* –**tacitly,** *adv.* –**tacitness,** *n.*

taciturn /ˈtæsətɜn/ *adj.* inclined to silence, or reserved in speech; not inclined to conversation. –**taciturnity** /tæsəˈtɜnəti/, *n.* –**taciturnly,** *adv.*

tack¹ /tæk/ *n.* **1.** a short, sharp-pointed nail or pin, usually with a flat and comparatively large head. **2.** a stitch, especially a long stitch used in fastening seams, etc., preparatory to a more thorough sewing. **3.** a fastening, especially in a temporary manner. **4.** the quality of being tacky; stickiness. **5.** *Naut.* **a.** the direction or course of a ship in relation to the position of its sails: *the starboard tack* (when close-hauled with the wind on the starboard side); *the port tack* (when close-hauled with the wind on the port side). **b.** a course taken obliquely against the wind. **c.** one of the series of straight runs which make up the zigzag course of a ship proceeding to windward. **6.** a course of action or conduct, especially one differing from some preceding or other course. **7.** one of the movements of a zigzag course on land. **8.** the equipment collectively which relates to the saddling and harnessing of horses; saddlery. –*v.t.* **9.** to fasten by a tack or tacks: *to tack a rug.* **10.** to secure by some slight or temporary fastening. **11.** *Naut.* **a.** to change the course of (a ship) to the opposite tack. **b.** to navigate (a ship) by a series of tacks. –*v.i.* **12.** *Naut.* **a.** to change the course of a ship by bringing its head into the wind and then causing the ship to fall off on the other side: *we were ordered to tack at once.* **b.** to change course in this way, as a ship. **c.** to proceed to windward by a series of courses as close to the wind as the vessel will sail, the wind being alternately on one bow and then on the other. **13.** to follow a zigzag course or route. –*phr.* **14. on the wrong tack,** following a false line of reasoning; under a wrong impression. **15. tack on,** (sometimes fol. by *to*) to attach as something supplementary; append or annex. –**tacker,** *n.* –**tackless,** *adj.*

tack² /tæk/ *n.* food; fare: *hard tack.*

tackle /ˈtækəl/ *n.* **1.** apparatus or gear, especially for fishing. **2.** a mechanism or apparatus, such as a rope and block or a combination of ropes and blocks, for lifting, lowering, moving objects or materials. **3.** *Naut.* the gear and rigging used in handling a ship, especially that used in working the sails, etc. **4.** the act of tackling, as in football. –*v.t.* **5.** to undertake to deal with, master, solve, etc. **6.** *Soccer, Hockey, etc.* to (attempt) to get the ball from (an opponent). **7.** *Rugby, etc.* to seize and pull down (an opponent having the ball). –**tackler,** *n.*

tacky¹ /ˈtæki/ *adj.* (**-kier, -kiest**) adhesive; sticky, as a paint, varnish, or the like, when partly dry. –**tackiness,** *n.*

tacky² /ˈtæki/ *adj.* (**-kier, -kiest**) *Colloq.* **1.** shabby; dowdy. **2.** superficially attractive but lacking quality or craftsmanship. **3.** in bad taste; vulgar. –**tackiness,** *n.* –**tackily,** *adv.*

taco /ˈtakoʊ, ˈtækoʊ/ *n.* a tortilla, usually fried so that it is crisp, folded around a savoury filling.

tact /tækt/ *n.* **1.** a keen sense of what to say or do to avoid giving offence; skill in dealing with difficult or delicate situations. **2.** touch; the sense of touch. –**tactful,** *adj.* –**tactless,** *adj.*

tactic /ˈtæktɪk/ *n.* **1.** (*pl.*) → **tactics. 2.** a system or a detail of tactics. **3.** a plan or procedure for achieving a desired end. –**tactical,** *adj.*

tactics /ˈtæktɪks/ *pl. n.* **1.** (*construed as sing.*) the art or science of disposing military or naval forces for battle

and manoeuvring them in battle. **2.** the manoeuvres themselves. **3.** mode of procedure for gaining advantage or success. –**tactician** /tækˈtɪʃən/, *n.*

tactile /ˈtæktaɪl/ *adj.* **1.** of or relating to the organs or sense of touch; endowed with the sense of touch. **2.** perceptible to the touch; tangible. –**tactility** /tækˈtɪləti/, *n.*

tad /tæd/ *phr.* **a tad, 1.** a small amount: *it won't make a tad of difference.* **2.** to a small extent: *a tad too salty.*

tadpole /ˈtædpoʊl/ *n.* the aquatic larva or immature form of frogs, toads, etc., especially after the enclosure of the gills and before the appearance of the forelimbs and the resorption of the tail.

tae bo /taɪ ˈboʊ/ *n.* an aerobic exercise regime using martial arts sequences at a rapid pace.

taffeta /ˈtæfətə/ *n.* **1.** a lustrous silk or rayon fabric of plain weave. **2.** any of various other fabrics of silk, linen, wool, etc., in use at different periods.

tag¹ /tæg/ *n.* **1.** a piece or strip of strong paper, leather, or the like, for attaching by one end to something as a mark or label. **2.** any small hanging or loosely attached part or piece; tatter. **3.** a loop of material sewn on a garment so that it can be hung up. **4.** a point or binding of metal, plastic, or other hard substance at the end of a cord, lace, or the like. **5.** a tag end. **6.** the refrain of a song or poem. **7.** the last words of a speech in a play, etc., as a curtain line or cue. **8.** (in popular music) a coda. **9.** an addition to a speech or writing, as the moral of a fable. **10.** a trite quotation or cliché, especially one in Latin. **11.** a word or phrase applied as characteristic of a person or group. **12.** a curlicue in writing. **13.** the identifying mark or signature of a graffitist. **14.** a lock of hair. **15.** a matted lock of wool on a sheep. **16.** *Computers* a type of marker used in a markup language, usually one of a pair which open and close the element, by which elements of a document, database, etc., can be recognised by a parser. **17.** *Internet* a caption to a digital photograph viewed online. –*v.t.* (**tagged, tagging**) **18.** to furnish with a tag or tags; to attach a tag to. **19.** (of a graffitist) to identify (graffiti) with a tag (def. 13). **20.** to append as a tag to something else. **21.** to apply as characteristic a word or phrase to (a person or group). **22.** *Colloq.* to follow closely. **23.** to attach a price tag to; to price. **24.** to identify (a digital picture viewed online) with a caption. –*phr.* **25. tag along,** *Colloq.* to follow closely; go along or about as a follower.

tag² /tæg/ *n.* **1.** a children's game in which one player chases the others until he or she touches one of them, who then takes his or her place as pursuer. **2.** *Wrestling* an act of touching hands over the top rope by two teammates in tag wrestling. –*adj.* **3.** of or relating to a form of professional wrestling in which two teams of two compete one at a time but with partners interchanging. –*v.t.* (**tagged, tagging**) **4.** to touch in or as in the game of tag.

tagine /taˈʒin/ *n.* **1.** (in Moroccan cookery) a slow-cooked stew, usually featuring meat or poultry with vegetables and spices, traditionally cooked in a shallow earthenware dish with a tall, cone-shaped lid; often served with couscous. **2.** the cooking dish itself. Also, **tajine.**

tag question *n. Gram.* a question in the form of a statement followed by a short question, as in *It is cold today, isn't it?* or *We must leave immediately, do you agree?*

tai chi /taɪ ˈtʃi/ *n.* a form of stylised exercises based on Chinese martial arts which emphasises the smooth transition of one movement into another while retaining balance.

tail /teɪl/ *n.* **1.** the hindmost part of an animal, especially when forming a distinct flexible appendage to the trunk. **2.** something resembling or suggesting this in shape or position: *the tail of a kite.* **3.** the hinder, bottom, or concluding part of anything; the rear. **4.** the rear of a mob of sheep or cattle. **5.** the small piece of electrical wiring from a meter or mains to which wiring from a house is attached. **6.** the final or concluding part of anything, as in cricket, the last people to bat. **7.** the inferior or refuse part of anything. **8.** *Astron.* the luminous stream of dust and gas particles extending from the head of a comet. **9.** (*pl.*) *Colloq.* the reverse of a coin. **10.** (*pl.*) (in two-up) the falling of the coins so that both tails are upward. **11.** an arrangement of objects or persons which extends like a tail. **12.** a downward stroke, as of a printed or written letter, the stem of a musical note, etc. **13.** *Aeronautics* the stabilising and control surfaces at the after end of an aircraft. **14.** (*pl.*) **a.** a man's dress coat having the lower part cut away over the hips and descending in a pair of tapering skirts behind. **b.** full-dress attire. **15.** *Printing, Bookbinding* the bottom of a page or book. **16.** *Colloq.* a person who follows another, especially one who is employed to do so in order to observe or hinder escape. **17.** *Colloq.* the buttocks. *–adj.* **18.** coming from behind: *a tail thrust.* **19.** being at the back or rear: *a tail light. –v.t.* **20.** to form or furnish with a tail. **21.** to form or constitute the tail or end of (a procession, etc.). **22.** to terminate; follow like a tail. **23.** to join or attach (one thing) at the tail or end of another. **24.** to tend or herd (sheep or cattle). **25.** to dock the tail of: *tailed lambs.* **26.** *Bot.* to remove the style (def. 10) of. **27.** *Colloq.* to follow in order to hinder escape or to observe: *to tail a suspect. –v.i.* **28.** to form or move in a line or continuation suggestive of a tail: *hikers tailing up a narrow path.* **29.** (of a boat, etc.) to have or take a position with the stern in a particular direction. **30.** *Colloq.* to follow close behind. *–phr.* **31. a bit** (or **piece**) **of tail**, *Colloq.* a person considered as a sexual object. **32. chase one's tail**, *Colloq.* to be very busy trying to catch up with tasks which have accumulated. **33. tail away** (or **off**), to decrease gradually; decline. **34. tail in**, *Building Trades* **a.** to fasten (a beam, etc.) by building one of its ends into a wall. **b.** (of a beam, etc.) to be fastened by the end built into a wall. **35. tail out**, to guide (timber) as it comes off the saw. **36. tail them**, *Two-up* to throw the coins with the result that both fall tails upward. **37. turn tail, a.** to turn the back, as in aversion or fright. **b.** to run away; flee. **38. with one's tail between one's legs**, in a state of utter defeat or humiliation; abjectly. **–tailless,** *adj.*

tailgate /'teɪlgeɪt/ *n.* **1.** Also, **tailboard.** the board at the back of a truck, wagon, etc., which can be removed or let down for convenience in loading and unloading. **2.** *Jazz* the flamboyant style of trombone-playing characteristic of traditional New Orleans jazz, so called because in processions the trombonist sat at the rear of a lorry. *–v.t.* **3.** to drive close behind (another vehicle). **–tailgating,** *n.*

tailor /'teɪlə/ *n.* **1.** someone whose business is to make or mend outer garments, especially for men. **2.** Also, **tailer, taylor.** an Australian sportfish, *Pomatomus saltatrix*, which has a scissor-like meshing of its teeth. *–v.i.* **3.** to do the work of a tailor. *–v.t.* **4.** to make by tailor's work. **5.** to fit or furnish with clothing. **6.** to design for a particular need or taste: *to tailor prices for the market.* **–tailorless,** *adj.*

tailplane /'teɪlpleɪn/ *n.* a horizontal surface at the rear end of an aircraft providing longitudinal stability; horizontal stabiliser.

tailwind /'teɪlwɪnd/ *n.* a favourable wind blowing from behind an aircraft or vessel, etc., thus increasing its speed.

taint /teɪnt/ *n.* **1.** a touch of something unpleasant or harmful. **2.** a trace of infection, dishonour, etc. *–v.t.* **3.** to infect as if by a touch of something unpleasant or

harmful. **4.** to make bad or evil; infect or corrupt. **5.** to spoil; tarnish. *–v.i.* **6.** to become tainted. **–taintless,** *adj.*

taipan /'taɪpæn/ *n.* a long-fanged, highly venomous snake, *Oxyuranus scutellatus*, of northern Australia and New Guinea, brownish in colour, with a long head and slender body, averaging 2 to 2.5 metres in length.

take /teɪk/ *verb* (**took, taken, taking**) *–v.t.* **1.** to get into one's hands or possession by force or artifice. **2.** to seize, catch, or capture. **3.** to grasp, grip, or hold. **4.** to get into one's hold, possession, control, etc., by one's own action but without force or artifice. **5.** to select; pick out from a number: *take a chocolate from a box.* **6.** to receive or accept willingly. **7.** to receive by way of payment or charge. **8.** to obtain by making payment: *to take a house in Paddington.* **9.** to get or obtain from a source; derive. **10.** to receive into the body or system, as by swallowing or inhaling: *to take food.* **11.** to eat or use habitually, as a foodstuff, flavouring, etc.: *to take sugar in tea.* **12.** to quote, especially without acknowledgement: *this writer has taken whole pages from Eliot.* **13.** to remove by death. **14.** to subtract or deduct: *to take 2 from 5.* **15.** to carry or convey: *take your lunch with you.* **16.** to convey or transport: *we took the children to the beach by car.* **17.** to have recourse to (a vehicle, etc.) as a means of progression or travel: *to take a bus to the top of the hill.* **18.** to effect a change in the position or condition of: *his ability took him to the top.* **19.** to conduct or lead: *where will this road take me?* **20.** to attempt to get over, through, round, etc. (something that presents itself), or succeed in doing this: *the horse took the hedge with an easy jump.* **21.** (of a disease, illness, or the like) to attack or affect: *to be taken with a fit.* **22.** to become affected by: *a stone which will take a high polish.* **23.** to absorb or become impregnated with (a colour, etc.). **24.** to surprise; detect; come upon: *to take a thief in the act of stealing.* **25.** to receive or adopt (a person) into some specified or implied relation: *to take a man in marriage.* **26.** to have sexual intercourse with. **27.** to secure regularly by payment: *to take a magazine.* **28.** to adopt and enter upon (a way, course, etc.); proceed to deal with in some manner: *to take a matter under consideration.* **29.** to proceed to occupy: *to take a seat.* **30.** to receive in a specified manner. **31.** to avail oneself of (an opportunity, etc.). **32.** to obtain or exact (satisfaction or reparation). **33.** to receive, or be the recipient of (something bestowed, administered, etc.): *to take first prize.* **34.** to have, undergo, enjoy, etc., as for one's benefit: *to take a bath; take a rest.* **35.** to occupy, use up, or consume (space, material, time, etc.). **36.** to attract and hold: *a well-dressed shop window takes one's eye.* **37.** to captivate or charm: *a pretty ring takes one's fancy.* **38.** to assume or adopt (a symbol, badge, or the like): *to take the veil.* **39.** to make, put forth, etc.: *to take exception.* **40.** to write down (notes, a copy, etc.): *to take a record of a speech.* **41.** to go onto (a place of action): *to take the stage; to take the field.* **42.** to make (a reproduction, picture, or photograph of something). **43.** to make a figure or picture, especially a photograph, of (a person or thing). **44.** to ascertain by inquiry, examination, measurement, scientific observation, etc.: *to take a reading; to take someone's pulse.* **45.** to begin to have (a certain feeling or state of mind); experience or feel (delight, pride, etc.). **46.** to form and hold in the mind: *to take a gloomy view.* **47.** to understand in a specified way: *how do you take this?* **48.** to regard or consider: *he was taken to be wealthy.* **49.** to assume or undertake (a function, duty, responsibility, etc.). **50.** to assume the obligation of (a vow, pledge, etc.); perform or discharge (a part, service, etc.). **51.** to assume or adopt as one's own (a part or side in a contest, etc.); assume or appropriate as if by right: *to take the credit for something; to take a liberty.* **52.** to grasp or apprehend, understand, or comprehend. **53.** to do, perform, execute, etc.: *to take a walk.* **54.** to accept and comply with (advice, etc.). **55.** to suffer or undergo: *to take insults.* **56.** to enter into the enjoyment of (recreation, a holiday, etc.). **57.** to employ for some specified or implied purpose: *to take measures to check an evil.* **58.** to require: *it takes courage to do that.* **59.** *Cards, Chess, etc.* to capture or win (a trick, piece, etc.). **60.** *Gram.* to have by usage, either as part of itself or with it in construction (a particular form, accent, etc., or a case, mood, etc.): *'police' takes a plural verb.* –*v.i.* **61.** to catch or engage, as a mechanical device. **62.** to strike root, or begin to grow, as a plant. **63.** to adhere, as ink, etc. **64.** to win favour or acceptance, as a play. **65.** to have the intended result or effect, as a medicine, inoculation, etc. **66.** to admit of being taken (out, apart, etc.): *the box takes apart easily.* **67.** *Angling* (of a fish) to bite. –*v. (copular)* **68.** to become (sick or ill). –*n.* **69.** an act or instance of taking. **70.** that which is taken. **71.** the quantity of fish, etc., taken at one time. **72.** money taken; gross profit; takings. **73.** *Film, etc.* **a.** a scene or a portion of a scene photographed at one time without any interruption or break. **b.** an instance of such continuous operation of the camera. **74.** *Recording* a single uninterrupted sequence of recorded sound. **75.** *Colloq.* a cheat; swindle. **76.** *Med.* a successful inoculation, vaccination, or the like. **77.** *Mining* a two-month period for which tributers would work on a pitch of ore at a set percentage. **78.** *Mining* a mineral-bearing area which a miner is permitted to work; a holding. –*phr.* **79. on the take,** *Colloq.* accepting bribes or benefits. **80. take aback,** to surprise; disconcert; startle. **81. take after, a.** to resemble (a parent, etc.). **b.** *US* to pursue. **82. take away, a.** to carry off or remove. **b.** to subtract (a number): *take away the number you first thought of.* **c.** minus: *four take away two is two.* **83. take back, a.** to retrieve; regain possession of. **b.** to retract or withdraw. **c.** to allow to return: *she would not take back her erring husband.* **d.** to return for exchange, etc.: *the radio was faulty so we took it back.* **84. take care,** to act or think cautiously. **85. take care of,** to look after; protect. **86. take down, a.** to pull down. **b.** to remove by pulling apart or taking apart. **c.** to write down. **d.** to take advantage of (someone); cheat; swindle. **87. take down a peg (or two),** to humble: *I'll take him down a peg or two.* **88. take for,** to believe or assume to be, especially mistakenly: *I took him for the postman.* **89. take for a ride,** *Colloq.* **a.** to deceive or cheat. **b.** to kidnap and murder. **90. take for granted, a.** to accept or assume without question. **b.** to fail to ascribe credit, merit, worth, or the like to: *it is very upsetting to have one's work taken for granted.* **91. take from,** to detract from or reduce: *he may behave foolishly, but that does not take from the value of his work.* **92. take in, a.** to receive and accommodate; provide lodging for. **b.** to alter (a garment) in order to make it smaller; reduce the size or measurement of. **c.** to include; encompass. **d.** to comprehend; understand; grasp the meaning of. **e.** to deceive, trick, or cheat. **93. take it, a.** *Colloq.* to endure pain, misfortune or the like with fortitude. **b.** to react in a manner specified: *when I broke the news, he took it very badly.* **c.** to assume: *I take it from your silence that this is true.* **94. take it or leave it, a.** to accept or reject the current offer, proposition, article for sale, etc. **b.** to consider something with indifference. **95. take it out,** *Colloq.* **a.** to serve a period of time in jail instead of paying a fine. **b.** to have sexual intercourse with a tradesperson, creditor, etc., in lieu of paying an account. **96. take it out of,** to exhaust; sap the strength or energy of. **97. take it out on,** to vent wrath, anger, or the like on. **98. take off, a.** to remove, as of clothing. **b.** to lead off or away. **c.** to set off; take one's departure; go away. **d.** *Surfing* to begin to ride a wave.

e. to withdraw or remove from: *to take oysters off the menu because of the polluted river.* **f.** to spend as holiday time: *to take three days off.* **g.** to deduct: *I'll take off $20 if you pay cash.* **h.** to become popular: *the internet took off in the 1980s.* **i.** to leave the ground, as an aeroplane. **j.** to escalate: *prices took off.* **k.** to become excited. **l.** to reach a level of excellence, success, flair, etc.: *the play took off in the last act.* **m.** to imitate so as to caricature or ridicule. **99. take on, a.** to hire (workers). **b.** to undertake to handle. **c.** to acquire: *to take on a new aspect.* **d.** to start a quarrel or fight with: *take on someone your own size.* **e.** to stand up to in a situation of conflict, especially political. **f.** to win popularity: *yoyos took on rapidly with children.* **g.** to show great excitement, grief, or other emotion. **100. take on board,** *Colloq.* to accept and use: *they took that idea on board.* **101. take out, a.** to extract: *to take out a tooth.* **b.** to escort or accompany (someone) assuming responsibility for the arrangements: *he took the children out yesterday.* **c.** to treat (someone) to dinner at a restaurant, an entertainment, etc. **d.** to obtain; apply for and get: *to take out an insurance policy.* **e.** to vent: *to take out one's rage on the dog.* **f.** to destroy; eliminate; render harmless: *to take out a military installation by bombing.* **g.** *Aust., NZ* to win (a prize): *to take out the cup.* **102. take over, a.** to assume complete control: *in any activity she takes over.* **b.** to assume or acquire control of: *to take over a company.* **103. take possession,** to enter into ownership, as of an estate. **104. take place,** to happen; occur. **105. take someone off,** *Colloq.* to imitate or mimic someone. **106. take someone up on,** to accept someone's offer of. **107. take the bull by the horns,** to act directly and promptly, particularly in a difficult situation. **108. take to, a.** to apply, devote, or addict oneself to: *to take to drink.* **b.** to respond (as specified, or if unspecified, favourably) to, as to: *to take to one's bed.* **d.** to resort to; have recourse to: *to take to one's heels.* **e.** to attack: *he took to his brother with a hairbrush.* **109. take up, a.** to lift; pick up. **b.** to occupy oneself with; adopt the practice or study of: *to take up Greek.* **c.** to occupy (time, space, or the like). **d.** to resume or continue: *to take up where one left off.* **e.** to accept (an offer). **f.** to commence (a job). **g.** to possession as owner or tenant of (a grant of Crown land). **h.** *Mining Colloq.* to reopen and mine (an abandoned mine). **110. take upon oneself,** to assume the responsibility for. **111. take up with,** to begin to associate with. –**taker,** *n.*

takeaway /'teɪkəweɪ/ *n.* **1.** food or beverage purchased for consumption elsewhere **2.** a place where takeaway food is sold. –*adj.* **3.** of or relating to such a meal or the place where it is sold.

take-off *n.* **1.** the leaving of the ground, as in leaping or jumping. **2.** the place or point at which one leaves the ground, as in jumping. **3.** the initial phase of an aeroplane flight in which the plane leaves the ground. **4.** *Colloq.* an imitating or mimicking; caricature.

takeover /'teɪkoʊvə/ *n.* **1.** acquisition of control, especially of a business company, by the purchase of the majority of its shares. **2.** the acquisition of control over another country, usually by means of force. –*adj.* **3.** of or relating to such acquisition: *a takeover bid.*

talc /tælk/ *n.* **1.** Also, **talcum** /'tælkəm/ a soft greenish grey mineral, hydrous magnesium silicate, $Mg_3Si_4O_{10}(OH)_2$ or $3MgO.4SiO_2.H_2O$, unctuous to the touch, and occurring usually in foliated, granular, or fibrous masses, used in making lubricants, talcum powder, electrical insulation, etc. **2.** → **talcum powder.** –*v.t.* (**talcked** *or* **talced** /tælkt/, **talcking** *or* **talcing** /'tælkɪŋ/) **3.** to treat or rub with talc. –**talcose,** *adj.*

talcum powder /'tælkəm paʊdə/ *n.* powdered talc or soapstone, usually perfumed for toilet use.

tale /teɪl/ *n.* **1.** a narrative purporting to relate the facts about some real or imaginary event, incident, or case; a story. **2.** a literary composition having the form of such a narrative: *Chaucer's 'Canterbury Tales'.* **3.** a falsehood; lie. **4.** a rumour or piece of gossip, especially when malicious.

talent /'tælənt/ *n.* **1.** a special natural ability or aptitude: *a talent for drawing.* **2.** a capacity for achievement or success; natural ability: *young men of talent.* **3.** persons of ability. **4.** (in television, film, or radio) anyone who is either invited as a guest or employed as a performer on a particular program. **5.** *Colloq.* at a party, dance, etc., women or men viewed as possible sexual partners. –**talented**, *adj.*

talisman /'tælɪzmən/ *n.* (*pl.* **-mans**) **1.** a stone, ring, or other object engraved with figures or characters under certain superstitious observances of the heavens and supposedly possessing occult powers; often worn as an amulet or charm. **2.** any amulet or charm. **3.** anything of almost magic power. –**talismanic** /tælɪz'mænɪk/, **talismanical** /tælɪz'mænɪkəl/, *adj.*

talk /tɔk/ *v.i.* **1.** to speak or converse; perform the act of speaking. **2.** to make known or interchange ideas, information, etc., by means of spoken words. **3.** to consult or confer. **4.** to gossip. **5.** to reveal information: *to make a spy talk.* **6.** to communicate ideas by other means than speech, as by writing, keying, signs, or signals. **7.** (of computers) to communicate; to be compatible in terms of software so that information can be exchanged and processed. –*v.t.* **8.** to express in words; utter: *to talk sense.* **9.** to use as a spoken language; speak: *he can talk French.* **10.** to discuss: *to talk politics.* –*n.* **11.** the act of talking; speech; conversation, especially of a familiar or informal kind. **12.** a lecture or informal speech. **13.** a conference. **14.** report or rumour; gossip. **15.** a subject or occasion of talking, especially of gossip. **16.** mere empty speech. **17.** a way of talking: *baby talk.* **18.** language, dialect, or lingo. –*phr.* **19. be talking ...**, to nominate (a concept) as the essential element in a discussion, situation, proposition, etc.: *I'm talking republicanism here; we're talking major dag.* **20. talk about ...**, *Colloq.* used to emphasise the magnitude of the attribute or action specified: *talk about laugh.* **21. talk back**, (sometimes fol. by *to* or *at*) to reply sharply or rudely. **22. talk big**, *Colloq.* to speak boastfully. **23. talk down**, to make appear less important: *the prime minister talked down the events in parliament.* **24. talk down to**, to speak condescendingly to. **25. talk off the top of one's head**, **a.** to speak without prior preparation. **b.** to speak nonsense. **26. talk out**, **a.** to resolve (differences) by discussion: *unions and management usually attempt to talk out their differences before resorting to industrial action.* **b.** *Parliamentary Procedure* to thwart the passage of (a piece of legislation) by prolonging discussion until the adjournment. **27. talk over**, to discuss. **28. talk round**, **a.** to discuss generally and discursively, without coming to the essential point. **b.** to persuade; bring around to one's own way of thinking. **29. talk someone down**, **a.** to override someone in argument by speaking in a loud, persistent manner. **b.** *Aeronautics* to radio landing instructions to a pilot when landing is difficult. **30. talk someone into**, to persuade someone to do (something), especially against their original intention. **31. talk someone out of**, to persuade someone not to do (something), especially against their original intention. **32. talk through the back of one's neck**, *Colloq.* to talk nonsense. **33. talk tough**, *Colloq.* to be forceful and uncompromising in putting forward one's views or intentions or in assessing a situation, with the aim of overcoming opposition. **34. talk to the hand**, *Colloq.* (a contemptuous expression indicating that the speaker is ignoring what is being said.) **35. talk up**, to boost the

performance of (shares, the economy, etc.) by making confident assessments and predictions. **36. the talk of the town**, the subject of admiring discussion generally: *you'll be the talk of the town in that outfit.* –**talkable**, *adj.* –**talkative**, *adj.* –**talker**, *n.*

talkback radio /tɔkbæk 'reɪdioʊ/ *n.* a type of radio program in which listeners are encouraged to contribute their comments by telephone.

tall /tɔl/ *adj.* **1.** having a relatively great stature; of more than average height: *tall grass.* **2.** having stature or height as specified: *a man 1.9 metres tall.* **3.** *Colloq.* high, great, or large in amount: *a tall price.* **4.** *Colloq.* extravagant; difficult to believe: *a tall story.* **5.** *Colloq.* difficult to accomplish: *a tall order.* –**tallish**, *adj.* –**tallness**, *n.*

tallboy /'tɔlbɔɪ/ *n.* **1.** a tall chest of drawers supported on a low stand. **2.** a tall chimneypot. **3.** a tall-stemmed glass for wine, etc.

tallow /'tæloʊ/ *n.* **1.** the fatty tissue or suet of animals. **2.** the harder fat of sheep, cattle, etc., separated by melting from the fibrous and membranous matter naturally mixed with it, and used to make candles, soap, etc. **3.** any of various similar fatty substances: *vegetable tallow.* –*v.t.* **4.** to smear with tallow. –*v.i.* **5.** to produce tallow. –**tallowy**, *adj.*

tall poppy *n.* (*pl.* **-pies**) *Aust., NZ Colloq.* someone with outstanding ability, wealth or status.

tally /'tæli/ *n.* (*pl.* **-lies**) **1.** (formerly) a stick of wood with notches cut to show the amount of a debt or payment. **2.** an account or reckoning; a record of debit and credit, of the score of a game, etc. **3.** the number or group of objects recorded, such as the number of sheep shorn in a given period. –*verb* (**-lied**, **-lying**) –*v.t.* **4.** to mark or enter on a tally; register; record. **5.** to count or reckon up. –*v.i.* **6.** to agree or accord: *does his story tally with John's?* –**tallier**, *n.*

Talmud /'tælmʊd/ *n.* the writings which form the basis of Jewish law and tradition. –**Talmudic**, *adj.*

talon /'tælən/ *n.* **1.** a claw, especially of a bird of prey. **2.** *Colloq.* a finger or fingernail, especially when regarded as grasping or attacking. **3.** (in a lock) the shoulder on the bolt against which the key presses in shooting the bolt. –**taloned**, *adj.*

tamarind /'tæmərənd/ *n.* **1.** the fruit of a large tropical tree, *Tamarindus indica*, a pod containing seeds enclosed in a juicy acid pulp that is used in beverages and food. **2.** Also, **tamarind tree**. the tree, cultivated throughout the tropics for its fruit, fragrant flowers, shade, and timber.

tambourine /tæmbə'rin/ *n.* a small drum consisting of a circular wooden frame with a skin stretched over it and several pairs of jingles (metal discs) inserted into the frame, played by striking with the knuckles, shaking, etc. –**tambourinist**, *n.*

tame /teɪm/ *adj.* **1.** changed from the wild state; domesticated: *a tame bear.* **2.** (of an animal) gentle, fearless, or without shyness. **3.** easily lead or controlled; tractable; docile; submissive. **4.** lacking in life or spirit; dull; insipid: *a tame existence.* **5.** only mildly risqué; weak or relatively inoffensive: *a tame joke.* –*v.t.* **6.** to make tame; domesticate; subdue. **7.** to take away courage, eagerness, or interest from. **8.** to soften; tone down. **9.** to bring under control or make manageable, especially for domestic or human use: *to tame the natural resources of a country.* –**tameability**, **tamability** /teɪmə'bɪləti/, **tameableness**, **tamableness**, *n.* –**tameable**, **tamable**, *adj.* –**tamely**, *adv.* –**tameness**, *n.* –**tamer**, *n.*

tam-o'-shanter /tæm-ə-'ʃæntə/ *n.* a cap, of Scottish origin, with a flat crown larger in diameter than the headband. Also, **tam**, **tammy**.

tamp /tæmp/ *v.t.* **1.** to force in or down by repeated, somewhat light strokes. **2.** (in blasting) to fill (the hole made by the drill) with earth, etc., after the powder or explosive has been introduced.

tamper /'tæmpə/ *v.i.* **1.** to engage secretly or improperly in something. *–phr.* **2. tamper with, a.** to meddle with, especially for the purpose of altering, damaging, misusing, etc.: *to tamper with a lock.* **b.** to undertake underhand or corrupt dealings with, as in order to influence improperly: *to tamper with a witness.* **–tamperer,** *n.*

tampon /'tæmpɒn/ *n.* **1.** a plug of cotton or the like inserted into an orifice, wound, etc., as to stop haemorrhage. **2.** a similar device used internally to absorb menstrual flow. *–v.t.* **3.** to fill or plug with a tampon.

tan¹ /tæn/ *verb* **(tanned, tanning)** *–v.t.* **1.** to change (a hide) into leather, especially by soaking in a bath prepared from wattle bark, etc., or synthetically. **2.** to make brown by exposure to ultraviolet rays, especially of the sun. **3.** *Colloq.* to beat or thrash: *I'll tan your hide! –v.i.* **4.** to become tanned: *she tans easily. –n.* **5.** the brown colour given to the skin by exposure to the sun; suntan. **6.** a yellowish brown colour. *–adj.* **7.** of the colour of tan; yellowish brown. **8.** used in or relating to tanning processes, materials, etc. **–tanned,** *adj.* **–tanner,** *n.*

tan² /tæn/ *n. Maths* tangent.

tanbark /'tænbak/ *n.* **1.** bark used in tanning; tan. **2.** such bark, after the tanning process is completed, broken up in chips and used as a ground cover, as in playgrounds, landscape gardening, etc.

tandem /'tændəm/ *adv.* **1.** one behind another; in single file: *to drive horses tandem. –adj.* **2.** having animals, seats, parts, etc., arranged tandem, or one behind another: *a tandem bicycle. –n.* **3.** a bicycle for two riders, having twin seats, pedals, etc. **4.** a team of horses harnessed in tandem. **5.** any mechanism having a tandem arrangement. *–phr.* **6. in tandem,** one behind the other.

tandoori /tæn'duəri/ *adj.* (in Indian cookery) of or relating to dishes, usually chicken, beef, or vegetables, flavoured with exotic spices and traditionally cooked in a clay oven.

tandoor oven /ˌtændɔr 'ʌvən/ *n.* a cylindrical clay oven which is heated to a high temperature by burning wood or charcoal, used in Indian cookery. Also, **tandoori oven.**

tang /tæŋ/ *n.* **1.** a strong taste or flavour. **2.** the distinctive flavour or quality of a thing. **3.** a pungent or distinctive smell. **4.** a smack, touch, or suggestion of something. **5.** a long and slender projecting strip, tongue, or prong forming part of an object, as a chisel, file, knife, etc., and serving as a means of attachment for another part, as a handle or stock. **–tangy,** *adj.*

tangent /'tændʒənt/ *adj.* **1.** touching. **2.** *Geom.* touching, especially of a straight line in relation to a curve or surface. **3.** *Geom.* in contact along a single line or element, such as a plane with a cylinder. *–n.* **4.** *Geom.* a tangent line or plane. **5.** *Maths* a trigonometric function, defined for an acute angle in a right-angled triangle as the ratio of the opposite side to the adjacent side, and defined for angles of any size as the ratio of the sine of the angle to the cosine of the angle. *Abbrev.:* tan **6.** a sudden new direction: *to fly off at a tangent.* **–tangency,** *n.* **–tangential,** *adj.*

tangerine /tændʒə'rin/ *n.* **1.** a small, loose-skinned variety of mandarin. See **mandarin** (def. 5). **2.** deep orange; reddish orange. *–adj.* **3.** of a deep orange colour.

tangible /'tændʒəbəl/ *adj.* **1.** capable of being touched; discernible by the touch; material or substantial. **2.** real or actual, rather than imaginary or visionary. **3.** definite; not vague or elusive: *no tangible grounds for suspicion. –n.* **4.** *(usu. pl.)* something capable of being possessed or realised. **–tangibility** /tændʒə'bɪləti/, **tangibleness,** *n.* **–tangibly,** *adv.*

tangle /'tæŋgəl/ *v.t.* **1.** to bring together into a mass of confusedly interlaced or intertwisted threads, strands, or other like parts; snarl. **2.** to involve in something that hampers, obstructs, or overgrows: *bushes tangled with vines.* **3.** to catch and hold in, or as in, a net or snare. *–v.i.* **4.** to be or become tangled. *–n.* **5.** a tangled condition. **6.** a tangled or confused mass or assemblage of something. **7.** a confused jumble: *a tangle of contradictory statements.* **8.** *Colloq.* a conflict, quarrel, or disagreement. *–phr.* **9. tangle with,** *Colloq.* to conflict, quarrel, or argue with. **–tangler,** *n.* **–tangly,** *adj.*

tango /'tæŋgoʊ/ *n.* *(pl.* **-gos)** **1.** a dance of Spanish-American origin, danced by couples, and having many varied steps, figures, and poses. **2.** music for this dance. *–v.i.* **(-goed, -going) 3.** to dance the tango. **–tangoist,** *n.*

tanh /θæn, tæn'eɪtʃ/ *n.* See **hyperbolic function.**

tank /tæŋk/ *n.* **1.** a receptacle or structure for holding water or other liquid or a gas: *fish tank; petrol tank.* **2.** a large, closed container made of corrugated, galvanised iron, or of concrete, for storing rainwater above ground. **3.** a large, open container made of concrete for storing matter in the ground. **4.** *Aust.* (mainly in rural areas) an artificial water storage site made by excavating a hole in flat ground, sometimes with excavated soil used as a retaining wall; dam. **5.** *Mil.* an armoured, self-propelled combat vehicle, armed with cannon and machine-guns, and moving on caterpillar tracks. *–v.t.* **6.** to put or store in a tank. **7.** *Colloq.* to lose (a sporting match) deliberately. *–v.i. Colloq.* **8.** to move like a tank: *a footballer tanking down the wing.* **9.** to be a disaster; fail; flop: *his latest film tanked. –phr.* **10. on the tank,** on a drinking spree. **11. tank up, a.** to fill the tank of a motor vehicle with fuel. **b.** *Colloq.* to drink heavily. **–tankless,** *adj.*

tanked /tæŋkt/ *adj. Colloq.* intoxicated, especially with beer.

tanker /'tæŋkə/ *n.* **1.** a ship, aircraft, road or rail vehicle designed to carry oil or other liquid in bulk. **2.** *Colloq.* a person who deliberately loses a sporting match. **3.** *Colloq.* a failure.

tankini /tæŋ'kini/ *n.* a bikini-style swimming costume in which the top is similar to a tank top.

tannin /'tænən/ *n.* any of a group of astringent vegetable principles or compounds, as that which gives the tanning properties to wattle bark, or that which, in grape skins, stalks, and seeds, gives a distinctive tannin taste to some wines.

tantalise /'tæntəlaɪz/ *v.t.* to torment with, or as with, the sight of something desired but out of reach; tease by arousing expectations that are repeatedly disappointed. Also, **tantalize. –tantalisation** /tæntəlaɪ'zeɪʃən/, *n.* **–tantaliser,** *n.* **–tantalising,** *adj.* **–tantalisingly,** *adv.*

tantamount /'tæntəmaʊnt/ *adj.* equivalent, as in value, force, effect, or signification.

tantrum /'tæntrəm/ *n.* **1.** a sudden burst of ill humour; a fit of ill temper or passion. *–phr.* **2. throw a tantrum,** to exhibit a fit of temper.

Taoism /'daʊɪzəm, 'taʊɪzəm/ *n.* a philosophical system advocating a discipline of nonintervention with the course of nature and of absolute sincerity and honesty. **–Taoist,** *n., adj.* **–Taoistic,** *adj.*

tap¹ /tæp/ *verb* **(tapped, tapping)** *–v.t.* **1.** to strike with slight blows. **2.** to make, put, etc., by tapping. **3.** to strike (the hand, foot, etc.) lightly upon or against something. *–v.i.* **4.** to strike lightly so as to attract attention. **5.** to strike light blows. *–n.* **6.** a light, fast blow that can be heard. **7.** the sound made by this. **8.** the smallest amount; skerrick: *no one had done a tap of work. –phr.* **9. tap on the shoulder,** a notification or alert of some kind given to an individual. **10. tap**

someone on the shoulder, **a.** to nominate someone for a role or position. **b.** to indicate to someone that they should resign from a role or position. –**tappable**, *adj.*

tap² /tæp/ *n.* **1.** any device for controlling the flow of liquid from a pipe or the like by opening or closing an orifice; a cock. **2.** a cylindrical stick, long plug, or stopper for closing an opening through which liquid is drawn, as in a cask; a spigot. **3.** *Surg.* withdrawal of gas or fluid. **4.** an instrument for cutting the thread of a female screw. **5.** a hole made in tapping, as one in a pipe to furnish connection for a branch pipe. **6.** *Elect.* a connection brought out of a winding at some point between its extremities. **7.** a connection, usually secretly made, to a telephone line, which enables interested parties to overhear or record the conversations on that line. –*v.t.* (**tapped, tapping**) **8.** to draw off (liquid) by drawing out or opening a tap, or by piercing the container; draw liquid from (any vessel or reservoir). **9.** to draw the tap or plug from, or pierce (a cask, etc.). **10.** to penetrate, reach, etc., for the purpose of drawing something off: *to tap one's resources.* **11.** *Surg.* to penetrate for the purpose of drawing off fluid or gas: *tap the abdomen.* **12.** *Colloq.* to extract money from, especially in a crafty manner. **13.** to gain or effect secret access to: *to tap telephone wires to hear conversations.* **14.** to cut a female screw thread in (a hole, etc.). **15.** to open outlets from (power lines, roads, pipes, etc.). –*phr.* **16. on tap, a.** ready to be drawn off and served, as drink, especially beer, in a cask. **b.** ready for immediate use. **17. tap someone for information,** *Colloq.* to get information from someone, especially in an informal way. –**tappable**, *adj.*

tape /teɪp/ *n.* **1.** a long narrow strip of linen, cotton, or the like, used for tying garments, etc. **2.** a long narrow strip of paper, metal, etc. **3.** a tape measure. **4.** → **magnetic tape. 5.** a string or the like stretched across the finishing line in a race and broken by the winning contestant. **6.** *Horseracing* the starting line of a race when no barrier stalls are used, as in trotting, picnic races, etc. –*v.t.* **7.** to furnish with a tape or tapes. **8.** to tie up or bind with tape. **9.** to tape-record. –*phr. Colloq.* **10. have someone taped,** to understand someone thoroughly, especially their weakness or guile. **11. have something taped,** to be in complete control of or be easily able to do something. –**taper**, *n.* –**tapeless**, *adj.*

tape deck *n.* a tape recorder without built-in amplifiers or speakers, used as a component in a high fidelity sound system.

tape machine *n.* (formerly) a telegraphic instrument which automatically prints share prices, market reports, etc., on a tape (**ticker tape**).

tape measure *n.* a long strip or ribbon, as of linen or steel, marked with subdivisions of the foot or metre for measuring. Also, *Chiefly US,* **tapeline.**

taper /ˈteɪpə/ *v.i.* **1.** to become gradually thinner towards one end. **2.** to gradually grow thin. –*v.t.* **3.** to make gradually thinner towards one end. **4.** to gradually make thin. –*n.* **5.** a gradual decrease of width, thickness, power, force or capacity. **6.** a very thin candle. –**taperer**, *n.* –**taperingly**, *adv.*

tape recorder *n.* a device for recording an electrical signal, especially one produced by sound, in which a magnetic tape moves past an inductance coil which magnetises the tape in relation to the input signal. The signal is recovered from the magnetised tape by a playback circuit and can be erased by demagnetising the tape. Also, **tape-recorder.**

tapestry /ˈtæpəstri/ *n.* (*pl.* **-ries**) **1.** a fabric consisting of a warp upon which coloured threads are woven by hand to produce a design, often pictorial, and used for wall hangings, furniture coverings, etc. **2.** a machine-woven reproduction of true tapestry.

tapeworm /ˈteɪpwɜːm/ *n.* any of various flat or tape-like worms of the class Cestoda, lacking any alimentary canal, and parasitic when adult in the alimentary canal of humans and other vertebrates, usually characterised by having the larval and adult stages in different hosts.

tapioca /tæpiˈoʊkə/ *n.* a granular farinaceous food substance prepared from cassava starch by drying while moist on heated plates, used for making puddings, thickening soups, etc.

tappet /ˈtæpət/ *n.* (in a machine or engine) a projecting part, arm, or the like which intermittently comes in contact with another part to which it communicates, or from which it receives an intermittent motion.

taproot /ˈtæpruːt/ *n. Bot.* a main root descending from the radicle and giving off small lateral roots.

tar¹ /tɑː/ *n.* **1.** any of various dark-coloured viscid products obtained by the destructive distillation of certain organic substances, such as coal, wood, etc. **2.** coal-tar pitch. –*adj.* **3.** made of or covered with tar. –*v.t.* (**tarred, tarring**) **4.** to smear or cover with, or as with, tar. –*phr.* **5. tar and feather,** to punish or have revenge on (someone) by or as by covering them with tar and feathers. **6. tarred with the same brush,** having similar faults.

tar² /tɑː/ *n. Colloq.* a sailor.

tarantula /təˈræntʃələ/ *n.* (*pl.* **-las** *or* **-lae** /-liː/) **1.** in Australia, a huntsman spider of the genus *Isopoda,* especially the large, swift *Isopoda immanis,* which often seeks shelter in houses during rain; a triantelope. **2.** a large spider of southern Europe, *Lycosa tarantula,* whose bite was formerly supposed to cause an uncontrollable impulse to dance. **3.** any large spider, especially one of the family Theraphosidae of America. **4.** a name given to several animals which are thought to be venomous, as certain snakes and lizards.

tardy /ˈtɑːdi/ *adj.* (**-dier, -diest**) **1.** moving or acting slowly; slow; sluggish. **2.** late. **3.** delaying through reluctance. –**tardily**, *adv.* –**tardiness**, *n.*

tare¹ /tɛə/ *n.* **1.** the weight of the wrapping, receptacle, or conveyance containing goods. **2.** a deduction from the gross weight to allow for this. **3.** the weight of a vehicle without cargo, passengers, etc. **4.** *Chem.* a counterweight used to balance the weight of a container. –*v.t.* (**tared, taring**) **5.** to ascertain, note, or allow for the tare of.

tare² /tɛə/ *n.* any of various vetches, especially *Vicia sativa.*

target /ˈtɑːɡət/ *n.* **1.** an object, usually marked with concentric circles, to be aimed at in shooting practice or contests. **2.** anything fired at or aimed at. **3.** a goal to be reached. **4.** the object of attack, scorn, laughter, etc.; butt. **5.** *Hist.* a small round shield or buckler. –*v.t.* (**-geted** *or* **-getted, -geting** *or* **-getting**) **6.** to have as a target: *police are targeting speeding drivers.* –**target-less**, *adj.*

tariff /ˈtærəf/ *n.* **1.** an official list or table showing the duties or customs imposed by a government on imports or, less commonly, exports. **2.** any duty in such a list or system. **3.** any table of charges, fees, etc. **4.** (a list of) the prices charged for rooms, meals, etc., at a hotel or restaurant. –**tariffless**, *adj.*

tarmac /ˈtɑːmæk/ *n.* **1.** → **tarmacadam. 2.** a road or other area made of tarmacadam. **3.** the apron area adjoining airport buildings where aeroplanes are loaded, boarded, etc.

tarmacadam /tɑːməˈkædəm/ *n.* a road-surfacing mixture consisting of small stones or gravel bound together with tar or a mixture of tar and bitumen.

tarnish /ˈtɑːnɪʃ/ *v.t.* **1.** to dull or change the surface shine of (metal) by contact with the air; discolour. **2.** to lessen or destroy the purity of; stain; sully. –*v.i.* **3.** to grow dull or discoloured; lose lustre. **4.** to become stained.

–*n.* **5.** a tarnished coating. **6.** a tarnished condition; discolouration; alteration of the lustre. **7.** a stain or mark; blemish. **–tarnishable**, *adj.* **–tarnisher**, *n.*

tarot /'tærou/ *n.* **1.** one of a pack of 78 cards, made up of four suits of 14 cards each, with 22 trump cards. **2.** Also, **tarot trump**. a trump card in such a pack, bearing a symbolic or mythological character, now chiefly used in cartomancy. –*adj.* **3.** of or relating to the tarots, especially the trump cards.

tarpaulin /ta'pɔlən/ *n.* **1.** a protective covering of canvas or other material waterproofed with tar, paint, or wax. **2.** a hat, especially a sailor's made of or covered with such material.

tarragon /'tærəgən/ *n.* **1.** a plant, *Artemisia dracunculus*, thought to be native to Russia but now widely cultivated for its aromatic leaves used for flavouring. **2.** the leaves themselves.

tarry[1] /'tæri/ *v.i.* (**-ried, -rying**) **1.** to remain or stay, as in a place; sojourn. **2.** to delay or be tardy in acting, starting, coming, etc.; linger or loiter. **3.** to wait. **–tarrier**, *n.*

tarry[2] /'tari/ *adj.* of or like tar; smeared with tar. **–tarriness**, *n.*

tarsus /'tasəs/ *n.* (*pl.* **-si** /-saɪ/) *Anat.* the bones of the ankle joint and instep. **–tarsal**, *adj.*

tart[1] /tat/ *adj.* **1.** sharp to the taste; sour or acid: *tart apples*. **2.** sharp in character, spirit, or expression; cutting; caustic: *a tart remark*. **–tartish**, *adj.* **–tartishly**, *adv.* **–tartly**, *adv.* **–tartness**, *n.*

tart[2] /tat/ *n.* a small saucer-shaped shell of pastry with a sweet or savoury filling and no top crust. **–tarty**, *adj.*

tart[3] /tat/ *Colloq.* –*n.* **1.** (*derog.*) a promiscuous woman. **2.** a female prostitute. **3.** any woman. –*phr.* **4. tart up**, to adorn; make attractive, especially with cheap ornaments and cosmetics.

tartan /'tatn/ *n.* **1.** a woollen or worsted cloth woven with stripes of different colours and widths crossing at right angles, worn chiefly by the Scottish Highlanders, each clan having its distinctive pattern. **2.** a design of such a plaid known by the name of the clan wearing it. **3.** any plaid. –*adj.* **4.** relating to or resembling tartan. **5.** made of tartan.

tartar /'tatə/ *n.* **1.** a hard substance deposited on the teeth by the saliva, consisting of calcium phosphate, mucus, etc. **2.** the deposit from wines; potassium bitartrate. **3.** the partially purified product midway between the crude form (argol) and the further purified form (cream of tartar). **–tartaric** /ta'tærɪk/, *adj.*

tar-vine *n.* any species of the genus *Boerhavia*, of inland Australia, especially *B. diffusa*, a widespread weed.

taser /'teɪzə/ (*from trademark*) –*n.* Also, **taser gun**. **1.** a form of stun gun which fires projectiles with a wire attached through which an electric current passes. –*v.t.* **2.** to use a taser gun on. **–tasered**, *adj.*

task /task/ *n.* **1.** a definite piece of work assigned or falling to a person; a duty. **2.** any piece of work. **3.** a matter of considerable labour or difficulty. –*phr.* **4. take to task**, to call to account, as for fault; blame or censure. **–tasker**, *n.* **–taskless**, *adj.*

Tasmanian blue gum *n.* a tall smooth-barked species of *Eucalyptus*, *E. globulus*, native to Tasmania and Victoria but widely cultivated; the floral emblem of Tasmania.

Tasmanian devil /tæzmeɪniən 'dɛvəl/ *n.* a carnivorous marsupial of the family Dasyuridae, *Sarcophilus harrisii*, of Tasmania, having a black coat with white markings.

Tasmanian scallop *n. Chiefly NSW* → **scallop** (def. 3).

Tasmanian tiger *n.* → **thylacine**.

Tasmanian wolf *n.* (*pl.* **Tasmanian wolves**) → **thylacine**.

tassel /'tæsəl/ *n.* **1.** a hanging ornament, usually a bunch of threads or small cords hanging from a roundish knob

or head. **2.** something like this, e.g. the flower of certain plants, especially that at the top of a stalk of sugar cane, maize, etc. **–tasselly**, *adj.*

taste /teɪst/ *verb* (**tasted, tasting**) –*v.t.* **1.** to try the flavour or quality of (something) by taking some into the mouth: *to taste food*. **2.** to eat or drink a little of: *he hadn't tasted food for three days*. **3.** to perceive or distinguish the flavour of: *to taste the wine in a sauce*. **4.** to have or get experience, especially a slight experience, of. –*v.i.* **5.** to try the flavour or quality of something. **6.** to perceive or distinguish the flavour of anything. **7.** to have experience, or make trial in experience, of something. –*v.* (*copular*) **8.** to have a flavour as specified: *the milk tastes sour*. –*n.* **9.** the act of tasting food, drink, or the like. **10.** the sense by which the flavour or savour of things is perceived when they are brought into contact with special organs of the tongue. **11.** sensation, flavour, or quality as perceived by these organs. **12.** a small quantity tasted; a morsel, bit, or sip. **13.** a relish, liking, or predilection for something: *a taste for music*. **14.** the sense of what is fitting, harmonious, or beautiful; the perception and enjoyment of what constitutes excellence in the fine arts, literature, etc. **15.** manner, style, or general character as showing perception, or lack of perception, of what is fitting or beautiful; characteristic or prevailing style. **16.** a slight experience or a sample of something. –*phr.* **17. taste of**, **a.** to eat or drink a little of. **b.** to smack or savour of. **18. to someone's taste**, agreeable or pleasing to someone: *he couldn't find a tie to his taste*. **–tasteless**, *adj.* **–tasteful**, *adj.*

tastebud /'teɪstbʌd/ *n. Physiol.* any of a number of small, flask-shaped bodies in the epithelium of the tongue, etc., the special organs of taste.

tasty /'teɪsti/ *adj.* (**-tier, -tiest**) **1.** pleasing to the taste; savoury; appetising. **2.** *Colloq.* having or showing good taste. **–tastily**, *adv.* **–tastiness**, *n.*

tat /tæt/ *verb* (**tatted, tatting**) –*v.t.* **1.** to make by tatting. –*v.i.* **2.** to do tatting.

tatter /'tætə/ *n.* **1.** a torn piece hanging loose from the main part, as of a garment, etc. **2.** a separate torn piece. **3.** (*pl.*) torn or ragged clothing. –*v.t.* **4.** to tear or wear to tatters. –*v.i.* **5.** to become ragged.

tatting /'tætɪŋ/ *n.* **1.** the process or work of making a kind of knotted lace of cotton or linen thread with a shuttle. **2.** such lace.

tattle /'tætl/ *v.i.* **1.** to let out secrets. **2.** to chatter, prate, or gossip. –*v.t.* **3.** to utter idly; disclose by gossiping. –*n.* **4.** the act of tattling. **5.** idle talk; chatter; gossip. **–tattlingly**, *adv.*

tattler /'tætlə/ *n.* **1.** someone who tattles; a telltale. **2.** any of various sandpipers with a vociferous cry, having mainly grey plumage, breeding in Canada and Siberia and spending the northern winter in Australia and South-East Asia.

tattoo[1] /tæ'tu/ *n.* (*pl.* **-toos**) **1.** a signal on a drum, bugle, or trumpet at night, for soldiers or sailors to retire to their quarters. **2.** any similar beating or pulsation. **3.** an outdoor military pageant or display.

tattoo[2] /tæ'tu/ *n.* (*pl.* **-toos**) **1.** the act or practice of marking the skin with indelible patterns, pictures, legends, etc., by making punctures in it and inserting pigments. **2.** a pattern, picture, legend, etc., so made. –*v.t.* (**-tooed, -tooing**) **3.** to mark with tattoos. **–tattooer**, *n.* **–tattooist**, *n.*

tatty /'tæti/ *adj.* (**-tier, -tiest**) untidy; shabby; tawdry.

taught /tɔt/ *v.* past tense and past participle of **teach**.

taunt /tɔnt/ *v.t.* **1.** to reproach in a sarcastic or insulting manner. **2.** to provoke by taunts; mock. –*n.* **3.** an insulting gibe or sarcasm; scornful reproach or challenge. **–taunter**, *n.* **–tauntingly**, *adv.*

taupe /tɒp, toʊp/ n. dark grey usually slightly tinged with brown, purple, yellow, or green.

Taurus /ˈtɔrəs/ n. the second sign of the zodiac, which the sun enters about 20 April; the Bull. –**Taurean**, n., adj.

taut /tɔt/ adj. **1.** tightly drawn; tense; not slack. **2.** in good order or condition; tidy; neat. –**tautly**, adv. –**tautness**, n.

tauto- a word element meaning same, as in tautonym.

tautology /tɔˈtɒlədʒi/ n. (pl. **-gies**) **1.** needless repetition of an idea, especially in other words in the immediate context, without imparting additional force or clearness, as to descend down. **2.** an instance of this. **3.** Logic a proposition that can be shown to be true because it includes every possibility: either Smith owns a car or he doesn't own a car. –**tautological** /tɔtəˈlɒdʒɪkəl/, adj. –**tautologically** /tɔtəˈlɒdʒɪkli/, adv. –**tautologist**, n.

tavern /ˈtævən/ n. premises where food and alcoholic drink are served, but where no accommodation is provided.

taw /tɔ/ n. **1.** a choice or fancy playing marble with which to shoot. **2.** (pl.) a game of marbles. **3.** the line from which the players shoot. –phr. **4. go back to taws** or **start from taws**, Aust. Colloq. to begin at the beginning.

tawdry /ˈtɔdri/ adj. (**-drier, -driest**) (of finery, etc.) gaudy; showy and cheap. –**tawdrily**, adv. –**tawdriness**, n.

tawny /ˈtɔni/ adj. (**-nier, -niest**) **1.** of a dark yellowish or yellowish brown colour. –n. **2.** a shade of brown tinged with yellow; dull yellowish brown. **3.** a sweet, fortified wine made in Australia, which is blended and matured in wood, thus turning to a golden-brown as a result of slight oxidation. Also, **tawney**. –**tawniness**, n.

tawny frogmouth n. a medium-sized endemic and widely distributed Australian frogmouth, Podargus strigoides, with variously coloured, mottled plumage and a low but penetrating call.

tax /tæks/ n. **1.** a compulsory contribution of money, demanded by a government for its support, and imposed on incomes, property, goods purchased, etc. **2.** a heavy or unwanted charge, duty, or demand. –v.t. **3.** to put a tax on (income, people, etc.). **4.** to lay a burden on; make serious demands: this job taxes my skills. **5.** to scold; censure; reprove. –**taxability** /tæksəˈbɪləti/, **taxableness**, n. –**taxably**, adv. –**taxer**, n. –**taxless**, adj.

taxation /tækˈseɪʃən/ n. **1.** the act of taxing. **2.** the fact of being taxed. **3.** a tax imposed. **4.** the revenue raised by taxes.

tax avoidance n. the taking of lawful measures to minimise one's tax liabilities. Compare **tax evasion**.

tax-deductible /ˈtæks-dədʌktəbəl/ adj. of or relating to any expense, loss, etc., which can be legally claimed as a deduction from taxable income.

tax evasion n. the illegal non-payment or underpayment of taxes, as by making inaccurate declarations of taxable income or expenditure. Compare **tax avoidance**.

tax file number n. a unique identification number allocated by the government to each taxpayer. Abbrev.: TFN

taxi /ˈtæksi/ n. (pl. **taxis**) Also, **taxicab**. **1.** a car for public hire, especially one fitted with a taximeter. –v.i. (**taxied, taxiing** or **taxying**) **2.** (of a plane) to move over the surface of the ground or water under its own power, especially when preparing to take off or just after landing.

taxidermy /ˈtæksədɜmi/ n. the art of preparing and preserving the skins of animals, and stuffing and mounting them in lifelike form. –**taxidermal** /tæksəˈdɜməl/, **taxidermic** /tæksəˈdɜmɪk/, adj. –**taxidermist**, n.

tax indexation n. the indexing of tax scales in accordance with certain economic variables such as the consumer price index.

taxis /ˈtæksəs/ n. **1.** arrangement, order, as in one of the physical sciences. **2.** Biol. the movement of an organism in a particular direction in response to an external stimulus. **3.** Surg. the replacing of a displaced part, or the reducing of a hernial tumour or the like, by manipulation without cutting.

-taxis a word element meaning 'arrangement', as in chemotaxis.

taxonomy /tækˈsɒnəmi/ n. (pl. **-mies**) **1.** classification, especially in relation to its principles or laws. **2.** the department of science, or of a particular science, which deals with classification. –**taxonomic** /tæksəˈnɒmɪk/, **taxonomical** /tæksəˈnɒmɪkəl/, adj. –**taxonomically** /tæksəˈnɒmɪkli/, adv. –**taxonomist**, **taxonomer**, n.

tax return n. a statement of personal income required annually by tax authorities, used in assessing a person's tax liability.

tax shelter n. an investment, allowance, etc., used by a person or company to reduce or avoid tax liability.

-taxy variant of **-taxis**, as in heterotaxy.

TB /ti ˈbi/ n. tuberculosis.

T cell n. a white blood cell derived from or processed by the thymus, responsible for cellular immune reactions.

T cell count n. a count of the T cells in the blood as an indication of the state of the immune system.

tea /ti/ n. **1.** the dried and prepared leaves of the shrub, Camellia sinensis (formerly Thea sinensis), from which a somewhat bitter, aromatic beverage is made by infusion in boiling water. **2.** the shrub itself, which is extensively cultivated in China, Japan, India, etc., and has fragrant white flowers. **3.** the beverage so prepared, served hot or iced. **4.** any of various infusions prepared from the leaves, flowers, etc., of other plants, used as beverages or medicines. **5.** any kind of leaves, flowers, etc., so used, or any plant yielding them. **6.** → **beef tea**. **7.** a light meal taken in the late afternoon. **8.** the main evening meal. **9.** Colloq. marijuana. –phr. **10. be one's cup of tea**, Colloq. to be a task, topic, person, or object, etc., well suited to one's experience, taste, or liking: that show is more like my cup of tea. **11. not for all the tea in China**, not at all; in no way. –**tealess**, adj.

teach /titʃ/ verb (**taught, teaching**) –v.t. **1.** to impart knowledge of or skill in; give instruction in: he teaches mathematics. **2.** to impart knowledge or skill to; give instruction to: he teaches a large class. –v.i. **3.** to impart knowledge or skill; give instruction. –**teacher**, n.

teak /tik/ n. **1.** a large tree native to India and South-East Asia, Tectona grandis, with a hard, durable, yellowish brown, resinous wood, used for shipbuilding, making furniture, etc. **2.** the wood of this tree. **3.** any of various similar trees or woods as Flindersia australis.

teal /til/ n. **1.** any of various small freshwater ducks of the genus Anas, typically having a greenish band on the wing, as the **grey teal**, Anas gracilis, a wideranging bird of Australia, Indonesia, New Zealand, and Pacific islands. **2.** Also, **teal green**. a deep greenish-blue colour. –adj. **3.** of the colour of teal.

tea light n. a small candle, often in a metal or plastic casing.

team /tim/ n. **1.** a number of persons associated in some joint action, especially one of the sides in a match: a team of football players. **2.** two or more horses, oxen, or other animals harnessed together to draw a vehicle, plough, or the like. –v.t. **3.** to join together in a team. **4.** to use, wear, etc., together, especially for effect: team a red blouse with your new skirt. **5.** US to convey or transport by means of a team. –v.i. **6.** US to drive a team. **7.** to work together in or as if in a team. –phr. **8. take one for the team**, Colloq. to make a sacrifice for the sake of another or others. **9. team up with**, to work together with; collaborate with.

team spirit *n.* the camaraderie and loyalty which members of a team display towards each other.

teamster /ˈtimstə/ *n.* **1.** someone who drives a team, especially as an occupation. **2.** *US* someone who drives a truck, especially as an occupation; haulier.

tear[1] /tɪə/ *n.* **1.** a drop of the limpid fluid secreted by the lachrymal gland, appearing in or flowing from the eye, chiefly as the result of emotion, especially of grief. **2.** something resembling or suggesting a tear, as a drop of a liquid or a tear-like mass of a solid substance. **3.** *(pl.)* grief; sorrow. –*phr.* **4. in tears**, weeping. **5. tear up**, to experience a welling up of tears in the eyes. –**tearful**, **teary**, *adj.* –**tearless**, *adj.*

tear[2] /tɛə/ *verb* (**tore**, **torn**, **tearing**) –*v.t.* **1.** to pull apart or in pieces by force, especially so as to leave ragged or irregular edges. **2.** to pull or pluck violently or with force. **3.** to distress greatly: *a heart torn with anguish.* **4.** to rend or divide: *a country torn by civil war.* **5.** to wound or injure by, or as by, rending; lacerate. **6.** to produce or effect by rending: *to tear a hole in one's coat.* **7.** to remove by force: *to be unable to tear oneself away from a place.* –*v.i.* **8.** to become torn. **9.** to make a tear or rent. **10.** *Colloq.* to move or go with violence or great haste. –*n.* **11.** the act of tearing. **12.** a rent or fissure. **13.** *Colloq.* a drinking spree: *on the tear.* –*phr.* **14. tear at**, to pluck violently at; attempt to tear. **15. tear down**, to pull down; destroy; demolish. **16. tear into**, *Colloq.* to attack violently, either physically or verbally. **17. tear off**, **a.** to pull or pluck away violently. **b.** *Colloq.* to perform or do, especially rapidly or casually. **c.** to leave hurriedly. **18. tear strips off**, *Colloq.* to reprove severely. **19. tear up**, **a.** to tear into small pieces. **b.** to cancel; annul.

tear gas *n.* a gas used in warfare or in riots, which makes the eyes smart and water, thus producing a temporary blindness.

tease /tiz/ *v.t.* **1.** to worry or irritate by persistent petty requests, trifling raillery, or other annoyances often in jest. **2.** to pull apart or separate the adhering fibres of, as in combing or carding wool; comb or card (wool, etc.); shred. **3.** to raise a nap on (cloth) with teasels; teasel. **4.** to give height and body to a hairdo by combing (the hair) from the end towards the scalp. **5.** to flirt with, especially insincerely. –*v.i.* **6.** to worry or disturb a person, etc., by importunity or persistent petty annoyance. –*n.* **7.** a person or thing that teases someone: *Julie is a terrible tease.* –*phr.* **8. tease out**, to separate or extricate (tangled or intricately connected parts): *to tease out some of the threads in a story.* –**teasingly**, *adv.*

teaspoon /ˈtispun/ *n.* **1.** the small spoon commonly used to stir tea, coffee, etc. **2.** a teaspoonful.

teat /tit/ *n.* **1.** the protuberance on the breast or udder in female mammals (except the monotremes), where the milk ducts discharge; a nipple or mamilla. **2.** something resembling a teat, especially for feeding a baby from a bottle.

tea-tree *n.* any of various species of shrubs or small trees of the genera *Leptospermum* or *Melaleuca*, native to Australia and New Zealand, often having white, pink, or red flowers; certain varieties yield an oil used as a germicide and fungicide. Also, **ti-tree**.

tech /tɛk/ *n. Colloq.* **1.** a technical college or school. **2.** → **techie**.

techie /ˈtɛki/ *n. Colloq.* someone with a professional or passionate interest in technology, especially computing. Also, **tech head**, **tech**.

technical /ˈtɛknɪkəl/ *adj.* **1.** belonging or relating to an art, science, or the like: *technical skill.* **2.** peculiar to or characteristic of a particular art, science, profession, trade, etc.: *technical details.* **3.** using terms or treating a subject in a manner peculiar to a particular field, as a

writer or a book. **4.** relating to or connected with the mechanical or industrial arts and the applied sciences: *a technical school.* **5.** so considered from a strictly legal point of view or a rigid interpretation of the rules: *a military engagement ending in a technical defeat.* –*phr.* **6. get technical**, *Colloq.* to propound or apply a strict interpretation of the rules. –**technically**, *adv.* –**technicalness**, *n.*

technical college *n.* a state institution providing technical education at the tertiary level.

technicality /tɛknəˈkæləti/ *n.* (*pl.* **-ties**) **1.** technical character. **2.** the use of technical methods or terms. **3.** something that is technical; a technical point, detail, or expression. **4.** a literal, often narrow-minded interpretation of a rule, law, etc.; quibble: *he was ruled ineligible on a technicality.*

technician /tɛkˈnɪʃən/ *n.* **1.** someone who has expert knowledge of the technicalities of a subject. **2.** someone skilled in the technique of an art, as music or painting. **3.** a person considered from the point of view of his or her technical skill: *a good technician; a bad technician.* **4.** someone skilled and knowledgeable in a particular technical area: *a telephone technician.*

technicolour /ˈtɛknɪkʌlə, -nə-/ *n.* **1.** a process of making cinema films in colour by superimposing the three primary colours to produce a final coloured print. –*adj.* **2.** bright, vivid, especially of colours: *a technicolour dream.* Also, **technicolor**.

technique /tɛkˈnik/ *n.* **1.** method of performance; way of accomplishing. **2.** technical skill, especially in artistic work.

techno- a word element referring to 'technic', 'technology'.

technocracy /tɛkˈnɒkrəsi/ *n.* **1.** a theory and movement (prominent about 1932) advocating control of industrial resources and reorganisation of the social system, based on the findings of technologists and engineers. **2.** a system of government which applies this theory. **3.** people who occupy senior positions in various technical fields, as engineering, science, economics, etc., considered as a class exercising a strong influence over society as a whole. –**technocrat** /ˈtɛknəkræt/, *n.* –**technocratic** /tɛknəˈkrætɪk/, *adj.*

technology /tɛkˈnɒlədʒi/ *n.* (*pl.* **-gies**) **1.** the branch of knowledge that deals with science and engineering, or its practice, as applied to industry; applied science. **2.** equipment of a technologically sophisticated nature, such as computers, internet connections, audiovisual equipment, etc.: *the technology has failed us in this demonstration.* –**technologist**, *n.* –**technological** /tɛknəˈlɒdʒɪkəl/, *adj.*

technology park *n.* an industrial park devoted to high-technology industries. Also, **high technology park**.

tectonic /tɛkˈtɒnɪk/ *adj.* **1.** of or relating to building or construction; constructive; architectural. **2.** *Geol.* **a.** of or relating to the structure of the earth's crust. **b.** of or relating to the forces or conditions within the earth that cause movements of the crust such as earthquakes, folds, faults, and the like. –**tectonically**, *adv.*

tectonic plate *n. Geol.* a section of the earth's crust and uppermost part of the mantle, which moves in relation to the other plates; there are seven main plates and a number of minor plates and microplates; movement at the boundaries can cause earthquakes, volcanoes, mountain-building and the formation of oceanic trenches. Also, **crustal plate**.

teddy /ˈtɛdi/ *n.* (*pl.* **-dies**) a woman's one-piece undergarment combining a top with underpants.

teddy bear *n.* a stuffed toy bear.

tedious /ˈtidiəs/ *adj.* **1.** marked by tedium; long and tiresome: *tedious tasks; a tedious journey.* **2.** prolix so as to cause weariness, as a speaker. **–tediously,** *adv.* **–tediousness,** *n.*

tedium /'tidiəm/ *n.* the state of being wearisome; irksomeness; tediousness.

tee[1] /ti/ *n.* **1.** the letter T, t. **2.** something shaped like a T, as a three-way joint used in fitting pipes together. **3.** the mark aimed at in various games, as curling. *–adj.* **4.** having a crosspiece at the top; shaped like a T.

tee[2] /ti/ *n. Golf* **1.** Also, **teeing ground.** the starting place, usually a hard mound of earth, at the beginning of each fairway. **2.** a small heap of sand, or a rubber, plastic, or wooden object, on which the ball is placed and from which it is driven at the beginning of a hole. *–v.t.* **(teed, teeing) 3.** to place (the ball) on a tee. *–phr.* **4. tee off,** *Golf* to strike the ball from a tee. **5. tee up,** *Colloq.* to organise; plan. **6. to a tee,** perfectly; exactly: *it suits you to a tee.*

teem[1] /tim/ *v.i.* (sometimes fol. by *with*) to abound or swarm; be prolific or fertile. **–teemer,** *n.*

teem[2] /tim/ *v.i.* **1.** to empty or pour out; discharge. **2.** to rain very hard. *–v.t.* **3.** to empty liquid from (a vessel), as molten steel from a crucible.

teen /tin/ *Colloq. –adj.* **1.** teenage. *–n.* **2.** a teenager.

-teen a termination forming the cardinal numerals from 13 to 19.

teenager /'tineidʒə/ *n.* a person in his or her teens. **–teenage,** *adj.*

teens /tinz/ *pl. n.* the period of one's life between the ages of 12 and 20.

teeny /'tini/ *adj.* **(-nier, -niest)** tiny.

teeny-bopper /'tini-bopə/ *n.* a young teenager (12–15 years) who conforms to the style of dress, music, etc., of current pop groups.

teepee /'tipi/ *n.* a tent or wigwam of the indigenous people of North America. Also, **tepee, tipi.**

teeter /'titə/ *v.i.* **1.** to seesaw. **2.** to move unsteadily.

teeth /tiθ/ *pl. n.* **1.** plural of **tooth. 2.** the punitive sections of a legislation, ruling, etc., meant to ensure its enforcement: *give a regulation teeth. –phr.* **3. be fed (up) to the (back) teeth with,** *Colloq.* to be heartily sick of; have had more than enough of. **4. get one's teeth into,** to start to cope effectively with (a problem, etc.). **5. grit (or set) one's teeth,** to prepare to endure pain or emergency with fortitude. **6. have (or take) the bit in (or between) one's teeth, a.** to tackle a task, problem, etc., in a determined and energetic fashion. **b.** to throw off control; rush headlong. **7. in someone's teeth, a.** in direct conflict or opposition to someone. **b.** to someone's face; openly. **8. in the teeth of, a.** so as to face or confront; straight against. **b.** in defiance of; in spite of. **c.** in the face or presence of. **9. scarce (or rare) as hen's teeth,** *Colloq.* very rare. **10. set someone's teeth on edge,** to cause someone a disagreeable sensation or strong feelings of antipathy: *the noise of chalk on blackboard sets my teeth on edge.* **11. to the teeth,** fully: *armed to the teeth.*

teethe /tið/ *v.i.* to grow teeth; cut one's teeth.

teetotal /'titoutl, ti'toutl/ *adj.* of or relating to total abstinence from intoxicating drink. **–teetotally,** *adv.*

telco /'tɛlkou/ *n.* a telecommunications company.

tele- **1.** a word element meaning 'distant', especially 'transmission over a distance', as in *telegraph.* **2.** a word element referring to television, as in *telemovie, teletext.* **3.** a word element referring to the use of telecommunications, as in *telecommute, telebanking.*

telecast /'tɛləkast, 'tɛli-/ *verb* **(-cast** *or* **-casted, -casting)** *–v.i.* **1.** to broadcast by television: *this station first telecast in 1965. –v.t.* **2.** to broadcast (programs, etc.) by television: *which network is telecasting the Olympics? –n.* **3.** a television broadcast.

telecommunication /ˌtɛləkəmjunəˈkeiʃən, ˌtɛli-/ *n.* the process by which communication of audio, video or digital information is carried out over a distance by means of a transmission line or by radio.

telecommute /tɛlikəˈmjut/ *v.i.* → **telework. –telecommuter,** *n.* **–telecommuting,** *n.*

teleconference /'tɛlikɒnfərəns/ *n.* **1.** a conference in which people at locations remote from each other can take part using teleconferencing. *–v.i.* **(-ced, -cing) 2.** to conduct a meeting via teleconferencing.

teleconferencing /tɛliˈkɒnfərənsɪŋ/ *n.* the process of conducting a meeting between separated groups of people making use of audio and sometimes video telecommunications systems.

telefraud /'tɛlifrɔd/ *n.* the swindling of people by scams that involve contact by telephone.

telegram /'tɛləgræm/ *n.* a communication sent by telegraph; a telegraphic message. **–telegrammic** /tɛləˈgræmɪk/, **telegrammatic** /tɛləgrəˈmætɪk/, *adj.*

telegraph /'tɛləgræf, -graf/ *n.* **1.** an apparatus, system, or process for transmitting messages or signals to a distance, especially by means of an electrical device consisting essentially of a transmitting or sending instrument and a distant receiving instrument connected by a conducting wire, or other communications channel, the making and breaking of the circuit at the sending end causing a corresponding effect, as on a sounder, at the receiving end. **2.** a telegraphic message. *–v.t.* **3.** to transmit or send (a message, etc.) by telegraph. **4.** to send a message to (a person) by telegraph. **5.** *Sport Colloq.* to give prior indication of (one's plans or intentions), especially to an opponent. *–v.i.* **6.** to send a message by telegraph. *–phr.* **7. telegraph one's punches,** *Colloq.* to give prior indication of one's plans or intentions, especially to an opponent. **–telegraphy** /təˈlɛgrəfi/, *n.* **–telegrapher** /təˈlɛgrəfə/, **telegraphist** /təˈlɛgrəfəst/, *n.* **–telegraphic** /tɛləˈgræfɪk/, *adj.* **–telegraphical** /tɛləˈgræfɪkəl/, *adj.* **–telegraphically** /tɛləˈgræfɪkli/, *adv.*

telemarketing /'tɛlimakətɪŋ/ *n.* the selling of goods or services by contacting potential customers on the telephone. **–telemarketer,** *n.*

teleology /tili'ɒlədʒi, tɛl-/ *n.* **1.** the doctrine that the universe is directed towards a final purpose, and that there is evidence of this in nature which is proof of the existence of the being who established what this purpose should be. **2.** such design or purpose. **3.** the doctrine in vitalism that phenomena are guided not only by mechanical forces but also by the ends towards which they move. **–teleological** /tiliəˈlɒdʒɪkəl/, *adj.* **–teleologically** /tiliəˈlɒdʒɪkli/, *adv.* **–teleologist** /tili'ɒlədʒəst/, *n.*

telepathy /təˈlɛpəθi/ *n.* communication of one mind with another by some means other than the normal use of the senses. **–telepathic** /tɛləˈpæθɪk/, *adj.* **–telepathically** /tɛləˈpæθɪkli/, *adv.* **–telepathist,** *n.*

telephone /'tɛləfoun/ *n.* **1.** a system or process for the transmission of sound or speech converted into electrical or radio signals to a distant point. **2.** an electrical device consisting of a microphone and a receiver with a handset, used to connect to this system. *–v.t.* **3.** to initiate telephone communications with (someone). **4.** to send (a message, etc.) by telephone. *–v.i.* **5.** to communicate with someone by telephone. *–phr.* **6. on the telephone,** engaged in a telephone conversation. Also, **phone. –telephoner,** *n.* **–telephonic** /tɛləˈfɒnɪk/, *adj.* **–telephonically** /tɛləˈfɒnɪkli/, *adv.* **–telephonist,** *n.*

telephoto lens /ˌtɛləfoutou 'lɛnz/ *n.* a lens used in or attached to a camera for producing an enlarged image of a distant object.

teleprinter /'tɛliprɪntə, 'tɛlə-/ *n.* an instrument having a typewriter keyboard which transmits and receives messages by telegraphic transmission, or to and from a computer. Also, **teletype.**

teleprocessing /ˈtɛliˌprousɛsɪŋ/ n. the processing of information held at another place, by means of an online computer.

telescope /ˈtɛləskoup/ n. **1.** an optical instrument for making distant objects appear nearer and larger. There are two principal forms, one (**refracting telescope**) consisting essentially of a lens or object glass for forming an image of the object and an eyepiece or combination of lenses for magnifying this image, and the other (**reflecting telescope**) having a similar arrangement but containing a concave mirror or speculum instead of an object glass. **Astronomical telescopes** are used for viewing objects outside the earth; **terrestrial telescopes** are used for viewing distant objects on the earth's surface. –adj. **2.** consisting of parts which fit and slide one within another. –v.t. **3.** to force together, one into another, or force into something else, in the manner of the sliding tubes of a jointed telescope. **4.** to condense; shorten. –v.i. **5.** to slide together, or into something else in the manner of the tubes of a jointed telescope. **6.** to be driven one into another, as railway carriages in a collision. –**telescopic** /tɛləˈskɒpɪk/, adj.

teletype /ˈtɛlitaɪp, ˈtɛlə-/ n. (from trademark) → **teleprinter.**

televise /ˈtɛləvaɪz/ v.t. to broadcast by television.

television /ˈtɛləvɪʒən/ n. **1.** the broadcasting of a still or moving image, usually with accompanying sound signal, via radio waves to receivers which project it electronically on a screen for viewing at a distance from the point of origin. **2.** the process used. **3.** a television receiver; television set. **4.** the programs transmitted: to watch too much television. **5.** the field of broadcasting by television. –**televisional** /tɛləˈvɪʒənəl/, **televisionary** /tɛləˈvɪʒənri/, adj.

television station n. **1.** a combination of devices for television transmission and/or receiving. **2.** a complete installation for television broadcasting, including transmitting apparatus, television studios, etc. **3.** an organisation engaged in broadcasting, on a fixed channel, programs of news, entertainment, propaganda, etc.

telework /ˈtɛliwɜk/ v.i. to work at a distance from one's employer's premises, usually at home, communicating via equipment such as computers and telephones. Also, **telecommute.** –**teleworking,** n. –**teleworker,** n.

telex /ˈtɛlɛks/ n. **1.** an international two-way communications system which uses the public telecommunications network to link teleprinters at remote locations. **2.** → **teleprinter. 3.** a message received or sent by teleprinter. –v.t. **4.** to send (someone) a message by telex. **5.** to send (a message) by telex.

tell /tɛl/ verb (**told, telling**) –v.t. **1.** to give an account or narrative of; narrate; relate (a story, tale, etc.): to tell one's life story. **2.** to make known by speech or writing (a fact, news, information, etc.); communicate. **3.** to utter (the truth, a lie, etc.). **4.** to express in words (thoughts, feelings, etc.). **5.** to reveal or divulge (something secret or private). **6.** to say plainly or positively: he won't tell me if it's true or not. **7.** to discern (a distant person or thing) so as to be able to identify or describe: can you tell who that is over there? **8.** to recognise or distinguish: you could hardly tell the difference between them. **9.** to inform or apprise (a person, etc.) of something. **10.** to assure emphatically: I won't, I tell you! **11.** to bid, order, or command: tell him to stop. **12.** to count or enumerate, as votes. –v.i. **13.** to give an account or report: she told about her experience. **14.** to disclose something secret or private. **15.** to know; be certain: how can we tell if there is a life after death? **16.** to have force or effect; operate effectively: a contest in which every stroke tells. **17.** to produce a marked or severe effect. –phr. **18. tell of,** to

give evidence or be an indication of: to tell of wonders. **19. tell off, a.** to mention one after another, as in enumerating. **b.** to count or set one by one or in exact amount: to tell off five metres. **c.** to separate from the whole, a group, etc., and assign to a particular task. **d.** Colloq. to scold; rebuke. **20. tell on,** Colloq. to inform on. **21. tell tales (out of school),** to report the misdemeanours, true or fictitious, of one's friends, peers, relatives, etc. –**tellable,** adj.

teller /ˈtɛlə/ n. **1.** a narrator. **2.** someone employed in a bank to receive or pay out money over the counter. **3.** someone appointed to count votes, as in a parliamentary division. –**tellership,** n.

telling /ˈtɛlɪŋ/ adj. **1.** having force or effect; effective; striking: a telling blow. **2.** indicative of one's feelings; revealing: a telling blush. –**tellingly,** adv.

telltale /ˈtɛlteɪl/ n. Also, **telltale-tit. 1.** someone who thoughtlessly and sometimes cruelly reveals private matters; tattler. –adj. **2.** that reveals what is not intended to be known: a telltale blush.

tellurian /tɛlˈjuriən, tə'lu-/ adj. **1.** of or characteristic of the earth or an inhabitant of the earth. –n. **2.** an inhabitant of the earth.

temerity /təˈmɛrəti/ n. reckless boldness; rashness. –**temerarious** /tɛməˈrɛəriəs/, adj.

temp¹ /tɛmp/ Colloq. –n. **1.** → **temporary** (def. 3). –v.i. **2.** to work as a temporary member of staff.

temp² /tɛmp/ n. Colloq. → **temperature** (def. 2).

temper /ˈtɛmpə/ n. **1.** a particular state of mind or feelings. **2.** habit of mind, especially with respect to irritability or impatience, outbursts of anger, or the like. **3.** heat of mind or passion, shown in outbursts of anger, resentment, etc. **4.** a substance added to something to modify its properties or qualities. **5.** Metallurgy the particular degree of hardness and elasticity imparted to steel, etc., by tempering. –v.t. **6.** to moderate or mitigate. **7.** to soften or tone down. **8.** to bring to a proper, suitable, or desirable state by, or as by, blending or admixture. **9.** to moisten, mix, and work up into proper consistency, as clay or mortar. **10.** to heat and cool or quench (metal) in order to bring to the proper degree of hardness, elasticity, etc. **11.** to produce internal stresses in (glass) by sudden cooling from low red heat; toughen. **12.** to tune (a keyboard instrument, as a piano, organ, etc.) so as to make the notes available in different keys or tonalities. –v.i. **13.** to be or become tempered. –phr. **14. keep one's temper,** to remain calm or patient, especially despite provocation. **15. lose one's temper,** to become suddenly angry or enraged. –**temperable,** adj. –**temperability** /tɛmpərəˈbɪləti/, n. –**temperer,** n.

tempera /ˈtɛmpərə/ n. paint made from pigment ground in water and mixed with an emulsion of egg yolk or some similar substance.

temperament /ˈtɛmprəmənt/ n. **1.** the individual peculiarity of physical organisation by which the manner of thinking, feeling, and acting of every person is permanently affected; natural disposition. **2.** unusual personal make-up manifested by peculiarities of feeling, temper, action, etc., with disinclination to submit to ordinary rules or restraints. **3.** the combination of the four cardinal humours, the relative proportions of which were supposed to determine physical and mental constitution. **4.** Music the tuning of a keyboard instrument as the piano, organ, etc., so that it can be played in all keys.

temperamental /tɛmprəˈmɛntl/ adj. **1.** having or exhibiting a strongly marked individual temperament. **2.** moody, irritable, or sensitive. **3.** liable to behave erratically; unstable; unreliable. **4.** of or relating to temperament; constitutional. –**temperamentally,** adv.

temperance /ˈtɛmpərəns, ˈtɛmprəns/ n. **1.** moderation or self-restraint in action, statement, etc.; self-control.

2. habitual moderation in the indulgence of a natural appetite or passion, especially in the consumption of alcoholic drink. **3.** total abstinence from alcoholic drink.

temperate /'tɛmpərət, 'tɛmprət/ *adj.* **1.** moderate or self-restrained; not extreme in opinion, etc. **2.** moderate as regards indulgence of appetite or passion, especially in the consumption of alcoholic drink. **3.** not excessive in degree, as things, qualities, etc. **4.** moderate in respect of temperature. –**temperately**, *adv.* –**temperateness**, *n.*

temperate climate *n.* a climate without extremes of temperature or precipitation.

temperate rainforest *n.* a coniferous or broadleaf forest occurring in coastal mountains with high rainfall, as in the south-east of the Australian mainland and Tasmania. See **cool temperate rainforest**, **warm temperate rainforest**. Compare **tropical rainforest**.

Temperate Zone *n.* either of two regions, the **North Temperate Zone**, between the Arctic Circle and the Tropic of Cancer, and the **South Temperate Zone**, between the Antarctic Circle and the Tropic of Capricorn.

temperature /'tɛmprətʃə/ *n.* **1.** a measure of the degree of hotness or coldness of a body or substance which determines the rate at which heat will be transferred to or from it. See **thermometer**. **2.** *Pathol.*, *Physiol.* **a.** Also, **body temperature.** the degree of heat of a living body, especially the human body. **b.** the excess of this above the normal (which in the adult human being is about 37°C or about 98.4°F). **3.** the degree of heat of the climatic conditions: *the temperature reached 40° today.*

tempest /'tɛmpəst/ *n.* **1.** an extensive current of wind rushing with great velocity and violence, especially one attended with rain, hail, or snow; a violent storm. **2.** a violent commotion, disturbance, or tumult. –**tempestuous**, *adj.*

template /'tɛmplət, -leɪt/ *n.* **1.** a formula or exemplum. **2.** a document which is designed to have certain basic information in it, other parts being added to suit individual instances or applications. **3.** a pattern, mould, or the like, usually consisting of a thin plate of wood, metal, or plastic, used as a guide in mechanical work or for transferring a design onto a work surface, etc. **4.** *Building Trades* a horizontal piece of timber, stone, or the like, in a wall, to receive and distribute the pressure of a girder, beam, etc. **5.** *Shipbuilding* either of two wedges in each of the temporary blocks forming the support for the keel of a ship while building. Also, **templet**.

temple[1] /'tɛmpəl/ *n.* **1.** an edifice or place dedicated to the service or worship of a deity or deities. **2.** any place or object regarded as occupied by the Divine Presence, as the body of a Christian. **3.** a building, usually large or pretentious, devoted to some public use: *a temple of music.* –**temple-like**, *adj.*

temple[2] /'tɛmpəl/ *n.* **1.** the flattened region on either side of the human forehead. **2.** a corresponding region in lower animals.

tempo /'tɛmpoʊ/ *n.* (*pl.* **-pos** *or* **-pi** /-piː/) **1.** *Music* relative rapidity or rate of movement (usually indicated by such terms as adagio, allegro, etc., or by reference to the metronome). **2.** characteristic rate, rhythm, or pattern of work or activity: *the tempo of city life.*

temporal[1] /'tɛmpərəl, 'tɛmprəl/ *adj.* **1.** of or relating to time. **2.** of or relating to the present life or this world; worldly. **3.** enduring for a time only; temporary; transitory. **4.** *Gram.* **a.** relating to or expressing time: *a temporal adverb.* **b.** of or relating to the tenses of a verb. **5.** secular, lay, or civil. –**temporally**, *adv.* –**temporality** /tɛmpə'ræləti/, *n.*

temporal[2] /'tɛmpərəl, 'tɛmprəl/ *Anat.* –*adj.* **1.** of, relating to, or situated near the temple or a temporal bone. –*n.*

2. any of several parts in the temporal region, especially the temporal bone.

temporary /'tɛmpri, -prəri/, *Orig. US* /'tɛmpərɛri/ *adj.* **1.** lasting, existing, serving, or effective for a time only; not permanent: *a temporary need.* **2.** (of an employee) not on the permanent staff and therefore not enjoying job security or fringe benefits, such as superannuation. –*n.* (*pl.* **-ries**) Also, **temp. 3.** a temporary member of an office staff, especially a secretary. –**temporarily**, *adv.* –**temporariness**, *n.*

temporise /'tɛmpəraɪz/ *v.i.* **1.** to act indecisively or evasively to gain time or delay matters. **2.** to comply with the time or occasion; yield temporarily or ostensibly to the current of opinion or circumstances. –*phr.* **3. temporise between**, to effect a compromise between. **4. temporise with**, **a.** to treat or parley with so as to gain time. **b.** to come to terms with. Also, **temporize**. –**temporisation** /tɛmpəraɪ'zeɪʃən/, *n.* –**temporiser**, *n.* –**temporisingly**, *adv.*

tempt /tɛmpt/ *v.t.* **1.** to induce or persuade by enticement or allurement. **2.** to allure, appeal strongly to, or invite: *the offer tempts me.* **3.** to render strongly disposed (to do something). **4.** to try to dispose or incite; assail with enticements, especially to evil. **5.** to put to the test in a venturesome way; risk provoking; provoke: *to tempt one's fate.* –*phr.* **6. tempt fortune**, to embark on a course of action which involves certain risk. –**temptable**, *adj.* –**temptation**, *n.* –**tempter**, *n.*

tempura /tɛm'pʊrə/ *n.* a Japanese dish in which seafood or vegetables are coated in a light batter and deep-fried in oil.

ten /tɛn/ *n.* **1.** a cardinal number, nine plus one $(9 + 1)$. **2.** the symbol for this number, as 10 or X. –*adj.* **3.** amounting to ten in number: *ten apples.* –*pron.* **4.** ten people or things: *ten came to the party.* –**tenth**, *adj.*

tenable /'tɛnəbəl/ *adj.* capable of being held, maintained, or defended, as against attack or objection: *a tenable theory.* –**tenability** /tɛnə'bɪləti/, **tenableness**, *n.* –**tenably**, *adv.*

tenacious /tə'neɪʃəs/ *adj.* **1.** holding fast; characterised by keeping a firm hold. **2.** highly retentive: *a tenacious memory.* **3.** pertinacious, persistent, stubborn, or obstinate. **4.** adhesive or sticky; viscous or glutinous. **5.** holding together; cohesive; not easily pulled apart; tough. –**tenaciously**, *adv.* –**tenacity** /tə'næsəti/, **tenaciousness**, *n.*

tenant /'tɛnənt/ *n.* **1.** someone who holds land, a house, or the like, from the owner for a period of time, as a lessee or occupant for rent. **2.** an occupant or inhabitant of any place. –*v.t.* **3.** to hold or occupy as a tenant; dwell in; inhabit. –**tenancy**, *n.* –**tenantable**, *adj.* –**tenantless**, *adj.*

tencel /'tɛnsɛl/ *n.* (*from trademark*) a fibre produced from cellulose obtained from wood pulp, used to make fabrics.

tend[1] /tɛnd/ *v.i.* **1.** to be disposed or inclined in action, operation, or effect (to do something): *the particles tend to unite.* **2.** to be disposed towards a state of mind, emotion, quality, etc. **3.** to incline in operation or effect; lead or conduce, as to some result or resulting condition: *measures tending to improved working conditions; governments are tending towards democracy.* **4.** to be directed or lead (in a specified direction), as a journey, course, road, etc.

tend[2] /tɛnd/ *v.t.* **1.** to attend to by work or services, care, etc.: *to tend a fire.* **2.** to look after; watch over and care for; minister to or wait on with service. **3.** *Naut.* to handle or watch (a line, etc.). –*phr.* **4. tend to**, to attend by action, care, etc.

tendency /'tɛndənsi/ *n.* (*pl.* **-cies**) natural or prevailing disposition to move, proceed, or act in some direction or towards some point, end, or result: *the tendency of falling bodies towards the earth.*

tendentious /tɛnˈdɛnʃəs/ *adj.* having or showing a definite tendency, bias, or purpose; described or written so as to influence in a desired direction or present a particular point of view: *a tendentious novel.* **–tendentiously**, *adv.* **–tendentiousness**, *n.*

tender¹ /ˈtɛndə/ *adj.* 1. soft or delicate in substance; not hard or tough: *a tender steak.* 2. weak or delicate in constitution; not strong or hardy. 3. *Wool* of wool fibres that have a weakness at a certain point of the staple such that if tension is applied the staple will break. 4. young or immature: *children of tender age.* 5. gentle. 6. soft-hearted. 7. acutely or painfully sensitive. 8. readily made uneasy, as the conscience. 9. of a delicate or ticklish nature; requiring careful or tactful handling: *a tender subject.* –*phr.* 10. **tender of,** considerate or careful of. **–tenderly**, *adv.* **–tenderness**, *n.*

tender² /ˈtɛndə/ *v.t.* 1. to present formally or offer for acceptance: *to tender one's resignation.* 2. *Law* to offer (money or goods) in payment of a debt or other claim. *–n.* 3. an offer of something for acceptance. 4. *Commerce* an offer made in writing by one party to another to carry out certain work, supply certain goods, etc., at a given cost. 5. *Law* an offer, as of money or goods, in payment of a debt, etc. **–tenderer**, *n.*

tender³ /ˈtɛndə/ *n.* 1. someone who tends; someone who attends to or takes charge of something. 2. an auxiliary vessel used to attend one or more other vessels, as for supplying provisions. 3. a small rowing boat or motorboat carried or towed by a yacht, usually used for transport to and from the shore. 4. a wagon attached to a steam locomotive, for carrying coal, water, etc.

tenderfoot /ˈtɛndəfʊt/ *n.* (*pl.* **-foots** *or* **-feet** /-fit/) a raw, inexperienced person; a novice.

tendon /ˈtɛndən/ *n. Anat.* a cord or band of dense, tough, inelastic, white fibrous tissue, serving to connect a muscle with a bone or part; a sinew.

tendril /ˈtɛndrəl/ *n. Bot.* a filiform leafless organ of climbing plants, often growing in spiral form, which attaches itself to or twines round some other body, so as to support the plant. **–tendrillar, tendrilous**, *adj.*

tenement /ˈtɛnəmənt/ *n.* 1. any house or building; dwelling house. 2. a portion of a house or building occupied by a tenant as a separate dwelling. 3. → **tenement house.** 4. any habitation, abode, or dwelling place. 5. *Law* **a.** any species of permanent property, as lands, houses, rents, an office, a franchise, etc., that may be held of another. **b.** (*pl.*) freehold interests in things immovable considered as subjects of property. **–tenemental** /tɛnəˈmɛntl/, **tenementary** /tɛnəˈmɛntəri/, *adj.*

tenement house *n.* a house divided into flats, especially one in the poorer, crowded parts of a large city.

tenet /ˈtɛnət/ *n.* any opinion, principle, doctrine, dogma, or the like, held as true.

tennis /ˈtɛnəs/ *n.* a game, played on a tennis court, in which two players, or two pairs of players, hit a ball backwards and forwards with racquets over a centrally placed net.

tenon /ˈtɛnən/ *n.* 1. a projection shaped on an end of a piece of wood, etc., for insertion in a corresponding cavity (mortice) in another piece, so as to form a joint. *–v.t.* 2. to shape so as to fit into a mortice. 3. to join securely.

tenor /ˈtɛnə/ *n.* 1. the course of thought or meaning which runs through something written or spoken; purport; drift. 2. continuous course, progress, or movement. 3. *Music* **a.** the highest natural male voice. **b.** a part sung by or written for such a voice, especially the next to the lowest part in four-part harmony. **c.** a singer with such a voice. **d.** an instrument of a range between alto and baritone. **e.** the lowest-toned bell of a peal. *–adj.* 4. *Music* of or relating to the tenor; having the compass of a tenor. **–tenorless**, *adj.*

tense¹ /tɛns/ *adj.* (**tenser, tensest**) 1. stretched tight, as a cord, fibre, etc.; drawn taut; rigid. 2. in a state of mental or nervous strain, as a person. 3. characterised by a strain upon the nerves or feelings: *a tense moment.* 4. *Phonetics* pronounced with relatively tense muscles. *–verb* (**tensed, tensing**) *–v.t.* 5. to make tense. *–v.i.* 6. to become tense. **–tensely**, *adv.* **–tenseness**, *n.*

tense² /tɛns/ *n. Gram.* a category of verb inflection found in some languages which specifies the time and length of occurrence of the action or state expressed by the verb.

tensile /ˈtɛnsaɪl/ *adj.* 1. of or relating to tension: *tensile stress.* 2. capable of being stretched or drawn out; ductile. **–tensility** /tɛnˈsɪləti/, *n.*

tension /ˈtɛnʃən/ *n.* 1. the act of stretching or straining. 2. the condition of being stretched or strained. 3. a strained feeling of anxiety or excitement. 4. a strained relationship between individuals, groups, countries, etc. 5. *Mechanics* a condition in which a body is stretched in size in one direction with a decrease in size in the perpendicular direction. 6. voltage. 7. a device to hold the proper tension on the material being woven in a loom. **–tensional**, *adj.* **–tensionless**, *adj.*

tent /tɛnt/ *n.* a portable shelter made of a strong material, formerly usually canvas, supported by one or more poles or a collapsible frame, and usually anchored by ropes fastened to pegs in the ground. **–tentless**, *adj.* **–tentlike**, *adj.*

tentacle /ˈtɛntəkəl/ *n.* 1. *Zool.* any of various slender, flexible processes or appendages in animals, especially invertebrates, which serve as organs of touch, prehension, etc.; a feeler. 2. *Bot.* a sensitive filament or process, as one of the glandular hairs of the sundew. **–tentacle-like**, *adj.* **–tentacular** /tɛnˈtækjələ/, *adj.*

tentative /ˈtɛntətɪv/ *adj.* 1. of the nature of, or made or done as, a trial, experiment, or attempt; experimental. 2. hesitant; cautious; diffident. **–tentatively**, *adv.* **–tentativeness**, *n.*

tenuous /ˈtɛnjuəs/ *adj.* 1. thin or slender in form. 2. thin in consistency; rare or rarefied. 3. of slight importance or significance; unsubstantial. 4. flimsy; lacking a firm or sound basis; weak; vague. **–tenuously**, *adv.* **–tenuousness, tenuity** /təˈnjuəti/, *n.*

tenure /ˈtɛnjə/ *n.* 1. the holding or possessing of anything: *the tenure of an office.* 2. **a.** a period of office or employment that terminates, possibly subject to certain conditions, only on resignation or retirement. **b.** the holding of such an office or employment. 3. *Law* the holding of property, especially real property, of a superior in return for services to be rendered. 4. the period or terms of holding something. **–tenurial** /tɛnˈjuriəl/, *adj.* **–tenurially** /tɛnˈjuriəli/, *adv.*

tepee /ˈtipi/ *n.* → **teepee.**

tepid /ˈtɛpəd/ *adj.* moderately warm; lukewarm. **–tepidity** /təˈpɪdəti/, **tepidness**, *n.* **–tepidly**, *adv.*

teppanyaki /tɛpənˈjaki/ *n.* a Japanese dish in which pieces of meat or fish are roasted on a hot plate, thus flavouring the oil in which vegetables are then cooked.

tequila /təˈkilə/ *n.* a Mexican drink produced by distillation of a fermented mash of agave.

tercentenary /tɜsənˈtinəri, -ˈtɛn-/ *adj.* 1. of or relating to a 300th anniversary. *–n.* (*pl.* **-ries**) 2. a 300th anniversary.

teriyaki /tɛriˈjaki/ *n.* a Japanese dish consisting of meat, chicken or seafood, marinated in a mixture containing soy sauce, and grilled.

term /tɜm/ *n.* 1. any word or expression used to name something, especially as used in some particular field of knowledge, as *atom* in physics, *free will* in theology, or *monkey wrench* in mechanics. **2.** any word or expression considered as a member of a construction or utterance. **3.** the time or period through which something lasts. **4.** a period of time to which limits have been set: *elected for a term of four years.* **5.** each of certain stated periods of the year into which instruction is regularly organised for students or pupils in universities, colleges, and schools. **6.** an appointed or set time or date, as for the payment of rent, interest, wages, etc.; tenor. **7.** (*pl.*) conditions with regard to payment, price, charge, rates, wages, etc.: *reasonable terms.* **8.** (*pl.*) conditions or stipulations limiting what is proposed to be granted or done: *the terms of a treaty.* **9.** (*pl.*) footing or standing: *on good terms with a person.* **10.** *Algebra, Arithmetic, etc.* each of the members of which an expression, a series of quantities, or the like is composed, as one of two or more parts of an algebraic expression. **11.** *Logic* **a.** the subject or predicate of a categorical proposition. **b.** the word or expression denoting the subject or predicate of a categorical preposition. **12.** *Law* **a.** an estate or interest in land, etc., to be enjoyed for a fixed period: *a term of years.* **b.** the duration of an estate. **c.** each of the periods during which certain courts of law hold their sessions. **13.** the normal completion of the period of pregnancy. **14.** *Aust. Rules* → **quarter** (def. 8). *–v.t.* **15.** to apply a particular term or name to; name; call; designate. *–phr.* **16. a contradiction in terms,** a statement which is self-contradictory. **17. bring to terms,** to compel to agree to stated conditions; force into submission. **18. come to terms,** to reach agreement. **19. come to terms with, a.** to reach agreement with. **b.** to become accustomed or resigned to.

termagant /ˈtɜməgənt/ *n.* **1.** a violent, turbulent, or brawling woman. *–adj.* **2.** violent; turbulent; brawling; shrewish.

terminal /ˈtɜmənəl/ *adj.* **1.** situated at or forming the end of something. **2.** relating to or lasting for a term or definite period. **3.** relating to, situated at, or forming the end of a bus or rail route. **4.** happening at or causing the end of life: *a terminal illness.* **5.** (of a person) having reached the point in the course of a disease where death from the disease is certain. *–n.* **6.** a terminal part or structure. **7.** the end of a railway line, shipping route, etc., at which large scale loading and unloading of passengers, goods, etc., takes place. **8.** *Elect.* **a.** a mechanical device by means of which an electrical connection to an apparatus is established. **b.** the point at which current enters or leaves any conducting part in an electric circuit. **9.** → **computer terminal**.

terminally /ˈtɜmənəli/ *adv.* **1.** at the end: *situated terminally.* **2.** incurably: *terminally ill.* **3.** *Colloq.* incessantly: *terminally cheerful.*

terminate /ˈtɜməneɪt/ *v.t.* **1.** bring to an end; put an end to. **2.** to occur at or form the conclusion of. **3.** to bound or limit spatially; form or be situated at the extremity of. **4.** to end (a pregnancy) by causing the fetus to be expelled before it is viable. **5.** to dismiss (someone) from employment. *–v.i.* **6.** to end, conclude, or cease. **7.** (of a train, bus, etc.) to complete a scheduled journey at a certain place. *–phr.* **8. terminate in,** to issue or result in. **–termination** /tɜməˈneɪʃən/, *n.* **–terminative** /ˈtɜmənətɪv/, *adj.* **–terminatively,** *adv.*

terminating building society *n. Finance* an association of individuals who make regular payments to a common fund, from which each obtains a housing loan, the order usually being determined by ballot; the society is terminated when the last house is paid for.

terminology /tɜməˈnɒlədʒi/ *n.* (*pl.* **-gies**) **1.** the system of terms belonging to a science, art, or subject; nomenclature: *the terminology of botany.* **2.** the systematic science of terms, as in particular sciences or arts.

–terminological /tɜmənəˈlɒdʒɪkəl/, *adj.* **–terminologically** /tɜmənəˈlɒdʒɪkli/, *adv.* **–terminologist,** *n.*

terminus /ˈtɜmənəs/ *n.* (*pl.* **-nuses** *or* **-ni** /-naɪ/) **1.** the end or extremity of anything. **2.** the station or town at the end of a railway line, bus route, etc. **3.** the point to which anything tends; goal or end. **4.** a boundary or limit.

termite /ˈtɜmaɪt/ *n.* any of the pale-coloured, soft-bodied, mainly tropical, social insects constituting the order Isoptera, some of which are very destructive to buildings, furniture, household stores, etc.; white ant.

tern /tɜn/ *n.* any bird of the subfamily Sterninae, family Laridae, comprising numerous aquatic species which are allied to the gulls but usually with a more slender body and bill, smaller feet, a long and deeply forked tail, and a more graceful flight, such as those constituting the genera *Sternula* and *Thalasseus*.

ternary /ˈtɜnəri/ *adj.* **1.** consisting of or involving three; threefold; triple. **2.** third in order or rank. **3.** based on the number three.

terrace /ˈtɛrəs/ *n.* **1.** a raised bank of earth with a level top, especially one of a series formed across a slope, mountain side, etc. **2.** *Geol.* a nearly level strip of land (once a flood plain) with a more or less sudden descent along the edge of a sea, lake or river. **3.** an open area connected with a house and serving as an outdoor living area. **4.** (a house in) a row of adjoining, identical houses, each built to its side boundaries, and usually of 19th-century construction or design, often with two storeys and iron lace decoration. **5.** a city street. *–v.t.* (**-raced, -racing**) **6.** to form into or supply with a terrace or terraces.

terracotta /tɛrəˈkɒtə/ *n.* **1.** a hard, usually unglazed earthenware of fine quality, used for architectural decorations, statuettes, vases, etc. **2.** a brownish orange colour like that of much terracotta.

terra firma /tɛrə ˈfɜmə/ *n.* firm or solid earth; dry land, as opposed to water or air.

terrain /təˈreɪn/ *n.* a tract of land, especially as considered with reference to its natural features, military advantages, etc.

terrarium /təˈrɛəriəm/ *n.* (*pl.* **-ariums** *or* **-aria** /-ˈrɛəriə/) **1.** a closed glass container in which moisture-loving plants are grown. **2.** a container or small enclosure in which small animals, as lizards, turtles, etc., are kept.

terrazzo /təˈratsoʊ, -ˈraz-/ *n.* a floor material of chippings of broken stone and cement, polished when in place.

terrestrial /təˈrɛstriəl/ *adj.* **1.** relating to, consisting of, or representing the earth: *a terrestrial globe.* **2.** of or relating to the land as separate from the water. **3.** *Zool.* living on the ground. **–terrestrially,** *adv.*

terrible /ˈtɛrəbəl/ *adj.* **1.** very bad: *a terrible performance.* **2.** very great: *a terrible liar.* **3.** exciting or fitted to excite terror or great fear; dreadful; awful. **–terribleness,** *n.* **–terribly,** *adv.*

terrier /ˈtɛriə/ *n.* one of a variety of dogs, typically small, with a propensity to pursue prey, as the fox, etc., into its burrow, occurring in many breeds including the fox terrier, Irish terrier, Australian terrier.

terrific /təˈrɪfɪk/ *adj.* **1.** extraordinarily great, intense, etc.: *terrific speed.* **2.** *Colloq.* very good: *terrific food, fishing.* **3.** causing terror; terrifying. **–terrifically,** *adv.*

terrify /ˈtɛrəfaɪ/ *v.t.* (**-fied, -fying**) to fill with terror; make greatly afraid. **–terrifier,** *n.*

terrine /təˈrin/ *n.* **1.** an earthenware cooking dish. **2.** a pâté of meat or game served in such a dish. **3.** a tureen.

territory /ˈtɛrətri, -təri/, *Orig. US* /-tɔri/ *n.* (*pl.* **-ries**) **1.** any area of land; region or district: *enemy territory.* **2.** the land and waters belonging to or under the control of a state, sovereign, etc. **3.** (*sometimes upper case*) **a.** (in Australia) an area of land under the jurisdiction of the federal government, distinguished from a state by its limited self-government. **b.** a region politically dependent (fully or partially) on an external government or externally appointed administrator. **4.** a field of action, thought, etc.: *giving legal advice is not in my territory.* **5.** an area which an animal claims as its own and defends against intruders. –**territorial**, *adj.*

terror /ˈtɛrə/ *n.* **1.** intense, sharp, overpowering fear: *to be frantic with terror.* **2.** a feeling, instance or cause of intense fear: *to be a terror to evildoers.* **3.** (*upper case*) a period when a political group uses violence to maintain or achieve supremacy, as that during the French Revolution. **4.** *Colloq.* a person or thing that is a particular nuisance: *that boy is a little terror.* –**terrorless**, *adj.*

terrorise /ˈtɛrəraɪz/ *v.t.* **1.** to fill or overcome with terror. **2.** to dominate or coerce by intimidation. Also, **terrorize**. –**terrorisation** /tɛrəraɪˈzeɪʃən/, *n.* –**terroriser**, *n.*

terrorism /ˈtɛrərɪzəm/ *n.* the use of methods to induce terror, especially the use of violence to achieve political ends. –**terrorist**, *n.*, *adj.* –**terroristic** /tɛrəˈrɪstɪk/, *adj.*

terry /ˈtɛri/ *n.* (*pl.* -**ries**) **1.** the loop formed by the pile of a fabric when left uncut. –*adj.* **2.** having the pile loops uncut: *terry velvet.*

terse /tɜs/ *adj.* **1.** neatly or effectively concise; brief and pithy, as language. **2.** abrupt or bad-tempered, especially in one's speech. –**tersely**, *adv.* –**terseness**, *n.*

tertiary /ˈtɜʃəri/ *adj.* **1.** of the third order, rank, formation, etc.; third. **2.** *Educ.* denoting or relating to tertiary education. **3.** (*upper case*) *Geol.* relating to a geological period or a system of rocks which precedes the Quaternary and constitutes the earlier principal division of the Cainozoic era. **4.** *Eccles.* denoting or relating to a branch (third order) of certain religious orders which consists of lay members living in community (**regular tertiaries**) or living in the world (**secular tertiaries**).

terylene /ˈtɛrəlin/ *n.* (*from trademark*) a synthetic polyester fibre, used in the manufacture of clothing, etc., made from ethylene glycol and terephthalic acid.

tesla /ˈtɛslə/ *n.* the SI derived unit of magnetic flux density, or magnetic intensity, defined as a magnetic flux of one weber per square metre (Wb/m²). *Symbol:* T

tessellate *v.t.* /ˈtɛsəleɪt/ **1.** to form into small squares or blocks, as floors, pavements, etc.; form or arrange in a chequered or mosaic pattern. **2.** *Maths* to cover (a plane surface) with a repeated shape without gaps or overlays. –*adj.* /ˈtɛsələt, -leɪt/ **3.** like a mosaic; tessellated. –**tessellation** /tɛsəˈleɪʃən/, *n.*

test¹ /tɛst/ *n.* **1.** a trial by which the presence, quality, or genuineness of anything is determined. **2.** a particular process or method of doing this: *this was a difficult test to carry out.* **3.** *Educ.* a form of examination for determining the performance and abilities of a student or class. **4.** *Chem.* **a.** a process of detecting the presence of an element in a compound, etc., or of determining the nature of a substance, usually by addition of a reagent. **b.** the reagent used. **c.** the result of the above process. **5.** a cup-like vessel for refining or refining metals. **6.** *Sport* → **test match**. –*v.t.* **7.** to subject to a test of any kind; try: *to test the water for heat.* **8.** to examine or refine in a test. –*v.i.* **9.** to conduct a test. –**testable**, *adj.* –**tester**, *n.*

test² /tɛst/ *n.* *Zool.* the hard covering of certain invertebrates, as molluscs, arthropods, tunicates, etc.; shell.

testament /ˈtɛstəmənt/ *n.* **1.** *Law* **a.** a formal declaration, usually in writing, of a person's wishes as to the disposition of his or her property after his or her death. **b.** a disposition to take effect upon death and relating to personal property. **2.** a covenant, especially between God and human beings. **3.** (*upper case*) either of the two main divisions of the Bible: **a.** the Mosaic or old covenant or dispensation. **b.** the Christian or new covenant or dispensation. –*phr.* **4.** (**a**) **testament to**, evidence of: *a testament to his good sense.*

testate /ˈtɛsteɪt, ˈtɛstət/ *adj.* *Law* having made and left a valid will.

testator /tɛsˈteɪtə/ *n.* *Law* **1.** someone who makes a will. **2.** someone who has died leaving a valid will.

testes /ˈtɛstiz/ *pl. n.* plural of **testis**.

testicle /ˈtɛstɪkəl/ *n.* the male sex gland, either of two oval glands situated in the scrotal sac. –**testicular** /tɛsˈtɪkjələ/, *adj.* –**testiculate** /tɛsˈtɪkjələt/, *adj.*

testify /ˈtɛstəfaɪ/ *verb* (**-fied, -fying**) –*v.i.* **1.** to give evidence; bear witness. **2.** *Law* to give a statement under solemn promise as to its truth, usually in court. –*v.t.* **3.** to state as fact or truth: *I testify that he lied.* **4.** to give evidence of in any manner: *the barren land testifies to a hard winter.* **5.** to declare, claim, or acknowledge openly. **6.** *Law* to state under solemn oath, usually in court. –**testifier**, *n.* –**testification** /tɛstəfəˈkeɪʃən/, *n.*

testimonial /tɛstəˈmoʊniəl/ *n.* **1.** a writing certifying to a person's character, conduct, or qualifications, or to a thing's value, excellence, etc.; a letter or written statement of recommendation. **2.** something given or done as an expression of esteem, admiration, or gratitude. –*adj.* **3.** relating to or serving as testimony.

testimony /ˈtɛstəməni/, *Orig. US* /-moʊni/ *n.* (*pl.* -**nies**) **1.** *Law* the statement or declaration of a witness under oath or affirmation, usually in court. **2.** evidence in support of a fact or statement; proof. **3.** open declaration or profession, as of faith.

testis /ˈtɛstəs/ *n.* (*pl.* -**tes** /-tiz/) → **testicle**.

test match *n.* a match or one of a series of matches, especially in cricket, between two nationally representative teams.

test tube *n.* a hollow cylinder of thin glass with one end closed, used in chemical tests.

test-tube baby *n.* **1.** a child born as a result of artificial insemination. **2.** a child conceived artificially outside a mother's body under simulated conditions suitable for its survival and then implanted in the womb.

testy /ˈtɛsti/ *adj.* (**-tier, -tiest**) irritably impatient; touchy. –**testily**, *adv.* –**testiness**, *n.*

tetanus /ˈtɛtnəs, ˈtɛtənəs/ *n.* **1.** *Pathol.* **a.** an infectious, often fatal disease, due to a specific microorganism, the **tetanus bacillus**, which gains entrance to the body through wounds, characterised by more or less violent tonic spasms and rigidity of many or all the voluntary muscles, especially those of the neck and lower jaw. **b.** the microorganism, *Clostridium tetami*, which causes this disease. **2.** *Physiol.* tonic contractions of a skeletal muscle induced by rapid stimulation. –**tetanoid**, *adj.*

tete-a-tete /teɪt-a-ˈteɪt/ *n.* **1.** a private conversation or interview, usually between two people. –*adv.* **2.** (of two persons) together in private: *to sit tete-a-tete.* Also, **tête-à-tête**.

tether /ˈtɛðə/ *n.* **1.** a rope, chain, or the like, by which an animal is fastened, as to a stake, so that its range of movement is limited. –*v.t.* **2.** to fasten or confine with or as with a tether. **3.** *Communications* to use a mobile phone or other internet-enabled mobile device as a modem for (another device), as a PDA, by cable or wireless connection. –*phr.* **4. the end of one's tether**, the limit of one's possibilities, patience, or resources.

tetra- a word element meaning 'four' as in *tetrabasic*.

tetragon /ˈtɛtrəgən, -gɒn/ *n.* *Geom.* a plane figure having four angles; a quadrangle; a quadrilateral.

tetrahedron /tɛtrəˈhidrən/ *n.* (*pl.* -**drons** *or* -**dra** /-drə/) *Geom.* a solid contained by four plane faces; a triangular pyramid.

text /tɛkst/ *n.* **1.** the main body of matter in a book or manuscript, not including notes, appendices, etc. **2.** the original words of an author as opposed to a translation, paraphrase, commentary, etc. **3.** the actual wording of anything written or printed. **4.** → **textbook**. **5.** a short passage of Scripture, especially one chosen as the subject of a sermon, etc. −*v.t.* **6.** to send (someone) a text message: *he texted me from Cairo.* **7.** to send (information) by text message: *I'll text the address of the party to you tomorrow.* −**textless**, *adj.* −**textual**, *adj.* −**texter**, *n.*

textaholic /ˈtɛkstəˈhɒlɪk/ *n. Colloq.* someone who sends an excessive number of text messages. −**textaholism**, *n.*

textbook /ˈtɛkstbʊk/ *n.* a book used by students as a standard work for a particular branch of study.

textile /ˈtɛkstaɪl/ *n.* **1.** any material that is woven. **2.** a material suitable for weaving. −*adj.* **3.** woven or capable of being woven: *textile fabrics.* **4.** of or relating to weaving: *the textile industries.*

text message *n.* a message sent by mobile phone using SMS. Also, **SMS message**, **SMS**. −**text messaging**, *n.*

texture /ˈtɛkstʃə/ *n.* **1.** the characteristic arrangement of the interwoven threads, etc., which make up a textile fabric. **2.** the characteristic appearance or basic quality of something, especially as sensed by touch: *the rough texture of concrete.* −**textural**, *adj.* −**textured**, *adj.* −**texturally**, *adv.*

-th[1] a noun suffix referring to condition, quality, or action, added to words (*warmth*) and to stems related to words (*depth, length*).

-th[2] the suffix of ordinal numerals (*fourth, tenth, twentieth*), the form *-th* being added in one or two cases to altered stems of the cardinal (*fifth, twelfth*).

thalidomide /θəˈlɪdəmaɪd/ *n.* a crystalline solid, $C_{13}H_{10}N_2O_4$, formerly used as a sedative until it was discovered that it could affect the normal growth of the fetus if taken during pregnancy.

thallophyte /ˈθæləfaɪt/ *n.* any member of the Thallophyta, a phylum of plants (including the algae, fungi, and lichens) in which the plant body of larger species is typically a thallus. −**thallophytic** /θæləˈfɪtɪk/, *adj.*

thallus /ˈθæləs/ *n.* (*pl.* **thalli** /ˈθælaɪ/ *or* **thalluses**) *Bot.* a simple vegetative plant body undifferentiated into true leaves, stem, and root, being the plant body of typical thallophytes.

than /ðæn/, *weak form* /ðən/ *conj.* **1.** a particle used after comparative adjectives and adverbs and certain other words, such as *other, otherwise, else*, etc., to introduce the second member of a comparison: *he is taller than I am.* −*prep.* **2.** in comparison with: *he is taller than me.*

thane /θeɪn/ *n.* **1.** *English Hist.* a member of any of several classes of men ranking between earls and ordinary freeman, and holding lands from the king or lord by military service. **2.** *Scot Hist.* a person, ranking with an earl's son, holding lands from the king; the chief of a clan, who became one of the king's barons.

thank /θæŋk/ *v.t.* **1.** to give thanks to; express gratitude to. −*phr.* **2. have oneself to thank**, to be oneself responsible or at fault. **3. have someone to thank for**, to rightly place blame or responsibility for (something) on someone. −**thanker**, *n.* −**thankful**, *adj.* −**thankless**, *adj.*

thanks /θæŋks/ *pl. n.* **1.** acknowledgement of gratitude for a benefit or favour, by words or otherwise: *to return a borrowed book with thanks.* −*interj.* **2.** an expression used in acknowledging a favour, service, courtesy, or the like. −*phr.* **3. thanks a million** (or **a bunch**), (*often ironic*) an emphatic expression of thanks. **4. thanks but no thanks**, (*sometimes ironic*) an expression of polite rejection. **5. thanks to**, **a.** thanks be given to. **b.** as a result or consequence of. **6. vote of thanks**, a formal expression of appreciation, usually on behalf of a group of people.

thank you *interj.* the customary expression of gratitude or acknowledgement. Also, **thankyou**.

thankyou /ˈθæŋkju/ *n.* **1.** the act of expressing thanks: *have you said your thankyous?* −*adj.* **2.** expressing thanks: *a thankyou letter.*

that /ðæt/, *weak form* /ðət/ *pron. (demonstrative)* **1.** used to indicate a person, thing, idea, etc., as pointed out or present, as before mentioned or supposed to be understood, as about to be mentioned, or by way of emphasis: *that's my choice.* **2.** used to indicate the one of two or more persons, things, etc., already mentioned, that is more remote in place, time, or thought. **3.** used to indicate one of two or more persons, things, etc., already mentioned, implying contradistinction, opposed to *this.* −*pron. (relative)* **4.** used as the subject or object of a relative clause, especially one defining or restricting the antecedent, sometimes replaceable by *who, whom*, or *which*: *the man that arrived*; *the man that I saw.* **5.** used as the object of a preposition, the preposition being at the end of the relative clause: *the man that I spoke of.* **6.** used in various special or elliptical constructions: *fool that he is.* −*adj. (demonstrative)* (*pl.* **those**) **7.** used to indicate a person, place, thing, idea, etc., as pointed out or present, as before mentioned or supposed to be understood, or by way of emphasis: *we want that help especially.* **8.** used to indicate, of two or more persons, things, etc., already mentioned, the one more remote in place, time, or thought. **9.** used to indicate one of two or more persons, things, etc., already mentioned, implying contradistinction (opposed to *this*). −*adv.* **10.** used with adjectives and adverbs of quantity or extent to indicate precise degree or extent: *that much*; *that far.* **11.** *Colloq.* used with other adjectives and adverbs to indicate extent or degree, or for emphasis: *poor lad, he was that weak!* −*conj.* **12.** used to introduce a clause as the subject or object of the principal verb or as the necessary complement to a statement made, or a clause expressing cause or reason, purpose or aim, result or consequence, etc.: *that he will come is certain*; *I know that you will do it.* **13.** used elliptically, to introduce a sentence or clause expressing desire, surprise, or indignation: *that you could do such a thing!* −*phr.* **14. and** (**all**) **that**, *Colloq.* and other related items: *the drawer was full of pencils and that.* **15. at that**, additionally; besides: *it's an idea, and a good one at that.* **16. that is**, more precisely (in clarification or example). **17. that's that**, that is the end of the matter; the matter is closed or finished (used dismissively). **18. with that**, thereupon; immediately afterwards.

thatch /θætʃ/ *n.* **1.** a material, as straw, rushes, leaves, or the like, used to cover roofs, haystacks, etc. **2.** *Colloq.* the hair covering the head. −*v.t.* **3.** to cover with or as with thatch. −**thatcher**, *n.* −**thatchless**, *adj.* −**thatchy**, *adj.*

thaw /θɔ/ *v.i.* **1.** to pass from a frozen to a liquid or semiliquid state; melt. **2.** to become less cold, formal, or reserved. **3.** to become less hostile, or aggressive: *relations between Russia and the US have thawed.* −*v.t.* **4.** to cause to thaw. −*n.* **5.** the act or process of thawing.

the[1] /ðɪ/ *before a vowel*, /ðə/ *before a consonant definite article* a word used especially before nouns **1.** with a limiting or specifying effect (opposed to *a* or *an*). **2.** with or as part of a title or name: *the Duke of Wellington*; *the Alps.* **3.** to mark a noun as being used to identify a class or type, etc.: *the dog is a quadruped.* **4.** in place of a possessive pronoun, to show a part of the body or a personal belonging: *to hang the head and weep.* **5.** to specify one of a class or type: *I saw it on the TV.* **6.** to show that there is enough of something: *I don't have the money to buy a car.*

the[2] /ðɪ/ *before a vowel*, /ðə/ *before a consonant adv.* a word used to modify an adjective or adverb in the comparative degree **1.** signifying 'in or by that', 'on that account', 'in or by so much', or 'in some or any degree': *he is taking more care of himself, and looks the better.* **2.** used correlatively, in one instance with relative force and in the other with demonstrative force, and signifying 'by how much … by so much' or 'in what degree … in that degree': *the more the merrier.*

theatre /ˈθɪətə, ˈθɪətə/ *n.* **1.** a building or room built or fitted for the presentation of dramatic performances, stage entertainments, etc. **2.** any area used for dramatic presentations, etc., as one in the open air. **3.** a cinema. **4.** dramatic works collectively, as of a nation, period, or author. **5.** a room or hall, fitted with tiers of seats rising like steps, used for lectures, etc. **6.** a room in a hospital in which surgical operations are performed: *an operating theatre.* **7.** a place of action: *theatre of war.*

theatrical /θiˈætrəkəl/ *adj.* Also, **theatric**. **1.** of or relating to the theatre, or dramatic or scenic representations: *theatrical performances.* **2.** suggestive of the theatre or of acting; artificial, pompous, spectacular, or extravagantly histrionic: *a theatrical display of grief.* –*n.* **3.** (*pl.*) dramatic performances, now especially as given by amateurs. –**theatricalism**, *n.* –**theatricality** /θi,ætrəˈkæləti/, **theatricalness**, *n.* –**theatrically**, *adv.*

theatrics /θiˈætrɪks/ *n.* **1.** (*construed as pl.*) dramatic performances. **2.** (*construed as pl.*) exaggerated or overblown expressions of emotion. **3.** (*construed as sing.*) the art of staging plays.

thee /ðiː/ *pron.* **1.** *Archaic* the objective case of **thou**[1]. **2.** a form of *thou* used, with a verb in the third person, by the Friends or Quakers.

theft /θɛft/ *n.* **1.** the act of stealing; the wrongful taking and carrying away of the personal goods of another; larceny. **2.** an instance of this.

their /ðɛə/ *adj.* **1.** the possessive form of **they**. **2.** (used with singular force in informal contexts, and increasingly in formal contexts, in place of a gender-specific form when the sex of the antecedent is not determined): *who has left their pen on my desk?*

theirs /ðɛəz/ *pron.* (*possessive*) **1.** the possessive form of **they**, used predicatively or absolutely: *the glory is all theirs; theirs not to reason why; a book of theirs.* **2.** (used with singular force in informal contexts, and increasingly in formal contexts, in place of a gender-specific form when the sex of the antecedent is not determined): *does anybody recognise this pen as theirs?*

theism /ˈθiːzəm/ *n.* **1.** the belief in one God as the creator and ruler of the universe, without rejection of revelation (distinguished from *deism*). **2.** belief in the existence of a God or gods (opposed to *atheism*). –**theist**, *n.*, *adj.* –**theistic** /θiˈɪstɪk/, **theistical** /θiˈɪstɪkəl/, *adj.* –**theistically** /θiˈɪstɪkli/, *adv.*

them /ðɛm/, *weak form* /ðəm/ *pron.* (*personal*) **1.** the objective case of **they**. **2.** used with singular force in informal contexts, and increasingly in formal contexts, in place of a gender-specific form where the sex of the antecedent is not determined: *if anyone calls, tell them I'm busy.* –*adj.* **3.** *Colloq.* (*non-standard*) those: *take them things out of here.*

theme /θiːm/ *n.* **1.** a subject of discourse, discussion, meditation, or composition; a topic. **2.** a short, informal essay, especially a school composition. **3.** *Music* **a.** a principal subject in a musical composition. **b.** a short subject from which variations are developed. **4.** *Gram.* the element common to all or most of the forms of an inflectional paradigm, often consisting in turn of a root with certain formative elements or modifications. –**thematic** /θəˈmætɪk/, *adj.* –**themeless**, *adj.* –**themed**, *adj.*

theme party *n.* a party in which the food, decor, guests' clothing, etc., is dictated by the choice of a particular theme.

themselves /ðəmˈsɛlvz/ *pl. pron.* **1.** the reflexive form of *them*: *they hurt themselves.* **2.** an emphatic form of *them* or *they* used: **a.** as object: *they used it for themselves.* **b.** in apposition to a subject or object: *they did it themselves.* **3.** their proper or normal selves; their usual

state of mind (used after *be, become,* or *come to*): *they are themselves again.* **4.** Also, **themself**. used with singular force in informal contexts, and increasingly in formal contexts, in place of a gender-specific form when the sex of the antecedent is not determined: *someone is deceiving themselves.*

then /ðɛn/ *adv.* **1.** at that time: *prices were lower then.* **2.** immediately or soon afterwards: *he stopped, and then began again.* **3.** next in order of time. **4.** at another time. **5.** next in order of place. **6.** in the next place; in addition; besides. **7.** in that case; in those circumstances. **8.** since that is so; therefore; consequently. –*adj.* **9.** being; being such; then existing: *the then prime minister.* –*n.* **10.** that time: *till then.* –*phr.* **11. but then**, but at the same time; but on the other hand.

thence /ðɛns/ *adv.* **1.** from that place. **2.** from that time; thenceforth. **3.** from that source; for that reason; therefore.

theo- a word element meaning 'relating to the gods', 'divine'. Also, (*before vowels*), **the-**.

theocracy /θiˈɒkrəsi/ *n.* (*pl.* **-cies**) a form of government in which God or a deity is recognised as the supreme civil ruler, his laws being interpreted by the ecclesiastical authorities.

theodolite /θiˈɒdəlaɪt/ *n.* *Surveying* an instrument for measuring horizontal or vertical angles. –**theodolitic** /θi,ɒdəˈlɪtɪk/, *adj.*

theology /θiˈɒlədʒi/ *n.* (*pl.* **-gies**) **1.** the science that deals with God, his attributes, and his relations to the universe; the science or study of divine things or religious truth; divinity. **2.** a particular form, system, or branch of this science or study. –**theologian** /θiəˈloʊdʒən/, *n.* –**theological** /θiəˈlɒdʒəkəl/, *adj.*

theorem /ˈθɪərəm/ *n.* **1.** *Maths* a statement embodying for proof established according to the axioms of a formal system of reasoning. **2.** *Maths* a rule or law, especially one expressed by an equation or formula. **3.** *Logic* a proposition which can be deduced from the premises or assumptions of a system. –**theorematic** /θɪərəˈmætɪk/, *adj.*

theoretical /θiəˈrɛtɪkəl/ *adj.* **1.** of, relating to, or consisting in theory; not practical. **2.** existing only in theory; hypothetical. **3.** given to, forming, or dealing with theories; speculative. Also, **theoretic**. –**theoretically**, *adv.* –**theoretician**, *n.*

theorise /ˈθɪəraɪz/ *v.i.* **1.** to form a theory or theories. **2.** to speculate or conjecture. Also, **theorize**. –**theorisation** /θɪəraɪˈzeɪʃən/, *n.* –**theoriser**, *n.*

theory /ˈθɪəri/ *n.* (*pl.* **-ries**) **1.** a logical group of statements used as principles to explain something: *Newton's theory of gravitation.* **2.** a suggested explanation not yet established as fact: *a theory about ghosts.* **3.** that part of a science or art which deals with principles and methods rather than with practice. **4.** opinion; conjecture. –**theorist**, *n.*

theosophy /θiˈɒsəfi/ *n.* **1.** any of various forms of philosophical or religious thought in which claim is made to a special insight into the divine nature or to a special divine revelation. **2.** the system of belief and doctrine, based largely on Brahmanic and Buddhistic ideas, of the Theosophical Society (founded in New York in 1875). –**theosophic** /θiəˈsɒfɪk/, **theosophical** /θiəˈsɒfɪkəl/, *adj.* –**theosophically** /θiəˈsɒfɪkli/, *adv.* –**theosophist**, *n.*

therapy /ˈθɛrəpi/ *n.* (*pl.* **-pies**) **1.** the treatment of disease, disorder, defect, etc., as by some remedial or curative process. **2.** a curative power or quality. –**therapeutic**, *adj.* –**therapeutically**, *adv.* –**therapist**, *n.*

there /ðɛə/ *adv.* **1.** in or at that place. **2.** at that point in an action, speech, etc. **3.** in that matter, particular, or respect. **4.** into or to that place; thither. **5.** used less definitely and also unemphatically as by way of calling the attention to something: *there they go.* **6.** used for emphasis with a demonstrative, after the noun: *that man there.* –*adj.* **7.** *Colloq.* used for emphasis between a demonstrative and the noun: *that there man.* –*pron.* **8.** that place: *he comes from there too.* **9.** used to introduce a sentence or clause in which the verb comes before its subject: *there is no hope.* **10.** used in interjectional phrases: *there's a good boy.* –*interj.* **11. a.** an exclamation used to express satisfaction, etc.: *there! it's done!* **b.** an exclamation used to give consolation: *there, there, don't cry.* **c.** an exclamation used to draw attention to something: *there! the jug's broken.* –*phr.* **12. all there, a.** of sound mind. **b.** shrewd; quick-witted. **13. so there,** an exclamation expressing opposition, defiance, etc.: *I will go, so there!* **14. there you are, a.** an expression indicating that all is well or as expected. **b.** an expression used when handing someone something which they expect to receive. **15. there you go, a.** an expression indicating resignation, acceptance of the way things are, etc. **b.** an expression used when handing someone something which they expect to receive.

there- a word element meaning 'that (place)', 'that (time)', etc., used in combination with certain adverbs and prepositions.

thereabouts /ðɛərə'bauts, 'ðɛərəbauts/ *adv.* **1.** about or near that place or time. **2.** about that number, amount, etc. Also, **thereabout.**

thereby /ðɛə'baɪ, 'ðɛəbaɪ/ *adv.* **1.** by that; by means of that. **2.** in that connection or relation: *thereby hangs a tale.* **3.** by or near that place.

therefore /'ðɛəfɔ, ðɛə'fɔ/ *conj.* in consequence of that; as a result; consequently.

thereupon /ðɛərə'pɒn, 'ðɛərəpɒn/ *adv.* **1.** immediately following that. **2.** in consequence of that. **3.** upon that or it. **4.** with reference to that.

therm /θɜm/ *n.* a unit of heat in the imperial system, used as a basis for the selling of gas; equal to 100 000 British thermal units, or about 105.5×10^6 J.

therm- a word element representing **thermal.** Also, **thermo-.**

thermal /'θɜməl/ *adj.* Also, **thermic. 1.** of or relating to heat or temperature: *thermal energy.* –*n.* **2.** *Aeronautics, Meteorol.* an ascending current of air caused by local heating, used by glider pilots to attain height. –**thermally,** *adv.*

thermodynamics /ˌθɜmoʊdaɪ'næmɪks/ *n.* the science concerned with the relations between heat and mechanical energy or work, and the conversion of one into the other. –**thermodynamic, thermodynamical,** *adj.* –**thermodynamically,** *adv.*

thermometer /θə'mɒmətə/ *n.* an instrument for measuring temperature, as by means of the expansion and contraction of mercury or alcohol in a capillary tube and bulb. –**thermometry,** *n.* –**thermometric** /θɜmə'mɛtrɪk/, **thermometrical** /θɜmə'mɛtrɪkl/, *adj.* –**thermometrically** /θɜmə'mɛtrɪkli/, *adv.*

thermonuclear /ˌθɜmoʊ'njukliə/ *adj.* designating, or capable of producing, extremely high temperatures resulting from, caused by, or associated with nuclear fusion.

thermonuclear reaction *n.* a nuclear fusion reaction that takes place between atomic nuclei which form part of a substance which has been heated to a temperature of several million degrees centigrade.

thermos /'θɜmɒs, -məs/ *n.* (*from trademark*) a double-walled container used to keep substances that are hotter or colder than their surroundings at a constant temperature. Also, **thermos flask.**

thermosphere /'θɜməsfɪə/ *n.* the region of the earth's atmosphere lying beyond the mesosphere, at an altitude

of 80 km to more than 100 km from the earth, in which the temperature increases with altitude.

thermostat /'θɜməstæt/ *n.* a device, including a relay actuated by thermal conduction or convection, which establishes and maintains a desired temperature automatically, or signals a change in temperature for manual adjustment. –**thermostatic** /θɜmə'stætɪk/, *adj.* –**thermostatically** /θɜmə'stætɪkli/, *adv.*

-thermy a word element referring to heat.

thesaurus /θə'sɔrəs, -'zɔ-/ *n.* (*pl.* **-ruses** /-raɪ, -'zɔ-/) **1.** a storehouse or repository, as of words or knowledge; a dictionary, encyclopedia, or the like, especially a dictionary of synonyms and antonyms. **2.** a treasury.

these /ðiz/ *pron., adj.* plural of **this.**

thesis /'θisəs/ *n.* (*pl.* **theses** /'θisiz/) **1.** a proposition laid down or stated, especially one to be discussed and proved or to be maintained against objections. **2.** a subject for a composition or essay. **3.** a dissertation, as one presented by a candidate for a diploma or degree, especially a postgraduate degree.

thespian /'θɛspiən/ (*also upper case*) –*adj.* **1.** relating to tragedy or to the dramatic art in general; tragic; dramatic. –*n.* **2.** an actor.

thew /θju/ *n.* **1.** (*usu. pl.*) muscle or sinew. **2.** (*pl.*) physical strength. –**thewy,** *adj.*

they /ðeɪ/ *pron. (personal), third person, pl., subjective* (*objective* **them**) **1.** plural of **he, she,** and **it. 2.** people in general: *they say he is rich.* **3.** used with singular force in informal contexts, and increasingly in formal contexts, in place of a gender-specific form where the sex of the antecedent is not determined: *if anybody cheats they will be disqualified.*

thiamine /'θaɪəmin/ *n.* a white crystalline solid forming part of the vitamin B complex, $C_{12}H_{17}ClN_4OS$; a vitamin (B_1) required by the nervous system, absence of which causes beri-beri and other disorders. Also, **thiamin.**

thick /θɪk/ *adj.* **1.** having relatively great extent from one surface or side to its opposite; not thin: *a thick slice.* **2.** measuring as specified between opposite surfaces, or in depth, or in a direction perpendicular to that of the length and breadth: *a board one centimetre thick.* **3.** set close together; compact; dense: *a thick forest.* **4.** numerous, abundant, or plentiful. **5.** having relatively great consistency; viscous: *a thick syrup.* **6.** husky, hoarse, muffled, or not clear in sound: *a thick voice.* **7.** (of an accent or dialect) very pronounced. **8.** (of mist, smoke, etc.) having the component particles densely aggregated. **9.** sluggish; heavy-headed, as after dissipation. **10.** slow of mental apprehension; stupid; dull; slow-witted. **11.** *Colloq.* close in friendship; intimate. **12.** *Colloq.* disagreeably excessive: *his demands are a bit thick.* –*adv.* **13.** in a thick manner. **14.** closely; near together: *flowers growing thick beside a wall.* –*n.* **15.** that which is thick. **16.** the thickest, densest, or most crowded part; the place, time, stage, etc., of greatest activity or intensity: *in the thick of the fight.* –*phr.* **17. as thick as thieves,** very close friends. **18. a thick ear,** a swollen ear. **19. lay it on thick,** *Colloq.* to be extravagant in flattery, praise, or the like. **20. thick with,** filled or covered with: *tables thick with dust.* **21. through thick and thin,** under all circumstances; unwaveringly. –**thicken,** *v.* –**thickish,** *adj.* –**thickly,** *adv.* –**thickness,** *n.*

thicket /'θɪkət/ *n.* a thick or dense growth of shrubs, bushes, or small trees; a thick coppice.

thickset /'θɪksɛt/ *adj.* **1.** set thickly or in close arrangement; dense: *a thickset hedge.* **2.** set, studded, or covered thickly: *a sky thickset with stars.* **3.** of thick form or build; heavily or solidly built. –*n.* **4.** → **thicket.**

thick-skinned *adj.* **1.** having a thick skin. **2.** not sensitive to criticism, reproach, rebuff, etc.

thief /θif/ *n.* (*pl.* **thieves**) someone who steals, especially secretly or without open force; someone guilty of theft or larceny. –**thieve**, *v.*

thigh /θaɪ/ *n.* **1.** the part of the leg between the hip and the knee in humans. **2.** a homologous or apparently corresponding part of the hind limb of other animals; the region of the femur. **3.** (in birds) **a.** the true femoral region, buried in the general integument of the body. **b.** the segment below, containing the fibula and tibia. **4.** → femur.

thimble /'θɪmbəl/ *n.* **1.** a small cap, usually of metal, worn on the finger to push the needle in sewing. **2.** *Machinery* any of various devices or attachments likened to this. **3.** a short length of pipe encasing one of smaller diameter, as where a stovepipe passes through a wooden roof. **4.** *Naut.* a metal ring with a concave groove on the outside, used to line the inside of a ring of rope forming an eye.

thin /θɪn/ *adj.* (**thinner**, **thinnest**) **1.** having relatively little extent from one surface or side to its opposite; not thick: *thin ice.* **2.** of small cross-section in comparison with the length; slender: *a thin wire.* **3.** having little flesh; spare; lean. **4.** having the constituent or individual parts relatively few and not close together: *thin vegetation.* **5.** not dense; sparse; scanty. **6.** having relatively slight consistency, as a liquid; fluid; rare or rarefied, as air, etc. **7.** without solidity or substance; unsubstantial. **8.** easily seen through, transparent, or flimsy: *a thin excuse.* **9.** lacking fullness or volume, as sound; weak and shrill. **10.** faint, slight, poor, or feeble. **11.** lacking body, richness, or growth. –*adv.* **12.** so as to be thin: *slice it thin.* –*phr.* (*v.* **thinned**, **thinning**) **13.** (**as**) **thin as a rake** (or **rail**) (or **lath**), *Colloq.* extremely lean; having little bodily flesh. **14. thin down**, to become thin or thinner. **15. thin down** (or **out**), to make thin or thinner. **16. thin off**, to become reduced or diminished. **17. thin on the ground**, few in number; scarce. –**thinly**, *adv.* –**thinness**, *n.*

thine /ðaɪn/ *Archaic* –*pron.* (*possessive*) **1.** the possessive form of **thou**[1], used predicatively or absolutely: *thine be the glory.* –*adj.* **2.** thy (before a noun beginning with a vowel sound): *thine eyes.* Compare **thy.**

thing /θɪŋ/ *n.* **1.** a material object without life or consciousness; an inanimate object. **2.** some entity, object, or creature which is not or cannot be specifically designated or precisely described: *the stick had a brass thing on it.* **3.** that which is or may become an object of thought, whether material or ideal, animate or inanimate, actual, possible, or imaginary. **4.** a matter or affair: *things are going well now.* **5.** a fact or circumstance: *it is a curious thing.* **6.** an action, deed, or performance: *to do great things.* **7.** a particular or respect: *perfect in all things.* **8.** what is desired or required: *just the thing.* **9.** (*pl.*) clothes or apparel, especially articles of dress added to ordinary clothing when going outdoors. **10.** (*pl.*) *Colloq.* implements, utensils, or other articles used for a particular activity, occasion, etc.: *to help with the breakfast things.* **11.** (*pl.*) *Colloq.* personal possessions or belongings, often such as one carries along on a journey. **12.** *Law* anything that may be the subject of a property right. **13.** that which is signified or represented, as distinguished from a word, symbol, or idea representing it. **14.** a living being or creature: *poor thing!; she was just a little thing.* –*phr.* **15. a good thing**, something warranting support. **16. do one's (own) thing**, *Colloq.* to act in a characteristic manner; to do what is most satisfying to oneself. **17. do the right** (or **handsome**) **thing by**, to treat generously. **18. have a thing about**, *Colloq.* **a.** to have an unaccountable feeling of fear or aversion toward: *I have a thing about walking under ladders.* **b.** to have a particular liking or fondness for: *I have a thing about French films.* **19. how's things?**, *Colloq.*

a form of greeting. **20. (just) one of those things**, an event which was unavoidable or which is no longer remediable, and so must be accepted as part of life. **21. just the thing**, exactly what is needed: *thank you, that's just the thing.* **22. know a thing or two**, *Colloq.* to be shrewd. **23. make a good thing out of**, to obtain an advantage from. **24. make a thing of**, *Colloq.* to exaggerate the significance of: *OK, so I made a mistake, but there's no need to make a thing of it.* **25. not get a thing out of**, **a.** to fail to elicit something desired, as information, from. **b.** to fail to enjoy, appreciate, etc.: *I went to a performance of a play in Czech, but didn't get a thing out of it.* **26. old thing**, *Colloq.* a familiar form of address. **27. on a good thing**, **a.** (in betting on horses, dogs, etc.) backing a likely winner at favourable odds. **b.** engaged in a project which promises to be successful. **28. the (done) thing**, behaviour which is considered to conform to acceptable standards of propriety and good taste. **29. the (in) thing**, whatever is deemed fashionable at the time. **30. the thing**, **a.** that which is important or necessary. **b.** the point of a matter: *this is the thing.*

think /θɪŋk/ *verb* (**thought**, **thinking**) –*v.t.* **1.** to form or conceive in the mind; have in the mind as an idea, conception, or the like. **2.** to turn over in the mind; meditate; ponder: *he was thinking what it could mean.* **3.** to have the mind full of (a particular subject or the like). **4.** to form or have an idea or conception of (a thing, fact, circumstance, etc.). **5.** to bear in mind, recollect, or remember. **6.** to have in mind, intent, or purpose. **7.** to hold as an opinion; believe; suppose: *they thought that the earth was flat.* **8.** to consider (something) to be (as specified): *she thought the lecture was very interesting.* **9.** to anticipate or expect: *I did not think to find you here.* **10.** to bring by thinking. –*v.i.* **11.** to use the mind, especially the intellect, actively; cogitate or meditate. **12.** to reflect upon the matter in question: *think carefully before you begin.* **13.** to have a belief or opinion as indicated. **14.** to have an opinion as indicated: *he thought fit to act alone.* –*n.* **15.** *Colloq.* an act or process of thinking: *go away and have a good think.* –*phr.* **16. think about**, to hold as an opinion concerning (someone or something): *what do you think about abortion?* **17. think aloud**, to utter one's thoughts without considering all implications or putting them into a formal pattern. **18. think better of**, to decide against (an original intention). **19. think little of**, to have a poor or low opinion of. **20. think nothing of**, **a.** to have a very low opinion of. **b.** to reckon to be of no account. **21. think of**, **a.** to form or have an idea or mental image of. **b.** to remember: *I can't think of his name.* **c.** to have consideration or regard for: *to think of others first.* **d.** to make mental discovery of; form or have a plan of: *he thought of it first.* **e.** to have an anticipation or expectation of. **22. think ... of**, to have a specified opinion of (someone or something): *to think well of someone.* **23. think out**, **a.** to finish or complete in thought. **b.** to understand or solve by process of thought. **c.** to devise or contrive by thinking. **24. think over**, to consider carefully and at leisure. **25. think through**, to consider carefully. **26. think twice**, to consider with great care (before taking action). **27. think up**, to form as a concept; devise. –**thinkable**, *adj.* –**thinker**, *n.*

think tank *n.* a group, usually of highly qualified specialists, dedicated to the solving of particular problems and the generating of productive ideas.

thinner /'θɪnə/ *n.* a volatile liquid added to paints or varnishes to facilitate application and to aid penetration by lowering the viscosity.

third /θɜd/ *adj.* **1.** next after the second in order, time, value, quality, etc. (the ordinal of 3). **2.** one out of every three: *every third Monday.* –*n.* **3.** someone or something that comes next after the second. **4.** a third part, especially of one ($^1/_3$). **5.** (*usu. pl.*) *Law* the third part of the personal property of a dead husband, which in certain circumstances goes totally to the widow. **6.** *Music* the third note in a scale from a given note (counted as the first): *E is a third above C.* –**thirdly,** *adv.*

third degree *n.* the use of bullying or torture by the police (or others) in some countries in examining a person in order to extort information or a confession: *to give one the third degree.*

third-degree *adj.* of a degree which is at the extreme end of a scale, either as the lowest (*third-degree murder*) or the highest (*third-degree burns*).

third man *n. Cricket* the player in a fielding position near the boundary on the off side behind the wicket of the person batting.

third party *n.* any person other than the principals to some transaction, proceeding, or agreement.

third-party *adj.* denoting an insurance policy against liability caused by the insurer or his or her employees to the property or person of others.

third person *n.* See **person** (def. 10).

third-person shooter *n.* a type of shooter game in which the game world is rendered as if viewed from above and behind the main character. *Abbrev.*: TPS Compare **first-person shooter**.

Third Way *n.* a political strategy which tries to find a middle path between the left and right wings and seeks consensus on individual issues.

Third World *n.* (*also lower case*) **1.** developing countries collectively, especially in Africa, South America, and South-East Asia, which are not heavily industrialised, have a low standard of living, and which usually did not have a strong political alignment with either the Communist bloc or the capitalist West. –*adj.* **2.** relating to or inhabiting countries considered to be part of the Third World.

thirst /θɜst/ *n.* **1.** an uneasy or painful sensation of dryness in the mouth and throat caused by need of drink. **2.** the physical condition resulting from this need. **3.** strong or eager desire; craving: *a thirst for knowledge.* –*v.i.* **4.** to feel thirst; be thirsty. **5.** to have a strong desire. –**thirster,** *n.* –**thirstless,** *adj.* –**thirsty,** *adj.* –**thirstily,** *adv.*

thirteen /θɜ'tin/ *n.* **1.** a cardinal number, ten plus three. **2.** a symbol for this number, as 13 or XIII. –*adj.* **3.** amounting to thirteen in number. –*pron.* **4.** thirteen people or things. –**thirteenth,** *adj.*

thirty /'θɜti/ *n.* (*pl.* -**ties**) **1.** a cardinal number, ten times three. **2.** a symbol for this number, as 30 or XXX. **3.** (*pl.*) the numbers from 30 to 39 of a series, especially with reference to the years of a person's age, or the years of a century, especially the twentieth. –*adj.* **4.** amounting to thirty in number. –*pron.* **5.** thirty people or things. –**thirtieth,** *adj.*

this /ðɪs/ *pron.* (*pl.* **these**) **1.** used to indicate a person, thing, idea, etc., as pointed out, present, or near, as before mentioned or supposed to be understood, as about to be mentioned, or by way of emphasis: *this is right.* **2.** used to indicate the one of two or more persons, things, etc., already mentioned, that is nearer in place, time, or thought. **3.** used to indicate one of two or more persons, things, etc., already mentioned, implying contradistinction; opposed to *that.* –*adj.* (*demonstrative*) (*pl.* **these**) **4.** used to indicate a person, place, thing, idea, etc., as pointed out, present, or near, as before mentioned or supposed to be understood, or by way of emphasis: *this point is important.* **5.** used to indicate one of two or more persons, things, etc., already mentioned, the one nearer in place, time, or thought. **6.** used to indicate one of two or more persons,

things, etc., already mentioned, implying contradistinction (opposed to *that*). –*adv.* **7.** used with adjectives and adverbs of quantity or extent to indicate precise degree or extent: *this much.* –*phr.* **8. with this,** hereupon; immediately after this.

thistle /'θɪsəl/ *n.* **1.** any of various prickly plants of the genus *Cirsium*, as *C. vulgare*, the **spear thistle. 2.** any prickly plant of related genera, as *Carduus*, *Carlina*, and *Onopordum.* **3.** any of various other prickly plants. –**thistlelike,** *adj.* –**thistly,** *adj.*

thither /'ðɪðə/ *adv.* Also, **thitherwards** /'ðɪðəwədz/, **thitherward. 1.** to or towards that place or point. –*adj.* **2.** on the side or in the direction away from the person speaking; farther; more remote.

thong /θɒŋ/ *n.* **1.** a narrow strip of hide or leather, used as a fastening, as the lash of a whip, etc. **2.** a similar strip of some other material. **3.** *Aust.* a sandal held loosely on the foot by two strips of leather, rubber, etc., passing between the first and second toes and over either side of the foot. **4.** *US* → **G-string.**

thorax /'θɔræks/ *n.* (*pl.* **thoraces** /'θɔrəsiz, θɔ'reisiz/ *or* **thoraxes**) **1.** *Anat.* (in humans and the higher vertebrates) the part of the trunk between the neck and the abdomen, containing the cavity (enclosed by the ribs, etc.) in which the heart, lungs, etc., are situated; the chest. **2.** *Zool.* a corresponding part in other animals. **3.** *Entomology* the portion of the body between the head and the abdomen. –**thoracic** /θɔ'ræsɪk/, *adj.*

thorn /θɔn/ *n.* **1.** a sharp excrescence on a plant, especially a sharp-pointed aborted branch; a spine; a prickle. **2.** any of various thorny shrubs or trees, especially of the genus *Crataegus*, as *C. monogyna*, the common hawthorn, often planted for hedges. **3.** their wood. **4.** something that wounds, or causes discomfort or annoyance. **5.** the character Þ, þ for *th* (formerly in the English alphabet; still used in Iceland). –*phr.* **6. thorn in someone's flesh** (or **side**), a source of continual annoyance, discomfort, or the like. –**thornless,** *adj.* –**thornlike,** *adj.*

thornbill /'θɔnbɪl/ *n.* any of various small birds of the genus *Acanthiza*, family Pardalotidae, of Australia and New Guinea, with small but stout and sharp bills, as the **yellow-rumped thornbill,** *A. chrysorrhoa.*

thorny /'θɔni/ *adj.* (**-nier, -niest**) **1.** having or characterised by thorns; spiny; prickly. **2.** thornlike. **3.** overgrown with thorns or brambles. **4.** painful; vexatious. **5.** full of points of dispute; difficult: *a thorny question.* –**thorniness,** *n.*

thorny devil *n.* a spiny agamid lizard, *Moloch horridus*, occurring in lowland as well as mountain regions of southern, central, and western Australia; moloch; mountain devil. Also, **thorn devil, thorn lizard.**

thorough /'θʌrə/ *adj.* **1.** carried out through the whole of something; fully executed; complete or perfect: *a thorough search.* **2.** being fully or completely (such): *a thorough fool.* **3.** thoroughgoing in action or procedure; leaving nothing undone. –**thoroughly,** *adv.* –**thoroughness,** *n.*

thoroughbred /'θʌrəbrɛd/ *adj.* **1.** of pure or unmixed breed, stock, or race, as a horse or other animal. **2.** (of human beings) having qualities characteristic of pure breeding; high-spirited; mettlesome; elegant or graceful. –*n.* **3.** a thoroughbred animal. **4.** (*upper case*) a horse of the English breed of racehorses, developed by crossing domestic and Middle Eastern strains. **5.** a well-bred or thoroughly trained person.

thoroughfare /'θʌrəfɛə/ *n.* **1.** a road, street, or the like, open at both ends, especially a main road. **2.** a passage or way through: *no thoroughfare.* **3.** a strait, river, or the like, affording passage.

those /ðoʊz/ *pron., adj.* plural of **that.**

thou[1] /ðaʊ/ *pron. (personal),* second person, *sing., subjective (objective* **thee**) *Archaic* used to denote the person or thing spoken to; formerly in general use, often as indicating equality, familiarity, or intimacy, superiority on the part of the speaker, or contempt or scorn for the person addressed, but now little used (being regularly replaced by *you,* which is in origin plural, and takes a plural verb) except in poetry or elevated prose, in addressing the Deity, and by the Friends or Quakers.

thou[2] /θaʊ/ *n. Colloq.* **1.** a thousand (dollars, kilometres, etc.). **2.** one thousandth (of an inch, etc.).

though /ðoʊ/ *conj.* **1.** (introducing a subordinate clause, which is often marked by ellipsis) notwithstanding that; in spite of the fact that: *though she was widowed, she was happy*; *he is active though disabled.* **2.** even if; granting that. **3.** yet, still, or nevertheless (introducing an additional statement restricting or modifying a principal one): *I will go though I fear it will be useless.* **4.** (usu. in *as though*) if. *–adv.* **5.** for all that; however. Also, *Poetic,* **tho'**.

thought /θɔt/ *v.* **1.** past tense and past participle of **think**. *–n.* **2.** the product of mental activity; that which one thinks. **3.** a single act or product of thinking; an idea, notion, or consideration: *to collect one's thoughts.* **4.** the act or process of thinking; mental activity. **5.** the capacity or faculty of thinking. **6.** meditation: *lost in thought.* **7.** intention, design, or purpose, especially a half-formed or imperfect intention: *we had some thought of going.* **8.** consideration, attention, care, or regard: *taking no thought for her appearance.* **9.** a judgement, opinion, or belief. **10.** the intellectual activity or the ideas, opinions, etc., characteristic of a particular place, class, or time: *Greek thought. –phr.* **11. have second thoughts,** to be reconsidering. *–***thoughtful,** *adj. –***thoughtless,** *adj.*

thought police *n. Colloq.* (*derog.*) authoritarians who wish to regulate the way people think, especially in relation to political correctness.

thousand /ˈθaʊzənd/ *n.* (*pl.* **-sands**, *as after a numeral,* **-sand**) **1.** a cardinal number, ten times one hundred. **2.** a symbol for this number, as 1000 or M. **3.** (*pl.*) a great number or amount. *–adj.* **4.** amounting to one thousand in number. *–pron.* **5.** one thousand people or things. *–phr.* **6. one in a thousand,** exceedingly good; exceptional; outstanding. *–***thousandth,** *adj.*

thrall /θrɔl/ *n.* **1.** someone who is in bondage; a bondman or slave. **2.** someone who is in bondage to some power, influence, or the like. **3.** thraldom.

thrash /θræʃ/ *v.t.* **1.** to beat soundly by way of punishment; administer a beating to. **2.** to defeat thoroughly. **3.** *Naut.* to force (a ship) forward against the wind, etc. **4.** *Colloq.* to drive (a vehicle, etc.) at high speed without regard to its condition. **5.** to thresh (wheat, grain, etc.). *–v.i.* **6.** to beat, toss, or plunge wildly or violently about. **7.** *Naut.* to make way against the wind, tide, etc.; beat. **8.** to thresh wheat, grain, etc. *–n.* **9.** the act of thrashing; a beating; a blow. **10.** *Swimming* the upward and downward movement of the legs, as in freestyle. **11.** heavy-metal music influenced by punk rock, characterised by powerful amplification and a very heavy beat. *–adj.* **12.** of or relating to thrash (def. 11). *–phr.* **13. thrash along,** *Colloq.* to proceed at high speed. **14. thrash out,** to discuss (a matter) exhaustively; solve (a problem, etc.) by exhaustive discussion.

thread /θrɛd/ *n.* **1.** a fine cord of flax, cotton, or other fibrous material spun out to considerable length, especially such a cord composed of two or more filaments twisted together. **2.** twisted fibres of any kind used for sewing. **3.** one of the lengths of yarn forming the warp and woof of a woven fabric. **4.** a filament or fibre of glass or other ductile substance. **5.** something having

the fineness or slenderness of a thread, as a thin continuous stream of liquid, a fine line of colour, or a thin seam of ore. **6.** the helical ridge of a screw. **7.** that which runs through the whole course of something, connecting successive parts, as the sequence of events in a narrative. **8.** (*pl.*) *Colloq.* clothes. **9.** *Internet* a newsgroup posting and its set of replies, forming a group of related messages. *–v.t.* **10.** to pass the end of a thread through the eye of (a needle). **11.** to fix (beads, etc.) upon a thread that is passed through; string. **12.** to form a thread on or in (a bolt, hole, etc.). *–v.i.* **13.** to make one's way, as through a passage or between obstacles. **14.** to move in a threadlike course; wind or twine. **15.** *Cookery* (of boiling syrup) to form a fine thread when dropped from a spoon. *–phr.* **16. hang by a thread,** to be in a dangerous or precarious position. **17. lose the thread,** to cease to understand through inattention at some stage. *–***threader,** *n. –***threadless,** *adj. –***threadlike,** *adj.*

threadbare /ˈθrɛdbɛə/ *adj.* **1.** having the nap worn off so as to lay bare the threads of the warp and woof, as a fabric, garment, etc. **2.** meagre, scanty, or poor. **3.** hackneyed or trite: *threadbare arguments.* **4.** wearing threadbare clothes; shabby: *the threadbare little old man.*

threading /ˈθrɛdɪŋ/ *n.* **1.** the passing of a thread through something, as a needle. **2.** the process of forming a thread. **3.** a beauty treatment for the removal of unwanted hair so as to improve an untidy hairline, in which hairs are caught and pulled out by a twisted cotton thread which is rolled over them.

threadworm /ˈθrɛdwɜm/ *n.* any of various nematode worms, especially a pinworm.

threat /θrɛt/ *n.* **1.** a declaration of an intention or determination to inflict punishment, pain, or loss on someone in retaliation for, or conditionally upon, some action or course; menace. **2.** an indication of probable evil to come; something that gives indication of causing evil or harm. *–***threaten,** *v. –***threatless,** *adj.*

three /θri/ *n.* **1.** a cardinal number, two plus one $(2 + 1)$. **2.** a symbol for this number, e.g. 3 or III. **3.** a set of this many people or things. *–adj.* **4.** amounting to three in number: *three apples. –pron.* **5.** three people or things: *three came to the party.*

3D /θri ˈdi/ *adj.* **1.** three-dimensional: *3D films. –n.* **2.** a three-dimensional form or appearance. Also, **3-D.**

three-dimensional /θri-dəˈmɛnʃənəl/ *adj.* **1.** having, or seeming to have, the dimension of depth as well as height and breadth. **2.** realistic; lifelike.

3D printing *n.* a process by which a three-dimensional solid object can be produced from a digital model by laying down successive layers of liquid, powder, paper, or sheet material to form the required shape. *–***3D printer,** *n.*

3G /θri ˈdʒi/ *n. Telecommunications* the third generation of wireless services, with faster transmission speeds allowing for high-quality audio and video.

three-quarter *adj.* **1.** consisting of or involving three quarters of a whole. *–n.* **2.** *Rugby Football* one of the four players in the three-quarter line.

three R's /θri ˈaz/ *pl. n.* reading, (w)riting, and (a)rithmetic, traditionally regarded as the fundamentals of education.

thresh /θrɛʃ/ *v.t.* **1.** to separate the grain or seeds from (a cereal plant, etc.) by some mechanical means, as by beating with a flail or by the action of a threshing machine. *–v.i.* **2.** to thresh wheat, grain, etc. **3.** to deliver blows as if with a flail.

threshold /ˈθrɛʃhoʊld/ *n.* **1.** the sill of a doorway. **2.** the entrance to a house or building. **3.** any place or point of entering or beginning: *the threshold of a new career.* **4.** *Psychol., Med.* the point at which a stimulus becomes noticeable, or strong enough to produce an effect: *the threshold of pain.* **5.** *Physics* the lowest value of any signal, stimulus, etc., which will produce a particular effect, as a threshold frequency.

threw /θruː/ *v.* past tense of **throw**.

thrice /θraɪs/ *adv.* three times, as in succession; on three occasions.

thrift /θrɪft/ *n.* **1.** economical management; economy; frugality. **2.** vigorous growth, as of a plant. **–thrifty**, *adj.* **–thriftless**, *adj.* **–thriftlessly**, *adv.* **–thriftlessness**, *n.*

thrill /θrɪl/ *v.t.* **1.** to affect with a sudden wave of keen emotion, so as to produce a tremor or tingling sensation through the body. *–v.i.* **2.** to affect one with a wave of emotion or excitement; produce a thrill. **3.** to be stirred by a thrill of emotion or excitement. *–n.* **4.** a tremor or tingling sensation passing through the body as the result of sudden keen emotion or excitement. **5.** thrilling property or quality, as of a story. *–phr.* **6. thrill to bits**, to delight. **–thrilling**, *adj.*

thriller /ˈθrɪlə/ *n.* **1.** something thrilling. **2.** a book, play, or film dealing with crime, mystery, etc., in an exciting or sensational manner.

thrive /θraɪv/ *v.i.* (**thrived** or **throve**, **thrived** or **thriven** /ˈθrɪvən/, **thriving**) **1.** to prosper; be fortunate or successful; increase in property or wealth; grow richer or rich. **2.** to grow or develop vigorously; flourish. **–thriver**, *n.* **–thrivingly**, *adv.*

throat /θrəʊt/ *n.* **1.** the passage from the mouth to the stomach or to the lungs; the fauces, pharynx, and oesophagus; the larynx and trachea. **2.** some analogous or similar narrowed part or passage. **3.** the front of the neck below the chin and above the collarbones. *–phr.* **4. cut one's (own) throat**, to pursue a course of action which is injurious or ruinous to oneself. **5. have someone** (or **something**) **by the throat**, *Colloq.* to have complete control over, or be in complete command of (a person or situation). **6. jump down someone's throat**, *Colloq.* to deliver a strong verbal attack on someone. **7. ram** (or **thrust**) **something down someone's throat**, *Colloq.* to force something on someone's attention. **8. stick in one's throat**, **a.** to be difficult to express or utter. **b.** to be difficult to resign oneself to. **–throatless**, *adj.*

throaty /ˈθrəʊti/ *adj.* (**-tier**, **-tiest**) produced or modified in the throat, as sounds; hoarse; guttural. **–throatily**, *adv.* **–throatiness**, *n.*

throb /θrɒb/ *v.i.* (**throbbed**, **throbbing**) **1.** (of the heart, etc.) to beat with increased force or speed; palpitate. **2.** to feel or show emotion: *to throb with excitement.* **3.** to beat; pulsate: *his head began to throb with pain.* *–n.* **4.** the act of throbbing. **5.** a violent beat, as of the heart. **6.** any beat or pulsation: *the throb of the engines.* **–throbber**, *n.* **–throbbingly**, *adv.*

throes /θrəʊz/ *pl. n.* **1.** any violent convulsion or struggle, as in the agony of death or the pains of childbirth. *–phr.* **2. in the throes of**, engaged in; fully preoccupied with.

thrombosis /θrɒmˈbəʊsəs/ *n.* *Pathol.* intravascular coagulation of the blood in any part of the circulatory system, as in the heart, arteries, veins, or capillaries. **–thrombotic** /θrɒmˈbɒtɪk/, *adj.*

throne /θrəʊn/ *n.* **1.** the chair or seat occupied by a sovereign, bishop, or other exalted personage on ceremonial occasions, usually raised on a dais and covered with a canopy. **2.** the office or dignity of a sovereign. **3.** *Theology* a member of the third order of angels. See **angel** (def. 1). **4. the throne**, *Colloq.* the toilet. *–v.t.* **5.** to set on or as on a throne. **–throneless**, *adj.*

throng /θrɒŋ/ *n.* **1.** a multitude of people crowded or assembled together; a crowd. **2.** a great number of things crowded or considered together. *–v.i.* **3.** to assemble, collect, or go in large numbers; crowd. *–v.t.*

4. to crowd or press upon; jostle. **5.** to fill by crowding or pressing into.

throttle /ˈθrɒtl/ *n.* **1.** a lever, pedal, or other device to control the amount of fuel being fed to an engine. *–v.t.* **2.** to strangle. **3.** to stop the breath of in any way; choke. **4.** to silence or check as if by choking. **5.** *Machinery* to block the flow of (steam, etc.) by means of a throttle valve, etc. **–throttler**, *n.*

through /θruː/ *prep.* **1.** in at one end, side, or surface, and out at the other, of: *to pass through a tunnel.* **2.** past: *the car went through the traffic lights without stopping.* **3.** between or among the individual members or parts of: *to swing through the trees.* **4.** over the surface of or within the limits of: *to travel through a country.* **5.** during the whole period of; throughout: *to work through the night.* **6.** having reached the end of: *to be through one's work.* **7.** having finished successfully: *to get through an examination.* **8.** by the means or instrumentality of: *it was through him they found out.* **9.** by reason of or in consequence of: *to run away through fear.* **10.** *US* up to and including: *from Monday through Thursday.* *–adv.* **11.** in at one end, side, or surface and out at the other: *to push a needle through.* **12.** all the way; along the whole distance: *this train goes through to Flinders St.* **13.** throughout: *wet through.* **14.** from the beginning to the end: *to read a letter through.* **15.** to the end: *to carry a matter through.* **16.** to a favourable or successful conclusion: *to pull through.* **17.** having completed an action, process, etc.: *he is not yet through.* *–adj.* **18.** passing or extending from one end, side, or surface to the other. **19.** that extends, goes, or conveys through the whole of a long distance with little or no interruption, obstruction, or hindrance: *a through train.* *–phr.* **20. go through**, to wear out: *he's gone through ten pairs of shoes.* **21. through and through**, **a.** through the whole extent or substance; from beginning to end. **b.** in all respects; thoroughly. **22. through with**, **a.** finished or done with. **b.** at an end of all relations or dealings with.

throughout /θruːˈaʊt/ *prep.* **1.** in or to every part of; everywhere in. **2.** from the beginning to the end of. *–adv.* **3.** in every part. **4.** at every moment or point.

throw /θrəʊ/ *verb* (**threw**, **thrown**, **throwing**) *–v.t.* **1.** to project or propel forcibly through the air by a sudden jerk or straightening of the arm; propel or cast in any way. **2.** to hurl or project (a missile), as a gun does. **3.** to project or cast (light, a shadow, etc.). **4.** to project (the voice). **5.** to make (a voice) appear to be coming from a place other than its source, as a ventriloquist does. **6.** to direct (words, a glance, etc.). **7.** to cause to go or come into some place, position, condition, etc., as if by throwing: *to throw a man into prison; to throw a bridge across a river; to throw troops into action.* **8.** to put hastily: *to throw a shawl over one's shoulders.* **9.** *Machinery* **a.** to move (a lever, etc.) in order to connect or disconnect parts of an apparatus or mechanism. **b.** to connect, engage, disconnect, or disengage by such a procedure. **10.** to shape on a potter's wheel. **11.** to bring to bear or exert (influence, authority, power, etc.). **12.** to deliver (a blow or punch). **13.** *Cards* **a.** to play (a card). **b.** to discard (a card). **14.** to cause to fall to the ground; bring to the ground, as an opponent in wrestling or as an animal for branding. **15.** Also, **throw off.** (of a wine) to produce (a sediment). **16.** to cast (dice). **17.** to make (a cast) at dice. **18.** (of a horse, etc.) to cause (a rider) to fall off. **19.** (of domestic animals) to bring forth (young). **20.** *Textiles* to wind or twist (silk, etc.) into threads. **21.** to arrange or host (a social event): *she threw a party last Saturday.* **22.** *Orig. US Colloq.* to permit an opponent to win (a race, contest, or the like) deliberately, as for a bribe. **23.** *Colloq.* to astonish; disconcert; confuse. *–v.i.* **24.** *Cricket* (of a bowler) to bowl with a bent arm; chuck. **25.** to cast, fling, or hurl a missile, etc. *−n.* **26.** an act of throwing or casting; a cast or fling. **27.** a turn in a game involving throwing, as ball games, etc. **28.** the distance to which anything is or may be thrown: *a stone's throw.* **29.** *Cricket* an illegal delivery in which there is a straightening of the elbow joint at any time after the arm has reached shoulder height. **30.** a venture or chance: *it was his last throw.* **31.** *Machinery* **a.** the movement of a reciprocating part or the like from its central position to its extreme position in either direction, or the distance traversed (equivalent to one half of the travel or stroke). **b.** the arm or the radius of a crank or the like; the eccentric, or the radius of a crank to which an eccentric is equivalent, being equal to the distance between the centre of the disc and the centre of the shaft. **c.** the complete movement of a reciprocating part or the like in one direction, or the distance traversed (equivalent to the travel or stroke). **32.** a light blanket, as for use when reclining on a sofa. **33.** a cast at dice. **34.** a number thrown. **35.** *Wrestling* the act, instance, or method of throwing an opponent. **36.** *Geol., Mining* the amount of vertical displacement produced by a fault. *−phr.* **37. throw away, a.** to discard; dispose of. **b.** to squander; waste. **c.** to fail to use; miss (an opportunity, chance, etc.). **38. throw back,** to revert to a type found in one's ancestors; show atavism. **39. throw in, a.** to add as an extra, especially in a bargain. **b.** to interpose; interpolate; contribute (a remark, etc.). **40. throw in the towel** (or **sponge**), to give in; accept defeat. **41. throw it in,** *Colloq.* **a.** to accept defeat. **b.** to cease an activity. **42. throw off, a.** to free oneself from. **b.** to elude, escape from (a pursuer, etc.). **c.** to discard or remove hastily. **d.** to recover from (a cold, etc.). **e.** to utter, write, compose, etc., with ease. **43. throw off at,** *Aust. Colloq.* to criticise or belittle. **44. throw oneself at someone,** to give someone an unusual amount of attention, flattery, etc., in order to win their regard or love. **45. throw oneself into,** to work enthusiastically at. **46. throw oneself on** (or **upon**), to entrust oneself to the mercy of; commit oneself completely to. **47. throw open, a.** to open wide. **b.** to permit general access to. **48. throw out, a.** to discard; cast away. **b.** to emit; give forth. **c.** to utter casually or indirectly (a remark, hint, etc.). **d.** to expel; eject; remove forcibly. **e.** to reject; refuse to accept. **f.** to cause to make a mistake. **49. throw over,** to abandon; forsake; desert. **50. throw together, a.** to assemble in a hasty or haphazard manner. **b.** to bring together; cause to associate. **51. throw up, a.** to give up; abandon. **b.** to build hastily. **c.** *Colloq.* to vomit.

throwback /ˈθroʊbæk/ *n.* **1.** reversion to an ancestral type or character. **2.** a setback or check. **3.** an act of throwing back.

thru /θruː/ *prep., adv., adj.* (*often used in advertising*) → **through.**

thrum /θrʌm/ *v.i.* (**thrummed, thrumming**) **1.** to play on a stringed instrument, as a guitar, by plucking the strings, especially in an idle, monotonous, or unskilful manner. **2.** to sound when thrummed on, as a guitar, etc. **3.** to drum or tap idly with the fingers. *−n.* **4.** the act or sound of thrumming; dull, monotonous sound. **−thrummer,** *n.*

thrush[1] /θrʌʃ/ *n.* any of numerous birds belonging to the family Muscicapidae (formerly Turdidae), most of which are moderate in size, migratory, gifted as songsters, and not brightly coloured, as the European **song thrush,** *Turdus philomelus,* which has been introduced into Australia, or the native **Bassian thrush,** *Zoothera lunulata,* of eastern and southern Australia. **−thrush-like,** *adj.*

thrush[2] /θrʌʃ/ *n.* **1.** *Pathol.* a disease characterised by whitish spots and ulcers on the membranes of the mouth, fauces, vagina, etc., due to a parasitic fungus, *Candida albicans;* monilia. **2.** *Vet. Science* (in horses) a diseased condition of the frog of the foot.

thrust /θrʌst/ *verb* (**thrust, thrusting**) *−v.t.* **1.** to push with force; shove: *he thrust a dagger into her back.* **2.** to put with force into some position, condition, etc.: *to thrust someone into danger.* *−v.i.* **3.** to push against something. **4.** to push or force one's way: *to thrust through the crowd.* **5.** to make a stab at something; lunge. *−n.* **6.** the act of thrusting; a push; a lunge. **7.** *Mechanics* the driving force generated by an engine. **8.** *Geol.* a pressure in the crust of the earth, which produces a fault.

thud /θʌd/ *n.* **1.** a dull sound, as of a heavy blow or fall. *−v.i.* (**thudded, thudding**) **2.** to make a dull heavy sound. *−phr.* **3. come a thud,** *Colloq.* to be disappointed in an expectation.

thug /θʌg/ *n.* **1.** a brutal, vicious, or murderous ruffian, robber, or gangster. **2.** a bully, especially one who is overbearing and threatens violence. **−thuggery,** *n.* **−thuggish,** *adj.*

thumb /θʌm/ *n.* **1.** the short, thick inner digit of the human hand, next to the forefinger. **2.** the corresponding digit in other animals; the pollex. **3.** that part of a glove, etc., which covers the thumb. *−v.t.* **4.** to soil or wear with the thumbs in handling, as the pages of a book. **5.** (of a hitchhiker) to solicit or obtain (a ride) by pointing the thumb in the direction in which one wishes to travel. *−phr.* **6. all thumbs,** clumsy; awkward. **7. thumb one's nose, a.** to put one's thumb to one's nose and extend the fingers in a gesture of defiance or contempt. **b.** to have a defiant or mocking attitude: *to thumb one's nose at everyone in authority.* **8. thumb through,** to run through (the pages of a book, etc.) quickly. **9. under someone's thumb,** controlled or dominated by someone. **−thumbless,** *adj.* **−thumblike,** *adj.*

thumb drive *n.* (*from trademark*) → **USB drive.**

thumbnail /ˈθʌmneɪl/ *n.* **1.** the nail of the thumb. **2.** Also, **thumbnail sketch. a.** a concise or rudimentary drawing. **b.** a brief description of a person or account of an event **3.** a small computer graphics image which offers a preview of a full-size image.

thump /θʌmp/ *n.* **1.** a heavy blow. **2.** the sound made by such a blow. *−v.t.* **3.** to strike or beat with something thick and heavy so as to make a dull sound; pound: *to thump a drum.* **4.** to strike against (something) heavily and noisily. **5.** *Colloq.* to punch. *−v.i.* **6.** to strike or beat heavily, with a dull sound; pound. **7.** to walk with heavy-sounding steps. **8.** (of the heart) to beat violently. **−thumper,** *n.*

thunder /ˈθʌndə/ *n.* **1.** the loud noise which happens with a flash of lightning, due to a violent disturbance of the air by a discharge of electricity. **2.** any loud, booming noise: *the thunder of applause.* *−v.i.* **3.** to give forth thunder: *it thundered last night.* **4.** to make a loud noise like thunder: *the horses thundered down the track.* **5.** to make a loud, threatening speech: *the preacher thundered from the pulpit.* *−phr.* **6. steal someone's thunder,** to appropriate or use another's idea, plan, etc. **−thunderous, thundery,** *adj.* **−thunderless,** *adj.*

thunderbird /ˈθʌndəbɜːd/ *n.* **1.** any of a number of Australian birds that call in response to sudden loud noises, as the rufous whistler, *Pachycephala rufiventris.* **2.** (in the mythology of certain Native American peoples) a huge bird capable of producing thunder, lightning, and rain.

thunderbolt /ˈθʌndəboʊlt/ *n.* **1.** a flash of lightning with the accompanying thunder. **2.** an imaginary bolt or dart conceived as the material destructive agent cast to earth in a flash of lightning. **3.** something very destructive, terrible, severe, sudden, or startling. **4.** someone who acts with fury or with sudden force.

Thursday /ˈθɜːzdeɪ, -di/ *n.* the fifth day of the week, following Wednesday.

thus /ðʌs/ *adv.* **1.** in the way just indicated; in this way. **2.** in the following manner; in the manner now indicated. **3.** accordingly; consequently. **4.** to this extent or degree: *thus far.*

thwack /θwæk/ *v.t.* **1.** to strike or beat vigorously with something flat; whack. *–n.* **2.** a sharp blow with something flat; whack. **–thwacker**, *n.*

thwart /θwɔt/ *v.t.* **1.** to oppose successfully; prevent from accomplishing a purpose; frustrate (a purpose, etc.); baffle. *–n.* **2.** a seat across a boat, especially one used by a rower. *–adj.* **3.** passing or lying crosswise or across; cross; transverse. *–prep.* **4.** across; athwart. **–thwarter**, *n.*

thy /ðaɪ/ *adj.* the possessive form of **thou**[1].

thylacine /ˈθaɪləsɪn/ *n.* a carnivorous, wolf-like marsupial now thought to be extinct, *Thylacinus cynocephalus*, of Tasmania, tan-coloured, with black stripes across the back. Also, **Tasmanian wolf**, **Tasmanian tiger**.

thyme /taɪm/ *n.* any of the plants of the mint family constituting the genus *Thymus*, as *T. vulgaris*, a low shrub with aromatic leaves used for seasoning, or a wild creeping species, *T. serpyllum* (**wild thyme**).

thymus /ˈθaɪməs/ *n. Anat.* a glandular body or ductless gland of uncertain function found in vertebrate animals, in humans lying in the thorax near the base of the neck and becoming vestigial in the adult. Also, **thymus gland**.

thyroid /ˈθaɪrɔɪd/ *adj.* **1.** indicating or relating to the thyroid gland. **2.** indicating or relating to the principal cartilage of the larynx, known in men as the Adam's apple. *–n.* **3.** → **thyroid gland**. **4.** a preparation made from the thyroid glands of certain animals, used in treating an underactive thyroid.

thyroid gland *n. Anat.* a bilobate ductless gland lying on either side of the windpipe or trachea and connected below the larynx by a thin isthmus of tissue. Its internal secretion is important in regulating the rate of metabolism and, consequently, body growth.

ti /ti/ *n.* (*pl.* **tis**) any of several species of tropical palmlike plants of the genus *Cordyline*, as *C. terminalis* of eastern Asia, or *C. australis* of New Zealand. Also, **ti-palm**, **ti-tree**.

TIA /ti aɪ ˈeɪ/ *n. Pathol.* transient ischaemic attack; a small ischaemic stroke, usually caused by a temporary disruption in the flow of blood to the brain tissue, the symptoms being minor and temporary but sometimes being an indicator that a more severe stroke will follow; ministroke.

tiara /tiˈɑːrə/ *n.* **1.** a jewelled ornamental coronet worn by women. **2.** a diadem worn by the pope, surmounted by the mound (or orb) and cross of sovereignty, and surrounded with three crowns. **3.** the papal position or dignity. **4.** a headdress or turban worn by the ancient Persians and others.

tibia /ˈtɪbiə/ *n.* (*pl.* **tibias** *or* **tibiae** /ˈtɪbiiː/) **1.** *Anat.* the inner of the two bones of the lower leg, extending from the knee to the ankle, and articulating with the femur and the astragalus; the shinbone. **2.** *Zool.* a corresponding bone in the hind limb of other animals. **3.** *Entomology* the fourth segment of the leg, between the femur and tarsus. **–tibial**, *adj.*

tic /tɪk/ *n. Pathol.* a sudden, painless, purposeless muscular contraction in the face or extremities.

tick[1] /tɪk/ *n.* **1.** a slight, sharp recurring click or beat, as of a clock. **2.** *Colloq.* a moment or instant: *hang on just a tick.* **3.** a small mark, as a hooked, sloping dash (formed by two strokes at an acute angle) serving to draw attention to something, to indicate that an item on a list, etc., has been noted or checked, or to indicate the correctness of something, as a written work. *–v.i.* **4.** to emit or produce a tick, like that of a clock. **5.** to pass as with ticks of a clock: *the hours ticked by.* *–v.t.* **6.** to

mark (an item, etc.) with a tick, as to indicate examination or correctness. *–phr.* **7. on the tick**, punctually. **8. tick off**, to mark (an item, etc.) with a tick, as to indicate examination or correctness. **9. tick over**, **a.** (of an internal-combustion engine) to run slowly with the gears disengaged. **b.** to be inactive, often in preparation for action. **10. tick someone off**, *Colloq.* to rebuke; scold. **11. what makes someone tick**, what motivates someone's behaviour.

tick[2] /tɪk/ *n.* **1.** any member of a group of bloodsucking mite-like animals (Acarina) of the families Ixodidae and Argasidae, provided with a barbed proboscis which it buries in the skin of vertebrate animals. **2.** any of the dipterous insects of the family Hippoboscidae, often wingless, which are parasitic on certain animals, as sheep, camels, bats, pigeons.

ticker /ˈtɪkə/ *n. Colloq.* **1.** a watch. **2.** the heart. **3.** courage; bravery.

ticket /ˈtɪkət/ *n.* **1.** a slip, usually of paper or cardboard, serving as evidence of the holder's title to some service, right, or the like: *a railway ticket*; *a theatre ticket.* **2.** a written or printed slip of paper, cardboard, etc., affixed to something to indicate its nature, price, or the like; a label or tag. **3.** a list of candidates nominated or put forward by a political party, faction, etc. **4.** *Colloq.* a certificate. **5.** *Colloq.* discharge from the armed forces: *to get one's ticket.* **6.** *Aust. Hist.* → **ticket of leave**. **7.** a summons issued for a traffic or parking offence. *–v.t.* **8.** to attach a ticket to; distinguish by means of a ticket; label. **9.** to furnish with a ticket. *–adj.* **10.** *Aust. Hist.* relating to someone who had a ticket of leave: *ticket man.* *–phr.* **11. be the ticket**, *Colloq.* to be the correct, right, or proper thing: *that's the ticket!* **12. have tickets on oneself**, *Aust., NZ Colloq.* to be conceited. **13. the hot ticket**, *Colloq.* something which is extremely popular.

ticket of leave *n. Aust. Hist.* a document which entitled a convict to freedom of occupation and lodging within a given district of a colony until the original sentence expired or a pardon was obtained. Also, **ticket-of-leave**.

tickle /ˈtɪkəl/ *v.t.* **1.** to touch or stroke lightly with the fingers, a feather, etc., so as to excite a tingling or itching sensation in; titillate. **2.** to poke in some sensitive part of the body so as to excite spasmodic laughter. **3.** to excite agreeably; gratify: *to tickle someone's vanity.* **4.** to excite amusement in. *–v.i.* **5.** to be affected with a tingling or itching sensation, as from light touches or strokes. **6.** to produce such a sensation. *–n.* **7.** the act of tickling. **8.** a tickling sensation. *–phr. Colloq.* **9. tickled pink**, greatly pleased or amused. **10. tickled to bits**, delighted. **11. tickle someone's fancy**, to amuse someone. **12. tickle the ivories**, to play the piano. **13. tickle the peter**, to rob the till.

ticklish /ˈtɪklɪʃ/ *adj.* **1.** sensitive to tickling. **2.** requiring careful handling or action; risky; difficult: *a ticklish situation.* **3.** unstable or easily upset, as a boat; unsteady. **–ticklishly**, *adv.* **–ticklishness**, *n.*

tidal power *n.* the energy which can be harvested from the tides in the ocean by trapping water at high tide and running it through a turbine system as the tide goes out. Also, **tidal energy**.

tidal wave *n.* **1.** (*in non-technical use*) a tsunami. **2.** Also, **tidal surge**. a large wave caused by the combination of floods and high tides caused by a cyclone. **3.** either of the two great wavelike swellings of the ocean surface (due to the attraction of the moon and sun) which move round the earth on opposite sides and give rise to tide. **4.** any overwhelmingly widespread or powerful movement, opinion, or the like: *a tidal wave of popular indignation.*

tiddler /ˈtɪdlə/ n. **1.** a very small fish, especially a stickleback or minnow. **2.** *Colloq.* a small child, especially one who is undersized.

tiddly¹ /ˈtɪdli/ adj. **(-lier, -liest)** *Colloq.* slightly drunk; tipsy.

tiddly² /ˈtɪdli/ adj. **(-lier, -liest)** *Colloq.* very small.

tiddlywinks /ˈtɪdliwɪŋks/ n. a game, the object of which is to flick small discs into a cup placed some distance away. Also, **tiddleywinks**.

tide /taɪd/ n. **1.** the periodic rise and fall of the waters of the ocean and its inlets, about every 12 hours and 26 minutes, due to the attraction of the moon and sun. **2.** the inflow, outflow, or current of water at any given place resulting from the tidal changes. **3.** a stream or current. **4.** anything that alternately rises and falls, increases and decreases, etc. **5.** a tendency, trend, current, etc., as of events, ideas, public opinion, etc. –*phr.* **6.** (*v.* **tided, tiding**) **tide someone over,** to get someone over a period of difficulty, distress, etc.; enable someone to cope temporarily. **7. turn the tide,** to reverse the course of events, a game, etc. –**tidal,** *adj.* –**tideless,** *adj.* –**tidelike,** *adj.*

tidings /ˈtaɪdɪŋz/ *pl. n.* news, information, or intelligence: *sad tidings.*

tidy /ˈtaɪdi/ adj. **(-dier, -diest) 1.** neat; trim; orderly: *a tidy room.* **2.** *Colloq.* considerable: *a tidy sum.* –*verb* **(-died, -dying)** –*v.t.* **3.** to make tidy or neat. –*v.i.* **4.** to put things in order; make things neat. –*n.* (*pl.* **-dies**) **5.** any of various articles for keeping things tidy, as a receptacle or box; a rubbish tin or wastepaper basket. –*phr.* **6. tidy up, a.** to make (a room, etc.) neat and tidy: *tidy your room up before you go.* **b.** to neaten things: *I'll just finish tidying up.* –**tidily,** *adv.* –**tidiness,** *n.*

tie /taɪ/ *verb* **(tied, tying)** –*v.t.* **1.** to bind or fasten with a cord, string, or the like, drawn together and knotted. **2.** to draw together the parts of with a knotted string or the like: *to tie a bundle.* **3.** to fasten by tightening and knotting the string or strings of: *to tie one's shoes.* **4.** to draw together into a knot, as a cord. **5.** to form by looping and interlacing, as a knot or bow. **6.** to fasten, join, or connect in any way. **7.** to bind or join closely or firmly. **8.** *Colloq.* to unite in marriage. **9.** to confine, restrict, or limit. **10.** to bind or oblige, as to do something. **11.** *Music* to connect (notes) by a tie. –*v.i.* **12.** to make a tie, bond, or connection. **13.** to make the same score; be equal in a contest. **14.** (of a ship) to moor. –*n.* **15.** that with which anything is tied. **16.** a cord, string, or the like, used for tying or fastening something. **17.** a narrow, decorative band, as of cotton or silk, worn round the neck, commonly under a collar, and tied in front. **18.** anything that fastens, secures, or unites. **19.** a link, bond, or connection of kinship, affection, mutual interest, etc. **20.** something that restricts one's freedom of action. **21.** a state of equality in points, votes, etc., as among competitors: *the game ended in a tie.* **22.** a match or contest in which this occurs. **23.** anything, as a beam, rod, etc., connecting or holding together two or more things or parts. **24.** *Civil Eng.* a member of a framework which is required to take only a tensile load. **25.** *Music* a curved line connecting two notes on the same line or space to indicate that the sound is to be sustained for their joint value, not repeated. **26.** *US* → **sleeper** (def. 1). –*phr.* **27. tie down, a.** to fasten down by tying. **b.** to hinder; confine; restrict; curtail. **28. tie in, a.** (of a fact, belief, etc.) to fit in; be in accord with the whole: *that ties in with his deprived childhood.* **b.** to coordinate (two activities or events): *to tie in the publication with the Book Fair.* **29. tie the knot,** *Colloq.* to get married. **30. tie up, a.** to fasten securely by tying. **b.** to bind or wrap up. **c.** to hinder. **d.** to bring to a stop or pause. **e.** to invest or place (money) in such a way as to make it unavailable for other purposes. **f.** to place

(property) under such conditions or restrictions as to prevent sale or alienation. **g.** to occupy or engage completely. **31. tie up (the) loose ends,** to complete the details of a project, enterprise, etc., once the main purpose is accomplished. **32. tie up with,** to be closely connected or associated with.

tier /tɪə/ n. **1.** a row, range, or rank. **2.** one of a series of rows or ranks rising one behind or above another, as of seats in an amphitheatre, of boxes in a theatre, or of oars in an ancient galley. **3.** a layer or level. **4.** (*oft. pl.*) a range of mountains.

tiff /tɪf/ n. **1.** a slight or petty quarrel. **2.** a slight fit of ill humour.

TIFF /tɪf/ *Computers* –n. **1.** a data format for bitmapped image files. **2.** a file stored in this format. –*adj.* **3.** of or relating to this format or a file stored in this format. Also, **TIF, tif**; (*in filenames*) **.tif, .tiff**.

tiger /ˈtaɪgə/ n. **1.** a large wild cat, *Panthera tigris*, of Asia, tawny-coloured, striped with black, formerly widespread but now existing in several isolated races in coastal western Siberia, India, southern China, continental South-East Asia, and Sumatra. **2.** the puma, jaguar, thylacine, or other animal resembling the tiger. **3.** someone who resembles a tiger in fierceness, courage, etc. **4.** *Aust.* a shearer.

tiger lily n. **1.** a lily, *Lilium tigrinum*, with flowers of a dull orange colour spotted with black, and small bulbs or bulbils in the axils of the leaves. **2.** any lily, especially *L. pardalinum*, of similar colouration.

tiger mother n. a demanding mother who pushes her children to excel, setting high goals for them, and encouraging a competitive spirit, so as to ensure success in adult life.

tiger shark n. a large voracious striped shark, *Galeocerdo cuvieri* (family Carcharinidae), of tropical oceans.

tiger snake n. any of several highly venomous snakes (*Notechis* species) found in southern mainland Australia, Tasmania, and Bass Strait islands, of various shades of brown, tan, olive, or grey, sometimes with creamy bands, and averaging about 1.5 metres in length.

tight /taɪt/ adj. **1.** firmly fixed in place; secure: *a tight knot.* **2.** drawn or stretched; taut. **3.** fitting closely, especially too closely: *tight trousers.* **4.** difficult to deal with: *to be in a tight corner.* **5.** strict; firm; rigid: *tight discipline.* **6.** closely packed; full. **7.** working well together as a unit: *a tight organisation.* **8.** (of a performance) at a high level of intensity, focus, skill, etc. **9.** *Colloq.* close; nearly even: *a tight race.* **10.** *Colloq.* mean in giving or spending; stingy; parsimonious. **11.** *Colloq.* drunk; tipsy. –*adv.* **12.** in a tight manner; firmly; securely: *to draw a knot tight.* –**tighten,** *v.* –**tightly,** *adv.*

-tight a suffix meaning 'impervious to', as in *watertight*.

tightrope /ˈtaɪtroʊp/ n. **1.** a rope or wire stretched tight, on which acrobats perform feats of balancing. –*phr.* **2. walk a tightrope, a.** to walk along a tightrope as an acrobatic performance. **b.** to be in a precarious situation.

tights /taɪts/ *pl. n.* **1.** a close-fitting, finely woven garment covering the body from the waist downwards, and the legs. **2.** pantihose.

tike¹ /taɪk/ n. *Colloq.* → **tyke**¹.

tike² /taɪk/ n. *Colloq.* (*derog.*) → **tyke**².

tiki /ˈtiki/ n. a carved image representing an ancestor, worn as an amulet in some Polynesian cultures.

tilde /ˈtɪldə/ n. a diacritical mark (~) placed over a letter, as over the letter 'n' in Spanish to indicate a palatal nasal sound, as in *señor*.

tile /taɪl/ n. **1.** a thin slab or shaped piece of baked clay, sometimes glazed and ornamented, used for covering roofs, lining walls, paving floors, draining land, in ornamental work, etc. **2.** any of various similar slabs or pieces, as of stone, metal, lino, cork, slate, etc. **3.** a small, usually square or rectangular piece of plastic, wood, ceramic, etc., marked with some symbol and used in certain games, as Scrabble, mahjong, etc. **4.** a pottery tube or pipe used for draining land. **5.** a hollow or cellular block used as a wall unit in masonry construction. *–v.t.* **6.** to cover with or as with tiles. **7.** *Computers* to arrange (different windows) on a computer screen so that you can see their content side by side. *–phr.* **8. on the tiles**, *Colloq.* having a wild, riotous, or debauched night's entertainment. **–tiler**, *n.* **–tilelike**, *adj.*

till¹ /tɪl/ *prep.* **1.** up to the time of; until: *to fight till death.* **2.** (*with a negative*) before: *he did not come till today.* *–conj.* **3.** to the time that or when; until. **4.** (*with a negative*) before: *he won't leave till you get here.*

till² /tɪl/ *v.t.* to labour, as by ploughing, harrowing, etc., upon (land) for the raising of crops; cultivate. **–tillable**, *adj.* **–tillage**, *n.*

till³ /tɪl/ *n.* (in a shop, etc.) a container as a box, drawer, or the like, usually having separate compartments for coins and notes of different denominations, in which cash for daily transactions is temporarily kept.

tiller /'tɪlə/ *n.* a bar or lever fitted to the head of a rudder, to turn the rudder in steering. **–tillerless**, *adj.*

tilt /tɪlt/ *v.t.* **1.** to cause to lean, incline, slope, or slant. **2.** to rush at or charge, as in a joust. *–v.i.* **3.** to move into or assume a sloping position or direction. **4.** to engage in a joust, tournament, or similar contest. *–n.* **5.** an act or instance of tilting. **6.** the state of being tilted; a sloping position. **7.** a slope. **8.** a joust or any other contest. *–phr.* **9.** (**at**) **full tilt**, with full force or speed. **10. tilt at**, to strike at, thrust at, or charge with a lance or the like. **11. tilt at windmills**, to fight imaginary enemies. **–tilter**, *n.*

timber /'tɪmbə/ *n.* **1.** wood cut for building and carpentry, joinery, etc. **2.** wood of growing trees suitable for use in building. **3.** the trees themselves. **4.** *Naut.* (in a ship's frame) a curved piece of wood; a rib. **–timberless**, *adj.*

timber line   *n.* → **tree line.**

timbre /'tɪmbə, 'tæmbə/ *n.* **1.** *Acoustics, Phonetics* the characteristic quality of a sound, independent of pitch and loudness, from which its source or manner of production can be inferred. The saxophone and the clarinet have different timbres, and so do the vowels of *bait* and *boat.* Timbre depends on the relative strengths of the components of different frequencies, which are determined by resonance. **2.** *Music* the characteristic quality of sound produced by a particular instrument or voice; tone colour. **–timbral**, *adj.*

time /taɪm/ *n.* **1.** the system of those relations which any event has to any other as past, present, or future; indefinite continuous duration regarded as that in which events succeed one another. **2. a.** a system or method of measuring or reckoning the passage of time: *Greenwich Mean Time.* **b.** (*humorous*) such a system proposed as characteristic of a specified group, country, etc., and used to explain lateness: *Bali time; South American time.* **3.** a limited extent of time, as between two successive events: *a long time.* **4.** a particular period considered as distinct from other periods: *for the time being.* **5.** (*oft. pl.*) a period in the history of the world, or contemporary with the life or activities of a notable person: *ancient times.* **6.** (*oft. pl.*) the period or era now (or then) present. **7.** (*oft. pl.*) a period considered with reference to its events or prevailing conditions, tendencies, ideas, etc.: *hard times.* **8.** a prescribed or allotted period, as of one's life, for payment of a debt, etc. **9.** the normal or expected moment of death. **10.** the natural termination of the period of gestation. **11.** a period with reference to personal experience of a

specified kind: *to have a good time.* **12.** a period of work of an employee, or the pay for it. **13.** the period necessary for or occupied by something: *to ask for time to consider.* **14.** leisure or spare time: *to have no time.* **15.** a particular or definite point in time: *what time is it?* **16.** a particular part of a year, day, etc.: *Christmas time.* **17.** an appointed, fit, due, or proper time: *there is a time for everything.* **18.** the particular moment at which something takes place: *opening time.* **19.** an indefinite period in the future: *time will tell.* **20.** the period in which an action is completed, especially a performance in a race: *the winner's time was just under four minutes.* **21.** the right occasion or opportunity: *to watch one's time.* **22.** each occasion of a recurring action or event: *to do a thing five times.* **23.** (*pl.*) → **times. 24.** *Music, etc.* **a.** tempo; relative rapidity of movement. **b.** the metrical duration of a note or rest. **c.** proper or characteristic tempo. **d.** the general movement of a particular kind of musical composition with reference to its rhythm, metrical structure, and tempo. **e.** the movement of a dance or the like to music so arranged: *waltz time.* **25.** *Mil.* the rate of marching, calculated on the number of paces taken per minute: *quick time.* *–v.t.* **26.** to ascertain or record the time, duration, or rate of: *to time a race.* **27.** to fix the duration of. **28.** to fix or regulate the intervals between (actions, movements, etc.). **29.** to regulate as to time, as a train, a clock, etc. **30.** to appoint or choose the moment or occasion for. **31.** to mark the rhythm or measure of, as in music. *–phr.* **32. against time**, in an effort to finish something within a certain period. **33. ahead of one's time**, having ideas more advanced than those of the age in which one lives. **34. ahead of time**, before the time due; early. **35. at one time**, formerly. **36. at the same time**, nevertheless. **37. at times**, occasionally; at intervals. **38. behind the times**, old-fashioned. **39. do time**, *Colloq.* to serve a prison sentence. **40. for the time being**, temporarily. **41. from time to time**, occasionally, at intervals. **42. gain time**, **a.** (of a clock) to run too quickly. **b.** Also, **make up time**. (of a plane, traveller, etc.) to travel more quickly so that arrival is sooner: *we gained time after Singapore.* **c.** to achieve delay or postponement by slowing the proceedings: *she spoke in great detail to gain time, hoping Brown would get there soon.* **d.** (of a musician, performance, etc.) to move at a faster tempo, often in just one part of the piece: *the pianist began to gain time in the recapitulation.* **43. have no time for**, to have a very low opinion of. **44. have (some) time for**, to have a good opinion of. **45. in good time**, **a.** punctually; at the right time. **b.** early; with time to spare. **46. in no time**, very quickly. **47. in time**, **a.** soon or early enough. **b.** eventually; after a lapse of time. **c.** following the correct rhythm or tempo. **48. keep time**, **a.** to function accurately, as a clock. **b.** to observe the tempo or rhythm. **c.** to perform movements in unison in the same rhythm. **49. kill time**, to occupy oneself in some manner so as to make the time pass quickly. **50. many a time**, often; frequently. **51. no time**, a very short time. **52. on time**, punctually. **53. pass the time of day**, to have a brief conversation. **54. take one's time**, to be slow or leisurely. **55. take time out**, **a.** to pause in an activity. **b.** to spare the time or make the effort (to do something). **56. the time of one's life**, *Colloq.* a very enjoyable experience. **57. time after time**, often; repeatedly. **58. time and (time) again**, often; repeatedly; again and again.

time clause   *n.* **1.** *Law* a clause in a contract which limits it or some aspect of it to a certain time period. **2.** *Gram.* a subordinate clause which specifies the time at which the action of the main clause takes place, as in *When you arrive, go straight to bed.*

timekeeper /'taɪmkipə/ *n.* **1.** (in a sports contest, etc.) someone who observes and records the time taken by competitors in a race, the duration of an event, etc. **2.** → **timepiece**. **3.** someone employed to keep account of the hours of work done by others and, sometimes, to pay them. **4.** someone who beats time in music.

timeless /'taimləs/ *adj.* **1.** eternal; unending. **2.** referring to no particular time. –**timelessly**, *adv.* –**timelessness**, *n.*

timely /'taimli/ *adj.* (-**lier**, -**liest**) **1.** occurring at a suitable time; seasonable; opportune; well-timed: *a timely warning*. –*adv.* **2.** seasonably; opportunely. –**timeliness**, *n.*

timepiece /'taimpis/ *n.* **1.** an apparatus for measuring and recording the progress of time; a chronometer. **2.** a clock or a watch.

time-poor *adj.* Also, **time poor**. **1.** short of time to spend as one wishes outside of work hours, although often not handicapped by lack of funds. –*n.* **2. the time-poor**, those who are in this situation. Compare **time-rich**.

time-rich *adj.* Also, **time rich**. **1.** with plenty of time to devote to whatever one chooses to do, although not necessarily with the funds to do it. –*n.* **2. the time-rich**, those in this situation. Compare **time-poor**.

times /taimz/ *pl. n.* **1.** used as a multiplicative word in phrasal combinations expressing how many instances of a quantity or factor are taken together: *four times five. Symbol:* × **2.** an expression of a quantitative comparison between two states, qualities, dimensions, etc.: *four times closer; five times better.*

time-sharing *n.* **1.** the handling by a computer of several programs at the same time. **2.** occupancy for a period of time each year in a resort dwelling by persons owning shares in the dwelling.

time sheet *n.* a sheet or card recording the hours worked by an employee. Also, **timesheet**.

timeshift /'taimʃift/ *v.t.* **1.** to record a radio or television program so as to listen or view it at a time of one's own convenience. –*v.t.* **2.** to record (a program) in this way. –**timeshifting**, *n.*

timetable /'taimteibəl/ *n.* **1.** a schedule showing the times at which railway trains, buses, aeroplanes, etc., arrive and depart. **2.** a schedule of times of classes, lectures, etc., in a school, university, etc. **3.** any plan listing the times at which certain things are due to take place. –*v.t.* **4.** to incorporate into a timetable.

timid /'timəd/ *adj.* **1.** subject to fear; easily alarmed; timorous; shy. **2.** characterised by or indicating fear. –**timidity** /tɪ'mɪdəti/, **timidness**, *n.* –**timidly**, *adv.*

timing /'taimiŋ/ *n.* **1.** *Theatre* **a.** a synchronising of the various parts of a production for theatrical effect. **b.** the result or effect thus achieved. **c.** (in acting) the act of adjusting one's tempo of reading and movement for dramatic effect. **2.** *Sport* the control of the speed of an action in order that it may reach its maximum at the proper moment. **3. a.** the mechanism which ensures that the valves in an internal-combustion engine open and close at the correct time. **b.** the process of adjusting this mechanism so that it operates correctly.

timorous /'timərəs/ *adj.* **1.** full of fear; fearful. **2.** subject to fear; timid. **3.** characterised by or indicating fear. –**timorously**, *adv.* –**timorousness**, *n.*

timpani /'timpəni/ *pl. n.* (*sing.* -**no** /-noʊ/) a set of kettledrums. Also, **tympani**. –**tympanist**, *n.*

tin /tin/ *n.* **1.** a low-melting, silver-coloured, metallic element used in making alloys and plating. *Symbol:* Sn; *atomic number:* 50; *relative atomic mass:* 118.69. **2.** thin sheet iron or sheet steel coated with tin. **3.** any shallow metal pan, especially one used in baking. **4.** a sealed container for food, especially one made of tin plate; can. **5.** any container made of tin plate. **6.** the contents of a tin; can. –*adj.* **7.** made of tin or tin plate. –*v.t.* (**tinned**, **tinning**) **8.** to cover or coat with a thin

layer of tin. **9.** to pack or preserve in tins: *to tin fruit.* –**tinlike**, *adj.*

tincture /'tɪŋktʃə/ *n.* **1.** *Pharmaceutical* a solution of a medicinal substance in alcohol. **2.** a trace; a smattering; tinge. –*v.t.* **3.** to give a dye or colour to; tinge.

tinder /'tɪndə/ *n.* **1.** a material or preparation formerly used for catching the spark from a flint and steel struck together for fire or light. **2.** any dry substance that readily takes fire from a spark. –**tinder-like**, *adj.*

tine /tain/ *n.* a sharp projecting point or prong, as of a fork or deer's antler. Also, **tyne**.

tinea /'tiniə/ *n.* any of several contagious skin diseases affecting various parts of the body and caused by related fungi which spread outward from small spots to form distinctive ring-shaped red patches, especially athlete's foot. Also, **ringworm**.

ting /tiŋ/ *v.t.* **1.** to make a high, clear, ringing sound. –*v.i.* **2.** to cause to make a high, clear, ringing sound. –*n.* **3.** a tinging sound.

tinge /tɪnʒ/ *v.t.* (**tinged**, **tingeing** *or* **tinging**) **1.** to impart a trace or slight degree of some colour to; tint. **2.** to impart a slight taste or smell to. –*n.* **3.** a slight degree of colouration. **4.** a slight admixture, as of some qualifying property or characteristic.

tingle[1] /'tɪŋɡəl/ *v.i.* **1.** to have a sensation of slight stings or prickly pains, from a sharp blow or from cold. **2.** to cause such a sensation. –*n.* **3.** a tingling sensation. **4.** the tingling action of cold, etc. **5.** *Colloq.* a telephone call. –**tingler**, *n.* –**tinglingly**, *adv.* –**tingly**, *adj.*

tingle[2] /'tɪŋɡəl/ *n.* either of two species of timber tree native to WA, as the **red tingle**, a tall evergreen tree, *Eucalyptus jacksonii*, with reddish-brown fibrous bark and creamy white flowers, one of WA's tallest trees, or the **yellow tingle**, an evergreen tree, *Eucalyptus guilfoylei*, of medium height with dark grey, fibrous bark and creamy white flowers. Also, **tingle tingle**.

tingle tingle *n.* → **tingle**[2].

tinker /'tɪŋkə/ *n.* **1.** (formerly) a person who mends pots, kettles, pans, etc., usually a wanderer. **2.** an act or instance of tinkering: *to have a tinker.* –*v.i.* **3.** (formerly) to do the work of a tinker. **4.** to busy oneself with improving the workings of various tools and machinery: *to tinker in the shed.* –*phr.* **5. tinker with**, **a.** to make minor improvements in the working of (a device). **b.** to make minor adjustments to: *to tinker with the team selection.* –**tinkerer**, *n.*

tinkle /'tɪŋkəl/ *v.i.* **1.** to make a succession of short, light, ringing sounds; jingle. –*v.t.* **2.** to cause to tinkle. –*n.* **3.** a tinkling sound. –**tinkling**, *n.*, *adj.*

tinnie /'tɪni/ *n.* *Aust. Colloq.* **1.** a can of beer. **2.** a small aluminium boat. Also, **tinny**.

tinnitus /'tɪnətəs, tə'naɪtəs/ *n.* a ringing or similar sensation of sound in the ears, due to disease of the auditory nerve, etc.

tinny[1] /'tɪni/ *adj.* (-**nier**, -**niest**) **1.** of or like tin. **2.** containing tin. **3.** characteristic of tin, as sounds; lacking resonance. **4.** not strong or durable. **5.** having the taste of tin. –*n.* **6.** → **tinnie**. –**tinnily**, *adv.* –**tinniness**, *n.*

tinny[2] /'tɪni/ *adj.* (-**nier**, -**niest**) *Aust., NZ Colloq.* lucky.

tin plate *n.* thin sheet iron or sheet steel coated with tin.

tinsel /'tɪnsəl/ *n.* **1.** a cheap glittering metallic substance, as copper, brass, etc., used in pieces, strips, threads, etc., to produce a sparkling effect. **2.** anything showy or attractive with little or no real worth. –*adj.* **3.** made of or containing tinsel. **4.** showy; gaudy; tawdry. –**tinsel-like**, *adj.*

tint /tint/ *n.* **1.** a colour, or a variety of a colour. **2.** a colour diluted with white (as opposed to a *shade*, which is produced by adding black). **3.** a delicate or pale colour. **4.** a dye for the hair. –*v.t.* **5.** to apply a tint or tints to; colour slightly; tinge. –**tinter**, *n.*

tiny /'taini/ *adj.* (-**nier**, -**niest**) very small; minute; wee.

-tion a composite suffix used to form abstract nouns consisting of the final consonant of participial and other stems, plus -ion, used to express an action (revolution, commendation), or a state (contrition, volition), or associated meanings (relation, temptation). Also, **-ation, -cion, -ion, -sion, -xion.**

tip¹ /tɪp/ n. **1.** a slender or pointed end of something: the tips of the fingers. **2.** the top; summit or apex. –v.t. (**tipped, tipping**) **3.** to put a tip on to: to tip shoes with metal. **4.** to mark or form the tip of: snow tipped the mountains. –**tipless**, adj.

tip² /tɪp/ verb (**tipped, tipping**) –v.t. **1.** to cause to assume a slanting or sloping position; incline; tilt. **2.** to take off or lift (the hat) in salutation. **3.** to dispose of (rubbish, etc.) by dumping. –v.i. **4.** to assume a slanting or sloping position; incline. **5.** to tilt up at one end and down at the other. **6.** to be overturned or upset. –n. **7.** the act of tipping. **8.** the state of being tipped. **9.** Also, **rubbish tip.** a place where waste material is deposited; dump; rubbish dump. –phr. **10. tip over** (or **up**), **a.** to tumble or topple. **b.** to overthrow, overturn, or upset.

tip³ /tɪp/ n. **1.** a small present of money given to someone, as a waiter, porter, etc., for performing a service; a gratuity. **2.** a piece of private or secret information, as for use in betting, speculation, etc. **3.** a useful hint or idea. –verb (**tipped, tipping**) –v.t. **4.** to give a small present of money to. **5.** Colloq. to guess: I tipped who it was. –v.i. **6.** to give a gratuity. –phr. **7. tip off, a.** to give private or secret information to; inform. **b.** to warn of impending trouble, danger, etc. **8. tip someone the wink,** to pass on secret information to someone, especially in warning.

tip⁴ /tɪp/ n. **1.** a light, smart blow; a tap. –v.t. (**tipped, tipping**) **2.** to strike or hit with a light, smart blow; tap. **3.** Cricket, etc. to strike (the ball) with a glancing blow.

tipple /'tɪpəl/ v.t. **1.** to drink (wine, spirits, etc.), especially repeatedly, in small quantities. –v.i. **2.** to drink alcoholic drink, especially habitually or to some excess. –n. **3.** intoxicating liquor. –**tippler**, n.

tipsy /'tɪpsi/ adj. (**-sier, -siest**) **1.** slightly intoxicated. **2.** characterised by or due to intoxication: a tipsy lurch. **3.** tripping, unsteady, or tilted, as if from intoxication. –**tipsily**, adv. –**tipsiness**, n.

tiptoe /'tɪptoʊ/ v.i. (**-toed, -toeing**) **1.** to move or go on tiptoe, as with caution or stealth. –phr. **2. on tiptoe, a.** on the tips of the toes collectively: to walk on tiptoe. **b.** eagerly expectant. **c.** cautious; stealthy.

tirade /taɪ'reɪd, tə'reɪd/ n. **1.** a prolonged outburst of denunciation. **2.** a long, vehement speech. **3.** a passage dealing with a single theme or idea, as in poetry.

tire¹ /'taɪə/ v.t. **1.** Also, **tire out.** to reduce or exhaust the strength of, as by exertion; make weary; fatigue. **2.** to exhaust the interest, patience, etc., of, as by long continuance or by dullness. –v.i. **3.** to have the strength reduced or exhausted, as by labour or exertion; become fatigued. **4.** to have one's appreciation, interest, patience, etc., exhausted. –phr. **5. tire of,** to become weary of. –**tired**, adj. –**tireless**, adj.

tire² /'taɪə/ n. US → **tyre.**

tiresome /'taɪəsəm/ adj. **1.** such as to tire one; wearisome. **2.** annoying or vexatious. –**tiresomely**, adv.

'tis /tɪz/ Archaic contraction of it is.

tissue /'tɪʃu/ n. **1.** Biol. **a.** the substance of which an organism or part is composed. **b.** an aggregate of cells and cell products forming a definite kind of structural material in an animal or plant: muscular tissue. **2.** a woven fabric, especially one of light or gauzy texture, originally woven with gold or silver. **3.** any of several kinds of soft gauze-like papers used for various purposes. **4.** a paper handkerchief. **5.** an interwoven or interconnected series or mass: a tissue of lies.

tit¹ /tɪt/ n. **1.** any of various small Australian birds, especially a thornbill. **2.** any of various birds of the family Paridae, as the **blue tit,** Parsus caeruleus, or of the family Aegithalidae, as the **long-tailed tit,** Aegithalos caudatus. **3.** any of various other small birds.

tit² /tɪt/ n. **1.** a nipple. **2.** Colloq. a female breast.

titanic /taɪ'tænɪk/ adj. of enormous size, strength, etc.; gigantic.

titbit /'tɪtbɪt/ n. **1.** a delicate bit of food. **2.** a choice or pleasing bit of anything. Also, US, **tidbit.**

tithe /taɪð/ n. **1.** (oft. pl.) the tenth part of the yearly produce of agriculture, etc., due or paid as a tax to the church. **2.** a tenth part of anything. –v.t. (**tithed, tithing**) **3.** to give or pay a tithe. **4.** to make (someone) pay a tithe. –**tithable**, adj. –**titheless**, adj. –**tither**, n.

titian /'tɪʃən, 'ti-/ n. a reddish or reddish brown colour.

titillate /'tɪtɪleɪt/ v.t. **1.** to tickle; excite a tingling or itching sensation in, as by touching or stroking lightly. **2.** to excite agreeably: to titillate the fancy. –**titillation** /tɪtə'leɪʃən/, n. –**titillator**, n. –**titillative** /'tɪtɪleɪtɪv/, adj.

titivate /'tɪtəveɪt/ v.i. **1.** to make oneself smart or spruce. –v.t. **2.** to make smart or spruce. Also, **tittivate.** –**titivation** /tɪtə'veɪʃən/, n. –**titivator**, n.

title /'taɪtl/ n. **1.** the name of a book, poem, picture, piece of music, etc. **2.** a descriptive heading of a chapter, or other part of a book. **3.** a name given to a person describing occupation, qualifications, rank, etc., e.g. Doctor, Mr, Reverend, Lady. **4.** Sport the championship: he lost the title. **5.** an established right to something. **6.** Law the legal right to the possession of property, especially houses, land: he holds the title to our house. –v.t. (**-tled, -tling**) **7.** to give a title to; entitle.

title deed n. Law a deed or document containing or constituting evidence of ownership.

ti-tree /'ti-tri/ n. **1.** → **ti. 2.** → **tea-tree.**

titter /'tɪtə/ v.i. **1.** to laugh in a low, half-restrained way, as from nervousness or in ill-suppressed amusement. –n. **2.** a tittering laugh. –**titterer**, n. –**titteringly**, adv.

tittle /'tɪtl/ n. **1.** a dot or other small mark in writing or printing, used, for example, as a diacritic. **2.** a very small part or quantity; a particle, jot, or whit.

tittle-tattle /'tɪtl-tætl/ n. **1.** gossip; telltale. –v.i. (**-tled, -tling**) **2.** to reveal private or confidential matters in idle gossip; act as a tale-bearer. –**tittle-tattler**, n.

titular /'tɪtʃələ/ adj. **1.** of or relating to a title. **2.** having a title, especially of rank. **3.** being in title only: a titular prince. –**titularly**, adv.

tizz /tɪz/ n. Colloq. frantic but ineffectual activity; commotion. –phr. **2. in a tizz,** in a state of somewhat hysterical confusion and anxiety: don't get in a tizz. Also, **tizzy.**

tizzy /'tɪzi/ Colloq. –n. (pl. **-zies**) **1.** → **tizz.** –adj. (**-zier, -ziest**) **2.** gaudy, vulgar; tinselly.

TNT /ti ɛn 'ti/ n. trinitrotoluene; a high explosive set off by detonators, but not affected by ordinary friction or shock.

to /tu/, weak form /tə/ prep. **1.** expressing motion or direction towards something: from north to south. **2.** indicating limit of movement or extension: rotten to the core. **3.** expressing contact or contiguity: apply varnish to the surface. **4.** expressing a point or limit in time: to this day. **5.** expressing time until and including: Monday to Friday. **6.** expressing aim, purpose, or intention: going to the rescue. **7.** expressing destination or appointed end: sentenced to death. **8.** indicating result or consequence: to her dismay. **9.** indicating state or condition: he tore it to pieces. **10.** indicating the object of inclination or desire: they drank to her health. **11.** expressing the object of a right or claim: claimants to an estate. **12.** expressing limit in degree or amount: punctual to the minute; goods to the value of $100. **13.** indicating addition or amount: adding insult to *injury.* **14.** expressing attachment or adherence: *the paper stuck to the wall*; *she held to her opinions.* **15.** indicating an accompanying item or concomitant: *they danced to music*; *they arrived to the sound of cheers.* **16.** expressing comparison or opposition: *the score was 9 to 5.* **17.** expressing agreement or accordance: *a position to one's liking.* **18.** expressing reference or relation: *what will he say to this?* **19.** expressing relative position: *one line parallel to another.* **20.** indicating proportion or ratio: *one teacher to every thirty students.* **21.** supplying the place or sense of the dative case in other languages, connecting transitive verbs with their indirect or distant objects, and adjectives, nouns, and intransitive or passive verbs with a following noun which limits their action or application. **22.** used as the ordinary sign or accompaniment of the infinitive. *–adv.* **23.** towards a person, thing, or point implied or understood. **24.** to a contact point or closed position: *pull the shutters to.* **25.** to a matter; to action or work: *we turned to with a will.* **26.** to consciousness; to one's senses: *after she came to. –phr.* **27. to and fro, a.** to and from some place or thing. **b.** in opposite or different directions alternately.

toad /toʊd/ *n.* **1.** the terrestrial species of tailless (i.e., frog-like) amphibians of the genus *Bufo* and allied genera. **2.** any of various tailless amphibians (order Salientia). **3.** any of various other animals, as certain lizards. **4.** a person or thing as an object of disgust or aversion. **–toadlike,** *adj.*

toadstool /ˈtoʊdstuːl/ *n.* **1.** any of various fleshy, usually poisonous, fungi, like a mushroom, having a stalk with an umbrella-like cap. **2.** any of various other fleshy fungi, as the puffballs, coral fungi, etc.

toady /ˈtoʊdi/ *n.* (*pl.* **-dies**) **1.** an obsequious sycophant; a fawning flatterer. *–verb* (**-died, -dying**) *–v.t.* **2.** to be the toady to. *–v.i.* **3.** to be a toady. **–toadyish,** *adj.* **–toadyism,** *n.*

toast¹ /toʊst/ *n.* **1.** bread in slices browned on both surfaces by heat. *–v.t.* **2.** to brown, as bread or cheese, by exposure to heat. **3.** to heat or warm thoroughly at a fire. *–v.i.* **4.** to become toasted. **–toaster,** *n.*

toast² /toʊst/ *n.* **1.** a person or thing to whose health others drink. **2.** a call on another or others to drink to some person or thing. **3.** the act of drinking in this way. **4.** words of congratulation, etc., spoken before drinking. **5.** a person who is suddenly very popular or famous: *she was the toast of the town. –v.t.* **6.** to propose as a toast. **7.** to drink to the health of, or in honour of. *–v.i.* **8.** to propose or drink a toast.

toastmaster /ˈtoʊstmɑːstə/ *n.* **1.** someone who presides at a dinner and introduces the after-dinner speakers. **2.** someone who proposes or announces toasts. **–toastmistress,** *fem. n.*

tobacco /təˈbækoʊ/ *n.* (*pl.* **-baccos** *or* **-baccoes**) **1.** any plant of the genus *Nicotiana*, especially one of those species, as *N. tabacum*, whose leaves are prepared for smoking or chewing or as snuff. **2.** the leaves so prepared. **3.** any of various similar plants of other genera.

tobacconist /təˈbækənəst/ *n.* someone who retails tobacco, cigarettes, and other items connected with smoking.

toboggan /təˈbɒɡən/ *n.* **1.** a light sledge with low runners. **2.** a long, narrow, flat-bottomed sledge made of a thin board curved upwards and backwards at the front end, used originally for transport over snow. *–v.i.* **3.** to use, or coast on, a toboggan. **–tobogganer, tobogganist,** *n.* **–tobogganing,** *n.*

today /təˈdeɪ/ *n.* **1.** this present day. **2.** this present time or age. *–adv.* **3.** on this present day. **4.** at the present time; in these days.

toddle /ˈtɒdl/ *v.i.* **1.** to go with short, unsteady steps, as a child or an old person. *–n.* **2.** the act of toddling. **3.** an

unsteady gait. *–phr.* **4. toddle off,** *Colloq.* to take one's leave; depart.

toddy /ˈtɒdi/ *n.* (*pl.* **-dies**) **1.** a drink made of spirits and hot water, sweetened and sometimes spiced with cloves. **2.** the drawn sap, especially when fermented, of various species of palm (**toddy palms**), used as a drink.

to-die-for *adj. Colloq.* extremely desirable: *the biggest to-die-for hunk at school; that outfit is to-die-for.*

to-do /təˈduː/ *n.* (*pl.* **to-dos**) bustle; fuss.

toe /toʊ/ *n.* **1.** (in humans) one of the terminal members or digits of the foot. **2.** an analogous part in other animals. **3.** a part, as of a stocking or shoe, to cover the toes. **4.** the outer end of the hitting surface of a golf club or hockey stick. **5.** *Machinery* **a.** a journal or part placed vertically in a bearing, as the lower end of a vertical shaft. **b.** an arm or projecting part on which a cam or the like strikes. **6.** *Colloq.* strength; speed: *do the fast bowlers have enough toe? –v.t.* (**toed, toeing**) **7.** to touch or reach with the toes. **8.** to kick with the toe. **9.** *Golf* to strike (the ball) with the toe of the club. *–phr.* **10. dig one's toes in, a.** to refuse to move or change. **b.** to maintain a decision, opinion, etc., despite all opposition. **11. go toe to toe,** *Colloq.* to adopt a combative stance: *to go toe to toe with the opposition in question time.* **12. hit the toe,** *Colloq.* **a.** to move out; depart. **b.** *Prison* to attempt to escape. **13. on one's toes,** prepared to act; wide-awake. **14. toe in** (or **out**), to adjust (the wheels of a motor car) so that each pair is at the angle of convergence or divergence required. **15. toe the line,** to behave according to the rules; conform; obey. **16. tread on someone's toes,** to offend someone, especially by ignoring their area of responsibility. **17. turn up one's toes,** *Colloq.* to die. **–toeless,** *adj.* **–toelike,** *adj.*

toey /ˈtoʊi/ *adj. Colloq., Aust.* **1.** *NZ* anxious; apprehensive. **2.** *NZ* raring to go, keen. **3.** → **randy** (def. 2). **4.** *NZ* (of a horse) having an excitable temperament; fast.

toff /tɒf/ *n. Colloq.* (*often derog.*) a rich, upper-class, usually well-dressed person. **–toffy,** *adj.*

toffee /ˈtɒfi/ *n.* a sweet made of sugar or treacle boiled down, often with butter, nuts, etc. Also, *US,* **taffy.**

tofu /ˈtoʊfuː/ *n.* a curd made from white soybeans, usually formed into small blocks, used in Asian cookery; bean curd.

toga /ˈtoʊɡə/ *n.* (*pl.* **-gas**) **1.** the loose outer garment of the citizens of ancient Rome when appearing in public in time of peace. **2.** a robe of office, a professional gown, or some other distinctive garment. **–togaed** /ˈtoʊɡəd/, *adj.*

together /təˈɡeðə/ *adv.* **1.** into or in one place, gathering, company, mass, or body: *to call the people together.* **2.** into or in union, contact, or collision, as two or more things: *to sew things together.* **3.** into or in relationship, association: *to bring strangers together.* **4.** taken or considered collectively: *this one cost more than all the others together.* **5.** (of a single thing) into or in a condition of unity, compactness, or coherence: *to squeeze a thing together; the argument does not hang together well.* **6.** at the same time; simultaneously: *you cannot have both together.* **7.** without interruption; continuously: *for days together.* **8.** with united action; in cooperation: *to undertake a task together. –adj.* **9.** *Colloq.* capable and calm: *he is quite together these days.*

toggle /ˈtɒɡl/ *n.* **1.** a pin, bolt, or rod placed through an eye of a rope, the link of a chain, etc., for various purposes. **2.** a small wooden bar around which a loop is passed, to fasten the front of some coats. *–adj.* **3.** *Computers* of or relating to a key or command that has the reverse effect on each successive use. *–v.t.* **4.** to equip with a toggle or toggles.

togs /tɒɡz/ *pl. n. Colloq.* clothes: *football togs; work togs.*

toil /tɔɪl/ *n.* **1.** hard and continuous labour or effort. **2.** a laborious task. *–v.i.* **3.** to engage in severe and continuous work; labour arduously. **4.** to move or travel with difficulty, weariness, or pain. *–v.t.* **5.** to bring or effect by toil. **–toiler,** *n.* **–toilful, toilsome,** *adj.*

toile /twal/ *n.* **1.** a type of transparent linen. **2.** the made-up pattern in a cheap cloth of an exclusively designed garment before this is made in its intended material.

toilet /ˈtɔɪlət/ *n.* **1.** a disposal apparatus of any type used for urination and defecation, especially a water closet. **2.** a room or booth fitted with a water closet or urinal, often with means for washing face and hands. **3.** Also, **toilette** /twaˈlɛt/ the act or process of dressing, including bathing, arranging the hair, etc. **4.** *Surg.* the cleansing of the part or wound after an operation, especially in the peritoneal cavity. *–phr.* **5. go to the toilet,** (*euphemistic*) to defecate or urinate: *to go to the toilet behind a tree.* **–toileting,** *n.*

toiletry /ˈtɔɪlətri/ *n.* (*pl.* **-tries**) an article or substance used in dressing or hygiene, as a soap, deodorant, shaving lotion, etc.

token /ˈtoʊkən/ *n.* **1.** something serving to represent or indicate some fact, event, feeling, etc.; sign: *to wear black as a token of mourning.* **2.** a characteristic mark or indication; symbol. **3.** a memento; a keepsake. **4.** something used to indicate authenticity, authority, etc. **5.** a ticket, metal disc, etc., certified as having a particular value, for payment or exchange, as for ferry fares, at a nominal value much greater than its commodity value. **6.** anything of only nominal value similarly used, as paper currency. **7.** a particular act or event, especially as an instance of a class or type: *each subject in the experiment pronounced six tokens of the key word.* *–adj.* **8.** of or relating to a person included in a group to give the appearance of fairness or merely to satisfy a ruling: *the committee had the inevitable lonely token female.* See **tokenism.** *–phr.* **9. by the same token,** in the same way; similarly. **10. in token of,** as a sign or evidence of.

tokenism /ˈtoʊkənɪzəm/ *n.* the policy of avoiding a real solution to a problem by a superficial gesture intended to impress and to distract attention from the real issues. **–tokenistic,** *adj.*

told /toʊld/ *v.* **1.** past tense and past participle of **tell.** *–phr.* **2. all told,** in all.

tolerable /ˈtɒlərəbəl/ *adj.* **1.** able to be tolerated; endurable. **2.** fairly good; not bad. **–tolerableness,** *n.* **–tolerably,** *adv.*

tolerable daily intake *n.* an estimate of the quantity of a particular substance in food or water which can be ingested each day over a lifetime without posing a significant risk to health; used of contaminants, rather than deliberately added substances. *Abbrev.:* TDI Compare **acceptable daily intake.**

tolerance /ˈtɒlərəns/ *n.* **1.** the disposition to be patient and fair towards those whose opinions or practices differ from one's own; freedom from bigotry. **2.** the disposition to be patient and fair to opinions which are not one's own. **3.** the ability to endure disagreeable circumstances. **4.** *Med.* **a.** the ability to endure the action of a drug, without adverse effects. **b.** physiological resistance to poison. **5. a.** *Machinery* an allowable variation in the dimensions of a machined article or part. **b.** an allowable variation in some other characteristic of an article as weight, quality, etc. **–tolerant,** *adj.*

tolerate /ˈtɒləreɪt/ *v.t.* **1.** to allow to be, be practised, or be done without prohibition or hindrance; permit. **2.** to bear without repugnance; put up with. **3.** *Med.* to endure or resist the action of (a drug, poison, etc.). **–toleration,** *n.* **–tolerative** /ˈtɒlərətɪv/, *adj.* **–tolerator,** *n.*

toll[1] /toʊl/ *v.t.* **1.** to make (a bell) sound with single, slow, and regular strokes. **2.** to sound (the hour, a death knell, etc.) by such strokes. *–v.i.* **3.** (of a bell) to sound with single, slow and regular strokes. *–n.* **4.** the act or sound of tolling.

toll[2] /toʊl/ *n.* Also, **tollage.** a payment exacted by the state, the local authorities, etc., for some right or privilege, as for passage along a road or over a bridge. **2.** a tax, duty, or tribute; a price. **3.** exaction, cost or the like, especially in terms of death or loss: *the accident took a heavy toll of lives.*

toluene /ˈtɒljuin/ *n.* a colourless liquid hydrocarbon, $C_6H_5CH_3$, obtained from tolu, coal tar, etc., used as a solvent and in the manufacture of coal-tar substances, as TNT.

tom /tɒm/ *n.* the male of various animals (often used in composition, as in *tomcat*).

tomahawk /ˈtɒməhɔk/ *n.* **1.** a small, short-handled axe for use with one hand; hatchet. **2.** a light axe used by the indigenous people of North America as a weapon and tool, and serving as a token of war. *–v.t.* **3.** to strike, cut, or kill with or as with a tomahawk. **4.** to shear (a sheep) roughly, as if with a tomahawk.

tomato /təˈmatoʊ/ *n.* (*pl.* **-toes**) **1.** a widely cultivated plant, *Lycopersicon esculentum*, bearing a slightly acid, pulpy fruit, commonly red, sometimes yellow, used as a vegetable. **2.** the fruit itself. **3.** any plant of the same genus. **4.** its fruit.

tomb /tum/ *n.* **1.** an excavation in earth or rock for the reception of a corpse. **2.** a grave or mausoleum. **3.** any sepulchral structure. **4.** the state of death. **–tombless,** *adj.* **–tomblike,** *adj.*

tomboy /ˈtɒmbɔɪ/ *n.* an adventurous, athletic girl. **–tomboyish,** *adj.* **–tomboyishness,** *n.*

tombstone /ˈtumstoʊn/ *n.* a stone, usually bearing an inscription, set to mark a tomb or grave.

tomcat /ˈtɒmkæt/ *n.* a male cat.

tome /toʊm/ *n.* **1.** a volume forming a part of a larger work. **2.** any volume, especially a ponderous one.

-tome a word element referring to cutting, used especially in scientific terms, as *microtome, osteotome.*

tomfoolery /tɒmˈfuləri/ *n.* (*pl.* **-ries**) **1.** foolish or silly behaviour. **2.** a silly act, matter, or thing.

tomorrow /təˈmɒroʊ/ *n.* **1.** the day after this day: *tomorrow will be fair.* **2.** a day immediately following or succeeding another day. **3.** some future day or time. *–adv.* **4.** on the morrow; on the day after this day: *come tomorrow.*

tom-tom /ˈtɒm-tɒm/ *n.* **1.** an African drum of indefinite pitch. **2.** a dully repetitious drumbeat or similar sound.

-tomy a word element forming a noun termination meaning a 'cutting', especially relating to a surgical operation, as in *appendectomy, lithotomy, phlebotomy,* or sometimes a division, as in *dichotomy.*

ton /tʌn/ *n.* **1.** a unit of mass in the imperial system equal to 2240 lb. (**long ton**), or approximately 1016 kg, and, in the US, 2000 lb. (**short ton**), or approximately 907 kg. **2.** a unit of freight equal to 1000 kg or, formerly, 40 cubic feet (**freight ton**). **3.** a unit of displacement of ships in the imperial system equal to 35 cubic feet of salt water (**displacement ton** or **shipping ton**), or approximately 0.99 cubic metres. **4.** a unit of internal capacity of ships in the imperial system, equal to 100 cubic feet, or approximately 2.83 cubic metres (**gross ton**). **5.** → **tonne. 6.** *Colloq.* a heavy weight: *that book weighs a ton.* **7.** (*pl.*) *Colloq.* very many; a good deal: *tons of things to see.*

-ton noun suffix, as in *simpleton, singleton.*

tonality /toʊnˈæləti/ *n.* **1.** *Music* **a.** the sum of relations, melodic and harmonic, existing between the notes of a scale or musical system; key. **b.** particular scale or system of notes; a key. **2.** *Painting, etc.* the system of tones or tints, or the colour scheme, of a picture, etc.

tone /toʊn/ *n.* **1.** any sound considered with reference to its quality, pitch, strength, source, etc.: *shrill tones.* **2.** quality or character of sound. **3.** vocal sound; the sound made by vibrating muscular bands in the larynx. **4.** a particular quality, way of sounding, modulation, or intonation of the voice as expressive of some meaning, feeling, spirit, etc.: *a tone of command.* **5.** an accent peculiar to a person, people, locality, etc., or a characteristic mode of sounding words in speech. **6.** *Phonetics* a vowel pitch or pitch modulation that distinguishes a particular phoneme in a tonal language, as in Chinese. **7.** *Music* **a.** an interval equivalent to two semitones; a whole tone. **b.** any of the nine plainsong melodies or tunes, to which the psalms are sung (called **Gregorian tones**). **c.** *Chiefly US* → **note. 8.** a variety of colour; a tint; a shade. **9.** hue; that distinctive quality by which colours differ from one another in addition to their differences indicated by chroma, tint, shade; a slight modification of a given colour: *green with a yellowish tone.* **10.** *Art* the prevailing effect of harmony of colour and values. **11.** *Physiol.* **a.** the state of tension or firmness proper to the organs or tissues of the body. **b.** that state of the body or of an organ in which all its animal functions are performed with healthy vigour. **c.** healthy sensitivity to stimulation. **12.** a particular state or temper of the mind; spirit, character, or tenor. **13.** prevailing character or style, as of manners or morals. **14.** style, distinction, or elegance. *–v.t.* **15.** to sound with a particular tone. **16.** to give the proper tone to (a musical instrument). **17.** to modify the tone or general colouring of. **18.** to give the desired tone to (a painting, etc.). **19.** *Photography* to change the colour of (a print), usually by chemical means. **20.** to render (as specified) in tone or colouring. **21.** to modify the tone or character of. **22.** to give physical or mental tone to. *–v.i.* **23.** to take on a particular tone; assume colour or tint. *–phr.* **24. tone down, a.** *Painting* to subdue; make (a colour) less intense in hue. **b.** to lower the strength, intensity, etc., of; soften; moderate. **c.** to become softened or moderated. **25. tone (in) with,** to harmonise with in tone or colour. **26. tone up, a.** to give a higher or stronger tone to. **b.** to make stronger or more vigorous: *walking tones up the muscles.* **c.** to gain in tone or strength. *–***tonal,** *adj.* *–***tonally,** *adv.* *–***toneless,** *adj.* *–***tonelessly,** *adv.* *–***tonelessness,** *n.* *–***toner,** *n.*

tongs /tɒŋz/ *pl. n.* (*sometimes construed as sing.*) any of various implements consisting of two arms hinged, pivoted, or otherwise fastened together, for seizing, holding, or lifting something.

tongue /tʌŋ/ *n.* **1.** an organ in humans and most vertebrates occupying the floor of the mouth and often protrusible and freely movable, being the principal organ of taste, and, in humans, of articulate speech. **2.** *Zool.* an organ in the mouth of invertebrates, frequently of a rasping nature. **3.** the tongue of an animal, as an ox, reindeer, or sheep, as used for food, often prepared by smoking or pickling. **4.** the human tongue as the organ of speech. **5.** the faculty or power of speech: *to find one's tongue*; *to lose one's tongue.* **6.** manner or character of speech: *a flattering tongue.* **7.** the language of a particular people, country, or locality: *the Hebrew tongue.* **8.** a strip of leather under the lacing or fastening of a shoe. **9.** a suspended piece inside a bell that produces a sound on striking against the side. **10.** a vibrating reed or the like in a musical instrument. **11.** *Carpentry* a projecting strip along the centre of the edge of a board, for fitting into a groove in another board. **12.** a narrow strip of land extending into a body of water. **13.** *Machinery* a long, narrow projection on a machine. **14.** the pin of a buckle, brooch, etc. *–verb* (**tongued, tonguing**) *–v.t.* **15.** to articulate

(the notes of a flute, cornet, etc.) by strokes of the tongue. **16.** *Carpentry* **a.** to cut a tongue on (a board). **b.** to join or fit together by a tongue-and-groove joint. **17.** to touch with the tongue. *–v.i.* **18.** to tongue the notes of a flute, etc. *–phr.* **19. give tongue, a.** to speak out, especially loudly. **b.** (of a hunting dog) to bark or bay loudly when the scent has been picked up or the quarry sighted. **20. hold one's tongue,** to be quiet. **21. mind one's tongue,** to be careful what one says. **22. on the tip of one's tongue,** on the verge of being remembered and uttered. **23. slip of the tongue,** an inadvertent remark. **24. with one's tongue in one's cheek,** not seriously; facetiously; ironically. *–***tongued,** *adj.* *–***tongueless,** *adj.*

tongue-in-cheek *adj.* not serious; facetious; ironic.

tongue kiss *n.* a kiss in which the tongue enters the partner's mouth. Also, **French kiss.**

tongue-kiss *v.i.* **1.** to participate in a tongue kiss. *–v.t.* **2.** to kiss (someone) in this manner. *–***tongue-kisser,** *n.* *–***tongue-kissing,** *n.*

tonic /ˈtɒnɪk/ *n.* **1.** a medicine that gives health and strength. **2.** anything that gives new strength or energy: *his success was a tonic to his spirits.* **3.** *Music* the first note or degree of the scale. *–adj.* **4.** giving health, strength, or energy. **5.** *Med.* **a.** relating to tension, as of the muscles. **b.** marked by continued muscular tension: *a tonic spasm.* **6.** relating to tone or accent in speech. **7.** *Music* relating to or founded on the tonic of a scale: *a tonic chord.*

tonic water *n.* effervescent water with quinine, often added to spirits.

tonight /təˈnaɪt/ *adv.* **1.** on this present night; on the night of this present day. *–n.* **2.** this present or coming night; the night of this present day.

tonnage /ˈtʌnɪdʒ/ *n.* **1.** the carrying capacity of a vessel expressed in gross tons. See **gross tonnage, register tonnage. 2.** ships collectively considered with reference to their carrying capacity or together with their cargoes. **3.** a duty on ships or boats at so much per ton of cargo or freight, or according to the capacity in tons.

tonne /tɒn/ *n.* a unit of mass equal to 1000 kilograms; metric ton. *Symbol*: t

tonsil /ˈtɒnsəl/ *n. Anat.* either of two prominent oval masses of lymphoid tissue situated one on each side of the fauces. *–***tonsillar,** *adj.*

tonsillectomy /tɒnsəˈlɛktəmi/ *n.* (*pl.* **-mies**) the surgical excision of one or both tonsils.

tonsillitis /tɒnsəˈlaɪtəs/ *n.* inflammation of a tonsil or the tonsils. *–***tonsillitic** /tɒnsəˈlɪtɪk/, *adj.*

tonsure /ˈtɒnʃə/ *n.* **1.** the act of shaving the hair on top of the head, especially formerly as a sign of becoming a priest or monk. **2.** the shaved top of the head. *–***tonsured,** *adj.*

too /tu/ *adv.* **1.** in addition; also; furthermore; moreover: *young, clever, and rich too.* **2.** to an excessive extent or degree; beyond what is desirable, fitting, or right: *too long.* **3.** an intensifier, especially after *only* or a negative: *only too glad to help you*; *not too bad.* **4.** *Colloq.* an intensifier: *I did too!* *–phr. Colloq.* **5. too right,** an emphatic expression of agreement. **6. too, too ...,** exaggeratedly: *he was too, too charming.*

took /tʊk/ *v.* past tense of **take.**

tool /tul/ *n.* **1.** an instrument, especially one held in the hand, for performing or facilitating mechanical operations, as a hammer, saw, file, etc. **2.** any instrument of manual operation. **3.** that part of a lathe, planer, drill, or similar machine, which performs the cutting or machining operation. **4.** the machine itself; a machine tool. **5.** anything used like a tool to do work or effect some result. **6.** anything used regularly in the course of a particular profession or occupation: *Words are the tools of the writer's trade.* **7.** any skill, resource, etc., seen as necessary or useful to a particular undertaking: *Assertiveness techniques can be a useful tool in dealing with difficult people.* **8.** someone used by another for that person's own ends; a cat's paw. **9.** the design or ornament impressed upon a book cover. **10.** *Colloq.* the penis. **11.** *Colloq.* a stupid person. *−v.t.* **12.** to work or shape with a tool. **13.** to work decoratively with a hand tool; to ornament with a bookbinder's tool, as on book covers. **14.** *Colloq.* to drive (a vehicle). *−v.i.* **15.** to work with a tool or tools. **16.** *Colloq.* to drive or ride in a vehicle. *−phr.* **17. tool up**, to equip, as a workshop for a particular job. **−tooler**, *n.*

toolbar /ˈtulbɑ/ *n.* *Computers* a rectangular bar, usually located at the top of a computer screen, containing a series of buttons marked with icons or words which can be activated to access specific functions of a particular computer program.

toolkit /ˈtulkɪt/ *n.* **1.** a collection of tools kept together and usually so comprehensive that it contains all the tools likely to be needed generally by its owner for some particular work such as plumbing, electrical repair, etc. **2.** the toolbox, sheath or any other storage device for holding such tools. Also, **kit**.

toot[1] /tut/ *v.i.* **1.** (of a horn) to give forth its characteristic sound. **2.** to make a sound resembling that of a horn or the like. **3.** to sound or blow a horn or other wind instrument. **4.** (of grouse) to give forth a characteristic cry or call. *−v.t.* **5.** to cause (a horn, etc.) to sound by blowing it. **6.** to sound (notes, etc.) on a horn or the like. *−n.* **7.** an act or sound of tooting. **−tooter**, *n.*

toot[2] /tut/ *n.* *Aust. Colloq.* a toilet.

tooth /tuθ/ *n.* (*pl.* **teeth** /tiθ/) **1.** (in most vertebrates) one of the hard bodies or processes usually attached in a row to each jaw, serving for the prehension and mastication of food, as weapons of attack or defence, etc., and in mammals typically composed chiefly of dentine surrounding a sensitive pulp and covered on the crown with enamel. **2.** (in invertebrates) any of various similar or analogous processes occurring in the mouth or alimentary canal, or on a shell. **3.** one of the projections of a comb, rake, saw, etc. **4.** one of a series of projections (cogs) on the edge of a wheel, etc., which engage with corresponding parts of another wheel or body. *−phr.* **5. a sweet tooth**, a liking for sweet things. **6. long in the tooth**, *Colloq.* elderly. **7. tooth and nail**, vigorously, and with determination. See **teeth**. **−toothed**, *adj.* **−toothless**, *adj.* **−toothlike**, *adj.*

tootle[1] /ˈtutl/ *v.i.* **1.** to toot gently or repeatedly on a flute or the like. *−n.* **2.** the sound itself.

tootle[2] /ˈtutl/ *v.i.* *Colloq.* to go, walk, or drive.

top[1] /tɒp/ *n.* **1.** the highest point or part of anything; the apex; the summit. **2.** the uppermost or upper part, surface, etc., of anything. **3.** the higher end of anything on a slope. **4.** a part considered as higher: *the top of a street.* **5.** the part of a plant above ground, as distinguished from the root. **6.** (*usu. pl.*) one of the tender tips of the branches or shoots of plants. **7.** that part of anything which is first or foremost; the beginning. **8.** the highest or leading place, position, rank, etc.: *at the top of the class.* **9.** the highest point, pitch, or degree: *to speak at the top of one's voice.* **10.** someone or something that occupies the highest or leading position. **11.** (*usu. pl.*) *Aust., NZ* one of the peaks or ridges of a high mountain range: *Barrington Tops.* **12.** a covering or lid, as of a box, motor car, carriage, etc. **13.** a blouse, T-shirt, jumper, jacket or other outer garment, sometimes with sleeves, to cover the torso. **14.** *Motor Vehicles* a transmission gear providing the highest forward speed ratio, usually turning the drive shaft at the same rate as the engine crankshaft. **15.** *Chem.* that part of a mixture under distillation which volatilises first. **16.** *Golf, etc.* **a.** a stroke above the centre of the ball, usually failing to give any height, distance, or accuracy. **b.** the forward spin given to the ball by such a stroke. *−adj.* **17.** relating to, situated at, or forming the top; highest; uppermost; upper: *the top shelf.* **18.** highest in degree; greatest: *to pay top prices.* **19.** foremost, chief, or principal: *to win top honours in a competition.* **20.** *Colloq.* the best; excellent: *he's a top bloke.* **21.** denoting or relating to the highest forward gear on a vehicle. *−verb* (**topped**, **topping**) *−v.t.* **22.** to furnish with a top; put a top on. **23.** to be at or constitute the top of. **24.** to reach the top of. **25.** to rise above: *the sun had topped the horizon.* **26.** to exceed in height, amount, number, etc. **27.** to surpass, excel, or outdo: *that tops everything!* **28.** to surmount with something specified. **29.** to complete by or as by putting the top on or constituting the top of. **30.** to remove the top of; crop; prune. **31.** to get or leap over the top of (a fence, etc.). **32.** *Chem.* to distil off only the most volatile part of a mixture. **33.** *Golf, etc.* **a.** to hit (the ball) above the centre. **b.** to make (a stroke, etc.) by hitting the ball in this way. **34.** to top-dress (land). *−v.i.* **35.** to rise aloft. **36.** *Golf, etc.* to hit the ball above the centre. *−phr.* **37. be top of the pops**, *Colloq.* to be extremely fashionable, popular, etc. **38. blow one's top**, *Colloq.* to lose one's temper. **39. from the top**, from the beginning. **40. off the top of one's head**, in an impromptu or improvised fashion. **41. on top**, successful; victorious; dominant. **42. on top of**, **a.** upon. **b.** close upon; following upon. **c.** displaying mastery of: *it took me weeks to get on top of the backlog.* **d.** depressing or discouraging: *sometimes things just get on top of me.* **43. over the top**, **a.** *Mil.* over the top of a parapet, as in charging the enemy. **b.** *Colloq.* extreme or excessive; beyond normal restraints or limits: *his reaction was over the top.* **44. (the) tops**, *Colloq.* the very best: *that book really is the tops.* **45. top off**, **a.** (sometimes fol. by *with*) to complete with success. **b.** to fatten (livestock) for market. **46. top oneself**, *Colloq.* to commit suicide. **47. top someone off**, *Colloq.* to inform or tell on someone. **48. top out at**, *Colloq.* to peak at: *temperatures will top out at 30°.* **49. top up**, **a.** to fill by adding liquid to (a partly filled container). **b.** to make an additional deposit of money into (an account) to make sure it does not fall into arrears: *to top up a mobile phone account.* **50. up top**, *Colloq.* **a.** at the topmost end. **b.** in a position of authority: *those up top will take change.* **c.** *Aust.* in the NT: *tourism up top.* **d.** in the head: *grow up top.*

top[2] /tɒp/ *n.* **1.** a child's toy, often inversely conical, with a point on which it is made to spin. *−phr.* **2. sleep like a top**, to sleep very soundly.

top- variant of **topo-**, before vowels, as in *toponym.*

topaz /ˈtoʊpæz/ *n.* **1.** a mineral, a type of silicate of aluminium, usually occurring in crystals of various colours, and used as a gem (**true topaz** or **precious topaz**). **2.** a yellow variety of sapphire (**oriental topaz**). **3.** a yellow variety of quartz (**false topaz** or **common topaz**).

top dressing *n.* **1.** a dressing of manure, soil, fertiliser, etc., on the surface of lawns, crops, etc. **2.** the action of someone who top-dresses. **3.** a top layer of gravel, crushed rock, etc., on a roadway. **4.** any superficial treatment or surface covering.

topee /ˈtoʊpi/ *n.* (in India) a helmet of sola pith. Also, **topi**.

top end *n.* *Colloq.* (*sometimes upper case*) the northern part of a geographical division, especially the top end of the NT of Australia. **−top-ender**, *n.*

top fermentation *n.* a brewing method using a strain of yeast that rises to the top of the vessel at the completion of fermentation, producing old beer or ale. Compare **bottom fermentation**.

top hat *n.* a man's tall silk hat.

topiary /ˈtoupiəri/ *adj.* **1.** (of hedges, trees, etc.) clipped or trimmed into (fantastic) shapes. *–n.* (*pl.* **-iaries**) **2.** topiary work; the topiary art. **–topiarian** /toupiˈɛəriən/, *adj.* **–topiarist**, *n.*

topic /ˈtɒpɪk/ *n.* **1.** a subject of conversation or discussion: *to provide a topic for discussion.* **2.** the subject or theme of a discourse or of one of its parts.

topical /ˈtɒpɪkəl/ *adj.* **1.** relating to or dealing with matters of current or local interest. **2.** relating to the subject of a discourse, composition, or the like. **3.** of a place; local. **4.** *Med.* relating or applied to a particular part of the body. **–topicality** /tɒpəˈkæləti/, *n.* **–topically**, *adv.*

topless /ˈtɒpləs/ *adj.* **1.** without a top. **2.** having the breasts bare. **3.** allowing the breasts to be exposed, as a garment.

topnotch /ˈtɒpnɒtʃ/ *adj. Colloq.* first-rate: *a topnotch job.* **–topnotcher**, *n.*

topo- a word element meaning 'place', as in *topography.* Also, **top-**.

topography /təˈpɒgrəfi/ *n.* (*pl.* **-phies**) **1.** the detailed description and analysis of the features of a relatively small area, district, or locality. **2.** the detailed description of particular localities, as cities, towns, estates, etc. **3.** the relief features or surface configuration of an area. **–topographer**, *n.* **–topographic** /tɒpəˈgræfɪk/, **topographical** /tɒpəˈgræfɪkəl/, *adj.* **–topographically** /tɒpəˈgræfɪkli/, *adv.*

topology /təˈpɒlədʒi/ *n. Maths* the branch of geometry that deals with those properties of geometric forms that remain invariant under certain transformations, as bending, stretching, etc. **–topologic** /tɒpəˈlɒdʒɪk/, **topological** /tɒpəˈlɒdʒɪkəl/, *adj.* **–topologically** /tɒpəˈlɒdʒɪkli/, *adv.*

top paddock *n.* **1.** the paddock farthest from the homestead. *–phr.* **2. have kangaroos (loose) in the top paddock**, *Colloq.* to be crazy.

topple /ˈtɒpəl/ *v.i.* **1.** to fall forwards as having too heavy a top; pitch or tumble down. **2.** to lean over or jut, as if threatening to fall. *–v.t.* **3.** to cause to topple.

topside /ˈtɒpsaɪd/ *n.* **1.** the upper side. **2.** (*usu. pl.*) the upper part of a boat's or ship's side, above the main deck. **3.** the top section of a butt of beef, without bone, below the rump.

topsoil /ˈtɒpsɔɪl/ *n.* the surface or upper part of the soil.

topsy-turvy /tɒpsiˈtɜvi/ *adv.* **1.** with the top where the bottom should be; upside down. **2.** in or into a state of confusion or disorder. *–adj.* **3.** turned upside down; inverted; reversed. **4.** confused or disorderly. **–topsy-turvily**, *adv.* **–topsy-turviness**, *n.*

tor /tɔ/ *n.* a rocky eminence; a hill.

Torah /ˈtɔrə/ *n.* the literature containing the teaching and judgements of the early Jewish priests. Also, **Tora**.

torch /tɔtʃ/ *n.* **1.** a small portable electric lamp powered by dry batteries. **2.** a light to be carried in the hand, consisting of some combustible substance, as resinous wood, or of twisted flax or the like soaked with tallow or other flammable substance. **3.** any of various lamp-like devices which produce a hot flame and are used for soldering, burning off paint, etc.; an oxyacetylene torch. **4.** *Colloq.* a person who, for a fee, sets fire to someone's property so that the owner may collect the insurance money. *–v.t.* **5.** *Colloq.* to destroy (a building, etc.) by setting fire to it: *someone had torched the shop.* *–phr.* **6. carry a torch for**, to suffer unrequited love for. **–torchless**, *adj.*

tore /tɔ/ *v.* past tense of **tear**[2].

toreador /ˈtɔriədɔ/ *n.* a Spanish bullfighter.

torment *v.t.* /tɔˈmɛnt/ **1.** to give great bodily or mental suffering to; torture: *to be tormented with violent headaches.* **2.** to worry or annoy greatly: *she tormented him with questions.* **3.** to stir into violent movement: *the wind tormented the trees.* *–n.* /ˈtɔmɛnt/ **4.** a state of great bodily or mental suffering; agony; misery. **5.** something that causes great bodily or mental pain or suffering. **6.** a source of trouble, worry, or annoyance. **–tormentor**, *n.* **–tormentingly**, *adv.*

torn /tɔn/ *v.* **1.** past participle of **tear**[2]. *–phr.* **2. that's torn it**, everything is ruined. **3. torn between**, unable to choose between (conflicting desires, duties, etc.).

tornado /tɔˈneɪdoʊ/ *n.* (*pl.* **-does** *or* **-dos**) **1.** *Meteorol.* **a.** a violent whirlwind of small radius, advancing over the land, in which winds of destructive force circulate round a centre. It is characterised by strong ascending currents and is generally made visible by a funnel-shaped cloud. **2.** a violent squall or whirlwind of small extent. **2.** a violent outburst, as of emotion or activity. **–tornadic** /tɔˈnædɪk/, *adj.* **–tornado-like**, *adj.*

torpedo /tɔˈpidoʊ/ *n.* (*pl.* **-does** *or* **-dos**) **1.** a self-propelled cigar-shaped missile containing explosives which is launched from a tube in a submarine, torpedo boat, or the like, or from an aircraft, and explodes upon impact with the ship fired at. **2.** any of various other explosive devices. **3.** any of the fishes of the genus *Torpedo*, relatives of the rays and sharks, characterised by their ability to give electric shocks to aggressors. *–verb* (**-doed, -doing**) *–v.t.* **4.** to attack, hit, damage, or destroy with a torpedo or torpedoes. *–v.i.* **5.** to attack, damage, or sink a ship with torpedoes.

torpor /ˈtɔpə/ *n.* **1.** a state of suspended physical powers and activities. **2.** sluggish inactivity or inertia. **3.** dormancy, as of a hibernating animal. **4.** lethargic dullness or indifference; apathy. **–torpid**, *adj.* **–torporific**, *adj.*

torque /tɔk/ *n.* **1.** *Mechanics* that which produces or tends to produce torsion or rotation; the moment of a system of forces which tends to cause rotation. **2.** *Machinery* the turning power of a shaft. **3.** *Optics* the rotational effect on plane-polarised light passing through certain liquids or crystals. **4.** a collar, necklace, or similar ornament consisting of a twisted narrow band, usually of precious metal, worn especially by the ancient Gauls and Britons. *–v.t.* (**torqued, torquing**) **5.** *Mechanics* to apply torque to.

Torrens title /ˈtɔrənz taɪtl/ *n.* (in Australia) a system whereby title to land is evidenced by one document issued by a government department.

torrent /ˈtɒrənt/ *n.* **1.** a stream of water flowing with great rapidity and violence. **2.** a rushing, violent, or abundant and unceasing stream of anything: *a torrent of lava.* **3.** a violent downpour of rain. **4.** a violent, tumultuous, or overwhelming flow: *a torrent of abuse.*

torrent file *n.* a file created using software which sets up a network of peer-to-peer file sharers who each supply a small part of the file, greatly increasing the speed of delivery.

torrid /ˈtɒrəd/ *adj.* **1.** subject to parching or burning heat, especially of the sun, as regions, etc. **2.** oppressively hot, parching, or burning, as climate, weather, air, etc. **3.** ardent; passionate. **–torridity** /təˈrɪdəti/, **torridness**, *n.* **–torridly**, *adv.*

Torrid Zone *n.* the part of the earth's surface between the Tropics of Cancer and Capricorn.

torsion /ˈtɔʃən/ *n.* **1.** the act of twisting. **2.** the resulting state. **3.** *Mechanics* **a.** the twisting of a body by two equal and opposite torques. **b.** the internal torque so produced. **–torsional**, *adj.* **–torsionally**, *adv.*

torso /ˈtɔsoʊ/ *n.* (*pl.* **-sos**) **1.** the trunk of the human body. **2.** a sculptured form representing the trunk of a nude female or male figure. **3.** something mutilated or incomplete.

tort /tɔt/ *n. Law* **1.** any wrong other than a criminal wrong, as negligence, defamation, etc. **2.** (*pl.*) the field of study of wrongs other than criminal wrongs.

torte /tɔt/ *n.* a large, highly decorated cake containing cream and other rich ingredients, usually served on festive occasions.

tortilla /tɔ'tijə/ *n.* (in Mexico, etc.) a thin, round, unleavened pancake of corn meal, cooked on a flat plate of iron, earthenware, or the like.

tortoise /'tɔtəs/ *n.* **1.** any terrestrial or freshwater turtle, having toed feet rather than flippers, as *Testudo chelodina*. **2.** a very slow person or thing.

tortoiseshell /'tɔtəʃɛl/ *n.* **1.** the horny substance, with a mottled or clouded yellow-and-brown colouration, composing the plates or scales that cover the marine **tortoiseshell turtle**, of the genus *Eretmochelys*, formerly used for making combs and other articles, inlaying, etc. **2.** the shell of a tortoise. **3.** any synthetic substance made to appear like natural tortoiseshell. **4.** Also, **tortoiseshell cat.** a domestic cat with black, brownish, and cream colouring. —*adj.* **5.** mottled or variegated like tortoiseshell, especially with yellow and black and sometimes other colours. **6.** made of tortoiseshell.

tortuous /'tɔtʃuəs/ *adj.* **1.** full of twists, turns, or bends; twisting, winding, or crooked. **2.** not direct or straightforward as in a course of procedure, thought, speech, or writing. **3.** deceitfully indirect or morally crooked, as proceedings, methods, policy, etc. —**tortuously,** *adv.* —**tortuousness,** *n.*

torture /'tɔtʃə/ *n.* **1.** the act of causing severe pain, especially from cruelty, or to get information from the victim. **2.** a method of causing such pain. **3.** (*oft. pl.*) the pain or suffering caused or undergone. **4.** (a cause of) agony of body or mind. —*v.t.* **5.** to cause severe bodily or mental pain to. **6.** to twist, force, or bring into some unnatural position or form. **7.** to twist or distort (language, etc.). —**torturer,** *n.* —**torturous,** *adj.*

toss /tɒs/ *v.t.* **1.** to throw, pitch, or fling, especially to throw lightly or carelessly: *to toss a piece of paper into the wastepaper basket.* **2.** to throw or send (a ball, etc.) from one to another, as in play. **3.** to throw or pitch with irregular or careless motions; fling or jerk about: *a ship tossed by the waves; a tree tosses its branches in the wind.* **4.** to throw, raise, or jerk upwards suddenly: *she tossed her head disdainfully.* **5.** to throw (a coin, etc.) into the air in order to decide something by the side turned up when it falls. **6.** (of an animal) to throw (someone or something) up into the air or to the ground. —*v.i.* **7.** to pitch, rock, sway, or move irregularly, as a ship on a rough sea, or a flag or plumes in the breeze. **8.** to fling or jerk oneself or move restlessly about, especially on a bed or couch: *to toss in one's sleep.* **9.** to throw something. **10.** *Colloq.* to go with a fling of the body: *to toss out of a room.* —*n.* **11.** the act of tossing. **12.** a pitching about or up and down. **13.** a throw or pitch. **14.** a tossing of a coin or the like to decide something; a toss-up. **15.** a sudden fling or jerk of the body, especially a quick upward or backward movement of the head. —*phr.* **16. argue the toss, a.** to go on arguing after a dispute has been settled. **b.** to debate or discuss, especially at length. **17. not give a toss,** *Colloq.* to be unconcerned; not care. **18. take a toss,** *Colloq.* to fall from a horse. **19. toss back** (or **down**), *Colloq.* to drink very quickly: *she tossed back a shot of bourbon.* **20. toss it in,** *Colloq.* to abandon an enterprise, project, job, etc. **21. toss off,** *Colloq.* **a.** to drink or eat very quickly: *he tossed off a few drinks and then left.* **b.** to produce easily and quickly: *she tossed off a few ideas.* **c.** (*taboo*) (of a male) to ejaculate; have an orgasm. **d.** (*taboo*) (of a male) to masturbate. **22. toss up,** to throw a coin or other object into the air in order to decide something by the way it falls.

tosser /'tɒsə/ *n.* **1.** someone or something that tosses. **2.** *Colloq.* a stupid person.

toss-up *n.* **1.** the tossing up of a coin or the like to decide something by the side on which it falls. **2.** *Colloq.* an even chance. **3.** *Colloq.* a situation in which there is very little to choose between two alternatives.

tot¹ /tɒt/ *n.* **1.** a small child. **2.** a small portion of drink. **3.** a small quantity of anything.

tot² /tɒt/ *phr.* **tot up,** *Colloq.* to add up.

total /'toutl/ *adj.* **1.** constituting or comprising the whole; entire; whole: *the total expenditure.* **2.** of or relating to the whole of something: *a total eclipse.* **3.** complete in extent or degree; absolute; unqualified; utter: *a total failure.* —*n.* **4.** the total amount; sum; aggregate: *to add the several items to find the total.* **5.** the whole; a whole or aggregate: *the costs reached a total of $200.* —*v.t.* (**-talled** *or,* *US,* **-taled,** **-talling** *or,* *US,* **-taling**) **6.** to bring to a total; add up. **7.** to reach a total of; amount to. **8.** *Colloq.* to crash (a motor vehicle) in such a way that it becomes irreparably damaged. —*phr.* **9. total to,** to amount to.

totalisator /'toutəlaɪˌzeɪtə/ *n.* **1.** an apparatus for registering and indicating the total of operations, measurements, etc. **2. a.** a system of betting, as on horseraces, in which those who bet on the winners divide the bets or stakes, less a percentage for the management, taxes, etc. **b.** the apparatus that records the bets in such a system. Also, **totalizator.**

totalitarian /touˌtælə'tɛəriən/ *adj.* **1.** of or relating to a centralised government in which those in control grant neither recognition nor tolerance to parties of differing opinion. —*n.* **2.** an adherent of totalitarian principles. —**totalitarianism,** *n.*

totality /tou'tæləti/ *n.* (*pl.* **-ties**) **1.** the state of being total; entirety. **2.** the total amount.

totally /'toutəli/ *adv.* **1.** wholly; entirely; completely. **2.** (*used with the present continuous form of a verb*) *Colloq.* definitely: *I am totally going to the party.*

tote¹ /tout/ *Colloq.* —*v.t.* **1.** to carry, as on the back or in the arms, as a burden or load. **2.** to carry or have on the person: *to tote a gun.* **3.** to transport or convey, as in a vehicle or boat. —*n.* **4.** the act or course of toting. **5.** something that is toted.

tote² /tout/ *n.* → **totalisator** (def. 2).

totem /'toutəm/ *n.* an object or natural phenomenon, often an animal, assumed as the token or emblem of a clan, family, or related group. —**totemic** /tou'tɛmɪk/, **totemistic,** *adj.* —**totemist,** *n.*

totter /'tɒtə/ *v.i.* **1.** to walk or go with faltering steps, as if from extreme weakness. **2.** to sway or rock on the base or ground, as if about to fall: *a tottering tower; a tottering government.* **3.** to shake or tremble: *a tottering load.* —*n.* **4.** the act of tottering; an unsteady movement or gait. —**totterer,** *n.* —**totteringly,** *adv.* —**tottery,** *adj.*

toucan /'tukæn/ *n.* any of various fruit-eating birds, family Ramphastidae, of tropical America, with an enormous beak and usually a striking colouration.

touch /tʌtʃ/ *v.t.* **1.** to put the hand, finger, etc., on or into contact with (something) to feel it. **2.** to come into contact with and perceive (something), as the hand or the like. **3.** to bring (the hand, finger, etc., or something held) into contact with something. **4.** to give a slight tap or pat to with the hand, finger, etc.; strike or hit gently or lightly. **5.** to hurt or injure. **6.** to come into or be in contact with. **7.** *Geom.* (of a line or surface) to be tangent to. **8.** to be adjacent to or border on. **9.** to come up to; reach; attain. **10.** to attain equality with; compare with (usually with a negative): *they can't touch her for speed.* **11.** to mark or relieve slightly, as with colour: *a grey dress touched with blue.* **12.** to strike the strings, keys, etc., of (a musical instrument) so as to cause it to sound. **13.** to treat or affect in some way by contact. **14.** to affect as if by contact; tinge; imbue. **15.** to affect with some feeling or emotion, especially tenderness, pity, gratitude, etc.: *his heart was touched by their sufferings.* **16.** to handle, use, or have to do with (something) in any way: *he won't touch another drink.* **17.** to begin to eat; eat a little of: *he hardly touched his food.* **18.** to deal with or treat in speech or writing. **19.** to refer or allude to. **20.** to relate or pertain to: *a critic in all affairs touching the kitchen.* **21.** to be a matter of importance to; make a difference to. **22.** *Colloq.* to apply to for money, or succeed in getting money from; to beg. –*v.i.* **23.** to place the hand, finger, etc., on or in contact with something. **24.** to come into or be in contact. –*n.* **25.** the act of touching. **26.** the state or fact of being touched. **27.** that sense by which anything material is perceived by means of the contact with it of some part of the body. **28.** the sensation or effect caused by touching something, regarded as a quality of the thing: *an object with a slimy touch.* **29.** a coming into or being in contact. **30.** a close relation of communication, agreement, sympathy, or the like: *to be in touch with public opinion.* **31.** a slight stroke or blow. **32.** a slight attack, as of illness or disease: *a touch of rheumatism.* **33.** a slight added action or effort in doing or completing any piece of work. **34.** manner of execution in artistic work. **35.** the act or manner of touching or fingering a musical instrument, especially a keyboard instrument, so as to bring out the tone. **36.** the mode of action of the keys of an instrument. **37.** a detail in any artistic work: *a nice touch; the finishing touches.* **38.** a slight amount of some quality, attribute, etc.: *a touch of sarcasm in his voice.* **39.** a slight quantity or degree: *a touch of salt.* **40.** a distinguishing characteristic or trait: *the touch of the master.* **41.** *Rugby Football, etc.* the area outside the field of play, including the touchlines. **42.** *Colloq.* **a.** the act of applying to a person for money, as a gift or loan. **b.** the money thus obtained. **c.** a person from whom such money can be obtained easily. –*phr.* **43. get in touch**, (sometimes fol. by *with*) to initiate communication. **44. into touch**, *Rugby Football, etc.* out of the field of play. **45. keep** (or **stay**) **in touch**, to maintain an association or friendship. **46. touch and go**, with an uncertain outcome; precariously close to disaster. **47. touch at**, to make a stop or a short call at (a place), as a ship or those on board. **48. touch base with someone**, *Colloq.* to make contact with someone. **49. touch down**, (of an aircraft) to land after a flight. **50. touch on** (or **upon**), **a.** to speak or write about briefly or casually in the course of a discourse, etc.: *he touched on his own travels.* **b.** to allude to briefly: *he touched on various tunes in the medley.* **51. touch up**, **a.** to modify or improve by adding a stroke of paint, etc., here and there. **b.** to put finishing touches to. **c.** to repair, renovate, or add points of detail to, as photographs. **d.** *Colloq.* to touch in amorous advances. –**touchable**, *adj.*

touch-and-go *adj.* **1.** hasty, sketchy, or desultory. **2.** precarious, risky: *a highly touch-and-go situation.* **3.** uncertain; hard to predict. Also, (*especially in predicative use*), **touch and go**.

touchdown /'tʌtʃdaʊn/ *n.* **1.** *American Football* **a.** the act of being on or behind the opponents' goal line while in possession of the ball, so as to score six points. **b.** the score made by this. **2.** the landing of an aircraft.

touché /tuˈʃeɪ, 'tuʃeɪ/ *interj.* **1.** *Fencing* an expression indicating a touch by the point of a weapon. **2.** an expression acknowledging a telling remark or rejoinder.

touching /'tʌtʃɪŋ/ *adj.* **1.** affecting; moving; pathetic. **2.** that touches. –*prep.* **3.** in reference or relation to; concerning; about. –**touchingly**, *adv.* –**touchingness**, *n.*

touchstone /'tʌtʃstoʊn/ *n.* **1.** a black siliceous stone used to test the purity of gold and silver by the colour of the streak produced on it by rubbing it with either metal. **2.** a test or criterion for the qualities of a thing.

touch-type *v.i.* to type without looking at the keys of a typewriter or computer keyboard.

touchy /'tʌtʃi/ *adj.* (**-chier, -chiest**) **1.** apt to take offence on slight provocation; irritable. **2.** risky, or ticklish, as a subject. –**touchily**, *adv.* –**touchiness**, *n.*

tough /tʌf/ *adj.* **1.** not easily broken or cut. **2.** not brittle or tender. **3.** difficult to masticate, as food. **4.** of viscous consistency, as liquid or semiliquid matter. **5.** capable of great endurance; sturdy; hardy. **6.** not easily influenced, as a person. **7.** hardened; incorrigible. **8.** difficult to perform, accomplish, or deal with; hard, trying, or troublesome. **9.** hard to bear or endure. **10.** vigorous; severe; violent: *a tough struggle.* **11.** rough, disorderly, or rowdyish. –*adv.* **12.** *Colloq.* aggressively; threateningly: *to act tough.* –*n.* **13.** a ruffian; a rowdy. –*interj.* **14.** *Colloq.* an exclamation of contemptuous lack of concern. –*phr.* **15. be tough on**, to make demands of: *to be tough on oneself.* **16. get tough**, **a.** (sometimes fol. by *with*) to deal harshly or strictly. **b.** to become hardened or inured. **17. hang tough**, *Colloq.* to persevere against the odds. **18. tough it out**, *Colloq.* to maintain an unyielding or unrepentant attitude throughout an episode, despite all criticism or blame. –**toughly**, *adv.* –**toughness**, *n.*

toupee /'tupeɪ/ *n.* a wig or patch of false hair worn to cover a bald spot. Also, **toupée**.

tour /tʊə, 'tuə, tɔ/ *v.i.* **1.** to travel from place to place. **2.** to travel from place to place giving musical or theatrical performances: *the band is touring this summer.* –*v.t.* **3.** to travel through (a place): *to tour Rome.* –*n.* **4.** (an organised) journey to or through a place or from place to place: *a tour of Sydney; a tour through the Snowy Mountains.* **5.** *Chiefly Mil.* a period of duty at one place.

Tourette syndrome /tuˈrɛt sɪndroʊm/ *n.* a disorder of the nervous system which manifests itself in involuntary body movements and vocalisations.

tourism /'tʊərɪzəm, 'tuə-, 'tɔ-/ *n.* **1.** the practice of touring, especially for pleasure. **2.** the occupation of providing local services, as entertainment, lodging, food, etc., for tourists.

tourist /'tʊərəst, 'tuə-, 'tɔ-/ *n.* **1.** someone who tours, especially for pleasure. **2.** a member of a touring international sporting team.

tournament /'tɔnəmənt/ *n.* **1.** a meeting for contests in athletic or other sports. **2.** a trial of skill in some game, in which competitors play a series of contests: *a chess tournament.* **3.** *Hist.* **a.** a contest or martial sport in which two opposing parties of mounted and armoured combatants fought for a prize, with blunted weapons and in accordance with certain rules. **b.** a meeting at an appointed time and place for the performance of knightly exercises and sports.

tourniquet /'tɔnəkeɪ, 'tʊə-/ *n.* *Med.* any device for arresting bleeding by forcibly compressing a blood vessel, as a pad pressed down by a screw, a bandage tightened by twisting, etc.

tousle /'taʊzəl/ *v.t.* **1.** to disorder or dishevel: *his hair was tousled.* **2.** to handle roughly.

tout /taʊt/ *v.i.* **1.** to try urgently or persistently to get business, employment, votes, etc. **2.** to spy on a racehorse, etc., to get (and sell) information for betting purposes. –*v.t.* **3.** to describe or declare, especially favourably: *to tout a politician as a friend of the people.* **4.** to watch; spy on. –*n.* **5.** someone who touts (see defs 1 and 2).

tow[1] /toʊ/ *v.t.* **1.** to drag or pull (a boat, car, etc.) by means of a rope or chain. –*n.* **2.** the act of towing. **3.** the thing being towed. **4.** a rope, chain, etc., for towing. –*phr.* **5. in tow**, **a.** in the condition of being towed. **b.** under guidance; in one's charge. **c.** in attendance; following or accompanying one around. **6. on** (or

under) **tow**, in the condition of being towed. –**towage**, n.

tow² /touˈ/ n. **1.** the fibre of flax, hemp, or jute prepared for spinning by beating. **2.** the coarse and broken parts of flax or hemp separated from the finer parts in combing. –adj. **3.** made of tow: tow cloth. **4.** resembling tow; pale yellow: tow-coloured hair.

toward adj. /ˈtouəd/ **1.** Archaic going on; in progress: when there is work toward. –prep. /təˈwɔd/ **2.** towards.

towards /təˈwɔdz, tɔdz/ prep. **1.** in the direction of (with reference to either motion or position): to walk towards the north. **2.** with respect to; as regards: one's attitude towards a proposition. **3.** nearly as late as; shortly before: towards two o'clock. **4.** as a help or contribution to: to give money towards a gift. Also, **toward**.

towel /ˈtauəl, taul/ n. **1.** a cloth or the like for wiping and drying something wet, especially one for the hands, face, or body after washing or bathing. –v.t. (**-elled** or, US, **-eled, -elling** or, US, **-eling**) **2.** to wipe or dry with a towel. –phr. **3. throw** (or **toss**) **in the towel**, to give up; admit defeat. **4. towel up**, Aust. Colloq. **a.** to defeat in competition, as at cards: we towelled you up last Friday. **b.** to thrash.

towelling /ˈtauəlɪŋ, ˈtaulɪŋ/ n. **1.** any of various absorbent fabrics used for towels, and also for beachwear and the like. **2.** a rubbing with a towel. **3.** Aust. Colloq. a thrashing. Also, Chiefly US, **toweling**.

tower /ˈtauə/ n. **1.** a building or structure high in proportion to its lateral dimensions, either isolated or forming part of any building. **2.** such a structure used as or intended for a stronghold, fortress, prison, etc. **3.** a tall, movable structure used in ancient and medieval warfare in storming a fortified place. –v.i. **4.** to rise or extend far upwards like a tower; rise aloft. –phr. **5. tower of strength**, a source of mental and physical support, as a person; someone who may be depended on. **6. tower over** (or **above**), **a.** to be higher and taller than. **b.** to surpass, as in ability, etc. –**towered**, adj. –**towerless**, adj. –**tower-like**, adj.

town /taun/ n. **1.** a small group of houses and other buildings thought of as a place, and given a name. **2.** a distinct densely populated area of considerable size, having some degree of self-government. **3.** Brit. a group of buildings, larger than a village and administratively more independent, but smaller than a city. **4.** US any of various administrative divisions, usually urban, and smaller and less elaborately organised than a city; a township. **5.** urban life, as opposed to rural: I prefer the town to the country. **6.** the particular town in question, as that in which one is. **7.** the nearest large town. **8.** the main shopping, business, or entertainment centre of a large town, contrasted with the suburbs. **9.** an urban community; the people of a town. –phr. **10. go to town, a.** to do something thoroughly. **b.** to do something enthusiastically; splash out. **c.** to overindulge or lose one's self-restraint. **d.** to celebrate. **11. go to town on**, Colloq. to berate; tell off. **12. man about town**, a sophisticated, pleasure-seeking, and usually sociable man of high social status. **13. on the town, a.** seeking amusement in the entertainments of a city or town. **b.** Obs. supported by the municipal authorities or public charity. **14. paint the town red**, Colloq. to indulge in riotous entertainment. **15. talk of the town**, the subject of general gossip or rumour. –**townish**, adj. –**townless**, adj.

town hall n. a hall or building belonging to a town, used for the transaction of the town's business, etc., and often also as a place of public assembly.

town house n. **1.** a house or mansion in a town or city, as distinguished from a country residence. **2.** Aust. a house designed as part of a small block of such, each with ground floor access.

townie /ˈtauni/ n. Colloq. (sometimes derog.) a person who lives in a town and is familiar with town ways. Compare **bushie** (def. 1).

township /ˈtaunʃɪp/ n. **1.** a small town or settlement. **2.** Hist. a tract of surveyed land; town site. **3.** (in South Africa) an area set aside for black Africans, as in an urban locality; a location.

tox- variant of **toxo-**, before vowels, as in toxaemia.

toxaemia /tɒkˈsimiə/ n. Pathol. entry into, and persistence in, the bloodstream of bacterial toxins absorbed from a local lesion, by which stream these poisons are borne by the circulation to all parts of the body. Also, **toxemia**.

toxic /ˈtɒksɪk/ adj. **1.** of, relating to, affected with, or caused by a toxin or poison. **2.** poisonous. **3.** detrimental to a good outcome; extremely disadvantageous: toxic assets; toxic debt. **4.** Colloq. harmful; destructive: a toxic relationship; a toxic personality. –**toxicity** /tɒkˈsɪsəti/, n. –**toxically**, adv.

toxic debt n. a debt which, although initially established as a legitimate business transaction, proves subsequently, as a result of changes in the fiscal environment, to be financially worthless to the lending body.

toxico- a combining form of **toxic**. Compare **toxo-**.

toxicology /tɒksəˈkɒlədʒi/ n. the branch of medical science that deals with poisons, their effects, antidotes, detection, etc. –**toxicological** /tɒksəkəˈlɒdʒɪkəl/, adj. –**toxicologically** /tɒksəkəˈlɒdʒɪkli/, adv. –**toxicologist**, n.

toxin /ˈtɒksən/ n. **1.** any of the specific poisonous products generated by pathogenic microorganisms and constituting the causative agents in various diseases, as tetanus, diphtheria, etc. **2.** any of various organic poisons produced in living or dead organisms. **3.** their products, as a venom, etc. Also, **toxine**.

toxo- a combining form representing **toxin**, or short for **toxico-**, as in toxoplasmosis.

toy /tɔɪ/ n. **1.** an object, often a small imitation of some familiar thing, for children or others to play with, or otherwise derive amusement; a plaything. **2.** a thing or matter of little or no value or importance. **3.** a small article of little real value, but prized for some reason; a knick-knack; a trinket. **4.** something diminutive. **5.** any of various breeds of dog bred or selected for their smallness; toy dog. –adj. **6.** of or like a toy, especially in size. **7.** made as a toy: a toy train. –v.i. **8.** to handle affectionately; play. **9.** to act idly, absent-mindedly, or without seriousness. –phr. **10. toy with**, to trifle with; deal with as unimportant. –**toyer**, n. –**toyless**, adj. –**toylike**, adj.

toy boy n. Colloq. the young male partner of an older woman.

trace¹ /treɪs/ n. **1.** a mark which shows that something has been present; vestige: a trace of blood on a dress; they didn't find a trace of the thieves. **2.** a very small amount: a trace of iron in the earth. **3.** (esp. pl.) a footprint or track. –v.t. (**traced, tracing**) **4.** to follow the footprints, track, or traces of. **5.** to follow or make out the course or line of: to trace a river to its source; to trace the history of the wool trade. **6.** to find by investigation; discover: the police traced the missing man. **7.** to copy (a drawing, plan, etc.) by following the lines of the original on a transparent sheet placed over it. **8.** to draw (a line, outline, figure, etc.). –**traceable**, adj. –**traceability** /treɪsəˈbɪləti/, **traceableness**, n. –**traceably**, adv.

trace² /treɪs/ n. **1.** each of the two straps, ropes, or chains by which a carriage, wagon, or the like is drawn by a harness horse or other draught animal. **2.** Machinery a piece in a machine, as a bar, transferring the movement of one part to another part, being hinged to each. **3.** Angling a short piece of gut or other strong material connecting the hook to a fishing line. –*phr.* **4. kick over the traces,** to reject discipline; to act in an independent manner.

trace element *n. Biochem.* any of some chemical elements found in plants and animals in minute quantities which is a critical factor in physiological processes.

trace gas *n.* a gas occurring naturally in very small quantities; altogether usually less than one per cent of the volume of the earth's atmosphere.

trace metal *n.* one of a number of metals that are present in animal and plant cells in extremely small quantities.

tracery /'treɪsəri/ *n.* (*pl.* **-ries**) **1.** ornamental work consisting of ramified ribs, bars, or the like, as in the upper part of a Gothic window, in panels, screens, etc. **2.** any delicate interlacing of lines, threads, etc., as in carving, embroidery, etc.; network.

trachea /trə'kiə/ *n.* (*pl.* **tracheas** or **tracheae** /trə'kii/) **1.** (in air-breathing vertebrates) the tube extending from the larynx to the bronchi, serving as the principal passage for conveying air to and from the lungs; the windpipe. **2.** (in insects and other arthropods) one of the air-conveying tubes of the respiratory system. **3.** *Bot.* a duct formed by a row of cells which have perforated end walls as in xylem vessels.

trachoma /trə'koʊmə/ *n. Pathol.* a contagious inflammation of the conjunctiva of the eyelids. –**trachomatous** /trə'kɒmətəs, -'koʊmə-/, *adj.*

track /træk/ *n.* **1.** a road, path, or trail. **2.** the structure of rails, sleepers, etc., on which a railway train or the like runs; a railway line. **3.** the mark, or series of marks, left by anything that has passed along. **4.** (*esp. pl.*) a footprint or other mark left by an animal, a person, or a vehicle. **5.** a rough roadway or path, as one made or beaten by the feet of humans or animals. **6.** a line of travel or motion: *the track of a bird.* **7.** a route, usually only roughly defined, as one used for droving: *the Birdsville Track.* **8.** an endless jointed metal band which is driven by the wheels of a tracklaying vehicle to enable it to move, or pull loads, over rough ground. **9.** a course of action or conduct; a method of proceeding: *to go on in the same track year after year.* **10.** a path or course made or laid out for some particular purpose. **11.** a course laid out for running or racing. **12. a.** the sports which are performed on a track, collectively; athletics. **b.** both track and field sports as a whole. **13.** one of the distinct sections of a CD, DVD, etc., containing a piece, or section of music, etc. **14.** one of the bands of material recorded lengthwise beside other such bands on magnetic tape, hence *2-track tape recorder, 8-track tape recorder,* etc. **15.** (*pl.*) *Colloq.* → **track marks.** –*v.t.* **16.** to follow up or pursue the tracks, traces, or footprints of. **17.** to hunt by following the tracks of. **18.** to follow the course of, as by radar. **19.** to follow the progress of in terms of increased numbers, areas of interest, etc. –*v.i.* **20.** to follow up a track or trail. **21. a.** to run in the same track, as the wheels of a vehicle. **b.** to be in alignment, as one gearwheel with another. **22.** *Film, TV, etc.* (of the camera) to move bodily in any direction while in operation. Compare **pan²**. **23.** to make one's way. –*adj.* **24.** *Athletics* relating to those sports performed on a running track (contrasted with *field*). –*phr.* **25. down the track, a.** into the future: *success is a long way down the track.* **b.** along a path of progress: *two years down the track and we're beginning to make a profit.* **26. go down the same track,** to follow the same course or action or pattern of behaviour. **27. in one's tracks,** just where one is standing: *the shock stopped him in his tracks.* **28. in the tracks of,** following; pursuing. **29. keep track of,** to follow the course or progress of; keep sight or knowledge of. **30. lose track of,** to fail to

keep informed on or in view; fail to stay in touch with. **31. make tracks,** *Colloq.* (sometimes fol. by *for*) to leave or depart. **32. off the beaten track,** secluded, unusual, or little known. **33. off the track,** away from the subject in hand. **34. on the track of,** pursuing; on the scent of. **35. on the (wallaby) track,** *Colloq.* on the move; itinerant, most frequently with reference to a swagman, seasonal worker, etc. **36. on track,** proceeding on a course leading to the successful accomplishment of a goal: *on track for a new world record; on track to meet profit forecasts.* **37. the right track,** right idea, plan, interpretation, etc. **38. the wrong side of the tracks,** an area regarded as socially unacceptable because of the poverty and lack of respectability of the inhabitants. **39. the wrong track,** the wrong idea, plan, interpretation, etc. **40. track down,** to catch or find, after pursuit or searching. **41. track in,** *Film, TV* to move the camera towards the subject. **42. track out,** *Film, TV* to move the camera away from the subject. –**tracker,** *n.* –**trackless,** *adj.*

trackball /'trækbɔl/ *n. Computers* a ball suspended in a mouse (def. 3) which as it rolls moves the cursor on the screen.

track marks *pl. n. Colloq.* scars or marks on the arms or legs caused by habitual use of a hypodermic needle. Also, **tracks.**

track record *n.* **1.** an account of a racehorse's successes and defeats on the racecourse. **2.** an account of a person's successes or failures in a specific field.

tracksuit /'træksut/ *n.* a loose, two-piece overgarment worn by athletes in training, between events, etc.

tract¹ /trækt/ *n.* **1.** a stretch or extent of land, water, etc.; region. **2.** *Anat.* **a.** a definite region or area of the body, especially a group, series, or system of related parts or organs: *the digestive tract.* **b.** a bundle of nerve fibres having a common origin and destination. **3.** a space or extent of time; a period.

tract² /trækt/ *n.* a brief treatise or pamphlet suitable for general distribution, especially one dealing with some topic of practical religion.

tractable /'træktəbəl/ *adj.* **1.** easily managed, or docile, as persons, their dispositions, etc. **2.** able to be easily handled or dealt with, as metals; malleable. –**tractability** /træktə'bɪləti/, **tractableness,** *n.* –**tractably,** *adv.*

traction /'trækʃən/ *n.* **1.** the act of drawing or pulling or the state of being drawn. **2.** the pulling of a body, car, etc., along a surface. **3.** a force that prevents a wheel slipping: *these tyres have good traction.* **4.** the medical treatment of applying tension to a limb or bone by means of weights and pulleys. **5.** a form or type of power used for pulling: *steam traction.* –**tractional,** *adj.* –**tractive,** *adj.*

tractor /'træktə/ *n.* **1.** a motor vehicle, usually fitted with tyres with deep treads, used to draw farm implements as the plough, seed drill, etc., and loads and also as a source of power for agricultural machinery, etc. **2.** Also, **tractor propeller.** a propeller mounted at the front of an aeroplane, thus exerting a pull.

trade /treɪd/ *n.* **1.** the buying and selling, or exchanging, of commodities, either by wholesale or by retail, within a country or between countries: *domestic trade; foreign trade.* **2.** a purchase, sale, or exchange. **3.** a form of occupation pursued as a business or calling, as for a livelihood or profit. **4.** a skilled occupation, especially one requiring manual labour: *the trade of a carpenter; the trade of a printer.* **5.** people engaged in a particular line of business: *a lecture of interest only to the trade.* **6.** traffic; amount of dealings: *a brisk trade in overcoats.* **7.** market: *the tourist trade.* **8.** commercial occupation (as against professional). **9.** (*pl.*) the trade winds. –*v.t.* **10.** to give in return; exchange; barter. **11.** to exchange: *to trade seats with a person.* –*v.i.*

12. to carry on trade. **13.** to make an exchange. *–adj.* **14.** of or relating to commerce, a particular trade or occupation, or trade as a whole. *–phr.* **15. trade in, a.** to give in part exchange, as in a transaction. **b.** to traffic in: *to trade in wheat.* **16. trade on,** to exploit or take advantage of, especially unfairly. **17. trade up,** to trade something in on something superior. *–tradeable, adj.*

trade gap *n. Econ.* the difference between the value of a country's imports and of its exports when the former is a larger figure.

trade-in *n.* **1.** goods given in whole or, usually, part payment of a purchase. *–adj.* **2.** of or relating to such goods or such a method of payment.

trademark /'treɪdmak/ *n.* **1.** the name, symbol, figure, letter, word, or mark adopted and used by a manufacturer or merchant in order to designate the goods he or she manufactures or sells, and to distinguish them from those manufactured or sold by others. Any mark entitled to registration under the provisions of a statute is a trademark. *–adj.* **2.** of or relating to any object, mannerism, etc., which is invariably associated with a particular person: *she was there with her trademark feather boa.* Also, **trade mark.**

trade name *n.* **1.** the name or style under which a commercial enterprise does business. **2.** a word or phrase used in trade whereby a business or enterprise or a particular class of goods is designated, but which is not technically a trademark, either because it is not susceptible of exclusive appropriation as a trademark or because it is not affixed to goods sold in the market. **3.** Also, **brand name.** the name by which an article or substance is known to the trade.

trade-off *n.* a concession made in a negotiation in return for one given.

trade price *n.* the price at which goods are sold to members of the same trade, or to retail dealers by wholesalers.

trader /'treɪdə/ *n.* **1.** someone who trades; a merchant or business person. **2.** a ship used in trade, especially in a limited sphere, as a chain of islands.

tradesman /'treɪdzmən/ *n.* (*pl.* **-men**) a person skilled in a trade (def. 4). *–tradeswoman, n.*

tradesperson /'treɪdzpɜsən/ *n.* (*pl.* **-people**) a person engaged in a trade (def. 4).

trade union *n.* an organisation of employees for mutual aid and protection, and for dealing collectively with employers. Also, **trades union.** *–trade unionism, n. –trade unionist, n.*

trading bank *n.* a bank which offers a wide variety of financial services to both individual and corporate customers, including cheque accounts, loans for commercial ventures, etc.

trading stamp *n.* a stamp with a certain value given as a premium by a seller to a customer, specified quantities of these stamps being exchangeable for various articles when presented to the issuers of the stamps.

trading stock *n.* stock not held for permanent investment.

tradition /trə'dɪʃən/ *n.* **1.** the handing down of statements, beliefs, legends, customs, etc., from generation to generation, especially by word of mouth or by practice: *a story that has come down to us by popular tradition.* **2.** something that is so handed down: *the traditions of the Maori.* **3.** *Theology* **a.** (in Judaism) an unwritten body of laws and doctrines, or any one of them, held to have been received from Moses and handed down orally from generation to generation. **b.** (in Christianity) a body of teachings, or any one of them, held to have been delivered by Christ and his apostles but not committed to writing. **c.** (in Islamic religion) the beliefs and customs of Islam supplementing the Koran, especially the Sunna. **4.** *Law* the act of handing over

something to another, especially in a formal legal manner; delivery; transfer. *–traditional, adj. –traditionally, adv.*

traditional custodian *n.* a person who is entitled, by Indigenous tradition, to have certain cultural knowledge.

traditional owner *n.* a person who has, in accordance with Indigenous tradition, social, economic, and spiritual affiliations with, and responsibilities for, the lands claimed or any part of them.

traduce /trə'djus/ *v.t.* (**-duced, -ducing**) to speak evil or maliciously and falsely of; slander, calumniate, or malign: *to traduce someone's character.* *–traducer, n. –traducingly, adv.*

traffic /'træfɪk/ *n.* **1.** the coming and going of people, cars, ships, etc., along a way, road or water route: *heavy traffic in a street.* **2.** the people, cars, etc., going along such a way. **3.** the business done by a railway or other carrier in the transportation of goods or passengers. **4.** trade or dealing in certain things or goods, often against the law: *traffic in drugs.* **5.** dealings or exchanges of anything between parties, people, etc. *–v.i.* (**-ficked, -ficking**) **6.** to carry on traffic, trade, or commercial dealings, especially of an illegal kind. *–trafficker, n. –trafficless, adj. –trafficable, adj.*

traffic island *n.* a defined area, usually at an intersection, from which traffic is excluded and which is used for control of vehicular movements and for pedestrian refuge.

traffic jam *n.* an acute congestion of motor vehicles, bringing traffic to a standstill.

traffic offence *n.* an offence committed by a person driving a motor vehicle, as driving over the speed limit, driving with more than the prescribed level of alcohol in the blood, driving without a current licence, or in an unregistered vehicle.

tragedian /trə'dʒidiən/ *n.* **1.** a writer of tragedy. **2.** an actor of tragedy.

tragedy /'trædʒədi/ *n.* (*pl.* **-dies**) **1.** a dramatic composition of serious or sombre character, with an unhappy ending: *Shakespeare's tragedy of 'Hamlet'.* **2.** any literary composition, as a novel, dealing with a sombre theme carried to a tragic conclusion. **3.** a lamentable, dreadful, or fatal event or affair; a disaster or calamity.

tragic /'trædʒɪk/ *adj.* Also, **tragical. 1.** characteristic or suggestive of tragedy: *tragic solemnity.* **2.** mournful, melancholy, or pathetic in the extreme: *a tragic expression.* **3.** dreadful, calamitous, or fatal: *a tragic death.* **4.** relating to or having the nature of tragedy: *the tragic drama.* **5.** acting in or composing tragedy. *–n.* **6.** *Colloq.* someone who is excessively devoted to a particular celebrity, sport, hobby, etc.: *a cricket tragic.* *–tragically, adv. –tragicalness, n.*

trail /treɪl/ *v.t.* **1.** to drag or let drag along the ground or other surface; to draw or drag along behind. **2.** to bring or have floating after itself or oneself: *to trail clouds of dust.* **3.** to follow the track or trail of; track. **4.** *US* to beat down or make a path or way through (grass, etc.). **5.** to follow along behind (another or others), as in a race. *–v.i.* **6.** to be drawn or dragged along the ground or some other surface, as when hanging from something moving: *her long gown trailed over the floor.* **7.** to hang down loosely from something. **8.** to stream or float from and after something moving, as dust, smoke, sparks, etc., do. **9.** to follow as if drawn along. **10.** to go slowly, lazily, or wearily along; straggle. **11.** to pass or extend in a straggling line. **12.** to fall behind the leaders, as a competitor in a race; be losing in a competition of any kind. **13.** (of a plant) to extend itself in growth along the ground and over objects encountered, resting on these for support rather than taking root or clinging by tendrils, etc. *–n.* **14.** a path or track made across a wild region, over rough country, or the like, by the passage of people or animals: *to follow the trail.* **15.** the track, scent, or the like, left by an animal, person, or thing, especially as followed by a hunter, hound, or other pursuer. **16.** something that is trailed or that trails behind, as the train of a skirt or robe. **17.** a stream of dust, smoke, light, people, vehicles, etc., behind something moving. **18.** *Astron.* **a.** a long bright tail seen in the sky in the wake of certain meteors. **b.** the trace left on a stationary photographic plate by a star during a long exposure. **19.** the act of trailing. *–phr.* **20. trail a coat,** to provoke a heated reaction by persistent antagonistic remarks, in order to bring suspected latent hostility into the open. **21. trail off,** to pass by gradual change, as into silence; diminish: *her voice trailed off.* **–trailless,** *adj.*

trail bike *n.* → **dirt bike.**

trailer /ˈtreɪlə/ *n.* **1.** a vehicle designed to be towed by a motor vehicle, and used in transporting loads. **2.** *Film* an advertisement for a forthcoming film, usually consisting of extracts from it. **3.** a trailing plant. **4.** *US* a caravan (def. 1).

train /treɪn/ *n.* **1.** a set of railway carriages joined together and driven by electric or diesel power, or pulled by a locomotive. **2.** → **locomotive** (def. 1). **3.** a line of people, cars, etc., travelling together. **4.** *Mil.* a crowd of vehicles, animals, and people accompanying an army, to carry supplies. **5.** *Mechanics* a series of connected parts, as wheels and pinions, through which movement is carried. **6.** something that is drawn along; a trailing part. **7.** a group of followers or attendants; retinue: *the king and his train entered.* **8.** a series of proceedings, events, circumstances, etc. **9.** a series of connected ideas; course of reasoning: *a train of thought.* **10.** aftermath: *war brings misery in its train.* *–v.t.* **11.** to teach (a person or animal) to know or do something; educate; drill. **12.** to make (a person, etc.) fit by proper exercise, diet, etc., for some sport or contest. **13.** to bring (a plant, branch, etc.) into a particular shape or position, by bending, pruning, etc. **14.** to bring (a gun, camera, glance, etc.) to bear on some object or point. *–v.i.* **15.** to give or undergo teaching, drill, practice, etc. **16.** to get oneself into condition by exercise, etc. **–trainable,** *adj.* **–trainless,** *adj.*

trainee /treɪˈniː/ *n.* **1.** someone receiving training. *–adj.* **2.** receiving training: *a trainee designer.*

trainer /ˈtreɪnə/ *n.* **1.** someone who trains others in a particular skill or activity. **2.** someone who prepares racehorses for racing. **3.** someone who trains athletes in a sport. **4.** equipment used in training, especially that which simulates the conditions of a sport. **5.** a shoe which is designed for use in sport.

train wreck *n.* **1.** the wreck of a train. **2.** *Colloq.* a complete disaster: *her life is a train wreck.*

traipse /treɪps/ *v.i. Colloq.* **1.** to walk so as to be, or having become, tired; trudge. **2.** to walk (about) aimlessly; gad about.

trait /treɪt, treɪ/ *n.* a distinguishing feature or quality; characteristic: *bad traits of character.*

traitor /ˈtreɪtə/ *n.* **1.** someone who betrays a person, a cause, or any trust. **2.** someone who betrays their country by violating their allegiance; someone guilty of treason. **–traitress** /ˈtreɪtrəs/, *fem. n.* **–traitorous,** *adj.*

trajectory /trəˈdʒɛktəri/ *n.* (*pl.* **-ries**) **1.** the curve described by a projectile in its flight. **2.** the path described by a body moving under the action of given forces. **3.** *Geom.* a curve or surface which cuts all the curves or surfaces of a given system at a constant angle.

tram /træm/ *n.* **1.** a passenger vehicle running on a tramway, having flanged wheels and, though originally powered by steam or cable, now usually powered by electricity taken by a current collector from an overhead conductor wire. **2.** the vehicle or cage of an overhead carrier. **–tramless,** *adj.*

trammel /ˈtræml/ *n.* **1.** (*usu. pl.*) anything that impedes or hinders free action; a restraint: *the trammels of custom.* **2.** an instrument for drawing ellipses. **3.** a three-layered fishing net. **4.** a contrivance hung in a fireplace to support pots, kettles, etc., over the fire. *–v.t.* (**-melled** *or, Chiefly US,* **-meled, -melling** *or, Chiefly US,* **-meling**) **5.** to involve or hold in trammels; hamper; restrain. **–trammeller,** *n.*

tramp /træmp/ *v.i.* **1.** to tread or walk with a firm, heavy, resounding step. **2.** to walk steadily; march; trudge. **3.** to go about as a vagrant or tramp. **4.** to hike. **5.** *NZ* → **bushwalk** (def. 1). *–v.t.* **6.** to tramp or walk heavily or steadily through or over. **7.** to traverse on foot: *tramp the streets.* **8.** to tread or trample underfoot. **9.** to travel over as a tramp. *–n.* **10.** the act of tramping. **11.** a firm, heavy, resounding tread. **12.** a long, steady walk; trudge. **13.** *Brit.* a walking excursion or expedition. **14.** someone who travels about on foot from place to place, especially a vagrant living on occasional jobs or gifts of money or food. **15.** *Colloq.* a promiscuous woman. **16.** Also, **tramp steamer.** a cargo boat which does not run regularly between ports, but goes wherever shippers desire. *–phr.* **17. tramp on** (or **upon**), to tread heavily on or trample: *to tramp on a person's toes.* **–tramper,** *n.* **–tramping,** *n.*

trample /ˈtræmpəl/ *v.i.* **1.** to tread or step heavily and noisily; stamp. **2.** to treat with contempt. *–v.t.* **3.** to tread heavily, roughly, or carelessly on or over; tread underfoot, etc. **4.** to treat with contempt. **5.** to domineer harshly over; crush: *to trample one's employees.* **6.** to put, force, reduce, etc., by trampling: *to trample out a fire.* *–n.* **7.** the act or sound of trampling. *–phr.* **8. trample on** (or **upon**), **a.** to tread heavily, roughly, or crushingly on, especially repeatedly. **b.** to treat in a harsh, domineering, or cruel way, as if treading roughly on: *to trample on an oppressed people.* **–trampler,** *n.*

trampoline /ˈtræmpəlin, træmpəˈliːn/ *n.* **1.** a sheet of canvas attached by resilient cords to a horizontal frame a metre or so above the floor; used as a springboard when performing acrobatics. *–v.i.* **2.** to jump on a trampoline.

trance /træns, trans/ *n.* **1.** a half-conscious or dazed state. **2.** the condition of being completely lost in thought. **3.** *Occult* a temporary state of unconsciousness in which a medium is controlled by an intelligence from without and used as a means of communication with the dead. **4.** Also, **trance music.** a type of dance music with a fast, steady 4/4 beat and repeated crescendos, designed for dancing while under the influence of drugs. **–trancelike,** *adj.*

trannie[1] /ˈtræni/ *n. Colloq.* a transistor radio.

trannie[2] /ˈtræni/ *n. Colloq.* a transparency (def. 3).

trannie[3] /ˈtræni/ *n. Colloq.* (*often derog.*) **1.** a transsexual. **2.** a transvestite. Also, **tranny.**

tranny /ˈtræni/ *n. Colloq.* (*often derog.*) → **trannie**[3]. Also, **trany.**

tranquil /ˈtræŋkwəl/ *adj.* (**-quiller** *or, Chiefly US,* **-quiler, -quillest** *or, Chiefly US,* **-quilest**) **1.** free from commotion or tumult; peaceful; quiet; calm: *a tranquil country place.* **2.** free from or unaffected by disturbing emotions; unruffled: *a tranquil life.* **–tranquilly,** *adv.* **–tranquilness, tranquillity** /træŋˈkwɪləti/, *n.*

tranquilliser /ˈtræŋkwəlaɪzə/ *n. Pharmacology* a drug that has a sedative or calming effect without inducing sleep. Also, *Chiefly US,* **tranquillizer, tranquilizer.** **–tranquillise,** *v.*

trans- **1.** a prefix meaning 'across', 'beyond', freely applied in geographical terms (*transcontinental, trans-Australian*), also found attached to stems not used as words, and in figurative meanings, as *transpire,* *transport, transcend.* **2.** a prefix meaning 'across' in the sense of changing from one state to another, as in *transgender, transsexual.*

transact /trænzˈækt/ *v.t.* **1.** to carry through (affairs, business, negotiations, etc.) to a conclusion or settlement. **2.** to perform. –**transactor**, *n.*

transaction /trænzˈækʃən/ *n.* **1.** the act of transacting. **2.** the fact of being transacted. **3.** an instance or process of transacting something. **4.** something that is transacted; an affair; a piece of business. **5.** *(pl.)* **a.** records of the doings of a learned society or the like. **b.** reports of papers read, addresses delivered, discussions, etc., at the meetings. –**transactional**, *adj.*

transcend /trænˈsɛnd/ *v.t.* **1.** to go or be above or beyond (a limit, something with limits, etc.); surpass or exceed. **2.** to go beyond in elevation, excellence, extent, degree, etc.; surpass, excel, or exceed. –*v.i.* **3.** to be transcendent; excel. –**transcendent**, *adj.*

transcendental /trænsɛnˈdɛntl/ *adj.* **1.** transcendent, surpassing, or superior. **2.** going beyond ordinary experience, thought, or belief; supernatural; metaphysical. **3.** abstract. **4.** *Philos.* belonging to every kind of thing, transcending all other distinctions. **5.** *Maths* (of a number) not algebraic; not able to be produced by the algebraic operations of addition, subtraction, multiplication, division, and the extraction of roots. For example, *pi* and *e* are transcendental numbers. –**transcendentalism**, *n.* –**transcendentally**, *adv.*

transcribe /trænˈskraɪb/ *v.t.* **1.** to make a copy of in writing: *to transcribe a document.* **2.** to reproduce in writing or print as from speech. **3.** to write out in other characters; transliterate: *to transcribe one's shorthand notes.* **4.** to make a transcription. **5.** *Music* to arrange (a composition) for a medium other than that for which it was originally written. –**transcriber**, *n.* –**transcription**, *n.* –**transcript**, *n.*

transept /ˈtrænsɛpt/ *n.* **1.** the transverse portion (or, occasionally, portions) of a cruciform church. **2.** either of the two armlike divisions of this, one on each side of the crossing. –**transeptal** /trænˈsɛptl/, *adj.* –**transeptally** /trænˈsɛptəli/, *adv.*

trans fat /ˈtræns fæt/ *n.* fat composed of trans fatty acid.

trans fatty acid *n.* a type of unsaturated fat occurring naturally in meat and dairy products but also created as a side effect of the hydrogenation of plant oils in the process of creating margarine; thought to increase the risk of coronary heart disease.

transfer *verb* /trænsˈfɜ/ (**-ferred, -ferring**) –*v.t.* **1.** to carry or send from one place, person, etc., to another. **2.** *Law* to make over; convey: *to transfer a title to land.* **3.** to take (a drawing, design, pattern, etc.) over from one surface to another. –*v.i.* **4.** to change over or be carried. –*n.* /ˈtrænsfɜ/ **5.** the act or means of transferring. **6.** the fact of being transferred. **7.** a drawing, pattern, etc., which may be put on to another surface, especially by direct contact. **8.** *Law* a making over, by sale or gift, of real or personal property to another. **9.** *Econ.* the act of having the ownership of a stock or registered bond transferred upon the books of the issuing company or its agent. **10.** *Econ.* a form filled in when stocks and shares change hands; share transfer. –**transferable** /trænsˈfɜrəbəl/, *adj.* –**transferability** /ˌtrænsfɜrəˈbɪləti/, *n.* –**transferral** /trænsˈfɜrəl/, **transference**, *n.*

transfigure /trænsˈfɪɡə/ *v.t.* **1.** to change in outward form or appearance; transform, change, or alter. **2.** to change so as to reach an exalted state: *to be transfigured by a divine revelation.* –**transfiguration**, *n.* –**transfigurement**, *n.*

transfix /trænsˈfɪks/ *v.t.* **1.** to pierce through, as with a pointed weapon, or as the weapon does. **2.** to fix fast with or on something sharp; thrust through. **3.** to make

motionless with amazement, terror, etc. –**transfixion** /trænsˈfɪkʃən/, *n.*

transform /trænsˈfɔm/ *v.t.* **1.** to change in form. **2.** to change in appearance, condition, nature, or character, especially completely or deeply: *to transform a desert into productive land.* **3.** *Chem.* to change (one substance, element, etc.) into another. **4.** *Maths* to change the form of (a figure, expression, etc.) without changing the value. **5.** *Physics* to change (one form of energy) into another. –*v.i.* **6.** to change in form, appearance, or character; become transformed. –**transformable**, *adj.* –**transformation**, *n.* –**transformative** /trænsˈfɔmətɪv/, *adj.*

transformer /trænsˈfɔmə/ *n. Elect.* an electric device, without continuously moving parts, which by electromagnetic induction transforms electric energy from one or more circuits to one or more circuits at the same frequency, usually with changed values of voltage and current.

transfuse /trænsˈfjuz/ *v.t.* **1.** to pour from one container into another. **2.** to transfer or transmit as if by pouring; instil; impart. **3.** to diffuse through something; infuse. **4.** *Med.* **a.** to transfer (blood) from the veins or arteries of one person or animal into those of another. **b.** to inject, as a saline solution, into a blood vessel. –**transfuser**, *n.* –**transfusible**, *adj.* –**transfusive** /trænsˈfjusɪv/, *adj.*

transfusion /trænsˈfjuʒən/ *n.* **1.** the act or process of transfusing. **2.** *Med.* **a.** the transferring of blood taken from one person or animal to another, as in order to renew a depleted blood supply. **b.** the injecting of some other liquid into the veins. **3.** an act of imparting, injecting, transmitting, or the like: *a transfusion of new capital into a business.*

transgender /trænzˈdʒɛndə/ *adj.* **1.** of or relating to a person whose gender identity is different from their physiological gender. –*n.* **2.** such a person. –**transgendered**, *adj.* –**transgenderism**, *n.*

transgress /trænzˈɡrɛs/ *v.t.* **1.** to pass over or go beyond (a limit, etc.): *to transgress the bounds of prudence.* **2.** to go beyond the limits imposed by (a law, command, etc.); violate; infringe; break. –*phr.* **3.** **transgress against**, to violate (a law, command, etc.); offend or sin against. –**transgressive**, *adj.* –**transgressively**, *adv.* –**transgressor**, *n.*

transient /ˈtrænziənt/ *adj.* **1.** passing with time; not lasting or enduring; transitory. **2.** remaining for only a short time, as a guest at a hotel. –*n.* **3.** someone who remains for only a short time; a transient guest, boarder, etc. –**transiently**, *adv.* –**transientness**, *n.*

transient ischaemic attack *n.* → **TIA**.

transistor /trænˈzɪstə/ *n.* **1.** *Electronics* a miniature solid-state device for amplifying or switching, using silicon or germanium semiconductors materials. **2.** a transistorised radio. –*adj.* **3.** equipped with transistors, as a radio or gramophone.

transit /ˈtrænzət/ *n.* **1.** the act or fact of passing across or through; passage from one place to another. **2.** conveyance from one place to another, as of persons or goods: *the problem of rapid transit in cities.* **3.** a transition or change. **4.** *Astron.* **a.** the passage of a heavenly body across the meridian of a place or through the field of a telescope. **b.** the passage of an inferior planet (Mercury or Venus) across the disc of the sun, or of a satellite or its shadow across the face of its primary. **5.** *US Surveying* a theodolite. –*verb* (**-sited, -siting**) –*v.t.* **6.** to pass across or through. **7.** *Surveying* to turn (the telescope of a theodolite) about its horizontal transverse axis so as to make it point in the opposite direction; reverse, invert, or plunge (the instrument). –*v.i.* **8.** to pass across or through a place or thing. –*phr.*

9. in transit, passing through a place; staying for only a short time.

transition /træn'zɪʃən/ n. **1.** passage from one position, state, stage, etc., to another. **2.** a passage or change of this kind. **3.** *Music* **a.** a passing from one key to another; modulation. **b.** a passage serving as a connecting link between two more important passages. –v.t. **4.** to move (someone) in a gradual and planned way from one role, position, or stage of life, to another. –**transitional, transitionary**, adj. –**transitionally**, adv.

transitive /'trænzətɪv/ adj. **1.** *Gram.* having the nature of a transitive verb. **2.** characterised by or involving transition; transitional; intermediate. –n. **3.** *Gram.* a transitive verb. –**transitively**, adv. –**transitiveness**, n.

transitive verb n. **1.** a verb which can only be used with a direct object. **2.** a verb used with a direct object, as *drink* in the sentence *he drinks water* where *water* is the direct object. Compare **intransitive verb**.

transit lane n. a traffic lane which is restricted to particular categories of vehicles, often during certain periods of the day.

transitory /'trænzətri/ adj. **1.** passing away; not lasting, enduring, permanent, or eternal. **2.** lasting for a short time; brief; transient. –**transitorily**, adv. –**transitoriness**, n.

translate /trænz'leɪt/ v.t. **1.** to turn (something written or spoken) from one language into another: *to translate Arrernte into English*. **2.** to change into another form; transform; convert. **3.** to carry or remove from one place, position, condition, etc., to another; transfer. **4.** to express in other terms; interpret; explain. **5.** *Physics* to cause (a body) to move without sideways rotation or angular displacement. –v.i. **6.** to turn or be turned from one language into another. –**translatable**, adj. –**translation**, n. –**translator**, n.

transliterate /trænz'lɪtəreɪt/ v.t. to change (letters, words, etc.) into corresponding characters of another alphabet or language: *to transliterate the Greek X as ch*. –**transliteration** /ˌtrænzlɪtə'reɪʃən/, n. –**transliterator**, n.

translucent /trænz'lusənt/ adj. transmitting light diffusely or imperfectly, as frosted glass. –**translucence, translucency**, n. –**translucently**, adv.

transmigrate /trænzmaɪ'greɪt/ v.i. **1.** to remove or pass from one place to another. **2.** to migrate from one country to another in order to settle there. **3.** (of the soul) to be reborn with the same soul in another body, either immediately upon death or after a purgatorial or waiting period. –v.t. **4.** to cause to transmigrate, as a soul. –**transmigrator**, n. –**transmigratory**, adj.

transmission /trænz'mɪʃən/ n. **1.** the act of transmitting. **2.** the fact of being transmitted. **3.** something that is transmitted. **4.** the sending and receiving of analogue and digital information through either wire or wireless means. **5. a.** an instance of broadcasting a television or radio program. **b.** such a program. **6.** *Machinery* **a.** the transmitting or transferring of motive force. **b.** a device for this purpose, especially the mechanism or gearing for transmitting the power from the revolutions of the engine shaft in a motor vehicle to the driving wheels, at the varying rates of speed and direction of drive as selected in gear changes. –**transmissive** /trænz'mɪsɪv/, adj.

transmit /trænz'mɪt/ v.t. (**-mitted, -mitting**) **1.** to send over or along, such as to a person or place. **2.** to pass on or communicate (information, news, etc.). **3.** to pass on or hand down to heirs, successors, etc. **4.** to pass on (a disease, etc.). **5.** to broadcast (a radio or television program). **6.** *Physics* to cause or permit (light, heat, sound, etc.) to pass through a medium. –**transmittable, transmittible**, adj. –**transmitter**, n.

transmogrify /trænz'mɒgrəfaɪ/ v.t. (**-fied, -fying**) to change as by magic; transform. –**transmogrification** /trænzˌmɒgrəfə'keɪʃən/, n.

transmute /trænz'mjut/ v.t. to change from one nature, substance, or form into another; transform. –**transmutable**, adj. –**transmutability** /ˌtrænzmjutə'bɪləti/, **transmutableness**, n. –**transmutably**, adv. –**transmuter**, n.

transnational /trænz'næʃənəl/ adj. **1.** operating on a nationwide basis. **2.** (especially of a business) operating in more than one country; multinational.

transom /'trænsəm/ n. **1.** a crosspiece separating a door, window, etc., from a window above it. **2.** a window above a door; fanlight. –**transomed**, adj.

transparency /træns'pɛərənsi, -'pær-/ n. (pl. **-cies**) **1.** Also, **transparence**. the property or quality of being transparent. **2.** something which is transparent; a picture, design, etc., on glass or some translucent substance, made visible by light shining through from behind. **3.** a transparent positive photographic image used for projection. **4.** (of a government or other organisation) the policy or practice of making all operations clearly manifest, and of being accountable to the public for all such operations.

transparent /træns'pɛərənt, -'pær-/ adj. **1.** having the property of sending rays of light through its substance so that objects situated beyond or behind can be clearly seen (opposed to *opaque*). **2.** (of material) allowing light to pass through. **3.** open, or candid: *transparent honesty*. **4.** open to public scrutiny, as government or business dealings. **5.** easily seen through or understood: *transparent excuses*. –**transparently**, adv. –**transparentness**, n.

transpire /træns'paɪə/ v.i. **1.** to occur, happen, or take place. **2.** to become apparent. **3.** to emit or give off waste matter, etc., through the surface, as of the body, of leaves, etc. **4.** to escape as through pores, as moisture, smell, etc. –v.t. **5.** to emit or give off (waste matter, watery vapour, a smell, etc.) through the surface, as of the body, of leaves, etc. –**transpirable**, adj. –**transpiration** /trænspə'reɪʃən/, n. –**transpiratory** /træns-'paɪrətri/, adj.

transplant v.t. /træns'plænt, -'plant/ **1.** to remove (a plant) from one place and plant it in another. **2.** *Surg.* to transfer (an organ or a portion of tissue) from one part of the body to another or from one person or animal to another. **3.** to remove (something) from one place to another. **4.** to bring (people, culture, etc.) from one country to another for settlement. –n. /'trænsplænt, -plant/ **5.** the act of transplanting. **6.** something transplanted, such as an organ of the body or a seedling. –**transplantable** /træns'plæntəbəl/, adj. –**transplantation** /trænsplæn'teɪʃən/, n. –**transplanter** /træns'plæntə/, n.

transport v.t. /træns'pɔt, 'trænspɔt/ **1.** to carry from one place to another; convey. **2.** to carry away by strong emotion. **3.** (formerly) to carry or send (a criminal, etc.) to a penal colony. –n. /'trænspɔt/ **4.** an act or method of transporting; conveyance. **5.** a system of transporting passengers or goods: *public transport*. **6.** a ship, aircraft or other vehicle providing a means of transporting or conveying, especially one employed for transporting soldiers or military stores. **7.** a large truck. **8.** strong emotion, such as joy, delight, etc. –**transportable** /træns-'pɔtəbəl/, adj. –**transportability** /ˌtrænspɔtə'bɪləti/, n. –**transportation**, n.

transpose /træns'pouz/ v.t. **1.** to alter the relative position or order of (a thing in a series, or a series of things). **2.** to cause (two or more things) to change places; interchange. **3.** to alter the order of (letters in a word, or words in a sentence). **4.** *Algebra* to bring (a term) from one side of an equation to the other, with change of the plus or minus sign. **5.** *Music* to reproduce in a different key, by raising or lowering in pitch. –**transposable**, *adj.* –**transposer**, *n.* –**transposition**, *n.*

transputer /trænzˈpjutə/ *n.* a microprocessor chip of great power and small size, comprising a 32 bit microprocessor containing the equivalent of 200 000 transistors condensed into a piece of silicon 9 mm square and capable of handling 10 mips.

transsexual /trænzˈsekʃuəl/ *adj.* **1.** of or relating to someone who has changed sex. **2.** of or relating to the medical procedures by which sex changes are effected. –*n.* **3.** someone who has undergone a sex change operation. **4.** someone who feels himself or herself, though physically of one sex, to be of the other sex in psychological disposition. Also, **transexual**.

transversal /trænzˈvɜsəl/ *n. Geom.* a line intersecting two or more lines.

transverse /ˈtrænzvɜs, trænzˈvɜs/ *adj.* **1.** lying or being across or in a crosswise direction; athwart. **2.** (of a flute) held across the body, and having a mouth hole in the side of the tube, near its end, across which the player's breath is directed. –*n.* **3.** something which is transverse. –**transversely**, *adv.*

transvestism /trænzˈvestɪzəm/ *n.* the desire to wear clothing typical of the opposite sex. –**transvestite**, *n.*

trap /træp/ *n.* **1.** a contrivance used for taking game or other animals, as a mechanical device that springs shut suddenly; a pitfall, or a snare. **2.** any device, stratagem, or the like for catching one unawares. **3.** an ambush. **4.** any of various mechanical contrivances for preventing the passage of steam, water, etc. **5.** an arrangement in a pipe, as a double curve or a U-shaped section, in which liquid remains and forms a seal, for preventing the passage or escape of air or gases through the pipe from behind or below. **6.** a device for suddenly releasing or tossing into the air objects to be shot at, as pigeons or clay targets. **7.** a carriage, especially a light two-wheeled one. **8.** a trapdoor. **9.** *Colloq.* the mouth. –*verb* (**trapped, trapping**) –*v.t.* **10.** to catch in a trap: *to trap foxes*. **11.** to take by stratagem; lead by artifice or wiles. **12.** to furnish or set with traps. **13.** to provide (a drain, etc.) with a trap. **14.** to stop and hold by a trap, as air in a pipe. –*v.i.* **15.** to set traps for game: *he was busy trapping*. **16.** to engage in catching animals in traps for their furs. –*phr.* **17. (a) round the traps**, *Aust. Colloq.* in public places, especially places where gossip and information is commonly circulated. **18. a trap for young players**, a danger or risk to the inexperienced. **19. go round the traps**, *Aust. Colloq.* to visit places where people gather and talk, as hotels, clubs, etc., in the hope of getting information.

trapdoor /ˈtræpdɔ/ *n.* **1.** a door or the like, flush, or nearly so, with the surface of a floor, ceiling, roof, etc. **2.** the opening which it covers.

trapdoor spider *n.* any of various burrowing spiders of the family Ctenizidæ that construct silk-lined tunnels in the ground, sometimes fitted with a lid, as the **brown trapdoor spider**, *Dyarcyops fuscipes*, of eastern Australia.

trapeze /trəˈpiz/ *n.* **1.** an apparatus for gymnastics consisting of a short horizontal bar attached to the ends of two suspended ropes. **2.** (on a small sailing boat) a device resembling this by which one may lean almost completely outboard. **3.** *Geom.* → **trapezium**.

trapezium /trəˈpiziəm/ *n.* (*pl.* **-ziums** *or* **-zia** /-ziə/) **1.** *Geom.* (as originally used by Euclid) any rectilinear quadrilateral plane figure not a parallelogram. **2.** a quadrilateral plane figure in which only one pair of opposite sides is parallel. Also, **trapeze**. –**trapezial**, *adj.*

trappings /ˈtræpɪŋz/ *pl. n.* **1.** articles of equipment or dress, especially of an ornamental character. **2.** conventional or characteristic articles of dress or adornment. **3.** that which necessarily accompanies or adorns:

the trappings of power. **4.** a covering for a horse, especially when ornamental in character.

traps /træps/ *pl. n. Colloq.* personal belongings; luggage.

trapshooting /ˈtræpʃutɪŋ/ *n.* the sport of shooting at live pigeons released from, or clay targets, etc., thrown into the air by, a trap (def. 6). –**trapshooter**, *n.*

trash /træʃ/ *n.* **1.** anything worthless or useless; rubbish. **2.** foolish ideas, talk, or writing; nonsense. **3.** people regarded as worthless. –*v.t. Colloq.* **4.** to destroy utterly, especially as an act of vandalism. **5.** to subject to scathing criticism. –*adj.* **6.** of low quality: *a trash record.* **7.** (of a person) despicable or disreputable. –**trasher**, *n.*

trauma /ˈtrɔmə/ *n.* (*pl.* **-mas** *or* **-mata** /-mətə/) **1.** *Pathol.* **a.** a bodily injury produced by violence, or any thermal, chemical, etc., extrinsic agent. **b.** the condition produced by this; traumatism. **c.** the injurious agent or mechanism itself. **2.** *Psychol.* a startling experience which has a lasting effect on mental life; a severe shock. –**traumatise, traumatize**, *v.* –**traumatic**, *adj.* –**traumatically**, *adv.*

travail /ˈtræveɪl/ *n.* **1.** physical or mental toil or exertion, especially when painful. **2.** the labour and pain of childbirth. –*v.i.* **3.** to suffer the pangs of childbirth; be in labour.

travel /ˈtrævəl/ *verb* (**-elled** *or, Chiefly US,* **-eled, -elling** *or, Chiefly US,* **-eling**) –*v.i.* **1.** to go from one place to another; make a journey. **2.** to move or advance in any way. **3.** to go from place to place as a representative of a business firm. **4.** *Colloq.* to move with speed. **5.** (of a mechanical part, etc.) to move in a fixed course. **6.** (of light, sound, etc.) to pass, or be transmitted. –*v.t.* **7.** to journey through or over (a country, area, road, etc.). **8.** to journey (a particular distance). –*n.* **9.** (*pl.*) journeys. **10.** *Mechanics* a complete movement of a moving part in one direction, or the distance covered; a stroke. **11.** movement or passage in general. –**traveller**, *n.*

travel advisory *n.* a notice, especially one issued by a government authority, giving advice on the degree of risk involved in travelling to certain parts of the world affected by war, diseases, etc.

travelogue /ˈtrævəlɒg/ *n.* **1.** a documentary film describing a country, travels, etc. **2.** a lecture describing travel, usually illustrated, as with photographs, slides, etc.

traverse /trəˈvɜs, ˈtrævɜs/ *v.t.* **1.** to pass across, over, or through. **2.** to go back and forwards over or along. **3.** to extend across. **4.** to examine or survey carefully. **5.** *Law* to deny formally. –*n.* **6.** the act of traversing, or passing across. **7.** something that traverses or lies across, such as a crossbar or a barrier. **8.** a place where a person may traverse or cross; crossing. **9.** *Naut.* the zigzag course taken by a vessel during tacking. –*adj.* **10.** lying, extending, or passing across; transverse. –**traversable**, *adj.* –**traverser**, *n.*

travesty /ˈtrævəsti/ *n.* (*pl.* **-ties**) **1.** any grotesque or debased likeness or imitation: *a travesty of justice.* **2.** a literary composition characterised by burlesque or ludicrous treatment of a serious work or subject. –*v.t.* (**-tied, -tying**) **3.** to make a travesty on; turn (a serious work or subject) to ridicule by burlesque imitation or treatment. **4.** to be a travesty of.

trawl /trɔl/ *n.* Also, **trawl net**. **1.** a strong net dragged along the sea bottom to catch fish. –*v.i.* **2.** to fish with such a net. –*v.t.* **3.** to catch (fish) with such a net.

trawler /ˈtrɔlə/ *n.* **1.** any of various types of vessels used in fishing with a trawl net. **2.** someone who trawls.

tray /treɪ/ *n.* **1.** any of various flat, shallow containers or receptacles of wood, metal, etc., with slightly raised edges used for carrying, holding, or exhibiting articles and for various other purposes. **2.** a removable receptacle of this shape in a cabinet, box, trunk, or the like, sometimes forming a drawer. **3.** (on a motor truck) a shallow open compartment behind the cab for holding and carrying goods. **4.** a tray and what is in it.

treachery /ˈtrɛtʃəri/ n. (pl. **-ries**) violation of faith; betrayal of trust; treason. **–treacherous**, adj.

treacle /ˈtrikəl/ n. the dark, viscous, uncrystallised syrup obtained in refining sugar. **–treacly** /ˈtrikli/, adj. **–treacliness**, n.

tread /trɛd/ verb (**trod, trodden** or **trod, treading**) –v.t. **1.** to step or walk on, about, in, or along. **2.** to trample or crush underfoot. **3.** to put into some position or condition by trampling: to tread grapes. **4.** to domineer harshly over; crush. **5.** to execute by walking or dancing: to tread a measure. **6.** (of male birds) to copulate with. –v.i. **7.** to set down the foot or feet in walking; step; walk. **8.** (of a male bird) to copulate. –n. **9.** a treading, stepping, or walking, or the sound of this. **10.** manner of treading or walking. **11.** a single step as in walking. **12.** any of various things or parts on which a person or thing treads, stands, or moves. **13.** the horizontal upper surface of a step in a stair, on which the foot is placed. **14.** the width of this from front to back. **15.** that part of a wheel, tyre, or runner which bears on the road, rail, etc. –phr. **16. tread on** (or **upon**), to step, walk, or trample on. **17. tread the boards,** to be a professional actor. **18. tread warily** (or **softly**), to proceed with great caution. **19. tread water,** Swimming to move the arms and legs in such a way as to keep the body in an upright position with the head above water. **–treader**, n.

treadle /ˈtrɛdl/ n. a lever or the like worked by the foot to impart motion to a machine.

treadmill /ˈtrɛdmɪl/ n. **1.** an apparatus for producing rotary motion by the weight of humans or animals, treading on a succession of moving steps that form a kind of continuous path, as around the periphery of a horizontal cylinder. **2.** a monotonous or wearisome round, as of work or life.

treason /ˈtrizən/ n. violation by a subject of his or her allegiance to his or her sovereign or to the state; high treason.

treasure /ˈtrɛʒə/ n. **1.** wealth or riches stored or accumulated, especially in the form of precious metals or money. **2.** any thing or person greatly valued or highly prized: this book was his chief treasure. –v.t. **3.** to put away for security or future use, as money; lay up in store. **4.** to retain carefully or keep in store, as in the mind. **5.** to regard as precious; prize; cherish. **–treasureless**, adj.

treasurer /ˈtrɛʒərə/ n. **1.** someone who is in charge of treasure or a treasury. **2.** someone who has charge of the funds of a company, private society, or the like. **3.** an officer of a state, city, etc., entrusted with the receipt, care, and disbursement of public money. **4.** (oft. upper case) the government minister responsible for the Treasury. **–treasurership**, n.

treasury /ˈtrɛʒəri/ n. (pl. **-ries**) **1.** a place where public revenues, or the funds of a company, etc., are deposited, kept, and disbursed. **2.** the funds or revenue of a state or a public or private company, etc. **3.** (upper case) the department of government which has control over the collection, management, and disbursement of the public revenue. **4.** a building, room, chest, or other place for the preservation of treasure or valuable objects. **5.** a repository or a collection of treasures of any kind; a thesaurus.

Treasury bond n. a security issued by the federal government through the Reserve Bank and actively traded in the money market; terms range from two years to twenty years depending on economic circumstances.

Treasury note n. a short-term security issued by the Reserve Bank on behalf of the Australian government, to acknowledge a borrowing obligation.

treat /trit/ v.t. **1.** to act or behave towards in some specified way: to treat someone with respect. **2.** to look upon, consider, or regard in a specified aspect, and deal with accordingly: to treat a matter as unimportant. **3.** to deal with (a disease, patient, etc.) in order to relieve or cure. **4.** to deal with in speech or writing; discuss. **5.** to deal with, develop, or represent artistically, especially in some specified manner or style: to treat a theme realistically. **6.** to subject to some agent or action in order to bring about a particular result: to treat a substance with an acid. **7.** to entertain with food, drink, amusement, etc. **8.** to regale (another) at one's own expense. –v.i. **9.** to deal with a subject in speech or writing, or discourse. **10.** to give, or bear the expense of, a treat. **11.** to carry on negotiations with a view to a settlement, discuss terms of settlement, or negotiate. –n. **12.** an entertainment of food, drink, amusement, etc., given by way of compliment or as an expression of friendly regard. **13.** anything that affords particular pleasure or enjoyment. **14.** the act of treating. **15.** one's turn to treat. –phr. **16. a (fair) treat,** Colloq. very well; attractively. **17. stand treat,** to bear the expense of an entertainment. **–treatable**, adj. **–treater**, n.

treatise /ˈtritəs/ n. **1.** a book or writing dealing with some particular subject. **2.** one containing a formal or methodical exposition of the principles of the subject.

treatment /ˈtritmənt/ n. **1.** the act or manner of treating. **2.** action or behaviour towards a person, etc. **3. a.** the application of medicines, surgery, psychotherapy, etc., to a patient to cure a disease or condition: asthma treatment. **b.** the application of a cosmetic preparation: skin treatment; hair treatment. **4.** literary or artistic handling, especially with reference to style. **5.** subjection to some agent or action. –phr. **6. the treatment,** Colloq. punishment; severe handling; thorough criticism: the unions are getting the treatment from the media.

treaty /ˈtriti/ n. (pl. **-ties**) **1.** a formal agreement between two or more independent states in reference to peace, alliance, commerce, or other international relations. **2.** any agreement or compact.

treble /ˈtrɛbəl/ adj. **1.** three times as great: treble pay. **2.** threefold; triple. **3.** Music (of a voice part, voice, singer, or instrument) of the highest pitch or range. –n. **4.** Music a treble voice, part, singer, or instrument. **5.** a set of three, as three wins or goals in a sporting contest. **6.** a form of multiple betting on three horseraces. –verb (**-bled, -bling**) –v.t. **7.** to make three times as much or as many; triple. –v.i. **8.** to become three times as much or as many; triple. **–trebly** /ˈtrɛbli/, adv.

tree /tri/ n. **1.** a plant having a permanent, woody, self-supporting main stem or trunk, usually growing to a considerable height, and usually developing branches at some distance from the ground. **2.** any of various shrubs, bushes, etc., such as the banana, similar to a tree in form or size. **3.** something similar to a tree in shape, such as a family tree, etc. **4.** Maths a network with no loops. **–treeless**, adj. **–treelessness**, n. **–treelike**, adj.

tree change n. a move from a city environment to a rural location away from the coast, as part of a lifestyle change, usually to escape stress and other deleterious aspects of city life. **–tree changer**, n.

tree line n. **1.** (on a mountain) the line above which no trees will grow. **2.** the line which marks the beginning of tree growth in the hills or mountains rising from a valley. Also, **timber line**.

tree preservation order *n.* an order to protect single trees or groups of trees, especially in urban areas. *Abbrev.*: TPO

tree-rat *n.* any member of a distinctive group of native rodents of the genera *Mesembriomys* and *Conilurus*, occurring mostly in northern Australia, usually living and nesting in trees.

trefoil /'trɛfɔɪl/ *n.* **1.** any of the herbs constituting the leguminous genus *Trifolium*, usually having digitate leaves of three leaflets, and reddish, purple, yellow, or white flower heads, and including the common clovers. **2.** an ornamental figure or structure resembling a tri-foliolate leaf.

trek /trɛk/ *v.i.* (**trekked**, **trekking**) **1.** to travel or migrate, especially with difficulty. *–n.* **2.** a journey, especially a difficult one. *–***trekker**, *n.*

trellis /'trɛləs/ *n.* **1.** a frame or structure of latticework; a lattice. **2.** a framework of this kind used for the support of growing vines, etc. *–***trellis-like**, *adj.*

trematode /'trɛmətoʊd, 'trimə-/ *n.* any of the Trematoda, a class or group of platyhelminths or flatworms, having one or more suckers, and living as ectoparasites or endoparasites on or in various animals; fluke.

tremble /'trɛmbəl/ *v.i.* **1.** (of people, the body, the voice, etc.) to shake from fear, excitement, weakness, cold, etc.; quiver. **2.** to be affected by a feeling of fear, etc. **3.** (of things) to shake with short, quick movements; vibrate. *–n.* **4.** the act of trembling. **5.** (*pl.*) a condition or disease marked by continued trembling, such as malaria. *–***trembler**, *n.* *–***trembly**, *adj.* *–***tremblingly**, *adv.*

tremendous /trə'mɛndəs/ *adj.* **1.** extraordinarily great in size, amount, degree, etc. **2.** dreadful or awful, as in character or effect. **3.** *Colloq.* extraordinary; unusual; remarkable. *–***tremendously**, *adv.* *–***tremendousness**, *n.*

tremolo /'trɛməloʊ/ *n.* (*pl.* **-los**) *Music* a tremulous or vibrating effect produced on certain instruments and in the human voice, as to express emotion.

tremor /'trɛmə/ *n.* **1.** involuntary shaking of the body or limbs, as from fear, weakness, etc.; a fit of trembling. **2.** any tremulous or vibratory movement; a vibration. **3.** a trembling or quivering effect, as of light, etc. **4.** a tremulous sound or note. *–***tremorless**, *adj.*

tremulous /'trɛmjələs/ *adj.* **1.** (of persons, the body, etc.) characterised by trembling, as from fear, nervousness, weakness, excitement, etc. **2.** (of things) vibratory or quivering. *–***tremulously**, *adv.* *–***tremulousness**, *n.*

trench /trɛntʃ/ *n.* **1.** a long, narrow ditch dug in the ground, the earth from which is thrown up in front to serve as a shelter from the enemy's fire, etc. **2.** (*pl.*) a system of ditches which formed the front line of battle in Europe in World War I. **3.** a deep ditch, furrow, or cut. **4.** a long, deep depression in the ocean floor. *–v.t.* **5.** to cut a trench or trenches in. *–v.i.* **6.** to dig a trench or trenches.

trenchant /'trɛntʃənt/ *adj.* **1.** incisive or keen, as language or a person; cutting: *trenchant wit.* **2.** thoroughgoing, vigorous, or effective: *a trenchant policy.* **3.** clearly or sharply defined, as an outline. *–***trenchancy**, *n.* *–***trenchantly**, *adv.*

trencher /'trɛntʃə/ *n.* **1.** → **mortarboard** (def. 2). **2.** a rectangular or circular flat piece of wood on which meat, or other food, was formerly served or carved.

trend /trɛnd/ *n.* **1.** the general course, drift, or tendency: *the trend of events.* **2.** the general direction which a road, river, coastline, or the like, tends to take. **3.** style; fashion. *–v.i.* **4.** to have a general tendency, as events, discussions, etc. **5.** (of a topic on a social network) to appear at an increasingly high level of frequency: *the election is trending on Twitter.*

trendy /'trɛndi/ *Colloq. –adj.* (**-dier**, **-diest**) **1.** forming part of or influenced by fashionable trends; ultrafashionable. *–n.* (*pl.* **-dies**) **2.** someone who embraces an

ultrafashionable lifestyle. **3.** someone who adopts a set of avant-garde social or political viewpoints. *–***trendiness**, **trendyism**, *n.*

trepidation /trɛpə'deɪʃən/ *n.* **1.** tremulous alarm or agitation; perturbation. **2.** vibratory movement; a vibration. **3.** *Pathol.* rapid, repeated, muscular flexion and extension of muscles of the extremities or lower jaw; clonus.

trespass /'trɛspəs/ *n.* **1.** *Law* **a.** an unlawful act causing injury to the person, property, or rights of another, committed with force or violence, actual or implied. **b.** a wrongful entry upon the lands of another. **2.** an encroachment or intrusion. **3.** an offence, sin, or wrong. *–v.i.* **4.** *Law* to commit a trespass. *–phr.* **5.** **trespass on** (or **upon**), to make an improper inroad on (a person's presence, time, etc.); encroach or infringe on. *–***trespasser**, *n.*

tress /trɛs/ *n.* (*usu. pl.*) any long lock or curl of hair, especially of a woman, not plaited or braided.

-tress a suffix forming some feminine agent-nouns, corresponding to masculine nouns in *-ter, -tor*, as *actor, actress*, etc. See **-ess**.

trestle /'trɛsəl/ *n.* **1.** a frame used as a support, consisting typically of a horizontal beam or bar fixed at each end to a pair of spreading legs. **2.** *Civil Eng.* **a.** a supporting framework composed chiefly of vertical or inclined pieces with or without diagonal braces, etc., used for various purposes, as for carrying tracks across a gap. **b.** a bridge or the like of such structure.

trevally /trə'væli/ *n.* (*pl.* **-ly** *or* **-lies**) any of numerous species of Australian sport and food fishes, especially of the genus *Caranx*, typically fast-swimming with streamlined bodies tapering sharply towards a forked or lunate tail.

tri- a word element meaning 'three', as in *triacid.*

triad /'traɪæd/ *n.* **1.** a group of three, especially of three closely related or associated persons or things. **2.** any of various Chinese secret organisations, often involved in criminal activities. **3.** *Chem.* an element, atom, or radical having a valency of three. **4.** *Music* a chord of three notes, especially one consisting of a given note with its major or minor third and its perfect, augmented, or diminished fifth. *–***triadic**, *adj.*

triage /'triaʒ/ *n.* **1.** the sorting at the battle front of casualties according to the urgency of treatment required. **2.** a similar procedure in a hospital casualty or disaster situation. *–v.t.* (**triaged**, **triaging**) **3.** to put (a patient) through a triage procedure.

trial /'traɪəl, traɪl/ *n.* **1.** *Law* **a.** the examination before a judicial tribunal of the facts put in issue in a cause (often including issues of law as well as of fact). **b.** the determination of a person's guilt or innocence by due process of law. **2.** the act of trying or testing, or putting to the proof. **3.** a contest or competition: *car trial*; *a trial of arms.* **4.** test; proof. **5.** an attempt or effort to do something. **6.** tentative or experimental action in order to ascertain results; an experiment. **7.** the state or position of a person or thing being tried or tested; probation. **8.** subjection to suffering or grievous experiences; affliction: *comfort in the hour of trial.* **9.** an affliction or trouble. **10.** a trying, distressing, or annoying thing or person. **11.** *Ceramics* a piece of ceramic material used to try the heat of the kiln and the progress of the firing of its contents. **12.** a competition, usually over rough terrain and roads in which competitors are required to keep to an average speed; motor trial. *–v.t.* (**trialled**, **trialling**) **13.** to put (a plan, procedure, etc.) into operation, often on a small scale, to test its feasibility. *–adj.* **14.** relating to trial or a trial. **15.** done or used by way of trial, test, proof, or experiment. *–phr.* **16. on trial, a.** undergoing a trial before a court of law. **b.** undergoing a test; on approval.

trial balance *n. Accounting* a statement of all the open debit and credit items, made preliminary to balancing a double-entry ledger.

triangle /ˈtraɪæŋgəl/ *n.* **1.** a geometrical plane figure formed by three (usually) straight lines which meet two by two in three points, thus forming three angles. **2.** any three-cornered or three-sided figure, object, or piece: *a triangle of land.* **3.** *Music* an instrument of percussion, made of a steel rod bent into the form of a triangle open at one of the corners, and sounded by being struck with a small, straight steel rod. **4.** a group of three; triad. **–triangular** /traɪˈæŋgjələ/, *adj.*

triathlon /traɪˈæθlɒn/ *n.* an athletic contest comprising three long-distance events, usually running, swimming, and cycling, one immediately after the other. **–triathlete**, *n.*

tribe /traɪb/ *n.* **1.** a group of people united by such features as descent, language or land ownership. **2.** a group of animals living together. **3.** *Zool., Bot.* **a.** a classificatory group of animals or plants, ranking between a family and a genus. **b.** any group of plants or animals. **4.** *Colloq.* (*humorous*) a family or class of people. **–tribal**, *adj.* **–tribesman**, *n.* **–tribeless**, *adj.*

tribulation /trɪbjəˈleɪʃən/ *n.* grievous trouble; severe trial or experience.

tribunal /traɪˈbjunəl/ *n.* **1.** a body set up to investigate and resolve disputes. **2.** a court of justice. **3.** a place or seat of judgement.

tribune /ˈtrɪbjun/ *n.* a raised platform, or dais; a rostrum or pulpit.

tributary /ˈtrɪbjətri/ *n.* (*pl.* **-taries**) **1.** a stream flowing into a larger stream or other body of water. **2.** a ruler or state paying tribute (def. 2). *–adj.* **3.** (of a stream) flowing into a larger stream or other body of water. **4.** giving aid; contributory. **5.** paying or required to pay tribute (def. 2). **–tributarily**, *adv.*

tribute /ˈtrɪbjut/ *n.* **1.** a personal offering, testimonial, compliment, or the like given as if due, or in acknowledgement of gratitude, esteem, or regard. **2.** a stated sum or other valuable consideration paid by one sovereign or state to acknowledgement of submission or as the price of peace, security, protection, or the like. **3.** a rent, tax, or the like, as that paid by a subject to a sovereign. **4.** anything paid as under exaction or by enforced contribution. **5.** (in opal mining) one's share when working on a partnership basis. **–tributer**, *n.*

trice¹ /traɪs/ *n.* a very short time; a moment; an instant: *to come back in a trice.*

trice² /traɪs/ *v.t. Naut.* to haul up and fasten with a rope. Also, **trice up.**

triceps /ˈtraɪsɛps/ *n. Anat.* a muscle having three heads, or points of origin, especially the extensor muscle at the back of the upper arm.

trick /trɪk/ *n.* **1.** a crafty or fraudulent device, expedient, or proceeding; an artifice, stratagem, ruse, or wile. **2.** a deceptive or illusory appearance; mere semblance. **3.** a roguish or mischievous performance; prank: *to play a trick on someone.* **4.** *Colloq.* an odd or eccentric person, often one providing amusement for others: *he looked a real trick in his weird uniform.* **5.** a foolish, disgraceful, or mean performance or action. **6.** a clever device or expedient, dodge, or ingenious shift: *a rhetorical trick.* **7.** the art or knack of doing something. **8.** a clever or dexterous feat, as for exhibition or entertainment: *tricks in horsemanship.* **9.** a feat of jugglery, magic, or legerdemain. **10.** a particular habit or way of acting; characteristic quality, trait, or mannerism. **11.** *Cards* the cards collectively which are played and won in one round. **12.** a turn, especially to relieve another operator: *a trick at the wheel.* **13.** *Colloq.* an act of sexual intercourse performed by a prostitute: *to turn a trick. –adj.* **14.** relating to or having the nature of

tricks. **15.** made for tricks. *–v.t.* **16.** to deceive by trickery. *–v.i.* **17.** to practise trickery or deception; cheat. *–phr.* **18. do the trick,** to achieve the desired result. **19. how's tricks?,** *Colloq.* a form of greeting. **20. not to be able to take a trick,** to have no success at all. **21. trick into,** to beguile into by trickery. **22. trick or treat,** *Chiefly US* that part of Halloween celebrations when children visit neighbouring households to play a trick unless they are given a treat. **23. trick out of,** to cheat or swindle out of. **24. trick out** (or **up**), to dress, array, or deck. **25. trick to,** to become aware of, especially of something previously concealed. **26. not** (or **never**) **miss a trick,** *Colloq.* **a.** never to fail to exploit an opportunity, press an advantage, etc. **b.** never to fail to notice what is happening around one. **–tricker, trickster**, *n.* **–trickery**, *n.* **–trickless**, *adj.*

trickle /ˈtrɪkəl/ *v.i.* **1.** to flow or fall by drops, or in a small, broken, or gentle stream: *tears trickled down her cheeks.* **2.** to come, go, pass, or proceed bit by bit, slowly, irregularly, etc.: *subscriptions are trickling in. –v.t.* **3.** to cause to trickle. *–n.* **4.** a trickling flow or stream. **5.** a small, slow, or irregular quantity of anything coming, going, or proceeding: *a trickle of visitors.*

trickle-down *adj.* permeating slowly from the top echelons of a society, community, organisation, etc., to the lowest or most marginal: *trickle-down politics*; *trickle-down feminism.*

tricky /ˈtrɪki/ *adj.* (**-kier, -kiest**) **1.** given to or characterised by deceitful or clever tricks; clever; wily. **2.** deceptive, uncertain or ticklish to deal with or handle. **–trickily**, *adv.* **–trickiness**, *n.*

tricolour /ˈtraɪkʌlə, ˈtrɪkələ/ *adj.* Also, **tricoloured.** **1.** having three colours. *–n.* **2.** a tricolour flag or the like. Also, **tricolor.**

tricycle /ˈtraɪsɪkəl/ *n.* **1.** a cycle with three wheels (usually one in front and one on each side behind) propelled by pedals or hand levers. *–adj.* **2.** having three wheels, usually one in front and two behind: *tricycle landing gear.*

trident /ˈtraɪdnt/ *n.* a three-pronged instrument or weapon.

tried /traɪd/ *v.* **1.** past tense and past participle of **try.** *–adj.* **2.** tested; proved; having sustained the tests of experience.

triennial /traɪˈɛniəl/ *adj.* **1.** lasting three years. **2.** occurring every three years. **–triennially**, *adv.*

trifecta /traɪˈfɛktə/ *n.* a form of betting in which the punter is required to nominate the first three placegetters in a race in the correct order.

trifle /ˈtraɪfəl/ *n.* **1.** an article or thing of small value. **2.** a small, inconsiderable, or trifling sum of money. **3.** (*pl.*) articles made of pewter of medium hardness. **4.** a dish typically consisting of sponge cake soaked in wine or liqueur, with jam, fruit, jelly, or the like topped with custard and whipped cream and (sometimes) almonds. *–v.i.* **5.** to pass time idly or frivolously; waste time; idle. *–phr.* **6. trifle away,** to pass (time, etc.) idly or frivolously. **7. trifle with, a.** to deal with lightly or without due seriousness or respect: *he was in no mood to be trifled with.* **b.** to play or toy with by handling or fingering: *he sat trifling with a pen.* **c.** to amuse oneself or dally with. **–trifler**, *n.*

trigger /ˈtrɪgə/ *n.* **1.** (in firearms) a small projecting tongue which when pressed by the finger liberates the mechanism and discharges the weapon. **2.** a device, as a lever, the pulling or pressing of which releases a spring. **3.** *Electronics* any circuit which is used to set a system in operation by the application of a single pulse. **4.** a stimulus or cause: *the trigger for a general election. –v.t.* Also, **trigger off. 5.** to start or precipitate (something), as a chain of events or a scientific reaction. –**triggerless**, *adj.*

trigonometry /trɪɡəˈnɒmətri/ *n.* the branch of mathematics that deals with the relations between the sides and angles of triangles (plane or spherical), and the calculations, etc., based on these. –**trigonometric** /trɪɡənəˈmɛtrɪk/, **trigonometrical** /trɪɡənəˈmɛtrɪkəl/, *adj.* –**trigonometrically** /trɪɡənəˈmɛtrɪkli/, *adv.*

trilby /ˈtrɪlbi/ *n.* (*pl.* **-bies**) a man's soft felt hat with an indented crown. Also, **trilby hat**.

trill /trɪl/ *n.* **1.** *Music* a vibrating sound, or a rapid alternation of two consecutive notes, in singing or in instrumental music. **2.** a similar sound, or series of sounds, made by a bird, an insect, a frog, a person laughing, etc. **3.** the pronunciation, as of the letter 'r' in some languages, performed by the rapid vibration of a speech organ, such as the tongue tip. –*v.i.* **4.** to sound, sing, etc., with a trill.

trillion /ˈtrɪljən/ *n.* (*pl.* **-lions**, *as after a numeral*, **-lion**) **1.** a million times a million, or 10^{12}. **2.** (*becoming obsolete*) a million times a million times a million, or 10^{18}. **3.** *Colloq.* a very large amount. –*adj.* **4.** amounting to one trillion in number. –**trillionth**, *n.*, *adj.*

trilogy /ˈtrɪlədʒi/ *n.* (*pl.* **-gies**) **1.** a series or group of three related dramas, operas, novels, etc. **2.** a group of three related things.

trim /trɪm/ *verb* (**trimmed**, **trimming**) –*v.t.* **1.** to reduce to a neat or orderly state by clipping, paring, pruning, etc.: *to trim a hedge.* **2.** to modify (opinions, etc.) according to expediency. **3.** *Carpentry* to bring (a piece of timber, etc.) to the required smoothness or shape. **4.** *Aeronautics* to level off (an aircraft in flight). **5.** *Naut.* **a.** to distribute the load of (a vessel) so that it sits well on the water. **b.** to adjust (the sails or yards) with reference to the direction of the wind and the course of the ship. **6.** to position a surfboard on a wave. **7.** to decorate or deck with ornaments, etc.: *to trim a Christmas tree.* **8.** to upholster and line the interior of motor cars, etc. **9.** to prepare (a lamp, fire, etc.) for burning. –*v.i.* **10.** *Naut.* **a.** to assume a particular position or trim in the water, as a vessel. **b.** to adjust the sails or yards with reference to the direction of the wind and the course of the ship. **11.** to accommodate oneself, or adjust one's principles, etc., to the prevailing climate of opinion. –*n.* **12.** proper condition or order: *to find everything out of trim.* **13.** condition or order of any kind. **14.** *Naut.* the set of a ship in the water, especially the most advantageous one. **15.** dress, array, or equipment. **16.** material used for decoration; decorative trimming. **17.** a trimming by cutting, clipping, or the like. **18.** a haircut which neatens the appearance of the hair without changing the style. **19.** something that is eliminated or cut off. **20.** *Aeronautics* the attitude of an aeroplane with respect to the three axes at which balance occurs in forward flight with free controls. **21.** *Carpentry* the visible woodwork of the interior of a building. **22. a.** the upholstery, knobs, handles, and other equipment inside a car. **b.** ornamentation on the exterior of a car, especially in chromium or a contrasting colour. –*adj.* (**trimmer**, **trimmest**) **23.** pleasingly neat or smart in appearance: *trim lawns.* **24.** in good condition or order. **25.** healthily slim. –*adv.* Also, **trimly. 26.** in a trim manner. –*phr.* **27. trim off**, to remove by clipping, paring, pruning, or the like: *to trim off loose threads from a ragged edge.* –**trimness**, *n.*

trimaran /ˈtraɪməræn/ *n.* a boat with a main middle hull and two outer hulls (usually smaller) acting as floats to provide transverse stability.

trimmer /ˈtrɪmə/ *n.* *NZ Colloq., Aust.* someone or something excellent.

trimming /ˈtrɪmɪŋ/ *n.* **1.** anything used or serving to trim or decorate: *the trimmings of a Christmas tree.* **2.** (*pl.*)

Colloq. agreeable accompaniments or additions to plain or simple dishes or food. **3.** (*pl.*) pieces cut off in trimming, clipping, paring, or pruning. –*phr.* **4. all the trimmings**, *Colloq.* all the optional extras, accessories, paraphernalia, etc.

trinity /ˈtrɪnəti/ *n.* (*pl.* **-ties**) **1.** a group of three; triad. **2.** the state of being threefold or triple. **3.** (*upper case*) (in Christian belief) the union of three persons or modes of being (Father, Son, and Holy Spirit) in one Godhead.

trinket /ˈtrɪŋkət/ *n.* **1.** any small fancy article, bit of jewellery, or the like, usually of little value. **2.** anything trifling.

trio /ˈtrioʊ/ *n.* (*pl.* **trios**) **1.** a musical composition for three voices or instruments. **2.** a company of three singers or players. **3.** any group of three persons or things.

trip /trɪp/ *n.* **1.** a journey or voyage. **2.** a journey, voyage, or run made by a boat, train, or the like, between two points. **3.** a journey made for pleasure; excursion. **4.** *Colloq.* **a.** a period under the influence of a hallucinatory drug. **b.** a quantity of LSD prepared in some form for sale. **5.** a specified activity or way of life: *a health trip; an exercise trip.* **6.** a stumble. **7.** a sudden impeding or catching of a person's foot so as to throw them down, especially in wrestling. **8.** a slip, mistake, or blunder. **9.** an act of stepping lightly; a light or nimble movement of the feet. **10.** *Machinery* **a.** a projecting part, catch, or the like for starting or checking some movement. **b.** a sudden starting or releasing. –*verb* (**tripped**, **tripping**) –*v.i.* **11.** to stumble: *to trip over a child's toy.* **12.** to make a slip or mistake, as in a statement; make a wrong step in conduct. **13.** to step lightly or nimbly; skip; dance. **14.** to tip or tilt. **15.** Also, **trip out**. *Colloq.* **a.** to hallucinate under the influence of LSD or other drugs. **b.** to have an exhilarating experience similar to hallucination. –*v.t.* **16.** cause to fail; hinder; overthrow. **17.** to catch in a slip or error. **18.** to perform with a light or tripping step, as a dance. **19.** to dance upon (ground, etc.). **20.** to tip or tilt. **21.** *Naut.* **a.** to break out (an anchor) by turning it over or lifting it from the bottom by a tripping line. **b.** to tip or turn (a yard) from a horizontal to a vertical position. **22.** to operate, start, or set free (a mechanism, weight, etc.) by suddenly releasing a catch, clutch, or the like. **23.** *Machinery* to release or operate suddenly (a catch, clutch, etc.). –*phr.* **24. trip up**, **a.** to stumble. **b.** to cause to stumble: *the rug tripped him up.* **c.** to make an error. **d.** to cause to make a slip or error: *to trip up a witness by artful questions.*

tripartite /traɪˈpɑːtaɪt/ *adj.* **1.** divided into or consisting of three parts. **2.** participated in by three parties, as a treaty. –**tripartitely**, *adv.* –**tripartism**, *n.*

tripe /traɪp/ *n.* **1.** the first and second divisions of the stomach of a ruminant, especially of the ox kind, prepared for use as food. **2.** *Colloq.* anything poor or worthless, especially written work; nonsense; rubbish.

triple /ˈtrɪpəl/ *adj.* **1.** three times as great: *triple pay.* **2.** consisting of three parts; threefold: *a triple knot.* –*n.* **3.** an amount, number, etc., three times as great as another. –*verb* (**-pled**, **-pling**) –*v.t.* **4.** to make triple. –*v.i.* **5.** to become triple. –**triply** /ˈtrɪpli/, *adv.*

triplet /ˈtrɪplət/ *n.* **1.** one of three children born at one birth. **2.** (*pl.*) three offspring born at one birth. **3.** any group of three. **4.** a thin bar of opal set between two layers of plastic, or one layer each of potch and crystal. **5.** three rhyming lines of poetry, usually forming a stanza. **6.** *Music* a group of three notes to be performed in the time of two ordinary notes of the same kind.

triplicate *v.t.* /ˈtrɪpləkeɪt/ **1.** to make threefold; triple. **2.** to make or produce a third time or in a third instance. –*adj.* /ˈtrɪpləkət/ **3.** threefold; triple; tripartite.

−n. /ˈtrɪpləkət/ **4.** one of three identical things. **−tripli-cation** /trɪpləˈkeɪʃən/, *n.*

tripod /ˈtraɪpɒd/ *n.* **1.** a stool, pedestal, or the like with three legs. **2.** a three-legged stand, as for a camera.

triptych /ˈtrɪptɪk/ *n.* **1.** *Art* a set of three panels or compartments side by side, bearing pictures, carvings, or the like. **2.** a hinged or folding three-leaved writing tablet.

trite /traɪt/ *adj.* hackneyed by constant use or repetition; commonplace: *a trite saying.* **−tritely,** *adv.* **−triteness,** *n.*

triton /ˈtraɪtn/ *n.* **1.** any of various marine gastropods constituting the family Tritonidae (especially of the genus *Triton*), having a large, spiral, often beautifully coloured shell. **2.** the shell of a triton

triumph /ˈtraɪʌmf, ˈtraɪəmf/ *n.* **1.** the act or fact of being victorious; victory. **2.** a great success; notable achievement. **3.** the joy of victory or success. **4.** the ceremonial entrance into ancient Rome of a victorious commander with his army, spoils, captives, etc. *−v.i.* **5.** to gain a victory; be victorious. **6.** to achieve success. **7.** to rejoice over victory or success. **−triumphal,** *adj.* **−triumpher,** *n.*

triumphant /traɪˈʌmfənt/ *adj.* **1.** having achieved victory or success; victorious; successful. **2.** exulting over victory; rejoicing over success; exultant. **−triumphantly,** *adv.*

triumvir /ˈtraɪəmvɪə/ *n.* one of three persons associated in any office. **−triumvirate** /traɪˈʌmvərət/, *n.* **−triumviral** /traɪˈʌmvərəl/, *adj.*

trivet /ˈtrɪvət/ *n.* **1.** a small metal plate with short legs put under a hot platter or dish at the table. **2.** a three-footed or three-legged stand or support, especially one of iron placed over a fire to hold cooking vessels or the like.

trivia /ˈtrɪviə/ *pl. n.* **1.** inessential, unimportant, or inconsequential things; trivialities. **2.** inconsequential and often arcane items of information.

trivia game *n.* a quiz in which contestants attempt to answer questions on areas of general knowledge such as literature, science, entertainment, sport and popular culture.

trivial /ˈtrɪviəl/ *adj.* **1.** of little importance; trifling; insignificant. **2.** commonplace; ordinary. **3.** *Biol.* (of names of animals and plants) specific, as distinguished from *generic.* **−triviality** /trɪviˈæləti/, *n.* **−trivially,** *adv.*

-trix a suffix of feminine agent-nouns, as in *executrix.* Compare **-or²**.

trochee /ˈtrəʊki/ *n. Prosody* a metrical foot of two syllables, a long followed by a short, or an accented followed by an unaccented. **−trochaic** /trəʊˈkeɪk/, *adj.*

trod /trɒd/ *v.* past tense and past participle of **tread**.

trodden /ˈtrɒdn/ *v.* past participle of **tread**.

troglodyte /ˈtrɒɡlədaɪt/ *n.* **1.** a cave-dweller, especially one of those people thought to have lived in caves in prehistoric times. **2.** someone living in seclusion. **3.** *Colloq.* someone thought to be primitive, barbaric, unintelligent, or insensitive. **−troglodytic** /trɒɡləˈdɪtɪk/, **troglodytical** /trɒɡləˈdɪtɪkəl/, *adj.*

troika /ˈtrɔɪkə/ *n.* **1.** a Russian vehicle drawn by a team of three horses abreast. **2.** a team of three horses driven abreast. **3.** any group of three persons acting together for a common purpose.

troll¹ /trəʊl/ *v.t.* **1.** to fish with a moving line, as one worked up and down in fishing for pike with a rod, or one trailed behind a boat. **2.** *Obs.* to roll; turn round and round. *−n.* **3.** the fishing line containing the lure and hook for use in trolling. **4.** *Internet* **a.** someone who, protected by online anonymity, posts messages in a discussion forum, chat room, etc., which are designed to disrupt the normal flow of communication by being inflammatory or puzzling. **b.** such a message. **−troller,** *n.*

troll² /trɒl/ *n.* (in Scandinavian folklore) one of a race of supernatural beings, sometimes conceived as giants and sometimes as dwarfs, inhabiting caves or subterranean dwellings.

trolley /ˈtrɒli/ *n.* (*pl.* **-leys**) **1.** any of various kinds of low carts or vehicles. **2.** a frame on wheels, used for carrying dishes, serving food, etc., as at a hospital or restaurant. **3.** Also, **hospital trolley.** a bed-like device on wheels used for transporting an ill or injured person. **4.** → **shopping trolley. 5.** a low truck running on rails, used on railways, in factories, mines, etc. **6.** a pulley travelling on an overhead track, or grooved metallic wheel or skid carried on the end of a sprung pole (**trolley pole**) by an electric tram or trolley bus and held in contact with an overhead conductor, usually a suspended wire (**trolley wire**), from which it collects the current for the propulsion of the vehicle. **7.** a trolley bus. **8.** *US* a tram. *−v.t.* **9.** to convey by trolley. *−v.i.* **10.** to go by trolley. *−phr.* **11. off one's trolley,** *Colloq.* crazy; mad; insane. Also, *Chiefly US,* **trolly. −trolley-less,** *adj.*

trolley bus *n.* an electric bus, whose motor draws current from two overhead wires by means of twin trolley poles. Also, **trolley-bus.**

trollop /ˈtrɒləp/ *n.* **1.** an untidy or slovenly woman; slattern. **2.** an immoral woman; prostitute.

trombone /trɒmˈbəʊn/ *n.* a musical wind instrument consisting of a cylindrical metal tube expanding into a bell and bent twice in U shape, usually equipped with a slide. **−trombonist,** *n.*

troop /trup/ *n.* **1.** a group of people, animals or things; a company, band, herd, etc. **2.** a great number. **3.** (*pl.*) *Mil.* a body of soldiers, marines, etc. **4.** an individual member of the military services. *−v.i.* **5.** to go or come in great numbers. **6.** to walk as if on a march. *−v.t.* **7.** *Mil.* to carry (the flag or colours) in a ceremonial way before troops: *trooping the colour.*

trooper /ˈtrupə/ *n.* **1.** a cavalry soldier. **2.** *Aust. Hist.* a mounted police officer. **3.** *Colloq.* a loyal, hardworking companion. *−phr.* **4. swear like a trooper,** to swear vigorously.

trope /trəʊp/ *n. Rhetoric* a figure of speech.

-trope a word element referring to turning, as in *heliotrope.*

trophy /ˈtrəʊfi/ *n.* (*pl.* **-phies**) **1.** anything taken in war, hunting, etc., especially when preserved as a memento; a spoil or prize. **2.** anything serving as a token or evidence of victory, valour, skill, etc. **3.** any memento or memorial. *−adj.* **4.** of or relating to a possession or association that is valued solely as an indication to others of one's wealth and superiority: *trophy home*; *trophy wife.* **−trophyless,** *adj.*

-trophy a word element denoting nourishment, as in *hypertrophy.*

tropic /ˈtrɒpɪk/ *n.* **1.** *Geog.* **a.** either of two corresponding parallels of latitude on the terrestrial globe, one (**Tropic of Cancer**) about 23½° north, and the other (**Tropic of Capricorn**) about 23½° south of the equator, being the boundaries of the Torrid Zone. **b. the tropics,** the regions lying between and near these parallels of latitude; the Torrid Zone and neighbouring regions. **2.** *Astron.* **a.** either of two circles on the celestial sphere, parallel to the celestial equator, one (**Tropic of Cancer**) about 23½° north of it, and the other (**Tropic of Capricorn**) about 23½° south of it. **b.** (formerly) either of the two solstitial points, at which the sun reaches its greatest distance north and south of the celestial equator. *−adj.* **3.** relating to the tropics. **−tropical,** *adj.*

-tropic an adjectival word element corresponding to **-trope, -tropism,** as in *geotropic.*

tropical climate *n.* a group of climate regions characterised by high temperatures throughout the year and pronounced wet and dry seasons.

tropical rainforest *n.* rainforest occurring in tropical areas, as in northern Australia. Compare **temperate rainforest**.

tropism /'troupizəm/ *n. Biol.* the response, usually an orientation, of a plant or animal, as in growth, to the influences of external stimuli. –**tropistic** /trou'pistik/, *adj.*

-tropism a word element referring to tropism, as in *heliotropism.*

tropo- a word element referring to turning or change.

tropopause /'tropəpɔz/ *n.* the transition layer between the troposphere and the stratosphere.

troposphere /'tropəsfiə/ *n.* the inner layer of atmosphere, from earth's surface to an altitude varying from about 10 to 16 km, within which there is a steady fall of temperature with increasing altitude of about 2°C per 300 metres, and within which nearly all cloud formations occur and weather conditions manifest themselves. –**tropospheric**, *adj.* –**tropospherically**, *adv.*

troppo /'tropou/ *adj. Aust., NZ Colloq.* mentally disturbed.

trot /trot/ *verb* (**trotted, trotting**) –*v.i.* **1.** (of a horse, etc.) to go at a gait between a walk and a run, in which the legs move in diagonal pairs, but not quite simultaneously, so that when the movement is slow one foot at least is always on the ground, and when fast all four feet are momentarily off the ground at once. **2.** to go at a quick, steady gait; move briskly, bustle, or hurry. –*v.t.* **3.** to cause to trot. –*n.* **4.** the gait of a horse, dog, etc., when trotting. **5.** a jogging gait between a walk and a run. **6.** (in harness racing) a race for trotters. –*phr.* **7. a bad trot,** *Aust. Colloq.* a run of bad luck. **8. a good trot,** *Aust., NZ Colloq.* a run of good luck. **9. on the trot,** *Colloq.* **a.** in a state of continuous activity. **b.** one after another, in quick succession: *he won three races on the trot.* **10. the trots, a.** races for trotting or pacing horses; a trotting meeting. **b.** *Colloq.* diarrhoea. **11. trot out,** *Colloq.* **a.** to bring forward for or as for inspection. **b.** to give voice to in a trite or boring way.

troth /trouθ/ *n. Archaic* one's word or promise, especially in engaging oneself to marry.

trotter /'trotə/ *n.* **1.** an animal which trots. **2.** someone who moves about briskly and constantly. **3.** the foot of an animal, especially of a sheep or pig, used as food.

troubadour /'trubədɔ/ *n.* a minstrel or ballad singer.

trouble /'trʌbəl/ *v.t.* **1.** to disturb in mind; distress; worry. **2.** to put to inconvenience, exertion, pains, or the like: *may I trouble you to shut the door?* **3.** to cause bodily pain or inconvenience to, as a disease or ailment does. **4.** to annoy, vex, or bother. **5.** to disturb or agitate, or stir up so as to make turbid, as water, etc. –*v.i.* **6.** to put oneself to inconvenience. **7.** to worry. –*n.* **8.** molestation, harassment, annoyance, or difficulty: *to make trouble for someone.* **9.** unfortunate position or circumstances; misfortunes. **10.** disturbance; disorder; unrest: *industrial trouble*; *political troubles.* **11.** physical derangement or disorder: *heart trouble.* **12.** disturbance of mind, distress, or worry. **13.** inconvenience endured, or exertion or pains taken, in some cause or in order to accomplish something. **14.** something that troubles; a cause or source of annoyance, difficulty, distress, or the like. **15.** a personal habit, characteristic, etc., which is disadvantageous or a source of anxiety or distress. –*phr.* **16. in trouble, a.** suffering or liable to suffer punishment, affliction, etc.; in difficulties. **b.** *Colloq.* pregnant while unmarried. –**troubler**, *n.* –**troublemaker**, *n.* –**troublesome**, *adj.*

troubleshooter /'trʌbəlʃutə/ *n.* an expert in discovering and eliminating the cause of trouble in the operation of something, in settling disputes, etc. –**troubleshooting**, *n.*

trough /trof/ *n.* **1.** an open, boxlike receptacle, usually long and narrow, as for containing water or food for animals, or for any of various other purposes. **2.** any receptacle of similar shape, especially one used for washing clothes: *a laundry trough.* **3.** a channel or conduit for conveying water, as a gutter under the eaves of a building. **4.** any long depression or hollow, as between two ridges or waves. **5.** *Meteorol.* an elongated area of relatively low pressure. –**troughlike**, *adj.*

trounce /trauns/ *v.t.* **1.** to beat or thrash severely. **2.** to punish. **3.** to defeat convincingly.

troupe /trup/ *n.* a troop, company, or band, especially of actors, singers, or the like. –**trouper**, *n.*

trousers /'trauzəz/ *pl. n.* **1.** an outer garment covering the lower part of the trunk and each leg separately, extending to the ankles. –*phr.* **2. wear the trousers,** *Colloq.* to have control, as of the dominant partner in a marriage.

trousseau /'trusou/ *n.* (*pl.* **-seaux** *or* **-seaus** /-souz/) a bride's outfit of clothes, linen, etc., which she brings with her at marriage.

trout /traut/ *n.* (*pl.* **trouts** *or, especially collectively,* **trout**) **1.** any fish of the genus *Salmo* or *Oncorhynchus* too small to be a salmon. The European **brown trout** and the North American **rainbow trout** have been introduced in Australia. **2.** any American fish of the salmon family of the genera *Salvelinus* and *Cristivomer*, known in Europe as chars, and including several American species, as the **brook trout**, introduced into NSW and Tasmania.

trowel /'trauəl/ *n.* **1.** any of various tools consisting of a plate of metal or other material, usually flat, fitted into a short handle, used for spreading, shaping, or smoothing plaster or the like. **2.** a similar tool with a curved, scoop-like blade, used in gardening for taking up plants, etc. –*v.t.* (**-elled** *or, Chiefly US,* **-eled, -elling** *or, Chiefly US,* **-eling**) **3.** to apply, shape, or smooth with or as with a trowel. –**troweller**, *n.*

troy weight /trɔɪ 'weɪt/ *n.* an imperial system for measuring the mass of precious metals and gems, in which 24 grains = 1 pennyweight and 20 pennyweights = 1 troy ounce.

truant /'truənt/ *n.* **1.** a student who stays away from school without permission. **2.** someone who shirks or neglects their duty. –*adj.* **3.** staying away from school without permission. **4.** relating to or characteristic of a truant. –*v.i.* **5.** to play truant. –*phr.* **6. play truant,** to be absent from school, etc., without permission. –**truancy**, *n.*

truce /trus/ *n.* **1.** a suspension of hostilities, as between armies, by agreement, for a specified period; an armistice. **2.** an agreement or treaty establishing this. **3.** respite or freedom, as from trouble, pain, etc. –**truceless**, *adj.*

truck¹ /trʌk/ *n.* **1.** any of various vehicles for carrying goods, etc. **2.** a motor vehicle with cab (def. 3) and tray or compartment for carrying goods; a lorry. **3.** any of various wheeled frames for moving heavy articles, as a barrow with two very low front wheels used to move heavy luggage, etc. **4.** a low rectangular frame on which heavy boxes, etc., are moved. **5.** *Mining* a wheeled car of various design used for haulage. **6.** a group of two or more pairs of wheels in a frame, for supporting a locomotive body, trailer, etc. –*v.t.* **7.** to transport by a truck or trucks. **8.** to put on a truck. –*v.i.* **9.** to convey articles or goods on a truck. **10.** to drive a truck. –*phr.* **11. fall off the back of a truck,** *Colloq.* (*humorous*) a phrase used to suggest that something has been stolen or acquired dishonestly: *I suppose your new TV set fell off the back of a truck.*

truck² /trʌk/ *n.* **1.** *Rare* trading by exchange of commodities; barter. **2.** payment of wages in goods, etc., instead of money. *–phr.* **3. have no truck with,** to have no dealings with.

truckie /'trʌki/ *n. Colloq.* a truck driver.

truckle¹ /'trʌkəl/ *phr.* **truckle to,** to submit to or yield to obsequiously or tamely. **–truckler,** *n.* **–trucklingly,** *adv.*

truckle² /'trʌkəl/ *n.* → **truck.**

truculent /'trʌkjələnt/ *adj.* **1.** fierce; cruel; brutal; savage. **2.** scathing; harsh; vitriolic. **3.** aggressive; belligerent. **–truculence, truculency,** *n.* **–truculently,** *adv.*

trudge /trʌdʒ/ *verb* (**trudged, trudging**) *–v.i.* **1.** to walk laboriously or wearily. *–v.t.* **2.** to walk laboriously or wearily along or over: *he trudged the streets. –n.* **3.** a long laborious walk. **–trudger,** *n.*

true /tru/ *adj.* (**truer, truest**) **1.** being in accordance with the actual state of things; conforming to fact; not false: *a true story.* **2.** real or genuine: *true gold.* **3.** free from deceit; sincere: *a true interest in someone's welfare.* **4.** firm in allegiance; loyal; faithful; trusty. **5.** being or indicating the essential reality of something. **6.** agreeing with or conforming to a standard, pattern, rule, or the like: *a true copy.* **7.** exact, correct, or accurate: *a true balance.* **8.** (of a scientific measurement) corrected to allow for factors, such as the observer's height, which affect the measurement. **9.** of the right kind; such as it should be; proper: *to arrange things in their true order.* **10.** properly so called; rightly answering to a description: *true statesmanship.* **11.** legitimate or rightful: *the true heir.* **12.** reliable, unfailing, or sure: *a true sign.* **13.** exactly or accurately shaped, formed, fitted, or placed, as a surface, instrument, or part of a mechanism. **14.** *Biol.* belonging to a particular group; conforming to the norm; typical. **15.** *Stock Breeding* purebred. **16.** *Navig.* (of a bearing) fixed in relation to the earth's axis rather than the magnetic poles: *true north. –n.* **17.** exact or accurate formation, position, or adjustment: *to be out of true. –adv.* **18.** in a true manner; truly or truthfully. **19.** exactly or accurately. **20.** in agreement with the ancestral type: *to breed true. –v.t.* (**trued, truing**) **21.** to make true; shape, adjust, place, etc., exactly or accurately. *–phr.* **22. come true,** to happen in reality as desired, expected, dreamed, etc.: *if dreams came true.* **–trueness,** *n.* **–truly,** *adv.*

true-blue *adj.* **1.** unchanging; unwavering; staunch; true. **2.** staunchly conservative. Also, (*especially in predicative use*), **true blue.**

true north *n.* the north axis of the earth. Compare **grid north, magnetic north.**

truffle /'trʌfəl/ *n.* **1.** any of various subterranean edible fungi of the genus *Tuber* of the class Ascomycetes. **2.** any of various similar fungi of other genera. **3.** a confection consisting of a ball of ganache coated with chocolate, cocoa, etc. **–truffled,** *adj.*

truism /'truɪzəm/ *n.* a self-evident, obvious truth. **–truistic** /tru'ɪstɪk/, **truistical** /tru'ɪstɪkəl/, *adj.*

trump¹ /trʌmp/ *n.* **1.** *Cards* **a.** any playing card of a suit that for the time outranks the other suits, such as a card being able to take any card of another suit. **b.** (*pl., US sometimes sing.*) the suit itself. **c.** a tarot card not belonging to any of the four suits; a major arcanum. **2.** *Colloq.* a person in authority; boss. *–v.t.* **3.** *Cards* to take with a trump. **4.** to excel; surpass; be better than; beat. *–v.i. Cards* **5.** to play a trump. **6.** to take a trick with a trump. *–phr.* **7. come** (or **turn**) **up trumps,** to perform very much better than indicated by initial efforts. **8. trump up,** to invent deceitfully or dishonestly, as an accusation; fabricate. **–trumpless,** *adj.*

trump² /trʌmp/ *n. Poetic* a trumpet.

trumpery /'trʌmpəri/ *n.* (*pl.* **-ries**) **1.** something showy but of little intrinsic value; worthless finery; useless stuff. **2.** rubbish; nonsense.

trumpet /'trʌmpət/ *n.* **1.** *Music* **a.** any of a family of musical wind instruments with a penetrating, powerful tone, consisting of a tube, now usually metallic, and commonly once or twice curved round upon itself, having a cup-shaped mouthpiece at one end and a flaring bell at the other. **b.** an organ stop having a tone resembling that of a trumpet. **c.** a trumpeter. **2.** the loud cry of the elephant or some other animal. *–v.i.* **3.** to blow a trumpet. **4.** to emit a sound like that of a trumpet, as an elephant. *–v.t.* **5.** to sound on a trumpet. **6.** to proclaim loudly or widely. *–phr.* **7. blow one's own trumpet,** to praise oneself.

truncate /trʌŋ'keɪt, 'trʌŋkeɪt/ *v.t.* **1.** to shorten by cutting off a part; cut short; mutilate. *–adj.* **2.** *Biol.* **a.** square or broad at the end, as if cut off transversely. **b.** lacking the apex, as certain spiral shells. **–truncation,** *n.*

truncheon /'trʌnʃən/ *n.* **1.** a short club carried by a police officer. **2.** a baton, or staff of office or authority.

trundle /'trʌndəl/ *v.t.* **1.** to cause (a ball, hoop, etc.) to roll along; roll. *–v.i.* **2.** to move or run on a wheel or wheels.

trunk /trʌŋk/ *n.* **1.** the main stem of a tree, as distinct from the branches and roots. **2.** a box or chest for holding clothes and other articles, as for use on a journey. **3.** the body of a human being or of an animal, excluding the head and limbs. **4.** → **trunk line. 5.** the long, flexible snout of the elephant. *–adj.* **6.** showing or relating to the main line of a railway, road, etc. **–trunkless,** *adj.*

trunk line *n.* **1.** *Telecommunications* a telephone line or channel between two exchanges in different parts of a country or of the world, which is used to provide connections between subscribers making long-distance calls. **2.** a main railway line. Also, **trunkline.**

trunks /trʌŋks/ *pl. n.* **1.** (especially formerly) a man's swimming costume, especially one in the style of shorts. **2.** *Obs.* men's shorts, either tight-fitting or loose, worn by athletes, etc.

truss /trʌs/ *v.t.* **1.** to tie, bind, or fasten. **2.** to make fast with skewers or the like, as the wings of a fowl preparatory to cooking. **3.** *Building Trades, etc.* to furnish or support with a truss or trusses. **4.** to confine or enclose, as the body, by something fastened closely around. *–n.* **5.** *Building Trades, etc.* **a.** a combination of members, as beams, bars, ties, or the like, so arranged, usually in a triangle or a collection of triangles, as to form a rigid framework, and used in bridges (**bridge truss**), roofs (**roof truss**), etc., to give support and rigidity to the whole or a part of the structure. **b.** any framework consisting of a number of members connected together and loaded principally at the joints so that the stresses in the members are essentially simple tensions or compressions. **6.** *Med.* an apparatus for maintaining a hernia in a reduced state. **7.** a collection of things tied together or packed in a receptacle; a bundle; a pack. **–trusser,** *n.*

trust /trʌst/ *n.* **1.** reliance on the integrity, justice, etc., of a person, or on some quality or attribute of a thing; confidence. **2.** confident expectation of something; hope. **3.** confidence in the ability or intention of a person to pay at some future time for goods, etc.; credit: *to sell goods on trust.* **4.** one on whom or that on which one relies. **5.** the state of being relied on, or the state of someone to whom something is entrusted. **6.** the obligation or responsibility imposed on one in whom confidence or authority is placed: *a position of trust.* **7.** the condition of being confided to another's care or guard: *to leave something in trust with a person.* **8.** something committed or entrusted to one, as an office, duty, etc. **9.** *Law* **a.** a fiduciary relationship in which one person (the trustee) holds the title to property (the **trust estate** or **trust property**) for the benefit of another (the beneficiary). **b.** Also, **trust fund.** a fund of securities, cash or other assets, held and administered under such a relationship. **10.** *Commerce* **a.** a combination of industrial or commercial companies having a central committee or board of trustees, controlling a majority or the whole of the stock of each of the constituent companies, thus making it possible to manage the concerns so as to economise expenses, regulate production, defeat competition, etc. **b.** a monopolistic organisation or combination in restraint of trade whether in the form of a trust (def. 10a), contract, association or otherwise. *–adj.* **11.** *Law* of or relating to trusts or a trust. *–v.i.* **12.** to have confidence; hope. *–v.t.* **13.** to have trust or confidence in; rely on. **14.** to believe. **15.** to expect confidently, hope (usually followed by a clause or an infinitive). **16.** to commit or consign with trust or confidence. **17.** to permit to be in some place, position, etc., or to do something, without fear of consequences: *he will not trust it out of his sight.* *–phr.* **18. trust in,** to have or place trust, reliance, or confidence in. **19. trust to,** to depend on; rely on. **–truster,** *n.* **–trustful, trusting,** *adj.* **–trusty,** *adj.*

trustee /trʌsˈtiː/ *n. Law* **1.** someone, usually one of a body of persons, appointed to administer the affairs of a company, institution, etc. **2.** someone who holds the title to property for the benefit of another.

trustworthy /ˈtrʌstwɜːði/ *adj.* worthy of trust or confidence; reliable. **–trustworthily,** *adv.* **–trustworthiness,** *n.*

truth /truːθ/ *n.* **1.** that which is true; the true or actual facts of a case: *to tell the truth.* **2.** conformity with fact or reality; verity: *the truth of a statement.* **3.** a verified or indisputable fact, proposition, principle, or the like: *mathematical truths.* **4.** the state or character of being true. **5.** genuineness, reality, or actual existence. **6.** agreement with a standard, rule, or the like. **7.** accuracy, as of position or adjustment. *–phr.* **8. in truth,** in fact; in reality; truly. **–truthful,** *adj.* **–truthless,** *adj.*

try /traɪ/ *verb* **(tried, trying)** *–v.t.* **1.** to attempt to do or accomplish: *it seems easy until you try it.* **2.** to test the effect or result of: *to try a new method.* **3.** to endeavour to ascertain by experiment: *to try one's luck.* **4.** to test the quality, value, fitness, accuracy, etc., of: *to try a new brand of soap powder.* **5.** to attempt to open (a door, window, etc.) in order to find out whether it is locked. **6.** *Law* to examine and determine judicially, as a cause; determine judicially the guilt or innocence of (a person). **7.** to put to a severe test; strain the endurance, patience, etc., of; subject to grievous experiences, affliction, or trouble. **8.** Also, **try out.** to melt (fat, etc.) to obtain the oil; render. *–v.i.* **9.** to make an attempt or effort: *try harder next time.* *–n.* (pl. **tries**) **10.** an attempt, endeavour, or effort: *to have a try at something.* **11.** *Rugby Football* **a.** the act of a player applying downward pressure on the ball, causing the ball to touch the ground in the opponents' in-goal area. **b.** a score of four points in Rugby League, five in Rugby Union, earned for this. *–phr.* **12. try it on,** *Colloq.* to attempt to hoodwink or test the patience of, especially impudently. **13. try on,** to put on (clothes, etc.) to see if they fit. **14. try out, a.** to test; experiment with. **b.** to compete (for a position, etc.). **–trier,** *n.*

trying /ˈtraɪɪŋ/ *adj.* annoying; distressing; irritating; testing one's patience. **–tryingly,** *adv.* **–tryingness,** *n.*

tryst /trɪst/ *n.* an appointment, especially between lovers, to meet at a certain time and place; rendezvous. **–tryster,** *n.*

tsar /zɑː/ *n.* **1.** an emperor or king. **2.** (*usu. upper case*) the emperor of Russia (until 1917). **3.** (*oft. upper case*) an

autocratic ruler or leader. Also, **czar, tzar.** **–tsardom** /ˈzɑːdəm/, *n.* **–tsarist,** *n.*

tsetse fly /ˈtsɛtsi flaɪ, ˈsɛtsi flaɪ/ *n.* any of the bloodsucking flies of the African genus *Glossina,* some of which transmit protozoan parasites (trypanosomes) which cause sleeping sickness and other serious diseases. Also, **tsetse, tzetze.**

T-shirt /ˈtiː-ʃɜːt/ *n.* a collarless, short-sleeved top, made from a knitted fabric. Also, **t-shirt, tee-shirt.**

T square *n.* a T-shaped ruler used in mechanical drawing to make parallel lines, etc., the short crosspiece sliding along the edge of the drawing board as a guide.

tsunami /suˈnami, sə-, tsu-, tsə-/ *n.* **1.** a large, often destructive sea wave or series of waves caused by an underwater earthquake, landslide, or volcanic eruption. **2.** an overwhelmingly widespread or powerful movement, reaction, etc.: *a tsunami of public outrage; a tsunami of comments on social media.*

tuan /ˈtjuən/ *n.* any of certain Australian brush-tailed, carnivorous marsupials, rat-sized and largely arboreal, of the dasyurid genus *Phascogale.*

tub /tʌb/ *n.* **1.** a large, round, open, flat-bottomed container made of wood or metal used for bathing, washing clothes, etc. **2.** any container shaped like a tub: *a tub of margarine.* **3.** *Colloq.* a slow, clumsy ship or boat. **–tubbable,** *adj.* **–tubber,** *n.* **–tublike,** *adj.*

tuba /ˈtjuːbə/ *n.* (pl. **-bas** or **-bae** /-biː/) **1.** a brass wind instrument of low pitch equipped with valves. **2.** an organ reed stop of large scale with notes of exceptional power.

tubal ligation /tjuːbəl laɪˈgeɪʃən/ *n.* the operation of applying a ligature to the fallopian tubes, to prevent conception.

tubby /ˈtʌbi/ *adj.* **(-bier, -biest)** short and fat: *a tubby man.* **–tubbiness,** *n.*

tube /tjuːb/ *n.* **1.** a hollow usually cylindrical body of metal, glass, rubber, or other material, used for conveying or containing fluids, and for other purposes. **2.** a small, collapsible, metal or plastic cylinder closed at one end and having the open end provided with a cap, for holding paint, toothpaste, or other semiliquid substance to be squeezed out by pressure. **3.** *Aust. Colloq.* a can or bottle of beer. **4.** *Anat., Zool.* any hollow, cylindrical vessel or organ: *the bronchial tubes.* **5.** *Surfing* the hollow of a wave as it breaks. **6.** (pl.) → **fallopian tube. 7.** *Bot.* any hollow, elongated body or part. **8. the,** (*sometimes upper case*) *Brit. Colloq.* **a.** the London underground railway system: *delays on the tube.* **b.** Also, **tube train.** a railway train running as part of this system. **c.** one of the tunnels through which these trains pass. **9.** *Colloq.* a television set. *–v.t.* **10.** to furnish with a tube or tubes. *–phr.* **11. go down the tube(s),** *Colloq.* to suffer a defeat; fail. **12. have one's tubes tied,** *Med.* (of a woman) to be made sterile by blocking of the Fallopian tubes. **–tubeless,** *adj.* **–tubelike,** *adj.* **–tubal,** *adj.* **–tubular,** *adj.*

tuber /ˈtjuːbə/ *n.* **1.** *Bot.* a fleshy, usually oblong or rounded thickening or outgrowth (as the potato) of a subterranean stem or shoot, bearing minute scale-like leaves with buds or eyes in their axils, from which new plants may arise. **2.** *Anat., etc.* a rounded swelling or protuberance; a tuberosity; a tubercle. **–tuberous,** *adj.*

tubercle /ˈtjuːbəkəl/ *n.* **1.** a small rounded projection or excrescence, as on a bone, on the surface of the body in various animals, or on a plant. **2.** *Pathol.* **a.** a small, firm, rounded nodule or swelling. **b.** such a swelling as the characteristic lesion of tuberculosis.

tuberculosis /təbɜːkjəˈloʊsəs/ *n. Pathol.* **1.** an infectious disease affecting any of various tissues of the body, due to the tubercle bacillus, and characterised by the production of tubercles. **2.** this disease when affecting the lungs; pulmonary phthisis; consumption.

tuberose /tjubə'rouz, 'tjubərouz/ *n.* a bulbous plant, *Polianthes tuberosa*, cultivated for its spike of fragrant, creamy white, lily-like flowers.

tuck /tʌk/ *v.t.* **1.** to thrust into some narrow space or close or concealed place: *tuck this in your pocket.* **2.** to thrust the edge or end of (a garment, covering, etc.) closely into place between retaining parts or things: *he tucked his napkin under his chin.* **3.** to cover snugly in or as in this manner: *to tuck a child into bed.* **4.** to draw up in folds or a folded arrangement: *to tuck one's legs under a chair.* **5.** *Sewing* to sew tucks in. –*v.i.* **6.** to draw together; contract; pucker. **7.** *Sewing* to make tucks. –*n.* **8.** a tucked piece or part. **9.** *Sewing* a fold, or one of a series of folds, made by doubling cloth upon itself, and stitching parallel with the edge of the fold. **10.** *Naut.* the part of a vessel where the after ends of the outside planking or plating unite at the sternpost. **11.** *Sport* (in diving) a dive in which the knees are bent and pulled in close to the chest, the body being straightened again before hitting the water. –*phr.* **12. tuck away**, to fold away neatly, especially to conceal from view. **13. tuck in** (or **up**), to cover (someone, usually a child) with bedclothes and make snug, as a preliminary to sleep. **14. tuck into** (or **away**), to consume (a meal, etc.) greedily.

tucker¹ /'tʌkə/ *n. NZ Colloq., Aust.* food.

tucker² /'tʌkə/ *phr.* **tucker out**, *Colloq.* to weary; tire; exhaust: *they were quite tuckered out.*

tuckshop /'tʌkʃɒp/ *n.* → **canteen** (def. 2).

-tude a suffix forming abstract nouns (generally from Latin adjectives or participles) in words of Latin origin, as in *latitude*, *fortitude*, but sometimes used directly as an English formative element.

Tuesday /'tjuzdeɪ, -di/ *n.* the third day of the week, following Monday.

tuffet /'tʌfət/ *n.* **1.** a hillock; mound. **2.** a footstool; hassock.

tuft /tʌft/ *n.* **1.** bunch of small, usually soft and flexible things, as feathers, hairs, grass, etc., fixed at the base with the upper part loose. –*v.t.* **2.** to provide with or arrange in a tuft or tufts. –*v.i.* **3.** to form a tuft or tufts. –**tufted**, *adj.* –**tufty**, *adj.*

tug /tʌg/ *verb* (**tugged**, **tugging**) –*v.t.* **1.** to pull at with force or effort. **2.** to move by pulling forcibly; drag; haul. **3.** to tow (a vessel, etc.) by means of a tugboat. –*v.i.* **4.** to pull with force or effort: *to tug at an oar.* **5.** to strive hard, labour, or toil. –*n.* **6.** act of tugging; a strong pull. **7.** → **tugboat**. –**tugger**, *n.* –**tugless**, *adj.*

tugboat /'tʌgboʊt/ *n.* a strongly-built vessel with a powerful engine, designed for towing other vessels.

tuition /tju'ɪʃən/ *n.* **1.** teaching or instruction, as of pupils. **2.** the charge or fee for instruction.

tulip /'tjuləp/ *n.* **1.** any of the plants constituting the genus *Tulipa*, cultivated in many varieties, and having large, showy, usually erect, cup-shaped or bell-shaped flowers of various colours. **2.** a flower or bulb of such a plant.

tulle /tjul/ *n.* a thin silk or nylon net, used in millinery, dressmaking, etc.

tumble /'tʌmbəl/ *v.i.* **1.** to roll or fall over or down as by losing footing, support, or equilibrium: *to tumble down the stairs.* **2.** to fall rapidly, as stock market prices. **3.** to perform leaps, springs, somersaults, or other feats of bodily agility, as for exhibition or sport. **4.** to roll about by turning one way and another; pitch about; toss. **5.** to go, come, get, etc., in a precipitate or hasty way. –*v.t.* **6.** to send falling or rolling; throw over or down. **7.** to move or toss about, or turn over, as in handling, searching, etc. **8.** to put in disorder by or as by tossing about. **9.** to throw, cast, put, send, etc., in a precipitate, hasty, or rough manner. **10.** to subject to the action of a tumbling box. –*n.* **11.** an act of tumbling; a fall; a

downfall. **12.** tumbled condition; disorder or confusion. **13.** a confused heap. –*phr.* **14. tumble over**, to stumble or fall. **15.** (**take a**) **tumble to someone**, *Colloq.* to understand the motives of someone suddenly. **16.** (**take a**) **tumble to something**, *Colloq.* to become suddenly alive to some fact, circumstance, or the like.

tumbler /'tʌmblə/ *n.* drinking glass without handle or stem.

tumbleweed /'tʌmblwid/ *n.* **1.** any of various plants of North America, as *Amaranthus albus*, whose branching upper part becomes detached from the roots in autumn and is driven about by the wind. **2.** any of various plants in Australia which are similarly blown about by the wind.

tumbrel /'tʌmbrəl/ *n.* one of the carts used during the French Revolution to convey victims to the guillotine. Also, **tumbril**.

tumefy /'tjuməfaɪ/ *verb* (**-fied**, **-fying**) –*v.t.* **1.** to make swollen or tumid. –*v.i.* **2.** to become swollen or tumid. –**tumefaction** /tjumə'fækʃən/, *n.* –**tumefacient** /tjumə'feɪʃənt/, *adj.*

tumescent /tju'mɛsənt/ *adj.* swelling; slightly tumid. –**tumescence**, *n.*

tumid /'tjuməd/ *adj.* **1.** swollen, or affected with swelling, as a part of the body. **2.** pompous, turgid, or bombastic, as language, literary style, etc. –**tumidity** /tju'mɪdəti/, **tumidness**, *n.* –**tumidly**, *adv.*

tummy /'tʌmi/ *n.* (*pl.* **-mies**) *Colloq.* stomach. Also, **tum**.

tumour /'tjumə/ *n.* **1.** a swollen part; a swelling or protuberance. **2.** *Pathol.* an abnormal or morbid swelling in any part of the body, especially a more or less circumscribed morbid overgrowth of new tissue which is autonomous, differs more or less in structure from the part in which it grows, and serves no useful purpose. Also, **tumor**. –**tumorous**, *adj.*

tumult /'tjumʌlt/ *n.* **1.** the commotion or disturbance of a multitude, usually with noise; an uproar. **2.** a popular outbreak or uprising; commotion, disturbance, or violent disorder. **3.** agitation of mind; a mental or emotional disturbance. –**tumultuous** /tju'mʌltʃuəs/, *adj.*

tuna /'tjunə/ *n.* **1.** any of various species of large, fast-swimming, marine food fishes, having red flesh, and related to and resembling the mackerel; widely distributed throughout warmer ocean waters, as the bluefin tuna or the yellowfin tuna of the eastern coast of Australia. **2.** any of various fishes of the tuna family as the albacore, bonito, etc. Also, **tunny**.

tundra /'tʌndrə/ *n.* one of the vast, nearly level, treeless plains of the arctic regions of Europe, Asia, and North America.

tune /tjun, tʃun/ *n.* **1.** a succession of musical sounds forming an air or melody, with or without the harmony accompanying it. –*v.t.* **2.** Also, **tune up**. to adjust (a musical instrument) to a correct or given standard of pitch. **3.** to bring into harmony. **4.** Also, **tune up**. to adjust (an engine, machine or the like) for proper or improved running. **5.** *Radio* **a.** to adjust (a circuit, etc.) so as to bring it into resonance with another circuit, a given frequency, or the like. **b.** to adjust (a receiving apparatus) so as to make it in accord in frequency with a sending apparatus whose signals are to be received. **c.** to adjust a receiving apparatus so as to receive (the signals of a sending station). **6.** to put into a proper or a particular condition, mood, etc. –*phr.* **7. call the tune**, to be in a position to give orders, dictate policy, etc. **8. change one's tune** or **sing another** (or **a different**) **tune**, to change one's mind; reverse previously held views, attitudes, etc. **9. in tune**, **a.** at the correct pitch: *to sing in tune.* **b.** agreeing in pitch; in unison; in harmony. **c.** in due agreement, as of radio instruments or circuits with respect to frequency. **d.** in accord; in agreement. **10. in tune with**, in a state of harmony or rapport with: *to be in tune with nature*. **11. to the tune of**, to the amount of. **12. tune in**, to adjust a radio so as to receive signals. **13. tune out**, to adjust a radio so as to avoid the signals of a sending station. **14. tune up**, to put a musical instrument, etc., in tune, especially with another instrument. –**tuneful**, *adj*. –**tuneless**, *adj*. –**tuner**, *n*.

tune-up *n*. a check or adjustment of working order or condition, as an adjustment of the carburettor, ignition timing, etc., of a motor vehicle for maximum efficiency or power.

tungsten /'tʌŋstən/ *n*. a rare metallic element having a bright grey colour, a metallic lustre, and a high melting point (3410°C), found in wolframite, tungstite, and other minerals, and used to make high-speed steel cutting tools, for electric-lamp filaments, etc.; wolfram. *Symbol*: W; *relative atomic mass*: 183.85; *atomic number*: 74; *density*: 19.3. –**tungstenic** /tʌŋ'stɛnɪk/, *adj*.

tunic /'tjunɪk/ *n*. **1.** coat worn as part of military or other uniform. **2.** loose, sleeveless dress, especially as worn by girls as part of a school uniform or for gymnastics, dancing, etc. **3.** garment like a shirt or gown, worn by both sexes among the ancient Greeks and Romans.

tunnel /'tʌnəl/ *n*. **1.** underground passage. **2.** passageway, as for trains, motor vehicles, etc., through or under a mountain, town, harbour, etc. **3.** passage made by an animal; burrow. –*verb* (**-nelled** *or, Chiefly US*, **-neled**, **-nelling** *or, Chiefly US*, **-neling**) –*v.t.* **4.** to make or form as or like a tunnel: *to tunnel a passage under a river*. –*v.i.* **5.** to make a tunnel: *to tunnel through the Snowy Mountains*. –**tunneller**, *n*.; *US*, **tunneler**, *n*.

tunny /'tʌni/ *n*. (*pl*. **-nies** *or, especially collectively,* **-ny**) **1.** any of a number of widely distributed, important, marine food fishes, genus *Thunnus*, of the mackerel family, especially *T. thynnus*, occurring in the warmer parts of the Atlantic and Pacific oceans, sometimes reaching a weight of 350 kg or more. **2.** → **tuna**.

turban /'tɜbən/ *n*. **1.** a form of headdress of Muslim origin worn by men chiefly in parts of northern Africa, and south-western and southern Asia, consisting of a scarf of silk, linen, cotton, or the like, wound directly round the head or around a cap. **2.** any headdress resembling this. **3.** a small hat, either brimless or with a brim turned up close against the crown, worn by women. –**turbaned**, *adj*. –**turbanless**, *adj*.

turbid /'tɜbəd/ *adj*. **1.** (of liquids) opaque or muddy with particles of extraneous matter. **2.** not clear or transparent; thick, as smoke or clouds; dense. **3.** disturbed; confused; muddled. –**turbidity** /tɜ'bɪdəti/, **turbidness**, *n*. –**turbidly**, *adv*.

turbine /'tɜbaɪn/ *n*. **1.** any of a class of hydraulic motors in which a vaned wheel or runner is made to revolve by the impingement of a free jet of fluid (**impulse turbine** or **action turbine**) or by the passage of fluid which completely fills the motor (**reaction turbine** or **pressure turbine**). **2.** any of certain analogous motors using other fluids, as steam (**steam turbine**), products of combustion (**gas turbine**), or air (**air turbine**).

turbo- an adjective prefix indicating: **1.** driven by a turbine. **2.** of or relating to a turbine.

turbocharged /'tɜboʊtʃadʒd/ *adj*. **1.** (of an engine) fitted with a turbocharger. **2.** (of a computer game) programmed to operate at high speed. **3.** (of an activity) conducted at an accelerated pace.

turbocharger /'tɜboʊtʃadʒə/ *n*. a supercharger which uses an exhaust-driven turbine to boost the air-intake pressure in an internal-combustion engine.

turbojet /'tɜboʊdʒɛt/ *n*. **1.** an engine in which the power is developed by a turbine driving a compressor which supplies air to a fuel burner, through the turbine to a thrust-producing exhaust nozzle. **2.** any vehicle propelled by such an engine.

turboprop /'tɜboʊprɒp/ *n*. *Aeronautics* **1.** a gas-turbine engine coupled to a propeller, forming a propulsive unit of an aircraft. **2.** an aeroplane driven by one or more of such units. Also, **propjet**.

turbot /'tɜbət/ *n*. (*pl*. **-bots** *or, especially collectively,* **-bot**) a European flatfish, *Psetta maxima*, with a diamond-shaped body.

turbulent /'tɜbjələnt/ *adj*. **1.** disposed or given to disturbances, disorder, or insubordination; violent; unruly. **2.** marked by or showing a spirit of disorder or insubordination: *a turbulent period*. **3.** disturbed; agitated; troubled; stormy. –**turbulently**, *adv*. –**turbulence**, *n*.

turd /tɜd/ *n*. *Colloq*. (*taboo*) **1.** a piece of excrement. **2.** an unpleasant person.

tureen /tə'rin, tju-/ *n*. a large deep dish with a cover, for holding soup, etc., at the table.

turf /tɜf/ *n*. (*pl*. **turfs** *or* **turves** /tɜvz/) **1.** the covering of grass, etc., with its matted roots, forming the surface of grassland. **2.** a piece cut or torn from the surface of grassland, with the grass, etc., growing on it; a sod. **3.** a block or piece of peat dug for fuel. **4.** peat as a substance for fuel. **5.** the functional domain or sphere of influence of an organisation, group or individual: *to defend one's turf*. **6.** *Colloq*. territory belonging to a gang. –*v.t.* **7.** to cover with turf or sod. –*phr*. **8. the turf**, **a.** the grassy course or other track over which horseraces are run. **b.** the practice or institution of racing horses. **c.** the racing world. **9. turf out**, *Colloq*. to throw out; eject. –**turfless**, *adj*. –**turfy**, *adj*.

turgid /'tɜdʒəd/ *adj*. **1.** pompous or bombastic, as language, style, etc. **2.** swollen; distended; tumid. –**turgidity** /tɜ'dʒɪdəti/, **turgidness**, *n*. –**turgidly**, *adv*.

turkey /'tɜki/ *n*. (*pl*. **turkeys** *or, especially collectively,* **turkey**) **1.** a large gallinaceous bird of the family Meleagrididae, especially *Meleagris gallopava*, of America, which is domesticated in most parts of the world. **2.** an Australian native bird judged to be similar, as the *brush turkey*, *plain turkey*. **3.** the flesh of such birds, especially *Meleagris gallopava*, used as food. **4.** *Colloq*. **a.** something which is unsuccessful, especially a theatrical production; a flop. **b.** something which fails to operate adequately, as a machine. **5.** *Colloq*. a foolish person, especially one who is noticeably inept or boorish. –*phr*. **6. talk turkey**, *Colloq*. **a.** to talk seriously; deal in hard facts. **b.** to negotiate a business deal.

turkey quail *n*. → **plains-wanderer**.

Turkish bath /tɜkɪʃ 'baθ/ *n*. a form of steam bath, in which, after copious perspiration in a heated room, the body is washed, massaged, etc.

Turkish bread *n*. → **pide** (def. 1).

Turkish coffee *n*. an extremely strong black coffee beverage made with finely ground coffee beans and usually sweetened.

Turkish delight *n*. a cubed, gelatine-stiffened confection covered with icing sugar.

Turkish pizza *n*. → **pide** (def. 2).

turmeric /'tɜmərɪk, 'tjumərɪk/ *n*. **1.** the aromatic rhizome of *Curcuma longa*, a tropical Asian plant of the family Zingiberaceae. **2.** a powder prepared from it, used as a condiment (especially in curry powder), a yellow dye, a medicine, etc.

turmoil /'tɜmɔɪl/ *n*. a state of commotion or disturbance; tumult; agitation; disquiet.

turn /tɜn/ *v.t.* **1.** cause to move round on an axis or about a centre; rotate: *to turn a wheel*. **2.** to cause to move round or partly round, as for the purpose of opening, closing, tightening, etc.: *to turn a key*. **3.** to reverse the position or posture of: *to turn a page*. **4.** to bring the underparts of (sod, soil, etc.) to the surface, as in ploughing. **5.** to change the position of, by, or as by, rotating; to move into a different position. **6.** to change or alter the course of; to divert; deflect. **7.** to change or alter the nature, character, or appearance of. **8.** to render or make by some change. **9.** to change the colour of (leaves, etc.). **10.** to cause to become sour, ferment, or the like: *warm weather turns milk*. **11.** to cause (the stomach) to reject food or anything swallowed. **12.** to change from one language or form of expression to another; translate. **13.** to put or apply to some use or purpose: *to turn a thing to good use*. **14.** to go or pass round or to the other side of: *to turn a street corner*. **15.** to get beyond or pass (a certain age, time, amount, etc.): *he has just turned forty*. **16.** to direct, aim or set going towards or away from a specified person or thing, or in a specified direction: *to turn towards the north*. **17.** to direct (the eyes, face, etc.) another way; avert. **18.** to shape (a piece of metal, etc.) into rounded form with a cutting instrument while rotating in a lathe. **19.** to bring into a rounded or curved form in any way. **20.** to shape artistically or gracefully, especially in rounded form. **21.** to form or express gracefully: *to turn a sentence*. **22.** to direct (thought, desire, etc.) towards or away from something. **23.** to cause to go; send; drive: *to turn a person from one's door*. **24.** to maintain a steady flow or circulation of (money or articles of commerce). **25.** to reverse (a garment, etc.) so that the inner side becomes the outer. **26.** to remake (a garment) by putting the inner side outwards. **27.** to curve, bend, or twist. **28.** to bend back or blunt (the edge of a knife, etc.). **29.** to execute, as a somersault, by rotating or revolving. **30.** to disturb the mental balance of, or make mad, distract; derange. **31.** to make (a profit); earn: *it's hard to turn a profit in this economic climate; just trying to turn a quid*. **32.** to throw into disorder or confusion; upset: *the thief turned the room upside down.* –*v.i.* **33.** to move round on an axis or about a centre; rotate. **34.** to move partly round in this manner, as a door on a hinge. **35.** to direct the face or gaze towards or away from something, or in a particular direction. **36.** to direct or set one's course towards or away from something or in a particular direction. **37.** to direct one's thought, attention, desire, etc., towards or away from something. **38.** to change or reverse the course so as to go in a different or the opposite direction: *to turn to the right*. **39.** to change position so as to face in a different or the opposite direction. **40.** to change or reverse position or posture as by a rotary motion. **41.** to shift the body about as if on an axis: *to turn on one's side in sleeping*. **42.** to assume a curved form; bend. **43.** to be affected with nausea, as the stomach. **44.** to have a sensation of whirling, or be affected with giddiness, as the head. **45.** to change one's position in order to resist or attack: *the dog turned on me*. **46.** to change or alter, as in nature, character, or appearance. **47.** to become sour, fermented, or the like, as milk, etc. **48.** to become of a different colour, as leaves, etc. **49.** to put about or tack, as a ship. –*v. (copular)* **50.** to change so as to be; become: *to turn pale*. –*n.* **51.** a movement of rotation, whether total or partial: *a slight turn of the handle*. **52.** the act of changing or reversing position or posture as by a rotary movement: *a turn of the dice*. **53.** the time for action or proceeding which comes in due rotation or order to each of a number of persons, etc. **54.** the act of changing or reversing the course: *to make a turn to the right*. **55.** a place or point at which such a change occurs. **56.** a place where a road, river, or the like turns. **57.** a single revolution, as of a wheel. **58.** the act of turning so as to face or go in a different direction. **59.** direction, drift, or trend: *the conversation took an interesting turn*. **60.** change or a change in nature, character, condition, circumstances, etc. **61.** the point or time of

change. **62.** the time during which a worker or a set of workers is at work in alternation with others. **63.** that which is done by each of a number of persons acting in rotation or succession. **64.** a passing or twisting of one thing round another as of a rope round a mast. **65.** the condition or manner of being twisted. **66.** a single round, as of a wound or coiled rope. **67.** style, as of expression or language. **68.** a distinctive form or style imparted: *a happy turn of expression*. **69.** a short walk, ride, or the like which includes a going and a returning, especially by different routes. **70.** natural inclination, bent, tendency, or aptitude. **71.** a spell or period of work; shift. **72.** a spell or bout of action. **73.** an attack of illness or the like. **74.** requirement, exigency, or need: *this will serve your turn*. **75.** *Colloq.* a nervous shock, as from fright or astonishment. **76.** *Stock Exchange* the difference between the stockjobber's buying and selling price. **77.** *Music* a melodic embellishment or grace, commonly consisting of a principal note with two auxiliary notes, one above and the other below it. **78.** an individual stage performance, especially in a music hall, cabaret, etc. **79.** the performer in such an entertainment. **80.** a contest or round; a bout. **81.** *Colloq.* a display of anger, hostility, etc.: *to stack on a turn*. **82.** Also, **turnout.** *Aust. Colloq.* a social entertainment; party: *it was a great turn on Friday.* –*phr.* **83. a bad** (or **ill**) **turn,** an unkind act of disservice towards someone. **84. a good turn,** an act done to help or benefit someone. **85. at every turn,** constantly; in every case. **86. by turns,** one after another; alternately; in rotation. **87. in turn,** in due order of succession. **88. on the turn, a.** in the process of or about to turn or change. **b.** (of milk, meat, fruit, etc.) about to go sour or bad. **89. out of turn, a.** out of proper order. **b.** at the wrong time; at an unsuitable moment; indiscreetly; tactlessly. **90. take turns,** to do in succession; alternate. **91. to a turn,** to just the proper degree; perfectly. **92. turn and turn about,** by turns; alternately. **93. turn away, a.** to look or face in a different direction. **b.** to refuse to help; rebuff. **c.** to refuse admission to. **94. turn against, a.** to make hostile towards; cause to be prejudiced against: *to turn a son against his father*. **b.** to take up an attitude of hostility or opposition: *to turn against a person*. **95. turn back, a.** to go back; return. **b.** to cause to go back or return. **c.** to fold back or over. **96. turn down, a.** to fold. **b.** to lessen the intensity of; moderate. **c.** to refuse or reject (a person, request, etc.). **97. turn in, a.** *Colloq.* to go to bed. **b.** *Colloq.* to hand over; deliver; surrender. **c.** to give back. **d.** to submit; hand in. **98. turn into** (or **to**), **a.** to change or convert: *to turn water into ice*. **b.** to be changed, transformed, or converted to. **99. turn it up,** *Colloq.* a peremptory request for peace, etc. **100. turn off, a.** to stop the flow of (water, gas, etc.) as by closing a valve, etc. **b.** to switch off (a radio, light, etc.). **c.** to branch off; diverge; change direction. **d.** to arouse antipathy or revulsion in: *his teaching turns me off*. **e.** to lose interest in or sympathy with; develop a dislike for: *I've turned off gardening*. **f.** *Aust.* to consign (livestock) to market. **101. turn on, a.** to cause (water, gas, etc.) to flow as by opening a valve, etc. **b.** *Aust., NZ Colloq.* to provide (refreshments, especially alcoholic liquor). **c.** to switch on (a radio, light, etc.). **d.** to become suddenly hostile to; attack without warning. **e.** to show or display suddenly: *to turn on the charm*. **f.** *Colloq.* to excite or interest (a person): *that jazz really turns me on!* **g.** *Colloq.* to arouse sexually. **h.** *Colloq.* to become sexually aroused. **i.** *Colloq.* to experience heightened awareness under the influence of a drug (usually illegal), as marijuana or LSD. **j.** *Colloq.* to take such a drug. **102. turn on** (or **upon**), to hinge or depend on: *the question turns on this point*. **103. turn out, a.** to extinguish or put out (a light, etc.). **b.** to produce as the result of labour; manufacture; make. **c.** to drive out; expel;

send away; dismiss; discharge. **d.** to clear or empty (a cupboard, pocket, drawer, etc.) of contents. **e.** to equip; fit out. **f.** to result or issue. **g.** to come to be; become ultimately. **h.** to be found or known; prove. **i.** *Colloq.* to get out of bed. **j.** *Colloq.* to assemble; gather: *the whole street turned out to meet her.* **k.** to cause to assemble; muster; parade. **104. turn over, a.** to move or be moved from one side to another. **b.** to reverse the position of; invert. **c.** to meditate; ponder; reflect. **d.** to start (an engine). **e.** (of an engine) to start. **f.** hand over; transfer. **g.** *Commerce* to purchase and then sell (goods or commodities). **h.** *Commerce* to do business or sell goods to the amount of (a specified sum). **i.** *Commerce* to invest or recover (capital) in some transaction or in the course of business. **j.** *Sport* to lose (the ball) to the opposing team. **105. turn to, a.** to apply to for help, advice, etc.; appeal to. **b.** to set oneself to a task; attend to. **c.** to apply one's efforts, interest, etc., to something; devote oneself to something: *she turned to the study of music.* **106. turn up, a.** to fold, especially so as to shorten, as a garment. **b.** to dig up; bring to the surface by digging; expose. **c.** to find; bring to light; uncover. **d.** to increase the intensity of. **e.** to happen; occur. **f.** to arrive; come. **g.** to come to light; be recovered. **h.** (of a person's nose, or the like) to point slightly upwards at the end.

turncoat /ˈtɜnkoʊt/ *n.* someone who changes his or her party or principles; renegade.

turner /ˈtɜnə/ *n.* someone who fashions objects on a lathe.

turning point *n.* a point at which a decisive change takes place; a critical point; a crisis.

turnip /ˈtɜnəp/ *n.* **1.** the thick, fleshy, edible root of the cruciferous plant *Brassica rapa*, the common **white turnip**, or of *B. napus*, the **swedish turnip** or swede. **2.** the plant itself. **3.** the root of this plant used as a vegetable.

turnkey /ˈtɜnˌki/ *n.* (*pl.* **-keys**) someone who has charge of the keys of a prison; a prison keeper.

turn-off *n.* **1.** a branch of a road leading from a major road, especially an exit from a highway. **2.** the junction of such roads. **3.** an act or instance of turning off. **4.** *Colloq.* a repellent thing or person.

turnout /ˈtɜnaʊt/ *n.* **1.** body of people who come to a meeting, show, concert, etc. **2.** quantity produced; output. **3.** act of turning out. **4.** manner or style in which a person or thing is dressed, equipped, etc. **5.** an outfit. **6.** *Aust.*, *Colloq.* a party, show, entertainment, etc.

turnover /ˈtɜnoʊvə/ *n.* **1.** act or result of turning over; upset. **2.** total number of worker replacements in a given period in a given business or industry. **3.** number of times that capital is invested and reinvested in a line of goods during a particular period of time. **4.** total amount of business done in a given time. **5.** rate at which items are sold or stock used up and replaced. **6.** small pastry made by putting fruit, preserves, or some other filling on one half of a circular piece of pastry, folding the other half over, and then baking it. **7.** *Sport* an instance in which the ball is lost to the opposing team.

turnpike /ˈtɜnpaɪk/ *n.* **1.** (formerly) **a.** a barrier set across a road to stop passage until toll was paid. **b.** a road on which a turnpike operated. **2.** *US* a road for fast traffic, especially one maintained by tolls.

turnstile /ˈtɜnstaɪl/ *n.* a structure usually consisting of four arms at right angles to each other, revolving horizontally on top of a post, and set in a gateway or opening in a fence, to allow the passage of people one at a time after a fee has been paid.

turntable /ˈtɜnteɪbəl/ *n.* **1.** the rotating disc on which the record in a record-player rests. **2.** the rotating plate on which food is placed in a microwave oven. **3.** *Railways* a rotating, track-bearing platform pivoted in the centre,

used for turning round locomotives and other rolling stock.

turn-up *n.* **1.** something that is turned up or that turns up. **2.** *Colloq.* a fight, row, or disturbance. **3.** Also, **turn-up for the books.** *Colloq.* a surprise; an unexpected reversal of fortune. **4.** the attendance at a meeting, sporting event, concert, etc. –*adj.* **5.** that is or may be turned up: *a turn-up sleeve.*

turpentine /ˈtɜpəntaɪn/ *n.* **1.** an oleoresin exuding from the Mediterranean tree *Pistacia terebinthus*. **2.** any of various oleoresins derived from coniferous trees, especially the longleaf pine, *Pinus palustris*, and yielding a volatile oil and a resin when distilled. **3.** any of various substitutes for these, especially white spirits. **4.** a tall rough barked tree common in eastern Australia, *Syncarpia glomulifera*, with dark green leaves, woolly underneath, and cream flowers clustered in dense fluffy balls; provides insect-resistant and water-resistant timber.

turpitude /ˈtɜpətjud, -tʃud/ *n.* **1.** shameful depravity. **2.** a depraved or shameful act.

turps /tɜps/ *Colloq.* –*n.* **1.** → **turpentine** (def. 3). –*phr.* **2. on the turps,** drinking intoxicating liquor excessively.

turquoise /ˈtɜkwɔɪz/ *n.* **1.** a sky blue or greenish blue compact opaque mineral, essentially a hydrous phosphate of aluminium containing a little copper and iron, much used in jewellery. **2.** Also, **turquoise blue.** a greenish blue or bluish green.

turret /ˈtʌrət/ *n.* **1.** a small tower, usually one forming part of a larger structure. **2.** a small tower at an angle of a building, frequently beginning some distance above the ground. **3.** Also, **turrethead.** *Machinery* a pivoted attachment on a lathe, etc., for holding a number of tools, each of which can be presented to the work in rapid succession by a simple rotating movement. **4.** *Navy*, *Mil.* a low, tower-like, heavily armoured structure, usually revolving horizontally, within which guns are mounted. –**turretless,** *adj.*

turtle /ˈtɜtl/ *n.* **1.** any of the Chelonia, an order or group of reptiles having the body enclosed in a shell consisting of a carapace and a plastron, from between which the head, tail, and four legs protrude. **2.** a marine species of turtle, as distinguished from freshwater and terrestrial tortoises, which possess toed feet rather than turtle flippers. –*phr.* **3. turn turtle,** to capsize.

turtle-dove /ˈtɜtl-dʌv/ *n.* a small, slender dove, *Streptopelia turtur*, having a long, graduated tail which is conspicuous in flight. Also, **turtledove, turtle dove.**

turtleneck /ˈtɜtlnɛk/ *n.* **1.** a high, close-fitting neck on a jumper, etc. **2.** a jumper, etc., with such a neck. –*adj.* **3.** (of a jumper, etc.) having such a neck.

tusk /tʌsk/ *n.* **1.** (in certain animals) a tooth developed to great length, usually as one of a pair, as in the elephant, walrus, wild boar, etc., but singly in the narwhal. **2.** a long, pointed, or protruding tooth. **3.** a projecting part resembling the tusk of an animal. –*v.t.* **4.** to dig, tear, or gore with the tusks or tusk. –*v.i.* **5.** to dig up or lunge at the ground with the tusks or tusk. –**tusked** /tʌskt/, *adj.*

tussive /ˈtʌsɪv/ *adj.* of or relating to a cough.

tussle /ˈtʌsəl/ *v.i.* **1.** to struggle or fight roughly or vigorously; wrestle; scuffle. –*n.* **2.** a rough struggle as in fighting or wrestling; a scuffle. **3.** any vigorous conflict or contest.

tussock /ˈtʌsək/ *n.* **1.** a tuft or clump of growing grass or the like. **2.** Also, **tussock grass.** any of various grasses of the genus *Poa*. **3.** any of a number of grass or sedge species as serrated tussock.

tutelage /ˈtjutəlɪdʒ/ *n.* **1.** the office or function of a guardian; guardianship. **2.** instruction. **3.** the state of being under a guardian or a tutor.

tutor /ˈtjutə/ *n.* **1.** someone employed to instruct another in some branch or branches of learning, especially a private instructor. **2.** a university teacher who oversees the studies of certain undergraduates. **3.** (in some universities and colleges) teacher of academic rank lower than lecturer. −*v.t.* **4.** to act as a tutor to; teach or instruct, especially privately. −*v.i.* **5.** to act as a tutor or private instructor. −**tutorless**, *adj.* −**tutorship**, *n.* −**tutorage**, *n.*

tutorial /tjuˈtɔriəl/ *adj.* **1.** relating to or exercised by a tutor: *tutorial functions; tutorial authority.* −*n.* **2.** a period of instruction given by a university tutor to an individual student or a small group of students.

tutti /ˈtoti/ *adj. Music* all; all the voices or instruments together (used as a direction).

tutti-frutti /tuti-ˈfruti/ *n.* **1.** a preserve of chopped mixed fruits, often with brandy syrup. **2.** a variety of fruits (usually candied and minced), used in ice-cream, confections, etc.

tutu /ˈtutu/ *n.* a short, full, ballet skirt, usually made of several layers of tulle.

tuxedo /tʌkˈsidoʊ/ *n.* (*pl.* **-dos**) **1.** a dinner jacket. **2.** Also, **tuxedo suit.** a men's formal suit comprising such a jacket, sometimes including vest, cummerbund, bow tie, and shirt; dinner suit.

TV /ti ˈvi/ *n.* television.

twaddle /ˈtwɒdl/ *n.* trivial, feeble, silly or tedious talk or writing. −**twaddler**, *n.*

twain /tweɪn/ *n. Archaic* two: *never the twain; cut in twain.*

twang /twæŋ/ *v.i.* **1.** to give out a sharp, ringing sound, such as that made by the string of a musical instrument when plucked. **2.** to have a sharp, nasal tone, as the human voice. −*v.t.* **3.** to cause to make a sharp, ringing sound, like the string of a musical instrument. **4.** to speak with a sharp, nasal tone. −*n.* **5.** sharp, ringing sound produced by plucking or suddenly releasing a tense string. **6.** sound like this. **7.** sharp, nasal tone, as of the human voice. −**twangy**, *adj.*

twat /twɒt/ *n. Colloq.* (*taboo*) **1.** the vagina and external female genitalia. **2.** a despicable or unpleasant person.

tweak /twik/ *v.t.* **1.** to seize and pull with a sharp jerk and twist: *to tweak someone's ear.* **2.** to make minor adjustments to for best effect or maximum performance. −**tweaky**, *adj.*

twee /twi/ *adj. Colloq.* affected; precious; excessively dainty; coy.

tweed /twid/ *n.* **1.** a coarse wool cloth in a variety of weaves and colours, either hand-spun and hand-woven in Scotland, or reproduced, often by machine, elsewhere. **2.** (*pl.*) garments made of this cloth. −**tweedy**, *adj.*

tweeny /ˈtwini/ *n.* (*pl.* **-nies**) a child, especially a girl, between the ages of 8 or 9 and 13 or 14. Also, **tweenie, tween, tweener.**

tweet¹ /twit/ *n.* **1.** the weak chirp of a young or small bird. −*v.i.* **2.** to utter a tweet or tweets.

tweet² /twit/ *v.i.* **1.** to post a message on the social network site Twitter. −*v.t.* **2.** to post such a message to (someone). −*n.* **3.** such a message.

tweeter¹ /ˈtwitə/ *n.* a small loudspeaker designed for the reproduction of high audio frequencies (opposed to *woofer*).

tweeter² /ˈtwitə/ *n.* someone who posts a message or messages on the social network site Twitter.

tweezers /ˈtwizəz/ *pl. n.* small pincers or nippers for plucking out hairs, taking up small objects, etc.

twelve /twelv/ *n.* **1.** a cardinal number, ten plus two. **2.** a symbol for this number, as 12 or XII. **3.** a set of this many persons or things. −*adj.* **4.** amounting to twelve in number. −*pron.* **5.** twelve people or things. −**twelfth**, *adj.*

twenty /ˈtwɛnti/ *n.* (*pl.* **-ties**) **1.** cardinal number, ten times two (10×2). **2.** symbol for this number, as 20 or XX. **3.** set of this many people or things. **4.** (*pl.*) the numbers from 20 to 29 of a series, especially with reference to the years of a person's age, or the years of a century, especially the 20th. −*adj.* **5.** amounting to twenty in number: *twenty apples.* −*pron.* **6.** twenty people or things: *twenty came to the party.* −**twentieth**, *adj.*

24/7 /twɛnti-fɔ ˈsɛvən/ *Colloq.* −*adv.* **1.** continuously; uninterruptedly: *this channel broadcasts news 24/7.* −*adj.* **2.** uninterrupted; constant: *24/7 broadcasting of tennis.* Also, **24-7, twenty-four seven.**

Twenty20 /twɛnti ˈtwɛnti/ *adj.* of or relating to a format for a cricket game in which each side is given 20 overs, with a format encouraging a faster pace. *Abbrev.*: T20

twi- a word element meaning 'two', or 'twice', as in *twibill.*

twice /twaɪs/ *adv.* **1.** two times, as in succession; on two occasions: *I asked him twice; write twice a week.* **2.** in twofold quantity or degree; doubly: *twice as much.* −*phr.* **3. look twice,** *Colloq.* **a.** to pay greater attention, as to something hard to make out or something which arouses one's sense of danger. **b.** (sometimes fol. by *at*) to be extremely favourably impressed.

twiddle /ˈtwɪdl/ *v.t.* **1.** to turn round and round, especially with the fingers. −*v.i.* **2.** to play with something idly, as by touching or handling. **3.** to turn round and round; twirl. −*n.* **4.** the act of twiddling; a twirl. −*phr.* **5. twiddle one's thumbs** (or **fingers**), **a.** to keep turning one's thumbs or fingers idly about each other. **b.** to do nothing; be idle. −**twiddler**, *n.*

twig¹ /twɪg/ *n.* **1.** a slender shoot of a tree or other plant. **2.** a small dry, woody piece fallen from a branch: *a fire of twigs.* **3.** *Anat.* one of the minute branches of a blood vessel or nerve. −*phr.* **4. hop** (or **fall off**) **the twig,** *Colloq.* to die. −**twiggy**, *adj.* −**twigless**, *adj.*

twig² /twɪg/ *verb* (**twigged, twigging**) *Colloq.* −*v.t.* **1.** to look at; observe. **2.** to catch sight of; perceive. **3.** to understand. −*v.i.* **4.** to understand; catch on: *she finally twigged.*

twilight /ˈtwaɪlaɪt/ *n.* **1.** the light from the sky when the sun is below the horizon, especially in the evening. **2.** the time during which this light prevails. **3.** a condition or period preceding or succeeding full development, glory, etc.

twill /twɪl/ *n.* **1.** a fabric woven with the weft threads so crossing the warp as to produce an effect of parallel diagonal lines, as in serge. **2.** the characteristic weave of such fabrics.

twin /twɪn/ *n.* **1.** (*pl.*) two children or animals brought forth at a birth. **2.** one of two such children or animals. **3.** (*pl.*) either of two people or things closely related or closely looking like each other. −*adj.* **4.** being two, or one of two, children or animals born at the same birth: *twin sisters.* **5.** consisting of two similar parts or elements joined or connected: *a twin vase.* −*verb* (**twinned, twinning**) −*v.t.* **6.** to pair or couple. −*v.i.* **7.** to be paired or coupled.

twine /twaɪn/ *n.* **1.** a strong thread or string composed of two or more strands twisted together. **2.** a twined or twisted thing or part; a fold, convolution, or coil. **3.** a twist or turn. **4.** a knot or tangle. −*v.t.* **5.** to twist together; intertwine. **6.** to form by or as by twisting strands: *to twine a wreath.* **7.** to twist (one strand, thread, or thing) with another. **8.** to bring (*in, into*, etc.) by or as by twisting or winding. **9.** to encircle or wreathe with something wound about. −*v.i.* **10.** to become twined or twisted together, as two things, or as one thing with another. **11.** to wind in a sinuous or meandering course. **12.** (of plants, stems, etc.) to grow in convolutions about a support. –*phr.* **13. twine about** (or **around**), **a.** to put or dispose by or as by winding. **b.** to wind itself around. –**twiner**, *n.*

twinge /twɪndʒ/ *n.* a sudden, sharp pain (in body or mind): *a twinge of rheumatism*; *a twinge of remorse.*

twinkle /ˈtwɪŋkəl/ *v.i.* **1.** to shine with quick, flickering, gleams of light, as stars, distant lights, etc. **2.** (of the eyes) to be bright with amusement, pleasure, etc. **3.** to appear or move as if with little flashes of light. –*v.t.* **4.** to give out (light) in little gleams or flashes. –*n.* **5.** sparkle. **6.** twinkling brightness in the eyes. **7.** time needed for a wink; twinkling. **8.** wink of the eye. –**twinkling**, *n.*, *adj.* –**twinkler**, *n.*

twirl /twɜl/ *v.t.* **1.** to cause to turn rapidly; spin; whirl; swing circularly. **2.** to wind aimlessly, usually about something. –*v.i.* **3.** to spin rapidly; whirl; rotate. **4.** to turn quickly so as to face or point another way. –*n.* **5.** a twirling or a being twirled; spin; whirl; twist. **6.** something twirled; curl; convolution. –**twirler**, *n.*

twist /twɪst/ *v.t.* **1.** to combine, as two or more strands or threads, by winding together; intertwine. **2.** to form by or as by winding strands together. **3.** to entwine (one thing) with or in another; wind or twine (something) about a thing. **4.** to encircle (a thing) with something wound about. **5.** to alter in shape, as by turning the ends in opposite directions, so that parts previously in the same straight line and plane are situated in a spiral curve. **6.** to wring out of shape or place; contort or distort. **7.** to turn sharply and put out of place; sprain: *when I fell I twisted my ankle.* **8.** to change the proper form or meaning; pervert. **9.** to form into a coil, knot, or the like by winding, rolling, etc.: *to twist the hair into a knot.* **10.** to bend tortuously. **11.** to cause to move with a rotary motion, as a ball pitched in a curve. **12.** to turn in another direction. –*v.i.* **13.** to be or become intertwined. **14.** to wind or twine about something. **15.** to writhe or squirm. **16.** to take a spiral form or course; wind, curve, or bend. **17.** to turn or rotate, as on an axis; revolve, as about something. **18.** to turn so as to face in another direction. **19.** to change shape with a spiral or screwing movement of parts. **20.** to move with a progressive rotary motion, as a ball pitched in a curve. **21.** to dance the twist (def. 43). –*n.* **22.** a curve, bend, or turn. **23.** a turning or rotating as on an axis; rotary motion; spin. **24.** anything formed by or as by twisting or twining parts together. **25.** the act or the manner of twisting strands together, as in thread, yarn, or rope. **26.** a wrench. **27.** a twisting awry. **28.** a changing or perverting, of meaning. **29.** spiral disposition, arrangement, or form. **30.** spiral movement or course. **31.** an irregular bend; a crook or kink. **32.** a peculiar bent, bias, or the like, as in the mind or nature. **33.** the altering of the shape of anything by or as by turning the ends in opposite directions. **34.** the stress causing this alteration. **35.** the resulting state. **36.** a sudden, unexpected alteration to the course of events, as in a play. **37.** *Baseball, Cricket, etc.* **a.** a spin given to a ball in pitching, etc. **b.** a ball having such a spin. **38.** a twisting or torsional action, force, or stress. **39.** a kind of strong twisted silk thread, heavier than ordinary sewing silk, used for working buttonholes and for other purposes. **40.** a loaf or roll of dough twisted and baked. **41.** a kind of tobacco manufactured in the form of a rope or thick cord. –*phr.* **42. round the twist**, *Colloq.* insane. **43. the twist**, a vigorous dance performed by couples and characterised by strongly rhythmic gyrations of the body and movements of the arms and legs in time to heavily accented music. **44. twist someone's arm**, *Colloq.* to persuade or coerce someone: *you've twisted my arm, I'll do it.* –**twister**, *n.* –**twistability**, *n.* –**twistable**, *adj.* –**twistingly**, *adv.*

twit[1] /twɪt/ *v.t.* (**twitted**, **twitting**) **1.** to taunt, gibe at, or banter by references to anything embarrassing. **2.** to reproach or upbraid. –**twitter**, *n.*

twit[2] /twɪt/ *n. Colloq.* a fool; twerp. –**twitty**, *adj.*

twitch[1] /twɪtʃ/ *v.t.* **1.** to give a short, sudden pull or tug at; jerk. **2.** to pull or draw with a hasty jerk. **3.** to move (a part of the body) with a jerk. **4.** to pinch and pull sharply; nip. –*v.i.* **5.** to move or be moved in a quick, jerky way. –*n.* **6.** a quick, jerky movement of the body, or of some part of it. **7.** a short, sudden pull or tug; a jerk. **8.** a twinge (of body or mind). **9.** a loop or noose, attached to a handle, for drawing tightly about the muzzle of a horse to bring it under control. –*phr.* **10. the twitches**, *Colloq.* a state of nerves causing muscular spasms. **11. twitch at**, to give a short, sudden pull or tug at; tug. –**twitcher**, *n.* –**twitchingly**, *adv.* –**twitchy**, *adj.*

twitch[2] /twɪtʃ/ *n.* a pest grass of cultivation and pasture areas, *Agropyron repens*, with underground rhizomes, native to Europe and Asia.

twitter[1] /ˈtwɪtə/ *v.i.* **1.** to utter a succession of small, tremulous sounds, as a bird. **2.** to titter; giggle. **3.** to tremble with excitement or the like; be in a flutter. –*n.* **4.** a state of tremulous excitement. –**twittery**, *adj.* –**twitteringly**, *adv.*

twitter[2] /ˈtwɪtə/ (*also upper case*) (*from trademark*) –*v.i.* **1.** to post a message on the Twitter website; tweet. –*v.t.* **2.** to post a message to (someone) on the Twitter website; tweet. –**twitterer**, *n.* –**twittering**, *n.*, *adj.*

two /tu/ *n.* **1.** a cardinal number, one plus one. **2.** a symbol for this number, as 2 or II. **3.** a set of this many persons or things. **4.** a playing card, die face, etc., with two pips. –*adj.* **5.** amounting to two in number: *two apples.* –*pron.* **6.** two people or things: *sleeps two; give me two.* –*phr.* **7. in two**, in two pieces; apart: *to break in two.* **8. put two and two together**, to draw a conclusion from certain circumstances. **9. two men and a dog**, *Colloq.* very few people.

two-bit *adj. Chiefly US Colloq.* **1.** cheap; worthless. **2.** petty; insignificant.

two-dimensional /tu-dəˈmɛnʃənəl/ *adj.* having two dimensions, as height and width.

two-faced /ˈtu-feɪst/ *adj.* **1.** having two faces. **2.** deceitful; hypocritical. –**two-facedly** /tu-ˈfeɪsədli/, *adv.* –**two-facedness**, *n.*

two-time *Colloq.* –*v.t.* **1.** to deceive or doublecross. **2.** to deceive (someone, especially a spouse or lover) by having a similar relationship with another. –*v.i.* **3.** to deceive or doublecross someone. **4.** to deceive a spouse, lover, etc., by having a similar relationship with another. –**two-timer**, *n.*

two-up *n.* (in Australia and NZ) a gambling game in which two coins are spun in the air and bets are laid on whether they will fall heads or tails; swy.

-ty[1] a suffix of numerals denoting multiples of ten, as in *twenty.*

-ty[2] a suffix of nouns denoting quality, state, etc., as *unity, enmity.*

tycoon /taɪˈkun/ *n.* a businessman having great wealth and power.

tyke[1] /taɪk/ *n. Colloq.* **1.** a mischievous or troublesome child. **2.** any small child. Also, **tike.**

tyke[2] /taɪk/ *n. Colloq.* (*derog.*) a Roman Catholic. Also, **tike.**

tympanic membrane *n.* a membrane separating the tympanum or middle ear from the passage of the external ear; the eardrum.

tympanum /ˈtɪmpənəm, tɪmˈpanəm/ *n.* (*pl.* **-nums** *or* **-na** /-nə/) **1.** *Anat., Zool.* the middle ear. **2.** → **tympanic membrane.** **3.** drum or similar instrument. –**tympanic** /tɪmˈpænɪk/, *adj.*

type /taɪp/ *n.* **1.** kind, class, or group as marked by a particular characteristic. **2.** person or thing representing the characteristic qualities of a kind, class, or group; representative specimen. **3.** general form, style, or character marking a particular kind, class or group. **4.** *Biol.* **a.** the general form or plan of structure common to a group of animals, plants, etc. **b.** genus or species which most nearly serves as an example of the main characteristics of a higher group and frequently gives the latter its name. See **genus, species. 5.** pattern or model from which something is made. **6.** *Printing* **a.** rectangular piece or block, now usually of metal, having on its upper surface a letter or character that stands out from its background. **b.** such pieces or blocks grouped together. **c.** a similar piece or pieces in a typewriter, etc. **d.** printed character(s): *a headline in large type.* –*v.t.* **7.** to produce (a document, etc.) by means of a computer or typewriter. **8.** to represent by a symbol; symbolise. –*v.i.* **9.** to write by means of a typewriter or keyboard.

-type a word element representing 'type', as in *prototype*, especially used of photographic processes, as in *ferrotype*.

typecast /ˈtaɪpkast/ *v.t.* (**-cast, -casting**) **1.** to cast (an actor, etc.) continually in the same kind of role, especially because of some physical characteristic. –*adj.* **2.** (of an actor) having acquired a particular image through frequent casting in similar roles.

typeface /ˈtaɪpfeɪs/ *n.* → **face** (def. 16b).

type 1 diabetes *n.* See **diabetes** (def. 1).

typescript /ˈtaɪpskrɪpt/ *n.* **1.** a typewritten copy of a literary composition, a document, or the like. **2.** typewritten material, as distinguished from handwriting or print.

typeset /ˈtaɪpsɛt/ *Printing* –*v.t.* (**-set, -setting**) **1.** to set in type. –*adj.* **2.** set in type. –**typesetter,** *n.* –**typesetting,** *n.*

type 2 diabetes *n.* See **diabetes** (def. 1).

typewriter /ˈtaɪpraɪtə/ *n.* a machine for writing mechanically in letters and characters, either operated by hand (**manual typewriter**) or powered by electricity (**electric typewriter**).

typho- a word element representing **typhus** and **typhoid,** as in *typhogenic.*

typhoid /ˈtaɪfɔɪd/ *n.* **1.** → **typhoid fever.** –*adj.* **2.** of or relating to typhoid fever. –**typhoidal** /taɪˈfɔɪdl/, *adj.*

typhoid fever *n. Pathol.* an infectious febrile disease, sometimes fatal if untreated, characterised by intestinal inflammation and ulceration, due to the typhoid bacillus, *Salmonella typhi,* which is usually introduced with contaminated food or drink in situations where hygiene is lacking.

typhoon /taɪˈfun/ *n.* a tropical cyclone or hurricane of the western Pacific area, the Indian Ocean and the China seas. –**typhonic** /taɪˈfɒnɪk/, *adj.*

typhus /ˈtaɪfəs/ *n. Pathol.* an acute infectious disease marked by great prostration, severe nervous symptoms, and a characteristic eruption of reddish spots on the body, now regarded as due to a specific microorganism transmitted by lice and fleas. Also, **typhus fever.** –**typhous,** *adj.*

typical /ˈtɪpɪkəl/ *adj.* **1.** relating to, of the nature of, or serving as a type or emblem; symbolic. **2.** of the nature of or serving as a type or representative specimen. **3.** conforming to the type. **4.** *Biol.* exemplifying most nearly the essential characteristics of a higher group in natural history, and forming the type: *the typical genus of a family.* **5.** relating or belonging to a representative specimen; characteristic or distinctive. Also, *Rare,* **typic.** –**typically,** *adv.* –**typicalness,** *n.*

typify /ˈtɪpəfaɪ/ *v.t.* (**-fied, -fying**) **1.** to serve as the typical specimen of; exemplify. **2.** to serve as a symbol or emblem of; symbolise; prefigure. **3.** to represent by a type or symbol. –**typification** /tɪpəfəˈkeɪʃən/, *n.* –**typifier,** *n.*

typist /ˈtaɪpəst/ *n.* someone who operates a typewriter.

typo /ˈtaɪpoʊ/ *n.* (*pl.* **typos**) *Colloq.* a typographical or keying error.

typography /taɪˈpɒgrəfi/ *n.* **1.** the art or process of printing with types. **2.** the work of setting and arranging types and of printing from them. **3.** the general character or appearance of printed matter. –**typographer,** *n.* –**typographical** /taɪpəˈgræfɪkəl/, **typographic** /taɪpəˈgræfɪk/, *adj.*

tyranny /ˈtɪrəni/ *n.* (*pl.* **-nies**) **1.** complete or unchecked exercise of power; despotic abuse of authority. **2.** government or rule of a tyrant or ruler with total power. **3.** state ruled by a tyrant or ruler holding total power. **4.** unjustly severe government. **5.** undue severity or cruelty. **6.** tyrannical act or undertaking. –**tyrannise, tyrannize,** *v.*

tyrant /ˈtaɪrənt/ *n.* **1.** a ruler who exercises power oppressively or unjustly. **2.** any person who exercises power despotically. –**tyrannical,** *adj.*

tyre /ˈtaɪə/ *n.* a band of metal or rubber, fitted round the rim of a wheel as a running surface. The inflated rubber **pneumatic tyre** provides good adhesion and resistance to shock. Also, *US,* **tire.**

tyro /ˈtaɪroʊ/ *n.* (*pl.* **-ros**) a beginner in learning anything; a novice. Also, **tiro.**

tzar /zɑ/ *n.* → **tsar.**

U u

U, u /juː/ *n.* a vowel, the 21st letter of the English alphabet.

U /juː/ *adj. Colloq.* appropriate to or characteristic of the upper class. Compare **non-U**.

U-bend /ˈjuːbɛnd/ *n.* a piece of plumbing pipe in the shape of a U, designed to trap water in the lowest part of the bend so as to prevent noxious fumes from coming back up the pipe.

uber /ˈuːbə/ *adj. Colloq.* extreme: *an uber example of greed.*

uber- /ˈuːbə-/ **1.** a prefix denoting the greatest or most extreme example of its kind: *uberbabe; ubernerd.* **2.** a prefix used as an intensifier: *uberfit.*

ubiquity /juːˈbɪkwəti/ *n.* the state or capacity of being everywhere at the same time; omnipresence. **–ubiquitous,** *adj.*

U-boat /ˈjuːbəʊt/ *n.* a German submarine, especially as used in World War I or World War II.

udder /ˈʌdə/ *n.* a mamma or mammary gland, especially when pendulous and with more than one teat, as in cows. **–udderless,** *adj.*

udon /ˈuːdɒn/ *n.* (in Japanese cookery) a thick noodle, round or square and made from wheat or cornflour; usually served hot in soup.

U-ey /ˈjuː-i/ *n.* **1.** *Colloq.* a U-turn. **–***phr.* **2. chuck a U-ey,** to do a U-turn. Also, **U-ie, Uey.**

UFO /juː ɛf ˈəʊ, ˈjuːfəʊ/ *n.* (*pl.* **UFOs** *or* **UFO's**) unidentified flying object.

ugg boot /ˈʌg bʊt/ *n. Aust.* a boot with an upper made from sheepskin with the fleece tanned into the skin, the fleece being on the inside of the boot and the leather on the outside. Also, **ug boot, ugh boot.**

ugly /ˈʌgli/ *adj.* (**-lier, -liest**) **1.** nasty or displeasing in appearance; offensive to the sense of beauty: *an ugly building.* **2.** morally displeasing: *an ugly sin.* **3.** of a troublesome nature; threatening disadvantage or danger: *ugly symptoms.* **4.** unpleasantly or dangerously rough: *ugly weather.* **5.** ill-natured; quarrelsome; vicious: *an ugly disposition.* **–uglily,** *adv.* **–ugliness,** *n.*

UHT /juː eɪtʃ ˈtiː/ *adj.* (of milk products) treated by being heated briefly to a high temperature and then packaged in hermetically sealed containers; long-life.

ukulele /juːkəˈleɪli/ *n.* a small musical instrument of the guitar kind, much used in the Hawaiian Islands. Also, **ukelele.**

ulcer /ˈʌlsə/ *n.* **1.** *Pathol.* a sore open either to the surface of the body or to a natural cavity, and accompanied by the disintegration of tissue and the formation of pus, etc. **2.** a corrupting influence or element. **–ulcerate,** *v.* **–ulceration,** *n.* **–ulcerous,** *adj.*

-ule a diminutive suffix of nouns, as in *globule.*

-ulent an adjective suffix meaning 'full of' (some thing or quality), as in *fraudulent, purulent.*

ulna /ˈʌlnə/ *n.* (*pl.* **-nae** /-niː/ *or* **-nas**) **1.** *Anat.* the one of the two bones of the forearm which is on the side opposite to the thumb. **2.** a corresponding bone in the forelimb of other vertebrates. **–ulnar,** *adj.*

-ulose variant of **-ulous** in scientific terms, as in *granulose, ramulose.*

-ulous a suffix forming adjectives meaning 'tending to', as in *credulous, populous.*

ulterior /ʌlˈtɪəriə/ *adj.* **1.** being beyond what is seen or avowed; intentionally kept concealed: *ulterior motives.*

2. coming at a subsequent time or stage: *ulterior action.* **3.** being or situated beyond, or on the farther side: *ulterior regions.* **–ulteriorly,** *adv.*

ultimate /ˈʌltəmət/ *adj.* **1.** forming the final aim or object: *his ultimate goal.* **2.** coming at the end, as of a course of action, a process, etc.; final; decisive: *ultimate lot in life.* **3.** beyond which it is impossible to proceed, as by investigation or analysis; fundamental; elemental: *ultimate principles.* **4.** impossible to exceed or override: *ultimate weapon.* **5.** last, as in a series. **–***n.* **6.** the final point; final result. **7.** a fundamental fact or principle. **–***phr.* **8. the ultimate,** *Colloq.* the most successful, pleasing, handsome, etc. **–ultimately,** *adv.* **–ultimateness,** *n.*

ultimatum /ʌltəˈmeɪtəm/ *n.* (*pl.* **-tums** *or* **-ta** /-tə/) **1.** the final terms of one of the parties in a diplomatic relationship, the rejection of which by the other party may involve a rupture of relations or lead to a declaration of war. **2.** a final proposal or statement of conditions.

ultimo /ˈʌltəməʊ/ *adv.* in or of the month preceding the present: *on the 12th ultimo.* *Abbrev.*: ult. Compare **proximo.**

ultra /ˈʌltrə/ *adj.* going beyond what is usual or accepted.

ultra- a prefix meaning: **1.** beyond (in space or time) as in *ultraplanetary.* **2.** excessive; excessively, as in *ultraconventional.*

ultra high frequency *n.* **1.** any radiofrequency between 300 and 3000 megahertz. *Abbrev.*: UHF **–***adj.* **2.** (of a device) designed to transmit or receive such a frequency.

ultralight /ˈʌltrəlaɪt/ *adj.* **1.** extremely lightweight. **2.** of or relating to an ultralight aircraft. **–***n.* **3.** an ultralight aircraft.

ultralight aircraft *n.* a fixed-wing powered aircraft of limited weight, designed to carry not more than two people. Also, **ultralight, ultralight plane.**

ultramarine /ʌltrəməˈriːn/ *adj.* **1.** beyond the sea. **–***n.* **2.** a blue pigment consisting of powdered lapis lazuli. **3.** a similar artificial blue pigment. **4.** a deep blue colour.

ultrasonic /ʌltrəˈsɒnɪk/ *adj.* of or relating to ultrasound.

ultrasound /ˈʌltrəsaʊnd/ *n.* **1.** pressure waves similar in nature to soundwaves but whose frequencies, greater than 20 000 hertz, are above the audible limit. **2.** the diagnostic or therapeutic use of such waves, as in the imaging of internal organs of the body or in deep-heat treatment of joints. **3.** Also, **ultrasound scan.** an image obtained by ultrasound of an internal organ of the body or of a fetus in the uterus. **4.** the machine which performs such a scan.

ultraviolet /ʌltrəˈvaɪələt, -ˈvaɪlət/ *adj.* **1.** beyond the violet, as the invisible rays of the spectrum lying outside the violet end of the visible spectrum. **2.** relating to these rays: *ultraviolet light.*

ululate /ˈjuːljəleɪt/ *v.i.* **1.** to howl, as a dog or wolf. **2.** to lament loudly. **–ululant,** *adj.* **–ululation** /juːljəˈleɪʃən/, *n.*

-ulus a diminutive suffix of nouns, as in *homunculus, calculus.*

umami /uˈmɑːmi/ *n.* a taste category, distinguished from sweet, sour, salt, and bitter, which is described as being the taste of freshness common to savoury food such as meat, cheese, mushrooms, etc.; associated with Japanese cuisine.

umbel /ˈʌmbəl/ *n. Bot.* an inflorescence in which a number of flower stalks or pedicels, nearly equal in length, spread from a common centre, called a **simple umbel** when each pedicel is terminated by a single flower, and a **compound umbel** when each pedicel bears a secondary umbel. –**umbellate**, *adj.* –**umbelliferous**, *adj.*

umber /ˈʌmbə/ *n.* **1.** an earth consisting chiefly of a hydrated oxide of iron and some oxide of manganese, used in its natural state (**raw umber**) as a brown pigment, or after heating (**burnt umber**) as a reddish brown pigment. **2.** the colour of such a pigment; dark dusky brown or dark reddish brown. –*adj.* **3.** of such a colour. –*v.t.* **4.** to colour with or as with umber.

umbilical cord /ʌmˈbɪlɪkəl kɔd, ʌmbəˈlaɪkəl/ *n.* **1.** *Anat.* a cord or funicle connecting the embryo or fetus with the placenta of the mother, and transmitting nourishment from the mother. **2.** Also, **umbilical connector**. *Aerospace* **a.** an electrical cable or fluid pipeline conveying supplies and signals from the ground to a rocket before the launch. **b.** an air or oxygen line connecting an astronaut to the spacecraft during a walk in space. Also, **umbilical**.

umbilicus /ʌmˈbɪlɪkəs, ʌmbəˈlaɪkəs/ *n.* (*pl.* **-bilici** /-ˈbɪləsaɪ, -bəˈlaɪsaɪ/) **1.** *Anat.* the navel, or central depression in the surface of the abdomen indicating the point of attachment of the umbilical cord. **2.** *Bot., Zool., etc.* a navel-like formation, as the hilum of a seed. **3.** a central point or place. **4.** a small, navel-like depression. –**umbilical**, *adj.*

umbrage /ˈʌmbrɪdʒ/ *n.* **1.** offence given or taken; resentful displeasure. **2.** the foliage of trees, etc., affording shade.

umbrella /ʌmˈbrɛlə/ *n.* **1.** a portable shade or screen for protection from sunlight, rain, etc., in its modern form consisting of a light circular canopy of silk, cotton, or other material on a folding frame of bars or strips of steel, cane, etc. **2.** *Zool.* the saucer- or bowl-shaped gelatinous body of a jellyfish; bell. **3.** any general protection or cover. **4.** a sphere of control or influence: *under the umbrella of the finance department.* **5.** *Mil.* a covering force of aircraft protecting ground troops. –*adj.* **6.** covering or intended to cover a group or class of things, circumstances, etc.; all-embracing: *winter sports is an umbrella term for skiing, skating, tobogganing, etc.*

umlaut /ˈʊmlaʊt/ *n.* **1.** (of vowels in Germanic languages) assimilation in which a vowel is influenced by a following vowel or semivowel. **2.** a vowel which has resulted from such assimilation, especially when written *ä*, *ö*, or *ü* in German. **3.** two dots as a diacritic over a vowel to indicate a different vowel sound from that of the letter without the diacritic, especially as so used in German. –*v.t.* **4.** to modify by umlaut. **5.** to write the umlaut over.

umpire /ˈʌmpaɪə/ *n.* **1.** a person selected to see that a game is played in accordance with the rules. **2.** a person to whose decision a controversy between parties is referred; an arbiter or referee. –*v.t.* **3.** to act as umpire in (a game). –*v.i.* **4.** to act as umpire. –**umpirage**, *n.* **umpireship**, *n.*

un-¹ a prefix meaning 'not', freely used as an English formative, giving a negative or opposite force, in adjectives (including participial adjectives) and their derivative adverbs and nouns, as in *unfair, unfairly, unfairness, unfelt, unseen, unfitting, unformed, unheard-of, unget-at-able*, and less freely in certain other nouns, as in *unease, unrest, unemployment.* Note: Of the words in **un-¹**, only a selected number are separately entered, since in most formations of this class, the meaning, spelling, and pronunciation may readily be

determined by reference to the simple word from which each is formed.

un-² a prefix freely used in English to form verbs expressing a reversal of some action or state, or removal, deprivation, release, etc., as in *unbend, uncork, unfasten*, etc., or to intensify the force of a verb already having such a meaning, as in *unloose.*

unaccountable /ʌnəˈkaʊntəbəl/ *adj.* **1.** not to be accounted for or explained. **2.** not accountable or answerable. –**unaccountability** /ʌnəˌkaʊntəˈbɪləti/, **unaccountableness**, *n.* –**unaccountably**, *adv.*

unanimous /juˈnænəməs/ *adj.* of one mind; in complete accord; agreed. –**unanimously**, *adv.* –**unanimousness**, *n.*

unarguable /ʌnˈagjuəbəl/ *adj.* **1.** not capable of being supported or argued: *an unarguable theory.* **2.** not capable of being countered or denied: *an unarguable claim.* Also, **inarguable**. –**unarguably**, *adv.*

unassuming /ʌnəˈsjumɪŋ/ *adj.* unpretending; modest. –**unassumingly**, *adv.* –**unassumingness**, *n.*

unavailing /ʌnəˈveɪlɪŋ/ *adj.* ineffectual; useless. –**unavailingly**, *adv.*

unawares /ʌnəˈwɛəz/ *adv.* **1.** while not aware or conscious of a thing oneself; unknowingly or inadvertently. **2.** while another is not aware; unexpectedly: *to come upon someone unawares.*

unbalanced /ʌnˈbælənst/ *adj.* **1.** not balanced, or not properly balanced. **2.** lacking steadiness and soundness of judgement. **3.** mentally disordered or deranged.

unbecoming /ʌnbəˈkʌmɪŋ/ *adj.* **1.** not becoming; not appropriate; unsuited. **2.** (*oft. placed after the noun*) improper; unseemly: *conduct unbecoming to a gentleman.* **3.** (of clothing, etc.) unattractively inappropriate. –**unbecomingly**, *adv.* –**unbecomingness**, *n.*

unbend /ʌnˈbɛnd/ *v.t.* (**-bent** *or* **-bended, -bending**) **1.** to make or become less formal. **2.** to make or become straight.

unbending /ʌnˈbɛndɪŋ/ *adj.* **1.** not bending; rigid; unyielding; inflexible. **2.** stern; rigorous; resolute. –*n.* **3.** a relaxing or easing. –**unbendingly**, *adv.* –**unbendingness**, *n.*

unborn /ʌnˈbɔn/ *adj.* **1.** not yet born; yet to come; future: *ages unborn.* **2.** (of a baby) still in the womb.

unbosom /ʌnˈbʊzəm/ *v.t.* **1.** to disclose (one's thoughts, feelings, etc.) especially in confidence. –*phr.* **2.** **unbosom oneself**, to disclose one's thoughts, etc. to another person. –**unbosomer**, *n.*

unbridled /ʌnˈbraɪdld/ *adj.* **1.** unrestrained or uncontrolled. **2.** not having a bridle on, as a horse.

uncanny /ʌnˈkæni/ *adj.* **1.** such as to arouse superstitious uneasiness; unnaturally strange. **2.** preternaturally good: *uncanny judgement.* –**uncannily**, *adv.* –**uncanniness**, *n.*

uncertain /ʌnˈsɜtn/ *adj.* **1.** not definitely or surely known; doubtful. **2.** not confident, assured, or decided: *the applicant's uncertain manner was a point against him.* **3.** not fixed or determined. **4.** doubtful; vague; indistinct. **5.** not to be depended on. **6.** subject to change; variable; capricious: *a person of uncertain temper.* **7.** dependent on chance. **8.** unsteady or fitful, as light. –**uncertainly**, *adv.* –**uncertainness**, *n.* –**uncertainty**, *n.*

uncheck /ʌnˈtʃɛk/ *v.t.* → **untick**.

uncial /ˈʌnsiəl/ *adj.* of or relating to ancient majuscule letters distinguished from capital majuscules by relatively great roundness, inclination, and inequality in height. –**uncially**, *adv.*

uncle /ˈʌŋkəl/ *n.* **1.** a brother of one's father or mother. **2.** an aunt's husband. **3.** a familiar title applied to any elderly man.

unclean /ʌnˈklin/ *adj.* **1.** morally or spiritually impure. **2.** ceremonially or ritually defiled. **3.** (of food) unfit to be eaten; forbidden. **4.** physically defiled or defiling; foul; dirty.

unconscionable /ʌnˈkɒnʃənəbəl/ *adj.* **1.** unreasonably excessive. **2.** not in accordance with what is just or reasonable: *unconscionable behaviour.* **3.** not guided by conscience; unscrupulous. –**unconscionableness**, *n.* –**unconscionably**, *adv.*

unconscious /ʌnˈkɒnʃəs/ *adj.* **1.** not conscious; unaware. **2.** temporarily devoid of consciousness. **3.** not endowed with knowledge of one's own existence, etc. **4.** occurring below the level of conscious thought. **5.** unintentional: *an unconscious slight.* **6.** *Psychol.* relating to mental processes which the individual cannot bring into consciousness. –*phr.* **7. the unconscious**, *Psychol.* an organisation of the mind containing all psychic material not available in the immediate field of awareness. –**unconsciously**, *adv.* –**unconsciousness**, *n.*

uncouth /ʌnˈkuθ/ *adj.* **1.** awkward, clumsy, or unmannerly, as persons, behaviour, actions, etc. **2.** strange and ungraceful in appearance or form. **3.** unusual or strange. –**uncouthly**, *adv.* –**uncouthness**, *n.*

uncrossed /ʌnˈkrɒst/ *adj.* **1.** (of a cheque) not crossed; negotiable. **2.** not thwarted.

unction /ˈʌŋkʃən/ *n.* **1.** the act of anointing, especially for medical purposes or as a religious rite. **2.** something soothing or comforting. **3.** a professional, conventional, or affected earnestness or fervour in utterance. –**unctionless**, *adj.*

unctuous /ˈʌŋkʃuəs/ *adj.* **1.** of the nature of or characteristic of an unguent or ointment; oily; greasy. **2.** characterised by religious unction or fervour, especially of an affected kind; excessively smooth, suave, or bland. **3.** having an oily or soapy feel, as certain minerals. –**unctuosity** /ʌŋkʃuˈɒsəti/, **unctuousness**, *n.* –**unctuously**, *adv.*

uncut /ʌnˈkʌt/ *adj.* (of drugs, as heroin) not mixed with other substances; pure.

under /ˈʌndə/ *prep.* **1.** beneath and covered by: *under a table*; *under a tree.* **2.** below the surface of: *under the sea.* **3.** at a point or position lower than or farther down than: *to stand under a window.* **4.** in the position or state of bearing, supporting, sustaining, undergoing, etc.: *to sink under a load*; *a matter under consideration.* **5.** subject to: *under the influence of drink.* **6.** bearing as a crop: *land under barley.* **7.** beneath (a head, heading, or the like), as in classification. **8.** as designated, indicated, or represented by: *under a new name.* **9.** below in degree, amount, price, etc.; less than: *under age.* **10.** below in rank, dignity, or the like. **11.** subject to the rule, direction, guidance, etc., of: *under supervision*; *to study under a professor.* **12.** during the reign or rule of. **13.** subject to the influence, conditioning force, etc., of: *under these circumstances*; *born under Taurus.* **14.** with the favour or aid of: *under protection.* **15.** authorised, warranted, or attested by: *under one's hand*; *under seal.* **16.** in accordance with: *under the provisions of the law.* **17.** in the state or process of: *under repair.* –*adv.* **18.** beneath and covered by something. **19.** beneath the surface. **20.** in a lower place. **21.** in a lower degree, amount, etc. **22.** in a subordinate position or condition. **23.** in or into subjection or submission. **24.** in or into cover or submersion: *to send a boat under.* –*adj.* **25.** beneath. **26.** lower in position. **27.** lower in degree, amount, etc. **28.** lower in rank or condition. **29.** facing downwards: *the under fringe of a curtain.* –*phr.* **30. down under**, (*also upper case*) in or to Australia and New Zealand. **31. go under**, **a.** to sink in or as in water. **b.** to fail, especially of a business. **c.** *Colloq.* to be found guilty by a jury. **32. under way**, **a.** in motion or moving along,

as a ship that has weighed anchor. **b.** in progress, as an enterprise.

under- a prefixal attributive use of *under*, as to indicate: **1.** a place or situation below or beneath, as in *underbrush, undertow*, or lower in grade or dignity, as in *understudy.* **2.** a lesser degree, extent, or amount, as in *undersized.* **3.** an insufficiency, as in *underfeed.*

underachieve /ʌndərəˈtʃiv/ *v.i.* to fail to perform as well as one's innate ability suggests. –**underachiever**, *n.* –**underachievement**, *n.*

under-age *adj.* below the customary or required age, especially below the legal age, as for entering licensed premises, marrying, etc.

underarm /ˈʌndəram/ *adj.* **1.** under the arm: *an under-arm seam.* **2.** in the armpit: *underarm odour.* **3.** *Cricket, Tennis, etc.* executed with the hand below the shoulder as in bowling, service, etc. –*adv.* **4.** *Cricket, Tennis, etc.* with an underarm action.

undercapitalise /ʌndəˈkæpətəlaɪz/ *v.t.* to provide insufficient capital for (a business venture). Also, **undercapitalize.**

undercarriage /ˈʌndəkærɪdʒ/ *n.* **1.** the supporting framework beneath the body of a carriage, etc. **2.** Also, **landing gear.** the portions of an aeroplane beneath the body, serving as a support when on the ground or water or when taxiing off and alighting.

undercover /ˈʌndəkʌvə/ *adj.* working or done out of public sight; secret: *an undercover agent.*

undercurrent /ˈʌndəkʌrənt/ *n.* **1.** a current below the upper currents or below the surface. **2.** an underlying or concealed condition or tendency.

undercut *v.t.* /ʌndəˈkʌt/ (**-cut, -cutting**) **1.** to cut under or beneath. **2.** to sell or work at a lower price than. **3.** *Sport* to hit (the ball) so as to cause a backspin. **4.** to outwit or outmanoeuvre (a rival); undermine. –*n.* /ˈʌndəkʌt/ **5.** a cut, or a cutting away, underneath.

underdeveloped /ʌndədəˈvɛləpt/ *adj.* **1.** (of a country) → **developing** (def. 2). **2.** (of film) developed less than normal, producing a lack of contrast. **3.** less fully developed than average. –**underdevelopment**, *n.*

underdog /ˈʌndədɒg/ *n.* **1.** a victim of oppression. **2.** the loser or expected loser in a competitive situation, fight, etc.

underdone /ˈʌndədʌn/ *adj.* (of food, especially meat) cooked lightly or less than completely.

underfelt /ˈʌndəfɛlt/ *n.* a thick felt laid under a carpet to make it more resilient.

undergo /ʌndəˈgoʊ/ *v.t.* **1.** to be subjected to; experience; pass through. **2.** to endure; sustain; suffer.

undergraduate /ʌndəˈgrædʒuət/ *n.* **1.** a student in a university or college who has not completed a first degree. –*adj.* **2.** relating to, characteristic of, or consisting of undergraduates. –**undergraduateship**, *n.*

underground /ˈʌndəgraʊnd/ *adv.* **1.** beneath the surface of the ground. **2.** secretly; not openly. –*adj.* **3.** being or taking place beneath the surface of the ground: *an underground river.* **4.** used, or for use, underground. **5.** hidden or secret; not open. **6.** referring to a group, organisation, etc., that holds radical political views and does not work as part of the establishment, or to the publications, etc., of such a group. –*n.* **7.** a place or region beneath the surface of the earth. **8.** a railway running mainly through underground tunnels. –*phr.* **9. the Underground**, a secret organisation fighting the established government or occupation forces, especially in World War II.

underground economy *n.* an economy which exists alongside the official economy but which involves payments in cash which are not declared as taxable income and which do not therefore become part of official figures and statistics.

undergrowth /ˈʌndəɡroʊθ/ *n.* **1.** shrubs or small trees growing beneath or among large trees. **2.** condition of being undergrown or undersized.

underhand /ˈʌndəhænd/ *adj.* **1.** not open and above-board; secret and crafty or dishonourable. **2.** done or delivered underhand. –*adv.* **3.** with the hand below the shoulder, as in pitching or bowling a ball. **4.** *Tennis* with the racquet held below the wrist. **5.** secretly; stealthily; slyly.

underlie /ʌndəˈlaɪ/ *v.t.* (**-lay, -lain, -lying**) **1.** to lie under or beneath; be situated under. **2.** to be at the basis of; form the foundation of. –**underlying**, *adj.*

underline *v.t.* /ʌndəˈlaɪn/ **1.** to mark with a line or lines underneath; underscore. **2.** to emphasise or stress the importance of. –*n.* /ˈʌndəlaɪn/ **3.** a line drawn under-neath.

underling /ˈʌndəlɪŋ/ *n.* (*usually derog.*) a subordinate.

undermine /ʌndəˈmaɪn, ˈʌndəmaɪn/ *v.t.* **1.** to form a mine or passage under, as in military operations; make an excavation under. **2.** to render unstable by digging into or wearing away the foundations. **3.** to affect injuri-ously or weaken by secret or underhand means. **4.** to weaken insidiously; destroy gradually. –**underminer**, *n.*

underneath /ʌndəˈniθ/ *prep.* **1.** under; beneath. –*adv.* **2.** beneath; below. –*adj.* **3.** lower. –*n.* **4.** the under or lowest part or aspect.

underpants /ˈʌndəpænts/ *pl. n.* an undergarment, in the form of more or less close-fitting short trousers, with or without legs, and made of light cotton or the like; pants; drawers.

underpass /ˈʌndəpas/ *n.* a passage running underneath, especially a passage for vehicles or pedestrians, or both, crossing under a railway, road, etc.

underpin /ʌndəˈpɪn/ *v.t.* **1.** to pin or support underneath; place something under for support or foundation. **2.** to support; prop.

underplay /ʌndəˈpleɪ/ *v.t.* **1.** to act (a part) sketchily. **2.** to perform or deal with in a subtle or restrained manner. –*v.i.* **3.** to achieve an effect in acting with a minimum of emphasis. **4.** *Cards* to play a low card while retaining a higher. –**underplayed**, *adj.*

underprivileged /ʌndəˈprɪvəlɪdʒd/ *adj.* denied the en-joyment of the normal privileges or rights of a society because of poverty and low social status.

underproof /ˈʌndəpruf/ *adj.* containing a smaller proportion of alcohol than proof spirit does.

underscore *v.t.* /ʌndəˈskɔ/ **1.** to mark with a line or lines underneath; underline. **2.** to emphasise. –*n.* /ˈʌndəskɔ/ **3.** a line drawn beneath something written or printed, as for emphasis.

undersecretary /ʌndəˈsɛkrətri/ *n.* (*pl.* **-ries**) **1.** a secretary subordinate to a principal secretary. **2.** the permanent head in certain government departments. –**undersecretaryship**, *n.*

undersigned /ˈʌndəsaɪnd/ *adj.* **1.** having signed, as a person, at the end of a letter or document. **2.** signed, as a name. –*phr.* **3. the undersigned**, the person or per-sons undersigning a letter or document.

understand /ʌndəˈstænd/ *verb* (**-stood, -standing**) –*v.t.* **1.** to grasp the idea of; comprehend: *now I understand your plan.* **2.** to be thoroughly familiar with the char-acter or nature of: *she understands mathematics; she understands her husband well.* **3.** to get the idea of by knowing the meaning of the words used: *can you understand foreign broadcasts?* **4.** to grasp the possible results or importance of: *does he understand what war would mean?* **5.** to accept as a fact; learn or hear: *from what I understand, the charge is true.* **6.** to take the meaning of in a particular way: *you are to understand the phrase exactly as written.* **7.** to accept as being present or existing: *his loyalty is understood.* –*v.i.* **8.** to see what is meant. **9.** to have knowledge about

something: *to understand about a matter.* **10.** to accept sympathetically: *if you go away, I shall understand.*

understanding /ʌndəˈstændɪŋ/ *n.* **1.** the act of someone who understands; comprehension; personal interpreta-tion. **2.** intelligence; wit. **3.** superior intelligence; su-perior power of recognising the truth: *women of understanding.* **4.** a mutual comprehension of each other's meaning, thoughts, etc. **5.** a state of (good or friendly) relations between persons. **6.** a mutual agree-ment of a private or unannounced kind. –*adj.* **7.** that understands; possessing or showing intelligence or understanding. **8.** sympathetically discerning; tolerant. –*phr.* **9. on the understanding that**, on condition that. –**understandingly**, *adv.*

understate /ʌndəˈsteɪt/ *v.t.* to state or represent less strongly than is desirable or necessary; state with too little emphasis. –**understatement** /ˈʌndəsteɪtmənt/, *n.*

understudy /ˈʌndəstʌdi/ *n.* (*pl.* **-dies**) **1.** an actor who stands by to replace a performer when the latter is unable to appear. –*v.t.* (**-died, -dying**) **2.** to act as an understudy to (an actor). **3.** to be the understudy for (a particular role).

undertake /ʌndəˈteɪk/ *v.t.* **1.** to take on oneself (some task, performance, etc.); take in hand; essay; attempt. **2.** to take on oneself by formal promise or agreement; lay oneself under obligation to perform or execute. **3.** to warrant or guarantee: *to undertake that something will happen.*

undertaker /ˈʌndəteɪkə/ *n.* someone whose business is to prepare the dead for burial and to take charge of funerals; funeral director; mortician.

undertaking /ˈʌndəteɪkɪŋ/ *n.* **1.** the act of someone who undertakes any task or responsibility. **2.** a task, enter-prise, etc., undertaken. **3.** a promise; pledge; guarantee. **4.** the business of an undertaker or funeral director.

under-the-counter *adj.* relating to goods kept hidden for sale in some improper way, as on the black market.

undertone /ˈʌndətoʊn/ *n.* **1.** a low or subdued tone, as of utterance. **2.** an underlying quality, element, or ten-dency. **3.** a subdued colour; a colour modified by an underlying colour.

undertow /ˈʌndətoʊ/ *n.* **1.** the backward flow or draught of the water, below the surface, from waves breaking on a beach. **2.** any strong current below the surface of a body of water, moving in a direction different from that of the surface current.

underwear /ˈʌndəwɛə/ *n.* clothes worn under outer clothes, especially those worn next to the skin.

underworld /ˈʌndəwɜld/ *n.* **1.** the lower, degraded, or criminal part of human society. **2.** the lower or nether world. **3.** the place or region below the surface of the earth.

underwrite /ˈʌndəraɪt, ʌndəˈraɪt/ *v.t.* (**-wrote, -written, -writing**) **1.** to write (something) under a thing, espe-cially under other written matter. **2.** to sign one's name to (a document, etc.). **3.** to agree to meet the expense of; undertake to finance. **4.** to guarantee the sale of (shares or bonds to be offered to the public for subscription). **5.** *Insurance* to write one's name at the end of (a policy of insurance), thereby becoming liable in case of cer-tain losses specified therein.

undies /ˈʌndiz/ *pl. n. Colloq.* → **underwear**.

undo /ʌnˈdu/ *v.t.* (**-did, -done, -doing**) **1.** to unfasten and open (something closed, locked, etc.). **2.** to untie or loose (strings, etc.). **3.** to open (a parcel, sealed letter, etc.). **4.** to cause to be as if never done: *he undid all her good work.* **5.** to bring to ruin; destroy. –**undoer**, *n.*

undone[1] /ʌnˈdʌn/ *adj.* not done; not accomplished or completed; not finished.

undone[2] /ʌnˈdʌn/ *v.* **1.** past participle of **undo**. –*adj.* **2.** unfastened. **3.** reversed. **4.** brought to destruction or ruin. *–phr.* **5. come undone**, *Colloq.* (of a plan or a person) to fail due to unforeseen difficulties.

undress /ʌnˈdrɛs/ *v.t.* **1.** to remove the clothes from; disrobe. *–v.i.* **2.** to take off one's clothes. *–n.* **3.** state of having little or no clothes on. **4.** ordinary or informal dress.

undue /ʌnˈdju/ *adj.* **1.** unwarranted; excessive; too great: *undue haste.* **2.** not proper, fitting, or right; unjustified: *to exert undue influence.* **3.** not yet owing or payable.

undulate /ˈʌndʒəleɪt/ *v.i.* **1.** to have a wavy motion; rise and fall or move up and down in waves. **2.** to have a wavy form or surface; bend with successive curves in alternate directions. **–undulation**, *n.* **–undulatory**, *adj.*

unduly /ʌnˈdjuli/ *adv.* **1.** excessively. **2.** inappropriately; improperly; unjustifiably.

unearned income *n.* income earned other than through personal exertion, as from investments, inheritance, property, etc.; such income is sometimes taxed at a higher level than earned income.

unearth /ʌnˈɜθ/ *v.t.* **1.** to dig or get out of the earth; dig up. **2.** to uncover or bring to light by digging, searching, or discovery.

unearthly /ʌnˈɜθli/ *adj.* **1.** not of this earth or world. **2.** supernatural; ghostly; unnaturally strange; weird: *an unearthly scream.* **3.** *Colloq.* unreasonable; absurd: *to get up at an unearthly hour.* **–unearthliness**, *n.*

uneasy /ʌnˈizi/ *adj.* **(-sier, -siest) 1.** not easy in body or mind; uncomfortable; restless; disturbed; perturbed. **2.** not easy in manner; constrained. **–uneasily**, *adv.* **–uneasiness**, *n.*

unemployed /ʌnəmˈplɔɪd, -ɛm-/ *adj.* **1.** out of work, especially temporarily and involuntarily; without work or employment. **2.** not in productive or profitable use. *–phr.* **3. the unemployed**, those who are out of work, especially temporarily and involuntarily.

unemployment trap *n.* → **welfare trap**.

unencumbered /ʌnɛnˈkʌmbəd/ *adj.* **1.** not burdened in any way. **2.** *Law* free of encumbrance.

unequivocal /ʌniˈkwɪvəkəl, -əˈkwɪv-/ *adj.* not equivocal; not ambiguous; clear; plain: *an unequivocal reply.* **–unequivocally**, *adv.* **–unequivocalness**, *n.*

unerring /ʌnˈɜrɪŋ/ *adj.* **1.** not erring; not going astray or missing the mark; without error or mistake. **2.** unfailingly right, exact, or sure. **–unerringly**, *adv.* **–unerringness**, *n.*

unethical /ʌnˈɛθɪkəl/ *adj.* **1.** contrary to moral precept; immoral. **2.** in contravention of some code of professional conduct. **–unethically**, *adv.*

unexampled /ʌnəgˈzæmpəld/ *adj.* unlike anything previously known; without parallel; unprecedented: *unexampled kindness, unexampled lawlessness.*

unexplored /ʌnəkˈsplɔd/ *adj.* **1.** not explored; uncharted. **2.** not analysed; unknown.

unfailing /ʌnˈfeɪlɪŋ/ *adj.* **1.** not failing or giving way; totally dependable: *unfailing good humour.* **2.** never giving out; unceasing; continuous: *an unfailing supply.* **–unfailingly**, *adv.* **–unfailingness**, *n.*

unfair competition *n.* dishonest or deceptive methods of competition, as between business enterprises.

unfair dismissal *n.* the dismissal of an employee, as by sacking, making redundant, or forcing them to resign, in violation of their contract or agreement, and in a manner which is harsh and unreasonable.

unfaithful /ʌnˈfeɪθfəl/ *adj.* **1.** false to duty or promises; disloyal; perfidious; faithless. **2.** not faithfully accurate or exact, as a copy or description. **3.** having sexual intercourse with a person other than one's spouse or partner. **–unfaithfulness**, *n.*

unfeeling /ʌnˈfilɪŋ/ *adj.* **1.** not feeling; devoid of feeling; insensible or insensate. **2.** unsympathetic; callous; hard-hearted. **–unfeelingly**, *adv.* **–unfeelingness**, *n.*

unfit /ʌnˈfɪt/ *adj.* **1.** not fit; not adapted or suited; unsuitable; not deserving or good enough. **2.** unqualified or incompetent. **3.** not physically fit or in due condition. *–v.t.* **(-fitted, -fitting) 4.** to render unfit or unsuitable; disqualify. **–unfitly**, *adv.* **–unfitness**, *n.*

unflammable /ʌnˈflæməbəl/ *adj.* not flammable

unfold /ʌnˈfoʊld/ *v.t.* **1.** to spread or open out: *unfold your arms.* **2.** to develop: *the skills of an artist unfold with experience.* **3.** to reveal, display or explain. *–v.i.* **4.** to become unfolded or be revealed. **–unfolder**, *n.* **–unfoldment**, *n.*

unforeseen /ʌnfɔˈsin, -fə-/ *adj.* not predicted; unexpected.

unformed /ʌnˈfɔmd/ *adj.* **1.** not formed; not definitely shaped; shapeless or formless. **2.** undeveloped; crude. **3.** not trained or educated, as the mind. **4.** not made or created.

unfortunate /ʌnˈfɔtʃənət/ *adj.* **1.** not lucky. **2.** being a misfortune; regrettable; disastrous. **3.** likely to have undesirable results; unpropitious: *an unfortunate decision.* **4.** unsuitable; inept: *an unfortunate choice of words.* **5.** deserving of sympathy; sad. *–n.* **6.** an unfortunate person. **–unfortunately**, *adv.* **–unfortunateness**, *n.*

unfounded /ʌnˈfaʊndəd/ *adj.* without foundation; baseless: *unfounded suspicions.* **–unfoundedly**, *adv.* **–unfoundedness**, *n.*

unfriend /ʌnˈfrɛnd/ *v.t. Internet* to delete (someone) as a friend from a site on a social network. Also, **defriend.** **–unfriended**, *adj.* **–unfriending**, *n.*

unfrock /ʌnˈfrɒk/ *v.t.* to deprive of priestly status.

unfurl /ʌnˈfɜl/ *v.t.* **1.** to spread or shake out from a furled state, as a sail or a flag; unfold. *–v.i.* **2.** to become unfurled.

ungainly /ʌnˈgeɪnli/ *adj.* not graceful or shapely; awkward; clumsy; uncouth. **–ungainliness**, *n.*

ungodly /ʌnˈgɒdli/ *adj.* **1.** irreligious; impious; sinful. **2.** wicked. **3.** *Colloq.* dreadful; outrageous. *–phr.* **4. the ungodly**, wicked people. **–ungodlily**, *adv.* **–ungodliness**, *n.*

ungracious /ʌnˈgreɪʃəs/ *adj.* **1.** not gracious; lacking in gracious courtesy or affability. **2.** unacceptable; unwelcome. **–ungraciously**, *adv.* **–ungraciousness**, *n.*

unguent /ˈʌŋgwənt/ *n.* any soft preparation or salve, usually of butter-like consistency, applied to sores, etc.; an ointment. **–unguentary**, *adj.*

unhappy /ʌnˈhæpi/ *adj.* **(-pier, -piest) 1.** sad, miserable, or wretched. **2.** unfortunate; unlucky. **3.** unfavourable; inauspicious. **4.** infelicitous: *an unhappy remark.* **–unhappily**, *adv.* **–unhappiness**, *n.*

unhealthy /ʌnˈhɛlθi/ *adj.* **(-thier, -thiest) 1.** not healthy; not possessing health; not in a healthy or sound condition. **2.** characteristic of or resulting from bad health. **3.** hurtful to health; unwholesome. **4.** morally harmful; noxious. **5.** morbid: *an unhealthy interest in death.* **–unhealthily**, *adv.* **–unhealthiness**, *n.*

unheard-of /ʌnˈhɜd-ɒv/ *adj.* **1.** that was never heard of; unknown. **2.** such as was never known before; unprecedented.

unhinge /ʌnˈhɪndʒ/ *v.t.* **1.** to take (a door, etc.) off the hinges. **2.** to unbalance (the mind, etc.). **3.** to deprive of fixity or stability; throw into confusion or disorder.

uni /ˈjuni/ *n. Colloq.* a university.

uni- a word element meaning 'one', 'single', as in *unisexual.*

unicameral /juniˈkæmərəl/ *adj.* having, characterised by, or consisting of a single chamber, as a legislative assembly. Compare **bicameral**. **–unicameralism**, *n.* **–unicameralist**, *n.*

unicorn /ˈjunəkɔn/ n. **1.** a mythological animal with a single long horn, said to elude every captor save a virgin. –adj. **2.** having one horn.

uniform /ˈjunəfɔm/ adj. **1.** having always the same form or character; unvarying. **2.** without variation in appearance, colour, etc.; unbroken. **3.** (of a person, action, rule, etc.) consistent in action, opinion, effect, etc.: a uniform divorce law. **4.** agreeing with one another in form, character, appearance, etc.; alike. –n. **5.** dress of the same style, materials, and colour worn by and setting apart the members of a group, especially a military body, school, etc. **6.** a single suit of such dress. –v.t. **7.** to clothe with a uniform. –**uniformly**, adv. –**uniformity** /junəˈfɔməti/, **uniformness**, n.

uniform taxation n. (in Australia) the system of income taxation under which the federal government collects all income tax and makes reimbursement grants to the states.

unify /ˈjunəfaɪ/ v.t. (**-fied, -fying**) to form into one; make a unit of; reduce to unity. –**unifier**, n. –**unification**, n.

uni-joint /ˈjuni-dʒɔɪnt/ n. Machinery a universal joint.

unilateral /juniˈlætərəl, -ˈlætrəl, junə-/ adj. **1.** relating to, occurring on, or affecting one side only. **2.** leaning or tending to one side. **3.** affecting one side, party, or person only. **4.** undertaken or performed by one side only: unilateral disarmament. **5.** concerned with or considering only one side of a matter or question; one-sided. –**unilaterality** /ˌjunilætəˈræləti/, n. –**unilaterally**, adv.

unimpeachable /ˌʌnɪmˈpitʃəbəl/ adj. **1.** that cannot be doubted; beyond question. **2.** irreproachable; blameless. –**unimpeachability** /ˌʌnɪmpitʃəˈbiləti/, n. –**unimpeachably**, adv.

unimpressed /ˌʌnɪmˈprɛst/ adj. **1.** not impressed; unmoved: unimpressed by the sales pitch. **2.** (rhetorical understatement) extremely displeased: decidedly unimpressed with their behaviour.

unimproved /ˌʌnɪmˈpruvd/ adj. **1.** not made better, more useful, more efficient, etc. **2.** (of land) **a.** not built upon or developed. **b.** not cultivated; left in the wild state. **3.** not bred for better quality or productiveness, as crops, domestic animals, etc. **4.** not better, as health.

uninstall /ˌʌnɪnˈstɔl/ v.t. **1.** to remove from any office, position, place, etc. **2.** Computers to remove (a software application) from a digital device. –**uninstaller**, n.

uninterested /ʌnˈɪntrəstəd/ adj. **1.** having or showing no feeling of interest; indifferent. **2.** not personally concerned in something. –**uninterestedly**, adv. –**uninterestedness**, n.

union /ˈjunjən/ n. **1.** act or result of making 2 or more things into one. **2.** a number of people, societies, states, etc., associated for some common purpose. **3.** a uniting or being united, especially in marriage. **4.** → **trade union**. **5.** an association to further the interests of their members, support their wellbeing, etc.: a student union. **6.** (upper case) **a.** Rugby Union an organisation of Rugby Union clubs which acts as a regulatory body. **b.** the game, as opposed to (Rugby) League **7.** (upper case) a club offering dining and sporting services for the members of certain universities.

unionise /ˈjunjənaɪz/ v.t. to organise into a trade union; bring into or incorporate in a trade union. Also, **unionize**. –**unionisation** /ˌjunjənaɪˈzeɪʃən/, n.

unique /juˈnik/ adj. **1.** of which there is only one; sole. **2.** having no like or equal; standing alone in comparison with others; unequalled. **3.** remarkable, rare, or unusual: a unique experience. –**uniquely**, adv. –**uniqueness**, n.

unisex /ˈjunisɛks/ adj. of a style of dress, etc., which does not adhere to the traditional differentiations between the sexes.

unisexual /juniˈsɛkʃuəl/ adj. **1.** of or relating to one sex only. **2.** having only male or female organs in one individual, as an animal or a flower. –**unisexuality** /ˌjuniˌsɛkʃuˈæləti/, n. –**unisexually**, adv.

unison /ˈjunəsən/ n. **1.** coincidence in pitch of two or more notes, voices, etc. **2.** the theoretical interval between any note and a note of exactly the same pitch; a prime. **3.** a sounding together at the same pitch or in octaves, as of different voices or instruments performing the same part. **4.** a sounding together in octaves, especially of male and female voices or of higher and lower instruments of the same class. **5.** accord or agreement. –phr. **6. in unison**, in agreement, concordant; in perfect accord; simultaneously.

unissued capital n. the difference in the value of shares which a company is entitled to issue and the number which it has issued; that is, the difference between authorised capital and paid-up capital.

unit /ˈjunət/ n. **1.** person, thing, or group regarded as a single entity. **2.** a particular quantity (of length, volume, time, etc.) regarded as a single, undivided amount, especially when used as a standard against which other quantities are measured. **3.** Maths the lowest positive integer; one. **4.** Also, **home unit**. Aust., NZ one of a number of dwelling apartments in the same building, each owned under separate title, frequently by the occupier. Compare **flat²** (def. 1). **5.** Educ. a quantity of educational instruction, determined usually on hours of work and examinations passed: he has 3 units towards his degree. **6.** Med., Pharmacology the measured amount of a substance necessary to cause a certain effect: one hundred units of vitamin E. **7.** NZ a suburban electric multiple-unit train. –adj. **8.** of, relating to, equal to, containing, or forming a unit or units.

unite /juˈnaɪt/ v.t. **1.** to join in order to form one connected whole. **2.** to cause to hold together. **3.** to join in marriage. **4.** to join in action, interest, opinion, feeling, etc. –v.i. **5.** to become one in action, opinion, feelings, etc.; combine. –**united**, adj. –**uniter**, n.

unit price n. a price per agreed unit, as per kilogram, per dozen, etc.

unit trust n. Finance **1.** a trust whose management purchases shares from a number of companies. The portfolio of such shares is divided into equal units for sale to the public, whose interests are served by an independent trustee company. **2.** the units issued for sale by such a trust.

unity /ˈjunəti/ n. (pl. **-ties**) **1.** the state or fact of being one; oneness. **2.** one single thing; something complete in itself, or regarded as such. **3.** the oneness of a complex or organic whole or of an interconnected series; a whole or totality as combining all its parts into one. **4.** the fact or state of being united or combined into one, as of the parts of a whole. **5.** freedom from diversity or variety. **6.** unvaried or uniform character, as of a plan. **7.** oneness of mind, feeling, etc., as among a number of persons; concord, harmony, or agreement. **8.** Maths the number one; a quantity regarded as one. **9.** (in literature and art) a relation of all the parts or elements of a work constituting a harmonious whole and producing a single general effect. **10.** one of the three principles of dramatic structure, especially in neoclassical drama: **unity of time** (action taking place during 24 hours); **unity of place** (no extensive shifts in setting); **unity of action** (a single plot).

univalve /ˈjunivælv/ n. a mollusc having only one valve, or its shell.

universal /junəˈvɜsəl/ adj. **1.** covering, including, or coming from all or the whole (of something known or understood). **2.** affecting, concerning, or given to all: universal military training. **3.** used or understood by all: a universal language. **4.** existing everywhere.

5. *Mechanics, etc.* able to be used for all or various angles, sizes, etc. **6.** (of a joint, etc.) allowing free movement in all directions, within certain limits. *–n.* **7.** something that may be applied throughout the universe to many things, usually thought of as something which can be in many places at the same time (opposed to *particular*). **8.** a characteristic which can be possessed in common by many different things, such as *mortality*. **9.** *Philos.* (type referred to by) a general term or concept. **10.** *Mechanics* a universal joint, especially one at the end of the propeller shaft in a motor vehicle. **–universally,** *adv.* **–universality,** *n.* **–universalism, universalness,** *n.* **–universalist,** *n.*

universal health care *n.* a system of health care which aims to provide medical help to all who need it, without regard to their ability to pay.

universal service obligation *n.* (in Australia) the requirement that universal service providers make their services reasonably accessible to all citizens on an equitable basis wherever they may live. Also, **USO.**

universal service provider *n.* a telecommunications company which offers all or most of the usual means of telecommunications such as standard telephones, pay phones, internet access, etc., in a given area.

universal solvent *n.* **1.** a hypothetical substance capable of dissolving anything, once sought by alchemists. **2.** water, which is able to dissolve many things while not being a true universal solvent.

Universal Time *n.* **1.** a system of time measurement based on Greenwich Mean Time, but counted from 0 h, which is equivalent to midnight Greenwich Mean Time, introduced in 1928 and used internationally until the introduction of Coordinated Universal Time in 1972. **2.** → **Coordinated Universal Time.** *Abbrev.:* UT

universe /ˈjunəvɜs/ *n.* **1.** all of space, and all the matter and energy which it contains; the cosmos. **2.** the whole world; humankind generally: *the whole universe knows it.* **3.** a world or sphere in which something exists or prevails. **4.** a galaxy. **5.** *Logic* the collection of all the objects to which any discourse refers.

university /junəˈvɜsəti/ *n.* (*pl.* **-ties**) **1.** a place of higher learning, at which both teaching and research are carried on. **2.** members (teachers, undergraduates, graduate members, etc.) of a university. **3.** buildings of a university. **4.** governing body of a university.

Unix /ˈjunɪks/ *n. Computers* a multi-user operating system written in C. Also, **UNIX, unix.**

unkempt /ʌnˈkɛmpt/ *adj.* **1.** having the hair not combed or cared for. **2.** in an uncared-for, neglected, or untidy state. **–unkemptness,** *n.*

unleavened /ʌnˈlɛvənd/ *adj.* **1.** (of bread, etc.) not made to rise by the addition of leaven, as yeast or bicarbonate of soda. **2.** unmodified by the addition of some influence.

unless /ʌnˈlɛs, ən-/ *conj.* except on condition that; except if it be, or were, that; except when; if … not: *I shan't come unless you really want me to.*

unlettered /ʌnˈlɛtəd/ *adj.* not educated; illiterate; without knowledge of books.

unlike /ʌnˈlaɪk/ *adj.* **1.** not like; different or dissimilar; having no resemblance. *–prep.* **2.** different from; different from. **3.** uncharacteristic of: *it is unlike you to be so cheerful.* **–unlikeness,** *n.*

unlisted /ʌnˈlɪstəd/ *adj.* **1.** not listed; not entered in a list. **2.** (of stock exchange securities) not entered in the official list of those admitted for dealings. **3.** (of a telephone number) not in the directory.

unload /ʌnˈloʊd/ *v.t.* **1.** to take the load from; remove the burden, cargo, or freight from. **2.** to relieve of anything burdensome. **3.** to withdraw the charge from (a firearm). **4.** to remove or discharge (a load, etc.). **5.** to get rid or dispose of (stock, etc.) by sale. **6.** *Football* to pass

(the ball) to a teammate, often while being tackled. *–v.i.* **7.** to unload something; remove or discharge a load. **8.** *Football* to pass the ball to a teammate. **9.** *Colloq.* to express one's dissatisfaction forcefully as a means of relieving built-up resentment. **–unloader,** *n.*

unman /ʌnˈmæn/ *v.t.* **1.** to deprive of the character or qualities of a man or human being. **2.** to deprive of virility; emasculate. **3.** to deprive of manly courage or fortitude; break down the manly spirit of. **4.** to deprive of men: *to unman a ship.*

unmannerly /ʌnˈmænəli/ *adj.* not mannerly; ill-bred; rude; churlish. **–unmannerliness,** *n.*

unmask /ʌnˈmask/ *v.t.* **1.** to strip of a mask or disguise. **2.** to lay open (anything concealed); expose in the true character. **–unmasker,** *n.*

unmentionable /ʌnˈmɛnʃənəbəl/ *adj.* not mentionable; unworthy or unfit to be mentioned. **–unmentionableness,** *n.* **–unmentionably,** *adv.*

unmistakable /ʌnməsˈteɪkəbəl/ *adj.* not mistakable; admitting of no mistake; clear; plain; evident. Also, **unmistakeable. –unmistakableness,** *n.* **–unmistakably,** *adv.*

unmitigated /ʌnˈmɪtəgeɪtəd/ *adj.* **1.** not mitigated; not softened or lessened. **2.** unqualified or absolute; utter. **–unmitigatedly,** *adv.*

unmoved /ʌnˈmuvd/ *adj.* unaffected; calm; unemotional. **–unmovedly** /ʌnˈmuvədli/, *adv.*

unnatural /ʌnˈnætʃərəl, -ˈnætʃrəl/ *adj.* **1.** having or showing a lack of natural or proper instincts, feelings, etc. **2.** unusual, strange, or abnormal. **3.** artificial or affected; forced or strained. **4.** more than usually cruel or evil. **–unnaturally,** *adv.* **–unnaturalness,** *n.*

unnecessary /ʌnˈnɛsəsəri, -səsri/ *adj.* not necessary; superfluous; needless. **–unnecessarily,** *adv.* **–unnecessariness,** *n.*

unnerve /ʌnˈnɜv/ *v.t.* to deprive of nerve, strength, or physical or mental firmness; break down the self-control of; upset.

unofficial /ʌnəˈfɪʃəl/ *adj.* **1.** not official; informal. **2.** (of news) not confirmed by official sources. **3.** *Sport* (of a time or speed, or a record) not confirmed by an official body. **–unofficially,** *adv.*

unplaced /ʌnˈpleɪst/ *adj.* **1.** not assigned to, or put in, a particular place. **2.** *Horseracing* not among the first three (or sometimes four) runners.

unpleasant /ʌnˈplɛzənt/ *adj.* not pleasant; unpleasing; disagreeable. **–unpleasantly,** *adv.*

unpleasantness /ʌnˈplɛzntnəs/ *n.* **1.** the quality or state of being unpleasant. **2.** something unpleasant; an unpleasant state of affairs. **3.** a disagreement or quarrel.

unpopular /ʌnˈpɒpjələ/ *adj.* not popular; not liked by the public or by persons generally or by an individual. **–unpopularity** /ˌʌnpɒpjəˈlærəti/, *n.* **–unpopularly,** *adv.*

unprecedented /ʌnˈprɛsədɛntəd, -ˈpri-/ *adj.* having no precedent or preceding instance; never known before; unexampled. **–unprecedentedly,** *adv.*

unprepossessing /ʌnpripəˈzɛsɪŋ/ *adj.* not impressive; ordinary: *her unprepossessing appearance and manner hid a brilliant and creative mind.*

unprincipled /ʌnˈprɪnsəpəld/ *adj.* **1.** lacking sound moral principles, as a person. **2.** showing want of principle, as conduct, etc. *–phr.* **3. unprincipled in,** not instructed in the principles of. **–unprincipledness,** *n.*

unprintable /ʌnˈprɪntəbəl/ *adj.* **1.** unfit to be printed, as offending against taste, morals, the laws of libel, or the like. **2.** not able to be printed.

unprofessional /ʌnprəˈfɛʃənəl, -ˈfɛʃnəl/ *adj.* **1.** contrary to professional ethics; unbecoming in members of a profession. **2.** not professional; not relating to or connected with a profession. **3.** not belonging to a profession. **4.** not of professional quality; amateur. **–unprofessionally,** *adv.* **–unprofessionalism,** *n.*

unquestionable /ʌnˈkwɛstʃənəbəl/ *adj.* 1. not questionable; not open to question; beyond dispute or doubt; indisputable; indubitable. 2. beyond criticism; unexceptionable. **–unquestionability** /ʌnˌkwɛstʃənəˈbɪləti/, **unquestionableness**, *n.* **–unquestionably**, *adv.*

unravel /ʌnˈrævəl/ *verb* (**-elled** *or, Chiefly US,* **-eled, -elling** *or, Chiefly US,* **-eling**) *–v.t.* 1. to free from a ravelled or tangled state; disentangle; disengage the threads or fibres of (a woven or knitted fabric, a rope, etc.). 2. to free from complication or difficulty; make plain or clear; solve. *–v.i.* 3. to become unravelled. **–unraveller**, *n.* **–unravelment**, *n.*

unread /ʌnˈrɛd/ *adj.* 1. not read or perused, as a book. 2. not having gained knowledge by reading. *–phr.* 3. **unread in**, not having read (some subject or matter).

unreal /ʌnˈriːl/ *adj.* 1. not real; not substantial; imaginary; artificial; unpractical or visionary. 2. *Colloq.* **a.** unbelievably awful. **b.** unbelievably wonderful. **–unreality** /ʌnriˈæləti/, *n.* **–unreally**, *adv.*

unreasonable /ʌnˈriːzənəbəl/ *adj.* 1. not reasonable; not endowed with reason. 2. not guided by reason or good sense. 3. not agreeable to or willing to listen to reason. 4. not based on or in accordance with reason or sound judgement. 5. exceeding the bounds of reason; immoderate; exorbitant. **–unreasonableness**, *n.* **–unreasonably**, *adv.*

unredeemed /ʌnrəˈdimd, -ri-/ *adj.* 1. unmitigated, unrelieved, or unmodified, as by some good feature. 2. not recovered from pawn or by ransom.

unrelenting /ʌnrəˈlɛntɪŋ/ *adj.* 1. not relenting; not yielding to feelings of kindness or compassion. 2. not slackening in severity or determination. 3. maintaining speed or rate of advance. **–unrelentingly**, *adv.* **–unrelentingness**, *n.*

unrelieved /ʌnrəˈlivd/ *adj.* 1. not varied, moderated, or made less monotonous. 2. not provided with relief or aid. **–unrelievedly** /ʌnrəˈlivədli/, *adv.*

unremitting /ʌnrəˈmɪtɪŋ/ *adj.* not remitting or slackening; not abating for a time; incessant. **–unremittingly**, *adv.* **–unremittingness**, *n.*

unrepeatable /ʌnrəˈpiːtəbəl/ *adj.* 1. too vulgar, abusive, or otherwise unpleasant to be repeated. 2. unable to be repeated: *an unrepeatable offer of goods on sale.* **–unrepeatability** /ʌnrəˌpiːtəˈbɪləti/, *n.* **–unrepeatably**, *adv.*

unrequited /ʌnrəˈkwaɪtəd/ *adj.* (used especially of affection) not returned or reciprocated. **–unrequitedly**, *adv.* **–unrequitedness**, *n.*

unrest /ʌnˈrɛst/ *n.* 1. lack of rest; restless or uneasy state; disquiet. 2. strong, almost rebellious, dissatisfaction and agitation.

unrivalled /ʌnˈraɪvəld/ *adj.* having no rival or competitor; having no equal; peerless. Also, *Chiefly US,* **unrivaled.**

unruffled /ʌnˈrʌfəld/ *adj.* 1. (of a person) calm; undisturbed. 2. not physically ruffled or disturbed; not choppy, as the sea.

unruly /ʌnˈruːli/ *adj.* not submissive or conforming to rule; ungovernable; turbulent; refractory; lawless. **–unruliness**, *n.*

unsaturated /ʌnˈsætʃəreɪtəd/ *adj.* 1. not saturated; having the power to dissolve still more of a substance. 2. *Chem.* capable of taking on an element, etc., by direct chemical combination without the liberation of other elements or compounds, especially as a result of the presence of a double or triple bond between carbon atoms.

unsavoury /ʌnˈseɪvəri/ *adj.* 1. unpleasant in taste or smell. 2. socially or morally unpleasant or offensive. Also, **unsavory**. **–unsavourily**, *adv.* **–unsavouriness**, *n.*

unscathed /ʌnˈskeɪðd/ *adj.* not scathed; unharmed; uninjured physically or spiritually.

unscramble /ʌnˈskræmbəl/ *v.t.* 1. to bring out of a scrambled condition; reduce to order. 2. to restore (a scrambled telephone message, or the like) to intelligibility. **–unscrambler**, *n.*

unscrew /ʌnˈskruː/ *v.t.* 1. to draw the screw or screws from; unfasten by withdrawing screws. 2. to remove (the lid of a screw-top jar, etc.) by turning. 3. to loosen or withdraw (a screw, screwlike plug, etc.). *–v.i.* 4. to permit of being unscrewed. 5. to become unscrewed.

unscrupulous /ʌnˈskrupjələs/ *adj.* unrestrained by scruples; conscienceless; unprincipled. **–unscrupulously**, *adv.* **–unscrupulousness**, *n.*

unseat /ʌnˈsiːt/ *v.t.* 1. to throw from a saddle, as a rider. 2. to depose from an official seat or from office. 3. to displace from a seat.

unsecured /ʌnsəˈkjʊəd/ *adj.* 1. not made secure or fastened. 2. not insured against loss, as by a mortgage, bond, pledge, etc.

unseen /ʌnˈsiːn/ *adj.* 1. not seen; unperceived; unobserved; invisible. 2. (of passages of writing or music) not previously seen. *–n.* 3. an unprepared passage for translation, as in an examination.

unsettle /ʌnˈsɛtl/ *v.t.* to bring out of a settled state; cause to be no longer firmly fixed or established; render unstable; disturb; disorder. 2. to shake or weaken (beliefs, feelings, etc.); derange (the mind, etc.). *–v.i.* 3. to become unfixed or disordered.

unsettled /ʌnˈsɛtld/ *adj.* 1. not settled; not fixed in a place or abode. 2. not populated, as a region. 3. not fixed or stable, as conditions, opinions, etc.; without established order, as times. 4. liable to change, as weather. 5. undetermined, as a point at issue. 6. not adjusted, closed, or disposed of finally, as an account. **–unsettledness**, **unsettlement**, *n.*

unsightly /ʌnˈsaɪtli/ *adj.* not pleasing to the sight; forming an unpleasing sight. **–unsightliness**, *n.*

unskilled /ʌnˈskɪld/ *adj.* 1. of or relating to workers lacking specialised training or ability. 2. not skilled (in some activity). 3. not requiring or exhibiting skill.

unsociable /ʌnˈsoʊʃəbəl/ *adj.* not sociable; having, showing, or marked by a disinclination to friendly social relations. **–unsociability** /ˌʌnsoʊʃəˈbɪləti/, **unsociableness**, *n.* **–unsociably**, *adv.*

unsound /ʌnˈsaʊnd/ *adj.* 1. not sound; diseased, as the body or mind. 2. decayed, as timber or fruit; impaired or defective, as goods. 3. not solid or firm, as foundations. 4. not well-founded or valid; fallacious: *unsound argument.* 5. not financially strong; unreliable: *an unsound business.* **–unsoundly**, *adv.* **–unsoundness**, *n.*

unsparing /ʌnˈspeərɪŋ/ *adj.* 1. not sparing; liberal or profuse. 2. unmerciful. **–unsparingly**, *adv.* **–unsparingness**, *n.*

unspeakable /ʌnˈspiːkəbəl/ *adj.* 1. inexpressibly bad or objectionable. 2. impossible to express in words; unutterable; inexpressible. 3. not speakable; that may not be spoken. **–unspeakably**, *adv.*

unspoken /ʌnˈspoʊkən/ *adj.* 1. not spoken; not expressed aloud. 2. understood without needing to be uttered.

unstable /ʌnˈsteɪbəl/ *adj.* 1. not stable; not firm or firmly fixed; unsteady. 2. liable to fall, change, or cease. 3. not steadfast; inconstant; wavering. 4. lacking emotional stability. 5. *Chem.* denoting compounds which readily decompose. **–unstableness**, *n.* **–unstably**, *adv.*

unsteady /ʌnˈstɛdi/ *adj.* 1. not steady; not firmly fixed; not secure or stable. 2. fluctuating or wavering; unsteadfast. 3. irregular or uneven. *–v.t.* (**-died, -dying**) 4. to make unsteady. **–unsteadily**, *adv.* **–unsteadiness**, *n.*

unsubscribe /ʌnsəbˈskraɪb/ *v.i.* to have one's email address removed from an electronic mailing list.

unsubstantiated /ʌnsəbˈstænʃieɪtəd/ *adj.* without supporting evidence: *an unsubstantiated accusation.*

unsuited /ʌn'sutəd/ *adj.* **1.** not suited or fit; inappropriate: *unsuited to the purpose to which it is put.* **2.** badly matched; incompatible.

unsung /ʌn'sʌŋ/ *adj.* **1.** not sung; not uttered or rendered by singing. **2.** not celebrated in, or as if in, song.

unswerving /ʌn'swɜvɪŋ/ *adj.* steady; constant; not turning aside: *unswerving loyalty.* –**unswervingly,** *adv.*

untapped /ʌn'tæpt/ *adj.* **1.** not drawn on, as resources, potentialities, etc.: *an untapped fund of money.* **2.** not tapped.

untenable /ʌn'tɛnəbəl/ *adj.* **1.** incapable of being held against attack. **2.** incapable of being maintained against argument, as an opinion, scheme, etc. **3.** not fit to be occupied. –**untenability** /,ʌntɛnə'bɪləti/, *n.* –**untenably,** *adv.*

unthinkable /ʌn'θɪŋkəbəl/ *adj.* **1.** inconceivable; unimaginable. **2.** not to be considered; utterly out of the question. –**unthinkably,** *adv.*

unthinking /ʌn'θɪŋkɪŋ/ *adj.* **1.** not thinking; thoughtless; heedless. **2.** indicating lack of thought or reflection. **3.** not given to reflection; uncritical. **4.** not possessing the faculty of thought. –**unthinkingly,** *adv.* –**unthinkingness,** *n.*

untick /ʌn'tɪk/ *v.t. Computers* to alter the status of (an option) on the internet from ticked to blank by clicking on it. Also, **uncheck.**

untidy /ʌn'taɪdi/ *adj.* (**-tidier, -tidiest**) **1.** not tidy or neat; slovenly; disordered. –*v.t.* (**-tidied, -tidying**) **2.** to make untidy; disorder. –**untidily,** *adv.* –**untidiness,** *n.*

untie /ʌn'taɪ/ *v.t.* to loosen or unfasten (anything tied); let or set loose by undoing a knot.

until /ʌn'tɪl/ *conj.* **1.** up to the time that or when; till. **2.** (with negatives) before: *he did not come until the meeting was half over.* –*prep.* **3.** onward to, or till (a specified time); up to the time of (some occurrence). **4.** (with negatives) before: *he did not go until night.*

untimely /ʌn'taɪmli/ *adj.* **1.** not timely; not occurring at a suitable time or season; ill-timed or inopportune. **2.** premature; not fully mature or ripe. –*adv.* **3.** unseasonably. –**untimeliness,** *n.*

unto /'ʌntu/ *prep. Archaic* **1.** to (in its various uses, except as the accompaniment of the infinitive). **2.** until; till.

untold /ʌn'toʊld/ *adj.* **1.** not told; not related; not revealed. **2.** more than can be numbered or enumerated; uncounted. **3.** *Colloq.* unbelievable.

untouchable /ʌn'tʌtʃəbəl/ *adj.* **1.** that may not be touched; of a nature such that it cannot be touched; not palpable; intangible. **2.** too distant to be touched. **3.** vile or loathsome to the touch. **4.** unable to be equalled. –*n.* **5.** (*sometimes upper case*) a member of the lowest caste in India, whose touch was traditionally believed to defile a high-caste Hindu.

untoward /ʌntə'wɔd, ʌn'toʊəd/ *adj.* **1.** unfavourable or unfortunate. **2.** unseemly. –**untowardly,** *adv.* –**untowardness,** *n.*

untrue /ʌn'tru/ *adj.* **1.** not true, as to a person or a cause, to fact, or to a standard. **2.** unfaithful; false. **3.** incorrect or inaccurate. –**untrueness,** *n.* –**untruly,** *adv.*

unusual /ʌn'juʒuəl/ *adj.* not usual, common, or ordinary; uncommon in amount or degree; of an exceptional kind. –**unusually,** *adv.* –**unusualness,** *n.*

unutterable /ʌn'ʌtərəbəl, -'trəbəl/ *adj.* **1.** not communicable by utterance; incapable of being expressed. **2.** inexpressibly great or remarkable; unspeakable. **3.** incapable of being uttered; unpronounceable. –**unutterably,** *adv.*

unveil /ʌn'veɪl/ *v.t.* **1.** to remove a veil from; disclose to view. **2.** to disclose, as if by removing a veil; reveal. –*v.i.* **3.** to remove a veil; reveal oneself; become unveiled. –**unveiling,** *n.*

unwarranted /ʌn'wɒrəntəd/ *adj.* **1.** not justified, confirmed, or supported: *an unwarranted supposition.* **2.** not authorised, as actions. –**unwarrantedly,** *adv.*

unwieldy /ʌn'wildi/ *adj.* **1.** not wieldy; wielded with difficulty; not readily handled or managed in use or action, as from size, shape, or weight. **2.** ungainly; awkward. –**unwieldily,** *adv.* –**unwieldiness,** *n.*

unwind /ʌn'waɪnd/ *verb* (**-wound, -winding**) –*v.t.* **1.** to undo (something wound); loose or separate, as what is wound. **2.** to remove the windings from around (something). **3.** to disentangle. –*v.i.* **4.** to become unwound. **5.** to relax or calm down.

unwitting /ʌn'wɪtɪŋ/ *adj.* **1.** not witting or knowing; ignorant; unaware; unconscious. **2.** performed unintentionally or unknowingly; unpremeditated. –**unwittingly,** *adv.* –**unwittingness,** *n.*

unworldly /ʌn'wɜldli/ *adj.* **1.** not worldly; not seeking material advantage or gain; spiritually minded. **2.** naive; unsophisticated. **3.** not terrestrial; unearthly. –**unworldliness,** *n.*

unwritten /ʌn'rɪtn/ *adj.* **1.** not written; not reduced to or recorded in writing. **2.** not actually formulated or expressed; customary. **3.** containing no writing; blank.

unwritten law *n.* **1.** the body of law which rests for its authority on custom, convention, etc., as distinguished from law originating in written command, judicial decision, statute, or decree. **2.** a custom or social convention.

unzip /ʌn'zɪp/ *verb* (**-zipped, -zipping**) –*v.t.* **1.** to open the zip of (a garment). **2.** *Computers* → **decompress** (def. 2). –*v.i.* **3.** to become unzipped.

up /ʌp/ *adv.* **1.** to, towards, or in a more elevated position: *to climb up to the top of a ladder.* **2.** into the air: *to throw up a ball.* **3.** out of the ground: *to dig up potatoes.* **4.** to or in an erect position: *to stand up.* **5.** out of bed: *to get up.* **6.** above the horizon: *the moon came up.* **7.** to or at any point that is considered higher, as the north, a capital city, or the like. **8.** to or at a source, origin, centre, or the like: *to follow a stream up to its source.* **9.** to or at a higher point or degree in a scale, as of rank, size, value, pitch, etc. **10.** to or at a point of equal advance, extent, etc.: *to catch up in a race.* **11.** ahead; into a leading or more advanced position: *to move up into the lead.* **12.** well advanced or versed, as in a subject: *to keep up in nuclear physics.* **13.** in or into activity, operation, etc.: *to set up vibrations.* **14.** in or into a state of agitation or excitement: *worked up.* **15.** into existence, view, prominence, or consideration: *a problem has cropped up; the lost papers have turned up; his case comes up in court on Thursday.* **16.** to a state of maturity: *to bring up a child.* **17.** into or in a place of safekeeping, storage, retirement, etc.: *to lay up riches.* **18.** to a state of completion; to an end: *to finish something up.* **19.** in or into a state of union, contraction, etc.: *to add up a column of figures; to fold up a blanket.* **20.** to the required or final point: *to pay up one's debts; to burn up rubbish.* **21.** to a standstill: *to rein up; seize up.* **22.** *US* equally; each; apiece; all: *the score was seven points up.* **23.** *Naut.* towards or facing into the wind. –*prep.* **24.** to, towards, or at a higher place on or in: *up the stairs; up a tree.* **25.** to, towards, near, or at a higher station, condition, or rank in. **26.** to, towards, or at a farther or higher point of: *up the street.* **27.** towards the source, origin, etc., of: *up the stream.* **28.** towards or in the interior of (a region, etc.): *the explorers went up the mulga.* **29.** in a course or direction contrary to that of: *to sail up wind.* **30.** *Colloq.* towards or at: *up King's Cross; up the Junction.* –*adj.* **31.** upwards; going or directed upwards. **32.** travelling towards a terminus or centre: *an up train.* **33.** in an upright position or pointing upwards: *the signal is up.* **34.** standing and speaking: *the prime minister was up* *for three hours.* **35.** out of bed: *I have been up since six o'clock.* **36.** risen above the horizon: *the sun is up.* **37.** at a high point or full: *the tide is up.* **38.** in the air; above the ground: *the aeroplane is 2000 metres up.* **39.** on horseback; in the saddle. **40.** well informed or advanced, as in a subject: *to be up in mathematics.* **41.** in activity: *the wind is up.* **42.** (especially of a computer) operational. **43.** under consideration; on offer: *a candidate up for election.* **44.** appearing before a court or the like on some charge: *he is up for speeding again.* **45.** in the process of going on or happening, especially something amiss: *they wondered what was up.* **46.** in a state of agitation or excitement: *his anger was up.* **47.** impassable to wheeled traffic, as a road under repair. **48.** in a leading or advanced position: *to be up in social standing.* **49.** winning or having won money at gambling or the like: *he was $50 up after an hour in the casino.* **50.** *Games* winning or ahead of an opponent by a specified number of points, holes, etc. *–n.* **51.** an upward movement; an ascent. **52.** a rise of fortune, mood, etc.: *to have one's ups and downs.* *–verb* (**upped**, **upping**) *–v.t.* **53.** to put or take up. **54.** to make larger; step up: *to up output.* **55.** to raise; go better than (a preceding wager). **56.** *Naut.* to turn (the helm) to windward, thus turning the ship's head away from the wind. *–v.i.* **57.** to get or start up: *to up and leave.* *–interj.* **58.** a command to rise or stand up. *–phr.* **59. be up each other** or **be up one another**, *Aust. Colloq.* to be behaving in a sycophantic or toadying fashion to each other. **60. be up oneself**, *Aust., NZ Colloq.* to have an unjustifiably high opinion of oneself; be self-deluding. **61. be up someone**, *Colloq.* **a.** (*taboo*) (of a man) to be engaged in sexual intercourse with someone: *he was up her like a lizard up a log.* **b.** *Aust.* to be angry with someone: *she was up him for being late.* **62. get up someone**, *Colloq.* to have sexual intercourse with someone. **63. in two ups**, *Colloq.* in a very short time. **64. on the up and up**, **a.** tending upwards; improving; having increasing success. **b.** *Aust. Colloq.* honest, frank, or credible. **65. up ...**, an exclamation of strong support for the person, team, etc., specified: *up the mighty Blues!* **66. up against**, faced with: *they are up against enormous problems.* **67. up against it**, *Colloq.* in difficulties; in severe straits. **68. up and about**, active; out of bed, especially after recovering from an illness. **69. up at** (or **in**), at or in any place considered higher, in altitude (*up at the mountains it is snowing*), or away from the centre of population (*up here in the bush*). **70. up close and personal** (**with**), in an intimate relationship (with). **71. up for**, *Colloq.* **a.** liable to pay: *you'll be up for $100 if you break that.* **b.** willing to undertake or participate in (something challenging): *are you up for a game of squash?* **72. up sticks**, to move away from one's present location or place of residence. **73. up to**, **a.** engaged in; doing: *what are you up to?* **b.** incumbent upon, as a duty: *it is up to him to make the next move.* **c.** as many as and no more: *I will take up to eight pupils.* **d.** as far as and no farther: *he is up to his knees in water.* **e.** *Colloq.* capable of: *he is not up to the job.* **f.** to any place considered higher, in altitude, or being more northerly in geographical location. **74. up to mud** (or **putty**) (or **shit**), *Aust. Colloq.* broken down, worthless. **75. up with**, in a high or favourable position in relation to: *up with the leaders.* **76. up with ...**, an exclamation of strong support for something specified: *up with the revolution!* **77. up you** (**for the rent**), *Colloq.* an exclamation of insolent or abusive dismissal. **78. up your arse** or **up yours**, *Colloq.* (*taboo*) an exclamation of insolent or angry dismissal. **79. who's up who** (**and who's paying the rent**), *Colloq.* what are the alliances, economic, political or sexual, within a particular group of people.

up- a prefixal, attributive use of **up**, in its various meanings, as in *upland, upshot, upheaval.*

up-and-coming *adj.* about to become successful, popular, powerful, etc.: *an up-and-coming politician.* Also, (*especially in predicative use*), **up and coming**. **–up-and-comer**, *n.*

Upanishad /uˈpænɪʃəd, -ˈpʌn-, -ˈʃæd/ *n.* the chief religious writings of ancient Hinduism, giving in more detail the mystical knowledge contained in the earlier Vedas.

up-beat *–n.* **1.** *Music* **a.** the last beat of a bar, especially when the piece of music or section or phrase starts with a note on that beat. **b.** the introductory beat of a conductor when bringing in the orchestra. *–adj.* **2.** *Colloq.* optimistic; cheerful. Also, **upbeat**.

upbraid /ʌpˈbreɪd/ *v.t.* **1.** to reproach for some fault or offence; reprove severely; chide. **2.** to censure or find fault with (things). *–v.i.* **3.** to utter reproaches. **–upbraider**, *n.* **–upbraiding**, *n., adj.*

upbringing /ˈʌpbrɪŋɪŋ/ *n.* the bringing up or rearing of a person from childhood; care and training devoted to the young while growing up.

up-country *adj.* **1.** being or living remote from the coast or border; interior: *an up-country town.* **2.** (*derog.*) unsophisticated. *–n.* **3.** the interior of the country. *–adv.* **4.** towards or in the interior of a country.

update *v.t.* /ʌpˈdeɪt/ **1.** to bring up to date. *–n.* /ˈʌpdeɪt/ **2.** the act of updating: *an update on the file.* **3.** an updated version; revision: *an update of an earlier bulletin.* **–updateable, updatable**, *adj.* **–updateability, updatability**, *n.*

updo /ˈʌpdu/ *n.* a hairstyle in which the hair is arranged on the head instead of falling freely, as in a beehive, bun, chignon, ponytail, etc.

up-end *v.t.* **1.** to set on end, as a barrel. **2.** to upset or alter drastically. *–v.i.* **3.** to be turned on end.

UPF /ju pi ˈɛf/ *n.* a measure of the effectiveness of clinically treated cloth made up into clothing in protecting the skin from ultraviolet radiation. Compare **SPF**. Also, **ultraviolet protection factor**.

up-front *adj.* **1.** Also, **upfront**. placed in a position of leadership or responsibility: *the up-front leader.* **2.** straightforward; open. **3.** (of money) payable in advance: *an up-front fee.* *–adv.* **4.** in advance: *to pay up-front.*

upgrade *v.t.* /ʌpˈgreɪd/ **1.** to assign (a person, job, or the like) to a higher status, usually with a larger salary. **2.** to improve. **3.** to allocate to (someone) a seat on a plane, etc., in a class higher than the one ticketed. *–n.* /ˈʌpgreɪd/ **4.** such a seat reallocation: *to give someone an upgrade.* **5.** *Computers* a new version of a product, usually software, designed to replace a previous version of the product. **6.** *US* an uphill slope. *–adj., adv.* /ˈʌpgreɪd, ʌpˈgreɪd/ **7.** *US* → **uphill**. *–phr.* **8. on the upgrade**, improving; up-and-coming. **–upgrading, upgradation**, *n.* **–upgradeable, upgradable**, *adj.*

upheaval /ʌpˈhivəl/ *n.* **1.** the act of upheaving. **2.** the state of being upheaved. **3.** a thorough, violent, or revolutionary change or disturbance, especially in a society. **4.** *Geol.* an upward warping of a part of the earth's crust, forcing certain areas into a relatively higher position than before.

upheave /ʌpˈhiv/ *v.t.* **1.** to heave or lift up; raise up or aloft. **2.** to disturb or change violently or radically. *–v.i.* **3.** to be lifted up; rise as if thrust up.

uphill *adv.* /ʌpˈhɪl/ **1.** up, or as if up, the slope of a hill; upwards. *–adj.* /ˈʌphɪl/ **2.** going or tending upwards on or as on a hill. **3.** laboriously fatiguing or difficult. *–n.* /ˈʌphɪl/ **4.** an ascent or rise. *–phr.* **5. an uphill battle**, a task to be completed or objective to be reached only with great difficulty.

uphold /ʌpˈhoʊld/ v.t. (**-held, -holding**) **1.** to support, sustain, or preserve unimpaired: *to uphold the old order.* **2.** to keep up, or keep from sinking; support. **3.** to support or maintain, as by advocacy or agreement: *to uphold the decision of a lower court.* –**upholder,** n.

upholster /ʌpˈhoʊlstə/ v.t. **1.** to provide (stools, arm-chairs, sofas, etc.) with coverings, cushions, stuffing, springs, etc. **2.** to cover or cushion in the manner of upholstery. –v.i. **3.** to do upholstery work. –**uphol-sterer,** n. –**upholstery,** n.

upkeep /ˈʌpkip/ n. **1.** the process of keeping up or maintaining; the maintenance, or keeping in operation, due condition, and repair, of an establishment, a ma-chine, etc. **2.** the cost of this, including operating expenses, cost of renewal or repair, etc.

upland /ˈʌplənd/ n. an area of high ground; a stretch of hilly or mountainous country.

uplift v.t. /ʌpˈlɪft/ **1.** to lift up; raise. **2.** to raise socially or morally. **3.** to raise emotionally or spiritually. –n. /ˈʌplɪft/ **4.** the act of lifting up or raising. **5.** the work of improving socially or morally. **6.** a great emotional or spiritual lift. –**uplifter,** n. –**upliftment,** n.

upload /ˈʌploʊd/ *Computers* –v.t. **1.** to transfer or copy (data) from a computer to a larger system, as from a personal computer to a network or mainframe com-puter. –n. **2.** the act or process of uploading data. **3.** the data uploaded in such an operation.

up-market adj. **1.** of or relating to commercial services and goods of superior status, quality, and price. **2.** su-perior in style or production. See **down-market.**

upon /əˈpɒn/ prep. **1.** up and on; upwards so as to get or be on: *to climb upon a table.* **2.** in an elevated position on. **3.** on, in any of various senses (used as an equi-valent of *on* with no added idea of ascent or elevation, and preferred in certain cases only for euphonic or metrical reasons).

upper /ˈʌpə/ adj. **1.** higher (than something implied) or highest, as in place, or position, or in a scale: *the upper slopes of a mountain; upper register of a voice.* **2.** oc-cupying or consisting of high or rising ground, or far-ther into the interior. **3.** forming the higher of a pair of corresponding things or sets. **4.** (of a surface) facing upwards. **5.** superior, as in rank, dignity, or station. **6.** higher or highest in respect of wealth, rank, office, birth, influence, etc.: *the upper classes; the upper or-ders.* **7.** (*upper case*) *Geol.* denoting a later division of a period, system, or the like: *the Upper Devonian.* –n. **8.** anything which is higher (than another, as of a pair) or highest. **9.** the part of a shoe or boot above the sole, comprising the vamp and quarters. **10.** *Colloq.* a stimulant, as amphetamine, etc.: *uppers and downers.* **11.** *Colloq.* a pleasant or exhilarating experience. –phr. **12. be (down) on one's uppers,** *Colloq.* to be reduced to poverty or want.

upper case n. **1.** the capital form of the letters: *to put the heading in upper case.* **2.** *Printing* the upper half of a pair of cases, which contains the capital letters of the alphabet.

upper-case adj. **1.** (of a letter) capital. **2.** *Printing* re-lating to or belonging in the upper case.

upper chamber n. → **upper house.**

upper class n. the class of people socially and con-ventionally regarded as being higher or highest in the social hierarchy and commonly identified by wealth or aristocratic birth. –**upper-class,** adj.

uppercut /ˈʌpəkʌt/ n. a swinging blow directed upwards, as to an adversary's chin.

upper hand n. the dominating or controlling position; the advantage.

upper house n. one of two branches of a legislature, generally smaller and less representative than the lower branch, usually acting as a house of review, rarely

formulating legislation and lacking the constitutional power to initiate any financial legislation, as the Senate in the Australian Parliament. Also, **upper chamber.**

uppermost /ˈʌpəmoʊst/ adj. **1.** highest in place, order, rank, power, etc. **2.** topmost; predominant; foremost. –adv. **3.** in the highest or topmost place. **4.** in the foremost place in respect of rank or precedence.

uppity /ˈʌpəti/ adj. *Colloq.* affecting superiority; pres-umptuous; self-assertive. Also, **uppish.**

upright /ˈʌpraɪt/ adj. **1.** straight upward or vertical, in position or posture. **2.** raised or directed vertically. **3.** honest or just; righteous. –n. **4.** the state of being upright or vertical. **5.** (of timber, etc.) something standing straight upward. **6.** an upright piano. –adv. **7.** in an upright position or direction. –**uprightly,** adv. –**uprightness,** n.

uprising /ˈʌpraɪzɪŋ, ʌpˈraɪzɪŋ/ n. **1.** an insurrection or revolt. **2.** the act of rising. **3.** an ascent or acclivity.

uproar /ˈʌprɔ/ n. violent and noisy disturbance, as of a multitude; tumultuous or confused noise or din.

uproarious /ʌpˈrɔriəs/ adj. **1.** characterised by or in a state of uproar; tumultuous. **2.** making or given to making an uproar, or disorderly and noisy, as an as-sembly, persons, etc. **3.** confused and loud, as sounds, utterances, etc. **4.** expressed by or producing uproar. **5.** extremely funny. –**uproariously,** adv. –**uproarious-ness,** n.

uproot /ʌpˈrut/ v.t. **1.** to root up; tear up by or as if by the roots. **2.** to eradicate; remove utterly. **3.** to remove (people) from their native environment; displace. –**uprooter,** n.

upscale /ˈʌpskeɪl/ adj. *Colloq.* **1.** of high quality; su-perior: *an upscale restaurant; upscale decor.* **2.** affluent: *an upscale suburb.*

upsell /ˈʌpsɛl/ v.t. (**-sold, -selling**) to effect the sale of (a product) which is more expensive than the one the customer intended to buy. –**upselling,** n.

upset verb /ʌpˈsɛt/ (**-set, -setting**) –v.t. **1.** to overturn: *to upset the boat.* **2.** to spill by knocking over: *to upset the cup.* **3.** to throw into disorder: *to upset the pile of pa-pers.* **4.** to disturb (someone) mentally or emotionally; distress. **5.** to make ill, especially in the stomach. **6.** to make ineffective: *to upset someone's plans.* **7.** to defeat (a competitor or opponent), especially contrary to ex-pectation. –v.i. **8.** to become overturned. –n. /ˈʌpsɛt/ **9.** a physical upsetting or being upset. **10.** the act or fact of disordering (ideas, patterns, etc.). **11.** a slight illness, especially of the stomach. **12.** an emotional disturbance. **13.** a quarrel. **14.** a defeat, especially unexpected. –adj. /ˈʌpsɛt, ʌpˈsɛt/ **15.** emotionally disturbed. **16.** over-turned; capsized.

upshot /ˈʌpʃɒt/ n. **1.** the final issue, the conclusion, or the result. **2.** the conclusion (of an argument).

upside down adj. **1.** with the upper part undermost. **2.** in complete disorder; topsy-turvy.

upstage adv. /ʌpˈsteɪdʒ/ **1.** at or to the back of the stage. –adj. /ˈʌpsteɪdʒ/ **2.** of or relating to the back of the stage. **3.** coldly proud; haughty; aloof. –v.t. /ʌpˈsteɪdʒ/ (**-staged, -staging**) **4.** to steal attention from (another) by placing oneself in a more favourable position in word or action.

upstairs adv. /ʌpˈstɛəz/ **1.** up the stairs; to or on an upper floor. **2.** *Colloq.* into the air. **3.** *Colloq.* to or in a higher rank or office. –adj. /ˈʌpstɛəz/ **4.** on or relating to an upper floor. –n. /ˈʌpstɛəz/ **5.** an upper storey or storeys; that part of a building above the ground floor. –phr. **6. kick upstairs,** *Colloq.* to promote (someone) especially to a position of diminished power, in order to get them out of the way.

upstanding /ˈʌpstændɪŋ/ (*esp. in predicative use*) /ʌp-ˈstændɪŋ/ adj. **1.** standing erect; erect and tall, especially of persons or animals; erect, well grown and vigorous in body or form. **2.** straightforward, open, or independent; upright; honourable. **3.** standing up: *be upstanding and charge your glasses.*

upstart /ˈʌpstat/ *n.* **1.** someone who has risen suddenly from a humble position to wealth or power, or to assumed consequence; a parvenu. **2.** someone who is pretentious and objectionable through being thus exalted. –*adj.* **3.** (of persons, families, etc.) newly or suddenly risen to importance; without pedigree. **4.** lately come into existence or notice. **5.** characteristic of an upstart.

upstream *adv.* /ʌpˈstrim/ **1.** towards or in the higher part of a stream; against the current. –*adj.* /ˈʌpstrim/ **2.** situated farther up the stream. **3.** moving or facing upstream.

upsurge *v.i.* /ʌpˈsɜdʒ/ (**-surged, -surging**) **1.** to surge up. –*n.* /ˈʌpsɜdʒ/ **2.** a surging upwards. –**upsurgeance,** *n.*

upswell /ˈʌpswɛl/ *v.i.* **1.** to rise up by swelling or as by swelling. –*n.* **2.** such a rising up: *the upswell of the ocean*; *the upswell of emotion*; *the upswell of demand.*

uptake /ˈʌpteɪk/ *n.* **1.** the action of understanding or comprehension; mental grasp. **2.** the act of taking up. **3.** *Med.* absorption. **4.** a pipe or passage leading upwards from below, as for conducting smoke, a current of air, or the like. –*phr.* **5. quick on the uptake,** quick to grasp new or complicated ideas, or to learn. **6. slow on the uptake,** slow to grasp new or complicated ideas, or to learn.

up-tempo *n.* **1.** a fast rhythm. –*adj.* **2.** rhythmic; fast.

uptight /ˈʌptaɪt/ *adj. Colloq.* **1.** tense, nervous, or irritable. **2.** conforming to established conventions, especially despised conventions.

up-to-date *adj.* **1.** extending to the present time; including the latest facts: *an up-to-date record.* **2.** in accordance with the latest or newest standards, ideas, or style; modern. **3.** (of persons, etc.) keeping up with the times, as in information, ideas, methods, style, etc. Also, (*especially in predicative use*), **up to date.** –**up-to-dateness,** *n.*

uptrend /ˈʌptrɛnd/ *n.* **1.** an upward trend: *an uptrend in interest rates.* –*v.i.* **2.** to tend in an upward direction, as of rates, etc.

upturn *v.t.* /ʌpˈtɜn/ **1.** to turn up or over. **2.** to direct upwards. –*v.i.* /ʌpˈtɜn/ **3.** to turn upwards. –*n.* /ˈʌptɜn/ **4.** an upward turn, or a changing and rising movement, as in prices, business, etc.

upvalue /ˈʌpvælju/ *v.t.* to revalue (a currency) upwards. –**upvaluation** /ˌʌpvæljuˈeɪʃən/, *n.*

upward /ˈʌpwəd/ *adj.* **1.** directed, tending, or moving towards a higher point or level; ascending. –*adv.* **2.** upwards. –**upwardly,** *adv.*

upwards /ˈʌpwədz/ *adv.* **1.** towards a higher place or position; in a vertical direction. **2.** towards a higher level, degree, or standard, as of thought, feeling, distinction, rank, age, amount, etc. **3.** towards the source, as of a stream; towards the interior, as of a country; towards the centre, most important part, etc. **4.** so as to be uppermost; in or facing the highest position. **5.** to or into later life. –*phr.* **6. upwards of,** more than; above. Also, **upward.**

upwind *adv.* /ʌpˈwɪnd/ **1.** against the wind; contrary to the course of the wind. **2.** towards or in the direction from which the wind is blowing: *he was standing upwind of us and could be heard clearly.* –*adj.* /ˈʌpwɪnd/ **3.** tending, facing, or moving towards the direction from which the wind is blowing.

uranium /juˈreɪniəm/ *n.* a white, lustrous, radioactive, metallic element, having compounds which are used in photography and in colouring glass. The natural element consists of 99.28 per cent of the isotope U-238 and 0.71 per cent of the isotope U-235. The latter is capable of sustaining a nuclear chain reaction and is the basis of the atomic bomb and nuclear reactors. *Symbol:* U; *relative atomic mass*: 238.03; *atomic number*: 92; *density*: 19.05.

urano- a word element meaning 'heaven', as in *uranography.*

urban /ˈɜbən/ *adj.* **1.** of, relating to, or comprising a city or town. **2.** living in a city or cities. **3.** occurring or situated in a city or town. **4.** characteristic of or accustomed to cities; citified. –**urbanite,** *n., adj.*

urban consolidation *n.* the encouragement of development within existing urbanised areas, limiting development on non-urbanised land, so as to maximise the use of existing infrastructure.

urbane /ɜˈbeɪn/ *adj.* **1.** having the refinement and manners considered to be characteristic of city-dwellers; civilised; sophisticated. **2.** smoothly polite; suave or bland. **3.** exhibiting elegance, refinement, or courtesy, as in expression. –*n.* **4.** one of a minority group which, to further its aims, uses violence, as bombing, machine-gun attack, etc., in an urban situation. –**urbanely,** *adv.* –**urbaneness, urbanity** /ɜˈbænəti/, *n.*

urbanism /ˈɜbənɪzəm/ *n.* the study of cities, especially in relation to the social, economic, political, and cultural systems which develop within them and how these are influenced by the nexus between communities and the built environment and the hinterland. –**urbanist,** *n.*

urban sprawl *n.* the outer areas of a city, especially where development is considered to have been unplanned and undesirable.

urchin /ˈɜtʃən/ *n.* **1.** a small boy or youngster, especially one who is mischievous and impudent, or ragged and shabbily dressed. **2.** → **sea urchin.** –*adj.* **3.** being, resembling, or characteristic of an urchin (def. 1)

-ure a suffix of abstract nouns indicating action, result, and instrument, as in *legislature, pressure.*

urea /juˈriə, ˈjuriə/ *n.* a colourless crystalline substance, $CO(NH_2)_2$, occurring in urine, used in fertilisers and in making plastics and adhesives; the principal nitrogenous excretory product of mammals, amphibians, elasmobranch fishes, and some reptiles. –**ureal,** *adj.*

-uret a noun suffix in names of some chemical compounds, having the same force as **-ide,** as in *arseniuret.*

ureter /juˈritə/ *n. Anat., Zool.* a muscular duct or tube conveying the urine from a kidney to the bladder or cloaca. –**ureteral, ureteric** /jurəˈtɛrɪk/, *adj.*

urethr- variant of **urethro-** before vowels, as in *urethritis.*

urethra /juˈriθrə/ *n.* (*pl.* **-thrae** /-θri/ *or* **-thras**) *Anat.* the membranous tube which extends from the bladder to the exterior. In the male it conveys semen as well as urine. –**urethral,** *adj.*

urethro- a word element representing **urethra,** as in *urethroscope.* Also, **urethr-.**

urge /ɜdʒ/ *verb* (**urged, urging**) –*v.t.* **1.** to endeavour to induce or persuade, as by entreaties or earnest recommendations; entreat or exhort earnestly: *urge a person to take more care.* **2.** to press by persuasion or recommendation, as for acceptance, performance, or use; recommend or advocate earnestly: *urge a plan of action.* **3.** to press (something) upon the attention: *urge a claim.* **4.** to insist on, allege, or assert with earnestness: *urge the need for haste.* **5.** to push or force along; impel with force or vigour: *urge the cause along.* **6.** to drive with incitement to speed or effort: *urge dogs on with shouts.* **7.** to impel, constrain, or move to some action: *urged by necessity.* –*v.i.* **8.** to make entreaties or earnest recommendations. **9.** to exert a driving or impelling force; to give an impulse to haste or action: *hunger urges.* **10.** to press, push, or hasten (*on, onwards, along,* etc.). –*n.* **11.** the fact of urging or being urged; impelling action, influence, or force; impulse. **12.** an involuntary, natural, or instinctive impulse. –*phr.* **13. give**

someone an urge, *Aust. Colloq.* to let someone in ahead of one in a queue. –**urger**, *n.* –**urging**, *n.*

urgent /ˈɜdʒənt/ *adj.* **1.** pressing; compelling or requiring immediate action or attention; imperative. **2.** insistent or earnest in solicitation; importunate, as a person. **3.** expressed with insistence, as requests or appeals. –**urgently**, *adv.*

-urgy a word element meaning 'a technology', as in *metallurgy*.

-uria a word element meaning 'urine'.

urinal /ˈjurənəl, juˈraɪnəl/ *n.* **1.** a fixture, room, or building for males for discharging urine in. **2.** a glass or metallic receptacle for urine.

urinate /ˈjurəneɪt/ *v.i.* to pass or discharge urine. –**urination** /jurəˈneɪʃən/, *n.* –**urinative**, *adj.*

urine /ˈjurən, -aɪn/ *n.* the secretion of the kidneys (in mammals, a fluid), which in most mammals is conducted to the bladder by the ureter, and from there to the exterior by the urethra. –**urinary**, *adj.*

URL /ju ar ˈɛl/ *n. Internet* the address of a web page on the internet.

urn /ɜn/ *n.* **1.** a kind of vase, of various forms, especially one with a foot or pedestal. **2.** such a vase for holding the ashes of the dead after cremation. **3.** *Bot.* the spore-bearing part of the capsule of a moss, between lid and seta. **4.** a vessel or apparatus with a tap, used for heating water, tea, coffee, etc., in quantity.

uro-¹ a word element referring to urine and the urinary tract, as in *urochrome*.

uro-² a word element meaning 'tail', as in *urodele*.

urogenital /jurouˈdʒɛnətl/ *adj.* of or relating to the urinary and genital organs.

urology /juˈrɒlədʒi/ *n.* the branch of medical science dealing with urine and the urogenital tract, with special reference to the diagnostic significance of changes in its anatomy and physiology. –**urologic** /jurəˈlɒdʒɪk/, **urological** /jurəˈlɒdʒɪkəl/, *adj.* –**urologist**, *n.*

ursine /ˈɜsaɪn/ *adj.* **1.** of or relating to the bear. **2.** bear-like.

urticaria /ɜtəˈkɛəriə/ *n. Pathol.* a skin condition characterised by transient eruptions of itching or weals, usually due to ingestion or inhalation of an allergen; nettle rash; hives. –**urticarial**, **urticarious**, *adj.*

us /ʌs/, *weak forms* /əs, əz/ *pron. (personal)* **1.** the objective case of **we. 2.** (*in non-standard use*) used instead of *me* or *to me*: *give us that book; I can't reach it.* **3.** (*in non-standard use*) in place of *we* in apposition with a plural noun or number: *us kids; us two.*

usable /ˈjuzəbəl/ *adj.* **1.** that is available for use. **2.** that is in condition to be used. Also, **useable.** –**usability** /juzəˈbɪləti/, **usableness**, *n.*

usage /ˈjusɪdʒ, ˈjuzɪdʒ/ *n.* **1.** custom or practice: *the usages of the last 50 years.* **2.** customary or standard manner of using a language or any of its forms: *English usage.* **3.** a particular instance of this: *a usage borrowed from the French.* **4.** the body of rules or customs followed by a particular set of people. **5.** way of using or treating: *hard or rough usage.* Also, **useage.**

usance /ˈjuzəns/ *n.* **1.** *Commerce* the length of time, exclusive of days of grace, allowed by custom or usage for the payment of foreign bills of exchange. **2.** *Econ.* the income of benefits of every kind derived from the ownership of wealth.

USB /ju ɛs ˈbi/ *n. Computers* universal serial bus; a standard for connection sockets.

USB drive *n.* a small portable data storage device that plugs into the USB port of a computer; memory stick. Also, **USB, USB stick, flash drive.**

USB stick *n.* → **USB drive.**

use *verb* (**used, using**) –*v.t.* /juz/ **1.** to employ for some purpose; put into service; turn to account: *use a knife to cut; use a new method.* **2.** to avail oneself of; apply to one's own purposes: *use the front room for a conference.* **3.** to expend or consume in use: *his car uses a lot of oil.* **4.** to act or behave towards, or treat (a person) in some manner. **5.** to exploit (a person) for one's own ends. **6.** to operate or put into effect. **7.** *Archaic* to practise habitually or customarily; make a practice of. –*v.i.* **8.** /jus/ (*used in interrogative and negative constructions, with an infinitive*) to have been accustomed or usually found to be the case: *didn't you use to smoke?* **9.** /juz/ *Colloq.* to take drugs, especially heroin: *are you using, mate?* –*n.* /jus/ **10.** the act of employing or using, or putting into service: *the use of tools.* **11.** the state of being employed or used: *this book is in use.* **12.** an instance or way of employing or using something: *each successive use of the tool.* **13.** a way of being employed or used; a purpose for which something is used: *the instrument has different uses.* **14.** the power, right, or privilege of employing or using something: *to lose the use of the right eye.* **15.** service or advantage in or for being employed or used; utility or usefulness: *of no practical use.* **16.** help; profit; resulting good: *what's the use of doing that?* **17.** occasion or need, as for something to be employed or used: *have you any use for another calendar?* **18.** continued, habitual, or customary employment or practice; custom; practice: *follow the prevailing use of such occasions.* **19.** way of using or treating; treatment. **20.** consumption, as of food or tobacco. **21.** *Law, Hist.* **a.** the enjoyment of property, as by employment, occupation, or exercise of it. **b.** the benefit or profit of property (lands and tenements) in the possession of another who simply holds them for the beneficiary. **c.** the equitable ownership of land the legal title to which is held by another; a passive trust. –*phr.* **22. be (of) no use,** to be of no service, advantage, or help; be useless: *it's no use crying.* **23. be of use,** to be useful. **24. bring into use,** to introduce so as to become customary or generally employed. **25. come into use,** to become customary or generally employed. **26. have no use for, a.** to have no occasion or need for. **b.** to have no liking or tolerance for. **27. in use, a.** occupied; currently employed to some purpose. **b.** in general employment. **28. make use of,** to employ; put to use; use for one's own purposes or advantages. **29. out of use,** not in current or general employment. **30. put to use,** to employ. **31. use up, a.** to consume completely. **b.** to exhaust; tire out.

useable /ˈjuzəbəl/ *adj.* → **usable.** –**useability** /juzəˈbɪləti/, **useableness**, *n.*

use-by date /ˈjuz-baɪ deɪt/ *n.* **1.** the date by which the manufacturer of a product recommends that it should be used, usually stamped onto the packaging. –*phr.* **2. past one's use-by date,** *Colloq.* past the time in which one is considered useful, employable, etc.: *he's well past his use-by date as a broadcaster.*

used¹ /juzd/ *adj.* **1.** that has been made use of, especially as showing signs of wear. **2.** → **second-hand.** –*phr.* **3. used up,** completely consumed or exhausted.

used² /just/ *phr.* **used to, 1.** accustomed to; habituated to; inured to: *he is used to being treated that way.* **2.** (sometimes fol. by infinitive or infinitive implied) an auxiliary expressing habitual past action: *I used to sing; she plays now but she used not to.*

useful /ˈjusfəl/ *adj.* **1.** being of use or service; serving some purpose; serviceable, advantageous, helpful, or of good effect. **2.** of practical use, as for doing work; producing material results; supplying common needs: *the useful arts.* –**usefully**, *adv.* –**usefulness**, *n.*

useless /ˈjusləs/ *adj.* **1.** of no use; not serving the purpose or any purpose; unavailing or futile. **2.** without useful qualities; of no practical good. –**uselessly**, *adv.* –**uselessness**, *n.*

user /'juzə/ *n.* **1.** someone or something that uses something, usually as specified: *a road user; a computer user.* **2.** *Colloq.* a drug user, especially someone who takes heroin. **3.** *Colloq.* a person who selfishly exploits others.

user-friendly *adj.* of or relating to computer programs or equipment designed to provide minimal difficulty for the inexperienced operator. **–user-friendliness,** *n.*

user group *n.* a group of people linked by their use of a particular product, sometimes forming an association for the sharing of information about that product. Also, **usergroup.**

userid /'juzəraɪ'di/ *n.* a personal identification code entered into a computer when signing on. Also, **username.**

username /'juzəneɪm/ *n.* → **userid.**

user-pays *adj.* of or relating to the principle that a government service should be paid for, at least primarily, if not entirely, by the people who benefit from it.

user-pays principle *n.* the principle that the cost of a government service should be borne at least primarily, if not entirely, by the people who benefit from it.

usher /'ʌʃə/ *n.* **1.** someone who escorts persons to seats in a church, theatre, etc. **2.** an attendant who keeps order in a law court. *–v.t.* **3.** to conduct or escort, as an attendant does. *–phr.* **4.** to conduct or lead in. **b.** to introduce **5. usher out, a.** to conduct or lead out **b.** to be present at the end of: *to usher out the century.* **–usherless,** *adj.*

usual /'juʒuəl/ *adj.* **1.** habitual or customary: *his usual skill.* **2.** such as is commonly met with or observed in experience; ordinary: *the usual January weather.* **3.** in common use; common: *say the usual things. –n.* **4.** that which is usual or habitual. *–phr.* **5. as usual,** as is (or was) usual; in the customary or ordinary manner: *he will come as usual.* **–usually,** *adv.* **–usualness,** *n.*

usurp /ju'sɜp, ju'zɜp/ *v.t.* **1.** to seize and hold (an office or position, power, etc.) by force or without right. **2.** to appropriate or make use of (rights, property, etc.) not one's own. *–v.i.* **3.** to commit forcible or illegal seizure of an office, power, etc.; encroach. **–usurpation** /juz³-'peɪʃən/, *n.* **–usurper,** *n.* **–usurpingly,** *adv.*

usury /'juʒəri/ *n.* (*pl.* **-ries**) **1.** an exorbitant amount or rate of interest, especially in excess of the legal rate. **2.** the lending, or practice of lending money at an exorbitant rate of interest.

ute /jut/ *n. NZ, Aust.* → **utility** (def. 4).

utensil /ju'tɛnsəl/ *n.* **1.** any of the instruments or vessels commonly used in a household, especially in a kitchen. **2.** any instrument, vessel, or implement.

utero- a word element representing **uterus.**

uterus /'jutərəs/ *n.* (*pl.* **uteri** /'jutəraɪ/ *or* **uteruses**) *Anat.* a hollow organ in the pelvic cavity of female mammals in which the fertilised ovum implants itself and develops. Uterine contractions help expel the fetus at parturition; the womb. **–uterine,** *adj.*

utilise /'jutəlaɪz/ *v.t.* to put to use; turn to profitable account: *to utilise water power for driving machinery.* Also, **utilize. –utilisable,** *adj.* **–utilisation** /jutəlaɪ-'zeɪʃən/, *n.* **–utiliser,** *n.*

utilitarian /ju,tɪlə'tɛəriən/ *adj.* **1.** relating to or consisting in utility; concerning practical or material things. **2.** having regard to utility or usefulness rather than beauty, ornamentality, etc. **3.** of, relating to, or adhering to the doctrine of utilitarianism. *–n.* **4.** an adherent of utilitarianism. **5.** someone who is only concerned with practical matters, or who assumes a practical attitude.

utilitarianism /,jutɪlə'tɛəriə,nɪzəm/ *n.* the ethical and political philosophy that holds that virtue is based on utility, and that conduct should be directed towards promoting the greatest happiness of the greatest number of persons.

utility /ju'tɪləti/ *n.* (*pl.* **-ties**) **1.** the state or character of being useful. **2.** something useful. **3.** a public service, such as a bus or railway service, gas or electricity supply, etc. **4.** Also, **ute.** *Aust., NZ* a small truck with an enclosed cabin and open body which is sometimes covered with a tarpaulin. **5.** *Econ.* the ability of an object to satisfy a human want. *–adj.* **6.** provided, designed, bred, or made for usefulness rather than beauty.

utility program *n. Computers* a computer program designed to carry out certain routine processes, as sorting data, copying files, etc.

utmost /'ʌtmoʊst/ *adj.* **1.** of the greatest or highest degree, quantity, or the like; greatest: *of the utmost importance.* **2.** being at the farthest point or extremity; farthest: *the utmost boundary of the East. –n.* Also, **uttermost. 3.** the greatest degree or amount: *the utmost that can be said.* **4.** the highest, greatest, or best of one's power: *do your utmost.* **5.** the extreme limit or extent.

utopia /ju'toʊpiə/ *n.* (*sometimes upper case*) **1.** a place or state of ideal perfection. **2.** any visionary system of political or social perfection.

utopian /ju'toʊpiən/ (*sometimes upper case*) *–adj.* **1.** relating to or resembling a utopia. **2.** founded upon or involving imaginary or ideal perfection. **3.** given to dreams or schemes of such perfection. *–n.* **4.** an ardent but unpractical political or social reformer; a visionary; an idealist. **–utopianism,** *n.*

utter¹ /'ʌtə/ *v.t.* **1.** to speak or pronounce: *the words were uttered in my hearing.* **2.** to give expression to (a subject, etc.): *unable to utter her opinions.* **3.** to make publicly known; publish: *utter a libel.* **4.** (of coins, notes, etc., and especially counterfeit money) to place into general use. **–utterable,** *adj.* **–utterableness,** *n.* **–utterance,** *n.* **–utterer,** *n.*

utter² /'ʌtə/ *adj.* **1.** complete; total; absolute: *her utter abandonment to grief.* **2.** unconditional; unqualified: *an utter denial.* **–utterly,** *adv.*

U-turn /'ju-tɜn/ *n.* a sharp turn executed by the driver of a motor vehicle so that the vehicle faces the direction from which it was travelling.

UV index *n.* a measure of the strength of the ultraviolet radiation in the atmosphere, on a scale from 1 to 10.

uvula /'juvjələ/ *n.* (*pl.* **-las** *or* **-lae** /-li/) the small, fleshy, conical body projecting downwards from the middle of the soft palate.

uxorious /ʌk'sɔriəs/ *adj.* excessively or foolishly fond of one's wife; doting on a wife. **–uxoriously,** *adv.* **–uxoriousness,** *n.*

V v

V, v /vi/ *n.* **1.** a consonant, the 22nd letter of the English alphabet. **2.** (*sometimes lower case*) the Roman numeral for five. **3.** something shaped like the letter V.

vacant /ˈveɪkənt/ *adj.* **1.** empty; void. **2.** (of a chair, position, house, etc.) not occupied. **3.** free from work, business, etc.: *a vacant hour.* **4.** characterised by, showing, or coming from lack of thought or intelligence. –**vacancy,** *n.* –**vacantly,** *adv.*

vacant possession *n.* the right of immediate possession of a house or property, the prior occupant having departed.

vacate /vəˈkeɪt, veɪˈkeɪt/ *v.t.* **1.** to make vacant; cause to be empty or unoccupied. **2.** to give up the occupancy of. **3.** to give up or relinquish (an office, position, etc.). **4.** to render inoperative; deprive of validity; annul: *to vacate a legal judgement.* –*v.i.* **5.** to withdraw from occupancy or possession; leave; quit.

vacation /vəˈkeɪʃən, veɪˈkeɪʃən/ *n.* **1.** a part of the year when law courts, universities, etc., are suspended or closed. **2.** *Chiefly US* an extended period of exemption from work, or of recreation. **3.** the act of vacating. –*v.i.* **4.** to take or have a vacation or holiday. –**vacationless,** *adj.* –**vacationer,** *n.*

vaccinate /ˈvæksəneɪt/ *v.t.* **1.** to inoculate with the vaccine of cowpox, so as to render the subject immune to smallpox. **2.** to inoculate with the modified virus of any of various other diseases, as a preventive measure. –*v.i.* **3.** to perform or practise vaccination. –**vaccination** /væksəˈneɪʃən/, *n.* –**vaccinator,** *n.*

vaccine /ˈvækˈsin, ˈvæksin/ *n.* **1.** the virus of cowpox, obtained from the vesicles of an affected cow or person, and used in vaccination against smallpox. **2.** the modified virus of any of various other diseases, used for preventive inoculation. –*adj.* **3.** relating to cowpox or to vaccination. **4.** of, relating to, or derived from cows.

vacillate /ˈvæsəleɪt/ *v.i.* **1.** to sway unsteadily; waver; stagger. **2.** to fluctuate. **3.** to waver in mind or opinion; be irresolute or hesitant.

vacuous /ˈvækjuəs/ *adj.* **1.** empty; without contents. **2.** empty of ideas or intelligence; stupidly vacant. **3.** showing mental vacancy: *a vacuous look.* **4.** purposeless; idle. –**vacuity,** *n.* –**vacuously,** *adv.* –**vacuousness,** *n.*

vacuum /ˈvækjum/ *n.* (*pl.* **vacuums** *or* **vacua** /ˈvækjuə/) **1.** a space entirely void of matter (**perfect vacuum** or **complete vacuum**). **2.** an enclosed space from which air (or other gas) has been removed, as by an air pump (**partial vacuum**). **3.** the state or degree of exhaustion in such an enclosed space. **4.** empty space. **5.** → **vacuum cleaner.** –*adj.* **6.** relating to, employing, or producing a vacuum. **7.** (of a hollow container) partly exhausted of gas. **8.** relating to apparatuses or processes which utilise gas pressures below atmospheric pressure. –*v.t.* **9.** to clean with a vacuum cleaner or treat with any vacuum device.

vacuum cleaner *n.* an apparatus for cleaning carpets, floors, etc., by suction.

vagabond /ˈvægəbɒnd/ *adj.* **1.** wandering from place to place without being settled; nomadic. **2.** good-for-nothing; useless. –*n.* **3.** someone who is without a fixed home and who wanders from place to place, especially one thought to be idle or worthless; tramp; vagrant.

vagary /ˈveɪgəri/ *n.* (*pl.* **-ries**) **1.** an extravagant idea or notion. **2.** a wild, capricious, or fantastic action; a freak. **3.** uncertainty: *the vagaries of life.*

vagina /vəˈdʒaɪnə/ *n.* (*pl.* **-nas** *or* **-nae** /-ni/) **1.** *Anat.* **a.** the passage leading from the uterus to the vulva in a female mammal. **b.** a sheath-like part or organ. **2.** *Bot.* the sheath formed by the basal part of certain leaves where they embrace the stem. **3.** (*in non-technical use*) the female external genitalia; vulva. –**vaginal,** *adj.*

vagrant /ˈveɪgrənt/ *n.* **1.** someone who wanders from place to place and has no settled home or means of support; a tramp. –*adj.* **2.** wandering from place to place; nomadic. –**vagrancy,** *n.* –**vagrantly,** *adv.* –**vagrantness,** *n.*

vague /veɪg/ *adj.* (**vaguer, vaguest**) **1.** not clear or certain in statement or meaning: *vague promises.* **2.** (of ideas, feelings, etc.) not clear or exact. **3.** not clear or sharp to the senses: *vague forms seen through mist.* **4.** not definitely fixed or known; uncertain: *vague plans.* **5.** (of people, etc.) not clear in thought or understanding. –**vaguely,** *adv.* –**vagueness,** *n.*

vain /veɪn/ *adj.* **1.** without real value or importance; hollow, idle, or worthless. **2.** futile; useless; ineffectual. **3.** having an excessive pride in one's own appearance, qualities, gifts, achievements, etc.; conceited. **4.** proceeding from or showing personal vanity: *vain boasts.* –*phr.* **5. in vain, a.** without effect or avail; to no purpose. **b.** improperly; blasphemously: *to take God's name in vain.* –**vainly,** *adv.* –**vainness,** *n.*

vainglory /veɪnˈglɔri/ *n.* **1.** inordinate elation or pride in one's achievements, abilities, etc. **2.** vain pomp or show. –**vainglorious,** *adj.*

valance /ˈvæləns/ *n.* **1.** a short curtain or piece of hanging drapery, as at the edge of a canopy, from the frame of a bed to the floor, etc. **2.** → **pelmet.** –**valanced,** *adj.*

vale /veɪl/ *n. Chiefly Poetic* a valley.

valediction /væləˈdɪkʃən/ *n.* **1.** a bidding farewell; a leave-taking. **2.** an utterance, speech, etc., made at the time of or by way of leave-taking.

valedictory /væləˈdɪktəri/ *adj.* **1.** bidding farewell. **2.** of or relating to an occasion of leave-taking. –*n.* (*pl.* **-ries**) **3.** a valedictory speech.

valencia orange /vəˈlɛnsiə/ *n.* a common type of orange. Also, **valencia.**

valency /ˈveɪlənsi/ *n.* (*pl.* **-cies**) *Chem.* **1.** the quality which determines the number of atoms or radicals with which any single atom or radical will unite chemically. **2.** the relative combining capacity of an atom or radical compared with the standard hydrogen atom: *a valency of one* (the capacity to unite with one atom of hydrogen or its equivalent). Also, *Chiefly US*, **valence.**

-valent a word element meaning 'having worth or value', used especially in scientific terminology to refer to valency, as in *quadrivalent.*

valentine /ˈvæləntaɪn/ *n.* **1.** an amatory or sentimental (sometimes satirical or comic) card or the like, or some token or gift, sent by one person to another on St Valentine's Day. **2.** a sweetheart chosen on St Valentine's Day, 14 February.

valerian /vəˈlɛriən, -ˈlɪə-/ *n.* **1.** any of the perennial herbs constituting the genus *Valeriana*, as *V. officinalis*, a plant with white or pink flowers and a medicinal root.

2. a drug consisting of or made from the root, used as a nerve sedative and antispasmodic.

valet /'vælei, 'vælət/ *n.* **1.** a male servant who is his employer's personal attendant, caring for the employer's clothing, etc.; manservant. **2.** someone who performs similar services for patrons of a hotel, etc. **3.** any of various contrivances, as a rack or stand, for holding coats, hats, etc. –*verb* (**-leted, -leting**) –*v.t.* **4.** to work as a valet for (someone). –*v.i.* **5.** to attend or act as valet. –**valetless**, *adj.*

valet parking *n.* a service provided, as by a hotel, whereby patrons drive to the door and leave their cars for an attendant to park.

valetudinarian /ˌvælətjudə'nɛəriən/ *n.* **1.** an invalid. **2.** someone who is constantly or excessively concerned about the state of their health. –*adj.* **3.** in poor health; sickly; invalid. **4.** constantly or excessively concerned about the state of one's health. Also, **valetudinary**.

valiant /'væliənt/ *adj.* **1.** brave, courageous, or stouthearted, as persons. **2.** marked by or showing bravery or valour, as deeds, attempts, etc. –**valiantly**, *adv.* –**valiance, valiantness**, *n.*

valid /'væləd/ *adj.* **1.** sound, just, or well-founded: *a valid reason, a valid objection.* **2.** having force, weight, or cogency; authoritative. **3.** legally sound, effective, or binding; having legal force; sustainable in law. –**validate**, *v.* –**validation**, *n.* –**validly**, *adv.* –**validity**, *n.*

valise /və'liz, -'lis/ *n.* a traveller's case for holding clothes, toilet articles, etc., especially a small one for carrying by hand; a travelling bag.

valley /'væli/ *n.* (*pl.* **-leys**) **1.** an elongated depression, usually with an outlet, between uplands, hills, or mountains, especially one following the course of a stream. **2.** an extensive, more or less flat, and relatively low region drained by a great river system. **3.** any hollow or structure likened to a valley. **4.** the lower phase of a horizontal wave motion.

valour /'vælə/ *n.* boldness or firmness in braving danger; bravery or heroic courage, especially in battle. Also, **valor**. –**valorous**, *adj.*

valuable /'væljuəbəl, 'væljubəl/ *adj.* **1.** of monetary worth. **2.** representing a large market value: *valuable paintings.* **3.** of considerable use, service, or importance: *valuable information, valuable aid.* **4.** capable of having the value estimated. –*n.* **5.** (*usu. pl.*) a valuable article, as of personal property or of merchandise, especially one of comparatively small size. –**valuableness**, *n.* –**valuably**, *adv.*

valuation /vælju'eɪʃən/ *n.* **1.** an estimating or fixing of the value of a thing. **2.** a value estimated or fixed; estimated worth. –**valuational**, *adj.*

value /'vælju/ *n.* **1.** that property of a thing because of which it is esteemed, desirable, or useful, or the degree of this property possessed; worth, merit, or importance: *the value of education.* **2.** material or monetary worth, as in traffic or sale: *even the waste has value.* **3.** (*pl.*) *Mining* payable quantities of mineral. **4.** the worth of a thing as measured by the amount of other things for which it can be exchanged, or as estimated in terms of a medium of exchange. **5.** equivalent worth or equivalent return: *for value received.* **6.** estimated or assigned worth; valuation. **7.** force, import, or significance: *the value of a word or phrase.* **8.** *Maths* **a.** the magnitude of a quantity or measurement. **b.** (of a function) the number obtained when particular numbers are substituted for the variables. **9.** (*pl.*) *Sociology* the things of social life (ideals, customs, institutions, etc.) towards which the people of the group have an affective regard. These values may be positive, as cleanliness, freedom, education, etc., or negative, as cruelty, crime, or blasphemy. **10.** *Ethics* any object or quality desirable as a means or as an end in itself. **11.** *Music* the relative length or duration of a note. **12.** *Phonetics* **a.** quality.

b. the phonetic equivalent of a letter: *one value of the letter 'a' is the vowel sound in 'hat', 'sang', etc.* –*v.t.* (**-ued, -uing**) **13.** to estimate the value of; rate at a certain value or price; appraise. **14.** to consider with respect to worth, excellence, usefulness, or importance. **15.** to regard or esteem highly. –*phr.* **16. good value**, excellent in one's field; capable.

value-add *v.i.* to add to the value of a product or service at any stage of production. –**value-added**, *adj.* –**value-adding**, *n.*

valve /vælv/ *n.* **1.** any device, especially a hinge-like part, for closing or altering the passage through a pipe, outlet, etc., in order to control the flow of liquids, gases, etc. **2.** *Music* a device, as in the trumpet, for changing the length of the air column to alter the pitch of a note. **3.** *Zool.* one of the two or more separable pieces making up certain shells. **4.** *Bot.* one of the parts into which a dry fruit opens to release its seeds. **5.** *Elect.* a device consisting of two or more electrodes in an evacuated or gas-filled cylinder, which can be used for controlling a flow of electricity. –*v.t.* **6.** to provide with a means of control of fluid flow (as gas from a balloon), by supplying with a valve. –**valveless**, *adj.*

vamoose /və'mus/ *v.i. Chiefly US* to make off; decamp; depart quickly.

vamp[1] /væmp/ *n.* **1.** the front part of the upper of a shoe or boot. **2.** anything patched up or pieced together. **3.** *Music* an accompaniment, usually improvised, consisting of a succession of simple chords. –*v.t.* **4.** to furnish with a vamp, especially to repair with a new vamp, as a shoe or boot. **5.** to give an appearance of newness to. **6.** *Music* to improvise (an accompaniment or the like). –*v.i.* **7.** *Music* to improvise an accompaniment, tune, etc. –*phr.* **8. vamp up**, to patch up or repair; renovate. –**vamper**, *n.*

vamp[2] /væmp/ *n.* **1.** *Colloq.* a woman who uses her charms to seduce and exploit men. –*v.i.* **2.** *Colloq.* to act as a vamp. **3.** to stay up very late at night while engaging in social media, and other digital pursuits, in the privacy of one's room. –*v.t.* **4.** *Colloq.* (of a woman) to use one's charms or arts upon (a man). –**vamper**, *n.* –**vampish**, *adj.* –**vampishly**, *adv.*

vamping /'væmpɪŋ/ *n.* the practice, adopted by teenagers, of staying up very late at night while engaging in social media, and other digital pursuits, in the privacy of their rooms.

vampire /'væmpaɪə/ *n.* **1.** a preternatural being, in the common belief a reanimated corpse of a person improperly buried, supposed to suck blood of sleeping persons at night. **2.** someone who preys ruthlessly on others; an extortionist. **3.** Also, **vampire bat. a.** any of various South and Central American bats including *Desmodus rotundus, Diphylla ecaudata* and *Diaemus youngi*, the **true vampires**, which feed on the blood of animals including humans. **b.** any large South American bat of the genera *Phyllostomus* and *Vampyrus*, erroneously reputed to suck blood. –**vampiric** /væm'pɪrɪk/, **vampirish**, *adj.*

van[1] /væn/ *n.* **1.** *Archaic* the foremost division or the front part of an army, a fleet, or any body of individuals advancing, or in order for advancing. **2.** the forefront in any movement, course of progress, or the like. **3.** those who are in the forefront of a movement or the like.

van[2] /væn/ *n.* **1.** a covered vehicle, usually large in size, for moving furniture, goods, etc. **2.** a closed railway wagon.

vanadium /və'neɪdiəm/ *n.* a rare element occurring in certain minerals, and obtained as a light grey powder with a silvery lustre, used as an ingredient of steel to toughen it and increase shock resistance. *Symbol*: V; *relative atomic mass*: 50.942; *atomic number*: 23; *density*: 5.96.

vandal /ˈvændl/ *n.* **1.** someone who deliberately or ignorantly destroys or damages property, works of art, etc. *–adj.* **2.** characterised by vandalism. **–vandalise, vandalize,** *v.* **–vandalism,** *n.*

vane /veɪn/ *n.* **1.** a flat piece of metal, or some other device fixed upon a spire or other elevated object in such a way as to move with the wind and indicate its direction; a weathercock. **2.** a similar piece, or sail, in the wheel of a windmill, to be moved by the air. **3.** any plate, blade, or the like, attached to an axis, and moved by or in air or a liquid: *a vane of a screw propeller.* **–vaned,** *adj.* **–vaneless,** *adj.*

vanguard /ˈvænɡad/ *n.* **1.** the foremost division or the front part of an army; the van. **2.** the leading position in any field. **3.** the leaders of any intellectual or political movement.

vanilla /vəˈnɪlə/ *n.* **1.** any of the tropical climbing orchids constituting the genus *Vanilla,* especially *V. fragrans,* whose pod-like fruit (**vanilla bean**) yields an extract used in flavouring food, in perfumery, etc. **2.** the fruit or bean. **3.** the extract. *–adj.* **4.** flavoured with vanilla or a synthetic substitute: *vanilla ice-cream.* **5.** *Colloq.* standard; basic; without refinements or additions: *a vanilla computer system; vanilla sex.*

vanish /ˈvænɪʃ/ *v.i.* **1.** to disappear from sight, or become invisible, especially quickly. **2.** to disappear by ceasing to exist; come to an end; cease. **3.** *Maths* (of a number or quantity) to become zero. **–vanisher,** *n.*

vanity /ˈvænəti/ *n.* (*pl.* **-ties**) **1.** the quality of being personally vain; excessive pride in one's own appearance, qualities, gifts, achievements, etc. **2.** an instance or display of this quality or feeling. **3.** something about which one is vain. **4.** vain or worthless character; want of real value; hollowness or worthlessness. **5.** something vain or worthless. **6.** → **vanity unit.**

vanity unit *n.* an item of bathroom furniture consisting of a cabinet with a bench top and an inset basin. Also, **vanity.**

vanquish /ˈvæŋkwɪʃ/ *v.t.* **1.** to conquer or defeat in battle or conflict; reduce to subjection by superior force. **2.** to defeat in any contest. **3.** to overcome or overpower. **–vanquishable,** *adj.* **–vanquisher,** *n.* **–vanquishment,** *n.*

vantage /ˈvæntɪdʒ, ˈvan-/ *n.* **1.** position or condition affording superiority, as for action. **2.** opportunity likely to give superiority.

vantage point *n.* a position or place affording an advantageous or clear view or perspective.

vape /veɪp/ *v.i.* (**vaped, vaping**) to smoke an e-cigarette. **–vaper,** *n.*

vapid /ˈvæpəd/ *adj.* **1.** having lost life, sharpness, or flavour; insipid; flat. **2.** without animation or spirit; dull, uninteresting or tedious, as talk, writings, persons, etc. **–vapidity** /vəˈpɪdəti/, **vapidness,** *n.* **–vapidly,** *adv.*

vaporise /ˈveɪpəraɪz/ *v.t.* **1.** to cause to pass into the gaseous state. *–v.i.* **2.** to become converted into vapour. Also, **vaporize. –vaporiser,** *n.* **–vaporisable,** *adj.*

vapour /ˈveɪpə/ *n.* **1.** a visible cloud of a gas-like substance, as fog, mist, steam, etc. **2.** a gaseous state of a substance that is normally a liquid or solid. **3.** (*pl.*) *Archaic* low spirits. Also, **vapor. –vapourability** /veɪpərəˈbɪləti/, *n.* **–vapourer,** *n.* **–vapourable,** *adj.* **–vapourless,** *adj.* **–vapour-like,** *adj.*

vapourware /ˈveɪpəwɛə/ *n.* computer software which is announced to be in the making but which may never eventuate. Also, **vaporware.**

variable /ˈvɛəriəbəl/ *adj.* **1.** likely to vary or change; inconsistent; changeable: *variable weather; a variable person.* **2.** capable of being varied or changed; alterable: *the width of the waistband is variable.* **3.** *Biol.* (of a species or a specific character) departing from the usual type. **4.** something variable. **5.** *Maths* a symbol, or the quantity or function which it signifies, which may represent any one of a given set of numbers and

other objects. **–variability** /ˌvɛəriəˈbɪləti/, **variableness,** *n.* **–variably,** *adv.*

variance /ˈvɛəriəns/ *n.* **1.** the state or fact of varying; divergence or discrepancy. **2.** an instance of this; difference. **3.** *Statistics* the square of the standard deviation. **4.** *Law* **a.** a difference or discrepancy, as between two statements or documents in law which should agree. **b.** a departure from the cause of action originally stated in the complaint. **5.** a disagreement, dispute, or quarrel. *–phr.* **6. at variance, a.** in a state of difference, discrepancy, or disagreement, as things. **b.** in a state of controversy or dissension, as persons.

variant /ˈvɛəriənt/ *adj.* **1.** tending to change or alter; varying. **2.** being an altered form of something: *a variant spelling of a word. –n.* **3.** a variant form.

variation /vɛəriˈeɪʃən/ *n.* **1.** the act or process of varying; change in condition, character, degree, etc. **2.** an instance of this. **3.** amount or rate of change. **4.** a different form of something; a variant. **5.** *Music* **a.** the transformation of a melody or theme with changes or elaborations in harmony, rhythm, and melody. **b.** a varied form of a melody or theme, especially one of a series of such forms developing the capacities of the subject. *–phr.* **6. variations on a theme,** the same thing presented in many different ways. **–variational,** *adj.*

varicose /ˈværɪkoʊs, -kəs/ *adj.* **1.** abnormally or unusually enlarged, swollen, or dilated. **2.** relating to or affected with varicose veins, which often affect the superficial portions of the lower limbs.

varied /ˈvɛərid/ *adj.* **1.** made various, diversified; characterised by variety: *a varied assortment.* **2.** changed or altered: *a varied form of a word.* **3.** variegated, as in colour, as an animal. **–variedly,** *adv.* **–variedness,** *n.*

variegate /ˈvɛəriəɡeɪt, ˈvɛərə-/ *v.t.* **1.** to make varied in appearance; mark with different colours, tints, etc. **2.** to give variety to; diversify. **–variegated,** *adj.* **–variegation** /ˌvɛəriəˈɡeɪʃən, ˌvɛərə-/, *n.*

variety /vəˈraɪəti/ *n.* (*pl.* **-ties**) **1.** the state or character of being various or varied; diversity. **2.** a number of things of different kinds: *a variety of cakes to eat.* **3.** kind or sort: *this variety of wood burns well.* **4.** a different form, condition, or phase of something. **5.** a category within a species, based on some hereditary difference not considered great enough to distinguish species. **6.** *Theatre* entertainment of mixed character, including singing, dancing, etc. **7.** *Ling.* any systematic form of a language, such as a regional or social dialect or a dialect recognised as a national or standard form of the language. **–varietal** /vəˈraɪətl/, *adj.*

various /ˈvɛəriəs/ *adj.* **1.** differing one from another, or of different kinds, as two or more things. **2.** divers, several, or many: *in various parts of the world.* **3.** exhibiting or marked by variety or diversity. **4.** differing in different parts, or presenting differing aspects. **–variously,** *adv.* **–variousness,** *n.*

varlet /ˈvalət/ *n. Archaic* a rascal.

varnish /ˈvanɪʃ/ *n.* **1.** a preparation which consists of resinous matter (as copal, lac, etc.) dissolved in an oil (**oil varnish**) or in alcohol (**spirit varnish**) or other volatile liquid, and which, when applied to the surface of wood, metal, etc., dries and leaves a hard, glossy, usually transparent coating. **2.** the sap of certain trees, used for the same purpose (**natural varnish**). **3.** any of various other preparations similarly used, as one having rubber, pyroxylin, or asphalt for the chief constituent. **4.** a coating or surface of varnish. **5.** something resembling a coating of varnish; a gloss. **6.** a merely external show, or a veneer. *–v.t.* **7.** to lay varnish on. **8.** to invest with a glossy appearance. **9.** to give an improved appearance to; embellish; adorn. **10.** to cover with a specious or deceptive appearance. **–varnisher,** *n.*

vary /ˈvɛəri/ *verb* (**-ried, -rying**) *–v.t.* **1.** to change or alter in form, appearance, character, degree, etc.: *she will not* *vary her opinion.* **2.** to cause to be different, one from another: *she varied the lunches every day. –v.i.* **3.** to be different; show diversity or variation: *Opinions vary on this issue.* **4.** to undergo change in form, appearance, character, etc.: *the trees vary with the seasons.* **5.** (usu. fol. by *from*) to depart; deviate: *the ship varied from its course.* **–varier,** *n.* **–varying,** *adj.* **–varyingly,** *adv.*

vas /væs/ *n.* (*pl.* **vasa** /ˈveɪsə/) *Anat., Zool., Bot.* a vessel or duct.

vascular /ˈvæskjələ/ *adj.* relating to, composed of, or provided with vessels or ducts which convey fluids, as blood, lymph, or sap. Also, **vasculose, vasculous.** **–vascularity** /væskjəˈlærəti/, *n.* **–vascularly,** *adv.*

vas deferens /væs ˈdɛfərɛnz/ *n.* (*pl.* **vasa deferentia** /ˌveɪsə dɛfəˈrɛnʃiə/) *Anat.* the deferent duct of the testicle which transports the sperm from the epididymis to the penis.

vase /vaz/ *n.* a hollow vessel, generally higher than it is wide, made of glass, earthenware, porcelain, etc., now chiefly used as a flower container or for decoration.

vasectomy /vəˈsɛktəmi/ *n.* (*pl.* **-mies**) the surgical excision of the vas deferens, or of a portion of it.

vaseline /ˈvæsəlin, væsəˈlin/ *n.* (*from trademark*) → **petroleum jelly.**

vaso- a word element meaning 'vessel', as in *vasoconstrictor.*

vasoconstriction /ˌveɪzoʊkənˈstrɪkʃən/ *n.* constriction of the blood vessels, as by the action of a nerve. **–vasoconstrictor,** *n.*

vassal /ˈvæsəl/ *n.* **1.** (in the feudal system) a person holding lands by the obligation to render military service or its equivalent to his superior. **2.** a person holding some similar relation to a superior; a subject, follower, or retainer. **–vassalless,** *adj.*

vast /vast/ *adj.* **1.** of very great extent or area; very extensive, or immense. **2.** of very great size or proportions; huge; enormous. **3.** very great in number, quantity, or amount, etc.: *a vast army, a vast sum.* **4.** very great in degree, intensity, etc.: *in vast haste, vast importance.* **–vastly,** *adv.* **–vastness,** *n.*

vat /væt/ *n.* **1.** a large container for liquids. *–v.t.* (**vatted, vatting**) **2.** to put into or treat in a vat.

vaudeville /ˈvɔdəvɪl, ˈvɔdvɪl/ *n.* **1.** variety entertainment. **2.** a theatrical piece of light or amusing character, interspersed with songs and dances. **–vaudevillian,** *n.,* *adj.* **–vaudevillist,** *n.*

vault¹ /vɔlt, vɒlt/ *n.* **1.** an arched structure forming a ceiling or roof over a hall, room, sewer, etc. **2.** an arched space, room, or passage, especially underground. **3.** an underground room, especially one used as a cellar or strongroom. **4.** a room for burying the dead. **5.** something like an arched roof: *the vault of heaven. –v.t.* **6.** to build or cover with a vault. **–vaulted,** *adj.*

vault² /vɔlt, vɒlt/ *v.i.* **1.** to leap or spring, as to or from a position or over something. **2.** to leap with the aid of the hands supported on something, sometimes on a pole: *to vault over a fence or a bar. –v.t.* **3.** to leap or spring over: *to vault a fence. –n.* **4.** the act of vaulting. **5.** an apparatus, derived from the horse (def. 6) but with a larger flat, cushioned surface which is about parallel to the floor, sloping downwards at one end. **–vaulter,** *n.*

vaunt /vɔnt/ *v.t.* **1.** to speak boastfully of. *–n.* **2.** boastful utterance. **–vaunter,** *n.* **–vauntingly,** *adv.*

V-chip /ˈvi-tʃɪp/ *n.* a computerised device installed in a television set which responds to a signal accompanying a television program identified as being violent, and which can be activated to prevent the showing of the program.

VCR /vi si ˈa/ *n.* → **video cassette recorder.**

VD /vi ˈdi/ *n.* venereal disease.

VDU /vi di ˈju/ *n.* → **visual display unit.**

veal /vil/ *n.* the flesh of the calf as used for food.

vector /ˈvɛktə/ *n.* **1.** *Maths* a quantity which possesses both magnitude and direction. Two such quantities acting on a point may be represented by the two sides of a parallelogram, so that their resultant is represented in magnitude and direction by the diagonal of the parallelogram. **2.** *Computers* the address of an entry in a memory which is conceptually organised into position-dependent entries of fixed length. **3.** *Biol.* an insect or other organism transmitting germs or other agents of disease. **–vectorial** /vɛkˈtɔriəl/, *adj.*

Veda /ˈveɪdə, ˈvidə/ *n.* (*sometimes pl.*) the ancient sacred scriptures of Hinduism. **–Vedic,** *adj.* **–Vedaism,** *n.*

veejay /ˈvidʒeɪ/ *n.* → **V-jay.**

veer /vɪə/ *v.i.* **1.** to turn or shift to another direction; change from one direction or course to another. **2.** to change; alter; be variable or changeable; pass from one state to another. *–n.* **3.** a change of direction. **–veering,** *adj.* **–veeringly,** *adv.*

vegan /ˈvigən/ *n.* someone who follows a strict vegetarian diet which excludes any animal product.

vegemite /ˈvɛdʒəmaɪt/ *phr.* **happy little vegemite,** *Aust. Colloq.* (*from trademark*) a contented person.

vegetable /ˈvɛdʒtəbəl/ *n.* **1.** any herbaceous plant, annual, biennial, or perennial, whose fruits, seeds, roots, tubers, stems, leaves, or flower parts are used as food, as tomato, bean, beet, potato, asparagus, cabbage, etc. **2.** the edible part of such plants, as the fruit of the tomato or the tuber of the potato. **3.** any member of the vegetable kingdom; a plant. **4.** *Colloq.* a person who, due to physical injury or mental deficiency, is physically completely helpless or has no mental powers. *–adj.* **5.** of, consisting of, or made from vegetables that can be eaten: *a vegetable diet.* **6.** of or relating to plants: *vegetable kingdom; vegetable life.* **7.** obtained from plants: *vegetable fibre; vegetable oil; vegetable dye.*

vegetarian /vɛdʒəˈtɛəriən/ *n.* **1.** someone who on moral principle or from personal preference lives on vegetable food (refusing meat, fish, etc.), or maintains that vegetables and farinaceous substances constitute the only proper food for humans. *–adj.* **2.** of or relating to the practice or principle of living solely or chiefly on vegetable food. **–vegetarianism,** *n.*

vegetate /ˈvɛdʒəteɪt/ *v.i.* **1.** to live in an inactive, passive, or unthinking way. **2.** *Pathol.* (of a wart, polyp, etc.) to grow, or increase by growth, as an excrescence. **3.** *Obs.* to grow in the manner of plants; increase as if by vegetable growth. **–vegetative,** *adj.*

vegetation /vɛdʒəˈteɪʃən/ *n.* **1.** plants collectively; the plant life of a particular region considered as a whole. **2.** the act or process of vegetating. **3.** *Pathol.* a morbid growth or excrescence. **–vegetational,** *adj.*

vehement /ˈviəmənt/ *adj.* **1.** eager, impetuous, or impassioned. **2.** characterised by anger, bitterness, or rancour: *vehement opposition.* **3.** passionate, as feeling; strongly emotional: *vehement desire, vehement dislike.* **4.** (of actions) marked by great energy, exertion, or unusual force. **–vehemence,** *n.* **–vehemently,** *adv.*

vehicle /ˈviɪkəl, ˈviakəl/ *n.* **1.** anything, especially moving on wheels, on which people or goods may be carried, e.g. a car, truck, bicycle, etc. **2.** a means of carrying or sending: *air is the vehicle of sound; language is a vehicle for thought.* **–vehicular** /vəˈhɪkjələ/, *adj.*

V8 /vi ˈeɪt/ *n.* **1.** a reciprocating engine with eight cylinders in a V formation. **2.** a vehicle powered by such an engine.

veil /veɪl/ *n.* **1.** a piece of material worn over the head and face, as that worn over the head and shoulders by some Muslim women to conceal the face. **2.** a piece of material worn over the head and sometimes the face as an adornment, or to protect the face from the sun or wind: *bridal veil; dust veil.* **3.** a piece of material worn so as to fall over the head and shoulders on each side of the face, forming a part of the headdress of a nun. **4.** the life accepted or the vows made by a woman, when she makes either her novice's vows and takes the white veil, or her irrevocable vows and takes the black veil of a nun. **5.** something that covers, screens, or conceals: *a veil of smoke; a veil of mist.* **6.** a mask, disguise, or pretence. *–v.t.* **7.** to cover or conceal with or as with a veil. **8.** to hide the real nature of; mask; disguise. *–phr.* **9. take the veil,** to become a nun. **–veiled,** *adj.* **–veilless,** *adj.* **–veil-like,** *adj.*

vein /veɪn/ *n.* **1.** one of the system of branching vessels or tubes carrying blood from various parts of the body to the heart. **2.** (loosely) any blood vessel. **3.** one of the tubular, riblike thickenings in an insect's wing. **4.** one of the strands or bundles of vascular tissue forming the framework of a leaf. **5.** *Geol.* any body or stratum of ore, coal, etc., clearly separated or defined. **6.** a streak or marking of a different colour, running through marble, wood, etc. **7.** a strain or quality traceable in character or behaviour, writing, etc.: *a vein of stubbornness; to write in a poetic vein.* *–v.t.* **8.** to provide with veins. **9.** to mark with lines or streaks suggesting veins. **–veined,** *adj.* **–veinless,** *adj.* **–veiny,** *adj.*

velcro /ˈvɛlkroʊ/ *(from trademark) –n.* **1.** a type of tape used as a fastening, comprising two strips of fabric, one with a dense arrangement of two small nylon hooks and the other with a nylon pile, so that when the strips are pressed together one hooks into the other sufficiently firmly to hold the fastening together. *–adj.* **2.** of or relating to velcro. Also, **Velcro.**

veldt /vɛlt/ *n.* the open country, bearing grass, bushes, or shrubs, or thinly forested, characteristic of parts of southern Africa. Also, **veld.**

vellum /ˈvɛləm/ *n.* **1.** a sheet of calfskin prepared as parchment for writing or bookbinding. *–adj.* **2.** made of or resembling vellum.

velocity /vəˈlɒsəti/ *n.* (*pl.* **-ties**) **1.** rapidity of motion or operation; swiftness; quickness. **2.** *Physics* rate of motion, especially when the direction of motion is also specified.

velodrome /ˈvɛlədroʊm/ *n.* an arena with a suitably banked track for cycle races.

velour /vəˈlʊə/ *n.* any of various fabrics with a fine, raised finish. Also, **velours.**

velvet /ˈvɛlvət/ *n.* **1.** material of silk, silk and cotton, etc., with a thick, soft pile formed of loops of the warp thread either cut at the outer end (as in ordinary velvet) or left uncut (as in uncut or terry velvet). **2.** anything with the soft, furry quality of velvet. **3.** the soft covering of a growing antler. *–adj.* **4.** Also, **velveted.** made of velvet or covered with velvet. **5.** resembling velvet; smooth and soft. **–velvety,** *adj.*

velveteen /vɛlvəˈtin/ *n.* a cotton pile fabric with short pile.

velvet revolution *n.* a revolution which does not involve violence, especially the non-violent overthrow of communist rule in Czechoslovakia in 1989.

venal /ˈvinəl/ *adj.* **1.** ready to sell one's services or influence unscrupulously; accessible to bribery; corruptly mercenary. **2.** purchasable like mere merchandise, as things not properly bought and sold. **3.** characterised by venality: *a venal period; a venal agreement.* **–venality,** *n.* **–venally,** *adv.*

vend /vɛnd/ *v.t.* to dispose of by sale. **–vendor,** *n.*

vendetta /vɛnˈdɛtə/ *n.* **1.** a private feud in which the relatives of a murdered person seek to obtain vengeance by killing the murderer or a member of his or her family, especially as existing in Corsica and parts of Italy; blood feud. **2.** any prolonged or persistent quarrel, rivalry, etc. **3.** a firm stand taken on a particular issue,

and strictly enforced: *the police conducted a vendetta against drunken driving.* **–vendettist,** *n.*

veneer /vəˈnɪə/ *n.* **1.** a thin layer of wood or other material used for facing or overlaying wood. **2.** one of the several layers of plywood. **3.** an outwardly pleasing appearance or show: *a veneer of good manners.* *–v.t.* **4.** to overlay or face (wood) with thin sheets of some material, as a fine wood, ivory, tortoiseshell, etc. **5.** to cover (an object) with a thin layer of costly material to give an appearance of superior quality. **6.** to cement (layers of wood veneer) to form plywood. **7.** to give an outwardly pleasing appearance to. **–veneerer,** *n.*

venerable /ˈvɛnrəbəl, -nərəbəl/ *adj.* **1.** worthy of veneration or reverence, as on account of high character or office. **2.** commanding respect by reason of age and dignity of appearance. **3.** (of places, buildings, etc.) hallowed by religious, historic, or other lofty associations. **4.** impressive or interesting from age, antique appearance, etc. **5.** ancient: *a venerable error.* **–venerability** /vɛnrəˈbɪləti, -nərəˈbɪləti/, **venerableness,** *n.* **–venerably,** *adv.*

venerate /ˈvɛnəreɪt/ *v.t.* to regard with reverence, or revere. **–veneration,** *n.* **–venerator,** *n.*

venereal disease /vəˈnɪəriəl dəziz/ *n.* any of those diseases which are transmitted by sexual intercourse with an infected person, especially syphilis and gonorrhoea.

venetian blind /vəniʃən ˈblaɪnd/ *n.* a blind, as for a window, having overlapping horizontal slats that may be opened or closed, especially one in which the slats may be raised and drawn together above the window by pulling a cord.

vengeance /ˈvɛndʒəns/ *n.* **1.** the avenging of wrong, injury, or the like, or retributive punishment. **2.** infliction of injury or suffering in requital for wrong done or other cause of bitter resentment. *–phr.* **3. with a vengeance, a.** with force or violence. **b.** extremely. **c.** to a surprising or unusual degree. **–vengeful,** *adj.*

venial /ˈviniəl/ *adj.* **1.** eligible for forgiveness or pardon; not seriously wrong, as a sin. **2.** excusable, as an error or slip. **–veniality** /vini·ˈæləti/, **venialness,** *n.* **–venially,** *adv.*

venison /ˈvɛnəsən/ *n.* the flesh of a deer or similar animal.

Venn diagram /ˈvɛn daɪəgræm/ *n. Logic, Maths* a diagram which represents sets of elements as circles whose overlap indicates the overlap of the sets.

venom /ˈvɛnəm/ *n.* **1.** the poisonous fluid which some animals, as certain snakes, spiders, etc., secrete, and introduce into the bodies of their victims by biting, stinging, etc. **2.** something resembling or suggesting poison in its effect; spite or malice. **–venomer,** *n.* **–venomless,** *adj.* **–venomous,** *adj.*

venous /ˈvinəs/ *adj.* **1.** of, relating to, or of the nature of a vein or veins. **2.** relating to the blood of the veins which has given up oxygen and become charged with carbon dioxide, and, in the higher animals, is dark red in colour. **–venously,** *adv.* **–venosity, venousness,** *n.*

vent[1] /vɛnt/ *n.* **1.** an opening or aperture serving as an outlet for air, smoke, fumes, etc. **2.** the small opening at the breech of a gun by which fire is communicated to the charge. **3.** *Zool.* the anal or excretory opening of animals, especially of those below mammals, as birds and reptiles. **4.** a means of escaping or passing out; an outlet, as from confinement. **–ventless,** *adj.*

vent[2] /vɛnt/ *n.* **1.** expression or utterance: *to give vent to emotions; to give vent to complaints.* *–v.t.* **2.** to give free course or expression to (an emotion, passion, etc.): *glad of any excuse to vent her pique.* **3.** to give utterance to; publish or spread abroad. **4.** to relieve by giving vent to something. **5.** to let out or discharge (liquid, smoke, etc.). **6.** to furnish with a vent or vents. *–v.i.* **7.** *Colloq.* to express one's dissatisfaction forcefully as a means of relieving built-up frustration. **–venter,** *n.*

vent³ /vɛnt/ *n.* the slit in the back or sides of a coat.

ventilate /ˈvɛntəleɪt/ *v.t.* **1.** to provide (a room, mine, etc.) with fresh air in place of stale air. **2.** to introduce fresh air to: *the lungs ventilate the blood.* **3.** to express: *to ventilate opinions.* **4.** to provide (a building, room) with a vent or vents. **–ventilation** /vɛntəˈleɪʃən/, *n.* **–ventilator,** *n.*

ventral /ˈvɛntrəl/ *adj.* **1.** of or relating to the venter or belly; abdominal. **2.** situated on the abdominal side of the body. **3.** situated on the anterior or lower side or surface, as of an organ or part. **4.** *Bot.* of, relating to, or designating the lower or inner surface, as of a petal, etc. **–ventrally,** *adv.*

ventricle /ˈvɛntrɪkəl/ *n. Anat.* **1.** any of various hollow organs or parts in an animal body. **2.** one of the two main cavities of the human heart which receive the blood from the atria and propel it into the arteries. **3.** one of a series of connecting cavities of the brain.

ventriloquism /vɛnˈtrɪləkwɪzəm/ *n.* the art or practice of speaking or of uttering sounds with little or no lip movement, in such a manner that the voice appears to come not from the speaker but from some other source, as a dummy. Also, **ventriloquy. –ventriloquist,** *n.*

venture /ˈvɛntʃə/ *n.* **1.** a hazardous or daring undertaking; any undertaking or proceeding involving uncertainty as to the outcome. **2.** a business enterprise or proceeding in which loss is risked in the hope of profit; a commercial or other speculation. *–v.t.* **3.** to expose to hazard; risk. **4.** to take the risk of; brave the dangers of. **5.** to dare; presume; be so bold as; go so far as. *–v.i.* **6.** to make a venture; risk oneself. **7.** to dare or presume: *I venture to say. –phr.* **8. at a venture,** according to chance; at random. **9. venture on** (or **upon**), to take a risk with: *to venture on an ambitious project.* **–venturesome,** *adj.* **–venturer,** *n.*

Venturer /ˈvɛntʃərə/ *n.* (*sometimes lower case*) a member of a senior division (ages 15–17) of the Scout Association.

venturous /ˈvɛntʃərəs/ *adj.* **1.** disposed to venture; bold; daring; adventurous. **2.** hazardous; risky. **–venturously,** *adv.* **–venturousness,** *n.*

venue /ˈvɛnju/ *n.* **1.** the scene of any action or event, as a hall for a concert, meeting, etc. **2.** *Law* the county or place where a jury is gathered and a crime or cause tried.

Venus flytrap /vinəs ˈflaɪtræp/ *n.* a plant, *Dionæa muscipula,* native to the south-eastern US, whose leaves have two lobes which close like a trap when certain delicate hairs on them are irritated, as by a fly. Also, **Venus's flytrap.**

veracious /vəˈreɪʃəs/ *adj.* **1.** speaking truly; truthful or habitually observant of truth: *a veracious witness.* **2.** characterised by truthfulness; true: *a veracious statement*; *a veracious account.* **–veraciously,** *adv.* **–veraciousness,** *n.* **–veracity,** *n.*

verandah /vəˈrændə/ *n.* an open or partly open portion of a house or other building, outside its principal rooms, but roofed usually by the main structure. Also, **veranda.**

verb /vɜb/ *n. Gram.* **1.** one of the major form classes, or parts of speech, comprising words which express the occurrence of an action, existence of a state, and the like, and such other words as show similar grammatical behaviour, as English *discover, remember, write, be.* **2.** any such word. **3.** any word or construction of similar function or meaning. **–verbless,** *adj.*

verbal /ˈvɜbəl/ *adj.* **1.** of or relating to words: *verbal symbols.* **2.** made up of or in the form of words: *a verbal picture of a scene.* **3.** expressed in spoken words rather than writing; oral: *verbal tradition*; *a verbal message.* **4.** concerned with words only, rather than ideas, facts, or realities: *a purely verbal distinction.*

5. *Gram.* of, relating to, or coming from a verb. *–n.* **6.** *Colloq.* a spoken confession made to police. *–v.t.* (**-balled, -balling**) **7.** *Colloq.* to represent (an accused person) as having made a statement containing admissions and presenting it to a court as evidence. **–verbally,** *adv.*

verbalise /ˈvɜbəlaɪz/ *v.t.* **1.** to express (ideas, emotions, etc.) in words. **2.** *Gram.* to convert into a verb: *to verbalise 'butter' into 'to butter'. –v.i.* **3.** to use many words; be verbose. **4.** to express ideas, etc. in words. Also, **verbalize. –verbalisation** /ˌvɜbəlaɪˈzeɪʃən/, *n.* **–verbaliser,** *n.*

verbatim /vɜˈbeɪtəm/ *adv.* **1.** word for word, or in exactly the same words. *–adj.* **2.** corresponding word for word to an original.

verbena /vɜˈbinə/ *n.* any plant of the genus *Verbena,* comprising species characterised by elongated or flattened spikes of sessile flowers, some of which are much cultivated as garden plants.

verbiage /ˈvɜbiɪdʒ/ *n.* abundance of useless words, as in writing or speech; wordiness.

verbose /vɜˈboʊs/ *adj.* expressed in, characterised by the use of, or using many or too many words; wordy. **–verbosity,** *n.* **–verbosely,** *adv.* **–verboseness,** *n.*

verdant /ˈvɜdnt/ *adj.* green with vegetation; covered with growing plants or grass: *a verdant valley.* **–verdancy,** *n.* **–verdantly,** *adv.*

verdict /ˈvɜdɪkt/ *n.* **1.** *Law* the finding or answer of a jury given to the court concerning a matter submitted to their judgement. **2.** a judgement or decision: *the verdict of the public.*

verdure /ˈvɜdʒuə/ *n.* **1.** greenness, especially of fresh, flourishing vegetation. **2.** green vegetation, especially grass or herbage. **3.** freshness in general; flourishing condition. **–verdurous,** *adj.* **–verdureless,** *adj.*

verge¹ /vɜdʒ/ *n.* **1.** the edge, rim, or margin of something. **2.** the limit or point beyond which something begins or occurs: *to be on the verge of tears.* **3.** a limiting belt, strip, or border of something. **4.** the cleared levelled space bordering the edge of a sealed road. **5.** a grassed strip of land between the front boundary of a residential block and the edge of the road. **6.** space within boundaries; room or scope. **7.** an area or district subject to a particular jurisdiction. **8.** the edge of the roofing projecting over the gable. **9.** *Archit.* the shaft of a column; a small ornamental shaft. **10.** a rod, wand, or staff, especially one carried as an emblem of authority or ensign of office of a bishop, dean, and the like. *–v.i.* (**verged, verging**) **11.** to be on the verge or border, or touch at the border. *–phr.* **12. verge on** (or **upon**), to come close to, approach, or border on (some state or condition): *with respect verging on reverence.*

verge² /vɜdʒ/ *v.i.* **1.** to incline or tend; slope. *–phr.* **2. verge to** (or **towards**), to slope towards.

verger /ˈvɜdʒə/ *n.* **1.** an official who takes care of the interior of a church and acts as attendant. **2.** an official who carries the verge or other symbol of office before a bishop, dean, or other dignitary.

verify /ˈvɛrəfaɪ/ *v.t.* (**-fied, -fying**) **1.** to prove (something) to be true, as by evidence or testimony; confirm or substantiate. **2.** to ascertain the truth or correctness of, especially by examination or comparison: *to verify dates*; *to verify spelling*; *to verify a quotation.* **3.** to state to be true, especially, in legal use, formally or upon oath. **–verifiable,** *adj.* **–verification,** *n.*

verily /ˈvɛrəli/ *adv. Archaic* in very truth; truly; really; indeed.

verisimilar /vɛriˈsɪmələ/ *adj.* having the appearance of truth; likely or probable. **–verisimilitude** /ˌvɛrɪsəˈmɪlətʃud/, *n.* **–verisimilarly,** *adv.*

veritable /ˈvɛrətəbəl/ *adj.* being truly such; genuine or real: *a veritable triumph.* **–veritableness,** *n.* **–veritably,** *adv.*

verity /ˈvɛrəti/ n. (pl. **-ties**) **1.** quality of being true, or in accordance with fact or reality. **2.** a truth, or true statement, principle, belief, idea, or the like.

verjuice /ˈvɜːdʒuːs/ n. an acid liquor made from the sour juice of unripe grapes, crabapples, etc., used for culinary and other purposes.

vermi- a word element meaning 'worm', as in *vermiform*.

vermicelli /vɜːməˈsɛli, -ˈtʃɛli/ n. **1.** a kind of pasta in the form of long, very slender, solid threads, thinner than spaghetti. **2.** (in South-East Asian cookery) a type of thin noodle made from rice.

vermicology /vɜːməˈkɒlədʒi/ n. the study of worms in the ecosystem. **–vermicologist**, n.

vermicular /vɜːˈmɪkjələ/ adj. **1.** consisting of or characterised by sinuous or wavy outlines or markings, resembling the tracks of worms. **2.** relating to or resembling a worm or worms. **–vermicularly**, adv.

vermiculture /ˈvɜːməkʌltʃə/ n. the cultivation of worms to produce more worms, especially for composting. **–vermiculturist**, n.

vermiform /ˈvɜːməfɔːm/ adj. like a worm in form; long and slender.

vermiform appendix n. Anat. a narrow, blind tube protruding from the caecum, situated in the lower right-hand part of the abdomen in humans, and having no known useful function, its diameter being about that of a pencil and its length approximately 10 cm. Also, **appendix**.

vermilion /vəˈmɪljən/ n. **1.** brilliant scarlet red. **2.** a bright red pigment consisting of mercuric sulphide; cinnabar. **–adj. 3.** of the colour of vermilion. **–v.t. 4.** to colour with or as with vermilion.

vermin /ˈvɜːmən/ n. (pl. **vermin**) **1.** (construed as pl.) troublesome, destructive, or disease-carrying animals collectively, especially rodents and insects which prey on living animals or plants. **2.** (construed as pl.) animals which prey on corpses and livestock. **3.** (construed as pl.) unpleasant or obnoxious persons collectively. **4.** a single person of this kind. **–verminous**, adj.

vermivorous /vɜːˈmɪvərəs/ adj. worm-eating.

vermouth /ˈvɜːməθ, vəˈmuːθ/ n. an aromatised wine in which herbs, roots, barks, bitters, and other flavourings have been steeped.

vernacular /vəˈnækjələ/ adj. **1.** (of language or words) native or originating in the place of its use. **2.** expressed or written in the native language: *a vernacular text.* **3.** using such a language: *a vernacular writer.* **–n. 4.** the native speech or language of a place: *the Catholic liturgy is now in the vernacular instead of Latin.* **5.** the language used by a class or profession: *punters have their own vernacular.* **6.** everyday language, as opposed to formal or learned language. **–vernacularism**, n. **–vernacularly**, adv.

vernal /ˈvɜːnəl/ adj. **1.** of or relating to spring. **2.** of or relating to youth. **–vernally**, adv.

veronica /vəˈrɒnɪkə/ n. any plant of the genus *Veronica*, as the speedwell, and of related genera, especially (in former times), *Hebe*.

versatile /ˈvɜːsətaɪl/ adj. **1.** capable of or adapted for turning with ease from one to another of various tasks, subjects, etc.; many-sided in abilities. **2.** Bot. attached at or near the middle so as to swing freely, as an anther. **3.** Zool. turning either forwards or backwards: *a versatile toe.* **4.** variable or changeable, especially in feeling, purpose, policy, etc. **–versatilely**, adv. **–versatility** /vɜːsəˈtɪləti/, **versatileness**, n.

verse¹ /vɜːs/ n. **1.** (in non-technical use) a stanza or other subdivision of a metrical composition: *the first verse of a hymn.* **2.** a succession of metrical feet written or printed or orally composed as one line; one of the lines of a poem. **3.** a poem, or piece of poetry. **4.** a particular type of metrical composition: *iambic verse, elegiac*

verse. **5.** a short division of a chapter in the Bible, usually one sentence, or part of a long sentence.

verse² /vɜːs/ v.t. Sport Colloq. to play against in a game or competition: *who are we versing this week?*

versed /vɜːst/ phr. **versed in**, knowledgeable about; experienced in; practised in; skilled at: *to be versed in mathematics.* Also, **well versed**.

versify /ˈvɜːsəfaɪ/ verb (**-fied, -fying**) **–v.t. 1.** to relate or describe in verse; treat as the subject of verse. **2.** to turn into verse or metrical form. **–v.i. 3.** to compose verses. **–versification**, n. **–versifier**, n.

version /ˈvɜːʒən/ n. **1.** a particular account of some matter, as different from another: *her version of what happened seemed more likely.* **2.** a translation. **3.** a particular form or variant of anything. **–versional**, adj.

verso /ˈvɜːsoʊ/ n. (pl. **-sos**) **1.** Printing a left-hand page of a book or manuscript. **2.** the reverse, back, or other side of some object, as a coin or medal.

versus /ˈvɜːsəs/ prep. against (used especially in law to indicate an action brought by one party against another, and in sport to denote a contest between two teams or players). Abbrev.: v., vs.

vertebra /ˈvɜːtəbrə/ n. (pl. **-bras** or **-brae** /-bri, -breɪ/) Anat. any of the bones or segments composing the spinal column, consisting typically in humans and the higher animals of a more or less cylindrical body (centrum) and an arch (neural arch) with various processes, forming a foramen through which the spinal cord passes. **–vertebral**, adj.

vertebrate /ˈvɜːtəbrət, -breɪt/ n. **1.** a vertebrate animal. **–adj. 2.** having vertebrae; having a backbone or spinal column. **3.** belonging to or relating to the Vertebrata, a subphylum of the phylum Chordata, all members of which have backbones. **–vertebration**, n.

vertex /ˈvɜːtɛks/ n. (pl. **-tices** /-təsiz/ or **-texes**) **1.** the highest point of something; the apex; the top; the summit. **2.** Anat., Zool. the crown or top of the head. **3.** Maths the point farthest from the base. **4.** Geom. **a.** a point in a plane figure common to two or more sides. **b.** a point in a solid common to three or more sides.

vertical /ˈvɜːtɪkəl/ adj. **1.** at right angles or perpendicular to the horizon; upright; plumb. **2.** of, relating to, or situated at the vertex. **–n. 3.** a vertical line, plane, etc. **4.** a vertical or upright position. **–verticality** /vɜːtəˈkæləti/, **verticalness**, n. **–vertically**, adv.

vertical bar n. → **pipe¹** (def. 11).

vertical blinds pl. n. blinds which consist of a number of strips of a stiff fabric hung vertically, which can be adjusted as with venetian blinds to let in more or less light. Also, **vertical drapes**.

vertigo /ˈvɜːtəɡoʊ/ n. (pl. **vertigos** or **vertigines** /vɜːˈtɪdʒəniz/) a disordered condition in which an individual, or whatever is around him or her, seems to be whirling about; dizziness.

verve /vɜːv/ n. enthusiasm or energy, as in literary or artistic work; spirit, liveliness, or vigour: *her novel lacks verve.*

very /ˈvɛri/ adv. **1.** in a high degree; extremely; exceedingly. **2.** used as an intensifier: *the very best thing to be done; in the very same place.* **–adj. 3.** same or precise: *the very thing you should have done.* **4.** even (what is specified): *they grew to fear his very name.* **5.** mere: *the very thought is distressing.* **6.** actual: *caught in the very act.* **7.** true, genuine, or real: *the very President himself.*

very low level waste n. radioactive waste with very low levels of radioactivity, as lightly contaminated soil, metal, paper, plastic, etc., from a nuclear power station.

Vesak /ˈvesak/ n. a major Buddhist festival celebrating the life, enlightenment and death of the Buddha; falling in May or June. Also, **Wesak, Vaisakha, Vesakha, Visakha, Buddha Day**.

vesicle /ˈvɛsɪkəl/ n. **1.** a little sac or cyst. **2.** Anat., Zool. a small bladder-like cavity, especially one filled with fluid. **3.** *Pathol.* a circumscribed elevation of the epidermis containing serous fluid. **4.** *Bot.* a small bladder, or bladder-like air cavity, especially one present in plants which float on water. **5.** *Geol.* a small, usually spherical cavity in a rock or mineral, due to gas or vapour. –**vesicular**, *adj.*

vesper /ˈvɛspə/ *n.* **1.** evening. **2.** (*upper case*) the evening star, especially Venus; Hesperus. **3.** an evening prayer, service, song, etc. **4.** a vesper bell; a bell rung at evening. –*adj.* **5.** of or relating to the evening. **6.** of or relating to vespers.

vespers /ˈvɛspəz/ *pl. n.* (*sometimes upper case*) a religious service held in the late afternoon or the evening.

vessel /ˈvɛsəl/ *n.* **1.** a craft for travelling on water, now especially one larger than an ordinary rowing boat; a ship or boat. **2.** a hollow or concave article, as a cup, bowl, pot, pitcher, vase, bottle, etc., for holding liquid or other contents. **3.** *Anat., Zool.* a tube or duct, as an artery, vein, or the like, containing or conveying blood or some other body fluid. **4.** *Bot.* a duct formed of connected cells which have lost their intervening partitions, containing or conveying sap, etc. **5.** a person regarded as a receptacle or container (chiefly in or influenced by biblical expressions).

vest /vɛst/ *n.* **1.** a short, warm undergarment with or without sleeves, usually worn next to the skin under a shirt; a singlet. **2.** a waistcoat. **3.** a similar garment, or a part or trimming simulating the front of such a garment, worn by women. –*v.t.* **4.** to clothe, dress, or robe. **5.** to invest or endow (a person, etc.) with something, especially with powers, functions, etc. –*v.i.* **6.** to put on ecclesiastical vestments. **7.** to become vested in a person or persons, as a right. **8.** to pass into possession; to devolve upon a person as possessor. –*phr.* **9. vest something in someone**, to place or settle something (especially property, rights, powers, etc.) in the possession or control of someone: *to vest an estate or a title in a person.* –**vestless**, *adj.*

vestal /ˈvɛstl/ *adj.* relating to or resembling a virgin; virginal; chaste.

vested /ˈvɛstəd/ *adj.* **1.** *Law* settled or secured in the possession of a person or persons, as a complete or fixed right, an interest sometimes possessory, sometimes future, which has substance because of its relative certainty. **2.** clothed or robed, especially in ecclesiastical vestments: *a vested choir.*

vestibule /ˈvɛstəbjul/ *n.* **1.** a passage, hall, or antechamber between the outer door and the interior parts of a house or building. **2.** *Anat., Zool.* any of various cavities or hollows regarded as forming an approach or entrance to another cavity or space: *the vestibule of the ear.* **3.** an enclosed space at the end of a railway carriage, affording entrance to the carriage from outside and from the next carriage. –**vestibular**, *adj.*

vestige /ˈvɛstɪdʒ/ *n.* **1.** a mark, trace, or visible evidence of something which is no longer present or in existence. **2.** a surviving evidence or memorial of some condition, practice, etc. **3.** a very slight trace or amount of something. **4.** *Biol.* a degenerate or imperfectly developed organ or structure having little or no utility, but which in an earlier stage of the individual or in preceding organisms performed a useful function. –**vestigial**, *adj.*

vestment /ˈvɛstmənt/ *n.* **1.** a garment, especially an outer garment, robe, or gown. **2.** an official or ceremonial robe. **3.** something that covers like a garment. –**vestmental** /vɛstˈmɛntl/, *adj.*

vestry /ˈvɛstri/ *n.* (*pl.* **-tries**) **1.** a room in or a building attached to a church, in which the vestments, and sometimes also the sacred vessels, etc., are kept; a sacristy. **2.** (in some churches) a room in or a building attached to a church, used as a chapel, for prayer meetings, for the Sunday school, etc. **3.** (in parishes of the Church of England) **a.** a meeting of all the parishioners, or of a committee of parishioners, held in the vestry for the dispatch of the official business of the parish. **b.** the body of parishioners so meeting; parish council.

vet[1] /vɛt/ *n.* **1.** a veterinary surgeon. –*verb* (**vetted, vetting**) –*v.t.* **2.** to examine or treat as a veterinary surgeon does. **3.** to check the aptitude, character, etc., of (a person): *we'll vet the applicants carefully.* **4.** to examine (a product, proposal, or the like) with a view to acceptance, rejection, or correction. –*v.i.* **5.** to work as a veterinary surgeon.

vet[2] /vɛt/ *n. Colloq.* a veteran.

vetch /vɛtʃ/ *n.* **1.** any of various leguminous plants, mostly climbing herbs, of the genus *Vicia*, as *V. sativa*, the common vetch, cultivated for forage and soil improvement. **2.** any of various allied plants, as *Lathyrus sativus*, of Europe, cultivated for its edible seeds and as a forage plant. **3.** the beanlike seed or fruit of any such plant.

veteran /ˈvɛtərən, ˈvɛtrən/ *n.* **1.** someone who has seen long service in any occupation or office. **2.** a soldier who has seen active service: *a veteran of the desert war.* –*adj.* **3.** experienced through long service or practice; having served for a long period; grown old in service. **4.** of, relating to, or characteristic of veterans. **5.** of or relating to cars built before 1918.

veterinary /ˈvɛtənri, ˈvɛtərənri/, *Orig. US* /ˈvɛtrənɛri/ *n.* (*pl.* **-ries**) **1.** a veterinary surgeon. –*adj.* **2.** of or relating to the medical and surgical treatment of animals, especially domesticated ones.

veterinary science *n.* the branch of medicine concerned with the study, prevention, and treatment of animal diseases. Also, **veterinary medicine**.

veterinary surgeon *n.* someone who practises veterinary science or surgery. Also, **veterinarian**.

veto /ˈvitoʊ/ *n.* (*pl.* **-tos** *or* **-toes**) **1.** the power or right of preventing action by a prohibition. **2.** a prohibition directed against some proposed or intended act. –*v.t.* (**-toed, -toing**) **3.** to prevent (a proposal, legislative bill, etc.) being put into action by exercising the right of veto. **4.** to refuse to consent to. –**vetoer**, *n.* –**vetoless**, *adj.*

vex /vɛks/ *v.t.* **1.** to irritate; annoy; provoke; make angry: *enough to vex a saint.* **2.** to torment; plague; worry: *want of money vexes many.* –**vexation**, *n.* –**vexer**, *n.* –**vexingly**, *adv.* –**vexatious**, *adj.*

VHS /vi eɪtʃ ˈɛs/ *adj.* (*from trademark*) of or relating to a unique format for coding and playing a videotape for a video cassette recorder.

via /ˈvaɪə/ *prep.* **1.** by way of; by a route that passes through: *go to Italy via Singapore.* **2.** by means of: *to reach a conclusion via three logical steps.*

viable /ˈvaɪəbəl/ *adj.* **1.** capable of living. **2.** practicable; workable. **3.** *Physiol.* (of a fetus) having reached such a stage of development as to permit continued existence, under normal conditions, outside the womb. **4.** *Bot.* able to live and grow. –**viability** /vaɪəˈbɪləti/, *n.*

viaduct /ˈvaɪədʌkt/ *n.* **1.** a bridge consisting of a series of narrow masonry arches with high supporting piers, for carrying a road, railway, etc., over a valley, ravine, or the like. **2.** a similar bridge of steel girders.

viagra /vaɪˈægrə/ *n. Colloq.* (*from trademark*) anything seen as having a beneficial effect on one's sexual performance: *the meal was culinary viagra.* Also, **Viagra**.

vial /ˈvaɪəl/ *n.* → **phial** (def. 1).

viand /ˈvaɪənd, ˈviənd/ *n.* **1.** an article of food. **2.** (*pl.*) articles or dishes of food, now usually of a choice or delicate kind.

vibes[1] /vaɪbz/ *pl. n. Colloq.* → **vibraphone**.

vibes[2] /vaɪbz/ *pl. n. Colloq.* the quality, mood, or atmosphere of a place or person, thought of as producing vibrations to which one unconsciously responds: *the vibes of that town were all wrong.*

vibrant /ˈvaɪbrənt/ *adj.* **1.** moving to and fro rapidly; vibrating. **2.** (of sounds) resonant. **3.** full of energy and vigour. **4.** exciting; producing a thrill. –**vibrancy**, *n.* –**vibrantly**, *adv.*

vibraphone /ˈvaɪbrəfoʊn/ *n.* a xylophone-like musical instrument with electronically operated resonators controlled by a pedal. Also, *US*, **vibraharp**. –**vibraphonist**, *n.*

vibrate /vaɪˈbreɪt/ *v.i.* **1.** to move to and fro, as a pendulum; oscillate. **2.** to move to and fro or up and down quickly and repeatedly; quiver; tremble. **3.** (of sounds) to produce or have a quivering or vibratory effect; resound. –*v.t.* **4.** to cause to move to and fro. **5.** to cause to quiver or tremble. –**vibration**, *n.* –**vibratory**, *adj.*

vibrato /vəˈbratoʊ/ *n.* (*pl.* **-tos**) *Music* a pulsating effect produced in the singing voice or in an instrumental tone by rapid small oscillations in pitch about the given note.

vibrator /vaɪˈbreɪtə, ˈvaɪbreɪtə/ *n.* **1.** any of various instruments or devices causing a vibratory motion or action. **2.** an appliance with a rubber or other tip of variable shape, made to oscillate very rapidly, used in vibratory massage, sometimes for the purpose of erotic stimulation. **3.** *Elect.* **a.** a device containing a vibrating member for converting a direct current into an oscillating current. **b.** a device for producing electrical oscillations.

vicar /ˈvɪkə/ *n.* **1.** (in some Anglican churches) a member of the clergy acting as priest of a parish. **2.** an ecclesiastic representing the pope or a bishop. **3.** the pope as the representative on earth of God or Christ. –**vicarship**, *n.*

vicarage /ˈvɪkərɪdʒ/ *n.* **1.** the residence of a vicar. **2.** the benefice of a vicar. **3.** the office or duties of a vicar.

vicarious /vəˈkɛəriəs, vaɪ-/ *adj.* **1.** performed, exercised, received, or suffered in place of another: *vicarious pleasure.* **2.** taking the place of another person or thing; acting or serving as a substitute. **3.** relating to or involving the substitution of one for another. –**vicariously**, *adv.* –**vicariousness**, *n.*

vice[1] /vaɪs/ *n.* **1.** wickedness or evil in general. **2.** evil or immoral behaviour, especially in the criminal use of sex, drugs, etc. **3.** a particular example of evil behaviour; sin: *the vice of envy.* **4.** a fault; defect; imperfection: *a vice of literary style.* **5.** any bad habit.

vice[2] /vaɪs/ *n.* **1.** any of various devices used to hold an object firmly while work is being done on it, usually having two jaws which may be brought together or separated by means of a screw, lever, or the like. –*v.t.* (**viced**, **vicing**) **2.** to hold, press, or squeeze with or as with a vice. Also, *US*, **vise**. –**vice-like**, *adj.*

vice[3] /ˈvaɪsi/ *prep.* instead of; in the place of.

vice- a prefix denoting a substitute, deputy, or subordinate: *vice-chairman, viceroy, vice-regent.*

vice-chancellor /vaɪs-ˈtʃænsələ, -ˈtʃan-/ *n.* **1.** the executive head of a university. **2.** a substitute, deputy, or subordinate chancellor. –**vice-chancellorship**, *n.*

viceroy /ˈvaɪsrɔɪ/ *n.* **1.** someone appointed to rule a country or province as the deputy of the sovereign: *the 19th-century viceroys of India.* **2.** anyone to whom rank or authority has been delegated. –**viceroyship**, *n.*

vice squad *n.* the section of the police force concerned with enforcement of laws relating to prostitution, gambling, etc.

vice versa /vaɪsə ˈvɜsə, vaɪs ˈvɜsə, vaɪsi ˈvɜsə/ *adv.* conversely; the order being changed (from that of a preceding statement): *A distrusts B, and vice versa.*

vicinity /vəˈsɪnəti/ *n.* (*pl.* **-ties**) **1.** the region near or about a place; the neighbourhood or vicinage. **2.** the state or fact of being near in place; proximity; propinquity.

vicious /ˈvɪʃəs/ *adj.* **1.** cruel; spiteful or malignant: *a vicious attack.* **2.** unpleasantly severe: *a vicious headache.* **3.** faulty; defective: *vicious reasoning.* **4.** (of a horse, dog, etc.) having bad habits or a bad temper. –**viciously**, *adv.* –**viciousness**, *n.*

vicious circle *n.* a situation in which an attempt to solve or escape from one problem creates further difficulties, and usually exacerbates or makes chronic the original problem. Also, **vicious cycle**.

vicissitude /vəˈsɪsətjud, -tʃud/ *n.* **1.** a change or variation, or something different, occurring in the course of something. **2.** interchange or alternation, as of states or things. **3.** (*pl.*) changes, variations, successive or alternating phases or conditions, etc., in the course of anything. **4.** regular change or succession of one state or thing to another. **5.** change, mutation, or mutability. –**vicissitudinary** /vəsɪsəˈtjudənəri/, **vicissitudinous** /vəsɪsəˈtjudənəs/, *adj.*

victim /ˈvɪktəm/ *n.* **1.** a sufferer from any destructive, injurious, or adverse action or agency: *victims of disease*; *victims of oppression.* **2.** a dupe, as of a swindler. **3.** a person or animal sacrificed, or regarded as sacrificed. **4.** a living creature sacrificed in religious rites. –**victimhood**, *n.*

victim impact statement *n.* a statement made to a court by the victim of a crime or by their family before the offender is sentenced, expressing the impact which the crime has had on them.

victimise /ˈvɪktəmaɪz/ *v.t.* **1.** to make a victim of. **2.** to discipline or punish selectively, especially as a result of an industrial dispute: *four men were victimised by management after the strike.* **3.** to punish unfairly. **4.** to dupe, swindle, or cheat: *to victimise poor widows.* **5.** to slay as or like a sacrificial victim. Also, **victimize**. –**victimisation** /ˌvɪktəmaɪˈzeɪʃən/, *n.* –**victimiser**, *n.*

victor /ˈvɪktə/ *n.* **1.** someone who has vanquished or defeated an adversary; a conqueror. **2.** a winner in any struggle or contest.

victory /ˈvɪktəri, -tri/ *n.* (*pl.* **-ries**) **1.** the ultimate and decisive superiority in a battle or any contest. **2.** a success or triumph won over the enemy in battle or war, or an engagement ending in such a triumph: *naval victories.* **3.** any success or successful performance achieved over an adversary or opponent, opposition, difficulties, etc. –**victorious**, *adj.*

victual /ˈvɪtl/ *n.* **1.** (*pl.*) articles of food prepared for use. –*verb* (**-ualled** *or*, *Chiefly US*, **-ualed**, **-ualling** *or*, *Chiefly US*, **-ualing**) –*v.t.* **2.** to supply with victuals. –*v.i.* **3.** to obtain victuals. –**victualless**, *adj.* –**victualler**, *n.*

vide /ˈvideɪ, ˈvaɪdi/ *v.* see (used especially in making reference to parts of a text).

video /ˈvɪdioʊ/ *adj.* **1.** *TV* relating to or employed in the transmission or reception of televised material as displayed on television screens or visual display units. –*n.* (*pl.* **videos**) **2.** a video recording. **3.** a video cassette. **4.** a video cassette recorder. –*v.t.* (**videoed**, **videoing**) **5.** to make a video recording of. –*phr.* **6. on video**, on a video recording: *a film on video; caught on video.*

video call *n.* a phone call made on a videophone.

video camera *n.* a camera designed for filming on videotape. Also, **video-camera**.

video cassette *n.* a cassette enclosing a length of videotape for video recording or playback. Also, **videocassette**.

video cassette recorder *n.* a videotape recorder which allows for play-back through or recording from a television set, the videotape being held in a video cassette. Also, **VCR**.

video clip *n.* a short video recording, as one showing a performance of a popular song, spectacular news event, etc.

video game *n.* an electronic game which is played on a television or computer screen. –**video gaming**, *n.*

videogram /ˈvɪdioʊgræm/ *n.* a video for publication on the internet.

videography /vɪdiˈɒgrəfi/ *n.* the making of a video recording of proceedings, as in court hearings. –**videographer**, *n.*

videophone /ˈvɪdioʊfoʊn/ *n.* a telephone which allows visual, as well as verbal, communication.

video recorder *n.* a tape recorder which records both images and sounds, usually on magnetic tape. Also, **video tape recorder**.

video referee *n. Sport* a referee who adjudicates with the aid of video footage of the game.

videostreaming /ˈvɪdioʊstrimɪŋ/ *n.* the streaming of video data. See **streaming**.

videotape /ˈvɪdioʊteɪp/ *n.* **1.** magnetic tape upon which a video-frequency signal is recorded; used for storing a television program or film. –*v.t.* **2.** to record on videotape.

video terminal *n.* a computer terminal in which information is displayed on a television screen.

videotext /ˈvɪdioʊtɛkst/ *n.* any of various cable and broadcast alphanumeric and graphic data systems using video displays.

vie /vaɪ/ *v.i.* to strive in competition or rivalry with another; to contend for superiority.

vienna /viˈɛnə/ *n.* **1.** → **vienna loaf. 2.** → **vienna coffee.**

vienna coffee *n.* a coffee beverage consisting of black coffee served with whipped cream on top. Also, **vienna**.

vienna loaf *n.* a cigar-shaped loaf of white bread. Also, **vienna**.

view /vju/ *n.* **1.** a seeing or beholding; an examination by the eye. **2.** sight or vision: *exposed to view.* **3.** range of sight or vision: *objects in view.* **4.** a sight or prospect of some landscape, scene, etc. **5.** a picture of a scene. **6.** the aspect, or a particular aspect, of something. **7.** mental contemplation or examination; a mental survey. **8.** contemplation or consideration of a matter with reference to action: *a project in view.* **9.** aim, intention, or purpose. **10.** prospect or expectation: *with no view of success.* **11.** a general account or description of a subject. **12.** a particular way of regarding something. **13.** a conception, notion, or idea of a thing; an opinion or theory. **14.** a survey or inspection. –*v.t.* **15.** to see or behold. **16.** to watch (a television program). **17.** to look at, survey, or inspect. **18.** to contemplate mentally; consider. **19.** to regard in a particular light or as specified. –*v.i.* **20.** to inspect a prospective purchase or the like. **21.** to watch television or a television program. –*phr.* **22. a dim view,** an unfavourable opinion. **23. in view, a.** within range of vision. **b.** under consideration. **c.** near to realisation. **24. in view of, a.** in sight of. **b.** in prospect or anticipation of. **c.** in consideration of. **d.** on account of. **25. on view,** in a place for public inspection; on exhibition. **26. with a view to, a.** with an aim or intention directed to. **b.** with an expectation or hope of. **c.** in consideration of. **d.** with regard to.

viewpoint /ˈvjupɔɪnt/ *n.* **1.** a place affording a view of something. **2.** a point of view; an attitude of mind: *the viewpoint of an artist.*

vigil /ˈvɪdʒəl/ *n.* **1.** a keeping awake for any purpose during the normal hours of sleep. **2.** a watch kept by night or at other times; a course or period of watchful attention. **3.** a period of wakefulness from inability to sleep. **4.** *Eccles.* **a.** a devotional watching, or keeping awake, during the customary hours of sleep. **b.** (*oft. pl.*) a nocturnal devotional exercise or service, especially on the eve before a church festival. **c.** the eve, or day and night, before a church festival, especially an eve which is a fast.

vigilant /ˈvɪdʒələnt/ *adj.* **1.** keenly attentive to detect danger; wary: *a vigilant sentry.* **2.** ever awake and alert; sleeplessly watchful. –**vigilantly**, *adv.* –**vigilance**, **vigilantness**, *n.*

vigilante /vɪdʒəˈlænti/ *n.* a private citizen who, usually as one of a group of such citizens, assumes the role of guardian of society in maintaining law and order, punishing wrongdoers, etc.

vigneron /ˈvɪnjərən, ˈvɪnjərɔ̃/ *n.* a person who owns or leases a vineyard.

vignette /vɪnˈjɛt/ *n.* **1.** an engraving, drawing, photograph, or the like, shading off gradually at the edges; a design without a borderline. **2.** decorative work representing meandering branches, leaves, or tendrils, as in architecture or in manuscripts. **3.** any small, pleasing picture or view. **4.** a small, graceful literary sketch. –*v.t.* (**-gnetted, -gnetting**) **5.** to finish (a picture, photograph, etc.) in the manner of a vignette. –**vignettist**, *n.*

vigoro /ˈvɪgəroʊ/ *n.* a team game with 12 players a side, combining elements of baseball and cricket.

vigour /ˈvɪgə/ *n.* **1.** active strength or force, as of body or mind. **2.** healthy physical or mental energy or power. **3.** energy; energetic activity. **4.** force of healthy growth in any living matter or organism, as a plant. **5.** active or effective force. Also, **vigor**. –**vigorous**, *adj.*

vile /vaɪl/ *adj.* **1.** wretchedly bad: *vile weather*; *clothes of vile quality.* **2.** highly offensive; obnoxious; objectionable: *vile behaviour*; *vile language.* **3.** morally bad; base; depraved: *vile thoughts.* **4.** low; humiliating; ignominious: *vile servitude*; *a vile task.* –**vilely**, *adv.* –**vileness**, *n.*

vilify /ˈvɪləfaɪ/ *v.t.* (**-fied, -fying**) to speak evil of; defame; traduce. –**vilification** /vɪləfəˈkeɪʃən/, *n.* –**vilifier**, *n.*

villa /ˈvɪlə/ *n.* **1.** a country residence, usually of some size and pretensions, especially one in a Mediterranean country. **2.** *Aust.* a small house, often one of a set of connected dwellings.

village /ˈvɪlɪdʒ/ *n.* **1.** a small assemblage of houses in a country district, larger than a hamlet and smaller than a town. **2.** the inhabitants collectively. **3.** an assemblage of animal dwellings or the like, resembling a village. **4.** a group of small, sometimes fashionable and exclusive shops, servicing a suburb. –*adj.* **5.** of, belonging to, or characteristic of a village; rustic. –**villager**, *n.* –**villageless**, *adj.*

villain /ˈvɪlən/ *n.* **1.** a wicked person; scoundrel. **2.** → **villein. 3. the villain of the piece,** the person or thing held responsible for everything that goes wrong. –**villainous**, *adj.*

villein /ˈvɪlən/ *n.* a member of a class of half-free persons under the feudal system who were serfs with respect to their lord but had the rights and privileges of freemen with respect to others. Also, **villain.**

vim /vɪm/ *n.* force; energy; vigour in action.

vinaigrette /vɪnəˈgrɛt/ *n.* Also, **vinegarette. 1.** *Obs.* a small ornamental bottle or box containing a sponge soaked in an aromatic vinegar, smelling salts, or the like. –*adj.* **2.** served with a vinaigrette sauce.

vindicate /ˈvɪndəkeɪt/ *v.t.* **1.** to clear, as from a charge, imputation, suspicion, or the like. **2.** to afford justification for: *subsequent events vindicated his policy.* **3.** to uphold or justify by argument or evidence. **4.** to assert, maintain, or defend (a right, cause, etc.) against opposition. **5.** to lay claim to, for oneself or another. –**vindication**, *n.* –**vindicable**, *adj.* –**vindicator**, *n.*

vindictive /vɪnˈdɪktɪv/ *adj.* **1.** disposed or inclined to revenge; revengeful: *a vindictive person.* **2.** proceeding from or showing a revengeful spirit. –**vindictively**, *adv.* –**vindictiveness**, *n.*

vine /vaɪn/ *n.* **1.** a long, slender stem that trails or creeps on the ground or climbs by winding itself around a support or holding fast with tendrils or claspers. **2.** a plant bearing such a stem. **3.** any of the climbing plants constituting the genus *Vitis*, having a woody stem and bearing grapes, especially *V. vinifera*, the common European species; a grapevine. –**vineless**, *adj.*

vinegar /'vɪnəgə, 'vɪnɪgə/ n. **1.** a sour liquid consisting of dilute and impure acetic acid, obtained by acetous fermentation from wine, cider, beer, ale, or the like, and used as a condiment, preservative, etc. **2.** *Pharmacology* a solution of a medicinal substance in dilute acetic acid, or vinegar. **3.** sour or crabbed speech, temper, or countenance. *–v.t.* **4.** to apply vinegar to. **–vinegarish**, *adj.*

vineyard /'vɪnjəd, 'vɪnjad/ n. a plantation of grapevines, for producing grapes for winemaking, etc. **–vineyardist**, *n.*

vintage /'vɪntɪdʒ/ n. **1.** a harvest or crop of grapes of a single year. **2.** the wine produced from a particular harvest. **3.** a very fine wine from the crop of a good year, labelled and sold as such. **4.** *Colloq.* the style of a particular period of production of anything: *a hat of last year's vintage.* *–adj.* **5.** (of wines) labelled and sold as the produce of a particular year. **6.** of high quality (often from, or in the manner of the past): *the actor gave a vintage performance.* **7.** indicating a motor vehicle built between 1918 and 1930, or a racing car more than ten years old. **8.** from a past period; old-fashioned.

vintner /'vɪntnə/ n. a dealer in wine; a wine merchant.

vinyl /'vaɪnəl/ n. **1.** any of various vinyl polymers, especially that used in the making of gramophone records. **2.** *Colloq.* records viewed collectively: *I've got vinyl and no CDs.* *–adj.* **3.** *Chem.* of or relating to, or consisting of, or containing the univalent group $CH_2=CH-$, formally derived from ethylene: *vinyl polymer.* *–phr.* **4. on vinyl**, *Colloq.* available as a record: *this song is out on vinyl.*

vinyl polymer n. one of a group of compounds derived from vinyl compounds such as vinyl acetate, styrene, etc., by polymerisation, forming plastics and resins of high molecular weight.

viol /'vaɪəl/ n. a bowed musical instrument, differing from the violin in having deeper ribs, sloping shoulders, a greater number of strings (usually 6) and frets, common in the 16th and 17th centuries in various sizes from the **treble viol** to the **bass viol**.

viola¹ /vi'oʊlə/ n. a four-stringed musical instrument of the violin family, slightly larger than the violin; a tenor or alto violin.

viola² /'vaɪələ, vaɪ'oʊlə/ n. **1.** any of a genus of plants, *Viola*, including the violet and the pansy, bearing irregular flowers on axillary peduncles. **2.** a pansy, *V. cornuta*, cultivated as a garden plant.

violate /'vaɪəleɪt/ v.t. **1.** to break (a law, rule, agreement, promise, etc.). **2.** to break in upon rudely: *to violate privacy; to violate the peace; to violate one's personal space.* **3.** to do violence to, especially by raping. **4.** to deal with or treat (something sacred) in a violent or irreverent way; desecrate; profane. **–violator**, *n.* **–violation**, *n.*

violence /'vaɪələns/ n. **1.** rough force: *the violence of the wind.* **2.** rough force that is used to injure or harm: *to die by violence.* **3.** any wrongful use of force or power, as against rights, laws, etc. **4.** intensity of feeling, language, etc.; fury.

violent /'vaɪələnt/ adj. **1.** acting with or characterised by uncontrolled, strong, rough force: *a violent blow; a violent explosion; a violent storm.* **2.** acting with, characterised by, or due to injurious or destructive force: *violent measures, a violent death.* **3.** intense in force, effect, etc.; severe; extreme: *violent heat; violent pain; violent contrast.* **4.** roughly or immoderately vehement, ardent, or passionate: *violent feeling.* **5.** furious in impetuosity, energy, etc.: *violent haste.* **–violently**, *adv.*

violet /'vaɪlət, 'vaɪələt/ n. **1.** any plant of the genus *Viola*, comprising chiefly low, stemless or leafy-stemmed herbs with purple, blue, yellow, white, or variegated flowers, as *V. hederacea*, and *V. odorata*, the much cultivated **English violet**. **2.** a bluish-purple colour. *–adj.* **3.** of the colour called violet; bluish-purple. *–phr.* **4. shrinking violet**, *Colloq.* a shy or retiring person.

violin /vaɪə'lɪn/ n. **1.** the treble of the family of modern bowed instruments, which is held nearly horizontal by the player's arm, with the lower part supported against the collarbone or shoulder; a fiddle. **2.** a violinist. **–violinist**, *n.* **–violinless**, *adj.*

violoncello /vaɪələn'tʃeloʊ/ n. (pl. **-los** or **-li** /-li/) → **cello**.

VIP /vi aɪ 'pi/ n. *Colloq.* very important person.

viper /'vaɪpə/ n. **1.** any of the venomous snakes of the genus *Vipera*, especially *V. berus*, a small European species; the adder. **2.** any snake of the highly venomous family Viperidae, found in Africa, Asia and Europe and including the common vipers, the puff adder, and various other types, all characterised by erectile venom-conducting fangs. **3.** any of various venomous or supposedly venomous snakes of allied or other genera, as the **horned viper**, *Cerastes cornutus*, a venomous species of Egypt, Palestine, etc., with a horny process above each eye. **4.** a venomous, malignant, or spiteful person. **5.** a false or treacherous person. **–viperine**, **viperish**, **viperous**, *adj.*

virago /və'ragoʊ/ n. (pl. **-goes** or **-gos**) **1.** a turbulent, violent, or ill-tempered, scolding woman; a shrew. **2.** *Obs.* a woman of masculine strength or spirit. **–viraginous** /və'rædʒənəs/, *adj.*

viral /'vaɪrəl/ adj. **1.** relating to or caused by a virus. *–phr.* **2. go viral**, to be disseminated rapidly and widely as one person alerts another in an ever-widening circle, especially using the internet.

virgin /'vɜdʒən/ n. **1.** a person, especially a woman, who has never had sexual intercourse. *–adj.* **2.** being a virgin. **3.** like or suggesting a virgin; pure; unsullied: *virgin snow.* **4.** untreated or unprocessed: *virgin gold; virgin wool.* **5.** untouched, untried, or unused: *virgin bush; virgin soil.* **6.** denoting the oil obtained as from olives, etc., by the first pressing without the application of heat. **–virginity**, *n.*

virginal¹ /'vɜdʒənəl/ adj. **1.** of, relating to, characteristic of, or befitting a virgin. **2.** continuing in a state of virginity. **3.** pure or unsullied; untouched; fresh. **4.** *Zool.* unfertilised. **–virginally**, *adv.*

virginal² /'vɜdʒənəl/ n. **1.** a small harpsichord of rectangular shape, with the strings stretched parallel to the keyboard, the earlier types placed on a table, common in the 16th and 17th centuries. **2.** (loosely) any harpsichord. Also, **virginals**, **pair of virginals**. **–virginalist**, *n.*

Virgo /'vɜgoʊ/ **1.** the sixth sign of the Zodiac, which the sun enters about 23 August; the Virgin. **2.** a person born under the sign of Virgo. *–adj.* **3.** of or relating to Virgo.

virile /'vɪraɪl/ adj. **1.** of, relating to, or characteristic of a man, as opposed to a woman or a child; masculine or manly; natural to or befitting a man. **2.** having or exhibiting in a marked degree masculine strength, vigour, or forcefulness. **3.** characterised by a vigorous masculine spirit: *a virile literary style.* **4.** relating to or capable of procreation. **–virility**, *n.*

virology /vaɪ'rɒlədʒi/ n. the branch of medical science that deals with viruses and the diseases caused by them. **–virological** /vaɪrə'lɒdʒɪkəl/, *adj.* **–virologically** /vaɪrə'lɒdʒɪkli/, *adv.* **–virologist**, *n.*

virtual /'vɜtʃuəl/ adj. **1.** being such in power, force, or effect, although not actually or expressly such: *he was reduced to virtual poverty.* **2.** *Optics* **a.** denoting an image formed by the apparent convergence of rays geometrically (but not actually) prolonged, as the image in a mirror (opposed to *real*). **b.** denoting a focus of a corresponding nature. **3.** *Computers* of or relating to an environment, object, etc., which exists only as an interactive computer representation, as opposed to a physical reality. —**virtuality**, *n*.

virtual community *n.* a community which is linked by a common interest and connected by the internet.

virtual computer *n.* a computer which is able to support a number of software systems using an emulator to translate and relay commands from each system to a single CPU and hard disk.

virtual courtroom *n.* a method of conducting legal proceedings in which videoconferencing technology is used to link parties separated by distance.

virtually /ˈvɜtʃuəli, ˈvɜtʃəli/ *adv.* 1. in effect, although not in name or in fact: *a licence for a television station is virtually a licence to print money.* 2. *Colloq.* almost.

virtual memory *n.* → **virtual RAM**.

virtual RAM *n. Computers* a method of programming a computer to use only those parts of a program which are required rather than the whole program, thus making the memory appear larger than it really is.

virtual reality *n.* 1. an artificial environment represented by a computer and intended to appear and feel real to the user, who, with the use of gloves, earphones and goggles connected to the computer, is able to interact with this environment as if it had a physical reality. 2. any artificial environment represented by a computer.

virtual site *n.* a website which presents a virtual reality.

virtual water *n.* water which is used in the production of a good or a service, as in the production of food, and in industrial processes such as the manufacture of textiles. Also, **embedded water**.

virtue /ˈvɜtʃu/ *n.* 1. moral excellence or goodness. 2. conformity of life and conduct to moral laws; uprightness; rectitude. 3. a particular moral excellence, the **cardinal virtues** being justice, prudence, temperance, and fortitude, and the **theological virtues** being faith, hope, and charity. 4. an excellence, merit, or good quality: *brevity is often a virtue.* 5. chastity. 6. effective force: *there is no virtue in such measures.* 7. a power or property of producing a particular effect. 8. inherent power to produce effects; potency or efficacy: *a medicine of sovereign virtue.* 9. *Theology* a member of the fifth order of angels. See **angel** (def. 1). —*phr.* 10. **by** (or **in**) **virtue of**, by reason of: *to act by virtue of authority conferred.*

virtuoso /vɜtʃuˈousou, -ˈouzou/ *n.* (*pl.* **-sos** *or* **-si** /-si, -zi/) 1. someone who has special knowledge or skill in any field, as in music. 2. someone who excels in musical technique or execution. 3. someone who has a cultivated appreciation of artistic excellence; a connoisseur of works or objects of art; a student or collector of objects of art, curios, antiquities, etc. —*adj.* 4. characteristic of a virtuoso. —**virtuosic**, *adj.* —**virtuosity**, *n.*

virtuous /ˈvɜtʃuəs/ *adj.* morally excellent or good; conforming or conformed to moral laws; upright; righteous; moral. —**virtuously**, *adv.* —**virtuousness**, *n.*

virulent /ˈvɪrələnt/ *adj.* 1. actively poisonous, malignant, or deadly: *a virulent poison, a virulent form of a disease.* 2. *Med.* highly infective; malignant or deadly. 3. *Bacteriol.* of the nature of an organism causing specific or general clinical symptoms. 4. violently or venomously hostile. 5. intensely bitter, spiteful, or acrimonious. —**virulence, virulency**, *n.* —**virulently**, *adv.*

virus /ˈvaɪrəs/ *n.* 1. a submicroscopic infective agent, inert outside a cell but able to reproduce within the host cell. 2. any disease caused by a virus. 3. Also, **computer virus**. a destructive program introduced into a computer system, sometimes to protect software from piracy, though mostly simply for malicious purposes. 4. a moral or intellectual poison; a corrupting influence. —**virus-like**, *adj.*

virus load *n. Med.* the level of a virus present in the body: *treatment to suppress virus load.*

visa /ˈvizə/ *n.* 1. an authority to enter a foreign country, usually for a temporary period, issued by the government of that country and usually stamped in a passport. —*v.t.* (**-saed, -saing**) 2. to put a visa on; examine and endorse, as a passport.

visage /ˈvɪzɪdʒ/ *n.* 1. the face, especially of a human being, and commonly with reference to shape, features, expression, etc.; the countenance. 2. aspect; appearance. —**visaged**, *adj.*

vis-a-vis /viz-a-ˈvi/ *prep.* 1. face to face with; opposite. 2. regarding; with relation to: *discussions with the treasurer vis-a-vis the finances of a proposal.* —*n.* (*pl.* **vis-a-vis**) 3. a person corresponding in status or function to another; opposite number. Also, **vis-à-vis**.

viscera /ˈvɪsərə/ *pl. n.* (*sing.* **viscus**) 1. the soft interior organs in the cavities of the body, including the brain, lungs, heart, stomach, intestines, etc., especially such of these as are confined to the abdomen. 2. (in popular use) the intestines or bowels. —**visceral**, *adj.*

viscid /ˈvɪsɪd/ *adj.* 1. sticky, adhesive, or glutinous; of a glutinous consistency; viscous. 2. *Bot.* covered by a sticky substance, as a leaf. —**viscidity** /vəˈsɪdəti/, **viscidness**, *n.* —**viscidly**, *adv.*

viscose /ˈvɪskouz, -ous/ *n.* 1. a viscous solution prepared by treating cellulose with caustic soda and carbon disulphide; used in manufacturing regenerated cellulose fibres, sheets, or tubes, as rayon or cellophane. —*adj.* 2. relating to or made from viscose.

viscount /ˈvaɪkaunt/ *n.* a nobleman next below an earl or count and next above a baron. —**viscountcy, viscountship**, *n.*

viscountess /ˈvaɪkauntɪs/ *n.* 1. the wife or widow of a viscount. 2. a woman holding in her own right a rank equivalent to that of a viscount.

viscous /ˈvɪskəs/ *adj.* 1. sticky, adhesive, or glutinous; of a glutinous character or consistency; thick. 2. having the property of viscosity. —**viscosity**, *n.* —**viscously**, *adv.* —**viscousness**, *n.*

Vishnu /ˈvɪʃnu/ *n. Hinduism* 1. 'the Pervader', one of a half-dozen solar deities in the Rig-Veda. 2. (in later Hinduism) 'the Preserver', the second member of an important trinity, together with Brahma the Creator and Shiva the Destroyer. 3. (in popular Hinduism) a deity believed to have descended from heaven to earth in several incarnations, or avatars; most important human incarnation is the Krishna of the Bhagavad-gita.

visibility /vɪzəˈbɪləti/ *n.* (*pl.* **-ties**) 1. the state or fact of being visible; capability of being seen. 2. the relative capability of being seen under given conditions of distance, light, atmosphere, etc.: *low visibility; high visibility.* 3. *Meteorol.* the greatest distance at which an object of specified characteristics can be seen and identified; visual range.

visible /ˈvɪzəbəl/ *adj.* 1. capable of being seen; perceptible by the eye; open to sight or view. 2. perceptible by the mind; apparent; manifest; obvious. 4. represented visually; prepared or converted for visual presentation: *visible sound* (an oscillograph of a soundwave). —**visibleness**, *n.* —**visibly**, *adv.*

vision /ˈvɪʒən/ *n.* 1. the act of seeing with the eye; power, or sense of sight. 2. the act or power of perceiving what is not actually present to the eye, either by imagination, or intelligence: *she shows vision in dealing with great problems.* 3. a mental view or image, either of supernatural origin or imaginary, of what is not actually present in place or time: *visions of the future; visions of God.* 4. something seen, especially in a dream, trance, etc. 5. someone or something of great beauty. 6. *Film, TV, etc.* recorded images on film or videotape (as opposed to *sound*). —**visionless**, *adj.*

visionary /'vɪʒənri/ *adj.* **1.** given to or concerned with seeing visions. **2.** belonging to or seen in a vision. **3.** unreal or imaginary: *visionary evils.* **4.** given to or based on imagination or theory; ideal; unpractical: *a visionary plan*; *a visionary thinker. –n. (pl. -ries)* **5.** someone who sees visions. **6.** someone who is given to ideas or plans which are not immediately practical; a dreamer, theorist, or enthusiast. **–visionariness**, *n.*

vision-impaired *adj.* **1.** *Med.* deficient in sight, ranging from complete blindness to partial vision. **2.** of or relating to a person with partial vision (opposed to *blind*). **–visually-impaired**, *adj.*

visit /'vɪzət/ *v.t.* **1.** to go or call on to see (a person, family, place, etc.). **2.** to stay with as a guest. **3.** to come upon or afflict: *the plague visited London in 1665.* **4.** *Internet* to access (a website). *–v.i.* **5.** to visit someone or something. *–n.* **6.** the act of visiting. **–visitor**, *n.*

visitant /'vɪzətənt/ *n.* **1.** a visitor; a guest; a temporary resident. **2.** a supernatural visitor; an apparition; a ghost. **3.** someone who visits a place of interest, a shrine, etc., for sightseeing, on a pilgrimage, or the like. **4.** a migratory bird, or other animal, at a temporary feeding place, etc., or on its nesting ground (**summer visitant**) or wintering ground (**winter visitant**). *–adj.* **5.** visiting; paying a visit.

visitation /vɪzə'teɪʃən/ *n.* **1.** a visit, especially for the purpose of making an official inspection, etc. **2.** a giving by God of a reward, or punishment, or an event or experience regarded as such. **–visitational**, *adj.*

visor /'vaɪzə/ *n.* **1.** the movable front parts of a helmet, covering the face, especially the uppermost part which protects the eyes. **2.** any disguise or means of concealment. **3.** a small shield attached to the inside roof of a car, which may be swung down to protect the driver's eyes from glare or sunlight. *–v.t.* **4.** to protect or mask with a visor; shield. Also, **vizor. –visored**, *adj.* **–visorless**, *adj.*

vista /'vɪstə/ *n.* **1.** a view or prospect, especially one seen through a long, narrow avenue or passage, as between rows of trees, houses, or the like. **2.** such an avenue or passage. **3.** a mental view of a far-reaching kind: *vistas of thought.* **4.** a mental view extending over a long time or a stretch of remembered, imagined, or anticipated experiences, etc.: *dim vistas of the past or the future.* **–vistaed** /'vɪstəd/, *adj.* **–vistaless**, *adj.*

visual /'vɪʒuəl/ *adj.* **1.** of or relating to sight. **2.** able to be seen; visible. *–n.* **3.** an object having a visual effect, such as a photograph, film, slide, etc.; an image. **–visually**, *adv.*

visual display unit *n.* → **monitor** (def. 4c). Also, **VDU**.

visualise /'vɪʒuəlaɪz/ *v.i.* **1.** to call up or form mental images or pictures. *–v.t.* **2.** to make visual or visible. **3.** to form a mental image of. **4.** to make perceptible to the mind or to the imagination. Also, **visualize**. **–visualisation** /vɪʒuələr'zeɪʃən/, *n.* **–visualiser**, *n.*

vital /'vaɪtl/ *adj.* **1.** of or relating to life: *vital functions.* **2.** having life, or living. **3.** having great energy, enthusiasm, etc.: *a vital personality.* **4.** being necessary to life: *the vital organs.* **5.** necessary; indispensable; essential: *it is vital that we act now.* **6.** of basic importance: *vital problems. –n.* **7.** *(pl.)* the essential parts of anything. **–vitally**, *adv.* **–vitalness**, *n.*

vitality /vaɪ'tæləti/ *n. (pl. -ties)* **1.** energy; vigour. **2.** the power to live; vital force. **3.** the power of continued existence.

vital statistics *pl. n.* **1.** statistics concerning human life or the conditions affecting human life and the maintenance of population. **2.** *Colloq.* the measurements of a woman's figure, as at the bust, waist, and hips.

vitamin /'vaɪtəmən, 'vɪt-/ *n.* any of a group of food factors essential in small quantities to maintain life, but not themselves using energy. The absence of any one of them results in a characteristic deficiency disease.

vitiate /'vɪʃieɪt/ *v.t.* **1.** to impair the quality of; make faulty; mar. **2.** to contaminate; corrupt; spoil. **3.** to make legally defective or invalid; invalidate. **–vitiation** /vɪʃi-'eɪʃən/, *n.* **–vitiator**, *n.*

viticulture /'vɪtikʌltʃə/ *n.* **1.** the culture or cultivation of the grapevine; grape-growing. **2.** the study or science of grapes and their culture. **–viticultural** /vɪti'kʌltʃərəl/, *adj.* **–viticulturer** /vɪti'kʌltʃərə/, **viticulturalist** /vɪti'kʌltʃərələst/, **viticulturist** /vɪti'kʌltʃərəst/, *n.*

vitreous /'vɪtriəs/ *adj.* **1.** resembling glass, as in transparency, brittleness, hardness, etc.; glassy: *vitreous china.* **2.** of or relating to glass. **3.** obtained from glass. **–vitreously**, *adv.* **–vitreousness, vitreosity** /vɪtri'ɒsəti/, *n.*

vitri- a word element meaning 'glass', as in *vitriform*.

vitrify /'vɪtrəfaɪ/ *verb* **(-fied, -fying)** *–v.t.* **1.** to convert into glass. **2.** to make vitreous. *–v.i.* **3.** to be converted into glass. **4.** to become vitreous. **–vitrifiable**, *adj.* **–vitrifiability** /ˌvɪtrəfaɪə'bɪləti/, *n.*

vitriol /'vɪtriɒl/ *n.* **1.** *Chem.* any of certain metallic sulphates of glassy appearance, as of copper (**blue vitriol**), or iron (**green vitriol**), or zinc (**white vitriol**), etc. **2.** sulphuric acid. **3.** something highly caustic, or severe in its effects, as criticism. *–v.t.* **(-olled** *or, Chiefly US,* **-oled, -olling** *or, Chiefly US,* **-oling) 4.** to injure or burn with vitriol or sulphuric acid.

vituperate /və'tjupəreɪt, vaɪ-/ *v.t.* **1.** to find fault with abusively. **2.** to address abusive language to; revile; objurgate. *–v.i.* **3.** to use abusive language. **–vituperation**, *n.* **–vituperative**, *adj.* **–vituperator**, *n.*

viva[1] /'vivə/ *interj.* *(used in phrases of acclamation)* long live (the person or idea named)!

viva[2] /'vaɪvə/ *n. Colloq.* → **viva voce** (def. 2).

vivacious /və'veɪʃəs/ *adj.* lively, animated, or sprightly: *a vivacious manner or style, vivacious conversation.* **–vivaciously**, *adv.* **–vivaciousness, vivacity**, *n.*

viva voce /vaɪvə 'voʊtʃeɪ/ *adv.* **1.** by word of mouth; orally. *–n.* Also, **viva**. **2.** an examination where questions are asked and answered orally rather than by a written paper. **–viva-voce**, *adj.*

vivid /'vɪvəd/ *adj.* **1.** strikingly bright, as colour, light, etc. **2.** lively; full of life: *a vivid personality.* **3.** presenting the appearance, freshness, etc, of life: *a vivid picture.* **4.** strong and clear: *a vivid impression; a vivid memory.* **5.** forming clear and striking mental images: *a vivid imagination.* **–vividly**, *adv.* **–vividness**, *n.*

vivify /'vɪvəfaɪ/ *v.t.* **(-fied, -fying) 1.** to give life to; quicken. **2.** to enliven; render lively or animated; brighten. **–vivification** /vɪvəfə'keɪʃən/, *n.* **–vivifier**, *n.*

viviparous /və'vɪpərəs/ *adj.* **1.** *Zool.* bringing forth living young (rather than eggs), as most mammals and some reptiles and fishes. **2.** *Bot.* producing seeds that germinate on the plant. **–viviparity** /vɪvə'pærəti/, **viviparousness**, *n.* **–viviparously**, *adv.*

vivisect /'vɪvəsɛkt, vɪvə'sɛkt/ *v.t.* **1.** to dissect the living body of. *–v.i.* **2.** to practise vivisection. **–vivisection**, *n.* **–vivisector**, *n.*

vixen /'vɪksən/ *n.* **1.** a female fox. **2.** an ill-tempered or quarrelsome woman; a spitfire. **–vixenish, vixenly**, *adj.* **–vixenishly**, *adv.* **–vixenishness**, *n.*

viyella /vaɪ'ɛlə/ *n. (also upper case) (from trademark)* a soft fabric made of cotton and wool, used especially for blouses, shirts, and children's clothing.

VJ /'vi dʒeɪ/ *n.* → **V-jay**.

V-jay /'vi-dʒeɪ/ *n.* a presenter of music video clips. Also, **VJ, veejay**.

vlog /vlɒg/ *n.* a blog with video streaming. **–vlogging**, *n.* **–vlogger**, *n.*

VLSI /vi ɛl ɛs 'aɪ/ *n. Computers* the process or technology which facilitates the concentration of many thousands of semiconductor devices on a single integrated circuit.

vocabulary /ˈvoʊˈkæbjələri, və-/, *Orig. US* /-lɛri/ *n.* (*pl.* **-ries**) **1.** the stock of words used by a people, or by a particular class or person. **2.** a list or collection of the words of a language, book, author, branch of science, or the like, usually in alphabetical order and defined; a wordbook, glossary, dictionary, or lexicon. **3.** the words of a language. **4.** a range of stylised artistic forms, as in music, architecture, etc.: *she is a versatile composer with a large musical vocabulary.*

vocal /ˈvoʊkəl/ *adj.* **1.** of or relating to the voice: *the vocal organs.* **2.** spoken with the voice; oral. **3.** sung, or intended for singing: *the vocal score.* **4.** having a voice: *a vocal being.* **5.** able to or inclined to express oneself clearly in speech. –*n.* **6.** a vocal sound. **7.** (*usu. pl.*) (in pop, rock, etc.) the musical part written for or performed by a singer. –**vocality** /voʊˈkæləti/, **vocalness,** *n.* –**vocally,** *adv.*

vocal cords *pl. n. Anat.* folds of mucous membrane projecting into the cavity of the larynx, the edges of which can be drawn tense and made to vibrate by the passage of air from the lungs, thus producing vocal sound; vocal folds.

vocalic /voʊˈkælɪk/ *adj.* **1.** of or relating to a vowel or vowels; vowel-like. **2.** containing many vowels.

vocalise[1] /ˈvoʊkəlaɪz/ *v.t.* **1.** to express with the voice; speak or sing. –*v.i.* **2.** to use the voice; speak or sing. Also, **vocalize.** –**vocalisation** /voʊkəlaɪˈzeɪʃən/, *n.* –**vocaliser,** *n.*

vocalise[2] /voʊkəˈliz/ *n.* a piece of music to be sung on vowel sounds without words; often a training exercise.

vocalist /ˈvoʊkəlɒst/ *n.* a singer.

vocation /voʊˈkeɪʃən/ *n.* **1.** a particular occupation, business, or profession; a trade or calling. **2.** a calling or summons, as to a particular activity or career. **3.** a divine call to God's service or to the Christian life. **4.** a function or station to which one is called by God. –**vocational,** *adj.*

vocative /ˈvɒkətɪv/ *adj.* **1.** *Gram.* (in some inflected languages) designating a case that indicates the person or thing addressed. **2.** relating to or used in calling. –*n.* **3.** *Gram.* the vocative case. –**vocatively,** *adv.*

vociferate /vəˈsɪfəreɪt/ *v.i.* **1.** to cry out loudly or noisily; shout; bawl. –*v.t.* **2.** to utter in a loud cry. –**vociferation,** *n.* –**vociferant,** *n., adj.* –**vociferator,** *n.*

vociferous /vəˈsɪfərəs/ *adj.* **1.** crying out noisily; clamorous. **2.** of the nature of vociferation; uttered with clamour. –**vociferously,** *adv.* –**vociferousness,** *n.*

vodcasting /ˈvɒdkæstɪŋ/ *n.* the online delivery of video on demand.

vodka /ˈvɒdkə/ *n.* an alcoholic drink of Russian origin, distilled originally from wheat, but now from corn, other cereals, and potatoes.

vogue /voʊɡ/ *n.* **1.** the fashion, as at a particular time: *a style in vogue fifty years ago.* **2.** popular currency, acceptance, or favour: *the book had a great vogue in its day.*

voice /vɔɪs/ *n.* **1.** the sound or sounds uttered through the mouth of living creatures, especially of human beings in speaking, shouting, singing, etc. **2.** the sounds naturally uttered by a single person in speech or vocal utterance, often as characteristic of the utterer. **3.** such sounds considered with reference to their character or quality: *a deep voice; a loud voice.* **4.** the condition of the voice for speaking or singing, especially effective condition: *he was in poor voice.* **5.** the ability to sing well: *she has a wonderful voice.* **6.** the faculty of uttering sounds through the mouth, especially articulate sounds; utterance; speech. **7.** expression in spoken or written words, or by other means: *to give voice to one's disapproval by writing a letter.* **8.** expressed opinion or choice: *his voice was for compromise.* **9.** the right to express an opinion or choice; vote; suffrage: *have no voice in a matter.* **10.** musical sound created by the

vibration of the vocal cords and amplified by oral and other throat cavities; tone produced in singing. **11.** *Phonetics* the sound produced by vibration of the vocal cords, as air from the lungs is forced through between them. **12.** *Gram.* **a.** (in some languages, as Latin) a group of categories of verb inflection denoting the relationship between the action expressed by the verb and the subject of the sentence (e.g., as acting or as acted upon). **b.** (in some other languages) one of several contrasting constructions with similar functions. **c.** any one of such categories or constructions in a particular language, as the *active* and *passive* voices in Latin. **13.** a singer. **14.** a voice part. –*v.t.* (**voiced, voicing**) **15.** to give voice, utterance, or expression to (an emotion, opinion, etc.); express; declare; proclaim: *to voice one's discontent.* **16.** *Phonetics* to utter with vibration of the vocal cords. –*phr.* **17. with one voice,** in chorus; unanimously. –**voicer,** *n.*

voice-activated *adj.* activated by a spoken command: *a voice-activated light switch.*

voice actor *n.* an actor who speaks a part for an animated character in a film or television show.

voicemail /ˈvɔɪsmeɪl/ *n.* **1.** a system for recording messages over the telephone for later playback. **2.** a message received on such a system. Also, **voice mail.**

voice messaging *n.* a system which records a spoken message for replay later, now often integrated in computer transfer of spoken information as well as data.

voice recognition *n.* **1.** Also, **speaker recognition.** the identifying by a computer of a particular voice which it has been programmed to learn to recognise with the purpose of allowing the owner of the voice to operate any machine, system of admission, etc., which the computer controls, merely by speaking. **2.** → **speech recognition.**

void /vɔɪd/ *adj.* **1.** *Law* without legal force or effect; not legally binding or enforceable. **2.** useless; ineffectual; vain. **3.** without contents. **4.** without an incumbent, as an office. –*n.* **5.** an empty space: *the void of heaven.* **6.** a place without the usual or desired occupant: *his death left a void among us.* **7.** a gap or opening, as in a wall. **8.** emptiness; vacancy. –*v.t.* **9.** to make void or of no effect; invalidate; nullify. **10.** to empty or discharge the contents of; evacuate: *to void the bowels.* –*v.i.* **11.** to empty the bowels: *the patient must void before undergoing the procedure.* –*phr.* **12. void of,** completely empty of; devoid of; destitute of: *void of hope.* –**voider,** *n.* –**voidness,** *n.*

voile /vɔɪl/ *n.* a semitransparent dress fabric of wool, silk, rayon, or cotton, with an open weave.

volatile /ˈvɒlətaɪl/ *adj.* **1.** evaporating rapidly; passing off readily in the form of vapour: *a volatile oil.* **2.** easily provoked to violence or anger. **3.** likely to change suddenly and unpredictably: *volatile interest rates; a volatile election campaign.* **4.** light and changeable (of mind; frivolous; flighty. **5.** fleeting; transient. **6.** (of wine) pricked; vinegary. **7.** *Computers* relating to information in the memory bank of a computer which is lost when power is disconnected. –**volatility** /vɒləˈtɪləti/, **volatileness,** *n.*

volcano /vɒlˈkeɪnoʊ/ *n.* (*pl.* **-noes** *or* **-nos**) **1.** an opening in the earth's crust through which molten rock (lava), steam, ashes, etc., are expelled from within, either continuously or at irregular intervals, gradually forming a conical heap (or in time a mountain), commonly with a cup-shaped hollow (crater) around the opening. **2.** a mountain or hill having such an opening and formed wholly or partly of its own lava. –**volcanic,** *adj.*

volcanology /vɒlkəˈnɒlədʒi/ *n.* the scientific study of volcanoes and volcanic phenomena. Also, **vulcanology.** –**volcanological** /vɒlkənəˈlɒdʒɪkəl/, *adj.* –**volcanologist,** *n.*

vole /voʊl/ *n.* any of the rodents of the genus *Microtus* and allied genera, resembling and belonging to the same family as the common rats and mice, and usually of heavy build and having short limbs and tail.

volition /vəˈlɪʃən/ *n.* **1.** the act of willing; exercise of choice to determine action. **2.** a determination by the will. **3.** the power of willing; will. –**volitional, volitionary,** *adj.* –**volitionally,** *adv.*

volley /ˈvɒli/ *n.* (*pl.* **-leys**) **1. a.** the firing of a number of guns or other weapons together. **b.** the missiles fired. **2.** a burst or outpouring of many things at once or close together: *a volley of words*; *a volley of blows.* **3.** *Tennis, etc.* a return of the ball before it touches the ground. –*verb* (**-leyed, -leying**) –*v.t.* **4.** to fire in a volley. **5.** *Tennis, Soccer, etc.* to return, kick, etc., (the ball) before it strikes the ground. –*v.i.* **6.** to fly or be fired together. **7.** to move, proceed, or sound with great rapidity, as in a volley. –**volleyer,** *n.*

volleyball /ˈvɒlibɔl/ *n.* **1.** a game, played outdoors or in a gymnasium, the object of which is to prevent a large ball from touching the ground by striking it from side to side over a high net with the hands or arms. **2.** the ball used in this game. –**volleyballer,** *n.*

volt /voʊlt/ *n.* the derived SI unit of electric potential or electromotive force, defined as the difference of potential between two points of a conducting wire carrying a constant current of one ampere, when the power dissipated between these points is one watt. *Symbol*: V

voltage /ˈvoʊltɪdʒ/ *n.* electromotive force or potential expressed in volts.

voluble /ˈvɒljəbəl/ *adj.* characterised by a ready and continuous flow of words, as a speaker or his or her tongue or speech; glibly fluent: *a voluble talker.* –**volubility** /vɒljəˈbɪləti/, **volubleness,** *n.* –**volubly,** *adv.*

volume /ˈvɒljum/ *n.* **1.** a collection of written or printed sheets bound together and forming a book. **2.** a book forming one of a related set or series. **3.** the size, measure, or amount of anything in three dimensions; the space occupied by a body or substance measured in cubic units. **4.** mass, amount, or quantity, especially a large quantity, of anything: *volumes of smoke*; *volumes of abuse*; *the volume of traffic increases in the evening.* **5.** loudness or softness.

volumetric /vɒljəˈmɛtrɪk/ *adj.* of or relating to measurement by volume. Also, **volumetrical.** –**volumetrically,** *adv.* –**volumetry** /vɒlˈjumətri/, *n.* –**volumetrics,** *n.*

voluminous /vəˈlumənəs, -ˈlju-/ *adj.* **1.** forming, filling, or writing a large volume or book, or many volumes: *a voluminous author.* **2.** sufficient to fill a volume or volumes: *a voluminous correspondence.* **3.** of great volume, size, or extent; in great volumes: *a voluminous flow of lava.* **4.** of ample size, fullness, or fullness, as garments, draperies, etc. –**voluminously,** *adv.* –**voluminousness, voluminosity** /vəlumaˈnɒsəti/, *n.*

voluntary /ˈvɒləntri, -ləntəri/, *Orig. US* /-tɛri/ *adj.* **1.** done, made, brought about, etc., by free will or choice: *a voluntary contribution.* **2.** acting of one's own will or choice: *a voluntary helper.* **3.** relating to or depending on voluntary action or help. **4.** controlled by the will: *voluntary muscles.* **5.** having the power of willing or choosing: *a voluntary agent.* –*n.* (*pl.* **-taries**) **6.** a piece of music, often improvised, especially a piece of organ music performed before, during, or after a church service. –**voluntarily,** *adv.* –**voluntariness,** *n.*

voluntary euthanasia *n.* euthanasia practised at the wish of a person with a terminal illness.

volunteer /vɒlənˈtɪə/ *n.* **1.** someone who enters into any service, or offers to do something, of his or her own free will for no financial gain. –*adj.* **2.** being a volunteer or consisting of volunteers: *a volunteer soldier*; *a volunteer force.* –*v.i.* **3.** to offer to do something. **4.** to enter a service, especially the armed forces, as a volunteer. –*v.t.* **5.** to offer (one's services, etc., or oneself) for some duty or purpose. **6.** to offer to give without being asked: *to volunteer advice*; *to volunteer an explanation.*

volunteerism /vɒlənˈtɪərɪzəm/ *n.* the system of volunteer participation in activities of benefit to the community.

voluptuary /vəˈlʌptʃuəri/ *n.* (*pl.* **-aries**) **1.** someone given up to luxurious or sensuous pleasures. –*adj.* **2.** relating to or characterised by luxurious or sensuous pleasures: *voluptuary habits.*

voluptuous /vəˈlʌptʃuəs/ *adj.* **1.** full of, suggesting, or producing sensual, especially sexual, pleasure: *a voluptuous dance.* **2.** arising from enjoyment of the pleasures of the senses: *the voluptuous pleasure of a warm bath.* **3.** (of the female figure) full and shapely. –**voluptuously,** *adv.* –**voluptuousness, voluptuosity,** *n.*

volute /vəˈljut/ *n.* **1.** a spiral or twisted formation or object. **2.** *Archit.* a spiral scroll-like ornament, especially one forming the distinctive feature of the Ionic capital or a more or less important part of the Corinthian and Composite capitals. **3.** *Zool.* **a.** a turn or whorl of a spiral shell. **b.** any of the Volutidae, a family of tropical marine gastropods, many species of which have shells prized for their beauty. –*adj.* **4.** in the form of a volute; rolled up. –**volution** /vəˈljuʃən/, *n.*

vomit /ˈvɒmət/ *v.i.* **1.** to throw out the contents of the stomach by the mouth. **2.** to be sent out with force or violence. –*v.t.* **3.** to throw out from the stomach through the mouth. **4.** to send out with force or violence. –*n.* **5.** the act of vomiting. **6.** the matter thrown out in vomiting. –**vomiter,** *n.* –**vomitive,** *adj.*

voodoo /ˈvudu/ *n.* (*pl.* **-doos**) **1.** an animistic religion practised chiefly in certain parts of the Caribbean, involving rituals of sorcery and communication with ancestors, and based on a combination of Roman Catholic ritual elements and animistic beliefs of African origin. **2.** someone who practises such rites. **3.** a fetish or other object of voodoo worship. –*adj.* **4.** relating to, associated with, or practising voodoo or voodooism. –*v.t.* (**-dooed, -dooing**) **5.** to affect by or as by voodoo sorcery or conjuration. –**voodooism,** *n.*

voracious /vəˈreɪʃəs/ *adj.* **1.** devouring or craving food in large quantities: *a voracious appetite.* **2.** greedy in eating; ravenous. **3.** eager and indefatigable: *she is a voracious reader.* –**voraciously,** *adv.* –**voracity** /vəˈræsəti/, **voraciousness,** *n.*

-vorous a word element meaning 'eating', as in *carnivorous, herbivorous, omnivorous.*

vortex /ˈvɔtɛks/ *n.* (*pl.* **-texes** *or* **-tices** /-təsiz/) **1.** a whirling mass of water, air, fire, etc. **2.** a state of affairs likened to this for violent activity, irresistible force, etc.

votary /ˈvoʊtəri/ *n.* (*pl.* **-ries**) **1.** someone who is bound by a vow, especially one bound by vows to a religious life; a monk or a nun. **2.** a devotee of some form of religious worship; a devoted worshipper; as of God, a saint, etc. **3.** someone devoted to some pursuit, study, etc. **4.** a devoted follower or admirer. Also, **votarist.**

vote /voʊt/ *n.* **1.** a formal expression of will, wish, or choice in some matter, whether of a single individual, as one of a number interested in common, or of a body of individuals, signified by voice, by ballot, etc. **2.** the means by which such expression is made, as a ballot, ticket, etc. **3.** the right to such expression; suffrage. **4.** the decision reached by voting, as by a majority of ballots cast. **5.** a number of votes (or expressions of will) collectively: *the Labor vote*; *a light vote was polled.* **6.** an expression of feeling, as approval, or the like: *they gave him a vote of confidence.* **7.** an award, grant, or the like, voted: *a vote of $100 000 for a new building.* –*v.i.* **8.** to express or signify choice in a matter undergoing decision, as by a voice, ballot, or otherwise; give or cast a vote or votes: *for whom will you vote at the election?* –*v.t.* **9.** to enact, establish, or determine by vote; bring or put (*in, out, down*, etc.) by vote; grant by vote: *to vote an appropriation for a new school.* **10.** to support by one's vote: *to vote Liberal.* **11.** to advocate by or as by one's vote: *to vote that the report be accepted.* **12.** to declare by general consent: *they voted the trip a success. –phr.* **13.** **vote with one's feet,** *Colloq.* to express one's disapproval by leaving.

vote rigging *n.* the subversion of an election by altering the numbers of votes cast or other dishonest means of achieving a desired result.

votive /'vootiv/ *adj.* **1.** offered, given, dedicated, etc., in accordance with a vow: *a votive offering.* **2.** performed, undertaken, etc., in consequence of a vow. **3.** of the nature of or expressive of a wish or desire. **4.** *Roman Catholic Church* optional; not prescribed, as in *votive mass* (a mass which does not correspond with the office of the day, but is said at the choice of the priest). **–votively,** *adv.* **–votiveness,** *n.*

vouch /vautʃ/ *v.t.* **1.** to warrant; attest; confirm. **2.** to sustain or uphold by some practical proof or demonstration, or as such proof does. **3.** to affirm or declare as with warrant; vouch for. **4.** to adduce or quote in support, as extracts from a book or author; cite in warrant or justification, as authority, instances, facts, etc. **5.** to support or authenticate with evidence. *–phr.* **6.** **vouch for, a.** to answer for as being true, certain, reliable, justly asserted, etc.: *she does know how to keep a secret, that I can vouch for.* **b.** to give warrant or attestation on behalf of; give one's own assurance for, as surety or sponsor: *I can vouch for him.*

voucher /'vautʃə/ *n.* **1.** a document, receipt, stamp, or the like, which proves the truth of a claimed expenditure. **2.** a ticket used as a substitute for cash, as a gift voucher, luncheon voucher, etc.

vouchsafe /vautʃ'seɪf/ *v.t.* **1.** to grant or give, by favour, graciousness, or condescension: *to vouchsafe a reply.* **2.** to allow or permit, by favour or graciousness. *–v.i.* **3.** to condescend; deign; have the graciousness (to do something). **–vouchsafement,** *n.*

vow /vaʊ/ *n.* **1.** a solemn promise, pledge, or personal engagement: *marriage vows*; *a vow of secrecy.* **2.** a solemn or earnest declaration. **3.** a solemn, religiously binding promise made to God or to any deity or saint, as to perform some act, make some offering or gift, or enter some service or condition. **4.** a promise, limited in duration and in subject, made at the novitiate by one seeking to become a member of a religious community (**simple vow**). **5.** a promise, binding for life, and usually undertaking absolute chastity, total poverty, and unquestioning obedience, made at the profession of a religious when the habit is taken (**solemn vow**). *–v.t.* **6.** to make a vow of; promise by a vow, as to God or a saint: *to vow a crusade*; *to vow a pilgrimage.* **7.** to pledge oneself to do, make, give, observe, etc.; make a solemn threat or resolution of: *I vowed revenge.* **8.** to declare solemnly or earnestly; assert emphatically, or asseverate (often with a clause as object). **9.** to make (a vow). **10.** to dedicate or devote by a vow: *to vow oneself to the service of God. –v.i.* **11.** to make a solemn or earnest declaration; bind oneself by a vow. *–phr.* **12.** **take vows,** to enter a religious order or house. **–vower,** *n.* **–vowless,** *adj.*

vowel /'vaʊəl/ *n.* **1.** *Phonetics* a voiced speech sound during the articulation of which air from the lungs is free to pass out through the middle of the mouth without causing undue friction. **2.** *Gram.* a letter which usually represents a vowel, as in English, *a, e, i, o,* and *u,* and sometimes *y. –adj.* **3.** relating to a vowel. **–vowelless,** *adj.*

vox populi /vɒks 'pɒpjəlaɪ/ *n.* the voice or opinion of the people.

voyage /'vɔɪdʒ/ *n.* **1.** a passage, or course of travel, by sea or water, especially to a distant place. **2.** a flight through air or space, as a journey in an aeroplane. **3.** (*oft. pl.*) a voyage as the subject of a written account, or the account itself. *–verb* (**-aged, -aging**) *–v.i.* **4.** to make or take a voyage; travel by sea or water. *–v.t.* **5.** to traverse by a voyage. **–voyager** /'vɔɪədʒə/, *n.*

voyeur /vɔɪ'ɜ, vwa'jɜ/ *n.* someone who attains sexual gratification by looking at sexual objects or situations.

V6 /vi 'sɪks/ *n.* **1.** a reciprocating engine with six cylinders in a V formation. **2.** a vehicle powered by such an engine.

V12 /vi 'twɛlv/ *n.* **1.** a reciprocating engine with twelve cylinders in a V formation. **2.** a vehicle powered by such an engine.

vulcanise /'vʌlkənaɪz/ *v.t.* to treat (rubber) with sulphur or some compound of sulphur, and subject to a moderate heat (110°–140°C), in order to render it nonplastic and give greater elasticity, durability, etc., or when a large amount of sulphur and a more extensive heat treatment are used, in order to make it very hard, as in the case of vulcanite. Also, **vulcanize. –vulcanisable** /vʌlkə'naɪzəbəl/, *adj.* **–vulcanisation** /vʌlkənaɪ'zeɪʃən/, *n.* **–vulcaniser,** *n.*

vulcanology /vʌlkə'nɒlədʒi/ *n.* → **volcanology. –vulcanological** /vʌlkənə'lɒdʒɪkəl/, *adj.* **–vulcanologist,** *n.*

vulgar /'vʌlgə/ *adj.* **1.** marked by lack of good taste; coarse; crude: *vulgar manners*; *vulgar clothes.* **2.** offensively sexual; indecent: *a vulgar joke.* **3.** belonging to the common people of society: *vulgar superstitions.* **4.** spoken by or being in the language spoken by the people generally; vernacular: *a vulgar translation of the Greek text of the New Testament* **–vulgarly,** *adv.* **–vulgarity,** *n.*

vulgar fraction *n.* → **common fraction.**

vulnerable /'vʌlnrəbəl, -nərəbəl/ *adj.* **1.** susceptible to being wounded; liable to physical hurt. **2.** not protected against emotional hurt; highly sensitive. **3.** not immune to moral attacks, as of criticism or calumny, or against temptations, influences, etc. **4.** (of a place, fortress, etc.) open to attack or assault; weak in respect of defence. **–vulnerability** /vʌlnrə'bɪləti, -nərə-/, **vulnerableness,** *n.* **–vulnerably,** *adv.*

vulnerable species *n.* a threatened species that is facing a high risk of extinction in the wild in the medium-term future. Compare **endangered species, critically endangered species.**

vulpine /'vʌlpaɪn/ *adj.* relating to, like, or characteristic of a fox.

vulture /'vʌltʃə/ *n.* **1.** any of various large, carrion-eating birds of the family Accipitridae, native to Africa, Asia and southern Europe and related to the eagles, kites, hawks, falcons, etc., but having less powerful toes and straighter claws and usually a naked head, as the **Egyptian vulture,** *Neophron percnopterus,* of Eurasia and Africa. **2.** any of various large, carrion-eating American birds of the family Ciconiidae, related to the storks, though superficially resembling African and Eurasian vultures, as the **turkey vulture,** *Cathartes aura,* and the **black vulture,** *C. atratus.* **3.** a person who gets satisfaction or advantage from the misfortune of others.

vulva /'vʌlvə, 'vʊlvə/ *n.* (*pl.* **-vae** /-vi/ *or* **-vas**) the external female genitalia, specifically, the two pairs of labia and the cleft between them. **–vulval, vulvar,** *adj.* **–vulviform,** *adj.*

vying /'vaɪɪŋ/ *adj.* that vies; competing: *men vying with one another for attention.* **–vyingly,** *adv.*

W

W, w /ˈdʌbəlju/ *n.* the 23rd letter of the English alphabet.

wad /wɒd/ *n.* **1.** a small mass or lump of anything soft. **2.** a ball or mass of something squeezed together: *a wad of folded paper.* **3.** a roll or bundle, especially of banknotes. –*phr.* **4. have wads of ...**, *Colloq.* to be well supplied with ...: *have wads of cash; have wads of style.* –**wadder**, *n.*

wadding /ˈwɒdɪŋ/ *n.* **1.** any fibrous or soft material for stuffing, padding, packing, etc., especially carded cotton in specially prepared sheets. **2.** material for wads for guns, etc. **3.** a wad or lump.

waddle /ˈwɒdl/ *v.i.* **1.** to walk with short steps and swaying or rocking from side to side, as a duck. **2.** to move with a similar movement. –*n.* **3.** the act of waddling; a waddling gait. –**waddler**, *n.* –**waddlingly**, *adv.*

waddy /ˈwɒdi/ *n.* (*pl.* **-dies**) **1.** an Aboriginal heavy wooden war club. **2.** *Aust.* a heavy stick or club of any kind. –*v.t.* (**-died, -dying**) **3.** *Aust.* to beat or strike with a waddy.

wade /weɪd/ *v.i.* **1.** to walk through any substance, as water, snow, sand, etc., that impedes free motion: *wading in mud; wading through high grass.* **2.** to make one's way with labour or difficulty. –*v.t.* **3.** to pass through or cross by wading; ford: *to wade a stream.* –*n.* **4.** the act of wading. –*phr.* **5. wade in** (or **into**), *Colloq.* **a.** to begin energetically. **b.** to attack strongly.

wader /ˈweɪdə/ *n.* **1.** any of various long-legged birds, as cranes, herons, storks, sandpipers, plovers, etc., that wade in water in search of food. **2.** a high waterproof boot used for wading.

wadi /ˈwɒdi/ *n.* (*pl.* **-dies**) (in Arabia, Syria, northern Africa, etc.) the channel of a watercourse which is dry except during periods of rainfall.

wafer /ˈweɪfə/ *n.* **1.** a thin, crisp cake or biscuit, variously made, and often sweetened and flavoured, usually eaten with ice-cream. **2.** a thin piece, usually a disc, of unleavened bread, commonly used in the celebration of the Eucharist. **3.** any of various other thin, flat cakes, sheets, or the like. **4.** a thin disc of dried paste, gelatine, adhesive paper, or the like, used for sealing letters, attaching paper, etc. **5.** *Computers* a thin layer of silicon which forms the basis of a microchip. –**wafery**, *adj.*

waffle¹ /ˈwɒfəl/ *n.* a batter cake with deep indentations formed by baking it in a waffle iron.

waffle² /ˈwɒfəl/ *Colloq.* –*v.i.* **1.** to speak or write vaguely, pointlessly, and at considerable length. –*n.* **2.** verbosity in the service of superficial thought. **3.** nonsense; twaddle. –**waffly**, *adj.*

waft /wɒft/ *v.t.* **1.** to bear or carry through the air or over water: *the gentle breeze wafted the sound of voices.* **2.** to bear or convey lightly as if in flight: *he wafted her away.* –*v.i.* **3.** to float or be carried, especially through the air. –*n.* **4.** a sound, smell, etc., carried through the air: *a waft of bells.* **5.** a wafting movement; current or gust: *a waft of wind.* –**wafter**, *n.*

wag¹ /wæg/ *verb* (**wagged, wagging**) –*v.t.* **1.** to move from side to side, forwards and backwards, or up and down, especially rapidly and repeatedly: *a dog wagged its tail.* **2.** to move (the tongue) in talking. **3.** to shake (a finger) at someone, especially in reproval, reproach, or admonition. **4.** *Colloq.* to be absent from (school,

etc.) without permission. –*v.i.* **5.** to be moved from side to side or one way and the other, especially rapidly and repeatedly, as the head or the tail. **6.** (of the tongue) to move busily, especially in idle or indiscreet talk. **7.** to get along; travel; proceed: *how the world wags.* –*phr.* **8. wag it** or **play the wag**, *Colloq.* to deliberately stay away from school, work, etc., without permission.

wag² /wæg/ *n.* **1.** a humorous person; joker. –*phr.* **2. play the wag**, to entertain with jokes, silly antics, etc. –**waggery**, *n.* –**waggish**, *adj.* –**waggishly**, *adv.* –**waggishness**, *n.*

wage /weɪdʒ/ *n.* **1.** (*oft. pl.*) that which is paid for work or services, as by the day or week; hire; pay. **2.** (*pl.*) *Econ.* the share of the products of industry received by labour for its work, as distinguished from the share going to capital. **3.** (*usu. pl., sometimes construed as sing.*) recompense or result: *the wages of sin is death.* –*v.t.* (**waged, waging**) **4.** to carry on (a battle, war, conflict, etc.): *to wage war against a nation.* –**wageless**, *adj.*

wager /ˈweɪdʒə/ *n.* **1.** something staked or hazarded on an uncertain event; a bet. **2.** the act of betting. **3.** the subject of a bet. –*v.t.* **4.** to hazard (something) on the issue of a contest or any uncertain event or matter; stake; bet. –*v.i.* **5.** to make or offer a wager; bet. –**wagerer**, *n.*

waggle /ˈwægəl/ *v.t.* **1.** to wag (something) with short, quick movements: *she waggled her finger.* –*v.i.* **2.** to wag with short, quick movements: *her finger waggled.* –*n.* **3.** a waggling motion. –**waggly**, *adj.* –**wagglingly**, *adv.*

wagon /ˈwægən/ *n.* **1.** any of various kinds of four-wheeled vehicles, especially one designed for the transport of heavy loads, delivery, etc. **2.** Also, **railway wagon**. a railway truck, especially one for carrying goods, stock, etc. –*phr.* **3. on the (water) wagon**, *Colloq.* abstaining from alcoholic drink. Also, **waggon**. –**wagoner**, *n.* –**wagonless**, *adj.*

wagtail /ˈwægteɪl/ *n.* **1.** any of numerous small, chiefly Eurasian birds of the family Motacillidae, having a slender body with a long, narrow tail which is habitually wagged up and down. **2.** any of various fantails, as the willie wagtail.

Wagyu /ˈwægju/ *n.* **1.** one of a breed of cattle from Japan, with a genetic tendency to fine marbling of the meat. **2.** the beef obtained from such cattle.

wahine /waˈhini/ *n.* *NZ* a Maori woman, especially a wife or girlfriend.

waif /weɪf/ *n.* **1.** a person without home or friends, especially a child. **2.** a stray thing or article. **3.** something found, of which the owner is not known, as an animal. –**waifish**, *adj.* –**waiflike**, *adj.*

wail /weɪl/ *v.i.* **1.** to utter a long, mournful cry (in grief or suffering): *the child wailed when he fell over.* –*v.t.* **2.** to wail over; lament: *to wail the dead.* –*n.* **3.** the act of wailing. **4.** a cry of grief or pain. –**wailer**, *n.* –**wailingly**, *adv.*

wainscot /ˈweɪnskət, -kɒt/ *n.* **1.** oak or other wood, usually in panels, serving to line the walls of a room, etc. **2.** the lower portion of a wall surfaced in a different manner or material from the upper portion.

waist /weɪst/ *n.* **1.** the part of the human body between the ribs and the hips. **2.** the part of a garment covering the waist. **3.** the part of an object, especially a central or middle part, which bears some analogy to the human waist: *the waist of a violin.* **4.** *Entomology* the narrow part or petiole of the abdomen of certain insects, as the wasp. **–waisted**, *adj.* **–waistless**, *adj.*

waistcoat /ˈweɪstkoʊt/ *n.* **1.** a close-fitting, sleeveless garment for men which reaches to the waist and buttons down the front, and is designed to be worn under a jacket. **2.** a similar garment sometimes worn by women. **–waistcoated**, *adj.*

wait /weɪt/ *v.i.* **1.** (sometimes fol. by *for, till,* or *until*) to stay or rest in expectation; remain in a state of quiescence or inaction, as until something expected happens: *waiting for him to go.* **2.** (of things) to be in readiness: *a letter waiting for you.* **3.** to remain neglected for a time: *a matter that can wait.* **4.** to postpone or delay something or to be postponed or delayed. *–v.t.* **5.** to continue stationary or inactive in expectation of; await: *to wait one's turn in a queue.* **6.** to defer or postpone in expectation of the arrival of someone: *to wait dinner for the guests. –n.* **7.** the act of waiting or awaiting; delay; halt. **8.** a period or interval of waiting. *–phr.* **9. lie in wait,** to wait in ambush. **10. wait on** (or **upon**), **a.** to perform the duties of an attendant or servant for. **b.** to supply the wants of (a person) at table. **c.** to call upon or visit (a person, especially a superior): *to wait on the emperor in his palace.* **d.** to attend as an accompaniment or consequence. **11. wait table,** to wait at table; serve. **12. wait up,** (sometimes fol. by *for*) to delay going to bed to await someone's arrival.

waiter /ˈweɪtə/ *n.* **1.** someone, especially a man, who waits at table, as in a restaurant, hotel, etc. **2.** a tray on which dishes, etc., are carried; salver. **3.** someone who waits or awaits.

waitress /ˈweɪtrəs/ *n.* a woman who waits at table, as in a restaurant, hotel, etc. **–waitressing,** *n.*

waive /weɪv/ *v.t.* **1.** to forbear to insist on; relinquish; forgo: *to waive one's rank, to waive honours.* **2.** *Law* to relinquish (a known right, etc.) intentionally. **3.** to put aside for the time; defer. **4.** to put aside or dismiss from consideration or discussion: *waiving my attempts to explain.*

waiver /ˈweɪvə/ *n.* **1.** an intentional relinquishment of some right, interest, or the like. **2.** an express or written statement of such relinquishment.

wakame /waˈkami/ *n.* (in Japanese cookery) a variety of kelp which is dried or salted and used in soups and salads.

wake¹ /weɪk/ *verb* (**woke** *or, Chiefly US,* **waked, woken** *or, Chiefly US,* **waken, waking**) *–v.i.* **1.** Also, **wake up.** to become roused from sleep; awake. **2.** to be or continue awake. **3.** to remain awake for some purpose, duty, etc. **4.** to become roused from a quiescent or inactive state. **5.** (sometimes fol. by *to*) to become alive, as to something perceived; become aware. *–v.t.* Also, **wake up. 6.** to rouse from sleep or as from sleep; awake. *–n.* **7.** a watching, or a watch kept, especially for some solemn or ceremonial purpose. **8.** a watch, especially at night, near the body of a dead person before burial, often accompanied by drinking and feasting. **9.** (*sometimes humorous*) a party to celebrate a doleful occasion: *a wake for the old car.* **10.** the state of being awake: *between sleep and wake. –phr.* **11. wake up to oneself,** *Aust. Colloq.* to adopt a more sensible and responsible attitude. **12. wake up to someone** (or **something**), *Colloq.* to become aware of the true nature, etc., of someone (or of a situation, etc.): *she's finally woken up to him; it's time she woke up to reality.* **–wakeful,** *adj.* **–waken,** *v.* **–waker,** *n.*

wake² /weɪk/ *n.* **1.** the track left by a ship or other object moving in the water. **2.** the path or course of anything that has passed or preceded. *–phr.* **3. in the wake of,** **a.** following behind. **b.** following as a result or consequence of.

walk /wɔk/ *v.i.* **1.** to go or travel on foot at a moderate pace; to proceed by steps, or by advancing the feet in turn, at a moderate pace (in bipedal locomotion, so that there is always one foot on the ground, and in quadrupedal locomotion, so that there are always two or more feet on the ground). **2.** to go about or travel on foot for exercise or pleasure. **3.** to go about on the earth, or appear to living persons, as a ghost. **4.** (of things) to move in a manner suggestive of walking, as through repeated vibrations or the effect of alternate expansion and contraction. **5.** *Baseball, Softball* to go to first base after the pitcher has thrown four balls (**ball¹** def. 5). **6.** *Cricket* (of a person batting) to acknowledge dismissal by leaving the wicket without waiting for the umpire's decision. *–v.t.* **7.** to proceed through, over, or upon by walking: *walking Sydney streets by night.* **8.** to cause to walk; lead, drive, or ride at a walk, as an animal: *walking their horses towards us.* **9.** to force or help to walk, as a person. **10.** to conduct or accompany on a walk: *he walked them about the park.* **11.** to move (an object, as a box or a trunk) in a manner suggestive of walking, as by a rocking motion. **12.** to examine, measure, etc., by traversing on foot: *to walk a track. –n.* **13.** the act or course of walking, or going on foot. **14.** a spell of walking for exercise or pleasure: *to take a walk.* **15.** a distance walked or to be walked, often in terms of the time required: *ten minutes' walk from the station.* **16.** the gait or pace of a person or animal that walks. **17.** manner of walking: *impossible to mistake her walk.* **18.** *Athletics* a walking race. **19.** a way for pedestrians at the side of a street or road; a path or pavement. **20.** a place prepared or set apart for walking. **21.** a path in a garden or the like. *–phr.* **22. walk about,** to wander as a nomad, especially of Aboriginal people. **23. walk all over someone,** *Colloq.* to behave in a domineering and aggressive fashion towards someone. **24. walk away from,** **a.** to abandon (one's responsibilities): *you can't just walk away from us like that.* **b.** to escape from without injury: *the driver walked away from the wreck.* **25. walk away with,** to win easily. **26. walk into,** to encounter unwittingly: *he walked into my trap.* **27. walk off,** **a.** to get rid of by walking: *to walk off a headache.* **b.** to quit a property, as a farm, etc., on which, as a result of economic circumstances, one can no longer make a living. **28. walk off the job,** to go on strike. **29. walk off with,** **a.** to remove without permission; steal. **b.** to win easily, as in a competition. **30. walk on air,** to be extremely pleased, excited, etc. **31. walk out,** **a.** to go on strike. **b.** to leave in protest; leave angrily. **32. walk out on,** to abandon; forsake; desert. **33. walk out with,** to court, woo, or be courted or wooed by. **34. walk over,** **a.** (of an unopposed contestant) to go over (the course) at walking pace and thus be judged the winner. **b.** to win easily. **35. walk the board,** *Surfing* to walk along the board while riding a wave, usually as a means of controlling the board's performance. **36. walk the streets,** **a.** to wander about the streets, especially as a result of being homeless. **b.** to be a prostitute, especially one who solicits on the streets. **37. walk the talk,** *Colloq.* to experience at first hand the situation in which one is issuing commands and directing other people. **38. walk the walk (and talk the talk),** *Colloq.* to behave in a manner that is in keeping with the status and responsibilities of a position. **39. walk up,** **a.** to ascend; go upstairs. **b.** to approach on foot; draw near. **–walkable,** *adj.* **–walker,** *n.*

walkabout /ˈwɔkəbaʊt/ *n.* **1.** a period of wandering as a nomad, often as undertaken by Aboriginal people who feel the need to leave the place where they are in contact with white society, and return for spiritual replenishment to their traditional way of life. **2. a.** a short walk or inspection, often to see what is going on: *I'll* *just take a walkabout and see what I can find.* **b.** a short walk undertaken by a public celebrity in a crowded place to meet the people informally: *a royal walkabout.* *–phr.* **3. go walkabout, a.** to wander around the country in a nomadic manner. **b.** to be misplaced or lost. **c.** *Colloq.* to go on a holiday.

walkie-talkie /wɔki-'tɔki/ *n.* a combined radio transmitter and receiver, light enough to be carried by one person, developed originally for military use in World War II and subsequently widely used by police, medical services, etc.

walking bus *n.* a group of schoolchildren who walk to each other's houses and then on to school under the supervision of a parent at the front and one at the tail of the group.

walking frame *n.* a frame designed to be used for support by a person whose ability to walk is impaired.

walking stick *n.* **1.** a stick used to aid in walking; a cane. **2.** *US, NZ* → **stick insect.**

walkman /'wɔkmən/ *n.* (*from trademark*) a small portable transistor radio, cassette player, etc., with earphones, designed to facilitate listening to music, etc., while moving about. Also, **Walkman.**

walkout /'wɔkaʊt/ *n.* **1.** a strike by workers, especially one called suddenly. **2.** the act of leaving or boycotting a conference, meeting, etc., especially as an act of protest.

walkover /'wɔkoʊvə/ *n.* **1.** *Racing* a going over the course at a walk or otherwise by a contestant who is the only starter. **2.** *Colloq.* an unopposed or easy victory.

walk shorts *pl. n.* men's tailored shorts, often worn with a belt, knee-high socks and shoes.

wall /wɔl/ *n.* **1.** an upright work or structure of stone, brick, or similar material, serving for enclosure, division, support, protection, etc., as one of the upright enclosing sides of a building or a room, or a solid fence of masonry. **2.** (*usu. pl.*) a rampart raised for defensive purposes. **3.** a wall-like enclosing part, thing, mass, etc.: *a wall of fire; wall of troops.* **4.** an embankment to prevent flooding. **5.** the external layer of structural material surrounding an object, as an organ of the body or a plant or animal cell. **6.** *Mountaineering* a vertical or nearly vertical stretch of unbroken rock. *–v.t.* **7.** to fill up (a doorway, etc.) with a wall. *–phr.* **8. be wall to wall with,** to be crowded with; be covered with. **9. go to the wall, a.** to give way or suffer defeat in a conflict or competition. **b.** to fail in business, or become bankrupt. **10. hit the wall, a.** (of an athlete) to reach a point of complete physical exhaustion as a result of the depletion of glycogen in the liver and muscles, usually occurring after prolonged exertion as during a marathon. **b.** *Colloq.* to reach a state of complete exhaustion; be in a state of collapse. **c.** *Colloq.* to reach a point where it is impossible to continue. **11. up the wall,** *Colloq.* in or into a state of exasperation, confusion, etc.: *washing dishes drives me up the wall.* **12. wall in,** to enclose with or as with a wall. **13. wall off,** to shut off or separate with or as with a wall. **14. wall up,** to shut up within walls; entomb; immure. **15. with one's back to the wall,** in a very difficult predicament. **–walled,** *adj.* **–wall-less,** *adj.* **–wall-like,** *adj.*

wallaby /'wɔləbi/ *n.* (*pl.* **-bies** *or, especially collectively,* **-by**) **1.** any of various smaller members of the family Macropodidae, many resembling kangaroos, belonging to a number of different genera. *–phr.* **2. on the wallaby** (**track**), *Aust., NZ Colloq.* on the move; itinerant, most frequently with reference to a swagman, seasonal worker, etc.

wallah /'wɔlə/ *n. Indian English* (used especially in combination) someone identified as being employed at or concerned with a specified place or activity: *laundry wallah; cleaning wallah.* Also, **walla.**

wallaroo /wɔlə'ruː/ *n.* **1.** any of several large, shaggy-coated macropods of the genus *Macropus.* **2.** a stocky, coarse-haired kangaroo, *Macropus robustus,* widely distributed throughout mainland Australia in rocky ranges and gullies; euro.

Walla Rugby /wɔlə 'rʌɡbi/ *n.* → **Mini Rugby.**

wallet /'wɔlət/ *n.* **1.** a small, book-like folding case for carrying papers, paper money, etc., in the pocket. **2.** a bag for holding food, clothing, toilet articles, or the like, as for use on a journey.

wall-eyed *adj.* **1.** having eyes in which there is an abnormal amount of the white showing, because of divergent strabismus. **2.** having an eye or the eyes presenting little or no colour, as the result of a light-coloured or white iris or of white opacity of the cornea. **3.** having large, staring eyes, as some fishes.

wallflower /'wɔlflaʊə/ *n.* **1.** a European perennial, *Cheiranthus cheiri,* growing wild on old walls, cliffs, etc., and also cultivated in gardens, with sweet-scented flowers, commonly yellow or orange but in cultivation varying from pale yellow to brown, red, or purple. **2.** any plant of the brassicaceous genera *Cheiranthus* and *Erysimum.* **3.** *Colloq.* a person, especially a woman, who looks on at a dance, especially from failure to obtain a partner.

wallop /'wɔləp/ *Colloq.* *–v.t.* **1.** to beat hard and thoroughly; thrash. **2.** to defeat thoroughly, as in a game. *–n.* **3.** a vigorous blow. **–walloping,** *adj.*

walloper /'wɔləpə/ *n. Colloq.* **1.** someone or something that wallops. **2.** a person or thing of unusually large size. **3.** a police officer.

wall oven *n.* an oven which is designed to fit into a built-in kitchen cupboard at shoulder height.

wallow /'wɔloʊ/ *v.i.* **1.** to roll the body about, or lie, in water, snow, mud, dust, etc.: *pigs wallow in the mud.* **2.** to live or behave self-indulgently: *to wallow in luxury; to wallow in self-pity.* *–n.* **3.** the act of wallowing. **4.** a place to which animals, such as buffaloes, go to wallow. **–wallower,** *n.*

wallpaper /'wɔlpeɪpə/ *n.* **1.** paper, commonly with printed decorative patterns in colour, for pasting on and covering the walls or ceilings of rooms, etc. **2.** *Computers* a picture or design forming the background image on a computer screen. *–v.t.* **3.** to put wallpaper on; furnish with wallpaper.

walnut /'wɔlnʌt/ *n.* **1.** the edible nut of trees of the genus *Juglans,* of temperate North America, south east Europe, and Asia. **2.** a tree bearing this nut, as *J. regia* (**common walnut**), or *J. nigra* (**black walnut**), which yields both a valuable timber and a distinctively flavoured nut. **3.** the wood of such a tree. **4.** any of various fruits or trees resembling the walnut, as those of the genus *Beilschmiedia.* **5.** a shade of brown, as that of the heartwood of the black walnut tree.

walrus /'wɔlrəs, 'wɒlrəs/ *n.* (*pl.* **-ruses** *or, especially collectively,* **-rus**) either of two large marine mammals of the genus *Odobenus,* of arctic seas, related to the seals, and having flippers, a pair of large tusks, and a thick, tough skin.

waltz /wɔls, wɒls/ *n.* **1.** a ballroom dance in triple time, in which the dancers move in a series of circles, taking one step to each beat. **2.** a piece of music for, or in the rhythm of, this dance. *–adj.* **3.** of, relating to, or of the quality of the waltz: *waltz music; waltz rhythm.* *–v.i.* **4.** to dance in the movement of a waltz. **5.** *Colloq.* to take easily: *he waltzed off with the first prize.* *–v.t.* **6.** to cause to waltz; accompany in a waltz: *He waltzed her around the floor.* *–phr.* **7. waltz in,** to enter, disregarding the fact that one's presence may be unwelcome or inappropriate. **8. waltz Matilda,** *Aust. Obs. Colloq.* to wander about as a tramp with a swag. **–waltzer,** *n.*

wan /wɒn/ *adj.* (**wanner, wannest**) **1.** of an unnatural or sickly pallor; pallid: *his wan face flushed.* **2.** pale in colour or hue: *wan cowslips.* **3.** showing or suggesting ill health, worn condition, unhappiness, etc.: *a wan look*; *a wan smile.* –**wanly,** *adv.* –**wanness,** *n.*

wand /wɒnd/ *n.* **1.** a slender stick or rod, especially one used by a conjurer, or supposedly by a magician or fairy to work magic. **2.** a rod or staff borne as an ensign of office or authority. **3.** a slender shoot, stem, or branch of a shrub or tree. **4.** an electronic device, in the form of a handheld rod, that optically scans coded data, as on products in a shop or ID cards in a library.

wander /'wɒndə/ *v.i.* **1.** to go around without having to be in or go to a particular place; ramble; roam; rove: *to wander over the earth.* **2.** to go without purpose or casually: *he wandered into the next room.* **3.** (of the hand, pen, eyes, mind, etc.) to move or turn idly. **4.** to go away from a path, place, companions, rules, etc.: *he can't have wandered far.* –*v.t.* **5.** *Poetic* to wander over or through: *to wander the hills.* –*n.* **6.** a stroll; ramble. –**wanderer,** *n.* –**wanderingly,** *adv.*

wanderlust /'wɒndəlʌst/ *n.* an instinctive impulse to rove or travel about.

wane /weɪn/ *v.i.* **1.** (of the moon) to decrease periodically in the extent of its illuminated portion after the full moon (opposed to *wax*). **2.** to decline in power, importance, prosperity, etc. **3.** to decrease in strength, intensity, etc.: *daylight waned, and night came on.* **4.** to draw to a close. –*n.* **5.** gradual decline in strength, intensity, power, etc. **6.** the waning of the moon. –*phr.* **7. on the wane,** decreasing; diminishing.

wangle /'wæŋgəl/ *v.t. Colloq.* **1.** to bring about, accomplish, or obtain by contrivance, scheming, or often, indirect or insidious methods. **2.** to fake; falsify; manipulate. –**wangler,** *n.*

wank /wæŋk/ *Colloq.* –*v.i.* **1.** (*taboo*) to masturbate. –*n.* **2.** (*taboo*) an act or instance of masturbation. **3.** a hobby: *flying is his wank.* **4.** behaviour which is self-indulgent or egotistical. –**wanker,** *n.*

wannabe /'wɒnəbi/ *n. Colloq.* someone who aspires to be something or to be like someone specified, but who is unlikely to be successful: *a Madonna wannabe.*

want /wɒnt/ *v.t.* **1.** to feel a need or a desire for; wish for: *to want one's dinner*; *always wanting something new.* **2.** to wish or desire: *I want to see you*; *she wants to be notified.* **3.** *Colloq.* ought; need: *you want to take more exercise.* **4.** to be without or be deficient in: *to want judgement*; *to want knowledge.* **5.** to require or need: *the car wants cleaning.* –*v.i.* **6.** to wish; like; feel inclined: *they can go out if they want.* **7.** to be in a state of destitution or poverty. **8.** to be lacking or absent, as a part or thing necessary to completeness. –*n.* **9.** something wanted or needed; a necessity. **10.** a need or requirement: *the wants of humankind.* **11.** absence or deficiency of something desirable or requisite; lack. **12.** the state of being without something desired or needed; need: *to be in want of an assistant.* **13.** the state of being without the necessities of life; destitution; poverty. **14.** a sense of lack or need of something. –*phr.* **15. want for,** to be deficient in: *if you want for anything, let me know.* **16. want out,** *Colloq.* (sometimes fol. by *of*) to wish to withdraw, as from a difficult situation, obligation, etc. –**wanter,** *n.* –**wantless,** *adj.*

wanted /'wɒntəd/ *adj.* (of a suspected criminal, etc.) sought by the police.

wanting /'wɒntɪŋ/ *adj.* **1.** lacking or absent: *an apparatus with some of the parts wanting.* **2.** deficient in some part, thing, or respect: *to be wanting in courtesy.* –*prep.* **3.** lacking; without. **4.** less; minus: *a century, wanting three years.*

wanton /'wɒntən/ *adj.* **1.** done or behaving in an uncontrolled, selfish way, with bad results: *wanton attacker*; *wanton cruelty.* **2.** uncontrolled in sexual behaviour; loose; lascivious. **3.** *Poetic* (of children, young animals, etc.) playful; frolicsome. –*n.* **4.** a wanton or lustful person, especially a woman. –**wantonly,** *adv.* –**wantonness,** *n.*

war /wɔ/ *n.* **1.** a conflict carried on by force of arms, as between nations or states, or between parties within a state; warfare (by land, by sea, or in the air). **2.** a contest carried on by force of arms, as in a series of battles or campaigns. **3.** active hostility or contention; conflict; contest: *a war of words.* **4.** armed fighting, as a department of activity, a profession, or an art: *war is our business.* –*v.i.* (**warred, warring**) **5.** to make or carry on war; fight. **6.** to carry on active hostility or contention: *to war with evil.* **7.** to be in a state of strong opposition: *the two political parties are constantly warring over the economy.* –*adj.* **8.** of, belonging to, used in, or due to war. –*phr.* **9. at war,** in a state of hostility or active military operations. **10. in the wars,** *Colloq.* involved in a series of misfortunes or minor injuries. –**warless,** *adj.* –**warlike,** *adj.*

waratah /wɒrə'ta, 'wɒrətə/ *n.* a shrub or small tree of the eastern Australian genus *Telopea*, especially *T. speciosissima*, the floral emblem of NSW, which has a dense globular head of red flowers surrounded by red bracts.

warble /'wɔbəl/ *v.i.* **1.** to sing with trills, quavers, or melodic embellishments. –*v.t.* **2.** to sing with trills, quavers, or melodious turns; carol. –*n.* **3.** a warbled song.

warbler /'wɔblə/ *n.* **1.** any of the small, chiefly Eurasian songbirds constituting the family Sylviidae, represented in Australia by a few species, as the clamorous reed-warbler. **2.** *Obs.* a gerygone. **3.** any of various small, insectivorous American birds of the family Parulidae, many of which are brightly coloured.

war chest *n.* **1.** funds set aside to finance a military campaign. **2.** any funds set aside to finance a contest, as in business, politics, etc.

ward /wɔd/ *n.* **1.** a division or district of a municipality, city or town, as for administrative or representative purposes. **2.** a division of a hospital or the like, as for a particular class of patients: *a convalescent ward.* **3.** each of the separate divisions of a prison. **4.** *Law* **a.** a person, especially a minor, who has been legally placed under the care or control of a legal guardian. **b.** the state of being under the care or control of a legal guardian. **c.** guardianship over a minor or some other person legally incapable of managing his or her own affairs. **5.** the state of being under restraining guard or in custody. **6.** someone who is under the protection or control of another. **7.** a curved ridge of metal inside a lock, forming an obstacle to the passage of a key which does not have a corresponding notch. **8.** the notch or slot in the bit of a key, into which such a ridge fits. **9.** the act of keeping guard or protective watch: *watch and ward.* –*v.t.* **10.** to place in a ward, as of a hospital. –*phr.* **11. ward off,** to avert, repel, or turn aside, as danger, an attack, assailant, etc.: *to ward off a blow.* –**wardless,** *adj.*

-ward an adjectival and adverbial suffix indicating direction, as in *onward, seaward, backward.*

warden /'wɔdn/ *n.* **1.** someone who is given the care or responsibility of something; a keeper. **2.** a public official in charge of a place, such as a port, prison, etc. **3.** the head of certain colleges, schools, hospitals, youth hostels, etc. **4.** *Mining* a government official in charge of a mineral field. –**wardenship,** *n.*

warder¹ /'wɔdə/ *n.* **1.** → **prison officer. 2.** someone who wards or guards something. –**wardership,** *n.*

warder[2] /'wɔdə/ n. a truncheon or staff of office or authority, used in giving signals.

wardrobe /'wɔdroʊb/ n. **1.** a stock of clothes or costumes, as of a person or of a theatrical company. **2.** a piece of furniture for holding clothes, now usually a tall, upright, cupboard fitted with hooks, shelves, etc. **3.** a room or place for keeping clothes or costumes in. **4.** the department of a royal or other great household charged with the care of wearing apparel.

-wards an adverbial suffix indicating direction, as in *onwards, seawards, backwards.* Also, *Chiefly US,* **-ward.**

ware /wɛə/ n. **1.** (*usu. pl.*) articles of merchandise or manufacture, or goods: *a pedlar selling his wares.* **2.** pottery, or a particular kind of pottery: *Delft ware.*

-ware a word part meaning 'a product' with **1.** the substance from which it is made specified, as in *silverware, tinware.* **2.** the kind or class specified, as in *freeware.* **3.** the location of use specified, as in *homeware, kitchenware.*

warehouse n. /'wɛəhaʊs/ **1.** a storehouse for wares or goods. **2.** the building in which a wholesale dealer's stock of merchandise is kept. *–v.t.* /'wɛəhaʊz, -haʊs/ (**-housed, -housing**) **3.** to deposit or store in a warehouse. **4.** to place in a government or bonded warehouse, to be kept until duties are paid.

warfare /'wɔfɛə/ n. **1.** the act of waging war. **2.** armed conflict. **3.** military operations.

warhead /'wɔhɛd/ n. the forward section of a self-propelled missile, bomb, torpedo, etc., containing explosives, chemical or biological agents, or inert materials intended to inflict damage.

warlock /'wɔlɒk/ n. someone who practises magic arts by the aid of the devil; a sorcerer or wizard.

warm /wɔm/ adj. **1.** having or communicating a moderate degree of heat, as perceptible to the senses. **2.** of or at a moderately high temperature; characterised by comparatively high temperature: *a warm climate.* **3.** having a sensation of bodily heat: *to be warm from fast walking.* **4.** keeping or maintaining warmth: *warm clothes.* **5.** (of colour, effects of colour, etc.) suggestive of warmth; inclining towards red or orange, as yellow (rather than towards green or blue). **6.** characterised by or showing lively feelings, passions, emotions, sympathies, etc.: *a warm heart; warm interest.* **7.** strongly attached, or intimate: *warm friends.* **8.** cordial or hearty: *a warm welcome.* **9.** heated; irritated, or angry: *to become warm when contradicted.* **10.** animated, lively, brisk, or vigorous: *a warm debate.* **11.** strong or fresh: *a warm scent.* **12.** *Colloq.* relatively close to something sought, as in a game. **13.** *Colloq.* uncomfortable or unpleasant. *–v.t.* **14.** to make warm; heat: *to warm one's feet;* warm up a room. **15.** to heat, as cooked food for re-use. **16.** to excite ardour, enthusiasm, or animation in. **17.** to inspire with kindly feeling; affect with lively pleasure. *–phr.* **18. warm a seat,** *Colloq.* to occupy a position, usually in a temporary capacity, and without actively discharging its responsibilities. **19. warm down,** *Sport* to perform light exercise or stretches after strenuous exercise. **20. warm to,** to become ardent, enthusiastic, or animated about (something). **21. warm to** (or **towards**), to grow kindly, friendly, or sympathetically disposed to (someone): *my heart warms towards him.* **22. warm up, a.** (of an engine) to idle or run at low speed prior to being actively engaged. **b.** to run (an engine) prior to use, so as to produce efficient working conditions: *wait while I warm up the engine.* **c.** to prepare for a musical or theatrical performance, etc. **d.** (in sport) to prepare for strenuous exercise by performing preliminary light exercise or stretching. **e.** to become warm: *the day warmed up.* **f.** to make warm: *to warm up a room.* **–warmth,** n. **–warmer,** n.

–warming, n., adj. **–warmish,** adj. **–warmly,** adv. **–warmness,** n.

warm-blooded /'wɔm-blʌdəd/ adj. **1.** *Zool.* denoting or relating to animals, as mammals and birds, whose blood ranges in temperature from about 36° to 44°C, and remains relatively constant, irrespective of the temperature of the surrounding medium. **2.** ardent, impetuous, or passionate: *young and warm-blooded valour.*

warm front n. *Meteorol.* the contact surface between two air masses where the warmer mass is advancing against and over the cooler mass.

warmonger /'wɔmʌŋgə/ n. someone who advocates war or seeks to bring it about.

warm temperate rainforest n. an evergreen broadleaved forest favoured by a mild climate and steady rainfall, exhibiting great diversity; in Australia dominated by evergreen eucalypts, with green ferns and moisture-loving conifers also present. Compare **cool temperate rainforest.** Also, **warm temperate forest.**

warn /wɔn/ v.t. **1.** to give notice or intimation to (a person, etc.) of danger, impending evil, possible harm, or anything unfavourable: *to warn a person of a plot against them; warned that she was in danger.* **2.** to urge or advise to be on one's guard; caution: *to warn a foolhardy person.* **3.** to admonish or exhort as to action or conduct: *to warn a person to be on time.* **4.** to notify, apprise, or inform: *to warn a person of an intended visit.* **5.** to give notice to (a person, etc.) to go, stay, or keep (away, off, etc.): *to warn trespassers off private grounds.* **6.** to give authoritative or formal notice to, order, or summon. *–v.i.* **7.** to give a warning: *to warn of impending disaster.* **–warner,** n.

warning /'wɔnɪŋ/ n. **1.** the act of warning, giving notice, or cautioning. **2.** something serving to warn, give notice, or caution. *–adj.* **3.** that warns. **–warningly,** adv.

warp /wɔp/ v.t. **1.** to bend or twist out of shape: *rain has warped this timber.* **2.** to bend or turn from the natural direction. **3.** to bend from truth or right; bias or pervert: *hatred warps the mind.* *–v.i.* **4.** to become bent or twisted out of shape: *the wood has warped.* **5.** *Geol.* (of the earth's crust) to undergo a slow bending process without forming definite folds or displacements. *–n.* **6.** a bend or twist in something. **7.** a twist or bias of the mind. **8.** the lengthwise fibres in weaving, placed across the weft (or woof) and interlaced with it. **–warper,** n.

warrant /'wɒrənt/ n. **1.** a giving of authority to do something: *a treasury warrant.* **2.** something which says formally that something is quite certain; guarantee. **3.** *Law* a written authority to do some act, e.g. to make an arrest, make a search, etc. **4.** (in the armed forces) a certificate of appointment given to a non-commissioned officer. **5.** a written authorisation for the payment or receipt of money: *a treasury warrant; dividend warrant.* **6.** *Stock Exchange* a long-dated option that is itself tradeable, issued in the form of a security by a third party that is not the stock exchange. *–v.t.* **7.** to give authority to; authorise. **8.** to show that there is need for; justify: *the circumstances warrant such measures.* **9.** to give one's word for; vouch for: *I'll warrant he did!* **10.** to give a formal promise for; guarantee: *to warrant safe delivery.* **–warrantable,** adj. **–warrantably,** adv. **–warrantless,** adj.

warrant officer n. a member of the armed forces holding, by warrant, an intermediate rank between that of commissioned and non-commissioned officers.

warranty /'wɒrənti/ n. (pl. **-ties**) **1.** the act of warranting; warrant; assurance. **2.** *Law* an engagement, express or implied, in assurance of some particular in connection with a contract, as of sale: *an express warranty of the quality of goods.*

warren /ˈwɒrən/ *n.* **1.** a place where rabbits breed or abound. **2.** a colony of small animals such as rabbits, rats, wombats, etc. **3.** a building, district, etc., containing many poor people living in overcrowded conditions. **4.** a building or a district with many intersecting passages or routes. Also, **rabbit warren**.

warrigal /ˈwɒrəgəl/ *Aust.* –*n.* **1.** a dingo. **2.** a wild horse. **3.** an Aboriginal person living in the traditional manner, as opposed to one who has become assimilated into the white community. –*adj.* **4.** wild; untamed.

warrior /ˈwɒriə/ *n.* **1.** someone engaged or experienced in warfare; soldier. **2.** a person who is fearless and courageous in support of a cause, issue, etc.: *a peace warrior.*

wart /wɔt/ *n.* **1.** a small, usually hard, abnormal elevation on the skin, caused by a filterable virus. **2.** a small protuberance.

wary /ˈwɛəri/ *adj.* (**-rier, -riest**) **1.** watchful, or on one's guard, especially habitually; on the alert; cautious; careful. **2.** characterised by caution. –**warily,** *adv.* –**wariness,** *n.*

was /wɒz/, *weak form* /wəz/ *v.* first and third person singular past tense indicative of **be**.

wash /wɒʃ/ *v.t.* **1.** to apply water or some other liquid to for the purpose of cleansing; cleanse by dipping, rubbing, or scrubbing in water, etc. **2.** *Shearing.* to clean (sheep) by dipping in sheep wash prior to shearing. **3.** to wet with water or other liquid, or as water does. **4.** to flow over or against: *a shore or cliff washed by waves.* **5.** to carry or bring (*up, down,* or *along*) with water or any liquid, or as the water or liquid does: *the storm washed seaweed high on the beach.* **6.** to form (a channel, etc.), as flowing water does. **7.** *Mining, etc.* **a.** to subject (earth, etc.) to the action of water in order to separate valuable material. **b.** to separate (valuable material, as gold) thus. **8.** to purify (a gas or gaseous mixture) by passage through or over a liquid. **9.** to cover with a watery or thin coat of colour. **10.** to overlay with a thin coat or deposit of metal: *to wash brass with gold.* –*v.i.* **11.** to wash oneself: *time to wash for dinner.* **12.** to wash clothes. **13.** to cleanse anything with or in water or the like. **14.** *Colloq.* to stand being put to the proof; bear investigation. **15.** to be carried or driven (along, ashore, etc.) by water. **16.** to flow or beat with a lapping sound, as waves on a shore. **17.** to move along in or as in waves, or with a rushing movement, as water. –*n.* **18.** the act of washing with water or other liquid. **19.** a quantity of clothes, etc., washed, or to be washed, at one time. **20.** a liquid with which something is washed, wetted, coloured, overspread, etc. **21.** the flow, sweep, dash, or breaking of water. **22.** the sound made by this: *listening to the wash of the Atlantic.* **23.** water moving along in waves or with a rushing movement. **24.** the rough or broken water left behind a moving ship, etc. **25.** *Aeronautics* the disturbance in the air left behind by a moving aeroplane or any of its parts. **26.** any of various liquids for toilet purposes: *a hair wash.* **27.** a medicinal lotion. **28.** earth, etc., from which gold or the like can be extracted by washing. **29.** the wearing away of the shore by breaking waves. **30.** a tract of land washed by the action of the sea or a river. **31.** a shallow arm of the sea or a shallow part of a river. **32.** a depression or channel formed by flowing water. **33.** alluvial matter transferred and deposited by flowing water. **34.** a broad, thin layer of colour applied by a continuous movement of the brush, as in watercolour painting. **35.** a thin coat of metal applied in liquid form. **36.** waste liquid matter, refuse food, etc., from the kitchen, as for pigs. **37.** washy or weak drink or liquid food. **38.** the fermented wort from which the spirit is extracted in distilling. –*phr.* **39. come out in the wash,** *Colloq.* to be revealed eventually; become known. **40. wash away, a.** to remove (dirt, stains, paint,

or any matter) by or as by the action of water, or as water does. **b.** to wear, as water does, by flowing over or against a surface. **c.** to be worn by the action of water, as a hill. **41. wash down, a.** to clean completely by washing. **b.** to swallow (food) with the aid of liquid. **42. wash out, a.** to remove or get rid of by washing. **b.** to cause (an arrangement, sporting event, etc.) to be cancelled or abandoned. **43. wash up,** to wash (dishes, saucepans, etc.) after a meal, etc.

washed-out *adj.* **1.** faded, especially during washing. **2.** *Colloq.* tired-looking; pale; wan.

washed-up *adj. Colloq.* **1.** having failed completely; finished; ruined. **2.** exhausted.

washer /ˈwɒʃə/ *n.* **1.** someone who washes. **2.** a machine or apparatus for washing something. **3.** a flat ring or perforated piece of leather, rubber, metal, etc., used to give tightness to a joint, to prevent leakage, and to distribute pressure (as under the head of a bolt, under a nut, etc.). **4.** → **face washer. 5.** Also, **washrag, washcloth.** a cloth used for washing dishes, etc.

washing /ˈwɒʃɪŋ/ *n.* **1.** clothes, etc., washed or to be washed, especially those washed at one time. **2.** matter removed in washing something. **3.** material, as gold dust, obtained by washing washing earth, etc. **4.** a placer or other superficial deposit so washed. **5.** a thin coating or covering applied in liquid form.

washout /ˈwɒʃaʊt/ *n.* Also, **washaway.** a washing out of earth, etc., by water, as from an embankment or a roadway by heavy rain or a freshet. **2.** the hole or break produced. **3.** *Sport* the cancellation or abandoning of a game because of heavy rain. **4.** *Colloq.* a failure or fiasco. Also, **wash-out.**

wasn't /ˈwɒzənt/ *v.* contraction of *was not.*

wasp /wɒsp/ *n.* **1.** any of numerous hymenopterous, stinging insects, included for the most part in two superfamilies, Sphecoidea and Vespoidea. Their habits vary from a solitary life to colonial organisation. **2.** a waspish person. –**wasplike, waspy,** *adj.*

WASP /wɒsp/ *n.* **1.** a member of the establishment conceived as being white, Anglo-Saxon, and Protestant. –*adj.* **2.** of or relating to this establishment. –**WASPish,** *adj.* –**WASPishness,** *n.*

waspish /ˈwɒspɪʃ/ *adj.* **1.** like or suggesting a wasp. **2.** quick to resent a trifling affront or injury; snappish. **3.** showing irascibility or petulance: *waspish writing.* **4.** having a slender waist, like a wasp. –**waspishly,** *adv.* –**waspishness,** *n.*

wassail /ˈwɒsəl, -seɪl/ *n.* **1.** a festivity or revel with drinking of healths. **2.** alcoholic drink for toasting on festive occasions, especially spiced ale, as on Christmas Eve and Twelfth night. –*v.i.* **3.** to drink healths; revel with drinking. –*v.t.* **4.** to drink to the health or success of. –**wassailer,** *n.*

wastage /ˈweɪstɪdʒ/ *n.* loss by use, wear, decay, wastefulness, etc.

waste /weɪst/ *verb* (**wasted, wasting**) –*v.t.* **1.** to consume, spend, or employ uselessly or without adequate return; use to no avail; squander: *to waste money; to waste time; to waste effort; to waste words.* **2.** to fail or neglect to use, or let go to waste: *to waste an opportunity.* **3.** to destroy or consume gradually, or wear away. **4.** to wear down or reduce in bodily substance, health, or strength; emaciate; enfeeble: *to be wasted by disease or hunger.* **5.** to destroy, devastate, or ruin: *a country wasted with fire and sword.* **6.** *Colloq.* to murder. –*v.i.* **7.** to be consumed or spent uselessly or without being fully utilised. **8.** to become gradually consumed, used up, or worn away: *a candle wastes in burning.* **9.** Also, **waste away.** to lose flesh or strength, or become emaciated or enfeebled. **10.** Also, **waste away.** to diminish gradually, or dwindle, as wealth, power, etc. –*n.* **11.** useless consumption or expenditure, or use without adequate return: *waste of material*; *a waste of money*; *a waste of time*. **12.** neglect, instead of use: *waste of opportunity*. **13.** gradual destruction, impairment, or decay: *the waste and repair of bodily tissue*. **14.** devastation or ruin, as from war, fire, etc. **15.** a region or place laid waste or in ruins. **16.** anything unused, unproductive, or not properly utilised. **17.** an uncultivated tract of land. **18.** a tract of wild land, desolate country, or desert. **19.** *Law* positive damage to, or neglect of land by a tenant. **20.** an empty, desolate, or dreary tract or extent: *a waste of snow*. **21.** anything left over or superfluous, as excess material, by-products, etc., not of use for the work in hand. **22.** remnants from the working of cotton, etc., used for wiping machinery, absorbing oil, etc. **23.** *Building Trades* **a.** sullage. **b.** a pipe or conduit for draining sullage from a fitting or a floor, as floor waste. **24.** *Physiol.* material unused by or unusable to an organism, especially such material voided by the body as excrement: *bodily waste*; *animal waste*. *–adj.* **25.** not used or in use: *waste energy*. **26.** (of land, regions, etc.) uninhabited and wild, desolate and barren, or desert. **27.** (of regions, towns, etc.) in a state of desolation and ruin, as from devastation or decay. **28.** left over or superfluous: *to utilise waste products of manufacture*. **29.** having served a purpose and no longer of use. **30.** rejected as useless or worthless, or refuse: *waste products*. **31.** *Physiol.* relating to material unused by or unusable to the organism. **32.** intended to receive, hold, or carry away refuse or surplus material, etc. *–phr.* **33. a waste of space**, *Colloq.* a useless person. **34. go to waste**, to be wasted; fail to be used. **35. lay waste**, to destroy; devastate; ruin.

wasted /'weɪstəd/ *adj.* **1.** worn; emaciated. **2.** *Colloq.* exhausted, as a result of taking drugs or alcohol.

wasteful /'weɪstfəl/ *adj.* **1.** characterised by useless consumption or expenditure: *wasteful methods*. **2.** squandering, or grossly extravagant. **3.** devastating or destructive: *wasteful war*.

wastewater /'weɪstwɔtə/ *n.* water that has been used in residences, businesses, factories, caravans, etc., containing waste such as faeces, chemicals, etc. Compare **greywater**. Also, **waste water**.

wastrel /'weɪstrəl/ *n.* **1.** a wasteful person; spendthrift. **2.** an idler, or good-for-nothing.

watch /wɒtʃ/ *v.i.* **1.** to be on the lookout, look attentively, or be closely observant, as to see what comes, is done, happens, etc. **2.** to be careful or cautious. **3.** to keep awake, especially for a purpose; keep a vigilant watch as for protection or safekeeping. **4.** to keep vigil, as for devotional purposes. **5.** to keep guard. *–v.t.* **6.** to keep under attentive view or observation, as in order to see or learn something; view attentively or with interest: *to watch a game of cricket*. **7.** to contemplate or regard mentally: *to watch her progress*. **8.** to look or wait attentively and expectantly for. **9.** to guard for protection or safekeeping. **10.** to be careful of; pay attention to: *watch what you're doing*. *–n.* **11.** close, constant observation for the purpose of seeking or discovering something. **12.** a lookout, as for something expected: *to be on the watch*. **13.** vigilant guard, as for protection, restraint, etc. **14.** a keeping awake for some special purpose: *a watch beside a sickbed*. **15.** a period of time for watching or keeping guard. **16.** a small, portable timepiece. **17.** *Naut.* **a.** a period of time (usually four hours) during which one part of a ship's crew is on duty, taking turns with another part. **b.** a certain part (usually half) of the officers and crew of a vessel who together attend to working it for an allotted period of time. **18.** a watchman, or a body of watchmen. *–phr.* **19. keep watch**, to maintain a vigil over something or someone. **20. watch for**, to look or wait for attentively and expectantly: *to watch for a signal*; *to watch for an opportunity*. **21. watch it**, an exclamation calling

someone else's attention to some event, danger, etc. **22. watch out**, to be on one's guard; be alert or cautious. **23. watch out for**, **a.** to beware of; avoid. **b.** to look for with anticipation. **24. watch over**, to guard; protect. *–watcher*, *n.*

watchful /'wɒtʃfəl/ *adj.* **1.** vigilant or alert; closely observant. **2.** characterised by vigilance or alertness. *–watchfully*, *adv.* *–watchfulness*, *n.*

watchlist /'wɒtʃlɪst/ *n.* **1.** a list of people to keep under observation for political or legal reasons. **2.** *Finance* a list of securities to keep under observation.

watchword /'wɒtʃwɜd/ *n.* **1.** a word or short phrase to be communicated, on challenge, to a sentinel or guard; a password; a countersign. **2.** a word or phrase expressive of a principle or rule of action. **3.** a rallying cry of a party, etc.; a slogan.

water /'wɔtə/ *n.* **1.** the liquid which in a more or less impure state constitutes rain, oceans, lakes, rivers, etc., and which in a pure state is a transparent, odourless, tasteless liquid, a compound of hydrogen and oxygen, H_2O, freezing at 32°F or 0°C, and boiling at 212°F or 100°C. **2.** a special form or variety of this liquid, as rain. **3.** (*oft. pl.*) the liquid obtained from a mineral spring. **4.** *Rural* the allocated amount of water that can be used by irrigation farmers in their scheduled timeslot. **5.** the water of a river, etc., with reference to its relative height, especially as dependent on tide: *high water*; *low water*. **6.** the surface of water: *below water*; *on the water*. **7.** (*pl.*) flowing water, or water moving in waves. **8.** (*pl.*) a body of water as a sea or seas bordering a particular country or situated in a particular region. **9.** a liquid solution or preparation: *toilet water*. **10.** any of various solutions of volatile or gaseous substances in water: *ammonia water*. **11.** any liquid or aqueous organic secretion, exudation, humour, or the like, as tears, perspiration, urine, the amniotic fluids, etc. **12.** a wavy, lustrous pattern or marking, as on silk fabrics, metal surfaces, etc. **13.** the degree of transparency and brilliance of a diamond or other precious stone. *–v.t.* **14.** to sprinkle, moisten, or drench with water: *to water a road*. **15.** to supply (animals) with water for drinking. **16.** to furnish with a supply of water, as a ship. **17.** to furnish water to (a region, etc.), as by streams; supply (land, etc.) with water, as by irrigation. **18.** to produce a wavy lustrous pattern, marking, or finish on (fabrics, metals, etc.). *–v.i.* **19.** to discharge, fill with, or secrete water or liquid, as the eyes, or as the mouth at the sight or thought of tempting food. **20.** to drink water, as an animal. **21.** to take in a supply of water, as a ship. *–adj.* **22.** of or relating to water in any way. *–phr.* **23. above water**, out of embarrassment or trouble, especially of a financial nature. **24. by water**, by ship or boat. **25. go to water**, to lose courage; abandon one's resolve. **26. in deep** (or **hot**) **water**, **a.** in trouble; in a difficult situation. **b.** touching on an area of consideration which is contentious. **27. like water**, abundantly; freely: *to spend money like water*. **28. make one's mouth water**, *Colloq.* to be extremely appetising. **29. make water**, to urinate. **30. of the first water**, of the finest quality or rank: *a literary critic of the first water*. **31. take water**, (of a ship or boat) to fill with water flowing in from leaks. **32. test the water(s)**, to make a preliminary assessment of a situation. **33. throw cold water on**, **a.** to dampen the enthusiasm of (a person); discourage. **b.** to dampen enthusiasm for (a plan, etc.). **34. water down**, **a.** to dilute or adulterate with water: *to water down the soup*. **b.** to weaken: *to water down a protest*. **35. water the horse**, *Colloq.* to urinate. **36. water under the bridge**, over and finished with: *that's water under the bridge now*. *–waterer*, *n.* *–waterless*, *adj.*

waterbed /'wɔtəbɛd/ *n.* a heavy durable plastic bag filled with water, used as a mattress often in a supporting wooden frame.

waterboarding /ˈwɔtəbɔdɪŋ/ n. a torture technique in which the victim is immobilised on their back with the head inclined downwards and a cloth covering their face while water is poured over their face and into the breathing passages producing the sensation of drowning.

water bomb n. 1. a balloon filled with water, used as a missile in play. 2. a large amount of water or fire retardant dropped from an aircraft over a bushfire. Also, **waterbomb**.

water-bomb v.t. 1. to fight (a bushfire) by means of water bombing. 2. to throw a balloon filled with water at (someone) as in play. –n. 3. → **water bomb**. Also, **waterbomb**. **–water-bomber**, n. **–water-bombing**, n.

water bombing n. a firefighting procedure in which large volumes of water are dropped from the air onto strategic points in a bushfire.

water buffalo n. the largest species of buffalo, *Bubalus bubalis*, originally from India but now domesticated and widely used as a draught animal; feral in northern Australia. Also, **water ox**.

water chestnut n. 1. any of the aquatic plants constituting the genus *Trapa*, bearing an edible, nutlike fruit, especially *T. natans*, native to Europe and Asia. 2. the fruit.

water closet n. 1. a receptacle in which human excrement is flushed down a drain by water from a cistern; toilet. 2. a room fitted with a water closet. Also, **WC**.

watercolour /ˈwɔtəkʌlə/ n. 1. a pigment dispersed in water-soluble gum. 2. the art or method of painting with such pigments. 3. a painting or design executed by this method. –adj. 4. of or relating to watercolour or a watercolour painting. Also, **watercolor**. **–watercolourist**, n.

water cooler n. a vessel for holding drinking water which is cooled and drawn off for use by a tap.

water-cooler topic n. *US* a topic of general interest and concern.

watercourse /ˈwɔtəkɔs/ n. 1. a stream of water, as a river or brook. 2. the bed of such a stream. 3. a natural channel conveying water. 4. a channel or canal made for the conveyance of water.

watercraft /ˈwɔtəkraft/ n. (pl. **-craft**) 1. skill in boating and water sports. 2. any boat or ship. 3. boats and ships collectively.

watercress /ˈwɔtəkrɛs/ n. 1. a perennial cress, *Rorippa nasturtium-aquaticum*, usually growing in clear, running water, and bearing pungent leaves. 2. the leaves, used for salads, soups, and as a garnish.

water diabetes n. → **diabetes** (def. 2).

water diviner n. someone who uses a divining rod to discover water in the ground. Also, **waterfinder**.

waterfall /ˈwɔtəfɔl/ n. a steep fall or flow of water from a height; a cascade.

water footprint n. the amount of fresh water, both virtual and visible, used by a country, business, organisation, or individual.

waterfront /ˈwɔtəfrʌnt/ n. 1. land abutting on a body of water. 2. a part of a city or town so abutting, especially an area where ships dock at a wharf or wharves: *industrial unrest on the waterfront*. –adj. 3. of or relating to or located on a waterfront. 4. of or relating to the stevedoring industry. **–waterfrontage**, n.

water gum n. 1. any of several myrtaceous trees growing near water, being species of the genus *Tristania*, especially *Tristaniopsis laurina*, a medium tree with deep green laurel-like leaves and clusters of yellow flowers in summer; kanooka. 2. any of several other species of myrtaceous tree growing near water.

waterhole /ˈwɔtəhoʊl/ n. a natural hole or hollow in which water collects, as a spring in a desert, a cavity in the dried-up course of a river, etc.

water hyacinth n. a floating plant of Central and South America, *Eichhornia crassipes*, which has become a serious pest of watercourses in some warm countries.

waterlily /ˈwɔtəlɪli/ n. (pl. **-lilies**) 1. any of the aquatic plants constituting the genus *Nymphaea*, having floating leaves and showy, often fragrant, flowers as *N. gigantea*. 2. any plant of the genus *Nuphar* of the same family (**yellow waterlily** or **yellow pond-lily**). 3. any member of the family Nymphaeaceae. 4. the flower of any such plant.

waterlog /ˈwɔtəlɒg/ v.t. (**-logged**, **-logging**) 1. to cause (a ship, etc.) to become unmanageable as a result of flooding. 2. to soak or saturate with water. **–waterlogged**, adj.

waterloo /wɔtəˈlu/ n. a final and complete defeat.

watermark /ˈwɔtəmak/ n. 1. a mark indicating the height to which water rises or has risen, as in a river, etc. 2. a figure or design impressed in the fabric in the manufacture of paper and visible when the paper is held to the light. 3. → **digital watermark**. –v.t. 4. to identify with a watermark. 5. to impress (a design, etc.) as a watermark.

watermelon /ˈwɔtəmɛlən/ n. 1. the large, roundish or elongated fruit of a trailing vine, *Citrullus lanatus*, having a hard, green rind and a (usually) pink or red pulp which abounds in a sweetish, watery juice. 2. the plant or vine.

water police n. a civil force whose function is to police waterways, coordinating incidents involving vessels on the water, dealing with criminal activity and assisting in rescue operations, security operations, etc.

water polo n. a water game played by two teams, each having seven swimmers, in which the object is to dribble or shoot the ball over the opponents' goal line.

waterproof /ˈwɔtəpruf/ adj. 1. impervious to water. 2. rendered impervious to water by some special process, as coating or treating with rubber or the like. –n. 3. any of several coated or rubberised fabrics which will hold water. 4. an outer garment of waterproof material. –v.t. 5. to make waterproof. **–waterproofing**, n.

water rat n. 1. a large, aquatic, native rat, *Hydromys chrysogaster*, having soft dense fur and webbed hind feet, found near rivers and streams throughout Australia. 2. any of several different rodents of aquatic habits, as the water vole, *Arvicola amphibius*.

watershed /ˈwɔtəʃɛd/ n. 1. the ridge or crest line dividing two drainage areas; divide. 2. a turning point; a crucial event or time in a career, venture, etc.

waterside worker /ˈwɔtəsaɪd ˌwɜkə/ n. a wharf labourer. Also, **watersider**.

water slide n. a feature at an amusement park consisting of a large slippery slide, often with many curves and twists, leading to a pool, with water running along the slide into the pool. Also, **waterslide**.

water snake n. 1. any of the harmless snakes of the genus *Natrix*, found in or near fresh water. 2. any of various other snakes living in or frequenting water.

water splitting n. the separation of water into its constituent molecules of hydrogen and oxygen, a chemical reaction required to produce hydrogen fuel.

water supply n. 1. the system of dams, pipes, etc., by which water is supplied to a community. 2. the supply of water to a community or region.

watertable /ˈwɔtəteɪbəl/ n. 1. in an aquifer, the upper limit of the portion of ground saturated with water. 2. *Archit.* a projecting string-course or similar member placed to throw off or divert water.

water taxi n. a small boat which operates as part of a taxi service over the water.

watertight /ˈwɔtətaɪt/ adj. 1. impervious to water. 2. without fault; irrefutable; flawless: *a watertight argument*; *a watertight alibi*. **–watertightness**, n.

water tower *n.* **1.** a tower holding a tank into which water is pumped to obtain the required pressure; a standpipe. **2.** a fire-extinguishing apparatus throwing a stream of water on the upper parts of a tall burning building.

water vapour *n.* gaseous water, especially when diffused and below the boiling point, distinguished from steam. Also, **water vapor**.

waterway /'wɒtəweɪ/ *n.* **1.** a river, canal, or other body of water as a route or way of travel or transport. **2.** a channel for vessels, especially a fairway in a harbour, etc.

waterwise /'wɒtəwaɪz/ *adj.* knowledgeable about water conservation stratagems and thorough in implementing them.

waterworks /'wɒtəwɜːks/ *pl. n.* **1.** (*sometimes construed as sing.*) an aggregate of apparatus and structures by which water is collected, preserved, and distributed for domestic and other purposes, as for a town. **2.** *Colloq.* tears, or the source of tears. **3.** *Colloq.* the bladder or its functioning. *–phr.* **4. turn on the waterworks**, *Colloq.* to cry loudly and profusely, often for the sake of gaining sympathy or getting one's own way.

watery /'wɒtəri/ *adj.* **1.** relating to, like, or in water: *a watery fluid.* **2.** full of or containing too much water: *watery soup.*

watt /wɒt/ *n.* the derived SI unit of power, defined as one joule per second. *Symbol*: W **–wattage**, *n.*

wattle /'wɒtl/ *n.* **1.** any of the many Australian types of acacia, being shrubs or trees with spikes or globe-shaped heads of yellow or cream flowers. **2.** (*pl. or sing.*) rods interwoven with twigs or branches of trees, used for making fences, walls, roofs, etc. **3.** a fleshy part or lobe hanging down from the throat or chin of certain birds, such as the hen, turkey, etc., or from the neck of certain breeds of pigs, sheep and goats. *–v.t.* **4.** to form (a structure) by interweaving twigs or branches: *to wattle a fence. –adj.* **5.** built or roofed with wattles. **–wattled**, *adj.*

wattle and daub *n.* wattles (interwoven rods) plastered with mud or clay and used as a building material.

wattlebird /'wɒtlbɜːd/ *n.* **1.** any of several large endemic Australian honeyeaters of the genus *Anthochaera* having pendulous wattles on each side of the throat, as the **red wattlebird**, *A. carunculata.* **2.** any of several New Zealand birds of the family Callaeidae.

WAV /wæv/ *n.* an audio file format for IBM-compatible PCs, widely used to distribute sound over the internet.

wave /weɪv/ *n.* **1.** a movement of the surface of a liquid body, such as the sea or a lake, in the form of a ridge or swell. **2.** any movement or part like a wave of the sea. **3.** a swell or rush, especially of feeling, excitement, etc.: *a wave of anger swept over him*; *a wave of anti-Americanism.* **4.** one of a succession of movements of people moving into an area, country, etc. **5.** an outward curve, or one of a number of such curves, in a surface or line; undulation. **6.** *Physics* a regular vibrational disturbance travelling through a medium such as air, without corresponding movement forward of the medium itself, as in sound or electromagnetic energy. **7.** a sign made by waving the hand, a flag, etc. *–v.i.* **8.** to move loosely to and fro or up and down; flutter. **9.** to curve in a line, etc., like a wave; have an undulating form. **10.** to be moved, especially first in one direction and then in the opposite: *the lady's handkerchief waved in encouragement.* **11.** to give a signal by waving something: *she waved to me as I left. –v.t.* **12.** to cause to move loosely to and fro or up and down. **13.** to cause to curve up and down or in and out. **14.** to give a wave or wavy appearance or pattern to (the hair, silk, etc.). **15.** to move, especially first in one direction and then in the opposite: *to wave the hand.* **16.** to direct by a

waving movement: *to wave a train to a halt.* **17.** to express by a waving movement: *to wave a last goodbye. –phr.* **18. make waves**, to cause a disturbance; upset existing standards or notions. **19. wave down**, to stop (a motor vehicle) by means of hand signals, in order to get assistance, a lift, etc. **–waver**, *n.* **–waveless**, *adj.* **–wavelike, wavy**, *adj.*

waveband /'weɪvbænd/ *n.* a range of radio wavelengths or frequencies in which the waves have similar propagation characteristics.

wavelength /'weɪvlɛŋθ/ *n.* **1.** *Physics* the distance, measured in the direction of propagation of a wave, between two successive points that are characterised by the same phase of vibration. **2.** *Radio* the wavelength (def. 1) of the carrier wave of a particular radio transmitter or station. **3.** a mode of thinking or understanding: *the teacher was obviously not on the same wavelength as his pupils.*

waver /'weɪvə/ *v.i.* **1.** to sway to and fro; flutter: *leaves wavered in the breeze.* **2.** to become unsteady or begin to fail or give way: *his mind is wavering; his voice is wavering.* **3.** to feel or show doubt or indecision; vacillate: *he wavered in his determination.* **–waverer**, *n.* **–wavering**, *adj.* **–waveringly**, *adv.*

wax¹ /wæks/ *n.* **1.** any of a group of amorphous solids consisting of esters of alcohols and long-chain, fatty acids, e.g. beeswax. **2.** any of various other similar substances, as spermaceti, the secretions of certain insects (**wax insects**), and the secretions (**vegetable wax**) of certain plants. **3.** any of a group of solid, non-greasy, insoluble substances which have a low melting or softening point, especially mixtures of the higher hydrocarbons, as paraffin wax. **4.** a resinous substance used by shoemakers for rubbing their thread. **5.** Also, **waxflower**. any of various shrubs of the genus *Chamelaucium*, family Myrtaceae, of WA, having waxy flowers. **6.** something suggesting wax as being readily moulded, worked upon, handled, managed, etc.: *helpless wax in their hands. –v.t.* **7.** to rub, smear, stiffen, polish, etc., with wax; treat with wax: *waxed moustaches, a waxed floor. –adj.* **8.** made of or resembling wax. **–waxer**, *n.* **–waxlike, waxy**, *adj.*

wax² /wæks/ *v.i.* (**waxed, waxed** *or, Poetic,* **waxen, waxing**) **1.** to increase in extent, quantity, intensity, power, etc.: *discord waxed daily.* **2.** (of the moon) to increase in the extent of its illuminated portion before the full moon (opposed to *wane*). **3.** to grow or become (as stated). *–phr.* **4. wax lyrical**, to speak in an enthusiastic and sometimes exaggeratedly poetic manner, in praise or in support of a person, scheme, etc.

waxen /'wæksən/ *adj.* **1.** made of or covered with wax. **2.** resembling or suggesting wax: *his face had an unhealthy waxen appearance.* **3.** weak or impressionable, as a person or their character.

waxflower /'wæksflauə/ *n.* **1.** any of various Australian shrubs of the genus *Eriostemon*, family Rutaceae, as Bendigo waxflower, *E. obovalis*, of south-eastern Australia. **2.** → **wax¹** (def. 5).

wax plant *n.* **1.** any of the climbing or trailing plants of the genus *Hoya*, natives of tropical Asia and Australia, having glossy leaves and umbels of pink, white, or yellowish waxy flowers. **2.** any of several Western Australian species of the genus *Chamelaucium*, especially *C. uncinatum.* **3.** any of the shrubs of the genus *Eriostemon* of eastern Australia, especially *E. australasicum*. Also, **waxplant**.

waxwork /'wækswɜːk/ *n.* **1.** figures, ornaments, etc., made of wax, or one such figure. **2.** (*pl. construed as sing.*) an exhibition of wax figures, ornaments, etc.

way /weɪ/ *n.* **1.** manner, mode, or fashion: *a new way of looking at a matter*; *to reply in a polite way.* **2.** characteristic or habitual manner: *that is only his way.* **3.** a course, plan, or means for attaining an end. **4.** respect or particular: *a plan defective in several ways.* **5.** direction: *look this way.* **6.** passage or progress on a course: *to make one's way on foot; to lead the way.* **7.** distance: *a long way off.* **8.** a path or course leading from one place to another. **9.** a road, route, passage, or channel (usually used in combination): *a highway; a waterway; a doorway.* **10.** *Law* a right of way. **11.** any line of passage or travel used or available: *blaze a way through dense woods.* **12.** space for passing or advancing: *he cleared a way through the throng of people.* **13.** (*oft. pl.*) a habit or custom: *I don't like his ways at all.* **14.** the course of mode or action which one prefers or upon which one is resolved: *to have one's own way.* **15.** condition, as to health, prosperity, etc.: *in a bad way.* **16.** course of life, action, or experience: *the way of transgressors is hard.* **17.** (*pl.*) (in shipbuilding) the timbers on which a ship is launched. **18.** *Machinery* a longitudinal strip, as in a planer, guiding a moving part along a surface. **19.** *Naut.* movement or passage through the water. **20.** a long distance: *we've still got a way to go yet.* –*adv.* **21.** very far: *she is way out in the surf.* **22.** to a great extent; much: *way too late; way out of sync.* **23.** *Colloq.* extremely: *she's way cool; open till way late.* –*phr.* **24. be by the way**, to be of superficial relevance but of no importance. **25. by the way**, incidentally; in the course of one's remarks: *by the way, have you received that letter yet?* **26. by way of, a.** by the route of; via; through. **b.** as a method or means of. **c.** having a reputation for; ostensibly (being, doing, etc.): *he is by way of being an authority on the subject.* **27. come someone's way**, to come to someone; happen to someone. **28. give way, a.** to withdraw; retreat. **b.** to yield; break down; collapse. **c.** (of a vehicle or driver of a vehicle) to accord right of way to another vehicle: *the rule is to give way to the right.* **29. give way to, a.** to yield to. **b.** to lose control of (one's emotions, etc.). **c.** to be replaced by. **d.** (of traffic) to accord right of way to (another vehicle). **30. go out of one's way,** to make a special effort; inconvenience oneself. **31. have a way with**, to have a skill in dealing with: *she has a way with children.* **32. have a way with one**, to have a charming or persuasive manner. **33. have one's (own) way**, to achieve one's objective in a situation of conflict. **34. have one's way with**, to seduce: *the local Don Juan was reputed to have had his way with numerous young women.* **35. have it both ways**, to gain or succeed by each of two contrary means, situations, etc. **36. in a way**, to a certain extent; after a fashion: *in a way he's a pleasant person.* **37. in a bad way**, *Colloq.* seriously ill or in difficulties. **38. in the way**, forming an obstruction or hindrance. **39. lead the way, a.** to proceed in advance of others. **b.** to take the initiative; show by example. **40. make one's way, a.** to proceed. **b.** to achieve advancement, recognition, or success: *to make one's way in the world.* **41. make way for, a.** to allow to pass. **b.** to give up or retire in favour of: *the manager resigned to make way for a younger person.* **42. no way**, not at all; never. **43. on the way out, a.** becoming obsolete; ready for rest or retirement. **b.** losing popularity. **44. out of the way, a.** so as not to obstruct or hinder. **b.** disposed of; dealt with. **c.** murdered: *to put a person out of the way.* **d.** out of the frequented way; off the beaten track. **e.** unusual; extraordinary. **45. pay one's (or its) way**, to remain solvent or financially self-supporting. **46. under way, a.** in motion or moving along, as a ship that has weighed anchor. **b.** in progress, as an enterprise. **47. way to go**, *Colloq.* an exclamation of encouragement, praise, etc.

wayback /ˈweɪbæk/ *Aust., NZ* –*adv.* **1.** in the outback or remote rural districts. –*adj.* **2.** remote; outback. –*phr.* **3. the wayback**, the outback or remote rural districts.

waybill /ˈweɪbɪl/ *n.* **1.** a list of goods sent by a common carrier, as a railway, with directions. **2.** (on a bus, etc.) a list showing the number of passengers carried or tickets sold.

wayfarer /ˈweɪfɛərə/ *n.* a traveller, especially on foot.

wayfinding /ˈweɪfaɪndɪŋ/ *n.* **1.** the finding of one's way to a specified location. **2.** the science which studies the strategies and intuitions which people bring to bear when finding their way so as to implement appropriate signage, mapping, etc.

waylay /weɪˈleɪ/ *v.t.* (**-laid, -laying**) **1.** to fall upon or assail from ambush, as in order to rob, seize, or slay. **2.** to await and accost unexpectedly. –**waylayer**, *n.*

way-out *adj. Colloq.* **1.** advanced in technique, style, etc. **2.** unusual; odd; eccentric.

-ways a suffix of manner creating adverbs, as in *sideways, lengthways.* See **-wise**.

wayside /ˈweɪsaɪd/ *n.* **1.** the side of the way; the border or edge of the road or highway. –*adj.* **2.** being, situated, or found at or along the wayside: *a wayside inn.* –*phr.* **3. fall by the wayside**, **a.** to drop out of some endeavour, as a contest, etc. **b.** to fail in an attempt.

wayward /ˈweɪwəd/ *adj.* **1.** turned or turning away from what is right or proper; perverse: *a wayward son.* **2.** swayed or prompted by caprice, or capricious: *a wayward fancy*; *a wayward impulse.* **3.** turning or changing irregularly; irregular: *a wayward stream*; *a wayward breeze.* –**waywardly**, *adv.* –**waywardness**, *n.*

WC /dʌbəlju ˈsi/ *n.* a toilet. Also, **wc**.

we /wi/ *pron. (personal), first person, pl., subjective* (*objective* **us**) **1.** used by a speaker or writer to denote two or more people, including himself or herself: *we usually take our holidays in August.* **2.** used by a sovereign when alluding to himself or herself in formal speech: *we are not amused.* **3.** used by an editor or other writer to give an impersonal tone: *we deplore the present economic situation.* **4.** used as a term of encouragement or cajolery where the second person is meant: *we really should work a little harder.*

weak /wik/ *adj.* **1.** likely to yield, break, or fall down under pressure or strain; fragile; frail; not strong: *a weak spot in the armour.* **2.** lacking in bodily strength or health; feeble; infirm: *a weak old man.* **3.** lacking in political strength, or authority: *a weak ruler.* **4.** lacking in force or effectiveness; impotent, ineffectual, or inadequate: *a weak heart.* **5.** lacking in logical or legal force or soundness: *a weak argument.* **6.** lacking in mental power, intelligence, or judgement: *a weak mind.* **7.** lacking in moral strength: *weak compliance.* **8.** lacking in amount, volume, loudness, strength, etc.; faint; slight: *a weak current of electricity.* **9.** unstressed (of a syllable, word, etc.). **10.** (of Germanic verbs) inflected with suffixes, without change of the root or original vowel, as in English *work, worked.* –**weaken**, *v.* –**weakish**, *adj.* –**weakly**, *adv.* –**weakness**, *n.*

weakling /ˈwiklɪŋ/ *n.* **1.** a weak or feeble creature (physically or morally). –*adj.* **2.** weak; not strong.

weal /wil/ *n.* **1.** a small burning or itching swelling on the skin, as from a mosquito bite or from urticaria. **2.** a wale or welt.

wealth /wɛlθ/ *n.* **1.** a great store of valuable possessions, property, or riches: *the wealth of a city.* **2.** a rich abundance or profusion of anything: *a wealth of imagery.* **3.** *Econ.* **a.** all things having a value in money, in exchange, or in use. **b.** anything having utility and capable of being appropriated or exchanged. **4.** rich or valuable contents or produce: *the wealth of the soil.* **5.** the state of being rich; affluence: *persons of wealth and standing.* –**wealthy**, *adj.*

wealth creation *n.* the development of assets to create wealth.

wean /wiːn/ *v.t.* **1.** to accustom (a child or animal) to food other than its mother's milk. *–phr.* **2. wean off** (or **from**), to induce to give up dependence on (a substance, habit, or activity). **3. wean on**, to expose to at an early age: *I was weaned on cricket.* **4. wean on to**, to induce to abandon a substance, habit, activity, etc., in favour of (something deemed better): *to wean a heroin addict on to methadone.* *–weaner, n.*

weapon /ˈwɛpən/ *n.* **1.** any instrument for use in attack or defence in combat, fighting, or war, as a sword, rifle, cannon, bomb, etc. **2.** anything serving as an instrument for making or repelling an attack: *the deadly weapon of meekness.* *–weaponry, n. –weaponed, adj. –weaponless, adj.*

weapon of mass destruction *n.* a biological, chemical or nuclear weapon capable of killing a great number of people. *Abbrev.*: WMD

weapons-grade *adj.* (of nuclear material) of a quality suitable for use in weapons.

wear /wɛə/ *verb* (**wore, worn, wearing**) *–v.t.* **1.** to carry or have on the body or about the person as a covering, equipment, ornament, or the like: *wear a coat*; *wear a watch*; *wear a disguise.* **2.** to have or use on a person habitually: *wear a beard.* **3.** to bear or have in the aspect or appearance: *wear a smile*; *wear an air of triumph.* **4.** to show or fly: *the ship wore its colours.* **5.** to impair (garments, etc.) by wear: *gloves worn at the fingertips.* **6.** to impair, deteriorate, or consume gradually by use or any continued process: *a well-worn volume.* **7.** to waste or diminish gradually by rubbing, scraping, washing, etc.: *rocks worn by the waves.* **8.** to make (a hole, channel, way, etc.) by such action. **9.** to weary or exhaust: *worn with toil.* **10.** *Colloq.* to accept, tolerate, or be convinced by: *he told me a lie but I wouldn't wear it. –v.i.* **11.** to hold out or last under wear, use, or any continued strain: *materials that will wear.* **12.** to become; grow gradually: *my patience is wearing thin. –n.* **13.** the act of wearing; use, as of a garment: *I have had very good wear from this dress.* **14.** the state of being worn, as on the person. **15.** clothing, garments, or other articles for wearing. **16.** style of dress, adornment, etc., especially for a particular time, activity, etc.: *evening wear*; *beach wear.* **17.** gradual impairment, wasting, diminution, etc., as from use: *the carpet shows wear. –phr.* **18. wear away**, **a.** to pass (time, etc.) gradually or tediously. **b.** to undergo gradual impairment, diminution, reduction, etc., from wear, use, attrition, or other causes. **19. wear away** (or **on**), to pass, as time, etc., especially slowly or tediously. **20. wear down**, **a.** to overcome the resistance of (someone). **b.** to reduce gradually by attrition: *to wear down the steps.* **21. wear off**, to diminish in effect, as of altered physical states, over a period of time: *the hunger has worn off.* **22. wear out**, **a.** to wear or use until no longer fit for use: *to wear out tools.* **b.** to exhaust by continued use, strain, or any gradual process: *to wear out patience.* **c.** to use up. **d.** to become unserviceable over time: *the fridge has worn out. –wearer, n.*

weariless /ˈwɪərɪləs/ *adj.* unwearying; tireless.

wearing /ˈwɛərɪŋ/ *adj.* **1.** relating to or made for wear. **2.** gradually impairing or wasting. **3.** wearying or exhausting. *–wearingly, adv.*

wearisome /ˈwɪərɪsəm/ *adj.* **1.** causing weariness; fatiguing: *a difficult and wearisome march.* **2.** tiresome or tedious: *a wearisome person*; *a wearisome day*; *a wearisome book. –wearisomely, adv. –wearisomeness, n.*

weary /ˈwɪəri/ *adj.* (**-rier, -riest**) **1.** exhausted physically or mentally by labour, exertion, strain, etc.; fatigued; tired: *weary eyes*; *weary feet*; *a weary brain.* **2.** characterised by or causing fatigue: *a weary journey.*

3. characterised by or causing such impatience or dissatisfaction; tedious; irksome: *a weary wait.* *–verb* (**-ried, -rying**) *–v.t.* **4.** to make weary; fatigue or tire. *–v.i.* **5.** to become weary; fatigue or tire. *–phr.* **6. weary of**, impatient or dissatisfied at excess or overlong continuance of: *weary of excuses. –wearily, adv. –weariness, n.*

weasel /ˈwizəl/ *n.* **1.** any of certain small Eurasian and American carnivores of the genus *Mustela*, family Mustelidae, having a long, slender bodies, short legs and rounded ears, and feeding mainly on small rodents. **2.** a cunning, sneaky person. **3.** a tracked vehicle used in snow; a kind of tractor. *–weaselly, adj.*

weather /ˈwɛðə/ *n.* **1.** the state of the atmosphere with respect to wind, temperature, cloudiness, moisture, pressure, etc. **2.** windy or stormy weather. *–v.t.* **3.** to expose to the weather; to dry, season, or otherwise affect by exposure to the air or atmosphere. **4.** to discolour, disintegrate, or affect injuriously, as by atmospheric agencies. **5.** to bear up against and come safely through (a storm, danger, trouble, etc.). *–v.i.* **6.** to undergo change, as discolouration or disintegration, as the result of exposure to atmospheric conditions. **7.** to endure or resist exposure to the weather. *–adj.* **8.** of or relating to the side or part, as of a ship, that is exposed to the wind: *the weather bow. –phr.* **9. make heavy weather of**, to have a lot of difficulty coping with. **10. under the weather**, *Colloq.* **a.** indisposed; ill; ailing. **b.** drunk. **11. weather through**, to go or come safely through a storm, danger, trouble, etc.

weatherboard /ˈwɛðəbɔd/ *n.* **1.** one of a series of thin boards, usually thicker along one edge than the other, nailed on an outside wall or a roof in overlapping fashion to form a protective covering which will shed water. **2.** a building whose exterior walls are constructed from weatherboards. *–v.t.* **3.** to cover or furnish with weatherboards. *–weather-boarded, adj.*

weathervane /ˈwɛðəveɪn/ *n.* a vane for indicating the direction of the wind; a weathercock.

weave[1] /wiv/ *verb* (**wove** or **weaved, woven** or **weaved, weaving**) *–v.t.* **1.** to interlace (threads, yarns, strips, fibrous material, etc.) so as to form a fabric or texture. **2.** to form by interlacing threads, yarns, strands, or strips of some material: *to weave a basket, to weave cloth.* **3.** to form by combining various elements or details into a connected whole: *to weave a tale*; *to weave a plot.* **4.** to introduce as an element or detail into a connected whole: *to weave a melody into a musical composition. –v.i.* **5.** to weave cloth, etc. **6.** to become woven or interwoven. *–n.* **7.** a manner of interlacing yarns: *plain weave*; *twill weave*; *satin weave. –weaver, n.*

weave[2] /wiv/ *verb* (**weaved** or **wove, weaving**) *–v.t.* **1.** to follow in a winding course; to move from side to side: *to weave one's way through traffic. –v.i.* **2.** to move repeatedly from side to side. **3.** to wind in and out of or through: *she weaved through the crowd. –phr.* **4. get weaving**, *Colloq.* to make a start, especially hurriedly, enthusiastically, etc.

web[1] /wɛb/ *n.* **1.** something formed as by weaving or interweaving. **2.** a thin silken fabric spun by spiders, and also by the larvae of some insects, as various caterpillars, etc.; cobweb. **3.** a woven fabric, especially a whole piece of cloth in the course of being woven or after it comes from the loom. **4.** a tangled intricate state of circumstances, events, etc.: *the web of intrigue.* **5.** *Zool.* **a.** a membrane which connects the digits of an animal. **b.** that which connects the toes of aquatic birds and aquatic mammals. *–v.t.* (**webbed, webbing**) **6.** to cover with or as with a web; envelop. *–webby, adj. –webless, adj. –weblike, adj.*

web² /wɛb/ n. Also, **World Wide Web. 1. the,** (*also upper case*) a large-scale, networked information system for documents in HTML released to users of the internet. –*adj.* **2.** (*also upper case*) of or relating to the web. –*phr.* **3. the dark web,** (*also upper case*) the data available on the web which cannot be accessed by general search engines, requiring specific software or authorisation for access, usually because the content is illegal. **4. the deep web,** (*also upper case*) the body of information available on the web which is not accessible through general search engines, but which may be accessed directly through specific web pages, as entries in an online telephone directory, etc.

web banner n. → **banner** (def. 5).

webbed /wɛbd/ *adj.* **1.** having the digits connected by a web, as the foot of a duck or a beaver. **2.** (of the digits) connected thus. **3.** formed like or with a web.

webbing /'wɛbɪŋ/ n. **1.** woven material of hemp, cotton, or jute, in bands of various widths, for use in belts and harnesses. **2.** such woven bands nailed on furniture under springs or upholstery, for support. **3.** *Zool.* the membrane forming a web or webs.

web browser n. → **browser**.

webcam /'wɛbkæm/ n. → **web camera**. Also, **web cam.**

web camera n. a digital video camera, the images from which are transmitted via the internet. Also, **webcam.**

webcast /'wɛbkast/ *verb* (**-cast** *or* **-casted, -casting**) –*v.i.* **1.** to broadcast live or delayed transmissions on the internet. –*v.t.* **2.** to broadcast (a program, event, etc.) on the internet in such a way. –*n.* **3.** such a broadcast on the internet. –**webcaster,** *n.* –**webcasting,** *n.*

web crawler n. an automated program that connects to computer web pages and gathers data, as web addresses, key information words, into a scalable index; robot.

weber /'veɪbə, 'weɪbə/ n. the derived SI unit of magnetic flux, defined as the flux which, linking a circuit of one turn, produces in it an electromotive force of one volt as it is reduced to zero at a uniform rate in one second. *Symbol:* Wb

web link n. *Internet* a link from one website to another.

webliography /wɛbli'ɒgrəfi/ n. (*pl.* **-graphies**) a list of resources on a particular subject available on the internet.

web log n. → **blog.** Also, **weblog.**

webmaster /'wɛbmastə/ n. a person, usually a male, responsible for the development and maintenance of a web server or website.

web page n. *Internet* an HTML file with a unique URL on the World Wide Web. Also, **webpage.**

web portal n. a website which offers information and sometimes direct links to other websites along with a range of services such as email, online shopping, etc. Also, **portal, portal site, internet portal.**

web server n. *Internet* **1.** the software running at a website which sends out web pages in response to remote browsers. **2.** a computer which connects a user's computer to the World Wide Web on request. Also, **webserver.**

website /'wɛbsaɪt/ n. *Internet* a location on the World Wide Web where there is a set of resources, as text files, images, etc. Also, **website.**

webzine /'wɛbzin/ n. a magazine published on the internet.

wed /wɛd/ *verb* (**wedded** *or* **wed, wedding**) –*v.t.* **1.** to bind oneself to (a person) in marriage; take for husband or wife. **2.** to unite (a couple) or join (one person to another) in marriage or wedlock; marry. **3.** to bind by close or lasting ties; attach firmly: *to be wedded to a theory.* –*v.i.* **4.** to contract marriage; marry. **5.** to become united as if in wedlock.

we'd /wid/ contraction of *we had, we should* or *we would.*

wedding /'wɛdɪŋ/ n. **1.** the act or ceremony of marrying; marriage; nuptials. **2.** a celebration of an anniversary of a marriage, as a silver wedding, celebrated on the 25th anniversary of a marriage.

wedge /wɛdʒ/ n. **1.** a device (one of the so-called simple machines) consisting of a piece of hard material with two principal faces meeting in a sharply acute angle. **2.** a piece of anything of like shape: *a wedge of pie*; *a cheese wedge.* **3.** Also, **potato wedge.** a thick wedge of potato, seasoned and fried. **4.** a shoe with a wedge heel. **5.** *Meteorol.* a region of relatively high pressure, extending from an anticyclone, with isobars in the shape of a wedge. **6.** a cuneiform character or stroke. **7.** something that serves to part, divide, etc.: *a disrupting wedge divided the loyalties of party members.* **8.** → **sand wedge.** –*verb* (**wedged, wedging**) –*v.t.* **9.** to cleave or split with or as with a wedge. **10.** to pack or fix tightly by driving in a wedge or wedges. **11.** to thrust, drive, or fix (in, between, etc.) like a wedge: *to wedge oneself through a narrow opening.* –*v.i.* **12.** to force a way (in, etc.) like a wedge. –*phr.* **13. thin end of the wedge,** something small or insignificant which is likely to lead to something large and important. –**wedgelike, wedgy,** *adj.*

wedge issue n. *Politics* an issue that is used in wedge politics.

wedge politics n. a political strategy whereby one group seeks to weaken opposing groups by forcing them to divide over a particular issue rather than form an alliance.

wedge-tailed eagle n. a very large, dark, long-tailed eagle, *Aquila audax*, of plains and forests throughout Australia and New Guinea; the largest of Australian birds of prey; eaglehawk. Also, **wedgetail eagle, wedgie.**

wedgie¹ /'wɛdʒi/ n. *Aust.* a wedge-tailed eagle.

wedgie² /'wɛdʒi/ n. *Colloq.* the experience of having one's pants pulled up so sharply as to cause discomfort, usually done as a prank.

wedlock /'wɛdlɒk/ n. the state of marriage; matrimony.

Wednesday /'wɛnzdeɪ, -di, 'wɛdn-/ n. the fourth day of the week, following Tuesday.

wee /wi/ *adj.* **1.** little; very small. –*phr.* **2. the wee (small) hours,** the hours immediately following midnight.

weed¹ /wid/ n. **1.** a plant growing wild, especially in cultivated ground to the exclusion or injury of the desired crop. **2.** any useless, troublesome, or noxious plant, especially one that grows profusely. **3.** *Colloq.* a cigar or cigarette. **4.** *Colloq.* a marijuana cigarette. **5.** a thin or weakly person, especially one regarded as stupid or infantile. **6.** a sorry animal, especially a horse unfit for racing or breeding purposes. –*v.t.* **7.** to free from weeds or troublesome plants: *to weed a garden.* **8.** to rid of what is undesirable or superfluous. –*v.i.* **9.** to remove weeds or the like. –*phr.* **10. the weed,** *Colloq.* **a.** tobacco. **b.** marijuana. **11. weed out, a.** to root out or remove (a weed): *to weed out the thistles.* **b.** to remove as being undesirable or superfluous: *to weed out undesirable members.* –**weeder,** *n.* –**weedless,** *adj.* –**weedlike,** *adj.* –**weedy,** *adj.*

weed² /wid/ n. a mourning band of black crepe or cloth, as on a man's hat or coat sleeve.

week /wik/ n. **1.** a period of seven successive days, commonly understood as beginning (unless otherwise specified or implied) with Sunday, followed by Monday, Tuesday, Wednesday, Thursday, Friday, and Saturday. **2.** Also, **working week.** the working days or working portion of the seven-day period. **3.** seven days after a specified day: *I shall come Tuesday week.* –*phr.* **4. week in, week out,** continuously; incessantly.

weekday /'wikdeɪ/ n. **1.** any day of the week, sometimes limited as **a.** (in a working week) any day except

Saturday and Sunday. **b.** (in a church calendar) any day except Sunday. *–adj.* **2.** of or on a weekday: *weekday occupations.*

weekend *n.* /ˈwikˈɛnd/ **1.** the end of the working week, especially the period from Friday night or Saturday to Sunday evening, as a time for recreation, visiting, etc. *–adj.* /ˈwikɛnd/ **2.** of, for, or on a weekend. *–v.i.* /ˈwikɛnd/ **3.** to pass the weekend, as at a place. *–phr.* **4. on** (or **at**) **the weekend,** during the weekend.

weekender /wikˈɛndə/ *n.* **1.** a holiday house. **2.** a person who regularly visits a certain place at weekends. **3.** a periodic detainee.

weekly /ˈwikli/ *adj.* **1.** done, happening, appearing, etc., once a week, or every week. **2.** continuing or staying for a week: *a weekly boarder. –adv.* **3.** once a week. **4.** by the week. *–n.* (*pl.* **-lies**) **5.** a magazine, paper, etc., appearing once a week.

weep /wip/ *verb* (**wept, weeping**) *–v.i.* **1.** to shed tears, as from sorrow, unhappiness, or any overpowering emotion; cry: *to weep for joy; to weep with rage.* **2.** to let fall drops of water or liquid; drip. **3.** to exude water or liquid, as soil, rock, a plant stem, a sore, etc. *–v.t.* **4.** to weep for; mourn with tears or other expression of sorrow: *he wept his dead brother.* **5.** to shed (tears, etc.). **6.** to let fall or give forth in drops: *trees weeping odorous gums.* **7.** to pass with the shedding of tears: *to weep the hours away. –n.* **8.** *Colloq.* weeping, or a fit of weeping. **9.** exudation of water or liquid. *–phr.* **10. weep one's eyes out,** to shed copious tears. **–weepy,** *adj.*

weeping /ˈwipɪŋ/ *adj.* **1.** that weeps. **2.** expressing sorrow by shedding tears. **3.** (of trees, etc.) having slender, drooping branches.

weevil /ˈwivəl/ *n.* **1.** any of the numerous beetles of the family Curculionidae, many of which are economically important, being destructive to nuts, grain, fruit, the stems of leaves, the pitch of trees, etc. **2.** any of the beetles of the family Lariidae, known as **seed weevils** or **bean weevils.**

weft /wɛft/ *n.* **1.** *Textiles* woof or filling yarns which interlace with warp running from selvage to selvage. **2.** a woven piece.

weigh¹ /wei/ *v.t.* **1.** to ascertain the weight of by means of a balance, scale, or other mechanical device: *to weigh gold; to weigh gases; to weigh oneself.* **2.** to hold up or balance, as in the hand, in order to estimate the weight. **3.** Also, **weigh up.** to balance in the mind; consider carefully in order to reach an opinion, decision, or choice: *to weigh facts or a proposal; to weigh up the pros and cons.* **4.** to raise or lift (now chiefly in the phrase **weigh anchor**). *–v.i.* **5.** to have weight or heaviness, often as specified: *to weigh little; to weigh 20 kilograms.* **6.** to have importance, moment, or consequence: *wealth weighs little in this case. –phr.* **7. weigh down,** to bear down by weight, heaviness, oppression, etc.: *weighed down with care; a bough weighed down by fruit.* **8. weigh in, a.** (of a boxer or wrestler) to be weighed before a fight. **b.** (of a jockey) to be weighed after a race. **9. weigh into, a.** to attack, physically or verbally. **b.** to begin to eat with hearty appetite. **10. weigh in with,** *Colloq.* to offer (an opinion, etc.). **11. weigh on** (or **upon**), to bear down as a weight or burden: *such responsibility weighed upon him.* **12. weigh one's words,** to consider and choose one's words carefully in speaking or writing. **13. weigh out,** to measure (a certain quantity of something) according to weight: *to weigh out 5 kg of sugar.* **–weighable,** *adj.* **–weigher,** *n.*

weigh² /wei/ *phr.* **under weigh,** *Naut.* in motion, as a ship that has weighed anchor.

weight /weit/ *n.* **1.** amount of heaviness; amount a thing weighs. **2.** *Physics* the force which gravitation exerts

upon a material body, varying with altitude and latitude. It is often taken as a measure of the mass, which does not vary, and is equal to the mass times the acceleration due to gravity. **3.** a system of units for expressing weight or mass: *avoirdupois weight.* **4.** a unit of weight or mass. **5.** a body of determinate mass, as of metal, for using on a balance or scale in measuring the weight or mass of (or weighing) objects, substances, etc. **6.** one of a series of standard divisions within which boxers or wrestlers fight, according to how much they weigh. **7.** a quantity of a substance determined by weighing: *a gram weight of gold dust.* **8.** any heavy mass or object, especially an object used because of its heaviness: *the weights of a clock.* **9.** pressure or oppressive force, as of something burdensome: *the weight of cares, sorrows.* **10.** a heavy load or burden: *that is such a weight I can't lift it.* **11.** a burden, as of care or responsibility: *to remove a weight from my mind.* **12.** importance, moment, consequence, or effective influence: *an opinion of great weight; men of weight.* **13. →** **stress** (def. 5). **14.** a measure of the relative importance of an item in a statistical population. **15.** (of clothing) the relative thickness as determined by the weather. **16.** *Printing* the degree of blackness of a typeface; the extent to which a bold typeface is heavier than its roman equivalent. *–v.t.* **17.** to add weight to; load with additional weight. **18.** to load (fabrics, threads, etc.) with mineral or other matter to increase the weight or bulk. **19.** to burden with or as with weight: *to be weighted with years.* **20.** *Statistics* to give a (statistical) weight to. *–phr.* **21. by weight,** according to weight measurement. **22. carry weight,** to have influence or importance. **23. correct weight,** *Horseracing* the confirmation that the contestants in a race did in fact carry the handicap weight allotted to them. **24. pull one's weight,** to do one's fair share of work. **25. throw one's weight around** (or **about**), **a.** to behave in an aggressive or selfish fashion. **b.** to use one's influence, personality, etc., to gain one's own ends without regard for others. **26. top weight,** *Horseracing* the maximum handicap. **–weightless,** *adj.*

weighting /ˈweitɪŋ/ *n.* **1.** an additional quantity or value attributed to any particular factor or factors in a complex situation: *a formula in which the weighting of different factors will determine future decisions.* **2.** an increased amount, as of salary or the like, to balance the higher cost of living in a particular area.

weightlessness /ˈweitləsnəs/ *n.* the state of being without apparent weight as experienced in free fall, due to the absence of any apparent gravitational pull; zero gravity.

weightlifting /ˈweitlɪftɪŋ/ *n.* the sport of lifting barbells of specified weights, in competition or for exercise. **–weightlifter,** *n.*

weight training *n.* exercises with weights to increase muscle strength. **–weight trainer,** *n.*

weighty /ˈweiti/ *adj.* (**-tier, -tiest**) **1.** having considerable weight; heavy; ponderous. **2.** burdensome or onerous: *the weighty cares of sovereignty.* **3.** important or momentous: *weighty negotiations.* **4.** influential: *a weighty financier.* **–weightily,** *adv.* **–weightiness,** *n.*

weir /wɪə/ *n.* **1.** a barrier in a river or stream to stop and raise the water, as for conducting it to a mill, for purposes of irrigation, etc. **2.** an obstruction placed across a stream thereby causing the water to pass through a particular opening or notch, thus measuring the quantity flowing. **3.** *Chiefly Brit.* a fence, as of brush, narrow boards, or a net, set in a stream, channel, etc., for catching fish.

weird /wɪəd/ *adj.* **1.** involving or suggesting the supernatural; unearthly or uncanny: *a weird scene; a weird light; a weird sound.* **2.** *Colloq.* startlingly or extraordinarily singular, odd, or queer: *a weird get-up.* **3.** concerned with fate or destiny. **–weirdly,** *adv.* **–weirdness,** *n.*

welch /wɛlʃ/ *v.t., v.i. Colloq.* → **welsh.** **–welcher,** *n.*

welcome /ˈwɛlkəm/ *interj.* **1.** a word of kindly greeting to a friend: *Welcome, friends!* *–n.* **2.** a kindly greeting or reception: *to give one a warm welcome.* *–v.t.* (**-comed, -coming**) **3.** to greet the coming of (a person, etc.) with pleasure or kindly politeness. **4.** to receive or regard, usually with pleasure: *to welcome a change.* *–adj.* **5.** gladly received: *a welcome visitor.* **6.** pleasing, such as something coming, happening, or experienced: *a welcome letter; a welcome rest.* **7.** given full right by the friendly consent of others: *he's welcome to anything he can find.* **8.** free to enjoy politeness, favours, etc., without being indebted (used in conventional response to thanks): *you are quite welcome.* **–welcomeless,** *adj.* **–welcomely,** *adv.* **–welcomeness,** *n.* **–welcomer,** *n.*

welcome swallow *n.* a swallow, *Hirundo neoxena,* with a swift, swooping flight, widely distributed throughout Australia, except in the north-west and the NT.

welcome to country *n.* a welcoming speech, performance, etc., given by a representative or representatives of the traditional Indigenous custodians of the land on which a public event, meeting, etc., is taking place.

weld /wɛld/ *v.t.* **1.** to unite or fuse (pieces of metal, etc.) by hammering, compression, or the like, especially after rendering soft or pasty by heat, and sometimes with the addition of fusible material like or unlike the pieces to be united. **2.** to bring into complete union. *–v.i.* **3.** to undergo welding; be capable of being welded. *–n.* **4.** a welded junction or joint. **5.** the act of welding. **–weldable,** *adj.* **–welder,** *n.*

welfare /ˈwɛlfɛə/ *n.* **1.** the state of faring well; wellbeing: *one's welfare, the physical or moral welfare of society.* **2.** Also, **welfare work.** work devoted to the welfare of persons in a community, especially the aged, sick, poor, etc. **3.** → **social service.**

welfare cheat *n.* a person who takes advantage of a welfare system to gain extra money or other advantages to which they are not entitled.

welfare state *n.* a nation or state in which the government undertakes the prime responsibility in areas such as social security, health and education, housing, and working conditions.

welfare trap *n.* an economic situation in which the benefit of taking paid work and securing an income is not much more than the benefit received from social welfare entitlements, thereby tending to encourage people to remain in the welfare system. Also, **unemployment trap.**

well[1] /wɛl/ *adv.* (**better, best**) **1.** in a satisfactory, favourable, or advantageous manner; fortunately or happily: *affairs are going well; to be well supplied; well situated.* **2.** in a good or proper manner: *he behaved very well.* **3.** commendably, meritoriously, or excellently: *to act, write, or reason well; good work well done.* **4.** with propriety, justice, or reason: *I could not well refuse.* **5.** in satisfactory or good measure; adequately or sufficiently: *think well before you act.* **6.** thoroughly or soundly: *shake well before using; beat well.* **7.** easily; clearly: *I can see it very well.* **8.** to a considerable extent or degree: *a sum well over the amount fixed; dilute the acid well.* **9.** personally; to a great degree of intimacy: *to know a person well.* *–adj.* (**better, best**) **10.** in good health, or sound in body and mind: *I am well; a well man.* **11.** satisfactory or good: *all is well with us.* **12.** proper or fitting. **13.** in a satisfactory position; well-off: *I am very well as I am.* *–interj.* **14.** used to express surprise, agreement: *well,*

who would have thought it? **15.** used as a preliminary to further speech: *well, as I was saying.* *–phr.* **16. all very well for someone,** (*ironic*) satisfactory; pleasing: *it's all very well for you, you don't have to worry about money.* **17. as well,** in addition: *she is bringing a friend as well.* **18. as well as,** in addition to; no less than: *he was handsome as well as rich.* **19. just as well,** preferable; more favourable; advisable: *it would be just as well if you went.* **20. very well, a.** with certainty; undeniably: *you know very well you are late.* **b.** a phrase used to indicate consent, often with reluctance: *very well, you may go, but not for long.* **–wellness,** *n.*

well[2] /wɛl/ *n.* **1.** a hole drilled into the earth, generally by boring, to obtain water, petroleum, natural gas, etc. **2.** a spring or natural source of water. **3.** a fountain, fountainhead, or source. **4.** a vessel, etc., for holding a liquid: *an inkwell.* **5.** any sunken or deep enclosed space, especially a shaft for air or light, or for stairs, a lift, etc., extending in an upright direction through the floors of a building. *–v.i.* **6.** (oft. fol. by *up, out,* or *forth*) to rise, spring, or gush from the earth or some source: *tears welled up in his eyes.* *–v.t.* **7.** to send welling up or out: *a fountain welling its pure water.*

we'll /wil/ contraction of *we will* or *we shall.*

well-appointed *adj.* comfortably and adequately equipped, decorated, furnished, etc., as a hotel, house, or the like. Also (*especially in predicative use*), **well appointed.**

wellbeing /ˈwɛlbiɪŋ/ *n.* good or satisfactory condition of existence; welfare. Also, **well-being.**

well-connected *adj.* **1.** having important, powerful, or influential relatives. **2.** having useful connections with influential people. Also (*especially in predicative use*), **well connected.**

well-covered *adj.* **1.** fully or satisfactorily covered. **2.** *Colloq.* (*euphemistic*) fat. Also (*especially in predicative use*), **well covered.**

well-heeled *adj. Colloq.* wealthy; prosperous. Also (*especially in predicative use*), **well heeled.**

wellington boot /wɛlɪŋtən ˈbʊt/ *n.* **1.** Also **wellington.** → **gumboot.** **2.** originally, a leather boot with the front reaching to above the knee.

well-mannered *adj.* polite; courteous. Also (*especially in predicative use*), **well mannered.**

well-meaning *adj.* **1.** meaning or intending well: *a well-meaning but tactless person.* **2.** proceeding from good intentions. Also (*especially in predicative use*), **well meaning.**

well-nigh *adv.* very nearly; almost.

well-off *adj.* **1.** in a satisfactory, favourable, or good position or condition. *–phr.* **2. comfortably well-off,** prosperous, though not exceedingly rich. Also (*especially in predicative use*), **well off.**

well-read /ˈwɛl-rɛd/ *adj.* **1.** having read much: *well-read in science.* **2.** having an extensive and intelligent knowledge of books or literature. Also (*especially in predicative use*), **well read** /wɛl ˈrɛd/.

well-spoken *adj.* **1.** having a cultured, refined accent. **2.** speaking well, fittingly, or pleasingly. **3.** polite in speech. **4.** spoken well, appropriately, etc. Also (*especially in predicative use*), **well spoken.**

well-to-do *adj.* having a sufficiency of means for comfortable living, well-off, or prosperous. Also (*especially in predicative use*), **well to do.**

welsh /wɛlʃ/ *Colloq. –v.i.* **1.** (sometimes fol. by *on*) to cheat by evading payment, especially of a gambling debt: *to welsh on one's partner.* *–phr.* **2. welsh on,** to inform or tell on (someone). Also, **welch.** **–welsher,** *n.*

welt /wɛlt/ *n.* **1.** a ridge or raised mark on the surface of the body, usually from the stroke of a stick or whip. **2.** strip of leather set in between the edges of the inner sole and upper and the outer sole of a shoe. **3.** a strengthening or ornamental finish along a seam, the edge of a garment, etc. **4.** a type of seam in which one edge is cut close to the stitching line and covered by the other edge which is stitched over it. −*v.t.* **5.** to beat soundly with a stick or whip. **6.** to supply with a welt or welts.

welter /ˈwɛltə/ *v.i.* **1.** *Archaic* to lie bathed or be drenched in something, especially blood. **2.** *Obs.* to roll or tumble about, or wallow, as animals. −*n.* **3.** a race in which the horses carry weights which are not less than 51 kg. −*phr.* **4. make a welter of it,** *Colloq.* to indulge in something to excess.

welterweight /ˈwɛltəweɪt/ *n.* **1.** a medium-to-heavy weight division in boxing. **2.** a boxer of this weight class.

wen /wɛn/ *n.* a benign encysted tumour of the skin, especially on the scalp, containing sebaceous matter; a sebaceous cyst.

wench /wɛntʃ/ *n.* **1.** a girl, or young woman. **2.** a rustic or working girl. −*v.i.* **3.** to consort with promiscuous women or prostitutes. −**wencher,** *n.*

wend /wɛnd/ *v.t.* (**wended** *or*, *Archaic*, **went**, **wending**) to direct or pursue (one's way, etc.): *he wended his way to the riverside.*

went /wɛnt/ *v.* past tense of **go**.

wept /wɛpt/ *v.* past tense and past participle of **weep**.

were /wɜ/, *weak form* /wə/ *v.* **1.** past tense indicative plural and subjunctive singular and plural of **be**. −*phr.* **2. as it were,** (an expression used to indicate that what is referred to is metaphorical or figurative); so to speak.

we're /wɪə, wɜ, wɛə/ contraction of *we are*.

weren't /wɜnt/ contraction of *were not*.

werewolf /ˈwɛəwʊlf/ *n.* (*pl.* **-wolves** /-wʊlvz/) (in old superstition) a human being turned preternaturally into a wolf, or capable of assuming the form of a wolf, while retaining human intelligence. Also, **werwolf**.

wert /wɜt/ *v. Archaic* 2nd person singular past tense indicative and subjunctive of **be**.

west /wɛst/ *n.* **1.** a cardinal point of the compass (90° to the left of north) corresponding to the point where the sun is seen to set. **2.** the direction in which this point lies. −*adj.* **3.** lying towards or situated in the west: *the west side.* **4.** directed or proceeding towards the west. **5.** coming from the west: *a west wind.* **6.** (*also upper case*) designating the western part of a region, nation, etc. **7.** *Eccles.* designating lying towards, or in that part of a church opposite to and farthest from the altar. −*adv.* **8.** in the direction of the sunset; towards or in the west. **9.** from the west (as of wind). −*phr.* **10. go west,** *Colloq.* **a.** (of a person) to die. **b.** (of an item) to disappear or be lost. **11. the west, a.** (*also upper case*) a quarter or territory situated in a western direction. **b.** (*usu. upper case*) the western part of the world as distinct from the East or Orient; the Occident. **c.** (*usu. upper case*) the countries of Western Europe, North America, and other countries with a Western European background, such as Australia and New Zealand, especially as contrasted historically, culturally, or politically with other parts of the world.

westerly /ˈwɛstəli/ *adj.* **1.** moving, directed, or situated towards the west. **2.** coming from the west: *a westerly gale.* −*adv.* **3.** towards the west. **4.** from the west. −*n.* (*pl.* **-lies**) **5.** a westerly wind.

western /ˈwɛstən/ *adj.* **1.** lying towards or situated in the west. **2.** directed or proceeding towards the west. **3.** coming from the west, as a wind. **4.** (*usu. upper case*) of or relating to the West (def. 6). −*n.* **5.** (*also upper case*) a story or film about frontier life in the American West during the latter half of the 19th century. −**westernise, westernize,** *v.*

Western red cedar *n.* See **red cedar** (def. 2).

wet /wɛt/ *adj.* (**wetter, wettest**) **1.** covered or soaked, wholly or in part, with water or some other liquid: *wet hands*; *a wet sponge.* **2.** moist, damp, or not dry: *wet ink*; *wet paint.* **3.** characterised by the presence or use of water or other liquid: *the wet method of chemical analysis.* **4.** rainy; having a rainy climate. **5.** characterised by or favouring allowance of the manufacture and sale of alcoholic beverages. **6.** *Colloq.* weak; feeble; spiritless. **7.** adhering to the policies of a wet (def. 14). **8.** (of sheep) having fleece too wet to be shorn. −*n.* **9.** that which makes wet, as water or other liquid; moisture. **10.** a wet state, condition, or place. **11.** rain. **12.** *US* someone who favours allowance of the manufacture and sale of alcoholic beverages. **13.** *Colloq.* a weak, usually dreary, person. **14.** someone within a political party, etc., who is opposed to a hard uncompromising fiscal policy (opposed to *dry*). −*verb* (**wet** *or* **wetted, wetting**) −*v.t.* **15.** to make wet. **16.** to make wet by urinating: *the child wet the bed.* −*v.i.* **17.** to become wet. −*phr.* **18. the wet,** the rainy season in central and northern Australia, usually from December to March. **19. wet behind the ears,** *Colloq.* naive; immature or inexperienced. **20. wet one's whistle,** *Colloq.* to satisfy one's thirst, usually with an alcoholic drink. −**wetly,** *adv.* −**wetness,** *n.* −**wetter,** *n.* −**wettish,** *adj.*

wet blanket *n.* a person or thing that dampens ardour or has a discouraging or depressing effect.

wet cell *n.* an electric cell whose electrolyte is in liquid form and free to flow.

wet dream *n.* a sexually exciting dream which causes a male to experience an involuntary orgasm while or just after sleeping

wether /ˈwɛðə/ *n.* a ram castrated when young.

wetland /ˈwɛtlænd, ˈwɛtlənd/ *n.* **1.** an area in which the soil is frequently or permanently saturated with or under water, as a swamp, marsh, etc. **2.** (*pl.*) an ecological system made up of such areas.

wet lease *n.* a leasing agreement on an aircraft under which the lessor supplies all operational aspects such as crew, maintenance, insurance, etc., along with the aircraft. −**wet leasing,** *n.*

wet nurse *n.* a woman hired to breastfeed another's infant.

wet-nurse *v.t.* **1.** to act as wet nurse to. **2.** *Colloq.* to cosset or pamper.

wet season *n.* the period of an annual cycle in the tropics when rainfall and humidity increase markedly, usually as a result of the change in the prevailing winds. Compare **dry season**.

wetsuit /ˈwɛtsut/ *n.* a set of tight-fitting upper and lower garments made of rubber, worn by scuba divers, surfers, canoeists, etc., to retain body heat while immersed in water.

wetware /ˈwɛtwɛə/ *n.* (*humorous*) **1.** the human brain, as opposed to computers. **2.** computer users, collectively.

we've /wiv/, *unstressed* /wəv/ contraction of *we have*.

whack /wæk/ *Colloq.* −*v.t.* **1.** to strike with a smart, resounding blow or blows. **2.** to put or place, especially roughly or quickly: *whack it down here*; *I'll just whack on a CD.* −*n.* **3.** a smart, resounding blow: *a whack with her hand.* **4.** a trial or attempt: *to take a whack at a job.* **5.** a portion or share. −*phr.* **6. out of whack,** not functioning correctly: *this metronome is out of whack.* **7. whack into,** put in; insert. −**whacker,** *n.*

whale¹ /weɪl/ *n.* (*pl.* **whales** *or*, *especially collectively,* **whale**) **1.** *Zool.* any of the larger marine mammals of the order Cetacea, which includes the large sperm and whalebone whales, and the smaller dolphins and porpoises. All have fishlike bodies, modified foreflippers, and a horizontally flattened tail. **2.** *Colloq.* something extraordinarily big, great, or fine of its kind: *a whale of a lot, a whale of a time.* **3.** *Aust. Colloq.* a Murray cod.

–v.i. **4.** to carry on the work of taking whales. **5.** *Aust. Colloq.* to fish for Murray cod.

whale² /weɪl/ *Colloq. –v.t.* **1.** to whip, thrash, or beat soundly. *–phr.* **2. whale into, a.** to throw oneself into (something) energetically. **b.** to beat up or bash (someone). **c.** to attack verbally; berate.

whalebone /ˈweɪlboʊn/ *n.* **1.** an elastic horny substance growing in place of teeth in the upper jaw of certain whales, and forming a series of thin, parallel plates on each side of the palate; baleen. **2.** a thin strip of this material, formerly used for stiffening corsets.

whale shark *n.* a huge, plankton-feeding shark, *Rhincodon typus*, of tropical and warm temperate oceans, growing to about eighteen metres.

wham /wæm/ *v.t.* to hit forcefully, especially with a single loud noise.

whare² /ˈfɒri, ˈwɒri/ *n.* **1.** a Maori hut. **2.** *NZ* any hut or makeshift home; bach; crib.

wharf /wɔf/ *n.* (*pl.* **wharves** *or* **wharfs**) **1.** a structure built on the shore of, or projecting out into, a harbour, stream, etc., so that vessels may be moored alongside to load or unload or to lie at rest; a quay; a pier. *–v.t.* **2.** to place or store on a wharf. **–wharfless,** *adj.*

wharfie /ˈwɔfi/ *n. Aust., NZ Colloq.* a wharf labourer. Also, **wharfy.**

what /wɒt/ *pron. (interrogative)* **1.** used to ask for the specifying of some impersonal thing: *what is your name?*; *what did he do?* **2.** used to inquire as to the nature, character, class, origin, etc., of a thing or person: *what is that animal?* **3.** used to inquire as to the worth, usefulness, force, or importance of something: *what is wealth without health?* **4.** used to ask, often elliptically, for repetition or explanation of some word or words used, as by a previous speaker: *you need five what? you claim to be what?* **5.** how much?: *what did it cost?* **6.** used to ask for the specifying of some thing or person: *what news?*; *what men?* **7.** used interjectionally to express surprise, disbelief, indignation, etc. **8.** used with intensive force in exclamatory phrases, preceding an indefinite article, if one is used: *what luck! what an idea! –pron. (relative)* **9.** that which: *this is what she says; I will send what was promised.* **10.** the kind of thing or person that, or such: *the book is just what it professes to be; the old man is not what he was.* **11.** anything that, or whatever: *say what you please; come what may.* **12.** (in parenthetic clauses) something that: *but she went, and, what is more surprising, gained a hearing.* **13.** (now regarded as non-standard) that, which, or who: *these are the tiles what Richard laid; that's the dog what bit me.* **14.** (used as a determiner) that or any ... which; such ... as: *take what time and what assistants you need. –adv.* **15.** to what extent or degree, or how much: *what does it matter? –phr.* **16. and what not** or **and what have you,** and the like: *friends, relatives, and what have you.* **17. do I what!,** *Colloq.* an affirmative exclamation expressing a positive response to a question asked: *Do you love me? Do I what!* **18. give someone what for,** *Colloq.* to administer severe treatment, punishment, or violence: *he hit me, so I gave him what for.* **19. know what it is to ...,** to have experience of ...: *to know what it is to be poor.* **20. know what's what,** to be in command of the facts of a situation and able to decide correctly what to do. **21. no matter what,** notwithstanding anything else that happens. **22. so what?,** *Colloq.* an exclamation of contempt, dismissal, or the like. **23. what about ...?,** a phrase used to make a suggestion: *what about a cup of tea?* **24. what for?,** for what reason or purpose? **25. what if,** *Colloq.* **a.** an interrogative pronoun which introduces the exploration of a possibility: *what if nobody comes?* **b.** a hypothetical possibility: *there are too many what ifs in this plan.* **26. what it takes,** the

necessary ability, personality, or the like: *he may look stupid, but he's got what it takes to hold the job down.* **27. what of it?,** (an exclamation of dismissal, etc.); what does it matter? **28. what say we ...?,** a phrase used to suggest an activity: *what say we have a picnic?* **29. what the hey** (or **heck**), *Colloq.* an expression of nonchalance, indifference, etc. **30. what with,** as a result of: *what with storms and sickness, his return was delayed.* **31. what's what,** the true position.

whatever /wɒtˈɛvə/ *pron. (relative)* **1.** anything that: *do whatever you like.* **2.** no matter what: *do it, whatever happens. –pron. (interrogative)* **3.** *Colloq.* (used to give force) what ever? what?: *whatever do you mean? –adj.* **4.** any ... that: *whatever worth the work has is to John's credit.* **5.** no matter what: *whatever blame he might receive, he'll still carry on.* **6.** what (who) ... it may be: *for whatever reason, he is unwilling; any person whatever. –interj.* **7.** a dismissive expression used to indicate indifference and sometimes scorn. Also, *Poetic,* **whate'er.**

whatnot /ˈwɒtnɒt/ *n.* **1.** a stand with shelves for bric-a-brac, books, etc. **2.** *Colloq.* an insignificant or unspecified article.

what's /wɒts/ contraction of *what is.*

wheat /wit/ *n.* **1.** the grain of a widely distributed cereal grass, genus *Triticum*, especially *T. aestivum* (*T. sativum*), used extensively in the form of flour for white bread, cakes, pastry, etc. **2.** the plant, which bears the edible grain in dense spikes that sometimes have awns (**bearded wheat**) and sometimes do not (**beardless wheat** or **bald wheat**). **–wheatless,** *adj.*

wheatgerm /ˈwitdʒɜm/ *n.* the vitamin-rich embryo of the wheat kernel which is removed when the wheat is milled and which is sold as a dietary supplement as it contains many B vitamins.

wheedle /ˈwidl/ *v.t.* **1.** to endeavour to influence (a person) by smooth, flattering, or beguiling words. **2.** to get by artful persuasions: *wheedling my money from me. –v.i.* **3.** to use beguiling or artful persuasions. **–wheedler,** *n.* **–wheedlingly,** *adv.*

wheel /wil/ *n.* **1.** a circular frame or solid disc arranged to turn on an axis, as in vehicles, machinery, etc. **2.** any instrument, machine, apparatus, etc., shaped like this, or having such a frame or disc as an essential feature: *a potter's wheel.* **3.** a circular frame with or without projecting handles and an axle connecting with the rudder, for steering a ship. **4.** an old instrument of torture in the form of a circular frame on which the victim was stretched while the limbs were broken with an iron bar. **5.** a circular firework which revolves while burning. **6.** (*pl.*) moving, propelling, or animating agencies: *the wheels of trade; the wheels of thought.* **7.** (*pl.*) *Colloq.* a motor vehicle. **8.** a wheeling or circular movement: *merrily whirled the wheels of the dizzying dances.* **9.** *Mil.* a change of direction. **10.** *Colloq.* a person of considerable importance or influence: *a big wheel. –v.t.* **11.** to cause to turn, rotate, or revolve, as on an axis. **12.** to cause (troops, etc.) to march in a circular or curving direction. **13.** to move, roll, or convey on wheels, castors, etc.: *to wheel the trolley around the supermarket.* **14.** to cause (a stampeding mob of cattle or horses) to turn away from their chosen direction. **15.** to provide (a vehicle, etc.) with a wheel or wheels. *–v.i.* **16.** to turn on or as on an axis or about a centre; rotate, revolve. **17.** *Mil.* to change direction while marching: *to wheel left.* **18.** to move in a circular or curving course: *pigeons wheeling above.* **19.** to roll along on, or as on, wheels; to travel along smoothly. *–phr.* **20. at the wheel, a.** at the steering wheel of a car, ship, etc. **b.** in command or control. **21. be on someone's wheel,** *Aust. Colloq.* to exert consistent pressure on someone; hound someone. **22. put one's shoulder to**

the wheel, to exert oneself greatly, as in a combined effort to achieve some end. **23. silly as a wheel**, *Aust. Colloq.* very silly. **24. wheel about** (or **around**), to turn or change in procedure or opinion. **25. wheel and deal**, to act as a wheeler-dealer. **26. wheels within wheels**, a complicated situation in which many different factors are involved. **–wheeled**, *adj.* **–wheelless**, *adj.*

wheelbarrow /ˈwilbæroʊ/ *n.* **1.** a frame or box for conveying a load, usually supported at one end by a wheel and at the other by two vertical legs above which are two horizontal shafts used in lifting the legs from the ground when the vehicle is pushed or pulled. **2.** a similar vehicle with more than one wheel. *–v.t.* **3.** to move or convey in a wheelbarrow.

wheelchair /ˈwiltʃeə/ *n.* a chair mounted on large wheels, used by invalids and those unable to walk.

wheeler-dealer /wilə-ˈdilə/ *n. Colloq.* **1.** *Chiefly US* someone in a position of power who controls and directs the actions of others. **2.** someone who actively pursues their own advancement by moving constantly from one profitable business transaction to another.

wheelie bin /ˈwili bɪn/ *n.* a large bin with wheels and a handle, used for household rubbish.

wheeze /wiz/ *v.i.* **1.** to breathe with difficulty and with a whistling sound: *wheezing with asthma. –v.t.* **2.** to utter such a sound. *–n.* **3.** a wheezing breath or sound. **4.** a theatrical gag. **–wheezer**, *n.* **–wheezy**, *adj.* **–wheezingly**, *adv.*

whelk /wɛlk/ *n.* any of various large spiral-shelled marine gastropods of the family Buccinidae, as the giant whelk *Verconella maxima* found along the continental shelf from SA to NSW.

whelp /wɛlp/ *n.* **1.** the young of the dog, or of the wolf, bear, lion, tiger, seal, etc. **2.** (*derog.*) a youth. **3.** *Machinery* **a.** any of a series of longitudinal projections or ridges of iron or the like on the barrel of a capstan, windlass, etc. **b.** one of the teeth of a sprocket wheel. *–v.t.* **4.** (of a bitch, lioness, etc.) to bring forth (young). *–v.i.* **5.** (of a bitch, lioness, etc.) to bring forth young.

when /wɛn/ *adv.* **1.** at what time: *when are you coming? –conj.* **2.** at what time: *to know when to be silent.* **3.** at the time that: *when we were young*; *when the noise stopped.* **4.** at any time, or whenever: *he gets impatient when he is kept waiting.* **5.** upon or after which; and then: *no sooner had she spoken when Mary came through the door.* **6.** while on the contrary; whereas: *you cover up the wound when you should clean it first. –pron.* (*interrogative*) **7.** what time: *since when have you known this? –pron.* (*relative*) **8.** which time: *they left on Monday, since when we have heard nothing. –n.* **9.** the time of anything: *the when and the where of an act. –phr.* **10. say when**, to tell someone when to stop, especially in pouring a drink.

whence /wɛns/ *adv. Archaic* **1.** from what place?: *whence comest thou?* **2.** from what source, origin, or cause?: *whence hath he wisdom? –conj.* **3.** from what place, source, cause, etc.: *he told whence he came.*

whenever /wɛnˈɛvə/ *conj.* **1.** at whatever time; at any time when: *come whenever you like. –adv.* **2.** (used emphatically) when: *whenever did she say that?*

where /wɛə/ *adv.* **1.** in or at what place?: *where is he?* **2.** in what position?: *where do you stand on this question?* **3.** in what particular respect, way, etc.?: *where does this affect us?* **4.** to what place, point, or end?: *where are you going?* **5.** from what source: *where did you get such an idea? –conj.* **6.** in, at, or to what place, part, point, etc.: *find where the trouble is*; *find out where he's gone.* **7.** in or at the place, part, point, etc., in or at which: *the book is where you left it.* **8.** in a position, case, etc., in which: *there are times where it is better not to know the truth.* **9.** in or at which place: *they came to the town, where they stayed for the night.*

10. *Colloq.* that: *I read where they are going to increase taxes. –pron.* **11.** what place: *where have you come from?* **12.** the place in which: *this is where we live.*

where- a word element meaning 'what' or 'which'.

whereabouts /ˈwɛərəbaʊts/, *interrogatively* /wɛərəˈbaʊts/ *adv.* Also, **whereabout**. **1.** about where? where? *–conj.* **2.** near or in what place: *seeing whereabouts in the world we were. –pl. n.* **3.** (sometimes construed as *sing.*) the place where a person or thing is; the locality of a person or thing: *no clue as to his whereabouts.*

whereas /wɛərˈæz/ *conj.* **1.** while on the contrary: *one came, whereas the others didn't.* **2.** it being the case that, or considering that (especially used in formal preambles). *–n.* (*pl.* **whereases**) **3.** a statement having 'whereas' as the first word: *to read the whereases in the will.*

whereby /wɛəˈbaɪ/ *conj.* by what or by which.

wherefore /ˈwɛəfɔ/ *adv.* **1.** for what? why? *–conj.* **2.** for what or which cause or reason. *–n.* **3.** the cause or reason.

whereupon /wɛərəˈpɒn/ *adv.* **1.** *Archaic* upon what? whereon? *–conj.* **2.** at or after which. **3.** upon what or upon which.

wherever /wɛərˈɛvə/ *conj.* **1.** in, at, or to whatever place. **2.** in any case or condition: *wherever it is heard of. –adv.* **3.** (used emphatically) where: *wherever did you find that?*

wherewithal /ˈwɛəwɪðɔl, -θɔl/ *n.* that wherewith to do something; means or supplies for the purpose or need, especially money: *the wherewithal to pay my rent.*

whet /wɛt/ *v.t.* (**whetted**, **whetting**) **1.** to sharpen (a knife, tool, etc.) by grinding or friction. **2.** to make keen or eager: *to whet the appetite*; *to whet the curiosity. –n.* **3.** the act of whetting. **4.** something that whets; an appetiser. **–whetter**, *n.*

whether /ˈwɛðə/ *conj.* **1.** used in dependent clauses or the like, to introduce the first of two or more alternatives, and sometimes repeated before the second or later alternative and used in correlation with *or*: *it matters little whether we go or whether we stay.* **2.** used to introduce a single alternative, the other being implied or understood, and hence some clause or element not involving alternatives: *see whether he has come (or not)*; *I doubt whether we can do any better. –phr.* **3. whether or no**, under whatever circumstances: *he threatens to go, whether or no.*

whetstone /ˈwɛtstoʊn/ *n.* **1.** a stone for sharpening cutlery or tools by friction. **2.** anything that sharpens: *a whetstone for dull wits.*

whey /weɪ/ *n.* milk serum, separating as a watery liquid from the curd after coagulation, as in cheese-making. **–wheyish**, **wheylike**, *adj.*

which /wɪtʃ/ *pron.* (*interrogative*) **1.** what one (of a certain number)?: *which of these do you want? –pron.* (*relative*) **2.** used as the subject or object of a relative clause: *how old is the car which was stolen?* **3.** what particular one or any one that: *she knows which she wants*; *choose which you like.* **4.** a thing that: *and, which is worse, your work is wrong. –adj.* **5.** what one of (a certain number): *which book do you want?* **6.** any … that: *go which way you please.* **7.** being previously mentioned: *it stormed all day, during which time the ship broke up.*

whichever /wɪtʃˈɛvə/ *pron.* **1.** any one (of those in question) that: *take whichever you like.* **2.** no matter which: *whichever you choose, the others will be offended. –adj.* **3.** no matter which: *whichever day*; *whichever person.* Also, *Poetic*, **whiche'er**.

whiff /wɪf/ *n.* **1.** a slight movement or puff: *a whiff of fresh air.* **2.** a slight smell. *–v.i.* **3.** (of wind, smoke, etc.) to blow lightly. **–whiffer**, *n.* **–whiffy**, *adj.*

while /waɪl/ *n.* **1.** a space of time: *a long while; a while ago.* *–conj.* Also, **whilst**. **2.** during or in the time that. **3.** throughout the time that, or as long as. **4.** at the same time that (implying opposition or contrast): *while she appreciated the honour, she could not accept the position.* *–phr.* (*v.* **whiled, whiling**) **5.** **once in a while**, occasionally. **6. the while**, during this time. **7. while away**, to cause (time) to pass, especially in some easy or pleasant manner. **8. worth one's while**, worth time, pains, or expense.

whilst /waɪlst/ *conj.* while.

whim /wɪm/ *n.* **1.** an odd or fanciful notion; a freakish or capricious fancy or desire. **2.** capricious humour: *to be swayed by whim.* **3.** *Mining* a large capstan or vertical drum turned by horsepower for raising coal, water, etc., from a mine.

whimper /ˈwɪmpə/ *v.i.* **1.** to cry with low, plaintive, broken sounds, as a child, a dog, etc. *–v.t.* **2.** to utter in a whimper. *–n.* **3.** a whimpering cry or sound. **–whimperer**, *n.* **–whimperingly**, *adv.*

whimsical /ˈwɪmzɪkəl/ *adj.* of an odd, quaint, or comical kind. **–whimsically**, *adv.* **–whimsicalness, whimsicality** /wɪmzəˈkælətɪ/, *n.*

whimsy /ˈwɪmzɪ/ *n.* (*pl.* **-sies**) **1.** an odd or fanciful notion. **2.** anything odd or fanciful; a product of playful fancy. Also, **whimsey**.

whine /waɪn/ *verb* (**whined, whining**) *–v.i.* **1.** to utter a nasal, complaining cry or sound, as from uneasiness, discontent, peevishness, etc. **2.** to complain in a feeble, plaintive way. **3.** to emit a high-pitched, monotonous sound, as of machinery, etc. *–v.t.* **4.** to utter with a whine. *–n.* **5.** a whining utterance, sound, or tone. **–whiner**, *n.* **–whiningly**, *adv.* **–whiny, adj.**

whinge /wɪndʒ/ *v.i.* (**whinged, whingeing**) to complain; whine. **–whingeing**, *adj.* **–whinger**, *n.*

whinny /ˈwɪnɪ/ *v.i.* (**-nied, -nying**) (of a horse) to utter its characteristic cry; neigh.

whio /ˈfiːoʊ/ *n.* → **blue duck** (def. 1).

whip /wɪp/ *verb* (**whipped, whipping**) *–v.t.* **1.** to strike with quick, repeated strokes of something slender and flexible; lash. **2.** to beat with a whip or the like, especially by way of punishment or chastisement; flog; thrash. **3.** to drive (*on, out, in*, etc.) by strokes or lashes. **4.** *Colloq.* to beat, outdo, or defeat, as in a contest. **5.** to pull, jerk, snatch, seize, put, etc., (*away, out, up, into*, etc.) with a sudden movement. **6.** to overlay or cover (cord, etc.) with cord, thread, or the like wound about it. **7.** to wind (cord, twine, thread, etc.) about something. **8.** to gather, or form into pleats by overcasting the turned edge with small stitches and then drawing up the thread. **9.** to beat (eggs, cream, etc.) to a froth with a whisk, fork, or other implement in order to incorporate air and produce expansion. *–v.i.* **10.** to move or go (*away, off, out, in*, etc.) quickly and suddenly; dart; whisk. **11.** to beat or lash about, as a pennant in the wind. *–n.* **12.** an instrument to strike with, as in driving animals or in punishing, typically consisting of a lash or other flexible part with a more rigid handle. **13.** a whipping or lashing strike or motion. **14.** someone who handles a whip; a driver of horses, a coach, etc. **15.** someone who has charge of the hounds in hunting. **16.** a party manager in a legislative body, who supplies information to members about the government business, secures their attendance for voting, supplies lists of members to serve on committees, and keeps the leaders informed as to the trend of party opinion. **17.** a dish made of cream or egg whites whipped to a froth with flavouring, etc., often with fruit pulp or the like: *prune whip.* **–phr. 18. be there when the whips are cracking**, *Aust., NZ Colloq.* to be at the scene of any action or crisis. **19. crack the whip**, *Colloq.* to urge greater effort. **20. fair crack of the whip**, *Colloq.* an

exhortation to be fair. **21. follow a whip**, *Parliamentary Procedure* to vote in accordance with a party decision as conveyed by the parliamentary whip. **22. whip in, a.** *Hunting* to prevent from wandering, as hounds. **b.** to exact obedience or obedience from (a group of people), as a party whip does. **23. whip into line**, to discipline into obedience. **24. whip off**, to take, steal. **25. whip (or flog) the cat**, *Aust., NZ* to reproach oneself. **26. whip round**, to make a collection of money. **27. whips of**, *Aust., NZ Colloq.* great quantities of. Compare **lashing**[1] (def. 3). **28. whip up, a.** to create quickly: *I whipped up a meal when I heard they were coming.* **b.** to arouse to fury, intense excitement, etc.: *his speech soon whipped up the crowd.* **29. under the whip**, (of a racehorse) driven on to extra effort by being whipped by the rider. **–whipper**, *n.*

whipbird /ˈwɪpbɜːd/ *n.* any of a number of birds the terminal note of whose call resembles the crack of a whip, especially the **eastern whipbird**, *Psophodes olivaceus*, of coastal and mountain forests and gullies of eastern Australia; coachman. Also, **coachman's whipbird**, **coach-whip bird**.

whiplash /ˈwɪplæʃ/ *n.* **1.** the lash of a whip. **2.** an injury to the spine, usually in the cervical area, caused by sudden movement forwards or backwards, as in a motor accident.

whippet /ˈwɪpət/ *n.* a dog of an English breed, probably a cross between the greyhound and the terrier, used especially in rabbit coursing and racing.

whippy[1] /ˈwɪpɪ/ *adj.* flexible as of a branch of a tree, riding crop, certain golf clubs, etc.

whippy[2] /ˈwɪpɪ/ *Aust.* *–n.* **1.** *Colloq.* **a.** a hiding place for money. **b.** a wallet. **2.** a place or object used as the home or base in hide-and-seek. *–phr.* **3. all in, the whippy's taken**, an expression used to signal the end of a round in certain games of hide-and-seek.

whipsaw /ˈwɪpsɔː/ *n.* any flexible saw, as a bandsaw.

whirl /wɜːl/ *v.i.* **1.** to turn round, spin, or rotate rapidly. **2.** to turn about or aside quickly. **3.** to move, travel, or be carried rapidly along on wheels or otherwise. **4.** to have the sensation of turning round rapidly. *–v.t.* **5.** to cause to turn round, spin, or rotate rapidly. **6.** to send, drive, or carry in a circular or curving course. **7.** to drive, send, or carry along with great or dizzying rapidity. *–n.* **8.** the act of whirling; rapid rotation or gyration. **9.** a whirling movement; a quick turn or swing. **10.** a short drive, run, walk, or the like, or a spin. **11.** something that whirls; a whirling current or mass. **12.** a rapid round of events, affairs, etc. **13.** a state marked by a dizzying succession or mingling of feelings, thoughts, etc. *–phr.* **14. give it a whirl**, *Colloq.* to try something out. **–whirler**, *n.*

whirlpool /ˈwɜːlpuːl/ *n.* a whirling eddy or current, as in a river or the sea, produced by irregularity in the channel or stream banks, by the meeting of opposing currents, by the interaction of winds and tides, etc.; a vortex of water.

whirlwind /ˈwɜːlwɪnd/ *n.* **1.** a mass of air rotating rapidly round and towards a more or less vertical axis, and having at the same time a progressive motion over the surface of the land or sea. **2.** anything resembling a whirlwind, as in violent activity. **3.** any circling rush or violent onward course.

whirr /wɜː/ *v.i.* (**whirred, whirring**) **1.** to go, fly, dart, revolve, or otherwise move quickly with a vibratory or buzzing sound. *–n.* **2.** the act or sound of whirring: *the whirr of wings.* Also, **whir**.

whisk[1] /wɪsk/ *v.t.* **1.** to sweep (dust, crumbs, etc., or a surface) with a brush, or the like. **2.** to draw, grab, move, carry, etc., lightly and quickly. *–v.i.* **3.** to sweep, pass, or go lightly and quickly. *–n.* **4.** a quick, sweeping stroke; light, rapid movement.

whisk[2] /wɪsk/ *v.t.* **1.** to whip (eggs, cream, etc.) to a froth with a whisk or beating implement. *−n.* **2.** a small bunch of grass, straw, hair, or the like, especially for use in brushing. **3.** an implement, in one form a bunch of loops of wire held together in a handle, for beating or whipping eggs, cream, etc.

whisker /'wɪskə/ *n.* **1.** (*pl.*) the beard generally. **2.** a single hair of the beard. **3.** (*pl.*) a moustache. **4.** one of the long, stiff, bristly hairs growing about the mouth of certain animals, as the cat, rat, etc. **5.** *Colloq.* a very small quantity or distance: *he won the race by a whisker.* *−phr.* **6.** **have whiskers on it**, *Colloq.* to be old-fashioned or useless: *that idea has whiskers on it.* *−***whiskered**, **whiskery**, *adj.*

whisky /'wɪski/ *n.* (*pl.* **-kies**) **1.** a distilled spirit made from grain, as barley, rye, oats, etc. **2.** a drink of whisky. *−adj.* **3.** of or relating to whisky. Also, *Irish*, **whiskey**.

whisper /'wɪspə/ *v.i.* **1.** to speak with soft, low sounds, using the breath, lips, etc., without vibration of the vocal cords. **2.** to talk softly and privately (often in telling tales, plotting, etc.). **3.** (of trees, water, breezes, etc.) to make a soft, rustling sound. *−v.t.* **4.** to utter (soft, low sounds), using the breath, lips, etc. **5.** to tell privately or secretly. *−n.* **6.** the type of utterance, or the voice, of someone who whispers. **7.** a sound, word, remark, etc., made by whispering. **8.** a soft, rustling sound. **9.** private information; rumour. *−***whisperer**, *n.*

whist /wɪst/ *n.* a card game played by four players, two against two, with 52 cards.

whistle /'wɪsəl/ *verb* (**whistled**, **whistling**) *−v.i.* **1.** to make a kind of clear musical sound, or a series of such sounds, by the forcible expulsion of the breath through a small orifice formed by contracting the lips, or through the teeth, together with the aid of the tongue. **2.** to make such a sound or series of sounds otherwise, as by blowing on a particular device. **3.** to produce a more or less similar sound by an instrument operated by steam or the like, or as such an instrument does. **4.** to emit somewhat similar sounds from the mouth, as birds. **5.** to move, go, pass, etc., with a high-pitched sound, as a bullet. *−v.t.* **6.** to produce or utter by whistling. **7.** to call, direct, or signal by or as by whistling. **8.** to send with a whistling or whizzing sound. *−n.* **9.** an instrument for producing whistling sounds as by the breath, steam, etc., as a small wooden or tin tube or a small pipe. **10.** a signal marking an event or stage, indicated by a whistle: *the full-time whistle.* **11.** a sound produced by or as by whistling: *a long-drawn whistle of astonishment.* *−phr.* **12.** **blow the whistle on**, *Colloq.* to report (a person, or a situation) to relevant authority, as reprehensible. **13.** **wet one's whistle**, *Colloq.* to satisfy one's thirst, usually with an alcoholic drink. **14.** **whistle for**, to ask or wish for (something) in vain. **15.** **whistle in** (or **against**) **the wind**, to protest in vain.

whistleblower /'wɪsəlbloʊə/ *n.* a person, usually an employee or member of an organisation, who alerts the public to some scandalous practice or evidence of corruption of that organisation. Also, **whistle-blower**.

whistler /'wɪslə/ *n.* **1.** something that sounds like a whistle. **2.** any of a large number of birds of the family Pachycephalidae, found in Australia, South-East Asia, New Guinea, and Oceania, having loud melodious calls.

whit /wɪt/ *n.* (*used esp. in negative phrases*) a particle; bit; jot: *not a whit better.*

white /waɪt/ *adj.* **1.** of the colour of pure snow, reflecting all or nearly all the rays of sunlight (see def. 21 below). **2.** light or comparatively light in colour. **3.** lacking colour; transparent. **4.** having a light skin; marked by comparatively slight pigmentation of the skin. **5.** denoting or relating to people with light-coloured skin, such as Europeans or people of the postulated Caucasian race. **6.** dominated by or exclusively for only people with light-coloured skin, such as Europeans or people of European descent. **7.** pallid or pale, as from fear or other strong emotion, or pain or illness. **8.** silvery, grey, or hoary: *white hair.* **9.** snowy: *a white Christmas.* **10.** (in some European countries) royalist, reactionary, or politically extremely conservative (opposed to *red*). **11.** blank, as an unoccupied space in printed matter. **12.** (of silverware) not burnished. **13.** wearing white clothing: *a white friar.* **14.** benevolent, beneficent, or good: *white magic.* **15.** auspicious or fortunate. **16.** free from spot or stain. **17.** pure or innocent. **18.** (of wines) made from white grapes, or red grapes with the skins removed, thus being light-coloured or yellowish (opposed to *red*). **19.** (of coffee or tea) with milk or cream. **20.** (of bread) made with white flour having a high gluten content. *−n.* **21.** an achromatic visual sensation of relatively high luminosity. A white surface reflects light of all hues completely and diffusely. **22.** the quality or state of being white. **23.** lightness of skin pigment. **24.** (*sometimes upper case*) a European or member of the postulated Caucasian race. **25.** something white, or a white part of something. **26.** a pellucid viscous fluid which surrounds the yolk of an egg; albumen. **27.** the white part of the eyeball. **28.** white wine. **29.** a type or breed which is white in colour. **30.** white fabric. **31.** (*pl.*) white or off-white clothing worn for sports, especially cricket. **32.** *Chess, Draughts* the men or pieces which are light-coloured. *−v.t.* Also, **white out**. **33.** *Printing* to make white by leaving blank spaces. *−phr.* **34.** **bleed white**, to deprive of resources. **35.** **in the white**, (of furniture or wood) unvarnished or unpainted. **36.** **white out**, to reduce the daylight visibility of, as a result of snow or fog. *−***whiteness**, *n.*

white ant *n.* any of various species of wood-eating isopterous insects which, like ants, exhibit social organisation and often form enormous moist colonies; destructive of trees, wooden fences, houses, etc.; termite.

white-ant *v.t. Colloq.* to subvert or undermine from within (an organisation or enterprise). *−***white-anter**, *n.* *−***white-anting**, *n.*

whitebait /'waɪtbeɪt/ *n.* any small delicate fish cooked whole without being cleaned.

white blindfold *adj.* of or relating to an interpretation of Australian history marked by Anglo-centrism and a disinclination to acknowledge the extent of past injustices and wrongs, especially those committed against Indigenous Australians. Compare **black armband** (def. 2).

white blood cell *n.* → **leukocyte**.

whiteboard /'waɪtbɔd/ *n.* a board with a white plastic surface on which one writes with an erasable felt pen, used for teaching or presentations.

whitecap /'waɪtkæp/ *n.* a wave with a broken white crest.

white cockatoo *n.* → **sulphur-crested cockatoo**.

white-collar *adj.* belonging or relating to non-manual workers, as those in professional and clerical work, who traditionally wore a suit, white shirt, and tie.

white elephant *n.* **1.** an abnormally whitish or pale elephant, found usually in Thailand; an albino elephant. **2.** an annoyingly useless possession. **3.** a possession of great value but entailing even greater expense.

white-eye *n.* any of the numerous small, chiefly tropical, singing birds of Australia, southern Asia, and some Pacific islands, constituting the family Zosteropidae, most species of which have a ring of white feathers round the eye.

white feather *n.* a symbol of cowardice, originally from a white feather in a gamecock's tail taken as a sign of inferior breeding and hence of poor fighting qualities.

white flag *n.* an all-white flag, used as a symbol of surrender, etc.

white gold *n.* any of several gold alloys possessing a white colour due to the presence of nickel or platinum. Commercial alloys contain gold, nickel, copper, and zinc.

whitegoods /ˈwaɪtɡʊdz/ *pl. n.* **1.** electrical goods as fridges, washing machines, etc. *–adj.* **2.** of or relating to such goods: *the whitegoods industry.*

white gum *n.* any of various eucalypts with smooth white bark.

white heat *n.* **1.** an intense heat at which a substance glows with white light. **2.** a stage of intense activity excitement, feeling, etc.: *to work at a white heat.*

white knight *n.* **1.** the champion of a good cause. **2.** a company or an individual who is friendly to a company under threat from a corporate raider and is willing to purchase its shares to protect the current ownership. Compare **black knight**.

white lie *n.* a lie uttered from polite, amiable, or pardonable motives; a harmless fib.

white light *n.* light which contains all the wavelengths of the visible spectrum at approximately the same intensity, as light from an incandescent white-hot solid.

white man's burden *n.* the supposed duty of white people to govern and educate other peoples, used especially in the context of European colonisation.

white meat *n.* any light-coloured meat, as veal, the breast of chicken, etc.

white noise *n.* an electronically produced noise used for experimental purposes as sound masking, etc., in which all frequencies are represented with equal energy in each equal range of frequencies, that is, with as much energy between 100 Hz and 200 Hz as between 200 Hz and 300 Hz, 1000 Hz and 1100 Hz, etc.

white oil *n.* a liquid hydrocarbon used as an insecticide for scale on citrus, roses and other shrubs.

white paper *n. Parliamentary Procedure* a statement of government policy on a particular issue, presented to parliament as a subject for discussion, usually prior to or accompanying the introduction of a relevant bill.

white pointer *n.* → **white shark**.

white sapote /waɪt səˈpouti/ *n.* **1.** a tree of the family Rutaceae native to central Mexico, *Casimiroa edulis*; casimiroa. **2.** the large round fruit of this tree with green, yellow or orange skin and a smooth-textured sweet pulp; casimiroa.

white shark *n.* a very large, aggressive shark of warm seas, *Carcharodon carcharias*. Also, **great white shark, white pointer**.

white slave *n.* a white woman who is sold or forced to serve as a prostitute, especially outside her native land. *–***white-slaver**, *n.* *–***white slavery**, *n.*

white spirits *pl. n.* a mixture of petroleum hydrocarbons in the boiling range 150°–200°C, used as a solvent for paints and varnishes as a substitute for turpentine. Also, **white spirit**.

white-throated gerygone /ˌwaɪt-θroʊtəd dʒəˈrɪɡəni/ *n.* a small bird, *Gerygone olivacea*, grey-brown with bright yellow underparts and a white throat, having a distinctive and beautiful voice, found in eastern and northern Australia and New Guinea.

white tie *n.* **1.** a white bow tie for men, worn with the most formal style of evening dress. **2.** Also, **white tie and tails**. the most formal style of evening dress for men, of which the characteristic garments are a white bow tie and a tail coat (distinguished from *black tie*).

whitewash /ˈwaɪtwɒʃ/ *n.* **1.** a composition, as of lime and water or of whiting, size, and water, used for whitening walls, ceilings, etc. **2.** anything used to cover up defects, gloss over faults or errors, or give a specious semblance of respectability, honesty, etc., especially a dishonest official investigation into malpractice which declares it to be acceptable. **3.** *Colloq.* (in various games) a defeat in which the loser fails to score. *–v.t.* **4.** to whiten with whitewash. **5.** to cover up or gloss over the defects, faults, errors, etc., of. *–***whitewasher**, *n.*

white water *n.* any stretch of water in which the surface is broken as in rapids or breakers, due to movement over a shallow bottom. *–***whitewater**, *adj.*

white wine *n.* a wine that is light-coloured or yellowish, made from light-coloured grapes or from dark grapes, the juice of which has been separated from the skins, pulp and seeds. Compare **red wine**.

whither /ˈwɪðə/ *adv. Archaic* to what place?

whiting¹ /ˈwaɪtɪŋ/ *n.* (*pl.* **whiting**) **1.** any of numerous Australian species of estuarine and surf fishes of the family Sillaginidae, highly prized for sport and table. **2.** any of several European species of the cod family, especially *Merlangus merlangus*. **3.** the American Atlantic hake (*Merluccins bilinearis*). **4.** a slender Atlantic shore fish of the genus *Menticirrhus*, of the croaker family (Sciaenidae).

whiting² /ˈwaɪtɪŋ/ *n.* pure white chalk (calcium carbonate) which has been ground and washed, used in making putty, whitewash, etc., and for cleaning silver, etc.

whitlow /ˈwɪtloʊ/ *n. Pathol.* an inflammation of the deeper tissues of a finger or toe, especially of the terminal phalanx, usually terminating in suppuration.

whittle /ˈwɪtl/ *v.t.* **1.** to cut, trim, or shape (a stick, piece of wood, etc.) by taking off bits with a knife. *–phr.* **2. whittle away at**, to reduce gradually over time. **3. whittle down**, to cut by way of reducing the amount of: *to whittle down expenses.* *–***whittler**, *n.*

whiz¹ /wɪz/ *v.i.* (**whizzed, whizzing**) **1.** to make a humming or hissing sound, as an object passing rapidly through the air. **2.** to move or rush with such a sound. *–n.* **3.** a swift movement producing such a sound. **4.** *Colloq.* an act of urination. Also, **whizz**.

whiz² /wɪz/ *n. Colloq.* someone who shows outstanding ability in a particular field or who is notable in some way; expert.

who /hu/ *pron.* (*interrogative*) (*objective* **whom**) **1.** what person: *who told you so?* **2.** (of a person) what as to character, origin, position, importance, etc.: *who is the man in uniform?* *–pron.* (*relative*) **3.** the or any person that; any person: *be it who it may.* **4.** with antecedent a person, or sometimes an animal or a personified thing: **a.** in clauses conveying an additional idea: *we saw men who were at work.* **b.** in clauses defining or restricting the antecedent: *one who tells the truth* *–phr.* **5. who's who**, the people who carry influence or importance.

whoa /woʊ/ *interj.* (used especially to horses) stop!

who'd /hud/ contraction of *who would*.

whodunnit /huˈdʌnət/ *n. Colloq.* → **murder mystery**. Also, **whodunit**.

whoever /huˈɛvə/ *pron.* (*relative*) (*objective* **whomever**) **1.** whatever person, or anyone that: *whoever wants it may have it.* *–pron.* (*interrogative*) **2.** (used emphatically) who: *whoever is that?*

whole /hoʊl/ *adj.* **1.** comprising the full quantity, amount, extent, number, etc., without diminution or exception; entire, full, or total. **2.** containing all the elements properly belonging; complete: *a whole set.* **3.** undivided, or in one piece: *to swallow a thing whole.* **4.** *Maths* integral, or not fractional: *a whole number.* **5.** uninjured, undamaged, or unbroken; sound; intact: *to get off with a whole skin.* **6.** sound; healthy. **7.** fully developed and balanced, in all aspects of one's nature: *educated to be a whole person.* **8.** being fully or entirely such: *whole brother.* –*n.* **9.** the whole assemblage of parts or elements belonging to a thing; the entire quantity, account, extent, or number. **10.** a thing complete in itself, or comprising all its parts or elements. **11.** an assemblage of parts associated or viewed together as one thing; a unitary system. –*phr.* **12. as a whole,** all things included or considered. **13. on** (or **upon**) **the whole, a.** on consideration of the whole matter, or in view of all the circumstances. **b.** as a whole or in general, without regard to exceptions. **14. out of whole cloth,** *US Colloq.* without foundation in fact: *a story out of whole cloth.* –**wholeness,** *n.*

wholehearted /'hoʊlhɑtəd/ *adj.* hearty; cordial; earnest; sincere. –**wholeheartedly,** *adv.* –**wholeheartedness,** *n.*

wholemeal /'hoʊlmil/ *adj.* prepared with the complete wheat kernel, as flour or the bread baked with it; wholewheat.

whole number *n. Maths* an integer as 0, 1, 2, 3, 4, 5, etc.

wholesale /'hoʊlseɪl/ *n.* **1.** the sale of commodities in large quantities, as to retailers or jobbers rather than to consumers directly (distinguished from *retail*). –*adj.* **2.** of, relating to, or engaged in sale by wholesale. **3.** extensive and indiscriminate: *wholesale discharge of workers.* –*adv.* **4.** in a wholesale way. –*v.t.* **5.** to sell by wholesale. –*v.i.* **6.** to sell goods, etc., by wholesale. –**wholesaler,** *n.*

wholesome /'hoʊlsəm/ *adj.* **1.** conducive to moral or general wellbeing; salutary; beneficial: *wholesome advice.* **2.** conducive to bodily health; healthful; salubrious: *wholesome food*; *wholesome air*; *wholesome exercise.* **3.** suggestive of health (physical or moral), especially in appearance. **4.** healthy or sound. –**wholesomely,** *adv.* –**wholesomeness,** *n.*

who'll /hʊl/ contraction of *who will* or *who shall.*

wholly /'hoʊli/ *adv.* entirely; totally; altogether.

whom /hum/ *pron.* objective case of **who.**

whoofy /'wʊfi/ *adj.* (**-fier, -fiest**) *Colloq.* smelly.

whoo hoo /wu 'hu/ *interj. Colloq.* → **woo hoo.**

whoop /wʊp/ *n.* **1.** a loud cry or shout, as one uttered by children or warriors. **2.** the whooping sound characteristic of whooping cough. –*v.i.* **3.** to utter a loud cry or shout (originally the syllable *whoop*, or *hoop*), as a call, or in enthusiasm, excitement, frenzy, etc. **4.** to cry as an owl, crane, or certain other birds. **5.** to make the characteristic sound accompanying the deep drawing in of breath after a series of coughs in whooping cough. –*v.t.* **6.** to utter with or as with a whoop or whoops. –*phr.* **7. whoop it** (or **things**) **up,** *Colloq.* **a.** to raise an outcry or disturbance. **b.** to have a party or celebration.

whoopee cushion /'wʊpi kʊʃən/ *n.* a small inflatable rubber cushion, which, hidden under the upholstery of a chair as a practical joke, emits the sound of a human breaking wind when sat upon.

whooping cough /'hupɪŋ kɒf/ *n. Pathol.* an infectious disease of the respiratory mucous membrane, especially of children, characterised by a series of short, convulsive coughs followed by a deep inspiration accompanied by a whooping sound; pertussis.

whoops /wʊps/ *interj.* an exclamation of mild surprise, dismay, etc., especially in reaction to an instance of stumbling, falling over, or bumping into someone or something, or in recognition of a mistake. Also, **whoops-a-daisy, woops, woops-a-daisy, whoopsie, whoopsie-daisy.**

whoosh /wʊʃ/ *n.* **1.** a loud rushing noise, as of water or air. –*v.i.* **2.** to move with a loud rushing noise.

whopper /'wɒpə/ *n. Colloq.* **1.** something uncommonly large of its kind. **2.** a big lie.

whore /hɔ/ *n.* **1.** a female prostitute. **2.** *Colloq.* (*derog.*) a promiscuous woman. –*verb* (**whored, whoring**) –*v.i.* **3.** to act as a whore. **4.** to consort with whores. –*v.t.* **5.** to make a whore of; debauch. –**whorish,** *adj.*

who're /'huə/ contraction of *who are.*

whorl /wɜl/ *n.* **1.** a circular arrangement of like parts, as leaves, flowers, etc., round a point on an axis; a verticil. **2.** one of the turns or volutions of a spiral shell. **3.** one of the principal ridge-shapes of a fingerprint, forming at least one complete circle (distinguished from *loop* and *arch*). **4.** *Anat.* one of the turns in the cochlea of the ear. **5.** anything shaped like a coil.

who's /huz/ contraction of *who is* or *who has.*

whose /huz/ *pron.* (*interrogative*) **1.** of, belonging, or relating to whom: *whose is this book?* –*pron.* (*relative*) **2.** of, belonging, or relating to whom or which: *the man whose book I borrowed*; *a pen whose point is broken.* –*adj.* (*interrogative*) **3.** of, belonging, or relating to whom: *whose name comes first?*

who've /huv/ contraction of *who have.*

wh-question /dʌbəlju'eɪtʃ-kwɛstʃən/ *n. Gram.* a question that begins with an interrogative word, such as *who, what, when, where, which,* or *how.*

why /waɪ/ *adv.* **1.** for what?; for what cause, reason, or purpose? –*conj.* **2.** for what cause or reason. **3.** for which (after *reason*, etc., to introduce a relative clause): *the reason why he refused.* **4.** the reason for which: *that is why I raised this question again.* –*n.* (*pl.* **whys**) **5.** the cause or reason. –*interj.* **6.** an expression of surprise, hesitation, etc.: *why, it is all gone!* –*phr.* **7. the whys and wherefores,** the underlying reasons.

wick /wɪk/ *n.* **1.** a bundle or loose twist or braid of soft threads, or a woven strip or tube, as of cotton, which in a candle, lamp, oil stove, or the like serves to draw up the melted tallow or wax or the oil or other flammable liquid to be burnt at its top end. –*phr.* **2. get on one's wick,** *Colloq.* to irritate.

wicked /'wɪkəd/ *adj.* **1.** evil or morally bad in principle or practice; iniquitous; sinful. **2.** playfully naughty. **3.** ill-natured: *a wicked horse.* –**wickedness,** *n.* –**wickedly,** *adv.*

wicker /'wɪkə/ *n.* **1.** a slender, pliant twig; an osier. –*adj.* **2.** consisting or made of wicker: *a wicker basket.*

wickerwork /'wɪkəwɜk/ *n.* work consisting of plaited or woven twigs or osiers; articles made of wicker.

wicket /'wɪkət/ *n.* **1.** a small door or gate, especially one beside, or forming part of, a larger one. **2.** a window or opening, often closed by a grating or the like, as in a door, or forming a place of communication in a ticket office or the like. **3.** → **turnstile. 4.** *Cricket* **a.** either of the two frameworks, each consisting of three stumps with two bails in grooves across their tops, at which the bowler aims the ball. **b.** the area between the wickets, especially with reference to the state of the ground. **c.** one end of the pitch, especially the area between the stumps and the popping crease. **d.** one player's turn at the wicket. **e.** the period during which two players bat together. **f.** the achievement of a player's dismissal by the fielding side. –*phr.* **5. a sticky wicket, a.** a wet or muddy wicket. **b.** *Colloq.* a difficult or disadvantageous situation or set of circumstances. **6. on a good wicket,** in an advantageous situation or set of circumstances.

wicketkeeper /'wɪkətkipə/ *n. Cricket* the player on the fielding side who stands immediately behind the wicket to stop balls that pass it.

wide /waɪd/ *adj.* **1.** having great extent from side to side; broad; not narrow. **2.** having a certain extent from side to side: *three metres wide.* **3.** of great range. **4.** open to the full or a great extent; expanded; distended: *to stare with wide eyes.* **5.** too far or too much to one side: *a wide ball in cricket.* –*adv.* **6.** to a great, or relatively great, extent from side to side: *open wide.* **7.** over a large space or area: *scattered far and wide*. **8.** to the full extent of opening: *to open the eyes wide*. **9.** fully: *to be wide awake*. *−n.* **10.** *Cricket* a bowled ball that passes outside the batter's reach, and counts as a run for the side batting. *−phr.* **11. go wide**, to go away from or to one side of a point, mark, purpose, etc.; go aside or astray: *the shot went wide*. **12. wide of the mark**, **a.** a long way off the target. **b.** badly in error. **−widely**, *adv.* **−wideness**, *n.* **−widish**, *adj.* **−widen**, *v.*

wide area network *n.* a computer network which connects computers over a wide area. *Abbrev.*: WAN Compare **local area network**.

wide boy *n. Chiefly Brit. Colloq.* a petty crook.

wideranging /ˈwaɪdreɪndʒɪŋ/ *adj.* covering all aspects; comprehensive. Also, **wide-ranging**.

widespread /ˈwaɪdsprɛd/ *adj.* **1.** spread over or occupying a wide space. **2.** distributed over a wide region, or occurring in many places or among many persons or individuals. Also, **widespreading**.

widget /ˈwɪdʒət/ *n.* **1.** *Colloq.* (*humorous*) a mechanical device or gadget, the name of which is not known or is temporarily forgotten. **2.** *Computers* a component of a graphical user interface that displays information or that responds in a specific way to a user action.

widow /ˈwɪdoʊ/ *n.* **1.** a woman who has lost her husband by death and has not married again. **2.** (used in combination) a woman whose husband is often absent, devoting his attention to some sport or other activity: *a golf widow*. **3.** *Cards* an additional hand or part of a hand, as one dealt to the table. *−v.t.* **4.** (*chiefly in past participle*) to make (someone) a widow.

widower /ˈwɪdoʊə/ *n.* a man whose wife has died and who has not married again.

widow's peak *n.* a point formed by the hair growing down in the middle of the forehead.

widow's weeds *pl. n.* mourning garments worn by a widow.

width /wɪdθ/ *n.* **1.** extent from side to side; breadth; wideness. **2.** a piece of the full wideness, as of cloth.

wield /wiːld/ *v.t.* **1.** to exercise (power, authority, influence, etc.), as in ruling or dominating. **2.** to manage (a weapon, instrument, etc.) in use; handle or use in action. **−wieldable**, *adj.* **−wielder**, *n.*

wife /waɪf/ *n.* (*pl.* **wives** /waɪvz/) **1.** a woman joined in marriage to a man as husband. **2.** *Archaic* (*except in compounds, as 'housewife' and 'midwife'*) a woman: *the wife of Bath*. **−wifedom, wifehood**, *n.* **−wifely**, *adj.* **−wifeless**, *adj.* **−wifelessness**, *n.*

wi-fi /ˈwaɪ-faɪ/ *n.* **1.** a communications networking standard which is used to create high-speed wireless local area networks. *−adj.* **2.** of, relating or conforming to, a wi-fi.

wig /wɪg/ *n.* **1.** an artificial covering of hair for the head, worn to conceal baldness, for disguise, theatricals, etc., or formerly as an ordinary head covering. **2.** real or synthetic hair covering or entwined with the wearer's own hair, worn to create a new hairstyle, for a change of hair colour, etc. **−wigged**, *adj.* **−wigless**, *adj.*

wiggle /ˈwɪgəl/ *v.i.* **1.** to move or go with short, quick, irregular movements from side to side; wriggle. *−v.t.* **2.** to cause to wiggle; move quickly and irregularly from side to side. *−n.* **3.** a wiggling movement or course. **4.** a wiggly line. **−wiggly**, *adj.* **−wiggler**, *n.*

wigwam /ˈwɪgwɒm/ *n.* a Native American hut or lodge, usually of rounded or oval shape, formed of poles overlaid with bark, mats, or skins.

wiki /ˈwɪki/ *n.* a website in which the contents are contributed and edited by visitors to the site.

wild /waɪld/ *adj.* **1.** living in a state of nature, as animals that have not been tamed or domesticated. **2.** growing or produced without cultivation or the care of humans,

as plants, flowers, fruit, honey, etc.: *wild mushrooms*. **3.** uncultivated, uninhabited, or waste, as land. **4. a.** native to Australia and New Zealand: *wild banana*. **b.** escaped to the wild: *wild cattle*. **5.** living in an uncivilised state. **6.** of unrestrained violence, fury, intensity, etc.; violent; furious: *wild fighting*; *wild storms*. **7.** characterised by or indicating violent excitement, as actions, the appearance, etc. **8.** frantic; distracted, crazy, or mad: *to drive someone wild*. **9.** violently excited: *wild with rage, fear, or pain*. **10.** undisciplined, unruly, lawless, or turbulent: *wild boys*; *a wild crew*. **11.** unrestrained, untrammelled, or unbridled: *wild gaiety*; *wild orgies*. **12.** disregardful of moral restraints as to pleasurable indulgence. **13.** unrestrained by reason or prudence: *wild schemes*. **14.** extravagant or fantastic: *wild fancies*. **15.** disorderly or dishevelled: *wild locks*. **16.** wide of the mark: *a wild throw*. **17.** *Colloq.* intensely eager or enthusiastic. **18.** *Cards* (of a card) having its value decided by the wishes of the players or the player who holds it. *−adv.* **19.** in a wild manner; wildly. *−n.* **20.** (*oft. pl.*) an uncultivated, uninhabited, or desolate region or tract; a waste; a wilderness; a desert. *−phr.* **21. in the wild**, in natural surroundings or habitat: *animals in the wild*. **22. run wild**, **a.** to grow without cultivation or check. **b.** to behave in an unrestrained or uncontrolled manner: *he allows his children to run wild*. **23. wild about**, *Colloq.* infatuated with: *wild about Harry*. **24. wild and woolly**, *Colloq.* **a.** rough; untidy; unkempt. **b.** uncivilised; unrestrained. **−wildly**, *adv.* **−wildness**, *n.*

wildcard /ˈwaɪldkad/ *n.* **1.** a playing card to which the holder may assign the value of any other card. **2.** *Computers* a non-alphanumeric character used especially in searches to represent any character or set of characters. **3.** *Sport* a player or team allowed into a competition without having to compete in qualifying matches. **4.** *Colloq.* an unpredictable person or thing. *−adj.* **5.** of or relating to a wildcard: *a wildcard search*; *a wildcard entry*. Also, **wild card**.

wildcat /ˈwaɪldkæt/ *n.* **1.** any of various Eurasian and African subspecies of the cat *Felis sylvestris*, probably the main source of the domesticated cat. **2.** a quick-tempered or fierce person. **3.** an exploratory well drilled in an effort to discover deposits of oil or gas. *−adj.* **4.** marked by or proceeding from irresponsible or unsafe business methods: *wildcat companies*. **5.** of or relating to an unauthorised undertaking or product. *−v.i.* (**-catted, -catting**) **6.** to search for oil, minerals, etc., as an independent prospector. **−wildcatting**, *n.*, *adj.*

wildcat strike *n.* a strike which has not been called or sanctioned by officials of a trade union; unofficial strike.

wildebeest /ˈwɪldəbist/ *n.* (*pl.* **-beests** *or, especially collectively,* **-beest**) any of several African antelopes constituting the genus *Connochaetes*, characterised by an oxlike head, curved horns, and a long, flowing tail; gnu.

wilderness /ˈwɪldənəs/ *n.* **1.** Also, **wilderness area**. a large tract of land remote at its core from mechanised access or settlement, substantially unmodified by modern technological society or capable of being restored to that state, and of sufficient size to make practicable the long-term protection of its natural systems. **2.** wild and uncultivated land, especially when of great natural beauty. **3.** any desolate or uninviting area of land. **4.** (*humorous*) a part of a garden in which plants grow with unchecked luxuriance. **5.** a bewildering mass or collection. *−phr.* **6. in the wilderness**, *Colloq.* **a.** in a state or place of isolation; away from the centre of things. **b.** out of political office.

wildflower /ˈwaɪldflaʊə/ *n.* **1.** the flower of an uncultivated plant. **2.** such a plant. Also, **wild flower**.

wildlife /'waıldlaıf/ *n.* a range of animals living in their natural habitat.

wile¹ /waıl/ *n.* **1.** a trick, artifice, or stratagem. **2.** (*oft. pl.*) an artful or beguiling procedure.

wile² /waıl/ *phr.* (**wiled, wiling**) **wile away**, to pass (time), especially in some easy or pleasant manner.

wilful /'wılfəl/ *adj.* **1.** willed, voluntary, or intentional: *wilful murder.* **2.** self-willed or headstrong; perversely obstinate or intractable. Also, *Chiefly US,* **willful.** —**wilfully,** *adv.* —**wilfulness,** *n.*

wilga /'wılgə/ *n.* a small shapely tree, *Geijera parviflora,* of inland eastern Australia, valuable as fodder in drought.

wilkintie /wıl'kınti/ *n.* the dusky hopping mouse, *Notomys fuscus,* of central Australia.

will¹ /wıl/, *weak forms* /wəl, l/ *v. (aux.)* **1.** am (is, are, etc.) about or going to: *I will cut his hair.* **2.** am (is, are, etc.) willing to: *I will help you.* **3.** am (is, are, etc.) expected or required to: *they will have me arrive on time.* **4.** may be expected or supposed to: *this will be right.* **5.** am (is, are, etc.) determined or sure to (used emphatically): *people will talk.* **6.** am (is, are, etc.) accustomed to: *he would write for hours at a time.* —*v.t., v.i.* **7.** to wish; desire; like: *as you will.*

will² /wıl/ *n.* **1.** the faculty of conscious and especially of deliberate action: *the freedom of the will.* **2.** the power of choosing one's own actions: *to have a strong will; a weak will.* **3.** the act of using this power. **4.** the process of willing, or volition. **5.** wish or desire: *to submit against one's will.* **6.** purpose or determination, often hearty determination: *to have the will to succeed.* **7.** the wish or purpose as carried out, or to be carried out: *to work one's will.* **8.** disposition (good or ill) towards another. **9.** *Law* **a.** a legal declaration of a person's wishes as to the disposition of his or her (real) property, etc., after death, usually in writing, and signed by the testator and attested by witnesses. **b.** the document containing such a declaration. —*verb* (**willed, willing**) —*v.t.* **10.** to give by will or testament; to bequeath or devise. **11.** to influence by exerting willpower. **12.** to wish or desire. **13.** to decide by act of will. **14.** to purpose, determine on, or elect, by act of will. —*v.i.* **15.** to exercise the will. **16.** to determine, decide, or ordain, as by act of will. —*phr.* **17. at will,** at one's discretion or pleasure: *to wander at will.* **18. a will of one's own,** a strong power of asserting oneself. **19. with a will,** willingly; readily; eagerly. **20. work one's will,** to do as one chooses. —**willer,** *n.*

willies /'wıliz/ *pl. n. Colloq.* feelings of uneasiness or fear: *that creaking door is giving me the willies.*

willie wagtail *n.* (*also upper case*) a common black and white fantail, *Rhipidura leucophrys,* noted for its habit of wagging its tail from side to side; found throughout Australia, the Maluku Islands, New Guinea and nearby islands. Also, **willie-wagtail, willy-wagtail.**

willing /'wılıŋ/ *adj.* **1.** disposed or consenting (without being particularly desirous): *willing to take what one can get.* **2.** cheerfully consenting or ready: *a willing worker.* **3.** done, given, borne, used, etc., with cheerful readiness. **4.** *Aust.* **a.** inclined to overcharge or make excessive demands: *that salesman is a bit willing.* **b.** of or relating to a situation in which such excessive demands are made: *that's a bit willing.* —**willingly,** *adv.* —**willingness,** *n.*

will-o'-the-wisp /'wıl-ə-ðə-wısp/ *n.* anything that deludes or misleads by luring on.

willow /'wıloʊ/ *n.* **1.** any of the trees or shrubs constituting the genus *Salix,* many species of which have tough, pliable twigs or branches which are used for wickerwork, etc. **2.** the wood of the willow. **3.** *Colloq.* something made of this, as a cricket bat. **4.** a machine consisting essentially of a cylinder armed with spikes

revolving within a spiked casing, for opening and cleaning cotton or other fibre. —*v.t.* **5.** to treat (cotton, etc.) with a willow.

willowy /'wıloʊi/ *adj.* **1.** pliant; lithe. **2.** gracefully slender and supple. **3.** bordered with or covered with willows.

willpower /'wılpaʊə/ *n.* **1.** control over one's impulses and actions. **2.** strength of will: *he has great willpower.*

willy-nilly /wıli-'nıli/ *adv.* **1.** willingly or unwillingly. **2.** in random order; in disarray. —*adj.* **3.** shillyshallying; vacillating.

willy-willy /'wıli-wıli/ *n.* (*pl.* **-willies**) *Aust.* a spiralling wind, often collecting dust, refuse, etc.

wilt¹ /wılt/ *v.i.* **1.** to become limp and drooping, as a fading flower; wither. **2.** to lose strength, vigour, assurance, etc. —*v.t.* **3.** to cause to wilt. —*n.* **4.** the act of wilting. **5.** a spell of depression, lassitude, or dizziness.

wilt² /wılt/ *v. Archaic* second person singular present indicative of **will¹.**

wily /'waıli/ *adj.* (**-lier, -liest**) full of, marked by, or proceeding from wiles; crafty; cunning. —**wilily,** *adv.* —**wiliness,** *n.*

wimp /wımp/ *Colloq.* —*n.* **1.** a weak, timorous, and ineffectual person. —*phr.* **2. wimp out,** to fail or renege on a commitment as a result of lack of character or determination. —**wimpish, wimpy,** *adj.*

wimple /'wımpəl/ *n.* a woman's headcloth drawn in folds about the chin, formerly worn outdoors, and still in use by some nuns.

win /wın/ *verb* (**won, winning**) —*v.i.* **1.** Also, **win out.** to succeed by striving or effort. **2.** to gain the victory. **3.** to be placed first in a race or the like. **4.** to get (*out, through, to,* etc., *free, loose,* etc.). —*v.t.* **5.** to get by effort, as through labour, competition, or conquest. **6.** to gain (a prize, fame, etc.). **7.** to be successful in (a game, battle, etc.). **8.** to make (one's way), as by effort, ability, etc. **9.** to attain or reach (a point, goal, etc.): *to win the shore in a storm.* **10.** to gain (favour, love, consent, etc.) as by qualities or influence. **11.** to gain the favour, regard, or adherence of. **12.** to persuade to love or marriage, or gain in marriage. **13.** *Mining* **a.** to obtain (ore, coal, etc.). **b.** to prepare (a vein, bed, mine, etc.) for working, by means of shafts, etc. —*n.* **14.** an act of winning; a success; a victory. **15.** the act or fact of finishing first, especially in a horserace. —*phr.* **16. win over** (or **round**), to bring over to favour, consent, etc.; persuade. —**winner,** *n.* —**winless,** *adj.* —**winnable,** *adj.*

wince /wıns/ *v.i.* (**winced, wincing**) **1.** to shrink, as in pain or from a blow; start; flinch. —*n.* **2.** a wincing or shrinking movement; a slight start. —**wincer,** *n.*

winch /wıntʃ/ *n.* **1.** the crank or handle of a revolving machine. **2.** a windlass turned by a crank, for hoisting, etc. **3.** any of a number of contrivances to crank objects by. —*v.t.* **4.** to hoist or haul by means of a winch. —**wincher,** *n.*

wind¹ /wınd/ *n.* **1.** air in natural motion, as along the earth's surface. **2.** a gale; storm; hurricane. **3.** any stream of air, as that produced by a bellows, a fan, etc. **4.** air impregnated with the scent of an animal or animals. **5.** a hint or intimation: *get wind of the scandal.* **6.** any tendency or likely course: *the wind of public opinion; wind of change.* **7.** breath or breathing; power of breathing freely, as during continued exertion. **8.** empty talk; mere words. **9.** vanity; conceitedness. **10.** gas generated in the stomach and bowels. **11.** *Colloq.* the solar plexus, where a blow may cause shortness of breath. **12.** *Music* **a.** a wind instrument or wind instruments collectively. **b.** (*oft. pl.*) the players on such instruments collectively. **13.** *Naut.* the point or direction from which the wind blows. —*v.t.* **14.** to make short of wind or breath, as by vigorous exercise. **15.** to deprive momentarily of breath, as by a blow. **16.** to let recover breath, as by resting after exertion. —*phr.* **17. before the**

wind, carried along by the wind; (of a ship) running with the wind astern. **18. between wind and water**, **a.** *Naut.* denoting the part of a ship, especially the deck of a heavily laden ship, which the waves wash over. **b.** in a vulnerable or precarious position. **19. break** (or **pass**) **wind**, to expel flatus through the anus; fart. **20. cast** (or **fling**) (or **throw**) **to the wind**(**s**), to throw off or discard recklessly or in an abandoned manner: *throw all caution to the winds.* **21. close to the wind**, **a.** *Naut.* sailing as near as possible to the direction from which the wind is blowing. **b.** taking a calculated risk. **c.** transgressing or nearly transgressing conventions of taste, propriety, or the like. **22. get the wind up**, *Colloq.* to take fright. **23. get wind of**, to receive news of; find out about. **24. how** (or **which way**) **the wind blows** (or **lies**), what the tendency or likelihood is. **25. in the teeth of the wind**, **a.** *Naut.* sailing directly against the wind. **b.** against opposition. **26. in the wind**, **a.** likely to happen; imminent. **b.** circulating as a rumour. **27. put the wind up**, *Colloq.* to frighten. **28. raise the wind**, *Colloq.* to obtain the necessary finances. **29. take the wind out of someone's sails**, to frustrate, disconcert, or deprive someone of an advantage.

wind² /waɪnd/ *verb* (**wound**, **winding**) –*v.i.* **1.** to change direction; bend; turn; take a frequently bending course; meander. **2.** to have a circular or spiral course or direction. **3.** to coil or twine about something. **4.** to undergo winding, or winding up. –*v.t.* **5.** to encircle or wreathe, as with something twined, wrapped, or placed about. **6.** Also, **wind up**. to roll or coil (thread, etc.) into a ball or on a spool or the like. **7.** to twine, fold, wrap, or place about something. **8.** Also, **wind up**. to adjust (a mechanism, etc.) for operation by some turning or coiling process: *to wind a clock.* **9.** Also, **wind up**. to haul or hoist by means of a winch, windlass, or the like. –*n.* **10.** a winding; a bend or turn. –*phr.* **11. wind down**, **a.** to relax after a period of tension or activity. **b.** (of a clock) to run down. **c.** to reduce the scope, intensity of (an operation). **d.** to lower by winding, as by a crank. **12. wind off**, to remove or take off by unwinding. **13. wind one's** (or **its**) **way**, to proceed in a winding or frequently bending course. **14. wind someone up**, *Colloq.* **a.** to bring someone to a state of great excitement or enthusiasm. **b.** to annoy or irritate someone, often deliberately. **15. wind up**, **a.** to conclude what one is doing or saying. **b.** *Colloq.* to end up: *wind up in the poorhouse.* **c.** to close down (a business, etc.) by making a final account of all financial dealings.

wind³ /waɪnd/ *v.t.* (**winded** or **wound**, **winding**) to blow (a horn, a blast, etc.).

windbag /ˈwɪndbæg/ *n.* **1.** *Colloq.* an empty, voluble, pretentious talker. **2.** the bag of a bagpipe.

windbreak /ˈwɪndbreɪk/ *n.* a growth of trees, a structure of boards, or the like, serving as a shelter from the wind.

windcheater /ˈwɪntʃitə/ *n.* (*from trademark*) a fleecy-lined garment for the upper part of the body designed to give protection against the wind.

wind energy *n.* energy derived from the wind, as by wind turbines in a wind farm.

windfall /ˈwɪndfɔl/ *n.* **1.** something blown down by the wind, as fruit. **2.** an unexpected piece of good fortune.

wind farm *n.* an array of wind generators set up in a windy location to produce electricity. Also, **windfarm**.

wind gauge *n.* → **anemometer** (def. 1).

wind generator *n.* an electric generator positioned on a tower and driven by the force of the wind on a rotor.

windhover /ˈwɪndhɒvə/ *n.* → **kestrel** (def. 2).

winding sheet /ˈwaɪndɪŋ ʃit/ *n.* a sheet in which a corpse is wrapped for burial.

wind instrument *n.* a musical instrument sounded by the player's breath or any current of air.

windjammer /ˈwɪndʒæmə/ *n.* a large sailing ship, especially a square-rigged ship.

windlass /ˈwɪndləs/ *n.* **1.** a device for raising weights, etc., usually consisting of a horizontal cylinder or barrel turned by a crank, lever, or the like, upon which a cable or the like winds, the outer end of the cable being attached directly or indirectly to the weight to be raised or the thing to be hauled or pulled. –*v.t.* **2.** to raise, haul, or move by means of a windlass.

windmill /ˈwɪndmɪl, ˈwɪnmɪl/ *n.* **1.** a mill or machine, as for grinding or pumping, operated by the wind, usually by the wind acting on a set of arms, vanes, sails, or slats attached to a horizontal axis so as to form a vertical revolving wheel. **2.** the wheel itself. **3.** an imaginary opponent, wrong, etc. (in allusion to Cervantes' *Don Quixote*): *to fight windmills.*

window /ˈwɪndoʊ/ *n.* **1.** an opening in the wall of a building, the cabin of a boat, etc., for the admission of air and light, commonly fitted with a frame containing panes of glass. **2.** anything like a window in appearance or function. **3.** *Computers* a defined area on a computer screen in which a particular program is run or data displayed. –**windowless**, *adj.*

window-dressing *n.* **1.** the act or fact of preparing a display in a shop window. **2.** the presentation of the most favourable aspect of something, especially when unpleasant facts are concealed. –**window-dresser**, *n.*

window-shop *v.i.* (**-shopped**, **-shopping**) to look at articles in shop windows instead of actually buying. –**window-shopper**, *n.* –**window-shopping**, *adj.*, *n.*

windpipe /ˈwɪndpaɪp, ˈwɪnpaɪp/ *n.* the trachea of an air-breathing vertebrate.

windscreen /ˈwɪndskrin, ˈwɪnskrin/ *n.* the sheet of glass which forms the front window of a motor vehicle. Also, *Chiefly US,* **windshield**.

windsock /ˈwɪndsɒk, ˈwɪnsɒk/ *n.* a wind-direction indicator, installed at airports and elsewhere, consisting of an elongated truncated cone of textile material, flown from a mast.

windsurfer /ˈwɪndsɜfə/ *n.* (*from trademark*) **1.** → **sailboard**. **2.** someone who windsurfs.

wind turbine *n.* a modern windmill, usually with blades designed like aeroplane wings, which drives a generator to produce electricity when wind turns the blades; varies in size from small domestic types to large computer-controlled machines feeding electricity into the national grid.

windward /ˈwɪndwəd/ *adv.* **1.** towards the wind; towards the point from which the wind blows. –*adj.* **2.** relating to, situated in, or moving towards the quarter from which the wind blows (opposed to *leeward*). –*n.* **3.** the point or quarter from which the wind blows. **4.** the side towards the wind. –*phr.* **5. get to the windward of**, to get the advantage of.

windy /ˈwɪndi/ *adj.* (**-dier**, **-diest**) **1.** accompanied by wind: *windy weather.* **2.** swept by the wind: *a windy hill.* **3.** towards the wind; windward. **4.** empty; unsubstantial. **5.** characterised by or causing flatulence. **6.** *Colloq.* frightened; nervous. –**windily**, *adv.* –**windiness**, *n.*

wine /waɪn/ *n.* **1.** the fermented juice of the grape, in many varieties (red, white, sweet, dry, still, sparkling, etc.) used as a drink, and in cookery, religious rites, etc. **2.** a particular variety of such fermented grape juice: *port and sherry wines.* **3.** the juice, fermented or unfermented, of various other fruits or plants, used as a drink, etc.: *gooseberry wine.* **4.** a dark reddish colour. **5.** something that cheers, or makes light-headed like wine. –*adj.* **6.** wine-coloured. –*v.t.* **7.** to entertain with wine. –*v.i.* **8.** to drink wine.

winemaking /ˈwaɪnmeɪkɪŋ/ *n.* the process of preparing wine from grapes or other fruit. –**winemaker**, *n.*

winery /ˈwaɪnəri/ *n.* (*pl.* **-ries**) an establishment for making wine.

wine-tasting *n.* **1.** the occupation of a wine-taster. **2.** a social or other gathering to sample various wines.

wing /wɪŋ/ *n.* **1.** either of the two anterior extremities, or appendages of the scapular arch or shoulder girdle, of most birds and of bats, which constitute the fore-limbs and correspond to the human arms, but are adapted for flight. **2.** either of two corresponding parts not adapted for flight in certain other birds, as ostriches and penguins. **3.** one of the thin, flat, movable, lateral extensions from the back of the mesothorax and the metathorax by means of which the insects fly. **4.** a similar structure with which gods, angels, demons, etc., are conceived to be provided for the purpose of flying. **5.** *Colloq.* an arm of a human being. **6.** a means or instrument of flight, travel, or progress. **7.** flight; departure: *to take wing.* **8.** *Aeronautics* **a.** that portion of a main supporting surface confined to one side of an aeroplane. **b.** any complete winglike structure; plane. **9.** *Archit.* a part of a building projecting on one side of, or subordinate to, a central or main part. **10.** either of a pair of fences running out from opposite sides of a stockyard so as to help funnel cattle into the yard. **11.** *Furniture* an extension on the side of the back of an armchair above the arms. **12. a.** *Navy* either of the two side portions of a fleet (usually called right wing and left wing, and distinguished from the centre); flank unit. **b.** either of the two side sections of a mob of cattle, sheep, etc. **13. a.** (in fighter command of the RAAF and certain other air forces) a number of squadrons, usually three, four, or five, operating together as a tactical unit. **b.** (in the US Air Force) an administrative and tactical unit consisting of two or more groups, a headquarters, and certain supporting and service units. **14.** (*pl.*) the insignia or emblem worn by a qualified pilot. **15. a.** *Aust. Rules* either of the two centre-line positions on each side of the centre. **b.** *Hockey, Rugby Football, Soccer, etc.* either of the two areas of the pitch near the touchline and ahead of the halfway line, known as the left and right wings respectively, with reference to the direction of the opposing goal. **c.** a player in one of these positions. **16.** *Theatre* **a.** the platform or space on the right or left of the stage proper. **b.** one of the long, narrow side pieces of scenery. **17.** *Anat.* an ala: *the wings of the sphenoid.* **18.** either of the parts of a double door, etc. **19.** a group within a political party: *right wing; left wing.* *–v.t.* **20.** to equip with wings. **21.** to enable to fly, move rapidly, etc.; lend speed or celerity to. **22.** to supply with a winglike part, a side structure, etc. **23.** to wound or disable (a bird, etc.) in the wing. **24.** to wound (a person) in an arm or other non-vital part. **25.** to bring down (an aeroplane, etc.) by a shot. **26.** *Theatre Colloq.* to perform (a part, etc.) relying on prompters in the wings. *–v.i.* **27.** to travel on or as on wings; fly; soar. *–phr.* **28. clip someone's wings**, to restrict someone's independence or freedom of action. **29. in the wings**, unobtrusively ready to take action when required; in reserve. **30. on a wing and a prayer**, *Colloq.* with very little to sustain one's performance. **31. on the wing**, **a.** in flight; flying. **b.** in motion; travelling; active. **c.** *Football, Hockey, etc.* playing in the position on the left or right extreme of the forward line. **32. take wing**, **a.** to fly off. **b.** to leave hastily. **33. under one's wing**, in or into one's care or protection. **–winglike**, *adj.*

wing commander *n.* *Air Force* **1.** a commissioned officer in the Royal Australian Air Force ranking below group captain and above squadron leader. **2.** the rank. *Abbrev.*: WGCDR

wing nut *n.* a nut which incorporates two flat projecting wings enabling it to be turned by thumb and forefinger. Also, **butterfly nut**.

wink /wɪŋk/ *v.i.* **1.** to close and open the eyes quickly. **2.** (of the eyes) to close and open thus; blink. **3.** to shine with little flashes of light, or twinkle. *–v.t.* **4.** to close and open (the eyes or an eye) quickly; execute or give (a wink). **5.** to drive or force (away, back, etc.) by winking: *to wink back one's tears.* **6.** to signal or convey by a wink. *–n.* **7.** the act of winking. **8.** a winking movement, especially of one eye as in giving a hint or signal. **9.** a hint or signal given by winking. **10.** the time required for winking once; an instant or twinkling. **11.** a little flash of light; a twinkle. **12.** *Colloq.* a bit (of sleep): *I didn't sleep a wink.* *–phr.* **13. forty winks**, *Colloq.* a short sleep or nap. **14. tip someone the wink**, *Colloq.* to give information or a vital hint to someone. **15. wink at**, **a.** to close and open one eye quickly as a hint or signal to, or with some sly meaning. **b.** to be purposely blind to, as if to avoid the necessity of taking action: *to wink at petty offences.*

winkle /ˈwɪŋkəl/ *n.* **1.** any of various marine gastropods; a periwinkle. *–phr.* **2. winkle out**, to prise out or extract, as a winkle from its shell with a pin.

winning /ˈwɪnɪŋ/ *n.* **1.** (*usu. pl.*) that which is won. **2.** *Mining* **a.** an opening of any kind by which coal is being, or has been, won. **b.** a bed of coal ready for mining. *–adj.* **3.** that wins; successful or victorious, as in a contest. **4.** engaging or charming, as of a personality, or as revealed in some expression of that personality: *a winning smile.* **–winningly**, *adv.* **–winningness**, *n.*

winnow /ˈwɪnoʊ/ *v.t.* **1.** to free (grain, etc.) from chaff, dirt, etc., by means of wind or driven air; fan. **2.** to blow upon, as the wind does upon grain in this process. **3.** to subject to some process of separating or distinguishing; analyse critically: *to winnow a mass of statements.* *–v.i.* **4.** to free grain from chaff by wind or driven air. *–n.* **5.** a device for winnowing grain, etc. **6.** the act of winnowing. **–winnower**, *n.*

winsome /ˈwɪnsəm/ *adj.* winning, engaging, or charming: *a winsome smile.* **–winsomely**, *adv.* **–winsomeness**, *n.*

wintarro /wɪnˈtaroʊ/ *n.* a short-nosed bandicoot, *Isoodon auratus*, of central Australia, distinguished by the golden brown fur on its back.

winter /ˈwɪntə/ *n.* **1.** the coldest season of the year. **2.** a whole year as represented by this season: *a man of sixty winters.* **3.** a period of decline, decay, inactivity, hardship, etc.: *the winter of life.* *–adj.* **4.** of, relating to, or characteristic of winter. **5.** suitable for wear or use in winter: *winter uniform.* **6.** (of fruit and vegetables) ripening in winter. *–v.i.* **7.** to spend the winter: *planning to winter in Cairns.* *–v.t.* **8.** to keep, feed, or manage (plants, cattle, etc.) during the winter. **–wintry**, *adj.* **–wintriness**, *n.* **–winterer**, *n.* **–winterless**, *adj.*

winter melon *n.* a long green vegetable, *Benincasa hispida*, with smooth, light green skin.

winter rose *n.* → **hellebore** (def. 1).

win-win *adj.* of or relating to a situation in which both parties to a dispute can achieve a satisfactory outcome.

wipe /waɪp/ *v.t.* **1.** to rub lightly with or on a cloth, towel, paper, the hand, etc., in order to clean or dry. **2.** to take (*away, off, out*, etc.) by rubbing with or on something. **3.** to remove as if by rubbing: *wipe the smile off your face.* **4.** to destroy or eradicate, as from existence or memory. **5.** *Colloq.* to refuse to have anything to do with. **6.** to rub or draw (something) over a surface, as in cleaning or drying. *–n.* **7.** the action of wiping. **8.** a rub, as of one thing over another. **9.** a disposable tissue soaked in a cleansing agent, as one used to cleanse the face, hands, etc., or one used to clean household surfaces. **10.** *Film* a technique in film editing by which the projected image of a scene appears to be pushed or wiped off the screen by the image that follows. *–phr.*

11. wipe out, to destroy completely. **12. wipe the floor with**, *Colloq.* to defeat utterly; overcome completely.

wipe-out *n. Colloq.* **1.** *Surfing* a fall from a surfboard because of loss of balance. **2.** a failure; fiasco. **3.** a blotting out of radio signals by atmospherics, jamming, etc. Also, **wipeout**.

wire /'waɪə/ *n.* **1.** a piece of slender, flexible metal, ranging from a thickness that can be bent by the hand only with some difficulty down to a fine thread, and usually circular in section. **2.** such pieces as a material. **3.** a length of such material used as a conductor of electricity, usually insulated in a flex. **4.** a hidden electronic device designed to enable conversations conducted by the wearer to be heard covertly by others: *the agent got the information by wearing a wire.* **5.** *US Colloq.* a telegram. **6.** *US Colloq.* the telegraphic system: *to send a message by wire.* **7.** (*pl.*) a system of wires by which puppets are moved. **8.** a metallic string of a musical instrument. **9.** a metal device used to snare rabbits, etc. **10.** *Horseracing Colloq.* the finish line originally indicated by a wire stretched over the track. *–adj.* **11.** made of wire; consisting of or constructed with wires. *–v.t.* **12.** to furnish with a wire or wires. **13.** to install an electric system of wiring, as for lighting, etc. **14.** to fasten or bind with wire. **15.** *US Colloq.* to send by telegraph, as a message. **16.** *US Colloq.* to send a telegraphic message to. **17.** to snare by means of a wire or wires. *–v.i.* **18.** *US Colloq.* to send a telegraphic message; telegraph. *–phr.* **19. go** (**down**) **to the wire**, *Colloq.* **a.** (of competitors) to be evenly matched until the very end. **b.** (of a competition) to involve competitors who are evenly matched until the end: *that race will go to the wire.* **20. have** (**or get**) **one's wires crossed**, *Colloq.* to become confused; misunderstand. **21. pull wires**, *Chiefly US* to exert hidden influence; pull strings. **22. take to the wire**, *Colloq.* (of one competitor, team, etc.) to push (opponents) to their very limit: *Norths will take Souths to the wire this Saturday.* **23. under the wire**, *Colloq.* at the very last minute; in the nick of time. *–***wirelike**, *adj.*

wired /'waɪəd/ *adj.* **1.** tied or affixed with a wire or wires. **2.** having or being connected to a wire or system of wires, as an electronic device. **3.** equipped with a (sometimes hidden) listening device, as a person, animal or room: *wired for sound.* **4.** *Colloq.* (of a person) stimulated or excited, especially excessively. **5.** *Colloq.* having up-to-date knowledge or awareness, especially with regard to modern technology.

wire grass *n.* any species of the widespread genus *Aristida*, a wiry grass characterised by a trifid awn.

wireless /'waɪələs/ *adj.* **1.** having no wire. **2.** of or relating to any of various devices which are operated with or set in action by electromagnetic waves. **3.** of or relating to radio. **4.** of or relating to telecommunications technology which operates independently of telephone lines, cables, etc. *–n.* **5.** a radio. **6.** a wireless telegraph or telephone, etc. *–v.t.* **7.** to telegraph or telephone by wireless. *–v.i.* **8.** to use wireless to telegraph or telephone.

wireless broadband *n.* a system of delivery for high-speed wireless internet access and data network access over a wide area.

wireless technology *n.* telecommunications technology which is independent of telephone lines, cables, etc.

wire tap *n.* a telephone tap. See **tap²** (def. 7). Also, **wiretap**.

wiry /'waɪəri/ *adj.* (**wirier**, **wiriest**) **1.** made of wire. **2.** resembling wire, as in form, stiffness, etc.: *wiry grass.* **3.** lean and sinewy. **4.** produced by or resembling the sound of a vibrating wire: *wiry tones.* *–n.* **5.** a beachworm, *Onuphis mariahirsuta*, growing up to

100 cm long and 1 cm wide, sometimes with dark brown pigment on its back, and with antennae longer than those of the kingworm or slimy. *–***wirily**, *adv.* *–***wiriness**, *n.*

wisdom /'wɪzdəm/ *n.* **1.** the quality or state of being wise; knowledge of what is true or right coupled with just judgement as to action; sagacity, prudence, or common sense. **2.** scholarly knowledge, or learning: *the wisdom of the schools.* **3.** wise sayings or teachings.

wisdom tooth *n.* the third molar, appearing usually between the ages of 17 and 25.

wise /waɪz/ *adj.* **1.** having the power of discerning and judging properly as to what is true or right. **2.** characterised by or showing such power; shrewd, judicious, or prudent. **3.** possessed of or characterised by scholarly knowledge or learning; learned; erudite: *wise in the law.* **4.** having knowledge or information as to facts, circumstances, etc.: *we are wiser for his explanations.* *–phr.* **5. be wise to**, *Colloq.* to be in the know about or alerted to: *they tried to keep it secret, but she was wise to them; I'm wise to your tricks.* **6. get wise**, *Colloq.* **a.** to face facts or realities. **b.** to learn something. **7. none the wiser**, still in ignorance or confusion. **8. put wise**, *Colloq.* **a.** to explain something to (someone, especially a naive person). **b.** to warn. **9. wise up**, *Colloq.* **a.** to make aware; inform; alert. **b.** to become aware, informed, or alerted; face the realities. **10. wise up to oneself**, *Colloq.* to be honest to oneself about oneself, especially about one's failings and limitations. *–***wisely**, *adv.*

-wise an adverbial suffix **1. a.** denoting attitude or direction: *lengthwise*; *clockwise*. **b.** meaning 'with reference to, in respect of': *moneywise*. **2.** See **-ways**.

wisecrack /'waɪzkræk/ *n. Colloq.* a smart, pungent, or facetious remark. *–***wisecracker**, *n.*

wish /wɪʃ/ *v.t.* **1.** to want; desire; long for (often with an infinitive or a clause as object): *I wish to see her; I wish that he would come.* **2.** to desire (a person or thing) to be (as specified): *to wish oneself elsewhere.* **3.** to entertain wishes of something, favourable or otherwise, for: *to wish one well or ill.* **4.** to bid, as in greeting or leave-taking: *to wish one a good morning.* **5.** to command, request, or entreat: *I wish him to come.* *–v.i.* **6.** to have a desire, longing, or yearning. **7.** to express a desire (for something), as in a magic ritual: *blow out the candles and wish.* *–n.* **8.** a distinct mental inclination towards the doing, obtaining, attaining, etc., of something; a desire, felt or expressed: *disregard the wishes of others.* **9.** an expression of a wish, often one of a kindly or courteous nature: *send one's best wishes.* **10.** that which is wished: *get one's wish.* **11.** an act of ritual wishing: *to make a wish.* *–phr.* **12. I wish**, *Colloq.* an emphatic negative expression indicating that one would wish that something stated were the case, but it is not: *He thought that Peugeot was my new car. I wish.* **13. wish on** (or **upon**), to perform a magic ritual, using (something) as a talisman or charm: *to wish upon a forked hazel twig.* **14. wish something on someone**, **a.** to force or impose something on someone: *it's a hard task you've wished on me.* **b.** to wish that someone be visited by something, usually unpleasant: *would you wish illness on any person?* **15. you wish!**, *Colloq.* an expression denoting that someone has unrealistic expectations or ideas: *Beat me in a race? Yeah right, you wish!* *–***wisher**, *n.*

wishbone /'wɪʃboʊn/ *n.* **1.** the forked bone (a united pair of clavicles) in front of the breastbone in most birds. **2.** something which resembles the wishbone of a bird, as a piece of machinery, electrical fitting, etc.

wishful /'wɪʃfəl/ *adj.* **1.** having or showing a wish; desirous; longing. *–phr.* **2. wishful thinking**, a belief that a thing will happen or is so, based on one's hopes rather than on reality.

wish list *n. Colloq.* an informal and usually unwritten list of things one would like to have or do. Also, **wishlist**.

wishy-washy /ˈwɪʃi-wɒʃi/ *adj.* **1.** washy or watery, as a liquid; thin and weak. **2.** lacking in substantial qualities; without strength or force; weak, feeble, or poor.

wisp /wɪsp/ *n.* **1.** a handful of straw, hay, etc. **2.** any small or thin bunch, lock, mass, etc.: *wisps of hair.* **3.** a thin column or trail of smoke, etc. **4.** a small or thin person. –**wisplike**, **wispy**, *adj.*

wisteria /wɪsˈtɪəriə, wəs-/ *n.* any of the climbing shrubs, with handsome pendent racemes of purple flowers, which constitute the leguminous genus *Wisteria*, as *W. sinensis* (**Chinese wisteria**), much used to cover verandahs and walls. Also, **wistaria** /wɪsˈtɛəriə, wəs-/.

wistful /ˈwɪstfəl/ *adj.* **1.** pensive or melancholy. **2.** showing longing tinged with melancholy; regretful; sad. –**wistfully**, *adv.* –**wistfulness**, *n.*

wit[1] /wɪt/ *n.* **1.** keen perception and cleverly apt expression of connections between ideas which may arouse pleasure and especially amusement. **2.** speech or writing showing such perception and expression. **3.** a person endowed with or noted for such wit. **4.** understanding, intelligence, or sagacity: *wit enough to come in out of the rain.* **5.** (*pl.*) mental abilities, or powers of intelligent observation, keen perception, ingenious contrivance, etc.: *to have one's wits about one.* **6.** (*pl.*) mental faculties, or senses: *to lose or regain one's wits.* –*phr.* **7. at one's wits' (or wit's) end**, at the end of one's powers of knowing, thinking, etc.; utterly at a loss or perplexed. **8. live by one's wits**, to gain a livelihood by resourcefulness and quick-wittedness rather than by hard work. **9. out of one's wits**, in or into a state of great fear or incoherence: *to frighten someone out of their wits.*

wit[2] /wɪt/ *phr.* **to wit**, that is to say; namely.

witch /wɪtʃ/ *n.* **1.** a person, especially a woman, who professes or is supposed to practise magic. **2.** (in folktales, children's literature, etc.) an old, ugly, evil woman who practises magic, conventionally depicted as wearing black clothes and a conical hat, riding on a broom. **3.** *Colloq.* an ugly or malignant old woman; a hag. **4.** *Colloq.* a fascinatingly attractive woman. –**witchlike**, *adj.*

witchcraft /ˈwɪtʃkraft/ *n.* the art or practices of a witch; sorcery; magic.

witchdoctor /ˈwɪtʃdɒktə/ *n.* (in various societies) a person possessing or supposedly possessing magical powers of healing or of harming; medicine man.

witchetty grub /ˈwɪtʃəti grʌb/ *n.* any of various large, white, edible, wood-boring grubs that are the larvae of certain Australian moths and beetles. Also, **witchety grub**.

witch-hazel *n.* **1.** a shrub, *Hamamelis virginiana*, of eastern North America, whose bark and leaves afford medicinal preparations used for inflammation, bruises, etc. **2.** a liquid medicinal preparation used externally for inflammation and bruises.

witch-hunt *n.* **1.** *Hist.* the searching out of people to be accused of, and executed for, witchcraft. **2.** an intensive effort to discover and expose disloyalty, subversion, dishonesty, or the like, usually based on slight, doubtful, or irrelevant evidence. –**witch-hunter**, *n.* –**witch-hunting**, *n.*, *adj.*

with /wɪð, wɪθ/ *prep.* **1.** accompanied by or accompanying: *I will go with you.* **2.** in some particular relation to (especially implying interaction, company, association, conjunction, or connection): *to deal, talk, sit, side, or rank with; to mix, compare, or agree with.* **3.** visiting; at the house of or in the company of: *he is with the doctor at the moment; she is with her cousin in the country.* **4.** expressing similarity or agreement: *in harmony with.* **5.** expressing equality or identity: *to be level with someone.* **6.** on the side of; in favour of: *are you with us or against us?* **7.** comprehending of: *are you with me?* **8.** of the same opinion as: *I'm with you on that subject.* **9.** in the same direction as: *with the stream; to cut timber with the grain.* **10.** in the same way as: *let us, with Solomon, be judicious.* **11.** characterised by or having: *a man with long arms.* **12.** carrying (a child or young), as a pregnant female. **13.** (of means or instrument) by the use of: *to line a coat with silk; to cut with a knife.* **14.** (of manner) using or showing: *to work with diligence.* **15.** in correspondence or proportion to: *their power increased with their number.* **16.** on the occasion or occurrence of; at the same time as, or immediately after: *to rise with the dawn; he swayed with every step he took.* **17.** in consequence of (the passage of time): *to alter with the years.* **18.** in regard to: *to be pleased with a thing.* **19.** in the estimation or view of: *if that's all right with you.* **20.** in the practice or experience of, or according to: *it's always the way with him.* **21.** expressing power or influence over: *to prevail with someone.* **22.** expressing subjection to power or influence: *to sway with the wind.* **23.** (of cause) owing to: *racked with pain.* **24.** in the region, sphere, or view of: *it is day with us while it is night with the British.* **25.** (of separation, etc.) from: *to part with a thing.* **26.** against, as in opposition or competition: *to fight or vie with.* **27.** in the hands, care, keeping or service of: *leave it with me.* –*phr.* **28. get with it**, **a.** to adopt the current fashion. **b.** an exhortation to someone to pay attention and to catch up with what others are doing. **29. get with someone**, to engage in sexual activity with someone, especially to have sexual intercourse with someone. **30. with it**, **a.** aware of a situation. **b.** concentrating. **c.** able to cope. **d.** fashionable or up-to-date.

with- limited prefixal use of *with*, separative or opposing, as in *withdraw, withstand*.

-with a suffix indicating conjunction: *herewith, therewith*.

withdraw /wɪðˈdrɔ, wɪθ-/ *verb* (**-drew**, **-drawn**, **-drawing**) –*v.t.* **1.** to draw back or away; take back; remove. **2.** to retract or recall: *to withdraw a charge.* –*v.i.* **3.** to retire; retreat; go apart or away. **4.** to retract a statement or expression. **5.** *Parliamentary Procedure* to remove an amendment, motion, etc., from consideration. –**withdrawal**, *n.* –**withdrawer**, *n.*

withdrawn /wɪðˈdrɔn, wɪθ-/ *v.* **1.** past participle of **withdraw**. –*adj.* **2.** shy, retiring, or reserved. **3.** secluded, as a place.

wither /ˈwɪðə/ *v.i.* **1.** to shrivel; fade; decay. **2.** Also, **wither away**. to deteriorate or lose freshness. –*v.t.* **3.** to make flaccid, shrunken, or dry, as from loss of moisture; cause to lose freshness, bloom, vigour, etc. **4.** to affect harmfully; blight: *reputations withered by scandal.* **5.** to abash, as by a scathing glance. –**withering**, *adj.*

withers /ˈwɪðəz/ *pl. n.* the highest part of a horse's or other animal's back, behind the neck.

withhold /wɪðˈhoʊld, wɪθ-/ *v.t.* (**-held**, **-holding**) **1.** to hold back; restrain or check. **2.** to refrain from giving or granting: *to withhold payment.* –**withholder**, *n.*

withholding tax *n.* a tax that is deducted from income at its source rather than from income in the hands of the taxpayer, as in the PAYG system.

within /wɪðˈɪn, wɪθˈɪn/ *adv.* **1.** in or into the inner part; inside. **2.** in the mind, heart, or soul; inwardly: *he rejoiced within.* –*prep.* **3.** in or into the interior of: *within a city.* **4.** not beyond: *within view; within one's lifetime.* **5.** at or to some amount not greater than: *within two* *degrees of freezing.* **6.** in the sphere or scope of: *within the family*; *within the law.*

with-it *adj. Colloq.* trendy, sophisticated, up to date: *with-it gear.*

without /wɪðˈaʊt, wɪθ-/ *prep.* **1.** not with; lacking: *without help.* **2.** free from; excluding: *without pain.* **3.** beyond the limits, range, etc., of (now used chiefly in opposition to *within*): *whether within or without the law.* *–adv.* **4.** *Archaic* outside. **5.** lacking: *we must take this or go without.* *–adj.* **6.** lacking money, goods, etc.; destitute: *to be without.*

withstand /wɪðˈstænd, wɪθ-/ *verb* (**-stood, -standing**) *–v.t.* **1.** to stand or hold out against; resist or oppose, especially successfully. *–v.i.* **2.** to stand in opposition. **–withstander**, *n.*

witless /ˈwɪtləs/ *adj.* lacking wits or intelligence; stupid; foolish. **–witlessly**, *adv.* **–witlessness**, *n.*

witness /ˈwɪtnəs/ *v.t.* **1.** to see or know by personal presence. **2.** to be present at (an occurrence) as a formal witness or otherwise: *he witnessed the shooting.* **3.** to bear witness to; testify to: *she witnessed that he was the killer.* **4.** to declare true by one's signature. **5.** to be the scene of: *this room witnessed many former parties.* *–v.i.* **6.** (also fol. by *to*) to bear witness; testify. *–n.* **7.** someone who, being present, personally sees or perceives a thing. **8.** a person or thing that gives evidence. **9.** someone who gives testimony in a court of law. **10.** someone who signs a document to declare the genuineness of other signatures on it. **11.** testimony or evidence: *to bear witness to the truth of a statement.* **–witnesser**, *n.*

witticism /ˈwɪtəsɪzəm/ *n.* a witty remark; a joke.

witty /ˈwɪti/ *adj.* (**-tier, -tiest**) **1.** possessing wit in speech or writing; amusingly clever in perception and expression. **2.** characterised by wit: *a witty remark.* **–wittily**, *adv.* **–wittiness**, *n.*

wives /waɪvz/ *pl. n.* plural of **wife.**

wizard /ˈwɪzəd/ *n.* **1.** someone who professes to practise magic; a magician or sorcerer. **2.** a person of exceptional or prodigious accomplishment (especially in a specified field). *–adj.* **3.** of or relating to a wizard. **–wizardry**, *n.*

wizened /ˈwɪzənd/ *adj.* dried-up; withered; shrivelled.

wobbegong /ˈwɒbɪɡɒŋ/ *n.* any of various sharks of the genus *Orectolobus*, having a flattened body and mottled colouring and living on the bottom of the sea, found along the eastern coast of Australia and other waters of the western Pacific as around Japan, especially the **spotted wobbegong**, *O. maculatus.* Also, **wobbygong, wobegong.**

wobble /ˈwɒbəl/ *v.i.* **1.** to move from one side and then to the other, because not properly balanced. **2.** to show unsteadiness; tremble; quaver: *his voice wobbled.* *–v.t.* **3.** to cause to wobble. *–n.* **4.** the act or fact of wobbling. **–wobbly**, *adj.* **–wobbler**, *n.* **–wobbling**, *adj.*

woe /woʊ/ *n.* **1.** grievous distress, affliction, or trouble. **2.** an affliction. *–interj.* Also, **woe is me. 3.** an exclamation of grief, distress, or lamentation. **–woeful**, *adj.*

woebegone /ˈwoʊbəɡɒn/ *adj.* **1.** beset with woe; mournful or miserable; affected by woe, especially in appearance. **2.** showing or indicating woe: *he had a perpetual woebegone look on his face.*

wog¹ /wɒɡ/ *n. Colloq.* (*derog.*) **1.** a person of Mediterranean extraction, or of similar complexion and appearance. **2.** *Chiefly Brit.* (especially in World War II) a person native to North Africa or the Middle East. **–woggy**, *adj.*

wog² /wɒɡ/ *n. Aust. Colloq.* **1.** a germ, especially one leading to a minor disease such as a cold or a stomach upset. **2.** such a cold, stomach upset, etc. **3.** a small insect.

wok /wɒk/ *n.* a large, shallow, round-bottomed, metal pan used especially in Chinese cookery.

woke /woʊk/ *v.* a past tense of **wake**¹.

woken /ˈwoʊkən/ *v.* past participle of **wake**¹.

wolf /wʊlf/ *n.* (*pl.* **wolves** /wʊlvz/) **1.** any of various wild members of the dog family, especially the **grey wolf**, *Canis lupus*, of Eurasia and North America, a large, highly social animal occupying a wide variety of habitats and hunting in packs. **2.** the fur of such an animal. **3.** some wolf-like animal not of the dog family, as the Tasmanian wolf. **4.** a cruelly rapacious person. **5.** *Colloq.* a man who is boldly flirtatious or amorous towards many women. *–v.t.* **6.** (oft. fol. by *down*) to eat ravenously. *–v.i.* **7.** to hunt for wolves. *–phr.* **8. cry wolf**, to give a false alarm, often on a number of occasions as a way of getting attention. **9. keep the wolf from the door**, to ward off or keep away poverty or hunger. **10. lone wolf**, a person or animal who prefers to be and act alone. **11. wolf in sheep's clothing**, someone who hides hostile or malicious intentions behind a harmless appearance.

wolframite /ˈwʊlfrəmaɪt/ *n.* a mineral, iron manganese tungstate, (Fe, Mn)WO₃, occurring in heavy, greyish to brownish black tabular or bladed crystals (*density:* 7.0–7.5), an important ore of tungsten. Also, **wolfram.**

wolves /wʊlvz/ *pl. n.* plural of **wolf.**

woma /ˈwoʊmə/ *n.* a large, non-venomous snake, *Aspidites ramsayi*, of inland Australia, regarded as a delicacy by local Aboriginal people.

woman /ˈwʊmən/ *n.* (*pl.* **women** /ˈwɪmən/) **1.** a female human being (as distinguished from *man*). **2.** an adult female person (as distinguished from *girl*). **3.** *Colloq.* a female lover, partner in a marriage or de facto relationship. **4.** a female servant, especially one who does domestic chores, such as cleaning, cooking, etc. **5.** feminine nature, characteristics, or feelings: *the woman in you.* *–adj.* **6.** female: *a woman doctor.* **7.** of, characteristic of, or belonging to women: *woman talk.* *–phr.* **8. kept woman**, a woman financially supported by a lover. **9. make someone an honest woman** or **make an honest woman of someone**, (*humorous*) to marry a woman with whom one has been having a sexual relationship: *he finally made an honest woman of her.* **10. the other woman**, the woman with whom a husband is having an adulterous affair: *did you know Gloria was the other woman?* **11. woman of easy virtue**, a woman who is easygoing in dispensing sexual favours. **12. woman of the world**, a sophisticated woman, versed in the ways and usages of the world and society. **–womanish, womanlike, womanly**, *adj.* **–womanless**, *adj.* **–womanliness**, *n.*

womanise /ˈwʊmənaɪz/ *v.i.* **1.** (of a man) to have numerous casual affairs; philander. *–v.t.* **2.** to cause to act or be like a woman; make effeminate. Also, **womanize.** **–womaniser**, *n.*

womb /wum/ *n.* **1.** the uterus of the human female and some of the higher mammalian quadrupeds. **2.** a hollow space. **3.** a place of origin, conception, etc.

wombat /ˈwɒmbæt/ *n.* **1.** any of several species of large, burrowing marsupials constituting the Australian family Vombatidae, heavily built with short legs and a rudimentary tail, and somewhat resembling small bears. **2.** *Aust. Colloq.* an uneducated or stupid person. *–phr.* **3. blind as a wombat**, *Aust. Colloq.* very short-sighted or completely blind.

women /ˈwɪmən/ *pl. n.* plural of **woman.**

women's business *n.* **1.** (in Aboriginal societies) matters, especially cultural traditions, which are the exclusive preserve of women, especially ceremonies which are only open to women. **2.** subjects such as menstruation, which women may prefer to discuss with other women rather than with men. **3.** *Colloq.*

(*humorous*) activities seen to be especially favoured or understood by women.

women's liberation *n.* the movement which seeks to free women from sexist discrimination and make available to them the opportunity to play any role in society they choose. Also, **women's lib.**

women's refuge *n.* a place which provides accommodation, usually temporary, for women (and their children) who have had to leave home because of some domestic crisis.

womera /'wɒmərə/ *n.* → **woomera.**

won /wʌn/ *v.* past tense and past participle of **win.**

wonder /'wʌndə/ *v.i.* **1.** to think or speculate curiously: *to wonder about a thing.* **2.** (sometimes fol. by *at*) to be affected with wonder; marvel. *−v.t.* **3.** to be curious about; be curious to know: *to wonder what happened.* **4.** to be in doubt about: *I wonder if she'll come.* **5.** to be surprised at: *I wonder that you went. −n.* **6.** something strange and surprising; a cause of surprise, astonishment, or admiration: *it is a wonder he declined such an offer.* **7.** the emotion excited by what is strange and surprising; a feeling of surprised or puzzled interest, sometimes tinged with admiration. **8.** a miracle, or miraculous deed or event. *−phr.* **9. nine day wonder,** a subject of general surprise and interest for a short time. **10. no wonder,** (it is) not at all surprising (that). **11. small wonder,** (it is) hardly surprising (that). **−wonderment,** *n.* **−wonderer,** *n.*

wonderful /'wʌndəfəl/ *adj.* **1.** excellent; delightful; extremely good or fine. **2.** of a kind to excite wonder; marvellous; extraordinary; remarkable. **−wonderfully,** *adv.* **−wonderfulness,** *n.*

wondrous /'wʌndrəs/ *adj.* **1.** wonderful; marvellous. *−adv.* **2.** in a wonderful or surprising degree; remarkably. **−wondrously,** *adv.* **−wondrousness,** *n.*

wonga pigeon /wɒŋgə 'pɪdʒən/ *n.* a large grounddwelling, endemic Australian pigeon, *Leucosarcia melanoleuca,* inhabiting heavily timbered areas of eastern Australia. Also, **wonga wonga.**

wonga wonga *n.* → **wonga pigeon.** Also, **wongawonga.**

wonga wonga vine *n.* a climbing plant, *Pandorea pandorana,* family Bignoniaceae, with cream spotted flowers found in eastern Australia. Also, **wonga vine.**

wonky /'wɒŋki/ *adj.* (**-kier, -kiest**) *Colloq.* **1.** shaky; unsound. **2.** askew; awry. **3.** unwell; upset.

wont /woʊnt, wɒnt/ *adj.* **1.** accustomed; used: *he is wont to digress; I rose early, as I am wont. −n.* **2.** custom; habit; practice.

won't /woʊnt/ *v.* contraction of *will not.*

won ton /'wɒn tɒn/ *n.* (in Chinese cookery) a ball of noodle dough filled with spicy minced pork, usually boiled and served in soup. Also, **wonton.**

woo /wu/ *v.t.* **1.** to seek the favour, affection, or love of, especially with a view to marriage. **2.** to seek to win: *to woo fame.* **3.** to invite (consequences, good or bad) by one's own action: *to woo one's own destruction.* **4.** to seek to persuade (a person, etc.), as to do something; solicit; importune. *−v.i.* **5.** to pay court to someone. **−wooer,** *n.* **−wooingly,** *adv.*

wood /wʊd/ *n.* **1.** the hard, fibrous substance composing most of the stem and branches of a tree or shrub, and lying beneath the bark; the xylem. **2.** the trunks or main stems of trees as suitable for architectural and other purposes; timber or lumber. **3.** firewood. **4.** the cask, barrel, or keg in which wine, beer, or spirits are stored, as distinguished from the bottle: *aged in the wood.* **5.** *Music* **a.** a wooden wind instrument. **b.** such instruments collectively in a band or orchestra; woodwind. **6.** (*oft. pl.*) a stretch of land on which the vegetation is dominated by trees, sometimes of one or few species, smaller than a forest. **7.** *Golf* a club with a wooden

head. **8.** *Tennis, etc.* the frame part of a racquet, usually made of wood. **9.** *Bowls* → **bowl²** (def. 1). *−adj.* **10.** made of wood; wooden. **11.** used to store or carry wood. **12.** used to cut, carve, or otherwise shape wood. **13.** dwelling or growing in woods: *a wood owl. −v.t.* **14.** to cover or plant with trees. **15.** to supply with wood; get supplies of wood for. *−v.i.* **16.** to take in or get supplies of wood. *−phr.* **17. have the wood on someone,** *Colloq.* to be in possession of evidence or information which can be used to damage someone. **18. not to see the wood for the trees,** to be unable to distinguish the essential or cardinal points of a problem, situation, or the like, from the mass of detail. **19. out of the wood(s),** disengaged or escaped from a series of difficulties or dangers. **20. touch wood,** a saying appended to a statement about something good, in the hope of averting the bad luck of the opposite happening: *I haven't had a single cold this winter, touch wood.* **−woodless,** *adj.* **−woody,** *adj.*

woodblock /'wʊdblɒk/ *n.* **1.** *Printing* **a.** a block of wood engraved in relief, for printing from; a woodcut. **b.** a print or impression from such a block. **2.** a wooden block or sett, as used for flooring, road making, etc. **3.** *Music* a hollow block used in the percussion section of an orchestra. *−adj.* **4.** printed with or made from a woodblock or blocks.

woodchip /'wʊdtʃɪp/ *n.* **1.** (*pl.*) small pieces of wood, made by mechanically reducing trees to fragments for subsequent industrial use. *−adj.* **2.** of or relating to an industry, company, etc., which deals in woodchips. **−woodchipping,** *n.* **−woodchipper,** *n.*

woodcut /'wʊdkʌt/ *n.* **1.** a carved or engraved block of wood for printing from. **2.** a print or impression from such a block.

wooden /'wʊdn/ *adj.* **1.** consisting or made of wood. **2.** stiff; ungainly; awkward: *a wooden manner of walking.* **3.** without spirit: *a wooden stare.* **4.** (of a sound) as if coming from a hollow wooden object when struck. **5.** (of a wedding anniversary, etc.), showing the fifth event of a series. **−woodenly,** *adv.* **−woodenness,** *n.*

wooden spoon *n.* **1.** a spoon made out of wood, as used in cooking. **2.** *Colloq.* the fictitious prize awarded to the individual or team coming last in a sporting competition.

woodpecker /'wʊdpɛkə/ *n.* any of numerous birds constituting the family Picidae, of Eurasia, Africa and the Americas, having a hard, chisel-like bill for boring into wood after insects, stiff tail feathers to assist in climbing, and usually a more or less boldly patterned plumage.

woodpigeon /'wʊdpɪdʒən/ *n.* a large wild pigeon, *Columba palumbus,* with two whitish patches on the neck, of Eurasia and Africa.

wood-turning *n.* the forming of wood articles upon a lathe. **−wood-turner,** *n.*

woodwind /'wʊdwɪnd/ *n.* (*sometimes construed as pl.*) the group of wind instruments which comprises the flutes, clarinets, oboes, bassoons, and occasionally, the saxophone.

woodwork /'wʊdwɜk/ *n.* **1.** objects or parts made of wood. **2.** the interior wooden fittings of a house or the like. **3.** the art or craft of working in wood; carpentry. *−phr.* **4. come out of the woodwork,** to appear unexpectedly or as though from nowhere.

woody pear *n.* **1.** a shrub or small tree, *Xylomelum pyriforme,* family Probeaceae, found growing on sandy soils in eastern Australia. **2.** the hard, beaked woody fruit of this plant. Also, **wooden pear.**

woof¹ /wʊf/ *n.* **1.** yarns which travel from selvage to selvage in a loom, interlacing with the warp; weft; filling. **2.** texture; fabric.

woof² /wʊf/ *n.* **1.** the sound of a dog barking, especially deeply and loudly. **2.** a sound in imitation of this; a deep, resonant sound. *–v.i.* **3.** to make any such sound.

woofer /ˈwʊfə/ *n.* a loudspeaker designed for the reproduction of low audio frequencies (opposed to *tweeter*).

woo hoo /wu ˈhu/ *interj. Colloq.* (*sometimes ironic*) an exclamation of delight, admiration, etc. Also, **whoo hoo.**

wool /wʊl/ *n.* **1.** the fine, soft, curly hair, characterised by minute, overlapping surface scales, to which its felting property is mainly due, that forms the fleece of sheep and certain other animals, that of sheep constituting one of the most important materials of clothing. **2.** a fibre produced from sheep's fleece or the like, that may be spun into yarn, or made into felt, upholstery materials, etc. **3.** any of various types of yarn spun from this, as worsted, tweed, etc. **4.** fabric made from sheep's wool. **5.** woollen yarn used for knitting, crocheting, ornamental needlework, etc. **6.** any of various substances used commercially as substitutes for the wool of sheep, etc. **7.** a kind of wool-like yarn or material made from cellulose by a process similar to that used in manufacturing rayon or artificial silk. **8.** any of certain vegetable fibres, such as cotton, flax, etc., so used, especially after preparation by special process (**vegetable wool**). **9.** any finely fibrous or filamentous matter suggestive of the wool of sheep: *glass wool.* **10.** *Colloq.* the human hair, especially when short, thick, and curly. *–phr.* **11. dyed in the wool,** inveterate. **12. in the wool,** (of sheep) ready or nearly ready for shearing. **13. keep one's wool,** *Colloq.* to keep one's temper; not become angry. **14. lose one's wool,** *Colloq.* to lose one's temper; become angry. **15. pull the wool over someone's eyes,** to deceive or hoodwink someone.

wool clip *n.* the amount of wool yielded from the annual shearing season (by a station, district, etc.). Also, **clip.**

wool-gathering *n.* **1.** indulgence in desultory fancies or a fit of abstraction. **2.** gathering of the tufts of wool as caught on bushes, etc., by passing sheep. **3.** idle speculation; undirected thought. *–adj.* **4.** inattentive; abstracted. **–wool-gatherer,** *n.*

woollen /ˈwʊlən/ *adj.* **1.** made of wool. **2.** of or relating to wool, or products made of wool, or their manufacture. *–n.* **3.** a fabric made from wool, especially a soft loose one. **4.** (*pl.*) knitted woollen clothing, especially jumpers. Also, *US,* **woolen.**

woolly /ˈwʊli/ *adj.* (**-lier, -liest**) **1.** consisting of or like wool. **2.** clothed or covered with wool or something like it. **3.** not clear or firm: *woolly thinking*; *a woolly outline.* *–n.* (*pl.* **-lies**) *Colloq.* **4.** an article of clothing made of wool. **5.** a sheep. Also, **wooly. –woollily,** *adv.* **–woolliness,** *n.*

woolly butt *n.* **1.** any of several species of *Eucalyptus* with thick fibrous bark present only on the lower part of the trunk, especially *E. longifolia* of NSW. **2.** any of several species of the genus *Eragrostis,* especially *E. eriopoda,* a tussocky native perennial, with bristly stems and a woolly covering on the roots and butt, growing in low rainfall areas of Australia.

woolshed /ˈwʊlʃɛd/ *n.* a large shed for shearing and baling of wool.

woomera /ˈwʊmərə/ *n.* a type of throwing stick with a notch at one end for holding a dart or spear, thus giving increased leverage in throwing, traditionally used by Australian Aboriginal people. Also, **womera.**

Woop Woop /ˈwʊp wʊp/ *n.* (*humorous*) any remote or backward town or district in the Australian outback. Also, **woop woop.**

woozy /ˈwuzi/ *adj.* (**-zier, -ziest**) *Colloq.* **1.** muddled, or stupidly confused. **2.** out of sorts physically, as with dizziness, nausea, or the like. **3.** slightly or rather drunk. **–woozily,** *adv.* **–wooziness,** *n.*

word /wɜd/ *n.* **1.** a sound or a combination of sounds, or its written or printed representation, used in any language as the sign of a concept. **2.** *Gram.* an element which can stand alone as an utterance, not divisible into two or more parts similarly characterised; thus *boy* and *boyish,* but not *-ish* or *boy band,* the former being less than a word, the latter more. **3.** a term used to describe or refer: *'blue' is not an accurate word for the sea.* **4.** speech or talk: *empty words*; *a quiet word.* **5.** an utterance or expression, usually brief: *a word of praise*; *a word of warning.* **6.** (*pl.*) the text or lyrics of a song as distinguished from the music. **7.** (*pl.*) contentious or angry speech; a quarrel. **8.** warrant, assurance, or promise: *to give one's word*; *to keep one's word.* **9.** intelligence or tidings. **10.** a verbal signal, as a password, watchword, or countersign. **11.** an authoritative utterance, or command: *his word was law.* **12.** a rumour; hint. **13.** *Computers* a unit of information, usually consisting of a number or of a group of alphanumeric characters, in the memory of a computer. *–v.t.* **14.** to express in words, or phrase; select words to express: *he words his speeches carefully to avoid causing offence.* *–phr.* **15. as good as one's word,** dependable; reliable; true to one's promises or stated intentions. **16. by word of mouth,** by means of spoken exchanges between people: *a reputation gained by word of mouth.* **17. eat one's words,** to retract something said or written. **18. have a word with,** to speak briefly to. **19. have words with,** *Colloq.* to remonstrate with; to argue with. **20. in a word, a.** in short; briefly. **b.** by way of summing up. **21. in so many words,** explicitly; unequivocally; without prevarication. **22. just say the word,** an expression indicating that the person spoken to has only to request a previously discussed course of action for it to be done at once. **23. my word, a.** *Aust.* an expression of agreement. **b.** an expression of surprise, mild annoyance, etc. **24. of few words,** taciturn or laconic; disinclined to talk. **25. of many words,** loquacious. **26. of one's word,** reliable; dependable: *she is a woman of her word.* **27. play on words,** a verbal construction making use of the peculiarities of words, especially ambiguities of meaning, spelling, or pronunciation, as a pun. **28. put in a (good) word for,** to recommend (someone); mention in a favourable way. **29. send word,** to communicate; send a message: *to send word from abroad.* **30. suit the action to the word,** to do what one has said one would do. **31. take someone at their word,** to act on the assumption that someone means what they say literally. **32. take the words out of someone's mouth,** to say exactly what another was about to say. **33. the last word, a.** the closing remark, as of an argument. **b.** the very latest, most modern, or most fashionable; the best, or most sophisticated: *this machine is the last word in automation.* **34. the word,** *Colloq.* news or information: *the hot word is that she'll be here soon.* **35. the ... word,** a euphemistic formula in which the first letter of a taboo word is specified, as *the f word* for *fuck, the r word* for *recession.* **36. word for word, a.** (of a repetition, report, etc.) using exactly the same words as the original; verbatim. **b.** translated by means of exact verbal equivalents rather than by general sense. **37. word of honour,** a promise. **38. word perfect,** knowing a lesson, part in a play, formula, etc., completely and correctly: *study this until you are word perfect.* **39. word up,** *Aust. Colloq.* to speak to, especially when informing beforehand: *he worded up the magistrate.*

wordbreak /ˈwɜdbreɪk/ *n.* the point of division in a word which runs over from one line to the next. The exact placing of the division is usually determined according to certain rules of sound, as not breaking words of one syllable, and of sense, as breaking words after a prefix.

word cloud *n.* a digital design produced by randomising selected words to form a pattern of text.

word processor *n.* a computer application designed for storing, editing and basic typesetting of text.

word wrap *n. Computers* the automatic formatting of lines of text to fit into a computer screen.

wordy /ˈwɜdi/ *adj.* (**-dier, -diest**) characterised by or given to the use of many, or too many, words; verbose. –**wordily**, *adv.* –**wordiness**, *n.*

wore /wɔ/ *v.* past tense of **wear**.

work /wɜk/ *n.* **1.** exertion directed to produce or accomplish something; labour; toil. **2.** that on which exertion or labour is expended; something to be made or done; a task or undertaking. **3.** productive or operative activity. **4.** manner or quality of working. **5.** *Physics* **a.** the product of the force acting upon a body and the distance through which the point of application of force moves. The derived SI unit of work is the joule. **b.** the transference of energy from one body or system to another. **6.** employment; a job, especially that by which one earns a living. **7.** materials, things, etc., on which one is working, or is to work. **8.** the result of exertion, labour, or activity; a deed or performance. **9.** a product of exertion, labour, or activity: *a work of art; literary works.* **10.** an engineering structure, as a building, bridge, dock, or the like. **11.** (*usu. pl.*) a building, wall, trench, or the like, constructed or made as a means of fortification. **12.** (*pl. oft. construed as sing.*) a place or establishment for carrying on some form of labour or industry: *iron works.* **13.** (*pl.*) the working parts of a mechanical contrivance. **14.** the piece being cut, formed, ground, or otherwise processed in a machine tool, grinder, punching machine, etc. –*adj.* **15.** of, for, or concerning work: *work clothes.* –*verb* (**worked** *or, Archaic except for defs 29–31,* **wrought, working**) –*v.i.* **16.** to do work, or labour; exert oneself. **17.** to be employed, as for one's livelihood **18.** to be active or operate, as a machine. **19.** to act or operate. **20.** to get (*round, loose,* etc.), as if by continuous effort. **21.** to move (*into, round, through,* etc.) gradually, carefully, or with effort: *to work carefully through a subject.* **22.** to have a desired effect or influence. **23.** to move in agitation, as the features under strong feeling. **24.** to make way with effort or difficulty: *a ship works to windward.* –*v.t.* **25.** to use or manage (an apparatus, contrivance, etc.) in operation. **26.** to put into effective operation. **27.** to operate (a mine, farm, etc.) for productive purposes. **28.** to carry on operations in (a district or region). **29.** to bring about (any result) by or as by work or effort: *to work a change.* **30.** to effect, accomplish, cause, or do. **31.** to make, fashion, or execute by work. **32.** to get, or cause (something or someone) to go or be (*in, into, up,* etc.) gradually, carefully, or with difficulty: *to work a broom up the chimney.* **33.** to herd (sheep or cattle). **34.** to achieve, win, or pay for by work or effort: *to work one's way through college.* **35.** to arrange or contrive. **36.** to keep (a person, a horse, etc.) at work. **37.** Also, **work up**. to move, stir, or excite in feeling, etc.: *he worked himself into a frenzy.* **38.** to make or decorate by needlework or embroidery. –*phr.* **39. at work, a.** at one's place of work. **b.** engaged in working: *danger, men at work.* **c.** operating; functioning: *strange forces have been at work in the neighbourhood.* **40. have one's work cut out,** to be hard pressed; have a difficult task. **41. make short work of,** to dispose of or deal with quickly. **42. out of work,** unemployed. **43. set to work,** to start; begin. **44. the works, a.** everything there is; the whole lot. **b.** *Colloq.* a violent assault. **45. work a point,** *Aust. Colloq.* to take an unfair advantage. **46. work at,** to attempt to achieve or master (something) with application and energy: *skating isn't easy, you've got to work at it.* **47. work back,** *Aust.* to remain at one's place of employment to work after hours. **48. work in, a.** to introduce, insert, or cause to penetrate, especially gradually: *work in the butter and sugar; he managed to work in the question of money.* **b.** to find room for or fit in, as into a program. **49. work in progress,** a developing but incomplete project. **50. work into, a.** to make one's way gradually into; penetrate slowly. **b.** to introduce or cause to mingle gradually, with care, etc. **c.** to get (something) into (somewhere) slowly, or with difficulty: *he worked his feet into his boots.* **51. work off, a.** to get rid of by working. **b.** to discharge (a debt) by one's labour. **52. work one's passage,** to pay for one's fare on a sea trip, or the like, by working as a member of the crew. **53. work out, a.** to effect or achieve by labour: *to work out a career in advertising.* **b.** to discharge (a debt, etc.) by one's labour. **c.** to solve (a problem) by a reasoning process. **d.** to find (the answer to a problem) by reasoning. **e.** to calculate (the best way of doing something, etc.). **f.** to amount to a total or calculated figure: *it works out at $10 a metre.* **g.** to cause to finish up, turn out, or culminate (satisfactorily, unless otherwise specified): *to work out one's difficulties.* **h.** to turn out; prove (effective or suitable, unless otherwise specified). **i.** to develop; elaborate: *he doesn't always work out his plots.* **j.** to exhaust (a mine, or the like). **k.** to expiate by or as by one's effort or labour. **l.** to exercise, usually intensively and regularly, as at a gym: *what a body! I'll bet he works out!* **54. work out of,** to operate from (a place): *she is now working out of Spain.* **55. work the crowd** (or **room**), (of politicians, etc.) to greet and talk to individuals at a gathering, in order to win their support. **56. work to rule** (or **regulations**), to operate or take part in a go-slow. **57. work up, a.** to excite or arouse: *to work up an appetite; to work up a temper.* **b.** to stir or excite (someone) into a state of anxiety, consternation, etc. **c.** to expand or elaborate (something). **d.** to move or cause to move gradually upwards. **e.** to rise gradually, as in intensity: *to work up to a climax.* **f.** to get gradually to something considered as higher, more important, etc.: *I was working up to that topic.* **58. work up a sweat,** to show evidence of hard work in one's perspiration. –**workless,** *adj.*

workable /ˈwɜkəbəl/ *adj.* **1.** practicable or feasible. **2.** capable of or suitable for being worked. –**workability** /wɜkəˈbɪləti/, **workableness,** *n.*

workaday /ˈwɜkədeɪ/ *adj.* **1.** of or befitting working days; working; practical; everyday. **2.** commonplace; humdrum.

workaholic /wɜkəˈhɒlɪk/ *n.* someone who is addicted to work. –**workaholism,** *n.*

workbox /ˈwɜkbɒks/ *n.* a box to hold instruments and materials for work, especially needlework.

worker /ˈwɜkə/ *n.* **1.** someone or something that works: *he's a good steady worker.* **2.** a lower-level employee, especially as contrasted with a manager or owner of a business. **3.** someone employed in manual or industrial labour (as opposed to an employer). **4.** someone who works in a particular occupation: *office workers; research workers.* **5.** *Zool.* the sterile or infertile female of bees, wasps, ants, or termites, which does the work of the colony. –**workerless,** *adj.*

workers compensation *n.* **1.** an insurance scheme for employers to cover compensation to employees suffering injury or disease in the course of or arising out of employment or during their journey to or from work. **2.** a payment made under such a scheme. Also, *Colloq.,* **workers comp.**

work experience *n.* experience of a real work situation, especially that provided to high-school students so that they can test their choice of career against firsthand observation.

workflow /'wɜkfloʊ/ *n.* the chain of events in a work process.

workforce /'wɜkfɔs/ *n.* the total of all those engaged in employment. Also, **work force**.

workhouse /'wɜkhaʊs/ *n.* (formerly) a publicly supported institution for the maintenance of able-bodied paupers who performed unpaid work.

working capital *n.* **1.** the amount of capital needed to carry on a business. **2.** *Accounting* current assets minus current liabilities. **3.** *Finance* liquid as distinguished from fixed capital assets.

working class *n.* the class of people composed chiefly of manual workers and labourers; the proletariat.

working-class *adj.* belonging or relating to, or characteristic of the working class; proletarian.

working memory *n. Computers* a high-speed memory unit used to hold intermediate results during a calculation.

workload /'wɜkloʊd/ *n.* the amount of work done or to be done in a specified time: *I have a very heavy workload this month.*

workmanship /'wɜkmənʃɪp/ *n.* **1.** the art or skill of a workman; skill in working or execution. **2.** quality or mode of execution, as of a thing made. **3.** the product or result of the labour and skill of a workman; work executed.

work-out *n.* **1.** a trial at running, boxing, a game, or the like, usually preliminary to and in preparation for a contest, exhibition, etc. **2.** any performance for practice or training, or as a trial or test. **3.** physical exercise.

workplace agreement *n.* a written formal agreement made between an employer and employees at a particular workplace about pay and other employment conditions.

work practice *n.* a procedure which is seen to be essential to the carrying out of a particular job: *safe work practices.*

works committee *n.* **1.** an elected body of employee representatives which deals with management regarding grievances, working conditions, wages, etc., and which is consulted by management in regard to labour matters. **2.** a joint council or committee representing employer and employees which discusses working conditions, wages, etc., within a factory or office. Also, **works council**.

workshop /'wɜkʃɒp/ *n.* **1.** a room or building in which work, especially mechanical work, is carried on (considered as smaller than a factory). **2.** a group meeting to exchange ideas and study techniques, skills, etc.: *writing workshop.*

workstation /'woksteɪʃən/ *n.* **1.** an area in an office which is assigned to a user of electronic equipment such as a computer terminal, etc. **2.** a powerful microcomputer with advanced graphics capabilities and high processing speeds. **3.** *Colloq.* a desk. Also, **work station**.

work-to-rule *n.* **1.** a deliberate curtailment of output by workers, by meticulous observation of rules, as an industrial sanction. **2.** → **go-slow**. Also, **work-to-regulation**.

world /wɜld/ *n.* **1.** the earth or globe. **2.** a particular division of the earth: *the New World.* **3.** the earth, with its inhabitants, affairs, etc., during a particular period: *the ancient world.* **4.** a particular section of the world's inhabitants: *the Third World.* **5.** the public generally: *the whole world knows it.* **6.** the class of persons devoted to the affairs, interests, or pursuits of this life: *the world worships success.* **7.** society; secular, social, or fashionable life, with its ways and interests: *to withdraw from the world.* **8.** a particular class of society, with common interests, aims, etc.: *the fashionable world.* **9.** any sphere, realm, or domain, with all that relates to it: *woman's world*; *the world of dreams*; *the* *insect world.* **10.** the totality of a person's immediate environment or context; one's physical and spiritual surroundings: *the world of high finance.* **11.** the entire system of created things; the universe; the macrocosm. **12.** one's life, conceived of as complete and separate from the rest of society; one's private mental universe. **13.** one of the three general groupings of physical nature, as the **animal world**, **mineral world**, **vegetable world**; *the world to come.* **15.** a very great quantity or extent: *to do a world of good.* **16.** any indefinitely great expanse or amount. **17.** all that is important, agreeable, or necessary to one's happiness: *you're the world to me.* –*phr.* **18. a world of one's own**, a state of being out of touch with other people. **19. bring into the world**, **a.** to bear (a child), as a mother. **b.** to deliver (a child), as a midwife. **20. come into the world**, to be born. **21. dead to the world**, *Colloq.* **a.** unaware of one's surroundings; sleeping heavily. **b.** totally drunk. **c.** utterly tired; exhausted. **22. for all the world**, **a.** for any consideration, no matter how great: *he wouldn't come for all the world.* **b.** in every respect, or precisely: *he looks for all the world like a drug addict.* **23. for the world** or **for worlds**, on any account. **24. in the world**, **a.** in the universe, or on earth anywhere. **b.** at all; ever: *nothing in the world will make me change my mind*; *where in the world did you get that hat?* **25. on top of the world**, elated; delighted; exultant. **26. out of this world**, excellent; supremely or sublimely good. **27. set the world on fire**, to be a great success. **28. think the world of**, to esteem very highly. **29. world without end**, through all eternity; forever.

world-class *adj.* sufficiently good to be acceptable anywhere in the world. Also, **worldclass**.

worldling /'wɜldlɪŋ/ *n.* someone devoted to the interests and pleasures of this world; a worldly person.

worldly /'wɜldli/ *adj.* (**-lier, -liest**) **1.** earthly or mundane. **2.** devoted to, directed towards, or connected with the affairs, interests, or pleasures of this world. **3.** secular. –*adv.* **4.** in a worldly manner. –**worldliness** /'wɜldlinəs/, *n.*

world music *n.* folk music or the music of different cultures and nationalities from around the world.

world-weary *adj.* no longer interested in taking an active part in life, or being tempted by its pleasures.

World Wide Web *n.* → **web²** (def. 1). *Abbrev.:* www

worm /wɜm/ *n.* **1.** *Zool.* any of the long, slender, soft-bodied bilateral invertebrates including the flatworms, roundworms, acanthocephalans, nemerteans, and annelids. **2.** (in popular language) any of numerous small creeping animals with more or less slender, elongated bodies, and without limbs or with very short ones, including individuals of widely differing kinds, as earthworms, tapeworms, insect larvae, adult forms of some insects, etc. **3.** woodworm, or its presence, as indicated by wormholes, etc. **4.** a shaft on which one or more helical grooves are cut, or a device in which this is the principal feature. **5.** the endless screw which engages with a worm wheel in a worm gear. **6.** a grovelling, abject, or contemptible person. **7.** a downtrodden or miserable person. **8.** something that penetrates, injures, or consumes slowly or insidiously, like a gnawing worm. **9.** (*pl.*) *Pathol.* any disease or disorder arising from the presence of parasitic worms in the intestines or other tissues. **10.** *Computers* a rogue program which, once it is loaded on a computer, replicates itself until it takes up all the available memory, bringing the whole system to a standstill. –*v.i.* **11.** to move or act like a worm; creep, crawl, or advance slowly or stealthily. –*v.t.* **12.** to make, cause, bring, etc., along by creeping or crawling, or by stealthy or devious advances. **13.** to free from worms. –*phr.* **14. a can of**

worms, *Colloq.* a situation, problem, etc., presenting many difficulties. **15. a worm's eye view**, *Colloq.* the perspective of an ordinary person with no power or influence in the action taking place. **16. worm into**, to get by insidious procedure. **17. worm out of**, **a.** to get from (someone) by persistent, insidious efforts: *to worm a secret out of a person*. **b.** to avoid (a difficulty or responsibility). –**wormer**, *n.* –**wormless**, *adj.* –**wormlike**, *adj.*

wormcast /'wɜmkast/ *n.* an irregular coil of compacted soil or sand voided on the surface by some annelid worms, as earthworms.

worm farm *n.* a waste recycling system in which food scraps and a base of shredded paper are placed in a container along with compost worms which eat the waste and produce worm castings which can be used as a garden fertiliser.

wormwood /'wɜmwʊd/ *n.* **1.** any plant of the genus *Artemisia*, as santonica and moxa. **2.** a bitter, aromatic herb, *Artemisia absinthium*, native to Europe, formerly much used as a vermifuge and a tonic, but now chiefly in making absinthe. **3.** *Obs.* something bitter, grievous, or extremely unpleasant; bitterness.

worn /wɒn/ *v.* **1.** past participle of **wear**. –*adj.* **2.** impaired by wear or use: *worn clothing*. **3.** Also, **worn out**. wearied or exhausted: *I'm feeling a bit worn*. –**worn-ness**, *n.*

worrisome /'wʌrisəm, 'wɒrisəm/ *adj.* **1.** worrying, annoying, or disturbing; causing worry. **2.** inclined to worry. –**worrisomely**, *adv.*

worry /'wʌri, 'wɒri/ *verb* (**-ried**, **-rying**) –*v.i.* **1.** to feel uneasy or anxious; fret; torment oneself with or suffer from disturbing thoughts. –*v.t.* **2.** to cause to feel uneasy or anxious; trouble; torment with annoyances, cares, anxieties, etc.; plague, pester, or bother. **3.** to seize (originally by the throat) with the teeth and shake or mangle, as one animal does another. **4.** to harass by repeated biting, snapping, etc. **5.** to cause to move, etc., by persistent efforts, in spite of difficulties. –*n.* (*pl.* **-ries**) **6.** worried condition or feeling; uneasiness or anxiety. **7.** a cause of uneasiness or anxiety, or a trouble. **8.** (*pl.*) difficulties or problems: *you'll have no worries with the neighbours about parking*. **9.** the act of worrying. **10.** a person who gives cause for anxiety. –*phr.* **11. no worries**, *Aust., NZ Colloq.* **a.** an expression of confidence that everything will go well: *I'll be there, no worries!* **b.** a cheerful response to an expression of gratitude: *'Thanks for your help'. 'No worries!'* **12. worry along** (or **through**), to progress by constant effort, in spite of difficulties. –**worrier**, *n.* –**worried**, *adj.*

worse /wɜs/ *adj.* (*comparative of* **bad**) **1.** bad or ill in a greater or higher degree; inferior in excellence, quality, or character. **2.** more faulty, unsatisfactory, or objectionable. **3.** more unfavourable or injurious. **4.** in poorer condition or health. **5.** more unpleasant or disagreeable. **6.** more unsuccessful, ineffective, or unskilful. –*n.* **7.** that which is worse. –*adv.* **8.** in a more disagreeable, evil, wicked, severe, or disadvantageous manner. **9.** with more severity, intensity, etc.; in a greater degree. **10.** in a less satisfactory, complete or effective manner. –*phr.* **11. for the worse**, so as to deteriorate: *a change for the worse*. **12. go from bad to worse**, to deteriorate. **13. none the worse for**, **a.** not harmed by. **b.** *Colloq.* positively benefited by. **14. the worse for wear**, **a.** showing signs of considerable wear; shabby or worn out. **b.** *Colloq.* drunk. **15. worse off**, in worse circumstances; poorer; less fortunate or well placed. –**worsen**, *v.* –**worseness**, *n.*

worship /'wɜʃəp/ *n.* **1.** deeply respectful honour paid to God, or to any person or thing regarded as sacred; adoration. **2.** the giving of such honour in formal ceremony, prayer, etc. **3.** great love or adoration; infatuation: *hero worship*. **4.** (*upper case*) a title of honour, prefixed by *Your*, *His*, *Her*, etc., used especially in addressing or mentioning magistrates in court. –*verb* (**-shipped** *or*, *Chiefly US*, **-shiped**, **-shipping** *or*, *Chiefly US*, **-shiping**) –*v.t.* **5.** to give religious adoration to (God). **6.** to feel great love or adoration for (any person or thing). –*v.i.* **7.** to give religious adoration. **8.** to go to religious services of worship; pray. **9.** to feel great love or adoration. –**worshipful**, *adj.* –**worshipable**, *adj.* –**worshipper**; *Chiefly US*, **worshiper**, *n.*

worst /wɜst/ *adj.* (*superlative of* **bad**) **1.** bad or ill in the greatest or highest degree. **2.** most faulty, unsatisfactory, or objectionable. **3.** most unfavourable or injurious. **4.** in the poorest condition or health. **5.** most unpleasant or disagreeable. **6.** most unsuccessful, ineffective, or unskilful. –*adv.* **7.** in the most disagreeable, evil, wicked, severe, or disadvantageous manner. **8.** with the most severity, intensity, etc.; in the greatest degree. **9.** in the least satisfactory, complete, or effective manner: *the worst-dressed girl in the room*. –*v.t.* **10.** to give (someone) the worst of a contest or struggle; defeat; beat. –*phr.* **11. come off worst** or **get the worst**, to be defeated (in a contest). **12. if (the) worst comes to (the) worst**, if the very worst happens. **13. one's worst**, the utmost, especially the utmost harm, that a person is capable of: *to do one's worst to someone*. **14. the worst**, someone or something that is worst or the worst part.

worsted¹ /'wʊstəd/ *n.* **1.** firmly twisted yarn or thread spun from combed long-staple wool, used for weaving, etc. **2.** wool cloth woven from such yarns, having a hard, smooth surface, and no nap. –*adj.* **3.** consisting or made of worsted.

worsted² /'wɜstəd/ *v.* past participle of **worst**.

wort¹ /wɜt/ *n.* the unfermented or fermenting infusion of malt which after fermentation becomes beer or mash.

wort² /wɔt, wɜt/ *n.* a plant; herb; vegetable (now used chiefly in combination, as in *liverwort*, *figwort*, etc.).

worth /wɜθ/ *adj.* **1.** good or important enough to justify (what is specified): *advice worth taking*; *a place worth visiting*. **2.** having a value of, or equal in value to, as in money. **3.** having property to the value or amount of. –*n.* **4.** excellence of character or quality as commanding esteem: *men of worth*. **5.** usefulness or importance, as to the world, to a person, or for a purpose. **6.** value, as in money. **7.** a quantity of something, of a specified value. **8.** wealth; the value of one's property. –*phr.* **9. for all one's worth**, with all one's might; to one's utmost. **10. for what it is worth**, in spite of possible doubts about the accuracy, veracity, or significance of what is said. **11. worth while**, deserving attention; repaying effort or outlay: *not worth while*; *well worth while*. –**worthless**, *adj.*

worthwhile /wɜθ'waɪl/ *adj.* such as to repay one's time, attention, interest, work, trouble, etc.: *a worthwhile book*; *do you think it is worthwhile waiting for the bus?*

worthy /'wɜði/ *adj.* (**-thier**, **-thiest**) **1.** of adequate merit or character. **2.** of commendable excellence or merit; deserving: *worthy of praise*; *worthy to be loved*. –*n.* (*pl.* **-thies**) **3.** a person of eminent worth or merit or of social importance. **4.** (*often humorous*) a person. –**worthily**, *adv.* –**worthiness**, *n.*

would /wʊd/, *weak forms* /wəd, d/ *v.* past tense of **will**¹ used: **1.** specially in expressing a wish: *I would it were true*. **2.** to express condition: *I would have come had you asked me*. **3.** often in place of *will*, to make a statement or question less direct or blunt: *that would scarcely be fair*; *would you be so kind?*

would-be *adj.* **1.** wishing or pretending to be: *a would-be wit*. **2.** intended to be: *a would-be kindness*.

wouldn't /'wʊdənt/ *v.* **1.** contraction of *would not*. –*phr.* **2. wouldn't it**, Also, **wouldn't it rot** (or **rotate**) (or **root**) **you.** *Aust., NZ Colloq.* (an exclamation indicating dismay, disapproval, disgust, etc.

wound[1] /wʊnd/ *n.* **1.** an injury to an organism, usually one involving division of tissue or rupture of the integument or mucous membrane, due to external violence or some mechanical agency rather than disease. **2.** a similar injury to the tissue of a plant. **3.** an injury or hurt to feelings, sensibilities, reputation, etc. *–v.t.* **4.** to inflict a wound upon; injure; hurt. *–v.i.* **5.** to inflict a wound or wounds. **–wounding,** *n.*, *adj.* **–woundingly,** *adv.* **–woundable,** *adj.* **–wounder,** *n.* **–woundless,** *adj.*

wound[2] /waʊnd/ *v.* past tense and past participle of **wind**[2] and **wind**[3].

wove /woʊv/ *v.* a past form of **weave**[1] and **weave**[2].

woven /'woʊvən/ *v.* past participle of **weave**[1].

wow /waʊ/ *Colloq.* *–n.* **1.** something that proves an extraordinary success. *–v.t.* **2.** to win approval, admiration from. *–interj.* **3.** an exclamation of surprise, wonder, pleasure, dismay, etc.

wow factor *n. Colloq.* a quality of a product, person, entertainment, etc., which excites instant admiration.

wowser /'waʊzə/ *n. Aust., NZ Colloq.* a prudish teetotaller; a killjoy. **–wowserism,** *n.* **–wowserish,** *adj.*

woylie /'wɔɪli/ *n.* a small bettong, *Bettongia penicillata*, of central and southern Australia, having a long prehensile tail covered with black hairs on the upper surface towards the tip.

wrack /ræk/ *n.* **1.** any brown seaweed of the genus *Fucus*, as the **bladderwrack,** *F. vesiculosus*, and the **serrated wrack,** *F. serratus*. **2.** any seaweed or marine vegetation cast ashore. **3.** wreck or wreckage. **4.** ruin or destruction; disaster; rack.

wraith /reɪθ/ *n.* **1.** a ghostly apparition of a living person, supposedly portending or indicating that person's death. **2.** a visible spirit. **3.** an insubstantial copy or replica of something. **4.** something pale, thin, and insubstantial, as a plume of vapour, smoke, or the like. **–wraithlike,** *adj.*

wrangle /'ræŋgəl/ *v.i.* **1.** to argue or dispute, especially in a noisy or angry manner. **2.** to engage in argument, debate, or disputation. *–v.t.* **3.** to influence, persuade, or otherwise affect by arguing. **4.** *US* to tend (horses). *–n.* **5.** a noisy or angry dispute; altercation. **–wrangler,** *n.*

wrap /ræp/ *v.t.* **1.** Also, **wrap up.** to enclose, envelop, or muffle in something wound or folded about. **2.** Also, **wrap up.** to enclose and make fast (an article, bundle, etc.) within a covering of paper or the like. **3.** Also, **wrap up.** to protect with coverings, outer garments, etc. **4.** to surround, envelop, shroud, or enfold. *–v.i.* **5.** to become wrapped, as about something; fold. *–n.* **6.** something to be wrapped about the person, especially in addition to the usually indoor clothing, as a shawl, scarf, or mantle. **7.** a food item in which various fillings are wrapped in a base such as lavash, pita bread, etc. **8.** *(pl.)* outdoor garments, or coverings, furs, etc. **9.** a wrapper, especially a plastic one: *the sausages were in a plastic wrap.* **10.** → **rap**[1] (def. 8). **11.** → **rap**[1] (def. 9). *–phr.* **12. under wraps,** not open to public scrutiny: *keep the project under wraps for a while.* **13. wrap around, a.** to wind, fold, or bind (something) about as a covering. **b.** *Computers* (of text on a screen) to move from one line to the next automatically when the cursor reaches the edge of the screen. **14. wrap up, a.** to fold or roll up. **b.** *Colloq.* to conclude or settle: *to wrap up a financial transaction.* **c.** to put on warm outer garments.

wrapped /ræpt/ *adj.* Also, **rapt.** **1.** *Aust. Colloq.* enthused: *I'm wrapped in Mahler.* *–phr.* **2. wrapped up,** *Colloq.* finished; concluded. **3. wrapped up in, a.** engrossed or absorbed in: *wrapped up in football.* **b.** intimately connected with: *their lives were wrapped*

up in the activities of the neighbourhood. **c.** dressed up with: *a simple story wrapped up in literary pretensions.*

wrasse /ræs/ *n.* any of various marine fishes of the family Labridae, having thick, fleshy lips, powerful teeth, and usually a brilliant colour, certain species being valued as food fishes, as the **hump-headed wrasse,** *Cheilinus undulatus*, of the Great Barrier Reef.

wrath /rɒθ/, *US* /ræθ/ *n.* **1.** strong, stern, or fierce anger; deeply resentful indignation; ire. **2.** vengeance or punishment, as the consequence of anger. **–wrathless,** *adj.*

wreak /rik/ *v.t.* **1.** to inflict or execute (vengeance, etc.). **2.** to carry out the promptings of (one's rage, ill humour, will, desire, etc.), as on a victim or object. *–phr.* **3. wreak havoc,** to cause great damage. **–wreaker,** *n.*

wreath /riθ/ *n.* (*pl.* **wreaths** /riðz/) **1.** something twisted or bent into a circular form; a circular band of flowers, foliage, or any ornamental work, for adorning the head or for any decorative purpose; a garland or chaplet. **2.** a garland of flowers, laurel leaves, etc., worn on the head as a mark of honour. **3.** such a circular band of flowers, foliage, etc., left at a grave, tomb, or memorial as a mark of respect or affection for the dead. **4.** any ringlike, curving, or curling mass or formation. **5.** any object having a helical path, as a rising curve in the handrail of a staircase. **–wreathless,** *adj.* **–wreathlike,** *adj.*

wreathe /rið/ *verb* (**wreathed, wreathing**) *–v.t.* **1.** to encircle or adorn with or as if with a wreath. **2.** to surround in curving or curling masses or form: *mist wreathed the valley.* **3.** to cover: *a face wreathed in smiles.* *–v.i.* **4.** to move in curving or curling masses, as smoke.

wreck /rɛk/ *n.* **1.** the ruin or destruction of a ship or aircraft in the course of navigation. **2.** any ship or aircraft in a state of ruin from disaster. **3.** anything brought to a state of ruin: *my car is just a wreck.* **4.** the ruin or destruction of anything: *the wreck of my hopes.* **5.** someone in very bad physical or mental health. *–v.t.* **6.** to cause the loss of (a ship, etc.); shipwreck. **7.** (*usu. passive*) to involve in a wreck: *the sailors were wrecked on a strange coast.* **8.** to ruin or destroy. **–wreckage,** *n.*

wren /rɛn/ *n.* **1.** any of a large number of small birds with long legs and long, almost upright tails, of the family Maluridae, especially the brightly coloured fairy-wrens, genus *Malurus*, and related genera, as the emu-wrens, *Stipiturus*, and the grasswrens, *Amytornis*. **2.** any of numerous small, active, birds constituting the family Troglodytidae, especially *Troglodytes troglodytes*, known as the wren in England and as the **winter wren** in America; and the common **house wren,** *T. aedon*, of North America. **3.** any of various similar birds of other families, as the **golden-crested wren,** *Regulus regulus*.

wrench /rɛntʃ/ *v.t.* **1.** to pull, jerk, or force by a violent twist. **2.** to overstrain or injure (the ankle, etc.) by a sudden, violent twist. **3.** to affect distressingly as if by a wrench: *wrenched by sorrow.* *–v.i.* **4.** to pull at something with a violent, twisting movement: *he wrenched at the door.* *–n.* **5.** a sudden, violent twist. **6.** a sharp, distressing strain to the feelings. **7.** a twisted or forced meaning. **8.** an adjustable spanner. **9.** a spanner.

wrest /rɛst/ *v.t.* **1.** to twist or turn; pull, jerk, or force by a violent twist. **2.** to take away by force. **3.** to get by effort: *to wrest a living from the soil.* **4.** to twist or turn from the proper course, application, use, meaning, or the like. *–n.* **5.** a wresting; a twist or wrench. **–wrester,** *n.*

wrestle /'rɛsəl/ *verb* (**-tled, -tling**) *–v.i.* **1.** to engage someone in wrestling. **2.** to struggle in a battle for mastery; grapple. **3.** to deal (with a subject) as a difficult task or duty. *–v.t.* **4.** to struggle with in wrestling.

–n. **5.** an act of or bout at wrestling. **6.** a struggle. **–wrestler,** *n.*

wrestling /ˈrɛslɪŋ/ *n.* an exercise or sport, subject to special rules, in which two persons struggle hand to hand, each striving to throw or force the other to the ground.

wretch /rɛtʃ/ *n.* **1.** a deplorably unfortunate or unhappy person. **2.** a person of despicable or base character.

wretched /ˈrɛtʃəd/ *adj.* **1.** very unfortunate in condition or circumstances; miserable; pitiable. **2.** characterised by or attended with misery. **3.** despicable, contemptible, or mean. **4.** poor, sorry, or pitiful; worthless: *a wretched blunderer, wretched little daubs.* **–wretchedly,** *adv.* **–wretchedness,** *n.*

wrick /rɪk/ *v.t.* **1.** to wrench or strain; rick. *–n.* **2.** a strain.

wriggle /ˈrɪgl/ *v.i.* **1.** to twist to and fro, writhe, or squirm. **2.** to move along by twisting and turning the body, as a worm or snake. **3.** to make one's way by shifts or expedients: *to wriggle out of a difficulty.* **4.** to insinuate oneself into a position of advantage; wheedle. *–v.t.* **5.** to cause to wriggle. **6.** to bring, get, make, etc., by wriggling. *–n.* **7.** an act of wriggling; a wriggling movement. **8.** a sinuous formation or course. *–phr.* **9. get a wriggle on,** *Colloq.* to hurry. **10. wriggle out of,** to avoid (a difficulty or responsibility). **–wriggler,** *n.* **–wriggly,** *adj.*

wright /raɪt/ *n.* a worker, especially one who constructs something (now chiefly in *wheelwright, playwright,* etc.).

wring /rɪŋ/ *verb* (**wrung, wringing**) *–v.t.* **1.** to twist forcibly, as something flexible. **2.** Also, **wring out.** to twist and compress, or compress without twisting, in order to force out moisture: *to wring one's clothes out.* **3.** to affect painfully by or as if by some contorting or compressing action; pain, distress, or torment. **4.** to force (*off,* etc.) by twisting. **5.** to extract or extort as if by twisting. *–v.i.* **6.** to perform the action of wringing something. **7.** to writhe, as in anguish. *–n.* **8.** a wringing; forcible twist or squeeze. *–phr.* **9. wring one's hands,** to clasp one's hands together, as in grief, etc. **10. wring (out) from,** to extract or expel from by twisting or compression. **11. wring someone's hand,** to clasp someone's hand fervently.

wringer /ˈrɪŋə/ *n.* **1.** an apparatus or machine which wrings water or the like out of anything wet; a mangle. *–phr.* **2. be put through** (or **go through**) **the wringer** (or **mangle**), *Colloq.* to be subjected to emotionally harrowing events.

wrinkle /ˈrɪŋkəl/ *n.* **1.** a ridge or furrow on a surface, due to contraction, folding, rumpling, or the like; corrugation; slight fold; crease. *–v.t.* **2.** to form a wrinkle or wrinkles in; corrugate; crease. *–v.i.* **3.** to become contracted into wrinkles; become wrinkled. **–wrinkleless,** *adj.* **–wrinkly,** *adj.*

wrist /rɪst/ *n.* **1.** the part of the arm between the forearm and the hand; technically, the carpus. **2.** the joint between the radius and the carpus (**wrist joint**). **3.** that part of an article of clothing which fits round the wrist.

writ /rɪt/ *n. Law* a formal order under seal, issued in the name of a sovereign, government, court, or other competent authority, enjoining the officer or other person to whom it is issued or addressed, to do or refrain from some specified act.

write /raɪt/ *verb* (**wrote, written, writing**) *–v.t.* **1.** to trace or form (characters, letters, words, etc.) on the surface of some material, as with a pen, pencil, or other instrument or means; inscribe. **2.** to express or communicate in writing; give a written account of. **3.** to fill in the blank spaces of (a form, etc.) with writing: *to write a cheque.* **4.** to execute or produce by setting down words, etc.: *to write two copies of a letter.* **5.** to compose and produce in words or characters duly set

down: *to write a letter to a friend.* **6.** to produce as author or composer. **7.** *US* to write a letter to (someone). **8.** (of a computer) to copy (information) from its primary storage area to a secondary device such as a magnetic tape or disk. *–v.i.* **9.** to trace or form characters, words, etc., with a pen, pencil, or other instrument or means, or as a pen or the like does. **10.** (of a writing implement) to produce characters, words, etc., in a specified manner: *this pen writes well.* **11.** to be a writer, journalist, or author for one's living. **12.** to express ideas in writing. **13.** to write a letter or letters, or communicate by letter. *–phr.* **14. have something written all over one** (or **it**), to show as a clear characteristic: *her face had delight written all over it.* **15. write down, a.** to set down in writing. **b.** to write in depreciation of; injure as by writing against. **c.** *Commerce* to reduce the book value of. **16. write down to,** to write in consciously simple terms for (a supposedly ignorant readership). **17. write for,** to request or apply for by letter. **18. write in, a.** to write a letter to a newspaper, business firm, or the like. **b.** *US Politics* (in a ballot) to add the name of a candidate not listed in the printed ballot. **19. write off, a.** to cancel, as an entry in an account, as by an offsetting entry. **b.** to treat as an irreparable or non-recoverable loss. **c.** to consider as dead. **20. write oneself off,** *Colloq.* **a.** to get very drunk. **b.** to have a motor accident. **c.** to give a poor account of oneself, as in an interview, examination, etc. **21. write out, a.** to put into writing. **b.** to write in full form. **c.** to remove (a character) from a film script, soap opera, etc. **22. write up, a.** to write out in full or in detail. **b.** to bring up to date or to the latest fact or transaction in writing. **c.** to present to public notice in a written description or account. **d.** to commend to the public by a favourable written description or account. **e.** *Accounting* to make an excessive valuation of (an asset). **–writer,** *n.*

write-off *n.* **1.** *Accounting* something written off from the books. **2.** *Colloq.* something not worth repairing, either because it is irreparably damaged or because it is too old or valueless to be worth restoring to use. **3.** *Colloq.* someone who is incapacitated through drunkenness, injury, etc. **4.** *Colloq.* an incompetent person; a no-hoper.

writer's block *n.* a drying up of creative ideas, commonly suffered by writers from time to time.

write-up *n.* a written description or account, as in a newspaper or magazine.

writhe /raɪð/ *verb* (**writhed, writhing**) *–v.i.* **1.** to twist the body about, or squirm, as in pain, violent effort, etc. **2.** to shrink mentally, as in acute discomfort, embarrassment, etc. *–v.t.* **3.** to twist or bend out of shape or position; distort; contort. **4.** to twist (oneself, the body, etc.) about, as in pain. *–n.* **5.** a writhing movement; a twisting of the body, as in pain. **–writher,** *n.* **–writhingly,** *adv.*

written /ˈrɪtn/ *v.* past participle of **write**.

wrong /rɒŋ/ *adj.* **1.** not in accordance with what is morally right or good. **2.** deviating from truth or fact; erroneous. **3.** not correct in action, judgement, opinion, method, etc., as a person; in error. **4.** not in accordance with a code, convention, or set of rules; not proper: *the wrong way to talk to one's betters.* **5.** not in accordance with needs or expectations: *to take the wrong road*; *the wrong way to hold a golf club.* **6.** out of order, awry, or amiss: *something is wrong with the machine.* **7.** not suitable or appropriate: *to say the wrong thing.* **8.** (of a fabric, etc.) relating to or constituting the side that is less finished, which forms the inner side of a garment, etc. *–n.* **9.** that which is wrong, or not in accordance with morality, goodness, justice, truth, or the like; evil. **10.** an unjust act; injury. **11.** *Law* an act in breach of civil or criminal law. *–adv.* **12.** in a wrong manner; not rightly; awry or amiss. –*v.t.* **13.** to do wrong to; treat unfairly or unjustly; injure or harm. **14.** impute evil to unjustly. **15.** to seduce. –*phr.* **16. get on the wrong side of,** to incur the hostility of. **17. get someone wrong,** to misunderstand someone. **18. get the wrong end of the stick,** to misunderstand. **19. get up on the wrong side (of bed),** to be in a bad temper. **20. in the wrong, a.** responsible for some error or accident; guilty; to blame. **b.** mistaken; in error. **21. in wrong with,** *Colloq.* in disfavour with. **22. wrong in the head,** *Colloq.* crazy; mad. –**wrongly,** *adv.* –**wrongful,** *adj.*

wrong-foot *v.t.* **1.** (in various sports, as football, tennis, etc.) to trick (an opponent) into moving the wrong way. **2.** to catch unprepared: *to wrong-foot the opposition in the campaign.*

wrongful dismissal *n.* the dismissal of an employee for reasons which are unlawful, as discrimination on the basis of race or religion, objection to the employee's union activities, etc. Compare **unfair dismissal.**

wrote /roʊt/ *v.* past tense of **write.**

wrought /rɔt/ *v.* **1.** a past tense and past participle of **work** (defs 29–31). **2.** *Archaic* a past tense and past participle of **work** (defs 16–28, 32–38). –*adj.* **3.** fashioned or formed; resulting from or having been subjected to working or manufacturing. **4.** produced or shaped by beating with a hammer, etc., as iron or silver articles. **5.** ornamented or elaborated. **6.** not rough or crude. –*phr.* **7. wrought havoc,** to have caused great damage.

wrought iron *n.* a comparatively pure form of iron (as that produced by puddling pig iron) which contains practically no carbon, and which is easily forged, welded, etc., and does not harden when suddenly cooled.

wrought-iron *adj.* made of, or used in the working or manufacture of, wrought iron.

wrought-up *adj.* excited; perturbed.

wrung /rʌŋ/ *v.* past tense and past participle of **wring.**

wry /raɪ/ *adj.* (**wryer** or **wrier, wryest** or **wriest**) **1.** (of a facial expression) showing dislike or discomfort: *she made a wry face when he suggested a picnic.* **2.** ironically or bitterly amusing: *wry humour.* **3.** abnormally bent or turned to one side; twisted or crooked: *a wry nose.* –**wryly,** *adv.* –**wryness,** *n.*

wrybill /ˈraɪbɪl/ *n.* a shorebird, *Anarhynchus frontalis,* of New Zealand, related to the plovers, and having its bill twisted to the right.

wuss /wʊs/ *n. Colloq.* an overly timid or ineffectual person, especially a male; wimp. –**wussy,** *adj.*

WYSIWYG /ˈwɪziwɪg/ *n.* **1.** a computer system which displays text and images on a video display unit screen exactly as it will appear in printed output, including underlines, typeface changes, line spacing, etc. –*adj.* **2.** of or relating to a computer screen display that is produced by WYSIWYG. Also, **what-you-see-is-what-you-get.**

X x

X, x /ɛks/ *n*. **1.** the 24th letter of the English alphabet. **2.** a term often used to designate a person, thing, agency, factor, or the like, whose true name is unknown or withheld. **3.** the Roman numeral for 10.

x /ɛks/ *Maths* **1.** → **abscissa**. **2.** an unknown quantity or a variable.

xanthorrhoea /zænθəˈriə/ *n*. any plant of the genus *Xanthorroea*, native to Australia, as the grass tree.

X-axis /ˈɛks-æksəs/ *n*. the horizontal reference axis in a two-dimensional Cartesian coordinate system.

X chromosome *n*. a sex chromosome, occurring as part of a homologous pair, or paired with an unlike or Y chromosome. In humans and most mammals the XX condition controls femaleness and XY maleness; in poultry and some insects the reverse is true.

xeno- a word element meaning 'alien', 'strange', 'foreign', as in *xenogenesis*. Also, *(before a vowel)*, **xen-**.

xenon /ˈzinɒn/ *n*. a heavy, colourless, chemically unreactive but not completely inert monatomic gaseous element present in the atmosphere, one volume in 170 000 000 volumes of air. *Symbol*: Xe; *relative atomic mass*: 131.3; *atomic number*: 54.

xenophobia /zɛnəˈfoʊbiə/ *n*. fear or hatred of foreigners. **–xenophobic**, *adj*. **–xenophobe**, *n*.

xenotransplant /zinoʊˈtrænsplænt/ *n*. **1.** the surgical transfer of cells, tissues or whole organs from one species to another. **2.** the cells, tissues, or organs transferred. **–xenotransplantation** /ˌzinoʊtrænsplænˈteɪʃən/, *n*.

Xer /ˈɛksə/ *n*. one of the generation X.

xero- a word element meaning 'dry', as in *xeroderma*. Also, *(before a vowel)*, **xer-**.

xerography /zɪəˈrɒɡrəfi/ *n*. a method of photographic copying in which an electrostatic image is formed on a surface coated with selenium when it is exposed to an optical image. A dark resinous powder is dusted onto this surface after exposure so that the particles adhere to the charged regions; the image so formed is transferred to a sheet of charged paper and fixed by heating. **–xerograph** /ˈzɪərəɡræf, -ɡraf/, *n*. **–xerographic** /zɪərəˈɡræfɪk/, *adj*.

xerophyte /ˈzɪərəfaɪt/ *n*. *Bot*. a plant adapted for growth under dry conditions. **–xerophytic** /zɪərəˈfɪtɪk/, *adj*.

xerox /ˈzɪərɒks/ *(from trademark)* **–n**. **1.** a xerographic process. **2.** a copy obtained by this process. **–v.t**. **3.** to obtain copies of by this process. **–v.i**. **4.** to use this process to obtain copies.

X generation *n*. → **generation X**.

-xion variant of **-tion**, as in *inflexion*, *flexion*.

XL /ɛks ˈɛl/ *adj*. (in clothing sizes) extra large.

Xmas /ˈɛksməs, ˈkrɪsməs/ *n*. Christmas.

XML /ɛks ɛm ˈɛl/ *n*. a computer markup language designed especially for the creation of documents for the internet, comprising a simplified version of SGML which enables users to create customised tags for various types of data.

X-ray /ˈɛks-reɪ, ɛks-ˈreɪ/ *n*. **1.** *(oft. pl.)* *Physics* electromagnetic radiation of very short wavelength (5×10^{-9} to 6×10^{-12} m) which can penetrate solids, ionise gases, and expose photographic plates; roentgen ray. **2.** an examination of the interior of the body of a person or animal or the interior of an opaque substance by means of an apparatus using X-rays. **3.** the photograph taken using the process. **–v.t**. **4.** to examine by means of X-rays. **5.** to make an X-ray of. **6.** to treat with X-rays.

xylem /ˈzaɪləm/ *n*. *Bot*. the woody tissue that is the mechanical supporting portion of a vascular bundle. See **phloem**.

xylo- a word element meaning 'wood', as in *xylograph*. Also, **xyl-**.

xylophone /ˈzaɪləfoʊn/ *n*. a musical instrument consisting of a graduated series of wooden bars, usually sounded by striking with small wooden hammers. **–xylophonic** /zaɪləˈfɒnɪk/, *adj*. **–xylophonist** /zaɪˈlɒfənəst/, *n*.

Y y

Y, y /waɪ/ *n.* **1.** the 25th letter of the English alphabet. **2.** something resembling the letter Y in shape.

y /waɪ/ *n. Maths* **1.** an ordinate. See **abscissa**. **2.** an unknown quantity or a variable.

-y¹ a suffix of adjectives meaning 'characterised by or inclined to' the substance or action of the word or stem to which the suffix is attached, as in *juicy, dreamy, chilly.* Also, **-ey.**

-y² a hypocoristic suffix, the same as **-ie**, used colloquially: **1.** (*with nouns*) as an endearment, or affectionately, especially with and among children: *doggy,* a dog; *littly,* a child. **2.** (*with nouns*) as a familiar abbreviation: *budgy,* a budgerigar; *conchy,* conscientious, or a conscientious objector; *mozzy,* a mosquito. **3.** (*with adjectives*) as a nominalisation: *lefty,* a left-handed person; *cheapy,* a cheap product. **4.** (*with adjectives*) as a familiar abbreviation: *comfy, exy, speccy.* Also, **-ey, -ie.**

-y³ a suffix forming action nouns from verbs, as in *inquiry,* also found in other abstract nouns, as *carpentry, infamy.*

yabber /ˈjæbə/ *Colloq.* −*v.i.* **1.** to talk; converse. −*n.* **2.** talk; conversation. **−yabberer,** *n.*

yabby /ˈjæbi/ *n.* (*pl.* **-bies**) **1.** either of two edible freshwater crayfish, *Cherax destructor* or *C. albidus,* native to central and eastern mainland Australia, and introduced for aquaculture into WA and Tasmania; crayfish. −*v.i.* **(-bied, -bying) 2.** to catch yabbies. Also, **yabbie. −yabbying,** *n.*

yacca /ˈjækə/ *n.* → **grass tree** (def. 1). Also, **yacka, yacka bush.**

yacht /jɒt/ *n.* a sailing vessel used for private cruising, racing, or other like non-commercial purposes.

yahoo /ˈjahu, jaˈhu/ *n.* **1.** a rough, coarse, or uncouth person. −*interj.* **2.** an exclamation expressing enthusiasm or delight. −*phr.* **3. yahoo around** (or **about**), to behave in a rough, uncouth manner.

yak¹ /jæk/ *n.* (*pl.* **yaks** *or, especially collectively,* **yak**) **1.** a long-haired wild bovine mammal, *Bos grunniens,* of the Tibetan highlands. **2.** a domesticated variety of the same species.

yak² /jæk/ *Colloq.* −*n.* **1.** empty conversation. −*v.i.* (**yakked, yakking**) **2.** to talk or chatter, especially pointlessly and continuously.

yakka /ˈjækə/ *n. Aust., NZ Colloq.* work. Also, **yacker, yacka, yakker, yacca.**

yam /jæm/ *n.* **1.** the starchy, tuberous root of any of various climbing vines of the genus *Dioscorea,* much cultivated for food in the warmer regions of both hemispheres. **2.** any of these plants. **3.** *Southern US* → **sweet potato.**

Yamatji /ˈjæmədʒi/ *n.* an Aboriginal person from mid-western WA. Compare **Anangu, Koori** (def. 1), **Murri, Nunga, Nyungar, Yolngu.** Also, **Yamaji, Yammagi.**

Yang /jæŋ/ *n.* one of the two fundamental principles of the universe in Chinese philosophy, regarded as masculine, active, and assertive. Compare **Yin.**

yank /jæŋk/ *Colloq.* −*v.t.* **1.** to pull with a sudden jerking motion; tug sharply. −*v.i.* **2.** to move with a sudden jerking motion. −*n.* **3.** a jerk or tug.

Yank /jæŋk/ *n. Colloq.* (*sometimes derog., racist*) an American.

yap /jæp/ *verb* (**yapped, yapping**) −*v.i.* **1.** to yelp; bark snappishly. **2.** *Colloq.* to talk snappishly, noisily, or foolishly. −*v.t.* **3.** to utter by yapping. −*n.* **4.** a yelp: a snappish bark.

yard¹ /jad/ *n.* **1.** a common unit of linear measure in the imperial system equal to 3 feet or 36 inches, defined as 0.9144 metres. **2.** *Naut.* a long cylindrical spar with a taper towards each end, slung crosswise to a mast and suspending a square sail, lateen sail, etc.

yard² /jad/ *n.* **1.** a piece of enclosed ground adjoining or surrounding a house or other building, or surrounded by it. **2.** a piece of enclosed ground for use as a garden, for animals, or for some other purpose. **3.** an enclosure within which any work or business is carried on: *a brickyard, a shipyard.* −*v.t.* **4.** to put into or enclose in a yard.

yardarm /ˈjadam/ *n. Naut.* either end of a yard of a square sail.

yardstick /ˈjadstɪk/ *n.* **1.** a stick a yard long, commonly marked with subdivisions, used to measure with. **2.** any standard of measurement.

yarmulke /ˈjamʊlkə/ *n.* a cap traditionally worn by Jewish males. Also, **yarmulka.**

yarn /jan/ *n.* **1.** a thread made by twisting fibres, such as nylon, cotton or wool, and used for knitting and weaving. **2.** *Colloq.* a story, especially a long one about unlikely events. **3.** a talk; chat. −*v.i.* **4.** *Colloq.* to tell stories. **5.** to talk; chat. −*phr.* **6. spin a yarn,** *Colloq.* **a.** to tell a tale. **b.** to tell a false or improbable story or version of an event.

yate /jeɪt/ *n.* any of several species of *Eucalyptus,* native to western Australia, especially *E. cornuta* of the south coastal region.

yaw /jɔ/ *v.i.* **1.** to deviate temporarily from the straight course, as a ship. **2.** (of an aircraft, rocket, etc.) to have a motion about its vertical axis. −*v.t.* **3.** to cause to yaw. −*n.* **4.** a motion of an aircraft, etc., about its vertical axis.

yawl /jɔl/ *n.* a fore-and-aft-rigged vessel with a large mainmast forward and a much smaller mast set far aft, usually abaft the rudderpost.

yawn /jɔn/ *v.i.* **1.** to open the mouth involuntarily with a long, deep intake of breath, as from sleepiness or boredom. **2.** to open wide like a mouth. **3.** to extend wide, as an open, deep space. −*n.* **4.** the act of yawning. **−yawning,** *adj.* **−yawningly,** *adv.* **−yawner,** *n.*

yaws /jɔz/ *n.* a contagious, non-sexually-transmitted disease, caused by the spirochaete, *Treponema pertenue,* prevalent in certain tropical regions, characterised in the early stages by eruption of raspberry-like excrescences, similar to the symptoms of syphilis, and in the later stages by bone and joint pain.

Y-axis /ˈwaɪ-æksəs/ *n. Maths* the vertical reference axis in a two-dimensional Cartesian coordinate system.

Y chromosome *n. Genetics* a sex chromosome, occurring in the heterozygous sex, paired with an X chromosome. In mammals the XY condition controls maleness.

ye /jɪ/ *pron.* *(personal) second person Archaic* **1.** (*pl.*, *subjective and objective*) you. **2.** (*sing.*, *subjective*) you.

yea /jeɪ/ *adv.* **1.** yes: *to say yea to a proposal.* −*n.* **2.** an affirmation; an affirmative reply or vote.

yeah /jɛə/ *Colloq.* −*adv.* **1.** yes. −*interj.* **2.** an exclamation of assent, agreement, etc. Also, **yair, yeh.**

yeah-no *interj. Colloq.* a discourse marker used to indicate emphatic agreement or polite disagreement, or to downplay the force of what has been put forward by the other speaker: *yeah-no, you're right about that.*

year /jɪə/ *n.* **1.** a period of 365 or 366 days, divided into 12 calendar months, based on the Gregorian calendar and now reckoned as beginning 1 January and ending 31 December (**calendar year**). **2.** a period of approximately the same length in other calendars. **3.** a space of 12 calendar months reckoned from any point: *he left on 15 May and he'll be away for a year.* **4.** a period consisting of 12 lunar months (**lunar year**). **5.** (in scientific use) the time interval between one vernal equinox and the next, or the period of one complete apparent circuit of the ecliptic by the sun, being equal to about 365 days, 5 hours, 48 minutes, 46 seconds (**tropical year, solar year, astronomical year**). **6.** the true period of the earth's revolution round the sun; the time it takes for the apparent travelling of the sun from a given star back to it again, being about 20 minutes longer than the tropical year, which is affected by the precession of the equinoxes (**sidereal year**). **7.** the time in which any planet completes a revolution round the sun. **8.** a full round of the seasons. **9.** a period out of every 12 months, devoted to a certain pursuit, activity, or the like: *the academic year.* **10.** a level or grade in an academic program, usually indicating one full year's study: *he's in fourth year science*; *she's in fifth year medicine.* **11.** Also, **class, form, grade. a.** a single division of a school containing pupils of about the same age or of the same level of scholastic progress. **b.** the pupils themselves in such a division. **12.** (*pl.*) age, especially of a person. **13.** (*pl.*) old age: *his years are beginning to tell.* **14.** (*pl.*) time, especially a long time. −*phr.* **15. a year and a day**, a period specified as the limit of time in various legal matters, as in determining a right or a liability, to allow for a full year by any way of counting. **16. year after year**, each year, every year: *year after year the bird returned.* **17. year in, year out**, occurring regularly year after year; continuously.

yearling /ˈjɪəlɪŋ/ *n.* **1.** an animal one year old or in the second year of its age. **2.** *Horseracing* a horse one year old, dating from August 1st of the year of foaling, but not yet two.

yearly /ˈjɪəli/ *adj.* **1.** done, made, happening, appearing, etc., once a year, or every year. **2.** continuing for a year. −*adv.* **3.** once a year; annually. −*n.* (*pl.* **-lies**) **4.** a publication appearing once a year.

yearn /jɜn/ *v.i.* **1.** to have an earnest or strong desire; long. **2.** to be moved or attracted tenderly.

yeast /jist/ *n.* **1.** a yellowish, somewhat viscid, semifluid substance consisting of the aggregated cells of certain minute fungi, which appears in saccharine liquids (fruit juices, malt worts, etc.), rising to the top as a froth (**top yeast** or **surface yeast**) or falling to the bottom as a sediment (**bottom yeast** or **sediment yeast**), employed to induce fermentation in the manufacture of alcoholic drink, especially beer, and as a leaven to render bread, etc., light and spongy, and also used in medicine. **2.** a commercial substance made of living yeast cells and some meal-like material, used in raising dough for bread, etc.

yeeros /ˈjɪərɒs/ *n.* → **yiros.**

yell /jɛl/ *v.i.* **1.** to cry out with a strong, loud, clear sound. **2.** to scream with pain, fright, etc. −*v.t.* **3.** to utter or tell by yelling. −*n.* **4.** a cry uttered by yelling. **5.** *US* a cry or shout of fixed sounds or words, as one adopted by a school or college. −**yeller,** *n.*

yellow /ˈjɛloʊ/ *adj.* **1.** of a bright colour like that of butter, lemons, etc.; between green and orange in the spectrum. **2.** (*derog.*) (*racist*) of or relating to people of Asian origin, regarded as having a yellowish skin colour. **3.** *Colloq.* cowardly. −*n.* **4.** a yellow colour. **5.** a yellow pigment or dye. −*v.t.* **6.** to make yellow. −*v.i.* **7.** to become yellow. −**yellowish, yellowy,** *adj.* −**yellowness,** *n.*

yellowcake /ˈjɛloʊkeɪk/ *n.* uranium oxide in an unprocessed form, which has low radioactivity.

yellow card *n.* a yellow card shown by the referee to a player who has committed a foul as an indication that the player has been cautioned. Compare **red card.**

yellow fever *n. Pathol.* an infectious febrile disease, sometimes fatal if untreated, due to a filterable virus transmitted by a mosquito, *Aëdes* (or *Stegomyia*) *calopus*, and characterised by jaundice, vomiting, haemorrhages, etc.; occurring mainly in warm climates, especially tropical areas of Africa and South America.

yellow pages *pl. n.* (*from trademark*) (*sometimes construed as sing.*) a telephone directory listing businesses, professional people, organisations, etc., grouped according to the nature of their services.

yellow spot *n.* → **macula** (def. 2).

yelp /jɛlp/ *v.i.* **1.** to give a quick, sharp, shrill cry, as dogs, foxes, etc. **2.** to call or cry out sharply. −*v.t.* **3.** to utter or express by, or as by, yelps. −*n.* **4.** a quick, sharp bark or cry. −**yelper,** *n.*

yen[1] /jɛn/ *n.* (*pl.* **yen**) the principal monetary unit of Japan.

yen[2] /jɛn/ *n.* **1.** desire; longing. −*v.i.* (**yenned, yenning**) **2.** to desire.

yeoman /ˈjoʊmən/ *n.* (*pl.* **-men**) **1.** *Brit. Hist.* a countryman, especially one of some social standing, who cultivates his own land. **2.** *Navy* (formerly) a petty officer.

yep /jɛp/ *interj. Colloq.* → **yes.**

yes /jɛs/ *interj.* **1.** used to express affirmation or assent. −*n.* (*pl.* **yeses**) **2.** an affirmative reply.

yes-man *n.* (*pl.* **yes-men**) *Colloq.* someone who always agrees with his superiors; an obedient or sycophantic follower.

yesterday /ˈjɛstədeɪ, -di/ *adv.* **1.** on the day preceding this day. **2.** a short time ago. −*n.* **3.** the day preceding this day. **4.** time in the immediate past.

yet /jɛt/ *adv.* **1.** at the present time: *don't go yet.* **2.** up to a particular time, or thus far: *he had not yet come.* **3.** in the time still remaining, or before all is done: *there is yet time.* **4.** now or then as previously; still: *he is here yet.* **5.** in addition, or again: *yet once more.* **6.** moreover: *he won't do it for you nor yet for me.* **7.** even or still (with comparatives): *a yet milder tone.* **8.** though the case may be such; nevertheless: *strange and yet true.* −*conj.* **9.** and yet, but yet, nevertheless: *it is good, yet it could be improved.* −*phr.* **10. as yet,** up to the present time.

yeti /ˈjɛti/ *n.* a humanoid creature supposed to inhabit the snows of Tibet (Xizang AR), a region north of the Himalayas.

yew /ju/ *n.* **1.** an evergreen coniferous tree, of the genus *Taxus*, found throughout most of the Northern Hemisphere, of moderate height and having a thick, dark foliage and a fine-grained elastic wood. **2.** the wood of such a tree. **3.** a bow for shooting, made of this wood.

Y generation *n.* → **generation Y.**

yield /jild/ *v.t.* **1.** to give forth or produce by a natural process or in return for cultivation. **2.** to produce or furnish as payment, profit, or interest. **3.** to give up, as to superior power or authority. **4.** to give up or over, relinquish, or resign. −*v.i.* **5.** to give a return, as for labour expended; produce or bear. **6.** to surrender or submit, as to superior power. **7.** to give way to influence, entreaty, argument, or the like. **8.** to give way to force, pressure, etc., so as to move, bend, collapse, or the like. *−n.* **9.** the action of yielding or producing. **10.** something that is yielded. **11.** the quantity or amount yielded. **12.** *Chem.* the ratio of the product actually formed in a chemical process to that theoretically possible, usually expressed as a percentage. **13.** *Stock Exchange* dividend return on investment outlet, usually expressed as a percentage. **14.** *Mil.* the explosive force of a nuclear weapon. *−phr.* **15. yield oneself up to,** to give up or surrender oneself to. **16. yield to,** to give place or precedence to.

Yin /jɪn/ *n.* one of the two fundamental principles of the universe in Chinese philosophy, regarded as feminine, passive, and yielding. Compare **Yang**.

yiros /ˈjɪərɒs/ *n.* a Greek dish consisting of slices of meat, usually cut from a vertical spit, rolled in pita bread with salad. Also, **yeeros**.

-yl a suffix used to indicate a chemical radical, as in *ethyl.*

yobbo /ˈjɒboʊ/ *n. Colloq.* **1.** an unrefined, uncultured, slovenly young man. **2.** a hooligan or lout. Also, **yob**.

yocto- /ˈjɒktoʊ/ a prefix denoting 10⁻²⁴, as in *yoctohertz.* *Symbol:* y See **yotta-**.

yodel /ˈjoʊdl/ *verb* (**-delled** *or, Chiefly US,* **-deled,** **-delling** *or, Chiefly US,* **-deling**) *−v.i.* **1.** to sing with frequent changes from the natural voice to falsetto and back again, in the manner of the Swiss and Tyrolean mountaineers. *−v.t.* **2.** to sing (something) in a yodelling manner. *−n.* **3.** a song, refrain, etc., so sung. *−*yodeller, *n.*

yoga /ˈjoʊgə/ *n.* any of various systems of discipline in the Hindu philosophical system concerned with achieving the union of the mind and body with the Universal Spirit, employing practices such as physical control of the body through the use of unfamiliar movements or postures, etc. *−*yogic, *adj.*

yoghurt /ˈjoʊgət, ˈjɒgət/ *n.* a prepared food of custard-like consistency, sometimes sweetened or flavoured, made from milk that has been curdled by the action of enzymes or other cultures. Also, *Chiefly Brit.,* **yogurt,** **yoghourt.**

yogi /ˈjoʊgi/ *n.* (*pl.* **-gis** /-giz/) someone who practises yoga.

yoke /joʊk/ *n.* **1.** a device for joining a pair of oxen, etc., usually consisting of a crosspiece with a bow-shaped piece at each end, each bow enclosing the head of an animal. **2.** (*pl.* **yokes** *or* **yoke**) a pair of animals fastened together by a yoke. **3.** something like a yoke, such as a frame fitting the neck and shoulders of a person, for carrying a pair of buckets, etc. **4.** a shaped piece in a garment, fitted about the neck, shoulders, or hips, from which the rest of the garment hangs. **5.** something that binds; bond or tie: *the yoke of servitude.* *−v.t.* **6.** to put a yoke on; join by means of a yoke. **7.** to harness (a draught animal) to a plough or vehicle. **8.** to harness a draught animal to (a plough or vehicle). **9.** to join, link, or unite. *−v.i.* **10.** to be or become joined, linked, or united. *−*yokeless, *adj.*

yokel /ˈjoʊkəl/ *n.* a country person or rustic; a country bumpkin.

yolk /joʊk/ *n.* **1.** the yellow and principal substance of an egg, as distinguished from the white. **2.** *Biol.* that part of the contents of the egg of an animal which enters directly into the formation of the embryo (**formative yolk** or **archiblast**), together with any material which nourishes the embryo during its formation (**nutritive yolk, deutoplasm** or **parablast**); distinguished from a mass of albumen (the white of the egg) which may surround it, and from the membrane or shell enclosing the whole. **3.** the essential part; the inner core. **4.** a natural grease exuded from the skin of sheep. *−*yolkless, *adj.* *−*yolky, *adj.*

Yolngu /ˈjɒlŋu/ *n.* an Aboriginal person from north-eastern Arnhem Land. Compare **Anangu, Koori** (def. 1), **Murri, Nunga, Nyungar, Yamatji.**

Yom Kippur /jɒm ˈkɪpə/ *n.* the Day of Atonement, an annual Jewish fast day.

yonder /ˈjɒndə/ *adj.* **1.** being the more distant, or farther. **2.** being in that place or over there, or being that or those over there. *−adv.* **3.** at, in, or to that place (specified or more or less distant); over there.

yonks /jɒŋks/ *n. Colloq.* a long time: *I haven't been there for yonks.*

yore /jɔ/ *phr.* **of yore,** in time long past: *the knights of yore.*

yorker /ˈjɔkə/ *n. Cricket* a ball so bowled that it pitches directly under the bat.

Yorkshire pudding /jɔkʃə ˈpʊdɪŋ/ *n.* a baked pudding made from batter and served with gravy before or with roast beef.

yotta- /ˈjɒtə/ a prefix denoting 10²⁴, as in *yottahertz.* *Symbol:* Y See **yocto-.**

you /ju/, *weak form* /jə/ *pron. (personal), second person, sing. and pl., subjective and objective* **1.** used to refer to the person addressed. **2.** one; anyone; people in general: *as you might think.*

you-beaut *adj. Aust. Colloq.* wonderful; amazing; excellent.

you'd /jud/, *weak form* /jəd/ contraction of *you had* or *you would.*

you'll /jul/, *weak form* /jəl/ contraction of *you will* or *you shall.*

young /jʌŋ/ *adj.* **1.** being in the first or early stage of life, or growth; youthful; not old. **2.** having the appearance, freshness, vigour, or other qualities of youth. **3.** of or relating to youth: *in one's young days.* **4.** relating to the young generation of a place: *young Australia was not impressed.* **5.** not far advanced in years in comparison with another or others. **6.** junior (applied to the younger of two persons of the same name). **7.** being in an early stage generally, as of existence, progress, operation, etc.; new; early. **8.** representing or advocating recent or progressive tendencies, policies, or the like. *−n.* **9.** young offspring. *−phr.* **10. the young,** young people collectively. **11. with young,** pregnant. *−*youngish, *adj.*

youngster /ˈjʌŋstə/ *n.* **1.** a child. **2.** a young person. **3.** a young horse or other animal.

your /jɔ/, *weak form* /jə/ *adj.* **1.** the possessive form of **you. 2.** used to indicate all members of a particular group: *your suburban housewife*; *your typical old-age pensioner.* Compare **yours.**

you're /jɔ/, *weak form* /jə/ contraction of *you are.*

yours /jɔz/ *pron. (possessive)* the possessive form of **you,** used predicatively or absolutely: *they had yours; yours was overlooked; a book of yours.*

yourself /jɔˈsɛlf/ *pron.* (*pl.* **-selves**) **1.** the reflexive form of **you:** *you've cut yourself.* **2.** an emphatic form of *you* used **a.** as object: *you took it for yourself.* **b.** in apposition to a subject or object: *you did it yourself.* **3.** your proper or normal self; your usual state of mind: *you'll soon be yourself again.*

youth /juθ/ *n.* **1.** the condition of being young; youngness. **2.** the appearance, freshness, energy, etc., that marks someone who is young. **3.** the time of being young, especially period of adolescence. **4.** the first or early period of anything. **5.** young people collectively: *the youth of today.* **6.** (*pl.* **youths** /juðz/) a young person, especially a young man. *−*youthful, *adj.*

youth hostel *n.* a simple lodging place for young travellers.

you've /juv/ contraction of *you have.*

yowl /jaʊl/ *v.i.* **1.** to utter a long distressful or dismal cry, as an animal or a person; howl. *−n.* **2.** a yowling cry; a howl.

yo-yo /ˈjoʊ-joʊ/ (*from trademark*) –*n.* (*pl.* **yo-yos**) **1.** a toy, consisting of a round, flat-sided block of wood, plastic, etc., with a groove round the edge, in which a string is wound. The yo-yo is spun out and reeled in by the string, one end of which remains attached to the finger. –*v.i.* (**yo-yoed** *or* **yo-yo'd**, **yo-yoing** *or* **yo-yo'ing**) **2.** *Colloq.* to repeatedly change from one position to another; fluctuate: *the price of petrol continued to yo-yo.* Also, **yoyo**.

yo-yo diet *n.* **1.** any diet in which rapid weight loss alternates with rapid weight gain. –*v.i.* **2.** to diet in such a way. –**yo-yo dieter**, *n.* –**yo-yo dieting**, *n.*

yuan /ˈjuːən/ *n.* the principal monetary unit of China.

yucca /ˈjʌkə/ *n.* any plant of the genus *Yucca*, of the warmer regions of America, having pointed, usually rigid leaves, and whitish flowers in terminal central racemes.

yucky /ˈjʌki/ *adj.* (**-kier, -kiest**) *Colloq.* disgusting; unpleasant; repulsive. Also, **yukky**.

Yule /juːl/ *n.* Christmas, or the Christmas season.

Yulefest /ˈjuːlfɛst/ *n.* **1.** a celebration or festival held at or near Christmas. **2.** → **Christmas in July**.

yum cha /jʌm ˈtʃɑː/ *n.* a form of Chinese meal in which diners choose individual serves from selections arranged on trolleys.

yummy /ˈjʌmi/ *adj.* (**-mier, -miest**) *Colloq.* (especially of food) very good. Also, **yum**.

yuppie /ˈjʌpi/ *n.* a young urban professional person, typified as having a good income and available cash to spend on luxury consumer goods. Also, **yuppy**.

yuppify /ˈjʌpəfaɪ/ *v.t.* (**-fied, -fying**) to make suit the taste and style of yuppies: *the suburb has been yuppified.* –**yuppification**, *n.*

Z z

Z, z /zɛd/, *Chiefly US* /zi/ *n.* a consonant, the 26th letter of the English alphabet.

z *n. Maths* **1.** an unknown quantity or a variable. **2.** a complex number or variable.

zack /zæk/ *n.* **1.** *Aust., NZ Colloq.* (formerly) a sixpence. **2.** *Aust. Colloq.* a five cent piece.

zany /'zeɪni/ *adj.* (**-nier, -niest**) **1.** extremely comical; clownish. **2.** slightly crazy; fantastic or ludicrous. *–n.* (*pl.* **-nies**) **3.** an apish buffoon; clown. **4.** a silly person; simpleton. **–zanyism,** *n.*

zap /zæp/ *Colloq. –verb* (**zapped, zapping**) *–v.t.* **1.** to bombard with electric current as from a laser. **2.** to give an electric shock: *the toaster zapped me.* **3.** to cook or heat in a microwave oven. **4.** to attack with a sudden burst of violence; annihilate **5.** to remove or delete, especially quickly. **6.** *TV* to change channels quickly, using the remote control. **7.** to move (something) quickly. *–v.i.* **8.** to move quickly. *–n.* **9.** vitality; lively action. *–phr.* **10. zap up,** to make livelier and more interesting.

zapped /zæpt/ *Colloq. –v.* **1.** past participle of **zap.** *–adj.* **2.** tired to the point of exhaustion.

zeal /zil/ *n.* ardour for a person, cause, or object; eager desire or endeavour; enthusiastic diligence.

zealot /'zɛlət/ *n.* **1.** someone who displays zeal. **2.** someone carried away by excess of zeal. **3.** a religious fanatic. **–zealotry,** *n.*

zealous /'zɛləs/ *adj.* full of, characterised by, or due to zeal; ardently active, devoted, or diligent. **–zealously,** *adv.* **–zealousness,** *n.*

zebra /'zɛbrə/; *US, Brit. also* /'zibrə/ *n.* a wild, horse-like animal, fully and regularly striped with dark bands on a light ground, or with alternating dark and light bands, occurring in three species, each with its own characteristic pattern of markings: the **mountain zebra,** *Equus zebra,* of southern Africa; the **common zebra,** *E. burchelli,* of southern, central, and eastern Africa; and Grevy's zebra, *E. grevyi,* of north-eastern Africa. **–zebrine** /'zɛbraɪn, 'zibraɪn/, *adj.*

zebra crossing *n.* a pedestrian crossing marked with broad black and white or black and yellow stripes parallel to the kerb.

zebra finch *n.* a small finch *Taeniopygia guttata,* having black and white banded rump feathers, found in south-eastern Indonesia and throughout most of mainland Australia.

zenith /'zɛnəθ/ *n.* **1.** *Astron.* the point of the celestial sphere vertically above any place or observer, and diametrically opposite to the nadir. **2.** the highest point or state; culmination. **–zenithal,** *adj.*

zephyr /'zɛfə/ *n.* **1.** a soft, mild breeze. **2.** (*upper case*) *Poetic* the west wind personified. **3.** any of various things of fine, light quality, as a fabric, yarn, etc.

zeppelin /'zɛpələn/ *n.* a large rigid airship consisting of a long, cylindrical, covered framework containing compartments or cells filled with gas, and of various structures for holding the engines, passengers, etc.

zepto- /'zɛptoʊ/ a prefix denoting 10^{-21} of a given unit, as in *zeptohertz. Symbol:* z See **zetta-.**

zero /'zɪəroʊ/ *n.* (*pl.* **-ros** *or* **-roes**) **1.** the figure or symbol 0, which stands for the absence of quantity in the Arabic notation for numbers; a cipher. **2.** the origin of any kind of measurement; line or point from which all divisions of a scale (as a thermometer) are measured in either a positive or a negative direction. **3.** naught or nothing. **4.** the lowest point or degree. **5.** *Gram.* a hypothetical affix or other alteration of an underlying form to derive a complex word, not present in the phonemic shape of the word but functioning in the same way as other affixes or alterations in the language; for example, the plural of *deer* is formed by adding a zero ending (that is, by adding nothing). *–v.t.* (**-roed, -roing**) **6.** *Chiefly US* to adjust (any instrument or apparatus) to a zero point or to an arbitrary reading from which all other readings are to be measured. *–phr.* **7. zero in,** to adjust the sight settings of (a rifle) by calibrated firing on a standard range with no wind blowing. **8. zero in on, a.** to move directly and rapidly towards as a target. **b.** to focus attention on. **c.** to arrive at by a process of elimination: *they zeroed in on the conservatory as the site of the murder.*

zero-emission vehicle *n.* a vehicle which does not emit any pollutant gases. Also, **ZEV.**

zero gravity *n.* → **weightlessness.**

zero hour *n.* **1.** *Mil.* the time set for the beginning of an attack. **2.** *Colloq.* the time at which any contemplated move is to begin.

zero population growth *n.* a population growth rate at which the rate of births and immigrations remains at that needed to maintain the existing population.

zero tolerance *n.* the refusal to accept any criminal, antisocial, or other prohibited type of behaviour, usually manifested in very strict application of the law by police, etc.: *zero tolerance on drugs.* **–zero-tolerance,** *adj.*

zest /zɛst/ *n.* **1.** anything added to give flavour or enjoyment. **2.** an agreeably sharp flavour. **3.** a quality that excites or awakens sharp interest; piquancy. **4.** keen enjoyment; gusto. **5.** the peel of citrus fruits, used as a flavouring. **–zestless,** *adj.* **–zesty, zestful,** *adj.*

zetta- /'zɛtə/ a prefix denoting 10^{21} of a given unit, as in *zettahertz. Symbol:* Z See **zepto-.**

Z generation /'zɛd dʒɛnəˌreɪʃən/ *n.* → **generation Z.**

zhoosh /ʒʊʃ, ʒuʃ/ *v.t. Colloq.* to enhance the appearance of, often with minor changes: *to zhoosh one's hair before a performance.* Also, **zhush, zhoozh** /ʒʊʒ, ʒuʒ/, **zhuzh** /ʒʊʒ, ʒuʒ/.

zigzag /'zɪgzæg/ *n.* **1.** a line, course, or progression marked by sharp turns first to one side and then to the other. *–adj.* **2.** moving or formed in a zigzag. *–adv.* **3.** with frequent sharp turns from side to side. *–verb* (**-zagged, -zagging**) *–v.t.* **4.** to make zigzag, as in form or course. *–v.i.* **5.** to proceed in a zigzag line or course.

zika virus /'zikə vaɪrəs/ *n.* a virus transmitted by the Aedes mosquito, causing symptoms similar to dengue fever; thought to cause the condition of having an abnormally small head in the offspring of women who contract the virus when pregnant.

zilch /zɪltʃ/ *n. Chiefly US Colloq.* nothing.

zillion /'zɪljən/ *n. Colloq.* an unimaginably large number.

zillionaire /zɪljə'nɛə/ *n. Colloq.* a very wealthy person.

Zimmer frame /'zɪmə freɪm/ *n.* (*from trademark*) → **walking frame.**

zinc /zɪŋk/ *n.* **1.** *Chem.* a bluish-white metallic element occurring combined as the sulphide, oxide, carbonate, silicate, etc., resembling magnesium in its chemical relations, and used in making galvanised iron, alloys such as brass and die-casting metal, etc., as an element in voltaic cells, and, when rolled out into sheets, as a protective covering for roofs, etc. *Symbol*: Zn; *relative atomic mass*: 65.37; *atomic number*: 30; *density*: 7.14 at 20 °C. **2.** a piece of this metal used as an element in a voltaic cell. –*v.t.* (**zincked** *or* **zinced** /zɪŋkt/, **zincking** *or* **zincing** /ˈzɪŋkɪŋ/) **3.** to coat or cover with zinc. –**zincic** /ˈzɪŋkɪk/, **zincky**, **zincous**, *adj.*

zine /ziːn/ *n. Colloq.* a magazine, especially one about an alternative subculture, or one in electronic form published on the internet. Also, **zeen**, **'zine**.

zing /zɪŋ/ *n.* **1.** a sharp singing sound. **2.** *Colloq.* vitality; enthusiasm: *she has lots of zing*. –*interj.* **3.** used to imitate a sharp singing sound. –*v.i.* **4.** to move quickly, as if to produce such a sound. **5.** *Colloq.* to exhibit vitality. –**zingy**, *adj.*

zinnia /ˈzɪnɪə/ *n.* any of the annual plants of the genus *Zinnia*, especially the colourful, cultivated varieties of *Z. elegans*, native to Mexico.

Zionism /ˈzaɪənɪzəm/ *n.* a worldwide movement founded with the purpose of establishing a national home for the Jewish people in Palestine, which now provides support to the state of Israel. –**Zionist**, *n.*, *adj.* –**Zionistic** /zaɪənˈɪstɪk/, *adj.*

zip[1] /zɪp/ *n.* **1.** Also, **zipper**, **zip-fastener**. a fastener consisting of an interlocking device set along two edges to unite (or separate) them when an attached piece sliding between them is pulled, and used in place of buttons, hooks, or the like, on clothing, bags, etc. **2.** *Colloq.* a sudden, brief hissing sound, as of a bullet. **3.** *Colloq.* energy or vigour. –*verb* (**zipped**, **zipping**) –*v.i.* **4.** *Colloq.* to move with zip; hurry. **5.** to proceed with energy. –*v.t.* **6.** Also, **zip up**. to fasten with a zip. **7.** *Computers* → **compress** (def. 2). –*phr.* **8. zip it**, (*oft. in the imperative*) *Colloq.* to stop talking. **9. zip someone up**, to do up a zipper on an article of clothing someone is putting on, especially when it is in an awkward position. –**zippy**, *adj.*

zip[2] /zɪp/ *n. Chiefly US Colloq.* zero; nothing.

zip drive *n. Computers* a small portable disk drive used for backing up and archiving files.

zip file *n. Computers* a compressed version of a file. Also, (*in filenames*), **.zip**.

zipper /ˈzɪpə/ (*from trademark*) –*n.* **1.** → **zip**[1] (def. 1). –*v.t.* **2.** to provide with a zipper.

zircon /ˈzɜːkɒn/ *n.* a common mineral, zirconium silicate, $ZrSiO_4$, occurring in square prismatic crystals or grains of various colours, usually opaque, used as a refractory when opaque and as a gem when transparent.

zit /zɪt/ *n. Colloq.* a pimple.

zither /ˈzɪðə/ *n.* a musical folk instrument consisting of a flat soundbox with numerous strings stretched over it, which is placed on a horizontal surface and played with a plectrum and the fingertips. –**zitherist**, *n.*

-zoa plural combining form naming zoological groups as in *Protozoa*.

zodiac /ˈzoʊdiæk/ *n.* **1.** *Astron.* an imaginary belt of the heavens, extending about 8° on each side of the ecliptic, within which are the apparent paths of the sun, moon, and principal planets. It contains twelve constellations and hence twelve divisions (called *signs*), each division, however, because of the precession of the equinoxes, now containing the constellation west of the one from which it took its name. **2.** a circular or elliptical diagram representing this belt, and usually containing pictures of the animals, etc., which are associated with the constellations and signs. –**zodiacal** /zoʊˈdaɪəkəl/, *adj.*

zombie /ˈzɒmbi/ *n.* **1.** a dead body supposedly brought to life by a supernatural force. **2.** (*derog.*) a person having no independent judgement, intelligence, etc. **3.** → **zombie PC**. Also, **zombi**. –**zombiism**, *n.*

zombie PC *n.* a home computer infected by a trojan horse, enabling it to be used by hackers and spammers as a platform for sending viruses and spam.

zone /zoʊn/ *n.* **1.** any continuous area, which differs in some respect, or is marked off for some purpose, from surrounding areas, or within which certain special circumstances exist: *a military zone*; *an industrial zone*. **2.** *Geog.* any of the five divisions of the earth's surface, bounded by imaginary lines parallel to the equator, and named according to the prevailing temperature (the Torrid Zone, the North Temperate Zone, the South Temperate Zone, the North Frigid Zone, and the South Frigid Zone). **3.** *Ecol.* an area lived in by a particular set of organisms, which is determined by a particular set of environmental conditions. **4.** *Geol.* a geological horizon. –*v.t.* **5.** to divide into zones, according to existing characteristics, or for some purpose, use, etc. –*phr. Colloq.* **6. in the zone**, performing with effortless skill. **7. zone out**, to go into a trancelike state where one is oblivious of one's surroundings. –**zonal**, *adj.* –**zonally**, *adv.*

zoning /ˈzoʊnɪŋ/ *n.* the marking out of an area of land with respect to its use.

zonked /zɒŋkt/ *adj. Colloq.* exhausted; faint with fatigue. Also, **zonked-out**.

zoo /zuː/ *n.* a park or other large enclosure in which live animals are kept for public exhibition; a zoological garden.

zoo- a word element meaning 'living being', as in *zoochemistry*.

zoogamy /zoʊˈɒɡəmi/ *n.* reproduction by means of gametes; sexual reproduction. –**zoogamous**, *adj.*

zooid /ˈzoʊɔɪd/ *n.* **1.** *Biol.* any organic body or cell which is capable of spontaneous movement and of an existence more or less apart from or independent of the parent organism. **2.** *Zool.* **a.** any animal organism or individual capable of separate existence, and produced by fission, gemination, or some method other than direct sexual reproduction. **b.** one of the individuals, as certain free-swimming medusas, which intervene in the alternation of generations between the products of proper sexual reproduction. **c.** any one of the recognisably distinct individuals or elements of a compound or colonial animal, whether detached or detachable or not. –*adj.* Also, **zooidal** /zoʊˈɔɪdl/ **3.** being or resembling an animal.

zoological garden *n.* (*oft. pl.*) a zoo.

zoology /zoʊˈɒlədʒi, zuˈɒlədʒi/ *n.* (*pl.* **-gies**) **1.** the systematic study of animals or the animal kingdom. **2.** a treatise on this subject. **3.** the animals existing in a particular region. –**zoological** /zoʊəˈlɒdʒɪkəl/, *adj.* –**zoologist**, *n.*

zoom /zuːm/ *v.i.* **1.** to make a continuous humming sound. **2.** to move with this sound: *he zooms along in his new car*. **3.** (of prices) to rise rapidly. **4.** *Aeronautics* to gain height in an aircraft, in a sudden climb, using the kinetic energy of the aircraft. –*v.t.* **5.** to cause (an aeroplane) to zoom. **6.** to fly over (an obstacle) by zooming. –*n.* **7.** the act of zooming. –*phr. TV, Film, etc.* **8. zoom in**, to use a zoom lens so as to make an object appear to approach the viewer. **9. zoom out**, to use a zoom lens so as to make an object appear to recede from the viewer.

-zoon a combining form referring to a single individual in a compound organism.

zoophile /ˈzoʊəfaɪl/ *n.* someone who loves animals, especially someone who is opposed to vivisection or other such experimentation. –**zoophilism** /zoʊˈɒfəlɪzəm/, *n.*

zooter /ˈzutə/ n. Cricket a deceptive type of wrist-spin delivery, in which the ball does not deviate after pitching, with the aim of producing an l.b.w. Also, **zoota**.

Zoroastrianism /zɒrouˈæstriənɪzəm/ n. a strongly ethical code which teaches a continuous struggle between Good (Ormazd), and Evil (Angra Mainyu). Also, **Zoroastrism**.

zot /zɒt/ Colloq. −verb (**zotted**, **zotting**) −v.i. **1.** to go (off, round, through, etc.) quickly. −v.t. **2.** to knock, or kill: quickly, zot that fly. −interj. **3.** an exclamation expressing suddenness: when suddenly, zot, out jumped a red kangaroo.

zounds /zaʊndz, zundz/ interj. Archaic a minced oath, often used as a mere emphatic exclamation, as of surprise, indignation, or anger.

zucchini /zəˈkini, zu-/ n. (pl. **-ni** or **-nis**) a small marrow (def. 4), usually harvested when very young; baby marrow; courgette.

zygote /ˈzaɪgoʊt, ˈzɪgoʊt/ n. Biol. the cell produced by the union of two gametes. −**zygotic** /zaɪˈgɒtɪk, zɪ-/, adj.

COMMON ABBREVIATIONS

Punctuation note: There are different conventions regarding the punctuation of abbreviations. In Australia, contractions (abbreviations from which the middle is omitted, rather than the end, such as **Dr**, **Cwlth**) are not usually given full stops. In the following list, initialisms consisting only of capital letters (such as **AAVE**, **TER**, etc.) are not given full stops, but abbreviations containing lower-case letters (such as **Jan.**, **tbsp.**, etc.) do have full stops (unless they are contractions). However, other conventions may be adopted, such as placing full stops between the letters of an initialism (**A.A.V.E.**, **T.E.R.**, etc.), using full stops only for abbreviations which consist entirely of lower-case letters (so **Jan**, but **tbsp.**, etc.), or abandoning full stops altogether (**AAVE**, **SARS**, **Jan**, **tbsp**).

Note that symbols, such as **cm** for *centimetre*, **Cu** for *copper*, etc., are not generally given full stops, regardless of the case of their letters.

A	ampere	**add.**	addendum
Å	angstrom	**ADF**	approved deposit fund
AAVE	African American Vernacular English	**ADHD**	attention deficit hyperactivity disorder
AB	Able Seaman	**ADI**	acceptable daily intake
ab., abt	about	**adj.**	adjective
abb., abbr., abbrev.	abbreviation	**ad lib.**	at pleasure; to the extent desired (L: *ad libitum*)
ABE	American Black English	**ad loc.**	at the place (L: *ad locum*)
ABN	Australian Business Number	**ADML**	Admiral
ABW	activity-based working	**admin.**	administration
ac	acre	**ADO**	accrued (or accumulated) day off
a.c., AC	alternating current	**ADP**	automatic data processing; adenosine diphosphate
a/c	account; air-conditioning		
Ac	actinium	**ADR**	Australian Design Rules
AC	Companion of the Order of Australia; Aircraftman	**adv., advb**	adverb
		advert, advt	advertisement
A/C	account; account current	**ADVO**	apprehended domestic violence order
ACC	anthropogenic climate change		
acc.	acceleration; accent; acceptance; according; account; accusative	**AE**	Australian English
		AEDT	Australian Eastern Daylight Time
accel.	(*Music*) quickening (It.: *accelerando*)	**AEST**	Australian Eastern Standard Time
		AeT	aerobic threshold
accom.	accommodation; accompaniment	**AEWC**	airborne early warning and control
ACDT	Australian Central Daylight Time		
ACM	Air Chief Marshal	**AF**	absent fail; Anglo-French; audio frequency
ACN	Australian Company Number		
ACR	Aircraftman Recruit	**AFSM**	Australian Fire Service Medal
ACST	Australian Central Standard Time	**aft.**	after; afternoon
ACW	Aircraftwoman	**aftn**	afternoon
ACWR	Aircraftwoman Recruit	**Ag**	silver (L: *argentum*)
AD	in the year of our Lord (L: *Anno Domini*); Australian Democrats; Dame of the Order of Australia	**AGL**	above ground level
		AGM	annual general meeting
		agric.	agriculture
adag.	(*Music*) leisurely (It.: *adagio*)	**a.h., AH**	after hours
ADD	attention deficit disorder	**AHD**	Australian Height Datum

AI	artificial intelligence; artificial insemination	**ASBV**	Australian sheep breeding value
		ASD	autism spectrum disorder
AIDS	acquired immune deficiency syndrome	**ASIC**	Australian Standard Industrial Classification
AIRCDRE	Air Commodore	**ASL**	above sea level; American Sign language
AK	Knight of the Order of Australia		
Al	aluminium	**ASLT**	Acting Sub Lieutenant
alg.	algebra	**ASMR**	autonomous sensory meridian response
al seg.	(*Music*) to the sign (It.: *al segno*)		
a.m.	before noon (L: *ante meridiem*)	**Assn, assn**	association
Am	americium	**assoc.**	associate; associated; association
AM	Member of the Order of Australia; (*Radio*) amplitude modulation	**asst**	assistant
		astr., astron.	astronomy; astronomical; astronomer
AMD	acid mine drainage		
AMDG	for the greater glory of God (L: *ad majorem Dei gloriam*)	**astrol.**	astrology; astrological; astrologer
		ASX	Australian Stock Exchange
amen.	amenities	**At**	astatine
amt	amount	**AT**	appropriate technology; anaerobic threshold; algorithmic training
anat.	anatomy; anatomical		
and.	(*Music*) moderately slow (It.: *andante*)	**ATAR**	Australian Tertiary Admission Rank
ann.	annual	**atm**	standard atmosphere
anniv.	anniversary	**ATM**	automatic teller machine
anon.	anonymous	**at. no.**	atomic number
ans.	answer	**attrib.**	attributed
anth.	anthology	**at. wt**	atomic weight
AO	Officer of the Order of Australia	**Au**	gold (L: *aurum*)
Ap., Apl, Apr.	April	**AU**	astronomical unit
AP	Anangu Pitjantjatjara	**AUC**	ab urbe condita
APC	armoured personnel carrier	**AUD**	Australian dollar
APF	absolute pollen frequency	**Aug.**	August
API	application programming interface	**Aus., Aust.**	Australian
		AUV	autonomous underwater vehicle
app.	appended; appendix; appointed; approval	**av., avg., avge**	average
		Av., Ave	Avenue
APP	amyloid precursor protein	**AV**	audio-visual
approx.	approximate; approximately	**AVM**	Air Vice-Marshal
APY	Anangu Pitjantjatjara Yankunytjatjara	**AVO**	apprehended violence order
		AWD	all-wheel drive
AQI	Australian question intonation	**AWL**	absent without leave
Ar	argon	**AWOL**	(*Chiefly US*) absent without leave
arch.	architect; architecture; archipelago	**AWST**	Australian Western Standard Time
ARG	alternate reality game		
arith.	arithmetic	**b.**	born; (*Cricket*) bowled; breadth; blend of; blended; bedroom; billion
arr.	arranged; arrival; arrives; arrived		
ART	assisted reproductive technology		
ARV	antiretroviral	**B**	boron
As	arsenic	**Ba**	barium
AS	Anglo-Saxon; Australian Standards	**BA**	building application; Bachelor of Arts
		bal.	balance
ASAP, a.s.a.p.	as soon as possible	**B & B**	bed and breakfast
ASBO	(in the UK) anti-social behaviour order	**B & D**	bondage and discipline

B & W	black and white	**Bro.**	brother
Bapt.	Baptist	**Bros**	brothers
BAS	Business Activity Statement	**BSc**	Bachelor of Science
BAU	business as usual	**Btu**	British thermal unit
BBQ	barbecue	**B2B**	business-to-business
BC	Before Christ	**B2C**	business-to-consumer
bcc	blind carbon copy; (in emails) blind courtesy copy	**bus.**	bushel
		BVDV, BVD	bovine viral diarrhoea virus
BCC	basal cell carcinoma	**B/W**	black and white
BCE	Before the Common Era	**BYO**	bring your own
bch	beach; branch	**BYOG**	bring your own grog
b/d	(*Accounting*) brought down		
BDD	body dysmorphic disorder	**c.**	(*Cricket*) caught; cent; centigrade; century; (preceding dates) about (L: *circa*)
Bde	Brigade		
bdg	binding; building		
BDR	Bombardier	**C**	Cape; carbon; Celsius; Centigrade; century; (*Music*) common time; coulomb
b/e, B/E	bill of exchange		
Be	beryllium		
BEF	bovine ephemeral fever	**C/–**	care of
BeV	billion electronvolts	**Ca**	calcium
b/f	(*Accounting*) brought forward	**CAD**	computer-aided design
BFF	best friend forever	**CAE**	computer-aided engineering; College of Advanced Education
Bh	bohrium		
BH	business hours	**cal**	calorie (gram calorie)
b.h.p.	brake horsepower	**cal.**	calibre; (*Music*) slowing gradually and decreasing in volume (It.: *calando*)
bi, b/i, BI	built-in		
Bi	bismuth		
Bib.	Bible; Biblical	**Cal**	calorie (kilogram calorie)
BIF	branded iron formation	**CALD**	culturally and linguistically diverse
biol.	biology; biological; biologist		
bir, BIR	built-in robe	**CAM**	computer-aided manufacturing
bk	bank; book	**Cantab.**	of Cambridge (L: *Cantabrigiensis*)
Bk	berkelium		
bldg	building	**Cap., Capt., CAPT**	Captain
Blvd, Boul.	Boulevard		
BMI	body mass index	**cap.**	capital letter
BMR	basal metabolic rate	**cas.**	casual
BO	body odour	**Cath.**	Catholic
BOD	biochemical oxygen demand	**CAVMAN**	Cavalryman
bot.	botany; botanical; botanist; bottle	**CB**	citizen band (radio)
bp	(*Genetics*) base pair	**CBA**	central borrowing authority
bps	bits per second; bytes per second	**CBD**	central business district
BP	Before Present (before 1950, in dating system used in geology, archaeology, etc.)	**CBT**	cognitive behaviour therapy
		CBU	(of vehicles) completely built-up
		cc	cubic capacity; cubic centimetre(s); carbon copy; (in emails) courtesy copy
bpm	(*Music*) beats per minute		
Bq	becquerel	**CC**	closed captioning
Br	bromine	**CCS**	carbon capture and storage
Br.	Brother	**CCTV**	closed-circuit television
BRIC	Brazil, Russia, India, and China	**CCV**	credit card verification (number)
BRIG	Brigadier	**cd.**	candela
Brisb.	Brisbane	**c/d**	(*Accounting*) carried down; carry down
Brit.	Britain; British		

Cd	cadmium	c/o	care of
CD	compact disc	Co	cobalt
CDE	carbon dioxide equivalent	Co., Coy	company
CDMA	(*Telecom.*) code-division multiple access	CO	commanding officer
		COB	close of business
CDRE	Commodore	COD	cash on delivery
CD-ROM	compact disc read-only memory	co-ed	co-educational
CDT	Central Daylight Time	C of E	Church of England
Ce	cerium	COL	Colonel
CE	Common Era; conductive education	col.	colour
		COLA	covered outdoor learning area
cent.	centigrade; central; century	colloq.	colloquial
CEO	chief executive officer	Comm.	Commonwealth
cert.	certain; certificate; certified	comp.	compiled; composition; compound
cf.	compare (L: *confer*)		
c/f	(*Accounting*) carried forward; carry forward	compl.	complimentary
		conj.	conjunction
Cf	californium	cont., contd	continued
CFC	chlorofluorocarbon	co-op	co-operative
CFL	compact fluorescent light bulb	COPD	chronic obstructive pulmonary disease
CFO	chief financial officer		
CFS	chronic fatigue syndrome	Corp.	corporation; Corporal
cg	centigram	COTS	crown-of-thorns starfish
CGI	common gateway interface	Cp	copernicium
CGS	centimetre-gram-second; Chief of General Staff	CPA	certified practising accountant; continuous partial attention
CGT	capital gains tax	CPAP	continuous positive airway pressure
ch., chap.	chapter		
Chap.	chaplain	CPI	Consumer Price Index
ChST	Chamorro Standard Time	CPL	Corporal
chq.	cheque	CPO	Chief Petty Officer
C-in-C	Commander-in-Chief	CPR	cardiopulmonary resuscitation
C/I	certificate of insurance	CPRS	carbon pollution reduction scheme
CiP	cataloguing-in-publication		
CIP	carbon-in-pulp	CPU	central processing unit
circ.	about (L: *circa*)	Cr	chromium; Councillor
cit.	citation; cited (L: *citato*)	cres.	(*Music*) gradually louder (It.: *crescendo*)
CJD	Creutzfeldt-Jakob disease		
CKD	(of vehicles) completely knocked down	Cres.	Crescent
		CRO	cathode-ray oscilloscope
cl	centilitre	CRP	C-reactive protein
Cl	chlorine	CRT	cathode-ray tube; *Victoria* casual relief teacher
CLL	crop lower limit		
Cllr	Councillor	c/s	cycles per second
CLOB	Central Limit Order Book	Cs	caesium
cm	centimetre	CSG	coal seam gas
Cm	curium	CSP	Commonwealth Supported Place
CM	(metric) carat	CST	Central Standard Time
CMDR	Commander	ct	carat; (*Cricket*) caught; circuit; court
CMO	career medical officer		
CMS	content management system	CTE	chronic traumatic encephalopathy
CMT	cash management trust	CTF	controlled traffic farming
cnr	corner	C2B	consumer-to-business

C2C	consumer-to-consumer; creator-to-consumer	**DOVAP**	doppler velocity and position
cu.	cubic	**doz.**	dozen
Cu	copper	**DP**	displaced person
CUP	cancer of unknown primary	**DPN**	diphosphopyridine nucleotide
CV	curriculum vitae; Cross of Valour	**DPP**	Director of Public Prosecutions
CWE	coal worker's pneumoconiosis	**dpt**	department
Cwlth, Cwth	Commonwealth	**Dr**	Doctor
cwt	hundredweight	**Dr.**	Drive (in street names)
		DRM	digital rights management
d.	daughter; density; diameter	**d.s.e.**	designated spouse equivalent
D	deuterium	**dup.**	duplicate
DA	development application; (in the US) district attorney	**Ds**	darmstadtium
		DST	daylight saving time
Dan.	Danish; (*Bible*) Daniel	**DTP**	desktop publishing
dbl., dble	double	**DTV**	digital TV
dB	decibel	**DUL**	drained upper limit
Db	dubnium	**DV**	God willing (L: *Deo volente*)
dbh	diameter at breast height	**DVI**	Disaster Victim Identification
DBS	deep brain stimulation	**DVR**	digital video recorder
d.c.	direct current	**DVT**	deep vein thrombosis
DC	direct current; (*Music*) repeat (It.: *da capo*); Double Certificated	**d/w**	dishwasher
		DW	data warehouse
DDH	developmental dysplasia of the hip	**dwt**	pennyweight
		dyn.	dyne
DDS	Doctor of Dental Surgery; digital data storage	**DX**	document exchange
		Dy	dysprosium
deb.	debenture		
dec.	deceased; (*Music*) becoming softer (It.: *decrescendo*)	**E**	east; eastern
		ea.	each
Dec.	December	**Eccl.**	(*Bible*) Ecclesiastes
deg.	degree	**ECG**	electrocardiogram; electrocardiograph
dep.	departure; departs; departed; deposit; depot; deputy	**ecol.**	ecology; ecological
		econ.	economy; economics; economist
Dept, dept	department	**ECT**	electroconvulsive therapy
Deut.	(*Bible*) Deuteronomy	**ed., edit.**	edited; edition; editor
DFTD	devil facial tumour disease	**EDP**	electronic data processing
DIB	development impact bond	**EDT**	Eastern Daylight Time
dict.	dictionary	**EEG**	electroencephalogram; electroencephalograph
DID	dissociative identity disorder		
dip.	diploma	**EEO**	Equal Employment Opportunity
Dip. Ed.	Diploma of Education	**EER**	energy efficiency ratio; energy efficiency rating
disc.	discount		
DIY	do-it-yourself	**EEZ**	Exclusive Economic Zone
DLUG	double lock-up garage	**EFBD**	European foul brood disease
DME	distance measuring equipment	**EFI**	electronic fuel injection
DMSO	dimethyl sulfoxide	**EFL**	English as a foreign language
DMZ	demilitarised zone	**EFT**	electronic funds transfer
DNA	deoxyribonucleic acid	**EFTPOS**	electronic funds transfer at point of sale
DNR	do not resuscitate		
DNS	domain name system	**e.g.**	for example (L: *exempli gratia*)
DOB	date of birth	**eGH**	equine growth hormone
DON	Director of Nursing	**EGM**	extraordinary general meeting

EI	equine influenza	**exch.**	exchange; exchequer
EIA	environmental impact assessment	**excl.**	excluding; exclusive
EIS	environmental impact statement	**exec.**	executive; executor
ELE	extinction-level event	**ex lib.**	from the library of (L: *ex libris*)
ELT	extremely large telescope; English language teaching	**Exod.**	(*Bible*) Exodus
ELV	extra low-voltage	**exp.**	expenses; experienced; export; express
EMF, **e.m.f.**	electromotive force	**ext.**	external
EMG	electromyography	**Ezek.**	(*Bible*) Ezekiel
EMP	environmental management plan		
EMU	emergency medical unit	**f.**	folio; following; franc; (*Music*) loud (It.: *forte*)
EN	enrolled nurse		
enc., **encl.**	enclosed; enclosure	**f.**, **fem.**	feminine; female
enl.	enlarged	**F**	Fahrenheit; farad; fluorine
ENL	English as a native language	**FADM**	Admiral of the Fleet
ens.	ensuite	**f.a.q.**	fair average quality
ENSO	El Niño-Southern Oscillation	**FAQ**	frequently asked question; fair average quality
ENT	(*Medicine*) ear, nose and throat		
ENTER	Equivalent National Tertiary Entrance Rank	**FAS**, **f.a.s.**	free alongside ship
		FBT	fringe benefits tax
env.	envelope	**fcp**	foolscap
EOD	end of day	**Feb.**	February
EOI	expression of interest	**FDI**	Fire Danger Index
EPNS	electroplated nickel silver	**Fe**	iron (L: *ferrum*)
EPO	erythropoietin	**ff**	folios; following; fully furnished; (*Music*) very loud (It.: *fortissimo*)
equiv.	equivalent		
Er	erbium		
ERMP	environmental risk management plan	**FF**	fast forward
		fict.	fiction
ERP	enterprise resource planning	**FID**	financial institutions duty
		FIE	feline infectious enteritis
Es	einsteinium	**fi. fa.**	fieri-facias
ESA	exchange settlement account	**FIFO**	fly-in fly-out
ESL	English as a second language	**fig.**	figure; figurative
esp.	especially	**figs**	figures
ESP	extrasensory perception	**FIO**	for information only; (*Shipping*) free in and out
Esq.	Esquire		
est.	established; estimated	**fl.**	flourished
EST	Eastern Standard Time	**fl dr**	fluid drachm
estab.	established	**FLGOFF**	Flying Officer
ETA	estimated time of arrival	**fl oz**	fluid ounce
et al.	and others (L: *et alii*)	**flr**	floor
etc.	and so on (L: *et cetera*)	**FLTLT**	Flight Lieutenant
ETD	estimated time of departure	**fm**	fathom
ETP	eligible termination payment	**Fm**	fermium
ETS	emissions trading scheme (or system)	**FM**	(*Radio*) frequency modulation; Field Marshal
et seq.	and that which follows (L: *et sequens*)	**FMCG**	fast-moving consumer goods
		FMD	farm management deposit
Eu	europium	**FMS**	fibromyalgia syndrome
eV	electronvolt	**FO**	foreign order
exc.	except; excellent	**FOB**, **f.o.b.**	free on board
Exc.	Excellency	**FOI**	freedom of information

fol.	folio; following	**GI**	glycaemic index
FOO	(*Agric.*) feed on offer	**GID**	gender identity disorder
FP	Field Position	**GIFT**	gamete intrafallopian transfer
FPP	first-past-the-post	**GIS**	geographical information systems
FPS	first-person shooter	**GLBT**	gay, lesbian, bisexual, transgender
Fr	francium	**GLBTI**	gay, lesbian, bisexual, transgender, intersex
FSGT	Flight Sergeant		
FSR	floor-space ratio	**GLBTIQ**	gay, lesbian, bisexual, transgender, intersex, queer (or questioning)
4WD	four-wheel drive		
Fr	Father		
Fr.	Friday	**GLBTQ**	gay, lesbian, bisexual, transgender, queer (or questioning)
freq.	frequent; frequently		
Fri., Frid.	Friday	**gloss.**	glossary
ft	foot	**GM**	genetically-modified; general manager
f.t.	full time		
FTE	full-time equivalent	**GMO**	genetically-modified organism
FTSE 100	Financial Times Stock Exchange 100	**GMT**	Greenwich Mean Time
		GNP	Gross National Product
fur	furlong	**GNR**	Gunner
fwd	forward	**GORD**	gastro-oesophageal reflux disease
FWD	four-wheel drive	**Gov.**	Governor
FYI	for your information	**Govt, govt**	government
		GP	general practitioner
g	gram	**GPCAPT**	Group Captain
G	gigabyte; (*Film classification*) general viewing	**GPG**	giant Parramatta grass
		GPO	General Post Office
Ga	gallium	**GPR**	ground-penetrating radar
gal.	gallon	**GPS**	global positioning system; Greater Public Schools
GB	gigabyte		
GBH	grievous bodily harm	**gr.**	grain(s); grade; gross
GC	gas chromatography	**gr. wt**	gross weight
GCS	Glasgow Coma Scale	**GST**	goods and services tax
Gd	gadolinium	**GUT**	grand unified theory
Gdns	Gardens	**GWP**	global warming potential
GDP	Gross Domestic Product		
gds	goods	**h.**	height; hour
Ge	germanium	**H**	henry; hydrogen
GE	genetic engineering; genetically engineered	**ha**	hectare
		HAPE	high altitude pulmonary oedema
gen.	general; genus; gender	**HAV**	hepatitis A virus
Gen.	(*Military*) General; (*Bible*) Genesis	**HCA**	hydroxycitric acid
		h.c.f.	highest common factor
GEN	(*Military*) General	**HCFC**	hydrochlorofluorocarbon
geog.	geography; geographical; geographer	**HCG**	human chorionic gonadotropin
		hcp	handicap
geol.	geology; geological; geologist	**HDL**	high-density lipoprotein
geom.	geometry; geometrical	**hdqrs**	headquarters
ger.	gerund; gerundive	**He**	helium
GF	grand final	**HECS**	Higher Education Contribution Scheme
GFC	global financial crisis		
G-G, GG	Governor-General	**HELP**	Higher Education Loan Program
GHG	greenhouse gas	**HEV**	hepatitis E virus
GHQ	General Headquarters		

h.f.	high frequency	**ILS**	(*Aeronautics*) instrument landing system
Hf	hafnium		
HFC	hydrofluorocarbon; hydrogen fuel cell	**ILW**	intermediate level waste
		imp.	imperial; import
HFMD	hand, foot and mouth disease	**Imp.**	Emperor (L: *Imperator*); Empress (L: *Imperatrix*)
Hg	mercury (L: *hydrargyrus*)		
HGH	human growth hormone	**IMP**	(*Bridge*) international match point
HGP	hormonal growth promotant	**imperf.**	imperfect; imperforate
hist.	history; historical	**in**	inch
HIV	human immunodeficiency virus	**In**	indium
HLW	high level waste	**inc.**	included; including; inclusive; increase
HM	Her (or His) Majesty		
HMAS	Her (or His) Majesty's Australian Ship	**Inc.**	Incorporated
		incr., inc.	increase
		ind.	independent
HMR	home meal replacement	**inHg**	inch of mercury
Ho	holmium	**init.**	initially
HO	Head Office	**in loc. cit.**	in the place cited (L: *in loco citato*)
HOA	home owners association		
Hon.	honourable; honorary	**ins.**	insurance
hosp.	hospital	**Insp.**	Inspector
HP	hire purchase	**inst.**	in or of the present month
hp	horsepower	**int., intl**	internal
hPa	hectopascal	**intro., introd.**	introduced; introduction
HPV	human papillomavirus	**I/O**	input/output
HQ	headquarters	**IOD**	Indian Ocean Dipole
hr	hour	**IOU**	I owe you
HR	human resources; House of Representatives	**IP**	intellectual property; internet protocol
HRT	hormone replacement therapy	**IPA**	International Phonetic Alphabet
HRH	Her (or His) Royal Highness	**IPO**	initial public offering
Hs	hassium	**Ir**	iridium
HSC	Higher School Certificate	**IR**	industrial relations
HT	(*Electricity*) high-tension	**IRC**	internet relay chat
Hts	Heights	**IRP**	integrated resource planning
hwy	highway	**Is., is., isl.**	Island; Isle
Hz	hertz	**ISBN**	International Standard Book Number
I	iodine	**ISD**	International Subscriber Dialling
IB	International Baccalaureate	**ISP**	internet service provider
ibid.	in the same place (L: *ibidem*)	**ISSN**	International Standard Serial Number
IBS	irritable bowel syndrome		
i/c	in charge; in command	**Isth., isth.**	Isthmus
IC	integrated circuit	**IT**	information technology
ICT	information and communications technology	**ital.**	italics (type)
		IU	International Unit
id.	the same (L: *idem*)	**IUD**	intra-uterine device
ID	identification	**IUS**	intra-uterine system
i.e.	that is (L: *id est*)	**IVF**	in-vitro fertilisation
IED	improvised explosive device	**IWB**	interactive whiteboard
IGT	impaired glucose tolerance		
illus.	illustrated; illustration	**J**	journal; joule; Judge; Justice
		Jan., Ja.	January

Jas	(*Bible*) James	**LACW**	Leading Aircraftwoman
Jer.	(*Bible*) Jeremiah	**LAN**	local area network
JI	Jemaah Islamiah	**lang.**	language
JIA	juvenile idiopathic arthritis	**LARP**	live-action role-playing
Jn	(*Bible*) John	**lat.**	latitude
Jn., Jun.	June	**lb**	pound
jnr, jr	junior	**lbf**	pound-force
Jon.	(*Bible*) Jonah	**LBM**	lean body mass
Josh.	(*Bible*) Joshua	**LBO**	leveraged buy-out
JP	Justice of the Peace	**l.b.w.**	(*Cricket*) leg before wicket
Jud., Judg.	(*Bible*) Judges	**l.c.**	lower case
Jul., Jl., Jy	July	**LC**	Legislative Council; locus ceruleus
k	kilometre; kilobyte	**l.c.d.**	lowest common denominator
K	thousand; kilometre; kilobyte; kelvin; king; Knight; (*Bible*) Kings; (*Music*) Köchel; potassium (L: *kalium*)	**LCD**	liquid crystal display
		LCDR	Lieutenant Commander
		l.c.m.	lowest common multiple
Kb, kb	kilobit	**LCPL**	Lance Corporal
KB, Kb, kb	kilobyte	**LDL**	low-density lipoprotein
kbps	kilobits per second	**LED**	light-emitting diode
kBps	kilobytes per second	**LEP**	local environment plan
kbyte	kilobyte	**LEUT**	(*Navy*) Lieutenant
kd	killed	**LEV**	low-emission vehicle
KDR	knock down rebuild	**Levit.**	(*Bible*) Leviticus
kg	kilogram	**LFP**	lead-free petrol
kHz	kilohertz	**LGB**	laser-guided bomb
KIF	knowledge interchange format	**LGBT**	lesbian, gay, bisexual, transgender
kit.	kitchen	**LGBTI**	lesbian, gay, bisexual, transgender, intersex
kJ	kilojoule		
kL, kl	kilolitre	**LGBTIQ**	lesbian, gay, bisexual, transgender, intersex, queer (or questioning)
km	kilometre		
km/h	kilometres per hour		
KMS	knowledge management systems	**LGBTQ**	lesbian, gay, bisexual, transgender, queer (or questioning)
KO	knockout		
Knt	Knight		
kPa	kilopascal	**lge**	large
k.p.h.	kilometres per hour	**l.h.s.**	left-hand side
KPI	key performance indicator	**Li**	lithium
Kr	krypton	**lic'd**	licensed
Kt	knight	**Lieut.**	Lieutenant
K-12	*NSW, ACT* kindergarten to year 12	**LLW**	low level waste
		lm	lumen
kW	kilowatt	**LMO**	living modified organism
kWh	kilowatt hour	**LNG**	liquefied natural gas
		loc. cit.	in the place cited (L: *loco citato*)
l	litre	**log.**	logarithm
l.	left; length	**long.**	longitude
L	learner (driver); litre; lambert; (*Electricity*) inductance; Lake	**LOTE**	languages other than English
		lox	liquid oxygen
La	lambert; lanthanum	**LPG**	liquefied petroleum gas
LA	Legislative Assembly	**Lr**	lawrencium
LAC	Leading Aircraftman	**LS**	Leading Seaman

l.s.d.	pounds, shillings and pence (L: *librae, solidi, denarii*)	**m.f.**	medium frequency
LSL	long service leave	**mfd**	manufactured
Lt	Lieutenant	**mfg**	manufacturing
LT	(*Electricity*) low-tension; (*Army*) Lieutenant	**MFN**	most favoured nation
		mfr	manufacture; manufacturer
LTCOL	Lieutenant Colonel	**mg**	milligram
Ltd	Limited	**Mg**	magnesium
LTGEN	Lieutenant General	**Mgr, mgr**	Manager
Lu	lutetium	**MHA**	Member of the House of Assembly
LUG	lock-up garage		
lx	lux	**MHR**	Member of the House of Representatives
l.y.	light-year		
		MHz	megahertz
m	metre	**mid.**	middle; midnight
m.	male; masculine; married; mass; million; minute; month; noon (L: *meridiem*)	**MIDN**	Midshipman
		mil.	military
		mill.	million
		min.	minute; minimum
M	(*Film classification*) mature; medium	**MIS**	management investment scheme
		misc.	miscellaneous
MA	Master of Arts; (*Film classification*) mature accompanied	**MKS**	metre-kilogram-second (system)
		MJ	megajoule
		ML	megalitre
MAJ	Major	**ml, mL**	millilitre
MAJGEN	Major General	**MLA**	Member of the Legislative Assembly
MAP	modified atmosphere packaging		
Mar., Mch	March	**MLC**	Member of the Legislative Council
masc.	masculine		
math., maths	mathematical; mathematics	**mm**	millimetre
matric.	matriculation	**MMA**	mixed martial arts
max.	maximum	**MMBM**	mandatory mob-based movement
mb	millibar	**Mn**	manganese
Mb	megabit	**mo.**	month
MB	megabyte	**Mo**	molybdenum
MBO	management buy-out	**MO**	mail order; money order; Medical Officer
MBP	Munchausen syndrome by proxy		
Mbps	megabits per second	**mod.**	modern; moderate; (*Music*) moderately; in moderate time (It.: *moderato*)
MBps	megabytes per second		
mbyte	megabyte		
m.c.	medical certificate	**MOG, MoG**	machinery of government
MC	Master of Ceremonies; Military Cross	**Mon.**	Monday
		MOR	(*Music*) middle-of-the-road
MCFC	molten carbonate fuel cell	**MOS**	mild ovarian stimulation
Md	mendelevium	**mp**	(*Music*) moderately soft (It.: *mezzo-piano*)
MD	Doctor of Medicine		
ME	myalgic encephalomyelitis	**MP**	Member of Parliament; Military Police
med.	medical; medicine; medium		
MERS	Middle East respiratory syndrome	**m.p.g.**	miles per gallon
Messrs	Gentlemen (F: *Messieurs*)	**m.p.h.**	miles per hour
met.	metropolitan	**m.p.s.**	miles per second
meth.	methylated	**MRAAF**	Marshal of the Royal Australian Air Force
mf	(*Music*) rather loud (It.: *mezzo-forte*)		
		MRI	magnetic resonance imaging
		mRNA	messenger RNA

MS	manuscript; multiple sclerosis	**NTCE**	Northern Territory Certificate of Education
MSBP	Munchausen syndrome by proxy		
MSG	monosodium glutamate	**NUM**	nursing unit manager
Msgr	Monsignor	**Num.**	(*Bible*) Numbers
MSL	mean sea level	**NW**	north-west; north-western
MSS	manuscripts		
mSv	millisievert	**O**	ohm; oxygen
Mt	meitnerium; Mount; Mountain	**OA**	Order of Australia
Mt.	(*Bible*) Matthew	**OAE**	otoacoustic emission
mus.	music; musical; musician; museum	**OAET**	otoacoustic emission test
		OAM	Medal of the Order of Australia
MUSN	(*Military*) Musician	**OBOE**	off-by-one error
MV	Merchant Vessel; Motor Vessel	**obs.**	observation; observatory; obsolete
MVP	most valued player		
MW	megawatt	**OC**	Officer Commanding; opportunity class
MYR	Malaysian ringgit		
		occas.	occasion
n.	born (L: *natus*)	**OCD**	obsessive-compulsive disorder
N	nitrogen; north; northern; newton	**OCDT**	Officer Cadet
n/a, n.a.	not applicable; not available	**Oct.**	October
NAIRU	non-accelerating inflation rate of unemployment	**O/D**	overdraft; overdrawn; on demand
		ODD	oppositional defiant disorder
NAM	Northern Australian Monsoon	**ODP**	ozone depletion potential
nat.	national; native; natural	**ODS**	ozone depleting substance
naut.	nautical	**off.**	office; officer; official
nav.	navigation; navy; naval	**OHMS**	On Her (or His) Majesty's Service
navig.	navigation; navigator	**OHS, OH&S**	occupational health and safety
Nb	niobium	**o.h.v.**	overhead valve
NB	note well (L: *nota bene*)	**OMG**	Oh, my God!
NBT	next big thing	**o.n.o.**	or near(est) offer
Nd	neodymium	**OOS**	occupational overuse syndrome
NDE	near-death experience	**OOSH**	out of school hours
Ne	neon	**op. cit.**	in the work cited (L: *opere citato*)
NE	north-east; north-eastern	**op.**	operation; opus
neg.	negation; negative	**OP**	overproof rum; out of print; (*Qld Education*) overall position; (*Theatre*) opposite prompt
NET	New Earth Time		
NGO	non-government organisation		
Ni	nickel	**opp.**	opposite
NL	no-liability company	**opt.**	option
NLIS	National Livestock Identification System	**orch.**	orchestra
		ord.	order; ordinary
NLP	natural language processing; neuro-linguistic programming	**orig.**	origin; original
		Orth.	Orthodox
no., No.	number	**o.s.**	overseas
No	nobelium	**o/s**	out of stock
nos, Nos	numbers	**Os**	osmium
Nov.	November	**OS**	outsize; operating system; Ordinary Seaman
Np	neptunium		
nr	near	**o/t**	overtime
NRMI	nuclear magnetic resonance imaging	**OT**	(*Bible*) Old Testament; occupational therapy; occupational therapist; Overland Telegraph (Line)
NSU	non-specific urethritis		
NT	(*Bible*) New Testament		

OTC	over-the-counter	**PI**	private investigator
Oxon.	of Oxford (L: *Oxoniensis*)	**PIC**	property identification code
oz	ounce	**PID**	pelvic inflammatory disease
		PINOP	person in need of protection
p.	page; (*Music*) softly (It.: *piano*)	**PIR**	parallel import restriction
P	phosphorus; provisional (driver's licence)	**pizz.**	(*Music*) plucked strings (It.: *pizzicato*)
p.a.	yearly (L: *per annum*)	**PjBL**	project-based learning
Pa	protactinium	**Pk**	Park
P & C	Parents and Citizens Association	**pkt**	packet
para.	paragraph	**PKU**	phenylketonuria
Parl., Parlt	Parliament	**Pl.**	Place (in street names)
partn.	partnership	**pl., plur.**	plural
pass.	passenger; passive	**P/L**	Proprietary Limited
pax	passenger(s)	**PLC**	(*British*) public limited company
PAYE	pay-as-you-earn	**PLR**	public lending right
PAYG	pay-as-you-go	**PLTOFF**	Pilot Officer
Pb	lead (L: *plumbum*)	**p.m.**	afternoon (L: *post meridiem*)
PB	personal best	**Pm**	promethium
PBL	problem-based learning	**PM**	prime minister
PBS	Pharmaceutical Benefits Scheme	**PMG**	postmaster-general
pc	parsec	**PMS**	premenstrual syndrome
p.c.	per cent	**PMT**	premenstrual tension
PC	personal computer; politically correct; personnel carrier	**PND**	postnatal depression
PCA	patient-controlled analgesia	**PO**	postal order; Post Office; Petty Officer
PCB	printed circuit board	**pop.**	population
p.c.m.	per calendar month	**POP**	Post Office Preferred
PCP	pneumocystis carinii pneumonia	**pos.**	position
pd	paid	**POV**	point of view
p.d.	per day (L: *per diem*); potential difference	**POW**	prisoner of war
Pd	palladium	**pp.**	pages; (*Music*) very softly (It.: *pianissimo*)
PDA	personal digital assistant; public display of affection	**PPP**	public–private partnership
PDS	product disclosure statement	**PPS**	additional postscript (L: *post post scriptum*)
PE	physical education; probable error	**pr**	pair
PED	performance-enhancing drug	**Pr**	praseodymium
Pen.	Peninsula	**PR**	public relations; permanent residence; proportional representation
perm.	permanent		
PET	positron emission tomography; polyethylene terephthalate	**pref.**	preference; preferred
PEX	cross-linked polyethylene	**prelim.**	preliminary
PFD	personal flotation device	**prep.**	preposition; preparation
PG	(*Film classification*) parental guidance recommended	**Pres.**	President
		pro tem.	for the time being (L: *pro tempore*)
pg., p.	page	**Prof.**	Professor
PhD	Doctor of Philosophy (L: *Philosophiae Doctor*)	**prop.**	proprietor
photog.	photography; photographic	**prox.**	in or of the next or coming month (L: *proximo*)
phr.	phrase		
phys. ed.	physical education	**PS**	postscript (L: *post scriptum*)
phys.	physical; physics	**PSA**	prostate specific antigen

PSE	pseudoephedrine
PSP	progressive supranuclear palsy
psi	pounds per square inch
PSO	protective service officer
psychol.	psychology; psychological
pt	point; pint
p.t.	part-time
Pt	platinum
PT	physical training; personal training
PTD	personal tracking device
PTE	Private
PTO, p.t.o.	please turn over
PTSD	post-traumatic stress disorder
P-10	*Victoria*, *Tasmania* preparatory class to year 10
p2p	(*Computers*) peer-to-peer
Pty	Proprietary
Pu	plutonium
PUA	potential unauthorised arrival
PUFA	polyunsaturated fatty acid
PVA	polyvinyl acetate
PVC	polyvinyl chloride
PVS	post-viral syndrome
p.w., pw, p/w	per week
PWC	personal watercraft
PWD	people with disabilities; person with disability
q	quintal
q.	quarto; question
Q	Queen
qubit	quantum bit
QC	Queen's Counsel
QCD	quantum chromodynamics
QCE	Queensland Certificate of Education
QE	quantitative easing
QED	which was to be proved (L: *quod erat demonstrandum*)
QM	quartermaster
QMS	quartermaster sergeant
qq.	questions
qr	quarter
qt.	quantity
qto	quarto
qtr	quarter; quarterly
qual.	qualified; quality
quot.	quotation
q.v.	which see (L: *quod vide*)

r.	radius; right; (*Cricket*) runs
R	(*Film classification*) restricted (to those aged 18 and over); roentgen; (*Electricity*) resistance
Ra	radium
rad	radian
RADM	Rear Admiral
rall.	(*Music*) becoming gradually slower (It.: *rallentando*)
RAM	random-access memory
R & B	rhythm and blues
Rb	rubidium
RBL	reasonable benefit limit
RBT	random breath test(ing)
RC	Roman Catholic; (*Film classification*) refused classification
RCT	(*Navy*) Recruit
Rd	Road
RD	rural delivery (used in addresses)
RDI	recommended dietary intake; recommended daily intake
RDO	rostered day off
RDT	random drug test(ing)
Re	rhenium
rec.	receipt
REC	(*Army*) Recruit
recd	received
ref.	reference; referee
reg.	registration; registered; regulation
Regt	Regiment
relig.	religion; religious
rep.	representative
retd	retired
Rev., Revd	Reverend
RFG	reformulated gasoline
RFID	radiofrequency identification
Rg	roentgenium
Rh	Rhesus; rhodium
RHDV	rabbit haemorrhagic disease virus
r.h.s.	right-hand side
RIB	rigid inflatable boat
RIP	may he or she (or they) rest in peace (L: *requiescat in pace*)
rit., ritard.	(*Music*) slower; holding back (It.: *ritardando*)
riv.	river
RLS	restless leg syndrome
rm	room
RMB	Roadside Mail Box
RMO	resident medical officer
Rn	radon

RN	registered nurse	**sen., snr, sr**	senior
RNA	ribonucleic acid	**sep., separ.**	separate
RNase	ribonuclease	**Sep., Sept.**	September
ROI	return on investment	**Sergt, Sgt,**	Sergeant
Rom.	Roman; Romanic; (*Bible*) Romans	**SGT**	
		SES	State Emergency Service
ROW	right of way; Rest of World	**sf., sfz.**	(*Music*) with force (It.: *sforzando*)
RP	Received Pronunciation	**SFA**	saturated fatty acid
RPF	relative pollen frequency	**SFN**	Superannuation Fund Number
r.p.m.	revolutions per minute	**s.g.**	specific gravity
r.p.s.	revolutions per second	**Sg**	seaborgium
RPV	remotely piloted vehicle	**SG**	Star of Gallantry
RSCT	regenerative stem cell technology	**SGC**	superannuation guarantee charge
RSS	(*Telecom.*) really simple syndication	**shd**	should
		shpt	shipment
RSVP	please reply (F: *répondez s'il vous plaît*)	**shr.**	share
		Si	silicon
Rt Hon.	Right Honourable	**SI**	International System of Units (Fr.: *Système International d'Unités*)
R-12	*SA* reception class to year 12		
Ru	rutherfordium		
RV	recreational vehicle; residual value	**SIEV**	suspected illegal entry vessel
		sig.	signature
RWUE	rural water use efficiency	**SIG**	(*Military*) Signaller
Rx	prescription (L: *recipe*)	**sing.**	singular
		SKD	(of vehicles) semi-knocked down
s.	singular; second(s)	**Sm**	samarium
S	south; southern; siemens; sulphur; small	**SM**	stipendiary magistrate
		SMN	Seaman
SACE	South Australian Certificate of Education	**SMN***	Seaman Star
		SMS	short messaging service
s.a.e., SAE	stamped addressed envelope; self-addressed envelope	**SMSF**	self-managed superannuation fund
SAE	South Asian English	**Sn**	tin (L: *stannum*)
SAM	surface-to-air missile	**snr, sr**	senior
S & M	sadism and masochism	**Soc.**	Society
SARS	severe acute respiratory syndrome	**SOB**	start of business
SASE	self-addressed stamped envelope	**SOHO**	small office home office
Sat.	Saturday	**SOI**	Southern Oscillation Index
Sb	antimony (L: *stibium*)	**sop.**	soprano
SBLT	Sub Lieutenant	**sp. gr.**	specific gravity
SBS	shadow banking system	**sp.**	special; species
SC	Senior Counsel	**spec., sp.**	special
Sc	scandium	**SPF**	sun protection factor
s/c	self-contained	**spp.**	species (plural)
sch.	school	**SPQR**	the Senate and the People of Rome (L: *Senatus Populusque Romanus*)
sci-fi, SF	science fiction		
SCM	supply chain management		
Se	selenium	**SPR**	Sapper
SE	south-east; south-eastern	**SPUD**	single person urban dwelling
sec.	second; secondary; secretary; section; secure	**Sq.**	Square (in street names)
		SQNLDR	Squadron Leader
sect.	section	**sr**	steradian
secy, sec.	secretary	**Sr**	Senior; Sister; strontium

SRC	Students' Representative Council	**TEE**	Tertiary Entrance Examination
SS	steamship	**tel.**	telephone
SSCE	Senior Secondary Certificate of Education	**telecom.**	telecommunications
SSRI	selective serotonin reuptake inhibitor	**temp.**	temporary; temperature
SSSB	small solar-system body	**TER**	Tertiary Entrance Rank
St	Street; Saint; Strait	**TES**	Tertiary Entrance Statement; Tertiary Entrance Score
STB	set-top box	**TESOL**	teaching English to speakers of other languages
STD	sexually transmitted disease; subscriber trunk dialling	**TFN**	tax file number
STEM	*Education* science, technology, engineering, and mathematics	**TGIF**	Thank God it's Friday
ster.	sterling	**theat.**	theatre; theatrical
Sth	south	**Th**	thorium
Sthn	southern	**Thu., Thurs.**	Thursday
STMM	short-term money market	**Ti**	titanium
stn	station	**TIA**	trans-ischaemic attack
sub.	subeditor; subject	**TK CMAN**	Tank Crewman
subj.	subject	**Tl**	thallium
SUDEP	sudden unexplained death in epilepsy	**Tm**	thulium
SUDS	sudden unexplained death syndrome	**TM**	transcendental meditation
Sun., Sund.	Sunday	**Tn**	thoron
SUP	stand-up paddleboard	**TNT**	trinitrotoluene
Super.	Superintendent	**TO**	Technical Officer
surg.	surgery; surgical; surgeon	**TPO**	tree preservation order
SUV	sports utility vehicle	**TPR**	Trooper
Sv	Sverdrup; sievert	**TPS**	third-person shooter
SW	south-west; south-western	**TPV**	temporary protection visa
sym.	symbol; symbolic; symmetrical; symphony	**tr.**	transitive; translate; translated; translator
sz.	size	**TR**	(*Military*) Trainee
		trad.	traditional
t	tonne	**trans.**	transcript; translated; translation; translator
T	tesla	**trig.**	trigonometric; trigonometry
Ta	tantalum	**trop.**	tropical
TAFE	Technical and Further Education	**tsp., t.**	teaspoon
TAI	International Atomic Time (F: *Temps Atomique International*)	**T-12**	*NT* transition to year 12
Tb	terbium	**Tues., Tue., Tu.**	Tuesday
TBA	to be announced	**TWI**	trade-weighted index
TBC	to be confirmed	**2LT**	Second Lieutenant
tbs., tbsp.	tablespoon		
Tc	technetium	**u**	atomic mass unit
TCE	Tasmanian Certificate of Education; trichloroethylene	**U**	Union; United; University; uranium
TD	traveller's diarrhoea	**UAI**	Universities Admission Index
TDI	tolerable daily intake	**UAV**	unmanned aerial vehicle
Te	tellurium	**u.c.**	upper case
tech.	technical; technology	**u/c**	under cover
		UCC	ultra-clean coal
		UCP	undercover parking
		UHF, u.h.f.	ultra high frequency
		UHT	ultra heat treated

1003

ult., ulto	in or of the preceding month (L: *ultimo*)	**WBP**	world's best practice
		w.c.	without charge
univ.	university	**WC**	toilet (water closet)
UPF	ultraviolet protection factor	**wd**	word; would
USB	(*Computers*) universal serial bus	**Wed.**	Wednesday
USD	US dollar	**WGCDR**	Wing Commander
UT	universal time	**wir**	walk-in robe
UTC	universal time coordinated	**wk**	week; work
UV	ultraviolet	**wkly**	weekly
UVA	ultraviolet A	**wkt**	wicket
UVB	ultraviolet B	**WMD**	weapon of mass destruction
		WO	(*Navy*) Warrant Officer
v.	verb; verse; versus; volume; velocity	**WOFF**	(*Air Force*) Warrant Officer
		WO1	(*Army*) Warrant Officer Class One
V	vanadium; volt		
vac.	vacancy; vacant; vacation	**WO2**	(*Army*) Warrant Officer Class Two
var.	variant; variation; variety		
VAT	value added tax	**w.p.b.**	wastepaper basket
vb	verb	**w.p.m.**	words per minute
VBIED	vehicle-borne improvised explosive device	**WST**	Western Standard Time
		wt	weight
VC	Victoria Cross; vice-chairman; vice-chancellor	**WUE**	water use efficiency
		ww	wall-to-wall
VCE	Victorian Certificate of Education	**www**	World Wide Web
VCR	video cassette recorder		
VDT	visual display terminal	**X**	Cross; (*Film classification*) restricted (to age 18 and over; contains sexually explicit material)
VDU	visual display unit		
vel.	velocity		
VET	Vocational Education and Training		
		Xe	xenon
VG	valuer general; vicar-general	**XL**	(in clothing sizes) extra large
VHF, v.h.f.	very high frequency	**XLPE**	cross-linked polyethylene
Vic.	Victoria	**Xmas**	Christmas
vid.	see (L: *vide*)	**XP**	extreme programming
viz.	namely (L: *videlicet*)	**X ref.**	cross-reference
VJ	video journalist	**XS**	(in clothing sizes) extra small
VMO	visiting medical officer	**XXS**	(in clothing sizes) extra, extra small
VOD	video on demand		
VoIP	voice over IP	**XXL**	(in clothing sizes) extra, extra large
vol.	volume		
VP	vice-president		
VPN	virtual private network	**y.**	year
vs.	versus; verse	**Y, Yt**	yttrium
vv.	verses	**Yb**	ytterbium
		yd	yard
		yo, y/o	year(s) old
w.	week; weight; wide; width; with	**yr**	year
W	tungsten (wolfram); west; western; watt	**yrs**	yours
WACE	Western Australian Certificate of Education	**ZEV**	zero-emission vehicle
		Zn	zinc
WAN	wide area network	**zool.**	zoology
WASP	white Anglo-Saxon Protestant	**Zr**	zirconium
Wb	weber		

COUNTRIES OF THE WORLD

Country	People	Official/main language	Capital	Main unit of currency	Internet address suffix
Afghanistan	Afghan, Afghani	Pashto, Dari (Persian)	Kabul	afghani	af
Albania	Albanian	Albanian	Tirana	lek	al
Algeria	Algerian, Algerine	Arabic	Algiers	Algerian dinar	dz
Andorra	Andorran	Catalan, French, Spanish	Andorra la Vella	euro	ad
Angola	Angolan	Portuguese	Luanda	kwanza	ao
Antigua and Barbuda	Antiguan	English	St John's	East Caribbean dollar	ag
Argentina	Argentine, Argentinian	Spanish	Buenos Aires	Argentine peso	ar
Armenia	Armenian	Armenian	Yerevan	dram	am
Australia	Australian	English	Canberra	Australian dollar	au
Austria	Austrian	German	Vienna	euro	at
Azerbaijan	Azerbaijani	Azerbaijani	Baku	manta	az
Bahamas, the	Bahamian	English	Nassau	Bahamian dollar	bs
Bahrain	Bahraini	Arabic	Manama	Bahraini dinar	bh
Bangladesh	Bangladeshi	Bengali	Dhaka	taka	bd
Barbados	Barbadian	English	Bridgetown	Barbados dollar	bb
Belarus	Belarusian	Belarusian	Minsk	Belarusian rouble	by
Belgium	Belgian	Dutch, French, German	Brussels	euro	be
Belize	Belizean	English, Spanish, Carib, Maya	Belmopan	Belize dollar	bz
Benin	Beninese	French	Porto-Novo	CFA franc	bj
Bermuda	Bermudan	English	Hamilton	Bermuda dollar	bm
Bhutan	Bhutanese	Dzongkha	Thimphu	ngultrum	bt
Bolivia	Bolivian	Spanish, Quechua, Aymará	Sucre (judicial), La Paz (legislative)	boliviano	bo
Bosnia and Herzegovina	Bosnian	Bosnian	Sarajevo	convertible marka	ba
Botswana	Botswanan	Tswana, English	Gaborone	pula	bw
Brazil	Brazilian	Portuguese	Brasília	real	br
Brunei	Bruneian	Malay, English	Bandar Seri Begawan	Brunei dollar	bn
Bulgaria	Bulgarian	Bulgarian	Sofia	lev	bg
Burkina Faso	—	French, Mossi	Ouagadougou	CFA franc	bf
Burma, *see* Myanmar					
Burundi	Burundian	French, Kirundi	Bujumbura	Burundi franc	bi

Country	People	Official/main language	Capital	Main unit of currency	Internet address suffix
Cambodia	Cambodian	Khmer, French	Phnom Penh	riel	kh
Cameroon	Cameroonian	French, English	Yaoundé	CFA franc	cm
Canada	Canadian	English, French	Ottawa	Canadian dollar	ca
Cape Verde	Cape Verdean	Portuguese	Praia	Cape Verde escudo	cv
Central African Republic	–	French, Sango	Bangui	CFA franc	cf
Chad	Chadian	French, Arabic	N'Djamena	CFA franc	td
Chile	Chilean	Spanish	Santiago	Chilean peso	cl
China	Chinese	Chinese (Mandarin)	Beijing	(renminbi) yuan	cn
Colombia	Colombian	Spanish	Bogotá	Colombian peso	co
Comoros	Comorian, Comoran	French, Arabic, Comorian	Moroni	Comorian franc	km
Congo, Democratic Republic of	Congolese	French, English	Kinshasa	Congolese franc	cd
Congo, Republic of	Congolese	French	Brazzaville	CFA franc	cg
Costa Rica	Costa Rican	Spanish	San José	Costa Rican colón	cr
Côte d'Ivoire (Ivory Coast)	Ivorian	French	Abidjan, Yamoussoukro	CFA franc	ci
Croatia	Croat, Croatian	Croatian	Zagreb	kuna	hr
Cuba	Cuban	Spanish	Havana	Cuban peso	cu
Cyprus	Cypriot	Greek, Turkish	Nicosia	euro	cy
Czech Republic	Czech	Czech	Prague	koruna	cz
Denmark	Dane	Danish	Copenhagen	Danish krone	dk
Djibouti	Djibouti	Arabic, French	Djibouti	Djibouti franc	dj
Dominica	Dominican	English	Roseau	East Caribbean dollar	do
Dominican Republic	Dominican	Spanish	Santo Domingo	Dominican peso	dm
East Timor	East Timorese	Tetum, Portuguese	Dili	US dollar	tp
Ecuador	Ecuadorian	Spanish, Quechua	Quito	US dollar	ec
Egypt	Egyptian	Arabic	Cairo	Egyptian pound	eg
El Salvador	Salvadoran	Spanish	San Salvador	US dollar	sv
Equatorial Guinea	Guinean	Spanish	Malabo	CFA franc	gq
Eritrea	Eritrean	Tigrinya	Asmara	nakfa	er
Estonia	Estonian	Estonian	Tallinn	euro	ee
Ethiopia	Ethiopian	Amharic	Addis Ababa	birr	et
Fiji	Fijian	English, Fijian, Hindi	Suva	Fiji dollar	fj
Finland	Finn, Finlander, Finnish	Finnish, Swedish	Helsinki	euro	fi
France	French	French	Paris	euro	fr

Country	Nationality	Language	Capital	Currency	Code
Gabon	Gabonese	French, Fang	Libreville	CFA franc	ga
Gambia, The	Gambian	English	Banjul	dalasi	gm
Georgia	Georgian	Georgian	Tbilisi	lari	ge
Germany	German	German	Berlin	euro	de
Ghana	Ghanian	English	Accra	cedi	gh
Greece	Greek	Greek	Athens	euro	gr
Grenada	Grenadian	English	St George's	East Caribbean dollar	gd
Guatemala	Guatemalan	Spanish	Guatemala City	quetzal	gt
Guinea	Guinean	French	Conakry	Guinean franc	gn
Guinea-Bissau	Guinean	Portuguese	Bissau	CFA franc	gw
Guyana	Guyanan	English	Georgetown	Guyanese dollar	gy
Haiti	Haitian	French, Haitian Creole	Port-au-Prince	gourde	ht
Honduras	Honduran	Spanish, English	Tegucigalpa	lempira	hn
Hungary	Hungarian	Hungarian	Budapest	forint	hu
Iceland	Icelandic	Icelandic	Reykjavik	króna	is
India	Indian	Hindi, English	New Delhi	Indian rupee	in
Indonesia	Indonesian	Bahasa Indonesia	Jakarta	rupiah	id
Iran	Iranian	Farsi (Persian)	Teheran	Iranian rial	ir
Iraq	Iraqi	Arabic, Kurdish	Baghdad	Iraqi dinar	iq
Ireland, Republic of	Irish	Irish (Gaelic), English	Dublin	euro	ie
Israel	Israeli	Hebrew, Arabic	Jerusalem	new shekel	il
Italy	Italian	Italian	Rome	euro	it
Jamaica	Jamaican	English	Kingston	Jamaican dollar	jm
Japan	Japanese	Japanese	Tokyo	yen	jp
Jordan	Jordanian	Arabic	Amman	Jordanian dinar	jo
Kazakhstan	Kazakh	Kazakh	Astana	tenge	kz
Kenya	Kenyan	Swahili, English	Nairobi	Kenyan shilling	ke
Kiribati	–	I-Kiribati, English	Bairiki	Australian dollar	ki
Korea, North	North Korean	Korean	Pyongyang	North Korean won	kp
Korea, South	South Korean	Korean	Seoul	South Korean won	kr
Kosovo	Kosovan	Albanian, Serbian	Priština	euro	
Kuwait	Kuwaiti	Arabic	Kuwait City	Kuwaiti dinar	kw
Kyrgyzstan	Kyrgyz	Kyrgyz, Russian	Bishkek	som	kg
Laos	Laotian	Lao	Vientiane	kip	la
Latvia	Latvian	Latvian	Riga	euro	lv
Lebanon	Lebanese	Arabic	Beirut	Lebanese pound	lb
Lesotho	–	English, Sesotho	Maseru	loti	ls

Country	People	Official/main language	Capital	Main unit of currency	Internet address suffix
Liberia	Liberian	English	Monrovia	Liberian dollar	lr
Libya	Libyan	Arabic	Tripoli	Libyan dinar	ly
Liechtenstein	Liechtensteiner	German (Alemannic)	Vaduz	Swiss franc	li
Lithuania	Lithuanian	Lithuanian	Vilnius	euro	lt
Luxembourg	Luxembourger	French, German	Luxembourg	euro	lu
Macedonia	Macedonian	Macedonian	Skopje	denar	mk
Madagascar	Madagascan	Malagasy, French	Antananarivo	ariary	mg
Malawi	Malawian	English, Chichewa	Lilongwe	Malawian kwacha	mw
Malaysia	Malaysian	Malay, English	Kuala Lumpur	ringgit	my
Maldives	Maldivian	Divehi	Malé	rufiyaa	mv
Mali	Malian	French	Bamako	CFA franc	ml
Malta	Maltese	Maltese, English	Valletta	euro	mt
Marshall Islands	Marshallese	Marshallese, English	Majuro	US dollar	mh
Mauritania	Mauritanian	French, Arabic	Nouakchott	ouguiya	mr
Mauritius	Mauritian	English, French Creole	Port Louis	Mauritian rupee	mu
Mexico	Mexican	Spanish	Mexico City	Mexican peso	mx
Micronesia, Federated States of	Micronesian	English	Palikir	US dollar	fm
Moldova	Moldovan	Romanian	Chişinău	Moldovan leu	md
Monaco	Monacan, Monegasque	French	Monaco-Ville	euro	mc
Mongolia	Mongolian	Khalkha Mongolian	Ulaanbaatar	tugrik	mn
Montenegro	Montenegrin	Montenegro Serbian	Cetinje, Podgorica (administrative centre)	euro	
Morocco	Moroccan	Arabic	Rabat	Moroccan dirham	ma
Mozambique	–	Portuguese	Maputo	metical	mz
Myanmar	–	Myanmar (Burmese)	Nay Pyi Taw	kyat	mm
Namibia	Namibian	English	Windhoek	Namibian dollar	na
Nauru	Nauruan	Nauruan, English	Nauru	Australian dollar	nr
Nepal	Nepalese, Nepali	Nepali	Katmandu	Nepalese rupee	np
Netherlands, the	Dutch	Dutch	Amsterdam	euro	nl
New Zealand	New Zealander	English, Maori	Wellington	NZ dollar	nz
Nicaragua	Nicaraguan	Spanish	Managua	córdoba	ni
Niger	Nigerien	French	Niamey	CFA franc	ne
Nigeria	Nigerian	English	Abuja	naira	ng

Country	Adjective	Capital	Language	Currency	Code
Norway	Norwegian	Oslo	Norwegian	Norwegian krone	no
Oman	Omani	Muscat	Arabic	rial Omani	om
Pakistan	Pakistani	Islamabad	Urdu	Pakistani rupee	pk
Palau	Palauan	Koror	Palauan, English	US dollar	pw
Panama	Panamanian	Panama City	Spanish	balboa	pa
Papua New Guinea	Papua New Guinean	Port Moresby	Neo-Melanesian, Pidgin, Motu, English	kina	pg
Paraguay	Paraguayan	Asunción	Spanish, Guaraní	guaraní	py
Peru	Peruvian	Lima	Spanish, Quechua, Aymara	nuevo sol	pe
Philippines, the	Filipino	Manila	Pilipino, English	Philippine peso	ph
Poland	Pole, Polish	Warsaw	Polish	zloty	pl
Portugal	Portuguese	Lisbon	Portuguese	euro	pt
Qatar	Qatari	Doha	Arabic	Qatar riyal	qa
Romania	Romanian	Bucharest	Romanian	Romanian leu	ro
Russia	Russian	Moscow	Russian	rouble	ru
Rwanda	Rwandan	Kigali	French, Rwanda	Rwandan franc	rw
Samoa	Samoan	Apia	Samoan, English	tala	ws
San Marino	San Marinese	San Marino	Italian	euro	sm
São Tomé and Príncipe	–	São Tomé	Portuguese	dobra	st
Saudi Arabia	Saudi Arabian, Saudi	Riyadh	Arabic	Saudi riyal	sa
Senegal	Senegalese	Dakar	French	CFA franc	sn
Serbia	Serb, Serbian	Belgrade	Serbian	Serbian dinar	cs
Seychelles	–	Victoria	English, French, Creole	Seychelles rupee	sc
Sierra Leone	Sierra Leonean	Freetown	English	leone	sl
Singapore	Singaporean	Singapore	Malay, Chinese, English, Tamil	Singapore dollar	sg
Slovakia	Slovak, Slovakian	Bratislava	Slovak	euro	sk
Slovenia	Slovene, Slovenian	Ljubljana	Slovene	euro	si
Solomon Islands	Solomon Islander	Honiara	English, Neo-Melanesian, Pidgin	Solomon Islands dollar	sb
Somalia	Somali, Somalian	Mogadishu	Somali, Arabic, English, Italian	Somali shilling	so
South Africa	South African	Pretoria, Cape Town, and Bloemfontein	English, Afrikaans, and 9 other official African languages	rand	za
South Sudan	South Sudanese	Juba	Arabic, English	Sudanese pound	ss
Spain	Spaniard, Spanish	Madrid	Spanish	euro	es
Sri Lanka	Sri Lankan, Sinhalese	Colombo, and Sri Jayawardenapura Kotte	Sinhalese, Tamil, English	Sri Lankan rupee	lk
St Kitts and Nevis	–	Basseterre	English	East Caribbean dollar	kn
St Lucia	St Lucian	Castries	English	East Caribbean dollar	lc

Country	People	Official/main language	Capital	Main unit of currency	Internet address suffix
St Vincent and the Grenadines	–	English	Kingstown	East Caribbean dollar	vc
Sudan	Sudanese	Arabic	Khartoum	Sudanese pound	sd
Suriname	Surinamese	Dutch, English	Paramaribo	Suriname dollar	sr
Swaziland	Swazi	English, Swazi	Mbabane, Lobamba	lilangeni	sz
Sweden	Swede, Swedish	Swedish	Stockholm	krona	se
Switzerland	Swiss	German, French, Italian	Bern	Swiss franc	ch
Syria	Syrian	Arabic	Damascus	Syrian pound	sy
Tajikistan	Tajik	Tajik	Dushanbe	somoni	tj
Tanzania	Tanzanian	Swahili, English	Dodoma	Tanzanian shilling	tz
Thailand	Thai	Thai	Bangkok	baht	th
Togo	Togolese	French	Lomé	CFA franc	tg
Tonga	Tongan	Tongan, English	Nuku'alofa	pa'anga	to
Trinidad and Tobago	Trinidadian	English	Port of Spain	Trinidad and Tobago dollar	tt
Tunisia	Tunisian	Arabic, French	Tunis	Tunisian dinar	tn
Turkey	Turk, Turkish	Turkish	Ankara	Turkish lira	tr
Turkmenistan	Turkmen	Turkmen	Ashgabat	Turkmen manta	tm
Tuvalu	Tuvaluan	Tuvaluan, English	Vaiaku (on Funafuti atoll)	Australian dollar, Tuvaluan dollar	tv
Uganda	Ugandan	Swahili, English	Kampala	Ugandan shilling	ug
Ukraine	Ukrainian	Ukrainian	Kiev	hryvnia	ua
United Arab Emirates	–	Arabic	Abu Dhabi	UAE dirham	ae
United Kingdom	Briton, British	English	London	pound sterling	uk
United States of America	American	English	Washington	US dollar	
Uruguay	Uruguayan	Spanish	Montevideo	peso uruguayo	uy
Uzbekistan	Uzbek	Uzbek	Tashkent	sum	uz
Vanuatu	Vanuatuan	Bislama, French, English	Vila	vatu	vu
Venezuela	Venezuelan	Spanish	Caracas	bolívar	ve
Vietnam	Vietnamese	Vietnamese	Hanoi	dông	vn
Yemen	Yemeni	Arabic	Sana'a	Yemeni rial	ye
Zambia	Zambian	English	Lusaka	Zambian kwacha	zm
Zimbabwe	Zimbabwean	English, and Bantu languages	Harare	various	zw

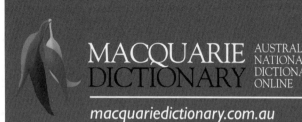